THE EUROPA WORLD YEAR BOOK 2011

VOLUME 2

KAZAKHSTAN–ZIMBABWE

LONDON AND NEW YORK

First published 1926

© **Routledge 2011**
Albert House, 1–4 Singer Street, London, EC2A 4BQ, United Kingdom
(Routledge is an imprint of the Taylor & Francis Group, an Informa business)

All rights reserved. No part of this
publication may be photocopied, recorded,
or otherwise reproduced, stored in a retrieval
system or transmitted in any form or by any
electronic or mechanical means without the
prior permission of the copyright owner.

ISBN: 978-1-85743-589-4 (The Set)
978-1-85743-591-7 (Vol. 2)
ISSN: 0956-2273

Publisher: Joanne Maher

Senior Editor, Statistics: Philip McIntyre

Regional Editors: Lynn Daniel, Iain Frame, Imogen Gladman,
Dominic Heaney, Neil Higgins, Juliet Love, Christopher Matthews, Jacqueline West

International Organizations Editors: Catriona Appeatu Holman, Helen Canton

Statistics Researchers: Abhinav Srivastava (Lead Researcher), Anuj Aggarwal, Mohd Khalid Ansari,
Prerna Kumra, Jasmeet Singh, Varun Wadhawan

Directory Researchers: Arijit Khasnobis (Lead Researcher), Esha Banerjee, Shubha Banerjee, Rima Kar,
Surmeet Kaur, Birendra Pratap Nayak, Thoithoi Pukhrambam,
Tessy Margaret Rajappan, C. Sandhya, K. Nungshithoibi Singha

Contributors: Christopher Bell, Rebecca Bomford, Lucy Dean, David Gruar,
Kirstie Macdonald, Catriona Marcham, Katharine Murison,
Jillian O'Brien, Elizabeth Salzman, Anna Thomas, Kristina Wischenkämper

Editorial Director: Paul Kelly

Typeset in New Century Schoolbook

Typeset by Data Standards Limited, Frome, Somerset

Printed and bound in Great Britain by Polestar Wheatons, Exeter

FOREWORD

THE EUROPA WORLD YEAR BOOK was first published in 1926. Since 1960 it has appeared in annual two-volume editions, and has become established as an authoritative reference work, providing a wealth of detailed information on the political, economic and commercial institutions of the world.

Volume 1 contains a comprehensive listing of some 1,900 international organizations, commissions and specialized bodies, and the first part of the alphabetical survey of countries of the world, from Afghanistan to Jordan. Volume 2 contains countries from Kazakhstan to Zimbabwe. An Index of Territories covered in both volumes is to be found at the end of Volume 2.

The International Organizations section gives extensive coverage to the United Nations and its related agencies and bodies. There are also detailed articles concerning other major international and regional organizations; entries for many affiliated organizations appear within these articles. In addition, the section includes briefer details of some 1,500 other international organizations. A comprehensive Index of International Organizations is included at the end of Volume 1.

Each country is covered by an individual chapter, containing: an introductory survey including contemporary political history, economic affairs, constitution and government, regional and international co-operation, and public holidays; a statistical survey presenting the latest available figures on demographics, labour force, health and welfare, agriculture, forestry, fishing, mining, industry, currency and exchange rates, government finance, international reserves and the monetary sector, cost of living, national accounts, balance of payments, external trade, railways, roads, shipping, civil aviation, tourism, media and telecommunications, and education; and a directory section listing names, addresses and other useful facts about organizations in the fields of government, election commissions, political parties, diplomatic representation, judiciary, religions, the media, telecommunications, banking, insurance, trade and industry, development organizations, chambers of commerce, industrial and trade associations, utilities, trade unions, transport, tourism, defence, and education.

The entire content of the print edition of THE EUROPA WORLD YEAR BOOK is available online at www.europaworld.com. This prestigious resource incorporates sophisticated search and browse functions as well as specially commissioned visual and statistical content. An ongoing programme of updates of key areas of information ensures currency of content, and enhances the richness of the coverage for which THE EUROPA WORLD YEAR BOOK is renowned.

Readers are referred to the nine titles in the Europa Regional Surveys of the World series: AFRICA SOUTH OF THE SAHARA, CENTRAL AND SOUTH-EASTERN EUROPE, EASTERN EUROPE, RUSSIA AND CENTRAL ASIA, THE FAR EAST AND AUSTRALASIA, THE MIDDLE EAST AND NORTH AFRICA, SOUTH AMERICA, CENTRAL AMERICA AND THE CARIBBEAN, SOUTH ASIA, THE USA AND CANADA, and WESTERN EUROPE, available both in print and online, offer comprehensive analysis at regional, sub-regional and country level. More detailed coverage of international organizations is to be found in THE EUROPA DIRECTORY OF INTERNATIONAL ORGANIZATIONS.

The content of THE EUROPA WORLD YEAR BOOK is extensively revised and updated by a variety of methods, including direct mailing to all the institutions listed. Many other sources are used, such as national statistical offices, government departments and diplomatic missions. The editors thank the innumerable individuals and organizations world-wide whose generous co-operation in providing current information for this edition is invaluable in presenting the most accurate and up-to-date material available.

May 2011

ACKNOWLEDGEMENTS

The editors gratefully acknowledge particular indebtedness for permission to reproduce material from the following sources: the United Nations' statistical databases and *Demographic Yearbook*, *Statistical Yearbook*, *Monthly Bulletin of Statistics*, *Industrial Commodity Statistics Yearbook* and *International Trade Statistics Yearbook*; the United Nations Educational, Scientific and Cultural Organization's *Statistical Yearbook* and Institute for Statistics database; the *Human Development Report* of the United Nations Development Programme; the Food and Agriculture Organization of the United Nations' statistical database; the statistical databases of the World Health Organization; the statistical databases of the UNCTAD/WTO International Trade Centre; the International Labour Office's statistical database and *Yearbook of Labour Statistics*; the World Bank's *World Bank Atlas*, *Global Development Finance*, *World Development Report* and *World Development Indicators*; the International Monetary Fund's statistical database, *International Financial Statistics* and *Government Finance Statistics Yearbook*; the World Tourism Organization's *Compendium* and *Yearbook of Tourism Statistics*; the US Geological Survey; the International Telecommunication Union; the International Road Federation's *World Road Statistics*; IHS Fairplay's *World Fleet Statistics* and *The Military Balance 2011*, a publication of the International Institute for Strategic Studies, Arundel House, 13–15 Arundel Street, London WC2R 3DX. Statistics Canada information is used with the permission of Statistics Canada. Users are forbidden to copy this material and/or redisseminate the data, in an original or modified form, for commercial purposes, without the expressed permission of Statistics Canada. Information on the availability of the wide range of data from Statistics Canada can be obtained from Statistics Canada's Regional Offices, its website at www.statcan.ca, and its toll-free access number 1-800-263-1136.

HEALTH AND WELFARE STATISTICS: SOURCES AND DEFINITIONS

Total fertility rate Source: WHO Statistical Information System (part of the Global Health Observatory). The number of children that would be born per woman, assuming no female mortality at child-bearing ages and the age-specific fertility rates of a specified country and reference period.

Under-5 mortality rate Source: WHO Statistical Information System. Defined by WHO as the probability of a child born in a specific year or period dying before the age of five, if subject to the age-specific mortality rates of that year or period.

HIV/AIDS Source: UNAIDS. Estimated percentage of adults aged 15 to 49 years living with HIV/AIDS. < indicates 'fewer than'.

Health expenditure Source: WHO Statistical Information System.
US $ per head (PPP)
International dollar estimates, derived by dividing local currency units by an estimate of their purchasing power parity (PPP) compared with the US dollar. PPPs are the rates of currency conversion that equalize the purchasing power of different currencies by eliminating the differences in price levels between countries.
% of GDP
GDP levels for OECD countries follow the most recent UN System of National Accounts. For non-OECD countries a value was estimated by utilizing existing UN, IMF and World Bank data.
Public expenditure
Government health-related outlays plus expenditure by social schemes compulsorily affiliated with a sizeable share of the population, and extrabudgetary funds allocated to health services. Figures include grants or loans provided by international agencies, other national authorities, and sometimes commercial banks.

Access to water and sanitation Source: WHO/UNICEF Joint Monitoring Programme on Water Supply and Sanitation (JMP) (Progress on Drinking Water and Sanitation, 2010 Update). Defined in terms of the percentage of the population using improved facilities in terms of the type of technology and levels of service afforded. For water, this includes house connections, public standpipes, boreholes with handpumps, protected dug wells, protected spring and rainwater collection; allowance is also made for other locally defined technologies. Sanitation is defined to include connection to a sewer or septic tank system, pour-flush latrine, simple pit or ventilated improved pit latrine, again with allowance for acceptable local technologies. Access to water and sanitation does not imply that the level of service or quality of water is 'adequate' or 'safe'.

Carbon dioxide emissions Source: World Bank, World Development Indicators database, citing the Carbon Dioxide Information Analysis Center (sponsored by the US Department of Energy). Emissions comprise those resulting from the burning of fossil fuels (including those produced during consumption of solid, liquid and gas fuels and from gas flaring) and from the manufacture of cement.

Human Development Index (HDI) Source: UNDP, *Human Development Report* (2010). A summary of human development measured by three basic dimensions: prospects for a long and healthy life, measured by life expectancy at birth; knowledge, measured by adult literacy rate and a combination of mean years of schooling and expected years of schooling; and standard of living, measured by GNP per head (PPP US $). The index value obtained lies between zero and one. A value above 0.8 indicates high human development, between 0.5 and 0.8 medium human development, and below 0.5 low human development. A centralized data source for all three dimensions was not available for all countries. In some cases other data sources were used to calculate a substitute value; however, this was excluded from the ranking. Other countries, including non-UNDP members, were excluded from the HDI altogether. In total, 169 countries were ranked for 2010.

CONTENTS

Abbreviations	Page ix
International Telephone Codes	xiii
Kazakhstan	2571
Kenya	2591
Kiribati	2616
The Democratic People's Republic of Korea (North Korea)	2625
The Republic of Korea (South Korea)	2654
Kosovo	2689
Kuwait	2702
Kyrgyzstan	2723
Laos	2743
Latvia	2759
Lebanon	2777
Lesotho	2808
Liberia	2822
Libya	2840
Liechtenstein	2864
Lithuania	2872
Luxembourg	2892
The former Yugoslav republic of Macedonia	2904
Madagascar	2923
Malawi	2942
Malaysia	2959
The Maldives	2998
Mali	3010
Malta	3028
The Marshall Islands	3039
Mauritania	3048
Mauritius	3064
Mexico	3080
The Federated States of Micronesia	3110
Moldova	3118
Monaco	3139
Mongolia	3146
Montenegro	3171
Morocco	3180
Mozambique	3205
Myanmar	3223
Namibia	3253
Nauru	3271
Nepal	3280
The Netherlands	3306
Netherlands Dependencies:	
Netherlands Special Municipalities:	
Bonaire	3332
Saba	3334
Sint Eustatius	3334
Netherlands Autonomous Countries:	
Aruba	3336
Curaçao	3343
Sint Maarten	3350

New Zealand	Page 3354
New Zealand's Dependent Territories:	
Ross Dependency	3380
Tokelau	3380
New Zealand's Associated States:	
The Cook Islands	3385
Niue	3393
Nicaragua	3400
Niger	3418
Nigeria	3436
Norway	3463
Norwegian External Territories:	
Svalbard	3487
Jan Mayen	3489
Norwegian Dependencies	3489
Oman	3491
Pakistan	3507
Palau	3554
Palestinian Autonomous Areas	3562
Panama	3592
Papua New Guinea	3611
Paraguay	3634
Peru	3652
The Philippines	3676
Poland	3718
Portugal	3742
Qatar	3768
Romania	3786
The Russian Federation	3811
Rwanda	3853
Saint Christopher and Nevis	3871
Saint Lucia	3880
Saint Vincent and the Grenadines	3891
Samoa	3900
San Marino	3910
São Tomé and Príncipe	3917
Saudi Arabia	3927
Senegal	3952
Serbia	3976
Seychelles	4001
Sierra Leone	4009
Singapore	4026
Slovakia	4053
Slovenia	4072
Solomon Islands	4088
Somalia	4103
South Africa	4122
South Sudan (see Sudan)*	
Spain	4156
Spanish External Territories:	
Ceuta	4195
Melilla	4200

*At the time of going to press, in late May 2011, the Republic of South Sudan was scheduled to become an independent state on 9 July.

CONTENTS

Sri Lanka	Page 4206
Sudan	4235
Suriname	4260
Swaziland	4272
Sweden	4287
Switzerland	4313
Syria	4339
Taiwan	4367
Tajikistan	4399
Tanzania	4418
Thailand	4438
Timor-Leste	4473
Togo	4492
Tonga	4510
Trinidad and Tobago	4521
Tunisia	4539
Turkey	4559
Turkmenistan	4596
Tuvalu	4613
Uganda	4620
Ukraine	4640
The United Arab Emirates	4670
The United Kingdom	4690
United Kingdom Crown Dependencies:	
The Channel Islands	4752
The Isle of Man	4759
United Kingdom Overseas Territories:	
Anguilla	4764
Bermuda	4770
The British Antarctic Territory	4778
The British Indian Ocean Territory	Page 4778
The British Virgin Islands	4779
The Cayman Islands	4786
The Falkland Islands	4793
Gibraltar	4799
Montserrat	4806
The Pitcairn Islands	4812
Saint Helena, Ascension and Tristan da Cunha	4815
South Georgia and the South Sandwich Islands	4820
The Turks and Caicos Islands	4821
The United States of America	4828
United States Commonwealth Territories:	
The Northern Mariana Islands	4901
Puerto Rico	4908
United States External Territories:	
American Samoa	4920
Guam	4926
The United States Virgin Islands	4934
Other United States Territories	4940
Uruguay	4942
Uzbekistan	4961
Vanuatu	4979
The Vatican City	4992
Venezuela	5002
Viet Nam	5028
Yemen	5059
Zambia	5085
Zimbabwe	5102
Index of Territories	5127

ABBREVIATIONS

AB	Aktiebolag (Joint-Stock Company); Alberta
Abog.	Abogado (Lawyer)
Acad.	Academician; Academy
ACP	African, Caribbean and Pacific (countries)
ACT	Australian Capital Territory
AD	anno Domini
ADB	African Development Bank; Asian Development Bank
ADC	aide-de-camp
Adm.	Admiral
admin.	administration
AEC	African Economic Community; African Economic Conference
AfDB	African Development Bank
AG	Aktiengesellschaft (Joint-Stock Company)
AGOA	Africa Growth and Opportunity Act
AH	anno Hegirae
a.i.	ad interim
AID	(US) Agency for International Development
AIDS	acquired immunodeficiency syndrome
AK	Alaska
Al.	Aleja (Alley, Avenue)
AL	Alabama
ALADI	Asociación Latinoamericana de Integración
Alt.	Alternate
AM	Amplitude Modulation
a.m.	ante meridiem (before noon)
amalg.	amalgamated
Apdo	Apartado (Post Box)
APEC	Asia-Pacific Economic Co-operation
approx.	approximately
Apt	Apartment
AR	Arkansas
ARV	advanced retroviral
AŞ	Anonim Şirketi (Joint-Stock Company)
A/S	Aktieselskab (Joint-Stock Company)
ASEAN	Association of South East Asian Nations
asscn	association
assoc.	associate
ASSR	Autonomous Soviet Socialist Republic
asst	assistant
AU	African Union
Aug.	August
auth.	authorized
av., Ave	Avenija, Avenue
Av., Avda	Avenida (Avenue)
Avv.	Avvocato (Lawyer)
AZ	Arizona
b.b.	bez broja (without number)
BC	British Columbia
BC	before Christ
Bd	Board
Bd, Bld, Blv., Blvd	Boulevard
b/d	barrels per day
BFPO	British Forces' Post Office
Bhd	Berhad (Public Limited Company)
Bldg	Building
blk	block
Blvr	Bulevar
BP	Boîte postale (Post Box)
br.(s)	branch(es)
Brig.	Brigadier

BSE	bovine spongiform encephalopathy
BSEC	(Organization of the) Black Sea Economic Co-operation
bte	boîte (box)
Bul.	Bulvar (boulevard)
bulv.	bulvarīs (boulevard)
C	Centigrade
c.	circa; cuadra(s) (block(s))
CA	California
CACM	Central American Common Market
Cad.	Caddesi (Street)
CAP	Common Agricultural Policy
cap.	capital
Capt.	Captain
CAR	Central African Republic
CARICOM	Caribbean Community and Common Market
CBSS	Council of Baltic Sea States
CCL	Caribbean Congress of Labour
Cdre	Commodore
CEMAC	Communauté économique et monétaire de l'Afrique centrale
Cen.	Central
CEO	Chief Executive Officer
CET	common external tariff
CFA	Communauté Financière Africaine; Coopération Financière en Afrique centrale
CFE	Treaty on Conventional Armed Forces in Europe
CFP	Common Fisheries Policy; Communauté française du Pacifique; Comptoirs français du Pacifique
Chair.	Chairman/person/woman
Chih.	Chihuahua
CI	Channel Islands
Cia	Companhia
Cía	Compañía
Cie	Compagnie
c.i.f.	cost, insurance and freight
C-in-C	Commander-in-Chief
circ.	circulation
CIS	Commonwealth of Independent States
CJD	Creutzfeldt-Jakob disease
cm	centimetre(s)
cnr	corner
CO	Colorado
Co	Company; County
c/o	care of
Coah.	Coahuila
Col	Colonel
Col.	Colima; Colonia
COMESA	Common Market for Eastern and Southern Africa
Comm.	Commission; Commendatore
Commdr	Commander
Commdt	Commandant
Commr	Commissioner
Cond.	Condominio
Conf	Confederation
confs	conferences
Cont.	Contador (Accountant)
COO	Chief Operating Officer
COP	Conference of (the) Parties
Corp.	Corporate
Corpn	Corporation
CP	Case Postale, Caixa Postal, Casella Postale (Post Box); Communist Party
C por A	Compañía por Acciones (Joint Stock Company)
CPOB	Central Post Office Box

CPSU	Communist Party of the Soviet Union
Cres.	Crescent
CSCE	Conference on Security and Cooperation in Europe
CSTAL	Confederación Sindical de los Trabajadores de América Latina
CT	Connecticut
CTCA	Confederación de Trabajadores Centro-americanos
Cttee	Committee
cu	cubic
cwt	hundredweight
DC	District of Columbia; Distrito Capital; Distrito Central
d.d.	delniška družba, dioničko društvo (joint stock company)
DE	Delaware; Departamento Estatal
Dec.	December
Del.	Delegación
Dem.	Democrat; Democratic
Dep.	Deputy
dep.	deposits
Dept	Department
devt	development
DF	Distrito Federal
Dgo	Durango
Diag.	Diagonal
Dir	Director
Div.	Division(al)
DM	Deutsche Mark
DMZ	demilitarized zone
DNA	deoxyribonucleic acid
DN	Distrito Nacional
Doc.	Docent
Dott.	Dottore/essa
DPRK	Democratic People's Republic of Korea
Dr	Doctor
Dr.	Drive
Dra	Doctora
Dr Hab.	Doktor Habilitowany (Assistant Professor)
DRC	Democratic Republic of the Congo
DR-CAFTA	Dominican Republic-Central American Free Trade Agreement
Drs	Doctorandus
DU	depleted uranium
dwt	dead weight tons
E	East; Eastern
EAC	East African Community
EBRD	European Bank for Reconstruction and Development
EC	European Community
ECA	(United Nations) Economic Commission for Africa
ECE	(United Nations) Economic Commission for Europe
ECF	Extended Credit Facility
ECLAC	(United Nations) Economic Commission for Latin America and the Caribbean
ECO	Economic Co-operation Organization
Econ.	Economics; Economist
ECOSOC	(United Nations) Economic and Social Council
ECOWAS	Economic Community of West African States
ECU	European Currency Unit

ix

ABBREVIATIONS

Edif.	Edificio (Building)
edn	edition
EEA	European Economic Area
EFTA	European Free Trade Association
e.g.	exempli gratia (for example)
EIB	European Investment Bank
EMS	European Monetary System
EMU	Economic and Monetary Union
eMv	electron megavolt
Eng.	Engineer; Engineering
EP	Empresa Pública
ERM	Exchange Rate Mechanism
ESACA	Emisora de Capital Abierto Sociedad Anónima
Esc.	Escuela; Escudos; Escritorio
ESCAP	(United Nations) Economic and Social Commission for Asia and the Pacific
ESCWA	(United Nations) Economic and Social Commission for Western Asia
esq.	esquina (corner)
est.	established; estimate; estimated
etc.	et cetera
EU	European Union
eV	eingetragener Verein
excl.	excluding
exec.	executive
Ext.	Extension
F	Fahrenheit
f.	founded
FAO	Food and Agriculture Organization
f.a.s.	free alongside ship
FDI	foreign direct investment
Feb.	February
Fed.	Federal; Federation
feds	federations
FL	Florida
FM	frequency modulation
fmr(ly)	former(ly)
f.o.b.	free on board
Fr	Father
Fr.	Franc
Fri.	Friday
FRY	Federal Republic of Yugoslavia
ft	foot (feet)
FTA	free trade agreement/area
FYRM	former Yugoslav republic of Macedonia
g	gram(s)
g.	gatve (street)
GA	Georgia
GATT	General Agreement on Tariffs and Trade
GCC	Gulf Co-operation Council
Gdns	Gardens
GDP	gross domestic product
GEF	Gobal Environment Facility
Gen.	General
GeV	giga electron volts
GM	genetically modified
GmbH	Gesellschaft mit beschränkter Haftung (Limited Liability Company)
GMO(s)	genetically modified organism(s)
GMT	Greenwich Mean Time
GNI	gross national income
GNP	gross national product
Gov.	Governor
Govt	Government
GPOB	General Post Office Box
Gro	Guerrero
grt	gross registered tons
GSM	Global System for Mobile Communications
Gto	Guanajuato
GWh	gigawatt hour(s)
ha	hectares
HD	high-definition
HDI	Human Development Index
HDTV	high-definition television
HE	His/Her Eminence; His/Her Excellency
hf	hlutafelag (Limited Company)
HI	Hawaii
HIPC	heavily indebted poor country
HIV	human immunodeficiency virus
hl	hectolitre(s)
HLTF	High Level Task Force
HM	His/Her Majesty
Hon.	Honorary, Honourable
HPAI	highly pathogenic avian influenza
HQ	Headquarters
HRH	His/Her Royal Highness
HSC	Harmonized System Classification
HSH	His/Her Serene Highness
Hwy	Highway
IA	Iowa
IBRD	International Bank for Reconstruction and Development
ICC	International Chamber of Commerce; International Criminal Court
ICRC	International Committee of the Red Cross
ICT	information and communication technology
ICTR	International Criminal Tribunal for Rwanda
ICTY	International Criminal Tribunal for the former Yugoslavia
ID	Idaho
IDA	International Development Association
IDB	Inter-American Development Bank
IDPs	internally displaced persons
i.e.	id est (that is to say)
IFC	International Finance Corporation
IGAD	Intergovernmental Authority on Development
IHL	International Humanitarian Law
IL	Illinois
ILO	International Labour Organization/Office
IMF	International Monetary Fund
IML	International Migration Law
in (ins)	inch (inches)
IN	Indiana
Inc, Incorp. Incd	Incorporated
incl.	including
Ind.	Independent
INF	Intermediate-Range Nuclear Forces
Ing.	Engineer
Insp.	Inspector
Int.	International
Inzå.	Engineer
IP	intellectual property
IPU	Inter-Parliamentary Union
Ir	Engineer
IRF	International Road Federation
irreg.	irregular
Is	Islands
ISIC	International Standard Industrial Classification
IT	information technology
ITU	International Telecommunication Union
ITUC	International Trade Union Confederation
Iur.	Lawyer
IUU	illegal, unreported and unregulated
Jal.	Jalisco
Jan.	January
Jnr	Junior
Jr	Jonkheer (Esquire); Junior
Jt	Joint
Kav.	Kaveling (Plot)
kg	kilogram(s)
KG	Kommandit Gesellschaft (Limited Partnership)
kHz	kilohertz
KK	Kaien Kaisha (Limited Company)
km	kilometre(s)
kom.	komnata (room)
kor.	korpus (block)
k'och.	k'ochasi (street)
KS	Kansas
küç	küçasi (street)
kv.	kvartal (apartment block); kvartira (apartment)
kW	kilowatt(s)
kWh	kilowatt hour(s)
KY	Kentucky
LA	Louisiana
lauk	laukums (square)
lb	pound(s)
LDCs	Least Developed Countries
Lic.	Licenciado
Licda	Licenciada
LLC	Limited Liability Company
LNG	liquefied natural gas
LPG	liquefied petroleum gas
Lt, Lieut	Lieutenant
Ltd	Limited
m	metre(s)
m.	million
MA	Massachusetts
Maj.	Major
Man.	Manager; managing
MB	Manitoba
mbH	mit beschränkter Haftung (with limited liability)
MD	Maryland
MDG	Millennium Development Goal
MDRI	multilateral debt relief initiative
ME	Maine
Me	Maître
mem.(s)	member(s)
MEP	Member of the European Parliament
Mercosul	Mercado Comum do Sul (Southern Common Market)
Mercosur	Mercado Común del Sur (Southern Common Market)
Méx.	México
MFN	most favoured nation
mfrs	manufacturers
Mgr	Monseigneur; Monsignor
MHz	megahertz
MI	Michigan
MIA	missing in action
Mich.	Michoacán
MIGA	Multilateral Investment Guarantee Agency
Mil.	Military
Mlle	Mademoiselle
mm	millimetre(s)
Mme	Madame
MN	Minnesota
mnt.	mante (road)
MO	Missouri
Mon.	Monday
Mor.	Morelos
MOU	memorandum of understanding
movt	movement
MP	Member of Parliament
MS	Mississippi
MSS	Manuscripts
MT	Montana
MW	megawatt(s); medium wave
MWh	megawatt hour(s)

x

ABBREVIATIONS

N	North; Northern	pl.	platz; place; ploshchad (square)	SAECA	Sociedad Anónima Emisora de Capital Abierto
n.a.	not available	PLC	Public Limited Company	SAR	Special Administrative Region
nab.	naberezhnaya (embankment, quai)	PLO	Palestine Liberation Organization	SARL	Sociedade Anônima de Responsabilidade Limitada (Joint-Stock Company of Limited Liability)
NAFTA	North American Free Trade Agreement	p.m.	post meridiem (after noon)		
nám.	náměstí (square)	PMB	Private Mail Bag		
Nat.	National	PNA	Palestinian National Authority		
NATO	North Atlantic Treaty Organization	POB	Post Office Box	SARS	Severe Acute Respiratory Syndrome
		pp.	pages		
Nay.	Nayarit	PPP	purchasing-power parity	Sat.	Saturday
NB	New Brunswick	PQ	Québec	SC	South Carolina
NC	North Carolina	PR	Puerto Rico	SD	South Dakota
NCD	National Capital District	pr.	prospekt, prospekti (avenue)	Sdn Bhd	Sendirian Berhad (Private Limited Company)
NCO	non-commissioned officer	Pres.	President		
ND	North Dakota	PRGF	Poverty Reduction and Growth Facility	SDR(s)	Special Drawing Right(s)
NE	Nebraska; North-East			SE	South-East
NEPAD	New Partnership for Africa's Development	Prin.	Principal	Sec.	Secretary
		Prof.	Professor	Secr.	Secretariat
		Propr	Proprietor	Sen.	Senior; Senator
NGO	non-governmental organization	Prov.	Province; Provincial; Provinciale (Dutch)	Sept.	September
NH	New Hampshire			SER	Sua Eccellenza Reverendissima (His Eminence)
NJ	New Jersey				
NL	Newfoundland and Labrador, Nuevo León	prov.	provulok (lane)	SFRY	Socialist Federal Republic of Yugoslavia
		PRSP	Poverty Reduction Strategy Paper		
NM	New Mexico			SGP	Stability and Growth Pact
NMP	net material product	PSI	Policy Support Instrument, Poverty Strategies Initiative	Sin.	Sinaloa
no	numéro, número (number)			SIS	Small(er) Island States
no.	number	pst.	puistotie (avenue)	SITC	Standard International Trade Classification
Nov.	November	PT	Perseroan Terbatas (Limited Company)		
NPT	Non-Proliferation Treaty			SJ	Society of Jesus
nr	near	Pte	Private; Puente (Bridge)	SK	Saskatchewan
nrt	net registered tons	Pty	Proprietary	Skt	Sankt (Saint)
NS	Nova Scotia	p.u.	paid up	SLP	San Luis Potosí
NSW	New South Wales	publ.	publication; published	SMEs	small and medium-sized enterprises
NT	Northwest Territories	Publr	Publisher		
NU	Nunavut Territory	Pue.	Puebla		
NV	Naamloze Vennootschap (Limited Company); Nevada	Pvt	Private	s/n	sin número (without number)
				Soc.	Society
				Sok.	Sokak (Street)
NW	North-West	QC	Québec	Son.	Sonora
NY	New York	QIP	Quick Impact Project	Șos.	Șosea (Road)
NZ	New Zealand	Qld	Queensland	SP	São Paulo
		Qro	Querétaro	SpA	Società per Azioni (Joint-Stock Company)
		Q. Roo	Quintana Roo		
OAPEC	Organization of Arab Petroleum Exporting Countries	q.v.	quod vide (to which refer)	Sq.	Square
				sq	square (in measurements)
OAS	Organization of American States			Sr	Senior; Señor
OAU	Organization of African Unity	Rag.	Ragioniere (Accountant)	Sra	Señora
Oax.	Oaxaca	Rd	Road	Srl	Società a Responsabilità Limitata (Limited Company)
Oct.	October	R(s)	rand; rupee(s)		
OECD	Organisation for Economic Cooperation and Development			SRSG	Special Representative of the UN Secretary-General
		REC	regional economic communities		
OECS	Organisation of Eastern Caribbean States	reg., regd	register; registered	SSR	Soviet Socialist Republic
		reorg.	reorganized	St	Saint, Sint; Street
Of.	Oficina (Office)	Rep.	Republic; Republican; Representative	Sta	Santa
OH	Ohio			Ste	Sainte
OIC	Organization of the Islamic Conference			STI(s)	sexually transmitted infection(s)
		Repub.	Republic	str.	strada, stradă (street)
		res	reserve(s)	str-la	stradelă (street)
OK	Oklahoma	retd	retired	subs.	subscribed; subscriptions
ON	Ontario	Rev.	Reverend	Sun.	Sunday
OPEC	Organization of the Petroleum Exporting Countries	RI	Rhode Island	Supt	Superintendent
		RJ	Rio de Janeiro	SUV	sports utility vehicle
opp.	opposite	Rm	Room	sv.	Saint
OR	Oregon	RN	Royal Navy	SW	South-West
ORB	OPEC Reference Basket	ro-ro	roll-on roll-off		
Org.	Organization	RP	Recette principale		
ORIT	Organización Regional Interamericana de Trabajadores	Rp.(s)	rupiah(s)		
		Rpto	Reparto (Estate)		
		RSFSR	Russian Soviet Federative Socialist Republic	Tab.	Tabasco
OSCE	Organization for Security and Cooperation in Europe			Tamps	Tamaulipas
		Rt	Right	TAŞ	Turkiye Anonim Șirketi (Turkish Joint-Stock Company)
				Tas	Tasmania
p.	page	S	South; Southern; San	TD	Teachta Dàla (Member of Parliament)
p.a.	per annum	SA	Société Anonyme, Sociedad Anónima (Limited Company); South Australia		
PA	Palestinian Authority; Pennsylvania			tech., techn.	technical
				tel.	telephone
Parl.	Parliament(ary)	SAARC	South Asian Association for Regional Co-operation	TEU	20-ft equivalent unit
per.	pereulok (lane, alley)			Thur.	Thursday
PE	Prince Edward Island	SACN	South American Community of Nations	TN	Tennessee
Perm. Rep.	Permanent Representative			tř	třída (avenue)
PF	Postfach (Post Box)	SADC	Southern African Development Community	Treas.	Treasurer
PICTs	Pacific Island countries and territories			Tue.	Tuesday
		SA de CV	Sociedad Anónima de Capital Variable (Variable Capital Company)	TV	television
PK	Posta Kutusu (Post Box)			TWh	terawatt hour(s)
Pl.	Plac, Plads (square)			TX	Texas

ABBREVIATIONS

u.	utca (street)	UNODC	United Nations Office on Drugs and Crime	Vn	Veien (Street)
u/a	unit of account			vol.(s)	volume(s)
UAE	United Arab Emirates	UNRWA	United Nations Relief and Works Agency for Palestine Refugees in the Near East	VT	Vermont
UEE	Unidade Económica Estatal			vul.	vulitsa, vulytsa (street)
UEMOA	Union économique et monetaire ouest-africaine	UNWTO	World Tourism Organization		
UK	United Kingdom	Urb.	Urbanización (District)	W	West; Western
ul.	ulica, ulitsa (street)	US	United States	WA	Washington (State); Western Australia
UM	ouguiya	USA	United States of America		
UN	United Nations	USAID	United States Agency for International Development	Wed.	Wednesday
UNAIDS	United Nations Joint Programme on HIV/AIDS			WEU	Western European Union
		USSR	Union of Soviet Socialist Republics	WFP	World Food Programme
UNCTAD	United Nations Conference on Trade and Development			WFTU	World Federation of Trade Unions
		UT	Utah		
UNDP	United Nations Development Programme			WHO	World Health Organization
				WI	Wisconsin
UNEP	United Nations Environment Programme	VA	Virginia	WSSD	World Summit on Sustainable Development
		VAT	value-added tax		
UNESCO	United Nations Educational, Scientific and Cultural Organization	VEB	Volkseigener Betrieb (Public Company)	WTO	World Trade Organization
				WV	West Virginia
		v-CJD	new variant Creutzfeldt-Jakob disease	WY	Wyoming
UNHCHR	UN High Commissioner for Human Rights				
		Ven.	Venerable		
UNHCR	United Nations High Commissioner for Refugees	Ver.	Veracruz	yr	year
		VHF	Very High Frequency	YT	Yukon Territory
UNICEF	United Nations Children's Fund	VI	(US) Virgin Islands	Yuc.	Yucatán
Univ.	University	Vic	Victoria		

INTERNATIONAL TELEPHONE CODES

To make international calls to telephone and fax numbers listed in *The Europa World Year Book*, dial the international access code of the country from which you are calling, followed by the appropriate country code for the organization you wish to call (listed below), followed by the area code (if applicable) and telephone or fax number listed in the entry.

	Country code	+ or − GMT*
Afghanistan	93	+4½
Åland Islands	358	+2
Albania	355	+1
Algeria	213	+1
American Samoa	1 684	−11
Andorra	376	+1
Angola	244	+1
Anguilla	1 264	−4
Antigua and Barbuda	1 268	−4
Argentina	54	−3
Armenia	374	+4
Aruba	297	−4
Ascension Island	247	0
Australia	61	+8 to +10
Austria	43	+1
Azerbaijan	994	+5
Bahamas	1 242	−5
Bahrain	973	+3
Bangladesh	880	+6
Barbados	1 246	−4
Belarus	375	+2
Belgium	32	+1
Belize	501	−6
Benin	229	+1
Bermuda	1 441	−4
Bhutan	975	+6
Bolivia	591	−4
Bonaire	599	−4
Bosnia and Herzegovina	387	+1
Botswana	267	+2
Brazil	55	−3 to −4
British Indian Ocean Territory (Diego Garcia)	246	+5
British Virgin Islands	1 284	−4
Brunei	673	+8
Bulgaria	359	+2
Burkina Faso	226	0
Burundi	257	+2
Cambodia	855	+7
Cameroon	237	+1
Canada	1	−3 to −8
Cape Verde	238	−1
Cayman Islands	1 345	−5
Central African Republic	236	+1
Ceuta	34	+1
Chad	235	+1
Chile	56	−4
China, People's Republic	86	+8
Christmas Island	61	+7
Cocos (Keeling) Islands	61	+6½
Colombia	57	−5
Comoros	269	+3
Congo, Democratic Republic	243	+1
Congo, Republic	242	+1
Cook Islands	682	−10
Costa Rica	506	−6
Côte d'Ivoire	225	0
Croatia	385	+1
Cuba	53	−5
Curaçao	599	−4
Cyprus	357	+2
Czech Republic	420	+1
Denmark	45	+1
Djibouti	253	+3

	Country code	+ or − GMT*
Dominica	1 767	−4
Dominican Republic	1 809	−4
Ecuador	593	−5
Egypt	20	+2
El Salvador	503	−6
Equatorial Guinea	240	+1
Eritrea	291	+3
Estonia	372	+2
Ethiopia	251	+3
Falkland Islands	500	−4
Faroe Islands	298	0
Fiji	679	+12
Finland	358	+2
France	33	+1
French Guiana	594	−3
French Polynesia	689	−9 to −10
Gabon	241	+1
Gambia	220	0
Georgia	995†	+4
Germany	49	+1
Ghana	233	0
Gibraltar	350	+1
Greece	30	+2
Greenland	299	−1 to −4
Grenada	1 473	−4
Guadeloupe	590	−4
Guam	1 671	+10
Guatemala	502	−6
Guernsey	44	0
Guinea	224	0
Guinea-Bissau	245	0
Guyana	592	−4
Haiti	509	−5
Honduras	504	−6
Hong Kong	852	+8
Hungary	36	+1
Iceland	354	0
India	91	+5½
Indonesia	62	+7 to +9
Iran	98	+3½
Iraq	964	+3
Ireland	353	0
Isle of Man	44	0
Israel	972	+2
Italy	39	+1
Jamaica	1 876	−5
Japan	81	+9
Jersey	44	0
Jordan	962	+2
Kazakhstan	7	+6
Kenya	254	+3
Kiribati	686	+12 to +13
Korea, Democratic People's Republic (North Korea)	850	+9
Korea, Republic (South Korea)	82	+9
Kosovo	381‡	+3
Kuwait	965	+3
Kyrgyzstan	996	+5
Laos	856	+7
Latvia	371	+2
Lebanon	961	+2
Lesotho	266	+2
Liberia	231	0
Libya	218	+1

xiii

INTERNATIONAL TELEPHONE CODES

	Country code	+ or – GMT*
Liechtenstein	423	+1
Lithuania	370	+2
Luxembourg	352	+1
Macao	853	+8
Macedonia, former Yugoslav republic	389	+1
Madagascar	261	+3
Malawi	265	+2
Malaysia	60	+8
Maldives	960	+5
Mali	223	0
Malta	356	+1
Marshall Islands	692	+12
Martinique	596	–4
Mauritania	222	0
Mauritius	230	+4
Mayotte	262	+3
Melilla	34	+1
Mexico	52	–6 to –7
Micronesia, Federated States	691	+10 to +11
Moldova	373	+2
Monaco	377	+1
Mongolia	976	+7 to +9
Montenegro	382	+1
Montserrat	1 664	–4
Morocco	212	0
Mozambique	258	+2
Myanmar	95	+6½
Namibia	264	+2
Nauru	674	+12
Nepal	977	+5¾
Netherlands	31	+1
New Caledonia	687	+11
New Zealand	64	+12
Nicaragua	505	–6
Niger	227	+1
Nigeria	234	+1
Niue	683	–11
Norfolk Island	672	+11½
Northern Mariana Islands	1 670	+10
Norway	47	+1
Oman	968	+4
Pakistan	92	+5
Palau	680	+9
Palestinian Autonomous Areas	970 or 972	+2
Panama	507	–5
Papua New Guinea	675	+10
Paraguay	595	–4
Peru	51	–5
Philippines	63	+8
Pitcairn Islands	872	–8
Poland	48	+1
Portugal	351	0
Puerto Rico	1 787	–4
Qatar	974	+3
Réunion	262	+4
Romania	40	+2
Russian Federation	7	+2 to +11
Rwanda	250	+2
Saba	599	–4
Saint-Barthélemy	590	–4
Saint Christopher and Nevis	1 869	–4
Saint Helena	290	0
Saint Lucia	1 758	–4
Saint-Martin	590	–4
Saint Pierre and Miquelon	508	–3
Saint Vincent and the Grenadines	1 784	–4
Samoa	685	–11§
San Marino	378	+1
São Tomé and Príncipe	239	0

	Country code	+ or – GMT*
Saudi Arabia	966	+3
Senegal	221	0
Serbia	381	+1
Seychelles	248	+4
Sierra Leone	232	0
Singapore	65	+8
Sint Eustatius	599	–4
Sint Maarten	599	–4
Slovakia	421	+1
Slovenia	386	+1
Solomon Islands	677	+11
Somalia	252	+3
South Africa	27	+2
Spain	34	+1
Sri Lanka	94	+5½
Sudan	249	+2
Suriname	597	–3
Svalbard	47	+1
Swaziland	268	+2
Sweden	46	+1
Switzerland	41	+1
Syria	963	+2
Taiwan	886	+8
Tajikistan	992	+5
Tanzania	255	+3
Thailand	66	+7
Timor-Leste	670	+9
Togo	228	0
Tokelau	690	–10
Tonga	676	+13
Trinidad and Tobago	1 868	–4
Tristan da Cunha	290	0
Tunisia	216	+1
Turkey	90	+2
'Turkish Republic of Northern Cyprus'	90 392	+2
Turkmenistan	993	+5
Turks and Caicos Islands	1 649	–5
Tuvalu	688	+12
Uganda	256	+3
Ukraine	380	+2
United Arab Emirates	971	+4
United Kingdom	44	0
United States of America	1	–5 to –10
United States Virgin Islands	1 340	–4
Uruguay	598	–3
Uzbekistan	998	+5
Vanuatu	678	+11
Vatican City	39	+1
Venezuela	58	–4½
Viet Nam	84	+7
Wallis and Futuna Islands	681	+12
Yemen	967	+3
Zambia	260	+2
Zimbabwe	263	+2

* The times listed compare the standard (winter) times in the various countries. Some countries adopt Summer (Daylight Saving) Time—i.e. +1 hour—for part of the year.

† Telephone numbers for Abkhazia use the country code for Russia and Kazakhstan (7).

‡ Mobile telephone numbers for Kosovo use either the country code for Monaco (377) or the country code for Slovenia (386).

§ Legislation was pending in 2011 to advance to GMT +13, effective from the end of that year.

Note: Telephone and fax numbers using the Inmarsat ocean region code 870 are listed in full. No country or area code is required, but it is necessary to precede the number with the international access code of the country from which the call is made.

KAZAKHSTAN

Introductory Survey

LOCATION, CLIMATE, LANGUAGE, RELIGION, FLAG, CAPITAL

The Republic of Kazakhstan extends 1,900 km (1,200 miles) from the Volga river in the west to the Altai mountains in the east, and about 1,300 km (800 miles) from the Siberian plain in the north to the Central Asian deserts in the south. To the south it borders Turkmenistan, Uzbekistan and Kyrgyzstan. To the east the border is with the People's Republic of China. There is a long border in the north with Russia and a coastline of 2,320 km (1,400 miles) on the Caspian Sea in the south-west. The climate is of a strongly continental type, but there are wide variations throughout the territory. Average temperatures in January range from −18°C (0°F) in the north to −3°C (27°F) in the south. In July average temperatures are 19°C (66°F) in the north and 28°C–30°C (82°F–86°F) in the south. Average annual rainfall in mountainous regions reaches 1,600 mm (63 ins), whereas in the central desert areas it is less than 100 mm (4 ins). The state language is Kazakh; however, Russian is employed officially in state and local government bodies. The predominant religion is Islam, most ethnic Kazakhs being Sunni Muslims of the Hanafi school. Other ethnic groups have their own religious communities, notably the (Christian) Russian Orthodox Church, which is attended mainly by Slavs. The national flag (proportions 1 by 2) consists of a light blue field, at the centre of which is a yellow sun (a disc surrounded by 32 rays), framed by the wings of a flying eagle, also in yellow, with a vertical stripe of national ornamentation in yellow near the hoist. In November 1997 the capital was moved from Almatı to Aqmola (formerly Tselinograd); the city was renamed Astana in 1998.

CONTEMPORARY POLITICAL HISTORY

Historical Context

After the February Revolution and the Bolshevik coup in Russia in 1917, there was civil war throughout Kazakhstan, which had come under Russian control in the first half of the 18th century. Bolshevik forces finally overcame those of the White Army, foreign interventionists and local nationalists. In 1920 the Kyrgyz Autonomous Soviet Socialist Republic (ASSR) was created within the Russian Soviet Federative Socialist Republic (the Russian Federation): the Kazakhs were known to the Russians as Kyrgyz, to distinguish them from the unrelated Cossacks. In 1925 the Kyrgyz ASSR was renamed the Kazakh ASSR; the Karakalpak region (Qoraqalpog'iston, now in Uzbekistan) was detached in 1930, and became an autonomous republic within the Uzbek Soviet Socialist Republic (SSR) in 1936. In December 1936 the Kazakh ASSR became a full Union Republic of the USSR, as the Kazakh SSR.

Under Soviet rule parts of Kazakhstan were heavily industrialized. However, more than 1m. people were estimated to have died as a result of the starvation that accompanied the campaign in the early 1930s to collectivize agriculture and settle nomadic peoples. Many of those deported from parts of the USSR during the Second World War (including Germans, Crimean Tatars, Baltic and Caucasian peoples) were sent to the Republic. During Nikita Khrushchev's period in office as Soviet leader (1953–64) large areas of previously uncultivated land in Kazakhstan were transformed into arable land. This, along with intensive industrialization, and the development of nuclear-testing sites and the Baikonur space centre brought large numbers of ethnic Russians to Kazakhstan; the proportion of Russians increased from 19.7% of the population in 1926 to 42.7% in 1959.

In June 1989 Nursultan Nazarbaev, Chairman of the republican Council of Ministers since March 1984, was appointed First Secretary of the Communist Party of Kazakhstan (CPK). Political and administrative changes were instituted in September 1989: a permanent Supreme Kenges (Supreme Council or Supreme Soviet—legislature) was to be established, and elections were to be conducted on a multi-candidate basis. The state duties hitherto held by the First Secretary of the CPK were transferred to the Chairman of the Supreme Kenges, to which post Nazarbaev was elected in February 1990. Many candidates stood unopposed at elections to the Supreme Kenges in March, and the system of reserved seats for CPK-affiliated organizations was retained, resulting in a substantial communist majority. In April the body elected Nazarbaev the first President of Kazakhstan.

On 25 October 1990 the Supreme Kenges declared its sovereignty, asserting republican control over natural resources and the economy. Nazarbaev strongly supported a redefinition of the respective all-Union and republican powers, and the Kazakhstani Government participated in discussions on the new Union Treaty in early 1991, although Nazarbaev also sought economic sovereignty for Kazakhstan, where some 90% of enterprises were under all-Union control.

In the referendum on the future of the USSR conducted in nine Soviet republics in March 1991, almost 90% of the electorate voted in Kazakhstan, of whom 94% endorsed the proposal to preserve the USSR as a 'union of sovereign states'. In June the Supreme Kenges voted, in principle, to adopt a draft union treaty. Kazakhstan was to sign the treaty in August, but the event was forestalled by an attempted coup, led by conservative communists, in Moscow, the Soviet and Russian capital. As the coup attempt collapsed, Nazarbaev resigned from the Politburo and Central Committee of the Communist Party of the Soviet Union (CPSU), in protest at the open support granted to the putschists by the CPSU leadership. The CPK was ordered to cease activities in state and government organs, and in September the party withdrew from the CPSU; elements from the party went on to form the Socialist Party of Kazakhstan (SPK).

On 1 December 1991 Nazarbaev was elected unopposed as President of Kazakhstan in direct popular elections. On 8 December the leaders of Russia, Ukraine and Belarus signed an agreement establishing the Commonwealth of Independent States (CIS, see p. 238). On 16 December Kazakhstan became the last of the republics to declare independence from the USSR, as the Republic of Kazakhstan. The country became a co-founder of the CIS on 21 December, when the leaders of 11 former Soviet republics met in Almatı.

Domestic Political Affairs

The Constitution, adopted in January 1993, invoked legislation adopted in September 1989, denoting Kazakh as the state language and Russian as a language of inter-ethnic communication. The document required that the President be fluent in Kazakh. Meanwhile, increased emigration, particularly by ethnic Germans (more than 300,000 of whom left Kazakhstan in the early 1990s) and Russians, was accompanied, albeit on a much smaller scale, by the return of ethnic Kazakhs from Kyrgyzstan, Mongolia, Tajikistan and Turkmenistan.

In June 1992 some 5,000 people demonstrated in Almatı against continued communist predominance in the Government and Supreme Kenges, demanding the formation of a new, coalition administration. In October the three most prominent nationalist opposition parties (the Freedom—Azat movement, the Republican Party and the Jeltoqsan National Democratic Party) united to form the Republican Party—Freedom (RP—F). The Union of National Unity of Kazakhstan was established in February 1993, with the declared aim of promoting social harmony and countering radical nationalism. Nazarbaev (who held no party affiliation) became Chairman of the Union, which was reorganized as a political party, the People's Unity Party (PUP), later in 1993.

In December 1993 the Supreme Kenges voted to dissolve itself and to grant Nazarbaev the power to rule by decree pending elections to a new, smaller, legislature. Kazakhstan's first multiparty elections were duly held on 7 March 1994, with the participation of 74% of the electorate; a number of irregularities were reported by international observers. The PUP obtained 33 seats, which, when combined with the 42 seats won by candidates from the so-called 'President's List' (candidates nominated by Nazarbaev) and those of pro-Nazarbaev independents, ensured that Nazarbaev's supporters emerged as the strongest force in the 177-member assembly. The Confederation of Kazakhstani Trade Unions (CKTU) won 11 seats, the People's Congress Party of Kazakhstan (PCPK) nine and the SPK eight.

KAZAKHSTAN

The CPK was granted legal status in March. In that month the CKTU, the SPK and the PCPK formed an opposition bloc in the Supreme Kenges.

In May 1994 some 96 members of the Supreme Kenges endorsed a motion expressing no confidence in the Government's economic, social and legal policies, and in June Nazarbaev announced a major government reorganization. The Government of Sergei Tereshchenko (premier since 1991) resigned in October 1994, admitting its failure to reform the economy. Akejan Kajegeldin, an economist and First Deputy Prime Minister in the outgoing Council of Ministers, was appointed premier.

In February 1995 the Constitutional Court declared the results of the 1994 general election to be invalid, owing to procedural irregularities. In March the Government was forced to tender its resignation, on the grounds that it had been approved by an unconstitutional parliament (although it was subsequently reinstated virtually unchanged). Nazarbaev was thereby effectively empowered to rule by decree pending further legislative elections. At a national referendum on 29 April more than 95% of voters endorsed the extension of Nazarbaev's five-year mandate until 1 December 2000.

In May 1995 Nazarbaev ordered the establishment of a special council to prepare a new constitution. The final draft, which was approved by 89.1% of the electorate in a referendum on 30 August, preserved the President's extensive executive powers. The Supreme Kenges was replaced by a bicameral Parliament, comprising a 47-member Senat (Senate, 40 members of which were to be elected by regional administrations and seven appointed by the President) and a directly elected 67-member Majlis (Assembly). The Constitutional Court was replaced by a Constitutional Council, the rulings of which were to be subject to a presidential right of veto.

Indirect elections to the Senat took place on 5 December 1995. Direct elections were held to the Majlis on 9 December, with the participation of 80.7% of the electorate; further rounds of voting took place later in the month and in February 1996. Foreign observers reported procedural violations.

Popular dissatisfaction with the Government's economic and social policies became more pronounced in 1996. In April a new opposition movement, Citizen (Azamat), was established. Prolonged delays in payments of wages, owing to the insolvency of numerous state-owned enterprises, were a principal cause of strikes and unauthorized demonstrations throughout 1997 and early 1998, as was the ongoing reform of pensions legislation.

Meanwhile, in late 1996 the relocation of civil servants from Almatı to the northern city of Aqmola marked the beginning of the transfer of the capital city (in July 1994 the Supreme Kenges had approved a proposal by Nazarbaev to transfer the capital to Aqmola by 2000). In November 1997 the new capital was officially inaugurated by Nazarbaev, and a joint session of both chambers of Parliament was held for the first time in Aqmola in the following month. A ceremony was held in June 1998 to mark the official opening of the capital under the new name of Astana.

In March 1997, while Kajegeldin was out of the country, Nazarbaev undertook a major reorganization and rationalization of the state apparatus. The Ministry of Petroleum and Natural Gas was abolished and replaced by a new state company, KazakhOil. Seven government institutions, including the Ministries of Defence and of Internal Affairs, were directly subordinated to the President, and the structure of regional government was reorganized. In October Kajegeldin's resignation, ostensibly for health reasons, was announced; in the previous month a Russian newspaper had published an admission by Kajegeldin of his involvement, in the late 1980s, with the former Soviet state security service (KGB). Nazarbaev appointed Nurlan Balgymbaev, hitherto head of KazakhOil, as his replacement.

In January 1998 17 political parties and movements signed a 'memorandum on mutual understanding and co-operation', pledging their support for the President. In September Nazarbaev outlined proposals for political reforms, including amendments to electoral procedures and enhanced legislative powers. In October, however, a joint session of Parliament rejected Nazarbaev's proposed constitutional reforms, and instead voted to schedule a presidential election before the expiry of Nazarbaev's extended mandate in 2000 and to decrease the quota of votes required by parties in order to secure representation in the legislature, from 10% to 7%.

During November 1998 several opposition figures were deemed ineligible to contest the presidency by the Central Electoral Commission, in accordance with a presidential decree, enacted in May, which prevented those convicted of an administrative offence in the 12 months prior to an election from registering as a candidate. The most prominent disqualification was that of Kajegeldin, who had been widely regarded as Nazarbaev's principal rival, after he attended a meeting of an unauthorized political organization. Kajegeldin subsequently established a new political party, the Republican People's Party of Kazakhstan (RPPK). A number of other opposition parties were formed in late 1998 and early 1999, although many were prevented from registering. Among those to be accorded official status was the pro-presidential Fatherland party (Otan).

Nursultan Nazarbaev re-elected as President

The Organization for Security and Co-operation in Europe (OSCE, see p. 385) was among international bodies to express serious concern at the conduct of the presidential election, contested by four candidates on 10 January 1999. Nazarbaev was elected to a further term, with 81.0% of the votes cast by 88.3% of the registered electorate. A new Government, headed by Balgymbaev, was appointed later in the month.

In August 1999 the President of KazakhOil, Nurlan Kaparov, was dismissed, having been accused by Nazarbaev of having exceeded his powers. Earlier that month the Minister of Defence, Gen. Mukhtar Altynbaev, and the Chairman of the National Security Committee (KNB), Nurtai Abykaev, had been dismissed, after admitting responsibility for the attempted illegal sale of military aircraft to the Democratic People's Republic of Korea. In September Kajegeldin, who had been charged with tax evasion in April, was arrested at an airport in Moscow, but released following criticism of his detention by the OSCE. Owing to the outstanding charges against him, Kajegeldin, together with two other leading members of the RPPK, was barred from registering as a candidate for the parliamentary elections in October. (Further charges were brought against him in February 2000.)

In late September 1999 the RPPK announced that it would boycott the forthcoming elections to the Majlis, in protest at the severe restrictions imposed on opposition parties by the President, although some of the party's members were to stand as independents. In early October Balgymbaev resigned from the premiership and resumed his former position as President of KazakhOil. He was replaced as Prime Minister by Kasym-Jomart Tokaev, a former Minister of Foreign Affairs. A government reorganization followed. Elections to the Majlis (as well as to municipal and local councils) were held on 10 October. Sixty-five candidates from nine political parties contested 10 seats allocated, for the first time, according to a party-list system, while almost 500 candidates contested the remaining 67 single-mandate constituency seats. All of the 10 party-list seats were filled at the first round (four by Fatherland, and two by each of the CPK, the Agrarian Party of Kazakhstan—APK and the Civic Party of Kazakhstan), but only 20 of the 67 directly elected seats were filled, and a second round of voting was held on 24 October. Final results indicated that Fatherland was to be the largest political grouping in the new Majlis, with 23 seats; the Civic Party held 13. Three other parties achieved representation, and 34 independent candidates were elected. The rate of participation by voters was reported to be 62.6%. Observers from the OSCE cited numerous breaches of electoral law.

In June 2000 a law (confirmed by the Constitutional Court in July) was approved awarding Nazarbaev certain lifetime guarantees and rights. In September 2001 Kajegeldin, who had been tried *in absentia* on charges of abuse of power, tax evasion and the illegal possession of weapons, was sentenced to 10 years' imprisonment. In November Nazarbaev approved the resignation of Rahat Aliev (the husband of Nazarbaev's daughter, Darigha Nazarbaeva) as Deputy Chairman of the KNB, amid accusations of abuse of power. Persistent reports that Aliev and Nazarbaeva controlled the majority of Kazakhstan's media outlets and influenced their output prompted the Akim (Governor) of Pavlodar Oblast, Galymjan Jakiyanov, and a number of other prominent political and business figures, including the Deputy Prime Minister, Oraz Jandosov, to form a new political movement, the Democratic Choice of Kazakhstan (DCK), in late November. The DCK, which aimed to revive democratic reform, criticized the concentration of power among members of Nazarbaev's family and a small group of leading entrepreneurs. Tokaev subsequently announced that two attempts to assassinate the President had been averted, and threatened to tender his resignation from the premiership unless the President dismissed ministers whom he denounced as disloyal, owing to their involvement in the formation of the DCK. Jandosov and Alixan Baymenov (the Minister of Labour and Social Security) resigned shortly afterwards; Nazarbaev dismissed Jakiyanov on the same day. In December Altynbaev was reappointed Minister of Defence. In early 2002 the United Democratic Party was formed by the merger of the Citizen (Azamat) Democratic Party, the PCPK and the RPPK.

In January 2002 amendments to media legislation came into effect, which required 50% of all radio and television programmes to be broadcast in Kazakh, restricted the rebroadcast of foreign (mainly Russian) television programmes, and was intended to subject internet sites to the same controls as print media. In late January Tokaev announced his resignation. On 31 January a new Government, led by a former Deputy Prime Minister, Imangali Tasmagambetov, was installed; Tokaev was appointed State Secretary and Minister of Foreign Affairs. Meanwhile, divisions emerged within the DCK, prompting a number of its founding members, including Jandosov and Jakiyanov, to form a new party, the Bright Road Democratic Party of Kazakhstan (Bright Road—Ak Jol).

Also in March 2002 a warrant was issued for the arrest of Jakiyanov, on charges of abuse of power during his tenure as Akim of Pavlodar Oblast. He subsequently sought refuge in the French embassy until April, when agreement was reached between the Government and the ambassadors of France, Germany, the United Kingdom and the USA that Jakiyanov would be permitted to go free until an investigation into the allegations had been carried out. However, he was arrested shortly afterwards, in contravention of the agreement. In mid-May it was reported that Jakiyanov had been admitted to hospital following interrogation by security officials. Jakiyanov's trial commenced in July, and he was sentenced to a seven-year term in August.

In July 2002 Nazarbaev signed into law new legislation on political parties, which required a party to demonstrate that it had at least 50,000 members (rather than the previous 3,000), representing every administrative region of the country, in order to qualify for registration. In the same month a former Minister of Energy, Industry and Trade and founding member of the DCK, Mukhtar Ablyazov, was sentenced to six years' imprisonment, having been found guilty of abuse of office. In late August Nazarbaev reorganized the Government. On 8 October partial elections to fill 16 seats in the Senate were conducted; Fatherland remained the largest grouping in the chamber, accounting for 18 of the 47 senators.

In January 2003 it was reported that Jandosov had been appointed as an aide to President Nazarbaev, suggesting to many observers that Bright Road was in fact supportive of the incumbent leadership. In the same month the DCK's party registration was annulled by the Ministry of Justice, and in mid-January the establishment of a new opposition bloc, Democracy-Elections-Kazakhstan, was announced, with the aim of uniting those parties prevented from re-registering by the new legislation on political parties. By the end of the re-registration period in April, only seven parties had satisfied the criteria for registration.

In late January 2003 Sergei Duvanov, an independent journalist, was convicted of rape and sentenced to more than three years' imprisonment. He had been arrested in October 2002, shortly before he was due to travel to the USA to speak about press freedoms and human rights issues in Kazakhstan. Duvanov's conviction prompted the US embassy to express concern about judicial procedure during his trial. In February 2003 the European Parliament adopted a resolution condemning the sentences imposed on Duvanov and the opposition politicians Ablyazov and Jakiyanov, and demanding that an independent investigation into their trials be carried out. Ablyazov was pardoned in May, and subsequently announced his withdrawal from politics. (Duvanov was released in August 2004, and Jakiyanov was released on parole in January 2006.)

In May 2003 the Government defeated a parliamentary vote of no confidence. However, on 9 June Tasmagambetov tendered his resignation, after it emerged that the results of the no confidence vote had been falsified by supporters of the Government. A new Government, led by Danial Axmetov, a former Akim of Pavlodar Oblast, was appointed in June, which included most of the ministers of the outgoing administration.

In September 2003 Zautbek Turisbekov was appointed as Minister of Internal Affairs, after Nazarbaev decreed that the heads of the law-enforcement and security bodies should be civilian appointments. Elections to local councils took place on 20 September, with further rounds of voting in October–November. The OSCE was again critical of the conduct of the electoral process.

In October 2003 a new party, Mutual Help (Asar), led by Darigha Nazarbaeva, was officially registered. In March 2004 Nurtai Abykayev was appointed as Chairman of the Senat. In early May four political parties that had not been granted official registration were declared invalid by a court ruling: Kazakh Ely, the Republican People's Party of Kazakhstan, the Azamat Party and the People's Congress of Kazakhstan. However, in mid-June the Ministry of Justice officially registered the Communist People's Party of Kazakhstan and the Democratic Party of Kazakhstan (DPK).

The 2004 legislative elections

On 19 September 2004 elections took place to the Majlis, with 'run-off' elections held on 3 October in 22 constituencies. Fatherland emerged as the largest grouping, with 42 seats, giving it an absolute majority in the chamber. An electoral coalition formed by the APK and the Civic Party of Kazakhstan won 11 seats, while Mutual Help obtained four seats. Bright Road and the DPK each obtained one seat, and 18 non-partisan candidates were elected. The rate of participation by the electorate was 56.7% in the first round of voting and 45.2% in the second round. Monitors from the OSCE criticized the conduct of the polls and media electoral coverage. Baymenov, now a member of Bright Road, and who was effectively the only opposition representative elected to the new legislature, subsequently announced that he would not take up his seat in the Majlis, alleging that the results of the elections had been falsified. The Chairman of the outgoing legislature, Jarmakhan Tuyakbay, resigned from Fatherland in mid-October in order to protest against the conduct of the elections. At the inaugural session of the new Majlis, held on 3 November, Oral Muxamejanov was elected Chairman.

In January 2005, following a declaration by the DCK in the previous month that it regarded the Kazakhstani Government to be illegitimate and urged non-violent civil disobedience, a court ordered that the party be dissolved, on the grounds that it had breached national security laws. Later in the month an unsanctioned rally was organized by Bright Road, the DCK and the CPK to protest against the closure of the party; in October 2004 the three parties had established a Co-ordinating Council of Opposition Democratic Forces of Kazakhstan, which aimed to draft a new constitution and create a more influential democratic movement in the country. In February 2005 the Co-ordinating Council of Opposition Democratic Forces of Kazakhstan announced that it was to establish a new national movement, to be known as For a Just Kazakhstan. In late March former members of the DCK announced the establishment of a new grouping, Forward (Alga), led by Asylbek Kojaxmetov. (However, in February 2006 the party was refused registration.) In late April 2005 another new party, Real Bright Road (Naghyz Ak Jol), held its founding congress, following divisions within Bright Road.

Meanwhile, in early December 2004 President Nazarbaev had issued a decree allowing village akims to be elected, and providing for 'experimental' elections of akims (who had hitherto been appointed) in several oblasts. Elections were duly held in villages and in four oblasts during 2005. Opposition representatives criticized the small number of administrative units covered, while the conduct of the elections to the oblast posts (in which all the incumbent candidates were returned to office, and in which all candidates had been nominated by the local authorities) was also criticized.

In April 2005 a law was introduced prohibiting demonstrations both during and immediately after elections. Concern was expressed at an announcement in July that the security agencies were preparing to use force against any popular unrest that might arise around the time of the forthcoming presidential election: the Minister of Internal Affairs, Turisbekov, asserted that the country would not allow a repetition of the events that had taken place in 2003–05 in Georgia, Ukraine and Kyrgyzstan (where popular revolts, following disputed elections, had led to the collapse of the incumbent regimes). In early August 2005 the For a Just Kazakhstan coalition, led by Tuyakbay, and comprising the CPK, Forward, the Generation Pensioners' Movement and Real Bright Road, was officially registered with the Ministry of Justice.

On 19 August 2005 partial elections to the Senate, originally scheduled to be held in December, took place. Fatherland secured 10 of the 16 seats contested; three seats were won by other pro-Nazarbaev parties and three by independents. In September the Majlis confirmed that a presidential election would be held in December, one year earlier than had been anticipated. Later in September the For a Just Kazakhstan movement elected Tuyakbay to stand as its single opposition candidate in the election.

In the presidential ballot, conducted on 4 December 2005, Nazarbaev was re-elected as President, with 91.2% of the votes cast, according to official results; his candidacy was supported by an electoral bloc, the Popular Coalition, which included Fatherland, Mutual Help, the DPK, the APK and the Civic Party of Kazakhstan. Of the four other candidates, Nazarbaev's closest rival was Tuyakbay, who received 6.6% of the votes. The rate of participation was 76.8%. Monitors from the OSCE declared that the conduct of the election had not satisfied international standards of democracy. On 18 January both chambers of Parliament unanimously approved Nazarbaev's nomination of Axmetov as Prime Minister. On the following day Nazarbaev approved a new Government, which retained most members of the previous administration. New appointments included those of Kärım Mäsımov, a longstanding presidential aide and prominent economist, as Deputy Prime Minister and Natalya Korzhova as Minister of Finance.

In February 2006 Altynbek Sarsenbaev, one of the leaders of Real Bright Road and a prominent supporter of Tuyakbay's presidential campaign, was shot dead in Almatı. A special commission was established to investigate the killing, which opposition representatives claimed had been politically motivated. Those detained on suspicion of involvement in the case included five KNB officials and the head of the administration of the Senat, Erjan Utembaev. The head of the KNB, Nartai Dutbaev, subsequently resigned as a result of the investigation. An unsanctioned protest rally was held in Almatı in late February, at which demonstrators urged the authorities to end the persecution of opposition representatives and to bring the perpetrators to trial. In March Real Bright Road was granted official registration.

In April 2006 Nazarbaev appointed Mäsımov to the additional post of Minister of the Economy and Budgetary Planning. (He was replaced in this position by Aslan Musin in October.) In June the trial began of 10 suspects charged with involvement in the killing of Sarsenbaev, including Utembaev. The conviction of the 10 defendants in August attracted international criticism; a former security officer received the death sentence, while Utembaev was sentenced to 20 years' imprisonment. In June the Majlis adopted a number of controversial legislative amendments designed to enforce greater regulation over media outlets, which, despite strong criticism from the OSCE, were endorsed by the Senat on 29 June and signed into law by the President on 4 July. Also in July, at an extraordinary Fatherland party congress in Astana, the party merged with Nazarbaeva's Mutual Help party, thereby consolidating support for Nazarbaev in the Majlis prior to forthcoming legislative elections. In December the APK and Civic Party also merged with Fatherland; the new party, known as Light Of The Fatherland (Nur Otan) controlled 57 seats in the Majlis.

Constitutional amendments and the 2007 elections

On 8 January 2007 Axmetov tendered his resignation as Prime Minister; it was reported that Nazarbaev had continually criticized him for poor organization and budget planning. On 10 January the Majlis voted to approve the President's nomination of Mäsımov as premier. Musin was appointed as Deputy Prime Minister (retaining the portfolio of the economy and budget planning), while Axmetov became Minister of Defence. Tokaev became Chairman of the Senat. In May Parliament approved extensive constitutional amendments, proposed by President Nazarbaev, strengthening the powers of an expanded Majlis, which was henceforth to approve prime ministerial appointments. The presidential term of office was to be reduced from seven to five years with effect from 2012, while the restriction on the incumbent President to two terms in office was to be removed.

In June 2007 Rahat Aliev, by then the Kazakhstani ambassador to Austria, was arrested in that country, after the Kazakhstani Government issued an arrest warrant against him in May for his alleged involvement in the kidnapping of two banking associates; Kazakhstan officially requested his extradition. (In January 2008 a district court in Almatı imposed in absentia a 20-year sentence of imprisonment on Aliev, who had claimed asylum in Austria, for his involvement in the creation of an organized criminal group and the abductions of the banking officials. In March, at a second trial in absentia, a military court sentenced Aliev to another 20 years' imprisonment for illegal possession of armaments and ammunition, misappropriation of property and planning a coup.)

On 20 June 2007 President Nazarbaev dissolved the Majlis and announced that legislative elections were to be brought forward to 18 August (two years earlier than scheduled). At the elections Light Of The Fatherland won 88.4% of votes cast, securing all 98 contested seats in the enlarged 107-member Majlis. None of the other six parties participating in the poll achieved the 7% minimum of votes required to gain representation in the chamber; the newly established National Social Democratic Party (NSDP) received 4.5% and Bright Road 3.1% of the votes cast. The leaders of the NSDP, Bright Road and the Communist People's Party refused to acknowledge the results and demanded that the poll be repeated. The OSCE announced that, despite some improvements, the poll had failed to meet international standards. In accordance with the amended Constitution, the Assembly of Nations of Kazakhstan (representing minority ethnic groups) elected the remaining nine deputies to the Majlis on 20 August. A reorganized Government was approved at the first session of the new Parliament on 2 September; most of the incumbent ministers retained their posts. Omırzaq Şökeev, hitherto Akim of Southern Kazakhstan Oblast, became the new Deputy Prime Minister, succeeding Musin, who was elected Chairman of the Majlis. In November a new Minister of Finance, Bolat Jämişev, was appointed, while Vladïmïr Bojko, hitherto First Deputy Chairman of the KNB, replaced the incumbent Minister of Emergency Situations, who had been dismissed over his suspected involvement in a corrupt land agreement during his tenure as Akim of Almatı. In February 2008, during a party congress, Real Bright Road was renamed Freedom (Azat).

In April 2008 Axmetjan Esımov, the hitherto Minister of Agriculture, was replaced by his deputy and was appointed Mayor of Almatı. In June public access to the Kazakh-language website of Radio Free Europe/Radio Liberty, which had been suspended by the authorities in April, was restored, following pressure from the OSCE, the USA, and other international representatives. In September it was reported that a former head of KazMunaiGaz and associate of Rahat Aliev, Şerik Burkitbaev, had been arrested and was to be charged with embezzlement. In the same month Alnur Musaev, formerly the head of the National Security Committee and an associate of Rahat Aliev, who had also received asylum in Austria after being sentenced in absentia to a 20-year term of imprisonment in the previous March, claimed there had been an abduction attempt against him. Elections were held to one-half of the 32 indirectly elected seats in the Senat on 4 October. In November the Majlis approved legislation restricting freedom of religious worship, which included provisions penalizing religious associations without registration, despite government pledges that the legislation would be drafted in consultation with the OSCE. In December several journalists associated with independent publications were assaulted.

In early 2009 former opposition leader Ablyazov fled to the United Kingdom, where he subsequently claimed political asylum, after the Kazakhstani authorities issued an arrest warrant against him for embezzlement in his previous post as Chairman of BTA Bank. In February plans by Freedom to organize a nationwide day of protests to demand the resignation of the Government were obstructed by refusal of the authorities to grant permission for the staging of demonstrations outside Almatı (where a rally proceeded); leaders of the party had proposed alternative economic stabilization proposals in response to the Government's perceived failure to address the effects of the international financial crisis. Also in February the Constitutional Court revoked the legislation on religion approved in November, after a report by the OSCE Office for Democratic Institutions and Human Rights criticized it as being incompatible with both democratic standards and Kazakhstan's commitments towards the OSCE (in view of its forthcoming assumption of the body's chairmanship). In early March a number of significant appointments of government ministers and other public officials were effected. Şökeev received the post of First Deputy Prime Minister, while Serık Axmetov, hitherto Minister of Transport, became a Deputy Prime Minister. In early April new appointments were announced to the posts of Minister of Justice and Minister of Internal Affairs. In April Nurlan Iskakov, a former Minister of Environmental Protection, and several other prominent senior officials were detained on suspicion of corruption. (In October Iskakov received a term of four years' imprisonment, having been convicted on charges of misusing state financial resources.) In May a book published by Aliev in Austria was banned in Kazakhstan, on the grounds that it was deemed to breach state secrecy. Later that month the KNB confirmed the arrest of the long-serving Chairman of the state-owned nuclear company Kazatomprom, Muxtar Jagishev, and three of his deputies; Jagishev was later charged with financial mismanagement and embezzlement. The removal of Danïal Axmetov as Minister of Defence in June was believed to be connected to a contract agreed between the ministry and an Israeli company in 2007, which had resulted in a substantial loss of government funds and had prompted the arrest of various senior officials on corruption charges. Adılbek Jaqsibekov, hitherto ambassador to Russia, was appointed as the new Minister of Defence. In September Qanatbek Sawdabaev was appointed as Minister of Foreign Affairs to succeed Marat Täjïn, who had been designated as an aide to the President.

In June 2009 Parliament adopted amendments to legislation on information and communications networks, under which all online resources were to be considered mass media, thus allowing officials to block websites deemed to be in violation of existing media regulations and to prosecute their owners. Although the OSCE urged Nazarbaev to veto the new provisions, they were enacted on 10 July. In September a sentence of four years' imprisonment imposed on human rights activist Yevgeny Jovtis, after he had been convicted of manslaughter resulting from a car accident, prompted protests from domestic and international human rights groups, and from the OSCE. Later that month the deputy leader of Light Of The Fatherland urged the adoption of legislation that would permit Nazarbaev to remain as President indefinitely. At a unification congress in October Freedom and the NSDP agreed to form a single party, to be known as the Freedom National Social Democratic Party, which was to be headed jointly by the leaders of the two constituent parties. In November a number of Kazakhstani non-governmental organizations issued statements criticizing Kazakhstan's assumption of the OSCE chairmanship, citing the recently revoked legislation restricting religious practice, the regulation of online information outlets, and restrictions on freedom of assembly. In November Serık Axmetov resigned from the post of Deputy Prime Minister, following his appointment as Akim of Qarağandi Oblast.

In March 2010 a substantial reorganization of the Government and other state agencies was implemented; as part of a reallocation of responsibilities, four new ministries, of Communication and Information, Economic Development and Trade, Industry and New Technologies, and of Oil and Gas, were established, while the Ministries of the Economy and Budgetary Planning, Industry and Trade, and Energy and Mineral Resources were abolished. Additionally, responsibility for relations between the Government and religious bodies was transferred from the Ministry of Justice to the Ministry of Culture. The hitherto Minister of Industry and Trade, Aset Isekeşev, was appointed to the posts of Deputy Prime Minister and Minister of Industry and New Technologies, while Sawat Miñbaev, hitherto the Minister of Energy and Mineral Resources became the Minister of Oil and Gas. In May both parliamentary chambers approved legislation awarding Nazarbaev the title 'Leader of the Nation', while also granting him and his relatives immunity from prosecution, and making it a criminal offence to utter or publish insulting remarks about the President. Although Nazarbaev formally refused to sign the legislation into law, it automatically entered into force on 15 June. In September Nazarbaev indicated his intention to contest the next presidential election in 2012.

Recent developments: 2011 presidential election

On 29 December 2010 both chambers of the Parliament adopted a motion, which had initially been proposed by a citizen's group, in favour of cancelling the next two presidential elections and thereby extending Nazarbaev's term in office until 2020, subject to approval at a national referendum. On 6 January 2011 Nazarbaev issued a decree vetoing the proposal (which had attracted particular criticism from the US Administration, as well as from the domestic opposition). On 14 January 2011 both parliamentary chambers voted unanimously to amend the Constitution to permit the referendum, following the submission of a petition of some 5m. signatures in its support. However, Nazarbaev subsequently refused to sign the constitutional amendments into force, instead referring them to the Constitutional Court for consideration. On 31 January the Constitutional Court ruled against the organization of a national referendum on extending the presidential term (thereby invalidating the constitutional amendments); Nazarbaev announced his acceptance of the Court's decision and proposed that an early presidential election be conducted (which he subsequently scheduled for 3 April). At a party congress in February, the Freedom National Social Democratic Party announced that it would boycott the forthcoming presidential election; the three opposition candidates who finally secured registration to contest the poll all declared their support for Nazarbaev. In an initial report issued in March, the OSCE, which again dispatched monitors to observe the elections, criticized inconsistencies in the application of a mandatory language test for prospective candidates.

Nazarbaev was overwhelmingly returned to office at the presidential election on 3 April 2011, securing some 95.6% of votes cast, according to preliminary official results; an exceptionally high voter turn-out of 89.9% was officially recorded. The OSCE released a statement referring to a continued failure of the authorities to implement democratic reform, citing the absence of creditable opposition candidates, lack of media freedom and serious irregularities noted by the observer mission during the conduct of the election. Nazarbaev was inaugurated for a further five-year term on 8 April, when, in response to the international criticism of the electoral process, he issued pledges to increase anti-corruption efforts and institutional reforms (which included commitments that other political parties than Light Of The Fatherland be represented in the Majlis). On the same day Nazarbaev's reappointment of Mäsımov as premier was approved by the Majlis. Nazarbaev subsequently reorganized the Government, notably replacing Sawdabaev as Minister of Foreign Affairs with a former ambassador to the UN, Erjan Qazixanov, and appointing Qayrat Kelımbetov as Minister of Economic Development and Trade. A new Minister of Internal Affairs, Qalmuxanbet Qasimov was also appointed, while a new ministerial position, of Economic Integration, was created and allocated to the former Minister of Economic Development and Trade (to whose ministry the new position was answerable), Janar Aytjanova. Meanwhile, on 15 April Nazarbaev appointed the incumbent Prosecutor-General, Kayrat Mami to the Senat, of which he was elected Chairman on the same day. A new Prosecutor-General was appointed on 15 April, and one day later Nazarbaev dismissed six judges of the Supreme Court, who were suspected of corrupt activity and who were under investigation by the office of the Prosecutor-General.

Foreign Affairs
Regional relations

The question of the legal status of the Caspian Sea—and the division of the substantial mineral resources believed to be located in the seabed—has been a source of tension between the five littoral states: Azerbaijan, Iran, Kazakhstan, Russia and Turkmenistan. In July 1998 Nazarbaev and the Russian President, Boris Yeltsin, signed a bilateral agreement on the delineation of their countries' respective boundaries of the Caspian seabed, by which Russia for the first time formally recognized Kazakhstan's claim to, and right to exploit, its offshore petroleum resources, prompting particular criticism from Iran, which continued to assert that partitioning of the seabed required the consensus of all five littoral states. In October 2000 Nazarbaev and the President of Russia, Vladimir Putin, signed an additional agreement, on the definition of the legal status of the Caspian Sea, and the 1998 agreement was further augmented in May 2002, when an accord was signed on the equal division of three oilfields in the northern Caspian. Russia and Kazakhstan have also signed a Treaty of Eternal Friendship and Co-operation, which provides for mutual military assistance in the event of aggression by a third party. In November 2001 Kazakhstan concluded a bilateral agreement with Azerbaijan on the two countries' respective mineral rights in the Caspian Sea, prompting further protests from Iran. In May 2003 Azerbaijan, Kazakhstan and Russia signed a trilateral agreement. In November representatives of Azerbaijan, Iran, Kazakhstan, Russia and Turkmenistan, meeting in Tehran, Iran, signed a UN-sponsored framework Convention for the Protection of the Marine Environment of the Caspian Sea, which sought to alleviate environmental damage in the Caspian Sea region. In mid-January 2005 Nazarbaev and Putin signed a treaty in Moscow defining the 7,500-km land border between their two countries. In May 2008 newly installed Russian President Dmitrii Medvedev made his first official international visit to Kazakhstan, where he discussed bilateral co-operation with President Nazarbaev. In September Medvedev and Nazarbaev met in the north-western town of Aqtöbe to discuss security issues. In March 2010 Putin (now Russian premier) and Mäsımov, meeting in Moscow,

KAZAKHSTAN

reiterated earlier pledges to expand their countries' mutual co-operation in the areas of the economy and energy. Meeting in the Azerbaijani capital, Baku (Bakı), in November 2010, the Heads of State of Azerbaijan, Iran, Kazakhstan, Russia and Turkmenistan signed an agreement on security co-operation, and pledged to resolve outstanding issues on the legal status of the Caspian Sea at a further summit in 2011. In January 2011 Kazakhstan announced the establishment of a joint regional air defence agreement with Russia, under which the Russian Government was to supply the country with advanced missile defence systems.

In the early 1990s the question of the formerly Soviet, subsequently Russian-controlled, nuclear warheads deployed in Kazakhstan was the focus of international concern. In September 1992 the Kazakhstani legislature ratified the first Strategic Arms Reduction Treaty, signed by the USA and the USSR in July 1991. In December 1993 the Kazakhstani legislature ratified the Treaty on the Non-Proliferation of Nuclear Weapons. By April 1995 all nuclear warheads had been transferred to Russia, and in September 1996 Russia and Kazakhstan signed a final protocol governing the withdrawal of military units linked to the Russian nuclear weapons facilities in Kazakhstan. In November 2001 the Kazakhstani legislature ratified the Comprehensive Nuclear Test Ban Treaty.

In May 2001 the signatories of the CIS Collective Security Treaty (Armenia, Belarus, Kazakhstan, Kyrgyzstan, Russia and Tajikistan) agreed to form a Collective Rapid Response Force, based in Bishkek, Kyrgyzstan, to combat Islamist militancy in Central Asia. An anti-terrorism centre became operational in Bishkek in August 2001. In April 2003 the signatories of the Treaty formally inaugurated the Collective Security Treaty Organization (CSTO, see p. 459), to which Uzbekistan subsequently acceded. Kazakhstan ratified an agreement to join the Collective Rapid Response Force in February 2010.

In 1992 Kazakhstan joined the Economic Co-operation Organization (ECO, see p. 264), founded by Iran, Pakistan and Turkey. In 1994 Kazakhstan, Kyrgyzstan and Uzbekistan formed a trilateral economic area, and in February 1995 an Interstate Council was established to supervise its implementation. Several agreements to expand economic co-operation were signed by the three countries in 1996. Two years later Tajikistan joined the alliance, which was renamed the Central Asian Co-operation Organization (CACO) in 2002. Meanwhile, Kazakhstan signed a treaty with Russia, Belarus and Kyrgyzstan in 1996, which envisaged a common market and a customs union between the four countries; Tajikistan signed the agreement in April 1998. In October 2000 a new economic body, the Eurasian Economic Community (EURASEC, see p. 447), was established, and this organization merged with CACO in January 2006. In October 2007 EURASEC leaders approved the legal basis for the establishment of a new customs union that was initially to comprise Belarus, Kazakhstan and Russia. President Nazarbaev and the President of Uzbekistan, Islam Karimov, signed a bilateral agreement in September 2002 on the delimitation of all disputed sectors of their countries' common border. A border agreement with Turkmenistan, which had been signed in July 2001, was ratified by the Senat in June 2003, and in July Nazarbaev signed a number of laws confirming the delimitation of Kazakhstan's borders with Kyrgyzstan, Turkmenistan and Uzbekistan. In June 2009, at a trilateral meeting of Heads of State, it was announced that Russia, Kazakhstan and Belarus were to establish a customs union at the beginning of 2010, prior to submitting a co-ordinated application for membership of the World Trade Organization (WTO, see p. 430). Mäsimov and other government members subsequently expressed doubts concerning the potential economic benefits to Kazakhstan; however, in late November the Heads of State of Russia, Kazakhstan and Belarus met in Minsk to sign final agreements on the establishment of the customs union. Russia, Kazakhstan and Belarus accordingly introduced unified customs tariffs on 1 January 2010, and the customs union officially entered into force in July. (However, the co-partners in the customs union subsequently agreed to apply separately to the WTO.)

In 1995 Nazarbaev made an official visit to the People's Republic of China, where an agreement was signed to improve long-term stability between the two countries, following concerns about Chinese underground nuclear tests near the border with eastern Kazakhstan. Bilateral relations were further strengthened by two accords concluded in 1997, which granted China permission to exploit two of the largest oilfields in Kazakhstan and provided for the construction of a petroleum pipeline connecting the two countries. (Construction of the pipeline, at an estimated cost of US $700m., was completed in late 2005.) In November 1998 Nazarbaev made a state visit to China, which resulted in the signature of a communiqué on the full settlement of outstanding border issues, and of an agreement outlining future bilateral relations. In July 2005 Nazarbaev and Chinese President Hu Jintao signed an agreement on the establishment of a strategic partnership between the two countries. China and Kazakhstan belonged to the so-called Shanghai Five (also comprising Kyrgyzstan, Russia and Tajikistan), which aimed to promote economic co-operation and regional co-ordination on border and security issues. Members of the alliance, which became the Shanghai Co-operation Organization (SCO, see p. 462) upon the accession of Uzbekistan in 2001, signed the Shanghai Convention on Combating Terrorism, Separatism and Extremism in June 2001. In July 2005, at a summit meeting in Astana, members of the SCO approved anti-terrorist measures, and signed a declaration advocating non-interference in the affairs of sovereign states. Several bilateral co-operation agreements were signed during a Chinese official visit in November 2007; a second stage in construction of the petroleum pipeline system linking Kazakhstan with China commenced in December. Construction of the pipeline section was completed and entered into operation in July 2009. During an official visit to China in February 2011, Nazarbaev signed a number of major economic and energy agreements with Hu Jintao, including a memorandum of understanding to support the construction of a modernized rail link between Astana and Almatı.

Other external relations

Following the suicide attacks on the USA on 11 September 2001, President Nazarbaev expressed his support for US-led military action against the al-Qa'ida militant Islamist organization and the regime of its hosts, the Taliban, in Afghanistan (see the chapters on Afghanistan and the USA). Kazakhstan offered the USA the use of airports, airspace and military bases. In February 2006 it was announced that US forces were to participate in Kazakhstani-British military exercises in Kazakhstan in September. Meanwhile, Nazarbaev's links with US petroleum companies were subject to legal scrutiny from March 2003, when James H. Giffen, a US businessman and former adviser to Nazarbaev, was indicted in the USA under the 1977 Foreign Corrupt Practices Act, which prohibits US companies or individuals from offering financial inducements to foreign officials in order to secure an agreement. He was accused of offering bribes to prominent Kazakhstani politicians, including Nazarbaev, in return for securing valuable contracts for US petroleum companies. In April 2004 a US federal court indicted Giffen and an executive of the petroleum company, ExxonMobil, on charges of corrupt business practices. Legal proceedings were subsequently delayed over permission from the US Central Intelligence Agency for Giffen to use classified information in his defence as evidence that the US Government had endorsed his actions. In September 2006 Nazarbaev met US President George W. Bush during an official visit to Washington, DC, USA. Despite criticism by the OSCE of the conduct of elections in August 2007 and continuing international concerns over human rights in the country (see above), on 1 January 2010 Kazakhstan assumed the OSCE rotating chairmanship for the period of twelve months. Amid considerable publicity, which was designed to improve Kazakhstan's international reputation, the authorities convened an OSCE summit meeting (the first since 1999) in Astana in December; Nazarbaev met US Secretary of State Hillary Clinton for discussions on the occasion of the summit. In March 2011, despite continuing criticism of its record by human rights groups, Kazakhstan submitted an application for membership of the UN Human Rights Council.

CONSTITUTION AND GOVERNMENT

Under the terms of the 1995 Constitution (as subsequently amended), the President of the Republic is Head of State and commander-in-chief of the armed forces, and holds broad executive powers. The President is directly elected by universal adult suffrage. Under constitutional amendments approved in 2007, the presidential term was reduced from seven to five years, with effect from 2012. The Government, headed by the Prime Minister, is responsible to the President. The supreme legislative organ is the bicameral Parliament, comprising the Senat (Senate, upper chamber) and the Majlis (Assembly, lower chamber). The Senat comprises 47 members, of whom 32 are elected by regional assemblies, while the remaining 15 deputies are appointed by the President. The Majlis comprises 107 deputies, of whom

98 are directly elected; the remaining nine deputies are elected by the Assembly of Nations of Kazakhstan (a 350-member body representing the country's minority ethnic groups). The Senat's term is six years, and that of the Majlis is five years. One-half of the elected deputies in the Senate are subject to election every three years. Judicial power is exercised by local courts and the Supreme Court. For administrative purposes, Kazakhstan is divided into 16 units (14 regions and the cities of Almatı and Astana). The city of Leninsk (now Turatam) serving the Baikonur space centre, and formerly one of Kazakhstan's administrative units, was transferred to Russian jurisdiction in August 1995. In January 2004 President Nazarbaev and the Russian President, Vladimir Putin, signed an agreement permitting Russia's continued use of the Baikonur space centre until 2050.

REGIONAL AND INTERNATIONAL CO-OPERATION

Kazakhstan is a founder member of the Commonwealth of Independent States (CIS, see p. 238) and participates in the Collective Security Treaty Organization (CSTO), and in the Customs Union of Belarus, Russia and Kazakhstan, which entered into effect in July 2010. It is also a member of the Organization for Security and Co-operation in Europe (OSCE, see p. 385), of which it assumed the rotating chairmanship in 2010. Kazakhstan is a member of the Economic Co-operation Organization (ECO, see p. 264), the Eurasian Economic Community (EURASEC, see p. 447) and the Shanghai Co-operation Organization (SCO, see p. 462).

Kazakhstan joined the UN in 1992.

ECONOMIC AFFAIRS

In 2009, according to estimates by the World Bank, Kazakhstan's gross national income (GNI), measured at average 2007–09 prices, was US $107,125m., equivalent to $6,740 per head (or $10,270 per head on an international purchasing-power parity basis). During 2000–09, it was estimated, the population increased at an average annual rate of 0.7%, while gross domestic product (GDP) per head increased, in real terms, by an average of 7.6% per year. Overall GDP increased, in real terms, at an average annual rate of 8.4% in 2000–09. Real GDP increased by 1.2% in 2009.

Agriculture (including forestry and fishing) contributed 6.2% of GDP and provided 29.4% of total employment in 2009. There are large areas of land suitable for agriculture, and Kazakhstan is a major producer and exporter of agricultural products. The principal crops include fruit, sugar beet, vegetables, potatoes, cotton and, most importantly, cereals. Livestock-breeding is also important, and Kazakhstan is a significant producer of karakul and astrakhan wools. According to the World Bank, the GDP of the agricultural sector increased, in real terms, by an average of 6.4% per year in 2000–09. Agricultural GDP increased by 6.6% in 2009.

Industry (including mining, manufacturing, construction, and power) contributed 39.0% of GDP and 18.9% of total employment in 2009. The principal branches of industry include the fuel industry and metal-processing. According to World Bank figures, industrial GDP increased, in real terms, at an average annual rate of 9.9% in 2000–09. The GDP of the sector increased by 5.5% in 2009.

Mining and quarrying contributed 18.1% of GDP and provided 2.5% of employment in 2009. Kazakhstan possesses immense mineral wealth, and large-scale mining and processing industries have been developed. There are major coalfields, as well as substantial deposits of iron ore, lead, zinc ore, titanium, magnesium, chromium, tungsten, molybdenum, gold, silver, copper and manganese. Petroleum is extracted, and Kazakhstan possesses substantial reserves of natural gas. In January 2004 the state-owned hydrocarbons company KazMunaiGaz awarded the Russian energy company LUKoil a 50% stake in a 40-year production-sharing contract for the development of the Tyub-Karagan field in the Caspian Sea, which has petroleum reserves of an estimated 100m. metric tons. In January 2005 the Kazakhstani and Russian Presidents signed an agreement confirming the equal rights of both countries to the Imashevskoye natural gas field, the second largest natural gas field in Kazakhstan, which was to be developed jointly by KazMunaiGaz and the Russian energy company Gazprom. Also in 2005 a subsidiary of KazMunaiGaz signed a production-sharing agreement with the Russian state-owned petroleum companies Zarubezhneft and Rosneft to develop the offshore Kurmanagazy oilfield, estimated to contain recoverable reserves of petroleum of between 900m. and 1,000m. metric tons. At the end of 2009 Kazakhstan's proven total reserves (on shore and off shore) of petroleum and natural gas were estimated at 39,828m. barrels and 1,822,443m. cu m, respectively.

Manufacturing contributed 11.0% of GDP and provided 7.2% of employment in 2009. The GDP of the manufacturing sector increased at an average annual rate of 7.6% in 2000–09, according to the World Bank. This sector's GDP increased by 3.0% in 2009.

The construction sector contributed 8.0% of GDP and engaged 7.0% of the employed labour force in the 2009. During 2000–08, according to UN estimates, the GDP of the sector increased at an average annual rate of 20.4%. Construction GDP increased by 4.0% in 2008.

In 2007 coal-fired thermal power stations provided about 70.3% of annual domestic electricity production, while natural gas accounted for 10.7% of production and hydroelectric power stations for a further 10.7%. In 2008 mineral products accounted for 10.1% of total imports.

The services sector contributed some 54.8% of GDP and provided 51.7% of employment in 2009. According to World Bank figures, the GDP of the services sector increased, in real terms, at an average annual rate of 9.8% during 2000–09. Services GDP increased by 5.5% in 2009.

In 2009 Kazakhstan recorded a visible trade surplus of US $15,158.8m., but there was a deficit of $4,248.5m. on the current account of the balance of payments. In 2009 the principal source of imports was Russia, which accounted for 31.3% of total imports. Other major suppliers were the People's Republic of China, Ukraine, Germany and Italy. The principal market for exports in that year was Italy, which accounted for 15.5% of total exports. Other important purchasers of exports were the People's Republic of China, Russia, France, Switzerland-Liechtenstein and the Netherlands. The main exports were mineral products and base metals, manufactured goods and inedible crude materials except fuels (chiefly metalliferous ore and metal scrap). The principal imports in that year were machinery and electrical equipment, manufactured goods, petroleum and related products, machinery and transport equipment and parts and road vehicles.

In 2009 Kazakhstan recorded a budgetary deficit of some 437,739.5m. tenge (equivalent to around 2.6% of GDP). Kazakhstan's general government gross debt was 1,739,377m. tenge in 2009, equivalent to 10.9% of GDP. At the end of 2008 Kazakhstan's external debt amounted to US $107,595m. of which only $1,915m. was external debt, public and publicly guaranteed. In that year the cost of debt-servicing was equivalent to 41.8% of the value of exports of goods, services and income. The annual rate of inflation averaged 8.9% during 2000–08, according to ILO. Consumer prices increased by 10.8% in 2007 and by 17.0% in 2008. In 2009 6.6% of the labour force were unemployed.

In 1998 the economy was severely affected by the economic crises in Russia and Asia, and the subsequent decline in prices for Kazakhstan's principal exports. However, by 2000 Kazakhstan had repaid all debts owed to the IMF, seven years ahead of schedule. A National Oil Fund was created in 2001, to protect the country against sudden declines in petroleum prices. Petroleum exports increased significantly following the official opening, in November 2001, of a 1,500-km petroleum pipeline, connecting the onshore Tengiz field in western Kazakhstan with Novorossiisk, on the Russian Black Sea coast. In May 2005 the BTC pipeline, linking Baku, Azerbaijan, via Tbilisi, Georgia, to Ceyhan, Turkey, which was principally intended to transport petroleum from Azerbaijan and Central Asia to Western markets, was officially inaugurated. In December 2007 Kazakhstan, Russia and Turkmenistan signed a formal agreement for the construction of a Caspian natural gas pipeline to transport Central Asian gas supplies to Russia. In late 2008 it was reported that petroleum from Kazakhstan had for the first time been transported by the BTC pipeline to Western markets. From the latter part of that year adverse conditions resulting from the international financial crisis required that the authorities initiate an 'anti-crisis' programme, under which savings from the National Oil Fund were drawn to stabilize the banking system and other affected sectors. In mid-2009 it was announced that Russia, Kazakhstan and Belarus were to implement long-standing plans for the establishment of a customs union. International observers expressed concerns that the removal of trade restrictions and Kazakhstan's underdeveloped domestic industry, might result in a sharp increase in inflation and potential losses for domestic producers. In January 2010, none the less, Kazakhstan, Belarus and Russia adopted a unified tariff policy, and the

KAZAKHSTAN

customs union officially entered into effect in July. Kazakhstan was expected to benefit from the immediate imposition of a tariff on petroleum exports, adopted in co-ordination with Russia. At the end of 2010 the IMF assessed that Kazakhstan's economy had begun to recover (with an increase in GDP growth of more than 5% expected in that year), although activity in the construction and real estate sectors, which had been particularly adversely affected by the global economic crisis, remained lower than previously, and the resolution of persistent weaknesses in the banking system was considered a priority for the authorities. In February 2011 President Nursultan Nazarbaev announced plans to list a 5% stake in a subsidiary of national oil company KazMunaiGaz on the domestic stock exchange, available for purchase only to Kazakhstani citizens, which was to be followed by offerings of shares in many of the largest state enterprises; the decision was designed further to increase Nazarbaev's popularity prior to an early presidential election (see Contemporary Political History), and to promote an improved business environment. Following his re-election in April, Nazarbaev pledged to increase anti-corruption measures, particularly with regard to the protection of private property rights, and to stimulate the development of small and medium-sized enterprises.

PUBLIC HOLIDAYS

2012: 1–2 January (New Year), 7 January (Russian Orthodox Christmas), 8 March (International Women's Day), 21–23 March (Nauryz Meyramy, Spring Holiday), 1 May (Day of Unity of the Peoples of Kazakhstan), 9 May (Victory Day, Day of Remembrance), 6 July (Day of the Capital City), 30 August (Constitution Day), 25 October* (Kurban Bayram, Id al-Adha or Feast of the Sacrifice), 16 December (Independence Day).

* This holiday is dependent on the Islamic lunar calendar and may vary by one or two days from the date given.

Statistical Survey

Source (unless otherwise stated): Statistical Agency of the Republic of Kazakhstan, 050009 Almatı, Abay kosh. 125; tel. (727) 261-13-23; fax (727) 242-08-24; e-mail stat@mail.online.kz; internet www.stat.kz.

Area and Population

AREA, POPULATION AND DENSITY

Area (sq km)	2,724,900*
Population (census results)	
25 February–4 March 1999	14,953,126
25 February–6 March 2009	
Males	7,712,200
Females	8,297,400
Total	16,009,600
Population (official estimate at 1 January)	
2010	16,036,075†
Density (per sq km) at 1 January 2010	5.9

* 1,049,150 sq miles.
† Preliminary estimate, not revised to take account of results of 2009 census.

POPULATION BY AGE AND SEX
('000, official estimates at 1 January 2010)

	Males	Females	Total
0–14	1,999.2	1,903.1	3,902.3
15–64	5,323.6	5,664.8	10,988.4
65 and over	395.9	749.5	1,145.4
Total	7,718.7	8,317.4	16,036.1

Note: Population estimates are preliminary, not revised to take account of the results of the 2009 census.

PRINCIPAL ETHNIC GROUPS
(at 2009 census)

	Number ('000)	%
Kazakh	10,096.8	63.1
Russian	3,793.8	23.7
Uzbek	457.0	2.9
Ukrainian	333.0	2.1
Uygur (Uighur)	224.7	1.4
Tatar	204.2	1.3
German	178.4	1.1
Others	721.7	4.5
Total	16,009.6	100.0

ADMINISTRATIVE DIVISIONS
(1 January 2010, official estimates)

	Area (sq km)	Population	Density (per sq km)	Capital city
Oblasts				
Almatı	224,000	1,692,951	7.56	Taldykorgan
Aqmola	146,200	738,010	5.05	Kökşetaw
Aqtöbe	300,600	718,870	2.39	Aqtöbe
Atiraw	118,600	513,363	4.33	Atiraw
Eastern Kazakhstan	283,200	1,418,784	5.01	Öskemen
Jambil	144,300	1,043,843	7.23	Taraz
Mañğystaw	165,600	446,265	2.70	Aktaw
Northern Kazakhstan	98,000	643,302	6.56	Petropavl
Pavlodar	124,800	750,853	6.02	Pavlodar
Qarağandi	428,000	1,352,037	3.16	Qarağandi
Qizilorda	226,000	689,749	3.05	Qizilorda
Qostanay	196,000	886,284	4.52	Qostanay
Southern Kazakhstan	117,300	2,429,137	20.71	Chimkent
Western Kazakhstan	151,300	624,280	4.13	Oral
Cities				
Almatı	700	1,404,329	2,006.14	—
Astana (capital)	300	684,018	2,280.00	—
Total	2,724,900	16,036,075	5.89	—

Note: Population estimates are preliminary, not revised to take account of the results of the 2009 census.

PRINCIPAL TOWNS
(population at 1999 census)

Almatı	1,129,400	Petropavl	203,500
Qarağandi	436,900	Oral	195,500
Chimkent	360,100	Temirtaw	170,500
Taraz	330,100	Qizilorda	157,400
Astana (capital)	313,000	Aktaw	143,400
Öskemen	311,000	Atiraw	142,500
Pavlodar	300,500	Ekibastuz	127,200
Semey	269,600	Kökşetaw	123,400
Aqtöbe	253,100	Rudniy	109,500
Qostanay	221,400		

Mid-2009 (incl. suburbs, UN estimate): Astana (capital) 649,818 (Source: UN, *World Urbanization Prospects: The 2009 Revision*).

Mid-2010 (incl. suburbs, UN estimate): Almatı 1,383,158 (Source: UN, *World Urbanization Prospects: The 2009 Revision*).

KAZAKHSTAN

IMMIGRATION AND EMIGRATION

	2007	2008	2009
Immigrants	365,137	390,777	406,251
Emigrants	354,175	389,660	398,749

BIRTHS, MARRIAGES AND DEATHS

	Registered live births Number	Rate (per 1,000)	Registered marriages Number	Rate (per 1,000)	Registered deaths Number	Rate (per 1,000)
2002	227,171	15.3	98,986	6.7	149,381	10.1
2003	247,946	16.6	110,414	7.4	155,277	10.4
2004	273,028	18.2	114,685	7.6	152,250	10.1
2005	278,977	18.4	123,045	8.1	157,121	10.4
2006	301,756	19.7	137,204	9.0	157,210	10.3
2007	321,963	20.8	146,379	9.5	158,297	10.2
2008	356,555	22.8	135,280	8.6	152,706	9.7
2009	357,552	22.0	140,785	8.0	142,780	8.0

Life expectancy (years at birth, WHO estimates): 64 (males 59; females 70) in 2008 (Source: WHO, *World Health Statistics*).

ECONOMICALLY ACTIVE POPULATION
(labour force survey, annual averages, '000 persons)

	2007	2008	2009
Agriculture, forestry and fishing	2,382.8	2,369.8	2,326.4
Mining and quarrying	193.5	200.3	197.9
Manufacturing	569.8	572.9	570.6
Electricity, gas and water supply	162.7	164.8	170.8
Construction	517.9	548.9	551.8
Wholesale and retail trade; repair of motor vehicles, motor cycles and personal and household goods	1,070.9	1,150.3	1,170.6
Hotels and restaurants	100.0	103.1	101.6
Transport, storage and communications	552.9	588.9	586.4
Financial intermediation	87.7	96.2	96.6
Real estate, renting and business activities	354.6	378.1	394.3
Public administration and defence; compulsory social security	343.7	352.5	373.1
Education	732.9	754.3	769.5
Health and social work	335.9	347.3	351.4
Community, social and personal services	197.4	205.4	220.9
Households with employed persons	28.4	24.4	21.4
Extra-territorial organizations and bodies	0.1	0.1	0.1
Total employed	7,631.1	7,857.2	7,903.4
Unemployed	597.1	557.8	554.5
Total labour force	8,228.3	8,415.2	8,457.9
Males	4,167.3	4,244.2	n.a.
Females	4,061.0	4,171.0	n.a.

Statistical Survey

Health and Welfare

KEY INDICATORS

Total fertility rate (children per woman, 2008)	2.3
Under-5 mortality rate (per 1,000 live births, 2008)	30
HIV/AIDS (% of persons aged 15–49, 2007)	0.1
Physicians (per 1,000 head, 2006)	3.9
Hospital beds (per 1,000 head, 2006)	7.8
Health expenditure (2007): US $ per head (PPP)	405
Health expenditure (2007): % of GDP	3.7
Health expenditure (2007): public (% of total)	66.1
Access to water (% of persons, 2008)	95
Access to sanitation (% of persons, 2008)	97
Total carbon dioxide emissions ('000 metric tons, 2007)	227,208.3
Carbon dioxide emissions per head (metric tons, 2007)	14.7
Human Development Index (2010): ranking	66
Human Development Index (2010): value	0.714

For sources and definitions, see explanatory note on p. vi.

Agriculture

PRINCIPAL CROPS
('000 metric tons)

	2007	2008	2009
Wheat	16,466.9	12,538.2	17,052.0
Rice, paddy	294.4	254.7	307.0
Barley	2,441.2	2,058.6	2,519.0
Maize	421.2	420.2	471.0
Rye	68.5	39.9	75.0
Oats	229.7	137.8	204.0
Millet	31.0	27.4	31.0
Buckwheat	81.4	16.6	62.0
Potatoes	2,414.8	2,354.4	2,755.6
Sugar beet	309.4	130.2	181.3
Beans, dry	0.8	0.7	1.0
Peas, dry	48.5	34.9	51.0*
Soybeans	83.3	88.7	151.0*
Sunflower seed	205.8	185.8	367.9
Safflower seed	43.9	45.7	78.0*
Seed cotton	441.7	317.5	270.0
Cabbages and other brassicas	337.7	361.1	389.0*
Tomatoes	515.2	549.3	592.0*
Cucumbers and gherkins	251.7	268.0	289.0*
Aubergines (Eggplants)	51.1	44.3	48.0*
Chillies and peppers, green	79.0	82.0	88.0*
Onions, dry	341.4	376.8	406.0*
Carrots and turnips	283.5	271.1	292.0*
Watermelons	476.7	653.9	641.0*
Apples	101.7	94.7	112.0*
Pears	11.1	8.0	11.0*
Cherries	11.4	9.9	13.0*
Plums and sloes	4.8	3.9	5.0*
Grapes	43.1	33.5	55.7
Tobacco, unmanufactured	11.0	9.0*	9.0†

* Unofficial figure(s).
† FAO estimate.

Aggregate production ('000 metric tons, may include official, semi-official or estimated data): Total cereals 20,090.0 in 2007, 15,541.5 in 2008, 20,785.1 in 2009; Total roots and tubers 2,414.8 in 2007, 2,354.4 in 2008, 2,755.6 in 2009; Total vegetables (incl. melons) 2,858.7 in 2007, 3,150.1 in 2008, 3,310.1 in 2009; Total fruits (excl. melons) 205.4 in 2007, 177.0 in 2008, 234.4 in 2009.

Source: FAO.

KAZAKHSTAN

LIVESTOCK
('000 head, year ending September)

	2007	2008	2009
Horses	1,235.6	1,291.1	1,370.5
Asses*	30	30	30
Cattle	5,660.4	5,840.9	5,991.6
Buffaloes*	10.0	10.0	10.0
Camels	138.6	143.2	148.3
Pigs	1,304.9	1,352.7	1,347.3
Sheep	12,813.7	13,470.1	14,126.1
Goats	2,536.6	2,609.9	2,644.3
Chickens†	28,100	29,400	30,000
Turkeys†	100	130	150

* FAO estimates.
† Unofficial figures.
Source: FAO.

LIVESTOCK PRODUCTS
('000 metric tons)

	2007	2008	2009
Cattle meat	385.9	400.1	396.1
Sheep meat	104.3	110.4	113.9
Goat meat	19.3	20.6	21.0*
Horse meat	65.3	66.3	71.5
Pig meat	193.9	206.2	208.9
Chicken meat	64.3	65.3	79.5
Cows' milk	5,038.1	5,162.7	5,267.0*
Sheeps' milk*	26.0	26.5	26.5
Goats' milk*	9.1	9.5	104.0
Hen eggs*	148.3	166.4	184.2
Wool, greasy	34.2	35.2	36.4

* Unofficial figure(s).
Source: FAO.

Forestry

ROUNDWOOD REMOVALS
(unofficial figures, cubic metres, excl. bark)

	2005	2006	2007
Sawlogs, veneer logs and logs for sleepers	513,600	38,800	158,300
Pulpwood	64,200	4,900	19,800
Other industrial roundwood	64,200	4,900	19,800
Fuel wood	210,000	69,200	49,600
Total	852,000	117,800	247,500

2008–09: Figures assumed to be unchanged from 2007 (FAO estimates).
Source: FAO.

SAWNWOOD PRODUCTION
(cubic metres, incl. railway sleepers)

	2005*	2006	2007
Coniferous (softwood)	113,275	144,000	108,000
Broadleaved (hardwood)	25,425	5,000	3,000
Total	138,700	149,000	111,000

* Unofficial figures.
2008–09: Figures assumed to be unchanged from 2007 (FAO estimates).
Source: FAO.

Fishing
('000 metric tons, live weight)

	2006	2007	2008
Capture	34.6	41.2	55.6
Freshwater bream	17.2	18.8	21.3
Common carp	0.1	0.1	0.1
Crucian carp	2.2	2.7	3.8
Roaches	2.0	2.3	4.8
Asp	1.0	1.0	5.2
Northern pike	0.8	1.2	1.9
Wels (Som) catfish	1.9	2.2	3.4
Pike-perch	3.5	4.9	9.8
Aquaculture	0.5	0.4	0.3
Total catch	35.1	41.6	55.9

Source: FAO.

Mining
('000 metric tons unless otherwise indicated)

	2007	2008	2009
Hard coal	98,384	111,072	100,854
Brown coal (incl. lignite)			
Crude petroleum*	67,125	70,671	76,483
Natural gas (million cu m)	29,562	32,889	35,942
Iron ore (gross weight)	23,834	21,486	22,281
Bauxite	4,943	5,160	5,130
Lead ore (metal content)	40	39	34
Zinc ore (metal content)	386	387	398
Manganese ore	2,482	2,485	2,457
Chromite	231	349	4,678
Silver ore (metal content, metric tons)	722,927	645,627	618,141
Gold (metal content, kg)	30,721	29,030	33,118
Asbestos	293	230	230

* Including gas condensate.

Industry

SELECTED PRODUCTS
('000 metric tons, unless otherwise indicated)

	2007	2008	2009
Wheat flour	3,080	3,375	3,725
Raw sugar	393	508	385
Wine ('000 hectolitres)	194	133	172
Beer ('000 hectolitres)	4,110	3,607	3,615
Cigarettes (million)	31,507	28,483	26,789
Woven cotton fabrics (metric tons)	43,325	43,480	35,491
Motor spirit (petrol)	2,633	2,505	2,613
Kerosene	385	402	374
Gas-diesel (distillate fuel) oils	4,295	4,375	4,261
Residual fuel oils (Mazout)	2,584	3,204	3,261
Cement	5,699	5,837	5,694
Crude steel	4,784	4,243	n.a.
Copper (unrefined, metric tons)	406,921	398,411	312,767
Electric energy (million kWh)	76,621	80,348	78,729

KAZAKHSTAN

Statistical Survey

Finance

CURRENCY AND EXCHANGE RATES

Monetary Units
100 tein = 1 tenge.

Sterling, Dollar and Euro Equivalents (31 December 2010)
£1 sterling = 230.911 tenge;
US $1 = 147.500 tenge;
€1 = 197.089 tenge;
1,000 tenge = £4.33 = $6.78 = €5.07.

Average Exchange Rate (tenge per US $)
2008   120.299
2009   147.497
2010   147.355

Note: The tenge was introduced on 15 November 1993, replacing the old Russian (formerly Soviet) rouble at an exchange rate of 1 tenge = 500 roubles. On 18 November the rate was adjusted to 250 roubles per tenge. In April 1999 the tenge was allowed to 'float' on foreign exchange markets.

STATE BUDGET
(million tenge)

Revenue*	2007	2008	2009
Tax revenue	2,356,040.3	2,819,509.7	2,228,681.8
Other current revenue	181,066.9	85,539.9	136,175.5
Capital revenue	92,685.9	56,939.6	35,887.4
Official transfers	258,045.3	1,072,421.3	1,104,600.0
Total	2,887,838.4	4,034,410.5	3,505,344.7

Expenditure†	2007	2008	2009
General public services	164,743.8	224,012.3	166,062.7
Defence	166,646.3	185,358.4	187,615.3
Public order and security	240,992.8	271,467.4	316,189.7
Education	455,430.1	572,403.0	660,917.1
Health care	299,380.5	363,209.9	450,892.5
Social security and social assistance	502,381.4	622,016.7	758,308.4
Housing and communal services	199,937.0	233,925.5	304,048.8
Recreation and cultural activities	122,209.9	163,968.6	173,618.1
Agriculture, forestry, water management, fishing and environmental protection	100,919.4	170,364.8	168,117.9
Transport and communications	289,653.9	332,709.1	337,511.5
Other expenditure	135,949.6	254,627.8	223,558.0
Total	2,678,244.6	3,394,063.5	3,746,840.2

* Excluding grants received (million tenge): 8,102.0 in 2007; 42,460.8 in 2008; 27,476.5 in 2009.
† Excluding net expenditure minus repayments (million tenge): 416,786.8 in 2007; 931,125.0 in 2008; 223,720.5 in 2009.

Source: Ministry of Finance, Astana.

INTERNATIONAL RESERVES
(US $ million at 31 December)

	2008	2009	2010
Gold	2,000.7	2,500.7	3,052.2
IMF special drawing rights	1.4	540.2	530.6
Reserve position in IMF	0.0	0.0	0.0
Foreign exchange	17,870.1	20,179.6	24,707.9
Total	19,872.2	23,220.5	28,290.7

Source: IMF, *International Financial Statistics*.

MONEY SUPPLY
(million tenge at 31 December)

	2008	2009	2010
Currency outside depository corporations	857,842	913,443	1,148,489
Transferable deposits	1,359,522	2,266,473	2,657,054
Other deposits	4,049,837	4,307,390	4,740,838
Broad money	6,267,201	7,487,306	8,546,381

Source: IMF, *International Financial Statistics*.

COST OF LIVING
(Consumer Price Index at December; base: December of previous year = 100)

	2008	2009	2010
Food and beverages	110.8	103.0	110.1
Other consumer goods	105.7	108.6	105.5
Services	111.4	108.4	106.8
All items	109.5	106.2	107.8

NATIONAL ACCOUNTS

Expenditure on the Gross Domestic Product
(million tenge at current prices)

	2007	2008	2009
Final consumption expenditure	7,215,845	8,624,674	10,037,360
Households	5,641,241	6,871,432	7,912,607
Non-profit institutions serving households	154,198	117,691	141,164
General government	1,420,406	1,635,551	1,983,589
Gross capital formation	4,565,108	4,415,594	5,002,725
Gross fixed capital formation. Acquisitions, less disposals of valuables	3,857,192	4,308,793	4,726,718
Changes in inventories	707,916	106,801	276,007
Total domestic expenditure	11,780,952	13,040,268	15,040,085
Exports of goods and services	6,352,917	9,190,284	7,150,140
Less Imports of goods and services	5,493,380	5,962,624	5,751,669
Statistical discrepancy	209,304	−215,009	569,091
GDP in market prices	12,849,794	16,052,919	17,007,647

Gross Domestic Product by Economic Activity

	2007	2008	2009
Agriculture, hunting, forestry and fishing	727,336	853,342	1,045,441
Mining and quarrying	1,934,762	3,003,647	3,036,306
Manufacturing	1,476,648	1,890,053	1,849,098
Electricity, gas and water supply	223,716	268,939	309,398
Construction	1,213,217	1,298,700	1,341,489
Wholesale and retail trade; repair of motor vehicles, motorcycles and personal and household goods	1,164,740	1,965,681	2,076,034
Hotels and restaurants	114,474	132,041	143,302
Transport, storage and communication	1,481,636	1,769,082	1,874,361
Financial intermediation	761,616	848,500	843,974
Real estate, renting and business activities	1,896,242	2,404,820	2,707,388
Public administration and defence; compulsory social security	249,747	272,332	348,557
Education	418,933	452,238	550,690
Health and social work	213,357	237,392	304,916
Other community, social and personal services	244,745	282,266	334,094
Sub-total	12,544,164	15,679,033	16,765,046
Less Financial intermediation services indirectly measured	613,955	751,370	539,682
Gross value added in basic prices	11,930,209	14,927,664	16,225,364
Taxes, less subsidies, on products	919,585	1,125,255	782,283
GDP in market prices	12,849,794	16,052,919	17,007,647

KAZAKHSTAN

BALANCE OF PAYMENTS
(US $ million)

	2007	2008	2009
Exports of goods f.o.b.	48,351.1	71,970.8	43,972.0
Imports of goods f.o.b.	−33,260.2	−38,452.0	−28,813.2
Trade balance	15,091.0	33,518.8	15,158.8
Exports of services	3,564.3	4,428.4	4,286.4
Imports of services	−11,729.8	−11,119.2	−10,064.1
Balance on goods and services	6,925.5	26,828.1	9,381.1
Other income received	3,463.5	3,242.1	2,500.3
Other income paid	−16,551.4	−22,806.0	−15,229.8
Balance on goods, services and income	−6,162.4	7,264.2	−3,348.4
Current transfers received	903.8	1,104.2	855.3
Current transfers paid	−3,063.3	−2,088.8	−1,755.4
Current balance	−8,321.9	6,279.5	−4,248.5
Capital account (net)	24.6	−12.6	−29.5
Direct investment abroad	−3,153.1	−996.6	−3,118.5
Direct investment from abroad	11,119.0	15,779.8	13,619.3
Portfolio investment assets	−4,101.3	−7,222.7	1,851.9
Portfolio investment liabilities	−481.8	−2,099.9	1,137.2
Financial derivatives assets	−614.0	−369.7	367.2
Financial derivatives liabilities	247.3	550.5	−310.4
Other investment assets	−11,910.9	−3,554.6	−830.5
Other investment liabilities	17,129.7	1,222.5	−4,680.7
Net errors and omissions	−2,966.4	−7,387.4	−1,300.3
Overall balance	−3,028.7	2,188.8	2,457.1

Source: IMF, *International Financial Statistics*.

External Trade

PRINCIPAL COMMODITIES
(distribution by SITC, US $ million)

Imports c.i.f.	2007	2008	2009
Food and live animals	1,737.5	2,266.2	1,918.8
Mineral fuels, lubricants and related materials	3,639.1	5,431.0	2,834.8
Petroleum and related products	3,003.5	4,518.0	2,341.1
Chemicals and related products	2,716.7	3,207.3	2,838.6
Manufactured goods classified chiefly by material	6,888.8	8,619.3	7,525.1
Iron and steel	2,731.2	4,158.7	3,893.1
Machinery and transport equipment	14,464.6	14,172.8	10,523.5
Machinery specialized for particular industries	2,228.1	2,608.7	1,704.2
General industrial machinery, equipment and parts	2,510.4	3,799.5	2,987.7
Electrical machinery, apparatus, appliances and parts	1,841.1	1,881.1	1,588.3
Road vehicles	4,311.2	2,438.1	1,444.1
Passenger cars and other passenger vehicles	2,392.1	1,228.3	771.3
Miscellaneous manufactured articles	2,161.0	2,121.1	1,926.4
Total (incl. others)	32,686.6	37,815.4	28,408.7

Exports f.o.b.	2007	2008	2009
Food and live animals	1,937.7	2,871.7	1,520.1
Crude materials (inedible) except fuels	2,960.4	4,414.7	2,580.6
Metalliferous ore and metal scrap	2,494.4	3,537.3	2,262.8
Mineral fuels, lubricants and related materials	31,518.6	48,910.9	30,027.2
Petroleum and related products	29,778.5	45,965.7	27,632.6
Manufactured goods classified chiefly by material	8,556.7	11,058.6	5,938.8
Iron and steel	3,502.6	5,881.2	2,866.3
Non-ferrous metals	4,537.7	4,507.2	2,598.7
Copper	2,774.8	2,866.1	1,494.0
Total (incl. others)	47,747.9	71,172.0	43,195.8

Source: UN, *International Trade Statistics Yearbook*.

PRINCIPAL TRADING PARTNERS
(distribution by SITC, US $ million)

Imports c.i.f.	2007	2008	2009
Belarus	396.0	396.2	367.1
China, People's Republic	3,507.3	4,565.1	3,569.5
Finland	307.4	506.0	309.7
France (incl. Monaco)	705.5	813.0	460.4
Germany	2,585.7	2,572.0	2,041.9
Italy	1,129.9	1,239.8	1,915.3
Japan	1,369.7	979.3	635.1
Korea, Republic	625.9	423.2	373.9
Netherlands	375.7	275.8	319.1
Norway	103.5	695.0	274.9
Poland	397.0	426.4	421.6
Russia	11,573.8	13,753.8	8,896.6
Sweden	311.2	301.6	262.2
Switzerland-Liechtenstein	248.5	164.6	156.2
Turkey	958.8	970.8	570.9
Ukraine	1,517.5	2,104.8	2,131.6
United Kingdom	737.0	688.9	702.3
USA	1,623.9	1,930.8	1,393.6
Uzbekistan	538.5	516.1	304.4
Total (incl. others)	32,686.6	37,815.4	28,408.7

Exports f.o.b.	2007	2008	2009
Canada	420.5	398.2	1,385.4
China, People's Republic	5,635.9	7,676.6	5,888.6
France (incl. Monaco)	3,982.7	5,388.7	3,381.5
Germany	392.3	614.2	898.1
Iran	2,451.4	2,039.5	1,279.0
Israel	1,058.8	2,226.5	1,121.5
Italy	7,774.2	11,920.3	6,686.8
Japan	382.6	803.9	247.5
Netherlands	2,464.3	4,638.7	2,222.5
Poland	257.0	461.5	835.8
Portugal	394.6	561.5	274.4
Romania	686.5	1,010.8	840.3
Russia	4,658.9	6,227.0	3,547.0
Spain	775.9	896.6	580.3
Switzerland-Liechtenstein	7,475.9	11,281.3	2,668.2
Turkey	934.4	1,903.8	791.8
Ukraine	1,113.1	2,003.3	1,289.2
United Kingdom	1,133.2	1,811.2	1,235.1
USA	419.7	569.6	612.6
Uzbekistan	871.7	1,272.0	891.8
Total (incl. others)	47,747.9	71,172.0	43,195.8

Source: UN, *International Trade Statistics Yearbook*.

Transport

RAILWAYS
(estimated traffic)

	2008	2009	2010
Paying passengers (million journeys)	17.5	17.7	19.1
Passenger-km (million)	14,131	14,520	15,800
Freight carried ('000 metric tons)	271,548	247,407	265,663
Freight net ton-km (million)	215,111	194,918	210,713

ROAD TRAFFIC
('000 motor vehicles in use at 31 December)

	2007	2008	2009
Passenger cars	2,183.1	2,576.6	2,656.8
Lorries and vans	359.2	414.3	410.8
Buses and coaches	83.4	89.2	94.8

SHIPPING

Merchant Fleet
(registered at 31 December)

	2007	2008	2009
Number of vessels	63	76	99
Total displacement (grt)	54,291	60,292	77,093

Source: IHS Fairplay, *World Fleet Statistics*.

CIVIL AVIATION
(traffic on scheduled services)

	2008	2009	2010
Passengers carried (million)	2.8	2.8	3.4
Passenger-km (million)	5,550.0	5,313.3	6,516.9
Total ton-km (million)	69.4	68.1	93.8

Tourism

FOREIGN TOURIST ARRIVALS

Country of residence	2006	2007	2008
China, People's Republic	117,279	171,753	172,083
Kyrgyzstan	1,018,524	1,076,478	1,045,781
Russia	1,385,964	1,339,506	1,105,981
Tajikistan	301,971	552,999	394,125
Uzbekistan	1,352,879	1,534,990	1,495,249
Total (incl. others)	4,706,742	5,310,582	4,721,456

Tourism receipts (US $ million, incl. passenger transport): 973 in 2006; 1,213 in 2007; 1,255 in 2008.

Source: World Tourism Organization.

Communications Media

	2007	2008	2009
Telephones ('000 main lines in use)	3,236.9	3,458.4	3,762.9
Mobile cellular telephones ('000 subscribers)	12,322.7	14,910.6	14,995.3
Internet users ('000)	620.0	1,707.0	5,300.0
Broadband subscribers ('000)	270.4	660.8	1,367.8

Book production (titles, incl. pamphlets, 1999): 1,223.
Book production (copies, 1996): 21,014,000.
Daily newspapers (1996): Titles 3; Average circulation 500,000.
Radio receivers ('000 in use, 1997): 6,470.
Television receivers ('000 in use, 2001): 5,440.

Sources: UNESCO, *Statistical Yearbook*; UN, *Statistical Yearbook*; International Telecommunication Union.

Education

(state educational institutions, 2009/10)

	Institutions	Teachers	Students ('000)
Pre-primary	1,852	29,862	274.9
Primary *and* Secondary: general*	7,811	282,254	2,534.0
Secondary: vocational	480	33,096	495.2
Professional-technical schools	306	7,110	115.5
Higher	148	39,155	610.3

* Excluding secondary-general evening schools.

Note: There were, additionally: 155 private primary and secondary-general schools, with 20,000 students; 179 private secondary-vocational schools, with 88,700 students; and 134 non-governmental higher education institutes, with 297,900 students, in 2003/04.

Pupil-teacher ratio (primary education, UNESCO estimate): 16.4 in 2008/09 (Source: UNESCO Institute for Statistics).

Adult literacy rate (UNESCO estimates): 99.7% (males 99.8%; females 99.5%) in 2008 (Source: UNESCO Institute for Statistics).

Directory

The Government

HEAD OF STATE

President: NURSULTAN A. NAZARBAEV (elected indirectly 24 April 1990; elected unopposed 1 December 1991; term extended by referendum 29 April 1995; re-elected 10 January 1999; re-elected 4 December 2005; inaugurated 11 January 2006; re-elected 3 April 2011; inaugurated 8 April 2011).

GOVERNMENT
(May 2011)

Prime Minister: KÄRIM Q. MÄSIMOV.
First Deputy Prime Minister: ÖMIRZAQ E. ŞÖKEEV.
Deputy Prime Minister: ERBOL T. ORINBAEV.
Deputy Prime Minister, Minister of Industry and New Technologies: ÄSET Ö. İSEKEŞEV.
Minister of Internal Affairs: QALMUXANBET N. QASIMOV.
Minister of Health: SALİDAT Z. QAYIRBEKOVA.
Minister of Foreign Affairs: ERJAN X. QAZIXANOV.
Minister of Culture: MUXTAR A. QUL-MUXAMMED.
Minister of Defence: ÄDILBEK R. JAQSIBEKOV.
Minister of Education and Science: BAQITJAN T. JUMAĞULOV.
Minister of Agriculture: ASILJAN S. MAMITBEKOV.

KAZAKHSTAN

Minister of Transport and Communications: BERIK S. KAMA-LIEV.
Minister of Emergency Situations: VLADIMIR K. BOJKO.
Minister of Environmental Protection: NURĠALI S. ÄŞIMOV.
Minister of Labour and Social Security: GÜLŞARA N. ÄBDIQALI-QOVA.
Minister of Tourism and Sport: TALĠAT A. ERMEGIYAEV.
Minister of Finance: BOLAT B. JÁMIŞEV.
Minister of Economic Development and Trade: QAYRAT N. KELIMBETOV.
Minister of Justice: RAŞID T. TÜSIPBEKOV.
Minister of Oil and Gas: SAWAT M. MIŃBAEV.
Minister of Communication and Information: ASQAR Q. JUMA-ĠALIEV.
Minister of Economic Integration: JANAR S. AYTJANOVA.

MINISTRIES

Office of the President: 010000 Astana, Beibitshilik kosh. 11; tel. (7172) 32-13-99; fax (7172) 32-61-72; e-mail egov@nitec.kz; internet www.akorda.kz.
Office of the Prime Minister: 010000 Astana, Beibitshilik kosh. 11; tel. (7172) 74-54-00; fax (7172) 32-40-89; internet www.government.kz.
Ministry of Agriculture: 010000 Astana, Kenesary kosh. 36; tel. and fax (7172) 55-59-95; e-mail mailbox@minagri.kz; internet www.minagri.kz.
Ministry of Communication and Information: 010000 Astana; tel. (7172) 74-01-34; fax (7172) 74-10-04; e-mail mci.gov@gmail.com; internet bam.gov.kz.
Ministry of Culture: 010000 Astana, Soljagaw, Ministrilkter uyi, 15 kireberis, 3rd floor, office 305; tel. (7172) 74-01-07; fax (7172) 50-30-51; e-mail mkis@mki.kz; internet www.mki.gov.kz.
Ministry of Defence: 010000 Astana, Soljagaw, AEA, 2-ui Barlyk kukyktar korgalgan; tel. (7172) 24-15-51; fax (7172) 24-15-95; internet www.mod.gov.kz.
Ministry of Economic Development and Trade: 010000 Astana, 35 kosh. 7; tel. (7172) 74-28-09; e-mail info@minplan.kz; internet www.minplan.kz.
Ministry of Education and Science: 010000 Astana, Orynbor kosh. 8; tel. (7172) 33-33-25; fax (7172) 33-34-12; e-mail pressa@edu.gov.kz; internet www.edu.gov.kz.
Ministry of Emergency Situations: 010000 Astana, Beibitshilik kosh. 22; tel. (7172) 60-21-28; fax (7172) 94-48-32; e-mail mchs@emer.kz; internet www.emer.kz.
Ministry of Environmental Protection: 010000 Astana, Soljagaw, ui. Ministrigi 35-8/14; tel. (7172) 74-00-75; fax (7172) 59-19-73; internet www.eco.gov.kz.
Ministry of Finance: 010000 Astana, Zhenis d-ly 11; tel. (7172) 71-77-64; fax (7172) 71-77-85; e-mail info@minfin.kz; internet www.minfin.kz.
Ministry of Foreign Affairs: 010000 Astana, Soljagaw, Tauelsizdik kosh. 31; tel. (7172) 72-05-18; fax (7172) 72-05-16; e-mail midrk@mid.kz; internet www.mfa.kz.
Ministry of Health: 010000 Astana, Soljagaw, Ministrilkter uyi, 5 kireberis; tel. (7172) 74-32-43; e-mail zdrav@mz.gov.kz; internet www.mz.gov.kz.
Ministry of Industry and New Technologies: 010000 Astana, Kabanbai batyr d-ly. 49, 'Transport Tauer'; tel. (3172) 24-16-42; fax (3172) 24-12-13; internet www.mit.kz.
Ministry of Internal Affairs: 010000 Astana, Tauelsizdik d-ly 1; tel. (7172) 71-40-10; fax (7172) 34-17-38; e-mail kense@mvd.kz; internet www.mvd.kz.
Ministry of Justice: 010000 Astana, Soljagaw, Orynbor kosh. 8, Ministrilkter uyi, 13 kireberis; tel. (7172) 74-07-37; fax (7172) 74-09-54; e-mail news@minjust.kz; internet www.minjust.kz.
Ministry of Labour and Social Security: 010000 Astana, Orynbor kosh. 8, Ministrilkter uyi, 6 kireberis; tel. (7172) 71-28-51; fax (7172) 74-36-08; e-mail mintrud@enbek.kz; internet www.enbek.gov.kz.
Ministry of Oil and Gas: 010000 Astana, Kabanbai batyr kosh. 19; tel. (7172) 97-68-83; fax (7172) 97-68-88; e-mail ayan@memr.kz; internet www.memr.gov.kz.
Ministry of Tourism and Sport: 010000 Astana, Abay d-ly 33; tel. (7172) 75-30-10; fax (7172) 75-34-30; e-mail kense@komtur.kz; internet www.mts.gov.kz.
Ministry of Transport and Communications: 010000 Astana, Kabanbai batyra d-ly 47; tel. (7172) 24-13-12; fax (7172) 24-14-19; e-mail mtc@mtc.gov.kz; internet www.mtk.gov.kz.

Directory

President

Presidential Election, 3 April 2011

Candidates	Votes	%
Nursultan A. Nazarbaev	7,850,958	95.55
Gani E. Kasymov	159,036	1.94
Jambyl A. Ahmetbekov	111,924	1.36
Mels H. Yeleussizov	94,452	1.15
Total	**8,216,370**	**100.00**

Legislature

Parliament is a bicameral legislative body, comprising the Senat and the Majlis (Assembly).

Majlis

010000 Astana, Parliament House; tel. (7172) 15-30-19; fax (7172) 33-30-99; e-mail www@parlam.kz; internet www.parlam.kz.
Chairman: ORAL B. MUXAMEJANOV.

General Election, 18 August 2007

Parties	Votes	%	Seats
Light Of The Fatherland (Nur Otan)	5,247,720	88.41	98
National Social Democratic Party	269,310	4.54	—
Bright Road Democratic Party of Kazakhstan (Ak Jol)	183,346	3.09	—
Village Kazakhstani Social Democratic Party (Auyl)	89,855	1.51	—
Communist People's Party of Kazakhstan	76,799	1.29	—
Others	68,595	1.16	—
Total	**5,935,625**	**100.00**	**107***

* Including nine deputies elected by the Assembly of the Nations of Kazakhstan (a body representing the country's minority ethnic groups) on 20 August 2007.

Senat

010000 Astana, Abay d-ly 33, Parliament House; tel. (7172) 15-33-76; fax (7172) 33-31-18; e-mail smimazh@parlam.kz; internet www.parlam.kz.
Chairman: KAYRAT A. MAMI.

The 47-member Senat is the upper chamber of Parliament. Elections are held every three years for one-half of the 32 seats elected by special colleges (comprising members of local councils) in Kazakhstan's 14 regions and two cities; the term of office for members of the Senat is six years. Under constitutional amendments adopted on 18 May 2007, the number of deputies appointed by the President increased from seven to 15; the additional eight members were officially appointed to the Senat by presidential decree in August. Partial elections to the Senat were conducted on 4 October 2008.

Election Commission

Ortalyk Sailau Komissiyasy (Central Election Commission): 010000 Astana, Beibitshilik kosh. 4; tel. (7172) 75-21-21; fax (7172) 33-33-i88; e-mail info@election.kz; internet www.election.kz; Chair. KUANDYK T. TURGANKULOV.

Political Organizations

A new law was introduced in July 2002, which required all parties to have a minimum of 50,000 members from among all the country's regions in order to qualify for official registration. In 2008 the following nine parties were registered.

Bright Road Democratic Party of Kazakhstan (Ak Jol) (Kazakstannyn 'Ak Jol' Demokratiyalyk Partiyasy): 010000 Astana, Ualihanova kosh. 9/1; tel. (7172) 20-05-85; fax (7172) 21-37-50; e-mail akzholpress@mail.ru; internet www.akzhol.kz; f. 2002 by former members of the Democratic Choice of Kazakhstan; merged with Justice Democratic Party (Adilet) in 2007; Chair. ALIXAN M. BAYMENOV; 175,862 mems (2007).

Communist Party of Kazakhstan (CPK) (Kazakstan Kommunistik Partiyasy): 010000 Astana, Beibitshilik kosh. 27/49; tel. and fax (7172) 21-32-97; e-mail pravdakz@list.ru; f. 1937; suspended Aug. 1991, re-registered Aug. 1998 and March 2003; contested 2004 legislative elections in alliance with Democratic Choice of Kazakhstan; mem. of For a Just Kazakhstan opposition bloc formed in 2005; Chair. SERIKBOLSYN A. ABDILDIN; Sec. JAMBYL A. AHMETBEKOV; 54,246 mems (2007).

Communist People's Party of Kazakhstan (Kazakstan Kommunistik Khalyk Partiyasy): 010000 Astana, Karasai batyr 14/7; tel. and fax (7172) 24-06-09; e-mail knpkastana@gmail.com; internet www.knpk.kz; f. 2004 by fmr mems of the Communist Party of Kazakhstan; Sec. of the Central Cttee VLADISLAV B. KOSAREV; 90,000 mems (2007).

Freedom National Social Democratic Party (Azat JSDP) ('Azat' Jalpyulttyk Sotsial Demokratiyalyk Partiyasy): 050000 Almatı, Kabanbai batyr kosh. 58; tel. (727) 266-36-40; fax (727) 266-36-43; e-mail ocdp@mail.ru; internet www.osdp.kz; f. 2009 by merger of Freedom and National Social Democratic Party; supports construction of a democratic, secular, social government and the rule of law, and an open society; Chair. JARMAKHAN A. TUYAKBAY; 400,000 mems (2009).

Light Of The Fatherland People's Democratic Party (Nur Otan) ('Nur Otan' Khalyktyk Demokratiyalyk Partiyasy): 050000 Almatı, Kunaev kosh. 12/1; tel. (7172) 55-55-62; fax (727) 279-40-66; e-mail partyotan@nursat.kz; internet www.ndp-nurotan.kz; f. 2006 by merger of Fatherland, Civic Party of Kazakhstan and Agrarian Party of Kazakhstan; supports administration of President Nazarbaev; Chair. NURSULTAN A. NAZARBAEV; First Deputy Chair. NURLAN Z. NYGMATULIN; 607,557 mems (2007).

Party of Patriots of Kazakhstan (PPK) (Kazakstan Patriottary Partiyasy): 050000 Almatı, Jibek-joly kosh. 76/318; tel. and fax (7172) 22-98-34; f. 2000; Chair. GANI E. KASYMOV; 172,000 mems (2007).

Spirituality Party ('Ruxaniyat' Partiyasy): 010000 Astana, Saryarka kosh. 5; tel. and fax (7172) 97-73-80; e-mail kazayelder@nursat.kz; f. 1995 as Renaissance Party of Kazakhstan; re-registered under new name 2003; supports Govt of President Nazarbaev; Chair. ALTYNSHASH K. JAGANOVA; 72,000 mems (2007).

Village Kazakhstani Social Democratic Party (Auyl) ('Auyl' Kazakstandyk Sotsial-Demokratiyalyk Partiyasy): 010000 Astana, Beibitshilik kosh. 46/109; tel. and fax (7172) 31-71-57; e-mail kaliev@parlam.kz; internet auyl.by.ru; registered in 2002; seeks to strengthen government support for the agricultural sector; Chair. GANI A. KALIEV; 61,043 mems (2007).

Diplomatic Representation

EMBASSIES IN KAZAKHSTAN

Afghanistan: 010000 Astana, Karaotel kosh. 3; tel. (7172) 57-14-42; fax (7172) 24-04-54; e-mail af_embassyalmaty@yahoo.com; internet www.afghanembassy.kz; Ambassador SOHRAB ALI SAFARI.

Armenia: 010000 Astana, Komsomolskii kosh. 73; tel. (7172) 40-20-15; fax (7172) 40-19-70; e-mail armeniaemb.kz@gmail.com; Ambassador VASILY KAZARIAN.

Austria: 010000 Astana, Kosmonavtov kosh. 62; tel. (7172) 97-78-69; fax (7172) 97-78-50; e-mail astana-ob@bmeia.gv.at; Ambassador URSULA FAHRINGER.

Azerbaijan: 010000 Astana, Diplomatiyalyk kalashyk B-6; tel. (7172) 24-15-81; fax (7172) 24-15-32; e-mail astana@azembassy.kz; internet www.azembassy.kz; Ambassador ZAKIR HASHIMOV.

Belarus: 010000 Astana, Kenesary kosh. 35; tel. and fax (7172) 32-48-29; e-mail kazakhstan@belembassy.org; internet kazakhstan.belembassy.org; Ambassador VALERY BRYLEV.

Belgium: 010000 Astana, Kosmonavtov kosh. 62; tel. (7172) 97-44-85; fax (7172) 97-78-49; e-mail embassy.astana@diplobel.fed.be; internet www.diplomatie.be/astana; Ambassador DANIEL BERTRAND.

Brazil: 010000 Astana, Kabanbai batyr kosh. 6/1, Kaskad; tel. (7172) 24-46-84; fax (7172) 24-47-43; e-mail brasemb.astana@itamaraty.gov.br; internet www.brasembastana.kz; Ambassador FREDERICO S. DUQUE ESTRADA MEYER.

Bulgaria: 010000 Astana, Saryarka kosh. 15; tel. (7172) 90-15-15; fax (7172) 90-18-19; e-mail astanabulemb@mail.bg; internet www.mfa.bg/bg/112/; Ambassador STOYAN RIZOV.

Canada: 050010 Almatı, Karasai batyr kosh. 34; tel. (727) 250-11-51; fax (727) 258-24-93; e-mail almat@international.gc.ca; internet www.canadainternational.gc.ca/kazakhstan; Ambassador STEPHEN MILLAR.

China, People's Republic: 010000 Astana, Kabanbai batyr d-ly 28/5; tel. (7172) 79-35-64; fax (7172) 79-35-65; e-mail chinaemb_kz@mfa.gov.cn; internet kz.china-embassy.org; Ambassador ZHOU LI.

Cuba: 010000 Astana, Kabanbai batyr d-ly 27/2; tel. and fax (7172) 24-24-67; fax (7172) 24-26-38; e-mail natembacu@mail.online.kz; Ambassador ABELARDO HERNÁNDEZ FERRER.

Czech Republic: 010000 Astana, Saryarka kosh. 6, Biznes-Tsentr Arman, 13th floor; tel. (7172) 66-04-72; fax (7172) 66-01-42; e-mail astana@embassy.mzv.cz; internet www.mzv.cz/astana; Ambassador BEDŘICH KOPECKÝ.

Egypt: 010000 Astana, Sarayshyk kosh. 30; tel. (7172) 28-60-67; fax (7172) 28-60-50; e-mail embassy.astana@mfa.gov.eg; Ambassador ABDALLAH OMAR ELARNOSI.

France: 010000 Astana, Kosmonavtov kosh. 62; tel. (7172) 79-51-00; fax (7172) 79-51-01; e-mail ambafrance@mail.online.kz; internet ambafrance-kz.org; Ambassador JEAN-CHARLES BERTHONNET.

Georgia: 010000 Astana, Diplomatiyalyk kalashyk C-4; tel. (7172) 24-32-58; fax (7172) 24-34-26; e-mail astana.emb@mfa.gov.ge; internet www.kazakhstan.mfa.gov.ge; Ambassador PAATA KALANDADZE.

Germany: 010000 Astana, Kosmonavtov kosh. 62; tel. (7172) 79-12-00; fax (7172) 79-12-13; e-mail info@astana.diplo.de; internet www.astana.diplo.de; Ambassador RAINER EUGEN SCHLAGETER.

Greece: 010000 Astana, Karaotkel sh-a 2, 109; tel. (7172) 24-12-66; fax (7172) 24-47-76; e-mail gremb.ast@mfa.gr; Ambassador EVANGELOS DENAXAS.

Holy See: 010000 Astana, Zelenaya Alleya kosh. 20; tel. (7172) 24-12-69; fax (7172) 24-16-04; e-mail nuntius_kazakhstan@lycos.com; Apostolic Nuncio Most Rev. MIGUEL MAURY BUENDÍA (Titular Archbishop of Italica).

Hungary: 010000 Astana, Kosmonavtov kosh. 62; tel. (7172) 55-03-23; fax (7172) 55-03-24; e-mail mission.ast@ku.hu; internet www.mfa.gov.hu/emb/astana; Ambassador IMRE LASZLÓCZKI.

India: 010000 Astana, Kabanbai batyr kosh. 6/1, Kenselik ortalygy 'Kaskad', 5th Floor; tel. (7172) 92-57-00; fax (7172) 92-57-16; e-mail amb.astana@mea.gov.in; internet www.indembassy.kz; Ambassador ASHOK KUMAR SHARMA.

Iran: 050000 Almatı, Diplomatiyalyk kalashyk B-7; tel. (727) 24-25-11; fax (727) 24-15-37; e-mail iranembassy@itte.kz; Ambassador GORBAN SEIFI.

Iraq: 010000 Astana, Konaev kosh. 19; tel. (7127) 28-60-92; fax (7172)-28-60-96; e-mail astemb@iraqmfamail.com; Ambassador RAGEH SABER AL-MOUSSAWI ABBOUD.

Israel: 010000 Astana, Auezov kosh. 8; tel. (7172) 68-87-39; fax (7172) 68-87-35; e-mail info@astana.mfa.gov.il; internet astana.mfa.gov.il; Ambassador ISRAEL MEI-AMI.

Italy: 010000 Astana, Shuba sh-a, Kosmonavtov kosh. 62; tel. (7172) 24-33-90; fax (7172) 24-36-86; e-mail ambasciata.astana@esteri.it; internet www.ambastana.esteri.it; Ambassador BRUNO ANTONIO PASQUINO.

Japan: 010000 Astana, Chubar sh-a, Kosmonavtov kosh. 62; tel. (7172) 97-78-43; fax (7172) 97-78-42; e-mail kobun@null.kz; internet www.kz.emb-japan.go.jp/jp/index_r.htm; Ambassador YUZO HARADA.

Jordan: 010000 Astana, Novostroitel kosh. 8/2; tel. (7172) 24-52-54; fax (7172) 24-52-53; e-mail astana@fm.gov.jo; Ambassador SLAIMAN ARABIAT.

Korea, Republic: 010000 Astana, Karasai batyr d-ly 6/1/91–93; tel. (7172) 92-55-91; fax (7172) 92-55-96; e-mail koreaemb-kz@mofat.go.kr; internet kaz.mofat.go.kr; Ambassador LEE BYUNG-HWA.

Kyrgyzstan: 010000 Astana, Diplomatiyalyk kalashyk B-5; tel. (7172) 24-20-24; fax (7172) 24-24-14; e-mail kz@mail.online.kz; Ambassador JANUSH RUSTENBEKOV.

Latvia: 010000 Astana, Kabanbai batyr d-ly 6/1/122, Kaskad Business Centre; tel. (7172) 92-53-17; fax (7172) 92-53-19; e-mail embassy.kazakhstan@mfa.gov.lv; Ambassador JURIS MAKLAKOVS.

Lebanon: 010000 Astana, Tauelsyzdyk 2, 13th floor; tel. (7172) 79-35-15; fax (7172) 79-35-16; e-mail embassylebanon-kz@hotmail.com; Ambassador VAZKEN KAVLAKIAN.

Libya: 010000 Astana, Karaokel sh-a, 36-8 kosh. 6; tel. (7172) 56-37-65; fax (7172) 56-37-23; e-mail lpb_ast@yahoo.com; Ambassador AHMED EDDEB.

Lithuania: 050059 Almatı, Gornyi Gigant sh-a, Eskandir kosh. 15; tel. (727) 263-10-40; fax (727) 263-19-75; e-mail amb.kz@urm.lt; internet kz.mfa.lt; Ambassador ROKAS BERNOTAS.

Malaysia: 050051 Almatı, Rubenshtein kosh. 9A; tel. (727) 333-44-83; fax (727) 387-28-25; e-mail mwalmaty@nursat.kz; internet www.kln.gov.my/web/kaz_almaty; Ambassador (vacant).

Mongolia: 050000 Almatı, Musabaev kosh. 1; tel. (727) 269-35-36; fax (727) 258-17-27; e-mail info@mongemb.kz; Ambassador KHARAAVCHIIN AYUURZANA.

Netherlands: 010000 Astana, Kosmonavtov kosh. 62; tel. (7172) 55-54-50; fax (7172) 55-54-74; e-mail ast@minbuza.nl; internet www.netherlands-embassy.kz; Ambassador FRANS POTUYT.

Oman: 010000 Astana, Chubar sh-a, Novostroitel kosh. 1; tel. (7172) 24-18-61; fax (7172) 24-18-63; e-mail astana@mofa.gov.om; Ambassador SAID AL-AMRI.

KAZAKHSTAN

Pakistan: 050004 Almatı, Tulebaev kosh. 25; tel. (727) 273-15-02; fax (727) 273-13-00; e-mail parepalmaty@hotmail.com; Ambassador MOHAMMAD AKHTAR TUFAIL.

Poland: 010000 Astana, Saryarka kosh. 15; tel. (7172) 90-10-11; fax (7172) 90-10-12; e-mail amb@poland.kz; internet www.astana.polemb.net; Ambassador JACEK KLUCZKOWSKI.

Qatar: 010000 Astana, Saraishyk kosh. 20A; tel. (7172) 28-61-23; fax (7172) 28-61-33; Ambassador NASSER BIN RASHID AL-NUAIMI.

Romania: 010000 Astana, Saraishyk kosh. 28; tel. (7172) 28-62-01; fax (7172) 28-62-03; e-mail amb@rom.ricc.kz; Ambassador EMIL RAPCEA.

Russia: 010000 Astana, Baraev kosh. 4; tel. (7172) 22-24-83; fax (7172) 22-38-49; e-mail rfe@nursat.kz; internet www.rfembassy.kz; Ambassador MIKHAIL N. BOCHARNIKOV.

Saudi Arabia: 010000 Astana, Akyn Sary kosh. 19; tel. (7172) 92-57-52; fax (7172) 92-57-62; e-mail kzemb@mofa.gov.sa; Ambassador ABDUL MAZHID KHAKIM.

Slovakia: 010000 Astana, Karaotkel sh-a 2, 5; tel. (7172) 24-11-91; fax (7172) 24-20-48; e-mail emb.astana@mzv.sk; internet www.mzv.sk/astana; Ambassador Dr DUŠAN PODHORSKÝ.

South Africa: 010000 Astana, Kabanbai batyr d-ly 6/1; tel. (7172) 92-53-27; fax (7172) 92-53-29; e-mail astana@foreign.gov.za; Chargé d'affaires a.i. JURGENS YOUNG.

Spain: 010000 Astana, Kenesary kosh. 47/25; tel. (7172) 20-15-35; fax (7172) 20-03-17; e-mail emb.astana@maec.es; Ambassador ALBERTO ANTÓN CORTÉS.

Switzerland: 010000 Astana, Kosmonavtov kosh. 62; tel. (7172) 97-98-92; fax (7172) 97-98-94; e-mail ast.vertretung@eda.admin.ch; internet www.eda.admin.ch/astana; Ambassador STEFAN NELLEN.

Tajikistan: 010000 Astana, Chubar sh-a, Marsovaya kosh. 15; tel. and fax (7172) 24-09-29; e-mail embassy_tajic@mbox.kz; Ambassador BAHROM M. HOLNAZAROV.

Turkey: 010000 Astana, Karasai batyr d-ly 6/1/23/101; tel. (7172) 92-58-70; fax (7172) 92-58-74; e-mail astanaturkbe@gmail.com; Ambassador LALE ÜLKER.

Turkmenistan: 010000 Astana, Otyrar kosh. 64; tel. and fax (7172) 21-08-82; e-mail tm_emb@astanatelecom.kz; Ambassador MAGTYMGULY AKMYRADOV.

Ukraine: 010000 Astana, Kenesary kosh. 41; tel. (7172) 32-60-42; fax (7172) 32-68-11; e-mail embassy_ua@kepter.kz; internet www.mfa.gov.ua/kazakhstan; Ambassador OLEH DYOMIN.

United Arab Emirates: 010000 Astana, Diplomatiyalyk kalashyk C-15; tel. (7172) 24-36-75; fax (7172) 24-36-76; e-mail emaratembassy_kz@yahoo.com; Ambassador IBRAHIM HASSAN SAIF.

United Kingdom: 010000 Astana, Shubar sh-a, Kosmonavtov kosh. 62; tel. (7172) 55-62-00; fax (7172) 55-62-11; e-mail britishembassy@mail.online.kz; internet www.ukinkz.fco.gov.uk; Ambassador DAVID MORAN.

USA: 010010 Astana, Ak Bulak 4/23-22/3; tel. (7172) 70-21-00; fax (7172) 34-08-90; e-mail info@usembassy.kz; internet kazakhstan.usembassy.gov; Chargé d'affaires a.i. JOHN M. ORDWAY.

Uzbekistan: 050010 Almatı, Beribaev kosh. 36; tel. (727) 291-78-86; fax (727) 291-10-55; e-mail emb-uzbekistan@mail.ru; Ambassador FARRUH TURSUNOV.

Viet Nam: 010000 Astana, Saryarka kosh. 6; tel. (7172) 99-03-75; fax (7172) 66-03-79; Ambassador VU THE HIEP.

Judicial System

Supreme Court of the Republic of Kazakhstan (Kazakstan Respublikasynyn Zhogargy Soty): 010000 Astana, Soljagaw, Tauelsizdik kosh. 39; tel. (7172) 74-75-00; fax (7172) 74-78-13; e-mail ms@supcourt.kz; internet www.supcourt.kz; Chair. BEKTAS BEKNAZAROV.

Constitutional Council of the Republic of Kazakhstan (Kazakstan Respublikasy Konstitutsiyalyk Keneci): 010000 Astana, Soljagaw, Tauelsizdik kosh. 39; tel. (7172) 74-79-56; fax (7172) 74-76-51; e-mail liaison@constcouncil.kz; internet www.constcouncil.kz; f. 1995; seven mems; Chair. IGOR I. ROGOV.

Prosecutor-General: ASKAT K. DAUYLBAEV, 010000 Astana, Seifullin kosh. 37; e-mail gp-rk@mail.online.kz; internet www.procuror.kz.

Religion

The major religion of the Kazakhs is Islam. They are almost exclusively Sunni Muslims of the Hanafi school. The Russian Orthodox Church is the dominant Christian denomination; it is attended mainly by Slavs. There are also Protestant Churches (mainly Baptists), as well as a Roman Catholic presence and a Jewish community.

In mid-2005 legislation was introduced, which required all religious organizations and communities to register with the state authorities.

ISLAM

The Kazakhs were converted to Islam only in the early 19th century, and for many years elements of animist practices remained. Over the period 1985–90 the number of mosques in Kazakhstan increased from 25 to 60. By 1991 there were an estimated 230 Muslim religious communities functioning in Kazakhstan and an Islamic institute had been opened in Almatı. The Islamic revival intensified following Kazakhstan's independence from the USSR, and during 1991–94 some 4,000 mosques were reported to have been opened.

Religious Administration of Muslims of Kazakhstan (Kazakstan musylmandary dini baskarmasy): 050000 Almatı; tel. (727) 230-63-65; fax (727) 297-94-23; e-mail susaev@bk.ru; internet www.muftyat.kz; Chair. Chief Mufti ABSATTAR B. Haji DERBISALI.

CHRISTIANITY

The Roman Catholic Church

The organization of the Roman Catholic Church in Kazakhstan comprises one archdiocese, two dioceses and one apostolic administration. Most Catholics in Kazakhstan are enrolled in the Latin Rite, and there are also a number of Byzantine Rite communities. There were an estimated 173,710 adherents at 31 December 2007.

Catholic Bishops' Conference of Kazakhstan: 010010 Astana, Tashenov kosh. 3, POB 622; tel. (7172) 37-25-53; e-mail Bishops-Conf.KZ@mail.ru; internet www.catholic-kazakhstan.org; f. 2003; Pres. Rt Rev. TOMASZ PETA (Archbishop of the Archdiocese of the Most Holy Virgin Mary at Astana).

Archbishop of the Archdiocese of the Most Holy Virgin Mary at Astana: Rt Rev. TOMASZ PETA, 010010 Astana, Tashenov kosh. 3, POB 622; tel. (7172) 37-29-35; fax (7172) 37-29-27; e-mail catholic_astana@mail.ru; internet www.catholic-kazakhstan.org.

Apostolic Administrator of Atiraw: Most Rev. JANUSZ KALETA (Titular Bishop of Phelbes), 060009 Atiraw, Avangard 3/34 A; tel. (7122) 28-16-86; fax (7122) 28-16-84; e-mail catholic.atyrau@gmail.com.

The Russian Orthodox Church

The Russian Orthodox Church of the Moscow Patriarchate in Kazakhstan is represented by a Metropolitan District, established in 2003, comprising three dioceses. In 2009 there were 112 parishes.

Metropolitan District of Kazakhstan: 010000 Astana, pl. Respubliki 12; tel. (7172) 28-60-49; fax (7172) 28-69-84; e-mail cross@orthodox.kz; internet www.mitropolia.kz; f. 2003; three dioceses (of Astana and Almatı, Chimkent and Aqmola, and Oral and Guriyev—Atiraw) Metropolitan of Astana and Almatı ALEKSANDR (MOGILEV).

JUDAISM

Mitsva Association of Kazakhstan: Almatı; tel. (727) 273-54-49; fax (727) 258-34-59; e-mail contact@mitsva.kz; internet www.mitsva.kz; f. 1992; unites Jewish communities across Kazakhstan; Pres. ALEKSANDR BARON.

Rabbi of Almatı: Rabbi MENACHEM GERSHOVICH.

The Press

PRINCIPAL DAILY NEWSPAPERS

Aikyn/Liter (Travel Warrant): 050029 Almatı, Mukanova kosh. 223B; tel. (727) 295-24-52; fax (727) 315-24-57; e-mail info@liter.kz; internet www.aikyn.kz; internet www.liter.kz; f. 2004; five a week; Kazakh and Russian edns; weekly arts and information supplement, *Aikyn apta/Liter nedelya* (Thursdays); Editor-in-Chief LEV TARAKOV; circ. 39,300 (Kazakh edn, *Aikyn*), 33,600 (Russian edn, *Liter*).

Almaty Herald: 050000 Almatı, Rozybakiev kosh. 37; tel. (727) 241-45-69; fax (727) 241-40-78; e-mail herald@nursat.kz; Editor-in-Chief OLESSYA IVANOVA.

Egemen Kazakhstan (Sovereign Kazakhstan): Astana, Egemen Kazakhstan kosh. 5/13; tel. (7172) 37-65-27; e-mail egemenkz@mail.online.kz; internet www.egemen.kz; f. 1919; 6 a week; organ of the Govt; in Kazakh; Pres. SAUYTBEK ABDRAXMANOV; Editor-in-Chief JANBOLAT AUPBAEV.

Ekspress-K: 010000 Almatı, Kabanbai-batyr kosh. 30A; tel. (727) 259-24-27; fax (727) 259-24-02; e-mail daily@express-k.kz; internet www.express-k.kz; f. 1920; 5 a week; in Russian; Editor-in-Chief TLEPBERGEN BEKMAGANBETOV; circ. 19,500.

Kazakhstanskaya Pravda (Kazakhstani Truth): 010000 Astana, Jenis kosh. 18A; tel. (727) 232-17-29; fax (727) 250-18-73; e-mail kpam@kaznet.kz; internet www.kazpravda.kz; f. 1920; 5 a week;

KAZAKHSTAN

publ. by the Govt; in Russian; Editor-in-Chief TATIANA V. KOSTINA; circ. 100,000 (2010).

Vechernii Almaty (Evening Almaty): 050016 Almatı, Abylai-xan d-ly 2; tel. and fax (727) 279-28-90; e-mail info@vecher.kz; internet www.vecher.kz; f. 1968; in Russian; Editor-in-Chief NIKOLAI N. ZHOROV.

Vremya (Time): 050000 Almatı, Raiymbek d-ly 115; tel. (727) 259-71-96; e-mail info@time.kz; internet www.time.kz; f. 1999; in Russian; general; Editor-in-Chief VADIM N. BOREIKO; circ. 250,000 (2004).

OTHER PUBLICATIONS

Akikat (Justice): 050044 Almatı, Gogol kosh. 39; tel. (727) 273-84-03; f. 1921; monthly; social and political.

Ana Tili (Native Language): 050044 Almatı, Dostyk d-ly 7; tel. (727) 233-22-21; fax (727) 233-34-73; f. 1990; weekly; in Kazakh; Editor-in-Chief J. BEISENBAY-ULI; circ. 11,073.

Dala Men Qala: 050029 Almatı, Abilaijan kosh. 79; tel. (727) 315-06-86; fax (727) 315-06-89; e-mail dalamenkala@mail.ru; internet dmk.kz; f. 2003; weekly; politics, society; Editor-in-Chief SAPARBAY PARMANKULOV.

Delovaya Nedelya (Business Week): 050044 Almatı, Jibek-joly d-ly 64; tel. (727) 250-62-72; fax (727) 273-91-48; e-mail info@dn.kz; internet www.dn.kz; f. 1992; weekly; business, politics, finance of Kazakhstan and Central Asia; in Russian; Editor-in-Chief S. A. KORJUMBAEV; circ. 15,000.

Delovoi Kazakhstan (Business Kazakhstan): 050013 Almatı, pl. Respubliki 15/553, POB 388; tel. (727) 250-72-68; fax (727) 295-23-02; e-mail dk@intelsoft.kz; internet www.dknews.kz; in Russian; weekly; f. 2006; Chief Editor SERIK KORJUMBAEV; circ. 15,000 (2009).

Druzhnye Rebyata (Friendly Chaps): 050009 Almatı, Abay d-ly 143/508; tel. (727) 242-77-89; e-mail jorken@mail.ru; f. 1933 as *Pioner Kazakhstana* (Kazakhstani Pioneer); present name adopted 1956; weekly; in Russian; for children.

Ekologicheskii Kuryer int (Ecological Courier International): 050000 Almatı, Panfilov kosh. 106A; tel. (727) 261-12-23; fax (727) 261-12-10; e-mail ecocourier@nursat.kz; every two weeks; in Russian; environmental concerns; Editor EDUARD MATSKEVICH; circ. 3,000.

Ekspert Kazakhstan: 05000 Almatı, Furmanov kosh. 122; tel. (727) 272-73-69; fax (727) 295-28-33; e-mail skir@expert.ru; internet www.expert.ru/printissues/kazakhstan; f. 2003; weekly; business and economics; in Russian; Chief Editor YURII DOROKHOV; circ. 10,000 (2011).

Jas Alash (Young Generation): 050002 Almatı, Jibek-joly kosh. 50; tel. (727) 273-75-59; fax (727) 273-87-55; e-mail zhasalash2010@mail.ru; internet www.zhasalash.kz; f. 1921; publ. by the Kazakhstan Youth Union; two a week; in Kazakh; Editor-in-Chief RYSBEK SARSENBAY.

Karavan (Caravan): 050000 Almatı, pl. Respubliki 13; tel. (727) 258-36-24; fax (727) 258-36-25; e-mail kaztag@caravan.kz; internet www.caravan.kz; f. 1991; weekly; in Russian; Editor-in-Chief ADIL IBRAEV; circ. 250,000.

Kazak Adebiety (Kazakh Literature): 050000 Almatı, Ablai-xan kosh. 105; tel. and fax (727) 269-54-62; f. 1934; weekly; organ of the Union of Writers of Kazakhstan; in Kazakh; Editor-in-Chief A. JAKSYBAEV; circ. 7,874.

Kazakhstan: 050044 Almatı, Jibek-joly d-ly 50; tel. (727) 233-13-56; f. 1992; weekly; analytical publication on the extractive industry intended for an audience of international investors; in Russian and English; Editor-in-Chief N. ORAZBEKOV.

Kazakstan Aielderi (Women of Kazakhstan): 050044 Almatı, Jibek-joly d-ly 50; tel. (727) 233-06-23; fax (727) 246-15-53; f. 1925; monthly; culture and housekeeping; in Kazakh; Editor-in-Chief ALTYNSHASH K. JAGANOVA; circ. 15,200.

Kazakstan Mektebi (Kazakhstan School): 050004 Almatı, Ablai-xan d-ly 34; tel. (727) 239-76-65; f. 1925; monthly; publ. by the Ministry of Education and Science; in Kazakh; Editor-in-Chief S. ABISHEVA; circ. 10,000.

Kazakstan Zaman (Kazakh Time): 050002 Almatı, Dostyk d-ly 106G; tel. (727) 265-07-39; e-mail info@kazakzaman.kz; internet www.kazakzaman.kz; f. 1992; in Kazakh and Turkish; weekly; Gen. Dir ERTAY AIGALYEVICH; circ. 15,000.

Kazakstannyn zher resurstary/Zemelnye Resursy Kazakhstana (Land Resources of Kazakhstan): 010000 Astana, 8 Orynbor kosh., 12 kireberis, 5th floor; tel. and fax (7172) 74-16-52; e-mail info@auzr.kz; internet www.auzr.kz; every two months; Kazakh and Russian edns; publication of Republican Agency for the Management of Land Resources; Chair of Editorial Bd ALJANBAY SHAYAHMETOV.

Kontinent (Continent): 050000 Almatı, POB 271; tel. (727) 250-10-39; fax (727) 250-10-41; e-mail bzchyt@kaznet.kz; f. 1999; every two weeks; policy and society journal; Editor-in-Chief ANDREI KUKUSHKIN; circ. 10,000.

Korye Ilbo (Korean News): 050044 Almatı, Jibek-joly d-ly 50; tel. (727) 233-90-10; fax (727) 263-25-46; f. 1923; weekly; in Korean and Russian; Editor-in-Chief YAN WON SIK.

Kredo (Credo): 100029 Qarağandi, Oktyabrskaya 25; tel. (721) 222-38-40; e-mail credogazeta@gmail.com; internet www.catholic-kazakhstan.org/credo; f. 1995; monthly; Catholic; in Russian; Chief Editor N. MAMAEV.

Megapolis (Megalopolis): 050060 Almatı, P. Tajibaevoy kosh. 155; tel. and fax (727) 315-09-87; e-mail info@megapolis.kz; internet www.megapolis.kz; f. 2000; general; weekly; Gen. Dir RINAT ASKAROV; Chief Editor IGOR SHAXNOVICH.

Novoye Pokoleniye (New Generation): 050091 Almatı, Bogenbai batyr kosh. 156A/505; tel. (727) 334-09-11; fax (727) 250-95-46; e-mail np@np.kz; internet www.np.kz; f. 1998; weekly; economic and political affairs of Kazakhstan and the CIS, with supplement on the arts; in Russian; Editor-in-Chief SERGEI APARIN; circ. 40,000.

Panorama: 050013 Almatı, pl. Respubliki 15/647; tel. (727) 291-50-46; fax (727) 291-50-36; e-mail panorama@intelsoft.kz; internet www.panorama.kz; f. 1992; weekly; analytical coverage of politics, economics, business and international relations; in Russian; Dir ALEKSANDR NESUKANNYI; Editor-in-Chief LERA TSOY; circ. 20,000.

Petroleum of Kazakhstan: 050000 Almatı, Nauryzbai batyr kosh. 58; tel. (727) 258-28-38; fax (727) 250-50-82; e-mail office@petroleumjournal.kz; internet www.petroleumjournal.kz; every two months; in Russian and English; Editor-in-Chief OLEG C. CHERVINSKY; circ. 1,000.

Pro Sport Kazakhstan: 050008 Almatı, Dostyk/Bogenbay batyr kosh. 34A/87A; tel. and fax (727) 250-90-30; two a week; in Russian; sport.

Rukh-Miras (Heritage Movement): 050013 Almatı, Abay d-ly 14; tel. (727) 267-28-83; e-mail ieshua@front.ru; internet www.nlrk.kz; f. 2004; quarterly; literature, fine arts; in Kazakh and Russian; Chair of Bd of Editors MURAT AUEZOV; Chief Editor TALASBEK ASEMKULOV.

Russkii Yazyk i Literatura v Kazakhskoye Shkole (Russian Language and Literature in the Kazakh School): 050091 Almatı, Abylai-xan kosh. 34; tel. (727) 239-76-68; f. 1962; every two months; in Russian; Editor-in-Chief B. S. MUKANOV.

Strana i Mir (The Country and The World): 050029 Almatı, Abylai-xan kosh. 79; tel. (727) 315-06-85; fax (727) 315-06-89; e-mail reklamanyr@liter.kz; internet sim.kz; politics; weekly; in Russian; f. 2003; Editor-in-Chief RASHID GARIPOV.

Turkistan: 050009 Almatı, Abay kosh. 143; tel. (727) 394-42-51; fax (727) 394-41-80; e-mail turkestan_gazeta@mail.ru; internet www.turkystan.kz; f. 1994; weekly; political analysis; in Kazakh; Editor-in-chief SHAMSHIDIN A. PATTEEV; circ. 10,000.

Uigur Avazi (Uigur Voice): 050044 Almatı, Jibek-joly d-ly 50; tel. (727) 233-84-59; f. 1957; two a week; publ. by the Govt; socio-political; in Uigur; Editor-in-Chief I. AZAMATOV; circ. 9,000.

Ulan (Man Alive): 050044 Almatı, Jibek-joly d-ly 50; tel. (727) 233-80-03; f. 1930; weekly; in Kazakh; for children and teenagers; Editor-in-Chief S. KALIEV; circ. 183,014.

Zerde (Intellect): 050044 Almatı, Jibek-joly d-ly 50; tel. (727) 233-83-81; f. 1960; monthly; popular, scientific, technical; in Kazakh; Editor-in-Chief E. RAUSHAN-ULY; circ. 68,600.

NEWS AGENCY

National Information Agency 'Kazinform': 010000 Astana, Beibitshilik kosh. 10; tel. and fax (7172) 32-75-67; e-mail product@inform.kz; internet www.inform.kz; f. 1997; 100% state-owned open jt-stock co; provides information on govt activities in Kazakhstan and abroad; Chair. of Bd DAUREN DIYAROV.

Publishers

Gylym (Science): 050010 Almatı, Pushkin kosh. 111–113; tel. (727) 291-18-77; fax (727) 261-88-45; f. 1946; books on natural sciences, humanities and scientific research journals; Dir S. G. BAIMENOV.

Kainar (Spring): 050009 Almatı, Abay d-ly 143; tel. (727) 242-27-96; e-mail kainar_baspasy@mail.ru; f. 1962; agriculture, history, culture, religion; Dir ORAZBEK S. SARSENBAEV.

Kazakhskaya Entsiklopediya (Kazakh Encyclopedia): 050000 Almatı; tel. (727) 262-55-66; f. 1968; Editor-in-Chief R. N. NURGALIEV.

Kazakhstan Publishing House: 050000 Almatı, Abay d-ly 143; tel. and fax (727) 242-29-29; f. 1920; political science, economics, medicine, general and social sciences; Dir E. X. SYZDYKOV; Editors-in-Chief M. D. SITKO, M. A. RASHEV.

Mektep: 050009 Almatı, Abay d-ly 143; tel. (727) 242-26-24; fax (727) 277-85-44; e-mail mektep@mail.ru; internet www.mektep.kz;

KAZAKHSTAN

f. 1947; mainly literature for educational institutions; dictionaries, phrase books, children's textbooks, teaching materials, reference books; publishes books in Kazakh, Russian, Uigur and Uzbek; Gen. Dir E. SATYBALDIEV.

Oner (Art): 050000 Almatı, Abay d-ly 143; tel. (727) 242-08-88; f. 1980; Dir S. S. ORAZALINOV; Editor-in-Chief A. A. ASKAROV.

Zhazushy (Writer): 050000 Almatı, Abay d-ly 143; tel. (727) 242-28-49; f. 1934; literature, literary criticism, essays and poetry; Dir D. I. ISABEKOV; Editor-in-Chief A. T. SARAEV.

Broadcasting and Communications

GOVERNMENT AGENCY

Republican Agency for Information and Communications: 010000 Astana, Ministry Bldg, Soljagaw, Ishim; tel. (7172) 74-01-35; fax (7172) 74-10-03; e-mail press@aic.gov.kz; internet www.aic.gov.kz; Chair. KUANYSHBEK B. YESEKEEV.

TELECOMMUNICATIONS

Altel: 050000 Almatı, Jurgenev kosh. 9; tel. (727) 230-16-30; fax (727) 230-01-43; e-mail info@altel.kz; internet www.altel.kz; f. 1994; provides mobile cellular communications in Kazakhstan (under the brand names City, Dalacom, Jet and PAThWORD).

GSM Kazakhstan (Kcell): 050013 Almatı, Timiriyazev kosh. 2G; tel. (727) 258-11-48; fax (727) 258-89-11; e-mail info@kcell.kz; internet www.kcell.kz; f. 1998; 51% owned by TeliaSonera (Sweden), 49% by Kazakhtelecom; provides mobile cellular telecommunications services (as Kcell and Activ) in 1,449 settlements across Kazakhstan; 7.5m. subscribers (May 2009); Chief Exec. VEYSEL ARAL.

KaR-tel (K-Mobile): 050000 Almatı, Tole bi 55; tel. (727) 250-60-60; fax (727) 295-23-97; e-mail csales@kartel.kz; internet www.k-mobile.kz; f. 1999; 100% subsidiary of VympelKom-Bilain (Russia); provides mobile cellular telecommunications services (as K-Mobile, Excess and Beeline) in more than 100 settlements and along principal roads across Kazakhstan; Gen. Dir DMITRII KROMSKII; 1.6m. subscribers (mid-2005).

Kazakhtelekom: 050000 Almatı, Abylai-xan d-ly 86; tel. (727) 262-05-41; fax (727) 263-93-95; internet www.telecom.kz; f. 1994; telecommunications services; public limited co; Pres. SERIK BURKITBAEV.

KazTransCom: 050012 Almatı, Baitursynov kosh. 46A; tel. (727) 270-13-10; fax (727) 270-13-18; e-mail ktc@kaztranscom.kz; jt-stock co; provides telecommunications services to the petroleum and natural gas sectors; won licence in 2004 to provide long-distance and international telephone calls country-wide, becoming Kazakhstan's second long-distance provider.

BROADCASTING

Private radio and television stations began operating in Kazakhstan in the 1990s.

Kazakh State Television and Radio Broadcasting Corpn: 050013 Almatı, Jeltoksan kosh. 175A; tel. (727) 263-37-16; f. 1920; Pres. YERMEK TURSUNOV.

Radio

Kazakh Radio: 050013 Almatı, Jeltoksan kosh. 175A; tel. (727) 263-19-68; fax (727) 265-03-87; e-mail kazradio@astel.kz; internet www.radio.kz; f. 1921; broadcasts in Kazakh, Russian, Uigur, German and other minority languages; Gen. Dir TOREXAN DANIYAR.

Radio 31: 050060 Almatı, Tajibaevoi kosh. 155; tel. (727) 315-29-31; e-mail radio@31.kz; internet www.31.kz; f. 1994; news and music; Dir SABIT SULEIMENOV.

Television

Khabar News Agency: 050013 Almatı, pl. Respubliki 13; tel. (727) 263-83-69; fax (727) 250-63-45; e-mail naz@khabar.almaty.kz; internet www.khabar.kz; f. 1959; international broadcasts in Kazakh, Uigur, Russian and German; two television channels; Chair. of the Bd of Dirs MAULEN ASHIMBAEV; Dir GULNAR IKSANOVA.

KTK (Kazakh Commercial Television): 050013 Almatı, pl. Respubliki 13; tel. (727) 263-44-28; fax (727) 250-66-25; e-mail ktkao@kzaira.com; f. 1990; independent; Gen. Dir ANDREI SHUXOV; Pres. SHOKAN LAUULIN.

NTK (Association of TV and Radio Broadcasters of Kazakhstan): 050013 Almatı, pl. Respubliki 13, 6th Floor; tel. (727) 270-01-83; fax (727) 270-01-85; e-mail kaztvradio@nursat.kz; f. 2000; privately owned; Pres. AIDAR JUMABAEV.

STV: 050010 Almatı, Karasai batyr kosh. 88; tel. (727) 292-74-74; internet www.rakhattv.kz; f. 1994; privately owned; fmrly Rakhat-TV, present name adopted 2009; information and entertainment broadcasts to Aktau, Almatı, Astana, Atiraw, Pavlodar, Petropavl and Toldykurgan, also available on cable networks and satellite.

Finance

(cap. = capital; res = reserves; dep. = deposits; m. = million; brs = branches; amounts in tenge, unless otherwise indicated)

BANKING

Central Bank

National Bank of Kazakhstan (NBK): 050040 Almatı, Koktem-3 21; tel. (727) 270-45-91; fax (727) 250-60-90; e-mail hq@nationalbank.kz; internet www.nationalbank.kz; f. 1990; cap. 20,000.0m., res 668,713.7m., dep. 2,555,829.3m. (Dec. 2009); Gov. GRIGORII A. MARCHENKO; 19 brs.

Major Commercial Banks

Alliance Bank: 050000 Almatı, Kunaev kosh. 32; tel. (727) 258-40-40; fax (727) 259-67-87; e-mail info@alb.kz; internet www.alb.kz; f. 1999; cap. 96,380m., res 3,216m., dep. 789,794m. (Dec. 2008); Chair. DAUREN KEREIBAEV.

ATF Bank: 050000 Almatı, Furmanov kosh. 100; tel. (727) 250-30-40; fax (727) 250-19-95; e-mail info@atfbank.kz; internet www.atfbank.kz; f. 1995; present name adopted 2002; cap. 106,878.5m., res 14,884.2m., dep. 535,330.1m. (Dec. 2009); Chair. TIMUR ISSATAEV; 10 brs.

Bank Centercredit: 050000 Almatı, Panfilov kosh. 98; tel. (727) 259-85-98; fax (727) 258-45-10; e-mail info@centercredit.kz; internet www.centercredit.kz; f. 1988; present name adopted 1996; 30.5% owned by Kookmin Bank (Rep. of Korea); cap. 52,710m., res −10m., dep. 1,022,193m. (Dec. 2009); Chair. of Bd BAXYTBEK R. BAYSEITOV; 19 brs.

BTA Bank: 050051 Almatı, Samal 2, Joldasbekov kosh. 97; tel. (727) 250-40-70; fax (727) 250-02-24; e-mail post@bta.kz; internet www.bta.kz; f. 1997 as Bank TuranAlem; name changed as above 2008; 75.1% state-owned; cap. 515,551m., res −47,981m., dep. 3,571,518m. (Dec. 2009); Chair. of Bd of Dirs ARMAN G. DUNAEV; Chair. of Managing Bd ANVAR G. SAIDENOV; 23 brs.

Development Bank of Kazakhstan: 010000 Astana, pl. Respublika 32; tel. (7172) 58-02-60; fax (7172) 58-02-76; e-mail info@kdb.kz; internet www.kdb.kz; f. 2001; wholly state-owned; cap. 255,975.9m., res 52,883.4m., dep. 575,226.3m. (Dec. 2009); Chair. of Bd NURLAN KUSSAINOV.

Eurasian Bank (Yevraziiskii Bank): 050002 Almatı, Kunaev kosh. 56; tel. (727) 250-77-05; fax (727) 250-86-50; e-mail info@eurasian-bank.kz; internet www.eurasian-bank.kz; f. 1994; cap. 24,210.2m., res 5,986.9m., dep. 253,693.9m. (Dec. 2009); Chair. MICHAEL EGGLETON; 18 brs.

Eurasian Development Bank: 050000 Almatı, Panfilov kosh. 98; tel. (727) 244-40-44; fax (727) 244-65-70; e-mail info@eabr.org; internet www.eabr.org; f. 2006; cap. US $1,500.6m., res $48.7m., dep. $849.7m. (Dec. 2009); Chair. IGOR FINOGENOV.

Halyk Bank: 050046 Almatı, Rozybakiev kosh. 97; tel. (727) 259-00-00; fax (727) 259-02-71; e-mail halykbank@halykbank.kz; internet www.halykbank.kz; f. 1936 as br. of Savings Bank of USSR; fully privatized in Nov. 2001; cap. 143,695m., res 136,907m., dep. 1,713,869m. (Dec. 2009); Chair. and Chief Exec. UMUT SHAYAKHMETOVA.

HSBC Bank Kazakhstan: 050010 Almatı, Dostyk d-ly 43; tel. (727) 259-69-00; fax (727) 259-69-02; e-mail info@hsbc.kz; internet www.hsbc.kz; f. 1998; 100% owned by HSBC Bank PLC (United Kingdom); cap. 3,360.0m., res 1,314.8m., dep. 147,468.5m. (Dec. 2009); Chair. of Bd of Dirs DEREK P. LUNT.

Kaspi Bank: 050012 Almatı, Adi Sharipov kosh. 90; tel. (727) 250-18-00; fax (727) 250-95-96; e-mail office@bankcaspian.kz; internet www.bc.kz; 96% owned by Caspian Group (Netherlands); fmrly Caspian Bank; present name adopted 2008; cap. 17,315.8m., res 2,888.6m., dep. 253,480.6m. (Dec. 2009); Chair. MIXEIL LOMTADZE; 17 brs.

KazInvestBank: 050051 Almatı, Dostyk d-ly 176; tel. (727) 261-90-60; fax (727) 259-86-58; e-mail info@kib.kz; internet www.kib.kz; f. 1993; open jt-stock co; cap. 9,437,9m., res 1,224.3m., dep. 59,843.7m. (Dec. 2009); Chair. ADNAN ALLY AGHA; 3 brs.

Kazkommertsbank (KKB): 050060 Almatı, Gagarin kosh. 135; tel. (727) 258-53-01; fax (727) 258-51-61; e-mail mailbox@kkb.kz; internet www.kkb.kz; f. 1991; cap. 9,031m., res 380,780m., dep. 1,985,233m. (Dec. 2009); Chair. NURJAN S. SUBXANBERDIN; Man. Dir ANDREI I. TIMCHENKO; 23 brs.

Nurbank: 050010 Almatı, Dostyk d-ly 38; tel. (727) 259-97-10; fax (727) 250-16-09; e-mail bank@nurbank.kz; internet www.nurbank

KAZAKHSTAN

.kz; f. 1992; cap. 31,677.7m., res 854.0m., dep. 252,214.8m. (Dec. 2009); Chair. Nurmuxamed Bektemissov; 56 brs.

Temirbank: 050008 Almatı, Abay d-ly 68/74; tel. (727) 257-88-88; fax (727) 250-62-41; e-mail board@temirbank.kz; internet www.temirbank.kz; f. 1992; owned by Samryk-Kazyna National Welfare Fund; cap. 34,568.5m., res −107.1m., dep. 275,860.9m. (Dec. 2009); Chair. Ablaxat Kebirov; 15 brs.

Tsesnabank: 010000 Astana, Jengis d-ly 29; tel. (7172) 77-07-70; fax (7172) 77-01-95; e-mail info@tsb.kz; internet www.tsb.kz; f. 1992; cap. 15,500.0m., res 2,409.4m., dep. 151,571.6m. (Dec. 2009); Chair. Yerkegali Yedenbaev; 9 brs.

Bankers' Organization

Bank Association of Kazakhstan: 010000 Almatı, Panfilov kosh. 98; tel. (727) 273-16-89; fax (727) 273-90-85; Pres. Baxytbek Baiseitov.

STOCK EXCHANGES

Kazakhstan Stock Exchange (KASE): 050020 Almatı, Dostyk 291/3a; tel. (727) 237-53-00; fax (727) 296-64-02; e-mail info@kase.kz; internet www.kase.kz; f. 1993; Pres. Kadyrzhan Damitov.

Regional Financial Centre of Almaty City: 050059 Almatı, Al-Farabi kosh. 17/1, Biznes-Tsentr 'Nurly-Taw' 4b, 9th Floor; tel. (727) 311-09-31; fax (727) 311-09-42; e-mail info@rfca.kz; internet www.rfca.kz; f. 2007; Chair. of Management Dauren B. Utkelbaev.

INSURANCE

Almaty International Insurance Group: 050000 Almatı, Kabanbai batyr kosh. 112; tel. and fax (727) 250-12-31; f. 1994; Chair. Suren Ambartsumian.

Centras Insurance: 050008 Almatı, Manas kosh. 32a; tel. (727) 259-77-55; fax (727) 259-77-66; e-mail insurance@centras.kz; internet www.cic.kz; f. 1997; non-life insurance and reinsurance; Chair. Talgat Usenov.

Dynasty Life Insurance Co: 050000 Almatı, Seifullin kosh. 410; tel. (727) 250-73-95; e-mail dynasty@bta.nursat.kz; Chair. Serik Temirgaleev.

Industrial Insurance Group (IIG): 050046 Almatı, Nauryzbai-batyr kosh. 65–69; tel. (727) 250-96-95; fax (727) 250-96-98; e-mail iig@kaznet.kz; f. 1998; Pres. Ivan Mixailov.

Interteach Kazakhstani Health and Medical Insurance Corpn: 050059 Almatı, Furmanov kosh. 275d; tel. and fax (727) 320-02-00; e-mail interteach@interteach.kz; internet www.interteach.kz; f. 1989; medical and travel insurance, health care, accident and employee liability insurance; 290 employees; 48 brs; Gen. Dir Ernst M. Kurleutov.

KazAgroPolits Insurance Co: 050000 Almatı, Nauryzbai-batyr kosh. 49–61; tel. (727) 232-13-24; fax (727) 232-13-26; e-mail kazagropolise@mail.banknet.kz; Chair. Yermek Uspanov.

Kazakhinstrakh (Kazakh International Insurance Co): 050044 Almatı, Jibek-joly d-ly 69; tel. (727) 233-73-49; fax (727) 250-74-37; e-mail kiscentr@nursat.kz; Chair. Nurlan Moldaxmetov.

Kazkommerts-Polits Insurance Co: 050013 Almatı, Satpaev kosh. 24; tel. (727) 258-48-08; fax (727) 292-73-97; e-mail info@kkp.kz; internet www.kkp.kz; f. 1996; non-life; Chair. Meiram B. Sergazin; Dir Talgat K. Ussenov.

Trade and Industry

GOVERNMENT AGENCY

Republican Agency for the Regulation of Natural Monopolies: 010000 Astana, Bukei-xan kosh. 14; tel. (7172) 59-16-77; fax (7172) 21-54-73; e-mail info@arem.kz; internet www.regulator.kz; Chair. Nurlan Sh. Aldabergenov.

CHAMBERS OF COMMERCE

Union of Chambers of Commerce and Industry of Kazakhstan: 050000 Almatı, Masanchi kosh. 26; tel. (727) 292-00-52; fax (727) 250-70-29; e-mail tpprkaz@online.ru; internet www.ccikaz.kz; f. 1959; Chair. Ablai Myrzaxmetov.

Almatı City Chamber of Commerce and Industry: 050000 Almatı, Tole bi 45; tel. (727) 262-03-01; e-mail alcci@nursat.kz; internet www.atpp.marketcenter.ru; Chair. Ablai Myrzaxmetov.

Astana City Chamber of Commerce and Industry: 010000 Astana, Auezov kosh. 66, POB 1966; tel. (7172) 32-38-33; e-mail akmcci@dan.kz; internet www.chamber.kz; Chair. Tatyana I. Kononova.

Jambil Oblast Chamber of Commerce and Industry: 080012 Jambil obl., Taraz, Karaxan kosh. 2; tel. (7262) 43-05-98; Chair. Adilxan Japarbekov.

Qarağandi Oblast Chamber of Commerce and Industry: 100000 Qarağandi, bulv. Mira 31; tel. (7212) 30-06-84; fax (7212) 30-05-05; e-mail karcci@mail.ru; internet www.karcci.kz; f. 1959; Chair. of Presidium Nessip Seitova.

Southern Kazakhstan Oblast Chamber of Commerce and Industry: 160000 Southern Kazakhstan obl., Chimkent, Taukexan kosh. 31; tel. (7252) 21-14-05; Chair. Syrlybaj Ordabekov.

EMPLOYERS' ORGANIZATIONS

Confederation of Employers of the Republic of Kazakhstan (KRRK): 050022 Almatı, Abay d-ly 42/44; tel. (727) 293-07-42; fax (727) 292-27-68; e-mail krrk@krrk.kz; internet www.krrk.kz; Pres. Kadyr Bayikenov.

Kazakhstan Petroleum Association: 050010 Almatı, Dostyk d-ly 43/517; tel. (727) 250-18-16; fax (727) 250-18-17; e-mail kpa@arna.kz; internet www.kpakz.kz; f. 1998; Chair. Nurjan Kamalov; 40 mem. cos.

UTILITIES

Electricity

KEGOS—Kazakhstan Electricity Grid Operating Co (Elektr zhelilerin baskaru zhanindegi Kazakstan kompaniyasy): 050000 Almatı, Kozybaev kosh. 23; tel. (727) 271-93-59; internet www.kegoc.kz; f. 1997; technical electricity network operator; Pres. Almasadam M. Satkaliev.

Water

Almatı Vodokanal: 050057 Almatı, Jarokov kosh. 196; tel. (727) 274-84-02; fax (727) 274-98-41; e-mail vk.prm@itte.kz; f. 1936; state-owned; responsible for water supply and sewerage in Almatı and surrounding villages; Gen. Dir Vladislav Galiev.

STATE HYDROCARBONS COMPANIES

KazMunaiGaz: 010000 Astana, Kabanbai-batyr kosh. 22; tel. (7172) 97-60-00; fax (7172) 97-60-01; e-mail info@kmg.kz; internet www.kmg.kz; f. 2002 by merger of KazakhOil and Transneftegas; national jt-stock co; subsidiaries include petroleum-transportation co KazTransOil, and gas-transportation co KazTransGas; CEO Askar Baljanov.

Munaigaz: 010000 Astana, Jeltoksan kosh. 7/1; tel. and fax (7172) 39-03-11; e-mail info@munaygas.com; internet www.munaygas.com; f. 2004; petroleum and gas prospecting and producing; Pres. Ye. V. Belyaev.

TRADE UNIONS

Confederation of Free Trade Unions of Kazakhstan: f. 1991; fmrly Independent Trade Union Centre of Kazakhstan; 9 regional brs with 2,200 mems; Chair. Sergei Belkin.

Confederation of Free Trade Unions of Coal and Mining Industries: 050000 Almatı; Chair. V. Gaipov.

Federation of Trade Unions of Kazakhstan: 010000 Astana, pr. Abay 38; tel. (7172) 216-68-14; fax (7172) 21-68-35; e-mail fprkastana@fprk.kz; internet www.fprk.kz; 26 affiliated unions with 2,047,185 mems (2009); Chair. Siyazbek Mukashev.

Transport

RAILWAYS

In 2003 the total length of rail track in use was 13,601 km (3,661 km of which were electrified). Much of the rail network is in the north of the country, where it joins the rail lines of Russia. There are also connections with Kyrgyzstan, Uzbekistan and the People's Republic of China.

An underground railway under construction in Almatı was scheduled to open to passengers in December 2011. In Astana the construction of a rapid transit system was planned.

Kazakstan Temir Joly (Kazakhstan Railways): 010011 Astana, Jengis d-ly 98; tel. (7172) 93-44-00; fax (7172) 32-82-30; e-mail temirzhol@railways.kz; internet www.railways.kz; f. 1991; Pres. Askar U. Mamin.

ROADS

In 2004 Kazakhstan's total road network was 90,018 km, including 23,055 km of main roads.

INLAND WATERWAYS

Kazakhstan has an inland waterway network extending over some 4,000 km. The main navigable river is the Ertis (Irtysh).

Committee of Transport and Railways (Ministry of Transport and Communications): 010000 Astana, Abay d-ly 47; tel. (7172) 24-10-79; fax (7172) 24-12-98; e-mail pr_ktps@mtc.gov.kz; f. 2008; Chair. BERIK UANDYKOV.

SHIPPING

A ferry port was inaugurated on the Caspian Sea at Aktaw in 2001, with services operating to Azerbaijan, Iran and Russia. At 31 December 2009 Kazakhstan's merchant fleet comprised 99 vessels, with a combined displacement of 77,093 grt.

Aktau International Commercial Sea Port: 130000 Mañğystaw obl., Aktaw akimat, Ömırzaq; tel. (7292) 51-45-49; fax (7292) 44-51-01; e-mail aktauport@aktauport.kz; internet www.portaktau.kz; f. 1963; Dir TALGAT B. ABYLGAZIN; 609 employees.

CIVIL AVIATION

There are 18 domestic airports and four airports with international services, located at Aktaw, Almatı, Astana and Atıraw.

Department of Aviation (Ministry of Transport and Communications): 010000 Astana, Abay d-ly 47; tel. (7172) 24-26-05; fax (7172) 24-31-65; e-mail kga@mtc.gov.kz; Chair. RADILBEK ADIMOLDA.

Air Astana: 050000 Almatı, Biznes Tsentr Samal Tauers, Joldasbekov kosh. 97; tel. (7172) 58-41-35; fax (7172) 59-87-01; internet www.airastana.com; f. 2001 jointly by the Samruk-Kazyna National Welfare Fund (51%) and BAE Systems (United Kingdom—49%); domestic and international flights; Pres. PETER FOSTER.

Tourism

Tourism is not widely developed in Kazakhstan. In 2008 there were 4.7m. tourist arrivals in Kazakhstan, and receipts from tourism (including passenger transport) amounted to US $1,255m.

Kazakhstan Tourist Association (KTA): 050022 Almatı, Abay d-ly 42/44/302; tel. (727) 292-53-31; fax (727) 292-48-53; e-mail kta@mail.kz; f. 1999.

Defence

Kazakhstan was one of the four former Union Republics to become a nuclear power in succession to the USSR, but dismantled its final nuclear-testing capabilities at Semey (Semipalatinsk) in July 2000. In mid-1992 Kazakhstan signed a Collective Security Treaty with five other members of the Commonwealth of Independent States (CIS); in May 2001 it was announced that the signatory countries were to form a Collective Rapid Reaction Force to combat Islamist militancy in Central Asia. In April 2003 the Collective Security Treaty Organization (CSTO) was inaugurated as the successor to the CIS collective security system, comprising Armenia, Belarus, Kazakhstan, Kyrgyzstan, Russia and Tajikistan. Kazakhstan participates, with Russia and Azerbaijan, in the operation of the Caspian Sea Flotilla, based at Astrakhan, Russia, and established its own navy in 2003. In May 1994 Kazakhstan joined the North Atlantic Treaty Organization's (NATO) 'Partnership for Peace' programme of military co-operation. As assessed at November 2010, the country's total armed forces numbered some 49,000, with an army of 30,000, an air force of 12,000 a navy of 3,000 and 4,000 joint troops answerable to the Ministry of Defence. There were also 31,500 paramilitary troops, including 20,000 internal security troops under the command of the Ministry of Internal Affairs, a 2,000–strong Presidential Guard, a 500–member Government Guard, and 9,000 state border protection forces answerable to the Ministry of Internal Affairs. Conscripts serve for a period of 24 months.

Chairman of Joint Chiefs of Staff: Gen.-Col SAKEN A. JASUZAKOV.

Defence Expenditure: Budgeted at 165,000m. tenge in 2010.

Education

General education (pre-primary, primary and secondary) is compulsory, and is fully funded by the state. Since 2010 primary education, which begins at seven years of age and lasts for four years, has been preceded by one year of pre-primary education, while secondary education continues for a further seven years. In 2007/08 total enrolment at primary schools included 90% of children in the relevant age-group, while the comparable ratio for secondary enrolment was 86%. In 2009/10 there were 7,811 state general schools. After completing general education, pupils may continue their studies at vocational secondary schools; there were 480 such schools in the state sector in 2009/10. In addition, there were 306 professional-technical schools.

In 2009/10 there was a total of 148 state higher schools (including universities), attended by 610,300 students, and in 2003/04 there were 134 non-governmental higher education institutes, attended by 297,900 students. Government expenditure on education in 2009 was 660,917.1m. tenge (17.6% of total spending).

KENYA

Introductory Survey

LOCATION, CLIMATE, LANGUAGE, RELIGION, FLAG, CAPITAL

The Republic of Kenya lies astride the equator on the east coast of Africa, with Somalia to the north-east, Ethiopia and Sudan to the north, Uganda to the west and Tanzania to the south. The climate varies with altitude: the coastal region is hot and humid, with temperatures averaging between 20°C and 32°C (69°F–90°F), while inland, at more than 1,500 m (5,000 ft) above sea-level, temperatures average 7°C–27°C (45°F–80°F). The highlands and western areas receive ample rainfall (an annual average of 1,000 mm–1,250 mm) but most of northern Kenya is very dry (about 250 mm). Kiswahili is the official language, while English is widely spoken and 22% and 13% of the population, respectively, speak Kikuyu and Luo as their mother tongue. Most of the country's inhabitants follow traditional beliefs. There is a sizeable Christian community, while Muslims form a smaller proportion of the population. The national flag (proportions 2 by 3) has three broad horizontal stripes, of black, red and green, separated by two narrow white stripes. Superimposed in the centre is a red shield, with black and white markings, upon crossed white spears. The capital is Nairobi.

CONTEMPORARY POLITICAL HISTORY

Historical Context

Formerly a British colony (inland) and protectorate (along the coast), Kenya became independent, within the Commonwealth, on 12 December 1963, and a republic exactly one year later. Jomo Kenyatta, a Kikuyu, and leader of the Kenya African National Union (KANU), was appointed Prime Minister in June 1963 and became the country's first President in December 1964. (He was subsequently re-elected to the presidency, unopposed, in 1969 and 1974.)

Kenyatta died in August 1978; the Vice-President, Daniel arap Moi, was proclaimed President in October, and was the sole candidate at a presidential election held (concurrently with a KANU-only general election) in November 1979. In June 1982 the National Assembly officially declared Kenya a one-party state. Moi was returned unopposed in presidential elections in 1983 and 1988.

Domestic Political Affairs

By the early 1990s pressure for political reform had grown and in November 1991 several members of the Forum for the Restoration of Democracy (FORD), an outlawed political movement, were arrested prior to a planned pro-democracy rally in Nairobi, which was suppressed by the security forces. The Kenyan authorities were condemned internationally and bilateral and multilateral creditors suspended aid to Kenya indefinitely, pending the acceleration of both economic and political reforms. In December a special conference of KANU delegates acceded to the demands for reform, resolving to introduce a multi-party political system. The National Assembly subsequently endorsed appropriate amendments to the Constitution. Former Vice-President Mwai Kibaki resigned as Minister of Health later in the month, in protest against alleged electoral malpractice by KANU, and founded the Democratic Party (DP).

During the first half of 1992 some 2,000 people were reportedly killed in tribal clashes in western Kenya. In March the Government banned all political rallies, and restrictions were placed on the activities of the press. Following a two-day general strike in April, organized by FORD, the Government ended the ban on political rallies. In August FORD split into two opposing factions, which were registered in October as separate political parties, FORD—Asili and FORD—Kenya, respectively led by Kenneth Matiba and Oginga Odinga.

At multi-party presidential and legislative elections held in December 1992 Moi was elected for a fourth term of office as President, winning 36.3% of the votes cast, ahead of Matiba (26.0%), Kibaki (19.5%) and Odinga (17.5%). Of the 188 elective seats in the National Assembly, KANU won 100 (including 16 uncontested); FORD—Asili and FORD—Kenya secured 31 seats each, and the DP took 23. Votes were cast predominantly in accordance with ethnic affiliations, with the two largest tribes, the Kikuyu and Luo, overwhelmingly rejecting KANU. An extensive reorganization of cabinet posts was subsequently effected. In 1993 the international donor community agreed to resume the provision of aid to Kenya, in response to what it recognized as the Government's progress in implementing political and economic reforms.

During the mid-1990s Kenya's human rights record came under intense domestic and international scrutiny. In April 1995 the country's Roman Catholic bishops accused the Government of eroding judicial independence and of condoning police brutality and endemic corruption. In December the human rights organization Amnesty International alleged that the security forces were systematically torturing criminal suspects and opposition activists. In response to its critics, the Moi administration provisionally withdrew controversial draft legislation in January 1996 that would have severely restricted the freedom of the press and, in July, inaugurated a human rights committee to investigate alleged humanitarian abuses.

Divisions within opposition parties continued to undermine efforts to present a cohesive challenge to Moi and KANU prior to the 1997 elections. A renewed attempt to establish a coalition of opposition organizations, initiated in November 1995, was short-lived. Meanwhile, following an unsuccessful attempt to assume the leadership of FORD—Kenya, Raila Odinga (the son of Oginga Odinga, who died in January 1994, and a prominent opposition activist) left that party and subsequently became leader of the National Development Party (NDP). In October 1997 Matiba's faction of FORD—Asili registered as an independent party, the Forum for the Restoration of Democracy for the People (FORD—People). During the mid-1990s several opposition deputies, disaffected by these internal rivalries, defected to KANU. Within KANU itself rivalries also began to emerge, not least because the Constitution permitted Moi to stand for only one further term as President.

In August 1997 the IMF suspended assistance to Kenya, pending the implementation of decisive action to eliminate official corruption and to improve the system of revenue collection; the Government consequently announced the inauguration of an anti-corruption body. In the following month the National Assembly approved legislation that amended the Constitution with the stated aim of ensuring free and fair democratic elections. All political parties were granted equal access to the media, and detention without trial was prohibited. In addition, the new legislation enabled the opposition to participate in selecting the 12 nominated members of the National Assembly and 10 of the 12 members of the supervisory Electoral Commission.

The presidential and legislative elections, which took place concurrently on 29 December 1997, were undermined by allegations of widespread fraud, as well as by logistical difficulties. Moi was re-elected President, winning 40.6% of the valid votes cast, while Kibaki came second, with 31.5% of the votes cast. KANU secured 107 of the 210 elected seats in the enlarged National Assembly, and the remainder were divided between nine opposition parties, with the DP taking 39 seats, the NDP 21, FORD—Kenya 17 and the Social Democratic Party 15. Moi was inaugurated for a fifth (and final) term as President in January 1998. Shortly afterwards Moi appointed a new Cabinet. However, he postponed the designation of a new Vice-President, evidently in order not to give an indication of his preferred successor to the presidency.

In early 1998 inter-ethnic violence erupted once again in the volatile Rift Valley. The Moi administration blamed the conflict on bitterness in the Kikuyu and Luo communities at the outcome of the elections, while the latter alleged persecution both by the security forces and by smaller tribal groups that had voted predominantly for Moi and KANU. Tension between the Kikuyu and Kalenjin communities in the Rift Valley persisted especially over disputed land vacated by the Kikuyu during the clashes.

In early August 1998 a car-bomb exploded at the US embassy in central Nairobi, concurrently with a similar attack on the US mission in Dar es Salaam, Tanzania. Some 254 people were killed in Nairobi, and more than 5,000 suffered injuries. The attacks were believed to have been co-ordinated by international Islamist terrorists, and, in mid-August, the USA retaliated by launching air-strikes against targets in Afghanistan and Sudan. Four men were convicted of involvement in the bombings by a court in New York, USA, in May 2001 and were later sentenced to life imprisonment. Osama bin Laden, the fugitive Saudi-born Islamist activist whom the US authorities held ultimately responsible for the bombings, was killed by US forces in Pakistan in May 2011.

In July 2000 the civil service commenced the reduction of its work-force as part of a programme of reforms to be effected over three years. Meanwhile, a parliamentary anti-graft committee sought the adoption by the National Assembly of a report in which the alleged perpetrators of corruption were named. (The Government later deleted the addendum containing the list of names, causing widespread outrage.) The committee also proposed legislation on economic crimes that would allow the anti-corruption authority (which had been established in 1997 at the insistence of the IMF) to prosecute alleged perpetrators of corruption without seeking permission from the Attorney-General. As a result of these measures, the IMF announced that it was to resume lending to Kenya. However, less than one month after the resumption of aid the High Court temporarily halted the retrenchment of civil servants, pending the final determination of a lawsuit on the issue, and ruled that all civil servants who had already been retrenched should be reinstated. In January 2001 the IMF and the World Bank expressed concern over the setbacks in the reforms, particularly the failure to approve legislation on public service ethics and economic crimes, and suspended aid to Kenya until the situation could be resolved. In August Kenyan deputies again refused to approve anti-corruption legislation, and the IMF suspended aid to Kenya indefinitely. Moi subsequently created a new police body to combat corruption.

In January 2001 Odinga, on behalf of the Luo-dominated NDP, signed a memorandum of understanding with KANU, which allowed Moi to appoint ministers from the NDP. In June Moi reorganized the Cabinet and appointed Odinga as Minister of Energy, thereby creating the first coalition Government in Kenya's history. Moi reshuffled the Cabinet again in November, introducing younger KANU ministers in an apparent attempt to provide suitable candidates for his succession; most notably Uhuru Kenyatta (son of the late President Jomo Kenyatta) was appointed as Minister for Local Government.

The NDP was dissolved and absorbed into KANU in mid-March 2002, despite opposition from elements within both parties; Moi was elected as party Chairman, while Odinga became Secretary-General. In July some 12 opposition parties, including the DP, FORD—Kenya and the National Party of Kenya, formed an electoral alliance, the National Alliance Party of Kenya (NAK).

The 2002 elections

In August 2002 Moi publicly announced that he favoured Uhuru Kenyatta as KANU's presidential candidate. However, several senior KANU members, including the Vice-President, Prof. George Saitoti, and Odinga, subsequently announced their intention to seek the party's presidential nomination and formed the Rainbow Alliance (RA) to campaign within KANU for a democratic vote to select its candidate. Moi responded by dismissing Saitoti. In mid-October, in protest against Moi's attempts to impose his preferred successor, members of the RA resigned from their posts in the Government and from KANU, together with some 30 KANU deputies. The RA subsequently boycotted the KANU conference, at which Kenyatta's presidential candidacy was endorsed. Later in October the RA established a new party, the Liberal Democratic Party (LDP), and joined with the NAK to form the National Rainbow Coalition (NARC), with Kibaki as its presidential candidate.

At the presidential and legislative elections, held concurrently on 27 December 2002, the opposition secured an emphatic victory, with Kibaki winning 62.3% of the votes cast in the presidential election, and the NARC securing 125 of the 210 elected seats in the National Assembly, while Kenyatta received 31.2% of the votes cast for the presidency, and KANU won 64 seats in the legislature. The NARC was allocated a further seven appointed seats, increasing their representation to 132, and KANU a further four seats, bringing their total to 68. The electoral turnout was 56.1%.

Following his inauguration as President on 30 December 2002, Kibaki promised reforms, including the adoption of a new constitution, under which certain powers would be transferred from the President to the legislature, the adoption of anti-corruption legislation, the privatization of state-owned companies and the dismissal of corrupt civil servants. In January 2003 Kibaki appointed a new Cabinet; however, divisions within the ruling coalition soon became apparent, as a group of 25 LDP deputies accused Kibaki of breaching a power-sharing agreement signed by the constituent parties of the NARC prior to the elections. In May the Anti-Corruption and Economic Crimes Act, which provided for the establishment of the Kenya Anti-Corruption Commission (KACC), and the Public Service (Code of Conduct and Ethics) Act, requiring elected officials and senior civil servants to declare their wealth, came into effect.

In February 2003 Kibaki appointed a commission of inquiry into the Goldenberg financial scandal, in which public funds had been paid to the company Goldenberg International in 1990–93 as subsidies for non-existent exports of gold and diamonds. Evidence presented at the inquiry indicated that Goldenberg had initially received some Ks. 13,500m. (around US $180m.) under the Government's export compensation scheme. After thousands of transfers, including dubious foreign-exchange transactions, made with the alleged complicity of officials at the central bank, the payments to Goldenberg increased to Ks. 25,000m. ($600m.), equivalent to more than 10% of Kenya's annual GDP, although it was estimated that the total amount misappropriated could reach $4,000m. The scandal had also contributed to an IMF decision to suspend the disbursement to Kenya of loans worth some $500m. in 1997. Public hearings ended in November 2004, and the commission's findings were reported to Kibaki in February 2005. It had initially been expected that prosecutions would follow from the report; however, the Minister of Justice and Constitutional Affairs, Martha Karua, stated that further investigations were necessary before any charges could be brought.

Meanwhile, a constitutional review conference opened in April 2003, but divisions persisted over the proposed post of Prime Minister. The LDP advocated an executive Prime Minister with powers to appoint the Cabinet, while Kibaki and his supporters sought to maintain a strong presidency. The ensuing tensions between the NAK and LDP factions of the NARC threatened to split the ruling coalition. In August the death of Vice-President Michael Wamalwa, who had been regarded as a moderating influence within the Government, led to an intensification of the power struggle. President Kibaki faced demands for a successor both from Wamalwa's Luhya ethnic group and from the Luo, who proposed the appointment of Odinga to the vice-presidency. In late September Kibaki named the Minister of Home Affairs, Arthur Moody Awori (a Luhya), as Vice-President and effected a minor government reshuffle. In March 2004 the constitutional review conference voted to reduce the powers vested in the presidency and to create the new post of executive Prime Minister following the next elections, which were scheduled to be held in December 2007. Under the recommendations adopted by the conference, greater power was to be accorded to the National Assembly. The Government withdrew from the conference in protest; however, the draft constitution was successfully presented to the Attorney-General, after which it was to be considered by the National Assembly. The High Court subsequently ruled that before the document could enter into force it required the approval of a simple majority at a referendum.

The draft constitution, which was approved by the National Assembly in July 2005, confirmed the retention of the executive functions of the President, who would have the power to appoint and dismiss a non-executive Prime Minister. Devolution was to be on two levels (national and provincial), rather than the four levels originally envisaged, while the National Assembly was to remain unicameral.

There followed several months of campaigning punctuated by often violent demonstrations. Seven ministers announced their opposition to the proposed new constitution, including, most notably, Raila Odinga, whose LDP split from the NARC coalition and joined with KANU to form the Orange Democratic Movement (ODM). At the referendum, held on 21 November 2005, the draft constitution was rejected by 58.1% of voters. Some 53% of the electorate participated in the poll. Kibaki conceded defeat but ignored demands from Odinga and the ODM to hold legislative elections. Instead Kibaki moved swiftly to dismiss the entire Cabinet, and in early December he announced a new administration, from which those ministers who had opposed the draft constitution were removed. Those NARC members who maintained their support for Kibaki subsequently formed a new coalition party, the National Rainbow Coalition—Kenya (NARC—Kenya), as a vehicle for contesting the 2007 elections.

Corruption

In 2004 it became increasingly apparent that corruption remained endemic in Kenya, despite the NARC Government's pledge to take measures to combat it. Four senior civil servants were suspended in May following their involvement in awarding contracts to supply passport printing equipment to a fictitious British company, Anglo Leasing Ltd. In July the British High Commissioner, Sir Edward Clay, claimed that corruption had cost Kenya some Ks. 15,000m. since Kibaki took office and warned that it could lead to a reduction in donor assistance—indeed, later that month the European Union (see p. 270) withheld substantial aid. Clay subsequently produced a dossier of some 20 allegedly dubious contracts involving corruption in four ministries, and in February 2005 reiterated his criticisms, urging Kibaki to remove corrupt ministers in order that investigations could proceed unhindered.

As public resentment increased, the issue of corruption became the subject of further attention in February 2005 when the Permanent Secretary for Governance and Ethics in the Office of the President, John Githongo, resigned citing his inability to continue working for the Government. Kibaki did not appoint a replacement for Githongo, and in November disbanded the Office of Governance and Ethics. Following Githongo's resignation, the USA and Germany announced that they would withhold anti-corruption aid, and the United Kingdom imposed travel restrictions on government ministers and others implicated in corruption. Awori admitted that there was massive corruption at senior levels, and there were demands from within the Government for the resignations of corrupt ministers. Kibaki subsequently reorganized the Cabinet, dismissing several high-ranking civil servants and effectively demoting a key presidential aide, the Minister of State for Provincial Administration and National Security in the Office of the President, Christopher Murungaru, to the Ministry of Transport. Kibaki also ordered the KACC to investigate procurement procedures in the National Security department.

Meanwhile, in February 2005 the Kenya Law Society announced that it was to prosecute senior figures on corruption charges, including Awori, the Attorney-General, Amos Wako, and the Minister of Finance, David Mwiraria. It was also revealed that the four senior civil servants suspended in May 2004 had agreed to act as prosecution witnesses and to testify that they had received instructions from government ministers to pursue the transactions for which they were being prosecuted. However, Wako invoked a provision in the Constitution granting him the power to take over private prosecutions initiated by individuals or institutions and entered a *nolle prosequi* to terminate the case.

In November 2005 Githongo presented Kibaki with a dossier detailing his investigations into corruption in Kenya and death threats made against him, as well as accounts of his meetings with allegedly corrupt senior officials. Awori, Mwiraria, Murungaru and Kiraitu Murungi (the Minister of Energy) were implicated by Githongo in the Anglo Leasing scandal. Githongo claimed that, in total, the four intended to defraud the exchequer of US $700m. through false military and security contracts. He further alleged that two ministers had admitted that the money was to be used for party political campaigning. Awori, Mwiraria, Murungaru and Murungi were subsequently summoned to appear before the KACC; they all denied the allegations.

In January 2006 Githongo, who considered that Kibaki had failed to act upon the information supplied, released a copy of his dossier to the British media. (Githongo remained in exile in the United Kingdom.) He also released a recording of a meeting with Murungi in which the latter allegedly attempted to impede Githongo's investigation. Following Githongo's disclosure, a delegation of deputies representing the parliamentary Public Accounts Committee (PAC) travelled to the United Kingdom and interviewed Githongo at the Kenyan High Commission in London. In early February Mwiraria resigned from the Cabinet. Pressure increased on the Government and later that month Kibaki announced the resignations of Murungi and Saitoti, the Minister of Education. (Saitoti had also been implicated in the Goldenberg scandal—see above.) All three denied any wrongdoing. Kibaki reshuffled the Cabinet following the resignations, with Amos Kimunya assuming the finance portfolio, although Awori retained his position as Vice-President despite growing demands for his resignation. The PAC began questioning Awori, Mwiraria, Murungi and Saitoti in late February. In March Saitoti was also questioned by the police about his role in the Goldenberg affair, but the High Court of Kenya later rejected recommendations that he be charged. In a further cabinet reorganization in November, he was readmitted to the Government as Minister of Education, alongside Murungi, who resumed responsibility for the energy portfolio.

Division among the main parties intending to contest the forthcoming presidential and legislative elections emerged during 2007. In June NARC—Kenya indicated that Kibaki was to be named as its presidential candidate, although this was not immediately confirmed. Dissension was also reported among ODM members and in May the party postponed for a fifth time the deadline for the submission of presidential nomination papers; however, Odinga emerged as the frontrunner for that party's presidential candidature. In October Minister of Health Charity Kaluki Nguli was dismissed after she attended a rally at which Odinga launched his election campaign. Primary elections were held in November with Kibaki defecting from the ruling NARC—Kenya and choosing to contest the elections under his newly established Party of National Unity (PNU). Odinga was named the presidential candidate for the ODM.

Violence follows elections

At the legislative elections, held on 27 December 2007, the ODM secured 99 of the 210 seats in the National Assembly, the PNU won 43, the ODM—Kenya, which had broken away from the main party in August, 16 and KANU 14. Results in three constituencies were not released. The presidential election was held concurrently and the Electoral Commission of Kenya (ECK) announced that, despite indications prior to the vote that Odinga had garnered greater popular support, Kibaki had narrowly been re-elected to the presidency with 4,584,721 votes; Odinga was reported to have secured 4,352,993 votes. Official figures detailing the total number of votes cast were not immediately made available. Odinga and other opposition candidates vehemently denounced the results, while independent international observers expressed scepticism regarding the credibility of the election, which had taken place amid allegations of widespread procedural violations. The results led to an upsurge in tribal conflict between Kibaki's Kikuyu supporters and Odinga's Luo followers. Nevertheless, on 30 December Kibaki was sworn in for a second term.

By mid-January 2008 some 600 people were reported to have been killed and more than 250,000 displaced, as a result of the unrest. A mediation effort undertaken from 8 January by President John Kufuor of Ghana, in his capacity as Chairperson of the African Union (AU) Assembly, failed to bring about direct talks between Kibaki and Odinga. On that day Kibaki had announced the partial composition of his new Cabinet; despite the ODM having secured the largest number of seats in the legislature, no representatives from that party were included in the new Government. Further proposed AU-sponsored mediation was rejected by the Kenyan Government, and on 16 January the ODM, defying a ban on public demonstrations, commenced nation-wide protests scheduled to last for three days. These were violently dispersed by the security forces, resulting in additional fatalities.

On 29 January 2008 the former UN Secretary-General, Kofi Annan, formally launched a further round of negotiations, but observers believed that it would take time to resolve the deep-rooted ethnic problems that underpinned the political crisis, including the issue of land distribution. Ethnic fighting intensified and two senior ODM officials were killed. As a result Annan suspended discussions temporarily and the ODM appealed for calm. Talks resumed in early February and a proposal was made regarding the establishment of a power-sharing transitional government. Odinga had insisted that the elections be re-run, but signalled his willingness to consider this measure, which would allow for new elections to be conducted within a year. Negotiations continued haltingly throughout February with both parties reluctant to compromise. However, on 28 February Kibaki and Odinga signed an agreement on the division of power and the creation of the posts of Prime Minister and two Deputy Prime Ministers, pending a full constitutional review to be carried out within 12 months. Odinga conceded the presidency to Kibaki and accepted the role of Prime Minister. Despite the agreement, attacks were carried out in early March ahead of the opening of a new parliamentary session during which members were to debate the legislation required to legalize the power-sharing agreement. The National Accord and Reconciliation Act, which provided, *inter alia*, for the creation of the position of Prime Minister and allowed a new coalition government to begin to implement a recovery programme and to assist the numerous internally displaced persons (IDPs) across the country in returning to their homes, was ratified by the National Assembly later that month. The total number of IDPs was estimated to have reached 600,000 (and over 1,000 people had been killed); in May the Government commenced 'Operation Rudi Nyumbani', which sought to return home all those IDPs dispersed throughout hundreds of refugee camps, mainly in the Rift Valley.

Meanwhile, following prolonged negotiations, in mid-April 2008 Kibaki named a new coalition Government, comprising members of the PNU, the ODM and ODM—Kenya, including Kenyatta as Deputy Prime Minister and Minister of Trade and Wycliffe Musalia Mudavadi as Deputy Prime Minister and Minister of Local Government; Stephen Kalonzo Musyoka, who had been appointed as Vice-President and Minister of Home Affairs in January, and Moses Wetangula, who assumed responsibility for the foreign affairs portfolio at the same time, retained their positions in the new 40-member Cabinet. It was agreed that a commission of inquiry to investigate the causes and perpetrators of the post-election violence should be established with immediate effect, which would be chaired by Appellate Judge Philip Waki. However, divisions soon emerged within the Cabinet as Odinga and ministers allied to the ODM sought an amnesty for all those arrested in the violence: Saitoti, who had been appointed Minister of State in the Office of the President, and Minister of Justice, National Cohesion and Constitutional Affairs Martha Karua were among the members of the Government who opposed the amnesty, and it was ultimately rejected. Waki's report, published in mid-October, recommended the establishment of a tribunal, to be known as the Special Tribunal for Kenya, to 'seek accountability against persons bearing the greatest responsibility for crimes, particularly crimes against humanity' relating to the 2007 elections. It also recommended that a comprehensive reform of the Kenya Police Service be undertaken, involving a complete audit of the current police management, structures, policies, practices and procedures. Kibaki and Odinga agreed to the establishment of the Special Tribunal in December 2008 and the following month legislation providing for its creation was introduced before the National Assembly.

Election inquiry

On 10 June 2008 the Minister of Roads, Kipkalya Kones, and the Assistant Minister of Home Affairs, Lorna Laboso, died when the aircraft they were travelling in crashed in the Enoosupkia Forest (near the Maasai Mara game reserve) killing all those on board. The Minister of Public Works, Chris Obure, assumed the roads portfolio on an acting basis. The following day by-elections were held for five seats in the National Assembly: the killings of two ODM deputies and the failure to announce the results in two Rift Valley constituencies during the unrest that followed the 2007 elections had left four seats vacant; the remaining seat was to be contested as it had previously been occupied by Kenneth Marende, who was elected speaker of the National Assembly. The by-elections were held in a largely peaceful atmosphere, despite fears of further unrest, with the ODM winning three of the seats and the PNU securing two, taking their total representations in the legislature to 102 and 45 seats, respectively.

The issue of corruption remained significant for the Government during 2008. In July Kimunya resigned from his position as Minister of Finance, owing to the commencement of an investigation into claims that he had given false information regarding the sale of a hotel to Libyan investors, although a government inquiry later cleared him of any wrongdoing. In January 2009 Kimunya was named as Minister of Trade in a minor government reorganization. At the same time Kenyatta was appointed as the new Minister of Finance (retaining the deputy premiership), while Franklin Bett assumed the roads portfolio. Meanwhile, in August 2008 the KACC initiated the prosecution of seven deputies (both former and serving), including Minister of Information Samuel Poghisio, for accepting fraudulent allowance payments.

In September 2008 a report was published by the independent commission of inquiry, chaired by Johann Kriegler, a South African judge and the former Chairperson of that country's Independent Electoral Commission, set up to investigate the disputed elections in December 2007. It concluded that the conduct of the elections made it impossible to verify results reliably, and recommended that the ECK should undergo major reforms or be replaced by a new body. In December 2008 the ECK was disbanded and provision was made for its replacement by a new nine-member body, the Interim Independent Electoral Commission.

In February 2009 the UN Special Rapporteur on Extrajudicial, Summary or Arbitrary Executions, Philip Alston, issued a report in which he accused Kenya's security forces of widespread extrajudicial killings, and demanded the removal of Kenya's Police Commissioner, Hussein Ali, and Attorney-General Wako, who he described as the 'embodiment in Kenya of the phenomenon of impunity'. The report concluded that death squads had been formed on the orders of senior police officials to exterminate members of the Mungiki (an illegal religious sect allegedly responsible for a number of murders and involved in extortion), although the Kenyan Government rejected the findings. In early March Oscar Kamau Kingara, the Chief Executive of the Oscar Foundation, a civil rights advocacy group, and another senior member of the organization, John Paul Oulowere, were killed by unidentified gunmen; a government spokesman had recently accused the organization of having links with the Mungiki. Prior to the murders the Oscar Foundation had led demonstrations in the capital, expressing anger at government corruption and accusing the Kenyan police of brutality and widespread extrajudicial killings and arrests, especially of suspected Mungiki members. The deaths of the two activists precipitated further demonstrations in which one student was shot dead, and on 10 March there were violent protests in Nairobi as thousands of people, mainly students and the unemployed, took to the streets. This was regarded by many analysts as evidence of the increasing frustration with the coalition Government, which many Kenyans believed had not met expectations and had failed to implement any significant reforms; notably, corruption remained a serious problem. The Government suffered a further reverse later in March when Karua announced her resignation, citing Kibaki's appointment of judges without her knowledge as the main reason for her departure. In May Mutula Kilonzo was named Minister of Justice, National Cohesion and Constitutional Affairs in a minor governmental reorganization.

In July 2009 the Kenya National Commission on Human Rights (KNCHR) named 219 people suspected of involvement in the violence that took place after the 2007 elections; included on the KNCHR's list were Deputy Prime Minister and Minister of Finance Uhuru Kenyatta and a number of other government ministers. In the same month former UN Secretary-General Kofi Annan submitted a list of 10 suspects to be investigated by the International Criminal Court (ICC) with regard to their involvement in the post-election violence and, while the list was not made public, it was believed to include high-ranking government officials. (Also in July 2009 President Kibaki announced the formation of a nine-member Kenya Truth, Justice, and Reconciliation Commission to investigate a number of 'injustices' including land allocation and regional imbalances. The Commission was chaired by Bethuel Kiplagat and would serve for a period of two years.) The Kenyan authorities were divided on whether suspects would be tried at a local tribunal or at the ICC, in The Hague, Netherlands. Although international observers advocated the establishment of a local tribunal, the National Assembly announced that it was willing to co-operate with the ICC on the conduct of the trials.

In November 2009 a new draft constitution was made public, under which the Prime Minister would become the Head of Government, a role currently undertaken by the President. The new constitution would also provide for a decentralized government with the creation of regional and county authorities, limitations on the number of government ministers and the establishment of a Senate. However, following further discussions, in January 2010 it was confirmed that Kenyan legislators had agreed to recommend removing the post of Prime Minister from the draft document, which was submitted for debate in the National Assembly in mid-March. It was envisaged that a national referendum on the proposed new basic law would be held in June.

Meanwhile, it was reported that five people had been killed during violent demonstrations in the mainly Somali Nairobi suburb of Eastleigh against the detention of a radical, Jamaican-born Muslim cleric, Sheikh Abdullah al-Faisal, in mid-January 2010. Al-Faisal had entered Kenya from Tanzania in late 2009 with the intention of carrying out a preaching tour, but was arrested in early January 2010 after the Kenyan Government stated that he was a threat to national security. Some 328 people were believed to have been arrested in the days following the protests, including a number of citizens with alleged links to a Somali militant Islamist group, al-Shabaab ('The Youth'), and

Al-Amin Kimathi, the Chairman of Kenya's Muslim Human Rights Forum. Kimathi was among eight of those charged with incitement to violence later in January. Al-Faisal was deported to Jamaica on 22 January.

In mid-February 2010 President Kibaki suspended a number of senior officials from the National Cereals and Produce Board and the permanent secretaries in the agriculture, education and special programmes ministries, after inquiries into the work of a subsidized maize scheme and Kenya's free primary education programme revealed corrupt practices. Shortly afterwards Prime Minister Odinga announced the suspension of Minister of Agriculture William Ruto (who had also featured on the KNCHR list of those suspected of major involvement in the post-election violence) and Minister of Education Samson Ongeri to allow independent investigations into the corruption allegations to proceed. However, Kibaki overturned Odinga's decision, maintaining that he had not been consulted on the matter and that Odinga did not have the constitutional powers to suspend the two ministers. (In April Ruto was removed as Minister of Agriculture and appointed Minister of Higher Education.)

In early March 2010 the Chief Prosecutor of the ICC, Luis Moreno-Ocampo, presented evidence relating to the potential prosecution of 20 people (whose identities remained confidential) for their role in the post-election violence in which more than 1,100 people had been killed, stating that senior political and business leaders from both the ODM and the PNU had organized and financed post-election attacks against civilians in 2008. At the end of March the ICC's pre-trial chamber, at Moreno-Ocampo's recommendation, announced that it was to initiate an investigation into the alleged crimes against humanity.

Recent developments: new Constitution

On 1 April 2010 the National Assembly unanimously approved the text of a draft constitution, which was presented to the Attorney-General later that month. In May the draft was officially published and a referendum on its adoption was scheduled to take place in August. On 4 August the new Constitution was endorsed by 66.9% of votes cast, according to official results released by the Interim Independent Electoral Commission, with a participation rate of 72.2%. However, ethnic differences over the issue were prominent, reflecting the continued divisions in the country. In Central and Nyanza provinces, dominated by the Kikuyu and Luo, respectively, an overwhelming majority voted in favour of the new Constitution, which had been supported by Odinga and Kenyatta; however, in Rift Valley, dominated by the Kalenjin, a significant majority had voted against it, following a campaign led by former President Moi and William Ruto. The new Constitution notably provided for the abolition of the post of Prime Minister and creation of a deputy presidency, and the devolution of some powers to 47 new counties, which were to be represented by a second legislative chamber, the Senate. On 16 August a ministerial reorganization was announced. On the following day the Government established a committee, to be chaired by Kibaki and Odinga, which was to supervise the implementation of the constitutional reforms (the full enactment of which was expected to be prolonged). The new Constitution was officially signed into law by President Kibaki on 27 August.

In October 2010 Ruto was suspended as Minister of Higher Education, following a court ruling that he be tried on charges of illegally selling forest land when he held the agriculture portfolio. Later that month the Minister of Foreign Affairs, Moses Wetangula, submitted his resignation, after being implicated in allegedly irregular property agreements conducted by Kenyan embassies overseas. In November Kiplagat was obliged to resign as Chairman of the Kenya Truth, Justice, and Reconciliation Commission, after he was accused of being implicated in a 1984 massacre by security forces. In December Moreno-Ocampo issued indictment requests formally naming six principal suspects accused of organizing the post-election violence, the most notable being Deputy Prime Minister and Minister of Finance Kenyatta. The other accused were: the Cabinet Secretary and close associate of Kibaki, Francis Muthaura; Ruto, who had travelled to the ICC in The Hague shortly beforehand in an effort to reach a compromise agreement; Henry Kosgey, the Chairman of the ODM and Minister of Industrialization; a former police commissioner, Mohammed Hussein Ali; and a radio broadcaster, Joshua Arap Sang. The announcement of the high-level suspects (all of whom denied the charges) prompted public controversy and later in December, following a motion submitted by Ruto, the National Assembly voted overwhelmingly for Kenya to withdraw from the jurisdiction of the ICC. The Minister of Justice and 13 foreign envoys subsequently urged Kibaki and Odinga to ignore the recommendation by the legislature for Kenya to sever its relations with the ICC. Prior to the announcement, the Government had indicated that it was prepared to establish a local tribunal to try the suspects. In early 2011 Kosgey resigned from the post of Minister of Industrialization, following allegations of corruption against him. On 8 March the ICC issued summonses for the six accused to appear before the Court on 7 April and confirmation hearings were scheduled to commence in September.

Foreign Affairs

Following the seizure of power by the National Resistance Army in Uganda in January 1986, President Daniel arap Moi offered full co-operation to the new Ugandan President, Yoweri Museveni. In September, however, Ugandan authorities claimed that Kenya was harbouring anti-Museveni rebels, and stationed troops at the two countries' common border. These claims were denied, and in December, when Ugandan troops allegedly entered Kenya in pursuit of rebels, Ugandan and Kenyan armed forces exchanged fire across the border for several days; at least 15 people were reported to have been killed. Later in December Moi and Museveni agreed to withdraw troops from either side of the border. Moi visited Museveni in August 1990, indicating improved relations between Kenya and Uganda. In November 1994 Moi, Museveni and Mwinyi met in Arusha, Tanzania, and established a commission for co-operation; in March 1996 the Secretariat of the Permanent Tripartite Commission for East African Co-operation was formally inaugurated, with a view to reviving the East African Community (EAC), which had been dissolved in 1977. A treaty for the re-establishment of the EAC, providing for the promotion of free trade between the member states, the development of the region's infrastructure and economy and the creation of a regional legislative assembly and court, was ratified by the Kenyan, Tanzanian and Ugandan Heads of State in November 1999. The new EAC (see p. 447) was officially inaugurated in Arusha in January 2001. Talks on integrating the economies of the three EAC members followed, and in March 2004 President Mwai Kibaki, Museveni and President Benjamin Mkapa of Tanzania signed a protocol on the creation of a customs union, eliminating most duties on goods traded within the Community, which took effect from January 2005. In November 2009 the Heads of State of Tanzania, Kenya, Uganda, Rwanda and Burundi signed a common market protocol in Arusha (Rwanda and Burundi having joined the EAC in 2007), allowing the free movement of goods, services, people and capital within the EAC. The common market protocol entered into force in July 2010.

Relations between Kenya and Sudan deteriorated in mid-1988, as the two countries made mutual accusations of aiding rebel factions. In early 1989 Sudan renewed a long-standing dispute with Kenya over the sovereignty of territory on the Kenyan side of the two countries' common border, known as the 'Elemi triangle'. During the late 1990s Kenya hosted a series of peace talks between the Sudanese Government and opposition leaders, under the auspices of the Intergovernmental Authority on Development (IGAD, see p. 336), in an attempt to resolve the conflict in southern Sudan. Further negotiations were held in Nairobi in September 2000 and June 2001, and in July 2002 the Sudanese Government and the opposition Sudan People's Liberation Movement (SPLM) signed an accord in Machakos, Kenya, which provided for the holding of a referendum on self-determination for southern Sudan after a transitional period of six years. In September 2003 Kenya and Sudan agreed to form a joint border committee. Talks aimed at achieving a final peace settlement between the Sudanese Government and the SPLM continued in Kenya throughout 2003 and 2004 (see the chapter on Sudan), and in January 2005 the Sudanese Government and southern rebels signed a peace accord in Nairobi, which officially ended the 21-year civil war. Relations with the Government of Southern Sudan (GOSS), which the Kenyan Government accused of oppressing its citizens, became strained in late 2009. Continued tensions regarding border disputes between the north and south of Sudan were also a concern, and, following the abduction of Kenyan medical staff while attempting to rescue a young girl allegedly raped by Sudanese military personnel, the Kenyan Government threatened to sever relations with the GOSS.

Somalia has traditionally laid claim to part of north-eastern Kenya. During 1989 tension developed between the Kenyan authorities and ethnic Somalis from both sides of the Kenya–Somalia border, when Somalis were alleged to have been largely

KENYA

responsible for wildlife-poaching and banditry in north-eastern Kenya. In September Moi protested strongly to the Somali Government, following an incursion into Kenya by Somali troops (reportedly pursuing Somali rebels), which resulted in the deaths of four Kenyans. In that month the Kenyan Minister of Foreign Affairs and International Co-operation stated that, while the Government supported the peace process in Somalia, it had not, as had been reported, officially declared recognition of the interim Somali President, Abdulkasim Hasan, or his Government. Moi later agreed to mediate between the interim Government and opposing rebel factions in Somalia. In July 2001 Kenya closed the border after numerous clashes were reported on the Somali side, which threatened to spill over into Kenya. However, Moi agreed to reopen the border in November. An IGAD-sponsored Somali reconciliation conference opened in the Kenyan town of Eldoret in October 2002 and was moved to Nairobi in February 2003; the talks continued throughout 2003 and early 2004, despite various disruptions, and in January 2004 representatives from more than 20 factions in attendance reached agreement on the establishment of a new Somali parliament, which was based in Nairobi until mid-2005 (see the chapter on Somalia). During 2009, as instability in Somalia persisted, the Kenyan authorities became increasingly concerned with the security of the border region. While Somalia repeated its request for international support to contain the fighting, the Kenyan Government remained divided on its position on military intervention, despite reiterating its active support for the transitional Somali administration.

Relations between the Kenyan and Ethiopian Governments became strained in 1997, owing to an increased incidence of cross-border cattle-rustling, including an attack in March during which 16 members of the Kenyan security forces were killed. A number of communiqués were subsequently signed by representatives of the two countries, agreeing to reinforce border security, to take measures to prevent the smuggling of arms and drugs, and to enhance trade. In November 1998 some 189 people (mainly Somalis) were found to have been massacred in north-eastern Kenya; Ethiopian guerrillas were widely believed to be responsible. In January 1999 the Kenyan Government protested to the Ethiopian authorities, following an incursion into Kenya by Ethiopian security forces, who were alleged to be in pursuit of Ethiopian rebels. Kenya deployed additional troops at the two countries' common frontier in May, following a series of land-mine explosions in the region, which had resulted in several fatalities. Bilateral relations deteriorated further during late 2000 after it was reported that some 50 Kenyans had been killed, allegedly by Ethiopian militia forces, in cross-border clashes. In January 2001 representatives from both countries met in Nairobi and agreed to initiate measures aimed at ending border disputes. In April 2006 Kenya closed part of its border with Ethiopia when militia forces allegedly entered Kenyan territory and fighting ensued. Seven people were reported to have been killed in further fighting that broke out in August.

In October 1995, despite strong condemnation from foreign governments, the Kenyan authorities refused to permit the international tribunal that was investigating war crimes committed in Rwanda during 1994 access to alleged Rwandan perpetrators of genocide who had fled to Kenya. In June 1996 the Moi Government closed the Rwandan embassy in Nairobi in protest against the Rwandan Government's refusal to waive diplomatic immunity for an embassy official who was suspected of plotting a murder in Kenya; the diplomat was deported. In September, however, the first arrest in Kenya was made of a Rwandan Hutu suspected of involvement in genocide. Kenya strongly denied accusations, in November, of supplying arms to Rwandan Hutu rebels operating from within Zaire (now the Democratic Republic of the Congo). Relations between the Kenyan and Rwandan Governments improved during 1997, when further Rwandan Hutus were arrested by the Kenyan security forces to stand trial on charges of genocide at the UN tribunal in Arusha. During a visit by Moi to Rwanda in May 2000 the two countries agreed to reopen the Kenyan embassy in Kigali and to establish a joint commission for bilateral relations.

In 1995 Kenya was reportedly sheltering about 200,000 refugees from the conflict in Somalia. The Moi Government, which claimed that the refugees placed an intolerable burden on the country's resources, repeatedly requested that the UN repatriate the total refugee population. By mid-1998 an estimated 155,000 Somalis had been repatriated from Kenya, with assistance from the office of the UN High Commissioner for Refugees (UNHCR). However, continuing instability in Somalia resulted in further influxes of refugees to Kenya. In late 2010 UNHCR urged the Kenyan authorities to halt the forced return of Somali refugees. According to UNHCR, in 2010 the majority of the some 404,000 refugees and asylum-seekers in Kenya were from Somalia, with the rest mainly from Ethiopia and Sudan.

CONSTITUTION AND GOVERNMENT

Under the terms of the Constitution approved at a national referendum on 4 August 2010 and which entered into force on 27 August, legislative power is vested in and exercised by Parliament, which consists of the National Assembly and the Senate. Members of Parliament serve concurrent five-year terms. The National Assembly consists of 290 members, each elected by the registered voters of single member constituencies; 47 women (one elected in each county); 12 members nominated by parliamentary political parties according to their proportion of members of the National Assembly to represent special interests including the youth, persons with disabilities and workers; and the Speaker, who is an ex officio member. The Senate consists of 47 members each elected by the registered voters of the counties, each county constituting a single member constituency; 16 women members who shall be nominated by political parties according to their proportion of members of the Senate; two members representing the youth; two members representing persons with disabilities; and the Speaker, who is an ex officio member. The President is the Head of State and Government and exercises the executive authority of the Republic, with the assistance of the Deputy President and Cabinet Secretaries. The Cabinet consists of the President, the Deputy President), the Attorney-General and not fewer than 14 and not more than 22 Cabinet Secretaries.

REGIONAL AND INTERNATIONAL CO-OPERATION

Kenya is a member of the Common Market for Eastern and Southern Africa (see p. 228) and, with Burundi, Rwanda, Tanzania and Uganda, of the East African Community (see p. 447). The International Tea Promotion Association (see p. 444) is based in Kenya.

Kenya became a member of the UN in 1963. As a contracting party to the General Agreement on Tariffs and Trade, Kenya joined the World Trade Organization (WTO, see p. 430) on its establishment in 1995. Kenya participates in the Group of 15 (G15, see p. 447) and the Group of 77 (G77, see p. 447) developing countries.

ECONOMIC AFFAIRS

In 2009, according to estimates by the World Bank, Kenya's gross national income (GNI), measured at average 2007–09 prices, was US $30,686m., equivalent to $770 per head (or $1,570 per head on an international purchasing-power parity basis). During 2000–09, it was estimated, the population increased at an average annual rate of 2.7%, while gross domestic product (GDP) per head increased, in real terms, by an average of 1.2% per year. Overall GDP increased, in real terms, at an average annual rate of 3.9% in 2000–09. Real GDP increased by 2.2% in 2009.

Agriculture (including forestry and fishing) contributed 26.7% of GDP in 2008 and accounted for 17.8% of workers engaged in paid employment in the formal sector in 2007. (According to FAO, some 70.1% of the labour force was employed in the agriculture sector in mid-2011.) The principal cash crops are coffee (which contributed 24.9% of total export earnings in 2009) and tea. Horticultural produce (Kenya is the world's fourth largest exporter of cut flowers), pyrethrum, sisal, sugar cane and cotton are also important. Maize is the principal subsistence crop. There is a significant dairy industry for domestic consumption and export. During 2000–09, according to the World Bank, agricultural GDP increased at an average annual rate of 2.5%. Agricultural GDP increased by 3.0% in 2009.

Industry (including mining, manufacturing, construction and power) contributed 18.6% of GDP in 2008 and employed an estimated 19.3% of workers engaged in paid employment in the formal sector in 2007. During 2000–09, according to the World Bank, industrial GDP increased at an average annual rate of 4.9%. Industrial GDP increased by 5.0% in 2009.

Mining contributed 0.8% of GDP in 2008 and employed an estimated 0.3% of those in paid formal sector employment in 2007. Soda ash is the principal mineral export. Fluorspar, iron ore, salt, limestone, gold, gemstones (including rubies and sapphires), vermiculite and lead are also mined. Kenya has substantial reserves of titanium. According to the African

Development Bank (AfDB), the GDP of the sector grew by 3.2% in 2008.

Manufacturing contributed 11.9% of GDP in 2008 and employed an estimated 13.7% of workers engaged in paid employment in the formal sector in 2007. During 2000–09, according to the World Bank, manufacturing GDP increased at an average annual rate of 4.1%. Manufacturing GDP increased by 5.0% in 2009.

Construction contributed 4.3% of GDP in 2008 and employed an estimated 4.3% of workers engaged in paid employment in the formal sector in 2007. GDP of the construction sector grew by 8.3% in 2008, according to the AfDB.

Hydroelectric power accounted for 51.4% of total electricity generated in 2007. It had accounted for an average of 81.9% during 1990–98, whereafter recurrent droughts began to affect hydroelectric production. This shortfall was taken up by petroleum, which accounted for 28.8% in 2007 (as opposed to an average of 9.2% during 1990–98). Kenya does not produce electricity from coal, natural gas or nuclear power. Energy for domestic use is derived principally from fuel wood and charcoal. The prolonged drought led to severe power shortages in 2000 and threatened to affect hydroelectric production in 2005–06. In February 2004 it was announced that the Kenyan and Tanzanian national grids were to be connected to that of Zambia under a cross-border energy project; the first phase of the project, which was to cost some US $300m., was commissioned in 2007, followed by a second phase in 2012. In 2009 imports of mineral fuels and lubricants (including crude petroleum intended for refining) comprised 21.4% of the value of total imports.

The services sector contributed 54.7% of GDP in 2008 and employed an estimated 62.9% of workers engaged in paid employment in the formal sector in 2007. Tourism makes an important contribution to Kenya's economy and has been the country's principal source of foreign exchange since 1987. Following terrorist attacks in 2001, however, and subsequent warnings against travel to Kenya by the United Kingdom and the USA, the tourism industry experienced difficulties. By 2008, according to the provisional figures, tourist arrivals had recovered to total 1,203,000 (receipts from tourism in that year amounted to US $1,398m.), although the industry was adversely affected by the violence that followed the 2007 elections. The GDP of the services sector increased at an average annual rate of 3.4% in 2000–09, according to the World Bank. Services GDP decreased by 1.5% in 2009.

In 2009 Kenya recorded a visible trade deficit of US $4,989.3m., and there was a deficit of $1,661.1m. on the current account of the balance of payments. In 2009 the principal source of imports was the United Arab Emirates (which supplied 11.4% of total imports in that year); other major suppliers were India, the People's Republic of China, South Africa, the USA, and Japan. Uganda was the principal market for Kenya's exports (purchasing 13.4%) in that year; other important purchasers were the United Kingdom, Tanzania, the Netherlands and the USA. The principal exports in 2009 were coffee, tea, vegetables and fruit, cut flowers and foliage, basic manufacturers, and chemicals and related products. The principal imports in that year were machinery and transport equipment, petroleum and petroleum products, chemicals and related products, basic manufacturers, and food and live animals.

In the financial year ending 30 June 2010 there was a budgetary deficit of Ks. 156,400m. Kenya's general government gross debt was Ks. 1,118.08m. in 2009, equivalent to 49.2% of GDP.

The country's external debt was US $7,441m. at the end of 2008, of which $6,268m. was public and publicly guaranteed debt. In that year the cost of debt-servicing was equivalent to 4.5% of the value of exports of goods, services and income. According to the IMF, the annual rate of inflation averaged 13.5% in 2003–09; consumer prices increased by 26.3% in 2008 and rose by a further 9.2% in 2009. Some 23% of the labour force were estimated to be unemployed in late 2000.

Kenya's economy is reasonably diversified, although most employment is dependent on agriculture, and the country is highly vulnerable to fluctuations in international prices for its cash crops, most notably tea and coffee. Poverty is widespread, with population growth considerably higher than growth in GNI per head, and the revelation in the mid-2000s that large-scale corruption remained endemic in Kenya adversely affected business confidence and investment and led international donors to withhold aid. Nevertheless, in late 2006 President Kibaki stated intentions to transform the country into a middle-income nation within 25 years, with a focus of the initiative being sustained annual economic growth of 10%. A potential positive development towards this goal was the signing in mid-2009 of an agreement with the Canadian firm Africa Oil Corpn and the Dubai-based East Exploration Ltd on the joint exploration of oilfields in both Kenya and Ethiopia. However, severe food shortages in 2008 were exacerbated by worsening drought conditions in early 2009, followed by excessive rainfall in early 2010, which caused widespread flooding. High international prices for fertilizer and fuel resulted in further pressure on the economy in general and on the primary sector in particular, and the UN World Food Programme commenced a relief operation in April 2009. Following the economic slowdown resulting from the global financial crisis, GDP growth increased in 2010 to more than 5%, compared with 2.6% in 2009, according to the IMF. This was generated principally by a recovery in the agricultural sector (which had benefited from improved weather conditions) and an increase in construction activity. Numerous allegations of high-level corruption continued; however, the formal adoption of a new Constitution in August 2010, which provided for the introduction of reforms on fiscal decentralization, public expenditure, and land ownership, was welcomed by the IMF, with the expectation that it would stimulate private investment. Kenya had begun to benefit from the ratification of East African Community (see p. 447) common market protocol in July. In January 2011 the IMF approved a three-year Extended Credit Facility (ECF) arrangement, totalling US $508.7m., for Kenya (with an immediate disbursement of $107.1m.), which was intended to support the Government's implementation of political and economic reforms contained in the new Constitution. The Government's economic programme under the ECF principally focused on increased infrastructural investment (notably in geo-thermal power generation in response to climate change issues).

PUBLIC HOLIDAYS

2012: 1 January (New Year's Day), 6–9 April (Easter), 1 May (Labour Day), 1 June (Madaraka Day, anniversary of self-government), 18 August* (Id al Fitr, end of Ramadan), 10 October (Moi Day), 20 October (Kenyatta Day), 12 December (Independence Day), 25–26 December (Christmas).

*This holiday is determined by the Islamic lunar calendar and may vary by one or two days from the date given.

KENYA

Statistical Survey

Source (unless otherwise stated): Kenya National Bureau of Statistics, POB 30266, Nairobi; tel. (20) 317583; fax (20) 315977; e-mail director@knbs.go.ke; internet www.knbs.or.ke.

Area and Population

AREA, POPULATION AND DENSITY

Area (sq km)	
Land area	571,416
Inland water	11,230
Total	582,646*
Population (census results)†	
24 August 1999	28,686,607
24 August 2009	
Males	19,192,458
Females	19,417,639
Total	38,610,097
Population (UN estimates at mid-year)‡	
2010	40,862,900
2011	41,947,728
Density (per sq km) at mid-2011§	73.4

* 224,961 sq miles.
† Excluding adjustment for underenumeration.
‡ Source: UN, *World Population Prospects: The 2008 Revision*; estimates not adjusted to take account of results of 2009 census.
§ Land area only.

POPULATION BY AGE AND SEX
(UN estimates at mid-2011)

	Males	Females	Total
0–14	9,033,720	8,925,739	17,959,459
15–64	11,440,161	11,441,458	22,881,619
65 and over	505,989	600,661	1,106,650
Total	20,979,870	20,967,858	41,947,728

Source: UN, *World Population Prospects: The 2008 Revision*.

PRINCIPAL ETHNIC GROUPS
(census of August 1989)

African	21,163,076		European	34,560
Arab	41,595		Other*	115,220
Asian	89,185		Total	21,443,636

* Includes persons who did not state 'tribe' or 'race'.

POPULATION BY PROVINCE
(2010, projected estimates)

Nairobi	3,240,155		Nyanza	5,201,996
Central	3,908,907		Rift Valley	9,101,524
Coast	3,205,175		Western	4,552,522
Eastern	5,587,781		Total	36,287,423
North-Eastern	1,489,363			

Note: Projections not adjusted to take account of 2009 census results.

PRINCIPAL TOWNS
(estimated population at census of August 1999)

Nairobi (capital)	2,143,020		Meru	78,100
Mombasa	660,800		Kitale	63,245
Nakuru	219,366		Malindi*	53,805
Kisumu*	194,390		Nyeri*	46,969
Eldoret*	167,016		Kericho	30,023
Thika	82,665		Kisii	29,634

* Boundaries extended between 1979 and 1989.

Mid-2010 (incl. suburbs, UN estimates): Nairobi (capital) 3,523,349; Mombasa 1,002,833 (Source: UN, *World Urbanization Prospects: The 2009 Revision*).

BIRTHS AND DEATHS
(annual averages, UN estimates)

	1995–2000	2000–05	2005–10
Birth rate (per 1,000)	38.2	38.8	39.0
Death rate (per 1,000)	11.3	12.9	11.7

Source: UN, *World Population Prospects: The 2008 Revision*.

Life expectancy (years at birth, WHO estimates): 54 (males 53; females 55) in 2008 (Source: WHO, *World Health Statistics*).

EMPLOYMENT
(labour force survey, selected urban and rural settlements, '000s)*

	2005	2006	2007†
Agriculture and forestry	327.1	334.6	339.9
Mining and quarrying	5.8	6.0	6.3
Manufacturing	248.4	254.9	261.3
Electricity and water	20.2	19.5	19.0
Construction	78.2	79.9	81.3
Wholesale and retail trade	175.4	185.9	195.8
Transport and communications	113.7	130.8	149.0
Finance, insurance, real estate and business services	88.9	92.3	95.0
Community, social and personal services	751.0	755.8	759.6
Total	1,808.7	1,859.7	1,907.2

* Data are for salaried employees in the formal sector only, and therefore exclude self-employed and unpaid family workers and a vast number of workers in the informal sector (almost 6.5m. in 2005, according to official estimates). According to ILO, the 1999 census recorded an employed population of 14,474,200.
† Provisional figures.

Health and Welfare

KEY INDICATORS

Total fertility rate (children per woman, 2008)	4.9
Under-5 mortality rate (per 1,000 live births, 2008)	128
HIV/AIDS (% of persons aged 15–49, 2005)	6.1
Physicians (per 1,000 head, 2002)	0.1
Hospital beds (per 1,000 head, 2006)	1.4
Health expenditure (2007): US $ per head (PPP)	72
Health expenditure (2007): % of GDP	4.7
Health expenditure (2007): public (% of total)	42.0
Access to water (% of persons, 2008)	59
Access to sanitation (% of persons, 2008)	31
Total carbon dioxide emissions ('000 metric tons, 2007)	11,226.5
Carbon dioxide emissions per head (metric tons, 2007)	0.3
Human Development Index (2010): ranking	128
Human Development Index (2010): value	0.470

For sources and definitions, see explanatory note on p. vi.

Agriculture

PRINCIPAL CROPS
('000 metric tons)

	2006	2007	2008
Wheat	329.2	322.3	288.6
Barley	81.1	45.0*	44.6
Maize	3,247.2	2,928.8	2,367.2
Millet	79.2	119.6	38.5
Sorghum	131.2	147.4	54.3
Potatoes	783.8	850.0*	600.0*
Sweet potatoes	724.6	811.5	894.8
Cassava (Manioc)	656.3	397.7	751.0
Sugar cane	4,932.8	5,204.2	5,112.0
Beans, dry	531.8	429.8	265.0
Cow peas, dry	87.8	83.3	48.0
Pigeon peas	110.8	95.6	84.2
Cashew nuts*	10.0	10.0	10.0
Coconuts	61.1	61.9	59.7
Seed cotton*	34.5	38.3	38.3
Cottonseed	22.5	25.0	25.0*
Cabbages and other brassicas	492.3	609.3	609.3*
Tomatoes	503.7	559.7	559.7*
Onions, dry	106.5	118.6	118.6*
Carrots and turnips	41.7	62.7	62.7*
Bananas	618.9†	593.4†	593.4*
Plantains	618.9†*	593.3†	593.3*
Guavas, mangoes and mangosteens	248.5	384.5	384.5*
Avocados	103.9	93.6	93.6*
Pineapples	417.9	429.1	429.1*
Papayas*	86.0	86.0	86.0
Coffee, green	48.3	53.4	42.0
Tea (made)	310.6	369.6	345.8
Tobacco, unmanufactured	17.6	11.2	11.2*
Sisal	26.4	24.8	22.6

* FAO estimate(s).
† Unofficial figure.

2009: Wheat 129.2; Barley 42.1; Maize 2,439.0; Millet 54.0; Sorghum 99.0; Potatoes 400.0; Sweet potatoes 930.8; Cassava (Manioc) 820.0; Sugar cane 5,610.7; Cottonseed 25.0 (FAO estimate); Coffee, green 57.0; Tea (made) 314.1.

Aggregate production ('000 metric tons, may include official, semi-official or estimated data): Total cereals 3,936.7 in 2006, 3,614.3 in 2007, 2,860.5 in 2008, 2,804.5 in 2009; Total roots and tubers 2,195.9 in 2006, 2,082.2 in 2007, 2,267.9 in 2008, 2,170.8 in 2009; Total vegetables (incl. melons) 1,880.5 in 2006, 2,102.9 in 2007–09; Total fruits (excl. melons) 2,405.7 in 2006, 2,467.7 in 2007–09.

Source: FAO.

LIVESTOCK
('000 head, year ending September)

	2007	2008	2009
Cattle	12,900.3	13,522.5	12,490.1
Sheep	9,428.7	9,907.3	9,903.3
Goats	13,966.0	14,478.3	13,872.3
Pigs	304.2	330.0	350.0*
Camels	1,006.3	1,132.5	947.2
Chickens	27,495	29,615	28,574

* FAO estimate.
Source: FAO.

LIVESTOCK PRODUCTS
('000 metric tons)

	2007	2008	2009
Cattle meat	445.0	365.0	n.a.
Sheep meat*	33.6	33.6	33.3
Goats' meat*	45.1	46.2	44.3
Pig meat	16.2	17.2*	18.2*
Chicken meat	24.0	24.0*	n.a.
Game meat*	14.0	14.0	n.a.
Camel meat*	27.0	27.0	n.a.
Cows' milk	4,230.0	3,990.0	4,070.0
Sheep's milk*	31.0	31.0	31.0
Goats' milk*	130.0	110.0	110.0
Camels' milk*	32.5	27.0	27.0
Hen eggs*	68.6	69.0	70.0
Honey	25.0*	25.0*	n.a.

* FAO estimate(s).
Source: FAO.

Forestry

ROUNDWOOD REMOVALS
('000 cubic metres, excluding bark)

	2006	2007*	2008*
Sawlogs, veneer logs and logs for sleepers	607.0	607.0	607.0
Pulpwood	450.0	450.0	450.0
Other industrial wood	189.0	189.0	189.0
Fuel wood	26,400.0	26,400.0	21,140.9
Total	27,646.0	27,646.0	22,386.9

* FAO estimates.

2009: Figures assumed to be unchanged from 2008 (FAO estimates).
Source: FAO.

SAWNWOOD PRODUCTION
('000 cubic metres, including railway sleepers)

	2004	2005	2006
Coniferous (softwood)	70	116	121
Broadleaved (hardwood)	8	20	21
Total	78	136	142

2007–09: Production assumed to be unchanged from 2006 (FAO estimates).
Source: FAO.

Fishing

('000 metric tons, live weight)

	2006	2007	2008
Capture	158.7	131.8	133.3
Silver cyprinid	57.9	49.5	49.4
Nile tilapia	19.0	10.1	12.7
Nile perch	55.7	47.6	45.0
Aquaculture	1.0	4.2	4.6
Total catch	159.7	136.0	137.7

Note: Figures exclude crocodiles, recorded by number rather than by weight. The number of Nile crocodiles caught was: 8,710 in 2006; 6,354 in 2007; 4,504 in 2008.

Source: FAO.

KENYA

Mining

('000 metric tons)

	2007	2008	2009
Soda ash	386.6	513.4	404.9
Fluorspar	82.0	98.2	15.7
Salt	11.6	24.3	24.1
Limestone flux	41.0	42.0	38.0*

* Estimated production.

Source: US Geological Survey.

Industry

SELECTED PRODUCTS
('000 metric tons, unless otherwise indicated)

	2005	2006	2007
Wheat flour	363.3	392.8	370.3
Raw sugar	392.4	417.1	520.4
Beer ('000 hectolitres)	2,662.6	3,115.6	3,934.2
Cigarettes (million)	7,324.0	10,261.6	12,203.7
Cement	2,181.6	2,405.9	2,615.0
Jet fuel	205	226	223
Motor gasoline	266	179	207
Gas-diesel oils	374	368	397
Residual fuel oils	549	596	534
Electric energy (million kWh)	6,737	7,323	6,773

Source: UN Industrial Commodity Statistics Database.

Finance

CURRENCY AND EXCHANGE RATES

Monetary Units
100 cents = 1 Kenya shilling (Ks.).
Ks. 20 = 1 Kenya pound (K£).

Sterling, Dollar and Euro Equivalents (30 November 2010)
£1 sterling = Ks. 125.74;
US $1 = Ks. 80.97;
€1 = Ks. 105.25;
Ks. 1,000 = £7.95 sterling = $12.35 = €9.50.

Average Exchange Rate (Ks. per US $)
2007   67.318
2008   69.175
2009   77.352

Note: The foregoing information refers to the Central Bank's mid-point exchange rate. However, with the introduction of a foreign exchange bearer certificate (FEBC) scheme in October 1991, a dual exchange rate system is in effect. In May 1994 foreign exchange transactions were liberalized and the Kenya shilling became fully convertible against other currencies.

BUDGET
(Ks. million, year ending 30 June)

Revenue	1999/2000	2000/01	2001/02*
Tax revenue	151,359.5	160,771.6	160,394.2
Taxes on income and profits	53,317.0	53,428.9	55,861.9
Taxes on goods and services	69,437.3	78,538.9	82,948.6
Value-added tax	40,944.2	50,220.9	50,871.7
Excise duties	28,493.1	28,317.9	32,076.9
Taxes on international trade	28,605.2	28,803.7	21,583.7
Import duties	28,605.2	28,803.7	21,583.7
Non-tax revenue	27,585.1	26,306.1	25,399.4
Property income	6,482.4	4,786.1	4,105.5
Administrative fees and charges	21,538.1	21,538.1	21,293.9
Total (incl. others)	184,550.9	192,221.0	187,863.8

Expenditure	1999/2000	2000/01	2001/02*
General administration	44,080.7	62,943.3	57,584.5
Defence	10,427.2	14,202.8	16,268.2
Social services	59,670.4	67,611.1	71,953.1
Education	47,726.8	49,611.3	54,653.0
Health	9,188.6	15,629.3	14,336.5
Economic services	28,481.1	39,362.3	38,069.4
General administration	5,101.3	14,085.6	12,696.2
Agriculture, forestry and fishing	8,115.4	8,269.6	7,850.1
Roads	8,848.5	9,458.4	8,856.7
Interest on public debt	28,917.8	24,425.5	29,850.9
Total	171,577.2	208,545.7	213,726.2

* Forecasts.

2008/09 (Ks. '000 million, year ending 30 June, estimates): *Revenue:* Income tax 184.4; Import duty 36.2; Value-added tax 126.9; Excise duty 69.9; Non-tax revenue 68.2; Total (incl. statistical discrepancy) 487.9 (excluding grants 19.7). *Expenditure:* Recurrent expenditure 435.5 (Interest payments 47.3; Wages and benefits 155.2); Development and net lending 166.3; Total 601.8 (Source: IMF, *Kenya: Request for a Three-Year Arrangement Under the Extended Credit Facility—Staff Report; Press Release on the Executive Board Discussion; and Statement by the Executive Director for Kenya*—February 2011).

2009/10 (Ks. '000 million, year ending 30 June, estimates): *Revenue:* Income tax 209.1; Import duty 41.3; Value-added tax 142.0; Excise duty 74.1; Non-tax revenue 81.6; Total 548.1 (excluding grants 20.7). *Expenditure:* Recurrent expenditure 504.3 (Interest payments 63.5; Wages and benefits 172.6; Defence 56.9); Development and net lending 214.7; Drought expenditures 6.2; Total 725.2 (Source: IMF, *Kenya: Request for a Three-Year Arrangement Under the Extended Credit Facility—Staff Report; Press Release on the Executive Board Discussion; and Statement by the Executive Director for Kenya*—February 2011).

2010/11 (Ks. '000 million, year ending 30 June, projections): *Revenue:* Income tax 252.0; Import duty 48.6; Value-added tax 168.7; Excise duty 86.2; Non-tax revenue 128.7; Total 684.2 (excluding grants 32.3). *Expenditure:* Recurrent expenditure 602.3 (Interest payments 74.9; Wages and benefits 197.7; Defence 63.7); Development and net lending 281.9; Civil contingency fund 2.0; Drought expenditures 2.0; Constitutional reform 4.0; Total (incl. others) 892.3 (Source: IMF, *Kenya: Request for a Three-Year Arrangement Under the Extended Credit Facility—Staff Report; Press Release on the Executive Board Discussion; and Statement by the Executive Director for Kenya*—February 2011).

INTERNATIONAL RESERVES
(excl. gold, US $ million at 31 December)

	2007	2008	2009
IMF special drawing rights	0.2	3.1	350.6
Reserve position in IMF	20.2	19.8	20.2
Foreign exchange	3,334.6	2,855.7	3,478.1
Total	3,355.0	2,878.5	3,849.0

2010: IMF special drawing rights 318.5; Reserve position in IMF 20.0.

Source: IMF, *International Financial Statistics*.

MONEY SUPPLY
(Ks. million at 31 December)

	2007	2008	2009
Currency depository corporations	95,985	93,739	100,850
Transferable deposits	348,677	430,097	427,532
Other deposits	331,042	372,685	515,682
Securities other than shares	175	—	—
Broad money	775,880	896,520	1,044,064

Note: Reporting methodology was revised in July 2008, therefore data for 2008 and 2009 are not strictly comparable with those for 2007.

Source: IMF, *International Financial Statistics*.

KENYA

COST OF LIVING
(Consumer Price Index at December; base: October 1997 = 100)

	2000	2001	2002
Food and non-alcoholic beverages	136.3	134.8	142.5
Alcohol and tobacco	120.8	136.3	137.1
Clothing and footwear	109.9	109.8	110.7
Housing	121.6	129.3	133.9
Fuel and power	143.1	154.1	165.8
Household goods and services	117.6	119.0	120.8
Medical goods and services	134.1	152.6	158.8
Transport and communications	128.4	127.7	130.8
Recreation and education	120.2	129.6	132.8
Personal goods and services	118.2	120.5	122.8
All items (incl. others)	129.0	131.1	136.7

Source: IMF, *Kenya: Statistical Appendix* (July 2003).

All items (Consumer Price Index, annual averages; base 2005 = 100): 81.2 in 2003; 90.7 in 2004; 114.5 in 2006; 125.6 in 2007; 158.6 in 2008; 173.2 in 2009; 180.1 in 2010 (Source: IMF, *International Financial Statistics*).

NATIONAL ACCOUNTS
(Ks. million at current prices)

Expenditure on the Gross Domestic Product

	2006	2007	2008
Government final consumption expenditure	283,236	337,560	360,569
Private final consumption expenditure	1,222,570	1,383,366	1,572,761
Changes in inventories	−18,383	−6,240	−6,095
Gross fixed capital formation	309,592	354,248	408,327
Total domestic expenditure	1,797,015	2,068,934	2,335,561
Exports of goods and services	437,376	484,642	551,264
Less Imports of goods and services	613,764	691,220	876,550
Statistical discrepancy	1,807	−36,395	89,524
GDP at market prices	1,622,434	1,825,960	2,099,798

Gross Domestic Product by Economic Activity

	2006	2007	2008
Agriculture, forestry and fishing	386,251	401,970	499,421
Mining and quarrying	7,884	12,904	14,630
Manufacturing	166,777	190,165	223,353
Electricity, gas and water	28,477	27,111	30,805
Construction	63,928	69,280	80,135
Wholesale and retail trade, restaurants and hotels	175,775	207,066	234,535
Transport, storage and communications	171,991	194,011	214,983
Finance, insurance, real estate and business services	152,267	182,718	206,029
Public administration and defence	86,973	105,582	104,828
Other services	219,034	239,514	263,306
Sub-total	1,459,357	1,630,321	1,872,025
Less Financial intermediation services indirectly measured	15,376	19,490	19,761
Indirect taxes, less subsidies	178,453	215,129	247,535
GDP in market prices	1,622,434	1,825,960	2,099,798

BALANCE OF PAYMENTS
(US $ million)

	2007	2008	2009
Exports of goods f.o.b.	4,132.3	5,039.8	4,502.3
Imports of goods f.o.b.	−8,388.3	−10,689.0	−9,491.6
Trade balance	−4,256.0	−5,649.2	−4,989.3
Exports of services	2,930.6	3,250.8	2,911.4
Imports of services	−1,670.8	−1,870.2	−1,822.1
Balance on goods and services	−2,996.2	−4,268.6	−3,900.0
Other income received	160.6	176.2	181.9
Other income paid	−304.8	−221.4	−239.7
Balance on goods, services and income	−3,140.4	−4,313.8	−3,957.9
Current transfers received	2,148.8	2,419.3	2,379.7
Current transfers paid	−40.4	−88.1	−82.9

—*continued*	2007	2008	2009
Current balance	−1,032.0	−1,982.6	−1,661.1
Capital account	156.8	94.5	260.9
Direct investment abroad	−36.0	−43.8	−46.0
Direct investment from abroad	729.0	95.6	140.5
Portfolio investment assets	−25.5	−35.9	−23.7
Portfolio investment liabilities	0.8	9.8	2.8
Other investment assets	−346.7	−631.6	547.2
Other investment liabilities	1,614.8	1,701.3	2,049.7
Net errors and omissions	−249.9	297.4	−152.3
Overall balance	811.3	−495.3	1,118.0

Source: IMF, *International Financial Statistics*.

External Trade

PRINCIPAL COMMODITIES
(distribution by SITC, US $ million)

Imports c.i.f.	2007	2008	2009
Food and live animals	552.5	688.9	1,117.0
Cereals and cereal preparations	293.5	421.7	811.4
Crude materials (inedible) except fuels	229.6	225.3	224.2
Mineral fuels, lubricants, etc.	1,917.5	3,029.4	2,187.1
Petroleum, petroleum products, etc.	1,876.6	2,976.7	2,138.7
Crude petroleum oils	731.5	1,176.5	705.8
Refined petroleum products	1,120.1	1,769.6	1,399.2
Animal and vegetable oils, fats and waxes	346.0	496.8	356.9
Chemicals and related products	1,150.8	1,454.0	1,325.7
Medicinal and pharmaceutical products	236.9	301.6	297.8
Plastics in primary forms	298.1	341.0	288.4
Basic manufactures	1,428.5	1,602.3	1,408.8
Iron and steel	398.9	512.9	437.3
Machinery and transport equipment	2,745.3	3,110.1	3,097.3
Power-generating machinery and equipment	142.5	350.8	317.2
Machinery specialized for particular industries	328.3	365.5	339.3
General industrial machinery, equipment and parts	233.6	329.6	272.0
Electrical machinery, apparatus, etc.	145.3	185.1	196.5
Road vehicles and parts	766.5	817.7	785.2
Passenger motor cars (excl. buses)	297.3	311.9	296.0
Motor vehicles for goods transport and special purposes	185.4	190.8	165.3
Aircraft, associated equipment and parts	499.7	235.5	349.5
Miscellaneous manufactured articles	447.9	431.5	417.2
Total (incl. others)	8,989.3	11,127.8	10,202.0

KENYA

Exports f.o.b.	2007	2008	2009
Food and live animals	1,517.1	1,827.7	1,681.1
Vegetables and fruit	402.0	451.6	358.9
Fresh or simply preserved vegetables	257.7	274.1	224.7
Coffee, tea, cocoa and spices	874.6	1,098.8	1,110.4
Tea	698.6	931.8	894.1
Crude materials (inedible) except fuels	568.8	763.1	638.3
Cut flowers and foliage	390.3	527.4	422.5
Mineral fuels, lubricants, etc.	174.0	197.7	187.5
Petroleum, petroleum products, etc.	170.9	192.3	183.9
Refined petroleum products	164.6	173.3	177.9
Chemicals and related products	354.3	574.0	457.2
Basic manufactures	534.6	654.1	547.8
Iron and steel	125.5	158.4	118.1
Miscellaneous manufactured articles	467.8	510.6	429.5
Total (incl. others)	4,080.8	5,000.9	4,463.4

Source: UN, *International Trade Statistics Yearbook*.

PRINCIPAL TRADING PARTNERS
(US $ million)

Imports c.i.f.	2007	2008	2009
Bahrain	146.5	198.8	97.9
Belgium	92.6	119.7	91.2
China, People's Repub.	678.7	932.2	965.2
Egypt	165.9	157.4	124.3
France (incl. Monaco)	245.3	237.6	206.8
Germany	329.4	389.7	294.4
India	844.5	1,309.5	1,078.1
Indonesia	278.8	335.7	243.1
Ireland	54.4	21.5	n.a.
Italy	196.5	181.7	179.9
Japan	611.2	649.3	632.7
Korea, Repub.	127.7	119.3	138.6
Netherlands	138.3	192.1	225.9
Pakistan	74.4	81.4	100.4
Russia	97.5	166.2	63.3
Saudi Arabia	261.4	373.1	356.4
Singapore	138.9	360.7	342.2
South Africa	525.3	678.2	913.8
Thailand	99.3	131.4	91.6
United Arab Emirates	1,329.0	1,655.7	1,161.8
United Kingdom	437.1	402.6	473.2
USA	661.6	402.3	649.1
Total (incl. others)	8,989.3	11,127.8	10,202.0

Exports f.o.b.	2007	2008	2009
Belgium	38.6	40.9	43.9
Burundi	36.0	50.5	59.5
Congo, Democratic Repub.	123.5	143.6	146.5
Egypt	135.4	224.7	153.8
Ethiopia	51.0	63.9	55.9
France (incl. Monaco)	63.2	72.1	56.1
Germany	88.4	89.3	95.1
India	86.7	98.2	66.5
Italy	38.3	43.3	31.3
Netherlands	325.7	380.1	340.7
Pakistan	201.0	202.3	196.3
Rwanda	86.2	130.4	123.4
Somalia	123.8	186.7	145.1
Sudan	172.3	204.6	165.1
Tanzania	331.7	424.9	389.3
Uganda	498.9	614.7	598.3
United Arab Emirates	128.2	109.8	138.7
United Kingdom	427.7	550.6	498.1
USA	285.8	299.6	226.1
Zambia	74.1	79.9	62.5
Total (incl. others)	4,080.8	5,000.9	4,463.4

Source: UN, *International Trade Statistics Yearbook*.

Transport

RAILWAYS
(traffic)

	2000	2001	2002*
Passenger-km (million)	302	216	288
Freight ton-km (million)	1,557	1,603	1,538

* Provisional figures.

ROAD TRAFFIC
(motor vehicles in use)

	2000	2001	2002*
Motor cars	244,836	255,379	269,925
Light vans	159,450	162,603	166,811
Lorries, trucks and heavy vans	57,796	58,501	59,835
Buses and mini-buses	38,930	42,629	46,606
Motorcycles and autocycles	44,894	46,004	47,451
Other motor vehicles	31,820	32,255	32,724

* Provisional figures.

2004: Motor cars 307,772; Buses 55,705; Lorries and vans 243,612; Motorcycles 53,508.

2007 (motor vehicles in use): Passenger cars 562,376; Buses and coaches 20,085; Vans and lorries 210,891; Motorcycles and mopeds 180,764 (Source: IRF, *World Road Statistics*).

SHIPPING

Merchant Fleet
(registered at 31 December)

	2007	2008	2009
Number of vessels	36	36	32
Total displacement ('000 grt)	15.1	15.1	14.4

Source: IHS Fairplay, *World Fleet Statistics*.

International Sea-borne Freight Traffic
('000 metric tons)

	1999	2000	2001*
Goods loaded	1,845	1,722	1,998
Goods unloaded	6,200	7,209	8,299

* Provisional figures.

Freight handled ('000 metric tons at Kenyan ports): 11,931 in 2003; 12,920 in 2004; 13,282 in 2005; 14,402 in 2006; 15,962 in 2007; 16,415 in 2008 (provisional).

CIVIL AVIATION
(traffic on scheduled services)

	2004	2005	2006
Kilometres flown (million)	43	48	51
Passengers carried ('000)	2,005	2,424	2,548
Passenger-km (million)	5,310	6,540	7,268
Total ton-km (million)	674	850	953

Source: UN, *Statistical Yearbook*.

2007: Passengers carried ('000) 2,857.5 (Source: World Bank, World Development Indicators database).

2008: Passengers carried ('000) 2,880.5 (Source: World Bank, World Development Indicators database).

KENYA

Tourism

FOREIGN TOURIST ARRIVALS
(number of visitors by country of origin)

	2001	2002	2003
Austria	19,929	20,054	22,954
France	47,802	48,101	55,057
Germany	156,414	157,394	180,156
India	23,858	24,007	27,479
Italy	53,328	53,662	61,428
Sweden	34,376	34,591	39,593
Switzerland	39,081	39,326	45,013
Tanzania	111,735	112,435	128,695
Uganda	69,781	70,218	80,373
United Kingdom	153,968	154,933	177,339
USA	65,191	65,599	75,086
Total (incl. others)	993,600	1,001,297	1,146,099

Tourism receipts (US $ million, incl. passenger transport): 1,181 in 2006; 1,514 in 2007; 1,398 in 2008.

Source: World Tourism Organization.

Total arrivals ('000): 1,361 in 2004; 1,479 in 2005; 1,601 in 2006; 1,817 in 2007; 1,203 in 2008 (provisional).

Communications Media

	2007	2008	2009
Telephones ('000 main lines in use)	464	646	664
Mobile cellular telephones ('000 subscribers)	11,349	16,304	19,365
Internet users ('000)	3,000	3,360	3,996
Broadband subscribers ('000)	17.7	3.3	8.3

Personal computers: 492,000 (13.7 per 1,000 persons) in 2005.

Source: International Telecommunication Union.

Television receivers ('000 in use, 2000): 768.

Radio receivers ('000 in use, 1999): 6,383.

Daily newspapers (2004): 5 titles (average circulation 310,000 copies in 2000).

Book production (titles, 1994): 300 first editions (excl. pamphlets).

Sources: UNESCO, *Statistical Yearbook*; UN, *Statistical Yearbook*.

Education

(2008/09 unless otherwise indicated)

	Institutions	Teachers	Pupils
Pre-primary	23,977[1]	92,555	1,914,222
Primary	17,611[1]	152,848	7,150,259
Secondary:			
general secondary	3,057[1]	106,033	3,188,707
technical	36[2]	1,937	15,672
teacher training	26[3]	808[4]	18,992[5]
Higher	n.a.[6]	n.a.[6]	167,983

[1] 1998/99 figures.
[2] 1988 figure.
[3] 1995 figure.
[4] 1985 figure.
[5] 1992 figure.
[6] In 1990 there were four universities, with 4,392 teachers.

Sources: Ministry of Education, Nairobi; UNESCO Institute for Statistics.

2005 ('000, estimates): Enrolment in primary schools 7,592; Enrolment in secondary schools 928; Enrolment in universities 90.

2006 ('000, estimates): Enrolment in primary schools 7,632; Enrolment in secondary schools 1,030; Enrolment in universities 112.

2007 ('000): Enrolment in primary schools 8,330; Enrolment in secondary schools 1,180; Enrolment in universities 118.

2008 ('000, provisional): Enrolment in primary schools 8,564; Enrolment in secondary schools 1,382; Enrolment in universities 123.

Pupil-teacher ratio (primary education, UNESCO estimate): 46.8 in 2008/09 (Source: UNESCO Institute for Statistics).

Adult literacy rate (UNESCO estimates): 86.5% (males 90.3%; females 82.8%) in 2008 (Source: UNESCO Institute for Statistics).

Directory

The Government

HEAD OF STATE

President: MWAI KIBAKI (took office 30 December 2002; re-elected 27 December 2007).

CABINET
(May 2011)

The Government is formed by a coalition of the Party of National Unity, the Orange Democratic Movement, and the Orange Democratic Movement—Kenya.

Prime Minister: RAILA AMOLLO ODINGA.

Vice-President and Minister of Home Affairs: STEPHEN KALONZO MUSYOKA.

Deputy Prime Minister and Minister of Finance: UHURU KENYATTA.

Deputy Prime Minister and Minister of Local Government: WYCLIFFE MUSALIA MUDAVADI.

Minister of the East African Community and Acting Minister of Higher Education, Science and Technology: Prof. HELEN JEPKEMOI SAMBILI.

Minister of State in the Office of the President responsible for Provincial Administration and Internal Security and Acting Minister of Foreign Affairs: Prof. GEORGE SAITOTI.

Minister of Justice, National Cohesion and Constitutional Affairs: MUTULA KILONZO.

Minister of Nairobi Metropolitan Development: NJERU GITHAE.

Minister of Public Works: CHRIS OBURE.

Minister of Trade: CHIRAU ALI MWAKWERE.

Minister of Water and Irrigation: CHARITY KALUKI NGULI.

Minister of Regional Development Authorities: FREDRICK OMULO GUMO.

Minister of Information and Communications: SAMUEL LESRON POGHISIO.

Minister of Energy: KIRAITU MURUNGI.

Minister of Lands: AGGREY JAMES ORENGO.

Minister of the Environment and Mineral Resources: JOHN MICHUKI.

Minister of Forestry and Wildlife: NOAH WEKESA.

Minister of Tourism: MOHAMED NAJIB BALALA.

Minister of Agriculture: Dr SALLY JEPNGETICH KOSGEY.

Minister of Livestock Development: MOHAMED ABDI KUTI.

Minister of Fisheries Development: AMASON JEFFAH KINGI.

Minister of the Development of Northern Kenya and Other Arid Lands: IBRAHIM ELMI MOHAMED.

Minister of Co-operative Development: JOSEPH NYAGAH.

Minister of Industrialization: (vacant).

KENYA

Minister of Housing: PETER SOITA SHITANDA.
Minister of State for Special Programmes: ESTHER MURUGI MATHENGE.
Minister of Gender, Children and Social Development: Dr NAOMI NAMSI SHABAN.
Minister of Public Health and Sanitation: BETH WAMBUI MUGO.
Minister of Medical Services: Prof. PETER ANYANG' NYONG'O.
Minister of Labour: JOHN KIONGA MUNYES.
Minister of Youth and Sports: Dr PAUL NYONGESA OTUOMA.
Minister of Education: SAMSON KEGEO ONGERI.
Minister of Roads: FRANKLIN BETT.
Minister of Transport: AMOS KIMUNYA.
Minister of State in the Office of the President, responsible for Defence: YUSUF MOHAMED HAJI.
Ministers of State in the Office of the Vice-President: GERALD OTIENO KAJWANG' (Immigration and Registration of Persons), WILLIAM OLE NTIMAMA (National Heritage and Culture).
Ministers of State in the Office of the Prime Minister: WYCLIFFE AMBETSA OPARANYA (Planning, National Development and Vision 2030), DALMAS ANYANGO OTIENO (Public Service).
Attorney-General: AMOS WAKO.

MINISTRIES

Office of the President: Harambee House, Harambee Ave, POB 62345, 00200 Nairobi; tel. (20) 2227411; e-mail president@statehousekenya.go.ke; internet www.cabinetoffice.go.ke.

Office of the Vice-President and Ministry of Home Affairs: Jogoo House 'A', Taifa Rd, POB 30478, 00100 Nairobi; tel. (20) 228411; fax (20) 243620; internet www.homeaffairs.go.ke.

Office of the Prime Minister: Treasury Bldg, 14th Floor, Harambee Ave, POB 74434, 00200 Nairobi; tel. (20) 252299; e-mail info@primeminister.go.ke; internet www.primeminister.go.ke.

Office of the Deputy Prime Minister and Ministry of Finance: Treasury Bldg, Harambee Ave, POB 30007, Nairobi; tel. (20) 2252299; fax (20) 310833; e-mail info@treasury.go.ke; internet www.treasury.go.ke.

Office of the Deputy Prime Minister and Ministry of Local Government: Jogoo House 'A', Taifa Rd, POB 30004, Nairobi; tel. (20) 2217475; fax (20) 217869; internet www.localgovernment.go.ke.

Ministry of Agriculture: Kilimo House, Cathedral Rd, POB 30028, Nairobi; tel. (20) 2718870; internet www.kilimo.go.ke.

Ministry of Co-operative Development and Marketing: NSSF Bldg, Block 'A', Eastern Wing, Bishop Rd, POB 30547, 00100, Nairobi; tel. (20) 2731531; fax (20) 2731511; internet www.cooperative.go.ke.

Ministry of the Development of Northern Kenya and Other Arid Lands: Kenya Int. Conference Centre, 13th Floor, Harambee Ave, POB 53547, 00200 Nairobi; tel. (20) 2227223; fax (20) 2227982.

Ministry of the East African Community: Co-operative House, 16th Floor, Haile Selassie Ave, POB 8846, 00200 Nairobi; tel. (20) 2245741; fax (20) 2229650; e-mail ps@meac.go.ke; internet www.meac.go.ke.

Ministry of Education: Jogoo House 'B', Harambee Ave, POB 30040, 00100 Nairobi; tel. (20) 318581; fax (20) 214287; e-mail info@education.go.ke; internet www.education.go.ke.

Ministry of Energy: Nyayo House, 23rd Floor, Kenyatta Ave, POB 30582, 00100 Nairobi; tel. (20) 310112; fax (20) 228314; e-mail info@energy.go.ke; internet www.energy.go.ke.

Ministry of the Environment and Mineral Resources: NHIF Bldg, Ragati Rd, POB 30126, 00100 Nairobi; tel. (20) 2730808; fax (20) 2725707; internet www.environment.go.ke.

Ministry of Fisheries Development: Maji House, Ngong Rd, POB 58187, 00200 Nairobi; tel. (20) 2716103; fax (20) 316731; e-mail fisheries@kenya.go.ke; internet www.fisheries.go.ke.

Ministry of Foreign Affairs: Old Treasury Bldg, Harambee Ave, POB 30551, 00100 Nairobi; tel. (20) 318888; fax (20) 240066; e-mail press@mfa.go.ke; internet www.mfa.go.ke.

Ministry of Forestry and Wildlife: NHIF Bldg, Ragati Rd, POB 30126, Nairobi; tel. (20) 2730808; internet www.forestryandwildlife.go.ke.

Ministry of Gender, Children and Social Development: NSSF Bldg, Block 'A', Eastern Wing, 6th Floor, Bishop Rd, POB 16936, 00100 Nairobi; tel. (20) 2727980; fax (20) 2734417; e-mail information@gender.go.ke; internet www.gender.go.ke.

Ministry of Higher Education, Science and Technology: Jogoo House 'B', Harambee Ave, POB 9583, 00200 Nairobi; tel. (20) 318581; e-mail info@scienceandtechnology.go.ke; internet www.scienceandtechnology.go.ke.

Ministry of Housing: Ardhi House, Ngong Rd, POB 30119, 00100 Nairobi; tel. (20) 2710451; fax (20) 2721248; e-mail ps@housing.go.ke; internet www.housing.go.ke.

Ministry of Industrialization: Teleposta Towers, GPO 11th Floor, POB 30418, 00100 Nairobi; tel. (20) 315001; e-mail info@industrialization.go.ke; internet www.tradeandindustry.go.ke.

Ministry of Information and Communications: Teleposta Towers, Kenyatta Ave, POB 30025, 00100 Nairobi; tel. (20) 2251152; fax (20) 315147; internet www.information.go.ke.

Ministry of Justice, National Cohesion and Constitutional Affairs: Cooperative Bank House, Haile Selassie Ave, POB 56057, 00200 Nairobi; tel. (20) 224029; e-mail info@justice.go.ke; internet www.justice.go.ke.

Ministry of Labour: Social NSSF Bldg, Block 'C', Bishop Rd, POB 40326, 00100 Nairobi; tel. (20) 2729800; fax (20) 2726497; e-mail info@labour.go.ke; internet www.labour.go.ke.

Ministry of Lands: Ardhi House, Ngong Rd, POB 30450, 00100 Nairobi; tel. (20) 2718050; fax (20) 2721248; internet www.ardhi.go.ke.

Ministry of Livestock Development: Kilimo House, Cathedral Rd, POB 34188, 00100 Nairobi; tel. (20) 2718870; fax (20) 2711149; e-mail info@livestock.go.ke; internet www.livestock.go.ke.

Ministry of Medical Services: Afya House, Cathedral Rd, POB 30016, 00100 Nairobi; tel. (20) 2717077; fax (20) 2713234; e-mail enquiries@health.go.ke; internet www.medical.go.ke.

Ministry of Nairobi Metropolitan Development: Kenya Int. Conference Centre, 25th Floor, Harambee Ave, POB 30130, 00100 Nairobi; tel. (20) 317224; fax (20) 317226; e-mail info@nairobimetro.go.ke; internet www.nairobimetro.go.ke.

Ministry of Public Health and Sanitation: Medical HQ, Afya House, Cathedral Rd, POB 30016, 00100 Nairobi; tel. (20) 2717077; fax (20) 2713234; e-mail psph@health.go.ke; internet www.publichealth.go.ke.

Ministry of Public Works: Ministry of Works Bldg, Ngong Rd, POB 30260, Nairobi; tel. (20) 2723101; e-mail ps@publiworks.go.ke; internet www.works.go.ke.

Ministry of Regional Development Authorities: NSSF Bldg, Block 'A', Eastern Wing, 21st Floor, Bishop Rd, POB 10280, 00100 Nairobi; tel. (20) 2724646; fax 2737693; e-mail psmrd@regional-dev.go.ke; internet www.regional-dev.go.ke.

Ministry of Roads: Ministry of Works Bldg, Ngong Rd, POB 30260, Nairobi; tel. (20) 2723101; fax (20) 720044; internet www.publicworks.go.ke.

Ministry of Special Programmes: Comcraft House, 5th Floor, Haile Selassie Ave, POB 40213, 00100 Nairobi; tel. (20) 247880; fax (20) 227622; e-mail info@sprogrammes.go.ke; internet www.sprogrammes.go.ke.

Ministry of Tourism: Utalii House, off Uhuru Hwy, POB 30027, Nairobi; tel. (20) 313010; fax (20) 318045; e-mail info@tourism.go.ke; internet www.tourism.go.ke.

Ministry of Trade: Teleposta Towers, Kenyatta Ave, POB 30430, 00100 Nairobi; tel. (20) 315001; fax (20) 252896; e-mail info@trade.go.ke; internet www.trade.go.ke.

Ministry of Transport: Transcom House, Ngong Rd, POB 52692, 00200 Nairobi; tel. (20) 2729200; fax (20) 2730330; e-mail ps@transport.go.ke; internet www.transport.go.ke.

Ministry of Water and Irrigation: Maji House, Ngong Rd, POB 49720, 00100 Nairobi; tel. (20) 2716103; fax (20) 2727622; e-mail pro@water.go.ke; internet www.water.go.ke.

Ministry of Youth and Sports: Kencom House, 3rd Floor, Moi Ave, POB 34303, 00100 Nairobi; tel. (20) 240068; fax (20) 312351; e-mail infor@youthaffairs.go.ke; internet www.youthaffairs.go.ke.

President and Legislature

PRESIDENT

Election, 27 December 2007*

Candidate	Votes
Mwai Kibaki (PNU)	4,584,721
Raila Odinga (ODM)	4,352,993
Stephen Kalonzo Musyoka (ODM—Kenya)	879,903
Others	59,411†

* Results released by the Office of the Government Spokesperson. The figure for the total number of votes cast at the election was not immediately made available.
† There were six other candidates.

KENYA

NATIONAL ASSEMBLY

Speaker: KENNETH OTIATO MARENDE.
General Election, 27 December 2007

Party	Seats
ODM	99
PNU	43
ODM—Kenya	16
KANU	14
Safina	5
NARC—Kenya	4
FORD—People	3
NARC	3
New FORD—Kenya	2
CCU	2
PICK	2
DP	2
SKS	2
Others	10
Vacant	3*
Total	**210†**

* Results in three constituencies were not immediately made available and a further two seats were made vacant with the deaths of members of the National Assembly. Following by-elections in five constituencies held on 11 June 2008, the ODM held 102 seats, while the PNU held 45. All other part representations remained unchanged.

† In addition to the 210 directly elected seats, 12 are held by nominees. The Attorney-General and the Speaker are, ex officio, members of the National Assembly.

Election Commission

Interim Independent Electoral Commission (IIEC): Loita St, Anniversary Towers, 6th Floor, POB 45371, 00100 Nairobi; tel. (20) 2769000; e-mail info@iiec.or.ke; internet www.iiec.or.ke; f. 2009 to replace Electoral Commission of Kenya which was disbanded following disputed elections in 2007; Chair. AHMED ISSACK HASSAN.

Political Organizations

Chama Cha Uma (CCU): Nairobi; Founder Dr PATRICK LUMUMBA.

Dawa Ya Wakenya (Remedy for Kenya): f. 2007 by politicians from the North-Eastern region and the north of the Rift Valley to defend the rights of the inhabitants of those areas and to campaign for improved infrastructure, social services and security; Chair. HASSAN HAJI; Gen. Sec. MORU SHAMBARU.

Democratic Party of Kenya (DP): Gitanga Rd, POB 53695, 00200 Nairobi; tel. 722794736 (mobile); f. 1991; Leader JOSEPH MUNYAO; rival faction led by NGENGI MUIGAI.

Forum for the Restoration of Democracy—Asili (FORD—Asili): 58 Duplex Apt, Upper Hill, POB 69564, 00400 Nairobi; e-mail fordasili@gmail.com; tel. (20) 2712214; f. 1992; Chair. JANE ELIZABETH OGWAPIT.

Forum for the Restoration of Democracy—Kenya (FORD—Kenya): Odinga House, Argwings Kodhek Rd, POB 43591, 00100 Nairobi; tel. (20) 3869338; e-mail fordkenya@yahoo.com; f. 1992; predominantly Luo support; Chair. MUSIKARI KOMBO.

Forum for the Restoration of Democracy for the People (FORD—People): Muchai Dr., off Ngong Rd, POB 5938, 00200 Nairobi; tel. (20) 2737015; f. 1997 by fmr mems of FORD—Asili; Nat. Chair. REUBEN OYONDI.

Growth and Development Party of Kenya (GDP): Nairobi; e-mail info@gdp.co.ke; internet www.gdp.co.ke; f. 2007; Chair. AURELIO REBELO.

Kenya African National Union (KANU): Yaya Center, Chania Rd, POB 72394, 00200 Nairobi; tel. (20) 6751284; fax (20) 3573115; internet www.kanuonline.com; f. 1960; sole legal party 1982–91; absorbed the National Development Party (f. 1994) in 2002; Chair. UHURU KENYATTA.

Kenya National Congress (KNC): Gatundu Rd. Kileleshwa, POB 61215, 00200 Nairobi; tel. 722754814 (mobile); f. 1992; Chair. NANCY MUNGAI.

Kenya National Democratic Alliance (KENDA): Int. Casino Complex, Museum Hill, Westlands, POB 10135, 00400 Nairobi; tel. 720841184 (mobile); f. 1991; Chair. KAMLESH PATTNI; Sec.-Gen. BERNARD KALOVE.

Kenya Social Congress (KSC): POB 55318, Nairobi; f. 1992; Chair. GEORGE MOSETI ANYONA; Sec.-Gen. KASHINI MALOBA FAFNA.

Labour Party Democracy: POB 7905, Nairobi; Chair. GEOFFREY MBURU; Sec. DAVID MBURI NGACHURA.

Liberal Democratic Party (LDP): Nairobi; f. 2002 by fmr mems of KANU; Chair. DAVID MUSHA; Sec.-Gen. J. J. KAMOTHO.

Liberal Party: Chair. WANGARI MAATHAI.

Mazingira Green Party of Kenya (MPK): POB 14832, Nairobi; tel. 737444901 (mobile); f. 2007; campaigns for the equitable sharing of wealth, sustainable use of natural resources, women's rights and the defence of Kenyan cultural values; Leader WANGARI MAATHAI.

National Party of Kenya (NPK): Nairobi; internet nationalpartyofkenya.org; f. 1992; Chair. CHARITY KALUKI NGILU; Sec.-Gen. FIDELIS MWEKE.

National Rainbow Coalition (NARC): Mwenge House, Ole Odume Rd, off Gitanga Rd and near Methodist Guest House, Nairobi; tel. (20) 571506; f. 2002; Chair. CHARITY NGILU KALUKI.

National Rainbow Coalition—Kenya (NARC—Kenya): Woodlands Rd, off Lenana Rd, Kilimani, POB 34200, 00100 Nairobi; tel. (20) 2726783; fax (20) 2726784; e-mail narckenya06@yahoo.com; internet www.narckenya.org; f. 2006 by former mems of NARC; Chair. MARTHA KARUA.

New FORD—Kenya: Kikombe House, Joseph Kangethe Rd, Woodley, POB 67404, 00200 Nairobi; tel. 721399626 (mobile); f. 2007; Chair. SOITA SHITANDA.

New Kenya African National Union (New—KANU): Nairobi; f. 2006 by former members of KANU; Pres. NICHOLAS BIWOTT.

Orange Democratic Movement (ODM): Orange House, Menelik Rd, Kilimani Area, POB 2478, 00202 Nairobi; tel. (20) 2053481; f. 2005; split in August 2007; Leader RAILA AMOLO ODINGA.

Orange Democratic Movement—Kenya (ODM—Kenya): Chungwa House, Othaya Rd, POB 403, 00100 Nairobi; tel. (20) 2726385; fax (20) 2726391; f. 2007 following split in the ODM; Leader STEPHEN KALONZO MUSYOKA.

Party of Independent Candidates of Kenya (PICK): Uganda House, 2nd Floor, Kenyatta Ave, POB 21821, 00400 Nairobi; tel. (20) 3513899; e-mail pickenya@yahoo.com; Chair. G. N. MUSYIMI.

Party of National Unity (PNU): Lenana Rd, opp. CVS Plaza, POB 5751, 00100 Nairobi; tel. 722510733 (mobile); f. 2007; coalition of 14 parties including: KANU, the SPK, the SKS, Safina, NARC—Kenya, the DP, New FORD—Kenya, FORD—People, FORD—Asili, FORD—Kenya and the MPK; Chair. MWAI KIBAKI.

Patriotic Pastoralist Alliance of Kenya: f. 1997; represents the interests of northern Kenyan pastoralist communities; Leaders KHALIF ABDULLAHI, IBRAHIM WOCHE, JACKSON LAISAGOR.

People's Alliance for Change in Kenya (PACK): Nairobi; f. 1999; aims to unite diverse ethnic groups; Sec.-Gen. OLANG SANA.

Safina ('Noah's Ark'): Safina Place, Jamhuri Cres., off Ngong Rd, POB 14746, 00100 Nairobi; tel. (20) 3864242; fax (20) 3864242; f. 1995; aims to combat corruption and human rights abuses and to introduce proportional representation; Chair. PAUL MUITE.

Shirikisho Party of Kenya (SPK): Githere Plaza, Haille Selassie Ave, POB 84648, 80100 Mombasa; f. 1997; Sec.-Gen. YUSUF MAHMOUD ABOUBAKAR.

Sisi Kwa Sisi (SKS): Nairobi; f. 2001; Sec.-Gen. JULIUS MWANGI.

Social Democratic Party of Kenya (SDP): 404 Summit House, Moi Ave, Monrovia Lane, POB 4403, 00100 Nairobi; tel. 722620953 (mobile); f. 1992; Chair. MWANDAWIRO MGHANGA.

United Agri Party of Kenya: f. 2001; Chair. GEORGE KINYUA; Sec.-Gen. SIMON MITOBIO.

United Democratic Movement: Mararo Ave, APA Insurance Arcade, POB 60064, 00200 Nairobi; tel. (20) 3862337; e-mail udmafya@gmail.com; Chair. Rev. PAUL CHEBOI; Sec.-Gen. MARTIN OLE KAMWARO.

United Patriotic Party of Kenya: POB 115, Athi River; Chair. JOSEPHAT GATHUA GATHIGA; Sec. MICHAEL NJUGUNA KIGANYA.

The following organizations are banned:

February Eighteen Resistance Army: believed to operate from Uganda; Leader Brig. JOHN ODONGO (also known as STEPHEN AMOKE).

Islamic Party of Kenya (IPK): Mombasa; f. 1992; Islamist fundamentalist; Chair. Sheikh KHALIFA MUHAMMAD (acting); Sec.-Gen. ABDULRAHMAN WANDATI.

KENYA

Diplomatic Representation

EMBASSIES AND HIGH COMMISSIONS IN KENYA

Algeria: Mobil Plaza, POB 64140, 00620 Nairobi; tel. (20) 3755559; fax (20) 3755560; e-mail algerianembassy@wananchi.com; Ambassador ALI BENZERGA.

Argentina: Kitisuru Rd, POB 30283, 00100 Nairobi; tel. (20) 4183119; fax (20) 4183054; e-mail ekeny@bidii.com; Ambassador DANIEL CHUBURU.

Australia: ICIPE House, Riverside Dr., off Chiromo Rd, POB 39341, 00623 Nairobi; tel. (20) 4277100; fax (20) 4277139; e-mail australian.hc.kenya@dfat.gov.au; internet www.kenya.embassy.gov.au; High Commissioner GEOFFREY PETER TOOTH.

Austria: City House, 2nd Floor, Wabera St, POB 30560, 00100 Nairobi; tel. (20) 319076; fax (20) 342290; e-mail nairobi-ob@bmeia.gv.at; internet www.bmeia.gv.at/botschaft/nairobi; Ambassador CHRISTIAN HASENBICHLER.

Bangladesh: Lenana Rd, POB 41645, Nairobi; tel. (20) 8562816; fax (20) 8562817; e-mail bdhc@bdootnairobi.com; High Commissioner A. K. M. SHAMSUDDIN.

Belgium: Muthaiga, Limuru Rd, POB 30461, 00100 Nairobi; tel. (20) 7122011; fax (20) 7123050; e-mail nairobi@diplobel.fed.be; internet www.diplomatie.be/nairobi; Ambassador JAN MUTTON.

Brazil: Tanar Center, UN Crescent Rd, UN Close, Gigiri, POB 30754, 00100 Nairobi; tel. (20) 7125765; fax (20) 7125767; e-mail geral@kenbrem.co.ke; Ambassador (vacant).

Burundi: Coop Trust Plaza, Upper Hill, off Bunyala Rd, POB 61165, 00200 Nairobi; tel. (20) 2719200; fax (20) 2719211; e-mail embunai@yahoo.fr; Ambassador (vacant).

Canada: Limuru Rd, Gigiri, POB 1013, 00621 Nairobi; tel. (20) 3663000; fax (20) 3663900; e-mail nrobi@international.gc.ca; internet www.canadainternational.gc.ca/kenya; High Commissioner DAVID COLLINS.

Chile: Riverside Dr. 66, Riverside, POB 45554, 00100 Nairobi; tel. (20) 4452950; fax (20) 4443209; e-mail echile@echile.co.ke; Ambassador KONRAD PAULSEN.

China, People's Republic: Woodlands Rd, Kilimani District, POB 30508, Nairobi; tel. (20) 2722559; fax (20) 2726402; e-mail chinaemb_ke@mfa.gov.cn; internet ke.china-embassy.org; Ambassador LIU GUANGYUAN.

Colombia: Int. House, 6th Floor, Mam Ngina St, POB 48494, 00100 Nairobi; tel. (20) 246770; fax (20) 246772; e-mail emkenia@colombia.or.ke; Ambassador MARÍA VICTORIA DÍAZ DE SUÁREZ.

Congo, Democratic Republic: Electricity House, 12th Floor, Harambee Ave, POB 48106, 00100 Nairobi; tel. (20) 2229772; fax (20) 3754253; e-mail ambardckenyal@yahoo.com; Ambassador TADUMI ON'OKOKO.

Cuba: International House, Mama Ngina St, 13th Floor, POB 41931, 00606 Nairobi; tel. (20) 2241003; fax (20) 2241023; e-mail embacuba@swiftkenya.com; internet emba.cubaminrex.cu/kenyaing; Ambassador JULIO CÉSAR GONZÁLEZ MARCHANTE.

Cyprus: Eagle House, 5th Floor, Kimathi St, POB 30739, 00100 Nairobi; tel. (20) 2220881; fax (20) 312202; e-mail cyphc@nbnet.co.ke; High Commissioner AGIS LOIZOU.

Czech Republic: Jumia Pl., Lenana Rd, POB 48785, 00100 Nairobi; tel. (20) 2731010; fax (20) 2731013; e-mail nairobi@embassy.mzv.cz; internet www.mzv.cz/nairobi; Ambassador MARGITA FUCHSOVÁ.

Denmark: 13 Runda Dr., Runda, POB 40412, 00100 Nairobi; tel. (20) 7122848; fax (20) 7120638; e-mail nboamb@um.dk; internet www.ambnairobi.um.dk; Ambassador BO JENSEN.

Djibouti: Comcraft House, 2nd Floor, Haile Selassie Ave, POB 59528, Nairobi; tel. (20) 339640; Ambassador ADEN HOUSSEIN ABDILLAHI.

Egypt: Othaya Rd, Kileleshwa, POB 30285, 00100 Nairobi; tel. (20) 3870360; fax (20) 3870383; Ambassador SAHER HASANEEN TAWFEEK HAMZA.

Eritrea: New Rehema House, 2nd Floor, Westlands, POB 38651, Nairobi; tel. (20) 4443164; fax (20) 4443165; Ambassador BEYENE RUSSOM.

Ethiopia: State House Ave, POB 45198, 00100 Nairobi; tel. (20) 2732052; fax (20) 2732054; e-mail ethiopian22embassy@yahoo.com; Ambassador DISSASA DIRBISSA WINSA.

Finland: Eden Sq., Blk 3, 6th Floor, Greenway Rd, off Westlands Rd, POB 30379, 00100 Nairobi; tel. (20) 3750721; fax (20) 3750714; e-mail sanomat.nai@formin.fi; internet www.finland.or.ke; Ambassador HELI SIRVE.

France: Barclays Plaza, 9th Floor, Loita St, POB 41784, 00100 Nairobi; tel. (20) 2778000; fax (20) 2778180; e-mail ambafrance.nairobi@diplomatie.gouv.fr; internet www.ambafrance-ke.org; Ambassador ETIENNE DE PONCINS.

Germany: Ludwig Krapf House, Riverside Dr. 113, POB 30180, Nairobi; tel. (20) 4262100; fax (20) 4262129; e-mail info@nairobi.diplo.de; internet www.nairobi.diplo.de; Ambassador MARGIT HELLWIG-BÖTTE.

Greece: Nation Centre, 13th Floor, Kimathi St, POB 30543, 00100 Nairobi; tel. (20) 340722; fax (20) 2216044; e-mail gremb.nai@mfa.gr; Ambassador DIMITRI LOUNDRAS.

Holy See: 151 Manyani Rd West, Waiyaki Way, POB 14326, 00800 Nairobi; tel. (20) 4442975; fax (20) 4446789; e-mail nunciokenya@nunciokenya.org; Apostolic Nuncio Most Rev. ALAIN PAUL CHARLES LEBEAUPIN (Titular Archbishop of Vico Equense).

Hungary: Kabarsiran Ave, off James Gichuru Rd, Lavington, POB 61146, Nairobi; tel. (20) 4442612; fax (20) 4442101; e-mail mission.nai@kum.hu; internet www.mfa.gov.hu/kulkepviselet/ke; Ambassador SÁNDOR JUHÁSZ.

India: Jeevan Bharati Bldg, 2nd Floor, Harambee Ave, POB 30074, Nairobi; tel. (20) 2225104; fax (20) 316242; e-mail hcindia@kenyaweb.com; internet www.hcinairobi.co.ke; High Commissioner SIBABRATA TRIPATHI.

Indonesia: Menengai Rd, Upper Hill, POB 48868, Nairobi; tel. (20) 2714196; fax (20) 2713475; e-mail indonbi@indonesia.or.ke; internet www.indonesia.or.ke; Ambassador BUDI BOWOLEKSONO.

Iran: Dennis Pritt Rd, POB 49170, Nairobi; tel. (20) 711257; fax (20) 339936; Ambassador Dr SEYED ALI SHARIFI SADATI.

Israel: Bishop's Rd, POB 30354, 00100 Nairobi; tel. (20) 2722182; fax (20) 2715966; e-mail info@nairobi.mfa.gov.il; internet nairobi.mfa.gov.il; Ambassador GIL HASKELL.

Italy: Int. House, 9th Floor, Mama Ngina St, POB 30107, 00100 Nairobi; tel. (20) 2247750; fax (20) 2247086; e-mail ambasciata.nairobi@esteri.it; internet www.ambnairobi.esteri.it; Ambassador PIERANDREA MAGISTRATI.

Japan: Mara Rd, Upper Hill, POB 60202, 00200 Nairobi; tel. (20) 2898000; fax (20) 2898531; e-mail jinfocul@eojkenya.org; internet www.ke.emb-japan.go.jp; Ambassador TOSHIHISA TOKATA.

Korea, Republic: Anniversary Towers, 15th Floor, University Way, POB 30455, 00100 Nairobi; tel. (20) 2220000; fax (20) 2217772; e-mail emb-ke@mofat.go.kr; internet ken.mofat.go.kr; Ambassador (vacant).

Kuwait: Muthaiga Rd, POB 42353, Nairobi; tel. (20) 761614; fax (20) 762837; Ambassador YAQOUB YOUSEF EID AL-SANAD.

Libya: Jamahiriya House, Loita St, POB 47190, Nairobi; tel. (20) 250380; fax (20) 243730; e-mail jamahiriyanbi@wananchi.com; Chargé d'affaires HESHAM ALI SHARIF.

Malaysia: 58 Red Hill Rd, Gigiri, POB 42286, 00200 Nairobi; tel. (20) 7123373; fax (20) 7123371; e-mail malnairobi@kln.gov.my; High Commissioner ZAINOL RAHIM ZAINUDDIN.

Mexico: Kibagare Way, off Loresho Ridge, POB 14145, 00800 Nairobi; tel. (20) 4182593; fax (20) 4181500; e-mail mexico@embamex.co.ke; internet www.sre.gob.mx/kenia; Ambassador LUIS JAVIER CAMPUZANO PINA.

Morocco: UN Ave, Gigiri, POB 617, 00621 Nairobi; tel. (20) 7120765; fax (20) 7120817; e-mail sifmanbi@clubinternetk.com; Ambassador ABDELILAH BENRYANE.

Mozambique: Bruce House, 3rd Floor, Standard St, POB 66923, Nairobi; tel. (20) 221979; fax (20) 222446; e-mail embamoc.quenia@minec.gov.mz; High Commissioner MANUEL JOSÉ GONCALVES.

Netherlands: Riverside Lane, off Riverside Dr., POB 41537, 00100 Nairobi; tel. (20) 4288000; fax (20) 4288264; e-mail nlgovnai@africaonline.co.ke; internet kenia.nlembassy.org; Ambassador LAETITIA VAN DEN ASSUM.

Nigeria: Lenana Rd, Hurlingham, POB 30516, Nairobi; tel. (20) 3864116; fax (20) 3874309; e-mail ng@nigeriahighcom.org; High Commissioner Dr CHIJIOKE WILCOX WIGWE.

Norway: Lion Pl., 1st Floor, Wayiaki Way, POB 46363, 00100 Nairobi; tel. (20) 4251000; fax (20) 4451517; e-mail emb.nairobi@mfa.no; internet www.norway.or.ke; Ambassador PER LUDVIG MAGNUS.

Pakistan: St Michel Rd, Westlands Ave, POB 30045, 00100 Nairobi; tel. (20) 4443911; fax (20) 4446507; e-mail parepnairobi@iwayafrica.com; internet www.pakistanafrica.org; High Commissioner MANSOOR A. JUNEJO.

Poland: 58 Red Hill Rd, POB 30086, 00100 Nairobi; tel. (20) 7120019; fax (20) 7120106; e-mail ambnairo@kenyaweb.com; internet www.nairobi.polemb.net; Ambassador ANNA M. GRUPIŃSKA.

Portugal: Reinsurance Plaza, 10th Floor, Aga Khan Walk, POB 34020, 00100 Nairobi; tel. (20) 313203; fax (20) 214711; e-mail portugalnb@jambo.co.ke; Ambassador LUIS LORUÁO.

Romania: Eliud Mathu St, Runda, POB 63240, 00619 Nairobi; tel. (20) 7123109; fax (20) 7122061; e-mail secretariat@romanianembassy.co.ke; Chargé d'affaires a.i. DUMITRU NEAGU.

Russia: Lenana Rd, POB 30049, Nairobi; tel. (20) 2728700; fax (20) 2721888; e-mail russembkenya@mail.ru; Ambassador (vacant).

Rwanda: International House, 12th Floor, Mama Ngina St, POB 48579, Nairobi; tel. (20) 560178; fax (20) 561932; internet kenya.embassy.gov.rw; High Commissioner GEORGE WILLIAM KAYONGA.

Saudi Arabia: Muthaiga Rd, POB 58297, Nairobi; tel. (20) 762781; fax (20) 760939; Ambassador NBEEL KHALAF A. ASHOUR.

Serbia: State House Ave, POB 30504, 00100 Nairobi; tel. (20) 2710076; fax (20) 2714126; e-mail nairobi@embassyofserbia.or.ke; internet www.embassyofserbia.or.ke; Ambassador ZDRAVKO BISIĆ.

Slovakia: Milimani Rd, POB 30204, Nairobi; tel. (20) 2721896; fax (20) 2717291; e-mail slovakembassy@jambo.co.ke; Ambassador MILAN ZACHAR.

Somalia: POB 30769, Nairobi; tel. (20) 580165; fax (20) 581683; internet www.kenya.somaligov.net; Ambassador MOHAMMED ALI NUR.

South Africa: Roshanmaer Place, Lenana Rd, POB 42441, 00100 Nairobi; tel. (20) 2827100; fax (20) 2827236; e-mail nairobi@foreign.gov.za; High Commissioner NDUMISO NDIMA NTSHINGA.

Spain: CBA Bldg, Mara and Ragati Rds, Upper Hill, POB 45503, 00100 Nairobi; tel. (20) 2720222; fax (20) 2720226; e-mail emb.nairobi@maec.es; Ambassador NICOLÁS MARTÍN CINTO.

Sri Lanka: Lenana Rd, POB 48145, Nairobi; tel. (20) 3872627; fax (20) 3872141; e-mail slhckeny@africaonline.co.ke; High Commissioner JAYANTHA DISSANAYAKE.

Sudan: Kabarnet Rd, off Ngong Rd, POB 48784, 00100 Nairobi; tel. (20) 3875159; fax (20) 3878187; e-mail embassy@sudanebassyke.org; internet www.sudanembassyke.org; Ambassador BEDHEREDIN ABDALLAH.

Sweden: Lion Pl., 3rd Floor, Waiyaki Way, Westlands, POB 30600, 00100 Nairobi; tel. (20) 4234000; fax (20) 4452008; e-mail ambassaden.nairobi@foreign.ministry.se; internet www.swedenabroad.com/nairobi; Ambassador ANN DISMORR.

Switzerland: Int. House, 7th Floor, Mama Ngina St, POB 30752, 00100 Nairobi; tel. (20) 2228735; fax (20) 2217388; e-mail nai.vertretung@eda.admin.ch; Ambassador JACQUES PITTELOUD.

Tanzania: Re-Insurance Plaza, 9th Floor, Taifa Rd, POB 47790, 0100 Nairobi; tel. (20) 312027; fax (20) 2218269; e-mail highcom@tanzaniahc.or.ke; High Commissioner Maj.-Gen. NYASUGARA P. KADEGE.

Thailand: Rose Ave, off Denis Pritt Rd, POB 58349, 00200 Nairobi; tel. (20) 2715243; fax (20) 2715801; e-mail thainbi@thainbi.or.ke; internet www.thaiembassy.org/nairobi; Ambassador APICHIT ASATTHAWASI.

Turkey: Gigiri Rd, off Limuru Rd, POB 64748, 00620 Nairobi; tel. and fax (20) 7126929; e-mail tcbenair@accesskenya.co.ke; internet www.nairobi.emb.mfa.gov.tr; Ambassador TUNCER KAYALAR.

Uganda: Uganda House, 1st Floor, Kenyatta Ave, POB 60853, 00200 Nairobi; tel. (20) 4449096; fax (20) 4443772; e-mail info@ugandahighcommission.co.ke; High Commissioner Brig. (retd) MATAYO KYALIGONZA.

Ukraine: POB 63566, 00619 Nairobi; tel. (20) 3748922; fax (20) 3756028; e-mail emb_ke@mfa.gov.ua; Ambassador VOLODYMYR BUTYAGA.

United Kingdom: Upper Hill Rd, POB 30465, 00100 Nairobi; tel. (20) 2844000; fax (20) 2844088; e-mail bhcinfo@jambo.co.ke; internet ukinkenya.fco.gov.uk; High Commissioner ROBERT NIGEL PAUL MACAIRE.

USA: UN Ave, Village Market, POB 606, 00621 Nairobi; tel. (20) 3636000; fax (20) 3633410; internet nairobi.usembassy.gov; Ambassador JONATHAN SCOTT GRATION.

Venezuela: Int. House, 3rd Floor, Mama Ngina St, POB 34477, 00100 Nairobi; tel. (20) 340134; fax (20) 248105; e-mail embavene@swiftkenya.com; Ambassador MARÍA JACQUELINE MENDOZA.

Yemen: cnr Ngong and Kabarnet Rds, POB 44642, Nairobi; tel. (20) 564379; fax (20) 564394; Ambassador AHMAD MAYSARI.

Zambia: Nyerere Rd, POB 48741, Nairobi; tel. (20) 7224850; fax (20) 2718494; e-mail zambiacom@swiftkenya.com; High Commissioner ENESS CHISHALA CHIYENGE.

Zimbabwe: 2 Westlands Close, Westlands, POB 30806, 00100 Nairobi; tel. (20) 3744052; fax (20) 3748079; e-mail zimna@africaonline.co.ke; Ambassador KELEBERT NKOMANI.

Judicial System

The superior courts are the Supreme Court, the Court of Appeal and the High Court.

Chief Justice: JOHNSON EVANS GICHERU.

Supreme Court: Nairobi; comprises the Chief Justice, who shall be the president of the court, the Deputy Chief Justice and five other judges; has jurisdiction to hear and determine disputes relating to the elections to the office of President and appellate jurisdiction to hear and determine appeals from the Court of Appeal and any other court or tribunal as prescribed by national legislation.

Court of Appeal: POB 30187, Nairobi; comprises not fewer than 12 judges; the final court of appeal for Kenya in civil and criminal process; sits at Nairobi, Mombasa, Kisumu, Nakuru and Nyeri.

High Court: Between Taifa Rd and City Hall Way, POB 30041, Nairobi; tel. (20) 221221; e-mail hck-lib@nbnet.co.ke; has unlimited criminal and civil jurisdiction at first instance; jurisdiction to determine the question whether a right or fundamental freedom in the Bill of Rights has been denied, violated, infringed or threatened; jurisdiction to hear an appeal from a decision of a tribunal appointed under the Constitution to consider the removal of a person from office; and jurisdiction to hear any question respecting the interpretation of this Constitution.

The subordinate courts are the Magistrates courts, the Kadhis' courts, the Courts Martial and any other court or local tribunal as may be established by an Act of Parliament.

Resident Magistrates' Courts: have country-wide jurisdiction, with powers of punishment by imprisonment for up to five years or by fines of up to K£500. If presided over by a chief magistrate or senior resident magistrate, the court is empowered to pass any sentence authorized by law. For certain offences, a resident magistrate may pass minimum sentences authorized by law.

District Magistrates' Courts: of first, second and third class; have jurisdiction within districts and powers of punishment by imprisonment for up to five years, or by fines of up to K£500.

Kadhis' Courts: have jurisdiction within districts, to determine questions of Islamic law; comprises a Chief Kadhi and no fewer than three other Kadhis.

Religion

According to official government figures, Protestants, the largest religious group, represent approximately 38% of the population. Approximately 25% of the population is Roman Catholic, 7% of the population practises Islam, 1% practises Hinduism and the remainder follow various traditional indigenous religions or offshoots of Christian religions. There are very few atheists. Muslim groups dispute government estimates; most often they claim to represent 15% to 20% of the population, sometimes higher. Members of most religious groups are active throughout the country, although certain religions dominate particular regions. Muslims dominate North-Eastern Province, where the population is chiefly Somali. Muslims also dominate Coast Province, except for the western areas of the Province, which are predominantly Christian. Eastern Province is approximately 50% Muslim (mostly in the north) and 50% Christian (mostly in the south). The rest of the country is largely Christian, with some persons following traditional indigenous religions. Many foreign missionary groups operate in the country, the largest of which are the African Inland Mission (Evangelical Protestant), the Southern Baptist Church, the Pentecostal Assembly of Kenya, and the Church Missionary Society of Britain (Anglican). The Government generally has permitted these missionary groups to assist the poor and to operate schools and hospitals. The missionaries openly promote their religious beliefs and have encountered little resistance.

CHRISTIANITY

National Council of Churches of Kenya: Jumuia Pl., POB 45009, 00100 Nairobi; tel. (20) 2711862; fax (20) 2724183; e-mail gsoffice@ncck.org; internet www.ncck.org; f. 1943 as Christian Council of Kenya; 24 mem. churches and 18 Christian orgs; Chair. Rev. JOSEPH WAITHONGA; Sec.-Gen. Rev. Canon PETER KARANJA MWANGI.

The Anglican Communion

Anglicans are adherents of the Church of the Province of Kenya, which was established in 1970. It comprises 28 dioceses, and has about 2.5m. members.

Archbishop of Kenya and Bishop of Nairobi: Most Rev. Dr DAVID M. GITARI, POB 40502, Nairobi; tel. (20) 2714755; fax (20) 2718442; e-mail davidgitari@insightkenya.com.

Greek Orthodox Church

Archbishop of East Africa: NICADEMUS OF IRINOUPOULIS, Nairobi; jurisdiction covers Kenya, Tanzania and Uganda.

KENYA

The Roman Catholic Church

Kenya comprises four archdioceses, 20 dioceses and one Apostolic Vicariate. Some 25% of the total population are adherents of the Roman Catholic Church.

Kenya Episcopal Conference

Kenya Catholic Secretariat, POB 13475, Nairobi; tel. (20) 443133; fax (20) 442910; e-mail csk@users.africaonline.co.ke; internet www.catholicchurch.or.ke.

f. 1976; Pres. Cardinal JOHN NJUE (Archbishop of Nairobi).

Archbishop of Kisumu: Most Rev. ZACCHAEUS OKOTH, POB 1728, 40100 Kisumu; tel. (57) 2020725; fax (57) 2022203; e-mail archdiocese-kisumu@africaonline.co.ke.

Archbishop of Mombasa: Most Rev. BONIFACE LELE, Catholic Secretariat, Nyerere Ave, POB 84425, Mombasa; tel. (41) 2311801; fax (41) 2228217; e-mail catholicsecretariat@msarchdiocese.org.

Archbishop of Nairobi: Cardinal JOHN NJUE, Archbishop's House, POB 14231, 00800 Nairobi; tel. (20) 241391; fax (20) 4447027; e-mail arch-nbo@wananchi.com.

Archbishop of Nyeri: Most Rev. PETER J. CAIRO, POB 288, 10100 Nyeri; tel. (61) 2030446; fax (61) 2030435; e-mail adn@wananchi.com.

Other Christian Churches

Africa Gospel Church: Kericho; tel. (52) 20123; internet www.agckenya.org; Bishop Rev. Dr JOSEPH RONO.

African Christian Church and Schools: POB 1365, Thika; e-mail accsheadoffice@yahoo.com; f. 1948; Moderator Rt Rev. JOHN NJUNGUNA; Gen. Sec. Rev. SAMUEL MWANGI; 50,000 mems.

African Church of the Holy Spirit: POB 183, Kakamega; f. 1927; 20,000 mems.

African Israel Nineveh Church: Nineveh HQ, POB 701, Kisumu; f. 1942; High Priest Rt Rev. JOHN KIVULI, II; Gen. Sec. Rev. JOHN ARAP TONUI; 350,000 mems.

Baptist Convention of Kenya: POB 14907, Nairobi; Pres. Rev. ELIUD MUNGAI.

Church of God in East Africa: Pres. Rev. Dr BYRUM MAKOKHA.

Evangelical Fellowship of Kenya: Co-ordinator Rt Rev. ARTHUR GITONGA; Sec.-Gen. Dr WASHINGTON NG'ENG'I.

Evangelical Lutheran Church in Kenya: POB 44685, 00100 Nairobi; tel. and fax 38131231; e-mail bishopobarewa@yahoo.com; Presiding Bishop Most Rev. WALTER OBARE OMWANZA; Gen. Sec. Rev. JOHN HALAKHE; 100,000 mems (2010).

Kenya Evangelical Lutheran Church: POB 54128, 00200 City Sq., Jogoo Rd, off Nile Rd, Nairobi; tel. and fax (20) 78-04-54; e-mail info@kelc.or.ke; internet www.kelc.or.ke; Bishop ZACHARIAH W. KAHUTHU; 44,000 mems (2010).

Methodist Church in Kenya: POB 47633, 00100 Nairobi; tel. (20) 2724828; fax (20) 2729790; e-mail mckconf@insightkenya.com; internet www.methodistchurchkenya.org; f. 1862; autonomous since 1967; Presiding Bishop Rev. Dr STEPHEN KANYARU M'IMPWII; 900,000 mems (2005).

Presbyterian Church of East Africa: POB 27573, 00506 Nairobi; tel. (20) 608848; fax (20) 609102; e-mail info@pcea.or.ke; internet www.pcea.or.ke; Moderator Rt Rev. Dr DAVID GITHII; Sec.-Gen. Rev. SAMUEL MURIGYH.

Other denominations active in Kenya include the African Brotherhood Church, the African Independent Pentecostal Church, Africa Inland Church in Kenya, the African Interior Church, the Episcopal Church of Kenya, the Free Pentecostal Fellowship of Kenya, the Full Gospel Churches of Kenya, the National Independent Church of Africa, the Pentecostal Assemblies of God, the Pentecostal Evangelistic Fellowship of God and the Reformed Church of East Africa.

BAHÁ'Í FAITH

National Spiritual Assembly: POB 47562, Nairobi; tel. (20) 725447; e-mail nsakenya@yahoo.com; mems resident in 9,654 localities.

ISLAM

Supreme Council of Kenyan Muslims (SUPKEM)

POB 45163, Nairobi; tel. and fax (20) 243109; Nat. Chair. Prof. ABD AL-GHAFUR AL-BUSAIDY; Sec.-Gen. MOHAMMED KHALIF.

Chief Kadhi: NASSOR NAHDI.

The Press

PRINCIPAL DAILIES

Business Daily: Nation Center, 2nd Floor, Kimathi St, POB 49010, 00100 Nairobi; tel. (20) 3288104; fax (20) 211130; internet www.businessdailyafrica.com; Man. Editor NICK WACHIRA.

Daily Nation: Nation Centre, Kimathi St, POB 49010, 00100 Nairobi; tel. (20) 3288000; fax (20) 2337710; e-mail newsdesk@nation.co.ke; internet www.nation.co.ke; f. 1960; English; owned by Nation Media Group; Editor-in-Chief WANGETHI MWANGI; Editorial Dir JOSEPH ODINDO; circ. 195,000.

Kenya Leo: POB 30958, Nairobi; tel. (20) 332390; f. 1983; Kiswahili; KANU party newspaper; Group Editor-in-Chief AMBOKA ANDERE; circ. 6,000.

Kenya Times: POB 30958, Nairobi; tel. (20) 2336611; fax (20) 2927348; internet www.timesnews.co.uk; f. 1983; evening; English; KANU party newspaper; Group Editor-in-Chief AMBOKA ANDERE; circ. 10,000.

The People: POB 10296, 00100 Nairobi; tel. (20) 2249686; fax (20) 2228503; e-mail info@people.co.ke; internet www.people.co.ke; f. 1993; Man. Editor MUGO THEURI; circ. 40,000.

The Standard: Mombasa Rd, POB 30080, 00100 Nairobi; tel. (20) 3222111; fax (20) 214467; e-mail ads@standardmedia.co.ke; internet www.standardmedia.co.ke; f. 1902 as African Standard; renamed East African Standard before adopting present name in 2004; Editor OKETCH KENDO; circ. 59,000.

Taifa Leo: POB 49010, Nairobi 00100; tel. (20) 3288419; e-mail taifa@ke.nationmedia.com; Kiswahili; f. 1960; daily and weekly edns; Kiswahili; owned by Nation Media Group; Man. Editor NICHOLAS MUEMA; circ. 15,000.

Kenya has a thriving vernacular press, but titles are often short-lived. Newspapers in African languages include:

Kihooto (The Truth): Kikuyu; satirical.

Mwaria Ma (Honest Speaker): Nyeri; f. 1997; Publr Canon JAMLICK M. MIANO.

Mwihoko (Hope): POB 734, Muranga; f. 1997; Roman Catholic.

Nam Dar: Luo.

Otit Mach (Firefly): Luo.

SELECTED PERIODICALS

Weeklies and Fortnightlies

The Business Chronicle: POB 53328, Nairobi; tel. (20) 544283; fax (20) 532736; f. 1994; weekly; Man. Editor MUSYOKA KYENDO.

Coastweek: Oriental Bldg, 2nd Floor, Nkrumah Rd, POB 87270, Mombasa; tel. (41) 2230125; fax (41) 2225003; e-mail coastwk@africaonline.co.ke; internet www.coastweek.com; f. 1978; English, with German section; Friday; Editor ADRIAN GRIMWOOD; Man. Dir SHIRAZ D. ALIBHAI; circ. 54,000.

Diplomat East Africa: Vision Plaza, Ground Floor, Suite 37, Mombasa Rd, POB 23399, Nairobi; tel. (20) 2525253; e-mail editor@diplomateastafrica.com; internet www.diplomateastafrica.com.

The East African: POB 49010, 00506 Nairobi; tel. (20) 3288000; fax (20) 2213946; e-mail newsdesk@nation.co.ke; internet www.theeastafrican.co.ke; f. 1994; weekly; English; owned by Nation Media Group; Editor-in-Chief JOE ODINDO; Man. Editor MBATAU WA NGAI.

The Herald: POB 30958, Nairobi; tel. (20) 332390; English; sponsored by KANU; Editor JOB MUTUNGI; circ. 8,000.

Kenrail: POB 30121, Nairobi; tel. (20) 2221211; fax (20) 2340049; quarterly; English and Kiswahili; publ. by Kenya Railways Corpn; Editor J. N. LUSENO; circ. 20,000.

Kenya Gazette: POB 30746, Nairobi; tel. (20) 334075; internet www.kenyalaw.org/KenyaGazette; f. 1898; official notices; weekly; circ. 8,000.

Kenya Today: c/o Office of Public Communications, KICC Bldg, 3rd Floor, POB 45617, 00100 Nairobi; e-mail comms@comms.go.ke; f. 2009; govt-owned; weekly; Dir JERRY OKUNGU.

Post on Sunday: Nairobi; weekly; independent; Editor-in-Chief TONY GACHOKA.

Sunday Nation: POB 49010, Nairobi; f. 1960; English; owned by Nation Media Group; Man. Editor BERNARD NDERITU; circ. 170,000.

Sunday Standard: POB 30080, Nairobi; tel. (20) 552510; fax (20) 553939; English; Man. Editor DAVID MAKALI; circ. 90,000.

Sunday Times: POB 30958, Nairobi; tel. (20) 337798; Group Editor AMBOKA ANDERE.

Taifa Jumapili: POB 49010, Nairobi; tel. (20) 3288419; e-mail taifa@ke.nationmedia.com; f. 1987; Kiswahili; owned by Nation Media Group; Man. Editor NICHOLAS MUEMA; circ. 15,000.

KENYA

Taifa Weekly: POB 49010, Nairobi; tel. (20) 337691; f. 1960; Kiswahili; Editor ROBERT K. MWANGI; circ. 68,000.

Trans Nzoia Post: POB 34, Kitale; weekly.

The Weekly Review: Stellacom House, POB 42271, Nairobi; tel. (20) 2251473; fax (20) 2222555; f. 1975; English; Man. Dir JAINDI KISERO; circ. 16,000.

What's On: Rehema House, Nairobi; tel. (20) 27651; Editor NANCY KAIRO; circ. 10,000.

Monthlies

Africa Law Review: Tumaini House, 4th Floor, Nkrumah Ave, POB 53234, Nairobi; tel. (20) 330480; fax (20) 230173; e-mail alr@africalaw.org; f. 1987; English; Editor-in-Chief GITOBU IMANYARA.

East African Medical Journal: POB 41632, 00100 Nairobi; tel. (20) 2712010; fax (20) 2724617; e-mail eamj@ken.healthnet.org; English; f. 1923; Editor-in-Chief Prof. WILLIAM LORE; circ. 4,500.

East African Report on Trade and Industry: POB 30339, Nairobi; journal of Kenya Asscn of Mfrs; Editor GORDON BOY; circ. 3,000.

Executive: POB 47186, Nairobi; tel. (20) 530598; fax (20) 557815; e-mail spacesellers@wananchi.com; f. 1980; business; Publr SYLVIA KING; circ. 25,000.

Kenya Farmer (Journal of the Agricultural Society of Kenya): c/o English Press, POB 30127, Nairobi; tel. (20) 20377; f. 1954; English and Kiswahili; Editor ROBERT IRUNGU; circ. 20,000.

Kenya Yetu: POB 8053, Nairobi; tel. (20) 250083; fax (20) 340659; f. 1965; Kiswahili; publ. by Ministry of Information and Communications; Editor M. NDAVI; circ. 10,000.

Nairobi Handbook: POB 30127, Accra Rd, Nairobi; Editor R. OUMA; circ. 20,000.

News from Kenya: POB 8053, Nairobi; tel. (20) 253083; fax (20) 340659; publ. by Ministry of Information and Communications.

PC World (East Africa): Gilgil House, Monrovia St, Nairobi; tel. (20) 246808; fax (20) 215643; f. 1996; Editor ANDREW KARANJA.

Presence: POB 10988, 00400 Nairobi; tel. (20) 577708; fax (20) 4948840; f. 1984; economics, law, women's issues, fiction.

Sparkle: POB 47186, Nairobi; tel. (20) 530598; fax (20) 557815; e-mail spacesellers@wananchi.com; f. 1990; children's; Editor ANNA NDILA NDUTO.

Today in Africa: POB 60, Kijabe; tel. (25) 64210; English; Man. Editor MWAURA NJOROGE; circ. 13,000.

Other Periodicals

African Ecclesiastical Review: POB 4002, 30100 Eldoret; tel. (53) 2061218; fax (53) 2062570; e-mail gabapubs@africaonline.co.ke; internet www.gabapublications.org; f. 1969; scripture, religion and devt; 4 a year; Editor and Dir Sister JUSTIN C. NABUSHAWO; circ. 2,500.

Afya: POB 30125, Nairobi; tel. (20) 501301; fax (20) 506112; e-mail amrefkco@africaonline.co.ke; journal for medical and health workers; quarterly.

Azania: POB 30710, 00100 Nairobi; tel. (20) 4343190; fax (20) 4343365; f. 1966; annual (Dec.); English and French; history, archaeology, ethnography and linguistics of East African region; circ. 650.

Defender: AMREF, POB 30125, Nairobi; tel. (20) 201301; f. 1968; quarterly; English; health and fitness; Editor WILLIAM OKEDI; circ. 100,000.

East African Agricultural and Forestry Journal: POB 30148, Nairobi; f. 1935; English; quarterly; Editor J. O. MUGAH; circ. 1,000.

Economic Review of Agriculture: POB 30028, Nairobi; tel. (20) 728370; f. 1968; publ. by Ministry of Agriculture; quarterly; last issue 1999; Editor OKIYA OKOITI.

Finance: Nairobi; monthly; Editor-in-Chief NJEHU GATABAKI.

Inside Kenya Today: POB 8053, Nairobi; tel. (20) 340010; fax (20) 340659; English; publ. by Ministry of Tourism; quarterly; Editor M. NDAVI; circ. 10,000.

Kenya Statistical Digest: POB 30007, Nairobi; tel. (20) 338111; fax (20) 330426; publ. by Ministry of Finance; quarterly.

Safari: Norwich Bldg, 4th Floor, Mama Ngina St, POB 30339, Nairobi; tel. (20) 2246612; fax (20) 2215127; 6 a year; English.

Target: POB 72839, Nairobi; f. 1964; English; 6 a year; religious; Editor FRANCIS MWANIKI; circ. 17,000.

NEWS AGENCY

Kenya News Agency (KNA): Information House, POB 8053, Nairobi; tel. (20) 223201; internet www.kenyanewsagency.go.ke; f. 1963; Dir S. MUSANDU.

Publishers

Academy Science Publishers: POB 24916, Nairobi; tel. (20) 884401; fax (20) 884406; e-mail asp@africaonline.co.ke; f. 1989; part of the African Academy of Sciences; Editor-in-Chief Prof. KETO E. MSHIGENI.

AMECEA Gaba Publications: Amecea Pastoral Institute, POB 4002, 30100 Eldoret; tel. (53) 2061218; fax (53) 2062570; e-mail gabapubs@africaonline.co.ke; internet www.gabapublications.org; f. 1958; anthropology, religious; owned by AMECEA Bishops; Editor and Dir Sister JUSTINE C. NABUSHAWO.

Camerapix Publishers International: POB 45048, GPO 00100, Nairobi; tel. (20) 4448923; fax (20) 4448818; e-mail rukhsana@camerapix.co.ke; internet www.camerapix.com; f. 1960; travel, topography, natural history; Man. Dir RUKHSANA HAQ.

East African Educational Publishers: cnr Mpaka Rd and Woodvale Grove, Westlands, POB 45314, 00100 Nairobi; tel. (20) 4444700; fax (20) 4448753; e-mail eaep@eastafricanpublishers.com; internet www.eastafricanpublishers.com; f. 1965 as Heinemann Kenya Ltd; present name adopted 1992; academic, educational, creative writing; some books in Kenyan languages; Chair. Dr HENRY CHAKAVA; Gen. Man. KIARIE KAMAU.

Evangel Publishing House: Lumumba Drive, off Kamiti Rd, Thika Rd, Private Bag 28963, 00200 Nairobi; tel. (20) 8560839; fax (20) 8562050; e-mail info@evangelpublishing.org; internet www.evangelpublishing.org; f. 1952; Christian literature; current backlist of about 300 titles; marriage and family, leadership, Theological Education by Extension (TEE); Gen. Man. BARINE A. KIRIMI.

Kenway Publications Ltd: POB 45314, Nairobi; tel. (20) 4444700; fax (20) 4451532; e-mail sales@eastafricanpublishers.com; internet www.eastafricanpublishers.com/kenway/defult.htm; f. 1981; general, regional interests; Chair. HENRY CHAKAVA.

Kenya Literature Bureau: Bellevue Area, Popo Rd, off Mombasa Rd, POB 30022, 00100 Nairobi; tel. (20) 600839; fax (20) 601474; e-mail customer@kenyaliteraturebureau.com; f. 1947 as East African Literature Bureau; name changed as above in 1980; educational and general books; CEO E. A. OBARA.

Jomo Kenyatta Foundation: Industrial Area, Enterprise Rd, POB 30533, 00100 Nairobi; tel. (20) 557222; fax (20) 531966; e-mail publish@jomokenyattaf.com; internet www.jkf.co.ke; f. 1966; primary, secondary, university textbooks; Man. Dir NANCY W. KARIMI.

Longman Kenya Ltd: Banda School, Magadi Rd, POB 24722, Nairobi; tel. (20) 8891220; fax (20) 8890004; e-mail bandaschool@swiftkenya.com; internet www.bandaschool.com; f. 1966.

Moran (EA) Publishers Ltd: Judda Complex, Forest Rd, POB 30797, 00100 Nairobi; tel. (20) 2013580; fax (20) 2013583; e-mail info@moranpublishers.co.ke; internet www.macmillankenya.com; f. 1970; as Macmillan Kenya Publishers Ltd; renamed as above in 2010; atlases, children's educational, guide books, literature; Man. Dir DAVID MUITA.

Newspread International: POB 46854, Nairobi; tel. (20) 331402; fax (20) 607252; f. 1971; reference, economic devt; Exec. Editor KUL BHUSHAN.

Oxford University Press (Eastern Africa): Waiyaki Way, ABC Place, POB 72532, Nairobi; tel. (20) 440555; fax (20) 443972; f. 1954; children's, educational and general; Regional Man. ABDULLAH ISMAILY.

Paulines Publications Africa: POB 49026, 00100 Nairobi; tel. (20) 447202; fax (20) 442097; e-mail publications@paulinesafrica.org; internet www.paulinesafrica.org; f. 1985; African bible, theology, children's, educational, religious, psychology, audio CDs, tapes, videos; Pres. Sister MARIA KIMANI; Dir Sister TERESA MARCAZZAN.

Transafrica Press: Kenwood House, Kimathi St, POB 48239, Nairobi; tel. (20) 331762; f. 1976; general, educational and children's; Man. Dir JOHN NOTTINGHAM.

GOVERNMENT PUBLISHING HOUSE

Government Printing Press: POB 30128, Nairobi; tel. (20) 317840.

PUBLISHERS' ORGANIZATION

Kenya Publishers' Association: POB 42767, 00100 Nairobi; tel. (20) 3752344; fax (20) 3754076; internet www.kenyapublishers.org; f. 1971; organizes Nairobi International Book Fair each Sept.; Chair. DAVID MUITA.

KENYA

Broadcasting and Communications

TELECOMMUNICATIONS

Airtel Kenya: Parkside Towers, Mombasa Rd, Nairobi; tel. (20) 6910000; e-mail info.africa@airtel.com; internet africa.airtel.com/kenya; f. 2004; mobile cellular telephone network provider; fmrly Celtel; name changed as above in 2010; Man. Dir RENE MEZA.

Essar Telecom Kenya Ltd: Brookside Grove, Muguga Green Lane, Westlands, POB 45742, 00100 Nairobi; tel. (20) 750100100; internet www.yu.co.ke; f. 2008; owner of yu brand; Country Man. ATUL CHATURVEDI.

Telkom Kenya Ltd: Teleposta Towers, Kenyatta Ave, POB 41951, Nairobi; tel. (20) 2221000; e-mail service@telkom.co.ke; internet www.telkom.co.ke; f. 1999; 51% owned by France Telecom; operates a national fixed telephone network; Man. Dir SAMMY KIRUI.

Safaricom Ltd: Safaricom House, Waiyaki Way, Westlands, POB 66827, 00800 Nairobi; tel. (20) 4273272; e-mail info@safaricom.co.ke; internet www.safaricom.co.ke; f. 1999; owned by Telkom Kenya Ltd and Vodafone Airtouch (UK); operates a national mobile cellular telephone network; Chair. NICHOLAS NG'ANG'A; CEO ROBERT WILLIAM COLLYMORE.

Regulatory Authority

Communications Commission of Kenya (CCK): Waiyaki Way, POB 14448, 00800 Westlands, Nairobi; tel. (20) 4242000; fax (20) 4451866; e-mail info@cck.go.ke; internet www.cck.go.ke; f. 1999; Chair. Eng. PHILIP OKUNDI; Dir-Gen. CHARLES J. K. NJOROGE.

BROADCASTING

Radio

Kenya Broadcasting Corpn (KBC): Broadcasting House, Harry Thuku Rd, POB 30456, Nairobi; tel. (20) 223757; fax (20) 220675; e-mail md@kbc.co.ke; internet www.kbc.co.ke; f. 1989; state corpn responsible for radio and television services; Chair. CHARLES MUSYOKI MUOKI; Man. Dir DAVID WAWERU.

   Radio: National service (Kiswahili); General service (English); Vernacular services (Borana, Burji, Hindustani, Kalenjin, Kikamba, Kikuyu, Kimasai, Kimeru, Kisii, Kuria, Luo, Luhya, Rendile, Somali, Suba, Teso and Turkana).

Capital FM: Lonrho House, 19th Floor, City Sq., POB 74933, Nairobi; tel. (20) 2210020; fax (20) 340621; e-mail info@capitalfm.co.ke; internet www.capitalfm.co.ke; f. 1999; commercial station broadcasting to Nairobi and environs; Man. Dir LYNDA HOLT.

Easy FM: Nation Centre, Kimathi St, POB 49010, Nairobi; tel. (20) 32088801; fax (20) 241892; e-mail info@nation.co.ke; internet www.nationmedia.com; f. 1999; commercial radio station broadcasting in English and Kiwahili; fmrly Nation FM; owned by Nation Media Group; Man. Dir IAN FERNANDES.

IQRA Broadcasting Network: Kilimani Rd, off Elgeyo Marakwet Rd, POB 21186, 00505 Nairobi; tel. (20) 3861542; fax (20) 4443978; e-mail iqrafm@swiftkenya.com; Islamic radio station broadcasting religious programmes in Nairobi; Man. Dir SHARIF HUSSEIN OMAR.

Kameme FM: Longonot Pl., Kijabe St, POB 49640, 00100 Nairobi; tel. (20) 2217963; fax (20) 2249781; e-mail info@kamemefm.com; internet www.kameme.co.ke; commercial radio station broadcasting in Kikuyu in Nairobi and its environs; Man. Dir ROSE KIMOTHO.

Kitambo Communications Ltd: Bishop's Tower, 4th Floor, Bishop's Rd, POB 56155, Nairobi; tel. (20) 4244000; commercial radio and television station broadcasting Christian programmes in Mombasa and Nairobi; Man. Dir Dr R. AYAH.

Radio Africa Ltd (KISS FM): 2nd Floor, Lion Pl., Waiyaki Way, POB 74497, 00200 Nairobi; tel. (20) 4244000; Man. Dir KIPRONO KITTONY.

Radio Citizen: Communication Centre, Maalim Juma Rd, off Dennis Pritt Rd, POB 7468, Nairobi; tel. (20) 2721415; fax (20) 2724220; e-mail citizen@royalmedia.co.ke; internet radiocitizen.co.ke; commercial radio station broadcasting in Nairobi and its environs; owned by Royal Media Services Ltd; Chair. SAMUEL KAMAU MACHARIA.

Sauti ya Rehema RTV Network: Gulab Lochab Bldg, Oginga Odinga St, POB 4139, Eldoret; tel. (20) 2045239; e-mail elirop2003@gmail.com; f. 1999; Christian, broadcasts in Eldoret and its environs; Man. Dir Rev. ELI ROP.

Television

Kenya Broadcasting Corpn (KBC): see Radio.

   Television: KBC–TV; services in Kiswahili and English; operates three channels—KBC1, KBC2 and Metro TV.

Citizen TV: Communication Centre, Maalim Juma Rd, off Dennis Pritt Rd, POB 7468, Nairobi; tel. (20) 2721415; fax (20) 2724220; e-mail citizen@royalmedia.co.ke; internet www.royalmediaservices.co.ke; f. 1999, relaunced 2006; commercial station broadcasting in Nairobi and its environs; Chair. SAMUEL KAMAU MACHARIA.

Family Media: Dik Dik Gardens, off Gatundu Rd, Kileleshwa, POB 2330, Nairobi; tel. (20) 4200000; fax (20) 4200100; e-mail info@familykenya.com; internet www.familykenya.com; f. 1999; Gen. Man. PAUL COOGAN.

Kenya Television Network (KTN–TV): Nyayo House, 22nd Floor, POB 56985, Nairobi; tel. (20) 3222111; fax (20) 215400; e-mail news@ktnkenya.com; internet www.ktnkenya.tv; f. 1990; commercial station operating in Nairobi and Mombasa; Man. Dir D. J. DAVIES.

NTV: POB 49010, Nairobi; e-mail ntv@nation.co.ke; internet www.nationmedia.com/ntv; f. 1999 as Nation TV; commercial station; owned by Nation Media Group; Man. Dir IAN FERNANDES.

Stellagraphics TV (STV): NSSF Bldg, 22nd Floor, POB 42271, Nairobi; tel. (20) 218043; fax (20) 222555; f. 1998; commercial station broadcasting in Nairobi; Gen. Man. KANJA WARURU.

Finance

(cap. = capital; res = reserves; dep. = deposits; m. = million; brs = branches; amounts in Kenya shillings)

BANKING

At the end of 2010 there were 43 licensed commercial banks and one mortgage finance company operating in Kenya, of which 31 were locally owned and 13 were foreign owned.

Central Bank

Central Bank of Kenya (Banki Kuu Ya Kenya): City Sq., Haile Selassie Ave, POB 60000, 00200 Nairobi; tel. (20) 22863000; fax (20) 2250783; e-mail info@centralbank.go.ke; internet www.centralbank.go.ke; f. 1966; bank of issue; cap. 5,000m., res 34,005m., dep. 125,637m. (June 2009); Gov. Prof. NJUGUNA NDUNG'U.

Commercial Banks

African Banking Corpn Ltd: ABC-Bank House, Mezzanine Floor, Koinange St, POB 46452, Nairobi; tel. (20) 2223922; fax (20) 2222437; e-mail headoffice@abcthebank.com; internet www.abcthebank.com; f. 1984 as Consolidated Finance Co; converted to commercial bank and adopted present name 1995; cap. 525.0m., res 5.5m., dep. 7,505.3m. (Dec. 2009); Chair. ASHRAF SAVANI; CEO SHAMAZ SAVANI; 7 brs.

Bank of Africa—Kenya: Re-Insurance Plaza, Taifa Rd, POB 69562, 00400 Nairobi; tel. (20) 3275000; fax (20) 2214166; e-mail bkofkenya@boakenya.com; internet www.boakenya.com; f. 2004; cap. 2,000.0m., res 364.3m., dep. 20,829.1m. (Dec. 2009); Chair. PAUL DERREUMAUX; Man. Dir KWAME AHADZI.

Barclays Bank of Kenya Ltd: 8th Barclays Plaza, Loita St, POB 30120, 00100 Nairobi; tel. (20) 2214270; fax (20) 2213915; e-mail barclays.kenya@barclays.com; internet www.barclays.com/africa/kenya; f. 1978; cap. 2,716m., res 4,612m., dep. 131,654m. (Dec. 2009); Chair. SAMUEL O. J. AMBUNDO; Man. Dir ADAN MOHAMMED; 87 brs.

CFC Stanbic Bank Ltd: CFC Centre, Chiromo Rd, Westlands, POB 3550, 00100 Nairobi; tel. (20) 3268000; fax (20) 3752905; e-mail customercare@stanbic.com; internet www.cfcstanbicbank.co.ke; formed by merger of CFC Bank Ltd and Stanbic Bank Kenya Ltd in June 2008; 100% owned by CFC Stanbic Holdings Ltd; cap. 2,441.3m., res 1,177.8m., dep. 82,799.7m. (Dec. 2009); Man. Dir GREG BRACKENRIDGE.

Chase Bank (Kenya) Ltd: Riverside Mews, Ring Rd Riverside and Riverside Westlane, POB 66015, 00800 Nairobi; tel. (20) 2774000; fax (20) 4454816; e-mail info@chasebank.co.ke; internet www.chasebankkenya.co.ke; cap. 1,000.0m., res 85.4m., dep. 10,863.7m. (Dec. 2009); Chair. OSMAN MURGIAN; Man. Dir and Pres. MOHAMED ZAFRULLAH KHAN.

Commercial Bank of Africa Ltd: Commercial Bank Bldg, Upper Hill, cnr Mara and Ragati Rds, POB 30437, Nairobi; tel. (20) 2884000; fax (20) 335827; e-mail cba@cba.co.ke; internet www.cba.co.ke; f. 1962; owned by Kenyan shareholders; cap. 4,515.4m., res 2,334.9m., dep. 57,492.7m. (Dec. 2009); Chair. MIRABEAU H. DA GAMA-ROSE; Pres. and Man. Dir ISAAC O. AWUONDO; 12 brs.

Consolidated Bank of Kenya Ltd: Consolidated Bank House, Koinange St, POB 51133, 00200 Nairobi; tel. (20) 340551; fax (20) 340213; e-mail headoffice@consolidated-bank.com; internet www.consolidated-bank.com; f. 1989; state-owned; cap. 1,119.5m., res 186.8m., dep. 5,678.3m. (Dec. 2009); Chair. EUNICE W. KAGANE; Man. Dir DAVID NDEGWA WACHIRA.

Dubai Bank Kenya Ltd: ICEA Bldg, Kenyatta Ave, POB 11129-00400, Nairobi; tel. (20) 311109; fax (20) 2245242; e-mail info@dubaibank.co.ke; internet www.dubaibank.co.ke; 20% owned by World of Marble and Granite, Dubai (United Arab Emirates), 22.4%

KENYA

owned by Abdul Hassan Ahmed, 16% owned by Hassan Bin Hassan Trading Co LLC, Dubai (United Arab Emirates), 17.6% owned by Ahmed Mohamed; cap. 411.4m., res 12.0m., dep. 986.2m. (Dec. 2009); Chair. Hassan Ahmed Zubeidi; Man. Dir Mayank Sharma.

Ecobank Kenya Ltd: Ecobank Towers, 5th Floor, Muindi Mbingu St, POB 49584, 00100 Nairobi; tel. (20) 22883000; fax (20) 22883304; e-mail eke-fedhamgr@ecobank.com; internet www.ecobank.com; f. 1972 as Akiba Bank Ltd, present name adopted 2008; cap. 2,519.3m., res 161.7m., dep. 11,308.5m. (Dec. 2009); Chair. N. P. G. Warren; Man. Dir Tony Okpanachi; 3 brs.

Equatorial Commercial Bank Ltd: Nyerere Rd, POB 52467, Nairobi; tel. (20) 2710455; fax (20) 2710700; e-mail Customerservice@ecb.co.ke; internet www.equatorialbank.co.ke; cap. 600m., res 41.1m., dep. 3,702.0m. (Dec. 2009); Chair. Dan Ameyo; Man. Dir Peter Harris.

Equity Bank: 14th Floor, NHIF Bldg, Ragati Rd, POB 75104, 00200 Nairobi; tel. (20) 2262000; fax (20) 2737276; e-mail info@equitybank.co.ke; internet www.equitybank.co.ke; f. 1984; Chair. Peter Munga; CEO James Mwangi.

Family Bank: Fourways Tower, Muindi Mbingu St, POB 74145, 00200 Nairobi; tel. (20) 318173; fax (20) 318174; e-mail info@familybank.co.ke; internet www.familybank.co.ke; f. 1984; Chair. Titus K. Muya; CEO Peter Kinyanjui.

Fidelity Commercial Bank Ltd: IPS Bldg, 7th Floor, Kimathi St, POB 34886, Nairobi; tel. (20) 2242348; fax (20) 2243389; e-mail customerservice@fidelitybankkenya.com; internet www.fidelitybank.co.ke; f. 1993 as Fidelity Finance; present name adopted 1996; cap. 323.5m., res 101.9m., dep. 3,820.1m. (Dec. 2008); Exec. Dir Sultan Khimji; Man. Dir Rana Sengupta.

Fina Bank Ltd: Fina House, Kimathi St, POB 20613, 00200 Nairobi; tel. (20) 2246943; fax (20) 2247164; e-mail banking@finabank.com; internet www.finabank.com; f. 1986 as The Finance Institute of Africa Ltd; converted to commercial bank as above in 1996; cap. 528.3m., res 239.8m., dep. 15,932.4m. (Dec. 2009); Chair. Dhanji Hansraj Chandaria; Man. Dir Tim Marshall.

Giro Commercial Bank Ltd: POB 46739, Giro House, Kimathi St, 00100 Nairobi; tel. (20) 22217776; fax (20) 22230600; e-mail info@girobankltd.com; f. 1992 as Giro Bank Ltd; name changed as above in 1999 after merging with Commerce Bank Ltd; 21.76% owned by Blandford Investments Ltd, Nairobi; cap. 309.5m., res 218.0m., dep. 4,959.3m. (Dec. 2007); Chair. Chandan Jethanand Gidoomal; Man. Dir T. K. Krishnan.

Gulf African Bank (GAB): Geminia Insurance Plaza, Kilimanjaro Ave, Upper Hill, POB 43683, Nairobi; tel. (20) 2740000; fax (20) 2729031; e-mail info@gulfafricanbank.com; internet www.gulfafricanbank.com; f. 2007; 20% owned by Bank Muscat International (BMI), 10% owned by the International Finance Corpn (IFC); cap. 250m., res 1,547m., dep. 6,425m. (Dec. 2009); Chair. Suleiman Said Shahbal; CEO Najmul Hassan.

Imperial Bank Ltd: Bunyala Rd, Upper Hill, POB 44905, 00100 Nairobi; tel. (20) 22719612; fax (20) 22719498; e-mail info@imperialbank.co.ke; internet www.imperialbank.co.ke; f. 1992 as Imperial Finance and Securities Company; converted to a bank and name changed as above in 1995; 100% owned by Kenyan shareholders; cap. 1,085.0m., res 205.2m., dep. 12,862.2m. (Dec. 2009); Chair. Alnashir Popat; Man. Dir Abdulmalek Janmohamed.

Kenya Commercial Bank Ltd: Kencom House, Moi Ave, POB 48400, 00100 Nairobi; tel. (20) 3270000; fax (20) 2216405; e-mail kcbhq@kcb.co.ke; internet www.kcb.co.ke; f. 1970; 23.1% state-owned; cap. 2,217.8m., res 18,368.3m., dep. 169,212.9m. (Dec. 2009); Chair. Peter W. Muthoka; CEO Martin Oduor-Otieno; 123 brs and sub-brs.

Middle East Bank Kenya Ltd: Mebank Tower, Milimani Rd, POB 47387, 00100 Nairobi; tel. (20) 2723120; fax (20) 343776; e-mail ho@mebkenya.com; internet www.mebkenya.com; f. 1981; 25% owned by Banque Belgolaise SA (Belgium), 75% owned by Kenyan shareholders; cap. 506.8m., res 31.0m., dep. 2,199.4m. (Dec. 2009); Chair. A. A. K. Esmail; Man. Dir Philip B. Ilako; 2 brs.

National Bank of Kenya Ltd (Banki ya Taifa La Kenya Ltd): National Bank Bldg, Harambee Ave, POB 72866, Nairobi; tel. (20) 2226471; fax (20) 311444; e-mail info@nationalbank.co.ke; internet www.nationalbank.co.ke; f. 1968; 42% owned by National Social Security Fund, 22.5% state-owned; cap. 6,675.0m., res 906.9m., dep. 34,347.0m. (Dec. 2008); Chair. M. E. G. Muhindi; Man. Dir Reuben M. Marambii; 23 brs.

Oriental Commercial Bank Ltd: POB 14357, Apollo Centre, Ring Rd, 00800 Nairobi; tel. (20) 3743289; fax (20) 3743270; e-mail info@orientalbank.co.ke; internet www.orientalbank.co.ke; f. 1991; name changed as above in 2003; cap. 1,643.8m., res 10.4m., dep. 822.9m. (Dec. 2007); Chair. Shanti Shah; Man. Dir and CEO R. B. Singh; 4 brs.

Paramount Universal Bank Ltd: Sound Plaza, 4th Floor, Woodvale Grove, Westlands, POB 14001, 00800 Nairobi; tel. (20) 44492668; fax (20) 4449265; e-mail info@paramountbank.co.ke; internet www.paramountbank.co.ke; f. 1993 as Combined Finance Ltd; name changed as above in 2000; 25% owned by Tormount Holdings Ltd, St Helier, 25% owned by Anwarali Merali, 25% owned by Tasneem Padamshi; Chair. Anwarali Merali; Man. Dir Ayaz Merali.

Standard Chartered Bank Kenya Ltd: Stanbank House, Moi Ave, POB 30003, Nairobi; tel. (20) 32093000; fax (20) 2214086; e-mail mds.office@ke.standardchartered.com; internet www.standardchartered.com/ke; f. 1987; 74.5% owned by Standard Chartered Holdings (Africa) BV (Netherlands); cap. 1,639.8m., res 4,191.7m., dep. 67,750.5m. (Dec. 2006); Chair. Harrington Awori; CEO Richard M. Etemesi; 29 brs.

Trans-National Bank Ltd: Transnational Plaza, 2nd Floor, Mama Ngina St, POB 34353, 00100 Nairobi; tel. (20) 2224235; fax (20) 339227; e-mail info@tnbl.co.ke; internet www.tnbl.co.ke; f. 1985; cap. 583.7m., res 19.5m., dep. 1,907.1m. (Dec. 2008); Chair. Michael Cherwon; CEO Dhirendra Rana; 9 brs.

Merchant Banks

Diamond Trust Bank Ltd: Nation Centre, 8th Floor, Kimathi St, POB 61711, 00200 Nairobi; tel. (20) 2849000; fax (20) 2245495; e-mail info@dtbkenya.co.ke; internet www.dtbafrica.com; f. 1945; cap. 652.1m., res 2,670.8m., dep. 45,853.3m. (Dec. 2008); Chair. Mahmood Manji; Man. Dir Nasim Mohamed Devji.

National Industrial Credit Bank Ltd (NIC): NIC House, Masaba Rd, POB 44599, 00100 Nairobi; tel. (20) 718200; fax (20) 718232; e-mail info@nic-bank.com; internet www.nic-bank.com; cap. 412m. (Dec. 2001); Chair. J. P. M. Ndegwa; Man. Dir James Macharia.

Co-operative Bank

Co-operative Bank of Kenya Ltd: Co-operative Bank House, Haile Selassie Ave, POB 48231, Nairobi; tel. (20) 3276100; fax (20) 2219831; e-mail md@co-opbank.co.ke; internet www.co-opbank.co.ke; f. 1968; cap. 2,856.5m., res 1,596.9m., dep. 56,198.0m., total assets 65,708.9m. (Dec. 2007); Chair. Stanley C. Muchiri; Man. Dir Gideon Muriuki; 29 brs.

Development Banks

Development Bank of Kenya Ltd: Finance House, 16th Floor, Loita St, POB 30483, 00100 Nairobi; tel. (20) 340426; fax (20) 2250399; e-mail dbk@devbank.com; internet www.devbank.com; f. 1963 as Development Finance Co of Kenya; current name adopted 1996; owned by Industrial and Commercial Devt Corpn (89.3%), the Commonwealth Development Corpn (10.7%); cap. 347.5m., res 884.7m., dep. 3,774.0m. (Dec. 2008); Chair. Prof. Haroun Ngeny Kipkemboi Mengech; CEO Victor J. O. Kidiwa.

East African Development Bank: Rahimtulla Tower, 2nd Floor, Upper Hill Rd, POB 47685, Nairobi; tel. (20) 340642; fax (20) 2731590; e-mail cok@eadb.org; internet www.eadb.org; Dirs J. Kinyua, F. Karuiru.

IDB Capital Ltd: National Bank Bldg, 18th Floor, Harambee Ave, POB 44036, Nairobi; tel. (20) 247142; fax (20) 334594; e-mail idbkenya@swiftkenya.com; internet www.idbkenya.com; f. 1973 as Industrial Development Bank Ltd; adopted present name in 2005; 49% state-owned; cap. 272m., res 83m., dep. 190m. (Dec. 2002); Chair. David Langat; Man. Dir James B. Ochami.

STOCK EXCHANGE

Nairobi Stock Exchange (NSE): Nation Centre, 1st Floor, Kimathi St, POB 43633, 00100 Nairobi; tel. (20) 2831000; fax (20) 2224200; e-mail info@nse.co.ke; internet www.nse.co.ke; f. 1954; Chair. Edward Njoroge; CEO Peter Mwangi.

INSURANCE

In 2009 there were 52 insurance companies operating in Kenya

Insurance Regulatory Authority: Zep-Re Place, off Mara Road, Upper Hill, POB 43505, 00100 Nairobi; tel. 20-4996000; fax (20) 2710126; internet www.ira.go.ke; f. 2006; Steve O. Mainda; CEO Sammy Mutua Makove.

Africa Merchant Assurance Co Ltd: Transnational Plaza, 2nd Floor, Mama Ngina St, POB 61599, 00200 Nairobi; tel. (20) 312121; fax (20) 340022; e-mail marketing@amaco.co.ke; internet www.amaco.co.ke; f. 2000; Gen. Man. Kennedy Abincha.

APA Insurance Ltd: Ring Rd Parklands, Westlands, POB 30065, 00100 Nairobi; tel. (20) 2862000; e-mail info@apainsurance.org; internet www.apainsurance.org; f. 2003; Chair. John P. N. Simba; Man. Dir Ashok K. M. Shah.

Apollo Life Assurance Ltd: Apollo Centre, 3rd Floor, Vale Close, off Ring Rd, Westlands, POB 30389, 00100 Nairobi; tel. (20) 223562; fax (20) 339260; e-mail insurance@apollo.co.ke; internet www.apollo

KENYA

.co.ke; f. 1977; life and general; Chair. BUDHICHAND M. SHAH; CEO PIYUSH SHAH.

Blue Shield Insurance Co Ltd: Blue Shield Towers, Upper Hill, Hospital Rd, off Mara Rd, POB 49610, 00100 Nairobi; tel. (20) 2712600; fax (20) 2712625; e-mail info@blueshield.co.ke; internet www.blueshield.co.ke; f. 1983; life and general; Chair. BETH MUIGAI; Man. Dir KULOVA WANJALA.

British-American Insurance Co: Mara and Ragati Rds Junction, Upper Hill, POB 30375, 00100 Nairobi; tel. (20) 2710927; e-mail insurance@british-american.co.ke; internet www.british-american.co.ke; f. 1965; Man. Dir STEPHEN WANDERA.

Cannon Assurance (Kenya) Ltd: Gateway Business Park, Mombasa Rd, Block D, POB 30216, Nairobi; tel. (20) 3966000; fax (20) 829075; e-mail info@cannonassurance.com; internet www.cannonassurance.com; f. 1964; life and general; Man. Dir MAINA MUKOMA.

CfC Life Assurance Co Ltd: CfC House, Mamlaka Rd, POB 30364, 00100 Nairobi; tel. (20) 2866000; fax (20) 2718365; e-mail cfclife@cfclife.co.ke; internet www.cfclife-kenya.com; f. 1964; life and general; Man. Dir ABEL MUNDA.

Chartis Kenya Insurance Co Ltd: Eden Sq. Complex, Chiromo Rd, POB 49460, 00100 Nairobi; tel. (20) 3676000; fax (20) 3676001; e-mail chartiskenya@chartisinsurance.com; internet www.chartisinsurance.com; Man. Dir JAPH OLENDE.

The Co-operative Insurance Co of Kenya Ltd: Mara Rd, Upper Hill, POB 59485, 00200 Nairobi; tel. (20) 2823000; fax (20) 2823333; e-mail cic@cic.co.ke; internet www.cic.co.ke; Chair. JAPHETH ANAVILA MAGOMERE; Man. Dir NELSON C. KURIA.

East Africa Reinsurance Co Ltd: EARe House, 98 Riverside Dr., POB 20196, 00200 Nairobi; tel. (20) 4443588; fax (20) 4455391; e-mail info@eastafricare.com; internet www.eastafricare.com; Chair. J. P. M. NDEGWA; Man. Dir HAROON MOTARA.

Fidelity Shield Insurance Ltd: 4th Floor, Rank Xerox House, Parklands Rd, Westlands, POB 47435, 00100 Nairobi; tel. (20) 4443063; fax (20) 4445699; e-mail info@fidelityshield.com; internet www.fidelityshield.com; Man. Dir SHEHNAZ SUMAR.

First Assurance Co Ltd: Gitanga Rd, Lavington, POB 30064, 00100, Nairobi; tel. (20) 3867374; fax (20) 3872204; f. 1979 as Prudential Assurance Co. of Kenya Ltd; present name adopted 1991; life and general; Chair. M. H. DA GAMA ROSE; Man. Dir STEPHEN GITHIGA.

General Accident Insurance Co Ltd: GA Insurance House, 4th Floor, Ralph Bunche Rd, POB 42166, 00100 Nairobi; tel. (20) 2711633; fax (20) 2714542; e-mail insure@gakenya.com; internet www.gakenya.com; general; Chair. SURESH B. R. SHAH; CEO VIJAY SRIVASTAVA.

Heritage Insurance Co Ltd: CFC House, Mamlaka Rd, POB 30390, 00100 Nairobi; tel. (20) 2783000; fax (20) 2727800; e-mail info@heriaii.com; internet www.heritageinsurance.co.ke; f. 1976; general; Chair. J. G. KIEREINI; Man. Dir JOHN H. D. MILNE.

Insurance Co of East Africa Ltd (ICEA): ICEA Bldg, Kenyatta Ave, POB 46143, Nairobi; tel. (20) 221652; fax (20) 338089; e-mail hof@icea.co.ke; internet www.icea.co.ke; life and general; Man. Dir J. K. NDUNGU.

Jubilee Insurance Co Ltd: Jubilee Insurance House, 5th Floor, Wabera St, POB 30376, 00100 Nairobi; tel. (20) 3281000; fax (20) 3281150; e-mail jic@jubileekenya.com; internet www.jubileeafrica.com; f. 1937; long term (life and pensions) and short term (general and medical) insurance; Chair. NIZAR JUMA; Gen. Man. PATRICK TUMBO NYAMEMBA.

Kenindia Assurance Co Ltd: Kenindia House, 11th Floor, Loita St, POB 40512, Nairobi; tel. (20) 316099; fax (20) 218380; e-mail kenindia@kenindia.com; internet www.kenindia.com; f. 1978; life and general; Chair. M. N. MEHTA; Man. Dir SADASIV MISHRA.

Kenya Reinsurance Corpn Ltd (KenyaRe): Reinsurance Plaza, Taifa Rd, POB 30271, Nairobi; tel. (20) 2240188; fax (20) 339161; e-mail kenyare@kenyare.co.ke; internet www.kenyare.co.ke; f. 1970; Chair. NELLIUS KARIUKI; Man. Dir JADIAH MWARANIA (acting).

Lion of Kenya Insurance Co Ltd: Williamson House, Jubilee Insurance Bldg, Kirem Arcade, 4 Ngong Ave, POB 30190, 00100 Nairobi; tel. (20) 710400; fax (20) 711177; e-mail insurance@lionofkenya.com; internet www.lionofkenya.com; f. 1978; general; Chair. C. W. OBURA; CEO JOHN K. KIMEU.

Madison Insurance Co Kenya Ltd: Upper Hill Rd, POB 47382, 00100 Nairobi; tel. (20) 2721970; e-mail madison@madison.co.ke; internet www.madison.co.ke; life and general; Chair. SAMUEL G. NGARUIYA; Man. Dir F. MUCHIRI; 14 brs.

Mercantile Insurance Co Ltd: Fedha Towers, 16th Floor, Muindi Mbingu St, Nairobi; tel. (20) 2219486; fax (20) 215528; e-mail mercantile@mercantile.co.ke; internet www.mercantile.co.ke; Chair. N. P. G. WARREN; Man. Dir SUPRIYO SEN.

Monarch Insurance Co Ltd: Prudential Assurance Bldg, 4th Floor, Wabera St, POB 44003, Nairobi; tel. (20) 310032; fax (20) 340691; e-mail info@themonarchsco.com; internet www.themonarchsco.com; f. 1975; life and general; Man. Dir CHARLES MAKONE.

Pan Africa Life Assurance Ltd: Pan Africa House, Kenyatta Ave, POB 44041, 00100 Nairobi; tel. (20) 247600; fax (20) 217675; e-mail insure@pan-africa.com; internet www.panafrica.co.ke; f. 1946; life and general; Chair. JOHN SIMBA; CEO TOM GITOGO.

Phoenix of East Africa Assurance Co Ltd: Ambank House, 17th and 18th Floors, University Way, POB 30129, 00100 Nairobi; tel. (20) 2251350; fax (20) 2211848; e-mail general@phoenix.co.ke; general; Gen. Man. KAUSHAL KUMAR.

PTA Reinsurance Co (ZEP-RE): Zep-Re Pl., Longonot Rd, Upper Hill, POB 42769, Nairobi; tel. (20) 212792; fax (20) 224102; e-mail mail@zep-re.com; internet www.zep-re.com; f. 1992; Chair. MICHAEL GONDWE; Man. Dir RAJNI VARIA.

REAL Insurance Co: Royal Ngao House, Hospital Rd, POB 40001, 00100 Nairobi; e-mail general@realinsurance.co.ke; tel. (20) 717888; fax (20) 712620; internet www.realinsurance.co.ke; f. 1979; general; Chair. S. K. KAMAU; CEO JOSEPH W. KIUNA.

Standard Assurance (Kenya) Ltd: POB 42996, Nairobi; tel. (20) 224721; fax (20) 224862; Man. Dir WILSON K. KAPKOTI.

UAP Provincial Insurance Co of East Africa Ltd: Bishop Garden Towers, Bishops Rd, POB 43013, 00100 Nairobi; tel. (20) 850000; fax (20) 719030; e-mail uapinsurance@uapkenya.com; f. 1980; general; Chair. FRANCIS OGUTU; CEO JAMES WAMBUGU.

Insurance Association

Association of Kenya Insurers (AKI): Victoria Towers, 3rd Floor, Kilimanjaro Ave, Upper Hill, POB 45338, 00100 Nairobi; tel. (20) 2731330; fax (20) 2731339; e-mail info@akinsure.com; internet www.akinsure.or.ke; Chair. STEPHEN WANDERA.

Trade and Industry

GOVERNMENT AGENCIES

Export Processing Zones Authority: Administration Bldg, Viwanda Rd, Athi River Export Processing Zone, off Nairobi-Namanga Highway, Athi River, POB 50563, Nairobi; tel. (45) 26421; fax (45) 26427; e-mail info@epzakenya.com; internet www.epzakenya.com; established by the Govt to promote investment in Export Processing Zones; Chief Exec. J. O. B. AKARA.

Export Promotion Council: Anniversary Towers, 1st and 16th Floors, University Way, POB 40247, Nairobi; tel. (20) 228534; fax (20) 218013; e-mail chiefexe@epc.or.ke; internet www.epckenya.org; f. 1992; Chair. Prof. PETER NJERU NDWIGA; CEO RUTH MWANIKI.

Kenya Investment Authority: Railways HQ, Block D, 3rd Floor, Workshops Rd, POB 55704, 00200 Nairobi; tel. (20) 2221401; fax (20) 2243862; e-mail info@investmentkenya.com; internet www.investmentkenya.com; f. 1986; promotes and facilitates local and foreign investment; Man. Dir SUSAN KIKWAI.

Kenya National Trading Corpn Ltd: Yarrow Rd, off Nanyuki Rd, POB 30587, Nairobi; tel. (20) 543121; fax (20) 532800; f. 1965; promotes national control of trade in both locally produced and imported items; exports coffee and sugar; CEO S. W. O. OGESSA.

DEVELOPMENT ORGANIZATIONS

Agricultural Development Corpn: Development House, 10th Floor, POB 47101, Nairobi; tel. (20) 250695; fax (20) 243571; e-mail info@adc.co.ke; internet www.adc.co.ke; f. 1965 to promote agricultural devt and reconstruction; Chair. L. W. WARUINGI; CEO WILLIAM K. KIRWA.

Agricultural Finance Corpn: POB 30367, Nairobi; tel. (20) 317199; fax (20) 219390; e-mail info@agrifinance.org; internet www.agrifinance.org; a statutory organization providing agricultural loans; Man. Dir OMUREMBE IYADI.

Horticultural Crops Development Authority: POB 42601, Nairobi; tel. (20) 8272601; fax (20) 827264; e-mail md@hcda.or.ke; internet www.hcda.or.ke; f. 1968; invests in production, dehydration, processing and freezing of fruit and vegetables; exports of fresh fruit and vegetables; Chair. JOSEPH G. KIBE; Man. Dir ALFRED SEREM.

Housing Finance Co of Kenya Ltd: Rehani House, cnr Kenyatta Ave and Koinange St, POB 30088, 00100 Nairobi; tel. (20) 317474; fax (20) 340299; e-mail housing@housing.co.ke; internet www.housing.co.ke; f. 1965; Chair. STEVE MAINDA; Man. Dir FRANK M. IRERI.

Industrial and Commercial Development Corpn: Uchumi House, 17th Floor, Aga Khan Walk, POB 45519, Nairobi; tel. (20) 229213; fax (20) 317456; e-mail info@icdc.co.ke; internet www.icdc.co

KENYA

.ke; f. 1954; govt-financed; assists industrial and commercial devt; Chair. MARTIN KARIUKI MURAGU; Exec. Dir PETER KIMURWA.

Kenya Industrial Estates Ltd: Nairobi Industrial Estate, Likoni Rd, POB 78029, Nairobi; tel. (20) 651348; fax (20) 651355; e-mail admin@kie.co.ke; internet www.kie.co.ke; f. 1967 to finance and develop small-scale industries; Chair. AHMED MOHAMMED; Man. Dir JULIUS OBARE MOKOGI.

Kenya Industrial Research and Development Institute: POB 30650, Nairobi; tel. (20) 603842; fax (20) 607023; e-mail info@kirdi.go.ke; internet www.kirdi.go.ke; f. 1942; reorg. 1979; restructured 1995; research and devt in industrial and allied technologies including engineering, agro-industrial, mining and environmental technologies; Chair. Prof. TUIKONG D. K. SEREM; Dir Dr CHARLES M. Z. MOTURI.

Kenya Tea Development Agency: Moi Ave, POB 30213, Nairobi; tel. and fax (20) 3227000; e-mail info@ktdateas.com; internet www.ktdateas.com; f. 1964 as Kenya Tea Development Authority to develop tea growing, manufacturing and marketing among African smallholders; operates 51 factories; privatized in 2000; Chair. STEPHEN M. IMANYARA; CEO LERIONKA TIAMPATI.

CHAMBER OF COMMERCE

Kenya National Chamber of Commerce and Industry: Ufanisi House, Haile Selassie Ave, POB 47024, Nairobi; tel. (20) 220867; fax (20) 334293; internet www.kncci.org; f. 1965; 69 brs; Nat. Chair. DAVID M. GITHERE; Chief Exec. TITUS G. RUHIU.

INDUSTRIAL AND TRADE ASSOCIATIONS

Central Province Marketing Board: POB 189, Nyeri.

Coffee Board of Kenya: Coffee Plaza, 10th Floor, Exchange Lane, off Haile Selassie Ave, POB 30566, Nairobi; tel. and fax (20) 315754; fax (20) 311079; e-mail info@coffeeboard.co.ke; internet www.coffeeboard.co.ke; f. 1947; Chair. JOHN KAGEMA MWANGI; Man. Dir LOISE W. NJERU.

East African Tea Trade Association (EATTA): Tea Trade Centre, Nyerere Ave, POB 85174, 80100 Mombasa; tel. (41) 2220093; fax (41) 2225823; e-mail info@eatta.co.ke; internet www.eatta.com; f. 1957; organizes Mombasa weekly tea auctions; Chair. FRANCIS KIRAGU; Man. Dir KIPKIRUI LANG'AT; 280 mems in 12 countries.

Fresh Produce Exporters' Association of Kenya (FPEAK): New Rehema House, 4th Floor, Rhapta Rd, Westlands, POB 40312, 00100 Nairobi; tel. (20) 4451488; fax (20) 445189; e-mail info@fpeak.org; internet www.fpeak.org; Chair. RICHARD COLLINS; CEO Dr STEPHEN MBITHI MWIKYA.

Kenya Association of Manufacturers (KAM): Mwanzi Rd, off Peponi Rd, Westlands, POB 30225, Nairobi; tel. (20) 3746005; fax (20) 3746028; e-mail kam@users.africaonline.co.ke; internet www.kam.co.ke; Chair. JASWINDER BEDI; Exec. Sec. LUCY MICHENI; 200 mems.

Kenya Dairy Board: NSSF Bldg, 10th and 11th Floors, Bishops Rd, POB 30406, Nairobi; tel. (20) 310559; fax (20) 244064; e-mail info@kdb.co.ke; internet www.kdb.co.ke; f. 1958; Chair. MARTHA MULWA; Man. Dir MACHIRA GICHOHI.

Kenya Fish Processors' and Exporters' Association: 5th Floor, New Rehema House, Raphta Rd, Westlands, POB 345, 00606 Nairobi; tel. and fax (20) 4440858; e-mail info@afipek.org; internet www.afipek.org; f. 2000; Chair. NADIR JESSA; CEO BETH WAGUDE.

Kenya Flower Council: Muthangari Gardens, off Gitanga Rd, POB 56325, 00200 Nairobi; tel. and fax (20) 3876597; e-mail info@kenyaflowercouncil.org; internet www.kenyaflowercouncil.org; regulates production of cut flowers; CEO JANE NGIGE.

Kenya Meat Commission: POB 30414, Nairobi; tel. (45) 6626041; fax (45) 6626520; e-mail info@kenyameat.co.ke; internet www.kenyameat.co.ke; state-owned; f. 1953; purchasing, processing and marketing of beef livestock; Man. Commr ALI HASSAN MOHAMMED.

Kenya Planters' Co-operative Union Ltd: Nairobi; e-mail gm@kpcu.co.ke; coffee processing and marketing; Chair. J. M. MACHARIA; Gen. Man. RUTH MWANIKI.

Kenya Sisal Board: Mutual Bldg, Kimathi St, POB 41179, Nairobi; tel. (20) 248919; fax (20) 240091; e-mail kensisal@sisalboardkenya.go.ke; internet www.sisalboardkenya.go.ke; f. 1946; Man. Dir CHARLES K. KAGWIMI (acting).

Kenya Sugar Board: Sukari Plaza, off Waiyaki Way, POB 51500, Nairobi; tel. (20) 2023316; fax (20) 593273; e-mail info@kenyasugar.co.ke; internet www.kenyasugar.co.ke; f. 2002 to succeed the Kenya Sugar Authority; Chair. OKOTH OBADO; CEO ROSEMARY MKOK.

Mild Coffee Trade Association of Eastern Africa (MCTA): Nairobi; Chair. F. J. MWANGI.

National Cereals and Produce Board (NCPB): POB 30586, Nairobi; tel. (20) 536028; fax (20) 542024; e-mail info@ncpb.co.ke; internet www.ncpb.co.ke; f. 1995; grain marketing and handling, provides drying, weighing, storage and fumigation services to farmers and traders, stores and manages strategic national food reserves, distributes famine relief; Chair. JIMNAH MBARU; Man. Dir ALFRED BUSOLO.

Pyrethrum Board of Kenya (PBK): POB 420, Nakuru; tel. (51) 2211567; fax (51) 2210466; e-mail pbk@pyrethrum.co.ke; internet www.kenya-pyrethrum.com; f. 1935; 14 mems; Chair. SOLOMON BOIT; Man. Dir ISAAC MULAGOLI.

Tea Board of Kenya: Naivasha Rd, off Ngong Rd, POB 20064, 00200 Nairobi; tel. (20) 3874446; fax (20) 3862120; e-mail info@teaboard.or.ke; internet www.teaboard.or.ke; f. 1950; regulates tea industry on all matters of policy, licenses tea processing, carries out research on tea through **Tea Research Foundation of Kenya**, monitors tea planting and trade through registration, promotes Kenyan tea internationally; Chair. TITUS G. KIPYAB; Man. Dir SICILY K. KARIUKI.

EMPLOYERS' ORGANIZATIONS

Federation of Kenya Employers (FKE): Waajiri House, Argwings Kodhek Rd, POB 48311, Nairobi; tel. (20) 2721929; fax (20) 2721990; e-mail fkehq@fke-kenya.org; internet fke-kenya.org; Chair. PATRICK OBATH; Exec. Dir JACQUELINE MUGO.

Association of Local Government Employers (ALGAE): POB 52, Muranga; Chair. SAMUEL NYANGESO.

Kenya Association of Hotelkeepers and Caterers: Heidelberg House, 2nd Floor, Mombasa Rd, POB 9977, 00100 Nairobi; tel. (20) 604419; fax (20) 602539; e-mail info@kahc.co.ke; internet www.kahc.co.ke; f. 1944; CEO MIKE MACHARIA.

Kenya Bankers' Association: POB 73100, Nairobi; tel. (20) 221792; e-mail kba@kenyaweb.com; Chair. MARTIN ODUOR-OTIENO.

Kenya Coffee Producers' Association (KCPA): Wakulima House, 4th Floor, Room 408, Haile Selassie Ave, Ronald Ngala, POB 8100, 00300 Nairobi; tel. (20) 311235; e-mail info@kcpa.or.ke; internet www.kcpa.or.ke; f. 2009; Chair. JAMES K. GITAO.

Kenya Tea Growers' Association: POB 320, Kericho; tel. (20) 21010; fax (20) 32172; Chair. M. K. A. SANG.

Kenya Vehicle Manufacturers' Association: POB 1436, Thika; tel. (20) 350309; fax (67) 31434; e-mail kvm@kvm.co.ke; internet www.kvm.co.ke; f. 1974; name changed as above in 1989; Chair. KENNETH KEBAARA.

Motor Trade and Allied Industries Employers' Association: POB 48311, Nairobi; tel. (20) 721929; fax (20) 721990; Exec. Sec. G. N. KONDITI.

Sisal Growers' and Employers' Association: POB 47523, Nairobi; tel. (20) 720170; fax (20) 721990; Chair. A. G. COMBOS.

UTILITIES

Electricity

Energy Regulatory Commission (ERC): Integrity Centre, 1st Floor, cnr Valley and Milimani Rds, POB 42681, 00100 Nairobi; tel. (20) 2717627; fax (20) 2717603; e-mail info@erc.go.ke; internet www.erc.go.ke; f. 1997 as Energy Regulatory Board; present name assumed in 2007; govt-owned; regulates the generation, distribution, supply and use of electric power; Chair. HINDPAL SINGH JABBAL; Dir-Gen. Eng. KABURU MWIRICHIA.

Kenya Electricity Generating Co Ltd (KenGen): Stima Plaza, Phase 3, Kolobot Rd, Parklands, POB 47936, Nairobi; tel. (20) 3666000; fax (20) 248848; e-mail comms@kengen.co.ke; internet www.kengen.co.ke; f. 1997 as Kenya Power Co; present name adopted 1998; generates 82% of Kenya's electricity requirements; partially privatized in 2006; Chair. TITUS KITILI MBATHI; Man. Dir and CEO EDWARD NJOROGE.

Kenya Power and Lighting Co (KPLC): Electricity House, Harambee Ave, POB 301779, Nairobi; tel. (20) 221251; fax (20) 337351; e-mail custcare@kplc.co.ke; internet www.kplc.co.ke; partially privatized in 2006; 4% owned by Transcentury Group; co-ordinates electricity transmission and distribution; Man. Dir JOSEPH K. NJOROGE.

TRADE UNIONS

Central Organization of Trade Unions (Kenya) (COTU): Solidarity Bldg, Digo Rd, POB 13000, Nairobi; tel. (20) 6761375; fax (20) 6762695; e-mail info@cotu-kenya.org; internet www.cotu-kenya.org; f. 1965 as the sole trade union fed.; Chair. RAJABU W. MWONDI; Sec.-Gen. FRANCIS ATWOLI.

Amalgamated Union of Kenya Metalworkers: Avon House, Mfangano St, POB 73651, Nairobi; tel. (20) 211060; e-mail aukmw@clubinternetk.com; Gen. Sec. MAERO TINDI.

Bakers', Confectionery Manufacturing and Allied Workers' Union (Kenya): Lengo House, 3rd Floor, Room 20, Tom Mboya St,

KENYA

opposite Gill House, POB 57751, 00200 Nairobi; tel. (20) 330275; fax (20) 222735; e-mail bakers@form-net.com.

Communication Workers' Union of Kenya: Hermes House, Tom Mboya St, POB 48155, Nairobi; tel. (20) 219345; e-mail cowuk@clubinternet.com.

Dockworkers' Union (DWU): Dockers House, Kenyatta Ave, POB 98207, Mombasa; tel. (41) 2491974; f. 1954; Gen. Sec. SIMON SANG.

Kenya Airline Pilots' Association: KALPA House, off Airport North Rd, POB 57505, 00200 Nairobi; tel. (20) 820354; fax (20) 820410; internet www.kalpa.co.ke.

Kenya Building, Construction, Timber, Furniture and Allied Industries Employees' Union: Munshiram Bldg, POB 49628, 00100 Nairobi; tel. (20) 223434; fax (20) 244779; e-mail kbctfaieu@yahoo.com; Gen. Sec. FRANCIS KARIMI MURAGE.

Kenya Chemical and Allied Workers' Union: Hermes House, Tom Mboya St, POB 73820, Nairobi; tel. (20) 249101; Gen. Sec. WERE DIBI OGUTO.

Kenya Electrical Trades Allied Workers' Union: Aqua Plaza, Murang'a Rd, POB 47060, Nairobi; tel. (20) 3752087; e-mail ketawuhq@todays.co.ke.

Kenya Engineering Workers' Union: Simla House, Tom Mboya St, POB 73987, Nairobi; tel. (20) 311168; Gen. Sec. JUSTUS MULEI.

Kenya Game Hunting and Safari Workers' Union: Comfood Bldg, Kilome Rd, POB 47509, Nairobi; tel. (20) 25049; Gen. Sec. J. M. NDOLO.

Kenya Jockey and Betting Workers' Union: Kirim and Sons Bldg, 3rd Floor, POB 55094, Nairobi; tel. (20) 332120.

Kenya Local Government Workers' Union: Dundee House, Country Rd, POB 55827, Nairobi; tel. (20) 217213; Gen. Sec. WASIKE NDOMBI.

Kenya Petroleum Oil Workers' Union (KPOWU): KCB Bldg, 4th Floor, Jogoo Rd, POB 10376, Nairobi; tel. (20) 55549; Gen. Sec. JACOB OCHINO.

Kenya Plantation and Agricultural Workers' Union: Co-operative House, Kenyatta St, POB 1161, 20100 Nakuru; tel. and fax (51) 2212310; e-mail kpawu@africaonline.co.ke; Gen. Sec. FRANCIS ATWOLI.

Kenya Quarry and Mine Workers' Union: Coffee Plaza, Exchange Line Off Hailesellasie Ave, POB 48125, Nairobi; tel. (20) 229774; f. 1961; Gen. Sec. WAFULA WA MUSAMIA.

Kenya Railway Workers' Union (KRWU): RAHU House, Mfangano St, POB 72029, Nairobi; tel. (20) 340302; f. 1952; Nat. Chair. FRANCIS O'LORE; Sec.-Gen. JOHN T. CHUMO.

Kenya Scientific Research, International Technical and Allied Institutions Workers' Union: Ngumba House, Tom Mboya St, POB 55094, Nairobi; tel. (20) 215713; Sec.-Gen. FRANCIS D. KIRUBI.

Kenya Shipping, Clearing and Warehouse Workers' Union: Yusuf Ali Bldg, 4th Floor, POB 84067, Mombasa; tel. (11) 312000.

Kenya Shoe and Leather Workers' Union: NACICO Plaza, 3rd Floor, POB 49629, Nairobi; tel. (20) 252788; Gen. Sec. JAMES AWICH.

Kenya Union of Commercial, Food and Allied Workers: Comfood Bldg, POB 2628, 00100 Nairobi; tel. (20) 245054; fax (20) 313118; e-mail info@kucfaw.org; Sec.-Gen. HANNINGTON OKOTH KOROMBO.

Kenya Union of Domestic, Hotel, Educational Institutions, Hospitals and Allied Workers (KUDHEIHA): Sonalux House, 4th Floor, POB 41763, 00100 Nairobi; tel. (20) 241509; fax (20) 243806; e-mail kudheihaworkers@hotmail.com; f. 1952; workers; Sec.-Gen. ALBERT NJERU.

Kenyan Union of Entertainment and Music Industry Employees: Coffee Plaza, 4th Floor, POB 8305, Nairobi; tel. (20) 243249.

Kenya Union of Journalists: POB 47035, 00100 Nairobi; tel. (20) 250888; fax (20) 250880; e-mail info@kujkenya.org; f. 1962; Gen. Sec. and CEO ERIC ORINA; Chair. TERVIL OKOKO.

Kenya Union of Printing, Publishing, Paper Manufacturers and Allied Workers: Meru South House, 5th Floor, Tom Mboya St, POB 72358, Nairobi; tel. (20) 215981; e-mail kupripupa04@yahoo.com; Gen. Sec. JOHN BOSCO.

Kenya Union of Sugar Plantation Workers: POB 19019, Kisumu; tel. (57) 2021595; e-mail kuspw@swiftkisumu.com; Gen. Sec. FRANCIS BUSHURU WANGARA.

National Seamen's Union of Kenya: Mombasa; tel. (11) 312106; Gen. Sec. I. S. ABDALLAH MWARUA.

Transport and Allied Workers' Union: NACICO Plaza, 3rd Floor, POB 45171, Nairobi; tel. (20) 545317; Gen. Sec. JULIAS MALII.

Independent Union

Kenya National Union of Teachers: POB 30407, 00100 Nairobi; tel. (20) 2220387; fax (20) 2222701; e-mail knut@nbnet.co.ke; internet www.knut.or.ke; f. 1957; Sec.-Gen. DAVID OKUTAH OSIANY.

Transport

RAILWAYS

In 2004 there were some 1,920 km of track open for traffic. In 2006 the Rift Valley Railways consortium assumed management of the Kenya Railways Corpn. In 2009 plans were announced to construct a railway line connecting Mombasa with Malaba, with a possible extension to Kampala, Uganda. The project was expected to start in late 2011 and be completed in 2016. In 2010 a new railway project was under way to connect Jomo Kenyatta International Airport (JKIA) with Embakasi and the Nairobi city centre to relieve congestion on the road system.

Kenya Railways Corpn: POB 30121, Nairobi; tel. (20) 221211; fax (20) 224156; internet www.krc.co.ke; f. 1977; management of operations assumed by Rift Valley Railways consortium in Nov. 2006; Chair. JONATHAN D. MTURI; Man. Dir NDUVA MULI.

ROADS

At the end of 2004 there were an estimated 63,265 km of classified roads, of which 6,527 km were main roads and 18,885 km were secondary roads. Only an estimated 14.1% of road surfaces were paved. An all-weather road links Nairobi to Addis Ababa, in Ethiopia, and there is a 590-km road link between Kitale (Kenya) and Juba (Sudan). The rehabilitation of the important internal road link between Nairobi and Mombasa (funded by a US $165m. loan from the World Bank) was undertaken during the late 1990s.

Akamba Public Road Services: Industrial Area, POB 40322, Nairobi; tel. (20) 556062; fax (20) 559885; e-mail info@akambabus.com; internet www.akambabus.com; operates bus services from Nairobi to all major towns in Kenya and to some major towns in Uganda and Tanzania.

East African Road Services Ltd: Nairobi; tel. (20) 764622; f. 1947; operates bus services from Nairobi to all major towns in Kenya; Chair. S. H. NATHOO.

Kenya Bus Service Management Ltd: Utali Lane, View Park Towers, 10th Floor, Rm 1010, POB 41001, 00100 Nairobi; tel. (20) 2223235; fax (20) 2223110; e-mail info@kenyabus.net; internet kenyabus.net; promotes and develops transport enterprises; Man. Dir EDWINS MUKABANAH.

Kenya Roads Board: Kenya Re Towers, 3rd Floor, Ragati Rd, Upper Hill, POB 73718, Nairobi; tel. (20) 722865; internet www.krb.go.ke; f. 2000 to co-ordinate maintenance, rehabilitation and devt of the road network; Chair. ALFRED JUMA.

Speedways Trans-Africa Freighters: POB 75755, Nairobi; tel. (20) 544267; private road haulier; CEO HASSAN KANYARE.

SHIPPING

The major international seaport of Mombasa has 16 deep-water berths, with a total length of 3,044 m, and facilities for the off-loading of bulk carriers, tankers and container vessels. Kenyan ports handled some 16.4m. metric tons of cargo in 2008.

Kenya Maritime Authority: White House, Moi Ave, Mombasa; tel. (41) 2318398; fax (41) 2318397; e-mail info@maritimeauthority.co.ke; internet www.maritimeauthority.co.ke; f. 2004; regulates, co-ordinates and oversees maritime affairs; Chair. Col. JOSEPH NGURU; Dir-Gen. NANCY W. KARIGITH.

Kenya Ports Authority: POB 95009, Mombasa; tel. (41) 2112999; fax (41) 311867; internet www.kpa.co.ke; f. 1978; sole operator of coastal port facilities; also operates two inland container depots at Nairobi and Kisumu; Chair. SHUKRI BARAMADI; Man. Dir JAMES MLEWA.

Inchcape Shipping Services Kenya Ltd: Inchcape House, Archbishop Makarios Cl., off Moi Ave, POB 90194, 80100 Mombasa; tel. (41) 2314245; fax (41) 2314662; e-mail mail@iss-shipping.com; internet www.iss-shipping.com; covers all ports in Kenya and Tanzania; Man. Dir DAVID MACKAY.

Mackenzie Maritime Ltd: Maritime Centre, Archbishop Makarios Close, POB 90120, Mombasa; tel. (11) 221273; fax (11) 316260; e-mail mml@africaonline.co.ke; shipping agents; Man. Dir M. M. BROWN.

Marship Ltd: Mombasa; tel. (11) 314705; fax (11) 316654; f. 1986; shipbrokers, ship management and chartering agents; Man. Dir MICHELE ESPOSITO.

Mitchell Cotts Kenya Ltd: Voi St, Shimanzi, POB 42485, 80100 Mombasa; tel. (20) 2315780; fax (20) 2226181; e-mail sales@mitchellcotts.co.ke; internet www.mitchellcottskenya.com; f. 1926;

transport and shipping agents; freight handling and distribution; warehousing; Man. Dir Daniel Tanui.

Motaku Shipping Agencies Ltd: Motaku House, Tangana Rd, POB 80419, 80100 Mombasa; tel. (41) 2229065; fax (41) 2220777; e-mail motaku@motakushipping.com; f. 1977; ship managers and shipping agents, freight broker and charter; Man. Dir Karim Kudrati.

PIL (Kenya) Ltd: Liberty Plaza, Mombasa Rd, POB 40109, Nairobi; tel. (20) 825082; fax (20) 821086; e-mail admin@nbo.pilship.com; internet www.pilship.com.

Shipmarc Ltd: POB 99553, Mombasa; tel. (41) 229241; fax (41) 221390; e-mail info@shipmarckenya.com.

Southern Line Ltd: POB 90102, 80107 Mombasa; tel. (11) 229241; fax (11) 221390; e-mail shipmarc@africaonline.co.ke; operating dry cargo and tanker vessels between East African ports, Red Sea ports, the Persian (Arabian) Gulf and Indian Ocean islands.

Spanfreight Shipping Ltd: Cannon Towers, Moi Ave, POB 99760, Mombasa; tel. (11) 315623; fax (11) 312092; e-mail a23ke464@gncomtext.com; Exec. Dir Dilipkumar Amritlal Shah.

Star East Africa Co: POB 86725, Mombasa; tel. (11) 314060; fax (11) 312818; shipping agents and brokers; Man. Dir Yeuda Fisher.

CIVIL AVIATION

Jomo Kenyatta International Airport (JKIA), in south-eastern Nairobi, and Moi International Airport, at Mombasa, both service international flights. Wilson Airport, in south-western Nairobi, Eldoret Airport (which opened in 1997) and airports at Malindi and Kisumu handle internal flights. Kenya has about 150 smaller airfields. The rehabilitation and expansion of JKIA and Moi International Airport was undertaken during the late 1990s. A new cargo handling facility, The Nairobi Cargo Centre, opened at JKIA in June 1999, increasing the airport's capacity for storing horticultural exports.

Kenya Airports Authority: Jomo Kenyatta International Airport, POB 19001, Nairobi; tel. (20) 825400; fax (20) 822078; e-mail info@kenyaairports.co.ke; internet www.kenyaairports.co.ke; f. 1991; state-owned; responsible for the provision, management and operation of all airports and private airstrips; Man. Dir George Muhoho.

Aero Kenya: Shelter Afrique House, Mamlaka Rd, Nairobi; tel. (20) 2719091; fax (20) 2719264; e-mail info@aerokenya.com; f. 1997; operates domestic charter and schedule services; Man. Dir Capt. Charles K. Muthama.

African Express Airways: Airport North Rd, Jomo Kenyatta International Airport, POB 19202, 00501 Nairobi; tel. (20) 2014746; fax (20) 2049888; e-mail afex@africanexpress.co.ke; internet www.africanexpress.co.ke.

Airkenya Express Ltd: Wilson Airport, POB 30357, 00100 Nairobi; tel. (20) 605745; fax (20) 602951; e-mail info@airkenya.com; internet www.airkenya.com; f. 1985; operates internal scheduled and charter passenger services; Gen. Man. Dino Bisleti.

Blue Bird Aviation Ltd: Wilson Airport, Langata Rd, POB 52382, Nairobi; tel. (20) 602338; fax (20) 602337.

Eagle Aviation (African Eagle): POB 93926, Mombasa; tel. (11) 434502; fax (11) 434249; e-mail eaglemsa@africaonline.co.ke; f. 1986; scheduled regional and domestic passenger and cargo services; Chair. Raja Tanuj; CEO Capt. Kiran Patel.

Five Forty Aviation Ltd (fly540.com): ABC Pl. Westlands, POB 10293, Nairobi; tel. (20) 4453252; fax (20) 4453257; e-mail info@fly540.com; internet www.fly540.com; f. 2006; low-cost airline operating domestic and regional flights; COO Neil Steffen.

Jetlink Express: Unit 3, Jomo Kenyatta International Airport, Nairobi; tel. (20) 827915; e-mail customercare@jetlink.co.ke; internet www.jetlink.co.ke; f. 2006; provides internal services and also operates flights to Juba (Sudan), Goma (DRC) and Kigali (Rwanda); Man. Dir and CEO Capt. Elly Aluvale.

Kenya Airways Ltd (KQ): Airport North Road, Jomo Kenyatta International Airport, POB 19142, Nairobi; tel. (20) 6422000; fax (20) 823488; e-mail contact@kenya-airways.com; internet www.kenya-airways.com; f. 1977; in private sector ownership since 1996; passenger services to Africa, Asia, Europe and Middle East; freight services to Europe; internal services from Nairobi to Kisumu, Mombasa and Malindi; also operates a freight subsidiary; Chair. Evanson Mwaniki; Man. Dir and CEO Titus Naikuni.

CIVIL AVIATION AUTHORITY

Kenya Civil Aviation Authority: Jomo Kenyatta International Airport, POB 30163, 00100 Nairobi; tel. (20) 827470; e-mail info@kcaa.or.ke; internet www.kcaa.or.ke; f. 2002; regulatory and advisory services for air navigation; Dir-Gen. C. A. Kuto.

Tourism

Kenya's main attractions for visitors are its wildlife, with 25 National Parks and 23 game reserves, the Indian Ocean coast and an equable year-round climate. In 2008 there were 1.2m. foreign visitors. Earnings from the sector totalled US $1,398m. in that year.

Kenya Tourism Board: Kenya-Re Towers, Ragati Rd, POB 30630, 00100 Nairobi; tel. (20) 271126; fax (20) 2719925; e-mail info@kenyatourism.org; internet www.magicalkenya.com; f. 1997; promotes Kenya as a tourist destination, monitors the standard of tourist facilities.

Kenya Tourist Development Corpn: Utalii House, 11th Floor, Uhuru Highway, POB 42013, Nairobi; tel. (20) 2229751; fax (20) 2227817; e-mail info@ktdc.co.ke; internet www.ktdc.co.ke; f. 1965; Chair. Charles Wachira Ngundo; Man. Dir Obondo Kajumbi.

Defence

As assessed at November 2010, Kenya's armed forces numbered 24,120, comprising an army of 20,000, an air force of 2,500 and a navy of 1,620. Military service is voluntary. The paramilitary police general service unit was 5,000 strong.

Defence Expenditure: Budgeted at Ks. 55,900m. for 2011.
Commander-in-Chief of the Armed Forces: Pres. Mwai Kibaki.
Chief of General Staff: Gen. Jeremiah M. Kianga.
Army Commander: Lt-Gen. Jackson K. Tuwei.
Air Force Commander: Maj.-Gen. Harold M. Tangai.
Navy Commander: Maj.-Gen. Samson J. Mwathethe.

Education

The Government provides, or assists in the provision of, schools. In 2007/08 enrolment at pre-primary level was 26% (26% of boys; 26% of girls). Primary education, which is compulsory, is provided free of charge. The education system involves eight years of primary education (beginning at six years of age), four years at secondary school and four years of university education. According to UNESCO estimates, in 2008/09 enrolment at primary schools included 83% of pupils in the relevant age-group (males 82%; females 83%), while enrolment at secondary schools included 50% of children in the relevant age-group (males 51%; females 48%). Tertiary enrolment in 2001/02 included just 3% of those in the relevant age-group (4% males; 2% females), according to UNESCO estimates. There are six state universities and seven private universities, with a total of 167,983 enrolled students in 2008/09. In 2004 spending on education represented 29.2% of total budgetary expenditure.

KIRIBATI

Introductory Survey

LOCATION, CLIMATE, LANGUAGE, RELIGION, FLAG, CAPITAL

The Republic of Kiribati (pronounced 'Kir-i-bas') comprises 32 atolls, in three principal groups, scattered within an area of about 5m. sq km (2m. sq miles) in the mid-Pacific Ocean, and the island of Banaba (formerly Ocean Island). The country extends about 3,870 km (2,400 miles) from east to west and about 2,050 km (1,275 miles) from north to south. Its nearest neighbours are Nauru, to the west, and Tuvalu and Tokelau, to the south. The climate varies between maritime equatorial in the central islands and tropical in the north and south, with daytime temperatures varying between 26°C (79°F) and 32°C (90°F). There is a season of north-westerly trade winds from March to October and a season of rains and gales from October to March. However, average annual rainfall varies greatly, from 3,000 mm (118 ins) in the northern islands to 1,500 mm (59 ins) in Tarawa and 700 mm (28 ins) in the Line Islands. Droughts often occur in the central and southern islands. The principal languages are I-Kiribati (Gilbertese) and English, and the islands' inhabitants are mostly Christians. The national flag (proportions 1 by 2) depicts a golden frigate bird in flight, on a red background, above a rising sun and six alternating wavy horizontal lines of blue and white, representing the sea. The capital is the island of Bairiki, in Tarawa Atoll.

CONTEMPORARY POLITICAL HISTORY

Historical Context

In 1892 the United Kingdom established a protectorate over the 16 atolls of the Gilbert Islands and the nine Ellice Islands (now Tuvalu). The two groups were administered together by the Western Pacific High Commission (WPHC), which was based in Fiji until its removal to the British Solomon Islands (now Solomon Islands) in 1953. The phosphate-rich Ocean Island (now Banaba), west of the Gilberts, was annexed by the United Kingdom in 1900. The Gilbert and Ellice Islands were annexed in 1915, effective from January 1916, when the protectorate became a colony. The local representative of the WPHC was the Resident Commissioner, based on Tarawa Atoll in the Gilbert group. Later in 1916 the new Gilbert and Ellice Islands Colony (GEIC) was extended to include Ocean Island and two of the Line Islands, far to the east. Christmas Island (now Kiritimati), another of the Line Islands, was added in 1919, and the eight Phoenix Islands (then uninhabited) in 1937. The Line and Phoenix Islands, south of Hawaii, were also claimed by the USA. A joint British-US administration for two of the Phoenix group, Canton (now Kanton) and Enderbury, was agreed in April 1939. During the Second World War the GEIC was invaded by Japanese forces, who occupied the Gilbert Islands in 1942–43. Tarawa Atoll was the scene of some of the fiercest fighting in the Pacific between Japan and the USA.

In 1963, to prepare the GEIC for self-government, the first of a series of legislative and executive bodies was established. In 1972 a Governor of the GEIC was appointed to assume almost all the functions previously exercised in the colony by the High Commissioner. The five uninhabited Central and Southern Line Islands, previously administered directly by the High Commissioner, became part of the GEIC at this time. In 1974 the Legislative Council was replaced by a House of Assembly, with 28 elected members and three official members. The House elected Naboua Ratieta as Chief Minister.

In October 1975 the Ellice Islands were allowed to secede from the GEIC to form a separate territory, Tuvalu (q.v.). The remainder of the GEIC was renamed the Gilbert Islands, and the House of Assembly's membership was reduced. The Gilbert Islands obtained internal self-government on 1 January 1977. Later in that year the number of elected members in the House of Assembly was increased to 36, and provision was subsequently made for a member appointed by the Rabi Council of Leaders. Following a general election in 1978, Ieremia Tabai, Leader of the Opposition in the previous House, was elected Chief Minister. On 12 July 1979 the Gilbert Islands became an independent republic within the Commonwealth, under the name of Kiribati. The House of Assembly was renamed the Maneaba ni Maungatabu, and Ieremia Tabai became the country's first President (Beretitenti). In September Kiribati signed a treaty of friendship with the USA, which relinquished its claim to the Line and Phoenix Islands, including Kanton and Enderbury. Kiribati did not become a member of the UN until September 1999, although it had previously joined some of the organization's agencies.

In 1975, meanwhile, the United Kingdom refused to recognize as legitimate a demand for independence by the people of Ocean Island (Banaba), who had been in litigation with the British Government since 1971 over revenues derived from exports of phosphate. Open-cast mining had adversely affected the island's environment to such an extent that most Banabans had been resettled on Rabi Island, 2,600 km (1,600 miles) away in Fiji. The Banabans rejected the British Government's argument that phosphate revenues should be distributed over the whole territory of the Gilbert Islands. In 1976 the High Court in London dismissed the Banabans' claim for unpaid royalties but upheld that for damages. An offer made by the British Government in 1977 of an *ex gratia* payment of $A10m., without admission of liability and on condition that no further judicial appeal would be made, was rejected. In 1981, however, the Banaban community on Rabi decided to accept the British Government's *ex gratia* offer of compensation, although it continued to seek self-government. The 1979 Constitution provided for the establishment of an independent commission of inquiry to review the political status of the Banabans three years after Kiribati had achieved independence; however, the inquiry was not commissioned until 1985. (In mid-2009 it was reported that rehabilitation work was being undertaken on Banaba. The work was expected to cost $A50m. and to take 20 years to complete, whereupon the Banaban community hoped to return to the island. In mid-2010 Banabans appealed to Australia, New Zealand, Japan and the United Kingdom for additional funding for the project.)

As part of the United Kingdom's programme to develop its own nuclear weapons, the first test of a British hydrogen bomb was conducted near Christmas Island in May 1957. Two further thermonuclear tests in the same vicinity followed later in the year. Serious concerns with regard to the monitoring of radioactivity levels in the area were subsequently raised. In addition to the potential effects on the health of both islanders and service personnel, millions of birds were reported to have died as a direct result of the high-altitude tests. The USA also operated a test programme, conducting 26 nuclear experiments in the vicinity of Christmas Island in 1962. The United Kingdom announced its withdrawal from the Christmas Island base in 1964. Despite various 'clean-up' operations, including one financed by the British Government in 2005–06, concerns arising from the environmental impact of the testing programmes remained, not only in the Pacific region but also in the Indian Ocean. Legal action against the British Government was instigated in 2007 (see Australian External Territories—Christmas Island).

Domestic Political Affairs

The first general election since independence took place in March–April 1982. The members of the new Maneaba all sat as independents. In accordance with the 1979 Constitution, the legislature nominated from among its members candidates for the country's first presidential election, to be held on the basis of direct popular vote. President Ieremia Tabai was confirmed in office at the election in May 1982. The Government resigned in December, after the Maneaba had twice rejected proposals to increase the salaries of civil servants. The legislature was dissolved, and a fresh general election took place in January 1983. The formation of the new Maneaba necessitated a further presidential election in February, at which Tabai was re-elected for a third term of office. He was returned to office in May 1987 (following a general election in March). The May 1991 legislative election was followed by a presidential election in July, at which the former Vice-President, Teatao Teannaki, narrowly defeated Roniti Teiwaki to replace Tabai, who had served the maximum number of presidential terms permitted by the Constitution.

In May 1994 the Government was defeated on a motion of confidence, following opposition allegations that cabinet ministers had misused travel allowances. The Maneaba was dissolved, and at a legislative election in July five ministers lost their seats. Of the newly elected members, 13 were supporters of the Maneaban Te Mauri (Protect the Maneaba), while only eight were known to support the previously dominant National Progressive Party grouping. At the presidential election in September Teburoro Tito, of the Maneaban Te Mauri, was elected, receiving 51.1% of the total votes cast by the electorate. The new President declared that reducing Kiribati's dependence on foreign aid would be a major objective for his Government. He also announced his intention to pursue civil and criminal action against members of the previous administration for alleged misuse of public funds while in office.

In 1995 a committee was created with the aim of assessing public opinion regarding possible amendments to the Constitution. In March 1998 more than 200 delegates attended a Constitutional Review Convention in Bairiki to consider the recommendations of a report presented to the Government in 1996, which included equalizing the status of men and women with regard to the citizenship rights of foreigners marrying I-Kiribati and changes to the structure of the Council of State.

A general election, held in September 1998 and contested by a record 191 candidates, failed to produce a conclusive result, necessitating a second round of voting one week later, at which the Government and opposition each lost seven seats. The new Maneaba convened in October, when it selected three presidential candidates. At a presidential election in November, Tito was re-elected with 52.3% of total votes cast, defeating Dr Harry Tong, who obtained 45.8% of votes, and Ambreroti Nikora (1.8%).

Controversy continued in 1999 regarding the renamed Millennium Island (previously known as Caroline Island). Following an adjustment to the International Date Line, the island had been renamed in 1997 in an attempt to promote it as a tourist destination for the year 2000. However, despite expenditure of more than $A1m., the Government failed to attract the predicted numbers to the island's millennium celebrations.

In late 1999 a New Zealand journalist working for Agence France-Presse was banned from entering Kiribati. The Government claimed that articles by the correspondent, published in a regional magazine and unfavourable to Kiribati, were biased and sensationalist. In December former President Ieremia Tabai and a former member of the Maneaba, Atiera Tetoa, were fined, having been convicted of importing telecommunications equipment without a permit. They had launched Newair FM, an independent commercial radio station, 12 months previously; it had been immediately suspended. Tabai subsequently established Kiribati's first private newspaper, the *Kiribati Newstar*, in an attempt to reduce the Government's control over the media in the islands.

In November 2000 the Vice-President and Minister for Home Affairs and Rural Development, Tewarika Tentoa, collapsed while addressing the Maneaba and died. The post of Vice-President was subsequently combined with the cabinet portfolio of finance and economic planning.

Campaigning for the general election during November 2002 was characterized by numerous allegations of improper conduct. Observers noted that officials from the Chinese embassy in Tarawa, accompanied by government candidates, had been donating gifts to the local community in the weeks preceding the election. (The Government had recently amended the Elections Act to allow gifts to be distributed to the public by candidates during their electoral campaigns, a practice that had been banned hitherto.) Moreover, under a newly amended Newspaper Registration Act, President Tito ordered police to seize opposition election pamphlets in November. Further allegations that the Government was attempting to stifle freedom of expression were made by former President Ieremia Tabai, whose private radio station was finally granted a licence to broadcast in December, following delays totalling almost four years in issuing the permit.

A total of 176 candidates contested the general election held on 29 November 2002. The Government suffered significant losses, with 14 of its supporters (including seven ministers) failing to retain their seats. The presidential election was postponed from its original date and finally took place on 25 February 2003. At the poll Tito received 14,160 votes, while opposition candidate Taberanang Timeon secured 13,613. Tito was sworn in for his third term as President on 28 February and many of his former opponents in the legislature were expected to cross the floor to support him. However, in late March Tito was narrowly defeated in a motion of no confidence and his Government was replaced by an interim administration, the Council of State (comprising the Speaker, the Chief Justice and the Public Service Commissioner). In accordance with the Constitution, another general election was held on 9 and 14 May, when supporters of Tito secured a majority of seats. A presidential election took place in early July at which the opposition candidate, Anote Tong, narrowly defeated his brother, Harry Tong. Anote Tong's electoral campaign, which had focused on his pledge to review the lease of the Chinese satellite-tracking station on South Tarawa (opened in 1997), had been characterized by a series of personal criticisms of his brother.

In November 2003 several hundred people staged a protest in Tarawa against the Government's decision to establish diplomatic relations with Taiwan, in place of the People's Republic of China, claiming that it had been made in return for Taiwanese funding of Anote Tong's election campaign. The President strongly denied this allegation, but did confirm that Taiwan had offered extensive development funds to Kiribati for adopting its position (see Regional Affairs).

Recent developments: the 2007 election and other events

A legislative election, contested by a total of 146 candidates, was held on 22 August 2007. Decisive majorities were achieved by candidates in only 18 constituencies, thus resulting in a second round of voting on 30 August. The ministers of the incumbent Government, with one exception, were re-elected to the Maneaba. The Boutokan Te Koaua (Pillars of Truth) grouping of Anote Tong secured 18 seats, defeating the Maneaban Te Mauri grouping, which won seven. Anote Tong defeated three other candidates to be re-elected to the post of President on 17 October, having received almost twice as many votes as his nearest rival, Nabuti Mwemwenikarawa. Prior to the presidential election, members of the opposition grouping protested against the omission of their candidates from the contest following their failure to gain sufficient parliamentary support. Anote Tong subsequently appointed a new Cabinet, retaining Teima Onorio in the position of Vice-President with additional responsibility for commerce, industry and co-operatives, and other erstwhile ministers, including Natan Teewe, who became Minister for Finance and Economic Development.

In May 2008 the Minister for Communications, Transport and Tourism Development, Patrick Tatireta, was forced to resign after a motion of no confidence was raised against him in the Maneaba. Controversy surrounded the Minister's dismissal of the chairman, along with members of the board of directors, of the country's shipping corporation, owing to their refusal to authorize payment for the completion of the purchase of a new ship. Deemed unseaworthy not only by the board of Kiribati Shipping Services Ltd (KSSL) but also by a maritime inspector, the vessel was to have been purchased from the WKK Shipping Line, a company owned by a close associate of Tatireta. President Tong announced that a commission of inquiry was to be established to investigate the affair. Tatireta was replaced in his ministerial role by Temate Eriateiti. However, in April 2009 the High Court of Kiribati ruled that KSSL was to honour the agreement to purchase the ship from the WKK Shipping Line, and ordered that a payment of US $390,000 be made.

A four-member parliamentary select committee, which was to investigate the operations of foreign investors in the country, was established in June 2009. Amid allegations of the involvement of government officials in corrupt practices, the committee stated its intention to focus on the activities of the Chinese business community, which in recent years had expanded considerably in Kiribati.

In August 2009 there was an outbreak of violence on the island of Maiana between the two ruling bodies, Te Bau Ni Maiana (the traditional elders' association) and the democratically elected council. The Mayor and the elected council refused to comply with an order from Te Bau Ni Maiana to vacate their seats in order to permit the holding of a fresh election. Following a High Court ruling in favour of the council, the Mayor's house was destroyed in an arson attack. The council subsequently acceded to Te Bau Ni Maiana's demands. The Minister for Environment, Lands and Agricultural Development, Tetabo Nakara, resigned in response to criticism of the Government's handling of the issue.

An inquiry by the Social Welfare Division of the Ministry for Internal and Social Affairs into domestic abuse published its report in December 2009. It found that nearly 70% of women in Kiribati had experienced abuse by their husbands, close relatives or others; of those, 19% were under 15 years of age. In response to the report, human rights organizations urged the Government to take action to address the problem.

Environmental Concerns and Other Issues
In addition to the legacies of phosphate-mining operations and of the testing of hydrogen bombs, by the end of the 20th century the impact of climate change on the islands had begun to assume major significance. In 1989 a UN report on the greenhouse effect (the heating of the earth's atmosphere, and a resultant rise in sea-level, as a consequence of pollution) listed Kiribati as one of the countries that would completely disappear beneath the sea in the 21st century, unless drastic action were taken. None of the land on the islands was more than 3m above sea-level, making the country extremely vulnerable to the potential effects of climate change. It was feared that a rise in sea-level would not only cause flooding but would also upset the balance between sea and fresh water (below the coral sands), rendering water supplies undrinkable. By the early 21st century increasingly high 'king tides' were causing regular flooding in Kiribati. A report released by the World Bank in 2000 listed the flooding and loss of low-lying areas, more intense cyclones and droughts, the failure of subsistence crops and coastal fisheries, the death of coral reefs and the spread of mosquito-borne diseases such as malaria and dengue fever as consequences of climate change on Pacific island nations. Meanwhile, a state of emergency was declared in Kiribati in early 1999, owing to one of the worst droughts ever recorded in the islands. In mid-1999 it was announced that two of the country's uninhabited coral reefs had been submerged as a result of rising sea-levels. Concern among the islanders intensified in early 2001 when many of the causeways linking villages on Tarawa atoll were flooded by high tides. Shortages of drinking water were also reported, and by 2009 were reported to be approaching critical levels. The UN Development Programme (UNDP, see p. 60) signed an agreement with the Government of Kiribati in September 2009 to assist in the implementation of environmental projects, for which UNDP was to provide financial support. In July 2010 technicians completed a project involving the drilling of boreholes on Tarawa atoll to measure the extent of the underground fresh water supply and assist in preventing contamination by salt water. The work was undertaken as part of the Kiribati Adaptation Program (KAP), financed by the World Bank, Australia and New Zealand. In September President Tong declared that his Government lacked the funds to combat coastal erosion caused by rising sea levels. With further international support, the planting of mangroves to alleviate the problem was subsequently undertaken, and in March 2011 it was reported that more than 37,000 mangroves had been planted. Beach mining (to extract materials for the production of concrete) was also identified as a cause of erosion, and in January 2011 the feasibility of dredging material from the lagoon sea-bed instead was being studied.

In late 1997 President Tito strongly criticized the Australian Government's refusal, at the Conference of the Parties to the Framework Convention on Climate Change (under the auspices of the UN Environment Programme, see p. 65) in Kyoto, Japan, to reduce its emission of gases known to contribute to the greenhouse effect. In April 2001 the USA's decision to reject the Kyoto Protocol to the UN's Framework Convention on Climate Change was widely criticized. Kiribati continued to urge the UN to work towards a co-ordinated response to the challenge of global warming. In December 2007 the new Australian Government of Kevin Rudd reversed the country's previous position, immediately signing the Kyoto Protocol. In early 2009, furthermore, the incoming US Administration of Barack Obama also confirmed its commitment to addressing the issue. President Anote Tong attended the UN Climate Change Conference in the Danish capital of Copenhagen in December. In his address to delegates he criticized the lack of agreement among nations on the issue. President Tong drew attention to the state of crisis approaching Kiribati and expressed profound disappointment when the conference failed to reach consensus on a legally binding agreement to reduce carbon emissions. In November 2010 Kiribati hosted a conference on climate change, at which the 19 countries and numerous organizations represented drew up a declaration to be submitted at the next UN conference on climate change, held in Cancún, Mexico, in December. The declaration urged the adoption of definite measures to prevent disastrous levels of global warming, and emphasized the need for funding to combat the effects of climate change in vulnerable developing countries.

In 2003 the UN Children's Fund (UNICEF) established a field office in Kiribati as part of a wider strategy to increase the UN's presence in the region. In July 2007 the efforts of a team of Cuban doctors were reported to have resulted in an 80% decrease in infant mortality rates. In September 2008, furthermore, President Anote Tong became the first leader of a Pacific nation to undertake a state visit to Cuba. President Tong had discussions with Cuban President Raúl Castro concerning co-operation between their respective countries in the area of medical training and assistance. Following the completion of the training in Cuba of more than 20 I-Kiribati medical students, the Cuban doctors were withdrawn from Kiribati. President Tong then proceeded to the US city of Boston where, in recognition of his leadership in establishing a large marine reserve, he received an international conservation award from the New England Aquarium. Tong also travelled to New York, to deliver an address to the UN General Assembly. In December the Kiribati Government signed a maritime security agreement with the USA, which permitted US patrol boats to operate in Kiribati waters. Kiribati's law enforcement officers were to be allowed on board in the event of the discovery of illegal activity. The Government welcomed the arrangement, stating that it would assist in the protection of the country's maritime resources.

Owing to Kiribati's high rate of annual population growth and, in particular, the situation of overpopulation on South Tarawa with associated social and economic problems, in 1988 it was announced that nearly 5,000 inhabitants were to be resettled on outlying atolls, mainly in the Line Islands. In November 2004 the Government announced a major new initiative, supported by UNDP and the Asian Development Bank, to establish up to four new urban areas in the outer islands as part of ongoing efforts to ease the overcrowding on South Tarawa. In September 2010, however, it was reported that efforts to resettle people on the island of Kiritimati were being hindered by the shortage of water on the island.

In 1976 a Japanese company established a satellite-tracking station on Kiritimati, the management of which was subsequently transferred to the Japan Aerospace Exploration Agency (JAXA). A Chinese satellite-tracking station was opened on South Tarawa in late 1997 but was dismantled in late 2003, following the suspension of diplomatic relations between Kiribati and the People's Republic of China. Sea Launch, an international consortium led by the US Boeing Commercial Space Company, also announced plans to undertake a rocket-launching project from a converted oil-rig near the islands. A prototype satellite was launched in March 1999, and commercial operations began later in the year. Kiribati, which, together with the South Pacific Regional Environment Programme (SPREP, see p. 457), had expressed concerns regarding the potential adverse environmental impact of the site, was not expected to benefit financially from the project, as the consortium had sought to carry out its activities in international waters near the outer limits of the islands' exclusive economic zone. The US authorities dismissed environmental concerns about the negative impact of the site (particularly the dumping of large quantities of waste fuel in the islands' waters), which were expressed by both the Government of Kiribati and SPREP in 1998. These fears were compounded in March 2000 after a rocket launched from the site crashed, and, furthermore, Sea Launch refused to disclose where it had landed.

In March 2006 President Anote Tong announced that a large marine reserve was to be established in Kiribati. Commercial fishing was to be banned in the Phoenix Islands Protected Area (PIPA), which would afford protection to more than 500 species of fish, along with other marine life such as coral and birds. The New England Aquarium, a leading US institute located in Boston, and an international conservation group were to assist in the creation of the reserve. In September 2009 the Governments of Kiribati and the USA agreed to establish a partnership to facilitate co-operation in the protection of their respective marine reserves, the latter having created a similar protected area. In August 2010 PIPA, which covered an area of 408,250 sq km, was designated by UNESCO as a World Heritage site.

Regional Affairs
Following its accession to independence in 1979, Kiribati maintained good relations with other island nations of the Pacific region, as well as with Australia and New Zealand, both of which continued to provide significant development assistance and support in various fields. Through the Pacific Patrol Boat Pro-

gram, for example, Australia supported Kiribati in the area of maritime surveillance. In January 2009 Australia signed a new partnership development agreement with Kiribati and Solomon Islands, which would assist in improving education, work-force skills and economic growth and management. In September a programme to provide training for I-Kiribati nursing students in Australia was also announced.

In June 2008 President Anote Tong embarked upon a state visit to New Zealand, where he attended World Environment Day celebrations. Tong met with Prime Minister Helen Clark, and the two leaders signed a declaration that envisaged increased political and economic links. Discussions focused on New Zealand's bilateral aid to Kiribati. New Zealand confirmed its support for the Marine Training Centre, where an expansion of facilities was planned. The Kiribati Sustainable Towns Programme was also discussed. Recently established in order to address the issue of rapid urbanization, particularly on South Tarawa, New Zealand intended to allocate $NZ15m. to this programme over a five-year period. In July 2009 the New Zealand Minister of Foreign Affairs, Murray McCully, undertook an official visit to several of the Pacific islands, his itinerary including Kiribati. During another visit, in August 2010, McCully undertook to double New Zealand's annual aid for Kiribati, emphasizing the need to improve water supplies and sanitation. In March 2011 it was confirmed that New Zealand's additional financial support was to be used in the fisheries sector and for the improvement of the islands' transport network (see Economic Affairs).

In November 2003 President Anote Tong announced the establishment of diplomatic relations with Taiwan. The Government's decision to transfer its recognition from the People's Republic of China to Taiwan caused considerable controversy, prompting a demonstration in Tarawa in protest against the decision. By late November it was reported that Chinese technicians were dismantling the satellite-tracking station, which had played an important role in China's recent first manned space flight. However the Chinese embassy remained open while China requested that Kiribati reconsider its decision. Despite its efforts, which many observers believed were motivated largely by the islands' strategic importance, in late November China suspended its diplomatic relations with Kiribati. In the same week the police in Kiribati announced that they were beginning an investigation into death threats received by President Tong, believed to have come from a Chinese source.

Following Kiribati's transfer of diplomatic allegiance, a Taiwanese embassy was opened in Tarawa in January 2004. In May 2005, as part of a diplomatic tour of Pacific nations, President Chen Shui-bian of Taiwan reportedly became the first foreign head of state to visit Kiribati in an official capacity. During a reciprocal visit by President Tong to Taiwan in May 2006, President Chen described Kiribati as a 'staunch ally' and drew attention to the bilateral projects instigated since the establishment of diplomatic relations. In March 2010 President Ma Ying-jeou of Taiwan visited Kiribati. The impact of global climate change was among the matters that he discussed with President Tong. With bilateral co-operation having included collaboration in the areas of fisheries and aquaculture, Ma also inspected a fish-breeding facility, established with Taiwanese assistance. Tong reciprocated the visit in June 2010.

Relations with Japan have been tested by various issues. In 1992 the legislature approved an opposition motion urging the Government to seek compensation from Japan for damage caused to the islands during the Second World War. The intention to seek compensation was reiterated by President Teburoro Tito in late 1994. As a result of discussions held at the Pacific Islands Forum (see p. 413) summit meeting in Kiribati in October 2000, Japan announced that it was willing to negotiate compensation claims. Furthermore, a six-day visit by President Tito to Japan in February 2001 resulted in a number of informal agreements aimed at enhancing relations between the two countries, particularly regarding the contentious issues of tuna fishing, whaling and nuclear fuel shipments. Tito also appeared to modify his position on nuclear energy following the visit to Japan, stating that emissions of harmful greenhouse gases could be reduced by replacing fossil with nuclear fuel. In June 2010 the Kiribati Government denied allegations published by a British newspaper that Kiribati had accepted financial assistance from Japan in return for voting, at that month's annual meeting of the International Whaling Commission (IWC), in favour of an end to the moratorium on commercial whaling that had been imposed by the IWC with effect from 1986.

In June 2010 President Tong affirmed his Government's intention to maintain cordial bilateral relations with Fiji, despite the latter's exclusion from the Pacific Islands Forum (from May 2009) because of its failure to restore democratic rule. In July 2010 Tong attended a conference of Pacific island leaders, entitled 'Engaging Fiji', convened by the Government of Fiji after the cancellation of a meeting of the Melanesian Spearhead Group which the Fijian interim Prime Minister, Frank Bainimarama, had been due to chair (see the chapter on Fiji). In January 2011 a delegation from Fiji visited Kiribati with the aim of developing the two countries' co-operation in economic and environmental matters.

CONSTITUTION AND GOVERNMENT

Under the Constitution of 1979, legislative power is vested in the unicameral Maneaba ni Maungatabu. It has 42 members elected by universal adult suffrage for four years (subject to dissolution), one nominated representative of the Banaban community and, if he is not an elected member, the Attorney-General as an ex-officio member. The Head of State is the Beretitenti (President), who is also Head of Government. The President is elected by direct popular vote. The President governs with the assistance of the Vice-President and Cabinet, whom he appoints from among members of the Maneaba. Executive authority is vested in the Cabinet, which is responsible to the Maneaba.

REGIONAL AND INTERNATIONAL CO-OPERATION

Kiribati is a member of the Pacific Community (see p. 410), the Pacific Islands Forum (see p. 413) and the Asian Development Bank (ADB, see p. 202). The country is an associate member of the UN's Economic and Social Commission for Asia and the Pacific (ESCAP, see p. 37) and is a signatory to the South Pacific Regional Trade and Economic Co-operation Agreement (SPARTECA, see p. 414).

Kiribati became a member of the UN in 1999. It is a signatory to the Lomé Conventions and successor Cotonou Agreement (see p. 327) with the European Union.

ECONOMIC AFFAIRS

In 2009, according to estimates by the World Bank, Kiribati's gross national income (GNI), measured at average 2007–09 prices, was US $185m., equivalent to $1,890 per head (or $3,350 on an international purchasing-power parity basis). During 2000–09, it was estimated, the population increased at an average annual rate of 1.7% per year, while gross domestic product (GDP) per head rose, in real terms, by an estimated average of 0.4% per year. Overall GDP increased, in real terms, at an average annual rate of 2.2% in 2000–09. According to the Asian Development Bank (ADB), GDP contracted by 0.7% in 2009.

Agriculture and fishing contributed an estimated 27.4% of GDP in 2009. In 2005, according to official estimates, agriculture engaged 7.4% of the economically active population (excluding subsistence workers). According to FAO projections, 22.5% of the population was expected to be engaged in agriculture in 2011. The principal cash crop is coconut, yielding copra as well as coconut oil. In 2007 exports of crude coconut oil accounted for 45.7% of the country's total receipts from exports and re-exports. Export revenue from copra and copra cake reached almost $A1.7m. in 2007, accounting for 14.4% of the total. Bananas, taro, screw-pine (*Pandanus*), breadfruit and papaya are cultivated as food crops. The cultivation of seaweed began in the mid-1980s. In 2007 seaweed provided 1.9% of total export earnings. Pigs and chickens are kept. The sale of fishing licences to foreign fleets (notably from South Korea, Japan, the People's Republic of China, Taiwan and the USA) has provided an important source of income. In September 2006 a new six-year agreement with the European Union (EU) entered into force: 16 Spanish vessels were permitted to fish for tuna in Kiribati waters, while the EU's annual financial contribution was to remain at US $0.6m. Revenue from the sale of fishing licences reached a record $A52m. in 2001 but declined in subsequent years. However, receipts from fishing licences rose from $A25.4m. in 2007 to $A32.2m. in 2008, accounting for 20% of total government revenue in the latter year. According to ADB data, the GDP of the agricultural sector increased at an average annual rate of 1.9% in 2000–09. Agricultural GDP increased by 1.8% in 2008 and by 1.4% in 2009.

Industry (including manufacturing, construction and utilities) contributed an estimated 9.1% of GDP in 2009. The sector engaged 8.7% of the economically active population in 2005. Industrial GDP contracted by an average of 2.9% per year in

KIRIBATI

2000–09. Compared with the previous year, industrial GDP was estimated by the ADB to have contracted by 7.1% in 2008 and by 1.6% in 2009.

Mining of phosphate rock on the island of Banaba, which ceased in 1979, formerly provided some 80% of export earnings. Interest from a phosphate reserve fund, the Revenue Equalization Reserve Fund (RERF, which was established in 1956) became an important source of income (see below). The production of solar-evaporated salt for export to other islands of the Pacific (for use on fishing vessels with brine refrigeration systems) began on Kiritimati in 1985.

Manufacturing, which contributed an estimated 5.9% of GDP in 2009, is confined to the small-scale production of coconut-based products, soap, foods, handicrafts, furniture, leather goods and garments. Manufacturing GDP increased by an annual average of 3.5% in 2000–09, according to ADB figures. Compared with the previous year, the GDP of the manufacturing sector increased by 0.9% in 2008 and by 4.6% in 2009.

The construction sector contributed 1.5% of GDP in 2009. The sector engaged 3.9% of the economically active population in 2005. Construction GDP decreased by an annual average of 8.0% in 2000–09, according to figures from the ADB. Compared with the previous year, the GDP of the construction sector decreased by 27.5% in 2008, but increased by 9.0% in 2009.

Production of electrical energy increased from 15.1m. kWh in 2001 to 22.2m. kWh in 2009. Mineral fuels accounted for an estimated 24.9% of total import costs in 2007. The use of solar energy is of increasing significance.

The services sector provided 63.4% of GDP in 2009. Services engaged 83.9% of the economically active population in 2005. Although impeded by factors such as the high costs of transport to Kiribati, the tourism sector makes a significant contribution to the economy. Receipts from tourism totalled $3.0m. in 2001. Details of a five-year plan to revitalize the country's tourism sector, which aimed to increase the number of visitors to 10,000 annually by 2015, were announced in December 2009, and a new promotional campaign was launched in April 2010. In comparison with the previous year, international visitor arrivals were reported to have increased by 19.2% in 2010 to total 4,701. The GDP of the services sector increased at an average annual rate of 2.6% in 2000–09. According to the ADB, the services sector's GDP expanded by 2.6% in 2008 but contracted by 2.2% in 2009.

In 2009, according to the ADB, Kiribati recorded a trade deficit of US $56m., and there was a deficit of $4m. on the current account of the balance of payments. The ADB estimated that the deficit on the current account was equivalent to 13.7% of GDP in 2010. Kiribati depends on imports for almost all essential commodities, and import duties are a major source of government revenue. In 2009 the principal sources of imports were Fiji (39.7%), Australia (25.7%) and Japan (10.5%). The principal recipients of exports in 2009 were Ecuador (29.1%), Thailand (27.0%) and Japan (20.8%). The major imports in 2007 were food and live animals, mineral fuels, manufactures, beverages and tobacco, and chemicals. The major exports in 2007 included coconut oil, copra and copra cake, and seaweed.

Current budgetary expenditure for 2007/08 reached almost $A82.7m., while revenue totalled $A61.8m. Budgetary deficits continued to be financed by drawdowns from the RERF. However, it was feared that the Government's repeated recourse to such drawdowns, estimated at $A25m. in 2008, would be unsustainable in the longer term (see below). The country is reliant on foreign assistance for its development budget. Australia is a major provider of development assistance, with emphasis on the management of human resources, training, governance, health, education and improved customs procedures, within the framework of a new co-operation strategy. In 2010/11 aid from Australia was projected at $A23.9m. Aid from New Zealand was expected to total $NZ8.0m. in 2010/11. Through the ADB, Taiwan has provided aid to finance various development projects, as has Japan. Kiribati's total external debt was estimated by the ADB to total US $10m. in 2009. The cost of debt-servicing was estimated to be the equivalent of 2.1% of the value of goods and services in 2008. The annual rate of inflation averaged 3.4% in 2000–09. Consumer prices rose by 8.4% in 2009 and by an estimated 5.4% in 2010. About 6.1% of the labour force were unemployed in 2005. Opportunities for formal employment are limited, the majority of jobs available being in the public sector.

With its isolated location and extremely limited export base, Kiribati is one of the world's least developed nations. In November 2008 Kiribati and Australia signed a memorandum of understanding whereby the latter would grant temporary employment permits for islanders to work in the Australian horticultural industry. However, the subsequent decline in the global economy resulted in the availability of fewer employment opportunities than anticipated. None the less, remittances from Kiribati's emigrant workers, the majority of whom are seafarers employed on foreign ships, remained a vital source of income for many families, reaching an estimated US $8m. in 2008. About 20% of I-Kiribati seafarers reportedly lost their jobs in 2009. Meanwhile, the IMF predicted that the RERF would be depleted by 2030, in view of the substantial drawdowns of recent years. Having exceeded $A637m. in mid-2007, the value of the RERF was reported to have declined by 10% in 2009 to stand at $A571m. A drawdown of $A15m. was effected in 2010. The Government also holds substantial offshore assets through the Kiribati Provident Fund. The 2008–11 National Sustainable Development Strategy focused on the strategic areas of economic growth, the reduction of poverty, health and education, the environment, improved governance and the upgrading of the country's infrastructure. Aid from New Zealand was to be substantially increased in 2011/12. With an allocation of US $23m., the programme was to provide financial assistance for various development projects. Having been identified as an area of major potential, the fisheries sector was to receive support for training programmes and the upgrading of facilities. (In February 2010 Kiribati joined seven other Pacific nations in a new campaign to secure a greater portion of proceeds from the region's tuna-fishing industry.) Other schemes included the upgrading of basic services on Tarawa and the improvement of port and airport facilities on Kiritimati. GDP growth was estimated by the ADB at just 0.5% in 2010, mainly owing to a decrease in receipts from exports of copra, as well as the decline in opportunities for I-Kiribati seafarers. An increase in GDP of 2.0% was forecast by the ADB for 2011. In May of that year it was announced that the World Bank was to provide US $2m. in emergency food aid to residents of the outer islands.

PUBLIC HOLIDAYS

2012 (provisional): 2 January (for New Year), 6–9 April (Easter), 18 April (National Health Day), 11 July (National Church Day), 12–16 July (National Day Celebrations), 7 August (for Youth Day), 11 December (Human Rights and Peace Day), 25–26 December (Christmas).

Statistical Survey

Source (unless otherwise stated): Statistics Office, Ministry of Finance and Economic Development, POB 67, Bairiki, Tarawa; tel. 21082; fax 21307; e-mail statistics@mfep.gov.ki; internet www.spc.int/prism/country/KI/Stats.

AREA AND POPULATION

Area: 810.5 sq km (312.9 sq miles). *Principal Atolls* (sq km): Banaba (island) 6.3, Tarawa 31.0 (North 15.3, South 15.8), Abemama 27.4, Tabiteuea 37.6 (North 25.8, South 11.9), Total Gilbert group (incl. others) 285.5; Kanton (Phoenix Is) 9.2, Tabuaeran (Fanning—Line Is) 33.8, Kiritimati (Christmas—Line Is) 388.4, Total Line and Phoenix group 525.0 (Line Is 496.0, Phoenix Is 29.0).

Population: 84,494 at census of 7 November 2000; 92,533 (males 45,612, females 46,921) at census of 7 November 2005. *Principal Atolls* (2005): Banaba (island) 301; Abaiang 5,502; Tarawa 45,989 (North 5,678, South 40,311); Tabiteuea 4,898 (North 3,600, South 1,298); Total Gilbert group (incl. others) 83,683; Kanton (Phoenix Is) 41; Kiritimati 5,115; Total Line and Phoenix Group (incl. others) 8,850. *Mid-2011* (Secretariat of the Pacific Community estimate): 102,697 (Source: Pacific Regional Information System).

Density (mid-2010): 124.4 per sq km.

Population by Age and Sex (Secretariat of the Pacific Community estimates at mid-2011): *0–14:* 35,828 (males 18,439, females 17,389); *15–64:* 63,285 (males 31,120, females 32,165); *65 and over:* 3,584

KIRIBATI

(males 1,417, females 2,167); *Total* 102,697 (males 50,976, females 51,721) (Source: Pacific Regional Information System).

Ethnic Groups (census of 2000): Micronesians 83,452; Polynesians 641; Europeans 154; Others 247; Total 84,494.

Principal Villages: (population at 2005 census): Betio 12,509; Bikenibeu 6,170; Teaoraereke 3,939; Bairiki (capital) 2,766; Eita 2,399; Bonriki 2,119; Temwaiku 2,011. Note: All of the listed villages are in South Tarawa atoll.

Births, Marriages and Deaths (Secretariat of the Pacific Community estimates, 2010, unless otherwise indicated): Registered live births 2,774 (birth rate 27.8 per 1,000); Marriages (registrations, 1988) 352 (marriage rate 5.2 per 1,000); Registered deaths 827 (death rate 8.3 per 1,000) (Source: mainly Pacific Regional Information System).

Life Expectancy (years at birth, WHO estimates): 67 (males 65; females 70) in 2008. Source: WHO, *World Health Statistics*.

Economically Active Population (paid employees aged 15 years and over, 2005 census): Agriculture, hunting, forestry and fishing 936; Manufacturing 305; Electricity, gas and water 293; Construction 511; Trade, restaurants and hotels 1,873; Transport, storage and communications 1,473; Financing, insurance, real estate and business services 356; Public administration 6,953; *Sub-total* 12,700; Activities not adequately defined 433; *Total employed* 13,133 (males 8,095, females 5,038); Unemployed 2,254 (males 1,130, females 1,124); *Total cash labour force* 15,387 (males 9,225, females 6,162). Note: Subsistence workers (not included) numbered 21,582 (males 10,788, females 10,794). *Mid-2011:* Agriculture, etc. 11,000; Total labour force 49,000 (Source: FAO).

HEALTH AND WELFARE

Key Indicators

Total Fertility Rate (children per woman, 2008): 3.1.

Under-5 Mortality Rate (per 1,000 live births, 2008): 48.

Physicians (per 1,000 head, 2004): 0.2.

Hospital Beds (per 1,000 head, 2005): 1.5.

Health Expenditure (2007): US $ per head (PPP): 358.

Health Expenditure (2007): % of GDP: 19.1.

Health Expenditure (2007): public (% of total): 84.0.

Access to Water (% of persons, 2006): 65.

Access to Sanitation (% of persons, 2006): 33.

Total Carbon Dioxide Emissions ('000 metric tons, 2007): 33.0.

Total Carbon Dioxide Emissions Per Head (metric tons, 2007): 0.3.

For sources and definitions, see explanatory note on p. vi.

AGRICULTURE, ETC.

Principal Crops ('000 metric tons, 2008, FAO estimates): Taro (Cocoyam) 2.2; Other roots and tubers 8.2; Coconuts 131.3; Vegetables 6.2; Bananas 5.8. Note: No data were available for 2009.

Livestock ('000 head, year ending September 2008, FAO estimates): Pigs 12.6; Chickens 480. Note: No data were available for 2009.

Livestock Products (metric tons, 2009, unless otherwise indicated, FAO estimates): Pig meat 888; Poultry meat 539; Hen eggs 287 (2008).

Fishing (metric tons, live weight, 2008): Capture 34,300* (Emperors 2,550*; Mullets 700*; Snappers and jobfishes 2,500*; Jacks and crevalles 1,170*; Skipjack tuna 12,175; Yellowfin tuna 5,906; Other marine fishes 4,829*; Marine molluscs 3,300*); Aquaculture 5; Total catch 34,305*. Figures exclude aquatic plants (metric tons, FAO estimate): 2,000 (all aquaculture).
* FAO estimate.

Source: FAO.

INDUSTRY

Copra Production (processed, metric tons): 9,686 in 2006; 8,808 in 2007; 9,135 in 2008.

Electric Energy (million kWh): 23.61 in 2007; 22.45 in 2008; 22.19 in 2009.

Sources: Asian Development Bank; UN Industrial Commodity Statistics Database.

FINANCE

Currency and Exchange Rates: Australian currency: 100 cents = 1 Australian dollar ($A). *Sterling, US Dollar and Euro Equivalents* (31 December 2010): £1 sterling = $A1.540; US $1 = $A0.984; €1 = $A1.315; $A100 = £64,92 = US $101.63 = €76.06. *Average Exchange Rate* (Australian dollars per US $): 1.1922 in 2008; 1.2822 in 2009; 1.0902 in 2010.

Budget (central government operations, $A '000, year ending 30 June 2008): *Revenue*: Current 61,831 (Direct taxes 29,835, Entrepreneurial income 121, Property income 25,822, Fees, etc. 5,981, Other 72); Capital receipts 9; Total 61,840. *Current Expenditure*: General public services 10,571; Public order and safety 7,988; Education 20,533; Health 13,106; Welfare and environment 2,686; Community and culture 2,729; Agriculture, etc. 1,890; Construction affairs 2,749; Communications 3,177; Commerce 1,100; Labour affairs 3,071; Other 13,079; Total 82,679.

Cost of Living (Consumer Price Index; base: 2000 = 100): All items 108.3 in 2006; 112.9 in 2007; 125.3 in 2008. Source: ILO.

Gross Domestic Product ($A '000 at constant 1996 prices): 100,213 in 2006; 100,184 in 2007; 103,971 in 2008.

Expenditure on the Gross Domestic Product ($A million at current prices, 2009): Government final consumption expenditure 117.0; Private final consumption expenditure 150.6; Gross fixed capital formation 138.6; Change in stocks 1.2; *Total domestic expenditure* 407.4; Exports of goods and services 28.3; *Less* Imports of goods and services 267.9; *GDP in purchasers' values* 167.9. Source: UN Statistics Division, National Accounts Main Aggregates Database.

Gross Domestic Product by Economic Activity ($A '000 at current prices, 2009): Agriculture and fishing 43,758; Mining 48; Manufacturing 9,487; Electricity, gas and water 2,657; Construction 2,394; Wholesale and retail trade 9,276; Transport and communications 16,552; Financial intermediation 11,493; Government administration 25,753; Other community, social and personal service activities 38,067; *Sub-total* 159,485; *Less* Imputed bank service charge 6,581; Indirect taxes, less subsidies 11,221; *GDP in purchasers' values* 164,125. Source: Asian Development Bank.

Balance of Payments ($A '000, 2007): Exports of goods 12,096.0; Imports of goods –83,861.4; *Trade balance* –71,765.4; Exports of services and income 85,767.8; Imports of services and income –55,586.7; *Balance on goods, services and income* –41,584.3; Current transfers received 59,517.8; Current transfers paid –11,986.5; *Current balance* 5,947.0 (incl. adjustments); Capital account (net) 36,963.0; Direct investment (net) 363.9; Portfolio investment (net) –4,319.0; Other investments (net) –32,260.9; Net errors and omissions –3,688.6; *Overall balance* 3,005.3. *2009:* Exports of goods 8,084; Imports of goods –85,386; Trade balance –77,302; Exports of services and income 103,991; Imports of services and income –75,575; Current balance –48,886. Source: Asian Development Bank.

EXTERNAL TRADE

Principal Commodities ($A '000, 2007): *Imports:* Food and live animals 26,429; Beverages and tobacco 5,434; Crude materials (excl. fuels) 1,327; Mineral fuels, lubricants, etc. 20,849; Chemicals 3,681; Basic manufactures 10,081; Machinery and transport equipment 10,841; Miscellaneous manufactured articles 4,254; Total (incl. others) 83,632. *Exports (incl. re-exports):* Copra 769; Copra cake (meal) 904; Coconut oil (crude) 5,331; Seaweed 220; Total (incl. others) 11,655 (Re-exports 2,218).

Principal Trading Partners (US $ '000, 2009): *Imports:* Australia 19,152; Fiji 29,578; Japan 7,827; New Zealand 3,847; Total (incl. others) 74,542. *Exports:* Ecuador 9,708; Japan 6,957; Thailand 9,013; USA 1,400; Total (incl. others) 33,360. Source: mainly Asian Development Bank.

TRANSPORT

Road Traffic (motor vehicles registered on Tarawa, 2004): Motor cycles 634; Passenger cars 610; Buses 7; Trucks 502; Minibuses 299; Others 18; Total 2,070.

Shipping: *Merchant Fleet* (registered, at 31 December 2009): 104 vessels; total displacement 547,062 grt. (Source: IHS Fairplay, *World Fleet Statistics*). *International Sea-borne Freight Traffic* ('000 metric tons, 1990): Goods loaded 15; Goods unloaded 26 (Source: UN, *Monthly Bulletin of Statistics*).

Civil Aviation (traffic on scheduled services, 1998): Passengers carried 28,000; Passenger-km 11 million; Total ton-km 2 million. Source: UN, *Statistical Yearbook*.

TOURISM

Foreign Tourist Arrivals: 2,004 in 2006; 3,599 in 2007; 3,380 in 2008.

Tourist Arrivals by Country of Residence (by air at Tarawa, 2008): Australia 876; Fiji 561; Japan 192; Nauru 28; New Zealand 319; Solomon Islands 55; Tuvalu 134; USA 35; Total (incl. others) 3,380.

Tourism Receipts ($A million): 2.1 in 1999; 2.2 in 2000; 3.0 in 2001.

KIRIBATI

COMMUNICATIONS MEDIA

Radio Receivers (1997): 17,000 in use.
Television Receivers (1997): 1,000 in use.
Telephones (main lines in use, 2009): 4,000.
Mobile Cellular Telephones (subscribers, 2009): 1,000.
Personal Computers (2005): 1,000.
Internet Users (2009): 7,800.
Non-daily Newspapers: 2 (estimated combined circulation 3,600) in 2002; 3 in 2004.

Sources: UNESCO, *Statistical Yearbook*; UN, *Statistical Yearbook*; International Telecommunication Union; Australian Press Council.

EDUCATION

Primary (2008): 91 schools; 16,123 students (males 8,044, females 8,079); 645 teachers (males 119, females 526).
Secondary (2005 unless otherwise indicated): 40 schools in 2008; 7,487 students (males 3,716, females 3,771); 665 teachers (males 350, females 315).
Teacher-training (2001): 198 students; 22 teachers.
Vocational (2001): 1,303 students; 17 teachers.
Pupil-teacher Ratio (primary education, UNESCO estimate): 25.0 in 2007/08. Source: UNESCO Institute for Statistics.
Adult Literacy Rate (UNESCO estimates): 92.5% (males 93%; females 92%) in 2001. Source: UNESCO, *Assessment of Resources, Best Practices and Gaps in Gender, Science and Technology in Kiribati*.

Directory

The Government

HEAD OF STATE

President (Beretitenti): ANOTE TONG (elected 4 July 2003; re-elected 17 October 2007).
Vice-President (Kauoman-ni-Beretitenti): TEIMA ONORIO.

CABINET
(May 2011)

Minister for Foreign Affairs and Immigration: TESSIE LAMBOURNE.
Minister for the Civil Service: TEREREI ABETE-REEMA.
Minister for Public Works and Utilities: KIRABUKE TEIAUA.
Minister for Education, Youth and Sports Development: TOAKAI KORIRINTETAAKE.
Minister for Communications, Transport and Tourism Development: TEMATE ERIATEITI.
Minister for Health and Medical Services: Dr KAUTU TENANAUA.
Minister for Environment, Lands and Agricultural Development: AMBEROTI NIKORA.
Minister for Internal and Social Affairs: KOURAITI BENIATO.
Minister for Finance and Economic Development: NATAN TEEWE.
Minister for Fisheries and Marine Resource Development: TABERANNANG TIMEON.
Minister for the Line and Phoenix Islands: TAWITA TEMOKU.
Minister for Labour and Human Resource Development: IOTEBA REDFERN.
Attorney-General: TITABU TABANE.

MINISTRIES

Office of the President (Beretitenti): POB 68, Bairiki, Tarawa; tel. 21183; fax 21145.
Ministry of Commerce, Industry and Co-operatives: POB 510, Betio, Tarawa; tel. 26158; fax 26233; e-mail enquiry@mcic.gov.ki; internet www.mcic.gov.ki.
Ministry of Communications, Transport and Tourism Development: POB 487, Betio, Tarawa; tel. 26003; fax 26193.
Ministry of Education, Youth and Sports Development: POB 263, Bikenibeu, Tarawa; tel. 28091; fax 28222.
Ministry of Environment, Lands and Agricultural Development: POB 234, Bikenibeu, Tarawa; tel. 28507; fax 28334.
Ministry of Finance and Economic Development: POB 67, Bairiki, Tarawa; tel. 21801; fax 21307; e-mail account@mfep.gov.ki; internet www.mfep.gov.ki.
Ministry of Fisheries and Marine Resource Development: POB 64, Bairiki, Tarawa; tel. 21099; fax 21120.
Ministry of Foreign Affairs and Immigration: POB 68, Bairiki, Tarawa; tel. 21342; fax 21466; e-mail mfa@tskl.net.ki.
Ministry of Health and Medical Services: POB 268, Bikenibeu, Tarawa; tel. 28100; fax 28152; e-mail mhfp@tskl.net.ki.
Ministry of Internal and Social Affairs: POB 75, Bairiki, Tarawa; tel. 21092; fax 21133; e-mail homeaffairs@tskl.net.ki.
Ministry of Labour and Human Resource Development: POB 69, Bairiki, Tarawa; tel. 21097; fax 21452; internet www.labour.gov.ki.
Ministry of the Line and Phoenix Islands: Kiritimati Island; tel. 81211; fax 81278.
Ministry of Public Works and Utilities: POB 498, Betio, Tarawa; tel. 26192; fax 26172.

President and Legislature

PRESIDENT

Election, 17 October 2007

Candidate	Votes	% of votes
Anote Tong	15,676	64.3
Nabuti Mwemwenikarawa	8,151	33.4
Patrick Tatireta	356	1.5
Timon Aneri	198	0.8
Total	24,381	100.0

MANEABA NI MAUNGATABU
(House of Assembly)

This is a unicameral body comprising 42 elected members (most of whom formally present themselves for election as independent candidates), and one nominated representative of the Banaban community, along with the Attorney-General in an ex officio capacity (if the latter is not elected). An election was held on 22 August 2007, with a second round of voting conducted on 30 August.

Speaker: TAOMATI IUTA.

Election Commission

Election Commission: Tarawa; Electoral Commr RINE UEARA.

Political Organizations

Political organizations in Kiribati are not conventional organized bodies but loose groupings of individuals supporting similar policies. In addition to the groupings listed below, also in existence are: the National Progressive Party, led by Teatao Teannaki, and the Liberal Party, led by Tewareka Tentoa.

Boutokan Te Koaua (Pillars of Truth): c/o Maneaba Ni Maungatabu, Tarawa; tel. 21880; fax 21278; mems affiliated to Anote Tong.
Maneaban Te Mauri: c/o Maneaba Ni Maungatabu, Tawara; tel. 21880; fax 21278; mems affiliated to Teburoro Tito and Harry Tong.
Maurin Kiribati Party: c/o Maneaba Ni Maungatabu, Tawara; Sec. NABUTI MWEMWENIKARAWA.

Diplomatic Representation

EMBASSY AND HIGH COMMISSIONS IN KIRIBATI

Australia: POB 77, Bairiki, Tarawa; tel. 21184; fax 21904; e-mail ahc.tarawa@dfat.gov.au; internet www.kiribati.embassy.gov.au; High Commissioner BRETT ALDAM.

New Zealand: POB 53, Bairiki, Tarawa; tel. 21400; fax 21402; e-mail nzhc@tskl.net.ki; High Commissioner ROBERT KAIWAI.

Taiwan (Republic of China): Bairiki, Tarawa; tel. 22557; fax 22535; e-mail Kir@tmofa.gov.tw; Ambassador BENJAMIN HO.

Judicial System

There are 24 Magistrates' Courts (each consisting of one presiding magistrate and up to eight other magistrates) hearing civil, criminal and land cases. When hearing civil or criminal cases, the presiding magistrate sits with two other magistrates, and when hearing land cases with four other magistrates. A single magistrate has national jurisdiction in civil and criminal matters. Appeal from the Magistrates' Courts lies, in civil and criminal matters, to a single judge of the High Court, and, in matters concerning land, divorce and inheritance, to the High Court's Land Division, which consists of a judge and two Land Appeal Magistrates.

The High Court of Kiribati is a superior court of record and has unlimited jurisdiction. It consists of the Chief Justice and a Puisne Judge. Appeal from a single judge of the High Court, both as a Court of the First Instance and in its appellate capacity, lies to the Kiribati Court of Appeal, which is also a court of record and consists of a panel of three judges.

All judicial appointments are made by the Beretitenti (President).

Chief Justice of the High Court: Sir JOHN BAPTIST MURIA, POB 501, Betio, Tarawa; tel. 26007; fax 26149.

Judges of the Kiribati Court of Appeal: Sir ROBERT SMELLIE, Sir DAVID TOMPKINS, ROBERT FISHER.

Religion

CHRISTIANITY

Most of the population are Christians: 53.4% Roman Catholic and 39.2% members of the Kiribati Protestant Church, according to the 1990 census.

The Roman Catholic Church

Kiribati forms part of the diocese of Tarawa and Nauru, suffragan to the archdiocese of Suva (Fiji). At 31 December 2007 the diocese contained an estimated 60,686 adherents. The Bishop participates in the Catholic Bishops' Conference of the Pacific, based in Suva (Fiji).

Bishop of Tarawa and Nauru: Most Rev. PAUL EUSEBIUS MEA KAIUEA, Bishop's House, POB 79, Bairiki, Tarawa; tel. 21279; fax 21401; e-mail diocesetarawa@tskl.net.ki.

The Anglican Communion

Kiribati is within the diocese of Polynesia, part of the Anglican Church in Aotearoa, New Zealand and Polynesia. The Bishop in Polynesia is resident in Fiji.

Protestant Church

Kiribati Protestant Church: POB 80, Bairiki, Tarawa; tel. 21195; fax 21453; e-mail kpc@tskl.net.ki; f. 1988; Moderator Rev. BAITEKE NABETARI; Gen. Sec. Rev. TIAONTIN ARUE; 29,432 mems in 1998.

Other Churches

Seventh-day Adventist, Church of God and Assembly of God communities are also represented, as is the Church of Jesus Christ of Latter-day Saints (Mormon).

BAHÁ'Í FAITH

National Spiritual Assembly: POB 269, Bikenibeu, Tarawa; tel. and fax 28074; e-mail emi@tskl.net.ki; 2,400 mems resident in 100 localities in 1995.

The Press

Butim'aea Manin te Euangkerio: POB 80, Bairiki, Tarawa; tel. 21195; e-mail kpc@tskl.net.ki; f. 1913; Protestant Church newspaper; weekly; a monthly publication *Te Kaotan te Ota* is also produced; Editor Rev. TOOM TOAKAI.

Kiribati Business Link: Bairiki, Tarawa; English.

Kiribati Newstar: POB 10, Bairiki, Tarawa; tel. 21652; fax 21671; f. 2000; independent; weekly; English and I-Kiribati; Editor-in-Chief NGAUEA UATIOA.

Te Itoi ni Kiribati: POB 231, Bikenibeu, Tarawa; tel. 28138; fax 21341; f. 1914; Roman Catholic Church newsletter; monthly; circ. 2,300.

Te Mauri: Protestant Church newspaper; Editor BATIRI BATAUA.

Te Uekera: Broadcasting and Publications Authority, POB 78, Bairiki, Tarawa; tel. 21162; fax 21096; e-mail bpa_admin@tskl.net.ki; f. 1945; bi-weekly; English and I-Kiribati; Editor ROOTI TERUBEA; circ. 2,000.

Broadcasting and Communications

TELECOMMUNICATIONS

Telecom Kiribati Ltd: Bairiki, Tarawa; govt-owned; Gen. Man. ENOTA INGINTAU.

Telecom Services Kiribati Ltd: POB 72, Bairiki, Tarawa; tel. 20700; fax 21424; e-mail ceo@tskl.net.ki; internet www.tskl.net.ki; f. 1990; Chair. ELLIOT ALI; CEO BARANIKO TONGANIBEIA.

BROADCASTING

Regulatory Authority

Broadcasting and Publications Authority: POB 78, Bairiki, Tarawa; tel. 21187; fax 21096.

Radio

Radio Kiribati: Broadcasting and Publications Authority, POB 78, Bairiki, Tarawa; tel. 21187; fax 21096; f. 1954; statutory body; station Radio Kiribati broadcasting on SW and MW transmitters; programmes in I-Kiribati (90%) and English (10%); some advertising; Gen. Man. TANIERI TEIBUAKO.

Television

Television Kiribati Ltd: Betio, Tarawa; tel. 26036; fax 26045; internet www.tkl.com.ki; f. 1987; CEO TAOM KAITARA.

Finance

(cap. = capital; dep. = deposits; res = reserves)

BANKING

ANZ Bank (Kiribati) Ltd: POB 66, Bairiki, Tarawa; tel. 21095; fax 21200; e-mail anzkiribati@anz.com; internet www.anz.com/kiribati; f. 1984; 75% owned by ANZ Bank, 25% by Govt of Kiribati; fmrly The Bank of Kiribati Ltd, name changed as above 2009; Chair. JOHN MORSCHEL; Man. Dir TERRENCE LOW; 4 brs.

Development Bank of Kiribati: POB 33, Bairiki, Tarawa; tel. 21345; fax 21297; e-mail dbk@tskl.net.ki; f. 1986; took over the assets of the National Loans Board; identifies, promotes and finances small-scale projects; auth. cap. $A2m.; Gen. Man. KIETAU TABWEBWEITI; 5 brs.

A network of lending entities known as 'village banks' operates throughout the islands, as do a number of credit unions under the management of the Credit Union League.

INSURANCE

Kiribati Insurance Corpn: POB 509, Betio, Tarawa; tel. 253367; fax 25338; e-mail enquire@kic.org.ki; internet www.kic.org.ki; f. 1981; govt-owned; sole insurance co; reinsures overseas; Chair. IEETE ROUATU.

Trade and Industry

GOVERNMENT AGENCIES

Kiribati Copra Mill Co Ltd: POB 607, Betio, Tarawa; tel. 26831; fax 26635; e-mail kcmc@tskl.net.ki; internet www.kcmcl.ki; f. 2001.

Kiribati Housing Corporation: Bairiki, Tarawa; tel. 21092; operates the Housing Loan and Advice Centre; Chair. TOKOREAUA KAIRORO.

Kiribati Provident Fund: POB 76, Bairiki, Tarawa; tel. 21153; fax 21300; internet www.kpf.com.ki; f. 1977; Chair. TEKIERA ABERA.

CHAMBER OF COMMERCE

Kiribati Chamber of Commerce: POB 550, Betio, Tarawa; tel. 26351; fax 26332; Pres. MARTIN TOFINGA.

KIRIBATI

UTILITIES

Public Utilities Board: POB 443, Betio, Tarawa; tel. 26292; fax 26106; e-mail ceo.pub@tskl.net.ki; f. 1977; govt-owned; provides electricity, water and sewerage services in Tarawa; CEO TABOIA METUTERA.

Solar Energy Company (SEC): POB 493 Betio, Tarawa; tel. 26058; fax 26210; e-mail sec@tskl.net.ki; a co-operative administering and implementing solar-generated electricity projects in North Tarawa and the outer islands.

CO-OPERATIVE SOCIETIES

Co-operative societies dominate trading in Tarawa and enjoy a virtual monopoly outside the capital, except for Banaba and Kiritimati.

Bobotin Kiribati Ltd (BKL): POB 485, Betio, Tarawa; tel. 26092; fax 26224; replaced Kiribati Co-operative Wholesale Society; govt-owned; Gen. Man. AKAU TIARE.

The Kiribati Copra Co-operative Society Ltd: POB 489, Betio, Tarawa; tel. 26534; fax 26391; e-mail kccs@tskl.net.ki; f. 1976; the sole exporter of copra; seven cttee mems; 29 mem. socs; Chair. RAIMON TAAKE; CEO RUTIANO BENETITO.

TRADE UNIONS

Kiribati Trades Union Congress (KTUC): POB 166, Bairiki, Tarawa; tel. 28157; fax 28712; e-mail ktc@tskl.net.ki; f. 1982; unions and asscns affiliated to the KTUC include: Fishermen's Union, Co-operative Workers' Union, Seamen's Union, Teachers' Union, Nurses' Asscn, Public Employees' Asscn, Bankers' Union, Butaritari Rural Workers' Union, Christmas Island Union of Federated Workers, Pre-School Teachers' Asscn, Makim Island Rural Workers' Org., Nanolelei Retailers' Union, Plantation Workers' Union of Fanning Island and Overseas Fishermen's Union; 2,500 mems; Pres. TATOA KAITEIE; Gen. Sec. TAMARETI TAAU.

Transport

ROADS

Wherever practicable, roads are built on all atolls, and connecting causeways between islets are also being constructed as funds and labour permit. Kiribati has about 670 km of roads that are suitable for motor vehicles; all-weather roads exist in Tarawa and Kiritimati. In March 2011 it was announced that, with a loan of US $12m. from the Asian Development Bank, the road network in South Tarawa was to be upgraded.

SHIPPING

A major project to rehabilitate the port terminal and facilities at Betio, with finance totalling some US $22m. from Japan, was completed in 2000. There are other port facilities at Banaba, Kanton and English Harbour.

Kiribati Shipping Services Ltd (KSSL): POB 495, Betio, Tarawa; tel. 26195; fax 26204; e-mail kssl@tskl.net.ki; govt-owned; operates three passenger/freight vessels on inter-island services connecting Kiribati, Nauru, Tuvalu, the Wallis and Futuna Islands, and Suva (Fiji), and one landing craft and multi-purpose cargo vessels between Fiji, Tuvalu, Nauru and Marshall Islands; Gen. Man. Capt. ITIBWINNANG AIAIMOA.

Nikoraoi Shipping: Betio, Tarawa; tel. 26536; fax 26367.

CIVIL AVIATION

There are five international airports (Bonriki on South Tarawa, Cassidy on Kiritimati, Antekana on Butaritari, as well as two others on Kanton and Tabuaeran) and several other airfields in Kiribati. Air Pacific, the Fijian carrier, operates services to Tarawa and Kiritimati, with links to Nadi (Fiji) and Honolulu (Hawaii, USA).

Air Kiribati Ltd: POB 274, Bonriki, Tarawa; tel. 28533; fax 29716; e-mail admin@airkiribati.net; internet www.airkiribati.com.au; f. 1977; fmrly Air Tungaru; national airline; operates scheduled services to outer islands; Chair. TINIAN REIHER; CEO Capt. IOSABATA NAMAKIN.

Tourism

Kiribati's attractions include fishing and bird-watching opportunities, as well as the sites of Second World War battles. In 1997 Caroline Island, situated close to the recently realigned International Date Line, was renamed Millennium Island, in an attempt to maximize its potential for attracting visitors. The Phoenix Islands Protected Area (PIPA), a 408,250 sq km expanse of marine and terrestrial habitats, was inscribed by UNESCO on its World Heritage List in 2010. PIPA contains about 800 species of fauna, including 200 coral species, 500 fish species, 18 marine mammals and 44 bird species. The objectives of the 2010–15 plan for the development of the tourism sector included an increase in the annual number of visitors to 10,000 by the end of the plan period. A campaign to attract more visitors was launched in April 2010. International visitor arrivals reportedly increased by more than 19% in 2010 to reach 4,701, largely supported by the US, New Zealand and Taiwanese markets.

Kiribati National Tourism Office: Ministry of Communications, Transport and Tourism Development, POB 487, Betio, Tarawa; tel. 25573; fax 26193; e-mail sto@mict.gov.ki; internet www.visit-kiribati.com; Sec. DAVID YEETING; Senior Tourist Officer (vacant).

Defence

Kiribati has no professional defence forces. Assistance is provided by Australia and New Zealand. In 2008 expenditure by Kiribati on the islands' defence totalled nearly $A8.0m. (equivalent to 9.7% of central government spending).

Education

Education is compulsory for children between six and 15 years of age. This generally involves six years at a primary school and at least three years at a secondary school. Every atoll is provided with at least one primary school. In 2008 there were 91 primary schools and 40 secondary schools. There were 16,123 pupils enrolled at primary schools in 2008; 7,487 pupils attended secondary schools in 2005. Teaching staff at primary level numbered 645 in 2008; in 2005 there were 665 secondary-school teachers. In 2001/02 enrolment at primary schools reached 97.4% of pupils in the relevant age-group. In 2006/07 enrolment at secondary schools was equivalent to 87% of students in the relevant age-group. The tertiary sector is based on Tarawa, except for one of the two private colleges, which is based on Abemama. The Government administers a technical college and training colleges for teachers, nurses and seafarers (the last, the Marine Training Centre, trains about 200 students each year for employment by overseas shipping companies). There were 198 students enrolled in teacher-training and 1,303 in other vocational training in 2001. An extra-mural centre of the University of the South Pacific (based in Fiji) is also located on South Tarawa. In 1999 plans for the establishment of a college of advanced education were announced. In 2008 government expenditure on education totalled $A20.5m. (equivalent to 24.8% of total recurrent budgetary expenditure).

THE DEMOCRATIC PEOPLE'S REPUBLIC OF KOREA

Introductory Survey

LOCATION, CLIMATE, LANGUAGE, RELIGION, FLAG, CAPITAL

The Democratic People's Republic of Korea (North Korea) occupies the northern part of the Korean peninsula, bordered to the north by the People's Republic of China and, for a very short section to the north-east, by the Russian Federation, and to the south by the Republic of Korea. The climate is continental, with cold, dry winters and hot, humid summers; temperatures range from $-6°C$ to $25°C$ ($21°F$ to $77°F$). The language is Korean. Buddhism, Christianity and Chundo Kyo are officially cited as the principal religions. The national flag (proportions 33 by 65) is red, with blue stripes on the upper and lower edges, each separated from the red by a narrow white stripe. Left of centre is a white disc containing a five-pointed red star. The capital is Pyongyang.

CONTEMPORARY POLITICAL HISTORY

Historical Context

Korea was formerly an independent monarchy. It was occupied by Japanese forces in 1905 and annexed by Japan in 1910, when the Emperor was deposed. Following Japan's surrender in August 1945, ending the Second World War, Korea was divided at latitude 38°N into military occupation zones, with Soviet forces in the North and US forces in the South. A Provisional People's Committee, led by Kim Il Sung of the Korean Communist Party (KCP), was established in the North in February 1946 and accorded government status by the Soviet occupation forces. In July the KCP merged with another group to form the North Korean Workers' Party. In 1947 a legislative body, the Choe Ko In Min Hoe Ui (Supreme People's Assembly—SPA), was established, and Kim Il Sung became Premier. A new Assembly was elected in August 1948, and the Democratic People's Republic of Korea (DPRK) was proclaimed on 9 September. In the same year the Republic of Korea (q.v.) was proclaimed in the South. Initially, the DPRK was recognized only by the USSR and other communist countries. Soviet forces withdrew from North Korea in December 1948. In the following year, as a result of a merger between communists in the North and South, the Korean Workers' Party (KWP) was formed, under the leadership of Kim Il Sung. The KWP continued to hold power in the 21st century.

The two republics each claimed to have legitimate jurisdiction over the whole Korean peninsula. North Korean forces crossed the 38th parallel in June 1950, precipitating a three-year war between North and South. The UN mounted a collective defence action in support of South Korea, and the invasion was repelled. North Korean forces were supported by the People's Republic of China from October 1950. The heavy bombardment of the North resulted in a high number of civilian casualties. Peace talks began in July 1951 and an armistice agreement was concluded in July 1953. The cease-fire line, which approximately followed the 38th parallel, became the frontier between North and South Korea, with a demilitarized zone (DMZ), supervised by UN forces, separating the two countries.

Domestic Political Affairs

Through the 'personality cult' of Kim Il Sung (the 'Great Leader') and of his son Kim Jong Il (the 'Dear Leader'), and a policy of strict surveillance of the entire population, overt opposition to the KWP was effectively eliminated. The only organized opposition to the regime (albeit in exile) appeared to be the Salvation Front for the Democratic Unification of Chosun, established by former military and other officials of the DPRK in the early 1990s, with branches in Russia, Japan and China. International human rights organizations indicated that they believed there to be a number of concentration camps in North Korea, in which as many as 200,000 political prisoners were being held.

A new Constitution, adopted in December 1972, created the office of President, and Kim Il Sung was duly elected to the post. Kim Jong Il was appointed to several key positions within the KWP in 1980. In July 1984 Radio Pyongyang referred to Kim Jong Il, for the first time, as the 'sole successor' to his father, but there were reports of opposition to the President's heir, particularly among older members of the KWP.

Following elections to the eighth SPA, in November 1986 (when the 655 members were returned unopposed), Kim Il Sung was re-elected President, and a new Administration Council (cabinet) was formed. In March 1990 Kim Il Sung was returned to the post of President, and Kim Jong Il was appointed to his first state (as distinct from party) post, as First Vice-Chairman of the National Defence Commission. In February 1991 it was rumoured that there had been an unsuccessful military coup against Kim Jong Il. In December he was appointed Supreme Commander of the Korean People's Army (KPA), in place of his father, and in January 1992 he was reported to have been given control of foreign policy. In April Kim Jong Il was appointed to the rank of Marshal, while his father assumed the title of Grand Marshal.

In what was interpreted as a partial attempt to adapt to the change in international conditions following the collapse of communist regimes world-wide, the SPA (according to South Korean reports) made several amendments to the DPRK's Constitution in April 1992. Principal among these were the deletion of all references to Marxism-Leninism, and the promotion of 'economic openness' to allow limited foreign investment in the DPRK (although the KWP's guiding principle of *Juche*, or self-reliance, was strongly emphasized). In September measures to address the deteriorating economic situation included a drastic devaluation of the national currency. At the fifth session of the ninth SPA in April 1993 Kim Jong Il was elected Chairman of the National Defence Commission. In July Kim Il Sung's younger brother, Kim Yong Ju, unexpectedly returned to political life after a 17-year absence, and was subsequently elevated to the position of Vice-President and to membership of the Central Committee of the KWP's Political Bureau (Politburo).

The death of Kim Il Sung and rise of Kim Jong Il

Kim Il Sung died of heart failure on 8 July 1994. One hundred days of national mourning were observed, but, contrary to expectations, Kim Jong Il was not appointed to the leading post of President of the DPRK. Kim Jong Il did not appear in public during this period, reviving earlier speculation that he was either in poor health or that a struggle for power was taking place. It was thought that Kim Song Ae, the widow of Kim Il Sung and stepmother of Kim Jong Il, favoured her eldest son, Kim Pyong Il, for the presidency. In February 1995 the Minister of the People's Armed Forces, Marshal O Jin U, died; O had been a significant supporter within the military of Kim Jong Il's succession. Scheduled elections to the SPA did not take place in April 1995, and no session of the Assembly was convened in 1996.

Meanwhile, from the mid-1990s, the influence of the KPA expanded significantly, as Kim Jong Il increasingly relied upon the military to maintain his power, and the policy of *Songun* ('military first') was emphasized as the regime's central doctrine. The 50th anniversary of the establishment of the KWP in October 1995 was dominated by the military rather than the party, and several generals were promoted. However, Kim Jong Il did not assume any new posts. In February 1996 Sung Hye Rim, a former consort of Kim Jong Il and mother of his eldest son, defected to a Western European country. In February 1997 Premier Kang Song San, who had made no public appearance since early 1996, was dismissed, and replaced on an acting basis by Hong Song Nam. Deepening social unrest was indicated by an increase in the rate of defections. In February 1997 Hwang Jang Yop, a close adviser to Kim Jong Il, sought political asylum in the South Korean embassy in China while returning from an official visit to Japan, and warned that the DPRK was preparing to launch a military assault on South Korea. Hwang's defection appeared to precipitate significant changes in the KWP and military high command, as did the deaths of the Minister of the

THE DEMOCRATIC PEOPLE'S REPUBLIC OF KOREA (NORTH KOREA)

Introductory Survey

People's Armed Forces, Marshal Choe Kwang, and of his deputy, Kim Kwang Jin. Many senior officials were replaced, and some 123 generals, including many allies of Kim Jong Il, were promoted in rank in April. In August two senior North Korean diplomats, including the ambassador to Egypt, defected to the USA. There were also rumours of unrest and coup attempts, and several senior officials disappeared from public view without explanation. The official mourning period for Kim Il Sung was formally declared to be at an end in July 1997, on the third anniversary of his death. It was announced that, henceforth, the country was to use the *Juche* calendar, with 1912, the year of Kim Il Sung's birth, designated the first year of the new calendar. On 8 October 1997 Kim Jong Il was elected General Secretary of the KWP.

Elections to the SPA finally took place in July 1998, at which the single list of candidates received 100% of the votes cast. Some two-thirds of the 687 deputies were newcomers to the Assembly, while the military reportedly doubled its representation. The first session of the 10th SPA was convened in September. However, the anticipated appointment of Kim Jong Il as President of the DPRK did not occur, as the post was effectively abolished under major amendments to the Constitution that extensively revised the structure of government. The deceased Kim Il Sung was designated 'Eternal President', thus remaining *de jure* Head of State, while Kim Jong Il, who had been re-elected Chairman of the National Defence Commission (now apparently the highest office in the state hierarchy), was reported to have assumed the role of de facto Head of State. Vice-Marshal Jo Myong Rok, the Director of the General Political Bureau of the KPA, was appointed First Vice-Chairman of the Commission, becoming the de facto second-ranking official in the DPRK. The Cabinet, as the Administration Council was redesignated, assumed many of the functions of the Central People's Committee, which was abolished. A new Presidium of the SPA was established, the President of which was to represent the State in diplomatic affairs; Kim Yong Nam, hitherto Minister of Foreign Affairs, was appointed to this position. Hong Song Nam was formally appointed Premier of the new Cabinet. Jo Chang Dok and Kwak Pom Gi, were appointed as Vice-Premiers.

In October 2000 the Minister of Finance, Rim Kyong Suk, and the President of the Central Bank of the DPRK, Jong Song Thaek, were dismissed. They were replaced, respectively, by Mun Il Bong and Kim Wan Su. The replacement of the Minister of Foreign Trade in December was similarly unexplained. The Minister of Agriculture was replaced in March 2001.

In January 2001 the Government urged a 'new way of thinking' to address the country's economic problems and to complement the *Kangsong Taeguk* ('prosperous and powerful nation') philosophy. Meanwhile, the number of people defecting from the North to the South continued to increase, with nearly 650 such persons having settled in the latter since 1996. Several senior officials died or were replaced during 2001, including Ri Song Bok, a senior aide to Kim Jong Il and Secretary-General of the KWP Central Committee, who died in May. At the fifth session of the 10th SPA held in March 2002, a new land planning law was adopted. Premier Hong Song Nam also urged improved trade and economic co-operation, including joint ventures with other countries. In April Kim Jong Il promoted some 55 military leaders, including Jang Song U, the elder brother of Kim's brother-in-law, Jang Song Thaek.

The question of the succession of the next generation of leadership became increasingly important following Kim Jong Il's 60th birthday in February 2002. Kim was initially believed to have been preparing his eldest son, Kim Jong Nam, who had served in the Ministry of Public Security and as head of the country's information technology (IT) industry since the late 1990s; however, in May 2001 he was detained in Tokyo, on charges of entering Japan with a false passport, and subsequently deported to China. Thenceforth it was reported that Kim Jong Il was preparing for leadership Kim Jong Chol, the elder son of Ko Yong Hui, described as Kim Jong Il's unofficial wife. Kim Jong Nam spent much of 2002 in Russia, where his mother, Sung Hye Rim, died in July.

In September 2002 the Government designated the city of Sinuiju a 'Special Administrative Region' designed to attract foreign investment, and appointed Yang Bin, a Chinese-born Dutch citizen, as its first governor. However, within days of his appointment, Yang was arrested by the Chinese authorities on corruption charges, and he was unable to assume his post. In late 2004 there were indications that the Sinuiju project had been abandoned, although in July 2006 it was reported that DPRK loyalists and foreign-currency management groups were being moved into the area. In mid-2007 it was reported that 3,000 families were being relocated from Pyongyang to Sinuiju, which had apparently been declared a special economic.

In late 2002 the Government also established a special industrial zone in Kaesong, and a special tourist zone in the region of Mount Kumgang, although these did not have the same special status as Sinuiju. A meeting of senior law enforcement officials was held in Pyongyang in December during which Premier Hong urged the elimination of 'non-socialist elements'. In early 2003 it was reported that travel restrictions within the country had been reintroduced.

Kim Jong Il did not attend the sixth session of the 10th SPA, held in March 2003. Having reportedly disappeared from public view for 50 days, Kim reappeared in April, in which month celebrations were organized in Pyongyang to mark the 10th anniversary of Kim's election as Chairman of the National Defence Commission. Further celebrations took place in July to commemorate the 50th anniversary of the Korean War truce (celebrated as a triumph for the DPRK by the country's media). In August elections were held to form the 11th SPA. Voter turn-out was reported to be have been 99.9%, and all 687 candidates were elected unopposed. At the first session of the 11th SPA in September, Kim Jong Il was re-elected as Chairman of the National Defence Commission. The appointment of Pak Pong Ju, hitherto Minister of Chemical Industry, as Premier was endorsed. Two new Vice-Premiers, Jon Sung Hun (previously Minister of Metal and Machine-Building Industries) and Ro Tu Chol, were appointed. Other cabinet changes included the transfer of the Chairman of the State Planning Commission, Pak Nam Gi, to the SPA budget committee and his replacement by Kim Kwang Rin. The portfolios of agriculture, of the power and coal industry, and of culture were also reallocated. In October Kim Yong Sun, a member of the KWP Secretariat and Chairman of the Korea Asia-Pacific Peace Committee, died, reportedly as a result of a traffic accident.

In April 2004 more than 150 people were killed and 1,300 injured by a massive explosion on a railway line at Ryongchon, a town near the border with China. Many children were among the victims of the accident, apparently caused when electric cables ignited chemical and other materials being transported by rail, only hours after a train carrying Kim Jong Il had travelled through the area. The North Korean authorities withheld information on the accident for two days, but subsequently accepted international humanitarian aid, including a donation (made through the Red Cross) from the USA.

In July 2004 Ju Sang Song was appointed as Minister of People's Security, replacing Choe Ryong Su. Choe had been removed from his post only one year after being appointed, and the reason for his removal was unclear. Also in July the 10th anniversary of the death of Kim Il Sung was commemorated. In August Ko Yong Hui, the mother of two of Kim Jong Il's sons, was reported to have died. In November there was speculation that Kim's power might be weakening, following reports that portraits of him had been removed from public locations. It was also noted that official news reports no longer referred to Kim by the honorific title of 'Dear Leader'. Some sources claimed that Kim himself was attempting to diminish the personality cult surrounding him. However, there were tentative suggestions throughout 2004 that a power struggle was taking place in Pyongyang. It was believed that in April Kim had removed his brother-in-law, Jang Song Thaek, from his position as vice-director of the KWP Central Committee and placed him under house arrest. Later in the year Jang's wife, Kim Jong Il's sister Kim Kyong Hui, was injured in a traffic incident, which was believed to have been a deliberate attack. Meanwhile, in April Kim's eldest son, Kim Jong Nam, reportedly survived an assassination attempt in Austria.

In May 2005 South Korean media reported that the North Korean Minister of Post and Telecommunications, Ri Kum Bom, had been dismissed, apparently as a result of his failure to control the revelation of information earlier in the year disclosing that the DPRK was in the process of combating outbreaks of avian influenza ('bird flu'). In July it was announced that his replacement was Ryu Yong Sop. In August an unspecified number of prisoners were granted an amnesty to mark the 60th anniversary of the liberation of the Korean peninsula from Japanese rule. In October the 60th anniversary of the KWP was celebrated. North Korean citizens were reportedly granted four public holidays in honour of the event. On 9 October, the day before the anniversary, the KWP held a national meeting

THE DEMOCRATIC PEOPLE'S REPUBLIC OF KOREA (NORTH KOREA)

Introductory Survey

in Pyongyang, at which the primacy of the *Songun* policy was reaffirmed, as was the need for economic development in order to achieve the objective of *Kangsong Taeguk*. The anniversary itself was commemorated with a large military parade in Pyongyang. In late October it was reported that Yon Hyong Muk, a Vice-Chairman of the National Defence Commission, who was regarded as a close adviser to Kim Jong Il, had died. North Korean media reports in November indicated that Ri Kwang Nam had been replaced as Minister of Extractive Industries by Kang Min Chol, while a report in December implied that Kim Jin Song had become Minister of Culture, replacing Choe Ik Kyu. In January 2006 Jang Song Thaek made his first public appearance since 2003, prompting speculation that he had been rehabilitated following his apparent removal from favour in 2004.

While thousands took to the streets in October 2006 for mass rallies to celebrate the nuclear test (see the North Korean Nuclear Programme), in November a rare protest against the authorities occurred in a town in North Hamgyong Province. Although the number of protesters was said to be little more than 100, the demonstration was highly significant, private mass activities being forbidden by North Korean law. According to a report on *Daily NK*, a website maintained by a group campaigning for democracy in the DPRK, residents of Hoiryeong were demonstrating against 'refurbishment fees' for a local market imposed on them by the town's officials. North Korean refugees arriving in China also reported growing discontent towards the regime, with 90% of the 1,300 refugees questioned by the bipartisan US Committee on Human Rights in North Korea agreeing that North Koreans were expressing their concerns about persistent food shortages.

In January 2007 the Minister of Foreign Affairs, Paek Nam Sun, was reported to have died of cancer. He was replaced by Pak Ui Chun, a former ambassador to Russia, in May. At the fifth session of the 11th SPA in mid-April, Premier Pak Pong Ju was replaced by Kim Yong Il, hitherto Minister of Land and Marine Transport. Although no official explanation was given, observers later suggested that Pak had unsuccessfully attempted to introduce economic reforms, including allowing greater autonomy for state enterprises. At the same time Vice-Marshal Kim Yong Chun, hitherto Chief of General Staff of the KPA, was appointed as a Vice-Chairman of the National Defence Commission, filling the vacancy left by the death of Yon Hyong Muk in October 2005. Gen. Kim Kyok Sik became the new KPA Chief of General Staff. The permanent staff of the National Defence Commission was expanded as part of a further reorganization of senior military officials in May 2007, with the appointment of Gen. Ri Myong Su, the former operations director of the KPA, as a standing member. The changes at the National Defence Commission were generally interpreted as an attempt to enhance its role and powers. Rumours suggesting that Kim Jong Il's health was deteriorating prompted renewed speculation regarding his successor, which intensified in August following reports that Kim's eldest son, Kim Jong Nam, had returned from exile to work in the organization and guidance bureau of the KWP. Thae Jong Su was appointed as a Vice-Premier later in that month. In November it was reported that Jang Song Thaek had been promoted from the position of vice-director within the KWP to the directorship of the party's department responsible for state internal security, while Kim's second eldest son, Kim Jong Chol, had been appointed as a vice-director of another department of the KWP.

Recent developments: the future leadership question

Several government changes were reported to have been implemented at senior level in 2008. In March Rim Kyong Man was said to have been replaced by Ri Ryong Nam in the position of Minister of Foreign Trade. It emerged in October that Jon Kil Su had been appointed as Minister of Railways, following the departure of Kim Yong Sam, while Kim Kwang Yong had succeeded Sok Kun Su as Minister of Forestry. Also in October, a senior member of the KWP Politburo, Pak Song Chol, died. In January 2009 three further cabinet appointments were revealed: Ho Taek was the new Minister of Electric Power Industry, and Kim Chang Sik and Kim Thae Bong had assumed responsibility for the agriculture and metal industry portfolios, respectively. Meanwhile, elections to the new SPA, originally due to be held in August 2008, were postponed, thereby further increasing speculation about the health of Kim Jong Il, who failed to attend a parade commemorating the country's 60th anniversary in early September and was not seen in public for three months subsequently. Although he had resumed his public duties by the beginning of 2009, Kim Jong Il did not appear to be in robust health, and it was widely concluded that he had suffered a stroke.

In January 2009 it was announced that the elections for the 12th SPA would take place on 8 March. A total of 687 candidates were duly elected unopposed; 316 deputies were reported to be entering the SPA for the first time, fewer than the number of new members elected in 2003. The level of voter participation was declared to have been 99.98%. Observers noted that the list of incoming deputies included none of Kim Jong Il's three sons, the youngest of whom, Kim Jong Un, had become the subject of much speculation with regard to the succession issue. (Kim Jong Un was the younger son of Ko Yong Hui.) In February 2009 Gen. Ri Yong Ho replaced Kim Kyok Sik as KPA Chief of General Staff. Various changes to the leadership were effected at the first session of the SPA, which opened on 9 April. Notable appointments were those of Kim Wan Su as Minister of Finance and Ri Kwang Gon as President of the Central Bank, who exchanged responsibilities. Ro Tu Chol remained as a Vice-Premier, in addition being appointed as Chairman of the State Planning Commission. O Su Yong relinquished the electronics industry portfolio upon his appointment as a Vice-Premier, in place of Jon Sung Hun. Kim Jong Il's influential brother-in-law, Jang Song Thaek, became a member of the National Defence Commission, of which Vice-Marshal O Kuk Ryol (a former Chief of General Staff of the KPA) was appointed a Vice-Chairman, as was the Minister of the People's Armed Forces, Vice-Marshal Kim Yong Chun. Also joining the National Defence Commission were Gen. U Tong Chuk Chuk (the deputy director of the State Security Agency) and Ju Kyu Chang, a senior party official and aide of Kim Jong Il.

Also in April 2009 the SPA adopted the text of a revised Constitution (although this was not published until the end of September): for the first time, this gave official recognition to the Chairman of the National Defence Commission (the post held by Kim Jong Il) as the 'supreme leader' of the nation, and added a reference to *Songun* alongside *Juche* as guiding principles. In June South Korean media quoted intelligence reports that Kim Jong Un had formally been declared his father's successor; however, this was not confirmed in the North Korean state media, and it appeared likely that Kim Jong Un's youth (he was believed to be only 27 or 28 years of age) would be an obstacle to his acceptance by the political establishment. In September Pak Su Gil replaced Kim Wan Su as Minister of Finance and was also appointed as a Vice-Premier; the appointment of another Vice-Premier, Pak Myong Son, was also announced.

In early December 2009 the Government announced a revaluation of the currency, obliging North Koreans to exchange existing bank-notes for new notes worth 1% of the old currency. A limit on the amount per family that could be exchanged meant that savings above a modest level became worthless. The aim of the revaluation was apparently to reduce inflation and to eliminate profiteering by unofficial traders; however, it resulted in price rises, disruption to the distribution of goods and food shortages. Furthermore, there were reports of considerable public resentment. In February 2010 it was reported that the official responsible for the revaluation, Pak Nam Gi (the director of the KWP's department for planning and finance), had been dismissed, and in March he was reported to have been executed.

In January 2010 An Tong Chun (hitherto chairman of the central committee of the Korean Writers' Union) was appointed Minister of Culture. Between April and June the deaths of three senior members of the KWP were reported, namely: Ri Yong Chol, deputy director of the party's organization and guidance department, with responsibility for the supervision of military organization; Ri Je Gang, a senior deputy director of the same department, who died in a car crash in June; and Kim Jung Rin, responsible for workers' organizations. In addition, the retirement was reported in May of Kim Il Chol, a member of the National Defence Commission and hitherto the Vice-Minister of the People's Armed Forces. Also in May, the Government condemned as a 'fabrication' a report by international experts that concluded that the sinking of a South Korean naval vessel in March had been caused by a North Korean torpedo (see Inter-Korean Relations), leading to speculation by observers that the attack might have been perpetrated by officers who had not been duly authorized, or alternatively that the attack had been deliberately ordered by the Government in an attempt to associate the possible future leader, Kim Jong Un, with a successful military action.

In an unusual development, after its regular meeting in April 2010 the SPA convened for a second session in June, when the appointment of Choe Yong Rim (hitherto chief secretary of the KWP's Pyongyang city committee) as Premier was announced, replacing Kim Yong Il, possibly because the latter had presided over the unsuccessful currency revaluation at the end of the previous year. Six new Vice-Premiers were appointed and three recalled; several cabinet portfolios were reallocated. The appointments as Vice-Premier included that of Jo Pyong Ju, retaining his previous post as Minister of Machine-Building Industries, and Han Kwang Bok, retaining her previous post as Minister of the Electronics Industry; the four other new Vice-Premiers were Kang Nung Su (hitherto chairman of the State Film Commission), Kim Rak Hui, Ri Tae Nam and Jon Ha Chol (senior KWP officials reportedly specializing in agricultural management, steel production and financial planning, respectively). Other appointments were to the ministries responsible for light industry (An Song Ju), foodstuff and daily necessities industry (Jo Yong Chol), and physical culture and sports (Pak Myong Chol). The promotion of Jang Song Thaek, Kim Jong Il's brother-in-law, to the powerful position of a Vice-Chairman of the National Defence Commission was also announced. Both Jang and Choe Yong Rim were reported to be supporters of Kim Jong Un as a successor to his father.

In late June 2010 there was speculation in the South Korean media that Kim Jong Un had been a member of the SPA, under a pseudonym, since the 2009 election. In August 2010 the former Premier, Pak Pong Ju, was described as a First Deputy Director of the KWP Central Committee, having apparently been reinstated after his demotion in 2007; Pak was believed to be a close ally of Jang Song Thaek. In September 2010 Kang Sok Ju, a cousin of Kim Jong Il and hitherto the Vice-Minister of Foreign Affairs, was promoted to Vice-Premier, while two senior negotiators in the six-nation talks on the DPRK's nuclear policy, Kim Kye Gwan and Ri Yong Ho (as distinct from Gen. Ri, the Chief of General Staff of the armed forces), became Vice-Ministers of Foreign Affairs. Later in September a delegates' conference of the KWP was convened, the first such meeting since 1980. Widespread speculation that the conference would be the setting for the official appearance of Kim Jong Un as Kim Jong Il's heir appeared to be confirmed when, shortly beforehand, Kim Jong Un (who had no record of military service) was awarded the rank of general. The same rank was conferred on Kim Kyong Hui (the sister of Kim Jong Il and wife of Jang Song Thaek), and on two other civilians, Choe Ryong Hae (whose father, Choe Hyon, had been a close colleague of Kim Il Sung), and Kim Kyong Ok (deputy director of the KWP's organization and guidance department).

At the conference itself, Kim Jong Il was re-elected General Secretary of the KWP. Kim Jong Un was appointed a Vice-Chairman of the KWP's Central Military Commission (a newly created post), and a member of the party's Central Committee; however, he was not given membership of the Politburo or the National Defence Commission. The KPA Chief of General Staff, Gen. Ri Yong Ho, was promoted to the rank of Vice-Marshal and became a member of the Politburo, and was also, alongside Kim Jong Un, appointed Vice-Chairman of the KWP's Central Military Commission. Jang Song Thaek was elected an alternate member of the Politburo and a member of the KWP's Central Military Commission, while his wife, Kim Kyong Hui, was also elected to the KWP's Politburo. Reports and photographs of Kim Jong Un published after the conference were believed to represent the first time that he had been mentioned by name in the North Korean media.

The 'Young General', as Kim Jong Un was often called, appeared with Kim Jong Il at a large military parade held in Pyongyang in October 2010 to celebrate the 65th anniversary of the KWP, and was subsequently reported to be accompanying his father on various official visits. In November Kim Jong Un was reported to be in charge of an investigation into corrupt officials. In the same month Jo Myong Rok, the First Vice-Chairman of the National Defence Commission, died, and there was speculation that Kim Jong Un might shortly be appointed to this post. Observing the year's events, analysts generally concluded that, in the event of Kim Jong Il's death or incapacity, while Kim Jong Un might be his nominal successor, the latter's youth and inexperience would mean that real power would be exercised collectively by older party members, in particular Jang Song Thaek, Kim Kyong Hui, and Vice-Marshal Ri Yong Ho. In January 2011 Yi Kyong Sik replaced Kim Chang Sik as Minister of Agriculture, a post Yi was reported to have held previously between 2003 and 2008. Following a meeting of the SPA in April 2011 there were, contrary to expectations, no announcements of any new appointment for Kim Jong Un. A Vice-Premier, Ri Tae Nam, left his post for reasons of health. Ri Myong Su was appointed as Minister of People's Security, a position vacated in March by Ju Sang Song, also owing to ill health. Pak To Chun, an alternate member of the KWP Politburo, joined the membership of the National Defence Commission, replacing Jon Pyong Ho who was transferred to another post.

Humanitarian Issues

The DPRK's economic difficulties and widespread food shortages were exacerbated by unusually serious flooding in 1995 and 1996, forcing the country to appeal to the UN and other international organizations for emergency food aid and flood relief. Assistance was provided by the USA, the Republic of Korea and Japan in 1995, but in early 1996 further shipments of cereals were halted, pending a positive response by the DPRK to US proposals for peace negotiations (see Relations with the USA). Renewed appeals for emergency aid were issued by the UN in mid-1996, to which the USA, South Korea and Japan responded on humanitarian grounds. In January 1997 it was reported that China had agreed to provide 500,000 metric tons of rice annually for five years. This was followed, in February, by an unprecedented admission from the DPRK that the country was experiencing 'temporary food problems' and that it had only one-half of the cereals necessary to feed its people.

In April and July 1997 the UN's World Food Programme (WFP, see p. 107) issued two further appeals for food and medical supplies. UN representatives sent to the DPRK to assess the extent of the crisis confirmed that chronic malnutrition was widespread, particularly among infants, and that the medical system was no longer able to provide even basic health care. In that year severe drought devastated most of the North Korean maize crop, and in January 1998 WFP issued the largest appeal in the organization's history, requesting emergency aid of US $380m. Agreement was reached with the DPRK whereby additional UN staff were to be permitted to enter the country in order to monitor the distribution of aid, following allegations that previous supplies had been diverted to the army. Despite the provision of aid, severe food shortages persisted during 1998 and malnutrition was widespread among children. In mid-1999 WFP announced that increased aid had prevented starvation in the country for the time being, although poor infrastructure continued to hamper food distribution, and entry to 49 of the country's 211 counties was still forbidden. In August serious flooding destroyed large areas of farmland.

Severe weather conditions during 2000 and 2001, including both drought and flooding, exacerbated the situation. Although the harvest was believed to have improved somewhat in 2002, a large cereals deficit was envisaged for 2002/03. In February 2001 WFP agreed to provide US $93m. in aid and 810,000 tons of food, and in May South Korea began deliveries of 200,000 tons of agricultural fertilizer. In November 2003 the UN made a new appeal for humanitarian assistance for the DPRK. A survey conducted by WFP in 2004 concluded that 37% of North Korean children aged six years and under were chronically malnourished. In November the UN stated that, despite relatively good harvests in 2004, 6.4m. people would remain in need of food aid in 2005, owing in part to a dramatic increase in food prices as a consequence of price reforms in 2002. In January 2005 it was reported that government food rations, upon which approximately two-thirds of the population were believed to depend, were to be reduced from 300 g of grains per day to 250 g. In June the USA pledged to supply 50,000 tons of food aid, its third successive annual donation. In September, however, the North Korean Government announced that it had asked humanitarian aid agencies operating in the DPRK to terminate food aid programmes and withdraw the majority of their foreign staff by the end of the year. The Government asserted that, following a harvest that year reported to be the best in a decade, it was able to feed its people without assistance, and expressed a desire to progress from humanitarian to developmental aid. (Analysts speculated that the Government of the DPRK preferred to rely on food aid from China and the Republic of Korea, as the distribution of aid from these countries was monitored less closely and the political implications of allowing Westerners access to the country were thereby avoided.) WFP operations in North Korea were temporarily suspended in early 2006.

Severe flooding in July 2006 prompted the North Korean Government to seek further humanitarian aid, and by October WFP was warning of renewed famine conditions. The shortage of food was exacerbated by the reluctance of donor nations to give aid to the DPRK following its missile tests in July and October. A report published by FAO in January 2007 estimated that the number of malnourished people in the DPRK had risen to 7.9m. in the period 2001–03. The DPRK suffered further severe flooding in August 2007, which led to 600 deaths and left more than 100,000 people homeless, as well as causing widespread damage to infrastructure and losses of cereal crops. In response, the UN and the Red Cross launched international appeals for funding, while WFP announced plans to provide emergency food aid for 215,000 people over a three-month period. South Korea, which had resumed deliveries of fertilizer to the North in March and of food aid in June, pledged aid worth US $47.5m. A typhoon in September led to further flooding of farm land and the destruction of buildings. FAO estimated that the import of more than 1m. metric tons of cereals would be required during 2007/08.

In April 2008 WFP warned of a humanitarian crisis, the food deficit for the coming year having been revised upwards to 1.66m. metric tons, more than double the shortfall of 2007. By May 2008 reports were emerging of deaths in certain provinces, prompting fears that a crisis on the scale of the famine of the 1990s was developing. The scope of WFP activities in the DPRK was to be increased under an agreement concluded with the North Korean Government in June. In September, following an appeal from the DPRK, WFP initiated an emergency operation, envisaging expenditure of US $504m. In March 2009, however, it was revealed that WFP operations in the country had been substantially scaled down, owing to serious funding difficulties, and that aid had reached only 15% of the extent originally planned. Of the 6.2m. vulnerable people scheduled to receive WFP support, only 2m. were in fact receiving food assistance, with many rations being incomplete. The revaluation of the currency in December (see above) led to further hardship, with widespread food shortages being reported. In February 2010 it was estimated that the previous year's cereals harvest had fallen short of requirements by some 1.3m. tons.

In July 2010 the human rights organization Amnesty International published a report, based on evidence from North Koreans who had left the country, describing seriously inadequate health facilities there; however, the report was criticized as being outdated by the World Health Organization. In August and September heavy flooding, followed by typhoon damage, was reported; the South Korean Red Cross offered aid worth US $8.4m. for the victims. In early 2011 an outbreak of foot-and-mouth disease among North Korean livestock was expected to lead to the deaths of thousands of animals, exacerbating food shortages. In January the Government of the DPRK asked WFP to conduct a new survey of food requirements, citing the effects of a severe winter, and in February North Korean embassies were ordered to request food aid from foreign governments; however, most were only willing to provide this under UN supervision, owing to concerns that the food would be reserved for the armed forces. In March the UN reported that more than 6m. North Koreans were in urgent need of food aid, recommending the provision of 430,000 metric tons.

Inter-Korean Relations

After the consolidation of power in the North by Kim Il Sung, the DPRK's relations with the Republic of Korea remained tense. In 1971 discussions took place for the first time between the Red Cross Societies of North and South Korea. However, negotiations were suspended in 1973, and hopes for better relations were undermined by a series of clashes between North and South Korean vessels in disputed waters during 1974. Propaganda campaigns, suspended by agreement in 1972, were resumed by both sides. In October 1978 the UN Command (UNC—under which troops were stationed in South Korea) accused the DPRK of threatening the 1953 truce, after the discovery of an underground tunnel (the third since 1974) beneath the DMZ. During the 1980s the increasing prominence of Kim Jong Il, who advocated an uncompromising policy towards the South, appeared to aggravate the situation. In 1983 some 17 South Koreans, including four government ministers, were killed in a bomb explosion in Burma (now Myanmar), in what appeared to be an assassination attempt on the South Korean President, Chun Doo-Hwan. The DPRK was held responsible for the attack, and Burma severed relations with the country. In January 1984, none the less, the DPRK suggested tripartite discussions on reunification, involving North and South Korea and the USA, but the proposal was rejected by South Korea, which favoured bilateral talks. The DPRK's propaganda campaign was moderated, and in September North Korea provided emergency relief to flood-stricken areas of the South. In November the first discussions, on possible economic co-operation, were held, and negotiations continued in 1985. However, in February 1986, during the annual South Korean-US 'Team Spirit' military manoeuvres, North Korea suspended all negotiations with the South. The DPRK denied accusations of involvement in the explosion of a South Korean airliner over Burma in November 1987, despite the subsequent confession of an alleged North Korean agent. In August 1988 three sessions of talks were held at the 'peace village' of Panmunjom (in the DMZ) between delegates of the legislatures of North and South Korea, although the discussions (the first formal contact between the two countries since 1986) produced no conclusive results. Further negotiations in 1989 were suspended by the DPRK.

Inter-Korean discussions resumed in mid-1990, and in September the DPRK Premier visited the South Korean capital, Seoul, for discussions with his counterpart, the most senior-level bilateral contact since the end of the Korean War. Subsequent discussions culminated in the signing of an 'Agreement on Reconciliation, Non-aggression and Exchanges and Co-operation between the South and the North', in Seoul in December 1991. Both states pledged, *inter alia*, to desist from mutual slander, vilification and sabotage; to promote economic and other co-operation; to facilitate the reunion of families separated by the war; and to work towards a full peace treaty to replace the 1953 armistice agreement. In November 1992, however, the DPRK threatened a complete suspension of contacts with the South, in protest against the latter's decision to resume the 'Team Spirit' military exercises in March 1993. (The 1992 exercises had been cancelled, owing to the improvement in relations between the two states.) Relations had also been seriously impaired by the South's announcement, in October 1992, that an extensive North Korean espionage network had been discovered in South Korea, and by the North's repeated refusals to agree to simultaneous nuclear inspections in both countries.

While the controversy surrounding the DPRK's suspected nuclear programme continued, inter-Korean relations were strained by the DPRK's withdrawal in May 1994 of its mission to the Military Armistice Commission (the Panmunjom-based body overseeing the maintenance of the 1953 truce). Following discussions between Kim Il Sung and former US President Jimmy Carter, who visited the DPRK in June 1994, it was announced that the first summit meeting at presidential level between the two Korean states would be held in Pyongyang in July. However, the death of Kim Il Sung led to the indefinite postponement of the meeting. The signature of the US-DPRK nuclear accord in October caused South Korea to make renewed efforts to resume the inter-Korean negotiations, and in February 1995 the South announced the cancellation of the annual 'Team Spirit' manoeuvres (for the second consecutive year).

Tension increased markedly in April 1996, when the DPRK announced its decision to abandon the 1953 armistice. North Korean troops subsequently made a number of incursions into the DMZ, thereby violating the provisions of the agreement. Later in the month, in an attempt to revitalize the peace process and replace the armistice agreement with a formal peace treaty, President Bill Clinton of the USA and President Kim Young-Sam of the Republic of Korea proposed four-way talks, involving the two Koreas, the USA and China. China responded positively, but the DPRK declared its willingness to hold discussions only with the USA. In September 1996 a submarine from North Korea was discovered abandoned in South Korean waters. One of the two surviving crew members claimed that this was the fourth such mission by armed North Koreans. South Korea suspended all contact with the DPRK; the UN Security Council expressed 'serious concern' at the incident. Following mediation by the USA, an unprecedented apology was broadcast in South Korea by the official North Korean news agency.

After exploratory talks in March 1997 involving delegates from the DPRK, the Republic of Korea and the USA, the DPRK announced that its participation in full quadripartite negotiations was conditional upon the receipt of substantial food aid. In May representatives of the Red Cross organizations of North and South Korea reached agreement on the provision of grain to the DPRK. Negotiations were concluded in October to allow foreign airlines, including those from South Korea, to use North Korean airspace.

Despite a military confrontation between North and South Korean troops in the DMZ in July 1997, full quadripartite negotiations, aimed at concluding a peace treaty between North and South Korea, finally opened in Geneva, Switzerland, in December. A second round of full discussions was held in March 1998, but proved unsuccessful, since the DPRK continued to

THE DEMOCRATIC PEOPLE'S REPUBLIC OF KOREA (NORTH KOREA) *Introductory Survey*

insist on the inclusion on the agenda of the withdrawal of US troops from the Korean peninsula. In December 1997, meanwhile, negotiations in the Chinese capital of Beijing between the South and North Korean Red Cross organizations foundered, owing to North Korea's reluctance to allow South Korean officials access to the DPRK to monitor the distribution of food aid. At a subsequent meeting, in March 1998, the provision of additional food aid was agreed.

Following the inauguration of the new South Korean President, Kim Dae-Jung, in February 1998, the DPRK urged 'dialogue and negotiation' with the South Korean administration. Nevertheless, a ministerial-level meeting held in Beijing in April, to discuss the provision of fertilizer to North Korea (the first such direct contact for four years), failed when the South Koreans insisted that the DPRK enter into negotiations on the reunion of families. In that month, however, as part of Kim Dae-Jung's 'sunshine' policy of co-operation with the DPRK, the South Korean Government announced measures to encourage inter-Korean economic contacts, allowing the transfer of private funds to the North and relaxing legislation on investment. In June, in an historic development, Chung Ju-Yung, the founder of the South Korean conglomerate Hyundai, was permitted to cross the DMZ to deliver a gift of cattle to his home town; proposals for several joint ventures were also discussed, including a plan to operate tour boats to Mount Kumgang, just north of the border. This improvement in relations seemed to be in jeopardy when, during the visit, a North Korean submarine was caught in the nets of a South Korean fishing boat; all nine crew members were found dead inside the vessel. The UNC condemned the incursion during a meeting with North Korean army officers in Panmunjom, the first such discussions to be held in seven years. A further delivery of cattle was made by Chung Ju-Yung in October, when he also met with Kim Jong Il, and in November some 800 tourists from South Korea participated in the first tour to Mount Kumgang. In December, during Chung's third visit to North Korea, a proposal for the construction of an industrial complex at Haeju was approved. Following further visits in early 1999, it was announced that these would continue on a monthly basis. In December 1998, meanwhile, South Korean naval forces sank a suspected North Korean spy boat, after pursuing it into international waters.

In June 1999 a week-long confrontation between North and South Korean naval forces in the Yellow Sea resulted in a brief gun battle, during which one North Korean torpedo boat was sunk. Two rounds of bilateral discussions in Beijing in June and July ended in failure. In September the DPRK declared invalid the Northern Limit Line (the maritime border that had separated the territorial waters of the two Koreas since 1953), in protest against the UNC's refusal to renegotiate its demarcation. Meanwhile, no discernible progress had been achieved at sessions of the quadripartite discussions held in April and August 1999. None the less, Hyundai proceeded with its plans for a number of projects in North Korea: in October the company concluded an agreement with the DPRK on the construction of the proposed industrial complex, which, it was envisaged, would eventually comprise about 850 businesses, employing 220,000 people, and would be capable of producing export goods worth an estimated US $3,000m. annually. In December another major South Korean company, Samsung Electronics, announced that it had signed a contract with the DPRK for the joint development of computer software and the manufacture of electronic products. In February 2000 the construction of a motor vehicle assembly plant, in a joint venture with the Pyonghwa Motor Company of South Korea, began in Nampo, south-west of Pyongyang. According to South Korean estimates, inter-Korean trade increased by 50.2% in 1999.

The summit meeting of 2000 and subsequent events

In June 2000 an historic summit meeting took place between Kim Jong Il and Kim Dae-Jung in Pyongyang, following which detailed agreements were signed pledging the promotion of economic co-operation, the building of mutual trust and the resolution of reunification issues. In July ministerial-level delegations from both countries met in Seoul. This was the first visit to the South by North Korean officials since 1991. A joint communiqué was issued allowing for, *inter alia*, the reopening of liaison offices at Panmunjom, which had been closed in 1996, and the reconnection of the inter-Korean Kyongui railway line. The construction of a highway to run alongside the railway from North to South was subsequently agreed. In September 2000 Kim Dae-Jung formally inaugurated the project to remove thousands of land-mines and rebuild the railway line and adjacent highway. Meanwhile, in August 100 North Korean families travelled to Seoul and 100 South Korean families visited Pyongyang simultaneously to meet with relatives from whom they had been separated by the Korean War. The second ministerial meeting between the two sides was held in Pyongyang later in that month. It was agreed to hold more cross-border family reunions and to commence discussions on economic co-operation.

In a symbolic display of unity, in September 2000 the two countries marched under the same flag in the opening ceremony of the Olympic Games in Sydney, Australia. In late September the DPRK's Minister of the People's Armed Forces, Vice-Marshal Kim Il Chol, visited the South and met his counterpart, Cho Seong-Tae, the first such ministerial meeting ever held. In October Kim Dae-Jung was awarded the Nobel Peace Prize in recognition of his reunification efforts. Further sessions of inter-ministerial, military and economic talks took place during 2000 and early 2001, and further family reunions were arranged by the North and South Korean Red Cross organizations. However, in its annual defence policy document published in December 2000, South Korea described the North as its main enemy and alleged that the DPRK had expanded its military capacity along the DMZ. The North Korean Government was also displeased by the approval of a resolution in the South Korean legislature to demand the repatriation of prisoners of war who, it alleged, remained in detention in the North.

In early 2001 the uncompromising attitude displayed by the new US Administration of President George W. Bush towards North Korea threatened to undermine the reconciliation process. In March the DPRK unilaterally postponed scheduled cabinet-level discussions following a visit to the USA by Kim Dae-Jung, and in April North Korea denounced joint US-South Korean military exercises as a betrayal of the goodwill surrounding the June 2000 summit meeting. Ministerial discussions resumed in Seoul in September 2001, the sixth round of which was concluded in November without any agreement—the first such unsuccessful round since the presidential summit meeting.

President Bush's reference in January 2002 to North Korea as part of an 'axis of evil' threatened seriously to damage inter-Korean relations. However, in April the North received Kim Dae-Jung's special envoy, Lim Dong-Won. Following the visit, during which Lim met Kim Jong Il, the two sides agreed to further reunions for separated families and to continuing discussions on economic co-operation. The DPRK also agreed to Lim's request that it renew dialogue with the USA and Japan. In May Park Geun-Hye, a South Korean legislator and the daughter of former President Park Chung-Hee, visited the North and met Kim Jong Il. The visit was remarkable because North Korean agents had killed Park's mother in 1974 in an attempt to assassinate her father. Despite the cordial visit, North Korea cancelled economic co-operation discussions with the South in May 2002. Also in May, the increasing number of defectors from the North received international attention as several groups sought asylum at Canadian, Japanese and South Korean diplomatic buildings in China. They were eventually allowed to travel to the South, via the Philippines.

At the end of June 2002 a gun battle between North and South Korean vessels in the Yellow Sea resulted in the sinking of a Southern patrol boat and the deaths of six crew members. South Korean military sources estimated that 30 North Korean crewmen were also killed in the confrontation, which had started when two North Korean vessels accompanying a fishing boat reportedly crossed the Northern Limit Line. Following the incident, in July South Korea suspended rice shipments to the North and economic co-operation projects, reflecting widespread public anger. None the less, Kim Dae-Jung maintained his 'sunshine' policy towards the North.

In August 2002 North and South Korea held a seventh round of ministerial discussions in Seoul, aimed at improving relations in the aftermath of the latest naval confrontation, and focusing on the issue of future family reunions, railway links and cultural exchanges. In September the first inter-Korean military 'hotline' was inaugurated to allow for improved communications during sensitive occasions.

The eighth round of ministerial talks was held in Pyongyang in October 2002 and mainly focused on economic co-operation issues, despite the fact that the USA had earlier revealed the existence of a secret nuclear weapons programme in the North. At the end of that month a North Korean economic delegation began a nine-day tour of the South, including several major industrial facilities in the itinerary. The delegation included Jang Song Thaek, Kim Jong Il's brother-in-law and reportedly one of his most trusted advisers, and also Kim Hi Thaek, the first deputy head of the KWP's Central Committee. At the end of December the South Korean Ministry of National Defence published a 'white paper', which, for the first time, excluded any reference to the North as its main enemy.

The election in December 2002 of Roh Moo-Hyun, the candidate of Kim Dae Jung's party, as President of the Republic of Korea heralded a continuation of Kim's 'sunshine' policy. However, during 2003 relations between the DPRK and the USA deteriorated over the issue of the former's nuclear weapons programme, and in May North Korea announced that it no longer recognized a Joint Declaration of the Denuclearization of the Korean Peninsula, signed with the South in 1992. North Korea warned that the South would risk 'unspeakable disaster' if it became too confrontational in co-operating with the USA on the nuclear issue (the threat followed a summit meeting between Roh and US President George W. Bush). Attempts to develop inter-Korean relations were also complicated by confirmation in June 2003 by South Korean investigators that former President Kim Dae-Jung had arranged for the Korea Development Bank to give a Hyundai affiliate substantial funds to transfer to the North in order to finance the historic inter-Korean summit meeting of 2000. In August 2003 the suicide of Hyundai official Chung Mong-Hun, who had been indicted in connection with the illegal payments to the North, further undermined the credibility of the 'sunshine' policy.

In April 2004, following a major railway accident in North Korea at Ryongchon, the DPRK accepted emergency supplies and assistance from South Korea. In May senior-level military discussions took place between the two sides, at which the establishment of a radio communication line between the North and South Korean navies was agreed. It was believed that the new communication line would reduce naval conflicts between the two sides, although later in the year there were none the less incidents of warning shots being fired by the South Korean navy at North Korean vessels considered to have intruded across the maritime border, amid accusations that in some instances South Korean navy officials had failed to report North Korean radio messages. In July more than 450 North Korean defectors arrived in Seoul. The DPRK subsequently accused South Korean officials of kidnapping its citizens and suspended bilateral dialogue. By the end of 2004 the number of North Koreans who had defected to South Korea had reportedly exceeded 6,000.

In May 2005 South Korea undertook to provide 200,000 metric tons of fertilizer to ease the DPRK's food supply problems. Three North Korean freighters reportedly docked at Ulsan in South Korea to load the fertilizer later in the month, this being the first time since 1984 that North Korean ships had docked in a South Korean port. In July 2005 the 15th ministerial discussions between North and South Korea, held in Seoul, concluded with a 12-point joint statement in which the two sides pledged, *inter alia*, to reopen military talks, continue reunions for separated families and hold North-South Red Cross discussions on the question of South Korean soldiers and civilians allegedly abducted to North Korea during and after the 1950–53 war, more than 1,000 of whom, according to the South Korean Government, remained in detention in the North. Further ministerial discussions were held in September and December. Meanwhile, a sizeable delegation from the DPRK, headed by Kim Ki Nam, a member of the KWP Politburo's Secretariat, travelled to Seoul in August to participate in celebrations commemorating the 60th anniversary of the liberation of the Korean peninsula from Japanese rule. In November it was announced that North and South Korea would present joint teams at the 2006 Asian Games in Doha, Qatar, and at the 2008 Olympic Games in Beijing, China. In March 2006 military negotiations were held between the two Koreas in the DMZ, following a break of some two years; these were reportedly the most senior-level military talks between the two sides since the 1953 armistice. However, the Government of the DPRK postponed the scheduled 18th round of ministerial discussions between the two sides in protest against the South's conduct of joint military exercises with the USA.

Relations between the two Koreas were strained further throughout 2006, mainly as a result of the DPRK's missile tests (see The North Korean Nuclear Programme). The testing of the intercontinental *Taepo Dong 2* missile on 5 July prompted the Republic of Korea to announce an indefinite suspension of food aid; however, it insisted that business co-operation, notably at Kaesong and Mount Kumgang, would not be affected. In response, the DPRK suspended family reunions. Aid was resumed after North Korea suffered severe flooding later in that month, with the South Korean Government granting US $10.5m. to the North via non-governmental organizations (NGOs) in August, followed by supplies of rice and equipment. However, the testing of a nuclear device by the North on 9 October placed this emergency aid programme in jeopardy. While again pledging to continue its economic co-operation in Kaesong and Mount Kumgang (despite express US pleas for these links to be severed), the South Korean Government announced an indefinite suspension of humanitarian aid. (However, NGOs continued to provide relief shipments.) Although the South Korean Minister of Foreign Affairs, Ban Ki-Moon, reportedly stated that the DPRK deserved sanctions under the UN Security Council Resolution, he also urged a resumption of dialogue. The South Korean Government refused to join the US-led Proliferation Security Initiative, which provided for the stopping and searching of North Korean ships that were suspected of carrying materials for use in nuclear, chemical or biological weapons, and in early November President Roh undertook to continue his policy of engagement with the North Korean Government. None the less, in a reversal of previous policy, in mid-November the Republic of Korea supported a UN resolution condemning the DPRK's human rights record (in previous votes it had been absent or abstained). Furthermore, a South Korean defence policy document published at the end of December described the DPRK as a 'serious threat' to the South—the most strongly worded assessment since the inception of the latter's policy of engagement in 2000. It was reported in February 2007 that the number of defectors from North to South Korea since 1953 had reached 10,000.

Following the progress made in mid-February 2007 at six-party talks on North Korea's nuclear programme, North and South Korea held ministerial discussions later in that month, and in late March South Korea shipped 12,500 metric tons of fertilizer to the North. Family reunions were resumed, by video conference in late March and in person at Mount Kumgang in May. Inter-Korean talks on economic co-operation were held in Pyongyang in April, shortly after North Korea had failed to meet a deadline agreed in February for the closure of its nuclear reactor at Yongbyon. South Korea agreed to revive its food aid programme to the North, with the provision of 400,000 metric tons of rice, but only on condition that the DPRK demonstrate some progress in complying with its commitments under the February six-party accord. Senior-level military talks at Panmunjom in mid-May resulted in agreement on a trial run of trains along reinstated cross-border rail links and, in principle, on the creation of a joint fishing zone in the disputed Yellow Sea, where naval clashes had previously occurred. However, ministerial discussions in Seoul in late May and early June ended without progress, as South Korea continued to refuse to dispatch any rice to the North while the latter's pledge to shut down the Yongbyon reactor remained unfulfilled. In late June, as inspectors of the International Atomic Energy Agency (IAEA, see p. 118) were permitted to enter North Korea for the first time since December 2002, South Korea announced the resumption of food aid to the North with a first shipment of rice; the remainder of the promised 400,000 tons was delivered over the following six-month period. In accordance with the agreement of February 2007, the first instalment of a promised total of 50,000 tons of heavy fuel oil followed in July. None the less, senior-level military talks ended in late July without agreement on the disputed maritime boundary, the Northern Limit Line, which the DPRK refused to recognize, and in early August North and South Korean soldiers exchanged gunfire across the DMZ.

In early October 2007, in only the second meeting between the two countries' leaders since the Korean War, Kim Jong Il welcomed President Roh to Pyongyang for a three-day summit. Kim and Roh, who was approaching the end of his term of office, issued a declaration, in which they committed North and South Korea, *inter alia*, to working towards the replacement of the 1953 armistice agreement with a peace treaty; to making joint efforts for the smooth implementation of the six-party nuclear agreements; to creating a special 'peace zone' around Haeju; to establishing the planned joint fishing zone in the Yellow Sea; to expanding co-operation on economic and humanitarian projects; and to developing co-operation in a wide range of other areas (including education and technology). Several bilateral ministerial exchanges followed. A three-day visit to Seoul by Premier Kim Yong Il took place in mid-November 2007. During the first bilateral prime ministerial discussions since 1992 Kim and the South Korean Prime Minister, Han Duck-Soo, agreed on a timetable for resuming cross-border freight rail services and on the establishment of a joint committee to advance the creation of the 'peace zone' at Haeju.

Increasing tensions on the Korean peninsula

The conservative Lee Myung-Bak, who was elected President of South Korea in December 2007, advocated the adoption of a more uncompromising approach towards North Korea than that pursued over the preceding 10 years by Presidents Kim Dae-Jung and Roh Moo-Hyun: he demanded increased progress on denuclearization in return for the continuation of economic co-operation. In January 2008 President Lee announced plans to review the agreements reached at the inter-Korean summit in the previous October, and the Ministry of Unification was reduced in importance. None the less, Lee proposed the creation of a 37,500m. won investment fund for the DPRK if it abandoned its nuclear weapons programme, with the aim of raising the North's per caput income to US $3,000 within 10 years. In March North Korea expelled South Korean officials from Kaesong and test-fired missiles in the Yellow Sea. The North Korean Government was reportedly dissatisfied with Lee's association of humanitarian assistance with preconditions on nuclear disarmament and human rights. Tensions rose further in July, when a female South Korean tourist was shot dead by a North Korean soldier at Mount Kumgang, having allegedly crossed into a restricted area. In response, the South Korean Government halted tours to the area, while the North refused to participate in a joint investigation into the death, warning that it would expel all 'unnecessary' South Korean nationals from the resort. In November South Korea acted as the co-sponsor of a UN resolution criticizing human rights violations in the DPRK. Later in that month the North announced the suspension of non-military telephone connections with the South, as well as the closure of the border. In early March 2009, in their first, albeit brief, meeting since 2002, North Korean officials and UNC representatives had discussions at Panmunjom, in an attempt to reduce tensions.

In early March 2009 the North Korean Government again closed the border, in response to the holding of joint US-South Korean military exercises. Unable to cross the frontier, 80 South Korean workers were stranded at the Kaesong industrial estate. The border was then partially reopened only to be closed again without explanation. Similar, seemingly arbitrary closures of the border followed. In the same month a South Korean worker at Kaesong was arrested by the North Korean authorities for allegedly criticizing the DPRK. In May, following North Korea's testing of a nuclear device, South Korea undertook to join the Proliferation Security Initiative, whereupon North Korea declared that it no longer considered itself bound by the armistice agreement with the South, and would respond with military action if any of its vessels were seized and searched. In August, however, following a meeting between Kim Jong Il and the chairwoman of the Hyundai group, the DPRK Government announced that it would reopen the border and permit tourism and family reunions to resume, as well as release the Kaesong worker who had been detained since March. The first family reunions since 2007 duly took place in September 2009. It was reported that in October, during further discussions on family reunions, the DPRK requested 100,000 metric tons of food aid, but South Korea agreed to provide only about 20,000 tons.

In November 2009 North and South Korean naval vessels exchanged fire across the disputed maritime boundary (the first such incident for seven years), and in January 2010 there was a further exchange of land-based artillery fire across the maritime boundary. In March a South Korean naval vessel, the *Cheonan*, exploded and sank near the boundary, with the loss of 46 lives. The South Korean Government did not immediately accuse the DPRK of deliberately causing the disaster, and it was initially suggested that a mine dating from the 1950–53 war might have caused the explosion. However, in May a multinational team of experts concluded that the only plausible explanation for the explosion was that it had been caused by a torpedo from a North Korean submarine (see the chapter on the Republic of Korea). This was vehemently denied by the North Korean Government, which threatened to respond aggressively to any retaliation. Joint naval exercises undertaken by South Korea and the USA in July were described as an 'intolerable provocation' by the DPRK. In September, following severe flooding in the North, South Korea offered food aid, although the amount was criticized as inadequate by the Government of the DPRK. In the same month the DPRK suggested the organizing of further family reunions (which took place in late October). Also in September, discussions took place at Panmunjom between senior military officers, for the first time in two years, but they ended without agreement, reportedly after the South Korean representatives urged the North to apologize for the sinking of the *Cheonan* and to punish those responsible.

In May 2010 the Government of the DPRK denied allegations that it had dispatched agents to South Korea on a mission to murder Hwang Jang Yop, who to date remained the most senior North Korean defector. Two suspects had been arrested in connection with the alleged plot in the previous month. The elderly Hwang died in October, apparently of natural causes.

In November 2010 the DPRK fired artillery shells at the South Korean island of Yeonpyeong, where South Korean forces had been conducting a military exercise. The bombardment killed four people, including two civilians, injured several more and caused widespread damage. In the same month South Korea and the USA conducted further (previously planned) naval exercises in the Yellow Sea. South Korea announced the suspension of the aid that it had promised to the DPRK in September, after the floods. In February 2011 further discussions between military officers at Panmunjom again failed to lead to agreement on a possible meeting at a more senior level.

Economic and other co-operation with South Korea

As the DPRK's financial situation worsened, economic issues played an important part in inter-Korean relations from 2000. In January 2001 it was reported that the DPRK's energy shortages had reached crisis point, and that the country was desperately researching alternative power sources. A summit meeting took place between the two Koreas in February, at which the DPRK requested immediate and substantial electricity supplies to alleviate its needs. Frustration resulted from South Korean insistence on the necessity of on-site investigations prior to the commencement of deliveries. Meanwhile, in August 2000 Hyundai agreed to establish a technologically advanced industrial compound in Kaesong in the DPRK. However, financial problems at Hyundai delayed the implementation of the project. In March 2001 the future of the Mount Kumgang tourist initiative was jeopardized by its lack of profitability, and Hyundai appealed to the South Korean Government for assistance; the Government subsequently pledged 90,000m. won to maintain the tourist cruises. Progress on economic co-operation in Kaesong was made from 2002, with Kaesong being declared a special industrial zone in November of that year (see also Economic Affairs). In June 2003 the DPRK announced regulations for the development of the zone, as well as plans to develop an area of 3.3 sq km in a first phase of development extending to 2007. A South Korean company, Korea Land, was to invest around US $184m. in the project. These plans were finalized at a meeting of North and South Korean economic officials in November 2003. Although inter-Korean trade increased steadily, reportedly amounting to $700m. in 2003, South Korea shared international concerns over North Korea's suspected illicit trade in weapons and narcotics. It was reported that in April 2004 some 1,600 South Korean companies had applied for a lease in the Kaesong special industrial zone, and in June Korea Land selected the first 15 companies that were to be permitted to conduct business in the zone. In March 2005 the Korea Electric Power Corporation (KEPCO), of South Korea, began to supply electricity to Kaesong, representing the first cross-border flow of electricity since the peninsula's partition. In July the South Korean Minister of Unification reportedly proposed to Kim Jong Il that South Korea compensate the North with 2,000 MW of energy assistance if the latter were to abandon its nuclear weapons programme. However, the DPRK rejected the offer. In October the first joint governmental office operated by both North and South Korea, to handle cross-border economic projects, was opened in Kaesong, and in December the first commercial telephone link between Kaesong and Seoul opened.

The construction of the major infrastructural facilities at Kaesong, which began in June 2003, was completed in October 2007, marking the end of the development phase. The complex was scheduled to be fully operational by the end of 2010, when it was anticipated that some 450 companies, employing a total of 100,000 North Koreans, would be conducting business there. By November 2007 the number of companies from the Republic of Korea operating in Kaesong had reached 52, according to the South Korean Ministry of Unification, with more than 20,000 North Koreans working at the complex; by December 2009 there were reported to be 116 South Korean companies in Kaesong, employing about 42,000 North Korean workers. The construction of living quarters for 15,000 North Korean workers in Kaesong was scheduled to begin in 2008; however, as a result

THE DEMOCRATIC PEOPLE'S REPUBLIC OF KOREA (NORTH KOREA)

of the deterioration in relations between the two sides, the intermittent imposition of restrictions on cross-border travel impeded the development of the facilities. In June 2009 the DPRK demanded a quadrupling of workers' wages (which were paid directly to the North Korean Government), a payment of US $500m. for the use of the land, and the imposition of annual land-use fees with effect from 2010. In September 2009 it was announced that the two sides had agreed on a much smaller pay rise (of 5%) and were to reopen their joint administrative office in Kaesong, which had been closed since December 2008. In May 2010 South Korea suspended trade with the North, and several South Korean officials were expelled from Kaesong, after the conclusion by an international inquiry that the DPRK had been responsible for the earlier sinking of the South Korean naval vessel, the *Cheonan*; in January 2011 the DPRK offered to readmit the officials, but the South Korean Government stated that it would not send them back without a guarantee for their safety and an undertaking not to expel them again.

In the area of infrastructural development, negotiations to re-establish the inter-Korean rail link continued during 2001. It was hoped that such a link would create a new Eurasian transport corridor that would reduce the cost and time involved in the transit of goods from North-East Asia to European markets from 25 days to about 15 days, bringing economic benefits to all participants. Ground-breaking ceremonies for the reconnection of rail and road links were held on both sides of the DMZ in September 2002, and South Korea released a loan to the North to assist the funding of the work. In February 2003 the first road reconnecting the North with the South was completed, on the eastern coast of the Korean peninsula. In June rail links between the two Koreas were officially opened, although the connections remained largely symbolic, as construction on the North Korean side to link the new railways with wider networks was yet to be completed. In December 2004 it was reported that the road link along the eastern coast of the two Koreas had been opened to traffic. By late 2005 two major rail links between North and South Korea along the west and east coasts, with adjacent roads, were believed to be complete; however, the DPRK cancelled scheduled trial runs along the cross-border rail links in May 2006, citing military security issues. South Korea had also pledged to assist the DPRK in constructing several railway stations. Following senior-level military talks at Panmunjom, in May 2007 cross-border rail links were finally completed when, for the first time in more than 50 years, passengers were conveyed on trains travelling in each direction. At the inter-Korean summit held in October, it was decided to resume a cross-border freight rail service. A daily freight service, connecting the South with Kaesong, was duly launched in December, although North Korea continued to oppose the introduction of regular passenger services. Inter-Korean talks on improving rail links, which were held in January 2008, resulted in agreement on the need to repair the North Korean section of the reconnected railway. However, the rail service between the two sides was discontinued by the North in November.

The Inception of the DPRK's Nuclear Programme

In the early 1990s there was growing international concern that the DPRK had intensified its clandestine nuclear programme at Yongbyon, north of Pyongyang, and would soon be capable of manufacturing a nuclear weapon. During 1991 pressure was applied, by the USA and Japan in particular, for the DPRK to sign the Nuclear Safeguards Agreement (NSA) with the IAEA. This was required by the DPRK's signature, in 1985, of the Treaty on the Non-Proliferation of Nuclear Weapons (the Non-Proliferation Treaty—NPT), in order that IAEA representatives might be permitted to inspect the country's nuclear facilities. However, the DPRK consistently refused to allow such inspections to take place unless there was to be a simultaneous inspection (or withdrawal) of US nuclear weapons sited in South Korea. Tension was eased considerably by the USA's decision, in October 1991, to remove all its tactical nuclear weapons from South Korea, and by South Korea's subsequent declaration that it would not manufacture, deploy or use nuclear, chemical or biological weapons. In December the South Korean Government stated that all US nuclear weapons had been withdrawn, and proposed that simultaneous inspections of military bases in the South and nuclear facilities in the North be conducted. Later in the month the two Korean states concluded an agreement 'to create a non-nuclear Korean peninsula', and in January 1992 the DPRK signed the NSA. In March delegates of North and South, meeting at Panmunjom, agreed to form a Joint Nuclear Control Commission (JNCC) to permit inter-Korean nuclear inspections.

In May 1992 IAEA inspectors were permitted to visit North Korean nuclear facilities (the first in a series of official visits during that year). Despite the findings of the inspectors (who concluded that the Yongbyon plant was 'primitive' and far from completion, although potentially capable of producing plutonium), suspicions persisted regarding North Korean nuclear ambitions. Moreover, the DPRK repeatedly failed to agree to separate nuclear inspections by the JNCC, finally announcing in January 1993 its intention to boycott all future inter-Korean nuclear talks (in protest against the imminent resumption of the joint US-South Korean 'Team Spirit' military manoeuvres). In February the DPRK refused to allow IAEA inspections of two 'undeclared' sites near Yongbyon, claiming that these were military installations unrelated to nuclear activities. The DPRK announced in March that it was to withdraw from the NPT. In May the UN Security Council adopted a resolution urging the DPRK to reconsider its decision to withdraw from the NPT and to allow an inspection by the IAEA of the country's nuclear facilities. Following negotiations with the USA, the DPRK agreed to suspend its withdrawal from the NPT; in return, the USA agreed to assist the DPRK in the development of its non-military nuclear programme. International concern regarding the North Korean weapons programme was further heightened by the successful testing of a medium-range missile in May.

In February 1994, following further discussions between the DPRK and the USA, an agreement was reached whereby the IAEA would be allowed to visit all the country's declared nuclear facilities. In March, however, the inspectors were impeded in their efforts to remove samples from nuclear installations, and it was discovered that seals placed on nuclear materials by IAEA representatives during previous visits had been broken, leading the IAEA to conclude that the DPRK had, in all probability, produced more plutonium than had been admitted. In June the DPRK again threatened to withdraw from the NPT, and also to declare war against the Republic of Korea, if economic sanctions were imposed by the UN. In August the USA and the DPRK reached an agreement on the replacement of the latter's existing nuclear reactors by two light-water reactors, which were considered to be less easily adapted to the production of nuclear weaponry. The agreement also recommended the establishment of a restricted form of diplomatic representation between the two countries. Further negotiations in October led to the signing of an Agreed Framework whereby the USA undertook to establish an international consortium to finance and supply the light-water reactors, while the DPRK agreed to suspend operation of its existing reactors and halt construction at two further sites. To compensate for the DPRK's consequent shortfall in energy production until the new reactors were fully operational, the USA agreed to donate to the DPRK 500,000 metric tons annually of heavy fuel oil. IAEA inspectors travelled to Pyongyang to oversee the suspension of the country's nuclear programme.

In March 1995 several countries, led by the USA, the Republic of Korea and Japan, created the Korean Peninsula Energy Development Organization (KEDO). In December the DPRK and KEDO reached agreement on the details of implementing the October 1994 accord. In January 1996 the DPRK announced its willingness to permit routine inspections of its nuclear installations by the IAEA. In March KEPCO was commissioned by KEDO as the principal contractor for the construction of the light-water reactors. Discussions between KEDO and the DPRK to negotiate the terms of repayment by the latter of the construction costs of the light-water reactors were successfully concluded in April 1997.

Meanwhile, US energy experts began the sealing of spent fuel rods at the DPRK's nuclear facilities. However, North Korea's continued refusal to grant IAEA inspectors access to several contentious laboratories again provoked concern that the DPRK was developing its nuclear programme. Preparation of the nuclear-reactor site at Sinpo formally began in August 1997. Negotiations held in early 1998 between the participants in KEDO (which the European Union—EU—had joined in mid-1997) concerning the financing of the light-water reactors (estimated at US $5,170m.) proved difficult, and were further complicated by South Korea's financial problems, raising fears that progress on the project would be hindered. In June 1998 the North Korean Government admitted to having sold nuclear missiles abroad, claiming that such exports were necessary, given ongoing US economic sanctions against the DPRK. In September the DPRK agreed to resume sealing of spent fuel rods (which had been suspended earlier that year), while the USA promised to deliver the delayed shipment of heavy fuel oil. However, the US Congress was increasingly reluctant to approve financing for the purchase of fuel oil, obliging President Bill Clinton personally to authorize the disbursement of funds in October, in order to safeguard the 1994 nuclear accord.

Talks held during mid-1999 between the USA and the DPRK culminated in September in a decision by the USA to ease several long-standing economic sanctions (principally on non-military trade, travel and banking) against the DPRK. In return, the country agreed to suspend missile test-firing for the duration of negotiations with the USA. Discussions aimed at improving US-North Korean relations were held in Beijing in November 1999 and January 2000. Meanwhile, in November 1999 it was reported that the IAEA was supervising the final stage of the sealing of spent fuel rods at Yongbyon. After several months of delays caused by disputes over the division of the costs of the project, in December KEDO and KEPCO finally signed the contract for the construction of the two light-water reactors; in February 2000 it was reported that construction of the reactors was unlikely to be completed before 2007, some four years later than scheduled. In November 2000 North Korea, frustrated by the delay, threatened to restart missile testing unless construction of the reactors was accelerated. The DPRK denied the IAEA's claim that delays were due to the former's refusal to allow nuclear inspections.

In June 2000 the North Korean Government confirmed its moratorium on test flights of ballistic missiles. In July the USA rejected the DPRK's demand for annual payments from the USA of US $1,000m. in return for the curtailment of weapons exports. The fundamental issues of missile development and export remained unresolved. A planned visit to Pyongyang by the outgoing US President, Bill Clinton, was cancelled in December when the DPRK rejected a US proposal that the two sides prepare a draft missile accord to form a basis for talks. In early 2001 the new Administration of George W. Bush adopted a less conciliatory stance towards the DPRK, refusing to grant economic aid unless transparency in North Korea's missile production and export was assured and verified. Since the late 1990s elements in Bush's Republican Party had been strongly arguing in favour of a planned 'national missile defence' (NMD) system to protect the USA from long-range missile attack, and had frequently cited North Korea as a developer and exporter of such missiles; it was feared that the DPRK had developed an intercontinental ballistic missile, the *Taepo Dong 2*, capable of striking the west coast of the USA. Bush's commitment to develop NMD was denounced by the DPRK, which responded by threatening to abandon the 1994 framework, and to resume ballistic missile testing. In June 2001 President Bush sought to broaden discussions with North Korea about its missile programme to include nuclear technology and a reduction of the country's conventional forces. The North responded that discussions on the latter would take place only following the withdrawal of the 37,000 US troops from the South, and that it was also seeking financial compensation for the delay in building KEDO's two light-water reactors, which were now not expected to be completed until 2008 at the earliest. In October 2001 the North rejected suggestions by the head of the IAEA and later by US officials that inspections of its nuclear facilities were necessary; however, in December it agreed to limited international access to certain laboratories. (See Relations with the USA for subsequent developments.)

Foreign Affairs

The DPRK's international relations have been dominated by its hostility to the USA and to perceived US influence in South Korea, resulting in belligerent official rhetoric and actions, despite the country's chronic need for economic assistance. China, North Korea's principal ally, has played an important role in persuading the DPRK to take part in international negotiations. The DPRK's unilateral application for UN membership, first announced in May 1991, represented a radical departure from its earlier insistence that the two Koreas should occupy a single UN seat. This development was welcomed by the Republic of Korea, and both countries were admitted separately to the UN in September of that year. In September 1999, for the first time in seven years, the North Korean Minister of Foreign Affairs attended and addressed the annual session of the UN General Assembly, in what was perceived as an attempt to end the DPRK's diplomatic isolation.

Relations with China

The DPRK's relations with the People's Republic of China remained a crucial focus of North Korean foreign policy. During the years of the so-called Sino-Soviet dispute the DPRK fluctuated in its allegiance to each of its powerful northern neighbours, China and the USSR. Kim Il Sung made several official visits to China in the late 1980s, which were interpreted by some Western observers as an attempt to establish closer relations in view of the erosion of communist power in many Eastern European countries. However, the DPRK was aggrieved at China's establishment of full diplomatic relations with the Republic of Korea in August 1992. China appeared largely conciliatory with regard to North Korea's nuclear programme, and during 1993 and the first months of 1994 indicated that it would veto any attempt by the UN Security Council to impose economic sanctions on the DPRK. In 1997 China agreed to provide substantial food aid to the DPRK to alleviate the effects of flooding. Later in that year China accepted US and South Korean proposals for quadripartite negotiations with North Korea to conclude a new peace agreement with the South, and between December 1997 and August 1999 it participated in all six rounds of these negotiations. A senior North Korean delegation visited China in June 1999. During the visit China announced that it would provide the country with 150,000 metric tons of food aid and 400,000 tons of coke over the following months. In October 1999 the Chinese Minister of Foreign Affairs participated in celebrations held in Pyongyang to commemorate the 50th anniversary of the establishment of diplomatic relations between the two countries.

In late 1999 international attention was focused on the uncertain situation of the large number of North Koreans (estimated at some 30,000 by South Korean sources and at 200,000 by the voluntary organization Médecins Sans Frontières) who had crossed the border into China in recent years. In early 2000 it was reported that China had returned some 10,000 escapees to the DPRK during 1999. The number of migrants was thought to fluctuate, according to the season.

In February 2000 China permitted the DPRK to open a consulate-general in Hong Kong. In May Kim Jong Il visited China, his first official trip abroad for 17 years. In January 2001 the North Korean leader paid a second visit to the People's Republic. During this visit Kim had extensive discussions with Chinese leaders in Beijing, and also toured the new business zones of Shanghai and Shenzhen. In September the Chinese President, Jiang Zemin, undertook an official visit to North Korea, the first such visit since 1990. Jiang promised an additional 200,000 metric tons of food aid and 30,000 tons of diesel oil to alleviate North Korea's economic crisis.

During 2002 the DPRK and China continued to seek the reconnection of the inter-Korean railway lines and their subsequent linking to China's own railway system. In May, however, China's forcible removal of North Korean refugees from South Korean embassy premises in the People's Republic again brought the issue of the refugees to international attention. Several groups of North Korean refugees had, in 2002, fled to Western, Japanese and South Korean diplomatic offices in China, embarrassing the latter, since the Chinese Government had signed a treaty with the DPRK providing for the repatriation of refugees. In June China allowed 24 North Korean refugees who had been concealed in the embassy of the Republic of Korea to leave for that country. After that incident, China began an operation against South Korean activists and missionaries who had been helping North Koreans to flee via China. It was estimated that as many as 300,000 North Korean refugees were already residing in China, with US sources stating that as many as 50,000 had fled to China in 2001 alone.

In February 2003 the President of the DPRK's SPA Presidium, Kim Yong Nam, visited Beijing and undertook to maintain strong bilateral relations. In March China suspended its oil supply to the DPRK via a pipeline from Liaoning Province for three days, following North Korean missile tests. In April China hosted and participated in senior-level meetings between the DPRK and the USA over the North Korean nuclear weapons programme. Immediately prior to the discussions, Vice-Marshal Jo Myong Rok, the DPRK's second highest ranking official, led a military delegation to China, and held meetings with President Hu Jintao and senior military leaders. Chinese diplomatic efforts played a major role in ensuring North Korean participation in the first round of six-party talks on the nuclear issue that were held in Beijing in August (as well as in subsequent rounds—see above). In April 2004 Kim Jong Il made a secretive visit to China, where he held talks with President Hu and other officials. Topics

THE DEMOCRATIC PEOPLE'S REPUBLIC OF KOREA (NORTH KOREA) *Introductory Survey*

under discussion included the nuclear issue, with China reportedly urging the DPRK to modify its stance, and economic matters. During 2004 repeated instances of defectors from the DPRK seeking refuge in foreign embassies in Beijing posed a dilemma for China, which as an official ally of the DPRK continued to refuse to grant refugee status to such persons. Many defectors were none the less able to travel to Seoul via a third country. In November, however, China forcibly repatriated a group of 70 North Korean nationals. It was believed that they would be imprisoned and possibly executed upon their return to the DPRK. In March 2005 the North Korean Premier, Pak Pong Ju, visited Beijing and Shanghai. Chinese diplomacy received considerable credit for the achievement of the joint draft agreement at the end of the fourth round of six-party talks in September. In October President Hu made his first official visit to Pyongyang, in advance of the fifth round of discussions in November. In January 2006 reports emerged that Kim Jong Il had travelled incognito to the People's Republic and was again visiting the special economic zone of Shenzhen, to observe China's economic modernization. The visit was confirmed by North Korean media only after Kim's return.

The DPRK's relations with China deteriorated in October 2006, however, following the North Korean nuclear weapon test. The test embarrassed the Chinese Government, which had repeatedly urged the DPRK to forgo its plans. Somewhat unexpectedly, China agreed to UN sanctions against the country, while ensuring that they did not contain a threat of military action. Moreover, the Chinese Government indicated that North Korean refugees being sheltered in a US consulate in northeastern China would be allowed to travel to the Republic of Korea or the USA (a transfer that China had originally opposed), and stated that it would no longer object to Japan raising the issue of the abduction of Japanese citizens by North Korea at the six-party talks. China helped to broker another diplomatic advance at the end of October, when the DPRK indicated that it was willing to rejoin the six-way nuclear talks. China was also reported to have permitted the release of funds from the accounts of DPRK officials held in Banco Delta Asia the following month. In September 2007 China provided North Korea with 50,000 metric tons of fuel oil, in accordance with the agreement reached in February at the six-party talks, which China continued to host. Following the DPRK's failure to meet the deadline for the disablement of its nuclear facilities and disclosure of its nuclear activities, in late January 2008 the head of the Chinese Communist Party's international liaison department visited Pyongyang to urge Kim Jong Il to comply with his commitments under the six-party agreement. During a visit to Beijing in late February US Secretary of State Condoleezza Rice urged the Chinese Government to use its influence to persuade the DPRK to implement the agreement fully. The newly appointed Chinese Vice-President, Xi Jinping, who was frequently described as a potential successor to President Hu Jintao, chose North Korea as the destination for his first official visit, meeting with Kim Jong Il and other senior officials in June 2008.

Following the DPRK's launch of a long-range ballistic missile, purporting to be a satellite, in April 2009, China joined the UN Security Council's unanimous condemnation of the launch, but expressed opposition to any new sanctions that might exacerbate the situation. After the DPRK tested its second nuclear device in late May, China stated that it was resolutely opposed to the test, urged the DPRK to return to negotiations, and concurred with the UN Security Council's resolution on stricter sanctions, agreed in June. In October Chinese Premier Wen Jiabao visited the DPRK, and it was reportedly his influence that led Kim Jong Il to announce, during the visit, that the DPRK was ready to return to the six-party negotiations on its nuclear programme. In May 2010, in what was believed to be his first departure from the DPRK since 2006, Kim Jong Il embarked upon a visit to China, travelling by train to the Chinese city of Dalian and thence to Beijing. Following the visit, during which Kim had discussions with both the Chinese President and Prime Minister, it was reported that the North Korean leader had declared his commitment to ending the country's nuclear programme and expressed his intention to create conditions favourable to the resumption of the six-party talks. Kim Jong Il paid another visit to China in August 2010, reportedly accompanied by his son, Kim Jong Un, and in November the Premier of the DPRK, Choe Yong Rim, spent eight days touring various industrial sites in China, particularly in Jilin Province, adjoining North Korea. Meanwhile, despite the conclusion by international investigators in May that the sinking of a South Korean naval vessel in March had been caused by a North Korean torpedo (see Inter-Korean Relations), China had refused to support a UN Security Council resolution condemning the action: China merely referred to the incident as unfortunate, and described subsequent joint South Korean and US naval exercises as unnecessarily confrontational. Following the bombardment of the South Korean island of Yeonpyeong by the DPRK in November, China expressed concern and urged both countries to display restraint.

Relations with Japan

The DPRK's relations with Japan have been characterized by continuing hostility towards the latter as a result of the atrocities committed in Korea during the Japanese occupation of 1910–45. The North Korean Government had demanded thousands of millions of dollars in compensation from Japan, before normal relations could be restored. In the 1980s, following the testimony of defectors, Japan began to suspect that North Korean agents had kidnapped a number of Japanese citizens during the late 1970s and early 1980s. Japan imposed sanctions on the DPRK after North Korean agents were accused of attempting to assassinate the South Korean President in Burma in 1983. Following the destruction of a South Korean aircraft in 1987, allegedly by North Korean agents posing as Japanese citizens (see above), Japan reimposed sanctions during 1988; the DPRK then severed diplomatic contacts with Japan, although mutual trade continued. From late 1990 there was a significant rapprochement between the DPRK and Japan, and in January 1991 a Japanese government delegation visited Pyongyang for discussions concerning the possible normalization of diplomatic relations. The Japanese delegation offered apologies, on behalf of its Government, for Japanese colonial aggression on the Korean peninsula between 1910 and 1945. Moreover, the Japanese Government expressed its willingness to make reparations for Japanese abuses of human rights in Korea during this period. However, subsequent negotiations in 1991 foundered, owing to the DPRK's demand for reparations for damage inflicted after 1945 (which the Japanese Government denied) and to Japan's insistence that North Korea's nuclear installations be opened to outside inspection; normalization talks collapsed in November 1992, as the North Korean delegation abandoned the proceedings. Relations with Japan were further strained after the DPRK's testing of the *Rodong-1* missile in the Sea of Japan (also known as the East Sea) in May 1993. The missile, according to US intelligence reports, would be capable of reaching most of Japan's major cities (and possibly of carrying either a conventional or a nuclear warhead). None the less, Japan, like the Republic of Korea, opposed the possible imposition of international economic sanctions on the DPRK in response to North Korea's refusal to allow inspections of its nuclear facilities. In March 1995 a Japanese parliamentary group visited the DPRK and reached an agreement for the resumption of normalization talks later in that year. In May Japan agreed to North Korea's request for emergency rice aid, and later in the year Japan provided aid to help the DPRK overcome the effects of serious flooding. In early 1996 Japan provided a shipment of fuel oil to alleviate the DPRK's energy shortfall.

Relations were complicated in 1997 by Japanese allegations that North Korea had abducted several Japanese citizens during the 1970s. However, in August 1997, for the first time since 1992, negotiations opened on the restoration of normal bilateral relations. An agreement was signed whereby some 1,800 Japanese women married to North Koreans, who had never been permitted to leave the DPRK, were to be allowed to visit their relatives in Japan for short periods; the first such visits took place in November 1997 and January 1998. Moreover, in October 1997 the Japanese Government resumed the provision of aid to North Korea, suspended since mid-1996, donating food and medical supplies in response to the renewed appeals issued by the UN. In mid-1998, however, the North Korean Government cancelled a third visit of the Japanese women to their homeland, following Japan's rejection of a North Korean investigation into the alleged abduction of Japanese nationals. The testing by the DPRK of a suspected *Taepo Dong* missile over Japanese territory in August prompted Japan to break off normalization talks, suspend food aid and postpone its contribution to the KEDO project. The DPRK subsequently claimed that the object launched was in fact a satellite.

In March 1999 Japanese naval forces pursued and opened fire on suspected North Korean spy ships that had infiltrated Japanese waters. However, relations improved following the DPRK's agreement with the USA, in September, to suspend its reported plans to test a new long-range missile. In December, following a successful visit to the DPRK by a group of Japanese parliamentarians, Japan announced an end to its ban on food aid. Later in that month intergovernmental preparatory discussions on re-establishing diplomatic relations were held in Beijing. Progress was achieved by the Japanese and North Korean Red Cross Societies at a meeting in March 2000. It was reported that the DPRK had agreed to co-operate in a further investigation into the fate of some 10 missing Japanese nationals, while Japan had agreed to a search for Korean citizens who had disappeared prior to 1945. In addition, visits to their homeland by Japanese women married to North Koreans were to resume, and Japan was to provide some 100,000 metric tons of rice to the DPRK through WFP. In late April 2000 Japanese charter flights to North Korea resumed. Following informal contacts between the North Korean and Japanese Governments, full normalization talks commenced in April; further rounds of discussions took place during the year.

In September 2000 the long-delayed third visits home by the Japanese wives of North Korean men took place. In October Japan decided, on humanitarian grounds, to provide 500,000 metric tons of rice to North Korea. In December the DPRK reiterated that normal relations with Japan could be restored only after the latter delivered an apology and compensation for its earlier colonial rule. In May 2001 Japan deported Kim Jong Nam, son of Kim Jong Il, for entering the country on a false passport. In December a suspected North Korean spy vessel was sunk by Japanese coastguard forces after it had been expelled from Japan's exclusive economic zone. The DPRK condemned the incident, accusing Japan of seeking to mislead world opinion. In February 2002 the DPRK released a Japanese journalist who had been detained on spying charges since December 1999.

In an unexpected development, Junichiro Koizumi visited Pyongyang in September 2002, becoming the first incumbent Japanese Prime Minister to do so. His one-day visit, during which he held discussions with Kim Jong Il, elicited the latter's admission that North Korean agents had abducted 12 Japanese citizens in the 1970s and 1980s, of whom five were still alive. Kim apologized for the incidents, attributing them to rogue elements within the security services. The surviving captives were temporarily allowed to return to Japan in October 2002, although they had to leave behind any spouses or children. Among the abductees allowed to return was Hitomi Soga, the wife of Charles Jenkins, a US soldier who in 1965 was believed to have defected to the DPRK where he had since remained. The Japanese authorities then refused to allow the abductees to return to the DPRK.

In October 2002 the alleged admission by North Korean officials to their visiting US counterparts that the DPRK was pursuing a secret nuclear weapons programme greatly alarmed Japan. In separate incidents in February and March 2003, the DPRK test-launched two short-range ground-to-ship missiles in the Sea of Japan, and in April tested a third missile in the Yellow Sea. However, it refrained from testing longer-range ballistic missiles, which Japan considered a threat to its security. In March the DPRK Government condemned Japan's launching of two spy satellites, believed to be part of a programme of intelligence-gathering on the DPRK initiated following the suspected testing of the North Korean *Taepo Dong* missile over Japan in 1998. In October 2003 the DPRK announced that it did not wish Japan to participate in future negotiations on its nuclear weapons programme.

In January 2004 the Japanese House of Representatives approved legislation to permit the imposition of economic sanctions on the DPRK; in April legislation was approved requiring all ships entering Japanese ports from March 2005 to be insured against oil damage. This in practice amounted to a ban on entry of all but 16 of an estimated 100 North Korean ships that were involved in trade with Japan. Following a second visit by Japanese Prime Minister Koizumi to Pyongyang in May 2004, five children of the abductees who had returned to Japan in 2002 (see above) were permitted to fly to Tokyo. Their release had been secured in return for pledges of food aid and medical supplies. However, suspicions remained over the fate of other missing Japanese nationals. In July 2004 the former US soldier Charles Jenkins, husband of the Japanese abductee Hitomi Soga, travelled to Indonesia with his two daughters and was reunited with his wife.

In November 2004 the DPRK relinquished human remains, which it claimed were those of Megumi Yokota, who had been kidnapped by North Korean agents in 1977. The DPRK claimed that she had committed suicide. However, subsequent DNA tests indicated that the remains were not those of Megumi Yokota. North Korea refused to accept the results of the tests. The Japanese Government subsequently suspended its food aid.

Japan remained reluctant to impose direct economic sanctions on the DPRK, not wishing to jeopardize negotiations on the nuclear weapons programme. The six-party agreement of September 2005 contained a clause whereby the two countries undertook to 'take steps to normalize their relations'. In February 2006 inconclusive bilateral discussions incorporated the issues of the alleged abductions of Japanese citizens, the development of ballistic missiles by the DPRK and the resumption of the nuclear negotiations.

In June 2006 the Japanese legislature enacted the North Korean Human Rights Act, which expressly linked the imposition of sanctions to issues of human rights in the DPRK. The Act stated that economic sanctions would be imposed unless the DPRK worked to resolve human rights issues, including the abduction of Japanese nationals. When the DPRK conducted missile tests in July, Japan was one of its most vehement critics, announcing unilateral sanctions against the DPRK in September. The Japanese sanctions provided for the freezing of transfers of funds to the DPRK by groups suspected of having links to the country's nuclear weapons or missiles programmes; this affected 15 groups and one individual. These followed more limited sanctions imposed in the immediate aftermath of the July missile tests, which included the banning of a North Korean trade ferry from Japanese ports and a moratorium on charter flights from Pyongyang.

When Shinzo Abe became Japanese Prime Minister in September 2006, he adopted a firmer stance on the North Korean issue. Abe appointed a prime ministerial adviser on the issue of Japanese abductees, and also established a special government panel on the subject. Following the North Korean nuclear test on 9 October, Japan was among the strongest supporters of stringent sanctions. Not only did Japan support sanctions under the UN Security Council, but it also imposed firm measures of its own, banning all North Korean imports and prohibiting North Korean ships from entering Japanese waters. In November the Japanese Government approved a ban on the export of luxury goods to the DPRK. However, the restoration of normal relations between the DPRK and Japan was one of the tenets of the agreement reached during six-party talks in February 2007, and a working group was established to conduct negotiations. The first bilateral discussions between the two countries for more than a year were held in Viet Nam in March, but they broke down over the issue of the Japanese abductees. In July the North Korean Ministry of Foreign Affairs issued a memorandum accusing Japan of attempting to obstruct the talks on the normalization of bilateral relations and to disrupt the six-party process with its refusal to provide energy aid and its insistence on the resolution of the abduction issue, which North Korea claimed had already been settled. In October Japan announced that it would not resume aid to North Korea and extended its ban on North Korean imports and the entry of North Korean ships into Japanese waters for a further six months, citing a continued lack of progress in the dispute over the abductees. Japan renewed its sanctions against the DPRK in April 2008. In June the DPRK and Japan attended bilateral talks in Beijing, with the former agreeing to carry out another investigation into the abduction issue in exchange for the withdrawal of certain Japanese sanctions, including restrictions on port visits by North Korean vessels carrying humanitarian cargo. In October, with little progress having been made on the abduction issue, Japan sought to withhold aid for the DPRK under the six-party agreement.

In March 2009, following the revelation that the DPRK was shortly to launch a satellite (widely believed to be a long-range missile), Japan mobilized its missile interceptors, in the country's first deployment of this technology. The Japanese Government reiterated its warning that it would attempt to destroy any North Korean missile or debris that threatened Japanese territory. In June, following North Korea's testing of a nuclear device in the previous month, Japan banned all exports to North Korea. In May 2010, following the conclusion by multinational investigators that the DPRK had been responsible for the sinking of a South Korean naval vessel in March (see Inter-Korean Relations), the Japanese Government expressed its support for South Korea and stated that it would consider imposing additional sanctions on the DPRK.

Other regional relations

In April 2000 the DPRK formally applied to join the Association of Southeast Asian Nations (ASEAN, see p. 206). Following the

THE DEMOCRATIC PEOPLE'S REPUBLIC OF KOREA (NORTH KOREA) — Introductory Survey

DPRK's admittance to the ASEAN Regional Forum (ARF), a meeting in Thailand in July was attended for the first time by the North Korean Minister of Foreign Affairs, Paek Nam Sun, who held unprecedented meetings with his South Korean, Japanese and US counterparts. In November the Asia-Pacific Economic Co-operation (APEC, see p. 197) forum supported the DPRK's guest status in that organization.

In May 2000 Australia restored diplomatic links with the DPRK. Diplomatic relations were established with the Philippines in 2000 and with New Zealand in 2001. In July 2001 the President of the Presidium of the SPA, Kim Yong Nam, visited Viet Nam, Laos and Cambodia. In March 2002 Kim undertook a visit to Thailand and Malaysia, where he discussed mainly trade issues. Prime Minister Mahathir bin Mohamad of Malaysia accepted an invitation to visit the DPRK, and Indonesian President Megawati Sukarnoputri visited the country at the end of March. Kim Yong Nam reciprocated Megawati's visit in July of that year. The President of Viet Nam, Tran Duc Luong, visited the DPRK in May and signed several economic and legal co-operation agreements. Relations with Timor-Leste were established in late 2002. In 2003 there were reports that military relations with Myanmar were being developed; diplomatic relations were re-established (after a hiatus of 25 years) in April 2007. In November 2005 it was reported that the Government of Thailand was investigating claims that a Thai woman missing since 1978 had been kidnapped by North Korean agents and was now living in the DPRK. North Korea denied that its agents had abducted the woman. However, in August 2007 the Thai Minister of Foreign Affairs announced that his North Korean counterpart had agreed to co-operate on investigations into the case. In late October and early November Premier Kim Yong Il led a senior-level delegation of North Korean officials to South-East Asia, visiting Cambodia, Laos, Malaysia and Viet Nam. In June 2009 ASEAN leaders, attending a summit meeting in Seoul, condemned the DPRK's recent testing of a nuclear device, urging the elimination of nuclear weapons on the Korean peninsula and the DPRK's return to the six-party negotiations. In July 2010 the North Korean Minister of Foreign Affairs, Pak Ui Chun, visited Myanmar, one of the countries to which, according to a UN report released in November, the DPRK was supplying nuclear-related technology.

Relations with the USA and multilateral talks

From the time of the Korean War, the DPRK continued to depict the USA as its main enemy and repeatedly accused the Republic of Korea of being a US 'puppet' state. Relations deteriorated after the DPRK seized a US naval vessel, the *USS Pueblo*, in 1968 and detained its crew for several months. In 1969 the DPRK shot down a US reconnaissance aircraft, which had apparently violated North Korean airspace, resulting in the deaths of 31 US servicemen. In 1987, in response to alleged North Korean involvement in the bombing of a South Korean airliner, the USA placed the DPRK on its list of countries supporting terrorism, and restricted contacts between US and North Korean diplomats. From the 1990s relations with the USA were largely dominated by the DPRK's nuclear ambitions. In December 1994 it was announced that agreement had been reached to establish liaison offices in Washington, DC, and Pyongyang in 1995, in preparation for an eventual resumption of full diplomatic relations. However, the USA insisted that normal relations would be restored only when the DPRK ceased to export ballistic missiles and withdrew its troops from the border with South Korea; the DPRK, in turn, stated that liaison offices could only be opened when light-water nuclear reactors, in accordance with the October 1994 agreement between the DPRK and the USA, had been supplied. Relations faltered following the shooting-down of a US army helicopter, which had apparently entered North Korean airspace; the DPRK initially refused to negotiate, but, after direct bilateral discussions in December, the pilot was repatriated. In January 1995 the DPRK opened its ports to US commercial shipping and removed restrictions on the import of goods from the USA. Following the severe flooding in the DPRK in 1995 and 1996, the USA provided relief aid.

The issue of four-way talks dominated relations between the USA and the DPRK in 1996, but parallel negotiations were conducted concerning the estimated 8,100 US soldiers who were listed as 'missing in action' following the Korean War. The USA agreed to provide funds to assist in locating the remains. In December, following the issuing of a (US-brokered) apology by the DPRK for the submarine incursion into South Korean waters in September, it was reported that the USA was prepared partially to revoke its economic sanctions against North Korea, and to allow the gradual expansion of bilateral trade. In early 1997 the USA responded to a renewed appeal issued by the UN for food aid and humanitarian assistance for North Korea, as a result of which the DPRK announced its intention to take part in exploratory discussions about the proposed quadripartite talks. Bilateral discussions with the USA focused on the establishment of liaison offices, missile non-proliferation and procedures for the exhumation of the US servicemen listed as 'missing in action'. In August, however, the defection to the USA of two North Korean diplomats (the most senior officials yet to seek asylum in North America) resulted in the suspension of the third round of missile non-proliferation talks. The DPRK was unsuccessful in attempting to make its participation in full quadripartite talks conditional upon the withdrawal of US forces from the Korean peninsula and upon the provision of food aid. None the less, the USA responded positively, on humanitarian grounds, to two further UN appeals for food aid during the year. Relations with the USA were dominated by nuclear issues and other concerns regarding the DPRK's missile development programme in 1998 and 1999. The exhumation of US soldiers listed as 'missing in action' proceeded, with the remains of more than 40 soldiers being returned in 1998–2000.

In October 2000 Kim Jong Il's special envoy, Vice-Marshal Jo Myong Rok, paid a state visit to the USA, the most senior North Korean official ever to do so. The US Secretary of State, Madeleine Albright, reciprocated the visit and met Kim Jong Il, who agreed in principle to halt his country's long-range missile-testing programme. However, tension arose when two US fighter aircraft participating in a US-South Korean joint manoeuvre briefly crossed the military demarcation line into the airspace of the DPRK, which protested to the UN.

Relations between the DPRK and the USA deteriorated during 2001 following the inauguration of George W. Bush as US President. Bush adopted a more hostile position towards the DPRK than that of his predecessor, and this also adversely affected inter-Korean relations. The DPRK condemned the joint US-South Korean military exercises held in April. In May a non-governmental delegation from the USA visited the DPRK to examine evidence of atrocities committed by US troops during the Korean War. In June Bush stated that he was willing to resume negotiations with the DPRK, albeit linking these to a reduction in North Korea's missile programme and military deployments—terms rejected by the North.

Following the terrorist attacks on the USA in September 2001, the US Administration paid increasing attention to the possibility of North Korea having developed biological, chemical and nuclear weapons. In October the US Department of State released its annual report on religious freedom, which included the DPRK on a list of countries suppressing such beliefs. Despite signing two UN treaties against terrorism in November, the DPRK remained on the USA's list of states sponsoring terrorism.

In January 2002 President Bush referred to North Korea as forming an 'axis of evil' with Iran and Iraq. Bush's comments were believed to reflect concern that the DPRK was exporting weapons technology to countries the USA considered to be 'rogue states'. (During the 1990s the DPRK had exported missiles and related technology to Egypt, Iran, Libya, Pakistan and Syria, allegedly earning up to US $1,000m. a year.) In April the North accepted a South Korean request to reopen dialogue with the USA, and invited a US envoy, Jack Pritchard, to discuss outstanding issues. At the same time the USA announced that it would release $95m. to the DPRK in order to accelerate the building of replacement nuclear reactors—construction of which finally began in August 2002.

In October 2002 the USA revealed that senior North Korean officials had confirmed to the visiting US Assistant Secretary of State for East Asian and Pacific Affairs US intelligence reports that the DPRK was pursuing a secret nuclear weapons programme. The clandestine programme was allegedly based on uranium extraction, whereas the suspended programme had been based on plutonium extraction. Officials of the DPRK later denied that they had made such an admission. Within days the USA declared the agreement concluded in October 1994 to be null and void and placed renewed pressure on the DPRK to halt its nuclear activities. The DPRK responded by stating that it would consider halting its nuclear programme if the USA would sign a non-aggression treaty guaranteeing it sovereignty, a demand rejected by the USA. In November 2002 the USA finally halted petroleum shipments to North Korea, citing the latter's violation of the 1994 framework. It was widely reported that

THE DEMOCRATIC PEOPLE'S REPUBLIC OF KOREA (NORTH KOREA)

Pakistan had provided the technical expertise for North Korea's nuclear programme in exchange for ballistic missiles.

In December 2002 the DPRK announced that it would restart its nuclear reactor at Yongbyon and removed the IAEA's monitoring and surveillance equipment from the facility. Security analysts, meanwhile, concluded that the DPRK already possessed between two and five nuclear devices. The IAEA reported that North Korean technicians had transferred 1,000 fuel rods (of the 8,000 necessary to reactivate it) to the Yongbyon reactor, ostensibly for the production of electricity, but probably for the production of plutonium required to manufacture nuclear devices. The DPRK expelled the two remaining IAEA inspectors at the end of the year.

In January 2003 the DPRK announced its withdrawal from the NPT, and the IAEA responded by adopting a resolution condemning the country's recent behaviour. However, President Bush indicated that the USA would resume petroleum deliveries if the DPRK abandoned its nuclear weapons programme. In February the DPRK stated that the Yongbyon reactor was operating normally, and that any US military build-up in the region could lead the North to launch a pre-emptive strike on US forces anywhere in the world.

In March 2003 the USA and South Korea began their annual joint military exercises, as usual incurring condemnation by the North, which announced at the end of the month that it was severing military contacts with the USA at the liaison office in the DMZ. Also in early March four North Korean fighter aircraft intercepted a US reconnaissance aircraft in international airspace and closely pursued its flight, the first such incident in 32 years. Between late February and the beginning of April the DPRK also test-fired three short-range missiles, although it refrained from testing its longer-range ballistic missiles. By early April the USA had imposed new sanctions on the DPRK's Government and its Changgwang Sinyong Corporation, for exporting ballistic missiles to Pakistan. However, the sanctions were largely symbolic, since the USA had minimal economic links with the DPRK. The seizure by Australian authorities of a North Korean ship carrying 50 kg of heroin confirmed US claims that the DPRK was involved in drugs-trafficking. Also in April, the UN Security Council held its first discussions on the North Korean crisis. The DPRK had stated that the imposition of economic sanctions through the Security Council would be tantamount to a declaration of war.

In June 2003 the DPRK for the first time publicly defended its nuclear weapons strategy, declaring that the development of nuclear weapons was a 'deterrent'. In July there were new indications from US and Asian intelligence sources that the DPRK was operating a second secret nuclear facility, in addition to the plant at Yongbyon. At the end of July it was announced that the DPRK had agreed to take part in multilateral talks on its nuclear weapons programme with the USA, the Republic of Korea, Japan, China and Russia. The six-party talks duly took place in Beijing in August, but little progress was achieved, the USA insisting that the DPRK unconditionally abandon its nuclear weapons programme, while the DPRK reiterated that it would continue to develop its nuclear capacity unless the USA provided a guarantee of non-aggression.

Following the six-party talks in Beijing, it was reported in September 2003 that President Bush had authorized his Assistant Secretary of State for East Asia and the Pacific, James Kelly, to abandon the USA's insistence on the full dismantling of the North Korean weapons programme before any concessions could be made. It was indicated that verifiable progress on dismantling might be sufficient. However, Kelly stated that a bilateral non-aggression treaty, as desired by the DPRK, was not a possibility, and that any guarantee would involve China, Russia, the Republic of Korea and Japan, as well as the USA. In October the North Korean state news agency claimed that the DPRK had successfully completed the reprocessing of 8,000 spent fuel rods, thus generating sufficient plutonium to build a nuclear bomb. In November the Central Intelligence Agency (CIA) reported to the US Congress that it believed the DPRK had the technology to turn its nuclear fuel into functioning weapons. In early December KEDO (the international consortium established in 1995 following the 1994 agreement with the USA on assistance for energy development in the DPRK in return for nuclear non-proliferation) announced that it would be suspending for one year its construction in the DPRK of two non-military nuclear reactors. Also in December 2003, the USA rejected an offer from the DPRK to freeze its nuclear programme in return for concessions on security and energy aid.

In January 2004 there was speculation about the existence of a second nuclear programme for enriching uranium (in addition to the plutonium-reprocessing activities at Yongbyon). In February and June further six-party talks took place, but no significant resolutions were reached, with the DPRK continuing to deny the existence of a uranium enrichment programme. In August it was reported that North Korea was developing a new sea-based long-range missile system, which would possibly be capable of targeting the USA. A fourth round of six-party talks scheduled for September 2004 was suspended when the DPRK refused to attend, citing US hostility. Tensions in relations with the USA increased further following the re-election of George W. Bush as US President in November. Later in that month KEDO announced its intention to suspend plans for the construction in the DPRK of two non-military nuclear reactors.

In January 2005 the North Korean Government was angered by a description of the DPRK by Condoleezza Rice, the recently appointed US Secretary of State, as an 'outpost of tyranny'. Subsequently, in a state radio broadcast in February, the DPRK for the first time explicitly stated that it possessed nuclear weapons, and that it intended to postpone its participation in six-party negotiations for an indefinite period. Subsequent suggestions by the DPRK for bilateral discussions with the USA were rejected by the latter. In May the DPRK test-fired a ballistic missile into the Sea of Japan, while Mohammad el-Baradei, Director-General of the IAEA, stated that he believed the DPRK possessed enough weapons-grade plutonium for five or six nuclear devices. However, an apparent improvement in relations in June included a US pledge of 50,000 metric tons of food aid, and the fourth round of six-party talks began in Beijing in late July. Meanwhile, bilateral discussions were held between the representatives of the DPRK and the USA in the hope of finding a compromise between their respective opening positions. The USA continued to insist that the restoration of normal relations, removal of sanctions and guarantees of security could only follow the 'complete, verifiable and irreversible dismantling' of the DPRK's nuclear weapons programme, while the latter reiterated that only after the normalization of relations, including the signing of a peace treaty ending the Korean War, and the removal of US nuclear weapons from South Korea (the presence of which the US side denied) would the North agree to abandon its military nuclear aspirations. (The USA had indicated that, for the purpose of these talks, it was prepared to disregard the issue of the possible existence of a uranium enrichment programme in the DPRK.) The discussions went into recess in early August; their resumption was postponed until mid-September as a mark of protest by the DPRK at the annual joint military exercises performed by South Korea and the USA.

In mid-September 2005 a draft joint agreement was signed by all sides in the six-party negotiations, in which the DPRK committed itself to dismantling its nuclear weapons programme, returning to the NPT and permitting IAEA inspectors to visit its nuclear facilities. In return, the USA declared that it maintained no nuclear weapons on the Korean peninsula and had no intention of attacking the DPRK. The DPRK's right to peaceful nuclear energy was acknowledged, and it was envisaged that the provision of a civilian light-water nuclear reactor to North Korea would be discussed 'at an appropriate time'. The other five parties also undertook to provide the DPRK with energy assistance. Although significant, the agreement was compromised almost immediately when the North Korean Government insisted that it would take no steps towards dismantling its nuclear weapons programme until provided with a light-water reactor as specified in the agreement. The USA insisted that concessions such as the provision of the reactor could be expected to come into force only after the DPRK had fulfilled its dismantlement obligations. The fifth round of talks, which began in Beijing in November, was intended to discuss means of implementing the September accord, but ended without agreement and without any setting of a date for the next round. Later in November KEDO announced that it was considering the termination of its light-water reactor construction project in the DPRK, which had been suspended since 2003. (All workers were withdrawn from KEDO's construction site in Kumho, DPRK, in January 2006, and in December KEDO's executive board signed an agreement to terminate the project.)

Meanwhile, the resumption of the six-party nuclear negotiations appeared to be jeopardized by US allegations of financial crimes on the part of the DPRK. In September 2005 the US Government had ordered that all transactions with Banco Delta Asia in the Chinese Special Administrative Region of Macao be

THE DEMOCRATIC PEOPLE'S REPUBLIC OF KOREA (NORTH KOREA) *Introductory Survey*

terminated, in relation to suspected money-laundering activities conducted with the bank by the North Korean Government, and had also frozen the assets of eight North Korean companies, which it accused of proliferating weapons of mass destruction. In October the US Department of Justice accused the DPRK of having forged millions of US dollars' worth of counterfeit $100 bills since 1989, and in December 2005 the US ambassador to the Republic of Korea publicly described the DPRK as a 'criminal regime'. Although the US Administration insisted that the sanctions were purely a legal matter and had no political connection to the nuclear issue, the North Korean Government declared that no further six-party negotiations could be held until sanctions against it were removed. In April 2006 the US Administration rejected North Korean overtures for bilateral discussions in Tokyo, to coincide with a regional security forum at which all six participants in the nuclear discussions were present, insisting that communication between the two sides was only possible within the context of the six-party talks.

By mid-2006 speculation was rife that the DPRK was soon to test-launch an intercontinental ballistic missile, thus breaking the moratorium on tests imposed in 1999. The US Secretary of State, Condoleezza Rice, warned that a test would be regarded as a provocative act. Japan threatened stern action should a test missile be launched. However, the DPRK continued to insist that it might be prepared to halt the planned test should the USA agree to direct bilateral talks, a request that the US Government once again rejected. Instead, the USA announced that it would deploy advanced *Patriot* missiles (capable of intercepting North Korean ballistic missiles, as well as cruise missiles and aircraft) on Japanese soil for the first time. The DPRK's decision to test seven missiles on 5 July 2006 was regarded as a deliberate attempt to provoke the USA. Of the missiles tested, at least one was a *Taepo Dong 2* missile, thought to be capable of reaching Alaska; although the US Department of State claimed that the *Taepo Dong 2* failed in mid-air after about 42 seconds of flight, the North Korean Government hailed the tests as a success, announcing that more test launches were planned.

While the international community broadly condemned the tests, harsh criticism from the USA and Japan was tempered by the more cautious stance adopted by China, Russia and the Republic of Korea. The USA and Japan urged the UN Security Council to adopt sanctions against the DPRK, while Russia and China, which as permanent members of the Council held the power of veto, emphasized the importance of the resumption of dialogue. The UN Security Council adopted Resolution 1695 on 15 July 2006, requiring member states to ban the import and export of missile-related material to and from the DPRK. The USA attempted once more to revive the six-party talks in September, but reiterated that its position had not changed.

In defiance of international opinion and despite a 'grave warning' from the South Korean Government, the DPRK conducted a nuclear test on 9 October 2006, reportedly from a test site near Kimchaek city in North Hamgyong Province. The South Korean Minister for Unification, Lee Jong-Seok, denounced the test as a clear challenge to world peace and stability. Although the size of the nuclear device tested was thought to be very small, the detection of airborne radiation by US analysts confirmed that the device was nuclear in nature. The test prompted an emergency meeting of the UN Security Council in New York, amid strong condemnation from the international community.

On 14 October 2006 the UN Security Council approved a unanimous resolution imposing sanctions on the DPRK, with Russia and China unexpectedly agreeing to a range of sanctions, albeit measures that were purely economic and commercial, rather than military, in nature. Resolution 1718 urged the DPRK to suspend immediately its ballistic weapons programme and further nuclear tests and to return to the six-party talks without precondition. Sanctions included provision for the inspection of cargo entering and leaving North Korean ports, a ban on weapons-related imports, a travel ban on North Korean officials thought to be involved in the weapons programme and a freezing of their assets, and also a ban on the import of luxury goods. At the end of October the DPRK indicated that it would return to the six-party talks, following discussions among Chinese, US and North Korean officials. While the DPRK set no conditions for its return to the discussions, it expressed the hope that one of the topics would be the removal of financial sanctions and the release of North Korean assets. In mid-November, however, a draft UN resolution condemned the DPRK's human rights record, and in the following week leaders from the APEC forum, meeting in the Vietnamese capital of Hanoi, issued a statement expressing their strong concern over the nuclear weapons test.

Intense diplomatic activity resulted in the resumption of the six-party talks in December 2006. However, the DPRK stated that it would consider halting its nuclear programme only if the USA removed both its financial sanctions and the UN sanctions. The country also reiterated demands for a nuclear reactor to generate electricity. The US negotiators, meanwhile, were reported by South Korean sources to have offered a fresh programme of incentives, which would give the DPRK aid and security guarantees if it agreed to declare all its nuclear-related programmes and place them under permanent external inspection. However, the DPRK rejected the US overture, and the discussions ended without agreement.

Nevertheless, discreet negotiations continued to take place. The six-party talks held in February 2007 resulted in the DPRK's agreement to permit IAEA inspections and to shut down its nuclear reactor at Yongbyon within 60 days in exchange for the equivalent of 50,000 metric tons of heavy fuel oil and the assurance of negotiations on the restoration of normal relations with Japan and the USA, with the latter notably agreeing to begin the process of ending the designation of the DPRK as a state sponsoring terrorism. Five working groups were to be established to address North Korean relations with both Japan and the USA, economic and energy co-operation, denuclearization of the Korean peninsula, and the establishment of a North-East Asia peace and security mechanism. The DPRK was given an incentive of a further 950,000 tons of heavy fuel oil for immobilizing its nuclear facilities and providing a complete declaration of all its nuclear programmes as part of the next phase of the agreement. Although the formal accord did not directly mention the North Korean funds in the Banco Delta Asia in Macao that had been frozen by the USA in 2005, this issue was covered by a reference to 'resolving pending bilateral issues', and the USA subsequently agreed to return the funds. Mohammad el-Baradei's visit to the DPRK in mid-March 2007 was an indication of further progress, with the head of the IAEA confirming the DPRK's evident commitment to the dismantling of its nuclear programme. However, a few days later, a further round of six-party talks faltered over delays to the release of the North Korean funds in Macao, and the DPRK missed the 14 April closure deadline for the Yongbyon reactor. As progress on the implementation of the February 2007 agreement remained stalled, with commercial banks reportedly unwilling to transfer the Banco Delta Asia funds, North Korea test-fired three short-range missiles in late May and early June.

US Assistant Secretary of State Christopher Hill visited Pyongyang for the first time in late June 2007. Shortly afterwards North Korea confirmed that it had received the Banco Delta Asia funds, which amounted to US $25m. and had been transferred via a Russian bank, and on the following day IAEA inspectors arrived in North Korea for discussions on the closure of the Yongbyon reactor. On their first visit to the DPRK since their expulsion in December 2002, the inspectors were given unlimited access to the nuclear site. In mid-July 2007 the DPRK announced that it had shut down Yongbyon, and this was subsequently verified by the IAEA. Participants in the six-party talks met in Beijing a few days later, but failed to agree upon a timetable for the second phase of the February accord, i.e. the disclosure and disablement of all North Korea's nuclear facilities. Following the discussions, the DPRK renewed its demands for a light-water reactor in exchange for immobilizing its Yongbyon nuclear reactor. Working groups established by the six nations involved in the talks on ending North Korea's nuclear weapons programme held meetings in Panmunjom in August to discuss the technical details of the next stage of the process. Following talks between the DPRK and the USA on improving their bilateral relations, which were held in Geneva in early September, Hill announced that North Korea had agreed to declare and disable all its nuclear facilities by the end of the year. The DPRK claimed that the US delegation had agreed to its removal from the US list of countries supporting terrorism and to lift economic sanctions, but Hill denied this.

A new round of six-party talks, which was held in Beijing in late September 2007, resulted in formal agreement on a deadline of 31 December for the completion of the second phase of the February accord, under which North Korea would receive a further 900,000 metric tons of heavy fuel oil (100,000 tons having already been supplied by South Korea and China). In mid-October a US team of government officials and nuclear experts spent a week in North Korea discussing detailed plans for disablement. Work on immobilizing the Yongbyon reactor, which was to entail the removal of 8,000 fuel rods, commenced in early November under US supervision. Following a visit to North Korea in early December, Hill reported that disablement was progressing well. Meanwhile, in a personal letter to Kim Jong Il delivered by Hill, President Bush urged the DPRK to fulfil its pledge to provide a full and complete declaration of its nuclear programmes. However, North Korea failed to meet the deadline to disclose details of its nuclear activities. The disablement of the country's nuclear facilities had also not been completed by the end of 2007, although this was attributed to technical difficulties.

At discussions between US and North Korean negotiators, held in February 2008, disagreement remained over the DPRK's continued denial of US claims of the existence of a covert North Korean nuclear programme for enriching uranium; this was followed in April by the USA's contention that the DPRK had passed sensitive nuclear information to Syria. An historic concert in Pyongyang by the New York Philharmonic orchestra in February, involving the largest US presence in the country since the Korean War, was hailed as a significant act of cultural diplomacy. In May the DPRK submitted an 18,000-page report on its nuclear weapons programme to US delegates. In the same month the DPRK accepted the USA's offer of substantial amounts of food aid, the bulk of which was to be delivered by WFP. Further documentation on the nuclear programme was provided in late June, prompting President Bush to announce that the DPRK would be removed from the USA's list of state sponsors of terrorism and that US trade sanctions would be withdrawn. Soon afterwards, the cooling tower of the Yongbyon reactor was destroyed by the North Korean authorities. However, further movement on the terms of the agreement was slow, owing to disputes over the method of authentication of the North Korean progress reports and delays to the DPRK's official redesignation as a non-terrorist nation. In August these disagreements resulted in an announcement from the DPRK that it would stop dismantling its Yongbyon reactor, and, in early September, that the reactor was to be restarted. The impasse appeared to have been resolved in October, when the USA implemented the redesignation of the DPRK in return for the latter's assurance of compliance with nuclear inspections, albeit with conditions. However, the issue of the verification procedure continued to impede progress when the six-party talks resumed in Beijing in December.

After Barack Obama had taken office as President of the USA in January 2009, his Secretary of State, Hillary Clinton, declared that if the DPRK were to eliminate its nuclear weapons programme 'genuinely and verifiably' the new Administration would be prepared to establish normal diplomatic relations and provide economic assistance. In March, however, following the closure of the border in response to South Korea's participation in its customary joint military exercises with the USA, and as speculation mounted with regard to the precise nature of an imminent satellite launch announced by the DPRK, the North Korean Government refused to accept any further supplies of US food aid and instructed five US aid groups to leave the country by the end of the month. In mid-March two US television journalists were arrested by North Korean guards near the border with China. The North Korean authorities confirmed that the two women were being held pending an investigation into their apparent intrusion into the DPRK.

The DPRK's announcement of its forthcoming launch of a communications satellite aroused much concern. The US, South Korean and Japanese Governments suspected that the operation might prove to be a long-range ballistic missile test. On 5 April 2009 the DPRK proceeded to launch its rocket, in defiance of international warnings. The rocket dropped a booster stage to the west of Japan before flying over the country towards the Pacific Ocean, where a second booster stage was released. The DPRK announced that the launch had permitted the placement of a communications satellite into orbit; however, this was contested by the US military, which asserted that the rocket's payload had landed in the Pacific Ocean. The Japanese Government requested an emergency session of the UN Security Council. The session ended without agreement after divisions emerged with regard to the response to the launch. Chinese and Russian envoys urged restraint, while the USA and Japan advocated a reinforcement of sanctions against the DPRK. However, on 13 April the Security Council released a statement condemning the rocket launch and the violation of the ban on missile tests by the DPRK. The country then expelled all UN nuclear inspectors and announced its withdrawal from the six-party talks and the resumption of its nuclear programme.

On 25 May 2009 the DPRK exploded an underground nuclear device, believed to be larger than the one tested in October 2006. On the same day three short-range ballistic missiles were also fired, followed by several more in the ensuing days. The nuclear test was condemned by the USA, China, Russia and numerous other countries, and in June 2009 the UN Security Council unanimously approved a resolution condemning the test 'in the strongest terms', demanding that the DPRK not conduct any further nuclear test or any launch using ballistic missile technology, urging the country to reverse its withdrawal from the NPT and strengthening the sanctions that had been imposed on the DPRK in 2006: the resolution prohibited the export of all weapons from the DPRK and the import of all except minor weapons, and urged member states to inspect North Korean cargo ships and aircraft for materials related to the production of nuclear weapons. The DPRK responded by firing several short-range and medium-range ballistic missiles in early July 2009. Later in July the Security Council's committee on sanctions nominated five companies and five individuals to be subject to a freeze of financial assets and a ban on foreign travel, including North Korea's General Bureau of Atomic Energy and its director, and three trading companies.

In June 2009 the two US journalists who had been detained in March were tried, convicted of illegal entry into the country and 'hostile acts', and sentenced to 12 years' labour. In August, however, the former US President, Bill Clinton, travelled to Pyongyang (reportedly at the indirect invitation of the North Korean Government) and secured the release of the two women: his visit, although unofficial, included a meeting with Kim Jong Il. In October, during a visit to Pyongyang by the Chinese Premier, Wen Jiabao, Kim Jong Il expressed readiness to resume multilateral talks on the nuclear programme, depending on the outcome of bilateral discussions with the USA. The Obama Administration, for its part, stated that bilateral dialogue was acceptable, provided that it led to a resumption of the six-party talks, and in November it was announced that a special US envoy to the DPRK, Stephen Bosworth, had been appointed. During a visit to South Korea in that month, President Obama offered economic assistance to the DPRK if it demonstrated an irreversible halt to its development of nuclear weapons. Bosworth paid a visit to Pyongyang in December, but no date for a subsequent meeting was announced.

In April 2010 the DPRK's principal negotiator on nuclear affairs, Kim Kye Gwan, was reported to have been refused entry to the USA for bilateral discussions, since no North Korean undertaking to resume the six-party talks had been made. In May, following the conclusion by expert investigators that the DPRK had been responsible for the sinking of the South Korean naval vessel *Cheonan* in March (see Inter-Korean Relations), the US Government condemned the incident as an unacceptable provocation. In the same month a preliminary report by a group of experts, commissioned by the UN, reported that the DPRK had been exporting nuclear technology to Iran, Myanmar and Syria, in defiance of sanctions imposed by the UN Security Council. In June President Obama announced an extension of US sanctions against the DPRK. In July the DPRK reacted with outrage to four days of large-scale joint naval exercises by South Korea and the USA, in international waters off North Korea. In August Jimmy Carter, the former US President, visited the DPRK in a successful attempt to secure the freedom of a US citizen who had been imprisoned after entering the country illegally in January; although the visit was private, Carter met Kim Kye Gwan and Kim Yong Nam (a senior member of the KWP and the country's titular head of state), and the latter was reported by the North Korean media to have expressed willingness to resume the six-party negotiations. Later in August the US Government imposed new sanctions and travel bans on North Korean organizations and individuals, including a clandestine branch of the KWP, known as Office 39, which was alleged to have been dealing in illicit drugs, and the Green Pine Corporation, which was believed to export weapons. In September Bosworth visited South Korea, China and Japan to discuss the resumption of the six-party talks. In November a senior US nuclear scientist visited the DPRK and reported that he had been shown an advanced uranium enrichment facility, which was much more extensive and up-to-date than expected; the facility was intended to supply a new light-water reactor that was under construction at Yongbyon, ostensibly for the peaceful production of electricity. Later in November, after the DPRK's bombardment of the South Korean island of Yeonpyeong, President Obama reaffirmed the USA's commitment to South Korea's defence, and the two countries again undertook joint naval exercises in the Yellow Sea. In January 2011 the US Secretary of Defense, Robert Gates, visited China, Japan and South Korea to discuss regional security, and warned that within five years the DPRK was likely to be capable of deploying missiles that would directly threaten US territory (namely the state of Alaska).

Other external relations

In the mid-1980s the DPRK placed increased emphasis on its relations with the USSR. The DPRK's diplomatic isolation became more pronounced in the early 1990s, as former communist bloc countries attempted to foster relations with the Republic of Korea. Furthermore, the USSR announced that, from January 1991, its barter trading system with the DPRK would be abolished in favour of trade in convertible currencies at world market prices. However, an agreement was reported to have been signed in May 1993 by the DPRK and the Russian Federation (which, following the dissolution of the USSR, had assumed responsibility for many of the USSR's international undertakings) on technological and scientific co-operation. Discussions on the rescheduling of the terms of repayment of North Korea's debt to Russia took place in October 1997. In March 1999 a new bilateral treaty of friendship, good neighbourliness and co-operation was initialled in Pyongyang (to replace a 1961 bilateral treaty); a formal signing followed in February 2000, during a visit to Pyongyang by the Russian Minister of Foreign Affairs, Igor Ivanov. The treaty was ratified by the DPRK in April. In July President Vladimir Putin became the first Russian (or Soviet) leader to visit North Korea. Following Putin's visit, co-operation between Russia and the DPRK placed a strong emphasis on connecting the latter's rail system to the Trans-Siberian railway, and in March 2001 the two countries signed a railway co-operation agreement.

In April 2001 the DPRK's Minister of the People's Armed Forces, Vice-Marshal Kim Il Chol, visited Moscow and reportedly negotiated the acquisition of defensive weaponry, in addition to signing a military co-operation protocol. In August Kim Jong Il undertook a 24-day visit across Russia to Moscow, where he and President Putin signed a new declaration of co-operation in politics, the economy, military matters, science and technology, and culture. However, Russia also urged the DPRK to settle the latter's outstanding bilateral debt of as much as US $5,500m.

In April 2002 two separate Russian delegations visited Pyongyang to discuss co-operation in all fields, particularly business. In May the Minister of Foreign Affairs, Paek Nam Sun, visited Moscow, in the first such visit in 15 years. In July the Russian Minister of Foreign Affairs, Igor Ivanov, visited Pyongyang, and in August Kim Jong Il visited the Russian city of Vladivostok, where he held discussions with Putin, mainly focusing on the reconnection of railway links across the Korean peninsula. The DPRK and the Russian Oblast of Amur signed a co-operation agreement on agriculture and forestry. In October two North Korean military delegations visited Russia.

As the diplomatic crisis over the DPRK's nuclear weapons programme intensified in January 2003, Russia sought to defuse the situation by sending the Deputy Minister of Foreign Affairs, Aleksandr Losyukov, to Pyongyang, where he held discussions with Kim Jong Il. Losyukov, who had earlier visited China and subsequently the USA, urged a three-stage formula whereby the international community would accept a nuclear-free Korean peninsula, guarantees for the regime's security, and a resumption of aid. The DPRK reiterated that the crisis could be resolved only through discussions with the USA.

In July 2006, following the North's missile tests, Russia and China ensured that attempts by the UN Security Council to impose sanctions on the DPRK were obstructed. However, Russia modified its strong anti-sanctions policy following the nuclear test of 9 October, like China using its power of veto and ensuring that UN Security Council Resolution 1718 did not include the threat of military action. The Russian authorities assisted in the process of transferring previously frozen North Korean funds from the Banco Delta Asia in Macao to North Korea via a Russian bank in June 2007, thus removing the main obstacle to the implementation of the February agreement on the DPRK's nuclear programme. In January 2008 Russia provided North Korea with 50,000 metric tons of fuel oil as part of its commitment under the six-party agreement on the dismantling of North Korea's nuclear facilities. In April Russia and the DPRK signed an agreement to restore an existing railway line between Khasan on the Russian border and Rajin in the DPRK. Russia condemned the DPRK's launch of a long-range missile in April 2009, but opposed the imposition of stricter sanctions; however, after the DPRK had conducted a nuclear test in the following month, Russia agreed to accept the new sanctions imposed by the UN Security Council. Following the conclusion by an expert inquiry in May 2010 that the sinking of a South Korean naval vessel in March had been caused by a torpedo fired by a North Korean submarine, the Russian Government undertook to 'closely consult' South Korea, and urged restraint on both sides.

The DPRK has maintained close relations with a number of Middle Eastern countries, including Egypt, Libya, Syria and Iran. The President of the Presidium of the SPA, Kim Yong Nam, visited Libya and Syria in July 2002. The DPRK retained long-standing links with many African nations, and reportedly had military advisers working in some 12 of that continent's countries in 2005. In January 2004 the Vice-President of the Presidium of the SPA, Yang Hyong Sop, visited Nigeria to discuss an agreement on military technology. In May it was reported that an IAEA investigation of uranium delivered to the USA by Libya in late 2003 had revealed that the material had been supplied to Libya by the DPRK through an illicit nuclear technology procurement network operated by a Pakistani nuclear scientist, Abdul Qadeer Khan. Following the revelation, in early 2004 the Pakistani scientist confessed to his role in the DPRK's sale of nuclear secrets. Further evidence concerning the transfer of nuclear material from the DPRK to Libya emerged in early 2005. In January 2007 North Korea was reported to have agreed to share its data from the October 2006 nuclear test with scientists from Iran. The alleged agreement reportedly followed a meeting between North Korean and Iranian nuclear scientists in the previous November. However, the DPRK strongly denied the allegations. In September 2007 the DPRK similarly rejected claims that it was assisting Syria to develop a nuclear weapons programme. In that month the United Arab Emirates announced that it had established diplomatic relations with North Korea at ambassadorial level. In March 2008, accompanied by the Ministers of Foreign Affairs, of Foreign Trade and of Public Health, Kim Yong Nam travelled to Namibia, where his visit prompted speculation regarding the DPRK's interest in the country's uranium resources. Kim Yong Nam and his delegation also visited Angola, the Democratic Republic of the Congo and Uganda. In September of the same year the DPRK and Kenya established diplomatic relations at ambassadorial level.

In January 2000 Italy became the first member of the Group of Seven (G7) Western industrialized nations (and the sixth member of the EU) to establish diplomatic relations with the DPRK. Diplomatic relations were established with the United Kingdom in December 2000. During 2001 the DPRK further expanded its range of diplomatic partners, opening relations with the EU and several European countries, including Germany and Spain, and also with Canada, Brazil and Turkey. In May 2003 the DPRK opened an embassy in the United Kingdom, amid protests from human rights activists. Relations with Ireland were established in December. During 2007 diplomatic links with several countries, including Myanmar (see above), were formed or restored.

CONSTITUTION AND GOVERNMENT

Under the Constitution of 1972, the highest organ of state power is the unicameral Supreme People's Assembly (SPA), with 687 members, elected (unopposed) for five years by universal adult suffrage. The SPA elects, for its duration, the Chairman of the National Defence Commission, who, since the effective abolition of the presidency in September 1998, holds the most senior accessible office of state. This position was designated as that of 'supreme leader' in 2009. The SPA elects the Premier and, on the latter's recommendation, appoints other Ministers to form the Cabinet. The President of the SPA Presidium, the members of which are elected by the SPA, represents the State in its relations with foreign countries.

Political power is held by the communist Korean Workers' Party (KWP), which is the most influential party in the Democratic Front for the Reunification of the Fatherland (comprising the KWP and two minor parties). The Front presents an approved list of candidates for elections to representative bodies. The KWP's highest authority is the Party Congress, which elects a Central Committee to supervise party work. The Committee elects a Political Bureau (Politburo) to direct policy. The Presidium of the Politburo is the KWP's most powerful policy-making body.

The DPRK comprises nine provinces and two cities, each with an elected Local People's Assembly.

THE DEMOCRATIC PEOPLE'S REPUBLIC OF KOREA (NORTH KOREA)

REGIONAL AND INTERNATIONAL CO-OPERATION

The DPRK formally applied to join the Association of Southeast Asian Nations (ASEAN, see p. 206) in 2000, and the country was subsequently admitted to the ASEAN Regional Forum (ARF). The country has guest status in the Asia-Pacific Economic Co-operation (APEC, see p. 197) forum. The DPRK is a member of the UN's Economic and Social Commission for Asia and the Pacific (ESCAP, see p. 37), having been admitted to the UN in 1991.

ECONOMIC AFFAIRS

In 2009, according to the Bank of Korea (the South Korean central bank), the gross national income (GNI) of the DPRK was estimated to total US $28,635m., equivalent to about $1,225 per head. According to UN estimates (based on a different method of calculation), the DPRK's GNI per head declined from $555 in 2008 to $500 in 2009. During 2000–09, according to estimates by the World Bank, the population increased by an annual average of 0.5%. In 2000–09, according to UN estimates, GDP grew at an average annual rate of 1.3%. According to estimates published by the South Korean central bank, the DPRK's GDP contracted by 1.2% in 2007. Growth of 3.7% was reported for 2008, followed by a decline of 0.9% in 2009.

Agriculture (including hunting, forestry and fishing) contributed 20.9% of GDP in 2009, according to UN estimates, and 36.0% of the employed population were engaged in the sector at the time of the 2008 census, according to official figures. The principal crops are rice, maize and potatoes. The DPRK is not self-sufficient in food, and imports substantial amounts of wheat, rice and maize annually. Intermittent food shortages became a serious problem from the mid-1990s, and considerable support has been provided by the World Food Programme (WFP—see Contemporary Political History). According to FAO estimates, cereal production increased from 4.4m. metric tons in 2007 to 4.7m. tons in 2008–09. Potato production was 1.5m. tons in 2008, compared with 2.0m. metric tons in 2006, according to estimates. The raising of livestock (principally cattle and pigs), forestry and fishing are important. During 2000–09, according to UN estimates, agricultural GDP increased by an average of 1.9% per year. Agricultural GDP declined by 9.1% in 2007, but expanded by 8.0% in 2008. In 2009, however, the sector's GDP was estimated to have decreased by 1.0%. An outbreak of foot-and-mouth disease was confirmed in February 2011.

In 2009, according to UN estimates, industry (including mining, manufacturing, construction and utilities) contributed 46.9% of GDP, and 34.3% of the employed population were engaged in the sector at the time of the 2008 census, according to official figures. During 2000–09, according to estimates from the UN, industrial GDP was estimated to have increased by an annual average of 1.5%. Industrial GDP increased by 2.7% in 2008 but decreased by 1.5% in 2009.

Mining contributed 12.7% of GDP in 2009, according to South Korean estimates. At the time of the 2008 census 5.9% of the employed population were engaged in the sector, according to official estimates. The DPRK possesses considerable mineral wealth, with large deposits of coal, iron, lead, copper, zinc, tin, silver and gold. Output of hard coal totalled an estimated 25.0m. metric tons in 2009. There are unexploited offshore deposits of petroleum and natural gas. South Korean sources estimated that the output of the mining sector increased by 1.5% in 2007 and by 2.4% in 2008, before decreasing by 0.9% in 2009.

In 2009, according to UN estimates, the manufacturing sector contributed 22.1% of GDP, and 23.7% of the employed population were engaged in the sector at the time of the 2008 census, according to official figures. In the 1990s industrial development concentrated on heavy industry (metallurgy—notably steel production, machine-building, cement and chemicals). The textiles industry has provided significant exports. According to UN estimates, the GDP of the manufacturing sector increased at an average annual rate of 1.1% in 2000–09. Manufacturing GDP increased by 2.6% in 2008 but declined by 3.0% in 2009.

Construction, according to UN estimates, contributed 8.0% of GDP in 2009. The sector engaged 3.0% of the employed population at the time of the 2008 census, according to official figures. The GDP of the construction sector was estimated to have increased at an average annual rate of 1.5% in 2000–09. Following a contraction of 1.5% in 2007, the sector's GDP increased by 1.1% in 2008 and by 0.8% in 2009. Under the 2011 budget, the Government's allocation to the construction sector was stated to have been increased by 15.1% in comparison with the previous year.

In 2007 it was estimated that 61.7% of the DPRK's energy supply was derived from hydroelectricity, followed in importance by coal (34.8%) and petroleum (3.5%). A 30-MW nuclear reactor was believed to have been inaugurated in 1987. From the 1990s the DPRK experienced increasing power shortages, as generation declined and transmission infrastructure deteriorated. Furthermore, the production of hydroelectric power was adversely affected by intermittent drought. In 2007 the DPRK's electricity production totalled 21,523m. kWh, compared with 22,436m. kWh in 2006. Fuel oil shipments to the DPRK have been intermittently suspended owing to international concerns with regard to the country's nuclear programme (see Contemporary Political History).

According to UN estimates, the services sector contributed 32.1% of GDP in 2009, and the sector engaged 29.6% of the employed population at the time of the 2008 census, according to official figures. The GDP of the services sector was estimated to have increased at an average annual rate of 0.7% in 2000–09; services GDP increased by 0.7% in 2008 and by 0.1% in 2009.

According to South Korean sources, in 2008 total exports, excluding trade with the Republic of Korea, reached US $113m. and imports totalled $269m. The DPRK's principal source of imports in 2005 (again excluding the Republic of Korea) was the People's Republic of China, which accounted for 54% of total imports, followed by Russia (11%). China was the DPRK's principal market for exports in 2005, purchasing 50% of goods, followed by Japan (13%). China was a source of crude petroleum (imports of this commodity were sourced exclusively from China in 2008, when the cost of petroleum imports greatly increased, by 46.9% to reach $414.3m.), food and vehicles, while Japan was a destination for industrial and agricultural goods. The principal exports in 2008 were mineral products (an increase of 33.5% in the value of exports compared with the previous year, and, at $465.4m., accounting for 41.3% of the total value of exports), non-ferrous minerals (16.8%), textiles (10.6%), chemical plastics (7.6%), and machinery and electrical equipment. The principal imports in 2008 were mineral products (25.9% of the value of total imports), textile fibres (11.9%), machinery and electrical equipment (11.5%), and processed food items (8.8%). In 2009, according to data from the Bank of Korea, in comparison with the previous year inter-Korean trade decreased by 7.8%, to total $1,680m.

The Government planned an increase in overall budgetary spending in 2010 of 8.3%, while revenue was projected to rise by 6.3%. The 2011 budget, endorsed in April of that year, provided for expenditure of 567,000m. won. Of this total, 15.8% was allocated to defence, declared to be the same percentage as in the previous year (albeit regarded by many observers as a substantial understatement). By 2008, according to one source, the DPRK's total external debt was estimated to have reached US $18,000m. Following the introduction of market-orientated reforms in 2002, the inflation rate was believed to have reached 4,000% in that year. Between mid-2007 and mid-2008 the prices of staple foods reportedly increased by 100% in Pyongyang. The revaluation of the currency in December 2009 had major repercussions (see Contemporary Political History), and prices of basic commodities were reported to have risen substantially in 2010.

In a report released in February 2009, the US Department of State reiterated its belief that activities such as the forging of US currency and the counterfeiting of brand cigarettes remained significant sources of revenue for the North Korean Government, along with trade in illicit drugs and the sale of weapons. In July 2010, in collaboration with Interpol, US investigators were reported to have identified 200 bank accounts, opened around the world under assumed names, that were allegedly connected to such illegal economic activities. The establishment of a special industrial zone at Kaesong contributed to a substantial increase in inter-Korean trade, but political tensions with South Korea hampered operations (see Inter-Korean Relations). Following a revaluation of the currency in December 2009 with the apparent aim of reducing inflation (see Domestic Political Affairs), the price of rice was subsequently reported to have increased 40-fold within a year. Investment from China reportedly rose from $1.1m. in 2003 to $41.0m. in 2008. In January 2010 the establishment of a state investment group, with the task of forming a state development bank to attract foreign investment, was reported. The economic contraction of 2009 was believed to be largely due to a decline in production of agricultural commodities such as maize, owing to adverse weather, while the manufacturing sector was constrained by shortages of electricity and a lack of raw materials. A report released by WFP in November 2010 suggested that there remained a significant shortfall in

THE DEMOCRATIC PEOPLE'S REPUBLIC OF KOREA (NORTH KOREA)

cereal production. The food deficit was estimated at 237,000 metric tons by WFP, and the situation appeared likely to be exacerbated by low production of winter vegetables. Meanwhile, the DPRK's five-year plan for 2008–12, announced in April 2008, accorded priority to improvements in the areas of science and technology. In January 2011, however, the State Strategy Plan for Economic Development, a new 10-year plan encompassing the period to 2020, was revealed. Amid suggestions that the authorities had tacitly acknowledged the need for more realistic targets, the new plan focused on projects in 12 areas, including agricultural development; petroleum and energy development; and the improvement of the transport network.

PUBLIC HOLIDAYS

The *Juche* calendar was introduced in the DPRK in 1997; 1912, the year of the late Kim Il Sung's birth, was designated the first year of the new calendar.

2012: 1 January (New Year), 16–17 February (Kim Jong Il's Birthday), 8 March (International Women's Day), 15 April (Day of the Sun, Kim Il Sung's Birthday), 1 May (May Day), 15 August (Anniversary of Liberation), 9 September (Independence Day), 10 October (Anniversary of the foundation of the Korean Workers' Party), 27 December (Anniversary of the Constitution).

Statistical Survey

Area and Population

AREA, POPULATION AND DENSITY*

Area (sq km)	122,762†
Population (census results)	
31 December 1993	21,213,378
1 October 2008‡	
Males	11,722,403
Females	12,328,815
Total	24,051,218
Population (UN estimates at mid-year)§	
2009	23,906,070
2010	23,990,703
2011	24,073,514
Density (per sq km) at mid-2011	196.1

* Excluding the demilitarized zone between North and South Korea, with an area of 1,262 sq km (487 sq miles).
† 47,399 sq miles.
‡ Provisional figures.
§ Source: UN, *World Population Prospects: The 2008 Revision*.

POPULATION BY AGE AND SEX
(UN estimates at mid-2011)

	Males	Females	Total
0–14	2,553,709	2,429,838	4,983,547
15–64	8,432,874	8,242,689	16,675,563
65 and over	911,908	1,502,496	2,414,404
Total	11,898,491	12,175,023	24,073,514

Source: UN, *World Population Prospects: The 2008 Revision*.

ADMINISTRATIVE DIVISIONS
(population at 2008 census)

	Area (sq km)	Population ('000)	Density (per sq km)
Chagang Province	16,968	1,299,830	76.6
Hamgyong North Province*	17,570	2,327,362	132.5
Hamgyong South Province	18,970	3,066,013	161.6
Hwanghae North Province	9,262	2,113,672	228.2
Hwanghae South Province	8,002	2,310,485	288.7
Kangwon Province	11,152	1,477,582	132.5
Pyongan North Province	12,191	2,728,662	223.8
Pyongan South Province	12,330	4,051,696	328.6
Yanggang (Ryanggang) Province	14,317	719,269	50.2
Pyongyang City	2,000	3,255,288	1,627.6
Total	122,762	24,051,218†	195.9

* Includes Najin-Sonbong, which enjoys the administrative status of Special City.
† Total includes population living in military camps.

Source: partly Thomas Brinkhoff, *City Population* (www.citypopulation.de).

PRINCIPAL TOWNS
(population at 2008 census)*

Pyongyang (capital)	2,581,076	Sariwon	271,434
Hamhung	703,610	Kaechon	262,389
Chongjin	614,892	Kanggye	251,971
Sinuiju	334,031	Sunchon	250,738
Wonsan	328,467	Haeju	241,599
Nampo	310,531	Tanchon	240,873

* Population for urban areas of cities, as enumerated at census.

BIRTHS AND DEATHS
(annual averages, UN estimates)

	1995–2000	2000–05	2005–10
Birth rate (per 1,000)	18.1	15.1	13.8
Death rate (per 1,000)	7.9	9.3	9.9

Source: UN, *World Population Prospects: The 2008 Revision*.

2008 census (12 months ending 1 October 2008): Live births 345,630; deaths 216,616.

Life expectancy (years at birth, WHO estimates): 67 (males 65; females 69) in 2008 (Source: WHO, *World Health Statistics*).

EMPLOYMENT
(persons aged 16 years and over at 2008 census)

	Males	Females	Total
Agriculture, forestry and fishing	2,082,297	2,304,598	4,386,895
Mining and quarrying	458,484	259,711	718,195
Manufacturing	1,507,014	1,375,968	2,882,982
Electricity, gas and water	161,098	55,184	216,282
Construction	285,941	81,709	367,650
Wholesale and retail trade; repair of motor vehicles	173,962	383,393	557,355
Transport, storage and communications	337,983	144,175	482,158
Hotels and restaurants	26,591	114,614	141,205
Finance and insurance activities	12,374	13,854	26,228
Professional, scientific and technical activities	80,574	37,558	118,132
Administrative and support service activities	287,951	163,385	451,336
Public administration and defence; compulsory social security	439,586	284,592	724,178
Education	263,635	284,497	548,132
Health and social welfare	134,306	196,396	330,702
Arts, entertainment and recreation	72,290	58,292	130,582
Other services	35,852	66,856	102,708
Total employed	6,359,938	5,824,782	12,184,720

Note: Of the remaining total population aged 16 years and over, 940,886 were studying, 155,093 were disabled, 3,147,553 were retired, 921,191 were engaged in housework and 17,326 were described as 'other'.

THE DEMOCRATIC PEOPLE'S REPUBLIC OF KOREA (NORTH KOREA)

Statistical Survey

Health and Welfare

KEY INDICATORS

Total fertility rate (children per woman, 2008)	1.9
Under-5 mortality rate (per 1,000 live births, 2008)	55
HIV/AIDS (% of persons aged 15–49, 1994)	<0.01
Physicians (per 1,000 head, 2003)	3.3
Health expenditure (2006): US $ per head (PPP)	1
Health expenditure (2006): % of GDP	3.5
Health expenditure (2006): public (% of total)	85.6
Access to sanitation (% of persons, 2004)	59
Total carbon dioxide emissions ('000 metric tons, 2007)	70,652.9
Carbon dioxide emissions per head (metric tons, 2007)	3.0

For sources and definitions, see explanatory note on p. vi.

Agriculture

PRINCIPAL CROPS
('000 metric tons)

	2006	2007	2008
Wheat*	199	195	175
Rice, paddy	2,479	1,870	2,862*
Barley*	77	75	65
Maize	1,750*	1,587*	1,411
Rye	60*	60*	60†
Oats	15*	15*	15†
Millet	64*	61*	61†
Sorghum	32*	30*	30†
Potatoes	2,000†	1,900†	1,520
Sweet potatoes†	360	370	380
Beans, dry†	300	300	300
Soybeans (Soya beans)*	345	345	345
Cabbages and other brassicas†	680	700	700
Tomatoes†	68	65	65
Pumpkins, squash and gourds†	85	80	80
Cucumbers and gherkins†	65	66	66
Aubergines (Eggplants)†	45	46	46
Chillies and peppers, green†	58	60	60
Onions and shallots, green†	95	98	98
Onions, dry†	86	84	84
Garlic†	93	95	95
Apples†	665	635	635
Pears†	130	125	125
Peaches and nectarines†	120	120	120
Watermelons†	100	95	95
Cantaloupes and other melons†	115	110	110
Tobacco, unmanufactured†	65	63	63

* Unofficial figure(s).
† FAO estimate(s).

Note: No data were available for individual crops in 2009.

Aggregate production ('000 metric tons, may include official, semi-official or estimated data): Total cereals 4,676 in 2006, 4,373 in 2007, 4,679 in 2008–09; Total roots and tubers 2,360 in 2006, 2,270 in 2007, 1,900 in 2008–09; Total vegetables (incl. melons) 3,876 in 2006, 3,756 in 2007–09; Total fruits (excl. melons) 1,405 in 2006, 1,370 in 2007–09.

Source: FAO.

LIVESTOCK
('000 head)

	2006*	2007*	2008
Horses	48	47	48*
Cattle	575	576	576
Pigs	3,300	3,400	2,178
Sheep	169	168	167
Goats	3,090	3,260	3,441
Chickens	18,000	17,000	15,548
Ducks	6,000	6,000	5,878

* FAO estimate(s).

Note: No data were available for 2009.

Source: FAO.

LIVESTOCK PRODUCTS
('000 metric tons, FAO estimates)

	2006	2007	2008
Cattle meat	21.6	21.8	21.8
Goat meat	12.7	13.4	14.1
Pig meat	170.0	175.0	180.0
Chicken meat	34.7	33.6	31.9
Cows' milk	96.0	96.0	96.0
Hen eggs	142.0	142.0	140.0

2009: Figures assumed to be unchanged from 2008 (FAO estimates).

Source: FAO.

Forestry

ROUNDWOOD REMOVALS
('000 cubic metres, excl. bark, FAO estimates)

	2007	2008	2009
Sawlogs, veneer logs and logs for sleepers	1,000	1,000	1,000
Other industrial wood	500	500	500
Fuel wood	5,873	5,911	5,949
Total	7,373	7,411	7,449

Sawnwood production ('000 cubic metres, incl. railway sleepers): 280 (coniferous 185, broadleaved 95) per year in 1970–2009 (FAO estimates).

Source: FAO.

Fishing

('000 metric tons, live weight, FAO estimates)

	2000	2001	2002
Capture	212.9	206.5	205.0
Freshwater fishes	8.0	4.9	5.0
Alaska pollock	60.0	60.0	60.0
Other marine fishes	112.2	109.0	107.6
Marine crustaceans	15.6	16.2	16.0
Squids	9.5	9.5	9.5
Aquaculture	66.7	63.7	63.7
Molluscs	63.0	60.0	60.0
Total catch	279.6	270.2	268.7

Note: Figures exclude aquatic plants (FAO estimates, '000 metric tons, aquaculture only): 401.0 in 2000; 391.0 in 2001; 444.3 in 2002.

2003–08: Figures assumed to be unchanged from 2002 (FAO estimates).

Source: FAO.

THE DEMOCRATIC PEOPLE'S REPUBLIC OF KOREA (NORTH KOREA)

Statistical Survey

Mining

('000 metric tons, unless otherwise indicated, estimates)

	2007	2008	2009
Hard coal	24,100	25,060	25,000
Iron ore: gross weight	5,130	5,316	5,300
Iron ore: metal content	1,400	1,488	1,500
Copper ore*	12	12	12
Lead ore*	13	13	13
Zinc ore*	70	70	70
Tungsten concentrates (metric tons)*	250	350	350
Silver (metric tons)*	20	20	20
Gold (kg)*	2,000	2,000	2,000
Magnesite (crude)	55,000	150,000	150,000
Phosphate rock†	300	300	300
Fluorspar‡	13	13	13
Salt (unrefined)	500	500	500
Graphite (natural)	30	30	30
Talc, soapstone and pyrophyllite	50	50	50

* Figures refer to the metal content of ores and concentrates.
† Figures refer to gross weight.
‡ Metallurgical grade.

Note: No recent data were available for the production of molybdenum ore and asbestos.

Source: US Geological Survey.

Industry

SELECTED PRODUCTS
('000 metric tons, unless otherwise indicated)

	2005	2006	2007
Motor spirit (petrol)	159	122	146
Kerosene	31	24	29
Gas-diesel (distillate fuel) oils	171	131	157
Residual fuel oils	98	75	90
Cement*	5,700	6,160	6,415
Pig-iron*	900	900	900
Crude steel*	1,070	1,180	1,230
Refined copper (primary and secondary metal)*	15	15	15
Refined lead (primary and secondary metal)*	9	9	9
Zinc (primary and secondary metal)	72	72	75
Electric energy (million kWh)	22,913	22,436	21,523

* US Geological Survey estimates.

Source: mostly UN Industrial Commodity Statistics Database.

2008 ('000 metric tons, estimates): Cement 6,415; Pig-iron 900; Crude steel 1,279; Refined copper (primary and secondary metal) 15; Refined lead (primary and secondary metal) 9; Refined zinc (primary and secondary metal) 75 (Source: US Geological Survey).

2009 ('000 metric tons, estimates): Cement 6,400; Pig-iron 900; Crude steel 1,300; Refined copper (primary and secondary metal) 15; Refined lead (primary and secondary metal) 9; Refined zinc (primary and secondary metal) 75 (Source: US Geological Survey).

Finance

CURRENCY AND EXCHANGE RATES

Monetary Units
100 chon (jun) = 1 won.

Sterling, Dollar and Euro Equivalents (31 December 2010)
£1 sterling = 153.575 won;
US $1 = 98.100 won;
€1 = 131.081 won;
1,000 won = £6.51 = $10.19 = €7.62.

Note: In August 2002 it was reported that a currency reform had been introduced, whereby the exchange rate was adjusted from US $1 = 2.15 won to $1 = 150 won: a devaluation of 98.6%. In November 2009 reports of further currency reform emerged; a 'currency exchange' was believed to have been implemented in December, whereby denominations of the former currency were exchanged for new currency at a rate of 100 old won for 1 new won. In January 2010 it was reported that an exchange rate of US $1 = 96.9 won had been established by some financial institutions.

BUDGET
(million won, projected)

	1992	1993	1994
Revenue	39,500.9	40,449.9	41,525.2
Expenditure	39,500.9	40,449.9	41,525.2
Economic development	26,675.1	27,423.8	28,164.0
Socio-cultural sector	7,730.6	7,751.5	8,218.3
Defence	4,582.1	4,692.2	4,816.9
Administration and management	513.1	582.4	326.0

1998 (million won, estimates): Total revenue 19,790.8; Total expenditure 20,015.2.

1999 (million won, estimates): Total revenue 19,801.0; Total expenditure 20,018.2.

2000 (million won, estimates): Total revenue 20,955.0; Total expenditure 20,903.0.

2001 (million won, projected): Total revenue 21,571.0; Total expenditure 21,571.0.

2002 (million won, projected): Total revenue 22,174.0; Total expenditure 22,174.0.

2003: Exact figures not made available following price reforms of August 2002.

2004 (million won, reported): Total revenue 337,546; Total expenditure 348,807.

2005 (million won, reported): Total expenditure 419,700.

2006 (million won, reported): Total expenditure 388,950.

2007 (million won, reported, estimate): Total expenditure 440,200 (Defence 69,200).

2008 (million won, reported): Total expenditure 451,500 (Defence 71,300).

2009 (million won, reported): Total expenditure 482,600 (Defence 76,300).

NATIONAL ACCOUNTS
(million won, UN estimates)

Expenditure on the Gross Domestic Product

	2007	2008	2009
Total domestic expenditure	2,102,142.4	1,951,407.1	1,761,724.5
Exports of goods and services	118,806.2	108,924.2	97,858.0
Less Imports of goods and services	221,791.3	206,516.3	186,696.3
GDP in purchasers' values	1,999,157.4	1,853,815.0	1,672,886.2
GDP in constant 2005 prices	1,761,880.2	1,816,468.5	1,799,957.3

THE DEMOCRATIC PEOPLE'S REPUBLIC OF KOREA (NORTH KOREA)

Statistical Survey

Gross Domestic Product by Economic Activity

	2007	2008	2009
Agriculture, hunting, forestry and fishing	423,821.4	400,424.0	349,633.2
Mining, manufacturing and utilities	719,696.7	704,449.7	650,752.7
Manufacturing	399,831.5	417,108.4	369,707.8
Construction	175,925.8	153,866.6	133,830.9
Services	681,712.7	596,928.4	536,996.5
Sub-total	2,001,156.5	1,855,668.8	1,671,213.3
Indirect taxes (net)*	−1,999.1	−1,853.8	1,672.9
GDP in purchasers' values	1,999,157.4	1,853,815.0	1,672,886.2

* Figures obtained as a residual.
Source: UN National Accounts Main Aggregates Database.

External Trade

PRINCIPAL COMMODITIES
(US $ million)*

Imports	2000	2001	2002
Live animals and animal products	20.3	73.9	103.4
Vegetable products	159.0	221.0	118.4
Animal or vegetable fats and oils; prepared edible fats; animal or vegetable waxes / Prepared foodstuffs; beverages, spirits and vinegar; tobacco and manufactured substitutes	89.1	89.9	72.3
Mineral products	171.2	231.1	235.9
Products of chemical or allied industries	108.4	123.4	122.1
Plastics, rubber and articles thereof	67.5	66.0	66.0
Textiles and textile articles	171.9	203.9	158.5
Base metals and articles thereof	85.2	100.4	88.2
Machinery and mechanical appliances; electrical equipment; sound and television apparatus	205.1	243.8	234.7
Vehicles, aircraft, vessels and associated transport equipment	146.2	88.4	76.1
Total (incl. others)	1,406.5	1,620.3	1,525.4

Exports	2000	2001	2002
Live animals and animal products	97.9	158.4	261.1
Vegetable products	30.3	42.0	27.5
Mineral products	43.2	50.5	69.8
Products of chemical or allied industries / Plastics, rubber and articles thereof	44.9	44.6	42.4
Wood, cork and articles thereof; wood charcoal; manufactures of straw, esparto, etc.	10.9	5.6	10.2
Textiles and textile articles	140.0	140.5	123.1
Natural or cultured pearls, precious or semi-precious stones, precious metals and articles thereof; imitation jewellery; coin	9.8	14.1	14.6
Base metals and articles thereof	43.9	60.2	57.4
Machinery and mechanical appliances; electrical equipment; sound and television apparatus	105.2	97.9	85.6
Total (incl. others)	565.8	650.2	735.0

* Excluding trade with the Republic of Korea (US $ million): *Imports:* 272.8 in 2000; 226.8 in 2001; 370.2 in 2002. *Exports:* 152.4 in 2000; 176.2 in 2001; 271.6 in 2002.

Source: Korea Trade-Investment Promotion Agency (KOTRA), Republic of Korea.

2005 (US $ million, unofficial estimates): *Excluding Republic of Korea:* Total imports 200; Total exports 100. *Republic of Korea only:* Total imports 715.5; Total exports 340.3 (Source: Bank of Korea, Republic of Korea).

2006 (US $ million, unofficial estimates): *Excluding Republic of Korea:* Total imports 205; Total exports 95. *Republic of Korea only:* Total imports 830.2; Total exports 519.5 (Source: Bank of Korea, Republic of Korea).

2007 (US $ million, unofficial estimates): *Excluding Republic of Korea:* Total imports 202; Total exports 92. *Republic of Korea only:* Total imports 1,032.6; Total exports 765.3 (Source: Bank of Korea, Republic of Korea).

2008 (US $ million, unofficial estimates): *Excluding Republic of Korea:* Total imports 269; Total exports 113. *Republic of Korea only:* Total imports 888.1; Total exports 932.3 (Source: Bank of Korea, Republic of Korea).

PRINCIPAL TRADING PARTNERS
(US $ million)*

Imports	2001	2002	2003
China, People's Republic	570.7	467.3	627.6
Germany	82.1	140.4	n.a.
Hong Kong	42.6	29.2	n.a.
India	154.8	186.6	157.9
Japan	249.1	135.1	91.5
Netherlands	9.1	27.6	n.a.
Russia	63.8	77.0	115.6
Singapore	112.3	83.0	n.a.
Spain	31.6	n.a.	n.a.
Thailand	106.0	172.0	203.6
United Kingdom	40.7	n.a.	n.a.
Total (incl. others)	1,620.3	1,525.4	1,614.4

Exports	2001	2002	2003
Bangladesh	38.0	32.3	n.a.
China, People's Republic	166.8	270.9	395.3
Germany	22.8	27.8	n.a.
Hong Kong	38.0	21.9	n.a.
India	3.1	4.8	1.6
Japan	225.6	234.4	173.8
Netherlands	10.4	6.4	n.a.
Russia	4.5	3.6	2.8
Spain	12.6	n.a.	n.a.
Thailand	24.9	44.6	50.7
Total (incl. others)	650.2	735.0	777.0

*Excluding trade with the Republic of Korea (US $ million): *Imports:* 226.8 in 2001; 370.2 in 2002; 435.0 in 2003. *Exports:* 176.2 in 2001; 271.6 in 2002; 289.3 in 2003.

Source: Korea Trade-Investment Promotion Agency (KOTRA).

2004 (US $ million): *Imports:* China, People's Republic 800; Japan 89; Korea, Republic 439; Total (incl. others) 2,280. *Exports:* China, People's Republic 586; Japan 163; Korea, Republic 258; Total (incl. others) 1,280 (Source: Ministry of Unification, Republic of Korea).

Trade with Republic of Korea (US $ million, unofficial estimates): *Total imports:* 715.5 in 2005; 830.2 in 2006; 1,032.6 in 2007; 888.1 in 2008. *Total exports:* 340.3 in 2005; 519.5 in 2006; 765.3 in 2007; 932.3 in 2008 (Source: Bank of Korea, Republic of Korea).

Transport

SHIPPING

Merchant Fleet
(registered at 31 December)

	2007	2008	2009
Number of vessels	301	296	252
Total displacement ('000 grt)	985.6	982.8	870.8

Source: IHS Fairplay, *World Fleet Statistics*.

International Sea-borne Freight Traffic
(estimates, '000 metric tons)

	1988	1989	1990
Goods loaded	630	640	635
Goods unloaded	5,386	5,500	5,520

Source: UN, *Monthly Bulletin of Statistics*.

CIVIL AVIATION
(traffic on scheduled services)

	2004	2005	2006
Kilometres flown (million)	1	1	1
Passengers carried ('000)	94	101	105
Passenger-km (million)	39	42	43
Total ton-km (million)	6	6	6

Source: UN, *Statistical Yearbook*.

Tourism

	1996	1997	1998
Tourist arrivals ('000)	127	128	130

Source: World Tourism Organization.

Communications Media

	1994	1995	1996
Radio receivers ('000 in use)	2,950	3,000	3,300
Television receivers ('000 in use)	1,000	1,050	1,090
Telefax stations (number in use)	3,000*	n.a.	n.a.
Daily newspapers:			
number	11	11*	3
average circulation ('000 copies)*	5,000	5,000	4,500

*Estimate(s).

1997 ('000 in use): Radio receivers 3,360; Television receivers 1,200.

Daily newspapers (number of titles): 15 in 2004.

Main telephones lines ('000 in use): 1,000 in 2006; 1,180 in 2007–09.

Mobile cellular telephones ('000 subscribers): 69.3 in 2009.

Sources: UNESCO, *Statistical Yearbook*; UN, *Statistical Yearbook*; International Telecommunication Union.

Education

(2000)

	Institutions	Students
Kindergartens	14,167	748,416
Primary	4,886	1,609,865
Senior middle schools	4,772	2,181,524

Source: mainly Government of the Democratic People's Republic of Korea, *UNESCO Education for All Assessment Report 2000*.

Universities and Colleges: The *UNESCO Education for All Assessment Report 2000* identified more than 300 universities and colleges with 1.89m. students and academics.

Teachers (1987/88, UNESCO estimates): Pre-primary 35,000, Primary 59,000, Secondary 111,000, Universities and colleges 23,000, Other tertiary 4,000 (Source: UNESCO, *Statistical Yearbook*).

Directory

The Government

HEAD OF STATE

President: President KIM IL SUNG died on 8 July 1994 and was declared 'Eternal President' in September 1998.

Chairman of the National Defence Commission: Marshal KIM JONG IL.

Titular Head of State: KIM YONG NAM.

CABINET
(May 2011)

The Government is formed by the Korean Workers' Party (KWP).

Premier: CHOE YONG RIM.

Vice-Premiers: KANG NUNG SU, KIM RAK HUI, JON HA CHOL, KANG SOK JU.

Vice-Premier and Chairman of the State Planning Commission: RO TU CHOL.

Vice-Premier and Minister of Finance: PAK SU GIL.

Vice-Premier and Minister of the Electronics Industry: HAN KWANG BOK.

Vice-Premier and Minister of Machine-Building Industries: JO PYONG JU.

Minister of Foreign Affairs: PAK UI CHUN.

Minister of People's Security: RI MYONG SU.

THE DEMOCRATIC PEOPLE'S REPUBLIC OF KOREA (NORTH KOREA)

Minister of Electric Power Industry: Ho Taek.
Minister of the Coal Industry: Kim Hyong Sik.
Minister of the Mining Industry: Kang Min Chol.
Minister of the Oil Industry: Kim Hui Yong.
Minister of the Metal Industry: Kim Thae Bong.
Minister of Construction and Building Materials Industries: Tong Jong Ho.
Minister of Railways: Jon Kil Su.
Minister of Land and Marine Transport: Ra Tong Hui.
Minister of Agriculture: Yi Kyong Sik.
Minister of Chemical Industry: Ri Mu Yong.
Minister of Light Industry: An Jong Su.
Minister of Foreign Trade: Ri Ryong Nam.
Minister of Forestry: Kim Kwang Yong.
Minister of Fisheries: Pak Thae Won.
Minister of Urban Management: Hwang Hak Won.
Minister of Land and Environmental Protection: Kim Chang Ryong.
Minister of State Construction Control: Pae Tal Jun.
Minister of Commerce: Kim Pong Chol.
Minister of Food Procurement and Administration: Mun Ung Jo.
Minister of Education: Kim Yong Jin.
Minister of Higher Education: Song Ja Rip.
Minister of Post and Telecommunications: Ryu Yong Sop.
Minister of Culture: An Tong Chun.
Minister of Labour: Jong Yong Su.
Minister of Public Health: Choe Chang Sik.
Minister of State Inspection: Kim Ui Sun.
Minister of Capital City Construction: Kim Ung Gwan.
Minister of the Foodstuff and Daily Necessities Industry: Jo Yong Chol.
Minister of Physical Culture and Sports: Pak Myong Chol.
President of the National Academy of Sciences: Pyon Yong Rip.
President of the Central Bank: Paek Ryong Chon.
Director of the Central Statistical Board: Kim Chang Su.
Director of the Secretariat of the Cabinet: Kim Yong Ho.
Note: the Minister of People's Armed Forces is not a member of the Cabinet (see under Defence).

MINISTRIES
All Ministries and Commissions are in Pyongyang.

Legislature

CHOE KO IN MIN HOE UI
(Supreme People's Assembly)

The 687 members of the 12th Supreme People's Assembly (SPA) were elected unopposed for a five-year term on 8 March 2009. The SPA's permanent body is the Presidium.
Chairman: Choe Tae Bok.
President of the Presidium: Kim Yong Nam.
Vice-Presidents of the Presidium: Yang Hyong Sop, Kim Yong Dae.

Political Organizations

Democratic Front for the Reunification of the Fatherland: Pyongyang; f. 1946; vanguard org. comprising political parties and mass working people's orgs seeking the unification of North and South Korea; Dir Kim Yang Gon.

The component parties are:

Chondoist Chongu Party: Pyongyang; tel. (2) 334241; f. 1946; follows the guiding principle of *Innaechon* (the realization of 'heaven on earth'); satellite party of the KWP; Chair. Ryu Mi Yong.

Korean Social Democratic Party (KSDP) (Joson Sahoeminju-dang): Pyongyang; tel. (2) 5591323; fax (2) 3814410; f. 1945; advocates national independence and a democratic socialist society; satellite party of the KWP; Chair. Kim Yong Dae; First Vice-Chair. Sin Pyong Chol.

Korean Workers' Party (KWP): Pyongyang; f. 1945; merged with South Korean Workers' Party in 1949; follows the guiding principle of *Juche*, based on the concept that man is the master and arbiter of all things; most significant political entity in the DPRK; Central Cttee of 124 full mems and 105 alternate mems; 3m. mems; Gen. Sec. Marshal Kim Jong Il.

SEVENTH CENTRAL COMMITTEE OF THE KWP
General Secretary: Marshal Kim Jong Il.

POLITICAL BUREAU (POLITBURO) OF THE KWP
Presidium: Marshal Kim Jong Il, Kim Yong Nam, Choe Yong Rim, Vice-Marshal Ri Yong Ho.
Full Members: Marshal Kim Jong Il, Kim Yong Nam, Choe Yong Rim, Vice-Marshal Ri Yong Ho, Kim Yong Chun, Jon Pyong Ho, Kim Kuk Thae, Kim Ki Nam, Choe Thae Bok, Yang Hyong Sop, Kang Sok Ju, Pyon Yong Rip, Ri Yong Mu, Ju Sang Song, Hong Sok Hyong, Kim Kyong Hui.
Alternate Members: Kim Yang Gon, Kim Yong Il, Pak To Chun, Choe Ryong Hae, Jang Song Thaek, Ju Kyu Chang, Ri Tae Nam, Kim Rak Hui, Thae Jong Su, Kim Phyong Hae, U Tong Chuk, Kim Jong Gak, Kim Chang Sop, Mun Kyong Dok.
Secretariat: Marshal Kim Jong Il, Kye Ung Tae, Jon Pyong Ho, Han Song Ryong, Choe Tae Bok, Kim Ki Nam, Kim Kuk Tae, Jong Ha Chol.

The component mass working people's organizations (see under Trade Unions) are:

General Federation of Trade Unions of Korea (GFTUK).
Kim Il Sung Socialist Youth League.
Korean Democratic Women's Union (KDWU).
Union of Agricultural Working People of Korea.

Diplomatic Representation

EMBASSIES IN THE DEMOCRATIC PEOPLE'S REPUBLIC OF KOREA

Cambodia: Munsudong, Taedongkang District, Pyongyang; tel. (2) 3817283; fax (2) 3817625; e-mail recpyongyang@gmail.com; Ambassador Chhorn Hay.

China, People's Republic: Kinmauldong, Moranbong District, Pyongyang; tel. (2) 3823316; fax (2) 3813425; e-mail chinaemb_kp@mfa.gov.cn; internet kp.china-embassy.org; Ambassador Liu Hongcai.

Cuba: Munsudong, Taedongkang District, POB 5, Pyongyang; tel. (2) 3817370; fax (2) 3817703; e-mail embacuba@rpdc.embacuba.cn; Ambassador José Manuel Galego Montano.

Czech Republic: Taedongkang Guyok 38, Taehakgori, Puksudong, Pyongyang; tel. (2) 3817021; fax (2) 3817022; e-mail pyongyang@embassy.mzv.cz; internet www.mzv.cz/pyongyang; Ambassador Dušan Strauch.

Egypt: 39 Munsudong, Taedongkang District, Pyongyang; tel. (2) 3817414; fax (2) 3817410; e-mail embassy.pyongyang@mfa.gov.eg; Ambassador Ismail Abdelrahman Ghoneim Hussein.

Ethiopia: Munsudong, Taedongkang District, POB 55, Pyongyang; tel. (2) 3827554; fax (2) 3827550; Chargé d'affaires Fekade S. G. Meskel.

Germany: Munsudong, Pyongyang; tel. (2) 3817385; fax (2) 3817397; e-mail info@pjoe.diplo.de; Ambassador Gerhard Thiedemann.

India: 6 Taehak St, Munsudong, Taedongkang District, Pyongyang; tel. (2) 3817274; fax (2) 3817619; e-mail amb.pyongyang@mea.gov.in; Ambassador Pratap Singh.

Indonesia: 5 Foreigners' Bldg, Munsudong, Taedongkang District, Pyongyang; tel. (2) 3827439; fax (2) 3817620; e-mail kompyg2@public2.bta.net.cn; Ambassador Nasri Gustaman.

Iran: Munhungdong, Monsu St, Taedongkang District, Pyongyang; tel. (2) 3817214; fax (2) 3817612; e-mail embpyong@mfa.gov.ir; Ambassador Morteza Moradian.

Laos: Munhungdong, Taedongkang District, Pyongyang; tel. (2) 3827363; fax (2) 3817722; Ambassador Chaleune Warinthrasak.

Libya: Munsudong, Taedongkang District, Pyongyang; tel. (2) 3827544; fax (2) 3817267; Secretary of People's Bureau Bashir Ramadan Khalifa Abu Janah.

Malaysia: Munhungdong Diplomatic Enclave, Pyongyang; tel. (2) 3817125; fax (2) 3817845; e-mail malpygyang@kln.gov.my; Ambassador Rahimi bin Harun.

Mali: Pyongyang; Ambassador Nakounte Diakité.

Mongolia: 17 Taehak St, Munsudong, Taedongkang District, Pyongyang; tel. (2) 3827322; fax (2) 3817616; e-mail mon-emb@kcckp.net; Ambassador SODOVJAMTSYN KHÜRELBAATAR.

Nigeria: Munsudong, Taedongkang District, POB 535, Pyongyang; tel. (2) 3827558; fax (2) 3817293; e-mail empngrdprk@yahoo.com; Ambassador Gen. (retd) YUSUF ABUBAKAR.

Pakistan: 23, Blk 66, Munsudong, Taedongkang District, Pyongyang; tel. (2) 3827479; fax 3817622; e-mail parep.pyongyang@kcckp.net; internet www.mofa.gov.pk/northkorea; Ambassador ARIF MAHMOOD.

Poland: Munsudong, Taedongkang District, Pyongyang; tel. (2) 3817325; fax (2) 3817634; e-mail phenian.amb.sekretariat@msz.gov.pl; internet www.phenian.polemb.net; Ambassador EDWARD PIETRZYK.

Romania: Munhungdong, Taedongkang District, Pyongyang; tel. (2) 3827336; fax (2) 3817336; e-mail ambrophe@gmail.com; Chargé d'affaires a.i. IANCU RIVIU OVIDIU.

Russia: Sinyangdong, Central District, Pyongyang; tel. (2) 3813101; fax (2) 3813427; e-mail rusembdprk@yahoo.com; internet www.dprk.mid.ru; Ambassador VALERII SUKHININ.

Sweden: Munsudong, Taedongkang District, Pyongyang; tel. (2) 3817485; fax (2) 3817663; e-mail ambassaden.pyongyang@foreign.ministry.se; Ambassador BARBRO ELM.

Syria: Munsudong, Taedongkang District, Pyongyang; tel. (2) 3827473; fax (2) 3817635; Chargé d'affaires a.i. SUHAIL HAIDER.

United Kingdom: Munsudong Diplomatic Compound, Pyongyang; tel. (2) 3817980; fax (2) 3817985; e-mail postmaster.PYONX@fco.gov.uk; Ambassador PETER HUGHES.

Viet Nam: 7 Munsudong, Taedongkang District, Pyongyang; tel. (2) 3817358; fax (2) 3817649; e-mail vnembassydprk@mofa.gov.vn; internet www.vietnamembassy-pyongyang.org; Ambassador LE QUANG BA.

Judicial System

The judicial organs include the Central (Supreme) Court—the highest judicial organ, which supervises the work of all courts—the Court of the Province (or city under central authority) and the People's Court. Each court is composed of judges and people's assessors.

The Central Procurator's Office, headed by the Procurator-General, supervises the work of procurator's offices in provinces, counties and cities. Procurators supervise the ordinances and regulations of all ministries and the decisions and directives of local organs of state power to ensure that they conform to the Constitution, laws and decrees, as well as to the decisions and other measures of the Cabinet. Procurators bring suits against criminals in the name of the State, and participate in civil cases to protect the interests of the State and citizens.

President of the Central Court: KIM PYONG RYUL.
First Vice-President of the Central Court: KANG SOK JU.
Procurator-General: RI KIL SONG.

Religion

The religions that are officially reported to be practised in the DPRK are Buddhism, Christianity and Chundo Kyo, a religion peculiar to Korea combining elements of Buddhism and Christianity. Religious co-ordinating bodies are believed to be under strict state control. The exact number of religious believers is unknown.

Korean Religious Believers Council: Pyongyang; f. 1989; brings together members of religious organizations in North Korea; Chair. JANG JAE ON.

BUDDHISM

In 2002 it was reported that there were an estimated 300 Buddhist temples in the DPRK; the number of believers was estimated at about 10,000 in 2003.

Korean Buddhists Federation: POB 77, Pyongyang; tel. (2) 43698; fax (2) 3812100; f. 1945; Chair. Cen. Cttee SHIM SANG JIN; Sec. JONG SO JONG.

CHRISTIANITY

In 2003 it was reported that there were approximately 13,000 Protestants and 3,000 Catholics in the country, many of whom worshipped in house churches (of which there were said to be about 500 in 2002). The construction of North Korea's first Russian Orthodox church was completed in August 2006.

Korean Christians Federation: Pyongyang; f. 1946; Chair. Cen. Cttee KANG YONG SOP; Sec. O KYONG U.

The Roman Catholic Church

For ecclesiastical purposes, North and South Korea are nominally under a unified jurisdiction. North Korea contains two dioceses (Hamhung and Pyongyang), both suffragan to the archdiocese of Seoul (in South Korea), and the territorial abbacy of Tokwon (Tokugen), directly responsible to the Holy See.

Diocese of Hamhung: Catholic Mission, Hamhung; 134-1 Waekwan-dong Kwan Eub, Chil kok kun, Gyeongbuk 718-800, Republic of Korea; tel. (545) 970-2000; Bishop (vacant); Apostolic Administrator of Hamhung and of the Abbacy of Tokwon Fr PLACIDUS DONG-HO RI.

Diocese of Pyongyang: Catholic Mission, Pyongyang; Bishop Rt Rev. FRANCIS HONG YONG HO (absent); Apostolic Administrator Most Rev. NICHOLAS CHEONG JIN-SUK (Archbishop of Seoul, South Korea).

Korean Catholics Association: Changchung 1-dong, Songyo District, Pyongyang; tel. (2) 23492; f. 1988; Chair. Cen. Cttee JANG JAE ON; Vice-Chair. MUN CHANG HAK.

CHUNDO KYO

According to officials quoted in 2002, there were approximately 40,000 practitioners of Chundo Kyo in the DPRK.

Korean Chundoists Association: Pyongyang; tel. (2) 334241; f. 1946; Chair. of Central Guidance Cttee RYU MI YONG.

The Press

PRINCIPAL NEWSPAPERS

Choldo Sinmun: Pyongyang; f. 1947; every two days.

Joson Inmingun (Korean People's Army Daily): Pyongyang; f. 1948; daily; Editor-in-Chief RI TAE BONG.

Kyowon Sinmun: Pyongyang; f. 1948; publ. by the Education Commission; weekly.

Minju Choson (Democratic Korea): Pyongyang; f. 1946; govt organ; 6 a week; Editor-in-Chief KIM JONG SUK; circ. 200,000.

Nongup Kunroja: Pyongyang; publ. of Cen. Cttee of the Union of Agricultural Working People of Korea.

Pyongyang Sinmun: Pyongyang; f. 1957; general news; 6 a week; Editor-in-Chief SONG RAK GYUN.

Rodong Chongnyon (Working Youth): Pyongyang; f. 1946; organ of the Cen. Cttee of the Kim Il Sung Socialist Youth League; 6 a week; Editor-in-Chief RI JONG GI.

Rodong Sinmun (Labour Daily): Pyongyang; internet www.kcna.co.jp/today-rodong/rodong.htm; f. 1946; organ of the Cen. Cttee of the Korean Workers' Party; daily; Editor-in-Chief KIM KI RYONG; circ. 1.5m.

Rodongja Sinmun (Workers' Newspaper): Pyongyang; f. 1945; organ of the Gen. Fed. of Trade Unions of Korea; Editor-in-Chief RI SONG JU.

Saenal (New Day): Pyongyang; f. 1971; publ. by the Kim Il Sung Socialist Youth League; 2 a week; Deputy Editor CHOE SANG IN.

Sonyon Sinmun: Pyongyang; f. 1946; publ. by the Kim Il Sung Socialist Youth League; 2 a week; circ. 120,000.

Tongil Sinbo: Kangan 1-dong, Youth Ave, Songyo District, Pyongyang; f. 1972; non-affiliated; weekly; Chief Editor PAK JIN SIK; circ. 300,000.

PRINCIPAL PERIODICALS

Chollima: Pyongyang; popular magazine; monthly.

Choson (Korea): Pyongyang; social, economic, political and cultural; bi-monthly.

Choson Minju Juuiinmin Gonghwaguk Palmyonggongbo (Official Report of Inventions in the DPRK): Pyongyang; 6 a year.

Choson Munhak (Korean Literature): Pyongyang; organ of the Cen. Cttee of the Korean Writers' Union; monthly.

Choson Yesul (Korean Arts): Pyongyang; organ of the Cen. Cttee of the Gen. Fed. of Unions of Literature and Arts of Korea; monthly.

Economics: POB 73, Pyongyang; fax (2) 3814410; quarterly.

History: POB 73, Pyongyang; fax (2) 3814410; quarterly.

Hwahakgwa Hwahakgoneop: Pyongyang; organ of the Hamhung br. of the Korean Acad. of Sciences; chemistry and chemical engineering; 6 a year.

Jokook Tongil: Kangan 1-dong, Youth Ave, Songyo District, Pyongyang; organ of the Cttee for the Peaceful Unification of Korea; f. 1961; monthly; Chief Editor LI MYONG GYU; circ. 70,000.

Korean Medicine: POB 73, Pyongyang; fax (2) 3814410; quarterly.

THE DEMOCRATIC PEOPLE'S REPUBLIC OF KOREA (NORTH KOREA)

Kunroja (Workers): 1 Munshindong, Tongdaewon, Pyongyang; f. 1946; organ of the Cen. Cttee of the Korean Workers' Party; monthly; Editor-in-Chief RYANG KYONG BOK; circ. 300,000.

Kwahakwon Tongbo (Bulletins of the Academy of Science): POB 73, Pyongyang; fax (2) 3814410; organ of the Standing Cttee of the Korean Acad. of Sciences; 6 a year.

Mulri (Physics): POB 73, Pyongyang; fax (2) 3814410; quarterly.

Munhwao Haksup (Study of Korean Language): POB 73, Pyongyang; fax (2) 3814410; publ. by the Publishing House of the Acad. of Social Sciences; quarterly.

Philosophy: POB 73, Pyongyang; fax (2) 3814410; quarterly.

Punsok Hwahak (Analysis): POB 73, Pyongyang; fax (2) 3814410; organ of the Cen. Analytical Inst. of the Korean Acad. of Sciences; quarterly.

Ryoksagwahak (Historical Science): Pyongyang; publ. by the Acad. of Social Sciences; quarterly.

Saengmulhak (Biology): Pyongyang; fax (2) 3814410; publ. by the Korea Science and Encyclopedia Publishing House; quarterly.

Sahoekwahak (Social Science): Pyongyang; publ. by the Acad. of Social Sciences; 6 a year.

Suhakkwa Mulli: Pyongyang; organ of the Physics and Mathematics Cttee of the Korean Acad. of Sciences; quarterly.

FOREIGN LANGUAGE PUBLICATIONS

The Democratic People's Republic of Korea: Korea Pictorial, Pyongyang; f. 1956; illustrated news; Korean, Russian, Chinese, English, French, Arabic and Spanish edns; monthly; Editor-in-Chief HAN POM CHIK.

Foreign Trade of the DPRK: Foreign Trade Publishing House, Potonggang District, Pyongyang; economic developments and export promotion; English, French, Japanese, Russian and Spanish edns; monthly.

Korea: Pyongyang; f. 1956; illustrated; Korean, Arabic, Chinese, English, French, Spanish and Russian edns; monthly.

Korea Today: Foreign Languages Publishing House, Pyongyang; current affairs; Chinese, English, French, Russian and Spanish edns; monthly; Vice-Dir and Editor-in-Chief HAN PONG CHAN.

Korean Women: Pyongyang; English and French edns; quarterly.

Korean Youth and Students: Pyongyang; English and French edns; monthly.

The Pyongyang Times: Sochondong, Sosong District, Pyongyang; tel. (2) 51951; English, Spanish and French edns; weekly.

NEWS AGENCY

Korean Central News Agency (KCNA): Potonggangdong 1, Potonggang District, Pyongyang; e-mail eng-info@kcna.co.jp; internet www.kcna.co.jp; f. 1946; sole distributing agency for news in the DPRK; publs daily bulletins in English, Russian, French and Spanish; Dir-Gen. KIM PYONG HO.

PRESS ASSOCIATION

Korean Journalists Union: Pyongyang; tel. (2) 36897; f. 1946; assists in the ideological work of the Korean Workers' Party; Chair. Cen. Cttee KIM SONG GUK.

Publishers

Academy of Sciences Publishing House: Nammundong, Central District, Pyongyang; tel. (2) 51956; f. 1953.

Academy of Social Sciences Publishing House: Pyongyang; Dir CHOE KWAN SHIK.

Agricultural Press: Pyongyang; labour, industrial relations; Pres. HO KYONG PIL.

Central Science and Technology Information Agency: Pyongyang; f. 1963; Dir JU SONG RYONG.

Education Publishing House: Pyongyang; f. 1945; Pres. KIM CHANG SON.

Foreign Language Press Group: Sochondong, Sosong District, Pyongyang; tel. (2) 841342; fax (2) 812100; f. 1949; Dir CHOE KYONG GUK.

Foreign Language Publishing House: Oesong District, Pyongyang; Dir KIM YONG MU.

Higher Educational Books Publishing House: Pyongyang; f. 1960; Pres. PAK KUN SONG.

Kim Il Sung University Publishing House: Pyongyang; f. 1965.

Korea Science and Encyclopedia Publishing House: POB 73, Pyongyang; tel. (2) 18111; fax (2) 3814410; publishes numerous periodicals and monographs; f. 1952; Dir-Gen. KIM JUNG HYOP; Dir of International Co-operation JEAN BAHNG.

Korean People's Army Publishing House: Pyongyang; Pres. YUN MYONG DO.

Korean Social Democratic Party Publishing House: Pyongyang; tel. (2) 5591709; fax (2) 3814410; f. 1946; publishes quarterly journal *Joson Sahoemingjudang* (in Korean) and *KSDP Says* (in English); Dir RI KANG SIK.

Korean Workers' Party Publishing House: Pyongyang; f. 1945; fiction, politics; Dir RYANG KYONG BOK.

Kumsong Youth Publishing House: Pyongyang; f. 1946; Dir HAN JONG SOP.

Literature and Art Publishing House: Pyongyang; f. by merger of Mass Culture Publishing House and Publishing House of the Gen. Fed. of Literary and Art Unions; Dir-Gen. RI PHYO U.

Transportation Publishing House: Namgyodong, Hyongjaesan District, Pyongyang; f. 1952; travel; Editor PAEK JONG HAN.

Working People's Organizations Publishing House: Pyongyang; f. 1946; fiction, government, political science; Dir MIN SANG HYON.

WRITERS' UNION

Korean Writers' Union: Pyongyang; Chair. Cen. Cttee KIM PYONG HUN.

Broadcasting and Communications

In October 2001 North Korea launched its first e-mail service provider in co-operation with China-based company Silibank.com, which was used for business and trade purposes. However, access to the internet remained severely limited, with information flow within North Korea still being conducted mainly via a closed intranet system (the Kwangmyong, meaning 'light', system). Although a mobile telephone network was established in 2002, the use of mobile telephones was banned in 2004, and it was reported that handsets had been confiscated by the authorities. However, the ban was subsequently removed, and Orascom Telecom Holding, a provider based in Egypt, was permitted to establish an operation in North Korea. In January 2008 Cheo Technology, a subsidiary of Orascom, was granted a licence to provide a mobile telephone service. By the end of 2010 the number of subscribers was reported to have reached 431,919.

TELECOMMUNICATIONS

Korea Post and Telecommunications Co: Pyongyang; Dir KIM HYON JONG.

BROADCASTING

Regulatory Authorities

DPRK Radio and Television Broadcasting Committee: see Radio, below.

Pyongyang Municipal Broadcasting Committee: Pyongyang; Chair. KANG CHUN SHIK.

Radio

DPRK Radio and Television Broadcasting Committee: Jonsungdong, Moranbong District, Pyongyang; tel. (2) 3816035; fax (2) 3812100; programmes relayed nationally with local programmes supplied by local radio cttees; loudspeakers are installed in factories and in open spaces in all towns; home broadcasting 22 hours daily; foreign broadcasts in Russian, Chinese, English, French, German, Japanese, Spanish and Arabic; Chair. (vacant).

Television

General Bureau of Television: Gen. Dir CHA SUNG SU.

DPRK Radio and Television Broadcasting Committee: see Radio.

Kaesong Television: Kaesong; broadcasts five hours on weekdays, 11 hours at weekends.

Korean Central Television Station: Ministry of Post and Telecommunications, Pyongyang; broadcasts five hours daily; satellite broadcasts commenced Oct. 1999.

Mansudae Television Station: Mansudae, Pyongyang; f. 1983; broadcasts nine hours of cultural programmes, music and dance, foreign films and news reports at weekends.

THE DEMOCRATIC PEOPLE'S REPUBLIC OF KOREA (NORTH KOREA) *Directory*

Finance

(cap. = capital; res = reserves; dep. = deposits; m. = million; br(s) = branch(es); amounts in won)

BANKING

The entry into force of the Joint-Venture Act in 1984 permitted the establishment of joint-venture banks, designed to attract investment into North Korea by Koreans resident overseas. The Foreign Investment Banking Act was approved in 1993. In early 2010 the establishment of a state development bank was reported.

Central Bank

Central Bank of the DPRK: Munsudong, Seungri St 58-1, Central District, Pyongyang; tel. (2) 3338196; fax (2) 3814624; e-mail kcb_idkb@co.chesin.com; f. 1946; bank of issue; supervisory and control bank; Pres. PAEK RYONG CHON; 13 brs.

State Banks

Credit Bank of Korea: Chongryu 1-dong, Munsu St, Otandong, Central District, Pyongyang; tel. (2) 3818285; fax (2) 3817806; f. 1986; est. as International Credit Bank, name changed 1989; Pres. LI SUN BOK; Vice-Pres. SON YONG SUN.

Foreign Trade Bank of the DPRK: FTB Bldg, Jungsongdong, Seungri St, Central District, Pyongyang; tel. (2) 3815270; fax (2) 3814467; e-mail ftb@co.chesin.com; f. 1959; deals in international settlements and all banking business; Pres. and Chair. O KWANG CHOL; 12 brs.

International Industrial Development Bank: Jongpyong-dong, Pyongchon District, Pyongyang; tel. (2) 3818610; fax (2) 3814427; f. 2001; Pres. SHIN DOK SONG.

Korea Daesong Bank: Segoridong, Gyongheung St, Potonggang District, Pyongyang; tel. (2) 3818221; fax (2) 3814576; f. 1978; cap. 158,205.8m., res 25,917.6m., dep. 1,990,582.5m. (Dec. 2006); Pres. RI GYONG HA.

Koryo Bank: Ponghwadong, Potonggang District, Pyongyang; tel. (2) 18333; fax (2) 3814410; e-mail krbankpy@co.chesin.com; f. 1989; est. as Koryo Finance Joint Venture Co, name changed 1994; co-operative, devt, regional, savings and universal bank; Pres. PAK YONG CHIL.

Kumgang Bank: Jungsongdong, Central District, Pyongyang; tel. (2) 3818532; fax (2) 3814467; f. 1979; Chair. KIM JANG HO.

Private Banks

Bank of East Land: BEL Bldg, Jonseung-dong, Moranbong District, POB 32, Pyongyang; tel. (2) 3818923; fax (2) 3814410; f. 2001; commercial, investment, merchant, private and retail banking; Pres. PAK HYONG GIL.

Tanchon Commercial Bank: Saemaeul 1-dong, Pyongchon District, Pyongyang; tel. (2) 18111999; fax (2) 3814793; e-mail cbktm828@co.chesin.com; f. 1983; fmrly Changgwang Credit Bank, merged with Samchon-ri Bank and named as above Nov. 2003; cap. 50,043.9m., res 93,817.9m., dep. 875,021.9m. (Dec. 2003); Chair. KIM CHOL HWAN; Pres. KYE CHANG HO.

Joint-Venture Banks

Korea Joint Bank (KJB): Ryugyongdong, Potonggang District, Pyongyang; tel. (2) 3818151; fax (2) 3814410; f. 1989; est. with co-operation of Fed. of Korean Traders and Industrialists in Japan; 50% owned by Korea Int. General Jt Venture Co, 50% owned by Gen. Asscn of Koreans in Japan; Gen. Man. O HO RYOL; 6 domestic brs, 1 br. in Tokyo.

Korea Joint Financial Co: f. 1988; jt venture with Koreans resident in the USA.

Korea Nagwon Joint Financial Co: f. 1987; est. by Nagwon Trade Co and a Japanese co.

Korea Rakwon Joint Banking Co: Pyongyang; Man. Dir HO POK DOK.

Korea United Development Bank: Central District, Pyongyang; tel. (2) 3814165; fax (2) 3814483; e-mail kudb888@yahoo.com; f. 1991; 51% owned by Zhongce Investment Corpn (Hong Kong), 49% owned by Osandok Gen. Bureau; Pres. KIM SE HO.

Koryo Commercial Bank: tel. (2) 3812060; fax (2) 3814441; f. 1988; jt venture with Koreans resident in the USA.

Foreign Investment Banks

Daedong Credit Bank: Potonggang Hotel, 401 Ansan-dong, Pyongchon District, Pyongyang; tel. (2) 3814866; fax (2) 3814723; internet www.daedongcreditbank.com; f. 1996; est. as Peregrine-Daesong Devt Bank; jt venture between Oriental Commercial Holdings Ltd (Hong Kong) and Korea Daesong Bank; Gen. Man. and CEO NIGEL COWIE.

Golden Triangle Bank: Rajin-Sonbong Free Economic and Trade Zone; f. 1995.

INSURANCE

State Insurance Bureau: Central District, Pyongyang; tel. (2) 38196; handles all life, fire, accident, marine, hull insurance and reinsurance.

Korea Foreign Insurance Co (Chosunbohom): Central District, Pyongyang; tel. (2) 3818024; fax (2) 3814464; f. 1974; conducts marine, motor, aviation and fire insurance, reinsurance of all classes, and all foreign insurance; brs in Chongjin, Hungnam and Nampo, and agencies in foreign ports; overseas representative offices in Chile, France, Germany, Pakistan, Singapore; Pres. RI JANG SU.

Korea International Insurance Co: Pyongyang; Dir PAEK MYONG RON.

Korea Mannyon Insurance Co: Pyongyang; Pres. PAK IL HYONG.

Trade and Industry

GOVERNMENT AGENCIES

DPRK Committee for the Promotion of External Economic Co-operation: Jungsongdong, Central District, Pyongyang; tel. (2) 333974; fax (2) 3814498; Chair. PAEK HONG BONG.

DPRK Committee for the Promotion of International Trade: Central District, Pyongyang; Pres. RI SONG ROK; Chair. KIM YONG JAE.

Economic Co-operation Management Bureau: Ministry of Foreign Trade, Pyongyang; f. 1998; Dir KIM YONG SUL.

Korea International Joint Venture Promotion Committee: Pyongyang; Chair. CHAE HUI JONG.

Korean Association for the Promotion of Asian Trade: Pyongyang; Pres. RI SONG ROK.

Korean International General Joint Venture Co: Pyongyang; f. 1986; promotes jt economic ventures with foreign countries; Man. Dir RO TU CHOL.

CHAMBER OF COMMERCE

DPRK Chamber of Commerce: Jungsongdong, Central District, POB 89, Pyongyang; tel. (2) 3815926; fax (2) 3815827; e-mail micom@co.chesin.com.

INDUSTRIAL AND TRADE ASSOCIATIONS

Korea Building Materials Trading Co: Tongdaewon District, Pyongyang; tel. (2) 18111-3818085; fax (2) 3814555; chemical building materials, woods, timbers, cement, sheet glass, etc.; Dir SHIN TONG BOM.

Korea Cereals Export and Import Corpn: Jungsongdong, Central District, Pyongyang; tel. (2) 18111-3818278; fax (2) 3813451; high-quality vegetable starches, etc.

Korea Chemicals Export and Import Corpn: Central District, Pyongyang; petroleum and petroleum products, raw materials for the chemical industry, rubber and rubber products, fertilizers, etc.

Korea Daesong General Trading Corpn: Pulgungori 1-dong, Potonggang District, Pyongyang; tel. (2) 18111; fax (2) 3814432; e-mail Daesong@silibank.com; Gen. Dir CHOE JONG SON.

Korea Daesong Jei Trading Corpn: Pulgungori 1-dong, Potonggang District, Pyongyang; tel. (2) 18111-3818213; fax (2) 3814431; machinery and equipment, chemical products, textiles, agricultural products, etc.

Korea Daesong Jesam Trading Corpn: Pulgungori 1-dong, Potonggang District, Pyongyang; tel. (2) 18111-3818562; fax (2) 3814431; remedies for diabetes, tonics, etc.

Korea Ferrous Metals Export and Import Corpn: Potonggang 2-dong, Potonggang District, Pyongyang; tel. (2) 18111-3818078; fax (2) 3814581; steel products.

Korea Film Export and Import Corpn: Taedongmundong, Central District, POB 113, Pyongyang; tel. (2) 180008034; fax (2) 3814410; f. 1956; feature films, cartoons, scientific and documentary films; Dir-Gen. CHOE HYOK U.

Korea First Equipment Export and Import Co: Central District, Pyongyang; tel. (2) 334825; f. 1960; export and import of ferrous and non-ferrous metallurgical plant, geological exploration and mining equipment, communication equipment, machine-building plant, etc.; construction of public facilities such as airports, hotels, tourist facilities, etc.; jt-venture business in similar projects; Pres. CHAE WON CHOL.

Korea Foodstuffs Export and Import Corpn: Kangan 2-dong, Songyo District, Pyongyang; tel. (2) 18111-3818289; fax (2) 3814417; cereals, wines, meat, canned foods, fruits, cigarettes, etc.

Korea Fruit and Vegetables Export Corpn: Central District, Pyongyang; tel. (2) 35117; vegetables, fruit and their products.

Korea General Corpn for External Construction (GENCO): Sungri St 25, Jungsongdong, Central District, Pyongyang; tel. (2) 18111-3818090; fax (2) 3814611; e-mail gen122@co.chesin.com; f. 1961; construction of dwelling houses, public establishments, factories, hydroelectric and thermal power stations, irrigation systems, ports, bridges, transport services, technical services; Gen. Dir CHOE BONG SU.

Korea General Machine Co: Tongsin 3-dong, Tongdaewon, Pyongyang; tel. (2) 18555-3818102; fax (2) 3814495; Dir RA IN GYUN.

Korea Hyopdong Trading Corpn: Othan-dong, Kangan St, Central District, Pyongyang; tel. (2) 18111-3818011; fax (2) 3814454; fabrics, glass products, ceramics, chemical goods, building materials, foodstuffs, machinery, etc.

Korea Industrial Technology Co: Jungsongdong, Central District, Pyongyang; tel. (2) 18111-3818025; fax (2) 3814537; Pres. KWON YONG SON.

Korea International Chemical Joint Venture Co: Pyongyang; Chair. RYO SONG GUN.

Korea Jangsu Trading Co: Kyogudong, Central District, Pyongyang; tel. (2) 18111-3818834; fax (2) 3814410; medicinal products and clinical equipment.

Korea Jeil Equipment Export and Import Corpn: Jungsongdong, Central District, Pyongyang; tel. (2) 334825; f. 1960; ferrous and non-ferrous metallurgical plant, geological exploration and mining equipment, power plant, communications and broadcasting equipment, machine-building equipment, railway equipment, construction of public facilities; Pres. CHO JANG DOK.

Korea Koryo Trading Corpn: Jongpyongdong, Pyongchon District, Pyongyang; tel. (2) 18111-3818104; fax (2) 3814646; Dir KIM HUI DUK.

Korea Kwangmyong Trading Corpn: Jungsongdong, Central District, Pyongyang; tel. (2) 18111-3818111; fax (2) 3814410; dried herbs, dried and pickled vegetables; Dir CHOE JONG HUN.

Korea Light Industry Import-Export Co: Juchetab St, Tongdaewon District, Pyongyang; tel. (2) 37661; exports silk, cigarettes, canned goods, drinking glasses, ceramics, handbags, pens, plastic flowers, musical instruments, etc.; imports chemicals, dyestuffs, machinery, etc.; Dir CHOE PYONG HYON.

Korea Machine Tool Trading Corpn: Tongdaewon District, Pyongyang; tel. (2) 18555-381810; fax (2) 3814495; Dir KIM KWANG RYOP.

Korea Machinery and Equipment Export and Import Corpn: Potonggang District, Pyongyang; tel. (2) 333449; f. 1948; metallurgical machinery and equipment, electric machines, building machinery, farm machinery, diesel engines, etc.

Korea Mansu Trading Corpn: Chollima St, Central District, POB 250, Pyongyang; tel. (2) 43075; fax (2) 812100; f. 1974; antibiotics, pharmaceuticals, vitamin compounds, drugs, medicinal herbs; Dir KIM JANG HUN.

Korea Marine Products Export and Import Corpn: Central District, Pyongyang; canned, frozen, dried, salted and smoked fish, fishing equipment and supplies.

Korea Minerals Export and Import Corpn: Central District, Pyongyang; minerals, solid fuel, graphite, precious stones, etc.

Korea Namheung Trading Co: Sinri-dong, Tongdaewon District, Pyongyang; tel. (2) 18111-3818974; fax (2) 3814623; high-purity reagents, synthetic resins, vinyl films, essential oils, menthol and peppermint oil.

Korea Non-ferrous Metals Export and Import Corpn: Potonggang 2-dong, Potonggang District, Pyongyang; tel. (2) 18111-3818247; fax (2) 3814569.

Korea Okyru Trading Corpn: Kansongdong, Pyongchon District, Pyongyang; tel. (2) 18111-3818110; fax (2) 3814618; agricultural and marine products, household goods, clothing, chemical and light industrial products.

Korea Ponghwa Contractual Joint Venture Co: Pyongyang; Dir MUN YONG OK.

Korea Ponghwa General Trading Corpn: Jungsongdong, Central District, Pyongyang; tel. (2) 18111-3818023; fax (2) 3814444; machinery, metal products, minerals and chemicals.

Korea Publications Export and Import Corpn: Yokjondong, Yonggwang St, Central District, Pyongyang; tel. (2) 3818536; fax (2) 3814404; f. 1948; export of books, periodicals, postcards, paintings, cassettes, videos, CDs, CD-ROMs, postage stamps and records; import of books; Pres. RI YONG.

Korea Rungra Co: Sinwondong, Potonggang District, Pyongyang; tel. (2) 18111-3818112; fax (2) 3814608; Dir CHOE HENG UNG.

Korea Rungrado Trading Corpn: Segori-dong, Potonggang District, Pyongyang; tel. (2) 18111-3818022; fax (2) 3814507; food and animal products; Gen. Dir PAK KYU HONG.

Korea Ryongaksan General Trading Corpn: Pyongyang; Gen. Dir HAN YU RO.

Korea Samcholli General Corpn: Pyongyang; Dir JONG UN OP.

Korea Technology Corpn: Jungsongdong, Central District, Pyongyang; tel. (2) 18111-3818090; fax (2) 3814410; scientific and technical co-operation.

Korea Unha Trading Corpn: Rungra 1-dong, Taedongkang District, Pyongyang; tel. (2) 18111-3818236; fax (2) 3814506; clothing and fibres.

Korea Yonghung Trading Co: Tongan-dong, Central District, Pyongyang; tel. (2) 18111-3818223; fax (2) 3814527; e-mail greenlam@co.chesin.com; f. 1979; export of freight cars, vehicle parts, marine products, electronic goods; import of steel, chemical products; Pres. CHOE YONG DOK.

Pyongsu JV Co Ltd: Pyongyang; f. 2004; pharmaceutical mfr, medical products incl. analgesics; jt venture with Interpacific/Zuellig Pharma (Switzerland).

TRADE UNIONS

General Federation of Trade Unions of Korea (GFTUK): Dongmun-dong, Taedongkang District, POB 333, Pyongyang; fax (2) 3814427; f. 1945; 1.6m. mems (2003); seven affiliated unions (2003); Pres. RYOM SUN GIL.

Trade Union of Construction and Forestry Workers of Korea: Pyongyang; f. 1945; 160,000 mems (2003); Pres. WON HYONG GUK.

Trade Union of Educational and Cultural Workers: Dongmun-dong, Taedongkang District, POB 333, Pyongyang; fax (2) 3814427; f. 1946; 89,800 mems (2003); Pres. KIM YONG DO.

Trade Union of Light and Chemical Industries of Korea: Pyongyang; f. 1945; 372,500 mems (2003); Pres. RI JIN HAK.

Trade Union of Metal and Engineering Industries of Korea: Pyongyang; f. 1945; 332,800 mems (2003); Pres. CHOE GWANG HYON.

Trade Union of Mining and Power Industries of Korea: Pyongyang; f. 1945; 221,000 mems (2003); Pres. SON YONG JUN.

Trade Union of Public Employees and Service Workers of Korea: Pyongyang; f. 1945; 305,900 mems (2003); Pres. KIM GANG HO.

Trade Union of Transport and Fisheries Workers of Korea: Pyongyang; f. 1945; 119,800 mems (2003); Pres. CHOE RYONG SU.

General Federation of Agricultural and Forestry Technique of Korea: Chung Kuyuck Nammundong, Pyongyang; f. 1946; 523,000 mems.

General Federation of Unions of Literature and Arts of Korea: Pyongyang; f. 1946; seven br. unions; Chair. Cen. Cttee CHANG CHOL.

Kim Il Sung Socialist Youth League: Pyongyang; fmrly League of Socialist Working Youth of Korea; First Sec. KIM GYONG HO.

Korean Architects' Union: Pyongyang; f. 1954; 500 mems; Chair. Cen. Cttee PAE TAL JUN.

Korean Democratic Lawyers' Association: Ryonhwa 1, Central District, Pyongyang; fax (2) 3814644; f. 1954; Chair. HAM HAK SONG.

Korean Democratic Scientists' Association: Pyongyang; f. 1956.

Korean Democratic Women's Union: Jungsongdong, Central District, Pyongyang; fax (2) 3814416; f. 1945; Chief Officer RO SONG SIL.

Korean General Federation of Science and Technology: Jungsongdong, Seungri St, Central District, Pyongyang; tel. (2) 3224389; fax (2) 3814410; f. 1946; 550,000 mems; Chair. Cen. Cttee CHOE HUI JONG.

Korean Medical Association: Pyongyang; f. 1970; Chair. CHOE CHANG SHIK.

Union of Agricultural Working People of Korea: Pyongyang; f. 1965; est. to replace fmr Korean Peasants' Union; 2.4m. mems; Chair. Cen. Cttee RI MYONG GIL.

Transport

RAILWAYS

In 2005 the total length of track was estimated at 5,214 km, of which some 70% was electrified. There are international train services to Moscow (Russia) and Beijing (People's Republic of China). Construction work on the reconnection of the Kyongui (West Coast, Sinuiju to Seoul, in South Korea) and East Coast Line (Wonsan–Seoul) began in

September 2002. The two lines were officially opened in June 2003, but were not yet open to traffic, as construction work on the Northern side remained to be completed. The lines were reportedly completed in 2005, and in May 2007 the first cross-border trial runs were conducted. In the long term, the two were to be linked to the Trans-China and Trans-Siberian railways, respectively, greatly enhancing the region's transport links.

There is an underground railway system in Pyongyang, with two public lines serving 17 stations. Unspecified plans to expand the system were announced in February 2002.

ROADS

In 2006 the road network was estimated at 25,554 km. Road links between the DPRK and the Republic of Korea were reported to have opened in late 2005. As part of the Government's 10-year plan, an additional 3,000 km of expressways were to be constructed by 2020.

INLAND WATERWAYS

In 2005 the total length of inland waterways was estimated at 2,253 km, most of which was navigable only by small craft. The Yalu (Amnok-gang), Taedong, Tumen and Ryesong are the most important commercial rivers. Regular passenger and freight services: Nampo–Chosan–Supung; Chungsu–Sinuiju–Dasado; Nampo–Jeudo; Pyongyang–Nampo.

SHIPPING

The principal ports are Nampo, Wonsan, Chongjin, Rajin, Hungnam, Songnim and Haeju. At 31 December 2009 North Korea's merchant fleet comprised 252 vessels, with a combined displacement of 870,800 grt.

Bochon Shipping Co: Pyongchon District, Pyongyang.

Chon Song Shipping Co Ltd: Sochang-dong, Potonggang District, Pyongyang.

Korea Ansan Shipping Co: Nampo.

Korea Chartering Corpn: Central District, Pyongyang; arranges cargo transport and chartering.

Korea Daehung Shipping Co: Ansan 1-dong, Pyongchon District, Pyongyang; tel. (2) 18111, ext. 8695; fax (2) 3814508; f. 1994; owns 6 reefers, 3 oil tankers, 1 cargo ship.

Korea East Sea Shipping Co: Pyongyang; Dir RI TUK HYON.

Korea Foreign Transportation Corpn: Central District, Pyongyang; arranges transport of cargoes for export and import (transit goods and charters).

Korea Myohyang Shipping Co: Ryonhwadong Changgoan St, Chung District, Pyongyang; tel. (3) 8160590; fax (3) 8146420.

Korea Myongsang Shipping Co: Chongpyong-dong, Pyongchon District, Pyongyang; tel. (2) 3815842; fax (2) 3815942.

Korea Tonghae Shipping Co: Changgwang St, Central District, POB 120, Pyongyang; tel. (2) 345805; fax (2) 3814583; arranges transport by Korean vessels.

Korea Undok Shipping Co Ltd: Nampo.

Korean-Polish Shipping Co Ltd: Moranbong District, Pyongyang; tel. (2) 3814384; fax (2) 3814607; f. 1967; maritime trade mainly with Polish and Far East ports.

Ocean Maritime Management Co Ltd: Tonghungdong, Central District, Pyongyang.

Ocean Shipping Agency of the DPRK: Moranbong District, POB 21, Pyongyang; tel. (2) 3818100; fax (2) 3814531; Pres. O JONG HO.

CIVIL AVIATION

The international airport is at Sunan, 24 km from Pyongyang.

Chosonminhang/General Civil Aviation Bureau of the DPRK: Sunan Airport, Sunan District, Pyongyang; tel. (2) 37917; fax (2) 3814625; f. 1954; internal services and external flights by Air Koryo to Beijing and Shenyang (People's Republic of China), Bangkok (Thailand), Macao, Nagoya (Japan), Kuala Lumpur (Malaysia), Moscow, Khabarovsk and Vladivostok (Russia), Sofia (Bulgaria) and Berlin (Germany); charter services are operated to Asia, Africa and Europe; Pres. KIM YO UNG.

Tourism

Tourism is permitted only in officially accompanied parties. In 1999 there were more than 60 international hotels (including nine in Pyongyang) with 7,500 beds. Mount Kumgang has been developed as a tourist attraction, as part of a joint venture between North Korea and Hyundai, the South Korean conglomerate. Other tourist destinations include Mount Chilbo, Mount Kuwol, Mount Jongbang and the Ryongmum Cave. In 2000 plans were announced for the development, jointly with the People's Republic of China, of the western part of Mount Paekdu, Korea's highest mountain, as a tourist resort. In 2003 it was estimated that around 1,500 Western tourists visited North Korea annually. It was estimated that more than 101,700 South Koreans visited the North in 2006 (of whom about 88,000 were business travellers to Kaesong), excluding visitors to Mount Kumgang.

Korea International Tourist Bureau: Pyongyang; Pres. HAN PYONG UN.

Korean International Youth Tourist Co: Mankyongdae District, Pyongyang; tel. (2) 73406; f. 1985; Dir HWANG CHUN YONG.

Kumgangsan International Tourist Co: Central District, Pyongyang; tel. (2) 31562; fax (2) 3812100; f. 1988.

Ryohaengsa (Korea International Travel Company): Central District, Pyongyang; tel. (2) 3817201; fax (2) 3817607; f. 1953; has relations with more than 200 tourist companies throughout the world; Pres. CHO SONG HUN.

State General Bureau of Tourism: Jungsongdong, Central District, Pyongyang; Pres. KIM DO JUN.

Defence

The estimated total strength of the armed forces as assessed at November 2010 was 1,190,000: army 1,020,000, air force 110,000, and navy 60,000. Security and border troops numbered 189,000, and there was a workers' and peasants' militia ('Red Guards') numbering about 5.7m. Military service is selective: army for five to 12 years; navy for five to 10 years; and air force for three to four years. Reserve forces were estimated to total 6m. in 2010.

Defence Expenditure: total expenditure was estimated at 76,300m. won in 2009.

Supreme Commander of the Korean People's Army and Chairman of the National Defence Commission: Marshal KIM JONG IL.

First Vice-Chairman of the National Defence Commission: (vacant).

Vice-Chairman of the National Defence Commission and Minister of the People's Armed Forces: Vice-Marshal KIM YONG CHUN.

Vice-Chairmen of the National Defence Commission: Vice-Marshal RI YONG MU, Vice-Marshal O KUK RYOL, JANG SONG THAEK.

Chief of General Staff of the Korean People's Army: Vice-Marshal RI YONG HO.

Commander of the Air Force: Col-Gen. RI PYONG CHOL.

Commander of the Navy: Gen. KIM YUN SHIM.

Education

Universal, compulsory primary and secondary education were introduced in 1956 and 1958, respectively, and are provided at state expense. Free and compulsory 11-year education in state schools was introduced in 1975. Children enter kindergarten at five years of age, and primary school at the age of six. After four years, they advance to senior middle school for six years. In 1988 the Government announced the creation of new educational establishments, including one university, eight colleges, three factory colleges, two farmers' colleges and five special schools. English is compulsory as a second language from the age of 14. A report submitted to UNESCO by the North Korean Government in 2000 stated that there were 27,017 nurseries for 1,575,000 pupils, 14,167 kindergartens for 748,416 pupils, 4,886 primary schools for 1,609,865 pupils, 4,772 senior middle schools for 2,181,524 pupils, and more than 300 universities and colleges with 1.89m. students and academics. The adult literacy rate was reported by UNESCO in 2003 to be 98%. In 2001 the Ministry of Education announced plans for the establishment of a university of information science and technology in Pyongyang, in co-operation with a South Korean education foundation: the Pyongyang University of Science and Technology (PUST) was expected to open in 2010. In June 2010 it was reported that the Ministry of Education was to be reorganized as the Education Commission, comprising the Ministry of Higher Education and the Ministry of Common Education.

THE REPUBLIC OF KOREA

Introductory Survey

LOCATION, CLIMATE, LANGUAGE, RELIGION, FLAG, CAPITAL

The Republic of Korea (South Korea) forms the southern part of the Korean peninsula, in eastern Asia. To the north, separated by a frontier that roughly follows the 38th parallel, is the country's only neighbour, the Democratic People's Republic of Korea (North Korea). To the west is the Yellow Sea, to the south is the East China Sea, and to the east is the Sea of Japan. The climate is marked by cold, dry winters, with an average temperature of −6°C (21°F), and hot, humid summers, with an average temperature of 25°C (77°F). The language is Korean. Confucianism, Mahayana Buddhism, and Chundo Kyo are the principal traditional religions. Chundo Kyo is peculiar to Korea, and combines elements of Shaman, Buddhist and Christian doctrines. There are some 17.5m. Christians, of whom about 83% are Protestants. The national flag (proportions 2 by 3) comprises, in the centre of a white field, a disc divided horizontally by an S-shaped line, red above and blue below, surrounded by four configurations of parallel, broken and unbroken black bars. The capital is Seoul.

CONTEMPORARY POLITICAL HISTORY

Historical Context

(For more details of the history of Korea up to 1953, including the Korean War, and subsequent bilateral relations see the chapter on the Democratic People's Republic of Korea—DPRK.)

UN-supervised elections to a new legislature, the National Assembly (Kuk Hoe), took place in May 1948. The Assembly adopted a democratic Constitution, and South Korea became the independent Republic of Korea on 15 August 1948, with Dr Syngman Rhee, leader of the Liberal Party, as the country's first President. He remained in the post until his resignation in April 1960. Elections in July were won by the Democratic Party, led by Chang Myon, but his Government was deposed in May 1961 by a military coup, led by Gen. Park Chung-Hee. Power was assumed by the Supreme Council for National Reconstruction, which dissolved the National Assembly, suspended the Constitution and disbanded all existing political parties. In January 1963 the military leadership formed the Democratic Republican Party (DRP). Under a new Constitution, Gen. Park became President of the Third Republic in December.

Domestic Political Affairs

Opposition to Park's regime led to the imposition of martial law in October 1972. A Constitution for the Fourth Republic, giving the President greatly increased powers, was approved by national referendum in November. A new body, the National Conference for Unification (NCU), was elected in December. The NCU re-elected President Park for a six-year term, and the DRP obtained a decisive majority in elections to the new National Assembly. In May 1975 opposition to the Government was effectively banned, and political trials followed. Elections to the NCU were held in May 1978, and the President was re-elected for a further six-year term in July. In October 1979 serious rioting erupted when Kim Young-Sam, the leader of the opposition New Democratic Party (NDP), was accused of subversive activities and expelled from the National Assembly. On 26 October Park was assassinated in an alleged coup attempt, led by the head of the Korean Central Intelligence Agency. Martial law was reintroduced, and in December the Prime Minister, Choi Kyu-Hah, was elected President by the NCU. A military coup in December was led by the head of the Defence Security Command, Lt-Gen. Chun Doo-Hwan, who arrested the Army Chief of Staff and effectively took power. Nevertheless, President Choi was inaugurated on 21 December to complete his predecessor's term of office (to 1984).

Choi promised liberalizing reforms, but in May 1980 demonstrations by students and confrontation with the army led to the arrest of about 30 political leaders, including Kim Dae-Jung, former head of the NDP. Martial law was extended throughout the country, the National Assembly was suspended, and all political activity was banned. Almost 200 people were killed when troops stormed the southern city of Gwangju, which had been occupied by students and dissidents. In August Choi resigned, and Gen. Chun was elected President. Acting Prime Minister Nam Duck-Woo formed a new State Council (cabinet) in September. In the same month the sentencing to death of Kim Dae-Jung for plotting rebellion was condemned internationally. (This sentence was subsequently suspended.) In October a new Constitution was overwhelmingly approved by referendum.

Martial law was ended in January 1981, and new political parties were formed. In the following month President Chun was re-elected: the start of his new term, in March, inaugurated the Fifth Republic. Chun's Democratic Justice Party (DJP) became the majority party in the new National Assembly, which was elected shortly afterwards. Amid opposition demands for liberalization, Chun pledged that he would retire at the end of his term in 1988, thus becoming the country's first Head of State to transfer power constitutionally.

During 1984, following an escalation of student unrest, the Government adopted a more flexible attitude towards dissidents. Several thousand prisoners were released, and the political 'blacklist' was finally abolished in March 1985. In January 1985 the New Korea Democratic Party (NKDP) was established by supporters of Kim Young-Sam and Kim Dae-Jung. At the general election to the National Assembly held in February, the DJP retained its majority, but the NKDP emerged as the major opposition force, boosted by the return from exile of Kim Dae-Jung. The new party secured 67 of the Assembly's 276 seats, while the DJP won 148 seats. Chun appointed a new State Council, with Lho Shin-Yong as Prime Minister. Before the opening session of the new National Assembly many deputies defected to the NKDP.

In April 1987 internal divisions within the NKDP led to the formation of a new opposition party, the Reunification Democratic Party (RDP); Kim Young-Sam was elected to its presidency in May. In April Chun unexpectedly announced the suspension of the process of reform until after the Olympic Games (due to be held in Seoul in September 1988). While confirming that he would leave office in February 1988, Chun indicated that his successor would be elected by the existing electoral college system, precipitating violent clashes between anti-Government demonstrators and riot police.

In June 1987 Roh Tae-Woo was nominated as the DJP's presidential candidate. However, Roh subsequently informed Chun that he would relinquish both the DJP chairmanship and his presidential candidature if the principal demands of the opposition for constitutional and electoral reform were not satisfied. Under international pressure, Chun acceded, and negotiations on constitutional amendments were announced. In August the DJP and the RDP announced that a bipartisan committee had agreed a draft constitution. Among its provisions were the reintroduction of direct presidential elections by universal suffrage, and the restriction of the presidential mandate to a single five-year term; the President's emergency powers were also to be reduced, and serving military officers were to be prohibited from taking government office. Having been approved by the National Assembly, the amendments were endorsed in a national referendum in October, and the amended Constitution was promulgated shortly thereafter.

Kim Dae-Jung joined the RDP in August 1987; however, in November he became President of a new Peace and Democracy Party (PDP), and declared himself a rival presidential candidate. At the election, in December, Roh Tae-Woo won some 36% of the votes, while Kim Dae-Jung and Kim Young-Sam each achieved about 27%. Roh Tae-Woo was inaugurated as President on 25 February 1988, whereupon the Sixth Republic was established. At the general election to the National Assembly, in April, the DJP failed to achieve an overall majority, securing 125 of the 299 seats. The PDP achieved 70 seats, thus becoming the main opposition party; the remainder went to the RDP and the New Democratic Republican Party (NDRP—the revived and renamed DRP), led by Kim Jong-Pil.

In February 1990 the DJP merged with the RDP and the NDRP to form the Democratic Liberal Party (DLP). Roh was

THE REPUBLIC OF KOREA (SOUTH KOREA)

subsequently elected President of the DLP, while Kim Young-Sam and Kim Jong-Pil were elected as two of the party's three Chairmen. The DLP thus controlled more than two-thirds of the seats in the National Assembly. The PDP, effectively isolated as the sole opposition party, condemned the merger and demanded new elections. In March a new opposition group, the Democratic Party (DP), was formed, largely comprising members of the RDP who had opposed the merger.

In July 1990 a large rally was held in Seoul to denounce the adoption by the National Assembly of several items of controversial legislation, including proposals to restructure the military leadership and to reorganize the broadcasting media. In protest, all the opposition members of the National Assembly tendered their resignations. Although the Assembly's Speaker refused to accept the resignations, the PDP deputies returned to the National Assembly only in November, following an agreement with the DLP that local council elections would take place in the first half of 1991, to be followed by gubernatorial and mayoral elections in 1992. The DLP also agreed to abandon plans for the transfer, by constitutional amendment, of executive powers to the State Council. The local elections (the first to be held in the Republic of Korea for 30 years) took place in March and June 1991, and resulted in a decisive victory for the DLP.

Meanwhile, in April 1991 the PDP merged with the smaller opposition Party for New Democratic Alliance to form the New Democratic Party (NDP). In September the NDP and the DP agreed to merge (under the latter's name) to form a stronger opposition front. A further opposition group, the Unification National Party (UNP), was established in January 1992 by Chung Ju-Yung, the founder and honorary chairman of the powerful Hyundai industrial conglomerate.

At elections to the National Assembly in March 1992, the DLP unexpectedly failed to secure an absolute majority, obtaining a total of 149 of the 299 seats. The remainder of the seats were won by the DP (97), the UNP (31) and independent candidates (21). In May Kim Young-Sam was chosen as the DLP's candidate for the presidential election, scheduled for December, and in August he replaced Roh as the party's President; divisions within the DLP led to defections from the party by opponents of Kim Young-Sam.

The presidency of Kim Young-Sam

The presidential election, on 18 December 1992, was won by Kim Young-Sam, with some 42% of the votes cast. Kim (who was inaugurated on 25 February 1993) was the first South Korean President since 1960 without military connections. In February 1993 Chung Ju-Yung resigned as President of the United People's Party (UPP—as the UNP had been renamed), following allegations that he had embezzled Hyundai finances to fund his election campaign; he was given a three-year suspended sentence in November. Kim Young-Sam appointed Hwang In-Sung as Prime Minister, and a new State Council was formed.

Kim Young-Sam acted swiftly to honour his campaign pledge to eliminate corruption in business and politics; in all, during 1993, Kim's anti-corruption measures were reported to have resulted in the dismissal of, or disciplinary action against, some 3,000 business, government and military officials, and new regulations to restrict the activities of the country's industrial conglomerates (*chaebol*) were announced.

Hwang In-Sung resigned as Prime Minister in December 1993 and was succeeded by Lee Hoi-Chang, hitherto Chairman of the Board of Audit and Inspection (BAI). However, he resigned in April 1994 and was replaced by Lee Yung-Duk, latterly the Deputy Prime Minister responsible for national unification.

In July 1994 the UPP and a smaller opposition party, the New Political Reform Party, merged to form the New People's Party (NPP). In October the Government announced that its inquiry into the role played by former Presidents Chun and Roh in the 1979 coup had found that both had participated in a 'premeditated military rebellion'. In December 1994 Lee Hong-Koo (hitherto the Deputy Prime Minister responsible for national unification) was appointed Prime Minister, as part of a major restructuring of the State Council.

The DLP fared badly at elections for gubernatorial, mayoral and other municipal and provincial posts in May 1995, in contrast to the success of a new party, the United Liberal Democrats (ULD), established in March by defectors from the DLP and led by Kim Jong-Pil (who had resigned as DLP Chairman earlier in the year). In September Kim Dae-Jung returned to politics, establishing his own party, the National Congress for New Politics (NCNP). The DP was severely undermined when many of its members left to join the NCNP.

A major scandal erupted in October 1995, when Roh Tae-Woo admitted in a televised address that he had amassed a large sum of money during his term of office. He was arrested in the following month; at his trial, which opened in December, Roh confessed to having received donations from South Korean businesses, but denied that these constituted bribes. Many senior politicians and business leaders were also detained and interrogated in connection with the affair. Kim Dae-Jung, meanwhile, unexpectedly admitted that his campaign for the 1992 presidential election had been supported by a donation of money from Roh's 'slush fund'. Kim Young-Sam denied opposition allegations that he too had benefited from a similar donation. In December 1995, in an effort to distance his party from the deepening scandal, Kim Young-Sam changed the DLP's name to the New Korea Party (NKP). A major reorganization of the State Council was effected, in which Lee Hong-Koo was replaced as Prime Minister by Lee Soo-Sung, the President of Seoul National University.

In late 1995 it was announced that Roh Tae-Woo and Chun Doo-Hwan were to be prosecuted for their involvement in the 1979 coup and the 1980 Gwangju massacre. Chun was arrested in December 1995, and in the following month he was additionally accused of accumulating a huge political 'slush fund'. At the opening of his trial for corruption in February 1996, Chun denied charges that the fund had been amassed as a result of bribe-taking. Legal proceedings in connection with the events of 1979 and 1980 opened in March 1996: Chun was charged with mutiny for his organization of the 1979 coup, and with sedition in connection with the Gwangju massacre, while Roh was charged with aiding Chun. Roh and Chun were convicted as charged in August 1996. For their role in the coup and the Gwangju massacre, Chun was sentenced to death and Roh to 22½ years' imprisonment, subsequently commuted on appeal to life imprisonment and 17 years, respectively; each was heavily fined in the corruption cases. Several others were also convicted for their part in the events of 1979 and 1980.

Elections to the National Assembly took place in April 1996. Contrary to widespread predictions, the NKP only narrowly failed to retain its parliamentary majority, winning a total of 139 of the 299 seats. One factor contributing to the NKP's success was believed to have been the recent incursions into the demilitarized zone (DMZ, separating North and South Korea) by North Korean troops, which, although apparently intended to destabilize the electoral proceedings, in fact caused many voters to favour the ruling party out of concern for national security. The NCNP performed less well than had been expected, taking 79 seats; moreover, the party's leader, Kim Dae-Jung, failed to win a seat. By the time the National Assembly convened in June, the NKP had secured a working majority with the support of several opposition and independent members.

The revision of the country's labour laws, to introduce greater flexibility into the employment market (a condition of the Republic of Korea's impending membership of the Organisation for Economic Co-operation and Development—OECD, see p. 376), was initiated in May 1996. Reforms proposed by the Government in early December were severely criticized by trade unions and opposition parties. Many thousands of factory workers, as well as public sector employees, participated in a strike called by the country's principal workers' confederation, the Federation of Korean Trade Unions (FKTU), after the Government convened a dawn session of the National Assembly, which approved the labour reform bill in the absence of opposition deputies. Anti-Government demonstrators in Seoul and other major cities repeatedly clashed with riot police, and warrants were issued for the arrest of several leaders of the Korean Confederation of Trade Unions (KCTU). Concern was expressed that President Kim might be resorting to a more authoritarian style of leadership, particularly when it was alleged that the DPRK was lending its support to the striking workers (a tactic used by the South Korean authorities in the past to justify the suppression of domestic dissent). By mid-January 1997 support for the strikes was abating; the KCTU suggested that it might accept a modification of the labour law, having previously insisted on its complete annulment. OECD issued a severe rebuke to the Government for failing to honour its pledges on labour reform, and, in a significant concession, Kim agreed to meet the leaders of the opposition parties to discuss amendments to the law; warrants for the arrest of union leaders were also suspended. In March the National Assembly approved a revised version of the legislation, whereby the implementation of certain proposals was delayed for two years, while the KCTU was granted immediate official recognition.

Meanwhile, bribery scandals persisted, prompting several government resignations during 1996. The infiltration of a North Korean submarine into South Korean waters in September (see below) resulted in the dismissal of the Minister of Defence, Lee Yang-Ho. He was subsequently charged with divulging classified information and with receiving bribes in connection with the procurement of helicopters for the army, and in December was sentenced to four years' imprisonment.

In January 1997 a further major scandal erupted when Hanbo, one of the country's largest steel and construction conglomerates, was declared bankrupt. Allegations were made that Hanbo had bribed the Government to exert pressure on banks to provide substantial loans to the conglomerate. The chief executives of several large Korean banks were arrested on charges of receiving bribes, and in February the Minister of Home Affairs, Kim Woo-Suk, resigned following allegations that he too had accepted payments from the company. President Kim issued an official apology for the loan scandal, and in March Lee Soo-Sung resigned as Prime Minister in a gesture of contrition. He was replaced by Goh Kun, hitherto President of Myongju University. The repercussions of the Hanbo affair widened further, implicating, among others, Kim Soo-Han, the Speaker of the National Assembly, and President Kim himself, whose 1992 election campaign was alleged to have been funded partially by the conglomerate. In June 1997 the former Chairman of Hanbo and several senior banking officials and politicians, including Kim Woo-Suk, were convicted on charges relating to the scandal.

In July 1997 Lee Hoi-Chang, former Prime Minister and Chairman of the NKP, was nominated as the ruling party's candidate for the presidential election, scheduled for December. Lee's candidacy was severely affected by various scandals surrounding the NKP and his family. Moreover, Rhee In-Je, the defeated challenger in the contest for the NKP nomination, decided to contest the presidency, subsequently forming his own political organization, the New Party by the People. In September Lee was elected President of the NKP, replacing Kim Young-Sam, who subsequently resigned from the party in order to ensure his neutrality in the forthcoming election. In October the NCNP and the ULD established an alliance, uniting behind the NCNP presidential nominee, Kim Dae-Jung. In November the NKP announced its merger with the DP, to form the Grand National Party (GNP).

However, internal party politics were overshadowed by the crisis experienced by the Korean economy in the latter half of 1997 and the revelation that many of the *chaebol* had amassed huge debts. Following the rejection by the legislature of the Government's financial liberalization measures, President Kim dismissed Kang Kyung-Shik, the Deputy Prime Minister and Minister of Finance and the Economy, in November, replacing him with Lim Chang-Yul, latterly Minister of Trade, Industry and Energy. An economic stabilization programme failed to curb the depreciation of the national currency, and the Government was forced to request the assistance of the IMF, a decision that was condemned by opposition politicians and the media as a 'national shame'. In December the IMF agreed to allocate substantial funds to prevent the Republic of Korea from defaulting on its repayments of external debt, subject to the implementation of a programme of extensive reforms.

The presidency of Kim Dae-Jung

The presidential election, held on 18 December 1997, was narrowly won by Kim Dae-Jung. Supporters of the ruling NKP were divided between Lee Hoi-Chang and Rhee In-Je, thus assuring victory for the NCNP-ULD alliance and the first peaceful transfer of power to an opposition politician in the Republic of Korea's history. Four other candidates contested the election. In a gesture to promote a sense of national unity, former Presidents Chun Doo-Hwan and Roh Tae-Woo were granted a presidential pardon and released from prison.

Legislation for financial reforms, to comply with the terms of the IMF agreement, was approved by the National Assembly in late December 1997. Discussions with South Korea's overseas creditors to renegotiate the terms of the country's debt repayments were successfully concluded at the end of January 1998. Compulsory reform of the *chaebol*, which had been widely criticized for contributing to the debt-repayment crisis through their extensive borrowing, and legislation to allow foreign investors to acquire majority shareholdings in South Korean companies, were among reform measures promulgated in early 1998.

Kim Dae-Jung was formally inaugurated as President in late February 1998. Despite resistance from the opposition, Kim Dae-Jung designated Kim Jong-Pil, the leader of the ULD, as acting Prime Minister, and a cabinet was formed in early March, with the ministries divided equally between the NCNP and the ULD. Various administrative reforms were implemented, including the abolition of the two posts of Deputy Prime Minister, the merger of the Ministries of Home Affairs and Government Administration, and a reduction in the powers of the Ministry of Finance and the Economy. The number of cabinet ministers was reduced to 17 (excluding the Prime Minister).

At the beginning of May 1998 a large rally organized by the KCTU in protest against job losses ended in violent clashes with riot police. Later in that month a two-day strike was called to demand that the Government fully honour its pledge to improve unemployment benefits and to reform the *chaebol*; according to the KCTU, some 120,000 workers supported the first day of the strike. The NCNP and the ULD performed well in local elections in June, although the turn-out was low. As the economic recession deepened, labour unrest increased. Tens of thousands participated in strikes in July to protest against rising unemployment, the Government's privatization proposals and plans from Hyundai Motor and Daewoo Motor for mass redundancies.

In August 1998 the National Assembly formally confirmed Kim Jong-Pil as Prime Minister, following months of legislative inactivity, during which the GNP had refused to support his nomination. However, the GNP boycotted parliamentary sessions throughout September and into October, further delaying the consideration of urgent economic reforms, in protest against a government anti-corruption campaign, which it claimed was partisan and aimed at dividing the opposition. Several GNP members were placed under investigation on suspicion of illegally raising electoral campaign funds. In late October three former aides to Lee Hoi-Chang were charged in connection with an alleged attempt to bribe North Korean officials to organize a border incursion into the DMZ in December 1997, with the aim of aiding Lee's campaign for the presidency. The dispute escalated in December 1998, when a number of opposition deputies entered a room in the assembly buildings, which was being used by the intelligence agency, and removed confidential documents on 44 politicians. The GNP claimed that the agency had been carrying out surveillance of opposition deputies and subsequently boycotted legislative proceedings. In early January 1999, as the boycott continued, the ruling parties unilaterally endorsed 130 bills without debate, including legislation on banking reform and a controversial fishing agreement with Japan (see below). In mid-January, however, the ruling and opposition parties agreed that all issues relating to the affair be referred to the National Assembly's steering committee. In May a major reorganization of the State Council was effected. However, in June corruption scandals led to the replacement of the newly appointed Ministers of Justice and of the Environment.

As the next legislative elections approached, in January 2000 Kim Jong-Pil resigned as Prime Minister to chair the ULD, nominating Park Tae-Joon, the founder of Pohang Iron and Steel Company, as his successor. Kim Dae-Jung reorganized the State Council, as a number of ministers resigned to concentrate on campaigning for parliamentary seats. Lee Hun-Jai, hitherto the Chairman of the Financial Supervisory Commission, was appointed as Minister of Finance and the Economy. Kim Dae-Jung established a new party, the Millennium Democratic Party (MDP), to succeed the ruling NCNP, having reportedly failed in attempts to effect a merger with the ULD. In February the National Assembly approved revisions to the election law, which reduced the number of legislative seats from 299 to 273 (227 directly elected and 46 allocated by proportional representation), and reversed a ban on campaigning by civic groups against candidates. Lee Han-Dong, recently elected as President of the ULD, subsequently announced the party's withdrawal from the ruling coalition, claiming that the MDP had failed to fulfil its electoral pledges, although Prime Minister Park was to remain in the Government.

The elections to the National Assembly were held on 13 April 2000. The GNP, which won 133 of the 273 seats, retained its position as the largest party in the Assembly, but remained four seats short of a majority. The ruling MDP secured 115 seats, while the ULD suffered a serious reverse, taking only 17 seats (compared with 50 in the 1996 elections). Only two seats were won by the Democratic People's Party (DPP), which had been formed in February by defectors from the GNP who had failed to

THE REPUBLIC OF KOREA (SOUTH KOREA)

be nominated as parliamentary candidates by their former party. In mid-May Park resigned as Prime Minister, amid increasing controversy over allegations of tax evasion. The designation of Lee Han-Dong as Park's successor indicated a restoration of MDP-ULD co-operation. Amid criticism that reform of the *chaebol* was proceeding too slowly, President Kim Dae-Jung effected a major government reorganization in August, which primarily concerned the economic portfolios.

President Kim enjoyed increasing respect within the international community, in October 2000 being awarded the Nobel Peace Prize for his contribution to democracy and human rights (and particularly for his successful attempts at reconciliation with the DPRK). However, his pursuit of reunification was criticized domestically by those who felt that, with its own economic problems, the Republic of Korea could ill afford assistance to the DPRK.

In November 2000 Kim Yong-Kap, a GNP member of the National Assembly, described the ruling MDP as 'a subsidiary' of the (North) Korean Workers' Party. The comments shocked and embarrassed both the MDP and the GNP, and the National Assembly was suspended. However, shortly after the legislature reconvened on the following evening, the GNP walked out in protest at an MDP motion to dismiss Kim Yong-Kap from his seat. A few days later the GNP walked out again, this time prompted by the MDP's obstruction of a motion to impeach the Prosecutor-General, Park Soon-Yong, for alleged bias in the investigation of irregularities during the April elections. The GNP returned to the session one week later.

During 2000 and early 2001 dissatisfaction with the Government manifested itself on numerous occasions in the form of industrial and agricultural unrest. Strike action by doctors over legislation depriving physicians of their right to prescribe drugs took place in June 2000 and again in October. In the following month farmers held a strike to demand that their debts be cancelled and that the Government intervene on their behalf at the World Trade Organization (WTO, see p. 430). Meanwhile, as the Daewoo Motor Company had been declared bankrupt, some 15,000 workers protested in November in Seoul against government-led corporate restructuring, which it was feared would result in large-scale retrenchment.

In January 2001 a minor reorganization of the State Council was effected, when changes included Jin Nyum's elevation to the post of Deputy Prime Minister for Finance and the Economy. Simultaneously, a government organization law came into effect that conferred the status of Deputy Prime Minister on the portfolios of Finance and Economy and of Education and Human Resources; a Ministry of Gender Equality was also created. In March there was a major reorganization of the State Council, following the resignation of the Minister of Foreign Affairs and Trade, Lee Joung-Binn, who had caused controversy by signing a joint statement with Russia criticizing the USA's planned 'national missile defence' (NMD) system. Han Seung-Soo, a member of the DPP, replaced him. The former Minister of Culture, Park Jie-Won, who had resigned in September 2000 following allegations of corruption, was appointed chief presidential policy adviser. Park had organized the historic inter-Korean summit in June 2000 (see below).

In early April 2001 the minor opposition DPP joined the ruling MDP-led coalition, despite protests from within the MDP. Later in that month the MDP suffered a defeat in local by-elections, and by May Kim Dae-Jung's popularity had declined sharply, as voters grew disillusioned by his failure to implement political reforms. President Kim had also received criticism for his appointment of ministers and advisers from his home region of Jeolla, in the south-west, thereby antagonizing the south-eastern Gyeongsang region.

In August 2001 the Minister of Unification, Lim Dong-Won, came under heavy criticism from the opposition after delegates from several South Korean non-governmental organizations (NGOs) travelled to the North to mark the anniversary of Korean liberation from Japanese rule, on 15 August. In September Lim was forced to resign after the National Assembly approved a motion of no confidence in him, organized by the GNP and supported by the MDP's coalition partner, the ULD. The latter's actions effectively dissolved the ruling coalition, and President Kim appointed four new ministers. Lim was immediately appointed presidential adviser on reunification, national security and foreign affairs, reaffirming Kim's confidence in him.

In October 2001 the GNP won three by-elections, increasing its seats in the National Assembly to 136—just one short of a majority. The opposition victory created new rifts within the ruling MDP between younger reformers and party veterans, and President Kim resigned from the party presidency in November, ostensibly in order to administer state affairs without being involved in party disputes. He was succeeded, on an interim basis, by Han Kwang-Ok.

In late January 2002 President Kim again reorganized the State Council, dismissing the Minister of Unification, Hong Soon-Young (who had been appointed only in September 2001), and reallocating seven other posts, as well as the positions of six of the eight senior presidential secretaries and his chief of staff. Park Jie-Won returned as Kim's special aide for policy, emphasizing his close relationship with the President. The changes were intended to strengthen Kim's authority during his final year in office. Within days, the Minister of Foreign Affairs and Trade, Han Seung-Soo, was also dismissed, owing to the country's strained relations with the USA.

A power struggle within the opposition GNP resulted in the departure of the party's Vice-President, Park Geun-Hye (daughter of former President Park Chung-Hee). In May 2002 Park established a new party, the Korean Coalition for the Future (KCF), serving as its Chairwoman; the KCF merged with the GNP in November.

Meanwhile, in mid-2001 and early 2002 strike action was taken by employees of several sectors, notably airline pilots, nurses, railway staff and energy workers, who were protesting against various issues, including the decline in real wage levels, privatization plans and shortened working hours. Intermittent strike action continued.

By late April 2002 Roh Moo-Hyun had secured the MDP presidential nomination, while the GNP remained mired in internal disputes; the party's eight vice-presidents all resigned on 24 March in order to 'renew the face of the party', and were succeeded by a collective leadership. Meanwhile, Lee Hoi-Chang had secured the GNP's nomination for the national presidency. Also in mid-April President Kim replaced the Deputy Prime Minister for Finance and the Economy, Jin Nyum, with Jeon Yun-Churl, hitherto the chief of staff to the President.

President Kim and six of his ministers resigned from the MDP in May 2002, in order to focus on state affairs during the final months of Kim's presidency. Kim had become increasingly embarrassed by corruption scandals involving his second and third sons, Kim Hong-Up and Kim Hong-Gul, respectively, and he publicly apologized for their behaviour. In June Kim Hong-Gul was charged with bribery and tax evasion, and subsequently went on trial. Kim Hong-Up was arrested later that month, accused of receiving bribes from businessmen. Both were subsequently sentenced to prison terms, although the two-year sentence of the latter was suspended for three years. The scandals adversely affected the MDP's performance in local elections held in mid-June.

In July 2002 President Kim announced a cabinet reorganization, nominating Chang Sang, hitherto President of Ewha Woman's University, as the country's first female Prime Minister. At the same time, six ministers were replaced. However, at the end of the month the National Assembly rejected Chang's appointment on the grounds of dubious property dealings and the fact that her son had adopted US citizenship. In her place, President Kim nominated Chang Dae-Whan, a former newspaper proprietor, but he too was rejected by the National Assembly in late August on the grounds of questionable financial practices. A third nominee, Kim Suk-Soo, a former Supreme Court judge and previously Head of the National Election Commission, was finally accepted by the National Assembly in October, thus ending months of political paralysis.

The MDP suffered further set-backs in by-elections held in August 2002 when the GNP won 11 out of 13 seats contested, giving it an overall majority in the National Assembly. In September Chung Mong-Joon (the sixth son of Hyundai founder Chung Ju-Yung), who was President of the Korean Football Association, announced that he was standing for the country's presidency. Chung's popularity had risen sharply following the Republic of Korea's successful co-hosting of the 2002 football World Cup. In November Chung formally established his 'National Unity 21' party, receiving support from a broad political spectrum. However, later in that month Chung and Roh agreed to present a joint candidate for the presidency, namely the latter, in order to prevent Lee Hoi-Chang's election as President in December. Under the terms of the Roh-Chung partnership, there was to be a constitutional amendment whereby the powers of the presidency would be reduced in favour of those of the Prime Minister. In the final months of 2002 the

THE REPUBLIC OF KOREA (SOUTH KOREA)

ruling MDP became mired in further scandals. In October it emerged that President Kim and Chung Mong-Joon had arranged for a Hyundai subsidiary to transfer a substantial sum of money to North Korea via the (South Korean) state-owned Korea Development Bank prior to the historic inter-Korean summit of June 2000 (see below), effectively 'buying' the meeting.

The presidency of Roh Moo-Hyun

None the less, the presidential election, held on 19 December 2002, was narrowly won by Roh Moo-Hyun, who received 48.9% of the votes cast, against Lee Hoi-Chang's 46.6%. The level of participation was estimated at 70.8%. Roh's victory, despite the late withdrawal of Chung Mong-Joon's support, was generally attributed to his uncompromising stance in favour of a foreign policy more independent from the USA, whereas Lee was widely seen as having very close relations with the US Government. The MDP accused the USA of supporting Lee in the election, citing a meeting between him and the US ambassador.

In January 2003 President-elect Roh began making various appointments. Goh Kun, hitherto the president of Transparency International Korea, an anti-corruption agency, and himself a former Prime Minister, was reappointed to that post, while Moon Hee-Sang, an MDP legislator, was appointed chief of staff, and concurrently Chairman of the Civil Service Commission. Roh was inaugurated on 25 February and promptly appointed a new cabinet. President Roh also reorganized the military and intelligence services, appointing Gen. Kim Jong-Hwan as Chairman of the Joint Chiefs of Staff, and Ko Young-Koo, a human rights lawyer, as director of the National Intelligence Service (NIS). The latter appointment reflected Roh's determination to depoliticize the agency, which had been responsible for surveillance of political figures even after the transition to democracy.

President Roh confronted immediate challenges on assuming office, most notably a diplomatic crisis between the DPRK and the USA. Other issues included the ongoing scandal surrounding Hyundai and the inter-Korean summit meeting of 2000. In March 2003 Roh appointed a special counsel to investigate the alleged transfer of funds by Hyundai to the DPRK in connection with the 2000 presidential summit meeting (see below). In the longer term Roh aimed to address regional imbalances and the disparity between rich and poor, to reduce corruption in business and the economy, and to improve living standards and labour management.

In April 2003 the GNP won two out of three seats in by-elections to the National Assembly, raising its total representation to 153. However, the victory of a reformist ally of the MDP, Rhyu Si-Min, was welcomed by the Government as an indication of support for the reform process. Also in April, the National Assembly voted in favour of the dispatch of South Korean troops to support US military action in Iraq in a non-combat capacity. Despite his independent stance on relations with the USA, President Roh justified the decision in terms of strengthening Korean-US relations. Several hundred South Korean military medical and engineering personnel were sent to Iraq in May, despite widespread public opposition to the deployment.

In June 2003 two aides of former President Kim Dae-Jung, former Minister of Unification Lim Dong-Won and former Minister of Culture and Tourism Park Jie-Won, were charged in connection with illegal payments made through the Hyundai group to the DPRK to arrange the 2000 presidential summit meeting (Lim received an 18-month prison sentence in September, and Park was sentenced to 12 years' imprisonment in December). Also implicated in the scandal was Hyundai heir Chung Mong-Hun, who committed suicide in August.

In September 2003 a faction of the MDP announced its intention to form a new party, owing to internal divisions over corruption and other issues. President Roh subsequently relinquished his membership of the MDP, although he did not commit himself to joining the new organization, which was named the Uri (meaning 'our') Party in October. A large number of MDP legislators, including MDP Chairman Chyung Dai-Chul, joined the Uri Party, thus leaving the MDP with only 62 seats in the National Assembly. The Uri Party was officially inaugurated in November under a temporary leadership (Chung Dong-Young was elected Uri Party Chairman in early 2004). Another development in September 2003, meanwhile, was the resignation of the Minister of Home Affairs, Kim Doo-Kwan, following an incident in which protesters had infiltrated a US base in Pocheon. In October there was renewed public protest over the country's involvement in Iraq, which intensified in late 2003 following the killing there of two South Korean engineers.

President Roh's declining popularity was further undermined in October 2003 by the investigation and subsequent arrest of his former aide Choi Do-Sul, who was accused of having received illegal funds from the SK Group, a major *chaebol*, following the 2002 presidential election. In an attempt to restore his popularity, Roh announced proposals for a referendum to be held on the issue of his presidency later in the year. However, the proposed referendum prompted further political instability, with Prime Minister Goh Kun and other government ministers offering their resignations (which were rejected by President Roh). Both the GNP and the MDP dismissed the referendum proposal as unconstitutional.

Official investigations into illegal campaign funding from leading *chaebol* during the 2002 presidential election, involving both the MDP and the GNP, were instigated in October 2003. Initially focusing on donations from the SK Group, the investigation widened in November, with forcible searches taking place at the offices of other *chaebol*, including Hyundai, LG Group and Samsung. At the end of November President Roh vetoed a bill, already approved by the National Assembly, which urged an independent investigation into the funding allegations. In December the National Assembly voted to rescind the veto, in the first reversal of a presidential decision since 1954. An independent investigator was subsequently appointed. In the same month President Roh announced that he would step down if the MDP were found by the investigation to have received one-tenth of the illegal funding taken by the GNP. In a further development in December 2003, the GNP's Lee Hoi-Chang, Roh's rival in the 2002 election, publicly admitted that his party had accepted US $42m. in illegal donations.

In January 2004 the Minister of Foreign Affairs and Trade, Yoon Young-Kwan, relinquished his post, reportedly following a dispute related to President Roh's policy on independence from the USA over issues such as the North Korean nuclear weapons programme, but there was also a suggestion that Yoon Young-Kwan's departure was due to unrelated internal divisions. Yoon Young-Kwan was replaced by Ban Ki-Moon. There were further government changes in February, following the resignation of Kim Jin-Pyo, the Deputy Prime Minister for Finance and the Economy, in order to stand as a Uri Party candidate in the legislative elections scheduled for April. Kim was replaced as Deputy Prime Minister by Lee Hun-Jai, and three further new ministers were appointed in the same month. Also in February, the National Assembly approved the deployment of an additional 3,000 non-combat troops to Iraq (the deployment was later delayed owing to security concerns—see below).

Meanwhile, investigations into political corruption continued in early 2004, and both the former MDP Chairman, Chyung Dai-Chul (now of the Uri Party), and the former Secretary-General of the GNP, Kim Young-Iel, were arrested. In February there was also speculation that Park Geun-Hye had received undeclared funds from the GNP for the purposes of a merger with her KCF. In March it was reported that President Roh's MDP election campaign had received 12,500m. won in illicit funds, amounting to one-seventh of the 84,000m. allegedly received by the GNP and thus to more than the proportion of one-tenth that Roh had previously stated would prompt his resignation. At the end of March it was confirmed that Roh's former aide Choi Do-Sul (see above) had received US $530,000 in illegal funding.

As the legislative election of April 2004 approached, there were dramatic developments in mid-March when President Roh was impeached over the issue of his support for the pro-Government Uri Party, whereby he had allegedly violated electoral law. A total of 193 legislators, mostly from the GNP and Roh's former party, the MDP, voted in favour of the impeachment. There were vehement protests from supporters of President Roh in the National Assembly and members of the public following the vote, with opinion polls indicating that around 70% of the population did not support the impeachment. President Roh's position was to be reviewed by the Constitutional Court within six months, with Prime Minister Goh Kun becoming acting head of state for this period.

At the elections to the National Assembly on 15 April 2004, the Uri Party won a narrow majority in the legislature, securing 152 seats of the total of 299 in the newly expanded chamber (243 of which were determined by direct election and the remainder by proportional representation). The GNP, now under the leadership of Park Geun-Hye, secured 121 seats. Roh's former party, the MDP, won only nine seats. The success of the Uri Party was seen as a victory for Roh and an expression of public disapproval of his impeachment. In May Roh was reinstated following the decision of the Constitutional Court to dismiss the case for impeachment. He became a formal member of the Uri Party in the same month.

Following the reinstatement of President Roh, Prime Minister Goh Kun resigned from his post; Lee Hae-Chan, a former education minister, was approved by the National Assembly as Prime Minister in June 2004. Three new ministerial appointments were then made, including that of Chung Dong-Young as Minister of Unification. Also in June, the Government announced that the deployment of 3,000 South Korean troops to Iraq, originally approved in February (see above), would take place in August. Public opposition to this decision increased dramatically a few days later when a South Korean translator, Kim Sun-Il, who had been taken hostage in Iraq, was beheaded by his captors. In July the Minister of National Defence, Cho Young-Kil, resigned, taking responsibility for an incident in which a South Korean ship had fired warning shots at a North Korean vessel believed to be intruding in South Korean waters, with naval staff reportedly having failed to report radio communication with the North Korean ship. Cho was replaced by Yoon Kwang-Woong. Meanwhile, during mid-2004 there were various instances of labour unrest, including strikes by subway workers and by employees of a major oil company. In August President Roh announced that investigations were to be held into the past conduct of politicians during the period of Japanese rule and of dictatorial governments extending into the 1980s. The first senior politician to be adversely affected by these investigations was Shin Ki-Nam, who had replaced Chung Dong-Young as leader of the Uri Party in May 2004; he was forced to resign after it was found that his father had committed human rights abuses as a police officer during the period of Japanese colonization. Shin was replaced by Lee Bu-Young. In September controversy arose over the anti-communist national security law, which dated back to the country's pre-democratic era. Human rights groups, supported by President Roh, claimed that the law was outdated and subject to abuse. However, proposals to abolish the law were rejected by the Supreme Court. In November there were further instances of labour unrest in protest against government plans to reform labour legislation to prohibit strikes by public sector workers and to allow employers to hire staff on a temporary basis. In December the National Assembly approved a proposal for South Korean troops in Iraq to remain there until the end of 2005, despite continuing strong public opposition to the deployment.

A number of government changes took place in January 2005. In March the Deputy Prime Minister for Finance and the Economy, Lee Hun-Jai, resigned as a result of controversy over his wife's real-estate investments. He was replaced by Han Duck-Soo, hitherto the Minister of Government Policy Co-ordination. Further government changes took place in June, when Roh appointed Chun Jung-Bae as Minister of Justice and Lee Jae-Yong as Minister of the Environment.

In January 2005 Lee Bu-Young resigned from the leadership of the Uri Party, citing his party's failure to realize its reform aims such as the abolition of the anti-communist national security law. Moon Hee-Sang was elected party leader in April. The Uri Party had lost its majority in the National Assembly in the previous month when the Supreme Court upheld the convictions of two party legislators for malpractice in the election of April 2004, thereby depriving them of their seats and reducing the party's representation to 146. In all, six of the legislators elected in April 2004 had subsequently lost their seats as a result of malpractice convictions, temporarily reducing the National Assembly to 293 seats. At by-elections held in late April 2005 to fill these vacancies, the opposition GNP took five of the six contested seats, with the sixth being won by an independent candidate. In May it was announced that the MDP was changing its name to the Democratic Party (DP). Another round of by-elections was held in October to replace two legislators from the Uri Party and two from the GNP who had lost their seats, again owing to convictions for electoral malpractice. The GNP won all four contested seats, thereby further reducing the Uri Party's parliamentary representation to 144 and prompting the resignation of the party's senior leadership, including Chairman Moon. Chung Sye-Kyun was appointed acting Chairman pending a leadership election in February 2006. Former party Chairman Chung Dong-Young resigned as Minister of Unification in December 2005 in order to stand in the leadership election, as did Kim Geun-Tae, the Minister of Health and Welfare.

Consequently, in January 2006 President Roh effected a government reorganization. Notably, Rhyu Si-Min was appointed Minister of Health and Welfare, while Lee Jong-Seok became Minister of Unification and acting Uri Party Chairman Chung Sye-Kyun was appointed Minister of Commerce, Industry and Energy. At the Uri Party's national convention in February, Chung Dong-Young was elected to the post of Chairman for a second time. Another series of ministerial nominations was announced in March, to replace government members who subsequently resigned in order to stand at the forthcoming mayoral and gubernatorial elections scheduled for May. Also in March a scandal developed with regard to the conduct of the Prime Minister, Lee Hae-Chan, after he chose to play golf rather than oversee the Government's reaction to the first day of a national strike. Furthermore, objections were raised to his choice of golfing partners, who reportedly included a businessman with a criminal record for the manipulation of share prices. Lee resigned in mid-March. Roh's nomination of Han Myeong-Sook as Lee's successor was approved by a vote in the National Assembly in mid-April, and she was thus appointed as the country's first female Prime Minister.

None the less, the appointment of a new Prime Minister failed to improve the fortunes of the Uri Party. (Conversely, the resignation of the Secretary-General of the GNP, Choi Yeon-Hee, following charges of sexual harassment, did little to boost the Uri Party's popularity.) Local elections held at the end of May 2006 resulted in victory for the GNP, which garnered 54.5% of the votes cast nation-wide, compared with just 21.2% received by the Uri Party. Significantly, of the 16 provincial governor and city mayoral positions, the Uri Party took only one, while the GNP secured 12, the DP two and an independent candidate the remaining one. In June, taking responsibility for the party's disastrous election performance, Chairman Chung Dong-Young resigned and was replaced by Kim Kun-Tae. By-elections held in July further emphasized the Uri Party's declining popularity: the GNP won three of the four seats contested, while the DP took the fourth.

Also in July 2006, President Roh effected a minor cabinet reorganization, appointing Kwon O-Kyu as Deputy Prime Minister for Finance and the Economy, Chang Byoung-Wan as Deputy Prime Minister for Planning and Budget, and Kim Byong-Joon as Deputy Prime Minister for Education and Human Resources Development. (However, Kim resigned just 13 days after his appointment, amid allegations of plagiarism in his university thesis; he was replaced by Kim Shin-Il.) All three of the new appointees were widely perceived as being close allies of Roh. In the following month Kim Sung-Ho, hitherto deputy head of the Commission Against Corruption, was named as Minister of Justice, replacing Chun Jung-Bae.

The North Korean nuclear test on 9 October 2006 (see below) resulted in a further ministerial reorganization. Both the Minister of Unification, Lee Jong-Seok, and the Minister of National Defence, Yoon Kwang-Woong, resigned amid both domestic and international criticism of the South Korean Government's continuing policy of engagement with the North. The new Minister of Unification was Lee Jae-Joung, a former Uri Party legislator, while the Army Chief of Staff, Kim Jang-Soo, took the defence portfolio. Another new appointment was that of Song Min-Soon, who was nominated to the post of Minister of Foreign Affairs and Trade (a position vacated by Ban Ki-Moon, following his appointment as UN Secretary-General).

Parliamentary by-elections and local elections held in October 2006 resulted in defeat for the Uri Party's candidates. While some members of the Uri Party remained staunch supporters of the embattled President, others began to indicate that they might establish a new party, and the party's parliamentary leader, Kim Han-Gill, warned Roh to confine himself to economic and diplomatic issues rather than becoming involved in party politics.

In addition to the issue of engagement with North Korea, public dissatisfaction with President Roh's handling of the economy also increased; house prices had risen rapidly and the education system had undergone a controversial restructuring. Many South Koreans were also deeply suspicious of the Government's plans to sign a free trade agreement (FTA) with the USA, and in November 2006 thousands took to the streets to protest against the proposed deal, leading to violent clashes with the police (see below).

By late 2006 preparations for the next presidential election, due to be held in December 2007, were well under way. Park Geun-Hye, the former GNP chairwoman, thought to be popular among conservative voters, had declared her intention to stand. Also entering the contest was her GNP colleague Lee Myung-

Bak, the former mayor of Seoul and CEO of Hyundai Engineering and Construction Company.

In January 2007 the Uri Party formally announced that it would disband and establish a new party. Initial reports suggested that the party would seek an alliance with the DP (defectors from which had originally formed the Uri Party in 2003), and that a number of Uri Party legislators had already switched their party allegiance to the DP. However, in February 2007, before these plans could be implemented, 23 legislators announced their defection from the Uri Party, joining six others who had resigned in the previous fortnight. Following this mass defection, the GNP held 127 seats and the Uri Party 110 in the National Assembly. President Roh finally announced his departure from the Uri Party, in the hope of reversing its decline in popularity. This decision forced the President to engage more deeply with the GNP and other parties; without their support, the Roh administration would be unable to secure the approval of important legislation.

In March 2007, after only 10 months in office, Prime Minister Han Myeong-Sook resigned and was succeeded by Han Duck-Soo, who had been special adviser to the President on free trade affairs since being replaced as Deputy Prime Minister for Finance and the Economy in July 2006. Further government changes followed in mid-April 2007. New appointees included Kim Jong-Min as Minister of Culture and Tourism and Kang Moo-Hyun as Minister of Maritime Affairs and Fisheries.

The GNP suffered a reverse in by-elections held in late April 2007, securing only one of the three seats contested. It was defeated by the recently formed People First Party and the DP in the other two constituencies, where the Uri Party had opted not to field candidates, instead supporting the minor opposition parties, with which it hoped to form a 'grand alliance' in advance of the forthcoming presidential and legislative elections. The polls were marked by a particularly low turn-out of 27.7%. Moreover, the GNP lost five of six mayoral and gubernatorial posts being contested concurrently. The poor performance of the GNP, which some observers attributed to bribery allegations connected with the nomination of candidates, prompted the resignation of several senior officials from the party's leadership, although its Chairman, Kang Jae-Seop, remained in his post. The party was also damaged by the extreme antagonism between its two rival presidential contenders, Park Geun-Hye and Lee Myung-Bak, while the latter's reputation was also undermined by allegations that he had been involved in fraudulent business transactions. None the less, the GNP elected Lee as its presidential candidate by a narrow margin in mid-August.

Meanwhile, the disintegration of the Uri Party continued, with a series of further defections in June and July 2007, including that of former Chairman Chung Dong-Young, which left the party with only 58 seats in the National Assembly. In early August Chung and 79 other former legislators of the Uri Party joined with five defectors from the DP to form the United New Democratic Party (UNDP). Later that month the Uri Party finally disbanded and merged into the UNDP, thus making the new party the largest in the National Assembly, with 143 seats.

In early August 2007 Roh announced a minor government reorganization, in which Chung Soung-Jin, hitherto Chairman of the Commission Against Corruption, was allocated the justice portfolio, replacing Kim Sung-Ho, who had resigned following disagreements with the President. Also appointed to the State Council were Im Sang-Gyu as Minister of Agriculture and Forestry and Yoo Young-Hwan as Minister of Information and Communication.

Chung Dong-Young was elected as the UNDP's presidential candidate in October 2007. In early November, in a development that threatened to split the conservative vote, former Prime Minister Lee Hoi-Chang unexpectedly announced that he was leaving the GNP to stand as an independent candidate, in a third attempt to secure the country's presidency.

A major corruption scandal at Samsung arose in late October 2007, when the former head of its legal department, Kim Yong-Chul, claimed that senior executives at the *chaebol* had regularly bribed politicians, government officials and prosecutors using a 'slush fund' totalling 200,000m. won. In late November the National Assembly approved legislation authorizing an independent investigation into Kim's allegations, which Samsung vigorously denied. Also to be examined were claims that the conglomerate had made improper payments to candidates in the 2002 presidential election. (The investigation commenced in January 2008. In April, having been charged with tax evasion and breach of trust, the Chairman of Samsung, Lee Kun-Hee, resigned, and in July he was convicted on the former charge and given a three-year suspended prison sentence. He was pardoned by President Lee Myung-Bak in December 2009.) Meanwhile, the head of the National Tax Service and two of Roh's former presidential aides were also arrested on various corruption charges. These developments proved embarrassing for Roh, who had pledged to reduce corruption.

Corruption allegations against Lee Myung-Bak gained renewed momentum in mid-November 2007, when the extradition from the USA to the Republic of Korea of one of his former business partners, to answer charges of embezzlement and money-laundering, prompted speculation that Lee himself might be implicated in the case. In early December prosecutors concluded that there was no evidence to link Lee to the financial crimes with which his former associate had been charged, but later in that month, only two days before the presidential election, the National Assembly voted to appoint an independent counsel to reinvestigate fraud claims against Lee, following the emergence of a video that purported to show the presidential candidate stating that he had established the investment company at the centre of the allegations. Lee denied any involvement in the scandal.

The presidency of Lee Myung-Bak

At the presidential election, which was held on 19 December 2007, the GNP's Lee Myung-Bak achieved a decisive victory, securing 48.7% of the votes cast, despite the allegations that had overshadowed the electoral campaign. Of the nine other candidates, his nearest rivals were Chung Dong-Young, with 26.1% of the votes, and Lee Hoi-Chang, with 15.1%. However, the level of voter participation, at 62.9%, was very low. Lee's win (by the largest margin since the reintroduction of direct elections in 1987) was attributed to a combination of the electorate's dissatisfaction with the achievements of the incumbent centre-left administration and its attraction to the new President-elect's focus on the economy. During the election campaign he had pledged to improve the country's economic prospects with his so-called '7.4.7' vision: achieving annual growth of 7%, raising average annual income per caput to US $40,000 and making the Republic of Korea one of the world's seven largest economies by 2017. More controversially, Lee also proposed the construction of a 540-km inland canal, traversing the country from Seoul in the north-west to the port city of Busan in the south-east, at a cost of 14,000,000m. won, with the aim of easing road and rail congestion, creating employment and improving growth.

Lee Myung-Bak was inaugurated as President on 25 February 2008. Four days previously he had been exonerated by the independent counsel re-examining the accusations of financial impropriety against him. The National Assembly subsequently approved Lee's nomination of Han Seung-Soo for the post of Prime Minister. An experienced politician and diplomat, Han had previously held various cabinet positions and was currently serving as a UN special envoy on climate change. The other members of the State Council were also designated in February, although several nominees, including Lee's choice to head the Ministry of Unification, Nam Joo-Hong, withdrew following criticism of misconduct in property dealings, of tax evasion and of malpractice in other areas. Among the nominees subsequently confirmed were Kang Man-Soo as Minister of Strategy and Finance; Kim Ha-Joong as Minister of Unification; and Yu Myung-Hwan as Minister of Foreign Affairs and Trade. The position of Deputy Prime Minister was terminated. Meanwhile, there was some realignment of political parties in early 2008 in advance of the forthcoming legislative election. Lee Hoi-Chang created the Liberty Forward Party, which later absorbed the People First Party, and the UNDP and the DP merged to form the United Democratic Party (UDP).

At the legislative election conducted on 9 April 2008, the GNP secured a narrow majority, winning 153 of the 299 seats in the National Assembly. The UDP garnered 81 seats and the Liberty Forward Party 18 seats, while the pro-Park coalition (comprising former GNP members allied to the party's defeated presidential nominee, Park Geun-Hye) took 14 seats. A total of 245 candidates were directly elected, with the remaining seats being determined by proportional representation. The rate of participation by voters, at some 46%, was the lowest ever recorded at a general election. The success of the GNP was expected to facilitate the enactment of legislation relating to the new President's programme of economic reform, although the party's lack of a strong majority was likely to curtail its power. The presence of more than 50 supporters of Park Geun-Hye within the GNP contin-

THE REPUBLIC OF KOREA (SOUTH KOREA)

gent, as well as the pro-Park coalition and independents, was another possible constraint on Lee's ambitions.

One of President Lee's first challenges emerged in April 2008, when he agreed to rescind the country's ban on beef imports from the USA, reportedly to improve bilateral relations and expedite the FTA process. Amid widespread public fear of bovine spongiform encephalopathy (BSE) contamination, daily demonstrations were attended by thousands of South Koreans; although initially peaceful, the protests subsequently escalated into violence, prompting the Government to offer concessions, such as a restriction on imports of cattle older than 30 months. As the protests continued, the issue became symbolic of wider public dissatisfaction with major government initiatives, including Lee's plans for the transnational canal system (which was subsequently reported to have been abandoned) and the privatization of several state-owned businesses. The GNP's defeat at local elections in early June, when it secured only 10 of 52 positions (in comparison with the 22 won by the UDP, now known as the DP), was a further sign of this decline in popularity. With the BSE affair rapidly becoming a national crisis, the members of the State Council offered to resign. In July President Lee responded by effecting a cabinet reorganization, replacing the Minister of Food, Agriculture, Forestry and Fisheries, Chung Woon-Chun, with Jang Tae-Pyoung.

President Lee implemented another cabinet reorganization in January 2009, appointing Hyun In-Taek to succeed Kim Ha-Joong as Minister of Unification and dismissing Kang Man-Soo as Minister of Strategy and Finance, to be replaced by Yoon Jeung-Hyun. In the same month Won Sei-Hoon, the Minister of Public Administration and Security, was transferred to a senior intelligence position; Lee Dal-Gon was nominated to replace him. By-elections for five seats in the National Assembly were held in April. In a rebuke to the ruling GNP, voters elected three independents (including former UNDP presidential candidate Chung Dong-Young) and one DP member to the Assembly, while the New Progressive Party, which had been founded in the previous year by a breakaway faction of the Democratic Labour Party, secured its first seat in the legislature.

Former President Roh Moo-Hyun became embroiled in a corruption scandal in April 2009, when he was questioned by prosecutors in connection with allegations that he had accepted US $6m. in bribes from a businessman Park Yeon-Cha. Park stated that he had given the money to Roh's wife and nephew-in-law 'at the request of the former President', and it was alleged that in return Roh had granted special treatment to Park's business interests. Roh's wife, Kwon Yang-Sook, was also summoned for questioning. She stated that the $1m. that she had received from Park was for the purpose of settling a personal debt, while it was argued that the $5m. transferred to Roh's nephew-in-law was a business investment. Roh denied any knowledge of the payments, and his supporters claimed that the investigation was motivated by political factors. With the former President's indictment believed to be imminent and his reputation severely damaged (combating corruption had been a central tenet of his presidency), Roh committed suicide on 23 May. Meanwhile, in August two former senior aides to Roh were sentenced to prison terms of three-and-a-half years and six years, respectively, after being convicted on bribery charges. In December former Prime Minister Han Myeong-Sook, appointed by Roh in 2006, was arrested on charges of accepting bribes. She was acquitted in April 2010, describing her trial as having been politically motivated; however, she was indicted in July on further charges of accepting bribes, and her trial on these charges began in December.

In July 2009, despite a DP-led opposition boycott and amid scuffles in the National Assembly, the GNP deputies in the legislature approved controversial reforms permitting newspaper companies to own stakes in broadcasting concerns. The Government argued that this was vital to the sector's competitiveness, but the opposition asserted that the reforms would lead to a conservative monopoly of the broadcasting industry. (The Constitutional Court upheld the approval of the reforms in October despite acknowledging that procedural violations, highlighted by the DP, had occurred during the parliamentary vote.)

President Lee announced a major reorganization of the State Council in September 2009, which included the nomination (approved at the end of the month despite DP protests) of a new Prime Minister, Chung Un-Chan, hitherto president of Seoul National University and a vocal critic of Lee's economic policies. Gen. Kim Tae-Young, the former Chairman of the Joint Chiefs of Staff, was appointed as Minister of National Defence,

Introductory Survey

Lee Kwi-Nam was allocated the justice portfolio, and Joo Ho-Young became the Minister for Special Affairs, a new position created to enhance cross-party co-operation. In October by-elections were held for five seats in the National Assembly: the DP won three seats and the GNP secured the remaining two. In the same month Chung Mong-Joon assumed the chairmanship of the GNP, replacing Park Tee-Hae, who had resigned in order to contest a seat at the by-elections.

The 2010 budget was approved unilaterally in December 2009, following another boycott of the National Assembly by the DP. Controversially, the budget incorporated significant funding for the President's plan to rehabilitate South Korea's four main rivers. Critics had expressed concern about the cost of the scheme and potential environmental damage, while many believed that Lee's ultimate objective was to revive his ambitious scheme for a national canal network.

Recent developments: further resignations

The GNP performed poorly in local elections held on 2 June 2010, securing only six of the 16 contested mayoral and gubernatorial posts, compared with seven for the DP; this was despite predictions that the GNP would benefit from President Lee's firm stance on the DPRK following the sinking of the *Cheonan* warship in March (see Relations with North Korea). Chung Mong-Joon resigned as GNP Chairman along with the party's entire Supreme Council in response to the electoral defeats; Ahn Sang-Soo was elected to replace Chung in July. Meanwhile, Lee announced a review of his policy priorities and a reorganization of his administrative office, including the appointment of Yim Tae-Hee, hitherto Minister of Labour, as presidential chief of staff.

The results of eight by-elections to the National Assembly on 28 July 2010 represented a significant improvement in the fortunes of the GNP, which won five seats in comparison with the DP's three. None the less, on the following day Chun Un-Chan announced his resignation as Prime Minister, claiming responsibility for a series of reverses suffered by the Government during his 10 months in office: in particular, he cited his failure to secure legislative approval for the Government's revised development plan for Sejong City, a new town under construction in the Chungcheong region. President Roh Moo-Hyun had originally proposed establishing the city as a new capital, before modifying the plan to entail transferring a limited number of ministries and government agencies from Seoul; the Lee administration had proposed abandoning Roh's plan and instead turning Sejong City into an industrial and scientific centre. Following the National Assembly's defeat of Lee's proposal in June, in mid-July the Government announced that 35 state agencies would relocate to Sejong by the end of 2014.

In early August 2010 President Lee nominated Kim Tae-Ho for the premiership, also naming seven other ministers (although the principal portfolios remained unchanged) and other senior officials. However, during August Kim and several of the other nominees were subjected to fierce criticism from opposition legislators at their confirmation hearings before the National Assembly, amid allegations of impropriety. At the end of the month Kim resigned as Prime Minister-designate, having failed to refute claims that he had accepted bribes from Park Yeon-Cha while he was Governor of South Gyeongsang province in 2004–09; Kim was one of several leading politicians, in addition to former President Roh, who had been implicated in the corruption scandal surrounding Park. The Ministers-designate of Culture, Sports and Tourism and of Knowledge Economy also resigned after admitting unethical conduct. In mid-September Lee nominated Kim Hwang-Sik, the Chairman of the Board of Audit and Inspection, for the post of Prime Minister, and his nomination was finally confirmed by the National Assembly in early October. Shortly afterwards Kim Sung-Hwan was appointed Minister of Foreign Affairs and Trade, filling a vacancy left in early September by Yu Myung-Hwan: Yu had tendered his resignation after being accused of nepotism following the revelation that his daughter had secured a mid-level job at his ministry, having previously been rejected for the post.

Sohn Hak-Kyu was elected Chairman of the DP at the party's convention in October 2010, defeating Chung Dong-Young, the former UNDP presidential candidate, and Chung Sye-Kyun, the outgoing Chairman. Chung Sye-Kyun had submitted his resignation following the DP's poor performance at the by-elections in July.

The Government was severely criticized by both opposition and GNP politicians for its hesitant response to the fatal shelling of Yeonpyeong island by North Korean artillery in November

THE REPUBLIC OF KOREA (SOUTH KOREA)

2010 (see Relations with North Korea), and for the armed forces' apparent lack of preparedness for the attack. The incident prompted the resignation as Minister of National Defence of Kim Tae-Young, whose earlier offer to resign in March over the sinking of the *Cheonan* had been refused by the President; he was replaced by Kim Kwan-Jin, a former Chairman of the Joint Chiefs of Staff. At the end of December President Lee finally nominated Choung Byoung-Gug as Minister of Culture, Sports and Tourism, and Choi Joong-Kyung as Minister of Knowledge Economy, both roles having remained unfilled since August. However, Choi's appointment once again encountered opposition at confirmation hearings before the National Assembly in January 2011, during which DP legislators questioned his professional competence and his wife's investment ethics; the DP refused to allow the Assembly to endorse his nomination. None the less, Lee disregarded the lack of legislative approval and appointed Choi to the post in late January. Meanwhile, the severe political polarization under Lee's presidency was once again manifested in the near-unilateral approval by GNP legislators of the 2011 budget in December 2010, following scuffles in the National Assembly and amid another DP boycott.

In a major cabinet reorganization in May 2011, President Lee proposed the replacement of five ministers. Bahk Jae-Wan, hitherto Minister of Employment and Labour, was nominated for the post of Minister of Strategy and Finance, while Bahk was to be replaced by Lee Chae-Pil. Other appointments, pending confirmation by the National Assembly, included that of Kwon Do-Yup as Minister of Land, Transport and Maritime Affairs.

Relations with North Korea

After the end of the Korean War in 1953 relations between the Republic of Korea and the DPRK continued to be characterized by mutual suspicion. Various attacks on South Korean interests were attributed to the DPRK. These included a bomb explosion in Burma (now Myanmar) in October 1983, in which four South Korean government ministers were killed. A South Korean airliner in flight over Burma was destroyed in November 1987, allegedly by a bomb that had been concealed aboard the aircraft by North Korean agents. In April 1996 the DPRK's announcement that it was abandoning the 1953 armistice agreement was followed by a series of incursions by North Korean troops into the DMZ, and in September a North Korean submarine was found abandoned near the South Korean coast. Other confrontations included a gun battle in June 2002 between North and South Korean vessels in the Yellow Sea, which resulted in the sinking of a South Korean patrol boat and the deaths of six crew members. South Korean military sources estimated that 30 North Korean crewmen had also been killed in the incident, which had started when two North Korean vessels accompanying a fishing boat reportedly crossed the Northern Limit Line (the maritime border separating the territorial waters of the two Koreas). Subsequent major confrontations included the sinking of the *Cheonan* and an attack on the South Korean island of Yeonpyeong in 2010 (see below).

Bilateral and multilateral discussions regarding the situation on the Korean peninsula took place intermittently. Roh Tae-Woo's appointment as South Korean President in 1988 led to an improvement in relations with the DPRK. In September 1990 the North Korean Premier travelled to Seoul for a meeting with his South Korean counterpart, the highest level of bilateral contact since 1953. The DPRK's abandonment in 1991 of its long-standing position that the two Koreas should occupy a single seat at the UN was regarded as a significant concession. Further prime-ministerial negotiations resulted in late 1991 in the signature of an agreement on reconciliation. In the hope ultimately of concluding a peace treaty, quadripartite negotiations, involving the two Koreas, the USA and the People's Republic of China, opened in Switzerland in December 1997.

In 1998 a significant improvement in relations between North and South Korea followed the newly appointed President Kim Dae-Jung's inauguration of a 'sunshine' policy of engagement with the North. In October 1999 Hyundai concluded an agreement with the DPRK on the construction of an industrial complex at Kaesong, located just north of the border, while a resort for South Korean tourists was developed at Mount Kumgang. As the DPRK's financial situation worsened, economic issues played an increasingly important part in inter-Korean relations from 2000. Many South Koreans had begun to question the wisdom of the allocation of extensive aid without firm preconditions, regarding the process of engagement as being increasingly unbalanced to the detriment of the South. An historic summit meeting took place between Kim Dae-Jung and the North Korean leader, Kim Jong Il, in June, during a visit by the South Korean President to the North Korean capital of Pyongyang. In December a resolution was approved by the South Korean legislature demanding the repatriation of prisoners of war who were alleged to remain in detention in the North, despite the DPRK's denial of the existence of such prisoners. In late 2002 it was revealed that Kim Dae-Jung had arranged for the transfer of substantial funds from a Hyundai affiliate to the DPRK in order to convene the summit meeting of 2000. Although the election in December 2002 of Roh Moo-Hyun as South Korean President heralded a continuation of the 'sunshine' policy, in August 2003 the suicide of Hyundai official Chung Mong-Hun, who had been indicted in connection with the illegal payments to the North, further undermined the credibility of the policy.

Meanwhile, family reunions were arranged under the auspices of the North and South Korean Red Cross organizations, which co-ordinated the exchange of lists of potential candidates, separated since the Korean War. In addition to 'face-to-face' reunions, the first private telephone line between North and South Korea since partition in 1945 was opened in July 2005, in preparation for video conference family reunions. In early 2006 the DPRK reportedly agreed to resolve the issue of South Korean prisoners of war and abductees held in the North.

In April 2005 the South Korean Prime Minister, Lee Hae-Chan, met Kim Yong Nam, the President of the Presidium of the North Korean Supreme People's Assembly, in Indonesia. However, bilateral relations deteriorated sharply in 2006 when the DPRK conducted two sets of missile tests: the first in July and the second (of a nuclear device) in October. The tests placed the 'sunshine' policy, which was by now coming under heavy criticism from the South Korean public, in serious jeopardy. The Uri Party continued to emphasize the importance of dialogue, and in November the Government announced that it would not take part in the Proliferation Security Initiative (PSI), a US-led scheme to stop and search suspect North Korean ships. (The South Korean Government nevertheless agreed to comply with the sanctions imposed by the UN Security Council, and announced that North Koreans thought to be involved in the weapons programme would be banned from travelling to the South.) The GNP took the opposite stance, insisting (like the USA) that the Kaesong and Mount Kumgang projects be brought to an immediate halt. In December 2006 the Republic of Korea prompted severe condemnation from the DPRK when prosecutors indicted five people, including one US citizen of Korean origin, on charges of spying for the North. The DPRK denounced the action as a 'calculated plot' against the North. Two of those arrested were members of the minor Democratic Labour Party. (In April 2007 the five defendants were convicted of espionage and sentenced to prison terms ranging from four to nine years.) Despite the continuing tensions, the new Minister of Unification, Lee Jae-Joung (who had been criticized by the GNP for his allegedly pro-DPRK views), described eventual unification with the North as a primary objective. None the less, the Republic of Korea remained concerned over the DPRK's military ambitions; a defence policy document published at the end of December 2006 described the DPRK as a 'serious threat' to the South—the most strongly worded assessment since the inception of the latter's policy of engagement in 2000.

In February 2007 significant progress appeared to have been made at the six-party talks (with discussions now including representatives from Japan and Russia, in addition to those from the USA and China) when the DPRK pledged to shut down its nuclear reactor in exchange for energy aid. In October President Roh and Kim Jong Il held a three-day summit meeting in Pyongyang. Following the meeting, Kim and Roh issued a declaration committing North and South Korea, *inter alia*, to working towards the replacement of the 1953 armistice agreement with a peace treaty and to making joint efforts for the smooth implementation of the six-party nuclear agreements. President Lee Myung-Bak, who assumed office in February 2008, adopted a firmer stance towards the DPRK than his two immediate predecessors, linking the continuation of economic co-operation to greater progress on denuclearization. Lee announced plans to review the agreements reached at the inter-Korean summit meeting in October 2007. None the less, Lee proposed the creation of a 37,500m. won investment fund for the DPRK if it abandoned its nuclear weapons programme.

In protest against joint South Korean-US military exercises, the DPRK closed the border several times in March 2009, thus stranding South Korean workers at the Kaesong industrial plant. In the following month bilateral talks at Kaesong between

THE REPUBLIC OF KOREA (SOUTH KOREA)

officials lasted just 22 minutes, with tension subsequently increasing when the North Korean Government alleged that South Korea had moved a border marker post. In May the DPRK unilaterally suspended all contracts at the Kaesong complex, after the South Korean authorities refused to accept North Korean wage demands and large increases in leasing fees. In May the DPRK provoked international outrage after it tested a second, larger nuclear weapon, followed by further missile tests, amid threats of war if the Republic of Korea joined the US-initiated naval blockade of shipments of weapons of mass destruction to and from the DPRK. The Republic of Korea announced its participation in the blockade on the following day, and in response the DPRK abjured the 1953 truce.

Despite this increase in tension, bilateral relations showed signs of improvement in August 2009. Agreement was reached on the revival of family reunion visits, in abeyance since 2007, and on the relaxation of cross-border transport regulations, introduced by the DPRK in 2008, while a North Korean delegation attended the funeral of former President Kim Dae-Jung. However, this amelioration in relations was undermined in September 2009 by the unannounced release of water from a North Korean dam on the Imjin river, which resulted in flash flooding across the border and the deaths of six South Koreans. The DPRK expressed regret for the incident and promised to provide advance warning of any future discharges from the dam. Relations were strained further in November when shots were exchanged between South and North Korean vessels on the maritime border in the Yellow Sea (a demarcation that was unrecognized by the DPRK). The Republic of Korea declared that the clash had occurred after a North Korean patrol boat entered into its territorial waters and opened fire, in response to South Korean warning shots; these claims were denied by the DPRK, which blamed the South for the skirmish. A further confrontation occurred in January 2010, when, as part of a military exercise, the DPRK launched artillery fire into the Yellow Sea near the maritime border, which was countered by warning shots from a nearby South Korean military base.

The sinking of the Cheonan and the assault on Yeonpyeong

In March 2010 a South Korean warship, the *Cheonan*, sank near the disputed Yellow Sea border following an explosion, resulting in the deaths of 46 sailors. The South Korean Government did not immediately attribute responsibility for the disaster to the DPRK, which denied any involvement, but President Lee subsequently referred to the incident as a 'grave international issue involving inter-Korean relations'. A preliminary investigation attributed the disaster to an external explosion. In May the South Korean Minister of Foreign Affairs and Trade declared North Korean involvement in the incident to be 'obvious', stating that there was sufficient evidence for the matter to be referred to the UN Security Council. On the following day an international team of investigators published a report confirming that a torpedo of North Korean manufacture, part of which had been discovered on the sea-bed, had been responsible for the sinking of the warship. In response to the report (which was denounced as a fabrication by the North Korean authorities), Lee demanded an apology from the DPRK and announced the severing of all trade links between the two Koreas (although the Kaesong complex was to continue operating). In addition, the Republic of Korea closed its territorial waters to North Korean merchant shipping and announced that it was to resume the broadcasting of propaganda by radio and loudspeaker to the North, suspended since 2004. In the following months the Republic of Korea continued to insist on an apology for the *Cheonan* incident before it would agree to the resumption of the stalled six-party talks on the North's nuclear programme. None the less, in October the two Koreas agreed to hold a further round of family reunions.

In November 2010 the South Korean island of Yeonpyeong, in the Yellow Sea close to the maritime border, was subjected to heavy shelling by North Korean artillery, resulting in the deaths of two South Korean marines and two civilian residents. The DPRK maintained that the attack was directed at a military base on the island and alleged that it was provoked by fire directed at the North by a South Korean military exercise in the area; however, the Republic of Korea insisted that its fire had been directed towards the open sea during the exercise. The Government subsequently announced an increase in military deployment to the Yeonpyeong island group, and in the following month the Minister-designate of National Defence, Kim Kwan-Jin, declared that he would counter any subsequent attack with aerial bombardment of the North. Despite the sharp escalation in tensions, in January 2011 the Republic of Korea accepted a North Korean offer to engage in talks between senior military officers, which were to include discussion of the sinking of the *Cheonan* and the Yeonpyeong shelling. However, these talks ended without agreement in February, and no date was set for any future meeting; it was reported that the DPRK had again refused to meet the South's demand for an apology over the two recent confrontations, and continued to deny any responsibility for the first.

(For full details of relations between North and South Korea, see the chapter on the Democratic People's Republic of Korea, Inter-Korean Relations.)

Foreign Affairs

The foreign policy of the Republic of Korea has been dominated by its relations with the major powers of Japan, China, the USA and Russia, owing to its geographical position, and by the quest for stability on the Korean peninsula.

Relations with Japan

Relations between the Republic of Korea and Japan, which had long been strained, were eased by President Chun's official visit to Japan in September 1984 (the first such visit undertaken by a South Korean Head of State), during which Emperor Hirohito and Prime Minister Yasuhiro Nakasone formally expressed their regret for Japanese aggression in Korea in the past. In May 1990, during President Roh's visit to Japan, Emperor Akihito offered official apologies for the cruelties of Japanese colonial rule in Korea. In January 1992 the Japanese Prime Minister, Kiichi Miyazawa, visited the Republic of Korea, where he publicly expressed regret at the enslavement during the Second World War of an estimated 100,000 Korean women, who were used by the Japanese military for sexual purposes ('comfort women'). In late 1994 the Japanese Government announced that it would not make compensation payments directly to individuals, but would finance a programme to construct vocational training centres for the women concerned. In August 1995, on the 50th anniversary of the end of the Second World War, the Japanese Prime Minister, Tomiichi Murayama, issued a statement expressing 'deep reflection and sincere apologies' for Japanese colonial aggression. At the end of a summit meeting with President Kim Young-Sam in June 1996, the Japanese Prime Minister, Ryutaro Hashimoto, issued a public apology to the 'comfort women'. However, the South Korean Government regarded Japanese proposals to provide compensation through private sources of funding, rather than government money, as tantamount to a denial of moral responsibility. The conclusion of new defence co-operation guidelines between Japan and the USA in September 1997 was of concern for the Republic of Korea, which feared an expansion in Japanese military capability. Negotiations for a new fisheries agreement, under way since mid-1996, were unilaterally terminated by Japan in January 1998, following the continuing disagreement regarding sovereignty of the Dokdo islands (or 'Takeshima' in Japanese, located between South Korea and Japan in the East Sea—also known as the Sea of Japan), to which both countries laid claim. In April 1998 the South Korean Government announced its intention to make payments itself to surviving 'comfort women'.

Relations with Japan improved considerably in October 1998, during a four-day state visit to Tokyo by President Kim Dae-Jung. A joint declaration was signed, in which Japan apologized for the suffering inflicted on the Korean people during Japanese colonial rule. In addition, the Republic of Korea agreed to revoke a ban on the import of various Japanese goods, while Japan promised financial aid to the Republic of Korea in support of its efforts to stimulate economic recovery. In November the two countries concluded negotiations on the renewal of their bilateral fisheries agreement, which came into effect in January 1999, despite the objections of the main South Korean opposition party, which protested that it failed positively to affirm the Republic of Korea's claim to sovereignty over the disputed Dokdo islands. Differences over the accord and its implementation continued to create tension in early 1999, particularly in the Republic of Korea, where protests from fishermen, who were apparently suffering heavy losses because of the revised agreement, forced the resignation of the Minister of Maritime Affairs and Fisheries. In March increasing co-operation between the two countries was highlighted during a visit to the Republic of Korea by the Japanese Prime Minister, Keizo Obuchi, despite protests against Japan's military links with the USA and failure fully to compensate the 'comfort women'. Both countries agreed to strengthen bilateral economic relations, and Japan pledged a further US $1,000m. in aid to the Republic of Korea. The Japanese Prime Minister, Yoshiro Mori, visited Seoul in May 2000 and met with Kim Dae-Jung.

During 2001 relations with Japan deteriorated owing to the publication in February of new Japanese history textbooks, which sought to justify Japan's aggression towards its Asian neighbours during the Second World War, and neglected to mention the forced prostitution of Asian (mainly Korean) 'comfort women' by the Japanese army and the forcible transfer and use of Koreans as slave labour in Japan. Large-scale protests were held in Seoul, and the Japanese ambassador was summoned to the Ministry of Foreign Affairs and Trade. In April the Republic of Korea temporarily withdrew its ambassador from Japan. The South Korean Ministry of Foreign Affairs and Trade demanded 35 major revisions to the books, but in July Japan's Ministry of Education ruled out any further significant changes, prompting Kim Dae-Jung to refuse to receive a visiting Japanese delegation and the suspension of bilateral military co-operation. In August the Republic of Korea was further outraged by the visit of the Japanese Prime Minister, Junichiro Koizumi, to the controversial Yasukuni Shrine in Tokyo honouring Japan's war dead. Amid popular protests, Koizumi visited Seoul in October and delivered an apology for the suffering of Koreans under Japanese rule. He was forced to cancel a visit to the National Assembly owing to the hostile sentiment of some legislators.

Along with China and North Korea, South Korea condemned Koizumi's visits to the Yasukuni Shrine in April 2002 and January 2003. However, in March 2002 Koizumi and Kim Dae-Jung agreed to begin discussions on a possible bilateral FTA, and in May Koizumi attended the opening ceremony of the 2002 football World Cup being co-hosted in Seoul. Also in attendance were Prince Takamado and his wife, who were making the first official visit to the Republic of Korea by a member of the Japanese Imperial family. Any remaining mutual hostility between the two countries was outweighed in 2002 by the need for co-operation in engaging with the North, and in December Koizumi and South Korean President-elect Roh Moo-Hyun agreed to co-ordinate their policies in this regard. In June Roh made his first state visit to Japan and had discussions with Koizumi on the issue of North Korea's nuclear weapons programme. Although both leaders opposed any development of nuclear weapons in North Korea, Roh urged dialogue with the DPRK, whereas Koizumi favoured stricter measures towards the DPRK. Japan and the Republic of Korea continued efforts towards reaching an FTA from 2003, but negotiations faltered in November 2004, reportedly over disagreement regarding the liberalization of trade in agricultural and fisheries products.

In February 2005 tensions arose over a statement by the Japanese ambassador to the Republic of Korea, Toshiyuki Takano, implying that the Dokdo islands belonged to Japan. The issue of the Dokdo islands renewed tensions in March when the local legislature of Japan's Shimane Prefecture, which claimed the islands as part of its territory, voted to establish a 'Takeshima Day'. In response, the South Korean Minister of Foreign Affairs and Trade, Ban Ki-Moon, cancelled a scheduled visit to Japan, while protests were held outside the Japanese embassy in Seoul. Further public demonstrations took place in April in reaction to the approval for use in Japanese schools of history textbooks, including one first published in 2001 (see above), which were regarded by Koreans (and Chinese) as failing to address the true nature of Japanese wartime conduct. Another visit to the Yasukuni Shrine by Prime Minister Koizumi in October 2005 provoked condemnation from the Republic of Korea, and prompted President Roh to cancel a scheduled visit to Japan in December. Throughout 2006 the Republic of Korea's continued requests for the shrine visits to end were disregarded by the Japanese Government. On 15 August (Liberation Day in Korea) Koizumi made another visit to the shrine, and the South Korean Ministry of Foreign Affairs and Trade issued a statement declaring that the visit would strain bilateral relations and obstruct regional co-operation and friendship. In the following month no progress was forthcoming during bilateral discussions in Seoul, particularly with regard to the disputed Dokdo islands. The Republic of Korea had antagonized the Japanese authorities in July when it had conducted a survey of the waters around the islands, against the express wishes of Japan (which, in turn, had announced plans to conduct a similar survey in April, prompting the South Korean Government to declare a five-year plan to develop facilities on the islands and to explore the area's marine and mineral resources).

Relations deteriorated further in early 2007 after the new Japanese Prime Minister, Shinzo Abe, made comments inferring that there was no direct evidence to prove that South Korean 'comfort women' had been coerced into sexual servitude. Despite public outrage in the Republic of Korea, the Japanese Prime Minister refused to apologize for his comments. However, in April he decided not to emulate his predecessor with regard to visits to the Yasukuni Shrine (despite a clandestine visit in the previous year). Instead, Abe sent a sacred plant to the shrine, thereby appeasing both South Koreans and opponents within his own Government. In early May the Republic of Korea declared its intention to seize assets secured by nine alleged collaborators during Japanese colonial rule. Land, worth some US $3.9m. and belonging to the descendants of the collaborators, would be seized in an effort to 'restore South Korean people's dignity'. The proceeds were to be used to assist former combatants, while other land was allocated for the purposes of commemorating the Korean independence movement.

Yasuo Fukuda, who succeeded Abe as Japanese Prime Minister in September 2007, identified strengthening relations with the Republic of Korea as a priority, notably pledging not to visit the controversial Yasukuni Shrine. The election of Lee Myung-Bak as South Korean President in December was also regarded as a positive development for the bilateral relationship. Fukuda attended Lee's inauguration in February 2008, following which the two leaders agreed to undertake regular reciprocal visits and to promote the resumption of negotiations on the establishment of an FTA (stalled since late 2004). Lee and Fukuda reaffirmed these intentions during Lee's official visit to Japan in April 2008. Meanwhile, in January, in a gesture of reconciliation, the relatives of 101 South Koreans who had been forced to fight for the Japanese army during the Second World War were invited to a memorial service in Tokyo to mark the return of their remains. In July 2008 the dispute over the Dokdo islands re-emerged when the Japanese Government announced that the islands would be described as Japanese in teachers' materials. The announcement provoked severe criticism from the South Korean Government and the recall of its ambassador to Japan, in addition to demonstrations in Seoul. A defence document reiterating Japan's stance placed further strain on bilateral relations in September.

During a visit to the Republic of Korea in February 2010 the Japanese Minister for Foreign Affairs, Katsuya Okada, apologized for the colonial occupation of Korea by Japan during the first half of the 20th century. However, in contrast to earlier suggestions by Okada in October 2009 that a joint regional history textbook be published to address controversial events in Asian history, new textbooks defining the Dokdo islands as Japanese territory—and as 'illegally occupied' by South Korea in one textbook—were endorsed by the Japanese authorities in March 2010. A foreign affairs report was issued by Japan shortly afterwards, reiterating its claim to the islands and again alleging an 'illegal' South Korean occupation. In April the Republic of Korea issued a formal complaint to a senior diplomat at the Japanese embassy, and the National Assembly denounced Japan's renewed territorial assertions. Furthermore, the South Korean Minister of Education, Science and Technology announced plans to teach students from an earlier age about South Korea's claim to the islands. Bilateral relations showed signs of improvement in August 2010, when the new Japanese Prime Minister, Naoto Kan, issued a renewed public apology for his country's occupation of Korea. In a statement made in advance of the centenary of Japan's annexation of the peninsula and directed specifically towards the Republic of Korea, Kan expressed 'deep remorse' for the period of colonial rule and announced the repatriation to South Korea of a number of cultural artefacts seized during the occupation. However, the Japanese Government's annual defence review published in September once again reiterated Japan's claim to the Dokdo islands, prompting protests by the Republic of Korea. The approval by the Japanese authorities in March 2011 of further school textbooks laying claim to the islands also elicited South Korean condemnation.

Other regional relations

Full diplomatic relations with the People's Republic of China were established in 1992 (a development that was denounced by the DPRK, of which China had been the principal ally hitherto). Relations with China were strengthened in November 1998, when South Korean President Kim Dae-Jung paid an official

THE REPUBLIC OF KOREA (SOUTH KOREA)

visit to the Chinese capital of Beijing, meeting with President Jiang Zemin and Premier Zhu Rongji. In August 1999 the first visit of a South Korean defence minister to China took place; a reciprocal visit to the Republic of Korea by the Chinese Minister of National Defence, Chi Haotian, took place in January 2000. The South Korean Government requested Chi's assistance in resolving the issue of seven North Korean defectors, who had recently been repatriated by China, despite South Korean protests. In October 2000 relations improved further when, during a visit to Seoul by Zhu Rongji, agreement was reached on the resumption of the quadripartite conference, incorporating the two Koreas, China and the USA, with the aim of establishing a peace mechanism for the Korean Peninsula (see the chapter on the Democratic People's Republic of Korea). Later in the month, following strong opposition from China, the Republic of Korea refused to grant a visa to the Dalai Lama, Tibet's spiritual leader, on the grounds that it would be 'inappropriate'.

A diplomatic dispute arose between the Republic of Korea and China in October 2001, following the execution in China of a South Korean national and the alleged torture of another Korean prisoner, both convicted of drugs-trafficking. In November the ministers of economics, finance and foreign affairs from China, the Republic of Korea and Japan agreed to hold regular meetings to foster closer co-operation. In mid-2002 the Chinese authorities sought to prevent North Korean refugees from seeking asylum in various diplomatic buildings in China, including the South Korean embassy in Beijing. In September senior politician Lee Hoi-Chang visited China and met President Jiang Zemin.

The growing diplomatic crisis over North Korea's nuclear programme from late 2002 led South Korea to seek China's assistance in persuading the North to work towards a peaceful solution. President Roh Moo-Hyun made a four-day state visit to Beijing in July. Chinese diplomatic efforts subsequently played a major role (see the chapter on the Democratic People's Republic of Korea). In August 2004, however, relations between the Republic of Korea and China were damaged by controversy over the issue of the historical kingdom of Koguryo, which had covered the area of modern North Korea and part of South Korea, as well as areas of northern China. Following the deletion of references to Koguryo from the Chinese Ministry of Foreign Affairs website, the South Korean Government feared that China was planning to claim Koguryo as part of Chinese, rather than Korean, history, and to use this historical 'distortion' as a basis for present-day expansionism. In September, however, the Chinese Ministry of Foreign Affairs issued a statement declaring that its reference to Koguryo as an ancient Chinese province had been a mistake. The issue of Koguryo dominated discussions between President Roh and Chinese Prime Minister Wen Jiabao held in September 2006, not least because China was in the process of applying to the UN to register Mount Paekdu (half of which belonged to North Korea, half to China, and regarded by Korean nationalists as a sacred symbol) as an historic site. By early 2011 South Korea's negotiations with China on a bilateral FTA, initiated in 2007, had not progressed beyond the preliminary stages.

In November 2000, after eight years' suspension, the 25th Joint Conference of Korea-Taiwan Business Councils took place in Seoul. It was agreed that henceforth annual conferences would be held alternately in the respective capitals of Seoul and Taipei. In the same month a Korean passenger aircraft flew from Seoul to Taipei for the first time since 1992, when diplomatic relations had been severed. The Republic of Korea also maintained close relations with South-East Asian countries, and Minister of Defence Kim Dong-Shin and Prime Minister Lee Han-Dong visited Viet Nam in December 2001 and April 2002, respectively. Security, economic and trade issues were the main topics of discussions. Viet Nam had already become the principal recipient of South Korean aid. In early 2003 a South Korean newspaper funded the opening of a peace park in southern Viet Nam, as a gesture of atonement for atrocities committed by South Korean soldiers, some 300,000 of whom had fought on behalf of South Viet Nam during the Viet Nam war. In October 2009 President Lee visited Viet Nam, where he met with Nguyen Minh Triet, the country's President; the two leaders pledged to bolster trade links, and agreement was reached on a 'strategic co-operative partnership', while preliminary proposals for a bilateral FTA were mooted. Meanwhile, in 2006 trade negotiations commenced between South Korea and India, and in August 2009 a Comprehensive Economic Partnership Agreement (a less stringent FTA) was signed by both countries. The South Korean

Introductory Survey

National Assembly ratified the agreement in November, and it entered into effect in January 2010.

An agreement on free trade in merchandise goods was reached between the Republic of Korea and nine of the 10 members of the Association of Southeast Asian Nations (ASEAN, see p. 206) in August 2006. Under the agreement, which was ratified by the South Korean National Assembly in May 2007 and took effect on 1 June, 97% of South Korean products exported to the nine ASEAN countries were exempt from tariffs or would carry tariffs of less than 5% by 2010. The South Korean Government thus envisaged a substantial increase in its trade surplus with the nine South-East Asian signatories. Although more commonly known as the South Korea-ASEAN FTA, the arrangement did not include Thailand, which refused to participate in protest against the Republic of Korea's insistence on the exclusion of rice from the agreement. However, several rounds of free trade negotiations were held between the two countries during 2007, and in January 2008 it was reported that an agreement had been reached whereby Thailand would be allowed more flexibility in reducing or waiving its tariffs compared with the other ASEAN nations. Meanwhile, in November 2007 the Republic of Korea and all 10 members of ASEAN signed an agreement on free trade in services; a further accord, covering investment, was also envisaged.

Relations with the USA

Relations between the Republic of Korea and the USA were frequently strained from the late 1970s, in particular by the proposal to withdraw US ground troops from South Korea (which was abandoned in 1979) and by the trial of Kim Dae-Jung (see above). Disputes between the Republic of Korea and the USA in the late 1980s over trade issues had subsided by mid-1991. President George Bush of the USA visited the country in January 1992, and it was agreed to cancel that year's 'Team Spirit' joint military exercises. In December 1991 it had been announced that all US nuclear weapons had been withdrawn from South Korean territory. The 'Team Spirit' exercises were resumed in 1993. In July, during a visit to Seoul, US President Bill Clinton affirmed his country's continuing commitment to the defence of the Republic of Korea. In January 1994 it was announced that the USA was to deploy air-defence missiles on South Korean territory. In April 1996, during a visit to Seoul, President Clinton issued a joint US-South Korean proposal for quadripartite negotiations with the DPRK and the People's Republic of China (see above). In October 1997 the US Government asked the South Korean administration to reconsider its decision to order an air-defence missile system from France. However, the Republic of Korea was seeking to reduce its dependence on the USA for military technology. Later in that year the USA pledged financial support for the Republic of Korea, following the conclusion of an agreement with the IMF.

President Kim Dae-Jung was warmly received on a state visit to the USA in June 1998, during which he outlined his 'sunshine' policy of engagement with North Korea. A reciprocal visit was made by President Clinton to Seoul in November. In March 1999 the South Korean Government welcomed a major advance in negotiations between the DPRK and the USA on US access to a suspected nuclear site in North Korea (see the chapter on the Democratic People's Republic of Korea). During a second visit by Kim Dae-Jung to the USA, in July, the US Administration reaffirmed its support for the 'sunshine' policy. In October the US and South Korean Governments began investigations into the alleged massacre of as many as 300 Korean refugees by US troops near Nogun-ri, in the South Korean province of North Chungcheong, shortly after the beginning of the Korean War. Revelations of the use of defoliants in the DMZ in the late 1960s created further controversy in November 1999. The herbicides, which had apparently been provided by the USA but applied by South Korean troops, included Agent Orange, which had later been found to be highly toxic. The South Korean Government announced that it was prepared to compensate both soldiers and civilians adversely affected by the defoliants, but the USA reportedly refused to accept any liability. In December a lawsuit was filed against seven US chemical companies by a group of Koreans demanding compensation for damage they claimed to have suffered as a consequence of the herbicides. (In January 2006, in the first such ruling, a South Korean court ordered the US manufacturers to pay 68,000m. won in compensation to 6,800 individuals.)

In May 2000 there was further tension between the two countries when a US aircraft accidentally released several bombs close to a village south-west of Seoul, causing minor

THE REPUBLIC OF KOREA (SOUTH KOREA)

injuries and damage to property. Violent protests were held outside the US embassy in Seoul, and the USA subsequently agreed to cease using the Koon-ni range for such training missions. (Operations subsequently resumed, the USA citing a lack of suitable alternative facilities.) Following the incident, opposition politicians demanded a review of the Status of Forces Agreement (SOFA), which governed the 37,000 US troops stationed in South Korea. In August negotiations were held on the issue, and resulted in partial agreement. Further discussions held in December successfully revised the agreement, which was signed in January 2001. However, South Korean civic groups protested that the partnership between the two countries remained biased in favour of the USA. A missile accord was signed between the Republic of Korea and the USA, permitting the former to develop missiles with greatly increased ranges and payloads. Also in January outgoing US President Bill Clinton made an unprecedented statement of regret for the massacre near Nogun-ri, but many South Koreans were angry that no apology was forthcoming.

The Republic of Korea immediately pledged support to the USA following terrorist attacks on the latter in September 2001, and in December the National Assembly endorsed the deployment of non-combat troops to assist the US-led campaign in Afghanistan, mainly in a logistical capacity. Meanwhile, in November the USA and the Republic of Korea agreed to a major 'land-swap' whereby existing US bases would relocate to other areas within the country, allowing a consolidation of bases and training facilities over the next 10 years.

Relations between the Republic of Korea and the USA deteriorated noticeably after an accident in June 2002 in which a US army vehicle killed two teenaged Korean girls. The US military charged two US soldiers with negligent homicide, and the South Korean authorities subsequently requested their submission for trial at a local court, but this was rejected by the US army. In November the two soldiers were acquitted by a US military court, leading to a significant increase in anti-US sentiment among the public. Although President George W. Bush apologized for the incident, in December hundreds of thousands of people attended anti-US rallies in Seoul and across the country. Although precipitated by the issue of the acquittals, the rallies became a forum of protest against the country's dependency on the USA and that country's policy towards North Korea. Meanwhile, in October a new joint base pact came into force whereby the US military would reduce the number of its bases from 41 to 23 and return 50% of the land it used to South Korea. However, there had yet to be changes to the SOFA that governed the conduct of US troops in Korea—amendments to which had long been demanded by South Koreans. Public anger towards the USA was further raised by the crash of a reconnaissance plane in January 2003.

The election of Roh Moo-Hyun as President raised fears that the Republic of Korea's relations with the USA would be further undermined, as Roh had campaigned for a foreign policy more independent from the USA. However, in January 2003 he indicated a more conciliatory stance, but nevertheless warned the USA against attacking North Korea, instead urging the USA to resume dialogue with the DPRK. He also instructed the military to prepare contingency plans for the possible withdrawal of US troops, and in March the US Secretary of Defense, Donald Rumsfeld, stated that the troops could be reduced in number or withdrawn completely. The USA announced that it planned to remove its 15,000 troops stationed between Seoul and the DMZ and deploy them in the south of the country. In February the commander of the United States Forces Korea, Gen. Leon LaPorte, stated that the USA and South Korea would review their 1953 Mutual Defense Treaty, with the possibility of ending provisions under the 'Combined Forces Command' for the transfer of control over South Korea's military to the USA in wartime. However, it was noted that South Korea still remained dependent on the USA for military intelligence. In April 2003 the US military announced that it would move its main base away from Seoul as part of a global redeployment of forces. The USA envisaged eventually consolidating its forces in two major hubs: the Osan-Pyeongtaek and Daegu-Busan regions. Despite domestic protests, meanwhile, Roh arranged to send 700 non-combatant troops to Iraq in support of the US-led military operation.

In June 2003, plans were confirmed to withdraw US troops to locations 120 km south of the DMZ, as part of a wider reorganization of US forces in South Korea. In January 2004 the two countries agreed to relocate US troops out of Seoul. In September it was announced that US troops would withdraw from the DMZ by the end of October (South Korean forces duly assumed responsibility for patrolling the border zone from the beginning of November). In October an agreement for the planned withdrawal of one-third of all US troops in South Korea was reached, to take place in three phases extending to 2008.

Meanwhile, the deployment of 3,000 South Korean troops to Iraq at the request of the USA, which had been approved by the National Assembly in February 2004, went ahead in August despite public outrage at the beheading of a South Korean hostage in that country in June. In December 2004, following a vote in the National Assembly, it was announced that South Korean troops in Iraq (now numbering around 3,600) would remain there throughout 2005. In December 2005 the National Assembly voted to reduce the number of South Korean troops in Iraq to 2,300 and to extend their deployment until the end of 2006. In January 2006, meanwhile, a court in Seoul ordered the US pharmaceutical companies responsible for producing the toxic Agent Orange to pay compensation to those South Koreans affected by the herbicide while serving alongside the US military during the Viet Nam war (see above).

In February 2007, at a meeting in Washington, DC, the South Korean Minister of National Defence, Kim Jang-Soo, and the US Secretary of Defense, Robert Gates, agreed to transfer operational control of South Korean military forces from the USA to South Korea in the event of war and to disband the Combined Forces Command in April 2012 (three years later than the USA had proposed). A new 'supporting-supported command relationship' was to be established, under which the United States Forces Korea would continue to support the South Korean military. Kim and Gates also reaffirmed earlier agreements on the relocation of US forces from Seoul to the Osan-Pyeongtaek and Daegu-Busan regions and on a reduction in the number of US troops stationed in the Republic of Korea from around 30,000 to 25,000 by 2008. The election of Lee Myung-Bak as South Korean President in December 2007 prompted speculation that the new administration might attempt to renegotiate the arrangement on the transfer of wartime military control. The GNP remained staunchly opposed to the agreement concluded under Roh earlier in the year. Lee pledged to forge closer relations with the USA, asserting that the Republic of Korea continued to require US protection. The National Assembly voted to extend the deployment of South Korean troops in Iraq until the end of 2008, but to reduce their number from around 1,250 to 650. The South Korean Government had come under pressure from the Bush Administration to maintain its military presence in Iraq, despite continued domestic public opposition to the deployment. In December 2008 South Korea withdrew its remaining soldiers from Iraq.

Meanwhile, in February 2006 it was announced that discussions had commenced with regard to an important FTA between the Republic of Korea and the USA. However, as negotiations proceeded in July an estimated 30,000 demonstrators took to the streets of Seoul to protest against what they described as 'economic subjugation'. South Korean farmers, in particular, were concerned that the proposed FTA might prove detrimental to their livelihoods. Major corporations expressed reservations with regard to US demands that trade-related legislation, including fair trade laws, be applied to the South Korean *chaebol*. A further obstacle was the pharmaceutical sector, owing to the USA's strong objections to a new South Korean drug-pricing system intended to ensure that medicines were available at reasonable cost to those on low incomes. Another fundamental issue was the South Korean policy of engagement towards the DPRK. The USA insisted that goods produced in the North Korean industrial complex of Kaesong should be exempt from the trade pact, while the South Korean Government regarded Kaesong as a symbol of reconciliation, serving to promote peace and stability on the Korean Peninsula. As public opposition to the proposed FTA increased, in November at least 65,000 protesters took to the streets across South Korea, as part of a general strike organized by the KCTU, to demonstrate their disapproval. Further demonstrations later in the month were severely curtailed by a heavy police presence. None the less, an estimated 5,000 farmers and their supporters defied a police ban to hold a protest in early December, to coincide with the start of the fifth round of FTA negotiations. The sixth round of discussions, which took place in early 2007, drew further protests, with up to 8,000 farmers and workers taking to the streets of Seoul.

In April 2007 the Republic of Korea and the USA finally reached a compromise on the terms of the FTA. The principal elements of the agreement included wider access to the US market for South Korean carmakers, a reduction of taxes payable by television and mobile phone manufacturers and the cessation of duties levied on beef imports. Critics claimed that these measures would have a drastic impact on South Korean farmers, although the agreement did not encompass rice imports, as the Republic of Korea objected to the liberalization of that particular market. The conclusion of the FTA led to renewed protests by various sections of South Korean society. Many argued that increased US imports would render local businesses uncompetitive, thus threatening numerous livelihoods. Several senior opposition politicians joined the protests when they began a hunger strike. However, the Government took a more positive view of the agreement, regarding it as the most important bilateral development since the two nations signed the military alliance in 1953. None the less, the FTA remained subject to ratification by both countries' legislatures. Several amendments to the FTA, incorporating stricter labour and environmental provisions, were agreed before it was formally signed at the end of June 2007, mainly in order to facilitate the ratification process in the US Congress. Tens of thousands of workers participated in several days of strike action organized by the Korean Metal Workers' Union in that month in protest against the agreement. The situation in the USA was also problematic, and was further complicated by US demands that the Republic of Korea remove restrictions on the import of US beef, which had been imposed in late 2003 in response to the detection of BSE at a US cattle farm. In April 2008, however, prior to a visit to the USA by the newly elected President Lee Myung-Bak, the South Korean Government agreed to relax the restrictions on imports of US beef. The decision prompted large-scale public protests in mid-2008 and, along with other factors, was responsible for a sharp decline in support for Lee (see above). In April 2009 a parliamentary committee approved a bill to allow the ratification of the FTA; however, the process of ratification subsequently stalled in both the South Korean National Assembly and the US Congress (which had expressed concern that the FTA would negatively affect the troubled US car industry). In December 2010, following talks between Lee and US President Barack Obama in the previous month, the two countries signed a revised version of the FTA that sought to address some of the concerns raised by both legislatures, in particular by delaying the elimination of tariffs on vehicle imports. By May 2011 the agreement was yet to be ratified by either legislature.

Following President Lee's visit to the USA in June 2009, President Obama travelled to South Korea in November and held discussions with Lee on the resumption of the six-party talks to address the issue of North Korea's nuclear programme (see Relations with North Korea); Obama reiterated that the USA's commitment to the defence of the Republic of Korea had 'never been stronger'. The US Secretary of State, Hillary Clinton, visited the DMZ together with Secretary of Defense Gates in July 2010, when she reaffirmed the USA's commitment to the Republic of Korea's defence in the aftermath of the sinking of the *Cheonan* in March; the visit coincided with the annual joint US-South Korean naval exercises.

Other external relations

The Republic of Korea established full diplomatic relations with the USSR in 1990. In 1991 the Republic of Korea extended a substantial loan to the USSR; this debt was subsequently transferred to the Russian Federation (Russia) following the disintegration of the USSR later in that year. In September 1993 it was announced that the Republic of Korea and Russia were to participate in joint naval exercises, and in 1994 it was reported that Russia was to supply 'defensive missiles' in order to repay a part of its debt to the Republic of Korea. Further arrangements were made concerning the settlement of Russia's debt, through the provision of commodities, in July 1997.

Relations were severely tested in mid-1998 by a diplomatic dispute, provoked by Russia's expulsion of a South Korean diplomat following allegations of espionage and bribery, which culminated in the resignation of the South Korean Minister of Foreign Affairs and Trade, Park Chung-Soo. During a state visit to Russia in May 1999 Kim Dae-Jung held a summit meeting with President Boris Yeltsin. Issues discussed included South Korea's engagement policy with North Korea. The Russian Minister of Defence visited Seoul in September 1999, and the two countries conducted their first joint naval exercises in April 2000. President Vladimir Putin of Russia paid a three-day state visit to the Republic of Korea in February 2001, when he agreed to proceed with a tripartite framework of co-operation between Russia and both Koreas. Arrangements were made for Russia to supply weapons to the Republic of Korea, which were to be partially paid for by the cancellation of some Soviet-era debt. The Republic of Korea and Russia also issued a joint statement supporting the 1972 Anti-Ballistic Missile (ABM) treaty; however, US displeasure with this led to the resignation of the Minister of Foreign Affairs and Trade, Lee Joung-Binn. In December 2002 the South Korean Government agreed to accept military equipment worth US $534m. from Russia as part of a 1995 agreement to repay its $2,000m. debt to the Republic of Korea.

There were indications that Roh Moo-Hyun would seek to improve relations with Russia during his presidency, as part of a broader policy of reducing dependency on the USA. In March 2003 Roh revived the idea of building a 4,000-km pipeline that would provide the DPRK with Russian natural gas from Sakhalin in exchange for the abandonment of its nuclear weapons programme. At a summit meeting in Bangkok, Thailand, in October 2003 Roh and Putin agreed to co-operate on the North Korean nuclear issue. In September 2004 President Roh visited Russia. A significant agreement between state-owned oil companies of the two countries (Korean National Oil Corporation—KNOC—and Russia's Rosneft) was signed. In April 2005 the Minister of Defence, Yoon Kwang-Woong, visited Russia, where he met his Russian counterpart, Sergei Ivanov, to discuss the provision of Russian 'advanced weapons technology' by way of further repaying the Russian debt to the Republic of Korea.

Taliban militants seized a group of 23 South Korean Christians in Afghanistan in mid-July 2007. Following the killing of two of the hostages later in that month, direct talks between South Korean officials and the Taliban were held in August. By the end of August the Taliban had released the remaining 21 hostages, who claimed to have been undertaking aid work rather than missionary activities. The South Korean authorities refused to confirm or deny speculation that a ransom had been paid to the Taliban, but stated that it had agreed to withdraw its troops from Afghanistan by the end of the year, as scheduled, and to prevent missionary groups from travelling to the country. The withdrawal of South Korea's 210-strong contingent (comprising military medical and engineering personnel) in the International Security Assistance Force in Afghanistan was completed by mid-December. None the less, in February 2010 the GNP-dominated National Assembly approved the deployment of some 350 troops to Afghanistan to protect the South Korean Provincial Reconstruction Team, in spite of a DP boycott of the parliamentary vote, demonstrations outside the National Assembly Building and a warning by Taliban insurgents of 'bad consequences' if the deployment were carried out. The troops began operating in Afghanistan in July and were expected to withdraw by the end of 2012.

As the country continued to sign various bilateral accords providing for free trade, in May 2007 the Republic of Korea and the European Union (EU) commenced negotiations on the establishment of an FTA; the final agreement (the second largest in the world after the North American Free Trade Agreement) was signed in October 2009. Despite the opposition of the EU's vehicle-manufacturing industry and South Korean farmers, the FTA was ratified by the European Parliament in February 2011 and by the South Korean National Assembly in May; it was scheduled to enter into force in July. Meanwhile, an FTA between the Republic of Korea and Peru was signed in March 2011. Negotiations aimed at concluding an FTA between the Republic of Korea and Canada, which commenced in July 2005, continued in mid-2011.

In March 2009 President Lee Myung-Bak embarked upon a state visit to Australia, where he and Prime Minister Kevin Rudd signed a pact relating to closer co-operation in the area of security, including counter-terrorism strategies and the combating of transnational crime. The commencement of formal negotiations on an FTA between the two countries was also announced, and discussions were ongoing in mid-2011.

CONSTITUTION AND GOVERNMENT

Under the Constitution of the Sixth Republic (adopted in October 1987), executive power is held by the President, who is directly elected for one term of five years by universal suffrage. The President appoints and governs with the assistance of the State Council (cabinet), led by the Prime Minister. Legislative power is vested in the unicameral National Assembly (Kuk Hoe), popularly elected for a four-year term. The Assembly has 299 members.

THE REPUBLIC OF KOREA (SOUTH KOREA)

REGIONAL AND INTERNATIONAL CO-OPERATION

The Republic of Korea is a member of the Asian Development Bank (ADB, see p. 202), Asia-Pacific Economic Co-operation (APEC, see p. 197), the Colombo Plan (see p. 446) and the UN's Economic and Social Commission for Asia and the Pacific (ESCAP, see p. 37). In 1991 the Republic of Korea was accepted as a dialogue partner of the Association of Southeast Asian Nations (ASEAN, see p. 206), subsequently becoming one of the three additional partners of ASEAN + 3.

The Republic of Korea joined the UN in 1991. As a contracting party to the General Agreement on Tariffs and Trade (GATT), the country joined the World Trade Organization (WTO, see p. 430) upon its establishment in 1995. The Republic of Korea is also a member of the Organisation for Economic Co-operation and Development (OECD, see p. 376).

ECONOMIC AFFAIRS

In 2009, according to estimates by the World Bank, the Republic of Korea's gross national income (GNI), measured at average 2007–09 prices, was US $966,600m., equivalent to $19,830 per head (or $27,310 per head on an international purchasing-power parity basis). During 2000–09, it was estimated, the population increased at an average annual rate of 0.4%, while gross domestic product (GDP) per head increased, in real terms, by an average of 3.5% per year. Overall GDP increased, in real terms, at an average annual rate of 3.9% in 2000–09. According to the Asian Development Bank (ADB), GDP rose by only 0.2% in 2009 but by 6.1% in 2010.

Agriculture (including forestry and fishing) contributed an estimated 2.6% of GDP in 2009, and the sector engaged 6.6% of the employed labour force in 2010. The principal crop is rice, but barley, potatoes, sweet potatoes and fruit are also important, as is the raising of livestock (principally poultry, pigs and cattle). Fishing provides food for domestic consumption, as well as a substantial surplus for export. South Korea is one of the world's leading ocean-fishing nations. During 2000–08, according to figures from the World Bank, the GDP of the agricultural sector increased by an average of 1.8% per year. Agricultural GDP rose by 1.6% in 2009 but declined by 4.9% in 2010, according to the ADB.

Industry (including mining and quarrying, manufacturing, utilities and construction) contributed an estimated 36.7% of GDP in 2009. The industrial sector engaged 17.0% of the employed labour force in 2010. Industry is dominated by large conglomerate companies (*chaebol*), with greatly diversified interests, especially in construction and manufacturing. According to figures from the World Bank, during 2000–08 industrial GDP increased at an average annual rate of 5.5%. The sector's GDP contracted by 0.6% in 2009 but expanded by 11.1% in 2010, according to the ADB.

South Korea is not richly endowed with natural resources. Mining and quarrying contributed an estimated 0.2% of GDP in 2009, employing a negligible percentage of the labour force. There are deposits of coal (mainly anthracite). Other minerals include iron ore, lead, zinc, silver, gold and limestone. Substantial offshore reserves of natural gas have been discovered.

Manufacturing contributed an estimated 27.7% of GDP in 2009. The sector engaged 16.9% of the employed labour force in 2010. The most important branches of manufacturing include electrical machinery, transport equipment (mainly road motor vehicles and shipbuilding), non-electrical machinery, chemicals, food products, iron and steel, and textiles. During 2000–08 manufacturing GDP increased by an average of 6.3% per year, according to figures from the World Bank; the sector's GDP expanded by 7.2% in 2007 and by 3.1% in 2008.

Construction contributed an estimated 6.9% of GDP in 2009, and the sector engaged 7.7% of the employed labour force in 2008. During 2000–08, according to ADB data, the sector's GDP grew at an average annual rate of 2.7%. Construction GDP grew by 2.6% in 2007, but it contracted by 2.4% in 2008.

Energy is derived principally from nuclear power and coal. In 2007 33.6% of total electricity output was generated by nuclear power and 40.1% from coal, while petroleum and hydroelectric power provided 5.9% and 0.9%, respectively. At the end of 2005 there were 20 nuclear units in operation in the country. The Republic of Korea also produces liquefied natural gas for domestic and industrial consumption. Imports of petroleum and its products comprised an estimated 20.6% of the value of merchandise imports in 2010.

The services sector contributed an estimated 60.7% of GDP in 2008. The sector engaged 76.4% of the employed labour force in 2010. Receipts from tourism are significant, totalling US $12,783m. in 2008. In comparison with the previous year, the number of visitor arrivals was reported to have risen by 12.5% in 2010, to reach 8.8m. During 2000–08, according to figures from the World Bank, the GDP of the services sector increased at an average annual rate of 4.0%. The GDP of the services sector increased by 1.0% in 2009 and by 3.5% in 2010, according to the ADB.

In 2009 the Republic of Korea recorded a visible trade surplus of US $56,128m., and there was a surplus of $42,668m. on the current account of the balance of payments. The People's Republic of China (accounting for 16.8%) and Japan (15.1%) were the principal sources of imports in 2010; other important suppliers were the USA and Saudi Arabia. China was the principal market for exports in 2010 (purchasing 25.1%), followed by the USA. Other important markets included Japan, Hong Kong, Singapore, India and Taiwan. The main exports are electrical machinery (particularly telecommunications and sound equipment), basic manufactures, and chemical products. The principal imports in that year were machinery and transport equipment (especially electrical machinery), petroleum and petroleum products, basic manufactures and chemical products.

The Republic of Korea recorded a budget deficit of 17,6210,000m. won in 2009, equivalent to 1.7% of GDP in that year. The general government gross debt was 346,109,000m. in 2009, equivalent to 32.6% of GDP. At the end of 2010, according to the ADB, the total external debt reached US $359,985m. In that year the cost of debt-servicing was equivalent to 9.1% of the value of exports of goods and services. The average annual rate of inflation was 3.2% in 2000–10. Consumer prices increased by 2.9% in 2010. The average rate of unemployment was 3.7% in 2010.

Strong growth in both domestic consumption and private investment (notably in the manufacturing sector) prevailed until the deterioration in global economic conditions in mid-2008. Attempting to raise levels of inter-bank lending and thus improve the availability of credit to businesses, in February 2009 (in the sixth reduction within four months) the central bank decreased its interest rate to an historically low level of 2.0%. From November 2008 the Government introduced a series of fiscal stimulus measures, which included reductions in corporate and personal taxation and a programme of job creation. Although external demand weakened considerably in the latter part of 2008, resulting in a substantial decline in the value of exports in 2009, the sector was sustained by demand from China (South Korea's leading market), particularly for electronic goods. The greater diversification of the South Korean manufacturing sector in recent years also afforded a higher degree of resilience to changing global conditions. The export sector was further assisted by the depreciation of the South Korean currency in 2009, when the won was reported to have declined in value by nearly 13% in comparison with the previous year. Following the minimal GDP growth of 2009, a robust recovery ensued in 2010, propelled by continued growth in exports, increased investment and revitalized domestic consumption. At 6.1%, the expansion in GDP in 2010 represented the largest increase since 2002. However, the rapid economic recovery, combined with rising global food and energy prices, was responsible for a steady increase in inflation during 2010, prompting the central bank to effect a series of interest rate rises from September; by March 2011 the official rate stood at 3.0%. The ADB forecast a more moderate economic growth rate of 4.6% for 2011. Inflationary pressures were predicted to remain high. Strong demand for South Korean exports from China was expected to continue. The implementation of a free trade agreement (FTA) with the European Union, scheduled for July 2011, was expected to yield major benefits to the South Korean economy. Meanwhile, an FTA with the USA awaited ratification. Furthermore, a trilateral trade agreement with China and Japan, which together accounted for nearly one-third of South Korean trade, was under consideration in 2011.

PUBLIC HOLIDAYS

2012 (provisional): 2 January (for New Year's Day), 23–24 January (Lunar New Year), 1 March (Sam Il Jol, Independence Movement Day), 5 May (Children's Day), 10 May (Buddha's Birthday), 6 June (Memorial Day), 15 August (Liberation Day), 11–13 September (Juseok, Korean Thanksgiving Day), 3 October (National Foundation Day), 25 December (Christmas).

THE REPUBLIC OF KOREA (SOUTH KOREA)

Statistical Survey

Source (unless otherwise stated): Statistics Korea, Bldg III, Government Complex-Daejeon 920, Dunsan-dong, Seo-gu, Daejeon 302-701; tel. (42) 481-2120; fax (42) 481-2460; internet kostat.go.kr.

Area and Population

AREA, POPULATION AND DENSITY*

Area (sq km)	99,646†
Population (census results)	
1 November 2005	47,041,434
1 November 2010‡	
Males	24,045,000
Females	24,174,000
Total	48,219,000
Density (per sq km) at 2010 census	483.9

* Excluding the demilitarized zone between North and South Korea, with an area of 1,262 sq km (487 sq miles).
† 38,474 sq miles. The figure indicates territory under the jurisdiction of the Republic of Korea, surveyed on the basis of land register in 2005.
‡ Preliminary results, rounded figures.

POPULATION BY AGE AND SEX
(official estimates at mid-2011)

	Males	Females	Total
0–14	3,978,912	3,664,502	7,643,414
15–64	18,337,401	17,470,946	35,808,347
65 and over	2,276,143	3,260,929	5,537,072
Total	24,592,456	24,396,377	48,988,833

Note: Data not adjusted to take account of results of 2010 census.

ADMINISTRATIVE DIVISIONS
(population at census of 1 November 2010)

Province	Area (sq km)	Population ('000)*	Density (per sq km)
Seoul	605.4	9,708	16,035.7
Busan	764.4	3,403	4,451.9
Daegu	884.5	2,444	2,763.1
Incheon	994.1	2,638	2,653.7
Gwangju	501.4	1,469	2,929.8
Daejeon	539.8	1,495	2,769.5
Ulsan	1,057.1	1,082	1,023.6
Gyeonggi-do	10,130.9	11,270	1,112.4
Gangwon-do	16,613.5	1,456	87.6
Chungcheongbuk-do	7,431.4	1,504	202.4
Chungcheongnam-do	8,600.5	2,010	233.7
Jeollabuk-do	8,054.6	1,755	217.9
Jeollanam-do	12,073.5	1,719	142.4
Gyeongsangbuk-do	19,026.0	2,583	135.8
Gyeongsangnam-do	10,520.8	3,154	299.8
Jeju-do	1,848.3	528	285.7
Total	99,646.2	48,219	483.9

* Preliminary figures.

PRINCIPAL TOWNS
(population at 1995 census)

Seoul (capital)	10,231,217	Jeonju (Chonju)	563,153
Busan (Pusan)	3,814,325	Jeongju (Chongju)	531,376
Daegu (Taegu)	2,449,420	Masan	441,242
Incheon (Inchon)	2,308,188	Jinju (Chinju)	329,886
Daejeon (Taejon)	1,272,121	Kunsan	266,559
Gwangju (Kwangju)	1,257,636	Jeju (Cheju)	258,511
Ulsan	967,429	Mokpo	247,452
Seongnam (Songnam)	869,094	Chuncheon (Chunchon)	234,528
Suwon	755,550		

2000 census: Seoul 9,853,972; Busan 3,655,437; Daegu 2,473,990; Incheon 2,466,338; Daejeon 1,365,961; Gwangju 1,350,948; Ulsan 1,012,110.

Mid-2010 (incl. suburbs, UN estimates): Seoul 9,772,717; Busan 3,425,291; Incheon 2,582,967; Daegu 2,458,372; Daejeon 1,509.201; Gwangju 1,475,655; Suwon 1,131,704; Ulsan 1,081,119; Goyang 960,983; Seongnam 954,787 (Source: UN, *World Urbanization Prospects: The 2009 Revision*).

BIRTHS, MARRIAGES AND DEATHS*

	Registered live births Number	Rate (per 1,000)	Registered marriages Number	Rate (per 1,000)	Registered deaths Number	Rate (per 1,000)
2003	490,543	10.2	302,503	6.3	244,506	5.1
2004	472,761	9.8	308,598	6.4	244,217	5.0
2005	435,031	8.9	314,304	6.5	243,883	5.0
2006	448,153	9.2	330,634	6.8	242,266	5.0
2007	493,189	10.0	343,559	7.0	244,874	5.0
2008	465,892	9.4	327,715	6.6	246,113	5.0
2009	444,849	9.0	309,759	6.2	246,942	5.0
2010	469,900	9.4	n.a.	n.a.	255,100	5.1

* Owing to late registration, figures are subject to continuous revision.

Life expectancy (years at birth, WHO estimates): 80 (males 76; females 83) in 2008 (Source: WHO, *World Health Statistics*).

ECONOMICALLY ACTIVE POPULATION*
(labour force survey, '000 persons aged 15 years and over)

	2006	2007	2008
Agriculture, forestry and fishing	1,785	1,779	1,686
Mining and quarrying	18	18	23
Manufacturing	4,167	4,014	3,963
Electricity, gas and water	76	86	90
Construction	1,835	1,849	1,812
Wholesale and retail trade, repair of motor vehicles and personal and household goods	3,713	3,673	3,631
Restaurants and hotels	2,049	2,049	2,044
Transport, storage and communications	1,470	1,498	1,875
Financial intermediation	786	806	821
Real estate, renting and business activities	2,168	2,350	2,219
Public administration and defence; compulsory social security	801	797	840
Education	1,658	1,740	1,784
Health and social work	686	740	842
Other community, social and personal service activities	1,781	1,845	1,782
Households with employed persons	138	161	150
Extra-territorial organizations and bodies	20	15	16
Statistical discrepancy	—	13	—
Total employed	23,151	23,433	23,577
Unemployed	827	783	769
Total labour force	23,978	24,216	23,346
Males	13,978	14,124	14,208
Females	10,000	10,092	10,139

* Excluding armed forces.

Source: ILO.

2009 ('000 persons aged 15 years and over): Agriculture, forestry and fishing 1,648; Industry 3,859 (Manufacturing 3,836); Services 17,998; *Total employed* 23,506; Unemployed 889; *Total labour force* 24,395.

2010 ('000 persons aged 15 years and over): Agriculture, forestry and fishing 1,566; Industry 4,048 (Manufacturing 4,028); Services 18,214; *Total employed* 23,829; Unemployed 920; *Total labour force* 24,749.

THE REPUBLIC OF KOREA (SOUTH KOREA)

Statistical Survey

Health and Welfare

KEY INDICATORS

Total fertility rate (children per woman, 2008)	1.2
Under-5 mortality rate (per 1,000 live births, 2008)	5
HIV/AIDS (% of persons aged 15–49, 2007)	<0.1
Physicians (per 1,000 head, 2003)	1.6
Hospital beds (per 1,000 head, 2006)	8.6
Health expenditure (2007): US $ per head (PPP)	1,688
Health expenditure (2007): % of GDP	6.3
Health expenditure (2007): public (% of total)	54.9
Access to water (% of persons, 2008)	98
Total carbon dioxide emissions ('000 metric tons, 2007)	502,909.6
Carbon dioxide emissions per head (metric tons, 2007)	10.4
Human Development Index (2010): ranking	12
Human Development Index (2010): value	0.877

For sources and definitions, see explanatory note on p. vi.

Agriculture

PRINCIPAL CROPS
('000 metric tons)

	2006	2007	2008
Rice, paddy	6,411.0	6,038.0	6,919.2
Barley	148.0	168.9	170.1
Maize	64.6	83.5	92.8
Potatoes	631.1	574.4	604.6
Sweet potatoes	285.8	352.3	329.4
Beans, dry	6.4	7.6	7.6
Chestnuts	82.5	77.5	75.2
Soybeans (Soya beans)	156.4	114.2	132.7
Sesame seed	15.5	17.5	19.5
Cabbages and other brassicas	3,068.1	2,537.6	2,901.9
Lettuce and chicory	160.3	154.8	154.8*
Spinach	103.7	81.5	93.4
Tomatoes	433.2	479.9	408.2
Pumpkins, squash and gourds	322.0	330.0	327.5
Cucumbers and gherkins	389.6	330.2	383.9
Chillies and peppers, green	353.0	414.1	385.8
Onions and shallots, green	543.0	488.0	505.1
Onions, dry	889.6	1,213.4	1,035.1
Garlic	331.4	347.5	375.5
Carrots and turnips	130.4	76.7	99.6
Mushrooms	27.4	28.7	28.4
Watermelons	778.4	741.9	856.8
Cantaloupes and other melons	219.7	205.4	220.4
Tangerines, mandarins, clementines and satsumas	620.3	777.5	636.4
Apples	407.6	435.7	470.9
Pears	431.5	467.4	470.7
Peaches and nectarines	193.8	184.5	189.1
Plums and sloes	64.4	64.8	66.7
Strawberries	205.3	203.2	203.2*
Grapes	330.0	328.7	333.6
Persimmons	352.8	395.6	430.5
Tobacco, unmanufactured*	34.0	35.5	35.5

* FAO estimate(s).

2009: Soybeans (Soya beans) 139.0 (unofficial figure); Sesame seed 20.0 (FAO estimate).

Aggregate production ('000 metric tons, may include official, semi-official or estimated data): Total cereals 6,647 in 2006, 6,312 in 2007, 7,203 in 2008–09; Total vegetables (incl. melons) 11,308 in 2006, 10,718 in 2007, 11,278 in 2008–09; Total fruits (excl. melons) 2,722 in 2006, 2,966 in 2007, 2,909 in 2008–09.

Source: FAO.

LIVESTOCK
('000 head)

	2006	2007	2008
Cattle	2,484	2,654	2,894
Pigs	9,382	9,606	9,153
Goats	467	372	266
Chickens	119,181	119,365	119,784

Note: No data were available for 2009.

Source: FAO.

LIVESTOCK PRODUCTS
('000 metric tons)

	2006	2007	2008
Cattle meat	200.0	219.0	246.0
Pig meat*	1,000.0	1,043.0	1,056.0
Chicken meat	510.0*	513.0*	488.0
Duck meat*	53.0	57.0	54.0
Cows' milk	2,184.0	2,188.0	2,200.0
Goats' milk†	5.2	5.2	4.2
Hen eggs	537.4	543.8	566.1
Other poultry eggs†	28.0	28.5	28.5
Honey	22.9	26.5	26.0†

* Unofficial figure(s).
† FAO estimate(s).

2009: Goats' milk 4.2 (FAO estimate).

Source: FAO.

Forestry

ROUNDWOOD REMOVALS
('000 cubic metres, excl. bark)

	2007	2008	2009
Sawlogs, veneer logs and logs for sleepers	440	456	451
Pulpwood	1,643	1,757	1,919
Other industrial wood	597	489	806
Fuel wood*	2,472	2,475	2,477
Total	**5,152**	**5,177**	**5,653**

* FAO estimates.

Source: FAO.

SAWNWOOD PRODUCTION
('000 cubic metres, incl. sleepers)

	2002	2003	2004
Coniferous (softwood)	4,209	4,200	4,200*
Broadleaved (hardwood)	201	180	166†
Total	**4,410**	**4,380**	**4,366***

* FAO estimate.
† Unofficial figure.

2005–09: Figures assumed to be unchanged from 2004 (FAO estimates).

Source: FAO.

THE REPUBLIC OF KOREA (SOUTH KOREA)

Fishing

('000 metric tons, live weight)

	2006	2007	2008
Capture	1,757.5	1,869.8	1,943.9
Croakers and drums	49.0	44.0	39.6
Japanese anchovy	265.3	221.1	261.5
Skipjack tuna	206.5	214.9	187.3
Chub mackerel	101.7	145.0	188.2
Largehead hairtail	63.7	66.0	72.9
Argentine shortfin squid	138.8	193.7	157.8
Japanese flying squid	197.1	174.5	186.2
Aquaculture	513.6	606.1	473.8
Pacific cupped oyster	283.3	321.3	250.0
Total catch	2,271.1	2,476.0	2,417.7

Note: Figures exclude aquatic plants ('000 metric tons): 779.4 (capture 13.8, aquaculture 765.6) in 2006; 811.2 (capture 18.2, aquaculture 793.0) in 2007; 934.9 (capture 13.9, aquaculture 921.0) in 2008. Also excluded are aquatic mammals, recorded by number rather than by weight; the number of dolphins and whales caught was: 544 in 2006; 610 in 2007; 728 in 2008.

Source: FAO.

Mining

('000 metric tons unless otherwise indicated)

	2007	2008	2009
Hard coal (Anthracite)	2,886	2,773	2,519
Iron ore: gross weight	291	366	455
Iron ore: metal content	163	205*	200*
Lead ore (metric tons)†	12	449	2,064
Zinc ore (metric tons)†	4,067	3,672	—
Kaolin	688	955	695
Feldspar	398.5	344.3	622.7
Salt (unrefined)	249.5	384.3	382.3
Mica (metric tons)	42,385	49,474	27,078
Talc (metric tons)	9,557	6,438	5,996
Pyrophyllite	798.1	892.6	617.4

* Estimate.
† Figures refer to the metal content of ores.

Source: US Geological Survey.

Industry

SELECTED PRODUCTS

('000 metric tons, unless otherwise indicated)

	2005	2006	2007
Wheat flour	1,837	1,850	1,760
Refined sugar	1,322	1,317	n.a.
Beer (million litres)	17,489	17,400	18,200
Cigarettes (million)	107,247	119,966	124,570
Cotton yarn—pure and mixed	253	217	216
Plywood ('000 cu m)	651	736	716
Newsprint	1,630	1,654	1,666
Rubber tyres ('000)*	65,655	65,231	68,771
Caustic soda	1,455	1,477	1,578
Liquefied petroleum gas	3,213	3,098	2,927
Naphtha	20,800	n.a.	n.a.
Kerosene	5,791	5,410	3,827
Gas-diesel (distillate fuel oil)	31,508	32,392	34,314

—continued	2005	2006	2007
Residual fuel oil	31,305	30,793	27,363
Cement	52,224	55,021	58,188
Pig-iron	27,309	27,559	29,437
Crude steel	46,123	48,259	51,003
Television receivers ('000)	5,843	n.a.	n.a.
Passenger cars—produced ('000 units)	3,356	3,489	n.a.
Lorries and trucks—produced (number)	218,902	n.a.	n.a.
Electric energy (million kWh)	389,390	n.a.	n.a.
Carbon black†	471.7	484.3	497.2
Products of petroleum refineries ('000 barrels)†	919,627	717,493	770,523

* Tyres for passenger cars and commercial vehicles.
† Source: US Geological Survey.

Shipbuilding (merchant ships launched, '000 grt): 8,977 in 1999; 11,211 in 2000; 8,385 in 2001.

Source: mostly UN, *Industrial Commodity Statistics Yearbook*.

2008 ('000 metric tons unless otherwise indicated): Cement 51,653; Crude steel 53,322; Pig-iron 31,043; Carbon black 484.0 (estimate); Products of petroleum refineries ('000 barrels) 747,827 (Source: US Geological Survey).

Finance

CURRENCY AND EXCHANGE RATES

Monetary Units
100 chun (jeon) = 10 hwan = 1 won.

Sterling, Dollar and Euro Equivalents (31 December 2010)
£1 sterling = 1,794.22 won;
US $1 = 1,146.10 won;
€1 = 1,531.42 won;
10,000 won = £5.57 = $8.73 = €6.53.

Average Exchange Rate (won per US $)
2008   1,102.05
2009   1,276.93
2010   1,156.19

BUDGET

('000 million won)

Revenue	2004	2005	2006
Current revenue	177,432	190,165	208,091
Tax revenue	140,643	152,371	165,359
Non-tax revenue	36,788	37,794	42,733
Capital revenue	1,329	1,281	1,482
Total	178,760	191,447	209,573

Expenditure	2004	2005	2006
Current expenditure	145,148	160,274	173,688
General public services	11,909	14,743	17,208
Defence	19,995	21,976	23,428
Education	22,113	27,467	28,457
Social security and welfare	15,125	16,716	18,536
Economic services	30,753	28,250	30,115
Transport and communications	14,458	14,041	13,903
Capital expenditure	26,992	24,648	26,493
Net lending	1,398	3,024	5,746
Total	173,538	187,946	205,928

2007: Total revenue 243,633 (Current 241,693, Capital 1,940); Total expenditure and net lending 209,810 (Current 169,658, Capital 33,045, Net lending 7,107).

2008: Total revenue 250,713 (Current 248,809, Capital 1,904); Total expenditure and net lending 238,834 (Current 196,879, Capital 36,475, Net lending 5,480).

2009: Total revenue 255,252 (Current 252,720, Capital 2,532); Total expenditure and net lending 272,873 (Current 209,689, Capital 45,134, Net lending 18,049).

Source: partly Bank of Korea, Seoul.

THE REPUBLIC OF KOREA (SOUTH KOREA)

INTERNATIONAL RESERVES
(US $ million at 31 December)

	2007	2008	2009
Gold (national valuation)	74.3	75.7	79.0
IMF special drawing rights	68.7	85.6	3,745.5
Reserve position in IMF	310.8	579.8	985.2
Foreign exchange	261,770.7	200,479.1	265,202.3
Total	262,224.5	201,220.2	270,012.0

Source: IMF, *International Financial Statistics*.

MONEY SUPPLY
('000 million won at 31 December)

	2007	2008	2009
Currency outside banks	23,937	25,323	31,209
Demand deposits at deposit money banks	62,034	63,203	72,953
Total money (incl. others)	86,677	92,143	105,398

Source: IMF, *International Financial Statistics*.

COST OF LIVING
(Consumer Price Index; base: 2005 = 100)

	2008	2009	2010
Food and non-alcoholic beverages	108.2	116.3	123.8
Alcoholic beverages and cigarettes	100.8	101.9	102.3
Housing, water and fuels	109.7	110.9	113.6
Furnishings and household goods	111.2	116.3	117.3
Clothing and footwear	108.1	113.6	116.9
Health	105.8	108.1	110.2
Education	117.2	120.1	122.8
Communication	95.3	95.2	94.3
Transport	117.9	113.7	119.3
All items (incl. others)	109.7	112.8	116.1

NATIONAL ACCOUNTS
('000 million won at current prices)

National Income and Product

	2007	2008	2009
Compensation of employees	448,993.8	474,953.8	490,710.0
Operating surplus	284,555.9	295,368.0	312,662.3
Domestic factor incomes	733,549.7	770,321.8	803,372.3
Consumption of fixed capital	128,904.2	135,876.4	142,461.4
Gross domestic product (GDP) at factor cost	862,453.9	906,198.2	945,833.7
Indirect taxes, *less* subsidies	112,559.2	120,253.6	117,225.3
GDP in purchasers' values	975,013.0	1,026,451.8	1,063,059.0
Net factor income from abroad	1,800.9	7,663.6	5,595.1
Gross national income	976,813.9	1,034,115.4	1,068,654.1
Less Consumption of fixed capital	128,904.2	135,876.4	142,461.4
National income in market prices	847,909.7	898,239.0	926,192.7

Expenditure on the Gross Domestic Product

	2007	2008	2009
Final consumption expenditure	673,526.3	718,571.6	747,660.3
Households	516,536.3	546,734.2	561,675.1
Non-profit institutions serving households	13,727.9	14,893.3	15,729.6
General government	143,262.2	156,944.1	170,255.6
Gross capital formation	286,917.6	320,368.8	275,542.3
Gross fixed capital formation	278,167.9	300,794.1	311,593.6
Changes in inventories	8,749.7	19,574.7	−36,051.2
Total domestic expenditure	960,443.9	1,038,940.4	1,023,202.6
Exports of goods and services	408,754.1	544,110.7	530,470.6
Less Imports of goods and services	394,026.2	556,197.9	488,825.4
Statistical discrepancy	−158.9	−401.4	−1,788.8
GDP in market prices	975,013.0	1,026,451.8	1,063,059.1

Gross Domestic Product by Economic Activity

	2007	2008	2009
Agriculture, forestry and fishing	25,208.8	24,686.0	24,928.8
Mining and quarrying	2,001.2	2,336.0	2,170.3
Manufacturing	238,610.9	256,209.4	265,783.0
Electricity, gas and water	19,155.3	12,298.6	17,412.8
Construction	64,979.0	64,612.2	66,472.3
Wholesale and retail trade, restaurants and hotels	93,405.5	100,419.3	105,343.0
Transport, storage and communications	79,268.6	81,279.9	82,340.6
Financial intermediation	61,114.0	65,132.2	66,283.3
Real estate, renting and business activities	114,491.7	121,791.9	124,044.2
Public administration and defence, compulsory social security	55,515.9	59,396.8	64,430.5
Education	55,554.4	60,940.1	63,430.9
Health and social work	35,451.6	38,452.1	43,080.3
Other service activities	30,025.2	32,133.5	32,511.3
Gross value added at basic prices	874,782.0	919,688.0	958,231.4
Taxes, less subsidies, on products	100,231.0	106,763.8	104,827.7
Total	975,013.0	1,026,451.8	1,063,059.1

Source: Bank of Korea.

BALANCE OF PAYMENTS
(US $ million)

	2007	2008	2009
Exports of goods f.o.b.	379,045	432,922	373,584
Imports of goods f.o.b.	−350,877	−427,253	−317,457
Trade balance	28,168	5,669	56,128
Exports of services	63,349	77,179	58,513
Imports of services	−83,116	−93,851	−75,716
Balance on goods and services	8,400	−11,003	38,925
Other income received	19,782	23,117	15,705
Other income paid	−18,780	−17,217	−11,151
Balance on goods, services and income	9,403	−5,103	43,479
Current transfers received	11,158	14,070	12,459
Current transfers paid	−14,685	−14,744	−13,269
Current balance	5,876	−5,777	42,668
Capital account (net)	−2,388	109	1,187
Direct investment abroad	−15,621	−18,943	−10,572
Direct investment from abroad	1,784	3,311	1,506
Portfolio investment assets	−56,436	23,484	1,300
Portfolio investment liabilities	30,378	−25,890	49,382
Financial derivatives assets	12,109	54,978	44,393
Financial derivatives liabilities	−6,665	−69,748	−49,931
Other investment assets	−16,763	−13,742	385
Other investment liabilities	60,727	−3,643	−11,199
Net errors and omissions	2,125	−586	−58
Overall balance	15,128	−56,446	69,061

Source: IMF, *International Financial Statistics*.

THE REPUBLIC OF KOREA (SOUTH KOREA)

External Trade

PRINCIPAL COMMODITIES
(distribution by SITC, US $ million)*

Imports c.i.f.	2008	2009	2010
Food and live animals	16,405.5	13,438.4	16,335.1
Crude materials (inedible) except fuels	28,272.1	20,310.1	30,632.2
Mineral fuels, lubricants, etc.	145,514.8	91,669.2	122,596.2
Petroleum, petroleum products, etc.	104,812.6	64,527.6	87,676.7
Gas (natural and manufactured)	24,892.6	17,146.7	21,788.7
Chemicals and related products	36,658.2	31,504.9	41,147.7
Organic chemicals	10,978.5	8,907.4	12,136.9
Basic manufactures	64,983.5	43,250.4	56,142.6
Iron and steel	33,554.9	17,430.2	22,726.5
Machinery and transport equipment	114,541.8	96,881.6	123,316.7
Machinery specialized for particular industries	13,336.8	9,634.3	18,148.8
General industrial machinery, equipment and parts	13,193.4	12,367.7	13,779.1
Office machines and automatic data-processing machines	7,526.5	6,443.6	8,855.1
Telecommunications and sound equipment	10,560.6	8,631.0	10,486.6
Other electrical machinery, apparatus, etc.	48,655.5	41,913.0	48,856.3
Thermionic valves and tubes, microprocessors, transistors, etc.	29,781.1	25,261.4	28,637.0
Miscellaneous manufactured articles	28,644.1	23,292.6	31,597.6
Total (incl. others)	435,274.7	323,084.5	425,212.2

Exports f.o.b.	2008	2009	2010
Mineral fuels, lubricants, etc.	38,454.7	23,786.0	32,579.7
Petroleum, petroleum products, etc.	38,311.3	23,663.4	32,375.2
Chemicals and related products	42,709.9	37,414.7	48,951.5
Organic chemicals	15,560.5	12,847.5	16,531.1
Plastics in primary forms	15,524.3	13,874.9	17,817.3
Basic manufactures	59,559.9	48,114.5	60,430.1
Textile yarn, fabrics, etc.	10,370.9	9,155.4	10,967.7
Iron and steel	25,037.8	17,468.0	24,432.9
Machinery and transport equipment	233,688.1	206,334.1	263,902.6
Office machines and automatic data-processing machines	10,688.0	8,991.8	12,889.8
Automatic data-processing machines and units, etc.	2,791.9	2,377.2	2,987.5
Parts and accessories for office machines and automatic data-processing equipment	6,161.1	5,074.9	8,266.8
Telecommunications and sound equipment	49,192.8	41,226.4	40,403.0
Other electrical machinery, apparatus, etc.	49,180.2	47,500.1	70,194.3
Thermionic valves and tubes, microprocessors, transistors, etc.	28,189.2	26,957.9	43,291.1
Road vehicles	48,099.2	36,294.6	53,209.0
Motor cars and other motor vehicles	31,287.5	22,399.1	31,781.7
Other transport equipment	42,170.4	43,592.6	48,617.7
Ships, boats and floating structures	40,967.6	42,483.4	46,735.3
Miscellaneous manufactured articles	37,223.3	36,906.7	46,860.0
Total (incl. others)	422,007.3	363,533.6	466,383.8

* Excluding trade with the Democratic People's Republic of Korea.

Source: Korea International Trade Association.

PRINCIPAL TRADING PARTNERS
(US $ million)*

Imports c.i.f.	2008	2009	2010
Australia	18,000.3	14,756.1	20,456.2
Brazil	4,380.5	3,743.5	4,712.1
Canada	4,403.5	3,535.3	4,350.9
China, People's Republic	76,930.3	54,246.1	71,573.6
France	4,877.4	4,006.1	4,283.5
Germany	14,769.1	12,298.5	14,304.9
Hong Kong	2,222.7	1,487.2	1,945.9
India	6,581.2	4,141.6	5,674.4
Indonesia	11,320.3	9,264.1	13,985.8
Iran	8,223.1	5,745.7	6,940.2
Iraq	4,227.6	3,812.2	4,427.7
Italy	4,151.4	3,512.9	3,723.3
Japan	60,956.4	49,427.5	64,296.1
Kuwait	12,128.8	7,991.5	10,850.1
Malaysia	9,909.1	7,574.1	9,531.0
Oman	5,694.7	4,124.5	4,095.9
Philippines	3,099.5	2,651.6	3,488.1
Qatar	14,374.6	8,386.5	11,915.5
Russia	8,340.1	5,788.7	9,899.5
Saudi Arabia	33,781.5	19,736.8	26,820.0
Singapore	8,361.8	7,871.8	7,849.5
Taiwan	10,642.9	9,851.4	13,647.1
Thailand	4,281.7	3,238.6	4,168.8
United Arab Emirates	19,248.5	9,310.0	12,170.1
United Kingdom	3,637.1	2,895.8	3,265.5
USA	38,364.8	29,039.5	40,402.7
Total (incl. others)	435,274.7	323,084.5	425,212.2

Exports f.o.b.	2008	2009	2010
Australia	5,171.3	5,243.1	6,641.6
Brazil	5,925.9	5,311.2	7,752.6
Canada	4,057.2	3,439.6	4,101.9
China, People's Republic	91,388.9	86,703.2	116,837.8
France	3,495.5	2,910.6	3,004.3
Germany	10,522.7	8,820.9	10,702.2
Hong Kong	19,771.9	19,661.1	25,294.3
India	8,977.1	8,013.3	14,830.6
Indonesia	7,933.6	5,999.9	8,897.3
Iran	4,342.6	3,991.9	4,596.7
Italy	3,545.6	2,797.3	3,569.1
Japan	28,252.5	21,770.8	28,176.3
Liberia	2,801.5	4,884.6	5,401.7
Malaysia	5,794.5	4,324.8	6,114.8
Mexico	9,089.9	7,132.8	8,845.5
Netherlands	6,405.6	4,527.5	5,306.2
Philippines	5,016.3	4,567.3	5,838.0
Russia	9,478.0	4,194.1	7,759.8
Singapore	16,293.0	13,617.0	15,244.2
Spain	3,192.5	1,737.1	1,858.0
Taiwan	11,462.0	9,501.1	14,830.5
Thailand	5,779.1	4,528.2	6,459.8
Turkey	3,772.6	2,660.7	3,752.9
United Arab Emirates	5,748.5	4,977.8	5,487.0
United Kingdom	5,936.2	3,796.6	5,555.1
USA	46,376.6	37,649.9	49,816.1
Viet Nam	7,804.8	7,149.5	9,652.1
Total (incl. others)	422,007.3	363,533.6	466,383.8

* Excluding trade with the Democratic People's Republic of Korea.

Source: Korea International Trade Association.

Trade with the Democratic People's Republic of Korea (US $ million, unofficial estimates): *Total imports:* 519.5 in 2006; 765.3 in 2007; 932.3 in 2008. *Total exports:* 830.2 in 2006; 1,032.6 in 2007; 888.1 in 2008 (Source: Bank of Korea, Republic of Korea).

THE REPUBLIC OF KOREA (SOUTH KOREA)

Transport

RAILWAYS
(traffic)

	2003	2004	2005
Passengers carried ('000)	894,620	921,223	950,995
Passenger-km (million)	27,228	28,459	31,004
Freight ('000 metric tons)	47,110	44,512	41,669
Freight ton-km (million)	11,057	10,641	10,108

ROAD TRAFFIC
(motor vehicles in use at 31 December)

	2002	2003
Passenger cars	9,737,428	10,278,923
Goods vehicles	2,894,412	3,016,407
Buses and coaches	1,275,319	1,246,629
Motorcycles and mopeds	1,708,457	1,730,193

2006 (motor vehicles in use at 31 December): Passenger cars 11,606,971; Goods vehicles 3,182,627; Buses and coaches 1,105,636; Motorcycles and mopeds 1,747,925 (Source: IRF, *World Road Statistics*).

2007 (motor vehicles in use at 31 December): Passenger cars 12,020,730; Goods vehicles 4,189,042; Buses and coaches 182,132; Motorcycles and mopeds 1,821,323 (Source: IRF, *World Road Statistics*).

SHIPPING
Merchant Fleet
(registered at 31 December)

	2007	2008	2009
Number of vessels	2,946	3,001	3,009
Total displacement ('000 grt)	13,102.0	14,144.7	12,892.5

Source: IHS Fairplay, *World Fleet Statistics*.

Sea-borne Freight Traffic
('000 metric tons)*

	2002	2003	2004
Goods loaded	319,570	340,527	317,799
Goods unloaded	615,555	616,326	593,361

* Including coastwise traffic loaded and unloaded.

CIVIL AVIATION*

	2003	2004	2005
Passengers ('000)	42,839	45,824	46,841
Passenger-km (million)	82,231	96,583	101,664
Freight ('000 metric tons)	2,632	2,978	2,989
Freight ton-km (million)	11,696	13,810	13,597

* Domestic and international flights.

Tourism

FOREIGN VISITOR ARRIVALS*

Country of residence	2006	2007	2008
China, People's Republic	896,969	1,068,925	1,167,891
Hong Kong	142,786	140,138	160,325
Japan	2,338,921	2,235,963	2,378,102
Philippines	248,262	263,799	276,710
Russia	144,611	140,426	136,342
Taiwan	338,162	335,224	320,244
Thailand	128,555	146,792	160,687
USA	555,704	587,324	610,083
Total (incl. others)	6,155,046	6,448,240	6,890,841

* Including same-day visitors (excursionists) and crew members from ships; also including Korean nationals resident abroad.

Receipts from tourism (US $ million, incl. passenger transport): 8,508 in 2006; 8,947 in 2007; 12,783 in 2008.

Source: World Tourism Organization.

Communications Media

	2007	2008	2009
Telephones ('000 main lines in use)	23,006.7	23,390.3	25,949.4
Mobile cellular telephones ('000 subscribers)	44,369.2	46,516.2	48,671.2
Internet users ('000)*	37,794.1	38,998.5	39,439.6
Broadband subscribers ('000)	15,195.0	15,921.0	16,830.0
Registered daily newspapers (titles)	203	n.a.	n.a.

* Estimates based on percentage.

Radio receivers ('000 in use): 47,500 in 1997.

Television receivers ('000 in use): 17,229 in 2000.

Book production: 27,527 titles (82,097,000 copies) in 2004.

Personal computers: 27,886,536 (575.5 per 1,000 persons) in 2007.

Sources: mainly UNESCO, *Statistical Yearbook*; UN, *Statistical Yearbook*; International Telecommunication Union; and Korean Association of Newspapers.

Education

(2007)

	Institutions	Teachers	Pupils
Kindergarten	8,294	33,504	541,550
Primary schools	5,756	167,182	3,829,998
Middle schools	3,032	107,986	2,063,159
General high schools	1,457	83,662	1,347,363
Vocational high schools	702	36,549	494,011
Junior colleges	148	11,685	795,519
Teachers' colleges	11	855	25,834
Universities and colleges	175	52,763	1,919,504
Graduate schools	1,042	2,895	296,576

Pupil-teacher ratio (primary education, UNESCO estimate): 24.1 in 2007/08 (Source: UNESCO Institute for Statistics).

Adult literacy rate (UNESCO estimates): 97.9% (males 99.2%; females 96.6%) in 2001 (Source: UN Development Programme, *Human Development Report*).

THE REPUBLIC OF KOREA (SOUTH KOREA)

Directory

The Government

HEAD OF STATE

President: LEE MYUNG-BAK (took office 25 February 2008).

STATE COUNCIL
(May 2011)

The Government is formed by the Grand National Party (GNP).
Prime Minister: KIM HWANG-SIK.
Minister of Strategy and Finance: BAHK JAE-WAN (designate).
Minister of Unification: HYUN IN-TAEK.
Minister of Foreign Affairs and Trade: KIM SUNG-HWAN.
Minister of Justice: LEE KWI-NAM.
Minister of National Defence: KIM KWAN-JIN.
Minister of Public Administration and Security: MAENG HYUNG-KYU.
Minister of Education, Science and Technology: LEE JU-HO.
Minister of Culture, Sports and Tourism: CHOUNG BYOUNG-GUG.
Minister of Food, Agriculture, Forestry and Fisheries: SUH KYU-YONG (designate).
Minister of Knowledge Economy: CHOI JOONG-KYUNG.
Minister of Health, Welfare and Family Affairs: CHIN SOO-HEE.
Minister of Environment: YOO YOUNG-SOOK (designate).
Minister of Employment and Labour: LEE CHAE-PIL (designate).
Minister of Gender Equality: PAIK HEE-YOUNG.
Minister of Land, Transport and Maritime Affairs: KWON DO-YUP (designate).
Minister for Special Affairs: LEE JAE-OH.

MINISTRIES

Office of the President: Chong Wa Dae (The Blue House), 1, Sejong-no, Jongno-gu, Seoul; tel. (2) 730-5800; e-mail foreign@president.go.kr; internet www.bluehouse.go.kr.

Office of the Prime Minister: 55, Sejong-no, Jongno-gu, Seoul 110-760; tel. (2) 2100-2114; fax (2) 739-5830; e-mail webmaster@pmo.go.kr; internet www.pmo.go.kr.

Office of the Minister for Special Affairs: c/o Office of the Prime Minister, 55, Sejong-no, Jongno-gu, Seoul 110-760.

Ministry of Culture, Sports and Tourism: 42, Sejong-no, Jongno-gu, Seoul 110-703; tel. (2) 3704-9114; fax (2) 3704-9119; e-mail webadmin@www.mct.go.kr; internet www.mcst.go.kr.

Ministry of Education, Science and Technology: 77-6, Sejong-no, Jongno-gu, Seoul 110-760; tel. (2) 6222-6060; fax (2) 2100-6133; e-mail webmaster@mest.go.kr; internet www.mest.go.kr.

Ministry of Employment and Labour: Govt Complex, 1, Jungang-dong, Gwacheon City, Gyeonggi Prov. 427-718; tel. (2) 2110-7497; fax (2) 503-6623; internet www.molab.go.kr.

Ministry of Environment: 88, Gwanmunro, Gwacheon City, Gyeonggi Prov. 427-729; tel. (2) 2110-6546; e-mail webmaster@me.go.kr; internet www.me.go.kr.

Ministry of Food, Agriculture, Forestry and Fisheries: Govt Complex, 1, Jungang-dong, Gwacheon City, Gyeonggi Prov.; tel. (2) 503-7200; fax (2) 503-7249; e-mail wmaster@maf.go.kr; internet www.mifaff.go.kr.

Ministry of Foreign Affairs and Trade: 37, Sejong-no, Seoul 110-787; tel. (2) 2100-2114; fax (2) 2100-7999; e-mail web@mofat.go.kr; internet www.mofat.go.kr.

Ministry of Gender Equality: Premiere Place Bldg, 96, Mugyo-dong, Jung-gu, Seoul 100-777; tel. (2) 2075-4500; fax (2) 2075-4780; e-mail webadmin@moge.go.kr; internet www.moge.go.kr.

Ministry for Health, Welfare and Family Affairs: 75, Yulgong-ro, Jongno-gu, Seoul 110-793; internet www.mohw.go.kr.

Ministry of Justice: 88, Gwanmunro, Gwacheon City, Gyeonggi Prov. 427-720; tel. (2) 2110-3009; fax (2) 503-7113; e-mail webmaster@moj.go.kr; internet www.moj.go.kr.

Ministry of Knowledge Economy: 88, Gwanmunro, Gwacheon City, Gyeonggi Prov. 427-723; tel. (2) 1577-0900; e-mail webmke@mke.go.kr; internet www.mke.go.kr.

Ministry of Land, Transport and Maritime Affairs: 1, Jungang-dong, Gwacheon City, Gyeonggi Prov. 427-712; tel. (2) 1599-0001; fax (2) 2150-1000; e-mail webmaster@mltm.go.kr; internet www.mltm.go.kr.

Ministry of National Defence: 1, 3-ga, Yeongsan-dong, Yeongsan-gu, Seoul 140-701; tel. (2) 795-0071; fax (2) 703-3109; e-mail cyber@mnd.go.kr; internet www.mnd.go.kr.

Ministry of Public Administration and Security: Govt Complex, 77-6, Sejong-no, 1-ga, Jongno-gu, Seoul 110-760; tel. (2) 2100-3399; e-mail unah88@mopas.go.kr; internet www.mopas.go.kr.

Ministry of Strategy and Finance: Govt Complex II, 88, Gwanmunro, Gwacheon City, Gyeonggi Prov. 427-725; tel. (2) 2150-2450; fax (2) 503-9070; e-mail fppr@mosf.go.kr; internet www.mosf.go.kr.

Ministry of Unification: Govt Complex, 77-6, Sejong-no, Jongno-gu, Seoul 110-760; tel. (2) 2100-5747; fax (2) 2100-5727; e-mail hanabyun@unikorea.go.kr; internet www.unikorea.go.kr.

President and Legislature

PRESIDENT

Election, 19 December 2007

Candidate	Votes	% of total
Lee Myung-Bak (Grand National Party)	11,492,389	48.7
Chung Dong-Young (United New Democratic Party)*	6,174,681	26.1
Lee Hoi-Chang (Independent)	3,559,963	15.1
Moon Kook-Hyun (Creative Korea Party)	1,375,498	5.8
Kwon Young-Gil (Democratic Labour Party)	712,121	3.0
Rhee In-Je (Democratic Party)*	160,708	0.7
Huh Kyung-Young (Economic Republican Party)	96,756	0.4
Geum Min (Korea Socialist Party)	18,223	0.1
Chung Kun-Mo (True Owner Coalition)	15,380	0.1
Chun Kwan (Chamsaram Society Full True Act)	7,161	0.0
Total (incl. others)	23,732,854	100.0

* In 2008 the United New Democratic Party merged with the Democratic Party to form the United Democratic Party, subsequently known as the Democratic Party.

LEGISLATURE

**Kuk Hoe
(National Assembly)**

1 Yeouido-dong, Yeongdeungpo-gu, Seoul 150-701; tel. (2) 788-2001; fax (2) 788-3375; e-mail webmaster@assembly.go.kr; internet www.assembly.go.kr.

Speaker: KIM HYONG-O.

General Election, 9 April 2008

Party	Elected	Proportional	Total
Grand National Party	131	22	153
United Democratic Party*	66	15	81
Liberty Forward Party	14	4	18
Pro-Park Coalition†	6	8	14
Democratic Labour Party	2	3	5
Creative Korea Party	1	2	3
Independents	25	—	25
Total	245	54	299

* Later renamed the Democratic Party.
† Comprising supporters of Park Geun-Hye, former Chairwoman of the GNP.

Election Commission

National Election Commission: 2-3 Junggang-dong, Gwacheon-si, Gyeonggi-do 427-727; tel. (2) 503-1114; e-mail e_nec@nec.go.kr; internet www.nec.go.kr; Chair. YANG SUNG-TAE.

THE REPUBLIC OF KOREA (SOUTH KOREA) *Directory*

Political Organizations

Centrist Reformists Democratic Party: 25-4, Yeouido-dong, Yeongdeungpo-gu, Seoul; tel. (2) 784-7007; fax (2) 780-4074; internet minjoo.org.kr; f. 2005; fmrly Millennium Democratic Party; Pres. RHEE IN-JE.

Creative Korea Party (CKP): Unit 601, 484-74, Bulgwang-dong, Eunpyeong-gu, Seoul 122-860; tel. (2) 784-4701; fax (2) 784-4705; e-mail master@ckp.kr; internet www.ckp.kr; f. 2007; Pres. SONG YOUNG-OH.

Democratic Labour Party (DLP): Jongdo Bldg, 1st and 2nd Floors, 25-1, Moonrae-dong, Yeongdeungpo-gu, Seoul 150-092; tel. (2) 2139-7777; fax (2) 2139-7890; e-mail kdlpinter@hotmail.com; internet www.kdlp.org; f. 2000; Pres. KANG KI-GAP.

Democratic Party (DP): 13-17, Yeouido-dong, Yeongdeungpo-gu, Seoul 150-701; tel. (2) 1577-7667; fax (2) 2630-0145; e-mail help@undp.kr; internet minjoo.kr; est. as United New Democratic Party in 2007 by defectors and mems of the Uri Party and the Democratic Party; name changed to United Democratic Party following merger with Democratic Party in Feb. 2008; name changed as above in mid-2008; Chair. SOHN HAK-KYU.

Grand National Party (GNP) (Hannara Party): 14-31, Yeouido-dong, Yeongdeungpo-gu, Seoul 156-768; tel. (2) 3786-3000; fax (2) 3786-3610; internet www.hannara.or.kr; f. 1997; est. by merger of the original Democratic Party (f. 1990) and New Korea Party; Chair. AHN SANG-SOO; Sec.-Gen. WON HEE-RYONG.

Korea Socialist Party: Nagyeong Bldg, 11th Floor, 115-62, Gongdeok-dong, Mapo-gu, Seoul 121-801; tel. (2) 711-4592; fax (2) 706-4118; internet sp.or.kr; f. 1998; Pres. GEUM MIN.

Liberty Forward Party (LFP): Yeongsan Bldg, 3rd Floor, 14-14, Yeouido-dong, Yeoungdeungpo-gu, Seoul; tel. (2) 780-3988; fax (2) 780-3983; e-mail webmaster@jayou.or.kr; internet www.jayou.or.kr; conservative; Leader LEE HOI-CHANG.

New Progressive Party (NPP): Daeha Bldg, Unit 801, 14-11, Yeouido-dong, Yeoungdeungpo-gu, Seoul; tel. (2) 6004-2000; fax (2) 6004-2001; e-mail newjinbo@gmail.com; internet www.newjinbo .org; f. 2008; left-wing; est. by splinter group of DLP; Pres. ROH HOE-CHAN; Sec.-Gen. LEE SUNG-HWA.

People's Participation Party: Dongbok Bldg, 4th Floor, 5-5, Changjeon-dong, Mapo-gu, Seoul 121-880; tel. (2) 1670-2010; fax (2) 784-2091; e-mail admin@handypia.org; internet www.handypia .org; f. 2010; est. by fmr members of Uri Party; Chair. RHYU SI-MIN.

Other parties that presented candidates for the 2007 presidential election were the Economic Republican Party, the True Owner Coalition and the Chamsaram Society Full True Act.

Civic groups play an increasingly significant role in South Korean politics. These include: the People's Solidarity for Participatory Democracy (Dir JANG HASUNG); the Citizens' Coalition for Economic Justice (Sec.-Gen. PARK BYEONG-OK); and the Citizens' Alliance for Political Reform (Leader KIM SOK-SU).

Diplomatic Representation

EMBASSIES IN THE REPUBLIC OF KOREA

Afghanistan: 27-2, Hannam-dong, Yeongsan-gu, Seoul 140-210; tel. (2) 793-3535; fax (2) 795-2662; e-mail info@afghanistanembassy.or .kr; internet www.afghanistanembassy.or.kr; Ambassador MOHAMMAD KARIM RAHIMI.

Algeria: 2-6, Itaewon 2-dong, Yeongsan-gu, Seoul 140-857; tel. (2) 794-5034; fax (2) 794-5040; e-mail sifdja01@kornet.net; internet www.algerianemb.or.kr; Ambassador HOCINE SAHRAOUI.

Angola: 737-11, Hannam 2-dong, Yeongsan-gu, Seoul 140-212; tel. (2) 792-8463; fax (2) 792-8467; e-mail embassy@angolaembassy.or .kr; internet www.angolaembassy.or.kr; Chargé d'affaires a.i. ALFREDO DOMBE.

Argentina: Chun Woo Bldg, 5th Floor, 534, Itaewon-dong, Yeongsan-gu, Seoul 140-861; tel. (2) 793-4062; fax (2) 792-5820; e-mail info@argentina.or.kr; internet www.argentina.or.kr; Chargé d'affaires a.i. FEDERICO LUIS MORCHIO.

Australia: Kyobo Bldg, 19th Floor, 1, Jongno 1-ga, Jongno-gu, Seoul 110-714; tel. (2) 2003-0100; fax (2) 2003-0196; e-mail seoul-inform@dfat.gov.au; internet www.southkorea.embassy.gov.au; Ambassador SAM GEROVICH.

Austria: Kyobo Bldg, 21st Floor, 1-1, Jongno 1-ga, Jongno-gu, Seoul 110-714; tel. (2) 732-9071; fax (2) 732-9486; e-mail seoul-ob@bmeia .gv.at; internet www.bmeia.gv.at/seoul; Ambassador Dr JOSEF MÜLLNER.

Azerbaijan: Hannam Tower, Annex Bldg, 3rd Floor, 730, Hannam-dong, Yeongsan-gu, Seoul 140-893; tel. (2) 797-1765; fax (2) 797-1767; e-mail info@azembassy.co.kr; internet www.azembassy.co.kr; Ambassador ROVSHAN JAMSHIDOV.

Bangladesh: 310-22, Dongbinggo-dong, Yeongsan-gu, Seoul; tel. (2) 796-4056; fax (2) 790-5313; e-mail bdootseoul@kornet.net; internet www.bdembseoul.org; Ambassador MOHAMMAD SHAHIDUL ISLAM.

Belarus: 432-1636, Sindang 2-dong, Jung-gu, Seoul 100-835; tel. (2) 2237-8171; fax (2) 2237-8174; e-mail korea@belembassy.org; internet www.korea.belembassy.org; Ambassador ALEKSANDR GURYANOV.

Belgium: 737-10, Hannam-dong, Yeongsan-gu, Seoul 140-893; tel. (2) 749-0381; fax (2) 797-1688; e-mail seoul@diplobel.fed.be; internet www.belgium.or.kr; Ambassador PIERRE CLÉMENT DUBUISSON.

Brazil: Ihn Gallery Bldg, 4th and 5th Floors, 141, Palpan-dong, Jongno-gu, Seoul; tel. (2) 738-4970; fax (2) 738-4974; e-mail braseul@kornet.net; internet www.brasemb.or.kr; Ambassador EDMUNDO SUSSUMU FUJITA.

Brunei: 39-1, Cheongun-dong, Jongno-gu, Seoul 110-030; tel. (2) 790-1078; fax (2) 790-1084; e-mail kbnbd_seoul@yahoo.com; Ambassador Dato' Paduka Haji HARUN BIN Haji ISMAIL.

Bulgaria: 723-42, Hannam 2-dong, Yeongsan-gu, Seoul 140-894; tel. (2) 794-8626; fax (2) 794-8627; e-mail seoul_bg@yahoo.co.uk; internet www.mfa.bg/seoul; Ambassador KOSSIO KITIPOV.

Cambodia: 653-110, Hannam-dong, Yeongsan-gu, Seoul 140-887; tel. (2) 3785-1041; fax (2) 3785-1040; e-mail info@cambodiaemb.kr; internet www.cambodiaemb.kr; Ambassador LIM SAMKOL.

Canada: 16-1, Jeong-dong, Jung-gu, CPOB 6299, Seoul 100-662; tel. (2) 3783-6000; fax (2) 3783-6239; e-mail seoul@international.gc.ca; internet www.canadainternational.gc.ca/korea-coree; Ambassador TED LIPMAN.

Chile: Coryo Daeyungak Tower, Unit 1801, 25-5, Chungmoro 1-ga, Jung-gu, Seoul 100-706; tel. (2) 779-2610; fax (2) 779-2615; e-mail echilekr@yahoo.co.kr; internet www.coreachile.org; Ambassador ADOLFO CARAFÍ MELERO.

China, People's Republic: 54, Hyoja-dong, Jongno-gu, Seoul 110-033; tel. (2) 738-1038; fax (2) 738-1046; e-mail chinaemb_kr@mfa.gov .cn; internet www.chinaemb.or.kr; Ambassador ZHANG XINSEN.

Colombia: Korea Tourism Org. Bldg, 7th Floor, 40, Cheonggyecheon-no, Jung-gu, Seoul 100-180; tel. (2) 720-1369; fax (2) 725-6959; e-mail eseul@cancilleria.gov.co; internet www.cancilleria.gov.co/wps/portal/embajada_corea; Chargé d'affaires a.i. MANUEL HERNANDO SOLANO SOSSA.

Congo, Democratic Republic: Daewoo Complex Bldg, Unit 702, 167, Naesu-dong, Jongno-gu, Seoul 110-070; tel. (2) 722-7958; fax (2) 722-7998; e-mail congokoreaembassy@yahoo.com; Ambassador N. CHRISTOPHE NGWEY.

Costa Rica: Iljin Bldg, Unit 8, 50-1, Dohwa-dong, Mapo-gu, Seoul 121-040; tel. (2) 707-9249; fax (2) 707-9255; e-mail embajadacr@ecostarica.or.kr; internet www.ecostarica.or.kr; Ambassador FERNANDO BORBÓN ARIAS.

Côte d'Ivoire: Chungam Bldg, 2nd Floor, 794-4, Hannam-dong, Yeongsan-gu, Seoul 140-894; tel. (2) 3785-0561; fax (2) 3785-0564; e-mail acisel1@hanafos.com; internet cotedivoireembassy.or.kr; Ambassador KOUASSI FLORENT EKRA.

Czech Republic: 1-121, Sinmun-no 2-ga, Jongno-gu, Seoul 110-062; tel. (2) 725-6765; fax (2) 734-6452; e-mail seoul@embassy.mzv.cz; internet www.mzv.cz/seoul; Ambassador JAROSLAV OLŠA, Jr.

Denmark: Namsong Bldg, 5th Floor, 260-199, Itaewon-dong, Yeongsan-gu, Seoul 140-200; tel. (2) 795-4187; fax (2) 796-0986; e-mail selamb@um.dk; internet www.ambseoul.um.dk; Ambassador PETER L. HANSEN.

Dominican Republic: Taepyeong-no Bldg, 19th Floor, 310, Taepyeong-no 2-ga, Jung-gu, Seoul; tel. (2) 756-3513; fax (2) 756-3514; e-mail embadom@kornet.net; internet www.embadom.or.kr; Ambassador HÉCTOR GALUÁN.

Ecuador: SC First Bank Bldg, 19th Floor, 100, Gongpyeong-dong, Jongno-gu, Seoul 110-702; tel. (2) 739-2401; fax (2) 739-2355; e-mail mecuadorcor1@kornet.net; Ambassador JOSÉ ENRIQUE NÚÑEZ TAMAYO.

Egypt: 46-1, Hannam-dong, Yeongsan-gu, Seoul 140-210; tel. (2) 749-0787; fax (2) 795-2588; e-mail embassyegyptkorea@yahoo.com; internet www.mfa.gov.eg/Missions/southkorea/seoul/embassy/en-GB/default.htm; Ambassador MOHAMED ABDEL RAHIM EL-ZORKANY.

El Salvador: Samsung Life Insurance Bldg, 20th Floor, 150, Taepyeong-no 2-ga, Jung-gu, Seoul 100-716; tel. (2) 753-3432; fax (2) 753-3456; e-mail koresal@kornet.net; Ambassador ZOILA DEL CARMEN AGUIRRE DE MAY.

Finland: Kyobo Bldg, 18th Floor, 1, Jongno 1-ga, Jongno-gu, Seoul 110-714; tel. (2) 732-6737; fax (2) 723-4969; e-mail sanomat.seo@formin.fi; internet www.finland.or.kr; Ambassador PEKKA WUORISTO.

THE REPUBLIC OF KOREA (SOUTH KOREA)

France: 30, Hap-dong, Seodaemun-gu, Seoul 120-030; tel. (2) 3149-4300; fax (2) 3149-4310; e-mail ambafrance@hanafos.com; internet www.ambafrance-kr.org; Ambassador Elisabeth Laurin.

Gabon: Yoosung Bldg, 4th Floor, 738-20, Hannam-dong, Yeongsan-gu, Seoul; tel. (2) 793-9575; fax (2) 793-9574; e-mail amgabsel@unitel.co.kr; Ambassador Jean-Pierre Sole-Emane.

Germany: 308-5, Dongbinggo-dong, Yeongsan-gu, Seoul 140-816; tel. (2) 748-4114; fax (2) 748-4161; e-mail info@seoul.diplo.de; internet www.seoul.diplo.de; Ambassador Dr Hans-Ulrich Seidt.

Ghana: 5-4, Hannam-dong, Yeongsan-gu, CPOB 3887, Seoul 140-884; tel. (2) 3785-1427; fax (2) 3785-1428; e-mail ghana3@kornet.net; internet www.ghanaembassy.or.kr; Ambassador Margaret Clarke-Kwesie.

Greece: Hanwha Bldg, 27th Floor, 1, Janggyo-dong, Jung-gu, Seoul 100-797; tel. (2) 729-1401; fax (2) 729-1402; e-mail greekemb@kornet.net; Ambassador Petros Avierinos.

Guatemala: 614, Lotte Hotel, 1, Sogong-dong, Jung-gu, Seoul 100-635; tel. (2) 771-7582; fax (2) 771-7584; e-mail embcorea@minex.gob.gt; Ambassador Rafael A. Salazar.

Holy See: 2, Gungjeong-dong, Jongno-gu, Seoul 110-031 (Apostolic Nunciature); tel. (2) 736-5725; fax (2) 739-5738; e-mail apnunkr@yahoo.com; Apostolic Nuncio Most Rev. Osvaldo Padilla (Titular Archbishop of Voli).

Honduras: Jongno Tower Bldg, 22nd Floor, 6, Jongno 2-ga, Jongno-gu, Seoul 110-160; tel. (2) 738-8402; fax (2) 738-8403; e-mail hondseul@kornet.net; Ambassador Michel Idiaquez Baradat.

Hungary: 1-103, Dongbinggo-dong, Yeongsan-gu, Seoul 140-230; tel. (2) 792-2105; fax (2) 792-2109; e-mail mission.sel@kum.gov.hu; internet www.mfa.gov.hu/emb/seoul; Ambassador Miklós Lengyel.

India: 37-3, Hannam-dong, Yeongsan-gu, CPOB 3466, Seoul 140-210; tel. (2) 798-4257; fax (2) 796-9534; e-mail eoiseoul@sinbiro.com; internet www.indembassy.or.kr; Ambassador Skand R. Tayal.

Indonesia: 55, Yeouido-dong, Yeongdeungpo-gu, Seoul 150-010; tel. (2) 783-5675; fax (2) 780-4280; e-mail konsuler@indonesiaseoul.org; internet www.indonesiaseoul.org; Ambassador Nicholas Tandi Dammen.

Iran: 1-93, Dongbinggo-dong, Yeongsan-gu, Seoul 140-809; tel. (2) 793-7751; fax (2) 792-7052; e-mail iranssy@chol.com; internet www.iranembassy.or.kr; Ambassador Mohammad Reza Bakhtiari.

Iraq: 1-94, Dongbinggo-dong, Yeongsan-gu, Seoul 140-811; tel. (2) 790-4202; fax (2) 790-4206; e-mail sulemb@iraqmfamail.com; Chargé d'affaires Mustafa Musa Taufik.

Ireland: Leema Bldg, 13th Floor, 146-1, Susong-dong, Jongno-gu, Seoul 110-755; tel. (2) 774-6455; fax (2) 774-6458; e-mail seoulembassy@dfa.ie; internet www.irelandhouse-korea.com; Ambassador Eamonn McKee.

Israel: Cheonggye 11 Bldg, 18th Floor, 149, Seorin-dong, Jongno-gu, Seoul 110-726; tel. (2) 3210-8500; fax (2) 3210-8555; e-mail info@seoul.mfa.gov.il; internet seoul.mfa.gov.il; Ambassador Tuvia Israeli.

Italy: Ilshin Bldg, 3rd Floor, 714, Hannam-dong, Yongsan-gu, Seoul 140-894; tel. (2) 796-0491; fax (2) 797-5560; e-mail embassy.seoul@esteri.it; internet www.ambseoul.esteri.it; Ambassador Sergio Mercuri.

Japan: 18-11, Junghak-dong, Jongno-gu, Seoul 110-150; tel. (2) 2170-5200; fax (2) 734-4528; e-mail info@japanem.or.kr; internet www.kr.emb-japan.go.jp; Ambassador Masatoshi Muto.

Kazakhstan: 271-5, Hannam-dong, Yeongsan-gu, Seoul 140-885; tel. (2) 379-9714; fax (2) 395-9719; e-mail kazkor@chollian.net; internet www.kazembassy.org; Ambassador Darkhan Berdaliyev.

Kenya: 243-36, Itaewon-dong, Yeongsan-gu, Seoul 140-200; tel. (2) 3785-2903; fax (2) 3785-2905; e-mail info@kenya-embassy.or.kr; internet www.kenya-embassy.or.kr; Ambassador Ngovi Kitau.

Kuwait: 309-15, Dongbinggo-dong, Yeongsan-gu, Seoul; tel. (2) 749-3688; fax (2) 749-3687; e-mail kuwaitembassykorea@hotmail.com; Ambassador Muteb al-Mutoteh.

Kyrgyzstan: Namsong Bldg, Unit 403, 260-199, Itaewon-dong, Yeongsan-gu, Seoul 140-200; tel. (2) 379-0951; fax (2) 379-0953; e-mail seoulembassykg@gmail.com; internet www.kyrgyzembassy.com; Ambassador Tuigunaaly Abdraimov.

Laos: 657-9, Hannam-dong, Yeongsan-gu, Seoul 140-887; tel. (2) 796-1713; fax (2) 796-1771; e-mail laoseoul@korea.com; Ambassador Soukthavone Keola.

Lebanon: 310-49, Dongbinggo-dong, Yeongsan-gu, Seoul 140-230; tel. (2) 794-6482; fax (2) 794-6485; e-mail emleb@lebanonembassy.net; internet www.lebanonembassy.net; Ambassador Issam Mustapha.

Malaysia: 4-1, Hannam-dong, Yeongsan-gu, Seoul 140-884; tel. (2) 2077-8600; fax (2) 794-5480; e-mail malseoul@kln.gov.my; internet www.malaysia.or.kr; Ambassador Dato' Ramlan bin Ibrahim.

Mexico: 33-6, Hannam 1-dong, Yeongsan-gu, Seoul 140-885; tel. (2) 798-1694; fax (2) 790-0939; e-mail embajada@embamexcor.org; internet portal.sre.gob.mx/corea; Ambassador Martha Ortiz de Rosas Gómez.

Mongolia: 33-5, Hannam-dong, Yeongsan-gu, Seoul 140-885; tel. (2) 794-1350; fax (2) 794-7605; e-mail mongol6@kornet.net; internet www.mongolembassy.com; Ambassador Dorjpalamyn Gerel.

Morocco: Hannam Tower, Annex Bldg, 4th Floor, 730, Hannam-dong, Yeongsan-gu, Seoul; tel. (2) 793-6249; fax (2) 792-8178; e-mail sifamase@kornet.net; Ambassador Mohamed Chraïbi.

Myanmar: 724-1, Hannam-dong, Yeongsan-gu, Seoul 140-210; tel. (2) 790-3814; fax (2) 790-3817; e-mail myanmar@kotis.net; Ambassador Nyo Win.

Nepal: 244-143, Huam-dong, Yeongsan-gu, Seoul; tel. (2) 3789-9770; fax (2) 736-8848; e-mail info@nepembseoul.gov.np; internet www.nepembseoul.gov.np; Ambassador Kamal Koirala.

Netherlands: KPOB 509, Seoul 110-605; tel. (2) 737-9514; fax (2) 735-1321; e-mail seo@minbuza.nl; internet southkorea.nlembassy.org; Ambassador Hans Heinsbroek.

New Zealand: Kyobo Bldg, 15th Floor, 1, Jongno 1-ga, Jongno-gu, KPOB 2258, Seoul 110-110; tel. (2) 3701-7700; fax (2) 3701-7701; e-mail nzembsel@kornet.net; internet www.nzembassy.com/korea; Ambassador Richard Mann.

Nigeria: 310-19, Dongbinggo-dong, Yeongsan-gu, CPOB 3754, Seoul 140-230; tel. (2) 797-2370; fax (2) 796-1848; e-mail chancery@nigerianembassy.or.kr; internet www.nigerianembassy.or.kr; Ambassador Desmond Akawor.

Norway: 258-8, Itaewon-dong, Yeongsan-gu, Seoul 140-200; tel. (2) 795-6850; fax (2) 798-6072; e-mail emb.seoul@mfa.no; internet www.norway.or.kr; Ambassador Didrik Tønseth.

Oman: 309-3, Dongbinggo-dong, Yeongsan-gu, Seoul; tel. (2) 790-2431; fax (2) 790-2430; e-mail omanembs@kornet.net; Ambassador Mohamed Salim al-Harthy.

Pakistan: 124-13, Itaewon-dong, Yeongsan-gu, Seoul 140-200; tel. (2) 796-8252; fax (2) 796-0313; e-mail consular@pkembassy.or.kr; internet www.pkembassy.or.kr; Ambassador Murad Ali.

Panama: Gwanghwamun Platinum Bldg, Unit 709, 7th Floor, 156, Jeokseon-dong, Jongno-gu, Seoul; tel. (2) 734-8610; fax (2) 734-8613; e-mail panaemba@kornet.net; Ambassador Jaime Lasso del Castillo.

Papua New Guinea: Doosan We've Pavilion Bldg, Unit 210, 58, Soosong-dong, Jongno-gu, Seoul 110-858; tel. (2) 2198-5771; fax (2) 2198-5779; e-mail ambassador@kunduseoul.kr; Ambassador Kuma Aua.

Paraguay: Hannam Tower, Annex Bldg, 3rd Floor, 730, Hannam-dong, Yeongsan-gu, Seoul; tel. (2) 792-8335; fax (2) 792-8334; e-mail pyemc2@kornet.net; internet www.embaparcorea.org; Ambassador Ceferino Adrian Valdez Peralta.

Peru: Daeyungak Bldg, Unit 2002, 25-5, Jungmu-no 1-ga, Jung-gu, Seoul 100-706; tel. (2) 757-1735; fax (2) 757-1738; e-mail lpruseul@uriel.net; internet www.embassyperu.or.kr; Ambassador Marcela López Bravo.

Philippines: 5-1, Itaewon 2-dong, Yeongsan-gu, Seoul; tel. (2) 796-7387; fax (2) 796-0827; e-mail seoulpe@philembassy-seoul.com; internet www.philembassy-seoul.com; Ambassador Luis Teodoro Cruz.

Poland: 70, Sagan-dong, Jongno-gu, Seoul; tel. (2) 723-9681; fax (2) 723-9680; e-mail embassy@polandseoul.org; internet www.seul.polemb.net; Ambassador Marek Całka.

Portugal: Wonseo Bldg, 2nd Floor, 171, Wonseo-dong, Jongno-gu, Seoul 110-280; tel. (2) 3675-2251; fax (2) 3675-2250; e-mail portcoreia@hotmail.com; Ambassador Henrique Silveira Borges.

Qatar: 309-5, Dongbinggo-dong, Yeongsan-gu, Seoul 140-817; tel. (2) 790-2444; fax (2) 790-1027; e-mail qatarembassy@koreamail.com; Ambassador Ali Hamad Mubarak al-Marri.

Romania: 1-104, Dongbinggo-dong, Yongsan-gu, Seoul 140-809; tel. (2) 797-4924; fax (2) 794-3114; e-mail ambseul@uriel.net; Chargé d'affaires a.i. Sever Cotu.

Russia: 34-16, Jeong-dong, Jung-gu, Seoul 100-120; tel. (2) 318-2116; fax (2) 754-0417; e-mail rusemb@uriel.net; internet www.russian-embassy.org; Ambassador Konstantin Vnukov.

Rwanda: Sooyong Bldg, Unit 503, 64-1, Hannam-dong, Yeongsan-gu, Seoul 140-889; tel. (2) 798-1052; fax (2) 798-1054; e-mail info@rwanda-embassy.or.kr; internet rwanda-embassy.or.kr; Chargé d'affaires Eugene S. Kayihura.

Saudi Arabia: 36-37, Itaewon 1-dong, Yeongsan-gu, Seoul 140-201; tel. (2) 739-0631; fax (2) 739-0041; e-mail embassysaudi@yahoo.co.kr; Ambassador Ahmed bin Yunus al-Barrak.

Senegal: Coryo Daeyungak Tower, 13th Floor, Unit 1302, 25-5, Chungmuro 1-ga, Jung-gu, Seoul 100-706; tel. (2) 745-5554; fax (2)

THE REPUBLIC OF KOREA (SOUTH KOREA)

745-5524; e-mail ambassenseoul@hotmail.com; Ambassador AMADOU DABO.

Serbia: 730, Hannam-dong, Yeongsan-gu, Seoul; tel. (2) 797-5109; fax (2) 790-6109; e-mail emserbseul@yahoo.com; internet www.embserb.or.kr; Ambassador SLOBODAN MARINKOVIĆ.

Singapore: Seoul Finance Bldg, 28th Floor, 84, Taepyeong-no 1-ga, Jung-gu, Seoul 100-101; tel. (2) 774-2464; fax (2) 773-2463; e-mail singemb_seo@sgmfa.gov.sg; internet www.mfa.gov.sg/seoul; Ambassador CHUA THAI KEONG.

Slovakia: 389-1, Hannam-dong, Yeongsan-gu, Seoul 140-210; tel. (2) 794-3981; fax (2) 794-3982; e-mail emb.seoul@mzv.sk; internet www.mzv.sk/seoul; Ambassador DUSAN BELLA.

South Africa: 1-37, Hannam-dong, Yeongsan-gu, Seoul 140-885; tel. (2) 792-4855; fax (2) 792-4856; e-mail general@southafrica-embassy.or.kr; internet www.southafrica-embassy.or.kr; Ambassador HILTON ANTHONY DENNIS.

Spain: 726-52, Hannam-dong, Yeongsan-gu, Seoul 140-894; tel. (2) 794-3581; fax (2) 796-8207; e-mail emb.seul@maec.es; internet www.mae.es/embajadas/seul; Ambassador JUAN BAUTISTA LEÑA CASAS.

Sri Lanka: 229-18, Itaewon-dong, Yeongsan-gu, Seoul 140-202; tel. (2) 735-2966; fax (2) 737-9577; e-mail lankaemb@kornet.net; internet www.srilankaembassy.net; Chargé d'affaires LAKSHITHA RATNAYAKE.

Sudan: Vivien Bldg, 3rd Floor, 4-52, Seobinggo-dong, Yeongsan-gu, Seoul 140-240; tel. (2) 793-8692; fax (2) 793-8693; e-mail sudanseoul@yahoo.com; internet www.sudanembassy.co.kr; Ambassador MOHAMMED SALAH ELDIN ABBAS.

Sweden: Danam Bldg, 8th Floor, 120, Namdaemunro 5-ga, Jung-gu, CPOB 3577, Seoul 100-635; tel. (2) 3703-3700; fax (2) 3703-3701; e-mail embassy@swedemb.or.kr; internet www.swedenabroad.com/seoul; Ambassador LARS VARGÖ.

Switzerland: 32-10, Songwol-dong, Jongno-gu, CPOB 2900, Seoul 110-101; tel. (2) 739-9511; fax (2) 737-9392; e-mail seo.vertretung@eda.admin.ch; internet www.eda.admin.ch/seoul; Ambassador THOMAS KUPFER.

Thailand: 653-7, Hannam-dong, Yeongsan-gu, Seoul 140-210; tel. (2) 795-3098; fax (2) 798-3448; e-mail rteseoul@kornet.net; internet www.thaiembassy.or.kr; Ambassador Dr CHAIYONG SATJIPANON.

Timor-Leste: Hannam Tower Bldg II, Unit 405, 725-23, Hannam-dong, Yeongsan-gu, Seoul 140-894; tel. (2) 797-6151; fax (2) 797-6152; e-mail tlembseoul@gmail.com; Ambassador JOÃO VIEGAS CARRASCALÃO.

Tunisia: 1-17, Dongbinggo-dong, Yeongsan-gu, Seoul 140-809; tel. (2) 790-4334; fax (2) 790-4333; e-mail ambtnkor@kornet.net; Ambassador MUSTAPHA KHAMMARI.

Turkey: Vivien Corpn Bldg, 4th Floor, 4-52, Seobinggo-dong, Yeongsan-gu, Seoul 140-240; tel. (2) 794-0255; fax (2) 797-8546; e-mail turkemb.seoul@hotmail.com; internet www.seul.be.mfa.gov.tr; Ambassador ERDOĞAN IŞCAN BÜYÜKELÇI.

Ukraine: 1-97, Dongbinggo-dong, Yeongsan-gu, Seoul; tel. (2) 790-5696; fax (2) 790-5697; e-mail emb_kr@mfa.gov.ua; internet www.mfa.gov.ua/korea; Ambassador BELASHOV VOLODYMYR.

United Arab Emirates: 5-5, Hannam-dong, Yeongsan-gu, Seoul 140-884; tel. (2) 790-3235; fax (2) 790-3238; e-mail uaeemb@kornet.net; Ambassador ABDULLAH MUHAMMAD AL-MAAINAH.

United Kingdom: Taepyeong-no 40, 4, Jeong-dong, Jung-gu, Seoul 100-120; tel. (2) 3210-5500; fax (2) 725-1738; e-mail postmaster.seoul@fco.gov.uk; internet www.ukinkorea.fco.gov.uk; Ambassador SCOTT WIGHTMAN (designate).

USA: 32, Sejong-no, Jongno-gu, Seoul 110-710; tel. (2) 397-4114; fax (2) 397-4080; e-mail embassyseoulpa@state.gov; internet seoul.usembassy.gov; Ambassador KATHLEEN STEPHENS.

Uruguay: LIG Kangnam Bldg, 14th Floor, 708-6, Yeoksam-dong, Gangnam-gu, Seoul 135-919; tel. (2) 6245-3179; fax (2) 6245-3181; e-mail uruseul@embrou.or.kr; Ambassador NELSON YEMIL CHABEN.

Uzbekistan: Diplomatic Center, Unit 701, 1376-1, Seocho 2-dong, Seocho-gu, Seoul; tel. (2) 574-6554; fax (2) 578-0576; e-mail uzbek001@yahoo.co.kr; internet www.uzbekistan.or.kr; Ambassador VITALI V. FEN.

Venezuela: SC First Bank Bldg, 16th Floor, 100, Gongpyeong-dong, Jongno-gu, CPOB 10043, Seoul 110-702; tel. (2) 732-1546; fax (2) 732-1548; e-mail emvesel@soback.kornet.net; internet www.venezuelaemb.or.kr; Chargé d'affaires a.i. WOLFGANG GONZÁLEZ.

Viet Nam: 28-58, Samcheong-dong, Jongno-gu, Seoul 140-210; tel. (2) 738-2318; fax (2) 739-2064; e-mail vndsq@yahoo.com; internet www.vietnamembassy-seoul.org; Ambassador TRAN TRONG TOAN.

Judicial System

SUPREME COURT

The Supreme Court is the highest court, consisting of 14 Justices, including the Chief Justice. The Chief Justice is appointed by the President, with the consent of the National Assembly, for a term of six years. Other Justices of the Supreme Court are appointed for six years by the President on the recommendation of the Chief Justice. The appointment of the Justices of the Supreme Court also requires the consent of the National Assembly. The Chief Justice may not be reappointed. The Supreme Court is empowered to receive and decide on appeals against decisions of the High Courts, the Patent Court, and the appellate panels of the District Courts or the Family Court in civil, criminal, administrative, patent and domestic relations cases. It is also authorized to act as the final tribunal to review decisions of courts-martial and to consider cases arising from presidential and parliamentary elections.

Chief Justice: LEE YONG-HOON, 219, Seocho-dong, Seocho-gu, Seoul; tel. (2) 533-2824; fax (2) 533-1911; e-mail webmaster@scourt.go.kr; internet www.scourt.go.kr.

Justices: CHA HAN-SUNG, YANG SEUNG-TAE, YANG CHANG-SOO, PARK SI-HWAN, KIM JI-HYUNG, PARK ILL-HOAN, KIM NUNG-HWAN, JEON SOO-AHN, AHN DAI-HEE, SHIN YOUNG-CHUL, MIN IL-YOUNG, LEE IN-BOK, PARK BYOUNG-DAE (designate).

CONSTITUTIONAL COURT

The Constitutional Court is composed of nine adjudicators appointed by the President, of whom three are chosen from among persons selected by the National Assembly and three from persons nominated by the Chief Justice. The Court adjudicates the following matters: constitutionality of a law (when requested by the other courts); impeachment; dissolution of a political party; disputes between state agencies, or between state agencies and local governments; and petitions relating to the Constitution.

President: LEE KANG-KUK, 15 Gahoero, Jongno-gu, Seoul 110-250; tel. (2) 708-3460; e-mail interdiv@ccourt.go.kr; fax (2) 708-3566; internet www.ccourt.go.kr.

HIGH COURTS

There are five courts, situated in Seoul, Daegu, Busan, Gwangju and Daejeon, with five chief, 78 presiding and 145 other judges. The courts have appellate jurisdiction in civil and criminal cases and can also pass judgment on administrative litigation against government decisions.

PATENT COURT

The Patent Court opened in Daejeon in March 1998, to deal with cases in which the decisions of the Intellectual Property Tribunal are challenged. The examination of the case is conducted by a judge, with the assistance of technical examiners.

DISTRICT COURTS

District Courts are established in 13 major cities; there are 13 chief, 241 presiding and 966 other judges. They exercise jurisdiction over all civil and criminal cases in the first instance.

MUNICIPAL COURTS

There are 103 Municipal Courts within the District Court system, dealing with small claims, minor criminal offences, and settlement cases.

FAMILY COURT

There is one Family Court, in Seoul, with a chief judge, four presiding judges and 16 other judges. The court has jurisdiction in domestic matters and cases of juvenile delinquency.

ADMINISTRATIVE COURT

An Administrative Court opened in Seoul in March 1998, to deal with cases that are specified in the Administrative Litigation Act. The Court has jurisdiction over cities and counties adjacent to Seoul, and deals with administrative matters, including taxes, expropriations of land, labour and other general administrative matters.

COURTS-MARTIAL

These exercise jurisdiction over all offences committed by armed forces personnel and civilian employees. They are also authorized to try civilians accused of military espionage or interference with the execution of military duties.

THE REPUBLIC OF KOREA (SOUTH KOREA)

Religion

BUDDHISM

Korean Mahayana Buddhism has about 80 denominations. The Chogye-jong is the largest Buddhist order in Korea, having been introduced from China in AD 372. The Chogye Order accounts for almost two-thirds of all Korean Buddhists. Won Buddhism combines elements of Buddhism and Confucianism.

Korean United Buddhist Association (KUBA): 46-19, Soosong-dong, Jongno-gu, Seoul 110-140; tel. (2) 732-4885; 28 mem. Buddhist orders; Pres. SONG WOL-JOO.

CHRISTIANITY

National Council of Churches in Korea: Christian Bldg, Rm 706, 136-46, Yeonchi-dong, Jongno-gu, Seoul 110-736; tel. (2) 744-3717; fax (2) 744-6189; e-mail kncc@kncc.or.kr; internet www.kncc.or.kr; f. 1924; est. as National Christian Council; present name adopted 1946; eight mem. churches; Gen. Sec. Rev. PAIK DO-WOONG.

The Anglican Communion

South Korea has three Anglican dioceses, collectively forming the Anglican Church of Korea (founded as a separate province in April 1993), under its own Primate, the Bishop of Seoul.

Bishop of Pusan (Busan): Rt Rev. SOLOMON JONG-MO YOON, 455-2, Oncheon-1-dong, Dongnae-gu, Busan 607-061; tel. (51) 554-5742; fax (51) 553-9643; e-mail adbusan@yahoo.co.kr; internet www.pusan1.net.

Bishop of Seoul: Most Rev. FRANCIS KYUNG JO-PARK, 3, Jeong-dong, Jung-gu, Seoul 100-120; tel. (2) 738-6597; fax (2) 723-2640; e-mail 44kyung@hanmail.net.

Bishop of Taejon (Daejeon): Rt Rev. ANDREW SHIN, 88-1, Sonhwa 2-dong, POB 22, Daejeon 300-600; tel. (42) 256-9987; fax (42) 255-8918.

The Roman Catholic Church

For ecclesiastical purposes, North and South Korea are nominally under a unified jurisdiction. South Korea comprises three archdioceses, 12 dioceses and one military ordinate. At 31 December 2007 some 4,821,020 people were adherents of the Roman Catholic Church.

Bishops' Conference

Catholic Bishops' Conference of Korea, 643-1, Junggok-dong, Gwangjin-gu, Seoul 143-912; tel. (2) 460-7500; fax (2) 460-7505; e-mail cbck@cbck.or.kr; internet www.cbck.or.kr.

f. 1857; Pres. Most Rev. PETER KANG (Bishop of Cheju—Jeju).

Archbishop of Kwangju (Gwangju): Most Rev. ANDREAS CHOI CHANG-MOU, Archdiocesan Office, 5-32, Im-dong, Buk-gu, Gwangju 500-868; tel. (62) 510-2838; fax (62) 525-6873; e-mail biseo@kjcatholic.or.kr.

Archbishop of Seoul: Cardinal NICHOLAS CHEONG JIN-SUK, Archdiocesan Office, 1, 2-ga, Myeong-dong, Jung-gu, Seoul 100-022; tel. (2) 727-2114; fax (2) 773-1947; e-mail ao@seoul.catholic.or.kr.

Archbishop of Daegu (Taegu): THADDEUS CHO HWAN-KIL, Archdiocesan Office, 225-1, Namsan 3-dong, Jung-gu, Daegu 700-804; tel. (53) 253-7011; fax (53) 253-9441; e-mail taegu@tgcatholic.or.kr.

Protestant Churches

Korean Methodist Church: 64-8, 1-ga, Taepyeong-no, Jung-gu, Seoul 100-101; KPO Box 285, Seoul 110-602; tel. (2) 399-4300; fax (2) 399-4307; e-mail bishop@kmcweb.or.kr; internet www.kmcweb.or.kr; f. 1885; 1,534,504 mems (2007); Bishop Dr KO SOO-CHUL.

Presbyterian Church in the Republic of Korea (PROK): Academy House, San 76, Suyu 6-dong, Kangbuk-ku, Seoul 142-070; tel. (2) 3499-7600; fax (2) 3499-7630; e-mail prok3000@chollian.net; internet www.prok.org; f. 1953; 337,570 mems (2007); Gen. Sec. Rev. BAE TAE-JIN.

Presbyterian Church of Korea (PCK): The Korean Church Centennial Memorial Bldg, 135, Yunji-dong, Jongno-gu, Seoul 110-470; tel. (2) 741-4350; fax (2) 766-2427; e-mail thepck@pck.or.kr; internet www.pck.or.kr; 2,395,323 mems (Dec. 2003); Moderator Rev. YOUNG TAE-KIM; Gen. Sec. Rev. SEONGI CHO.

There are some 160 other Protestant denominations in the country, including the Korea Baptist Convention and the Korea Evangelical Church.

OTHER RELIGIONS

Chundo Kyo, a religion indigenous and unique to Korea, combines elements of Shaman, Buddhist, and Christian doctrines. Confucianism also has a significant number of followers. Taejong Gyo is Korea's oldest religion, dating back 4,000 years, and comprising beliefs in the national foundation myth, and the triune god, Hanul. By the 15th century the religion had largely disappeared, but a revival began in the late 19th century.

The Press

NATIONAL DAILIES
(In Korean, unless otherwise indicated)

Chosun Ilbo: 61, 1-ga, Taepyeong-no, Jung-gu, Seoul 100-756; tel. (2) 724-5114; fax (2) 724-5059; e-mail englishnews@chosun.com; internet www.chosun.com; f. 1920; morning, weekly and children's edns; independent; Korean, English, Chinese and Japanese; Exec. Editor BYUN YONG-SHIK; circ. 2,470,000.

Daily Sports Seoul: 25, 1-ga, Taepyeong-no, Jung-gu, Seoul; tel. (2) 721-5114; fax (2) 721-5396; internet www.seoul.co.kr; f. 1985; morning; sports and leisure; Pres. LEE HAN-SOO; Man. Editor SON CHU-WHAN.

Dong-A Ilbo: 139-1, 3-ga, Sejong-no, Jongno-gu, Seoul 100-715; tel. (2) 2020-0114; fax (2) 2020-1239; e-mail newsroom@donga.com; internet www.donga.com; f. 1920; morning; independent; Publr and CEO KIM JAE-HO; Editor-in-Chief LEE HYUN-NAK; circ. 2,150,000.

Han-Joong Daily News: 91-1, 2-ga, Myeong-dong, Jung-gu, Seoul; tel. (2) 776-2801; fax (2) 778-2803; Chinese.

Hankook Ilbo: 14, Junghak-dong, Jongno-gu, Seoul; tel. (2) 724-2114; fax (2) 724-2244; internet www.hankooki.com; f. 1954; morning; independent; Pres. CHANG CHAE-KEUN; Editor-in-Chief YOON KOOK-BYUNG; circ. 2,000,000.

Hankuk Kyungje Shinmun (Korea Economic Daily): 441, Junglim-dong, Jung-gu, Seoul 100-791; tel. (2) 360-4114; fax (2) 779-4447; e-mail hkinfo@hankyung.com; internet www.hankyung.com; f. 1964; morning; Pres. and CEO KIM KI-WOONG; Man. Dir and Editor-in-Chief CHOI KYU-YOUNG.

Hankyoreh Shinmun (One Nation): 116-25, Gongdeok-dong, Mapo-gu, Seoul 121-020; tel. (2) 710-0114; fax (2) 710-0210; internet www.hani.co.kr; f. 1988; centre-left; Korean, English; CEO and Publr CHUNG TAE-KI; Editor-in-Chief SUNG HAN-PYO; circ. 500,000.

Ilgan Sports (The Daily Sports): 14, Junghak-dong, Jongno-gu, Seoul 110-792; tel. (2) 724-2114; fax (2) 724-2299; internet www.dailysports.co.kr; morning; f. 1969; Pres. CHANG CHAE-KEUN; Editor KIM JIN-DONG; circ. 600,000.

Jeil Economic Daily: 146, Ssangrin-dong, Jung-gu, Seoul; tel. (2) 6325-3114; e-mail ysk@jed.co.kr; internet www.jed.co.kr; f. 1988; morning; Pres. PARK JUNG-GU; Editor-in-Chief JANG CHANG-YONG.

JoongAng Ilbo (JoongAng Daily News): 7, Soonhwa-dong, Jung-gu, 100-759 Seoul; tel. (2) 751-9215; fax (2) 751-9219; e-mail iht@joongang.co.kr; internet joongangdaily.joins.com; f. 1965; morning; Korean and English; Publr LHO CHOL-SOO; Exec. Dir KIM DONG-KYUN; circ. 2,300,000.

Kookmin Ilbo: Kookmin Ilbo Bldg, 5/F, 12, Yeouido-dong, Yeongdeungpo-gu, Seoul; tel. (2) 781-9114; fax (2) 781-9781; e-mail kimyh@kmib.co.kr; internet www.kukminilbo.co.kr; Pres. RO SEUNG-SOOK; Editorial Dir KIM Y. H.

Korea Daily News: 25, 1-ga, Taepyeong-no, Jung-gu, Seoul; tel. (2) 2000-9000; fax (2) 2000-9659; e-mail webmaster@seoul.co.kr; internet www.kdaily.com; f. 1945; morning; independent; Publr and Pres. SON CHU-HWAN; Man. Editor LEE DONG-HWA; circ. 700,000.

The Korea Herald: 1-17, Jeong-dong, Jung-gu, Seoul; tel. (2) 727-0205; fax (2) 727-0670; e-mail editor@heraldm.com; internet www.koreaherald.co.kr; f. 1953; morning; English; independent; Pres. WOOK HONG-JUNG; Man. Editor CHON SHI-YONG; circ. 150,000.

The Korea Times: 43, Chungmuro 3-ga, Chung-gu, Seoul 100-013; tel. (2) 724-2859; fax (2) 723-1623; e-mail webmaster@koreatimes.co.kr; internet www.koreatimes.co.kr; f. 1950; morning; English; independent; Pres. PARK MOO-JONG; Man. Editor SAH DONG-SEOK; circ. 100,000.

Kyung-hyang Shinmun: 22, Jeong-dong, Jung-gu, Seoul; tel. (2) 3701-1114; fax (2) 737-6362; internet www.khan.co.kr; f. 1946; evening; independent; Pres. HONG SUNG-MAN; Exec. Editor KIM JI-YOUNG; circ. 350,000.

Maeil Business Newspaper: 30-1, 1-ga, Bil-dong, Jung-gu, Seoul 100-728; tel. (2) 2000-2114; fax (2) 2269-6200; internet www.mk.co.kr; f. 1966; evening; economics and business; Korean, English; Pres. CHANG DAE-WHAN; Chief Editor JANG YONG-SUNG; circ. 235,000.

Munhwa Ilbo: 68, 1-ga, Chungjeong-no, Jung-gu, Seoul 110-170; tel. (2) 3701-5114; fax (2) 3701-5566; internet www.munhwa.co.kr; f. 1991; evening; Pres. and Publr LEE BYUN-KYU; Editor-in-Chief KANG SIN-KU.

Naeway Economic Daily: 1-12, 3-ga, Hoehyon-dong, Jung-gu, Seoul 100; tel. (2) 727-0114; fax (2) 727-0661; f. 1973; morning; Pres. KIM CHIN-OUK; Man. Editor HAN DONG-HEE; circ. 300,000.

THE REPUBLIC OF KOREA (SOUTH KOREA)

Segye Times: 550-15, Gasan-dong, Seoul; tel. (2) 2000-1160; fax (2) 2000-1349; e-mail webmaster@segye.com; internet www.segyetimes.co.kr; f. 1989; morning; Pres. SA KWANG-KEE; Editor MOK JUNG-GYUM.

Seoul Kyungje Shinmun (Seoul Economic Daily): 14, Junghak-dong, Jongno-gu, Seoul; tel. (2) 724-2114; fax (2) 732-2140; e-mail webmaster@hanooki.com; internet economy.hankooki.com; f. 1960; morning; Pres. LIM KONG-JON; Man. Editor LEE JONG-WHAN; circ. 500,000.

Sports Chosun: 61, 1-ga, Taepyeong-no, Jung-gu, Seoul; tel. (2) 3219-8114; fax (2) 724-6979; e-mail readers@sportschosun.com; internet www.sportschosun.com; f. 1964; Publr BANG SANG-HOON; circ. 400,000.

LOCAL DAILIES

Chungcheong Daily News: 304, Sachang-dong, Hungduk-gu, Cheongju, N. Chungcheong Prov.; tel. (43) 279-5000; fax (43) 279-5050; e-mail webmaster@ccilbo.com; internet www.ccilbo.com; f. 1946; morning; Pres. SEO JEONG-OK; Editor IM BAIK-SOO.

Daegu Ilbo: 177-10, Sincheon 2-dong, Dong-gu, Daegu; tel. (53) 757-5700; fax (53) 757-5757; internet www.idaegu.com; f. 1953; morning; Pres. LEE TAE-YEUL; Editor KIM KYUNG-PAL.

Daejon Ilbo: 1-135, Munhwa 1-dong, Jung-gu, Daejeon; tel. (42) 251-3311; fax (42) 253-3320; f. 1950; evening; Pres. CHO JOON-HO; Editor KWAK DAE-YEON.

Halla Ilbo: 568-1, Samdo 1-dong, Jeju; tel. (64) 750-2114; fax (64) 750-2520; e-mail webmaster@ihalla.com; internet www.ihalla.com; f. 1989; evening; Chair. KANG YONG-SOK; Man. Editor HONG SONG-MOK.

Incheon Ilbo: 18-1, 4-ga, Hang-dong, Jung-gu, Incheon; tel. (32) 763-8811; fax (32) 763-7711; e-mail webmaster@itimes.co.kr; internet www.itimes.co.kr; f. 1988; evening; Chair. MUN PYONG-HA; Man. Editor LEE JAE-HO.

Jeju Daily News: 2324-6, Yeon-dong, Jeju; tel. (64) 740-6114; fax (64) 740-6500; e-mail webmaster@jejunews.com; internet www.jejunews.com; f. 1945; evening; Pres. KIM DAE-SUNG; Man. Editor KANG BYUNG-HEE.

Jeonbuk Domin Ilbo: 417-62, 2-ga, Deokjin-dong, Deokjin-gu, Jeonju, N. Jeolla Prov.; tel. (63) 251-7113; fax (63) 251-7127; internet www.domin.co.kr; f. 1988; morning; Pres. LIM BYOUNG-CHAN; Man. Editor YANG CHAE-SUK.

Jeonbuk Ilbo: 710-5, Kumam-dong, Deokjin-gu, Jeonju, N. Jeolla Prov.; tel. (63) 250-5500; fax (63) 250-5550; f. 1950; evening; Chair. SUH CHANG-HOON; Man. Editor LEE KON-WOONG.

Jeonju Ilbo: 568-132, Sonosong-dong, Deokjin-gu, Jeonju, N. Jeolla Prov.; tel. (63) 285-0114; fax (63) 285-2060; f. 1991; morning; Chair. KANG DAE-SOON; Man. Editor SO CHAE-CHOL.

Jeonnam Ilbo: 700-5, Jungheung-dong, Buk-gu, Gwangju 500-758; tel. (62) 527-0015; fax (62) 510-0436; f. 1989; morning; Pres. PARK KEE-JUNG; Editor-in-Chief KIM YONG-OK.

Joongdo Ilbo: 274-7, Galma-dong, Seo-gu, Daejeon; tel. (42) 530-4114; fax (42) 535-5334; f. 1951; morning; CEO KIM WOK-SIK; Man. Editor SONG HYOUNG-SOP.

Kangwon Ilbo: 23, Jungang-no, Chuncheon, Gangwon Prov.; tel. (33) 258-1000; fax (33) 258-1114; internet www.kwnews.co.kr; f. 1945; evening; Pres. CHOI SEUNG-IK; Editor-in-Chief KIM SUNG-KEE.

Kookje Daily News: 76-2, Goje-dong, Yeonje-gu, Busan 611-702; tel. (51) 500-5114; fax (51) 500-4274; e-mail jahwang@ms.kookje.co.kr; internet www.kookje.co.kr; f. 1947; morning; Pres. ROH KI-TAE; Editor-in-Chief JEONG WON-YOUNG.

Kwangju Ilbo: 20-2, Geumnam-no, Dong-gu, Gwangju; tel. (62) 222-8111; fax (62) 227-9500; e-mail kwangju@kwangju.co.kr; internet www.kwangju.co.kr; f. 1952; evening; Chair. KIM CHONG-TAE; Man. Editor CHO DONG-SU.

Kyeonggi Ilbo: 452-1, Songjuk-dong, Changan-gu, Suwon, Gyeonggi Prov.; tel. (31) 250-3333; fax (31) 250-3306; e-mail webmaster@ekgib.co.kr; internet www.kgib.co.kr; f. 1988; evening; Pres. SHIN CHANG-GI; Man. Editor LEE CHIN-YONG.

Kyeongin Ilbo: 1276, Maetan-dong, Yeongtong-gu, Suwon, Gyeonggi-do; tel. (31) 231-5114; fax (31) 232-1231; e-mail webmaster@kyeongin.com; internet www.kyeongin.com; f. 1960; evening; Pres. WOO JE-CHAN; Man. Editor KIM HWA-YANG.

Kyungnam Shinmun: 100-5, Sinwol-dong, Changwon, S. Gyeong-sang Prov.; tel. (55) 283-2211; fax (55) 210-6048; internet www.knnews.co.kr; f. 1946; morning; Pres. KIM DONG-KYU; Editor PARK SUNG-KWAN.

Maeil Shinmun: 71, 2-ga, Gyesan-dong, Jung-gu, Daegu; tel. (53) 255-5001; fax (53) 255-8902; e-mail imaeil@msnet.co.kr; internet www.imaeil.com; f. 1946; evening; Pres. CHO HWAN-KIL; Editor LEE YONG-KEUN; circ. 300,000.

Pusan Daily News: 1-10, Sujeong-dong, Dong-gu, Busan 601-738; tel. (51) 461-4114; fax (51) 463-8880; internet www.pusanilbo.co.kr; f. 1946; Pres. JEONG HAN-SANG; Man. Editor AHN KI-HO; circ. 427,000.

Yeongnam Ilbo: 111, Sincheon-dong, Dong-gu, Daegu; tel. (53) 756-8001; fax (53) 756-9011; internet www.yeongnam.co.kr; f. 1945; morning; Chair. PARK CHANG-HO; Man. Editor KIM SANG-TAE.

SELECTED PERIODICALS

Academy News: 50, Unjung-dong, Bundang-gu, Seongnam, Gyeonggi Prov. 463-791; tel. (31) 709-8111; fax (31) 709-9945; organ of the Acad. of Korean Studies; Pres. HAN SANG-JIN.

Eumak Dong-A: 139, Sejong-no, Jongno-gu, Seoul 110-715; tel. (2) 781-0640; fax (2) 705-4547; f. 1984; monthly; music; Publr KIM BYUNG-KWAN; Editor KWON O-KIE; circ. 85,000.

Han Kuk No Chong (FKTU News): 35, Yeouido-dong, Yeong-deungpo-gu, Seoul 150-885; tel. (2) 6277-0026; fax (2) 6277-0068; internet www.fktu.or.kr; f. 1961; labour news; circ. 20,000.

Hyundae Munhak: Seoul; tel. (2) 516-3770; fax (2) 516-5433; e-mail webmaster@hdmh.co.kr; internet www.hdmh.co.kr; f. 1955; literature; Publr KIM SUNG-SIK; circ. 200,000.

Korea Business World: Yeouido, POB 720, Seoul 150-607; tel. (2) 532-1364; fax (2) 594-7663; f. 1985; monthly; English; Publr and Pres. LEE KIE-HONG; circ. 40,200.

Korea Buyers Guide: Rm 2301, Korea World Trade Center, 159, Samseong-dong, Gangnam-gu, Seoul; tel. (2) 551-2376; fax (2) 551-2377; e-mail info@buyersguide.co.kr; internet www.buykorea21.com; f. 1973; monthly; consumer goods; quarterly, hardware; Pres. YOU YOUNG-PYO; circ. 30,000.

Korea Journal: Korean National Commission for UNESCO, CPOB 64, Seoul 100-600; tel. (2) 695-84112; fax (2) 6958-4252; e-mail kj@unesco.or.kr; internet www.ekoreajournal.net; f. 1961; quarterly; organ of the Korean National Commission for UNESCO; focus on Korean Studies; Editor KIM MIN-A; Publr CHUN TAEK-SOO.

Korea Newsreview: 1-12, 3-ga, Hoehyeon-dong, Jung-gu, Seoul 100-771; tel. (2) 756-7711; weekly; English; Publr and Editor PARK CHUNG-WOONG.

Korea and World Affairs: Rm 1723, Daewoo Center Bldg, 5-541, Namdaemun-no, Jung-gu, Seoul 100-714; tel. (2) 777-2628; fax (2) 319-9591; organ of the Research Center for Peace and Unification of Korea; Pres. CHANG DONG-HOON.

Korean Business Review: FKI Bldg, 28-1, Yeouido-dong, Yeong-deungpo-gu, Seoul 150-756; tel. (2) 3771-0114; fax (2) 3771-0138; monthly; publ. by Fed. of Korean Industries; Publr KIM KAK-CHOONG; Editor SOHN BYUNG-DOO.

Literature and Thought: Seoul; tel. (2) 738-0542; fax (2) 738-2997; f. 1972; monthly; Pres. LIM HONG-BIN; circ. 10,000.

Monthly Travel: Cross Bldg, 2nd Floor, 46-6, 2-ga, Namsan-dong, Jung-gu, Seoul 100-042; tel. (2) 757-6161; fax (2) 757-6089; e-mail kotfa@unitel.co.kr; Pres. SHIN JOONG-MOK; circ. 50,000.

News Maker: 22, Jung-dong, Jung-gu, Seoul 110-702; tel. (2) 3701-1114; fax (2) 739-6190; e-mail hudy@kyunghyang.com; internet www.kyunghyang.com/newsmaker; f. 1992; Pres. JANG JUN-BONG; Editor PARK MYUNG-HUN.

Reader's Digest: 295-15, Deoksan 1-dong, Geumcheon-gu, Seoul 153-011; tel. (2) 3670-5497; fax (2) 3670-5001; internet www.readersdigest.co.kr; f. 1978; monthly; general; Pres. YANG SUNG-MO; Editor PARK SOON-HWANG; circ. 115,000.

Shin Dong-A (New East Asia): 139, Chungjeong-no, Seodaemun-gu, Seoul 120-715; tel. (2) 361-0974; fax (2) 361-0988; e-mail hans@donga.com; internet shindonga.donga.com; f. 1931; monthly; general; Publr KIM JAE-HO; Editor LEE HYUNG-SAM; circ. 150,000.

Taekwondo: Joyang Bldg 113, 4/F, Samseong-dong, Gangnam-gu, Seoul; tel. (2) 566-2505; fax (2) 553-4728; e-mail wtf@wtf.org; internet www.wtf.org; f. 1973; annual; organ of the World Taekwondo Federation; Pres. Dr CHOUE CHUNG-WON.

Vantage Point: 85-1, Susong-dong, Jongno-gu, Seoul, 110-140; tel. (2) 398-3114; fax (2) 398-3539; e-mail master@yna.co.kr; internet www.yonhapnews.co.kr; f. 1978; monthly; developments in North Korea; Editor KWAK SEUNG-JI.

Weekly Chosun: 61, Taepyeong-no 1, Jung-gu, Seoul; tel. (2) 724-5114; fax (2) 724-6199; weekly; Publr BANG SANG-HOON; Editor CHOI JOON-MYONG; circ. 350,000.

The Weekly Hankook: 14, Junghak-dong, Jongno-gu, Seoul; tel. (2) 732-4151; fax (2) 724-2444; f. 1964; Publr CHANG CHAE-KUK; circ. 400,000.

Wolgan Mot: 139, Sejong-no, Jongno-gu, Seoul 110-715; tel. (2) 733-5221; f. 1984; monthly; fashion; Publr KIM SEUNG-YUL; Editor KWON O-KIE; circ. 120,000.

Women's Weekly: 14, Junghak-dong, Jongno-gu, Seoul; tel. (2) 735-9216; fax (2) 732-4125.

THE REPUBLIC OF KOREA (SOUTH KOREA)

Yosong Dong-A (Women's Far East): 139, Sejong-no, Jongno-gu, Seoul 110-715; tel. (2) 721-7621; fax (2) 721-7676; f. 1933; monthly; women's magazine; Publr KIM BYUNG-KWAN; Editor KWON O-KIE; circ. 237,000.

NEWS AGENCY

Yonhap News Agency: 85-1, Susong-dong, Jongno-gu, Seoul; tel. (2) 398-3114; fax (2) 398-3567; e-mail ldm@yna.co.kr; internet www.yonhapnews.co.kr; f. 1980; Pres. KIM KUN.

PRESS ASSOCIATIONS

Journalists Association of Korea (JAK): Korea Press Center Bldg, 25 1-ga, Taepyeong-no, Jung-gu, Seoul; tel. (2) 737-2483; fax (2) 738-1003; e-mail jakmaster@journalist.or.kr; internet www.journalist.or.kr; Pres. JANG KYUNG-WOO.

Korean Association of Newspapers: Korea Press Center, 13th Floor, 25, 1-ga, Taepyeong-no, Jung-gu, Seoul 100-745; tel. (2) 733-2251; fax (2) 720-3291; e-mail iwelcome@presskorea.or.kr; internet www.presskorea.or.kr; f. 1962; 48 mems; Pres. JAE-HO; Sec.-Gen. MOON HAN-KWON.

Korean Newspaper Editors' Association: Korea Press Center, 13th Floor, 25, 1-ga, Taepyeong-no, Jung-gu, Seoul; tel. (2) 732-1726; fax (2) 739-1985; f. 1957; 416 mems; Pres. SEONG BYONG-WUK.

Seoul Foreign Correspondents' Club: Korea Press Center, 18/F, 1-ga, Taepyeong-no, Jung-gu, Seoul; tel. (2) 734-3272; fax (2) 734-7712; e-mail master@sfcc.or.kr; internet www.sfcc.or.kr; f. 1956; Pres. RYOJI ITO.

Publishers

Ahn Graphics Ltd: 260-288, Seongbuk-dong, Seongbuk-gu, Seoul 136-823; tel. (2) 743-8065; fax (2) 744-3251; e-mail lbr@ag.co.kr; internet www.ag.co.kr; f. 1985; computer graphics; Pres. KIM OK-CHUL.

Bak-Young Publishing Co: 13-31, Pyeong-dong, Jongno-gu, Seoul; tel. (2) 733-6771; fax (2) 736-4818; f. 1952; sociology, philosophy, literature, linguistics, social science; Pres. AHN JONG-MAN.

BIR Publishing Co Ltd: 4/F, Gangnam Publishing Culture Center, 506 Sinsa-dong, Gangnam-Gu, Seoul 135-887; tel. (2) 3443-4318; fax (2) 3442-4661; e-mail bir@bir.co.kr; internet www.bir.co.kr; children's books.

Bobmun Sa Publishing Co: Hanchung Bldg, 4th Floor, 161-7, Yomni-dong, Mapo-gu, Seoul 121-090; tel. (2) 703-6541; fax (2) 703-6594; internet www.bobmunsa.co.kr; f. 1954; law, politics, philosophy, history; Pres. BAE HYO-SEON.

Bookhouse Publishing Co Ltd: 6/F, Dongsomun Bldg, Seoul 136-034; tel. (2) 924-4736; fax (2) 924-4738; e-mail editor@bookhouse.co.kr; internet www.bookhouse.co.kr; business, foreign novels, health.

Bumwoo Publishing Co: 525-2, Paju Book City, Munbal-ri, Gyoha-eup, Paju-si, Gyeonggi-do; tel. (31) 955-6900; fax (31) 955-6905; e-mail help@bumwoosa.co.kr; internet www.bumwoosa.co.kr; f. 1966; philosophy, religion, social science, technology, art, literature, history; Pres. YOON HYUNG-DOO.

Chaeksesang Publishing Co (Book World): tel. (2) 704-1251; fax (2) 719-1258; e-mail webmaster@bkworld.co.kr; internet www.bkworld.co.kr; f. 1975.

Chajaknamu: 21-1, Sangsoo-dong, Seoul 121-160; tel. (2) 3142-9150; fax (2) 3142-9160; humanities.

Changhae Publishing: 336-10, Ahyun 2-dong, Seoul 121-012; tel. (2) 313-3200; fax (2) 313-3204; e-mail nanal21@changhae.com; internet www.changhae.com.

Cheong Moon Gak Publishing Co Ltd: 486-9, Kirum 3-dong, Seongbuk-gu, Seoul 136-800; tel. (2) 985-1451; fax (2) 988-1456; e-mail cmgbook@cmgbook.co.kr; internet www.cmgbook.co.kr; f. 1974; science, technology, business; subsidiaries HanSeung Publishers, Lux Media; Pres. KIM HONG-SEOK; Man. Dir HANS KIM.

Crayon House Co Ltd: 5/F, Crayon House Bldg, Seoul; tel. (2) 3436-1711; fax (2) 3436-1410; e-mail crayong@korea.com; internet www.crayonhouse.co.kr; f. 1996; children's books.

Dai Won Publishing Co: 40-456, Hangangno 3-ga, Yeongsan-gu, Seoul 140-880; tel. (2) 2071-2000; fax (2) 793-8994; e-mail int@daiwon.co.kr; internet www.daiwon.co.kr; f. 1990; comics.

Design House Publishing Co: Paradise Bldg, 186-210, Jangchung-dong, 2-ga, Jung-gu, Seoul 100-392; tel. (2) 2275-6151; fax (2) 2275-7884; internet www.design.co.kr; f. 1987; social science, art, literature, languages, children's periodicals; Pres. LEE YOUNG-HEE.

Dong-A Publishing Co Ltd: 295-15, Toksan-dong, Seoul 140-100; tel. (2) 866-8800; fax (2) 862-0410; f. 1945; children's books, arts, humanities.

Dong-Hwa Publishing Co: 130-4, 1-ga, Wonhyoro, Yeongsan-gu, Seoul 140-111; tel. (2) 713-5411; fax (2) 701-7041; f. 1968; language, literature, fine arts, history, religion, philosophy; Pres. LIM IN-KYU.

Dongmoonsun Publishing Co: 4, Kwanhum-dong, Jongno-gu, Seoul 110-300; tel. (2) 733-4901; fax (2) 723-4518; e-mail dmoonsun@netsgo.com; humanities.

Doosan Corporation Publishing BG: 14-34, Yeouido-dong, Yeongdeungpo-gu, Seoul; tel. (2) 2167-0601; fax (2) 2167-0668; e-mail dudvkf@doosan.com; internet www.bookdonga.com; f. 1951; general works, school reference, social science, periodicals; Pres. CHOI TAE-KYUNG.

E*Public Co: 923-11, Mok 1-dong, Yangcheon-gu, Seoul 158-051; tel. (2) 653-5131; fax (2) 653-2454; e-mail skliu@panmun.co.kr; internet www.panmun.co.kr; f. 1955; social science, pure science, technology, medicine, linguistics; Pres. and CEO LIU SUNG-KWON.

Ehak Publishing Co Ltd: 17-1, Anhuk-dong, Jongno-gu, Seoul 110-240; tel. (2) 720-4572; fax (2) 720-4573; e-mail legosum@dreamwiz.com.

Eulyoo Publishing Co Ltd: 46-1, Susong-dong, Jongno-gu, Seoul 110-603; tel. (2) 733-8151; fax (2) 732-9154; e-mail eulyoo@chollian.net; f. 1945; linguistics, literature, social science, history, philosophy; Pres. CHUNG CHIN-SOOK.

Gilbut Publishing Co Ltd: 380-15, Seogyo-dong, Mapo-gu, Seoul; tel. (2) 332-0931; fax (2) 323-0586; internet www.gilbut.co.kr; f. 1991.

Gimm-Young Publishers Inc: 17, Kahoe-dong, Jongno-gu, Seoul 110-260; tel. (2) 3668-3202; fax (2) 745-4827; e-mail marketing@gimmyoung.com; f. 1979; current affairs, humanities, history, religion, children's books.

Hainaim Publishing Co Ltd: 5/F, Hainaim Bldg, 368-4, Seogyo-dong, Mapo-gu, Seoul; tel. (2) 326-1600; fax (2) 326-1624; e-mail hainaim@chollian.net; internet www.hainaim.com; f. 1983; philosophy, literature, children's; Pres. SONG YOUNG-SUK.

Haksan Publishing Co: Haksan Bldg, 777-1, Sangdo-dong, Dongjak-gu, Seoul 156-830; tel. (2) 828-8988; fax (2) 828-8890; internet www.haksanpub.co.kr; f. 1995; children's books, comics, magazines.

Hakwon Publishing Co Ltd: Seocho Plaza, 4th Floor, 1573-1, Seocho-dong, Seocho-gu, Seoul; tel. (2) 587-2396; fax (2) 584-9306; f. 1945; general, languages, literature, periodicals; Pres. KIM YOUNG-SU.

Hangilsa Corpn: 520-11, Paju Book City, Munbal-ri, Gyoha-eup, Paju-si, Gyeonggi-do; tel. (31) 955-2000; fax (31) 955-2005; e-mail hangilsaone@hangilsa.co.kr; internet www.hangilsa.co.kr; f. 1976; social science, history, literature; Pres. KIM EOUN-HO.

Hanul Publishing Company: 3/F Seoul Bldg, 105-90 Gongdeok-dong, Mapo-gu, Seoul 121-801; tel. (2) 336-6183; fax (2) 333-7543; internet www.hanulbooks.co.kr; f. 1980; general, philosophy, university books, periodicals; Pres. KIM CHONG-SU.

Hollym Corporation: 13-13, Gwancheol-dong, Jongno-gu, Seoul 110-111; tel. (2) 735-7551; fax (2) 730-5149; e-mail info@hollym.co.kr; internet www.hollym.co.kr; f. 1963; academic and general books on Korea in English; Pres. HAM KI-MAN.

Hyang Mun Sa Publishing Co: 645-20, Yeoksam-dong, Gangnam-gu, Seoul 135-081; tel. (2) 538-5672; fax (2) 538-5673; f. 1950; science, agriculture, history, engineering, home economics; Pres. NAH JOONG-RYOL.

Hyonam Publishing Co Ltd: 627-5, Ahyun 3-dong, Mapo-gu, Seoul 121-013; tel. (2) 365-5056; fax (2) 365-5251; e-mail lawhyun@chollian.net; f. 1951; general, children's, literature, periodicals; Pres. CHO KEUN-TAE.

Hyungseul Publishing Co: 33, Tongeui-dong, Jongno-gu, Seoul; tel. (2) 738-6052; fax (2) 736-7134; e-mail hs@hyungseul.co.kr; internet www.hyungseul.co.kr.

Il Jin Sa Publishing Co: 5-104, Hyochang-dong, Yeongsan-gu, Seoul; tel. (2) 704-1616; fax (2) 715-3536; e-mail webmaster@iljinsa.com; internet www.iljinsa.com; f. 1956; literature, social sciences, juvenile, fine arts, philosophy, linguistics, history; Pres. KIM SUNG-JAE.

Ilchokak Publishing Co Ltd: 1-335, Sinmunno 2-ga, Jongno-gu, Seoul 110-062; tel. (2) 733-5430; fax (2) 738-5857; e-mail ilchokak@hanmail.net; internet www.ilchokak.co.kr; f. 1953; history, literature, sociology, linguistics, medicine, law, engineering; Pres. KIM SI-YEON.

Jigyungsa Publishers Ltd: 790-14, Yeoksam-dong, Gangnam-gu, Seoul 135-080; tel. (2) 557-6351; fax (2) 557-6352; e-mail jigyung@uriel.net; internet www.jigyung.co.kr; f. 1979; children's, periodicals; Pres. KIM BYUNG-JOON.

Jihak Publishing Co Ltd: 180-20, Dongkyo-dong, Mapo-gu, Seoul 121-200; tel. (2) 330-5200; fax (2) 325-4488; e-mail webmaster@jihak.co.kr; internet www.jihak.co.kr; f. 1965; philosophy, language, literature, Pres. KWON BYONG-IL.

THE REPUBLIC OF KOREA (SOUTH KOREA)

Jimoondang: 95, Waryon-dong, Jongno-gu, Seoul 110-360; tel. (2) 743-0227; fax (2) 742-4657; e-mail plan@jipmoon.co.kr; internet www.jimoon.co.kr; f. 1970; scholarly books on Korean history, society, language, literature, religion, art, folklore, politics and economy; Pres. LIM SAM-KYU.

Jisik Sanup Publications Co Ltd: 35-18, Dongui-dong, Jongno-gu, Seoul 110-040; tel. (2) 734-1978; fax (2) 720-7900; e-mail jsp@jisik.co.kr; internet www.jisik.co.kr; f. 1969; religion, social science, art, literature, history, children's; Pres. KIM KYUNG-HEE.

Joongang Publishing Co Ltd: 172-11, Yomni-dong, Mapo-gu, Seoul 121-090; tel. (2) 717-2111; fax (2) 716-1369; f. 1972; study books, children's; Pres. KIM DUCK-KI.

Kemongsa Publishing Co Ltd: 772, Yeoksam-dong, Gangnam-gu, Seoul 135-080; tel. (2) 531-5335; fax (2) 531-5520; internet www.kemongsa.co.kr; f. 1946; picture books, juvenile, encyclopaedias, history, fiction; Pres. RHU SEUNG-HEE.

Kookminbooks Co Ltd: 514-4, Paju Book City, Munbal-ri, Gyoha-eup, Paju-si, Gyeonggi-do; tel. (31) 955-7861; fax (31) 955-7855; internet www.kmbooks.com; f. 1961; children's books.

Korea Britannica Corpn: 117, 1-ga, Jungchung-dong, Seoul 100-391; tel. (2) 272-2151; fax (2) 278-9983; f. 1968; encyclopaedias, dictionaries; Pres JANG HO-SANG, SUJAN ELEN TAPANI.

Korea University Press: 5-1, Anam-dong, 5-ga, Seongbuk-gu, Seoul 136-701; tel. (2) 3290-4231; fax (2) 923-6311; e-mail kupress@korea.ac.uk; internet www.kupress.com; f. 1956; philosophy, history, language, literature, Korean studies, education, psychology, social science, natural science, engineering, agriculture, medicine; Pres. EUH YOON-DAE.

Kum Sung Publishing Co: 242-63, Gongdeok-dong, Mapo-gu, Seoul 121-022; tel. (2) 713-9651; fax (2) 718-4362; e-mail webmaster@kumsungpub.co.kr; internet www.kumsung.co.kr; f. 1965; literature, juvenile, social sciences, history, fine arts; Pres. KIM NAK-JOON.

Kyohak-sa Publishing Co Ltd: 105-67, Gongdeok-dong, Mapo-gu, Seoul 121-020; tel. (2) 707-5110; fax (2) 707-5160; internet www.kyohak.co.kr; f. 1952; dictionaries, educational, children's; Pres. YANG CHEOL-WOO.

Kyung Hee University Press: 1, Hoeki-dong, Dongdaemun-gu, Seoul 130-701; tel. (2) 961-0106; fax (2) 962-8840; f. 1960; general, social science, technology, language, literature; Pres. CHOE YOUNG-SEEK.

Kyungnam University Press: 28-42, Samchung-dong, Jongno-gu, Seoul 110-230; tel. and fax (2) 3700-0700; e-mail ifes@kyungnam.ac.kr; internet ifes.kyungnam.ac.kr; Pres. PARK JAE-KYU.

Minumsa Publishing Co Ltd: 5/F Kangnam Publishing Culture Centre, 506, Sinsa-dong, Gangnam-gu, Seoul 135-120; tel. (2) 515-2000; fax (2) 515-2007; e-mail michellenam@minumsa.com; internet www.minumsa.com; f. 1966; literature, philosophy, linguistics, pure science; Pres. PARK MAENG-HO.

Munhakdongne Publishing Co Ltd: 513-8, Paju Book City, Munbal-ri, Gyoha-eup, Paju-si, Gyeonggi-do 413-832; tel. (31) 955-8888; fax (31) 955-8855; e-mail editor@munhak.com; internet www.munhak.com; f. 1993; art, literature, science, philosophy, non-fiction, children's, periodicals; Pres. KANG BYUNG-SUN.

Sakyejul Publishing Ltd: 1513-3, Paju Book City, Munbal-ri, Gyoha-eup, Paju-si, Gyeonggi-do; tel. (31) 955-8558; fax (31) 955-8596; e-mail kec@sakyejul.co.kr; internet www.sakyejul.co.kr; f. 1982; social sciences, art, literature, history, children's; Pres. KANG MAR-XILL.

Sam Joong Dang Publishing Co: 261-23, Soke-dong, Yeongsan-gu, Seoul 140-140; tel. (2) 704-6816; fax (2) 704-6819; f. 1931; literature, history, philosophy, social sciences, dictionaries; Pres. LEE MIN-CHUL.

Sam Seong Dang Publishing Co: 101-14, Non Hyun-dong, Gangnam-gu, Seoul 135-010; tel. (2) 3442-6767; fax (2) 3442-6768; e-mail kyk@ssdp.co.kr; f. 1968; literature, fine arts, history, philosophy; Pres. KANG MYUNG-CHAE.

Sam Seong Publishing Co Ltd: 1516-2, Seocho-dong, Seocho-gu, Seoul 137-070; tel. (2) 3470-6900; fax (2) 597-1507; f. 1951; literature, history, juvenile, philosophy, arts, religion, science, encyclopaedias; Pres. KIM JIN-YONG.

Samsung Publishing Co Ltd: Samsung Publishing Bldg, 1516-2, Seocho 3-dong, Seocho-gu 137-871; tel. (2) 3470-6900; fax (2) 521-8534; e-mail lisababy@ssbooks.com; internet www.samsungbooks.com; children's books, comics, cooking, parenting, health, travel; f. 1951; Chief Editor BOSUNG KONG.

Segyesa Publishing Co Ltd: 217-1 Poi-dong, Gangnam-gu, Seoul 135-260; tel. (2) 577-2341; fax (2) 576-9853; f. 1988; general, philosophy, literature, periodicals; Pres. CHOI SUN-HO.

Se-Kwang Music Publishing Co: 232-32, Seogye-dong, Yeongsan-gu, Seoul 140-140; tel. (2) 719-2652; fax (2) 719-2656; f. 1953; music, art; Pres. PARK SEI-WON; Chair. PARK SHIN-JOON.

Seong An Dang Publishing Co: 4579, Singil-6-dong, Yeongdeungpo-gu, Seoul 150-056; tel. (2) 3142-4151; fax (2) 323-5324; f. 1972; technology, text books, university books, periodicals; Pres. LEE JONG-CHOON.

Seoul National University Press: San 56-1, Sillim-dong, Gwanak-gu, Seoul; tel. (2) 880-0434; fax (2) 888-4148; e-mail snubook@snu.ac.kr; internet www.snupress.com; f. 1961; philosophy, engineering, social science, art, literature; Pres. LEE KI-JUN.

Si-sa-young-o-sa, Inc: 55-1, 2-ga, Jongno, Jongno-gu, Seoul 110-122; tel. (2) 274-0509; fax (2) 271-3980; internet www.ybmsisa.co.kr; f. 1959; language, literature; Pres. CHUNG YOUNG-SAM.

Sogang University Press: 1, Sinsu-dong, Mapo-gu, Seoul 121-742; tel. (2) 705-8212; fax (2) 705-8612; f. 1978; philosophy, religion, science, art, history; Pres. LEE HAN-TAEK.

Sookmyung Women's University Press: 53-12, 2-ga, Jongpa-dong, Yeongsan-gu, Seoul 140-742; tel. (2) 710-9162; fax (2) 710-9090; f. 1968; general; Pres. LEE KYUNG-SOOK.

Sungkyunkwan University Press: 53, Myeongnyun-dong 3-ga, Jongno-gu, Seoul; tel. (2) 760-1252; fax (2) 762-7452; internet www7.skku.ac.kr/skkupress.

Sungshin Women's University Press: 249-1, Dongsun-dong 3-ga, Seongbuk-gu, Seoul; tel. (2) 920-7327; fax (2) 920-7326; internet www.sungshin.ac.kr/press.

Tam Gu Dang Publishing Co: 158, 1-ga, Hanggangno, Yeongsan-gu, Seoul 140-011; tel. (2) 3785-2271; fax (2) 3785-2272; f. 1950; linguistics, literature, social sciences, history, fine arts; Pres. HONG SUK-WOO.

Woongjin Think Big Co Ltd: Jongno Tower 23/F, Jongno 2-ga, Jongno-gu, Seoul; tel. (2) 3670-1832; fax (2) 766-2722; e-mail lois.kim@email.woongjin.com; internet www.woongjin.com; children's; Pres. YOON SUCK-KEUM.

Yearimdang Publishing Co Ltd: Yearim Bldg, 153-3, Samseong-dong, Gangnam-gu, Seoul 135-090; tel. (2) 566-1004; fax (2) 567-9610; e-mail yearim@yearim.co.kr; internet www.yearim.co.kr; f. 1973; children's; Pres. NA CHOON-HO.

Yonsei University Press: 134, Sincheon-dong, Seodaemun-gu, Seoul 120-749; tel. (2) 361-3380; fax (2) 393-1421; e-mail ysup@yonsei.ac.kr; f. 1955; philosophy, religion, literature, history, art, social science, pure science; Pres. KIM BYUNG-SOO.

Youl Hwa Dang: Paju Book City, 520-10, Munbal-li, Gyoha-eup, Paju-si, Gyeonggi-do 413-832; tel. (31) 955-7000; fax (31) 955-7010; e-mail yhdp@youlhwadang.co.kr; internet www.youlhwadang.co.kr; f. 1971; art; Pres. YI KI-UNG.

Younglim Cardinal Inc: Hyecheon Bldg, 831, Yeoksam-dong, Gangnam-gu, Seoul 135-792; tel. (2) 553-8516; fax (2) 552-0436; e-mail edit@ylc21.co.kr; internet www.ylc21.co.kr; f. 1987.

PUBLISHERS' ASSOCIATION

Korean Publishers' Association: 105-2, Sagan-dong, Jongno-gu, Seoul 110-190; tel. (2) 735-2702; fax (2) 738-5414; e-mail kpa@kpa21.or.kr; internet www.kpa21.or.kr; f. 1947; Pres. BAEK SOK-GHEE; Sec.-Gen. KO HUNG-SIK.

Broadcasting and Communications

TELECOMMUNICATIONS

Korea Telecom: 206 Jungja-dong, Bundang-gu, Seongnam-si, Gyeonggi Prov. 463-711; tel. (2) 727-0114; fax (2) 750-3994; internet www.kt.co.kr; domestic and international telecommunications services and broadband internet services; privatized in June 2002; CEO JOONG SOO-NAM.

Korea Telecom (KT) Freetel: Seoul; internet www.ktf.co.kr; subsidiary of Korea Telecom; 10m. subscribers (2002); CEO JOONG SOO-NAM.

LG Dacom Corpn: Dacom Bldg, 706-1, Yeoksam-dong, Gangnam-gu, Seoul 135-610; tel. (2) 6220-0220; fax (2) 6220-0702; internet www.lgdacom.net; f. 1982; domestic and international long-distance telecommunications services and broadband internet services; CEO PARK JONG-WOOK.

LG Telecom: LG Gangnam Tower, 19th Floor, 679 Yeoksam-dong, Gangnam-gu, Seoul 135-985; tel. (2) 2005-7114; fax (2) 2005-7505; e-mail englishweb@lgtel.co.kr; internet www.lgtelecom.com; subsidiary of LG Corpn; mobile telecommunications and wireless internet services; commenced commercial CDMA2000 1x service in May 2001; 4m. subscribers (2002); CEO JUNG IL-JAE.

Onse Telecom: 192-2, Gumi-dong, Bundang-gu, Seongnam-si, Gyeonggi Prov. 463-500; tel. and fax (31) 738-6000; internet www.onse.net; domestic and international telecommunications services; Pres. and CEO HWANG KYU-BYUNG.

THE REPUBLIC OF KOREA (SOUTH KOREA)

SK Telecom Co Ltd: 11, Euljiro, 2-ga, Jung-gu, Seoul 100-999; tel. (2) 6100-2114; fax (2) 2121-3999; e-mail webmaster@sktelecom.com; internet www.sktelecom.com; cellular mobile telecommunications and wireless internet services; merged with Shinsegi Telecom in Jan. 2002; 16m. subscribers (2002); Pres. and CEO SHIN BAE-KIM.

BROADCASTING

Regulatory Authority

Broadcasting and Communications Commission: KBS Bldg, 923-5, Mok-dong, Yangcheon-gu, Seoul 158-715; tel. (2) 3219-5117; fax (2) 3219-5371; e-mail admin@kbc.go.kr; internet www.kbc.go.kr; Chair. CHOI SI-JUNG.

Radio

Korean Broadcasting System (KBS): 18, Yeouido-dong, Yeongdeungpo-gu, Seoul 150-790; tel. (2) 781-1000; fax (2) 781-4179; internet www.kbs.co.kr; f. 1926; publicly owned corpn with 26 local broadcasting and 855 relay stations; overseas service in Korean, English, German, Indonesian, Chinese, Japanese, French, Spanish, Russian and Arabic; Pres. LEE BYUNG-SOON.

Buddhist Broadcasting System (BBS): 140, Mapo-dong, Mapo-gu, Seoul 121-050; tel. (2) 705-5114; fax (2) 705-5229; e-mail webmaster@bbsfm.co.kr; internet www.bbsfm.co.kr; f. 1990; Pres. CHO HAE-HYONG.

Christian Broadcasting System (CBS): 917-1, Mok-dong, Yangcheon-gu, Seoul 158-701; tel. (2) 650-0500; fax (2) 654-0505; e-mail changsoo@cbs.co.kr; internet www.cbs.co.kr; f. 1954; independent religious network with 14 network stations, incl. Seoul, Daegu, Busan and Gwangju; also satellite, cable and digital media broadcasting; programmes in Korean; Pres. LEE JEONG-SIK.

Educational Broadcasting System (EBS): 92-6, Umyeon-dong, Seocho-gu, Seoul 137-791; tel. (2) 526-2000; fax (2) 526-2179; e-mail hotline@ebs.co.kr; internet www.ebs.co.kr; f. 1990; Pres. Dr PARK HEUNG-SOO.

Far East Broadcasting Co (FEBC): 89, Sangsu-dong, Mapo-gu, Seoul 121-707; tel. (2) 320-0114; fax (2) 320-0229; e-mail febcadm@febc.net; internet www.febc.net; Christian programmes; nine local stations; Pres. KIM EUN-GI.

Radio Station HLAZ: MPO Box 88, Seoul 121-707; tel. (2) 320-0114; fax (2) 320-0129; e-mail febcadm@febc.net; internet www.febc.net; f. 1973; religious, educational service operated by Far East Broadcasting Co; programmes in Korean, Chinese, Russian and Japanese; Pres. Dr BILLY KIM.

Radio Station HLKX: MPO Box 88, Seoul 121-707; tel. (2) 320-0114; fax (2) 320-0129; e-mail febcadm@febc.net; internet www.febc.net; f. 1956; religious, educational service operated by Far East Broadcasting Co; programmes in Korean, Chinese and English; Pres. Dr BILLY KIM.

Munhwa Broadcasting Corpn (MBC): 31, Yeouido-dong, Yeongdeungpo-gu, Seoul 150-728; tel. (2) 784-2000; fax (2) 784-0880; e-mail mbcir@imbc.com; internet www.imbc.com; f. 1961; public; Pres. and CEO OHM KI-YOUNG.

Pyong Hwa Broadcasting Corpn (PBC): 2-3, 1-ga, Jeo-dong, Jung-gu, Seoul 100-031; tel. (2) 270-2114; fax (2) 270-2210; internet www.pbc.co.kr; f. 1990; religious and educational programmes; Pres. Rev. PARK SHIN-EON.

Seoul Broadcasting System (SBS): 10-2, Yeouido-dong, Yeongdeungpo-gu, Seoul 150-010; tel. (2) 786-0792; fax (2) 780-2530; internet www.sbs.co.kr; f. 1991; Pres. HA KUM-LOUL.

US Forces Network Korea (AFN Korea): Seoul; tel. (2) 7914-6495; fax (2) 7914-5870; e-mail info@afnkorea.net; internet afnkorea.com; f. 1950; six originating stations and 19 relay stations; 24 hours a day.

Television

Educational Broadcasting System (EBS): see Radio.

Jeonju Television Corpn (JTV): 656-3, Sonosong-dong, Deokjin-gu, Jeonju, N. Jeolla Prov.; tel. (63) 250-5231; fax (63) 250-5249; e-mail jtv@jtv.co.kr; f. 1997.

Korean Broadcasting System (KBS): 18, Yeouido-dong, Yeongdeungpo-gu, Seoul 150-790; tel. (2) 781-1000; fax (2) 781-4179; internet www.kbs.co.kr; f. 1961; publicly owned corpn with 25 local broadcasting and 770 relay stations; Pres. JUNG YUN-JOO.

Munhwa Broadcasting Corpn (MBC-R/TV): 31, Yeouido-dong, Yeongdeungpo-gu, Seoul 150-728; tel. (2) 789-2851; fax (2) 782-3094; e-mail song@mbc.co.kr; internet www.imbc.com; f. 1961; public; owned by the Foundation for Broadcast Culture (70%) and the Chung-Soo Scholarship Foundation (30%); includes terrestrial, cable and satellite TV stations, regional stations and radio stations; Pres. and CEO CHOI MOON-SOON.

Seoul Broadcasting System (SBS): see Radio.

US Forces Network Korea (AFN Korea): Seoul; tel. (2) 7914-2711; fax (2) 7914-5870; f. 1950; main transmitting station in Seoul; 19 rebroadcast transmitters and translators; 168 hours weekly.

Finance

(cap. = capital; res = reserves; dep. = deposits; m. = million; brs = branches; amounts in won, unless otherwise indicated)

REGULATORY AUTHORITIES

Financial Services Commission: 97, Yeouido-dong, Yeongdeungpo-gu, Seoul 150-743; tel. (2) 2156-8000; internet www.fsc.go.kr; f. 1998; deliberates on and resolves financial supervision issues; oversees Financial Supervisory Service; Chair. KIM SEOK-DONG.

Financial Supervisory Service: 97, Yeouido-dong, Yeongdeungpo-gu, Seoul 150-743; tel. (2) 3145-5114; fax (2) 785-3475; e-mail fssintl@fss.or.kr; internet www.fss.or.kr; f. 1999; examines and supervises financial institutions; Gov. KWON HYOUK-SE.

BANKING

In 2003 there were 59 commercial banks in South Korea, comprising eight nation-wide banks, six regional commercial banks, five specialized banks and 40 branches of foreign banks. In mid-2006 there were 32 foreign banks operating in South Korea. The Financial Supervisory Service oversees the operations of commercial banks and the financial services sector.

Central Bank

Bank of Korea: 110, 3-ga, Namdaemun-no, Jung-gu, Seoul 100-794; tel. (2) 759-4114; fax (2) 759-4060; e-mail bokdplp@bok.or.kr; internet www.bok.or.kr; f. 1950; bank of issue; res 3,342m., dep. 283,785m. (Dec. 2009); Gov. KIM CHOONG-SOO; Sr Dep. Gov. LEE JU-YEOL; 16 domestic brs, 6 overseas offices.

Commercial Banks

Citibank Korea Inc: 39, Da-dong, Jung-gu, Seoul 100-180; tel. (2) 3455-2114; fax (2) 3455-2966; internet www.citibank.co.kr; f. 1983; fmrly KorAm Bank, name changed as above 2004; acquired by Citigroup in 2004; cap. 1,518,322m., res 1,187,253m., dep. 34,637,975m. (Dec. 2009); CEO and Chair. HA YUNG-KU; 222 brs.

Hana Bank: 101-1, 1-ga, Ulchi-no, Jung-gu, Seoul 100-191; tel. (2) 2002-1111; fax (2) 775-7472; e-mail webmaster@hanabank.co.kr; internet www.hanabank.co.kr; f. 1991; merged with Boram Bank in Jan. 1999; merged with Seoulbank in Dec. 2002; cap. 1,147,404m., res 7,790,795m., dep. 89,884,425m. (Dec. 2009); Chair. and CEO KIM JUNG-TAE; 604 brs.

Kookmin Bank: 9-1, 2-ga, Namdaemun-no, Jung-gu, CPOB 815, Seoul 100-703; tel. (2) 2073-7114; fax (2) 2073-3296; e-mail corres@kookminbank.com; internet www.kookminbank.com; f. 1963; est. as Citizen's National Bank, renamed 1995; re-est. Jan. 1999, following merger with Korea Long Term Credit Bank; merged with H & CB in Nov. 2001; cap. 2,481,896m., res 7,810,968m., dep. 170,385,878m. (Dec. 2009); Chair. EUH YOON-DAE; Pres. and CEO MIN BYUNG-DUK; 1,122 domestic brs, 6 overseas brs.

Korea Exchange Bank: 181, 2-ga, Ulchi-no, Jung-gu, Seoul 100-793; tel. (2) 729-0114; fax (2) 775-2565; internet www.keb.co.kr; f. 1967; merged with Korea International Merchant Bank in Jan. 1999; cap. 3,224,534m., res 1,234,496m., dep. 56,951,887m. (Dec. 2009); Chair. and CEO LARRY A. KLANE; 345 domestic brs, 19 overseas brs.

Shinhan Bank: 120, 2-ga, Taepyeong-no, Jung-gu, Seoul 100-102; tel. (2) 756-0505; fax (2) 774-7013; e-mail corres@shinhan.com; internet www.shinhan.com; f. 1982; merged with Chohung Bank in April 2006; cap. 7,928,078m., res 1,502,360m., dep. 159,041,712m. (Dec. 2009); Pres. and CEO EUNG CHAN RA; 957 domestic brs, 12 overseas brs.

Standard Chartered First Bank Korea Limited: 100, Gongpyeong-dong, Jongno-gu, Seoul 110702; tel. (2) 3702-3114; fax (2) 3702-4934; e-mail webmaster@scfirstbank.com; internet www.scfirstbank.com; f. 1929; acquired by Standard Chartered Bank in Jan. 2005, name changed from Korea First Bank to above in Sept. 2005; cap. 1,313,043m., res 978,767m., dep. 46,300,583m. (Dec. 2009); Chair. ROBERT T. BARNUM; Pres. and CEO RICHARD HILL; 367 domestic brs, 2 overseas brs.

Woori Bank: 203, 1-ga, Hoehyeon-dong, Jung-gu, Seoul; tel. (2) 2002-3000; fax (2) 2002-5687; internet www.wooribank.com; f. 2002; est. by merger of Hanvit Bank and Peace Bank of Korea; 78% govt-owned; privatization plans deferred in 2008; cap. 3,829,783m., res 1,948,126m., dep. 147,541,287m. (Dec. 2009); CEO LEE SOON-WOO; 712 domestic brs.

THE REPUBLIC OF KOREA (SOUTH KOREA)

Development Banks

Export-Import Bank of Korea: 16-1, Yeouido-dong, Yeongdeungpo-gu, Seoul 150-996; tel. (2) 3779-6114; fax (2) 3779-6750; e-mail iro@koreaexim.go.kr; internet www.koreaexim.go.kr; f. 1976; cap. 5,008,755m., res 350,392m. (Dec. 2009); Chair. and Pres. KIM YONG-HWAN; 11 brs.

Korea Development Bank: 16-3, Yeouido-dong, Yeongdeungpo-gu, Seoul 150-973; tel. (2) 787-6934; fax (2) 787-6991; e-mail KDBir@kdb.co.kr; internet www.kdb.co.kr; f. 1954; cap. 9,241,861m., res 797,919m., dep. 15,582,933m. (Dec. 2009); Chair. KANG MAN-SOO; 40 domestic brs, 6 overseas brs.

Specialized Banks

Industrial Bank of Korea: 50, 2-ga, Ulchi-no, Jung-gu, Seoul 100-758; tel. (2) 729-6114; fax (2) 729-6402; e-mail ifd@ibk.co.kr; internet www.ibk.co.kr; f. 1961; est. as the Small and Medium Industry Bank; 85.5% govt-owned; cap. 3,207,944m., res 5,297,187m., dep. 50,711,514m. (Dec. 2009); Chair. and CEO YOON YONG-RO; 417 domestic brs, 5 overseas brs.

Meritz Investment Bank: Seoul Financial Center, 5th Floor, 84, Taepyeong-no 1-ga, Jung-gu, Seoul 100-768; tel. (2) 777-7711; fax (2) 318-7060; internet home.imeritz.com; f. 1977; fmrly Korean-French Banking Corpn (SogeKo).

Provincial Banks

Daegu Bank Ltd: 118, 2-ga, Susong-dong, Susong-gu, Daegu 706-712; tel. (53) 756-2001; fax (53) 756-2095; internet www.daegubank.co.kr; f. 1967; cap. 660,625m., res 19,795m., dep. 17,641,673m. (Dec. 2009); Chair. and CEO HA CHUN-SOO; 209 brs.

Jeju Bank: 1349, Ido-1-dong, Jeju 690-021, Jeju Prov.; tel. (64) 720-0200; fax (64) 753-4132; internet www.e-jejubank.com; f. 1969; cap. 55,500m., res. 30,700m., dep. 1,044,100m. (2002); merged with Central Banking Co in 2000, joined the Shinhan Financial Group in 2002; Chair. and Pres. KANG JOON-HONG; 29 brs.

Jeonbuk Bank Ltd: 669-2, Geumam-dong, Deokjin-gu, Jeonju 561-711, N. Jeolla Prov.; tel. (63) 250-7114; fax (63) 250-7078; internet www.jbbank.co.kr; f. 1969; cap. 266,797m., res 14,310m., dep. 5,251,565m. (2009); Chair. and Pres. HONG SUNG-JOO; 74 brs.

Kwangju Bank Ltd: 7-12, Daein-dong, Dong-gu, Gwangju 501-719; tel. (62) 239-5000; fax (62) 239-5199; e-mail kbjint1@nuri.net; internet www.kjbank.com; f. 1968; cap. 247,069m., res 95,825m., dep. 12,314,239m. (Dec. 2009); Chair. JEONG TAE-SEOK; 124 brs.

Kyongnam Bank: 246-1, Sokjeon-dong, Hoewon-gu, Masan 630-010, Gyeongsang Prov.; tel. (551) 290-8000; fax (551) 294-9426; internet www.knbank.co.kr; f. 1970; est. as Gyeongnam Bank Ltd, name changed 1987; cap. 290,250m., res 120,728m., dep. 15,302,799m. (Dec. 2009); Pres. and CEO MOON DONG-SUNG; 110 brs.

Banking Association

Korea Federation of Banks: 4-1, 1-ga, Myeong-dong, Jung-gu, Seoul 100-021; tel. (2) 3705-5000; fax (2) 3705-5337; internet www.kfb.or.kr; f. 1928; Chair. SHIN DONG-KYU; Vice-Chair. KIM KONG-JIN.

STOCK EXCHANGE

Korea Exchange (KRX): Nulwon Bldg, 825-3, Beomil-dong, Dong-gu, Busan 601-720; tel. (51) 662-2000; fax (51) 662-2478; internet www.krx.co.kr; f. 2005; formed by merger of Korea Stock Exchange, Korea Futures Exchange, Kosdaq Stock Market, Korea Securities Dealers Association; Chair. and CEO KIM BONG-SOO.

INSURANCE

Principal Life Companies

Allianz Life Insurance Co Ltd: Allianz Tower, 45-21 Yeouido-dong, Yeongdeungpo-gu, Seoul 150-978; tel. (2) 3787-7000; e-mail webadmin@allianzlife.co.kr; internet www.allianzlife.co.kr; fmrly Allianz Jeil Life Insurance; formed in 2000 following acquisition of Jeil (First Life) by Allianz Group; renamed as above in 2002; Pres. and CEO MANUEL BAUER.

American International Assurance Korea: Shinil Bldg, 5/F, 64-5, 2-ga, Chungmu-ro, Jung-gu, Seoul; tel. (2) 3707-4800; fax (67) 725-0783; e-mail kr.webmaster@aia.com; internet www.aia.co.kr; f. 1977; CEO SANG LEE.

Dongbu Life Insurance Co Ltd: Dongbu Bldg, 7th Floor, 891-10, Daechi-dong, Gangnam-gu, Seoul 135-820; tel. (2) 1588-3131; fax (2) 3011-4100; internet www.dongbulife.co.kr; f. 1989; cap. 85,200m. (2003); CEO CHO JAE-HONG.

Green Cross Life Insurance Co Ltd: 395-68, Shindaebang-dong, Dongjak-gu, Seoul; tel. (2) 3284-7000; fax (2) 3284-7455; internet www.healthcare.co.kr; CEO LEE JUNG-SANG.

Hana HSBC Life Insurance Ltd: Hana Bank HQ Bldg, 17/F, 101-1 Ulchiro-1ga, Jung-gu, Seoul 100-191; tel. (2) 3709-7300; fax (2) 755-0668; internet www.hanahsbclife.co.kr; jt venture between HSBC Insurance (Asia-Pacific) Holdings Ltd and Hana Financial Group; CEO DAVID YOON.

Hungkuk Life Insurance Co Ltd: 226, Sinmun-no 1-ga, Jongno-gu, Seoul 100-061; tel. (2) 2002-7000; fax (2) 2002-7804; e-mail webmaster@hungkuk.co.kr; internet www.hungkuk.co.kr; f. 1958; CEO JIN HUN-JIN.

ING Life Insurance Co Korea Ltd: ING Center, 53 Sunhwa-dong, Jung-gu, Seoul 100-130; tel. (2) 3703-9500; fax (2) 734-3309; e-mail webmaster@inglife.co.kr; internet www.inglife.co.kr; f. 1991; cap. 64,820m. (2002); Pres. and CEO JOHN WYLIE.

KB Life Insurance Co Ltd: 2–5/F, 16-49, Hangangro-3 ga, Yongsan-gu, Seoul; tel. (2) 398-6800; fax (2) 398-6843; e-mail webmaster@kbli.co.kr; internet www.kbli.co.kr.

Korea Life Insurance Co Ltd: 60, Yeouido-dong, Yeongdeungpo-gu, Seoul 150-603; tel. (2) 789-5114; fax (2) 789-8173; internet www.korealife.com; f. 1946; cap. 3,550,000m. (2002); CEO SHIN EUN-CHUL.

Korean Reinsurance Company: 80, Susong-dong, Jongno-gu, Seoul 110-733; tel. (2) 3702-6000; fax (2) 739-3754; internet www.koreanre.co.kr; f. 1963; cap. 57,000m. (2010); Pres. PARK JONG-WON.

Kumho Life Insurance Co Ltd: 57, 1-ga, Sinmun-no, Jongno-gu, Seoul 110-061; tel. (2) 1588-4040; fax (2) 771-7561; internet www.kumholife.co.kr; f. 1988; acquired Dong-Ah Life Insurance in 2000; cap. 211,249m. (2002); Pres. CHOI BYEONG-GIL.

Kyobo Life Insurance Co Ltd: 1, 1-ga, Jongno, Jongno-gu, Seoul 110-714; tel. (2) 721-2121; fax (2) 737-9970; internet www.kyobo.co.kr; f. 1958; cap. 92,500m.; Chair. and CEO SHIN CHANG-JAE; 84 main brs.

Life Insurance Association of North America: Seoul City Tower, 14/F, 581, Namdaemunro-5-ga, Jung-gu, Seoul; tel. (2) 3781-1000; fax (2) 792-6063; internet www.lina.co.kr; f. 1987; CEO BENJAMIN HONG.

MetLife Insurance Co of Korea Ltd: Sungwon Bldg, 8/F, 141, Samseong-dong, Gangnam-gu, Seoul 135-716; tel. (2) 3469-9600; fax (2) 3469-9700; internet www.metlifekorea.co.kr; f. 1989; cap. 97,700m. (2002); Pres. STUART B. SOLOMON.

Mirae Asset Life Insurance: Times Sq. Bldg A, 442, 4-ga, Yeongdeungpo-dong, Seoul 150-034; tel. (2) 3271-4114; fax (2) 3271-4400; e-mail msp@miraeasset.com; internet www.miraeassetlife.com; f. 2005; CEO PARK HYEON-JOO.

New York Life Insurance Ltd: 10/F, Shinyoung Bldg, 68-5, Chung Dam-dong, Gangnam-gu, Seoul; tel. (2) 2107-4600; fax (2) 2107-4700; f. 1990.

PCA Life Insurance Co Ltd: PCA Life Tower, 706, Yeoksam-dong, Gangnam-gu, Seoul; tel. (2) 6960-1700; fax (2) 6960-1606; internet www.pcakorea.co.kr; f. 1990; cap. 52,100m. (2002); Pres. MIKE BISHOP.

Prudential Life Insurance Co of Korea Ltd: Prudential Bldg, Yeoksam-dong, Gangnam-gu, Seoul; tel. (2) 2144-2000; fax (2) 2144-2100; internet www.prudential.co.kr; f. 1989; cap. 26,400m.; Pres. HWANG OU-JIN.

Samsung Life Insurance Co Ltd: 150, 2-ga, Taepyeong-no, Jung-gu, Seoul 100-716; tel. (2) 751-8000; fax (2) 751-8100; e-mail samsunglife.ir@samsung.com; internet www.samsunglife.com; f. 1957; cap. 100,000m. (2002); Pres. LEE SOO-CHANG; 1,300 brs.

Shinhan Life Insurance Co Ltd: 120, 2-ga, Taepyeong-no, Jung-gu, Seoul 100-102; tel. (2) 3455-4000; fax (2) 775-3286; internet www.shinhanlife.co.kr; f. 1990; CEO GWEON JEUM-JOO.

Tong Yang Life Insurance Co Ltd: 185, Ulchi-no 2-ga, Jung-gu, Seoul 100-192; tel. (2) 728-9114; fax (2) 728-9563; internet www.myangel.co.kr; f. 1989; cap. 340,325m. (2002); Pres. KU JA-HONG.

Woori Aviva Life Insurance Co Ltd: Woori Aviva Life Insurance Bldg, Sujung 3-dong, Dong-gu, Busan 601-716; tel. (2) 2087-9337; fax (51) (2) 2087-9329; internet www.wooriaviva.com; f. 1988; fmrly LIG Life Insurance Co Ltd; name changed as above after joint acquisition by Woori Finance Holdings Co Ltd and Aviva Life Insurance Co; Pres. SEON HWAN-KYU.

Non-Life Companies

American Home Insurance Co: Seoul Central Bldg, 15–18/F, 136 Seorin-dong, Jongno-gu, Seoul; tel. (2) 2260-6800; fax (2) 2260-6707; e-mail ask.chartis@chartisinsurance.com; internet www.chartisinsurance.com; f. 1947; operates under the brand name Chartis; Pres. BRAD BENNETT.

Dongbu Insurance Co Ltd: Dongbu Financial Center, 12/F, 891-10, Daechi-dong, Gangnam-gu, Seoul 135-840; tel. (2) 2262-3450; fax (2) 3001-3159; e-mail dongbu@dongbuinsurance.co.kr; internet www.idongbu.com; f. 1962; cap. 30,000m.; Pres. KIM JING-NAM.

THE REPUBLIC OF KOREA (SOUTH KOREA)

First Fire and Marine Insurance Co Ltd: 12-1, Seosomun-dong, Jung-gu, CPOB 530, Seoul 100-110; tel. (2) 316-8114; fax (2) 771-7319; f. 1949; cap. 17,200m.; Pres. KIM WOO-HOANG.

Green Non-Life Insurance Co Ltd: Green Non-Life Insurance Co Bldg, 705-19, Yeoksam-dong, Gangnam-gu, Seoul; tel. (2) 3788-2000; fax (2) 774-8368; internet www.greenfire.co.kr; Pres. LEE YOUNG-DOO.

Heungkuk Fire and Marine Insurance Co Ltd: 226, Sinmun-no, 1-ga, Jongno-gu, Seoul; tel. (2) 724-9000; fax (2) 774-8368; e-mail sfmi@ssy.insurance.co.kr; internet www.insurance.co.kr; f. 1948; fmrly Ssangyong Fire and Marine Insurance Co; cap. 27,400m.; Pres. KIM YONG-GWON.

Hyundai Marine and Fire Insurance Co Ltd: 178, Sejongno, Jongno-gu, Seoul 110-731; tel. (2) 732-1212; fax (2) 732-5687; e-mail webpd@hdinsurance.co.kr; internet www.hi.co.kr; f. 1955; cap. 30,000m.; Pres. and CEO SEO TAI-CHANG.

Korean Reinsurance Co: 80, Susong-dong, Jongno-gu, Seoul 100-733; tel. (2) 3702-6000; fax (2) 739-3754; e-mail service@koreanre.co.kr; internet www.koreanre.co.kr; f. 1963; cap. 57,000m.; Pres. PARK JONG-WON.

Kyobo AXA General Insurance Co Ltd: 395-70, Sindaebang-dong, Dongjak-gu, Seoul; tel. (2) 3479-4900; fax (2) 3479-4800; internet www.kyobodirect.com; fmrly Kyobo Auto Insurance Co Ltd, name changed as above in 2007; Pres. GUY MARCILLAT.

LIG Insurance Co Ltd: 649-11, Yeoksam-dong, Gangnam-gu, Seoul; tel. (2) 310-2391; fax (2) 753-1002; e-mail webmaster@lginsure.com; internet www.lig.co.kr; f. 1959; fmrly LG Insurance Co; Pres. JANG NAM-SIK.

Lotte Insurance Co Ltd: 51-1, Namchang-dong, Jung-gu, Seoul 100-778; tel. (2) 1588-3344; fax (2) 754-5220; internet www.lotteins.co.kr; f. 1946; cap. 19,500m.; fmrly Daehan Fire and Marine Insurance Co Ltd, name changed as above in 2008; Pres. and CEO KIM CHANG-JAE.

Meritz Fire and Marine Insurance Co Ltd: 825-2, Yeoksam-dong, Gangnam-gu, Seoul 135-080; tel. (2) 3786-1910; fax (2) 3786-1940; e-mail ir@meritzfire.com; internet www.meritzfire.com; f. 1922; Vice-Chair. and CEO WOHN MYUNG-SOO.

Samsung Fire and Marine Insurance Co Ltd: Samsung Insurance Bldg, 87, 1-ga, Ulchi-no, Jung-gu, Seoul 100-191; tel. (2) 758-7948; fax (2) 758-7831; internet www.samsungfire.com; f. 1952; cap. 6,566m.; Pres. LEE SOO-CHANG.

Seoul Guarantee Insurance Co: 136-74, Yeonchi-dong, Jongno-gu, Seoul 110-470; tel. (2) 3671-7459; fax (2) 3671-7480; internet www.sgic.co.kr; f. 1969; CEO BAANG YOUNG-MIN.

Shindongah Fire and Marine Insurance Co Ltd: 43, 2-ga, Taepyeong-no, Jung-gu, Seoul; tel. (2) 6366-7000; fax (2) 755-8006; internet www.sdafire.com; f. 1946; cap. 60,220m.; CEO KWON CHU-SIN.

Insurance Associations

General Insurance Association of Korea: KRIC Bldg, 6th Floor, 80, Susong-dong, Jongno-gu, Seoul; tel. (2) 3702-8539; fax (2) 3702-8549; e-mail jhero@knia.or.kr; internet www.knia.or.kr; f. 1946; 16 corporate mems; fmrly Korea Non-Life Insurance Asscn; Chair. MOON JAE-WOO.

Korea Life Insurance Association: Kukdong Bldg, 16th Floor, 60-1, 3-ga, Jungmu-no, Jung-gu, Seoul 100-705; tel. (2) 2262-6600; fax (2) 2262-6580; e-mail info@klia.or.kr; internet www.klia.or.kr; f. 1950; Chair. LEE WOO-CHEOL.

Trade and Industry

GOVERNMENT AGENCIES

Fair Trade Commission: 217, Banpo-dong, Seocho-gu, Seoul; tel. (2) 2023-4248; fax (2) 2023-4241; e-mail kftc@korea.kr; internet www.ftc.go.kr; Chair. KIM DONG-SOO; Sec.-Gen. LEE DONG-KYU.

Federation of Korean Industries: FKI Bldg, 14/F, 28-2, Yeouido-dong, Yeongdeungpo-gu, Seoul 150-756; tel. (2) 3771-0354; fax (2) 3771-0110; e-mail webmaster@fki.or.kr; internet www.fki.or.kr; f. 1961; conducts research and survey work on domestic and overseas economic conditions and trends; advises the Govt and other interested parties on economic matters; exchanges economic and trade missions with other countries; sponsors business conferences; 366 corporate mems and 63 business asscns; Chair. HUH CHANG-SOO.

Korea Appraisal Board: 171-2, Samseong-dong, Gangnam-gu, Seoul; tel. (2) 2189-8000; fax (2) 561-6133; internet www.kab.co.kr; Chair. KWAN JIN-BONG.

Korea Asset Management Corpn (KAMCO): 450, Gangnam-daero, Gangnam-gu, Seoul; tel. (2) 3420-5000; fax (2) 3420-5030; e-mail irkamco@kamco.or.kr; internet www.kamco.or.kr; f. 1963; collection and foreclosure agency; appointed following Asian financial crisis as sole institution to manage and dispose of non-performing loans for financial institutions; Chair. and CEO CHANG YONG-CHUL.

Korea Export Industrial Corpn: 33, Seorin-dong, Jongno-gu, Seoul; tel. (2) 853-5573; f. 1964; encourages industrial exports, provides assistance and operating capital, conducts market surveys; Pres. KIM KI-BAE.

Korea Industrial Research Institutes: FKI Bldg, 28-1, Yeouido-dong, Yeongdeungpo-gu, Seoul; tel. (2) 780-7601; fax (2) 785-5771; f. 1979; analyses industrial and technological information from abroad; Pres. KIM CHAE-KYUM.

Korea Institute for Industrial Economics and Trade (KIET): 66 Hoegi-ro, Dongdaemun-gu, Seoul; tel. (2) 3299-3114; fax (2) 963-8540; e-mail webmaster@kiet.re.kr; internet www.kiet.re.kr; f. 1976; economic and industrial research; Pres. SONG BYOUNG-JUN.

Korea Land and Housing Corpn: 217, Jeongja-dong, Seongnam-shi, Gyeonggi-do; tel. (31) 738-7114; fax (31) 717-5431; internet www.lh.or.kr; f. 1975; land development; est. by merging Korea Land Corpn and Korea National Housing Corpn; CEO LEE JI-SONG.

Korea Resources Corpn (KORES): 606, Siheung-daero, Dongjak-gu, Seoul; tel. (2) 840-5600; e-mail csmaster@kores.or.kr; internet www.kores.or.kr; f. 1967; provides technical and financial support for the national mining industry; Pres. KIM SHIN-JONG.

Korea Trade Insurance Corpn: Seoul Central Bldg, 2/F, 136, Seorin-dong, Jongno-gu, Seoul 110-729; tel. (2) 399-6800; fax (2) 399-7439; internet www.ksure.or.kr; f. 1992; financial support services for traders; fmrly Korea Export Insurance Corpn; Chair. and Pres. RYU CHANG-MOO.

Korea Trade-Investment Promotion Agency (KOTRA): 300-9, Yeomgok-dong, Seocho-gu, Seoul; tel. (2) 3460-7114; fax (2) 3460-7777; e-mail digitalkotra@kotra.or.kr; internet www.kotra.or.kr; f. 1962; various trade promotion activities, market research, cross-border investment promotion, etc.; 102 overseas brs; Pres. CHO HWAN-EIK.

Korean Intellectual Property Office: Government Complex-Daejeon Bldg 4, 189, Cheongsa-ro, Seo-gu, Daejeon; tel. (42) 481-5071; fax (42) 472-9314; e-mail kipoicd@kipo.go.kr; internet www.kipo.go.kr; Commissioner LEE SOO-WON.

CHAMBER OF COMMERCE

Korea Chamber of Commerce and Industry: 45, 4-ga, Namdaemun-no, Jung-gu, Seoul 100-743; tel. (2) 6050-3114; fax (2) 6050-3400; e-mail webmaster@korcham.net; internet www.korcham.net; f. 1884; over 47,000 mems; 70 local chambers; promotes development of the economy and of international economic co-operation; Chair. SOHN KYUNG-SHIK.

INDUSTRIAL AND TRADE ASSOCIATIONS

Construction Association of Korea: Construction Bldg, 8th Floor, 71-2, Nonhyon-dong, Gangnam-gu, Seoul 135-701; tel. (2) 3485-0200; fax (2) 542-6264; internet www.cak.or.kr; f. 1947; national licensed contractors' asscn; 6,823 mem. firms (2006); Pres. KWON HONG-SA.

Korea Agro-Fisheries Trade Corpn (aT): aT Center, 232 Yangjae-dong, Seocho-gu, Seoul; tel. (2) 6300-1114; fax (2) 6300-1600; internet www.at.or.kr; f. 1967; fmrly Agricultural and Fishery Marketing Corpn; integrated devt for secondary processing and marketing distribution for agricultural products and fisheries products; Pres. JANG BAE-YOO; Exec. Vice-Pres. KIM JIN-KYU.

Korea Automobile Manufacturers Association (KAMA): 1461-15, Seocho 3-dong, Seocho-gu, Seoul 137-720; tel. (2) 3660-1854; fax (2) 3660-1900; e-mail webmaster@kama.or.kr; internet www.kama.or.kr/index.jsp; f. 1988; Chair. YOUN YEO-CHUL.

Korea Electronics Association: Digital Innovation Center, 11–12/F, 1599, Sangnam-dong, Mapo-gu, Seoul; tel. (2) 6388-6000; fax (2) 6388-6009; e-mail webmaster@gokea.org; internet www.gokea.org; f. 1976; 328 mems; Chair. YUN JONG-YONG.

Korea Federation of Textile Industries: Textile Center, 16/F, 944-31, Daechi 3-dong, Gangnam-gu, Seoul 135-713; tel. (2) 528-4052; fax (2) 528-4069; e-mail kofoti@kofoti.or.kr; internet www.kofoti.or.kr; f. 1980; 50 corporate mems; Chair. CHAN RO-HEE.

Korea Foods Industry Association: 1002-6, Bangbae-dong, Seocho-gu, Seoul; tel. (2) 3470-8100; fax (2) 3471-3492; internet www.kfia.or.kr; f. 1969; 104 corporate mems; Pres. CHUN MYUNG-KE.

Korea Importers Association (KOIMA): 218, Hangang-no, 2-ga, Yeongsan-gu, Seoul 140-875; tel. (2) 792-1581; fax (2) 785-4373; e-mail koima@koima.or.kr; internet www.koima.or.kr; f. 1970; 6,804 mems; Chair. Dr LEE JU-TAE.

Korea International Trade Association: 159-1, Samseong-dong, Gangnam-gu, Seoul; tel. (2) 6000-5114; fax (2) 6000-5115; e-mail kitainfo@kita.net; internet www.kita.org; f. 1946; private, non-profitmaking business org. representing all licensed traders in South

THE REPUBLIC OF KOREA (SOUTH KOREA)

Korea; provides foreign businesses with information, contacts and advice; 80,000 corporate mems; Chair. and CEO IL SAKONG.

Korea Iron and Steel Association: 19/F, Posteel Tower, 735-3, Yeoksam-dong, Gangnam-gu, Seoul; tel. (2) 559-3500; fax (2) 559-3508; internet www.kosa.or.kr; f. 1975; 39 corporate mems; Chair. YOO SANG-BOO.

Korea Oil Association: 28-1, Yeouido-dong, Yeongdeungpo-gu, Seoul; tel. (2) 555-8322; fax (2) 555-7825; e-mail oilassn@yahoo.co.kr; internet www.koreaoil.or.kr; f. 1980; Pres. CHOI DOO-HWAN.

Korea Productivity Center: 122-1, Jeokseon-dong, Jongno-gu, Seoul 110-751; tel. (2) 724-1114; fax (2) 736-0322; internet www.kpc.or.kr; f. 1957; services to increase productivity of industries, consulting services, education and training of specialized personnel; Chair. and CEO CHOI DONG-KYU.

Korea Sericultural Association: 17-9, Yeouido-dong, Yeongdeungpo-gu, Seoul; tel. (2) 783-6072; fax (2) 780-0706; e-mail jamsa@silktopia.or.kr; internet ksa.silktopia.or.kr; f. 1946; improvement and promotion of silk production; 50,227 corporate mems; Pres. PARK DONGCHUI.

Korea Shipbuilders' Association: Landmark Tower, 18/F, 837-36, Yeoksam-dong, Gangnam-gu, Seoul 135-937; tel. (2) 2112-8181; fax (2) 2112-8182; internet www.koshipa.or.kr; f. 1977; 9 mems; Chair. NAM SANG-TAE.

Korea Textiles Trade Association: Textile Center, 16/F, 944-31, Daechi 3-dong, Gangnam-gu, Seoul 135-713; tel. (2) 528-5158; fax (2) 528-5188; e-mail keat@kotis.net; internet www.textra.or.kr; f. 1981; 947 corporate mems; Pres. KANG TAE-SEUNG.

Korean Apparel Industry Association: Textile Center, 16/F, 944-31, Daechi 3-dong, Gangnam-gu, Seoul 135-713; tel. (2) 528-0114; fax (2) 528-0120; internet www.kaia.or.kr; f. 1993; 741 corporate mems; Chair. LEE IN-SUNG.

Mining Association of Korea: 35-24, Dongui-dong, Jongno-gu, Seoul 110; tel. (2) 737-7748; fax (2) 720-5592; f. 1918; 128 corporate mems; Pres. KIM SANG-BONG.

Spinners and Weavers Association of Korea: 43-8, Gwancheol-dong, Jongno-gu, Seoul 110; tel. (2) 735-5741; fax (2) 735-5749; internet www.swak.org; f. 1947; 20 corporate mems; Chair. KIM HYONG-SANG.

EMPLOYERS' ORGANIZATION

Korea Employers' Federation: KEF Bldg, 276-1, Daeheung-dong, Mapo-gu, Seoul 121-726; tel. (2) 3270-7310; fax (2) 3270-7431; e-mail admin@kef.or.kr; internet www.kef.or.kr; f. 1970; advocates employers' interests with regard to labour and social affairs; 13 regional employers' asscns, 20 economic and trade asscns, and 4,000 major enterprises; Chair. LEE HEE-BEOM.

UTILITIES

Electricity

Korea Electric Power Corpn (KEPCO): 167, Samseong-dong, Gangnam-gu, Seoul; tel. (2) 3456-3114; fax (2) 3456-3699; internet www.kepco.co.kr; f. 1961; transmission and distribution of electric power, and development of electric power sources; six power generation subsidiaries formed in 2001; CEO KIM SSANG-SOO.

Oil and Gas

Daegu City Gas Co Ltd: 2268-1, Namsan 4-dong, Jung-gu, Daegu; tel. (53) 606-1000; fax (53) 606-1004; e-mail kej@taegugas.co.kr; internet www.taegugas.co.kr; f. 1983; Pres. and CEO LEE CHONG-MOO.

Daehan City Gas: 27-1, Daechi-dong, Kangnam-gu, Seoul; tel. (2) 3410-8000; internet www.daehancitygas.com; f. 1978; supplies liquefied natural gas (LNG) to customers in Seoul and Gyeonggi Province; Co-CEOs NAH SEONG-HWA, KIM BOK-HWAN.

GS Caltex: GS Tower, 679 Yeoksam-dong, Gangnam-gu, Seoul; tel. (2) 2005-1114; internet www.gscaltex.com; subsidiary of GS Holdings Corpn; fmrly LG Caltex Oil, renamed as above March 2005; Chair. and CEO HUR DONG-SOO.

Hanjin City Gas: 711, Sanggye 6-dong, Nowon-gu, Seoul; tel. (2) 950-5000; fax (2) 950-5001; e-mail webmaster@hjcgas.com; internet www.hjcgas.com; f. 1985; supplies natural gas to Seoul and Gyeonggi; CEO LEE SEUNG-CHIL.

Incheon City Gas Corpn: 178-24, Gajoa-dong, Seo-gu, Incheon; tel. (32) 1600-0002; fax (32) 576-2710; internet www.icgas.co.kr; f. 1983; CEO PARK DAE-YONG.

Jungbu City Gas Co Ltd: Jungbu; fax (41) 533-6748; e-mail webmaster@jbcitygas.com; internet www.cbcitygas.co.kr; f. 1992.

Korea Gas Corpn: 215, Jeongja-dong, Bundang-gu, Seongnam, Gyeonggi-do; tel. (31) 710-0114; fax (31) 710-0117; e-mail kogasmaster@kogas.or.kr; internet www.kogas.or.kr; f. 1983; state-owned; privatization pending; Pres. and CEO CHOO KANG-SOO.

Korea National Oil Corpn (KNOC): tel. 380-2114; fax 387-9321; e-mail webmaster@knoc.co.kr; internet www.knoc.co.kr; CEO KANG YOUNG-WON.

KyungDong City Gas Co: 939, Jinjang-dong, Book-gu, Ulsan; tel. (52) 219-5300; internet www.kdgas.co.kr; distributes liquefied natural gas (LNG) to residential, commercial and industrial customers in Ulsan and Yangsan; CEO SONG JAE-HO.

Kyungnam Energy Co Ltd: 55-5, Ungnam-dong, Changwon, Gyeongsangnam-do 641-290; tel. (55) 260-4432; fax (55) 285-9861; e-mail admin@knenegy.co.kr; internet www.knenergy.co.kr; f. 1972; supplies natural gas to Changwon and the surrounding area; Pres. and CEO CHUNG YEUN-WOOK.

Samchully Co Ltd: 35-6, Yeouido-dong, Yeongdeungpo-gu, Seoul; tel. (2) 368-3300; fax (2) 783-1206; e-mail webmaster@samchully.co.kr; internet www.samchully.co.kr; f. 1966; gas supply co for Seoul metropolitan area and Gyeonggi Prov; Pres. and CEO CHUNG SOON-WON.

Seoul City Gas Co: 281, Yeomchang-dong, Gangseo-gu, Seoul 157-864; tel. (2) 810-8000; fax (2) 828-6740; internet www.seoulgas.co.kr; f. 1983; distributes gas in Seoul and Gyeonggi Province; Chair. and CEO KIM YOUNG-MIN.

SK E & S: 99, Seorin-dong, Jongno-gu, Seoul; tel. (2) 2121-3114; fax (2) 2121-3198; internet www.skens.net; f. 1999; jt venture between SK Corpn and Enron Corpn (USA); supplies natural gas through various cos, incl.: Chongju City Gas, Chonnam City Gas, Chungnam City Gas, Iksan City Gas, Iksan Energy, Kangwon City Gas, Kumi City Gas and Pusan City Gas; Pres. and CEO MOON DUK-KYU.

Yesco Co Ltd: 249-8, Yongdap-dong, Sungdong-gu, Seoul; tel. (2) 1644-0303; fax (2) 3390-3117; e-mail webmaster@lsyesco.com; internet www.gaspia.com; f. 1981; fmrly Kukdong City Gas Co; part of the LS Group; supplies liquefied natural gas (LNG) to the Seoul metropolitan area; CEO and Pres. CHOI KYUNG-HOON.

Water

Korea Water Resources Corpn: 6-2, Yeonchuk-dong, Daedeok-gu, Daejeon; tel. (42) 629-3114; fax (42) 623-0963; e-mail mwshi@kwater.or.kr; internet www.kowaco.or.kr; CEO KIM KUEN-HO.

Office of Waterworks, Seoul Metropolitan Govt: 27-1 Hapdong, Seodaemun-gu, Seoul; tel. (2) 390-7332; fax (2) 362-3653; internet arisu.seoul.go.kr; f. 1908; responsible for water supply in Seoul; Head SON JANG-HO.

Ulsan City Water and Sewerage Board: 646-4, Sin-Jung 1-dong, Nam-gu, Ulsan; tel. (52) 743-020; fax (52) 746-928; f. 1979; responsible for water supply and sewerage in Ulsan; Dir HO KUN-SONG.

CO-OPERATIVES

Korea Auto Industries Co-operative Association: 1638-3, Seocho-dong, Seocho-gu, Seoul 137-070; tel. (2) 587-0014; fax (2) 583-7340; e-mail kaica@kaica.or.kr; internet www.kaica.or.kr; f. 1962; Chair. SHIN DAL-CHUK.

Korea Computers Co-operative: 14-8, Yeouido-dong, Yeongdeungpo-gu, Seoul; tel. (2) 780-0511; fax (2) 780-7509; f. 1981; Pres. MIN KYUNG-HYUN.

Korea Federation of Knitting Industry Co-operatives: 586-1, Sinsa-dong, Gangnam-gu, Seoul; tel. (2) 548-2131; fax (2) 3444-9929; e-mail kts01@korea.com; internet www.knit.or.kr; f. 1962; Chair. JOUNG MAN-SUB.

Korea Federation of Non-ferrous Metal Industry Co-operatives: Backsang Bldg, Rm 715, 35-2, Yeouido-dong, Yeongdeungpo-gu, Seoul; tel. (2) 780-8551; fax (2) 784-9473; f. 1962; Chair. PARK WON-SIK.

Korea Federation of Plastic Industry Co-operatives: 146-2, Ssangrim-dong, Jung-gu, Seoul; tel. (2) 2280-8200; fax (2) 2277-3915; internet www.koreaplastic.or.kr; f. 1973.

Korea Federation of Small and Medium Business (Kbiz): 16-2, Yeouido-dong, Yeongdeungpo-gu, Seoul 150-740; tel. (2) 2124-3114; fax (2) 3775-1981; e-mail webmaster@kbiz.or.kr; internet www.kbiz.or.kr; f. 1962; Chair. KIM KI-MUN.

Korea Federation of Weaving Industry Co-operatives: tel. (2) 752-8097; fax (2) 755-6994; e-mail weaving3@hanmail.net; internet www.weaving.or.kr; f. 1964.

Korea Information and Communication Industry Co-operative: tel. (2) 711-2266; fax (2) 7111-2272; e-mail webmaster@kicic.or.kr; internet www.kicic.or.kr; f. 1962; CEO JOO DAE-CHULL.

Korea Metal Industry Co-operative: tel. (2) 780-4411; fax (2) 785-5067; e-mail master@koreametal.or.kr; internet www.koreametal.or.kr; f. 1962.

Korea Mining Industry Co-operative: 35-24, Dongui-dong, Jongno-gu, Seoul; tel. (2) 735-3490; fax (2) 735-4658; f. 1966; Chair. JEON HYANG-SIK.

THE REPUBLIC OF KOREA (SOUTH KOREA)

Korea Steel Industry Co-operative: 915-14, Bangbae-dong, Seocho-gu, Seoul; tel. (2) 587-3121; fax (2) 588-3671; internet www.kosic.or.kr; f. 1962; Pres. KIM DUK-NAM.

National Agricultural Co-operative Federation (NACF): Saemunangil 91, Jung-gu, Seoul; tel. (2) 2080-5114; fax (2) 1544-2100; internet www.nonghyup.com; f. 1961; international banking, marketing, co-operative trade, utilization and processing, supply, co-operative insurance, banking and credit services, education and research; Chair. CHOI WUN-BYUNG.

National Federation of Fisheries Co-operatives: 11-6, Sincheon-dong, Songpa-gu, Seoul; tel. (2) 2240-2114; fax (2) 2240-3024; e-mail webmaster@suhyup.co.kr; internet www.suhyup.co.kr; f. 1962; CEO LEE JONG-KOO.

TRADE UNIONS

Federation of Korean Trade Unions (FKTU): 35, Yeouido-dong, Yeongdeungpo-gu, Seoul 150-885; tel. (2) 6277-0026; fax (2) 6277-0068; e-mail fktu@fktu.or.kr; internet www.fktu.or.kr; f. 1941; Pres. LEE YONG-DEUK; affiliated to ITUC; 26 union federations are affiliated, including:

Federation of Korean Chemical Workers' Unions: FKTU Bldg 802, 35, Yeouido-dong, Yeongdeungpo-gu, Seoul 150-980; tel. (2) 6277-1234; fax (2) 6277-1235; e-mail fkcu@chollian.net; internet www.fkcu.or.kr; f. 1959; Pres. HAN KWANG-HO; 116,286 mems.

Federation of Korean Metal Workers Trade Unions: 208 Samsung IT Valley, 197-5, Guro-dong, Guro-gu, Seoul; tel. (2) 2028-1260; fax (2) 2028-1273; e-mail dykim@metall.or.kr; internet www.metall.or.kr; f. 1961; Pres. JANG SOEK-CHUN; 130,000 mems.

Federation of Korean Seafarers' Unions: 544, Donhwa-dong, Mapo-gu, Seoul; tel. (2) 716-2764; fax (2) 702-2271; e-mail zzoinn@naver.com; internet www.fksu.or.kr; f. 1961; Pres. BANG DONG-SIK; 60,037 mems.

Federation of Korean State-invested Corporation Unions: Sunwoo Bldg, 501, 350-8, Yangjae-dong, Seocho-gu, Seoul; tel. (2) 529-2268; fax (2) 529-2270; internet public.inochong.org; f. 1998; Pres. JANG DAE-IK; 19,375 mems.

Federation of Korean Taxi & Transport Workers' Unions: 415-7, Janan 1-dong, Dongdaemun-gu, Seoul; tel. (3) 633-0099; fax (3) 638-0090; internet www.ktaxi.or.kr; f. 1988; Pres. KWAN OH-MAN; 105,118 mems.

Korea Automobile & Transport Workers' Federation: 4-2, Yangjae 1-dong, Seocho-gu, Seoul 137-886; tel. (2) 554-0890; f. 1963; Pres. KANG SUNG-CHUN; 84,343 mems.

Korea Federation of Communication Trade Unions: 10th Floor, 106-6, Guro 5-dong, Guro-gu, Seoul; tel. (2) 864-0055; fax (2) 864-5519; f. 1961; Pres. OH DONG-IN; 18,810 mems.

Korea Federation of Food Industry Workers' Unions: 7-57, Yeongdeungpo-dong, Yeongdeungpo-gu, Seoul; tel. (2) 2679-6441; fax (2) 2679-6444; e-mail hpunion@hanmir.com; internet food.inochong.org; f. 2000; Pres. BAEK YOUNG-GIL; 19,146 mems.

Korea Federation of Port & Transport Workers' Unions: 19th Floor, Pyouk-San Bldg, 12-5 Dongja-dong, Yeongsan-gu, Seoul; tel. (2) 727-4741; fax (2) 727-4749; e-mail kfptwu@chollian.net; f. 1980; Pres. CHOI BONG-HONG; 33,347 mems.

Korea National Electrical Workers' Union: 167, Samseong-dong, Gangnam-gu, Seoul; tel. (2) 3456-6017; fax (2) 3456-6004; internet www.knewu.or.kr; f. 1961; Pres. KIM JU-YOUNG; 16,741 mems.

Korea Tobacco & Ginseng Workers' Unions: 100, Pyeongchon-dong, Daedeok-gu, Daejeon; tel. (42) 939-6884; fax (42) 939-6891; e-mail ktgson35@ktng.com; internet tobac.inochong.org; f. 1960; Pres. KANG TAE-HEUNG; 6,008 mems.

Korea Union of Teaching and Education Workers: tel. (2) 720-5334; fax (2) 720-5336; e-mail leemo@korea.com; internet www.kute.or.kr; f. 1999; 18,337 mems.

Korean Financial Industry Union: Dong-A Bldg, 9/F, 88, Da-dong, Chung-gu, Seoul; tel. (2) 2095-0000; fax (2) 2095-0018; e-mail accuchung@hanmail.net; internet www.kfiu.org; f. 1960; Pres. KIM MOON-HO.

Korean Government Employees' Union (KGEU): Rm 202, Hyundai Plaza Bldg, 49-1, 5-ga, Yeongdeungpo-gu, Seoul 150-986; tel. (70) 7728-4728; fax (2) 2631-1949; e-mail kgeu.inter@gmail.com; internet inter.kgeu.org; f. 2009; est. following merger of Fed. of Govt Employees' Union, United Municipal Education Civil Servants' Union and Fed. of Local Govt Employees' Union; Pres. YANG SUNG-YUN.

Korean Postal Workers' Union: 154-1, Seorin-dong, Jongno-gu, Seoul 110-110; tel. (2) 2195-1773; fax (2) 2195-1761; e-mail cheshin@chol.com; internet www.kpwu.or.kr; f. 1958; Pres. JUNG HYUN-YOUNG; 23,500 mems.

Korean Railway Workers' Union (KRWU): 40-504, 3-ga, Hangang-no, Yeongsan-gu, Seoul; tel. (2) 797-1126; fax (2) 790-2598; internet www.krwu.or.kr; f. 1947; Pres. KIM KI-TAE; 31,041 mems.

Korean Tourist Industry Workers' Federation: 749, 5-ga, Namdaemun-no, Jung-gu, Seoul 100-095; tel. (2) 779-1297; fax (2) 779-1298; f. 1970; Pres. JEONG YOUNG-KI; 27,273 mems.

Korean Confederation of Trade Unions: 5th Daeyoung Bldg, 139, 2-ga, Yeouido-dong, Yeongdeungpo-gu, Seoul 150-032; tel. (2) 2670-9234; fax (2) 2635-1134; internet www.kctu.org; f. 1995; legalized 1999; Chair. KIM YOUNG-HOON; 600,000 mems.

Transport

RAILWAYS

In 2008 there were 3,381 km of railways in operation. The first phase of construction of a new high-speed rail system connecting Seoul to Busan (412 km) via Cheonan, Daejeon, Daegu, and Gyungju, was completed in early 2004. The second phase, Daejeon–Busan, became operational in November 2010.

Korean National Railroad (Korail): 293-74 Soje-dong, Dong-gu, Daejeon 300-720; tel. (42) 472-3014; fax (42) 259-2197; e-mail admin@korail.com; internet www.korail.com; f. 1963; operates all railways under the supervision of the Ministry of Land, Transport and Maritime Affairs; Pres. and CEO HUH JOON-YOUNG.

City Underground Railways

Busan Subway: Gyotonggongsa 1-ro, Busanjin-gu, Busan 614-722; tel. (51) 640-7186; fax (51) 640-7010; e-mail ipsubway@buta.or.kr; internet www.subway.busan.kr; f. 1988; length of 71.6 km (2 lines, with a further line under construction); Pres. AN JUN-TAE.

Daegu Metropolitan Transit Corpn: 1500, Sangin 1-dong, Dalseo-gu, Daegu 704-808; tel. (53) 643-2114; fax (53) 640-2189; e-mail webmaster@daegusubway.co.kr; internet www.dtro.or.kr; length of 28.3 km (one line, with a further five routes totalling 125.4 km planned or under construction); CEO BAE SANG-MIN.

Daejeon Metropolitan Express Transit Corpn: tel. (42) 539-3114; fax (42) 539-3119; e-mail qnsdlqkr@hanmail.net; internet www.djet.co.kr; f. 2006; operates one line, with a further four lines planned.

Gwangju Metropolitan Rapid Transit Corpn: 529, Sangmu-no, Seo-gu, Gwangju 502-750; tel. (62) 604-8000; fax (62) 604-8069; internet www.gwangjusubway.co.kr; f. 2004; one line, with a further line planned; Pres. OH HAENG-WON.

Incheon Rapid Transit Corpn: 67-2, Gansok-dong, Namdong-gu, Incheon 405-233; tel. (32) 451-2290; fax (32) 451-2160; e-mail sehong4450@gmail.com; internet www.irtc.co.kr; length of 31.1 km (29 stations, 1 line), with two further lines planned; Pres. LEE KWANG-YUONG.

Seoul Metropolitan Rapid Transit Corporation: 133-783, Seongdong-gu, Yongdap-dong 223-3, Seoul; tel. (2) 6311-2200; e-mail eumsj@smrt.co.kr; internet www.smrt.co.kr; operates lines 5–8; Pres. EUM SEONG-JIK.

Seoul Metropolitan Subway Corpn: 447-7, Bangbae-dong, Seocho-gu, Seoul; tel. (2) 520-5020; fax (2) 520-5039; internet www.seoulsubway.co.kr; f. 1981; length of 134.9 km (115 stations, lines 1–4); Pres. KIM YOUNG-KEOL.

ROADS

At the end of 2006 there were 102,062 km of roads. A network of motorways (3,103 km) links all the principal towns, the most important being the 428-km Seoul–Busan motorway. Improvements in relations with North Korea resulted in the commencement of work on a four-lane highway to link Seoul and the North Korean capital, Pyongyang, in September 2000. In February 2003 a road link between the two countries was reportedly opened.

Korea Expressway Corpn: 293-1, Kumto-dong, Sujong-gu, Seongnam, Gyeonggi-do 461-703; tel. (822) 2230-4114; fax (822) 2230-4308; internet www.freeway.co.kr; f. 1969; responsible for construction, maintenance and management of toll roads; Pres. LIEU CHULLHO.

SHIPPING

In December 2009 South Korea's merchant fleet (3,009 vessels) had a total displacement of 12.8m. grt. Major ports include Busan, Incheon, Donghae, Masan, Yeosu, Gunsan, Mokpo, Pohang, Ulsan, Jeju and Gwangyang.

Busan Port Authority: 79-9, Jungangdong 4-ga, Junggu, Busan 600-817; tel. (2) 999-3000; fax (2) 988-8878; e-mail bpmaster@busanpa.com; internet www.busanpa.com; f. 2004; Pres. KI TAE-ROH.

Korea Shipowners' Association: Sejong Bldg, 10th Floor, 100, Dangju-dong, Jongro-gu, Seoul 110-071; tel. (2) 739-1551; fax (2) 739-

THE REPUBLIC OF KOREA (SOUTH KOREA)

1558; e-mail korea@shipowners.or.kr; internet www.shipowners.or.kr; f. 1960; 181 shipping co mems (March 2011); Chair. LEE JONG-CHUL.

Korea Shipping Association: 660-10, Dungchon 3-dong, Gangseo-gu, Seoul 157-033; tel. (2) 6096-2000; fax (2) 6096-2059; e-mail kimny@haewoon.co.kr; internet www.haewoon.co.kr; f. 1962; management consulting and investigation, mutual insurance; 1,189 mems; Chair. PARK HONG-JIN; CEO JUNG YOU-SUB.

Principal Companies

DooYang Line Co Ltd: 170-8, Samseong-dong, Gangnam-gu, Seoul 135-091; tel. (2) 569-7722; fax (2) 550-1777; internet www.dooyang.co.kr; f. 1984; world-wide tramping and conventional liner trade; Pres. CHO DONG-HYUN.

Hanjin Shipping Ltd: 25-11, Yeouido-dong, Yeongdeungpo-gu, Seoul; tel. (2) 3770-6114; fax (2) 3770-6748; e-mail micaela@hanjin.com; internet www.hanjin.com; f. 1977; marine transport, harbour service, warehousing, shipping and repair, vessel sales, harbour department and cargo service; Chair. and CEO CHOI EUN-YOUNG.

Hyundai Merchant Marine Co Ltd: 1-7, Yeonje-dong, Jongno-gu, Seoul 110-052; tel. (2) 3706-5114; fax (2) 778-4341; internet www.hmm.co.kr; f. 1976; Pres. and CEO KIM SEONG-MAN.

Korea Line Corpn: 135-878 KLC Bldg, 145-9, Samseong-dong, Gangnam-gu, Seoul; tel. (2) 3701-0114; fax (2) 733-1610; internet www.korealines.co.kr; f. 1968; world-wide transport service and shipping agency service; Pres. KIM CHANG-SHIK.

STX Pan Ocean Co Ltd: STX Namsan Tower, 631 Namdaemunno 5-ga, Jung-nu, Seoul; tel. (2) 316-5114; fax (2) 316-5296; e-mail panocean@stxpanocean.com; internet www.stxpanocean.co.kr; f. 1966; transport of passenger cars and trucks, chemical and petroleum products, dry bulk cargo; STX Shipbuilding Co Ltd became the majority shareholder in 2004; Chair. KANG DUK-SOO.

CIVIL AVIATION

There are international airports at Incheon (Seoul), Gimpo (Seoul), Busan, Jeongju, Daegu, Gwangju, Jeju and Yangyang. The main gateway into Seoul is Incheon International Airport, located 52 km from Seoul, which opened for service in 2001. The second phase of construction was completed in mid-2008.

Asiana Airlines Inc: 47, Osae-dong, Gangseo-gu, Seoul; tel. (2) 2669-8000; fax (2) 2669-8180; internet flyasiana.com; f. 1988; serves 12 domestic cities and 67 destinations in 20 countries; fmrly Seoul Air International; CEO YOON YOUNG-DOO.

Hansung Airlines: Jeongju; tel. (43) 1599-1090; fax (43) 210-0520; internet www.gohansung.com; f. 2004; operates low-cost flights between Jeongju and Jeju City; CEO HAN WOO-BONG.

Jeju Air: tel. (64) 746-7003; fax (64) 746-7011; internet www.jejuair.net; f. 2005; 25% owned by Jeju provincial govt, 75% by the Aekyung Group; operates low-cost flights between Jeju and the mainland; CEO KIM JONG-CHUL.

Jin Air Co Ltd: 653-25 Deungchon-dong, Gangseo-gu, Seoul; internet www.jinair.com; f. 2008; low-cost subsidiary of Korean Air; CEO KIM JAE-KUN.

Korean Air: 1370, Gonghang-dong, Gangseo-gu, Seoul 157-712; tel. (2) 2656-7857; fax (2) 656-7289; internet www.koreanair.com; f. 1962; est. by the Govt, privately owned since 1969; fmrly Korean Air Lines (KAL); operates domestic and regional services and routes to the Americas, Europe, the Far East and the Middle East, serving 116 cities in 39 countries; Chair. and CEO CHO YANG-HO.

Tourism

South Korea's mountain scenery and historic sites are the principal attractions for tourists. Jeju Island, located some 100 km off the southern coast, is a popular resort. In comparison with the previous year, the number of visitor arrivals reportedly increased by 12.5% in 2010, to reach nearly 8.8m. Japan and the People's Republic of China are the leading sources of visitors. Receipts from tourism in 2008 amounted to US $12,783m.

Korea Tourism Organization: KTO Bldg, 40, Cheonggyecheon-ro, Jung-gu, Seoul 100-180; tel. (2) 729-9600; fax (2) 757-5997; e-mail webmaster@mail.knto.or.kr; internet kto.visitkorea.or.kr; f. 1962; est. as International Tourism Corpn; name changed to Korea National Tourism Corpn in 1982 and to Korea National Tourism Organization in 1996, before present name was adopted; Chair. and CEO LEE CHARM.

Korea Tourism Association: KTO Bldg, 8th Floor, 40, Cheonggyecheon-ro, Jung-gu, Seoul 100-180; tel. (2) 757-7485; fax (2) 757-7489; internet www.koreatravel.or.kr; f. 1963; Chair. SHIN JOONG-MOK.

Defence

As assessed at November 2010, the strength of the active armed forces was 655,000 (including an estimated 140,000 conscripts): army 522,000, navy 68,000, air force 65,000. Paramilitary forces included a 3m.-strong civilian defence corps. Military service is compulsory and lasts for 26 months. In November 2010 US forces stationed in South Korea comprised 17,130 army personnel, 254 navy, 7,857 air force and 133 marines.

Defence Expenditure: Budgeted at 25,600,000m. won for 2011.

Chairman of the Joint Chiefs of Staff: Gen. HAN MIN-KOO.

Chief of Staff (Army): Gen. KIM SANG-KI.

Chief of Staff (Air Force): Gen. PARK JONG-HEON.

Chief of Naval Operations: Adm. KIM SUNG-CHAN.

Education

Education, available free of charge, is compulsory for nine years between the ages of six and 15 years. Primary education begins at six years of age and lasts for six years. In 2007/08 enrolment at primary schools included 99% of children in the appropriate age-group. Secondary education begins at 12 years of age and lasts for up to six years, comprising two cycles of three years each. Enrolment at secondary schools in 2007/08 included 95% of children in the relevant age group. In 2006 school pupils were granted two Saturdays off school every month; previously, they had attended school six days every week. The Government was reportedly planning the introduction of a five-day school week in 2007. In 2007 there were 175 colleges and universities, with a student enrolment of 1,919,504. There were 1,042 graduate schools in that year. In 2001, according to UNESCO estimates, the rate of adult literacy averaged 97.9% (males 99.2%, females 96.6%). Expenditure on education by the central Government in 2007 was projected at 30,395,000m. won, representing 19.7% of total projected spending.

KOSOVO

Introductory Survey

LOCATION, CLIMATE, LANGUAGE, RELIGION, FLAG, CAPITAL

The Republic of Kosovo (Kosova), formerly the province officially named Kosovo and Metohija within the Republic of Serbia, is situated in the central Balkan peninsula in south-eastern Europe. There are borders with Serbia in the north-west and north-east, the former Yugoslav republic of Macedonia in the south, Albania in the south-west, and Montenegro to the west. The climate is continental. Under a new Constitution, approved in April 2008, the official languages of Kosovo are Albanian and Serbian, while the Turkish, Bosnian and Roma languages are also accorded official status at municipal level. The principal religion in Kosovo is Islam. Serbs are principally adherents of Orthodox Christianity, as represented by the Serbian Orthodox Church. The state flag (proportions 2 by 3) is blue, with an arc of six white stars above a golden map of Kosovo. The capital is Prishtina (Prishtinë—Priština).

CONTEMPORARY POLITICAL HISTORY

Historical Context

Kosovo was part of the Serbian state established by the Nemanja dynasty in 1166. The Serbian Orthodox Patriarchate was established in Kosovo in the 13th century, and the territory was the location of the defeat of the Serbs by the Turkish Ottoman Empire at Fushë Kosovë (Kosovo Polje—'the Field of Blackbirds') in 1389. After continued Albanian resistance to Ottoman rule, the League of Prizren political organization was established in 1878. Kosovo remained under Ottoman rule until its annexation by Serbia during the First Balkan War in 1912. During the Second World War (1939–45) Kosovo was annexed by Albania (in personal union with the Italian Crown). Following the establishment of the Federative People's Republic of Yugoslavia, the 1946 Constitution provided for the establishment of Kosovo and Metohija (as the region was renamed) and the northern territory of Vojvodina as autonomous units within Serbia. In 1963 the autonomous region of Kosovo and Metohija was formally upgraded in status to that of an autonomous province, a status that was confirmed by the 1974 Constitution, which also renamed the territory simply as Kosovo and increased the powers of the two autonomous provinces at the federal level of the state.

From the mid-1980s increasing Serb nationalism, and the rise to power of Slobodan Milošević (President of Serbia in 1989–97), exacerbated tensions in the province. A new Serbian Constitution of 1990 revoked the autonomy of Kosovo and Vojvodina; this was confirmed by the April 1992 Constitution that created the Federal Republic of Yugoslavia (FRY). A republic-wide referendum on a new Serbian Constitution, largely boycotted by the ethnic Albanians, was conducted on 2 July 1990, when a majority of Serbs approved the new Constitution. It was formally promulgated on 28 September, whereupon the designation of Kosovo reverted to that of Kosovo and Metohija (although this designation continued to be unpopular with the ethnic Albanian population of Kosovo). Meanwhile, following the constitutional referendum, 114 of 180 deputies in the Kosovo Assembly (Kuvendi i Kosovës/Skupština Kosova) met and declared Kosovo independent of Serbia. On 5 July the Serbian authorities dissolved the provincial Assembly and Government. The Kosovo presidency resigned in protest, and Serbia introduced a special administration. On 7 September members of the old representative body declared the Kosovo Assembly to have been reconvened and subsequently proclaimed a basic law of a 'Republic of Kosovo'. Meanwhile, elections, declared illegal by the Serbian authorities, had been held in the province on 24 May. The Democratic Alliance of Kosovo (DAK) secured the most seats in the 130-member Assembly, and the DAK leader, Ibrahim Rugova, was elected President of the self-proclaimed 'Republic of Kosovo'.

Domestic Political Affairs

Throughout the mid-1990s there were reports of harassment of Kosovo Albanians by Serbian police. The situation deteriorated further in 1996 with the emergence, in February, of an ethnic Albanian militant organization, the Kosovo Liberation Army (KLA), which announced its intention to achieve independence for Kosovo through armed resistance against the Serbian authorities, and began attacks against security forces. Special Serbian security units undertook reprisals against the Albanian population.

Negotiations regarding the implementation of a cease-fire in Kosovo and the withdrawal of Serbian forces continued throughout 1998. In October, following a North Atlantic Treaty Organization (NATO, see p. 368) ultimatum, Milošević, President of the FRY (Serbia and Montenegro) since the previous year, agreed to the presence in Kosovo of an Organization for Security and Co-operation in Europe (OSCE, see p. 385) mission, which began deployment in early November. Nevertheless, armed clashes between Serbian forces and the KLA increased. In January 1999 the bodies of 45 Albanians were discovered in the village of Reçak (Račak), increasing international concerns of a humanitarian crisis. In February a peace conference in Rambouillet, France, attended by Serbian and ethnic Albanian delegations, including KLA representatives, commenced. Despite the reluctance of the KLA to accept conditions for disarmament, the Albanian delegation signed the peace agreement on 18 March. However, the Serbian delegation continued to present objections to the peace plan; on 23 March the Serbian legislature adopted a resolution condemning aggression against its country and opposing the deployment of NATO forces in Kosovo.

On 24 March 1999 a NATO-led aerial bombardment of military and civilian installations in the FRY commenced. Serbian security forces in Kosovo subsequently conducted mass expulsions and large-scale massacres of the Albanian civilian population, resulting in the continued exodus of refugees from the province. According to the UN High Commissioner for Refugees (UNHCR), a total of 848,100 Albanians fled or were expelled from Kosovo. On 3 June a peace agreement providing for the withdrawal of Serbian forces from Kosovo and the deployment of a joint NATO-Russian peace-keeping force was approved by the Serbian legislature. On 10 June, following a Military Technical Agreement between NATO and the Federal Government, the withdrawal of Serbian forces from Kosovo commenced, and NATO officially suspended its air operations. On the same day a UN Security Council resolution was approved, authorizing the deployment of international civil and security presences in Kosovo, and providing for the establishment of the UN Interim Administration Mission in Kosovo (UNMIK) as the supreme legal and executive authority in the region. On 12 June both Russian and NATO troops entered Kosovo. By 20 June the Serb withdrawal had been completed and the multinational NATO-led Kosovo Force (KFOR), which had an authorized strength of up to 50,000 personnel, was established. Some three weeks after the end of the conflict, an estimated 600,000 Albanians had returned to Kosovo. Over the same period some 180,000 Serbs and Roma fled the province.

Kosovo under UN administration

In February 2000 Rugova announced the dissolution of the 'Republic of Kosovo' and of the DAK. In local government elections, held in Kosovo on 28 October, Rugova's Democratic League of Kosovo (DLK—a successor organization to the DAK) secured 58% of the votes cast to 30 municipal councils, while the Democratic Party of Kosovo (DPK), led by a former KLA commander, Hashim Thaçi, won 27% of the votes. Elections to 100 seats of the 120-member Kosovo Assembly were conducted on 17 November 2001, under a UNMIK programme for establishing partial and provisional self-government in the province. (The remaining 20 seats were reserved for representatives of Serbs and other minority ethnic groups.) The DLK secured 47 seats, while the DPK won 26 seats and a coalition of Serb parties 22 seats. On 4 March 2002, following protracted inter-party discussions, Rugova was elected President of Kosovo. Under a coalition agreement, a member of the DPK, Bajram Rexhepi, became Prime Minister, and a 10-member Government (in which the DLK held four portfolios and the DPK a further two) was subsequently established. In April the Serb coalition agreed to join the administration.

In March 2004 the deaths of three Albanian boys, who had allegedly been pursued by a group of Serbs into the Ibar River, precipitated rioting in Mitrovicë (Kosovska Mitrovica), which escalated into several days of clashes between the Serbian and Albanian communities throughout Kosovo. Some 2,000 KFOR reinforcements were dispatched to quell the violence. Some 19 civilians (11 Albanians and eight Serbs) were killed in the clashes, while some 4,000 Serbs and Roma were forced to flee from their residences, after being attacked by Albanian rioters. At elections to the Kosovo Assembly on 23 October, the DLK secured 45.4% of the votes cast, retaining 47 seats in the 120-member legislature. The DPK won 28.9% of the votes cast, increasing its representation to 30 seats, while the Alliance for the Future of Kosovo (AFK) obtained 8.4% of the votes cast and nine seats. The DLK negotiated a coalition agreement, whereby the leader of the AFK, Ramush Haradinaj, became the new Prime Minister on 3 December. The election of Haradinaj, a former senior KLA leader who had been under investigation by the International Criminal Tribunal for the former Yugoslavia (ICTY, see p. 20) for alleged war crimes in Kosovo, was strongly criticized by Serbian parties. Although the overall rate of participation by voters in the province was recorded at some 53.6% of the registered electorate, only about 0.3% of the Serb community participated in the poll. (Serbs retained an allocation of 10 seats in the Assembly, but continued to boycott the provisional institutions.) On 8 March 2005 Haradinaj, having received an indictment from the ICTY on a total of 37 charges, resigned as Prime Minister and surrendered to the Tribunal. His indictment prompted widespread protests in the province (causing the dispatch of British military reinforcements). On 23 March a new Government, led by Bajram Kosumi, also of the AFK, was established. (In April 2008 the ICTY acquitted Haradinaj.)

Following a favourable report of the European Commission on Serbia and Montenegro (as the FRY had been reconstituted in 2003) in April 2005, the resolution of Kosovo's future status became an increasingly pressing issue. The European Commission pledged to continue support for the eventual integration of Kosovo into European institutions, provided that the Kosovo Government demonstrated commitment to reforms and democratic principles. In September delegations from the Governments of Serbia and Kosovo met in Vienna, Austria, for preliminary discussions. On 4 October a UN Special Envoy officially submitted a review to the Secretary-General of the organization, stating that the Kosovo Government had made significant progress towards establishing executive, legislative and judicial institutions. On 24 October the UN Security Council endorsed the initiation of final status negotiations on Kosovo. In November the Serbian Government adopted a resolution rejecting the independence of Kosovo, while the Kosovo Assembly approved a motion stating that it would accept only independence as the final status of the territory. Later that month former Finnish President Martti Ahtisaari, who had been appointed UN Special Envoy for the Future Status Process for Kosovo, commenced separate discussions with Serbian and Kosovo leaders. On 21 January 2006 Rugova died following a period of illness. Later that month the DLK nominated Fatmir Sejdiu to succeed Rugova; on 10 February Sejdiu was elected unopposed as the new President by the Kosovo Assembly. On 1 March Kosumi resigned as Prime Minister, and nine days later the Kosovo Assembly voted to approve Agim Çeku, a former KLA chief of staff, as his successor. Meanwhile, the first round of final status negotiations on Kosovo commenced in Vienna on 20–21 February. Direct high-level discussions, the first to involve the Presidents and Prime Ministers of Serbia and Kosovo since 1999, were conducted in Vienna in July; the Kosovo delegation reiterated demands for full independence for the province, while the Serbian Prime Minister, Vojislav Koštunica, maintained that Serbia would not accept a loss of territory. By the end of 2006 the two delegations had failed to reach any agreement.

On 2 February 2007 Ahtisaari presented his recommendations for the future status of Kosovo to the Serbian and Kosovo authorities and invited the delegations to engage in consultations on the draft in Vienna. The discussions, which commenced later that month, ended without success in March; Ahtisaari concluded that there was no further prospect of achieving a negotiated agreement. On 26 March Ahtisaari submitted to the UN Security Council the finalized Comprehensive Proposal for the Kosovo Status Settlement, which recommended independence for the province, initially under international military and civilian supervision. Kosovo was to adopt a constitution, flag and anthem, and be granted rights to membership of international organizations; the rights of all minority groups living in the province, particularly the Kosovo Serbs, were to be protected. Under the Proposal, an International Civilian Representative, operating under a UN and European Union (EU, see p. 270) mandate, would be appointed to supervise the implementation of the Settlement, and would be empowered to veto legislation and dismiss local officials. KFOR would continue to provide security in the province, while the EU would deploy a police mission to assist in the development of institutions of law enforcement. On 3 April Koštunica, speaking in a debate at the UN Security Council, declared that Serbia rejected the Proposal, confirming the result of a vote in the Serbian legislature in February. On 5 April Ahtisaari's Proposal was approved by 100 of the 101 votes cast in the Kosovo Assembly. During a visit to Belgrade later that month, the Russian Minister of Foreign Affairs reiterated previous statements that Russia (as a permanent member of the Security Council) would not support an imposed resolution on the status of Kosovo that was not acceptable to the Serbian Government. Prime Minister Çeku stated that Kosovo was prepared to declare unilateral independence in the event of a protracted delay. From late April intensive discussions on Ahtisaari's Proposal continued in the UN Security Council; however, in July it was announced that it had proved impossible to secure a resolution. In August a further series of negotiations began between Serbian and Kosovo delegations, with mediation by the USA, the EU and Russia, but again failed to resolve the impasse. On 10 December the UN Secretary-General was informed that an agreement could not be concluded.

Meanwhile, amid increasing expectations of a unilateral declaration of independence, legislative elections were conducted in Kosovo on 17 November 2007. According to official results, the DPK secured the highest number of votes cast, with 34.3% of the total, taking 37 seats in the Assembly, while the DLK received some 22.6% of the votes cast and 25 seats. With a further boycott of the elections by Serb parties, a rate of participation of about 43% of the electorate was recorded. After lengthy negotiations, the DPK and the DLK reached a coalition agreement. On 9 January 2008 a coalition Government, headed by Thaçi, and comprising eight members of the DPK, six members of the DLK, two representatives of Serb groups and one representative of the ethnic Turkish community, was approved by the Assembly. With both main parties in the administration in favour of independence, Thaçi confirmed to the Assembly that a declaration of independence was imminent, and would receive the support of the USA and most EU member states. On the same day Sejdiu was re-elected President in a third round of voting in the Assembly for a term that was, in an amendment to the existing Constitutional Framework for Provisional Government, extended to five years. Jakup Krasniqi of the DPK was elected President of the Assembly.

Declaration of independence

On 17 February 2008 the Assembly of Kosovo endorsed a declaration establishing the province as the Republic of Kosovo (Kosova), a sovereign state independent from Serbia, the resolution adopted being based on Ahtisaari's Comprehensive Proposal for the Kosovo Status Settlement and in accordance with UN Security Council Resolution 1244 (of 1999). Serbia immediately protested that the declaration of independence contravened international law and demanded that it be annulled. An emergency meeting of the UN Security Council failed to agree on a new resolution, with Russia, in continued strong support of Serbia, and the People's Republic of China opposing Kosovo's sovereignty among the permanent members of the Council. Several countries, including Albania, France, the USA and the United Kingdom, extended recognition to Kosovo on 18 February 2008, and were rapidly followed by a number of other states. On 28 February an International Steering Group appointed a Dutch diplomat, Pieter Feith, already the EU Special Representative, as an International Civilian Representative, to supervise the implementation of the Settlement. An EU Rule of Law Mission in Kosovo (EULEX), comprising some 1,900 foreign personnel, was to be deployed in Kosovo to support the authorities in maintaining public order. In March one member of UNMIK was killed in fierce clashes between Serb protesters and UNMIK and KFOR troops in Mitrovica. Serbia insisted that it intended to organize polls for its legislative and local elections (scheduled for 11 May) in the Serb-dominated municipalities in Kosovo. Also in March Serbia announced that it intended to submit a legal challenge against Kosovo's declaration of independence at the International Court of Justice (ICJ, see p. 23) in The Hague, Netherlands, and would apply for international support at the UN General Assembly. A new Constitution, which had been drafted by a Constitutional Commission in accordance with the principles of the Settlement, was adopted by the Assembly on 9 April, after being approved by Feith. The Constitution, which declared Kosovo to be an independent and sovereign state, was to enter into effect on 15 June, when UNMIK was officially to transfer its functions to the Kosovo authorities. However, during the transitional period it became evident that the deployment of EULEX would not proceed as envisaged, owing to the refusal of Kosovo Serbs and the Serbian Government to accept an EU mission. A report by the UN Secretary-General on developments in Kosovo, published at the beginning of April, stated that UNMIK's mandate would remain in force under Resolution 1244, pending a further decision by the UN Security Council.

The new Constitution entered into effect on 15 June 2008, as scheduled. Serbia, supported principally by Russia, continued to oppose the deployment of EULEX. Consequently, UN Secretary-General Ban Ki-Moon presented a plan to the Security Council, whereby UNMIK was to be reorganized and substantially reduced in size to allow an increased EU operational role. On 20 June an Italian diplomat, Lamberto Zannier, was appointed as the new Special Representative of the UN Secretary-General and head of UNMIK, replacing Joachim Rücker, who had held that position since September 2006. The NATO Secretary-General announced that the remaining KFOR contingent was to organize the dissolution of the Kosovo Protection Corps (KPC—formed in 1999 largely on the basis of the KLA) and the establishment of a 2,500-member multi-ethnic Kosovo Security Force. Following polls conducted among Kosovo Serbs on 11 May 2008, without the recognition of the Kosovo Government, on 28 June a parallel legislature comprising representatives of the Serb community from 26 municipalities, the 'Assembly of the Community of Municipalities of the Autonomous Province of Kosovo and Metohija', was convened in Mitrovica.

In early August 2008 Thaçi appointed Kosovo's first Minister of Defence. In September it was announced that Kosovo had appointed its first 10 envoys to countries that had recognized its statehood, while a number of diplomatic missions in Prishtina had become embassies. In October the decision of Montenegro and the former Yugoslav republic of Macedonia to extend recognition to Kosovo prompted strong protests from the Serbian Government, which expelled the ambassadors of both countries. In the same month the UN General Assembly, in support of Serbia, voted in favour of referring to the ICJ the question of whether Kosovo's unilateral declaration of independence from Serbia was in accordance with international law.

Following the continued refusal of Kosovo Serbs to accept the deployment of EULEX, in early November 2008 the UN Secretary-General presented an amended six-point plan on the reconfiguration of the international presence in Kosovo, under which police, customs officers and judges in the Serb-majority areas would receive directives from UNMIK, while those in Albanian-majority areas would be the responsibility of EULEX. (This followed an agreement in late October by the US Administration to participate in EU operations in Kosovo.) Despite international pressure, the Kosovo Government remained opposed to EULEX's deployment under the compromise plan, and protests were staged in Prishtina by ethnic Albanian groups in opposition to the EU presence. The Serbian Government insisted, as a precondition of its acceptance of EULEX, that the plan be officially approved by the UN Security Council, that it be neutral with regard to Kosovo's status and that it would not be mandated to implement Ahtisaari's Comprehensive Proposal. On 26 November the UN Security Council unanimously endorsed the six-point plan under the stipulated terms. On 9 December EULEX began deployment throughout the country, including Mitrovica, which proceeded without incidents of violence; the police component of UNMIK was subsequently reduced from 1,582 to 55 personnel; it was later confirmed that a reduced UNMIK presence was to continue in the country indefinitely under Resolution 1244.

In January 2009 the KPC was officially dissolved and replaced by the Kosovo Security Force, which was to be primarily responsible for crisis management, civil protection and mine clearance. Several thousand Serbs demonstrated in Mitrovica in protest at the establishment of the new body, claiming that it threatened regional stability. In February a Security Council, comprising the Prime Minister, Deputy Prime Ministers and a number of ministers, was established as Kosovo's highest body on security matters. Celebrations for the first anniversary of Kosovo's declaration of independence took place without incident; however, 80 opposition deputies of the Serbian legislature joined the Kosovo Serb 'Assembly' in approving a declaration affirming the constitutional status of Kosovo within Serbia and rejecting the activities of the Kosovo institutions.

Municipal elections

In late June 2009 former Prime Minister Agim Çeku was arrested in Bulgaria, under an international warrant issued by Serbia for alleged war crimes committed while he was a KLA military commander. The Serbian Government subsequently requested Çeku's extradition; however, he was released on the order of a Bulgarian court and at the end of June returned to Kosovo, after the Bulgarian prosecution decided not to appeal against the court's ruling. In August seven people were injured in clashes between Serbs and Albanians in Mitrovica, following Serb protests against the reconstruction of Albanian houses in the ethnically divided Brđani district of the town.

The first elections since independence to elect councils and mayors in Kosovo's 36 municipalities (which included six new municipalities) took place on 15 November 2009. The rate of participation by voters was recorded at about 45.4%, after a Serb boycott urged by the Serbian Government was only partially observed. A mission from the European Network of Election Monitoring Organizations released an initial report that concluded that the elections generally met international standards, but nevertheless emphasized a number of shortcomings. A second round of voting was conducted on 13 December in 21 municipalities where no candidate had secured more than 50% of the votes in the first round. According to the Central Election Commission (CEC), the DPK secured 16 municipalities, the DLK seven municipalities (including Prishtina, where it won 46.4% of the votes), the AFK five municipalities and the Independent Liberal Party (Samostalna liberalna stranka—SLS) three. Voting was repeated in two municipalities on 31 January 2010, and in a further constituency on 14 March, after allegations of irregularities were upheld.

At the beginning of December 2009 proceedings began at the ICJ to determine the legality of Kosovo's declaration of independence; 29 states, including Russia and the USA, presented statements on the case. In January 2010 Serbia's Minister of Kosovo and Metohija, Goran Bogdanović, was expelled from Kosovo, shortly before meeting local Serb representatives, on the grounds that he had intended to undertake illicit political activities. At the end of January NATO reduced the number of troops deployed in KFOR from some 14,000 to just under 10,000, in view of the improved security situation. In early February the Special Representative of the EU and International Civilian Representative in Kosovo, Pieter Feith, announced the initiation of preparations for the establishment of a Serb-majority municipality in northern Mitrovica, which was to be followed by the creation of three further Serb-majority municipalities, as part of a government strategy to establish institutional authority in northern Kosovo. Later in February Fejzullah Hasani was appointed President of the Supreme Court, and 21 other judges and prosecutors were nominated, as part of efforts to create an independent, multi-ethnic judiciary. At the end of March the DPK and the DLK agreed to the replacement of three ministers from each party in a government reorganization (which also included the creation of a new Ministry of Integration), following increasing concerns over the need for good governance to address public corruption; notably, former Prime Minister Bajram Rexhepi was appointed as the new Minister of Internal Affairs. On 30 May unauthorized elections were organized to the Serb 'Assembly' in Mitrovica, amid protests and tensions between Kosovo Serbs and Kosovo Albanians. In July two bombs were thrown into a crowd of Kosovo Serbs, who were demonstrating against the Government's plan to open an office in Mitrovica; one person was killed, and 11 others were injured. Later that month the appeals chamber of the ICTY overturned the acquittal of Haradinaj and an associate, Idriz Balaj, in April 2008, on the grounds that witnesses had been intimidated, and ordered their retrial on part of the original indictment.

Recent developments: early legislative elections

On 22 July 2010 the ICJ issued a non-binding, advisory opinion that Kosovo's declaration of independence had not breached international law, UN Security Council Resolution 1244, or the constitutional framework. The ruling prompted public celebrations in Prishtina, while Serbia reaffirmed its intention to continue to withhold recognition of the independence of Kosovo. In

KOSOVO

August Rexhepi accused the Serbian Government of encouraging the Kosovo Serb 'Assembly' to draft a declaration of independence. In early September the UN General Assembly adopted a resolution supported by Serbia and the 27 EU member states urging a direct dialogue between Serbia and Kosovo on ensuing issues. On 27 September Sejdiu tendered his resignation as President of Kosovo, following a ruling by the Constitutional Council that holding the office was incompatible with his chairmanship of the DLK. (He was subsequently replaced on an acting basis by parliamentary President Krasniqi.) In October Sejdiu withdrew the DLK from the coalition Government, which consequently lost its majority in the Assembly. In early November the Assembly adopted a motion of no confidence in the Government, after Thaçi urged DPK deputies to support it and thereby bring an end to the institutional crisis; early legislative elections were subsequently scheduled for 12 December. As a consequence of divisions within the DLK, two prominent party members, a former Minister of Health, Bujar Bukoshi, and Uke Rugova (son of former President Rugova), announced the establishment of an alternative candidate list to contest the elections. On 7 November the mayor of Prishtina, Isa Mustafa, was elected Chairman of the DLK at a party convention, replacing Sejdiu.

In December 2010 Swiss senator and Council of Europe rapporteur Dick Marty presented a report (which was subsequently adopted by the Parliamentary Assembly of the Council of Europe—PACE) claiming that human-organ trafficking operations had occurred during and after the 1999 conflict in Kosovo, and implicating Thaçi; EULEX was charged with investigating the allegations, which the Governments of Kosovo and Albania strenuously denied.

The legislative elections on 7 December 2010 were monitored by officials from embassies in Kosovo, under the co-ordination of Feith, together with a large number of local observers. Although Serb voters in the north of the country again boycotted the elections, greater numbers than previously participated in central and southern regions. Following allegations by all parties of voter intimidation and major irregularities during the elections, complaints were upheld in five municipalities, where polls were repeated on 9 January and (in the case of Mitrovica) on 23 January 2011. The final election results were released by the CEC on 7 February, following the resolution of appeals: the DPK, with 32.1% of the votes cast, secured 34 seats, while the DLK won 24.7% of the votes and 27 seats; an ethnic Albanian nationalist party that opposed international involvement in Kosovo, Self-Determination!, was third placed, with 12.7% of the votes and 14 seats, followed by the AFK, with 11.0% of votes and 12 seats, and a coalition led by the New Kosovo Alliance (Aleanca Kosova e Re—AKR), with 7.3% and eight seats. The rate of participation by the registered electorate was estimated at about 45%. On 22 February, under a coalition agreement reached between the DPK and the AKR, a construction industry magnate and President of the AKR, Behgjet Pacolli, was elected unopposed as the President of Kosovo in a third round of voting in the new Assembly (with opposition parties boycotting the session). On the same day Thaçi was re-elected Prime Minister and the appointment of a new coalition Government was approved. The five Deputy Prime Ministers in the new administration included for the first time a Kosovo Serb, the Chairman of the SLS, Slobodan Petrović. In early March Kosovo and Serbian delegations met in Brussels, Belgium, for EU-supported discussions reported to concern regional co-operation, freedom of movement and issues related to the rule of law; the dialogue was subsequently endorsed by a resolution adopted in the Kosovo Assembly. Following a challenge by the DLK, on 28 March the Constitutional Court ruled the election of Pacolli to be illegitimate, owing to the absence of the requisite parliamentary quorum; Pacolli resigned from the presidency on 30 March. Following an unprecedented agreement between the DPK, the DLK and the AKR on a consensus candidate, on 7 April the deputy director of the Kosovo police, Maj.-Gen. Atifete Jahjaga, was elected President with 80 of 100 votes cast in the Assembly, becoming the country's first female Head of State.

CONSTITUTION AND GOVERNMENT

A new Constitution entered into effect in Kosovo on 15 June 2008, largely supplanting the arrangements in place since the establishment of the UN Interim Administration Mission in Kosovo (UNMIK) as the supreme executive and legal authority in the territory in June 1999, the Kosovo Assembly (Kuvendi i Kosovës/Skupština Kosova) having adopted a declaration of independence on 17 February 2008. (The Constitution of Serbia continues to refer to Kosovo and Metohija as an integral part of that state.) This declaration was based on the Comprehensive Proposal for the Kosovo Status Settlement drawn up by the UN Special Envoy of the Secretary-General for the Future Status Process for Kosovo, Martti Ahtisaari, and in accordance with UN Security Council Resolution 1244 (of 1999). An International Civilian Representative, who is also the Special Representative of the European Union (EU, see p. 270), was appointed by an International Steering Group on 28 February 2008 to supervise the implementation of the Settlement. An EU Rule of Law Mission in Kosovo (EULEX), which became operational under the overall authority of the UN in December, was deployed in Kosovo to maintain public order and security, and to assist in the development of legal and judicial institutions. A reduced UNMIK presence was to continue in the country indefinitely under Resolution 1244. The International Steering Group was to conduct its first review of the implementation of the Status Settlement after a period of two years.

Under the Constitution, the Kosovo Assembly comprises 120 deputies, of whom 100 are directly elected (the remaining 20 seats are reserved for the elected representatives of specified minority ethnic communities, including eight allocated to Serbs). The Assembly has a nine-member Presidency. The President of Kosovo is elected by the Assembly for a five-year term (renewable only once). The President nominates a Prime Minister, who proposes a Government, for approval by the Assembly. Kosovo comprises seven regions, which are divided into 36 municipalities.

REGIONAL AND INTERNATIONAL CO-OPERATION

Following Kosovo's unilateral declaration of independence on 17 February 2008, a total of 75 UN member states, including 22 of the 27 member states of the European Union (EU, see p. 270), recognized Kosovo as an independent sovereign state by mid-May 2011. Kosovo joined the Central European Free Trade Agreement (CEFTA, see p. 446) in July 2007, and became a member of the Vienna Economic Forum (an organization promoting regional investment opportunities) in March 2009.

On 29 June 2009 Kosovo was formally admitted to both the World Bank and the IMF.

ECONOMIC AFFAIRS

In 2009, according to estimates by the UN, the gross national income (GNI) of Kosovo was US $5,842m., equivalent to $3,240 per head. During 2000–09, it was estimated, the population declined at an average annual rate of 0.7%. During 2000–09 gross domestic product (GDP) per head increased, in real terms, at an average annual rate of 5.2%. Overall GDP grew, in real terms, at an average annual rate of 5.9% in 2000–09; growth was 4.0% in 2009.

Agriculture (including hunting, forestry and fishing) contributed some 14.5% of GDP in 2007. In 2008 about 8.0% of the total employed labour force were engaged in the sector. Kosovo's principal crops are wheat, potatoes, maize and peppers. According to UN figures, agricultural production decreased at an average annual rate of 7.9% in 2000–09, but increased by 2.1% in 2009.

Industry (including mining, manufacturing, construction and power) contributed some 26.4% of GDP in 2007, and engaged 24.0% of the employed labour force in 2008. Industrial production decreased at an average annual rate of 0.6% in 2000–09, according to UN figures. Output increased by 3.7% in 2009.

The mining sector contributed some 0.9% of GDP in 2007, and mining and quarrying engaged 1.5% of the employed labour force in 2008. One of the principal minerals extracted is halloysite, a clay mineral used in the production of porcelain and bone china. More significantly, Kosovo has some 14.7m. metric tons of proven lignite reserves. Lead, zinc, chromium and bauxite are also mined.

Manufacturing and utilities together contributed some 13.5% of GDP in 2007. The manufacturing sector employed 8.7% of the population in 2008. Mining, manufacturing and utilities together declined at an average annual rate of 4.9% in 2000–09, according to UN figures, but increased by 1.8% in 2009.

The construction sector contributed some 12.0% of GDP in 2007, and engaged 8.6% of the employed labour force in 2008. The GDP of the sector declined at an average annual rate of 12.5% in 2000–09. Sectoral GDP decreased by 3.9% in 2008, but increased by 6.4% in 2009.

Energy in Kosovo is derived principally from coal (which contributes, on average, 97% of total electricity generated).

KOSOVO

Imports of mineral fuels accounted for 14.7% of the value of total imports to Kosovo in 2009.

Services contributed some 59.2% of GDP in 2007, and engaged 68.1% of the employed labour force in 2008. Important areas of the services sector include wholesale and retail trade, education and administration (which engaged 9.7% of the working population). According to UN estimates, GDP in the services sector increased at an average annual rate of 13.3% in 2000–09; sectoral GDP rose by 2.7% in 2009.

In 2008 Kosovo recorded a visible trade deficit of €1,634m. and there was a deficit of €732m. on the current account of the balance of payments. In 2009 the principal source of imports to Kosovo was the former Yugoslav republic of Macedonia (FYRM), accounting for 15.1% of the total; other major sources were Germany, Serbia, Turkey and the People's Republic of China. The principal market for exports in that year was Italy (taking 28.0% of total exports); other important purchasers were Albania, the FYRM and Switzerland. The main exports in 2009 were base metals (accounting for 53.4% of export trade), in particular iron and steel. Exports of mineral products, vegetable products and prepared foodstuffs, beverages, alcohol and tobacco were also significant. The principal imports in 2009 were mineral products (which accounted for 17.1% of imports), machinery and mechanical products, prepared foodstuffs, vehicles and transport equipment, base metals and chemical products.

In 2008 the overall budgetary deficit for Kosovo was €174.8m., equivalent to 5.1% of GDP. In 2002–10 the rate of inflation in Kosovo increased at an average annual rate of 1.6%. Consumer prices declined by 2.4% in 2009, but increased by 3.5% in 2010. The rate of unemployment in Kosovo was estimated at 47.5% in 2008.

Kosovo's economy was formerly concentrated in extractive industry, but much of the sector became inoperative as a result of the NATO bombardment in March–June 1999 (see Contemporary Political History), compounding long-term neglect and lack of investment. Post-conflict reconstruction was supported by substantial donor assistance. The UN Interim Administration Mission in Kosovo (UNMIK) introduced an external trade regime and customs administration, and extensive economic reforms were undertaken. The privatization of socially owned enterprises commenced in 2002. Following its declaration of independence in 2008, Kosovo remained one of the poorest territories in Europe and continued to be highly reliant upon remittances from abroad. The Government declared that efforts to combat 'grey' (semi-licit) market activity, corruption and organized crime were a priority. Kosovo was officially admitted to the IMF and the World Bank in June 2009. In a statement issued in that month, the IMF commended the Kosovo authorities' progress in improving the stability of the state, which had resulted in its rapid admission. The Government's principal objectives were improvements in tax administration and extensive reform of the energy sector, including the privatization of the publicly owned electricity company. The continuing inability of the Kosovo institutions to exert authority in northern Serb-dominated areas, or to obtain recognition for the independence of Kosovo from several important states internationally also presented substantial challenges to Kosovo's economic development. In early 2010 the announcement of a tender to construct a new thermal power plant represented part of the government strategy to resolve severe energy shortages and reduce the cost of electricity imports. In July the IMF approved an 18-month stand-by credit arrangement of US $139.6m. for Kosovo. The Fund considered that both exports and foreign remittances had begun to recover in 2010 (following the adverse affects of the international financial crisis in the previous year), while real GDP growth, which had slowed in 2009, was projected to increase slightly that year. In November, despite criticism from opposition parties, legislation providing for the rapid privatization of the state telecommunications entity was adopted as part of the planned restructuring of public enterprises. Early legislative elections were conducted in December, following the dissolution of the governing coalition. At the beginning of 2011 the IMF expressed concern at government commitments (under a pre-election pledge issued by the Prime Minister) to raise substantially the salaries of teachers and other public sector workers, in contravention of the terms of the Fund-supported financial programme for 2011.

PUBLIC HOLIDAYS

2012: 1–2 January (New Year's Day), 7 January (Orthodox Christmas), 17 February (Independence Day), 9 April (Constitution Day and Catholic Easter Monday), 1 May (Labour Day), 9 May (Europe Day), 18 August* (Small Bayram, end of Ramadan), 25 October* (Great Bayram, Feast of the Sacrifice), 25 December (Catholic Christmas).

* These holidays are dependent on the Islamic lunar calendar and may vary by one or two days from the dates given.

Statistical Survey

Source (unless otherwise indicated): Statistical Office of Kosovo, 10000 Prishtina, Rruga Zenel Salihu 4; tel. (38) 235111; fax (38) 235033; e-mail esk@ks-gov.net; internet www.ks-gov.net/esk.

Area and Population

AREA, POPULATION AND DENSITY

Area (sq km)	10,908*
Population (census results)	
31 March 1981	1,584,440
31 March 1991†	1,956,196
Population (official estimates at 31 December)‡	
2009	2,180,686
2010 (preliminary)	2,207,896
Density (per sq km) at 31 December 2010	202.4

* 4,212 sq miles.
† Assessment of the Office of Statistics of the Socialist Federal Republic of Yugoslavia.
‡ Assessment of the Statistical Office of Kosovo.

POPULATION BY ETHNIC GROUP
(official estimates at 1 January 2006)

Ethnic group	Population ('000)	%
Albanians	1,932	92.0
Serbs	111	5.3
Roma	24	1.1
Turks	8	0.4
Others	25	1.2
Total	**2,100**	**100.0**

1991 census ('000): Albanians 1,596 (81.6%); Serbs 194 (9.9%); Roma 46 (2.3%); Turks 10 (0.5%); Others 110 (5.6%).

KOSOVO

BIRTHS, MARRIAGES AND DEATHS

	Registered live births Number	Rate (per 1,000)	Registered marriages Number	Rate (per 1,000)	Registered deaths Number	Rate (per 1,000)
2002	36,136	18.2	18,280	9.2	5,654	2.8
2003	31,994	15.9	17,034	8.4	6,417	3.2
2004	35,063	17.2	16,989	8.3	6,399	3.1
2005	37,218	18.0	15,732	7.6	7,207	3.5
2006	34,187	16.3	15,825	7.5	7,479	3.6
2007	33,112	15.6	16,824	7.9	6,681	3.1
2008	34,399	16.0	17,950	8.3	6,852	3.2
2009	34,240	15.7	20,209	9.3	7,030	3.2

Life expectancy (years at birth, official estimates): 69 (males 67; females 71) in 2003.

EMPLOYMENT
(labour force survey, percentage distribution)

	2006	2007	2008
Agriculture, hunting, forestry and fishing	21.4	14.6	8.0
Mining and quarrying	1.5	1.0	1.5
Manufacturing	7.3	10.4	8.7
Electricity, gas and water supply	3.6	2.7	5.2
Construction	8.1	6.6	8.6
Wholesale and retail trade; repair of motor vehicles, motorcycles and personal and household goods	16.4	16.9	17.1
Hotels and restaurants	2.8	3.9	4.5
Transport, storage and communications	3.7	4.5	5.6
Financial intermediation	1.4	1.1	1.8
Real estate, renting and business activities	2.1	1.4	2.6
Public administration and defence; compulsory social security	7.8	9.6	9.7
Education	11.7	12.1	13.6
Health and social work	5.4	7.0	6.5
Other community, social and personal service activities	7.0	8.3	6.7

Note: Reliable estimates of the number of employed people were not available. According to the results of an official agricultural household survey conducted at the end of 2005, some 500,000 farm residents of working age were engaged in some level of farming activity (of which 135,000 were employed in this activity on a full-time basis). An official statistical overview of some 54,000 registered private sector businesses at the end of 2002 recorded 186,000 employees, while the number of people engaged in public administration at the end of 2005 totalled 74,081.

Registered unemployed (at 31 December 2008): 335,942. Note: According to official estimates, some 47.5% of the total labour force were unemployed in 2008.

Agriculture

PRINCIPAL CROPS
('000 metric tons)

	2005	2007	2008
Wheat	273.4	207.2	293.1
Barley	11.3	3.7	6.4
Oats	9.8	7.8	8.9
Maize (incl. mixed crops)	79.9	37.5	58.5
Potatoes	87.4	95.1	104.0
Tomatoes	15.0	14.7	20.6
Peppers	55.0	36.0	51.3
Pumpkins (incl. mixed crops)	8.3	5.0	11.6
Cabbages	18.9	15.4	19.0
Onions	11.0	10.9	16.0
Beans (incl. mixed crops)	7.5	2.5	6.2
Cucumbers	6.1	7.1	9.0
Watermelons	13.5	15.0	24.7
Apples	7.1	6.3	12.6
Pears	2.8	1.8	2.9
Plums	12.0	8.0	10.9
Vine grapes	2.2	2.8	1.9
Other grapes	3.5	3.5	8.6

Note: Data exclude second crops and autumn crops; production from state-owned enterprises is also excluded. Data for 2006 are not available.

LIVESTOCK
('000 head, October–December, unless otherwise indicated)

	2006	2007	2008
Horses	6.7	6.1	5.0
Cattle	382.0	321.6	341.6
Pigs	68.2	39.6	26.8
Sheep	100.8	139.2	124.1
Goats	12.1	12.6	8.9
Chickens	2,337.1	2,058.8	2,046.9
Other poultry	187.4	219.4	166.5

Note: Data exclude livestock belonging to state-owned enterprises.

LIVESTOCK PRODUCTS
(total value of products sold, € '000)

	2007	2008
Meat	2,955.5	2,331.4
Milk	15,266.4	20,995.6
Fat	85.8	343.9
Other dairy products	463.6	1,480.3
Eggs	616.6	1,389.7
Honey	871.6	958.7
Total (incl. others)	24,135.2	33,139.7

Note: Data exclude production by state-owned enterprises.

Forestry

FORESTRY REMOVALS
('000 cubic metres)

	2005	2007	2008
Fuel wood	393.1	468.9	451.7
Total (incl. others)	400.5	482.9	456.0

Note: Data exclude removals by state-owned enterprises. Data for 2006 are not available.

KOSOVO

Statistical Survey

Mining

('000 metric tons)

	2007	2008	2009
Coal	6,715.4	7,842.0	7,870.7

Industry

(million kWh)

	2007	2008	2009
Electric energy	4,309	4,506	5,349

Finance

CURRENCY AND EXCHANGE RATES

Monetary Units
100 cent = 1 euro (€).

Sterling, Dollar and Euro Equivalents (31 December 2010)
£1 sterling = 1.172 euros;
US $1 = 0.748 euros;
€10 = £8.54 = $13.36.

Average Exchange Rate (euros per US $)
2008 0.6827
2009 0.7198
2010 0.7550

BUDGET
(consolidated accounts, € million)

Revenue	2006	2007	2008
Tax revenue	621.5	716.2	786.7
Direct taxes	119.6	132.7	146.7
Indirect taxes	501.9	583.5	640.0
Value-added tax	258.6	313.8	362.0
Excise duties	161.9	191.4	205.2
Trade duties	82.3	81.2	80.7
Non-tax revenue	91.5	108.1	114.8
Statistical discrepancy	—	75.0	−12.9
Total	**713.1**	**899.3**	**888.6**

Expenditure	2006	2007	2008
Current expenditure	502.3	506.4	612.5
Wages and salaries	203.8	209.0	219.9
Goods and services	143.0	144.9	173.7
Subsidies and transfers	155.4	153.0	218.9
Capital expenditure and net lending	132.2	148.8	371.8
Statistical discrepancy	—	—	79.1
Total	**634.5**	**655.2**	**1,063.4**

2009: *Revenue:* Tax revenue 815.8; Non-tax revenue 130.0; Dividends 200.0; Total 1,145.9. *Expenditure:* Current 694.0 (wages and salaries 264.4, goods and services 172.7, subsidies and transfers 256.9); Capital 400.4; Total (incl. others) 1,109.9.

2010: *Revenue:* Tax revenue 890.5; Non-tax revenue 130.4; Dividends 85.0; Total 1,105.9. *Expenditure:* Current 730.7 (wages and salaries 299.2, goods and services 184.1, subsidies and transfers 247.4); Capital 494.8; Total (incl. others) 1,253.6.

Source: then Ministry of the Economy and Finance, Prishtina.

COST OF LIVING
(Consumer Price Index; base: May 2002 = 100)

	2008	2009	2010
All items	112.4	109.7	113.5

NATIONAL ACCOUNTS
(€ million at current prices)

Expenditure on the Gross Domestic Product

	2007	2008	2009
Government final consumption expenditure	641.6	674.4	670.5
Private final consumption expenditure	3,169.0	3,670.3	3,609.3
Gross fixed capital formation	744.3	937.9	1,026.5
Changes in inventories	148.3	156.0	140.0
Total domestic expenditure	**4,703.2**	**5,438.6**	**5,446.3**
Exports of goods and services	512.2	569.0	611.8
Less Imports of goods and services	1,821.7	2,156.1	2,145.8
GDP in market prices	**3,393.7**	**3,851.4**	**3,912.4**

Note: Data include contributions from UNMIK operations.

Gross Domestic Product by Economic Activity
(preliminary)

	2005	2006	2007
Agriculture, hunting, forestry and fishing	346.9	372.4	413.6
Mining	19.2	20.4	25.2
Manufacturing and utilities	401.9	411.3	384.8
Construction	257.8	284.2	342.4
Wholesale and retail trade; repair of motor vehicles, motorcycles and personal and household goods	313.7	326.0	323.6
Hotels and restaurants	22.7	24.5	25.6
Transport, storage and communications	127.8	145.5	122.7
Financial intermediation	77.6	96.1	149.7
Real estate, renting and business activities	392.5	408.7	425.2
Public administration and defence; compulsory social security	514.0	480.1	454.3
Education	84.6	89.2	91.8
Health and social work	52.8	41.9	36.9
Other community, social and personal service activities	41.8	41.9	53.6
Statistical discrepancy	—	—	−3.6
GDP at basic prices	**2,653.2**	**2,742.2**	**2,845.8**
Taxes, less subsidies, on products	415.2	449.5	587.8
GDP in purchasers' values	**3,068.4**	**3,191.7**	**3,433.6**

BALANCE OF PAYMENTS
(€ million)

	2006	2007	2008
Exports of goods f.o.b.	111	146	208
Imports of goods f.o.b.	−1,252	−1,506	−1,842
Trade balance	**−1,141**	**−1,360**	**−1,634**
Exports of services	175	197	216
Imports of services	−189	−214	−218
Balance on goods and services	**−1,155**	**−1,377**	**−1,636**
Income (net)	44	65	49
Balance on goods, services and income	**−1,111**	**−1,312**	**−1,587**
Transfers (net)	728	800	856
Current balance	**−383**	**−512**	**−732**

Capital and financial account: 12 in 2006 (Direct investments 248, Portfolio investments −128, Other investments −108); 105 in 2007 (Direct investments 420, Portfolio investments −69, Other investments −246); 529 in 2008 (Direct investments 461, Portfolio investments −76, Other investments 144).

Errors and omissions: 371 in 2006; 407 in 2007; 203 in 2008.

Source: then Ministry of the Economy and Finance, Prishtina.

KOSOVO

Statistical Survey

External Trade

PRINCIPAL COMMODITIES
(€ '000, distribution by Harmonized System)

Imports c.i.f.	2007	2008	2009
Live animals and animal products	61,211	85,426	84,598
Vegetable products	83,444	103,634	90,035
Prepared foodstuffs, beverages, alcohol and tobacco	222,156	261,917	241,566
Beverages, spirits and vinegar	48,155	53,267	49,102
Tobacco and manufactured tobacco substitutes	43,494	57,535	38,532
Mineral products	295,295	378,629	331,303
Mineral fuels, mineral oils and products of their distillation	258,420	343,687	283,846
Chemical products	119,858	138,783	142,902
Pharmaceutical products	28,290	33,901	37,997
Plastics, rubber and articles thereof	72,764	86,082	95,748
Plastics and articles thereof	60,737	71,891	78,640
Wood and articles of wood	35,429	41,685	44,922
Paper and paper articles	31,884	39,012	45,412
Textiles and textile articles	53,036	63,982	69,089
Articles of stone, plaster, ceramics and glass	63,028	67,195	73,465
Ceramic products	41,976	43,003	47,344
Base metals and articles thereof	144,346	179,625	159,368
Iron and steel	75,022	105,918	76,434
Machinery and mechanical appliances; electrical equipment; sound and television apparatus	203,422	239,927	278,689
Vehicles, aircraft, vessels and associated transport equipment	95,907	131,148	162,215
Total (incl. others)	1,576,186	1,928,236	1,935,541

Exports f.o.b.	2007	2008	2009
Vegetable products	9,111	8,986	9,484
Edible vegetables (incl. some roots and tubers)	3,473	3,643	4,175
Prepared foodstuffs, beverages, alcohol and tobacco	8,407	10,597	9,356
Beverages, spirits and vinegars	3,728	5,644	4,578
Mineral products	27,316	18,669	24,952
Ores, slag and ash	12,717	7,353	12,065
Mineral fuels, mineral oils and products of their distillation	12,595	8,313	7,213
Plastics, rubber and articles thereof	6,514	6,476	6,357
Leather and leather articles	6,488	4,861	4,454
Raw hides and skins (other than fur)	6,479	4,836	4,452
Base metals and articles thereof	74,122	124,774	88,363
Iron and steel	47,612	105,221	73,229
Articles of iron and steel	5,107	6,592	5,390
Copper and articles thereof	9,723	7,074	4,764
Aluminium and articles thereof	7,019	4,438	3,393
Machinery and mechanical appliances; electrical equipment; sound and television apparatus	21,326	8,789	7,206
Total (incl. others)	165,112	198,463	165,328

PRINCIPAL TRADING PARTNERS
(€ '000)

Imports c.i.f.	2007	2008	2009
Albania	35,262	59,632	58,385
Austria	26,842	30,953	38,886
Bosnia and Herzegovina	29,838	38,747	59,739
Brazil	30,282	43,499	37,888
Bulgaria	42,008	53,824	44,493
China, People's Rep.	104,951	121,059	128,318
Croatia	38,982	49,985	58,544
France	25,007	37,505	27,166
Germany	155,031	196,627	246,120
Greece	63,737	81,403	79,107
Hungary	25,537	37,694	26,892
Italy	57,678	74,385	87,646
Japan	10,120	10,759	15,794
Macedonia, former Yugoslav republic	237,895	346,536	291,837
Montenegro	15,063	13,789	13,059
Netherlands	9,711	20,112	30,926
Poland	14,067	22,223	24,146
Serbia	222,534	208,951	210,901
Slovenia	62,420	66,762	66,249
Spain	9,604	9,351	11,779
Switzerland	28,222	32,441	21,949
Turkey	101,827	128,249	141,545
Ukraine	16,267	11,730	6,355
United Kingdom	9,502	12,580	14,133
USA	14,698	23,610	26,703
Total (incl. others)	1,576,186	1,928,236	1,935,541

Exports f.o.b.	2007	2008	2009
Albania	20,799	21,113	26,182
Austria	2,005	2,072	1,978
Bosnia and Herzegovina	5,287	5,919	1,206
Bulgaria	10,005	2,632	2,709
Croatia	1,837	793	2,151
Germany	16,190	7,205	7,563
Greece	8,400	10,851	240
Italy	9,672	25,485	46,218
Macedonia, former Yugoslav republic	17,384	20,046	17,355
Montenegro	2,913	3,770	3,084
Netherlands	2,413	1,888	1,506
Serbia	19,280	9,893	3,504
Slovenia	4,290	6,304	2,882
Switzerland	12,937	7,380	10,510
Turkey	2,660	3,044	6,512
Total (incl. others)	165,112	198,463	165,328

Transport

RAILWAYS

	2005	2006
Passenger train journeys	3,427	5,662
Passenger train-kilometres	214,731	317,320
Freight train journeys	1,440	1,494
Freight train-kilometres	69,245	82,459
Total freight transported (metric tons)	297,555	354,835

Source: Kosovo Railways, *Annual Report 2006*.

ROAD TRAFFIC
(vehicles registered at 31 December)

	2004	2005	2006
Passenger cars	137,981	145,546	146,744
Buses and coaches	1,142	13,757	239
Lorries and vans	21,565	13,887	20,611
Heavy goods vehicles	7,213	4,769	6,457
Total (incl. others)	169,072	200,000	178,185

KOSOVO

CIVIL AVIATION
(traffic at Prishtina International Airport)

	2008	2009	2010
Aircraft movements	4,928	5,709	5,541
Passengers arrivals	551,990	578,451	641,406
Passenger departures	578,649	613,527	664,126

Education

(2009/10, unless otherwise indicated)

	Institutions*	Pupils	Teachers
Kindergarten	46	24,033	1,220
Primary	972	306,299	17,227
Secondary	121	104,806	5,519
Special	10	885	212
Primary	7	791	166
Secondary	3	94	46
University level	n.a.	37,839	1,015

* 2008/09.

Directory

The Government

HEAD OF STATE

President: ATIFETE JAHJAGA.

GOVERNMENT
(May 2011)

A coalition of the Democratic Party of Kosovo (DPK), the New Kosovo Alliance (AKR), the Independent Liberal Party (SLS), the Democratic League of Kosovo (DLK), the Justice Party (PD), the Social Democratic Party (PSD) and the Turkish Democratic Party of Kosovo (TDPK).

Prime Minister: HASHIM THAÇI (DPK).
Deputy Prime Minister and Minister of Justice: HAJREDIN KUÇI (DPK).
Deputy Prime Minister, and Minister of Trade and Industry: MIMOZA KUSARI-LILA (AKR).
Deputy Prime Minister and Minister of Local Government: SLOBODAN PETROVIĆ (SLS).
Deputy Prime Minister: BUJAR BUKOSHI (DLK).
Deputy Prime Minister: EDITA TAHIRI (DPK).
Minister of Finance: BEDRI HAMZA (DPK).
Minister of Foreign Affairs: ENVER HOXHAJ (DPK).
Minister of the Kosovo Security Force: AGIM ÇEKU (PSD).
Minister of Economic Development: BESIM BEQAJ (DPK).
Minister of Public Administration: MAHIR YAĞCILAR (TDPK).
Minister of Infrastructure: FEHMI MUJOTA (DPK).
Minister of Education, Science and Technology: RAMË BUJA (DPK).
Minister of Culture, Youth and Sports: MEMLI KRASNIQI (DPK).
Minister of Internal Affairs: BAJRAM REXHEPI (DPK).
Minister of the Environment and Spatial Planning: DARDAN GASHI (DLK).
Minister of Labour and Social Welfare: NENAD RAŠIĆ (ILP).
Minister of European Integration: VLORA ÇITAKU (DPK).
Minister of Health: FERID AGANI (PD).
Minister of Communities and Resettlement: RADOJICA TOMIĆ.
Minister of Agriculture, Forestry and Rural Development: BLERAND STAVILECI (DPK).

MINISTRIES

Office of the President: 10000 Prishtina, Rruga Nënë Terezë; tel. (38) 213222; fax (38) 211651; e-mail xh_beqiri@president-ksgov.net; internet www.president-ksgov.net.

Office of the Prime Minister: 10000 Prishtina, Rruga Nënë Terezë; tel. (38) 20114635; fax (38) 13814671; e-mail info_pmo@ks-gov.net; internet www.kryeministri-ks.net.

Ministry of Agriculture, Forestry and Rural Development: 10000 Prishtina; tel. (38) 211375; e-mail idriz.vehapi@ks-gov.net; internet www.ks-gov.net/mbpzhr.

Ministry of Communities and Resettlement: 12000 Fushë Kosova, Sheshi Nënë Terezë; tel. (38) 552045; e-mail sasa.rasic@ks-gov.net.

Ministry of Culture, Youth and Sports: 10000 Prishtina; tel. (38) 211557; fax (38) 211440; e-mail info@mkrs-ks.org; internet www.mkrs-ks.org.

Ministry of Economic Development: Prishtina.

Ministry of Education, Science and Technology: 10000 Prishtina, Rruga Musine Kokalari 18, Lagjja Dadania Blloku-III; tel. (38) 541035; e-mail masht@ks-gov.net; internet www.masht-gov.net.

Ministry of the Environment and Spatial Planning: 10000 Prishtina, Rruga Nazim Gafurri 31; tel. (38) 517800; fax (38) 517845; e-mail webmaster.mmph@ks-gov.net; internet www.ks-gov.net/mmph.

Ministry of European Integration: Prishtina; internet www.mei-ks.net.

Ministry of Finance: 10000 Prishtina, Sheshi Nënë Terezë; tel. (38) 20034101; e-mail abeqiri@mfe-ks.org; internet www.mef-rks.org.

Ministry of Foreign Affairs: 10000 Prishtina, Government Bldg, Rruga Nënë Terezë; tel. (38) 213963; fax (38) 213985; e-mail mfa@ks-gov.net; internet www.mfa-ks.net.

Ministry of Health: 10000 Prishtina, Rruga Zagrebi; tel. (38) 213886; e-mail faik.hoti@ks-gov.net.

Ministry of Infrastructure: Prishtina.

Ministry of Internal Affairs: 10000 Prishtina, Bulevardi Nënë Terezë, p.n. Objekti i Qeverisë; tel. (38) 213307; e-mail merita.vidishiq@ks-gov.net; internet www.mpb-ks.org.

Ministry of Justice: 10000 Prishtina, Ndërtesa e Kuvendit, Aneksi Jugor Kati II, Sheshi Nënë Terezë; tel. (38) 20018010; e-mail liridona.kozmaqi@ks-gov.net; internet www.md-ks.org.

Ministry of the Kosovo Security Force: 10000 Prishtina; tel. and fax (38) 211202; e-mail info_pmo@ks-gov.net; internet mksf-ks.org.

Ministry of Labour and Social Welfare: 10000 Prishtina, Rruga UÇK-së 1; tel. and fax (38) 212818; e-mail feim.osmani@ks-gov.net; internet www.mpms-ks.org.

Ministry of Local Government: 10000 Prishtina, Rruga Tirana; tel. and fax (38) 213716; e-mail lumnije.demi@ks-gov.net; internet www.ks-gov.net/mapl.

Ministry of Public Administration: 10000 Prishtina, Rruga Nënë Terezë, Zona A, Ndërtesa e Gërmisë; tel. (38) 20030020; e-mail info-mshp@ks-gov.net; internet www.ks-gov.net/mshp.

Ministry of Trade and Industry: 10000 Prishtina, Lagjja e Spitalit, Muharrem Fejza; tel. (38) 512164; fax (38) 512798; internet www.mti-ks.org.

INTERNATIONAL REPRESENTATIVES

Special Representative of the Secretary-General of the UN, Head of the UN Interim Administration Mission in Kosovo (UNMIK): LAMBERTO ZANNIER.

Special Representative of the European Union and International Civilian Representative in Kosovo: (vacant).

International Civilian Office (ICO): 10000 Prishtina, Rruga Ahmet Krasniqi, Blue Bldg; tel. (38) 2044100; fax (38) 2044210; e-mail office@ico-kos.org; internet www.ico-kos.org.

KOSOVO

Legislature

Kosovo Assembly
(Kuvendi i Kosovës/Skupština Kosova)

10000 Prishtina, Rruga Nënë Terezë; tel. (38) 211186; fax (38) 211188; e-mail info@assembly-kosova.org; internet www.assembly-kosova.org.

President: Jakup Krasniqi.

Election, 12 December 2010*

Parties and Coalitions	Votes	% of votes	Seats
Democratic Party of Kosovo	224,339	32.11	34
Democratic League of Kosovo	172,552	24.69	27
Self-Determination!	88,652	12.69	14
Alliance for the Future of Kosovo	77,130	11.04	12
New Kosovo Alliance-led coalition†	50,951	7.29	8
Independent Liberal Party	14,352	2.05	8
United Serbian List	6,004	0.86	4
Turkish Democratic Party of Kosovo	8,548	1.22	3
Vakat Coalition	5,296	0.76	2
New Spirit	15,156	2.17	—
Democratic League of Dardania	14,924	2.14	—
Others	20,847	2.98	8‡
Total	**698,751**	**100.00**	**120**

* Including the results of re-run elections, held in the municipalities of Skenderaj/Srbica Gllogovc/Glogovac and Deçan/Dečani and in certain polling stations in the municipalities of Malishevë/Mališevo and Lipjan/Lipljan on 9 January 2011, and in the municipality of Mitrovicë/Mitrovica on 23 January 2011. The figures shown in this table incorporate the results of voting to the 20 seats reserved for representatives of designated minority ethnic groups (10 seats are elected by Serbs, four by a constituency comprising Roma, Ashkali and 'Egyptian' Roma, three by Bosniaks, two by Turks and one by Gorani).

† An alliance of six parties, comprising: the New Kosovo Alliance; the Justice Party; the Social Democratic Party; the Pensioners' and Disabled People's Party; the Pensioners Party of Kosovo; and the Green Party of Kosovo.

‡ The other parties to obtain representation (one seat apiece) were: the Civic Initiative of Gora; the Democratic Ashkali Party of Kosovo; New Democratic Party; the New Democratic Initiative of Kosovo; the Serb Democratic Party of Kosovo and Metohija; the United Roma Party of Kosovo; the Bosniak Party of Democratic Action of Kosovo; and the Ashkali Party for Integration.

Election Commission

Central Election Commission (Komisioni Qendror i Zgjedhjeve): 10000 Prishtina, Str. Agim Ramadani p.n.; tel. (38) 246599; fax (38) 246602; e-mail kqz.sekretariati@cec-ko.org; internet www.kqz-ks.org; f. 2004; Chair. Valdete Daka.

Political Organizations

Albanian Christian Democratic Party of Kosovo (Partia Shqiptare Demokristane e Kosovës): 10000 Prishtina, Mustafa Kruja, Dorona; tel. (38) 221536; e-mail info@pshdk-ks.org; internet www.pshdk.org; f. 2000; Chair. Nikë Gjeloshi.

Alliance for the Future of Kosovo (AFK) (Aleanca për Ardhmërinë e Kosovës): 10000 Prishtina, Bulevardi i Dëshmorëve 49; tel. (38) 544188; e-mail info@aak-ks.com; internet www.aak-ks.com; f. 2001; Chair. Ramush Haradinaj.

Democratic League of Dardania (Lidhja Demokratike e Dardanisë): 10000 Prishtina, Rruga Isa Kastrati 117, Lagja Velania; tel. and fax (38) 248586; e-mail info@ldd-kosova.org; internet www.ldd-kosova.org; f. Jan. 2007 by fmr mems of Democratic League of Kosovo; Leader Nexhat Daçi.

Democratic League of Kosovo (DLK) (Lidhja Demokratike e Kosovës): 10000 Prishtina, Kompleksi Qafa; tel. (38) 242242; fax (38) 245305; e-mail ldk@ldk-kosova.eu; internet www.ldk-kosova.eu; f. 2000 as successor to the Democratic Alliance of Kosovo; Chair. Isa Mustafa.

Democratic Party of Kosovo (DPK) (Partia Demokratike e Kosovës): 10000 Prishtina, Rruga Nënë Terezë 20; tel. (44) 183445; e-mail pdk@pdk-ks.org; internet www.pdk-ks.org; f. 1999; est. as Party for the Democratic Progress of Kosovo; renamed as above 2000; Chair. Hashim Thaçi.

Independent Liberal Party (Samostalna liberalna stranka—SLS): 10000 Prishtina; internet www.sls-ks.org; f. 2006; represents Serb interests; Chair. Slobodan Petrović.

Justice Party (Partia e Drejtësisë—PD): 10000 Prishtina, Vellusha, Rruga Bajram Kelmendi 22; tel. and fax (44) 248920; internet www.drejtesia.org; f. 2000; Chair. Ferid Agani.

Liberal Party of Kosovo (Partia Liberale e Kosovës): 10000 Prishtina, Goleshi St 10/2; tel. and fax (38) 244780; e-mail info@plk-kosova.org; internet n.1asphost.com/mend/base; Chair. Prof. Gjergj Dedaj.

New Democracy (Nova Demokratija): 10000 Prishtina; f. 2007; represents Serb interests; Leader Branislav Grbić.

New Kosovo Alliance (Aleanca Kosova e Re—AKR): 10000 Prishtina, Rruga UÇK 55; tel. and fax (38) 247988; e-mail avdii@hotmail.com; internet www.akr-ks.eu; f. 2006; Pres. Behgjet Pacolli.

ORA Reformist Party (Partia Reformiste ORA): 10000 Prishtina, Ulpiana, Kati 10; tel. (44) 127526; e-mail info@ora-kosovo.org; internet www.ora-kosovo.org; Chair. Teuta Sahatqija.

Self-Determination! (Vetëvendosje!): 10000 Prishtina, Qyteza Pejton, Rruga Perandori Justinian 9; tel. (38) 222704; e-mail info@vetevendosje.org; internet www.vetevendosje.org; f. 2004; ethnic Albanian nationalist party; Leader Albin Kurti.

Serb List for Kosovo and Metohija (Srpska Lista za Kosovo i Metohiju): Mitrovicë; coalition of representatives of the Serbian Renewal Movement, the Democratic Party of Kosovo (q.v.) and the Social Democratic Party (q.v.); Leader Oliver Ivanović.

Social Democratic Party (Partia Social Demokrate—PSD): 10000 Prishtina, Rruga Rexhep Mala 5; tel. (38) 225645; internet www.psd-ks.org; Pres. Agim Çeku.

Socialist Party of Kosovo (Partia Socialiste e Kosovës): 10000 Prishtina, Rruga Thimi Mitko 6; tel. (44) 131832; e-mail info@ps-ks.org; internet www.ps-ks.org; f. 1982; Chair. Ilaz Kadolli.

Turkish Democratic Party of Kosovo (TDPK) (Kosova Demokratik Türk Partisi): 10000 Prizren, Sheshi e Lidhjes Cad. 47; tel. (29) 223959; fax (29) 242534; e-mail kdtp@kdtp.org; internet www.kdtp.org; Chair. Mahir Yağcılar.

Vakat Coalition (Koalicija Vakat): Dragaš; f. 2004; coalition of representatives of the Bosniak Democratic Party, the Fatherland (Vatan) Democratic Party and the Bosniak Party of Kosovo; Leader Sadik Idrizi.

Other political parties include: the **Democratic Ashkali Party of Kosovo** (Partia Demokratike e Ashkanlive të Kosovës); the **Serb Democratic Party of Kosovo and Metohija** (Srpska Demokratska Stranka Kosova i Metohije), led by Slaviša Petković; the **Party of Democratic Action** (Stranka Demokratske Akcije); the **Serb People's Party** (Srpska Narodna Stranka), led by Mihajl Šćepanović; the **Civic Initiative of Gora** (Građanska Inicijativa Gore); the **Serb Kosovo and Metohija Party** (Srpska Kosovsko-Metohijka Stranka), led by Dragiša Mirić; the **New Democratic Initiative of Kosovo** (Iniciativa e re Demokrarike e Kosovës), representing the 'Egyptian' Roma; the **Union of Independent Social Democrats of Kosovo and Metohija** (Savez Nezavisnih Socijaldemokrata Kosova i Metohije), led by Nebojša Živić; and the **United Roma Party of Kosovo** (Partia Rome e Bashkuar e Kosovës).

Diplomatic Representation

EMBASSIES IN KOSOVO

At May 2011 the following 75 countries officially recognized Kosovo: Afghanistan, Albania, Australia, Austria, Bahrain, Belgium, Belize, Bulgaria, Burkina Faso, Canada, Colombia, The Comoros, Costa Rica, Croatia, the Czech Republic, Denmark, Djibouti, the Dominican Republic, Estonia, Finland, France, The Gambia, Germany, Guinea-Bissau, Honduras, Hungary, Iceland, Ireland, Italy, Japan, Jordan, Kiribati, the Republic of Korea, Latvia, Liberia, Liechtenstein, Lithuania, Luxembourg, the former Yugoslav republic of Macedonia, Malawi, Malaysia, the Maldives, Malta, the Marshall Islands, Mauritania, the Federated States of Micronesia, Monaco, Montenegro, Nauru, the Netherlands, New Zealand, Norway, Oman, Palau, Panama, Peru, Poland, Portugal, Qatar, Samoa, San Marino, Saudi Arabia, Senegal, Sierra Leone, Slovenia, Somalia, Swaziland, Sweden, Switzerland, Turkey, Tuvalu, the United Arab Emirates, the United Kingdom, the USA and Vanuatu.

Albania: 10000 Prishtina, Qyteza Pejton, Rruga Mujo Ulqinaku 18; tel. (38) 248208; fax (38) 248209; e-mail embassy.pristina@mfa.gov.al; Ambassador Islam Lauka.

Austria: 10000 Prishtina, Fan Noli 22, Arbëria 1; tel. (38) 249284; fax (38) 249285; e-mail pristina-as@bmeia.gv.at; Ambassador Johann Brieger.

KOSOVO

Bulgaria: 10000 Prishtina, Arbëria 1, Rruga Ismail Qemali 12; tel. (38) 245540; fax (38) 245543; e-mail dbpristina@abv.gb; internet www.mfa.bg/bg/111; Ambassador BOBI BOBEV.

Croatia: 10000 Prishtina, Rruga Mujo Ulqinaku 20; tel. (38) 223978; fax (38) 223979; e-mail croemb.pristina@mvpei.hr; Ambassador ZORAN VODOPIJA.

Czech Republic: 10000 Prishtina, Dragodan, Rruga Ismail Qemali 31; tel. (38) 246676; fax (38) 248782; e-mail pristina@embassy.mzv.cz; Ambassador JIŘÍ DOLEŽEL.

Finland: 10000 Prishtina, Lagja Payton, Perandori Justiani 19; tel. (43) 737000; fax (43) 732863; e-mail sanomat.pri@formin.fi; internet www.finlandkosovo.org; Chargé d'affaires a.i. TARJA FERNÁNDEZ.

France: 10000 Prishtina, Dragodan, Rruga Ismail Qemali 67; tel. (38) 22458800; fax (38) 22458801; e-mail admin-etrangers.pristina-amba@diplomatie.gouv.fr; internet www.ambafrance-kosovo.org; Ambassador JEAN-FRANÇOIS FITOU.

Germany: 10000 Prishtina, Arbëri, Rruga Azem Jashanica 17; tel. (38) 254500; fax (38) 254536; e-mail info@pris.auswaertiges-amt.de; internet www.pristina.diplo.de; Ambassador HANS-DIETER STEINBACH.

Hungary: 10000 Prishtina, Arbëri, 24 Maj 23; tel. (38) 247763; fax (38) 247764; e-mail prs.missions@kum.gov.hu; internet www.mfa.gov.hu/pristina; Ambassador LÓRÁNT BALLA.

Italy: 10000 Prishtina, Dragodan, Rruga Azem Jashanica 5; tel. (38) 244925; fax (38) 244929; e-mail segretaria.pristina@esteri.it; Ambassador MICHAEL LOUIS GIFFONI.

Macedonia, former Yugoslav republic: 10000 Prishtina; Ambassador STOJAN KARAJANOV.

Netherlands: 10000 Prishtina, Velania, Xhemajl Berisha 12; tel. (38) 516101; fax (38) 516103; e-mail pri@minbuza.nl; internet kosovo.nlembassy.org; Ambassador ROBERT BOSCH.

Norway: 10000 Prishtina, Pejton, Sejdi Kryeziu 6; tel. (38) 23211100; fax (38) 23211120; e-mail embpri@mfa.no; internet www.norway-kosovo.no; Ambassador SVERRE JOHAN KVALE.

Slovenia: 10000 Prishtina, Anton Ceta 6; tel. (38) 246255; fax (38) 246256; e-mail mpi@gov.si; Ambassador JOŽEF HLEB.

Switzerland: 10060 Prishtina, Adrian Krasniqi 11; tel. (38) 248088; fax (38) 248078; e-mail pri.vertretung@eda.admin.ch; internet www.eda.admin.ch/pristina; Ambassador LUKAS BEGLINGER.

Turkey: 10000 Prishtina, Arbëri, Rruga Ismail Qemali 59; tel. (38) 226044; e-mail turkemb.prishtina@mfa.gov.tr; internet www.prishtina.emb.mfa.gov.tr; Ambassador SONGÜL OZAN BÜYÜKELÇI.

United Kingdom: 10000 Prishtina, Arbëri, Rruga Ismail Qemali 6; tel. (38) 254700; fax (38) 249799; e-mail britishoffice.pristina@fco.gov.uk; internet ukinkosovo.fco.gov.uk; Ambassador IAN CAMERON CLIFF.

USA: 10000 Prishtina, Arbëri, Nazim Hikmet 30; tel. (38) 593000; fax (38) 549890; e-mail papristina@state.gov; internet pristina.usembassy.gov; Ambassador CHRISTOPHER WILLIAM DELL.

Judicial System

The court system comprises a Supreme Court, Constitutional Court, district courts, municipal courts and minor offences courts.

Constitutional Court: 10000 Prishtina, Qyteteza Pejton; tel. (38) 220104; fax (38) 220105; e-mail info@gjk-ks.org; internet www.gjk-ks.org; f. 2009; Chair. Prof. ENVER HASANI; Dep. Chair. KADRI KRYEZIU.

Supreme Court: 10000 Prishtina; Pres. FEJZULLAH HASANI.

Religion

Most of the inhabitants of Kosovo are adherents of Islam, although most Serbs are Orthodox Christians, and several sites of historic importance to Serbian Orthodoxy are located within Kosovo. A significant minority of the Kosovo Albanian population are Roman Catholics.

ISLAM

Islamic Community: 10000 Prishtina; Pres. of the Mesihat Dr REDZEP BOJE.

CHRISTIANITY

The Eastern Orthodox Church

The Patriarchate of the Serbian Orthodox Church is located at Pej (Peć), in central Kosovo.

The Roman Catholic Church

At 31 December 2008 there were an estimated 65,000 Roman Catholics within the Apostolic Administration of Prizren. In the early 2010s a Catholic co-cathedral was under construction in Prishtina.

Apostolic Administrator of Prizren: GJERGJU DODË, 20000 Prizren, Rruga I. L. Ribar 7; tel. (29) 41933; fax (29) 41232; e-mail ipeshkvia_pz@yahoo.com.

The Press

PRINCIPAL DAILIES

Bota Sot (The World Today): 10000 Prishtina, Rruga Jakove Xoxa 18; tel. and fax (38) 226881; e-mail bota-sot@ipko.org; in Albanian; Editor IDRIZ MORINA.

Epoka e Re (The New Age): 10000 Prishtina, opp. UNMIK HQ; tel. (44) 127434; e-mail info@epokaere.com; internet www.epokaere.com; f. 1999; Man. MUHAMET MAVRAJ.

Express: 10000 Prishtina, Dardania 1/1; tel. (38) 767676; fax (38) 767678; e-mail info@gazetaexpress.com; internet www.gazetaexpress.com; f. 2005; in Albanian; seven a week; Chief Editor LEONARD KERQUKI.

Infopress: 10000 Prishtina, Shtypshkronja Rilindja; tel. (38) 222464; fax (38) 222510; e-mail info@infopress-rh.com; internet www.infopress-rh.com; popular; supports Democratic Party of Kosovo; Editor AVNI AZEMI.

Koha Ditore: 10000 Prishtina, Rruga Nëna Tereze, POB 202; tel. (38) 249104; fax (38) 249106; e-mail redaksia@kohaditore.com; internet www.kohaditore.com; in Albanian; Editor-in-Chief AGRON BAJRAMI.

Kosova Sot (Kosovo Today): 10000 Prishtina, Zona Industriale; tel. (38) 601007; fax (38) 601010; e-mail redaksia@kosova-sot.info; internet www.kosova-sot.info; f. 1998; in Albanian; Editor-in-Chief MARGARITA KADRIU.

Lajm (The News): 10000 Prishtina, UÇK 58; tel. (38) 243021; fax (38) 243009; e-mail redaksia@gazetalajm.info; internet www.gazetalajm.info; f. 2004; in Albanian; supports the New Kosovo Alliance; Chief Exec. BEHGJET PACOLLI.

Prishtina Post: 10000 Prishtina, Bulevardi Bil Klinton; tel. and fax (38) 555566; e-mail redaksia@prishtinapost.info; internet www.prishtinapost.info; in Albanian; Editor FATON ABDULLAHU.

PERIODICALS

Alem: 1000 Prishtina, Rruga Hajdar Dushi 1A; tel. (44) 185099; fax (38) 243800; e-mail info@alemnet.info; f. 2001; weekly; in Bosnian; Editor-in-Chief NADIRA A. VLASSI.

Drita: 20000 Prizren, Rruga I. L. Ribar 7; e-mail ipeshkvia_pz@yahoo.com; review publ. by Catholic Church in Kosovo; Editor Mgr LUSH GJERGJI.

Fokus Kosova/Fokus Kosovo/Focus Kosovo: 10000 Prishtina, UNMIK Administrative HQ; e-mail focuskosovo@un.org; f. 2001; publ. by UNMIK; Albanian, Serbian and English edns; seven a year; Publr ALEXANDER IVANKO; Editors MYRIAM DESSABLES (Albanian and Serbian edns), RICARDO Z. DUNN.

Gradanski Glasnik (The Civil Messenger): 10000 Prishtina, Tringe Ismaili 34A; tel. (44) 431106; e-mail jbjelica@yahoo.com; weekly; in Serbian; Editor-in-Chief JELENA BJELICA.

Official Gazette of the Republic of Kosovo (Gazeta Zyrtare e Republikës së Kosovës/Sluzbeni list Republike Kosova/Kosova Cumhuriyeti Resmi Gazetesi/Sluzbeni Novine Republike Kosova): 10000 Prishtina, Ndërtesa e re e Qeverisë; tel. (38) 20114039; e-mail info-gzk@ks-gov.net; internet www.ks-gov.net/GazetaZyrtare; f. 2005; monthly; publishes official text of laws adopted by the Kosovo Assembly as promulgated by the Special Representative of the Secretary-General, resolutions adopted by the Kosovo Assembly, secondary and other legislation issued by the Government and ministries of Kosovo, international agreements, etc.; edns in Albanian, Serbian, English, Turkish and Bosnian; administered by the Office of the Prime Minister; Editor MENTOR HOXHA.

Yeni Dönem (New Era): Prizren, Rruga Ceraviqa 13A; tel. (29) 630230; fax (29) 44788; e-mail yenidonem@hotmail.com; in Turkish; weekly.

Zëri (The Voice): 10000 Prishtina, Media House Annex II; tel. (38) 249071; fax (38) 222451; e-mail redaksia@zeri.info; f. 1945; in Albanian; weekly; Editor-in-Chief ASTRIT GASHI.

NEWS AGENCIES

Infosot: Prishtina; tel. (38) 776000; e-mail info@infosot.com; internet www.infosot.com.

KOSOVO

KosovaLive: 1000 Prishtina, Aneksi te Pallati i Shtypit, Kati II; tel. (38) 248276; fax (38) 248277; e-mail editor@kosovalive.com; internet www.kosovalive.com; f. 2000; Dir KELMEND HAPÇIU.

Kosovapress: 10000 Prishtina, Rruga Hamez Jashari 28/22A; tel. and fax (38) 248721; e-mail kryeredaktori@kosovapress.com; internet www.kosovapress.com; f. 1999; Dir and Editor SKENDER KRASNIQI.

Press Association

Press Council of Kosovo: 10000 Prishtina, Rruga Hajdar Dushi 17; tel. (44) 291810; e-mail presscouncil.kosovo@gmail.com; internet www.presscouncil-ks.org; self-regulatory body of the print media; Chair. of Bd WILLEM HOUWEN; Dir NEHAT ISLAMI.

Publishers

Dukagjini Publishing House: 10000 Pejë, Rruga Fehmi Agani 16; tel. (39) 432025; fax (39) 434281; internet books.dukagjinigroup.com; literature and contemporary philosophy; titles publ. in three series: Rozafa, Ballkan and Fryma; owned by Dukagjini Group; Pres. RAMADAN MEHMETI.

Gjon Buzuku Publishing House: 10000 Prishtina, Rruga Brigadat e Kosovës; tel. and fax (38) 530873; e-mail buzuku@prishtina.com; f. 1990; Pres. HANA ZENELI.

Panorama: 10000 Prishtina; f. 1994; publishes newspapers and journals in Serbian, Albanian and Turkish; Dir JORDAN RISTIĆ.

Rilindja Publishing House: 10000 Prishtina, Pallati i mediave, Dom štampe pa nr; tel. (38) 549675; popular science, literature, children's fiction, travel books, textbooks in Albanian; Dir DAUT DEMAKU.

Broadcasting and Communications

TELECOMMUNICATIONS

Regulatory Authority

Telecommunications Regulatory Authority (Kosovo) (ART) (Autoriteti Rregullativ i Telekomunikacionit): 10000 Prishtina; tel. (38) 212345; e-mail info@art-ks.org; internet www.art-ks.org; Chair. ANTON BERISHA.

Service Providers

iPKO: 10000 Prishtina, Rruga Nënë Terezë, ndërtesa e RTK-së, kati 5; tel. (38) 700000; e-mail portal@ipko.net; internet www.ipko.net; f. 1999; subsidiary of Telekom Slovenije (Slovenia); mobile cellular telecommunications services, and provider of internet and digital cable television.

PTK (Post and Telecommunications of Kosovo): 10100 Prishtina, Dardania pa nr, Kati VIII, zyra 808; tel. (38) 524583; e-mail postaekosoves@ptkonline.com; internet www.ptkonline.com; f. 1959; became jt-stock co in 2005; provides postal and telecommunications services in Kosovo, including mobile cellular telephone services operated under the brand name Vala; plans for privatization announced in 2008; CEO Dr SHYQYRI HAXHA.

BROADCASTING

Radio Televizioni i Kosovës (RTK) (Radio-Television Kosovo): 10000 Prishtina, Rruga Xhemail 12; tel. (38) 230102; fax (38) 235336; e-mail post@rtklive.com; internet www.rtklive.com; subsidiaries include Radio Kosova and Radio Blue Sky; Chair. Dr VJOSA DOBRUNA; Dir-Gen. AGIM ZATRIQI.

RadioTelevizioni21 (RTV21): 10000 Prishtina, Pallati i Mediave, Aneks II; tel. and fax (38) 550088; e-mail lajmet@rtv21.tv; internet www.rtv21.tv; radio and television broadcaster.

Finance

(cap. = capital; res = reserves; dep. = deposits; m. = million; amounts in euros; brs = branches)

BANKING

Regulatory Authority

Central Bank of the Republic of Kosovo (Banka Qendrore Republikës së Kosoves): 10000 Prishtina, Rruga Garibaldi 33; tel. (38) 222055; fax (38) 243763; e-mail publicrelations@cbak-kos.org; internet www.bqk-kos.org; f. 1999 as the Banking and Payments Authority of Kosovo; became Central Banking Authority of Kosovo 2006; total assets 1,113.2m. (Dec. 2008); Gov. HASHIM REXHEPI; Chair. GAZMEND LUBOTENI.

Registered Banks

In 2009 there were eight registered banks operating in Kosovo, of which six were foreign-owned.

Banka Kombëtare Tregtare: 10000 Prishtina, Qyteza Pejton, Rruga Kosta Novakoviç 9; tel. (38) 222910; fax (38) 222907; e-mail infobktkosova@bkt.com; internet www.bkt.com.al; f. 1993; total assets 18.3m. (Dec. 2008).

Bank for Business (Banka për Biznes—BpB): Prishtina, Rruga UÇK 41; tel. (38) 244666; fax (38) 243656; e-mail info@bpbbank.com; internet www.bpbbank.com; f. 2001; total assets 41.2m. (Dec. 2007); Dir-Gen. SELVINAZE SHEHOLLI.

Economic Bank: 10000 Prishtina, Rruga Migjeni 1; tel. (38) 225353; fax (38) 225454; e-mail bek@bekonomike.com; internet www.bekonomike.com; f. 2001; total assets 86.1m. (Dec. 2008); Pres. HAJRULLAH ZAITI.

Komercijalna Banka a.d. Beograd: 40000 Mitrovica, Rruga Kralja Petra Prvog 33; tel. (28) 423822; fax (28) 425295; e-mail posta@kombank.com; internet www.kombank.com; f. 1970; Chair. VLADISLAV CVETKOVIĆ.

NLB Prishtina: 10000 Prishtina, Rruga Rexhep Luci 5; tel. (38) 234111; fax (38) 246189; e-mail info@nlbprishtina-kos.com; internet www.nlbprishtina-kos.com; f. Jan. 2008 by merger of NLB Kasabank and NLB New Bank of Kosovo; 80.4% owned by NLB d.d; cap. 20.5m., dep. 256.0m., total assets 298.4m. (Dec. 2009); Gen. Man. ALBERT LUMEZI.

ProCredit Bank Kosova: 10000 Prishtina, Nënë Terezë 16; tel. (38) 555777; fax (38) 555776; e-mail info@procreditbank-kos.com; internet www.procreditbank-kos.com; f. 2000 as Micro Enterprise Bank; present name adopted 2003; cap. 28.0m., res 0.6m., dep. 639.8m. (Dec. 2009); CEO PHILIP SIGWART.

Raiffeisen Bank Kosovo: Rruga UÇK 51; tel. (38) 222222; e-mail info@raiffeisen-kosovo.com; internet www.raiffeisen-kosovo.com; fmrly American Bank of Kosovo; acquired by Raiffeisen International (Austria) and name changed in 2003; cap. 58.0m., res 0.3m., dep. 548,6m. (Dec. 2009); Chair. and CEO BOGDAN MERFEA; 43 brs.

TEB sh. a.: 10000 Prishtina, Rruga Agim Ramadani 15; tel. (38) 230000; fax (38) 224699; e-mail info@teb-kos.com; internet www.teb-kos.com; f. Jan. 2008; joint venture of TEB (Turkey) and BNP Paribas (France); cap. 17.5m., dep. 107.9m., total assets 117.1m. (Dec. 2009).

INSURANCE

In early 2009 there were 14 registered insurance companies operating in Kosovo.

Croatia Sigurimi-Kosovo: 10000 Prishtina, Rruga Luan Haradinaj 5D; tel. (38) 246956; fax (38) 426957; e-mail ivopcro@yahoo.com; owned by Croatia Sigurimi (Croatia); Dir IVICA PEZO.

Dardania Kompania e Sigurimeve (Dardania Insurance Co): 10000 Prishtina, Rruga Sylejman Vokshi 4; tel. (38) 244080; fax (38) 244081; e-mail info@dardaniainsurance.com; internet www.dardaniainsurance.com; Dir RYZA BICI.

Elsig: 10000 Prishtina, Rruga e Trepçës 15; tel. (38) 221112; fax (38) 221115; e-mail office@kselsig.com; internet www.kselsig.com; f. 2008; non-life; Dir REXHEP IDRIZAJ.

Illyria Insurance Co: 10000 Prishtina, Nëna Terezë 33; tel. (38) 225385; fax (38) 225384; e-mail fatgashi@hotmail.com; Dir FATMIR GASHI.

Insig Kosovo: 10000 Prishtina, Mujo Ulqinaku, Pejton 6; tel. (38) 249900; fax (38) 249901; e-mail shberisha@insig-ks.com; Dir ILDA KEKEZI.

Kompania e Sigurimeve Dukagjini (Dukagjini Insurance Co): 10000 Prishtina, Sheshi Nënë Terezë 33; tel. (38) 225385; fax (38) 225384; e-mail info@insurancedukagjini.com; internet www.insurancedukagjini.com; f. 2002; 51% owned by Sava Re (Slovenia); Dir EKREM LLUKA.

Kosova e Re Insurance Co (New Kosova Insurance Co): 10000 Prishtina, Lagja Kalabria 5/1B; tel. (38) 770777; fax (38) 770888; e-mail info@kosovaere.com; internet www.kosovaere.com; f. 2002; owned by Kürüm Holding; Dir VISAR RRUSTEMI.

Sigal Kosove: 10000 Prishtina, Rruga Vaso Pasha; tel. and fax (38) 240241; e-mail info@sigal-ks.com; internet www.sigal-ks.com; f. 2003; owned by Uniqa Group Austria; five main brs in Prishtina, Prizren, Peja, Ferizaj and Gjilan; two sub-brs in Gjakova and Mitrovica; more than 50 agencies throughout Kosovo; Dir SOFO LIMAJ.

Sigkos: 10000 Prishtina, Rruga Sylejman Vokshi, Pallati i Kuq; tel. (38) 240022; fax (38) 240222; e-mail info@sigkos.com; internet www.sigkos.com; f. 2006; Dir IBRAHIM KASTRATI.

KOSOVO

Sigma Kosovo: 10000 Prishtina, Qyteza Pejton, Rruga Pashko Vasa; tel. (38) 246301; fax (38) 246302; e-mail info@sigma-ks.net; internet www.sigma-ks.net; f. 2004; part of Vienna Insurance Gp; Dir ROLAND KACANI.

Siguria: 10000 Prishtina, Rruga Luan Haradinaj; tel. (38) 248848; fax (38) 248850; e-mail info@ks-siguria.com; internet www.ks-siguria.com; f. 2000; Dir RRAHIM PACOLLI.

Trade and Industry

GOVERNMENT AGENCIES

Investment Promotion Agency of Kosovo (IPAK): 10000 Prishtina, Rruga Muharrem Fejza; tel. and fax (38) 20036527; e-mail info@invest-ks.org; internet www.invest-ks.org; CEO MUSTAFË HASANI (acting).

Privatization Agency of Kosovo: 10000 Prishtina, Rruga Ilir Konushevci 8; tel. (38) 500400; fax (38) 248076; e-mail info@pak-ks.org; internet www.pak-ks.org; fmrly Kosovo Trust Agency, supervised by UNMIK; restructured as above in June 2008; Chair. TAMARA PERIČIĆ.

CHAMBERS OF COMMERCE

American Chamber of Commerce: 10000 Prishtina, Fehmi Agani 36/3; tel. (38) 246012; fax (38) 248012; e-mail info@amchamksv.org; internet www.amchamksv.org; f. 2004; Exec. Dir LEKË MUSA; 90 mem. cos.

Kosovo Chamber of Commerce (Oda Ekonomike e Kosovës): 10000 Prishtina, Rruga Nënë Terezë 20; tel. (38) 224741; fax (38) 224299; e-mail info@oek-kcc.org; internet www.oek-kcc.org; Pres. SAFET GËRXHALIU; Sec.-Gen. BERAT RUKIQI.

UTILITIES

Korporata Energetike e Kosovës/Energetska Korporacija Kosova (KEK) (Kosovo Energy Corpn): 10000 Prishtina; tel. (38) 240245; e-mail nezir.sinani@kek-energy.com; internet www.kek-energy.com; generation and distribution of electricity.

Prishtina Regional Water Company (Kompania Ujësjellësi Rajonal 'Prishtina'): 10000 Prishtina, Rruga Tahir Zajmi; tel. (38) 551010; e-mail info@kur-prishtina.com; internet www.kur-prishtina.com; f. 2007; offers services in central Kosovo, est. 550,000 customers; Dir SKENDER BUBLAKU.

TRADE UNIONS

Union of Independent Trade Unions of Kosovo (BSPK) (Bashkimi i Sindikatave të Pavarura të Kosovës): 38000 Prishtina, Rruga Nënë Terezë 35; tel. (38) 221782; fax (38) 223175; e-mail bspk@etuc.org; internet www.bskp.org; 120,000 mems in 18 federations (2006); Chair. HAXHI ARIFI.

Transport

RAILWAYS

In 2005 there were 436 km of railways and 33 railway stations in operation in Kosovo.

Hekurudhat e Kosovës/Kosovske Železnice (Kosovo Railways): Fushë Kosovë, Sheshi i lirisë pn; tel. (38) 536355; fax (38) 536307; e-mail info@kosovorailway.com; internet www.kosovorailway.com; f. 2005 to replace UNMIK Railway; jt-stock co; operates railway services within Kosovo and international services to Skopje, former Yugoslav republic of Macedonia; Man. Dir XHEVAT RAMOSAJ.

CIVIL AVIATION

There is an international airport at Prishtina.

Defence

Under an agreement between the North Atlantic Treaty Organization (NATO) and the Federal Government, reached in June 1999, and a subsequent UN resolution, the NATO-led Kosovo Force (KFOR—with a maximum authorized strength of 50,000 personnel) was deployed in the province of Kosovo, and the UN Interim Administration Mission in Kosovo (UNMIK) was installed. In September, following the disarmament of the Kosovo Liberation Army paramilitary organization, the movement was reconstituted as a 5,000-member civil emergency security force, the Kosovo Protection Corps. After Kosovo's declaration of independence in February 2008, an EU Rule of Law Mission (EULEX Kosovo), comprising some 1,900 foreign personnel and 1,100 local staff, became operational under the overall authority of the UN in December, with an initial mandate of two years. At the end of June 2008 UNMIK comprised 2,028 police officers and 39 military observers. A reduced UNMIK presence is to continue in the country indefinitely under UN Resolution 1244. In January 2009 the Kosovo Protection Corps was dissolved and a new multi-ethnic, 2,500 member Kosovo Security Force was launched. At November 2010 8,454 KFOR troops were maintaining security, in support of Kosovo's institutions.

Commander of KFOR: Maj.-Gen. ERHARD BÜHLER.

Education

Responsibility for education was transferred to the Ministry of Education, Science and Technology in 2002. The system of compulsory education was extended from eight to nine years in 2003/04. The education system comprises a five-year period of primary education, beginning at seven years, and two cycles of secondary education, lasting four years and three years, respectively. The higher education system operates through two state universities, the University of Prishtina, and the University of Mitrovica; a total of 37,839 students were enrolled in higher education in 2009/10.

KUWAIT

Introductory Survey

LOCATION, CLIMATE, LANGUAGE, RELIGION, FLAG, CAPITAL

The State of Kuwait lies at the north-west extreme of the Persian (Arabian) Gulf, bordered to the north-west by Iraq and to the south by Saudi Arabia. The State comprises a mainland region and nine small islands, of which the largest is Bubiyan and the most populous is Failaka. Immediately to the south of Kuwait, along the Gulf, lies a Neutral (Partitioned) Zone of 5,700 sq km, which is shared between Kuwait and Saudi Arabia. Much of Kuwait is arid desert, and the climate is generally hot and humid. Temperatures in July and August often exceed 45°C (113°F), and in the winter months are frequently above 20°C (68°F)—although there is often frost at night. Average annual rainfall is only 111 mm. The official language is Arabic, which is spoken by the majority of Kuwaiti nationals (estimated to have comprised 32.1% of Kuwait's population in 2009) and by many of the country's non-Kuwaiti residents. Apart from other Arabs, the non-Kuwaitis are mainly Iranians, Indians and Pakistanis. At the 1975 census 95.0% of the population were Muslims (of whom about 70% are now thought to belong to the Sunni sect), while 4.5% were Christians, Hindus or adherents of other faiths. The national flag (proportions 1 by 2) has three equal horizontal stripes, of green, white and red, with a superimposed black trapezoid at the hoist. The capital is Kuwait City.

CONTEMPORARY POLITICAL HISTORY

Historical Context

Kuwait became part of Turkey's Ottoman Empire in the 16th century. During the later years of Ottoman rule Kuwait became a semi-autonomous Arab monarchy, with local administration controlled by a Sheikh of the Sabah family, which is still the ruling dynasty. In 1899, fearing an extension of Turkish control, the ruler of Kuwait made a treaty with the United Kingdom, accepting British protection while surrendering control over external relations. Nominal Turkish suzerainty over Kuwait ended in 1918, with the dissolution of the Ottoman Empire.

Petroleum was first discovered in Kuwait in 1938, but exploration was interrupted by the Second World War. After 1945 drilling resumed on a large scale, and extensive deposits of petroleum were found. Sheikh Ahmad (ruler since 1921) was succeeded in 1950 by his cousin, Sheikh Abdullah al-Salim al-Sabah, who inaugurated a programme of public works and educational development, funded by petroleum revenues, which transformed Kuwait's infrastructure and introduced a comprehensive system of welfare services.

Domestic Political Affairs

Kuwait became fully independent on 19 June 1961, when the United Kingdom and Kuwait agreed to terminate the 1899 treaty. The ruler took the title of Amir and assumed full executive power. Kuwait was admitted to the League of Arab States (the Arab League, see p. 361) despite opposition from Iraq, which claimed that Kuwait was historically part of Iraqi territory. Kuwait's first election took place in December 1961, when voters chose 20 members of a Constituent Assembly (the other members being government ministers appointed by the Amir). The Assembly drafted a new Constitution, which was adopted in December 1962. A 50-member Majlis al-Umma (National Assembly) was elected, under a limited franchise (see Constitution and Government), in January 1963. In the absence of formal political parties (which remain illegal), candidates contested the poll as independents, although some known opponents of the Government were elected. In the same month the Amir appointed his brother, Sheikh Sabah al-Salim al-Sabah (the heir apparent), to be Prime Minister. Iraq renounced its claim to Kuwait in October, and diplomatic relations between the two countries were established.

In January 1965, following conflict between the paternalistic ruling family and the democratically inclined Majlis, the powers of the Council of Ministers were strengthened. The Amir died in November 1965, and Sheikh Sabah succeeded to the throne. He was replaced as Prime Minister by his cousin, Sheikh Jaber al-Ahmad al-Sabah, who was named heir apparent in May 1966. The Neutral (Partitioned) Zone between Kuwait and Saudi Arabia was formally divided between the two countries in 1969: revenues from oil production in the area are shared equally.

As Kuwait's petroleum sector expanded during the 1960s, the country became increasingly wealthy. The Government effected an extensive redistribution of income, through public expenditure and a land compensation scheme, but there was some popular discontent concerning corruption, and official manipulation of the media and the Majlis. A more representative legislature was elected in January 1971 (again under a limited franchise). A further general election took place in January 1975, but in August 1976 the Amir dissolved the Majlis, on the grounds that it was acting against the best interests of the State. Sheikh Sabah died in December 1977 and was succeeded by Crown Prince Jaber. In January 1978 the new Amir appointed Sheikh Saad al-Abdullah al-Salim al-Sabah to be his heir apparent. The new Crown Prince, hitherto Minister of Defence and the Interior, became Prime Minister in the following month. In accordance with an Amiri decree of August 1980, a new Majlis was elected in February 1981, although only one-half of the eligible 6% of the population registered to vote.

The collapse of Kuwait's unofficial stock exchange, the Souk al-Manakh, in September 1982 caused a prolonged financial crisis, and eventually led to the resignations of the Ministers of Finance (in 1983) and of Justice (in 1985). The Majlis subsequently opposed several government measures, including proposed price increases for public services, educational reforms and legislation to restrict the press, and questioned the competence of certain ministers. In July 1986 the Council of Ministers submitted its resignation to the Amir, who then dissolved the Majlis and suspended some articles of the Constitution, declaring his intention to rule by decree. The Crown Prince was immediately reappointed Prime Minister. An Amiri decree accorded the Council of Ministers greater powers of censorship, including the right to suspend publication of newspapers for up to two years.

In late 1989 the Amir refused to accept a petition, signed by more than 20,000 Kuwaiti citizens, seeking the restoration of the Majlis. In January 1990 police dispersed two pro-democracy demonstrations, although later in the month the Government agreed to relax press censorship. In June 62% of eligible voters participated in a general election for 50 members of a 'provisional' National Council; a further 25 members were appointed by the Amir. The election was boycotted by pro-democracy activists, who continued to demand the full restoration of the Majlis.

Of all the Gulf states, Kuwait has been most vulnerable to regional disruption. Immediately after independence British troops (soon replaced by an Arab League force) were dispatched to support the country against the territorial claim by Iraq. The force remained until 1963, and relations between Kuwait and Iraq were stable until 1973, when Iraqi troops occupied a Kuwaiti outpost on their joint border. Kuwait none the less supplied aid to Iraq from the outbreak of the Iran–Iraq War in 1980. As a result, Kuwaiti petroleum installations and shipping in the Persian (Arabian) Gulf were targeted intermittently by Iranian forces, and by pro-Iranian groups within Kuwait, for much of the 1980s. A large number of Iranians were among 27,000 expatriates deported in 1985–86, and in 1987 the Government initiated a five-year plan to reduce the number of expatriates in the Kuwaiti work-force. Kuwait resumed diplomatic relations with Iran following the 1988 cease-fire between Iran and Iraq.

Iraqi invasion of Kuwait

In July 1990 the Iraqi Government implicitly criticized Kuwait (among other states) for disregarding the petroleum production quotas stipulated by the Organization of the Petroleum Exporting Countries (OPEC, see p. 405). It also declared that Kuwait should cancel Iraq's war debt and compensate it for losses of revenue incurred during the war with Iran, and as a result of

Kuwait's overproduction of petroleum—to which Iraq attributed a decline in international oil prices. In addition, Iraq alleged that Kuwait had established military posts and drilled oil wells on Iraqi territory. Despite regional mediation efforts, Iraq subsequently began to deploy armed forces on the Kuwait-Iraq border. Direct negotiations in Jeddah, Saudi Arabia, at the end of the month between Kuwaiti and Iraqi officials collapsed, and on 2 August some 100,000 Iraqi troops invaded Kuwait (the total military strength of which was about 20,000); Iraq stated that it had entered at the invitation of insurgents who had overthrown the Kuwaiti Government. The Amir and other government members fled to Saudi Arabia, where they established a 'Government-in-exile', while Iraq declared that a provisional Government had been formed in Kuwait comprising Iraqi-sponsored Kuwaiti dissidents. The UN Security Council immediately adopted a series of resolutions, of which the first (Resolution 660) condemned the invasion, demanded the immediate and unconditional withdrawal of Iraqi forces from Kuwait, and appealed for a negotiated settlement of the conflict. A trade embargo was then imposed on Iraq and Kuwait. Meanwhile, the USA and member states of the European Community (now European Union—EU, see p. 270) froze all Kuwait's overseas assets to prevent their repatriation. Five days after the invasion US troops and aircraft were deployed in Saudi Arabia, with the stated aim of securing that country's borders with Kuwait in the event of further Iraqi territorial expansion. A number of European governments, together with some Arab League states, agreed to provide military support for the US forces. The Iraqi Government subsequently announced the formal annexation of Kuwait, and ordered the closure of foreign diplomatic missions there. At the end of August most of Kuwait was officially declared to be the 19th Governorate of Iraq, while a northern strip was incorporated into the Basra Governorate.

In the months following the invasion apparent attempts at demographic manipulation—by settling Iraqis and Palestinians in Kuwait and by forcing Kuwaitis to assume Iraqi citizenship—were documented. The population was estimated to have decreased from approximately 2m. prior to the invasion to some 700,000, of whom Kuwaitis constituted about 300,000, Palestinians 200,000, and the remainder comprised other Arab and Asian expatriates. Many Kuwaitis, and Arab and Asian expatriates, had fled Iraq and Kuwait into Jordan, while most European and US expatriates were detained as hostages; by the end of 1990 it was claimed that all hostages had been released.

UN Security Council Resolution 678, adopted in November 1990, authorized the multinational force by now stationed in Saudi Arabia and the Gulf region to use 'all necessary means' to liberate Kuwait. It was implied that should Iraq not begin, by 15 January 1991, to implement the terms of 10 resolutions hitherto adopted regarding the invasion, military action would ensue. Renewed international diplomatic attempts failed to avert a military confrontation. On the night of 16-17 January the US-led multinational force launched an intensive aerial bombardment of Iraq. Ground forces entered Kuwait during the night of 23-24 February, encountering relatively little effective Iraqi opposition. Within three days the Iraqi Government had agreed to comply with the terms of all Security Council resolutions concerning Kuwait, and on 28 February the USA announced a suspension of military operations. Resolutions 686 and 687, adopted by the UN Security Council in March and April respectively, dictated the terms to Iraq for a permanent cease-fire: Iraq was required to release all allied prisoners of war and Kuwaitis detained as hostages, repeal all laws and decrees concerning the annexation of Kuwait, and recognize the inviolability of the Iraq-Kuwait border. Iraq promptly announced its compliance with both resolutions. Resolution 689, adopted in April, provided for the establishment of a demilitarized zone, to be supervised by a UN Iraq-Kuwait Observation Mission (UNIKOM).

Meanwhile, in October 1990, at a conference in Jeddah of some 1,000 prominent Kuwaitis, the exiled Crown Prince Saad agreed to establish government advisory committees on political, social and financial matters, and pledged to restore the country's Constitution and legislature and to organize free elections after Kuwait's eventual liberation. In February 1991, however, the Government-in-exile excluded the possibility of early elections, maintaining that the need to rebuild and repopulate the country took precedence over that for political reform. Immediately following liberation an Amiri decree imposed martial law in Kuwait, and in March the formation of a state security committee was announced: its objectives included the investigation of individuals suspected of collaboration with the Iraqi authorities in Kuwait, the prevention of unofficial acts of reprisal and the identification of those civilians relocated to Kuwait by Iraq. Palestinians in Kuwait were a particular target of reprisals, and it was alleged by several human rights organizations that they were subject to torture by Kuwaiti security forces. Kuwait's Palestinian population, which had totalled around 400,000 prior to the Iraqi invasion, was estimated to have declined to less than 50,000 by early 1992.

The Amir, the Prime Minister and other members of the exiled regime returned to Kuwait in March 1991. The Council of Ministers resigned later that month, apparently in response to public discontent at the Government's failure to restore essential services. Although several specialists were appointed to strategic posts within the new Government named by Sheikh Saad in April (most notably to the finance, planning and oil portfolios), other important positions (including the foreign affairs, interior and defence ministries) were allocated to members of the al-Sabah family.

In May 1991 it was revealed that some 900 people were under investigation in Kuwait in connection with crimes committed during the Iraqi occupation; about 200 of these were accused of collaboration. The Government undertook to investigate alleged abuses documented by the human rights organization Amnesty International, which claimed that trials were being conducted without the provision of adequate defence counsel and that in some cases torture had been used to extract confessions. Martial law was ended in June, and 29 death sentences hitherto imposed on convicted collaborators were commuted to custodial terms. Outstanding trials relating to the occupation were to be referred to civilian courts, and in August a tribunal, said to guarantee defendants the right to greater legal protection as well as a right of appeal, was established to replace the martial law courts.

It was announced in May 1991 that a US military presence would remain in Kuwait until September, by which time, it was envisaged, a regional defence force would be established. However, little progress was achieved in negotiations for such a force, and in August the USA announced that it would maintain 1,500 troops in Kuwait for several more months. In September the US and Kuwaiti Governments signed a 10-year military co-operation agreement, permitting the storage of US supplies and equipment in Kuwait, and providing for joint military training and exercises. (The agreement was renewed for a further 10 years in February 2001.) Defence accords were signed with both the United Kingdom and France in 1992.

In June 1993 the State Security Court was reported to have issued death sentences against 17 people who had been found guilty of collaborating with Iraq in 1990-91; Alaa Hussein Ali, the leader of the provisional Government installed by Iraq in August 1990, was convicted *in absentia*. In February 1994 Amnesty International asserted that at least 120 alleged collaborators had been convicted by trials that failed to satisfy international minimum standards. Human rights organizations therefore welcomed the endorsement by the Majlis, in August 1995, of government proposals to abolish the State Security Court. In January 1997 the Government announced the creation of a new human rights committee within the Ministry of the Interior.

Political developments following the Gulf War

Press censorship was partially relaxed in January 1992. Elections to the new Majlis, on 5 October, were contested by some 280 candidates, many of whom (although nominally independent) were affiliated to one of several quasi-political organizations. The franchise was again restricted, with only about 81,400 men eligible to vote. Anti-Government candidates, notably those representing Islamist groups, were unexpectedly successful, securing 31 of the chamber's 50 seats. The Prime Minister subsequently formed a new Government, including six members of the Majlis, who were allocated, inter alia, the oil and justice portfolios; members of the ruling family retained control of foreign affairs, the interior and defence.

The Majlis voted in December 1992 to establish a commission of inquiry into the circumstances surrounding the 1990 invasion. The commission's report, published in May 1995, revealed profound negligence on the part of government and military officials, who had apparently ignored warnings of an imminent invasion. The report also claimed that the immediate flight of members of the royal family and the Council of Ministers had deprived the country of political leadership and military organization.

KUWAIT

In June 1994 the Majlis approved legislation extending the franchise to sons of naturalized Kuwaitis and in July 1995 it approved a bill reducing from 30 years to 20 the minimum period after which naturalized Kuwaitis would become eligible to vote. In July 1996 the Ministry of the Interior announced that an electorate of just over 107,000 men was entitled to vote in the forthcoming elections to the Majlis, scheduled for 7 October. Pro-Government candidates were the most successful, securing the majority of the 50 seats, and Sheikh Saad was reappointed Prime Minister.

In March 1998 Sheikh Saad submitted his Government's resignation, after members of the Majlis proposed a motion of no confidence in the Minister of Information, Sheikh Sa'ud Nasir al-Sa'ud al-Sabah, who had allowed what were deemed 'un-Islamic' publications to be exhibited at a book fair in Kuwait. The Amir immediately reappointed the Crown Prince as Prime Minister, and a new Government was named at the end of the month. The promotion of Sheikh Sa'ud to the post of Minister of Oil was controversial not only because of the recent action taken against him, but also because the oil portfolio was not customarily allocated to a member of the ruling family.

Confrontation persisted between the Government and the Majlis. In May 1999 the Amir dissolved the legislature and ordered fresh elections, after deputies had in the previous month questioned the Minister of Justice and of Awqaf (Religious Endowments) and Islamic Affairs over errors that had appeared in copies of the Koran printed and distributed by his ministry. Some 80% of an eligible electorate of 113,000 Kuwaiti men voted in the election, which took place on 3 July. Pro-Government candidates recorded the greatest losses, taking only 12 seats; Islamist candidates won 20 seats and liberals 14, with the remaining four seats won by independents. Sheikh Saad was again reappointed Prime Minister, and the ruling family retained control of the strategic foreign affairs, oil, interior and defence portfolios, although a number of liberal deputies joined the Government.

During the period between the dissolution of the Majlis and the election, the Government had promulgated some 60 decrees (subject to legislative approval), most notably one proposing that women should be allowed to contest and to vote in elections from 2003. However, the law on female suffrage was defeated by a considerable majority in the new Majlis in November 1999, as liberal deputies, who supported women's enfranchisement, registered their protest at what they considered to be the unconstitutionality of legislation by decree by joining Islamist and conservative deputies in voting against the measure. Liberal deputies immediately submitted identical legislation regarding women's suffrage, but this was narrowly defeated in a vote at the end of the month.

In January 2000 Alaa Hussein Ali, who had been in self-imposed exile since Kuwait's liberation, returned to Kuwait in order to appeal against the death sentence pronounced in June 1993 (see above). In May 2000 it was announced that Hussein had lost his appeal at the Court of First Instance, and that he planned a further challenge to his sentence. The Court of Appeal upheld the previous ruling in July, but in March 2001 commuted Hussein's death sentence to one of life imprisonment.

In July 2000 unrest was reported in the Al-Jahra region, where a community of *bidoun* ('stateless' Arabs) form the majority of the population. (About 100,000 *bidoun* reside in Kuwait, but the authorities refuse to recognize their claims to Kuwaiti nationality.) The unrest followed the approval, in May, of a draft amendment to the Citizenship Law that would grant only a small number of *bidoun* the right to Kuwaiti citizenship. Some 1,000 *bidoun* obtained Kuwaiti citizenship in early 2001, leading to protests by those whose applications had been refused.

Sheikh Saad tendered his Government's resignation in January 2001. The Crown Prince denied that this constituted an attempt to prevent parliamentary scrutiny of the Minister of Justice and of Awqaf and Islamic Affairs, Saad Jasem Yousuf al-Hashil, relating to allegations of inefficiency and corruption in his ministry. The Amir immediately reappointed Sheikh Saad as Prime Minister, and a new 15-member Government was named in February.

Meanwhile, during November 2000, as the crisis in Israeli–Palestinian relations deepened, 16 suspected Islamist militants (Kuwaitis and other Arab nationals) were arrested in Kuwait, accused of involvement in plotting bomb attacks on US military installations in the Gulf region in retaliation for perceived US support for Israel. In June 2001 a senior Kuwaiti military official was convicted of concealing weapons to be used for terrorist purposes; he received a 10-year prison sentence, but in December this was reduced to seven years.

In January 2002 four people died following a major explosion at Raudhatain, Kuwait's second largest oilfield, to the north of Kuwait City. Dr Adil Khalid al-Sabih immediately submitted his resignation as Minister of Oil, stating that he accepted responsibility for the incident. The Minister of Information, Sheikh Ahmad al-Fahd al-Ahmad al-Sabah, was subsequently named as acting Minister of Oil. Meanwhile, several members of the increasingly assertive Majlis demanded the resignation of the entire Government, alleging that the explosion at Raudhatain was the result of state corruption and mismanagement.

After a campaign that was overshadowed by the US-led military intervention in Iraq (which was largely conducted from Kuwaiti territory), parliamentary elections were held, as scheduled, on 5 July 2003. Islamist candidates secured 21 of the 50 seats in the Majlis, while pro-Government candidates won 14 seats, independents (regarded as being aligned with the Government) 12 and liberals three. The rate of voter participation was reported to be only 45% of the electorate (which comprised just 6% of the total population). The results were viewed as a major setback for those seeking political reform, and were widely interpreted as signalling popular dissatisfaction with the entire political process.

Sheikh Sabah appointed Prime Minister

Following the elections, in July 2003 the ailing Crown Prince relinquished the position of Prime Minister. The appointment of Sheikh Sabah al-Ahmad al-Sabah as his replacement represented an unprecedented separation between the post of Prime Minister and the position of Crown Prince, and provided some encouragement to reformists after their heavy electoral losses. A new Council of Ministers, including six new appointments, was also announced in mid-July. The most significant change was the merger of the oil portfolio with the Ministry of Electricity and Water to form the Ministry of Energy, to be headed by Sheikh Ahmad al-Fahd al-Ahmad al-Sabah.

In October 2003 and May 2004 the Council of Ministers approved legislation that would permit women to vote in and contest municipal and parliamentary elections, respectively. The Majlis gave provisional approval for the former piece of legislation in April 2005, but subsequently failed to ratify the legislation at a second vote in May. Both new laws were approved later in the month; however, this was too late to allow women to participate in the June municipal elections. By early 2006 it was reported that there were already considerably more women than men registered as voters. Kuwaiti women received their first opportunity to vote in and contest a municipal by-election on 4 April 2006, where two of the eight candidates were female. Some 28 women registered as candidates for legislative elections in June of the same year.

Meanwhile, in March 2004 the Minister of Finance, Mahmud Abd al-Khaliq al-Nuri, narrowly survived a vote of no confidence, having been heavily criticized by the Majlis for mismanagement during the sale of state property. Citing health reasons, al-Nuri resigned shortly after the vote; Bader Mishari al-Humaidhi was appointed as his replacement in April 2005. The day after the appointment of al-Humaidhi, the Minister of Health, Muhammad Ahmad al-Jarallah, resigned in advance of a parliamentary vote on a motion of no confidence accusing him of mismanagement; he thus became the third member of the Council of Ministers to resign in connection with hostile parliamentary questioning since the elections to the Majlis in July 2003 (the Minister of Information having stood down from his post in January 2005). Al-Jarallah's resignation was accepted by the Prime Minister in mid-April 2005, and the Minister of Energy, Sheikh Ahmad al-Fahd al-Sabah, assumed the health portfolio in an acting capacity. In June the Prime Minister appointed Dr Massouma Saleh al-Mubarak as Minister of Planning and Minister of State for Administrative Development Affairs, making her Kuwait's first female member of the Council of Ministers.

In the mean time, in February 2005 the Majlis approved legislation giving security agencies flexible new powers to search for and seize illegal firearms, following several confrontations between government forces and armed militants. Some of the violence was linked to reports of hostility towards Westerners, particularly US citizens, and al-Qa'ida was believed by some to be implicated in the violence. The new legislation was to be renewed on an annual basis.

KUWAIT

Introductory Survey

The accession of Sheikh Sabah

On 15 January 2006 the death of the Amir, Sheikh Jaber, was announced. He was automatically succeeded by the Crown Prince, Sheikh Saad. However, in an unprecedented development, on 24 January Sheikh Saad, who had yet to take the oath of office, was removed from the position of Amir on health grounds, following a formal request from the Council of Ministers that the Majlis debate the issue. Under the Constitution, the law of succession required a two-thirds' majority of Majlis deputies in order to dismiss an Amir, but, in the event, the vote in favour of replacing Sheikh Saad was unanimous. In the absence of a nominated Crown Prince, the Prime Minister, Sheikh Sabah, who was in any case regarded as the de facto ruler of the emirate, assumed the powers of the Amir pending the nomination of a permanent head of state by the Council of Ministers. Sheikh Sabah was duly sworn in as Amir on 29 January, after his widely predicted nomination had been unanimously approved by the Majlis. The sole controversy attached to Sheikh Sabah's accession was that, like the late Sheikh Jaber, he belonged to the al-Jaber branch of the ruling al-Sabah family, which, by tradition, alternated the position of Amir with the al-Salim branch of the family, of which Sheikh Saad was a member.

The new Amir accepted the resignation of the Council of Ministers in January 2006. In February Sheikh Sabah appointed Sheikh Nasser al-Muhammad al-Ahmad al-Sabah, a former diplomat and the Amir's nephew, as the new Prime Minister, and the erstwhile Deputy Prime Minister and Minister of the Interior, Sheikh Nawwaf al-Ahmad al-Jaber al-Sabah, the Amir's brother, as Crown Prince. The appointments, which maintained the post-2003 separation between the roles of premier and Crown Prince, emphasized the channelling of power towards the al-Jaber branch of the ruling family, although both men were respected for their extensive political experience. On the following day the Amir approved Sheikh Nasser's first Council of Ministers; a notable change was the addition of the interior portfolio to the responsibilities of the Minister of Defence, Sheikh Jaber Mubarak al-Hamad al-Sabah, who also became First Deputy Prime Minister.

A long-running campaign for electoral reform, which sought to reduce the number of electoral constituencies in Kuwait in order to diminish the opportunities for vote-buying, began to attract extensive popular support from May 2006. A proposal by the Government to reduce the number of constituencies from 25 to 10 was rejected by the opposition, which advocated a more comprehensive reduction, to just five constituencies. Following efforts by the Majlis to cross-examine the Prime Minister on the matter, the Amir dissolved parliament and called for elections to be held on 29 June, just over one year earlier than scheduled. A loose alliance of 29 pro-reform members of the outgoing legislature was formed to contest the elections, comprising candidates from across the political spectrum. Reformists made significant gains at the polls, winning 34 of the 50 seats contested. The remaining 16 seats were won by independents and pro-Government candidates; no female candidates were elected. Voter participation was reported to be 65% of those registered to vote; despite constituting 65% of the electorate, women accounted for only 35% of the total number of votes cast. A reform bill drafted by the new Majlis proposing the introduction of a five-constituency electoral system was passed into law in July. Meanwhile, in early July a new Council of Ministers was named under Prime Minister Sheikh Nasser. Although the key portfolios remained unchanged, the Minister of Energy, Sheikh Ahmad al-Fahd al-Sabah, failed to be reappointed, after he was accused by members of the opposition and pro-reformists of having interfered in the electoral process and of seeking to block reforms.

In December 2006 the Minister of Information, Muhammad Nasser al-Sanousi, resigned following a request by the increasingly confrontational Majlis to question him over allegations that he had curbed media freedom during the recent election campaign. In the following month deputies made a similar attempt to question the Minister of Health, Sheikh Ahmad Abdullah al-Ahmad al-Sabah, on four charges related to the mismanagement of, and deterioration in, the medical sector. Following the cross-examination of Sheikh Ahmad in February 2007, a motion of no confidence was filed against the minister; however, in early March, one day before the Majlis was due to debate the motion, the entire Council of Ministers resigned. A new Government, approved by the Amir in late March, excluded Sheikh Ahmad but retained most of the key ministers in the same posts. The reorganization also included the division of the recently created Ministry of Energy into the Ministry of Oil and the Ministry of Electricity and Water; the latter was to be headed by Muhammad Abdullah Hadi al-Olaim, spokesman of the Islamic Constitutional Movement. In June Sheikh Ali al-Jarrah al-Sabah, resigned as Minister of Oil; the Majlis had been scheduled to debate a motion of no confidence in the minister after members questioned him over allegations of corruption. Al-Olaim replaced Ali al-Sabah in an acting capacity. In October Prime Minister Sheikh Nasser instigated an extensive reorganization of the Council of Ministers, in an apparent attempt to prevent an escalation of the ongoing difficulties between the Government and the Majlis. New appointments included Sheikh Jaber Khalid al-Jaber al-Sabah as Minister of the Interior, Bader Mishari al-Humaidhi as Minister of Oil and Mustafa Jassem al-Shimali as Minister of Finance. However, in November al-Humaidhi resigned amid continuing controversy relating to his previous role as Minister of Finance (see above).

In January 2008 the liberal Minister of Education, Nouriya al-Subeeh, survived a no-confidence vote in the Majlis, having undergone a lengthy interrogation by Islamist and tribal deputies. The fact that political infighting was increasingly damaging Kuwait's prospects for economic and social development was said to be causing growing frustration among the population. On 17 March the entire Council of Ministers tendered its resignation, stating that relations with the Majlis had become untenable, and that the legislature was continuing to obstruct ministers' attempts to carry out their duties effectively. The immediate cause of the crisis involved a dispute concerning salary increases for state employees, with deputies asserting that the government pay rise was too low. Having cut short a visit to Morocco, on 19 March Sheikh Sabah ordered the dissolution of the Majlis in order for fresh elections to take place on 17 May. The elections would be the first to use the five-constituency system adopted into law in July 2006.

Meanwhile, in February 2008 tensions increased between Sunni and Shi'a Muslims in the emirate after several hundred people from the minority Shi'a community had held a rally to commemorate the death of a senior commander of the militant Shi'a organization Hezbollah in Lebanon. Imad Mughniyeh, who was killed in a bomb attack in the Syrian capital, Damascus, in that month, was described by the Kuwaiti Government as a 'terrorist', who, they claimed, had been responsible for the hijacking of a Kuwait Airways plane in 1988, in which two Kuwaiti passengers were murdered. A number of prominent Shi'a politicians and clerics were questioned by the authorities over their involvement in the rally, and many arrests were reported; Kuwaiti officials claimed that all of those under investigation were members of an illegal opposition group, Hezbollah Kuwait. In October 2008 it was reported that two prominent Shi'a members of the Majlis were among seven people acquitted by a court in Kuwait for their alleged membership of Hezbollah Kuwait.

Escalating tension between the Majlis and the Government following the election of May 2008

At the legislative election held, as scheduled, on 17 May 2008, Islamist candidates performed strongly, with Sunni Islamists winning 21 of the 50 seats in the Majlis and Shi'ite Islamists (including the Popular Action Bloc) nine; liberals and their allies garnered seven and the remaining 13 seats were won by independents. Of the 27 female candidates who stood for election, none secured a seat in the new Majlis. In spite of opposition from several parliamentarians, the Amir subsequently reappointed Sheikh Nasser to the post of Prime Minister. In late May Sheikh Nasser appointed a new Council of Ministers comprising 15 ministers, two of whom were women. The incumbent Ministers of Defence, Foreign Affairs, Finance and the Interior retained their posts in the new Council of Ministers, while al-Olaim, hitherto acting Minister for Oil, was appointed to the role in a permanent capacity (also retaining the electricity and water portfolios). It was immediately apparent, however, that the elections had done little to improve relations between the Majlis and the Government. At the first session of the new legislature, held in June, a number of members withdrew in protest against the composition of the new Council of Ministers.

In July 2008 hundreds of Bangladeshi workers protested about low and irregular wages and poor working conditions. The demonstration, which followed several similar ones in recent months, turned violent, and the police reportedly arrested and subsequently deported some 1,000 of the workers involved in the riot. The incident reignited international discussion of Kuwait's human rights record (a US State Department report on forced labour, published in June, had placed Kuwait in the 'worst offender' category). The Council of Ministers subsequently announced that it would introduce a minimum monthly wage of KD 40 (US $150) for workers employed by companies contracted by the Government. In October the Government announced its intention to draft legislation abolishing its much-criticized employee sponsorship system (which stipulates that foreign workers must be sponsored by a Kuwaiti employer); however, a package of labour market reforms aimed at improving the conditions of expatriate workers approved by the Majlis in December did not address this system, although the Government pledged in December 2010 to terminate the system during 2011.

Meanwhile, relations between the Majlis and the Council of Ministers deteriorated further in late 2008, as parliamentarians continued to express disquiet over the Prime Minister's handling of the Government and his alleged mismanagement of public funds. In early November three Sunni Islamist members of the Majlis submitted a request to question Sheikh Nasser over the decision to allow the controversial Iranian Shi'a cleric, Muhammad Baqer al-Fali, to visit Kuwait (al-Fali had been banned from entering Kuwait after being convicted of religious slurs that had offended Sunni Muslims and of 'threatening national unity'). To avert parliamentary questioning of the Prime Minister, on 25 November the entire Council of Ministers resigned; the Amir accepted its resignation on 1 December and asked Sheikh Nasser to form a new Government. The political upheaval jeopardized Kuwait's efforts to fortify and diversify its economy, which had suffered in 2008 in the wake of a growing global financial crisis.

On 12 January 2009 the Amir approved the formation of a new Council of Ministers. Prime Minister Sheikh Nasser retained his post, as did many of the ministers from the outgoing Government, although Al-Olaim did not secure reappointment. Several deputies walked out of the opening parliamentary session in protest at the lack of new appointments to the Council of Ministers, and the nomination of Sheikh Ahmad Abdullah al-Ahmad al-Sabah as Minister of Oil in early February further strained relations between the legislature and the Government: some members of the Majlis asserted that the appointment was unconstitutional, given that he had been subject to a motion of no confidence in his capacity as Minister of Health two years previously.

In March 2009 several Islamist members of the legislature sought to question the Prime Minister about allegations of mismanagement, misuse of public funds and the failure to adapt economic policy to the worsening global financial climate. The continued refusal by Sheikh Nasser to submit to scrutiny precipitated the resignation of the entire Council of Ministers on 16 March. Two days later the Amir ordered the dissolution of parliament; fresh elections were subsequently called for May. Meanwhile, in late March the Council of Ministers, which remained in office on an interim basis, finally approved a programme of economic stimulus, envisaging expenditure of up to US $5,200m. to support Kuwait's beleaguered financial markets. The initiative was ratified by the Amir and entered into effect in April.

An estimated 59% of eligible voters participated in parliamentary elections on 16 May 2009: Sunni Islamists retained only 11 seats in the 50-member Majlis, losing out to Shi'ite Islamists (who won nine seats) and liberals (eight seats), with the balance gained by the tribal-based independents. Although the main figures involved in the previous confrontations with the Government were returned to the Majlis, 20 new deputies were elected, many of whom were joining the legislature for the first time. Four deputies elected to the new Majlis were women, the first to be elected since women were allowed to participate in electoral politics in 2005. Most observers concluded that the new parliament would be more liberal in outlook, compared with its predecessor. Sheikh Nasser was reappointed Prime Minister and a new, 16-member Council of Ministers, including seven new appointees (among them Dr Massouma Saleh al-Mubarak, Kuwait's first female government minister), was named in late May 2009. However, members of the ruling family retained the key foreign affairs, oil, interior and defence portfolios, and Sheikh Ahmad Abdullah al-Ahmad al-Sabah, the Minister of Oil, assumed additional responsibility for information.

Recent developments: political events after the 2009 elections

In his speech at the inaugural session of the new legislature on 31 May 2009, the Amir stressed the urgent need for renewed co-operation at all levels of government in order to safeguard national unity and promote economic development. However, the session was boycotted by 14 Islamist and tribal deputies in protest at the composition of the new Council of Ministers. Several Islamist deputies also lodged objections against the presence of Dr Moudhi Abd al-Aziz al-Homoud, the Minister of Education and Higher Education, and two female members of parliament, who declined to wear the *hijab* (Islamic headscarf) during the opening session, accusing them of violating legislation requiring women to adhere to *Shari'a* (Islamic) law.

Tensions between the Majlis and the Council of Ministers resumed immediately, and it appeared that the recent government reorganization had failed to break the political impasse that had produced three dissolutions of parliament in as many years. Deputies launched scathing attacks against the ministers responsible for defence, finance and the interior during early sessions of the legislature in June 2009. Following allegations of corruption relating to the award of ministry tenders, and other financial irregularities, a motion of no confidence against the Minister of the Interior, Sheikh Jaber, was proposed in late June. However, in early July the motion was comfortably defeated.

In the second week of August 2009 security officials announced that they had discovered plans by an al-Qa'ida-linked terrorist group, comprising six Kuwaiti nationals, to launch bomb attacks against Camp Arifjan, the main US military base in Kuwait; further attacks against the Shuaiba oil refinery and a state security building were reportedly also planned. Five suspects were arrested that month, while a sixth was already in custody on other charges. In late August the suspects reportedly retracted their initial confessions, which they claimed had been extracted under torture. Trial proceedings commenced in December and included two further suspects, who were tried *in absentia*. However, the state prosecutor subsequently withdrew the charge of plotting to attack Camp Arifjan; charges of manufacturing explosives and possessing illegal weapons remained. All eight defendants were acquitted in May 2010, owing to insufficient evidence.

A legal petition seeking to invalidate the election of two female parliamentary deputies, on the grounds that they refused to wear the *hijab*, was rejected by the Constitutional Court in October 2009, which ruled that wearing the *hijab* was not compulsory by law and stressed that personal freedoms and freedom of religion were enshrined in the Constitution. In an unprecedented move, on 8 December Prime Minister Sheikh Nasser agreed to submit himself to formal scrutiny by members of parliament, concerning allegations of misuse of public funds; similar motions were lodged against three other senior government ministers. Following the interrogation of the Prime Minister and the Ministers of Defence, the Interior, and Public Works and Municipal Affairs in a closed parliamentary session on 9 December, 10 deputies proposed a motion of non-co-operation against Sheikh Nasser, which, if successful, would require his dismissal or the dissolution of parliament; a motion of no confidence was lodged against Sheikh Jaber, the Minister of the Interior. The Prime Minister comfortably survived the vote against him, which was conducted in the Majlis on 16 December, with 35 deputies voting in his support, 13 against and one abstaining. The no-confidence motion against Sheikh Jaber was also defeated on the same day.

In early 2010 renewed tension surfaced between the executive and the legislature over controversial legislation under which the Government would be required to purchase all personal loans in Kuwait, cancel the outstanding interest and reschedule repayments, at an estimated cost of US $23,000m. The initiative, which was to be financed from state deposits, gained parliamentary approval in January but was subsequently rejected by the Council of Ministers; Minister of Finance al-Shimali contended that the proposed legislation 'undermines the banking, financial and legal systems in the country, and reinforces a disrespect for contracts'. In June parliament voted against further discussion of the initiative, thereby thwarting the ambitions of certain elements within the legislature that had sought a second parliamentary vote on the legislation. Meanwhile, in an apparent political breakthrough, a four-year economic development plan proposed by the Government received parliamentary support in February, leading to renewed optimism concerning the introduction of much-needed economic reforms; the plan was duly implemented in April. (For further details, see Economic Affairs.) In the same month initial draft legislation that would allow the privatization of certain state assets was endorsed by members of the Majlis; the final legislation, which excluded privatization of the production of petroleum and natural gas, oil refineries and the health and education sectors, and stipulated that all privatized companies should be *Shari'a*-compliant, was approved by parliament in May. However, hopes of a rapprochement between the executive and the legislature were quashed in June when the Prime Minister was asked by parliament to submit to further questioning, following allegations of negligence in his official duties. In the event, the session was cancelled after deputies were unable to reach consensus on whether the questioning should take place during a closed or open parliamentary session.

Human rights issues continued to be a source of considerable anti-Government sentiment throughout 2010. In April Muhammad Abd al-Qader al-Jassem, a prominent Kuwaiti journalist, author and former editor of *Al-Watan* newspaper, was convicted of criticizing government policy and defaming Prime Minister Sheikh Nasser; he was sentenced to six months' imprisonment and ordered to pay a fine of US $17,500. In May al-Jassem, who had remained free pending an appeal, was ordered to be detained for further investigation into new charges, including inciting the overthrow of the Government, undermining the status of the Amir and damaging national interests. The charges were all reported to have been brought in response to criticism of Sheikh Nasser and the Government made by al-Jassem in three books on Kuwaiti politics, as well as articles posted on his internet site. Opposition and human rights groups urged the authorities to release al-Jassem, the charges against whom, they argued, were politically motivated. Al-Jassem, who had begun a hunger strike in protest against his detention, was released on bail in June, following protests from his supporters and human rights groups, who had voiced concerns about his health.

Al-Jassem's conviction for defaming the Prime Minister was overturned on appeal in July 2010, and later that month he was acquitted of further charges of defamation, as well as the charges of inciting the overthrow of the Government and undermining the status of the Amir, which human rights groups hailed as a triumph for freedom of expression and for the Kuwaiti judicial system. However, in the same month the Prime Minister and Minister of Information declared that public criticism of the Amir, Prime Minister, government ministers and countries with which Kuwait enjoyed close relations constituted a threat to national unity, and announced that the Government intended to amend the press and publications law accordingly. In November al-Jassem was convicted on a further charge of defaming the Prime Minister and was sentenced to one year's imprisonment; in the following month this was reduced to three months. Although al-Jassem was released in mid-January 2011, after the Supreme Court overturned his original conviction, a new series of similar charges was reported to have been levelled against the writer at the end of that month.

Meanwhile, Khalid al-Fadalah, the Secretary-General of the liberal National Democratic Alliance (NDA), was imprisoned for three months and fined KD 150 (US $500), having been convicted in June 2010 of defaming the Prime Minister at a public rally in December 2009; al-Fadalah was reported to have accused Sheikh Nasser of complicity in instances of money-laundering. Salah al-Mudhaf was appointed to replace al-Fadalah as NDA Secretary-General on an interim basis. Al-Fadalah was released after serving 10 days in prison, after the Court of Appeal ruled that the initial sentence had been too severe. In an attempt to clear his name, al-Fadalah subsequently appealed against the original verdict, insisting that he had committed no crime and was being targeted for his political views. However, in December 2010 it was announced that he was to be retried in early 2011, prompting criticism from human rights groups which appealed for his immediate acquittal.

Further claims that the Government was intent on suppressing freedom of expression were provoked by its decision to shut down the local offices of the Qatar-based broadcasting network Al Jazeera in mid-December 2010, accusing the network of interference in Kuwait's internal affairs; the Government withdrew Al Jazeera's media accreditation and barred the network's reporters from working in Kuwait. A few days previously Al Jazeera had broadcast video footage that purported to show Kuwaiti security forces using excessive force to disperse people attending a rally staged by the opposition in early December. At least 14 people, including four parliamentary deputies, were reported to have been injured in the resulting clashes. Opposition deputies attributed the blame for the violence to the Prime Minister, claiming that the authorities' response had represented an attempt to intimidate dissenters. In late December a motion of non co-operation was filed against Sheikh Nasser by members of a broad-based opposition grouping within the Majlis, which blamed the Prime Minister for the violence, claiming that the authorities' heavy-handed response had been 'premeditated' by the Government in an attempt to intimidate dissenters. Sheikh Nasser again survived the motion, voting on which was conducted in January 2011; however, unlike in December 2009, the motion against the Prime Minister was only narrowly defeated, with the opposition falling just four votes short of the required majority.

Opposition members pledged to continue to fight for the removal from office of the Prime Minister and Government, and tensions continued to escalate. In February 2011 the Deputy Prime Minister and Minister of the Interior, Sheikh Jaber, resigned from office in advance of parliamentary questioning over allegations that a man arrested by police in January had been tortured to death while in custody; he was replaced by Sheikh Ahmad al-Homoud al-Jaber al-Sabah. In early March a number of youth opposition groups began protests in the capital demanding the resignation of Sheikh Nasser and reform of the political system. Later that month parliamentarians filed requests to interrogate three government ministers—the Minister of Oil and Information, Ahmad Abdullah al-Ahmad, the Deputy Prime Minister for Economic Affairs and Minister of State for Development Affairs and for Housing Affairs, Dr Ahmad Fahad al-Ahmad al-Jaber al-Sabah, and the Deputy Prime Minister and Minister of Foreign Affairs, Sheikh Dr Muhammad Sabah al-Salim al-Sabah (all of whom were members of the ruling family). The first two ministers were required to submit to questioning related to allegations of corruption and financial mismanagement, while the third was to be questioned over his response to a broadcast by Bahraini state television which was deemed to be critical of Kuwait and its ruling family. On 1 April the Amir accepted the resignation of the Council of Ministers, which had been announced the previous day by the Prime Minister. However, Sheikh Nasser and his administration were instructed to remain in office on an interim basis pending the formation of a new government. Despite repeated calls from members of the opposition and protesters for Sheikh Nasser to be replaced, on 5 April the outgoing premier was reappointed to the role and instructed to form a new government—his seventh Council of Ministers since being appointed as Prime Minister in 2006. The new Council of Ministers was duly sworn in on 8 May 2011. Ali Fahd Rashid al-Rashid replaced Roudhan Abd al-Aziz Roudhan as Minister of State for Cabinet Affairs, while the Minister of State for Parliamentary Affairs, Muhammad Mohsen al-Busairi, additionally became Minister of Oil. The Minister of Social Affairs and Labour, Muhammad Mohsen Hassan al-Ifasi, assumed the additional roles of Deputy Prime Minister and Minister of Justice. Dr Ahmad Fahad al-Ahmad al-Jaber al-Sabah remained as a deputy prime minister and Minister of State for Housing Affairs, although the economic and development affairs roles were abolished. Members of the ruling family retained the key foreign affairs, interior and defence portfolios they had held in the outgoing administration.

Regional Relations

Friction between Kuwait and Iraq in the aftermath of the Gulf War was exacerbated by the issue of the demarcation of their joint border. The UN commission with responsibility for delineating the frontier formalized the land border as it had been defined by British administrators in 1932 (and officially agreed by Kuwait and Iraq in 1963). The boundary, the validity of which was now rejected by Iraq, was established some 570 m north of its pre-war position, dividing the Iraqi port of Umm Qasr, with the effect that Iraq retained the town and much of the harbour, while Kuwait was awarded hinterland that included an abandoned Iraqi naval base; the border also situated several Iraqi oil wells on Kuwaiti territory. In January 1993 the USA led air attacks on Iraq, and more than 1,000 US troops were dispatched to Kuwait, in response to a series of incursions by Iraqi forces into Kuwaiti territory in the days immediately preceding the designated entry into force of the new border; its formal delineation was completed in March, when the UN commission defined the maritime border along the median line of the Khawr Abd Allah waterway. Allegations made by Kuwait of Iraqi violations of the border, and of attempts to impede construction of a trench along the land border, intensified during the second half of 1993, and there were sporadic reports of exchanges of fire in the border region. In November a 775-strong armed UNIKOM reinforcement was deployed in northern Kuwait, with authorization (under specific circumstances) to use its weapons to assist the unarmed force already in the demilitarized zone.

In October 1994 Iraq deployed some 70,000 troops and 700 tanks near the border with Kuwait, in an apparent attempt to force an easing of UN economic sanctions. Kuwait immediately mobilized its army reserves, and dispatched some 20,000 troops to the border region. The USA committed almost 40,000 land, naval and air forces to the region; France and the United Kingdom deployed naval vessels, and the United Kingdom dispatched about 1,200 troops. Following Russian mediation, Iraq announced its willingness to recognize Kuwait's sovereignty and borders, on condition that the UN ease sanctions against Iraq after six months. However, the UN Security Council adopted a resolution (No. 949) requiring Iraq's unconditional recognition of Kuwait's sovereignty and borders and restricting the movement of Iraqi troops in the border area. In November Iraq officially recognized Kuwait's sovereignty, territorial integrity and political independence, as well as its UN-defined borders. Most of the US and British reinforcements deployed in the region in October had been withdrawn by the end of the year.

Kuwait's relations with Iraq deteriorated sharply in September 1996, after the Kuwaiti Government agreed to the deployment in Kuwait of US military aircraft and troops in support of a US operation to force the withdrawal of Iraqi armed forces from the Kurdish 'safe haven' in northern Iraq. In December the USA announced that some 4,200 US troops deployed in Kuwait during 1996 would be withdrawn by the end of the year, although the deployment of US F-117 *Stealth* fighter aircraft was to be extended.

As the crisis involving weapons inspections in Iraq by the UN Special Commission (see the Contemporary Political History of Iraq) deepened in February 1998, fears were expressed for Kuwait's security—in particular that an attack on Iraq might result in the use of chemical or other weapons of mass destruction against Kuwait. The USA, supported by the United Kingdom, undertook a military deployment in the Gulf region at this time: by the end of the month, when the UN Secretary-General and the Iraqi Government reached a compromise agreement regarding weapons inspections, some 6,000 US ground troops had been dispatched to Kuwait. Following a series of air-strikes against targets in Iraq by US and British forces from December 1998, Iraq accused Kuwait of collaborating in the air attacks, and frequently reiterated claims to Kuwaiti territory. In November 1999 the Majlis established a committee to examine future relations with Iraq, and in December the Kuwaiti Government welcomed UN Security Council Resolution 1284 (establishing a new weapons inspectorate for Iraq), which incorporated demands for: the repatriation of Kuwaiti and other prisoners from Iraq, Iraq's co-operation with the International Committee of the Red Cross (ICRC), and the return of Kuwaiti property seized during the occupation.

In September 2000 Iraq renewed its long-standing accusation that Kuwait was drilling oil wells on Iraqi territory, and accused Kuwait and Saudi Arabia of inflicting suffering on the Iraqi population through the maintenance of UN sanctions. In November 2001 Kuwait issued a formal complaint to the UN, following an alleged violation of its territory by Iraq. In January 2002 the Kuwaiti leadership was reported to have rejected attempts by the Arab League to persuade it to accept Iraqi proposals apparently aimed at improving bilateral relations: as part of Iraq's diplomatic offensive to secure the support of the Arab world in view of the threat of US-led military action against Saddam Hussain's regime, the Iraqi leader had conveyed an appeal to Arab states to set aside their differences. Later in the month it was reported that Iraq had announced its preparedness to allow a delegation from Kuwait to visit Iraq to verify that no Kuwaiti prisoners of war were being held. At the Arab League summit held in Beirut, Lebanon, in March 2002, however, it was announced that Kuwait and Iraq had reached agreement on the resolution of outstanding differences.

Relations with Iraq were profoundly affected by the political repercussions of the suicide attacks against New York and Washington, DC, in September 2001. Kuwait, which strongly condemned the attacks, thereafter assumed an important role in persuading other Gulf states to join the US-led 'coalition against terror'. US bases in Kuwait were subsequently used to provide logistical support to the US-led campaign against al-Qa'ida (held by the USA to be principally responsible for the suicide attacks) and its Taliban hosts in Afghanistan during late 2001. Meanwhile, in October the Kuwaiti authorities revoked the citizenship of the official spokesperson of al-Qa'ida, Sulayman Abu Ghaith, after remarks that he had made via Al Jazeera.

During the course of 2002 increased speculation that the US Administration of George W. Bush intended to extend the 'war on terror' to target the regime of Saddam Hussain in Iraq threatened to fuel opposition to a continued US presence in the region and exacerbate an increasingly tense political situation in Kuwait. In December some 12,000 US troops were stationed in Kuwait, and the entire northern half of Kuwait was designated a closed military zone from February 2003. In March an emergency meeting of the Arab League, hosted by Qatar, to discuss the deepening crisis descended into a bitter exchange of insults between, primarily, a senior Iraqi official and the Kuwaiti Minister of Information. Kuwait subsequently supported a proposal made by the President of the United Arab Emirates (UAE) for Saddam Hussain to go into exile in order to prevent a US-led war to remove his regime. At the outset of military action, which commenced in late March, US-led troops in Kuwait, the base for the main ground assault on Iraq, numbered some 140,000. Iraqi armed forces launched several missiles at Kuwaiti territory, although little damage was caused in the emirate during the course of the conflict. In the aftermath of the most intense period of fighting, which President Bush declared to have ended by early May, Kuwait renewed its financial demands against Iraq, while a number of Kuwaiti firms entered into agreements with the US-led occupying powers. In October the demilitarized zone between Iraq and Kuwait was ended and, having fulfilled its mandate, UNIKOM's operations were terminated.

The resumption of diplomatic relations between Iraq and Kuwait was announced in mid-2004. In 2005 Kuwait began the construction of a 200-km steel barrier along the border with Iraq, parts of which were destroyed by Iraqi militants who claimed that it was encroaching upon their land; however, in November 2006 Iraq agreed to allow the fence to be completed. In April 2007 the Kuwaiti Government expressed its hope that the two countries would open diplomatic missions in their respective capitals in the near future. This ambition was realized in July 2008, when Kuwait announced the appointment of an ambassador to Iraq—its first since the Iraqi invasion of mid-1990; Ali Muhammad al-Momen took up his post in the Iraqi capital, Baghdad, in October. (Iraq had earlier reopened its embassy in Kuwait, which was initially headed by a chargé d'affaires; Muhammad Hussain Bahr al-Ulum was subsequently appointed, in April 2010, as Iraq's first ambassador to Kuwait since the Iraqi invasion.) Further evidence of an improvement in relations between Kuwait and Iraq was provided in February 2009, when Deputy Prime Minister and Minister of Foreign Affairs, Sheikh Dr Muhammad Sabah al-Salim al-Sabah, visited Baghdad for talks with Iraqi Prime Minister Nuri al-Maliki. During the visit al-Maliki spoke of Iraq's desire to distance itself from the regime of Saddam Hussain, and sought to reassure Sheikh Dr Muhammad of the country's growing emphasis on 'security' and 'stability'.

In June 2009 Iraq's Permanent Representative to the UN, Hamid al-Bayati, lodged an official request with the Security Council requesting a reduction in the reparation payments owed to Kuwait (see below). In July the issue of reparations was the primary topic in talks between Prime Minister al-Maliki and UN Secretary-General Ban Ki-Moon in New York. However, later that month Sheikh Dr Muhammad Sabah al-Salim al-Sabah stated in a newspaper interview that Iraqi 'violations' of their common border continued to represent a serious threat to regional security and bilateral relations, and urged Iraq to respect all existing UN resolutions relating to the Gulf War. Bilateral negotiations aimed at resolving all outstanding differences between Kuwait and Iraq, under the auspices of the UN, continued throughout 2009–10. In January 2011 Prime Minister Sheikh Nasser paid an official visit to Baghdad, the first visit to Iraq by a Kuwaiti premier since the Gulf War. At the inauguration of a new building for the Kuwaiti embassy in Baghdad later that month, the Kuwaiti ambassador and Iraqi Minister of Foreign Affairs Hoshyar al-Zibari pledged to work toward resolving remaining issues of bilateral contention, notably issues pertaining to Iraqi reparation payments. However, a maritime border skirmish earlier in January, in which a Kuwaiti coast-guard official was fatally shot by a group of Iraqi fishermen, served as a tangible reminder of enduring bilateral tensions.

Meanwhile, in May 1994 the governing body of the UN Compensation Commission (UNCC), responsible for considering claims for compensation arising from the 1990–91 Gulf crisis, approved the first disbursements (to 670 families or individuals

KUWAIT

Introductory Survey

in 16 countries), totalling US $2.7m. By late 1996 payments amounting to $3,000m. (to be financed partly by Iraqi petroleum revenues) had been endorsed by the UN, which had yet to consider claims for a further $190,000m. In December international arbitrators recommended that a payment of $610m. should be made to the Kuwait Oil Company (KOC), in compensation for the cost of extinguishing oil wells set alight by retreating Iraqi troops in early 1991. In March 1997 the Kuwaiti general committee responsible for evaluating war damages stated that it was to begin compensation payments, initially to some 4,500 citizens who had incurred losses valued at less than $100,000. The disbursement of a further $84m. to some 33,800 individuals was authorized by the UN in February 1999. In September 2000 the UN Security Council approved the payment to the Kuwait Petroleum Corporation (which controls the KOC) of $15,900m. in compensation for lost petroleum revenues arising from the Iraqi occupation. However, the Security Council decided at the same time to reduce the share of Iraqi petroleum revenues to be paid into the compensation fund from 30% to 25%. France and Russia, which increasingly opposed the maintenance of sanctions against Iraq, had delayed a decision by the UNCC on the payment, and Russia had warned of its inclination to oppose Kuwaiti claims to reparations unless the levy on Iraqi petroleum revenues were reduced. By mid-2003 the majority of individual claimants (Kuwaitis and expatriates in Kuwait and Iraq during the Gulf war) had received compensation, with total disbursements being valued at some $17,600m. Meanwhile, the UNCC was considering a claim of $86,000m. by the Kuwait Investment Agency, principally in recompense for lost earnings during the conflict. However, in a deposition issued in June 2003, the UNCC rejected all but $1,500m. of the claim. In May 2003 UN Security Council Resolution 1483 had reduced the share of Iraqi petroleum revenue to be used for compensation payments from 25% to 5%, which was expected to result in outstanding compensation payments believed to total more than $30,000m. remaining unpaid for several decades. In January 2004, following similar announcements by the Governments of the UAE and Qatar, Sheikh Sabah stated that Kuwait was prepared to waive a 'significant proportion' of the estimated $16,000m. owed by Iraq. This did not, however, include any war reparations still claimed by the Government. In March 2005 the UN panel overseeing payments to victims of the Gulf crisis approved a further disbursement of $265m. to families of those who had died in Iraqi detention. At a final session of the UNCC governing body, held in June, a further $367m. in compensation was awarded to successful claimants. The claims assessment process was concluded thereafter, and payments to individuals ceased in 2007. In July 2009 payments worth $430m. were made by the UNCC, principally to Kuwaiti state-owned and private companies and government agencies for losses incurred as a result of the Iraqi invasion and occupation; a further disbursement of $610m. was issued in October. In July 2010 further reparations amounting to $650m. were paid by the UNCC to nine Kuwaiti companies and government agencies. A further $590m. was disbursed in October, while some $680m. was paid out in January 2011, taking the total value of payments issued by the UNCC since 1994 to around $31,400m.; according to the UNCC, some $21,000m. remained owing to Kuwait.

In July 2000 Kuwait and Saudi Arabia signed an agreement finalizing the delineation of their maritime borders. Kuwait subsequently commenced negotiations with Iran on the demarcation of respective rights to the continental shelf, following complaints by the Kuwaiti and Saudi authorities over Iran's decision to begin drilling for gas in a disputed offshore area. Iraq asserted that, as a concerned party, it should be included in the Kuwaiti-Iranian discussions. Iran suspended drilling pending the conclusion of the dispute; talks remained ongoing at early 2011.

Meanwhile, in December 2000 a defence agreement was signed by the six member states of the Co-operation Council for the Arab States of the Gulf (Gulf Co-operation Council—GCC, see p. 243). Kuwait opposes any military action being taken by the USA against Iran, and supports the Iranian Government's right to develop a peaceful nuclear energy programme. In July 2007 the US Administration unveiled a US $20,000m. package of military assistance and weapons sales to Kuwait and the other GCC member states, in an attempt to bolster security in the Gulf region and to encourage the GCC to side with the USA in its dispute with the Iranian regime regarding the latter's nuclear programme.

Prime Minister Sheikh Nasser made an official visit to Tehran in November 2009, the first such visit by a Kuwaiti premier since the foundation of the Islamic Republic of Iran in 1979. Sheikh Nasser, accompanied by a senior-level ministerial delegation, held talks encompassing economic co-operation and bilateral relations with Iranian First Vice-President Muhammad Reza Rahimi. The premier also met with Ayatollah Sayed Ali Khamenei, Iran's Supreme Religious Leader. Discussions on the possible construction of a sub-marine gas pipeline connecting Kuwait with Iran's gas network were also conducted between Kuwait's Minister of Oil and Information, Sheikh Ahmad Abdullah al-Ahmad al-Sabah, and his Iranian counterpart. In April 2010 a delegation of senior Kuwaiti officials concluded several bilateral co-operation agreements in Tehran, including understandings concerning the import of Iranian water and gas. However, relations were threatened by the discovery in the following month of an allegedly Iranian-led network of spies in Kuwait; seven people, including three Iranians, one Syrian, and one Kuwaiti soldier, were arrested on suspicion of belonging to the network. Several legislators demanded the expulsion of the Iranian ambassador in Kuwait, while Iranian officials denied any involvement in espionage in Kuwait, dismissing the case as an attempt to create 'a climate of fear towards Iran'. The seven were charged in early August with, inter alia, passing confidential military information to Iran's Islamic Revolutionary Guards Corps, and their trial commenced later that month. The defendants initially confessed to the charges against them, but their lawyer subsequently claimed that these confessions had been extracted under duress. At early 2011 their trial, which was conducted behind closed doors, remained ongoing.

CONSTITUTION AND GOVERNMENT

Under the 1962 Constitution, executive power is vested in the Amir, the Head of State (who is chosen by and from members of the ruling family), and is exercised through the Council of Ministers. The Amir appoints the Prime Minister and, on the latter's recommendation, other ministers. Legislative power is vested in the unicameral Majlis al-Umma (National Assembly), with 50 elected members who serve for four years (subject to dissolution), along with some 15 government ministers who sit as *ex officio* members. In May 2005 legislation was approved allowing women to vote in legislative and municipal elections for the first time. The country is divided administratively into six governorates.

REGIONAL AND INTERNATIONAL CO-OPERATION

Kuwait is a member of the Co-operation Council for the Arab States of the Gulf (Gulf Co-operation Council—GCC, see p. 243); the six GCC states established a unified regional customs tariff in January 2003, and agreed to create a single market and currency. The economic convergence criteria for the monetary union were agreed at a GCC summit in Abu Dhabi, the UAE, in December 2005, and in January 2008 the GCC launched its common market. Kuwait also participates in the League of Arab States (the Arab League, see p. 361) and the Organization of Arab Petroleum Exporting Countries (OAPEC, see p. 397).

Kuwait became a member of the UN in May 1963 and, as a contracting party to the General Agreement on Tariffs and Trade, joined the World Trade Organization (WTO, see p. 430) upon its establishment in 1995. The country is also a participant in the Organization of the Petroleum Exporting Countries (OPEC, see p. 405), the Organization of the Islamic Conference (OIC, see p. 400) and the Group of 77 developing countries (G77, see p. 447).

ECONOMIC AFFAIRS

In 2007, according to estimates by the World Bank, Kuwait's gross national income (GNI), measured at average 2005–07 prices, was US $116,984m., equivalent to $43,930 per head (or $53,590 on an international purchasing-power parity basis). During 2000–09, it was estimated, the population increased at an average annual rate of 2.7%, while gross domestic product (GDP) per head grew, in real terms, by an average of 4.3% per year in 2000–07. Overall GDP was estimated to have increased, in real terms, at an average annual rate of 7.2% in 2000–07. Real GDP rose by 4.4% in 2007.

Agriculture (including hunting, forestry and fishing) contributed 0.2% of GDP in 2009. The sector engaged 2.2% of the labour force in mid-2009. The principal crops are potatoes, tomatoes, cucumbers, aubergines and dates. Owing to scarcity of water, little grain is produced, and the bulk of food requirements is

KUWAIT

imported. (Imports of food and live animals accounted for 11.5% of merchandise imports in 2007.) Livestock, poultry and fishing are also important. Agricultural GDP increased, in real terms, by an average annual rate of 4.0% in 2000–07. The agricultural sector contracted by 8.8% in 2007.

Industry (including mining, manufacturing, construction and power) provided 51.7% of GDP in 2009, and employed 17.7% of the labour force in mid-2009. During 2000–07 industrial GDP increased, in real terms, at an average annual rate of 7.7%. The GDP of the sector increased by 4.8% in 2006, and by 2.7% in 2007.

Mining and quarrying contributed 43.5% of GDP in 2009, although the sector engaged only 0.4% of the labour force in mid-2009. The production of petroleum and its derivatives is the most important industry in Kuwait, providing an estimated 92.7% of export revenue in 2009. At the end of 2009 the country's proven recoverable reserves of petroleum were 101,500m. barrels, representing about 7.6% of world reserves. Kuwait's petroleum production averaged 2.48m. barrels per day (b/d) in 2009; the Government aimed to increase its production capacity to 4.0m. b/d by 2020. As a member of the Organization of the Petroleum Exporting Countries (OPEC, see p. 405), Kuwait is subject to production quotas agreed by the Organization's Conference. There are significant reserves of natural gas (1,780,000m. cu m at the end of 2009) associated with the petroleum deposits. Output was 12,800m. cu m in that year. Moreover, in March 2006 a major discovery of non-associated gas in the north of the country was announced. During 2000–07 the GDP of the mining sector increased, in real terms, at an average rate of 64.4% per year. The sector's GDP declined by 6.9% in 2006, and further fell by 8.0% in 2007.

Manufacturing provided 5.1% of GDP in 2009, and employed 6.8% of the labour force in mid-2009. Petroleum refineries accounted for 60.5% of manufacturing activity, measured by gross value of output, in 2004. Of the other branches of manufacturing, the most important are the production of building materials (and related activities such as aluminium extrusion), fertilizer production, food processing and the extraction of salt and chlorine. During 2000–07 manufacturing GDP increased, in real terms, at an average annual rate of 3.0%. Growth in the manufacturing sector was 1.6% in 2007.

Construction contributed 1.8% of GDP in 2009, and engaged 9.8% of the employed labour force in mid-2009. During 2000–07 construction GDP increased, in real terms, at an average annual rate of 9.0%. The GDP of the sector grew by 3.7% in 2007, compared with 18.5% in 2006.

Electrical energy is derived from Kuwait's own resources of petroleum (providing 72.3% of total electricity production in 2007) and both local and imported natural gas (27.7%).

Services contributed 48.1% of GDP in 2009, and employed 80.1% of the labour force in mid-2009. Kuwait's second most important source of revenue is investment abroad, both in petroleum-related ventures and in other industries, chiefly in the USA, Western Europe and Japan; many such investments are held by the Reserve Fund for Future Generations (RFFG—to which 10% of petroleum revenues must by law be contributed each year, and which is intended to provide an income after hydrocarbon resources have been exhausted) and managed by the Kuwait Investment Authority. As part of its efforts to diversify the economy, the Government plans to develop the islands of Bubiyan and Failaka into major tourist resorts. The combined GDP of the service sectors increased, in real terms, at an average rate of 10.2% per year during 2000–07. The services sector grew by 12.8% in 2007.

In 2009 Kuwait recorded a visible trade surplus of US $33,263m., and there was a surplus of $28,605m. on the current account of the balance of payments. In 2009 the principal sources of imports were Brazil and the People's Republic of China, which provided, respectively, 14.0% and 12.7% of total imports; other important suppliers in that year were the USA, Germany, Japan, Saudi Arabia and India. Details concerning the destination of Kuwait's petroleum exports are not available for recent years; however, the major markets for non-petroleum exports in 2009 included the UAE (11.6%), Saudi Arabia and India. The principal exports are petroleum and petroleum products. The principal imports are machinery and transport equipment (which accounted for 40.2% of total imports in 2009), basic manufactures and other manufactured goods, food and live animals, and chemicals and related products.

A budget surplus of KD 6,437.2m. was recorded for the financial year ending 30 June 2010. Kuwait's general government gross debt was KD 4.046m. in 2009, equivalent to 14.3% of GDP. Kuwait's total external debt in 2007 was estimated at US $26,300m., equivalent to 23.5% of GDP. The average annual rate of inflation in 2000–09 was 3.5%; according to the IMF, consumer prices increased by an estimated average of 4.0% in 2009. National unemployment among Kuwaitis was estimated at only 3.6% at June 2009; however, underemployment was unofficially reported to be up to 50%.

Despite its significant, oil-based wealth, Kuwait has a number of fundamental weaknesses in its economic structure: instability in its relations with Iraq have necessitated a high level of defence expenditure; reliance on petroleum revenues has impeded diversification into other industries; and its constitutional commitment to provide employment for all Kuwaitis has resulted in a heavy burden on government spending. Plans to allow foreign participation in a development project for the northern oilfields (known as 'Project Kuwait'), which aimed to increase national production from 2.5m. b/d to 4m. b/d by 2020, were first proposed by the Kuwait Petroleum Corpn (KPC) in 1997. However, the project was hampered by consistent opposition from the Majlis, as many deputies remained opposed to foreign involvement in the petroleum sector, which was exempted from legislation approved by parliament in April 2010 permitting the privatization of certain state assets. In the same month the Kuwait Oil Co signed a five-year agreement, worth almost US $800m., with Royal Dutch Shell of the Netherlands/United Kingdom to develop Kuwait's northern gasfields. (Despite significant reserves, Kuwait is a net importer of natural gas.) Kuwait's economic performance was adversely affected by the sharp fall in oil prices and the global financial crisis, which took hold from September 2008. The revelation, in January 2009, that Kuwait's banks had incurred a combined loss of $1,000m. through their exposure to distressed US assets undermined confidence in the financial system. The implementation of a fiscal stimulus package, which was to provide up to $5,200m. in state guarantees for new credit facilities, was effected in April. In February 2010 the Majlis approved a four-year economic development plan that envisaged expenditure of up to $125,000m. on energy, transport, social and utilities projects, with special provisions for private sector participation. The gradual recovery in oil prices from 2009 resulted in a higher than predicted budget surplus, of KD 6,437m., in 2009/10 and was expected to result in a significantly larger surplus in 2010/11; oil revenues in the nine months to 31 December 2010 amounted to KD 14,200m., while non-oil revenues totalled about KD 1,000m. The budget for 2010/11, approved by the Amir in July 2010, had envisaged a deficit of KD 6,591m. for 2010/11, with government expenditure projected at KD 16,310m. (representing an increase of some 33% on 2009/10 spending levels) and revenues budgeted at KD 9,719m., based on an assumed average oil price of $43 per barrel; however, at January 2011 the price of oil was about $91 per barrel. The IMF projected GDP growth of 4.4% for 2011, compared with growth of 2.3% anticipated in 2010.

PUBLIC HOLIDAYS

2012: 1 January (New Year's Day), 4 February* (Mouloud, Birth of the Prophet), 25 February (Kuwaiti National Day), 26 February (Liberation Day), 16 June* (Leilat al-Meiraj, Ascension of the Prophet), 18 August* (Id al-Fitr, end of Ramadan), 25 October* (Id al-Adha, Feast of the Sacrifice), 14 November (Muharram, Islamic New Year).

* These holidays are dependent on the Islamic lunar calendar and may vary by one or two days from the dates given.

KUWAIT

Statistical Survey

Sources (unless otherwise stated): Economic Research Department, Central Bank of Kuwait, POB 526, 13006 Safat, Kuwait City; tel. 22403257; fax 22440887; e-mail cbk@cbk.gov.kw; internet www.cbk.gov.kw; Central Statistical Office, POB 26188, 13122 Safat, Kuwait City; tel. 22454968; fax 22430464; e-mail salah@mop.gov.kw; internet cso.gov.kw.

Note: Unless otherwise indicated, data refer to the State of Kuwait as constituted at 1 August 1990, prior to the Iraqi invasion and annexation of the territory and its subsequent liberation. Furthermore, no account has been taken of the increase in the area of Kuwait as a result of the adjustment to the border with Iraq that came into force on 15 January 1993.

Area and Population

AREA, POPULATION AND DENSITY

Area (sq km)	17,818*
Population (census results)†‡	
20 April 1995	1,575,570
20 April 2005 (preliminary results)	
Males	1,310,067
Females	903,336
Total	2,213,403
Population (official estimate at mid-year)§	
2007	3,399,600
2008	3,441,800
2009	3,484,900‖
Density (per sq km) at mid-2009	195.6

* 6,880 sq miles.
† Figures include Kuwaiti nationals abroad. The total population at the 2005 census comprised 880,774 Kuwaiti nationals (433,977 males; 446,797 females) and 1,332,629 non-Kuwaitis (876,090 males; 456,539 females).
‡ Excluding adjustment for underenumeration.
§ Estimates based on new methodology used by the Public Authority for Civil Information. Source: partly IMF, *Kuwait: Statistical Appendix* (July 2010).
‖ Comprising 1,118,900 Kuwaitis (548,300 males; 570,600 females) and 2,366,000 non-Kuwaitis (1,591,900 males; 774,000 females).

POPULATION BY AGE AND SEX
(UN estimates at mid-2011)

	Males	Females	Total
0–14	365,796	356,279	722,075
15–64	1,434,766	882,487	2,317,253
65 and over	45,583	31,837	77,420
Total	1,846,145	1,270,603	3,116,748

Source: UN, *World Population Prospects: The 2008 Revision*.

GOVERNORATES
(population at 2005 census, preliminary)

Governorate	Area (sq km)*	Population	Density (per sq km)
Capital	199.8	261,013	1,306.4
Hawalli	}	487,514	
Mubarak al-Kabir	368.4	176,519	3,491.2
Farwaniya	}	622,123	
Al-Jahra	11,230.2	272,373	24.3
Al-Ahmadi	5,119.6	393,861	76.9
Total	16,918.0	2,213,403	130.8

* Excluding the islands of Bubiyan and Warba (combined area 900 sq km).

PRINCIPAL TOWNS
(population at 1995 census)

Kuwait City (capital)	28,747	Subbah al-Salem	54,608
Salmiya	129,775	Sulaibiah	53,639
Jaleeb al-Shuyukh	102,169	Farwaniya	52,928
Hawalli	82,154	Al-Kreen	50,689
South Kheetan	62,241	Subahiya	50,644

Mid-2010 (incl. suburbs, UN estimate): Kuwait City 2,305,404 (Source: UN, *World Urbanization Prospects: The 2009 Revision*).

BIRTHS, MARRIAGES AND DEATHS

	Registered live births		Registered marriages		Registered deaths	
	Number	Rate (per 1,000)	Number	Rate (per 1,000)	Number	Rate (per 1,000)
1993	37,379	25.6	10,077	6.9	3,441	2.4
1994	38,868	24.0	9,550	5.9	3,464	2.1
1995	41,169	22.8	9,515	5.3	3,781	2.1
1996	44,620	23.6	9,022	4.8	3,812	2.0
1997	42,817	21.6	9,610	4.9	4,017	2.0
1998	41,424	20.4	10,335	5.1	4,216	2.1
1999	41,135	19.5	10,847	5.1	4,187	2.0
2000	41,843	19.1	10,785	4.9	4,227	1.9

2004: Total births 47,274; Total deaths 4,793; Total marriages 12,359.
2005: Total births 50,941; Total deaths 4,784; Total marriages 12,419.
2006: Total births 52,759; Total deaths 5,247; Total marriages 12,584.
2007: Total births 53,587; Total deaths 5,293; Total marriages 13,315.
2008: Total births 54,571; Total deaths 5,701; Total marriages 12,649.

Life expectancy (years at birth, WHO estimates): 78 (males 78; females 79) in 2008 (Source: WHO, *World Health Statistics*).

ECONOMICALLY ACTIVE POPULATION
('000 persons aged 15 years and over, mid-2009)

	Kuwaitis	Non-Kuwaitis	Total
Agriculture, hunting and fishing	0.3	37.8	38.1
Mining and quarrying	4.6	1.7	6.2
Manufacturing	8.8	109.2	118.0
Electricity, gas and water	10.3	2.1	12.4
Construction	8.2	161.5	169.6
Wholesale and retail trade	11.5	308.5	320.0
Transport, storage and communications	8.7	58.4	67.1
Finance, insurance, real estate and business services	18.3	89.1	107.3
Public administration	247.0	648.8	895.7
Sub-total	317.5	1,416.9	1,734.5
Activities not adequately defined	34.0	324.8	358.7
Total labour force	351.5	1,741.7	2,093.2
Males	190.6	1,343.3	1,533.9
Females	160.8	398.4	559.2

Source: IMF, *Kuwait: Statistical Appendix* (July 2010).

Health and Welfare

KEY INDICATORS

Total fertility rate (children per woman, 2008)	2.2
Under-5 mortality rate (per 1,000 live births, 2008)	11
HIV/AIDS (% of persons aged 15–49, 1994)	<0.2
Physicians (per 1,000 head, 2005)	1.8
Hospital beds (per 1,000 head, 2005)	1.9
Health expenditure (2007): US $ per head (PPP)	814
Health expenditure (2007): % of GDP	2.2
Health expenditure (2007): public (% of total)	77.5
Access to water (% of persons, 2008)	99
Total carbon dioxide emissions ('000 metric tons, 2007)	86,074.7
Carbon dioxide emissions per head (metric tons, 2007)	32.3
Human Development Index (2010): ranking	47
Human Development Index (2010): value	0.771

For sources and definitions, see explanatory note on p. vi.

KUWAIT

Agriculture

PRINCIPAL CROPS
('000 metric tons)

	2005	2006	2007
Potatoes	20.7	20.7*	23.5*
Cabbages and other brassicas	9.5*	8.4*	13.7
Lettuce*	6.4	6.4	6.5
Tomatoes	64.0*	55.8	55.5*
Cauliflowers and broccoli*	7.0	6.9	7.3
Pumpkins, squash and gourds*	5.0	5.0	5.1
Cucumbers and gherkins*	34.0	34.0	35.0
Aubergines (Eggplants)*	15.0	15.0	15.5
Chillies and peppers, green*	7.0	7.0	8.0
Onions, dry	9.6*	7.2*	10.7
Dates	15.8*	16.0	14.5*

* FAO estimate(s).

2008: Production assumed to be unchanged from 2007 (FAO estimates).

Note: No data were available for individual crops in 2009.

Aggregate production ('000 metric tons, may include official, semi-official or estimated data): Total cereals 3.3 in 2005–06, 3.7 in 2007–08, 3.8 in 2009; Total roots and tubers 20.7 in 2005–06, 23.5 in 2007–09; Total vegetables (incl. melons) 212.6 in 2005, 200.9 in 2006, 213.4 in 2007–09; Total fruits (excl. melons) 16.7 in 2005, 17.0 in 2006, 15.5 in 2007–09.

Source: FAO.

LIVESTOCK
('000 head, year ending September)

	2006	2007	2008
Cattle*	28.0	28.0	28.0
Camels	5.8	5.8	5.8
Sheep*	900	900	900
Goats*	160.0	160.0	160.0
Chickens*	32,500	32,500	33,000

* FAO estimates.

2009 (FAO estimates): Camels 5.8; Chickens 33,500.

Source: FAO.

LIVESTOCK PRODUCTS
('000 metric tons)

	2004*	2005	2006
Cattle meat	2.7	2.2*	2.2*
Sheep meat	29.8	34.0	30.0*
Chicken meat	40.0	32.4	42.0*
Cows' milk	40.0	43.0	43.0
Goats' milk	4.0	4.5	4.9*
Hen eggs	22.0	26.0	22.0*

* FAO estimate(s).

2007–08: Figures assumed to be unchanged from 2006 (FAO estimates).

Source: FAO.

Fishing

(metric tons, live weight)

	2006	2007	2008*
Capture	5,635	4,373	4,373
Hilsa shad	136	78	78
Mullets	301	259	259
Groupers	148	169	169
Grunts and sweetlips	107	140	140
Croakers and drums	35	45	45
Yellowfin seabream	320	305	305
Indo-Pacific king mackerel	73	58	58
Carangids	124	92	92
Natantian decapods	2,245	1,540	1,540
Silver pomfret	175	101	101
Aquaculture	568	348	360
Nile tilapia	557	293	300
Total catch	**6,203**	**4,721**	**4,733**

* FAO estimates.

Source: FAO.

Mining

	2007	2008	2009
Crude petroleum ('000 metric tons)	129,950	137,176	121,309
Natural gas (million cu metres)	12,100	12,750	12,500

Source: BP, *Statistical Review of World Energy*.

Industry

SELECTED PRODUCTS
('000 metric tons, unless otherwise stated)

	2007	2008	2009
Bran and flour*	345.0	336.7	n.a.
Sulphur (by-product)†	830	830	830
Chlorine*	25.2	24.7	n.a.
Caustic soda (Sodium hydroxide)*	36.4	37.0	n.a.
Salt†	14.0	14.0	14.0
Nitrogenous fertilizers†‡	430	430	420
Motor spirit (petrol) (million barrels)†§	76	80	80
Kerosene (million barrels)†§	61	65	65
Gas-diesel (distillate fuel) oils (million barrels)†§	96	96	96
Residual fuel oils (mazout—million barrels)†§	75	69	69
Quicklime†	50	50	45
Cement†	2,200	2,200	2,000
Electric energy (million kWh)*§	48,800	51,700	n.a.

* Source: IMF, *Kuwait: Statistical Appendix* (July 2010).
† Source: US Geological Survey; estimates.
‡ Production in terms of nitrogen.
§ Including an equal share of production with Saudi Arabia from the Neutral (Partitioned) Zone.

Finance

CURRENCY AND EXCHANGE RATES

Monetary Units
1,000 fils = 10 dirhams = 1 Kuwaiti dinar (KD).

Sterling, Dollar and Euro Equivalents (31 December 2010)
£1 sterling = 439.28 fils;
US $1 = 280.60 fils;
€1 = 374.94 fils;
10 Kuwaiti dinars = £22.76 = $35.64 = €26.67.

Average Exchange Rate (fils per US $)
2008   268.8
2009   287.8
2010   286.7

From 1 January 2003 the official exchange rate was fixed within the range of US $1 = 289 fils to $1 = 310 fils (KD 1 = $3.4602 to KD 1 = $3.2258), but this 'peg' to the US dollar was abandoned in May 2007 in favour of a basket of currencies including the pound sterling, the euro and the yen.

GENERAL BUDGET
(KD million, year ending 30 June)

Revenue	2008/09	2009/10	2010/11
Tax revenue	349.1	296.4	307.9
International trade and transactions	214.7	190.8	223.2
Non-tax revenue	20,656.7	17,391.6	9,411.4
Oil revenue	19,710.7	16,584.9	8,616.6
Total operating revenue of government enterprises	517.8	566.3	636.2
Total	21,005.8	17,687.9	9,719.3

Expenditure	2008/09	2009/10	2010/11
Current expenditure	9,321.3	8,095.0	10,627.2
Land acquisitions	179.3	10.1	1.7
Capital expenditure	122.1	226.6	225.0
Construction expenditure	1,178.5	1,071.2	2,088.3
Other expenditure	7,460.9	1,847.8	3,367.8
Total	18,262.2	11,250.7	16,310.0

INTERNATIONAL RESERVES
(US $ million at 31 December)

	2007	2008	2009
Gold (national valuation)	116.3	115.0	110.7
IMF special drawing rights	231.0	234.2	2,261.3
Reserve position in IMF	143.5	267.7	397.8
Foreign exchange	16,285.6	16,611.0	17,608.4
Total	16,776.4	17,227.8	20,378.2

Source: IMF, *International Financial Statistics*.

MONEY SUPPLY
(KD million at 31 December)

	2007	2008	2009
Currency outside depository corporations	641.5	707.8	775.7
Transferable deposits	3,788.2	4,192.8	4,383.5
Other deposits	14,530.2	17,049.7	19,736.5
Broad money	18,959.9	21,950.2	24,895.8

Source: IMF, *International Financial Statistics*.

COST OF LIVING
(Consumer Price Index; base: 2000 = 100)

	2007	2008	2009
Food	129.9	145.0	149.6
Beverages and tobacco	122.3	145.6	159.1
Clothing and footwear	128.6	137.9	144.7
Housing	116.1	131.0	137.7
Transport and communication	110.2	115.0	114.9
Education and medical care	132.0	145.1	151.3
All items (incl. others)	118.3	130.8	136.0

Source: IMF, *Kuwait: Statistical Appendix* (July 2010).

NATIONAL ACCOUNTS
(KD million at current prices)

Expenditure on the Gross Domestic Product

	2007	2008	2009
Government final consumption expenditure	4,563.1	5,307.8	6,465.9
Private final consumption expenditure	9,917.6	11,139.0	11,724.7
Increase in stocks / Gross fixed capital formation	6,664.8	7,364.7	4,383.5
Total domestic expenditure	21,145.5	23,811.5	22,574.1
Exports of goods and services	20,661.0	26,450.0	17,755.0
Less Imports of goods and services	9,226.0	10,271.0	8,829.0
GDP in purchasers' values	32,580.5	39,990.5	31,500.1

Gross Domestic Product by Economic Activity

	2007	2008	2009
Agriculture, hunting, forestry and fishing	69.5	71.9	73.3
Mining and quarrying	17,094.4	23,653.5	14,232.4
Manufacturing	1,803.0	1,755.6	1,681.7
Electricity, gas and water	337.0	362.9	418.8
Construction	595.6	604.6	584.5
Trade	1,130.8	1,132.4	1,126.1
Restaurants and hotels	240.1	253.3	255.9
Transport, storage and communications	2,394.5	2,589.8	2,623.6
Finance, insurance, real estate and business services	6,307.1	6,348.1	6,115.9
Community, social and personal services	4,089.7	4,786.4	5,612.4
Sub-total	34,061.7	41,558.5	32,724.6
Import duties	215.7	217.1	226.3
Less Imputed bank service charges	−1,696.9	−1,785.1	−1,450.8
GDP in purchasers' values	32,580.5	39,990.5	31,500.1

BALANCE OF PAYMENTS
(US $ million)

	2007	2008	2009
Exports of goods f.o.b.	62,526	86,944	50,344
Imports of goods f.o.b.	−19,117	−22,939	−17,081
Trade balance	43,409	64,004	33,263
Exports of services	10,169	11,448	11,348
Imports of services	−13,344	−15,264	−13,598
Balance on goods and services	40,234	60,189	31,013
Other income received	16,327	13,962	10,227
Other income paid	−3,932	−3,219	−2,502
Balance on goods, services and income	52,629	70,932	38,739
Current transfers (net)	−10,453	−10,689	−10,133
Current balance	42,715	60,242	28,605

KUWAIT

—continued	2007	2008	2009
Capital account (net)	1,488	1,729	1,034
Direct investment abroad	-9,784	-9,091	-8,706
Direct investment from abroad	112	-6	145
Portfolio investment assets	-35,581	-32,084	8,485
Portfolio investment liabilities	677	3,955	-887
Other investment assets	-14,483	-18,821	-9,204
Other investment liabilities	24,178	4,215	-13,269
Net errors and omissions	-5,563	-10,032	-2,446
Overall balance	3,219	647	3,759

Source: IMF, *International Financial Statistics*.

External Trade

PRINCIPAL COMMODITIES
(KD million)

Imports c.i.f.	2007	2008	2009
Food and live animals	698	880	849
Chemicals and related products	484	558	571
Basic manufactures	1,394	1,478	973
Machinery and transport equipment	2,527	2,721	2,351
Miscellaneous manufactured articles	715	758	823
Total (incl. others)	6,062	6,679	5,852

Exports f.o.b.*	2007	2008	2009
Petroleum, petroleum products, etc.	16,780	22,200	13,415
Crude petroleum	10,941	15,492	8,567
Refinery products	5,285	5,976	4,386
Non-petroleum products	991	1,173	1,073
Plastics in primary forms	345	n.a.	n.a.
Road vehicles	194	n.a.	n.a.
Total	17,771	23,373	14,488

*Source: IMF, *Kuwait: Statistical Appendix* (July 2010); including re-exports (KD million): 342 in 2007; 402 in 2008; 310 in 2009.

PRINCIPAL TRADING PARTNERS
(KD million)*

Imports c.i.f.	2007	2008	2009
Australia	161.2	141.0	127.9
Brazil	61.6	162.5	781.8
Canada	56.8	93.1	50.0
China, People's Repub.	696.8	780.7	707.0
France (incl. Monaco)	162.9	136.8	160.4
Germany	452.0	489.1	445.7
India	252.3	302.7	315.5
Iran	110.6	58.8	35.3
Italy	365.9	322.8	261.2
Japan	517.2	641.1	419.4
Korea, Repub.	243.2	223.5	247.7
Malaysia	67.0	77.8	60.5
Netherlands	87.6	91.3	92.9
Saudi Arabia	365.6	374.6	346.8
Spain	77.6	64.7	59.7
Switzerland-Liechtenstein	85.6	102.1	91.8
Syria	26.7	25.3	32.3
Taiwan	49.5	52.3	106.7
Thailand	86.8	100.9	142.4
Turkey	78.0	152.1	76.3
United Arab Emirates	223.0	264.1	249.7
United Kingdom	206.4	190.2	188.4
USA	686.2	719.1	635.3
Total (incl. others)	6,061.5	6,678.7	5,852.2

Exports f.o.b.†	2007	2008	2009
Bahrain	25.2	45.2	41.2
Belgium-Luxembourg	3.6	2.3	5.1
China, People's Repub.	29.9	25.9	32.6
Egypt	16.9	20.4	23.3
India	110.4	143.9	94.4
Indonesia	52.3	56.4	41.8
Iran	39.3	34.5	26.8
Japan	0.8	8.7	2.1
Jordan	44.1	58.1	64.8
Korea, Repub.	4.7	4.1	3.4
Lebanon	14.9	13.9	13.4
Malaysia	11.1	9.3	10.1
Oman	12.7	16.0	18.9
Pakistan	42.8	69.1	37.0
Philippines	3.3	3.3	3.9
Qatar	56.2	55.9	42.3
Saudi Arabia	94.5	114.2	127.0
Spain	15.5	4.8	8.0
Syria	27.3	25.0	26.2
Taiwan	1.3	2.7	1.1
Turkey	11.7	34.3	65.9
United Arab Emirates	148.3	185.4	168.5
USA	74.9	125.8	51.8
Total (incl. others)	990.2	1,281.4	1,456.0

* Imports by country of production; exports by country of last consignment.
† Excluding petroleum exports.

Transport

ROAD TRAFFIC
(motor vehicles in use at 31 December)

	1995	1996	1997
Passenger cars	662,946	701,172	747,042
Buses and coaches	11,937	12,322	13,094
Goods vehicles	116,813	121,753	127,386

1999: Buses and coaches 12,775; Goods vehicles 97,706.

2000: Buses and coaches 10,974; Goods vehicles 80,378.

2001: Passenger cars 715,000; Commercial vehicles 226,000.

2004: Passenger cars, 858,055; Buses and coaches 37,789; Commercial vehicles 143,151.

2007: Passenger cars, 750,635; Buses and coaches 27,295; Vans and lorries 573,212; Motorcycles and mopeds 13,648 (Source: IRF, *World Road Statistics*).

SHIPPING

Merchant Fleet
(registered at 31 December)

	2007	2008	2009
Number of vessels	212	205	209
Displacement ('000 grt)	2,426.8	2,366.5	2,369.3

Source: IHS Fairplay, *World Fleet Statistics*.

International Sea-borne Freight Traffic
('000 metric tons)*

	1988	1989	1990
Goods loaded	61,778	69,097	51,400
Goods unloaded	7,123	7,015	4,522

* Including Kuwait's share of traffic in the Neutral (Partitioned) Zone.

Source: UN, *Monthly Bulletin of Statistics*.

Goods loaded ('000 metric tons): 89,945 in 1997.

Goods unloaded ('000 metric tons): 746 in 1991 (July–December only); 2,537 in 1992; 4,228 in 1993; 5,120 in 1994; 5,854 in 1995; 6,497 in 1996; 6,049 in 1997.

KUWAIT

CIVIL AVIATION
(traffic on scheduled services)

	2004	2005	2006
Kilometres flown (million)	44	43	42
Passengers carried ('000)	2,496	2,433	2,435
Passenger-km (million)	7,285	7,282	6,946
Total ton-km (million)	892	905	891

Source: UN, *Statistical Yearbook*.

Tourism

VISITOR ARRIVALS BY COUNTRY OF ORIGIN
(incl. excursionists)

	2006	2007	2008
Bahrain	99,133	108,216	112,910
Bangladesh	127,568	99,183	93,585
Egypt	421,152	508,434	532,753
India	560,951	653,392	673,671
Iran	96,597	93,248	90,839
Lebanon	94,522	110,289	117,055
Pakistan	188,223	196,631	214,427
Philippines	118,593	118,750	117,812
Saudi Arabia	1,158,775	1,349,441	1,425,049
Sri Lanka	71,952	83,457	90,896
Syria	251,764	289,848	304,605
Total (incl. others)	3,899,105	4,481,616	4,735,910

Tourism receipts (US $ million, incl. passenger transport): 508 in 2006; 530 in 2007; 610 in 2008.

Source: World Tourism Organization.

Communications Media

	2007	2008	2009
Telephones ('000 main lines in use)	529.0	541.0	553.5
Mobile cellular telephones ('000 subscribers)	2,773.7	2,907.0	3,876.0
Internet users ('000)	900	1,000	1,100
Broadband subscribers ('000)	35	40	45

1996: Daily newspapers 8 (average circulation 635,000 copies); Non-daily newspapers 78.

1999: Radio receivers 1,200,000 in use; Television receivers 910,000 in use; Facsimile machines 60,000 in use; Book titles published 219.

2000: Television receivers 930,000 in use.

2004: Daily newspapers 8; Non-daily newspapers 91.

Personal computers: 600,000 (236.6 per 1,000 persons) in 2005.

Sources: UNESCO, *Statistical Yearbook*; UN, *Statistical Yearbook*; International Telecommunication Union.

Education

(state-controlled schools, 2000/01)

	Schools	Teachers	Males	Females	Total
Kindergarten	153	3,379	22,142	22,128	44,270
Primary	184	8,151	48,796	49,322	98,118
Intermediate	165	9,073	47,955	47,509	95,464
Secondary	117	9,234	34,868	41,353	76,221
Religious institutes	7	351	n.a.	n.a.	2,454
Special training institutes	33	756	n.a.	n.a.	543

Private education (2007/08): 106 kindergarten schools (1,725 teachers, 30,111 students); 131 primary schools (4,306 teachers, 77,907 students); 122 intermediate schools (2,731 teachers, 46,218 students); 92 secondary schools (2,499 teachers, 26,945 students).

2000/01 (private education): 112 schools; 7,324 teachers; 128,204 students.

2008/09: *Teaching staff:* kindergarten 6,468, primary 24,605, secondary general 30,770, secondary technical/vocational 436, tertiary 3,329; *Student enrolment:* kindergarten 71,146 (2007/08), primary 210,665, secondary general 250,745; secondary technical/vocational 4,356; tertiary 61,920 (Source: UNESCO Institute for Statistics).

Pupil-teacher ratio (primary education, UNESCO estimate): 8.6 in 2008/09 (Source: UNESCO Institute for Statistics).

Adult literacy rate (UNESCO estimates): 94.5% (males 95.2%; females 93.1%) in 2007 (Source: UNESCO Institute for Statistics).

Directory

The Government

HEAD OF STATE

Amir of Kuwait: His Highness Sheikh SABAH AL-AHMAD AL-JABER AL-SABAH (acceded 29 January 2006).

COUNCIL OF MINISTERS
(May 2011)

Prime Minister: Sheikh NASSER AL-MUHAMMAD AL-AHMAD AL-SABAH.

First Deputy Prime Minister and Minister of Defence: Sheikh JABER MUBARAK AL-HAMAD AL-SABAH.

Deputy Prime Minister and Minister of the Interior: Sheikh AHMAD HOMOUD AL-JABER AL-SABAH.

Deputy Prime Minister and Minister of Foreign Affairs: Sheikh Dr MUHAMMAD SABAH AL-SALIM AL-SABAH.

Deputy Prime Minister and Minister of State for Housing Affairs: Sheikh AHMAD FAHAD AL-AHMAD AL-SABAH.

Deputy Prime Minister, Minister of Justice and of Social Affairs and Labour: Dr MUHAMMAD MOHSEN HASSAN AL-IFASI.

Minister of State for Cabinet Affairs: ALI FAHD RASHID AL-RASHID.

Minister of Finance: MUSTAFA JASSEM AL-SHIMALI.

Minister of Public Works and Minister of State for Municipal Affairs: Dr FADHIL SAFAR ALI SAFAR.

Minister of Oil and Minister of State for Parliamentary Affairs: Dr MUHAMMAD MOHSEN AL-AL-BUSAIRI.

Minister of Health: Dr HILAL MUSAED AL-SAYER.

Minister of Education and of Higher Education: AHMAD ABD AL-MOHSEN AL-MLAIFI.

Minister of Commerce and Industry: Dr AMANI KHALID BURESLI.

Minister of Electricity and Water: SALIM AL-UTHAINA.

KUWAIT

Minister of Information and of Communications: SAMI ABD AL-LATIF AL-NESEF.
Minister of Awqaf (Religious Endowments) and Islamic Affairs: MUHAMMAD ABBAS AL-NOMES.

MINISTRIES

Diwan of the Prime Minister: POB 1397, 13014 Kuwait City; tel. 22000000; fax 22223150; e-mail info@pm.gov.kw; internet www.pm.gov.kw.
Ministry of Awqaf (Religious Endowments) and Islamic Affairs: POB 13, 13001 Safat, Kuwait City; tel. 22487225; internet www.islam.gov.kw.
Ministry of Commerce and Industry: POB 2944, 13030 Safat, Kuwait City; tel. 2248000; fax 22424411; e-mail admin@moci.gov.kw; internet www.moci.gov.kw.
Ministry of Communications: POB 15, 13001 Safat, Kuwait City; tel. 24840606; internet www.moc.kw.
Ministry of Defence: POB 1170, 13012 Safat, Kuwait City; tel. 24848300; fax 24846059; e-mail it@mod.gov.kw; internet www.mod.gov.kw.
Ministry of Education: POB 7, 13001 Safat, Hilali St, Kuwait City; tel. 24839452; fax 22423676; e-mail webmaster@moe.edu.kw; internet www.moe.edu.kw.
Ministry of Electricity and Water: POB 12, 13001 Safat, Kuwait City; tel. 25371000; fax 25371420; internet www.mew.gov.kw.
Ministry of Finance: POB 9, 13001 Safat, al-Morkab St, Ministries Complex, Kuwait City; tel. 22480000; fax 22404025; e-mail webmaster@mof.gov.kw; internet www.mof.gov.kw.
Ministry of Foreign Affairs: POB 3, 13001 Safat, Gulf St, Kuwait City; tel. 22425141; fax 22420429; e-mail mofa.site@mofa.gov.kw; internet www.mofa.gov.kw.
Ministry of Health: POB 5, 13001 Safat, Arabian Gulf St, Kuwait City; tel. 24863840; fax 24863485; e-mail health@moh.gov.kw; internet www.moh.gov.kw.
Ministry of Higher Education: tel. 24925177; fax 24925260; e-mail info_minister@mohe.edu.kw; internet www.mohe.edu.kw.
Ministry of Information: POB 193, 13002 Safat, al-Sour St, Kuwait City; tel. 22415301; fax 22418605; e-mail info@moinfo.gov.kw; internet www.moinfo.gov.kw.
Ministry of the Interior: POB 11, 13001 Safat, Kuwait City; tel. 22430500; fax 24348821; e-mail contact@moi.gov.kw; internet www.moi.gov.kw.
Ministry of Justice: POB 6, 13001 Safat, al-Morkab St, Ministries Complex, Kuwait City; tel. 22486218; fax 22442257; e-mail info@moj.gov.kw; internet www.moj.gov.kw.
Ministry of Oil: POB 5077, 13051 Safat, Kuwait City; tel. 22406990; e-mail alnaft@moo.gov.kw; internet www.moo.gov.kw.
Ministry of Public Works: POB 8, 13001 Safat, Kuwait City; tel. 25385520; fax 25380829; e-mail undersecretary@mpw.gov.kw; internet www.mpw.gov.kw.
Ministry of Social Affairs and Labour: POB 563, 13006 Safat, Kuwait City; tel. 22480000; fax 22419877; internet www.mosal.gov.kw.

Legislature

Majlis al-Umma
(National Assembly)

POB 716, Safat 13008; tel. 22436336; fax 22436331; e-mail kwt-ipu-grp@majlesalommah.net; internet www.majlesalommah.net.
Speaker: JASEM AL-KHARAFI.

Elections to the 50-seat Majlis took place three years early on 16 May 2009, following the dissolution of the legislature by Sheikh Sabah in March (precipitated by a continuing dispute between the Government and parliament over the accountability of the Prime Minister). Sunni Islamists retained only 11 seats; Shi'ite Islamists took nine; liberals and their allies secured eight; and the remaining seats were won by independent candidates. Among the incoming deputies were four women, the first to win election to the Kuwaiti legislature.

Political Organizations

Political parties are not permitted in Kuwait. However, several quasi-political organizations are in existence. Among those that have been represented in the Majlis since 1992 are:

Islamic Constitutional Movement (Hadas): internet www.icmkw.org; f. 1991; Sunni Muslim; political arm of the Muslim Brotherhood; Sec.-Gen. NASSER AL-SANE.
Islamic Salafi Alliance: Sunni Muslim; Sec.-Gen. ALI AL-OMAIR (acting).
Justice and Peace Alliance: Shi'a Muslim; Leader HASSAN NASIR.
Kuwait Democratic Forum: f. 1991; loose asscn of secular, liberal and Arab nationalist groups; campaigned for the extension of voting rights to women.
National Action Bloc: liberal, nationalist.
National Democratic Alliance (NDA): f. 1997; secular, liberal; Sec.-Gen. SALAH AL-MUDHAF (acting).
National Islamic Alliance: Shi'a Muslim; Leader HUSSAIN AL-MA'TOUQ.
Popular Action Bloc: loose asscn of nationalists and Shi'a Muslims; Leader AHMAD AL-SAADOUN.

Diplomatic Representation

EMBASSIES IN KUWAIT

Afghanistan: POB 33186, 73452 Rawdah, Block 6, Surra St, Across Surra Co-op Society House 16, Kuwait City; tel. 25329461; fax 25326274; e-mail afg_emb_kuw@hotmail.com; Ambassador ABDUL RAHIM KARIMI.
Algeria: POB 578, 13006 Safat, Istiqlal St, Kuwait City; tel. 24820791; fax 24820853; e-mail ambalgkt@qualitynet.net; Ambassador MUHAMMAD BURUBA.
Argentina: POB 3788, 40188 Mishref, Kuwait City; tel. 25379211; fax 25379212; e-mail ekuwa@mrecic.gov.ar; Chargé d'affaires a.i. CARLOS MARCELO SALORD.
Armenia: Jabriya District, Fahaheel Expressway, Kuwait City; Ambassador FADEY CHARCHOGHLYAN.
Australia: Dar al-Awadi Complex (Level 12), Ahmad al-Jaber St, Sharq, Kuwait City; tel. 22322422; fax 22322430; e-mail austemb.kuwait@dfat.go.au; internet www.kuwait.embassy.gov.au; Ambassador GLENN MILES.
Austria: POB 15013, Daiyah, Area 3, Shawki St, House 10, 35451 Kuwait City; tel. 22552532; fax 22563052; e-mail kuwait-ob@bmaa.gv.at; Ambassador MARIAN VERBA.
Azerbaijan: al-Yarmouk, Block 2, St 1, Bldg 15, Kuwait City; tel. 25355247; fax 25355246; e-mail embazerbaijan@yahoo.com; internet www.azerembassy-kuwait.org; Ambassador TURAL RZAYEV.
Bahrain: POB 196, 13002 Safat, Area 6, Surra Rd, Villa 35, Kuwait City; tel. 25318530; fax 25330882; e-mail Kuwait.mission@mofa.gov.bh; Ambassador Sheikh KHALIFA BIN HAMAD AL KHALIFA.
Bangladesh: POB 22344, 13084 Safat, Khaldya, Block 6, Ali bin Abi Taleb St, House 361, Kuwait City; tel. 25316042; fax 25316041; e-mail bdoot@ncc.moc.kw; Ambassador SYED SHAHED REZA.
Belgium: POB 3280, Safat, Kuwait City; tel. 25384582; fax 25384583; e-mail kuwait@diplobel.fed.be; internet www.diplomatie.be/kuwait; Ambassador DAMIEN ANGELET.
Bhutan: POB 1510, 13016 Safat, Adailiya-Block 3, Issa Abd al-Rahman al-Assoussi St, Jadda 32, Villa 7, Kuwait City; tel. 22516640; fax 22516550; e-mail bhutankuwait@hotmail.com; Ambassador Dasho SHERUB TENZIN.
Bosnia and Herzegovina: POB 6131, 32036 Hawalli, Bayan, Block 3, St 1, House 46, Kuwait City; tel. 25392637; fax 25392106; Ambassador JASIN RAVAŠDE.
Brazil: POB 39761, 73058 Nuzha, Block 2, St 1, Jadah 1, Villa 8, Kuwait City; tel. 25328610; fax 25328613; e-mail brasemkw@qualitynet.net; internet www.brazil.org.kw; Ambassador MARIO DA GRAÇA ROITER.
Bulgaria: POB 12090, 71651 Shamiya, Jabriya, Block 11, St 107 and St 1, Villa 272, Kuwait City; tel. 25314458; fax 25321453; e-mail bgembkw@fasttelco.com; internet www.mfa.bg/en/46/; Ambassador ILKO SHIVACHEV.
Canada: POB 25281, 13113 Safat, Daiyah, Area 4, 24 al-Mutawakkel St, Kuwait City; tel. 22563025; fax 22560173; e-mail kuwait@international.gc.ca; internet www.canadainternational.gc.ca/kuwait-koweit; Ambassador J. REID HENRY.
China, People's Republic: POB 2346, 13024 Safat, Yarmouk, Sheikh Ahmad al-Jaber Bldgs 4 & 5, St 1, Villa 82, Kuwait City; tel. 25333340; fax 25333341; e-mail chinakwt@hotmail.com; Ambassador HUANG JIEMIN.
Czech Republic: Nuzha, Block 3, St 34, House 13, Kuwait City; tel. 22529018; fax 22529021; e-mail kuwait@embassy.mzv.cz; internet www.mzv.cz/kuwait; Ambassador MARTIN VÁVRA.

KUWAIT

Egypt: POB 11252, 35153 Dasmah, Istiqlal St, Kuwait City; tel. 22519955; fax 22563877; e-mail embassy.kuwait@mfa.gov.eg; Ambassador TAHER AHMED FARAHAT.

Eritrea: POB 53016, 73015 Nuzha, Jabriya, Block 9, St 21, House 9, Kuwait City; tel. 25317427; fax 26631304; Ambassador MAHMOUD OMAR CHURUM.

Ethiopia: POB 939, 45710 Safat, Jabriya, Block 10, St 107, Villa 30, Kuwait City; tel. 25330128; fax 25331179; e-mail ethiokwt@qualitynet.net; Ambassador MUHAMMAD GUDETA CHEBSA.

France: POB 1037, 13011 Safat, Mansouriah, Blk 1, St 13, Villa 24, Kuwait City; tel. 22582020; fax 22571058; e-mail cad.koweit-amba@diplomatie.gouv.fr; Ambassador JEAN-RENÉ GEHAN.

Georgia: Qurtoba, Block 2, Area 1, Ave 3, Villa 6, Kuwait City; tel. 25352909; fax 25354707; e-mail kuwait.emb@mfa.gov.ge; internet www.kuwait.mfa.gov.ge; Ambassador EKATERINE MEIERING-MIKADZE.

Germany: POB 805, 13009 Safat, Dahiya Abdullah al-Salem, Area 1, Ave 14, Villa 13, Kuwait City; tel. 22520827; fax 22520763; e-mail info@kuwait.diplo.de; internet www.kuwait.diplo.de; Ambassador FRANK M. MANN.

Greece: POB 23812, 13099 Safat, Khaldiya, Block 4, St 44, House 4, Kuwait City; tel. 24817100; fax 24817103; e-mail gremb.kuw@mfa.gr; Ambassador KONSTANTINOS DRAKAKIS.

Holy See: POB 29724, 13158 Safat, Kuwait City; tel. 22562248; fax 22562213; e-mail nuntiuskuwait@gmail.com; Apostolic Nuncio Most Rev. Archbishop PETAR RAJIČ (Titular Archbishop of Sarsenterum).

Hungary: POB 23955, 13100 Safat, Bayan, Block 13, St 13, Villa 381, Kuwait City; tel. 25379351; fax 25379350; e-mail mission.kwi@kum.hu; internet www.mfa.gov.hu/emb/kuwait; Ambassador FERENC CSILLAG.

India: POB 1450, 13015 Safat, Diplomatic Enclave, Arabian Gulf St, Kuwait City; tel. 22530600; fax 22525811; e-mail contact@indembkwt.org; internet www.indembkwt.org; Ambassador AJAI MALHOTRA.

Indonesia: POB 21500, 13076 Safat, Kaifan, Block 6, al-Andalus St, House 29, Kuwait City; tel. 24839927; fax 24819250; e-mail unitkom@kbrikuwait.org; internet www.kbrikuwait.org; Ambassador SUDIRMAN FAISAL ISMAIL.

Iran: POB 4686, 13047 Safat, Daiyah, Embassies Area, Block B, Kuwait City; tel. 22560694; fax 22529868; e-mail iranebassy@hotmail.com; Ambassador ALI JANNATI.

Iraq: Kuwait City; e-mail kuwemb@iraqmfamail.com; Ambassador MUHAMMAD HUSSAIN BAHR AL-ULUM.

Italy: POB 4453, 13045 Safat, Kuwait City; tel. 25356010; fax 25356030; e-mail ambasciata.alkuwait@esteri.it; internet www.ambalkuwait.esteri.it; Ambassador ENRICO GRANARA.

Japan: POB 2304, 13024 Safat, Jabriya, Area 9, Plot 496, St 101, Kuwait City; tel. 25309400; fax 25309401; e-mail info@embjp-kw.org; internet www.kw.emb-japan.go.jp; Ambassador YASUYOSHI KOMIZO.

Jordan: POB 39891, 73059 Kuwait City; tel. 22533261; fax 22533270; e-mail kujor@qualitynet.net; Ambassador JUMA AL-ABBADI.

Korea, Republic: POB 4272, Qourtoba Block 4, St 1, Jaddah 3, House 5, 13043 Safat, Kuwait City; tel. 25339601; fax 25312459; e-mail kuwait@mofat.go.kr; internet kwt.mofat.go.kr/index.jsp; Ambassador MOON YOUNG-HAN.

Lebanon: POB 253, 13003 Safat, Da'Yiah Diplomatic Area, Plot 6, Kuwait City; tel. 22562103; fax 22571682; Ambassador Dr BASSEM ABD AL-QADIR AL-NO'MANI.

Libya: POB 21460, 13075 Safat, 27 Istiqlal St, Kuwait City; tel. 22575183; fax 22575182; Ambassador MUHAMMAD AL-MUBARAK.

Malaysia: POB 4105, 13042 Safat, Daiya, Diplomatic Enclave, Area 5, Istiqlal St, Plot 5, Kuwait City; tel. 22550394; fax 22550384; e-mail malkuwait@kln.gov.my; internet www.kln.gov.my/perwakilan/kuwait; Chargé d'affaires a.i. MOHIUDDIN GHAZALI.

Morocco: Yarmouk, Block 2, St 2, Villa 14, Kuwait City; tel. 25312980; fax 25317423; e-mail ambkow@yahoo.fr; Ambassador MUHAMMAD BELAICHE.

Netherlands: POB 21822, 13079 Safat, Jabriya, Area 9, St 1, Plot 40A, Kuwait City; tel. 25312650; fax 25326334; e-mail kwe@minbuza.nl; internet www.netherlandsembassy.gov.kw; Ambassador TON BOON VAN OCHSSÉE.

Niger: POB 44451, 32059 Hawalli, Salwa Block 12, St 6, Villa 183, Kuwait City; tel. 25652943; fax 25640478; Ambassador ASSOUMANE GUIAOURI.

Nigeria: POB 6432, 32039 Hawalli, Surra, Area 1, St 14, House 24, Kuwait City; tel. 18278813; fax 18278896; Ambassador BALA AHMAD GUSAU.

Directory

Oman: POB 21975, 13080 Safat, al-Odeilia Block 3, St 3, Villa 25, Kuwait City; tel. 22561956; fax 22561963; Ambassador Sheikh SALIM BIN SUHAIL AL-MA'ASHANI.

Pakistan: POB 988, 13010 Safat, Jabriya, Police Station Rd, St 101, Plot 5, Block 11, Villa 7, Kuwait City; tel. 25327649; fax 25327648; e-mail parepkwt@yahoo.com; internet www.mofa.gov.pk/kuwait; Ambassador IFTEKHAR AZIZ.

Philippines: POB 26288, 13123 Safat, Area 7, No. 103, Villa 503, Jabriya, Kuwait City; tel. 25349099; fax 25329319; e-mail pe.kuwait@dfa.gov.ph; internet www.philembassykuwait.gov.kw; Ambassador SHULAN O. PRIMAVERA.

Poland: POB 5066, 13051 Safat, Jabriya, Plot 7, St 3, House 20, Kuwait City; tel. 25311571; fax 25311576; e-mail embassy@kuwejt.polemb.net; internet www.kuwejt.polemb.net; Ambassador JANUSZ SZWEDO.

Qatar: POB 1825, 13019 Safat, Diiyah, Istiqlal St, Kuwait City; tel. 22523107; fax 22513604; e-mail kuwait@mofa.gov.qa; Ambassador ABD AL-AZIZ BIN SAAD AL-FEHAID.

Romania: POB 11149, 35152 Dasmah, Keifan, Area 4, Moona St, House 34, Kuwait City; tel. 24845079; fax 24848929; e-mail ambsa@kems.net; Ambassador CONSTANTIN VOLODEA NISTOR.

Russia: POB 1765, Safat, Daya Diplomatic Area, Block 17, Kuwait City; tel. 22560427; fax 22524969; e-mail rusposkuw@mail.ru; internet www.kuwait.mid.ru; Ambassador ALEKSANDR KINSCHAK.

Saudi Arabia: POB 20498, 13065 Safat, Istiqlal St, Kuwait City; tel. 22550021; fax 22551858; Ambassador ABD AL-AZIZ AL-FAYEZ.

Senegal: POB 23892, 13099 Safat, Rawdah, Block 3, St 35, House 9, Kuwait City; tel. 22573477; fax 22542044; e-mail senegal_embassy@yahoo.com; internet www.diplomatie.gouv.sn/maeuase/ambassene_koweit.htm; Ambassador ABDOU LAHAD MBACKE.

Serbia: POB 20511, 13066 Safat, Jabriya, Block 7, St 12, Villa 3, Kuwait City; tel. 25327548; fax 25327568; e-mail embrskw@qualitynet.net; Chargé d'affaires a.i. ZLATAN MALTARIĆ.

Somalia: POB 22766, 13088 Safat, Bayan, St 1, Block 7, Villa 25, Kuwait City; tel. 25394795; fax 25394829; e-mail soamin1@hotmail.com; Ambassador ABDUL KHADIR AMIN SHEIKH ABUBAKER.

South Africa: POB 2262, 40173 Mishref, Salwa Block 10, St 1, Villa 91, Unit 3, Kuwait City; tel. 25617988; fax 25617917; e-mail kuwait.political@foreign.gov.za; Ambassador ASHRAF SULIMAN.

Spain: POB 22207, 13083 Safat, Surra, Block 3, St 14, Villa 19, Kuwait City; tel. 25325827; fax 25325826; e-mail emb.kuwait@mae.es; Ambassador MANUEL GÓMEZ DE VALENZUELA.

Sri Lanka: Jabriya, Block 10, St 107, Villa 1, Kuwait City; tel. 25339140; fax 25339154; e-mail lankaemb@qualitynet.net; internet www.slembkwt.org; Ambassador SARATH DISSANAYAKE.

Switzerland: POB 23954, 13100 Safat, Qortuba, Block 2, St 1, Villa 122, Kuwait City; tel. 25340172; fax 25340176; e-mail kow.vertretung@eda.admin.ch; internet www.eda.admin.ch/kuwait; Ambassador MICHEL GOTTRET.

Syria: POB 25600, 13116 Safat, Kuwait City; tel. 25396560; fax 25396509; Ambassador Brig.-Gen. BASSAM ABD AL-MAJID.

Thailand: POB 66647, 43757 Bayan, Block 6, St 8, Villa 1, Jabriya, Kuwait City; tel. 25317530; fax 25317532; e-mail thaiemkw@kems.net; internet www.mfa.go.th/web/1319.php?depid=217; Ambassador CHET DHERAPATTANA.

Tunisia: POB 5976, 13060 Safat, Nuzha, Plot 2, Nuzha St, Villa 45, Kuwait City; tel. 2542144; fax 2528995; e-mail tunemrku@ncc.moc.kw; Ambassador MUSTAPHA BAHIA.

Turkey: POB 20627, 13067 Safat, Block 16, Plot 10, Istiqlal St, Kuwait City; tel. 22531466; fax 22560653; e-mail turkiyebuyukelciligi@fasttelco.com; internet kuveyt.be.fscnet.net; Ambassador MEHMET HILMI DEDEOĞLU.

Ukraine: POB 7588, 32096 Hawalli, Jabriya, Block 10, St 6, House 5, Kuwait City; tel. 25318507; fax 25318508; e-mail emb_kw@mfa.gov.ua; internet www.mfa.gov.ua/kuwait; Ambassador VOLODYMYR TOLKACH.

United Arab Emirates: POB 1828, 13019 Safat, Plot 70, Istiqlal St, Kuwait City; tel. 22528544; fax 22526382; Ambassador HASSAN SALIM AL-KHAYYAL.

United Kingdom: POB 2, 13001 Safat, Arabian Gulf St, Kuwait City; tel. 22594320; fax 22594339; e-mail kuwait.generalenquiries@fco.gov.uk; internet ukinkuwait.fco.gov.uk; Ambassador FRANCIS RAYMOND (FRANK) BAKER.

USA: POB 77, 13001 Safat, Bayan, al-Masjed al-Aqsa St, Plot 14, Block 14, Kuwait City; tel. 22591001; fax 25380282; e-mail paskuwaitm@state.gov; internet kuwait.usembassy.gov; Ambassador DEBORAH K. JONES.

Uzbekistan: Mishref, Block 2, St 5, Villa 18A, Kuwait City; Ambassador ABDURAFIK A. HOSHIMOV.

KUWAIT

Venezuela: POB 24440, 13105 Safat, Block 5, St 7, Area 356, Surra, Kuwait City; tel. 25324367; fax 25324368; e-mail embavene@qualitynet.net; Ambassador ELOY FERNÁNDEZ AZUAJE.

Yemen: POB 7182, al-Jabriya St, Kuwait City; tel. 25349416; fax 25349415; Ambassador KHALED SHEIKH.

Zimbabwe: POB 36484, 24755 Salmiya, Kuwait City; tel. 25620845; fax 25621491; e-mail zimkuwait@hotmail.com; Ambassador MARK GREY MARONGWE.

Judicial System

SPECIAL JUDICIARY

Constitutional Court: Comprises five judges. Interprets the provisions of the Constitution; considers disputes regarding the constitutionality of legislation, decrees and rules; has jurisdiction in challenges relating to the election of members, or eligibility for election, to the Majlis al-Umma.

ORDINARY JUDICIARY

Court of Cassation: Comprises five judges. Is competent to consider the legality of verdicts of the Court of Appeal and State Security Court; Chief Justice MUHAMMAD YOUSUF AL-RIFA'I.

Court of Appeal: Comprises three judges. Considers verdicts of the Court of First Instance; Chief Justice RASHED AL-HAMMAD.

Court of First Instance: Comprises the following divisions: Civil and Commercial (one judge), Personal Status Affairs (one judge), Lease (three judges), Labour (one judge), Crime (three judges), Administrative Disputes (three judges), Appeal (three judges), Challenged Misdemeanours (three judges); Chief Justice MUHAMMAD AL-SAKHOBY.

Summary Courts: Each governorate has a Summary Court, comprising one or more divisions. The courts have jurisdiction in the following areas: Civil and Commercial, Urgent Cases, Lease, Misdemeanours. The verdict in each case is delivered by one judge.

There is also a **Traffic Court**, with one presiding judge.

Prosecutor-General: HAMED AL-OTHMAN.

Religion

ISLAM

The majority of Kuwaitis are Muslims of the Sunni or Shi'a sects. The Shi'ite community comprises about 30% of the total.

CHRISTIANITY

The Roman Catholic Church

Latin Rite

For ecclesiastical purposes, Kuwait forms part of the Apostolic Vicariate of Northern Arabia. At 31 December 2007 there were an estimated 300,000 adherents in the country.

Vicar Apostolic: CAMILLO BALLIN (Titular Bishop of Arna), Bishop's House, POB 266, 13003 Safat, Kuwait City; tel. 22434637; fax 22409981; e-mail vicariate_clergy@hotmail.com; internet www.catholic-church.org/kuwait.

Melkite Rite

The Greek-Melkite Patriarch of Antioch is resident in Damascus, Syria. The Patriarchal Exarchate of Kuwait had an estimated 800 adherents at 31 December 2005.

Exarch Patriarchal: Rev. BOUTROS GHARIB, Vicariat Patriarcal Greek-Melkite, POB 1205, Salwa Block 12, St 6, House 58, 22013 Salmiya, Kuwait City; tel. and fax 25652802; e-mail greekcatholickuwait@yahoo.com.

Syrian Rite

The Syrian Catholic Patriarch of Antioch is resident in Beirut, Lebanon. The Patriarchal Exarchate of Basra and the Gulf, with an estimated 325 adherents at 31 December 2007, is based in Basra, Iraq.

The Anglican Communion

Within the Episcopal Church in Jerusalem and the Middle East, Kuwait forms part of the diocese of Cyprus and the Gulf. The Anglican congregation in Kuwait is entirely expatriate. The Bishop in Cyprus and the Gulf is resident in Cyprus, while the Archdeacon in the Gulf is resident in Bahrain.

Other Christian Churches

National Evangelical Church in Kuwait: POB 80, 13001 Safat, Kuwait City; tel. 22407195; fax 22431087; e-mail elc@ncc.moc.kw; Rev. NABIL ATTALLAH (pastor of the Arabic-language congregation), Rev. JERRY A. ZANDSTRA (senior pastor of the English-speaking congregation); an independent Protestant Church founded by the Reformed Church in America; services in Arabic, English, Korean, Malayalam and other Indian languages; combined weekly congregation of some 20,000.

The Armenian, Greek, Coptic and Syrian Orthodox Churches are also represented in Kuwait.

The Press

Freedom of the press and publishing is guaranteed in the Constitution, although press censorship was in force between mid-1986 and early 1992 (when journalists adopted a voluntary code of practice). In February 1995 a ruling by the Constitutional Court effectively endorsed the Government's right to suspend publication of newspapers; however, legislation passed in 2006 rendered this illegal without a court order. The Government provides financial support to newspapers and magazines.

DAILIES

Al-Anbaa (The News): POB 23915, 13100 Safat, Kuwait City; tel. 24830322; fax 24832647; e-mail editorial@alanba.com.kw; internet www.alanba.com.kw; f. 1976; Arabic; general; Editor-in-Chief BIBI KHALID AL-MARZOOQ; circ. 85,000.

Arab Times: POB 2270, Airport Road, Shuwaikh, 13023 Safat, Kuwait City; tel. 24849144; fax 24818267; e-mail arabtimes@arabtimesonline.com; internet www.arabtimesonline.com; f. 1977; English; political and financial; no Fri. edn; Editor-in-Chief AHMAD ABD AL-AZIZ AL-JARALLAH; Man. Editor MISHAL AL-JARALLAH; circ. 41,922.

Al-Jarida (The Newspaper): POB 29846, 13159 Safat, Kuwait City; tel. 22257036; fax 22257035; e-mail info@aljarida.com; internet www.aljarida.com; f. 2007; Arabic; affiliated with the Nat. Democratic Alliance; Editor-in-Chief KHALID HILAL AL-MUTAIRI.

Kuwait Times: POB 1301, 13014 Safat, Kuwait City; tel. 24833199; fax 24835621; e-mail info@kuwaittimes.net; internet www.kuwaittimes.net; f. 1961; English, Malayalam and Urdu; political; Editor-in-Chief ABD AL-RAHMAN ALYAN; circ. 32,000.

Al-Qabas (Firebrand): POB 21800, 13078 Safat, Kuwait City; tel. 24812822; fax 24834355; e-mail info@alqabas.com.kw; internet www.alqabas.com.kw; f. 1972; Arabic; independent; Gen. Man. FOUZAN AL-FARES; Editor-in-Chief WALEED ABD AL-LATIF AL-NISF; circ. 60,000.

Al-Ra'i al-'Aam (Public Opinion): POB 761, 13008 Safat, Kuwait City; tel. 24817777; fax 24838352; e-mail editor@alraialaam.com; internet www.alraialaam.com; f. 1961; Arabic; political, social and cultural; Editor-in-Chief YOUSUF AL-JALAHMA; circ. 101,500.

Al-Seyassah (Policy): POB 2270, Shuwaikh, Kuwait City; tel. 24813566; fax 24846905; internet www.al-seyassah.com; f. 1965; Arabic; political and financial; Editor-in-Chief AHMAD ABD AL-AZIZ AL-JARALLAH; circ. 70,000.

Al-Watan (The Homeland): POB 1142, 13012 Safat, Kuwait City; tel. 24840950; fax 24818481; e-mail alwatan@alwatan.com.kw; internet www.alwatan.com.kw; f. 1962; Arabic; political; Editor-in-Chief Sheikh KHALIFA ALI AL-KHALIFA AL-SABAH; Gen. Man. DINA AL-MALLAK; circ. 91,726.

WEEKLIES AND PERIODICALS

Al-Balagh (Communiqué): POB 4558, 13046 Safat, Kuwait City; tel. 24818820; fax 24812735; e-mail albalagh5@yahoo.com; internet www.al-balagh.com; f. 1969; weekly; Arabic; general, political and Islamic affairs; Editor-in-Chief ABD AL-RAHMAN RASHID AL-WALAYATI; circ. 29,000.

Byzance: Kuwait City; f. 2007; bi-monthly; Arabic and French; lifestyle magazine, incl. features on fashion, jewellery, furniture and art; Man. Editor JEAN-PIERRE GUEIRARD; Exec. Editor-in-Chief ANTOINE DAHER.

Al-Dakhiliya (The Interior): POB 71655, 12500 Shamiah, Kuwait City; tel. 22410091; fax 22410609; e-mail moipr@qualitynet.net; monthly; Arabic; official reports, transactions and proceedings; publ. by Public Relations Dept, Ministry of the Interior; Editor-in-Chief Lt-Col AHMAD A. AL-SHARQAWI.

Dalal Magazine: POB 6000, 13060 Safat, Kuwait City; tel. 24832098; fax 24832039; internet www.dalal-kw.com; f. 1997; monthly; Arabic; family affairs, beauty, fashion; Editor-in-Chief AHMAD YOUSUF BEHBEHANI.

KUWAIT

Friday Times: POB 1301, 13014 Safat, Kuwait City; tel. 24833199; fax 24835627; e-mail info@kuwaittimes.net; internet www.kuwaittimes.net; f. 2005; weekend edn of *Kuwait Times*.

Al-Hadaf (The Objective): POB 2270, 13023 Safat, Kuwait City; tel. 24813566; fax 24816042; internet www.al-seyassah.com/alhadaf; f. 1964; weekly; Arabic; social and cultural; Editor-in-Chief AHMAD ABD AL-AZIZ AL-JARALLAH; circ. 268,904.

Al-Iqtisadi al-Kuwaiti (Kuwaiti Economist): POB 775, 13008 Safat, Kuwait City; tel. 1805580; fax 22404110; e-mail kcci@kcci.org.kw; internet www.kcci.org.kw; f. 1960; monthly; Arabic; commerce, trade and economics; publ. by Kuwait Chamber of Commerce and Industry; Editor MAJED B. JAMALUDDIN; circ. 6,000.

Journal of the Gulf and Arabian Peninsula Studies: POB 17073, 72451 Khaldiya, Kuwait University, Kuwait City; tel. 24833215; fax 24833705; e-mail jotgaaps@kuc01.kuniv.edu.kw; internet pubcouncil.kuniv.edu.kw/jgaps; f. 1975; quarterly; Arabic and English; publ. by Academic Publication Council of Kuwait Univ; Editor-in-Chief Dr FATIMA HUSSAIN ABD AL-RAZZAQ.

Al-Khaleej Business Magazine: POB 25725, 13118 Safat, Kuwait City; tel. 22433765; e-mail aljabriya@gulfweb.com; Editor-in-Chief AHMAD ISMAIL BEHBEHANI.

Kuwait Medical Journal (KMJ): POB 1202, 13013 Safat, Kuwait City; tel. 25316023; fax 25317972; e-mail kmj@kma.org.kw; internet www.kma.org.kw/KMJ; f. 1967; quarterly; English; publ. by the Kuwait Medical Asscn; original articles, review articles, case reports, short communications, letters to the editor and book reviews; Editor-in-Chief Prof. FOUAD ABDULLAH M. HASSAN; circ. 6,000.

Kuwait al-Youm (Kuwait Today): POB 193, 13002 Safat, Kuwait City; tel. 24842167; fax 24831044; e-mail info@ipd.gov.kw; internet www.ipd.gov.kw; f. 1954; weekly; Arabic; statistics, Amiri decrees, laws, govt announcements, decisions, invitations for tenders, etc.; publ. by the Ministry of Information; circ. 5,000.

Al-Kuwaiti (The Kuwaiti): Information Dept, POB 9758, 61008 Ahmadi, Kuwait City; tel. 23981076; fax 23983661; e-mail kocinfo@kockw.com; f. 1961; monthly journal of the Kuwait Oil Co; Arabic; Editor-in-Chief KHALED AL-KHAMEES; circ. 6,500.

The Kuwaiti Digest: Information Dept, POB 9758, 61008 Ahmadi, Kuwait City; tel. 23981076; fax 23983661; e-mail kocinfo@kockw.com; f. 1972; quarterly journal of Kuwait Oil Co; English; Editor-in-Chief KHALED AL-KHAMEES; circ. 7,000.

Al-Majaless (Meetings): POB 5605, 13057 Safat, Kuwait City; tel. 24841178; fax 24847126; e-mail qasem@almajaless.com; weekly; Arabic; current affairs; Editor-in-Chief QASIM ABD AL-QADIR; circ. 60,206.

Mejallat al-Kuwait (Kuwait Magazine): POB 193, 13002 Safat, Kuwait City; tel. 22415300; fax 22419642; f. 1961; monthly; Arabic; illustrated magazine; science, arts and literature; publ. by the Ministry of Information.

Mirat al-Umma (Mirror of the Nation): POB 1142, 13012 Safat, Kuwait City; tel. 24837212; fax 24838671; weekly; Arabic; Editor-in-Chief MUHAMMAD AL-JASSEM; circ. 79,500.

Al-Nahdha (The Renaissance): POB 695, 13007 Safat, Kuwait City; tel. 24813133; fax 24849298; f. 1967; weekly; Arabic; social and political; Editor-in-Chief THAMER AL-SALAH; circ. 170,000.

Osrati (My Family): POB 2995, 13030 Safat, Kuwait City; tel. 24813233; fax 24838933; e-mail info@osratimag.com; internet www.osratimag.com; f. 1964; weekly; Arabic; women's magazine; publ. by Fahad al-Marzouk Establishment; Editor GHANIMA F. AL-MARZOUK; circ. 10,500.

Al-Talia (The Ascendant): POB 1082, 13011 Safat, Kuwait City; tel. 24831200; fax 24840471; f. 1962; weekly; Arabic; politics and literature; Editor AHMAD YOUSUF AL-NAFISI; circ. 10,000.

Al-Yaqza (The Awakening): POB 6000, 13060 Safat, Kuwait City; tel. 24831318; fax 24832039; internet www.alyaqza.com; f. 1966; weekly; Arabic; political, economic, social and general; Editor-in-Chief AHMAD YOUSUF BEHBEHANI; circ. 91,340.

NEWS AGENCY

Kuwait News Agency (KUNA): POB 24063, 13101 Safat, Kuwait City; tel. 24834546; fax 24813424; e-mail kuna@kuna.net.kw; internet www.kuna.net.kw; f. 1979; public corporate body; independent; also publishes research digests on topics of common and special interest; Chair. and Dir-Gen. Sheikh MUBARAK AL-DUAIJ AL-SABAH.

PRESS ASSOCIATION

Kuwait Journalists Association: POB 5454, 13055 Safat, Kuwait City; tel. 24843351; fax 24842874; e-mail kja@kja-kw.com; internet www.kja-kw.com; Chair. AHMAD YOUSUF BEHBEHANI.

Publishers

Al-Abraj Translation and Publishing Co WLL: POB 26177, 13122 Safat, Kuwait City; tel. 22442310; fax 22407024; Man. Dir Dr TARIQ ABDULLAH.

Dar al-Seyassah Publishing, Printing and Distribution Co: POB 2270, 13023 Safat, Kuwait City; tel. 24813566; fax 24833628; internet www.dar-al-seyassah.com; publ. *Arab Times*, *Al-Seyassah* and *Al-Hadaf*.

Gulf Centre Publishing and Publicity: POB 2722, 13028 Safat, Kuwait City; tel. 22402760; fax 22458833; Propr HAMZA ISMAIL ESSLAH.

Kuwait National Advertising and Publishing Co (KNAPCO): POB 2268, Safat 13023, Kuwait City; tel. 25745776; fax 25745779; e-mail support@knapco.com; internet www.knapco.com; f. 1995; publ. annual commercial business directory, *Teledymag*.

Kuwait Publishing House Co: POB 1446, 13015 Safat, Kuwait City; tel. 22449686; fax 22436956; e-mail info@kuwaitpocketguide.com; f. 1970; Dir ESAM AS'AD ABU AL-FARAJ.

Kuwait United Co for Advertising, Publishing and Distribution WLL: POB 29359, 13153 Safat, Kuwait City; tel. 24817111; fax 24817797.

Al-Talia Printing and Publishing Co: POB 1082, Airport Rd, Shuwaikh, 13011 Safat, Kuwait City; tel. 24840470; fax 24815611; Man. AHMAD YOUSUF AL-NAFISI.

GOVERNMENT PUBLISHING HOUSE

Ministry of Information: see Ministries.

Broadcasting and Communications

TELECOMMUNICATIONS

National Mobile Telecommunications Co KSC (Wataniya Telecom): POB 613, 13007 Safat, Kuwait City; tel. 65805555; fax 22423369; e-mail info@wataniya.com; internet www.wataniya.com; f. 1999; Qatar Telecommunications Corpn (Q-Tel) acquired 51% stake 2007; Chair. and Man. Dir Sheikh ABDULLAH BIN MUHAMMAD BIN SAUD AL THANI; CEO and Gen. Man. SCOTT GEGENHEIMER.

VIVA: POB 181, Salmiya 22002, Kuwait City; tel. 55670000; fax 55676666; e-mail info@viva.com.kw; internet www.viva.com.kw; f. 2008; mobile cellular communications; commercial brand of Kuwait Telecom Co; Chair. ADEL MUHAMMAD AL-ROUMI; CEO NAJEEB AL-AWADI.

Zain Kuwait: POB 22244, 13083 Safat, Kuwait City; tel. 24644444; fax 24641111; e-mail info.kw@zain.com; internet www.kw.zain.com; f. 1983 as Mobile Telecommunications Co; in Sept. 2007 began operating under new global brand, Zain; group operates in 24 countries in the Middle East and Africa; 1.8m. subscribers in Kuwait, 69.5m. total group subscribers (30 June 2009); Chair. ASAAD AL-BANWAN; CEO NABEEL BIN SALAMAH.

BROADCASTING

Radio

Radio of the State of Kuwait: POB 397, 13004 Safat, Kuwait City; tel. 22423774; fax 22456660; e-mail info@moinfo.gov.kw; internet www.moinfo.gov.kw; f. 1951; broadcasts daily in Arabic, Farsi, English and Urdu, some in stereo; Dir of Radio Dr ABD AL-AZIZ ALI MANSOUR; Dir of Radio Programmes ABD AL-RAHMAN HADI.

Television

Kuwait Television: POB 193, 13002 Safat, Kuwait City; tel. 22415301; fax 22438403; e-mail info@moinfo.gov.kw; internet www.moinfo.gov.kw; f. 1961; transmission began privately in Kuwait in 1957; transmits in Arabic; colour television service began in 1973; has a total of five channels; Head of News Broadcasting MUHAMMAD AL-KAHTANI.

Al-Rai: Kuwait City; tel. 24817777; fax 24953002; e-mail alraitv@alrai.tv; internet www.alrai.tv; f. 2004; first private satellite television station in Kuwait; admin. offices in Kuwait and transmission facilities in Dubai (United Arab Emirates); owned by Al-Rai Media Group.

KUWAIT

Finance

(cap. = capital; res = reserves; dep. = deposits; m. = million; br(s) = branch(es); amounts in Kuwaiti dinars, unless otherwise stated)

BANKING

Central Bank

Central Bank of Kuwait: POB 526, 13006 Safat, Abdullah al-Salem St, Kuwait City; tel. 22449200; fax 22464887; e-mail cbk@cbk.gov.kw; internet www.cbk.gov.kw; f. 1969; cap. 5m., res 562m., dep. 3,369m. (March 2010); Governor Sheikh SALEM ABD AL-AZIZ SA'UD AL-SABAH.

National Banks

Al-Ahli Bank of Kuwait KSC (ABK): POB 1387, 13014 Safat, Ahmad al-Jaber St, Kuwait City; tel. 22400900; fax 22424557; e-mail marketing@abkuwait.com; internet www.eahli.com/abk; f. 1967; wholly owned by private Kuwaiti interests; cap. 115m., res 215m., dep. 2,577m. (Dec. 2009); Chair. AHMAD YOUSUF BEHBEHANI; Dep. Chair. and Man. Dir ALI HILAL AL-MUTAIRI; 25 domestic brs and 2 foreign brs.

Ahli United Bank KSC (BKME): POB 71, 13001 Safat, Joint Banking Centre, East Tower, Darwazat Abd al-Razzak, Kuwait City; tel. 22459771; fax 22461430; e-mail hayakom@bkme.com.kw; internet www.bkme.com; f. 1971; fmrly Bank of Kuwait and the Middle East KSC; current name adopted in April 2010 after acquiring Kuwaiti brs of British Bank of the Middle East; 75% owned by Ahli United Bank (Bahrain); cap. 97m., res 115m., dep. 1,988m. (Dec. 2009); Chair. and Man. Dir HAMAD ABD AL-MOHSEN AL-MARZOUQ; 26 brs.

BBK: POB 24396, 13104 Safat, Ahmad al-Jaber St, Kuwait City; tel. 22417140; fax 22440937; e-mail bbkp@batelco.com.bh; internet www.bbkonline.com; f. 1971 as Bank of Bahrain and Kuwait BSC; name changed as above in 2005; dep. BD 1,756.4m. (Dec. 2009); Chair. MURAD ALI MURAD; Chief Exec. ABD AL-KARIM AHMAD BUCHEERI.

Boubyan Bank KSC: POB 25507, 13116 Safat, Kuwait City; tel. 22325000; fax 22454263; e-mail info@bankboubyan.com; internet www.bankboubyan.com; f. 2004; cap. 116.5m., res 9.0m., dep. 865.7m. (Dec. 2009); Chair. IBRAHIM ALI AL-QADHI; Vice-Chair. and Man. Dir ADEL ABD AL-WAHAB AL-MAJID.

Burgan Bank SAK: POB 5389, 12170 Safat, Abd al-Haih al-Ahmad St, Kuwait City; tel. 22439000; fax 22461148; e-mail info@burgan.com; internet www.burgan.com; f. 1975; 33.9% owned by Kuwait Projects Co (Holding), Safat; cap. 104m., res 187m., dep. 3,402m. (Dec. 2009); Chair. MAJID EISA AL-AJEEL; CEO EDUARDO EGUREN LINSEN; 20 brs.

Commercial Bank of Kuwait SAK: POB 2861, 13029 Safat, Mubarak al-Kabir St, Kuwait City; tel. 22411001; fax 22464870; e-mail cbkinq@cbk.com; internet www.cbk.com; f. 1960 by Amiri decree; cap. 127m., res 220m., dep. 3,085m. (Dec. 2009); Chair. ALI YOUSEF AL-AWADHI; CEO ELHAM YOUSRI MAHFOUZ (acting); 51 brs.

Gulf Bank KSC: POB 3200, 13032 Safat, Mubarak al-Kabir St, Kuwait City; tel. 22449501; fax 22445212; e-mail customerservice@gulfbank.com.kw; internet www.e-gulfbank.com; f. 1960; cap. 250m., res 183m., dep. 4,158m. (Dec. 2009); Chair. ALI ABD AL-RAHMAN AL-RASHID AL-BADER; CEO and Chief Gen. Man. MICHEL ACCAD; 52 brs.

Industrial Bank of Kuwait KSC (IBK): POB 3146, 13032 Safat, Joint Banking Centre, Darwazzat Abd al-Razaq, Commercial Area 9, Kuwait City; tel. 22457661; fax 22406595; e-mail ibk@ibkuwt.com; internet www.ibkuwt.com; f. 1973; 31.4% state-owned; cap. 20m., res 162m., dep. 104m. (Dec. 2009); Chair. and Man. Dir ABD AL-MOHSEN YOUSUF AL-HANIF; Gen. Man. ALI ABD AL-NABI KHAJA.

Kuwait Finance House KSC (KFH): POB 24989, 13110 Safat, Abdullah al-Mubarak St, Kuwait City; tel. 22445050; fax 22455135; e-mail kfh@kfh.com; internet www.kfh.com; f. 1977; 45% state-owned; Islamic banking and investment co; cap. 230m., res 1,011m., dep. 8,722m. (Dec. 2009); Chair. SAMIR YACOUB AL-NAFISI; Chief Exec. MUHAMMAD SULAYMAN AL-OMAR; 44 brs.

Kuwait International Bank (KIB): POB 22822, 13089 Safat, West Tower, Joint Banking Centre, Mubarak al-Kabir St, Kuwait City; tel. 22458177; fax 22462516; e-mail contact@kib.com.kw; internet www.kib.com.kw; f. 1973 as Kuwait Real Estate Bank KSC; name changed as above upon conversion into an Islamic bank in 2007; wholly owned by private Kuwaiti interests; cap. 103m., res 77m., dep. 945m. (Dec. 2009); Chair. MUHAMMAD JARRAH AL-SABAH; Chief Exec. D. MAHMOUD ABUL; 11 brs.

National Bank of Kuwait SAK (NBK): POB 95, 13001 Safat, Abdullah al-Ahmad St, Kuwait City; tel. 22422011; fax 22462469; e-mail webmaster@nbk.com; internet www.nbk.com; f. 1952; cap. 297m., res 974m., dep. 10,869m. (Dec. 2009); Chair. MUHAMMAD ABD AL-RAHMAN AL-BAHAR; CEO IBRAHIM S. DABDOUB; 66 brs in Kuwait, 44 brs abroad.

INSURANCE

Al-Ahleia Insurance Co SAK: POB 1602, Ahmad al-Jaber St, 13017 Safat, Kuwait City; tel. 1888444; fax 22416495; e-mail aic@alahleia.com; internet www.alahleia.com; f. 1962; all forms of insurance; cap. 15.6m. (July 2007); Chair. and Man. Dir SULAYMAN HAMAD MUHAMMAD AL-DALALI.

Arab Commercial Enterprises WLL (Kuwait): POB 2474, 13025 Safat, Kuwait City; tel. 22413854; fax 22409450; e-mail acekwt@ace-ins.com; f. 1952; Man. SALIM ABOU HAIDAR.

First Takaful Insurance Co (FTIC): Abdullah al-Mubarak St, Alenma'a Tower, POB 5713, 13058 Safat, Kuwait City; tel. 21880055; fax 22444599; e-mail info@firsttakaful.com; internet www.firsttakaful.com; f. 2000; Islamic insurance; Chair. and Man. Dir KHALIL IBRAHIM MUHAMMAD AL-SHAMI; 5 brs.

Gulf Insurance Co KSC: POB 1040, 13011 Safat, Ahmad al-Jaber St, Kuwait City; tel. 1802080; fax 22961998; e-mail contacts@gulfins.com.kw; internet www.gulfins.com.kw; f. 1962; cap. 11.3m. (2002); all forms of insurance; Chair. FARKAD ABDULLAH AL-SANEA; CEO and Man. Dir KHALED SAOUD AL-HASSAN.

Al-Ittihad al-Watani Insurance Co for the Near East SAL: 4th Floor, Bahman Bldg, Ahmad al-Jaber St, POB 781, 13008 Safat, Kuwait City; tel. 22420390; fax 22420366; e-mail webmaster@alittihadalwatani.com.lb; Man. JOSEPH ZACCOUR.

Kuwait Insurance Co SAK (KIC): POB 769, 13008 Safat, Abdullah al-Salem St, Kuwait City; tel. 1884433; fax 22428530; e-mail info@kic-kw.com; internet www.kic-kw.com; f. 1960; cap. US $64.6m.; all life and non-life insurance; Chair. MUHAMMAD SALEH BEHBEHANI; Gen. Man. Dr ALI HAMAD AL-BAHAR.

Kuwait Reinsurance Co KSCC: POB 21929, 13080 Safat, Kuwait City; tel. 22432011; fax 22427823; e-mail kuwaitre@kuwaitre.com; internet www.kuwaitre.com; f. 1972; cap. 10.0m., total assets 59.3m. (2006); Chair. FAHED AL-IBRAHIM; Gen. Man. AMIR AL-MUHANNA.

Mohd Saleh Behbehani & Co: POB 341, 13004 Safat, Kuwait City; tel. 24721670; fax 24760070; e-mail msrybco@qualitynet.net; f. 1963; Pres. MUHAMMAD SALEH YOUSUF BEHBEHANI.

New India Assurance Co: 19th Floor, Behbehani Bldg, Jaber al-Mubarak St, Sharq, POB 370, 13004 Safat, Kuwait City; tel. 22404258; fax 22412089; e-mail newindia@qualitynet.net; f. 1919; Man. Dr G. VENKATAIAH.

The Oriental Insurance Co Ltd: 7th Floor, Osama Bldg, POB 22431, 13085 Safat, Kuwait City; tel. 22426218; fax 22424017; e-mail insurance@almullagroup.com; internet www.orientalinsurance.nic.in; Man. ANIL KUMAR PARASHER.

Sumitomo Marine & Fire Insurance Co (Kuwait Agency): POB 3458, 13035 Safat, Kuwait City; tel. 22433087; fax 22430853; Contact ABDULLAH BOUDROS.

Warba Insurance Co SAK: POB 24282, 13103 Safat, Kuwait City; tel. 22445140; fax 22466131; e-mail warba@warbaonline.com; internet www.warbaonline.com; f. 1976; cap. 7.7m. (2002); total assets 80.1m. (Dec. 2005); all forms of insurance; Chair. ANWAR JAWAD KHAMSEEN; Man. Dir TAWFIK SHAMLAN AL-BAHAR; 3 brs.

Wethaq Takaful Insurance Co: Khaled bin al-Waleed St, City Tower, Kuwait City; tel. 21866662; fax 22491280; f. 2000; Islamic insurance; Chair. ABDULLAH YOUSUF AL-SAIF; Gen. Man. MAJID Y. AL-ALI.

STOCK EXCHANGE

Kuwait Stock Exchange (KSE): POB 22235, 13083 Safat, Mubarak al-Kabir St, Kuwait City; tel. 22992000; fax 22420779; e-mail webmaster@kuwaitse.com; internet www.kuwaitse.com; f. 1983; 226 cos and one mutual fund listed (August 2009); Dir-Gen. SALEH MUBARAK AL-FALAH.

Markets Association

Kuwait Financial Markets Association (KFMA): 6th Floor, Deema Bldg, POB 25228, 13113 Safat, Block 3, St 64, Kuwait City; tel. 22498560; fax 22498561; e-mail kfma@kfma.org.kw; internet www.kfma.org.kw; f. 1977; represents treasury, financial and capital markets and their mems; Pres. AQEEL NASSER HABIB; Sec.-Gen. FERAS FAISAL AL-KANDARY.

Trade and Industry

GOVERNMENT AGENCY

Kuwait Investment Authority (KIA): POB 64, 13001 Safat, Kuwait City; tel. 22485600; fax 22454059; e-mail information@kia.gov.kw; internet www.kia.gov.kw; oversees the Kuwait Investment Office (London, United Kingdom); sovereign wealth fund; responsible for the Kuwaiti General Reserve; Chair. MUSTAFA JASSEM AL-SHIMALI (Minister of Finance); Man. Dir BADER MUHAMMAD AL-SAAD.

DEVELOPMENT ORGANIZATIONS

Arab Planning Institute (API): POB 5834, 13059 Safat, Kuwait City; tel. 24843130; fax 24842935; e-mail api@api.org.kw; internet www.arab-api.org; f. 1966; 15 Arab mem. states; publishes *Journal of Development and Economic Policies* (twice-yearly) and proceedings of seminars and discussion group meetings, offers research, training programmes and advisory services; Dir-Gen. ESSA AL-GHAZALI.

Industrial and Financial Investments Co (IFIC): POB 26019, 13121 Safat, Joint Banking Complex, 8th Floor, Industrial Bank Bldg, Derwaza Abd al-Razak, Kuwait City; tel. 22429073; fax 22448850; e-mail ific@ific.net; internet www.ific.net; f. 1983; privatized in 1996; invests directly in industry; Chair. and Man. Dir Dr TALEB AHMAD ALI.

Kuwait Fund for Arab Economic Development (KFAED): POB 2921, 13030 Safat, cnr Mubarak al-Kabir St and al-Hilali St, Kuwait City; tel. 22999000; fax 22999090; e-mail info@kuwait-fund.org; internet www.kuwait-fund.org; f. 1961; cap. KD 2,000m.; state-owned; provides and administers financial and technical assistance to developing countries; Chair. Sheikh Dr MUHAMMAD SABAH AL-SALIM AL-SABAH (Deputy Prime Minister and Minister of Foreign Affairs); Dir-Gen. ABD AL-WAHAB A. AL-BADER.

Kuwait International Investment Co SAK (KIIC): POB 22792, 13088 Safat, al-Salhiya Commercial Complex, Kuwait City; tel. 22438273; fax 22454931; 30% state-owned; domestic real estate and share markets; Chair. and Man. Dir JASEM MUHAMMAD AL-BAHAR.

Kuwait Investment Co SAK (KIC): POB 1005, 13011 Safat, 5th Floor, al-Manakh Bldg, Mubarak al-Kabir St, Kuwait City; tel. 65888852; fax 22444896; e-mail info@kic.com.kw; internet www.kic.com.kw; f. 1981; 88% state-owned, 12% owned by private Kuwaiti interests; cap. KD 50.0m. (2002); international banking and investment; Chair. and Man. Dir BADER NASSER AL-SUBAIEE.

Kuwait Planning Board: POB 15, 13001 Safat, Kuwait City; tel. 22428200; fax 22414734; f. 1962; supervises long-term devt plans; through its Central Statistical Office publishes information on Kuwait's economic activity; Dir-Gen. AHMAD ALI AL-DUAIJ.

Mega Projects Agency (MPA): c/o Ministry of Public Works, POB 8, 13001 Safat, Kuwait City; tel. 25385520; fax 25385234; e-mail hmansour@mpa.gov.kw; f. 2005; supervises the progress of Failaka and Bubiyan island devts; Chair. BADER AL-HUMAIDI.

Public Authority for Industry (PAI): POB 4690, 13047 Safat, Kuwait City; POB 10033, Shuaiba; tel. 25302222; fax 25302190; e-mail indust@pai.gov.kw; internet www.pai.gov.kw; f. 1997; successor to Shuaiba Area Authority (f. 1964); develops, promotes and supervises industry in Kuwait; CEO AMANI KHALID BURESLI (Minister of Commerce and Industry); Gen. Man. ALI FAHAD AL-MUDHAF.

CHAMBER OF COMMERCE

Kuwait Chamber of Commerce and Industry: POB 775, 13008 Safat, Chamber's Bldg, Abd al-Aziz Hamad al-Sager St, Kuwait City; tel. 1805580; fax 22404110; e-mail kcci@kcci.org.kw; internet www.kuwaitchamber.org.kw; f. 1959; 50,000 mems; Chair. ALI MUHAMMAD THUNAYAN AL-GHANIM; Dir-Gen. RABAH AL-RABAH.

STATE HYDROCARBONS COMPANIES

Supreme Petroleum Council (SPC): Kuwait City; f. 1974; highest energy decision-making body, responsible for national oil policy; Chair. Sheikh NASSER AL-MUHAMMAD AL-AHMAD AL-SABAH (Prime Minister).

Kuwait Petroleum Corpn (KPC): POB 26565, 13126 Safat, al-Salhiya Commercial Complex, Fahed al-Salem St, Kuwait City; tel. 22455455; fax 22467159; e-mail info@kpc.com.kw; internet www.kpc.com.kw; f. 1980; co-ordinating org. to manage the petroleum industry; Chair. Dr MUHAMMAD MOHSEN AL-BUSAIRI (Minister of Oil and Minister of State for Parliamentary Affairs); CEO FARUK HUSSAIN AL-ZANKI; subsidiaries include:

Kuwait Aviation Fuelling Co KSC (KAFCO): POB 1654, 13017 Safat, Kuwait City; tel. 24330507; fax 24330475; e-mail airfuel@kafco.com; internet www.kafco.com; f. 1963; Dep. Chair. and Gen. Man. NASSER BADER AL-MUDHAF; 70 employees.

Kuwait Foreign Petroleum Exploration Co KSC (KUFPEC): POB 5291, 13053 Safat, Kuwait City; tel. 1836000; fax 24921818; internet www.kufpec.com; f. 1981; state-owned; overseas oil and gas exploration and devt; Chair. and Man. Dir FAHED AL-AJMI; 169 employees.

Kuwait Gulf Oil Co KSC (KGOC): POB 9919, Ahmadi 61010; tel. 23980883; e-mail info@kgoc.com; internet www.kgoc.com; f. 2002 to take over Kuwait's interest in the Neutral (Partitioned) Zone's offshore operator, Khafji Joint Operations, and all of Kuwait's other offshore exploration and production activities; Chair. and Man. Dir BADER NASSER AL-KHASHTI.

Kuwait National Petroleum Co KSC (KNPC): POB 70, 13001 Safat, Ali al-Salem St, Kuwait City; tel. 23989900; fax 23986188; internet www.knpc.com.kw; f. 1960; oil refining, production of liquefied petroleum gas, and domestic marketing and distribution of petroleum by-products; Chair. and Man. Dir FAROUK HUSSAIN AL-ZANKI; 5,611 employees.

Kuwait Oil Co KSC (KOC): POB 9758, 61008 Ahmadi; tel. 23983661; fax 23984971; e-mail kocinfo@kockw.com; internet www.kockw.com; f. 1934; state-owned; Chair. and Man. Dir SAMI FAHED AL-RUSHAID; 4,815 employees.

Kuwait Petroleum International (Q8): POB 1819, 13019 Safat, Kuwait City; tel. 22332800; fax 22332776; e-mail info-kuwait@q8.com; internet www.q8.com; marketing division of KPC; controls 4,000 petrol retail stations in Europe, and European refineries with capacity of 235,000 b/d; Man. Dir HUSSEIN AL-ISMAIL.

UTILITIES

The Government planned to create regulatory bodies for each of Kuwait's utilities, with a view to facilitating their privatization.

Ministry of Electricity and Water: see Ministries; provides subsidized services throughout Kuwait.

TRADE UNIONS

Federation of Petroleum and Petrochemical Workers: Kuwait City; f. 1965; Chair. JASEM ABD AL-WAHAB AL-TOURA.

KOC Workers Union: Kuwait City; f. 1964; Chair. HAMAD SAWYAN.

Kuwait Trade Union Federation (KTUF): POB 5185, 13052 Safat, Kuwait City; tel. 25636389; fax 25627159; e-mail ktuf@hotmail.com; internet www.ktuf.org; f. 1967; central authority to which all trade unions are affiliated; KHALED M. ALAZEMI; Gen. Sec. FARRAJ A. AL-RASHEDI.

Transport

RAILWAYS

There are currently no railways in Kuwait. However, plans for a 518-km national rail network, which would be linked to a regional rail network, connecting Kuwait with member countries of the Co-operation Council for the Arab States of the Gulf (or Gulf Co-operation Council—GCC), were announced in early 2008. A contract to construct a four-line, 171-km metro system in Kuwait City, intended to ease traffic congestion, was expected to be awarded by the end of 2011. The project, the cost of which was projected at US $7,000m., was provisionally scheduled to commence operations in 2016.

ROADS

In 2004 the total road network was estimated at 5,749 km (613 km of motorways, 5,136 km of secondary roads), of which 85% was paved. Roads in the towns are metalled, and the most important are motorways or dual carriageways. There are metalled roads linking Kuwait City to Ahmadi, Mina al-Ahmadi and other centres of population in Kuwait, and to the Iraqi and Saudi Arabian borders. A 72-km Subiya–Jahra highway and a ring-road at Sabah al-Ahmad City are currently under construction; work on a 42-km, six-lane Nawaseeb Highway was expected to be completed in 2013. Bids for a US $3,700m. design-and-build contract for a causeway linking Kuwait City with Madinat al-Hareer (City of Silk—a new development under construction in Subiya) were submitted in late 2010, and in February 2011 a bid submitted by a consortium including Hyundai Engineering and Construction Co of the Republic of Korea (South Korea) was approved by Kuwait's Central Tenders Committee. However, by early May the contract had yet formally to be awarded.

Kuwait Public Transport Co SAK (KPTC): POB 375, 13004 Safat, Murghab, Safat Sq., Kuwait City; tel. 22469420; fax 22401265; e-mail info@kptc.com.kw; internet www.kptc.com.kw; f. 1962; state-owned; provides internal bus service; regular service to Mecca, Saudi Arabia; Chair. and Man. Dir MAHMOUD A. AL-NOURI.

SHIPPING

Kuwait has three commercial seaports. The largest, Shuwaikh, situated about 3 km from Kuwait City, comprises 21 deep-water berths, with a total length of 4 km, three shallow-water berths and three basins for small craft, each with a depth of 3.35 m. Shuaiba Commercial Port, 56 km south of Kuwait City, comprises 20 berths with a total length of 4 km. Since 2003 the port has been used by the US Army as a base for supplying its troops in Iraq. Expansion plans were announced in 2009. Doha, the smallest port, has 20 small berths, each 100 m long. An oil port at Mina al-Ahmadi, 40 km south of Kuwait City, comprises 12 tanker berths, one bitumen-carrier berth, two LPG export berths and bunkering facilities, and is able to load more than 2m. barrels of oil per day.

KUWAIT

Plans for the privatization of Kuwait's ports were under development in the late 2000s. In mid-2010 a contract for the construction of a new US $1,200m. international port at Bubiyan island was awarded to Hyundai Engineering and Construction Co.

At 31 December 2009 Kuwait's merchant fleet numbered 209 vessels, with a total displacement of 2,369,300 grt.

Port Authority

Kuwait Ports Authority: POB 3874, 13039 Safat, Kuwait City; tel. 24812622; fax 24819714; e-mail info@kpa.gov.kw; internet www.kpa.gov.kw; f. 1977; Dir-Gen. Dr SABER JABER AL-ALI AL-SABAH.

Principal Shipping Companies

Arab Maritime Petroleum Transport Co (AMPTC): POB 22525, 13086 Safat, Kuwait City; tel. 24959400; fax 24842996; e-mail amptc.kuwait@amptc.net; internet www.amptc.net; f. 1973; six crude petroleum tankers, four LPG carriers and one product carrier; owned by Algeria, Bahrain, Egypt, Iraq, Kuwait, Libya, Qatar, Saudi Arabia and the UAE; Gen. Man. SULAYMAN I. AL-BASSAM.

Heavy Engineering Industries and Shipbuilding Co (Heisco): POB 21998, 13080 Safat, Kuwait City; tel. 24835488; fax 24830291; e-mail heisco@heisco.com; internet www.heisco.com; f. 1974 as Kuwait Shipbuilding and Repairyard Co; name changed as above in 2003; ship repairs and engineering services, underwater services, maintenance of refineries, power stations and storage tanks; maintains floating dock for vessels up to 35,000 dwt; synchrolift for vessels up to 5,000 dwt with transfer yard; seven repair jetties up to 550 m in length and floating workshop for vessels lying at anchor; Chair. JUHAIL MUHAMMAD AL-JUHAIL.

KGL Ports Int. Co (KGL PI): POB 24565, 13106 Safat, Kuwait City; tel. 22245155; fax 22245166; e-mail bader.alkhaldi@kglpi.com; internet www.kglpi.com; f. 2005; subsidiary of Kuwait and Gulf Link Transport Co; port management and stevedoring; operates Shuaiba Commercial Port Container Terminal; also operations and management contracts with ports in United Arab Emirates and Saudi Arabia; Chair. and CEO FADHEL AL-BAGHLI.

Kuwait Maritime Transport Co KSC (KMTC): POB 22595, 13086 Safat, Nafisi and Khatrash Bldg, Jaber al-Mubarak St, Kuwait City; tel. 22449974; fax 22420513; f. 1981; Chair. YOUSUF AL-MAJID.

Kuwait Oil Tanker Co SAK (KOTC): POB 810, 13009 Safat, al-Salhiya Commercial Complex, Blks 3, 5, 7 and 9, Kuwait City; tel. 24625050; fax 24913597; e-mail nakilat@kotc.com.kw; internet www.kotc.com.kw; f. 1957; state-owned; operates eight crude oil tankers, 11 product tankers and five LPG vessels; sole tanker agents for Mina al-Ahmadi, Shuaiba and Mina al-Abdullah and agents for other ports; LPG filling and distribution; Chair. and Man. Dir NABIL M. BOURISLI.

United Arab Shipping Co SAG (UASC): POB 20722, 13068 Safat, Old Airport Rd, Kuwait City; tel. 24848190; fax 24831263; e-mail gencom.uasackwt@uasc.net; internet www.uasc.net; f. 1976; nat shipping co of six Arabian Gulf countries; services between Europe, Far East, Mediterranean ports, Japan and east coast of USA and South America, and ports of participant states on Persian (Arabian) Gulf and Red Sea; operates 42 vessels; subsidiary cos include: United Arab Shipping Agencies Co (Kuwait), Arab Transport Co (Aratrans), United Arab Chartering Ltd (United Kingdom), Middle East Container Repair Co (UAE), Arabian Chemicals Carriers (Saudi Arabia), United Arab Agencies Inc (USA) and United Arab Shipping Agencies Co (Saudi Arabia); Pres. and CEO JØRN HINGE.

CIVIL AVIATION

Kuwait International Airport opened in 1980, and by 2009 handled 8.1m. passengers, compared with 3.8m. in 2001. The airport is undergoing a major programme of expansion: the first phase of the project was to expand the airport's annual capacity to 20m. passengers and to modernize facilities, with a further final phase of development intended to achieve passenger capacity of 55m.

Directorate-General of Civil Aviation (DGCA): POB 17, 13001 Safat, Kuwait City; tel. 24335599; fax 24713504; Pres. FAWAZ AL-FARAH; Dir-Gen. Eng. BADER BOUTAIBAN.

Jazeera Airways: POB 29288, 13153 Safat, Kuwait City; e-mail helpdesk@jazeeraairways.com; internet www.jazeeraairways.com; f. 2005; low-cost airline owned by Boodai Group; serves 26 destinations in the Middle East, North Africa, Europe and Asia; Chair. MARWAN BOODAI; CEO STEFAN PICHLER.

Kuwait Airways Corpn (KAC): POB 394, Kuwait International Airport, 13004 Safat, Kuwait City; tel. 24345555; fax 24314118; e-mail info@kuwait-airways.com; internet www.kuwait-airways.com; f. 1954; scheduled and charter passenger and cargo services to the Arabian peninsula, Asia, Africa, the USA and Europe;

scheduled for privatization; Chair. and Man. Dir HAMAD A. LATIF AL-FALAH.

Tourism

Attractions for visitors include the Kuwait Towers leisure and reservoir complex, the Entertainment City theme park, the Kuwait Zoological Garden in Omariya and the Khiran Resort tourist village near the border with Saudi Arabia, as well as extensive facilities for sailing and other water sports. Foreign tourist arrivals totalled some 4.7m. in 2008, while tourism receipts of US $610m. were recorded in that year.

Department of Tourism: Ministry of Information, Tourism Affairs, POB 193, 13002 Safat, al-Sour St, Kuwait City; tel. 22457591; fax 22401540; e-mail tourism_kw@media.gov.kw.

Kuwait Tourism Services Co: POB 21774, 13078 Safat, Kuwait City; tel. 2451734; fax 2451731; e-mail ktsc@qualitynet.net; internet www.ktsc-q8.com; f. 1997; Chair. KHALID AL-DUWAISAN.

Touristic Enterprises Co (TEC): POB 23310, 13094 Safat, Kuwait City; tel. 24965555; fax 24965055; e-mail info@tec.com.kw; internet www.kuwaittourism.com; f. 1976; 92% state-owned; manages 23 tourist facilities; Chair. BADER AL-BAHAR; Vice-Chair. SHAKER AL-OTHMAN.

Defence

As assessed at November 2010, Kuwait's active armed forces numbered 15,500—a land army of 11,000, an air force of 2,500 and a navy of around 2,000—and there were reserve forces of 23,700. Paramilitary forces were estimated to comprise a 6,600-strong national guard and a 500-strong coastguard. Military service is voluntary. The defence, security and justice budget for 2009 was estimated at KD 1,860.0m. A US military force has been deployed in Kuwait as part of 'Operation Iraqi Freedom', launched in 2003 (see the chapter on Iraq), and there are also small contingents of troops from the United Kingdom and Japan.

Chief of Staff of Armed Forces: Lt-Gen. AHMAD AL-KHALED AL-HAMAD AL-SABAH.

Education

Compulsory education for children between six and 14 years of age was introduced in 1966–67. However, many children spend two years prior to this in a kindergarten, and go on to complete their general education at the age of 18 years. It is government policy to provide free education to all Kuwaiti children from kindergarten stage to the University. In 2000/01 a total of 269,803 pupils attended 466 government schools (184 primary, 165 intermediate and 117 secondary). In that year a total of 128,204 pupils attended 112 private schools.

Primary education lasts for four years between the ages of six and 10, after which the pupils move on to an intermediate school for another four years. Secondary education, which is optional and lasts between the ages of 14 and 18, is given mainly in general schools. There are also commercial institutes, a Faculty of Technological Studies, a health institute, religious institutes (with intermediate and secondary stages) and 11 institutes for handicapped children. In 2007/08 enrolment at primary schools included 88.2% of children in the relevant age-group, while at secondary schools the rate included 79.9% of children in the relevant age-group.

Scholarships are granted to students to pursue courses not offered by Kuwait University. Such scholarships are mainly used to study in Egypt, Lebanon, the United Kingdom and the USA. There are also pupils from Arab, African and Asian states studying in Kuwait schools on scholarships provided by the Kuwaiti Government. Kuwait University had about 20,000 students in 2006, and also provides scholarships for a number of Arab, Asian and African students. In May 1996 the Majlis approved a draft law to regulate students' behaviour, dress and activities, with regard to observance of the teachings of Shari'a (Islamic) law, and to eradicate co-educational classes at Kuwait University over a five-year period. A KD 1,000m. project to build a new university campus and to gather the institution's dispersed facilities onto one site was expected to be completed by 2025. In 2008/09 an estimated 61,920 students were enrolled in tertiary education. Expenditure on education by the central Government in 2008/09 totalled KD 1,448.3m. (12.3% of total expenditure).

KYRGYZSTAN

Introductory Survey

LOCATION, CLIMATE, LANGUAGE, RELIGION, FLAG, CAPITAL

The Kyrgyz Republic is a small, landlocked state situated in eastern Central Asia. It borders Kazakhstan to the north, Uzbekistan to the west, Tajikistan to the south and west, and the People's Republic of China to the east. There are distinct variations in climate between low-lying and high-altitude areas. In the valleys the mean July temperature is 28°C (82°F), falling to an average of −18°C (−0.5°F) in January. Annual rainfall ranges from 180 mm (7 ins) in the eastern Tien Shan mountains to 750 mm–1,000 mm (30 ins–39 ins) in the Farg'ona (Fergana) mountain range. In the settled valleys the annual average varies between 100 mm and 500 mm (4 ins–20 ins). The state language is Kyrgyz; Russian additionally has the status of an official language. The major religion is Islam, with the majority of ethnic Kyrgyz being Sunni Muslims of the Hanafi school. The national flag (proportions 3 by 5) consists of a red field, at the centre of which is a yellow sun, with 40 counter-clockwise rays surrounding a red-bordered yellow disc, on which are superimposed two intersecting sets of three red, curved, narrow bands. The capital is Bishkek.

CONTEMPORARY POLITICAL HISTORY

Historical Context

Following the October Revolution of 1917 in Russia, Kyrgyzstan (which had been formally incorporated into the Russian Empire in 1876) experienced civil war, with anti-Bolshevik forces, including the Russian White Army and local armed groups (*basmachi*), fighting against the Bolshevik Red Army. In 1918 the Turkestan Autonomous Soviet Socialist Republic (ASSR) was established within the Russian Soviet Federative Socialist Republic (the Russian Federation), and Soviet power was established in the region by 1919. In 1924 the Kara-Kyrgyz Autonomous Oblast (Region) was created. In 1925 the region was renamed the Kyrgyz Autonomous Oblast, and became the Kyrgyz ASSR in February 1926. On 5 December 1936 the Kyrgyz Soviet Socialist Republic (SSR) was established as a full union republic of the USSR.

During the 1920s considerable economic and social developments were made in Kyrgyzstan, when land reforms resulted in the settlement of many of the nomadic Kyrgyz. The agricultural collectivization programme implemented under Stalin (Iosif V. Dzhugashvili—Soviet leader in 1924–53) in the early 1930s was strongly opposed in the republic, and many so-called 'national communists' were expelled from the Kyrgyz Communist Party (KCP) and imprisoned or exiled, particularly during the late 1930s. Tensions with the all-Union (Soviet) authorities continued following the death of Stalin in 1953.

The election of Mikhail Gorbachev as Soviet leader in 1985, and his introduction of the policies of perestroika (restructuring) and glasnost (openness), led to the resignation of Turdakan Usubaliyev as First Secretary of the KCP and the dismissal from office of his allies by Absamat Masaliyev, his successor. The republic's Supreme Soviet (Jogorku Kenesh or Supreme Council—legislature) adopted Kyrgyz as the official language, although Russian was retained as a language of inter-ethnic communication. The conservative republican leadership opposed the development of unofficial quasi-political groups, although one such group, Ashar, was partially tolerated by the authorities and soon developed a wider political role. A notable group at this time was Osh Aymaghi, based in Osh Oblast of the Farg'ona (Fergana) valley (which is shared between Kyrgyzstan, Tajikistan and Uzbekistan). Osh Aymaghi attempted to obtain land and housing provision for Kyrgyz in the Uzbek-dominated region (where demands for the establishment of an Uzbek autonomous region). In 1990 disputes over land and homes developed into violent inter-ethnic confrontations. According to official reports, more than 300 people died, and a state of emergency and a curfew were introduced, the former remaining in force until 1995; the Uzbekistani–Kyrgyzstani border was also closed.

At elections to the 350-member Kyrgyzstani Supreme Soviet held in February 1990 KCP candidates won most seats unopposed, and in April Masaliyev was elected to the new office of Chairman of the Supreme Soviet. In October an extraordinary session of the Supreme Soviet was convened to elect the President. The growth in support for the opposition Democratic Movement of Kyrgyzstan (DMK), combined with the discrediting of Masaliyev as a consequence of the conflict in Osh meant that Masaliyev failed to be elected in the first round of voting. In a further round of voting a compromise candidate, Askar Akayev, the President of the Kyrgyz Academy of Sciences, was elected to the executive presidency. Akayev rapidly allied himself with reformist factions. In December Masaliyev resigned as Chairman of the Supreme Soviet, and was replaced by Medetkan Sherimkulov. (In April 1991 he also resigned as First Secretary of the KCP.) Also in December 1990, the Supreme Soviet voted to change the name of the republic from the Kyrgyz SSR to the Republic of Kyrgyzstan. In January 1991 Akayev replaced the Council of Ministers with a smaller, largely reformist, cabinet. In February the capital, Frunze, reverted to its pre-1926 name of Bishkek. In a referendum held in nine Soviet Union Republics in March, 87.7% of eligible voters in Kyrgyzstan approved the proposal to retain the USSR as a 'renewed federation'.

Domestic Political Affairs

In August 1991, when the conservative communist State Committee for the State of Emergency (SCSE) announced that it had assumed power in the Russian and Soviet capital, Moscow, there was an attempt to depose Akayev in Kyrgyzstan. Akayev dismissed the Chairman of the republican Committee of State Security (KGB) and ordered interior ministry troops to guard strategic buildings in Bishkek. Akayev publicly denounced the coup (which the KCP had supported) and issued a decree prohibiting activity by any political party in government or state bodies. After the coup had collapsed in Moscow, Akayev and republican Vice-President German Kuznetsov renounced their membership of the Communist Party of the Soviet Union, and the entire politburo and secretariat of the KCP resigned. On 31 August the Kyrgyzstani Supreme Soviet voted to declare independence from the USSR. Akayev (the sole candidate) was re-elected President of Kyrgyzstan by direct popular vote on 12 October, receiving 95% of the votes cast.

In October 1991 Akayev signed, with representatives of seven other republics, a treaty to establish a new economic community. On 21 December Kyrgyzstan was among the 11 signatories to the Almaty (Alma-Ata) Declaration, which formally established the Commonwealth of Independent States (CIS, see p. 238).

Discussions were held throughout 1992 to draft a new constitution. The Constitution, which was finally promulgated on 5 May 1993, provided for a parliamentary system of government, headed by a Prime Minister. Legislative power was to be vested in a 105-member Jogorku Kenesh, following a general election, to be held by 1995. Russian was accorded the status of a language of inter-ethnic communication. The country's official name was changed from the Republic of Kyrgyzstan to the less ethnically neutral Kyrgyz Republic. In July Akayev's attempts to encourage non-Kyrgyz to remain in the republic suffered a serious reverse when Kuznetsov, by this time the First Deputy Prime Minister, announced his decision to return to Russia. By mid-1993 it was estimated that some 145,000 Russians had left the republic since 1989.

Akayev's presidency was destabilized during 1993 by a series of corruption scandals. Two commissions of inquiry were established to investigate the business dealings of the Vice-President, Feliks Kulov, and to examine allegations that senior politicians—including the Prime Minister since February 1992, Tursunbek Chyngyshev—had been involved in unauthorized gold exports. In December 1993 Kulov resigned and the legislature subsequently held a vote of confidence in Chyngyshev's Government: the motion failed to secure the required two-thirds' majority and Akayev dismissed the entire cabinet. A new Government, headed by Apas Jumagulov (Chairman of the Council of Ministers in 1986–91), was approved later in the month. A referendum of confidence in the presidency was held (on Akayev's initiative) in January 1994, at which 96.2% of voters endorsed Akayev's leadership. In June, in an attempt to curb the rate of emigration, Akayev issued a decree promoting the use of Russian, simplifying the procedure of application for dual citizenship, and guaranteeing the equitable representation of ethnic Russians in the state administration.

In September 1994 more than 180 deputies demanded the dissolution of the Kenesh and the holding of fresh elections, in protest at the continuing obstruction of economic reforms. The Government tendered its resignation, and Akayev announced that fresh parliamentary elections would be held. The Government was promptly reinstated by Akayev, who announced the holding of a referendum in October on constitutional amendments, at which the majority of the electorate endorsed proposals for a bicameral Jogorku Kenesh, to comprise a 70-member El Okuldor Palatasy (People's Assembly—upper chamber) to represent regional interests at twice-yearly sessions and a permanent 35-member Myizam Chygaru Palatasy (Legislative Assembly—lower chamber) to represent the population as a whole. Elections to the two legislative chambers were held in February 1995. The two chambers of the Jogorku Kenesh held their inaugural sessions on 28 March. A new Government, again led by Jumagulov, was appointed in April.

In September 1995 the Myizam Chygaru Palatasy vetoed a proposal to hold a referendum on extending the President's term of office until 2000. On 24 December 1995 Akayev received 71.6% of the votes cast in a direct presidential election; Masaliyev (who had recently been reinstated as the leader of the revived KCP) won 24.4% of the votes. The rate of participation by the electorate was some 82%. Akayev was inaugurated on 30 December. Following a decree issued by Akayev, a referendum was held on 10 February 1996, at which the majority of the electorate endorsed amendments to the Constitution increasing presidential powers and decreasing those of the legislature. The Government resigned later that month; Jumagulov was reinstated as Prime Minister in March and Akayev approved a new Government shortly afterwards.

In January 1998 a new criminal code was promulgated. In March Jumagulov announced his retirement and the Jogorku Kenesh endorsed the appointment of Kuvachbek Jumaliyev as the new Prime Minister. In July the Constitutional Court ruled that Akayev was permitted to seek a third term in the presidential election due to be held in 2000. A referendum on several constitutional amendments took place on 17 October, with the participation of about 96% of the electorate, and some 90% of voters approved the following amendments: the number of deputies in the Myizam Chygaru Palatasy was to increase to 60, and representation in the El Okuldor Palatasy was to be reduced to 45; the electoral system was to be reformed; restrictions on parliamentary immunity were to be introduced; private land ownership was to be legalized; the presentation of unbalanced or unattainable budgets was to be banned; and the adoption of any legislation restricting freedom of speech or of the press was to be prohibited. The Jogorku Kenesh and the majority of political parties declared their opposition to the constitutional changes and, in particular, to the introduction of private land ownership. By mid-December some 383 government officials had been dismissed on grounds of corruption, and in late December the President dissolved the Government for its failure to address the country's economic problems. Jumabek Ibraimov was appointed Prime Minister and a new Government was formed, in which 10 ministers from the previous administration retained their portfolios. Akayev strengthened the Prime Minister's mandate, empowering him to appoint and dismiss ministers and heads of departments (hitherto the exclusive right of the President). Ibraimov died in April 1999, and Amangeldy Muraliyev was appointed as his successor.

The 2000 legislative and presidential elections

A new electoral law was introduced at the end of May 1999 whereby, henceforth, 15 seats in the Myizam Chygaru Palatasy were to be allocated on a proportional basis for those parties that secured a minimum of 5% of the votes; the legislation also banned the use of foreign funding in electoral campaigns. In June legislation came into effect, banning political organizations considered a threat to Kyrgyzstan's stability and ethnic harmony. In July two new opposition parties were established: the Dignity (Ar-Namys) Party, led by Kulov—by this time Mayor of Bishkek—and the Justice (Adilettuuluk) Party.

Two rounds of elections were held to both chambers of the Jogorku Kenesh on 20 February and 12 March 2000. In the first round, six parties surpassed the 5% threshold required to secure party-list seats in the Myizam Chygaru Palatasy. A number of electoral violations were reported by the Organization for Security and Co-operation in Europe (OSCE, see p. 385). Overall, nominally independent candidates took 73 of the 105 seats in the two chambers, while the Union of Democratic Forces achieved the greatest representation of any party or bloc in the combined Jogorku Kenesh, securing a total of 12 seats, compared with the KCP's six. Kulov (who contested the poll as an independent after Dignity was prohibited from participating) failed to win a seat, prompting opposition protests. Later in March Kulov was arrested on charges of abuse of office during his tenure as Minister of National Security in 1997–98. Although he was acquitted in August 2000, a retrial was ordered, and Kulov was sentenced to seven years' imprisonment in January 2001. An appeal was rejected in March, and in May 2002 Kulov was also found guilty of embezzlement.

Meanwhile, at the presidential election, held on 29 October 2000, Akayev was re-elected, securing 74.5% of the votes cast. His closest rival was Omurbek Tekebayev, the leader of the Fatherland Socialist Political Party (Ata-Meken), with 13.9%, while Almazbek Atambayev, the leader of the Social Democratic Party of Kyrgyzstan (SDPK), obtained 6.0% of the ballot. According to official figures, 74% of the electorate participated. On the day of the election a criminal case opened in Bishkek following the discovery, by international observers, of several hundred ballot papers, marked in favour of Akayev, before polling had begun officially. Moreover, opposition parties claimed that they had been prevented from participating in media broadcasts. The Chairman of the Central Commission for Elections and Referendums was forced to concede that electoral violations had taken place. Despite mass protests and demands for the election to be repeated, on 10 November the Constitutional Court formally endorsed the results.

Akayev was inaugurated for a third term on 9 December 2000 and on 21 December Kurmanbek Bakiyev, hitherto the Governor of Chui Oblast, was appointed Prime Minister; a new Government was announced at the beginning of January 2001. In April the leaders of nine opposition parties formally announced the establishment of an alliance, the People's Patriotic Movement, which was to seek to safeguard democracy and protect human and constitutional rights. The movement organized demonstrations against the erosion of the independent media and against the imprisonment of Kulov. In November opposition parties including Dignity, the Fatherland Socialist Political Party and the Liberty party announced the formation of a new People's Congress, and elected the imprisoned Kulov its Chairman. In the following month the President signed into law a constitutional amendment granting Russian the status of official language, in a further apparent attempt to halt the emigration of ethnic Russians from Kyrgyzstan.

In January 2002 the arrest of Azimbek Beknazarov, an opposition deputy, was denounced as politically motivated. In March 2002 six demonstrators were shot dead by security forces in the village of Aksy, in the southern Jalal-Abad region, where Beknazarov's trial was being held; the trial was subsequently suspended and was not resumed until January 2011, though it was later postponed. In May the Myizam Chygaru Palatasy ratified a controversial Sino-Kyrgyzstani border treaty signed in 1999 and of which Beknazarov had been a prominent opponent, prompting two weeks of anti-Government demonstrations, hunger strikes and civil disobedience. Protesters demanded that the Government accept responsibility for the violence of March, rescind the ratification of the border treaty (which they claimed had been signed illegally by President Akayev, since he had agreed to cede land to the People's Republic of China without the consent of the legislature), and close the criminal case against Beknazarov. Nevertheless, the El Okuldor Palatasy ratified the treaty later in May, and it was duly signed into law by the President.

As controversy continued about his alleged responsibility for ordering the killings by the security forces in Aksy in March, in May 2002 Prime Minister Bakiyev tendered his resignation. The First Deputy Prime Minister, Nikolai Tanayev, was appointed Prime Minister and a new Government was announced in June. Meanwhile, in May Beknazarov received a one-year, suspended prison sentence. Following an appeal and further large-scale demonstrations, Beknazorov's sentence was annulled (although the initial guilty verdict was upheld), enabling him to retain his parliamentary seat. In June the Myizam Chygaru Palatasy approved an amnesty, proposed by Tanayev for both protesters and law enforcement officials involved in the disturbances of March.

In January 2003 President Akayev announced that a referendum on several constitutional amendments was to be held on 2 February. The amendments, which provided for the introduction of a unicameral legislature with effect from 2005, in which all deputies were to be elected in single-member constituencies, were duly approved by 76.6% of the electorate, while 78.7% of voters supported Akayev's remaining in office until 2005; the reported rate of participation was 86.7%. The hasty scheduling of the referendum attracted international criticism, and there were also allegations of procedural violations.

A major government reorganization took place in February 2004. In April the President introduced a new law designating Kyrgyz the state language, and stipulating measures for its promotion, apparently in order to encourage bilingualism in Kyrgyz and Russian, which was to remain an official language. In May, in advance of legislative elections, opposition parties, including Dignity, the Fatherland Socialist Political Party and the SDPK, announced the formation of an electoral bloc, the Civic Union For Fair Elections. The formation of a larger electoral bloc, the People's Movement of Kyrgyzstan, was announced in September, under Bakiyev's leadership.

'The Tulip Revolution'

In January 2005 Roza Otunbayeva, a former ambassador to the United Kingdom, and the leader of the recently formed opposition Homeland Idealistic Democratic Party (Ata-Jurt), was refused permission to register as a candidate in the parliamentary elections, on the grounds that she had not been resident in the country for the previous five years. Campaigning for the elections officially began on 2 February. Protests against the exclusion of candidates and opposition rallies demanding free and fair parliamentary elections, or the impeachment of Akayev, continued throughout February. In the first round of legislative voting on 27 February the rate of participation by the electorate was reported to be 60%. Some 31 candidates (each of whom had received an absolute majority of votes cast in their respective electoral districts) were elected to the restructured, unicameral, 75-member Jogorku Kenesh. The majority of those elected were nominally independent candidates. Forward, Kyrgyzstan, established in 2003 and regarded as generally sympathetic to Akayev's administration, became the largest party faction to achieve representation, with 10 deputies. OSCE monitors concluded that the elections had not fully complied with democratic standards, while opposition and independent observers asserted that large-scale electoral fraud had taken place. Protests to dispute local polling results took place in various regions in advance of the second round of elections, held on 13 March, and media outlets supportive of the opposition or critical of the authorities were suppressed. Following the second round of voting, a further 37 candidates were elected (with a participation rate of 55%); only six opposition candidates obtained representation in the new legislature.

Dissatisfaction at the conduct and outcome of the elections resulted in large-scale protests in a number of cities, particularly in the south. From mid-March 2005 demonstrators occupied the regional governor's office in Jalal-Abad for several weeks and, later in the month, demonstrators took control of a government building in Osh. On 22 March the Central Commission for Elections and Referendums declared that the results of voting for 69 of the 75 seats were valid; investigations into the conduct of voting in the remaining six districts were to continue. The Supreme Court, however revoked the mandate of the newly elected Jogorku Kenesh, asserting that the previous bicameral legislature continued to hold authority. On 23 March Akayev dismissed the Prosecutor-General, Myktybek Abdyldayev, and the Minister of Internal Affairs, Bakirdin Subanbekov, who had declared that he would not use force to end the protests.

By 24 March 2005 demonstrations had spread to Bishkek, and protesters stormed the presidential palace and government buildings. Akayev fled the country, while maintaining that he remained Kyrgyzstan's Head of State, and Tanayev resigned as Prime Minister. Meanwhile, protesters freed Kulov from gaol. On the same day, at an emergency session, the lower chamber of the legislature elected in 2000 named Bakiyev acting Prime Minister (he automatically became acting President in Akayev's absence). On 25 March Bakiyev announced the appointment of several senior officials in the interim Government, including Otunbayeva as Minister of Foreign Affairs, Abdyldayev as Minister of Internal Affairs, Gen. Ismail Isakov as Minister of Defence, and Beknazarov as acting Prosecutor-General. Kulov was given responsibility for overseeing the country's law enforcement agencies and armed forces. After the Central Commission for Elections and Referendums announced that the powers of the bicameral legislature elected in 2000 were terminated, the lower and upper chambers dissolved themselves on 28 and 29 March, respectively, thereby effectively confirming the legitimacy of the recently elected legislature, and apparently overturning the ruling of the Supreme Court. Meanwhile, on 28 March the new Jogorku Kenesh voted to confirm Bakiyev as interim Prime Minister, and to elect Tekebayev as legislative Chairman. (In late April Tekebayev was also appointed as Chairman of the Constitutional Court.) On 30 March Kulov resigned his post, reportedly owing to disagreement with Bakiyev.

On 4 April 2005 Akayev, speaking at the Kyrgyzstani embassy in Moscow, announced his resignation as President (the decision was approved by the Jogorku Kenesh on 11 April). On 8 April Parliament voted to deprive Akayev of certain privileges associated with his status as a former president, and to remove immunity from prosecution from members of his family, allowing them to be investigated on corruption charges. The Jogorku Kenesh subsequently scheduled a presidential election for 10 July. From mid-April protests were staged outside the Supreme Court against aspects of the legislative elections, demanding, inter alia, the resignation of the Chairman of the Court, Kurmanbek Osmonov, who was regarded as an ally of Akayev. In mid-April the Court overturned Kulov's convictions. Although Osmonov submitted his resignation later in the month, Bakiyev rejected it. In mid-May Bakiyev reached an agreement with Kulov, who was considered to be Bakiyev's principal rival in the presidential contest, according to which Kulov agreed to withdraw his candidacy in return for a guarantee that Bakiyev would appoint him Prime Minister should he secure the presidency. Also in mid-May, Bakiyev dismissed acting Minister of Internal Affairs Abdyldayev and replaced him with Murat Sutalinov. Violent unrest in Bishkek was reported in June.

On 10 July 2005 Bakiyev won 88.7% of the votes cast in the presidential election, which was contested by six candidates. The OSCE reported some irregularities in the counting of votes. Bakiyev was inaugurated as President on 14 August, and on 1 September the Jogorku Kenesh confirmed Kulov's appointment as Prime Minister. In mid-September Bakiyev removed Beknazarov from his position as Prosecutor-General, together with his deputy, accusing them of negligence. Busurmankul Tabaldiyev was appointed to succeed Beknazarov on an acting basis; however, he resigned in October, and was replaced by Kambaraly Kongantiyev. Meanwhile, in late September the Jogorku Kenesh approved 10 of the 16 ministers proposed by Bakiyev. Many ministers in the outgoing interim administration retained their portfolios, notably Isakov as Minister of Defence and Akylbek Japarov as Minister of the Economy and Finance. Following the rejection by the legislature of Otunbayeva's nomination as Minister of Foreign Affairs, Alikbek Jekshenkulov was appointed to the post. Otunbayeva and Beknazarov subsequently became co-chairmen of the Banner (Asaba) Party of National Revival, although Otunbayeva resigned from this position shortly afterwards. Adakhan Madumarov was appointed Deputy Prime Minister and Marat Kaiypov became Minister of Justice. In October the Office of the Prosecutor-General charged former Prime Minister Tanayev, who was under house arrest in Bishkek, with abuse of power and corruption. (In May 2006 it was reported that the criminal case against Tanayev had been closed.) Also in October 2005 Bakiyev nominated Daniyar Usenov, an opponent of Kulov, as First Deputy Prime Minister, although the Jogorku Kenesh rejected this nomination in November, instead approving the appointment, in the following month, of Medetbek Kerimkulov. The Government was sworn in on 20 December.

Meanwhile, in September 2005 Bayaman Erkinbayev, a parliamentary deputy and businessman who had actively participated in Akayev's removal from power (and who was alleged to have links to criminal groups), was murdered in Bishkek; another parliamentary deputy had been assassinated in July. In October a further parliamentary deputy, Tynychbek Akmatbayev, was killed by inmates during an official visit to a gaol. Large rallies, led by Akmatbayev's brother, Ryspek, a prominent and controversial figure alleged to be involved in organized crime (see below), subsequently took place to demand the dismissal of Kulov, whom the protesters accused of having collaborated with prisoners to organize the killing of Akmatbayev.

In January 2006 President Bakiyev decreed that measures be taken to organize a referendum on the division of power between the President and parliament; Bakiyev had pledged to award the legislature increased powers following his election. Also in early January, representatives of 17 political movements and organizations agreed to establish an opposition bloc, the People's Coalition of Democratic Forces, which united those dissatisfied with the new regime. In late January Kulov demanded reform of the judicial system and the entire law enforcement system, and criticized the Chairman of the National Security Service (SNB), Tashtemir Aitbayev, for allowing criminal elements to infiltrate the organization. Although Bakiyev rejected demands by parliamentary deputies for Aitbayev's dismissal, in early February he removed the deputy head of the SNB, and accepted the resignation of the Deputy Secretary of the Security Council. Also in early February further tensions between the Jogorku Kenesh and the President arose when Bakiyev accused the legislature of fomenting political instability and exceeding its mandate, causing Tekebayev to tender his resignation from the parliamentary chairmanship. Although the Jogorku Kenesh initially rejected Tekebayev's resignation, leading to further strains between the legislature and the President, it was accepted in late February. Marat Sultanov was elected as the new Chairman of the Jogorku Kenesh in early March, and pledged to attempt to resolve disagreements with the executive without recourse to confrontation. In March President Bakiyev signed a decree officially suspending the Chairman of the National Bank, Ulan Sarbanov, from office, during his trial on charges of having illegally transferred some US $420,000 to former President Akayev in 1999. Meanwhile, in early March Bakiyev had signed a decree designating 24 March, the anniversary of Akayev's effective removal from power as a result of the so-called 'tulip revolution', a national holiday, to be known as the Day of the People's Revolution.

Parliamentary by-elections, scheduled to take place in three districts in April 2006, generated considerable controversy owing to the candidacy of Rysbek Akmatbayev. Akmatbayev, convicted twice during the 1990s for, inter alia, assault and robbery, had been tried, but acquitted, in early 2006 for the murder of a policeman; however, his acquittal was in the process of being appealed at the time of the polls, thus rendering his candidacy illegitimate under the terms of the Constitution. In protest at Akmatbayev's participation, thousands of demonstrators amassed in the streets of the capital on the eve of the by-elections, urging the Government to adopt a tougher stance against organized crime. The by-elections proceeded as planned on 9 April, and Akmatbayev secured a comfortable victory in the constituency that he contested. Another large-scale demonstration took place in the capital in late April when several thousand people gathered to protest against widespread corruption among state officials, demanding that Bakiyev implement the reforms that he had pledged during his election campaign. In May Akmatbayev was shot dead by unknown assailants in Bishkek.

Further evidence of a rift between the executive and the legislature emerged in late April 2006, when the Jogorku Kenesh voted to evaluate the performance of individual members of the Government: only Prime Minister Kulov, two ministers and the head of a state committee were given positive appraisals, and in early May 14 ministers resigned. Although President Bakiyev rejected their resignations and the ministers subsequently agreed to remain in their posts, Bakiyev effected a cabinet reorganization in mid-May, which included the appointment of Usenov as First Deputy Prime Minister. Also in mid-May Bakiyev dismissed Kombaraaly Kongantiyev as Prosecutor-General and Usen Sydykov as Chief of the Presidential Administration, and replaced Tashtemir Aitbayev as Chairman of the SNB with former Prosecutor-General Busurmankul Tabaldiyev. The Jogorku Kenesh rejected the nomination of Ishengul Boljurova as a Deputy Prime Minister in June.

Constitutional disputes

In November 2006 thousands of opposition supporters attended a rally in Bishkek demanding constitutional reform and the resignation of President Bakiyev. Following a week of mass protests, the Jogorku Kenesh approved a new Constitution on 8 November, which was to diminish the power afforded to the President and to augment that of the legislature, the capacity of which was to be enlarged to 90 members; the membership of governments was henceforth to be determined by the Jogorku Kenesh, rather than the President. Bakiyev signed the new Constitution into effect on 9 November. In mid-December Prime Minister Kulov tendered his resignation (together with that of his Government), with the stated aim of forcing early parliamentary elections and thereby addressing the ongoing political crisis.

At the end of December 2006 the legislature voted to adopt a number of amendments to the new Constitution, including the retraction of the legislature's power to appoint the Government, which was henceforth to be appointed by the President at the suggestion of the Prime Minister, without the need for legislative approval. These amendments were signed into law on 17 January 2007. In late January the Jogorku Kenesh formally approved President Bakiyev's nomination of Azim Isabekov as Prime Minister, having twice rejected the President's nomination of Kulov. In early February Isabekov formed a new Government, in which the majority of key posts were allocated to close associates of President Bakiyev, including: Usenov, who was re-appointed First Deputy Prime Minister; Ednan Karabayev, who was appointed Minister of Foreign Affairs, and Igor Chudinov, who was awarded the industry, energy and fuel resources portfolio. In the same month Kulov added his voice to opposition demands for the President's resignation, strongly suggesting that the appointment of a new Prime Minister and Government would do little to restore stability. On 29 March Isabekov resigned as premier, after Bakiyev reversed his decision, taken in response to continuing mass protests, to dismiss five government ministers. The appointment of Atambayev as Prime Minister, which was regarded as an attempt to satisfy opposition demands, was approved by the Jogorku Kenesh on the following day, and Usenov was dismissed in an ensuing governmental reorganization. Later in April large-scale protests in Bishkek, organized by Kulov's recently established opposition grouping, the United Front For A Worthy Future For Kyrgyzstan, were dispersed by the security forces, and an encampment of tents established by protesters in the city centre was removed; some 100 demonstrators were arrested and two prominent opposition leaders were detained on charges of inciting unrest.

In September 2007 the Constitutional Court ruled that the adoption of the Constitutions of both November 2006 and January 2007 had been illegal, since the drafts had not been submitted to a national referendum; consequently the Constitution in place prior to November 2006 again entered into force. Bakiyev subsequently announced that a further new constitutional text was to be proposed at a referendum on 21 October. In October Bakiyev established a political party, Bright Road (Ak Jol). The Constitution proposed at the national referendum on 21 October was endorsed by 76.1% of the electorate (with a voter turnout of 81.6%); henceforth, in legislative elections single-member constituencies were to be replaced by a proportional party list system, while the number of parliamentary deputies was to increase from 75 to 90. On the following day Bakiyev dissolved the Zhorgorku Kenesh; early legislative elections were subsequently scheduled for 16 December. The Government submitted its resignation on 24 October, remaining in office in an interim capacity.

On 29 November 2007 Bakiyev removed Atambayev from the premiership; on the same day he appointed Iskenderbek Aidaraliyev, hitherto Governor of Jalal-Abad Oblast, as First Deputy Prime Minister and also assigned him the role of acting Prime Minister. At the elections on 16 December Bright Road won 47.0% of votes cast, securing 71 seats in the 90-member Zhorgorku Kenesh, ahead of the SDPK, with 5.1% of the votes cast and 11 seats, and the Communist Party of Kyrgyzstan, with 5.1% of the votes cast and eight seats. The Fatherland Socialist Political Party, despite gaining 8.3% of votes overall, narrowly failed to qualify for representation, owing to a new electoral requirement that each party obtain at least 0.5% of the votes cast in each of the country's seven oblasts and two largest cities. Although this stipulation was particularly criticized by OSCE observers, who stated that the conduct of the elections failed to meet democratic standards, the electoral commission upheld the results. On 24 December Chudinov was appointed Prime Minister, while Adaham Madumarov of Bright Road was elected the legislative Chairman. A new Government, which retained the principal ministers of the former administration, was approved in the Zhorgorku Kenesh on 27 December.

On 26 May 2008 the head of the pro-presidential faction in the Jogorku Kenesh, Elmira Ibragimova, was appointed Deputy Prime Minister, succeeding Dosbol Nur uulu. On the same day Bakytbek Kalyev, hitherto the head of the State Border Guard Service, was appointed Minister of Defence, succeeding Isakov, who became Secretary of the National Security Council. On 29 May Madumarov resigned as Chairman of the Jogorku Kenesh, in response to a report that he had contravened regulations concerning expenditure; he was replaced by a relatively obscure parliamentarian regarded as a close ally of President Bakiyev, Aitibai Tagayev. In September, on the recommendation of the Prime Minister, Bakiyev dismissed the Minister of Justice, Marat Kaiyypov, and the head of the penal service, following an investigation into a prison riot, in which two officers had been killed. A hitherto deputy prosecutor-general, Nurlan Tursunkulov, was appointed as the new Minister of Justice. Later that month, the Chairman of the electoral commission, Klara Kabilova, fled the country, subsequently accusing Maksim Bakiyev, the son of the President and a prominent businessman, of intimidation and of issuing threats against her. In local elections, held on 5 October, observers from local non-governmental organizations (NGOs) alleged that numerous irregularities had enabled government candidates to win most seats in municipal councils, and contested the CEC's statement of a participation rate of 61.6%. The new electoral commission Chairman, Damir Lisovsky, denied widespread allegations of electoral fraud. In November the Minister of Industry, Energy and Fuel Resources was replaced, following criticism over energy shortages. Also in November restrictions were imposed on the operation of religious organizations; in order to obtain official registration, religious organizations were henceforth required to have a minimum of 200 members, compared with the previous requirement of 10, while the distribution of religious material was also to be subject to greater restrictions. The Government stated that a principal motive in the introduction of the legislation was a growth in support for extremist Islamist groups, particularly in the south of the country. In late December an alliance of the major opposition parties, the United People's Movement (UPM), was established to demand: the resignation of Bakiyev; an end to the appointment of leading officials based on clan and family; and the cancellation of the proposed privatization of various important facilities. Severe energy shortages, and other indications of a deterioration in the economy following the onset of the international financial crisis, led to an increase in anti-Government sentiment. In January 2009 Bakiyev removed a total of 17 ministers and senior government officials, regional officials and ambassadors. Aidaraliyev was transferred to the post of Minister of Agriculture, Water Resources and Processing Industry; he was succeeded as First Deputy Prime Minister by Omurbek Babanov (who resigned from the SDPK following his appointment). Kadyrbek Sarbayev, hitherto the ambassador to Mongolia, received the post of Minister of Foreign Affairs, replacing Karabayev.

The 2009 presidential election

Following the announcement of his decision (rescinded in mid-June) to close the Manas airbase (see Foreign Affairs, below) in February 2009, Bakiyev indicated his intention to seek a second term in office, and was reported to favour an early presidential election; several opposition leaders had appealed to the Constitutional Court to bring forward the next poll (due to take place in October 2010). Opposition parties threatened to begin a campaign of protests to demand that the Government end repressive measures against opposition leaders and activists. In early March 2009, shortly after Bakiyev had agreed to negotiate with opposition leaders, former Minister of Foreign Affairs and prominent opposition member Alikbek Jekshenkulov was arrested on suspicion of involvement in the killing of a Turkish businessman in 2007, prompting immediate speculation that his arrest had been prompted by his support of Tekebayev (who was believed to be a likely presidential candidate) and his involvement with the opposition For Justice Movement; Jekshenkulov was also charged with abuse of office while serving in the Government; his trial commenced in mid-June, and in August he was released from custody on remand, instead being placed under house arrest. He was sentenced to five years' imprisonment in March 2010. Also in March 2009 Medet Sadyrkulov, who had been replaced as the head of the presidential administration in January, was killed in an automobile collision; several opposition leaders immediately claimed that the circumstances of his death were suspicious and that he had intended to transfer support to opponents of Bakiyev. On 19 March the Constitutional Court issued a ruling that the next presidential election must take place no later than 25 October of that year; on the following day the Zhorgorku Kenesh voted in favour of the poll being conducted on 23 July. In late March the UPM, led by Beknazarov, staged large anti-Government demonstrations in Bishkek and other major towns; opposition leaders warned that they would organize further protests if major demands for the replacement of one-half of the officials in principal ministries and the CEC were not met by the Government. The UPM further announced its intention to present a single candidate to contest the forthcoming presidential election, and in April it announced that it had selected Atambayev as its candidate. In April a Bright Road deputy, Sanjarbek Kadyraliyev, was assassinated outside his home in Bishkek, becoming the fifth parliamentarian to have been killed since the start of the Bakiyev presidency. In early May Bright Road confirmed that it had nominated Bakiyev as its presidential candidate. In early July a journalist who had often criticized the Government for its social policies and failure to reduce unemployment, Almaz Tashiyev, was severely beaten by several police officers; he died a few days later, after falling into a coma.

In the presidential election, held as scheduled on 23 July 2009, Bakiyev was re-elected, obtaining 76.4% of the vote cast, according to official results. Shortly after polling began, the leading opposition candidate, Atambayev, announced his withdrawal from the election on the grounds that officials had perpetrated extensive fraud. None the less, he remained the second-placed candidate, with 8.4%. Some 79.1% of the electorate were recorded to have participated. Observers from the OSCE described the election as falling short of full democratic standards, noting various irregularities in voters lists and incidents of multiple voting, while it was reported that around 20 opposition supporters had been detained by the police on polling day. On 29 July clashes broke out between demonstrators protesting at the conduct of the election and police in Bishkek, precipitating the imposition of a ban, from the following day, of mass gatherings.

On 1 September 2009, in an address to the Jogorku Kenesh, Bakiyev proposed a series of administrative reforms, including the establishment of two bodies to improve communication and co-operation between the state and citizens that would replace the existing presidential advisory offices and the State Secretariat: a Supreme Assembly was to comprise representatives of NGOs, religious bodies and social movements, while a Presidential Council would include representatives of farmers', business and youth groups. These proposed reforms were opposed by Prime Minister Chudinov, who consequently resigned on 21 October. He was succeeded as premier on the same day by Daniyar Usenov, a close ally of Bakiyev, who had served as the Chairman of the Presidential Administration since January. A new Government was formed one day later, to which many members of the outgoing administration were reappointed. A significant change in the balance of power was the transfer of responsibility for foreign affairs to the Office of the President, with the post of Minister of Foreign Affairs being abolished. In early December Tursunkulov was appointed as Prosecutor-General; he was succeeded as Minister of Justice later in the month by Kurmuntai Abdiyev. In the same month Bakyt Torobayev succeeded Kamchybek Tashiyev as Minister of Emergency Situations. On 17 December legislative Chairman Tagayev was appointed as the Governor of Batken Oblast; several days later the Jogorku Kenesh voted for an independent deputy, Zainidin Kurmanov, as his successor.

On 22 December 2009 a prominent Kyrgyzstani journalist critical of the Bakiyev regime, Gennady Pavlyuk (also known as Ibragim Rustamek), was killed after he was thrown to the ground from a high-rise building in Almatı, Kazakhstan. The Kazakhstani police stated that they regarded Pavlyuk's death as murder, prompting speculation that his killing was politically motivated, particularly as Pavlyuk had recently been involved with negotiations with Atambayev on the establishment of an online news site. (Two other journalists operating in Kyrgyzstan were physically attacked during that month.) The European Union (EU, see p. 270) subsequently demanded that a full investigation into Pavlyuk's killing be conducted; two people were arrested in Almatı in October 2010 in connection with the killing, while a third, the prime suspect, was apprehended two months later and was reportedly to be tried in Kazakhstan. In March 2010 the Government imposed a number of measures that inhibited the freedom of the media; two opposition newspapers, *Achyk Sayasat* and *Nazar*, were ordered to close, and the rebroadcasting on local FM radio stations of the Kyrgyz programming of the Czech Republic-based (and US-funded) Radio Free Europe/Radio Liberty was halted, while access to two prominent independent online news websites was blocked. In early April a further newspaper, *Forum*, was ordered by a court in Bishkek to cease publication, after it had allegedly called for the overthrow by force of the Government.

KYRGYZSTAN

The April 2010 uprising

On 3 April 2010 UN Secretary-General Ban Ki-Moon visited Kyrgyzstan as part of a tour of the states of Central Asia. His visit was a focus for protests in Bishkek, led by members of civil rights organizations, who expressed concern about apparently systematic human rights abuses. Meanwhile, social tensions, which had remained prevalent as a result of high unemployment and widespread poverty, were exacerbated by a steep increase in fuel prices at the start of the month. On 6 April, following reports of the arrest of opposition leader Bolot Shernizayev, several thousand protesters, demanding the resignation of President Bakiyev, stormed the regional government offices in the northwestern town of Talas, holding the regional governor hostage, while rioting ensued throughout the town. (Smaller demonstrations against the Government also took place in various other cities.) A further cause of discontent was the recent appointment of a number of relatives of the President to various senior positions in the security services as well as, in particular, that of Maksim Bakiyev to the position of Chairman of a state committee responsible for the control of all financial inflows into the country and several major companies. Although the police succeeded in freeing the regional governor later in the day, the demonstrators regained control of the administrative building. On the same day Atambayev was arrested and accused of inciting the unrest in Talas. Several other prominent opposition leaders, including Tekebayev, were detained in Bishkek.

On 7 April 2010 demonstrations in Bishkek, which were attended by an estimated 5,000 people demanding the resignation of Bakiyev and expressing opposition to the increases in fuel tariffs and the arrest of opposition leaders, rapidly degenerated into widespread violent disorder, as unruly crowds undertook extensive looting of commercial and government premises in the city. The demonstrations appeared to have no clear leader. Supporters of the opposition gained control of the state TV channel and broadcast speeches in support of the uprising. The First Deputy Prime Minister Akylbek Japarov was taken hostage, and the Minister of the Interior Moldomusa Kongantiyev was severely beaten. On the same day anti-Bakiyev protesters seized control of government and police buildings in the provincial cities of Naryn and Tokmak. In Bishkek, police officers opened fire on demonstrators when they attempted to storm the principal government building. In the ensuing violence around 80 people were killed and more than 1,000 injured. Kazakhstan closed its border with the country, which remained closed until 20 May. By the end of the day the Government had effectively lost control, and President Bakiyev, having been forced to flee Bishkek, flew to Osh, from where he announced his refusal to resign from office. Meanwhile, Otunbayeva, now the leader of the parliamentary faction of the SDPK, declared herself to be the leader of a transitional administration, the Interim Government of National Trust (later designated simply the Interim Government), which would hold office for a period of six months prior to the organization of a presidential election. Other senior members of the transitional administration included Temir Sarayev, the leader of the White Falcon Political Party (Ak Shumkar), Atambayev, Tekebayev and Beknazarov. On 11 April, as the first decree of the transitional administration, the Jogorku Kenesh was dissolved and all legislative functions temporarily assumed by the interim administration.

On 12 April 2010 Bakiyev led a rally in Jalal-Abad, attended by around 4,000 people. On 15 April officials of the Interim Government announced that Bakiyev had resigned as President. Following negotiations between the transitional administration and the leaders of Kazakhstan, Russia and the USA, mediated by the OSCE, Bakiyev was provided with safe passage to Kazakhstan, from where he denied that he had resigned. Meanwhile, the Minister of Defence in the Bakiyev administration, Bakytbek Kalyyev, was arrested on charges related to the use of force against unarmed civilians in Bishkek during the uprising. On 22 April Tekebayev announced that a referendum on a new constitution, which would reduce presidential powers, would be held on 27 June, and that a presidential election would be scheduled for 10 October. Meanwhile, as sporadic unrest continued in various regions of the country, including attacks that targeted minority ethnic groups, most notably Meshketians (a Turkic people originally from southern Georgia), Otunbayeva declared that the state would take firm action to restore order. Meanwhile, the President of Belarus, Alyaksandr Lukashenka, announced that he had granted asylum to Bakiyev, who continued to state that he was the legitimate Head of State of Kyrgyzstan, and that his letter of resignation had been written under pressure and against his will, following a telephone conversation with the Russian Chairman of the Government, Vladimir Putin. On 4 May Otunbayeva signed an agreement seeking the extradition of Bakiyev, formally removing his immunity from prosecution (by affirming that he was no longer Head of State), and ordered the opening of a criminal investigation against him in connection with his involvement in the violent suppression of protests on 7 April. However, President Lukashenka of Belarus stated that he would not permit Bakiyev's extradition. On the same day an investigation began into alleged corruption by companies allegedly controlled by Maksim Bakiyev that were responsible for the supply of fuel to the US airbase at Manas. On 13 May supporters of the ousted President succeeded in bringing about the removal from office of the interim Governor of Jalal-Abad Oblast, Bektur Asanov; however he was restored to his post on the following day. On 17 May KCP leader Iskhak Masaliyev was charged with organizing mass protests in Osh, Batken and Jalal-Abad. Violent clashes erupted on 19 May between rival Kyrgyz and Uzbek groups in Jalal-Abad and Osh, in which two people died and more than 70 were injured; a state of emergency was declared in Jalal-Abad. Also on 19 May the Interim Government announced that Otunbayeva was to serve additionally as interim President until the end of 2011, and that she would be prohibited from contesting the subsequent presidential election (to be held in October 2011 and not, as previously announced, in 2010) and, in the mean time, from the membership of any political party. On 21 May the Interim Government published Kyrgyzstan's new draft constitution, which defined the country as a secular state with a parliamentary system of government. Voters in the referendum on the constitution would also be required to approve Otunbayeva as interim President until December 2011, while parliamentary elections were to be held on 10 October 2010.

Ethnic unrest and the 2010 Constitution

On 9–10 June 2010 there was renewed ethnic violence in Osh, after a fight broke out between ethnic Kyrgyz and Uzbek groups at a casino. A series of subsequent attacks against ethnic Kyrgyz resulted in reprisals against the city's Uzbek population, prompting the Interim Government to send troops to the region and to declare a state of emergency (which remained in force for more than two weeks). In the ensuing days the ethnic unrest spread to other cities, including Jalal-Abad, while tens of thousands of ethnic Uzbeks attempted to flee across the border into Uzbekistan. As it became clear that the regional authorities were unable to deal with the scale of the conflict, the Interim Government declared a partial mobilization of the armed forces and appealed to Russia for help in restoring peace to the region. On 14 June Uzbekistan closed its border to prevent any further influx of refugees. The UN stated that there was evidence that the violence was 'orchestrated, targeted and well-planned'. While the Interim Government accused supporters of Bakiyev of inciting the unrest, a subsequent report by the international organization Human Rights Watch stated that the Kyrgyzstani military had played a role in facilitating the attacks against the Uzbek population. At least 400 were officially reported to have died in the conflict, which lasted just four days (although Otunbayeva, following a visit to Osh, set the number as high as 2,000), and 400,000 people, of whom at least 100,000 had crossed into Uzbekistan, were displaced. On 17 June the Russian-led Collective Security Treaty Organization (CSTO) announced that it would not deploy a peace-keeping mission to Kyrgyzstan. The following week the USA announced that it intended to provide a total of more than US $48m. of aid to Kyrgyzstan and the border region of Uzbekistan, as many ethnic Uzbeks returned to their homes from refugee camps across the border. Meanwhile, officials in Jalal-Abad Oblast were reported to have detained 12 suspected organizers of the inter-ethnic violence. On 25 June 2010 it was reported that Sanjarbek Bakiyev, a nephew of the ousted president, had been detained on charges of organizing the ethnic unrest in Jalal-Abad in May. (He was found guilty and sentenced to 10 years in prison on 2 November and subsequently lost an appeal against the verdict.)

Despite the unrest, the Kyrgyzstani authorities proceeded with the scheduled referendum on the constitution on 27 June 2010, the conduct of which was praised by the OSCE as being 'largely transparent'. A total of 90.6% of participants voted in favour of the constitution, with voter participation estimated at 72%. The Constitution came into force on 2 July; one day later Otunbayeva was sworn in as interim President, while retaining the post of Prime Minister. Subsequently, several prominent members of the Interim Government, including deputy chairmen Atambayev, Tekebayev and Sarayev filed letters of resignation from the cabinet in order to participate in the upcoming legislative elections. On 14 July, when several other senior members of the Government were appointed, they were replaced by former Prime Minister Amangeldy Muraliyev, Aleksandr Kostyuk and Jantoro Satybaldiyev, while Kubatbek Baibolov succeeded Sherniyazov (who in the previous month announced that he had changed his surname to Sher) as Minister of the Interior. In mid-July Human Rights Watch reported that ethnic Uzbeks, who formed the vast majority of those detained after the conflict, were being maltreated in police custody in Osh, calling for the deployment of an international police force in the region. A further source of discontent was the lack of information regarding the dozens of people missing after the violence. On 15 July the Interim Government announced that it would set up a national commission to investigate the events of the previous month. The following week the OSCE approved sending a 52-strong police force to Osh and Jalal-Abad. The move was met with opposition from some of the region's inhabitants, including the mayor of Osh, Melisbek Myrzakmatov (a Bakiyev supporter whom some alleged had played a part in inciting the violence), some 1,500 of whom demonstrated on 26 July. Similar protests were subsequently held in other cities, including Bishkek. (Having postponed the deployment of the police force owing to security threats, in November the OSCE announced that mission would be scaled down to around 30 personnel.) Three days later Otunbayeva embarked on a tour of southern Kyrgyzstan, during which she met Myrzakmatov.

On 2 August 2010 the official investigation began into the ethnic violence that had occurred in June. On 5 August Urmat Baryktabasov (leader of the nationalist Flag of the Fatherland—Meken Tuu party) was arrested along with more than 20 others on charges of plotting a coup. Police used tear gas to disperse around 2,000 of Baryktabasov's supporters in Bishkek after officials banned a demonstration against his prosecution for economic crimes allegedly committed in Kazakhstan. On 10 August former premier Igor Chudinov was detained on unspecified charges. He was released from custody two days later. On 19 August, while Myrzakmatov was attending a conference in Bishkek, around 2,000 of his supporters gathered outside his office following rumours that he had been dismissed. On 15 September a prominent ethnic Uzbek human rights activist, Azimjan Askarov, and seven other Uzbeks were found guilty of the murder of a Kyrgyz policemen during the conflict in June. Askarov and four of his co-defendants were sentenced to life imprisonment. The verdict, which was criticized by several human rights groups, came amid growing concern that a disproportionately high number of Uzbeks were standing trial for atrocities committed during that time. An appeal hearing for Askarov commenced in October, in which the verdict was upheld.

Recent developments: the 2010 legislative elections

On 10 September 2010 the political campaigns for the legislative elections began. Two weeks later, in an apparent attempt to damage the reputation of Tekebayev, a key orchestrator of the new Constitution, a Russian television network broadcast a report that implicated him in an extramarital affair, citing video evidence that had first appeared on the internet two years previously. On 6 October around 100 people attacked the Bishkek offices of the Homeland Idealistic Democratic Party (Ata-Jurt), a nationalist party that enjoyed strong support among ethnic Kyrgyz in the south of the country, following reports (subsequently denied) that its leader, Kamchybek Tashiyev, had called for the return to power of Bakiyev. Many former members of Bakiyev's party, Bright Road (Ak-Jol), were reported to have joined the ranks of Homeland. A total of 29 political parties contested the elections to the new 120-seat legislature, which were duly held on 10 October and were widely reported to be free and fair. Of these parties, just five won the requisite number of votes (5% of the total registered electorate) for representation in the Jogorku Kenesh: the Homeland was unexpectedly successful, winning 15.3% of the valid votes cast (equivalent to 8.5% of the total registered electorate), obtaining 28 legislative seats; the SDPK, won 14.2% (26 seats); Dignity Party won 13.7% (25 seats); the Republic Political Party (Respublika), a new party led by Omurbek Babanov, won 12.5% (23 seats); and Tekebayev's Fatherland Socialist Political Party, which had been expected to gain considerable support, won just 9.9% (18 seats). The White Falcon Political Party also was also less successful than predicted, winning 4.7% of the votes cast and, therefore, no parliamentary seats. A total of 55.3% of the registered electorate participated in the ballot. Supporters of the United Kyrgyzstan Political Party (Butun Kyrgyzstan), which won 8.3% of the votes cast, and which also failed to obtain legislative representation, subsequently staged protests outside the parliamentary building in Bishkek and in Osh. On 24 October, following claims by Tashiyev that he had been the target of an assassination attempt by state security forces, hundreds of his supporters held a rally in the capital.

The final results of the legislative elections in Kyrgyzstan were not announced until 1 November 2010, owing to allegations of procedural irregularities and confusion over the number of voters. Despite its challenge to the results United Kyrgyzstan still failed to gain representation; the party was one of several had that filed official complaints at courts around Bishkek. The first session of the newly elected parliament was held on 10 November; at least 150 activists from the Martyrs of the Fatherland (Meken Sheyitteri) movement, comprised of relatives of those killed during the clashes between protesters and security forces on 7 April, attempted to prevent the delegates from entering the parliament building. Tashiyev was notable for his absence from the proceedings. The following day, with no coalition agreement having been made among the five parties represented in the Jogorku Kenesh, Otunbayeva issued a mandate to SDPK leader Atambayev to form a parliamentary coalition within 15 days.

Ethnic tensions resurfaced in Osh Oblast on 7 November 2010, when some 500 Kyrgyz illegally occupied land in the Uzbek-populated villages of Ishkevan and Kyzyl-Kyshtak, with the intention of dividing it into plots. The following day at least 20 Kyrgyz were arrested as several hundred activists joined the protesters; the rest were dispersed by the police. At a meeting on 9 November the regional governor promised representatives of the group, whose homes had been destroyed during the ethnic violence in June, that they would be allocated land in the suburbs of Osh. On 17 November the long-awaited trial of ousted President Bakiyev opened in Bishkek. Bakiyev, along with 27 of his aides, was being tried in absentia for ordering special forces to open fire on civilians during the protests on 7 April. However, the hearing was immediately adjourned after relatives of those killed in the violence disrupted proceedings. On 30 November a bomb exploded outside the sports stadium where the trial was being held, injuring at least three people. One day earlier four people alleged to have connections with the Islamic Movement of Uzbekistan (IMU) had been killed by security forces in Osh, while interior ministry officials announced that nine people suspected of planning to carry out terrorist attacks in Kyrgyzstan had been arrested the previous week in Bishkek. Some 15 kg of explosives had reportedly been confiscated during the operation.

On 30 November 2010 the SDPK formed a coalition with the Republic Political Party and the Fatherland Socialist Political Party. Atambayev was nominated as Prime Minister with Babanov as his deputy. Tekebayev was to become parliamentary speaker. Dignity declined to join the alliance. On 2 December, however, Tekebayev's nomination failed by just three votes to gain a majority in the Jogorku Kenesh and the coalition subsequently collapsed. Consequently, on 4 December Otunbayeva announced that she had instructed Babanov to form a government. On 15 December it was announced that the Republic Political Party was to join a coalition with the SDPK and the Homeland Idealistic Democratic Party. Atambayev was once again due to be nominated as Prime Minister and Babanov was expected to assume the post of First Deputy Prime Minister, while Akhmatbek Keldibekov was to be proposed as parliamentary speaker. On the same day the trial began of Akmat Bakiyev, brother of the ousted President, who had been arrested on 23 June and faced a number of charges, including in connection with the ethnic violence in the south of the country. On 16 December Amnesty International announced that ethnic Uzbeks were being disproportionately targeted in the investigations relating to the June unrest; by early November 271 people had been detained and the 'overwhelming majority' of those brought to trial had been Uzbeks, despite the fact that Uzbek casualties during the violence far exceeded those of ethnic Kyrgyz. The organization also reported that the trials of ethnic Uzbeks had been 'seriously flawed' and questioned the role of the security forces during the unrest.

In early December 2010 teachers in the southern regions of Osh and Jalal-Abad began industrial action demanding an immediate pay increase; by the middle of the month the strike had spread to many other areas of the country. On 10 December

KYRGYZSTAN

the trial began of Masaliyev, who had resigned from the leadership of the KCP in August. On 17 December parliament endorsed Keldibekov as speaker and Atambayev as Prime Minister. Kyrgyzstan's new Government was approved, which included Ruslan Kazakbayev of the SDPK as Minister of Foreign Affairs, Zarylbek Rysaliyev as Minister of Internal Affairs and Chorobek Imashev as Minister of Finance. President Otunbayeva congratulated Atambayev on his appointment and spoke of the many challenges facing his administration, including the country's chronic energy shortages, the threat of militant activities and the ongoing protests by teachers. On 25 December the Kyrgyzstani authorities announced that they had discovered a vehicle packed with explosives outside Bishkek's main police headquarters. Nine people were later arrested in connection with the planned attack. On 4 January 2011 three policemen were killed while carrying out identity checks in Bishkek; two suspects were killed and a third was detained by security forces the following day. Rysaliyev later announced that the men had been responsible for the recent bombing in Bishkek and the attempted car bomb, and had been planning further terrorist attacks.

On 11 January 2011 the national commission appointed to investigate the violence of June 2010 in southern Kyrgyzstan published its findings. In its report it stated that a combination of local Uzbek leaders, relatives of ousted President Bakiyev, drug dealers, Islamist extremists and 'outside forces' were responsible for the violence. The report also criticized several high-ranking officials serving in the Interim Government at the time of the crisis—including head of the National Security Committee Keneshbek Duishebayev, Minister of the Interior Sherniyazov and Prosecutor-General Baytemir Ibrayev—for failing to act with sufficient rapidity to curb the violence. Deputy Prime Minister Azimbek Beknazarov and Ismail Isakov, a special government representative, were also named as being partially responsible. (Isakov later announced his intention to sue the commission over its allegations.) Maksim Bakiyev and another prominent businessman, Kadyrjon Batyrov, an ethnic Uzbek, both of whom had left the country, were among those found to be implicated in initiating the violence. Additionally, the older brother of the former President, Janysh Bakiyev, was accused of having financed the unrest. On the same day the National Security Committee announced the arrest of a local leader of the clandestine, transnational, Islamist Hizb-ut-Tahrir al-Islami (Party of Islamic Liberation) in Jalal-Abad Oblast. At least four other members of the organization were apprehended in southern Kyrgyzstan in that month. On 26 January a former energy minister, Saparbek Balkybekov, who had served during President Bakiyev's term of office, was detained at the house of one of his relatives in Dublin, Ireland. He was wanted by the Kyrgyzstani authorities on charges of corruption, theft and financial mismanagement. The Prosecutor-General subsequently issued an official request to Ireland for Balkybekov's extradition. On 7 February eight alleged members of Hizb ut-Tahrir were detained in Osh region. On the same day several hundred people participated in rallies to demand the release of Masaliyev. In mid-February Otunbayeva appointed two non-partisan ministers to the Government; Melis Mambetjanov became Minister of Finance, while Aigul Ryskulova became Minister of Social Welfare. On 9 March two visiting deputies from the Russian State Duma accused First Deputy Prime Minister Omurbek Babanov of corruption in relation to Megacom, a mobile telecommunications service provider and one of Kyrgyzstan's leading companies, which was 51% owned by the Russian enterprise, Eventis Telecom. The event prompted Tashiyev to announce that his party would withdraw from the coalition should the allegations against Babanov be proven in court. On 13 April Atambayev agreed to Babanov's request that he be permitted to temporarily resign from office, for the period of one month, and with effect from the following day; Babanov also requested that the Zhogorku Kenesh form a special commission to investigate the accusations against him (which he denied) during that period. In mid-April 10 of the 25 parliamentary deputies of Dignity announced their support for the ruling coalition, saying that this support would strengthen the Government and so help to guarantee peace within the country. Kulov, the leader of the party, suggested that is would be necessary to remove membership of the party from these deputies as a result of their actions.

Introductory Survey

Foreign Affairs
Regional relations

In January 1994 Kyrgyzstan joined the economic zone newly established by Kazakhstan and Uzbekistan. Following the admission of Tajikistan, in May 1998 the zone was formally constituted as the Central Asian Economic Union (the Central Asian Co-operation Organization—CACO—from March 2002). Meanwhile, in March 1996 Kyrgyzstan signed a treaty with Russia, Belarus and Kazakhstan to create a 'community of integrated states'. In April 1998 Tajikistan joined the union, and in October 2000 it was superseded by a new economic body, the Eurasian Economic Community (EURASEC, see p. 447), which merged with CACO in January 2006. Kyrgyzstan did not participate in the first stage of a customs union to be established by Belarus, Kazakhstan and Russia in January 2010, although the administration of President Roza Otunbayeva, which came to power later in the year, confirmed the intention of Kyrgyzstan to join the union at a subsequent date.

In May 2001 the signatories of the CIS Collective Security Treaty—Armenia, Belarus, Kazakhstan, Kyrgyzstan, Russia and Tajikistan—agreed to form a Collective Rapid Reaction Force in Bishkek to combat Islamist militancy in Central Asia; in January 2002 it was announced that the force was ready to undertake combat missions. In April 2003 the Collective Security Treaty Organization (CSTO, see p. 459) was inaugurated to succeed the Collective Security Treaty.

Kyrgyzstan's campaign against Islamist extremism—particularly against the clandestine, transnational, Islamist Hizb-ut-Tahrir al-Islami (Party of Islamic Liberation)—intensified in mid-1999, when Islamist groups believed to be based in Uzbekistan and Tajikistan took hostages in separate instances near Osh. In August Kyrgyzstani and Uzbekistani forces launched airstrikes against Tajikistani militants in the Osh region. Later that month a senior Kyrgyzstani military commander was among more than 25 people kidnapped by a group of rebels, believed to be members of the Islamic Movement of Uzbekistan (IMU), which captured three villages near the Tajikistani border, demanding the release of Islamists imprisoned in Uzbekistan. After Kyrgyzstani troops undertook a large-scale military operation, in October the rebels were defeated and the hostages released (although one hostage, a police officer, was killed). From August 2000 Islamist militants made a further series of incursions from Tajikistan, leading to armed conflict with government forces. By the end of October the Government claimed that it had regained full control of the border regions.

In April 2001 a local government official accused Uzbekistan of laying land-mines along the border with Kyrgyzstan, and demanded the removal of Uzbekistani troops, deployed in an effort to combat the incursions of Islamist militants and drugs-traffickers, from Kyrgyzstani border territories. Meanwhile, reports in May indicated that Islamist rebels were increasingly recruiting from southern Kyrgyzstan. In July 2003 it was reported that Kyrgyzstan was to commence the unilateral removal of land-mines along the border with Uzbekistan.

Relations with Uzbekistan were further strained in mid-2005, when the Kyrgyzstani Government refused to return a large number of refugees who had fled Uzbekistan after violence broke out in Andijon in May (see the chapter on Uzbekistan). In August Uzbekistan annulled a bilateral agreement to supply natural gas to Kyrgyzstan, and in September issued a report accusing Kyrgyzstan of having permitted religious extremists to use bases in the south of the country to prepare to foment unrest in Andijon. In August 2006 the Kyrgyzstani authorities attracted international censure for the decision to repatriate to Uzbekistan a number of refugees from Andijon. In the same month Rafiq Qori Kamoluddin, a prominent imam in Kyrgyzstan and an ethnic Uzbek, was shot dead in an operation targeting alleged Islamist extremists conducted by the Kyrgyzstani and Uzbekistani national security services. Despite the large-scale ethnic unrest that occurred near the border with Uzbekistan in June 2010 and the subsequent influx into Uzbekistan of many thousands of refugees, the Uzbekistani Government did not actively intervene in the conflict, regarding it as an internal affair, although it did briefly close the border.

Kyrgyzstan endeavoured to maintain good relations with Russia. In June 1992 the Presidents of both countries signed a treaty of friendship, co-operation and mutual assistance, and a further declaration of partnership was signed in July 2000. An agreement concerning Russian-Kyrgyzstani military co-operation was concluded in October 1997, in accordance with which Russia was to lease four military installations in Kyrgyzstan in

KYRGYZSTAN

Introductory Survey

return for training Kyrgyzstani army recruits. In October 2003 a Russian airbase became operational at Kant, some 30 km from an airbase at Manas, occupied by the US-led coalition fighting in Afghanistan (see below); this was the first Russian military installation to be established outside Russia since the collapse of the USSR. In September the Russian Minister of Defence, Sergei Ivanov, declared that Russia was to provide Kyrgyzstan with several million US dollars in military aid. In February 2009 Russian President Dmitrii Medvedev agreed to extend funds equivalent to more than US $2,000m. to the Kyrgyzstani Government (of which some $1,700m. were designated for the development of a major hydroelectric project). Russia harshly criticized the decision of President Bakiyev, announced in June, to reverse the proposed closure of the US airbase at Manas. In August 2009 a summit meeting of the CSTO took place in Cholpon-Ata, in northern Kyrgyzstan, when Presidents Bakiyev and Medvedev signed a preliminary memorandum of understanding on the opening of a second Russian military base in Kyrgyzstan. This base, which was to operate under the auspices of the CSTO, was to be leased to Russia for a period of up to 49 years, extendable for subsequent 25-year periods, and all Russian personnel at the base were to be granted diplomatic immunity. Although final agreement on the base was to have been reached by 1 November, negotiations subsequently stalled, apparently owing to opposition from Uzbekistan. In mid-March 2011 President Otunbayeva announced that plans for Russia to establish a military training centre in Batken would proceed, although a firm schedule was not specified.

Russia appeared to be broadly sympathetic to the Interim Government of National Trust that came to power in Kyrgyzstan following the overthrow of President Bakiyev in April 2010, and was the first state to recognize the administration of Otunbayeva. One week after the regime came to power, Russia announced that it would provide financial aid to the sum of US $50m. in grants and loans. Observers also noted that Otunbayeva and other senior members of the interim administration had visited Russia prior to Bakiyev's overthrow, and had met Russian Chairman of the Government Vladimir Putin and other senior Russian officials. Following the ethnic unrest in southern Kyrgyzstan in June, however, the Russian Government was reluctant to accept that the proposed new parliamentary system of government in Kyrgyzstan would be the most effective at achieving stability. During the campaign for the October legislative elections several party leaders visited Moscow; of these Feliks Kulov, leader of the Dignity Party, was seen to be most closely allied with the Russian administration, particularly after he signed a co-operation agreement with United Russia on behalf of his party. In January 2011, in what was widely perceived to be an act of support for the new coalition Government, Russia agreed to abolish an export tax on fuel imposed during the final days of Bakiyev's administration. In mid-March, however, it was announced that finalization of the tariff-elimination agreement had been delayed, owing to a dispute over the nationalization of the Megacom telecommunications company (see Recent developments, above).

Kyrgyzstan reached a series of bilateral co-operation agreements with the People's Republic of China during 1996. A border treaty signed in August 1999 ceded almost 95,000 ha of disputed territory to China. Akayev signed the agreement without the consent of the legislature, prompting widespread protests prior to its ratification in 2002. Meanwhile, an agreement signed in April 1997 with China, Russia, Kazakhstan and Tajikistan (which, together with Kyrgyzstan, constituted the so-called Shanghai Five or Forum) aimed to improve joint border security. The alliance, renamed the Shanghai Co-operation Organization (SCO) upon the accession of Uzbekistan, signed the Shanghai Convention on Combating Terrorism, Separatism and Extremism in mid-2001. In August an SCO anti-terrorism centre became operational in Bishkek. The Presidents of Kazakhstan and Kyrgyzstan signed a border agreement in December. In August 2003 Kyrgyzstani forces participated in major anti-terrorist manoeuvres, hosted by China and Kazakhstan. In September 2004 Tanayev and the Chinese Prime Minister, Wen Jiabao, signed a 10-year co-operation agreement on combating terrorism, separatism and religious extremism, and a protocol on the demarcation of the border between the two countries.

Other external relations

Following the suicide attacks on the US cities of New York and Washington, DC, on 11 September 2001, President Akayev announced that he was prepared to give US military aircraft access to Kyrgyzstani airspace for the aerial bombardment of militants of the Islamist al-Qa'ida organization (which co-ordinated the attacks) and its Taliban hosts in Afghanistan. In late November the Government agreed to give the US-led coalition access to its military bases and, later, the airbase at Manas airport. Kyrgyzstan undertook joint exercises with US troops in February 2002, which aimed to facilitate attempts to counter insurgency in the country's mountainous regions. In September Akayev met the US President, George W. Bush, and the US Secretary of State, Colin Powell, in Washington, DC. Although Kyrgyzstan stated that it would permit the USA to use the Manas airbase until the situation in Afghanistan stabilized, in early 2006 Kyrgyzstan presented the USA with new conditions for the use of the facility, apparently proposing to increase the rent payable by the USA from US $2m. to $200m.; President Bakiyev maintained that the proposed charge was in accordance with international norms. In July Kyrgyzstan and the USA signed an agreement allowing the latter to continue using the airbase at Manas airport in exchange for 'assistance and co-operation' of some $150m. Nevertheless, in early 2008 President Bakiyev announced that the Kyrgyzstani Government planned to request the closure of the airbase and in February 2009 in early February Bakiyev announced that the airbase would be closed, owing to the inadequate levels of rent paid by the US Administration; his decision followed a visit to Moscow during which the Russian Government offered Kyrgyzstan assistance and loans equivalent to more than US $2,000m. to compensate for economic difficulties exacerbated by the onset of the international financial crisis. On 19 February the Jogorku Kenesh approved the closure of the airbase; US forces were to be required to withdraw from Kyrgyzstan within a period of 180 days after the US embassy received notice of the termination of the lease. However, in June Kyrgyzstan and the USA concluded an agreement to reverse the decision on the closure of the airbase, although the new agreement stipulated that the USA would use the site as a transit centre, rather than as a full military facility, while the rent charged was to be increased more than three-fold, to an annual rate of US $60m. The five-year agreement was approved by the Jogorku Kenesh on 25 June, and signed into law on 2 July.

Following the overthrow of President Bakiyev in April 2010, the new interim leader, Roza Otunbayeva—a former Ambassador to the USA—stated that Kyrgyzstan wished to maintain co-operative relations with the USA. The award by the US Administration in November 2010 of a $315m. fuel supply contract for the Manas Transit Center, as the airbase had been renamed, to the Gibraltar-based Mina Corporation was unpopular with the Interim Government, which at the time was investigating claims that the company had been involved in corrupt schemes during Akayev's and Bakiyev's terms in office. On assuming his post as Prime Minister in December, Almazbek Atambayev suggested that the Transit Center would close on the expiry of the agreement in July 2014. In February 2011 the Jogorku Kenesh approved the draft of a new leasing agreement under which a Kyrgyzstani state-owned enterprise, the Manas Refueling Complex, would share up to 50% of the fuel contract with Mina Corporation, with effect from no later than August of that year.

CONSTITUTION AND GOVERNMENT

Under the Constitution adopted on 2 July 2010, following a national referendum, presidential powers in Kyrgyzstan were substantially reduced. Legislative power is vested in the 120-seat Jogorku Kenesh, elected by universal adult suffrage for a term of five years. Executive power is vested in the President, who is directly elected for just one term of six years. The President appoints the members of the Government, including the Prime Minister. Judicial power is exercised by the Supreme Court and regional courts. For administrative purposes, Kyrgyzstan is divided into seven oblasts (regions) and the municipality of Bishkek (the capital).

REGIONAL AND INTERNATIONAL CO-OPERATION

Kyrgyzstan is a member of the Commonwealth of Independent States (CIS, see p. 238), and has also joined the Eurasian Economic Community (EURASEC, see p. 447), the Collective Security Treaty Organization (CSTO) and the Shanghai Co-operation Organization (SCO).

Kyrgyzstan joined the UN in 1992 and became a member of the World Trade Organization (WTO, see p. 430) in 1998.

KYRGYZSTAN

ECONOMIC AFFAIRS

In 2009, according to estimates by the World Bank, Kyrgyzstan's gross national income (GNI), measured at average 2007–09 prices, was US $4,613m., equivalent to $870 per head (or $2,200 per head on an international purchasing-power parity basis). During 2000–09, it was estimated, the population increased by an annual average of 0.9%, while gross domestic product (GDP) per head increased, in real terms, at an average annual rate of 3.6%. Overall GDP increased, in real terms, at an estimated average annual rate of 4.6% in 2000–09. Real GDP increased by 8.4% in 2008, and by 2.3% in 2009.

Agriculture (including forestry and fishing) contributed an estimated 23.9% of GDP in 2009, according to the Asian Development Bank (ADB), and engaged 32.4% of the employed labour force in that year, according to official figures. By tradition, the Kyrgyz are a pastoral nomadic people, and the majority of the population (some 63.3% in 2010, according to UN estimates) reside in rural areas. Livestock-rearing, once the mainstay of agricultural activity, is declining in importance. Only about 7% of the country's land area is arable; of this, some 70% depends on irrigation. The principal crops are grain, potatoes, vegetables and sugar beet. By 2002, according to government figures, collective farms accounted for only around 6% of agricultural production, while state farms accounted for just under 2%. According to the World Bank, the GDP of the agricultural sector increased, in real terms, by an average of 2.1% per year in 2000–08; according to the ADB, agricultural GDP grew by 15.8% in 2008 and by 23.4% in 2009.

Industry (comprising manufacturing, mining, utilities and construction) contributed 22.3% of GDP in 2009, according to the ADB, and provided 21.2% of employment in that year, according to official figures. According to the World Bank, real industrial GDP increased at an average annual rate of 1.7% in 2000–08; however, according to the ADB, the GDP of the sector increased by 18.9% in 2008 and by 41.6% in 2009.

In 2009 the mining and quarrying sector provided 0.7% of GDP, according to the ADB. The sector engaged 0.7% of the employed workforce in that year, according to official figures. Kyrgyzstan has considerable mineral deposits, including coal, gold, tin, mercury, antimony, zinc, tungsten and uranium. In May 2001 the Government announced the discovery of new deposits of petroleum, estimated to total 70m. barrels, in an oilfield in the west. Production of gold from the Kumtor mine, which is believed to contain the eighth largest deposit of gold in the world (over 200 metric tons), began in January 1997. As a result, by 2001 Kyrgyzstan had become the 10th largest extractor and seller of gold world-wide. The Kumtor mine reportedly produced almost 4.4m. ounces of gold between 1997 and the end of 2003. Production of gold from the Jeruy deposit commenced in 2002. In April 2006 an agreement was signed with a Kazakhstani company on the development of the Taldy Bulak Levoberezhny gold deposit. Gold production totalled 18.5 tons in 2008.

Manufacturing contributed 13.6% of GDP in 2009, according to the ADB. The manufacturing sector employed 7.8% of the workforce in that year, according to official figures. In 2005 the principal branches of manufacturing, measured by gross value of output, were metallurgy (50.6% of the total) and food products, beverages and tobacco (18.2%). Real manufacturing GDP declined by an average of 1.2% per year in 2000–08, according to the World Bank; according to ADB figures, the GDP of the sector increased by 30.8% in 2008 and by 31.7% in 2009.

Kyrgyzstan's principal source of domestic energy production (and a major export) is hydroelectricity (generated by the country's mountain rivers), which provided 85.9% of the country's total energy requirements in 2007. Kyrgyzstan has insufficient petroleum and natural gas to meet its needs, and substantial imports of hydrocarbons are thus required; Kyrgyzstan exports electricity to Kazakhstan and Uzbekistan in return for coal and natural gas, respectively. Imports of mineral products comprised 31.1% of the value of total recorded imports in 2010.

The construction sector contributed 6.2% of GDP in 2009, according to the ADB; the sector engaged 11.0% of the employed labour force in that year, according to official figures. During 2000–09, according to UN figures, the GDP of the sector increased at an average annual rate of 10.1%. However, construction GDP increased by 6.3% in 2009.

In 2009 the services sector contributed 53.8% of GDP, according to the ADB; the sector provided 46.4% of employment in that year, according to official figures. In 2000–08, according to the World Bank, the GDP of the sector increased, in real terms, by an average of 7.7% per year; according to the ADB, services GDP increased by 29.8% in 2008 and by 22.8% in 2009.

In 2009 Kyrgyzstan recorded a visible trade deficit of US $1,113.2m., and there was a deficit of $300.2m. on the current account of the balance of payments. In 2010 the principal source of imports (accounting for 33.2% of the total) was Russia; other major suppliers were the People's Republic of China, Kazakhstan and the USA. The main market for exports in that year was Switzerland (which accounted for 26.4% of all exports); other principal markets were the United Arab Emirates, Russia, Kazakhstan and USA. The main exports in 2010 were precious and semi-precious stones, chemical and related products, textiles, mineral products, and vegetable products. The principal imports in that year were mineral products (mostly petroleum and natural gas), machinery, chemical and related products, vehicle and transport equipment, prepared foodstuffs, textiles, and metals.

In 2010 Kyrgyzstan recorded an overall budgetary surplus of 22,420.2m. soms. Kyrgyzstan's general government gross debt was 116,548m. soms in 2009, equivalent to 59.4% of GDP. Kyrgyzstan's total external debt was US $2,463.7m. at the end of 2008, of which $1,962.9m. was public and publicly guaranteed debt. In that year the cost of debt-servicing was equivalent to 8.2% of the value of exports of goods, services and income. The annual rate of inflation averaged 7.3% in 2000–09. According to official figures, consumer prices increased by 6.8% in 2009. The average rate of unemployment was 8.4% in 2009.

An ambitious programme of economic reform was undertaken following independence in 1991, resulting in GDP growth in 1996–2001. GDP declined in 2002, largely owing to reduced industrial output after a landslide at the Kumtor gold mine, but growth resumed in 2003 and 2004, partly thanks to increased foreign trade and measures to tackle tax evasion. Political instability following the removal of President Askar Akayev in 2005, coupled with a decline in gold production, led to a contraction in GDP in that year. Although GDP growth was recorded thereafter (reaching 8.5% in 2007), the poverty rate remained relatively high (decreasing from 46% in 2004 to 35% in 2007), and the economy remained vulnerable to external shocks, as exemplified in 2008 when the dramatic rise in international commodity prices led to mid-year inflation of 32.5% and a widening of the current account deficit. The international financial crisis resulted in decreases in workers' remittances, domestic demand and revenue from exports, although the country none the less recorded positive GDP growth, of an estimated 2.3%, in 2009, according to the IMF, in part owing to the strong performance of the agricultural sector. Meanwhile, the country increased imports of fuel and electricity after power shortages at the Toktogul hydropower station, and the Government appealed for substantial grants and loans. In early 2009, following an announcement (rescinded later in the year) that the Government would close the Manas airbase (used by US and other forces for offensives in Afghanistan), it was announced that Russia had pledged Kyrgyzstan $2,150m. in aid and loans, including a $150m. grant and some $1,700m. for a planned hydroelectric project. A steep increase in consumer tariffs for electricity, fuel and water, as well as intensified concern about corruption, was a principal factor in generating support for protests in early 2010 that led, in April, to the overthrow of Bakiyev's regime. Shortly after it assumed power the Interim Government reversed the politically unpopular increase in energy tariffs and introduced key reforms to the energy sector aimed at improving transparency. The new administration also recovered $60.6m. of a $300m. loan from Russia (part of the $2,150 aid package agreed in 2009) that had allegedly been diverted by the Bakiyev regime. However, the political instability in Kyrgyzstan of 2010 had a serious effect on the country's economy, which contracted by an estimated 1.4% in that year, with a sharp decrease in agricultural production contributing to a massive rise in food prices. In February 2011 the IMF warned that inflation, which had reached 19.2% at the end of 2010, could result in widespread social unrest. Inflation was likely to be exacerbated by the Government's proposed pay increase for teachers and medical personnel in response to widespread industrial action at the start of 2011. In March the First Deputy Prime Minister, Omurbek Babanov, announced that on the adoption of the 2011 state budget the Government would grant $21m. in credits to private and state companies in order

KYRGYZSTAN

to boost agricultural production and combat rising food prices. In the same month petroleum prices, which had been reduced by around 25% following an agreement by Russia to reduce fuel import tariffs, was halted (see Foreign Affairs, above). In the short term, therefore, the maintenance of political and social stability was a principal prerequisite for the restoration of a healthy economy, while in the longer term the country would benefit from the creation of an environment attractive to investors (not least by reducing corruption), which would enable it to exploit resources such as gold and other minerals, and from reducing its dependence on Russia.

PUBLIC HOLIDAYS

2012: 1 January (New Year's Day), 7 January (Christmas), 8 March (International Women's Day), 21 March (Nooruz, Spring Holiday), 24 March (Day of the People's Revolution), 1 May (International Labour Day), 5 May (Constitution Day), 9 May (Victory Day), 18 August* (Orozo Ait, Id al-Fitr, end of Ramadan), 31 August (Independence Day), 25 October* (Kurban Ait, Id al-Adha, Feast of the Sacrifice).

* These holidays are dependent on the Islamic lunar calendar and may vary by one or two days from the dates given.

Statistical Survey

Source (unless otherwise stated): National Statistical Committee, 720033 Bishkek, Frunze 374; tel. (312) 22-63-63; fax (312) 22-07-59; e-mail zkudabaev@nsc.bishkek.su; internet www.stat.kg.

Area and Population

AREA, POPULATION AND DENSITY

Area (sq km)	199,900*
Population (census results)†	
24 March 1999	4,822,938
24 March 2009	
Males	2,645,921
Females	2,716,872
Total	5,362,793
Density (per sq km) at 2009 census	26.8

* 77,182 sq miles.

† The figures refer to *de jure* population. The *de facto* total was 4,850,700 at the 1999 census and 5,107,640 in 2009.

POPULATION BY AGE AND SEX
(official estimates at 1 January 2009)

	Males	Females	Total
0–14	812,262	777,752	1,590,014
15–64	1,692,583	1,730,330	3,422,913
65 and over	104,093	159,072	263,165
Total	2,608,938	2,667,154	5,276,092

Note: Preliminary estimates, not revised to take account of 2009 census results.

PRINCIPAL ETHNIC GROUPS
(at 2009 census)

	Number	%
Kyrgyz	3,804,788	71.0
Uzbek	768,405	14.3
Russian	419,583	7.8
Dungan	58,409	1.1
Uigur	48,543	0.9
Tajik	46,105	0.9
Turk	39,133	0.7
Kazakh	33,198	0.6
Tatar	31,424	0.6
Ukrainian	21,924	0.4
Others	91,281	1.7
Total	5,362,793	100.0

ADMINISTRATIVE DIVISIONS
(2009 census)

	Area (sq km)	Population	Density (per sq km)	Principal city
Oblasts (Regions)				
Batken	17,000	428,636	25.2	Batken
Chui	20,200	803,230	39.8	Tokmok
Jalal-Abad	33,700	1,009,889	30.0	Jalal-Abad
Naryn	45,200	257,768	5.7	Naryn
Osh	29,200	1,362,359	46.7	Osh*
Talas	11,400	226,779	19.9	Talas
Yssyk-Kul	43,100	438,389	10.2	Karakol
City				
Bishkek	100	835,743	8,357.4	—
Kyrgyzstan	199,900	5,362,793	26.8	

* The city of Osh also constitutes a separate administrative area, with a population numbering 258,111 at the 2009 census.

PRINCIPAL TOWNS
(population at census of March 1999)

Bishkek (capital)	750,327	Karakol	64,322
Osh	208,520	Tokmok	59,409
Jalal-Abad	70,401	Kara-Balta	53,887

2009 census: Bishkek (capital) 865,527; Osh 243,216.

BIRTHS, MARRIAGES AND DEATHS

	Registered live births		Registered marriages		Registered deaths	
	Number	Rate (per 1,000)	Number	Rate (per 1,000)	Number	Rate (per 1,000)
2002	101,012	20.2	31,240	6.3	35,235	7.1
2003	105,490	20.9	34,266	6.8	35,941	7.1
2004	109,939	21.6	34,542	6.8	35,061	6.9
2005	109,839	21.4	37,321	7.3	36,992	7.2
2006	120,737	23.3	43,760	8.4	38,566	7.4
2007	123,251	23.5	44,392	8.5	38,180	7.3
2008	127,332	24.1	44,258	8.4	37,710	7.1
2009	135,494	25.7	47,567	9.0	n.a.	n.a.

Life expectancy (years at birth, official estimates): 66 (males 62; females 69) in 2008.

IMMIGRATION AND EMIGRATION

	2007	2008	2009
Immigrants	3,960	3,497	3,829
Emigrants	54,608	41,287	33,380

KYRGYZSTAN

ECONOMICALLY ACTIVE POPULATION
(annual averages, '000 persons)

	2007	2008	2009
Agriculture, hunting forestry and fishing	742.4	743.0	718.6
Mining and quarrying	13.1	13.3	14.7
Manufacturing	179.8	178.0	172.6
Electricity, gas and water supply	38.3	37.8	38.8
Construction	205.3	221.9	244.0
Wholesale and retail trade; repair of motor vehicles, motor cycles and personal and household goods	316.9	319.4	316.0
Hotels and restaurants	58.4	66.2	82.2
Transport, storage and communications	133.3	133.8	144.9
Financial intermediation	9.7	12.2	15.8
Real estate, renting and business activities	45.8	49.7	55.3
Public administration and defence; compulsory social security	106.8	101.7	103.6
Education	156.6	156.1	164.3
Health and social work	86.2	86.2	79.4
Other services	60.3	65.1	66.2
Total employed	**2,152.7**	**2,184.3**	**2,216.4**
Unemployed	191.1	195.6	203.7
Total labour force	**2,343.8**	**2,379.9**	**2,420.1**
Males	n.a.	1,356.6	n.a.
Females	n.a.	1,023.3	n.a.

2007 (annual averages, '000 persons): Total males employed 1,251.6; total females employed 901.1.

2008 (annual averages, '000 persons): Total males employed 1,257.0; total females employed 927.3.

2009 (annual averages, '000 persons): Total males employed 1,292.1; total females employed 924.3.

Health and Welfare

KEY INDICATORS

Total fertility rate (children per woman, 2008)	2.5
Under-5 mortality rate (per 1,000 live births, 2008)	38
HIV/AIDS (% of persons aged 15–49, 2007)	0.1
Physicians (per 1,000 head, 2006)	2.4
Hospital beds (per 1,000 head, 2006)	5.1
Health expenditure (2007): US $ per head (PPP)	130
Health expenditure (2007): % of GDP	6.5
Health expenditure (2007): public (% of total)	54.0
Access to water (% of persons, 2008)	90
Access to sanitation (% of persons, 2008)	93
Total carbon dioxide emissions ('000 metric tons, 2007)	6,074.9
Carbon dioxide emissions per head (metric tons, 2007)	1.2
Human Development Index (2010): ranking	109
Human Development Index (2010): value	0.598

For sources and definitions, see explanatory note on p. vi.

Agriculture

PRINCIPAL CROPS
('000 metric tons)

	2007	2008	2009
Wheat	708.9	746.2	1,056.7
Rice, paddy	17.3	17.7	20.7
Barley	227.2	210.6	289.7
Maize	460.7	462.1	486.6
Potatoes	1,373.8	1,334.9	1,393.1
Sugar beet	155.4	98.0*	54.0
Sunflower seed	62.0	52.7	57.5
Cabbages and other brassicas	100.3	120.9	123.2
Tomatoes	180.3	187.2	194.2
Cucumbers and gherkins	58.5	63.8	68.4
Onions, dry	126.3	118.8	136.4
Garlic	28.5	29.3	32.0

—continued

	2007	2008	2009
Carrots and turnips	169.1	173.4	168.9
Apples†	122.0	135.0	146.0
Apricots†	15.2	16.6	18.0
Peaches and nectarines†	5.5	3.8	4.0
Grapes	14.9	10.5	6.1
Watermelons	119.1	124.4	137.2
Seed cotton	95.1	95.1	49.2
Tobacco, unmanufactured	14.4	13.6	12.0

* FAO estimate.
† Unofficial figures.

Aggregate production ('000 metric tons, may include official, semi-official or estimated data): Total cereals 1,411.8 in 2007, 1,434.2 in 2008, 1,851.2 in 2009; Total roots and tubers 1,373.8 in 2007, 1,334.9 in 2008, 1,393.1 in 2009; Total vegetables (incl. melons) 923.8 in 2007, 962.1 in 2008, 984.8 in 2009; Total fruits (excl. melons) 195.4 in 2007, 195.8 in 2008, 206.5 in 2009.

Source: FAO.

LIVESTOCK
('000 head at 1 January)

	2007	2008	2009
Horses	347.5	355.5	362.4
Asses*	44	44	n.a.
Cattle	1,116.7	1,168.0	1,224.6
Pigs	79.6	74.9	63.3
Sheep	3,197.1	3,379.1	3,605.8
Goats	849.9	872.7	896.9
Chickens†	4,088	4,194	3,990
Turkeys†	174	213	215

* FAO estimate.
† Unofficial figure.

Source: FAO.

LIVESTOCK PRODUCTS
('000 metric tons)

	2007	2008	2009
Cattle meat	90.8	93.3	96.5
Sheep meat	39.9	39.9	41.1
Goat meat	7.3	7.4	7.6
Pig meat	20.4	19.0	17.3
Horse meat	18.9	18.5	18.7
Chicken meat	5.3	5.8	4.0
Cows' milk	1,197.5	1,231.2	1,273.5
Hen eggs	20.8	20.6*	20.6*
Honey	1.2	1.3	1.4
Wool, greasy	10.1	10.8	11.0

* Unofficial figure.

Source: FAO.

Forestry

ROUNDWOOD REMOVALS
('000 cubic metres, excl. bark, unofficial figures)

	2002	2003	2004
Sawlogs, veneer logs and logs for sleepers	5.6	5.6	4.7
Other industrial wood	5.6	5.6	4.7
Fuel wood	24.7	24.9	18.0
Total	**35.9**	**36.1**	**27.4**

2005–09: Figures assumed to be unchanged from 2004 (FAO estimates).

Source: FAO.

SAWNWOOD PRODUCTION
('000 cubic metres, incl. railway sleepers, unofficial figures)

	2007	2008	2009
Coniferous (softwood)	26.0	30.0	44.0
Broadleaved (hardwood)	26.0	30.0	44.0
Total	**52.0**	**60.0**	**88.0**

Source: FAO.

KYRGYZSTAN

Fishing

(metric tons, live weight)

	2006*	2007	2008
Capture	8	34	8
Freshwater bream	2	1	—
Common carp	—	27	6
Silver carp	n.a.	2	1
Pike-perch	1	n.a.	n.a.
Goldfish	2	3	1
Whitefishes	1	1	n.a.
Aquaculture	20	107	92
Common carp	8	27	35
Grass carp	2	14	6
Silver carp	10	13	28
Total catch	28	141	100

* FAO estimates.
Source: FAO.

Mining

('000 metric tons, unless otherwise indicated)

	2007	2008	2009
Coal	395.6	491.8	605.0
Crude petroleum	68.5	71.0	77.8
Natural gas (million cu metres)	15.0	17.4	15.7

Gold (metric tons): 10.5 in 2007; 18.4 in 2008; 17.0 in 2009 (Source: Gold Fields Mineral Services, *Gold Survey 2010*).

Industry

SELECTED PRODUCTS
('000 metric tons unless otherwise indicated)

	2007	2008	2009
Vegetable oil	17.6	18.5	20.9
Refined sugar	36.8	10.9	5.8
Vodka ('000 hectolitres)	14.0	14.6	13.6
Beer ('000 hectolitres)	14.0	15.4	15.2
Cigarettes (million)	3,052.7	3,024.4	3,586.0
Textile fabrics ('000 sq metres)	1,323.0	1,943.1	n.a.
Footwear	3,097.9	5,691.1	n.a.
Motor spirit (petrol)	13.6	12.8	9.9
Gas-diesel (distillate fuel) oil	51.6	59.9	48.0
Residual fuel oils (mazout)	55.5	58.9	39.0
Cement	1,229.5	1,218.1	581.8
Electric energy (million kWh)	14,830.4	11,789.1	11,058.2

Finance

CURRENCY AND EXCHANGE RATES
Monetary Units
100 tyiyns = 1 som.

Sterling, Dollar and Euro Equivalents (31 December 2010)
£1 sterling = 73.734 soms;
US $1 = 47.099 soms;
€1 = 62.934 soms;
1,000 soms = £13.56 = $21.23 = €15.89.

Average Exchange Rate (soms per US $)
2008   36.575
2009   42.904
2010   45.964.

Note: In May 1993 Kyrgyzstan introduced its own currency, the som, replacing the Russian (former Soviet) rouble at an exchange rate of 1 som = 200 roubles.

BUDGET
(million soms)*

Revenue†	2008	2009	2010
Taxation	35,925.0	36,097.8	39,362.7
Corporate income taxes	2,603.1	2,661.6	2,407.9
Personal income taxes	3,929.9	5,657.1	6,338.6
Value-added tax	16,540.0	13,467.4	14,602.0
Excise taxes	1,575.0	1,668.6	1,689.3
Taxes on international trade and transactions	4,633.6	4,138.9	4,347.7
Other current revenue	8,154.8	9,061.4	10,999.8
Capital revenue	1,116.8	312.3	628.6
Total	45,196.6	45,471.5	50,991.1

Expenditure‡	2008	2009	2010
Current expenditure	36,944.0	50,034.3	61,583.2
General public services	6,754.5	8,333.4	8,191.5
Defence and public security	5,460.9	6,391.0	8,475.8
Economic affairs	2,243.3	8,008.1	10,801.8
Environmental protection	399.7	581.8	567.7
Education	9,616.6	11,498.4	11,993.6
Health care	4,376.2	5,809.8	6,413.3
Social insurance and security	4,659.2	5,587.5	11,075.2
Housing and public utilities	2,303.1	2,441.8	2,504.3
Cultural and religious activity	1,130.6	1,382.5	1,560.1
Capital expenditure	8,087.7	8,523.4	7,197.8
Total	45,031.7	58,557.7	68,781.1

* Figures represent a consolidation of the budgetary transactions of the central Government and local governments. The operations of extra-budgetary accounts, including the Social Fund (formed in 1994 by an amalgamation of the Pension Fund, the Unemployment Fund and the Social Insurance Fund), are excluded.
† Excluding grants received (million soms): 1,399.8 in 2008; 10,162.9 in 2009; 7,022.1 in 2010.
‡ Excluding lending minus repayments (million soms): −795.1 in 2008; 2,601.1 in 2009; 11,652.3 in 2010.

Source: National Bank of the Kyrgyz Republic.

INTERNATIONAL RESERVES
(US $ million at 31 December)

	2008	2009	2010
Gold	71.9	90.8	116.8
IMF special drawing rights	55.3	162.1	171.7
Foreign exchange	1,097.6	1,331.9	1,431.9
Total	1,224.8	1,584.8	1,720.4

Source: IMF, *International Financial Statistics*.

MONEY SUPPLY
(million soms at 31 December)

	2005	2006	2007
Currency outside banks	13,065	19,410	26,675
Demand deposits at banking institutions	2,123	3,655	5,669
Total money	15,188	23,065	32,343

Source: IMF, *International Financial Statistics*.

COST OF LIVING
(Consumer Price Index; base: previous year = 100)

	2007	2008	2009
Food and non-alcoholic drinks	131.5	120.9	92.6
Alcoholic drinks and tobacco products	109.1	113.0	105.2
Non-food products	109.8	116.0	110.4
Services	110.6	134.4	104.4
All items (incl. others)	120.1	120.0	100.0

KYRGYZSTAN

NATIONAL ACCOUNTS
(million soms at current prices)

Expenditure on the Gross Domestic Product

	2007	2008	2009
Government final consumption expenditure	24,268.8	30,441.7	37,798.1
Private final consumption expenditure	124,141.2	174,595.7	178,743.3
Changes in inventories	2,310.5	2,962.4	-17,392.3
Gross fixed capital formation	35,495.3	42,838.9	54,763.1
Total domestic expenditure	186,215.8	250,838.7	253,912.2
Exports of goods and services	75,082.3	104,554.5	110,369.6
Less Imports of goods and services	119,400.4	173,139.8	158,302.9
Statistical discrepancy	—	2,760.2	-9,555.8
GDP in market prices	141,897.7	185,013.6	196,423.1

Gross Domestic Product by Economic Activity

	2007	2008	2009
Agriculture, forestry and fishing	38,140.6	47,799.6	43,367.6
Mining	643.7	832.0	1,232.7
Manufacturing	14,074.9	20,852.2	24,577.0
Electricity, gas and water supply	3,882.8	4,121.2	3,334.0
Construction	5,070.4	5,789.3	11,235.3
Wholesale and retail trade; repair of motor vehicles, motorcycles and personal and household goods	25,445.2	34,449.9	32,205.2
Transport and communication	10,561.1	15,458.2	17,931.0
Financial intermediation	4,801.0	6,611.4	8,066.1
Public administration and defence; compulsory social security	6,137.6	7,859.9	12,322.3
Others*	17,678.1	21,980.3	26,879.3
Sub-total	126,435.4	165,754.0	181,150.5
Less Financial intermediation services indirectly measured	3,695.5	5,183.8	6,587.4
Gross value added in basic prices	122,739.9	160,570.2	174,563.1
Taxes, less subsidies, on products	19,157.8	24,443.4	21,860.0
GDP in market prices	141,897.7	185,013.6	196,423.1

* Including hotels and restaurants; real estate, renting and business activities; education; health and social work; and other community, social and personal services.

Source: Asian Development Bank.

BALANCE OF PAYMENTS
(US $ million)

	2007	2008	2009
Exports of goods f.o.b.	1,337.8	1,874.4	1,700.4
Imports of goods f.o.b.	-2,613.6	-3,753.5	-2,813.6
Trade balance	-1,275.8	-1,879.2	-1,113.2
Exports of services	684.8	896.1	859.8
Imports of services	-604.5	-992.9	-866.9
Balance on goods and services	-1,195.5	-1,975.9	-1,120.2
Other income received	42.6	41.7	21.7
Other income paid	-94.5	-243.3	-211.6
Balance on goods, services and income	-1,247.4	-2,177.6	-1,310.1
Current transfers received	1,065.2	1,507.7	1,095.0
Current transfers paid	-79.0	-80.5	-85.1
Current balance	-261.3	-750.3	-300.2
Capital account (net)	-74.9	-44.9	-14.0
Direct investment abroad	0.2	0.1	0.3
Direct investment from abroad	207.9	377.0	189.4
Portfolio investment assets	-19.2	-31.8	-21.7
Portfolio investment liabilities	1.5	6.2	0.7
Other investment assets	19.4	-362.7	-215.8
Other investment liabilities	154.1	230.0	495.1
Net errors and omissions	265.4	629.6	-67.0
Overall balance	293.1	53.2	66.8

Source: IMF, *International Financial Statistics*.

External Trade

PRINCIPAL COMMODITIES
(distribution by Harmonized System Classification, US $ million)

Imports c.i.f.	2008	2009	2010
Vegetable products	174.0	142.7	122.5
Prepared foodstuffs, beverages and tobacco	251.3	245.9	268.8
Mineral products	1,242.1	839.0	1,053.8
Products of chemical or allied industries	289.5	305.9	301.7
Plastics, rubber and articles thereof	108.0	99.1	119.8
Textiles and fabrics	260.8	189.1	196.8
Metals and articles thereof	233.4	185.4	183.8
Machinery, electrical equipment and parts	456.7	330.0	415.6
Vehicles and transport equipment	627.0	276.5	271.6
Total (incl. others)	4,072.4	3,040.2	3,385.8

Exports f.o.b.	2008	2009	2010
Vegetable products	95.6	86.2	103.8
Prepared foodstuffs, beverages and tobacco	37.1	36.4	45.2
Mineral products	451.9	236.3	123.6
Products of chemical or allied industries	131.3	258.5	166.8
Raw hides and skins, leather, fur, travel articles and bags	18.4	6.6	6.7
Textiles and fabrics	132.9	103.1	161.9
Natural and cultured pearls, precious and semi-precious stones, precious metals and products, and coins	483.6	533.7	649.4
Metals and articles thereof	47.8	19.0	38.3
Machinery, electrical equipment and parts	55.3	49.5	50.1
Vehicles and transport equipment	39.1	34.1	39.9
Total (incl. others)	1,617.6	1,443.5	1,468.4

PRINCIPAL TRADING PARTNERS
(US $ million)

Imports c.i.f.	2008	2009	2010
Belarus	42.5	74.0	93.8
Canada	30.8	19.3	24.8
China, People's Republic (incl. Hong Kong)	728.2	623.6	650.9
Germany	335.9	100.7	82.8
Kazakhstan	376.6	339.9	379.3
Korea, Republic	83.2	51.2	49.2
Netherlands	41.8	49.5	24.9
Russia	1,492.2	1,090.4	1,126.3
Turkey	91.1	72.8	84.8
Ukraine	94.1	89.3	81.7
USA	119.8	101.6	196.8
Uzbekistan	160.1	111.7	100.5
Total (incl. others)	4,072.4	3,040.2	3,385.8

Exports f.o.b.	2008	2009	2010
Afghanistan	45.9	18.8	10.9
China, People's Republic (incl. Hong Kong)	44.4	19.4	28.9
Kazakhstan	184.1	140.7	175.2
Russia	310.2	185.8	265.7
Switzerland	440.5	444.8	387.9
Tajikistan	27.0	15.8	15.2
Turkey	44.9	36.7	37.3
United Arab Emirates	50.7	101.7	279.9
Uzbekistan	232.1	167.6	39.9
Total (incl. others)	1,617.6	1,443.5	1,468.4

Transport

RAILWAYS
(traffic)

	2007	2008	2009
Paying passengers ('000 journeys)	435.5	646.4	751.5
Passenger-km (million)	59.9	90.2	106.1
Freight carried (million metric tons)	2.3	1.8	1.0
Freight net ton-km (million)	848.9	945.5	743.6

ROAD TRAFFIC
(vehicles in use at 31 December)

	2002	2003	2004
Passenger cars	188,711	188,900	196,339
Motorcycles and mopeds	12,288	11,221	10,172

CIVIL AVIATION
(traffic on scheduled services)

	2007	2008	2009
Passengers carried ('000)	279.1	370.8	357.8
Passenger-km (million)	509.3	635.3	571.9
Total ton-km (million)	47.1	59.4	48.3

Kilometres flown (million): 7 in 2004.

Tourism

FOREIGN TOURIST ARRIVALS
(selected countries)

Country of residence	2007	2008	2009
China, People's Republic	20,201	21,921	21,879
Germany	9,794	10,010	9,374
Kazakhstan	1,125,214	1,078,945	1,036,322
Korea, Republic	6,417	4,526	4,790
Russia	118,604	193,998	157,008
Turkey	17,110	15,611	12,265
Uzbekistan	283,396	758,423	474,751
Total (incl. others)	1,655,833	2,435,386	2,146,740

Tourism receipts (US $ million, incl. passenger transport): 94 in 2005; 189 in 2006; 392 in 2007 (Source: World Tourism Organization).

Communications Media

	2007	2008	2009
Telephones ('000 main lines in use)	482.0	494.5	498.3
Mobile cellular telephones ('000 subscribers)	2,168.3	3,394.0	4,487.1
Internet users ('000)	750.1	850.0	2,194.4
Broadband subscribers ('000)	3.1	18.9	15.3

Daily newspapers (2004): 2 (total average circulation 4,923).
Non-daily newspapers (2004): 212 (total average circulation 33,774.8).
Book production (2004): 703 titles; 1,600,300 copies.
Personal computers: 100,000 (19.4 per 1,000 persons) in 2005.
Sources: UNESCO and International Telecommunication Union.

Education

(2009)

	Institutions	Teachers	Students
Pre-primary	594	2,895	65,629
Primary and Secondary: general	2,191	71,172	1,041,564
Secondary: vocational	220	7,972	74,694
Higher (all institutions)	54	12,678	217,403

Pupil-teacher ratio (primary education, UNESCO estimate): 24.0 in 2008/09 (Source: UNESCO Institute for Statistics).
Adult literacy rate (UNESCO estimates): 99.3% (males 99.5%; females 99.1%) in 2008 (Source: UNESCO Institute for Statistics).

Directory

The Government

HEAD OF STATE

President: ROZA OTUNBAYEVA (appointed in acting capacity 19 May 2010, inaugurated 3 July 2010).

THE GOVERNMENT
(May 2011)

A coalition, principally comprising members of the Social Democratic Party of Kyrgyzstan (SDPK), the Republic Political Party (Respublika) and the Homeland Idealistic Democratic Political Party (Ata-Jurt).

Prime Minister: ALMAZBEK ATAMBAYEV (SDPK).
First Deputy Prime Minister: OMURBEK BABANOV (Respublika).
Deputy Prime Minister: IBRAGIM JUNUSOV (Ata-Jurt).
Deputy Prime Minister, General Director of the State Direction for the Reconstruction of the Cities of Osh and Jalal-Abad: JANTORO SATYBALDIYEV (SDPK).
Deputy Prime Minister, responsible for the Co-ordination of the Security Structures, Representative of the Kyrgyz Republic at the Eurasian Economic Community (EURASEC): SHAMIL ATAKHANOV (SDPK).
Minister, Head of the Government Staff: NURKHANBEK MOMUNALIYEV (SDPK).
Minister of Foreign Affairs: RUSLAN KAZAKBAYEV (SDPK).
Minister of Internal Affairs: ZARYLBEK RYSALIYEV (SDPK).
Minister of Justice: ABYLAI MUKHAMEJANOV (Ata-Jurt).
Minister of Labour, Employment and Migration: ALMASBEK ABYTOV (Ata-Jurt).
Minister of Transport and Communications: ERKIN ISAKOV (SDPK).
Minister of Natural Resources: ZAMIRBEK ESENAMANOV (Respublika).
Minister of Health: SABYR DJUMABEKOV (Respublika).
Minister of Finance: MELIS MAMBETJANOV (Independent).
Minister of Economic Regulation: UCHKUNBEK TASHBAYEV (Respublika).
Minister of State Property: NURDIN ILEBAYEV (Respublika).
Minister of Agriculture: TOROGUL BEKOV (Respublika).
Minister of Emergency Situations: BOLOT BORBIYEV (Ata-Jurt).

KYRGYZSTAN

Minister of Energy: ASKAR SHADIYEV (Respublika).
Minister of Education and Science: KANAT SADYKOV (SDPK).
Minister of Culture and Information: NURLAN SHAKIYEV (Ata-Jurt).
Minister of Youth Affairs: ALIYASBEK ALYMKULOV (SDPK).
Minister of Social Welfare: AIGUL RYSKULOVA (Independent).
Minister of Defence: ABIBILLA KUDAIBERDIYEV (Independent).
Chairman of the State National Security Service: KENESHBEK DUSHEBAYEV (Independent).
Chairman of the State Committee for Water Resources and Irrigation: ZIYADIN JAMALDINOV (Ata-Jurt).

MINISTRIES

Office of the President: 720003 Bishkek, Dom Pravitelstva; tel. (312) 63-91-17; fax (312) 63-86-88; e-mail PS@adm.gov.kg; internet www.president.kg.

Office of the Government: 720003 Bishkek, Dom Pravitelstva; tel. (312) 62-50-71; e-mail office@mail.gov.kg; internet www.gov.kg.

Ministry of Agriculture: 720040 Bishkek, Kiyevskaya 96 A; tel. (312) 66-20-25; fax (312) 62-36-22; e-mail agroprod@agroprod.kg; internet www.agroprod.kg.

Ministry of Culture and Information: 720040 Bishkek, Pushkina 78; tel. (312) 62-12-00; e-mail mincultkr@mail.ru; internet www.minculture.gov.kg.

Ministry of Defence: 720001 Bishkek, Logvinenko 261; tel. (312) 66-17-09; fax (312) 66-19-04; e-mail ud@bishkek.gov.kg.

Ministry of Economic Regulation: 720002 Bishkek, pr. Chui 106; tel. (312) 66-38-00; fax (312) 66-34-98; e-mail mert_kg@mail.ru; internet www.mert.kg.

Ministry of Education and Science: 720040 Bishkek, Tynystanova 257; tel. (312) 62-24-42; fax (312) 62-15-20; e-mail minedukg@gmail.com; internet edu.gov.kg.

Ministry of Emergency Situations: 720055 Bishkek, Toktonaliyeva 2/1; tel. (312) 54-79-86; fax (312) 25-60-77; e-mail mchs@elcat.kg; internet mes.kg.

Ministry of Energy: 720055 Bishkek, Akhunbayeva 119; tel. (312) 56-18-22; fax (312) 56-20-28; e-mail mptr_kg@mail.ru.

Ministry of Finance: 720040 Bishkek, bul. Erkindik 58; tel. (312) 66-12-27; fax (312) 66-16-45; e-mail minfin@mf.gov.kg; internet www.minfin.kg.

Ministry of Foreign Affairs: 720040 Bishkek, bul. Erkindik 57; tel. (312) 62-05-45; fax (312) 66-05-01; e-mail gendep@mfa.gov.kg; internet www.mfa.kg.

Ministry of Health: 720040 Bishkek, Moskovskaya 148; tel. (312) 62-26-80; fax (312) 66-07-17; e-mail mz@med.kg; internet www.med.kg.

Ministry of Internal Affairs: 720040 Bishkek, Frunze 469; tel. (312) 66-24-50; fax (312) 68-20-44; e-mail pressa@mail.mvd.kg; internet www.mvd.kg.

Ministry of Justice: 720010 Bishkek, M. Gandi 32; tel. (312) 65-64-90; fax (312) 65-65-02; e-mail admin@minjust.gov.kg; internet www.minjust.gov.kg.

Ministry of Labour, Employment and Migration: 720040 Bishkek, pr. Chui 106, POB 1485; tel. (312) 66-51-58; fax (312) 66-54-13; e-mail mz@mz.kg; internet www.mz.kg.

Ministry of Natural Resources: 720026 Bishkek, pr. Erkindik 2; tel. (312) 30-04-10; fax (312) 30-07-18; e-mail info@geo.gov.kg; internet www.geo.gov.kg.

Ministry of Social Welfare: 720000 Bishkek, Tynystanova 215; tel. (312) 66-34-00; e-mail bjekshenov@mlsp.kg; internet www.mlsp.kg.

Ministry of State Property: 720000 Bishkek, Moskovskaya 151; tel. (312) 61-51-87; fax (312) 61-51-96; e-mail goskomitet@ktnet.kg; internet spf.gov.kg.

Ministry of Transport and Communications: 720017 Bishkek, Isanova 42; tel. (312) 31-43-85; fax (312) 31-28-11; e-mail mtk@mtk.gov.kg; internet www.mtk.gov.kg.

Ministry of Youth Affairs: Bishkek.

President

Following an uprising in the capital city, Bishkek, on 7 April 2010, and the subsequent assumption of power by the Interim Government of National Trust, President KURMANBEK BAKIYEV (who had been elected in July 2005 and re-elected in July 2009) went into exile in Belarus, although he continued to insist that he remained the legitimate Head of State of the Kyrgyz Republic. On 19 May the Interim Government appointed ROZA OTUNBAYEVA, the Chairman of the Interim Government, additionally as acting President; she was to retain this position until December 2011, and was to be prohibited from contesting the subsequent presidential election. She was formally inaugurated as President on 3 July 2010, after these arrangements had been approved by referendum.

Legislature

Jogorku Kenesh
(Supreme Council)

720053 Bishkek, Abdymomunov 207; tel. (312) 61-16-04; fax (312) 62-50-12; e-mail zs@kenesh.gov.kg; internet www.kenesh.kg.

Chairman: AKHMATBEK KELDIBEKOV.

General Election, 10 October 2010

Parties	Votes	%*	Seats
Homeland Idealistic Democratic Political Party (Ata-Jurt)	257,100	15.31	28
Social Democratic Party of Kyrgyzstan	237,634	14.15	26
Dignity Political Party (Ar-Namys)	229,916	13.69	25
Republic Political Party (Respublika)	210,594	12.54	23
Fatherland Socialist Political Party (Ata-Meken)	166,714	9.93	18
United Kyrgyzstan Political Party	139,548	8.31	—
White Falcon Political Party (Ak Shumkar)	78,673	4.68	—
Zamandash Political Party	55,907	3.33	—
Harmonious Fatherland Party (Meken Yntymagy)	46,070	2.74	—
Others	246,715	14.69	—
Against all	10,839	0.65	
Total valid votes	**1,679,710**	**100.00**	**120**

* Parties were required to obtain the support of at least 5% of the total registered electorate (3,036,703 persons) in order to be eligible for legislative representation. (44.69% of the registered electorate either did not participate or cast invalid votes.) The results announced by the Central Commission for Elections and Referendums presented the share of the vote received by each party as a proportion of the total electorate, rather than of the valid votes cast. The five parties that obtained legislative representation received the support of the following share of the total electorate: Homeland Idealistic Democratic Political Party (Ata-Jurt) 8.47%; Social Democratic Party of Kyrgyzstan 7.83%; Dignity Political Party (Ar-Namys) 7.57%; Republic Political Party (Respublika) 6.93%; Fatherland Socialist Political Party (Ata-Meken) 5.49%.

Election Commission

Central Commission for Elections and Referendums (Shailoo Jana Referendum Otkoruu Boyuncha Borborduk Komissiyasy): 720040 Bishkek, ul. Razzakova 59; tel. (312) 62-68-25; fax (312) 66-58-60; e-mail cec@shailoo.gov.kg; internet www.shailoo.gov.kg; independent govt organ; one-third of mems nominated by President; Chair. AKYLBEK A. SARIYEV.

Political Organizations

At December 2007 some 50 political organizations were registered with the Central Election Commission. A total of 29 parties contested the legislative elections held in October 2010. The following were among the most important operating in 2011.

Bright Road People's Party (Ak Jol) (Ak Jol Eldik Partiyasy): 720000 Bishkek, Panfilov 152; tel. (312) 62-62-06; fax (312) 66-34-03; internet www.akjolnarod.kg; f. Oct. 2007; Chair. KURMANBEK S. BAKIYEV (in exile).

Dignity Political Party (Ar-Namys): 720033 Bishkek, Togolok Moldo 60A; tel. (312) 32-46-01; e-mail ar-namys@mail.kg; internet www.ar-namys.org; f. 1999; pro-democracy; mem. of political bloc For a Worthy Future of Kyrgyzstan United Front, formed Feb. 2007; Chair. FELIKS KULOV; c. 11,000 mems.

Fatherland Socialist Political Party (Ata Meken) (Ata Meken Sotsialisttik Partiyasy): 720040 Bishkek, Orozbekova 110A/2; tel. (312) 66-34-92; fax (312) 66-46-38; e-mail atameken@elcat.kg; internet www.atameken.kg; f. 1992; nationalist; supports state control of the economy; participated in 2005 legislative elections as mem. of For Fair Elections electoral bloc; supports parliamentary system of govt; mem. of the opposition United People's Movement

KYRGYZSTAN

formed in late 2008; supported Interim Govt that assumed power in April 2010; Chair. OMURBEK CH. TEKEBAYEV; more than 2,000 mems.

Great Unification National Democratic Party (Uluu Birimdik): Bishkek; f. 2005; moderate nationalist party; supported Interim Govt that assumed power in April 2010; Leader EMILBEK KAPTAGAYEV.

Harmonious Fatherland Party (Meken Yntymagy): Bishkek; f. 2010; represents interests of Kyrgyz diaspora; Leader TEMIRBEK ASANBEKOV.

Homeland Idealistic Democratic Political Party (Ata-Jurt): 720000 Bishkek, Ibraimova 100; tel. (312) 90-01-73; fax (312) 90-02-68; e-mail info@atajurt.kg; internet www.atajurt.kg; f. 2004; opposed fmr regime of President Akayev, and supported fmr regime of President Bakiyev; Chair. KAMCHYBEK TASHIYEV.

Party of Communists of Kyrgyzstan (KCP): 720001 Bishkek, pr. Chui 114/206; tel. (312) 62-49-99; fax (312) 67-02-55; e-mail anashparties@mail.ru; disbanded 1991, re-established 1992, re-registered 2007; successor to the Communist Party of Kyrgyz SSR; participated in 2005 legislative elections as mem. of People's Movement of Kyrgyzstan election bloc; Chair. BUMAYRAM MAMASEYITOVA; 20,000 mems.

Republic Political Party (Respublika): Bishkek; f. 2010; supportive of fmr Pres. Bakiyev; Leader OMURBEK BABANOV.

Social Democratic Party of Kyrgyzstan (SDPK) (Kyrgyzstandyn Sotsial-Demokratiyalyk Partiyasy): 720000 Bishkek, Alma-Atinskaya 4B/203; tel. (312) 53-33-23; fax (312) 53-00-01; e-mail sdpkkenesh@gmail.com; internet www.sdpk.kg; f. 1993; supports parliamentary system of govt; mem. of the opposition United People's Movement formed in late 2008; supported Interim Govt that assumed power in April 2010; Chair. ALMAZBEK SH. ATAMBAYEV.

United Kyrgyzstan Political Party (Butun Kyrgyzstan): 720000 Bishkek, Turusbekov 109/1; tel. (312) 39-40-48; fax (312) 39-40-70; e-mail pressa@bytyn.kg; internet bytyn.kg; f. 2010; supportive of former President Bakiyev; Chair. ADAHAN MADUMAROV.

White Falcon Political Party (Ak Shumkar): 720000 Bishkek, pr. Manasa 40; tel. (312) 31-17-54; e-mail p.akshumkar@gmail.com; internet www.akshumkar.kg; f. 2008; supported Interim Govt that assumed power in April 2010; Chair. TEMIR SARIYEV.

Zamandash Political Party (Zamadash Sayasiy Partiyasy): 720001 Bishkek, Turusbekov 118; tel. (312) 34-02-08; fax (312) 34-01-88; e-mail partiya.zamandash@gmail.com; internet zamandash.kg; f. 2010; represents interests of Kyrgyz diaspora; Leader MUKTARBEK OMURAKUNOV.

Diplomatic Representation

EMBASSIES IN KYRGYZSTAN

Azerbaijan: 720040 Bishkek, Shurukova 41; tel. (312) 51-07-70; fax (312) 51-31-72; e-mail bishkek@mission.mfa.az; Ambassador ARIF AGHAYEV.

Belarus: 720040 Bishkek, Moskovskaya 210; tel. (312) 35-28-23; fax (312) 35-34-33; e-mail kyrgyzstan@belembassy.org; internet www.kyrgyzstan.belembassy.org; Ambassador VIKTOR DENISENKO.

China, People's Republic: 720001 Bishkek, Toktogula 196; tel. (312) 31-74-09; fax (312) 59-74-84; e-mail chinaemb_kg@mfa.gov.cn; internet kg.chineseembassy.org; Ambassador WANG KAIWEN.

Germany: 720040 Bishkek, Razzakova 28; tel. (312) 90-50-00; fax (312) 66-66-30; e-mail info@bischkek.diplo.de; internet www.bischkek.diplo.de; Ambassador HOLGER GREEN.

India: 720044 Bishkek, Aeroportinskaya 15A; tel. (312) 54-92-14; fax (312) 54-32-45; e-mail indembas@infotel.kg; Ambassador JYOTI SWARUP PANDE.

Iran: 720026 Bishkek, Razzakova 36; tel. (312) 62-49-17; fax (312) 66-02-09; e-mail embiran@mail.kg; Ambassador MANOUCHEHR MORADI.

Japan: 720033 Bishkek, Frunze 503; tel. (312) 32-54-02; fax (312) 32-54-08; internet www.kg.emb-japan.go.jp; Ambassador SHIN MARUO.

Kazakhstan: 720040 Bishkek, pr. Mira 95A; tel. (312) 66-21-01; fax (312) 69-20-94; e-mail kaz_emb@kazemb.elcat.kg; internet www.kaz-emb.kg; Ambassador BEYBIT O. ISABAEV.

Korea, Republic: 720005 Bishkek, Matrosova 67/8; tel. (312) 56-02-71; fax (312) 57-60-04; e-mail koreanemb.kg@gmail.com; internet kgz.mofat.go.kr; Ambassador SURH SUNG-YOL.

Pakistan: 720040 Bishkek, Serova 37; tel. (312) 37-39-01; fax (312) 37-39-05; e-mail parepbishkek@elcat.kg; internet www.mofa.gov.pk/kyrgyzstan; Ambassador TANVEER AKHTAR KHASKHELI.

Russia: 720001 Bishkek, Manas 55; tel. (312) 61-09-05; fax (312) 90-33-84; e-mail rusemb@saimanet.kg; internet www.kyrgyz.mid.ru; Ambassador VALENTIN S. VLASOV.

Tajikistan: 720031 Bishkek, Karadarynskaya 36; tel. (312) 51-14-64; fax (312) 51-14-64; e-mail tjemb@ktnet.kg; internet www.tajikemb.kg; Ambassador ASOMUDIN A. SAIDOV.

Turkey: 720040 Bishkek, Moskovskaya 89; tel. (312) 62-23-54; fax (312) 66-05-19; e-mail biskbe@infotel.kg; internet bishkek.emb.mfa.gov.tr; Ambassador NEJAT AKÇAL.

Ukraine: 720040 Bishkek, bulv. Akhunbayeva 201; tel. (312) 25-17-67; fax (312) 25-17-80; e-mail emb_kg@mfa.gov.ua; internet www.mfa.gov.ua/kirgizia; Ambassador VOLODYMYR V. SOLOVEY.

USA: 720016 Bishkek, pr. Mira 171; tel. (312) 55-12-41; fax (312) 55-12-64; internet bishkek.usembassy.gov; Ambassador PAMELA SPRATLEN.

Uzbekistan: 720040 Bishkek, Tynystanova 213; tel. (312) 66-20-65; fax (312) 66-44-03; e-mail uzbembish@infotel.kg; internet www.uzbekistan.kg; Ambassador ZIYADULLA S. PULATKHOJAYEV.

Judicial System

Supreme Court: 720000 Bishkek, Orozbekova 37; tel. (312) 66-33-18; fax (312) 66-29-46; e-mail scourt@bishkek.gov.kg; to be reformed to include a Constitutional Chamber, in accordance with the 2010 Constitution, to replace the former Constitutional Court; Chair. FERUZ DJAMASHEV (acting).

Office of the Prosecutor-General: 720040 Bishkek; Prosecutor-General AIDA J. SALYANOVA.

Religion

ISLAM

The majority of Kyrgyz are Sunni Muslims (Hanafi school), as are the Uzbeks and Tajiks living in Kazakhstan.

Chief Mufti of the Muslims of Kyrgyzstan: Haji SUYUN AJY KOLUEV (acting), 720000 Bishkek.

International Islamic Centre of Kyrgyzstan: 714018 Osh; Pres. Haji SADYKJAN KAMALUDDIN.

CHRISTIANITY

Roman Catholic Church

The Church is represented in Kyrgyzstan by an Apostolic Administration, established in March 2006. There were an estimated 500 adherents in the country at 31 December 2007.

Apostolic Administrator of Kyrgyzstan: Most Rev. NIKOLAUS MESSMER (Titular Bishop of Carmeiano), 720040 Bishkek, Mayakovskogo 25; tel. (312) 28-50-03; fax (312) 67-03-92; e-mail nikmessmer@hotmail.com; internet www.catholic-kyrgyzstan.org.

Russian Orthodox Church (Moscow Patriarchate)

The Russian Orthodox Church (Moscow Patriarchate) in Kyrgyzstan comes under the jurisdiction of the Eparchy of Tashkent and Central Asia, based in Uzbekistan.

JUDAISM

At the 1989 census, around 6,000 Jews were enumerated as living within the Kyrgyz SSR, although around one-half of this number had emigrated, mostly to Israel, by 1993, and emigration continued subsequently.

Chief Rabbi: Rabbi ARIYE RAICHMAN, 720000 Bishkek, Sutombayev 193, Khabad Lyubavich Synagogue; tel. and fax (312) 68-19-66; e-mail arier@mail.ru.

The Press

In 2004 there were 83 non-daily newspapers, with an average circulation of 427,800 copies. Two daily newspapers were published in that year, with an average circulation of 21,000 copies.

PRINCIPAL NEWSPAPERS

Bishkek Observer: 720001 Bishkek, Ibraimova 105; tel. (312) 28-95-96; fax (312) 29-28-21; e-mail dssuri@elcat.kg; f. 2000; weekly; independent; in English; Editor AVTAR SINGH.

Bishkek Taims (Bishkek Times): 720040 Bishkek, Pushkina 70; tel. (312) 62-15-70; fax (312) 62-15-68; e-mail b-times@yandex.ru; internet www.presskg.com/bt; Editor-in-Chief NURALY KAPAROV.

Chuy Baayni/Chuyskiye Izvestiya (Chui News): 720300 Bishkek, Ibraimova 24; tel. (312) 42-83-31; weekly; organ of Chui Oblast administration; Kyrgyz and Russian edns; Editor (Kyrgyz edn) KURMANBEK RAMATOV; Editor (Russian edn) A. BLINDINA.

KYRGYZSTAN

Delo N°... (Case Number...): 720000 Bishkek, Sovetskaya 190; tel. (312) 22-84-62; fax (312) 66-36-03; e-mail cactus@elcat.kg; f. 1991; weekly; in Russian; independent; politics, crime; Editor Viktor Zapolskii; circ. 40,000.

Erkin Too (Free Mountain): 720040 Bishkek, Ibraimova 24; tel. (312) 59-15-30; fax (312) 59-16-31; f. 1991; 2 a week; organ of the Govt; publishes laws, presidential, parliamentary and govt decrees, and other legal documents; in Kyrgyz; Chief Editor Abduvakhab Moniyev; circ. 10,000.

Gazeta.kg: 720000 Bishkek; e-mail info@gazeta.kg; internet gazeta.kg; online only, in Russian and English; independent; politics and analysis of current affairs; culture; regional news; f. 2003; Chief Editor Anton Nosik.

Kyrgyz Madaniyaty (Kyrgyz Culture): 720301 Bishkek, Bokonbayeva 99; tel. (312) 26-14-58; f. 1967; weekly; organ of the Union of Writers; Editor Nuraly Kaparov; circ. 15,940.

Kyrgyz Rukhu: 720040 Bishkek, Abdymomunova 193; tel. (312) 62-76-60; fax (312) 66-11-60; f. 1991; weekly; in Kyrgyz; Editor-in-Chief Bakbyrbek Alenov; circ. 7,000.

Kyrgyz Tuusu (Flag of Kyrgyzstan): 720040 Bishkek, Abdymomunova 193; tel. (312) 62-20-29; fax (312) 62-20-25; e-mail tuusu@infotel.kg; f. 1924; fmrly *Sovettik Kyrgyzstan*; daily; organ of the Govt; in Kyrgyz; Chief Editor Kyaz Moldokasymov; circ. 20,000.

Limon (Lemon): 720040 Bishkek, Moskovskaya 189; tel. (312) 45-66-72; fax (312) 65-02-04; e-mail limon@akipress.org; internet www.limon.kg; f. 1994; in Russian; youth newspaper; independent; Editor-in-Chief Venera Jamona Kulova.

MSN—Moya Stolitsa—Novosti (My Capital City—News): 720001 Bishkek, Turusbekova 47; tel. (312) 48-62-15; fax (312) 48-61-24; e-mail city@infotel.kg; internet www.msn.kg; f. 2001; independent; 3 a week; in Russian; Editor-in-Chief Alexander Kim; circ. 5,000 (Tues. and Thurs.), 50,000 (Fri.).

Slovo Kyrgyzstana (Word of Kyrgyzstan): 720004 Bishkek, Abdymomunova 193; tel. (312) 66-60-88; fax (312) 66-59-28; e-mail slovo@infotel.kg; f. 1925; daily; organ of the Govt; in Russian; Chief Editor Tamara Slashcheva.

The Times of Central Asia: 720000 Bishkek, Abdrahmanova 175A/303–304; tel. (312) 66-17-37; fax (312) 66-50-86; e-mail edittimes@timesca.com; internet www.timesca.com; f. 1995; weekly; in English; also distributed in Kazakhstan, Turkmenistan, Tajikistan and Uzbekistan, and internationally; Publr Giorgio Fiacconi.

Vechernii Bishkek (Bishkek Evening News): 720021 Bishkek, Usenbayeva 2; tel. (312) 48-65-65; fax (312) 68-02-68; e-mail webmaster@vb.kg; internet www.vb.kg; f. 1974; daily; independent; in Russian; Editor-in-Chief Gennadii A. Kuzmin; circ. 700,000.

Zaman Kyrgyzstan (Herald of Kyrgyzstan): 720040 Bishkek, Ibraimova 24; tel. (312) 61-46-42; fax (312) 61-46-20; e-mail zamantur@hotmail.com; f. 1992; weekly; independent; in Kyrgyz, Turkish and English; Editor-in-Chief Mustafa Bashkurt; circ. 7,500.

PRINCIPAL PERIODICALS

AKIpress: 720010 Bishkek, Moskovskaya 189; tel. and fax (312) 45-54-38; e-mail admin@akipress.org; internet www.akipress.org; f. 1993; monthly; in Russian; independent; analysis of political and economic affairs; Editor-in-Chief Samagan Aitymbetov; circ. 1,000.

Kut Bilim (Good Knowledge): 720001 Bishkek, Tynystanova 257; tel. (312) 62-04-86; e-mail kutbilim@elcat.kg; internet kb.host.net.kg; f. 1953 as *Mugalimder Gazetasy*; current name adopted 1993; organ of the Ministry of Education and Science; weekly; in Kyrgyz; Editor-in-Chief Kubatbek Chekirov; circ. 6,000.

Literaturnyi Kyrgyzstan (Literary Kyrgyzstan): 720301 Bishkek, Pushkina 70; tel. (312) 626-16-01; e-mail literary_kyrgyzstan@rambler.ru; f. 1955; journal of the Union of Writers; fiction, literary criticism, journalism; monthly; in Russian; Editor-in-Chief A. I. Ivanov; circ. 3,000.

Zdravookhraneniye Kyrgyzstana (Health-care of Kyrgyzstan): 720005 Bishkek, Moskovskaya 148; tel. (312) 62-26-80; fax (312) 66-07-17; e-mail mz@med.kg; f. 1938; 4 a year; publ. by the Ministry of Health; health research; in Russian; Editor-in-Chief T. Abdraimov; circ. 3,000 (2007).

Zhany Agym (Current): 720021 Bishkek, Usenbayeva 2; tel. (312) 38-67-73; fax (312) 48-61-24; e-mail agym@vb.kg; internet presskg.com/agym; f. 1992 as Agym; renamed as above in 2010; 2 a week; in Kyrgyz; political; Editor-in-Chief Asker Sakybaeva.

NEWS AGENCY

Kabar Kyrgyz News Agency: 720011 Bishkek, Abdrahmanova 175; tel. (312) 62-05-74; fax (312) 62-05-43; e-mail kabar@kabar.kg; internet www.kabar.kg; f. 1937; Dir Kubanychbek A. Taabaldiev.

Publishers

Ilim (Science): 720071 Bishkek, pr. Chui 265A; tel. (312) 39-20-70; e-mail ilimph@mail.ru; f. 1954; state-owned; scientific and science fiction; Dir L. V. Tarasova.

Kyrgyz-Russian Slavic University Publishing House (Izdatelstvo Kyrgyzsko-Rossiiskogo slavyanskogo universiteta): 720000 Bishkek, Kiyevskaya 44; tel. (312) 25-53-60; internet www.krsu.edu.kg/Rus/EduIzd.htm; f. 1995; academic works of university staff; textbooks; Dir Larisa V. Tarasova.

Kyrgyzstan: 720000 Bishkek, Abdrakhmanova 170; tel. (312) 62-19-47; politics, science, economics, literature; Dir Berik N. Chalagyzov.

Tsentr Gosudarstvennogo Yazyka i Kyrgyzskoi Entsiklopedii (Centre for the State Language and the Kyrgyz Encyclopedia): 720040 Bishkek, bul. Erkindik 56; tel. (312) 62-50-72; fax (312) 62-50-03; e-mail gocst.ensk@mail.ru; dictionaries and encyclopedias; Dir Baktygul Kaldybayeva; Editor-in-Chief Usen A. Asanov.

Broadcasting and Communications

National Communications Agency of the Kyrgyz Republic: 720005 Bishkek, Baytik Baatyra 7B; tel. (312) 54-41-03; fax (312) 54-41-05; internet www.nas.kg; f. 1997; Dir Kubat S. Kydyraliyev.

TELECOMMUNICATIONS

BiMoKom: 720040 Bishkek, Razzakova 33/2; tel. (312) 90-52-21; fax (312) 90-52-40; internet www.megacom.kg; f. 2006; provides mobile cellular telecommunications services in Bishkek, Manas Airport, the shores of Lake Issyk-Kul and in Chui, Yssyk-Kul, Osh, Jalal-Abad, Naryn, Talas and Batken Oblasts under the Megacom brand name; Dir Andrei G. Silich; c. 600,000 subscribers (Jan. 2008).

Kyrgyztelekom AO: 720000 Bishkek, pr. Chui 96; tel. (312) 68-16-16; fax (312) 66-24-24; e-mail info@kt.kg; internet www.kt.kg; f. 1993, transformed into joint stock co in 1997; Chair. of the Bd of Dirs Damir A. Jumayev; Pres. of the Bd of Management Marat M. Mambetaliyev.

Sky Mobile: 720011 Bishkek, pr. Chui 121; tel. (312) 58-79-15; fax (312) 90-09-16; e-mail office@bitel.kg; internet www.bitel.kg; f. 1997; provides mobile cellular telecommunications services under the Bitel and Mobi brand names; Dir-Gen. D. V. Shershnev; over 1m. subscribers (Jan. 2008).

BROADCASTING

Radio and Television

National TV and Radio Broadcasting Corporation of the Kyrgyz Republic: 720010 Bishkek, Molodoi Gvardii 59; tel. (312) 65-56-77; fax (312) 65-10-64; e-mail ntrk@ntrk.kg; internet www.ntrk.kg; f. 1958; Dir Gen. Kaiyrgul Orozbai kyzy.

Kyrgyz Public Educational Radio and Television (Kyrgyzskoye Obshchestvennoye Obrazovatelnoye Radio i Televideniye—KOORT): 720031 Bishkek, Ibraimova 24; tel. (312) 54-77-27; fax (312) 54-77-15; e-mail office@koort.kg; f. 1997; broadcasts in Kyrgyz and Russian; educational programmes and entertainment; Gen. Dir Azima Abdimaminova; 103 employees.

Radio

Radio Azattyk: 720000 Bishkek; tel. (312) 66-88-17; fax (312) 66-68-14; internet www.azattyk.org; Kyrgyz language news broadcasts by Radio Free Europe/Radio Liberty (USA—based in the Czech Republic); Dir Tyntchtykbek Tchoroev; Bureau Chief Kubat Otorbaev.

Kyrgyz Radio: 720010 Bishkek, Molodoi Gvardii 59; tel. (312) 25-79-36; fax (312) 65-10-64; internet www.ktr.kg; f. 1931; broadcasts in Kyrgyz, Russian, English, German, Ukrainian, Uzbek, Dungan and Uigur; subsidiary of State National Television and Radio Broadcasting Corpn; Dir Baima Sutenova.

Radio Television Pyramid: 720300 Bishkek, Jantosheva 70; tel. and fax (312) 51-00-15; e-mail pyramid@tom.kg; f. 1992; privately owned; broadcasts to Bishkek and neighbouring regions; Pres. Mirbek Orozov.

There are several other private radio stations operating in Kyrgyzstan.

Television

Kyrgyz Television: 720300 Bishkek, Molodoi Gvardii 63; tel. (312) 25-79-36; fax (312) 25-79-30; internet www.ktr.kg; subsidiary of State National Television and Radio Broadcasting Corpn; Pres. Kyyas Moldokasymov.

KYRGYZSTAN

TV Pyramid: 720005 Bishkek; tel. and fax (312) 41-01-31; e-mail pyramid@ss5-22.kyrnet.kg; f. 1991; privately owned; broadcasts to Bishkek and neighbouring regions; Pres. ADYLBEK T. BIINAZAROV.

Finance

(cap. = capital; res = reserves; m. = million; brs = branches; amounts in soms, unless otherwise indicated)

BANKING

Central Bank

National Bank of the Kyrgyz Republic (Kyrgyz Respublikasynyn Uluttuk Banky): 720040 Bishkek, Umetaliyeva 101; tel. (312) 66-90-08; fax (312) 61-04-56; e-mail mail@nbkr.kg; internet www.nbkr.kg; f. 1991; name changed in 1992, and as above in 1993; cap. 300.0m., res 10,331.5m., dep. 27,047.0m. (Dec. 2009); Chair. MARAT O. ALAPAYEV.

Other Banks

AsiaUniversalBank: 720001 Bishkek, Toktogula 187; tel. (312) 55-44-44; fax (312) 31-31-00; e-mail reception@aub.kg; internet www.aub.com; f. 1997; present name adopted 2000; cap. 1,337.5m., res 458.3m., dep. 9,649.5m. (Dec. 2008); Chair. MIKHAIL NADEL; Chief Exec. NURDIN ABDRAZAKOV; 2 brs.

ATFBank-Kyrgyzstan: 720070 Bishkek, Jibek Jolu 493; tel. and fax (312) 67-04-71; e-mail bank@atfbank.kg; internet www.atfbank.kg; f. 1992; fmrly Energobank, present name adopted 2006; cap. 700.0m., res –5.5m., dep. 4,964.2m. (Dec. 2008); Chair. of Bd of Dirs MUHABBAT SEITOVA; 7 brs.

Bank Bakai: 720001 Bishkek, Isanov 77; tel. (312) 61-02-42; fax (312) 61-02-43; e-mail bank@bakai.kg; internet www.bakai.kg; f. 1998; cap. 200m., res 78m., dep. 955,276m. (Jan. 2010); Chair. BAKYT MURZALIEV (acting); Pres. SERGEI IBRAGIMOV; 5 brs.

BTA Bank: 720040 Bishkek, Moskovskaya 118; tel. (312) 90-50-50; fax (312) 62-45-65; e-mail info@ineximbank.com; internet www.bta.kg; f. 1996; name changed as above 2008; cap. 1,000.0m., res 216.8m., dep. 4,420.8m. (Dec. 2008); Chair.of Bd MURAT KUNAKUNOV; 4 brs.

Demir Kyrgyz International Bank (DKIB): 72001 Bishkek, pr. Chui 245; tel. (312) 61-06-10; fax (312) 66-64-44; e-mail demir@demirbank.kg; internet www.demirbank.kg; f. 1997; cap. 132.5m., res 2.5m., 3,211.5m. (Dec. 2009); Chair. ISMAIL HASAN AKCAKAYALIOGLU; Gen. Man. L. SEVKI SARILAR; 5 brs.

Kyrgyz Investment and Credit Bank: 720001 Bishkek, Ibraimova 115A, Dordoi Plaza Business Centre; tel. (312) 69-05-55; fax (312) 69-05-60; e-mail kicb@kicb.net; internet www.kicb.net; f. 2001; 21% owned by Aga Khan Fund for Economic Development, 18% by Habib Bank (Pakistan), 17% by Deutsche Investitions und Entwicklungsgesellschaft GmbH (Germany), 17% by European Bank for Reconstruction and Development (United Kingdom), 17% by International Finance Corpn; cap. US $10.0m., res $12.4m., dep. $78.1m. (Dec. 2009); Chief Exec. KUANG YOUNG CHOI; 8 brs.

Kyrgyzstan Bank: 720001 Bishkek, Togolok Moldo 54A; tel. (312) 21-95-98; fax (312) 61-02-20; e-mail akb@bankkg.kg; internet www.bankkg.kg; f. 1991; cap. 160.9m., res 4.2m., dep. 1,268.1m. (Dec. 2008); Chair. ABIROV NURBEK; 29 brs.

Tolubay Bank: 720040 Bishkek, Umetaliyeva 105; tel. (312) 65-88-88; fax (312) 25-63-14; e-mail tolubay@infotel.kg; internet www.tolubaybank.kg; f. 1996; cap. 63.0m., res 12.5m., dep. 293.1m. (Dec. 2006); Chair. JENISHBEK S. BAIGUTTIYEV; 1 br.

COMMODITY EXCHANGE

Kyrgyzstan Commodity and Raw Materials Exchange: 720001 Bishkek, Belinskaya 40; tel. (312) 22-13-75; fax (312) 22-27-44; f. 1990; Gen. Dir TEMIR SARIYEV.

STOCK EXCHANGE

Kyrgyz Stock Exchange (Kyrgyz Fonduluk Birjasy/ Kyrgyzskaya Fondovaya Birzha): 720010 Bishkek, Moskovskaya 172; tel. (312) 31-14-84; fax (312) 31-14-83; e-mail kse@kse.kg; internet www.kse.kg; f. 1994; privately owned; Pres. AIBEK TOLUBAEV.

INSURANCE

At 1 July 2005 there were 12 private insurance companies operating in Kyrgyzstan, including two that were partly Russian-owned and three that were entirely British-owned. In late 2007 there were 15 insurance companies operating in the country.

Anglo-Kyrgyz Insurance Co: 720000 Bishkek, ul. Akhunbaeva 100; tel. (312) 54-90-23; fax (312) 54-90-49; e-mail anglokgz@elcat.kg.

ATN Polis: 720000 Bishkek, ul. Isanova 42/1; tel. (312) 93-79-37; fax (312) 90-32-52; e-mail info@atnpolis.kg; internet www.atnpolis.kg; f. 2001; life and non-life.

Insurance Group of Central Asia: 720000 Bishkek, Baitik Baatyra 191, Hyatt Hotel, room 103; tel. (312) 68-12-21.

Kyrgyzinstrakh: 720001 Bishkek, pr. Chui 219; tel. (312) 61-45-88; fax (312) 61-46-45; e-mail kinstrakli@ingo.kg; internet www.ingo.kg; f. 1996 by the Russian joint-stock insurance company Investstrakh and the Kyrgyz Government to insure foreign investors; brs in Karakol and Osh; insurance and reinsurance; Chair. of Bd E. M. SEIDAKHMETOVA.

Kyrgyzstan Insurance Co: 720000 Bishkek, ul. Moskovskaya 76B; tel. (312) 28-28-15; e-mail office@insurance.kg; internet www.insurance.kg; f. 1991; Dir MARIYA ADENOVA.

Trade and Industry

GOVERNMENT AGENCIES

Centre for Standartization and Metrology: 720040 Bishkek, Panfilova 197; tel. (312) 62-68-70; fax (312) 66-13-67; e-mail nism@nism.gov.kg; internet www.nism.gov.kg; f. 1927 as the Division of the Chamber of Measures and Weights; present name adopted 2010; certification, control and testing of products and services; Dir ALIMBEK KURMANBAEV.

State Agency for Geology and Mineral Resources: 720739 Bishkek, pr. Erkindik 2; tel. (312) 66-49-01; fax (312) 66-03-91; e-mail mail@geoagency.bishkek.gov.kg; internet www.kgs.bishkek.gov.kg; Chair. SHEISHENALY MURZAGAZIYEV.

State Committee for Management of State Property: 720017 Bishkek, Moskovskaya 151; tel. (312) 62-68-52; fax (312) 66-02-36; e-mail mail@spf.bishkek.gov.kg; internet www.spf.gov.kg; f. 1991; responsible for the privatization of state-owned enterprises and deals with bankruptcies; Chair. TURSUN O. TURDUMAMBETOV.

CHAMBER OF COMMERCE

Chamber of Commerce and Industry of the Kyrgyz Republic: 720001 Bishkek, Kiyevskaya 107; tel. (312) 61-38-72; fax (312) 61-38-75; e-mail info@cci.kg; internet www.cci.kg; f. 1959; supports foreign economic relations and the development of small and medium-sized enterprises; regional brs in Balykchy, Batken, Jalal-Abad, Karakol, Naryn, Osh, Talas and Tokmok; Pres. NURJUNOV JUMASARLYK.

TRADE ASSOCIATION

Kyrgyzvneshtorg: 720033 Bishkek, Abdymomunova 276; tel. (312) 21-39-78; fax (312) 66-08-36; e-mail kvt@infotel.kg; f. 1992; export-import org.; Gen. Dir KADYRBEK K. KALIYEV.

UTILITIES

Electricity

NES Kyrgyzstana (National Electric Grid of Kyrgyzstan) (NESK): 720070 Bishkek, pr. Jibek Jolu 326; tel. (312) 66-10-01; fax (312) 66-16-09; e-mail nesk@elcat.kg; internet www.energo.kz; f. 2001; comprises six companies, including three regional distribution companies, Oshelektro, Jalabadelektro, Vostokelektro (a fourth, Severelektro, was privatized in 2010); one heating company, Bishkekteploset; 80.49% owned by State Cttee for State Property, 13.16% owned by Social Fund of the Kyrgyz Republic; cap. 1,597.4m. soms (June 2006); Gen. Dir RAIMBEK MAMYROV.

Severelektro: 720033 Bishkek, ul. Togolok Moldo 70A; tel. (312) 61-05-48; transferred to private ownership in 2010; 80% owned by Chakan GES; distribution of electricity in northern regions of Kyrgyzstan, including Bishkek, Chui and Talas Oblasts.

Gas

Kyrgyzgaz: 720661 Bishkek, Gorkogo 22; tel. (312) 53-45-10; fax (312) 53-00-33; e-mail admin@kg.elcat.kg; internet www.kyrgyzgaz.kg; state gas distributor; Dir-Gen. TURGUNBEK N. KULMURZAYEV.

TRADE UNIONS

Trade Unions Federation of Kyrgyzstan: 720032 Bishkek, Chui 207; tel. (312) 61-32-38; fax (312) 62-57-53; e-mail fpk.kg@mail.ru; f. 1925; affiliated with the General Confed. of Trade Unions; Chair. IMANKADYR RYSALIEV.

Transport

RAILWAYS

Kyrgyzstan's railway network consists of one main line (340 km) in northern Kyrgyzstan, which connects the country to Kazakhstan and Russia, and some local lines that connect Osh and Jalal-Abad with Uzbekistan.

Kyrgyz Railway Administration (Kyrgyz Temir Jolu): 720009 Bishkek, L. Tolstogo 83; tel. (312) 62-48-65; fax (312) 65-06-90; e-mail asoup@imfiko.bishkek.su; internet railway.aknet.kg; f. 1992; Pres. I. S. OMURKULOV.

ROADS

In 1999 Kyrgyzstan's road network totalled an estimated 18,500 km, including 140 km of motorway; in 1996 there were 3,200 km of main roads and 6,380 km of secondary roads. About 91% of roads were paved.

CIVIL AVIATION

There are three international airports at Bishkek (Manas), Osh and Tamchy (in the Yssyk-Kul region).

Aviakompaniya Kyrgyzstan: 720017 Bishkek, pr. Manasa 12A; tel. (312) 31-30-26; fax (312) 31-27-42; e-mail company@air.kg; internet www.air.kg; f. 2006 by merger of Altyn Air and Kyrgyzstan Airlines; state-owned; charter passenger services; Pres. EGEMBERDI B. MYRZABEKOV.

Tourism

In 2009 there were 2,146,740 foreign tourist arrivals, compared with 398,078 in 2004. Tourism receipts (including passenger transport) amounted to US $392m. in 2007.

State Committee for Tourism, Sport and Youth Policy: 720033 Bishkek, Togolok Moldo 17; tel. (312) 62-24-99; fax (312) 21-28-45; e-mail gktsm@gks.gov.kg; Chair. TURUSBEK CH. MAMASHEV.

Defence

Military service is compulsory, and lasts for 18 months. As assessed at November 2010, Kyrgyzstan's total armed forces numbered 10,900, comprising an army of 8,500 and an air force of 2,400. There were 9,500 paramilitary forces (comprising 5,000 border guards—including both Kyrgyzstani conscripts and Russian officers, 3,500 troops attached to the Ministry of Internal Affairs and a national guard of 1,000). About 500 Russian troops were deployed at the Kant airbase (established by Russia in October 2003). In 2009 August a preliminary memorandum of understanding was signed on the establishment of a second Russian military base in Kyrgyzstan for a period of up to 49 years. Meanwhile, in February 2009 the Kyrgyzstani legislature approved a government decision for the closure of the US military base at Manas airport (where some 1,000 US forces had been stationed); however, in June the legislature endorsed a bilateral agreement to maintain the US presence at Manas, although the facility's official legal status was to be amended to that of a logistics centre rather than an airbase.

Defence Expenditure: Budgeted at 4,390m. soms in 2010.

Chief of the General Staff: Col TALAIBEK OMURALIYEV.

Education

Compulsory education comprises four years of primary education (between the ages of seven and 10), followed by five years of lower secondary school (ages 11 to 15). Pupils may then attend upper secondary schools, specialized secondary schools or technical and vocational schools. In 2006/07 total enrolment at primary schools included 84% of children in the relevant age-group; enrolment at secondary schools included 81% of the school-age population. In 1993/94 some 63.6% of primary and secondary schools used Kyrgyz as the sole language of instruction, 23.4% Russian, 12.7% Uzbek and 0.3% Tajik. Russian, however, was the principal language of instruction in higher educational establishments. In 2009 there were 54 institutes of higher education in Kyrgyzstan, attended by 217,403 students. Government budgetary expenditure on education in 2010 was 11,993.6m. soms (representing 17.4% of total spending).

LAOS

Introductory Survey

LOCATION, CLIMATE, LANGUAGE, RELIGION, FLAG, CAPITAL

The Lao People's Democratic Republic is a land-locked country in South-East Asia, bordered by the People's Republic of China to the north, by Viet Nam to the east, by Cambodia to the south, by Thailand to the west and by Myanmar (formerly Burma) to the north-west. The climate is tropical, with a rainy monsoon season lasting from May to September. The temperature in the capital ranges between 23°C and 38°C in the hottest month, April, and between 14°C and 28°C in the coolest month, January. Laos comprises 47 ethnic groups. The official language, Lao or Laotian, is spoken by about two-thirds of the population. French is also spoken, and there are numerous tribal languages, including Meo. The principal religion is Buddhism. There are also some Christians and followers of animist beliefs. The national flag (proportions 2 by 3) has three horizontal stripes, of red, blue (half the total depth) and red, with a white disc in the centre. The capital is Vientiane (Viangchan).

CONTEMPORARY POLITICAL HISTORY

Historical Context

Laos was formerly a part of French Indo-China and comprised the three principalities of Luang Prabang, Vientiane and Champasak. These were merged in 1946, when France recognized Sisavang Vong, ruler of Luang Prabang since 1904, as King of Laos. In May 1947 the King promulgated a democratic constitution (although women were not allowed to vote until 1957). The Kingdom of Laos became independent, within the French Union, in July 1949, and full sovereignty was recognized by France in October 1953. The leading royalist politician was Prince Souvanna Phouma, who was Prime Minister in 1951–54, 1956–58, 1960 and in 1962–75. King Sisavang Vong died in October 1959, and was succeeded by his son, Savang Vatthana.

Domestic Political Affairs

From 1950 the Royal Government was opposed by the Neo Lao Haksat (Lao Patriotic Front—LPF), an insurgent movement formed by a group of former anti-French activists. The LPF's Chairman was Prince Souphanouvong, a half-brother of Prince Souvanna Phouma, but its dominant element was the communist People's Party of Laos (PPL), led by Kaysone Phomvihane. During the 1950s the LPF's armed forces, the Pathet Lao, gradually secured control of the north-east of the country with the assistance of the Vietnamese communists, the Viet Minh, who were engaged in war with the French (until 1954). Several agreements between the Royal Government and the LPF, attempting to end the guerrilla war and reunite the country, failed during the 1950s and early 1960s. By 1965 the de facto partition of Laos was established, with the LPF refusing to participate in national elections and consolidating its power over the north-eastern provinces.

During the 1960s, as the 'Ho Chi Minh Trail' (the communist supply route to South Viet Nam) ran through Pathet Lao-controlled areas, Laos remained closely involved with the war between communist forces and anti-communist troops (supported by the USA) in Viet Nam. In 1973 the Viet Nam peace negotiations included provisions for a cease-fire in Laos. A new Government was formed in April 1974 under Prince Souvanna Phouma, with royalist, neutralist and LPF participation; Prince Souphanouvong was appointed Chairman of the Joint National Political Council. However, the LPF increased its power and eventually gained effective control of the country. This was confirmed by election victories in October and November 1975. In November King Savang Vatthana abdicated, and Prince Souvanna Phouma resigned.

In December 1975 the National Congress of People's Representatives (264 delegates elected by local authorities) abolished the monarchy and elected a 45-member legislative body, the Supreme People's Council. Souphanouvong was appointed President of the renamed Lao People's Democratic Republic and President of the Supreme People's Council. Kaysone Phomvihane, who had become Secretary-General of the Phak Pasason Pativat Lao (Lao People's Revolutionary Party—LPRP, a successor to the PPL), was appointed Prime Minister. The former King, Savang Vatthana, was designated Supreme Counsellor to the President, but he refused to co-operate with the new regime and was arrested in March 1977. (He was subsequently stated to have died in a 're-education camp'.) The LPF was replaced in February 1979 by the Lao Front for National Construction (LFNC), under the leadership of the LPRP.

In October 1986 the ailing Souphanouvong announced his resignation from his duties as President of the Republic (while retaining the title) and of the Supreme People's Assembly (as the Supreme People's Council had been renamed). Phoumi Vongvichit, formerly a Vice-Chairman in the Council of Ministers, became acting President of the Republic, while Sisomphon Lovansai, a Vice-President of the Supreme People's Assembly and a member of the LPRP Political Bureau (Politburo), became acting President of the Assembly. In November Kaysone Phomvihane was re-elected Secretary-General of the LPRP. In September 1987 it was announced that Phoumi Vongvichit had also replaced Souphanouvong as Chairman of the LFNC.

In June 1988 elections (the first since the formation of the Lao People's Democratic Republic) took place to determine the members of 113 district-level People's Councils. The LFNC approved 4,462 candidates to contest 2,410 seats. Provincial prefectural elections took place in November, when 898 candidates contested 651 seats. At the legislative election of March 1989, 121 candidates contested 79 seats in the enlarged Supreme People's Assembly. At its inaugural session in May, Nouhak Phoumsavanh (a Vice-Chairman of the Council of Ministers) was elected President of the Assembly.

In June 1990 a draft Constitution, enshrining free-market principles, was published, and the Supreme People's Assembly approved legislation providing for the ownership of property, for inheritance rights and contractual obligations. In October three former government officials were arrested in connection with what were termed 'activities aimed at overthrowing the regime'. It was reported in Thailand that they had formed part of a 'Social Democrat Group', which was actively seeking the introduction of multi-party democracy. In November 1992 all three were sentenced to 14 years' imprisonment.

In March 1991, at the Fifth Congress of the LPRP, Souphanouvong retired from all his party posts. Phoumi Vongvichit and Sisomphon Lovansai also retired, and the three were appointed to a newly created advisory board to the LPRP Central Committee. Kaysone Phomvihane's title was altered to President of the LPRP, and his power was slightly enhanced following the abolition of the party Secretariat. A new Politburo and (younger) Party Central Committee were elected. Gen. Sisavat Keobounphan, the military Chief of the General Staff, was not re-elected to the Politburo. The leadership pledged a continuance of free-market economic reforms, but denied the need for political pluralism.

On 14 August 1991 the Supreme People's Assembly adopted a new Constitution, which provided for a National Assembly, confirmed the leading role of the LPRP, enshrined the right to private ownership and endowed the presidency with executive powers; new electoral legislation was also promulgated. Kaysone Phomvihane was appointed President of Laos. Gen. Khamtay Siphandone, a Vice-Chairman of the Council of Ministers, Minister of National Defence and Supreme Commander of the Lao People's Army, replaced Kaysone Phomvihane as Chairman of the Council of Ministers, the position being restyled Prime Minister.

Kaysone Phomvihane died in November 1992. He was replaced as President of the LPRP by Gen. Khamtay Siphandone, and a specially convened meeting of the Supreme People's Assembly elected Nouhak Phoumsavanh as the country's President. At elections to the new National Assembly in December, 99.33% of eligible voters participated in the polls, in which 154 LFNC-approved candidates contested 85 seats. In February 1993 the new National Assembly re-elected Nouhak Phoumsavanh as President, confirmed Khamtay Siphandone as Prime Minister, and implemented the most extensive reorganization of the Council of Ministers since the LPRP's accession to power in 1975. Phoumi Vongvichit died in January 1994, and Souphanouvong in January 1995.

Although the 20th anniversary of the beginning of communist rule was celebrated in 1995, the Laotian Government was gradually attempting to replace communist ideology with Lao nationalism, as Laos developed a market economy with increasing foreign participation. In July senior Buddhist monks were assembled in Vientiane (as Buddhism was deemed central to Laotian cultural identity) and were encouraged by the Government to lead a 'cultural renaissance'. Meanwhile, the Government urged the security forces to suppress social problems, particularly corruption and prostitution, perceived as arising from increasing external influences.

The outcome of the LPRP Congress at the end of March 1996 consolidated the country's apparent progress towards a form of military-dominated authoritarian government. The armed forces gained a majority of seats on the new Politburo; Khamtay Siphandone was elected as its President (replacing Nouhak Phoumsavanh, who retired from this post), and the Minister of National Defence and Commander-in-Chief of the armed forces, Lt-Gen. Choummali Saignason, was promoted to third position, after the President of the National Assembly, Lt-Gen. Saman Vignaket. The most significant development was the failure of Khamphoui Keoboualapha, a Deputy Prime Minister responsible for many of Laos's reforms, to be re-elected either to the Politburo or to the Central Committee. Lts-Gen. Choummali Saignason and Saman Vignaket were widely reported to be opposed to rapid economic and political reform.

At the opening session of the National Assembly in April 1996 Nouhak Phoumsavanh was, despite his retirement from the Politburo, confirmed as head of state until the end of his term of office in February 1998. Sisavat Keobounphan (who had been restored to the Politburo at the previous month's elections) was elected to the new office of Vice-President, in order to relieve Nouhak Phoumsavanh of a number of presidential duties. Contrary to expectation, Khamphoui Keoboualapha was retained as Deputy Prime Minister and Chairman of the State Committee for Planning and Co-operation. However, his influence was diminished both by his exclusion from the Politburo and by the establishment of a new State Planning Committee, which assumed some of the responsibilities hitherto exercised by Khamphoui's Committee.

Elections to the National Assembly took place on 21 December 1997, at which 159 LFNC-approved candidates, including 41 members of the outgoing legislature, contested 99 seats. The three members of the LPRP Politburo and 10 Central Committee members who stood for election were all successful; one of the four 'independent' candidates without affiliation to the LPRP was elected. The level of participation by voters was officially recorded as 99.37%. The first session of the new National Assembly was held in February 1998, when Gen. Khamtay was elected to succeed Phoumsavanh as President of Laos. The Assembly also endorsed the appointment of Sisavat Keobounphan as Prime Minister and of Oudom Khattigna in his place as Vice-President, re-elected Saman Vignaket as President of the National Assembly, and approved a redistribution of ministerial posts.

In March 2001 the Seventh Congress of the LPRP confirmed the military's control of the Politburo. In a further reorganization of the Council of Ministers, Oudom was replaced as the country's Vice-President by Lt-Gen. Choummali Saignason, who had withdrawn his candidacy for the premiership owing to ill health. Prime Minister Sisavat Keobounphan was forced to resign, in order to take responsibility for the mismanagement of the economy following the Asian financial crisis of 1997/98. His successor, the former Deputy Prime Minister and Minister of Finance, Boungnang Volachit, provided a civilian balance to the entirely military executive branch. The appointment of Thongloun Sisolit to the post of Deputy Prime Minister further increased the civilian representation on the Council of Ministers.

In February 2002 elections took place from among 166 LFNC-approved candidates for the 109 seats available in the National Assembly. Only one of the elected members was not affiliated to the LPRP, ensuring that the ruling party secured a comprehensive victory. In April, at the opening session of the National Assembly, the existing Council of Ministers was almost wholly re-elected. The former Minister of the Interior, Maj.-Gen. Asang Laoli, became Deputy Prime Minister and Maj.-Gen. Soudchai Thammasith subsequently assumed the interior portfolio. In January 2003 a cabinet reorganization was announced in an apparent attempt to strengthen the national economy. The former Governor of the Central Bank, Chansy Phosikham, was appointed Minister of Finance, Onneua Phommachanh became Minister of Industry and Handicrafts and Soulivong Daravong was placed in charge of the Ministry of Commerce and Tourism. In October Politburo member Bouasone Bouphavanh was appointed fourth Deputy Prime Minister, with responsibility for home affairs.

The 2006 legislative election

In February 2006 it was announced that a legislative election would be held at the end of April, almost a year ahead of schedule. President Khamtay Siphandone stated that the decision to hold early elections had been made in order to enable the new Council of Ministers and the incoming legislature to commence their respective terms of office within close proximity of one another, in order to facilitate the forging of a strong working relationship. In March the LPRP held its Eighth Party Congress, during which Gen. Khamtay tendered his resignation from the Politburo; he was replaced as party leader by Vice-President Lt-Gen. Choummali Saignason. Two new members were elected to the Politburo, including Pany Yathotou (a Vice-President of the National Assembly), the only female member of the Bureau. Elections for a new Central Committee were also held, at which 55 members were selected. The party Secretariat, comprising seven members, was revived.

The legislative election was duly conducted on 30 April 2006, when an estimated 2.7m. voters cast their ballot. The results showed that two nominally independent candidates (of the three who had contested the election) had been elected, alongside 113 members of the LPRP. However, some 71 of the incoming deputies had not previously been members of the National Assembly, and therefore were described by some commentators as constituting a new generation of legislators. The new National Assembly convened in June, electing Thongsing Thammavong, Politburo member and Governor of Vientiane, as its President. Lt-Gen. Choummali Saignason was chosen to succeed Gen. Khamtay as President of Laos. Boungnang Volachit became Vice-President, while Bouasone Bouphavanh was appointed to replace him as Prime Minister. Two women were among the new cabinet appointments; other notable changes included the transfer of the foreign affairs portfolio from Somsavat Lengsavat to Thongloun Sisolit, both of whom remained as Deputy Prime Ministers, as did Maj.-Gen. Asong Laoli. Lt-Gen. Douangchai Phichit retained the defence portfolio and was promoted to the position of Deputy Prime Minister. In a structural reorganization, the Ministries of Commerce and of Industry were combined to form one entity, and a new Ministry of Energy and Mining was established.

The National Assembly approved several ministerial changes proposed by Prime Minister Bouasone in July 2007. Chansy Phosikham was replaced as Minister of Finance by his deputy, Somdy Douangdy, and three new Ministers to the Office of the Prime Minister were appointed. Chansy succeeded Somphet Phetmala as Governor of Vientiane, with the latter becoming Deputy Minister of National Defence. The Assembly also adopted new legislation on public security. Addressing the legislature in the previous month, Bouasone had emphasized the need to combat rising corruption among government officials.

Recent developments: Thongsing's appointment as Prime Minister and the LPRP Congress of 2011

In mid-December 2010 Bouasone Bouphavanh unexpectedly announced his resignation as Prime Minister three months prior to the expiry of his term of office, citing 'family issues'. (He was reported to have been involved in an extra-marital relationship.) However, some observers speculated that the decision was more likely to have been due to a shift in the balance of power within the Politburo. Bouasone had been widely expected to be reappointed Prime Minister at the forthcoming Ninth Congress of the LPRP. Thongsing Thammavong was elected unanimously by the National Assembly as the new premier; he pledged to combat what he termed 'negative phenomena' among public sector workers and to transform Laos into a 'reliable partner' of foreign allies and international organizations. Thongsing was replaced as President of the National Assembly by Pany Yathotou, hitherto one of his deputies, who thus became the first Laotian woman to assume the role.

At a three-day congress held by the Vientiane Capital Administration in January 2011, a new executive committee for Vientiane was elected, together with representatives to attend the Ninth Party Congress. In the same month the country's first stock exchange was formally opened (see Economic Affairs), with just two companies initially listed: Electricité du Laos Generation Company and Banque pour le Commerce Extérieur Lao.

The Ninth Congress of the LPRP, which was convened in mid-March 2011, was attended by 576 delegates. Following the appointment of a new 61-member Central Committee, Choummali Saignason was re-elected as Secretary-General of the party for a further five-year term. Former Prime Minister Bouasone Bouphavanh was removed from both the Politburo and from the Central Committee. Another former Prime Minister, Sisavat Keobounphan, and Saman Vignaket retired from the Politburo. The incoming 11-member body thus incorporated three new members. A nine-member Secretariat was also appointed. Details of the Seventh National Socio-economic Development Plan, covering the period 2011–15, were also confirmed (see Economic Affairs). The social objectives of the Plan included the further reduction of household poverty and of illiteracy.

A legislative election was held on 30 April. As in previous polls, the LPRP was the sole party permitted to present candidates, although independent candidates were also eligible to stand. An indirect presidential poll was due to be conducted in June.

Increasing Unrest

Armed opposition to the Government persisted during the 1980s, particularly among hill tribes. In December 1989 the right-wing United Lao National Liberation Front (ULNLF) proclaimed the 'Revolutionary Provisional Government' of Laos. The self-styled Government, which was headed by Outhong Souvannavong (the former President of the Royal Council of King Savang Vatthana), claimed to have used military force to 'liberate' one-third of Laotian territory. Although there were reports of attacks by insurgent guerrillas in northern Laos at this time, it was widely assumed that the ULNLF's claims were exaggerated and that its proclamation was an attempt to elicit popular support. Responsibility for defence in the 'Revolutionary Provisional Government' was reportedly allocated to Gen. Vang Pao, a leader of the Hmong tribe who in the 1970s had been a commander of the Royalist army (and who had lived in exile in the USA since 1975); Somphorn Wang, also formerly a prominent Royalist, was described as secretary of state. In late 1992 Gen. Vang Pao reportedly travelled to Singapore to direct an unsuccessful military operation from Thailand. In October Gen. Vang Pao's brother, Vang Fung, and another Hmong rebel, Moua Yee Julan (who were allegedly preparing an incursion into Laos under Gen. Vang Pao's command), were arrested in Thailand. In September 1993 Thai troops launched an offensive against Gen. Vang Pao's forces, expelling 320 rebels from Thai territory.

From the mid-1990s uprisings against the Government became more frequent. In July 1995 an army unit based near Luang Prabang mutinied after its commander, a Hmong general, was passed over for promotion. Five members of the armed forces died in the rebellion, which was believed to be symptomatic of the resentment felt by hill tribes over the political and military dominance by the lowland Lao. About 2,000 troops were dispatched to Luang Prabang to restore order. In October a shipment of explosives, allegedly destined for Hmong insurgents, was intercepted on the Mekong River. Several incidents in the Luang Prabang region during late 1995 and 1996 were ascribed to Hmong rebels. Meanwhile, fund-raising by the Hmong community in the USA was reportedly a cause for concern within the Laotian Government.

In October 1999 an anti-Government demonstration by students and teachers was held in Vientiane. The protest, which constituted an extremely rare overt demonstration of public dissatisfaction, was reportedly swiftly dispersed by police. The Government subsequently denied that the demonstration had taken place; however, it was claimed that about 50 people suspected to have been involved in the protest had been arrested, and in March 2000 it was reported that the whereabouts of one professor and five students arrested during the protest remained unknown.

Civil unrest intensified throughout 2000, with a spate of bomb attacks. The first occurred in a restaurant in March, immediately drawing international attention as several tourists were injured in the explosion. Two further attacks took place in Vientiane in May, coinciding with the respective visits of the Thai Prime Minister, Chuan Leekpai, and his Minister of Foreign Affairs, Surin Pitsuwan. Two more attacks followed within a week of each other, bringing the total number of injured to more than 20, with at least two killed. The Government attributed the campaign to Hmong insurgents, claiming to have arrested two men (one Lao and one Hmong) carrying explosive devices in mid-June. However, the bombing operation continued unabated. A bomb was defused near the Vietnamese embassy in Vientiane at the end of July, lending credence to the suspicion that the action was part of an internal power struggle between pro-Chinese and pro-Vietnamese governmental factions. In total, at least nine bombs exploded between March 2000 and January 2001, including an attack prior to the meeting of the European Union and the Association of Southeast Asian Nations (see p. 206) (EU-ASEAN summit) in December 2000.

In November 2000 about 200 workers and students staged a pro-democracy demonstration in the southern province of Champasak. The protest was swiftly quelled, and 15 people were arrested. However, the timing of the demonstration exacerbated the increasing sense of instability, as less than two weeks previously Helen Clark, the Prime Minister of New Zealand, had confirmed that her Government had granted political asylum to Khamsay Souphanouvong, a minister attached to the Prime Minister's office and son of the first President of the Lao People's Democratic Republic.

In October 2001 five European activists, including Olivier Dupuis, a Belgian member of the European Parliament, were arrested for distributing pro-democracy leaflets at a peaceful protest in Vientiane. The protest was held to commemorate the second anniversary of the disappearance of the five students who had participated in the demonstration of October 1999. In November 2001, following expressions of concern at the conditions under which the detainees were being held, Romani Prodi, President of the European Commission, warned the Laotian authorities that the continued detention of the activists would threaten diplomatic relations with the EU. In the same month, following a swift trial, the prisoners were convicted of attempting to spread unrest and ordered to be deported. They were also fined and given two-year suspended prison terms.

In September 2002 a bomb exploded at the Si Muang temple in Vientiane, injuring two children. Fears that tourists might be deterred from visiting Laos were intensified by three separate attacks on buses, thought to have been perpetrated by Hmong rebels, in February, April and August 2003; the ambushes claimed the lives of at least 30 people, including several foreign nationals. In October three bombs exploded in Vientiane. A previously unknown group, the Free Democratic People's Government of Laos (FDPGL), claimed responsibility for the bombings, as well as for the spate of bomb attacks in the capital since 2000. It was believed that the group consisted of disaffected former members of the armed forces. However, a German-based organization, the Committee for Independence and Democracy in Laos, later claimed responsibility for the bombings, including two further attacks in February 2004—one in Vientiane, which killed two people, and one in the southern town of Savannakhet, where tourism ministers from ASEAN countries had convened.

In June 2003 it was reported that two European journalists, together with their Lao-US interpreter, had been arrested on suspicion of involvement in the murder of a Lao national and for contravening the terms of their tourist visas. The journalists had allegedly been researching the Hmong insurgency, which they had found to be almost exhausted and desperate for assistance. Following a summary trial, the three were sentenced to 15-year prison terms; three Hmong defendants were given 20-year prison sentences. However, following intense diplomatic pressure from their respective Governments, the three foreign nationals were released in the following month.

In March 2004 an official from the Ministry of National Defence claimed that some 700 Hmong, including five senior commanders, had recently surrendered to the authorities, having been offered amnesty. Five bomb attacks reportedly occurred in April and May, the most serious of which killed one person and injured six others in southern Laos. In September the human rights organization Amnesty International alleged that up to 40 government troops had murdered five Hmong children in the Xaysomboun special zone in northern Laos in May; the Government denied the accusations. Two minor bombs explosions occurred in a village near Vientiane in November, prompting a heightening of security in advance of the ASEAN summit meeting, which was held in the capital at the end of the month.

In June 2007 10 Hmong resident in the USA and a former officer of the California National Guard were arrested and charged in connection with an alleged plot to overthrow the Laos Government, which had been uncovered by US federal agents. Most of the 11 defendants, including Gen. Vang Pao, the purported leader of the group, were released on bail in July. The

Foreign Affairs

Regional relations

Laos was formally admitted as a full member of ASEAN at the organization's meeting of ministers responsible for foreign affairs in July 1997. Laos hosted the 10th summit meeting of the Association in November 2004 and the 38th Ministerial Meeting in July 2005. Despite bomb threats made to staff at the US embassy in Vientiane, apparently by groups opposed to the Laotian Government, in the period prior to the summit meeting in November 2004, both the meeting itself and the subsequent ministerial conference proceeded without incident and did much to raise the international profile of Laos. In February 2008 Laos ratified the new ASEAN Charter, which codified the principles and purposes of the Association and had been signed in November 2007 at the 13th summit meeting in Singapore.

Laos's closest regional partner for many years was Viet Nam. However, more recently, Vietnamese influence in Laos has begun to be eclipsed by that wielded by the People's Republic of China. From 1975 Laos was dependent on Vietnamese economic and military assistance, permitting the stationing of Vietnamese troops (estimated in 1987 to number between 30,000 and 50,000) on its territory. In 1977 a 25-year treaty of friendship between the two countries was signed, and Laos supported the Vietnamese-led overthrow of the Khmer Rouge regime in Kampuchea (Cambodia) in January 1979. Following the outbreak of hostilities between Viet Nam and China in that year, Laos allied itself with the former. Viet Nam withdrew its military presence from Laos during 1988. The two countries signed a protocol governing military co-operation in March 1994. In July 2001 Prime Minister Boungnang Volachit visited Viet Nam on his first foreign trip since assuming office in March. In May 2002 President Khamtay Siphandone paid an official friendship visit to Viet Nam, which was reciprocated in October by the Chairman of the Vietnamese National Assembly, Nguyen Van An. The visits affirmed the strength of relations between the two countries. In February 2006 a major border crossing was opened between Sekong province in Laos and Quang Nam province in Viet Nam. It was hoped that this would facilitate economic exchanges and help to control smuggling along the common border. Discussions held during an official visit to Laos by the Vietnamese President, Nguyen Minh Triet, in February 2007 also focused on the expansion of economic co-operation. Various joint activities were organized later in that year to celebrate the 45th anniversary of the establishment of diplomatic relations between Laos and Viet Nam and the 30th anniversary of the signing of the treaty of friendship. In February 2008 it was reported that Viet Nam had become the second largest foreign investor in Laos. An official visit to Laos in April 2010 by Nong Duc Manh, General Secretary of the Communist Party of Viet Nam, was reciprocated by a state visit to Viet Nam in September by Prime Minister Bouasone, accompanied by a senior-level ministerial delegation.

Relations with China improved from the mid-1980s. In December 1986 a Chinese delegation, led by the Deputy Minister of Foreign Affairs, made the first official Chinese visit to Laos since 1978. In December 1987, after an assurance that Chinese support would be withdrawn from Laotian resistance groups operating from within China, the two countries agreed to restore full diplomatic relations and to encourage bilateral trade. Relations between the LPRP and the Chinese Communist Party were fully restored in August 1989. In October 1991 the Laotian and Chinese Prime Ministers signed a border treaty, which established a framework for meetings of a Laotian-Chinese joint border committee. In January 1992 the committee adopted a resolution providing for the demarcation of the common border, and in June an agreement on the delineation of boundaries was signed. In November 1994 Laos and China signed a reciprocal agreement on the transport of passengers and goods on each other's sections of the Mekong River. In February 1996 Laos and China opened a section of their border to highway traffic. The first ever visit by a Chinese head of state to Laos was undertaken by President Jiang Zemin in November 2000.

As the volume of bilateral trade continued to increase, Laotian-Chinese relations were further strengthened by a state visit by Chinese President Hu Jintao to Vientiane in November 2006 and by a seven-day official visit to China by Laotian Prime Minister Bouasone Bouphavanh, during which six agreements on co-operation in a range of areas were signed. In March 2008 Chinese Premier Wen Jiabao undertook a three-day visit to Laos for discussions with Bouasone. The two leaders broadly agreed to increase exchanges, to collaborate closely on important projects and to promote strategic industries. However, China's increasing involvement in the economy of Laos, mainly in infrastructural development projects, had begun to concern the citizens of Laos. Many were perturbed by the influx of Chinese workers and business entrepreneurs, who, according to some estimates, totalled as many as 300,000 by 2008. In particular, in return for the granting of a concession to develop a large residential and economic zone in Vientiane, thousands of Chinese labourers were engaged to work on the construction of a new sports stadium. Financed by the China Development Bank, the national stadium was completed in time for the South-East Asian Games, hosted by Laos in December 2009. In April 2010 Laos and China signed a memorandum of understanding (MOU) agreeing to co-operate in the development of a railway from their joint border to Vientiane, from where it would connect to the rail network in Viet Nam; a long-term loan from the Chinese Government was expected to fund the US $4,000m. project. The railway prompted further consternation in Laos on account of the high number of Chinese workers expected to be involved (some 64,000, according to Laotian officials). In June Laos received a senior-level Chinese delegation; during its stay, the two countries signed 18 co-operation agreements on bilateral trade and development, among other fields. In the following month Laotian Deputy Prime Minister and Minister of National Defence Lt-Gen. Douangchai Phichit visited the Chinese capital, Beijing, where he signed a military co-operation agreement with his Chinese counterpart.

Following a visit to Japan in 1989 by LPRP Secretary-General Kaysone Phomvihane (his first official visit to a non-communist country), the Japanese Government agreed to increase grant aid to Laos. Japan resumed the provision of official loans to Laos in 1996. In January 2000 the Japanese Prime Minister, Keizo Obuchi, undertook an official visit to Laos, and in August a bridge over the Mekong, built with a 5,460m.-yen grant from the Japanese Government, was officially opened in Paksé. In September 2001 Japan agreed a further loan to fund the construction of the second Mekong Friendship Bridge. During a visit to Japan by Bouasone Bouphavanh in May 2007, the Laotian Prime Minister held a meeting with his Japanese counterpart, Shinzo Abe, who pledged to provide continued economic assistance to Laos; the financial aid was to include approximately US $1m. for the clearance of unexploded ordnance remaining from the Viet Nam War (see Other external relations), which was impeding development. Furthermore, it was hoped that a bilateral agreement on the liberalization, promotion and protection of investment, which was signed in January 2008, would encourage the participation of Japanese businesses in the Laotian economy. Bilateral relations were further strengthened by a five-day official visit to Japan by President Chounmali Saignason in March 2010; during his visit, which marked the 55th anniversary of the establishment of diplomatic relations between the two countries, Chounmali met with the Emperor of Japan, Akihito, and the Japanese Prime Minister, Yukio Hatoyama. Prime Minister Bouasone made an official visit to Japan in May, during which Japan pledged further aid for Laos, to be divested primarily towards poverty reduction measures.

In February 1993 Laos, Thailand, Viet Nam and Cambodia signed a joint communiqué providing for the resumption of co-operation in the development of the Mekong River. In April 1995 in Chiang Rai, Thailand, representatives of the four countries signed an agreement on the joint exploitation and development of the lower Mekong. The accord provided for the establishment of the Mekong River Commission (see p. 448) as a successor to the Committee for Co-ordination of Investigations of the Lower Mekong Basin. The first summit meeting of the Commission, the primary focus of which was to examine means of enhancing the sustainable use and development of the Mekong River, was held in the Thai resort of Hua Hin in April 2010, and was attended by Laotian Prime Minister Bouasone Bouphavanh and his Cambodian, Thai and Vietnamese counterparts. Meanwhile, in August 2008 Laos, Cambodia and Viet Nam signed a border-crossing agreement that defined the intersection point of their borders and affirmed their resolve to complete works related to the demarcation of their land borders. A joint Laotian-Cambodian border demarcation survey in an area between the Laotian province of Attapeu and the Cambodian province of Ratanakiri was conducted during the course of 2010. In November Laos and

Viet Nam commenced a joint border demarcation survey along the Mo River, and in December the two countries signed an agreement pledging to enhance border security co-operation. Some 256 border markers were reported to have been installed during 2010, and the Laotian-Vietnamese border demarcation process was expected to be completed in 2014.

Relations with Thailand from 1975 were characterized by mutual suspicion. Thailand intermittently closed its border to Laotian imports and exports, causing considerable hardship. Disputed sovereignty claims in border areas were a cause of friction, and led to clashes between Laotian and Thai troops in 1984. Further hostilities began in December 1987, resulting in hundreds of casualties. In February 1988 the two sides agreed to declare a cease-fire, to withdraw their troops from the combat area and to attempt to negotiate a peaceful solution. In March 1991 (following a military coup in Thailand) representatives of the two countries signed an agreement providing for the immediate withdrawal of troops from disputed areas. The Thai Government also undertook to suppress the activities of Laotian insurgents operating from Thai territory. In December Thailand and Laos signed a border co-operation agreement. In June 1992 about 300 guerrillas from a Thai-based rebel group, the Free Democratic Lao National Salvation Force, attacked three Laotian government posts, killing two people and causing significant damage. In the same month Laos refuted allegations made by a senior Thai military officer that a Laotian government unit was receiving training in chemical warfare from Cuban and Vietnamese experts, and also dismissed previous accusations by Laotian resistance fighters and Western aid agencies of its use of chemical warfare to suppress the activities of rebel groups. Bilateral relations improved in July, when the Thai authorities announced the arrest of 11 Laotian citizens accused of planning subversive activities against the Government in Vientiane.

The first bridge linking Laos and Thailand, the so-called 'Friendship Bridge', was opened in April 1994; the bridge (over the Mekong River) connected Vientiane and Nong Khai province in north-eastern Thailand. In September 1996 the countries' Joint Co-operation Commission agreed to establish a boundary commission, in an effort to resolve demarcation problems. Despite various diplomatic efforts to stimulate further co-operation between the two countries, such as the signing of an extradition treaty in January 2001, the relationship was strained by an assault launched from Thai territory on a customs outpost in the border town of Vang Tao, carried out by suspected royalist rebels. (In July 2004, following a lengthy legal dispute, Thailand handed over to the Laotian authorities 16 Lao nationals who were allegedly involved in the incursion, despite an earlier ruling by a Thai court rejecting their extradition; in October all were convicted of robbery in connection with the raid and sentenced to prison terms of between two and 12 years.) Meanwhile, the situation deteriorated further in August 2000 after Laotian troops occupied two islands in the Mekong River, evicting 65 Thai farming families. Laos claimed that, under a treaty of 1926, it had sovereignty over all the islands in the Mekong, while Thailand merely requested the withdrawal of the troops. Nevertheless, in April 2001 the Thai Minister of Foreign Affairs, Surakiart Sathirathai, visited Laos, affirming the beginning of a new era of friendly Lao-Thai relations based on shared cultural values. In June Thai Prime Minister Thaksin Shinawatra arrived in Vientiane on a two-day official visit intended further to consolidate relations. In late 2003, following a meeting of the Joint Co-operation Commission, the two countries pledged to resolve all outstanding border demarcation issues, and also agreed to collaborate on various social development initiatives.

In March 2004, for the first time, the Thai and Laotian Governments held a joint cabinet meeting to discuss bilateral co-operation. The meeting ended with Prime Ministers Thaksin and Boungnang Volachit presiding over a ceremony to lay the foundation stone for a second Mekong Friendship Bridge (the third bridge over the river in total), connecting Savannakhet in Laos to the Thai province of Mukdahan, which was officially opened in December 2006. In February 2008 Laos and Thailand agreed to complete the demarcation of their land border in that year, as the area remaining under dispute covered only 12 km, followed by that of the maritime border in 2010; however, by early 2011 demarcation of neither border had been completed. At the end of February 2008 the new Thai Prime Minister, Samak Sundaravej, visited Laos. In March 2009 the first rail link between Laos and Thailand was inaugurated; the route between Vientiane to Nong Khai province in north-eastern Thailand was promoted as marking 'the start of a new era of connectivity between the two neighbours'. Construction of a fourth Mekong bridge, between the Laotian province of Khammouane and the Thai province of Nakhon Pathom, commenced in May and was scheduled to be completed in November 2011. A fifth bridge over the Mekong, which would link the Laotian province of Bokeo and the northernmost Thai province, Chiang Rai, was originally scheduled for completion by 2011; however, following numerous delays, construction commenced in May 2010 and was expected to be completed by the end of 2014. The 480-m bridge would, for the first time, provide a direct road link from the Chinese province of Yunnan, through Laos, to the Thai capital of Bangkok. The project was to be financed jointly by the Laotian and Thai Governments, although the Chinese Government contributed US $20m. to the Laotian share of the cost. Also in May 2010 it was announced that Laos had secured financing of some $50m. for a sixth bridge over the Mekong, which would connect the Laotian province of Oudomxay with Thailand's Nan province; work on the project was scheduled to begin in the second half of 2011 and to be completed by 2015. At a meeting in October 2010 of the Joint Co-operation Commission, co-chaired by the Laotian Deputy Prime Minister and Minister of Foreign Affairs, Thongloun Sisolit, and by Thai Minister of Foreign Affairs Kasit Piromya, the two countries reiterated their commitment to expand bilateral co-operation; Thailand confirmed a prior agreement to purchase 7,000 MW of electricity from Laos by 2015.

During the 1970s and 1980s thousands of Laotian refugees fled to Thailand to escape from civil war and food shortages. In January 1989 an estimated 90,000 Laotian refugees remained in border camps in Thailand. The office of the UN High Commissioner for Refugees (UNHCR) began a programme of voluntary repatriation in 1980. By late 1990 fewer than 6,000 refugees had been repatriated under UNHCR supervision, while some 15,000 had returned independently, and others had been resettled abroad. In June 1991 UNHCR, Laos and Thailand signed an agreement guaranteeing the repatriation or resettlement in a third country of the remaining 60,000 Laotian refugees in Thailand by the end of 1994; however, this deadline was subsequently revised on several occasions. In December 1997 UNHCR announced that a final review of the status of the last remaining refugees at Ban Napho camp in Thailand would be completed by January 1998, whereupon they would be repatriated or resettled in a third country. Among the camp's 1,344 refugees were reportedly 964 Hmong, most of whom were unwilling to return to Laos. In December 2003 the USA agreed to accept around 15,000 Laotian Hmong refugees living in refugee camps in Thailand. The first group of refugees was resettled in the USA in June 2004, under the aegis of the International Organization for Migration.

In early 2006 tension arose between Laos and Thailand concerning 27 Hmong refugees (all but one of whom were children), who had been reported missing from a refugee camp in Phetchabun province, north-eastern Thailand, in December 2005. The group was subsequently discovered in Laos, allegedly having been forcibly repatriated by the Thai authorities. Laos and Thailand entered into negotiations regarding the possibility of reuniting the children with their parents at the Phetchabun refugee camp, although it was later reported that the children had disappeared. In June 2006 Thai police arrested some 270 Hmong migrants who had allegedly entered Thailand illegally from Laos; however, officials of the latter country denied that the migrants were necessarily Laotian citizens. In August officials from the respective Ministries of Foreign Affairs of Laos and Thailand declared that their countries were ready to co-operate in addressing the Hmong refugee issue, for which neither side took responsibility. Laotian Deputy Prime Minister Somsavat Lengsavat suggested in November that Laos might allow repatriation of Hmong refugees if they were proven to be of Laotian nationality, but reiterated that the Government had not persecuted the Hmong. In the following month UNHCR urged the Thai Government to abandon its plan for the forcible repatriation of 158 Hmong migrants (including 92 children, and all recognized by UNHCR as political refugees), arguing that they would be at risk if they returned to Laos. In response, the Thai Ministry of Foreign Affairs stated that Thai and Laotian immigration officials were determining the nationality of the migrants, who, it was stated, would not be repatriated against their will. In January 2007 the Thai Government agreed to halt the deportation process for the group of 158 Hmong after the USA, Canada, Australia and the Netherlands agreed to provide asylum to the migrants, some of whom had protested against repatriation by locking themselves inside the immigration detention centre in which they were being held.

Meanwhile, in December 2006 a meeting between the Laotian Prime Minister and his Thai counterpart reportedly resulted in an agreement to repatriate the more than 7,000 Hmong living in refugee camps in Thailand's Phetchabun province, who were alleged to be economic migrants (and to whom UNHCR did not have access), following verification of their origin. In January 2007 UNHCR expressed concern about reports that Thailand had returned to Laos 16 Hmong who had apparently not been screened to ascertain if they required international protection, urging the suspension of deportations pending the introduction of procedures to allow a proper assessment of the needs and claims of the Hmong. Thai and Laotian officials held further discussions on the repatriation of the Hmong in Phetchabun province in September, later confirming that around 200 Hmong had already been resettled in Laos in that year and that the process of verifying the identity of those remaining in Phetchabun was ongoing. A site in Kaxi district, some 150 km from Vientiane, had been prepared for those who could not return to their homes in Laos. In February 2008, following a visit to Laos, the Thai Minister of Foreign Affairs declared that the Thai authorities were nearing the completion of the screening process. Later in that month Thai defence officials announced that 10 Hmong were being repatriated from Phetchabun in advance of an official visit by the Thai Prime Minister to Laos; UNHCR sought reassurance that their return was voluntary, as claimed by the officials. Following a mass protest at the Ban Huay Nam Khao camp in Phetchabun in June, when more than 5,000 refugees marched some distance from the compound before being halted by the Thai security forces, the Thai authorities promptly deported 837 Hmong refugees to Laos. Although 3,700 of the protesters returned to the camp on the following day, 1,300 refugees remained unaccounted for after the incident. The 837 repatriations were described by the Thai army as voluntary, although concerns were raised by human rights organizations, including Amnesty International and Human Rights Watch. A total of 1,809 Hmong were deported from Thailand to Laos during 2008 (see the chapter on Thailand). In December 2009 the Thai Government forcibly deported to Laos more than 4,000 Hmong from the Ban Huay Nam Khao camp, as well as the 158 UNHCR-recognized political refugees being held in an immigration detention centre, despite protests by UNHCR, the USA and other members of the international community. Following the repatriation, the Thai Government stated that it had concerns for the safety of about 100 of those who had been deported but had been assured by the Laotian Government that they would be granted pardons upon their return to Laos. In February 2010 the Laotian Deputy Prime Minister and Minister of National Defence, Lt-Gen. Douangchai Phichit, visited a group of about 3,000 of the repatriated refugees, who had been resettled in Phonkham, a village built specifically for the refugees, in Bolikhamsai province; Douangchai was reported by local media to have warned the refugees of 'the tactics employed by subversive elements', widely perceived to be a reference to exiled Hmong leader Gen. Vang Pao (see Domestic Political Affairs). In July the USA urged the Laotian Government to allow the group of 158 UNHCR-recognized political refugees to leave Laos for a third country. However, the Laotian authorities claimed that the group wished to remain in Laos. Although foreign diplomats who had been allowed access to the refugees earlier in the year had stated that there was no evidence to suggest that the group had been mistreated, media reports indicated that the refugees' living conditions were extremely poor and that they were being kept under the constant supervision of armed guards, who had warned them to inform any visiting diplomats that they were being well looked after and did not wish to leave Laos. At early 2011 little was known of their whereabouts.

Other external relations

During the Viet Nam War US aircraft completed almost 600,000 bombing missions over Laos, leaving large amounts of undetonated explosives, which were estimated to have caused 50–100 fatalities per year in the 1990s and which continued to claim the lives of Laotians in the 21st century. The National Unexploded Ordnance Awareness and Clearance Programme was established in Laos in May 1995, with support from the UN. Following the adoption by 107 countries in May 2008 of the Convention on Cluster Munitions, banning the use, production, stockpiling and transfer of cluster bombs, the treaty was opened for signature in December. The First Meeting of States Parties to the Convention on Cluster Munitions was held in Vientiane in November 2010. About 1,200 foreign delegates attended the meeting, during which the Convention adopted the Vientiane Declaration, pledging the signatories' commitment to a 'new phase of implementation' and acknowledging the need to turn 'vision into action'. In order to facilitate the achievement of this objective, the Convention adopted a five-year action plan. The Declaration also pledged the Convention's resolve to foster greater international co-operation in order better to assist victims of cluster bombs and to accelerate efforts to destroy cluster munition stockpiles and clear buried remnants.

Relations with the USA have been dominated by the issue of the US soldiers listed as 'missing in action' in Laos during the Viet Nam war. In 1985 Laos agreed to co-operate with the USA in tracing missing soldiers. In August 1987 a US delegation visited Vientiane to discuss 'humanitarian co-operation' and agreed to provide Laos with aid. The first remains of US soldiers were passed to the US Government in February 1988; further operations to locate the remains of US soldiers took place in the 1990s and 2000s. In November 1991, in response to continued Laotian co-operation and the implementation of limited political and economic reforms, the US Government announced that diplomatic relations with Laos were to be upgraded to ambassadorial level. Following 17 months of hearings, in January 1993 a special US Senate panel concluded that (despite considerable public speculation to the contrary) there was 'no compelling evidence' of the survival of US servicemen in the region. In May 1995 the USA announced the ending of a 20-year embargo on aid to Laos. In November 1997 the US Deputy Secretary of State, Strobe Talbott, led the most senior-level US delegation to Laos since the mid-1970s. During the visit further US support was pledged for a programme to clear unexploded ordnance left behind from the Viet Nam war, which had been backed by the USA since 1996. In mid-1998 US officials agreed to extend financial and logistical support for the programme until September 1999. In December 2004, following its adoption by Congress, President George W. Bush of the USA signed legislation according normal trade relations (NTR) status to Laos: this status had been suspended in 1975. The US Senate had separately adopted a resolution condemning Laos's human rights record, concerns over which had delayed the approval of NTR status. A bilateral trade agreement signed by the USA and Laos in September 2003 consequently entered into force in February 2005; according to the US Department of State, trade between the two countries increased from US $25.4m. in 2007 to $60.7m. in 2008. A meeting in Washington, DC, between Deputy Prime Minister and Minister of Foreign Affairs Thongloun Sisolit and US Secretary of State Hillary Clinton in July 2010 represented the first official visit to the USA by a Laotian minister responsible for foreign affairs since the establishment of the Lao People's Democratic Republic in 1975. An air travel co-operation agreement was signed, which it was hoped would bolster bilateral tourism; other areas of discussion included US aid, and trade and military co-operation.

In April 2009 Ban Ki-Moon visited Vientiane, the first official visit to Laos by a UN Secretary-General for almost 25 years. During his visit, Ban Ki-Moon met with President Choummali Saignason and Deputy Prime Minister and Minister of Foreign Affairs Thongloun Sisolit. He praised the Laotian Government for its poverty reduction efforts (during the previous 10 years, the incidence of poverty had declined from 46% to 33% of the population), and pledged a continuance of UN support for Laos's goal of eliminating poverty by 2020.

Meanwhile, in November 2002 Indian Prime Minister Atal Bihari Vajpayee paid the first visit to Laos by an Indian head of government in more than 45 years. During his stay, bilateral agreements on defence co-operation and the control of drugs-trafficking were signed. The Indian Government also agreed to provide US $10m. of credit to Laos at low interest rates. Several meetings of the Laos-India Joint Commission for Bilateral Co-operation subsequently took place; a further meeting of the Joint Commission was held in February 2010, at which Deputy Prime Minister and Minister of Foreign Affairs Thongloun and Indian Minister of External Affairs S. M. Krishna signed an agreement intended to bolster collaboration in the fields of politics, economic affairs, trade and investment, health, education, culture, communications and tourism. During a visit to Laos by Indian President Pratibha Patil in September, the two countries signed an agreement whereby India would provide funding of $72.5m. for two Laotian power projects, as part of a wider programme of monetary and technical assistance for Laos across several fields. A free trade agreement signed between India and ASEAN in

LAOS

August 2009 was implemented between India and Laos in January 2011; as a result of the pact, the import duties of 80% of goods currently traded between the two countries were to be eliminated by 2019, with tariffs on chemicals, electronics, garments and machinery significantly reduced with immediate effect.

CONSTITUTION AND GOVERNMENT

Under the terms of the 1991 Constitution, executive power is vested in the President of State, while legislative power resides with the National Assembly. The President is elected for five years by the National Assembly. Members of the National Assembly are elected for a period of five years by universal adult suffrage. The Lao People's Revolutionary Party remains the sole legal political party. With the approval of the National Assembly, the President appoints the Prime Minister and members of the Council of Ministers, who conduct the government of the country. The President also appoints provincial governors and mayors of municipalities, who are responsible for local administration.

REGIONAL AND INTERNATIONAL CO-OPERATION

Laos is a member of the Association of Southeast Asian Nations (ASEAN, see p. 206), of the Asian Development Bank (ADB, see p. 202), of the UN's Economic and Social Commission for Asia and the Pacific (ESCAP, see p. 37), of the Colombo Plan (see p. 446), which promotes economic and social development in Asia and the Pacific, and of the Mekong River Commission (see p. 448).

Laos became a member of the UN in 1955. In early 2011 the country's negotiations for admission to the World Trade Organization (WTO, see p. 430) were approaching conclusion. Laos participates in the Group of 77 (G77, see p. 447) developing countries, and is a member of the International Labour Organization (ILO, see p. 138) and of the Non-aligned Movement (see p. 461).

ECONOMIC AFFAIRS

In 2009, according to estimates by the World Bank, Laos's gross national income (GNI), measured at average 2007–09 prices, was US $5,550m., equivalent to $880 per head (or $2,210 per head on an international purchasing-power parity basis). During 2000–09, it was estimated, the population increased at an average annual rate of 1.8%, while gross domestic product (GDP) per head increased, in real terms, by an average of 4.9% per year. Overall GDP increased, in real terms, at an average annual rate of 6.8% in 2000–09. According to the ADB, GDP expanded by 7.3% in 2009 and by 7.5% in 2010.

Agriculture (including forestry and fishing) contributed an estimated 32.8% of GDP in 2009. According to the ADB, an estimated 78.5% of the working population were employed in the sector in 2005; FAO projected that 74.7% of the labour force would be employed in the sector in mid-2011. Rice is the staple crop. Other crops include sweet potatoes, maize, cassava, sugar cane and fruit. Coffee, production of which reached an estimated 46,000 metric tons in 2009, is grown for export. In 2007 forest covered 69.3% of the country's total land area. Although declining, timber remained a significant export commodity in 2008, accounting for an estimated 8.0% of total export revenue in that year (compared with 13.6% in 2007). The illicit cultivation of narcotic drugs has been widespread. Although the UN Office on Drugs and Crime (UNODC) estimated that the area under opium poppy cultivation in Laos had declined from 26,800 ha in 1998 to 1,600 ha in 2008, a moderate rise was thought to have occurred in 2009, and in 2010 the area was estimated to have expanded by 58% to reach 3,000 ha. Calculated on the basis of the area under cultivation, the country's potential production of dry opium increased from an estimated 11.4 metric tons in 2009 to 18.0 tons in 2010. During 2000–09 agricultural GDP increased at an estimated average annual rate of 2.8%, according to figures from the ADB. The sector's rate of growth was estimated by the ADB at 2.3% in 2009 and at 2.0% in 2010.

Industry (including mining, manufacturing, construction and utilities) contributed an estimated 25.2% of GDP in 2009. According to the ADB, the sector employed 9.3% of the working population in 2003. During 2000–09 industrial GDP increased at an average annual rate of 9.6%, according to figures from the ADB. Growth in the industrial sector was estimated by the ADB at 17.0% in 2009 and at 18.0% in 2010.

Mining contributed an estimated 7.3% of GDP in 2009 (in comparison with just 1.5% in 2004). Laos has considerable mineral resources: copper, gold, tin, coal, iron ore, gemstones and gypsum are among the minerals that are exploited. Other mineral deposits include zinc, nickel, potash, lead, limestone and silver. Copper production rose to an estimated 64,100 metric tons in 2008. Exports of copper were estimated to have increased from US $446.0m. in 2007 to $620.3m. in 2008. The value of gold exports (including re-exports) rose from $93.2m. in 2007 to $118.9m. in 2008. During 2000–09 the GDP of the mining sector increased by an average of 58.6% per year. The start of gold production in 2003 greatly enhanced the sector's output. In comparison with the previous year, the mining sector expanded by 20.6% in 2008 and by 46.1% in 2009.

Manufacturing contributed an estimated 10.6% of GDP in 2009. The sector is mainly confined to the processing of raw materials (chiefly sawmilling) and agricultural produce, the production of garments (a significant export, accounting for an estimated 11.6% of total exports in 2008), and the manufacture of handicrafts and basic consumer goods for the domestic market. Manufacturing GDP increased at an estimated average annual rate of 9.4% in 2000–09. Manufacturing GDP grew by an estimated 9.6% in 2009.

Construction contributed an estimated 4.4% of GDP in 2009. In 2000–09 the GDP of the sector increased at an average annual rate of 4.1%. Growth in the construction sector reached 11.7% in 2009.

Electrical energy is principally derived from hydroelectric power. Electricity is exported to Thailand and Viet Nam, and is an important source of foreign exchange. Laos's total hydroelectric power potential was estimated at 25,000 MW in 2000. According to the ADB, electricity production reached 3,428m. kWh in 2009. The 1,088-MW Nam Theun 2 hydroelectric project was fully operational by early 2010, with several other power projects having been commissioned. Laos is dependent on imports, mainly from Thailand, for supplies of mineral fuels. Petroleum accounted for 15.0% of total import costs in 2008.

The services sector contributed an estimated 42.0% of GDP in 2009, and engaged 8.6% of the total labour force in 2003. Visitor arrivals were reported to have increased by 24.5% to exceed 2.5m. in 2010. In that year receipts from tourism were officially estimated to have reached US $360m. The country's first stock exchange commenced trading in early 2011 (see below). The GDP of the services sector increased at an estimated average annual rate of 9.6% in 2000–09. The GDP of the sector grew by 4.4% in 2009 and by 5.0% in 2010, according to the ADB.

In 2009 Laos recorded a visible trade deficit of US $408.2m., and there was a deficit of $132.2m. on the current account of the balance of payments. Remittances from relatives residing overseas are a significant source of income for many Lao. In 2009 Thailand was the principal source of imports, supplying an estimated 66.1% (including any goods in transit) of the total. The People's Republic of China was also an important source of imports (11.5%) in that year, along with Viet Nam, the Republic of Korea and Japan. The principal destination of exports from Laos in 2009 was Thailand, which purchased 29.0% (including any goods in transit) of the total. Other significant purchasers in that year were Viet Nam (15.0%) and China (also 15.0%). The main export in 2008 was copper, followed by garments, timber, gold and electricity. The principal imports were capital goods, petroleum and material for the garment industry.

An overall budget deficit (including grants) of 1,718,000m. new kips was recorded in the financial year ending 30 September 2009. In that year the ADB estimated the budget deficit (excluding grants) to be equivalent to 3.3% of GDP. Laos's general government gross debt was 29,322,407m. new kips in 2009, equivalent to 62.1% of GDP. At the end of 2010 the country's external debt totalled US $3,270m. In 2009 the cost of debt-servicing was equivalent to 6.5% of revenue from exports of goods and services. According to the ADB, consumer prices increased by an annual average of 7.8% in 2000–09. Consumer prices were reported to have risen by 3.9% in 2009 and were estimated to have increased by 5.8% in 2010. The unemployment rate was estimated by the ADB at 1.4% of the labour force in 2005.

The contraction in global economic activity during 2008/09, combined with substantial decreases in international commodity prices (particularly for copper, the country's leading export), had a significant impact on Laos. In response to the global downturn, credit facilities for small and medium-sized enterprises were expanded. In 2010 the country benefited from stronger commodity prices and from the increasing revenue from sales of electricity. Following the completion of the Nam Theun 2 hydroelectric scheme, earnings from exports of electricity were projected to reach US $300m. in 2010, in comparison with less than $115m. in

LAOS

2007. A resurgence in inflationary pressures, mainly owing to rising food prices, was reported in the latter part of 2010. In order to comply with the requirements of the World Trade Organization (WTO, see p. 430), which Laos hoped to join by the end of 2011, the Government continued to implement measures to improve trade and investment conditions. A new investment promotion law was approved in July 2009. However, foreign direct investment decreased from $769m. in 2009 to $394m. in 2010. The Government aimed to raise the funds required to finance wider development through the introduction in January 2010 of value-added tax (VAT), to be levied at a rate of 10%. It was also hoped that the Lao Securities Exchange, established in 2010 with financial support from the Republic of Korea, would raise $8,000m. in equity and bond sales, which would be used to fund investment in the country, as well as attract foreign investors. The Seventh National Socio-economic Development Plan, encompassing the period 2011–15, projected an annual economic growth rate of at least 8%. The Plan included among its objectives the reduction of poverty to less than 10% of households, the raising of annual rice production to 4.2m. metric tons and an increase in annual tourist arrivals to 2.5m. Priority was also to be accorded to the greater integration of Laos into the regional economy. Following the robust GDP growth of 2010, the ADB envisaged similarly strong expansion, of 7.7%, in 2011.

PUBLIC HOLIDAYS

2012 (provisional): 2 January (for New Year's Day), 6 January (Pathet Lao Day), 20 January (Army Day), 23 January (Chinese New Year), 8 March (Women's Day), 22 March (People's Party Day), 13–15 April (Lao New Year), 1 May (for Labour Day), 1 June (Children's Day), 13 August (for Free Laos Day), 23 August (Liberation Day), 12 October (Liberation from the French Day, Vientiane only), 3 December (for Independence Day),

Statistical Survey

Source (unless otherwise stated): National Statistics Centre, rue Luang Prabang, Vientiane; tel. (21) 214740; fax (21) 219129; e-mail nscp@laotel.com; internet www.nsc.gov.la.

Area and Population

AREA, POPULATION AND DENSITY

Area (sq km)	236,800*
Population (census results)	
1 March 1995	4,581,258
1 March 2005	
Males	2,800,551
Females	2,821,431
Total	5,621,982
Population (UN estimates at mid-year)†	
2009	6,320,429
2010	6,436,093
2011	6,552,093
Density (per sq km) at mid-2011	27.7

* 91,400 sq miles.
† Source: UN, *World Population Prospects: The 2008 Revision*.

POPULATION BY AGE AND SEX
(UN estimates at mid-2011)

	Males	Females	Total
0–14	1,207,617	1,160,894	2,368,511
15–64	1,959,669	1,984,038	3,943,707
65 and over	105,551	134,324	239,875
Total	3,272,837	3,279,256	6,552,093

Source: UN, *World Population Prospects: The 2008 Revision*.

PROVINCES
(population at mid-2005, official estimates)

	Area (sq km)	Population ('000)	Density (per sq km)
Vientiane (municipality)	3,920	698	178.1
Phongsali	16,270	166	10.2
Luang Namtha	9,325	145	15.5
Oudomxay	15,370	265	17.2
Bokeo	6,196	145	23.4
Luang Prabang	16,875	407	24.1
Houaphanh	16,500	281	17.0
Sayabouri	16,389	339	20.7
Xiangkhouang	15,880	230	14.5
Vientiane	18,526	389	21.0
Bolikhamsai	14,863	225	15.1
Khammouane	16,315	337	20.7
Savannakhet	21,774	826	37.9
Saravan	10,691	324	30.3
Sekong	7,665	85	11.1
Champasak	15,415	607	39.4
Attopu	10,320	112	10.9
Xaysomboun SR	4,506	39	8.7
Total	236,800	5,622	23.7

Note: In January 2006 the Xaysomboun special region was dissolved, and its administrative responsibilities were transferred to Vientiane and Xiangkhouang provinces.

PRINCIPAL TOWNS
(population at 1995 census)

Viangchan (Vientiane—capital)	160,000	Xam Nua (Sam Neua)	33,500
Savannakhet (Khanthaboury)	58,500	Luang Prabang	25,500
Pakxe (Paksé)	47,000	Thakhek (Khammouane)	22,500

Source: Stefan Helders, *World Gazetteer* (internet www.world-gazetteer.com).

Mid-2010 (incl. suburbs, UN estimate): Vientiane 831,472 (Source: UN, *World Urbanization Prospects: The 2009 Revision*).

LAOS

Statistical Survey

BIRTHS AND DEATHS
(annual averages, UN estimates)

	1995–2000	2000–05	2005–10
Birth rate (per 1,000)	36.5	29.1	27.6
Death rate (per 1,000)	9.7	8.1	7.1

Source: UN, *World Population Prospects: The 2008 Revision*.

Life expectancy (years at birth, WHO estimates): 62 (males 61; females 63) in 2008 (Source: WHO, *World Health Statistics*).

ECONOMICALLY ACTIVE POPULATION
('000 persons in 2003)

	Total
Agriculture, etc.	2,085
Industry	235
Services	217
Total employed	**2,537**
Unemployed	136
Total labour force	**2,673**

2005 ('000 persons): Agriculture 2,091; Total employed 2,664; Unemployed 38; Total labour force 2,701.

Source: Asian Development Bank.

Mid-2011 (estimates in '000): Agriculture, etc. 2,526; Total labour force 3,380 (Source: FAO).

Health and Welfare

KEY INDICATORS

Total fertility rate (children per woman, 2008)	3.5
Under-5 mortality rate (per 1,000 live births, 2008)	61
HIV/AIDS (% of persons aged 15–49, 2007)	0.2
Physicians (per 1,000 head, 2004)	0.4
Hospital beds (per 1,000 head, 2005)	1.2
Health expenditure (2007): US $ per head (PPP)	84
Health expenditure (2007): % of GDP	4.0
Health expenditure (2007): public (% of total)	18.9
Access to adequate water (% of persons, 2008)	57
Access to adequate sanitation (% of persons, 2008)	53
Total carbon dioxide emissions ('000 metric tons, 2007)	1,535.2
Carbon dioxide emissions per head (metric tons, 2007)	0.3
Human Development Index (2010): ranking	122
Human Development Index (2010): value	0.497

For sources and definitions, see explanatory note on p. vi.

Agriculture

PRINCIPAL CROPS
('000 metric tons)

	2007	2008	2009
Rice, paddy	2,710	2,927	3,145
Maize	620	947	849
Potatoes*	36	36	n.a.
Sweet potatoes	126	126*	n.a.
Cassava (Manioc)	233	262	153
Sugar cane	324	417	434
Watermelons	91	100	115
Cantaloupes and other melons*	36	36	n.a.
Bananas*	48	48	n.a.
Oranges*	28	28	n.a.
Tangerines, mandarins, clementines and satsumas*	25	25	n.a.
Pineapples*	31	33	46
Coffee, green	33	39	46
Tobacco, unmanufactured	42	50	48

* FAO estimate(s).

Aggregate production ('000 metric tons, may include official, semi-official or estimated data): Total cereals 3,331 in 2007, 3,874 in 2008, 3,993 in 2009; Total vegetables (incl. melons) 875 in 2007, 900 in 2008, 914 in 2009; Total fruits (excl. melons) 200 in 2007, 202 in 2008, 215 in 2009.

Source: FAO.

LIVESTOCK
('000 head, year ending September)

	2006	2007	2008
Horses*	31	31	31
Cattle	1,321	1,353	1,449
Buffaloes	1,108	1,123	1,155
Pigs	2,033	2,186	2,548
Goats	210	268	289
Chickens	20,803	20,453	21,983
Ducks*	3,200	3,200	3,200

* FAO estimates.

2009: Cattle 1,500.

Source: FAO.

LIVESTOCK PRODUCTS
('000 metric tons, FAO estimates)

	2007	2008	2009
Cattle meat	23.8	26.0	26.0
Buffalo meat	18.5	19.0	19.0
Pig meat	46.0	54.0	40.0
Chicken meat	16.0	17.2	17.2
Cows' milk	6.8	7.5	7.5
Hen eggs	13.4	14.5	n.a.

Source: FAO.

Forestry

ROUNDWOOD REMOVALS
('000 cubic metres, excl. bark, FAO estimates)

	2007	2008	2009
Sawlogs, veneer logs and logs for sleepers	62	91	86
Other industrial wood	132	132	132
Fuel wood	5,944	5,945	5,946
Total	**6,138**	**6,168**	**6,164**

Source: FAO.

SAWNWOOD PRODUCTION
('000 cubic metres, incl. railway sleepers)

	2003	2004	2005
Total (all broadleaved)	125	125	130

2006–09: Production assumed to be unchanged from 2005 (FAO estimate).

Source: FAO.

Fishing

('000 metric tons, live weight)

	2003*	2004*	2005
Capture	29.8	29.8	29.8*
Cyprinids	4.5	4.5	4.5*
Other freshwater fishes	25.3	25.3	25.3*
Aquaculture	64.9	64.9	78.0
Common carp	16.2	16.2	5.8
Roho labeo	2.7	2.7	5.3
Mrigal carp	2.7	2.7	4.7
Bighead carp	3.8	3.8	6.5
Silver carp	3.8	3.8	8.0
Nile tilapia	29.2	29.2	19.6
Total catch	**94.7**	**94.7**	**107.8**

* FAO estimate(s).

2006–08: Catch assumed to be unchanged from 2005 (FAO estimates).

Source: FAO.

LAOS

Mining

('000 metric tons unless otherwise indicated, estimates)

	2006	2007	2008
Coal (all grades)	233.0	620.0	600.0
Gemstones, sapphire ('000 carats)	1,200.0	1,200.0	1,200.0
Gold (kg)	6,088	4,161	4,300
Gypsum	775.0	775.0	775.0
Salt	35.0	35.0	35.0
Copper (metric tons)*	60,803	62,541	64,100
Tin (metric tons)*	450	700	700

* Figures refer to metal content.

Source: US Geological Survey.

Industry

SELECTED PRODUCTS

	2007	2008	2009
Beer ('000 hectolitres)	1,029	1,363	1,391
Soft drinks ('000 hectolitres)	257	270	273
Cigarettes (million packs)	124	136	137
Garments (million pieces)	47	53	51
Plastic products (metric tons)	7,383	7,625	7,750
Detergent (metric tons)	1,255	1,613	1,713
Agricultural tools ('000 metric tons)	n.a.	46,500	52,750
Nails (metric tons)	2,168	2,225	2,313
Bricks (million)	244	266	269
Hydroelectric energy (million kWh)	3,474	3,705	3,428
Tobacco (metric tons)	3,991	4,738	5,063
Plywood (million sheets)	952	996	1,009

Source: Ministry of Industry and Commerce, Vientiane.

Finance

CURRENCY AND EXCHANGE RATES

Monetary Units
100 at (cents) = 1 new kip.

Sterling, Dollar and Euro Equivalents (31 July 2010)
£1 sterling = 12,842.8 new kips;
US $1 = 8,245.2 new kips;
€1 = 10,741.9 new kips;
100,000 new kips = £7.79 = $12.13 = €9.31.

Average Exchange Rate (new kips per US $)
2007   9,603.2
2008   8,744.2
2009   8,516.1

Note: In September 1995 a policy of 'floating' exchange rates was adopted, with commercial banks permitted to set their rates.

GENERAL BUDGET
('000 million new kips, year ending 30 September)*

Revenue†	2006/07	2007/08	2008/09‡
Tax revenue	4,711	5,624	6,338
Profits tax	1,170	1,655	1,804
Income tax	252	333	364
Turnover tax	1,046	1,229	1,347
Excise tax	999	1,191	1,432
Import duties	573	674	834
Timber royalties	212	110	100
Non-tax revenue	749	811	975
Payment for depreciation or dividend transfers	157	293	482
Overflight	231	235	225
Other revenue	361	283	268
Total	5,460	6,436	7,313

Expenditure	2006/07	2007/08	2008/09‡
Current expenditure	3,445	4,621	5,702
Wages and salaries	1,534	2,057	2,793
Compensation and allowances, subsidies and transfers	806	1,013	1,327
Interest	277	361	388
Other recurrent expenditure	828	1,191	1,195
Capital expenditure and net lending	3,089	3,155	3,569
Domestically financed	833	984	1,485
Foreign-financed and net onlending	2,328	2,171	2,084
Debt repayment and contingency expenses	586	427	512
Total	7,120	8,202	9,783

* Since 1992 there has been a unified budget covering the operations of the central Government, provincial administrations and state enterprises.
† Excluding grants received ('000 million new kips): 674 in 2006/07; 599 in 2007/08; 752 in 2008/09 (budget).
‡ Budget forecasts.

Source: IMF, *Lao People's Democratic Republic: Statistical Appendix* (September 2009).

INTERNATIONAL RESERVES
(US $ million at 31 December)

	2007	2008	2009
Gold (national valuation)	7.35	9.90	9.90
IMF special drawing rights	15.47	15.10	80.06
Foreign exchange	517.09	613.64	622.80
Total	539.91	638.64	712.76

Source: IMF, *International Financial Statistics*.

MONEY SUPPLY
(million new kips at 31 December*)

	2006	2007	2008
Currency outside banks	1,230,590	1,837,920	2,223,230
Demand deposits at commercial banks	767,660	1,226,740	1,491,680
Total (incl. others)	1,998,320	3,064,720	3,715,330

* Figures rounded to the nearest ten million.

Source: IMF, *International Financial Statistics*.

COST OF LIVING
(Consumer Price Index; base: December 1999 = 100)

	2007	2008	2009
Food	208.6	231.9	237.3
Others	187.9	196.2	191.9
All items	197.3	212.1	212.4

Source: Asian Development Bank.

LAOS

NATIONAL ACCOUNTS

Gross Domestic Product by Economic Activity
('000 million new kips at current prices)

	2007	2008	2009
Agriculture, hunting, forestry and fishing	12,621.4	13,889.3	14,549.5
Mining and quarrying	4,245.3	4,595.0	3,220.4
Manufacturing	3,399.4	3,998.8	4,683.7
Electricity, gas and water	1,048.3	1,172.9	1,299.9
Construction	2,030.7	2,187.3	1,969.1
Wholesale and retail trade	7,517.9	8,741.8	9,324.1
Transport, storage and communications	1,723.6	2,120.0	2,317.8
Finance	1,126.4	1,483.5	1,820.3
Government services	1,609.9	2,123.7	2,171.9
Other services	2,509.0	2,812.7	2,963.8
Sub-total	37,831.9	43,125.0	44,320.5
Taxes on imports	2,635.2	3,089.7	3,246.1
GDP in purchasers' values	40,467.1	46,214.7	47,566.6

Source: Asian Development Bank.

BALANCE OF PAYMENTS
(US $ million)

	2007	2008	2009
Exports of goods f.o.b.	922.7	1,091.9	1,005.3
Imports of goods c.i.f.	−1,064.7	−1,403.2	−1,413.5
Trade balance	−142.0	−311.3	−408.2
Services and other income (net)	115.9	261.6	143.2
Balance on goods, services and income	−26.1	−49.7	−265.0
Current transfers (net)	102.3	140.9	132.9
Current balance	76.2	91.2	−132.2
Direct investment (net)	323.5	227.8	318.6
Other investments (net)	76.4	191.8	297.8
Net errors and omissions	−283.0	−410.3	−488.0
Overall balance	193.2	100.5	−3.7

Source: Asian Development Bank.

External Trade

PRINCIPAL COMMODITIES
(US $ million)

Imports c.i.f.	2006	2007	2008*
Petroleum	208.7	311.0	421.8
Capital goods	728.1	1,084.8	1,171.8
Materials for garments industry	98.7	80.3	143.7
Electricity	28.0	37.4	43.3
Total (incl. others)	1,589.3	2,156.1	2,816.1

Exports f.o.b.	2006	2007	2008*
Timber	195.6	179.0	131.4
Coffee	9.8	28.9	18.5
Garments	151.2	152.8	189.7
Electricity	122.6	114.1	118.3
Copper	409.3	446.0	620.3
Gold (incl. re-exports)	117.9	93.2	118.9
Total (incl. others)	1,132.6	1,320.7	1,638.6

* Estimates.

Source: IMF, *Lao People's Democratic Republic: Statistical Appendix* (September 2009).

PRINCIPAL TRADING PARTNERS
(US $ million)

Imports	2007	2008	2009
Australia	24.1	15.5	9.6
China, People's Republic	195.2	295.0	312.5
France	12.6	20.1	62.7
Germany	34.8	25.1	17.9
Hong Kong	14.7	23.4	18.5
Japan	41.7	69.1	83.5
Korea, Republic	61.2	58.5	51.7
Singapore	43.0	28.1	40.4
Thailand*	1,442.8	1,932.6	1,800.5
Viet Nam	120.7	164.8	145.5
Total (incl. others)	2,107.9	2,829.5	2,722.8

Exports	2007	2008	2009
Belgium	11.2	17.9	14.7
China, People's Republic	77.3	135.9	219.2
France	27.2	23.0	12.8
Germany	43.0	42.0	48.2
Korea, Republic	63.9	48.2	42.5
Malaysia	32.4	2.7	0.2
Thailand*	431.5	568.7	423.7
United Kingdom	42.3	54.5	62.3
USA	19.1	40.4	41.7
Viet Nam	192.1	248.3	219.3
Total (incl. others)	1,324.5	1,604.9	1,459.2

* Trade with Thailand may be overestimated, as it may include goods in transit to and from other countries.

Note: Data reflect the IMF's direction of trade methodology and, as a result, the totals may not be equal to those presented for trade in commodities.

Source: Asian Development Bank.

Transport

ROAD TRAFFIC
(motor vehicles in use at 31 December, estimates)

	1994	1995	1996
Passenger cars	18,240	17,280	16,320
Motorcycles and mopeds	169,000	200,000	231,000

2007: Passenger cars 12,822; Buses and coaches 6,411; Lorries and vans 108,984; Motorcycles and mopeds 506,454.

Source: IRF, *World Road Statistics*.

SHIPPING

Inland Waterways
(traffic)

	2002	2003	2004
Freight ('000 metric tons)	770.0	893.0	939.9
Freight ton-kilometres (million)	69.9	55.5	49.6
Passengers ('000)	2,025.0	2,203.0	2,183.5
Passenger-kilometres (million)	76.9	45.3	22.4

Source: Ministry of Communications, Transport, Post and Construction, Vientiane.

Merchant Fleet
(registered at 31 December)

	2007	2008	2009
Number of vessels	2	1	1
Displacement ('000 grt)	2.9	0.5	0.5

Source: IHS Fairplay, *World Fleet Statistics*.

LAOS

CIVIL AVIATION
(traffic on scheduled services)

	2004	2005	2006
Kilometres flown (million)	3	3	4
Passengers carried ('000)	272	293	327
Passenger-kilometres (million)	113	124	141
Total ton-kilometres (million)	12	13	14

Source: UN, *Statistical Yearbook*.

2007 ('000): Passengers carried 328 (Source: World Bank, World Development Indicators database).
2008 ('000): Passengers carried 323 (Source: World Bank, World Development Indicators database).

Tourism

FOREIGN VISITOR ARRIVALS
(incl. excursionists)

Country of nationality	2006	2007	2008
China, People's Republic	50,317	54,920	105,852
France	32,453	34,584	39,077
Japan	23,147	29,770	31,569
Thailand	675,845	949,452	891,448
United Kingdom	31,684	31,352	36,038
USA	46,829	45,691	54,717
Viet Nam	190,442	290,584	351,384
Total (incl. others)	1,215,107	1,623,943	1,736,787

Tourism receipts (US $ million, excl. passenger transport): 173 in 2006; 233 in 2007; 276 in 2008.

Source: World Tourism Organization.

Communications Media

	2007	2008	2009
Telephones ('000 main lines in use)	94.8	127.8	100.2
Mobile cellular telephones ('000 subscribers)	1,478.4	2,022.1	3,234.6
Internet users ('000)	99.9	220.0	379.2
Broadband subscribers ('000)	4.6	6.1	8.4

Personal computers: 100,000 (17.0 per 1,000 persons) in 2005.
Radio receivers ('000 in use): 730 in 1997.
Television receivers ('000 in use): 280 in 2001.
Book production (1995): Titles 88; copies ('000) 995.
Daily newspapers (2004): 6 (average circulation 14,558).
Non-daily newspapers (1988, estimates): 18 (average circulation 34,550).

Sources (unless otherwise specified): International Telecommunication Union; UNESCO, *Statistical Yearbook*.

Education

(2007/08)

	Institutions	Teachers	Students
Pre-primary	1,170	3,185	55,340
Primary	8,740	28,751	891,807
Secondary:			
lower	653	10,702	248,567
upper	29	5,497	151,509
vocational	50	1,369	24,378
University level	4	1,420	37,903
Other higher	56	1,610	39,514

Source: Ministry of Education, Vientiane.

Pupil-teacher ratio (primary education, UNESCO estimate): 30.5 in 2007/08 (Source: UNESCO Institute for Statistics).

Adult literacy rate (UNESCO estimates): 73.2% (males 80.0%; females 66.6%) in 2007 (Source: UNESCO Institute for Statistics).

Directory

The Government

HEAD OF STATE

President of State: Lt-Gen. CHOUMMALI SAIGNASON (elected 8 June 2006).
Vice-President: BOUNGNANG VOLACHIT.

COUNCIL OF MINISTERS
(May 2011)

The Council of Ministers comprises members of the Phak Pasason Pativat Lao (Lao People's Revolutionary Party—LPRP).

Prime Minister: THONGSING THAMMAVONG.
Deputy Prime Minister and Minister of Foreign Affairs: THONGLOUN SISOLIT.
Deputy Prime Minister and Minister of National Defence: Lt-Gen. DOUANGCHAI PHICHIT.
Deputy Prime Ministers: Maj.-Gen. ASANG LAOLI, SOMSAVAT LENGSAVAT.
Minister of Finance: SOMDY DOUANGDY.
Minister of Public Security: THONGBANH SENGAPHONE.
Minister of Justice: CHALEUN YIAPAOHEU.
Minister of Agriculture and Forestry: SITAHENG LATSAPHONE.
Minister of Communications, Transport, Post and Construction: SOMMATH PHOLSENA.
Minister of Industry and Commerce: Dr NAM VIYAKET.
Minister of Information and Culture: MOUNKEO OLABUN.
Minister of Labour and Social Welfare: ONECHANH THAMMAVONG.
Minister of Education: Prof. SOMKOT MANGNOMEK.
Minister of Public Health: Dr PONEMEKH DARALOY.
Minister of Energy and Mining: SOULIVONG DALAVONG.
Minister of Planning and Investment: Dr SINLAVONG KHOUTPHAYTHOUN.
Minister to the Office of the President: PHONGSAVATH BOUPHA.
Ministers to the Office of the Prime Minister: BOUNTIEM PHITSAMAY, ONNEUA PHOMMACHANH, KHAM-OUANE BOUPPHA, SAISENGLI TENGBRIAJU, KHAMLOUAT SITLAKON, CHEUANG SOMBOUNKHAN, BOUNPHENG MOUNPHOSAY, SOMPHONG MONGKONVILAI, KHEMPHENG PHOLSENA, PHOUTHONG SAENGAKHOM, DOUANGSAVAT SOUPHANAOUVONG, SOUBANH SRITHIRATH.
Governor of the Central Bank: PHOUPHET KHAMPHOUNVONG.

MINISTRIES

Office of the President: rue Lane Xang, Vientiane; tel. (21) 214200; fax (21) 214208.
Office of the Prime Minister: Ban Sisavat, Vientiane; tel. (21) 213653; fax (21) 213560.
Ministry of Agriculture and Forestry: Ban Phonxay, Vientiane; tel. (21) 412359; fax (21) 412344; internet www.maf.gov.la.
Ministry of Communications, Transport, Post and Construction: ave Lane Xang, Vientiane; tel. (21) 412251; fax (21) 414123.
Ministry of Education: 1 rue Lane Xang, BP 67, Vientiane; tel. (21) 216013; fax (21) 216006; e-mail esitc@moe.gov.la; internet www.moe.gov.la.
Ministry of Energy and Mining: rue Nongbone, Ban Hatsady, BP 4708, Vientiane.

Ministry of Finance: 23 rue Singha, BP 24, Ban Phonxay, Vientiane; tel. and fax (21) 900798; e-mail ict@mof.gov.la; internet www.mof.gov.la.

Ministry of Foreign Affairs: 23 rue Singha, Ban Phonxay, Vientiane; tel. (21) 413148; fax (21) 414009; e-mail cabinet@mofa.gov.la; internet www.mofa.gov.la.

Ministry of Industry and Commerce: rue Phonxay, BP 4107, Vientiane; tel. (21) 412009; fax (21) 412434; e-mail citd@moic.gov.la; internet www.moic.gov.la.

Ministry of Information and Culture: rue Setthathirath, Ban Xiengnyeun, Chanthaboury, BP 122, Vientiane; tel. (21) 212406; fax (21) 212408; e-mail email@mic.gov.la.

Ministry of Justice: Ban Phonxay, Vientiane; tel. (21) 414105.

Ministry of Labour and Social Welfare: rue Pangkham, Ban Sisaket, Vientiane; tel. (21) 213003.

Ministry of National Defence: rue Kaysone Phomvihane, Ban Phone Kheng, Vientiane; tel. (21) 911550; fax (21) 911118; e-mail kongthap@yahoo.com; internet www.kongthap.gov.la.

Ministry of Planning and Investment: rue Luang Prabang, Vientiane 01001; tel. (21) 218377; fax (21) 215491; internet www.investlaos.gov.la.

Ministry of Public Health: rue Samsenthai, Ban That Khao, Sisattanak, Vientiane; tel. (21) 214000; fax (21) 214003; e-mail contact@moh.gov.la.

Ministry of Public Security: rue Nongbone, Ban Hatsady, Vientiane; tel. (21) 212500.

Ministry of Public Works and Transport: ave Lane Xang, Vientiane; tel. (21) 452167; fax (21) 451826.

Legislature

At the election held on 30 April 2011 128 candidates of the Lao People's Revolutionary Party (LPRP) and four independents were elected to the National Assembly.

President of the National Assembly: PANY YATHOTOU.

Vice-President: Dr XAYSOMPHONE PHOMVIHANE.

Political Organizations

COMMUNIST PARTY

Phak Pasason Pativat Lao (Lao People's Revolutionary Party—LPRP): Vientiane; f. 1955; est. as People's Party of Laos; reorg. under present name in 1972; 191,700 mems (2011); Cen. Cttee of 61 full mems elected at Ninth Party Congress in March 2011; Sec.-Gen. Lt-Gen. CHOUMMALI SAIGNASON.

Political Bureau (Politburo)

Full members: Lt-Gen. CHOUMMALI SAIGNASON, THONGSING THAMMAVONG, BOUNGNANG VOLACHIT, Maj.-Gen. ASANG LAOLI, THONGLOUN SISOLIT, Lt-Gen. DOUANGCHAI PHICHIT, SOMSAVAT LENGSAVAT, PANY YATHOTOU, Dr BOUNTHONG CHITMANY, Dr BOUNPONE BOUTTANAVONG, Dr PHANKHAM VIPHAVANH.

OTHER POLITICAL ORGANIZATIONS

Lao Front for National Construction (LFNC): Thanon Khouvieng, Ban Sisakhet, Chanthaboury, Vientiane; tel. and fax (21) 213752; f. 1979; est. to replace Lao Liberal Front and Lao Patriotic Front; comprises representatives of various political and social groups, of which the LPRP is the dominant force; fosters national solidarity; Chair. Gen. SISAVAT KEOBOUNPHAN; Vice-Chair. SIHO BANNAVONG, KHAMPHOUI CHANTHASOUK, TONG YEUTHOR.

Numerous factions are in armed opposition to the Government. The principal groups are:

Democratic Chao Fa Party of Laos: led by PA KAO HER until his death in Oct. 2002; Pres. SOUA HER; Vice-Pres. TENG TANG.

Free Democratic Lao National Salvation Force: based in Thailand.

United Front for the Liberation of Laos: Leader PHOUNGPHET PHANARETH.

United Front for the National Liberation of the Lao People: f. 1980; led by Gen. PHOUMI NOSAVAN until his death in 1985.

United Lao National Liberation Front: Sayabouri Province; comprises an est. 8,000 mems, mostly Hmong (Meo) tribesmen; Sec.-Gen. VANG SHUR.

Diplomatic Representation

EMBASSIES IN LAOS

Australia: rue Thadeua, Ban Wat Nak, Km 4, Sisattanak, Vientiane; tel. (21) 353800; fax (21) 353801; e-mail austemb.laos@dfat.gov.au; internet www.laos.embassy.gov.au; Ambassador LYNDA WORTHAISONG.

Brunei: Unit 12, 30 Lao-Thai Friendship Rd, Ban Thoungkang, Sisattanak, Vientiane; tel. (21) 352294; fax (21) 352291; e-mail laosfeedbk@mfa.gov.bn; Ambassador Pengiran KASMIRHAN Pengiran Haji TAHIR.

Cambodia: rue Thadeua, Km 2, BP 34, Vientiane; tel. (21) 314952; fax (21) 314951; e-mail recamlao@laotel.com; Ambassador DAN YI.

China, People's Republic: rue Wat Nak, Sisattanak, BP 898, Vientiane; tel. (21) 315100; fax (21) 315104; e-mail chinaemb_la@mfa.gov.cn; Ambassador BU JIANGUO.

Cuba: Ban Saphanthong Neua 128, BP 1017, Vientiane; tel. (21) 314902; fax (21) 314901; e-mail embacuba@etllao.com; Ambassador WALDO REYES SARDINAS.

France: rue Setthathirath, BP 06, Vientiane; tel. (21) 267400; fax (21) 267439; e-mail contact@ambafrance-laos.org; internet www.ambafrance-laos.org; Ambassador FRANÇOIS SÉNÉMAUD.

Germany: rue Sok Paluang 26, Sisattanak, BP 314, Vientiane; tel. (21) 312110; fax (21) 351152; e-mail info@vientiane.diplo.de; internet www.vientiane.diplo.de; Ambassador PETER WIENAND.

India: 2 Ban Wat Nak, rue Thadeua, Km 3, Sisattanak, BP 225, Vientiane; tel. (21) 352301; fax (21) 352300; e-mail indiaemb@laotel.com; internet indemblao.nic.in; Ambassador Dr JITENDRA NATH MISRA.

Indonesia: ave Phone Keng, BP 277, Vientiane; tel. (21) 413909; fax (21) 214828; e-mail kbrivte@laotel.com; internet www.vientiane.deplu.go.id; Ambassador KRIA FAHMI PASARIBU.

Japan: rue Sisangvone, Vientiane; tel. (21) 414401; fax (21) 414406; internet www.la.emb-japan.go.jp; Ambassador JUNKO YOKOTA.

Korea, Democratic People's Republic: quartier Wat Nak, Vientiane; tel. (21) 315261; fax (21) 315260; Ambassador HAN PONG HO.

Korea, Republic: Lao-Thai Friendship Rd, Ban Wat Nak, Sisattanak, BP 7567, Vientiane; tel. (21) 352031; fax (21) 352035; e-mail laorok@etl.com; internet lao.mofat.go.kr; Ambassador LEE GUN-TAE.

Malaysia: 23 rue Singha, Ban Phonxay, BP 789, Vientiane; tel. (21) 414205; fax (21) 414201; e-mail mwvntian@laopdr.com; internet www.kln.gov.my/web/lao_vientiane; Ambassador ZAINAL ABIDIN AHMAD.

Mongolia: Ban Wat Nak, Km 3, BP 370, Vientiane; tel. (21) 315220; fax (21) 315221; e-mail embmong@laotel.com; Ambassador TOGTOKHBAYARYN BATBAATAR.

Myanmar: Lao-Thai Friendship Rd, Ban Wat Nak, Sisattanak, BP 11, Vientiane; tel. (21) 314910; fax (21) 314913; e-mail mevlao@laotel.com; Ambassador NYUNT HLAING.

Philippines: Ban Saphanthong Kang, Sisattanak, BP 2415, Vientiane; tel. (21) 452490; fax (21) 452493; e-mail pelaopdr@laotel.com; Ambassador MARILYN J. ALARILLA.

Russia: rue Thadeua, Ban Thaphalanxay, Km 4, BP 490, Vientiane; tel. (21) 312222; fax (21) 312210; e-mail embrus_lao@mail.ru; internet www.laos.mid.ru; Ambassador OLEG V. K. KABANOV.

Singapore: Unit 4, rue Thadeua, Ban Wat Nak, Km 3, Sisattanak, Vientiane; tel. (21) 353939; fax (21) 353938; e-mail singemb_vte@sgmfa.gov.sg; internet www.mfa.gov.sg/vientiane; Ambassador (vacant).

Thailand: ave Kaysone Phomvihane, Xaysettha, Vientiane; tel. (21) 214581; fax (21) 214580; e-mail thaivte@mfa.go.th; internet www.thaiembassy.org/vientiane; Ambassador VITAVAS SRIVIHOK.

USA: 19 rue Bartholonie, BP 114, That Dam, Vientiane; tel. (21) 267000; fax (21) 267190; e-mail conslao@state.gov; internet laos.usembassy.gov; Ambassador KAREN BREVARD STEWART.

Viet Nam: Unit 85, 23 rue Singha, Ban Phonxay, Xaysettha, Vientiane; tel. (21) 413409; fax (21) 413379; e-mail dsqvn@laotel.com; internet www.mofa.gov.vn/vnemb.la; Ambassador TA MINH CHAU.

Judicial System

President of the People's Supreme Court: KHAMMY SAYAVONG.

Vice-President: PASEUTH SAUKHASEUM.

People's Supreme Court Judges: NOUANTHONG VONGSA, NHOTSENG LITTHIDETH, PHOUKHONG CHANTHALATH, SENGSOUVANH CHANTHALOUNNAVONG, KESON PHANLACK, KONGCHI YANGCHY, KHAMPON PHASAIGNAVONG.

Public Prosecutor-General: SOMPHANE PHENGKHAMMY.

Religion

The 1991 Constitution guarantees freedom of religious belief. The principal religion of Laos is Buddhism.

BUDDHISM

Lao Unified Buddhists' Association: Maha Kudy, Wat That Luang, Vientiane; f. 1964; Pres. (vacant); Sec.-Gen. Rev. SIHO SIHAVONG.

CHRISTIANITY

The Roman Catholic Church

For ecclesiastical purposes, Laos comprises four Apostolic Vicariates. At 31 December 2007 an estimated 0.6% of the population were adherents.

Episcopal Conference of Laos and Cambodia
c/o Mgr Pierre Bach, Paris Foreign Missions, 254 Silom Rd, Bangkok 10500, Thailand; f. 1971; Pres. Most Rev. EMILE DESTOMBES (Titular Bishop of Altava).

Vicar Apostolic of Luang Prabang: (vacant), Evêché, BP 113, Luang Prabang.

Vicar Apostolic of Paksé: Mgr LOUIS-MARIE LING MANGKHANE-KHOUN (Titular Bishop of Proconsulari), Centre Catholique, BP 77, Paksé, Champasak; tel. (31) 212879; fax (31) 251439.

Vicar Apostolic of Savannakhet: Fr JEAN MARIE PRIDA INTHIRATH (Titular Bishop of Lemfocta), Centre Catholique, BP 12, Thakhek, Khammouane; tel. (51) 212184; fax (51) 213070.

Vicar Apostolic of Vientiane: Mgr JEAN KHAMSÉ VITHAVONG (Titular Bishop of Moglaena), Centre Catholique, BP 113, Vientiane; tel. (21) 216593; fax (21) 215085.

The Anglican Communion

Laos is within the jurisdiction of the Anglican Bishop of Singapore.

The Protestant Church

Lao Evangelical Church: BP 4200, Vientiane; tel. (21) 169136; Exec. Pres. Rev. KHAMPHONE KOUTHAPANYA.

BAHÁ'Í FAITH

National Spiritual Assembly: BP 189, Vientiane; tel. and fax (21) 216996; e-mail usme@laotel.com; f. 1956; Sec. SUSADA SENCHANTHISAY.

The Press

Aloun Mai (New Dawn): rue That Luang, Ban Nongbone, Xaysettha, Vientiane; tel. (21) 413029; fax (21) 413037; f. 1985; quarterly; theoretical and political organ of the LPRP; Editor-in-Chief SISOUK PHILAVONG.

Finance: rue That Luang, Ban Phonxay, Vientiane; tel. (21) 412401; fax (21) 412415; organ of Ministry of Finance.

Heng Ngan: 87 ave Lane Xang, BP 780, Vientiane; tel. (21) 212756; fax (21) 219750; fortnightly; organ of the Federation of Lao Trade Unions; Editor CHANSING KOKKEOBOUNMA.

Khao Tourakit (Business News): rue Sihom, Ban Sihom, Chanthaboury, Vientiane; tel. (21) 219244; fax (21) 219223; e-mail bsnews@laotel.com; f. 1999; fortnightly; organ of the Lao National Chamber of Commerce and Industry; Editor-in-Chief SOMCHIT THIPTHIENGTHAM.

Khaokila (Sports Daily News): Ban Mixay, Chanthaboury, Vientiane; tel. (21) 252908; fax (21) 252909; e-mail khaokila@hotmail.com; f. 1999; Editor-in-Chief SUKSAKHONE SIPRASEUTH.

Lao Dong (Labour): 87 ave Lane Xang, Vientiane; f. 1986; fortnightly; organ of the Federation of Lao Trade Unions; circ. 46,000.

Laos: 80 rue Setthathirath, BP 3770, Vientiane; tel. (21) 21447; fax (21) 21445; quarterly; published in Lao and English; illustrated; Editor V. PHOMCHANHEUANG; English Editor O. PHRAKHAMSAY.

Meying Lao: rue Manthatoarath, BP 59, Vientiane; e-mail chansoda@hotmail.com; f. 1980; monthly; women's magazine; organ of the Lao Women's Union; Editor-in-Chief VATSADY KHUTNGOTHA; Editor CHANSODA PHONETHIP; circ. 7,000.

Noum Lao (Lao Youth): rue Phonthan, Ban Phonthan Neua, Xaysettha, Vientiane; tel. (21) 951067; fax (21) 416727; f. 1979; fortnightly; organ of the Lao People's Revolutionary Youth Union; Editor KHANKAB BUDARAT; circ. 1,500.

Pasason Van Athit: rue Pangkham, Ban Xiengyeun Thong, Chanthaboury, Vientiane; tel. (21) 212471; fax (21) 212470; weekly; Editor THONGLITH LIEMXAYYACHAK; circ. 2,000.

Pasaxon (The People): 80 rue Setthathirath, BP 110, Vientiane; tel. (21) 212466; fax (21) 212470; e-mail infonews@pasaxon.org.la; internet www.pasaxon.org.la; f. 1940; daily; Lao; organ of the Cen. Cttee of the LPRP; Editor-in-Chief BOUALAPHANH THANPHILOM; circ. 28,000.

Pathet Lao: 80 rue Setthathirath, Vientiane; tel. (21) 212447; f. 2001; daily; Lao and English; organ of the Lao News Agency, Khao San Pathet Lao (KPL); Editor KHEMTHONG SANOUBAN.

Sciences and Technics: Science, Technology and the Environment Agency (STEA), BP 2279, Vientiane; f. 1991; est. as Technical Science Magazine; quarterly; organ of the Dept of Science and Technology; scientific research and development.

Siang Khong Gnaovason Song Thanva (Voice of the 2nd December Youths): Vientiane; monthly; youth journal.

Sieng Khene Lao: Vientiane; monthly; organ of the Lao Writers' Association.

Suksa Mai: Vientiane; monthly; organ of the Ministry of Education.

Valasan Khosana (Propaganda Journal): Vientiane; f. 1987; organ of the Cen. Cttee of the LPRP.

Vannasinh: Vientiane; monthly; literature magazine.

Vientiane Mai (New Vientiane): 36 rue Setthathirath, BP 989, Vientiane; tel. (21) 212623; fax (21) 215989; e-mail admin@vientianemai.net; internet www.vientianemai.net; f. 1975; morning daily; organ of the LPRP Cttee of Vientiane province and city; Editor SOMPHET INTHISARATH; circ. 2,500.

Vientiane Times: rue Pangkham, BP 5723, Vientiane; tel. (21) 216364; fax (21) 216365; e-mail info@vientianetimes.gov.la; internet www.vientianetimes.org.la; f. 1994; daily; English; Editor-in-Chief SAVANKHONE RAZMOUNTRY; circ. 3,000.

Vientiane Tourakit Sangkhom (Vientiane Business-Social): 36 rue Setthathirath, Vientiane; tel. (21) 2623; fax (21) 6365; weekly; publ. in conjunction with Vientiane Mai; Editor SOMPHET INTHISARATH; circ. 2,000.

There is also a newspaper published by the Lao People's Army, and several provinces have their own newsletters.

NEWS AGENCY

Khao San Pathet Lao (Lao News Agency—KPL): 80 rue Setthathirath, BP 3770, Vientiane; tel. (21) 215402; fax (210 212446; e-mail kplnews@yahoo.com; internet www.kplnet.net; f. 1968; dept of the Ministry of Information and Culture; news service for press, radio and television broadcasting; daily bulletins in Lao, English and French; Gen. Dir KHAMSENE PHONGSA; English Editor BOUNLERT LOUANEDOUANGCHANH.

PRESS ASSOCIATION

Lao Journalists' Association (LJA): BP 122, Vientiane; tel. (21) 212420; fax (21) 212408; Pres. Dr BOSENGKHAM VONGDARA; Sec.-Gen. KHAM KHONG KONGVONGSA.

Publishers

Khoualuang Kanphim: 2–6 Khoualuang Market, Vientiane.

Lao-phanit: Ministry of Education, Bureau des Manuels Scolaires, rue Lane Xang, Ban Sisavat, Vientiane; educational, cookery, art, music, fiction.

Pakpassak Kanphin: 9–11 quai Fa-Hguun, Vientiane.

Department of Publishing, Printing, Distribution and Libraries: Ministry of Information and Culture, BP 122, Vientiane; tel. (21) 212421; fax (21) 212408; oversees the State Publishing and Book Distribution House and the State Printing Enterprise; Dir NOUPHAY KOUNLAVONG.

Broadcasting and Communications

TELECOMMUNICATIONS

Entreprise de Télécommunications de Laos (ETL): rue Saylom, Ban Saylom, Chanthaboury, Vientiane; tel. (21) 215767; fax (21) 212779; e-mail csd@etllao.com; internet www.etllao.com; state enterprise, telephone, mobile and voice over internet protocol (VOIP) services; Dir-Gen. KHAMMOUANE XOMSIHAPANYA.

Lao Télécommunications Co Ltd: ave Lane Xang, BP 5607, 01000 Vientiane; tel. (21) 244212; fax (21) 241638; e-mail marketin@laotel.com; internet laotel.com; f. 1996; jt venture between a subsidiary of Shinawatra Group of Thailand and Entreprises des Postes et Télécommunications de Laos; awarded 25-year contract by Govt in 1996 to undertake all telecommunications projects in Laos; Dir-Gen. THANSAMAY KOMMASITH.

BROADCASTING

Radio

In mid-2010 there were 44 radio stations broadcasting throughout Laos.

Lao National Radio: rue Phangkham, Km 6, BP 310, Vientiane; tel. (21) 212468; fax (21) 212430; e-mail laonradio@lnr.org.la; internet www.lnr.org.la; f. 1960; state-owned; programmes in Lao, French, English, Thai, Khmer and Vietnamese; domestic and international services; Dir-Gen. SIPHA NONGLATH.

Television

A domestic television service began in December 1983.

Lao National Television (TVNL): rue Sivilay, BP 5635, Vientiane; tel. (21) 710067; fax (21) 710182; e-mail tnlinfo@tnl.gov.la; internet www.tnl.gov.la; f. 1983; colour television service; Dir-Gen. BOUMCHOM VONGPHET.

Laos Television 3: BP 860, Vientiane; tel. (21) 315449; fax (21) 215628; f. 1994; est. as IBC Channel 3; 30% govt-owned, 70% owned by Int. Broadcasting Corpn Co Ltd (Thailand); operated by latter; programmes in Lao.

Finance

(cap. = capital; dep. = deposits; br.(s) = branch(es); m. = million)

BANKING

The banking system was reorganized in 1988–89, ending the state monopoly of banking. Some commercial banking functions were transferred from the central bank and the state commercial bank to a new network of autonomous banks. The establishment of joint ventures with foreign financial institutions was permitted.

Central Bank

Banque de la RDP Lao: rue Yonnet, BP 19, Vientiane; tel. (21) 213109; fax (21) 213108; e-mail bol@bol.gov.la; internet www.bol.gov.la; f. 1959 as the bank of issue; became Banque Pathetlao 1968; took over the operations of Banque Nationale du Laos 1975; known as Banque d'Etat de la RDP Lao from 1982 until adoption of present name; dep. 394,017m. kips, total assets US $361m. (Dec. 2002); Gov. PHOUPHET KHAMPHOUNVONG.

Commercial Banks

Acleda Bank Lao: 372, cnr rues Dongpalane and Dongpaina, Unit 21, Ponesavanh, Sisattanak, Vientiane; tel. (21) 264994; fax (21) 264995; e-mail acledabank@acledabank.com.la; internet www.acledabank.com.la; f. 2008; cap. 100,000m. kips, dep. 122,152m. kips (Dec. 2009); Chair. CHEA SOK; Pres. and CEO PHON NARIN.

Agriculture Promotion Bank: 58 rue Hengboun, Ban Haysok, BP 5456, Vientiane; tel. (21) 241394; fax (21) 223714; e-mail apblao@laotel.com; internet www.apblaos.com; Dir BOUANGEUN PHONGSAVATH.

ANZ Vientiane Commercial Bank Ltd: 33 ave Lane Xang, Ban Hatsady, Chanthaboury, Vientiane; tel. (21) 222700; fax (21) 213513; e-mail vccbank@laotel.com; internet www.anz.com/laos/; f. 1993; renamed as above in 2007; private jt venture owned by Laotian, Thai, Taiwanese and Australian investors; Man. Dir KERROD THOMAS.

Banque pour le Commerce Extérieur Lao (BCEL): 1 rue Pangkham, Ban Xiengnheun, Chanthaboury, Vientiane; tel. (21) 213200; fax (21) 213202; e-mail bcelhqv@bcel.com.la; internet www.bcel.com.la; f. 1975; 100% state-owned; cap. 329,201m. kips, res 109,427m. kips, dep. 6,059,189m. kips (Dec. 2009); Chair. VIENGTHONG SYPHANDONE; Man. Dir SONEXAY SITPHAXAY.

International Commercial Bank: 127/07, rue Hatsady, Hatsady Tai, Chanthaboury, Vientiane; tel. (21) 250388; fax (21) 250479; e-mail enquiry@icb-lao.com; internet www.icb-lao.com; f. 2008; Man. Dir ZHUKIBLI KUAN.

Joint Development Bank: 82 ave Lane Xang, BP 3187, Vientiane; tel. (21) 213531; fax (21) 213530; e-mail jdb@jdbbank.com; internet www.jdbbank.com; f. 1989; the first jt venture bank between Laos and a foreign partner; 30% owned by Banque de la RDP Lao, 70% owned by Phrom Suwan Silo and Drying Co Ltd of Thailand; cap. US $4m.; Dir SAROGE SINGSOMBOON.

Lao Development Bank (LDB): BP 2700, Ban Sihome, Chanthaboury, Vientiane; tel. (21) 213300; fax (21) 213304; e-mail ldbhovte@ldblao.com; internet www.ldb.org.la; f. 1999; est. as Lao May Bank upon consolidation by the Govt of ParkTai Bank, Lao May Bank and Nakornluang Bank; merged with Lane Xang Bank Ltd in 2001; name changed as above in 2003; 100% govt-owned; lends mainly to SMEs; Man. Dir BOUNTA DALAVY; 18 brs.

Lao-Viet Bank (LVB): 44 ave Lane Xang, Ban Hatsady, Chanthaboury, Vientiane; tel. (21) 216316; fax (21) 212197; e-mail lvbho@laotel.com; f. 1999; jt venture between BCEL and Bank for Investment and Devt of Vietnam; cap. US $15m.; Chair. PHANSANA KHOUNNOUVONG; Man. Dir NGUYEN KIM DIEU; 3 brs.

Phongsavanh Bank: Unit 1, rue Kaisorn Phomvihane, Ban Phakhao, Xaythany, Vientiane; tel. (21) 215666; e-mail info@phongsavanhbank.com; internet www.phongsavanhbank.com; f. 2007; Man. Dir OD PHONGSAVANH; cap. US $10m. (2007).

STOCK EXCHANGE

Lao Securities Exchange (LSX): Ban Phonethan Neue, rue T4, Saysettha, Vientiane; internet www.lsx.com.la; f. 2010; establishment funded by Bank of Laos (51% of capital) and Republic of Korea (49%); Chair. and CEO DETHPHOUVANG MOULARAT.

INSURANCE

Assurances Générales du Laos (AGL): Vientiane Commercial Bank Bldg, 33 ave Lane Xang, BP 4223, Vientiane; tel. (21) 215903; fax (21) 215904; e-mail agl@agl-allianz.com; internet www.agl-allianz.com; f. 1990; jt venture between Laotian Govt (49%) and Assurances Générales de France (51%); Group Chair. Dr MICHAEL DIEKMANN; Man. Dir GUY APOVY.

Lane Xang Assurance Co (LAP): Vientiane; f. 2010; equal jt venture between Lao Development Bank and Post and Telecommunication Joint Venture Insurance Corpn; life and general.

Trade and Industry

GOVERNMENT AGENCY

National Economic Research Institute (NERI): ave Kaysone Phomvihan, Ban Sivilay, Xaythany, Vientiane; tel. and fax (21) 711181; e-mail nerilaos@yahoo.com; govt policy development unit; Dir SOUPHAN KEOMISAY.

DEVELOPMENT ORGANIZATIONS

Department of Domestic and Foreign Investment (DDFI): rue Luang Prabang, 01001 Vientiane; tel. (21) 222690; fax (21) 215491; e-mail fimc@laotel.com; internet invest.laopdr.org; fmrly Foreign Investment Management Committee (FIMC); provides information and assistance to existing and potential investors.

Department of Livestock and Fisheries: Ministry of Agriculture and Forestry, Ban Phonxay, BP 811, Vientiane; tel. (21) 416932; fax (21) 415674; e-mail eulaodlf@laotel.com; public enterprise; imports and markets agricultural commodities; produces and distributes feed and animals; Dir-Gen. BOUAPHAN KONEDAVONG.

National Agriculture and Forestry Research Institute (NAFRI): Nongviengkham, BP 7170, Vientiane; tel. (21) 770084; fax (21) 770047; e-mail bounthong@nafri.org.la; internet www.nafri.org.la; f. 1999; supports sectoral devt and formulation of strategies and programmes in accordance with govt policy; Dir-Gen. Dr BOUNTHONG BOUAHOM.

State Committee for State Planning: Office of the Prime Minister, Ban Sisavat, Vientiane; tel. (21) 213653; fax (21) 213560; Pres. SOULIVONG DARAVONG.

CHAMBER OF COMMERCE

Lao National Chamber of Commerce and Industry (LNCCI): ave Kaysone Phomvihane, Ban Phonphanao, Xaysettha, BP 4596, Vientiane; tel. (21) 452579; fax (21) 452580; e-mail lncci@laopdr.com; internet www.lncci.laotel.com; f. 1989; 800 mems; Pres. KISSANA VONGSAY; Sec.-Gen. KHAMPANH SENGTHONGKHAM.

TRADE ASSOCIATION

Société Lao Import-Export (SOLIMPEX): 43–47 ave Lane Xang, BP 2789, Vientiane; tel. (21) 213818; fax (21) 217054; Dir KANHKEO SAYCOCIE; Dep. Dir PHONGSAMOUTH VONGKOT.

UTILITIES

Electricity

Electricité du Laos (EDL): rue Nongbone, BP 309, Vientiane; tel. (21) 451519; fax (21) 416381; e-mail edlgmo@laotel.com; internet www.edl-laos.com; f. 1959; state-owned corpn; responsible for production and distribution of electricity; shares in subsidiary Electricité du Laos Generation Co offered in 2011; Chair. KHAMMONE PHONEKEO; Man. Dir KHAMMANY INTHIRATH.

Lao National Grid Co: Vientiane; responsible for Mekong hydro-electricity exports.

Water

Nam Papa Vientiane (Vientiane Water Supply Authority): rue Phone Kheng, Ban That Luang Neue, Xaysettha, Vientiane; tel. (21) 412880; fax (21) 414378; e-mail daophet@laotel.com; f. 1962; fmrly Nam Papa Lao; responsible for the water supply of Vientiane; Gen. Man. DAOPHET BOUAPHA.

Water Supply Authority (WASA): Dept of Housing and Urban Planning, Ministry of Public Works and Transport, ave Lane Xang, Vientiane; tel. and fax (21) 452167; fax (21) 451826; e-mail nvirabouth@yahoo.com; internet www.wasa.gov.la; f. 1998; Dir NOUPHEUAK VIRABOUTH.

STATE ENTERPRISES

Agricultural Forestry Development Import-Export and General Service Co: trading co of the armed forces.

Bolisat Phatthana Khet Phoudoi Import-Export Co: rue Khoun Boulom, Vientiane; tel. (21) 216234; fax (21) 215046; f. 1984; trading co of the armed forces.

Dao-Heuang Import-Export Co: 242-7 Route 13 South, Ban Thaluang, Paksé, Champasak Province; tel. (31) 212250; fax (31) 212438; e-mail daoheuangcafe@laopdr.com; internet www.daoheuangcoffee.com; f. 1990; imports and distributes whisky, beer, mineral water, coffee and foodstuffs; Pres. LEUANG LITDANG.

Lao Commodities Export Co Ltd (Lacomex): Ban Wattuang, Paksé, Champasak Province; tel. (31) 212552; fax (31) 212553; e-mail sisanouk@laotel.com; f. 1994; exports coffee under the Paksong Cafe Lao brand; Man. Dir SISANOUK SISOMBAT.

Lao Houng Heuang Export-Import Co: rue Nongbone, Vientiane; tel. (21) 217344; fax (21) 212107.

Lao State Material Import-Export Co (Lasmac): 59 Ban Hatsady Tai, Chanthaboury, Vientiane; tel. (21) 216578; fax (21) 217149; e-mail lasmac@laotel.com; internet www.lasmac.laopdr.com; f. 1983; mfr of wood products and woven plastic; exports agricultural and wood products; imports construction materials.

Luen Fat Hong Lao Plywood Industry Co: BP 83, Vientiane; tel. (21) 314990; fax (21) 314992; e-mail lfhsdsj@laotel.com; internet www.luenfathongyada.laopdr.com; devt and management of forests, logging and timber production.

CO-OPERATIVES

Central Leading Committee to Guide Agricultural Co-operatives: Vientiane; f. 1978; helps to organize and plan regulations and policies for co-operatives; by the end of 1986 there were some 4,000 co-operatives, employing about 74% of the agricultural labour force; Chair. (vacant).

TRADE UNION ORGANIZATION

Federation of Lao Trade Unions: 87 ave Lane Xang, BP 780, Vientiane; tel. (21) 212754; e-mail kammabanlao@pan-laos.net.la; f. 1956; 21-mem. Cen. Cttee and five-mem. Control Cttee; Pres. KHAMLA LORLONESY; 70,000 mems.

Transport

RAILWAYS

In 2003 the Thai Government agreed to finance a 3.5-km rail link from Tha Naleng (near Vientiane) to Nong Khai, in north-eastern Thailand; construction was completed in April 2008, and the first passenger train service commenced in March 2009. Proposals to extend the track, to link Tha Naleng with Vientiane and to extend southwards and eastwards to Vinh in Viet Nam via Thakhek in central Laos, were also announced.

ROADS

The Asian Development Bank has supported an extensive development programme for the road network in Laos. In 2006 there were an estimated 29,811 km of roads. The main routes link Vientiane and Luang Prabang with Ho Chi Minh City in southern Viet Nam and with northern Viet Nam and the Cambodian border, Vientiane with Savannakhet, Phongsali to the Chinese border, Vientiane with Luang Prabang and the port of Ha Tinh (northern Viet Nam), and Savannakhet with the port of Da Nang (Viet Nam). Laos, Thailand and China are linked by the Kunming–Bangkok Highway, 250 km of which traverse Laos. In February 2004 construction of a 245-km national road (Route 9) was completed, linking Laos with Thailand and Viet Nam.

A number of bridges across the Mekong River link Laos to Thailand. A bridge linking Khammouane in Laos with the Thai province of Nakhon Pathom was scheduled for completion in November 2011. Construction of a fifth bridge, between the Laotian province of Bokeo and the northernmost Thai province of Chiang Rai, was expected to be completed by 2014.

INLAND WATERWAYS

The Mekong River, which forms the western frontier of Laos for much of its length, is the country's greatest transport artery. However, the size of river vessels is limited by rapids, and traffic is seasonal. There are about 4,600 km of navigable waterways.

CIVIL AVIATION

Wattay airport, Vientiane, is the principal international airport. In 1998 Luang Prabang airport also gained formal approval to receive international flights. Construction of a new airport in Oudomxay Province was completed in the late 1990s. Savannakhet Airport was to be developed into an international facility, as part of plans for the east–west economic corridor project, a proposed transport network linking Laos with Myanmar, Thailand and Viet Nam.

Lao Civil Aviation Department: BP 119, Vientiane; tel. (21) 512163; fax (21) 520236; e-mail laodca@laotel.com; internet www.dca.mpwt.gov.la; Dir-Gen. YAKUA LOPANGKAO.

Lao Airlines: National Air Transport Co, 2 rue Pangkham, BP 6441, Vientiane; tel. (21) 212057; fax (21) 212065; e-mail laoairlines@laoairlines.com; internet www.laoairlines.com; f. 1975; state airline, fmrly Lao Aviation; operates internal and international passenger and cargo transport services within South-East Asia; CEO SOMPHONE DOUANGDARA.

Tourism

Laos has spectacular scenery and ancient pagodas. Luang Prabang was approved by UNESCO as a World Heritage site in 1995, as was the Wat Phu temple complex in southern Laos in 2001. Foreign visitor arrivals were reported to have increased by 24.5% in 2010 to exceed 2.5m. Receipts were estimated at US $360m. in 2010.

National Tourism Administration of Lao PDR: ave Lane Xang, BP 3556, Hatsady, Chanthaboury, Vientiane; tel. (21) 212251; fax (21) 212769; e-mail tmpd_lnta@yahoo.com; internet www.tourismlaos.org; parastatal org.;promotes Laos as a tourist destination and regulates the tourism industry; 17 provincial offices; Chair. SOMPHONG MONGKHONVILAY.

Defence

As assessed at November 2010, the total strength of the armed forces was an estimated 29,100: army 25,600 (including an army marine section of an estimated 600); air force 3,500. Conscription lasts a minimum of 18 months. Paramilitary forces comprise militia self-defence forces numbering about 100,000 men.

Defence Expenditure: Budgeted for 2009: 119,000m. kips.

Supreme Commander of the Lao People's Army (Commander-in-Chief): Lt-Gen. CHOUMMALI SAIGNASON.

Chief of the General Staff: Lt-Gen. SANYAHAK PHOMVIHANE.

Education

A comprehensive educational system is in force, and Lao is the medium of instruction.

In 2007/08 enrolment in pre-primary education included 14% of pupils in the relevant age-group (males 13%; females 14%). In the same year enrolment in primary education, which begins at six years of age and lasts for five years, included 82% of children in the relevant age-group (males 84%; females 81%). Secondary education, beginning at the age of 11, lasts for six years, comprising two three-year cycles. In 2006/07 enrolment in secondary education included 36% of pupils in the relevant age-group (males 39%; females 33%).

In the 2007/08 academic year there were 1,170 pre-primary institutions, which were attended by 55,340 children, and 8,740 primary schools, attended by 891,807 pupils. The 732 secondary schools provided education for a total of 424,455 students (including 50 vocational schools, at which 24,378 students were enrolled). There were 60 tertiary institutions, including four universities, at which 37,903 students were enrolled, while 39,514 were studying at other institutions of higher education. There are several regional technical colleges. The National University of Laos was founded in 1995. Enrolment in tertiary education in 2006 was equivalent to 9% of the relevant age-group (males 11%; females 7%). Government spending on education in 2006 reached an estimated 15.8% of total budgetary expenditure.

LATVIA

Introductory Survey

LOCATION, CLIMATE, LANGUAGE, RELIGION, FLAG, CAPITAL

The Republic of Latvia is situated in north-eastern Europe, on the east coast of the Baltic Sea. The country is bounded by Estonia to the north and by Lithuania to the south and south-west. To the east it borders Russia, and to the south-east Belarus. Owing to the influence of maritime factors, the climate is relatively temperate, but changeable. Average temperatures in January range from −2.8°C (26.6°F) in the western coastal town of Liepāja to −6.6°C (20.1°F) in the inland town of Daugavpils. Mean temperatures for July range from 16.7°C (62.1°F) in Liepāja to 17.6°C (63.7°F) in Daugavpils. Average annual rainfall in Rīga is 617 mm (24 ins). The official language is Latvian. The major religion is Christianity: most ethnic Latvians are traditionally Lutherans or Latin-rite Catholics, whereas ethnic Russians are mainly adherents of the Russian Orthodox Church. The national flag (proportions 1 by 2) has a maroon background, with a narrow white horizontal stripe superimposed across the central part. The capital is Rīga (Riga).

CONTEMPORARY POLITICAL HISTORY

Historical Context

In November 1917 representatives of Latvian nationalist groups elected a provisional national council, which informed the Russian Government of its intention to establish an independent Latvian state. On 18 November 1918 the Latvian National Council, which had been constituted on the previous day, proclaimed the independent Republic of Latvia, with Jānis Cakste as President. Independence, under the nationalist Government of Kārlis Ulmanis, was fully achieved after the expulsion of the Bolsheviks from Rīga in May 1919, with the aid of German troops, and from the eastern province of Latgale, with Polish and Estonian assistance, in January 1920. A Latvian-Soviet peace treaty was signed in August. Latvia's first Constitution was adopted in 1922. An electoral system based on proportional representation permitted many small parties to be represented in the Saeima (Parliament). As a result, there was little administrative stability, with 18 changes of government in 1922–34. None the less, under the dominant party, the Latvian Farmers' Union (LZS, led by Ulmanis), agrarian reforms were successfully introduced and agricultural exports flourished. The world-wide economic decline of the early 1930s, together with domestic political fragmentation, prompted a (bloodless) *coup d'état* in May 1934, led by Ulmanis. Martial law was introduced, the Saeima was dissolved and all political parties, including the LZS, were banned. A Government of National Unity, assumed the legislative functions of the Saeima, and Ulmanis (hitherto the Prime Minister) became President in 1936.

Under the Treaty of Non-Aggression signed by Germany and the USSR in August 1939, the incorporation of Latvia into the Soviet 'sphere of interests' was agreed by the two powers. A 'treaty of mutual aid' with the USSR allowed the establishment of Soviet military bases in Latvia, and in June 1940 Soviet forces occupied the country. A 'puppet' administration, under Augusts Kirhenšteins, was installed, and the election to the Saeima of Soviet-approved candidates took place in July. The new legislature proclaimed the Latvian Soviet Socialist Republic, which was formally incorporated into the USSR as a constituent union republic in August.

In the first year of Soviet rule almost 33,000 Latvians were deported to Russia and Kazakhstan, and a further 1,350 were killed. Latvian language, traditions and culture were also suppressed. In July 1941 Soviet rule in Latvia was interrupted by German occupation. Most German troops had withdrawn by 1944, although the Kurzeme region, in south-western Latvia, was retained by Germany until the end of the Second World War. Soviet Latvia was re-established in 1944–45 and the process of 'sovietization' was resumed. There were further mass deportations of Latvians to Russia and Central Asia. Independent political activities were prohibited and the Communist Party of Latvia (LKP) exercised exclusive political power, and industrialization encouraged significant and sustained Russian and other Soviet immigration into the republic. Under LKP First Secretary Arvīds Pelše—appointed in 1959—and his successor, Augusts Voss (1966–84), limited autonomy gained in the 1950s was reversed.

There was a revival in Latvian national culture from the late 1970s. In 1986 anti-Soviet demonstrations were suppressed by the police. In 1987 there were further demonstrations on the anniversaries of significant events in Latvian history. The LKP strongly opposed such movements, fostered by the greater freedom of expression permitted under the new Soviet policy of *glasnost* (openness). In 1988 opposition movements in Latvia began to unite, and in October representatives of the leading movements organized the inaugural congress of the Latvian Popular Front (LTF), at which delegates resolved to seek sovereignty for Latvia within a renewed Soviet federation. The LTF, chaired by Dainis Ivāns, rapidly became the largest and most influential political force in Latvia, with an estimated membership of 250,000 by the end of 1988.

In September 1988 Jānis Vagris was appointed First Secretary of the LKP, and the new leadership of the party came increasingly under the influence of members of the LTF. At the end of September Latvian was designated the state language. In March 1989 candidates supported by the LTF won 26 of the 34 contested seats in elections to the USSR's Congress of People's Deputies. On 28 July, following similar measures in Lithuania and Estonia, the Latvian Supreme Soviet (Supreme Council—legislature) adopted a declaration of sovereignty and economic independence. However, there was growing support within the republic for full independence, as advocated by the Latvian National Independence Movement (LNNK), formed in 1988, particularly among ethnic Latvians—who, however, were outnumbered by ethnic Slavs in Rīga and the other large cities in the republic as a result of the Soviet policy of large-scale immigration. In December 1989 candidates supported by the LTF won some 75% of seats contested in local elections.

In January 1990 the Latvian Supreme Soviet voted to abolish the constitutional provisions that guaranteed the LKP's political predominance. In February the Supreme Soviet adopted a declaration condemning the Latvian legislature's decision to request admission to the USSR in 1940, and the flag, state emblems and anthem of pre-1940 Latvia were restored to official use. At elections to the Supreme Soviet in March and April 1990, pro-independence candidates endorsed by the LTF won 131 of the 201 seats; the LKP and the anti-independence Interfront (International Front—dominated by members of the Russian-speaking population) together won 59 seats. The LKP subsequently split into two parties: the majority of delegates at an extraordinary congress rejected a motion to leave the Communist Party of the Soviet Union (CPSU), and elected Alfrēds Rubiks, an opponent of independence, as First Secretary.

The new Supreme Council, convened in early May 1990, elected Anatolijs Gorbunovs of the LKP as its Chairman (*de facto* president of the Republic). On 4 May the Supreme Council adopted a resolution that declared the incorporation of Latvia into the USSR in 1940 as unlawful, and announced the beginning of a transition towards full political and economic independence. Four articles of the 1922 Constitution, defining Latvia as an independent democratic state and asserting the sovereignty of the Latvian people, were restored, and were to form the basis of the newly declared Republic of Latvia's legitimacy. Ivars Godmanis, the Deputy Chairman of the LTF, was elected Prime Minister in a new Government. Meanwhile, a rival body to the Supreme Soviet had been convened at the end of April 1990. This Congress of Latvia had been elected in an unofficial poll, in which some 700,000 people were reported to have participated: only citizens of the pre-1940 republic and their descendants had been entitled to vote. The Congress, in which members of the LNNK predominated, declared Latvia to be an occupied country and adopted resolutions on independence and the withdrawal of Soviet troops.

The Supreme Council's resolutions, although more cautious than the independence declarations adopted in Lithuania and Estonia, severely strained relations with the Soviet authorities.

LATVIA

On 14 May 1990 the Soviet President, Mikhail Gorbachev, issued a decree annulling the Latvian declaration of independence as a violation of the USSR Constitution. The declaration was also opposed within the republic by some ethnic Slavs, who organized protest strikes and demonstrations. In December the Latvian Government claimed that special units (OMON) of the Soviet Ministry of Internal Affairs had caused a series of explosions in Rīga, and in January 1991 OMON troops seized the Rīga Press House. Later in January a 'Committee of Public Salvation', headed by Alfrēds Rubiks, declared itself as a rival Government to the Godmanis administration; on the same day five people died when OMON troops attacked the Ministry of the Interior in Rīga. (In November 1999 10 former Soviet officers were convicted of attempting to overthrow the Latvian Government in 1991; seven received suspended prison sentences of up to four years' duration.)

The attempted seizure of power by Rubiks reinforced opposition in Latvia to inclusion in the new union treaty being prepared by nine Soviet republics. Latvia refused to conduct the all-Union referendum on the future of the USSR, which was scheduled for 17 March 1991 (although some 680,000 people, mostly ethnic Russians and Ukrainians, did participate, unofficially). Instead, a referendum on Latvian independence took place on 3 March. Of those eligible to vote, 87.6% participated, of whom, according to official results, 73.7% endorsed proposals for a democratic, independent Latvian republic.

Domestic Political Affairs

During the attempted overthrow by conservative communists of the Gorbachev administration in the Russian and Soviet capital, Moscow, in August 1991, an emergency session of the Latvian Supreme Council was convened and the full independence of the country proclaimed. As the coup collapsed, the Godmanis Government banned the LKP and detained Rubiks. (In July 1995 Rubiks was found guilty of involvement in the coup attempt. He was released in November 1997.) On 6 September 1991 the USSR State Council formally recognized the independent Republic of Latvia, and the country was admitted to the UN later that month. In late 1991 the Supreme Council adopted legislation guaranteeing the right of citizenship to all citizens of the pre-1940 republic and their descendants. Other residents of Latvia were to be required to apply for naturalization after final legislation governing citizenship was determined by a restored Saeima.

The first legislative elections since the restoration of independence took place in June 1993, with the participation of about 90% of the electorate. Only citizens of pre-1940 Latvia and their descendants were entitled to vote; consequently, some 27% of the adult population (mainly ethnic Russians) were excluded from the elections. A total of 23 parties, movements and alliances contested the poll, of which eight secured representation in the 100-seat Saeima. Latvian Way (LC), a broadly-based movement, emerged as the strongest party, with more than 32% of the votes and 36 seats in the assembly. The results of the elections demonstrated strong popular support for the more moderate nationalist parties, while socialist-orientated parties (including the successor of the LKP, the Latvian Socialist Party—LSP) failed to win representation. The LTF also failed to secure any seats. Only 11 of the elected deputies were non-ethnic Latvians.

The new Saeima voted to restore the 1922 Constitution, and undertook to elect the President of the Republic from among three prominent deputies. At a third round of voting on 7 July 1993 Guntis Ulmanis (great-nephew of Kārlis Ulmanis) of the revived LZS succeeded in winning a majority, with 53 votes. He was inaugurated as President the following day, when he appointed Valdis Birkavs of LC as Prime Minister. The Cabinet of Ministers represented a coalition agreement between LC (the majority partner) and the LZS.

The requirements for naturalization proposed by the Government's draft citizenship law included a minimum of 10 years' permanent residence in Latvia, a knowledge of Latvian to conversational level and an oath of loyalty to the republic. In March 1994 the Saeima approved the establishment of the new post of State Minister for Human Rights, in an attempt to counter accusations of violations of minority rights. In July the Saeima amended the legislation on citizenship, which had the effect of placating some international criticism of Latvia.

Meanwhile, in July 1994 the LZS announced its withdrawal from the governing coalition, following disagreements with LC over economic and agricultural policy. A new Cabinet of Ministers was appointed in September. It, too, was dominated by LC members, including the Prime Minister, Māris Gailis; Birkavs became Deputy Prime Minister and Minister of Foreign Affairs. Latvia was admitted to the Council of Europe (see p. 250) in February 1995.

A general election was held on 30 September–1 October 1995. Nine parties and coalitions succeeded in obtaining the 5% of the votes required for legislative representation; as a result, the Saeima was highly fragmented. LC's share of the 100 seats was reduced significantly, to 17, while the largest number of seats (18) was won by the newly established, leftist Democratic Party Saimnieks (The Master—DPS). The People's Movement for Latvia (Zigerists' Party), an extreme nationalist party led by a German-Latvian, Joahims Zigerists, won 16 seats. In December the Saeima finally endorsed a Cabinet of Ministers led by Andris Šķēle (an entrepreneur with no party affiliation). The new Government was a broad coalition of the DPS, LC, the For Fatherland and Freedom Union (TB), the Latvian National Conservative Party (as the LNNK had been renamed), the LZS and the Latvian Unity Party (LVP). Former Prime Ministers Gailis and Birkavs were appointed to senior positions in the new Cabinet.

On 18 June 1996 the Saeima re-elected Ulmanis for a second three-year term as President. In July it was announced that the LVP was to merge into the DPS. In January 1997 Šķēle resigned as Prime Minister, but was swiftly reappointed by Ulmanis. Local elections conducted in March demonstrated a marked increase in support for the LZS.

By July 1997 the governing coalition had begun to disintegrate, not least because a series of corruption scandals had prompted the resignation of several ministers, and at the end of the month Šķēle's Government resigned. Ulmanis invited Guntars Krasts, the outgoing Minister of the Economy, to form a new administration. In August the Saeima approved Krasts' proposals for a five-party coalition, comprising his own party, the TB/LNNK (formed in the previous month by the merger of the TB and the LNNK—which had reverted to its former designation), the DPS, LC, the LZS and the Christian Democratic Union of Latvia. In early 1998 Krasts was accused of having been negligent, while serving as Minister of the Economy, with regard to a privatization proposal for the state power utility, Latvenergo. In March Krasts formally requested that the Saeima conduct a vote of confidence in his personal integrity, in order to confirm his mandate. The refusal of any parliamentary faction to organize such a vote was interpreted by the Prime Minister as an endorsement of his leadership. In that month Šķēle announced the formation of a new political party, later named the People's Party (TP).

In April 1998 the Minister of the Economy, Atis Sausnītis, was dismissed. Shortly afterwards the DPS withdrew from the governing coalition. Later in the month Krasts survived a parliamentary vote of no confidence proposed by the LZS and LC. At the same session the Saeima approved appointments to a new coalition Government, with members of the Cabinet of Ministers drawn from the LZS, LC, and an alliance of the Latvian National Reform Party and the Latvian Green Party.

In April 1998 draft amendments to the strict legislation regulating rights to citizenship were adopted, in response to recommendations made by the Organization for Security and Co-operation in Europe (OSCE, see p. 385). In June the Saeima approved the amendments, which removed the age-related system of naturalization that allocated dates for application by age-group, granted citizenship to stateless children permanently resident in Latvia born after the 1991 declaration of independence and relaxed the citizenship requirements for Russian-speakers. Although welcomed elsewhere in Europe, the amendments were deemed inadequate by Russia, and nationalist groups within the Latvian legislature secured sufficient support to force a delay to the enactment of the new legislation and the organization of a referendum on the subject. The referendum was conducted concurrently with legislative elections on 3 October; 52.5% of the votes were cast in favour of the amendments, which were promulgated later in the month.

At the legislative elections, Šķēle's TP was the most successful single party, taking 21.2% of the votes (and 24 of the 100 legislative seats), ahead of LC with 18.1% (21 seats) and the TB/LNNK with 14.7% (17 seats). Six parties secured the minimum 5% of the votes necessary for representation in the Saeima. In November 1998 the Saeima approved a minority coalition Government, headed by Vilis Krištopans of LC. The coalition, comprising LC, the TB/LNNK and the New Party (which held eight legislative seats), also drew support from the Latvian Social Democratic Alliance, which controlled 14 seats in the

Saeima. In February 1999 the Social Democrats formally joined the coalition with the appointment of one of their members to the Cabinet of Ministers.

On 17 June 1999 Vaira Viķe-Freiberga was elected President at a seventh round of voting in the Saeima, with the support of 53 deputies. Born in Latvia, but resident in Canada from the end of the Second World War until 1998, Viķe-Freiberga, a non-partisan figure who had trained as a psychologist, became the first female President in central or eastern Europe. At her inauguration on 8 July 1999 Viķe-Freiberga identified as priorities for her presidency Latvia's entry into the European Union (EU, see p. 270) and the North Atlantic Treaty Organization (NATO, see p. 368). Three days before her inauguration, Krištopans announced his Government's resignation, apparently in response to the recent signing by the TB/LNNK of a co-operation accord with the opposition TP. Viķe-Freiberga subsequently asked Šķēle to form a new government. Šķēle thus became Prime Minister for the third time, leading a coalition of his TP, the TB/LNNK and LC.

In July 1999 the Saeima adopted new language legislation, requiring all business and state- and municipally-organized gatherings to be conducted in Latvian. Russia denounced the legislation, which was also condemned by the OSCE, the Council of Europe, the European Commission and, within Latvia, by groups representing ethnic Slavs. Revised legislation, which incorporated amendments urged by the OSCE was approved in December and took effect in September 2000.

Šķēle resigned the premiership in April 2000, after LC withdrew from the governing coalition. President Viķe-Freiberga asked Andris Bērziņš, hitherto the Mayor of Rīga, to form a new government; a coalition administration, principally comprising the TP, LC and the TB/LNNK, was approved by the Saeima in early May. In November 2001 Einars Repše resigned as Governor of the Bank of Latvia, in order to found a new rightist political party, New Era (JL), of which he was elected Chairman in February 2002. In May a new Christian democratic party, the Latvian First Party (LPP), was formed.

In legislative elections, held on 5 October 2002, JL won 23.9% of the votes cast, obtaining 26 seats; the leftist, pro-Russian electoral bloc For Human Rights in a United Latvia (PCTVL), which included the People's Harmony Party (TSP) and the LSP, obtained 18.9% of the votes (25 seats); and the TP received 16.7% (20 seats). Other groups to achieve representation in the Saeima were the Greens' and Farmers' Union (ZZS—an alliance of the Centre Party, the LZS and the Latvian Green Party—LZP), with 12 seats, the LPP (10 seats) and the TB/LNNK (seven); LC failed to obtain a seat in the Saeima. The rate of participation by the electorate was some 72.5%. Repše formed a coalition government comprising members of JL, the LPP, the ZZS and the TB/LNNK, which was approved by the Saeima on 7 November. The Minister of Defence, Ģirts Kristovskis, was the only member of the Cabinet of Ministers to have retained his previous portfolio; a new post of Deputy Prime Minister was established, to which Ainārs Šlesers of the LPP was appointed. In late November Atis Slakteris replaced Šķēle as Chairman of the TP.

In February 2003 the TSP withdrew from the PCTVL alliance, apparently in order to pursue more moderate policies. In June the LSP also announced its withdrawal; the remainder of the PCTVL was officially reconstituted as a united organization later that year. On 20 June Viķe-Freiberga was re-elected unopposed to serve a second term of office as President; she was inaugurated on 8 July. In September tensions emerged within the Government, when its constituent parties (with the exception of JL) issued a statement expressing a lack of confidence in Repše as Prime Minister. A compromise agreement was reached, following inter-party discussions, and Repše remained in office. In January 2004 Repše dismissed Šlesers as Deputy Prime Minister; Šlesers alleged that his removal had been prompted by a proposal to establish a special investigative committee to examine the premier's property dealings. On 5 February, after the LPP had withdrawn from the Government, Repše announced the resignation of his administration. On 20 February President Viķe-Freiberga nominated the Co-Chairman of the LZP, Indulis Emsis, as premier. Emsis went on to secure the support of the ZZS, the LPP and the TP, and on 9 March the Saeima approved a new right-of-centre coalition Government, with the parliamentary support of the TSP.

After accession to the European Union

Following Latvia's accession to the EU on 1 May 2004 (see below), elections to the European Parliament were conducted on 13 June; the opposition TB/LNNK won four of the nine seats available, while its ally JL won two, and PCTVL, the LPP and LC each won one seat. Neither of the two major parties in the ruling coalition obtained representation. Rihards Piks resigned as Minister of Foreign Affairs in order to take his seat in the European Parliament; he was replaced by Artis Pabriks. On 28 October Saeima voted to reject the draft budget, precipitating the collapse of the ruling coalition. President Viķe-Freiberga nominated Aigars Kalvītis of the TP (which had led opposition to the proposed budget) to form a new government, and on 2 December, following prolonged negotiations, the Saeima approved the formation of a Government comprising members of the TP, JL, the ZZS and the LPP. Several members of the outgoing administration were retained in the same posts, including Pabriks and Oskars Spurdziņš (both of the TP), as Minister of Foreign Affairs and Minister of Finance, respectively. The new Government was able to command a majority of votes in the legislature, and a revised draft budget was approved on 20 December.

Local elections, held on 12 March 2005, were marred by allegations of electoral malpractice in Jūrmala and Rēzekne. In early July Jānis Jurkāns resigned as leader of the TSP, in protest at the party's decision, following electoral defeats at both European and local level, to form an alliance with the New Centre, the leader of which, Sergejs Dolgopolovs, had been expelled from the TSP in 2003. The new union, the Harmony Centre (SC) alliance, was joined by the LSP in December 2005. Meanwhile, in October LC and the LPP also formed a political alliance, in preparation for the legislative elections to be held in the following year. In November Jānis Urbanovičs was elected as leader of the TSP.

In October 2005 the Minister of the Interior, Ēriks Jēkabsons, tendered his resignation, after attracting criticism for his performance in office, and for his contacts with the controversial, self-exiled Russian businessman Boris Berezovskii. In November Jēkabsons was replaced by Dzintars Jaundzeikars of the LPP. In December Repše resigned as Minister of Defence, following the announcement of a criminal investigation into his property investments; he also resigned his parliamentary seat and withdrew from the leadership of JL. Linda Mūrniece succeeded Repše as Minister of Defence. In March 2006 Kalvītis dismissed Šlesers as Minister of Transport, after evidence emerged that implicated him in electoral malpractice in the 2005 municipal elections. In April 2006 the Ministry of the Interior launched an inquiry into allegations of financial misconduct by the JL Minister of the Economy, Krišjānis Kariņš. JL accused the LPP of misusing its control of the interior ministry and subsequently withdrew its seven representatives from the Government, after Kalvītis (of the TP) rejected its demand that the LPP be removed from the governing coalition. On 8 April the Saeima approved a three-party minority Government (excluding JL).

At elections to the Saeima on 7 October 2006 the TP won 19.6% of the votes cast and 23 seats, the ZZS alliance 16.7% (18 seats), JL 16.4% (18 seats), the SC alliance 14.4% (17 seats), the LPP, allied with LC, 8.6% (10 seats), the TB/LNNK 6.9% (eight seats) and PCTVL 6.0% (six seats). The outgoing governing coalition of the TP, the ZZS and the LPP thus secured a narrow parliamentary majority. Around 62.3% of the electorate participated in the elections, significantly less than had done so in 2002. Kalvītis invited the TB/LNNK to join the governing coalition in order to strengthen its parliamentary majority and subsequently formed a new, four-party administration, which was approved by the Saeima on 7 November. In December a congress of the TSP approved the consolidation of the SC alliance as a merged association (although the LSP retained its separate status as an affiliated party).

On 31 May 2007 the Saeima elected Valdis Zatlers, the candidate proposed by the ruling coalition, as President, to succeed Viķe-Freiberga. Zatlers (a medical doctor without political experience) was inaugurated on 8 July. In August the LPP officially merged with LC; the reconstituted LPP/LC was jointly chaired by Šlesers and Godmanis.

In mid-September 2007 Jurijs Strods of the TB/LNNK resigned as Minister of the Economy. On 22 September the Chairman of the Saeima, Emsis, resigned, after the opening of a criminal investigation into allegations that he had given false testimony in a case related to corruption in the city of Ventspils. He was succeeded by Gundars Daudze, a close ally of the controversial Mayor of Ventspils, Aivars Lembergs, who had been arrested for corruption and abuse of public office in March. In October Kalvītis dismissed the Minister of Regional Development and Local Government, who had voted against a government motion to remove the director of the anti-corruption bureau, Aleksejs Loskutovs, who had been suspended from his post in connection with accounting irregularities. Later in the month Artis Pabriks resigned as Minister of Foreign Affairs in protest at the suspension of Loskutovs, which opponents of Kalvītis claimed was motivated by the bureau's investigations into corruption allegations involving members of the ruling coalition. Although the crisis precipitated a mass anti-Government demonstration in Rīga, a motion of no confidence in the administration presented in the Saeima was defeated. At the end of October the Minister of Welfare resigned, following opposition to her proposed pensions reforms. In early December Kalvītis finally tendered the resignation of his Government. Zatlers, after rejecting an attempt by the TP to propose a further candidate as Prime Minister, nominated Godmanis (who had hitherto held the interior portfolio) to the premiership. On 20 December the Saeima approved a new coalition Government, comprising representatives of the TP, the LPP/LC, the ZZS and the TB/LNNK.

In April 2008 a new, centre-right political party, the Civic Union (PS), was founded by two prominent politicians, Sandra Kalniete (formerly a member of JL) and Valdis Kristovskis (formerly of the TB/LNNK). Also in April it was announced that at least 10% of the electorate had signed a petition in support of a constitutional amendment that would enable voters to dissolve the legislature by referendum, thereby requiring a national referendum to be held on the matter (The referendum was subsequently scheduled for 2 August). In June Loskutovs (who remained under investigation) was removed from his post by a vote in the Saeima. On 2 August the proposed constitutional amendment failed to secure sufficient support (a minimum of 50% of the registered electorate) at the referendum. However, Zatlers described the referendum result, which was equivalent to about 40.2% of the electorate voting in favour, as significant, and submitted a legal initiative to the Saeima for consideration of the amendment. In September public sector workers staged a large demonstration to demand improved salaries and conditions.

In November 2008 the severe impact of the international financial crisis upon Latvia (see Economic Affairs) obliged the Government to seek funding from international institutions, notably the International Monetary Fund (IMF, see p. 143), which demanded that Latvia increase levels of taxation and reduce public expenditure. In January 2009 around 10,000 people attended a demonstration in Rīga to protest against perceived economic mismanagement by the Government and in support of the holding of early legislative elections; after ensuing riots, some 100 protesters were arrested. On the following day Zatlers issued an ultimatum threatening to dissolve the Saeima in the event that it (and the Government) had not, by the end of March, implemented a number of political reforms (the adoption of a constitutional amendment on the dissolution of the legislature by a national referendum initiated by voters, the reformation of the electoral law, the appointment of a new director of the anti-corruption bureau, and the establishment of a committee to supervise the distribution of IMF funds). In early February the Government survived a parliamentary motion of no confidence, initiated by JL. However, following protests by farmers about increasing hardship in the sector, the Minister of Agriculture resigned. After the Cabinet of Ministers failed to adopt proposed measures to reduce the number of existing government ministries, Zatlers declared that he had lost confidence in Godmanis as Prime Minister. On 20 February, after the TP and the ZZS threatened to withdraw from the governing coalition, Godmanis tendered his resignation.

Recent developments: the Government of Valdis Dombrovskis

President Zatlers nominated Valdis Dombrovskis, a member of JL and a former Minister of Finance, as Prime Minister. Subsequently, JL invited all parties represented in the Saeima, except PCTVL, to enter into consultations on the formation of a new administration. On 12 March 2009 a new coalition Government, comprising representatives of JL, the TP, the ZZS alliance, the TB/LNNK and the PS and headed by Dombrovskis (who also held the portfolio of children, the family and social integration), was approved by the Saeima; new appointments included those of Repše as Minister of Finance and Artis Kampars of JL as Minister of the Economy. On the same day the Saeima appointed a new director of the anti-corruption bureau. In late March Zatlers announced that he would not act upon his threat to dissolve the Saeima, owing to the installation of a new Government and progress towards the adoption of political and economic reforms. On 8 April the Saeima approved amendments to two articles of the Constitution, enabling voters to initiate a referendum on the dissolution of the legislature during the second and third years of its term; the changes were to enter into effect following the next parliamentary elections.

On 6 June 2009 elections to the European Parliament took place. Of the eight seats allocated to Latvia, the PS and the SC both won two, while PCTVL, the LPP/LC, the TB/LNNK and JL each won one. On the same day local elections were held, prior to the introduction of a new, single-tier structure of local government across the country from the beginning of July. The SC performed strongly in the local elections, and secured just over one-third of the vote in Rīga. In mid-June the Minister of Health, Ivars Eglītis, resigned, in protest at spending reductions in the health sector, approved as part of efforts to satisfy conditions for the disbursement of EU funds. In August high-level tensions became evident, when the Governor of the Bank of Latvia, Ilmārs Rimševics, publicly disagreed with Dombrovskis during a televised broadcast of an interview with the Prime Minister, following media accusations that Rimševics' earnings were excessive. In March 2010 the founding congress was held for a new right-wing alliance, Unity, comprising JL, the PS and the Society for a Different Politics. (The admission of the TB/LNNK to the alliance, sought by the leadership of that party, was rejected.) In mid-March the TP withdrew its five ministers (including the Minister of Foreign Affairs) from the governing coalition, after Dombrovskis refused to sign an economic agreement with the party, accusing it of populism. After unsuccessful negotiations with the LPP/LC, Dombrovskis was expected to lead a minority Government until the legislative elections scheduled for 2 October. At the end of April Aivis Ronis, a former ambassador to the USA and to NATO, was appointed as the new Minister of Foreign Affairs. Meanwhile, another right-wing electoral coalition headed by Ulmanis, the Alliance for A Good Latvia, comprising the TP and the LPP/LC, was established.

At the legislative elections, held as scheduled on 2 October 2010, the Unity coalition was the most successful group, obtaining 31.9% of the votes cast and a total of 33 seats. The SC demonstrated an increase in support, receiving 26.6% and 29 seats. The ZZS alliance obtained 20.1% of the votes cast and 22 seats. A coalition of the nationalist All For Latvia party and the TB/LNNK obtained 7.8% of the votes cast and eight seats, and For A Good Latvia obtained 7.8% and eight seats. Despite the increase in support for the SC, which was strongly opposed to the austerity measures that had been introduced in recent months (including public sector wage cuts of up to 30%), Dombrovskis formed a coalition Government comprising the parties of the Unity coalition and the ZZS alliance, although attempts to negotiate the inclusion of the TB/LNNK proved unsuccessful. None the less, the administration held 55 of the 100 deputies in the Saeima. Among the principal appointments in the new Government were Ģirts Kristovskis of the PS as Minister of Foreign Affairs, Artis Kampars of JL as Minister of the Economy and Aigars Stokenbergs as Minister of Justice. Mūrniece was one of three ministers from the outgoing Government to be re-appointed, retaining her position as Minister of the Interior.

In December 2010 the Saeima voted to approve the budget for 2011, which (despite a return to economic growth) provided for further austerity measures, including both increases in taxation and reductions in public spending.

In mid-February 2011 Mūrniece tendered her resignation as Minister of the Interior, after persistent concerns about corruption within the police and security forces were exacerbated by an incident, in late January, in which a group of police officers (including members of a special police unit) were discovered robbing a casino in Jekabpils; one of the police officers dispatched to the casino to apprehend the criminals was shot dead, and two others were injured. Dombrovskis delayed the consideration of Mūrniece's resignation, and eventually requested that she remain in office.

Foreign Affairs
Regional relations

Latvia's post-independence relations with Russia were troubled by two questions. The first concerned the citizenship and linguistic rights of Latvia's large Russian-speaking community (see above). The second was the question of the 100,000 former Soviet troops still stationed in Latvia (jurisdiction over whom had been transferred, following the dissolution of the USSR, to Russia).

Following negotiations, withdrawal of the troops began in early 1992. The process was hampered by a series of disagreements, in particular concerning a Russian military radar station at Skrunda, in western Latvia, that the Russians wished to retain. In April 1994 agreements were concluded on the complete withdrawal of the remaining 10,000 Russian troops by the end of August, as well as on social guarantees for the estimated 22,000 Russian military pensioners residing in Latvia. Installations at the Skrunda base were subsequently dismantled.

Negotiations regarding the demarcation of the Latvian–Russian border, and Latvia's claim to some 1,640 sq km of land transferred from Latvia to Russia during the Soviet era, commenced in 1996. Latvia initially insisted that any future border agreement should include a reference to the 1920 treaty in which Russia recognized Latvia's independence. However, in 1997 the Latvian administration abandoned this demand, and agreed that claims to property in the disputed territory should be discussed separately from the main border agreement. In March a draft treaty on the demarcation of the border was agreed by the two countries, and full agreement on a border treaty was reached in October, although it remained unratified. In January 2007 Latvia agreed to remove a declaration from the draft treaty, which Russia had interpreted as making a territorial claim over the land that had formerly constituted part of Latvia, thereby providing for the official endorsement of the treaty. In February the Saeima approved legislation authorizing the Government to sign the border treaty with Russia. On 27 March Kalvītis and the Russian premier, Mikhail Fradkov, signed the treaty in Moscow. The treaty was endorsed by Viķe-Freiberga in May and by Russian President Vladimir Putin in October; a legal challenge against it, proposed by JL, was rejected by the Constitutional Court in November. In August 2008 Zatlers, together with the Presidents of Estonia, Lithuania and Poland, condemned a Russian military offensive in Georgia (see the chapter on Georgia).

Relations with Russia became further strained in March 1998, following the organization, in Rīga, of a rally of Latvian veterans of Nazi German *Waffen SS* units, who had fought Soviet forces during the Second World War; the participation of senior Latvian politicians and military personnel attracted particular criticism from the Russian authorities. Government officials and serving military officers were not permitted to participate in a further veterans' rally held in March 2000. Meanwhile, tensions arising from repeated Russian threats to impose economic sanctions against Latvia, if the Government did not promptly address perceived infringements of minority rights, were exacerbated by Latvia's new state language law (see above) in 1999. The revised language law, as approved by the Saeima in December, was again denounced by Russia. Economic issues threatened to raise further tensions between the two countries in early 2003, following Russia's decision to cease using the port of Ventspils for its petroleum exports, primarily owing to the opening of a new Russian petroleum terminal on the Baltic coast at Primorsk, Leningrad Oblast. Russia also condemned amendments to legislation on education, which took effect from September 2004, in accordance with which 60% of lessons in minority schools were to be taught in the Latvian language; in February thousands of ethnic Russians had protested in Rīga against the reforms.

On 9 May 2005 President Viķe-Freiberga travelled to Moscow to attend celebrations to commemorate the 60th anniversary of the end of the Second World War in Europe. (Notably, the Heads of State of Estonia and Lithuania declined to attend.) Three days later the Saeima adopted a declaration denouncing the Soviet occupation of Latvia and urging Russia to accept moral, legal and financial responsibility for the losses incurred by the Latvian people under Soviet rule. In late May the Saeima ratified the Council of Europe's Framework Convention for the Protection of National Minorities; however, a declaration was appended, stipulating that only Latvian citizens would be regarded as members of a national minority, thereby excluding large numbers of ethnic Slavs who had failed to obtain citizenship. In August a commission was established to calculate the economic damage and human loss sustained by Latvia under Soviet rule. Latvia (together with Estonia and Lithuania) was concerned at the signature in September of an agreement between Russia and Germany on the construction of a North European Gas Pipeline, which was to carry natural gas from Russia to Germany under the Baltic Sea, bypassing the Baltic countries. In August 2006 the Latvian authorities introduced a new citizenship law provision, stipulating that applicants who failed a Latvian language test three times would be disqualified permanently from obtaining citizenship.

Latvia enjoys close relations with Estonia and Lithuania, and the three countries have established institutions to promote co-operation, including the interparliamentary Baltic Assembly and the Baltic Council of Ministers (which meets twice yearly). In 1992 Latvia became a founder member, with Estonia, Lithuania and other countries of the region, of the Council of the Baltic Sea States, a principal aim of which was to assist the political and economic development of its former communist member states (including Russia). Differences arose in the mid-1990s between Latvia and its two closest Baltic neighbours, in particular concerning the demarcation of maritime borders. However, agreement on the delimitation of the sea border with Estonia was reached in May 1996, and the document was ratified by both countries' legislatures in August. A further agreement on fishing rights was concluded in 1997, in which year the demarcation of the land border between the two countries was completed. Negotiations between Latvia and Lithuania on their maritime border were complicated in 1996 by the Saeima's ratification of an agreement with two foreign petroleum companies to explore and develop offshore oilfields in disputed areas of the Baltic Sea. Although the two countries signed an agreement on the delimitation of their territorial waters in 1999, protests from the Latvian fishing industry prevented the Saeima from ratifying the agreement. In 2000 a protocol was signed on the re-demarcation of the land border between the two countries. In early 2006 the leaders of all three Baltic countries reached agreement on the construction of a new nuclear power plant to replace that at Ignalina, Lithuania, and on various other measures aimed at reducing Russian dominance in the supply of energy.

A priority of Latvian foreign policy was attaining full membership of the EU. Latvia applied for membership in October 1995, and formal negotiations on accession commenced in February 2000. In December 2002 Latvia, together with nine other countries, was formally invited to become a full member of the EU in 2004. A referendum on EU membership was held on 20 September 2003. Of the 72.5% of the electorate who participated in the plebiscite, 66.8% voted in support of Latvia's accession to the EU, although in certain areas of the country, particularly in the predominately Russian-speaking, south-eastern regions around the second city of Daugavpils, a majority of votes were cast against EU membership. The country became a full member on 1 May 2004. In December 2007 Latvia, together with eight other nations, implemented the EU's Schengen Agreement, enabling its citizens to travel to and from other member states, without border controls. On 8 May 2008 the Saeima voted to ratify the EU's Lisbon Treaty.

CONSTITUTION AND GOVERNMENT

Under the terms of the 1922 Constitution, which was restored in July 1993 and subsequently amended, Latvia is an independent democratic parliamentary republic. The supreme legislative body is the Saeima (Parliament), the 100 members of which are elected by universal adult suffrage for a four-year term. The President of the Republic, who is Head of State, is elected by a secret ballot of the Saeima, also for a period of four years. The President, who is also Head of the Armed Forces, may not serve for more than two consecutive terms. Executive power is held by the Cabinet of Ministers, which is headed by the Prime Minister. The Prime Minister is appointed by the President; the remaining members of the Cabinet are nominated by the Prime Minister. Judges are independent, and their appointment is confirmed by the Saeima. For administrative purposes, Latvia is divided into nine cities (including the capital, Rīga) and 109 municipalities.

REGIONAL AND INTERNATIONAL CO-OPERATION

Latvia is a member of the European Bank for Reconstruction and Development (EBRD, see p. 265), the Council of the Baltic Sea States (see p. 248), the Baltic Council (see p. 459), the Council of Europe (see p. 250) and the Organization for Security and Co-operation in Europe (see p. 385). In 2004 it acceded to the European Union (see p. 270).

Latvia joined the UN in 1991, and was admitted to the World Trade Organization (see p. 430) in 1999. The country joined the North Atlantic Treaty Organization (see p. 368) in 2004.

ECONOMIC AFFAIRS

In 2009, according to estimates by the World Bank, Latvia's gross national income (GNI), measured at average 2007–09 prices, was US $27,937m., equivalent to $12,390 per head (or $16,510 per

LATVIA

head on an international purchasing-power parity basis). During 2000–09, it was estimated, the population decreased by an annual average of 0.6%, while gross domestic product (GDP) per head increased at an average annual rate of 4.7%, in real terms. Overall GDP increased, in real terms, at an average annual rate of 4.1% in 2000–09; according to World Bank estimates, real GDP declined by 4.6% in 2008 and by 18.0% in 2009.

Agriculture (including hunting, forestry and fishing) contributed 3.3% of GDP and provided 9.0% of employment in 2009. The principal sectors are dairy farming and pig-breeding. Cereals, potatoes, sugar beet and fodder crops are the main crops grown. As part of the process of land reform and privatization, the dissolution of collective and state farms was undertaken in the early 1990s. Fishing makes an important contribution to the economy (an estimated 70% of the total annual catch is exported). Output of the forestry industry increased from 1996. According to UN estimates, agricultural GDP increased, in real terms, by an average of 3.0% per year in 2000–09; the real GDP of the sector increased by 3.4% in 2009.

Industry (comprising mining and quarrying, manufacturing, construction and utilities) contributed 20.6% of GDP and provided 23.3% of employment in 2009. According to UN estimates, industrial GDP increased, in real terms, at an average annual rate of 2.9% in 2000–09; the GDP of the industrial sector decreased, in real terms, by 22.4% in 2009.

Mining and quarrying contributed just 0.5% of GDP in 2009, and employed 0.3% of workers in 2008. Latvia has limited mineral resources, the most important being peat, dolomite, limestone, gypsum, amber, gravel and sand. Offshore and onshore petroleum reserves have been located.

The manufacturing sector contributed 9.9% of GDP and (along with utilities) provided 15.6% of employment in 2009. According to UN estimates, real manufacturing GDP increased by an average of 1.6% per year in 2000–09; the GDP of the sector decreased, in real terms, by 19.2% in 2009.

The construction sector contributed 6.6% of GDP and provided 7.7% of employment in 2009. During 2000–09, according to UN estimates, the GDP of the sector increased at an average annual rate of 5.3%. However, construction GDP declined by 2.6% in 2008 and a further decline of 33.6% was recorded in 2009.

Latvia is highly dependent on imported fuels to provide energy. In 2009 mineral products represented 17.2% of the total value of Latvia's imports. Electric energy is supplied primarily by Estonia and Lithuania, and petroleum products are supplied by Russia and Lithuania. In 2007 hydroelectric plants provided some 57.3% of annual domestic electricity production in Latvia; a further 40.3% was derived from natural gas.

The services sector contributed 76.1% of GDP and accounted for 67.7% of employment in 2009. According to UN estimates, the GDP of the sector increased, in real terms, by an annual average of 5.1% in 2000–09; real services GDP declined by 14.2% in 2009. The tourism sector expanded markedly in the mid-2000s, following a significant expansion in air services between Rīga and cities in central and western Europe. Total visitor arrivals numbered 753,875 in 2009, compared with 545,366 in 2004.

In 2009 Latvia recorded a visible trade deficit of US $1,822m., and there was a surplus of $2,284m. on the current account of the balance of payments. The principal source of imports in 2009 was Lithuania, which accounted for 17.0% of total imports; other major sources were Germany, Russia, Poland and Estonia. The main market for exports in that year was Lithuania, which accounted for 16.4% of the total; other significant purchasers were Estonia, Russia, Germany and Sweden. The principal exports in 2009 were wood and wood articles (accounting for 16.5% of total exports), followed by machinery and electrical equipment, base metals and manufactures, chemicals, foodstuffs, beverages and tobacco, mineral products, and textiles. The principal imports in that year were mineral products (accounting for 17.2% of total imports), machinery and electrical equipment, chemicals, foodstuffs, beverages and tobacco, textiles, base metals, and vehicles and transport equipment.

In 2009 there was a budgetary deficit of 1,183m. lats (equivalent to 9.0% of GDP). Latvia's general government gross debt was 4.295m. lats in 2009, equivalent to 32.8% of GDP. At the end of 2008 Latvia's external debt totalled US $42,108m., of which $2,258m. was public and publicly guaranteed debt. In that year the cost of debt-servicing was equivalent to 37.7% of the value of exports of goods and services. Annual consumer-price inflation averaged 5.1% in 2000–10. Consumer prices increased by 3.5% in 2009 and declined by 1.1% in 2010. According to official statistics, some 16.9% of the population were registered as unemployed in 2009.

Following its accession to the European Union (EU, see p. 270) in 2004, Latvia was admitted to the EU's exchange rate mechanism (ERM II) in 2005, in preparation for its planned adoption of the common European currency, the euro. After recording strong growth in 2000–06, GDP declined by 4.6% in 2008, as a consequence of the international financial crisis, which affected Latvia particularly severely. In December, after the legislature adopted a revised budget providing for extensive austerity measures, the IMF approved an economic stabilization programme, which was to be funded by a loan of €7,500m., financed by the EU, the IMF, and Sweden, Denmark and Norway. Disputes within the governing coalition resulted in the resignation of Prime Minister Ivars Godmanis in February and the installation of a new administration, under Valdis Dombrovskis. The Dombrovskis Government implemented further austerity measures, adopting a supplementary budget in June. In 2009 GDP declined by an estimated 18%, and the rate of unemployment reached 16.9%, increasing to around 20% by the following year. In February 2010 the IMF stated that the economic situation in Latvia appeared to have stabilized, and predicted a modest economic recovery from late that year, based on an incipient resurgence in export trade. Real GDP was predicted to decline by 4.0% in 2010, but to record an increase of 3.3% in 2011. In May 2010 the Constitutional Court ruled that a government decision to reduce pensions by 70% for retired people in employment, and by 10% for other pensioners, was unconstitutional; discussions on a temporary reduction in funding for the pensions system were ongoing in 2011. A new coalition Government, again led by Dombrovskis, which was returned to office following the legislative elections of October 2010, announced further reductions in expenditure and increases in taxation in the 2011 budget. By mid-2011 the Government maintained that the consequences of the austerity measures, in particular the reduction of the budgetary deficit (which was forecast to decline from 8.5% of GDP in 2010 to 5.5% in 2011), would permit Latvia to attain its target of adopting the euro in 2014.

PUBLIC HOLIDAYS

2012: 1 January (New Year's Day), 6–9 April (Easter), 1 May (Labour Day), 4 May (Declaration of Independence Day), 23–24 June (Midsummer Festival), 18 November (National Day, proclamation of the Republic), 25–26 December (Christmas), 31 December (New Year's Eve).

LATVIA

Statistical Survey

Source (unless otherwise stated): Central Statistical Bureau of Latvia, Lāčplēša iela 1, Rīga 1301; tel. 6736-6850; fax 6783-0137; e-mail csb@csb.lv; internet www.csb.lv.

Area and Population

AREA, POPULATION AND DENSITY

Area (sq km)	64,559*
Population (census results)†	
12 January 1989	2,666,567
31 March 2000	
Males	1,094,964
Females	1,282,419
Total	2,377,383
Population (official estimates at 1 January)	
2009	2,261,294
2010	2,248,374
2011‡	2,229,500
Density (per sq km) at 1 January 2011	34.5

* 24,926 sq miles.
† Figures refer to the resident population.
‡ Figure is rounded to the nearest 100 persons.

POPULATION BY AGE AND SEX
(official estimates at 1 January 2010)

	Males	Females	Total
0–14	158,056	151,098	309,154
15–64	752,167	796,844	1,549,011
65 and over	127,228	262,981	390,209
Total	1,037,451	1,210,923	2,248,374

POPULATION BY ETHNIC GROUP
(official estimates, 1 January 2010)

	Number	%
Latvian	1,335,646	59.4
Russian	620,017	27.6
Belarusian	80,259	3.6
Ukrainian	55,330	2.5
Polish	52,313	2.3
Lithuanian	29,916	1.3
Others	74,893	3.3
Total	2,248,374	100.0

PRINCIPAL TOWNS
(population at 1 January 2010, official estimates)

Rīga (Riga, capital)	706,413	Jūrmala		55,858
Daugavpils	103,922	Ventspils		42,734
Liepāja	84,074	Rēzekne		35,074
Jelgava	64,898			

BIRTHS, MARRIAGES AND DEATHS

	Registered live births		Registered marriages		Registered deaths	
	Number	Rate (per 1,000)	Number	Rate (per 1,000)	Number	Rate (per 1,000)
2002	20,044	8.6	9,738	4.2	32,498	13.9
2003	21,006	9.0	9,989	4.3	32,437	13.9
2004	20,334	8.8	10,370	4.5	32,024	13.8
2005	21,497	9.3	12,554	5.5	32,777	14.2
2006	22,264	9.7	14,616	6.4	33,098	14.5
2007	23,273	10.2	15,486	6.8	33,042	14.5
2008	23,948	10.6	12,946	5.7	31,006	13.7
2009	21,677	9.6	9,925	4.4	29,897	13.2

Life expectancy (years at birth, WHO estimates) 71 (males 66; females 77) in 2008 (Source: WHO, *World Health Statistics*).

IMMIGRATION AND EMIGRATION

	2008	2009	2010
Immigrants	3,465	2,688	1,974
Emigrants	6,007	7,388	10,107

ECONOMICALLY ACTIVE POPULATION
(annual averages, '000 persons aged 15–74 years)

	2006	2007	2008
Agriculture, hunting and forestry	117.8	107.5	87.3
Fishing	2.4	2.8	1.8
Mining and quarrying	3.8	6.6	2.8
Manufacturing	169.6	164.8	171.0
Electricity, gas and water	22.3	20.7	21.3
Construction	103.9	125.6	125.5
Wholesale and retail trade; repair of motor vehicles, motorcycles and personal and household goods	170.2	184.6	186.6
Hotels and restaurants	29.2	31.2	30.4
Transport, storage and communications	100.8	104.0	105.8
Financial intermediation	25.1	22.0	19.6
Real estate, renting and business activities	60.7	74.0	78.1
Public administration and defence, compulsory social security	88.2	83.9	86.6
Education	87.8	81.8	90.4
Health and social work	51.0	50.1	54.7
Other community, social and personal service activities	49.5	53.7	57.4
Sub-total	**1,082.3**	**1,113.3**	**1,119.3**
Activities not adequately defined	5.3	5.7	4.8
Total employed	**1,087.6**	**1,119.0**	**1,124.1**
Males	559.2	573.5	571.5
Females	528.5	545.5	552.6
Unemployed	79.9	72.1	91.6
Total labour force	**1,167.5**	**1,191.1**	**1,215.7**

2009: Agriculture, hunting, forestry and fishing 88.7; Manufacturing and electricity, gas and water supply 154.2; Construction 75.7; Wholesale and retail trade, and repair of motor vehicles, motorcycles and personal and household goods; hotels and restaurants 193.2; Transport, storage and communications 97.7; Financial intermediation, and real estate, renting and business activities 95.8; Public administration and defence, and compulsory social security 78.2; Education 88.2; Health and social work 53.5; Other activities 61.1; *Total employed* 986.7 (males 480.3, females 506.4); Unemployed 200.7; *Total labour force* 1,187.4.

Health and Welfare

KEY INDICATORS

Total fertility rate (children per woman, 2008)	1.4
Under-5 mortality rate (per 1,000 live births, 2008)	9
HIV/AIDS (% of persons aged 15–49, 2007)	0.8
Physicians (per 1,000 head, 2006)	3.1
Hospital beds (per 1,000 head, 2006)	7.6
Health expenditure (2007): US $ per head (PPP)	1,071
Health expenditure (2007): % of GDP	6.2
Health expenditure (2007): public (% of total)	57.9
Access to water (% of persons, 2008)	99
Access to sanitation (% of persons, 2008)	78
Total carbon dioxide emissions ('000 metric tons, 2007)	7,819.0
Carbon dioxide emissions per head (metric tons, 2007)	3.4
Human Development Index (2010): ranking	48
Human Development Index (2010): value	0.769

For sources and definitions, see explanatory note on p. vi.

LATVIA

Agriculture

PRINCIPAL CROPS
('000 metric tons)

	2007	2008	2009
Wheat	807.3	989.6	1,036.4
Barley	350.5	307.1	265.5
Rye	181.1	194.9	162.2
Oats	130.2	141.5	141.4
Triticale (wheat-rye hybrid)	37.9	35.2	33.3
Potatoes	642.1	673.4	525.4
Sugar beet	10.8	—	n.a.
Peas, dry	1.4	1.1	2.6
Rapeseed	196.9	198.5	204.7
Cabbages and other brassicas	51.5	53.4	61.9
Cucumbers and gherkins	4.5	0.8	0.6
Onions, dry	16.7	17.3	29.8
Carrots and turnips	30.4	36.4	43.3
Apples	30.5	28.9	12.8
Currants	2.1	0.5	0.4

Aggregate production ('000 metric tons, may include official, semi-official or estimated data): Total cereals 1,535.2 in 2007, 1,689.4 in 2008, 1,663.2 in 2009; Total roots and tubers 642.1 in 2007, 673.4 in 2008, 525.4 in 2009; Total vegetables (incl. melons) 156.4 in 2007, 131.6 in 2008, 170.9 in 2009; Total fruits (excl. melons) 40.3 in 2007, 35.7 in 2008, 18.3 in 2009.

Source: FAO.

LIVESTOCK
('000 head at 1 January)

	2007	2008	2009
Cattle	377	399	380
Pigs	417	414	384
Sheep	41	54	67
Goats	14	13	13
Horses	14	13	13
Chickens	4,097*	4,000*	4000†
Turkeys	660*	621*	630†

* Unofficial figure.
† FAO estimate.

Source: FAO.

LIVESTOCK PRODUCTS
('000 metric tons, unless otherwise indicated)

	2007	2008	2009
Cattle meat	22.8	21.4	20.5
Pig meat	40.4	40.7	38.8
Chicken meat	20.6	23.1	23.2
Cows' milk	838.4	832.1	828.1
Hen eggs	42.1	40.3	45.6

Source: FAO.

Forestry

ROUNDWOOD REMOVALS
('000 cubic metres, excl. bark)

	2007	2008	2009
Sawlogs, veneer logs and logs for sleepers	6,717	4,836	6,213
Pulpwood	3,268	2,461	1,701
Other industrial wood	1,160	910	759
Fuel wood	1,028	598	1,736
Total	12,173	8,806	10,409

Source: FAO.

SAWNWOOD PRODUCTION
('000 cubic metres, incl. railway sleepers)

	2007	2008	2009
Coniferous (softwood)	2,881	2,246	2,149
Broadleaved (hardwood)	579	299	351
Total	3,459	2,545	2,500

Source: FAO.

Fishing

('000 metric tons, live weight)

	2006	2007	2008
Capture	140.4	155.3	157.9
Atlantic cod	4.6	4.3	4.0
Jack and horse mackerels	17.8	22.5	31.3
Atlantic herring	21.8	22.4	22.5
Sardinellas	15.6	13.2	11.5
European sprat	54.6	60.5	57.3
Chub mackerel	3.6	8.9	8.1
Northern prawn	1.6	2.2	1.6
Aquaculture	0.6	0.7	0.6
Total catch	141.0	156.0	158.5

Source: FAO.

Mining

('000 metric tons)

	2006	2007	2008
Peat	1,000.0	541.2	865.5
Gypsum	235.7	346.1	349.1
Limestone	468.1	388.1	515.9

Industry

SELECTED PRODUCTS
('000 metric tons, unless otherwise indicated)

	2005	2006	2007
Sausages	44	45	43
Preserved fish	76	70	61
Yoghurt	57	65	80
Ice-cream (million litres)	13.9	14.4	12.4
Beer ('000 hectolitres)	1,285	1,383	1,414
Plywood ('000 cu metres)	267	277	318
Electric energy (million kWh)	4,905	4,891	4,771

Source: UN Industrial Commodity Statistics Database.

LATVIA

Finance

CURRENCY AND EXCHANGE RATES

Monetary Units
100 santimi = 1 lats.

Sterling, Dollar and Euro Equivalents (31 December 2010)
£1 sterling = 83.75 santimi;
US $1 = 53.50 santimi;
€1 = 71.49 santimi;
10 lats = £11.94 = $18.69 = €13.99.

Average Exchange Rate (lats per US $)
2008   0.4808
2009   0.5056
2010   0.5305

GOVERNMENT FINANCE
(general government operations, million lats)

Summary of Balances

	2006	2007	2008
Revenue	4,002.3	5,326.3	5,719.0
Less Expense	3,786.7	4,495.0	5,534.0
Net operating balance	215.6	831.2	185.0
Less Net acquisition of non-financial assets	245.9	736.5	724.0
Net lending/borrowing	−30.3	94.7	−539.0

Revenue

	2006	2007	2008
Tax revenue	2,340.5	3,098.2	3,335.0
Taxes on income, profits and capital gains	911.0	1,287.7	1,532.0
Taxes on goods and services	1,331.4	1,697.9	1,700.0
Taxes on property	66.4	74.3	71.0
Social contributions	958.5	1,265.0	1,402.0
Grants	267.9	461.5	431.0
Other revenue	435.4	501.6	551.0
Total	4,002.3	5,326.3	5,719.0

Expense/Outlays

Expense by economic type	2006	2007	2008
Compensation of employees	970.4	1,392.5	1,679.0
Use of goods and services	664.0	799.2	933.0
Interest	57.6	51.7	64.0
Subsidies	72.2	1,008.6	1,293.0
Grants	—	139.1	—
Social benefits	927.7	1,088.5	1,385.0
Other expense	1,094.8	15.5	180.0
Total	3,786.7	4,495.0	5,534.0

Outlays by function of government	2006	2007	2008
General public services	599.2	600.4	678.0
Defence	168.4	211.1	244.0
Public order and safety	247.7	369.2	357.0
Education	626.3	853.6	1,052.0
Health care	421.0	527.8	579.0
Social security and social welfare	1,010.6	1,200.5	1,515.0
Housing and community amenities	205.2	184.6	201.0
Recreation, sport, cultural and religious affairs	149.5	240.7	282.0
Economic affairs	604.7	901.6	1,183.0
Environmental protection	—	142.2	167.0
Total	4,032.6	5,231.6	6,258.0

Source: IMF, *Government Finance Statistics Yearbook*.

2009 (general government operations, million lats): Total revenue 4,499.9; Total expenditure 5,682.9.

INTERNATIONAL RESERVES
(US $ million at 31 December)

	2007	2008	2009
Gold (national valuation)	204.81	220.20	274.78
IMF special drawing rights	0.17	0.38	186.72
Reserve position in IMF	0.09	0.09	0.09
Foreign exchange	5,553.11	5,027.17	6,444.99
Total	5,758.18	5,247.84	6,906.58

Source: IMF, *International Financial Statistics*.

MONEY SUPPLY
(million lats at 31 December)

	2007	2008	2009
Currency outside depository corporations	900	866	667
Transferable deposits	3,034	2,478	2,313
Other deposits	2,308	2,620	2,816
Securities other than shares	69	74	77
Broad money	6,311	6,038	5,873

Source: IMF, *International Financial Statistics*.

COST OF LIVING
(Consumer Price Index; base: 2000 = 100)

	2008	2009	2010
Food and non-alcoholic beverages	189.4	189.3	188.7
Fuel and light	215.0	237.0	235.6
Clothing (incl. footwear)	108.7	103.0	96.9
Rent	208.7	179.3	154.3
All items (incl. others)	165.0	170.8	169.0

NATIONAL ACCOUNTS
(million lats at current prices)*

Expenditure on the Gross Domestic Product

	2007	2008	2009
Government final consumption expenditure	2,574.9	3,169.8	2,566.8
Private final consumption expenditure	9,196.1	10,181.3	8,053.8
Gross fixed capital formation	4,975.1	4,748.5	2,806.8
Changes in inventories	994.7	298.1	−150.9
Total domestic expenditure	17,740.9	18,397.7	13,276.5
Exports of goods and services	6,258.7	6,931.1	5,741.7
Less Imports of goods and services	9,219.7	9,140.6	5,935.3
GDP in market prices	14,779.8	16,188.2	13,082.8

LATVIA

Gross Domestic Product by Economic Activity

	2007	2008	2009
Agriculture, hunting and forestry	456.4	429.4	375.7
Fishing	11.2	12.9	12.7
Mining and quarrying	53.5	59.5	56.1
Manufacturing	1,487.3	1,563.0	1,171.4
Electricity, gas and water supply	319.2	414.1	425.8
Construction	1,176.9	1,309.4	780.8
Wholesale and retail trade; repair of motor vehicles, motorcycles and personal and household goods	2,577.7	2,486.1	1,792.9
Hotels and restaurants	239.6	240.9	162.7
Transport, storage and communications	1,334.4	1,546.7	1,341.9
Financial intermediation	804.5	873.3	721.7
Real estate, renting and business activities	2,108.2	2,533.4	2,354.5
Public administration and defence; compulsory social security	983.1	1,169.9	980.7
Education	611.2	744.6	649.7
Health and social work	361.0	463.2	389.6
Other community, social and personal service activities	535.6	673.5	572.1
GDP at basic prices	13,059.7	14,519.7	11,788.5
Taxes *less* subsidies on products	1,720.1	1,668.5	1,294.3
GDP in purchasers' values	14,779.8	16,188.2	13,082.8

* Figures revised in accordance with standard EU classification.

BALANCE OF PAYMENTS
(US $ million)

	2007	2008	2009
Exports of goods f.o.b.	8,227	9,634	7,387
Imports of goods f.o.b.	−15,125	−15,648	−9,209
Trade balance	−6,898	−6,014	−1,822
Exports of services	3,705	4,538	3,844
Imports of services	−2,703	−3,190	−2,278
Balance on goods and services	−5,896	−4,666	−255
Other income received	1,487	1,785	1,324
Other income paid	−2,396	−2,381	331
Balance on goods, services and income	−6,804	−5,261	1,400
Current transfers received	2,023	2,191	1,984
Current transfers paid	−1,644	−1,422	−1,100
Current balance	−6,425	−4,492	2,284
Capital account (net)	578	513	622
Direct investment abroad	−371	−265	57
Direct investment from abroad	2,316	1,357	94
Portfolio investment assets	−607	222	161
Portfolio investment liabilities	−52	151	11
Financial derivatives assets	334	325	639
Financial derivatives liabilities	−105	−392	−236
Other investment assets	−6,063	−504	−1,046
Other investment liabilities	11,590	2,361	−1,481
Net errors and omissions	−212	−577	180
Overall balance	982	−1,301	1,285

Source: IMF, *International Financial Statistics*.

External Trade

PRINCIPAL COMMODITIES
(million lats)

Imports c.i.f.	2007	2008	2009
Prepared foodstuffs; beverages spirits and vinegar; tobacco and manufactured substitutes	475.5	514.2	416.9
Mineral products	896.7	1,171.2	808.6
Products of chemical or allied industries	631.5	732.8	557.3
Plastics, rubber and articles thereof	371.9	356.3	237.8
Paper-making material; paper and paperboard and articles thereof	154.8	149.2	113.5
Textiles and textile articles	335.6	303.4	230.4
Base metals and articles thereof	747.8	775.2	379.7
Machinery and mechanical appliances; electrical equipment; sound and television apparatus	1,618.6	1,374.0	740.3
Vehicles, aircraft, vessels and associated transport equipment	1,136.2	807.8	304.6
Total (incl. others)	7,780.2	7,527.7	4,709.8

Exports f.o.b.	2007	2008	2009
Prepared foodstuffs; beverages spirits and vinegar; tobacco and manufactured substitutes	314.1	349.1	290.3
Mineral products	165.4	184.0	199.6
Products of chemical or allied industries	300.3	371.4	307.0
Wood, cork and articles thereof; wood charcoal; manufactures of straw, esparto, etc.	908.5	735.0	595.4
Textiles and textile articles	271.0	242.8	178.8
Base metals and articles thereof	589.7	738.9	447.8
Machinery and mechanical appliances; electrical equipment; sound and television apparatus	444.0	553.7	509.4
Miscellaneous manufactured articles	157.8	154.4	121.0
Total (incl. others)	4,040.3	4,428.9	3,602.2

PRINCIPAL TRADING PARTNERS
(million lats)*

Imports c.i.f.	2007	2008	2009
Austria	115.3	128.3	51.7
Belarus	256.7	250.0	163.3
Belgium	149.2	131.0	72.3
China, People's Rep.	179.2	174.7	99.5
Czech Republic	147.6	113.1	69.1
Denmark	207.7	218.0	126.6
Estonia	629.9	535.7	375.7
Finland	397.3	330.9	168.6
France	179.8	174.4	120.7
Germany	1,218.0	981.7	543.1
Hungary	83.7	87.2	64.1
Italy	285.9	252.9	160.7
Lithuania	1,080.6	1,241.4	800.9
Netherlands	250.6	273.7	190.5
Norway	80.8	57.6	66.6
Poland	544.0	540.7	397.2
Russia	653.5	801.3	505.7
Spain	108.1	80.7	63.8
Sweden	379.8	332.6	168.3
Switzerland	80.9	84.4	85.0
Ukraine	77.8	70.6	57.1
United Kingdom	126.9	107.9	64.5
USA	88.7	73.3	41.0
Total (incl. others)	7,780.2	7,527.7	4,709.8

LATVIA

Statistical Survey

Exports f.o.b.	2007	2008	2009
Belarus	92.6	98.0	92.2
Belgium	41.8	44.0	43.0
Denmark	161.1	202.1	148.6
Estonia	581.8	621.7	518.4
Finland	127.0	137.4	102.5
France	63.3	81.3	66.8
Germany	353.1	358.5	314.0
Ireland	44.3	50.4	16.2
Italy	61.9	76.2	58.2
Lithuania	638.6	739.8	590.4
Netherlands	85.5	103.9	92.6
Norway	101.5	114.0	94.7
Poland	146.0	165.5	138.3
Russia	386.2	442.2	316.4
Spain	56.8	66.2	38.4
Sweden	313.0	293.4	219.5
Switzerland	27.6	31.1	17.2
Ukraine	59.8	64.5	37.7
United Kingdom	277.1	166.7	115.3
USA	55.5	65.4	58.6
Total (incl. others)	4,040.3	4,428.9	3,602.2

* Imports by country of origin; exports by country of destination.

Transport

RAILWAYS
(traffic)*

	2007	2008	2009
Passenger journeys (million)	27.4	26.8	21.6
Passenger-kilometres (million)	983	951	756
Freight transported (million metric tons)	52.2	56.1	53.7
Freight ton-kilometres (million)	18,313	19,581	18,725

* Data relating to passengers include railway personnel, and data on freight include passengers' baggage, parcel post and mail.

ROAD TRAFFIC
(motor vehicles in use at 31 December)

	2007	2008	2009
Passenger cars	904,869	932,828	904,308
Buses and coaches	10,624	10,543	9,687
Lorries and vans (incl. road tractors)	129,614	129,805	120,571

SHIPPING

Merchant Fleet
(registered at 31 December)

	2007	2008	2009
Number of vessels	153	151	144
Total displacement ('000 grt)	261.8	289.7	263.9

Source: IHS Fairplay, *World Fleet Statistics*.

International Sea-borne Freight Traffic
('000 metric tons)

	2007	2008	2009
Goods loaded	55,178	57,654	57,565
Goods unloaded	7,256	5,995	4,415

CIVIL AVIATION
(traffic)

	2007	2008	2009
Passengers carried (million)	2.2	2.8	2.9
Passenger-kilometres (million)	2,766	3,498	3,474
Cargo carried ('000 metric tons)	11	12	14
Cargo ton-kilometres (million)	13	15	19

Tourism

FOREIGN TOURIST ARRIVALS*

Country of residence	2007	2008	2009
Denmark	15,986	17,100	12,686
Estonia	76,410	82,296	58,762
Finland	75,286	93,025	72,024
Germany	111,439	122,682	93,739
Italy	27,551	31,372	27,303
Lithuania	82,703	107,173	71,811
Norway	59,017	61,261	49,190
Poland	26,353	30,701	24,038
Russia	60,055	70,778	72,227
Sweden	58,823	62,830	55,609
United Kingdom	62,699	56,191	35,596
USA	17,055	20,261	14,829
Total (incl. others)	844,828	944,690	753,875

* Figures refer to the number of visitors arriving at accommodation establishments.

Tourism receipts (US $ million, incl. passenger transport): 622 in 2006; 880 in 2007; 1,134 in 2008 (Source: World Tourism Organization).

Communications Media

	2007	2008	2009
Telephones ('000 main lines in use)*	644	644	644
Mobile cellular telephones ('000 subscribers)	2,217	2,234	2,371
Internet users ('000)†	1,343	1,432	1,504
Broadband subscribers ('000)	320.7	379	419.2
Book production: titles	2,767	2,855	2,244
Book production: copies ('000)	5,300	5,200	3,500
Newspapers: number	259	262	244
Newspapers: average annual circulation (million copies)	211	176	153
Other periodicals: number	412	431	370
Other periodicals: average annual circulation (million copies)	46.3	44.1	35.4

* At 31 December.
† Estimates.

Personal computers: 748,000 (326.9 per 1,000 persons) in 2006.

Radio receivers ('000 in use): 1,760 in 1997.

Television receivers ('000 in use): 1,220 in 1997.

Sources: partly UNESCO, *Statistical Yearbook*; UN, *Statistical Yearbook*; and International Telecommunication Union.

Education

(2009/10 unless otherwise indicated)

	Institutions	Students
Pre-primary (children ages 3–6)	586	83,237
General schools*	846	226,034
Primary (Grades 1–4)	35	5,189
Basic (Grades 5–9)	374	50,361
Secondary (Grades 10–12)	374	161,578
Special	63	8,906
Vocational schools	85	36,660
Higher education institutions	61	112,567

* Full-time education.

Teachers (2002 unless otherwise indicated): Pre-primary 7,996 (2004); Primary (including basic schools) 9,252; Secondary 16,495; Special schools 1,837; Vocational 5,639; Higher 4,535 (2004).

Pupil-teacher ratio (primary education, UNESCO estimate): 11.1 in 2007/08 (Source: UNESCO Institute for Statistics).

Adult literacy rate (UNESCO estimates): 99.8% (males 99.8%; females 99.8%) in 2008 (Source: UNESCO Institute for Statistics).

LATVIA

Directory

The Government

HEAD OF STATE

President: Valdis Zatlers (inaugurated 8 July 2007).

CABINET OF MINISTERS
(May 2011)

A coalition of Unity—comprising the Civic Union (PS), New Era (JL) and the Society for a Different Politics (SCP)—and the Greens' and Farmers' Union (ZZS).

Prime Minister: Valdis Dombrovskis (JL).
Deputy Prime Minister and Minister of Defence: Artis Pabriks (SCP).
Minister of Foreign Affairs: Ģirts V. Kristovskis (PS).
Minister of the Economy: Artis Kampars (JL).
Minister of Finance: Andris Vilks (PS).
Minister of the Interior: Linda Mūrniece (JL).
Minister of Education and Science: Rolands Broks (ZZS).
Minister of Culture: Sarmīte Ēlerte (PS).
Minister of Welfare: Ilona Juršhevska (PS).
Minister of Transport: Uldis Augulis (ZZS).
Minister of Justice: Aigars Štokenbergs (SCP).
Minister of Health: Juris Bārzdiņš (ZZS).
Minister of the Environment and Regional Development: Raimonds Vējonis (ZZS).
Minister of Agriculture: Jānis Dūklavs (ZZS).

MINISTRIES

Chancery of the President: Pils lauk. 3, Rīga 1900; tel. 6709-2106; fax 6709-2157; e-mail info@president.lv; internet www.president.lv.
Office of the Cabinet of Ministers: Brīvības bulv. 36, Rīga 1520; tel. 6708-2800; fax 6728-0469; e-mail vk@mk.gov.lv; internet www.mk.gov.lv.
Ministry of Agriculture: Republikas lauk. 2, Rīga 1981; tel. 6702-7010; fax 6702-7512; e-mail zm@zm.gov.lv; internet www.zm.gov.lv.
Ministry of Culture: K. Valdemāra iela 11A, Rīga 1364; tel. 6733-0200; fax 6733-0293; e-mail pasts@km.gov.lv; internet www.km.gov.lv.
Ministry of Defence: K. Valdemāra iela 10–12, Rīga 1473; tel. 6733-5113; fax 6721-2307; e-mail kanceleja@mod.gov.lv; internet www.mod.gov.lv.
Ministry of the Economy: Brīvības iela 55, Rīga 1519; tel. 6701-3101; fax 6728-0882; e-mail pasts@em.gov.lv; internet www.em.gov.lv.
Ministry of Education and Science: Vaļņu iela 2, Rīga 1050; tel. 6722-6209; fax 6722-3905; e-mail info@izm.gov.lv; internet www.izm.gov.lv.
Ministry of the Environment and Regional Development: Peldu 25, Rīga 1494; tel. 6702-6448; fax 6782-0442; e-mail pasts@vidm.gov.lv; internet www.vidm.gov.lv.
Ministry of Finance: Smilšu iela 1, Rīga 1919; tel. 6709-5405; fax 6709-5503; e-mail info@fm.gov.lv; internet www.fm.gov.lv.
Ministry of Foreign Affairs: K. Valdemāra iela 3, Rīga 1395; tel. 6701-6201; fax 6782-8121; e-mail mfa.cha@mfa.gov.lv; internet www.mfa.gov.lv.
Ministry of Health: Brīvības iela 72, Rīga 1011; tel. 6787-6000; fax 6787-6002; e-mail vm@vm.gov.lv; internet www.vm.gov.lv.
Ministry of the Interior: Čiekurkalna 1, līnija 1, korp. 2, Rīga 1026; tel. 6721-9263; fax 6782-9686; e-mail kanceleja@iem.gov.lv; internet www.iem.gov.lv.
Ministry of Justice: Brīvības bulv. 36, Rīga 1536; tel. 6703-6801; fax 6728-5575; e-mail info@tm.gov.lv; internet www.tm.gov.lv.
Ministry of Transport: Gogoļa iela 3, Rīga 1743; tel. 6702-8205; fax 6721-7180; e-mail vards.uzvards@sam.gov.lv; internet www.sam.gov.lv.
Ministry of Welfare: Skolas iela 28, Rīga 1331; tel. 6702-1666; fax 6727-6445; e-mail lm@lm.gov.lv; internet www.lm.gov.lv.

President

In voting by members of the Saeima (Parliament), conducted on 31 May 2007, Valdis Zatlers was elected President, obtaining 58 votes, defeating Aivars Endziņš, who received 39 votes.

Legislature

Saeima
(Parliament)

Jekaba iela 11, Rīga 1811; tel. 6708-7111; fax 6708-7100; e-mail web@saeima.lv; internet www.saeima.lv.
Chairman: Solvita Āboltiņa.

General Election, 2 October 2010

Coalitions	Votes	%	Seats
Unity*	301,429	31.90	33
Harmony Centre†	251,400	26.60	29
Greens' and Farmers' Union‡	190,025	20.11	22
All for Latvia-For Fatherland and Freedom Union/Latvian National Independence Movement coalition	74,029	7.84	8
Alliance for a Good Latvia‖	73,881	7.82	8
Others	54,077	5.72	—
Total§	944,841	100.00	100

* Coalition comprising the Civic Union, New Era and Society for a Different Politics.
† Coalition comprising the Harmony Social Democratic Party and the Latvian Socialist Party.
‡ Comprising the Latvian Green Party and the Centre Party Latvian Farmers' Union.
‖ Coalition comprising the People's Party and the Latvian First Party/Latvian Way.
§ Excluding 20,697 invalid votes (2.14% of the total).

Election Commission

Central Election Commission (Centrālā vēlēšanu komisija—CVK): Smilšu iela 4, Rīga 1050; tel. 6732-2688; fax 6732-5251; e-mail cvk@cvk.lv; internet web.cvk.lv; Chair. Arnis Cimdars.

Political Organizations

The following are among the most influential political parties in Latvia:

All for Latvia (Visu Latvijai): Ģertrūdes iela 46/2, Rīga 1011; tel. 6727-2735; fax 2927-1030; e-mail solidaritate@visulatvijai.lv; internet www.visulatvijai.lv; f. 2006 as a political party; nationalist; Co-Chair. Imants Parādnieks, Raivis Dzintars.
Centre Party Latvian Farmers' Union (CP LZS) (Centriskā partija Latvijas Zemnieku savienība): Republikas lauk. 2, Rīga 1010; tel. 6702-7163; fax 6702-7467; e-mail lzs@latnet.lv; internet www.lzs.lv; f. 1990; rural, centrist; forms part of the Greens' and Farmers' Union; Chair. Augusts Brigmanis.
Civic Union (PS) (Pilsoniskā savienība): Aspazijas iela 24, Rīga 1050; tel. 6732-3325; fax 6732-3315; e-mail birojs@pilsoniska-savieniba.lv; internet pilsoniska-savieniba.lv; f. 2008; contested 2010 legislative elections as part of the Unity coalition; Chair. Ģirts Valdis Kristovskis.
For Fatherland and Freedom Union/Latvian National Independence Movement (TB/LNNK) (Apvienība 'Tēvzemei un Brīvībai'/Latvijas Nacionālās Neatkarības Kustība): Jēkaba iela 20/22–9, Rīga 1050; tel. and fax 6721-6762; e-mail tb@tb.lv; internet www.tb.lv; f. 1997 by merger; Chair. Roberts Zīle.
For Human Rights in a United Latvia (PCTVL/ZaPChEL) (Par cilvēka tiesībām vienotā Latvijā/ Za prava cheloveka v yedinoi Latvii): Rūpniecības iela 9, Rīga 1010; tel. and fax 6732-0290; e-mail pctvl@saeima.lv; internet www.pctvl.lv; f. 1998 as electoral alliance; became united party Nov. 2003; represents interests of Russian-speaking communities in Latvia; opposed to Latvian membership of NATO; Leaders Tatjana Ždanoka, Jakovs Pliners, Juris Sokolovskis.
Harmony Centre (SC) (Saskaņas Centrs/ Tsentr soglasiya): Jūra Alunana 8/3, Rīga 1010; tel. 6733-3515; e-mail office@saskanascentrs.lv; internet www.saskanascentrs.lv; formed in 2005 by merger of the National Harmony Party and the New Centre, subsequently joined by the Latvian Socialist Party (q.v.), the Social Democratic Union and by the Harmony Social Democratic Party (q.v.); Chair. Nils Ušakovs.
Harmony Social Democratic Party (SDPS) (Sociāldemokrātiskā Partija 'Saskaņa'): Jēkaba iela 16, Rīga 1050; f. 2010; contested 2010

legislative elections as part of the Harmony Centre alliance; absorbed Daugavpils City Party in 2011; Leader Jānis Urbanovičs.

Latvian First Party/Latvian Way (LPP/LC) (Latvijas Pirmā Partija/Latvijas ceļš): Darzauglu iela 1–70, Rīga 1012; tel. 26140059; e-mail info@lpplc.lv; internet www.lpplc.lv; f. 2007 by merger of Latvian First Party (f. 2002) and Latvian Way (f. 1993); Liberal democratic; contested 2010 legislative elections as part of Alliance for a Good Latvia coalition; Chair. Ainārs Šlesers.

Latvian Green Party (LZP) (Latvijas Zaļā partija): Kalnciema iela 30, Rīga 1046; tel. and fax 6761-4272; e-mail birojs@zp.lv; internet www.zp.lv; f. 1990; forms part of the Greens' and Farmers' Union; Co-Chair. Viesturs Silenieks, Raimonds Vējonis.

Latvian Social Democratic Workers' Party (LSDSP) (Latvijas Sociāl-demokrātiskā strādnieku partija): Aldaru iela 8, Rīga 1050; tel. 6735-6585; fax 6735-6588; e-mail lsdsp@lis.lv; internet www.lsdsp.lv; f. 1904; Chair. Jānis Dinevičs.

Latvian Socialist Party (LSP) (Latvijas Sociālistiskā partija/Sotsialisticheskaya partiya Latvii): Citadeles 2, Rīga 1010; tel. and fax 6755-5535; e-mail latsocpartija@inbox.lv; internet www.latsocpartija.lv; f. 1994; joined the Harmony Centre alliance in Dec. 2005, remained affiliated to Harmony Centre at 2006 and 2010 legislative elections; Chair. Alfrēds Rubiks.

New Era (JL) (Jaunais laiks): Zigfrīda Annas Meierovica bulv., Rīga 1050; tel. 6720-5472; fax 6720-5473; e-mail sekretare@jaunaislaiks.lv; internet www.jaunaislaiks.lv; f. 2002; right-wing; contested 2010 legislative elections as part of the Unity coalition; Chair. Solvita Āboltiņa; Sec.-Gen. Ēriks Skapars.

People's Party (TP) (Tautas partija): Zigfrīda Annas Meierovica iela 1, Rīga 1050; tel. 6750-8808; fax 6750-8684; e-mail birojs@tautaspartija.lv; internet www.tautaspartija.lv; f. 1998; contested 2010 legislative elections as part of Alliance for a Good Latvia coalition; Chair. Andris Šķēle.

Society for a Different Politics (SCP) (Sabiedrība citai politikai): Audēju iela 8, 2nd flr, Rīga 1050; tel. 6722-3001; fax 6722-3017; e-mail birojs@parmainas.lv; internet www.scp.lv; f. 2008; contested 2010 legislative elections as part of the Unity coalition; Chair. Aigars Štokenbergs.

Diplomatic Representation

EMBASSIES IN LATVIA

Austria: Elizabetes iela 15, Rīga 1010; tel. 6721-6125; fax 6721-6126; e-mail riga-ob@bmeia.gv.at; Ambassador Hermine Poppeller.

Azerbaijan: Raiņa bulv. 2–5, Rīga 1050; tel. 6714-2889; fax 6714-2896; e-mail office@azembassy.lv; internet www.azembassy.lv; f. 2005; Ambassador Elman Zeynalov.

Belarus: Jēzusbaznīcas iela 12, Rīga 1050; tel. 6722-2560; fax 6732-2891; e-mail latvia@belembassy.org; internet www.latvia.belembassy.org; Ambassador Alyaksandr Gerasimenka.

Belgium: Alberta iela 13, Rīga 1010; tel. 6711-4852; fax 6711-4855; e-mail riga@diplobel.be; internet www.diplomatie.be/riga; f. 2004; Ambassador Leopold Merckx.

Canada: Baznicas iela 20–22, Rīga 1010; tel. 6781-3945; fax 6781-3960; e-mail rigag@international.gc.ca; internet www.latvia.gc.ca; Ambassador Scott Heatherington.

China, People's Republic: Ganību dambis 5, Rīga 1045; tel. 6735-7023; fax 6735-7025; e-mail chinaemb_lv@mfa.gov.cn; internet lv.chineseembassy.org; Ambassador Hu Yeshun.

Czech Republic: Elizabetes iela 29A, Rīga 1010; tel. 6721-7814; fax 6721-7821; e-mail riga@embassy.mzv.cz; internet www.mfa.cz/riga; Ambassador Tomáš Pštross.

Denmark: Pils iela 11, Rīga 1863; tel. 6722-6210; fax 6722-9218; e-mail rixamb@um.dk; internet www.ambriga.um.dk; Ambassador Per Carlsen.

Estonia: Skolas iela 13, Rīga 1010; tel. 6781-2020; fax 6781-2029; e-mail embassy.riga@mfa.ee; internet www.estemb.lv; Ambassador Mati Vaarmann.

Finland: Kalpaka bulv. 1, Rīga 1605; tel. 6707-8800; fax 6707-8814; e-mail sanomat.rii@formin.fi; internet www.finland.lv; Ambassador Maria Serenius.

France: Raiņa bulv. 9, Rīga 1050; tel. 6703-6600; fax 6703-6616; e-mail webmastre.ambafrance-lv@diplomatie.gouv.fr; internet www.ambafrance-lv.org; Ambassador Chantal Poiret.

Georgia: Raiņa bulv. 3/2, Rīga 1050; tel. and fax 6721-3136; e-mail riga.emb@mfa.gov.ge; internet www.latvia.mfa.gov.ge; Ambassador Konstantin Korkelia.

Germany: Raiņa bulv. 13, Rīga 1050; tel. 6708-5100; fax 6708-5149; e-mail info@riga.diplo.de; internet www.riga.diplo.de; Ambassador Klaus Burkhardt.

Greece: Elizabetes iela 11/5, Rīga 1010; tel. 6735-6345; fax 6735-6351; e-mail gremb.rig@mfa.gr; Ambassador Chrysanthie Panayotopoulou.

Hungary: Alberta iela 4, Rīga 1010; tel. 6721-7500; fax 6721-7878; e-mail mission.rix@kum.hu; internet www.mfa.gov.hu/emb/riga; Ambassador Gábor Dobokay.

Ireland: Alberta iela 13, Rīga 1010; tel. 6703-9370; fax 6703-9371; e-mail rigaembassy@dfa.ie; internet www.embassyofireland.lv; Ambassador Aidan Kirwan.

Israel: Elizabetes iela 2, Rīga 1010; tel. 6763-5574; fax 6763-5555; e-mail press@rig.mfa.gov.il; internet riga.mfa.gov.il; Chargé d'affaires Naftali Tamir.

Italy: Teātra iela 9, Rīga 1050; tel. 6721-6069; fax 6721-6084; e-mail ambitalia.riga@esteri.it; internet www.ambriga.esteri.it; Ambassador Francesco Puccio.

Japan: K. Valdemāra iela 21, Rīga 1010; tel. 6781-2001; fax 6781-2004; e-mail eoj@latnet.lv; internet www.lv.emb-japan.go.jp; Ambassador Takashi Osanai.

Lithuania: Rūpniecibas iela 24, Rīga 1010; tel. 6732-1519; fax 6732-1589; e-mail lt@apollo.lv; internet lv.mfa.lt; Ambassador Antanas Valionis.

Moldova: Zigfrīda Annas Meierovica bulv. 14, Rīga 1050; tel. 6735-9160; fax 6735-9165; e-mail riga@moldovaembassy.lv; internet www.letonia.mfa.md; Ambassador Aleksei Cracan.

Netherlands: Torņu iela 4, Jēkaba Kazarmas 1A, Rīga 1050; tel. 6732-6147; fax 6732-6151; e-mail rig@minbuza.nl; internet www.netherlandsembassy.lv; Ambassador Jurriaan Kraak.

Norway: Zirgu iela 14, POB 181, Rīga 1050; tel. 6781-4100; fax 6781-4108; e-mail emb.riga@mfa.no; internet www.norvegija.lv; Ambassador Jāns Grēvstads.

Poland: Mednieku iela 6B, Rīga 1010; tel. 6703-1500; fax 6703-1549; e-mail ambpol@apollo.lv; internet www.ryga.polemb.net; Ambassador Jerzy Marek Nowakowski.

Portugal: Balasta Dambis 60, Ogļu iela, Ķīpsala, Rīga 1048; tel. 6782-1926; fax 6767-1626; e-mail embporturiga@gmail.com; Chargé d'affaires a.i. Virgínia Fragoso.

Russia: Antonijas iela 2, Rīga 1010; tel. 6733-2151; fax 6783-0209; e-mail rusembas@delfi.lv; internet www.latvia.mid.ru; Ambassador Aleksandr A. Veshnyakov.

Slovakia: Smilšu iela 8, Rīga 1050; tel. 6781-4280; fax 6781-4290; e-mail emb.riga@mzv.sk; internet www.mzv.sk/riga; Ambassador Dušan Krištofik.

Spain: Elizabetes iela 11, 3rd Floor, Rīga 1010; tel. 6732-0281; fax 6732-5005; e-mail emb.riga@maec.es; internet www.maec.es/Embajadas/Riga; Ambassador María Consuelo Femenía Guardiola.

Sweden: A. Pumpura iela 8, Rīga 1010; tel. 6768-6600; fax 6768-6601; e-mail ambassaden.riga@foreign.ministry.se; internet www.swedenemb.lv; Ambassador Mats Staffansson.

Switzerland: World Trade Centre, Elizabetes iela 2, Rīga 1340; tel. 6733-8351; fax 6733-8354; e-mail rig.vertretung@eda.admin.ch; internet www.eda.admin.ch/riga; Ambassador Gabriela Nützi Sulpizio.

Turkey: A. Pumpura iela 2, Rīga 1010; tel. 6782-1600; fax 6732-0334; e-mail turkemb.riga@mfa.gov.tr; internet riga.emb.mfa.gov.tr; Ambassador Ayşe Ayhan Asya.

Ukraine: Kalpaka bulv. 3, Rīga 1010; tel. 6724-3082; fax 6732-5583; e-mail emb_lv@mfa.gov.ua; internet www.mfa.gov.ua/latvia; Chargé d'affaires a.i. Oleksandr A. Kushnir.

United Kingdom: J. Alunāna iela 5, Rīga 1010; tel. 6777-4700; fax 6777-4707; e-mail british.embassy@apollo.lv; internet ukinlatvia.fco.gov.uk; Ambassador Dr Andrew Soper.

USA: Raiņa bulv. 7, Rīga 1510; tel. 6703-6200; fax 6782-0047; e-mail pas@usembassy.lv; internet riga.usembassy.gov; Ambassador Judith G. Garber.

Uzbekistan: Elizabetes iela 11/11, Rīga 1010; tel. 6732-2424; fax 6732-2306; e-mail posoluz@apollo.lv; Ambassador Kobiljon S. Nazarov.

Judicial System

Constitutional Court (Latvijas Republikas Satversmes tiesa): J. Alunāna iela 1, Rīga 1010; tel. 6721-0274; fax 6783-0770; e-mail tiesa@satv.tiesa.gov.lv; internet www.satv.tiesa.gov.lv; f. 1996; comprises seven judges, appointed by the Saeima for a term of 10 years; Chair. Gunārs Kūtris.

Supreme Court (Latvijas Republikas Augstākā tiesa): Brīvības bulv. 36, Rīga 1511; tel. 6702-0350; fax 6702-0351; e-mail at@at.gov.lv; internet www.at.gov.lv; Chair. Ivars Bičkovičs.

LATVIA

Office of the Prosecutor-General: Kalpaka bulv. 6, Rīga 1801; tel. 6704-4400; fax 6704-4449; e-mail una.brenca@lrp.gov.lv; internet www.lrp.gov.lv; Prosecutor-General ERIKS KALNMEIERS.

Religion

From the 16th century the traditional religion of the Latvians was Lutheran Christian, although there remained a substantial Roman Catholic population. Russian Orthodoxy is the religion of much of the Slavic population. During the period of Soviet rule many places of religious worship were closed. Following the restoration of independence in 1991, religious organizations regained their legal rights and property.

Board of Religious Affairs: Pils lauk. 4, Rīga 1050; tel. 6722-0585; e-mail zlp@zlp.gov.lv; f. 2000; govt agency, attached to the Ministry of Justice; Principal IRETA ROMANOVSKA.

CHRISTIANITY
Protestant Churches

Evangelical Lutheran Church of Latvia: M. Pils iela 4, Rīga 1050; tel. 6722-5406; fax 6722-5436; e-mail konsistorija@lutheran.lv; internet www.lutheran.lv; f. 1922; 250,000 mems; Archbishop JĀNIS VANAGS.

Latvian Conference of Seventh-day Adventists in Latvia: Baznīcas iela 12A, Rīga 1010; tel. and fax 6724-0013; e-mail viesturs@baznica.lv; internet www.adventistu.baznica.lv; f. 1920; Pres. of Council VIESTURS REĶIS.

Latvian Pentecostal Union: J. Asara iela 8, Jelgava 3001; tel. 6308-1401; fax 6308-1407; e-mail lvdaddf@hotmail.com; f. 1989; Bishop JĀNIS OZOLINKEVIČS.

Union of Baptist Churches in Latvia: Lāčplēša iela 37, Rīga 1011; tel. and fax 6722-3379; internet www.lbds.lv; e-mail kanceleja@lbds.lv; f. 1860; Bishop Dr PĒTERIS SPROĢIS.

United Methodist Church in Latvia: Klaipēdas iela 56, Liepāja 3401; tel. 6343-2161; fax 6346-9848; re-est. 1991; Supt ĀRIJS VĪKSNA.

The Roman Catholic Church

Latvia comprises one archdiocese and three dioceses. There were an estimated 444,548 adherents in the country (equivalent to 19.5% of the population).

Bishops' Conference
M. Pils iela 2A, Rīga 1050; tel. 6722-7266; fax 6722-0775; Pres. Cardinal JĀNIS PUJATS (Archbishop of Rīga).

Archbishop of Rīga: Cardinal JĀNIS PUJATS, Pils iela 2A, Rīga 1050; tel. 6722-7266; fax 6722-0775; e-mail curia@e-apollo.lv; internet www.catholic.lv.

The Orthodox Church

Although the Latvian Orthodox Church has close ties with the Moscow Patriarchate, it has administrative independence.

Latvian Orthodox Church (Moscow Patriarchate): Pils iela 14, Rīga 1050; tel. 6722-5855; fax 6722-4345; e-mail sinode@orthodoxy.lv; internet www.pareizticiba.lv; f. 1850; Metropolitan of Rīga and all Latvia ALEKSANDR (KUDRJASHOV).

Latvian Old Believer (Old Ritualist) Pomor Church: Krasta iela 73, Rīga 1003; tel. 6711-3083; fax 6714-4513; e-mail oldbel@junik.lv; f. 1760 in split from Moscow Patriarchate; Head of Central Council IVANS MIZOĻUBOVS.

JUDAISM

Jewish Religious Community of Rīga: Peitavas iela 6/8, Rīga 1050; tel. 6722-4549; f. 1764; Rabbi NATAN BARKAN.

The Press

The joint-stock company Preses nams (Press House—q.v.) is the leading publisher of newspapers and magazines in Latvia. In 2002 there were eight daily newspapers, with an average circulation of 183,000. In 2009 a total of 244 daily and non-daily newspapers and 370 other periodicals were published. The publications listed below are in Latvian, unless otherwise indicated.

DAILIES

Bizness & Baltiya (Business and the Baltics): K. Valdemāra iela 149, Rīga 1013; tel. 6703-3011; fax 6703-3010; e-mail media@bb.lv; internet www.bb.lv; f. 1991; 5 a week; in Russian; Editor-in-Chief ALEKSEI SHERBAKOV; circ. 12,000 (2007).

Directory

Chas (Hour): Peldu iela 15, Rīga 1050; tel. 6708-8733; fax 6721-1067; internet www.chas-daily.com; f. 1997; 5 a week; in Russian; Editor-in-Chief PAVEL KIRILLOV; circ. 13,100 (2010).

Diena (Day): Mūkusalas iela 15, Rīga 1004; tel. 6706-3300; fax 6706-3190; e-mail info@dienasmediji.lv; internet www.diena.lv; f. 1990; social and political issues; associated with free newspaper *5min*, launched in Sept. 2005; Editor-in-Chief GUNTIS BOJĀRS; circ. 85,000 (2009).

Neatkarīgā Rīta Avīze (Independent Morning Paper): Balasta dambis 3, Rīga 1081; tel. 6706-2462; fax 6706-2465; e-mail redakcija@nra.lv; internet www.nra.lv; f. 1990; Editor-in-Chief ALDIS BĒRZIŅŠ; circ. 40,000.

Rīgas Balss (RB) (Voice of Rīga): Rīga; tel. 6706-2420; fax 6706-2400; e-mail balss@rb.lv; internet www.rigasbalss.lv; f. 1957; city evening newspaper; Editor-in-Chief IVETA MEDIŅA; circ. 18,100 (Mon.–Thur.), 42,700 (Fri.).

Vakara Ziņas (The Evening News): Bezdelīgas iela 12, Rīga 1007; tel. 6761-7595; fax 6761-2383; e-mail vakara.zinas@vz.lv; internet www.vz.lv; f. 1993; popular; Editor-in-Chief AINĀRS VLADIMIROVS; circ. 53,000.

Vesti Segodnya (News Today): Martiņa 9, Rīga 1048; tel. 6706-6130; fax 6706-8131; e-mail sm@fenster.lv; internet www.ves.lv; f. 1945; in Russian; 6 a week; Editor-in-Chief ALEKSANDRS BĻINOVS; circ. 25,500.

OTHER NEWSPAPERS

The Baltic Times: Rupniciēbas iela 1–5, Rīga 1010; tel. 6722-9978; fax 6722-6041; e-mail editor@baltictimes.com; internet www.baltictimes.com; f. 1996; news from Estonia, Latvia and Lithuania; in English; Man. Dir SERGEI ALEKSEYEV; Editor-in-Chief DORIAN ZIEDONIS; circ. 12,000 (2007).

Dienas Bizness (Daily Business): Mūkusalas iela 15, Rīga 1004; tel. 6706-3100; fax 6706-3190; e-mail redakcija@db.lv; internet www.db.lv; f. 1992; Man. Editor INDRA LAZDIŅA; circ. 17,000.

Ieva (Eve): Stabu iela 34, Rīga 1880; tel. 6700-6102; fax 6700-6111; e-mail ieva@santa.lv; internet www.ieva.lv; f. 1997; weekly; illustrated journal for women; Editor-in-Chief INITA SILA; circ. 73,650.

Izglitība un Kultūra (Education and Culture): Marijas iela 2/5, Rīga 1050; tel. 6735-7585; fax 6735-7584; e-mail redakcija@izglitiba-kultura.lv; internet www.izglitiba-kultura.lv; f. 1948; Man. Editor VIOLETA BRENČEVA.

Latvijas Avīze (Latvian Newspaper): Dzirnavu iela 21, Rīga 1010; tel. 6709-6600; fax 6709-6645; e-mail redakcija@la.lv; internet www2.la.lv; f. 1987; fmrly *Lauku Avīze* (Country Newspaper); present name adopted 2004; 6 issues a week; popular; agriculture, politics and sport; Editor-in-Chief LINDA RASA; circ. 59,500.

Latvijas Vēstnesis (Latvian Herald): Bruņinieku iela 41, Rīga 1011; tel. 6729-8833; fax 6731-2190; e-mail info@lv.lv; internet www.lv.lv; f. 1993; official newspaper; 4 a week; Editor-in-Chief OSKARS GERTS; circ. 3,500.

Privātā Dzīve (Private Life): Stabu iela 34, Rīga 1011; tel. 6700-6104; fax 6700-6111; e-mail pdz@santa.lv; weekly; Man. Editor ZITA RAMMA; circ. 56,000 (2010).

Rīgas Viļņi (Riga Waves): Lāčplēša iela 20A, Rīga 1011; tel. 6784-2577; fax 6784-2578; e-mail info@rigasvilni.lv; internet www.abone.rigasvilni.lv; weekly.

PRINCIPAL PERIODICALS

Baltiskii Kurs/The Baltic Course: Lāčplēša iela 53, Rīga 1011; tel. 2926-9645; fax 2926-9645; e-mail olga.pavuk@baltic-course.com; internet www.baltic-course.com; f. 1996; quarterly; business; in Russian and English; Int. Editor EUGENE ETERIS; Editor-in-Chief OLGA PAVUK.

Karogs (Banner): Kuršu iela 24, Rīga 1006; tel. 6755-4128; fax 6755-4146; e-mail karogs@apollo.lv; internet www.ekarogs.lv; f. 1940; literary monthly; Editor-in-Chief IEVA KOLMANE; circ. 1,500.

Klubs (Club): Stabu iela 34, Rīga 1011; tel. 6700-6103; fax 6700-6111; e-mail klubs@santa.lv; internet www.klubs.lv; f. 1994; monthly; politics, business, fashion; Editor-in-Chief JURIS SLEIERS; circ. 17,000 (Jan. 2010).

Latvijas Ekonomists: Alūksnes iela 5, Rīga 1045; tel. 6779-0631; fax 6779-0619; e-mail birojs@ekonomists.lv; internet www.ekonomists.lv; f. 1992; monthly; in Latvian and Russian; Dir INESE LAPIŅA.

Māksla Plus (M+): Akadēmijas lauk. 1, a.k. 41, Rīga 1027; tel. 6722-0722; fax 6782-0608; e-mail makslap@latnet.lv; internet www.makslaplus.lv; cultural magazine (cinema, music, theatre, photography); Editor-in-Chief SANITA BUČINIECE.

Mans Mazais: Balasta dambis 3, Rīga 1081; tel. 6700-6100; fax 6700-6111; e-mail mansmazais@santa.lv; internet www

LATVIA

.mansmazais.lv; f. 1994; monthly; illustrated journal for parents; Editor-in-Chief TĪNA KEMPELE; circ. 20,000.

Mūsmājas (Our Home): Mūkusalas iela 15, Rīga 1004; tel. 6729-9105; fax 6729-2701; e-mail musmajas@musmajas.lv; internet www.musmajas.lv; f. 1993; monthly; home and family magazine; Editor-in-Chief AIVA KALVE; circ. 50,000.

Mūzikas Saule (Musical Sun): K. Barona iela 37/5, Rīga 1011; tel. 6731-0161; fax 2678-9826; e-mail saule@muzikassaule.lv; internet www.muzikassaule.lv; music; Editor-in-Chief IEVA ROZENTĀLE.

Rīgas Laiks (Rīga Times): Lāčplēša iela 25, Rīga 1011; tel. 6728-7922; fax 6728-2798; e-mail pasts@rigaslaiks.lv; internet www.rigaslaiks.lv; f. 1993; monthly; Editor-in-Chief ULDIS TĪRONS; circ. 10,000.

Santa: Stabu iela 34, Rīga 1011; tel. 6700-6103; fax 6700-6111; e-mail santa@santa.lv; internet www.zurnalssanta.lv; f. 1991; monthly; illustrated journal for women; Editor-in-Chief SANTA DANSBERGA-ANČA; circ. 42,000.

Zinātnes Vēstnesis (Scientific Herald): Akadēmijas lauk. 1, Rīga 1050; tel. 6721-2706; fax 6782-1109; e-mail lza@lza.lv; internet www.lza.lv/zv00.htm; f. 1989; published by the Latvian Scientific Council, the Latvian Academy of Science and the Latvian Society of Scientists; two a month; Man. Editor JURIS EKMANIS.

NEWS AGENCIES

Baltic News Service: DBerga Bazārs, Marijas iela 13/1 Rīga 1050; tel. 6708-8600; fax 6708-8601; e-mail bns@bns.lv; internet www.bns.lv; f. 1990; news from Latvia, Lithuania, Estonia and the CIS; in English, Russian and the Baltic languages; Dir SIGITA KIRILKA.

LETA Latvian News Agency: Marijas iela 2, Rīga 1050; tel. 6722-2509; fax 6722-3850; e-mail redaktori@leta.lv; internet www.leta.lv; independent; Chair. MĀRTIŅŠ BARKĀNS.

PRESS ASSOCIATION

Latvian Union of Journalists (Latvijas Žurnālistu savienība): K. Valdemāra iela 118–211, Rīga 1013; tel. 6721-1433; e-mail zurnalistu.savieniba@e-apollo.lv; internet www.zurnalistusavieniba.lv; f. 1992; 600 mems; Pres. JURIS PAIDERS.

Publishers

Izdevniecība AGB (AGB Publishing House): K. Barona iela 31, Rīga 1011; tel. 6728-0464; fax 6728-0356; e-mail info@izdevnieciba.com; internet www.izdevnieciba.com.

Avots (Spring): Puskina iela 1A, Rīga 1050; tel. 6721-1394; fax 6722-5824; e-mail avots@apollo.lv; f. 1980; non-fiction, dictionaries, crafts, hobbies, etc.; Pres. JĀNIS LEJA.

Elpa (Breath): Doma lauk. 1, Rīga 1050; tel. 6721-1776; fax 6722-6497; e-mail elpa@apollo.lv; f. 1990; books and newspapers; Pres. MAIRITA SOLIMA.

Jāņa sēta: Elizabetes iela 83–85, Rīga 1050; tel. 6709-2290; fax 6709-2292; e-mail janaseta@janaseta.lv; internet www.janaseta.lv; f. 1991; travel and culinary books; Dir AIVARS ZVIRBULIS.

Jumava: Dzirnavu iela 73, Rīga 1011; tel. and fax 6728-0314; e-mail jumava@parks.lv; internet www.jumava.lv; f. 1994; translations, dictionaries, fiction, etc.; Pres. JURIS VISOCKIS.

Kontinents: Elijas iela 17, Rīga 1050; tel. 6720-4130; fax 6720-4129; e-mail kontinent@ml.lv; internet www.kontinents.lv; f. 1991; translated fiction, non-fiction and colour children's books; Chair. of Bd OLEG MIHALEVICH.

Nordik: Daugavgrīvas 36–9, Rīga 1048; tel. 6760-2672; fax 6760-2818; e-mail nordik@nordik.lv; internet www.nordik.lv; f. 1992; sister co, Tapals, at same address; Dir JĀNIS JUŠKA; Editor-in-Chief IEVA JANAITE.

Preses nams (Press House): Balasta dambis 3, Rīga 1081; tel. 6246-5732; internet www.presesnams.lv; f. 1990; newspapers, magazines, encyclopedias and scientific literature; controlling interest owned by Ventspils Nafta; Dir EGONS LAPIŅŠ.

Smaile (Peak): Rīga; tel. 6731-5137; f. 1999; fiction, poetry, fine arts; Dir ANDREJS BRIMERBERGS.

Zinātne Publishers Ltd (Science): Akadēmijas lauk. 1, Rīga 1050; tel. 6721-2797; fax 6722-7825; e-mail zinatne@navigator.lv; f. 1951; non-fiction, text books, dictionaries, reference books; Dir INGRĪDA SEGLINA.

Zvaigzne ABC: K. Valdemāra iela 6, Rīga 1010; tel. 6750-8799; fax 6750-8798; e-mail info@zvaigzne.lv; internet www.zvaigzne.lv; f. 1966; privately owned; educational literature, textbooks, dictionaries, non-fiction for children and adults, fiction; Head of Bd VIJA KILBLOKA.

PUBLISHERS' ASSOCIATION

Latvian Publishers' Asscn (Latvijas Grāmatizdevēju asociācija): Rīga; tel. 6728-2392; fax 6728-0549; e-mail lga@gramatizdeveji.lv; internet www.gramatizdeveji.lv; f. 1993; 40 mems; Pres. JĀNIS LEJA.

Broadcasting and Communications

TELECOMMUNICATIONS

In 2006 there were 657,000 main telephone lines in use; 69% of lines were digital in 2001. In 2005 there were four providers of mobile telecommunications services.

Regulatory Organizations

Dept of Communications (Ministry of Transport): Gogoļa iela 3, Rīga 1190; tel. 6724-2321; fax 6782-0636; e-mail diana.ainep@sam.gov.lv; f. 1991; Dir INĀRA RUDAKA.

Public Utilities Commission (Sabiedrisko Pakalpojumu Regulēšanas Komisija): see Trade and Industry (Utilities) section.

Major Service Providers

Lattelecom SIA: Dzirnavu iela 105, Rīga 1011; tel. 6705-5222; fax 6705-5001; e-mail nils.melngailis@lattelecom.lv; internet www.lattelecom.lv; f. 1992; 51% state-owned, 49% by TeliaSonera AB (Sweden); CEO NILS MELNGAILIS; 3,000 employees.

Latvian Mobile Telephone Co (Latvijas Mobilais Telefons SIA—LMT): Ropazu iela 6, Rīga 1039; tel. 6777-3200; fax 6753-5353; e-mail info@lmt.lv; internet www.lmt.lv; f. 1992; 24.5% owned by Sonera Holding BV (Finland), 24.5% owned by TeliaSonera AB (Sweden), 23.0% owned by SIA Lattelekom, 23.0% owned by Digitālais Latvijas radio un televīzijas centrs; Gen. Man. JURIS BINDE.

SIA Radiokoms: Elizabetes iela 45–47, Rīga 1010; tel. 6733-3355; e-mail radiokoms@radiokoms.lv; internet www.radiokoms.lv; Dir JANA BALODE.

Tele2: Rīga; tel. 6706-0069; fax 6706-0176; internet www.tele2.lv; f. 1991; owned by Tele2 AB (Sweden); fmrly Baltkom GSM; Pres. BILL BUTLER; 110 employees.

BROADCASTING

Regulatory Organization

National Broadcasting Council of Latvia (Nacionālā Radio un Televizijas Padome): Smilšu iela 1/3, Rīga 1939; tel. 6722-1848; fax 6722-0448; e-mail nrtp@nrtp.lv; internet www.nrtp.lv; f. 1995; independent regulatory authority; Chair. ABRAMS KLECKINS.

Radio

Latvijas Radio (Latvian Radio): Doma lauk. 8, Rīga 1505; tel. 6720-6722; fax 6720-6709; e-mail radio@radio.org.lv; internet www.latvijasradio.lv; f. 1925; state-operated service; broadcasts in Latvian and Russian; Dir-Gen. DZINTRIS KOLATS.

Alise Plus: Raiņa iela 28, Daugavpils 5403; e-mail radio@aliseplus.eu; internet www.aliseplus.eu; 24-hour transmissions in Russian and Latvian.

European Hit Radio: Elijas iela 17, Rīga 1050; tel. 6957-5757; fax 6720-4407; e-mail radio@superfm.lv; internet www.europeanhitradio.com; f. 1994; 24-hour transmissions in Latvian, Russian, Estonian, Lithuanian and English; Pres. UGIS POLIS; Dir RICHARD ZAKSS.

Latvijas Kristīgais Radio (Latvian Christian Radio): Lāčplēša iela 37, Rīga 1011; tel. 6721-3704; fax 6782-0633; e-mail lkr@lkr.lv; internet www.lkr.lv; f. 1993; 24-hour transmissions in Latvian and Russian.

Radio Ef-Ei: Atbrvōsanas aleja 98, Rēzekne 4600; e-mail efei@mailbox.riga.lv; 24-hour transmissions in Russian and Latvian.

Radio Imanta: Tērbatas iela 1, Valmiera 4201; tel. 6420-7349; fax 6420-7350; e-mail radio.imanta@tl.lv; internet www.radioimanta.lv; 24-hour transmissions in Russian and Latvian; Chief Editor NILS INTERBERGS.

Radio Mix FM: L. Nometņu iela 62, Rīga 1002; 24-hour transmissions in Russian.

Radio Sigulda: L. Paegles iela 3, Sigulda 2150; tel. 6797-2678; fax 6797-3786; e-mail mail@radiosigulda.lv; internet www.radiosigulda.lv; f. 1991; 24-hour transmissions in Latvian; music radio; Dir AIVARS PLUCIS.

Radio SWH: Skanstes iela 13, Rīga 1013; tel. 6737-0067; fax 6782-8283; e-mail radio@radioswh.lv; internet www.radioswh.lv; Pres. ZITMARS LIEPINSCH.

LATVIA

Radio Trīs: Vaļņu iela 5, Cēsis 4101; tel. 6412-4566; fax 6412-7041; e-mail radio@radio3.lv; internet www.radio3.lv; f. 1994; Di EGILS VISKRINTS.

Radio Zemgale: Grāfa lauk. 6, Lecava 3913; e-mail rz@apollo.lv; f. 2000; 24-hour transmissions in Latvian; Dir DACE DUBKEVIČA.

Television

Latvijas Televīzija (Latvian Television): Zaķusalas krastmala 3, Rīga 1509; tel. 6720-0315; fax 6720-0025; internet www.ltv.lv; f. 1954; state-operated service; two channels in Latvian, LTV1 and LTV7 (LTV7 also includes programmes in Russian, English and French); Dir-Gen. EDGARS KOTS.

Latvijas Neatkariga Televizija (Latvian Independent Television—LNT): Elijas iela 17, Rīga 1050; tel. 6707-0200; fax 6782-1128; e-mail lnt@lnt.lv; internet www.lnt.lv; f. 1996; entertainment, news reports; Dir-Gen. ANDREJS ĒĶIS.

TV3 Latvia: Mūkusalas iela 72B, Rīga 1004; tel. 6762-9366; fax 6760-0599; e-mail tv3@tv3.lv; internet www.tv3.lv; owned by Modern Times Group–MTG (Sweden); affiliated with channel 3+, targeted at a Russian-speaking audience; Dir KASPARS OZOLINS.

Finance

(cap. = capital; res = reserves; dep. = deposits; m. = million; brs = branches; amounts in lats)

BANKING

Central Bank

Bank of Latvia (Latvijas Banka): K. Valdemāra iela 2A, Rīga 1050; tel. 6702-2300; fax 6702-2420; e-mail info@bank.lv; internet www.bank.lv; f. 1990; cap. 25.0m., res 163.5m., dep. 2,135.9m. (Dec. 2008); Gov. and Chair. of Council ILMĀRS RIMŠĒVIČS.

Commercial Banks

Aizkraukles Banka: Elizabetes iela 23, Rīga 1010; tel. 6777-5222; fax 6777-5200; e-mail bank@ab.lv; internet www.ab.lv; f. 1993; cap. 15.0m., res 54.6m., dep. 858.4m. (Dec. 2008); Chair. of Bd ALEKSANDRS BERGMANIS.

Citadele banka: Republikas laukums 2A, Rīga 1522; tel. 6701-0000; fax 6701-0001; e-mail info@parex.lv; internet www.citadele.lv; f. 1992 as Parex banka; name changed as above in Aug. 2010; cap. 65.0m., res −20.5m., dep. 3,261.7m. (Dec. 2008); 75% state-owned; 25% owned by the European Bank for Reconstruction and Development; Pres. and Chair. of Bd NILS MELNGAILIS; 72 brs.

DnB Nord Banka Latvija: Smilšu iela 6, Rīga 1803; tel. 6716-1112; fax 6732-3449; e-mail ib@nordlb.lv; internet www.dnbnord.lv; f. 1989; fmrly Rīgas Komercbanka PLC and AS NORD/LB Latvija; 99.76% owned by Bank DnB NORD (Denmark); cap. 99.1m., res 49.3m., dep. 1,738.9m. (Dec. 2008); Pres. and Chair. of Bd ANDRIS OZOLINS; 10 brs.

GE Money Bank: 13 Janvāra iela 3, Rīga 1050; tel. 6702-4747; fax 6782-0319; e-mail info@gemoneybank.lv; internet www.gemoneybank.lv; f. 2008 by merger of Baltic Trust Bank (BTB) and GE Money; 99.48% owned by Finstar Baltic Investments; cap. 15.6m., res 11.2m., dep. 238.7m. (Dec. 2007); Chair. RICHARD GASKIN; 31 brs.

Latvijas Biznesa Banka (Latvian Business Bank): 3 Antonijas iela, Rīga 1010; tel. 6777-5888; fax 6777-5849; e-mail info@lbb.lv; internet www.lbb.lv; f. 1992; present name adopted 2004; 99.87% owned by Bank of Moscow (Russia); cap. 10.8m., res 5.4m., dep. 113.9m. (Dec. 2008); Chair. and Pres. ANDREY BORODIN.

Latvijas Hipotēku un Zemes Banka (Hipotēku Banka) (Mortgage and Land Bank of Latvia): Doma lauk. 4, Rīga 1977; tel. 6800-0100; fax 6777-4152; e-mail banka@hipo.lv; internet www.hipo.lv; f. 1993; present name adopted in 2000; state-owned; cap. 48.5m., res −1.4m., dep. 841.6m. (Dec. 2008); Chair. of Bd ROLAND PAŅKO; 32 brs.

LTB Bank: Grēcinieku iela 22, Rīga 1050; tel. 6704-3510; fax 6704-3511; e-mail ltb@ltblv.com; internet www.ltblv.com; f. 1991; fmrly Latvijas Tirdzniecības banka (Latvian Trade Bank); owned by MDM Bank (Russian Federation); cap. 8.2m., res 24.4m., dep. 286.0m. (Dec. 2008); Chair. ARMANDS ŠTEINBERGS.

Norvik Banka: E. Birznieka-Upīša iela 21, Rīga 1011; tel. 6704-1100; fax 6704-1111; e-mail welcome@norvik.lv; internet www.norvik.lv; f. 1992; fmrly Lateko Bank; present name adopted 2006; cap. 40.5m., res 8.9m., dep. 551.0m. (Dec. 2007); Chair. of Bd ANDREJS SVIRČENKOVS; 15 brs.

PrivatBank: Terbatas iela 4, Rīga 1134; tel. 6704-1300; fax 6728-2981; e-mail info@privatbank.lv; internet www.privatbank.lv; f. 1992; fmrly Paritate Banka; present name adopted 2007; cap. 10.6m., res 3.7m., dep. 165.5m. (Dec. 2008); Chair. of Bd OLEKSANDR TRUBAKOV.

Rietumu Banka: Vesetas iela 7, Rīga 1013; tel. 6702-5555; fax 6702-5588; e-mail info@rietumu.lv; internet www.rietumu.lv; f. 1992; cap. 22.5m., res 6.6m., dep. 974.9m. (Dec. 2008); Pres. and Chair. of Exec. Bd ALEXANDER KALINOVSKI.

SEB Banka: SEB finanšu centrs, Meistaru iela 1, Valdlauci 1076; tel. 2777-8777; fax 6721-5335; e-mail info@seb.lv; internet www.seb.lv; f. 1993; fmrly SEB Latvijas Unibanka; present name adopted 2008; owned by SEB (Skandinaviska Enskilda Banken AB, Sweden); cap. 37.1m., res −7.4m., dep. 2,657.3m. (Dec. 2008); Chair. of the Bd AINĀRS OZOLS; 68 brs.

Svedbank Latvia: Balasta dambis 1A, Rīga 1048; tel. 6744-4444; fax 6744-4344; e-mail info@swedbank.lv; internet www.swedbank.lv; f. 1992; present name adopted 2008, following merger between Hansabank and Swedbank; cap. 406.0m., res 0.1m., dep. 4,515.2m. (Dec. 2008); Pres. and CEO MARIS MANCINSKIS; 86 brs.

Trasta komercbanka—TKB (Trust Commercial Bank): Miesnieku iela 9, Rīga 1050; tel. 6702-7777; fax 6702-7700; e-mail info@tkb.lv; internet www.tkb.lv; f. 1989; present name adopted 1996; cap. 6.3m., res 3.8m., dep. 173.6m. (Dec. 2008); Pres. and Chair. GUNDARS GRIEZE.

UniCredit Bank: Elizabetes iela 63, Rīga 1050; tel. 6708-5500; fax 6708-5507; e-mail info@unicreditbank.lv; internet www.unicreditbank.lv; f. 1997; fmrly Vereinsbank Rīga; present name adopted 2005; 100% owned by Bank Austria Creditanstalt AG (Austria); cap. 41.7m., res 0.0m., dep. 722.6m. (Dec. 2008); Chair. of Bd RALF CYMANEK.

Savings Bank

Latvijas Krājbanka (Latvian Savings Bank): Dalina iela 15, Rīga 1013; tel. 6709-2020; fax 6709-2070; e-mail info@lkb.lv; internet www.krajbanka.lv; f. 1924; present name adopted 1998; 76.65% owned by Snoras Bankas (Lithuania); cap. 12.1m., res 18.2m., dep. 624.1m. (Dec. 2008); Pres. IVARS PRIEDITIS; 10 brs.

Regulatory Authority

Financial and Capital Markets Commission (Finanšu un kapitāla tirgus komisija—FKTK): Kungu iela 1, Rīga 1050; tel. 6777-4800; fax 6722-5755; e-mail fktk@fktk.lv; internet www.fktk.lv; f. 2001; Chair. IRENA KRUMANE.

Banking Association

Association of Latvian Commercial Banks (Latvijas Komercbanku asociācija): Pērses iela 9–11, Rīga 1011; tel. 6728-4528; fax 6782-8170; e-mail asoc@bankasoc.lv; internet www.bankasoc.lv; f. 1992; 23 mems; Pres. ANDRIS TVERIJONS.

INSURANCE

At September 2004 there were 18 insurance companies in Latvia, of which six were involved in life insurance and 12 in non-life insurance operations.

Balta Insurance Co: Raunas iela 10/12, Rīga 1039; tel. 6708-2333; fax 6708-2345; e-mail balta@balta.lv; internet www.balta.lv; f. 1992; automobile, property, freight, travel, agricultural insurance; Chair. ANDREW KIRKLAND.

Balva: Vīlandes iela 14, Rīga 1010; tel. 6750-6955; fax 6750-6956; e-mail balva@balva.lv; internet www.balva.lv; f. 1992; partly owned by Ingosstrakh (Russia); non-life insurance; Chair. of Bd RUŽENA OZERNOVA; 31 brs.

BTA Apdrošināšana: K. Valdemāra iela 63, Rīga 1142; tel. 6702-5100; fax 6702-5190; e-mail bta@bta.lv; internet www.bta.lv; f. 1993; Chair. of Bd GINTS DANDZBERGS.

Colemont FKB Latvia: Dārzaugļu iela 1–50, Rīga 1012; tel. 6724-0066; fax 6720-1737; e-mail info@colemont.lv; internet www.colemont.lv; f. 2000; 60% owned by Colemont Insurance Brokers (USA); fmrly Finansu Konsultanti Un Brokeri (FKB); name changed in 2006; Chair. of Bd BEERH SURINDER KUMAR.

ERGO Latvija: Ūnijas iela 45, Rīga 1039; tel. 6708-1700; fax 6708-1715; e-mail info@ergo.lv; internet www.ergo.lv; owned by Alte Leipziger (Germany); life and non-life; Chair. of Bd THOMAS HANS SCHIRMER.

Estora Reinsurance Co: Elizabetes iela 14, Rīga 1010; tel. 6733-3335; fax 6733-3898; e-mail estora@estora.com; internet www.estora.com; f. 1992; reinsurance; Dir-Gen. JERGENIJS TOLOČKOVS.

SEB Dzīvības Apdrošināšana (SEB Life Insurance): Antonijas iela 9, Rīga 1010; tel. 6707-9800; fax 6707-9808; e-mail dziviba@seb.lv; internet www.seb.lv; f. 1940; present name adopted 2005; Chair. of Bd UĢIS VORONS.

Seesam Latvia: Vienības gatve 87H, Rīga 1004; tel. 6706-1000; fax 6706-1022; e-mail seesam@seesam.lv; internet www.seesam.lv; f. 1993; owned by Pohjola Group Plc (Finland); Chair. of Bd IVO KULDMÄE.

LATVIA

COMMODITY AND STOCK EXCHANGE

NASDAQ OMX Riga (NASDAQ OMX Riga AS): Vaļņu iela 1, Rīga 1050; tel. 721-2431; fax 722-9411; e-mail riga@nasdaqomx.com; internet www.nasdaqomxbaltic.com; f. 1993; owned by the NASDAQ OMX Group (USA); Chair. of Managing Bd DAIGA AUZIŅA-MELALKSNE.

Trade and Industry

GOVERNMENT AGENCY

Corruption Prevention and Combating Bureau (Korupcuas Novēršanas un Apkarošanas Birojs—KNAB): Brīvības iela 104, blk 2, Rīga 1001; tel. 6735-6161; fax 6733-1150; e-mail knab@knab.gov.lv; internet www.knab.gov.lv; f. 2002; ind. authority under government supervision; Deputy. Dir ALVIS VILKS.

Latvian Privatization Agency (Latvijas Privatizācijas agentūra): K. Valdemāra iela 31, Rīga 1887; tel. 6702-1358; fax 6783-0363; e-mail lpa@mail.bkc.lv; internet www.lpa.bkc.lv; f. 1994; became state joint-stock co in 2004; Dir-Gen. ARTIS KAMPARS.

DEVELOPMENT ORGANIZATIONS

Investment and Development Agency of Latvia (Latvijas Investīciju un Attīstības Agentūra—LIAA): Pērses iela 2, Rīga 1442; tel. 6703-9400; fax 6703-9401; e-mail liaa@liaa.gov.lv; internet www.liaa.gov.lv; f. 1993; promotion of business development in Latvia and foreign markets; Dir ANDRIS OZOLS.

CHAMBER OF COMMERCE

Latvian Chamber of Commerce and Industry (Latvijas Tirdzniecības un rūpniecības kamera): K. Valdemāra iela 35, Rīga 1010; tel. 6722-5595; fax 6782-0092; e-mail info@chamber.lv; internet www.chamber.lv; f. 1934; re-est. 1990; Pres. ANDRIS BĒRZIŅŠ; Chair. of Bd ŽANETA JAUNZEME GRENDE.

INDUSTRIAL AND TRADE ASSOCIATIONS

Employers' Confederation of Latvia: Baznicas iela 25-3, Rīga 1010; tel. 6722-5162; fax 6722-4469; e-mail lddk@lddk.lv; internet www.lddk.lv; f. 1993; Pres. VITĀLIJS GAVRILOVS.

Latvian Construction Contractors' Association (LCCA) (Latvijas būvnieku asociācija—LBA): Grēcinieku ielā 22/24, kab. 201, Rīga 1050; tel. 6722-8584; fax 6721-0023; e-mail lba@latnet.lv; internet www.building.lv/lba; f. 1996; Pres. VIKTORS PURIŅŠ; 6 brs.

Latvian Electrical Engineering and Electronics Industry Association (LETERA): Dzirnavu iela 93, Rīga 1011; tel. 6728-8360; fax 6728-8390; e-mail letera@latnet.lv; internet www.letera.lv; f. 1995; 50 mems (enterprises and education institutions); Pres. NORMUNDS BERGS.

Latvian Fuel Traders' Association (Latvijas Degvielas Tirgotāju Asociācija): Citadeles iela 7/43, Rīga 1010; tel. 6732-0229; fax 6732-0228; e-mail birojs@ldta.lv; internet www.ldta.lv; Chair. of Bd O. KARČEVSKIS; Exec. Dir U. SAKNE.

Latvian Information Technology and Telecommunications Association (Latvijas Informācijas un Komunikācijas Tehnoloģijas Asociācija—LIKTA): Stabu iela 47–1, Rīga 1011; tel. 6731-1821; fax 6731-5567; e-mail office@likta.lv; internet www.likta.lv; f. 1998; Pres. SIGNE BĀLIŅA.

Latvian Timber Exporters' Association (LTEA) (Latvijas Kokmateriālu Eksportētāju Asociācija): Skaistkalnes iela 1, Rīga 1004; tel. 6706-7369; fax 6786-0268; e-mail office@latvianwood.lv; internet www.latvianwood.lv; f. 1998; Pres. JANIS APSITIS.

UTILITIES

Regulatory Authority

Public Utilities Commission (PUC) (Sabiedrisko Pakalpojumu Regulēšanas Komisija): Brīvības iela 55, Rīga 1010; tel. 6709-7200; fax 6709-7277; e-mail sprk@sprk.gov.lv; internet www.sprk.gov.lv; f. 2001; multi-sector regulator overseeing electricity, gas, telecommunications, post and railway sectors; Chair. VALENTĪNA ANDRĒJEVA.

Electricity

Latvenergo: Pulkveža Brieža iela 12, Rīga 1230; tel. 6772-8222; fax 6772-8778; e-mail info@latvenergo.lv; internet www.latvenergo.lv; state-owned joint-stock co; transmits and distributes electricity and thermal energy; five regional subsidiary cos and two associated cos; Chair. of Bd KĀRLIS MIĶELSONS.

Rīgas Siltums AS: Cesu iela 3A, Rīga 1012; tel. 6701-7300; fax 6701-7363; e-mail siltums@rs.lv; internet www.rs.lv; f. 1996; production, distribution and sale of thermal energy, and also ensures technical maintenance of inner heat supply systems in buildings; Chair. of Bd EMĪLS JAKRINS.

Gas

Latvian Gas (Latvijas gāze): Vagonu iela 20, Rīga 1009; tel. 6704-1818; fax 6782-1604; e-mail latvijas_gaze@lg.lv; internet www.lg.lv; partially privatized in 2000–01; jt-stock co; 8% state-owned; Chair. ADRIAN DAVIS; 2,817 employees.

Water

Major suppliers include:

Aizkraukle Water Co (Aizkraukles ūdens): Torņu iela 1, Aizkraukle 5101; fax 6512-2150; e-mail udensall@inbox.lv.

Daugavpils Water Co (Daugavpils ūdens): Ūdensvada iela 3, Daugavpils 5401; tel. 6544-4608; fax 6542-5547; e-mail kontakti@daugavpils.udens.lv; internet www.daugavpils.udens.lv; f. 1889.

Liepāja Water Co (Liepājas ūdens): K. Valdemāra iela 12, Liepāja 3401; tel. 6541-1416; fax 6541-0769; e-mail dmeu@dpu.lv.

Rīga Water Co (Rīgas ūdens): Zigfrīda Annas Meierovica bulv. 1, Rīga 1495; tel. 6708-8555; fax 6722-2660; e-mail office@ru.lv; internet www.rw.lv; water supply and sewage treatment.

TRADE UNIONS

Free Trade Union Confederation of Latvia (Latvijas Brīvo Arodbiedrību Savienība—LBAS): Bruņinieku iela 29–31, Rīga 1001; tel. 6727-0351; fax 6727-6649; e-mail lbas@lbas.lv; internet www.lbas.lv; f. 1990; 21 branch or professional affiliated unions; Pres. PETERIS KRIGERS; 110,602 mems (2009).

Transport

RAILWAYS

In 2005 there were 2,270 km of railways on the territory of Latvia, of which 257 km were electrified. In 2007 Latvian railways carried 27.4m. passengers and 52.2m. metric tons of freight.

Latvian Railways (Latvijas Dzelzceļš): Gogoļa iela 3, Rīga 1547; tel. 6723-4940; fax 6782-0231; e-mail biruta.sakse@ldz.lv; internet www.ldz.lv; f. 1993; state joint-stock co; Chair. of Bd UGIS MAGONIS.

ROADS

In 2004 Latvia's total road network was 69,532 km, of which 6,963 km were main roads.

Latvian State Roads (Latvijas Valsts Ceļi): Gogoļa iela 3, Rīga 1050; tel. 6702-8169; fax 6702-8171; e-mail lad@lvceli.lv; internet www.lvceli.lv; f. 2004 to replace Latvian Road Administration; state joint-stock co; manages state road network, administers State Road Fund; Chair. TĀLIS STRAUME.

SHIPPING

At 31 December 2009 the Latvian-registered merchant fleet numbered 144 vessels, with a combined total displacement of 263,900 grt. In 2009 some 62.0m. metric tons of sea-borne freight were transported through the country's three main (Ventspils, Rīga and Liepāja) and seven smaller ports.

Maritime Department (Ministry of Transport): Gogoļa iela 3, Rīga 1743; tel. 6702-8198; fax 6733-1406; e-mail aigars.krastins@sam.gov.lv; internet www.sam.gov.lv; Dir AIGARS KRASTIŅŠ.

Port Authorities and Ports

The Freeport of Riga Authority (Rīgas Brīvostas Pārvalde): Kalpaka bulv. 12, Rīga 1010; tel. 6703-0800; fax 6703-0835; e-mail info@freeportofriga.lv; internet www.rop.lv; f. 1994; CEO LEONIDS LOGINOVS; Chair. of Bd AINARS SLESERS.

Liepāja Port Authority: Liepāja Special Economic Zone, Feniksa iela 4, Liepāja 3401; tel. 6342-7605; fax 6348-0252; e-mail authority@lsez.lv; internet www.lsez.lv; Man. Dir AIVARS BOJA.

Rīga Commercial Free Port SSC: Katrinas iela 5A, Rīga 1227; tel. 6732-9224; fax 6783-0215; e-mail rto@mail.bkc.lv; internet www.rto.lv; f. 1996.

Ventspils Commercial Port (Ventspils Tirdzniecības Ostā): Dzintaru iela 22, Ventspils 3602; tel. 6366-8706; fax 6366-8860; e-mail vcp@vto.lv; internet www.vcp.lv; Chair. of Bd VALERIJ PASHUTA.

Ventspils Free Port Authority (Ventspils brīvostas pārvalde): Jāņa iela 19, Ventspils 3601; tel. 6362-2586; fax 6362-1297; e-mail info@vbp.lv; internet portofventspils.lv; f. 1991; Chief Exec. IMANTS SARMULIS.

Shipping Company

Latvijas kugniecība (LASCO) (Latvian Shipping Co): Elizabetes iela 1, Rīga 1807; tel. 6702-0111; fax 6782-8106; e-mail lsc@lscgroup.lv; internet www.lk.lv; f. 1991; tanker, reefer, liquid petroleum gas and dry-cargo transportation; 49.94% owned by Ventspils Nafta; Pres. IMANTS SARMULIS.

CIVIL AVIATION

There is an international airport at Rīga.

airBaltic Corpn: Rīga Airport, Rīga 1053; tel. 6720-7069; fax 6720-7369; e-mail info@airbaltic.lv; internet www.airbaltic.com; f. 1995; 52.6% govt-owned; Pres. and Chief Exec. BERTOLT FLICK; Chair. of Bd VIGO LEGZDINS.

Civil Aviation Agency of Latvia (Latvijas Civilās Aviācijas Administrācija): Rīga Airport 1011, Rīga 1053; tel. 6783-0936; fax 6783-0967; internet www.caa.lv; Dir MĀRIS GORODCOVS.

Tourism

Among Latvia's principal tourist attractions are the historic centre of Rīga, with its medieval and art nouveau buildings, the extensive beaches of the Baltic coastline, and Gauja National Park, which stretches east of the historic town of Sigulda for nearly 100 km. Revenue from tourism was some US $1,134m. in 2008. Foreign tourist arrivals at accommodation establishments numbered 753,875 in 2009.

Latvian Tourism Development Agency: Pils lauk. 4, Rīga 1050; tel. and fax 6722-9945; fax 6735-8128; e-mail tda@latviatourism.lv; internet www.latviatourism.lv; f. 1993; Dir ULDIS VITOLINS.

Defence

A Latvian Ministry of Defence was established in November 1991. In August 1994 the withdrawal from Latvia of all former Soviet forces was completed. As assessed at November 2010, Latvia's total armed forces numbered 5,745, comprising an army of 1,058, a navy of 587, an air force of 319, joint staff of 3,202, and a national guard of 579. Army volunteer reservists, numbered 10,866. Conscription ended in 2006. Latvia joined the North Atlantic Treaty Organization's (NATO) 'Partnership for Peace' programme in February 1994, and became a full member of the Alliance on 29 March 2004.

Defence Expenditure: Budgeted at 134m. lats for 2010.

Commander of the National Armed Forces: Brig.-Gen. RAIMONDS GRAUBE.

Commander of the Air Force: Col ALEXSANDRS STEPANOV.

Commander in Chief of the Navy: Cmmdr ALEKSANDRS PAVLOVIČS.

Education

Primary education begins at seven years of age and lasts for four years. Secondary education, beginning at the age of 11, comprises a first cycle of five years and a second of three years. Only the first nine years of education are officially compulsory. In 2005 enrolment at primary schools included 87.8% of pupils in the relevant age-group; in that year enrolment at secondary schools was equivalent to 98.2% of pupils in the relevant age-group. In the 2004/05 academic year some 65% of school-age pupils were taught in Latvian-language schools and some 25% were taught in Russian-language schools; 10% were taught in schools offering instruction in both Latvian and Russian. In 2009/10 higher education was offered at 61 institutions and enrolment totalled 112,567 students. According to official figures, in 2008 consolidated central government expenditure on education amounted to 1,052.0m. lats (representing 16.8% of expenditure).

LEBANON

Introductory Survey

LOCATION, CLIMATE, LANGUAGE, RELIGION, FLAG, CAPITAL

The Republic of Lebanon lies in western Asia, bordered by Syria to the north and east, and by Israel and the Palestinian Autonomous Areas to the south. The country has a coastline of about 220 km (135 miles) on the eastern shore of the Mediterranean Sea. The climate varies widely with altitude. The coastal lowlands are hot and humid in summer, becoming mild (cool and damp) in winter. In the mountains, which occupy much of Lebanon, the weather is cool in summer, with heavy snowfalls in winter. Rainfall is generally abundant. The official language is Arabic, which is spoken by almost all of the inhabitants. French is widely used as a second language, while Kurdish and Armenian are spoken by small ethnic minorities. According to the UN Relief and Works Agency for Palestine Refugees in the Near East (UNRWA), at June 2010 there were 427,057 Palestinian refugees registered in Lebanon. The major religions are Islam and Christianity, and there is a very small Jewish community. In the early 1980s it was estimated that 57% of Lebanon's inhabitants were Muslims, with about 43% Christians; these figures were believed to have changed to 60% and 39%, respectively, by 2008. The principal Muslim sects are Shi'a and Sunni, while there is also a significant Druze community. By the 1980s it was generally considered that Shi'a Muslims, totalling an estimated 1.2m., constituted Lebanon's largest single community. Most Christians adhere to the Roman Catholic Church, principally the Maronite rite. In 1994 it was estimated that 29%–32% of the population of Lebanon were Shi'a Muslims, 25%–28% Maronites, 16%–20% Sunni Muslims and 3.5% Druzes. There are also Armenian, Greek and Syrian sects (both Catholic and Eastern Orthodox) and small groups of Protestants. The national flag (proportions 2 by 3) has three horizontal stripes, of red, white (half the depth) and red, with a representation of a cedar tree (in green and brown) in the centre of the white stripe. The capital is Beirut.

CONTEMPORARY POLITICAL HISTORY

Historical Context

Lebanon, the homeland of the ancient Phoenicians, became part of the Turkish Ottoman Empire in the 16th century, and following the dissolution of the Ottoman Empire after the First World War (1914–18), a Greater Lebanese state was created by the Allied powers. The new state was formed in order to meet the nationalist aspirations of the area's predominantly Christian population, but it also included largely Muslim-populated territories traditionally considered to be part of Syria. Lebanon was administered by France, under a League of Nations mandate, from 1920 until independence was declared on 26 November 1941. A republic was established in 1943, and full autonomy was granted in January 1944.

Religious and cultural diversity is Lebanon's defining feature. At the time of independence Christians formed a slight majority of the population, the largest single community (nearly 30% of the total) being the Maronite Christians, who mostly inhabited the north of the country and the capital, Beirut. Other Christian groups included Greek Orthodox communities, Greek Catholics and Armenians. The Muslim groups were the Sunnis, living mainly in the coastal towns of Sur (Tyre), Saida (Sidon) and Beirut, the Shi'ites, a predominantly rural community in southern Lebanon and the northern Beqa'a valley, and, in much smaller numbers, the Druzes, an ancient community in central Lebanon. The relative size of the various communities provided the basis for the unwritten 'national pact' of 1943, whereby executive and legislative posts were to be shared in the ratio of six Christians to five Muslims, and seats in the Chamber of Deputies (renamed the National Assembly in March 1979) were distributed on a religious, rather than a politico-ideological, basis. The convention according to this 'confessional' arrangement was that the President was a Maronite Christian, the Prime Minister a Sunni Muslim, and the President of the National Assembly a Shi'a Muslim.

Lebanon's first President, from 1943 until 1952, was Sheikh Bishara el-Khoury. His successor was Camille Chamoun, whose reforms included the enfranchisement of women. Following elections to the Chamber of Deputies in 1957 there was considerable unrest, mainly among Muslims who mistrusted Chamoun's pro-Western foreign policy and advocated Lebanon's closer alignment with Syria and Egypt. In July 1958 Chamoun appealed to the USA for military assistance; US forces remained in Beirut until October, by which time peace had been restored. Meanwhile, Chamoun was persuaded not to seek a further presidential term, and the Chamber elected Gen. Fouad Chehab as his successor. Chehab, who took office in September 1958, adopted a foreign policy of non-alignment, and introduced state provision of health, education and other services. In 1964 he was succeeded by Charles Hélou, who was faced by increasing controversy over the status of Palestinians in Lebanon.

After the establishment of Israel in 1948, and during the subsequent Arab–Israeli wars, thousands of Palestinians fled to Lebanon, where most were housed in refugee camps in the south of the country. Following the creation of the Palestine Liberation Organization (PLO) in 1964, military training centres for Palestinian guerrilla fighters were established in the camps. From 1968 these self-styled *fedayeen* ('martyrs') began making raids into Israel, provoking retaliatory attacks by Israeli forces. In 1969 there were clashes between Lebanese security forces and the *fedayeen*. Many Christians, particularly the Maronites, advocated strict government control over the Palestinians' activities, but the majority of Muslims strongly supported Palestinian operations against Israel.

Domestic Political Affairs

Charles Hélou's successor as President, Sulayman Franjiya, took office in 1970. In July 1971 a further influx of Palestinian fighters expelled from Jordan led to fierce fighting between Israeli forces and Palestinians based in Lebanon, while Christian groups began their own armed campaign against the *fedayeen*. In July 1974 Palestinian forces clashed with militia of the Phalangist Party (the Phalanges libanaises or al-Kataeb, a militant right-wing Maronite Christian group now also known as the Lebanese Social Democratic Party). From April 1975 the conflict between the Palestinians and Phalangists quickly descended into full-scale civil war between the Lebanese National Movement (LNM) of left-wing Muslims (including Palestinians), led by Kamal Joumblatt of the Parti socialiste progressiste (PSP, a mainly Druze-supported group), and conservative Christian groups, mainly the Phalangist militia. Constitutional matters overtook the status of Palestinians as the main divisive issue, with the LNM advocating an end to the 'confessional' system, claiming that this unduly favoured Christians (who by now were generally accepted as no longer forming a majority of the population). Despite diplomatic efforts by Arab and Western countries, no durable cease-fire was achieved until October 1976, largely as a result of intervention in the conflict (in order to prevent an outright LNM victory) by Syrian forces in mid-1976. Under the terms of the cease-fire, a 30,000-strong Arab Deterrent Force (ADF), composed mainly of Syrian troops, entered Lebanon.

President Franjiya was succeeded by Elias Sarkis in September 1976, and Prime Minister Rashid Karami by Selim al-Hoss in December. Legislative elections, due in April 1976, were postponed for an initial period of 26 months—the term of the Chamber of Deputies was subsequently extended further. Although the constitutional status quo remained intact, more than 30,000 people had already died in the civil war and the militias of the various warring factions controlled most of the country. East Beirut and much of northern Lebanon was controlled by the Lebanese Forces (LF), a coalition of Maronite militias formed in September 1976; west Beirut was controlled by Muslim groups; and Palestinians dominated much of southwest Lebanon.

In March 1978 Israeli forces advanced into southern Lebanon in a counter-attack against forces of Fatah (the Palestine National Liberation Movement), the main guerrilla group within the PLO. UN Security Council Resolution 425, adopted on 17 March, demanded an Israeli withdrawal from Lebanon (thereby respecting its territorial integrity, sovereignty and independence) and also established a UN Interim Force in Lebanon (UNIFIL, see p. 89), initially of 4,000 troops. Israeli forces withdrew in June, but transferred control of a border strip to the pro-Israeli Christian militia which in May 1980 became known as the South Lebanon Army (SLA). Meanwhile, in October 1978, following several months of renewed fighting in Beirut between Syrian troops of the ADF and right-wing Christian militias, the ADF states agreed on a peace plan (the Beiteddin Declaration), which aimed to restore the authority of the Lebanese Government and army. Attempts to implement the plan were unsuccessful, however, and Lebanon's fragmentation deepened.

Al-Hoss resigned the premiership in June 1980 and was replaced in October by Chafic al-Wazzan. In August 1982, in an election boycotted by most Muslim deputies, the renamed National Assembly designated Bashir Gemayel (the younger son of the founder of the Phalangist Party and commander of the LF) to succeed President Sarkis. The President-elect was assassinated in September, and his brother, Amin, was elected in his place. Following the assassination, Phalangist forces (with the apparent complicity of occupying Israeli forces) entered the Palestinian refugee camps of Sabra and Chatila, in west Beirut, killing some 2,000 refugees. Israeli forces had re-entered Lebanon in June 1982, with the declared aim of finally eliminating the PLO's military threat to Israel's northern border; they quickly defeated Palestinian forces in south-west Lebanon and surrounded the western sector of Beirut, trapping more than 6,000 Palestinian fighters. A US-led diplomatic initiative resulted in an agreement enabling the PLO fighters to disperse among several Arab states, and a multinational peace-keeping force was deployed in Beirut. (In September 1983 intense fighting between rival factions of Fatah resulted in a truce agreement, brokered by Saudi Arabia and Syria, which led to a second evacuation of some 4,000 Palestinian fighters, most notably of the PLO Chairman, Yasser Arafat, who was exiled to Tunisia.) Meanwhile, in May 1983 Lebanon and Israel agreed to end all hostilities (including the theoretical state of war that had existed between them since 1948) and to withdraw all foreign troops from Lebanon. However, Syria did not recognize the accord, leaving 40,000 of its own troops and 7,000 PLO fighters in the Beqa'a valley and northern Lebanon. Israel, meanwhile, redeployed a reduced force of 10,000 troops along the Awali river, south of Beirut. The SLA was to police southern areas as Israel's role lessened. Meanwhile, the multinational force in Beirut (comprising some 5,800 mainly French, Italian and US personnel) was drawn increasingly into the fighting, coming under frequent attack from Muslim militias who opposed its tantamount support for the Christian-led Government. In October 1983, 241 US and 58 French marines were killed in suicide bombings by Muslim groups.

The failure to conclude a peaceful settlement, and in particular the resumption of heavy fighting in February 1984 (which the reconstituted, US-trained Lebanese army was unable to suppress), led to the resignation of Prime Minister al-Wazzan, followed shortly afterwards by the withdrawal of the USA, Italy and the United Kingdom from the peace-keeping force. French troops were withdrawn in March. By this time successive defeats had left Gemayel's forces with effective control only in the mainly Christian-populated east Beirut. In March President Gemayel abrogated the May 1983 agreement with Israel, and in April 1984, with Syrian support, he formed a Government of national unity under former premier Rashid Karami. The Lebanese army failed to gain control of Beirut, and Gemayel's efforts to obtain approval for constitutional reform, already constrained by his fear of alienating his Christian supporters, were further undermined by divisions within the Cabinet.

The Israeli Government formed by Shimon Peres in September 1984 pledged to withdraw Israeli forces from Lebanon. However, while the Lebanese authorities demanded that UNIFIL police the Israeli–Lebanese border, by the time the Israeli withdrawal was completed, in June 1985, Israel had ensured that a narrow security zone, policed by the SLA, was in place along the border. With the Israeli presence in Lebanon reduced to a token force, Syria withdrew about one-third of its troops from the Beqa'a valley in July, leaving some 25,000 in position.

In December 1985 the leaders of the three main Lebanese militias (the Druze forces, Amal and the LF) signed an accord in the Syrian capital, Damascus, providing for an immediate cease-fire and for the cessation of the civil war within one year. The militias were to be disarmed and disbanded, and a new constitutional regime was to be introduced within three years. However, the militias of the Sunni Murabitoun and the Iranian-backed Shi'ite Hezbollah were not parties to the agreement, which was also opposed by influential Christian elements. Furthermore, there were clashes later in December between supporters of the agreement within the LF and those who resented the concessions made by their leader, Elie Hobeika. In January 1986 Hobeika was forced into exile and replaced as leader of the LF by Samir Geagea, who urged renegotiation of the Damascus accord.

During 1986 Palestinian guerrillas resumed rocket attacks on settlements in northern Israel, provoking retaliatory air attacks by Israel on targets in the Beqa'a valley and southern Lebanon. Meanwhile, Hezbollah escalated its attacks on SLA positions within the Israeli security zone, and also clashed with UNIFIL. Fighting between Palestinian guerrillas and Shi'ite Amal militiamen for control of the refugee camps in south Beirut escalated in May, before a cease-fire was imposed around the camps in June, as part of a Syrian-sponsored peace plan for Muslim west Beirut. The activities of the Amal, Druze and Sunni militias in west Beirut were temporarily curtailed by the deployment of Lebanese and Syrian troops, but fighting across the so-called 'Green Line', which had effectively divided the area from Christian east Beirut since early 1984, continued. By the time Amal and the PLO agreed in September 1987 to end hostilities, more than 2,500 people had died in the 'war of the camps'. Despite renewed fighting near Sidon in October, the Amal leader, Nabih Berri, in January 1988 announced an end to the siege of the Palestinian refugee camps in Beirut and southern Lebanon, avowedly as a gesture of support for the *intifada* (uprising) by Palestinians in the Israeli-occupied territories.

After Prime Minister Karami was killed in a bomb explosion in June 1987, Selim al-Hoss (Prime Minister in 1976–80) was appointed acting premier. In 1988 a political crisis developed as it proved impossible to find a successor to President Gemayel that was acceptable to all the warring factions. Sulayman Franjiya (President in 1970–76) was Syria's preferred candidate but was notably opposed by Geagea, who apparently ensured that the National Assembly was inquorate when it convened for the presidential election in August 1988. Gemayel's term of office expired later in the month, at which time the outgoing President appointed an interim military administration, comprising three Christians and three Muslims, with Gen. Michel Aoun (Commander-in-Chief of the Lebanese army) as Prime Minister. However, the three nominated Muslim officers immediately refused to serve in the new administration. The constitutional crisis, with two governments claiming legitimacy, was further complicated in November, when the Minister of Defence in the al-Hoss administration dismissed Aoun as army commander; however, Aoun retained the loyalty of large sections of the military and thus remained its de facto leader.

The Ta'if agreement

In September 1989, following six months of fighting in Beirut between Aoun's Lebanese army and Syrian forces, a Tripartite Arab Committee—formed in May by an emergency session of Arab leaders, and comprising King Hassan of Morocco, King Fahd of Saudi Arabia and President Chadli of Algeria—announced a peace plan whereby, most notably, the Lebanese National Assembly would meet to discuss a draft charter of national reconciliation. The Committee's charter was approved by the Syrian Government and the leaders of Lebanon's Muslim militias. Aoun initially rejected its terms, on the grounds that it did not provide for the withdrawal of Syrian forces, but he was forced to relent, in view of support for the charter by almost every Arab country, as well as the USA, the USSR, the United Kingdom and France; a cease-fire accordingly took effect. The National Assembly subsequently met in Ta'if, Saudi Arabia, to discuss the charter, which was finally approved (with some amendments) in October by 58 of the 62 attending deputies (of the 99 deputies elected in May 1972, only 73 survived); it became known as the 'Ta'if agreement'. The charter provided for the transfer of executive power from the presidency to a cabinet, with portfolios divided equally between Christian and Muslim ministers. The number of seats in the National Assembly was to be increased to 108, comprising equal numbers of Christian and Muslim deputies. Following the election of a President and the formation of a new government, all militias involved in the Lebanese conflict were to be disbanded within six months, while the internal security forces would be strengthened; the Syrian armed forces would assist the new Government in implementing the security plan for a maximum of two years.

The National Assembly elected René Mouawad, a Maronite Christian deputy and a former Minister of Education and Arts, as President in early November 1989. The Assembly also unanimously endorsed the Ta'if agreement. However, Aoun, who denounced the agreement as a betrayal of Lebanese sovereignty, declared the presidential election unconstitutional and its result null and void, proclaiming himself President. Mouawad was assassinated only 17 days after his election. The National Assembly again convened and elected Elias Hrawi as the new President; the legislature also voted to extend its own term until 1994. A new Cabinet was formed by al-Hoss in late November 1989.

The Christian communities were divided over the Ta'if agreement, and Geagea's refusal to reject it precipitated violent clashes between his LF and Aoun's forces in January 1990: by March more than 800 people had been killed in inter-Christian fighting. In August the National Assembly duly approved amendments to the Constitution, increasing the number of seats in the legislature to 108, to be divided equally between Muslims and Christians. On 21 September the Second Lebanese Republic was officially inaugurated when President Hrawi formally endorsed the amendments. In October Aoun and his forces were expelled from east Beirut by Syrian forces and units of the Lebanese army loyal to Hrawi; Aoun sought refuge in the French embassy. The Lebanese army began to deploy in Beirut in December, by which time all militia forces had withdrawn from the city. In the same month al-Hoss submitted his Government's resignation, and Hrawi invited Omar Karami to form a government of national unity, as stipulated by the Ta'if agreement. By early 1991 the Lebanese army was established in most major southern Lebanese towns; by September the militias had been largely disbanded (although Hezbollah maintained armaments in southern Lebanon and the Beqa'a valley). In May the National Assembly approved amendments to the electoral law, and in June the Cabinet appointed 40 deputies to fill the seats that had become vacant since the 1972 election as well as the nine new seats created under the Ta'if agreement. In August 1991 the National Assembly approved a general amnesty for crimes perpetrated during the civil war, although its terms excluded several specified crimes committed during 1975–90. Under a presidential pardon, Aoun was permitted to depart for exile in France.

In May 1991 Lebanon and Syria signed a bilateral treaty establishing formal relations in political, military and economic affairs, and confirming the role of the Syrian army as guarantor of the security plans enshrined in the Ta'if agreement. Israel immediately condemned the treaty as a further step towards the formal transformation of Lebanon into a Syrian protectorate, while its opponents within Lebanon denounced it as a threat to the country's independence. In September Lebanon and Syria concluded a mutual security agreement. Syrian forces began to withdraw from Beirut in March 1992, in preparation for their scheduled withdrawal to eastern Lebanon by September. Israel, meanwhile, reasserted its intention of maintaining a military presence in the security zone, and its support for the SLA, by launching fierce attacks on Palestinian bases in southern Lebanon in June 1991. Lebanese forces began to take up positions in Sidon in July. Initial resistance from Palestinians loyal to Arafat was swiftly overcome, and an agreement was concluded with the PLO to allow the Lebanese army to assume control of the area. The conflict escalated further in February 1992, following the assassination by the Israeli air force of the Secretary-General of Hezbollah, Sheikh Abbas Moussawi.

The deteriorating economic situation in early 1992, combined with allegations of government corruption and incompetence, and a series of general strikes, provoked the resignation of Karami and his Cabinet in May. Subsequent talks in Damascus between President Hrawi and the Syrian leadership led to the reappointment of Rashid Solh (Prime Minister in 1974–75) as premier. In July 1992 the National Assembly approved a new electoral law whereby the number of seats in the Assembly was raised from 108 to 128, to be divided equally between Christian and Muslim deputies.

The 1992 and 1996 elections to the National Assembly

Lebanon's first legislative elections for 20 years were held in three rounds, on 23 August (in the governorates of the North and the Beqa'a valley), 30 August (Beirut and Mount Lebanon) and 6 September 1992 (South and Nabatiyah). Electoral turn-out was low (averaging 32%), especially in Maronite districts where leaders had urged a boycott. Hezbollah, contesting the elections for the first time as a political party, enjoyed considerable success in southern constituencies. The Amal leader, Nabih Berri, was appointed President of the new National Assembly in October, and Hrawi invited Rafiq Hariri, a Lebanese-born Saudi Arabian business executive, to form a new government, amid hopes that he would restore some confidence in the Lebanese economy and oversee the country's reconstruction. Hariri's Cabinet was dominated by technocrats, and the system of distributing portfolios on an entirely 'confessional' basis was somewhat diluted.

In December 1992 the Lebanese army took up positions in southern suburbs of Beirut for the first time in eight years, apparently meeting no resistance from Hezbollah, which had hitherto effectively controlled the areas. From mid-1993 the Lebanese Government was said to be attempting to curtail the activities of the Damascus-based Popular Front for the Liberation of Palestine—General Command (PFLP—GC), which had begun to mount guerrilla attacks on Israeli military positions from bases in southern Lebanon. In July Israeli armed forces launched their heaviest artillery and air attacks on targets in southern Lebanon since 1982. The declared aim of 'Operation Accountability' was to eradicate the threat posed by Hezbollah and Palestinian guerrillas, and to create a flow of refugees so as to compel the Lebanese and Syrian authorities to take action against these groups. According to Lebanese sources, the week-long offensive displaced some 300,000 civilians towards the north and resulted in 128 (mainly civilian) deaths. Although a US-brokered cease-fire understanding took effect in July 1993, hostilities continued.

Hezbollah reported in June 1994 that 26 of its fighters had been killed in an Israeli air-strike on a training camp in the Beqa'a valley; its response was to launch rockets into the security zone and northern Israel. In October an Israeli attack on the town of Nabatiyah, in which seven civilians died, was apparently provoked by the deaths of 22 people in a bomb attack, attributed to Palestinian militants of the Islamic Resistance Movement (Hamas), in the Israeli city of Tel-Aviv: hitherto, Israeli operations in Lebanon had tended to be in reprisal for terrorist activity in the security zone. Clashes in southern Lebanon in December reportedly resulted in the killing by Hezbollah of several members of the Israeli military and SLA.

Meanwhile, in March 1994 the National Assembly approved legislation instituting the death penalty for 'politically motivated' murders. Shortly afterwards the Maronite LF was proscribed (on the grounds that it had sought the country's partition) and its leader, Samir Geagea, was arrested and charged, along with several of his associates, in connection with the murder, in October 1990, of Dany Chamoun, son of former President Camille Chamoun and the leader of the right-wing Maronite Parti national libéral (PNL), and with the bombing of a Maronite church outside Beirut in January 1994. In September Geagea was reportedly relieved of the organization's leadership and his recognition of the Ta'if agreement revoked; the LF command had also reportedly countermanded the formal dissolution of the organization's militia status. (A successor political organization, the Lebanese Forces Party, had been created in September 1990.) In June 1995 Geagea and a co-defendant were convicted of instigating the murder of Chamoun, and were (together with seven others convicted *in absentia*) sentenced to death; the sentences were immediately commuted to life imprisonment with hard labour. In July 1996 Geagea was acquitted of involvement in the Maronite church bombing. However, by mid-1997 Geagea had received another two death sentences (one for ordering the assassination of another Maronite rival in 1990, and the other for attempting to assassinate the Minister of Defence, Michel Murr, in 1991—both of which were later commuted to life imprisonment); another sentence of life imprisonment for orchestrating the death of Prime Minister Rashid Karami in 1987; and a 10-year prison term for attempting illegally to recruit and arm militiamen after 1991.

In October 1995 the National Assembly voted to amend the Constitution to extend President Hrawi's mandate for a further three years. Prime Minister Hariri had sought an extension of the presidential term in the stated interest of promoting stability in the economic reconstruction process, and the amendment had been facilitated following intervention by Syria to resolve a procedural dispute between Hariri and National Assembly President Berri.

Elections to the National Assembly took place in five rounds during August–September 1996. Pro-Hariri candidates enjoyed considerable success in the first three rounds of voting (in Mount

LEBANON

Lebanon, North Lebanon and Beirut governorates), with the Prime Minister himself winning the largest number of votes at the third round; there were, however, allegations of vote-buying involving Hariri's supporters in Beirut. In the fourth and fifth rounds (in the South and Nabatiyah, and in the Beqa'a valley) an electoral alliance led by Amal and Hezbollah was reported to have won all but one of the 46 seats. Prior to the fifth round Syria had effected the redeployment (delayed since 1992) of some 12,000 of its estimated 30,000 troops in Lebanon to the eastern Beqa'a valley. The overall rate of voter participation averaged about 45%. Berri was re-elected President of the legislature in October 1996, and in the following month a new Government was formed under Hariri.

In April 1996 Israel commenced a sustained military offensive (code-named 'Operation Grapes of Wrath') in southern Lebanon and suburbs to the south of Beirut, aimed at preventing rocket attacks by Hezbollah on settlements in northern Israel. Some 400,000 Lebanese were displaced northwards, and the shelling by Israeli forces of a UNIFIL base at Qana, which resulted in the deaths of more than 100 Lebanese civilians who had been sheltering there, and of four UNIFIL soldiers, provoked international condemnation. After more than two weeks of hostilities a cease-fire understanding took effect in late April. As in 1993, this was effectively a compromise confining the conflict to the area of the security zone, recognizing both Hezbollah's right to resist Israeli occupation and Israel's right to self-defence; the understanding also envisaged the establishment of an Israel-Lebanon Monitoring Group (ILMG), comprising representatives of Israel, Lebanon, Syria, France and the USA, to supervise the cease-fire. According to the Israeli authorities, the operation had resulted in no Israeli deaths, while 170–200 Lebanese civilians, in addition to some 50 fighters, were killed. Hezbollah claimed to have sustained minimal casualties, and its military capacity appeared largely undiminished.

A subsequent UN report on the killing of Lebanese civilians at Qana concluded that it was 'unlikely' that the shelling of the UNIFIL base had, as claimed by the Israelis, been the result of 'gross technical and/or procedural errors'. Prior to the first meeting of the ILMG, in July 1996, Israel and Hezbollah reportedly exchanged prisoners and bodies of members of their armed forces for the first time since 1991. However, despite the April 1996 cease-fire understanding, sporadic clashes continued during 1997–98. The extent of Israeli casualties as a result of the occupation of southern Lebanon prompted a vocal campaign within Israel for a unilateral withdrawal from the security zone. In April 1998 Israel's 'inner' Security Cabinet voted to adopt UN Security Council Resolution 425, but with the stipulation that Lebanon provide guarantees of the security of Israel's northern border. Lebanon, however, emphasized that Resolution 425 demanded an unconditional withdrawal, and stated that neither would it be able to guarantee Israel's immunity from attack, nor would it be prepared to deploy the Lebanese army in southern Lebanon for this purpose; furthermore, Lebanon could not support the continued presence there of the SLA. Concern was also expressed that a unilateral withdrawal from Lebanon in the absence of a comprehensive Middle East peace settlement might foment regional instability.

Voting in Lebanon's first municipal elections since 1963 took place in four rounds during May–June 1998. At the first round (in Mount Lebanon governorate), Hezbollah won convincing victories in Beirut's southern suburbs, while right-wing organizations opposed to the Government also took control of several councils. At the second round (in North Lebanon), efforts failed to achieve an inter-community balance in Tripoli, where a council comprising 23 Muslims and only one Christian was elected; elsewhere in the governorate there was notable success for candidates loyal to Samir Geagea. However, a joint list of candidates supported by Hariri and Berri won control of the Beirut council at the third round, while Berri's Amal gained overall control in Tyre. At the final round of voting (in the Beqa'a valley), Hezbollah candidates were largely defeated by their pro-Syrian secular rivals and by members of the governorate's leading families. Other than in Beirut, the rate of voter participation was high (about 70%). (Municipal elections did not take place in southern Lebanon until September 2001, following the withdrawal of Israeli troops in 2000.)

Emile Lahoud's accession to the presidency and the Israeli withdrawal from the south

As President Hrawi's mandate neared completion in 1998, the Commander-in-Chief of the Army, Gen. Emile Lahoud, emerged as a suitable successor: his firm stance on corruption and his success in having reconstructed the army following the civil war were expected to assist the process of political reform and economic regeneration. Moreover, despite his strong nationalist tendency, Lahoud's candidacy was endorsed by Syria. To enable his appointment, the National Assembly overwhelmingly adopted an exceptional amendment to Article 49 of the Constitution—which requires that senior civil servants resign their post two years prior to seeking political office—and Lahoud was duly elected President on 15 October, with the approval of all 118 National Assembly deputies present (the vote was boycotted by the Druze leader, Walid Joumblatt, and his supporters). Lahoud took office on 24 November. Hariri unexpectedly declined an invitation from him to form a new government, and at the beginning of December Selim al-Hoss (who had headed four administrations during the civil war) was designated Prime Minister. His new Cabinet, which was almost halved in size (to 16 members), included only two ministers from the previous administration—Michel Murr notably retained the post of deputy premier as well as the interior portfolio. Several reformists were appointed to the Cabinet, which excluded representatives of the various 'confessional' blocs and former militia leaders whose rivalries had frequently undermined previous governments. At the Cabinet's first session, held later in December, Gen. Michel Suleiman was appointed to succeed Lahoud as head of the armed forces.

Clashes persisted in southern Lebanon following Israel's 'adoption' of Resolution 425, amid continuing protests of violations of the April 1996 cease-fire understanding. In January 1999 Israel's Security Cabinet voted to respond to future Hezbollah offensives by targeting infrastructure in central and northern Lebanon, as well as suspected guerrilla bases in the south. Hostilities escalated in February, when Israeli forces annexed the village of Arnoun, just outside the security zone; Israel also launched intensive air attacks on Hezbollah targets, following an ambush in the security zone that had killed Brig.-Gen. Erez Gerstein, the commander of the Israeli army's liaison unit with the SLA. In July the Lebanese Government was angered by an announcement made by the new Israeli Prime Minister, Ehud Barak, that Palestinian refugees residing in Lebanon would under no circumstances be permitted to return to Israel. President Lahoud responded by demanding that any permanent peace agreement should guarantee the right of Palestinians to return home; he subsequently initiated legislation to prevent Palestinian refugees in Lebanon from being granted Lebanese citizenship.

During his election campaign Barak had pledged to withdraw Israeli forces from southern Lebanon by July 2000. In June 1999 the SLA completed a unilateral withdrawal from the enclave of Jezzine, in the north-east of the occupied zone. Following further Hezbollah attacks on northern Israel, in late June the outgoing administration of Binyamin Netanyahu ordered a series of air-strikes against infrastructure targets in central and southern Lebanon—the heaviest aerial bombardment since 'Operation Grapes of Wrath' in 1996. In December 1999 an 'understanding in principle' was reportedly reached between Israel and Syria in order to curb the fighting in southern Lebanon, although the informal cease-fire ended in January 2000 when a senior SLA commander was killed; moreover, the deaths of three Israeli soldiers led Israel to declare that peace talks with Syria (again postponed indefinitely) could resume only if Syria took action to restrain Hezbollah. In February, after suffering further military casualties in the security zone, Israel announced that its Prime Minister would henceforth be empowered to order immediate retaliatory raids against Hezbollah without discussion with the Security Cabinet. In March the Israeli Cabinet voted unanimously to withdraw its forces from southern Lebanon by July, even if no agreement had been reached on the Israeli-Syrian track of the Middle East peace process. In April, having released 13 Lebanese prisoners held without trial for more than a decade as 'bargaining counters' for Israeli soldiers missing in Lebanon, Israel gave the UN official notification that it intended to withdraw its forces from southern Lebanon 'in one phase' by 7 July. The Lebanese Government made the unprecedented admission that it would accept a UN peace-keeping force in southern Lebanon after the Israeli withdrawal.

On 23 May 2000 Israel's Security Cabinet voted to accelerate the withdrawal of its remaining troops from Lebanon, after Hezbollah had taken control of about one-third of southern Lebanon following the evacuation by the SLA of outposts transferred to its control by the Israeli army. Both the Israeli Government and the UN had expected the withdrawal to take place on 1 June; however, the rapid and chaotic withdrawal of Israeli forces from southern Lebanon was completed on 24 May, almost six weeks ahead of Barak's original deadline. In June the UN Security Council officially declared that the Israeli withdrawal had been completed. However, both the Lebanese Government and Hezbollah maintained that Israel was still required to depart from territory known as Shebaa Farms and to release all Lebanese prisoners. (The UN maintains that Shebaa Farms is part of territory captured by Israel from Syria, and as such must be considered under the Israeli-Syrian track of the peace process.) In July a limited contingent of UNIFIL troops assumed responsibility for the Lebanese border with Israel; they numbered some 5,600 by August. In that month a Joint Security Force of some 1,000 Lebanese troops and Internal Security Forces reportedly deployed in southern Lebanon (other than in the border area), charged with the provision of general security in the territory. By January 2001 an estimated 2,041 SLA militiamen were reported to have been convicted of having collaborated with Israel during its occupation of southern Lebanon.

Redefinition of Syria's role after the 2000 legislative elections

Elections to the National Assembly took place on 27 August (Mount Lebanon and North Lebanon) and 3 September 2000 (Beirut, the Beqa'a valley, Nabatiyah and the South). For the first time since 1972 Lebanese citizens in the former Israeli-occupied zone of southern Lebanon participated in the elections. Voting patterns in the first round swiftly indicated a rejection of al-Hoss's premiership, as the Druze leader, Walid Joumblatt (one of former premier Rafiq Hariri's staunchest allies), secured an overwhelming victory in Mount Lebanon governorate. Moreover, the election of Pierre Gemayel, son of Amin Gemayel, in the Maronite Northern Metn district (north-east of Beirut) was regarded as a considerable reverse for President Lahoud. At the second round of voting, Hariri's Al-Karamah (Dignity) list secured 18 of the 19 assembly seats in Beirut; al-Hoss lost his own seat in the legislature. In the south an alliance of Hezbollah and Amal candidates took all the governorate's 23 seats, while Hezbollah enjoyed similar successes in the Beqa'a valley. Independent monitors reported numerous instances of electoral malpractice. Overall, Hariri was reported to have the support of between 92 and 106 of the 128 seats in the new legislature. In October President Lahoud formally appointed Rafiq Hariri to the premiership. The composition of his radically altered Cabinet (newly expanded to 30 members) was announced a few days later, with Issam Fares named as Deputy Prime Minister and Elias Murr, the son-in-law of President Lahoud and a non-parliamentarian, replacing his father, Michel Murr, as Minister of the Interior and of Municipal and Rural Affairs. Hariri and President Lahoud were reported to have reached an informal power-sharing agreement, according to which Hariri would be responsible for economic policy and the President would take charge of defence and foreign affairs.

Divisions between pro- and anti-Syrian elements within Lebanon had become increasingly vocal in the aftermath of the Israeli withdrawal from southern Lebanon in May 2000 and the death of Syria's President Hafiz al-Assad in the following month. An unofficial visit to Beirut by his successor, Bashar al-Assad, for meetings with key Lebanese politicians shortly before the legislative elections appeared to indicate that he intended to continue his late father's role as power-broker in Lebanon. However, the decisive rejection of the Syrian-backed Government of Selim al-Hoss, combined with Joumblatt's electoral successes, suggested a redefinition of Syria's role in Lebanon. In September Maronite bishops issued a statement urging the departure of the Syrian military from Lebanon. While the Maronite community and other Christian groups maintained that the departure of Syrian forces was necessary in order for full Lebanese sovereignty to be attained, both President Lahoud and Prime Minister Hariri continued to defend Syria's military presence. In December Syria—which had never previously confirmed that it was holding Lebanese prisoners—freed 46 Lebanese political prisoners (including many Christians who had been detained by Syrian troops during 1975–90), apparently as a goodwill gesture. In January 2001 the Lebanese Government established a commission to examine the issue of Lebanese prisoners held in Syria. In April, following student protests demanding the withdrawal of Syrian troops, the Government banned all unlicensed demonstrations against Syria.

The outbreak of the so-called 'al-Aqsa *intifada*' in the Palestinian territories in September 2000 resulted in a renewed crisis in the Middle East, prompting uncertainty in Lebanon about the permanence of the Israeli withdrawal, particularly as Hezbollah had renewed its campaign against the Israeli military. In October Hezbollah fighters captured three Israeli soldiers in Shebaa Farms, with the demand that Israel release 19 Lebanese and tens of Palestinians from Israeli detention. The UN Secretary-General, Kofi Annan, visited Beirut for talks regarding the soldiers' release; however, in the following week a senior Israeli army reservist and businessman, Elhanan Tannenbaum, was kidnapped in Switzerland, apparently by Hezbollah (which claimed that the officer was working for Israeli intelligence). The killing of an Israeli soldier in Shebaa Farms at the end of November prompted Israel to launch air-strikes against suspected Hezbollah targets in southern Lebanon. In mid-November the UN Security Council had urged the Lebanese Government to comply with international law by deploying its armed forces on the Israeli border with southern Lebanon (where Hezbollah still controlled the line of withdrawal, or 'Blue Line'), but Lebanon rejected such a deployment until Israel had signed a comprehensive peace treaty with both Lebanon and Syria. In January 2001 the UN Security Council voted to extend UNIFIL's mandate in Lebanon until July, when its operational strength was to be reduced to about 4,500—the number of troops deployed prior to the Israeli withdrawal. In April 2001 Israel responded to the killing by Hezbollah of one of its soldiers in Shebaa Farms with the first military action against Syrian troops since 1996, launching air raids on a Syrian radar base to the east of Beirut. According to Syrian sources, at least one Syrian soldier died in the attack, which Israel claimed had been provoked by Syria's sponsorship of Hezbollah.

In June 2001 Syria withdrew an estimated 6,000–10,000 troops from the largely Christian eastern and southern suburbs of Beirut and from Mount Lebanon, and redeployed the majority to the Beqa'a valley. However, the withdrawal was widely regarded as merely symbolic since Syria retained 15 military bases in strategic parts of Beirut. In early August the Maronite patriarch, Cardinal Sfeir, and the Druze leader, Walid Joumblatt, held discussions, apparently to indicate a new era of reconciliation between the two communities. Within days, however, the mainly pro-Syrian army intelligence service began mass arrests of Maronite Christians (mostly members of the banned LF or supporters of the exiled Michel Aoun) who were again demanding a complete Syrian withdrawal from Lebanon. Many Christian and Muslim deputies condemned the detentions as 'unconstitutional'. Indeed, Hariri's political standing appeared to have been weakened by the security forces' actions, which had been undertaken when he was out of the country, as in mid-August the National Assembly approved legislation granting increased powers to President Lahoud.

Israel launched a further air attack on a Syrian radar station in eastern Lebanon at the beginning of July 2001, again apparently in response to an assault by Hezbollah against the Israeli military in Shebaa Farms. At the end of July the UN Security Council voted for an extension of UNIFIL's mandate for a further six months; prior to the expiry of this mandate, the status of the peace-keeping force—now numbering 3,600 troops—was downgraded to that of an observer mission. In October Israel alleged that Hezbollah was directly involved in the Palestinian *intifada*, and was supplying weapons to Palestinians in the West Bank and Gaza. (In March 2002 Hezbollah Secretary-General Sheikh Hasan Nasrallah admitted that two Lebanese militants detained in Jordan had been attempting to smuggle weapons into the West Bank, and in April 2006 he acknowledged for the first time that Hezbollah funded Palestinian militant groups.) In January 2002 the UN Security Council expressed concern regarding recent Israeli violations of Lebanese airspace, and criticized Hezbollah for its frequent interference with the freedom of movement of UNIFIL. The UN again urged the Lebanese Government to deploy its army along the Blue Line. The observer mission's mandate was extended for further six-month periods in January and July; by the end of 2002 the strength of the force had been reduced to some 2,000 troops.

In January 2002 Elie Hobeika, the former leader of the Christian LF militia, was killed (along with three aides and two bystanders) in a car bombing in Beirut. A previously unknown anti-Syrian group, the 'Lebanese for a Free and Independent Lebanon', claimed responsibility for the attack, alleging that Hobeika was a 'Syrian agent'. Israel denied in the strongest terms assertions made by some Lebanese sources that Israeli

LEBANON

interests had instigated the killing, since Hobeika had declared his willingness to give evidence to an investigation being carried out by a Belgian court into alleged 'crimes against humanity' by Israeli premier Ariel Sharon related to the massacre of Palestinians in the Sabra and Chatila refugee camps in 1982 (at which time Sharon had been Israel's Minister of Defence). Hobeika was the first prominent Lebanese politician to be assassinated since the civil war ended in 1990. (A Belgian appeals court judged the case against Sharon to be inadmissible in June 2002.)

It was feared in early 2002 that rising tensions between Israel and Lebanon might escalate into a 'second front' of Arab–Israeli conflict. In February Iran denied allegations made by Israeli officials that it was supplying Hezbollah with vast consignments of *Katyusha* rockets and had sent a number of its Revolutionary Guards to Lebanon. In March and August Hezbollah initiated cross-border mortar, missile and machine-gun attacks against Israeli military targets in Shebaa Farms, asserting that these were in retaliation for Israeli violations of Lebanese airspace. Israel responded by shelling suspected militant bases in southern Lebanon. In April the UN had condemned Hezbollah for increasing the instability along the Blue Line, and also for an incident in which five UNIFIL personnel allegedly came under attack by Hezbollah guerrillas near Shebaa Farms.

President Bashar al-Assad of Syria undertook an historic visit to Beirut in March 2002 for discussions with President Lahoud. This first official visit by a Syrian leader to Beirut since 1947 was welcomed by many Lebanese as a formal recognition by Syria of Lebanese sovereignty. The talks resulted in several agreements regarding closer economic co-operation. It was reported in April 2002 that Syrian troops were soon to redeploy from central Lebanon to the Beqa'a valley, thus fulfilling one of the requirements of the 1989 Ta'if agreement. However, hundreds of Syrian intelligence officers were likely to remain in central Lebanon.

In March 2002 Beirut hosted the annual summit meeting of the Council of the Arab League, at which the principal issue under discussion was a peace initiative for the Middle East proposed by Crown Prince Abdullah of Saudi Arabia. However, only 10 out of 22 Arab heads of state attended the summit, while President Mubarak of Egypt and King Abdullah of Jordan reportedly declined to participate in the discussions as a demonstration of solidarity with the President of the Palestinian (National) Authority (PA), Yasser Arafat, who was effectively blockaded by Israeli forces in the West Bank. At the conclusion of the summit Arab leaders unanimously endorsed the Saudi peace initiative. Incorporated in the Beirut Declaration, this required from Israel a complete withdrawal from all Arab territories occupied in June 1967, and what were termed 'territories still occupied in southern Lebanon', a 'just solution' to the issue of Palestinian refugees, and acceptance of the establishment of a sovereign Palestinian state in the West Bank and Gaza Strip with East Jerusalem as its capital. In return, the Arab states undertook to consider the Arab–Israeli conflict at an end, to sign a peace agreement with Israel, and to establish normal relations with Israel within this comprehensive peace framework. The initiative was, however, rejected by the Israeli Government, which maintained that it would lead to the destruction of the State of Israel.

Jihad Jibril, the head of the PFLP—GC's military operations and son of the group's leader, was killed by a car bomb in west Beirut in May 2002. The Lebanese security forces blamed intra-Palestinian rivalries for the assassination, although many PFLP—GC officials held the Israeli intelligence services responsible. In August two people were killed in the worst factional fighting at the Ain al-Hilweh Palestinian refugee camp for several years. Tensions had escalated following the arrest of an Islamist militant in the previous month by the Lebanese army, aided by Fatah. (The Israeli daily *Ha'aretz* subsequently alleged that the violence at Ain al-Hilweh was linked to the presence there of up to 200 members of the militant Islamist al-Qa'ida organization who had returned from the war in Afghanistan.) In September clashes between the Lebanese army and Palestinian militants at the al-Jalil refugee camp, near Ba'albak (Ba'albek), left one soldier and three Palestinians dead.

In November 2002 international donors attending a conference in Paris, France, agreed to provide Lebanon with an aid package worth some US $4,300m. to assist the country with its heavy burden of debt and to finance development projects. In April 2003, following weeks of reported disagreements between members of the Cabinet over economic and other domestic policies, the Prime Minister, Rafiq Hariri, tendered his resignation and that of his Government. However, after his premiership was endorsed by the Lebanese parliament, Hariri was asked by President Lahoud to form a new 30-member cabinet. The new Government, announced two days after Hariri's resignation, brought in 11 new ministers, including Jean Obeid, who replaced Mahmoud Hammoud as Minister of Foreign Affairs and Emigrants; Hammoud was named as the new Minister of National Defence. The new Cabinet was widely considered to be the most pro-Syrian for more than a decade; it contained no members of the Christian opposition, nor of Hezbollah. Syria was still believed to be exerting considerable influence over Lebanese domestic affairs, despite the decreasing Syrian military presence in the country: in February 2003 Syria had commenced the gradual redeployment of more than 4,000 troops stationed in northern Lebanon, under the terms of the Ta'if agreement.

It was reported in May 2003 that Lebanese security forces had arrested at least nine suspected al-Qa'ida operatives in Sidon. The suspects were accused of plotting to attack the US embassy in Beirut and to kidnap members of the Lebanese Cabinet. Moreover, they were believed to be linked to the al-Qa'ida militants thought to be in hiding in the Ain al-Hilweh refugee camp. In December 27 Lebanese were found guilty, and given varying prison sentences, on charges of carrying out bomb attacks against mostly US and British businesses in Lebanon between the end of 2002 and April 2003. However, a military court in Beirut acquitted three defendants of plotting to assassinate the US ambassador to Lebanon.

The Israeli Cabinet agreed in November 2003 to release more than 400 Palestinian, Lebanese (mostly Hezbollah) and other Arab prisoners in exchange for the remains of three soldiers kidnapped by Hezbollah in Shebaa Farms in 2000, as well as the return of the abducted Israeli businessman, Elhanan Tannenbaum. Israel also hoped to receive information on the fate of a missing Israeli airman, Ron Arad, who had been shot down over Lebanon in 1986, and was still believed to be held in Lebanese detention. Germany, which had mediated the negotiations between Israel and Hezbollah, oversaw the exchange, and in January 2004 the first 30 Lebanese and other Arab prisoners to be released by Israel were flown to the airport at Cologne, Germany, where they were exchanged for Tannenbaum and the remains of the Israeli soldiers. The other Palestinian prisoners, and the remains of 59 Lebanese militants held by Israel, were later released at Israeli border posts.

In January 2005 at least one Israeli officer and two UN observers were killed when Israeli soldiers retaliated against Hezbollah guerrilla attacks on an Israeli military vehicle patrolling Shebaa Farms. UN Secretary-General Kofi Annan criticized Israel's persistent violations of Lebanese airspace and also Hezbollah's recent launching of a drone (an unmanned aircraft) over Israel, both of which he considered to be provocative acts; moreover, he urged Lebanon to respect the Blue Line. In November Hezbollah launched what was apparently its heaviest attack on Israeli troops in the Shebaa Farms area since October 2000. Four Hezbollah militants were killed and 11 Israeli soldiers injured in the ensuing violence, in which the two sides exchanged heavy artillery fire across the border.

Meanwhile, four rounds of voting took place in municipal elections held in May 2004. At the first round (in Mount Lebanon governorate), Hezbollah and other pro-Syrian groups, such as the PSP and independent Christian candidates, defeated the primarily Christian opposition, which was reportedly suffering from internal divisions. At the second round, a list of candidates supported by Hariri won in Beirut (where turn-out was reportedly only 23%) against lists connected to the Parti communiste libanais (PCL) and the opposition Christian Free Patriotic Movement; in the Beqa'a valley Hezbollah took the majority of municipalities that it contested, again securing victory over its opposition, Amal. At the third round, Hezbollah achieved further success, particularly in the mostly Shi'a villages on the Israeli border, where elections took place for the first time since the withdrawal of Israeli troops. The list supported by Hariri suffered an overwhelming defeat in the region's capital and the Prime Minister's home town, Sidon, while Amal secured an unexpected victory over Hezbollah in some mainly Shi'a villages. At the final round of elections in north Lebanon, a candidate considered to be a potential rival to Hariri as Prime Minister, Najib Miqati (also the Minister of Public Works and Transport and a close friend of Syrian President Assad), achieved success.

In August 2004, in advance of the expiry of President Lahoud's six-year term of office in November, the Cabinet voted to amend the Constitution, which prevented Lahoud from seeking a second term, to extend Lahoud's mandate by three years. Both Muslim

LEBANON

and Christian politicians and Hariri protested against the decision, but Hariri eventually offered his support for the amendment after a meeting with Syrian politicians, including President Assad. The USA and France expressed their opposition to the move, and presented a resolution to the UN in early September in an attempt to forestall it. The UN subsequently adopted Resolution 1559, demanding that: Lebanon's sovereignty be respected; a 'free and fair' presidential election be held; the Government assert its power throughout the whole country; all foreign forces leave Lebanon; and all militias in the country, both Lebanese and non-Lebanese, disband and disarm. The resolution did not explicitly refer to Syria or its forces and agents, however. The Security Council gave Lebanon 30 days to comply with the resolution's demands, threatening to take measures against the country if it failed to meet them. Nevertheless, the National Assembly approved the constitutional amendment by 96 votes to 29, prompting the resignation of four cabinet ministers in protest.

The Syrian army responded to Resolution 1559 by redeploying about 3,000 special forces from positions to the south of Beirut, although some 14,000 Syrian troops remained in Lebanon. (Further redeployments of Syrian troops took place in December 2004, from the northern town of Batrun and from Beirut's southern suburbs and the airport to the Beqa'a valley.) In October 2004, after UN Secretary-General Kofi Annan had reported Lebanon's non-compliance with the resolution, the Security Council ordered Annan to provide a report every six months detailing steps towards its fulfilment. Hariri dissolved his Cabinet a day after the release of the statement, declaring that he would not attempt to head the next government. The following day he was replaced by Omar Karami, who revealed the composition of his Cabinet five days later (which for the first time included two women). The former Minister of Public Health, Sulayman Franjiya, assumed the post of Minister of the Interior and Municipalities, while Mahmoud Hammoud became Minister of Foreign Affairs and Emigrants; Hammoud's former national defence portfolio was allocated to Abd al-Rahim Mrad. The new Government, which received legislative approval in November, was considered to be still more favourable than its predecessor to continued Syrian influence in Lebanese affairs. The new Prime Minister criticized the recent UN Security Council resolution, asserting that: the fulfilment of its demands would lead to crises of security and stability in Lebanon; the resolution constituted external pressure on Syria and Lebanon; and the presence of Syrian troops in Lebanon was a matter only for the two countries involved. The USA exerted further pressure on Lebanon in January 2005, when it vowed to include Lebanon among its list of states deemed to sponsor terrorism if the country did not end its support for Hezbollah.

On 22 November 2004 (Independence Day) some 3,000 students from several universities and right-wing Christian activists demonstrated in Beirut against what they perceived to be Syria's dominance in Lebanon, in defiance of a government ban. At the end of the month the Government supported a march by over 100,000 demonstrators in Beirut in praise of Syria's influence in the country and rejecting the terms of UN Resolution 1559. In December parties opposed to the Lebanese Government's support of Syrian involvement in Lebanese affairs, including the main Christian opposition group, the Qornet Shehwan Gathering, Kamal Joumblatt's mainly Druze-supported PSP and the proscribed Lebanese Forces Party, issued a joint statement demanding a cessation of foreign interference in Lebanon and calling for the release of Lebanese Forces Party leader Samir Geagea, who had been imprisoned on murder charges in 1994. They also demanded an electoral law that would allow people of all political sensibilities to participate in governing the country.

The assassination of Rafiq Hariri

On 14 February 2005 a car bombing in Beirut killed former Prime Minister Rafiq Hariri and 22 other people; at least 100 were injured in the blast. The attack provoked condemnation from Syrian President Assad. However, the USA, emphasizing the problems caused by the Syrian military presence in Lebanon and the inability of the Syrian-dominated intelligence services to forestall the attack, removed its ambassador to Syria for consultations, and subsequently demanded that all Syrian troops and security forces withdraw from Lebanon. Later in the month Syria announced that it would redeploy its troops in Lebanon to the Beqa'a valley. On 28 February, following a general strike and mass protests in Beirut advocated by opposition parties, at which demonstrators demanded the complete withdrawal of Syrian troops from Lebanon and an end to Syrian influence in Lebanese politics, Karami dissolved his Cabinet and resigned as premier. Nevertheless, Lahoud requested that Karami and his ministers remain in office pending the appointment of a new government.

Lebanese opposition groups demanded in March 2005 that President Assad and the public prosecutor and senior security officials in Lebanon resign their posts in order to ensure that the investigation into Hariri's death be conducted legitimately and with integrity. They also announced their refusal to participate in any discussions on the formation of a new government until their demands were met. Assad and Lahoud agreed at a summit meeting to the withdrawal of Syrian troops to the Beqa'a valley by the end of the month; Syria later pledged to withdraw all troops prior to Lebanon's general election, scheduled to begin in May, and to provide the UN with a timetable for the withdrawal. Meanwhile, protests took place in Beirut in support of Syria's influence and military presence. Syria reportedly withdrew 4,000–6,000 of its soldiers and intelligence agents from Lebanon to Syria in mid-March; 8,000–10,000 troops remained in the Beqa'a valley. A UN report released later that month accused Syria of allowing political tension in Lebanon to be heightened before the murder of Hariri, and criticized Lebanon's initial attempts to investigate the incident. In April the UN Security Council approved Resolution 1595, establishing an International Independent Investigation Commission (UNIIIC) to investigate Hariri's murder; the commission was to be headed by a German prosecutor, Detlev Mehlis. After Syria declared that it had fulfilled its promise to withdraw all troops, military assets and intelligence apparatus, in May a UN team dispatched to Lebanon verified the absence of Syrian military personnel in areas that it had inspected.

President Lahoud reappointed Karami to the post of Prime Minister on 10 March 2005. Yet in the following month Karami, having failed to form a new administration, tendered his resignation for a second time, and Najib Miqati was appointed to the post of caretaker Prime Minister. Miqati named a new Cabinet (approved by the National Assembly on 27 April), which was to be responsible for the implementation of legislation facilitating a general election. Elias Murr was appointed Deputy Prime Minister and Minister of National Defence, while Mahmoud Hammoud retained responsibility for foreign affairs and emigrants. In late April three senior Lebanese security officials with close ties to Syria announced their resignations, and by mid-May a number of other pro-Syrian security officials, whose replacement had been demanded by the opposition, had been dismissed from their posts.

Elections to the National Assembly were held in four rounds between 29 May and 19 June 2005. The first round of voting took place in the Beirut region, where turn-out was a reported 28%. The anti-Syrian Rafiq Hariri Martyr List, headed by the Future Movement of Rafiq Hariri's son, Saad el-Din Hariri, and including the PSP, the Lebanese Forces Party—which now functioned legally—and the Qornet Shehwan Gathering, won all 19 seats. Four days later the prominent anti-Syrian journalist Dr Samir Kassir was killed in a car bombing in a Christian district of Beirut. The anti-Syrian opposition accused remaining Syrian intelligence agents of involvement in the murder, and again called on President Lahoud to resign. Syria, however, insisted that it had removed all its security personnel. An estimated 45% of registered voters participated in the second round of elections conducted on 5 June in southern Lebanon; as in the first round, turn-out was reportedly lower in Christian than in Muslim districts. The Resistance and Development Bloc, consisting of the pro-Syrian Shi'a organizations Amal and Hezbollah and their allies, secured all 23 seats. The third round was held on 12 June in Mount Lebanon, where candidates contested 35 seats and turn-out was unofficially estimated at 54%, and the Beqa'a valley, where an estimated 49% of registered voters elected deputies to 23 seats. Immediately prior to the poll, Michel Aoun allied himself with pro-Syrian factions as the Free Patriotic Movement (FPM), declaring that he was no longer hostile to Syria since it had withdrawn its troops from Lebanon. Aoun's alliance took 21 seats, while Hariri's list secured 25. However, in the final round in north Lebanon on 19 June, at which turn-out was officially estimated at 49%, Hariri's list won all 28 seats. Consequently, according to final results, the Rafiq Hariri Martyr List secured 72 of the National Assembly's 128 seats, allowing the Lebanese Forces Party to achieve parliamentary representation for the first time; the Resistance and Development Bloc won 35 seats; and the FPM took 21.

LEBANON

In June 2005 George Hawi, the former Secretary-General of the PCL and an outspoken critic of Syrian interference in Lebanese politics, was killed by a car bomb in Beirut. The anti-Syrian opposition attributed the attack to Syrian agents and their allies in the Lebanese security services. Further bomb explosions took place in the capital throughout 2005, causing a number of fatalities. In July two people were killed in an explosion that injured pro-Syrian Deputy Prime Minister Murr, and in December the anti-Syrian publisher of the daily newspaper *An-Nahar*, Gebran Tueni, and three others were killed in a car bombing.

Meanwhile, pro-Syrian Nabih Berri was re-elected President of the National Assembly in June 2005. Two days later President Lahoud appointed Fouad Siniora of the Future Movement, a close ally of Rafiq Hariri, as Prime Minister, and asked him to form a new government. In July Siniora announced the composition of a new Cabinet: Fawzi Sallouk was appointed Minister of Foreign Affairs and Emigrants, while Muhammad Fneish became the first representative of Hezbollah to hold cabinet office, assuming responsibility for energy and water. In the same month the National Assembly passed a law pardoning Lebanese Forces Party leader Samir Geagea, as demanded by some of the opposition (see above). Almost 40 Islamist militants, some of whom were allegedly linked to al-Qa'ida, were also released by parliamentary approval. Siniora met President Assad and the Syrian Prime Minister, Muhammad Naji Otari, in Damascus in August. The two states reportedly agreed to improve relations based on mutual respect, and Siniora emphasized Lebanon's support of Syria and its commitment to bilateral agreements.

UNIIIC began its inquiry into Rafiq Hariri's assassination in mid-June 2005, with a three-month mandate. In August UNIIIC arrested the three former security officials who had tendered their resignations in April for questioning regarding the assassination. A fourth security chief, who had retained his post after Hariri's murder, was also sought, and subsequently handed himself in to the organization; a former pro-Syrian parliamentary deputy was also detained. In October, shortly before UNIIIC issued its first report on the investigation, the Syrian Minister of the Interior, Maj.-Gen. Ghazi Kanaan, was found shot dead in his office. The official Syrian Arab News Agency announced that he had committed suicide. A former head of Syrian military intelligence in Lebanon, Kanaan had become Chief of Political Intelligence in Syria in 2002, and had been appointed Minister of the Interior in October 2004. Shortly before his apparent suicide, Kanaan had told a Lebanese radio station that he had been questioned by UNIIIC, but had not given any evidence against Syria. According to its report, issued in October 2005, UNIIIC had found evidence that Lebanese and Syrian intelligence and security services were directly involved in Hariri's assassination. Moreover, the report reasoned, the act was too complex and too well planned to have taken place without the approval of senior Syrian security officials and their Lebanese counterparts. UNIIIC expressed its extreme concern at the lack of co-operation by the Syrian authorities. Both Lebanon and Syria denounced the investigation's findings as being politically motivated, and Syria announced that it had established a special judicial commission to deal with all matters relating to UNIIIC's mission. The commission was granted an extension to its mandate until December.

The UN Security Council responded to the first UNIIIC report by adopting in October 2005 a resolution, sponsored by the USA, France and the United Kingdom, establishing measures against suspects in the assassination, including prohibitions on travel and the freezing of assets. The Security Council urged Syria to co-operate fully with the investigation commission and detain suspects identified by the inquiry, threatening unspecified 'further action' should Syria fail to comply with the resolution's demands by the stipulated deadline of 15 December. Syria reported in November that it had arrested six government officials for questioning. Meanwhile, in October the UN Special Envoy, Terje Rød-Larsen, issued his report on the implementation of UN Security Council Resolution 1559, in which he praised the withdrawal of Syrian troops from Lebanon, but noted that Lebanon had still not complied with the demands that Lebanese and non-Lebanese militias disarm and disband, and that government authority be extended throughout the country. Lebanon rejected the report, asserting that the Government would deal with armed groups through national dialogue.

In December 2005 UNIIIC began questioning five Syrian officials suspected of involvement in Hariri's assassination in Vienna, Austria. Mehlis presented his second report on the investigating body's work to the UN Security Council later in the month. While noting that Syria had presented the five officials to the commission for interrogation, the report again accused Syria of hindering the investigation. It stated that UNIIIC had found further evidence that the Lebanese and Syrian intelligence and security services had been involved in the assassination, and revealed that Mehlis had identified 19 suspects, six of whom were Syrian (including the five being questioned in Vienna). Mehlis resigned as the head of UNIIIC shortly afterwards, citing personal and professional reasons; he was replaced by Serge Brammertz, and UNIIIC's mandate was extended to 15 June 2006.

In January 2006 UNIIIC investigators declared that they wished to question Syrian President Assad and Minister of Foreign Affairs Farouk al-Shara' in relation to Hariri's murder. (A few days earlier the Vice-President of Syria, Abd al-Halim Khaddam, who had been living in exile in Paris, having resigned his post in June 2005, had accused Assad of personally threatening Hariri. He subsequently declared that, in his view, Assad had ordered Hariri's assassination, although he awaited the final decision of the investigating commission.) However, the following day the Syrian Minister of Information announced that Syria would not permit UNIIIC to interview Assad. Al-Shara' announced in March 2006 that he had reached an agreement with UNIIIC that provided for full Syrian co-operation with the investigation, while preserving the country's 'sovereignty and dignity'. UNIIIC's mandate was later extended until 15 June 2007.

Ministers from Hezbollah and Amal announced in February 2006 that they were ending a boycott of cabinet meetings begun in December in protest against the Government's decision to allow an international investigation into Hariri's assassination. The announcement came shortly after Prime Minister Fouad Siniora declared to the National Assembly that the Government had always considered Hezbollah to be a movement of national resistance rather than a militia (a further demand of the ministers).

The 2006 conflict with Israel

On 12 July 2006 Hezbollah soldiers conducted a cross-border raid in which three Israeli troops were killed and two were captured; five more Israeli soldiers were killed during an attempt to rescue the kidnapped men. Prime Minister Siniora denied Israeli claims that his Government had organized the soldiers' abduction, and insisted that he did not condone the raid. Later that same day Israel launched a series of air raids on a number of suspected Hezbollah positions across southern Lebanon. Further strikes during the night caused extensive damage to civilian infrastructure in the area. Hezbollah declared 'open war' on 14 July, firing barrages of rockets into northern Israel in response to Israeli airstrikes. On the same day the UN Security Council held an emergency meeting, which was reported to have been called by Lebanon and at which Lebanon accused Israel of instigating the violence.

Numerous strikes were exchanged between the two warring factions on a daily basis and, despite claims to the contrary from both sides, who insisted that they were targeting political and military targets exclusively, many civilians were killed or injured in the conflict and thousands of homes were destroyed. Israel systematically targeted Lebanese infrastructure—roads and bridges were destroyed, seaports were blockaded and Beirut International Airport was bombed, forcing all international flights to be diverted to Cyprus. An estimated 70% of civilians living in southern Lebanon fled to the north of the country to escape the worst of the violence. In late July 2006 at least 28 civilians, including 19 children, were reported to have been killed when a residential building in the Lebanese village of Qana was struck by missiles during an Israeli air raid. At an emergency session of the UN Security Council, convened on the following day, members issued a statement expressing 'extreme shock and distress' at the attack; UN Secretary-General Kofi Annan, while apportioning blame for the initial outbreak of the conflict to Hezbollah, denounced the Israeli response as excessive and as being responsible for 'death and suffering on a wholly unacceptable scale'. Nevertheless, in early August the Israeli Cabinet approved a plan to send a large number of ground troops further into Lebanon, as far as the Litani river (approximately 30 km north of the Israeli–Lebanese border).

The USA and France agreed at the beginning of August 2006 upon the content of a draft resolution to be submitted to the UN Security Council, which duly convened to discuss the proposed terms. (The USA had come under criticism for apparently blocking earlier attempts to impose a cease-fire, which had led to allegations that the Administration of President George W. Bush was implicitly encouraging Israel to wreak damage upon Hezbollah.) On 11 August the Security Council adopted Resolution 1701, which had been unanimously approved and which called for: an immediate and full cessation of hostilities; the extension of the Lebanese Government's authority over the whole country; and the delineation of Lebanese international boundaries, with particular regard to disputed sectors such as Shebaa Farms. The resolution was endorsed by the Lebanese Government on 12 August, and Sheikh Nasrallah announced that Hezbollah would honour the call for a cease-fire; however, 24 Israeli soldiers were killed on that same day—the greatest loss of life on any single day since the conflict began. Similarly, despite Israel's Cabinet approving the resolution on 13 August, on the following day Israeli troops launched an attack on a refugee camp in Sidon, killing an UNRWA staff member approximately one hour before the cease-fire was scheduled to take effect.

In late August 2006 Sheikh Nasrallah acknowledged that Hezbollah's kidnapping of the two Israeli soldiers that had triggered the conflict had, with hindsight, been deeply regrettable and that talks concerning their possible return, in exchange for Lebanese nationals detained by Israel, were ongoing. However, he remained defiant, claiming during a rally staged in Beirut in September that Hezbollah was stronger than it had been prior to the conflict and that the organization possessed in excess of 20,000 rockets in its arsenal. Earlier that month Israel had lifted its naval blockade of Lebanon and rescinded its restrictions on air travel to and from Lebanon, thereby formalizing the end of the conflict. However, much of southern Lebanon remained uninhabitable owing to the presence of unexploded cluster bombs. According to figures released by Lebanon's Higher Relief Council, an estimated 1,191 Lebanese civilians were killed during the conflict, and a further 4,410 were thought to have been injured. According to the Israeli Ministry of Foreign Affairs, 119 Israeli troops and 44 Israeli civilians had died in the fighting, and more than 530 Hezbollah members had also been killed. In November the findings of an official UN investigation into the conflict determined that Israel had fired artillery shells containing white phosphorus, an incendiary substance the use of which against civilians, or against legitimate military targets within residential areas, is banned under the terms of the Geneva Convention. However, the Israeli Government refuted the claim, insisting that the shells had been aimed solely at military targets in open ground. Meanwhile, in September 2006 the human rights group Amnesty International accused Hezbollah of having committed war crimes by deliberately targeting Israeli civilians in its missile launches during the recent conflict.

Increasing political and sectarian division

In October 2006 Sheikh Nasrallah demanded that Hezbollah be allocated one-third of the seats in an expanded national unity government, prompting accusations that he was attempting to attain the right of veto in order to protect the Syrian Government from prosecution in the ongoing investigation into the assassination of Rafiq Hariri. Nasrallah's demands were ignored, however, and in the following month five ministers—two members of Hezbollah and three from its ally, Amal—resigned from the Cabinet, thereby removing any Shi'a presence from the Government. A sixth resignation, that of a Christian pro-Syrian minister, followed soon afterwards. The assassination later in November of Pierre Gemayel, the Minister of Industry since 2005, rendered the political situation even more unstable. Gemayel was shot dead in his car in a suburb of Beirut, and many Lebanese leaders were quick to blame Syria for his murder. Since the Lebanese Constitution decrees that any government in which one-third of the ministers have vacated their posts must automatically be dissolved and a new government appointed, Gemayel's assassination meant that, should just one further minister leave the Cabinet for any reason, it would force the collapse of the Government.

In December 2006 thousands of demonstrators gathered in Beirut and erected tents in the capital's main square, besieging government buildings and proclaiming that the Cabinet was now constitutionally invalid. When the protests, aimed at pressurizing the Government into resigning, had failed to achieve any tangible results by late January 2007, the opposition intensified its efforts and called for a general strike, which brought commercial districts of the capital to a virtual standstill; at least three people were killed during clashes between protesters and the authorities. Yet, despite the Government's refusal to submit to the wishes of the opposition, the presence of two separate Lebanese delegations at the annual summit meeting of the Arab League, held in Saudi Arabia in March 2007, aptly symbolized the endemic divisions threatening the country's future stability.

Meanwhile, a disagreement between pro-Government Sunni and anti-Government Shi'a students at Beirut Arab University in January 2007 escalated into violent clashes; up to four people were killed and more than 150 injured. The incident fuelled concerns that Lebanon was about to spiral into full-scale sectarian conflict again; in an effort to prevent further violence, the Government imposed an overnight curfew in Beirut for the first time in a decade. In February two bombs were detonated on commuter buses travelling through Ein Alaq, a village to the north-east of Beirut, killing three people. The attacks, which took place on the eve of the second anniversary of Hariri's assassination, were thought to have been intended to deter people from travelling to Beirut to attend a rally to mark the occasion; however, amid tight security, tens of thousands of people congregated on the following day to honour their former leader. In March Minister of the Interior and Municipalities al-Sabaa announced that four Syrian members of Fatah al-Islam—a militant Islamist Palestinian group, inspired by al-Qa'ida and alleged by the Lebanese authorities to be supported by Syria—had been arrested on suspicion of involvement in the bus explosions.

In March 2007 UNIIIC released its latest report into the assassination of Rafiq Hariri, in which again it claimed to have made considerable progress in acquiring further evidence, but declined to give specific details. Brammertz did, however, state that UNIIIC had identified 250 individuals whom it wanted to question; 50 of these were to be interviewed within the next three months. UNIIIC's mandate was extended to 15 June 2008. Also in March 2007 recently appointed UN Secretary-General Ban Ki-Moon issued his report on the implementation of UN Security Council Resolution 1701, in which he rebuked both Israel and Lebanon for failing to adhere to all of its terms. However, he praised both sides' overall commitment to maintaining the cease-fire, and proposed the establishment of an independent assessment mission to assist with the monitoring of the Israeli–Lebanese border and thereby to facilitate the full implementation of the resolution.

In May 2007 the UN Security Council adopted Resolution 1757, authorizing the formation of an international tribunal to try suspects in Hariri's assassination. The Special Tribunal for Lebanon (STL) was to comprise 11 independent judges (or 14, should a second trial chamber be created), of whom seven were to be international judges and four Lebanese; should a second trial chamber be created, there were to be nine international and five Lebanese judges. While the creation of the STL was welcomed by the Siniora Government, the Hezbollah-led opposition was quick to challenge its validity. Sheikh Nasrallah insisted that any such tribunal not approved by the Lebanese legislature was illegitimate, suggesting that the new body would be unable to rely on the co-operation of Hezbollah should no agreement concerning its establishment be reached between the opposition and the Government.

Walid Eido, an anti-Syrian legislator and member of the Future Movement, was killed in a car bombing in Beirut in mid-June 2007; nine others, including Eido's son, also died. Once again, suspicions were immediately raised regarding Syria's involvement; however, Syrian officials vehemently denied the allegations. A few days later, following a request by Prime Minister Siniora, the UN Security Council announced that UNIIIC was to assist with the investigation into Eido's assassination. By-elections to select replacements for Eido, in Beirut's second district, and for Pierre Gemayel, in the Metn district, were held in August. The former seat was won comfortably by the pro-Government Muhammad Amin Itani, of the Future Movement, while the latter was secured by pro-Syrian Camille Khoury, of the FPM, in a very tight contest against his closest rival, former President Amin Gemayel. Khoury's victory was a considerable reverse for the Lebanese leadership, which had hoped to fill both seats with supporters of Siniora; since the assassination of Eido had reduced the number of pro-Government legislators to 68, the loss of just three more seats, for whatever reason, would result in the loss of the Siniora administration's majority quorum.

The sixth UNIIIC report compiled during the tenure of Serge Brammertz was released in mid-July 2007. It asserted that a 'number of persons' had now been identified who might have been involved in Hariri's assassination, and stated that Syria and other states had continued to provide a 'mostly positive response' to UNIIIC's requests for co-operation and information. Also in July Lebanese investigators concluded that Fatah al-Islam had been responsible for the killing of Pierre Gemayel. Meanwhile, the 10th UNIIIC report, and the first to be published since the appointment in early 2008 of Daniel Bellemare in place of Brammertz, was issued in March of that year. In the report, the UN body revealed that the evidence it had examined thus far indicated that a network of people was behind Hariri's murder, without mentioning specific individuals. A UN Security Council resolution issued in June extended UNIIIC's mandate until 31 December.

In September 2007 a 105-day siege of the Nahr al-Bared refugee camp in Tripoli was finally concluded when the Lebanese army seized control from Islamist militants. The siege had begun in May, after members of Fatah al-Islam had fled to the camp having conducted a bank robbery in the town of Amioun, south of Tripoli. In the ensuing weeks more than 300 people were believed to have been killed in fierce clashes between the army and militants within the camp, which forced an estimated 40,000 Palestinian refugees to flee the violence. The Syrian Government commended the efforts of the Lebanese army in ending the siege, and continued to deny ongoing claims that it in any way supported or condoned the activities of Fatah al-Islam. In March 2008 Fatah al-Islam's leader, Shaker al-Abassi (who was reported to have gone missing), was charged with incitement to murder, in connection with the bus explosions at Ein Alaq in February 2007.

The 2007 constitutional crisis

With the scheduled expiry, in November 2007, of Lahoud's presidential term, the attention of the Government and the opposition in the preceding months came increasingly to focus on the election of his successor. The first session of the National Assembly to elect a new president was duly arranged for 25 September 2007—the first time the legislature was to have met since October 2006. In a conciliatory overture, the President of the Assembly, Nabih Berri, proposed an initiative whereby the opposition would relinquish its long-standing demand for a national unity government if the rival factions could agree on a presidential candidate, although the response from Siniora and his supporters to the proposal was muted. The ambiguity of the Lebanese Constitution meant that, in the event of political divisions between the two camps preventing agreement on a common candidate, the likely eventuality remained deeply uncertain. According to the Constitution, if a new president was not elected by 23 November 2007, then Siniora and his Cabinet would automatically assume executive control. However, the Constitution also authorized the President to decree the resignation of the Cabinet, allowing Lahoud, should he have chosen, to appoint a new, opposition cabinet, which would almost certainly have elected a pro-Syrian, anti-Government president. Lebanon experienced a further political assassination in late September, just six days before the scheduled presidential election, when Antoine Ghanem, a Christian Phalangist legislator, was killed in a car bombing in a predominantly Christian district of Beirut; five others died in the explosion. Since the Government and opposition were unwilling to co-operate in order to elect a new president, leading to an opposition boycott, the National Assembly failed to achieve the requisite two-thirds' quorum of members on 25 September; a second vote was thus scheduled for 23 October. Speculation increased at this time about the possibility of a return to a dual-government system, effectively formalizing the intense divisions in Lebanon.

Following mediation by German diplomats and representatives of the International Committee of the Red Cross, Hezbollah and Israel carried out a limited exchange of prisoners and bodies in mid-October 2007—the first such exchange between the two sides since their conflict of the previous year. However, the two Israeli soldiers whose abduction by Hezbollah militants in July 2006 had apparently provoked the conflict were not included in the arrangement. In January 2008 Sheikh Nasrallah alleged that Hezbollah was holding the remains of a number of Israeli troops killed during the 2006 conflict. Indeed, the remains of several Israeli soldiers were handed over to Israel at the start of June 2008, when the Israeli authorities returned a Lebanese civilian who had served a six-year prison term for espionage. At the end of June the Israeli Cabinet controversially voted to exchange the bodies of the two soldiers abducted by Hezbollah in July 2006 (who it now transpired were certainly dead) for five Lebanese detainees. The exchange occurred in mid-July 2008, with a large crowd welcoming the prisoners back to Lebanon.

(One of the detainees, Samir Kuntar, was a militant of the Palestine Liberation Front, who had been handed down multiple life sentences for an attack on the Israeli town of Nahariya in April 1979.)

The second postponement of the scheduled ballot to elect a successor to President Lahoud was announced by Berri on 22 October 2007, the day before the vote was to take place; a new date of 12 November was declared. In early October US President Bush had warned the Syrian Government not to interfere in Lebanon's internal affairs, since it was a boycott of the National Assembly by pro-Syrian opposition members that had rendered the parliament inquorate. Thus began a seven-month period during which no fewer than 17 further postponements of the presidential election were ordered, owing to a failure by the opposing factions to agree first on a mutually acceptable candidate, and then on the exact nature of administration to be formed after a new president had been elected. When the parliamentary session scheduled for 23 November—at the end of which Lahoud's term of office expired—was postponed until 30 November, it meant that Lahoud was obliged to leave office without a successor having been appointed. Under the terms of the Constitution, therefore, presidential duties were assumed by the Siniora Government in an acting capacity, although, shortly before the expiry of his mandate, Lahoud had issued a statement asserting that, owing to conditions being present for a 'state of emergency', he would hand over responsibility for the country's security to the armed forces. (He and other representatives of the pro-Syrian opposition refused to recognize the legitimacy of the Government following the ministerial resignations of November 2006.) Yet Lahoud's stance was firmly rejected by the Prime Minister, who insisted that no Head of State could call a state of emergency without the approval of the Cabinet. This represented the first time that Lebanon had been without a president since the civil war ended in 1990.

Although the Commander-in-Chief of the Army, Gen. Michel Suleiman (a Maronite Christian), was chosen as a 'compromise candidate' acceptable to both pro-Government and pro-opposition politicians towards the end of November 2007, disagreements remained as to how to amend the Constitution in order to permit Suleiman, as a serving senior state official, to assume the office of Head of State. Amid a flurry of international and regional diplomatic meetings, the ministers responsible for the foreign affairs of Arab League member states, meeting in Cairo, Egypt, in early January 2008, approved details of a plan intended to bring to an end Lebanon's presidential vacuum. The three-phase proposals included the election of Suleiman as president, establishment of a Lebanese government of national unity (where Suleiman would have the deciding vote in any dispute) and approval of new electoral legislation. It was reported that the Arab League plan had received the support of both the Lebanese and Syrian administrations, but that Hezbollah and its principal allies continued to demand that they receive at least one-third of government portfolios in any new cabinet, thus granting them the right to veto important decisions. A National Assembly session to elect a president was postponed (for the 19th time) on 13 May. In April, meanwhile, Suleiman had announced his intention to retire from his military post in August, three months in advance of the scheduled date.

In December 2007 Brig.-Gen. François al-Hajj, the army's head of operations, was killed, along with three other people, in a car bomb attack in east Beirut. Al-Hajj had been widely expected to be promoted to Commander-in-Chief should Suleiman be elected as Lahoud's successor. It was, however, unclear as to which group had carried out the assassination, with Syria, Israel and Fatah al-Islam all being accused by various parties of responsibility for the blast. An explosion apparently aimed at US embassy officials in mid-January 2008 resulted in the deaths of four Lebanese bystanders. There was a further wave of unrest in the principally Shi'ite suburbs of southern Beirut in late January, which had been precipitated by popular frustration over power shortages; seven protesters were reported to have died in the ensuing clashes with security forces. A group of army officers was detained and charged by the authorities in February, amid criticism of the military's handling of the protests. Towards the end of January, meanwhile, Capt. Wissam Eid, a senior member of the police team charged with investigating the recent bombings and assassinations, was killed in another car bomb attack in a suburb of the capital; Eid's driver and up to 10 others also died in the explosion. In mid-February Imad Mughniyeh, one of Hezbollah's most senior militants, was killed in a car bombing in the Syrian capital. Hezbollah representatives immediately blamed Israel for Mughniyeh's death; however, Israeli officials rejected such claims. Mughniyeh had been implicated in a number of high-profile kidnappings of Western journalists, military personnel and religious envoys in Lebanon during the 1980s, as well as in several bomb attacks against principally US interests in the 1980s and 1990s.

Lebanon's political situation deteriorated rapidly in early May 2008, when a decision taken by the Government to shut down a private telecommunications network controlled by Hezbollah and to close Beirut International Airport (where Hezbollah was accused of using surveillance equipment to spy on pro-Government politicians) prompted fierce clashes between members of the Shi'a opposition group and government loyalists. Moreover, a general strike called by the opposition in protest against price increases and to demand higher salaries descended into violence. As Sheikh Nasrallah called the Government's actions against his organization a 'declaration of war', gunmen from Hezbollah and its allies besieged the Beirut offices of the media controlled by the Future Movement's Saad Hariri, while major roads were blocked. Observers noted that west Beirut was now effectively controlled by militants of the Hezbollah-led opposition. After several days of violent clashes, which spread to other cities such as Tripoli, at least 81 people had been killed, and up to 250 wounded, in Lebanon's worst period of unrest since the civil war. However, by mid-May the Government and army claimed to have regained control, and, following mediation by the Arab League, the Cabinet voted to revoke the measures that had provoked the recent violence—an outcome widely viewed as a demonstration of Hezbollah's growing military strength and influence. This development meant that the lengthy sit-in by demonstrators in the centre of Beirut came to an end and businesses that had been closed during the months of paralysis began to resume trading.

The Doha Agreement

On 21 May 2008 18 months of conflict between the Lebanese Government on one side and Hezbollah and its allies on the other was apparently ended through the signing of the Doha Agreement. The agreement was named after the Qatari capital, where—following effective mediation by the Qatari leadership under the auspices of the Arab League—the two sides finally agreed to seek to put aside their differences in order to restore national unity. The Doha Agreement encompassed: the election of a new president; formation of a national unity government, which would involve power-sharing with Hezbollah; and introduction of a new electoral law. A few days after the signing of the unity accord, Fouad Siniora was chosen by the National Assembly to remain as Prime Minister. Yet, notwithstanding the election of a new President (see below) and formation of a 30-member national unity Cabinet on 11 July (the administration consisted of 16 ministers of the Western-supported majority coalition, 11 linked to Hezbollah and its allies, and three appointed by President Suleiman), the security situation in Lebanon remained uneasy. Heavy fighting between supporters of the Government and pro-opposition activists was reported in the eastern Beqa'a valley and Tripoli, resulting in tens of fatalities. Michel Suleiman had been sworn in as President on 25 May 2008, having finally been elected by the National Assembly. Prior to Suleiman's election, the President of the Assembly, Nabih Berri, rejected the demands of some deputies that the Constitution needed to be amended to permit a serving official to become Head of State; this occasion was deemed exceptional since the presidency was actually vacant. The new Siniora Government secured a vote of confidence in the National Assembly on 12 August, and were to thus administer the country until the holding of fresh legislative elections in 2009. Elias Murr remained as Deputy Prime Minister and Minister of National Defence, Issam Abou Jamra was appointed as a second Deputy Prime Minister, Fawzi Salloukh returned to the Cabinet as Minister of Foreign Affairs and Emigrants (having resigned the post in November 2006) and Ziad Baroud was named as Minister of the Interior and Municipalities. At the end of August 2008 Brig.-Gen. Jean Kahwaji was chosen as Suleiman's successor as Commander-in-Chief of the Army.

A landmark agreement was reached between Lebanon and Syria in mid-July 2008, when the two countries announced that they were to enter into diplomatic relations and open embassies in one another's capitals for the first time since they had achieved independence in 1943 and 1945, respectively. The announcement was made by the French President, Nicolas Sarkozy, who welcomed Syria's President Assad and President Suleiman to Paris in advance of the summit convened to launch his Union for the Mediterranean initiative. Following the agreement to resume ties, it was revealed that the work of a committee to demarcate the Lebanese–Syrian border and to investigate the issue of missing persons since Lebanon's civil war would be resumed. Suleiman undertook an official visit to Damascus on 13–14 August 2008 for discussions with Assad, and the Lebanese Cabinet formally adopted a resolution to establish diplomatic relations with Syria on 22 August. On 16 March 2009 Michel al-Khoury duly arrived in Damascus to assume the post of Lebanese ambassador to Syria and on 24 March Syria opened its embassy in Beirut, with Ali Abd al-Karim Ali as ambassador.

However, the deployment of some 10,000 Syrian special forces along the border with northern Lebanon in late September 2008 caused concern among many Lebanese who were uneasy about Syria's long-term intentions towards their country and its sovereignty. The Syrian Government insisted that the presence of the troops merely constituted a campaign to prevent cross-border smuggling. Within Lebanon, meanwhile, there was a continuation of the violence being witnessed in Tripoli: in mid-August 18 people—including at least nine soldiers—died in a bomb explosion which targeted a military bus stop. At the end of September a second attack against a military bus in Tripoli resulted in seven deaths—up to five of them soldiers.

In September 2008 the National Assembly adopted new electoral legislation as required under the terms of the Doha Agreement, in preparation for the general election subsequently scheduled for 7 June 2009. The new law involved the redrawing of electoral boundaries and the staging of elections on one day, rather than over several days. In late October Sheikh Nasrallah and Saad el-Din Hariri held their first meeting since 2006, in advance of a second round of discussions between Lebanon's rival political factions as part of the national dialogue which had begun on 16 September 2008. The talks were held in early November and hosted by President Suleiman; however, they failed to achieve a breakthrough regarding the drafting of a national defence strategy, largely owing to a failure by the 14 participants (who represented each of Lebanon's parliamentary blocs) to agree on the issue of how to deal with Hezbollah's military arsenal. It was agreed that a third round of talks would be held in late December, at which the focus was on the formation of a committee of experts to examine the exact details of a potential national defence strategy. Further national reconciliation discussions were held during late January and early March 2009.

Meanwhile, the UN Secretary-General, Ban Ki-Moon, announced in late November 2008 that the STL established to try those charged with the assassination of former premier Rafiq Hariri in February 2005 would commence proceedings in the Netherlands on 1 March 2009. The 11 judges—four of whom were to be Lebanese—would be led by the Canadian general prosecutor, Daniel Bellemare, with a Lebanese deputy. In the 11th UNIIIC report, issued at the start of December 2008, the Commission asserted that it had discovered evidence of links between Hariri's assassination and other political attacks that had taken place in Lebanon. On 16 December the UN Security Council approved a resolution extending UNIIIC's mandate until 28 February 2009, although Bellemare pledged that the investigation would continue after the STL began operating in March. On 29 February three of the seven suspects being detained on suspicion of withholding information and misleading the investigation of Hariri's murder were released on bail. Four pro-Syrian army generals, including Maj.-Gen. Jamil Sayyed, former head of the General Security Directorate, suspected of involvement in that crime and other terrorist attacks in Lebanon remained in custody, although they had not been formally charged.

The UN-sponsored STL formally opened on 1 March 2009, with general prosecutor Daniel Bellemare emphasizing that the work of the tribunal 'must and will be above politics'. The STL had a renewable three-year mandate and there was a 60-day period during which Bellemare could request that the Lebanese Government hand over to the tribunal the four generals in Lebanese custody. However, it was unclear when exactly the tribunal proceedings would begin. In late March an Italian judge, Antonio Cassese, was named as President of the STL. There were reports in late April that a principal suspect in Hariri's murder, Muhammad Zuhair Siddiq (who was alleged to be a Syrian intelligence officer), had been arrested in Dubai, United Arab Emirates (UAE); the arrest was not confirmed by the UAE authorities. Also in late April the four pro-Syrian generals

LEBANON

held over Hariri's assassination were unexpectedly released from custody, after the STL ruled that there was insufficient evidence to charge them. (In December Maj.-Gen. Sayyed launched legal proceedings in Syria against several defendants in the case whom he accused of giving false evidence in order to implicate Syria and pro-Syrian Lebanese individuals in the crime.)

In mid-March 2009 the National Assembly approved a bill which reduced the voter eligibility age in Lebanese parliamentary elections from 21 to 18; the new legislation would not, however, take effect until after the general election due to be held on 7 June as, under the terms of the Constitution, the Cabinet had four months during which to endorse it. The change in electoral law satisfied a long-standing demand of Hezbollah and its ally, Amal, since it would affect the eligibility to vote of a substantial number of young Shi'a voters. Meanwhile, in May the German current affairs periodical *Der Spiegel* reported that the UNIIIC had discovered evidence indicating Hezbollah's involvement in Hariri's murder. The allegation was denounced by Hezbollah as part of a campaign to influence the result of the forthcoming elections. Hezbollah also claimed that a landmark visit to Beirut in late May by the US Vice-President, Joseph Biden, was intended to persuade Lebanese voters not to support the Shi'a group.

The 2009 legislative elections and 2010 municipal polls

Despite the failure of parliamentarians to approve electoral reforms proposed by the Cabinet, legislative elections were held as scheduled on 7 June 2009. The March 14 Alliance of Saad Hariri—notably including among its constituent parties Hariri's Future Movement, the PSP and the Lebanese Forces Party—retained its status as the largest group in the legislature, winning 71 of the 128 seats in the National Assembly. The March 8 Alliance, which included Amal, the FPM and Hezbollah, secured 57 seats; voter turn-out was recorded at 54%. The following day Hariri, as Prime Minister-designate, proposed a cabinet for the approval of President Suleiman; however, the proposal was denounced by Hezbollah leader Sheikh Nasrallah, who claimed that his party had not been consulted. Protracted negotiations ensued between the constituent parties of the two main electoral alliances, but negotiators failed to reach an agreement, partly owing to a dispute between the Future Movement and the FPM over the portfolios allocated to the latter. The process was further complicated in August when the leader of the PSP, Walid Joumblatt, announced his party's withdrawal from the March 14 Alliance, although he reiterated his support for the bloc. In early September Hariri resigned as Prime Minister-designate; however, the following week President Suleiman again instructed him to lead talks over the formation of a national unity coalition, and on 9 November a new, 30-member administration was sworn in by the President. In total, 12 cabinet portfolios were assigned to members of the March 14 Alliance, 10 to the March 8 Alliance and three to March 14-affiliated independents. Among the most notable appointments were those of Raya Haffar al-Hassan, of the Future Movement, as Minister of Finance and Amal's Ali Hussein Shamy as Minister of Foreign Affairs and Emigrants. In addition, five ministers were nominated by Suleiman, including Elias Murr and Ziad Baroud, who retained their respective posts of Deputy Prime Minister and Minister of National Defence, and Minister of the Interior and Municipalities. In mid-December Prime Minister Hariri visited Damascus to meet with President Assad, and, in what was regarded by some observers as a further indication of waning anti-Syrian sentiment among the March 14 parties and its allies, in late March 2010 Joumblatt also travelled to Damascus for talks with Assad.

Meanwhile, in August 2009 the mandate of UNIFIL was extended until August 2010, following a vote by the UN Security Council. The issue of integrating Hezbollah's weapons and fighters into the Lebanese armed forces, under the terms of the 2008 Doha Agreement, remained a cause for concern among the international community, amid increasing tensions along the Israeli-Lebanese border. (Cross-border rocket attacks on northern Israel had continued during 2009, although these were largely attributed to Palestinian militants.) Following reports that Hezbollah had acquired Scud missiles capable of reaching targets across Israel, in early April 2010 Israeli President Shimon Peres publicly accused Syria of supplying the weapons; however, both the Lebanese and Syrian Governments denied the allegations. In late April the US Secretary of Defense, Robert Gates, expressed his Administration's concerns that Syria and Iran were supplying Hezbollah with increasingly sophisticated weaponry. In May UNIFIL declared southern Lebanon to be free of Scud missiles. During discussions with Hariri in Washington, DC, in late May—the Lebanese premier's first official visit to the USA—the US President, Barack Obama, also raised the issue of arms-smuggling to Hezbollah militants.

Despite demands to postpone municipal elections scheduled for May 2010 until electoral reforms on proportional representation could be promulgated, in early April Baroud announced that the elections would be held as scheduled, over four consecutive weeks from 2–30 May. Despite many predictable results, there was evidence that some voters had switched their allegiance away from the principal March 14 or March 8 Alliances to support family and tribal representatives. At the first round (in Mount Lebanon governorate), Hezbollah and Aoun's FPM notably lost support to a coalition of the Lebanese Forces Party, Al-Kataeb, other March 14 parties and independents. At the second round, candidates supported by the March 14 Alliance and Hariri won all the seats in Beirut, after Aoun had boycotted this poll (resulting in the participation of only 21% of voters); in the Beqa'a valley joint lists of Hezbollah and Amal candidates secured most municipalities. At the third round in south Lebanon, Hariri's Future Movement fared well, as did the FPM, Hezbollah and Amal (in the Shi'a villages close to the Israeli border); other members of the March 14 coalition lost seats. At the final round of voting in north Lebanon, success for Hariri's list was mixed: although it won in Tripoli, the governorate's largest city, candidates backed by the Future Movement were defeated elsewhere, and the Lebanese Forces Party, FPM-supported candidates and March 14 parties also claimed successes in other towns of the region.

Recent developments: Renewed tension arising from developments in the Rafiq Hariri case

President Assad and King Abdullah of Saudi Arabia held a tripartite summit meeting with President Suleiman in Beirut on 30 July 2010, in an effort to dissuade Lebanon's competing Sunni and Shi'ite political factions from once again resorting to violence. This was the first visit to Lebanon by the Syrian leader since the Arab League summit of 2002, and the first by a Saudi monarch since 1957. The summit meeting was convened amid growing tensions in Lebanon over reports that an indictment by the STL was imminent, and that members of Hezbollah were likely to be named as culprits in the 2005 assassination of Rafiq Hariri. Sheikh Nasrallah insisted that his organization would reject such an outcome.

An exchange of gunfire between Lebanese and Israeli forces across their joint border on 3 August 2010 reportedly led to the deaths of at least two Lebanese soldiers and a journalist, and one Israeli commander. This was the most serious violence between the two sides since the conflict between Israel and Hezbollah in mid-2006. Both Israeli and Lebanese officials blamed the other's military for having been first to violate the terms of UN Security Council Resolution 1701; however, the UN urged both sides to exercise restraint. The foreign affairs committee of the US House of Representatives declared on 10 August 2010 that the US Administration had decided to suspend US $100m. of military assistance to Lebanon, and that this recent incident highlighted concerns among many in the USA that its weaponry might be employed by Lebanese troops, with the possible influence of Hezbollah, to attack Israeli targets. On 30 August the UN Security Council voted to extend the mandate of UNIFIL until 31 August 2011; the Council expressed the hope that an investigation by UNIFIL into the events of 3 August would ensure that they were not repeated.

Abd al-Rahman Awad, who was said to have assumed the leadership of Fatah al-Islam after the siege of the Palestinian refugee camp Nahr al-Bared in 2007, was reported to have been killed on 14 August 2010, along with his bodyguard, by Lebanese military intelligence forces in the Beqa'a valley. Two days later it was revealed by the pan-Arab daily newspaper *Al-Hayat* that Osama al-Shahabi had been appointed to replace Awad, although al-Shahabi's brother denied this. On 17 August the National Assembly approved legislation granting limited rights to Palestinian refugees resident in Lebanon, including the right to work legally in some areas of the private sector and to contribute to, and claim payments from, the state social security fund. The law was highly controversial and had required a number of amendments, since many of Lebanon's political factions (particularly Christian groups) were fearful of the consequences for the country's fragile sectarian balance of fully integrating Palestinian refugees into Lebanese society. Palesti-

LEBANON

Introductory Survey

nians would continue to be denied access to medical and educational services and the right to work in the public sector.

In September 2010 Prime Minister Saad Hariri stated in an interview with *Asharq al-Awsat*, a United Kingdom-based Arabic newspaper, that he had been mistaken in initially having accused the Syrian Government of involvement in his father's assassination. In mid-October the Iranian President, Mahmoud Ahmadinejad, appeared to increase sectarian divisions when he undertook a two-day state visit to Lebanon; Ahmadinejad was welcomed by thousands of Hezbollah supporters in southern Beirut and in the south of the country, where a mass rally was held in Bint Jbeil, near the Israeli border. At the end of that month Sheikh Nasrallah urged all Lebanese people to boycott the STL, stating that the UN-led tribunal was an 'Israeli project' created in order to defeat Hezbollah. In mid-November Israel announced that, in line with the terms of UN Security Council Resolution 1701, its military was preparing to withdraw from the northern part of the disputed village of Ghajar, just north of the Blue Line and thus inside Lebanese territory.

As the country awaited the issuing of the first indictment by the STL (see below), on 12 January 2011 the parties comprising the March 8 Alliance announced the withdrawal from the Cabinet of their 10 ministers, after Prime Minister Hariri refused to accede to Hezbollah demands that the Government end its co-operation with the STL; one of President Suleiman's five appointed ministers also resigned. The resignations of more than one-third of cabinet ministers (including the Minister of Foreign Affairs and Emigrants, Ali Shamy) thus prompted the collapse of the national unity Government after only 14 months in office. The previous day the Saudi and Syrian Governments were reported to have failed in their efforts to secure a compromise agreement for Lebanon. Some sources alleged that the USA had intervened to prevent a political deal being reached which allowed Hezbollah to avoid censure by the STL. Having instructed ministers to remain in office pending the approval of a new cabinet, on 25 January Suleiman invited Najib Miqati—who was briefly Prime Minister in 2005—to begin negotiations to form a new administration. The Prime Minister-designate had received support from the March 8 Alliance, but he was widely viewed a moderate politician, who claimed to be independent and who was acceptable to both the Saudi and Syrian leaderships. However, supporters of Hariri held large-scale protests in Beirut, Tripoli (Miqati's mainly Sunni home town), Sidon and other cities, amid widespread anger about Hezbollah's role in the collapse of the Government and Miqati's subsequent appointment.

On 17 January 2011 the UN prosecutor, Daniel Bellemare, submitted the first sealed indictment for the assassination of Rafiq Hariri to pre-trial judge Daniel Fransen; the latter was required to confirm the indictment before any arrest warrants could be issued. It was unclear at this stage whether Miqati would continue to co-operate with the STL, which reportedly aimed to begin pre-trial hearings later in the year, thereby ensuring that all indictments could be filed by February 2012. Meanwhile, in mid-February 2011 Saad Hariri announced formally that his March 14 Alliance would decline to join a cabinet under Prime Minister Miqati.

A growing movement of mainly young Lebanese, who sought to change the country's political system to reduce the level of sectarianism had been witnessed during 2010, and large-scale rallies began to be held from late February 2011. On 20 March a demonstration was held by thousands of protesters in Beirut, who demanded the abolition of Lebanon's 'sectarian regime' and the introduction of widespread political reforms, including the drafting of new electoral legislation. The President of the National Assembly, Nabih Berri, had angered some in the country's political establishment by urging members of his Amal movement to participate in the protests.

Meanwhile, the protracted negotiations concerning the formation of a new government were ongoing in mid-May 2011, although there was speculation that an announcement would be made by the end of that month. There were reports that the Syrian Government was exerting considerable pressure on Lebanese politicians to agree on a cabinet list without delay, particularly in light of the popular uprisings taking place in many countries of the Middle East and North Africa since January, which had spread to Syria itself by April. Tensions between the March 8 Alliance parties and the Future Movement increased in mid-April, following the broadcast on Syrian state television of a purported confession by members of a 'terrorist cell' which, it was claimed, had attempted to foment unrest in Syria; one of those interviewed stated that Future Movement parliamentarian Jamal al-Jarrah had financed and supplied arms to the group, a claim which al-Jarrah vehemently denied.

CONSTITUTION AND GOVERNMENT

The Constitution was promulgated on 23 May 1926 and amended by the Constitutional Laws of 1927, 1929, 1943, 1947 and 1990. Legislative power is held by the National Assembly (called the Chamber of Deputies until 1979), with 128 members elected by universal adult suffrage for four years (subject to dissolution), on the basis of proportional representation. Seats are allocated on a religious or 'confessional' basis (divided equally between Christians and Muslims); according to convention, the President of the Assembly is usually a Shi'a Muslim. The President of the Republic (who must be a Maronite Christian) is elected for six years by the National Assembly. The President, in consultation with deputies and the President of the National Assembly, appoints the Prime Minister (a Sunni Muslim) and other ministers to form the Cabinet, in which executive power is vested. The Ta'if agreement of October 1989 (see Contemporary Political History) stated that cabinet portfolios must be distributed equally between Christian and Muslim ministers.

REGIONAL AND INTERNATIONAL CO-OPERATION

Lebanon is a member of the League of Arab States (Arab League, see p. 361). A Euro-Mediterranean Association Agreement was signed with the European Union (EU, see p. 270) in 2002. Lebanon joined the UN on 10 October 1966, and was elected a non-permanent member of the UN Security Council for the years 2010–11. The country also participates in the Organization of the Islamic Conference (OIC, see p. 400). Lebanon has observer status at the World Trade Organization (WTO, see p. 430), membership of which organization was applied for in 1999.

ECONOMIC AFFAIRS

In 2009, according to estimates by the World Bank, Lebanon's gross national income (GNI), measured at average 2007–09 prices, was US $33,646m., equivalent to $7,970 per head (or $13,230 per head on an international purchasing-power parity basis). During 2000–09, it was estimated, the population increased at an average annual rate of 1.3%, while gross domestic product (GDP) per head grew, in real terms, by an average of 3.6% per year. Overall GDP increased, in real terms, at an average annual rate of 4.9% in 2000–09; GDP growth of some 8.0% was recorded in 2009.

Agriculture (including hunting, forestry and fishing) contributed an estimated 4.6% of GDP in 2009. Some 5.1% of the employed labour force were engaged in the sector in 2007. The principal crops are potatoes, tomatoes, cucumbers, citrus fruits and grapes. Viticulture is also significant. The cultivation of hashish is a notable, albeit illegal, activity in the Beqa'a valley, despite official efforts to eradicate crops and switch land to other production. According to World Bank estimates, the GDP of the agricultural sector increased at an average annual rate of 0.7% in 2000–09; agricultural GDP grew by 3.5% in 2009.

The industrial sector (including manufacturing, construction and power) contributed an estimated 18.3% of GDP in 2009. Some 25.9% of the labour force were employed in industry in 1997. Lebanon's only mineral resources consist of small reserves of lignite and iron ore, and their contribution to GDP is insignificant. According to World Bank estimates, the GDP of the industrial sector increased by an average of 3.6% per year in 2000–09; industrial GDP expanded by 3.0% in 2009.

Manufacturing contributed an estimated 7.1% of GDP in 2009. The sector employed about 10% of the labour force in 1985. The most important branches have traditionally been food-processing, petroleum-refining, textiles, and furniture and woodworking. According to World Bank estimates, manufacturing GDP increased at an average annual rate of 2.7% in 2000–09; the GDP of the sector grew by 3.0% in 2009.

Construction contributed an estimated 12.6% of GDP in 2009. The sector employed about 5.5% of the labour force in 1985.

Energy is derived principally from thermal power stations, mainly using imported petroleum (which accounted for 93.9% of total electricity production in 2007). Generating capacity is inadequate to meet Lebanon's peak requirements, and interruptions to supply are frequent. From 2009, following an agreement reached with Egypt in August 2008, Lebanon was to receive a supply of electricity from the regional power grid, and would also import natural gas from Egypt. In January 2010 Turkey agreed to supply electricity and natural gas to Lebanon via Syria;

LEBANON

Turkish officials indicated in October that the provision of electricity could begin immediately and that of natural gas by the end of 2011. Meanwhile, in June 2010 the Lebanese Government adopted a new strategy for the power sector, which aimed to improve infrastructure and to encourage the use of liquefied petroleum gas and renewable energy sources. In August legislation was approved permitting the exploration and drilling of potential oil and gas reserves off Lebanon's Mediterranean coast; the new law was likely to increase tensions with Israel since no formal maritime border exists between the two states. Imports of mineral products accounted for 20.5% of the value of total imports in 2009.

The services sector contributed an estimated 77.1% of GDP in 2009. In 1997 some 65.1% of the working population were employed in the sector. Financial services, particularly banking, withstood many of the disruptions inflicted on the economy by the civil conflict during 1975–90 (although trading on the Beirut Stock Exchange was suspended in 1983–96). The revival of tourism, which was of considerable importance prior to the civil conflict, remains vulnerable to the political and security situation. None the less, the sector experienced strong growth in 2008–09: arrivals of foreign tourists reached 1.3m. in 2008 and 1.9m. in 2009. According to World Bank estimates, the GDP of the services sector increased at an average annual rate of 3.5% in 2000–09; the sector's GDP expanded by 1.1% in 2009.

In 2009 Lebanon recorded a trade deficit of US $11,179m. and there was a deficit of $7,555m. on the current account of the balance of payments. The principal market for exports in 2008 was the United Arab Emirates (which took 10.0% of Lebanese exports); other significant purchasers included Switzerland, Syria, Saudi Arabia and Turkey. In 2009 the principal supplier of imports was the USA (10.9%); the People's Republic of China, France, Germany and Italy were also important suppliers. The principal exports in 2009 were pearls and precious or semi precious stones, machinery and electrical equipment, base metal and base metal products, food, beverages and tobacco, chemical products, and paper and paper products. The principal imports in that year were mineral products, vehicles and transport equipment, machinery and electrical equipment, chemical products, base metals and base metal products, and food, beverages and tobacco.

In 2009, according to official estimates, Lebanon recorded an overall budget deficit of £L4,462,000m, equivalent to an estimated 8.5% of GDP. Lebanon's general government gross debt was £L77,019,000m in 2009, equivalent to 148.0% of GDP. At the end of 2008 Lebanon's total external debt was US $24,395m., of which $20,561m. was public and publicly guaranteed debt. The cost of debt-servicing in that year was equivalent to 14.0% of the value of exports of goods, services and income. According to ILO, the annual rate of inflation averaged 4.7% in 2000–08. According to official figures, the annual rate of inflation declined to 3.4% in 2009, but increased to 4.6% in 2010. Some 9.2% of the adult labour force were unemployed in 2007.

Lebanon's economy performed strongly following the Doha Agreement of May 2008 and, according to the IMF in October 2010, demonstrated a 'remarkable resilience' to the impact of the global financial crisis. The Lebanese banking sector was particularly well placed due to its traditionally conservative management practices and a deposit-led finance structure. Despite an overall decline in the global tourism market, in 2009 Lebanon enjoyed a 39% rise in the number of foreign tourist arrivals compared with 2008, and a 27% increase was recorded in the first half of 2010. The World Tourism Organization estimated that tourism contributed 13.3% of GDP in 2009, and projected that this figure could reach 15.7% by 2020. In 2009 there was a record increase of 26% in capital inflow, from tourists, foreign direct investment and remittances from Lebanese abroad. After an initial disbursement by the IMF in 2007 under the Emergency Post-Conflict Assistance and a further US $37.6m. in November 2008, the organization in its 2009 report praised the Government's prudent macroeconomic policies that had led to the doubling of international reserves since 2007. It also noted that financial indicators, such as consistently growing commercial bank deposits, were pointing to an increasing economic confidence in Lebanon. In October 2010 the IMF forecast GDP growth to continue strongly, reaching an estimated 8% for that year—the same figure officially recorded for 2009. Economic growth was being driven largely by the construction, tourism, retail and financial services industries. High international prices for fuel and food during 2008, in conjunction with long-awaited increases in Lebanese public sector pay and pensions as well as rises in the minimum wage in the private sector, had placed upward pressure on consumer prices. Nevertheless, the rate of inflation slowed to 3.4% in 2009, although it rose to 4.6% in 2010. While efforts to reduce the debt-to-GDP ratio had, to late 2008, proceeded at a faster rate than envisaged under the Paris III programme, the ratio—148% of GDP at the end of 2009—remained one of the highest in the world. The IMF assessed that this figure could decline to 139% by the end of 2010. The Fund encouraged the national unity Government formed under Prime Minister Saad el-Din Hariri in late 2009 to relaunch the fiscal consolidation agenda to counteract the limited progress that had been made on structural reforms. However, by mid-2010 progress remained slow: the planned sale of the two state-owned mobile telephone networks had been deferred until after the legislative elections of June 2009, and in January 2009 the Government awarded one-year contracts (subsequently extended in 2010 and 2011) to allow Orascom Telecom of Egypt and Kuwait's Zain Group to operate the networks. Meanwhile, there were fears that the increase in sectarian tensions evident during late 2010, which led to the collapse of the Hariri Government in January 2011 (see Contemporary Political History), might have a negative impact on Lebanon's hitherto impressive rates of economic growth.

PUBLIC HOLIDAYS

2012: 1 January (New Year's Day), 6 January (Christmas Day—Armenian Orthodox Church only), 4 February* (Mouloud/Yum al-Nabi, birth of Muhammad), 9 February (Feast of St Maron), 25 March (Feast of the Annunciation), 8 April (Easter, Western Church), 13–16 April (Greek Orthodox Easter), 1 May (Labour Day), 2 May (Martyrs' Day), 17 May (Ascension Day, Western Church), 16 June* (Leilat al-Meiraj, ascension of Muhammad), 15 August (Assumption), 18 August* (Id al-Fitr, end of Ramadan), 25 October* (Id al-Adha, Feast of the Sacrifice), 1 November (All Saints' Day), 14 November* (Muharram, Islamic New Year), 22 November (Independence Day), 23 November* (Ashoura), 25 December (Christmas Day).

* These holidays are determined by the Islamic lunar calendar and may vary by one or two days from the dates given.

LEBANON

Statistical Survey

Sources (unless otherwise stated): Central Administration for Statistics, Beirut; internet www.cas.gov.lb; Direction Générale des Douanes, Beirut.

Area and Population

AREA, POPULATION AND DENSITY

Area (sq km)	10,452*
Population (official estimate) 15 November 1970†	
Males	1,080,015
Females	1,046,310
Total	2,126,325
Population (UN estimates at mid-year)‡	
2009	4,223,550
2010	4,254,583
2011	4,287,610
Density (per sq km) at mid-2011	410.2

* 4,036 sq miles.

† Figures are based on the results of a sample survey, excluding Palestinian refugees in camps. The total number of registered Palestinian refugees in Lebanon was 425,640 at 31 December 2009.

‡ Source: UN, *World Population Prospects: The 2008 Revision*.

2007 (official estimate): Total resident population 3,759,137 (males 1,857,662; females 1,901,475).

POPULATION BY AGE AND SEX
(UN estimates at mid-2011)

	Males	Females	Total
0–14	527,737	508,371	1,036,108
15–64	1,423,708	1,510,531	2,934,239
65 and over	147,107	170,156	317,263
Total	2,098,552	2,189,058	4,287,610

Source: UN, *World Population Prospects: The 2008 Revision*.

PRINCIPAL TOWNS
(population in 2003)*

Beirut (capital)	1,171,000	Jounieh	79,800
Tarabulus (Tripoli)	212,900	Zahle	76,600
Saida (Sidon)	149,000	Baabda	58,500
Sur (Tyre)	117,100	Ba'albak (Ba'albek)	29,800
Al-Nabatiyah al-Tahta (Nabatiyah)	89,400	Alayh	26,700

* Figures are rounded.

Source: Stefan Helders, *World Gazetteer* (internet www.world-gazetteer.com).

Mid-2010: Beirut 1,936,990 (Source: UN, *World Urbanization Prospects: The 2009 Revision*).

BIRTHS, MARRIAGES AND DEATHS
(annual averages, UN estimates)

	1995–2000	2000–05	2005–10
Birth rate (per 1,000)	22.6	17.6	15.8
Death rate (per 1,000)	7.1	7.0	6.9

Source: UN, *World Population Prospects: The 2008 Revision*.

Live births (numbers registered, official estimates): 73,900 in 2004; 73,770 in 2005; 72,790 in 2006; 78,944 in 2007; 84,823 in 2008; 90,388 in 2009.

Marriages (numbers registered, official estimates): 30,014 in 2004; 29,705 in 2005; 29,078 in 2006; 35,068 in 2007; 37,593 in 2008; 40,565 in 2009.

Deaths (numbers registered, official estimates): 17,774 in 2004; 18,012 in 2005; 18,787 in 2006; 19,399 in 2007; 21,048 in 2008; 22,260 in 2009.

Life expectancy (years at birth, WHO estimates): 72 (males 70; females 74) in 2008 (Source: WHO, *World Health Statistics*).

Employment
(ISIC major divisions)

	1975	1985*
Agriculture, hunting, forestry and fishing	147,724	103,400
Manufacturing	139,471	45,000
Electricity, gas and water	6,381	10,000
Construction	47,356	25,000
Trade, restaurants and hotels	129,716	78,000
Transport, storage and communications	45,529	20,500
Other services	227,921	171,000
Total	744,098	452,900

* Estimates.

1997 (provisional estimates at mid-year): Total employed 1,246,000; Unemployed 116,000; Total labour force 1,362,000.

2007 (household survey, persons aged 15 years and over): Total employed 1,033,572 (Agriculture and fishing 52,528, Unskilled 126,684, Skilled 188,168, Intermediate professions 108,051, Specialists 115,420, Office employees 84,269, Service sector workers and salespersons 131,950, General and corporate managers 132,761, Drivers 93,741). Note: Figures exclude members of the armed forces (84,224) and non-respondents (585).

Source: partly National Employment Office.

Mid-2011 ('000, estimates): Agriculture, etc. 27; Total labour force 1,583 (Source: FAO).

Health and Welfare

KEY INDICATORS

Total fertility rate (children per woman, 2008)	1.8
Under-5 mortality rate (per 1,000 live births, 2008)	13
HIV/AIDS (% of persons aged 15–49, 2007)	0.1
Physicians (per 1,000 head, 2005)	2.4
Hospital beds (per 1,000 head, 2005)	3.6
Health expenditure (2007): US $ per head (PPP)	921
Health expenditure (2007): % of GDP	8.8
Health expenditure (2007): public (% of total)	44.7
Access to sanitation (% of persons, 2006)	97
Total carbon dioxide emissions ('000 metric tons, 2007)	13,344.3
Carbon dioxide emissions per head (metric tons, 2007)	3.2
Human Development Index (2007): ranking	83
Human Development Index (2007): value	0.803

For sources and definitions, see explanatory note on p. vi.

Agriculture

PRINCIPAL CROPS
('000 metric tons)

	2006	2007	2008
Wheat	153	116	144
Barley	32	33	29
Potatoes	398	515	515*
Almonds, with shell	28	29	29*
Olives	177	76	76*
Cabbages and other brassicas	73	88	88*
Lettuce and chicory	21	22	22*
Tomatoes	291	305	305*
Cauliflowers and broccoli	25	24	24*
Pumpkins, squash and gourds	24	28	28*
Cucumbers and gherkins	50	143	143*
Aubergines (Eggplants)	24	24	24*
Onions, dry	45	46	46*
Garlic	3	3	3*
Beans, green	13	14	14*
Carrots and turnips	6	7	7*
Watermelons	58	54	54*
Cantaloupes and other melons	8	9	9*
Bananas	87	90	90*

LEBANON

—continued

	2006	2007	2008
Oranges	231	229	229*
Tangerines, mandarins, clementines and satsumas	35	35	35*
Lemons and limes	92	114	114*
Grapefruit and pomelos	16	15	15*
Apples	122	125	125*
Pears	36	34	34*
Apricots	29	32	32*
Sweet cherries	23	30	30*
Peaches and nectarines	37	41	41*
Plums and sloes	25	25	25*
Strawberries	3	3	3*
Grapes	112	119	119*
Figs	6	5	5*

* FAO estimate.

2009: Wheat 153; Barley 34.

Aggregate production ('000 metric tons, may include official, semi-official or estimated data): Total cereals 190 in 2006, 154 in 2007, 177 in 2008, 192 in 2009; Total roots and tubers 399 in 2006, 515 in 2007–09; Total vegetables (incl. melons) 690 in 2006, 820 in 2007–09; Total fruits (excl. melons) 908 in 2006, 950 in 2007–09.

Source: FAO.

LIVESTOCK
('000 head, year ending September)

	2006	2007	2008*
Horses	4†	4†	4
Asses	15†	15†	15
Mules	5†	5†	5
Cattle	77	77	77
Pigs	10	9	9
Sheep	370	324	330
Goats	484	435	450
Chickens	36,000*	36,700*	37,000

* FAO estimate(s).
† Unofficial figure.

Note: No data were available for 2009.

Source: FAO.

LIVESTOCK PRODUCTS
('000 metric tons)

	2005	2006	2007
Cattle meat*	61.5	51.9	46.5
Sheep meat*	7.7	7.3	8.0
Goat meat*	3.3	2.6	4.1
Pig meat*	1.1	1.0	0.9
Chicken meat	122.4	132.1	135.2
Cows' milk	189.8	166.8	183.6
Sheep's milk	22.8	19.7	24.7
Goats' milk	39.3	26.0	34.0
Hen eggs	45.5	40.2	45.7
Wool, greasy*	2.0	1.9	1.9

* FAO estimates.

2008: Figures assumed to be unchanged from 2007 (FAO estimates).

2009 (FAO estimates): Cattle meat 46.5; Sheep meat 8.0; Goat meat 4.1; Pig meat 0.9.

Source: FAO.

Forestry

ROUNDWOOD REMOVALS
('000 cubic metres, excluding bark, FAO estimates)

	2007	2008	2009
Sawlogs, veneer logs and logs for sleepers*	7.2	7.2	7.2
Fuel wood	80.1	79.5	78.9
Total	87.3	86.7	86.1

* Assumed to be unchanged since 1992.

Source: FAO.

SAWNWOOD PRODUCTION
('000 cubic metres, including railway sleepers)

	1991	1992	1993
Total (all broadleaved)	10.9	9.1	9.1*

* FAO estimate.

1994–2009: Figures assumed to be unchanged from 1993 (FAO estimates).

Source: FAO.

Fishing
(metric tons, live weight)

	2004	2005	2006
Capture	3,866	3,798	3,811
Groupers and seabasses	245	250	252
Porgies and seabreams	365	370	371
Surmullets (Red mullets)	200	190	190
Barracudas	250	240	240
Mullets	360	365	360
Scorpionfishes	125	110	115
Carangids	400	380	383
Clupeoids	600	580	580
Tuna-like fishes	400	385	389
Mackerel-like fishes	300	320	322
Marine crustaceans	60	55	57
Aquaculture	790	803	803
Rainbow trout	700	708	708
Total catch	4,656	4,601	4,614

2007–08: Catch assumed to be unchanged from 2006 (FAO estimates).

Source: FAO.

Mining
('000 metric tons, estimates)

	2004	2005
Gypsum	30	30
Salt (unrefined)	3.5	3.5
Phosphoric acid	175	180

2006–08: Production assumed to be unchanged from 2005 (estimates).

Source: US Geological Survey.

Industry

SELECTED PRODUCTS
('000 metric tons, unless otherwise indicated)

	2006	2007	2008
Flour and derivatives thereof	650	379	n.a.
Cigarettes (metric tons)	554.9	431.9	433.1
Cement	4,400	4,900	5,283
Bottled water and soda (million litres)	261*	497	532
Wine†	15	15	15
Electric energy (million kWh)	8,694	9,072	11,188

* Year to November.
† FAO estimates (Source: FAO).

2009: Cement 4,897,000 metric tons; Electric energy 11,909m. kWh.

LEBANON

Statistical Survey

Finance

CURRENCY AND EXCHANGE RATES

Monetary Units:
100 piastres = 1 Lebanese pound (£L).

Sterling, Dollar and Euro Equivalents (31 December 2010):
£1 sterling = £L2,360.0;
US $1 = £L1,507.5;
€1 = £L2,014.3;
£L10,000 = £4.24 sterling = $6.63 = €4.96.

Exchange Rate: The official exchange rate has been maintained at US $1 = £L1,507.5 since September 1999.

BUDGET
(£L '000 million)

Revenue	2007	2008	2009
Tax revenue	5,583	7,182	8,967
Taxes on income, profits and capital gains	1,308	1,564	1,839
Taxes on property	532	786	809
Domestic taxes on goods and services	2,224	2,895	3,206
Taxes on international trade	1,247	1,588	2,664
Other taxes	271	350	396
Non-tax revenue	2,511	2,613	3,069
Income from public enterprises	2,003	2,028	2,456
Administrative fees and charges	422	484	505
Fines and confiscations	6	7	7
Other	80	94	100
Treasury revenue	655	758	669
Total	**8,749**	**10,553**	**12,705**

Expenditure	2007	2008	2009
Personnel costs	3,583	3,970	4,936
Salaries and wages	2,473	2,676	3,325
Interest payments and financial charges	4,695	4,957	5,784
Foreign debt principal repayment	246	347	303
Materials and supplies	198	273	238
External services	84	106	114
Various transfers	563	568	717
Acquisitions of land, buildings, for the construction of roads, ports, airports and water networks	18	7	4
Equipment	41	33	35
Construction in progress	416	366	356
Maintenance	48	72	103
Other expenditures (including current capital and treasury expenditures)	2,563	4,125	4,425
Total	**12,587**	**14,957**	**17,167**

INTERNATIONAL RESERVES
(US $ million at 31 December)

	2007	2008	2009
Gold (national valuation)	7,639.8	8,031.7	10,062.0
IMF special drawing rights	36.1	33.7	328.9
Reserve position in IMF	29.8	29.0	29.5
Foreign exchange	12,844.1	20,181.8	28,744.5
Total	**20,549.8**	**28,276.2**	**39,164.9**

Source: IMF, *International Financial Statistics*.

MONEY SUPPLY
(£L '000 million at 31 December)

	2007	2008	2009
Currency outside banks	1,929.0	2,174.6	2,383.0
Demand deposits at commercial banks	1,601.8	2,057.5	2,410.3
Total money (incl. others)	**3,578.1**	**4,269.3**	**4,839.7**

Source: IMF, *International Financial Statistics*.

COST OF LIVING
(Consumer Price Index for Beirut; December of each year; base: December 2007 = 100)

	2008	2009
Food and non-alcoholic beverages	118.2	117.2
Alcoholic beverages and tobacco	100.1	107.8
Clothing and footwear	104.9	94.2
Water, electricity and gas	91.4	98.5
Housing	104.8	111.2
Health	104.4	106.6
Transport	101.1	118.9
All items (incl. others)	**105.5**	**109.1**

NATIONAL ACCOUNTS
(£L '000 million)

Expenditure on the Gross Domestic Product

	2007	2008	2009
Government final consumption expenditure	5,509	6,686	7,384
Private final consumption expenditure	31,311	38,018	41,659
Gross fixed capital formation / Changes in stocks	10,463	13,810	18,063
Total domestic expenditure	**47,283**	**58,514**	**67,106**
Exports of goods and services	8,694	11,077	10,728
Less Imports of goods and services	18,203	24,244	25,183
GDP in purchasers' values	**37,774**	**45,346**	**52,650**

Gross Domestic Product by Economic Activity

	2007	2008	2009
Agriculture, hunting, forestry and fishing	2,279	2,646	2,574
Manufacturing (including mining and quarrying)	3,325	3,545	3,947
Electricity, gas and water	−608	−1,341	−756
Construction	4,286	6,090	7,012
Wholesale and retail trade; repair of motor vehicles, motorcycles and personal and household goods	8,532	11,778	14,531
Hotels and restaurants	1,223	1,602	1,993
Transport, storage and communications	3,089	3,376	4,026
Financial intermediation	3,439	4,166	4,322
Real estate, renting and business activities	4,269	4,733	5,084
Government services	3,662	4,270	4,766
Education	3,509	3,837	4,105
Health	2,376	2,614	2,983
Other services	971	1,112	1,123
Sub-total	**40,352**	**48,428**	**55,710**
Less Financial intermediation services indirectly measured	2,579	3,084	3,061
GDP in purchasers' values	**37,774**	**45,346**	**52,650**

Note: Indirect taxes assumed to be distributed at origin.

Source: Presidency of the Council of Ministers, *Economic Accounts of Lebanon*.

BALANCE OF PAYMENTS
(US $ million)

	2007	2008	2009
Exports of goods f.o.b.	4,046	5,251	4,716
Imports of goods f.o.b.	−11,926	−16,261	−15,895
Trade balance	**−7,880**	**−11,010**	**−11,179**
Exports of services	12,755	17,574	16,884
Imports of services	−9,988	−13,464	−14,320
Balance on goods and services	**−5,114**	**−6,900**	**−8,615**

LEBANON

—continued	2007	2008	2009
Other income received	3,113	2,723	2,013
Other income paid	−2,373	−2,286	−2,780
Balance on goods, services and income	−4,373	−6,463	−9,382
Current transfers received	5,219	6,070	6,642
Current transfers paid	−2,450	−3,709	−4,815
Current balance	−1,605	−4,103	−7,555
Capital account (net)	590	410	18
Direct investment abroad	−848	−987	−1,126
Direct investment from abroad	3,376	4,333	4,804
Portfolio investment assets	−1,560	−566	−817
Portfolio investment liabilities	1,730	1,203	2,692
Other investment assets	529	7,819	5,027
Other investment liabilities	3,197	890	8,053
Net errors and omissions	−6,074	−1,664	−2,160
Overall balance	−665	7,336	8,935

Source: IMF, *International Financial Statistics*.

External Trade

PRINCIPAL COMMODITIES
(£L '000 million)

Imports c.i.f.	2007	2008	2009
Live animals and animal products	752.5	881.3	1,136.7
Vegetable products	843.5	1,058.8	948.3
Prepared foodstuffs; beverages, spirits and vinegar; tobacco and manufactured substitutes	1,139.6	1,282.7	1,442.7
Mineral products	4,061.8	6,448.8	5,015.3
Products of chemical or allied industries	1,660.4	1,941.0	2,063.9
Plastics, rubber and articles thereof	721.6	855.5	820.0
Textiles and textile articles	777.4	971.1	1,048.7
Natural or cultured pearls, precious or semi-precious stones, precious metals and articles thereof; imitation jewellery; coin	727.9	1,284.2	1,208.0
Base metals and articles thereof	1,452.9	1,970.8	1,569.8
Machinery and mechanical appliances; electrical equipment; sound and television apparatus	2,148.5	2,545.5	2,913.3
Vehicles, aircraft, vessels and associated transport equipment	1,497.9	2,586.9	3,632.2
Total (incl. others)	17,817.4	24,334.1	24,492.4

Exports f.o.b.	2007	2008	2009
Vegetable products	158.4	197.1	181.1
Prepared foodstuffs; beverages, spirits and vinegar; tobacco and manufactured substitutes	359.5	424.0	427.7
Mineral products	135.8	203.0	134.2
Products of chemical or allied industries	352.2	656.7	348.0
Plastics, rubber and articles thereof	177.8	226.3	188.1
Paper and paperboard and articles thereof	262.0	308.3	345.6
Textiles and textile articles	154.7	178.8	160.9
Natural or cultured pearls, precious or semi-precious stones, precious metals and articles thereof; imitation jewellery; coin	735.6	866.1	1,657.8
Base metals and articles thereof	745.1	798.5	473.0
Machinery and mechanical appliances; electrical equipment; sound and television apparatus	693.2	808.2	768.1
Total (incl. others)	4,246.8	5,245.3	5,254.4

PRINCIPAL TRADING PARTNERS
(£L '000 million)

Imports c.i.f.	2007	2008	2009
Belgium	274.8	398.2	389.5
Brazil	433.7	480.4	546.0
China, People's Republic	1,535.0	2,098.2	2,171.0
Egypt	789.7	691.0	634.3
France	1,331.7	2,012.7	2,368.4
Germany	1,130.9	1,549.0	1,866.0
Italy	1,597.2	1,672.1	1,846.8
Japan	595.0	934.6	1,011.3
Korea, Republic	217.3	360.8	500.2
Kuwait	445.4	737.0	438.2
Netherlands	228.2	253.1	368.7
Romania	194.2	404.9	283.7
Russia	531.3	759.3	627.4
Saudi Arabia	425.8	437.2	467.4
Spain	322.5	417.5	387.2
Switzerland	524.6	928.5	613.6
Syria	311.4	408.5	352.4
Turkey	610.9	1,053.4	985.0
Ukraine	181.0	389.1	331.9
United Arab Emirates	329.2	492.3	393.9
United Kingdom	678.4	688.4	736.5
USA	1,718.2	2,789.4	2,660.6
Total (incl. others)	17,817.4	24,334.1	24,492.4

Exports f.o.b.	2006	2007	2008
Belgium	70.5	131.1	123.8
Egypt	72.2	171.3	191.6
France	59.0	77.0	126.8
Germany	33.5	55.6	50.9
Greece	33.6	68.3	72.1
Iran	54.4	58.9	n.a.
Italy	40.9	51.4	79.2
Jordan	127.0	149.8	179.6
Korea, Republic	26.8	46.8	33.0
Kuwait	124.3	160.4	144.5
Netherlands	41.6	40.0	35.5
Nigeria	51.0	64.6	n.a.
Qatar	96.2	114.2	n.a.
Saudi Arabia	220.5	282.4	315.0
Spain	15.5	61.2	70.5
Switzerland	680.1	464.7	496.1
Syria	265.0	316.6	337.2
Turkey	154.3	165.2	311.9
United Arab Emirates	265.7	367.6	522.2
United Kingdom	47.6	111.4	88.8
USA	79.4	102.1	74.5
Total (incl. others)	3,442.1	4,246.8	5,245.3

2009: Total exports f.o.b. 5,254.4.

Transport

ROAD TRAFFIC
(motor vehicles in use)

	1995	1996*	1997*
Passenger cars (incl. taxis)	1,197,521	1,217,000	1,299,398
Buses and coaches	5,514	5,640	6,833
Lorries and vans	79,222	81,000	85,242
Motorcycles and mopeds	53,317	54,450	61,471

* Estimates.

Source: IRF, *World Road Statistics*.

Passenger cars ('000, incl. taxis): 1,370.6 in 1999; 1,370.8 in 2000; 1,370.9 in 2001 (Source: UN, *Statistical Yearbook*).

LEBANON

SHIPPING

Merchant Fleet
(registered at 31 December)

	2007	2008	2009
Number of vessels	58	56	54
Total displacement ('000 grt)	135.9	141.4	140.5

Source: IHS Fairplay, *World Fleet Statistics*.

International Sea-borne Freight Traffic
('000 metric tons)

	2007	2008	2009
Goods loaded	891	841	615
Goods unloaded	4,426	4,906	5,034

CIVIL AVIATION
(traffic on scheduled services)

	2004	2005	2006
Kilometres flown (million)	22	22	24
Passengers carried ('000)	1,087	1,076	969
Passenger-km (million)	2,197	2,168	1,940
Total ton-km (million)	292	291	257

Source: UN, *Statistical Yearbook*.

Tourism

FOREIGN TOURIST ARRIVALS
('000)*

Country of nationality	2006	2007	2008
Australia	31.9	29.9	40.9
Canada	48.3	47.2	66.8
Egypt	38.7	29.6	41.7
France	66.8	72.4	91.1
Germany	39.3	42.1	53.9
Iran	86.4	75.5	92.5
Iraq	60.4	83.2	72.8
Jordan	144.2	127.0	180.9
Kuwait	50.1	44.5	68.9
Philippines	26.1	17.4	28.0
Saudi Arabia	93.6	63.9	101.7
United Kingdom	29.9	29.6	38.1
USA	64.1	57.0	83.8
Total (incl. others)	**1,062.6**	**1,017.1**	**1,332.5**

* Figures exclude arrivals of Syrian nationals, Palestinians and students.

Tourism receipts (US $ million, incl. passenger transport): 5,457 in 2006; 6,046 in 2007; 7,690 in 2008.

Source: World Tourism Organization.

Total tourist arrivals ('000): 1,850.0 in 2009.

Communications Media

	2007	2008	2009
Telephones ('000 main lines in use)	697.5	750.0	803.7
Mobile cellular telephones ('000 subscribers)	1,260.0	1,427.0	2,390.3
Internet users ('000)	780	945	1,000
Broadband subscribers ('000)	200	211	222

Personal computers: 420,000 (101.8 per 1,000 persons) in 2006.

Radio receivers ('000 in use): 2,850 in 1997.

Television receivers ('000 in use): 1,170 in 2000.

Daily newspapers (number of titles): 13 in 2000.

Daily newspapers (total average circulation, estimates, '000 copies): 220 in 2000.

Non-daily newspapers (number of titles): 7 in 2000.

Book production (number of titles): 289 in 1998.

Sources: UNESCO Institute for Statistics; UNESCO, *Statistical Yearbook*; UN, *Statistical Yearbook*; and International Telecommunication Union.

Education

(2008/09, unless otherwise indicated)

	Institutions	Teachers	Students
Pre-primary	1,938*	9,507	152,740
Primary	2,160*	33,302	464,442
Secondary:			
general	n.a.	31,629	328,484
vocational	275†	10,863	62,603
Higher	n.a.	24,302	199,656

* 1996/97 figure.
† 1994 figure.

Sources: UNESCO Institute for Statistics; Banque du Liban, *Annual Report*.

Pupil-teacher ratio (primary education, UNESCO estimates): 13.9 in 2008/09 (Source: UNESCO Institute for Statistics).

Adult literacy rate (UNESCO estimates): 89.6% (males 93.4%; females 86.0%) in 2007 (Source: UNESCO Institute for Statistics).

Directory

The Government

HEAD OF STATE

President: Gen. MICHEL SULEIMAN (inaugurated 25 May 2008).

CABINET
(May 2011)

On 12 January 2011 the parties comprising the March 8 Alliance (which included Hezbollah, Amal, the Free Patriotic Movement, the Syrian Social Nationalist Party, the Baath Party, the Islamic Action Front, the El-Marada Movement, the Lebanese Democratic Party and independents) announced the withdrawal from the Cabinet of their 10 ministers. The resignation later that day of one of the five ministers nominated by President Michel Suleiman prompted the collapse of the national unity coalition Government, under the terms of the Constitution. However, President Suleiman instructed Prime Minister Saad Hariri and his outgoing Cabinet to remain in office on an interim basis pending the formation of a new government. On 25 January Najib Miqati, a former interim premier who had received support from the March 8 Alliance, was appointed as Prime Minister-designate.

Prime Minister: SAAD EL-DIN HARIRI (*ad interim*).

Deputy Prime Minister and Minister of National Defence: ELIAS MURR.

Minister of the Interior and Municipalities: ZIAD BAROUD.

Minister of Foreign Affairs and Emigrants: ALI HUSSEIN SHAMY.

Minister of Justice: IBRAHIM NAJJAR.

Minister of Industry: ABRAHAM DEDEYAN.

Minister of Energy and Water: GEBRAN BASSIL.

Minister of Public Works and Transportation: GHAZI ARIDI.

LEBANON

Minister of Finance: Raya Haffar al-Hassan.
Minister of Economy and Trade: Muhammad Safadi.
Minister of Education and Higher Education: Hassan Mneimneh.
Minister of Culture: Salim Wardeh.
Minister of Information: Tariq Mitri.
Minister of Tourism: Fadi Abboud.
Minister of Telecommunications: Charbel Nahhas.
Minister of Labour: Boutros Harb.
Minister of Agriculture: Hussein Hajj Hassan.
Minister of the Environment: Muhammad Rahhal.
Minister of Public Health: Muhammad Jawad Khalifa.
Minister of Social Affairs: Dr Salim al-Sayegh.
Minister of the Displaced: Akram Chehayeb.
Minister of Youth and Sports: Ali Hussein Abdullah.
Minister of State for Administrative Reform: Muhammad Fneish.
Minister of State for Parliamentary Afffairs: Michel Faroun.
Ministers of State: Wael Abu Faour, Adnan al-Kassar, Mona al-Dib Ofeish, Jean Oghassabian, Youssef Saadeh, Adnan Sayyed Hussein.

MINISTRIES

Presidency of the Republic of Lebanon: Presidential Palace, Baabda, Beirut; tel. (5) 920900; fax (5) 922400; e-mail president_office@presidency.gov.lb; internet www.presidency.gov.lb.
Office of the President of the Council of Ministers: Grand Sérail, place Riad el-Solh, Beirut; tel. (1) 746800; fax (1) 865630; internet www.pcm.gov.lb.
Ministry of Agriculture: Embassies St, Bir Hassan, Beirut; tel. (1) 849600; fax (1) 849620; e-mail ministry@agriculture.gov.lb; internet www.agriculture.gov.lb.
Ministry of Culture: Immeuble Hatab, rue Madame Curie, Verdun, Beirut; tel. (1) 744250; fax (1) 756303; e-mail omarhala_48@hotmail.com; internet www.culture.gov.lb.
Ministry of the Displaced: Minet el-Hosn, Starco Centre, Beirut; tel. (1) 366373; fax (1) 503040; e-mail modbeirut@hotmail.com; internet www.ministryofdisplaced.gov.lb.
Ministry of Economy and Trade: rue Artois, Hamra, Beirut; tel. (1) 982292; fax (1) 982293; e-mail sdabaghy@economy.gov.lb; internet www.economy.gov.lb.
Ministry of Education and Higher Education: Unesco Quarter, Habib Abi Chahla, Beirut; tel. (1) 789611; fax (1) 789606; e-mail info@higher-edu.gov.lb; internet www.higher-edu.gov.lb.
Ministry of Energy and Water: Beirut River Highway, Beirut; tel. (1) 565100; e-mail mew@terra.net.lb; internet www.energyandwater.gov.lb.
Ministry of the Environment: POB 11-2727, 7th and 8th Floors, Lazarieh Centre, Beirut; tel. (1) 976555; fax (1) 976530; e-mail webmaster@moe.gov.lb; internet www.moe.gov.lb.
Ministry of Finance: MOF Bldg, place Riad el-Solh, Beirut; tel. (1) 981001; fax (1) 981059; e-mail infocenter@finance.gov.lb; internet www.finance.gov.lb.
Ministry of Foreign Affairs and Emigrants: al-Sultana Bldg, al-Jnah, Sultan Ibrahim, Beirut; tel. (1) 8470767; fax (1) 840924; e-mail director@emigrants.gov.lb; internet www.emigrants.gov.lb.
Ministry of Industry: Ministry of Industry and Petroleum Bldg, ave Sami Solh, Beirut; tel. (1) 423338; fax (1) 427112; e-mail ministry@industry.gov.lb; internet www.industry.gov.lb.
Ministry of Information: rue Hamra, Beirut; tel. (1) 754400; fax (1) 754776.
Ministry of the Interior and Municipalities: Grand Sérail, place Riad el-Solh, Beirut; tel. (1) 751601; fax (1) 750084; e-mail info@moim.gov.lb; internet www.moim.gov.lb.
Ministry of Justice: rue Sami Solh, Beirut; tel. (1) 422112; fax (1) 427957; e-mail info@justice.gov.lb; internet www.justice.gov.lb.
Ministry of Labour: Shiah, Beirut; tel. (1) 556804; fax (1) 556806; e-mail mol@labor.gov.lb; internet www.labor.gov.lb.
Ministry of National Defence: Yarze, Beirut; tel. (5) 420000; fax (5) 951035; e-mail cmdarm@lebarmy.gov.lb; internet www.lebarmy.gov.lb.
Ministry of Public Health: Hussein Mansour Bldg, Museum St, Beirut; tel. (1) 615774; fax (1) 615771; e-mail ministry@public-health.gov.lb; internet www.moph.gov.lb.
Ministry of Public Works and Transportation: Shiah, Beirut; tel. (5) 456482; fax (5) 455840.

Ministry of Social Affairs: rue Badro, Beirut; tel. (1) 260611; fax (1) 242611; e-mail info@socialaffairs.gov.lb; internet www.socialaffairs.gov.lb.
Ministry of State for Administrative Reform: Immeuble Starco, rue Omar Daouk, Beirut; tel. (1) 371510; fax (1) 371599; e-mail webmaster@omsar.gov.lb; internet www.omsar.gov.lb.
Ministry of Telecommunications: 1st Floor, Ministry of Telecom Bldg, place Riad el-Solh, Beirut; tel. (1) 979161; fax (1) 979164; e-mail webmaster@mpt.gov.lb; internet www.mpt.gov.lb.
Ministry of Tourism: POB 11-5344, rue Banque du Liban 550, Beirut; tel. (1) 340940; fax (1) 340945; e-mail mot@inco.com.lb; internet www.destinationlebanon.gov.lb.
Ministry of Youth and Sports: rue Sami Solh, Beirut; tel. (1) 425770; fax (1) 424387; e-mail minijes@cyberia.net.lb.

Legislature

Majlis al-Nuab
(National Assembly)

Place de l'Etoile, Beirut; tel. (1) 982047; fax (1) 982059; e-mail lp@lp.gov.lb; internet www.lp.gov.lb.

The equal distribution of seats among Christians and Muslims is determined by law, and the Cabinet must reflect the level of representation achieved by the various religious denominations within that principal division. Deputies of the same religious denomination do not necessarily share the same political or party allegiances. The distribution of seats is as follows: Maronite Catholics 34; Sunni Muslims 27; Shi'a Muslims 27; Greek Orthodox 14; Druzes 8; Greek-Melkite Catholics 8; Armenian Orthodox 5; Alawites 2; Armenian Catholics 1; Protestants 1; Others 1.

President: Nabih Berri.

General Election, 7 June 2009

Party list	Seats
March 14 Alliance*	71
March 8 Alliance†	57
Total	128

* Electoral list comprising the Future Movement, Parti socialiste progressiste, Lebanese Forces Party, Al-Kataeb, Democratic Left, Parti national libéral, Ramgavar Party, Al-Jama'a al-Islamiya and independents.
† Electoral list comprising Amal, Hezbollah, the Free Patriotic Movement, Armenian Revolutionary Federation, Syrian Social Nationalist Party, Al-Baath, Islamic Action Front, El-Marada Movement, Lebanese Democratic Party and independents.

Political Organizations

Amal (Hope—Afwaj al-Muqawamah al-Lubnaniyyah—Lebanese Resistance Detachments): e-mail info@amal-movement.com; internet www.amal-movement.com; f. 1975 as a politico-military organization; Shi'ite political party; contested 2009 legislative elections as part of March 8 Alliance; Leader Nabih Berri.

Armenian Revolutionary Federation (ARF) (Tashnag): rue Spears, Beirut; internet www.arfd.am; f. 1890; principal Armenian party; historically the dominant nationalist party in the independent Armenian Republic of Yerevan of 1917–21, prior to its becoming part of the USSR; socialist ideology; contested 2009 legislative elections as part of March 8 Alliance; Leader Hrant Markarian.

Al-Baath (Baath Arab Socialist Party): Beirut; f. 1948; local branch of secular pro-Syrian party with policy of Arab union; contested 2009 legislative elections as part of March 8 Alliance; Leader Fayez Shuker.

Bloc national libanais (National Bloc): rue Pasteur, Gemmayze, Beirut; tel. (1) 584585; fax (1) 584591; f. 1943; right-wing Lebanese party with policy of power-sharing between Christians and Muslims and the exclusion of the military from politics; Pres. Carlos Eddé.

Free Patriotic Movement (FPM) (Tayar al-Watani al-Horr): Beirut; tel. (3) 122858; e-mail info@tayyar.org; internet www.tayyar.org; aims to recover sovereignty and complete independence for Lebanon; majority of leaders and supporters are from the Christian community, although is officially secular; largest party in the Change and Reform parliamentary bloc; contested 2009 legislative elections as part of March 8 Alliance; Leader Gen. Michel Aoun.

Future Movement (Tayar al-Mustaqbal): POB 123, Koraytem, Hamra, Beirut; tel. (3) 375442; fax (1) 375442; e-mail info@almustaqbal.org; internet www.almustaqbal.org; opposed to Syrian

LEBANON

influence in Lebanese affairs; contested 2009 legislative elections as largest party of the March 14 Alliance; Leader SAAD EL-DIN HARIRI.

Hezbollah (Party of God): Beirut; e-mail moqawama@moqawama.org; internet www.hizbollah.tv; f. 1982 by Iranian Revolutionary Guards who were sent to Lebanon; militant Shi'ite faction, which has become the leading organization of Lebanon's Shi'a community and a recognized political party; demands the withdrawal of Israeli forces from the occupied Shebaa Farms area of what it considers to be southern Lebanon (but which is designated by the UN as being part of Syria) and the release of all Lebanese prisoners from Israeli detention; contested 2009 legislative elections as part of March 8 Alliance; Chair. MUHAMMAD RA'D; Leader and Sec.-Gen. Sheikh HASAN NASRALLAH; Spiritual Leader Ayatollah MUHAMMAD HUSSAIN FADLALLAH.

Hizb-ut-Tahrir al-Islami (Party of Islamic Liberation): e-mail info@hizb-ut-tahrir.org; internet www.hizb-ut-tahrir.org; f. 1953; transnational org. granted a political parties licence in Lebanon in 2006; aims to establish Islamic caliphate throughout the world; denies claims that it is a militant group; Global Leader Sheikh ABU YASIN ATA IBN KHALIL ABU RASHTA, (Sheikh Ata Abu Rashta).

Al-Kataeb (Lebanese Social Democratic Party): POB 992, place Charles Hélou, Beirut; tel. (1) 584107; internet www.kataeb.org; f. 1936 as the Phalangist Party (Phalanges libanaises); nationalist, reformist, democratic social party; largest Maronite party, although is officially secular; contested 2009 legislative elections as part of March 14 Alliance; 100,000 mems; Pres. AMIN GEMAYEL.

Lebanese Democratic Party (LDP): Beirut; e-mail webmaster@ldparty.org; internet www.ldparty.org; f. 2001; contested 2009 legislative elections as part of March 8 Alliance; Leader TALAL ARSLAN.

Lebanese Forces Party: Beirut; internet www.lebanese-forces.org; political successor to the **Lebanese Forces** (f. 1976; coalition of Maronite Christian militias); launched as political party in 1989; proscribed by the Government in 1994; resumed activities as a legal party in 2005; contested 2009 legislative elections as part of March 14 Alliance, securing five seats; Leader SAMIR GEAGEA.

Lebanese Option Gathering: Beirut; tel. (1) 399344; e-mail ghadazoghbi@lebaneseoption.com; internet lebaneseoption.org; f. 2007; aims to contest Hezbollah's monopoly over Shi'ite political representation in Lebanon, and to reform and develop the south of the country; Leader AHMAD AL-ASSAD.

El-Marada Movement: Zgharta; internet elmarada.org; f. as the Marada Brigade, relaunched in 1996 as a political party; advocates Lebanese unity, sovereignty and independence; contested 2009 legislative elections as part of March 8 Alliance; Leader SULAYMAN FRANJIYA.

March 8 Alliance: contested 2009 legislative elections as an electoral bloc comprising Hezbollah, Amal, the Free Patriotic Movement, the Armenian Revolutionary Federation, the Syrian Social Nationalist Party, the Baath Party, the Islamic Action Front, the El-Marada Movement, the Lebanese Democratic Party and independents.

March 14 Alliance: contested 2009 legislative elections as an electoral bloc comprising Future Movement, Parti socialiste progressiste (PSP), the Lebanese Forces Party, Al-Kataeb and other smaller parties and independents; following disagreements over the formation of a new government, the PSP withdrew from the alliance in August 2009.

National Dialogue Party: POB 15-5060, First Floor, Immeuble Marj el-Zouhour, rue Donna Maria, Ras el-Nabeh, Beirut; tel. (1) 637000; fax (1) 631234; e-mail info@alhiwar.com; internet www.alhiwar.com; f. 2004; advocates a comprehensive national dialogue to bring about political, social and judicial reforms; also seeks to target corruption and to ensure that the State has authority over the whole of Lebanon; Founder and Chair. FOUAD MAKHZOUMI.

Parti communiste libanais (PCL) (Lebanese Communist Party): rue al-Bahatri, al-Watuat, Beirut; tel. and fax (1) 739615; e-mail lcparty@lcparty.org; internet www.lcparty.org; f. 1924; officially dissolved 1948–71; Marxist, with much support among intellectuals; Pres. MAURICE NOHRA; Sec.-Gen. KHALID HADDADEH.

Parti national libéral (PNL) (Al-Wataniyin al-Ahrar): POB 165576, rue du Liban, Beirut; tel. (1) 338000; fax (1) 200335; e-mail ahrar@ahrar.org.lb; internet www.ahrar.org.lb; f. 1958; liberal reformist secular party, although has traditionally had a predominantly Maronite Christian membership; contested 2009 legislative elections as part of March 14 Alliance; Pres. DORY CHAMOUN.

Parti socialiste progressiste (PSP) (Al-Takadumi al-Ishteraki): POB 11-2893, Beirut 1107 2120; tel. (1) 303455; fax (1) 301231; e-mail internationalrelation@psp.org.lb; internet www.psp.org.lb; f. 1949; progressive party, advocates constitutional road to socialism and democracy; over 25,000 mems; mainly Druze support; contested 2009 legislative elections as part of the March 14 Alliance; Pres. WALID JOUMBLATT; Sec.-Gen. SHARIF FAYAD.

Syrian Social Nationalist Party (al-Hizb al-Suri al-Qawmi al-Ijtima'i): internet www.ssnp.net; f. 1932 in Beirut; banned 1962–69; seeks creation of a 'Greater Syrian' state, incl. Lebanon, Syria, Iraq, Jordan, the Palestinian territories, Kuwait, Cyprus and parts of Egypt, Iran and Turkey; advocates separation of church and State, the redistribution of wealth and a strong military; supports Syrian involvement in Lebanese affairs; contested 2009 legislative elections as part of March 8 Alliance; Leader ASSAD HARDANE.

Al-Wa'ad (National Secular Democratic Party—Pledge): Beirut; f. 1986 by the late Elie Hobeika; pro-Syrian splinter group of Lebanese Forces; officially secular, although most supporters are Maronite Christians; aligned with March 8 Alliance; did not achieve parliamentary representation in June 2009 legislative elections.

Other parties include the **Independent Nasserite Movement** (Murabitoun; Sunni Muslim Militia; Leader IBRAHIM QULAYAT) and the **Lebanese Popular Congress** (Pres. KAMAL SHATILA). The **Nasserite Popular Organization** and the **Arab Socialist Union** merged in January 1987, retaining the name of the former. The **Islamic Amal** is a breakaway group from Amal, based in Ba'albek (Leader HUSSEIN MOUSSAVI). **Islamic Jihad** is a pro-Iranian fundamentalist guerrilla group. The **Popular Liberation Army** (f. 1985 by the late MUSTAFA SAAD) is a Sunni Muslim faction, active in the south of Lebanon. **Tawhid Islami** (the Islamic Unification Movement; f. 1982; Sunni Muslim) and the **Arab Democratic Party** (or the Red Knights; Alawites; pro-Syrian; Leader ALI EID) are based in Tripoli.

Diplomatic Representation

EMBASSIES IN LEBANON

Algeria: POB 4794, face Hôtel Summerland, rue Jnah, Beirut; tel. (1) 826712; fax (1) 826711; Ambassador AHMAD BOUTEHRI.

Argentina: 2nd Floor, Residence des Jardins, Immeuble Moutran, 161 rue Sursock, Achrafieh, Beirut; tel. (1) 210800; fax (1) 210802; e-mail embarg@cyberia.net.lb; Ambassador JOSÉ MAXWELL.

Armenia: POB 70607, rue Jasmin, Rabieh, Mtailob, Beirut; tel. (4) 402952; fax (4) 418860; e-mail armenia@dm.net.lb; Ambassador ASHOT KOCHARIAN.

Australia: Embassy Complex, Sérail Hill, Beirut; tel. (1) 960600; fax (1) 960601; e-mail austemle@dfat.gov.au; internet www.lebanon.embassy.gov.au; Ambassador LEX BARTLEM.

Austria: POB 11-3942, 8th Floor, Immeuble Tabaris, 812 ave Charles Malek, Achrafieh, Beirut; tel. (1) 217360; fax (1) 217772; e-mail beirut-ob@bmeia.gv.at; Ambassador EVA MARIA ZIEGLER.

Belgium: Bloc A, 10e étage, Immeuble Lazarie, rue Emir Béchir, Beirut; tel. (1) 976001; fax (1) 976007; e-mail beirut@diplobel.fed.be; internet www.diplomatie.be/beirut; Ambassador JOHAN VERKAMMEN.

Brazil: POB 40242, Baabda, Beirut; tel. (5) 921255; fax (5) 923001; e-mail braemlib@terra.net.lb; Ambassador EDUARDO AUGUSTO IBIAPINA DE SEIXAS.

Bulgaria: POB 11-6544, Sector 6, Mar-Takla, Hazmieh, Beirut; tel. (5) 452883; fax (5) 452892; e-mail bg_emblb@yahoo.com; internet www.mfa.bg/bg/48/; Ambassador (vacant).

Canada: POB 60163, 1er et 2e étage, Immeuble Coolrite, Autoroute Jal el-Dib 43, Beirut; tel. (4) 711664; fax (4) 710595; e-mail berut@international.gc.ca; internet www.lebanon.gc.ca; Ambassador HILARY CHILDS-ADAMS.

Chile: Nouvelle Naccache, 21 Bifurcation après La Belle Antique avant Carpacio, Beirut; tel. (4) 418670; fax (4) 418672; e-mail echilelb@dm.net.lb; internet chileabroad.gov.cl/libano; Ambassador PEDRO BARROS URZUA.

China, People's Republic: POB 11-8227, 72 rue Nicolas Ibrahim Sursock, Ramlet el-Baida, Beirut 1107 2260; tel. (1) 850314; fax (1) 822492; e-mail chinaemb_lb@mfa.gov.cn; internet lb.china-embassy.org; Ambassador WU ZEXIAN.

Colombia: 5th Floor, Mazda Centre, Jal el-Dib, Beirut; tel. (4) 712646; fax (4) 712656; e-mail ebeirut@minrelext.gov.co; Ambassador RIDA MARIETTE ALJURE-SALAME.

Cuba: Center Farrania, Saïd Freiha St, Mar-Takla, Hazmieh, Beirut 2901 6727; tel. (1) 459925; fax (1) 950070; e-mail libancub@cyberia.net.lb; internet www.embacubalebanon.com; Ambassador MANUEL MARÍA SERRANO ACOSTA.

Cyprus: Immeuble M.N.C., Debbas St, Achrafieh, Beirut; tel. (1) 326461; fax (1) 326471; e-mail info@cyprusembbeirut.org; internet www.cyprusembbeirut.org; Ambassador HOMER MAVROMMATIS.

Czech Republic: POB 40195, Baabda, Beirut; tel. (5) 929010; fax (5) 922120; e-mail beirut@embassy.mzv.cz; internet www.mzv.cz/beirut; Ambassador JAN ČÍŽEK.

LEBANON

Denmark: POB 11-5190, Army St, Sérail Hill, Beirut; tel. (1) 991001; fax (1) 991006; e-mail beyamb@um.dk; internet www.ambbeirut.um.dk; Ambassador JAN TOP CHRISTENSEN.

Egypt: POB 5037, rue Thomas Eddison, al-Ramla el-Baida, Beirut; tel. (1) 825566; fax (1) 859988; Ambassador AHMAD AL-BIDYAWI.

France: rue de Damas, Beirut; tel. (1) 420000; fax (1) 420013; e-mail ambafr@ciberia.net.lb; internet www.ambafrance-lb.org; Ambassador DENIS PIETTON.

Gabon: POB 11-1252, Riad el-Solh, Hadath, Beirut 1107 2080; tel. (5) 924649; fax (5) 924643; Ambassador SIMON NTOUTOUME EMANE.

Germany: POB 11-2820, Riad el-Solh, Beirut 1102 2110; tel. (4) 935000; fax (4) 935001; e-mail info@beirut.diplo.de; internet www.beirut.diplo.de; Ambassador BIRGITTA SIEFKER-EBERLE.

Greece: POB 11-0309, Immeuble Boukhater, rue des Ambassades, Nouvelle Naccache, Beirut; tel. (4) 418772; fax (4) 418774; e-mail gremb.bei@mfa.gr; internet www.mfa.gr/beirut; Ambassador PANAGIOTIS KALOGEROPOULOS.

Holy See: POB 1061, Jounieh (Apostolic Nunciature); tel. (9) 263102; fax (9) 264488; e-mail naliban@terra.net.lb; Apostolic Nuncio Most Rev. GABRIELE GIORDANO CACCIA (Titular Archbishop of Sepino).

Hungary: POB 113-5259, 9th Floor, Immeuble BAC, rue Justinien, Sanayeh, Beirut; tel. (1) 730083; fax (1) 741261; e-mail mission.bej@kum.hu; internet www.mfa.gov.hu/kulkepviselet/LB; Ambassador LÁSZLÓ VÁRADI.

India: POB 113-5240, Immeuble Sahmarani, rue Kantari 31, Hamra, Beirut; tel. (1) 373539; fax (1) 373538; e-mail amb.beirut@mea.gov.in; Ambassador RAVI THAPAR.

Indonesia: POB 40007, ave Palais Presidential, rue 68, Secteur 3, Baabda, Beirut; tel. (5) 924682; fax (5) 924678; e-mail kbri@kbri-beirut.org; internet kbri-beirut.org; Ambassador R. BAGAS HAPSORO.

Iran: POB 5030, Bir Hassan, Beirut; tel. (1) 821224; fax (1) 821229; Ambassador GHANDAFAR RUKUN ABADI.

Iraq: Beirut; tel. (1) 453209; fax (1) 459850; e-mail brtemb@iraqmofamail.net; Ambassador OMAR AL-BARZENJI.

Italy: rue du Palais Présidentiel, Baabda, Beirut; tel. (5) 954955; fax (5) 959616; e-mail amba.beirut@esteri.it; internet www.ambbeirut.esteri.it; Ambassador GIUSEPPE MORABITO.

Japan: POB 11-3360, Army St, Zkak al-Blat, Sérail Hill, Beirut; tel. (1) 989751; fax (1) 989754; e-mail japanemb@japanemb.org.lb; internet www.lb.emb-japan.go.jp; Ambassador YOSHIHISA KURODA.

Jordan: POB 109, Beirut 5113; tel. (5) 922500; fax (5) 922502; e-mail joremb@dm.net.lb; Ambassador ZIYAD MAJALI.

Korea, Republic: POB 40-290, Baabda, Beirut; tel. (5) 953167; fax (5) 953170; e-mail lbkor@hanmail.net; internet lbn.mofat.go.kr/eng/af/lbn/main/index.jsp; Ambassador LEE YOUNG-HA.

Kuwait: POB 4580, Rond-point du Stade, Bir Hassan, Beirut; tel. (1) 756100; fax (1) 842220; e-mail info@kuwaitinfo.net; internet www.kuwaitinfo.net; Ambassador ABD AL-AAL AL-QINAI.

Mexico: POB 70-1150, rue 53, Antélias, Beirut; tel. (4) 418871; fax (4) 418873; e-mail mail@embassyofmexicoinlebanon.org; internet www.embassyofmexicoinlebanon.org; Ambassador JORGE ÁLVAREZ FUENTES.

Morocco: Bir Hassan, Beirut; tel. (1) 859829; fax (1) 859839; e-mail sifmar@cyberia.net.lb; Ambassador ALI OUMLIL.

Netherlands: POB 167190, Netherlands Tower, ave Charles Malek, Achrafieh, Beirut; tel. (1) 204663; fax (1) 204664; e-mail bei@minbuza.nl; internet www.netherlandsembassy.org.lb; Ambassador G. DE BOER.

Norway: POB 113-7001, Immeuble Dimashki, rue Bliss, Ras Beirut, Hamra, Beirut 1103 2150; tel. (1) 960000; fax (1) 960099; e-mail emb.bey@mfa.no; internet www.norway-lebanon.org; Ambassador AUD LISE NORHEIM.

Pakistan: POB 135506, Immeuble Shell, 11e étage, Raoucheh, Beirut; tel. (1) 835634; fax (1) 864583; e-mail pakemblb@cyberia.net.lb; internet www.mofa.gov.pk/lebanon; Ambassador RAANA RAHIM.

Paraguay: 1er étage, Immeuble Kormali, rue Ambassade de France, Hazmieh, Beirut; tel. and fax (1) 5458502; e-mail embaparlibano@hotmail.com; Ambassador FERNANDO PARISI.

Philippines: POB 136631, ave Charles Malik, Achrafieh, Beirut; tel. (1) 212001; fax (1) 212004; e-mail beirutpe@dfa.gov.ph; Ambassador GILBERTO G. B. ASUQUE.

Poland: POB 40-215, Immeuble Khalifa, ave Président Sulayman Franjiya 52, Baabda, Beirut; tel. (5) 924881; fax (5) 924882; e-mail polamb@cyberia.net.lb; internet www.polambeirut.org; Ambassador TOMASZ NIEGODZISZ.

Qatar: POB 11-6717, 1er étage, Immeuble Deebs, Shouran, Beirut; tel. (1) 865271; fax (1) 810460; e-mail beirut@mofa.gov.qa; Ambassador SAAD BIN ALI AL-MUHANNADI.

Romania: Route du Palais Presidentiel, Baabda, Beirut; tel. (5) 924848; fax (5) 924747; e-mail romembey@inco.com.lb; internet beirut.mae.ro; Ambassador DANIEL TANASE.

Russia: POB 5220, rue Mar Elias el-Tineh, Wata Mseitbeh, Beirut; tel. (1) 300041; fax (1) 303837; e-mail rusembei@cyberia.net.lb; internet www.lebanon.mid.ru; Ambassador ALEKSANDR ZASYPKIN.

Saudi Arabia: POB 136144, Kuraitem, Beirut; tel. (1) 860351; fax (1) 861524; e-mail lbemb@mofa.gov.sa; Ambassador ALI BIN AWADH ASSERI.

Spain: POB 11-3039, Palais Chehab, Hadath Antounie, Beirut; tel. (5) 464120; fax (5) 464030; e-mail emb.beirut@maec.es; Ambassador JUAN CARLOS GAFO ACEVEDO.

Sri Lanka: 549 Immeuble Muhammad K. Awad, Beirut; tel. (5) 924765; fax (5) 924763; e-mail slemblbn@cyberia.net.lb; Ambassador MEER SAHIB MAHROOF.

Sudan: POB 2504, Hamra, Beirut; tel. (1) 350057; fax (1) 353271; Ambassador IDRIS SULEIMAN YUSUF MUSTAPHA.

Switzerland: POB 11-172, Immeuble Bourj al-Ghazal, ave Fouad Chehab, Achrafieh, Beirut 1107 2020; tel. (1) 324129; fax (1) 324167; e-mail bey.vertretung@eda.admin.ch; internet www.eda.admin.ch/beirut; Ambassador RUTH FLINT.

Syria: Makdessi St, Hamra, Beirut; Ambassador ALI ABD AL-KARIM ALI.

Tunisia: Mar-Takla, Hazmieh, Beirut; tel. (5) 457431; fax (5) 950434; Ambassador MUHAMMAD SAMIR ABDELLAH.

Turkey: POB 70-666, zone II, rue 1, Rabieh, Beirut; tel. (4) 520929; fax (4) 407557; e-mail trbebeyr@intracom.net.lb; internet beirut.emb.mfa.gov.tr; Ambassador INAN OZYILDIZ.

Ukraine: POB 431, Jardin al-Bacha, Jisr al-Bacha, Sin el-Fil, Beirut; tel. (1) 510527; fax (1) 510527; e-mail emb_lb@mfa.gov.ua; internet www.mfa.gov.ua/lebanon; Ambassador VOLODYMYR KOVAL.

United Arab Emirates: Immeuble Wafic Tanbara, Jnah, Beirut; tel. (1) 857000; fax (1) 857009; e-mail eembassy@uae.org.lb; Ambassador RAHMAN HUSSAIN AL-ZA'ABI.

United Kingdom: POB 11-471, Sérail Hill, Beirut Central District, Beirut; tel. (1) 960800; fax (1) 990420; e-mail chancery@cyberia.net.lb; internet ukinlebanon.fco.gov.uk; Ambassador FRANCES GUY.

USA: POB 70-840, Antélias; tel. (4) 542600; fax (4) 544136; e-mail pasbeirut@state.gov; internet lebanon.usembassy.gov; Ambassador MAURA CONNELLY.

Uruguay: POB 2051, Centre Stella Marris, 7e étage, rue Banque du Liban, Jounieh; tel. (9) 636529; fax (9) 636531; e-mail uruliban@dm.net.lb; internet www.embauruguaybeirut.org; Ambassador JORGE LUIS JURE.

Venezuela: POB 11-603, Immeuble Baezevale House, 5e étage, Zalka, Beirut; tel. (1) 888701; fax (1) 900757; e-mail embajadora@embavenelibano.com; internet www.embavenelibano.com; Ambassador ZOED KARAM.

Yemen: Bir Hassan, Beirut; tel. (1) 852688; fax (1) 821610; Ambassador (vacant).

Judicial System

Law and justice in Lebanon are administered in accordance with the following codes, which are based upon modern theories of civil and criminal legislation:

Code de la Propriété (1930).

Code des Obligations et des Contrats (1932).

Code de Procédure Civile (1933).

Code Maritime (1947).

Code de Procédure Pénale (Code Ottoman Modifié).

Code Pénal (1943).

Code Pénal Militaire (1946).

Code d'Instruction Criminelle.

The following courts are now established:

(a) Fifty-six **'Courts of First Instance'**, each consisting of a single judge, and dealing in the first instance with both civil and criminal cases; there are 17 such courts in Beirut and seven in Tripoli.

President of the Courts of First Instance of Beirut: Dr FADI ELIAS.

(b) Eleven **Courts of Appeal**, each consisting of three judges, including a President and a Public Prosecutor, and dealing with civil and criminal cases; there are five such courts in Beirut.

First President of the Courts of Appeal of Beirut: JEAN FAHD.

LEBANON

(c) Four **Courts of Cassation**, three dealing with civil and commercial cases and the fourth with criminal cases. A Court of Cassation, to be properly constituted, must have at least three judges, one being the President and the other two Councillors. If the Court of Cassation reverses the judgment of a lower court, it does not refer the case back but retries it itself.

General Prosecutor of Cassation: SAID MIRZA.

(d) **State Consultative Council**, which deals with administrative cases.

President of the State Consultative Council: SHUKRI SADER.

(e) The **Court of Justice**, which is a special court consisting of a President and four judges, deals with matters affecting the security of the State; there is no appeal against its verdicts.

In addition to the above, the **Constitutional Council** considers matters pertaining to the constitutionality of legislation, while the **Higher Judicial Council** considers matters involving members of the executive branch. Military courts are competent to try crimes and misdemeanours involving the armed and security forces. Islamic (*Shari'a*), Christian and Jewish religious courts deal with affairs of personal status (marriage, death, inheritance, etc.).

President of the Constitutional Council: ISSAM SULEIMAN.
President of the Higher Judicial Council: GHALEB GHANEM.
Chief of the Military Court: Brig.-Gen. MAHER SAFI EL-DIN.

Religion

Of all the regions of the Middle East, Lebanon probably presents the closest juxtaposition of sects and peoples within a small territory. Estimates for 1983 assessed the sizes of communities as: Shi'a Muslims 1.2m., Maronites 900,000, Sunni Muslims 750,000, Greek Orthodox 250,000, Druzes 250,000, Armenians 175,000. There is also a small Jewish community. In 1994 it was estimated that 29%–32% of the population of Lebanon were Shi'a Muslims, 25%–28% Maronites, 16%–20% Sunni Muslims and 3.5% Druzes. The Maronites, a uniate sect of the Roman Catholic Church, inhabited the old territory of Mount Lebanon, i.e. immediately east of Beirut. In the south, towards the Israeli frontier, Shi'a villages are most common, while between the Shi'a and the Maronites live the Druzes (divided between the Yazbakis and the Joumblatis). The Beqa'a valley has many Greek Christians (both Roman Catholic and Orthodox), while the Tripoli area is mainly Sunni Muslim.

CHRISTIANITY

The Roman Catholic Church

Armenian Rite

Patriarchate of Cilicia: Patriarcat Arménien Catholique, rue de l'Hôpital orthodoxe, Jeitawi, Beirut 2078 5605; tel. (1) 570555; fax (1) 570563; e-mail nerbed19@magnarama.com; f. 1742; est. in Beirut since 1929; includes patriarchal diocese of Beirut, with an estimated 12,000 adherents (31 December 2007); Patriarch Most Rev. NERSES BEDROS XIX TARMOUNI; Protosyncellus Rt Rev. VARTAN ACHKARIAN (Titular Bishop of Tokat—Armenian Rite).

Chaldean Rite

Diocese of Beirut: Evêché Chaldéen de Beyrouth, POB 373, Hazmieh, Beirut; tel. (5) 457732; fax (5) 457731; e-mail chaldepiscopus@hotmail.com; an estimated 10,000 adherents (31 December 2007); Bishop of Beirut MICHEL KASSARJI.

Latin Rite

Apostolic Vicariate of Beirut: Vicariat Apostolique, POB 11-4224, Riad el-Solh, Beirut 1107 2160; tel. (9) 236101; fax (9) 236102; e-mail vicariatlat@hotmail.com; an estimated 15,000 adherents (31 December 2007); Vicar Apostolic PAUL DAHDAH (Titular Archbishop of Arae in Numidia).

Maronite Rite

Patriarchate of Antioch and all the East: Patriarcat Maronite, Bkerké; tel. (9) 915441; fax (9) 938844; e-mail jtawk@bkerke.org.lb; includes patriarchal dioceses of Jounieh, Sarba and Jobbé; the Maronite Church in Lebanon comprises four archdioceses and six dioceses, with an estimated 1,498,677 adherents (31 December 2007); Patriarch Cardinal BÉCHARA BOUTROS RAÏ.

Archbishop of Antélias: Most Rev. JOSEPH MOHSEN BÉCHARA, Archevêché Maronite, POB 70400, Antélias; tel. (4) 410020; fax (4) 415872.

Archbishop of Beirut: Most Rev. PAUL YOUSUF MATAR, Archevêché Maronite, 10 rue Collège de la Sagesse, Achrafieh, Beirut; tel. (1) 561980; fax (1) 561930; e-mail maronitebeyrouth@yahoo.fr; also representative of the Holy See for Roman Catholics of the Coptic Rite in Lebanon.

Archbishop of Tripoli: Most Rev. GEORGES BOU-JAOUDÉ, Archevêché Maronite, POB 104, rue al-Moutran, Karm Sada, Tripoli; tel. (6) 624324; fax (6) 629393; e-mail rahmat@inco.com.lb.

Archbishop of Tyre: Most Rev. CHUCRALLAH-NABIL HAGE, Archevêché Maronite, Tyre; tel. (7) 740059; fax (7) 344891; e-mail abounacharbel@cyberia.net.lb.

Melkite Rite

Patriarch of Antioch: Patriarcat Grec-Melkite Catholique, POB 22249, 12 ave al-Zeitoon, Bab Charki, Damascus, Syria; tel. (11) 5441030; fax (11) 5417900; e-mail pat.melk@scs-net.org; internet www.pgc-lb.org; f. 1724; the Melkite Church in Lebanon comprises seven archdioceses, with an estimated 384,700 adherents (31 December 2007); Patriarch of Antioch and all the East, of Alexandria and of Jerusalem His Beatitude GREGORIOS III LAHAM.

Archbishop of Ba'albek: Most Rev. ELIAS RAHAL, Archevêché Grec-Catholique, Ba'albek; tel. (8) 370200; fax (8) 373986.

Archbishop of Baniyas: Most Rev. GEORGES NICOLAS HADDAD, Archevêché de Panéas, Jdeidet Marjeyoun; tel. and fax (3) 830007.

Archbishop of Beirut and Jbeil: JOSEPH KALLAS, Archevêché Grec-Melkite-Catholique, POB 11-901, 655 rue de Damas, Beirut; tel. (1) 616104; fax (1) 616109; e-mail agmcb@terra.net.lb.

Archbishop of Saida (Sidon): Most Rev. ELIE BÉCHARA HADDAD, Archevêché Grec-Melkite-Catholique, POB 247, rue el-Moutran, Sidon; tel. (7) 720100; fax (7) 722055; e-mail mhaddad.saida@hotmail.com.

Archbishop of Tripoli: Most Rev. GEORGE RIASHI, Archevêché Grec-Catholique, POB 72, rue al-Kanaess, Tripoli; tel. (6) 431602; fax (6) 441716.

Archbishop of Tyre: Most Rev. GEORGES BAKOUNY, Archevêché Grec-Melkite-Catholique, POB 257, Tyre; tel. (7) 740015; fax (7) 349180; e-mail pbacouni@yahoo.com.

Archbishop of Zahleh and Furzol: Most Rev. ANDRÉ HADDAD, Archevêché Grec-Melkite-Catholique, Saidat el-Najat, Zahleh; tel. (8) 800333; fax (8) 822406; e-mail info@catholiczahle.org; internet www.catholiczahle.org.

Syrian Rite

Patriarchate of Antioch: Patriarcat Syrien Catholique d'Antioche, rue de Damas, POB 116/5087, Beirut 1106 2010; tel. (1) 615892; fax (1) 616573; e-mail psc_lb@yahoo.com; jurisdiction over about 150,000 Syrian Catholics in the Middle East, incl. (at 31 December 2007) 14,700 in the diocese of Beirut; Patriarch Most Rev. IGNACE JOSEPH III YOUNAN; Protosyncellus Mgr GEORGES MASRI.

The Anglican Communion

Within the Episcopal Church in Jerusalem and the Middle East, Lebanon forms part of the diocese of Jerusalem (see the chapter on Israel).

Other Christian Groups

Armenian Apostolic Orthodox Church: Armenian Catholicosate of Cilicia, POB 70317, Antélias; tel. (4) 410001; fax (4) 419724; e-mail info@armenianorthodoxchurch.org; internet www.armenianorthodoxchurch.org; f. 301 in Armenia, re-established in 1293 in Cilicia (now in Turkey), transferred to Antélias, Lebanon, 1930; Leader His Holiness ARAM KESHISHIAN I (Catholicos of Cilicia); jurisdiction over an estimated 3.5m. adherents in Lebanon, Syria, Cyprus, Kuwait, Greece, Iran, Qatar, the United Arab Emirates, South America, the USA and Canada.

National Evangelical Synod of Syria and Lebanon: POB 70890, Antélias; tel. (4) 525030; fax (4) 411184; e-mail nessl@synod-sl.org; internet www.synod-sl.org; f. 1959; 20,000 adherents (2010); Gen. Sec. Rev. FADI DAGHER.

Patriarchate of Antioch and all the East (Greek Orthodox): Patriarcat Grec-Orthodoxe, POB 9, Damascus, Syria; tel. (11) 5424400; fax (11) 5424404; e-mail info@antiochpat.org; internet www.antiochpat.org; Patriarch His Beatitude IGNATIUS (HAZIM) IV.

Supreme Council of the Evangelical Community in Syria and Lebanon: POB 70/1065, rue Rabieh 34, Antélias; tel. (4) 525036; fax (4) 405490; e-mail suprcoun@minero.net; Pres. Rev. Dr SALIM SAHIOUNY.

Patriarchate of Antioch and all the East (Syrian Orthodox): Patriarcat Syrien Orthodoxe, Bab Toma, POB 22260, Damascus, Syria; tel. (11) 5951870; fax (11) 5951880; internet www.syrian-orthodox.com; Patriarch IGNATIUS ZAKKA I IWAS.

Union of the Armenian Evangelical Churches in the Near East: POB 11-377, Beirut; tel. (1) 565628; fax (1) 565629; e-mail uaecne@cyberia.net.lb; f. 1846 in Turkey; comprises about 30

LEBANON

Armenian Evangelical Churches in Syria, Lebanon, Egypt, Cyprus, Greece, Iran, Turkey and Australia; Pres. Rev. MEGRDICH KARAGOEZIAN; Gen. Sec. SEBOUH TERZIAN.

ISLAM

Shi'a Muslims: Leader Imam Sheikh SAYED MOUSSA AL-SADR (went missing during visit to Libya in August 1978); Vice-Pres. of the Supreme Islamic Council of the Shi'a Community of Lebanon ABD AL-AMIR QABALAN; Beirut.

Sunni Muslims: Grand Mufti of Lebanon, Dar el-Fatwa, rue Ilewi Rushed, Beirut; tel. (1) 422340; Leader Sheikh Dr MUHAMMAD RASHID QABBANI.

Druzes: Supreme Spiritual Leader of the Druze Community, Beirut; tel. (1) 341116; Supreme Spiritual Leader Sheikh AL-AQL BAHJAT GHAITH; Political Leader WALID JOUMBLATT.

Alawites: a schism of Shi'ite Islam; there are an estimated 50,000 Alawites in northern Lebanon, in and around Tripoli.

JUDAISM

A small Jewish community, numbering less than 200 people in 2009, remains in Lebanon.

Jewish Community: Leader Rabbi CHAHOUD CHREIM (Beirut).

The Press

DAILIES

Al-Akhbar (The News): POB 5963-113, 6th Floor, Concorde Centre, rue Verdun, Beirut; tel. (1) 759500; fax (1) 759597; internet www.al-akhbar.com; f. 2006; Arabic; independent; Editor KHALID SAGHIEH.

Al-Amal (Hope): POB 992, place Charles Hélou, Beirut; tel. (1) 382992; f. 1939; Arabic; organ of Al-Kataeb (Lebanese Social Democratic Party); Chief Editor ELIAS RABABI; circ. 35,000.

Al-Anwar (Lights): c/o Dar Assayad, POB 11-1038, Hazmieh, Beirut; tel. (5) 456374; fax (5) 452700; e-mail info@alanwar.com; internet www.alanwar-leb.com; f. 1959; Arabic; independent; supplement, Sunday; cultural and social; publ. by Dar Assayad SAL; Editors-in-Chief MICHEL RAAD, RAFIK KHOURY; circ. 14,419.

Aztag: POB 80-860, Shaghzoyan Cultural Centre, Bourj Hammoud; tel. (1) 258526; fax (1) 258529; e-mail info@aztagdaily.com; internet www.aztagdaily.com; f. 1927; Armenian; Editor-in-Chief SHAHAN KANDAHARIAN; circ. 6,500.

Al-Balad: Beirut; tel. (1) 494694; fax (1) 494894; e-mail crm@albaladonline.com; internet albaladonline.com; Arabic; Chair. AHMAD BADRANI; Man. Editor GEORGE JABARA.

Al-Bayrak (The Standard): Immeuble Dimitri Trad, rue Issa Maalouf, Achrafieh, Beirut; tel. (1) 216393; fax (1) 338928; e-mail dalwl@dm.net.lb; internet www.albayrakonline.com; f. 1913; Arabic; publ. by Dar Alf Leila wa Leila Publishing House; politics and society; Editor-in-Chief MELHEM KARAM; circ. 10,000.

Al-Charq (The East): POB 11-0838, rue Verdun, Riad el-Solh, Beirut; tel. (1) 810820; fax (1) 866105; e-mail info@elshark.com; internet www.elshark.com; f. 1926; Arabic; Gen. Dir and Editor-in-Chief AOUNI AL-KAAKI.

Daily Star: 6th Floor, Marine Tower, rue de la Sainte Famille, Achrafieh, Beirut; tel. (1) 587277; fax (1) 561333; e-mail editorial@dailystar.com.lb; internet www.dailystar.com.lb; f. 1952; English; Publr and Editor-in-Chief JAMIL K. MROUE; circ. 10,550.

Al-Diyar (The Homeland): al-Nahda Bldg, Yarze, Beirut; tel. (5) 923830; fax (5) 923773; e-mail info@addiyaronline.com; internet www.aldiyaronline.com; f. 1987; Arabic; Propr and Editor-in-Chief CHARLES AYYUB.

Al-Dunya (The World): Beirut; f. 1943; Arabic; political; Chief Editor SULIMAN ABOU ZAID; circ. 25,000.

Al-Hayat (Life): POB 11-1242, rue Maarad, place Riad el-Solh, Beirut; tel. (1) 987990; fax (1) 983921; e-mail information@alhayat.com; internet www.alhayat.com; f. 1946; Arabic; independent; Editor-in-Chief GHASSAN CHARBEL; circ. 196,800.

Lisan ul-Hal (The Organ): rue Châteaubriand, Beirut; e-mail lebanon@lissan-ul-hal.com; internet www.lissan-ul-hal.com; f. 1877; Arabic; Editor GEBRAN HAYEK; circ. 33,000.

Al-Liwa' (The Standard): POB 11-2402, Beirut; tel. (1) 735745; fax (1) 735749; e-mail events@aliwaa.com.lb; internet www.aliwaa.com; f. 1963; Arabic; Propr ABD AL-GHANI SALAM; Editor SALAH SALAM; circ. 26,000.

Al-Mustaqbal: POB 14-5426, Beirut; tel. (1) 797770; fax (1) 869264; e-mail rnakib@almustaqbal.com.lb; internet www.almustaqbal.com.lb; f. 1999; Dir RAFIQ NAKIB; Editor-in-Chief HANI HAMMOUD; circ. 20,000.

Directory

An-Nahar (The Day): Immeuble An-Nahar, place des Martyrs, Marfa', Beirut 2014 5401; tel. (1) 994888; fax (1) 996777; e-mail webmaster@annahar.com.lb; internet www.annahar.com; f. 1933; Arabic; independent; publ. by Editions Dar an-Nahar SAL; Chair. GHASSAN TUÉNI; Exec. Editor-in-Chief EDMOND SAAB; circ. 50,000.

Al-Nida (The Appeal): Beirut; f. 1959; Arabic; publ. by the Parti communiste libanais; Editor KARIM MROUÉ; circ. 10,000.

L'Orient-Le Jour: POB 11-2488, Kantari, Immeuble Kantari Corner, Beirut; tel. (1) 365365; fax (1) 375888; e-mail administration@lorientlejour.com; internet www.lorientlejour.com; f. 1942; French; independent; Pres. Dir MICHEL EDDÉ; Editor-in-Chief NAJUIB AOUN; circ. 23,000.

Sada Lubnan (Echo of Lebanon): Beirut; f. 1951; Arabic; pan-Arab; Editor MUHAMMAD BAALBAKI; circ. 25,000.

As-Safir: POB 113/5015, Immeuble as-Safir, rue Monimina, Hamra, Beirut 1103-2010; tel. (1) 350001; fax (1) 743602; e-mail mail@assafir.com; internet www.assafir.com; f. 1974; Arabic; political; Publr and Editor-in-Chief TALAL SALMAN; circ. 45,000.

Sawt al-Uruba (The Voice of Europe): POB 3537, Beirut; f. 1959; Arabic; organ of the Al-Najadeh Party.

Le Soir: POB 1470, rue de Syrie, Beirut; f. 1947; French; independent; Dir DIKRAN TOSBATH; Editor ANDRÉ KECATI; circ. 16,500.

Zartonk: POB 11-617, rue Nahr Ibrahim, Beirut; tel. and fax (1) 566709; e-mail info@zartonkdaily.com; internet www.zartonkdaily.com; f. 1937; Armenian, Arabic and English; official organ of Armenian Liberal Democratic Party; Man. Editor BAROUYR H. AGHBASHIAN.

WEEKLIES

Achabaka (The Net): c/o Dar Assayad SAL, POB 11-1038, Hazmieh, Beirut; tel. (5) 456373; fax (5) 452700; e-mail achabaka@achabaka.com; internet www.achabaka.com; f. 1956; Arabic; society and features; Founder SAID FREIHA; Editor ELHAM FREIHA; circ. 139,775.

Al-Alam al-Lubnani (The Lebanese World): POB 462, Beirut; f. 1964; Arabic, English, Spanish, French; politics, literature and social economy; Editor-in-Chief FAYEK KHOURY; Gen. Editor CHEIKH FADI GEMAYEL; circ. 45,000.

Al-Anwar Supplement: c/o Dar Assayad, POB 11-1038, Hazmieh, Beirut; tel. (5) 450406; fax (5) 452700; e-mail info@alanwar.com; internet www.alanwar.com; cultural and social; every Sun.; supplement to daily Al-Anwar; Editor ISSAM FREIHA; circ. 90,000.

Assayad (The Hunter): c/o Dar Assayad, POB 11-1038, Hazmieh, Beirut; tel. (5) 450933; fax (5) 452700; e-mail assayad@inco.com.lb; internet www.al-sayad.com; f. 1943; Arabic; political and social; Editor-in-Chief MOUNIR NAJJAR; circ. 76,192.

Attamaddon: POB 90, Tripoli; tel. (6) 441164; fax (6) 435252; e-mail info@attamaddon.com; internet www.attamaddon.com; f. 1972; political.

Al-Bayan: Karim Centre, Tripoli; tel. and fax (6) 425555; e-mail info@albayanlebanon.com; internet albayanlebanon.com; political.

Ad-Dabbour: place du Musée, Beirut; tel. and fax (1) 616771; e-mail addabbour@yahoo.com; internet www.addabbour.com; f. 1922; Arabic; CEO JOSEPH RICHARD MOUKARZEL; circ. 12,000.

Al-Hadaf (The Target): Beirut; tel. (1) 420554; f. 1969; organ of Popular Front for the Liberation of Palestine; Arabic; Editor-in-Chief SABER MOHI EL-DIN; circ. 40,000.

Al-Hawadeth (Events): POB 1281, rue Clémenceau, Beirut; tel. (1) 216393; fax (1) 200961; e-mail info@al-hawadeth.com; internet www.al-hawadeth.com; publ. from London, United Kingdom (183–185 Askew Rd, W12 9AX; tel. (20) 8740-4500; fax. (20) 8749-9781); f. 1911; Arabic; news; Editor-in-Chief MELHEM KARAM; circ. 120,000.

L'Hebdo Magazine: POB 11-1404, Immeuble Sayegh, rue Sursock, Beirut; tel. (1) 202070; fax (1) 202663; e-mail info@ediori.com.lb; internet www.magazine.com.lb; f. 1956; French; political, economic and social; publ. by Editions Orientales SAL; Pres. CHARLES ABOU ADAL; Editor-in-Chief PAUL KHALIFEH; circ. 18,000.

Al-Hiwar (Dialogue): rue Donna Maria, Beirut; tel. (1) 637000; fax (1) 631282; e-mail info@alhiwar.info; internet www.alhiwar.info; f. 2000; Arabic; publ. by the National Dialogue Party; Chair. FOUAD MAKHZOUMI; Editor-in-Chief SAM MOUNASSA.

Al-Hurriya (Freedom): Beirut; e-mail alhouriaa@hotmail.com; internet www.alhourriah.org; f. 1960; Arabic; organ of the Democratic Front for the Liberation of Palestine; Editor DAOUD TALHAME; circ. 30,000.

Al-Intiqad: internet www.alintiqad.com; Arabic; political; organ of Hezbollah; Editor IBRAHIM MOUSSAWI.

Al-Kifah al-Arabi (The Arab Struggle): POB 5158-14, Immeuble Rouche-Shams, Beirut; tel. (1) 809300; fax (1) 808281; e-mail editor@kifaharabi.com; internet www.kifaharabi.com; f. 1974; Arabic; political, socialist, pan-Arab; Publr WALID HUSSEINI.

LEBANON

Directory

Massis: Immeuble Eglise Ste Croix des Arméniens Catholiques, rue Zoghbi, Zalka, Beirut; tel. (4) 715263; e-mail hebdomassis@sodetel.net.lb; internet www.armeniancatholic.org; f. 1947; Armenian; Catholic; Editor-in-Chief Fr ANTRANIK GRANIAN; Dir SARKIS NADJARIAN; circ. 2,500.

Al-Moharrer (The Liberator): POB 136702, rue Hamra, Beirut; tel. (1) 750516; fax (1) 750515; e-mail almoharrer@almoharrer.net; internet www.almoharrer.net; f. 1962; Arabic; circ. 87,000; Gen. Man. WALID ABOU ZAHR.

Monday Morning: POB 165612, Immeuble Dimitri Trad, rue Issa Maalouf, Achrafieh, Beirut; tel. (1) 200961; fax (1) 335079; e-mail info@mmorning.com; internet www.mmorning.com; f. 1971; political and social affairs; publ. by Dar Alf Leila wa Leila; circ. 15,000; Editor-in-Chief MELHEM KARAM.

Al-Nass (The People): POB 4886, ave Fouad Chehab, Beirut; tel. (3) 376185; fax (8) 376610; f. 1959; Arabic; weekly news magazine; Editor-in-Chief HASSAN YAGHI; circ. 22,000.

Al-Ousbou' al-Arabi (Arab Week): POB 11-1404, Immeuble Sayegh, rue Sursock, Beirut; tel. (1) 202070; fax (1) 202663; e-mail info@arabweek.com.lb; internet www.arabweek.com.lb; f. 1959; Arabic; political and social; publ. by Editions Orientales SAL; Chair. and Editor-in-Chief CHARLES ABOU ADAL; circ. 88,407 (circulates throughout the Arab world).

Phoenix: POB 113222, Beirut; tel. (1) 363133; fax (1) 371186; e-mail dolfins@cyberia.net.lb; for women; publ. by Al-Khal.

La Revue du Liban (Lebanon Review): POB 165612, Immeuble Dimitri Trad, rue Issa Maalouf, Achrafieh, Beirut; tel. (1) 200961; fax (1) 338929; e-mail rdl@rdl.com.lb; internet www.rdl.com.lb; f. 1928; French; political, social, cultural; publ. by Dar Alf Leila wa Leila; Publr MELHEM KARAM; Gen. Man. MICHEL MISK; circ. 22,000.

Sabah al-Khair (Good Morning): Beirut; Arabic; publ. by the Syrian Socialist Nationalist Party.

Sahar: c/o Dar Assayad, POB 11-1038, Hazmieh, Beirut; tel. (5) 452700; fax (5) 452957; Arabic; for teenagers; publ. by Dar Assayad SAL.

Al-Shiraa (The Sail): POB 13-5250, Beirut; tel. (1) 703000; fax (1) 866050; e-mail alshiraa@alshiraa.com; internet www.alshiraa.com; Arabic; Editor HASSAN SABRA; circ. 40,000.

OTHER SELECTED PERIODICALS

Alam Attijarat (Business World): Immeuble Strand, rue Hamra, Beirut; f. 1965; monthly; commercial; Editor NADIM MAKDISI; international circ. 17,500.

Al Computer, Communications and Electronics (ACCE): c/o Dar Assayad, POB 1038, Hazmieh, Beirut; tel. (5) 450935; fax (5) 452700; e-mail assayad@inco.com.lb; internet www.darassayad.net; f. 1984; monthly; computer technology; publ. by Dar Assayad Int; Chief Editor ANTOINE BOUTROS; circ. 31,912 (Jan.–June 2006).

Arab Construction World: POB 13-5121, Chouran, Beirut 1102 2802; tel. (1) 352413; fax (1) 352419; e-mail info@acwmag.com; internet www.acwmag.com; f. 1985; monthly; English and Arabic; publ. by Chatila Publishing House; Pres. and Publr FATHI CHATILA; Editor-in-Chief MUHAMMAD RABIH CHATILA; circ. 10,100.

Arab Defence Journal: c/o Dar Assayad, POB 11-1038, Hazmieh, Beirut; tel. (5) 456374; fax (5) 452700; e-mail adj2004a@yahoo.com; internet www.arabdefencejournal.com; f. 1976; monthly; military; publ. by Dar Assayad Int; Chief Editor FAWZI ABOU FARHAT; circ. 24,831 (July–Dec. 2005).

Arab Water World: POB 13-5121, Chouran, Beirut 1102-2802; tel. (1) 748333; fax (1) 352419; e-mail editorial@awwmag.com; internet www.awwmag.com; f. 1977; monthly; English and Arabic; publ. by Chatila Publishing House; Pres., Publr and Editor-in-Chief FATHI CHATILA; circ. 8,400.

The Arab World: POB 567, Jounieh; tel. and fax (9) 935096; e-mail naamanculture@lynx.net.lb; internet www.naamanculture.com; f. 1985; 24 a yr; publ. by Dar Naamān lith-Thaqāfa (Maison Naaman pour la Culture); Editor NAJI NAAMAN.

Argus: POB 16-5403, 6 rue Arguse Sodeco, Beirut; tel. (1) 219113; fax (1) 219955; e-mail argus@cyberia.net.lb; monthly; Arabic, French and English; economics and law; circ. 1,000.

BusinessWeek Al-Arabiya: POB 11-4355, Beirut; tel. (1) 739777; fax (1) 749090; f. 2005; monthly; Arabic edn of US weekly business publ; publ. by InfoPro SA; distributed across 22 countries; Regional Dir SYLVIE GYURAN.

Le Commerce du Levant: Kantari, Immeuble Kantari Corner, 11e étage, Beirut 2021 2502; tel. (1) 362361; fax (1) 360379; e-mail lecommerce@inco.com.lb; internet www.lecommercedulevant.com; f. 1929; monthly; French; commercial and financial; publ. by Société de la Presse Economique; Chief Editor SIBYLLE RIZK; circ. 15,000.

Déco: POB 11-1404, Immeuble Sayegh, rue Sursock, Beirut; tel. (1) 202070; fax (1) 202663; e-mail info@decomag.com.lb; internet www.decomag.com.lb; f. 2000; quarterly; French; architecture and interior design; publ. by Editions Orientales SAL; Pres. CHARLES ABOU ADAL; circ. 14,000.

Fairuz International: Dar Assayad, POB 11-1038, Hazmieh, Beirut; tel. (5) 456373; fax (5) 450609; e-mail assayad@inco.com.lb; internet www.darassayad.net; f. 1982; monthly; Arabic; for women; publ. by Dar Assayad Int; Chief Editor ELHAM FREIHA; circ. 93,892 (July–Dec. 2005).

Al-Fares: c/o Dar Assayad, POB 11-1038, Hazmieh, Beirut; tel. (5) 450406; fax (5) 450609; e-mail assayad@inco.com.lb; internet www.darassayad.net; f. 1991; monthly; Arabic; men's interest; publ. by Dar Assayad Int; Chief Editor ELHAM FREIHA; circ. 79,237 (July–Dec. 2005).

Al-Idari (The Manager): c/o Dar Assayad, POB 11-1038, Hamzieh, Beirut; tel. (5) 450406; fax (5) 450609; e-mail assayad@inco.com.lb; internet www.darassayad.net; f. 1975; monthly; Arabic; business management, economics, finance and investment; publ. by Dar Assayad Int; Pres. BASSAM FREIHA; Gen. Man. ELHAM FREIHA; circ. 31,867.

Al-Intilak (Outbreak): Al-Intilak Printing and Publishing House, POB 4958, Beirut; tel. (1) 302018; e-mail tonehnme@cyberia.net.lb; f. 1960; monthly; Arabic; literary; Chief Editor MICHEL NEHME.

Al-Khalij Business Magazine: POB 11-8440, Beirut; tel. (1) 345568; fax (1) 602089; e-mail massaref@dm.net.lb; f. 1981; fmrly based in Kuwait; 6 a year; Arabic; Editor-in-Chief ZULFICAR KOBEISSI; circ. 16,325.

Lebanese and Arab Economy: POB 11-1801, Sanayeh, Beirut; tel. (1) 744160; fax (1) 353395; e-mail info@ccib.org.lb; internet www.ccib.org.lb; f. 1951; monthly; Arabic, English and French; publ. by Chamber of Commerce, Industry and Agriculture of Beirut and Mount Lebanon.

Lebanon Opportunities: POB 11-4355, rue Emile Eddé, Immeuble Salem, Beirut; tel. (1) 739777; fax (1) 749090; e-mail opportunities@infopro.com.lb; internet www.opportunities.com.lb; monthly; English; real estate, business and general finance and economy; publ. by InfoPro SA; Publr and Editor-in-Chief RAMZI EL-HAFEZ; Sr Editor SOHA YAMMINE.

Al-Mar'a: POB 11-1404, Immeuble Sayegh, rue Sursock, Beirut; tel. (1) 202070; fax (1) 202663; e-mail info@almara.com.lb; internet www.almara.com.lb; f. 2000; monthly; Arabic; for women; publ. by Editions Orientales SAL; Pres. CHARLES ABOU ADAL; circ. 20,000.

MENA Health World: POB 13-5121, Chouran, Beirut 1102 2802; tel. (1) 748333; fax (1) 352419; e-mail editorial@mhwmag.net; internet www.mhwmag.net; f. 1986 as Arab Health World magazine, but publ. suspended in 1993; relaunched as above 2006; bi-monthly; English and Arabic; publ. by Chatila Publishing House; Pres. and Publr FATHI CHATILA; Editor-in-Chief Dr RAJAA CHATILA ALAYLI.

Middle East Food: POB 13-5121, Chouran, Beirut 1102 2802; tel. (1) 352413; fax (1) 352419; e-mail info@mefmag.com; internet www.mefmag.com; f. 1985; monthly; publ. by Chatila Publishing House; Editor-in-Chief ROULA HAMDAN; circ. 8,650.

Qitāboul A'lamil A'rabi (The Arab World Book): POB 567, Jounieh; tel. and fax (9) 935096; e-mail naaman@lynx.net.lb; internet www.naamanculture.com; f. 1991; 6 a yr; Arabic; publ. by Dar Naamān lith-Thaqāfa (Maison Naaman pour la Culture); Editor NAJI NAAMAN.

Rijal al-Amal (Businessmen): Beirut; f. 1966; monthly; Arabic; business; Publr and Editor-in-Chief MAHIBA AL-MALKI; circ. 16,250.

Scoop: POB 165612, rue Issa Maalouf, Sioufi, Beirut; tel. (1) 482185; fax (1) 490307; weekly; general interest; publ. by La Régie Libanaise de Publicité; circ. 100,000.

Al-Sihāfa wal I'lām (Press and Information): POB 567, Jounieh; tel. and fax (9) 935096; e-mail naamanculture@lynx.net.lb; internet www.naamanculture.com; f. 1987; 12 a yr; Arabic; publ. by Dar Naaman lith-Thaqafa; Editor NAJI NAAMAN.

Siyassa was Strategia (Politics and Strategy): POB 567, Jounieh; tel. and fax (9) 935096; e-mail naamanculture@lynx.net.lb; internet www.naamanculture.com; f. 1981; 36 a year; Arabic; publ. by Dar Naaman lith-Thaqafa (Maison Naaman pour la Culture); Editor NAJI NAAMAN.

Tabibok (Your Doctor): POB 90434, Beirut; tel. (3) 604159; fax in Syria (963-11) 3738901; e-mail tabibokmag@mail.sy; internet www.tabibokmag.com; f. 1956; monthly; Arabic; medical, social, scientific; Editor Dr SAMI KABBANI; circ. 90,000.

Takarir Wa Khalfiyat (Background Reports): c/o Dar Assayad, POB 11-1038, Hazmieh, Beirut; tel. (5) 456374; fax (5) 452700; internet www.darassayad.net; f. 1976; monthly; Arabic; political and economic bulletin; publ. by Dar Assayad SAL; Editor-in-Chief HASSAN EL-KHOURY.

Al-Tarik (The Road): Beirut; monthly; Arabic; cultural and theoretical; publ. by the Parti communiste libanais; circ. 5,000.

Travaux et Jours (Works and Days): Rectorat de l'Université Saint-Joseph, rue de Damas, Beirut; tel. (1) 421157; fax (1) 421005; e-mail travauxetjours@usj.edu.lb; internet www.usj.edu.lb; f. 1961; publ.

twice a year; French; political, social and cultural; Editor MOUNIR CHAMOUN.

NEWS AGENCY

National News Agency (NNA): Hamra, Beirut; tel. (1) 754400; fax (1) 745776; e-mail akassas@nna-leb.gov.lb; internet www.nna-leb.gov.lb; state-owned; Dir LAURE SLEIMAN; Chief Editor ALI LAHHAM.

PRESS ASSOCIATION

Lebanese Press Order: POB 3084, ave Saeb Salam, Beirut; tel. (1) 865519; fax (1) 865516; e-mail mail@pressorder.org; internet www.pressorder.org; f. 1911; 18 mems; Pres. MUHAMMAD AL-BAALBAKI; Sec. ABD AL-KARIM EL-KHALIL.

Publishers

Dar al-Adab: POB 11-4123, Beirut; tel. (1) 795135; fax (1) 861633; e-mail d_aladab@cyberia.net.lb; internet www.adabmag.com; f. 1953; dictionaries, literary and general; Man. RANA IDRISS; Editor-in-Chief SAMAH IDRISS.

Arab Institute for Research and Publishing (Al-Mouasasah al-Arabiyah Lildirasat Walnashr): POB 11-5460, Beirut; tel. and fax (1) 751438; fax (1) 752308; e-mail info@airpbooks.com; internet www.airpbooks.com; f. 1969; works in Arabic and English; Dir MAHER KAYYALI.

Arab Scientific Publishers BP: POB 13-5574, Immeuble Ein al-Tenah Reem, rue Sakiet al-Janzir, Beirut; tel. (1) 786233; fax (1) 786230; e-mail asp@asp.com.lb; internet www.asp.com.lb; computer science, biological sciences, cookery, travel, politics, fiction, children's; Pres. BASSAM CHEBARO.

Dar Assayad Group (SAL and International): POB 11-1038, Hazmieh, Beirut; tel. (5) 450406; fax (5) 452700; e-mail assayad@inco.com.lb; internet www.darassayad.net; Dar Assayad SAL f. 1943; Dar Assayad Int. f. 1983 and provides publishing, advertising and distribution services; publishes in Arabic *Al-Anwar* (daily), *Assayad* (weekly), *Achabaka* (weekly), *Background Reports*, *Arab Defense Journal* (monthly), *Fairuz* (international monthly edition), *Al-Idari* (monthly), *Al Computer, Communications and Electronics* (monthly), *Al-Fares* (monthly); also publishes monthly background reports; has offices and correspondents in Arab countries and most parts of the world; CEO BASSAM FREIHA; Gen. Man. ELHAM FREIHA.

Chatila Publishing House: POB 13-5121, Chouran, Beirut 1102 2802; tel. (1) 352413; fax (1) 352419; e-mail info@cph.com.lb; internet www.chatilapublishing.com; f. 1977; publishes *Arab Construction World* (monthly), *Arab Health World* (monthly), *Arab Water World* (monthly), *Middle East Food* (monthly), *Middle East and World Construction Directory* (bi-annual), *Middle East and World Food Directory* (bi-annual), *Middle East and World Health Directory* (bi-annual), *Middle East and World Water Directory* (bi-annual); Pres. and Publr FATHI CHATILA; Gen. Man. MUHAMMAD RABIH CHATILA.

Edition Française pour le Monde Arabe (EDIFRAMO): POB 113-6140, Immeuble Elissar, rue Bliss, Beirut; tel. (1) 862437; Man. TAHSEEN S. KHAYAT.

Editions Orientales SAL: POB 11-1404, Immeuble Sayegh, rue Sursock, Beirut; tel. (1) 202070; fax (1) 202663; e-mail info@ediori.com.lb; internet www.ediori.com.lb; political and social newspapers and magazines; Pres. and Editor-in-Chief CHARLES ABOU ADAL.

GeoProjects SARL: POB 113-5294, Immeuble Barakat, 13 rue Jeanne d'Arc, Beirut; tel. (1) 344236; fax (1) 342217; e-mail info@geo-publishers.com; internet www.geo-publishers.com; f. 1978; cartographers, researchers, school textbook publrs; Dir-Gen. RIDA ISMAIL.

Dar el-Ilm Lilmalayin: POB 1085, Centre Metco, rue Mar Elias, Beirut 2045 8402; tel. (1) 306666; fax (1) 701657; e-mail info@malayin.com; internet www.malayin.com; f. 1945; dictionaries, encyclopaedias, reference books, textbooks, Islamic cultural books; CEO TAREF OSMAN.

InfoPro SARL: POB 11-4355, Immeuble Salem, rue Emile Eddé, Beirut; tel. (1) 739777; fax (1) 749090; e-mail infopro@infopro.com.lb; internet www.infopro.com.lb; f. 1997; information-based magazines, incl. *BusinessWeek Al-Arabiya* and *Lebanon Opportunities*, as well as reference books; Pres. RAMZI EL-HAFEZ.

Institute for Palestine Studies, Publishing and Research Organization (IPS): POB 11-7164, rue Anis Nsouli, off Verdun, Beirut 1107 2230; tel. (1) 868387; fax (1) 814193; e-mail ipsbrt@palestine-studies.org; internet www.palestine-studies.org; f. 1963; independent non-profit Arab research org., which promotes better understanding of the Palestine problem and the Arab–Israeli conflict; publishes books, reprints, research papers, etc.; Chair. Dr HISHAM NASHABE; Gen. Dir MAHMOUD SOUEID.

The International Documentary Center of Arab Manuscripts: POB 2668, Immeuble Hanna, Ras Beirut, Beirut; e-mail alafaq@cyberia.net.lb; f. 1965; publishes and reproduces ancient and rare Arabic texts; Propr ZOUHAIR BAALBAKI.

Dar al-Kashaf: POB 11-2091, rue Assad Malhamee, Beirut; tel. (1) 249952; e-mail dakashaf4@yahoo.com; f. 1930; publrs of *Al-Kashaf* (Arab Youth Magazine), maps, atlases and business books; printers and distributors; Propr M. A. FATHALLAH.

Dar al-Kitab al-Lubnani: POB 11-8330, Beirut; tel. (1) 735731; fax (1) 351433; e-mail info@daralkitabalmasri.com; internet www.daralkitabalmasri.com; f. 1929; publr of books on Islamic studies, history, sciences and literature; Man. Dir HASSAN EL-ZEIN.

Dar Alf Leila wa Leila: rue Issa Maalouf, Immeuble Dimitri Trad, Achrafieh, Beirut; tel. (1) 200961; fax (1) 334116; e-mail rdl@rdl.com.lb; internet www.rdl.com.lb; publishes *Al-Bayraq* (Arabic, daily), *Al-Hawadeth* (Arabic, weekly), *La Revue du Liban* (French, weekly), *Monday Morning* (English, weekly); Editor-in-Chief MELHEM KARAM.

Librairie du Liban Publishers: POB 11-9232, Beirut; tel. (9) 217735; fax (9) 217734; e-mail info@ldlp.com; internet www.ldlp.com; f. 1944; publr of children's books, dictionaries and reference books; distributor of books in English and French; Man. Dirs HABIB SAYEGH, PIERRE SAYEGH.

Dar al-Maaref Liban SARL: POB 2320, Riad el-Solh, Beirut; tel. (1) 931243; f. 1959; children's books and textbooks in Arabic; Man. Dir Dr FOUAD IBRAHIM; Gen. Man. JOSEPH NACHOU.

Dar al-Machreq SARL: POB 11-946, Beirut 1107 2060; tel. (1) 202423; e-mail machreq@cyberia.net.lb; internet www.darelmachreq.com; f. 1848; religion, art, Arabic and Islamic literature, history, languages, science, philosophy, school books, dictionaries and periodicals; Man. Dir SALAH ABOUJAOUDE.

Dar Naamān lith-Thaqāfa (Maison Naaman pour la Culture): POB 567, Jounieh; tel. and fax (9) 935096; e-mail naamanculture@lynx.net.lb; internet www.naamanculture.com; f. 1979; publishes *Mawsou'atul 'Alamil 'Arabiyyil Mu'asser* (Encyclopaedia of the Contemporary Arab World), *Mawsou'atul Waqa'e'il 'Arabiyya* (Encyclopaedia of Arab Events), *Qitāboul A'lamil A'rabi*, *Siyassa was Strategia*, *Al-Sahafa wal I'lam* in Arabic, and *The Arab World* in English; Propr NAJI NAAMAN; Exec. Man. MARCELLE AL-ASHKAR.

Editions Dar an-Nahar SAL: BP 11-226, 36 rue Andraos, Immeuble Media Centre, Beirut; tel. (1) 561687; fax (1) 561693; e-mail darannahar@darannahar.com; internet www.darannahar.com; f. 1967; pan-Arab publishing house; Pres. GHASSAN TUÉNI; Gen. Man. SAMIA SHAMI.

Naufal Group SARL: POB 11-2161, Immeuble Naufal, rue Sourati, Beirut; tel. (1) 354898; fax (1) 354394; e-mail naufalgroup@terra.net.lb; f. 1970; encyclopaedias, fiction, children's books, history, law and literature; subsidiary cos: Macdonald Middle East Sarl, Les Editions Arabes; Man. Dir TONY NAUFAL.

Publitec Publications: POB 16-6142, Beirut; tel. (1) 495401; fax (1) 493330; e-mail info@whoswhointhearabworld.info; internet www.whoswhointhearabworld.info; f. 1965; publishes *Who's Who in Lebanon* and *Who's Who in the Arab World* (both bi-annual); Pres. CHARLES GEDEON; Man. KRIKOR AYVAZIAN.

Dar al-Raed al-Lubnani: 11-6585, Beirut; tel. (1) 663109; e-mail info@al-raed.com; f. 1971; CEO RAYED SAMMOURI.

Rihani Printing and Publishing House: Beirut; tel. (1) 868380; f. 1963; Propr ALBERT RIHANI; Man. DAOUD STEPHAN.

Sader Publishers: POB 55530, Immeuble Sader, Dekwaneh, Beirut; tel. (1) 488776; e-mail sader@saderpublishers.com; internet www.saderpublishers.com; f. 1863; legal publr; Chair. JOSEPH SADER.

Samir Éditeur: POB 55542, Jisr al-Waty, Sin el-Fil, Beirut; tel. (1) 489464; fax (1) 482541; e-mail samir@samirediteur.com; internet www.samirediteur.com; children's books in Arabic, English and French.

World Book Publishing: POB 11-3176, 282 rue Emile Eddé, Sanayeh, Beirut; tel. (1) 349370; fax (1) 351226; e-mail info@wbpbooks.com; internet www.wbpbooks.com; f. 1926; literature, education, philosophy, current affairs, self-help, children's books; Chair. M. SAID EL-ZEIN; Man. Dir RAFIK EL-ZEIN.

Broadcasting and Communications

TELECOMMUNICATIONS

Regulatory Authority

Telecommunications Regulatory Authority (TRA): Marfaa Bldg 200, 2nd Floor, Beirut Central District, Beirut; tel. (1) 964300; fax (1) 964341; e-mail info@tra.gov.lb; internet www.tra.gov.lb; f. 2007; Chair. and CEO Dr IMAD HOBALLAH (acting).

LEBANON

Service Providers

OGERO (Organisme de Gestion et d'Exploitation de l'ex Radio Orient): POB 11-1226, Bir Hassan, Beirut 1107 2070; tel. (1) 840000; fax (1) 826823; internet www.ogero.gov.lb; f. 1972; 100% state-owned; plans for the incorporation of OGERO and two depts of the Ministry of Telecommunications into a single operator, Liban Télécom, were announced in 2005; preparations were stalled as a result of the conflict between Hezbollah and Israel in mid-2006, but have subsequently resumed; fixed-line operator.

In late 2008 it was announced that the planned privatization of Lebanon's two state-owned mobile telephone networks would be deferred until after the 2009 legislative elections. New management contracts to operate the Mobile Interim Company (MIC) networks until April 2010 were awarded with effect from February 2009 to Orascom Telecom Holding of Egypt (which was to operate the MIC1 network) and Zain Group of Kuwait (MIC2); the contracts were subsequently extended until February 2012.

Alfa: Palm Center, rond-point Chevrolet, Beirut; tel. (3) 391111; fax (3) 391109; e-mail customercare@alfamobile.com.lb; internet www.alfa.com.lb; managed by Orascom Telecom Holding (Egypt); operates the state-owned MIC1 mobile telephone network under licence to Feb. 2012; Chair. and CEO MARWAN HAYEK.

MTC Touch: POB 17-5051, Immeuble MTC Touch, ave Charles Helou, Beirut; tel. (3) 792000; e-mail info@mtc.com.lb; internet www.mtctouch.com.lb; managed by Zain Group (fmrly Mobile Telecommunications Co—Kuwait); operates the state-owned MIC2 mobile telephone network under licence to Feb. 2012; Gen. Man. CLAUDE BASSIL.

BROADCASTING

Radio

Radio Liban: rue Emile Edée, Sanayeh, Hamra, Beirut; tel. (1) 756185; fax (1) 347489; internet www.96-2.com; run by the Ministry of Information in conjunction with Radio France International; f. 1937; Arabic programmes broadcast on 98.1 FM and 98.5 FM; scheduled for privatization; Dir-Gen. FOUAD KABALAN HAMDAN; Dir of Programmes MICHÈLE DE FREIGE.

The Home Service broadcasts in Arabic on short wave, and the Foreign Service broadcasts in Portuguese, Armenian, Arabic, Spanish, French and English.

Television

Lebanese Broadcasting Corpn (LBC) Sat Ltd: POB 111, Zouk, Beirut 165853; tel. (9) 850850; fax (9) 850916; e-mail lbcsat@lbcsat.com.lb; internet www.lbcgroup.tv; f. 1985 as Lebanese Broadcasting Corpn Int. SAL; name changed 1996; operates satellite channel on Arabsat 2C, Arabsat 3A and Nilesat 102; programmes in Arabic, French and English; broadcasts to Lebanon, the Middle East, Europe, the USA and Australia; Chair. Sheikh PIERRE EL-DAHER.

Future Television (Al-Mustaqbal): POB 13-6052, White House, rue Spears, Sanayeh, Beirut; tel. (1) 355355; fax (1) 753434; e-mail future@future.com.lb; internet www.future.com.lb; f. 1993; privately owned; commercial; Gen. Man. NADIM AL-MONLA.

Al-Manar (Lighthouse): Bir Hassan, Beirut; tel. (1) 540440; fax (1) 553138; e-mail info@manartv.com.lb; internet www.almanar.com.lb; f. 1991; television station owned by Lebanese Communication Group; broadcasts to Arab and Muslim audiences worldwide; operates satellite channel since May 2000; partially controlled by Hezbollah; Chair. of Bd ABDALLAH KASSIR.

Murr Television: Naccache, Beirut; internet www.mtv.com.lb; f. 1991; closed down in 2002 for contravening electoral laws; relaunched April 2009; privately owned; CEO MICHEL EL-MURR.

Finance

(cap. = capital; dep. = deposits; res = reserves; m. = million; br(s) = branch(es); amounts in Lebanese pounds, unless otherwise stated)

BANKING

Beirut was, for many years, the leading financial and commercial centre in the Middle East, but this role was destroyed by the civil conflict during 1975–90. To restore the city as a regional focus for investment banking has been a key element of the reconstruction plans of successive governments.

Central Bank

Banque du Liban: POB 11-5544, rue Masraf Loubnane, Beirut; tel. (1) 750000; fax (1) 747600; e-mail bdlfx@bdl.gov.lb; internet www.bdl.gov.lb; f. 1964 as successor in Lebanon to the Banque de Syrie et du Liban; cap. and res 3,342,331m., dep. 63,932,268m. (Dec. 2009); Gov. RIAD T. SALAMEH; 9 brs.

Principal Commercial Banks

Ahli International Bank SAL: POB 11-5556, Riad el-Solh, Beirut 1107-2200; tel. (1) 970920; fax (1) 970944; e-mail gm@ahli.com.lb; internet www.ahli.com.lb; f. 1964 as Bank of Lebanon and Kuwait SAL; name changed as above in 2008; 97.9% owned by Jordan Ahli Bank; cap. 29,800m., res 39,692m., dep. 733,777m. (Dec. 2009); Gen. Man. MICHEL SAROUFIM; 9 brs.

Arab Finance House SAL (Islamic Bank) (AFH): POB 11-273, Riad el-Solh, Beirut 1107 2020; tel. (1) 706680; fax (1) 706684; e-mail info@arabfinancehouse.com; internet www.afh.com.lb; f. 2003 as Arab Finance House SAL; merged into Arab Finance Investment House SAL in 2005, when name changed as above; commercial and investment banking; cap. 30,000m., res 68,229m., dep. 96,236m. (Dec. 2009); Chair. and Gen. Man. MUHAMMAD ABD AL-LATIF AL-MANEH; 5 brs.

Audi Saradar Private Bank SAL: Immeuble Clover, ave Charles Malek, Achrafieh, Beirut 1107 2805; tel. (1) 205400; fax (1) 205480; e-mail contactus@audisaradarpb.com; internet www.audisaradarpb.com; f. 1948 as Banque Marius Saradar; succeeded by Banque Saradar SAL 1956; became part of Audi Saradar Group in 2004; name changed as above 2005; cap. 40,000m., res 85,415m., dep. 2,772,565m. (Dec. 2009); Chair. FADI G. AMATOURI; Gen. Man. TOUFIQ R. AOUAD; 1 br.

Bank Audi SAL—Audi Saradar Group: POB 11-2560, Riad el-Solh, Beirut 1107 2808; tel. (1) 994000; fax (1) 990555; e-mail contactus@banqueaudi.com; internet www.banqueaudi.com; f. 1962 as Bank Audi; acquired Orient Credit Bank 1997 and Banque Nasr 1998; absorbed into Audi Saradar Group in 2004; cap. 436,944m., res 2,246,927m., dep. 35,740,371m. (Dec. 2009); Chair. and Gen. Man. RAYMOND W. AUDI; CEO SAMIR HANNA; 78 brs in Lebanon, 11 brs in Jordan.

Bank of Beirut SAL: POB 11-7354, Bank of Beirut SAL Bldg, Foch St, Beirut Central District, Beirut; tel. (1) 983999; fax (1) 972972; e-mail contactus@bankofbeirut.com; internet www.bankofbeirut.com.lb; f. 1973; acquired Transorient Bank 1999, Beirut Riyad Bank 2002; cap. 60,560m., res 1,009,029m., dep. 8,147,665m. (Dec. 2009); Chair. and Gen. Man. SALIM G. SFEIR; 46 brs.

BankMed SAL: POB 11-0348, Centre Groupe Méditerranée, 482 rue Clémenceau, Beirut 2022 9302; tel. (1) 373937; fax (1) 362706; internet www.bankmed.com.lb; f. 1944 as Banque Naaman et Soussou; name changed to Eastern Commercial Bank 1955, Banque de la Méditerranée SAL 1970 and as above 2006; acquired Allied Bank SAL in 2006; cap. 680,750m., res 777,723m., dep. 13,519,628m. (Dec. 2009); Chair. and Gen. Man. MUHAMMAD HARIRI; 51 brs.

Banque Bemo SAL: POB 16-6353, Immeuble Bemo, place Sassine, ave Elias Sarkis, Achrafieh, Beirut 1100 2120; tel. (1) 200505; fax (1) 217860; e-mail bemosal@dm.net.lb; internet www.bemobank.com; f. 1964 as Future Bank SAL; name changed to BEMO (Banque Européenne pour le Moyen-Orient) SAL 1994 and as above 2006; cap. 16,000m., res 101,799m., dep. 1,574,203m. (Dec. 2009); Chair. and Gen. Man. RIAD BECHARA OBEGI; Man. Dir and Gen. Man. SAMIH H. SAADEH; 9 brs in Lebanon, 1 br. in Cyprus.

Banque de Crédit National SAL: POB 110-204, Immeuble Marfaa, 157 rue Saad Zaghloul, Beirut; tel. (1) 990808; fax (1) 975140; e-mail bncrena@dm.net.lb; f. 1920; cap. 18,091m., res 10,290m., dep. 23,862m. (Dec. 2009); Chair., Dir and Gen. Man. Dr MARWAN ISKANDAR.

Banque de l'Industrie et du Travail SAL (BIT Bank): POB 11-3948, Immeuble BIT, 89 Riad el-Solh, Beirut 1107 2150; tel. (1) 985680; fax (1) 985681; e-mail info@bitbank.com.lb; internet www.bitbank.com.lb; f. 1960; cap. 4,000m., res 50,996m., dep. 666,160m. (Dec. 2009); Chair. and Gen. Man. Sheikh FOUAD JAMIL EL-KHAZEN; Exec. Dir and Gen. Man. NABIL N. KHAIRALLAH; 12 brs.

Banque Libano-Française SAL: POB 11-0808, Tour Liberty, 5 rue de Rome, Beirut 1107 2804; tel. and fax (1) 791332; e-mail info@eblf.com; internet www.eblf.com; f. 1967; cap. 200,000m., res 550,367m., dep. 10,071,518m. (Dec. 2009); Chair. FARID RAPHAËL; 44 brs.

Banque Misr-Liban SAL: rue Riad el-Solh, Beirut 2011 9301; tel. (1) 986666; fax (1) 964296; e-mail mail@bml.com.lb; internet www.bml.com.lb; f. 1929 as Banque Misr Syrie Liban; name changed as above 1958; cap. 27,000m., res 32,140m., dep. 858,276m. (Dec. 2009); Chair. MUHAMMAD KAMAL EL-DIN BARAKAT; Exec. Gen. Man. HADI NAFFI; 14 brs.

Al-Baraka Bank SAL: POB 113-5683, 2nd Floor, Verdun 2000 Centre, Rashid Karameh St, Beirut; tel. (1) 808008; fax (1) 806499; e-mail info@al-baraka.com; internet www.al-baraka.com; f. 1992; as Al-Baraka Bank Lebanon SAL; name changed as above 2009; Islamic banking; owned by Al-Baraka Banking Group (ABG), Bahrain; Gen. Man. MUTASIM MAHMASSANI; 7 brs.

LEBANON

BBAC (Bank of Beirut and the Arab Countries) SAL: POB 11-1536, Immeuble de la Banque, 250 rue Clémenceau, Riad el-Solh, Beirut 1107 2080; tel. (1) 374299; fax (1) 365200; e-mail marketing@bbac.com.lb; internet www.bbacbank.com; f. 1956; cap. 147,375m., res 181,982m., dep. 5,105,689m. (Dec. 2009); Chair. and Gen. Man. GHASSAN T. ASSAF; 37 domestic brs and 1 foreign rep. office.

BLC Bank SAL: POB 11-1126, BLC Bldg, Adlieh Intersection, Beirut 2064 5809; tel. and fax (1) 429000; e-mail info@blcbank.com; internet www.blcbank.com; f. 1950; 97.51% owned by Fransabank SAL; cap. 152,700m., res 139,965m., dep. 3,462,417m. (Dec. 2009); Chair. and Gen. Man. MAURICE SEHNAOUI; 35 brs.

BLOM Bank SAL: POB 11-1912, Immeuble BLOM Bank, rue Rachid Karameh, Verdun, Beirut 1107 2807; tel. (1) 743300; fax (1) 738946; e-mail blommail@blom.com.lb; internet www.blom.com.lb; f. 1951 as Banque du Liban et d'Outre-Mer; name changed as above 2000; cap. 241,800m., res 1,775,169m., dep. 27,818,569m. (Dec. 2009); Chair. and Gen. Man. SAAD AZHARI; 62 domestic brs and 11 foreign brs.

Byblos Bank SAL: POB 11-5605, ave Elias Sarkis, Achrafieh, Beirut 1107 2811; tel. (1) 335200; fax (1) 339436; e-mail byblosbk@byblosbank.com.lb; internet www.byblosbank.com; f. 1959; merged with Banque Beyrouth pour le Commerce SAL 1997; acquired Byblos Bank Europe SA 1998, Wedge Bank Middle East SAL 2001 and ABN AMRO Bank Lebanon 2002; cap. 516,835m., res 1,106,420m., dep. 17,206,016m. (Dec. 2009); Chair. and Gen. Man. Dr FRANÇOIS S. BASSIL; 78 brs in Lebanon, 23 brs abroad.

Creditbank SAL: POB 16-5795, Immeuble Crédit Bancaire SAL, 680 blvd Bachir Gemayel, Achrafieh, Beirut 1100 2802; tel. (1) 485148; fax (1) 485245; e-mail info@creditbank.com.lb; internet www.creditbank.com.lb; f. 1981 as Crédit Bancaire SAL; name changed as above following merger with Crédit Lyonnais Liban SAL 2002; cap. 66,379m., res 78,459m., dep. 1,586,806m. (Dec. 2009); Chair. and Gen. Man. TAREK JOSEPH KHALIFÉ; Vice-Chair. SALAH FOUAD ZOGHBY; 15 brs.

Crédit Libanais SAL: POB 16-6729, Centre Sofil, 5e étage, ave Charles Malek, Beirut 1100 2811; tel. (1) 200028; fax (1) 325713; e-mail info@creditlibanais.com.lb; internet www.creditlibanais.com.lb; f. 1961; cap. 250,000m., res 316,461m., dep. 7,394,867m. (Dec. 2009); Chair. and Gen. Man. Dr JOSEPH M. TORBEY; 57 brs in Lebanon, 2 brs abroad.

Federal Bank of Lebanon SAL: POB 11-2209, Immeuble Renno, ave Charles Malek, St Nicolas, Beirut; tel. (1) 212307; fax (1) 215837; e-mail info@fbl.com.lb; internet www.fbl.com.lb; f. 1952; cap. 13,018m., res 43,407m., dep. 982,396m. (Dec. 2009); Chair. and Gen. Man. AYOUB FARID MICHEL SAAB; CEO MUHAMMAD YASSER MORTADA; 8 brs.

Fenicia Bank SAL: POB 113-6248, Immeuble Bellevue, Ain al-Tineh, Verdun, Beirut 1103 2110; tel. (1) 866306; fax (1) 865299; e-mail info@bkawbank.com; internet www.bkawbank.com; f. 1959; as Bank of Kuwait and the Arab World SAL; name changed as above 2010; 74% owned by Achour Group, 15% by Maacaron Group, 10% by Merhi Group and 1% by Dr Cheaib; cap. 50,000m., res 46,684m., dep. 1,387,463m. (Dec. 2009); Chair. and Gen. Man. ABD AL-RAZZAK ACHOUR; 14 brs in Lebanon.

First National Bank SAL: POB 11-0435, Immeuble 147, rue Allenby, Riad el-Solh, Beirut 2012 6004; tel. (1) 963000; fax (1) 973090; e-mail info@fnb.com.lb; internet www.fnb.com.lb; f. 1996; acquired Société Bancaire du Liban SAL 2002; cap. 137,605m., res 91,951m., dep. 2,922,936m. (Dec. 2009); Chair. and Gen. Man. RAMI REFAAT EL-NIMER; 21 brs.

Fransabank SAL: POB 11-0393, Riad el-Solh, Beirut 1107 2803; tel. (1) 745761; fax (1) 354572; e-mail fsb@fransabank.com; internet www.fransabank.com; f. 1978 as a result of merger between Banque Sabbag SAL and Banque Française por le Moyen Orient SAL; acquired Banque Tohmé SAL 1993, Universal Bank SAL 1999, United Bank of Saudi and Lebanon SAL 2001 and Banque de la Beka'a SAL 2003; Banque de la Beka'a was subsequently sold to Bank of Sharjah Ltd (United Arab Emirates) in July 2007; cap. 430,000.0m., res 831,013.6m., dep. 13,917,671.3m. (Dec. 2009); Chair. and Gen. Man. ADNAN KASSAR; 63 brs.

IBL Bank SAL: POB 11-5292, Immeuble Ittihadiah, ave Charles Malek, Beirut 1107 2190; tel. (1) 200350; fax (1) 204505; e-mail ibl@ibl.com.lb; internet www.ibl.com.lb; f. 1961 as Intercontinental Bank of Lebanon SAL; cap. 151,657m., res 97,041m., dep. 3,593,879m. (Dec. 2009); Chair. and Gen. Man. SALIM Y. HABIB; 17 brs.

Jammal Trust Bank SAL: POB 11-5640, Immeuble Jammal, rue Verdun, Beirut 1102 2110; tel. (1) 805702; fax (1) 864170; e-mail services@jammalbank.com.lb; internet www.jammalbank.com.lb/home.html; f. 1963 as Investment Bank SAL; cap. 58,000m., res 16,730m., dep. 664,920m. (Dec. 2009); Chair. and Gen. Man. ANWAR A. AL-JAMMAL; 22 brs in Lebanon, 3 rep. offices abroad.

Lebanese Canadian Bank: POB 11-2520, Immeuble Ghantous, blvd Dora, Riad el-Solh, Beirut 1107 2110; tel. and fax (1) 379922; e-mail lebcan@lebcanbank.com; internet www.lebcanbank.com; f. 1960 as Banque des Activités Economiques; name changed to The Royal Bank of Canada (Middle East) SAL 1970 and as above 1988; cap. 156,000m., res 299,118m., dep. 7,095,100m. (Dec. 2009); Chair. and Gen. Man. GEORGES ZARD ABOU JAOUDÉ; 35 brs in Lebanon, 1 rep. office in Canada.

Lebanese Swiss Bank SAL: POB 11-9552, Immeuble Hoss, 6e étage, rue Emile Eddé, place Hamra, Ras Beirut, Beirut; tel. (1) 354501; fax (1) 346242; e-mail lbs@t-net.com.lb; internet www.lebaneseswissbank.com; f. 1962; cap. 70,000m., res 31,679m., dep. 1,071,755m. (Dec. 2009); Chair. and Gen. Man. Dr TANAL SABBAH; 14 brs.

Lebanon and Gulf Bank SAL: POB 11-3360, 124 Allenby St, Beirut Central District, Beirut; tel. (1) 965000; fax (1) 965999; e-mail info@lgb.com.lb; internet www.lgb.com.lb; f. 1963 as Banque de Crédit Agricole; name changed as above 1980; cap. 100,000m., res 34,369m., dep. 2,219,766m. (Dec. 2009); Pres., Chair. and Gen. Man. ABD AL-HAFIZ MAHMOUD ITANI; 13 domestic brs, 1 foreign br.

MEAB SAL: POB 14-5958, Immeuble Hejeij, ave Adnan al-Hakim, Beirut 1105 2080; tel. (1) 826740; fax (1) 841190; e-mail meab@meabank.com; internet www.meabank.com; f. 1991 as Middle East and Africa Bank SAL; name changed as above 2003; cap. 41,000m., res 16,117m., dep. 784,937m. (Dec. 2009); Chair. HASSAN M. HEJEIJ; Man. Dir KASSEM HEJEIJ; Gen. Man. ADNAN YOUSSEF; 6 brs.

National Bank of Kuwait (Lebanon) SAL: POB 11-5727, BAC Bldg, Sanayeh Sq., Justinien St, Riad el-Solh, Beirut 1107 2200; tel. (1) 741111; fax (1) 747846; e-mail info@nbk.com.lb; internet www.nbk.com.lb; f. 1963 as Rifbank; name changed as above 1996; cap. 40,020m., res 29,069m., dep. 398,988m. (Dec. 2009); Chair. IBRAHIM DABDOUB; Gen. Man. HANY SHERIF; 10 brs.

Near East Commercial Bank SAL: POB 16-5766, SNA Bldg, Said Akl St, Tabaris, Achrafieh, Beirut 1100 2070; tel. and fax (1) 200770; fax (1) 339000; e-mail info@necbbank.com; internet www.necbbank.com; f. 1978; cap. 28,756m., res 4,269m., dep. 240,776m. (Dec. 2009); Chair. and Gen. Man. FOUAD BAIDA; Gen. Man. GEORGES TABET; 5 brs.

North Africa Commercial Bank SAL: POB 11-9575, Centre Aresco, rue Justinian, Beirut; tel. (1) 759000; fax (1) 346322; e-mail info@nacb.com.lb; internet www.nacb.com.lb; f. 1973; 99% owned by Libyan Foreign Bank; cap. 128,599m., res 6,559m., dep. 1,117,751m. (Dec. 2009); Pres. and Chair. ABOUBAKER ALI AL-SHARIF; 2 brs.

Société Générale de Banque au Liban (SGBL): POB 11-2955, rond-point Salomé, Sin el-Fil, Beirut; tel. (1) 499813; fax (1) 502820; e-mail sgbl@sgbl.com.lb; internet www.sgbl.com.lb; f. 1953 as Banque Belgo-Libanaise; name changed to Société Générale Libano Européenne de Banque SAL in 1969; present name adopted in 2001; cap. 12,532m., res 393,921m., dep 6,312,536m. (Dec. 2009); Pres. ANTOUN SEHNAOUI; 41 brs in Lebanon, 23 abroad.

Société Nouvelle de la Banque de Syrie et du Liban SAL (SNBSL): POB 11-957, rue Riad el-Solh, Beirut; tel. (1) 980080; fax (1) 980991; e-mail snbsl@snbsl.com.lb; internet www.bsl.com.lb; f. 1963; cap. 46,920m., res 55,986m., dep. 995,575m. (Dec. 2009); Chair. and Man. Dir RAMSAY A. EL-KHOURI; Gen. Man. SÉLIM STÉPHAN; 17 brs.

Standard Chartered Bank SAL: POB 70-216, Immeuble Standard Chartered Bank, Dbayeh Highway, Antélias; tel. (4) 542474; fax (4) 542494; e-mail aamir.hussain@standardchartered.com; internet www.standardchartered.com/lb; f. 1979 as Metropolitan Bank SAL; acquired by Standard Chartered Bank 2000; cap. 12,000m., res 9,136m., dep. 196,065m. (Dec. 2009); Chair. JONATHAN MORRIS; CEO PIK YEE FOONG; 3 brs.

Syrian Lebanese Commercial Bank SAL: SLCB Bldg, Makdessi St, Beirut; tel. (1) 741666; fax (1) 736629; e-mail hamra@slcbk.com; internet www.slcb.com.lb; f. 1974; cap. 125,000m., res 26,331m., dep. 516,142m. (Dec. 2009); Chair. and Gen. Man. Dr DOURAID AHMAD DERGHAM; Vice-Chair. MARCEL EL-KHOURY; 3 brs in Lebanon.

Development Bank

Audi Saradar Investment Bank SAL: POB 16-5110, Bank Audi Plaza, Omar al-Daouk St, Beirut; tel. (1) 994000; fax (1) 999406; e-mail contactus@asib.com; internet www.asib.com; f. 1974 as Investment and Finance Bank; name changed to Audi Investment Bank SAL 1996 and as above 2004; medium- and long-term loans, 100% from Lebanese sources; owned by Bank Audi SAL—Audi Saradar Group; cap. 25,075m., res 144,409m., dep. 833,596m. (Dec. 2009); Chair. and Gen. Man. Dr MARWAN M. GHANDOUR; Gen. Man. RAMZI N. SALIBA.

Supervisory Body

Banking Control Commission of Lebanon: POB 11-5544, rue Masraf Loubnane, Beirut; tel. (1) 350167; fax (1) 750040; internet www.bccl.gov.lb; f. 1967; Chair. OSAMA MEKDASHI.

Banking Association

Association of Banks in Lebanon: POB 976, Gouraud St, Saifi, Beirut; tel. (1) 970500; e-mail abl@abl.org.lb; internet www.abl.org.lb; f. 1959; serves and promotes the interests of the banking community in Lebanon; mems: 64 banks and 7 foreign rep. offices; Chair. JOSEPH TORBEY; Sec. RAYMOND AUDI.

STOCK EXCHANGE

Beirut Stock Exchange (BSE): POB 11-3552, 4e étage, Bloc O1, Immeuble Azareih, Beirut; tel. (1) 993555; fax (1) 993444; e-mail bse@bse.com.lb; internet www.bse.com.lb; f. 1920; recommenced trading in Jan. 1996; 10 cttee mems; Vice-Chair. GHALEB MAHMASSANI.

INSURANCE

About 80 insurance companies were registered in Lebanon in the late 1990s, although fewer than one-half of these were operational. An insurance law enacted in 1999 increased the required capital base for insurance firms and provided tax incentives for mergers within the sector.

Allianz SNA SAL: POB 16-6528, Immeuble Allianz SNA, Hazmieh, Beirut 1100 2130; tel. (1) 956600; fax (1) 956624; e-mail info@allianzsna.com; internet www.allianzsna.com; f. 1963 as Société Nationale d'Assurances SAL; renamed as above 2008; part of Allianz Group; cap. 13,264m. (2007); Chair. ANTOINE WAKIM; CEO XAVIER DENYS.

Arabia Insurance Co SAL: POB 11-2172, Arabia House, rue de Phénicie, Beirut; tel. (1) 363610; fax (1) 365139; e-mail arabia@arabia-ins.com.lb; internet www.arabiainsurance.com; f. 1944; cap. 51,000m.; Chair. WAHBÉ A. TAMARI; CEO FADY SHAMMAS.

Bankers Assurance SAL: POB 11-4293, Immeuble Capitole, rue Riad el-Solh, Beirut; tel. (1) 988777; fax (1) 984004; e-mail mail@bankers-assurance.com; internet www.bankers-assurance.com; f. 1972; Chair. SABA NADER; Gen. Man. EUGÈNE NADER.

Commercial Insurance Co (Lebanon) SAL: POB 11-4351, Centre Starco, North Block, 9th Floor, Beirut; tel. (1) 373070; fax (1) 373071; e-mail comins@commercialinsurance.com.lb; internet www.commercialinsurance.com.lb; f. 1962; cap. 6,000m. (March 2006); Chair. MAX R. ZACCAR; 2 brs.

Compagnie Libanaise d'Assurances SAL: POB 3685, rue Riad el-Solh, Beirut; tel. (1) 868988; e-mail lebanese@sodetel.net.lb; internet www.lebaneseinsurance.com; f. 1951; cap. 22,500m.; Chair. PEDRO ABOUJAOUDÉ; Gen. Man. JIHAD SAKR.

Al-Ittihad al-Watani: POB 11-1270, Jisr al-Wati, Immeuble Al-Ittihad al-Watani, Beirut; tel. (1) 426480; fax (1) 426486; e-mail webmaster@alittihadalwatani.com.lb; internet www.alittihadalwatani.com.lb; f. 1947; cap. 20.6m. (2005); Chair. and Gen. Man. TANNOUS FEGHALI.

Libano-Suisse Insurance Co SAL: POB 11-3821, Immeuble Commerce and Finance, Beirut 1107 2150; tel. (1) 374900; fax (1) 368724; e-mail libano-suisse@libano-suisse.com; internet www.libano-suisse.com; f. 1959; Chair. MICHEL PIERRE PHARAON; Gen. Man. LUCIEN LETAYEF, Jr.

Al-Mashrek Insurance and Reinsurance SAL: POB 16-6154, Immeuble Al-Mashrek, Antélias Main Rd, Rabieh, Beirut 1100 2100; tel. (4) 408666; fax (4) 417688; e-mail almashrek@almashrek.com.lb; internet www.almashrek.com.lb; f. 1962; Chair. and CEO ABRAHAM MATOSSIAN.

'La Phénicienne' SAL: POB 11-5652, Immeuble Hanna Haddad, rue Amine Gemayel, Sioufi, Beirut; tel. (1) 425484; fax (1) 424532; e-mail phenicienne@sodetel.net.lb; f. 1964; cap. 3,167m.; Chair. and Gen. Man. CAROLE FÉGHALI CHAMOUN.

Trade and Industry

DEVELOPMENT ORGANIZATIONS

Council for Development and Reconstruction (CDR): POB 116-5351, Tallet el-Serail, Beirut; tel. (1) 980096; fax (1) 981252; e-mail general@cdr.gov.lb; internet www.cdr.gov.lb; f. 1977; an autonomous public institution reporting to the Cabinet, the CDR is charged with the co-ordination, planning and execution of Lebanon's public reconstruction programme; it plays a major role in attracting foreign funds; Pres. NABIL ADNAN EL-JISR.

Investment Development Authority of Lebanon (IDAL): POB 113-7251, Azarieh Tower, 4th Floor, Emir Bechir St, Riad el-Solh, Beirut; tel. (1) 983306; fax (1) 983302; e-mail invest@idal.com.lb; internet www.idal.com.lb; f. 1994; state-owned; Chair. and Gen. Man. NABIL ITANI.

Société Libanaise pour le Développement et la Reconstruction de Beyrouth (SOLIDERE): POB 11-9493, 149 rue Saad Zaghoul, Beirut 2012-7305; tel. (1) 980650; fax (1) 980662; e-mail solidere@solidere.com.lb; internet www.solidere.com.lb; f. 1994; real estate co responsible for reconstruction of Beirut Central District after the civil war; Chair. NASSER CHAMMAA; Gen. Man. MOUNIR DOUAIDY.

CHAMBERS OF COMMERCE AND INDUSTRY

Federation of the Chambers of Commerce, Industry and Agriculture in Lebanon: POB 11-1801, Immeuble CCIAB, rue Justinian, Sanayeh, Beirut; tel. (1) 744702; fax (1) 349614; e-mail fccial@cci-fed.org.lb; internet www.cci-fed.org.lb; f. 1996; Pres. GHAZI KRAYTEM.

Chamber of Commerce, Industry and Agriculture of Beirut and Mount Lebanon: POB 11-1801, rue Justinian, Sanayeh, Beirut; tel. (1) 353390; fax (1) 353395; e-mail information@ccib.org.lb; internet www.ccib.org.lb; f. 1898; 32,000 mems; Pres. GHAZI KRAYTEM.

Chamber of Commerce, Industry and Agriculture of Tripoli and North Lebanon: POB 47, rue Bechara Khoury, Tripoli; tel. (6) 627162; fax (6) 442042; e-mail abdallahg@cciat.org.lb; internet www.cciat.org.lb; Chair. ABDALLAH GHANDOUR.

Chamber of Commerce, Industry and Agriculture in Sidon and South Lebanon: POB 41, rue Maarouf Saad, Sidon; tel. (7) 720123; fax (7) 722986; e-mail chamber@ccias.org.lb; internet www.ccias.org.lb; f. 1933; Pres. MUHAMMAD ZAATARI.

Chamber of Commerce, Industry and Agriculture of Zahleh and Beka'a: POB 100, Zahleh; tel. (8) 802602; fax (8) 800050; e-mail info@cciaz.org.lb; internet www.cciaz.org.lb; f. 1939; 2,500 mems; Pres. EDMOND JREISSATI.

EMPLOYERS' ASSOCIATION

Association of Lebanese Industrialists: POB 11-1520, Chamber of Commerce and Industry Bldg, 5e étage, rue Justinien, Sanayeh, Beirut; tel. (1) 350280; fax (1) 351167; e-mail ali@ali.org.lb; internet www.ali.org.lb; Pres. FADY ABBOUD; Gen. Man. SAAD S. OUEINI.

UTILITIES

Electricity

Electricité du Liban (EDL): POB 131, Immeuble de l'Electricité du Liban, 22 rue du Fleuve, Beirut; tel. (1) 442720; fax (1) 443828; e-mail info@edl.gov.lb; internet www.edl.gov.lb; f. 1954; state-owned; scheduled for privatization; Chair. and Dir-Gen. KAMAL F. HAYEK.

Water

Legislation introduced in 2000 allowed for the merging of 21 water authorities into four new regional establishments for water exploitation—Beirut and the Mount of Lebanon; North Lebanon; South Lebanon; and the Beka'a. Under the reorganization the new authorities were to operate under the supervision of the Ministry of Energy and Water.

North Lebanon Water Authority: Chair. and Gen. Man. JAMAL ABD AL-LATIF KARIM.

South Lebanon Water Authority: Chair. and Gen. Man. AHMAD HASSAN NIZAM.

Litani River Authority: rue Bechara el-Khoury, Beirut; tel. (1) 666662; fax (1) 660476; e-mail litani@litani.gov.lb; internet www.litani.gov.lb; f. 1954; responsible for water resources management, irrigation, and the devt of dams and hydroelectric facilities.

TRADE UNION FEDERATION

Confédération Générale des Travailleurs du Liban (CGTL): POB 4381, Beirut; f. 1958; 300,000 mems; only national labour centre in Lebanon and sole rep. of working classes; comprises 18 affiliated feds incl. all 150 unions in Lebanon; Pres. GHASSAN GHOSN.

Transport

RAILWAYS

Office des Chemins de Fer et des Transports en Commun (OCFTC): POB 11-109, Gare St Michel, Nahr, Beirut; tel. (1) 587211; fax (1) 447007; since 1961 all railways in Lebanon have been state-owned; the original network of some 412 km is no longer functioning; however, in 2004 work began on a project to reconstruct a section of the railway network between Tripoli and the Syrian border; Dir-Gen. and Pres. RADWAN BOU NASSER EL-DIN.

LEBANON

ROADS

In 2005 Lebanon had an estimated 6,970 km of roads, of which some 170 km were motorways. The two international motorways are the north–south coastal road and the road connecting Beirut with Damascus in Syria. Among the major roads are those crossing the Beqa'a and continuing south to Bent-Jbail and the Shtaura–Ba'albek road. It was reported that up to 80% of Lebanon's major roads, and almost all of its bridges, were destroyed as a result of the Israeli military offensive in mid-2006.

SHIPPING

In the 1990s a two-phase programme to rehabilitate and expand the port of Beirut commenced, involving the construction of an industrial free zone, a fifth basin and a major container terminal, at an estimated cost of US $1,000m.; the container terminal became operational in February 2005. Tripoli, the northern Mediterranean terminus of the oil pipeline from Iraq, is also a busy port, with good equipment and facilities. Jounieh, north of Beirut, is Lebanon's third most important port. A new deep-water sea port was to be constructed south of Sidon. The reconstructed port of al-Naqoura, in what was then the 'security zone' along the border with Israel, was inaugurated in June 1987. Several ports were bombed by Israeli forces during the conflict of mid-2006.

Port Authorities

Gestion et Exploitation du Port de Beyrouth: POB 1490, Beirut; tel. (1) 580211; fax (1) 585835; e-mail info@portdebeyrouth.com; internet www.portdebeyrouth.com; Pres., Dir-Gen. and Man. Dir Hassan Kamel Kraytem; Harbour Master Maroun Khoury.

Service d'Exploitation du Port de Tripoli: rond point Tripoli, rue Mina, Tripoli; tel. (6) 600413; fax (6) 220180; e-mail tport@terra.net.lb; f. 1959; Harbour Master Marwan Baroudi.

Principal Shipping Companies

Ets Paul Adem: Centre Moucarri, 6e étage, autostrade Dora, Bourj Hammoud, Beirut; tel. (1) 244610; fax (1) 244612; e-mail padco@inco.com.lb; f. 1971; ship owners, operators, maritime agents, brokers, consultants; Gen. Man. Paul Adem.

Ademar Shipping Lines: POB 175-231, rue Shafaka, al-Medawar, Beirut; tel. and fax (1) 444100; fax (1) 444101; e-mail ademar@ademarlb.com; internet www.ademarlb.com; f. 1982.

Amin Kawar & Sons (Jordan): POB 11-4230, Beirut; tel. (1) 352525; fax (1) 353802; e-mail amkawar@travelkawar.com; internet www.kawar.com; f. 1963; Chair. Tawfiq Amin Kawar; CEO Rudain Kawar.

Associated Levant Lines SAL: POB 110371, Immeuble Mercedes, autostrade Dora, Beirut; tel. (1) 255366; fax (1) 255362; e-mail tgf-all@dm.net.lb; Dirs T. Gargour, N. Gargour, H. Gargour.

Beirut Cargo Center: Kurban Bldg, Corniche al-Nahr, Beirut; tel. (1) 585582; fax (1) 585580; e-mail bcc@bcc.com.lb; internet www.bcc.com.lb; f. 1993; air, sea and land freight forwarder; Pres. Joseph Harb; Gen. Man. Elie Shamsy.

Consolidated Bulk Inc: POB 70-152, Centre St Elie, Bloc A, 6e étage, Antélias, Beirut; tel. (4) 410724; fax (4) 402842; e-mail info@bulkgroup.com; internet www.bulkgroup.com; f. 1978; Gen. Man. Sami P. Zacca.

Continental Shipping Agencies SARL: POB 17-5039, Immeuble Medawar, rue Pasteur, Saifi, Beirut; tel. (1) 567130; fax (1) 567132; e-mail info@csa-continental.com; internet www.csa-continental.com; f. 1991.

O. D. Debbas & Sons: POB 16-6678, Immeuble Debbas, 530 blvd Corniche du Fleuve, Ashrafieh, Beirut; tel. (1) 585253; fax (1) 587135; e-mail oddebbas@oddebbas.com; internet www.oddebbas.com; f. 1892; Man. Dir Oidih Elie Debbas.

Freight Leader SARL: POB 17-5530, 5th Floor, Immeuble Medawar, rue Pasteur, Saifi, Beirut; tel. (1) 581870; fax (1) 564387; e-mail info@freightleader.com; internet www.freightleader.com; f. 2001; transportation services and logistics; Exec. Man. Moussa Salamoun.

Gezairi Chartering and Shipping Co (GEZACHART): POB 11-1402, Immeuble Gezairi, place Gezairi, Ras Beirut 2034 0716; tel. (1) 783783; fax (1) 784784; e-mail gezairi@gezairi.com; internet www.gezairi.com; f. 1945; ship management, chartering, brokerage; Pres. and CEO Mona Bouazza Bawarshi.

Gulf Agency Co (Lebanon) Ltd: POB 11-4392, Riad el-Solh, Beirut 1107 2160; tel. (1) 446086; fax (1) 446097; e-mail lebanon@gacworld.com; internet www.gacworld.com/lebanon; f. 1969; Man. Dir Simon G. Bejjani.

Lebanese Navigators Co SARL: POB 17-5179, Immeuble Aleddine, blvd Ghobeiry, Beirut; tel. (3) 996789; e-mail navigators@navigators-lb.com; internet www.navigators-lb.com; Man. Dir Antoine Mouhayar.

Orient Shipping and Trading Co SARL: POB 11-2561, Immeuble Moumneh, no 72, rue Ain al-Mraisseh 54, Beirut; tel. (1) 364455; fax (1) 365570; e-mail ortship@inco.com.lb; internet orientgroup.net/lebanon.swf; Dirs Elie Zarouby, Emile Zarouby.

G. Sahyouni & Co SARL: POB 17-5452, Mar Mikhael, Beirut 1104 2040; tel. (1) 257046; fax (1) 241317; e-mail postmaster@georgesahyouni.com; internet www.georgesahyouni.com; f. 1989; agents for Baltic Control Lebanon Ltd, SARL, and Lloyds; Man. Dir George Sahyouni.

CIVIL AVIATION

In late 2001 a major expansion project at Beirut International Airport was completed, at an estimated cost of US $600m.; facilities included a new terminal building and two new runways, increasing handling capacity to 6m. passengers a year. In May 2005 the airport was renamed Beirut Rafiq Hariri International Airport in honour of the former Prime Minister who had been killed in February. The airport was targeted by Israeli armed forces in 2006, and was closed to commercial flights during the conflict between Israel and Hezbollah. Following extensive repairs to damaged runways and other infrastructure, the airport reopened to commercial operations in August. In 2008 some 4.1m. passengers used the airport.

MEA (Middle East Airlines, Air Liban SAL): POB 11-206, blvd de l'Aéroport, Beirut 1107 2801; tel. (1) 628888; fax (1) 629260; e-mail mikaouir@mea.com.lb; internet www.mea.com.lb; f. 1945; acquired Lebanese Int. Airways in 1969; privatization pending; regular services throughout Europe, the Middle East, N and W Africa, and the Far East; Chair. and Dir-Gen. Muhammad A. el-Hout; Commercial Man. Nizar Khoury.

Trans-Mediterranean Airways SAL (TMA): POB 30-1001, Beirut International Airport, Beirut; tel. (1) 629210; fax (1) 629219; e-mail cargo@tmacargo.com; internet www.tma.com.lb; f. 1953; cargo services covering Europe, the Middle East, Africa and the Far East; also provides handling, storage and maintenance services; Chair. and Pres. Mazen Bissat.

Tourism

Since the end of the civil conflict in 1990 Lebanon's scenic beauty, sunny climate and historic sites have once again attracted foreign visitors. The Government has chosen to concentrate its efforts on the promotion of cultural as well as conference and exhibition-based tourism, while the country is also being promoted as an 'eco-tourism' destination. Excluding Syrian visitors, the annual total of tourist arrivals increased from 177,503 in 1992 to some 1.28m. in 2004. The Lebanese tourism industry experienced a significant downturn in the aftermath of the conflict between Israel and Hezbollah in 2006. However, there was a marked revival in the sector following the Doha Agreement of May 2008, and in 2009 the tourism sector continued to expand significantly, with foreign tourist arrivals reaching some 1.9m. Receipts from tourism totalled US $7,690 in 2008.

Ministry of Tourism: see section on The Government—Ministries.

Defence

Commander-in-Chief of the Army: Brig.-Gen. Jean Kahwaji.
Chief of Staff of Armed Forces: Maj.-Gen. Shawki al-Masri.
Commander of the Air Force: Brig.-Gen. Samir Maalouli.
Commander of the Navy: Rear Adm. Ali al-Moallem.
Director-General of State Security Forces: Brig.-Gen. Elias Kaayketi.
Defence Budget (2010): £L1,740,000m.
Total armed forces (as assessed at November 2010): 59,100: army 57,000; air force 1,000; navy 1,100.

Paramilitary forces included an estimated 20,000 members of the Internal Security Force, attached to the Ministry of the Interior and Municipalities. Compulsory military service was formally abolished in February 2007. Hezbollah's active members numbered some 2,000, as assessed at November 2009.

Following conflict in Lebanon between Hezbollah and Israeli armed forces in July–August 2006, the UN Security Council unanimously adopted Resolution 1701, calling for a full cessation of hostilities, upon which Lebanon was to deploy government forces in southern Lebanon and the presence there of the UN Interim Force in Lebanon (UNIFIL) was to be expanded, to a maximum authorized strength of 15,000 troops, while Israel was to commence the parallel withdrawal of all its forces from that region. A formal cease-fire entered into effect on 14 August. At April 2011 there were 11,873 UNIFIL military personnel (incl. 50 military observers) deployed in Lebanon.

Education

Education is not compulsory. Primary education has been available free of charge in state schools since 1960, but private institutions still provide the main facilities for secondary and university education. Private schools enjoy almost complete autonomy, except for a certain number that receive government financial aid and are supervised by inspectors from the Ministry of Education and Higher Education. In the 2010 budget some £L1,293,000m. was allocated to the Ministry of Education and Higher Education (representing 5.9% of total budgetary expenditure).

Primary education begins at six years of age and lasts for five years. It is followed either by the four-year intermediate course or the three-year secondary course. The baccalaureate examination is taken in two parts at the end of the second and third years of secondary education, and a public examination is taken at the end of the intermediate course. Technical education is provided mainly at the National School of Arts and Crafts, which offers four-year courses in electronics, mechanics, architectural and industrial drawing, and other subjects. There are also public vocational schools providing courses for lower levels. In 2007/08 enrolment at primary schools included 83.2% of the relevant age-group, while the comparable rate for secondary schools was 73.5%. Higher education is provided by at least 14 institutions, including 12 universities, an arts academy and a school of theology. Some 199,656 students were enrolled in higher education institutes in 2008/09.

LESOTHO

Introductory Survey

LOCATION, CLIMATE, LANGUAGE, RELIGION, FLAG, CAPITAL

The Kingdom of Lesotho is a land-locked country, entirely surrounded by South Africa. The climate is generally mild, although cooler in the highlands: lowland temperatures range from a maximum of 32°C (90°F) in summer (October to April) to a minimum of −7°C (20°F) in winter. Rainfall averages about 725 mm (29 ins) per year, mostly falling in summer. The official languages are English and Sesotho; other languages spoken include Zulu and Xhosa. About 90% of the population are Christians. The largest denominations are the Roman Catholic, Lesotho Evangelical and Anglican Churches. The national flag (official proportions 2 by 3) has three horizontal stripes from top to bottom of blue, white and green, with a black traditional Basotho hat in the centre of the white stripe. The capital is Maseru.

CONTEMPORARY POLITICAL HISTORY

Historical Context

Lesotho was formerly Basutoland, which became a separate British colony in 1884 and was administered as one of the High Commission Territories in southern Africa (the others being the protectorates of Bechuanaland, now Botswana, and Swaziland). The British Act of Parliament that established the Union of South Africa in 1910 also provided for the possible inclusion in South Africa of the three High Commission Territories, subject to local consent: the native chiefs opposed requests by successive South African Governments for the transfer of the three territories.

Within Basutoland a revised Constitution, which established the colony's first Legislative Council, was introduced in 1956. A new document, granting limited powers of self-government, was adopted in September 1959. Basutoland's first general election, on the basis of universal adult suffrage, took place on 29 April 1965, and full internal self-government was achieved the following day. Moshoeshoe II, Paramount Chief since 1960, was recognized as King. The Basutoland National Party (BNP), a conservative group supporting limited co-operation with South Africa, narrowly won a majority of the seats in the new Legislative Assembly. The BNP's leader, Chief Leabua Jonathan, was appointed Prime Minister in July 1965. Basutoland became independent, as Lesotho, on 4 October 1966. The new Constitution provided for a bicameral legislature, comprising the 60-seat National Assembly and the 33-member Senate; executive power was vested in the Cabinet, which was presided over by the Prime Minister. The King was designated Head of State.

Domestic Political Affairs

The BNP, restyled the Basotho National Party, remained in power at independence. A general election was held in January 1970, at which the opposition Basotho Congress Party (BCP), a pan-Africanist group led by Dr Ntsu Mokhehle, appeared to have won a majority of seats in the National Assembly. Chief Jonathan declared a state of emergency, suspended the Constitution and arrested several BCP organizers. The election was annulled, and the legislature prorogued. King Moshoeshoe II was placed under house arrest and subsequently exiled, although he returned in December after accepting a government order banning him from participating in politics. The country was thus effectively under the Prime Minister's personal control. An interim National Assembly, comprising the former Senate (mainly chiefs) and 60 members nominated by the Cabinet, was inaugurated in April 1973 and the state of emergency was revoked in July. However, following a failed coup attempt in January 1974 by alleged supporters of the BCP, Chief Jonathan introduced stringent security laws. Mokhehle and other prominent members of the BCP went into exile abroad, and the party split into two factions, internal and external, the latter led by Mokhehle.

Although Lesotho was economically dependent on South Africa, and the Government's official policy during the 1970s was one of 'dialogue' with its neighbour, Chief Jonathan repeatedly criticized the apartheid regime, and supported the then banned African National Congress of South Africa (ANC). In December 1982 South African forces launched a major assault on the homes of ANC members in Maseru, killing more than 40 people. Lesotho's persistent refusal to sign a joint non-aggression pact led South Africa to impound consignments of armaments destined for Lesotho, and the imposition of a blockade on the common border from early 1986.

On 20 January 1986 Chief Jonathan's Government was overthrown in a coup led by Maj.-Gen. Justin Lekhanya, the head of the armed forces. A Military Council, chaired by Lekhanya, was established and executive and legislative powers were to be vested in King Moshoeshoe, assisted by the Military Council and a (mainly civilian) Council of Ministers. In March 1986 the Military Council suspended all formal political activity. In September the Council of Ministers was restructured, giving increased responsibility to Lekhanya, and the Military Council held discussions with the leaders of the five main opposition parties.

Although the South African Government denied having any part in the coup, the Lekhanya regime proved to be more amenable to South Africa's regional security policy. In March 1986 it was announced that the two countries had reached an informal agreement whereby neither would allow its territory to be used for attacks against the other. Moreover, the Lesotho Government did not join other African states in pressing for international economic sanctions against South Africa. In March 1988 Lesotho and South Africa reached final agreement on the Lesotho Highlands Water Project (LHWP), a major scheme to supply water to South Africa.

In May 1988 Mokhehle was allowed to return to Lesotho after 14 years of exile and by 1990 the two factions of the BCP had apparently reunited under Mokhehle's leadership.

In February 1990 Lekhanya dismissed three members of the Military Council and one member of the Council of Ministers, accusing them of 'insubordination'. When Moshoeshoe refused to approve new appointments to the Military Council, Lekhanya suspended the monarch's executive and legislative powers, which were assumed by the Military Council in March. Moshoeshoe (who remained Head of State) was exiled in the United Kingdom. Lekhanya announced that a general election would take place during 1992; however, party political activity remained outlawed. In June 1990 a National Constituent Assembly (including Lekhanya, members of the Council of Ministers, representatives of banned political parties, traditional chiefs and business leaders) was inaugurated to draft a new constitution. In October Lekhanya invited the King to return from exile. Moshoeshoe responded that his return would be conditional upon the ending of military rule and the establishment of an interim government, pending the readoption of the 1966 Constitution. On 6 November 1990 Lekhanya promulgated an order dethroning the King with immediate effect. Lesotho's 22 principal chiefs elected Moshoeshoe's elder son, Prince David Mohato Bereng Seeiso, as the new King; on 12 November he acceded to the throne, as King Letsie III, having undertaken to remain detached from politics.

On 30 April 1991 Lekhanya was deposed in a coup organized by disaffected army officers. Col (later Maj.-Gen.) Elias Phitsoane Ramaema succeeded Lekhanya as Chairman of the Military Council. Ramaema repealed the ban on party political activity, and by July the National Constituent Assembly had completed the draft Constitution. In May 1992 Lesotho and South Africa agreed to establish diplomatic relations at ambassadorial level. Following talks in the United Kingdom with Ramaema, former King Moshoeshoe returned from exile in July.

The general election was eventually held in March 1993. The BCP secured all 65 seats in the new National Assembly, winning 54% of the votes cast. In April Mokhehle was inaugurated as Prime Minister, and King Letsie swore allegiance to the new Constitution, under the terms of which he remained Head of State with no executive or legislative powers; executive authority was vested in the Cabinet.

Suspension of constitutional government

A mutiny by the Royal Lesotho Defence Force (RLDF) took place in November 1993 following which four senior army officers were reported to have resigned their posts. Skirmishes near Maseru in January 1994 escalated into more serious fighting between some 600 rebel troops and a 150-strong contingent of forces loyal to the Government, reportedly resulting in the deaths of at least five soldiers and three civilians. Following mediation efforts involving representatives of Botswana, South Africa, Zimbabwe, the Commonwealth (see p. 230), the Organization of African Unity (OAU, now the African Union, see p. 183—AU) and the UN, a truce entered into force, and at the beginning of February the rival factions surrendered their weapons and returned to barracks. In April, however, the Deputy Prime Minister, Selometsi Baholo (who also held the finance portfolio), was killed during an abduction attempt by disaffected troops.

A commission to investigate the armed forces unrest of January and April 1994 began work in July. In that month Mokhehle appointed a commission of inquiry into the dethronement of King Moshoeshoe II. On 17 August Letsie announced that he had dissolved the National Assembly, dismissed the Government and suspended sections of the Constitution, citing 'popular dissatisfaction' with the BCP administration. Although several thousand people gathered outside the royal palace in Maseru in support of the deposed Government, army and police support for Letsie's 'royal coup' was evident, and subsequent clashes between demonstrators and the security forces reportedly resulted in five deaths. A well-known human rights lawyer, Hae Phoofolo, was appointed Chairman of a transitional Council of Ministers, and the Secretary-General of the BNP, Evaristus Retselisitsoe Sekhonyana, was appointed Minister of Foreign Affairs. Phoofolo identified as a priority for his administration the amendment of the Constitution to facilitate the restoration of Moshoeshoe; in the mean time, King Letsie was to act as executive and legislative Head of State.

The suspension of constitutional government was widely condemned outside Lesotho. The Presidents of Botswana, South Africa and Zimbabwe led diplomatic efforts to restore the elected Government, supported by the OAU and the Commonwealth. The USA withdrew financial assistance, and several other countries threatened sanctions. Following negotiations in South Africa, in September 1994 King Letsie and Mokhehle signed an agreement, guaranteed by Botswana, South Africa and Zimbabwe, providing for the restoration of Moshoeshoe II as reigning monarch and for the restitution of the elected organs of government; the commission of inquiry into Moshoeshoe's dethronement was to be abandoned; all those involved in the 'royal coup' were to be immune from prosecution; the political neutrality of the armed forces and public service was to be guaranteed, and consultations were to be undertaken with the aim of broadening the democratic process. Moshoeshoe was restored to the throne on 25 January 1995, undertaking not to interfere in politics. Letsie took the title of Crown Prince.

King Moshoeshoe was killed in a motor accident on 15 January 1996. The College of Chiefs subsequently elected Crown Prince David to succeed his father, and the prince was restored to the throne, resuming the title King Letsie III, on 7 February. Letsie undertook not to involve the monarchy in any aspect of political life.

In June 1997, following a protracted struggle between rival factions for control of the party, Mokhehle resigned from the BCP and formed the Lesotho Congress for Democracy (LCD), to which he transferred executive power. Some 38 members of the National Assembly joined the LCD. In July Molapo Qhobela was elected leader of the BCP. There was further controversy in August, when the Speaker of the National Assembly designated the BCP as the official opposition party. In October members of the Senate (most of whom apparently refused to recognize the legitimacy of Mokhehle's Government) voted to suspend discussion of proposed legislation, pending the King's response to appeals for the dissolution of the National Assembly. At the first annual conference of the LCD, held in January 1998, Mokhehle resigned as leader, and was made Honorary Life President of the party. In February Deputy Prime Minister Bethuel Pakalitha Mosisili was elected to succeed him as party leader. (Mokhehle died in January 1999.)

Elections to an expanded National Assembly took place on 23 May 1998, at which the LCD secured an overwhelming victory, winning 78 of the Assembly's 80 seats; the BNP was the only other party to win representation. Voting for one seat was postponed, owing to the death of a candidate. The Independent Electoral Commission (IEC) and observers representing the Southern African Development Community (SADC, see p. 420) and the Commonwealth concluded that the polls had been generally free and fair. Mosisili was elected Prime Minister by the National Assembly in late May, and a new Government was appointed in June. However, later that month the BCP, the BNP and the Marematlou Freedom Party appealed to the High Court to annul the election results; in the following month the Court ordered the IEC to permit the opposition parties to inspect election documents.

In August 1998 opposition activists began a mass vigil outside the royal palace; within one week some 2,000 people were reported to have joined the protest against the outcome of the poll. Tensions escalated as LCD militants blocked access roads to the capital, in a stated attempt to prevent supplies of weapons to the protesters. Following consultations involving the Lesotho Government and the main opposition parties, with mediation by the Government of South Africa, Mosisili announced the establishment of an independent commission, comprising representatives of the SADC 'troika' of Botswana, South Africa and Zimbabwe, to investigate the conduct and results of the May election. The commission was to be chaired by Pius Langa, the Deputy President of South Africa's Constitutional Court.

Meanwhile, revelations that state funds had been used to purchase farmland for the Commander of the Lesotho Defence Force (LDF, as the RLDF had been redesignated), Lt-Gen. Makhula Mosakeng, fuelled opposition allegations of the Commander's complicity in corruption and vote-rigging. (Mosakeng stated that the land had been acquired for army, rather than personal, use.) However, Mosakeng later announced his resignation and stated that 26 members of the military command had been dismissed.

SADC intervention

The Langa Commission's report, which was finally released on 17 September 1998, expressed serious concerns at apparent irregularities and discrepancies in the conduct of the May general election, but the Commission was 'unable to state that the invalidity of the elections had been conclusively established'. On 22 September an SADC peace-keeping force, initially comprising 600 South African troops and 200 from Botswana, entered Lesotho. In response to criticism that he had not consulted King Letsie prior to requesting external military assistance, Mosisili stated that the monarch had, by harbouring opposition protesters in the palace grounds, contributed to the instability that had necessitated SADC intervention. (It was subsequently reported that the King had been prevented from making a broadcast to the nation.) Within Lesotho, there was widespread outrage at what was perceived as an effective 'invasion' by South Africa, and the SADC force encountered unexpectedly strong resistance. There was sustained fighting between the intervention force and rebel units of the LDF before strategic points, including military bases and the Katse Dam (part of the LHWP essential to the supply of water to South Africa), were secured, while rioting in Maseru and other towns targeted in particular South African interests and caused widespread destruction. Mosakeng and his officers, who had fled to South Africa earlier in the month, returned to resume the army command on 24 September: Mosakeng stated that his resignation had been exacted under duress and, since it had not been approved by the King, was invalid.

Following meetings with representatives of the SADC 'troika', in early October 1998 it was reported that the LCD and the main opposition parties had agreed in principle that fresh elections should be held within 15–18 months. In the mean time, the IEC was to be restructured, and the electoral system was to be reviewed, with the aim of ensuring wider inclusion in political affairs (many parties felt that the simple majority voting system was incompatible with the nature of Lesotho's political evolution). In mid-October agreement was reached on a transitional structure, designated the Interim Political Authority (IPA), to comprise representatives of 12 political parties, as well as government and parliamentary delegates, to oversee preparations for fresh elections to the National Assembly.

Multi-party talks took place in Pretoria, South Africa, during November 1998, but progress towards the establishment of the IPA was impeded after warrants were issued for the arrest, on murder charges, of several opposition activists, including two leading members of the BCP and BNP youth wings. The opposition parties stated that they would not co-operate in arrangements for the IPA until outstanding security matters, including the release of all rebel soldiers, had been expedited. A court martial in October 1999 ruled against the discharge of a total of 38 members of the LDF accused of mutiny.

The withdrawal of the SADC intervention force was completed in May 1999. This force was immediately succeeded by a new SADC mission, comprising some 300 military personnel from South Africa, Botswana and (subsequently) Zimbabwe, which remained until May 2000, assisting in the retraining and restructuring of the LDF.

Meanwhile, the 24-member IPA was inaugurated on 9 December 1998. After protracted consultations, it was announced that the number of seats in the National Assembly was to be increased by 50, to 130, effective from the elections scheduled for April 2000, with 80 seats to be allocated on the basis of simple majority in single-member constituencies, and 50 by proportional representation. The mandate of the IPA was to be extended until elections took place. In the mean time, the Presidents of South Africa, Botswana, Mozambique and Zimbabwe, together with the UN, the OAU and the Commonwealth Secretaries-General, were to act as guarantors to ensure the implementation of the accord. The elections were subsequently postponed due to delays in enacting legislation concerning voter registration and the electoral model.

In April 2000 the establishment of a commission of inquiry to investigate political events during July–November 1998 was announced. The commission, comprising three senior judges and chaired by Nigel Leon, met for the first time in June 2000 and heard evidence from several public figures. However, a number of opposition politicians criticized the commission, expressing doubts as to its impartiality. In August three LDF members were convicted by a court martial of participation in the mutiny of September 1998 and sentenced to a combined 29 years' imprisonment; a further 33 LDF members were convicted in November. The Leon commission of inquiry, which submitted its report to Prime Minister Mosisili in October 2001, rejected demands for a general amnesty to be granted to perpetrators of violence during the period under review, recommending the indictment of a number of opposition politicians and members of the armed forces.

In January 2001 a congress of the LCD re-elected Mosisili as leader of the party, for a five-year term. Shakhane Mokhehle, the incumbent and brother of the party's founder, was defeated in the election to the post of Secretary-General of the LCD by the Minister in the Prime Minister's Office, Sephiri Motanyane. In a minor cabinet reshuffle in July Mokhehle, who had disputed the results of the LCD elections, was dismissed as Minister of Justice, Human Rights and Rehabilitation, Law and Constitutional Affairs. Deputy Prime Minister Kelebone Maope resigned from the Government in September and broke away from the LCD, together with Mokhehle, to form a new opposition party, the Lesotho People's Congress (LPC), to prepare for forthcoming elections. By mid-October a total of 27 deputies had defected from the LCD to join the LPC, which was declared the main opposition party. Mosisili made new cabinet appointments in October, in an effort to consolidate his position ahead of the elections.

In mid-January 2002 a protracted dispute over the leadership of the BCP, which had been ongoing since the late 1990s, also appeared to be resolved, when the High Court ruled in favour of Tseliso Makhakhe's leadership of the party. Qhobela subsequently formed a new party, the Basutoland African Congress (BAC), which had been the name of the BCP in 1952–59.

Meanwhile, divisions over the electoral model, notably regarding the number of seats to be allocated by proportional representation, had continued to impede progress towards the elections. In January 2002 Parliament finally approved amendments to the electoral legislation, providing for the expansion of the National Assembly to 120 members, with 80 to be elected on a constituency basis and 40 selected by proportional representation.

The LCD won a resounding victory at the general election, which took place on 25 May 2002, retaining 77 of the 78 contested constituency seats, with 54.9% of the valid votes cast. The BNP became the second largest legislative party, securing 21 of the 40 seats allocated by proportional representation (known as compensatory seats), with 22.4% of the votes cast; the LPC won one constituency seat and four compensatory seats. Voting in two constituencies was postponed, owing to the deaths of candidates. Of the remaining 15 compensatory seats, the National Independent Party (NIP) secured five, the BAC and the BCP both won three, while four smaller parties each took one seat. Mosisili was re-elected Prime Minister by the National Assembly in early June and a new Cabinet was subsequently appointed.

In mid-October 2004 a 30-member committee, comprising government ministers and members of the National Assembly and the Senate, was established to direct a parliamentary reform programme. In mid-November the Cabinet was reorganized: Monyane Moleleki was appointed Minister of Foreign Affairs, the Deputy Prime Minister, Lesao Lehohola, also assumed the home affairs portfolio, and Mothejoa Metsing became the Minister of Justice, Human Rights and Rehabilitation, Law and Constitutional Affairs.

Recent developments: political realignments

In late January 2006 Khauhelo Raditapole and Kelebone Maope, the leaders of the BAC and the LPC, respectively, announced that their parties would form an alliance, following appeals by the BCP for reconciliation between political parties. Legislative elections took place on 17 February 2007, at which the LCD retained its parliamentary majority, although the party's total number of seats in the National Assembly was reduced from 77 to 61. The NIP took 21 of the 40 compensatory seats, thus becoming the second largest legislative party, while the All Basotho Convention (ABC) secured 17 constituency seats and the Lesotho Workers' Party (LWP) 10 compensatory seats. Voting in one constituency was postponed, owing to the death of a candidate. The Alliance of Congress Parties won one constituency seat and one compensatory seat, while five other parties each secured one compensatory seat. Observers from SADC and the AU declared the elections to have been free and fair. It emerged that an alliance had formed between the LCD and the NIP and that the NIP had fielded candidates from the LCD at the elections, giving the coalition a total of 82 seats in the National Assembly; a similar arrangement was made between the ABC and the LWP, resulting in that alliance securing 27 seats in total. Mosisili was reappointed Prime Minister later that month and in early March a new Cabinet was sworn in. Most notably, Mohlabi Tsekoa, hitherto Minister of Education and Training, was appointed Minister of Foreign Affairs; Mahase-Moiloa became Minister of Law and Constitutional Affairs.

During 2008 tensions had been building between the ruling and opposition parties over the formation of alliances for the 2007 legislative elections, and in January 2009 the ABC claimed that the coalition formed by the LCD and the NIP contravened the Constitution. Opposition parties argued that the allocation of compensatory seats to the LCD-NIP alliance had been unfair and appealed for SADC intervention in the matter.

In April 2009 Mosisili's residence was attacked by gunmen in an apparent assassination attempt. Four of the attackers were reported to have been killed and two men suspected of involvement in the incident were detained in South Africa; the Prime Minister escaped unharmed. Despite recent tensions, observers maintained that the prevailing situation in Lesotho was one of stability and a motive for the attack was not immediately clear. At a press conference in August it was announced that the mercenaries responsible for the shooting in April were from Mozambique. A further five assailants from that country were awaiting trial; four were detained in South Africa and one was arrested in Lesotho.

In an attempt to resolve the long-standing dispute over the distribution of compensatory seats following the 2007 elections, in February 2010 the SADC organ on political, defence and security co-operation requested that a 'road map' be drawn up to address the main points of disagreement among the country's political organizations and to examine the possibility of modifying the Constitution and the legislation governing elections. Several rounds of cross-party talks, mediated by the Christian Council of Lesotho, were conducted throughout 2010, but no substantive progress was reported.

Doubts were raised in April 2010 regarding the future viability of Lesotho as an independent nation following, in accordance with the AU's African Peer Review Mechanism, the presentation of a report detailing the dire social and economic conditions within the country. In the following month the People's Charter Movement (PCM) organized a march through the capital to present to the South African High Commission a document, signed by some 30,000 Basotho, appealing for annexation. The PCM's campaign gained further impetus in June following South Africa's imposition of new border restrictions, denying entry to Basotho without passports. The Government expressed its concerns about the border controls to the South African High Commissioner, while Lehohola travelled to South Africa to discuss the issue with high-ranking officials, but the restrictions remained in place, nevertheless.

Opposition threats to boycott the May 2010 local elections—in protest against, *inter alia*, proposed 'affirmative action' laws (which had been criticized for being too heavily weighted in favour of female candidates), constituency boundaries and the unreformed simple majority electoral system still employed in local ballots—led Parliament in April to postpone the vote until 2011. The decision to suspend the elections received cross-party support and was intended to facilitate the parliamentary approval of amendments to the existing legislation regulating local elections. The IEC implemented a restructuring of constituency boundaries in July 2010, although the leader of the ABC, Thomas Thabane, argued that the alterations would benefit the LCD, alleging that the IEC was 'directly working' for the ruling party.

Mosisili effected a cabinet reorganization in October 2010. The ministers responsible for trade, tourism, agriculture and employment—all of whom were believed to be members of an influential faction within the LCD reportedly led by Mothejoa Metsing, the Minister of Communications, Science and Technology—were replaced by close associates of the Prime Minister. Following the reorganization, supporters of the dismissed ministers besieged the LCD's headquarters in protest and accused Monyane Moleleki, the Minister of Natural Resources and alleged leader of a rival wing of the LCD, of pressuring Mosisili to remove Metsing's allies from the Cabinet. The discord within the ruling party was confirmed in November, when Mosisili publicly criticized the 'hatred and divisions' afflicting the LCD. Infighting was also evident within the opposition parties during 2010. The fragile ABC-LWP alliance ended in July due to continued disagreements between the leaders of the respective parties, precipitating a dispute over control of the compensatory seats allocated to the now-defunct coalition after the 2007 elections. Meanwhile, after losing a vote of confidence in December, BNP leader Justin Lekhanya was replaced by his deputy, Thesele Maseribane. Despite the factionalism undermining the LCD, most commentators agreed that the ruling party would easily defeat the weakened opposition in the 2012 elections, a point reinforced by the LCD's comfortable victory in three by-elections held in May 2010.

Foreign Affairs

As exemplified by South Africa's prominent role in the resolution of the 1994 constitutional crisis and by its intervention in the political crisis of September 1998, Lesotho's internal affairs continue to be strongly influenced by South Africa. Long-standing problems of border security and, in particular, the issue of disputed land in South Africa's Free State (formerly Orange Free State) have periodically caused friction between the two countries. Relations between the two countries were strained in August 2000 when Lesotho withdrew its support shortly before the scheduled signing of an agreement with Botswana, Namibia and South Africa on the management of water resources from the Orange river. In September an official at the South African High Commission was killed in Maseru. Representatives of both countries met in Pretoria in November and recommended increased co-operation in areas including education and criminal justice. During a visit to Lesotho by President Thabo Mbeki of South Africa in April 2001, it was agreed to replace an intergovernmental liaison committee that had been established following SADC intervention in 1998 (see above) with a joint binational commission at ministerial level, with the aim of enhancing bilateral relations. Relations between Lesotho and South Africa were further enhanced in May 2002, when their ministers of foreign affairs signed the Joint Bilateral Commission of Co-operation programme, which aimed to raise Lesotho from its current status as a 'least developed country'.

CONSTITUTION AND GOVERNMENT

Lesotho is an hereditary monarchy. Under the terms of the Constitution, which came into effect following the March 1993 election, the King, who is Head of State, has no executive or legislative powers. The College of Chiefs is theoretically empowered, under traditional law, to elect and depose the King by a majority vote. Executive power is vested in the Cabinet, which is headed by the Prime Minister. Legislative power is exercised by the National Assembly, which is elected, at intervals of no more than five years, by universal adult suffrage in the context of a multi-party political system. A system of mixed member proportional representation was introduced at the general election of May 2002, when the National Assembly was expanded to 120 members (80 elected by simple majority in single-member constituencies and 40 selected from party lists). The upper house, the Senate, comprises traditional chiefs and 11 nominated members. Lesotho comprises 10 administrative districts, each with an appointed district co-ordinator.

REGIONAL AND INTERNATIONAL CO-OPERATION

Lesotho is a member of the Common Monetary Area (with Namibia, South Africa and Swaziland), and a member of the Southern African Customs Union (SACU—with Botswana, Namibia, South Africa and Swaziland). Lesotho also belongs to the Southern African Development Community (SADC, see p. 420) and the African Union (see p. 183).

Lesotho became a member of the UN in 1966 and was admitted to the World Trade Organization (WTO, see p. 430) in 1995. Lesotho participates in the Group of 77 (G77, see p. 447) developing countries.

ECONOMIC AFFAIRS

In 2009, according to estimates by the World Bank, Lesotho's gross national income (GNI), measured at average 2007–09 prices, was US $2,139m., equivalent to $1,030 per head (or $1,950 per head on an international purchasing-power parity basis). During 2000–09, it was estimated, the population increased at an average annual rate of 1.0%, while gross domestic product (GDP) per head increased, in real terms, by an average of 2.6% per year. Overall GDP increased, in real terms, at an average annual rate of 3.7% in 2000–09; growth in 2009 was 2.1%.

Agriculture, forestry and fishing contributed just 7.8% of GDP in 2009, according to the African Development Bank (AfDB). The sector engaged some 39.0% of the labour force in mid-2011, according to FAO estimates. The principal agricultural export is tobacco. The main subsistence crops are potatoes, maize, sorghum and wheat. Lesotho remains a net importer of staple foodstuffs, largely owing to its vulnerability to adverse climatic conditions, especially drought. According to the World Food Programme, less than 10% of land is arable and there is no irrigation. According to the World Bank, during 2000–09 agricultural GDP declined at an average annual rate of 2.3%; the sector's GDP declined by 0.5% in 2008, but increased by 6.2% in 2009.

Industry (including mining, manufacturing, construction and power) provided 32.4% of GDP in 2009, according to the AfDB. The sector engaged 9.3% of the labour force in 1999. According to the World Bank, during 2000–09 industrial GDP increased by an average annual rate of 4.8% per year. Industrial GDP increased by 1.7% in 2008, but declined by 1.4% in 2009.

Mining contributed 7.6% of GDP in 2009. Lesotho has reserves of diamonds, which during the late 1970s provided more than 50% of visible export earnings, but large-scale exploitation of these ceased in 1982. The Lets'eng-la-Terae diamond mine reopened in April 2004 and by the time of its official inauguration in November gems with an estimated value of US $28m. had been recovered. Industrial mining at other sites was also envisaged, including a second diamond mine at Liqhobong. Lesotho also possesses deposits of uranium, lead and iron ore, and is believed to have petroleum deposits. According to the AfDB, the GDP of the mining sector declined by an average of 6.7% per year in 2000–08; GDP of the sector increased by 7.9% in 2009.

Manufacturing contributed 15.7% of GDP in 2009, according to the AfDB. The sector employed 3.5% of the total labour force in 1999. During 2000–09 manufacturing GDP increased by an average of 8.1% per year, according to the World Bank; it declined by 2.0% in 2008 and by 3.4% in 2009.

According to the AfDB, the construction sector contributed 4.9% of GDP in 2009. The sector engaged 4.8% of the employed labour force in 1999. According to the AfDB, during 2000–08 construction GDP declined by an average of 17.1% per year; the GDP of the sector increased by 13.9% in 2009.

The Lesotho Highlands Water Project (LHWP) provides hydroelectricity sufficient for all Lesotho's needs and for export to South Africa; phases 1A and 1B were inaugurated in 1998 and 2004, respectively. In late September 2005 an agreement was signed for a feasibility study concerning the location of the second phase of the project. The scheme was expected to be completed by about 2030. The R200m. (US $30m.) that Lesotho receives annually in royalties from South Africa for the LHWP represents the country's largest single source of foreign exchange. Prior to the LHWP more than 90% of Lesotho's energy requirements were imported from South Africa. Imports of mineral fuels and lubricants comprised only 4.4% of the total value of imports in 2005.

LESOTHO

Statistical Survey

The services sector contributed 59.8% of GDP in 2009, according to the AfDB. Only 18.3% of the labour force was employed in the services sector in 1999. During 2000–09 the GDP of the services sector increased at an average annual rate of 3.2%, according to the World Bank; the GDP of the sector increased by 4.3% in 2009.

In 2009 Lesotho recorded a visible trade deficit of US $951.7m., and there was a deficit of $32.0m. on the current account of the balance of payments. In 2007 the principal source of imports (85.4%) was the Southern African Customs Union (SACU—i.e. chiefly South Africa—see below), which was also the second largest market for exports (19.0%), behind the USA (59.7%); the European Union was also a significant market for exports (17.2%). The principal exports in that year were miscellaneous manufactured articles. The principal imports in 2005 were industrial supplies, food and beverages, and machinery and other capital equipment.

In the financial year ending 31 March 2008 there was an overall budgetary surplus of M1,835.4m. Lesotho's general government gross debt was M6,238m. in 2009, equivalent to 44.0% of GDP. Lesotho's external debt totalled US $682.3m. at the end of 2008, of which $652.7m. was public and publicly guaranteed debt. In that year the cost of debt-servicing was equivalent to 2.5% of the value of exports of goods, services and income. The annual rate of inflation averaged 6.6% in 2000–09; consumer prices increased by 7.2% in 2009. In 1999 231,742 people were registered as unemployed, equivalent to 27.3% of the labour force. In 2006 51,595 Basotho were employed as miners in South Africa, compared with 129,000 in 1989. The number was expected to continue to decrease in the coming years. According to the Central Bank of Lesotho, in 2004 Basotho miners' remittances amounted to M1,795.0m. and accounted for more than 70% of total earnings during the period 1997–2004. South African officials estimated that around 300,000 Basotho were employed in South Africa at any given time.

Impediments to economic development in Lesotho include vulnerability to drought and serious land shortages, combined with the country's dependence on South Africa (the Lesotho currency, the loti, is fixed at par with the South African rand, exposing Lesotho to fluctuations within the South African economy). The textile industry benefited considerably from the USA's African Growth and Opportunities Act (AGOA), for which Lesotho was first declared eligible in April 2001; under its terms, textiles and clothing made in Lesotho had unlimited access to the US market. Lesotho's qualification for the benefits of the AGOA attracted interest from foreign investors in Lesotho, notably Taiwanese textile manufacturers. However, faced with increasing competition from producers in Asia, between mid-2004 and January 2005 eight textile factories closed with the loss of more than 23,000 jobs. The textile and garment sector, having shown marked improvement in 2007, suffered in late 2008 and early 2009 as a result of the global financial crisis, as did the mining sector, resulting in redundancies and reduced production levels. Real GDP increased by just 0.9% in 2009, according to IMF estimates. In February 2010 the Lesotho authorities reaffirmed the commitments of the 'Vision 2020' long-term economic development programme, and announced preparations for a five-year National Development Plan, which was to commence in 2012. However, declining SACU revenues, which provide some 60% of the country's total income, and a proposed restructuring of SACU tariffs presented additional challenges for the Lesotho authorities in meeting the ambitious targets of these programmes. Meanwhile, in September 2009 the Government granted a 10-year lease of the Mothae kimberlite pipe, located in north-east Lesotho, to Canadian group Lucara Diamond Corpn, indicating a resurgence in the mining sector. A similar arrangement was concluded for the Kao kimberlite pipe (the largest in Lesotho) in January 2010, with a lease being granted to a consortium led by Namakwa Diamonds of South Africa. Increased diamond prices suggested the possibility of further mining companies recommencing operations in the near future. To bolster the Government's fiscal position, in June 2010 the IMF released US $11.4m. as part of an Extended Credit Facility package worth $61.4m. over the next three years. The IMF projected increased real GDP growth of 5.6% in 2010, and further expansion of 3.3% was forecast for 2011.

PUBLIC HOLIDAYS

2012: 1 January (New Year's Day), 11 March (Moshoeshoe Day), 6–9 April (Easter), 1 May (Workers' Day), 17 May (Ascension Day), 25 May (Africa Day and Heroes' Day), 17 July (King's Birthday), 4 October (National Independence Day), 25 December (Christmas Day), 26 December (Boxing Day).

Statistical Survey

Sources (unless otherwise stated): Bureau of Statistics, POB 455, Maseru 100; tel. 22323852; fax 22310177; internet www.bos.gov.ls; Central Bank of Lesotho, POB 1184, Maseru 100; tel. 22314281; fax 22310051; e-mail cbl@centralbank.org.ls; internet www.centralbank.org.ls.

Area and Population

AREA, POPULATION AND DENSITY

Area (sq km)	30,355*
Population (*de jure* census results)	
14 April 1996	1,862,275
9 April 2006	
Males	916,282
Females	964,379
Total	1,880,661
Population (UN estimates at mid-year)†	
2009	2,067,920
2010	2,084,182
2011	2,101,308
Density (per sq km) at mid-2011	69.2

* 11,720 sq miles.
† Source: UN, *World Population Prospects: The 2008 Revision*.

POPULATION BY AGE AND SEX
(UN estimates at mid-2011)

	Males	Females	Total
0–14	403,389	398,528	801,917
15–64	549,826	649,310	1,199,136
65 and over	41,591	58,664	100,255
Total	994,806	1,106,502	2,101,308

Source: UN, *World Population Prospects: The 2008 Revision*.

DISTRICTS
(population at 2006 census)

District	Population
Berea	256,496
Butha-Buthe	109,529
Leribe	298,352
Mafeteng	193,682
Maseru	429,823
Mohale's Hoek	174,924
Mokhotlong	96,340
Qacha's Nek	71,876
Quthing	120,502
Thaba-Tseka	129,137
Total	1,880,661

LESOTHO

PRINCIPAL TOWNS
(population at 1986 census)

Maseru (capital)	109,400	Hlotse	9,600
Maputsoa	20,000	Mohale's Hoek	8,500
Teyateyaneng	14,300	Quthing	6,000
Mafeteng	12,700		

Source: Stefan Helders, *World Gazetteer* (www.world-gazetteer.com).

Mid-2009 (including suburbs, UN estimate): Maseru 220,012 (Source: UN, *World Urbanization Prospects: The 2009 Revision*).

BIRTHS AND DEATHS
(annual averages, UN estimates)

	1995–2000	2000–05	2005–10
Birth rate (per 1,000)	34.0	31.2	29.1
Death rate (per 1,000)	12.0	16.5	16.9

Source: UN, *World Population Prospects: The 2008 Revision*.

Life expectancy (years at birth, WHO estimates): 47 (males 44; females 49) in 2008 (Source: WHO, *World Health Statistics*).

ECONOMICALLY ACTIVE POPULATION
(household survey, persons aged 10 years and over, 1999)

	Males	Females	Total
Agriculture	270,919	175,760	446,679
Fishing	125	—	125
Mining and quarrying	2,392	611	3,003
Manufacturing	7,957	13,839	21,795
Electricity, gas and water supply	1,722	1,541	3,263
Construction	18,947	10,548	29,495
Wholesale and retail trade; repair of motor vehicles, motorcycles and household goods	11,099	17,915	29,014
Hotels and restaurants	918	3,529	4,447
Transport, storage and communications	9,307	1,363	10,670
Financial intermediation	1,041	810	1,851
Real estate, renting and business activities	3,405	2,032	5,437
Public administration and defence; compulsory social security	5,181	2,395	7,576
Education	5,125	8,099	13,224
Health and social work	2,070	2,895	4,965
Other community, social and personal service activities	1,765	7,686	9,451
Households with employed persons	4,474	21,970	26,444
Extra-territorial organizations and bodies	126	—	126
Total employed	346,573	270,993	617,566
Unemployed	90,964	140,778	231,742
Total labour force	437,537	411,771	849,308

Source: ILO.

Mid-2011 (estimates in '000): Agriculture, etc. 353; Total labour force 906 (Source: FAO).

Health and Welfare

KEY INDICATORS

Total fertility rate (children per woman, 2008)	3.3
Under-5 mortality rate (per 1,000 live births, 2008)	79
HIV/AIDS (% of persons aged 15–49, 2007)	23.2
Physicians (per 1,000 head, 2003)	0.05
Hospital beds (per 1,000 head, 2006)	1.30
Health expenditure (2007): US $ per head (PPP)	92
Health expenditure (2007): % of GDP	6.2
Health expenditure (2007): public (% of total)	58.3
Access to water (% of persons, 2008)	85
Access to sanitation (% of persons, 2008)	29
Human Development Index (2010): ranking	141
Human Development Index (2010): value	0.427

For sources and definitions, see explanatory note on p. vi.

Agriculture

PRINCIPAL CROPS
('000 metric tons)

	2007	2008	2009
Wheat	4.0	3.7	7.4
Maize	60.3	59.7	57.1
Sorghum	7.8	10.2	10.2
Potatoes*	93.0	96.5	n.a.
Beans, dry	6.1	3.2	3.5
Peas, dry	1.3	1.0	1.4
Vegetables*	32	35	n.a.

* FAO estimates.
Source: FAO.

LIVESTOCK
('000 head, year ending September)

	2007	2008	2009
Cattle	688	616	616
Sheep	905	1,276	1,401
Goats	879	917	1,009
Pigs	216	95	84
Horses	69	78	75
Asses	172	136	144
Chickens	893	677	716

Source: FAO.

LIVESTOCK PRODUCTS
('000 metric tons, FAO estimates)

	2007	2008	2009
Cattle meat	10.9	11.4	11.4
Cows' milk	31.3	32.5	32.5
Pig meat	9.7	4.0	3.5
Chicken meat	2.3	2.3	2.3
Game meat	4.4	4.5	n.a.
Hen eggs	1.6	1.6	1.7
Wool, greasy	3.9	3.9	n.a.

Source: FAO.

Forestry

ROUNDWOOD REMOVALS
('000 cubic metres, excluding bark, FAO estimates)

	2007	2008	2009
Total (all fuel wood)	2,068.3	2,076.1	2,084.0

Source: FAO.

Fishing

(metric tons, live weight)

	2006	2007	2008
Capture	45	48	50
Common carp	12	16	16
North African catfish	3	2	2
Other freshwater fishes	30	30	32
Aquaculture	2	131	91
Common carp	2	1	1
Rainbow trout	—	130	90
Total catch	47	179	141

Source: FAO.

LESOTHO

Mining

(cubic metres, unless otherwise indicated)

	2006	2007	2008
Fire clay*	15,000	15,000	15,000
Diamond (carats)	231,324	454,014	450,000
Gravel and crushed rock*	300,000	300,000	300,000

* Estimated production.

2009 (estimates): Production assumed to be unchanged from 2008.

Source: US Geological Survey.

Finance

CURRENCY AND EXCHANGE RATES

Monetary Units
100 lisente (singular: sente) = 1 loti (plural: maloti).

Sterling, Dollar and Euro Equivalents (31 December 2010)
£1 sterling = 10.382 maloti;
US $1 = 6.632 maloti;
€1 = 8.861 maloti;
100 maloti = £9.63 = $15.08 = €11.29.

Average Exchange Rate (maloti per US $)
2008 8.2612
2009 8.4737
2010 7.3212

Note: The loti is fixed at par with the South African rand.

BUDGET
(million maloti, year ending 31 March)

Revenue*	2005/06	2006/07	2007/08
Tax revenue	1,696.4	1,840.9	2,232.1
Taxes on net income and profits	920.1	970.7	1,216.4
Company tax	192.0	199.6	293.7
Individual income tax	615.0	629.5	785.4
Other income and profit taxes	113.1	141.7	137.4
Taxes on goods and services	768.4	856.3	1,003.1
Value-added tax	655.7	714.6	847.9
Excise taxes	84.7	65.6	118.1
Other taxes	8.0	13.8	12.5
Non-tax revenue	487.2	561.8	664.2
Sales of goods and services	381.8	388.4	449.7
Water royalties	235.9	262.3	297.4
Property income	24.5	78.2	151.1
Fines and forfeits	6.8	17.1	0.8
Miscellaneous revenue	74.2	78.1	62.6
SACU	2,306.0	3,945.0	4,097.7
Total	**4,489.6**	**6,347.7**	**6,994.0**

Expenditure and net lending	2005/06	2006/07	2007/08
Wages and salaries	1,513.0	1,645.3	1,937.3
Goods and services	1,275.0	1,602.0	1,770.3
Subsidies	—	—	3.4
Interest payments	216.8	308.1	292.5
Grants	502.5	650.0	776.0
Social benefits	148.6	170.9	223.0
Other expenditures	306.2	305.4	332.0
Current transfers	281.3	280.8	289.1
Capital transfers	24.9	24.6	42.8
Total	**3,962.1**	**4,681.7**	**5,334.4**

* Excluding grants received (million maloti): 171.4 in 2005/06; 92.4 in 2006/07; 175.8 in 2007/8.

INTERNATIONAL RESERVES
(excl. gold, US $ million at 31 December)

	2004	2005	2006
IMF special drawing rights	0.62	0.44	0.22
Reserve position in IMF	5.53	5.15	5.45
Foreign exchange	495.35	513.52	652.74
Total	**501.50**	**519.11**	**658.41**

2007 (US $ million at 31 December): IMF special drawing rights 6.28; Reserve position in IMF 5.71.
2008 (US $ million at 31 December): IMF special drawing rights 5.53; Reserve position in IMF 5.57.
2009 (US $ million at 31 December): IMF special drawing rights 49.00; Reserve position in IMF 5.66.

Source: IMF, *International Financial Statistics*.

MONEY SUPPLY
(million maloti at 31 December)

	2007	2008	2009
Currency outside depository corporations	2,651.35	3,475.32	3,692.06
Transferable deposits	339.31	402.08	487.18
Other deposits	1,090.79	1,006.16	1,567.63
Broad money	**4,081.46**	**4,883.56**	**5,746.87**

Source: IMF, *International Financial Statistics*.

COST OF LIVING
(Consumer Price Index; base: April 1997 = 100)

	2007	2008	2009
Food (incl. non-alcoholic beverages)	231.5	267.7	291.4
Alcoholic beverages and tobacco	224.5	236.6	253.1
Housing, water, electricity, and other fuels	207.3	237.8	239.8
Clothing (incl. footwear)	162.0	172.4	182.2
All items (incl. others)	**200.8**	**222.3**	**238.2**

NATIONAL ACCOUNTS
(million maloti at current prices)

Expenditure on the Gross Domestic Product

	2007	2008	2009
Government final consumption expenditure	4,097	5,190	6,291
Private final consumption expenditure	10,901	12,450	13,911
Changes in inventories	145	35	—
Gross fixed capital formation	3,133	3,602	4,425
Total domestic expenditure	**18,276**	**21,277**	**24,627**
Exports of goods and services	6,138	7,546	7,021
Less Imports of goods and services	13,297	15,545	17,436
Statistical discrepancy	11	−103	—
GDP in purchasers' values	**11,128**	**13,175**	**14,212**

LESOTHO

Gross Domestic Product by Economic Activity

	2007	2008	2009
Agriculture	819	933	1,040
Mining and quarrying	820	1,198	1,016
Manufacturing	2,014	2,258	2,101
Electricity, gas and water	478	502	572
Construction	460	532	650
Wholesale and retail trade, restaurants and hotels	891	1,039	1,116
Transport and communication	662	766	883
Finance, insurance, real estate and business services	1,997	2,390	2,587
Public administration and defence	1,128	1,335	1,528
Other services	1,269	1,623	1,880
Sub-total	10,538	12,576	13,373
Less Imputed bank service charge	170	277	297
Indirect taxes, less subsidies	760	878	1,137
GDP in purchasers' prices	11,128	13,175	14,212

Source: African Development Bank.

BALANCE OF PAYMENTS
(US $ million)

	2007	2008	2009
Exports of goods f.o.b.	805.0	882.4	715.9
Imports of goods f.o.b.	−1,604.4	−1,650.3	−1,667.6
Trade balance	−799.4	−768.0	−951.7
Exports of services	76.2	57.9	72.9
Imports of services	−110.2	−111.1	−124.3
Balance on goods and services	−833.3	−821.2	−1,003.1
Other income received	525.2	536.8	479.0
Other income paid	−97.1	−29.5	−55.2
Balance on goods, services and income	−405.3	−313.9	−579.3
Current transfers received	628.7	519.4	551.7
Current transfers paid	−3.6	−4.0	−4.5
Current balance	219.8	201.5	−32.0
Capital account (net)	32.0	23.6	79.6
Direct investment from abroad	130.3	72.4	62.9
Other investment assets	−62.2	−75.3	−9.9
Other investment liabilities	17.3	22.4	67.2
Net errors and omissions	−67.4	28.8	−195.2
Overall balance	269.9	273.4	−27.5

Source: IMF, *International Financial Statistics*.

External Trade

PRINCIPAL COMMODITIES

Imports c.i.f. (US $ million)	2002	2003	2004
Food and live animals	142.7	179.1	183.1
Beverages and tobacco	32.3	28.2	26.2
Crude materials, inedible except fuels	13.2	18.5	18.2
Mineral fuels and lubricants	61.7	71.7	89.0
Animal and vegetable oils, fats and waxes	9.8	7.7	8.3
Chemicals and related products	99.2	83.3	66.8
Manufactured goods	186.1	283.4	287.5
Machinery and transport equipment	98.3	135.6	146.2
Miscellaneous manufactured articles	115.8	188.8	143.5
Total (incl. others)	799.6	1,115.0	1,399.4

Exports (million maloti)	2005	2006	2007
Foodstuffs, etc.	61.4	72.9	89.3
Cereals	6.2	6.8	7.5
Beverages and tobacco	50.4	61.2	74.6
Live animals	3.3	1.3	3.4
Livestock materials	12.1	7.9	10.5
Wool	10.3	6.1	7.4
Manufactures	3,565.7	4,039.7	4,75.7
Chemicals and petroleum	13.2	15.6	18.6
Telecommunication equipment	70.5	72.3	74.5
Machinery	12.3	8.8	10.2
Furniture and parts	2.3	5.6	6.2
Clothing, etc.	3,355.5	3,841.1	4,015.2
Footwear	65.8	60.2	85.6
Other manufactures	12.9	13.3	38.9
Total (incl. others)	4,138.1	4,736.7	5,663.8

Sources: UN, *International Trade Statistics Yearbook*; IMF, *Kingdom of Lesotho: Statistical Appendix* (January 2010).

Imports (2005, million maloti): Food and beverages 2,180; Industrial supplies 3,128; Fuels and lubricants 408; Machinery and other capital equipment 572; Parts and accessories 169; Transport equipment 321; Parts and accessories for transport equipment 232; Total (incl. others) 9,252.

PRINCIPAL TRADING PARTNERS
(million maloti)

Imports c.i.f.*	2005	2006	2007
Africa	7,709.9	8,574.3	10,473.7
SACU†	7,665.2	8,524.6	10,613.0
Asia	1,315.3	1,462.8	1,786.8
China, People's Repub.	238.9	265.7	324.5
Hong Kong	386.3	429.6	524.8
Taiwan	448.4	498.7	609.2
European Union	61.5	68.4	83.6
North America	38.1	42.3	51.7
USA	31.8	35.4	43.2
Total (incl. others)	9,135.7	10,160.0	12,420.7

Exports f.o.b.	2005	2006	2007
Africa	813.3	930.9	1,113.1
SACU†	714.2	817.5	1,077.5
European Union	711.0	813.8	973.1
North America	2,600.0	2,976.1	3,558.6
Canada	56.1	64.3	76.8
USA	2,543.8	2,911.8	3,381.7
Total (incl. others)	4,138.1	4,736.7	5,663.8

* Valuation exclusive of import duties. Figures also exclude donated food.
† Southern African Customs Union, of which Lesotho is a member; also including Botswana, Namibia, South Africa and Swaziland.

Source: IMF, *Kingdom of Lesotho: Statistical Appendix* (January 2010).

Transport

ROAD TRAFFIC
(motor vehicles in use at 31 December, estimates)

	1994	1995	1996
Passenger cars	9,900	11,160	12,610
Lorries and vans	20,790	22,310	25,000

Source: International Road Federation, *World Road Statistics*.

LESOTHO

CIVIL AVIATION
(traffic on scheduled services)

	1997	1998	1999
Kilometres flown (million)	0	1	0
Passengers carried ('000)	10	28	1
Passenger-km (million)	3	9	0
Total ton-km (million)	0	1	0

Source: UN, *Statistical Yearbook*.

Tourism

FOREIGN TOURIST ARRIVALS BY COUNTRY OF RESIDENCE

	2006	2007	2008
Botswana	1,903	1,679	1,796
Germany	5,901	5,778	3,349
South Africa	318,458	261,099	246,014
Swaziland	1,506	1,246	1,233
United Kingdom	4,937	4,168	2,245
USA	1,878	621	1,311
Zimbabwe	3,899	3,457	4,149
Total (incl. others)	356,913	300,350	293,073

Tourism receipts (US $ million, excl. passenger transport): 27 in 2006; 43 in 2007; 34 in 2008.

Source: World Tourism Organization.

Communications Media

	2007	2008	2009
Telephones ('000 main lines in use)	47.6	41.2	40.0
Mobile cellular telephones ('000 subscribers)	456.0	593.2	661.0
Internet users ('000)	70.0	73.3	76.8
Broadband subscribers	100	100	400

Personal computers: 5,000 (2.5 per 1,000 persons) in 2005.
Radio receivers ('000 in use): 104 in 1997.
Television receivers ('000 in use): 70 in 2001.
Non-daily newspapers (1996): 7 (average circulation 74,000 copies).
Sources: UNESCO Institute for Statistics; International Telecommunication Union.

Education

(2006/07, unless otherwise indicated)

	Institutions	Teachers	Males	Females	Total
Primary	1,455*	10,841	202,710	198,233	400,943
Secondary:					
general	240*	5,837	42,357	55,579	97,936
technical and vocational	8†	200	724	804	1,528*
teacher training	1†	108‡	n.a.	n.a.	2,335§
University	1†	638*	3,810*	4,690*	8,500*

* 2005/06.
† 2002/03.
‡ 2001/02.
§ 2004/05.

Source: partly UNESCO Institute for Statistics.

Pupil-teacher ratio (primary education, UNESCO estimate): 37.0 in 2006/07 (Source: UNESCO Institute for Statistics).

Adult literacy rate (UNESCO estimates): 89.5% (males 82.6%; females 95.1%) in 2008 (Source: UNESCO Institute for Statistics).

Directory

The Government

HEAD OF STATE

King: HM King LETSIE III (acceded to the throne 7 February 1996).

CABINET
(May 2011)

Prime Minister and Minister of Defence and National Security: BETHUEL PAKALITHA MOSISILI.
Deputy Prime Minister and Minister of Home Affairs and Public Safety and Parliamentary Affairs: ARCHIBALD LESAO LEHOHLA.
Minister of Natural Resources (Water, Lesotho Water Highlands Project, Energy and Mining): MONYANE MOLELEKI.
Minister of Gender, Youth, Sports and Recreation: 'MATHABISO LEPONO.
Minister of Foreign Affairs and International Relations: MOHLABI KENNETH TSEKOA.
Minister of Local Government and Chieftainship: Dr PONTŠO SUZAN 'MATUMELO SEKATLE.
Minister of Finance and Development Planning: Dr TIMOTHY THAHANE.
Minister of Education and Training: Dr 'MAMPHONO KHAKETLA.
Minister of Agriculture and Food Security: RALECHATE MOKOSE.
Minister of Justice, Human Rights and Correctional Services, Law and Constitutional Affairs: MPEO MAHASE-MOILOA.
Minister of Communications, Science and Technology: MOTHEJOA METSING.
Minister of Public Service: SEMANO SEKATLE.
Minister of Health and Social Welfare: Dr MPHU RAMATLAPENG.
Minister of Public Works and Transport: TS'ELE CHAKELA.
Minister of Trade, Industry, Co-operatives and Marketing: Dr LEKETEKETE KETSO.
Minister of Tourism, Environment and Culture: 'MANNETE RAMAILI.
Minister of Employment and Labour: 'MAPHOKA MOTOBOLI.
Minister of Forestry and Land Reclamation: KABELO MAFURA.

There were also four assistant ministers.

MINISTRIES

Office of the Prime Minister: POB 527, Maseru 100; tel. 22311000; fax 22320662; internet www.lesotho.gov.ls.
Ministry of Agriculture and Food Security: POB 24, Maseru 100; tel. 22316407; fax 22310186; e-mail minagric@leo.co.ls.
Ministry of Communications, Science and Technology: Moposo House, 3rd Floor, POB 36, Maseru 100; tel. 22324715; fax 22325682; e-mail m.makhorole@mcst.gov.ls.
Ministry of Defence and National Security: POB 527, Maseru 100; tel. 22311000; fax 22310518; e-mail nmokatsa@yahoo.co.uk.

LESOTHO

Ministry of Education and Training: POB 47, Maseru 100; tel. 22317900; fax 22326119; e-mail letsoelam@education.gov.ls; internet www.education.gov.ls.

Ministry of Employment and Labour: Private Bag A1164, Maseru 100; tel. 22322602; fax 22325163; e-mail infolabour@leo.co.ls; internet www.labour.gov.ls.

Ministry of Finance and Development Planning: POB 395, Maseru 100; tel. 22311101; e-mail hmf@finance.gov.ls; internet www.finance.gov.ls.

Ministry of Foreign Affairs and International Relations: POB 1387, Maseru 100; tel. 22311150; fax 22310178; e-mail information@foreign.gov.ls; internet www.foreign.gov.ls.

Ministry of Forestry and Land Reclamation: POB 92, Maseru 100; tel. 22313057; fax 22310515; e-mail lincmox@ilesotho.com.

Ministry of Gender, Youth, Sports and Recreation: POB 729, Maseru 100; tel. and fax 22311006; e-mail honsec@mgysr.gov.ls.

Ministry of Health and Social Welfare: POB 514, Maseru 100; tel. 22317707; fax 22321014; e-mail lesenyehom@health.gov.ls; internet www.health.gov.ls.

Ministry of Home Affairs and Public Safety and Parliamentary Affairs: POB 174, Maseru 100; tel. 22320017; fax 22310013; e-mail mohonoel@homeaffairs.gov.ls.

Ministry of Justice, Human Rights and Correctional Services, Law and Constitutional Affairs: POB 402, Maseru 100; tel. 22322683; fax 22311092; e-mail dps@justice.gov.ls; internet www.justice.gov.ls.

Ministry of Local Government and Chieftainship: POB 686, Maseru 100; tel. 22323415; fax 22327782; e-mail minmolg@leo.co.ls; internet www.localgovt.gov.ls.

Ministry of Natural Resources: POB 772, Maseru 100; tel. 22323163; fax 22310527.

Ministry of Public Service: POB 228, Maseru 100; tel. 22315946; fax 22310883; e-mail minister@mps.gov.ls.

Ministry of Public Works and Transport: POB 20, Maseru 100; tel. 22324697; fax 22310658; e-mail cio@mopwt.gov.ls.

Ministry of Tourism, Environment and Culture: POB 52, Maseru 100; tel. 22313034; fax 22310194; e-mail pmasita.mohale@mtec.gov.ls; internet www.mtec.gov.ls.

Ministry of Trade, Industry, Co-operatives and Marketing: POB 747, Maseru 100; tel. 22312938; fax 22310644; e-mail mafura@mticm.gov.ls; internet www.trade.gov.ls.

Legislature

PARLIAMENT

National Assembly

POB 190, Maseru; tel. 22323035; fax 22310023; internet www.parliament.ls/TheNationalAssembly/About.aspx.

Speaker: NTLHOI MOTSAMAI.

General Election, 17 February 2007

Party	Constituency seats	Compensatory seats*	Total seats
Lesotho Congress for Democracy	61	—	61
National Independent Party	—	21	21
All Basotho Convention	17	—	17
Lesotho Workers' Party	—	10	10
Basotho National Party	—	3	3
Alliance of Congress Parties	1	1	2
Basotho Batho Democratic Party	—	1	1
Basotho Congress Party	—	1	1
Basotho Democratic National Party	—	1	1
Maremaltou Freedom Party	—	1	1
Popular Front for Democracy	—	1	1
Total	**79†**	**40**	**119†**

* Allocated by proportional representation.
† Voting in Makhaleng constituency was postponed, owing to the death of a candidate. The Lesotho Congress for Democracy secured the seat at a by-election held on 30 June 2007.

Senate

POB 553, Maseru 100; tel. 22315338; fax 22310023; internet www.parliament.ls/Senate/AboutSenate.aspx.

Speaker: Chief SEMPE LEJAHA.

The Senate is an advisory chamber, comprising 22 traditional chiefs and 11 members appointed by the monarch.

Election Commission

Independent Electoral Commission (IEC): Moposo House, 7th Floor, POB 12698, Kingsway 100, Maseru; tel. 22314991; fax 22310398; internet www.iec.org.ls; f. 1997 as successor to the Constituency Delimitation Commission; Chair. LIMAKATSO MOKHOTHU.

Political Organizations

All Basotho Convention (ABC): Maseru; f. 2006 by fmr mems of the Lesotho Congress for Democracy; Pres. MOTSOAHAE TOM THABANE.

Basotho Batho Democratic Party: f. 2006.

Basotho Democratic Alliance (BDA): Maseru; f. 1984; Pres. S. C. NKOJANE.

Basotho Democratic National Party: e-mail joangmolapo@hotmail.com; internet bdnp.blogspot.com; f. 2006; Leader THABANG NYEOE; Sec.-Gen. PELELE LETSOALA.

Basotho National Party (BNP): POB 124, Maseru 100; f. 1958; Leader THESELE MASERIBANE; Sec.-Gen. RANTHOMENG MATETE; 280,000 mems.

Basutoland African Congress (BAC): Maseru; f. 2002 following split in the BCP; Leader Dr KHAUHELO RADITAPOLE; Sec.-Gen. MOHOPLO MACHELI.

Basutoland Congress Party (BCP): POB 111, Maseru 100; tel. 8737076; f. 1952; Leader THULO MAHLAKENG.

Khokanyana-Phiri Democratic Alliance: Maseru; f. 1999; alliance of opposition parties comprising:

Christian Democratic Party: Maseru.

Communist Party of Lesotho (CPL): Maseru; f. 1962; banned 1970–91; supported mainly by migrant workers employed in South Africa; Sec.-Gen. MOKHAFISI KENA.

Kopanang Basotho Party (KBP): Maseru; f. 1992; campaigns for women's rights; Leader LIMAKATSO NTAKATSANE.

National Independent Party (NIP): Maseru; f. 1984; Pres. ANTHONY CLOVIS MANYELI.

National Progressive Party (NPP): Maseru; f. 1995 following split in the BNP; Leader Chief PEETE NKOEBE PEETE.

Popular Front for Democracy (PFD): Maseru; f. 1991; leftwing; Leader LEKHETHO RAKUOANE.

Social Democratic Party: Maseru; Leader MASITISE SELESO.

Lesotho Congress for Democracy (LCD): POB 7, Mohole's Hoek; tel. 785207; f. 1997 as a result of divisions within the BCP; Leader BETHUEL PAKALITHA MOSISILI; Chair. MOEKETSI MOLETSANE; Sec.-Gen. MPHO MALIE; 200,000 mems.

Lesotho Labour Party (LLP): Maseru; f. 1991; Leader MUTHUTHULEZI TYHALI.

Lesotho People's Congress (LPC): f. 2001 following split in the LCD; Leader KELEBONE ALBERT MAOPE; Sec.-Gen. SHAKHANE MOKHEHLE.

Lesotho Workers' Party (LWP): Maseru; f. 2001; Leader MACAEFA BILLY.

Maremaltou Freedom Party (MFP): POB 0443, Maseru 105; tel. 315804; f. 1962 following merger between the Marema Tlou Party and Basutoland Freedom Party; Leader MOEKETSE MALEBO; Dep. Leader THABO LEANYA; 300,000 mems.

Sefate Democratic Union (SDU): Maseru; Leader BOFIHLA NKUEBE.

Senkatana Party: Maseru; f. 2009; breakaway party from the All Basotho Convention (ABC); Leader LEHLOHONOLO TS'EHLANA; Sec.-Gen. KARABO THLOELI.

United Democratic Party (UDP): POB 776, Maseru 100; f. 1967; Chair. BEN L. SHEA; Leader CHARLES DABENDE MOFELI; Sec.-Gen. MOLOMO NKUEBE; 26,000 mems.

United Party (UP): Maseru; Pres. MAKARA SEKAUTU.

LESOTHO

Diplomatic Representation

EMBASSIES AND HIGH COMMISSIONS IN LESOTHO

China, People's Republic: POB 380, Maseru 100; tel. 22316521; fax 22310489; e-mail chinaemb_ls@mfa.gov.cn; internet ls.china-embassy.org; Ambassador Hu Dingxian.
Ireland: Tona-Kholo Rd, Private Bag A67, Maseru 100; tel. 22314068; fax 22310028; e-mail maseruembassy@dfa.ie; internet www.embassyofireland.org.ls; Ambassador Gerry Gervin.
Libya: 173 Tona-Kholo Rd, Maseru West, POB 432, Maseru 100; tel. 22320148; fax 22327750; Ambassador Dr Yousef Algowizy.
South Africa: Lesotho Bank Tower, 10th Floor, Kingsway, Private Bag A266, Maseru 100; tel. 22315758; fax 22310128; e-mail sahcmas@lesoff.co.ls; High Commissioner Happy Mahlangu.
USA: 254 Kingsway, POB 333, Maseru 100; tel. 22312666; fax 22310116; e-mail infomaseru@state.gov; internet maseru.usembassy.gov; Ambassador Michele Thoren Bond.

Judicial System

HIGH COURT

The High Court is a superior court of record, and in addition to any other jurisdiction conferred by statute it is vested with unlimited original jurisdiction to determine any civil or criminal matter. It also has appellate jurisdiction to hear appeals and reviews from the subordinate courts. Appeals may be made to the Court of Appeal.
POB 90, Maseru; tel. 22312188; internet www.justice.gov.ls/judiciary/high_court.html.
Chief Justice: Mahapela Lehohla.
Judges: T. Nomngcongo, W. C. M. Maqutu, T. E. Monapathi, L. Chaka-Makhooane, G. Mofolo, S. Peete, M. Hlajoane, N. Majara, A. M. Hlajoane, M. Mahase.

COURT OF APPEAL

POB 90, Maseru; tel. 22312188; internet www.justice.gov.ls/judiciary/appeal.html.
President: (vacant).
Judges: John Smallberger, Hein Grosskopf, Graig Howie (acting), Geremy Gauntlett, Lionel Melunsky, Douglas Graham Scott.

SUBORDINATE COURTS

Each of the 10 districts possesses subordinate courts, presided over by magistrates.
Chief Magistrate: Molefi Makara.

JUDICIAL COMMISSIONERS' COURTS

These courts hear civil and criminal appeals from central and local courts. Further appeal may be made to the High Court and finally to the Court of Appeal.

CENTRAL AND LOCAL COURTS

There are 71 such courts, of which 58 are local courts and 13 are central courts which also serve as courts of appeal from the local courts. They have limited civil and criminal jurisdiction.

Religion

About 90% of the population profess Christianity.

CHRISTIANITY

African Federal Church Council (AFCC): POB 70, Peka 340; f. 1927; co-ordinating org. for 48 African independent churches.
Christian Council of Lesotho (CCL): POB 547, Maseru 100; tel. 22313639; fax 22310310; f. 1833; 112 congregations; 261,350 mems (2003); Chair. Rev. M. Mokhosi; Sec. Catherine Ramokhele.

The Anglican Communion

Anglicans in Lesotho are adherents of the Anglican Church of Southern Africa (formerly the Church of the Province of Southern Africa). The Metropolitan of the Province is the Archbishop of Cape Town, South Africa. Lesotho forms a single diocese, with an estimated 200,000 members.
Bishop of Lesotho: Mallane Adam Taaso, Bishop's House, POB 87, Maseru 100; tel. 22311974; fax 22310161; e-mail diocese@ilesotho.com.

The Roman Catholic Church

Lesotho comprises one archdiocese and three dioceses. Some 52% of the total population are Roman Catholics.

Lesotho Catholic Bishops' Conference

Catholic Secretariat, POB 200, Maseru 100; tel. 22312525; fax 22310294.
f. 1972; Pres. Rt Rev. Evaristus Thatho Bitsoane (Bishop of Qacha's Nek).
Archbishop of Maseru: Most Rev. Gerard Tlali Lerotholi, Archbishop's House, 19 Orpen Rd, POB 267, Maseru 100; tel. 22312565; fax 22310425; e-mail archmase@lesoff.co.za.

Other Christian Churches

At mid-2000 there were an estimated 279,000 Protestants and 257,000 adherents professing other forms of Christianity.
African Methodist Episcopal Church: POB 223, Maseru 100; tel. 22311801; fax 22310548; e-mail bishopsarah@leo.co.ls; f. 1903; Presiding Prelate Rt Rev. Sarah F. Davis; 15,000 mems.
Lesotho Evangelical Church: POB 260, Maseru 100; tel. 22323942; f. 1833; independent since 1964; Pres. Rev. John Rapelang Mokhahlane; Exec. Sec. Rev. A. M. Thebe; 230,000 mems (2003).

Other denominations active in Lesotho include the Apostolic Faith Mission, the Assemblies of God, the Dutch Reformed Church in Africa, the Full Gospel Church of God, Methodist Church of Southern Africa and the Seventh-day Adventists. There are also numerous African independent churches.

BAHÁ'Í FAITH

National Spiritual Assembly of the Bahá'ís of Lesotho: POB 508, Maseru 100; tel. 22312346; e-mail bahailesotho@leo.co.ls.

The Press

Lesotho does not have a daily newspaper.
Leseli ka Sepolesa (The Police Witness): Press Dept, Police Headquarters, Maseru CBD, POB 13, Maseru 100; tel. 22317262; fax 22310045; fortnightly; Sesotho; publ. by the Lesotho Mounted Police Services; Editor-in-Chief Clifford Molefe.
Leselinyana la Lesotho (Light of Lesotho): Morija Printing Works, POB 7, Morija 190; tel. 22360244; fax 22360005; e-mail mpw@lesoff.co.ls; f. 1863; fortnightly; Sesotho, with occasional articles in English; publ. by the Lesotho Evangelical Church; Editor Selborne Motlatsi Mohlalisi; circ. 10,000.
Lesotho Times: Maseru; tel. 22315335; fax 22315352; e-mail editor@lestimes.co.ls; internet www.lestimes.com.
Lesotho Today/Lentsoe la Basotho (Voice of the Lesotho Nation): POB 353, Maseru 100; tel. 22323561; fax 22322764; internet www.lesothotoday.co.ls; f. 1974; weekly; Sesotho; publ. by Ministry of Communications, Science and Technology; Editor Kahliso Lesenyane; circ. 14,000.
Makatolle: POB 111, Maseru 100; tel. 22850990; f. 1963; weekly; Sesotho; Editor M. Ramangoei; circ. 2,000.
MoAfrika: MoAfrika Broadcasting and Publishing Services, Carlton Centre Bldg, 1st Floor, POB 7234, Maseru 100; tel. 22321854; fax 22321956; f. 1990 as *The African*; weekly; Sesotho and English; Editor-in-Chief Prof. Sebononola R. K. Ramainoane; circ. 5,000.
Moeletsi oa Basotho: Mazenod Institute, POB 18, Mazenod 160; tel. 22350465; fax 22350010; e-mail mzpwrks@lesoff.co.za; f. 1933; weekly; Sesotho; publ. by the Roman Catholic Church; Editor Francis Khoaripe; circ. 20,000.
Mohahlaula: Allied Bldg, 1st Floor, Manonyane Centre, POB 14430, Maseru 100; tel. 22312777; fax 22320941; weekly; Sesotho; publ. by Makaung Printers and Publrs; Editor Willy Mollungoa.
Moloi: Cooperatives Bldg, Main North 1 Rd, POB 9933, Maseru 100; tel. 22312287; fax 22327912; f. 1997; Sesotho; organ of the Lesotho Congress for Democracy; Editor (vacant).
Mopheme (The Survivor): Allied Bldg, 1st Floor, Manonyane Centre, POB 14184, Maseru; tel. and fax 22311670; e-mail mopheme@lesoff.co.za; weekly; English and Sesotho; publ. by Newsshare Foundation; Owner and Editor Lawrence Keketso; circ. 2,500.
Public Eye/Mosotho: House No. 14A3, Princess Margaret Rd, POB 14129, Old Europa, Maseru 100; tel. 22321414; fax 22310614; e-mail editor@publiceye.co.ls; internet www.publiceye.co.ls; f. 1997; weekly; 80% English, 20% Sesotho; publ. by Voice Multimedia; also publ. *Eye on Tourism* and *Family Mirror* magazines; Editor-in-Chief Bethuel Thai; circ. 20,000 (Lesotho and South Africa).
Southern Star: POB 7590, Maseru; tel. 22312269; fax 22310167; e-mail ba-holdings@ilesotho.com; weekly; English; Editor Frank Boffoe; circ. 1,500.

PERIODICALS

Justice and Peace: Catholic Bishops' Conference, Our Lady of Victories Cathedral Catholic Centre, POB 200, Maseru 100; tel. 22312750; fax 22312751; quarterly; publ. by the Roman Catholic Church.

Moqolotsi (The Journalist): House No. 1B, Happy Villa, POB 14139, Maseru 100; tel. and fax 22320941; e-mail medinles@lesoff.co.za; monthly newsletter; English; publ. by the Media Institute of Lesotho (MILES).

NGO Web: 544 Hoohlo Extension, Florida, Maseru 100; tel. 22325798; fax 22317205; e-mail lecongo@lecongo.org.ls; quarterly; English and Sesotho; publ. of the Lesotho Council of NGOs; circ. 2,000.

Review of Southern African Studies: Institute of Southern African Studies, National University of Lesotho, PO Roma 180; tel. 22340247; fax 22340601; 2 a year; arts, social and behavioural sciences; Editor TANKIE KHALANYANE.

Shoeshoe: POB 36, Maseru 100; tel. 22323561; fax 22310003; quarterly; women's interest; publ. by Ministry of Communications, Science and Technology.

Other publications include *Mara LDF Airwing/Airsquadron* and *The Sun/Thebe*.

NEWS AGENCY

Lesotho News Agency (LENA): Lesotho News Agency Complex, Lerotholi St, opp. Royal Palace, POB 36, Maseru 100; tel. 22325317; fax 22324608; e-mail l_lenanews@hotmail.com; internet www.lena.gov.ls; f. 1985; Dir R. PHANGWA; Editor VIOLET MARAISANE.

Publishers

Longman Lesotho (Pty) Ltd: 104 Christie House, 1st Floor, Orpen Rd, Old Europa, POB 1174, Maseru 100; tel. 22314254; fax 22310118; e-mail connie.burford@pearsoned.com; Man. Dir SEYMOUR R. KIKINE.

Macmillan Boleswa Publishers Lesotho (Pty) Ltd: 523 Sun Cabanas Hotel, POB 7545, Maseru 100; tel. 22317340; fax 22310047; e-mail macmillan@lesoff.co.ls; Man. Dir PAUL MOROLONG.

Mazenod Institute: POB 39, Mazenod 160; tel. 22350224; f. 1933; Roman Catholic; Man. Fr B. MOHLALISI.

Morija Sesuto Book Depot: POB 4, Morija 190; tel. and fax 22360204; f. 1862; owned by the Lesotho Evangelical Church; religious, educational and Sesotho language and literature.

St Michael's Mission: The Social Centre, POB 25, Roma; tel. 22316234; f. 1968; religious and educational; Man. Dir Fr M. FERRANGE.

GOVERNMENT PUBLISHING HOUSE

Government Printer: POB 268, Maseru; tel. 22313023.

Broadcasting and Communications

TELECOMMUNICATIONS

Lesotho Communications Authority (LCA): Moposo House, 6th Floor, Kingsway Rd, POB 15896, Maseru 100; tel. 22224300; fax 22310984; e-mail lca@lca.org.ls; internet www.lca.org.ls; f. 2000; regulates telecommunications and broadcasting; Chief Exec. MONEHELA POSHOLI.

Telecom Lesotho: POB 1037, Maseru 100; tel. 22211000; fax 22310600; e-mail enquiries@telecom.co.ls; internet www.telecom.co.ls; 70% holding acquired by the Econet Wireless Group in 2007; 30% state-owned; Chair. PAKO PETLANE; CEO ANTHONY CARTER.

Vodacom Lesotho (Pty) Ltd: Block B, Development House, Kingsway Rd, POB 7387, Maseru 100; tel. 52212201; fax 22311079; internet www.vodacom.co.ls; f. 1996; jt venture between Telecom Lesotho and Vodacom (Pty) Ltd; fmrly VCL Communications; mobile cellular telecommunications provider; CEO PIETER UYS.

BROADCASTING

RADIO

The first licences for private radio stations were issued in 1998. Licences are issued by the Lesotho Telecommunications Authority. Radio Lesotho is the only station to broadcast nationwide; all the other stations are restricted to urban areas and their peripheries.

Catholic Radio FM: Our Lady of Victories Cathedral, Catholic Centre POB 200, Maseru 100; tel. 22323247; fax 22310294; f. 1999.

Harvest FM: Carlton Centre, 3rd Floor, Room No. 312, POB 442, Maseru 100; tel. 22313168; fax 22313858; e-mail mlekhoaba@harvestfm.co.ls; internet www.harvestfm.co.ls; operated by Harvest FM Trust; affiliated to United Christian Broadcasters Africa, South Africa; evangelical religious programming; Station Man. MARY MOSHOESHOE.

Joy FM: Lesotho Sun Hotel, Suites 2204–2206, Private Bag A457, Maseru 100; tel. 22310920; fax 22310104; internet www.joyfm.co.ls; f. 2001; Sesotho and English; relays Voice of America broadcasts.

Khotso FM: Institute of Extramural Studies, National University of Lesotho POB 180, Roma; Private Bag A47, Maseru 100; tel. 22322038; fax 22340000; community radio station; sister station of DOPE FM (f. 2004).

MoAfrika FM: Carlton Centre, 2nd Floor, Kingsway, POB 7234, Maseru 100; tel. and fax 22321956; e-mail info@moafrika.co.ls; internet www.moafrika.co.ls; affiliated to the *MoAfrika* newspaper; Sesotho, Xhosa and Mandarin; news and entertainment; Man. and Editor-in-Chief Prof. SEBONONOLA R. K. RAMAINOANE.

People's Choice Radio (PCFM): LNDC Centre, Development House, Level 9, Block D, POB 8800, Maseru 100; tel. 22322122; fax 22310888; internet www.pcfm.co.ls; f. 1998; news and entertainment; Man. Dir MOTLATSI MAJARA.

Radio Lesotho: Lesotho News Agency Complex, Lerotholi St, opp. Royal Palace, POB 36, Maseru 100; tel. and fax 22322714; e-mail enquiries@africanextension.com; internet www.radiolesotho.co.ls; f. 1964; state-owned; part of Lesotho Nat. Broadcasting Services; Sesotho and English; Dir of Broadcasting LEBOHANG DADA MOQASA.

TELEVISION

Lesotho Television (LTV): Lesotho News Agency Complex, Lerotholi St, opp. Royal Palace, POB 36, Maseru 100; tel. 22324735; fax 22310149; e-mail mfalatsa@yahoo.com; f. 1988 in association with M-Net, South Africa; state-owned; part of Lesotho Nat. Broadcasting Services; Sesotho and English.

Finance

(cap. = capital; res = reserves; dep. = deposits; m. = million; brs = branches; amounts in maloti)

BANKING

In 2008 there were four commercial banks in Lesotho.

Central Bank

Central Bank of Lesotho: cnr Airport and Moshoeshoe Rds, POB 1184, Maseru 100; tel. 22314281; fax 22310051; e-mail cbl@centralbank.org.ls; internet www.centralbank.org.ls; f. 1978 as the Lesotho Monetary Authority; present name adopted in 1982; bank of issue; cap. 25.0m., res 1,479.1m., dep. 5,093.2m. (Dec. 2009); Gov. and Chair. Dr M. SENAOANA.

Commercial Banks

First National Bank Lesotho: POB 11902, Maseru 100; tel. 22222200; f. 2004; CEO J. JORDAAN; 1 br.

Lesotho PostBank (LPB): Oblate House, Kingsway Rd, Private Bag A121, Maseru 100; tel. 22317842; fax 22313170; e-mail info@lpb.co.ls; internet www.lpb.co.ls; f. 2004; state-owned; Chair. TŠELISO MOKELA; CEO MPHO VUMBUKANI; 12 brs.

Nedbank (Lesotho) Ltd: 115–117 Griffith Hill, Kingsway St, POB 1001, Maseru 100; tel. 22312696; fax 22310025; e-mail georgego@nedcor.co.za; internet www.nedbank.co.ls; f. 1997; fmrly Standard Chartered Bank Lesotho Ltd; 100% owned by Nedbank Ltd (South Africa); cap. 20m., res 205m., dep. 1,969m. (Dec. 2009); Chair. SOPHIA MOHAPI; Man. Dir LAZARUS MURAHWA; 3 brs and 7 agencies.

Standard Lesotho Bank: Banking Bldg, 1st Floor, Kingsway Rd, Kingsway Town Centre, POB 1053, Maseru 100; tel. 22315737; fax 22317321; internet www.standardbank.co.ls; f. 2006 following merger between Lesotho Bank (1999) Ltd (f. 1972) and Standard Bank Lesotho Ltd (fmrly Stanbic Bank Lesotho Ltd); Chair. THABO MAKEBA; Man. Dir COLIN ADDIS; 11 brs.

INSURANCE

In 2008 there were five insurance companies in Lesotho.

Alliance Insurance Co Ltd: Alliance House, 4 Bowker Rd, POB 01118, Maseru West 105; tel. 22312357; fax 22310313; e-mail alliance@alliance.co.ls; internet www.alliance.co.ls; f. 1993; life and short-term insurance; Man. Dir ROB DUNCAN; Gen. Mans MOK'HAPHEK'HA LAZARO, THABISO MADIBA.

Lesotho National General Insurance Co Ltd (LNIG): Lesotho Insurance House, Kingsway, Private Bag A65, Maseru 100; tel. 22313031; fax 22310007; e-mail manager@lngic.com; f. 1977 as Lesotho National Insurance Group; 60% owned by Regent Insurance Co Ltd (South Africa), 20% state-owned, 20% owned by Molepe

LESOTHO

Investment Holdings (Pty) Ltd; part-privatized in 1995; incorporating subsidiaries specializing in life and short-term insurance; Chair. Dr TIMOTHY THAHANE; Man. Dir R. J. LETSOELA.

Metropolitan Lesotho Ltd: Metropolitan Bldg, Kingsway St, POB 645, Maseru 100; tel. 22222300; fax 22317278; internet www.metropolitan.co.ls; f. 2003; subsidiary of Metropolitan Holdings Ltd, South Africa; Man. Dir NKAU MATETE.

Trade and Industry

GOVERNMENT AGENCIES

Privatisation Unit: Privatisation Project, Lesotho Utilities Sector Reform Project, Ministry of Finance and Development Planning, Lesotho Bank Mortgage Division Bldg, 2nd Floor, Kingsway St, Private Bag A249, Maseru 100; tel. 22317902; fax 22317551; e-mail mntsasa@privatisation.gov.ls; internet www.privatisation.gov.ls; CEO MOSITO KHETHISA.

Trade Promotion Unit: c/o Ministry of Trade, Industry, Co-operatives and Marketing, POB 747, Maseru 100; tel. 322138; fax 310121; e-mail tradepu@lesoff.co.za.

DEVELOPMENT ORGANIZATIONS

Basotho Enterprises Development Corpn (BEDCO): POB 1216, Maseru 100; tel. 22312094; fax 22310455; e-mail admin@bedco.org.ls; internet www.bedco.org.ls; f. 1980; promotes and assists in the establishment and devt of Basotho-owned enterprises, with emphasis on small- and medium-scale; Chair. MOHLOMI D. RANTEKOA.

Lesotho Council of Non-Governmental Organizations: House 544, Hoohlo Extension, Private Bag A445, Maseru 100; tel. 22317205; fax 22310412; e-mail lecongo@lecongo.org.ls; internet www.lecongo.org.ls; f. 1990; promotes sustainable management of natural resources, socio-economic devt and social justice; Exec. Dir SEABATA MOTSAMAI.

Lesotho Highlands Development Authority (LHDA): Lesotho Bank Tower, 3rd Floor, Kingsway, POB 7332, Maseru 100; tel. 22311280; fax 22310665; e-mail lhwp@lhda.org.ls; internet www.lhda.org.ls; f. 1986 to implement the Lesotho Highlands Water Project, being undertaken jtly with South Africa; Chair. TEBOHO NKHAHLE; CEO MASILO PHAKOE (acting).

Lesotho National Development Corpn (LNDC): Development House, Block A, Kingsway, Private Bag A96, Maseru 100; tel. 22312012; fax 22310038; e-mail info@lndc.org.ls; internet www.lndc.org.ls; f. 1967; state-owned; total assets M477.5m. (March 2006); interests in manufacturing, mining, food-processing and leisure; Chair. MOHLOMI RANTEKOA; CEO MOTEBANG MOKOALELI (acting).

Lesotho Co-operative Handicrafts: Basotho Hat Bldg, Kingsway, PO Box 148, Maseru; tel. 22322523; e-mail lch@ilesotho.com; internet www.basothohat.co.ls; f. 1978; marketing and distribution of handicrafts; Gen. Man. KHOTSO MATLA.

CHAMBER OF COMMERCE

Lesotho Chamber of Commerce and Industry: Kingsway Ave, POB 79, Maseru 100; tel. 22316937; fax 22322794; Pres. SIMON KUENA PHAFANE.

INDUSTRIAL AND TRADE ASSOCIATIONS

Livestock Marketing Corpn: POB 800, Maseru 100; tel. 22322444; f. 1973; sole org. for marketing livestock and livestock products; liaises with marketing boards in South Africa; projects incl. an abattoir, tannery, poultry and wool and mohair scouring plants; Gen. Man. S. R. MATLANYANE.

EMPLOYERS' ORGANIZATION

Association of Lesotho Employers: 18 Bowker Rd, POB 1509, Maseru 100; tel. 22315736; fax 22325384; e-mail makeka@leo.co.ls; f. 1961; represents mems in industrial relations and on govt bodies, and advises the Govt on employers' concerns; Pres. R. LETSOELA; Exec. Dir THABO MAKEKA.

UTILITIES

Lesotho Electricity Authority (LEA): Moposo House, 6th Floor, Kingsway, Private Bag A315, Maseru; tel. 22312479; fax 22315094; e-mail secretary@lea.org.ls; internet www.lea.org.ls; f. 2004; Chair. ZOLA TSOTSI; Chief Exec. BATALATSANG KANETSI.

Lesotho Electricity Corpn (LEC): 53 Moshoeshoe Rd, POB 423, Maseru 100; tel. 22312236; fax 22310093; e-mail info@lec.co.ls; internet www.lec.co.ls; f. 1969; 100% state-owned; Man. Dir F. M. HLOAELE.

Lesotho Water and Sewerage Authority (WASA): POB 426, Maseru 100; tel. 22312449; fax 22312006; internet www.wasa.co.ls; Chair. REFILOE TLALI.

TRADE UNIONS

Congress of Lesotho Trade Unions (COLETU): POB 13282, Maseru 100; tel. 22320958; fax 22310081; f. 1998; Sec.-Gen. VUYANI TYHALI; 15,587 mems.

Construction and Allied Workers' Union of Lesotho (CAWULE): Manonyana Centre, 2nd Floor, Room 24, POB 132282, Maseru 100; tel. 63023484; fax 22321951; f. 1967; Pres. L. PUTSOANE; Sec. T. TLALE.

Factory Workers' Union (FAWU): Maseru; f. 2003 following split from the Lesotho Clothing and Allied Workers' Union; Pres. KHABILE TSILO; Sec.-Gen. BILLY MACAEFA.

Lesotho Association of Teachers (LAT): POB 12528, Maseru 100; tel. and fax 22317463; Exec. Sec. PAUL P. SEMATLANE.

Lesotho Clothing and Allied Workers' Union (LECAWU): LNDC Centre, 2nd Floor, Rm 12–14, Kingsway Rd, POB 11767, Maseru 100; tel. 22324296; fax 22320958; e-mail lecawu@lesoff.co.ls; Sec.-Gen. DANIEL MARAISANE; 6,000 mems.

Lesotho Congress of Democratic Unions (LECODU): POB 15851, Maseru 100; tel. and fax 22323559; f. 2004; Sec.-Gen. ELLIOT T. RAMOCHELA; 15,279 mems (2005).

Lesotho General Workers' Union: POB 322, Maseru 100; f. 1954; Chair. J. M. RAMAROTHOLE; Sec. T. MOTLOHI.

Lesotho Teachers' Trade Union (LTTU): POB 0509, Maseru West 105; tel. 22322774; fax 22311673; e-mail lttu@leo.co.ls; Gen. Sec. MALIMABE JOAKIM MOTOPELA.

Lesotho Transport and Allied Workers' Union: Maseru 100; f. 1959; Pres. M. BERENG; Gen. Sec. TSEKO KAPA.

Lesotho University Teachers' and Researchers' Union (LUTARU): Maseru; Pres. Dr FRANCIS MAKOA.

Transport

RAILWAYS

Lesotho is linked with the South African railway system by a short line (2.6 km in length) from Maseru to Marseilles, on the Bloemfontein–Natal main line.

ROADS

In 2000 Lesotho's road network totalled 5,940 km, of which 1,084 km were main roads and 1,950 km were secondary roads. About 18.3% of roads were paved. In 1996 the International Development Association granted US $40m. towards the Government's rolling five-year road programme. From 1996/97 an extra-budgetary Road Fund was to finance road maintenance. In March 2000 a major road network was opened, linking Maseru with the Mohale Dam.

CIVIL AVIATION

King Moshoeshoe I International Airport is at Thota-Moli, some 20 km from Maseru; in January 2002 the Government announced plans for its expansion. International services between Maseru and Johannesburg are operated by South African Airlink. The national airline company, Lesotho Airways, was sold to a South African company in 1997 as part of the Government's ongoing privatization programme; however, after two years of losses the company was liquidated in 1999.

Tourism

Spectacular mountain scenery is the principal tourist attraction, and a new ski resort was opened in 2003. Tourist arrivals totalled 293,073 in 2008. In that year receipts from tourism amounted to an estimated US $34m.

Lesotho Tourism Development Corpn (LTDC): cnr Linare and Parliament Rds, POB 1378, Maseru 100; tel. 22312238; fax 22310189; e-mail ltdc@ltdc.org.ls; internet www.ltdc.org.ls; f. 2000; successor to the Lesotho Tourist Board; Chair. MAMORUTI MALIE.

Defence

Military service is voluntary. As assessed at November 2010, the Lesotho Defence Force (LDF, formerly the Royal Lesotho Defence Force) comprised 2,000 men, including an air wing of 110 men. The creation of a new commando force unit, the first professional unit in

LESOTHO

the LDF, was announced in October 2001, as part of ongoing efforts to restructure the armed forces.

Defence Expenditure: Estimated at M452m. for 2009.

Commander of the Lesotho Defence Force: Lt-Gen. THUSO MOTANYANE.

Education

All primary education is available free of charge, and is provided mainly by the three main Christian missions (Lesotho Evangelical, Roman Catholic and Anglican), under the direction of the Ministry of Education. Education at primary schools is officially compulsory for seven years between six and 13 years of age. Secondary education, beginning at the age of 13, lasts for up to five years, comprising a first cycle of three years and a second of two years. According to UNESCO estimates, in 2006/07 total enrolment at primary schools included 73% of children in the appropriate age-group (71% of boys; 74% of girls); in that year enrolment at secondary schools included 25% of children in the relevant age-group (20% of boys; 31% of girls). Some 8,500 students were enrolled at the National University of Lesotho, at Roma, in 2005/06. Proposed expenditure on education in 2008 represented 23.7% of total government expenditure. In January 2006 17 new schools, constructed with the assistance of the Government of Japan, were opened; they were expected to accommodate some 14,000 pupils.

LIBERIA

Introductory Survey

LOCATION, CLIMATE, LANGUAGE, RELIGION, FLAG, CAPITAL

The Republic of Liberia lies on the west coast of Africa, with Sierra Leone and Guinea to the north, and Côte d'Ivoire to the east. The climate is tropical, with temperatures ranging from 18°C (65°F) to 49°C (120°F). English is the official language but the 16 major ethnic groups speak their own languages and dialects. Liberia is officially a Christian state, although some Liberians hold traditional beliefs. There are about 670,000 Muslims. The national flag (proportions 10 by 19) has 11 horizontal stripes, alternately of red and white, with a dark blue square canton, containing a five-pointed white star, in the upper hoist. The capital is Monrovia.

CONTEMPORARY POLITICAL HISTORY

Historical Context

Founded by liberated black slaves from the southern USA, Liberia became an independent republic in 1847. The leader of the True Whig Party (TWP), William Tubman, who had been President of Liberia since 1944, died in July 1971 and was succeeded by his Vice-President, William R. Tolbert, who was re-elected in October 1975.

In April 1980 Tolbert was assassinated in a military coup, led by Master Sgt (later Commander-in-Chief) Samuel Doe, who assumed power as Chairman of the newly established People's Redemption Council (PRC), suspending the Constitution and proscribing all political parties. The new regime attracted international criticism for its summary execution of 13 former senior government officials who had been accused of corruption and mismanagement. In July 1981 all civilian ministers received commissions, thus installing total military rule.

A draft Constitution was approved by 78.3% of registered voters in a national referendum in July 1984. In the same month Doe dissolved the PRC and appointed a 58-member Interim National Assembly. The ban on political organizations was repealed in the same month, to enable parties to secure registration prior to presidential and legislative elections, which were due to take place in October 1985. In August 1984 Doe established the National Democratic Party of Liberia (NDPL) and formally announced his candidature for the presidency. By early 1985 a total of 11 political associations had been formed; however, two influential parties, the Liberian People's Party (LPP) and the United People's Party (UPP), were proscribed, and apart from the NDPL only three parties—the Liberian Action Party (LAP), the Liberia Unification Party (LUP) and the Unity Party (UP)—were eventually permitted to participate in the elections. Doe won the presidential election, receiving 50.9% of the votes. At the concurrent elections to the bicameral National Assembly, the NDPL won 22 of the 26 seats in the Senate and 51 of the 64 seats in the House of Representatives. On 6 January 1986 Doe was inaugurated as President. He appointed a new Cabinet (which largely comprised members of the previous administration).

Domestic Political Affairs

In December 1989 an armed insurrection by rebel forces began in the north-eastern border region of Nimba County. In early 1990 several hundred deaths ensued in fighting between the Liberian army (the Armed Forces of Liberia—AFL) and the rebels, who claimed to be members of a hitherto unknown opposition group, the National Patriotic Front of Liberia (NPFL), led by a former government official, Charles Taylor. The fighting swiftly degenerated into a war between Doe's ethnic group, the Krahn, and the local Gio and Mano tribes, and many thousands of people took refuge in neighbouring Guinea and Côte d'Ivoire. Taylor's authority as self-proclaimed President of his own interim administration, known as the National Patriotic Reconstruction Assembly, was challenged by a faction of the NPFL, led by Prince Yormie Johnson, which rapidly secured control of parts of Monrovia in July. In the subsequent conflict both government and rebel forces were responsible for numerous atrocities against civilians. The Economic Community of West African States (ECOWAS, see p. 257) repeatedly failed to negotiate a cease-fire, and in late August it dispatched a military force to restore peace in the region. Doe and Johnson accepted this Monitoring Group (ECOMOG, see p. 261), but its initial occupation of the port area of Monrovia encountered armed opposition by Taylor's forces.

On 30 August 1990 exiled representatives of Liberia's principal political parties and other influential groups met at a conference convened by ECOWAS in the Gambian capital, Banjul, where they elected Dr Amos Sawyer, the leader of the LPP, as President of an Interim Government of National Unity (IGNU). Doe was taken prisoner by Johnson's rebel Independent National Patriotic Front of Liberia (INPFL) on 9 September, and was killed on the following day. In early October, following Taylor's rejection of a proposed peace settlement, ECOMOG began an offensive aimed at establishing a neutral zone in Monrovia separating the three warring factions. By mid-October ECOMOG had gained control of central Monrovia. On 22 November Sawyer was inaugurated as Interim President, under the auspices of ECOWAS, in Monrovia. By January 1991 all rebel forces had withdrawn from Monrovia, and in that month Sawyer nominated ministers to the IGNU. Legislative power was vested in a 28-member Interim National Assembly, which represented the principal political factions, including the INPFL; however, the NPFL refused to participate. On 19 April a national conference re-elected Sawyer as Interim President and appointed a member of the INPFL, Peter Naigow (a former minister in Doe's administration), as Vice-President. In June Sawyer nominated a new Council of Ministers, which was subsequently approved by the Interim National Assembly. In August, however, the INPFL representatives, including Naigow, resigned from the IGNU, after Sawyer denounced the execution, apparently at Johnson's instigation, of four members of the INPFL who had reportedly complied with arrangements to relinquish weapons to ECOMOG.

In April 1991, after members of the NPFL perpetrated several incursions into Sierra Leone, Sierra Leonean forces entered Liberian territory and launched retaliatory attacks, while the NPFL reportedly advanced within Sierra Leone. It was claimed that NPFL forces were supporting a Sierra Leonean resistance movement, the Revolutionary United Front (RUF), in hostilities against government forces of that country (see the chapter on Sierra Leone). In September members of a newly emerged rebel movement, comprising former supporters of Doe, the United Liberation Movement of Liberia for Democracy (ULIMO), began attacks from Sierra Leone against NPFL forces in north-western Liberia.

At the end of October 1991 a summit meeting between Sawyer and Taylor, which took place in Yamoussoukro, Côte d'Ivoire, resulted in a peace agreement whereby the troops of all warring factions were to be disarmed and restricted to camps, while the NPFL was to relinquish the territory under its control to ECOMOG. It was also agreed that all Liberian forces would be withdrawn from Sierra Leone, and that a demilitarized zone, under the control of ECOMOG, would be created along Liberia's border with Sierra Leone. In January 1992 the Interim Election Commission and Supreme Court were established, in accordance with the peace accord. At the end of April, in response to pressure from within the NPFL, Taylor agreed to withdraw NPFL troops from the border with Sierra Leone. In May ECOMOG began to disarm the rebel factions and to deploy troops in NPFL-controlled territory, and, despite continued fighting between ULIMO and NPFL forces, established a demilitarized zone along the border with Sierra Leone.

In August 1992 ULIMO launched a renewed offensive in western Liberia, gaining control of Bomi and Grand Cape Mount Counties. In October the NPFL claimed that Nigerian aircraft under ECOMOG command had bombed its bases at Kakata and Harbel (the site of the Robertsfield International Airport and the country's principal rubber plantation), and at Buchanan, following an NPFL attack on ECOMOG forces stationed near Monrovia. The NPFL subsequently seized a number of strategic areas on the outskirts of Monrovia. ECOMOG forces (who were supported by members of the AFL and militia loyal to the IGNU) began retaliatory attacks against NPFL positions around the capital. In late October ECOMOG units succeeded in capturing the INPFL base at Caldwell, near Monrovia, and forcing Johnson to surrender. (The INPFL was subsequently disbanded.) In November the UN Security Council adopted a resolution imposing a mandatory embargo on the supply of armaments to Liberia, and authorized the UN Secretary-General to send a special representative to the country. In December ECOMOG announced that it had regained control of the area surrounding Monrovia, and in early 1993 began to advance in south-eastern Liberia, recapturing Harbel, while ULIMO was reported to have gained control of Lofa County in the west. In March ULIMO accepted an invitation from Sawyer to join the IGNU; ULIMO forces in Monrovia were subsequently disarmed. Following a major offensive, ECOMOG announced in April that it had gained control of Buchanan (which was reopened to shipping later that year).

Installation of transitional institutions

In July 1993 a conference, attended by the factions involved in the hostilities, was convened (under the auspices of the UN and ECOWAS) in Geneva, Switzerland. Following several days of negotiations, the IGNU, the NPFL and ULIMO agreed to a cease-fire (to be monitored by a joint committee of the three factions, pending the deployment of UN observers and a reconstituted peace-keeping force), and to the establishment of a transitional administration. The peace accord was formally signed in Cotonou, Benin, on 25 July. Under its terms, the IGNU was to be replaced by the Liberian National Transitional Government (LNTG), with a five-member transitional Council of State and a 35-member Transitional Legislative Assembly (comprising 13 representatives of the IGNU, 13 of the NPFL and nine of ULIMO), pending elections. In response to demands by Taylor, the dominance in ECOMOG of the Nigerian contingent was to be reduced.

The cease-fire came into effect at the end of July 1993; however, ECOMOG subsequently accused the NPFL of violating the Cotonou accord by repeatedly entering territory under its control. In August the IGNU, the NPFL and ULIMO each appointed a representative to the Council of State, while a list of nine candidates, nominated by the three factions, elected the two remaining members (who were representatives of the IGNU and ULIMO, respectively) from among their number. Dr Bismark Kuyon, a member of the IGNU, was subsequently elected Chairman of the Council of State. Shortly afterwards, however, Kuyon announced that the inauguration of the Council of State (originally scheduled to take place on 24 August) was to be postponed, pending the clear implementation of the disarmament process.

In September 1993 the UN Security Council approved the establishment of a 300-member UN Observer Mission in Liberia (UNOMIL), which was to co-operate with ECOMOG and the Organization of African Unity (now the African Union, see p. 183) in monitoring the transitional process. In October the Transitional Legislative Assembly was established, in accordance with the peace agreement. Sawyer dismissed Kuyon (who had reportedly dissociated himself from the IGNU's refusal to relinquish power prior to disarmament) and appointed Philip Banks, hitherto Minister of Justice, in his place.

Meanwhile, it was feared that renewed hostilities in several areas of the country would jeopardize the peace accord. An armed faction styling itself the Liberia Peace Council (LPC), which reportedly comprised members of the Krahn ethnic group from Grand Gedeh County, joined by a number of disaffected AFL troops, emerged in September 1993 and subsequently entered into conflict with the NPFL in south-eastern Liberia. In December fighting between ULIMO and a newly formed movement, the Lofa Defence Force (LDF), was also reported in Lofa County. The NPFL denied involvement with the LDF, which occupied territory previously controlled by ULIMO in the north-west.

In February 1994 the Council of State elected David Kpomakpor, a representative of the IGNU, as its Chairman. In early March units belonging to UNOMIL and the new ECOMOG force (which had been reinforced by contingents from Tanzania and Uganda) were deployed, and the disarmament of all factions commenced. On 7 March the Council of State was inaugurated; it was envisaged that the presidential and legislative elections (originally scheduled for February) would take place in September. However, the disarmament process was subsequently impeded by an increase in rebel activity: in addition to continuing clashes involving the LDF and the LPC, more than 200 people were killed in fighting within ULIMO between members of the Krahn and Mandingo ethnic groups, particularly in the region of Tubmanburg (in Bomi County, where the movement was officially based). The hostilities were prompted by resentment among the Krahn at the predominance of the Mandingo in ULIMO's representation in the transitional institutions.

UNOMIL's mandate was renewed in April 1994. In May, following prolonged controversy over the allocation of principal portfolios, a 19-member Cabinet was installed, comprising seven representatives of the NPFL, seven of ULIMO and five of the former IGNU. In July, however, a faction known as ULIMO—K (led by Alhaji G. V. Kromah) launched an offensive to recapture Tubmanburg, which was under the control of Maj.-Gen. Roosevelt Johnson's forces (ULIMO—J). In early September (when the original mandate of the LNTG was due to expire) a meeting of the NPFL, the AFL and ULIMO—K took place in Akosombo, Ghana. On 12 September Taylor, Kromah and the Chief of Staff of the AFL, Lt-Gen. Hezekiah Bowen, signed a peace accord providing for the immediate cessation of hostilities and for the establishment later that month of a reconstituted Council of State, in which four of the five members were to be nominated, respectively, by the three factions and a civilian Liberian National Conference (LNC—which had been convened in Monrovia at the end of August). Meanwhile, following clashes between dissident members of the NPFL and troops loyal to Taylor, the dissidents' Central Revolutionary Council (CRC) announced that Taylor had been deposed and replaced by the Minister of Labour in the LNTG, Thomas Woewiyu, who indicated that he was not prepared to accept the Akosombo agreement. In mid-September disaffected members of the AFL, led by a former officer who had served in the Doe administration, Gen. Charles Julu, seized the presidential mansion, but were subsequently overpowered by ECOMOG forces. (Almost 80 members of the AFL, including Julu, were later arrested, and a further 2,000 troops were disarmed by ECOMOG.) Later that month the CRC, apparently in alliance with elements of the AFL, ULIMO, the LPC and the LDF, took control of Taylor's base at Gbarnga (in central Bong County); Taylor was reported to have fled to Côte d'Ivoire.

In October 1994 both the ECOMOG and UNOMIL contingents were reduced in size, in view of the lack of progress achieved in the peace process. Meanwhile, the NPFL had regained control of much of the territory, including Gbarnga, that the CRC had captured in September. In December a cease-fire entered into force and reaffirmed the terms of the Akosombo agreement, including provisions for the establishment of demilitarized zones throughout Liberia and for the installation of a reconstituted Council of State, to comprise a single representative of each of the NPFL, ULIMO, the 'Coalition Forces' (a loose alliance comprising the CRC, the LPC, the LDF and elements of the AFL), and the LNC, with a fifth member elected jointly by the NPFL and ULIMO from traditional rulers. At the end of December the UN Security Council extended the mandate of UNOMIL (now comprising some 90 observers) until April 1995, while the Nigerian Government reduced its ECOMOG contingent to 6,000 (from about 10,000).

Regional peace initiatives continue

Negotiations regarding the composition of the Council of State were impeded by Taylor's persistent demand to be granted its chairmanship. On 19 August 1995, following a further ECOWAS summit meeting in Abuja, Nigeria, the armed factions (the NPFL, ULIMO—K, the LPC, the CRC, the LDF, ULIMO—J and the AFL) finally signed a compromise agreement providing for the installation of a reconstituted Council of State, which was to remain in power, pending elections, for one year. An academic with no factional affiliations, Prof. Wilton Sankawulo, was to assume the office of Chairman, while the other seats were to be allocated to Taylor, Kromah, George Boley, the LNC representative, Oscar Quiah, and a traditional ruler who had been nominated by ULIMO and the NPFL, Chief Tamba Taylor. Later that month a cease-fire entered into force, in compliance with the terms of the peace accord. The Council of State was formally installed on 1 September, and was to remain in place pending elections, scheduled for 20 August 1996. The Council of State subsequently appointed a transitional Council of Ministers, comprising members of the seven factions that had signed the Abuja agreement. Later in September 1995 the UN Security Council extended UNOMIL's mandate until the end of January 1996.

In November 1995 a demilitarized zone was established between NPFL and ULIMO—K forces in the region of St Paul River (between Bong and Lofa Counties). Deployment of

ECOMOG forces commenced, in accordance with the Abuja peace terms, in December. Following continued clashes between the ULIMO factions, however, ULIMO—J attacked ECOMOG troops near Tubmanburg. ECOMOG suspended deployment of its forces, and launched a counter-offensive in an attempt to restore order. Hostilities continued in early 1996, with large numbers of civilians killed or displaced.

In February 1996 ULIMO—J officials stated that Johnson had been replaced as leader of the movement in the interests of the peace process. In March the Council of State announced his removal from the Council of Ministers. In subsequent clashes between the two factions of ULIMO—J, forces loyal to Johnson allegedly killed a supporter of the new leadership, prompting the Council of State to order that he be arrested on charges of murder. Johnson, however, refused to surrender to the authorities, and became effectively besieged in his private residence in Monrovia. In April government forces, led by Charles Taylor, engaged in hostilities with Johnson's supporters, in an effort to force him to surrender. The principal factions represented in the transitional authorities thus became involved in the conflict: elements of the LPC and AFL (which were predominantly Krahn) supported Johnson's forces, while the NPFL and ULIMO—K opposed them. Fighting rapidly intensified in central Monrovia and ECOMOG (which had refrained from military intervention) deployed its forces in the region, with the aim of negotiating between the warring factions. Following a lull in the fighting, however, some of Johnson's supporters launched attacks in the residential area of Mamba Point (where embassies and offices of humanitarian organizations were situated) and seized a number of civilians as hostages. Later in April a further cease-fire agreement was negotiated under the aegis of the US Government, the UN and ECOWAS, allowing the deployment of ECOMOG troops throughout Monrovia, while most of the remaining hostages were released by Johnson's supporters.

In May 1996, during the absence of Johnson (who had left the country under US protection, to attend a planned ECOWAS summit meeting), the NPFL launched a further attack against the Barclay Training Centre, prompting large numbers of civilians to flee to Monrovia Freeport. At the end of May the UN Security Council renewed the mandate of UNOMIL for a further three months, but warned the armed factions that international support would be withdrawn if fighting continued; UNOMIL was henceforth to comprise only the remaining five military and 20 civilian personnel, following the evacuation of the main mission of about 90 observers in April. In June Johnson's supporters agreed to disarm, while an ECOWAS arbitration mission commenced discussions with the faction leaders in an effort to restore the peace process.

In August 1996, at an ECOWAS conference in Abuja, the principal faction leaders (apart from Johnson, who remained abroad) signed a further peace agreement, whereby a reconstituted Council of State was to be installed by the end of that month, with a former senator, Ruth Perry, replacing Sankawulo as Chairman; Taylor and Boley were to remain members of the new administration. Under a revised schedule, elections were to take place at the end of May 1997, and power was to be transferred to an elected government by mid-June, following the dissolution of the armed factions by the end of January of that year. In order to implement the new timetable, ECOMOG (which then numbered 8,500) was to be reinforced by personnel from several West African states. At the end of August 1996 the mandate of UNOMIL was again extended.

Perry was inaugurated as Chairman of the Council of State in early September 1996; Johnson was again allocated a ministerial portfolio in a subsequent reorganization of the Cabinet. Following the expiry of the deadline for the completion of the disarmament process, which had been extended to early February 1997, ECOMOG announced that about 91% of the rebel forces (who numbered 30,000–35,000, according to revised estimates) had relinquished their armaments.

In January 1997 Taylor announced that the NPFL had been officially dissolved, in accordance with the peace agreement; the movement was subsequently reconstituted as a political organization, the National Patriotic Party (NPP). In the same month Kromah declared that ULIMO—K had also ceased to exist as a military organization, and was to be reconstituted as the All Liberian Coalition Party (ALCOP). In March Taylor, Kromah and Boley resigned from the Council of State, in compliance with the peace agreement, to allow their candidacy in the forthcoming elections. From March a number of West African countries began to dispatch additional contingents to reinforce ECOMOG (which was expected to be increased in size to about 16,000 personnel prior to the elections), with the USA providing logistical and financial assistance. In May, however, following a request by several political parties, the elections were postponed until 19 July to allow all the newly registered organizations sufficient time for preparation.

Charles Taylor elected President

A 10-day voter registration process commenced at the end of June 1997. A total of 13 presidential candidates had emerged by this time, among them Ellen Johnson-Sirleaf (a former minister in the Tolbert administration and subsequently a World Bank official, who was to contest the election on behalf of the UP). Despite demands for a further postponement, the elections proceeded on 19 July. The elections commission announced on 23 July that Taylor had been elected President, with 75.3% of votes cast; Johnson-Sirleaf (who had been widely expected to be Taylor's strongest opponent) received only 9.6% of the votes. In the concurrent elections to the bicameral legislature (at which seats were allocated on a proportionate basis), the NPP secured 49 seats in the 64-member House of Representatives and 21 seats in the 26-member Senate, the UP won seven seats in the House of Representatives and three in the Senate, while ALCOP obtained three seats in the House of Representatives and two in the Senate. Kromah (who had won only 4.0% of the votes) subsequently declared that serious irregularities had occurred, but international observers declared the conduct of the elections to have been 'free and fair'. Taylor's overwhelming victory was generally ascribed to the widely held perception that he was the candidate most likely to achieve long-term stability in the country.

Taylor was inaugurated as President on 2 August 1997, and subsequently nominated a 19-member Cabinet, which was approved by the Senate. The new Government retained several members of the previous transitional administration, including Johnson and Woewiyu. A nine-member National Security Council, comprising several government ministers, the Chief of Staff of the Armed Forces and the Commander of ECOMOG, was established with the aim of ensuring the maintenance of civil order.

At an ECOWAS summit meeting, convened in Abuja, at the end of August 1997, it was agreed that ECOMOG was to be reconstituted and would henceforth assist in the process of national reconstruction, including the restructuring of the armed and security forces, and the maintenance of security; it was further envisaged that the contingent's mandate (officially due to expire on 2 February 1998) would be extended in agreement with the Liberian Government. Following the military coup in Sierra Leone in May 1997, ECOMOG was authorized to enforce international sanctions against the new junta led by Maj. Johnny Paul Koroma (see the chapter on Sierra Leone). In October, however, Taylor announced that he opposed the use of military force to oust the Koroma regime, and that ECOMOG would no longer be permitted to launch offensives against Sierra Leone from Liberian territory. Taylor ordered the closure of Liberia's border with Sierra Leone in response to civil disorder within that country. At the end of October Taylor established a National Human Rights Commission, which was empowered to investigate complaints of human rights violations.

In November 1997 it was reported that some 30 members of ULIMO had been arrested in southern Guinea. The alleged presence of former Liberian factions in Guinea was discussed at a meeting between Taylor and the Guinean President, Gen. Lansana Conté, in December. Taylor subsequently appointed Kromah (who had taken up residence in Guinea following his electoral defeat in July) to the post of Chairman of a National Commission on Reconciliation.

By early 1998 the ECOMOG contingent had been reduced to about 5,000 and the Government had notified ECOWAS of its desire for ECOMOG to withdraw formally by 2 February, but had also requested that Nigeria, Ghana, Burkina Faso and Niger continue to provide military assistance. Following the seizure of the Sierra Leonean capital, Freetown, by ECOMOG troops, Taylor protested that the arrest by ECOMOG of about 25 senior members of Sierra Leone's ousted junta at James Spriggs Payne Airport was an infringement of Liberian territory. The Liberian Government recalled its ambassador in Nigeria for consultations, and subsequently submitted a formal complaint to ECOWAS.

In March 1998 violent clashes erupted in Monrovia between the security forces and Johnson's supporters; Johnson subsequently claimed that members of Taylor's special security forces had attacked his private residence. ECOMOG troops were deployed to prevent further violence, and, in an attempt to ease tension in the capital, Johnson was removed from the Cabinet and appointed ambassador to India. In the same month Kromah, who had expressed concern regarding his own safety, was removed from his position as Chairman of the National Commission on Reconciliation. Later that month the Government and ECOWAS signed an agreement revising ECOMOG's mandate in the country; the contingent was henceforth banned from intervening in civil disputes.

In September 1998 security forces attempted to arrest Johnson (who had not yet assumed his ambassadorial post), pursuing him to the US embassy compound, where he and a number of his supporters had taken refuge. The Government subsequently announced that Johnson, Kromah and 21 of their associates had been charged with treason, following an abortive coup attempt, and demanded that US embassy officials relinquish Johnson to Liberian authority. After discussions with the Liberian authorities, however, US officials transported Johnson to Sierra Leone. In response to an incursion by Liberian security forces into the US embassy compound during the fighting, the US Government temporarily closed the embassy and deployed a naval vessel near the Liberian coast to facilitate the evacuation of US nationals in the event of an escalation of violence in Monrovia. The Liberian Government subsequently issued a formal apology to the USA and announced that an investigation would be conducted into the incident, in co-operation with the US authorities. In October 32 people (several, including Johnson, *in absentia*) were formally charged with treason; their trial commenced in November.

Regional instability

By November 1998 most of the ECOMOG forces in Liberia had been redeployed in Sierra Leone, owing to increased rebel activity in that country, and to continued tension between the Liberian Government and ECOMOG officials. In December the Government closed Liberia's border with Sierra Leone, in response to the escalation in civil conflict in the neighbouring country, and pledged support for the administration of President Ahmed Kabbah. In January 1999 it was announced that further ECOMOG troops in Liberia were to be relocated to Sierra Leone, following a major offensive by RUF forces against Freetown. A small number of ECOMOG forces remained in Liberia to provide military assistance to the armed forces. In April 13 of the defendants on trial for treason were convicted and sentenced to 10 years' imprisonment.

In August 1999 members of a rebel movement reported to comprise former members of ULIMO—K, known as the Joint Forces for the Liberation of Liberia (JFLL), attacked principal towns in Lofa County from Guinea. Some 80 aid workers, including six foreign nationals, were taken hostage by the JFLL, but were released a few days later, following negotiations by humanitarian relief officials. Taylor ordered the closure of the border with Guinea and declared a temporary state of emergency in Lofa County. At an ECOWAS meeting on relations between Liberia and Guinea, which took place in Abuja in September, it was agreed that a commission would be established to address the issue of security at the border between Liberia, Guinea and Sierra Leone. The border was reopened in February 2000.

Reports of increased activity by Liberian dissidents in Sierra Leone, where rebels had allied with Kamajor militia, and in Guinea, resulted in a further deterioration in relations between the Liberian authorities and the Governments of those countries. In July 2000 rebel forces again launched an offensive from Guinean territory against Voinjama. Another hitherto unknown movement, Liberians United for Reconciliation and Democracy (LURD), believed to be a grouping of former members of the armed factions (particularly ULIMO—K), claimed responsibility for the attacks. Taylor and Conté subsequently conducted further discussions, with mediation from the Malian President, Alpha Oumar Konaré. In August Johnson-Sirleaf and a further 14 prominent opposition leaders (many of whom were abroad) were charged with alleged involvement with the LURD dissidents.

In January 2001 the Liberian Government withdrew its ambassador in Guinea, following further Guinean bombardment of towns in the Foya district of northern Liberia. In the same month a committee of the UN Security Council reported that the Liberian Government actively supported the RUF and proposed the imposition of UN sanctions against Liberia. In February the authorities announced that the Commander of the RUF, Sam Bockarie, had left the country, and that the rebels' liaison office had been closed. In March the UN Security Council renewed the embargo on the supply of armaments to Liberia and voted in favour of a 12-month ban on diamond exports from Liberia and restrictions on the foreign travel of senior government and military officials; these latter measures were, however, deferred for a period of two months to allow the Government time to comply with demands that it expel RUF members from Liberia and end financial and military aid to the rebels. (In October 2000 the US Government had announced the imposition of diplomatic sanctions against Taylor, his relatives and close associates, prohibiting them from entering the USA until Liberia withdrew support for the RUF.) In late March 2001 Taylor expelled the ambassadors of Guinea and Sierra Leone from Liberia, claiming that they had been engaged in activity incompatible with their office, and announced the closure of the border with Sierra Leone. The Sierra Leonean authorities subsequently retaliated by ordering the Liberian chargé d'affaires to leave the country.

In April 2001 François Massaquoi, the former leader of the LDF, and Minister of Youth and Sport since 1997, was killed, after LURD forces fired on the helicopter transporting him to Voinjama. The Government subsequently intensified operations to suppress the continuing insurgency in northern Lofa County, near the border with Guinea. In May, in response to Taylor's perceived failure to comply with UN demands, the embargo on exports of diamonds from Liberia, together with the travel restrictions on senior government and military officials, entered into effect. Taylor condemned the imposition of UN sanctions, claiming that he had ended all connections with the RUF, while a large demonstration was staged in Monrovia in protest against the measures.

In July 2001 Taylor offered a general amnesty to active rebel supporters and to opposition members in exile who had been charged with treason or associated crimes. In August the Government announced that its order of expulsion against the ambassadors of Guinea and Sierra Leone accredited to Liberia had been formally withdrawn, following a request by ECOWAS. In September Johnson-Sirleaf (who had been charged with supporting anti-Government activities) returned to Monrovia under the terms of the general amnesty. In October a five-member UN commission issued a report recommending the extension of the existing sanctions against Liberia. The UN report also stated that the Liberian Government continued to use revenue generated by the timber industry and maritime activities to finance illicit trade in armaments with the RUF, and proposed the imposition of additional sanctions on timber exports.

By early 2002 LURD forces had gained considerable territory from government troops, and continued to advance southwards towards Monrovia. In response, Taylor declared a national state of emergency on 8 February (which was subsequently ratified by the legislature, and was to be revised after three months). Later that month the Government announced that it was to establish a permanent security presence at the country's northern border with Sierra Leone and Guinea. At the beginning of March the leader of LURD, Sekou Damate Conneh, announced that his forces aimed to depose Taylor and install a transitional administration in Monrovia. The rebels declared a few days later that they were prepared to enter into dialogue with government officials, but demanded that Taylor be excluded from discussions, on the grounds that he was not the legitimate Head of State of Liberia. The Government insisted that it would not contemplate the negotiation of a power-sharing agreement with the movement. Later that month a meeting of representatives of the Liberian authorities and opposition was convened at Abuja, under the aegis of ECOWAS; however, representatives of LURD failed to attend the negotiations, purportedly owing to the logistical difficulties in travelling to Abuja. At the conclusion of the discussions delegates representing 29 political and civil society associations, including major opposition leaders, urged the Government and LURD forces to declare a cease-fire. Nevertheless, fighting continued, particularly at Liberia's northern border with Guinea. At the end of March ECOWAS imposed travel restrictions on the LURD leadership, on the grounds that the movement had renewed hostilities against the Government.

On 6 May 2002 the UN Security Council adopted a resolution extending the armaments and diamond embargoes, and the travel ban, for a further 12 months. Also in May the Liberian legislature extended for a further six months the national state of emergency, after LURD forces gained further territory, seizing control of Gbarnga, in Bong County. In September Taylor ended the national state of emergency and the ban on political demonstrations, announcing that government forces had regained control of much of the territory captured by LURD, including the significant town of Bopolu, 100 km north-west of Monrovia.

During early 2003 hostilities frequently crossed into the territory of Côte d'Ivoire, and reports emerged that Ivorian rebel groups, notably the Mouvement pour la justice et la paix (MJP) and the Mouvement populaire ivoirien du grand ouest (MPIGO), had become allied with LURD. In March LURD occupied Klay, followed by the Ricks Institute Camp for internally displaced civilians, only 20 km from Monrovia, causing large numbers of civilians to take refuge in the capital. Simultaneous heavy fighting for control of Gbarnga was reported; LURD forces had recaptured the town by April. Meanwhile, a new rebel faction, the Movement for Democracy in Liberia (MODEL), attacked and secured Zwedru in Grand Gedeh County. MODEL was believed to comprise former members of the AFL and Doe loyalists, who were mainly based in Côte d'Ivoire (and reportedly supported by the Ivorian Government). At the end of April Taylor and President Laurent Gbagbo of Côte d'Ivoire agreed to deploy joint border patrols. On 6 May the UN Security Council renewed the existing embargoes in force against Liberia for a further year, and imposed an additional ban on timber exports (which entered into effect in early July). Also in early May the Liberian authorities announced that Bockarie (who had been indicted by the Special Court established in Sierra Leone to try suspects of war crimes committed during the 10-year conflict in the country) had been killed in Liberia during an attempt to arrest him. (It was reported that he had been leading former RUF elements involved in the conflict in Liberia.) Subsequently, however, officials at the Special Court claimed that Bockarie and his immediate family had been captured and murdered by Liberian security forces to prevent him from testifying against prominent regional leaders.

Removal of Taylor

The international community repeatedly urged unconditional negotiations within the framework of a mediation process led by ECOWAS, and in March 2003 LURD finally agreed, in principle, to enter into dialogue with Taylor. LURD and MODEL halted their advances on Monrovia and Buchanan at the end of May and pledged to observe a cease-fire, provided that the Government also suspended attacks. Peace discussions, attended by Taylor and LURD, commenced in Accra, Ghana, on 4 June, but were disrupted by the announcement of Taylor's indictment for war crimes by the Special Court, in connection with his alleged long-standing involvement with the RUF. On the following day Taylor returned to Monrovia, where he immediately announced that the authorities had suppressed an attempted coup. On the same day LURD forces launched a major attack on Monrovia from the movement's base in Tubmanburg, and rapidly reached the capital's western outskirts, causing an exodus from refugee camps towards the city centre. LURD's political leadership issued an ultimatum demanding Taylor's resignation, and French military forces commenced the evacuation of foreign nationals in response to the increasingly critical situation. Following the arrival of a MODEL delegation, the peace discussions in Ghana resumed on 9 June. Repeated demands by LURD for Taylor's resignation as a precondition to the suspension of hostilities, and Taylor's insistence that his indictment by the Sierra Leone Special Court be withdrawn, impeded progress. On 17 June, however, a cease-fire agreement was signed by the LURD and MODEL leaders, and by the Minister of Defence, Daniel Chea, on behalf of the Liberian Government. Immediately beforehand, government troops recaptured Greenville, forcing LURD to withdraw to positions some 35 km from Monrovia. The cease-fire agreement required the deployment of a multinational stabilization force and a 30-day period of discussions to resolve outstanding issues, prior to the adoption of a comprehensive peace accord.

Shortly after the cease-fire agreement was signed in Accra, however, Taylor declared that he would remain in office at least until the end of his presidential term in January 2004, and rejected the Special Court indictment against him. Serious breaches of the cease-fire were reported, and on 26 June 2003, after the resumption of heavy fighting between government and rebel forces in and around Monrovia, in which about 300 civilians were killed, US President George W. Bush urged Taylor to resign. On the following day the rebel leadership declared a unilateral cease-fire (which was, however, rapidly abandoned). At the end of June the UN Secretary-General recommended to the Security Council that a multinational peace-keeping force be deployed in Liberia in response to the critical humanitarian situation, and urged US military intervention. On 6 July Taylor announced that he had accepted, in principle, an offer of asylum from the Nigerian Head of State, Olusegun Obasanjo, but stipulated that he would not leave the country until a peace-keeping operation was installed. Following continued appeals from Liberian civilians for foreign intervention to prevent a humanitarian disaster, a US mission of military observers was dispatched to Liberia. However, Bush indicated that he would only deploy peace-keeping troops in Liberia after Taylor had left the country and a West African mission had restored order. Later in July, after the rebel offensive to oust Taylor had reached the centre of the capital, the US embassy compound (in which some 10,000 Liberian civilians had taken refuge) was repeatedly bombarded. Some 100 US marines were flown in to defend the building, while US naval vessels were stationed off the Liberian coast. Meanwhile, following the resumption of discussions between the government, LURD and MODEL delegations in Accra, it was announced that a peace accord, based on the terms of the failed cease-fire agreement, had been drafted.

On 22 July 2003 a summit meeting of ECOWAS Heads of State was convened in the Senegalese capital, Dakar. Following pressure from the UN Secretary-General, the West African delegates agreed to dispatch an initial 1,300 Nigerian peace-keeping troops (including a battalion redeployed from neighbouring Sierra Leone) to Liberia. On 1 August the UN Security Council officially authorized the establishment of a multinational force with a maximum strength of 3,250 troops, to be known as the ECOWAS Mission in Liberia (ECOMIL), which was to restore security to allow the distribution of emergency humanitarian assistance, and prepare for the deployment of a longer-term UN stabilization force. On 11 August, following continued pressure from West African Governments and the international community, Taylor relinquished power to the Vice-President, Moses Zeh Blah, before leaving Liberia for exile in the town of Calabar, in south-eastern Nigeria. Blah was inaugurated as interim Head of State, pending the installation of a government of national unity, which was the subject of continuing negotiations between the government and rebel delegations in Accra. Taylor's departure fulfilled the main demand of the rebel leadership, who ceded control of Monrovia Freeport to ECOMIL, and a further 200 US military personnel arrived in Liberia to support the peace operation. On 18 August delegates of the incumbent Government, rebel factions, political opposition and civil organizations, under the aegis of the UN, reached a comprehensive peace agreement, which provided for the establishment of a transitional power-sharing government and legislature, to comprise representatives of the participating groupings. Under the accord, Blah was to transfer power to the new administration on 14 October, all armed militia were to be disbanded, and democratic elections were to be conducted by October 2005. On 21 August 2003 the delegations elected Gyude Bryant, a prominent church figure and leader of the LAP, as Chairman of the transitional administration. Perceived as being most neutral, Bryant defeated a further two candidates for the office, Johnson-Sirleaf and Rudolph Sherman of the TWP. By the end of August a UN Joint Monitoring Committee had been dispatched to Monrovia, and ECOMIL troops (then numbering 1,500) were slowly taking control of rebel-held territory.

The National Transitional Government

On 19 September 2003 the UN Security Council formally established the UN Mission in Liberia (UNMIL, see p. 91), which was mandated to support the transitional authorities and the implementation of the August peace agreement; the first contingent, of about 4,000, commenced deployment in the country (replacing ECOMIL) on 1 October. On 14 October, under the terms of the peace agreement, Bryant was officially inaugurated as Chairman of the two-year power-sharing administration, the National Transitional Government, while the leader of the UPP, Wesley Johnson, became Vice-Chairman. At the same time a 76-member unicameral legislature, the National Transitional Legislative Assembly (NTLA), comprising representatives of the groupings signatory to the August agreement and 15 deputies nominated by the counties, was installed. A prominent member of LURD, George Dweh, was subsequently elected Speaker of the new Assembly. Shortly before his inauguration, Bryant had signed an agreement for the resumption of diplomatic relations with the People's Republic of China (thereby ending links with Taiwan); the Chinese Government was expected to finance substantially reconstruction projects in the country. Later in October LURD and MODEL (which were each allocated five ministries in the National Transitional Government) submitted ministerial nominees for approval by the legislature. Of the former Taylor loyalists, Chea retained the post of Minister of Defence, while

LURD representatives were awarded the portfolios of justice and finance, and the leader of MODEL, Thomas Nimely Yaya, became Minister of Foreign Affairs. (However, the political opposition and civil society groups failed to agree on representatives for the remaining six portfolios divided between them.) In early December the International Criminal Police Organization (INTERPOL) issued an arrest notice against Taylor (who remained in Nigeria) for suspected war crimes.

On 22 December 2003 the UN Security Council adopted a resolution maintaining the embargoes on imports of armaments and on exports of timber and diamonds for a minimum of one year, but envisaged that these would be ended in response to progress in the peace process and in efforts by the National Transitional Government to prevent the illicit exploitation of resources. In January 2004 it was reported that Conneh's wife, Aisha, had ousted him from the leadership of LURD, with the support of other military commanders, resulting in the division of the movement. LURD and MODEL continued to demand Bryant's resignation from the chairmanship of the interim administration as a precondition to disarmament. On 23 March, after the remaining ministerial portfolios were finally designated, Bryant finally inaugurated the National Transitional Government. In mid-April UNMIL resumed the disarmament programme.

In May 2004 the Civil Society Organizations of Liberia, a grouping of pro-democracy and human rights organizations, presented a petition to the NTLA in support of the extradition of Taylor by the Nigerian Government. (Legal representatives of Taylor continued to plead at the Special Court in Sierra Leone that, as serving President at the time of his indictment, he was immune from prosecution.) In June, in a further struggle for leadership within LURD, the national executive council announced the removal of Sekou Conneh and his replacement by Chayee Doe (a brother of the former President). Conneh refused to acknowledge the statement, and continued to reject demands by his opponents within the movement for the replacement of the LURD Minister of Finance, Lusine Kamara. In September the International Criminal Court (ICC, see p. 340) announced that Liberia had ratified the signatory treaty, thereby allowing the Court jurisdiction to prosecute crimes committed during the civil conflict. On 17 September the UN Security Council adopted a resolution extending the mandate of UNMIL for a further year (while welcoming the progress made in the peace process).

The disarmament process, under which a total of some 96,000 former combatants had relinquished armaments, officially ended on 31 October 2004, with a ceremony at which the three former armed factions were also officially dissolved (although operations continued after that date). In December the UN Security Council conducted a review of the sanctions in force on Liberia and concluded that, following the report of an assessment mission to the country, the National Transitional Government had not met the requisite conditions. The sanctions on armaments, timber and travel were consequently renewed for a further year, while, in view of preparations by the authorities to introduce a certification system, the embargo on the export of diamonds was extended for six months (and again extended in mid-2005).

Electoral reform legislation, which had been submitted to the NTLA at the end of August 2004, became an issue of contention, following attempts by the NTLA to add an amendment requiring a prior population census to be conducted, which would effectively prevent the elections from taking place in October 2005 (as specified in the comprehensive peace agreement). Ensuing disputes over the legislation between the NTLA and the Government were resolved only by sustained pressure from Bryant and the US Ambassador, thereby delaying the adoption of the legislation until December 2004. Nevertheless, in February 2005 the National Elections Commission (NEC) announced that the presidential and legislative elections would be conducted on 11 October. Some 40 prospective presidential candidates had emerged, notably including George Manneh Weah, a Liberian national and an international association footballer. In mid-March NTLA Speaker Dweh, together with the Deputy Speaker and two parliamentary deputies, were suspended from office on suspicion of corruption, following a report by a parliamentary committee. Dweh denied the charges against him, insisting that his suspension was not legitimate, and the UNMIL presence in Monrovia was reinforced, amid concerns of renewed unrest.

The 2005 elections

At the first round of presidential voting on 11 October 2005, which was contested by a total of 22 candidates, Weah secured 28.3% of votes cast, while Johnson-Sirleaf won 19.8% of votes and Charles Brumskine of the Liberty Party (LP) 13.9% of votes. At the elections to the 64-member lower House of Representatives Weah's party, the Congress for Democratic Change (CDC), won 15 seats, the LP nine seats, an alliance known as the Coalition for the Transformation of Liberia (COTOL) eight seats and the UP eight seats. At the elections to the 30-member Senate the COTOL secured seven seats, while the CDC, the UP and the LP each received three seats. Some 74.9% of the registered electorate voted in the presidential ballot and 76.5% in the legislative elections. Since no presidential candidate had secured an absolute majority, a second round was conducted on 8 November: Johnson-Sirleaf defeated Weah by securing 59.4% of votes cast (with 61.0% of the electorate participating). On 23 November, despite claims of electoral malpractice, the NEC officially declared that Johnson-Sirleaf had won the presidential election. Violent demonstrations by Weah's supporters in Monrovia resulted in clashes with security forces and the arrest of some 40 protesters. In mid-December, following international pressure, however, Weah agreed to suspend his legal challenge to Johnson-Sirleaf's election at the Supreme Court, and subsequently announced that he would abandon his claim to the presidency in the interests of national reconciliation. Later that month the UN Security Council again extended the sanctions on armaments and travel for a further year and those on diamonds and timber for six months, and urged the establishment of a panel of experts to assess the authorities' compliance with requirements.

Johnson-Sirleaf was inaugurated as President on 16 January 2006, thereby becoming the first woman to be elected Head of State in Africa. The two legislative chambers were officially installed on the same day. The election of a close former associate of Taylor, Edwin Snowe, as Speaker of the House of Representatives attracted controversy. Johnson-Sirleaf nominated a number of ministers for approval by the Senate. In February Johnson-Sirleaf established a seven-member Truth and Reconciliation Commission (TRC), which was to investigate human rights abuses perpetrated during the civil conflict. In March the Nigerian Government announced that it had received an official request from Johnson-Sirleaf for Taylor's extradition. Later in March, shortly after President Obasanjo declared that Nigeria would agree his extradition, Taylor fled from his residence in Calabar; he was apprehended two days later in Borno State, near the border with Cameroon, and dispatched to Liberia, from where he was immediately extradited by UNMIL peace-keepers to the Special Court. In early April Taylor pleaded 'not guilty' to all charges at the Special Court. Tribunal officials subsequently requested that his trial be transferred to the ICC at The Hague, the Netherlands, (while remaining under the jurisdiction of the Special Court), in the interests of regional stability. The Dutch authorities acceded to that request on the condition that any sentence handed down to Taylor was served in another country. The United Kingdom subsequently agreed to host Taylor should he be imprisoned, and, following the unanimous approval of the UN Security Council, on 20 June Taylor was transferred to The Hague, where his trial commenced on 4 June 2007. (However, the proceedings were adjourned until January 2008 at the request of Taylor's defence counsel.)

In November 2006 the Minister of Information, Culture and Tourism, Johnny McClain, resigned from office citing insufficient funding and a lack of support from the Government. He was replaced by Rev. Dr Lawrence Bropleh. In August Johnson-Sirleaf implemented a major reorganization of the Government, in which Olubanke King Akerele replaced George W. Wallace as Minister of Foreign Affairs, and Philip Banks became Minister of Justice, replacing Frances Johnson-Morris, who assumed the commerce and industry portfolio.

In February 2007 Gyude Bryant was charged with misappropriating US $1.3m. during his period as Chairman of the National Transitional Government; his trial opened in March. In July former armed forces leader Julu was arrested, along with a number of other senior military officials, and charged with attempting a coup; they remained in custody pending trial. In July 2008 the House of Representatives approved new defence legislation following several amendments to the original draft; the new Act, which provided for the professionalization of the national armed forces, also prohibited citizens with a record of human rights violations from enlisting in the military.

LIBERIA

Meanwhile, in June Peter B. Jallah was named Minister of National Security.

In November 2008 Charles 'Chuckie' Taylor, Jr, son of the former President, was found guilty of torture and executions committed while he was head of an anti-terrorist unit during the civil conflict. He had been apprehended in Miami, USA, and taken into custody in 2006 under legislation allowing for the prosecution of such crimes committed abroad. In January 2009 he was sentenced to 97 years' imprisonment. In March the President of the Senate, Isaac Nyenabo (who had been suspended from the post in the previous August on grounds of incompetence), announced his resignation, following a sustained boycott of the Senate by many of its members and the adoption of a vote of no confidence in him. In April Bryant, former parliamentary Speaker and head of the Liberia Petroleum Refining Corporation (LPRC) Edwin Snowe, and three others charged with embezzling funds from the LPRC during Bryant's presidency were acquitted of all charges of corruption while holding public office.

On 1 July 2009 the TRC submitted its final report recommending the establishment of an Extraordinary Criminal Tribunal for Liberia, and the prosecution or investigation of a number of individuals, corporations and institutions for human rights violations. The Commission also recommended that some 50 people who had associated with or financed the warring factions should be barred from public office for a period of 30 years; they included Johnson-Sirleaf, following her admission to the Commission in February that she had supported Taylor's NPFL after its insurrection in 1989, and had donated US $10,000 to the movement. The proposed ban against Johnson-Sirleaf prompted domestic and international consternation, and speculation that it had been instigated in view of the forthcoming 2011 elections. The National Assembly was required to adopt a resolution on the TRC's report to allow its enactment; in late August 2009 the legislature announced that it would consult with the public for about one year before deciding whether or not to implement the Commission's recommendations. In September the National Assembly approved a resolution to amend several provisions of the Constitution, mainly concerning the electoral system, and providing for a change in the date of elections from October to November. Also in September the UN Security Council extended the mandate of UNMIL for a further year and authorized a reduction in its total strength to about 8,200 personnel (while maintaining the strength of its police component). In December the UN Security Council relaxed for a trial period of one year the armaments embargo imposed on Liberia to allow the Government and UNMIL to receive military supplies, in view of the progress made in national reconstruction; the freeze on the assets of former associates of Taylor and the travel embargo were extended for a further year.

Recent developments: preparations for the 2011 elections

In December 2009 the General Auditing Commission concluded that Minister of Information, Culture and Tourism Bropleh, who had been suspended from office pending investigations, had embezzled some US $358,000 and recommended his prosecution. (Cletus Sieh was subsequently appointed to replace Bropleh.) In January 2010 Johnson-Sirleaf announced that she intended to seek re-election in 2011, despite the proposed ban against her serving public office. In early February George Boley was arrested in the USA on grounds of lack of proper documentation. Later that month the Minister of Internal Affairs, Ambulai Johnson, resigned from his post, owing to his alleged mismanagement of the Social Development Fund; in April Johnson-Sirleaf appointed Harrison Kahnweah to replace him. In August the testimony in Taylor's ongoing trial of celebrity model Naomi Campbell (who affirmed that in 1997 he had given her diamonds allegedly mined illegally by the RUF in Sierra Leone) attracted international attention. In September 2010 the UN Security Council extended the mandate of UNMIL for a further year.

In July 2010 the National Assembly adopted legislation creating nine additional parliamentary seats to be distributed among the six most populated counties, thereby increasing the total number of seats in the House of Representatives to 73 (with effect from the next elections). In August the CDC, the NPP, the Progressive Democratic Party and the National Vision Party of Liberia agreed to form a coalition to contest the presidential and legislative elections scheduled for October 2011; the alliance was expected to present Weah as its presidential candidate. At the end of August 2010 the National Assembly approved four main constitutional amendments, that: the 10-year residency requirement for presidential candidates would be reduced to five years; Supreme Court justices would serve a life term (rather than retiring at 70 years of age); elections would be held in early November, rather than in October; and the two-round system used in legislative elections would be replaced by a single-round, first-past-the-post system. In September the NEC announced that the amendments were to be submitted for endorsement at a pre-election national referendum, which was scheduled for 23 August 2011. At a party convention in October 2010, Johnson-Sirleaf was nominated as the presidential candidate of the UP (which had previously merged with the LUP and LAP, under the chairmanship of former presidential candidate Varney Sherman); the incumbent Vice-President, Joseph Nyumah Boakai, was confirmed as the party's vice-presidential candidate. Former rebel leader Prince Johnson had also announced that he intended to contest the forthcoming presidential election. In November Johnson-Sirleaf dismissed her Government but subsequently reappointed most of the ministers; new appointments included the replacement of long-standing Minister of Lands, Mines, and Energy, Eugene Shannon, by a former ECOWAS official, Roosevelt Jayjay. A voter registration exercise was conducted in January 2011. Taylor's trial reached completion in March (despite a boycott of proceedings by Taylor and his defence counsel in February), and a judgment was expected by mid-2011.

CONSTITUTION AND GOVERNMENT

Under the Constitution of January 1986, legislative power is vested in the bicameral National Assembly, comprising the 64-member House of Representatives and the 30-member Senate. Members of the House of Representatives are elected by legislative constituency for a term of six years, while each county elects two members of the Senate (one for a term of nine years and one for six years). Executive power is vested in the President, who is elected to office for a six-year term (renewable only once), and who appoints the Government (subject to the approval of the Senate). Following a peace agreement in August 2003, a democratically elected administration was installed in January 2006 (replacing the power-sharing National Transitional Government). The country comprises 15 counties, which are divided into 64 districts.

REGIONAL AND INTERNATIONAL CO-OPERATION

Liberia is a member of the Economic Community of West African States (ECOWAS, see p. 257) and the Mano River Union (see p. 448), both of which aim to promote closer economic co-operation in the region. Liberia is also a member of the African Union (see p. 183)

Liberia was a founder member of the UN on its establishment in 1945, and has observer status at the World Trade Organization (WTO, see p. 430). Liberia participates in the Group of 77 (G77, see p. 447) developing countries.

ECONOMIC AFFAIRS

In 2009, according to the World Bank, Liberia's gross domestic product (GDP) was US $648m., equivalent to $160 per head (or $290 per head on an international purchasing-power parity basis). During 2000–09, it was estimated, the population increased at an average annual rate of 3.8%, while GDP per head declined by 3.2%. Overall GDP saw a negligible increase, in real terms, in 2000–09; however, real GDP increased by 7.1% in 2008 and by 4.6% in 2009.

Agriculture and forestry, measured at constant 1992 prices, contributed an estimated 61.9% of GDP in 2010. An estimated 26.7% of the formal labour force were employed in the sector in that year. The principal cash crops are rubber (which accounted for an estimated 74.8% of export earnings in 2010), cocoa beans and coffee. The principal food crops are cassava, rice, bananas, plantains, yams and sweet potatoes. Timber production traditionally represented an important source of export revenue, providing an estimated 50.1% of export earnings in 2003 (when, however, sanctions on timber exports were imposed). Agricultural GDP increased at an average annual rate of 7.0% in 2006–10. The GDP of the agricultural sector also increased by 7.0% in 2010.

Industry (including mining, manufacturing, construction and power), measured at constant 1992 prices, contributed 16.8% of GDP in 2008, and employed an estimated 4.8% of the formal labour force in 2010. Industrial GDP, according to African Development Bank (AfDB) figures, increased at an average annual rate of 5.2% in 2000–07; the GDP of the industrial sector increased by 8.0% in 2007.

The mining sector, measured at constant 1992 prices, contributed an estimated 0.2% of GDP in 2010, and engaged an estimated 1.2% of the formal labour force in the same year. Gold and diamonds are mined, and Liberia possesses significant amounts of barytes and kyanite. The production and export of mineral products were severely disrupted from 1990, as a result of the civil conflict. In 1997 total mineral reserves were estimated to include more than 10m. carats of diamonds and 3m. troy oz of gold. In January 2005 the Government prohibited diamond mining in order to support the enforcement of UN sanctions on the export of diamonds (imposed in 2001). However, mineral exports recommenced in 2007 (see below) and, in that year, foreign sales of gold accounted for 2.7% of total export revenue; diamonds contributed 1.3%. In 2010 these commodities contributed 6.8% and 5.3% of total exports, respectively. The GDP of the mining sector, increased at an average annual rate of 6.5% in 2006–10; mining GDP increased by 12.5% in 2010.

Manufacturing, measured at constant 1992 prices, provided an estimated 11.4% of GDP in 2010, and engaged an estimated 0.9% of the formal labour force in the same year. Manufacturing GDP increased at an average annual rate of 3.8% in 2006–10; the GDP of the manufacturing sector increased by 2.9% in 2010.

Construction, measured at constant 1992 prices, provided an estimated 3.2% of GDP in 2008, and engaged an estimated 2.7% of the formal labour force in 2010.

Energy is derived from the consumption of fossil fuels (62.2%) and from hydroelectric power (37.8%). In 2003 the authorities announced plans to restore power throughout the country by a programme to rehabilitate a major hydroelectric power installation, which had been damaged in the civil conflict. Liberia is dependent on imports of petroleum, which comprised an estimated 13.9% of the value of total imports in 2010.

The services sector, measured at constant 1992 prices, contributed 21.9% of GDP in 2008, and employed an estimated 68.5% of the formal labour force in 2010. The GDP of the services sector, according to AfDB figures, increased at an average annual rate of 2.3% in 2000–06; the GDP of the sector increased by 10.1% in 2006.

Liberia's large open-registry ('flag of convenience') merchant shipping fleet has become an increasingly significant source of foreign exchange. In 2007 revenue from Liberia's maritime programme accounted for an estimated 7.0% of total revenue.

In 2009 Liberia recorded an estimated visible trade deficit of US $379.0m., and there was a deficit of $541.1m. on the current account of the balance of payments. In 2004 the principal source of imports (37.8%) was the Republic of Korea. The principal market for exports in 2006 was the USA (73.7%); the other major purchaser was Belgium. The principal export in 2010 was rubber, accounting for 74.8% of total exports. The principal imports in that year were food (particularly rice) and live animals (31.6%), machinery and transport equipment, and petroleum.

Liberia's overall budgetary deficit was projected at US $14m. in 2008/09, according to IMF figures. Liberia's general government gross debt was L $1.97m. in 2009, equivalent to 224.1% of GDP. The country's external debt totalled $3,484m. at the end of 2008, of which $1,237m. was public and publicly guaranteed debt. In that year the cost of debt-servicing was equivalent to 131.3% of the value of exports of goods, services and income. The annual rate of inflation averaged 13.2% in 2001–09; consumer prices increased by 7.8% in 2009. In 2006 unemployment was estimated at about 85.0% of the labour force.

The inauguration of Ellen Johnson-Sirleaf, a former World Bank economist, as President in January 2006 marked a turning point in Liberia's economy, which had been ravaged by the civil conflict. She appealed for international support for reconstruction, and announced measures to end endemic corruption. UN sanctions on the export of timber were lifted in September and those on diamond exports in April 2007; shortly afterwards Liberia joined the Extractive Industries Transparency Initiative to ensure that part of the proceeds of extractive industries, including timber, would be used to improve living conditions for Liberians. In December the AfDB cancelled US $255.2m. of Liberia's debt, and in March 2008 the country cleared its long-standing overdue obligations with the IMF; the Fund fully restored Liberia's rights and designated it eligible for debt relief under the initiative for heavily indebted poor countries (HIPC). The Government instigated a three-year poverty reduction strategy, supported by an IMF credit facility arrangement, based on consolidating peace and security, strengthening governance and the rule of law, and rehabilitating infrastructure and delivering basic services. Notable advances were made in re-establishing the public financial management system and introducing measures to facilitate investment. Liberia experienced some adverse effects following the onset of the international financial crisis in late 2008, including a drop in exports and investment. In June 2010 the IMF and World Bank, having determined that Liberia had made the required progress in poverty reduction and stabilization to reach completion point under the HIPC initiative, approved $4,600m. of debt relief (of which $1,500m. was to be delivered by multilateral creditors and the remainder by bilateral and commercial creditors), thereby reducing the country's external debt by more than 90%. In December the IMF completed the fifth assessment of economic performance under the Government's programme supported by the Extended Credit Facility arrangement and approved a further disbursement. Following a slowdown in GDP growth in 2009, the rate was expected to increase to more than 6% in 2010 (according to IMF projections), assisted by a recovery in exports owing to rising rubber and timber production. Foreign investment in the country continued to increase, with the approval of several new concessions in the iron ore and palm oil sectors, and a concession for port management in Monrovia, while in late 2010 US corporation Chevron acquired a 70% interest in three offshore exploration areas. In early 2011 World Bank officials praised the considerable progress made by the Government in development since benefiting from debt relief, particularly with regard to investment in the rehabilitation of infrastructure.

PUBLIC HOLIDAYS

2012: 1 January (New Year's Day), 11 February (Armed Forces Day), 9 March (Decoration Day), 15 March (J. J. Robert's Birthday), 6 April (Good Friday), 13 April (Fast and Prayer Day), 14 May (National Unification Day), 25 May (Africa Day), 26 July (Independence Day), 24 August (Flag Day), 1 November (All Saints' Day), 12 November (National Memorial Day), 29 November (President Tubman's Birthday), 25 December (Christmas Day).

LIBERIA

Statistical Survey

Sources (unless otherwise stated): Liberia Institute of Statistics and Geo-Information Services, POB 629, Tubman Blvd, Sinkor, Monrovia; internet www.tlcafrica.com/lisgis/lisgis.htm; the Central Bank of Liberia, POB 2048, Corner of Warren and Carey St, Monrovia; tel. 6225685; fax 6226114; internet www.cbl.org.lr/index.php.

Area and Population

AREA, POPULATION AND DENSITY

Area (sq km)	97,754*
Population (census results)	
1 February 1984	2,101,628
21 March 2008	
Males	1,739,945
Females	1,736,663
Total	3,476,608
Population (UN estimates at mid-year)†	
2009	3,954,977
2010	4,101,767
2011	4,230,847
Density (per sq km) at mid-2011	43.3

* 37,743 sq miles.
† Source: UN, *World Population Prospects: The 2008 Revision*.

POPULATION BY AGE AND SEX
(UN estimates at mid-2011)

	Males	Females	Total
0–14	901,467	886,035	1,787,502
15–64	1,143,080	1,167,133	2,310,213
65 and over	59,237	73,895	133,132
Total	2,103,784	2,127,063	4,230,847

Source: UN, *World Population Prospects: The 2008 Revision*.

COUNTIES
(population at 2008 census)

Bomi	84,119		Margibi	209,923
Bong	333,481		Maryland	135,938
Gbarpolu	83,388		Montserrado	1,118,241
Grand Bassa	221,693		Nimba	462,026
Grand Cape Mount	127,076		Rivercess	71,509
Grand Gedeh	125,258		River Gee	66,789
Grand Kru	57,913		Sinoe	102,391
Lofa	276,863		**Total**	**3,476,608**

PRINCIPAL TOWNS
(2003)

Monrovia (capital)	550,200		Harbel	17,700
Zwedru	35,300		Tubmanburg	16,700
Buchanan	27,300		Gbarnga	14,200
Yekepa	22,900		Greenville	13,500
Harper	20,000		Ganta	11,200
Bensonville	19,600			

Source: Stefan Helders, *World Gazetteer* (internet www.world-gazetteer.com).

Mid-2010 ('000, incl. suburbs, UN estimate): Monrovia 1,185 (Source: UN, *World Urbanization Prospects: The 2007 Revision*).

BIRTHS AND DEATHS
(annual averages, UN estimates)

	1995–2000	2000–05	2005–10
Birth rate (per 1,000)	43.6	41.1	38.6
Death rate (per 1,000)	14.1	12.0	10.6

Source: UN, *World Population Prospects: The 2008 Revision*.

Life expectancy (years at birth, WHO estimates): 54 (males 53; females 55) in 2008 (Source: WHO, *World Health Statistics*).

ECONOMICALLY ACTIVE POPULATION
(formal sector only)

	2008	2009	2010*
Agriculture and forestry	22,616	34,882	38,615
Mining	1,421	1,907	1,691
Manufacturing	2,215	2,075	1,367
Construction	390	1,659	3,856
Wholesale and retail trade	10,028	10,998	7,536
Transport and communications	4,984	5,563	9,423
Banking and insurance	2,189	4,044	6,426
Business services	6,231	9,467	10,179
Social and community services	9,213	20,160	28,020
Government	47,681	34,000	37,532
Total	**106,968**	**124,755**	**144,647**

* Estimates.

Total employed in informal sector: 487,000 in 2008; 569,790 in 2009; 672,352 (estimate) in 2010.

Health and Welfare

KEY INDICATORS

Total fertility rate (children per woman, 2008)	5.1
Under-5 mortality rate (per 1,000 live births, 2008)	144
HIV/AIDS (% of persons aged 15–49, 2007)	1.7
Physicians (per 1,000 head, 2004)	0.03
Health expenditure (2007): US $ per head (PPP)	39
Health expenditure (2007): % of GDP	10.6
Health expenditure (2007): public (% of total)	26.2
Access to water (% of persons, 2008)	68
Access to sanitation (% of persons, 2008)	17
Total carbon dioxide emissions ('000 metric tons, 2007)	674.2
Carbon dioxide emissions per head (metric tons, 2007)	0.2
Human Development Index (2010): ranking	162
Human Development Index (2010): value	0.300

For sources and definitions, see explanatory note on p. vi.

LIBERIA

Agriculture

PRINCIPAL CROPS
('000 metric tons)

	2006	2007	2008
Rice, paddy*	164	232	295
Cassava (Manioc)	500*	550†	560†
Taro (Cocoyam)†	26	25	30
Yams†	20	19	21
Sweet potatoes†	20	20	21
Sugar cane†	255	265	265
Oil palm fruit	183*	183*	183†
Bananas†	116	120	120
Plantains†	42	43	43
Natural rubber*	101	106	81

* Unofficial figure(s).
† FAO estimate(s).

Aggregate production ('000 metric tons, may include official, semi-official or estimated data): Total cereals 164 in 2006, 232 in 2007, 295 in 2008–09; Total roots and tubers 566 in 2006, 614 in 2007, 632 in 2008–09; Total vegetables (incl. melons) 84 in 2006, 89 in 2007–09; Total fruits (excl. melons) 175 in 2006, 181 in 2007–09.

Source: FAO.

LIVESTOCK
('000 head, year ending September, FAO estimates)

	2006	2007	2008
Cattle	37	38	39
Pigs	150	173	200
Sheep	220	230	241
Goats	240	262	285
Chickens	5,600	5,920	6,250
Ducks	250	315	395

Source: FAO.

LIVESTOCK PRODUCTS
(metric tons, FAO estimates)

	2007	2008	2009
Pig meat	5,882	5,882	5,882
Chicken meat	9,480	10,000	10,000
Game meat	6,600	6,700	n.a.
Cows' milk	741	754	754
Hen eggs	4,750	4,750	5,000

Source: FAO.

Forestry

ROUNDWOOD REMOVALS
('000 cubic metres, excluding bark)

	2007	2008	2009
Sawlogs, veneer logs and logs for sleepers	180	240	240
Other industrial wood*	180	180	180
Fuel wood*	6,263	6,503	6,751
Total	6,623	6,923	7,171

* FAO estimates.
Source: FAO.

SAWNWOOD PRODUCTION
('000 cubic metres, including railway sleepers)

	2006	2007	2008
Total (all broadleaved)	60	60	80

2009: Figure assumed to unchanged from 2008 (FAO estimate).
Source: FAO.

Fishing

(metric tons, live weight of capture)

	2006	2007	2008
Freshwater fishes	2,400*	1,743	763
African sicklefish	98	150	185
Barracudas	419	356	126
Blue butterfish	159	n.a.	n.a.
Bobo croaker	300	201	260
Cassava croaker	369	381	229
Clupeoids	364	n.a.	1
Hammerhead sharks	100	332	n.a.
Mantas, devil rays	23	n.a.	n.a.
Marlins, sailfishes, etc.	n.a.	459	180
Sardinellas	508	1,599	626
Sharks, rays, skates, etc.	349	504	108
Snappers	1,194	243	251
Total catch (incl. others)	8,894*	14,488	7,890

* FAO estimate.
Source: FAO.

Mining

	2007	2008	2009
Diamonds ('000 carats)	22	61	37
Gold (kilograms)	311	624	524

Note: In addition to the commodities listed, Liberia produced significant quantities of a variety of industrial minerals and construction materials (clays, gypsum, sand and gravel, and stone), but insufficient information is available to make reliable estimates of output levels.

Source: US Geological Survey.

Industry

SELECTED PRODUCTS
(litres, unless otherwise indicated)

	2008	2009	2010*
Beverages	17,595,586	19,979,814	25,675,338
Cement (metric tons)	94,037	70,584	66,747
Paint (litres)	119,540	211,694	349,386
Candles (kilograms)	289,041	323,200	448,136
Bleach	456,534	529,396	677,038
Rubbing alcohol	118,964	231,060	797,758
Mattresses (number)	108,596	47,278	120,371
Treated (finished) water (million gallons)	1,446.0	299.7	1,510.4

* Estimates.

Electric energy (million kWh): 338 in 2005; 351 in 2006; 353 in 2007 (Source: UN Industrial Commodity Statistics Database).

LIBERIA

Finance

CURRENCY AND EXCHANGE RATES

Monetary Units
100 cents = 1 Liberian dollar (L $).

Sterling, Dollar and Euro Equivalents (30 September 2010)
£1 sterling = L $115.376;
US $1 = L $72.500;
€1 = L $98.948;
L $1,000 = £8.67 = US $13.79 = €10.11.

Average Exchange Rate (L $ per US $)
2007 61.2722
2008 63.2075
2009 68.2867

Note: The aforementioned data are based on market-determined rates of exchange. Prior to January 1998 the exchange rate was a fixed parity with the US dollar (L $1 = US $1).

BUDGET
(US $ million)

Revenue*	2005/06	2006/07	2007/08†
Tax revenue	81.0	140.0	149.5
Taxes on income and profits	25.1	42.5	48.6
Taxes on goods and services	20.3	26.1	26.9
Maritime revenue	12.1	11.8	13.0
Taxes on international trade and transactions	35.3	69.9	70.1
Other taxes	0.3	1.4	3.8
Non-tax revenue	3.6	6.9	36.2
Stumpage fees and land rental	0.0	0.1	2.2
Total	**84.6**	**146.8**	**185.7**

Expenditure‡	2005/06	2006/07	2007/08†
Current expenditure	67.2	106.4	167.6
Wages and salaries	32.5	40.6	67.5
Other goods and services	22.0	46.1	59.8
Subsidies, transfers and net lending	11.2	19.1	32.7
Interest on debt	1.4	0.5	7.6
Capital expenditure	6.3	16.6	21.1
Total	**73.5**	**123.0**	**188.7**

* Excluding grants received (US $ million): 1.0 in 2005/06; 1.5 in 2006/07; 0.0 in 2007/08 (budget projection).
† Budget projection.
‡ Includes net lending.

Source: IMF, *Liberia: Fourth Review of Performance Under the Staff-Monitored Program and Request for Three-Year Arrangement Under the Poverty Reduction and Growth Facility and the Extended Fund Facility—Staff Report; Press Release on the Executive Board Discussion* (March 2008).

2007/08 (US $ million, revised figures): Tax revenue 168.8 (Taxes on income and profits 52.6; Taxes on goods and services 34.9; Taxes on international trade and transactions 79.1); Non-tax revenue 32.0; Total revenue 200.8. Current expenditure 173.2 (Wages and salaries 68.0; Other goods and services 61.2; Subsidies, transfers and net lending 36.6; Interest on debt 7.5); Capital expenditure 23.9; Total expenditure and net lending 197.1 (Source: IMF, *Liberia: 2008 Article IV Consultation, First Review Under the Three-Year Arrangement Under the Poverty Reduction and Growth Facility, Financing Assurances Review, and Request for Waiver and Modification of Performance Criteria—Staff Report; Public Information Notice and Press Release on the Executive Board Discussion; and Statement by the Executive Director for Liberia*—January 2009).

2008/09 (US $ million): *Revenue:* Tax revenue 190.0 (Taxes on income, profits and capital gains 65.8; Taxes on goods and services 33.7; Taxes on international trade and transactions 87.9); Non-tax revenue 21.3; Total revenue 211.3 (excl. grants 23.6). *Expenditure:* Current expenditure 215.1 (Wages and salaries 91.4; Other goods and services 75.3; Subsidies, transfers and net lending 40.9; Interest on debt 7.5); Capital expenditure 33.8; Total expenditure and net lending 248.9 (Source: IMF, *Liberia: 2010 Article IV Consultation and Fifth Review Under the Three-Year Arrangement Under the Extended Credit Facility—Staff Report; Public Information Notice and Press Release on the Executive Board Discussion; and Statement by the Executive Director for Liberia*—December 2010).

INTERNATIONAL RESERVES
(US $ million at 31 December)

	2007	2008	2009
IMF special drawing rights	—	21.84	201.43
Reserve position in IMF	0.05	0.05	0.05
Foreign exchange	119.31	138.97	170.97
Total	**119.36**	**160.86**	**372.46**

2010: IMF special drawing rights 210.49; Reserve position in IMF 0.05.

Source: IMF, *International Financial Statistics*.

MONEY SUPPLY
(L $ million at 31 December)

	2007	2008	2009
Currency outside banks*	3,317.4	3,637.1	4,161.8
Demand deposits at commercial banks	5,541.7	9,110.8	14,189.1
Total money (incl. others)	**9,099.9**	**13,243.7**	**19,113.7**

* Figures refer only to amounts of Liberian coin in circulation. US notes and coin also circulate, but the amount of these in private holdings is unknown. The amount of Liberian coin in circulation is small in comparison to US currency.

Source: IMF, *International Financial Statistics*.

COST OF LIVING
(Consumer Price Index; base: May 1998 = 100)

	2003	2004	2005
Food	140.9	153.8	167.0
Fuel and light	154.4	217.6	342.1
Clothing	121.2	128.7	137.3
Rent	131.8	156.1	180.9
All items (incl. others)	**157.0**	**169.3**	**187.6**

Source: IMF, *Liberia: Selected Issues and Statistical Appendix* (May 2006).

All items (Consumer Price Index; base 2000 = 100): 167.6 in 2006; 186.7 in 2007; 219.4 in 2008; 236.5 in 2009 (Source: African Development Bank).

NATIONAL ACCOUNTS

Expenditure on the Gross Domestic Product
(US $ million at current prices)

	2007	2008	2009
Government final consumption expenditure	95.1	159.7	129.4
Private final consumption expenditure	1,488.3	1,678.1	1,578.5
Gross capital formation	130.6	165.9	171.2
Total domestic expenditure	**1,713.9**	**2,003.8**	**1,879.1**
Exports of goods and services	184.8	258.0	251.2
Less Imports of goods and services	1,246.0	1,432.1	1,274.4
GDP in purchasers' values	**652.8**	**829.7**	**855.9**
GDP at constant 2005 prices	**602.5**	**645.5**	**675.0**

Source: UN Statistics Division, National Accounts Main Aggregates Database.

LIBERIA

Gross Domestic Product by Economic Activity
(US $ million at constant 1992 prices)

	2006	2007	2008*
Agriculture	192.3	210.4	213.8
Forestry	74.1	81.1	97.5
Mining and quarrying	0.7	0.8	0.8
Manufacturing	55.5	60.7	64.3
Electricity and water	3.0	3.3	3.8
Construction	11.3	12.3	16.1
Trade, restaurants and hotels	29.2	31.9	36.7
Transport and communications	30.9	33.8	34.8
Financial institutions	10.8	11.8	11.9
Government services	10.4	11.4	11.3
Other services	14.9	16.3	16.2
GDP in purchasers' values	**433.2**	**473.9**	**507.1**

* Estimates.

2009 (US $ million at constant 1992 prices, preliminary): Agriculture 221.3; Forestry 105.4; Mining and quarrying 0.8; Manufacturing 62.7; Other 140.1; *GDP in purchasers' values* 530.3.

2010 (US $ million at constant 1992 prices, preliminary): Agriculture 229.9; Forestry 119.8; Mining and quarrying 0.9; Manufacturing 64.5; Other 149.5; *GDP in purchasers' values* 564.7.

BALANCE OF PAYMENTS
(US $ million)

	2007	2008	2009
Exports of goods f.o.b.	196.2	249.0	180.0
Imports of goods c.i.f.	−498.5	−728.8	−559.0
Trade balance	**−302.3**	**−479.8**	**−379.0**
Exports of services	346.2	509.6	274.1
Imports of services	−1,248.8	−1,411.1	−1,145.2
Balance on goods and services	**−1,204.9**	**−1,381.4**	**−1,250.1**
Other income received	19.9	22.4	18.1
Other income paid	−176.9	−170.7	−145.9
Balance on goods, services and income	**−1,361.9**	**−1,529.7**	**−1,377.9**
Current transfers (net)	966.8	911.5	836.8
Current balance	**−395.1**	**−618.2**	**−541.1**
Capital account (net)	n.a.	1,197.0	1,526.0
Direct investment from abroad	131.6	394.5	217.8
Other investment assets	−13.2	−33.2	200.4
Other investment liabilities	−4.9	−13.4	158.5
Net errors and omissions	2.4	−465.1	10.8
Overall balance	**−279.2**	**461.6**	**1,572.4**

Source: IMF, *International Financial Statistics*.

External Trade

PRINCIPAL COMMODITIES
(US $ million, estimates)

Imports c.i.f.	2008	2009	2010
Food and live animals	206.8	161.8	234.0
Rice	105.6	65.6	58.4
Beverages and tobacco	13.9	18.6	18.0
Mineral fuels and lubricants	13.2	10.5	82.5
Petroleum	147.2	68.5	103.0
Chemicals and related products	36.5	29.6	32.7
Basic manufactures	104.7	84.0	70.5
Machinery and transport equipment	215.2	125.1	137.4
Miscellaneous manufactured articles	60.1	27.0	47.3
Total (incl. others)	**813.5**	**551.6**	**740.5**

Exports f.o.b.	2008	2009	2010
Rubber	206.8	93.1	167.1
Cocoa beans and coffee	3.4	3.7	5.9
Diamonds	10.0	6.9	11.9
Gold	13.3	11.9	15.3
Iron ore	1.5	0.9	2.4
Total (incl. others)	**242.4**	**148.8**	**223.5**

PRINCIPAL TRADING PARTNERS
(US $ million)

Imports c.i.f.	1986	1987	1988
Belgium-Luxembourg	8.5	11.2	15.0
China, People's Repub.	7.1	14.7	4.8
Denmark	10.6	7.6	5.9
France (incl. Monaco)	6.5	6.4	4.7
Germany, Fed. Repub.	32.7	52.3	39.5
Italy	2.5	2.2	7.3
Japan	20.1	15.0	12.0
Netherlands	20.6	26.8	14.4
Spain	2.5	6.6	3.1
Sweden	2.4	0.6	4.6
United Kingdom	24.2	18.4	12.7
USA	42.5	58.0	57.7
Total (incl. others)	**259.0**	**307.6**	**272.3**

Source: UN, *International Trade Statistics Yearbook*.

Exports f.o.b.	2004	2005	2006*
Belgium	30.6	28.5	39.2
China, People's Repub.	5.5	1.2	n.a.
France	1.7	n.a.	n.a.
USA	63.7	96.8	133.3
Total (incl. others)	**103.8**	**131.8**	**180.8**

* Estimates.

Imports (US $ million): 813.5 in 2008; 551.6 in 2009; 740.5 in 2010 (preliminary).

Exports (US $ million): 242.4 in 2008; 148.8 in 2009; 223.4 in 2010 (preliminary).

Transport

RAILWAYS
(estimated traffic)

	1991	1992	1993
Passenger-km (million)	406	417	421
Freight ton-km (million)	200	200	200

Source: UN Economic Commission for Africa, *African Statistical Yearbook*.

ROAD TRAFFIC
(estimates, '000 vehicles in use at 31 December)

	1999	2000	2001
Passenger cars	15.3	17.1	17.1
Commercial vehicles	11.9	12.8	12.8

2002: Figures assumed to be unchanged from 2001.

Source: UN, *Statistical Yearbook*.

2007 (motor vehicles in use at 31 December): Passenger cars 7,428; Buses and coaches 554; Lorries and vans 2,772; Motorcycles and mopeds 333 (Source: IRF, *World Road Statistics*).

LIBERIA

SHIPPING

Merchant Fleet
(registered at 31 December)

	2007	2008	2009
Number of vessels	2,171	2,306	2,456
Displacement ('000 gross registered tons)	76,572.6	82,389.4	91,695.8

Source: IHS Fairplay, *World Fleet Statistics*.

International Sea-borne Freight Traffic
(estimates, '000 metric tons)

	1991	1992	1993
Goods loaded	16,706	17,338	21,653
Goods unloaded	1,570	1,597	1,608

Source: UN Economic Commission for Africa, *African Statistical Yearbook*.

CIVIL AVIATION
(traffic on scheduled services)

	1990	1991	1992
Passengers carried ('000)	32	32	32
Passenger-km (million)	7	7	7
Total ton-km (million)	1	1	1

Source: UN, *Statistical Yearbook*.

Communications Media

	2007	2008	2009
Telephones ('000 main lines in use)	2.0	2.0	2.0
Mobile cellular telephones ('000 subscribers)	563.0	732.0	842.0
Internet users ('000)	20	20	20

Source: International Telecommunication Union.

Radio receivers ('000 in use): 790 in 1997 (Source: UNESCO, *Statistical Yearbook*).

Television receivers ('000 in use): 70 in 1997 (Source: UNESCO, *Statistical Yearbook*).

Daily newspapers: 6 in 1998 (estimated average circulation 36,600); 3 in 2004 (Source: UNESCO Institute for Statistics).

Education

(2007/08 unless otherwise indicated)

	Teachers	Males	Females	Total
Pre-primary	11,778	251,049	240,515	491,564
Primary	22,253	286,584	253,303	539,887
Secondary	11,880	90,383	67,859	158,242
Secondary technical and vocational*	603	26,988	18,079	45,067
Post-secondary technical and vocational*	430	8,842	6,789	15,631
University	772†	25,236*	18,871*	44,107*

* 1999/2000.
† 2000/01.

Source: UNESCO Institute for Statistics.

Pupil-teacher ratio (primary education, UNESCO estimate): 24.3 in 2007/08 (Source: UNESCO Institute for Statistics).

Adult literacy rate (UNESCO estimates): 58.1% (males 63.3%; females 53.0%) in 2008 (Source: UNESCO Institute for Statistics).

Directory

The Government

HEAD OF STATE

President: ELLEN JOHNSON-SIRLEAF (inaugurated 16 January 2006).

THE CABINET
(May 2011)

Vice-President: JOSEPH NYUMAH BOAKAI.
Minister of Agriculture: Dr FLORENCE CHENOWETH.
Minister of Commerce and Industry: MIATTA BEYSOLOW.
Minister of Defence: BROWNIE SAMUKAI.
Minister of Education: OTHELLO GONGAR.
Minister of Finance: AUGUSTINE NGANFUAN.
Minister of Foreign Affairs: Dr TOGA GAYEWEA MCINTOSH.
Minister of Gender and Development: VARBAH GAYFLOR.
Minister of Health and Social Welfare: Dr WALTER GWENIGALE.
Minister of Information, Culture and Tourism: CLETUS SIEH.
Minister of Internal Affairs: HARRISON KAHNWEAH.
Minister of Justice: CHRISTIANA TAH.
Minister of Labour: JEREMIAH SULUNTEH.
Minister of Lands, Mines and Energy: ROOSEVELT JAYJAY.
Minister of National Security: VICTOR HELB.
Minister of Planning and Economic Affairs: AMARA KONNEH.
Minister of Posts and Telecommunications: FREDERICK NORKEH.
Minister of Public Works: SAMUEL KOFI WOODS.
Minister of Transport: WILLARD RUSSELL.
Minister of Youth and Sports: ETMONIA TARPEH.

MINISTRIES

Office of the President: Executive Mansion, POB 10-9001, Capitol Hill, 1000 Monrovia 10; e-mail rpailey@emansion.gov.lr; internet www.emansion.gov.lr.

Ministry of Agriculture: 19th St, Sinkor, POB 10-9010, 1000 Monrovia 10; tel. 226399; internet www.moa.gov.lr.

LIBERIA

Ministry of Commerce and Industry: Ashmun St, POB 10-9014, 1000 Monrovia 10; tel. 226283; internet www.moci.gov.lr.

Ministry of Defence: Benson St, POB 10-9007, 1000 Monrovia 10; tel. 226077; internet www.mod.gov.lr.

Ministry of Education: E. G. N. King Plaza, Broad St, POB 10-1545, 1000 Monrovia 10; tel. and fax 226216; internet www.moe.gov.lr.

Ministry of Finance: Broad St, POB 10-9013, 1000 Monrovia 10; tel. 47510680 (mobile); internet www.mof.gov.lr.

Ministry of Foreign Affairs: Mamba Point, POB 10-9002, 1000 Monrovia 10; tel. 226763; internet www.mofa.gov.lr.

Ministry of Gender and Development: Monrovia; internet www.mogd.gov.lr.

Ministry of Health and Social Welfare: Sinkor, POB 10-9004, 1000 Monrovia 10; tel. 226317; internet www.moh.gov.lr.

Ministry of Information, Culture and Tourism: Capitol Hill, POB 10-9021, 1000 Monrovia 10; tel. and fax 226269; internet www.micat.gov.lr.

Ministry of Internal Affairs: cnr Warren and Benson Sts, POB 10-9008, 1000 Monrovia 10; tel. 226346; internet www.moia.gov.lr.

Ministry of Justice: Ashmun St, POB 10-9006, 1000 Monrovia 10; tel. 227872; internet www.moia.gov.lr.

Ministry of Labour: Mechlin St, POB 10-9040, 1000 Monrovia 10; tel. 226291; internet www.mol.gov.lr.

Ministry of Lands, Mines and Energy: Capitol Hill, POB 10-9024, 1000 Monrovia 10; tel. 226281; internet www.molme.gov.lr.

Ministry of National Security: Monrovia.

Ministry of Planning and Economic Affairs: Broad St, POB 10-9016, 1000 Monrovia 10; tel. 226962; internet www.mopea.gov.lr.

Ministry of Posts and Telecommunications: Carey St, 1000 Monrovia 10; tel. 6433715 (mobile); e-mail ministryofposttelecommunication@yahoo.com.

Ministry of Presidential Affairs: Executive Mansion, Capitol Hill, 1000 Monrovia 10; tel. 228026; internet www.emansion.gov.lr.

Ministry of Public Works: Lynch St, POB 10-9011, 1000 Monrovia 10; tel. 227972; internet www.mopw.gov.lr.

Ministry of Transport: 1000 Monrovia 10; internet www.mopt.gov.lr.

Ministry of Youth and Sports: Monrovia; internet www.lys.gov.lr.

President and Legislature

PRESIDENT

Presidential Election, First Round, 11 October 2005

Candidate	Votes	% of votes
George Manneh Weah (Congress for Democratic Change)	275,265	28.26
Ellen Johnson-Sirleaf (Unity Party)	192,326	19.75
Charles Walker Brumskine (Liberty Party)	135,093	13.87
Winston A. Tubman (National Democratic Party of Liberia)	89,623	9.20
Harry Varney Gboto-Nambi Sherman (Coalition for the Transformation of Liberia)	76,403	7.85
Roland Chris Yarkpah Massaquoi (National Patriotic Party)	40,361	4.14
Joseph D. Z. Korto (Liberia Equal Rights Party)	31,814	3.27
Alhaji G. V. Kromah (All Liberian Coalition Party)	27,141	2.79
Togba-Nah Tipoteh (Alliance for Peace and Democracy)	22,766	2.34
Others	82,998	8.52
Total	**973,790**	**100.00**

Presidential Election, Second Round, 8 November 2005

Candidate	Votes	% of votes
Ellen Johnson-Sirleaf (Unity Party)	478,526	59.40
George Manneh Weah (Congress for Democratic Change)	327,046	40.60
Total	**805,572**	**100.00**

LEGISLATURE

House of Representatives

Speaker: ALEX JANEKAI TYLER.

General Election, 11 October 2005

Party	% of votes	Seats
Congress for Democratic Change	23.4	15
Liberty Party	14.1	9
Unity Party	12.5	8
Coalition for the Transformation of Liberia	12.5	8
Independents	10.9	7
Alliance for Peace and Democracy	7.8	5
National Patriotic Party	6.3	4
New Deal Movement	4.7	3
All Liberian Coalition Party	3.1	2
National Democratic Party of Liberia	1.6	1
United Democratic Alliance	1.6	1
National Reformation Party	1.6	1
Total	**100.0**	**64**

Senate

President: (vacant).

General Election, 11 October 2005

Party	% of votes	Seats
Coalition for the Transformation of Liberia	23.3	7
Congress for Democratic Change	10.0	3
Unity Party	10.0	3
Liberty Party	10.0	3
Alliance for Peace and Democracy	10.0	3
National Patriotic Party	10.0	3
Independents	10.0	3
National Democratic Party of Liberia	6.7	2
National Reformation Party	3.3	1
All Liberian Coalition Party	3.3	1
United Democratic Alliance	3.3	1
Total	**100.0**	**30**

Election Commission

National Elections Commission: Tubman Blvd, 16th St, Sinkor, Monrovia; internet www.necliberia.org; independent; Chair. JAMES M. FROMAYAN.

Political Organizations

A total of 30 political parties were granted registration prior to presidential and legislative elections in October and November 2005.

Alliance for Peace and Democracy (APD): Benson St, Monrovia; tel. 6918196 (mobile); e-mail karwease@go.metrostate.edu; internet www.members.tripod.com/tipoteh12/index.html; f. 2005; Leader TOGBA-NAH TIPOTEH; Chair. DUSTY WOLOKOLIE.

Liberian People's Party (LPP): Monrovia; f. 1984 by fmr mems of the Movement for Justice in Africa; Leader DUSTY WOLOKOLIE.

United People's Party (UPP): Monrovia; f. 1984 by fmr mems of the Progressive People's Party, which led opposition prior to April 1980 coup; Leader WESLEY JOHNSON.

All Liberian Coalition Party (ALCOP): Broad St, Monrovia; tel. 6524735; f. 1997 from elements of fmr armed faction the United Liberation Movement of Liberia for Democracy; Leader Alhaji G. V. KROMAH; Chair. JOHNSTON P. FANNEBRDE.

Congress for Democratic Change: Bernard Beach Compound, Monrovia; tel. 6513469 (mobile); internet www.cdcforliberia.org; f. 2004; Leader GEORGE MANNEH WEAH; Chair. J. BANGULA COLE.

Free Democratic Party (FDP): Center St, Monrovia; tel. 6582291 (mobile); Leader DAVID M. FARHAT; Chair. S. CIAPHA GBOLLIE.

Liberia Destiny Party (LDP): Congo Town Back Rd, Monrovia; tel. 6511531 (mobile); f. 2005; Leader MILTON NATHANIEL BARNES; Sec.-Gen. BORBOR B. KROMAH.

Liberia Equal Rights Party (LERP): Duala Gas Station, Bushrod Island, Opposite Duala Market, Monrovia; f. 2005; Leader JOSEPH D. Z. KORTO; Chair. SOLOMON KING.

LIBERIA

Liberty Party (LP): Old Rd, Sinkor Opposite Haywood Mission, POB 1340, Monrovia; tel. 6547921 (mobile); f. 2005; Leader CHARLES WALKER BRUMSKINE; Chair. ISRAEL AKINSANYA.

National Democratic Party of Liberia (NDPL): Capitol By-Pass, Monrovia; f. 1997 from the fmr armed faction the Liberia Peace Council; Chair. MICHAEL NAYOU.

National Patriotic Party (NPP): Sinkor, Tubman Bldg, Monrovia; tel. 6515312 (mobile); f. 1997 from the fmr armed faction the National Patriotic Front of Liberia; won the majority of seats in legislative elections in July 1997; Leader ROLAND CHRIS YARKPAH MASSAQUOI; Chair. LAWRENCE A. GEORGE.

National Reformation Party (NRP): Duala Market, Monrovia; tel. 6511531 (mobile); Chair. Rev. SAMUEL TORMETIEE.

New Deal Movement (NDM): Randall St, Monrovia; tel. 6567470 (mobile); e-mail info@newdealmovement.com; internet newdealmovement.com; f. 2002; Leader Prof. GEORGE KLAY KIEH, Jr; Chair. MOSES B. MADY-YUU (acting).

Progressive Democratic Party (PRODEM): McDonald St, Monrovia; tel. 6521091 (mobile); f. early 2005 by mems of fmr rebel movement, Liberians United for Reconciliation and Democracy (emerged 1999); Leader SEKOU DAMATE CONNEH.

Reformed United Liberia Party (RULP): 70 Ashmun St, POB 1000, Monrovia; tel. 571212; f. 2005; Leader WILLIAM VACANARAT SHADRACH TUBMAN.

United Democratic Alliance (UDA): Monrovia; f. 2005 by the Liberia National Union (LINU); led by HENRY MONIBA; the Liberia Education and Development Party (LEAD); and the Reformation Alliance Party (RAP), led by HENRY BOIMAH FAHNBULLEH.

Unity Party (UP): 86 Broad St, Monrovia; tel. 6512528 (mobile); e-mail info@theunityparty.org; f. 1984; Leader ELLEN JOHNSON-SIRLEAF; Chair. HARRY VARNEY GBOTO-NAMBI SHERMAN.

Diplomatic Representation

EMBASSIES IN LIBERIA

Algeria: Capitol By-Pass, POB 2032, Monrovia; tel. 224311; Chargé d'affaires a.i. MUHAMMAD AZZEDINE AZZOUZ.

Cameroon: 18th St and Payne Ave, Sinkor, POB 414, Monrovia; tel. 261374; Ambassador BENG'YELA AUGUSTINE GANG.

China, People's Republic: Tubman Blvd, Congotown, POB 5970, Monrovia; tel. 228024; fax 226740; e-mail Chinaemb_lr@mfa.gov.cn; internet lr.china-embassy.org; Ambassador ZHAO JIANHUA.

Congo, Democratic Republic: Spriggs Payne Airport, Sinkor, POB 1038, Monrovia; tel. 261326; Ambassador (vacant).

Côte d'Ivoire: Tubman Blvd, Sinkor, POB 126, Monrovia; tel. 261123; Ambassador ELISABETH TOURÉ KINANWONAMAN.

Cuba: 17 Kennedy Ave, Congotown, POB 3579, Monrovia; tel. 262600; Ambassador Dr MIGUEL GUSTAVO PÉREZ CRUZ.

Egypt: Coconut Plantation, Randal St, Mamba Point, POB 462, Monrovia; tel. 226226; fax 226122; Ambassador AMED MOHAMED YAKOUB.

France: German Compound, Congo Town, Monrovia; tel. 6579373 (mobile); e-mail ambafrance.liberia@yahoo.fr; Ambassador GÉRARD LARÔME.

Germany: Tubman Blvd, Monrovia; tel. 6438365 (mobile); e-mail info@monrovia.diplo.de; Ambassador Dr BODO SCHAFF.

Ghana: cnr 11th St and Gardiner Ave, Sinkor, POB 471, Monrovia; tel. 261477; Ambassador Maj.-Gen. FRANCIS ADU-AMANFOH.

Guinea: Monrovia; Ambassador ABDOULAYE DORÉ.

Lebanon: 12th St, Monrovia; tel. 262537; Ambassador MANSOUR ABDALLAH.

Libya: Monrovia; Ambassador MUHAMMAD UMARAT-TABI.

Morocco: Tubman Blvd, Congotown, Monrovia; tel. 262767; Ambassador MOHAMED LASFAR.

Nigeria: Tubman Blvd, Congotown, POB 366, Monrovia; tel. 6823638 (mobile); fax 226135; e-mail nigerianmonrovia@yahoo.com; Chargé d'affaires a.i. ESSESIEN NTEKIM.

Russia: Payne Ave, Sinkor, POB 2010, Monrovia; tel. 261304; Ambassador ANDREY V. POKROVSKII.

Senegal: Monrovia; Ambassador MOCTAR TRAORÉ.

Sierra Leone: Tubman Blvd, POB 575, Monrovia; tel. 261301; Ambassador Rev. MARIE J. BARNETT.

South Africa: Monrovia; Ambassador MASILO ESAU MEBETA.

USA: 111 United Nations Dr., Mamba Point, POB 98, Monrovia; tel. 77054826 (mobile); fax 77010370 (mobile); e-mail ConsularMonrovia@state.gov; internet monrovia.usembassy.gov; Ambassador LINDA THOMAS-GREENFIELD.

Judicial System

In February 1982 the People's Supreme Tribunal (which had been established following the April 1980 coup) was renamed the People's Supreme Court, and its Chairman and members became the Chief Justice and Associate Justices of the People's Supreme Court. The judicial system also comprised People's Circuit and Magistrate Courts. The five-member Supreme Court was established in January 1992 to adjudicate in electoral disputes.

Chief Justice of the Supreme Court of Liberia: JOHNNIE LEWIS.

Justices: KABINEH JA'NEH, FRANCIS KORPKPOR, GLADYS JOHNSON.

Religion

Liberia is officially a Christian state, although complete religious freedom is guaranteed. Christianity and Islam are the two main religions. There are numerous religious sects, and many Liberians hold traditional beliefs.

CHRISTIANITY

Liberian Council of Churches: 15th St, Sinkor, POB 10-2191, 1000 Monrovia; tel. 6517879 (mobile); e-mail liberiancouncil@yahoo.com; internet www.liberiancouncilofchurches.org; f. 1982; 11 mems, two assoc. mems, one fraternal mem.; Pres. Rev. Dr JOHN G. INNIS.

The Anglican Communion

The diocese of Liberia forms part of the Church of the Province of West Africa, incorporating the local Episcopal Church. Anglicanism was established in Liberia in 1836, and the diocese of Liberia was admitted into full membership of the Province in 1982. The Metropolitan of the Province is the Bishop of Koforidua, Ghana.

Bishop of Liberia: Rt Rev. JONATHAN BAU-BAU BONAPARTE HART, POB 10-0277, 1000 Monrovia 10; tel. 224760; fax 227519; e-mail bishop@liberia.net.

The Roman Catholic Church

Liberia comprises the archdiocese of Monrovia and the dioceses of Cape Palmas and Gbarnga. An estimated 9% of the total population were Roman Catholics.

Catholic Bishops' Conference of Liberia
POB 10-2078, 1000 Monrovia 10; tel. 227245; fax 226175.
f. 1998; Pres. Rt Rev. LEWIS ZEIGLER (Bishop of Gbarnga).

Archbishop of Monrovia: Most Rev. LEWIS ZEIGLER, Archbishop's Office, POB 10-2078, 1000 Monrovia 10; tel. 6519766 (mobile); fax 77003719 (mobile); e-mail apostolic_adm@yahoo.com.

Other Christian Churches

Assemblies of God in Liberia: POB 1297, Monrovia; f. 1908; 14,578 adherents, 287 churches; Gen. Supt JIMMIE K. DUGBE, Sr.

Lutheran Church in Liberia (LCL): POB 10-1046, 13th St, Payne Ave, Sinkor, 1000 Monrovia 10; tel. 226323; fax 380637; e-mail lutheranchurchinliberia@yahoo.com; f. 1947 as Evangelical Lutheran Church, reorg. in 1965 under indigenous leadership as LCL; Pres. Bishop SUMOWARD E. HARRIS; 71,196 mems (2010).

Providence Baptist Church: cnr Broad and Center Sts, Monrovia; tel. 6533941 (mobile); e-mail admin@providencebc.net; internet www.providencebc.net; f. 1821; 2,500 adherents, 300 congregations, 6 ministers, 8 schools; Pastor Rev. A. MOMOLUE DIGGS.

Liberia Baptist Missionary and Educational Convention, Inc: POB 390, Monrovia; tel. 222661; f. 1880; 72,000 adherents, 270 churches (2007); Pres. Rev. J. K. LEVEE MOULTON; Nat. Vice-Pres. Rev. J. GBANA HALL; Gen. Sec. CHARLES W. BLAKE.

United Methodist Church in Liberia: cnr 12th St and Tubman Blvd, POB 1010, 1000 Monrovia 10; tel. 223343; e-mail bishop.jinnis@liberiaumc.org; internet www.umcliberia.org; f. 1833; c. 168,300 adherents, 600 congregations, 700 ministers, 394 lay pastors; Resident Bishop Rev. Dr JOHN G. INNIS.

Other active denominations include the National Baptist Mission, the Pentecostal Church, the Presbyterian Church in Liberia, the Prayer Band and the Church of the Lord Aladura.

ISLAM

The total community numbers about 670,000.

National Muslim Council of Liberia: Monrovia; Leader Shaykh KAFUMBA KONNAH.

LIBERIA
Directory

The Press

NEWSPAPERS

Daily Observer: POB 1858, Monrovia; tel. 6513788 (mobile); e-mail editor@liberianobserver.com; internet www.liberianobserver.com; f. 1981; independent; daily; Dir KENNETH Y. BEST.

The Inquirer: POB 3600, Monrovia; tel. 6538573 (mobile); fax 227036; e-mail theinquirernews@yahoo.com; internet www.theinquirer.com.lr; New Era Publications, Ltd; daily; Man. Editor PHILIP WESSEH.

Monrovia Guardian: 58 Broad Street, POB 2131, Monrovia; weekly; independent; Editor B. IGNATIUS GEORGE.

News: ACDB Bldg, POB 10-3137, Carey Warren St, Monrovia; tel. 227820; independent; weekly; Chair. WILSON TARPEH; Editor-in-Chief JEROME DALIEH.

PERIODICALS

The Kpelle Messenger: Kpelle Literacy Center, Lutheran Church, POB 1046, Monrovia; Kpelle-English; monthly; Editor Rev. JOHN J. MANAWU.

Liberia Orbit: Voinjama; e-mail orbit@tekmail.com; internet www.liberiaorbit.org; national current affairs; Editor LLOYD SCOTT.

Liberian Post: e-mail info@liberian.org; internet www.liberian.org; f. 1998; independent internet magazine; tourist information; Publr WILLEM TIJSSEN.

New Democrat: Clay St, Central Town, Monrovia; tel. 5548626 (mobile); fax 77249415 (mobile); e-mail newdemnews@yahoo.com; internet www.newdemocratnews.com; national news and current affairs; Editor TOM KAMARA.

Patriot: Congo Town 1000, Monrovia; internet www.allaboutliberia.com/patriot.htm.

The People Magazine: Bank of Liberia Bldg, Suite 214, Carey and Warren Sts, POB 3501, Monrovia; tel. 222743; f. 1985; monthly; Editor and Publr CHARLES A. SNETTER.

PRESS ORGANIZATIONS

Liberia Institute of Journalism: Kashour Bldg, 2nd Floor, cnr Broad and Johnson Sts, POB 2314, Monrovia; tel. 227327; Dir VINICIUS HODGES.

Press Union of Liberia: Benson St, POB 20-4209, Monrovia; tel. and fax 227105; internet www.pressunionlib.net; f. 1985; Pres. PETER QUAQUA.

NEWS AGENCY

Liberian News Agency (LINA): POB 9021, Capitol Hill, Monrovia; tel. 222229; Dir-Gen. ERNEST KIAZOLY (acting).

Broadcasting and Communications

TELECOMMUNICATIONS

Cellcom: Haile Selassie Ave, Capitol By-Pass, Monrovia; tel. 77777008 (mobile); fax 77000101 (mobile); e-mail info@cellcomgsm.com; internet www.lr.cellcomgsm.com; mobile cellular telephone provider.

Comium: Comium Bldg, Congo Town, Monrovia; tel. 5600600 (mobile); fax 5600611 (mobile); e-mail info@comium.com.lr; internet www.comium.com.lr; mobile cellular telephone provider; Exec. Chair. MONIE R. CAPTAN.

LiberCell: Monrovia; e-mail info@awli.net; internet www.libercell.info; f. 2004; mobile cellular telephone provider; CEO AZZAM SBAITY; Gen. Man. MOHAMMED ALAWIE.

Liberia Telecommunications Corpn: 18th St and Tubman Blvd, Sinkor, Monrovia; tel. 25551000; fax 25551099; e-mail info@libtelco.com.lr; internet www.libtelco.com.lr; Man. Dir BEN WOLO.

Lonestar Cell: LBDI Bldg, Congo Town, Monrovia; tel. 6500000 (mobile); fax 6501101 (mobile); internet www.lonestarcell.com; f. 2001; mobile cellular telephone provider; subsidiary of Mobile Telephone Networks (Pty) Ltd, South Africa; CEO FRANS JOUBERT; Gen. Man. KHALED MIKKAWI.

BROADCASTING

Radio

Liberia Communications Network: Congo Town 1000, Monrovia; govt-operated; broadcasts information, education and entertainment 24 hours daily in English, French and several African languages; short-wave service.

Liberia Rural Communications Network: POB 10-02176, 1000 Monrovia 10; tel. 271368; f. 1981; govt-operated; rural devt and entertainment programmes; Dir J. RUFUS KAINE (acting).

Radio Veritas: POB 3569, Monrovia; tel. 4712834 (mobile); e-mail radioveritas@hotmail.com; internet radioveritas.org; f. 1981; Catholic; independent; nation-wide shortwave broadcasts; Dirs Fr ANTHONY BOWAH, LEDGERHOOD RENNIE.

Star Radio: 12 Broad St, Snapper Hill, Monrovia; tel. 77104411 (mobile); e-mail star@liberia.net; internet www.starradio.org.lr; independent news and information station; f. July 1997 by Fondation Hirondelle, Switzerland, with funds from the US Agency for International Development; broadcasts in English, French and 14 African languages; Man. JAMES K. MORLU.

Television

Liberia Broadcasting System: POB 594, Monrovia; tel. 224984; internet www.liberiabroadcastingsystem.com; govt-owned; Chair. ALHAJI KROMAH; Dir-Gen. DARRYL AMBROSE NMAH.

Finance

(cap. = capital; res = reserves; dep. = deposits; m. = million; br. = branch; amounts in Liberian dollars, unless otherwise indicated)

BANKING

In 2010 there were eight commercial banks in Liberia.

Central Bank

Central Bank of Liberia: cnr Warren and Carey Sts, POB 2048, 1000 Monrovia; tel. 6225685 (mobile); fax 6226114 (mobile); e-mail webmaster@cbl.org.lr; internet www.cbl.org.lr; f. 1974 as National Bank of Liberia; name changed March 1999; bank of issue; cap. 7,598.5m., res 3,817.4m., dep. 9,226.7m. (Dec. 2009); Gov. JOSEPH MILLS JONES.

Other Banks

AccessBank Liberia Ltd: Johnson St, Monrovia; tel. 77006688 (mobile); f. 2008; CEO MARY CLARE ODONG.

Ecobank Liberia Ltd: Ashmun and Randall Sts, POB 4825, Monrovia; tel. 6553919 (mobile); fax 227029; e-mail ecobanklr@ecobank.com; internet www.ecobank.com; commenced operations Aug. 1999; cap. and res US $2.1m., total assets US $10.2m. (Dec. 2001); Chair. G. PEWU SUBAH; Man. Dir KOLA ADELEKE.

First International Bank (Liberia) Ltd: Luke Bldg, Broad St, Monrovia; tel. 77026241 (mobile); e-mail info@fib-lib.com; internet www.fib-lib.com; f. April 2005; Chair. FRANCIS L. M. HORTON; Exec. Dir ARISA AWA.

Global Bank Liberia Ltd (GBLL): Ashmun and Mechlin Sts, POB 2053, Monrovia; tel. 6425760 (mobile); e-mail mail@globalbankliberia.com; internet www.globalbankliberia.com; f. 2005; Italian-owned; Pres. Dr RICCARDO SEMBIANTE.

Guaranty Trust Bank (Liberia) Ltd (GTBLL): United Nations Dr., Clara Town, Bushrod Island, POB 0382, Monrovia; tel. 77499992 (mobile); fax 77499995 (mobile); internet www.gtbanklr.com; f. 2007; Chair. TAYO ADERINOKUN; CEO DAN OROGUN.

International Bank (Liberia) Ltd: 64 Broad St, POB 10292, 1000 Monrovia; tel. 6557473 (mobile); fax 4074245 (mobile); e-mail customercare@ibliberia.com; internet www.ibliberia.com; f. 1948 as International Trust Co of Liberia; name changed April 2000; 75.5% owned by Liberian Financial Holdings; 19.1% Trust Bank Ltd (The Gambia); cap. 2m. (1989), dep. 96.4m. (Dec. 1996); CEO PATRICK ANUMEL (acting); Gen. Man. HENRY SAAMOI; 3 brs.

Liberian Bank for Development and Investment (LBDI): Ashmun and Randall Sts, POB 547, Monrovia; tel. 227140; fax 226359; e-mail lbdi@lbdi.net; internet www.lbdi.net; f. 1961; 18.7% govt-owned; cap. and res US $12.5m., total assets US $26.8m. (Dec. 2001); Chair. AUGUSTINE K. NGAFUAN; Pres. FRANCIS A. DENNIS, Jr.

United Bank for Africa Liberia Ltd: POB 4523, Monrovia; tel. 6569375 (mobile); e-mail ubaliberia@ubagroup.com; internet www.ubagroup.com/ubaliberia; f. 2006; CEO EBELE E. OGBUE.

Banking Association

Liberia Bankers' Association: POB 292, Monrovia; mems include commercial and devt banks; Pres. FRANCIS A. DENNIS, Jr.

INSURANCE

American Life Insurance Co: Carter Bldg, 39 Broad St, POB 60, Monrovia; f. 1969; life and general; Vice-Pres. ALLEN BROWN.

American National Underwriters, Inc: Carter Bldg, 39 Broad St, POB 180, Monrovia; tel. 114921; general; Gen. Man. S. B. MENSAH.

LIBERIA

Insurance Co of Africa: 2nd Floor, International Bank Building, 64 Broad St, Monrovia; tel. 6513281 (mobile); internet icaliberia.com; f. 1969; life and general; Pres. SAMUEL OWAREE MINTAH.

National Insurance Corpn of Liberia (NICOL): LBDI Bldg Complex, POB 1528, Sinkor, Monrovia; tel. 262429; f. 1983; state-owned; sole insurer for Govt and parastatal bodies; also provides insurance for the Liberian-registered merchant shipping fleet; Man. Dir MIATTA EDITH SHERMAN.

Royal Exchange Assurance: Ashmun and Randall Sts, POB 666, Monrovia; all types of insurance; Man. RONALD WOODS.

United Security Insurance Agencies Inc: Randall St, POB 2071, Monrovia; life, personal accident and medical; Dir EPHRAIM O. OKORO.

Trade and Industry

GOVERNMENT AGENCIES

Budget Bureau: Capitol Hill, POB 1518, Monrovia; tel. 226340; Dir-Gen. MATHEW DINGIE.

General Services Agency (GSA): Old USTC Compound, UN Dr., POB 10-9027, Monrovia; tel. 6901333 (mobile); e-mail info@gsa.gov.lr; internet www.gsa.gov.lr; Dir-Gen. ALPHONSO GAYE.

DEVELOPMENT ORGANIZATIONS

Forestry Development Authority: POB 10-3010, Kappa House, Eli Saleby Compound, Monrovia; tel. 224940; fax 226000; e-mail john.woods@fda.gov.lr; internet www.fda.gov.lr; f. 1976; responsible for forest management and conservation; Chair. EDWIN ZELEE; Man. Dir MOSES WOGBEH.

Liberia Industrial Free Zone Authority (LIFZA): One Free Zone, Monrovia; tel. 533671; e-mail mskromah@lifza.com; internet www.lifza.com; f. 1975; 98 mems; Man. Dir MOHAMMED S. KROMAH.

National Investment Commission (NIC): Fmr Executive Mansion Bldg, POB 9043, Monrovia; tel. 7873001 (mobile); internet www.nic.gov.lr; f. 1979; autonomous body negotiating investment incentives agreements on behalf of Govt; promotes agro-based and industrial devt; Chair. O'NATTY B. DAVIS; Exec. Dir CIATA BISHOP.

CHAMBER OF COMMERCE

Liberia Chamber of Commerce: Capitol Hill, POB 92, Monrovia; tel. 77857805 (mobile); e-mail secgen@chamberofcommerce.org.lr; internet www.chamberofcommerce.org.lr; f. 1951; Pres. MONIE RALPH CAPTAN; Sec.-Gen. DAVID G. FROMAYAN.

INDUSTRIAL AND TRADE ASSOCIATIONS

Liberian Produce Marketing Corpn: POB 662, Monrovia; tel. 222447; f. 1961; govt-owned; exports Liberian produce, provides industrial facilities for processing of agricultural products and participates in agricultural devt programmes; Man. Dir NYAH MARTEIN.

Liberian Resources Corpn (LIBRESCO): controls Liberia's mineral resources; 60% govt-owned; 40% owned by South African co, Amalia Gold.

EMPLOYERS' ASSOCIATION

National Enterprises Corpn: POB 518, Monrovia; tel. 261370; importer, wholesaler and distributor of foodstuffs, and wire and metal products for local industries; Pres. EMMANUEL SHAW, Sr.

UTILITIES

Electricity

Liberia Electricity Corpn (LEC): Waterside, UN Dr., Monrovia; tel. 6653650 (mobile); e-mail mlackay@libelcorp.com; internet www.libelcorp.com; Chair. DUNSTAN L. D. MACAULEY; Man. Dir JOSEPH MAYAH.

National Oil Co of Liberia (NOCAL): Episcopal Church Plaza, Ashmun and Randall Sts, 1000 Monrovia; internet www.nocal-lr.com; Chair. CLEMENCEAU B. UREY; Pres. and CEO CHRISTOPHER NEYOR.

TRADE UNION

Liberian Labor Congress: J. B. McGill Labor Center, Gardnersville Freeway, POB 415, Monrovia; f. 2008 following merger of Liberian Federation of Labor Unions and Congress of National Trade Unions; Pres. MOSES P. BARWROR, Jr; Sec.-Gen. MARCUS S. BLAMAH.

Transport

RAILWAYS

Railway operations were suspended in 1990, owing to the civil conflict. Large sections of the 480-km rail network were subsequently dismantled.

Bong Mine Railway: POB 538, Monrovia; tel. 225222; fax 225770; f. 1958; Gen. Man. HANS-GEORG SCHNEIDER.

ROADS

In 2000 the road network in Liberia totalled an estimated 10,600 km, of which about 657 km were paved. The main trunk road is the Monrovia–Sanniquellie motor road, extending north-east from the capital to the border with Guinea, near Ganta, and eastward through the hinterland to the border with Côte d'Ivoire. Trunk roads run through Tapita, in Nimba County, to Grand Gedeh County and from Monrovia to Buchanan. A bridge over the Mano river connects with the Sierra Leone road network, while a main road links Monrovia and Freetown (Sierra Leone). Although principal roads were officially reopened to commercial traffic in early 1997, following the 1989–96 armed conflict, much of the infrastructure remained severely damaged. In late 2003 the Liberian authorities announced plans for the extensive rehabilitation of the road network, including a highway linking Monrovia with Harper, which was to be funded by the People's Republic of China.

SHIPPING

In December 2009 Liberia's open-registry fleet (2,456 vessels), the second largest in the world (after Panama) in terms of gross tonnage, had a total displacement of 91.7m. grt. Commercial port activity in Liberia was frequently suspended from 1990, as a result of hostilities. At September 2004 only Monrovia Freeport had fully resumed operations and (compared with the corresponding period in 2003) experienced a rise in vessel traffic of 95.2%, owing to increasing commercial and humanitarian activities.

Bureau of Maritime Affairs: Tubman Blvd, Sinkor, POB 10-9042, 1000 Monrovia 10; tel. and fax 77206108 (mobile); e-mail info@bma-liberia.com; internet www.bma-liberia.com; Commissioner BINYAH C. KESSELLY.

Liberia National Shipping Line (LNSL): Monrovia; f. 1987; jt venture by the Liberian Govt and private German interests; routes to Europe, incl. the United Kingdom and Scandinavia.

National Port Authority: Freeport of Monrovia, Bushrod Island, Monrovia; tel. 6402906 (mobile); fax 77861997 (mobile); e-mail natportliberia@yahoo.com; internet www.nationalportauthorityliberia.org; f. 1967; administers Monrovia Freeport and the ports of Buchanan, Greenville and Harper; Chair. Dr C. WILLIAM ALLEN; Man. Dir MATILDA PARKER.

CIVIL AVIATION

Liberia's principal airports are Robertsfield International Airport, at Harbel, 56 km east of Monrovia, and James Spriggs Payne Airport, at Monrovia.

ADC Liberia Inc: Monrovia; f. 1993; services to the United Kingdom, the USA and destinations in West Africa.

Air Liberia: POB 2076, Monrovia; f. 1974; state-owned; scheduled passenger and cargo services; Man. Dir JAMES K. KOFA.

Tourism

Liberia's natural assets, especially its beaches and the Sapo National Park and other areas of primary tropical rainforest, have the potential to support both a beach-based and an eco-tourism industry. However, no such industry has ever been developed in Liberia and tourism has been entirely in abeyance since 1990 because of the almost continuous civil conflict since that time. The development of the country's tourist potential will be limited by high levels of violent crime and a tourism infrastructure that remains meagre or absent.

Defence

Following a major rebel offensive against the capital in June 2003, the UN Security Council on 1 August authorized the establishment of an Economic Community of West African States (ECOWAS) peace-keeping contingent, the ECOWAS Mission in Liberia (ECOMIL), which was to restore security and prepare for the deployment of a longer-term UN stabilization force. The UN Mission in Liberia (UNMIL), which was officially established on 19 September and replaced ECOMIL on 1 October, was mandated to support the implementation of a comprehensive peace agreement, and a two-year transitional administration. With a total authorized strength of up to 15,000, at the end of January 2009 UNMIL numbered 10,595 troops, 167 military observers and 1,201 civilian police, supported by 489 international civilian personnel, 975 local staff and 206 UN volunteers. Following the completion of the disarmament programme, in January 2005 a US military commission arrived in Liberia to assist in the restructuring of the armed forces, which was ongoing in the early 2010s. In June 2006 the armed forces began recruiting women as part of the reform process. A 3,500-member Liberia National Police force, trained by UNMIL was also established, although by early 2009 the force remained generally ineffective with little equipment. As assessed at November 2010, the total strength of the Liberian armed forces was 2,050.

Defence Expenditure: Estimated at US $110m. in 2009.

Chief of Staff of the Armed Forces of Liberia: Maj.-Gen. SURAJ ALAO ABDURRAHMAN.

Education

Education is provided by a mixture of government, private, church and mosque schools. The civil conflicts of 1989–1996 and 1999–2003 devastated the education system as buildings and equipment were damaged and looted, and teachers, parents and children became refugees or internally displaced. By September 2005 3,817 of the country's 4,500 schools were reported to be functioning again. Education in Liberia is officially compulsory for 10 years, between six and 16 years of age. Primary education begins theoretically at six years of age and lasts for six years (grades 1–6). Secondary education, beginning theoretically at 12 years of age, lasts for a further six years, and is divided into two three-year cycles, known in Liberia as 'junior high school' (grades 7–9) and 'senior high school' (grades 10-12). Pre-primary education is undertaken from the age of five or younger and is important for those students whose mother language is not English, since English is the language of instruction throughout the school system. School attendance is not enforced and in 2006 an estimated 61% of primary school age children were out of school (60% of boys and 61% of girls). Although the 1984 Liberian Constitution includes the aspiration to provide universal free education, and fees in public primary schools have been officially abolished, school attendance is discouraged by the poor quality of education offered, by the remaining school fees, by charges and by the cost of uniforms and travel. The higher education sector consists of the University of Liberia in Monrovia, Cuttington University College in Bong County, the Booker Washington Institute in Kakata, Margibi County, and the William V. S. Tubman College in Maryland County. According to UNESCO, a total of 44,107 students were enrolled in tertiary education in 1999–2000.

LIBYA

Introductory Survey

LOCATION, CLIMATE, LANGUAGE, RELIGION, FLAG, CAPITAL

The Great Socialist People's Libyan Arab Jamahiriya extends along the Mediterranean coast of North Africa. Its neighbours are Tunisia and Algeria to the west, Niger and Chad to the south, Egypt to the east, and Sudan to the south-east. The climate is very hot and dry. Most of the country is part of the Sahara, an arid desert, but the coastal regions are cooler. Average temperatures range from 13°C (55°F) to 38°C (100°F), but a maximum of 57.3°C (135°F) has been recorded in the interior. Arabic is the official language, although English and Italian are also used in trade. Almost all of the population are Sunni Muslims. The national flag (proportions 2 by 3) is plain green. The administrative capital was formerly Tripoli (Tarabulus), but under a decentralization programme announced in September 1988 most government departments and the legislature were relocated to Sirte (Surt), while some departments were transferred to other principal towns. However, some departments were subsequently moved back to Tripoli.

CONTEMPORARY POLITICAL HISTORY

Historical Context

Libya, formerly an Italian colony and occupied by British and French troops in 1942, attained independence as the United Kingdom of Libya on 24 December 1951. Muhammad Idris al-Sanusi, Amir of Cyrenaica, became King Idris of Libya. British and US forces maintained bases in Libya in return for economic assistance; however, the discovery of petroleum reserves in 1959 greatly increased the country's potential for financial autonomy.

King Idris was deposed in September 1969, in a bloodless revolution led by a group of young nationalist army officers. A Revolution Command Council (RCC) was established, with Col Muammar al-Qaddafi as Chairman, and a Libyan Arab Republic was proclaimed. British and US military personnel withdrew from Libya in 1970, and the following year British oil interests in Libya were nationalized.

The Arab Socialist Union (ASU) was established in June 1971 as the country's sole political party. People's Congresses and Popular Committees were formed, and an undertaking was made to administer the country in accordance with Islamic principles. The General National Congress of the ASU (which comprised members of the RCC, and leaders of the People's Congresses and Popular Committees, and of trade unions and professional organizations) held its first session in January 1976; it was subsequently restyled the General People's Congress (GPC).

In March 1977 the GPC endorsed constitutional changes, recommended by Qaddafi, whereby the official name of the country was changed to the Socialist People's Libyan Arab Jamahiriya. Power was vested in the people through the GPC and its constituent parts. The RCC was dissolved, and a General Secretariat of the GPC (with Qaddafi as Secretary-General) was established. The GPC elected Qaddafi as Revolutionary Leader of the new state. The Council of Ministers was replaced by a General People's Committee, initially with 26 members—each a secretary of a department.

In March 1979 Qaddafi resigned from the post of Secretary-General of the General Secretariat of the GPC to devote more time to 'preserving the revolution'. The creation in early 1984 of the post of Secretary for External Security and of an office, attached to the Secretariat for Foreign Liaison, to 'combat international terrorism', combined with repressive measures to curb the activity of dissidents, apparently reflected Qaddafi's increasing sensitivity to the growth of opposition groups—principally the National Front for the Salvation of Libya (NFSL), which he accused foreign governments of fostering. In 1986 the country's official name was changed to the Great Socialist People's Libyan Arab Jamahiriya.

Domestic Political Affairs

From 1988, in an apparent attempt to allay domestic dissatisfaction and international criticism, Qaddafi initiated a series of liberalizing economic and political reforms. In foreign policy he adopted a more pragmatic approach to his ambition of achieving Maghreb union (see below), and to his relations with other Arab and African countries. Within Libya he accused the 'revolutionary committees' (young, pro-Qaddafi activists) of murdering political opponents of his regime. Qaddafi encouraged the reopening of private businesses, in recognition of the inadequacy of state-sponsored supermarkets, and declared an amnesty for all prisoners, other than those convicted of violent crimes or of conspiring with foreign powers. Libyan citizens were guaranteed freedom to travel abroad, and the powers of the revolutionary committees were curbed. The GPC created a People's Court and People's Prosecution Bureau to replace the revolutionary courts, and approved a charter of human rights. In August Qaddafi announced that the army was to be replaced by a force of 'Jamahiri Guards', which would be supervised by 'people's defence committees'. In September it was decided to relocate all but two of the secretariats of the GPC, mostly to the town of Sirte (Surt), 400 km east of Tripoli, and in January 1989 Qaddafi announced that all state institutions, including the state intelligence service and the official Libyan news agency, were to be abolished.

In October 1990 the GPC implemented extensive changes to the General People's Committee, creating three new secretariats and electing a new Secretary-General, Abu Sa'id Omar Durdah, as well as 11 new secretaries. Three of the five-member General Secretariat of the GPC were replaced, and Abd al-Raziq al-Sawsa was appointed Secretary-General of the GPC; in November 1992 al-Sawsa was replaced by Muhammad al-Zanati. In the same month there was a further reorganization of the General People's Committee; the former Secretary for Economic Planning, Omar al-Muntasir, was named Secretary for Foreign Liaison and International Co-operation. Regarded as a moderate, al-Muntasir's appointment was viewed by some observers as a sign of Libya's willingness to resume dialogue with the West over the Lockerbie issue (see below).

Western media reported in October 1993 that elements loyal to Qaddafi had suppressed an attempted military *coup d'état*, and that Libya's second-in-command, Maj. Abd al-Salam Jalloud, was among many placed under house arrest. Qaddafi denied that a coup had been attempted, but the appointment of known loyalists to senior positions in the General People's Committee was announced in January 1994. Most notably, Abd al-Majid al-Aoud, a member of Qaddafi's closest personal entourage, replaced Durdah, a close associate of Jalloud, as Secretary-General.

At its annual convention in March 1997 the GPC made changes to the composition and structure of the General People's Committee. Muhammad Ahmad al-Manqush was appointed Secretary-General of the Committee in December, as part of a further reorganization. The Secretariat for Arab Unity was abolished in a restructuring of the General People's Committee in December 1998, in accordance with Qaddafi's recently stated intention to forge closer relations with African rather than Arab countries.

In January 2000 Qaddafi unexpectedly attended the opening session of the GPC, at the end of which he demanded that the budget for 2000 be redrafted, with a view to channelling petroleum revenues into education, health and public services. Furthermore, he urged that the current administrative system, based on General People's Committees, be abandoned in favour of an alternative form of government. Accordingly, a radical decentralization of the Government was announced in March, whereby almost all of the People's Committees were dissolved and their responsibilities devolved mainly to local level: only those areas described as 'sovereign' were to remain under the control of the General People's Committee, now led by Mubarak Abdallah al-Shamikh. Most notably, Ali Abd al-Salam al-Turayki was allocated the new post of Secretary for African Unity, being replaced as Secretary for Foreign Liaison and International Co-operation by Abd al-Rahman Muhammad Shalgam. Al-Ujayli Abd al-Salam Burayni replaced Muhammad Abdullah Bait al-Mal as Secretary for Finance in October, when a further restructuring of the General People's Committees was announced; it had been reported in July that Bait al-Mal, along with the President of the Central Bank of Libya and a further 22 senior Libyan bankers, had been implicated in allegations of financial impropriety.

In September 2000 clashes occurred throughout the country between Libyans and nationals of several other African countries. The confrontations were believed to reflect resentment within Libya at the increasing numbers of black African migrants entering the country. A large number of Chadians and Sudanese were reportedly killed in incidents in the town of al-Zawiyah, some 30 km west of Tripoli, and thousands more were interned in military camps. The Nigerian embassy in Tripoli was ransacked, and Libyan youths were also held responsible for an attack on a camp that had been razed to the ground. The GPC announced its intention formally to investigate the incidents, and in October the evacuation and deportation of migrant workers from Nigeria, Chad, Niger, Sudan and Ghana commenced. It was estimated that as a result of the clashes more than 100 Africans had been killed and as many as 30,000 migrants had left Libya. Qaddafi subsequently apportioned blame for the incidents on 'foreign hostile hands' opposed to his plans to create an African Union. In May 2001 two Libyans, four Nigerians and one Ghanaian were sentenced to death for their roles in the violence. A further 12 defendants were sentenced to life imprisonment.

A minor reorganization of the General People's Committee was announced in September 2001, including the creation of a new Secretariat for Infrastructure, Urban Planning and Environment. In November it was announced that more than 40 government and bank officials had been sentenced to varying terms of imprisonment for corruption and embezzlement; reportedly among those convicted was Secretary for Finance Burayni, who received a one-year prison sentence for negligence.

In January 2003 Libya was elected to chair the session of the UN Human Rights Commission scheduled to be held in March. It was the first time since the formation of the Commission in 1947 that the decision had been voted upon, with Libya securing 33 of the 53 votes, and 17 countries, including the United Kingdom, abstaining; the USA, Canada and Guatemala opposed the proposal. Libya's election was widely criticized by a number of international human rights organizations.

In June 2003 Qaddafi dismissed al-Shamikh from the post of Secretary of the General People's Committee, replacing him with Shukri Muhammad Ghanem, who was succeeded as Secretary for the Economy and Trade by Abd al-Qadir Balkheir. It was also announced that the Secretariat for African Unity had been merged with the Secretariat for Foreign Liaison and International Co-operation; Shalgam assumed responsibility for both portfolios. In March 2004 Qaddafi announced a further reorganization of the General People's Committee, which included the creation of four new secretariats (for national security, youth and sport, training and labour, and culture) and the restoration of the Secretariat for Energy, which had been abolished in 2000.

It was announced in October 2005 that 84 members of banned opposition group the Muslim Brotherhood, originally convicted and imprisoned in 2002, were to be retried, following the abolition in January 2005 of the unpopular People's Court, which had passed the original verdicts; the prisoners were subsequently released in March 2006. An extensive reorganization of the General People's Committee was announced that same month, including the creation of seven new secretariats. Ghanem was replaced as Secretary of the General People's Committee by the former Deputy Secretary for Production, Dr al-Baghdadi Ali al-Mahmoudi, and was allocated the role of Chairman of the National Oil Corporation, while Muhammad Ali al-Houeiz, hitherto Secretary for Finance, was promoted to Deputy Secretary. The Secretariat for Energy, only reinstated in March 2004, was restructured and renamed the Secretariat for Industry, Electricity and Mines.

In May 2006 the US-based organization Human Rights Watch (HRW) called for the immediate release of Fathi al-Jahmi, a political dissident detained since March 2004 for criticizing Qaddafi. The Libyan Government avowed that the trial of al-Jahmi, who faced the death sentence if convicted, had commenced in 2005; however, no details of the specific charges were made available. HRW urged the Libyan Government to build upon its recent renunciation of terrorism by allowing peaceful opponents freely to express their opinions. In June 2006 HRW also pressed the Libyan Government to allow a full, independent investigation into the deaths of hundreds of inmates at Abu Salim prison in Tripoli in 1996; the alleged massacre was reported to have been caused by security officers opening fire on prisoners protesting against poor living conditions. In September 2006 HRW released a report in which it claimed that the Libyan Government routinely subjected refugees and asylum-seekers to violence, arrest without due cause and forcible deportation; the report urged members of the European Union (EU, see p. 270) to apply pressure on Libya to protect the rights of the hundreds of thousands of foreigners residing therein.

In October 2006 Abu Salim prison was again the scene of controversy when one inmate was killed and a further 17 people were injured in clashes between prisoners and guards. The disturbance, reported predominantly to have involved detainees who were members of the Libyan Islamic Fighting Group (LIFG), followed the decision by a Tripoli court earlier that same day to uphold the convictions, on charges of having links with the LIFG, of 190 inmates housed at the prison. The Libyan People's Prosecution Bureau, however, indicated that the violence had erupted when guards moved to end a sit-in protest against delays in legal proceedings. The human rights organization Amnesty International appealed for a thorough independent investigation into the incident.

Meanwhile, in July 2006 Qaddafi claimed that Libya had come close to building a nuclear bomb before abandoning in December 2003 its programmes to produce weapons of mass destruction (see below). In November 2006 an official source in Tripoli announced that Qaddafi's second son, Seif al-Islam, a popular figure among Libyans on account of his ongoing efforts to effect political and economic change, was to leave the country to take up employment with an international economic institution. His departure from Libya, which many feared would severely lessen hopes of genuine, lasting reform, was widely perceived to have been orchestrated by the Government in reaction to his outspoken criticism of the regime during a speech at a youth activist rally in Sirte in August.

In a speech broadcast live on state television in August 2007, Seif al-Islam Qaddafi urged the drafting of a new constitution or 'social contract' that would establish, *inter alia*, an independent central bank and a free media and judiciary. He also criticized the Libyan political system for its lack of a freely elected legislature, its refusal to allow the creation of political parties and its ongoing intolerance of political dissent, and called for political power to be more widely distributed, beyond the GPC and the General People's Committee. While few observers questioned Seif al-Islam's commitment to these proposals, it was widely believed that his father would never allow such radical reforms to be implemented.

Meanwhile, a reorganization of the General People's Committee was announced in January 2007, including five new appointments. Notable changes included the appointment of Dr Abd al-Hafid Mahmud Zalitni as Deputy Secretary and the modification of the recently restructured Secretariat for Industry, Electricity and Mines, its responsibilities to be shared henceforth between the newly created Secretariats for Industry and Mineral Resources and for Electricity, Water and Gas.

In November 2007 an audio tape purporting to be from Dr Ayman al-Zawahiri, the deputy leader of the militant Islamist organization al-Qa'ida, was released; it included a message from Abu Laith al-Libi, the leader of al-Qa'ida in Afghanistan, who identified himself on the tape as also being a member of the LIFG. Al-Libi declared that the LIFG had pledged allegiance to al-Qa'ida. Al-Zawahiri's own message urged the overthrow of the Libyan, Algerian, Moroccan and Tunisian Governments, and criticized Qaddafi for surrendering Libya's nuclear weapons materials to 'crusader masters'. In early April 2008 it was reported that around 90 members of the LIFG had been released from a prison in Tripoli, after they had renounced violence.

Qaddafi effected a reorganization of the General Secretariat of the GPC and of the General People's Committee in March 2008. Changes to the former included the replacement of al-Zanati as Secretary by Muftah Muhammad Kaiba, and the appointment of Huda Fathi ben Amer to the position of Secretary for Women's Affairs; changes to the latter included the appointment of former General People's Committee Secretary Mubarak Abdallah al-Shamikh to the position of Deputy Secretary, and that of Gen. Abd al-Fattah Yunis al-Abaidi as the new Secretary for National Security. At the same time Qaddafi announced that he intended to abolish the majority of secretariats within the General People's Committee by the end of that year, in an effort to eliminate corruption and maladministration in what he termed the 'labyrinthine bureaucracy' of the Committee. Through a Wealth Distribution Programme (WDP), oil wealth would be redistributed by transferring the secretariats' powers to the people to enable them to manage their own affairs, requiring privatization of many sectors of Libyan society; only the secretariats for defence, internal security and foreign affairs would be retained, along with those responsible for strategic infrastructural projects, such as the Great Man-made River Project (see Economic Affairs). At the beginning of September Qaddafi reiterated his plans to dismantle most of the secretariats and redistribute oil revenues, asserting that the reforms would come into effect in early 2009. Meanwhile, in August 2008 Seif al-Islam, for some time considered to be Qaddafi's probable successor, announced his intention to withdraw from politics. In the months that followed public demonstrations took place in several locations across the country to demand his return.

In November 2008, meanwhile, there were protests by members of the Tebu tribe in the southern town of Kufra against what they claimed was discrimination practised by the Qaddafi Government against indigenous peoples (including a restriction of access to health and education services). Dozens of people were reported to have been killed in violent confrontations between the Libyan security forces and members of the Tebu tribe.

At a meeting of the General People's Congress held in Sirte at the beginning of March 2009, it was announced tthat he country's Basic People's Congresses had voted in the previous month to defer implementation of the WDP. At the Sirte meeting Qaddafi implemented a reorganization of the General Peoples's Committee. Notable changes included the appointment of Musa Kusa, hitherto head of Libya's foreign intelligence service, to replace Abd al-Rahman Muhammad Shalgam as Secretary for Foreign Liaison and International Co-operation, and the appointment of Abd al-Hafid Mahmoud Zlitni, the head of the Libyan Investment Authority, to the position of Secretary for Finance and Planning. The finance and planning secretariats were among several to be merged, and the position of Secretary for Manpower, Training and Employment was abolished. Meanwhile, Mubarak al-Shamikh was appointed as Secretary of the GPC, replacing Kaiba. The changes fell far short of the large-scale dismantling of secretariats that Qaddafi had previously outlined, but were none the less indicative of the ongoing programme of administrative retrenchment.

Increasing prominence of Seif al-Islam Qaddafi

In March 2009 it was announced that, following two years of talks between the Libyan Human Rights Association—chaired by Seif al-Islam Qaddafi—and the LIFG, 170 imprisoned members of the group were to be released; it was also revealed that 136 LIFG prisoners had already been freed, having completed a rehabilitation programme. The announcement was welcomed by HRW; however, concerns were expressed by some analysts that the prisoners' release was a means of buying peace from radical groups who had opposed the latest government reorganization. Signs of increased reconciliation between the LIFG and the Libyan authorities continued to be evident throughout 2009. In July the LIFG leadership announced that it was renouncing armed violence and reversed the 2007 decision to align the group with al-Qa'ida. In September 2009 the six imprisoned members of the LIFG ruling council published a document, described as a new 'code' for *jihad*, which denounced the ideologies of al-Qa'ida; some 45 LIFG members were subsequently released from prison. In March 2010 202 prisoners, including 34 LIFG members and a further 100 'with a direct relationship with groups operating in Iraq', were released by the Libyan authorities; Seif al-Islam stated his hope that their release would encourage other Islamist militants to renounce violence and enter into dialogue with the Government. Human Rights Watch welcomed the development as a positive step, but urged the Libyan authorities to release all those who were 'arbitrarily detained' in Libyan gaols, including many who continued to be imprisoned despite having served the full duration of their sentence or having being acquitted of all charges against them. A further 37 Islamist prisoners, including at least one former inmate of the US detention centre at Guantánamo Bay, Cuba, were released in late August.

Meanwhile, in October 2009 it was announced that Seif al-Islam would be appointed as co-ordinator of social and popular committees, a role that elevated Qaddafi's son to the second most powerful position in the Libyan leadership. The decision was widely interpreted as the formal approval by the Libyan authorities of Seif al-Islam as the successor to his father. In January 2010 Qaddafi effected a reorganization of the General Secretariat of the GPC, most notably appointing Muhammad Aboulghasem al-Zwai as Secretary, in place of al-Shamikh; the number of portfolios was reduced from 12 to seven, as part of the ongoing programme of administrative reform.

In December 2009 Seif al-Islam's Human Rights Association published a report detailing wide-ranging examples of the use of torture, wrongful imprisonment and other human rights abuses in Libya, and criticizing the state's dominance of the media. In an unprecedented press conference two days later, HRW announced the findings of its latest report on human rights in Libya. The report highlighted limited progress in areas such as freedom of expression and freedom of association, and described systemic human rights abuses. Despite significant opposition from human rights groups, Libya was elected to the UN Human Rights Council in May 2010, attracting 155 votes in support of its membership bid from the 192-member body. In early June Amnesty International condemned the execution in Libya of 18 people from Chad, Egypt and Nigeria, following their conviction on charges of murder; the human rights group voiced its concerns that the defendants had not been granted a fair trial and that foreign nationals were 'disadvantaged' within the Libyan judicial system, often not being allowed access to legal representation. A report published by Amnesty International in late June, which was severely critical of Libya's human rights record based on evidence collated during a fact-finding mission's visit to the country in May 2009, alleging that the Government was 'stall[ing] on reform', was strongly condemned by the Libyan Secretariat for Foreign Liaison and International Co-operation, which issued a statement denouncing the 'false information' contained in the report and inviting the organization to revisit Libya to 'see the reality'. The report detailed a wide array of rights violations that had allegedly been perpetrated by the Libyan Government, including indefinite detentions without trial, the use of torture to extract confessions from prisoners, the disappearance of numerous dissidents, and inhumane treatment of refugees and migrant workers. Meanwhile, in mid-June 2010 the Libyan Government ordered the closure of the office in Tripoli of the UN High Commissioner for Refugees (UNHCR), citing the fact that Libya was not a signatory to the 1951 convention on refugees and had not signed any co-operation agreement with the UNHCR, whose activities in Libya were therefore 'illegal'.

The Libyan authorities were reported to have arrested 20 journalists (15 Libyan citizens, and three Tunisian and two Egyptian nationals), during a four-day period in early November 2010, in what some interpreted as being symptomatic of an increasing 'power struggle' between Seif al-Islam and conservatives opposed to what they regarded as Qaddafi's son's reformist agenda. The detained journalists all worked for media entities controlled by Al-Ghad—a publishing company sponsored by Seif al-Islam—including the Libya Press news agency and the weekly publication *Oea*. According to a statement published by Libya Press, no reason was given by the authorities for the journalists' arrests and their immediate release was demanded. However, the arrests were widely seen to have been prompted by the publication in *Oea*, at the beginning of November, of an article urging a 'final assault' on the Government in response to its perceived failure effectively to combat official corruption; the authorities had suspended the publication of *Oea* immediately following the publication of the article. On the day after the journalists were arrested Col Qaddafi was reported personally to have ordered their release and a full inquiry into the incident.

The Qaddafi International Charity and Development Foundation, a charitable organization headed by Seif al-Islam, announced in mid-December 2010 that it was henceforth to cease advocating political reform and championing human rights causes, and would instead focus on its 'core charitable mission'—namely, the provision of aid and relief to disadvantaged populations, primarily in sub-Saharan Africa. Seif al-Islam insisted that the change of direction would allow the Foundation better to direct its efforts to this end, but others criticized the decision, contending that Qaddafi's son was merely seeking to protect himself from the ire of conservative forces within Libya, which had strongly objected to the Foundation's pro-reform stance.

Recent developments: anti-Qaddafi protests and NATO-led intervention

In mid-January 2010 crowds gathered in several Libyan cities, including Benghazi and Bani Walid, to protest against corruption and protracted delays in the transfer of government-subsidized residential buildings to their owners, who had already signed contracts and paid significant instalments on their new homes; protesters seized control of hundreds of vacant residential units in Benghazi and Bani Walid. The Libyan state media made no reference to the protests, but in late January the Government announced the establishment of a US $24,000m. investment fund, the aim of which was to provide affordable housing for lower-income families. Meanwhile, in mid-January the Government announced the elimination of all taxes on food products, in a move believed to be linked to popular unrest in Algeria and Tunisia over, among other things, increased food prices.

At the end of January 2011 a Libyan political writer, Jamal al-Hajji, who had previously been imprisoned for dissidence, posted an article on the internet urging Libyans to stage demonstrations 'in support of greater freedoms in Libya', seemingly inspired by recent events in Tunisia and Egypt that ultimately led to the removal of those countries' ruling regimes in mid-January and mid-February, respectively. Al-Hajji was arrested at the beginning of February and charged two days later with causing injury to another person while driving; however, human rights groups, including Amnesty International, alleged that al-Hajji had been targeted because of his political views and his appeal for the holding of protests. Qaddafi was reported to have met with prominent political activists and journalists shortly thereafter and to have threatened serious repercussions if they should in any way be involved in 'disturbing the peace or creating chaos in Libya'.

On 15 February 2011 protesters gathered outside the police headquarters in Benghazi, following the arrest earlier that day of Fathi Terbil, a prominent critic of the Government and a lawyer who had been campaigning for the release of hundreds of people detained in Abu Salim prison owing to their alleged involvement with militant Islamist groups, including the LIFG. Police officers dispersed the protesters, resorting to the use of violence against those who refused to leave; more than 40 people were reported to have been injured on that day. On 16 February Terbil was released, but the protests continued in Benghazi and spread to several other Libyan cities, including al-Bayda and al-Quba, with protesters demanding the resignation of Qaddafi and the Government. Police officers and soldiers used water cannons in an attempt to break up the protests; six people were reported to have been killed on 16 February. On the same day, in an apparent attempt to appease the protesters, the Government announced the release of 110 LIFG members.

In response to a 'day of revolt' staged by opposition forces on 17 February 2011, which saw protests take place in Tripoli for the first time, the Government was reported to have hired hundreds of mercenaries from several African countries, notably Chad, to swell the ranks of the Libyan army. The Libyan air force deployed fighter jets and helicopters to launch air-strikes against protesters; on 21 February two senior pilots flew to Malta, where they requested political asylum from the Qaddafi regime. Violent clashes continued between protesters and the authorities throughout the rest of February and into March, with many eyewitness reports attesting to the indiscriminate use of excessive force by the authorities. Some sources, including the Libyan League for Human Rights, estimated that by early March some 6,000 people had been killed as a result of the unrest. About 200,000 Libyans were estimated to have fled the country in order to escape the violence, and many countries launched rescue missions to help their nationals in Libya to return home. Libyan national flags on buildings were replaced by the flag of the former Libyan monarchy, while government and police buildings, banks, media premises, and construction sites in many towns were looted, set on fire or otherwise damaged, and the protesters seized control of the airport in Benghazi, which remained the opposition forces' stronghold.

By early March 2011 much of eastern Libya was reported to be under opposition control, including Benghazi and Tobruk, and the opposition had also pushed into the central and northern provinces, with a number of cities therein—including the port towns of Mersa Brega and Ras Lanuf—under rebel control, with significant numbers of police and army officers in the region defecting to the opposition. Many of Libya's foreign diplomats, including its ambassador in Washington, DC, USA, had also renounced the Qaddafi regime and urged the international community to take action to stop the violence. Several prominent government officials had also resigned, including Secretary for Justice Moustafa Muhammad Abu Jelil, on 21 February, and Secretary for Public Security Gen. Abd al-Fattah Yunis al-Abaidi, on 22 February.

On 20 February 2011 Seif al-Islam Qaddafi gave a televised address in which he blamed the ongoing unrest on 'foreign agents', primarily the Israeli Government, and pledged that the Libyan Government would 'fight to the last man and woman and bullet'. On 22 February Col Qaddafi made his first public statement in response to the protests, appearing briefly on state television to deny reports that he had fled to Venezuela, stating that he remained in Tripoli and warning Libyans not to trust foreign media 'dogs'. Also that day the UN Security Council issued a statement in which it condemned 'the use of force against civilians' and called for 'an immediate end to the violence and for steps to address the legitimate demands of the population'. Qaddafi appeared on state television on 23 February, talking at length this time, blaming foreign powers and the abuse of hallucinogenic drugs for the unrest, while insisting that, as he had no formal position from which to resign, he would remain the 'head of the revolution', and pledged to 'cleanse Libya house by house'. Qaddafi also condemned the US and British Governments, which he accused of attempting to 'destabilize' Libya and 'humiliate' its people. Seif al-Islam's reputation as a reformist within the Qaddafi regime was dealt an irrevocable blow when video footage materialized on 28 February that purported to show him inciting a crowd of pro-Government supporters to commit violence against the opposition forces, whom he dismissed as 'nothing' and as 'bums, brats and druggies', and promising to provide those loyal to his father with weapons. Nevertheless, in an interview broadcast on US television on the previous day, Seif al-Islam had denied that the Libyan regime had attacked any civilians.

Meanwhile, on 21 February 2011 Libya's deputy ambassador to the UN, Ibrahim Dabbashi, urged the UN Security Council to address the Libyan Government's violent response to the protests, and stated that he could no longer support the Qaddafi regime, which, he argued, was responsible for 'genocide'. Dabbashi's comments prompted the first UN Security Council meeting on the issue of the uprisings in the Middle East and North Africa since the beginning of Tunisia's revolution, unrest in Egypt, and the developing protests in Bahrain, Iran, the Palestinian Autonomous Areas and Yemen (q.v.); the Security Council condemned the Libyan Government's response to the protests and issued a statement demanding an immediate end to the violence. On 26 February the UN Security Council unanimously adopted Resolution 1970, which imposed sanctions including, inter alia, the referral of the situation in Libya to the Chief Prosecutor of the International Criminal Court (ICC), the institution of an embargo upon the sale and transport of arms to Libya, and the imposition of a travel ban and an asset freeze on senior members of the regime and on the Qaddafi family. At the beginning of March the UN General Assembly voted to suspend Libya's membership of the Human Rights Council in response to the Government's 'gross and systematic violations' of human rights, the first time that a member state had been excluded from the Council. Susan Rice, the US ambassador to the UN, stated that the 'unprecedented action' sent a 'clear warning' to Qaddafi and his supporters that they 'must stop the killing', while Mark Lyall Grant, the British ambassador to the UN, suggested that the Security Council was considering further action against the Qaddafi regime, declaring that the Council 'will look to take whatever measures we consider necessary to respond to events on the ground'.

On 1 March 2010 US Secretary of State Hillary Clinton announced that the Administration of US President Barack Obama was considering its legal options, following the claims by a number of defecting Libyan government officials, including former Secretary for Justice Abd al-Jelil, that the 1988 Lockerbie bombing had been carried out on the direct orders of Qaddafi. A few days previously Clinton had pledged 'any type of assistance', including aid, to those elements within Libya seeking to remove Qaddafi from power, and issued an unequivocal statement of the US Administration's position on events in that country: 'we want him to leave. We want him to end his regime and call off the mercenaries and forces loyal to him. How he manages that is up to him'. Also on 1 March British Prime Minister David Cameron had contested that Western countries could not tolerate the 'illegitimate' Qaddafi regime and should pursue active contact with the Libyan opposition in order to gain a greater understanding of their motivations and intentions; Cameron also controversially intimated that the United Kingdom might be prepared to furnish the Libyan rebels with weapons, suggested that the North Atlantic Treaty Organization (NATO, see p. 368) impose an air exclusion zone over Libya, and refused to rule out the possibility of a military invasion. However, protesters in Benghazi appeared to reject the offer of British assistance, unveiling banners emblazoned with the phrase 'No intervention', and Cameron's bellicose stance encountered considerable opposition from, inter alia, France, Russia and many within the British Government itself, while the Obama Administration publicly distanced itself from Cameron's proposals. On 6 March a British diplomat and a group of six British soldiers, believed to belong to the élite Special Air Service force, who had been accompanying him, were released after being captured by Libyan rebels two days previously near Benghazi; the group were reported to have been on their way to meet with Libyan opposition leaders when they were apprehended. In a statement released on 8 March, the Obama Administration stated that during a telephone conversation earlier that day Obama and Cameron had pledged their shared commitment to ensuring 'an immediate end to brutality and violence; the departure of Qaddafi from power as quickly as possible; and a transition that meets the Libyan peoples' aspirations' for freedom and a fully representative, democratically elected government. Meanwhile, it was reported that Qaddafi had appointed replacements for those members of the General People's Committee who had defected to the opposition in late February: Muhammad Ahmad al-Qamoud became Secretary for Justice, and Masoud Abd al-Hafiz Secretary for Public Security.

On 17 March 2011 the UN Security Council approved, by 10 votes to none (with five abstentions), Resolution 1973, which, among other measures, prohibited all flights in Libyan airspace, authorized member states to take 'all necessary measures ... to protect civilians and civilian populated areas under threat of attack' by forces loyal to Qaddafi, 'while excluding a foreign occupation force of any form on any part of Libyan territory', and demanded an immediate cease-fire by Libyan government forces. Despite the announcement by Libyan officials the following day of a cease-fire, it was reported in subsequent days that Qaddafi's forces continued to use violence to counter opposition groups that had taken control of Mersa Brega, Misurata, Ras Lanuf and Zawia. Air-strikes by Allied forces against strategic locations across Libya, including in the capital, Tripoli, commenced on 19 March, while on 22 March NATO warships were deployed to waters off the coast of Libya to enforce an arms embargo imposed against Qaddafi's forces. Two days later NATO members determined to enforce the UN-sanctioned air exclusion zone over Libya, alongside a military operation to prevent further attacks on civilians and civilian-populated areas, undertaken by a multinational coalition under British, French and US command, and on 27 March NATO members agreed to assume full command of operations.

At the end of March 2011 officials in the British Foreign and Commonwealth Office revealed that Kusa had arrived in the United Kingdom, whereupon he stated his intention to defect. Despite official denials of Kusa's defection by the Libyan Government, it emerged later that month that Kusa's former deputy, Abd al-Ati al-Obeidi, had been appointed to replace him. NATO air-strikes against government forces appeared initially to have emboldened opposition forces, but in early April the rebel groups were forced to abandon control of towns in Libya's central coastal area, including Mersa Brega and Ras Lanuf, as Qaddafi's forces continued to bombard opposition-held areas with heavy artillery. On 10 April an African Union (AU) delegation led by South African President Jacob Zuma arrived in Tripoli to present a proposal for a settlement of the conflict, which included, inter alia, an immediate cease-fire and negotiations between representatives of the regime and of the opposition over a gradual transition to political reform. It was reported that Qaddafi had indicated his approval, but that the plan had been rejected by opposition figures, who demanded Qaddafi's ouster as a prerequisite for talks. Meanwhile, government forces continued to launch attacks on opposition strongholds, particularly in Misurata, where it was reported that missiles had struck the port area, in an attempt to disrupt the supply by ship of aid to opposition fighters.

At the beginning of May 2011 it was reported that one of Qaddafi's sons, Seif al-Arab, and three of the Libyan leader's grandchildren had been killed in a NATO air-strike on Qaddafi's compound in central Tripoli. Libyan representatives claimed that the strike had been intended to assassinate the Libyan leader, who they stated had been in the building when the bombing occurred, although NATO commanders denied targeting Col Qaddafi and insisted that the building had been a 'military command and control' facility. Following the attack, large crowds of pro-Qaddafi demonstrators surrounded the residences of diplomats representing NATO members states; the British embassy was reported to have been set alight and others ransacked, prompting the British Secretary of State for Foreign and Commonwealth Affairs, William Hague, to order the expulsion of Libya's head of mission in the United Kingdom. On 16 May the Chief Prosecutor of the ICC, Luis Moreno Ocampo, ordered arrest warrants to be issued against Qaddafi and Seif al-Islam, as well as Libya's head of intelligence, Abdullah al-Sanoussi, in respect of crimes against humanity committed in Libya since initial protests began in February. The Office of the Chief Prosecutor was stated to have gathered direct evidence concerning orders issued by the Libyan leader, Seif al-Islam's role in the recruitment of mercenaries, and al-Sanoussi's participation in violent acts against demonstrators. On 17 May foreign media reported that the Chairman of the National Oil Corporation and former Secretary of the General People's Committee, Shukri Muhammad Ghanem, had fled to Tunisia, with the intention of defecting. However, the conflict between opposition forces and those remaining loyal to Qaddafi continued unabated, and the prospect of a peaceful outcome appeared distant.

Foreign Affairs
Relations with the USA and the United Kingdom

Libya's relations with the USA, which had been strained for many years, deteriorated significantly under the presidency of Ronald Reagan (1981–89), who accused the Libyan Government of sponsoring international terrorism. In January 1986 Reagan severed all economic and commercial relations with Libya, and in March Libyan forces fired missiles at US fighter aircraft, which were challenging Libya's attempts to enforce recognition of the whole of the Gulf of Sirte as its territorial waters. In retaliatory attacks in April, US military aircraft bombed military installations, airports and official buildings, as well as alleged terrorist training camps and communication centres, in Tripoli and Benghazi. A total of 101 people, including many civilians, were reported to have died in the raids. The US Administration claimed in justification to have irrefutable proof of Libyan involvement in terrorist attacks and plots against US targets in Europe and the Middle East.

In November 1991 the US and British Governments announced that they would seek to extradite two Libyan citizens, Abd al-Baset Ali Muhammad al-Megrahi (a former head of security at Libyan Arab Airlines) and Al-Amin Khalifa Fhimah (an employee of the airline), alleged to have been responsible for an explosion that destroyed a Pan American World Airways (Pan Am) passenger aircraft over Lockerbie, Scotland, in December 1988, resulting in the deaths of 270 people. The Libyan Government denied any involvement in the bombing, and recommended that the allegations be investigated by a neutral body. In January 1992 the UN Security Council adopted a resolution (No. 731) demanding Libya's compliance with requests for the extradition of its two nationals and its co-operation with a French inquiry into the bombing over Niger, in September 1989, of a UTA passenger airline, in which all 171 passengers and crew had been killed. Libya's offer to try on its own territory the two men accused of the Lockerbie bombing was rejected by the USA, the United Kingdom and France, which urged the UN to impose sanctions on Libya. On 31 March 1992 the UN Security Council adopted a resolution (No. 748) providing for the imposition of economic sanctions against Libya if it refused to comply with Resolution 731, and to commit itself to a renunciation of international terrorism, by 15 April. Sanctions, including the severance of international air links, the prohibition of trade in arms and the reduction of Libya's diplomatic representation abroad, were duly imposed on the specified date. In May, at Qaddafi's instigation, 1,500 People's Congresses were convened in Libya and abroad, to enable the country's citizens to decide the fate of the two Lockerbie suspects and their response to the UN sanctions. The GPC announced in the following month its decision to allow the two Lockerbie suspects to be tried abroad, provided that the proceedings were 'fair and just'.

In August 1993 the USA, the United Kingdom and France announced that they would request the UN Security Council to strengthen the sanctions in force against Libya if, by 1 October, Libya had still not complied with Resolutions 731 and 748. The Libyan Government rejected this ultimatum, but stated its willingness to commence discussions with those three countries on an appropriate venue for the trial of the two Lockerbie suspects. In October the UN Secretary-General, Dr Boutros Boutros-Ghali, met the Libyan Secretary for Foreign Liaison and International Co-operation, but failed to secure agreement on a timetable for the surrender of the two suspects to either the USA or the United Kingdom. (US and British officials remained convinced that there was sufficient evidence of Libyan involvement to continue to seek the suspects' extradition, despite various reports issued in the early 1990s that alleged that Iranian, Syrian and Palestinian agents—sometimes separately, sometimes in collaboration—had been responsible for the bombing.) In November the Security Council adopted a resolution (No. 883) providing for the strengthening of the economic sanctions in force against Libya in the event of the country's failure fully to comply with Resolutions 731 and 748 by 1 December. The sanctions, which were duly applied, included: the closure of all Libyan Arab Airlines' offices abroad; a ban on the sale of equipment and services for the civil aviation sector; the sequestration of all Libyan financial resources overseas; and a ban on the sale to Libya of specified items for use in the petroleum and gas industries.

In January 1994 the Scottish lawyer representing the two Lockerbie suspects stated that they might be willing to stand trial in The Hague, Netherlands; this was subsequently endorsed as an appropriate venue by Qaddafi. In February, however, US President Bill Clinton recommended that an embargo be imposed on Libya's sales of petroleum (which accounted for some 98% of its export earnings) if the country continued to defy the international community. In mid-1996, following its repeated failure to persuade the UN to agree yet more stringent sanctions against Libya, the US Congress approved unilateral 'secondary' sanctions against Libya (and Iran). The Iran-Libya Sanctions Act (ILSA) sought to penalize companies operating in US markets that were investing more than US $40m. (later amended to $20m.) in Libya's oil and gas industries.

In July 1997 the League of Arab States (Arab League, see p. 361), which had been criticized by Qaddafi for its lack of support, formally proposed that the two Libyan suspects in the Lockerbie case be tried by Scottish judges under Scottish law in a neutral country. In September the members of the League urged a relaxation of the air embargo on Libya and voted to defy UN sanctions by permitting aircraft carrying Qaddafi, and other flights for religious or humanitarian purposes, to land on their territory.

In August 1998 the United Kingdom and the USA proposed that the trial of the two Lockerbie suspects be held in the Netherlands under Scottish law and presided over by Scottish judges. The UN Security Council adopted a resolution (No. 1192) welcoming the initiative and providing for the suspension of sanctions upon the arrival in the Netherlands of the two suspects; additional sanctions were threatened if the Libyan authorities did not comply with the resolution.

In December 1998 the UN Secretary-General, Kofi Annan, held a meeting with Qaddafi in Libya in an attempt to expedite a trial of the Lockerbie suspects. Shortly afterwards, the GPC endorsed the principle of a trial, but requested that the USA and the United Kingdom remove 'all remaining obstacles'. In a bid to break the impasse arising from Qaddafi's demand that the trial include a panel of international judges, envoys from Saudi Arabia and South Africa were dispatched to Libya in January 1999 to negotiate with Qaddafi. In February it was reported that the envoys had reached an understanding with the Libyan leader whereby UN observers would be allowed to monitor the two Libyan suspects during the trial, to ensure that they were not questioned by US and British agents, and afterwards, if they were convicted and imprisoned in Scotland. The diplomatic initiative culminated in March with a visit by President Nelson Mandela of South Africa to Libya, during which Qaddafi undertook to surrender the suspects by 6 April. The two Libyans duly arrived for trial in the Netherlands on 5 April and were transferred to Camp Zeist, a former US airbase near Utrecht, designated Scottish territory for the purposes of the trial, where they were formally arrested and charged with murder, conspiracy to murder and contravention of the 1982 Aviation Security Act. The UN Security Council immediately voted to suspend sanctions against Libya indefinitely, although they were not to be permanently revoked until Libya had complied with other conditions stipulated in Resolution 1192 (including the payment of compensation to the families of victims of the Lockerbie bombing). The USA refused to remove the 'secondary' sanctions against Libya, but subsequently announced that it would permit the sale of food and medical items to Libya on a 'case-by-case' basis. In June 1999 the US and Libyan ambassadors to the UN participated in talks; this represented the first official contact between the two countries in 18 years.

The two Libyan suspects appeared before the Scottish court in the Netherlands for the first time in December 1999, at a pre-trial hearing to decide on the court's jurisdiction. The presiding Scottish judge ruled that the two suspects could be tried on all three charges, and that they could be described as members of the Libyan intelligence services. The trial of al-Megrahi and Fhimah eventually commenced on 3 May 2000; both pleaded not guilty to the charges brought against them, and defence lawyers accused a number of organizations, including militant Palestinian resistance groups, of perpetrating the bombing.

In January 2001 prosecution lawyers unexpectedly announced that they would no longer pursue charges of conspiracy to murder and contravention of the 1982 Aviation Security Act. Accordingly, the trial proceeded on the sole charge of murder. On 31 January 2001 the judges announced that they had unanimously found al-Megrahi guilty of the murder of 270 people and sentenced him to life imprisonment, with the recommendation that he serve a minimum of 20 years. The judges accepted that al-Megrahi was a member of the Libyan intelligence services, and, although they acknowledged their awareness of what they termed 'uncertainties and qualifications' in the case, they concluded that the evidence against him combined to form 'a real and convincing pattern' that left them with no reasonable doubt as to his guilt. Fhimah, however, was unanimously acquitted, owing to lack of proof, and freed to return to Libya. Despite mounting pressure from Arab League states, the British Government asserted that sanctions against Libya would not be permanently revoked until Libya accepted responsibility for the bombing and paid 'substantial' compensation. The newly inaugurated US President, George W. Bush, also indicated his support for this stance, and in July 2001 the ILSA was extended for a further five-year term.

Meanwhile, demands for further investigation into the bombing, and Qaddafi's role in it, were rejected by senior Scottish legal officials, who stated that there was insufficient evidence to justify any further proceedings against those alleged to have abetted al-Megrahi, despite the fact that he had apparently not acted alone. Lawyers for al-Megrahi subsequently lodged an appeal against his conviction; the hearing, before five Scottish judges, began at Camp Zeist in January 2002. Al-Megrahi's lawyers based their case on what they termed new 'strong circumstantial evidence', which raised the possibility that the bomb had been placed on the aircraft at London, United Kingdom, and not in Malta, as the trial judges had concluded. In February Seif al-Islam Qaddafi indicated that Libya would pay compensation to the families of those killed in the Lockerbie bombing, regardless of the outcome of the appeal. In March the appeal was unanimously rejected, and al-Megrahi was transferred to a prison in Scotland to begin his sentence.

In July 1999 Libya and the United Kingdom reached agreement on the full restoration of diplomatic relations, after Qaddafi issued a statement in which he accepted Libya's 'general responsibility' for the death of Yvonne Fletcher, a British policewoman who was shot outside the Libyan People's Bureau in London in 1984, and agreed to co-operate with the investigation into the killing. The payment by Libya, in November 1999, of compensation to the victim's family facilitated the reopening of the British embassy in Tripoli the following month. The normalization of relations between the United Kingdom and Libya continued to progress, and in March 2001 Libya appointed an ambassador to the United Kingdom for the first time in 17 years. In August 2002 a minister of the British Foreign and Commonwealth Office visited Libya for talks with Qaddafi.

In April 2003 it was confirmed that, following negotiations in London between senior British, US and Libyan representatives, Libya had agreed to accept civil responsibility for the actions of its officials in the Lockerbie case and would pay US $10m. in compensation to the families of the victims. Payment of the compensation was to be a three-stage process: $4m. would be paid to each family on the permanent lifting of UN sanctions; a further $4m. would follow upon the removal of unilateral US sanctions; and a final payment of $2m. would be made when Libya was removed from the list of countries that the USA deemed to support international terrorism. However, Libya would pay only an additional $1m. to each family if the USA did not complete the second and third stages.

After further negotiations, on 16 August 2003 Libya delivered a letter to the President of the UN Security Council stating that it: accepted 'responsibility for the actions of its officials' in the Lockerbie bombing; agreed to pay compensation to the families of the victims; pledged co-operation in any further Lockerbie inquiry; agreed to continue its co-operation in the 'war on terror'; and to take practical measures to ensure that such co-operation was effective. Following the transfer of US $2,700m. in compensation to the International Bank of Settlements, the United Kingdom submitted a draft resolution to the Security Council requesting the formal lifting of UN sanctions against Libya. It was feared, however, that France, which had demanded a similar amount of compensation for families of victims of the UTA bombing in 1989 (see above), would veto the resolution unless Libyan officials agreed to an additional payment. The United Kingdom, France and the USA eventually agreed to postpone the vote on the draft resolution to allow more time for such an agreement to be reached. On 12 September 2003 13 of the 15 members of the UN Security Council approved the lifting of the sanctions imposed against Libya; France and the USA abstained from the vote. Later that month Libya announced its intention to commence dialogue with the USA aimed at normalizing bilateral relations. Nevertheless, the US Administration continued to insist that unilateral sanctions would remain in place until the Libyan Government addressed ongoing US concerns such as the infringement of human rights in the country and the pursuit of weapons of mass destruction.

In September 2003, following an intervention by the French President, Jacques Chirac, the Libyan Government and the families of the UTA bombing reached partial agreement on the payment of additional compensation to the victims' relatives. Talks between Libya and France in October, aimed at reaching a final settlement regarding the issue of compensation for the UTA bombing, were suspended following a number of disagreements between the two sides. However, in January 2004 Libya agreed to pay an additional US $170m. to the relatives of the victims; the payment was to be made in four equal instalments, resulting in the families of each victim receiving an additional $1m.

Meanwhile, in October 2003 an official of the US Department of State accused Libya of having increased its efforts to purchase components for biological and chemical weapons since the lifting of UN sanctions the previous month, and warned that Libya would be added to the group of countries described by President Bush as forming an 'axis of evil'—comprising Iran, Iraq and the Democratic People's Republic of Korea (North Korea). In mid-December, however, in an unexpected development, the British Prime Minister, Tony Blair, announced that Libya had agreed to disclose and dismantle its programme to develop weapons of mass destruction and long-range ballistic missiles. The statement was the culmination of nine months of clandestine negotiations between Qaddafi and British and US diplomats, during which the Libyan authorities had reportedly shown evidence of a 'well advanced' nuclear weapons programme, as well as the existence of large quantities of chemical weapons and bombs designed to carry poisonous gas. Libya also agreed to adhere to the Chemical Weapons Convention and to sign an additional protocol allowing the International Atomic Energy Agency (IAEA) to carry out random inspections of its facilities. Upon visiting a number of sites in Tripoli in late December, in order to commence the process of dismantling Libya's weapons development projects, the Director-General of the IAEA, Dr Muhammad el-Baradei, insisted that these projects had been in the initial stages of development, contradicting the assessment given by the United Kingdom and the USA. In January 2004 the US Department of State confirmed that British and US intelligence agents had, in October 2003, intercepted a shipment of centrifuges capable of developing weapons-grade uranium destined for Tripoli. Also in January 2004 it was announced that Libya had ratified the IAEA's Comprehensive Nuclear Test Ban Treaty.

Further disagreements in January 2004 between the USA, the United Kingdom and the IAEA concerning their respective roles in the process of dismantling Libya's weapons facilities were finally resolved late that month: it was agreed that US and British officials would be responsible for destroying and removing the nuclear material and that the IAEA would verify that the dismantling process was complete. In February it was confirmed that an American diplomat had been stationed in the US interests section of the Belgian embassy in Tripoli, providing the USA with its first permanent diplomatic presence in Libya for 25 years. Also in February the Libyan Secretary for Foreign Liaison and International Co-operation, Abd al-Rahman Muhammad Shalgam, visited London for talks with his British counterpart and Prime Minister Blair; this represented the first meeting between cabinet-level ministers of the two countries in more than 20 years.

The Secretary of the General People's Committee, Shukri Muhammad Ghanem, caused controversy in late February 2004 when he claimed that compensation was being paid to the families of the Lockerbie victims in order to 'buy peace' and avoid sanctions, and that the country did not accept responsibility for the Lockerbie bombing; he also denied any Libyan involvement in the murder of Yvonne Fletcher. The following day, however, Shalgam issued a statement in which he announced his regret at Ghanem's comments and reiterated that Libya stood by its acceptance of responsibility for the Lockerbie bombing. The USA subsequently lifted the restrictions on its citizens travelling to Libya. In March Libya signed an additional IAEA protocol allowing the agency to carry out random inspections of its nuclear facilities; moreover, Libya commenced the destruction of its supplies of chemical weapons and transported all of its remaining nuclear weapons-related equipment to the USA. Later that month the Organisation for the Prohibition of Chemical Weapons verified that Libya's declaration of its chemical weapons inventory (submitted to the UN in early March) had been accurate, after a series of inspections carried out by the agency's officials. In May it was announced that Libya would no longer conduct military trade with those countries that it believed to be involved in the proliferation of weapons of mass destruction.

Meanwhile, in late March 2004 William Burns, the US Assistant Secretary of the Bureau of Near Eastern Affairs, became the highest-ranking US official to visit Libya in more than 30 years; the principal issues under discussion were further moves towards the lifting of US sanctions on Libya and the restoration of normal bilateral relations. In April the USA announced that it would remove the restrictions that prevented US petroleum companies and banks from conducting commercial activities in Libya; however, it also declared that all Libyan assets held in the USA would remain frozen. In June it was revealed that Libya had resumed exports of petroleum to the USA. At the end of the month formal diplomatic relations were re-established between the two countries when a US liaison office was opened in Tripoli, and it was reported that Libya was preparing to establish diplomatic representation in Washington, DC. In September President Bush lifted all travel restrictions for charter and commercial flights between Libya and the USA. He also announced that the US $1,300m. of Libyan assets held in the USA or in US banks abroad would be unfrozen. In February 2005 the US authorities lifted all restrictions on Libyan diplomats travelling within the USA.

Relations between Libya and the United Kingdom continued to improve in 2004. In March Blair visited Tripoli and held talks with Qaddafi, after which the British Prime Minister stated that there was genuine hope for a 'new relationship', while Qaddafi insisted that he was willing to join the international 'war on terror'. It was also announced that British police officers would travel to Libya in April to continue investigations into the murder of Fletcher. In October 2005 Libya signed a memorandum of understanding with the British Government, which allowed for the deportation from the United Kingdom of Libyans suspected of involvement in terrorist activities. (The United Kingdom is legally prevented from deporting foreign nationals to countries that it suspects of using inhumane or degrading treatment.) In May 2007 the British oil company BP (formerly British Petroleum) announced that it was to return to Libya, more than three decades after its expulsion from the country when Qaddafi had nationalized its assets in 1971; BP was granted onshore and offshore exploratory rights in a deal worth an estimated US $900m., a development welcomed by Blair as evidence of a 'transformed' bilateral relationship.

Meanwhile, in December 2004, with the unilateral sanctions imposed upon Libya by the USA having been lifted, Libya paid the second instalment of its compensation to the families of those killed in the Lockerbie explosion. In August 2005 the head of the Senate Foreign Relations Committee, Senator Richard Lugar, visited Libya to hold talks with Qaddafi; two months previously officials from the US Department of State had praised Libya for its co-operation in the fight against international terrorism. In May 2006 the US Secretary of State, Condoleezza Rice, announced the US Administration's intention to restore full diplomatic relations between the two countries in recognition of Libya's 'continued commitment to its renunciation of terrorism', a development regarded by observers as the natural culmination of a process initiated in 2003 by Qaddafi's decision to abandon Libya's nuclear weapons programme; the US liaison office in Tripoli was formally upgraded to an embassy at the end of that month. In June 2006 Libya was removed from the US Department of State's list of countries deemed to support international terrorism. The renewal of full ties was expected significantly to boost both political and economic co-operation between the two nations, and was extended by the Bush Administration as an implicit incentive to the Iranian and North Korean Governments to dismantle their respective nuclear programmes.

In June 2006 tensions arose when Libyan lawyers in the USA insisted that, as a result of the expiration in December 2004 of an agreement concerning the transfer of the final portion of compensation for families of the victims of the Lockerbie bombing, the Libyan Government was no longer obligated to pay the final US $2m. promised to each family. Nevertheless, in July the USA lifted all air transport sanctions against Libya. In March 2007 the Libyan Government announced that it had reached an agreement with the USA that would aid the development of Libya's programme of nuclear energy generation; US officials contested that negotiations had been restricted to the possible establishment of a nuclear medicine centre in Libya. In further evidence of the improving relationship between the two countries, Shalgam made an official visit to Washington, DC, in January 2008, and held discussions with Condoleezza Rice—the first official visit by a Libyan foreign secretary in almost four decades. Rice called on Libya to improve its human rights record and to resolve the problem of outstanding compensation payments to families of victims of the Lockerbie bombing. Following discussions between Libyan and US officials in London in May 2008, a statement was issued reiterating the commitment of both parties to resolving all outstanding compensation claims. In mid-August representatives of both countries, meeting in Tripoli, signed a joint agreement on the full and final settlement of mutual claims by victims or their relatives in respect of bombings involving the two countries. (In the USA, the Libyan Claims Resolution Act had been signed into law earlier in the month.) Visiting Libya in early September, Rice—the first US Secretary of State to visit the country since 1953—stated that the two countries had entered a new phase in their relations, although differences remained. In October 2008 Libya paid $1,500m. into an agreed compensation fund for the relatives of US victims of bombings covered by the agreement. In December, following Senate approval in the previous month, Gene A. Cretz was sworn in as the first US ambassador to Libya since 1972 (having been nominated to this post in July 2007). In January 2009 Ali Suleiman Aujali assumed the role of Libyan ambassador to the USA, following the upgrading of Libya's liaison office in Washington, DC, to a full embassy in May 2006. From 1 April 2009 the USA began accepting Libyan applications for visas; over 1,000 visas were reported to have been issued by July that year. In mid-September Qaddafi visited the USA for the first time to address the UN General Assembly in New York.

In August 2009 the Scottish Cabinet Secretary for Justice, Kenny MacAskill, announced that al-Megrahi would be freed on compassionate grounds the following day, following discussions between the British and Libyan authorities over al-Megrahi's declining health (al-Megrahi had been diagnosed with terminal cancer in September 2008). The decision provoked outrage from many of the families of the US victims of the Lockerbie bombing and official condemnation by the US authorities. The celebrations that greeted al-Megrahi's arrival at Tripoli airport and a subsequent televised meeting between al-Megrahi and Qaddafi shortly after his return to Libya prompted further criticism. The British Government attempted to distance itself from the controversy, insisting that al-Megrahi's release had been purely a Scottish decision. However, one of a series of leaked US diplomatic cables published in late 2010 by the WikiLeaks organization indicated that the Scottish decision had enjoyed the full support of the British Government, to which Qaddafi had made 'thuggish' threats and warned of 'enormous repercussions' for British-Libyan relations if al-Megrahi were not granted early release, including the potential severance of diplomatic ties and the immediate cessation of all British commercial activity in Libya; the personal safety of British diplomatic staff and expatriate workers in Libya was also implicitly threatened. Another leaked communiqué revealed that Cretz had warned the US Administration that public opposition to al-Megrahi's release could result in US interests being subject to similarly punitive measures.

Meanwhile, the signing in May 2010 of a trade and investment agreement between the USA and Libya appeared to suggest a thawing in relations between the two countries. The deal, which followed a visit to Libya in February by a US trade delegation, provided for the establishment of a bilateral trade and investment council; the USA also agreed to offer assistance in Libya's bid to accede to the World Trade Organization (WTO, see p. 430). However, the apparent amelioration in relations was severely undermined by the Qaddafi regime's response to the popular protests in Libya in early 2011, which prompted vociferous condemnation from the Obama Administration. (For US and British responses to the Libyan Government's handling of the protests, see Domestic Political Affairs.)

Regional relations

Various plans for pan-Arab unity led to the formation, in January 1972, of the Federation of Arab Republics, comprising Libya, Egypt and Syria. In 1972 Libya concluded an agreement with Egypt to merge the two countries in 1973. Neither union was effective, and proposals for union with Tunisia in 1974, Syria in 1980, Chad in 1981, Morocco in 1984, Algeria in 1987 and Sudan in 1990 also proved abortive.

Relations with Egypt, already tense following the failure of the Libya-Egypt union, deteriorated further when President Anwar Sadat launched the October 1973 war against Israel without consulting Qaddafi. In common with the other members of the League of Arab States (the Arab League, see p. 361), Libya strongly objected to Sadat's peace initiative with Israel, which culminated in the signing of the Camp David accords in 1978, and Libya also condemned the proposals for Middle East peace that were agreed by other Arab states in Fez, Morocco, in 1982. From the late 1980s, none the less, Egypt and Libya forged a close relationship, with Egypt acting as an intermediary between Libya and Western nations (particularly in negotiations resulting from the Lockerbie bombing—see above). Following the suspension of UN sanctions against Libya in April 1999, Egypt Air resumed regular flights to Tripoli in July 2000, and Libyan flights to Egypt recommenced later that month.

In 1973 Libyan forces occupied the 'Aozou strip', a reputedly mineral-rich region of 114,000 sq km in the extreme north of Chad, to which it laid claim on the basis of an unratified border treaty concluded by Italy and France in 1935. Thereafter, Libya became embroiled in the lengthy struggle for political control between rival forces in Chad (q.v.). In September 1987, however, the two countries agreed to observe a cease-fire sponsored by the Organization of African Unity (OAU, now African Union—AU, see p. 183), and in October 1988 Libya and Chad restored diplomatic relations. In August 1989, with Algerian mediation, Chad and Libya concluded an agreement to attempt to resolve the dispute over sovereignty of the 'Aozou strip' through a political settlement. Accordingly, the issue was submitted to the International Court of Justice in The Hague, Netherlands, which in February 1994 ruled against Libya's claim. All Libyan troops remaining in the 'Aozou strip' were withdrawn in May. In June Libya and Chad concluded a treaty of friendship, neighbourly terms and co-operation. In May 1998 Qaddafi made his first visit to Chad for 17 years, and in November the two countries officially opened two of their common border posts.

Libya's outspoken criticism of other Arab regimes, and perceived interference in the internal affairs of other countries, led to years of relative political isolation. However, in 1987 Qaddafi sought to realign Libyan policy with that of the majority of Arab states. Qaddafi was reconciled in March with Yasser Arafat's Fatah wing of the Palestine Liberation Organization (PLO—against which he had previously advocated revolt, owing to its more moderate policies) and attempted to reunite the opposing factions of the Palestinian movement. In September Libya re-established 'fraternal' links with Iraq, modifying its support for Iran in the Iran–Iraq War.

A summit meeting of North African heads of state, held in Morocco in February 1989, concluded a treaty proclaiming the Union du Maghreb arabe (UMA—Union of the Arab Maghreb, see p. 450), comprising Algeria, Libya, Mauritania, Morocco and Tunisia. The treaty envisaged: the establishment of a council of heads of state; regular meetings of ministers of foreign affairs; and the eventual free movement of goods, people, services and capital throughout the countries of the region. During 1989–92 the member states formulated 15 regional co-operation conventions. In February 1993, however, it was announced that, in view of the differing economic orientations of each signatory, no convention had actually been implemented, and the UMA's activities were to be limited.

During the late 1990s and 2000s Qaddafi oscillated between identifying Libya as an African nation on the one hand, and emphasizing Libya's links with the Arab world on the other, often to suit his own political aims. In mid-1998 Qaddafi announced his intention to ally Libya more closely with African rather than Arab countries. In October, as further evidence of his dissatisfaction with Arab states, Qaddafi changed the name of Libya's mission to the Arab League from 'permanent' to 'resident'. In September 1999, on the 30th anniversary of his seizure of power,

Qaddafi hosted an extraordinary OAU summit in Sirte, at which he presented his vision of a United States of Africa and demanded that Africa be given veto power on the UN Security Council. The 'Sirte Declaration', a final document adopted by the 43 attending heads of state and government, called for the strengthening of the OAU, the establishment of a pan-African parliament, African monetary union and an African court of justice. At a further extraordinary summit of the OAU in Sirte in March 2001, it was announced that the organization's member states had overwhelmingly endorsed the proposals to declare the formation of the AU. In July 2002 Qaddafi travelled to Durban, South Africa, for the 38th and final summit of the OAU, which saw the formal creation of the new AU, chaired by South African President Thabo Mbeki. During the summit Mbeki and numerous other African heads of state attempted to persuade Qaddafi to abandon his hostility towards the New Partnership for Africa's Development, a contract between Africa and the international community under which, in exchange for aid and investment, the African states agreed to strive towards democracy and good governance.

Qaddafi's growing influence in Africa was somewhat checked in January 2003, following the removal of some 300 Libyan troops from the Central African Republic, to the Government of which they had been providing protection. In the previous month an agreement between Libya and Zimbabwe that would have resulted in the exchange of Libyan fuel for Zimbabwean beef, sugar and tobacco was abandoned. Attempts to revive the trade pact in mid-2003, which would have resulted in Zimbabwe mortgaging its petroleum assets to Libya, proved unsuccessful, and the abolition of the Secretariat for African Unity was widely interpreted as evidence of the failure of Qaddafi's African policy. In June 2004 allegations were made that in mid-2003 Qaddafi had ordered the assassination of Crown Prince Abdullah of Saudi Arabia, the kingdom's de facto leader, following a dispute between the two leaders at the Arab League summit held in March. (Libya also reportedly accused Saudi Arabia of financing Libyan opposition groups that had attempted to assassinate Qaddafi.) Libyan officials strongly refuted these allegations; however, in December 2004 Saudi Arabia recalled its ambassador from Tripoli and dismissed the Libyan ambassador in the Saudi capital, Riyadh.

In May 2006 Sudanese President Omar Hassan Ahmad al-Bashir expressed gratitude to Qaddafi for the latter's role in finding a resolution to the crisis in Darfur and proposed the establishment of a tripartite committee, comprising representatives of the Libyan and Sudanese Governments and the Sudan Liberation Movement, to oversee the implementation of the peace agreement signed between the two latter parties on 5 May (see the chapter on Sudan). In October Qaddafi and Egyptian President Muhammad Hosni Mubarak met in Tripoli to discuss the situation in Darfur, whereupon they concurred on the importance of the AU in resolving the crisis, and urged a rejection of foreign intervention. In November Qaddafi accused the USA and other Western countries of involving themselves in the Darfur crisis not because of genuine compassion but in order to secure oil, and, by means of the deployment of UN troops, to effect the return of colonialism to Africa. In July 2007 Libya hosted an international conference on Darfur, co-chaired by the AU and the UN.

In June 2006 ministers responsible for foreign affairs from Algeria, Libya, Mauritania, Morocco and Tunisia convened in Tripoli to discuss efforts to revive the five-nation UMA, which had remained dormant for more than a decade, predominantely owing to Algerian–Moroccan disagreements concerning Western Sahara (see the chapters on Algeria and Morocco). This will to relaunch the UMA was restated in April 2008 during celebrations held in Morocco to mark the 50th anniversary of the summit at which the idea of a union of Arab Maghreb states had initially been proposed. A year later delegates responsible for foreign affairs from the UMA member states again met in Tripoli, where they reiterated their commitment to improving political and economic co-operation among the countries of North Africa.

In March 2007 Qaddafi announced his decision to boycott the Arab League summit meeting in Riyadh, insisting that Libya was an African nation and had 'turned its back to Arabs'. Later that year Qaddafi embarked upon a tour of West Africa, including visits to Côte d'Ivoire, Guinea, Mali and Sierra Leone, and culminating with his attendance in July at an AU summit meeting, held in the Ghanaian capital, Accra, which focused predominantly on proposals to establish a pan-African government. However, Qaddafi was reported to have left the session abruptly when the majority of those present rejected his call for the immediate creation of a United States of Africa, and in February 2008 he threatened to sever Libyan ties with Africa, pledging to transfer Libya's African investments to alternative destinations in Arab and European countries if his vision for African unity continued to be ignored. In February 2009 Qaddafi was, none the less, appointed to the chairmanship of the AU. Qaddafi immediately used this role once more to promote the concept of a United States of Africa. However, at an AU summit meeting in Addis Ababa, Ethiopia, in January 2010, attempts by Qaddafi to gain re-election to the chairmanship of the organization were unsuccessful.

In November 2010 Libya and Tunisia agreed to lift all administrative and financial restrictions on the movement of goods and people between the two countries, in a development that was hailed as an important step towards the achievement of greater Maghreb unity. The two countries also agreed to double the value of bilateral investment, to US $2,000m., and discussed the creation of a free economic zone.

The Arab League suspended Libya's membership of that body in mid-February 2011, citing its disapproval of the Libyan Government's response to the popular protests that commenced earlier that month. Following criticism levelled against the AU for remaining silent on the Qaddafi regime's violent handling of the protesters, the Chairman of the AU Commission issued a statement in late February condemning the Government's 'disproportionate use of force' against civilians, and demanding 'an immediate end of the repression and violence'.

Other external relations

Relations with the EU, and particularly with France, generally improved following talks in early 1996 between Libyan and EU representatives in Belgium. In July Qaddafi granted the French authorities investigating the 1989 bombing of the UTA passenger aircraft unprecedented access to Libyan evidence. This resulted in February 1998 in a judge's decision to try *in absentia* six Libyans suspected of involvement in the attack, and in March 1999 a French court sentenced the six suspects to life imprisonment. The French authorities issued international arrest warrants for the Libyans, and threatened to intensify sanctions against Libya if it did not impose the verdicts on the accused. In July Libya began payment of some US $31m. in compensation to the families of those killed in the bomb attack, although attempts by French lawyers on behalf of the victims' families to prosecute Qaddafi for complicity in the bombing of the aircraft were unsuccessful. Nevertheless, it was announced in January 2004 that Libya had agreed to pay an additional $170m. to the relatives of the victims (see above). During an official visit to Libya in November, French President Jacques Chirac affirmed his commitment to rebuilding diplomatic ties with Libya. In December 2005 the Libyan Government was ordered by a French court to pay an additional $4m. in compensation to families of victims of the 1989 bombing not included in the previous agreement. Despite the ongoing process of reparation, relations between the French and Libyan Governments improved in 2005, after France expressed its interest in assisting the development of civil nuclear technology in Libya. In March 2006 a deal on co-operation regarding the development of nuclear energy in Libya was signed by representatives of the two countries during a visit to Tripoli by the Director of France's Commissariat à l'énergie atomique. Meanwhile, in April 2004 Qaddafi, who was visiting Europe for the first time in 15 years, met with several senior EU politicians in Brussels, Belgium, and addressed the European Commission. The ending of economic sanctions and an arms embargo imposed on Libya by the European Economic Community (now EU) in 1986 was ratified by EU ministers in October 2004.

In December 2007 Qaddafi made an official visit to the French capital at the invitation of President Nicolas Sarkozy—the first such invitation from a Western country since Libya had abandoned its nuclear weapons programme in 2003, and interpreted by some as a reward for the Libyan leader's decision to release the Bulgarian medical workers earlier in 2007 (see below). The visit provoked strong censure from both French and Libyan opposition politicians, as well as international human rights groups, owing to Libya's questionable human rights record. While Sarkozy insisted that he had broached the issue of human rights with the Libyan leader, Qaddafi was reported as saying that human rights had not in fact been discussed. During Qaddafi's visit commercial agreements worth an estimated €10,000m. were signed between the two countries; Libya also expressed a keen interest in the future purchase of military equipment. Franco-Libyan relations were, however, once more strained in mid-2008 when Qaddafi criticized President Sarkozy's project to create a Union for the Mediterranean. Qaddafi, who had expressed concerns that French promotion of Mediterranean co-operation represented a reassertion of colonial dominance over former North African colonies, and also that the initiative would undermine the role of the AU, refused to attend the official inauguration of the Union in July. During a state visit to Libya in July 2010, Qaddafi and Sarkozy signed a memorandum of understanding intended to boost nuclear energy co-operation, providing for French access to Libya's uranium resources and the eventual construction of a nuclear desalination plant to provide drinking water to the Libyan population. However, following the onset of conflict in Libya in early 2011 (see Domestic Political Affairs), the French Government was among those countries that imposed measures against the Qaddafi regime, and in early March France became the first state officially to recognize the opposition Transitional National Council as the 'legitimate representative of the Libyan people'.

In October 1996, meanwhile, the German authorities announced that evidence existed to prove the Libyan Government's direct involvement in a bomb attack on a discothèque in Berlin in 1986. Arrest warrants were subsequently issued for the four Libyans suspected of carrying out the bombing, but in March 1997 a German parliamentary delegation recommended that regular contact between the German Parliament and the GPC should continue. In April 1998 Libya resolved to allow the German authorities to question the Libyan suspects. In May the two countries signed an agreement on economic co-operation. Following a lengthy trial, in November 2001 a court in Berlin sentenced four people, including a Libyan national, to between 12 and 14 years' imprisonment for their involvement in the bomb attack. Although Qaddafi's personal complicity in the incident could not be proven, the presiding judge stated that there was sufficient evidence to ascertain that the bombing had been carried out by members of the Libyan secret service and employees of the Libyan People's Bureau in the former East Germany.

In August 2003 the Qaddafi International Foundation for Charitable Associations (now the Qaddafi International Charity and Development Foundation), a charity run by Seif al-Islam Qaddafi, offered to compensate the relatives of the three victims of the Berlin bomb attack. While negotiations between the USA and Libya regarding this compensation continued, a new round of talks between Germany and Libya began in July 2004 to decide upon compensation payments for the non-US citizens injured in the attack. The talks were finalized in the following month, and the Libyan authorities signed a deal in September agreeing to pay US $35m. to compensate some 160 non-US victims. The agreement signalled the start of improved relations between Germany and Libya, and in October Chancellor Gerhard Schröder paid an official visit to Libya.

In July 1998 Italy formally apologized for its colonial rule of Libya, and commitments were made to improve bilateral relations. Following the suspension of international sanctions in April 1999, Italy's Prime Minister, Massimo D'Alema, travelled to Libya in December, thus becoming the first EU premier to visit the country since 1992, and in December 2000 officials from the two countries signed accords regarding political consultation, visas and the removal of landmines during talks in the Italian capital, Rome. In February 2004 the Italian Prime Minister, Silvio Berlusconi, became the first Western leader to meet with Qaddafi following the Libyan renouncement of its nuclear weapons programme. In August Berlusconi exerted pressure on Qaddafi to place stricter border controls on the country's northern coastline, following an influx of illegal immigrants into the Italian island of Lampedusa from Libya. In October, following a sudden increase in the number of illegal immigrants arriving from North Africa (up to 1,700 a week), the Italian Government began a mass expulsion of illegal immigrants to Libya. Having agreed to assist with the immigration problem, Libya returned some 1,000 of these people to Egypt. Also in October Qaddafi agreed to revoke a ban that prohibited some 20,000 Italian settlers who had been expelled from Libya in 1970 (following Qaddafi's rise to power) from visiting the country.

Diplomatic relations between Libya and Italy briefly soured, however, in early 2006. In February the Italian consulate in Benghazi and the residence of the consul were attacked and set alight by protesters, following the publication in numerous countries, including Italy, of cartoons originally printed in a Danish newspaper depicting the Prophet Muhammad, which were deemed to be offensive towards Islam. A day prior to the protests, an Italian government minister had appeared on Italian television wearing an item of clothing bearing one of the cartoons; it was claimed that the television appearance had provoked the disturbances in Benghazi, during which 11 people were killed. Libyan Secretary for National Security Nasser al-Mabrouk was suspended and referred for investigation over the conduct of security forces during the protests.

In August 2008, during a meeting with Qaddafi in Benghazi, Berlusconi issued an apology for the 'damage inflicted on Libya by Italy during the colonial era'. The two heads of state also signed a treaty of 'friendship, partnership and co-operation' (which was subsequently ratified in Sirte in February 2009), committing Italy to annual payments of US $200m. to Libya, over a period of 25 years, via investment and infrastructure projects in country. For its part, Libya agreed to co-operate more fully in efforts to combat illegal immigration, principally through the establishment of joint marine patrols of the Libyan coastline. This issue became particularly salient in early 2009, after a report published by the office of the UN High Commissioner for Refugees stated that the number of migrants arriving in Italy from Libya had risen to 33,000 in 2008 (from 20,000 in 2007). At the end of March 2009 more than 200 migrants were reported to have drowned after their boat, destined for Italy, capsized 30 miles off the Libyan coast. In an unprecedented move, Libya agreed in May to take back more than 200 migrants discovered off the Libyan coastline by Italian marine patrols. In June Qaddafi paid an official visit to Italy, indicating the strengthening relationship between the two countries. However, relations between Libya and Italy, France and Germany, together with most other European countries, were severely compromised in early 2011 as a result of the Libyan Government's response to the widespread popular protests (see Domestic Political Affairs and below). The Libyan-Italian 'friendship, partnership and co-operation' treaty was suspended by Italy in late February. However, the Italian Minister of Foreign Affairs, Franco Frattini, stressed that the treaty had been suspended, not revoked, and, while adhering to measures imposed against Libya by the EU, Italy was not expected to impose any unilateral measures against the Qaddafi regime, prompting some observers to speculate that the Italian Government was keen to remain on workable terms with Libya, which accounts for about one-quarter of Italy's supply of crude petroleum.

Meanwhile, Libya came under heavy criticism from EU officials in May 2004, after five Bulgarian nurses and a Palestinian doctor were sentenced to death for deliberately infecting more than 400 children at a Benghazi hospital in 1999 with blood containing the HIV virus. The trials were denounced by international human rights associations as being unfair, and the nurses stated that their confessions had been extracted through torture. In December 2004 it was announced that Libya would review the sentences, and later in the month Seif al-Islam Qaddafi reportedly stated that the medical workers would not be executed. By March 2005, however, the sentences remained in place and the six launched an official appeal. Meanwhile, Libya continued to reject calls from Bulgaria, the USA and the EU to release the detainees, and demanded compensation from Bulgaria for the families affected by the case. The Bulgarian Government refused, stating that any payment would constitute an admission of the medical workers' guilt. In November the Supreme Court announced that a judgment regarding the medical workers' appeal would be made in January 2006. However, in December 2005 the previous sentences were overturned by the Supreme Court and a retrial was ordered.

The retrial began in May 2006 but was immediately adjourned for procedural reasons until 13 June. Despite calls from the presiding judge to accelerate the pace of legal proceedings, the trial was beset by numerous subsequent delays and adjournments. Eventually, however, in December, notwithstanding data arising from genetic analysis that strongly suggested that the children had been infected with HIV prior to the defendants' arrival in Libya in 1998, the original verdict was upheld and the six death sentences were reinstated. The EU Commissioner for Justice, Franco Frattini, called for the ruling to be reviewed, branding it an 'obstacle' to comfortable EU-Libyan relations, while the office of the UN High Commissioner for Human Rights urged the Libyan Government to intervene, citing 'serious and credible concerns' about the legitimacy of the trial. A few days after the ruling, the Government declared that it would not succumb to international pressure to invalidate the verdict, insisting that the Supreme Court had sole jurisdiction in the matter.

In January 2007 Qaddafi denounced 'Western intervention and pressure', reiterating the Government's argument that the outcome of the trial was a strictly juridical matter. However, it was reported later that month that the Libyan Government had extended an offer to free the six medical staff in exchange for the release of Abd al-Baset Ali Muhammad al-Megrahi, convicted for his part in the Lockerbie bombing (see above). Qaddafi, who claimed that the infections had arisen as a result of illicit experiments conducted on the children at the hospital by either the US or Israeli state intelligence agencies, linked the HIV case with the Lockerbie attack on numerous occasions, and demanded compensation of US $2,700m. to be paid to the affected families—the same amount tendered by the Libyan Government to the families of Lockerbie victims. In February 2007 the defence filed an appeal against the verdict reached in December 2006, but this was rejected in July 2007 and the death sentences were upheld. A few days later, however, the High Judicial Court commuted the sentences to terms of life imprisonment, following the successful brokerage of a compensation deal, according to which the victims' families would receive a reported $1m. for each child infected. The Bulgarian Government urged Libya to allow the medical workers to complete their sentences in Bulgaria, and Benita Ferrero-Waldner, the EU Commissioner responsible for External Relations and European Neighbourhood Policy, and Cécilia Sarkozy, then the wife of French President Nicolas Sarkozy, both travelled to Tripoli to lobby the Libyan Government to this end. Libya finally acquiesced to the Bulgarian request, and the medical workers were duly released from Libyan custody on 24 July. Upon their return to Bulgaria, they were immediately pardoned by that country's President.

In the context of progress towards the full normalization of relations between Libya and the USA, and the release from prison of the six Bulgarian medical workers, in November 2008 formal negotiations on an EU-Libya Framework Agreement were inaugurated. The agreement, intended to encompass economic, political, social and cultural co-operation, would represent the first such partnership between the EU and Libya. It was also designed to achieve greater consensus regarding the issue of illegal immigration to EU countries via Libya: during a second round of negotiations held in Tripoli in February 2009, Libya was offered some €20m. in assistance to address illegal migration. Negotiations on the EU-Libya Framework Agreement and ongoing co-operation contracts between the EU and Libya were suspended on 22 February 2011, and on 28 February the EU imposed an arms embargo on Libya in line with the UN Security Council resolution adopted on 26 February that implemented an arms embargo and other sanctions against the Qaddafi regime owing to its use of force in response to the popular riots; the EU also prohibited trade with Libya in any equipment that might be used for internal repression and imposed a visa ban and an asset freeze on Qaddafi and other leading members of the regime.

Diplomatic tensions between Libya and Switzerland grew from mid-2008, when Qaddafi's youngest son, Hannibal, was arrested in the Swiss city of Geneva following allegations of assault made by two of his servants. The Swiss Federal Department of Foreign Affairs subsequently complained to the Libyan authorities that Libya had taken retaliatory measures against the country, including closing the offices of some Swiss companies in Libya. It was further revealed in October that Libya had blocked oil shipments to Switzerland. In August 2009 the President of the Swiss Confederation, Hans-Rudolf Merz, issued a formal apology to the Libyan people for the arrest of Hannibal Qaddafi, against whom all charges had been dropped; in the same month Hannibal Qaddafi was reported to have told diplomats in Tripoli that if he had nuclear weaponry he would 'sweep Switzerland off the map'. In December two Swiss businessmen who had been held in Libya since Hannibal Qaddafi's arrest were sentenced to 16 months' imprisonment on charges of tax evasion and visa irregularities; however, one of the businessmen, Rachid Hamdani, had his sentence overturned and was released in February 2010. The second businessman, Max Goeldi, who had been sheltering at the Swiss embassy in Tripoli, handed himself in to the Libyan officials later that month to commence his gaol sentence, which had been reduced on appeal to four months. On 25 February, in a speech in Benghazi, Col Qaddafi reportedly called for 'jihad' against Switzerland; it was widely believed that this declaration was triggered not only by Hannibal's arrest but also by a referendum held in Switzerland in November 2009, at which voters approved a proposal to outlaw the construction of minarets in that country. It was subsequently announced that senior Libyan officials, including Col Qaddafi, were to be banned from the 25 European countries signed up to the Schengen Agreement. In early February 2010 the Swiss Government was reported to have imposed visa restrictions on 188 high-ranking Libyans, including Qaddafi, thereby preventing the blacklisted persons from entering any signatory to the Schengen Agreement; under the terms of the accord, all Schengen signatories are obliged to refuse visas to those blacklisted by fellow members. In mid-February the Libyan Government imposed a ban on the issuing of visas to all of the signatories to the Schengen Agreement, a decision that was denounced by the European Commission as a 'unilateral and disproportionate' response. The ban was lifted in late March, after it was announced that the Swiss blacklist had been withdrawn. It was hoped that this, together with the release from prison in June of Goeldi, having served his full sentence, would bring an end to the protracted dispute between Libya and Switzerland. However, the Libyan Government's response to widespread popular protests in early 2011 prompted the Swiss Government to freeze assets in Swiss banks that it claimed belonged to Qaddafi in order to prevent the potential expropriation of Libyan state funds.

During a visit to Libya in April 2008 by the Russian President, Vladimir Putin, several agreements were signed on co-operation in energy, military and infrastructure projects. Putin agreed to cancel Libyan debts amounting to some US $4,500m. Qaddafi began his first visit to Russia in late October: the principal issues discussed during the visit were collaboration in energy projects, including Russian assistance for Libya's civilian nuclear programme, and military co-operation. In January 2010 the two countries concluded an agreement worth more than $2,000m. for Libya to purchase more than 20 Russian fighter jets.

Increasing cordial relations with the People's Republic of China have been evident in recent years, fuelled by Chinese interest in Libya's oil resources and Libya's continued adherence to the 'one-China' policy (see the chapter on the People's Republic of China). A number of high-level bilateral exchanges took place in 2009, culminating in the attendance of the Chinese Minister of Housing and Urban-Rural Development, Jiang Weixin, as the special envoy of President Hu Jintao, at celebrations in Tripoli to mark the 40th anniversary of Col Qaddafi's rule. During a visit to China in October 2010 Seif al-Islam Qaddafi reiterated Libya's adherence to the 'one-China' policy and pledged to strive for enhanced co-operation between Libya and China on a range of areas including infrastructural development, energy and telecommunications. China, together with Russia, supported in late February 2011 the UN Security Council resolution implementing an arms embargo and other sanctions against the Qaddafi regime owing to its use of force in response to the popular protests, and referring the actions of the regime to the ICC; however, both countries remained opposed to any military action against the regime.

A diplomatic incident arose between Libya and the Republic of Korea (South Korea) in June 2010, following the expulsion by Libya of a South Korean intelligence official on suspicion of espionage, and the closure of Libya's Economic Co-operation Bureau, which served as its de facto embassy, in the South Korean capital, Seoul. The official, who had been arrested in Tripoli earlier that month, was alleged to have been collating information about Qaddafi, his relatives and senior government officials, as well as attempting to gather information on defence industry contacts between Libya and North Korea. The South Korean Government dismissed the incident as a 'misunderstanding', and in early October dispatched a senior-level delegation to Tripoli; following a meeting with Qaddafi, the delegation's leader, Lee Sang-Deuk (a brother of the South Korean President), declared that the dispute had been resolved, and the Libyan Economic Co-operation Bureau was reopened a few days later. However, relations were again threatened as a result of the popular protests in Libya in early 2011; in February the South Korean Government urged its nationals to leave Libya, after three South Korean labourers were injured when the construction site on which they were working, in Zawia, near Tripoli, was attacked.

CONSTITUTION AND GOVERNMENT

Following the overthrow of King Idris I in 1969, a Constitutional Proclamation was issued by the Revolutionary Command Council (see Contemporary Political History). In 1977 a further document, the Declaration on the Establishment of the Authority of the People, was approved by the General People's Congress (GPC). Under the system set out in this document, power is vested in the people through People's Congresses, Popular Committees, Trade Unions, and Vocational Syndicates, and with the GPC and its General Secretariat. The head of state is the Revolutionary Leader, elected by the GPC; however, Col Muammar al-Qaddafi himself rejects this nomenclature and all other titles. Executive power is exercised by the General People's Committee. The country is divided into three provinces, 10 governorates and 1,500 administrative communes.

REGIONAL AND INTERNATIONAL CO-OPERATION

Libya is a member of the African Union (AU, see p. 183), the League of Arab States (Arab League, see p. 361), the Organization of Arab Petroleum Exporting Countries (OAPEC, see p. 397) and the Union du Maghreb arabe (UMA—Union of the Arab Maghreb, see p. 450). (Libya's membership of the Arab League was suspended in mid-February 2011.) The Community of Sahel-Saharan States (CEN-SAD, see p. 446) has its headquarters in Tripoli.

Libya joined the UN in September 1990. The country also participates in the Organization of the Petroleum Exporting Countries (OPEC, see p. 405). In 2004 the World Trade Organization (WTO, see p. 430) agreed to commence accession negotiations with Libya, which had applied for membership of the organization in 2001.

ECONOMIC AFFAIRS

In 2009, according to estimates by the World Bank, Libya's gross national income (GNI), measured at average 2007–09 prices, was US $77,185m., equivalent to $12,020 per head (or $16,430 on an international purchasing-power parity basis). During 2000–09, it was estimated, the population increased at an average annual rate of 2.1%, while gross domestic product (GDP) per head increased, in real terms, by an average of 2.2% per year. According to World Bank estimates, overall GDP increased, in real terms, at an average annual rate of 4.3% in 2000–09; GDP increased by 2.1% in 2009.

Agriculture (including forestry and fishing) contributed 2.7% of GDP in 2009, according to preliminary official figures, and engaged 7.6% of the employed labour force in 2007. The principal subsistence crops are wheat and barley; other crops include potatoes, olives, tomatoes, onions, watermelons, dates and citrus fruits. An aim of the Great Man-made River Project (GMR), in progress since 1984, is to reclaim some 130,000 ha of arable land; more than 70% of water to be delivered by the GMR is intended for agricultural use. The main agricultural activity is animal husbandry, with sheep and goats being the principal livestock. During 2004–09, according to preliminary official data, agricultural GDP increased at an average annual rate of 5.2%; the sector's GDP increased by 2.5% in 2009.

Industry (including mining, manufacturing, construction and power) contributed 70.8% of GDP in 2009, according to preliminary official figures, and engaged 16.6% of the employed labour force in 2007. Preliminary official data indicated that the GDP of the industrial sector increased at an average annual rate of 2.8% in 2004–09; industrial GDP declined by 4.4% in 2009, compared with an increase of 1.1% in 2008.

Mining contributed 54.3% of GDP in 2009, according to preliminary official figures, although the sector engaged just 3.1% of the employed labour force in 2007. Libya's economy is overwhelmingly reliant on its petroleum and natural gas resources. Hydrocarbons contributed 89.7% of total government revenue in 2008. At the end of 2009 proven recoverable reserves of petroleum were estimated at 44,300m. barrels, the largest proven reserves in Africa and sufficient to enable production to be maintained—at that year's levels, averaging 1.65m. barrels per day (b/d)—for almost 74 years. As a member of the Organization of the Petroleum Exporting Countries (OPEC, see p. 405), Libya is subject to production quotas agreed by the Organization's Conference. Libya's natural gas reserves are extensive (estimated at 1,540,000m. cu m at the end of 2009). Libya also has reserves of iron ore, salt, limestone, clay, sulphur and gypsum. According to preliminary official figures, the GDP of the mining sector increased, in real terms, at an average annual rate of 1.1% in 2004–09; mining GDP contracted by 7.6% in 2009.

Manufacturing contributed 6.3% of GDP in 2009, according to preliminary official figures, and engaged 7.9% of the employed labour force in 2007. The principal manufacturing activity is petroleum refining. Other important activities include the production of iron, steel and cement, chemicals-manufacturing, and the processing of agricultural products. Preliminary official figures indicated that the GDP of the manufacturing sector increased at an average annual rate of 4.1% during 2004–09; the sector's GDP increased by 3.5% in 2009.

According to preliminary official figures, construction contributed 8.7% of GDP in 2009. The sector engaged only 2.4% of the employed labour force in 2007. Preliminary official figures indicated that the GDP of the construction sector increased at an average annual rate of 13.3% during 2004–09; the sector's GDP increased by 9.0% in 2009.

Energy is derived principally from petroleum, which contributed 55.1% of total electricity output in 2007, and natural gas (44.9%). Libya is a net exporter of fuels.

Services contributed 26.5% of GDP in 2009, according to preliminary official figures, and engaged 75.9% of the employed labour force in 2007. Efforts to reform the financial sector, hitherto highly state-controlled, have notably included the sale, in 2007–08, of minority stakes in two banks to foreign interests. A stock exchange was established in 2007. The Government has invested heavily in recent years to expand and rehabilitate Libya's tourism infrastructure. Visitor arrivals neared 1m. in 2004. During 2004–09, according to preliminary official data, the GDP of the services sector increased at an average annual rate of 8.0%; services GDP increased by 5.7% in 2009.

In 2009 Libya recorded a visible trade surplus of US $15,053m., and there was a surplus of $9,381m. on the current account of the balance of payments. In 2007 the principal source of imports was Italy (which provided 8.1% of total imports); Japan, Egypt, the USA, Germany and the Republic of Korea (South Korea) were also important suppliers. The principal market for exports in 2007 was Italy (41.0%); Germany, France and Spain were also significant purchasers. The petroleum sector is overwhelmingly Libya's principal generator of exports revenue: according to balance of payments data published by the IMF, hydrocarbons (including foreign partners' share) accounted for some 96.2% of the value of merchandise exports in 2009. The principal imports in 2005 were plant and equipment, basic manufactures, and food and live animals.

An overall budgetary surplus of LD 8,306m. was recorded in 2009, equivalent to 10.6% of GDP. This was projected to reach LD 15,077m. in 2010, equivalent to 15.8% of GDP. According to the Central Bank of Libya, the annual rate of inflation averaged 4.0% in 2003–09; consumer prices increased by an estimated average of 2.4% in 2009, compared with an increase of 10.4% in 2008.

Strong GDP growth and robust budgetary and balance of payments surpluses in 2003–07 were achieved in the context of high international oil prices, in conjunction with the ending of international sanctions and the 'normalization' of Libya's external relations. The growth of the non-hydrocarbons sector was notably strong during this period, with the construction, transport and trade sectors registering particular expansion; this area of growth continued in 2008–09, despite the world-wide financial crisis. Several large construction projects were announced in 2009, including a plan valued at some US $54,400m. to develop two 'energy cities' at Ras Lanuf and Mersa Brega. The project, which was expected to create some 32,000 jobs and attract further foreign investment through a complete renovation of the existing energy facilities, was scheduled for completion in 2024. In February 2010, however, it was revealed that final approval from the Libyan Government had yet to be granted. A new sovereign wealth fund, the Libyan Investment Authority (LIA), which became operational in 2007, was established to manage state-allocated assets, including the Oil Reserve Fund, with the intention of creating a diversified investment portfolio (the bulk of investments were to be made overseas) as part of efforts to reduce the country's overwhelming reliance on petroleum exports. In 2009 the country's closer diplomatic ties with the West and falling property prices in Western European countries also allowed the LIA to make significant foreign investments, with a focus on tangible assets such as utilities and real estate. With the ending of international sanctions, Libya rapidly became a major centre for hydrocarbons exploration, and output of both oil and natural gas expanded rapidly. Furthermore, since large areas of Libyan territory remained hitherto unexplored, it was believed that reserves (already the largest in Africa) could be significantly higher than currently estimated. However, industry analysts considered that Libya's aim to increase oil production to 3m. b/d by the mid-2010s was unlikely to be

LIBYA

achieved. Moreover, oil exports were severely disrupted by the eruption of conflict between the regime of Col Muammar al-Qaddafi and anti-Government forces in early 2011. Despite reports that some facilities that had passed into opposition control continued to produce and export oil, the International Energy Agency indicated that output had declined by some 50% by early March. Meanwhile, much of Libya's foreign assets was blocked, following the imposition of sanctions by the UN, as well as other countries and organizations, including the USA and the European Union.

PUBLIC HOLIDAYS

2012: 4 February* (Mouloud, Birth of Muhammad), 2 March (Jamahiriya Day), 28 March (Evacuation Day), 11 June (Evacuation Day), 16 June* (Leilat al-Meiraj, Ascension of Muhammad), 18 August* (Id al-Fitr, end of Ramadan), 1 September (Revolution Day), 7 October (Evacuation Day), 25 October* (Id al-Adha, Feast of the Sacrifice), 14 November* (Muharram, Islamic New Year), 23 November* (Ashoura).

* These holidays are dependent on the Islamic lunar calendar and may vary by one or two days from the dates given.

Statistical Survey

Sources (unless otherwise stated): National Corporation for Information and Documentation; Census and Statistical Dept, Secretariat of Planning, Sharia Damascus 40, 2nd Floor, Tripoli; tel. (21) 3331731; Central Bank of Libya, POB 1103, Sharia al-Malik Seoud, Tripoli; tel. (21) 3333591; fax (21) 4441488; e-mail info@cbl.gov.ly; internet www.cbl.gov.ly.

Area and Population

AREA, POPULATION AND DENSITY

Area (sq km)	1,775,500*
Population (census results)†	
August 1995	4,404,986
August 2006	
Males	2,610,639
Females	2,687,513
Total	5,298,152
Population (official estimates at 31 March)	
2009	5,539,000
2010	6,100,000
Density (per sq km) at 31 March 2010	3.4

* 685,524 sq miles.
† Excluding non-Libyans: 409,326 in 1995 and 359,540 in 2006.
Source: partly National Authority for Information and Authentication.

POPULATION BY AGE AND SEX
(UN estimates at mid-2011)

	Males	Females	Total
0–14	1,024,851	978,318	2,003,169
15–64	2,269,404	2,100,930	4,370,334
65 and over	148,777	148,648	297,425
Total	3,443,032	3,227,896	6,670,928

Source: UN, *World Population Prospects: The 2008 Revision*.

POPULATION BY REGION
(population at 2006 census)

Al-Butnan	150,353	Misratah	511,628
Banghazi (Benghazi)	622,148	Nalut	87,772
Darnah	155,402	Al-Nuqat al-Khams	269,553
Ghat	21,329	Sabha	119,038
Al-Jabal al-Akhdar	192,689	Surt (Sirte)	131,786
Al-Jabal al-Gharbi	288,944	Tarabulus (Tripoli)	997,065
Al-Jifarah	422,999	Wadi al-Hayat	70,711
Al-Jufrah	46,899	Wadi al-Shati	73,443
Al-Kufrah	42,769	Al-Wahah	164,718
Al-Marqab	410,187	Al-Zawiyah (Zawia)	270,751
Al-Marj	175,455	**Total**	5,298,152
Marzuq	72,513		

Source: National Authority for Information and Authentication.

PRINCIPAL TOWNS
(population at census of 2006)

Tarabulus (Tripoli, the capital)	997,065	Al-Nuquat al-Khams	269,553
Banghazi (Benghazi)	622,148	Al-Jabal al-Akhdar	192,689
Misratah (Misurata)	511,628	Al-Marj	175,455
Al-Jifarah	422,999	Al-Wahah	164,718
Al-Marqab	410,187	Darnah	155,402
Al-Jabal al-Gharbi	288,944	Al-Butnan	150,353
Al-Zawiyah (Zawia)	270,751	Surt (Sirte)	131,786

Source: National Authority for Information and Authentication.

BIRTHS, MARRIAGES AND DEATHS

	Registered live births		Registered marriages		Registered deaths	
	Number	Rate (per 1,000)	Number	Rate (per 1,000)	Number	Rate (per 1,000)
2004	119,633	23.5	39,105	7.6	15,765	3.1
2005	120,999	23.3	43,979	8.4	16,425	3.2
2006	124,541	23.2	47,219	8.8	17,975	3.4
2007	128,337	23.7	59,583	11.0	20,045	3.7
2008	132,826	24.1	65,326	11.9	21,481	3.9

Source: National Authority for Information and Authentication.

Life expectancy (years at birth, WHO estimates): 73 (males 71; females 76) in 2008 (Source: WHO, *World Health Statistics*).

EMPLOYMENT
('000 persons)

	2005	2006	2007
Agriculture, forestry and fishing	117.0	125.8	135.7
Oil and gas extraction	29.3	31.0	32.8
Mining and quarrying	21.1	22.4	23.7
Manufacturing	131.1	136.3	141.8
Electricity, gas and water	50.4	53.3	56.4
Construction	47.0	44.6	42.4
Trade, restaurants and hotels	190.1	192.6	195.1
Transport and communications	121.9	130.5	140.8
Financing, insurance and real estate	35.8	38.4	41.2
Public administration	271.8	280.9	290.4
Education	453.2	468.4	484.2
Health services	196.3	202.9	209.7
Other services	0.1	0.2	0.3
Total	1,665.2	1,727.2	1,794.5
Libyans	1,479.1	1,543.3	1,613.6
Non-Libyans	186.1	183.9	180.9

Source: IMF, *Socialist People's Libyan Arab Jamahiriya: Statistical Appendix* (September 2008).

Mid-2011 ('000, estimates): Agriculture, etc. 69; Total labour force 2,471 (Source: FAO).

LIBYA

Health and Welfare

KEY INDICATORS

Total fertility rate (children per woman, 2008)	2.7
Under-5 mortality rate (per 1,000 live births, 2008)	17
HIV/AIDS (% of persons aged 15–49, 2003)	0.3
Physicians (per 1,000 head, 2004)	1.3
Hospital beds (per 1,000 head, 2006)	3.7
Health expenditure (2007): US $ per head (PPP)	453
Health expenditure (2007): % of GDP	2.7
Health expenditure (2007): public (% of total)	71.8
Access to water (% of persons, 2002)	72
Access to sanitation (% of persons, 2000)	97
Total carbon dioxide emissions ('000 metric tons, 2007)	57,286.6
Carbon dioxide emissions per head (metric tons, 2007)	9.3
Human Development Index (2010): ranking	53
Human Development Index (2010): value	0.755

For sources and definitions, see explanatory note on p. vi.

Agriculture

PRINCIPAL CROPS
('000 metric tons)

	2007	2008	2009
Wheat	104	104	n.a.
Barley	100	100	n.a.
Potatoes	290	290	n.a.
Broad beans, horse beans, dry	15	15	15*
Almonds, with shell*	25	25	n.a.
Groundnuts, with shell	23†	23†	23*
Olives	180†	180†	180*
Tomatoes	213	213	200*
Pumpkins, squash and gourds*	30	30	n.a.
Cucumbers and gherkins	12†	12†	12*
Chillies and peppers, green*	15	15	n.a.
Onions and shallots, green*	53†	53†	n.a.
Onions, dry	182†	182†	182*
Peas, green	6†	6†	6*
Carrots and turnips	25†	25†	25*
Watermelons	2188†	218†	220*
Cantaloupes and other melons	26†	26†	26*
Oranges*	45	45	n.a.
Tangerines, mandarins, etc.*	10	10	n.a.
Lemons and limes*	16	16	n.a.
Apples	20†	20†	20*
Apricots*	17	17	n.a.
Peaches and nectarines*	10	10	n.a.
Plums and sloes*	33	33	n.a.
Grapes	30†	30†	30*
Figs	10†	10†	10*
Dates	150†	150†	150*

* FAO estimate(s).
† Unofficial figure.

Aggregate production ('000 metric tons, may include official, semi-official or estimated data): Total cereals 213 in 2007–09; Total roots and tubers 290 in 2007–09; Total vegetables (incl. melons) 872 in 2007–08, 862 in 2009; Total fruits (excl. melons) 346 in 2007–09.

Source: FAO.

LIVESTOCK
('000 head, year ending September)

	2004*	2005*	2006
Horses	45	45	45
Asses	30	30	29
Cattle	130	150	185
Camels	48	49	50*
Sheep	5,200	5,500	6,000
Goats	2,100	2,300	2,500
Poultry	25,000	25,000	24,000

* FAO estimate(s).

2007–09: Figures assumed to be unchanged from 2006 (FAO estimates).

Source: FAO.

LIVESTOCK PRODUCTS
('000 metric tons)

	2006	2007	2008
Cattle meat*	10	10	10
Sheep meat*	26	25	28
Goat meat*	12	12	12
Chicken meat	94	120	120*
Cows' milk*	130	130	130
Sheep's milk*	56	56	56
Goats' milk	15	15	15
Hen eggs*	60	60	60
Wool, greasy*	9	9	9

* FAO estimate(s).

2009: Production assumed to be unchanged from 2008 (FAO estimates).

Source: FAO.

Forestry

ROUNDWOOD REMOVALS
('000 cubic metres, excl. bark, FAO estimates)

	2007	2008	2009
Sawlogs, veneer logs and logs for sleepers*	63	63	63
Other industrial wood	53	53	53
Fuel wood	914	926	939
Total	1,030	1,042	1,055

* Annual output assumed to be unchanged since 1978.

Source: FAO.

SAWNWOOD PRODUCTION
('000 cubic metres, incl. railway sleepers, FAO estimates)

	1976	1977	1978
Total (all broadleaved)*	9	21	31

* Annual output to 2009 assumed to be unchanged since 1978 (FAO estimates).

Source: FAO.

Fishing

(metric tons, live weight)

	2006	2007	2008
Capture	34,647*	31,921	47,645
Groupers	1,200*	896	1,537
Bogue	2,700*	2,708	4,009
Porgies and seabreams	3,000	n.a.	n.a.
Surmullet	1,400*	889	1,519
Jack and horse mackerels	4,700*	4,691	6,855
Sardinellas	12,000*	13,554	19,518
'Scomber' mackerels	3,800*	3,895	6,029
Aquaculture*	388	240	240
Total catch (incl. others)*	35,035	32,161	47,885

* FAO estimate(s).

Source: FAO.

LIBYA

Mining

('000 metric tons unless otherwise indicated, estimates)

	2007	2008	2009
Salt	40	40	40
Gypsum (crude)	240	260	300

Source: US Geological Survey.

Crude petroleum (million barrels): 642.8 in 2006; 653.8 in 2007; 643.6 in 2008; 592.5 in 2009.

Natural gas (incl. flared, '000 million cu ft): 948,100 in 2006; 1,024,400 in 2007; 1,070,100 in 2008; 1,035,500 in 2009.

Industry

SELECTED PRODUCTS
('000 metric tons)

	2007	2008	2009
Jet fuels (incl. kerosene)	1,470	1,511	1,876
Motor spirit (petrol)	813	775	751
Naphthas (raw)	2,677	2,575	2,474
Gas-diesel (distillate fuel) oil	4,137	3,845	4,178
Residual fuel oils	7,004	6,955	6,719

Cement (hydraulic, '000 metric tons, estimates): 5,500 in 2007; 6,000 in 2008; 6,500 in 2009 (Source: US Geological Survey).

Electric energy (million kWh): 22,317 in 2005; 23,992 in 2006; 25,694 in 2007 (Source: UN Industrial Commodity Statistics Database).

Finance

CURRENCY AND EXCHANGE RATES

Monetary Units:
1,000 dirhams = 1 Libyan dinar (LD).

Sterling, Dollar and Euro Equivalents (29 October 2010):
£1 sterling = 1.9575 dinars;
US $1 = 1.2294 dinars;
€1 = 1.7036;
100 Libyan dinars = £51.09 = $81.34 = €58.70.

Average Exchange Rate (Libyan dinar per US $):
2007 1.2626
2008 1.2236
2009 1.2535

BUDGET
(LD million)

Revenue	2008	2009*	2010*
Hydrocarbon budget allocation	65,365	41,632	50,630
Non-hydrocarbon	7,532	10,353	11,408
Non-hydrocarbon tax revenue	3,531	4,350	4,817
Taxes on income and profits	2,790	3,100	3,456
Taxes on international trade	499	1,000	1,080
Other tax revenue	241	250	280
Non-hydrocarbon non-tax revenue	4,002	6,002	6,591
Total	72,898	51,984	62,037

Expenditure	2008	2009*	2010*
Current	17,579	22,039	24,179
Expenditure on goods and services	10,593	12,324	13,494
Wages and salaries	7,764	8,874	9,717
Subsidies and other current transfers†	6,986	9,715	10,684
Capital	27,257	21,639	22,782
Development budget	22,610	18,500	19,333
Total‡	44,835	43,678	46,961

* Projections.
† Subsidies for 2007 include food and medicine only; from 2008 subsidies also include fuel, electricity and water.
‡ Including net lending (LD million): 1,350 in 2008; 850 in 2009 (projection); 650 in 2010 (projection).

Source: IMF, *Socialist People's Libyan Arab Jamahiriya: 2009 Article IV Consultation—Staff Report; Public Information Notice on the Executive Board Discussion; and Statement by the Executive Director for the Socialist People's Libyan Arab Jamahiriya* (September 2009).

INTERNATIONAL RESERVES
(US $ million at 31 December)

	2007	2008	2009
Gold (national valuation)	194	194	194
IMF special drawing rights	882	901	2,514
Reserve position in IMF	625	609	595
Foreign exchange	77,897	90,803	95,916
Total	79,598	92,507	99,219

Source: IMF, *International Financial Statistics*.

MONEY SUPPLY
(LD million at 31 December)

	2007	2008	2009
Currency outside banks	4,581.2	5,608.3	6,962.9
Demand deposits at commercial banks	16,375.1	27,055.8	29,582.9
Total money (incl. others)	22,013.8	33,323.1	37,380.5

Source: IMF, *International Financial Statistics*.

COST OF LIVING
(Consumer Price Index; base: 2003 = 100)

	2007	2008	2009
Personal services and others	111.2	120.9	123.5
Medical care	133.8	134.1	134.0
Recreation and education	91.1	94.1	100.0
Transport and communication	129.7	134.3	137.3
Clothing and shoes	92.5	94.7	98.1
Furniture	89.0	92.4	96.7
Housing	103.6	109.3	109.6
Food, beverages and tobacco	121.0	144.8	149.3
All items	112.0	123.7	126.7

LIBYA

NATIONAL ACCOUNTS
(LD million at current prices)

Expenditure on the Gross Domestic Product

	2007	2008	2009
Government final consumption expenditure	9,850.8	12,421.4	9,310.5
Private final consumption expenditure	28,571.1	35,400.3	26,964.7
Gross fixed capital formation	7,320.5	9,092.0	6,861.6
Changes in inventories	306.7	380.9	287.2
Total domestic expenditure	46,048.9	57,294.6	43,423.9
Exports of goods and services	54,368.4	68,875.4	50,139.0
Less Imports of goods and services	21,289.9	26,601.2	19,902.8
GDP in purchasers' values	79,127.5	99,568.9	73,660.1
GDP at constant 2005 prices	66,689.8	68,504.7	67,994.1

Source: UN National Accounts Main Aggregates Database.

Gross Domestic Product by Economic Activity
(preliminary figures)

	2007	2008	2009
Agriculture, forestry and fishing	1,905.3	2,247.9	2,382.7
Mining and quarrying (incl. hydrocarbons)	62,397.1	81,277.3	47,231.2
Manufacturing	4,032.1	4,888.8	5,447.6
Electricity, gas and water	1,019.1	1,204.5	1,334.6
Construction	4,198.4	5,994.5	7,577.5
Trade, restaurants and hotels	3,396.3	3,949.5	4,298.1
Transport, storage and communications	3,299.5	3,884.2	4,125.8
Financial intermediation	980.8	1,081.3	1,181.8
Real estate, renting and business activities	5,218.9	5,723.8	6,154.8
Education and health, etc.*	252.6	277.9	298.5
Government, defence and mandatory social insurance	6,507.3	6,670.7	6,870.8
Other services	69.4	82.3	91.0
Sub-total	93,276.9	117,282.6	86,994.4
Less Financial intermediation services indirectly measured	364.3	643.1	705.5
Total	92,693.6	116,639.6	86,288.9

* Private sector only.

BALANCE OF PAYMENTS
(US $ million)

	2007	2008	2009
Exports of goods f.o.b.	46,970	61,950	37,055
Imports of goods f.o.b.	−17,701	−21,658	−22,002
Trade balance	29,269	40,292	15,053
Exports of services	109	208	385
Imports of services	−2,665	−4,344	−5,063
Balance on goods and services	26,712	36,155	10,375
Other income received	4,517	4,471	2,462
Other income paid	−2,500	−3,885	−1,884
Balance on goods, services and income	28,729	36,742	10,953
Current transfers received	598	45	—
Current transfers paid	−817	−1,085	−1,572
Current balance	28,510	35,702	9,381
Direct investment abroad	−3,933	−5,888	−1,165
Direct investment from abroad	4,689	4,111	1,711
Portfolio investment assets	−1,440	−10,964	−3,352
Other investment assets	−8,947	−8,280	−3,952
Other investment liabilities	88	−19	1,573
Net errors and omissions	1,076	−1,715	993
Overall balance	20,044	12,948	5,188

Source: IMF, *International Financial Statistics*.

External Trade

PRINCIPAL COMMODITIES
(LD million)

Imports c.i.f.	2004	2005
Food and live animals	1,159.8	1,177.4
Beverages and tobacco	15.1	30.2
Animal and vegetable oils and fats	156.5	111.6
Crude materials (inedible) except fuels	118.1	145.8
Mineral fuels and related materials	56.4	30.0
Chemical materials	334.4	458.1
Basic manufactures	1,646.7	1,650.0
Plant and equipment	3,960.3	3,787.0
Miscellaneous products	807.9	563.1
Total	8,255.2	7,953.5

Exports f.o.b.*	2004	2005
Food and live animals	3.2	2.3
Mineral fuels and related products	20,085.6	30,312.2
Chemicals and related products	675.9	825.2
Basic manufactures	73.2	2.3
Machinery and transport equipment	8.9	2.5
Total (incl. others)	20,848.3	31,148.0

* Including re-exports.

2006 (LD million): Total imports c.i.f. 7,934.7; Total exports (incl. re-exports) 36,336.3.

2007 (LD million): Total imports c.i.f. 8,501.4; Total exports (incl. re-exports) 40,972.1.

2008 (LD million): Total imports c.i.f. 11,195.2; Total exports (incl. re-exports) 54,732.4.

PRINCIPAL TRADING PARTNERS
(US $ million)*

Imports c.i.f.	2003	2004
Argentina	25.7	99.6
Belgium	101.3	118.3
Brazil	50.7	81.2
Canada	37.2	114.4
China, People's Republic	85.1	207.3
Egypt	129.7	131.6
France (incl. Monaco)	274.3	255.4
Germany	486.2	760.8
Greece	47.7	40.9
India	12.8	162.6
Italy	925.9	1,156.7
Japan	321.9	525.4
Korea, Republic	96.5	471.2
Malta	160.6	78.0
Netherlands	69.9	72.0
Spain	64.4	92.7
Sweden	22.6	68.3
Switzerland-Liechtenstein	93.9	41.9
Tunisia	135.8	145.6
Turkey	92.1	111.3
United Arab Emirates	99.1	23.8
United Kingdom	300.8	260.2
USA	20.3	157.0
Total (incl. others)	4,322.5	6,317.6

LIBYA

Exports f.o.b.	1998	1999	2000
Austria	125.2	87.0	18.9
Egypt	97.6	94.1	57.1
France (incl. Monaco)	236.8	509.8	574.4
Germany	1,002.9	1,507.1	1,556.2
Greece	161.6	186.1	270.7
Italy	2,449.9	2,987.0	4,343.8
Netherlands	141.0	81.8	70.0
Portugal	29.6	20.6	49.9
Spain	685.9	1,084.5	1,555.0
Switzerland-Liechtenstein	0.9	105.2	18.4
Tunisia	303.6	320.6	423.2
Turkey	394.4	5.7	769.3
United Kingdom	158.0	104.4	233.6
Total (incl. others)	6,131.4	7,905.1	10,194.9

* Imports by country of origin; exports by country of destination. Figures exclude trade in gold.

Source: UN, *International Trade Statistics Yearbook*.

2005 (LD million): *Imports:* Egypt 295; France 414; Germany 743; Italy 947; Japan 248; Korea, Republic 568; Tunisia 171; United Kingdom 274; USA 237; Total (incl. others) 7,954. *Exports:* France 1,733; Germany 3,032; Greece 997; India 884; Italy 12,931; Netherlands 608; Portugal 615; Spain 3,103; Tunisia 615; Turkey 2,348; Total (incl. others) 31,148 (Source: National Authority for Information and Authentication).

2006 (LD million): *Imports:* Egypt 334; France 233; Germany 674; Italy 784; Japan 449; Korea, Republic 519; Tunisia 377; United Kingdom 291; USA 418; Total (incl. others) 7,935. *Exports:* France 1,747; Germany 3,560; Greece 1,440; India 108; Italy 15,456; Netherlands 1,099; Portugal 611; Spain 3,079; Tunisia 857; Turkey 1,620; Total (incl. others) 36,336 (Source: National Authority for Information and Authentication).

2007 (LD million): *Imports:* Egypt 578; France 256; Germany 503; Italy 690; Japan 600; Korea, Republic 437; Tunisia 158; United Kingdom 386; USA 536; Total (incl. others) 8,501. *Exports:* France 2,616; Germany 4,659; Greece 1,874; India 700; Italy 16,805; Netherlands 1,042; Portugal 1,079; Spain 2,379; Tunisia 817; Total (incl. others) 40,972 (Source: National Authority for Information and Authentication).

Transport

ROAD TRAFFIC
(motor vehicles in use at 31 December)

	2000	2001
Passenger cars	549,600	552,700
Commercial vehicles	177,400	195,500

Buses and coaches: 1,424 in 1995; 1,490 in 1996.

Motorcycles and mopeds: 1,078 in 1995; 1,112 in 1996.

2007: Passenger cars 1,388,165; Buses and coaches 91,327; Vans and lorries 310,511; Motorcycle and mopeds 36,531.

Sources: IRF, *World Road Statistics*; UN, *Statistical Yearbook*.

SHIPPING
Merchant Fleet
(registered at 31 December)

	2007	2008	2009
Number of vessels	141	152	161
Total displacement ('000 grt)	97.9	276.5	801.5

Source: IHS Fairplay, *World Fleet Statistics*.

International Sea-borne Freight Traffic
(estimates, '000 metric tons)

	1991	1992	1993
Goods loaded	57,243	59,894	62,491
Goods unloaded	7,630	7,710	7,808

Source: UN Economic Commission for Africa, *African Statistical Yearbook*.

CIVIL AVIATION
(traffic on scheduled services)

	2004	2005	2006
Kilometres flown (million)	9	18	17
Passengers carried ('000)	850	n.a.	1,152
Passenger-km (million)	985	1,572	1,507
Total ton-km (million)	82	142	137

Source: UN, *Statistical Yearbook*.

2007: Passengers carried ('000) 1,204.1 (Source: World Bank, World Development Indicators database).

2008: Passengers carried ('000) 1,213.9 (Source: World Bank, World Development Indicators database).

Tourism

VISITOR ARRIVALS*

Country of origin	2002	2003	2004
Algeria	70,416	71,657	73,459
Egypt	354,189	429,220	441,230
Morocco	19,076	19,120	20,803
Tunisia	329,145	346,331	366,871
Total (incl. others)	857,952	957,896	999,343

* Including same-day visitors (excursionists).

Tourism receipts (US $ million, incl. passenger transport): 244 in 2006; 99 in 2007–08.

Source: World Tourism Organization.

LIBYA
Directory

Communications Media

	2007	2008	2009
Telephones ('000 main lines in use)	969.0	920.4	1,063.3
Mobile cellular telephones ('000 subscribers)	4,500.0	7,379.1	9,534.1
Broadband subscribers ('000)	9.8	46.2	63.0
Internet users ('000)	291.3	323.0	353.9

Book production (titles): 26 in 1994.

Radio receivers ('000 in use): 1,350 in 1997.

Television receivers ('000 in use): 730 in 1997.

Daily newspapers: 4 in 2004 (estimated average circulation 71,100 in 1998).

Personal computers: 130,000 (21.9 per 1,000 persons) in 2005.

Sources: UNESCO, *Statistical Yearbook*; International Telecommunication Union.

Education

(1995/96, unless otherwise indicated)

	Institutions	Teachers	Students
Primary and preparatory: general	2,733*	122,020	1,333,679
Primary and preparatory: vocational	168	n.a.	22,490
Secondary: general	n.a.	17,668	170,573
Secondary: teacher training	n.a.	2,760†	23,919
Secondary: vocational	312	n.a.	109,074
Universities	13	n.a.	126,348

* 1993/94.
† 1992/93.

Source: partly UNESCO, *Statistical Yearbook*.

1998: 1,160,315 primary school students (Source: World Bank).

Students (UNESCO estimates, 2005/06 unless otherwise indicated): Pre-primary 22,246; Primary 755,338; Secondary 732,614; Tertiary 375,028 (2002/03) (Source: UNESCO Institute for Statistics).

Teachers (UNESCO estimates, 2005/06 unless otherwise indicated): Pre-primary 2,486; Primary 148,476; Secondary 152,338; Tertiary 15,711 (2002/03) (Source: UNESCO Institute for Statistics).

Adult literacy rate (UNESCO estimates): 88.4% (males 94.9%; females 81.3%) in 2008 (Source: UNESCO Institute for Statistics).

Directory

The Government

HEAD OF STATE

Revolutionary Leader: Col MUAMMAR AL-QADDAFI (took office as Chairman of the Revolution Command Council 8 September 1969).

GENERAL SECRETARIAT OF THE GENERAL PEOPLE'S CONGRESS
(May 2011)

Secretary: MUHAMMAD ABOULGHASEM AL-ZWAI.

Secretary for People's Congresses: IBRAHIM ABJAD.

Secretary for Popular Committees: Dr BASHIR ZIMBIL.

Secretary for the Apparatus of Inspection and People's Supervision: Dr HUDA FATHI BEN AMER.

Secretary for Foreign Affairs: SULEIMAN SASI AL-SHAHOUMI.

Secretary for Legal Affairs and Human Rights: HUSSEIN AL-WAHISHI AL-SADIQ.

Secretary for Women's Affairs: Dr SALMA ABD AL-JABAR.

GENERAL PEOPLE'S COMMITTEE
(May 2011)

Secretary: Dr AL-BAGHDADI ALI AL-MAHMOUDI.

Secretary for Foreign Liaison and International Co-operation: ABD AL-ATI AL-OBEIDI.

Secretary for Justice: MUHAMMAD AHMAD AL-QAMOUDI.

Secretary for Finance and Planning: Dr ABD AL-HAFID MAHMOUD ZLITNI.

Secretary for the Treasury: ALI AL-HESNAWI.

Secretary for Industry, the Economy and Trade: MUHAMMAD ALI AL-HOUEIJ.

Secretary for Health and Environment: MAHMOUD MUHAMMAD HIJAZI.

Secretary for Public Utilities: MAATUK MUHAMMAD MAATUK.

Secretary for National Planning: Dr BASHIR ALI ZENBIL.

Secretary for Agriculture, Animal Wealth and Marine Resources: ABD AL-HAMID AL-GAOUD.

Secretary for Public Security: MASOUD ABD AL-HAFIZ.

Secretary for Social Affairs: Dr IBRAHIM AL-ZARRUQ AL-SHARIF.

Secretary for Communication and Transport: MUHAMMAD ALI ZIDANE.

Secretary for Education and Research: ABD AL-KABIR AL-FAKHRI.

SECRETARIATS OF THE GENERAL PEOPLE'S COMMITTEE

Secretariat for Agriculture, Animal Wealth and Marine Resources: Tripoli; tel. (21) 3616727; e-mail m.ziyd@yahoo.com; internet gpca.gov.ly.

Secretariat for Communication and Transport: Tripoli; tel. (21) 3609011; e-mail contact@ctt.gov.ly; internet www.ctt.gov.ly.

Secretariat for Education and Research: Tripoli; tel. (21) 4630209; e-mail scholarship@edu.gov.ly; internet www.higheredu.gov.ly.

Secretariat for Finance and Planning: Tripoli; tel. (21) 3620136; e-mail amen@mof.gov.ly; internet www.mof.gov.ly.

Secretariat for Foreign Liaison and International Co-operation: Tripoli; tel. (21) 3400461; fax (21) 3402921; internet www.foreign.gov.ly.

Secretariat for Health and Environment: Sharia Omar Mukhtar, Tripoli; tel. (21) 3339369; fax (21) 3332951; e-mail info@health.gov.ly; internet www.health.gov.ly.

Secretariat for Industry, the Economy and Trade: POB 4779, Tripoli; tel. (21) 5826946; e-mail info@ect.gov.ly; internet www.ect.gov.ly.

Secretariat for Justice: Tripoli; tel. (21) 4808251; e-mail secretary@aladel.gov.ly; internet www.aladel.gov.ly.

Secretariat for Public Security: Tripoli; tel. (21) 3341315; internet www.almiezan.gov.ly.

Secretariat for Public Utilities: Tripoli; e-mail webmaster@utilities-gov-ly.com; internet www.utilities-gov-ly.com.

Secretariat for Social Affairs: Tripoli; tel. (21) 3614301; internet sa.gov.ly.

Legislature

General People's Congress

POB 2554, Tripoli; tel. (21) 3404848; fax (21) 3403705; internet www.gpcongress.gov.ly.

The Senate and House of Representatives were dissolved after the *coup d'état* of September 1969, and the provisional Constitution issued in December 1969 made no mention of elections or a return to parliamentary procedure. However, in January 1971 Col Qaddafi announced that a new legislature would be appointed, not elected; no date was mentioned. All political parties other than the Arab Socialist Union were banned. In November 1975 provision was made for the creation of the 1,112-member General National Congress of the Arab

LIBYA

Socialist Union, which met officially in January 1976. This later became the General People's Congress, which met for the first time in November 1976 and in March 1977 began introducing wide-ranging changes.

Secretary-General: MUHAMMAD ABOULGHASEM AL-ZWAI.

Political Organizations

In June 1971 the Arab Socialist Union (ASU) was established as the country's sole authorized political party. The General National Congress of the ASU held its first session in January 1976 and later became the General People's Congress (see Legislature).

The following groups are in opposition to the Government:

Ansarollah (Followers of God): f. 1996.

Islamic Martyrs' Movement (IMM): seeks to establish an Islamic republic; Leader ABU SHALTILAH; Spokesman ABDALLAH AHMAD.

Libyan Baathist Party.

Libyan Change and Reform Movement: breakaway group from NFSL.

Libyan Conservatives' Party: f. 1996.

Libyan Constitutional Grouping.

Libyan Democratic Authority: f. 1993.

Libyan Democratic Conference: f. 1992.

Libyan Democratic Movement: f. 1977; external group.

Libyan Islamic Fighting Group (LIFG): f. 1995; seeks to establish an Islamic regime; claimed responsibility for subversive activities in early 1996, and engaged in armed clashes with security forces in mid- to late 1990s; Leader ANAS SEBAI.

Libyan Movement for Change and Reform: POB 3423, London, NW6 7TZ, United Kingdom; f. 1994.

Libyan National Alliance: f. 1980 in Cairo, Egypt.

Libyan National Democratic Grouping: Leader MAHMOUD SULAYMAN AL-MAGHRABI.

Movement of Patriotic Libyans: f. 1997; aims to establish a 'free Libyan state' based on a market economy.

National Front for the Salvation of Libya (NFSL): e-mail nfsl@comcast.net; internet www.libyanfsl.com; f. 1981 in Khartoum, Sudan; aims to replace the existing regime by a democratically elected govt; Leader IBRAHIM ABD AL-AZIZ SAHAD.

Diplomatic Representation

EMBASSIES IN LIBYA

Afghanistan: POB 4245, Sharia Mozhar al-Aftes, Tripoli; tel. (21) 4841441; fax (21) 4841443; e-mail tripoli@afghanistan.mfa.net; Ambassador (vacant).

Algeria: Sharia Kairouan 12, Tripoli; tel. (21) 4440025; fax (21) 3334631; Ambassador ABDELHAMID BOUZAHER.

Argentina: POB 932, Gargaresh, Madina Syahia, Tripoli; tel. (21) 4781148; fax (21) 4782105; e-mail ELBIA@mrecic.gov.ar; Chargé d'affaires a.i. JAVIER MARIO MIGUEL GARCIA.

Austria: POB 3207, Sharia Khalid ibn al-Walid, Garden City, Tripoli; tel. (21) 4443379; fax (21) 4440838; e-mail tripolis-ob@bmeia.gv.at; Ambassador Dr DOROTHEA AUER.

Bangladesh: POB 5086, Hi Damasq, Tripoli; tel. (21) 4911198; fax (21) 4906616; e-mail bdtripoli@yahoo.com; Ambassador Rear Adm. MUSTAFIZUR RAHMAN.

Belarus: POB 1530, Tripoli; tel. (21) 3612555; fax (21) 3614298; e-mail libya@belembassy.org; internet libya.belembassy.org; Ambassador ANATOLIY STEPIEN.

Belgium: POB 91650, Jasmin St, Hay Andalus, Tripoli; tel. (21) 4782044; fax (21) 4782046; e-mail tripoli@diplobel.be; internet www.diplomatie.be/tripoli; Ambassador MICHAEL ARDUI.

Benin: POB 6676, Sharia Ghout al-Shaal, Tripoli; tel. (21) 4837663; fax (21) 834569; Ambassador LAFIA CHABI.

Bosnia and Herzegovina: POB 6946, Sharia Abd al-Melik bin Kutn, Tripoli; tel. (21) 4774327; fax (21) 4770652; Ambassador FERHAT SETA.

Brazil: POB 2270, Sharia Ben Ashour, Tripoli; tel. (21) 3614894; fax (21) 3614895; e-mail brcastripoli@ittnet.net; Ambassador GEORGE NEY FERNANDES.

Bulgaria: POB 2945, Sharia Selma Ben al-Ukua, Ben Ashour Area No. 58–56, Tripoli; tel. (21) 3605625; fax (21) 3609990; e-mail tripoli@embassy.transat.bg; internet www.mfa.bg/en/47/; Ambassador ALEXANDER OLSHEVSKI.

Burkina Faso: POB 81902, Route de Gargeresh, Tripoli; tel. (21) 4771221; fax (21) 4778037; e-mail ambafasolibye@yahoo.fr; Ambassador YOUSSOUF SANGARE.

Burundi: POB 2817, Sharia Ras Hassan, Tripoli; tel. (21) 608848; Ambassador RAPHAËL BITARIHO.

Canada: POB 93392, al-Fateh Tower Post Office, Tripoli; tel. (21) 3351633; fax (21) 3351630; e-mail trpli@international.gc.ca; internet www.dfait-maeci.gc.ca/libya; Ambassador SANDRA MCCARDELL.

Chad: POB 1078, Sharia Muhammad Mussadeq 25, Tripoli; tel. (21) 4443955; Ambassador DAOUSSA DEBY.

China, People's Republic: POB 5329, Sharia Menstir, Andalus, Gargaresh, Tripoli; tel. (21) 4832914; fax (21) 4831877; e-mail chinaemb_ly@mfa.gov.cn; Ambassador WANG WANGSHENG.

Croatia: Great al-Fatah Towers, Tower 2, 12th Floor, Rm 125, Tripoli; tel. (21) 3351097; fax (21) 3351486; e-mail tripoli@mvpei.hr; Ambassador JOVAN VEJNOVIĆ.

Cuba: POB 83738, Sharia Farj al-Eshbili, Tripoli; tel. (21) 4775216; fax (21) 4776294; e-mail embacuba.libia@lttnet.net; internet emba.cubaminrex.cu/libia; Ambassador VICTOR DANIEL RAMIREZ PEÑA.

Cyprus: POB 3284, Wassayat Ebderi, Fashloum, Tripoli; tel. (21) 3622610; fax (21) 3622613; e-mail cyprusembassy@lttnet.net; Ambassador PERICLES D. STIVAROS.

Czech Republic: POB 1097, Sharia Rewaifaa bin Thabet, Ben Ashour, Tripoli; tel. (21) 3615436; fax (21) 3615437; e-mail tripoli@embassy.mzv.cz; internet www.mzv.cz/tripoli; Ambassador JOSEF KOUTSKÝ.

Egypt: Sharia Omar el-Mokhtar, Tripoli; tel. and fax (21) 3339876; e-mail eg.emb_tripoli@mfa.gov.eg; internet www.mfa.gov.eg/missions/libya/tripoli/embassy/en-gb; Ambassador MUHAMMAD FATIHY REFA'A EL-TAHTAWI.

Equatorial Guinea: Tripoli.

Eritrea: POB 91279, Tripoli; tel. (21) 4773568; fax (21) 4780152; Ambassador ABDALLA MUSSA.

France: POB 312, Sharia Ben Khafaja, Hay Andalus, Tripoli; tel. (21) 4774891; fax (21) 4778266; e-mail tripoli-amba@diplomatie.gouv.fr; internet www.ambafrance-ly.org; Ambassador FRANÇOIS GOUYETTE.

Germany: POB 302, Sharia Hassan al-Mashai, Tripoli; tel. (21) 8552444; fax (21) 8968444; e-mail info@tripolis.diplo.de; internet www.tripolis.diplo.de; Ambassador MATTHIAS MEYER.

Ghana: POB 4169, Andalus 21A, nr Funduk Shati Gargaresh, Tripoli; tel. (21) 4772534; fax (21) 4773557; e-mail ghaemb@all-computers.com; Ambassador HODARI OKAE.

Greece: POB 5147, Sharia Jalal Bayar 18, Tripoli; tel. (21) 3338563; fax (21) 4441907; e-mail gremb.tri@mfa.gr; Ambassador ALEXIOS PAVLOS STEFANOU.

Guinea: POB 10657, Hay Andalus, Tripoli; tel. (21) 4772793; fax (21) 4773441; e-mail magatte@lttnet.net; Ambassador ABDUL AZIZ SOUMAH.

Holy See: Tripoli; Apostolic Nuncio Most Rev. CAPUTO TOMMASO (Titular Archbishop of Otricoli).

Hungary: POB 4010, Sharia Talha Ben Abdullah, Tripoli; tel. (21) 3618218; fax (21) 3618220; e-mail missions.tpi@kum.hu; Ambassador Dr BÉLA MARTON.

India: POB 3150, Fashloom Area, Nafleen, Tripoli; tel. (21) 3409288; fax (21) 3404843; e-mail amb.tripoli@mea.gov.in; Ambassador MORUGESAN MANIMEKALAI.

Indonesia: POB 5921, Tripoli; tel. (21) 4842067; fax (21) 4842069; e-mail tripoli.kbri@deplu.go.id; Ambassador MUHAMMAD SANUSI.

Iran: POB 6185, Tripoli; tel. (21) 3609552; fax (21) 3611674; e-mail iran_em_tripoli@hotmail.com; Chargé d'affaires ALI ASGHAR NASERI.

Italy: POB 912, Sharia Vahran 1, Tripoli; tel. (21) 3334131; fax (21) 3334132; e-mail ambasciata.tripoli@esteri.it; internet www.ambtripoli.esteri.it; Ambassador VINCENZO SCHIOPPA.

Japan: POB 3265, Sharia Jamal al-Din al-Waeli, Hay Andalus, Tripoli; tel. (21) 4781041; fax (21) 4781044; Ambassador AKIRA WATANABE.

Korea, Democratic People's Republic: Tripoli; Ambassador KIM TONG JE.

Korea, Republic: POB 4781, Sharia Gargaresh, Tripoli; tel. (21) 4831322; fax (21) 4831324; e-mail libya@mofat.go.kr; internet lby.mofat.go.kr; Ambassador CHANG DONG-HEE.

Kuwait: POB 2225, Beit al-Mal Beach, Tripoli; tel. (21) 4440281; fax (21) 607053; Ambassador MUBARAK ABDULLAH AL-ADWANI.

Lebanon: POB 927, Auss bin al-Arkam, Ben Ashour 10, Tripoli; tel. (21) 3615744; fax (21) 3611740; e-mail emblebanon_ly@hotmail.com; Chargé d'affaires a.i. NAZIH ACHOUR.

Lesotho: POB 5771, Hay Andalus, Tripoli; tel. (21) 4840900; fax (21) 4840901; e-mail lesotho-tripoli@foreign.gov.ls; Ambassador MALEFETSANE MOHAFA.

Madagascar: POB 652, al-Maidan Zajeir, Tripoli; tel. (21) 3408257; fax (21) 3408256; e-mail ambamtri@yahoo.fr; Ambassador Dieudonné Marie Michel Razafindrandriatsimaniry.

Malaysia: POB 6309, Hay Andalus, Sharia Gargaresh, Tripoli; tel. (21) 4830854; fax (21) 4831496; e-mail maltripoli@kln.gov.my; internet kln.gov.my/web/lby_tripoli; Ambassador Muhammad Zulkephli bin Muhammad Noor.

Mali: POB 2008, Sharia Jaraba Saniet Zarrouk, Tripoli; tel. (21) 4444924; Ambassador Ousmane Tandja.

Malta: POB 2534, Sharia Ubei Ben Ka'ab, Tripoli; tel. (21) 3611181; fax (21) 3611180; e-mail maltaembassy.tripoli@gov.mt; Ambassador Dr George J. Cassar.

Mauritania: Sharia Aïssa el-Wakwak, Tripoli; tel. (21) 4443223; Ambassador Yahia Muhammad el-Hadi.

Morocco: POB 908, Ave 7 Avril, Tripoli; tel. (21) 3617809; fax (21) 3614752; e-mail sifmatripo@hotmail.com; Ambassador Mehdi Alaoui.

Netherlands: POB 3801, Sharia Jalal Bayar 20, Tripoli; tel. (21) 4441549; fax (21) 4440386; e-mail tri@minbuza.nl; internet www.hollandembassy-libya.com; Ambassador Bart von Bartheld.

Niger: POB 2251, Fachloun Area, Tripoli; tel. (21) 4443104; Ambassador Amadou Tidjani Ali.

Nigeria: POB 4417, Sharia Bashir al-Ibrahim, Tripoli; tel. (21) 4443038; e-mail ambassador@nigeriantripoli.org; internet www.nigeriantripoli.org; Ambassador Isa Muhammad (recalled in March 2010).

Oman: Tripoli; tel. (21) 4772879; fax (21) 4773849; e-mail tripoli@mofa.gov.om; Ambassador Dr Qasim bin Muhammad bin Salem al-Salehi.

Pakistan: POB 2169, Sharia Huzayfa bin al-Yaman, Manshiya Ben Ashour, Tripoli; tel. (21) 3610937; fax (21) 3600412; e-mail pareptripoli@hotmail.com; Ambassador Jamil Ahmed Khan.

Philippines: POB 12508, Km 7, Sharia Gargaresh, Abu Nawas, Hay Andalus, Tripoli; tel. (21) 4833966; fax (21) 4836158; e-mail tripoli_pe76@lttnet.net; Ambassador Alejandrino A. Vicente.

Poland: POB 519, Sharia Ben Ashour 61, Tripoli; tel. (21) 3608569; fax (21) 3615199; e-mail poland@trypolis.polemb.net; internet www.trypolis.polemb.net; Ambassador Wojciech Stanisław Bożek.

Portugal: Zaid Bem Thabet, Sharia Ben Ashour, Tripoli; tel. (21) 3621352; fax (21) 3621351; Ambassador Rui Nogueira Lopes Aleixo.

Qatar: POB 6312, Libay, Tripoli; tel. (21) 4832431; fax (21) 4836660; e-mail tripoli@mofa.gov.qa; Ambassador Muhammad Abdullah al-Subaei.

Romania: POB 5085, Sharia Ali bin Talib, Ben Ashour, Tripoli; tel. (21) 3615295; fax (21) 3607597; e-mail ambaromatrip@hotmail.com; Ambassador Niculae Stan.

Russia: POB 4792, Sharia Mustapha Kamel, Tripoli; tel. (21) 3330545; fax (21) 4446673; e-mail embr@mail.ru; Ambassador (vacant).

Rwanda: POB 6677, Villa Ibrahim Musbah Missalati, Andalus, Tripoli; tel. (21) 72687; fax (21) 70317; Chargé d'affaires Christophe Habimana.

Saudi Arabia: Sharia Kairouan 2, Tripoli; tel. (21) 30485; Ambassador Muhammad ibn Abdullah al-Tasaji.

Senegal: POB 6392, el-Arabia Gotchalle 246/5, Gargaresh, Tripoli; tel. (21) 4836090; fax (21) 4838955; e-mail ambassene.tripoli@stcc.presidence.sn; Chargé d'affaires a.i. Diame Sarr.

Serbia: POB 1087, 14–16 Sharia Turkia, Tripoli; tel. (21) 3333392; fax (21) 3334114; e-mail serbianembassy_tripoli@yahoo.com; Ambassador Oliver Potezica.

Sierra Leone: Tripoli; Ambassador el Hadj Mohammed Samura.

Slovakia: POB 5721, Km 3, Gargaresh, Hay Andalus, Tripoli; tel. (21) 4781388; fax (21) 4781387; e-mail slovembtrp@slovembtrp.com; Ambassador Marián Záhora.

Spain: POB 2302, Sharia el-Amir Abd al-Kader al-Jazairi 36, Tripoli; tel. (21) 3620051; fax (21) 3620061; e-mail emb.tripoli@maec.es; internet www.maec.es/embajadas/tripoli; Ambassador Luis Francisco García Cerezo.

Sudan: POB 1076, Sharia Gargaresh, Tripoli; tel. (21) 4775387; fax (21) 4774781; e-mail sudtripoli@hotmail.com; Ambassador Osman M. O. Dirar.

Switzerland: POB 439, Sharia el-Moussawer Ben Maghzamah, off Sharia Ben Ashour, Tripoli; tel. (21) 3614118; fax (21) 3614238; e-mail tri.vertretung@eda.admin.ch; internet www.eda.admin.ch/tripoli; Ambassador (vacant).

Syria: POB 4219, Sharia Muhammad Rashid Reda 4, Tripoli (Relations Office); tel. (21) 3331783; fax (21) 3339030; Ambassador Hilal al-Atrash.

Togo: POB 3420, Sharia Khaled ibn al-Walid, Tripoli; tel. (21) 4449565; fax (21) 3332423.

Tunisia: POB 613, Sharia el-Bashir Ibrahimi, Medinat el-Hadaik, Tripoli; tel. (21) 3331051; fax (21) 4447600; High Representative Muhammad B'rahem.

Turkey: POB 947, Sharia Zaviya Dahmani, Tripoli; tel. (21) 3401140; fax (21) 3401146; e-mail turkemb.tripoli@mfa.gov.tr; internet tripoli.emb.mfa.gov.tr; Ambassador Salim Levent Şahinkaya.

Uganda: POB 80215, Sharia Jaraba, Tripoli; tel. (21) 3603083; fax (21) 3634471; e-mail info@ugembassylibya.org; internet www.ugembassylibya.org; Ambassador Moses Kiwa Sebunya.

Ukraine: POB 4544, Sharia Dhil, Ben Ashour, Tripoli; tel. (21) 3608665; fax (21) 3608666; e-mail emb_ly@mfa.gov.ua; internet www.mfa.gov.ua/libya; Ambassador Hennadiy Latiy.

United Kingdom: POB 4206, Tripoli; tel. (21) 3403644; fax (21) 3403648; e-mail tripoli.press@fco.gov.uk; internet ukinlibya.fco.gov.uk; Ambassador Richard Northern.

USA: Ben Ashour Area, Sharia Jraba, Tripoli; tel. (91) 2203239; e-mail TripoliPAO@state.gov; internet libya.usembassy.gov; Ambassador Gene A. Cretz.

Venezuela: POB 2584, Sharia Ben Ashour, Jamaa al-Sagaa Bridge, Tripoli; tel. (21) 3600408; fax (21) 3600407; e-mail embavenezlibia@hotmail.com; Ambassador Afif Tajeldine.

Viet Nam: POB 587, Sharia Gargaresh, Tripoli; tel. (21) 4901456; fax (21) 4901499; e-mail dsqvnlib@yahoo.com; internet www.vietnamembassy-libya.org; Ambassador Dao Duy Tien.

Yemen: POB 4839, Sharia Ubei Ben Ka'ab 36, Tripoli; tel. (21) 607472; Ambassador Ahmad Abdullah al-Majidi.

Judicial System

The judicial system is composed, in order of seniority, of the Supreme Court, Courts of Appeal, and Courts of First Instance and Summary Courts.

All courts convene in open session, unless public morals or public order require a closed session; all judgments, however, are delivered in open session. Cases are heard in Arabic, with interpreters provided for aliens.

The courts apply the Libyan codes, which include all the traditional branches of law, such as civil, commercial and penal codes, etc. Committees were formed in 1971 to examine Libyan law and ensure that it coincides with the rules of Islamic *Shari'a*. The proclamation of People's Authority in the Jamahiriya provides that the Holy Koran is the law of society.

Attorney-General: Muhammad Aqri al-Mahgoubi.

SUPREME COURT

The judgments of the Supreme Court are final. It is composed of the President and several Justices. Its judgments are issued by circuits of at least three Justices (the quorum is three). The Court hears appeals from the Courts of Appeal in civil, penal, administrative and civil status matters.

President: Abd al-Salam Bashir al-Toumi.

COURTS OF APPEAL

These courts settle appeals from Courts of First Instance; the quorum is three Justices. Each court of appeal has a court of assize.

COURTS OF FIRST INSTANCE AND SUMMARY COURTS

These courts are first-stage courts in the Jamahiriya, and the cases heard in them are heard by one judge. Appeals against summary judgments are heard by the appellate court attached to the court of first instance, the quorum of which is three judges.

Religion

ISLAM

The vast majority of Libyan Arabs follow Sunni Muslim rites, although Col Qaddafi has rejected the Sunnah (i.e. the practice, course, way, manner or conduct of the Prophet Muhammad, as followed by Sunnis) as a basis for legislation.

Chief Mufti of Libya: Sheikh Tahir Ahmad al-Zawi.

CHRISTIANITY

The Roman Catholic Church

Libya comprises three Apostolic Vicariates and one Apostolic Prefecture. At 31 December 2007 there were an estimated 106,000 adherents in the country.

LIBYA

Apostolic Vicariate of Benghazi: POB 248, Benghazi; tel. and fax (91) 9081599; e-mail apostvicar@yahoo.com; Vicar Apostolic Mgr SYLVESTER CARMEL MAGRO (Titular Bishop of Saldae).

Apostolic Vicariate of Derna: c/o POB 248, Benghazi; Vicar Apostolic (vacant).

Apostolic Vicariate of Tripoli: POB 365, Dahra, Tripoli; tel. (21) 3331863; fax (21) 3334696; e-mail bishoptripolibya@hotmail.com; internet www.catholicinlibya.com; Vicar Apostolic Mgr GIOVANNI INNOCENZO MARTINELLI (Titular Bishop of Tabuda).

The Anglican Communion

Within the Episcopal Church in Jerusalem and the Middle East, Libya forms part of the diocese of Egypt (q.v.).

Other Christian Churches

The Coptic Orthodox Church is represented in Libya.

The Press

Most newspapers and periodicals are published either by the Jamahiriya News Agency (JANA), by government secretariats, by the Press Service or by trade unions.

DAILIES

Al-Fajr al-Jadid (The New Dawn): POB 91291, Press Bldg, Sharia al-Jamahiriya, Tripoli; tel. (21) 3606393; fax (21) 3605728; e-mail info@alfajraljadeed.com; internet www.alfajraljadeed.com; f. 1969; publ. by JANA; also publishes bi-monthly English version; Editor AOUN ABDULLAH MADI.

Al-Jamahiriya: POB 4814, Tripoli; tel. (21) 3605731; e-mail info@aljamahiria.com; internet www.aljamahiria.com; f. 1980; Arabic; political; publ. by the revolutionary cttees.

Al-Shams: POB 82331, Al-Sahafa Bldg, Sharia al-Jamhouria, Tripoli; tel. (21) 4442524; fax (21) 609315; e-mail info@alshames.com; internet www.alshames.com; Editor MUHAMMAD M. IBRAHIM.

Az-Zahf al-Akhdar (The Green March): POB 14273, Al-Sahafa Bldg, Sharia al-Jamhouria, Tripoli; tel. (21) 4776890; fax (21) 4772502; e-mail info@azzahfalakhder.com; internet www.azzahfalakhder.com; f. 1980; ideological journal of the revolutionary cttees; Editor-in-Chief HAMID ABU SALIM.

PERIODICALS

Al-Amal (Hope): POB 4845, Tripoli; e-mail info@alamalmag.com; internet www.alamalmag.com; monthly; social, for children; publ. by the Press Service.

Al-Daawa al-Islamia (Islamic Call): POB 2682, Sharia Sawani, Km 5, Tripoli; tel. (21) 4800294; fax (21) 4800293; f. 1980; weekly (Wed.); Arabic, English, French; cultural; publ. by the World Islamic Call Society; Eds MUHAMMAD IMHEMED AL-BALOUSHI, ABDULAHI MUHAMMAD ABD AL-JALEEL.

Economic Bulletin: POB 2303, Tripoli; tel. (21) 3337106; monthly; publ. by JANA.

Al-Jarida al-Rasmiya (The Official Newspaper): Tripoli; irregular; official state gazette.

Libyan Arab Republic Gazette: Secretariat of Justice, NA, Tripoli; weekly; English; publ. by the Secretariat of Justice.

Risalat al-Jihad (Holy War Letter): POB 2682, Tripoli; tel. (21) 3331021; f. 1983; monthly; Arabic, English, French; publ. by the World Islamic Call Society.

Scientific Bulletin: POB 2303, Tripoli; tel. (21) 3337106; monthly; publ. by JANA.

Al-Thaqafa al-Arabiya (Arab Culture): POB 4587, Tripoli; f. 1973; weekly; cultural; circ. 25,000.

The Tripoli Post: POB 1159, Al-Fateh Tower, 1st Floor, Office No. 74, Tripoli; tel. (21) 3337422; fax (21) 3351740; e-mail editor@tripolipost.com; internet www.tripolipost.com; f. 1999; weekly; English; privately owned; Editor-in-Chief Dr SAID LASWAD.

Al-Usbu al-Thaqafi (The Cultural Week): POB 4845, Tripoli; weekly.

Al-Watan al-Arabi al-Kabir (The Greater Arab Homeland): Tripoli; f. 1987.

NEWS AGENCY

Jamahiriya News Agency (JANA): POB 2303, Sharia al-Fatah, Tripoli; tel. (21) 3402606; fax (21) 3402421; e-mail info@jananews.ly; internet www.jananews.ly; f. 1964; brs and correspondents throughout Libya and abroad; provides Arabic, English and French news services.

Publishers

Al-Dar al-Arabia Lilkitab (Maison Arabe du Livre): POB 3185, Tripoli; tel. (21) 4447287; f. 1973 by Libya and Tunisia.

Al-Dar al-Hikma Publishing House: Tripoli; tel. (21) 3606571; fax (21) 3606610; e-mail info@elgabooks.com.

Al-Fatah University, General Administration of Libraries, Printing and Publications: POB 13543, Tripoli; tel. (21) 4628034; fax (21) 4625045; e-mail m.alfituri@hotmail.com; f. 1955; academic books.

General Co for Publishing, Advertising and Distribution: POB 921, Sirte (Surt); tel. (54) 63170; fax (54) 62100; general, educational and academic books in Arabic and other languages; makes and distributes advertisements throughout Libya.

Ghouma Publishing: POB 80092, Tripoli; tel. (21) 3630864; e-mail ghoumapub@hotmail.com; f. 1993; book publishing, distribution and art production; Gen. Man. MUSTAFA FETOURI.

Broadcasting and Communications

TELECOMMUNICATIONS

General Telecommunications Authority (GTA): POB 866, Sharia Zawia, Tripoli; e-mail info@gta.ly; internet www.gta.ly; f. 2006; supervisory body reporting directly to the Gen. People's Cttee.

General Directorate of Posts and Telecommunications: POB 81686, Tripoli; tel. (21) 3604101; fax (21) 3604102; Dir-Gen. ABU ZAID JUMA AL-MANSURI.

General Post and Telecommunications Co (GPTC): POB 886, Sharia Zawia, Tripoli; tel. (21) 3617945; fax (21) 3619011; internet www.gptc.ly; f. 1984; operates and develops the postal and telecommunications networks; subsidiaries include Libyana Mobile Phone Co and Al-Madar Al-Jadeed (mobile cellular telecommunications operators), and Libya Telecom and Technology (internet service provider); Chair. MUHAMMAD MUAMMAR AL-QADDAFI.

Libyana Mobile Phone Co: POB 90071, Tripoli; tel. (21) 3406555; internet www.libyana.ly; f. 2004.

Al-Madar Al-Jadeed: Tripoli; internet www.almadar.ly; f. 1997; mobile telecommunications network operator; 1.2m. subscribers; Chief Exec. ABD AL-KHALEK BIN ASHOUR.

BROADCASTING

Radio

Great Socialist People's Libyan Arab Jamahiriya Broadcasting Corporation: POB 80237, Tripoli; tel. (21) 3402107; fax (21) 3403468; e-mail info@en.ljbc.net; internet www.ljbc.net; f. 1968; broadcasts in Arabic; additional satellite channel broadcast for 18 hours a day from 1982; Sec.-Gen. ABDULLAH MANSOUR.

Voice of Africa: POB 4677, Sharia al-Fateh, Tripoli; tel. (21) 4449209; fax (21) 4449875; f. 1973 as Voice of the Greater Arab Homeland; adopted current name in 1998; broadcasts in Arabic, French, English, Swahili and Hausa; Dir-Gen. ABDULLAH AL-MEGRI.

Television

People's Revolution Broadcasting TV: POB 80237, Tripoli; tel. (21) 3402107; fax (21) 3403468; e-mail info@en.ljbc.net; internet www.ljbc.net; f. 1957; broadcasts in Arabic; additional satellite channels broadcast for limited hours in English; Dir ABDULLAH MANSOUR.

Finance

(cap. = capital; res = reserves; dep. = deposits; m. = million; br(s) = branch(es); amounts in Libyan dinars, unless otherwise stated)

BANKING

The Libyan banking sector, hitherto highly state-controlled, was undergoing restructure in the late 2000s. Minority stakes in two state-owned commercial banks were sold to foreign banking interests in 2007–08. It was announced in early 2010 that the Central Bank of Libya (CBL) was to grant two licences to foreign banks for the creation of joint-venture banking operations with Libyan investors. However, in August the CBL announced that it had decided to grant just one licence, to UniCredit (Italy); bids from two other European banks and three from the Gulf region were rejected.

LIBYA   Directory

Central Bank

Central Bank of Libya (CBL): POB 1103, Sharia al-Malik Seoud, Tripoli; tel. (21) 3333591; fax (21) 4441488; e-mail info@cbl.gov.ly; internet www.cbl.gov.ly; f. 1955 as Nat. Bank of Libya; name changed to Bank of Libya 1963, to Cen. Bank of Libya 1977; state-owned; bank of issue and central bank carrying govt accounts and operating exchange control; commercial operations transferred to Nat. Commercial Bank 1970; cap. 500m., res 909m., dep. 108,079m. (Dec. 2009); Gov. and Chair. FARHAT OMAR BENGDARA.

Other Banks

Alwafa Bank: POB 84212, Sharia Alfallah, Tripoli; tel. (21) 4815123; fax (21) 4801247; e-mail info@alwafabank.com; internet www.alwafabank.com; f. 2003; private bank; Chair. and Gen. Man. HADI M. GITELI.

Gumhouria Bank: POB 685, Sharia Omar el-Mokhtar, Tripoli; tel. and fax (21) 4442541; e-mail gm@gumhouriabank.com.ly; internet www.gumhouria-bank.com.ly; f. 1969 as successor to Barclays Bank Int. in Libya; known as Masraf al-Jumhuriya until March 1977, and as Jamahiriya Bank until Dec. 2000; merger with Umma Bank SAL completed mid-2008; wholly owned subsidiary of the Cen. Bank; cap. 1,000m., res 39m., dep. 19,817m. (Dec. 2009); Chair. ABU BAKR EL-WADAN; Gen. Man. ABD AL-FATAH S. GHAFFAR; 122 brs.

Libyan Foreign Bank: POB 2542, Tower 2, Dat al-Imad Complex, Tripoli; tel. (21) 3350155; fax (21) 3350164; e-mail it@lafbank.com; internet www.lafbank.com; f. 1972 as Libyan Arab Foreign Bank; present name adopted 2005; 'offshore' bank wholly owned by Cen. Bank of Libya; cap. US $3,000.0m. (Feb. 2010), res $573m., dep. $10,166m. (Dec. 2009); Chair. Dr MUHAMMAD A. BEIT—ELMAAL; Gen. Man. MUHAMMAD M. BEN YOUSUF.

National Commercial Bank SAL: POB 543, Aruba Ave, al-Baida; tel. (21) 3610306; fax (21) 3612267; e-mail ncbly@lttnet.net; internet www.ncb.ly; f. 1970 to take over commercial banking division of Cen. Bank (then Bank of Libya) and brs of Aruba Bank and Istiklal Bank; wholly owned by Cen. Bank; cap. 100m., res 4,685m., dep. 6,317m. (Dec. 2008); Chair. BADER A. ABU AZIZA; Gen. Man. AHMAD F. BELKHEIR; 51 brs.

Sahara Bank SPI: POB 70, Sharia 1 September, Tripoli; tel. (21) 3340663; fax (21) 4443836; e-mail sahbankgm1@lttnet.net; internet saharabank.com.ly; f. 1964 to take over br. of Banco di Sicilia; the Govt sold a 19% stake to BNP Paribas (France) in July 2007; cap. and res 208.2m., total assets 1,951.8m. (March 2003); Chair. and Gen. Man. Dr ABD AL-LATIF ABD AL-HAFIZ EL-KIB; CEO CLAUDE RUFIN; 48 brs.

Wahda Bank: POB 452, Sharia Gamal Abd al-Nasser, Benghazi; tel. (61) 2261218; fax (21) 2224122; e-mail wahda@wahdabank.com; internet www.wahdabank.com; f. 1970 to take over Bank of North Africa, Commercial Bank SAL, Nahda Arabia Bank, Société Africaine de Banque SAL, and Kafila al-Ahly Bank; 19% stake acquired by Arab Bank PLC (Jordan) in April 2008; remainder owned by Cen. Bank of Libya; cap. 108.0m., res 107.5m., dep. 4,273.3m. (Dec. 2008); Chair. Dr ANTOINE SREIH; Gen. Man. SELIM K. IHMOUDA; 76 brs.

STOCK EXCHANGE

Libyan Stock Market: Sharia Omar el-Mokhtar, Tripoli; tel. (21) 3365026; fax (61) 9091097; e-mail info@lsm.gov.ly; internet www.lsm.ly; f. 2007; Sec. SULIMAN SALEM AL-SHOHOMIY.

INSURANCE

Libya Insurance Co: POB 80087, Aman Bldg, Sharia al-Taha, Tripoli; tel. (21) 4441499; fax (21) 4444176; e-mail infolt@libtamin.com; internet www.libtamin.com; f. 1964; merged with Al-Mukhtar Insurance Co in 1981; all classes of insurance; Man. ALI AMAR AL-RAGAYEE.

Trade and Industry

There are state trade and industrial organizations responsible for the running of industries at all levels, which supervise production, distribution and sales. There are also central bodies responsible for the power generation industry, agriculture, land reclamation and transport.

GOVERNMENT AGENCIES

Council for Oil and Gas Affairs: Tripoli; f. 2006; reports to the General People's Committee; holds ultimate responsibility for all matters involving oil, gas and their by-products; Chair. Dr AL-BAGHDADI ALI AL-MAHMOUDI.

Great Man-made River Water Utilization Authority (GMRA): POB 7217, Benghazi; tel. (61) 2230392; fax (61) 2230393; e-mail info@gmrwua.com; internet www.gmrwua.com; supervises construction of pipeline carrying water to the Libyan coast from beneath the Sahara desert, to provide irrigation for agricultural projects; Sec. for the Great Man-made River Project ABD AL-MAJID AL-AOUD.

Libyan Investment Authority (LIA): Tripoli; e-mail info@lia.ly; internet www.lia.ly; f. 2006, operations commenced 2007; sovereign wealth fund managing state-allocated assets, including Oil Reserve Fund; Chair. Dr ABD AL-HAFID MAHMOUD ZLITNI.

National Economic Development Board (NEDB): Tripoli; internet www.nedb.ly; f. 2007; charged with the drafting and execution of reform campaigns, and the facilitation of decision-making and action on critical economic issues; Chair. MAHMOUD GEBRIL.

DEVELOPMENT ORGANIZATIONS

Arab Organization for Agricultural Development: POB 12898, Zohra, Tripoli; tel. and fax (21) 3619275; e-mail arabagri@lycos.com; internet www.aoad.org; responsible for agricultural devt projects.

General National Organization for Industrialization: Sharia San'a, Tripoli; tel. (21) 3334995; f. 1970; public org. responsible for the devt of industry.

Kufra and Sarir Authority: Council of Agricultural Development, Benghazi; f. 1972 to develop the Kufra oasis and Sarir area in south-eastern Libya.

CHAMBERS OF COMMERCE

Benghazi Chamber of Commerce, Trade, Industry and Agriculture: POB 208 and 1286, Benghazi; tel. (61) 3372319; fax (61) 3380761; f. 1956; Pres. Dr BADIA; Gen. Man. Dr TAREK TARBAGHIA; 150,000 mems.

Tripoli Chamber of Commerce and Industry: POB 2321, Sharia Najed 6–8, Tripoli; tel. (21) 3336855; fax (21) 3332655; f. 1952; Chair. MUHAMMAD KANOON; Dir-Gen. ABD AL-MONEM H. BURAWI; 30,000 mems.

UTILITIES

Electricity

General Electricity Company of Libya (GECOL): POB 668, Tripoli; tel. (21) 4445068; fax (21) 4447023; e-mail gecol@gecol.net; internet www.gecol.ly; Sec. of Management Cttee Eng. ABU AL-GHASSIM ONEAS.

STATE HYDROCARBONS COMPANIES

Until 1986 petroleum affairs in Libya were dealt with primarily by the Secretariat of the General People's Committee for Petroleum. This body was abolished in March 1986, and sole responsibility for the administration of the petroleum industry passed to the national companies that were already in existence. The Secretariat of the General People's Committee for Petroleum was re-established in March 1989 and incorporated into the new Secretariat for the General People's Committee for Energy in October 1992. This was dissolved in March 2000, and responsibility for local oil policy was transferred to the National Oil Corporation, under the supervision of the General People's Committee. Since 1973 the Libyan Government has entered into participation agreements with some of the foreign oil companies (concession holders), and nationalized others. It has concluded 85%:15% production-sharing agreements with various oil companies.

National Oil Corporation (NOC): POB 2655, Sharia Bashier Sadawi, Tripoli; tel. (21) 3337141; fax (21) 3331390; e-mail info@noclibya.com; internet en.noclibya.com.ly; f. 1970 to: undertake jt ventures with foreign cos; build and operate refineries, storage tanks, petrochemical facilities, pipelines and tankers; take part in arranging specifications for local and imported petroleum products; participate in general planning of oil installations in Libya; market crude and refined petroleum and petrochemical products; and establish and operate oil terminals; from 2000 responsible for deciding local oil policy, under supervision of Gen. People's Cttee; Chair. and Dir-Gen. (vacant).

Arabian Gulf Oil Co (AGOCO): POB 263, Benghazi; tel. (61) 28931; fax (21) 49031; wholly owned subsidiary of the NOC; Chair. TAWSIG MESMARI.

Oilinvest International NV: Tripoli; f. 1988; wholly owned subsidiary of the NOC; Libya's foreign oil investment arm; Chair. and Gen. Man. AHMAD ABD AL-KARIM AHMAD.

Agip North Africa and Middle East Ltd—Libyan Branch: POB 346, Tripoli; tel. and fax (21) 3335135; Sec. of People's Cttee OMAR AL-SWEIFI.

LIBYA

Azzawiya Oil Refining Co (ARC): POB 6451, Tripoli; tel. (23) 610539; fax (23) 610543; e-mail infoazzawiya@azzawiyaoil.com; internet www.azzawiyaoil.com; f. 1976; Gen. Man. AL-MOAMARE A. SWEDAN.

Brega Oil Marketing Co: POB 402, Sharia Bashir al-Saidawi, Tripoli; tel. (21) 4440830; f. 1971; Chair. Dr DOKALI B. AL-MEGHARIEF.

International Oil Investments Co: Tripoli; f. 1988, with initial capital of US $500m. to acquire 'downstream' facilities abroad; Chair. MUHAMMAD AL-JAWAD.

National Drilling and Workover Co: POB 1454, 208 Sharia Omar Mukhtar, Tripoli; tel. (21) 3332411; f. 1986; Chair. IBRAHIM BAHI.

Ras Lanouf Oil and Gas Processing Co (RASCO): POB 1971, Ras Lanuf, Benghazi; tel. (21) 3605177; fax (21) 607924; f. 1978; Chair. ABULKASIM M. A. ZWARY.

Sirte Oil Co: POB 385, Marsa el-Brega, Tripoli; tel. (21) 607261; fax (21) 601487; internet www.soc.com.ly; f. 1955 as Esso Standard Libya, taken over by Sirte Oil Co 1982; absorbed Nat. Petrochemicals Co in Oct. 1990; exploration, production of crude petroleum, gas and petrochemicals, liquefaction of natural gas; Chair. ABD AL-BASET TAHER AL-REFAE.

Umm al-Jawaby Petroleum Co: POB 693, Tripoli; Chair. and Gen. Man. MUHAMMAD TENTTOUSH.

Waha Oil Co: POB 395, Tripoli; tel. (21) 3331116; fax (21) 3337169; e-mail infowaha@wahaoil.com; internet www.wahaoil.net; Chair. Dr BASHEER MUHAMMAD ELASHAHAB.

Zueitina Oil Co (ZOC): POB 2134, Tripoli; tel. (21) 3338011; fax (21) 3339109; e-mail info@zueitina-ly.com; f. 1986; Chair. of Management Cttee BASHIR BAZAZI.

TRADE UNIONS

General Federation of Producers' Trade Unions: POB 734, Sharia Istanbul 2, Tripoli; tel. (21) 4446011; f. 1952; affiliated to ITUC; Sec.-Gen. BASHIR IHWIJ; 17 trade unions with 700,000 mems.

General Union for Oil and Petrochemicals: Tripoli; Chair. MUHAMMAD MITHNANI.

Pan-African Federation of Petroleum Energy and Allied Workers: Tripoli; affiliated to the Organisation of African Trade Union Unity.

Transport

Department of Road Transport and Railways: POB 14527, Sharia al-Zawiyah, Tripoli; tel. and fax (21) 3605808; Dir-Gen. (Projects and Research) MUHAMMAD ABU ZIAN.

RAILWAYS

There are, at present, no railways in Libya. In 1998, however, the Government invited bids for the construction of a 3,170-km railway, comprising one branch, 2,178 km in length, running from north to south, and another, 992 km in length, running from east to west along the north coast. The railway may eventually be linked to other North African rail networks. Russian Railways OAO was awarded the contract to build a 554-km section of the network between Sirte and Benghazi in April 2008; construction work commenced in August. In 2008–09 a Chinese company was awarded contracts for a further three sections.

Railway Executive Board: Tripoli; tel. (21) 3609486; fax (21) 626054; e-mail info@libyanrailways.com; oversees the planning and construction of railways; Sec. SAEED RASHID.

ROADS

The most important road is the 1,822-km national coast road from the Tunisian to the Egyptian border, passing through Tripoli and Benghazi. It has a second link between Barce and Lamluda, 141 km long. Another national road runs from a point on the coastal road 120 km south of Misurata through Sabha to Ghat near the Algerian border (total length 1,250 km). There is a branch 247 km long running from Vaddan to Sirte. A 690-km road, connecting Tripoli and Sabha, and another 626 km long, from Ajdabiya in the north to Kufra in the south-east, were opened in 1983. The Tripoli–Ghat section (941 km) of the third, 1,352-km national road was opened in September 1984. There is a road crossing the desert from Sabha to the frontiers of Chad and Niger. As part of a wide-ranging agreement signed by Libya and Italy in August 2008, the latter agreed to fund construction of a new coastal motorway between the Tunisian and Egyptian borders. Construction work on the project commenced in mid-2009.

In addition to the national highways, the west of Libya has about 1,200 km of paved and macadamized roads and the east about 500 km. All the towns and villages of Libya, including the desert oases, are accessible by motor vehicle. In 2001 Libya had an estimated total road network of 83,200 km, of which 57,200 km was paved.

SHIPPING

The principal ports are Tripoli, Benghazi, Mersa Brega, Misurata and al-Sider. Zueitina, Ras Lanuf, Mersa Hariga, Mersa Brega and al-Sider are mainly oil ports. A pipeline connects the Zelten oilfields with Mersa Brega. Another pipeline joins the Sarir oilfield with Mersa Hariga, the port of Tobruk, and a pipeline from the Sarir field to Zueitina was opened in 1968. A port is being developed at Darnah, and plans were under way for the expansion of the port of Sirte. Libya also has the use of Tunisian port facilities at Sand Gabès, to alleviate congestion at Tripoli. At 31 December 2009 Libya's merchant fleet consisted of 161 vessels, with a combined displacement of 801,500 grt.

Principal Shipping Companies

General National Maritime Transport Co (GNMTC): POB 80173, el-Shaab Terminal, Tripoli; tel. and fax (21) 4808094; e-mail info@gnmtc.com; internet www.gnmtc.com; f. 1975 to handle all projects dealing with maritime trade; state-owned; Chair. Capt. ALI BELHAG AHMED.

Libya Shipping Agency: POB 4288, Tripoli; tel. (21) 3402528; fax (21) 3401928; e-mail info@libyashipping.com; internet www.libyashipping.com; provides chartering, land transportation and customs clearance services; Gen. Man. IMAD FELLAH.

CIVIL AVIATION

There are four international airports: Tripoli International Airport, situated at Ben Gashir, 34 km (21 miles) from Tripoli; Benina Airport 19 km (12 miles) from Benghazi; Sabha Airport; and Misurata Airport. There are a further 10 regional airports. A US $800m. programme to improve the airport infrastructure and air traffic control network was approved in mid-2001. In the mid-2000s plans were announced for the upgrade and expansion of Tripoli International Airport, which were to include the construction of two new terminals, following which the airport's annual passenger capacity was expected to increase to some 20m., compared with 3m. in 2007. Work on the project commenced in September 2007 and was scheduled for completion in 2011; however, by May 2011 progress was uncertain, following the outbreak of conflict earlier that year. Moreover, all commercial flights to Libya had been suspended owing to the imposition by international forces of an air exclusion zone over the country.

Civil Aviation Authority: Tripoli; tel. (21) 3605318; fax (21) 3605322; e-mail shlebik@lycaa.org; internet www.lycaa.org; Sec.-Gen. MUHAMMAD SHLEBIK.

Afriqiyah Airways: 1st Floor, Waha Bldg, Sharia Omar al-Mokhtar, Tripoli; tel. (21) 4449734; fax (21) 4449128; e-mail customerservice@afriqiyah.aero; internet www.afriqiyah.aero; f. 2001; state-owned; flights to 29 destinations in Africa, Asia, Europe and the Middle East; Chair. Capt. SABRI SAAD ABDALLAH SHADI; CEO RAMMAH ETTIR.

Buraq Air: Tripoli International Airport, Tripoli; e-mail lias@buraqair.com; internet www.buraqair.com; f. 2001; first privately owned Libyan airline; scheduled international passenger and cargo flights to Egypt, Morocco, Syria and Turkey; domestic flights from Tripoli, Benghazi and Sabha; Chair. and Man. Dir Capt. MUHAMMAD A. BUBEIDA.

Libyan Airlines: POB 2555, Ben Fernas Bldg, Sharia Haiti, Tripoli; tel. (21) 3614102; fax (21) 3614815; e-mail i.alwani@ln.aero; internet www.libyanairlines.aero; f. 1964 as Kingdom of Libya Airlines; reorg. in 1975 as Libyan Arab Airline; present name adopted 2006; passenger and cargo services from Tripoli, Benghazi and Sabha to destinations in Europe, North Africa, the Middle East and Asia; domestic services throughout Libya; Chair. and CEO Capt. MUHAMMAD M. IBSEM.

Tourism

The principal attractions for visitors to Libya are Tripoli, with its beaches and annual International Fair, the ancient Roman towns of Sabratha, Leptis Magna and Cyrene, and historic oases. There were 999,343 visitor arrivals in 2004; in 2007–08 receipts from tourism totalled US $99m.

General Board of Fairs: POB 891, Sharia Omar Mukhtar, Tripoli; tel. (21) 3332255; fax (21) 4448385; e-mail info@gbf.com.ly; internet gbf.com.ly; Head of Fairs GAMAL N. A. AL-AMOUSHI.

General Board of Tourism and Traditional Industries: POB 82063, Tripoli; tel. (21) 3334673; fax (21) 4445336; e-mail info@libyan-tourism.net; internet www.libyan-tourism.org; Chair. MUHAMMAD SEALNA.

Defence

Commander-in-Chief of Armed Forces: Brig. ABU-BAKR YOUNIS JABER.
Chief of Staff of Armed Forces: Brig. MUSTAPHA KHARROUBI.
Commander of the Navy: Rear Adm. HAMDI AL-SHABANI AL-SAWEHLI.
Estimated Defence Expenditure (2009): LD 2,140m.
Military Service: selective conscription; 1–2 years.
Total Armed Forces (as assessed at November 2010): 76,000: army 50,000, incl. (estimated) 25,000 conscripts; navy 8,000; air force 18,000.
People's Militia: (estimated) 40,000.

Education

Education is officially compulsory for nine years between six and 15 years of age. Primary education begins at the age of six and lasts for nine years. Secondary education, beginning at 15 years of age, lasts for a further three years. In 2005/06 some 755,338 students were enrolled in primary education. At the secondary level there were 732,614 students in the same year. The teaching of French was abolished in Libyan schools in 1983. Libya also has institutes for agricultural, technical and vocational training, of which there were 84 in 2004.

In 1958 the University of Libya opened in Benghazi with Faculties of Arts and Commerce, followed the next year by the Faculty of Science, near Tripoli. Faculties of Law, Agriculture, Engineering, Teacher Training, and Arabic Language and Islamic Studies have since been added to the University. In 1973 the University was divided into two parts, to form the Universities of Tripoli and Benghazi, later renamed Al-Fatah and Ghar Younis universities. The Faculty of Education at Al-Fatah University became Sabha University in 1983. There is a University of Technology (Bright Star) at Mersa Brega and the Al-Arab Medical University at Benghazi. In 1995 the number of public universities had reached 13. In 2002/03 some 375,028 students were enrolled in tertiary education.

LIECHTENSTEIN

Introductory Survey

LOCATION, CLIMATE, LANGUAGE, RELIGION, FLAG, CAPITAL

The Principality of Liechtenstein is in central Europe. The country lies on the east bank of the Upper Rhine river, bordered by Switzerland to the west and south, and by Austria to the north and east. Liechtenstein has an Alpine climate, with mild winters. The average annual temperature is about 10.5°C, while average annual rainfall is 996 mm. The official language is German, of which a dialect—Alemannish—is spoken. Almost all of the inhabitants profess Christianity, and about 79% are adherents of the Roman Catholic Church. The national flag (proportions 3 by 5) consists of two equal horizontal stripes, of royal blue and red, with a golden princely crown, outlined in black, in the upper hoist. The capital is Vaduz.

CONTEMPORARY POLITICAL HISTORY

Historical context

Liechtenstein has been an independent state since 1719, except while under French domination briefly in the early 19th century. It joined the German Confederation in 1815, but failed to realign itself with other German states upon the dissolution of the Confederation in 1866. In 1919 Switzerland assumed responsibility for Liechtenstein's diplomatic representation, replacing Austria. In 1920 a postal union with Switzerland was agreed, and in 1924 a treaty was concluded with Switzerland whereby Liechtenstein was incorporated in a joint customs union. Franz Josef II became Reigning Prince in 1938 and was succeeded by his son Prince Hans-Adam II in 1989.

Domestic Political Affairs

After 42 years as the dominant party in government, the Fortschrittliche Bürgerpartei (FBP—Progressive Citizens' Party) was defeated by the Vaterländische Union (VU—Patriotic Union) at a general election to the Landtag (parliament) in February 1970. Four years later the FBP regained its majority. At the general election in February 1978 the VU, led by Hans Brunhart, won a majority of seats. After protracted negotiations, Brunhart replaced the FBP's Dr Walter Kieber as Prime Minister in April 1978. At the general election in February 1982 the distribution of seats remained unchanged. Following a referendum in July 1984, women were granted the right to vote on a national basis. However, women were still not permitted to vote on communal affairs in three of Liechtenstein's 11 communes until April 1986, when they were finally accorded full voting rights. (An amendment to the Constitution, declaring equality between men and women, took effect in 1992.) In August 1984 Prince Franz Josef transferred executive power to his son, Prince Hans-Adam, although he remained titular Head of State until his death in November 1989, when he was succeeded by his son as Hans-Adam II.

The composition of the Landtag remained unchanged following a general election in February 1986, when women voted for the first time in a national poll. In January 1989 the Landtag was dissolved by Prince Hans-Adam, following a dispute between the VU and the FBP regarding the construction of a new museum to accommodate the princely art collection. At the subsequent general election, which took place in March, the number of seats in the Landtag was increased from 15 to 25; the VU retained its majority, securing 13 seats, while the FBP took the remaining 12 seats.

In October 1992 almost 2,000 people demonstrated in Vaduz to protest against a threat by Prince Hans-Adam that he would dissolve the Landtag if deputies did not submit to his wish to hold a proposed referendum to endorse Liechtenstein's entry to the nascent European Economic Area (EEA) shortly in advance of a similar vote in Switzerland. The Prince believed that the outcome of the Swiss poll might be prejudicial to that of the Liechtenstein vote, and that, in the event of voters' rejecting EEA membership at an early referendum, Liechtenstein might still be able to join other EFTA members in applying for admission to the European Community (EC, now European Union—EU, see p. 270). A compromise was reached, whereby the referendum was scheduled to take place shortly after the Swiss vote, while the Government agreed actively to promote a vote in favour of the EEA and to explore the possibility of applying to the EC should EEA membership be rejected. (The authorities subsequently decided that admission to the EU would not be beneficial to the Principality.) At the referendum in December, although Switzerland's voters had rejected accession to the EEA, Liechtenstein's membership was approved by 55.8% of those who voted; consequently, the two countries' joint customs union was renegotiated. In April 1995 a further national referendum was held, at which 55.9% of those who voted approved the revised customs arrangements. Liechtenstein joined the EEA in May.

At the general election in February 1993 the VU lost its majority, winning only 11 of the Landtag's 25 seats. The FBP retained 12 seats, and two seats were won by an environmentalist party, the Freie Liste (FL—Free List). Lengthy negotiations resulted in the formation of a new coalition between the FBP and the VU, in which the FBP was the dominant party, and Markus Büchel of the FBP became Prime Minister. In September, however, following a unanimous vote in the Landtag expressing no confidence in his leadership, Büchel was dismissed from his post, and Prince Hans-Adam dissolved the legislature. At a further general election, which was held in October, the VU regained its majority, winning 13 seats, while the FBP took 11 and the FL one. The VU became the dominant party in a new coalition with the FBP, with Mario Frick of the VU as Prime Minister.

In March 1996 the Landtag adopted a unanimous motion of loyalty to the hereditary monarchy, after Prince Hans-Adam offered to resign in response to continued tension between him and the legislature. At the next general election, which took place in February 1997, the VU retained its majority with 13 seats, while the FBP secured 10 and the FL two. Frick remained Prime Minister. In April the FBP withdrew from the ruling coalition, leaving a single party (the VU) to govern alone for the first time since 1938. The constitutional role of the Reigning Prince came under renewed scrutiny in 1997, when, against the wishes of the Landtag, Prince Hans-Adam refused to reappoint Dr Herbert Wille, a senior judge who had advocated that constitutional issues should be decided by the Supreme Court rather than the monarch. Wille subsequently presented a formal complaint to the European Court of Human Rights, which ruled, in November 1999, that Prince Hans-Adam had restricted Wille's right to free speech; the Prince was required to pay 100,000 Swiss francs in costs.

In December 1999 Prince Hans-Adam requested an Austrian prosecutor, Kurt Spitzer, to investigate allegations in the German press based on an unpublished report of April 1999 by the German secret service that international criminals were using financial institutions in Liechtenstein to launder the proceeds of organized crime. As a result, five people were placed under investigative arrest in May 2000, including the brother of one of the Principality's most senior judges; all five were later released without charge. In his final report, which was released in August, Spitzer concluded that Liechtenstein was no more culpable of money-laundering than other countries in Europe. He blamed the current problems on the Principality's over-bureaucratic and inefficient banking system and the poor application of existing legislation designed to combat economic crimes. In June the Financial Action Task Force on Money Laundering (FATF), a commission of the Organisation for Economic Co-operation and Development (OECD, see p. 376), included Liechtenstein on a list of countries considered unco-operative in international attempts to combat money-laundering. In an effort to improve the country's international reputation, the Liechtenstein Bankers' Association announced in July that anonymous accounts would be abolished. In the same month the Government approved the establishment of a new financial investigative unit within the police force and measures to accelerate legal assistance to foreign countries in money-laundering investigations. Legislation was promulgated in December requiring financial institutions to maintain tighter controls over accounts and transactions, including the abolition of anonymous accounts. Liechtenstein was removed from the FATF's list of unco-operative countries in 2001, and, in October of that year, the Government appointed the former head of the Swiss anti-money-laundering authority, Daniel Thelesklaf, to administer a new financial surveillance unit, which was to enforce new regulations requiring banks and lawyers to be able to verify the identity of their clients. However, Liechtenstein was among seven jurisdictions identified by OECD as 'unco-operative tax havens' lacking financial transparency in April 2002, under its initiative to abolish 'harmful tax practices'. Although four jurisdictions were subsequently removed from the list, Liechtenstein remained one of three countries so designated until May 2009 (see below).

At the general election that took place in February 2001 the VU lost its parliamentary majority, securing only 11 of the 25 seats in the Landtag, while the FBP won 13 seats and the FL obtained one. The VU administration's popularity had been adversely affected by an unresolved dispute with Prince Hans-Adam over his demands for constitutional changes, notably with regard to appointments in the judiciary (the Prince advocated that judges be nominated by the monarch rather than by parliamentary deputies); the Prince claimed that these amendments would benefit the people, while the VU regarded them as an attempt to extend the royal prerogative. A new Government comprising solely the FBP, under the leadership of Otmar Hasler, took office in April. The Prince had previously announced that if he failed to secure the support of the new Government for his proposed constitutional reforms, he would seek a national referendum; in December he also threatened to leave the Principality and take up residence in Austria.

The issue of constitutional reform was finally resolved by a national referendum, held on 14 and 16 March 2003, in which 64.3% of the votes cast were in favour of granting the Prince new powers; the voter participation rate was 87.7%. As a result of the referendum, the Prince gained the right to dismiss a government even if it retained parliamentary confidence, to appoint an interim administration pending elections, to preside over a panel to select judges, to veto laws by not signing them within a six-month period; and to adopt emergency legislation. Conversely, citizens could now force a referendum on any subject by collecting a minimum of 1,500 signatures. A compromise proposal put forward by a cross-party group that included former premier Frick (the Volksinitiative für Verfassungsfrieden—People's Initiative for Constitutional Peace), which suggested that a princely veto could be overruled by a referendum and sought to limit the Prince's use of emergency legislation to times of war, received the support of only 16.5% of the voters. The overwhelming support for the Prince's proposed changes was partially attributed to widespread fear that, if fulfilled, his threat of self-imposed exile as a symbolic monarch would cause economic decline and social upheaval. Prince Hans-Adam dismissed the findings of a commission established by the Council of Europe, which stated that the constitutional amendments would constitute a retrograde step for democracy and could lead to the isolation of Liechtenstein in Europe. On 15 August 2004 Prince Hans-Adam transferred his sovereign powers to his son, Prince Alois, in accordance with an announcement that he had made in August 2003. Prince Hans-Adam, however, remained Head of State.

At the general election held on 11 and 13 March 2005 the FBP failed to retain an absolute majority, winning 12 of the 25 seats. The VU won 10 seats, while the FL increased its representation from one seat to three. In April the FBP and the VU formed a coalition Government, which comprised three representatives of the FBP, including Hasler, who remained as Prime Minister, and two of the VU, with Dr Klaus Tschütscher becoming Deputy Prime Minister.

In August 2005 a conservative group known as the Volksinitiative für das Leben (People's Initiative For Life) submitted 1,889 signatures to the Government in support of its demands for a national referendum to be held on constitutional revisions. The group hoped to amend Article 14 of the Constitution so that the highest responsibility of the state would be 'to protect human life from conception until natural death' and also aimed to insert a reference to the state's responsibility to protect human dignity. The initiative was intended to address the potential legalization of abortion and, indirectly, the issues of euthanasia, genetic technology and stem-cell research. Having failed to secure sufficient support in the Landtag, the proposals were to be subject to a national referendum. Considering the initiative to be too restrictive, the FBP and VU jointly drafted a counterproposal to make the protection of life and human dignity a right for Liechtenstein citizens rather than a duty of the state. A further amendment was added explicitly prohibiting the death penalty (which had already been abolished by a revision of the criminal code in 1985). Following its approval by the Landtag in September, the counterproposal was presented to the referendum concurrently with the People's Initiative For Life. At the referendum, held on 25 and 27 November, the initiative, which opponents claimed would prevent abortion, birth control and assisted suicide, was rejected by 80.9% of the votes cast, while the counterproposal was adopted, with the support of 79.4% of voters.

At the general election that took place on 8 February 2009 the VU won an absolute majority, securing 13 of the 25 seats and replacing the FBP as the largest party in the Landtag; the rate of participation by eligible voters was 84.6%. The FBP won 11 seats, while the FL's representation declined from three seats to just one. Tschütscher, hitherto Deputy Prime Minister, was sworn in as Prime Minister on 25 March. Despite the VU's absolute majority, the VU and FBP continued to co-operate in a coalition Government; the new administration comprised three members of the VU (including Tschütscher, who also assumed the portfolios for general government affairs, finance, and family and equal opportunity) and two representatives of the FBP. Tschütscher undertook to improve the reputation of Liechtenstein's financial system by increasing co-operation with other countries in order to combat tax evasion (see Foreign Affairs, below).

Foreign Affairs

In 1950 Liechtenstein became a party to the Statute of the International Court of Justice (ICJ, see p. 23), in 1973 it joined the Organization for Security and Co-operation in Europe (see p. 385) and in 1978 it was admitted to the Council of Europe (see p. 250). Liechtenstein became a member of the UN in September 1990 (hitherto the country had been a member of some UN specialized agencies). In the following year Liechtenstein became a full member of the European Free Trade Association (EFTA, see p. 447). Liechtenstein participates in the European Economic Area (EEA), which from 1994 has incorporated Liechtenstein (together with Iceland and Norway) into the internal market of the European Union (EU, see p. 270).

In February 2008, following a meeting of EU ministers responsible for justice and home affairs in Brussels, Belgium, Liechtenstein became an associate member of the EU's Schengen agreement (which binds signatories to the abolition of border controls) and the Dublin Convention on Asylum (relating to common formal arrangements on asylum). Although the Landtag ratified the agreement in June, the EU process of ratification remained incomplete in early 2010, owing to ongoing negotiations between Liechtenstein and the EU on an anti-fraud agreement. Meanwhile, an interim solution to the issue of border control between Liechtenstein and Switzerland was put in place after the latter acceded to the Schengen agreement in December 2008.

Following the Second World War, Liechtenstein's relations with Czechoslovakia (from 1993 the Czech Republic and Slovakia) were strained. This stemmed from the expulsion of ethnic Germans from Czechoslovakia and the confiscation of their land (without compensation) after the war, under the controversial Beneš Decrees. The Liechtenstein princely family lost a large part of its estates during this time—including the castles of Feldsberg and Eisgrub, estimated to be worth some €100m. in 2003. Liechtenstein, which was a sovereign, neutral state throughout both the First and Second World Wars, claimed that it was unfairly grouped together with Germany under the terms of the Decrees. Czechoslovakia, however, considered the Liechtenstein princely family to have been collaborators with the Nazi regime in Germany during the Second World War, and that its action was thus legitimate. As a result of the dispute, Czechoslovakia refused to recognize Liechtenstein as a sovereign state. In October 2003 Prince Hans-Adam blocked the entry of the Czech Republic and Slovakia (along with that of the eight other EU accession states) into the EEA; the 10 countries were due to become members of the EU on 1 May 2004 and would, under normal circumstances, have automatically joined the EEA. Their accession to the EEA was delayed until November 2003, when Liechtenstein agreed to sign the enlargement treaty on the EEA; Slovakia subsequently agreed to establish diplomatic relations with Liechtenstein. Liechtenstein reiterated its demand that the Czech Republic and Slovakia acknowledge that the Principality was a sovereign, neutral state through both World Wars. To do so, however, would expose these two countries to the possibility of legal action being brought against them by

LIECHTENSTEIN

Liechtenstein for the illegal seizure of land. None the less, Liechtenstein established diplomatic relations with the Czech Republic in September 2009, although the two countries stressed that any resolution of the dispute over the confiscated property would be subject to separate negotiations. It was also agreed that a joint commission of historians would be established to investigate the background to the dispute. In December relations with Slovakia were also restored.

Liechtenstein also sought damages from Germany for assets that it claimed Germany had improperly awarded to Czechoslovakia after the Second World War as reparations. The German position was that the assets were seized by Czechoslovakia and that Germany was not responsible. In February 2005, however, the ICJ ruled that it was not competent to make a decision on the claim as it predated the 1980 agreement between the two countries that disputes between them should be settled by the ICJ.

Following a four-year investigation, in April 2005 an Independent Commission of Historians charged with examining Liechtenstein's role in the Second World War reported that no Jewish assets were confiscated and no forced labour was used during the war, and that while 165 refugees from Nazi-controlled Austria were turned away by Liechtenstein between 1933 and 1945, 400 others were taken in and thousands more allowed safe passage to Switzerland. The Commission was appointed by the Government in 2001 after the World Jewish Congress accused the Principality's financial institutions of having hidden plundered Jewish assets for the Nazis during the war.

Liechtenstein's banking secrecy laws were subject to increased international scrutiny in early 2008, following the revelation that the German Federal Intelligence Service had paid some €4m. to a former employee of Liechtenstein's LGT Bank for access to records detailing accounts held by German nationals. It appeared that members of Germany's business élite had avoided tax by channelling up to €4,000m. into secret foundations established by banks in Liechtenstein. Although Prince Alois condemned as unreasonable Germany's method of obtaining the information, the German Government demanded greater financial transparency in Liechtenstein, as well as greater co-operation regarding tax evasion. In the following months, several more countries (including the USA and the United Kingdom) began investigations into allegations of tax evasion through secret bank accounts held in the country. In response to growing international criticism, Prince Alois announced in August that the country would endeavour to co-operate more fully on matters pertaining to tax in the future, but that this should not be at the expense of the country's 'culture of privacy'. A bilateral agreement was reached with the USA in December, whereby Liechtenstein would co-operate with investigations into suspected tax evasion, while Liechtenstein banks would benefit from increased access to US financial markets. A bilateral accord was also signed with the United Kingdom in August 2009, under which Liechtenstein agreed to close the bank accounts of British investors who refused to disclose details of their Liechtenstein-held assets to the British tax authorities; at the same time, however, Liechtenstein offered favourable terms, including limits on penalties, to customers who voluntarily disclosed details of their unpaid tax, in the hope that tax evaders wishing to regularize their status would move their accounts to the country's banks in order to take advantage of the new arrangements. By the end of December 2010 Liechtenstein had concluded tax information exchange agreements with 19 countries and territories. Meanwhile, prior to the meeting in April 2009 of the Group of 20 major industrialized and systemically important emerging market nations (G20, see p. 451) in London, United Kingdom, Liechtenstein agreed in March to amend its secrecy laws to allow for greater transparency and to comply with rules on the sharing of bank data set by OECD to combat tax evasion. As a consequence of this commitment, in May OECD removed Liechtenstein from its list of 'unco-operative tax havens', and in November it recognized Liechtenstein as a jurisdiction which had implemented international co-operation standards in tax matters.

CONSTITUTION AND GOVERNMENT

Under the Constitution of 1921 (as amended in 1969, 1984, 2003 and 2005), the monarchy is hereditary in the male line. The Reigning Prince, who is constitutionally responsible for foreign affairs, exercises legislative power jointly with the Landtag (parliament). The Landtag comprises 25 members, who are elected by universal adult suffrage for a term of four years (subject to dissolution), on the basis of proportional representation. The country is divided into the two election districts of Oberland (Upper Country) and Unterland (Lower Country), which elect 15 and 10 members of the Landtag, respectively. A five-member collegial Government is nominated by the Reigning Prince, on the recommendation of the Landtag, for four years. Under constitutional changes approved by referendum in 2003, the Reigning Prince is empowered to dismiss governments (even if they retain parliamentary confidence), appoint an interim administration pending an election, approve judicial nominees, veto laws and invoke emergency legislation. Under the same constitutional changes, citizens can force a referendum on any subject, including the future of the monarchy, by collecting 1,500 signatures. On 15 August 2004 the sovereign rights pertaining to the Reigning Prince were transferred to the Hereditary (Crown) Prince, who was to exercise them as the representative of the Reigning Prince, who remained head of state.

REGIONAL AND INTERNATIONAL CO-OPERATION

Liechtenstein has important links with neighbouring Switzerland: the two countries are joined in a customs union, and Switzerland is responsible for Liechtenstein's diplomatic interests in countries where Liechtenstein is not directly represented. Liechtenstein is a member of the European Free Trade Association (EFTA, see p. 447) and participates in the European Economic Area (EEA), which incorporates Liechtenstein (together with Iceland and Norway) into the internal market of the European Union (EU, see p. 270). Liechtenstein became an associate member of the EU's Schengen agreement on border controls in 2008, but its accession to full membership remained subject to negotiations in 2011. It is also a member of the Council of Europe (see p. 250) and the Organization for Security and Co-operation in Europe (OSCE, see p. 385).

Liechtenstein joined the UN in 1990 and the World Trade Organization (WTO, see p. 430) in 1995.

ECONOMIC AFFAIRS

In 2008, according to estimates by the World Bank, Liechtenstein's gross national income (GNI), measured at average 2006–08 prices, was US $4,033.7m., equivalent to $113,210 per head (although as 50.1% of the work-force was domiciled abroad in 2008, this figure is not comparable with those for other countries). During 2000–09 the population increased at an average annual rate of 1.0%, while Liechtenstein's gross domestic product (GDP) per head increased, in real terms, by an average of 1.2% per year during 2000–08. Overall GDP increased, in real terms, at an average annual rate of 2.2% in 2000–08; GDP grew by 1.8% in 2009.

According to the UN, in 2009 the agricultural sector (together with forestry and fishing) accounted for 1.2% of GDP. Within the agricultural sector the emphasis is on cattle-breeding, dairy farming and market gardening. The principal crops are maize and potatoes. In addition, wine is produced, and forestry is a significant activity. In 2009 0.8% of those employed in Liechtenstein worked in agriculture (including forestry).

In 2009, according to the UN, industry (including production of goods) contributed some 26.8% of GDP, while 41.3% of those employed in Liechtenstein worked in industrial activity (including mining and quarrying, processing industries, energy and water supply, and construction) in that year.

According to the UN, in 2009, the manufacturing sector accounted for 19% of GDP. In that year 32.7% of those employed in Liechtenstein worked in the manufacturing sector. The principal branches of manufacturing are mechanical engineering, electrical machinery, vehicle components and dental instruments.

In 2009, according to the UN, the construction sector accounted for 5.6% of GDP. In that year, 7.5% of those employed in Liechtenstein worked in the construction sector.

In 2009 more than 91% of energy requirements were imported from other countries. In that year electricity supplied 27.9% of energy requirements, natural gas 23.4%, fuel oil 17.8%, motor fuel (petrol) 13.8%, and diesel 9.6%.

According to the UN, in 2009, 72.0% of GDP was generated by the services sector, while the sector engaged 57.9% of those employed in Liechtenstein in that year. Financial services are of great importance. Numerous foreign corporations, holding companies and foundations (estimated to number about 75,000) have nominal offices in Liechtenstein, benefiting from the Principality's stable political situation, tradition of bank secrecy (although stricter banking legislation was introduced in 1997, in 2000–02, and in 2009–10, partly to increase the transparency of the sector) and low fiscal charges. Following the Principality's accession to

LIECHTENSTEIN

Statistical Survey

the European Economic Area (EEA) in 1995, the registration of foreign banks was permitted. New legislation governing insurance companies was approved in 1996, and during the late 1990s the insurance sector expanded rapidly. The building and hotel trades and other service industries are also highly developed. The Government initiated a publicity campaign in 2004 to promote Liechtenstein, with the aim of increasing tourism and investment and further developing the Principality as a business centre. The new coalition Government formed in March 2009 announced its commitment to pursuing this objective.

With a very limited domestic market, Liechtenstein's industry is export-orientated. In 2009 total exports (excluding Switzerland) amounted to 3,081.0m. Swiss francs, while imports (excluding Switzerland) totalled 1,924.3m. Swiss francs. Switzerland is the principal trading partner. In 2005 Switzerland purchased 11.7% of total exports of members of the Liechtenstein Chamber of Commerce and Industry and the EEA accounted for 44.1%. Specialized machinery, dental technology, vehicle components and frozen food are important exports.

In 2009, according to official figures, Liechtenstein recorded a visible trade surplus of 1,157m. Swiss francs (excluding Switzerland). In 2009 there was a fiscal surplus of 59.2m. Swiss francs, compared with a fiscal deficit of 126.6m. Swiss francs in 2008. The average annual rate of inflation was 0.8% during 2005–08; consumer prices increased by 2.5% in 2008, but decreased in 2009 by 0.5%. Traditionally the unemployment rate has been negligible; in 2009 the rate of unemployment was 3.0%. More than one-third of Liechtenstein's population are resident foreigners, many of whom provide the labour for industry, while in 2009 16,704 workers crossed the borders (51% of workers in Liechtenstein), mainly from Austria and Switzerland each day, to work in the Principality.

During the first decade of the 21st century Liechtenstein's reputation as a financial centre and tax haven was challenged by foreign governments aiming to combat money-laundering and tax evasion. The widespread recession that affected most developed countries in 2008–09 increased governments' determination to recover the revenues that were due to them. From 2008 Liechtenstein concluded bilateral agreements on the exchange of tax information with the USA, the United Kingdom and a number of other countries. Liechtenstein's recognition by OECD in November 2009 as a jurisdiction which had implemented international co-operation standards in tax matters was described by the Prime Minister, Dr Klaus Tschütscher, as an important stage in the 'reorientation' of Liechtenstein as a business location.

In May 2010 Liechtenstein adopted reforms that aimed to simplify the country's own tax system and make it more transparent, while increasing its compatibility with EU law: the measures, which were to come into effect from the beginning of 2011, included a uniform corporate tax rate of 12.5%, while residents were to pay a reduced maximum income tax, also of 12.5%. As a result, the Government expected to receive an additional 66m. Swiss francs in revenue in 2011. Tschütscher expressed the hope that the reforms would enhance the attractiveness of Liechtenstein for investors and encourage sustainable growth. In August 2010 the Government introduced revisions to legislation concerning the financial markets, so as to ensure that Liechtenstein's practices would be consistent with international standards.

PUBLIC HOLIDAYS

2012: 1 January (New Year's Day), 2 January (St Berchtold's Day), 6 January (Epiphany), 2 February (Candlemas), 8 March (Shrove Tuesday), 19 March (St Joseph's Day), 6 April (Good Friday), 9 April (Easter Monday), 1 May (Labour Day), 17 May (Ascension Day), 28 May (Whit Monday), 7 June (Corpus Christi), 15 August (National Holiday and Assumption), 8 September (Nativity of the Virgin Mary), 1 November (All Saints' Day), 8 December (Immaculate Conception), 25 December (Christmas Day), 26 December (St Stephen's Day).

Statistical Survey

Source: Amt für Statistik, Gerberweg 5, 9490 Vaduz; tel. 2366111; fax 2366895; e-mail info.statistik@avw.llv.li; internet www.as.llv.li.

AREA AND POPULATION

Area: 160.5 sq km (62.0 sq miles).

Population: 36,010, incl. 11,934 resident aliens at 30 June 2010.

Density (at 30 June 2010): 224.4 per sq km.

Population by Age and Sex (official estimates at 30 June 2010): *0–14:* 5,854 (males 2,998, females 2,856); *15–64:* 25,207 (males 12,640, females 12,567); *65 and over:* 4,949 (males 2,179, females 2,770); *Total* 36,010 (males 17,817, females 18,193).

Municipalities (population at 30 June 2010): Schaan 5,799; Vaduz (capital) 5,195; Triesen 4,806; Balzers 4,550; Eschen 4,204; Mauren 3,959; Triesenberg 2,499; Ruggell 1,976; Gamprin 1,577; Schellenberg 1,024; Planken 421; Total 36,010.

Births, Marriages and Deaths (2008, provisional, unless otherwise indicated): Live births 350 (9.9 per 1,000); Marriages 114 (3.2 per 1,000) (2007); Deaths 205 (5.8 per 1,000). Source: UN, *Population and Vital Statistics Report*.

Economically Active Population (2009): Agriculture and forestry 261; Industry and skilled trades 13,582 (Mining and quarrying 50, Manufacturing 10,742, Energy and water supply 325, Construction 2,465); Services 19,034 (Retail, repairs, etc. 2,413, Hotels and restaurants 904, Transport and communications 1,729, Banking and insurance 3,135, Real estate, information, business and support services, etc. 2,645, Legal consultancy and trust management 2,598, Public administration 1,626, Education 1,011, Health and social services 1,798, Other services—incl. activities of extraterritorial organizations 1,175); *Total employed* 32,877; Unemployed 518; *Total labour force* 33,395.

HEALTH AND WELFARE

Key Indicators

Under-5 Mortality Rate (per 1,000 live births, 2004): 5.

Physicians (per 1,000 head, 1997): 1.31 (Source: Statistik des Fürstentums Liechtenstein, *Statistisches Jahrbuch—1998*).

For sources (unless specified) and definitions, see explanatory note on p. vi.

AGRICULTURE, ETC.

Note: Figures are for farms with a minimum of either 1 ha of arable land, 30 acres of specialized cultivation, 10 acres of protected cultivation, 8 sows, 80 porkers (or capacity for 80 porkers) or 300 head of poultry, and where livestock owners are covered by the *Tierseuchenfond* (insurance against epidemics).

Principal Crops (metric tons, 1987): Wheat 460; Oats 4; Barley 416; Silo-maize 27,880; Potatoes 1,040. *2009:* Grapes 200 metric tons (FAO estimate) (Source: partly FAO).

Livestock (2009): Cattle 6,078; Pigs 1,811; Horses 495; Sheep 3,963; Goats 452; Hens 12,003.

Dairy Produce (2008, metric tons): Milk delivered to dairies 13,401; Milk for consumption and pasteurization 1,007; Milk for processing 5,425; Cream 1,582; Yoghurt 561.

Forestry ('000 cubic metres, 2009): Roundwood removals (excl. bark) 25.0 (Sawlogs, veneer logs and logs for sleepers 10, Fuel wood 15). Source: FAO.

FINANCE

Currency and Exchange Rates: Swiss currency: 100 Rappen (centimes) = 1 Franken (Swiss franc). *Sterling, Dollar and Euro Equivalents* (31 December 2010): £1 sterling = 1.471 Franken; US $1 = 0.940 Franken; €1 = 1.255 Franken; 10 Franken = £6.80 = $10.64 = €7.96. For average exchange rate, see chapter on Switzerland.

Budget (million Swiss francs, 2009): *Revenue:* Current 1,120 (Taxes and duties 728; Revenues from assets 326); Capital 18; Total 1,138. *Expenditure:* Current 987.0 (Social welfare 219; Finance and taxation 362); Capital 88; Total 1,075.

Cost of Living (Consumer Price Index; base: May 2005 = 100, annual averages): All items 101.2 in 2007; 103.7 in 2008; 103.2 in 2009.

Gross Domestic Product (million Swiss francs at current prices, official estimates): 5,525 in 2007; 5,495 in 2008; 5,220 in 2009 (preliminary).

LIECHTENSTEIN

Expenditure on the Gross Domestic Product (million Swiss francs at current prices, 2009): Government final consumption expenditure 595.0; Private final consumption expenditure 3,045.9; Increase in stocks –43.9; Gross fixed capital formation 1,079.9; *Total domestic expenditure* 4,676.9; Exports of goods and services 2,714.0; Less Imports of goods and services 2,139.4; *GDP in purchasers' values* 5,251.6 (Source: UN, National Accounts Main Aggregates Database).

Gross Domestic Product by Economic Activity (million Swiss francs at current prices, 2009): Agriculture, forestry and fishing 64.1; Mining and utilities 121.7; Manufacturing 1,030.5; Construction 305.5; Retail trade and hotel and restaurants 853.6; Transport, storage and communication 342.6; Other services 2,718.3; *Total gross value added* 5,436.4; Net of taxes on products –184.8 (figure obtained as residual); *GDP in purchasers' values* 5,251.6 (Source: UN, National Accounts Main Aggregates Database).

EXTERNAL TRADE

Note: Imports and exports to and from Liechtenstein presented at Swiss customs, not including trade with Switzerland and goods traffic via Switzerland.

Principal Commodities ('000 Swiss francs, 2009): *Imports:* Food, animals and other products of agriculture 81,971; Raw materials, metals, construction and chemical products 168,532; Vehicles and transport equipment 95,966; Machinery and electrical products 703,912; Metal manufactures and other finished and semi-finished goods 451,617; Glass, ceramic and textile manufactures 191,565; Total 1,924,306. *Exports:* Food, animals and other products of agriculture 291,934; Raw materials, metals, construction and chemical products 308,532; Vehicles and transport equipment 282,785; Machinery and electrical products 1,281,476; Metal manufactures and other finished and semi-finished goods 574,762; Glass, ceramic and textile manufactures 217,698; Total (incl. others) 3,080,988.

Principal Trading Partners ('000 Swiss francs, 2009): *Imports:* Austria 673,634; China, People's Republic 34,107; France 30,210; Germany 790,276; Italy 80,637; Netherlands 26,658; Poland 35,403; United Kingdom 23,374; USA 38,390; Total (incl. others) 1,924,306. *Exports:* Austria 338,481; China, People's Republic 98,758; France 311,970; Germany 726,968; Hong Kong 47,204 Italy 200,094; Japan 56,180; Mexico 27,790; Poland 35,938; Russia 25,137; Singapore 61,228; Spain 79,473; Sweden 41,313; United Arab Emirates 44,674; United Kingdom 109,241; USA 349,485; Total (incl. others) 3,080,988.

TRANSPORT

Road Traffic (registered motor vehicles, 1 July 2010): Passenger cars 26,890; Commercial vehicles 3,665; Motorcycles 3,734; Total (incl. others) 35,291.

TOURISM

Arrivals by Country of Residence (arrivals at accommodation establishments, 2009): Austria 2,828; France 1,393; Germany 20,386; Italy 1,977; Switzerland 22,453; United Kingdom 2,664; USA 1,912; Total (incl. others) 72,428. Note: Total includes 5,921 residents of Liechtenstein.

COMMUNICATIONS MEDIA

Daily Newspapers (2004): 2 (total circulation 18,387 copies). Source: UNESCO Institute for Statistics.

Radio Receivers (1998): 12,451 in use.

Television Receivers (1998): 12,089 in use.

Telephones (2009): 19,600 main lines in use. Source: International Telecommunication Union.

Mobile Cellular Telephones (2009): 35,000 subscribers. Source: International Telecommunication Union.

Internet Users (2009): 23,000. Source: International Telecommunication Union.

Broadband Subscribers (2009): 27,000. Source: International Telecommunication Union.

EDUCATION

(2007/08, unless otherwise indicated*)

Kindergarten: 49 classrooms; 79 teachers (males 1, females 78); 711 pupils (males 371, females 340). *2008/09:* 82 teachers; 714 pupils.

Primary†: 138 classrooms; 262 teachers (males 63, females 199); 2,073 pupils (males 1,035, females 1,038). *2008/09:* 261 teachers; 2,134 pupils.

High School: 34 classrooms; 101 teachers (males 45, females 56); 412 pupils (males 221, females 191). *2008/09:* 101 teachers; 422 pupils.

Secondary: 45 classrooms; 127 teachers (males 60, females 67); 732 pupils (males 380, females 352). *2008/09:* 125 teachers; 842 pupils.

Optional 10th School Year: 5 classrooms; 19 teachers (males 10, females 9); 78 pupils (males 32, females 46). *2008/09:* 19 teachers; 77 pupils.

Vocational Training: 8 classrooms; 16 teachers (males 8, females 8); 124 pupils (males 84, females 40).

Grammar Schools (2004/05, unless otherwise indicated): 38 classrooms (2001/02); 103 teachers; 744 pupils.

Music (2004/05): 91 teachers; 2,519 pupils.

Higher Education (2004/05)‡: 527 students.

Pupil-teacher Ratio (primary education, UNESCO estimate): 6.5 in 2007/08 (Source: UNESCO Institute for Statistics).

* Excluding private institutions.
† Including pre-school and reception classes.
‡ Those studying in Liechtenstein only (931 students attended institutions abroad).

Directory

The Government

HEAD OF STATE

Reigning Prince: HSH Prince HANS-ADAM II (succeeded 13 November 1989).

On 15 August 2004 Prince Hans-Adam II transferred the execution of his sovereign powers to his son, Hereditary Prince Alois.

GOVERNMENT
(May 2011)

A coalition of the Vaterländische Union (VU—Patriotic Union) and the Fortschrittliche Bürgerpartei (FBP—Progressive Citizens' Party).

Prime Minister and Minister of General Government Affairs, of Finance and of Family and Equal Opportunity: Dr KLAUS TSCHÜTSCHER (VU).

Deputy Prime Minister and Minister of Economic Affairs, of Transport and of Construction and Public Works: Dr MARTIN MEYER (FBP).

Minister of Public Health, of Social Affairs and of Environmental Affairs, Land Use Planning, Agriculture and Forestry: RENATE MÜSSNER (VU).

Minister of Home Affairs, of Education and of Sports: HUGO QUADERER (VU).

Minister of Foreign Affairs, of Justice and of Cultural Affairs: Dr AURELIA FRICK (FBP).

Alternate Ministers: ROLAND MOSER (VU), ANDREA KLEIN (VU), Dr MAURO PEDRAZZINI (FBP), Dr PATRICK SCHÜRMANN (FBP), HUBERT BÜCHEL (VU).

GOVERNMENT OFFICES

Regierungsgebäude: Regierungsgebäude, Peter-Kaiser-Pl. 1, Postfach 684, 9490 Vaduz; tel. 2366111; fax 2366022; e-mail info@regierung.li; internet www.liechtenstein.li.

LIECHTENSTEIN

Legislature

LANDTAG

Landtagssekretariat des Fürstentums Liechtenstein: Peter-Kaiser-Pl. 3, Postfach 684, 9490 Vaduz; tel. 2366571; fax 2366580; e-mail info@landtag.li; internet www.landtag.li.
President: ARTHUR BRUNHART.
Vice-President: RENATE WOHLWEND.

General Election, 8 February 2009

Party	Votes*	% of votes	Seats
Vaterländische Union (VU)	95,219	47.60	13
Fortschrittliche Bürgerpartei (FBP)	86,951	43.47	11
Freie Liste (FL)	17,835	8.92	1
Total	200,005	100.00	25

* Each elector was permitted to vote for as many candidates as there were seats allocated to the respective electoral district (15 in Oberland and 10 in Unterland). The total number of valid ballots cast was 15,124.

Election Commissions

Hauptwahl- oder Hauptabstimmungskommission Oberland: c/o Postfach 684, 9490 Vaduz; independent; Chair. BECK HEINZ.
Hauptwahl- oder Hauptabstimmungskommission Unterland: c/o Postfach 684, 9490 Vaduz; independent; Chair. ELKUCH ROLAND.

Political Organizations

Fortschrittliche Bürgerpartei (FBP) (Progressive Citizens' Party): Aeulestr. 56, Postfach 1213, 9490 Vaduz; tel. 2377940; fax 2377949; e-mail marcus.vogt@fbp.li; internet www.fbp.li; f. 1918; Pres. ALEXANDER BATLINER.
Freie Liste (FL) (Free List): Landstr. 140, Postfach 254, 9494 Schaan; tel. 2311731; fax 2311733; e-mail info@freieliste.li; internet www.freieliste.li; f. 1985; social democratic and ecological party; Pres. WOLFGANG MARXER.
Vaterländische Union (VU) (Patriotic Union): Fürst-Franz-Josef-Str. 13, 9490 Vaduz; tel. 2398282; fax 2398289; e-mail vu@vu-online.li; internet www.vu-online.li; f. 1936 by merger of the People's Party (f. 1918) and the Heimatdienst movement; Pres. ADOLF HEEB; Sec.-Gen. HANS-JÖRG GOOP.

Diplomatic Representation

According to an arrangement concluded in 1919, Switzerland has agreed to represent Liechtenstein's interests in countries where it has diplomatic missions and where Liechtenstein is not represented in its own right. In so doing, Switzerland always acts only on the basis of mandates of a general or specific nature, which it may either refuse or accept, while Liechtenstein is free to enter into direct relations with foreign states or to establish its own additional missions. Liechtenstein has nine diplomatic missions abroad, comprising embassies in Berlin (Germany), Bern (Switzerland), Brussels (Belgium, including a permanent mission to the European Union), Washington, DC (USA) and Vienna (Austria, including permanent missions to the Organization for Security and Co-operation in Europe and the UN), as well as a non-resident ambassador to the Holy See, a permanent representative to the Council of Europe in Strasbourg (France), a permanent mission to the UN in New York (USA) and a permanent mission in Geneva (Switzerland).

Judicial System

CIVIL AND CRIMINAL COURTS

Landgericht (County Court): Spaniagasse 1, 9490 Vaduz; tel. 2366111; fax 2366539; e-mail benedikt.marxer@lg.liv.li; Court of First Instance; 1 presiding judge, and 13 other judges; Presiding Judge Dr BENEDIKT MARXER.
Kriminalgericht (Criminal Court): 9490 Vaduz; bench of 5 judges; Presiding Judge Lic. Iur. UWE ÖHRI.
Schöffengericht (Court of Assizes): 9490 Vaduz; for minor misdemeanours; bench of 3 judges; Presiding Judge Dr BENEDIKT MARXER.
Jugendgericht (Juvenile Court): 9490 Vaduz; bench of 3 judges; Presiding Judge Lic. Iur. UWE ÖHRI.
Obergericht (Superior Court): 9490 Vaduz; Court of Second Instance; divided into 3 senates, each with bench of 5 judges; Presiding Judge and Chair. of Second Senate Lic. Iur. RUDOLF FEHR; Chair. of First Senate Dr LOTHAR HAGEN; Chair. of Third Senate Dr GERHARD MISLIK.
Oberster Gerichtshof (Supreme Court): 9490 Vaduz; Court of Third Instance; bench of 5 judges; Presiding Judge Dr GERT DELLE-KARTH.

ADMINISTRATIVE COURTS

Verwaltungsgerichtshof (Administrative Court of Appeal): Peter-Kaiser Pl. 1, 9490 Vaduz; tel. 2366111; appeal against decrees and decisions of the Government may be made to this court; 5 members; Presiding Judge Lic. Iur. ANDREAS BATLINER.
Staatsgerichtshof (State Court): Peter-Kaiser Pl. 1, Postfach 729, 9490 Vaduz; tel. 2391010; fax 2391039; e-mail kontakt@stgh.li; internet www.stgh.li; 5 members; exists for the protection of Public Law; Presiding Judge Lic. Iur. MARZELL BECK.

Religion

CHRISTIANITY

The Principality comprises a single archdiocese, Vaduz, created in 1997, which is directly responsible to the Holy See. At 31 December 2006 there were an estimated 26,800 adherents of the Roman Catholic Church (some 78.8% of the population). The few Protestants (7.3%) belong to the parish of Vaduz.

Archdiocese of Vaduz: Erzbischöfliche Kanzlei, Fürst-Franz-Josef-Str. 112, Postfach 103, 9490 Vaduz; tel. 2332311; fax 2332324; e-mail erzbistum@powersurf.li; internet www.erzbistum-vaduz.li; f. 1997; Archbishop Most Rev. WOLFGANG HAAS.

The Press

Exclusiv: Aubündt 28, 9490 Vaduz; tel. 2328080; fax 2328081; e-mail info@exclusiv.li; internet www.exclusiv.li; f. 1996; monthly; Publr ALBERT MENNEL.
Liechtensteiner Vaterland: Austr. 81, 9490 Vaduz; tel. 2361616; fax 2361617; e-mail redaktion@vaterland.li; internet www.vaterland.li; f. 1913; publ. by Vaduzer Medienhaus AG; daily (Mon.–Sat.); organ of the VU; Editor-in-Chief GÜNTHER FRITZ; circ. 10,295.
Liechtensteiner Volksblatt: Im alten Riet 103, 9494 Schaan; tel. 2375151; fax 2375155; e-mail redaktion@volksblatt.li; internet www.volksblatt.li; f. 1878; daily (Mon.–Sat.); organ of the FBP; Editor-in-Chief HEINZ ZÖCHBAUER; circ. 9,000.
Liewo Sonntagszeitung: Austr. 81, 9490 Vaduz; tel. 2361616; fax 2361617; e-mail redaktion@liewo.li; internet www.liewo.li; f. 1993 as *Liechtensteiner Wochenzeitung*; publ. by Vaduzer Medienhaus AG; weekly (Sun.); Editor-in-Chief MICHAEL WINKLER; circ. 32,000.
Wirtschaft Regional: Austr. 81, 9490 Vaduz; tel. 2361616; fax 2361617; e-mail info@wirtschaftregional.li; internet www.wirtschaftregional.li; f. 2001; publ. by Vaduzer Medienhaus AG; weekly; Editor-in-Chief MATTHIAS HASSLER.

PRESS AGENCY

Presse- und Informationsamt (PIA) (Press and Information Office): St Florinsgasse 3, Postfach 684, 9490 Vaduz; tel. 2366721; fax 2366460; e-mail info@pia.llv.li; internet www.pia.llv.li; f. 1962; Dir DANIELA CLAVADETSCHER.

Publishers

Alpenland Verlag AG: Feldkircher Str. 13, 9494 Schaan; tel. 2395030; fax 2395031; e-mail office@buchzentrum.li; internet www.buchzentrum.li; Man. Dir MARCO NESCHER.
BONAFIDES Verlags-Anstalt: Auring 52, 9490 Vaduz; tel. 2654680; fax 3900594; e-mail bva-fl@adon.li.
BVD Druck+Verlag AG: Landstr. 153, 9494 Schaan; tel. 2361836; fax 2361840; e-mail bvd@bvd.li; internet www.bvd.li; Pres. KURT GÖPPEL.
van Eck Verlag: Haldenweg 8, 9495 Triesen; tel. 3923000; fax 3922277; e-mail info@vaneckverlag.li; internet www.vaneckverlag

LIECHTENSTEIN

.li; f. 1982; art, local interest, juvenile, golf, crime fiction; Man. Dirs Frank P. van Eck, Peter Göppel.

Ex Jure Verlagsanstalt: Aeulestr. 74, Postfach 86, 9490 Vaduz; tel. 2360404; fax 2360481; e-mail service@exjure.li; internet www.exjure.net; f. 1968; legal.

A. R. Gantner Verlag KG: Industriestr. 26, Postfach 131, 9491 Ruggell; tel. 3771808; fax 3771802; e-mail bgc@adon.li; internet www.gantner-verlag.com; f. 1966; botany; Dir Bruni Gantner-Caplan.

GMG Verlag AG: Landstr. 30, 9494 Schaan; tel. 2381166; fax 2381160; e-mail verlag@gmg.biz; internet www.gmg.biz; f. 1990; Man. Dir Arthur Gassner.

Lehrmittelverlag: Pflugstr. 30, 9490 Vaduz; tel. 2366390; fax 2366391; e-mail lehrmittelverlag@schulen.li; educational materials.

Verlag der Liechtensteinischen Akademischen Gesellschaft (LAG): In der Fina 26, Postfach 829, 9494 Schaan; tel. 2323028; fax 2331449; e-mail info@verlag-lag.li; internet www.verlag-lag.li; f. 1972; Dir Norbert Jansen.

Liechtenstein-Verlag AG: Landstr. 30, 9494 Schaan; tel. 2396010; fax 2396019; e-mail books@liechtensteinverlag.com; internet www.liechtensteinverlag.com; f. 1946; belles-lettres, legal and scientific books; agents for international literature; Man. Arthur Gassner.

Litag Anstalt—Literarische, Medien und Künstler Agentur: Industriestr. 26A, Postfach 131, 9491 Ruggell; tel. 3771808; fax 3771802; e-mail bgc@adon.li; f. 1956; Dir Bruni Gantner-Caplan.

MM-Verlag Buchhandlung Irmgard Meier: Pradafant 20, 9490 Vaduz; tel. 2329448; fax 2329449; e-mail mm.verlag@buchhandlung.li.

Neue Verlagsanstalt: In der Fina 18, Postfach 29, 9494 Schaan; tel. 2334381; fax 2334382; e-mail info@neue-verlagsanstalt.li; magazine publisher; Dir Janine Hillert.

Sändig Reprint Verlag Wohlwend: Am Schrägen Weg 12, 9490 Vaduz; tel. 2323627; fax 2323649; e-mail saendig@adon.li; internet www.saendig.com; f. 1981; natural sciences, linguistics, freemasonry, fiction, folklore, music, history; Dir Christian Wohlwend.

Topos Verlag AG: Industriestr. 105, 9491 Ruggell; tel. 3771111; fax 3771119; e-mail topos@supra.net; internet www.topos.li; f. 1977; law, politics, literature, social science, periodicals; Dir Graham A. P. Smith.

Broadcasting and Communications

TELECOMMUNICATIONS

Regulatory Authority

Amt für Kommunikation: Kirchstr. 10, Postfach 684, 9490 Vaduz; tel. 2366488; fax 2366489; e-mail info@ak.llv.li; internet www.ak.llv.li; f. 1999; national regulatory authority; Dir Kurt Bühler.

Major Service Providers

Mobilkom Liechtenstein AG: Äulestras. 20, Postfach 1514, 9490 Vaduz; tel. 7970077; fax 7970099; internet www.mobilkom.li; f. 2000; subsidiary of Mobilkom Austria AG; mobile cellular telephone operator; Dir Michael Amman.

Telecom Liechtenstein AG: Schaanerstr. 1, 9490 Vaduz; tel. 2377400; fax 2377499; e-mail telecom@telecom.li; internet www.telecom.li; f. 1999; fixed-line and mobile cellular telecommunications, broadband internet access, digital television; Pres. Oliver Gerstgrasser.

BROADCASTING

Radio Liechtenstein: Dorfstr. 24, 9495 Triesen; tel. 3991313; fax 3991366; e-mail admin@radio.li; internet www.radio.li; f. 1995; Pres. Clemens Laternser; Editor-in-Chief Martin Frommelt.

Finance

(cap. = capital; res = reserves; dep. = deposits; m. = million; brs = branches; amounts in Swiss francs)

REGULATORY AUTHORITY

Finanzmarktaufsicht Liechtenstein (FMA) (Financial Market Authority of Liechtenstein): Landstr. 109, Postfach 279, 9490 Vaduz; tel. 2367373; fax 2367374; e-mail info@fma-li.li; internet www.fma-li.li; f. 2005; independent authority under the auspices of the Landtag; regulates banks and credit institutions, insurance cos and Liechtensteinische Post AG (Liechtenstein Postal Service); Pres. Michael Lauber; CEO Mario Gassner.

BANKING

In mid-2010 there were 14 banks in Liechtenstein.

Bank Alpinum AG: Städtle 17, 9490 Vaduz; tel. 2396211; fax 2396221; e-mail info@bankalpinum.com; internet www.bankalpinum.com; fmrly NewCenturyBank, renamed as above April 2006; Chair. Wolfgang Seeger; CEO Urban B. Eberle.

Bank von Ernst (Liechtenstein) AG: Egertastr. 10, Postfach 112, 9490 Vaduz; tel. 2655353; fax 2655363; e-mail info@bve.li; internet www.bve.li; wholly owned by EFG Bank (Switzerland); cap. 25m., res 26m., dep. 282m. (Dec. 2008); Chair. Jean-Pierre Cuoni; CEO Ernst Weder.

Bank Frick & Co. AG: Landstr. 14, Postfach 43, 9496 Balzers; tel. 3882121; fax 3882122; e-mail bank@bfc.li; internet www.bfc.li; Chair. Mario Frick, Sr; CEO Jürgen Frick.

Bank Vontobel (Liechtenstein) AG: Pflugstr. 20, Postfach 786, 9490 Vaduz; tel. 2364111; fax 2364112; e-mail postmaster@vontobel.li; internet www.vontobel.li; f. 2000; Chair. Dr Urs Widmer; CEO Herbert J. Scheidt.

Banque Pasche (Liechtenstein) SA: Austr. 61, Postfach 832, 9490 Vaduz; tel. 2393333; fax 2393300; e-mail pasche.liechtenstein@pasche.li; internet www.pasche.li; fmrly Swissfirst Bank (Liechtenstein) AG; 52.5% owned by Banque Pasche CM-CIC Private Banking (Switzerland); Chair. Jean-François Kurz; CEO Daniel Brühwiler.

Centrum Bank AG: Kirchstr. 3, Postfach 1168, 9490 Vaduz; tel. 2383838; fax 2383839; e-mail info@centrumbank.com; internet www.centrumbank.com; f. 1993; cap. 20m., res 194m., dep. 1,280m. (Dec. 2008); Chair. Dr Peter Marxer; CEO Stephan Häberle.

Kaiser Ritter Partner Privatbank AG: Herrengasse 23, 9490 Vaduz; tel. 2378000; fax 2378001; e-mail bank@serica.com; internet www.kaiserritterpartner.com; f. 1999; cap. 10m., res 35m., dep. 681m. (Dec. 2008); Chair. Dr Peter Ritter; CEO Dr Thomas Trauth.

LGT Bank in Liechtenstein Ltd (LGT): Herrengasse 12, Postfach 85, 9490 Vaduz; tel. 2351122; fax 2351522; e-mail info@lgt.com; internet www.lgt.com; f. 1920; present name adopted 1996; cap. 291m., res 3m., dep. 17,471m. (Dec. 2008); Group CEO HSH Prince Maximilian.

Liechtensteinische Landesbank AG (State Bank): Städtle 44, Postfach 384, 9490 Vaduz; tel. 2368811; fax 2368822; e-mail llb@llb.li; internet www.llb.li; f. 1861; present name adopted 1955; cap. 154m., res −192m., dep. 21,081m. (Dec. 2008); Chair., Bd of Dirs Dr Hans-Werner Gassner; Chair., Management Bd Dr Josef Fehr; 4 brs.

Neue Bank AG: Marktgass 20, Postfach 1533, 9490 Vaduz; tel. 2360808; fax 2329260; e-mail info@neuebankag.li; internet www.neuebankag.li; f. 1992; cap. 40m., res 42m., total assets 1,257m. (Dec. 2007); Chair. Georg Vogt.

Raiffeisen Bank (Liechtenstein) AG: Austr. 51, Postfach 1621, 9490 Vaduz; tel. 2370707; fax 2370777; e-mail info@raiffeisen.li; internet www.raiffeisen.li; f. 1998; total assets 252m. (Dec. 2006); Chair. Günther Dapunt.

Valartis Bank (Liechtenstein) AG: Schaaner Str. 27, 9487 Gamprin-Bendern; tel. 2655656; fax 2655699; e-mail info@valartis.li; internet www.valartis.li; f. 1998 as Hypo Investment Bank (Liechtenstein); renamed 2009 following takeover by Valartis Group AG; CEO, Management Bd Dr Andreas Insam.

Verwaltungs- und Privat-Bank AG (VP Bank): Aeulestr. 6, 9490 Vaduz; tel. 2356655; fax 2356500; e-mail info@vpbank.com; internet www.vpbank.com; f. 1956; cap. 59m., res 557m., dep. 9,110m. (Dec. 2009); Chair. Hans Brunhart; CEO Roger H. Hartmann; 9 brs.

Volksbank AG: Feldkircher Str. 2, 9494 Schaan; tel. 2390404; fax 2390405; e-mail info@volksbank.li; internet www.volksbank.li; f. 1997; Man. Dir Gerhard Lehner.

Bankers' Association

Liechtensteinischer Bankverband: Austr. 46, Postfach 254, 9490 Vaduz; tel. 2301323; fax 2301324; e-mail info@bankenverband.li; internet www.bankenverband.li; f. 1969; Pres. Adolf E. Real; Dir Michael Lauber; 14 mems.

INSURANCE

In early 2010 there were 40 insurance companies in Liechtenstein.

Fortuna Lebens-Versicherungs-AG: Städtle 35, 9490 Vaduz; tel. 2361545; fax 2361546; e-mail fl.service@fortuna.li; internet www.fortuna.li; f. 1996; Man. Dir Heiner Keil.

Liechtensteinische AHV-IV-FAK: Gerberweg 2, Postfach 84, 9490 Vaduz; tel. 2381616; fax 2381600; e-mail ahv@ahv.li; internet www.ahv.li; state-owned; Chair. Peter Wolff; Dir Walter Kaufmann.

Swisscom Re AG: Kirchstr. 12, 9490 Vaduz; tel. 2301665; fax 2301666; Man. Dirs Bernhard Lampert, Urs Luginbühl, Marcel von Vivis, Thomas Wittbjer.

LIECHTENSTEIN

Swiss Life (Liechtenstein) AG: In der Specki 3, 9494 Schaan; tel. 3777000; fax 3777099; e-mail office@swisslife.li; internet www.swisslife.li; absorbed CapitalLeben Versicherung AG in 2007; life insurance; Chair. BRUNO GEHRIG.

Transmarine Insurance Co Ltd: Egertastr. 17, 9490 Vaduz; tel. 2334488; fax 2334489; f. 1996.

Valorlife Lebensversicherungs-AG: Heiligkreuz 43, 9490 Vaduz; tel. 3992950; fax 3992959; e-mail info@valorlife.com; internet www.valorlife.com; f. 1997; subsidiary of Vaudoise Versicherungsgruppe (Switzerland); Pres. ROLF MEHR; Dir SERGE HEDIGER.

Insurance Association

Liechtensteinischer Versicherungsverband eV (LVV): Austr. 46, Postfach 445, 9490 Vaduz; tel. 2374777; fax 2374778; e-mail office@versicherungsverband.li; internet www.versicherungsverband.li; f. 1998; Pres. Dr PHILIPPE MOSER; 25 mems.

Trade and Industry

CHAMBER OF COMMERCE

Liechtensteinische Industrie- und Handelskammer (Liechtenstein Chamber of Commerce and Industry): Altenbach 8, 9490 Vaduz; tel. 2375511; fax 2375512; e-mail info@lihk.li; internet www.lihk.li; f. 1947; Pres. KLAUS RISCH; Gen. Man. JOSEF BECK; 40 mems.

INDUSTRIAL ASSOCIATION

Vereinigung Bäuerlicher Organisationen im Fürstentum Liechtenstein (VBO) (Agricultural Union): Duxweg 14, Postfach 351, 9494 Mauren; tel. 3759050; fax 3759051; e-mail vbo@kba.li; Pres. THOMAS BÜCHEL.

UTILITIES

Electricity

Liechtenstein imported some 91% of its electricity in 2009, mainly from Switzerland.

Liechtensteinische Kraftwerke (LKW): Im alten Riet 17, 9494 Schaan; tel. 2360111; fax 2360112; e-mail lkw@lkw.li; internet www.lkw.li; Pres. PATRIK OEHRI; Dir-Gen. GERALD MARXER.

Gas

Liechtensteinische Gasversorgung (LGV): Im Rietacker 4, 9494 Schaan; tel. 2361555; fax 2361566; e-mail lgv@lgv.li; internet www.lgv.li; f. 1985; Dir ROLAND RISCH.

Water

Wasserversorgung Liechtensteiner Unterland (WLU): Industriestr. 36, 9487 Gamprin-Bendern; tel. 3732555; fax 3735136; e-mail info@wlu.li; supplies water to Eschen, Gamprin, Mauren, Ruggell, and Schellenberg; Pres. DONATH OEHRI.

Gruppenwasserversorgung Liechtensteiner Oberland (GWO): supplies water to Balzers, Planken, Schaan, Triesen, Triesenberg and Vaduz.

TRADE UNIONS

Liechtensteinischer ArbeitnehmerInnenverband (LANV) (Employees' Asscn): Dorfstr. 24, 9495 Triesen; tel. 3993838; fax 3993839; e-mail info@lanv.li; internet www.lanv.li; Pres. SIGI LANGENBAHN; Sec. CHRISTINE SCHÄDLER; 1,200 mems.

Liechtensteinische Ingenieur- und Architektenvereinigung (Engineers' and Architects' Asscn): Postfach 323, 9490 Vaduz; tel. 3751728; fax 3751729; e-mail office@lia.li; internet www.lia.li; Pres. HANSJÖRG VOGT; 153 mems.

Wirtschaftskammer Liechtenstein: Zollstr. 23, 9494 Schaan; tel. 2377788; fax 2377789; e-mail info@wirtschaftskammer.li; internet www.wirtschaftskammer.li; f. 1936; aims to protect the interests of Liechtenstein artisans and tradespeople; Pres. MATT ARNOLD; Gen. Man. JÜRGEN NIGG; 3,000 mems.

Transport

RAILWAYS

Liechtenstein is traversed by some 18.5 km of railway track, which is administered by Austrian Federal Railways. There is a station at Nendeln, as well as two halts at Schaan and Schaanwald. A local service connects Feldkirch in Austria and Buchs in Switzerland via Liechtenstein, and the Arlberg Express (Paris, France, to Vienna, Austria) passes through the Principality.

ROADS

Modern roads connect the capital, Vaduz, with all the towns and villages in the Principality. There are approximately 250 km of roads, all of which are paved. The Rhine and Samina valleys are connected by a tunnel 740 m long. Public transport is provided by a well-developed network of postal buses.

Liechtenstein Bus Anstalt (LBA): Städtle 38, 9490 Vaduz; tel. 2366310; fax 2366311; e-mail info.lba@tba.llv.li; internet www.lba.li; operates 42 buses on 13 routes over 105 km; Man. Dir ULRICH FEISST.

INLAND WATERWAYS

A canal of 26 km, irrigating the Rhine valley, was opened in 1943.

Tourism

Liechtenstein has an Alpine setting in the Upper Rhine area. The principal tourist attractions include a renowned postal museum, a National Museum and the Liechtenstein State Art Collection at Vaduz, as well as the Prince's castle (although this is closed to the public) and two ruined medieval fortresses at Schellenberg. Annually about two-fifths of foreign tourists visit the winter sports resort at Malbun, in the south-east of the Principality. For summer visitors there are some 400 km of hiking trails and an extensive network of cycling paths. In 2009 the number of foreign guests staying in accommodation establishments was 66,507.

Liechtenstein Tourismus: Postfach 139, Städtle 37, 9490 Vaduz; tel. 2396300; fax 2396301; e-mail info@tourismus.li; internet www.tourismus.li; Dir ROLAND BÜCHEL.

Defence

Although Liechtensteiners under the age of 60 years are liable to military service in an emergency, there has been no standing army since 1868 and there is only a small police force, with some 83 officers.

Education

Pre-primary education starts at the age of four and continues till the age of six. It is not compulsory and is provided free of charge. Compulsory education begins at six years of age. Basic instruction is given for five years at a primary school (*Primarschule*) till the age of 11, after which a pupil may transfer to a lower secondary school (*Oberschule*) or secondary school (*Realschule*) for four years, with the option of an additional year, or to the grammar school (*Liechtensteinisches Gymnasium*) for eight years. In 2007/08, enrolment at pre-primary level included 76% of children in the relevant age-group, while enrolment at primary level included 90% of the children in the relevant age group. There is limited provision for tertiary education in Liechtenstein: a state-run university, the *Hochschule Liechtenstein*, which offers degrees in architecture and business sciences; the *Private Universität im Fürstentum Liechtenstein* (Private University of the Principality of Liechtenstein), which runs courses in sciences and jurisprudence; a private institution, the *Liechtenstein-Institut*, a research and academic teaching centre; and the private International Academy of Philosophy. Many Liechtensteiners continue their studies at universities in Austria and Switzerland. Liechtenstein also has a music school, an art school, an adult education centre and a school for mentally disabled children. Government expenditure on education totalled 160.4m. Swiss francs in 2009 (15.1% of total expenditure).

LITHUANIA

Introductory Survey

LOCATION, CLIMATE, LANGUAGE, RELIGION, FLAG, CAPITAL

The Republic of Lithuania (formerly the Lithuanian Soviet Socialist Republic) is situated on the eastern coast of the Baltic Sea, in north-eastern Europe. It is bounded by Latvia to the north, by Belarus to the south-east, by Poland to the south-west and by the Russian exclave, Kaliningrad Oblast, to the west. Lithuania's maritime position moderates an otherwise continental-type climate. Temperatures range from an average of −4.9°C (23.2°F) in January to a July mean of 17.0°C (62.6°F). Rainfall levels vary considerably from region to region: in the far west the annual average is 700 mm–850 mm (28 ins–33 ins), but in the central plain it is about 600 mm (24 ins). The official language is Lithuanian. The predominant religion is Christianity. Most ethnic Lithuanians are Roman Catholics by belief or tradition, but there are small communities of Lutherans and Calvinists, as well as a growing number of modern Protestant denominations. Adherents of Russian Orthodoxy are almost exclusively ethnic Slavs, while most Tatars have retained an adherence to Islam. The national flag (proportions 3 by 5) consists of three equal horizontal stripes of yellow (top), green and red (bottom). The capital is Vilnius.

CONTEMPORARY POLITICAL HISTORY

Historical Context

Prior to annexation by the Russian Empire in 1795, Lithuania was united in a Commonwealth with Poland. In 1915, after the outbreak of the First World War, it was occupied by German troops. A 'Lithuanian Conference' was convened in September 1917, which demanded the re-establishment of an independent Lithuanian state and elected a 'Lithuanian Council', headed by Antanas Smetona; it proceeded to declare independence on 16 February 1918. The new state survived both a Soviet attempt to create a Lithuanian-Belarusian Soviet republic and a Polish campaign aimed at reincorporating Lithuania. In October 1920 Poland annexed the region of Vilnius, but was forced to recognize the rest of Lithuania as an independent state (with its provisional capital at Kaunas). Soviet Russia had recognized Lithuanian independence in the Treaty of Moscow, signed in July. Lithuania's first Constitution, which declared Lithuania a parliamentary democracy, was adopted in August 1922. In December 1926 Smetona seized power in a military coup and established an authoritarian regime, which endured until 1940.

According to the 'Secret Protocols' to the Treaty of Non-Aggression (the Molotov-Ribbentrop Pact), signed on 23 August 1939 by the USSR and Germany, Lithuania was to be part of the German sphere of influence. However, the Nazi-Soviet Treaty on Friendship and Existing Borders, agreed in September (following the outbreak of the Second World War), permitted the USSR to take control of Lithuania. In October Lithuania was compelled to agree to the stationing of 20,000 Soviet troops on its territory. In return, the USSR granted the city and region of Vilnius (which had been seized by Soviet troops in September) to Lithuania. In June 1940 the USSR dispatched a further 100,000 troops to Lithuania and forced the Lithuanian Government to resign. A Soviet-approved People's Government was formed. Elections to a People's Seim (parliament), which only pro-Soviet candidates were permitted to contest, took place in July. The Seim proclaimed the Lithuanian Soviet Socialist Republic on 21 July, and on 3 August Lithuania formally became a Union Republic of the USSR. The establishment of Soviet rule was followed by the arrest and imprisonment of many Lithuanian politicians and government officials.

Some 210,000 people, mainly Jews, were killed during the Nazi occupation of Lithuania (1941–44). The return of the Soviet Army, in 1944, was not welcomed by most Lithuanians, and anti-Soviet partisan warfare continued until 1952. Lithuanian agriculture was forcibly collectivized and rapid industrialization was implemented. Meanwhile, some 150,000 people were deported, many to Kazakhstan or to Russian Siberia and the Far East, and leaders and members of the Roman Catholic Church were persecuted and imprisoned. Lithuanian political parties were disbanded, and political power became the exclusive preserve of the Communist Party of Lithuania (CPL), the local branch of the Communist Party of the Soviet Union (CPSU). The leader (First Secretary) of the CPL in 1940–74 was Antanas Sniečkus.

A significant dissident movement was established during the 1960s and 1970s. With the introduction of the policy of glasnost (openness) by the Soviet leader, Mikhail Gorbachev, in the mid-1980s, a limited discussion of previously censored aspects of Lithuanian history appeared in the press. Dissident groups took advantage of a more tolerant attitude to political protests, organizing a demonstration in August 1987 to denounce the Nazi-Soviet Pact. However, in February 1988 security forces were deployed to prevent the public celebration of the 70th anniversary of Lithuanian independence. This, together with frustration among the intelligentsia at the slow pace of reform in the republic, led to the establishment in June of the Lithuanian Movement for Reconstruction (Sąjūdis). Sąjūdis organized mass demonstrations to protest against environmental pollution, the suppression of national culture and 'russification', and to condemn the signing of the Molotov-Ribbentrop Pact. The movement appealed to the CPL to support a declaration of independence and the recognition of Lithuanian as the state language. The latter demand was adopted by the Lithuanian Supreme Soviet (Supreme Council—legislature) in November, and traditional Lithuanian state symbols were restored. Other concessions made by the CPL during 1988 included the restoration of Independence Day as a public holiday and the return of buildings to the Roman Catholic Church.

Sąjūdis won 36 of the 42 popularly elected Lithuanian seats at elections to the all-Union Congress of People's Deputies in March 1989. Thereafter, the CPL began to adopt a more radical position, in an attempt to retain some measure of popular support. On 18 May the CPL-dominated Supreme Soviet approved a declaration of Lithuanian sovereignty, which asserted the supremacy of Lithuania's laws over all-Union legislation. Public debate concerning the legitimacy of Soviet rule in Lithuania intensified: a commission of the Lithuanian Supreme Soviet declared the establishment of Soviet power in 1940 to have been unconstitutional, and, in August, on the 50th anniversary of the signing of the Pact with Nazi Germany, more than 1m. people participated in a 'human chain' extending from Tallinn in Estonia, through Latvia, to Vilnius.

Despite denunciations of Baltic nationalism by the all-Union authorities, the Lithuanian Supreme Soviet continued to adopt reformist legislation, including the establishment of freedom of religion and the legalization of a multi-party system. In December 1989 the CPL declared itself an independent party, no longer subordinate to the CPSU, adopting a new programme and declaring support for multi-party democracy and independent statehood. Shortly afterwards a group of former CPL members who were opposed to independence formed a separate movement, the Lithuanian Communist Party on the CPSU Platform (LCP). Meanwhile, Algirdas Brazauskas, First Secretary of the CPL since October 1988, was elected Chairman of the Presidium of the Lithuanian Supreme Soviet, defeating three other candidates, including Romualdas Ozolas, a leading member of Sąjūdis. None the less, Sąjūdis remained the dominant political force in the republic, and its supporters won an overall majority in the elections to the Lithuanian Supreme Soviet in February–March 1990. This new, pro-independence parliament elected Vytautas Landsbergis, the Chairman of Sąjūdis, to replace Brazauskas as its Chairman (de facto President of Lithuania), and on 11 March declared the restoration of Lithuanian independence: Lithuania thus became the first of the Soviet republics to make such a declaration. The Supreme Council also restored the pre-1940 name of the country (the Republic of Lithuania) and suspended the USSR Constitution on Lithuanian territory. Kazimiera Danutė Prunskienė, a member of the CPL and hitherto a Deputy Chairman of the Council of Ministers, was appointed to be the first Prime Minister of the restored republic.

LITHUANIA

Domestic Political Affairs

The Lithuanian declarations were condemned by a special session of the all-Union Congress of People's Deputies as unconstitutional, and Soviet forces occupied CPL buildings in Vilnius. An economic embargo was imposed on Lithuania in April 1990, and vital fuel supplies were suspended; the embargo remained in force for more than two months, until Lithuania agreed to a six-month moratorium on the independence declaration, pending formal negotiations. However, talks, which began in August, were soon terminated by the Soviet Government, and in January 1991 Landsbergis revoked the suspension of the declaration of independence, since negotiations on Lithuania's status had not resumed. Tension increased in the republic when the Soviet authorities dispatched to Vilnius troops (led by the special OMON units of the Soviet Ministry of Internal Affairs), who occupied former CPSU properties that had been nationalized by the Lithuanian Government. Landsbergis mobilized popular support to help to defend the parliament building, which he believed to be under threat. In mid-January 13 people were killed and about 500 injured, when Soviet troops seized the broadcasting centre in Vilnius. (In August 1999 six former officers of the LCP were convicted of complicity in attempts to overthrow the Lithuanian Government in January 1991, and sentenced to between three and 12 years' imprisonment.)

The consolidation of independent statehood

Meanwhile, policy differences had arisen within the Lithuanian leadership, and earlier in January 1991 Prunskienė and her Council of Ministers had resigned after the Supreme Council refused to sanction proposed price increases. Gediminas Vagnorius, a member of the Supreme Council, was appointed Prime Minister. At a referendum on 9 February, 90.5% of voters expressed support for the re-establishment of an independent Lithuania and for the withdrawal of the Soviet army from the republic. In common with five other Soviet republics, Lithuania refused to conduct the all-Union referendum on the future of the USSR, which was held in March. (Voting did take place unofficially in predominantly Russian- and Polish-populated areas of Lithuania, where the majority endorsed the preservation of the USSR.)

A series of attacks by OMON forces on members of the nascent Lithuanian defence force and on the customs posts on the border with Belarus, combined with the seizure of power in Moscow, the Russian and Soviet capital, by the conservative communist 'State Committee for the State of Emergency' (SCSE) in August 1991, led to fears in Lithuania that there would be a renewed attempt to overthrow the Landsbergis administration and reimpose Soviet rule. Soviet military vehicles entered Vilnius, but did not prevent the convening of an emergency session of the Supreme Council, which condemned the SCSE and issued a statement supporting Boris Yeltsin, President of the Russian Federation. As the coup collapsed, the Lithuanian Government ordered the withdrawal of Soviet forces from the republic and banned the LCP. (The successor party to the CPL, the Lithuanian Democratic Labour Party—LDLP, was not banned.) The Government also began to assume effective control of the country's borders. The failed coup prompted the recognition of Lithuanian independence by other states, and on 6 September the USSR State Council recognized the independence of Lithuania and the other Baltic republics (Estonia and Latvia), all three of which were admitted to the UN and the Conference on (now Organization for) Security and Co-operation in Europe (OSCE, see p. 385) later in the month.

During the first half of 1992 there was an increasing polarity within the Supreme Council between Sąjūdis deputies and those of the mainly left-wing opposition parties, most prominently the LDLP, led by Brazauskas. In April 10 members of the Council of Ministers criticized Vagnorius's 'dictatorial' methods, and two ministers subsequently resigned. Vagnorius tendered his resignation as Prime Minister in May, but remained in the post until July, when the legislature approved a motion of no confidence in his leadership. The Seimas (Parliament—as the Supreme Council had been renamed) appointed Aleksandras Abišala, a close associate of Landsbergis, as Prime Minister; a new Council of Ministers was named shortly afterwards. Meanwhile, the growing division within the legislature had led to a boycott by pro-Sąjūdis deputies, rendering it frequently inquorate. In July, however, the Seimas approved a new electoral law, whereby Lithuania's first post-Soviet legislative elections, scheduled for late 1992, would be held under a mixed system of majority voting (for 71 seats) and proportional representation on the basis of party lists (70 seats).

The LDLP emerged as the leading party in the elections to the Seimas, which took place on 25 October and 15 November 1992, winning 73 of the 141 seats. The defeat of Sąjūdis (which, in alliance with the Citizens' Charter of Lithuania, secured 30 seats) was largely attributed to popular disenchantment with its management of economic reform. The Christian Democratic Party of Lithuania (CDPL), which was closely aligned with Sąjūdis, won 16 seats. Also on 25 October a referendum approved a new Constitution, which was adopted by the Seimas on 6 November. Pending an election to the new post of President of the Republic, Brazauskas was elected by the Seimas to be its Chairman and acting Head of State. In December Brazauskas appointed Bronislovas Lubys (hitherto a Deputy Prime Minister) as Prime Minister. Lubys formed a new coalition Council of Ministers, including only three representatives of the LDLP.

The presidential election on 14 February 1993 was won by Brazauskas, with some 60% of the votes cast. His only rival was Stasys Lozoraitis, Lithuania's ambassador to the USA. Brazauskas subsequently resigned from the LDLP. Adolfas Sleževičius replaced Lubys as Prime Minister in March, and was appointed Chairman of the LDLP in April. In May a new political organization, the Conservative Party of Lithuania (CP), also known as the Homeland Union (Lithuanian Conservatives), was formed. Mainly comprising former members of Sąjūdis, and chaired by Landsbergis, the CP rapidly established itself as the principal opposition party.

The Minister of the Economy resigned in October 1995, following the collapse of several small commercial banks and in view of the slow progress achieved in the privatization programme. In November the Government survived its second vote of no confidence, initiated by the conservative opposition, which accused the LDLP of economic mismanagement. The banking crisis culminated in December with the suspension of the operations of the country's two largest commercial banks, owing to insolvency. In January 1996 it was revealed that Sleževičius had withdrawn funds from the Lithuanian Joint Stock Innovation Bank (LJIB) only two days before the bank's suspension. Later in January Romasis Vaitekūnas, who had also withdrawn funds from the LJIB before its closure, resigned as Minister of the Interior, following public criticism of his handling of the crisis. Kazys Ratkevičius, the Chairman of the Bank of Lithuania (the central bank), also resigned. Sleževičius initially disregarded a presidential decree that he should leave office, which was upheld by the Seimas in February. He was replaced as Prime Minister by Laurynas Mindaugas Stankevičius, hitherto Minister of Government Reforms and Local Governments. Sleževičius also resigned as Chairman of the LDLP, and was succeeded by Česlovas Juršėnas, the Chairman of the Seimas.

A general election took place in two rounds on 20 October and 10 November 1996. The results confirmed the substantial loss of popular support for the LDLP, which retained only 12 seats in the Seimas. The CP obtained 70 seats, and the CDPL 16. The right-wing Lithuanian Centre Union won 13 seats and the Lithuanian Social Democratic Party (LSDP) 12. Some 53% of eligible voters participated in the first round, and about 40% took part in the second. Following the election, a coalition agreement was signed by the leaders of the CP and the CDPL. Landsbergis was elected Chairman of the Seimas in late November, and shortly afterwards the Seimas approved the appointment of Vagnorius as Prime Minister. His Government was dominated by members of the CP, with three representatives of the CDPL and two of the Centre Union. In January 1997 the Minister of Finance, Rolandas Matiliauskas, resigned, amid allegations of financial impropriety.

Valdas Adamkus elected as President

In the first round of voting in the presidential election held on 21 December 1997, none of the seven candidates won an overall majority of votes. In a second round on 4 January 1998, the second-placed candidate after the first round, Valdas Adamkus (a former environmental protection executive, who had been naturalized in the USA), narrowly defeated Artūras Paulauskas (a prominent lawyer and deputy Prosecutor-General, supported by the Lithuanian Liberal Union), with 50.4% of the votes. In April Paulauskas announced the formation of a new, centre-left political party, the New Union (Social Liberals—NU).

A serious conflict of interests between President Adamkus and Vagnorius intensified in April 1999, following the President's criticism of the Government's efforts to combat corruption in the public sector. Vagnorius secured the confidence of the Seimas in

LITHUANIA

a non-binding vote, but at the end of the month he announced his intention to resign. In mid-May Adamkus invited the Mayor of Vilnius, Rolandas Paksas (a member of the CP), to form a new government. His Council of Ministers, announced at the beginning of June, was again formed from a coalition led by the CP and the CDPL. In October Paksas indicated that he would not endorse an agreement to sell a one-third stake in the state-owned Mažeikiai Nafta petroleum refinery to a US oil company, Williams International, under the terms of which Lithuania would be required to provide long-term financing equivalent to more than twice the price paid by the US company, in order to offset the refinery's debts. None the less, the Council of Ministers endorsed the sale, which was strongly supported by Adamkus and the majority of the CP, prompting the resignations of the Ministers of National Economy and of Finance, and, in late October, of Paksas.

At the end of October 1999 Adamkus nominated Andrius Kubilius, the First Deputy Chairman of the Seimas, as Prime Minister. Kubilius's Council of Ministers, approved by the legislature in November, retained largely the same membership as the previous administration. Following the appointment of the new Government, the Lithuanian Centre Union announced that it was to become an opposition party, its leader, Ozolas, having resigned as a Deputy Chairman of the Seimas after criticizing Landsbergis (who chaired both the CP and the legislature). Paksas resigned from the CP in November, and was elected Chairman of the Lithuanian Liberal Union in December. Local elections in March 2000 resulted in considerable successes for parties of the left, most notably the NU. A lack of support for the CP apparently precipitated a split in the party, as several deputies established a 'moderate' faction in the Seimas, thus depriving the CP-CDPL coalition of an automatic majority in the legislature. In May the country's two largest left-wing parties, the LSDP and the LDLP, agreed to contest forthcoming legislative elections in alliance. The New Democracy Party and the Lithuanian Russians' Union subsequently joined the alliance, named the A. Brazauskas Social Democratic Coalition, after the former President, who had been elected Honorary Chairman.

Some 56.2% of eligible voters participated in legislative elections held on 8 October 2000, at which the CP won only nine seats (compared with 70 in 1996). The A. Brazauskas Social Democratic Coalition obtained the largest representation, with 51 seats. However, the Lithuanian Liberal Union (with 34 seats) and the NU (with 29), which had formed an informal alliance prior to the elections, subsequently signed a coalition agreement and were able to form a parliamentary majority with partners that included the Lithuanian Centre Union and the Modern Christian-Democratic Union. The new Council of Ministers, headed by Paksas, was approved in October; Paulauskas was elected Chairman of the Seimas. However, in subsequent months a number of ministers resigned from the cabinet, including the Minister of the Economy. The LDLP merged with the LSDP at a joint congress held in January 2001; the LSDP thereby became the largest single party in the Seimas, and Brazauskas was elected its Chairman. Further political consolidation took place in May, when the CDPL merged with the Christian Democratic Union to form the Lithuanian Christian Democrats (LCD).

In mid-June 2001 the six NU members of the Council of Ministers resigned their portfolios, following disagreements with the Lithuanian Liberal Union over privatization of the energy sector and economic reform, and criticism of the Prime Minister. Paksas was subsequently unable to form an alternative coalition government and resigned on 20 June. The NU sought a new alliance with the LSDP, and at the end of the month President Adamkus offered the post of Prime Minister to Brazauskas, who was confirmed on 3 July. The LSDP agreed to an informal accord, which granted the NU the same six ministerial positions from which it had withdrawn in June. In September Paksas resigned as Chairman of the Lithuanian Liberal Union, in compliance with intra-party demands; he was replaced by Gentvilas. In December Paksas and 10 other deputies left the parliamentary faction of the Lithuanian Liberal Union, owing, in part, to its failure to nominate Paksas as First Deputy Chairman of the Seimas; they were formally expelled from the party in January 2002, and founded the rightist Liberal Democratic Party (LDP) in March, with Paksas as its Chairman.

The results of the first round of voting in the presidential election, held on 22 December 2002, were inconclusive. In a second round, on 5 January 2003, Paksas obtained 54.7% of the votes cast, defeating Adamkus. Paksas was inaugurated as President on 26 February. In March Brazauskas was reappointed as Prime Minister; his Council of Ministers was substantially unchanged. Following the presidential election, Paksas resigned as Chairman of the LDP; Valentinas Mazuronis was elected as his successor. In May Kubilius was elected as Chairman of the CP, in succession to Landsbergis. In the same month the Lithuanian Centre Union, the Lithuanian Liberal Union and the Modern Christian-Democratic Union merged to form the Lithuanian Liberal and Centre Union, with Artūras Zuokas as Chairman. In June a faction of the Lithuanian Centre Union that did not support the merger founded the National Centre Party, and elected Ozolas its Chairman. In February 2004 the CP merged with the Lithuanian Union of Political Prisoners and Deportees to form the Homeland Union—Conservatives, Political Prisoners and Deportees, Christian Democrats (HU).

The impeachment of President Rolandas Paksas

Meanwhile, following the nomination by President Paksas of a new Director-General of the State Security Department, in October 2003 a classified departmental report was disclosed, which claimed to provide evidence of links between the presidential adviser on national security, Remigijus Acas, and Yurii Borisov, an ethnic Russian with alleged connections with organized crime groups, who had contributed significant funds to Paksas's presidential election campaign. It was revealed that in April Paksas had signed a presidential decree permitting Borisov to hold dual citizenship, despite warnings from the State Security Department that he was suspected of involvement in the illegal trading of weapons. In November an emergency session of the Seimas established a special parliamentary commission to investigate Paksas's alleged links with Russian organized crime and the associated threat to national security, and the Prosecutor-General launched a criminal investigation into Borisov. Paksas subsequently dismissed a number of his senior advisers, but refused to appear before the commission. In December the Seimas approved the commission's conclusion that the President's conduct had jeopardized national security, and the following day both Brazauskas and Paulauskas appealed for the President's resignation. On 18 December the Seimas approved a draft resolution to initiate impeachment proceedings against Paksas, and an investigative commission was subsequently established to consider the charges.

On 18 February 2004 the investigative commission endorsed six charges, which were to form the basis for the impeachment of the President: that Paksas represented a threat to national security; that he had failed to protect classified information; that he had attempted illegally to influence the operations of private companies; that he was unable to reconcile his public and private interests; that he had hindered the operations of state institutions; and that he had failed to prevent his advisers from abusing their positions. On the following day the Seimas voted to initiate formal impeachment proceedings and, in the mean time, agreed to seek a ruling from the Constitutional Court as to whether the charges constituted a breach of the Constitution. Paksas continued to deny the charges, and in late February he demanded that the Seimas initiate impeachment proceedings against the parliamentary Chairman, Paulauskas, whom he accused of the unauthorized disclosure of the confidential report that had been made public in October 2003 (the request was rejected, on the grounds that the Constitution provided only for the impeachment of deputies, and not of the parliamentary Chairman). On 31 March 2004 the Constitutional Court ruled that the President had severely violated the Constitution by: granting Borisov dual citizenship in exchange for financial support; failing to protect state secrets; and using his presidential office illegally to influence the actions of a company's shareholders. The ruling was followed by a parliamentary vote on Paksas's impeachment, which took place on 6 April. Paksas was removed from office, after the necessary three-fifths' majority in the Seimas supported impeachment on the three charges confirmed by the Constitutional Court. Paulauskas immediately assumed the presidency, in an acting capacity, pending a presidential election, and subsequently suspended his membership of the NU, in compliance with the Constitution. In May the Constitutional Court ruled that legislation recently approved by the Seimas, preventing an impeached head of state from seeking presidential office again, was in accordance with the Constitution, and Paksas was obliged to withdraw his candidacy from the forthcoming presidential election.

The first round of the presidential election, held on 13 June 2004 and contested by five candidates, proved inconclusive. In the second round, held on 27 June, Adamkus was narrowly elected to the presidency, receiving 52.6% of the votes cast, defeating Prunskienė. Meanwhile, Lithuania's first elections to the European Parliament, following the accession of the country to full membership of the European Union (EU, see p. 270) on 1 May (see below), were held concurrently with the first round of presidential voting, with the participation of 46% of the electorate. The recently founded Labour Party (LP), headed by a controversial, ethnically Russian business executive, Viktor Uspaskich, won five of the 13 mandates allocated to Lithuania; the governing LSDP, the Lithuanian Liberal and Centre Union and the HU each obtained two seats, while the LDP and the Peasants' and New Democracy Union (PNDU—led by Prunskienė) each won one seat. Adamkus was inaugurated on 12 July, and on the following day the Seimas approved his nomination of Brazauskas as Prime Minister.

Elections to the Seimas, held in two rounds on 10 and 24 October 2004, demonstrated that the LP had further consolidated its support. It became the largest single party in the Seimas, receiving 28.4% of the votes cast on the basis of party lists, and obtaining 39 of the 141 elective seats. A coalition of the LSDP and the NU, known as Working for Lithuania, received 20.7% of the votes cast on the basis of party lists, and 31 seats. The HU obtained 25 seats, and the Liberal and Centre Union 18. The Order and Justice coalition, comprising the LDP and the Lithuanian People's Union for a Free Lithuania, received 11 seats, while the PNDU obtained 10.

In October 2004 the Vilnius District Court effectively cleared Paksas of disclosing state secrets by ruling that there was no indisputable evidence that Borisov had learned from Paksas that his telephones were being monitored by the State Security Department. (However, this decision was overturned by the Court of Appeal in March 2005, when Paksas was ordered to pay a fine of 9,735 litai.) In December 2004 a congress of the LDP re-elected Paksas as the party's Chairman.

The Seimas approved a coalition Government of the LP, the LSDP, the NU and the PNDU in December 2004. Brazauskas remained Prime Minister, while several prominent members of the LSDP and the NU also retained the posts they had held in the outgoing administration. In April 2005 Algirdas Butkevičius resigned as Minister of Finance, after the governing coalition rejected a proposed tax reform programme. He was replaced by Zigmantas Balčytis, hitherto the Minister of Transport, in May. In December the Supreme Court ruled that Paksas was not guilty of divulging confidential state information, while Borisov was granted permission to remain resident in Lithuania.

In April 2006 Paulauskas, the Chairman of the NU, was removed from his position as parliamentary speaker, following a secret ballot in the Seimas, amid accusations that he had been aware of a scandal involving the unauthorized use of official vehicles by government employees. The NU immediately withdrew from the governing coalition. The remaining coalition members, the LSDP, the LP and the PNDU, signed a new agreement on the following day, and Viktoras Muntianas of the LP was subsequently elected as the new Chairman of the Seimas. At the end of April Paulauskas was re-elected as Chairman of the NU, which in early May declared itself to be in opposition to the Government.

The Government of Gediminas Kirkilas

In early May 2006 seven LP deputies renounced their party membership and defected to the newly reconstituted Civil Democracy Party (formerly the Citizens' Union), citing dissatisfaction with the LP leadership, in particular its Chairman, Uspaskich. The ruling coalition's number of seats in the 141-member Seimas was thereby reduced to just 62. Uspaskich, the subject of ongoing corruption allegations, tendered his resignation as party Chairman later that month. At the end of May the LP withdrew from the ruling coalition, effectively forcing the resignation of Prime Minister Brazauskas and of the Council of Ministers. Minister of Finance Balčytis was appointed Prime Minister in an acting capacity, but in July the Seimas approved the nomination of Gediminas Kirkilas, Vice-Chairman of the LSDP, as premier. The new Council of Ministers comprised six members of the LSDP, three members of the Lithuanian Peasant Nationalists' Union (LPNU), and two members each of the Civil Democracy Party and of the Liberal and Centre Union. Balčytis retained the finance portfolio, while Petras Vaitiekūnas of the LPNU was appointed Minister of Foreign Affairs.

Kęstutis Dauksys was elected Chairman of the LP in August 2006. Uspaskich, meanwhile, had fled to Russia, but was detained there in September, following the issuing of a European warrant for his arrest by the Lithuanian Office of the Prosecutor-General; he was subsequently released without charge. In January 2007 it was reported that Uspaskich had registered as an LP candidate to contest the municipal elections scheduled to take place in February (see below).

From August 2006 pressure mounted on Balčytis to resign from the Council of Ministers, amid claims that his son had abused office while an employee of the Lithuanian Business Support Agency, which was responsible for the distribution of EU funding. In the event Balčytis announced his resignation one day after his son was cleared of the charges against him.

The rate of participation at the municipal elections held on 25 February 2007 failed to exceed 40% of the electorate. The HU was placed first, with 17.1% of the votes cast, while the LSDP came a close second, with 16.3%; the LP ranked sixth, with 6.4% of the ballot. Uspaskich and Paksas won seats in Kedainiai and Vilnius, respectively. In May Prime Minister Kirkilas was elected Chairman of the LSDP, following the resignation of the incumbent, Brazauskas. Uspaskich returned to Lithuania from Russia in September, and was subsequently placed under house arrest. Having failed in an attempt to secure a seat in the Seimas at a by-election in October (losing to the HU candidate), Uspaskich was re-elected Chairman of the LP in November; he was released on bail in April 2008.

In November 2007 the Minister of the Interior and the head of the police service resigned, after a police official under the influence of alcohol fatally injured three children in an automobile accident. In January 2008 an agreement was signed on the expansion of the ruling coalition to include the NU, thereby giving it a majority in the Seimas, with 73 seats. Later that month NU Chairman Paulauskas joined the Government as Minister of the Environment; representatives of the NU were also offered posts at the head of parliamentary commissions.

In February 2008 the Seimas approved a controversial agreement signed between the Government and a private investor, NDX Energija, on the establishment of the Lithuanian Electricity Organization (LEO LT), which was to be responsible for projects in the energy sector, including the construction of a new nuclear power plant. Kirkilas narrowly survived a motion of no confidence in the Seimas in April, with the support of 68 deputies; the Prime Minister's removal from office had been favoured by 63 deputies, many of whom were opposed to the creation of LEO LT.

Česlovas Juršėnas of the LSDP was elected Chairman of the Seimas at the beginning of April 2008, following the resignation of Muntianas in response to media allegations of corruption. Also in early April the Minister of Education and Science, Roma Žakaitienė, tendered her resignation, following a series of strikes by teachers; she was replaced by Algirdas Monkevičius of the NU, a previous incumbent of the post, in late May. The HU merged with the LCD in May, to form the HU—LCD. Also that month a new political organization, the National Revival Party (NRP), was established by television presenter Arūnas Valinskas.

The HU—LCD became the largest party in the Seimas as a result of legislative elections held in two rounds on 12 and 26 October 2008, winning 19.7% of the votes cast on the basis of party lists and a total of 45 of the 141 seats. In second place, with a total of 25 seats, was Prime Minister Kirkilas's LSDP (which received 11.7% of the votes cast on the basis of party lists), followed by the NRP, with 16 seats, and the Order and Justice Party, with 15. The Liberal Movement of the Republic of Lithuania (which had been formed by a splinter group of the Liberal and Centre Union in 2006) secured 11 seats, while a coalition of the LP and the Youth party took 10, and the Liberal and Centre Union itself won eight; three other parties and four independents also obtained representation. In late October President Adamkus invited the Chairman of the HU—LCD, Andrius Kubilius, to form a government. The poor performance of the parties in the outgoing administration was attributed, in part, to a recent downturn in the economy, particularly a sharp rise in consumer prices (the inflation rate having reached 12.1% in the second quarter of the year). The rate of participation by the electorate was 48.6% in the first round, reportedly declining to 32.4% in the second. Uspaskich secured one of the LP's seats in the Seimas, gaining immunity from prosecution, but in December the legislature voted to remove his immunity, as well as that of two other deputies who were standing trial at the time of their election. Arūnas Valinskas, the leader of the NRP, was elected as Chairman of the Seimas in mid-November.

In late November 2008 the Seimas approved the nomination of Kubilius as Prime Minister, to head a four-party coalition Gov-

LITHUANIA

ernment controlling 80 seats in the Seimas. The new Council of Ministers, which took office in December, comprised six members of the HU—LCD, three members of the Liberal Movement of the Republic of Lithuania, two members each of the Liberal and Centre Union and of the NRP, and one independent. The HU—LCD assumed responsibility for the economy, finance and national defence portfolios, while Vygaudas Ušackas, hitherto ambassador to the United Kingdom, was appointed Minister of Foreign Affairs. Addressing the country's economic difficulties was identified as the Government's main priority by Kubilius, who proposed to reform the taxation system, to restructure public finances and to reduce levels of corruption. However, the introduction of austerity measures in January 2009 (see Economic Affairs) aroused public discontent, and a protest organized that month by trade union leaders in Vilnius became violent, with police reportedly forcibly dispersing demonstrators. In February Arvydas Sekmokas was appointed to the newly created post of Minister of Energy. In the following month the Constitutional Court ruled that legislation providing for the establishment of LEO LT violated the Constitution. The Government pledged to restructure LEO LT, but in December an agreement allowing the liquidation of the company was signed with NDX Energija.

The presidency of Dalia Grybauskaitė

Dalia Grybauskaitė, hitherto European Commissioner responsible for Financial Programming and the Budget, was elected as President of Lithuania in a first round of voting on 17 May 2009, receiving 69.1% of the valid votes cast. Her nearest rival among the six other candidates, with 11.8%, was Algirdas Butkevičius, who had succeeded Kirkilas as Chairman of the LSDP. A rate of electoral participation of 51.7% was recorded. Grybauskaitė's victory was attributed to her political independence and, amid increasing concern regarding the continued deterioration in economic conditions, to her financial experience. She took office on 12 July. Two government changes were effected in that month: Ingrida Simonytė was appointed as Minister of Finance, succeeding Algirdas Gediminas Šemeta, who had become Lithuania's representative at the European Commission, while Rimantas Jonas Dagys was replaced as Minister of Social Security and Labour by Donatas Jankauskas.

Meanwhile, elections to the European Parliament were conducted on 7 June 2009, with the participation of only 21.0% of the electorate. Of the 12 seats allocated to Lithuania, the HU—LCD won four (increasing its representation two-fold), the LSDP three and the Order and Justice Party two, while the LP (which had previously held five seats), Lithuanian Polish Electoral Action and the Liberal Movement of the Republic of Lithuania each obtained one seat.

The Seimas voted to dismiss Valinskas as its Chairman in September 2009 in response to allegations that he had links to an organized crime group. The claims, which Valinskas denied, had been made by Aleksandras Sacharukas, a former party colleague who had been excluded from the NRP in July, together with three other NRP deputies. Irena Degutienė, of the HU—LCD, was elected to chair the Seimas. In October, following several months of negotiations, the Government signed an agreement with trade unions and business associations on reductions in salaries and social security benefits.

The Minister of Foreign Affairs, Vygaudas Ušackas, resigned in January 2010. A day earlier the Seimas had approved the findings of a parliamentary investigation that had confirmed the existence in Lithuania of two secret detention centres operated by the USA's Central Intelligence Agency in 2002–06. Grybauskaitė remained unsure whether the facilities had been used to hold detainees (a fact that the investigation had not established), despite Ušackas's assertions that they had not. Audronius Ažubalis was subsequently appointed to replace Ušackas. In February 2010 the Minister of Health, Algis Čaplikas, of the Liberal and Centre Union, also announced his resignation, following criticism from members of the HU—LCD of his efforts in health care reform and the conviction of accepting a bribe of his former deputy, Artūras Skikas. Raimondas Sukys was appointed as the new Minister of Health in mid-March. In June Remigijus Vilkaitis resigned from his position as Minister of Culture, and was replaced by Arūnas Gelūnas the following month.

Recent developments: administrative reform

As part of a wider programme of administrative reform, in July 2010 10 governorships and their corresponding county divisions were abolished. Hitherto the highest level of local governance, county-level powers were redistributed to municipal bodies. On 27 February 2011 municipal elections took place, in which the electorate was able to vote for coalitions of independent candidates, as well as political parties, for the first time. According to the provisional results of the Central Electoral Committee, the LSDP secured the most votes (21.4%), followed by the CP (16.3%).

Meanwhile, in December 2010 the European Court of Human Rights (ECHR) had returned a verdict stating that the decision by the Constitutional Court to impose a 'permanent and irreversible' ban on the appointment of former President Paksas to a position that required an oath of office was disproportionate, and in contravention of the principals of the Convention for the Protection of Human Rights and Fundamental Freedoms. The ECHR recommended that amendments to Lithuania's Constitution be implemented. Although the ECHR emphasized that it had not assessed the validity of Paksas's 2004 impeachment, Paksas immediately sought to use the ruling as proof that it had been unconstitutional, and announced his intention to stand in the legislative elections scheduled for 2012. In response to the ECHR's ruling, Minister of Justice Remigijus Šimašius announced that a working group would be established to determine how to implement the ruling. In early March Dainius Kreivys resigned from his position as Minister of the Economy, owing to claims that he had transferred EU funds to a company that was partly owned by his mother; he was replaced by Rimantas Zylius. In April 2011 the Government approved a new National Anti-Corruption Programme for 2011–14, which focused on nine areas, including public procurement, legislative bodies and the activities of civil servants.

Minority Ethnic Groups and Citizenship Concerns

Whereas Lithuania's Baltic neighbours, Estonia and Latvia, have large national minorities, ethnic Lithuanians constitute much of the republic's population: in the 2001 census, ethnic Lithuanians represented some 84% of the total population, while the two largest minority groups, Poles and Russians, represented 7% and 6%, respectively. As a result, the requirements for the naturalization of non-ethnic Lithuanians were less stringent than in the neighbouring Baltic republics, where national identity was perceived in some quarters as being under threat. Under citizenship laws adopted in late 1989, all residents, regardless of ethnic origin, were eligible to apply for naturalization; by early 1993 more than 90% of the country's non-ethnic Lithuanian residents had been granted citizenship. None the less, the population of Lithuania declined by some 191,000 between 1989 and 2001. In an attempt to counter emigration (in particular to the USA), in September 2002 the Seimas approved legislation permitting Lithuanian citizens to hold dual citizenship, thereby facilitating the eventual return of Lithuanian nationals to the country. However, in November 2006 the Constitutional Court ruled that several provisions of this legislation contravened the Constitution, which only allowed dual citizenship to be held in exceptional cases. In July 2008 the Seimas adopted an amended law on citizenship (which was due to expire in January 2010), which notably permitted dual citizenship to be held by Lithuanian citizens who had left the country during the occupations of June 1940–March 1990, as well as their children and grandchildren. In December 2009 the Seimas extended the application of this law until July 2010, subsequently extended until January 2011. On 2 December 2010 the Seimas voted on the adoption of new legislation on citizenship, 65 members voting in favour of the proposed law, with amendments and supplements as provided by President Grybauskaitė, 21 voting against, and 40 abstaining. Grybauskaitė had previously vetoed two amended proposals; the Constitutional Court was expected to hear an appeal on the validity of the presidential vetoes.

Regional Affairs

Mainly because of its citizenship laws (see above), Lithuania's relations with Russia have generally been less strained than have those of Estonia and Latvia. Agreement was reached in September 1992 on the withdrawal of the estimated 38,000 former Soviet troops remaining in Lithuania, and the final troops left, as scheduled, on 31 August 1993, whereupon full state sovereignty was perceived as having been restored in Lithuania.

In November 1993 Lithuania and Russia signed several agreements, including an accord on most-favoured nation status in bilateral trade, and another concerning the transportation, via Lithuania, of Russian military equipment and troops from the Russian exclave of Kaliningrad Oblast, on the Baltic coast. In October 1997 President Brazauskas undertook the first official visit to Russia by a Baltic head of state since the disintegration of the former USSR: a state border delimitation treaty was signed by both sides, and bilateral co-operation agreements on joint economic zones, and on the Baltic continental shelf, were also concluded. The border treaty was ratified by the Seimas in October 1999, but was not ratified by Russia until May 2003. Lithuania expressed support for an agreement between the EU and Russia in late 2002, which proposed simplified visa arrangements for Russian citizens traversing Lithuania to reach Kaliningrad. New transit arrangements were implemented in Lithuania in February 2003.

All three Baltic Governments were concerned at an agreement signed between Russia and Germany, in September 2005, on the construction of a North European Gas Pipeline, which was to carry natural gas from Russia to Germany under the Baltic Sea, bypassing the Baltic countries, which would allow Russia to interrupt the supply of gas to the Baltic states without having to compromise supplies to Western Europe. In June 2006 Russian petroleum supplies to the Mažeikiai Nafta petroleum refinery were indefinitely suspended, on the grounds that its pipeline link had been damaged; Russia subsequently refused assistance to repair the pipeline, prompting speculation that the halt in pipeline exports was in reprisal for the majority acquisition in that year of the refinery by Polish enterprise PKN Orlen, rather than by a Russian company. In May 2008 Lithuania withdrew its earlier objections to the initiation of long-delayed talks between the EU and Russia on a new partnership agreement, after being assured that its concerns regarding the continued closure of the pipeline link to the Mažeikiai Nafta refinery and Russian policy towards Georgia and Moldova would be addressed. The pipeline remained closed at the end of 2010. Although PKN Orlen bid to purchase the refinery and build a new pipeline to service the facility, the Lithuanian Government refused the offer, amid concerns over national security. With the refinery experiencing economic difficulties, a number of major Russian oil companies expressed an interest in purchasing the site.

Meanwhile, relations between Lithuania and Russia were further strained in June 2008, when the Seimas adopted legislation prohibiting the public display of Soviet and Nazi symbols. In late June several hundred Lithuanian websites were subject to pro-Russian attacks, their content being replaced by the Soviet flag and anti-Lithuanian propaganda. A dispute over customs inspections arose in August 2009, when the Lithuanian Government accused Russian officials of deliberately delaying Lithuanian lorries attempting to enter Russia from neighbouring Latvia, but was resolved following the intervention of President Grybauskaitė. In February 2010, in the highest level bilateral meeting to take place since 2001, Grybauskaitė and Russian premier Vladimir Putin held talks in Helsinki, Finland to discuss co-operation in a number of areas, including energy.

In June 2010, at the Baltic Development Forum Summit held in Vilnius, Lithuania announced plans to build an offshore liquefied natural gas terminal in an effort to foster greater independence in energy supplies. This followed a reduction in gas supplies from Russia the previous month owing to a dispute between Russia and Belarus over payments, and Lithuania began to examine the possibility of importing gas via Latvia. In December the Lithuanian Government approved the construction of a gas pipeline between the river town of Jurbarkas and the main port of Klaipėda, which was scheduled to be operational before the scheduled completion of the new gas terminal in 2014. Meanwhile, relations between Lithuania and Belarus became warmer in 2010, and in October the two countries signed a cross-border agreement facilitating travel of residents living within 50 km of the Lithuania–Belarus border.

Lithuania's relations with neighbouring Poland were largely concerned with the status of the Polish minority in Lithuania. Following the failed coup attempt of August 1991 in Moscow, leaders of councils in Polish-populated regions of Lithuania were dismissed, in response to their alleged support for the coup, and direct rule was introduced. However, in January 1992 Lithuania and Poland signed a 'Declaration on Friendly Relations and Neighbourly Co-operation', which guaranteed the rights of the respective minority ethnic groups and also recognized the existing border between the two countries. A full treaty of friendship and co-operation was signed by the respective Heads of State in April 1994. The treaty, notably, did not include a condemnatory reference to Poland's occupation of the region of Vilnius in 1920–39 (a provision that had originally been demanded by Lithuania). In May 2005 the Chairmen of the national legislatures of Lithuania, Poland and Ukraine, meeting in Lutsk, Ukraine, signed a declaration establishing a new Inter-Parliamentary Assembly, which aimed to help fulfil Ukraine's objective of attaining membership of the EU and the North Atlantic Treaty Organization (NATO, see p. 368). In September 2006 President Adamkus made an official visit to the Polish capital, Warsaw, where he signed a joint declaration with President Lech Kaczyński on a plan to connect the electricity grids of Lithuania and Poland; a joint company to manage the project was formed in May 2008.

Lithuania enjoys close relations with Estonia and Latvia. Relations between the three states are co-ordinated through the consultative inter-parliamentary Baltic Assembly, the Council of the Baltic Sea States (see p. 248) and the Baltic Council (see p. 459). However, in the mid-1990s Lithuania's relations with Latvia came under strain, as a result of disagreement over the demarcation of the countries' maritime border. In October 1995 the Lithuanian Government protested against Latvia's signature of a preliminary agreement with two foreign petroleum companies to explore oilfields in the disputed waters. Tension increased following the ratification of the agreement by the Latvian parliament in October 1996, although in July 1999 the two countries signed an agreement on the Delimitation of the Territorial Sea, Exclusive Economic Zone and Continental Shelf in the Baltic Sea. However, protests from the Latvian fishing industry prevented the agreement from being ratified by the Latvian parliament. In December 2000 a protocol was signed for the re-demarcation of the land border between the two countries. In early 2008 Prime Minister Kirkilas welcomed a decision by the Latvian Government that ratification of the maritime border treaty would proceed separately to the signing of an economic co-operation agreement between the two countries. Meanwhile, in early 2006 the leaders of all three Baltic states had reached agreement on the construction of a new nuclear power plant to replace that at Ignalina (see Economic Affairs) and various other co-operative measures aimed at reducing Russian dominance in the supply of regional energy.

Lithuania pursued close co-operation with, and eventual integration into, the political, economic and defence systems of Western Europe, notably NATO and the EU. In December 1999 a summit meeting of EU Heads of State and Government endorsed proposals to begin accession talks with a number of countries, including Lithuania; formal negotiations commenced in February 2000. As a concession to achieve EU membership, the Government approved a draft national energy strategy in September 1999, which provided for the decommissioning of the first unit of the Ignalina nuclear power plant by 2005. In June 2002 Lithuania agreed to decommission the plant's remaining unit in 2009, in return for a significant contribution from the EU towards the cost of the endeavour. The plant eventually closed in 2010, and at early 2011 construction of a new plant was under way. In December 2002 Lithuania and nine other countries were formally invited to join the EU on 1 May 2004; at a national referendum, held on 10–11 May 2003, 90.0% of participants voted in favour of membership, and Lithuania duly acceded to the EU as scheduled. In December 2007 Lithuania, together with eight other nations, implemented the EU's Schengen Agreement, enabling its citizens to travel to and from other member states without border controls. In May 2008 the Seimas approved the ratification of the EU's Lisbon Treaty, which was designed to reform the Union's institutions and entered into force in December 2009. Meanwhile, in November 2002 Lithuania was one of seven countries invited to join NATO in 2004. Lithuania became a full member of the Alliance on 29 March 2004. In April 2011 US President Barack Obama met Heads of State and Government of Central and Eastern European countries in Prague, the Czech Republic, to discuss regional and global security issues and NATO matters.

CONSTITUTION AND GOVERNMENT

Under the terms of the Constitution that was approved in a national referendum on 25 October 1992, supreme legislative authority resides with the Seimas (Parliament), which has 141 members, elected by universal adult suffrage for a four-year term (71 deputies are directly elected by majority vote, with 70 being elected from party lists on the basis of proportional representation). The President of the Republic (who is Head of State) is elected by direct popular vote for a period of five years (and a maximum of two consecutive terms). Executive power is vested in the Council of Ministers, headed by the Prime Minister, who is appointed by the President with the approval of the Seimas. Judicial power is exercised by the Constitutional Court, the Supreme Court, the Court of Appeal and district and local courts.

LITHUANIA

For administrative purposes, Lithuania is divided into 10 counties. Until July 2010 Lithuania was divided into 10 counties. However, in a process of administrative reform, the counties were abolished and their powers were transferred to municipal bodies.

REGIONAL AND INTERNATIONAL CO-OPERATION

Lithuania is a member of the European Bank for Reconstruction and Development (EBRD, see p. 265), the Council of the Baltic Sea States (see p. 248), of the Baltic Council (see p. 459), of the Council of Europe (see p. 250), and of the Organization for Security and Co-operation in Europe (see p. 385). In 2004 it acceded to the European Union (see p. 270).

Lithuania joined the UN in 1991, and the World Trade Organization (see p. 430) in 2001. The country is also a member of the North Atlantic Treaty Organization (see p. 368).

ECONOMIC AFFAIRS

In 2009, according to estimates by the World Bank, Lithuania's gross national income (GNI), measured at average 2007–09 prices, was US $38,095m., equivalent to $11,410 per head (or $16,740 per head on an international purchasing-power parity basis). During 2000–09 the population decreased at an average annual rate of 0.5%, while gross domestic product (GDP) per head increased, in real terms, by an average of 5.2% per year. Overall GDP increased, in real terms, by an average of 4.6% annually during 2000–09. Real GDP grew by 2.8% in 2008, but declined by 15.0% in 2009.

Agriculture (including hunting, forestry and fishing) contributed 4.2% of GDP and engaged an estimated 9.2% of the employed population in 2009. The principal crops are cereals, sugar beet, potatoes and vegetables. Legislation approved in January 2003 authorized the sale of agricultural land to foreign owners, although its implementation was to be subject to a seven-year transition period. According to World Bank estimates, agricultural GDP increased, in real terms, at an average annual rate of 1.7% during 2000–08; the GDP of the sector increased by 13.3% in 2007, and by just 0.4% in 2008.

Industry (including mining, manufacturing, construction and power) contributed 26.7% of GDP and engaged an estimated 27.0% of the employed population in 2009. According to World Bank estimates, industrial GDP increased by an average of 9.0% per year during 2000–08; the GDP of the sector increased by 8.2% in 2007 and by 1.0% in 2008.

Mining and quarrying contributed 0.3% of GDP, and provided only an estimated 0.2% of employment in 2009. Lithuania has significant reserves of peat and materials used in construction (limestone, clay, dolomite, chalk, and sand and gravel), as well as small deposits of petroleum and natural gas. In terms of gross value added, the sector registered growth of 3.0% in 2004, according to official data.

The manufacturing sector contributed 16.3% of GDP and engaged 16.0% of the employed labour force in 2009. Based on the value of sales (excluding refined petroleum products), in 2008 the principal branches of manufacturing were food products (particularly dairy products), chemicals (including fertilizers), wood products (particularly furniture), and clothing. According to World Bank estimates, manufacturing GDP increased, in real terms, at an average annual rate of 8.4% during 2000–08; sectoral GDP increased by 4.8% in 2007 and by 1.6% in 2008.

The construction sector contributed 6.3% of GDP, and engaged 8.7% of the employed labour force in 2009.

In 2007 nuclear power accounted for 73.0% of gross electricity production, and natural gas accounted for 17.9%. Lithuania has substantial petroleum-refining and electricity-generating capacities, which enable it to export refined petroleum products and electricity. Lithuania has been a net exporter of electricity, although in June 2002 formal agreement was reached with the European Union (EU, see p. 270) on the closure of the Ignalina nuclear power plant. The plant's two reactors were decommissioned in 2004 and 2009, in return for substantial financial compensation from the EU. In February 2006 the Prime Ministers of Estonia, Latvia and Lithuania reached agreement on the construction of a new nuclear plant in Lithuania by 2015, and Poland became involved in the project in 2007. The connection of the Lithuanian electricity grid to those of Poland and Sweden was also planned. In 2009 imports of mineral fuels accounted for 27.9% of the total value of merchandise imports.

The services sector contributed 69.1% of GDP and provided 63.8% of total employment in 2009. The Baltic port of Klaipėda is a significant entrepôt for regional trade. According to World Bank estimates, the GDP of the services sector increased, in real terms, by an average of 7.1% per year in 2000–08; real services GDP increased by 10.5% in 2007 and by 3.9% in 2008.

According to IMF estimates, in 2009 Lithuania recorded a visible trade deficit of US $1,077.4m., and there was a surplus of $1,491.6m. on the current account of the balance of payments. In that year the principal source of imports was Russia (accounting for 30.1% of the total); other major sources were Germany, Poland and Latvia. Russia was also the main market for exports in that year (accounting for 13.2% of the total); other principal markets were Latvia, Germany, Poland and Estonia. In 2009 the principal exports were mineral products, machinery and electrical equipment, vehicles and transportation equipment, chemical products, plastics and rubber, and vegetable products. The principal imports were mineral products, machinery and electrical equipment (particularly nuclear reactors and boilers), chemical products, vehicles and transportation equipment, plastics and rubber, and base metals.

According to official sources, in 2009 there was a budgetary deficit of 8,210.1m. litai (equivalent to 8.9% of GDP). Lithuania's general government gross debt was 27,105m. litai in 2009, equivalent to 29.5% of GDP. Lithuania's total external debt was US $31,720m. in 2008, of which $5,329m. was public and publicly guaranteed debt. In that year the cost of debt-servicing was equivalent to 30.6% of the value of exports of goods and services. According to ILO estimates, annual inflation averaged 3.2% in 2000–09. The rate of inflation was 10.9% in 2008 and 4.5% in 2009. The average rate of unemployment was 4.3% in 2007, compared with 11.4% in 2004, but increased to 17.8% in 2010.

In February 2002 the national currency's fixed rate of exchange was linked to the common European currency, the euro, instead of the US dollar. Lithuania was admitted to the EU's exchange rate mechanism (ERM II) in June 2004. In May 2006 the European Commission rejected Lithuania's application to adopt the euro in 2007, owing to its rate of consumer price inflation. As a result of the impact of adverse economic conditions in 2008–09, in January 2009 the Government introduced a number of austerity measures, which included a 15% reduction in public sector salaries, pension reforms and an increase in value-added tax (VAT). A €1,470m. economic stimulus plan, approved in February, included measures to support the construction sector and to improve the provision of credit to businesses. The Government raised additional funds by issuing a €500m. five-year Eurobond in June and bonds worth US $1,500m. and $2,000m. in October 2009 and February 2010, respectively. The budget for 2010 outlined significant reductions in social security benefits and, with the aim of stimulating business activity and encouraging foreign investment, a reduction in the tax on corporate profits from 20% to 15%. Despite signs of recovery, in November the Seimas warned that austerity measures introduced in previous budgets could not be eased and that the budget for 2011 would maintain a tight control on spending. However, the focus would move to increasing revenue by reforming state-owned companies and introducing measures to combat illicit trade. In October 2010 the IMF commended the Government's objective of reducing public debt gradually from 8.1% of GDP in 2010 to 5.8% in 2011, and to some 3% in 2012, as stipulated by the EU, with the intention of adopting the euro in 2014. GDP contracted by 15.0% in 2009, with GDP in the construction sector decreasing by 43.3%. The IMF reported growth of just 1.3% in 2010, but forecast stronger growth, of 4.6% in 2011, based on anticipated increased demand for Lithuanian exports resulting from a recovery in the global economy. However, with global food and fuel prices continuing to rise, GDP growth could be lower than forecast. Reducing the rate of unemployment, which had reached 17.8% in 2010, before declining in the first quarter of 2011, to 13.6%, remained a priority.

PUBLIC HOLIDAYS

2012: 1 January (New Year's Day), 16 February (National Day), 11 March (Day of the Re-establishment of Independence), 9 April (Easter Monday), 1 May (Labour Day), 24 June (St John's Day), 6 July (Anniversary of the Coronation of Grand Duke Mindaugas), 15 August (Assumption), 1 November (All Saints' Day), 25–26 December (Catholic Christmas).

LITHUANIA

Statistical Survey

Statistical Survey

Source (unless otherwise indicated): Department of Statistics to the Government of Lithuania (Statistics Lithuania), Gedimino pr. 29, Vilnius 01500; tel. (5) 236-4800; fax (5) 236-4845; e-mail statistika@stat.gov.lt; internet www.stat.gov.lt.

Area and Population

AREA, POPULATION AND DENSITY

Area (sq km)	65,300*
Population (census results)	
12 January 1989†	3,674,802
6 April 2001	
Males	1,629,148
Females	1,854,824
Total	3,483,972
Population (official estimates at 1 January)	
2009	3,349,872
2010	3,329,039
2011	3,244,509
Density (per sq km) at 1 January 2011	49.7

* 25,212 sq miles.
† Figure refers to the *de jure* population. The *de facto* total was 3,689,779.

POPULATION BY AGE AND SEX
(official estimates at 1 January 2010)

	Males	Females	Total
0–14	256,043	243,256	499,299
15–64	1,111,291	1,184,048	2,295,339
65 and over	180,417	353,984	534,401
Total	1,547,751	1,781,288	3,329,039

POPULATION BY ETHNIC GROUP
('000 permanent inhabitants at 1 January 2010, official estimates)

	Number	%
Lithuanian	2,765.6	83.1
Polish	201.5	6.0
Russian	161.7	4.8
Belarusian	35.9	1.1
Others	164.3	5.0
Total	3,329.0	100.0

ADMINISTRATIVE DIVISIONS
(official estimates at 1 January 2011)

County	Area (sq km)	Population	Density (per sq km)
Alytus	5,425	167,262	30.8
Kaunas	8,089	647,509	80.0
Klaipėda	5,209	366,935	70.4
Marijampolė	4,463	173,686	38.9
Panevėžys	7,881	270,798	34.4
Šiauliai	8,540	329,063	38.5
Tauragė	4,411	120,692	27.4
Telšiai	4,350	166,322	38.2
Utena	7,201	163,351	22.7
Vilnius	9,731	838,891	86.2
Total	65,300	3,244,509	49.7

PRINCIPAL TOWNS
(official estimates at 1 January 2011)

Vilnius (capital)	543,071	Šiauliai	120,934
Kaunas	336,817	Panevėžys	109,034
Klaipėda	177,823	Alytus	63,651

BIRTHS, MARRIAGES AND DEATHS

	Registered live births		Registered marriages		Registered deaths	
	Number	Rate (per 1,000)	Number	Rate (per 1,000)	Number	Rate (per 1,000)
2003	30,598	8.9	16,975	4.9	40,990	11.9
2004	30,419	8.8	19,130	5.6	41,340	12.0
2005	30,541	8.9	19,938	5.8	43,799	12.8
2006	31,265	9.2	21,246	6.3	44,813	13.2
2007	32,346	9.6	23,065	6.8	45,624	13.5
2008	35,065	10.5	24,063	7.2	43,832	13.1
2009	36,682	11.0	20,542	6.2	42,032	12.5
2010	35,948	10.9	18,744	5.7	42,114	12.8

Life expectancy (years at birth, WHO estimates): 72 (males 66; females 78) in 2008 (Source: WHO, *World Health Statistics*).

IMMIGRATION AND EMIGRATION

	2007	2008	2009
Immigrants	8,609	9,297	6,487
Emigrants	13,853	17,015	21,970

ECONOMICALLY ACTIVE POPULATION
(annual averages, '000 persons)*

	2007	2008	2009
Agriculture, hunting, forestry and fishing	159.5	119.8	130.5
Mining and quarrying	5.3	4.0	3.1
Manufacturing	267.9	260.4	226.0
Electricity, gas and water	26.2	35.5	30.9
Construction	170.9	166.5	122.6
Wholesale and retail trade; repair of motor vehicles, motorcycles and personal and household goods	262.4	270.1	249.7
Hotels and restaurants	33.5	38.9	34.9
Transport, storage and communications	111.4	120.8	115.5
Financial intermediation	22.3	20.4	22.0
Real estate, renting and business activities	75.4	97.8	98.9
Public administration and defence; compulsory social security	83.5	83.1	84.9
Education	144.3	152.3	149.0
Health and social work	100.7	94.4	92.6
Other community, social and personal service activities	67.1	52.1	53.7
Private households with employed persons	3.9	3.7	1.5
Extra-territorial organizations and bodies	—	0.2	—
Total	1,534.2	1,520.0	1,415.9
Unemployed	69.0	94.3	225.1
Total labour force	1,603.2	1,614.3	1,640.9
Males	812.3	818.1	819.8
Females	790.8	796.1	821.1

* Official estimates based on results of 2001 census.

2010 ('000): Employed 1,343.7; Unemployed 291.1; Total labour force 1,634.8.

LITHUANIA

Health and Welfare

KEY INDICATORS

Total fertility rate (children per woman, 2008)	1.3
Under-5 mortality rate (per 1,000 live births, 2008)	7
HIV/AIDS (% of persons aged 15–49, 2007)	0.1
Physicians (per 1,000 head, 2006)	4.0
Hospital beds (per 1,000 head, 2006)	8.0
Health expenditure (2007): US $ per head (PPP)	1,109
Health expenditure (2007): % of GDP	6.2
Health expenditure (2007): public (% of total)	73.0
Total carbon dioxide emissions ('000 metric tons, 2007)	15,267.9
Carbon dioxide emissions per head (metric tons, 2007)	4.5
Human Development Index (2010): ranking	44
Human Development Index (2010): value	0.783

For sources and definitions, see explanatory note on p. vi.

Agriculture

PRINCIPAL CROPS
('000 metric tons)

	2007	2008	2009
Wheat	1,390.7	1,722.5	2,100.2
Barley	1,013.7	970.4	858.2
Rye	165.2	204.9	207.9
Oats	119.5	140.8	142.5
Triticale (wheat-rye hybrid)	227.6	311.0	426.0
Potatoes	576.1	716.4	662.5
Sugar beet	799.9	339.1	682.0
Peas, dry	24.2	29.1	50.3
Rapeseed	311.9	330.2	415.8
Cabbages and other brassicas	94.5	115.0	121.1
Onions, dry	17.6	30.0	20.6
Carrots and turnips	62.7	57.0	63.7
Apples	40.6	74.3	53.3

Aggregate production ('000 metric tons, may include official, semi-official or estimated data): Total cereals 3,017.0 in 2007, 3,421.9 in 2008, 3,806.6 in 2009; Total roots and tubers 576.1 in 2007, 716.4 in 2008, 662.5 in 2009; Total vegetables (incl. melons) 288.7 in 2007, 318.5 in 2008, 332.2 in 2009; Total fruits (excl. melons) 56.6 in 2007, 89.7 in 2008, 70.5 in 2009.

Source: FAO.

LIVESTOCK
('000 head at 1 January)

	2007	2008	2009
Horses	61	56	54
Cattle	839	788	771
Pigs	1,127	923	897
Sheep	37	43	48
Goats	21	20	17
Chickens	9,234	9,693	8,841
Turkeys	117	104	194

Source: FAO.

LIVESTOCK PRODUCTS
('000 metric tons)

	2007	2008	2009
Cattle meat	56.0	47.5	45.1
Pig meat	99.3	75.9	60.4
Chicken meat	63.2	65.4	66.6
Cows' milk	1,931.2	1,950.4	1,786.9
Hen eggs	55.0	54.8	47.8
Honey	1.6	1.9	1.6

Source: FAO.

Forestry

ROUNDWOOD REMOVALS
('000 cubic metres, excl. bark)

	2007	2008	2009
Sawlogs, veneer logs and logs for sleepers	3,330	2,881	2,742
Pulpwood	1,560	1,331	935
Fuel wood	1,305	1,382	1,783
Total	6,195	5,594	5,460

Source: FAO.

SAWNWOOD PRODUCTION
('000 cubic metres, incl. railway sleepers)

	2007	2008	2009
Coniferous (softwood)	905	644	635
Broadleaved (hardwood)	475	465	376
Total	1,380	1,109	1,011

Source: FAO.

Fishing

(metric tons, live weight)

	2006	2007	2008
Capture	154,548	187,513	182,763
Largehead hairtail	n.a.	n.a.	28
Atlantic redfishes	3,002	3,005	828
Jack and horse mackerels	47,064	45,648	50,321
Sardinellas	24,846	21,116	23,021
European sprat	10,814	19,745	18,296
European anchovy	25,791	18,072	20,610
Chub mackerel	6,681	11,893	17,768
Northern prawn	3,082	3,514	1,497
Aquaculture	2,224	3,377	3,008
Total catch	156,772	190,890	185,771

Source: FAO.

Mining

('000 metric tons, unless otherwise indicated)

	2006	2007	2008
Crude petroleum	181	154	128
Dolomite ('000 cubic metres)	1,300	1,595	1,848
Limestone	1,279	1,778	1,596
Clay ('000 cubic metres)	281	342	359
Peat	495	452	378

LITHUANIA

Industry

SELECTED PRODUCTS
('000 metric tons unless otherwise indicated)

	2006	2007	2008
Sausages and smoked meat products	76.7	71.7	80.8
Flour	214.4	252.3	249.3
Refined sugar	96.6	125.1	70.1
Beer ('000 hectolitres)	293.4	285.6	296.9
Wine ('000 hectolitres)	797	886	835
Cotton fabrics (million sq m)	20.4	4.1	0.4
Woollen fabrics (million sq m)	22.5	18.9	8.1
Fabrics of man-made fibres	19.4	17.7	13.5
Footwear—excl. rubber and plastic ('000 pairs)*	1,000	1,000	900
Plywood ('000 cubic metres)	47.1	64.2	43.5
Particle board ('000 cubic metres)	433.4	624.7	652.1
Paper and paperboard	119.2	125.0	119.7
Sulphuric acid	1,117	1,145	1,051
Cement*	1,100	1,100	1,100
Cast iron	10.0	11.3	10.8
Television sets ('000)	711.3	509.2	376.7
Refrigerators and freezers ('000)	434.9	468.2	376.6
Bicycles ('000)	330	405	389
Electric energy (million kWh)*	11,900	13,100	13,100

* Figures are rounded.

Finance

CURRENCY AND EXCHANGE RATES

Monetary Units
100 centas = 1 litas (plural: litai).

Sterling, Dollar and Euro Equivalents (31 December 2010)
£1 sterling = 4.086 litai;
US $1 = 2.610 litai;
€1 = 3.453 litai;
100 litai = £24.48 = $38.32 = €28.96.

Average Exchange Rate (litai per US $)
2008   2.3571
2009   2.4840
2010   2.6063

Note: An official mid-point exchange rate of US $1 = 4.00 litai was in operation from 1 April 1994 until 1 February 2002. From 2 February 2002 the litas was linked to the euro, with the exchange rate set at €1 = 3.4528 litai.

GOVERNMENT FINANCE
(general government transactions, million litai)

Revenue	2007	2008	2009
Taxes	20,481.7	23,185.4	15,992.5
Indirect taxes	11,381.8	12,763.6	10,467.7
Direct taxes	9,093.6	10,415.7	5,518.6
Capital taxes	6.3	6.1	6.1
Social contributions	8,775.4	10,404.0	11,080.9
Sales	1,247.3	1,510.4	1,501.9
Other current revenue	1,410.6	1,650.6	1,435.9
Grants and other capital transfers	1,451.4	1,241.8	1,518.8
Total	33,366.4	37,992.2	31,530.0

Expenditure	2007	2008	2009
Compensation of employees	9,786.2	11,991.5	11,774.1
Intermediate consumption	5,193.9	6,364.7	5,294.2
Interest	690.8	720.7	943.8
Subsidies	882.4	774.6	600.8
Social benefits	10,590.6	14,216.4	15,719.3
Other current expenditure	1,177.1	1,470.4	1,277.4
Capital transfers	918.8	508.6	544.5
Capital investments	5,127.5	5,592.2	3,586.0
Total	34,367.4	41,639.1	39,740.1

INTERNATIONAL RESERVES
(US $ million at 31 December)

	2007	2008	2009
Gold (national valuation)	155.36	161.47	206.43
IMF special drawing rights	0.11	0.11	215.26
Reserve position in IMF	0.05	0.05	0.05
Foreign exchange	7,565.61	6,279.58	6,237.91
Total	7,721.13	6,441.21	6,659.65

Source: IMF, *International Financial Statistics*.

MONEY SUPPLY
(million litai at 31 December)

	2007	2008	2009
Currency outside depository corporations	8,108	8,520	6,972
Transferable deposits	19,832	14,802	15,077
Other deposits	15,795	20,139	21,683
Securities other than shares	544	694	704
Broad money	44,279	44,155	44,436

Source: IMF, *International Financial Statistics*.

COST OF LIVING
(Consumer Price Index; base: 2000 = 100)

	2006	2007	2008
Food (incl. beverages)	111.7	124.3	144.1
Fuel and light	117.1	130.0	156.3
Clothing	83.7	81.2	78.0
Rent	123.1	138.8	163.3
All items (incl. others)	108.2	114.4	126.9

2009: Food (incl. beverages) 146.5; All items (incl. others) 132.6.
Source: ILO.

NATIONAL ACCOUNTS
(million litai at current prices)

National Income and Profit

	2007	2008	2009
Compensation of employees	42,558.9	49,047.6	41,909.3
Operating surplus and mixed income	33,964.4	36,499.6	27,133.9
Domestic primary incomes	76,523.3	85,547.2	69,043.2
Consumption of fixed capital	11,890.4	13,872.3	13,292.4
Gross domestic product (GDP) at factor cost	88,413.7	99,419.5	82,335.6
Taxes on production and imports	11,788.9	13,276.2	10,831.5
Less Subsidies	1,533.4	1,505.9	1,151.1
GDP in market prices	98,669.1	111,189.8	92,016.1
Primary incomes received from abroad	2,640.3	3,173.4	2,382.4
Less Primary incomes paid abroad	6,483.6	6,015.9	1,865.7
Gross national income (GNI)	94,825.8	108,347.3	92,532.9
Less Consumption of fixed capital	11,890.4	13,872.3	13,292.4
Net national income	82,935.4	94,475.0	79,240.4
Current transfers from abroad	4,006.8	4,347.5	4,038.6
Less Current transfers paid abroad	1,869.9	2,011.3	2,218.4
Net national disposable income	85,072.3	96,811.2	81,060.6

LITHUANIA

Expenditure on the Gross Domestic Product

	2007	2008	2009
Final consumption expenditure	81,375.1	93,871.6	82,954.9
Households	63,508.4	72,140.6	62,706.8
Non-profit institutions serving households	228.5	262.0	236.7
General government	17,638.2	21,469.0	20,011.4
Gross capital formation	30,459.5	30,036.0	10,077.4
Gross fixed capital formation	27,918.8	27,984.0	15,609.1
Changes in inventories	2,456.8	1,976.8	−5,562.2
Acquisitions, less disposals, of valuables	83.8	75.2	30.4
Total domestic expenditure	111,834.6	123,907.6	93,032.3
Exports of goods and services	53,371.8	66,974.9	49,527.7
Less Imports of goods and services	66,537.3	79,692.6	50,543.9
GDP in market prices	98,669.1	111,189.8	92,016.1

Gross Domestic Product by Economic Activity

	2007	2008	2009
Agriculture, hunting and forestry	3,420.0	4,280.4	3,401.1
Fishing	63.8	77.4	85.3
Mining and quarrying	407.6	434.5	249.6
Manufacturing	16,440.1	17,840.3	13,421.9
Electricity, gas and water supply	2,924.5	3,108.5	3,187.1
Construction	9,048.0	9,982.1	5,176.0
Wholesale and retail trade; repair of motor vehicles, motorcycles and personal and household goods	14,726.4	16,526.9	13,705.5
Hotels and restaurants	1,156.6	1,333.3	1,164.6
Transport, storage and communications	11,304.6	12,097.3	11,511.2
Financial intermediation	2,928.2	3,485.3	1,892.5
Real estate, renting and business activities	11,521.1	13,060.1	11,574.1
Public administration and defence; compulsory social security	5,716.2	6,649.3	6,165.2
Education	3,786.5	4,843.1	5,163.6
Health and social work	2,707.0	3,300.1	3,260.7
Other community, social and personal service activities	2,172.5	2,525.3	2,474.9
Private households with employed persons	88.3	96.1	78.8
Gross value added at basic prices	88,411.3	99,639.9	82,512.3
Taxes on products	11,298.2	12,800.8	10,371.0
Less Subsidies on products	1,040.4	1,250.9	867.2
GDP in market prices	98,669.1	111,189.8	92,016.1

BALANCE OF PAYMENTS
(US $ million)

	2007	2008	2009
Exports of goods f.o.b.	17,162.0	23,768.3	16,480.6
Imports of goods f.o.b.	−23,035.8	−29,507.1	−17,558.0
Trade balance	−5,873.8	−5,738.7	−1,077.4
Exports of services	4,025.0	4,825.9	3,791.4
Imports of services	−3,392.7	−4,251.9	−2,954.1
Balance on goods and services	−5,241.6	−5,164.7	−240.1
Other income received	793.5	1,030.7	754.3
Other income paid	−2,407.2	−2,569.6	−545.4
Balance on goods, services and income	−6,855.3	−6,703.6	−31.2
Current transfers received	2,071.2	2,157.1	2,614.7
Current transfers paid	−908.3	−1,080.1	−1,091.9
Current balance	−5,692.4	−5,626.5	1,491.6

	2007	2008	2009
Capital account (net)	690.1	870.4	1,261.5
Direct investment abroad	−608.4	−386.4	−200.7
Direct investment from abroad	2,017.0	1,769.7	306.7
Portfolio investment assets	−838.0	−33.1	−1,167.5
Portfolio investment liabilities	608.8	−146.3	2,189.9
Financial derivatives assets	4.8	40.4	61.6
Financial derivatives liabilities	−7.1	−25.6	−23.5
Other investment assets	−1,561.1	−841.5	−602.7
Other investment liabilities	6,656.0	3,400.9	−3,178.5
Net errors and omissions	−53.9	−183.5	6.0
Overall balance	1,215.7	−1,161.4	144.4

Source: IMF, *International Financial Statistics*.

External Trade

PRINCIPAL COMMODITIES
(million litai)

Imports c.i.f.	2007	2008	2009
Prepared foodstuffs; beverages, spirits and vinegar; tobacco and manufactured substitutes	2,553.5	3,045.7	2,677.5
Mineral products	10,569.7	21,552.6	13,218.8
Mineral fuels	9,984.3	20,154.4	12,590.7
Products of the chemical or allied industries	5,957.0	6,530.0	5,557.6
Plastics, rubber and articles thereof	3,145.6	3,055.2	2,051.1
Textiles and textile articles	2,961.5	2,916.0	2,278.4
Base metals and articles thereof	4,806.6	4,475.4	2,258.5
Machinery and mechanical appliances; electrical equipment; sound and television apparatus	10,984.6	10,485.1	5,934.7
Nuclear reactors, boilers, etc.	6,137.2	5,839.4	3,473.4
Electrical machinery, sound and television recorders and parts thereof	4,847.4	4,645.7	2,461.2
Vehicles, aircraft, vessels and associated transport equipment	10,060.9	8,978.7	2,865.5
Total (incl. others)	61,503.5	73,006.3	45,138.0

Exports f.o.b.	2007	2008	2009
Live animals and animal products	2,363.7	2,405.5	2,287.4
Vegetable products	2,195.5	3,366.2	2,650.9
Prepared foodstuffs; beverages, spirits and vinegar; tobacco and manufactured substitutes	2,661.7	2,905.8	2,894.2
Mineral products	5,901.8	13,824.5	8,744.4
Mineral fuels	5,790.7	13,678.0	8,676.3
Products of the chemical or allied industries	3,477.4	5,354.2	3,688.2
Fertilizers	2,130.9	3,519.0	1,803.5
Plastics, rubber and articles thereof	3,430.2	3,304.0	2,746.8
Wood, cork and articles thereof; wood charcoal; manufactures of straw, esparto, etc.	1,985.3	1,742.0	1,348.6
Textiles and textile articles	3,262.7	3,058.9	2,636.3
Articles of apparel and clothing accessories, not knitted	1,152.4	990.9	812.5
Base metals and articles thereof	2,261.8	2,647.3	1,809.0
Machinery and mechanical appliances; electrical equipment; sound and television apparatus	5,589.3	5,914.5	4,063.7
Vehicles, aircraft, vessels and associated transport equipment	4,557.4	4,756.6	2,957.2
Miscellaneous manufactured articles	2,954.9	2,894.8	2,593.1
Total (incl. others)	43,192.4	55,511.0	40,724.9

LITHUANIA

PRINCIPAL TRADING PARTNERS
(million litai)

Imports c.i.f.	2007	2008	2009
Austria	708.4	642.5	350.0
Belarus	1,220.4	1,247.0	748.7
Belgium	1,774.4	1,751.0	1,334.9
China, People's Republic	1,720.2	1,870.0	1,122.8
Czech Republic	959.3	1,086.1	829.9
Denmark	1,687.0	1,560.9	997.7
Estonia	2,198.3	2,115.7	1,184.5
Finland	1,720.5	1,525.5	834.7
France	2,153.1	2,088.7	1,127.8
Germany	9,221.5	8,647.8	5,040.3
Italy	2,451.1	2,598.2	1,723.2
Latvia	3,365.5	3,801.0	2,866.4
Netherlands	2,628.9	2,562.2	1,839.3
Poland	6,532.9	7,291.3	4,497.3
Russia	11,083.2	21,854.8	13,602.6
Spain	1,038.9	1,043.1	673.8
Sweden	2,301.9	2,170.1	1,224.0
Ukraine	847.9	1,017.4	427.7
United Kingdom	1,736.0	1,371.9	750.2
USA	1,356.2	1,275.0	504.8
Total (incl. others)	61,503.5	73,006.3	45,138.0

Exports f.o.b.	2007	2008	2009
Belarus	1,733.4	2,495.8	1,923.5
Belgium	728.3	916.5	705.4
Canada	192.0	672.7	215.0
Denmark	1,749.4	2,598.0	1,554.9
Estonia	2,513.7	3,169.0	2,913.4
France	1,580.0	2,682.4	1,306.3
Germany	4,534.4	3,974.6	3,944.3
Italy	981.3	884.0	815.4
Latvia	5,562.4	6,442.2	4,088.6
Netherlands	1,295.2	1,896.5	2,066.1
Norway	993.4	1,165.9	1,018.5
Poland	2,713.7	3,207.8	2,917.9
Russia	6,473.0	8,916.5	5,392.3
Singapore	197.5	240.4	83.8
Spain	609.2	906.9	674.8
Sweden	1,640.9	1,885.5	1,467.4
Ukraine	1,176.3	1,805.4	1,221.5
United Kingdom	1,968.0	2,567.8	1,790.0
USA	1,109.3	1,775.7	1,200.9
Total (incl. others)	43,192.4	55,511.0	40,724.9

Transport

RAILWAYS
(traffic)

	2007	2008	2009
Passenger journeys ('000)	5,186.0	5,063.1	5,403.2
Passenger-km (million)	408.7	397.5	428.7
Freight transported ('000 metric tons)	53,503.0	54,970.2	42,669.0
Freight ton-km (million)	14,373	14,748	11,888

ROAD TRAFFIC
(motor vehicles in use at 31 December)

	2006	2007	2008
Passenger cars	1,592,238	1,587,903	1,671,065
Buses and coaches	15,134	13,997	13,824
Lorries and vans	117,427	126,507	128,733
Motorcycles and mopeds	25,478*	35,270	45,617

* Motorcycles only.

INLAND WATERWAYS

	2007	2008	2009
Passenger journeys ('000)	2,331.9	2,371.6	2,014.9
Passenger-km (million)	3	3	3
Freight transported ('000 metric tons)	958.7	988.5	908.5
Freight ton-km (million)	11	13	4

SHIPPING

Merchant Fleet
(registered at 31 December)

	2007	2008	2009
Number of vessels	127	114	121
Total displacement ('000 grt)	425.8	423.7	433.7

Source: IHS Fairplay, *World Fleet Statistics*.

International Sea-borne Freight Traffic
('000 metric tons)

	2007	2008	2009
Goods loaded	19,604	22,218	21,550
Goods unloaded	12,335	16,733	14,705

CIVIL AVIATION
(traffic on scheduled services)

	2007	2008	2009
Passengers carried ('000)	755.3	1,161.1	715.2
Passenger-km (million)	1,522	2,424	1,528
Freight transported ('000 metric tons)	6.4	4.2	3.7
Freight ton-km (million)	5.8	4.5	1.9

Tourism

FOREIGN VISITORS BY COUNTRY OF ORIGIN
(arrivals at accommodation establishments)

	2007	2008	2009
Belarus	57,241	45,694	52,193
Estonia	39,946	41,058	30,340
Finland	36,613	40,639	30,211
France	22,321	24,456	21,641
Germany	129,828	130,327	110,163
Italy	27,772	27,081	20,689
Latvia	69,965	84,722	62,815
Poland	128,087	156,283	125,662
Russia	78,586	91,992	78,690
Sweden	23,387	22,158	19,101
United Kingdom	37,731	39,875	25,911
USA	22,598	20,129	16,961
Total (incl. others)	849,006	909,983	752,389

Receipts from tourism (US $ million, incl. passenger transport): 975 in 2005; 1,077 in 2006; 1,192 in 2007.

Source: World Tourism Organization.

LITHUANIA

Communications Media

	2007	2008	2009
Telephones ('000 main lines in use)	799.4	784.9	747.4
Mobile cellular telephones ('000 subscribers)	4,912.1	5,022.6	4,961.5
Internet users ('000)*	1,674.7	1,833.8	1,963.9
Broadband subscribers ('000)	507.6	590.1	633.8
Book titles (incl. brochures)	4,567	n.a.	n.a.
Newspapers: number	328	327	297
Newspapers: average circulation (million copies)	269.6	290.8	229.4
Magazines and other periodicals	581	587	589
Magazines and other periodicals: average circulation (million copies)	72.7	77.0	65.8

* Estimates.

Personal computers: 812,400 (241.9 per 1,000 persons) in 2008.

Sources: International Telecommunication Union, and Ministry of Education and Science, Vilnius.

Education

(2009/10, unless otherwise indicated)

	Institutions	Teachers	Students
General schools	1,364	39,842	440,504
Vocational schools	78	3,882	47,886
Professional college	1*	120†	16*
Colleges	23	3,922	56,704
Universities	23	9,275	144,301

* 2006/07.
† 2005/06.

Pupil-teacher ratio (primary education, UNESCO estimate): 13.0 in 2007/08 (Source: UNESCO Institute for Statistics).

Adult literacy rate (UNESCO estimates): 99.7% (males 99.7%; females 99.7%) in 2008 (Source: UNESCO Institute for Statistics).

Directory

The Government

HEAD OF STATE

President: DALIA GRYBAUSKAITĖ (inaugurated 12 July 2009).

COUNCIL OF MINISTERS
(May 2011)

A coalition comprising representatives of the Homeland Union—Lithuanian Christian Democrats (HU—LCD), the Liberal Movement of the Republic of Lithuania (LM), the Liberal and Centre Union (LCU), the National Revival Party (NRP) and the New Union (Social Liberals) (NU).

Prime Minister: ANDRIUS KUBILIUS (HU—LCD).
Minister of the Economy: RIMANTAS ŽYLIUS (Independent).
Minister of Finance: INGRIDA ŠIMONYTĖ (HU—LCD).
Minister of National Defence: RASA JUKNEVIČIENĖ (HU—LCD).
Minister of Energy: ARVYDAS SEKMOKAS (HU—LCD).
Minister of Culture: ARŪNAS GELŪNAS (NU).
Minister of Social Security and Labour: DONATAS JANKAUSKAS (HU—LCD).
Minister of Justice: REMIGIJUS ŠIMAŠIUS (LM).
Minister of Transport and Communications: ELIGIJUS MASIULIS (LM).
Minister of Health: RAIMONDAS ŠUKYS (LCU).
Minister of Foreign Affairs: AUDRONIUS AŽUBALIS (HU—LCD).
Minister of the Interior: RAIMUNDAS PALAITIS (LCU).
Minister of Agriculture: KAZIMIERAS STARKEVIČIUS (HU—LCD).
Minister of Education and Science: GINTARAS STEPONAVIČIUS (LM).
Minister of the Environment: GEDIMINAS KAZLAUSKAS (NRP).

MINISTRIES

Office of the President: S. Daukanto 3/8, Vilnius 01122; tel. (5) 266-4154; fax (5) 266-4145; e-mail ieva.baubinaite@president.lt; internet www.president.lt.

Office of the Prime Minister: Gedimino pr. 11, Vilnius 01103; tel. (5) 266-3711; fax (5) 266-3895; e-mail mptarnyba@lrv.lt; internet www.lrv.lt.

Ministry of Agriculture: Gedimino pr. 19, Vilnius 01103; tel. (5) 239-1111; fax (5) 239-1212; e-mail zum@zum.lt; internet www.zum.lt.

Ministry of Culture: J. Basanavičiaus 5, Vilnius 01118; tel. (5) 219-3400; fax (5) 262-3120; e-mail culture@lrkm.lt; internet www.lrkm.lt.

Ministry of the Economy: Gedimino pr. 38/2, Vilnius 01104; tel. (5) 262-5515; fax (5) 262-3974; e-mail kanc@ukmin.lt; internet www.ukmin.lt.

Ministry of Education and Science: A. Volano 2/7, Vilnius 01516; tel. (5) 219-1190; fax (5) 261-2077; e-mail smmin@smm.lt; internet www.smm.lt.

Ministry of Energy: Gedimino pr. 38/2, Vilnius 01104; tel. (5) 262-0549; fax (5) 261-5140; e-mail info@enmin.lt; internet www.enmin.lt.

Ministry of the Environment: A. Jakšto 4/9, Vilnius 01105; tel. (5) 266-3661; fax (5) 266-3663; e-mail info@am.lt; internet www.am.lt.

Ministry of Finance: Lukiškių g. 2, Vilnius 01512; tel. (5) 239-0000; fax (5) 279-1481; e-mail finmin@finmin.lt; internet www.finmin.lt.

Ministry of Foreign Affairs: J. Tumo-Vaižganto g. 2, Vilnius 01511; tel. (5) 236-2444; fax (5) 231-3090; e-mail urm@urm.lt; internet www.urm.lt.

Ministry of Health: Vilniaus g. 33, Vilnius 01506; tel. (5) 268-5110; fax (5) 266-1402; e-mail ministerija@sam.lt; internet www.sam.lt.

Ministry of the Interior: Šventaragio 2, Vilnius 01510; tel. (5) 271-7130; fax (5) 271-8551; e-mail bendrasisd@vrm.lt; internet www.vrm.lt.

Ministry of Justice: Gedimino pr. 30/1, Vilnius 01104; tel. (5) 266-2981; fax (5) 262-5940; e-mail rastine@tm.lt; internet www.tm.lt.

Ministry of National Defence: Totorių 25/3, Vilnius 01121; tel. (5) 273-5673; fax (5) 264-8517; e-mail pilieciuaptarnavimas@kam.lt; internet www.kam.lt.

Ministry of Social Security and Labour: A. Vivulskio 11, Vilnius 03610; tel. (5) 266-4201; fax (5) 266-4209; e-mail post@socmin.lt; internet www.socmin.lt.

Ministry of Transport and Communications: Gedimino pr. 17, Vilnius 01505; tel. (5) 261-2363; fax (5) 212-4335; e-mail transp@transp.lt; internet www.transp.lt.

President

Presidential Election, 17 May 2009

Candidates	Valid votes	%
Dalia Grybauskaitė	950,407	69.09
Algirdas Butkevičius	162,665	11.82
Valentinas Mazuronis	84,656	6.15
Valdemar Tomaševski	65,255	4.74
Kazimiera Danutė Prunskienė	53,778	3.91
Loreta Graužinienė	49,686	3.61
Česlovas Jezerskas	9,191	0.67
Total	**1,374,319**	**100.00**

LITHUANIA

Legislature

Seimas
(Parliament)

Gedimino pr. 53, Vilnius 01109; tel. (5) 239-6212; fax (5) 239-6330; e-mail priim@lrs.lt; internet www.lrs.lt.

Chairman: IRENA DEGUTIENĖ.

General Election, 12 and 26 October 2008

Parties and blocs	A*	B*	Total
Homeland Union—Lithuanian Christian Democrats	18	27	45
Lithuanian Social Democratic Party	10	15	25
National Revival Party	13	3	16
Order and Justice Party	11	4	15
Liberal Movement of the Republic of Lithuania	5	6	11
Labour Party–Youth	8	2	10
Liberal and Centre Union	5	3	8
Lithuanian Polish Electoral Action	—	3	3
Lithuanian Peasant Nationalists' Union	—	3	3
New Union (Social Liberals)	—	1	1
Independent candidates	—	4	4
Total	**70**	**71**	**141**

* Of the 141 seats in the Seimas, 70 (A) are awarded according to proportional representation on the basis of party lists, and 71 (B) are elected in single-mandate constituencies.

Election Commission

Lietuvos Respublikos Vyriausioji rinkimų komisija (Central Electoral Committee of the Republic of Lithuania): Gedimino pr. 53, Vilnius 8860715; tel. (5) 239-6969; fax (5) 239-6960; e-mail rinkim@vrk.lt; internet www.vrk.lt; Chair. ZENONAS VAIGAUSKAS.

Political Organizations

In 2008 38 political parties were officially registered. The following were among the most significant:

Christian Party (Krikščionių partija): Odminių g. 5, Vilnius 01122; tel. and fax (5) 212-6874; e-mail info@krikscioniupartija.lt; internet www.krikscioniupartija.lt; f. 2010 by merger of Christian-Conservative Social Union and Lithuanian Christian Democratic Party; Leader GEDIMINAS VAGNORIUS.

Civil Democracy Party (Pilietinės Demokratijos Partija): Kaštonų g. 4, Vilnius 01107; tel. (5) 204-0204; fax (5) 204-0205; e-mail pdpsekretoriatas@gmail.com; internet www.pdp.lt; f. 2006; fmrly Civic Union; joined by fmr members of the Labour Party and the Liberal Democratic Party in 2006; Chair. ALGIMANTAS MATULEVIČIUS.

Electoral Action of Poles in Lithuania (Akcja Wyborcza Polaków na Litwie): Pilies g. 16, Vilnius 01123; tel. (5) 233-3103; fax (5) 233-1266; e-mail info@awpl.lt; internet www.awpl.lt; f. 1994; Chair. WALDEMAR TOMASZEWSKI.

Homeland Union—Lithuanian Christian Democrats (HU—LCD) (Tėvynės Sąjunga—Lietuvos Krikščionys Demokratai—TS—LKD): L. Stuokos-Gucevičiaus g. 11, Vilnius 01122; tel. (5) 212-1657; fax (5) 278-4722; e-mail sekretoriatas@tsajunga.lt; internet www.tsajunga.lt; f. 1993 as the Conservative Party of Lithuania (Homeland Union); absorbed the Lithuanian Rightist Union in Nov. 2003; merger with the Lithuanian Union of Political Prisoners and Deportees in Feb. 2004; merged with the Lithuanian Christian Democrats in May 2008, and name changed as above; Chair. VINCI VIDEVUTIS MARGEVIČIENĖ; some 18,000 mems.

Labour Party (LP) (Darbo Partija): Ankštoji 3, Vilnius 01109; tel. (5) 210-7152; fax (5) 210-7153; e-mail info@darbopartija.lt; internet www.darbopartija.lt; f. 2003; Chair. VIKTOR USPASKICH; 12,956 mems.

Liberal and Centre Union (Liberalų Centro Sąjunga): Vilniaus g. 22/1, Vilnius 01119; tel. (5) 231-3264; fax (5) 261-9363; e-mail info@lics.lt; internet www.lics.lt; f. 2003 by a merger of the Lithuanian Centre Union, the Lithuanian Liberal Union and the Modern Christian-Democratic Union; Chair. GINTAUTAS BABRAVIČIUS; over 5,000 mems.

Liberal Movement of the Republic of Lithuania (Lietuvos Respublikos liberalų sąjūdis): Sėlių g. 48, Vilnius 08125; tel. and fax (5) 249-6959; e-mail info@liberalai.lt; internet www.liberalusajudis.lt; f. 2006; formed by a splinter group of the Liberal and Centre Union; Chair. ELIGIJUS MASIULIS.

Lithuanian Peasant Nationalists' Union (Lietuvos Valstiečių Liaudininkų Sąjunga—LVLS): Pamėnkalnio g. 26, Vilnius 01114; tel. (5) 212-0821; fax (5) 212-0822; e-mail info@lvls.lt; internet www.lvls.lt; f. 2001 by the merger of the New Democracy Party and the Lithuanian Peasants' (Farmers') Party; fmrly Peasants' (Farmers') and New Democratic Party Union (VNDS); present name adopted Feb. 2006; Chair. RAMŪNAS KARBAUSKIS; 1,500 mems.

Lithuanian Polish People's Party (Lietuvos Lenkų Liaudies Partija/Polska Partia Ludowa): Kauno g. 1A, Vilnius 03212; tel. (5) 216-2874; fax (5) 233-5467; e-mail lllp@zebra.lt; internet www.lllp.lt; f. 2002; Chair. ANTONINA POŁTAWIEC.

Lithuanian Russians' Union (Lietuvos rusų sąjunga/Soyuz Russkikh Litvy): Pamėnkalnio g. 3–27, Vilnius 01116; tel. and fax (5) 262-4248; e-mail sojuzru@tts.lt; internet sojuzru.tts.lt; f. 1995; Chair. SERGEI DMITRIYEV.

Lithuanian Social Democratic Party (LSDP) (Lietuvos Socialdemokratų Partija): Barboros Radvilaites g. 1, Vilnius 01124; tel. (5) 261-3907; fax (5) 261-5420; e-mail info@lsdp.lt; internet www.lsdp.lt; absorbed the Lithuanian Democratic Labour Party in 2001; Chair. ALGIRDAS BUTKEVIČIUS; 11,000 mems.

National Revival Party (NRP) (Tautos prisikėlimo partija): Pranciškonų g. 4A/10, Vilnius 01133; tel. (8) 686-82470; fax (5) 240-0493; e-mail bustine@prisikelimopartija.lt; internet www.prisikelimopartija.lt; f. 2008; Leader ARŪNAS VALINSKAS.

New Union (Social Liberals) (NU) (Naujoji sąjunga—Socialliberalai): Gedimino pr. 10/1, Vilnius 01103; tel. (5) 210-7600; fax (5) 210-7602; e-mail centras@nsajunga.lt; internet www.nsajunga.lt; f. 1998; centre-left; Chair. ARTŪRAS PAULAUSKAS.

Order and Justice Party (Partijos Tvarka ir teisingumas): Gedimino pr. 10/1, Vilnius 01103; tel. and fax (5) 269-1618; e-mail tt@tvarka.lt; internet www.tvarka.lt; f. 2002; fmrly Liberal Democratic Party (LDP); present name adopted 2008; right-wing; Chair. ROLANDAS PAKSAS; 6,500 mems (2007).

Diplomatic Representation

EMBASSIES IN LITHUANIA

Austria: Gaono g. 6, Vilnius 01131; tel. (5) 266-0580; fax (5) 279-1363; e-mail wilna-ob@bmaa.gv.at; internet www.bmeia.gv.at/wilna; Ambassador Dr HELMUT KOLLER.

Azerbaijan: Olimpiečių g. 5-7, Vilnius 02051; tel. (5) 219-0042; fax (5) 279-1504; e-mail info@azembassy.lt; Ambassador NAIRA SHAKHTAKHTINSKAYA.

Belarus: Mindaugo g. 13, Vilnius 03225; tel. (5) 266-2200; fax (5) 266-2212; e-mail emb@belarus.lt; internet www.lithuania.belembassy.org; Ambassador ULADZIMIR DRAZHIN.

Belgium: Kalinausko g. 2B, Vilnius 03107; tel. (5) 266-0820; fax (5) 212-6444; e-mail vilnius@diplobel.org; internet www.diplomatie.be/vilnius; Ambassador CHRISTIAN VERDONCK.

Bulgaria: Pylimo 8, Palangos 2, Vilnius 01118; tel. (5) 249-9274; fax (5) 261-9174; e-mail vilnius@bgembassy.lt; internet www.mfa.bg/vilnius; Ambassador IVAN P. DANTCHEV.

China, People's Republic: Algirdo g. 36, Vilnius 03218; tel. (5) 216-2861; fax (5) 216-2682; e-mail chinaemb_lithuania@mfa.gov.cn; internet www.chinaembassy.lt; Ambassador TONG MINGTAO.

Czech Republic: Birutės g. 16, Vilnius 08117; tel. (5) 266-1040; fax (5) 266-1066; e-mail vilnius@embassy.mzv.cz; internet www.mzv.cz/vilnius; Ambassador RADEK PECH.

Denmark: Kosciuškos g. 36, Vilnius 01100; tel. (5) 264-8760; fax (5) 231-2300; e-mail vnoamb@um.dk; internet www.ambvilnius.um.dk; Ambassador JØRGEN MOLDE.

Estonia: A. Mickevičiaus g. 4A, Vilnius 08119; tel. (5) 278-0200; fax (5) 278-0201; e-mail sekretar@estemb.lt; internet www.estemb.lt; Ambassador TIIT NABER.

Finland: Klaipėdos g. 24, Vilnius 03107; tel. (5) 266-8010; fax (5) 212-2441; e-mail sanomat.vil@formin.fi; internet www.finland.lt; Ambassador MARJA-LIISA KILJUNEN.

France: Švarco g. 1, Vilnius 01131; tel. (5) 219-9600; fax (5) 219-9613; e-mail ambafrance.vilnius@diplomatie.gouv.fr; internet www.ambafrance-lt.org; Ambassador FRANÇOIS LAUMONIER.

Georgia: Poškos g. 13, Vilnius 08123; tel. (5) 273-6959; fax (5) 272-3623; e-mail embassy@georgia.w3.lt; internet www.lithuania.mfa.gov.ge; Ambassador GEORGI KERDIKOSHVILI.

Germany: Z. Sierakausko g. 24/8, Vilnius 03105; tel. (5) 210-6400; fax (5) 210-6446; e-mail info@wilna.diplo.de; internet www.wilna.diplo.de; Ambassador HANS PETER ANNEN.

LITHUANIA

Greece: Didžioji 33/Rūdininkų 2, Vilnius 01132; tel. (5) 261-0526; fax (5) 261-0536; e-mail embassy@grembvil.w3.lt; Ambassador Constantine Catsambis.

Holy See: Kosciuškos g. 28, Vilnius 01100; tel. (5) 212-3696; fax (5) 212-4228; e-mail nuntiusbalt@aiva.lt; Apostolic Nuncio Most Rev. Luigi Bonazzi (Titular Archbishop of Glastonia).

Hungary: Jojailos g. 4, Vilnius 01116; tel. (5) 269-0038; fax (5) 269-0039; e-mail mission.vno@kum.hu; internet www.mfa.gov.hu/emb/vilnius; Ambassador Péter Noszkó-Horvath.

Ireland: Gedimino pr. 1, Vilnius 01103; tel. (5) 262-9460; fax (5) 262-9462; e-mail vilniusembassy@dfa.ie; internet www.embassyofireland.lt; f. 2005; Ambassador Philomena Murnaghan.

Italy: Vytauto g. 1, Vilnius 08118; tel. (5) 212-0620; fax (5) 212-0405; e-mail ambasciata.vilnius@esteri.it; internet www.ambvilnius.esteri.it; Ambassador Renato Maria Ricci.

Japan: M. K. Čiurlionio g. 82B, Vilnius 03100; tel. (5) 231-0462; fax (5) 231-0461; e-mail consular@emb-japan.lt; internet www.lt.emb-japan.go.jp; Ambassador Miyoko Akashi.

Kazakhstan: Birutės g. 20A/35, Vilnius 08117; tel. (5) 212-2123; fax (5) 231-3580; e-mail kazemb@iti.lt; internet kazakhstan.embassy.lt; Ambassador Galymzhan Koishybaev.

Latvia: M. K. Čiurlionio g. 76, Vilnius 03100; tel. (5) 213-1260; fax (5) 213-1130; e-mail embassy.lithuania@mfa.gov.lv; internet www.latvia.lt; Ambassador Martinš Virsis.

Moldova: Miglos g. 61A, Vilnius 08102; tel. (5) 260-7914; fax (5) 260-7915; e-mail vilnius@mfa.md; internet www.lituania.mfa.gov.md; Ambassador Igor Klipii.

Netherlands: Business Centre 2000, 4th Floor, Jogailos g. 4, Vilnius 01116; tel. (5) 269-0072; fax (5) 269-0073; e-mail vil@minbuza.nk; internet www.netherlandsembassy.lt; Ambassador Josephus Camille S. Wijnands.

Norway: Kalinausko g. 24/3, Vilnius 03107; tel. (5) 261-0000; fax (5) 261-0100; e-mail emb.vilnius@mfa.no; internet www.norvegija.lt; Ambassador Leif Arne Ulland.

Poland: Smėlio g. 20A, Vilnius 10323; tel. (5) 270-9001; fax (5) 270-9007; e-mail ampol@tdd.lt; internet www.wilno.polemb.net; Ambassador Janusz Skolimowski.

Portugal: Gedimino pr. 5, Vilnius 01103; tel. (5) 262-0511; fax (5) 262-0512; e-mail vilnius@embportugal.lt; Ambassador João Manuel da Cruz da Silva Leitão.

Romania: Vivulskio g. 19, Vilnius 03115; tel. (5) 231-0557; fax (5) 231-0652; e-mail ambromania@romania.lt; internet vilnius.mae.ro; Chargé d'affaires a.i. Mircea Costineanu.

Russia: Latvių g. 53/54, Vilnius 08113; tel. (5) 272-1763; fax (5) 272-3877; e-mail post@rusemb.lt; internet www.lithuania.mid.ru; Ambassador Vladimir V. Chkhikvadze.

Spain: Algirdo g. 4, Vilnius 03220; tel. (5) 231-3961; fax (5) 231-3962; e-mail emb.vilnius@mae.es; f. 2004; Ambassador Miguel Aria Estévez.

Sweden: Didžioji g. 16, Vilnius 01128; tel. (5) 268-5010; fax (5) 268-5030; e-mail ambassaden.vilnius@foreign.ministry.se; internet www.swedenabroad.com/vilnius; Ambassador Ulrika Eva Maria Cronenberg-Mossberg.

Turkey: Didžioji g. 37, Vilnius 01128; tel. (5) 264-9570; fax (5) 212-3277; e-mail turkemb.vilnius@mfa.gov.tr; internet vilnius.emb.mfa.gov.tr; Ambassador Ömer Altuğ.

Ukraine: Teatro g. 4, Vilnius 03107; tel. (5) 212-1536; fax (5) 212-0475; e-mail ukrembassy@post.5ci.lt; internet www.mfa.gov.ua/lithuania; Chargé d'affaires a.i. Serhiy Popyk.

United Kingdom: Antakalnio g. 2, Vilnius 10308; tel. (5) 246-2900; fax (5) 246-2901; e-mail be-vilnius@britain.lt; internet ukinlithuania.fco.gov.uk; Ambassador Simon John Butt.

USA: Akmenų g. 6, Vilnius 03106; tel. (5) 266-5300; fax (5) 266-5310; e-mail webemailvilnius@state.gov; internet vilnius.usembassy.gov; Ambassador Anne Elizabeth Derse.

Judicial System

The organs of justice are the Supreme Court, the Court of Appeal, district courts, local courts of administrative areas and a special court—the Commercial Court. The Seimas (Parliament) appoints and dismisses from office the judges of the Supreme Court in response to representations made by the President of the Republic (based upon the recommendation of the chairman of the Supreme Court). Judges of the Court of Appeal are appointed by the President with the approval of the Seimas (on the recommendation of the Minister of Justice), while judges of district and local courts are appointed and dismissed by the President. The Council of Judges submits recommendations to the President of the Republic concerning the appointment of judges, as well as their promotion, transfer or dismissal from office.

The Constitutional Court decides on the constitutionality of acts of the Seimas, as well as of the President and the Government. It consists of nine judges, who are appointed by the Seimas for a single term of nine years; one-third of the Court's members are replaced every three years.

The Office of the Prosecutor-General is an autonomous institution of the judiciary, comprising the Prosecutor-General and local and district prosecutors' offices, which are subordinate to him. The Prosecutor-General and his deputies are appointed for terms of seven years by the President, subject to approval by the Seimas, while the prosecutors are appointed by the Prosecutor-General. The Office of the Prosecutor-General incorporates the Department for Crime Investigation. The State Arbitration decides cases of business litigation. A six-volume Civil Code, in accordance with European Union and international law, came into effect in 2001, replacing the Soviet civil legal system, which had, hitherto, remained in operation.

Constitutional Court (Lietuvos Respublikos Konstitucinis Teismas): Gedimino pr. 36, Vilnius 01104; tel. (5) 261-1466; fax (5) 212-7975; e-mail mailbox@lrkt.lt; internet www.lrkt.lt; f. 1993; Pres. Romualdas Kęstutis Urbaitis.

Court of Appeal: Gedimino pr. 40/1, Vilnius 01503; tel. (5) 266-3685; fax (5) 266-3060; e-mail apeliacinis@vtr.lt; internet www.apeliacinis.lt; Chair. Egidijus Žironas.

Supreme Court (Lietuvos Aukščiausiasis Teismas): Gynėjų g. 6, Vilnius 01109; tel. (5) 261-0560; fax (5) 261-6813; e-mail lat@lat.lt; internet www.lat.lt; Chair. Gintaras Kryževičius.

Office of the Prosecutor-General: Rinktinės g. 5A, Vilnius 01515; tel. (5) 266-2305; fax (5) 266-2317; e-mail info@prokuraturos.lt; internet www.prokuraturos.lt; Prosecutor-General Darius Valys.

Religion

CHRISTIANITY

The Roman Catholic Church

Catholicism has been the principal religious affiliation in Lithuania since its adoption by the Lithuanian State in 1387. The Catholic Church in Lithuania comprises two archdioceses and five dioceses (all of the Latin rite). At 31 December 2008 there were an estimated 2.7m. adherents in Lithuania (equivalent to 77.3% of the population).

Bishops' Conference: Skapo 4, Vilnius 01122; tel. (5) 212-5455; fax (5) 212-0972; e-mail lvk@takas.lt; internet lvk.lcn.lt; f. 1965; Pres. Most Rev. Sigitas Tamkevičius (Archbishop of Kaunas).

Archbishop of Kaunas: Most Rev. Sigitas Tamkevičius, Rotušes 14A, Kaunas 44279; tel. (37) 409026; fax (37) 320090; e-mail kurija@kn.lcn.lt; internet www.kaunas.lcn.lt.

Archbishop of Vilnius: Cardinal Audrys Juozas Bačkis, Šventaragio 4, Vilnius 01122; tel. (5) 262-7098; fax (5) 212-2807; e-mail curia@vilnensis.lt; internet vilnius.lcn.lt.

Orthodox Churches

Russian Orthodox Church (Moscow Patriarchate)

The first Orthodox communities in Lithuania appeared during the 12th century. While Lithuania formed part of the Russian Empire (1795–1915), Orthodoxy was considered the state religion. There were an estimated 180,000 adherents in 2001.

Lithuanian Orthodox Church (Moscow Patriarchate): Aušros Vartų 10/3, Vilnius 01129; tel. (5) 212-7765; internet www.orthodoxy.lt; Metropolitan of Vilnius and Lithuania Chryzostom (Martishkin).

Lithuanian Old Believers Pomor Church

The first communities settled in Lithuania in 1679 and the Church was established in 1709. In 1996 there were approximately 34,000 adherents.

Supreme Council of the Old Believers Pomor Church in Lithuania: Naujininkų g. 20, Vilnius 02109; tel. (5) 269-5271; f. 1925; Chair. Mark Semionov (acting).

Protestant Churches

Lithuanian Evangelical Lutheran Church

The first parishes were established in 1539–69. The Lithuanian Evangelical Lutheran Church comprises one diocese. In 1998 there were approximately 30,000 adherents.

Consistory of the Lithuanian Evangelical Lutheran Church (Lietuvos Evangeliku-Liuteronu Bažnycia): Tumo-Vaižganto 50, Tauragė 72263; tel. and fax (446) 61145; e-mail redakcija@liuteronai.lt; internet www.liuteronai.lt; Bishop Mindaugas Sabutis.

Lithuanian Evangelical Reformed Church

The first parishes were established after 1563. At 1 January 1996 there were approximately 12,000 adherents.

Lithuanian Evangelical Reformed Church: POB 661, Vilnius 04008; tel. and fax (5) 245-0656; Pres. of Synodie Collegium POVILAS A. JAŠINSKAS.

ISLAM

Sunni Islam is the religion of the ethnic Tatars of Lithuania. The first Tatar communities settled there in the 14th century. The first mosque in Vilnius was erected in 1558. In 2001 there were an estimated 5,000 adherents.

JUDAISM

The first Jewish communities appeared in Lithuania in the 15th century. In the 15th–17th centuries Vilnius was an important centre of Jewish culture and religion. Before the Second World War approximately 200,000 Jews lived in Lithuania; an estimated 90% were murdered during the German occupation (1941–44). At 1 January 1996 there were five religious communities, with two synagogues (in Vilnius and Kaunas). There were an estimated 5,000 adherents in Lithuania in 2001. There is a small number of Karaites (Karaim), who originate from Crimea (now in Ukraine), and who speak a Turkic language and follow a form of Judaism, resident in Lithuania.

The Press

In 2009 there were 297 newspapers and 589 periodicals published in Lithuania.

The publications listed below are in Lithuanian, except where otherwise indicated.

PRINCIPAL NEWSPAPERS

Kauno diena (Kaunas Daily): Kęstučio g. 86, Kaunas 44296; tel. (37) 302250; fax (37) 423404; e-mail redakcija@kaunodiena.lt; internet www.kauno.diena.lt; f. 1945; 6 a week; Editor-in-Chief ŽILVINĖ PETRAUSKAITĖ; circ. 50,000.

Klaipėda: Naujojo Sodo g. 1A, K Centras, Klaipėda 92233; tel. (46) 397750; fax (46) 397700; e-mail redakcija@kl.lt; internet www.klaipeda.daily.lt; Editor-in-Chief SAULIUS POCIUS.

Kurier Wileński (Vilnius Courier): Birbynių g. 4A, Vilnius 02121; tel. and fax (5) 260-8444; e-mail r.mickiewicz@kurierwilenski.lt; internet www.kurierwilenski.lt; f. 1953; 5 a week; in Polish; Editor-in-Chief ROBERT MICKIEWICZ; circ. 8,000.

Lietuvos aidas (Lithuanian Echo): B. Radvilaitės g. 9, Vilnius 01124; tel. (52) 212-4876; e-mail algirdaspilvelis@gmail.com; internet www.aidas.lt; f. 1917; re-est. 1990; 5 a week; Editor-in-Chief ALGIRDAS PILVELIS; circ. 20,000.

Lietuvos rytas (Lithuanian Morning): Gedimino pr. 12A, Vilnius 01103; tel. (5) 274-3600; fax (5) 274-2000; e-mail daily@lrytas.lt; internet www.lrytas.lt; f. 1990; 6 a week, with 3 supplements per week; Editor-in-Chief RIMVYDAS VALATKA; circ. 65,000 (Mon.–Fri.), 200,000 (Sat.).

Lietuvos žinios (Lithuanian News): Kęstučio g. 4/14, Vilnius 08117; tel. (5) 249-2152; fax (5) 275-3131; e-mail red@lzinios.lt; internet www.lzinios.lt; 6 a week; Gen. Dir and Editor-in-Chief VALDAS VASILIAUSKAS.

Respublika (Republic): A. Smetonos g. 2, Vilnius 01115; tel. (5) 212-3112; fax (5) 212-3538; e-mail press@respublika.net; internet www.respublika.lt; f. 1988; 6 a week in Lithuanian, with 5 Russian editions per week; Editor-in-Chief VITAS TOMKUS; circ. 55,000.

Šiaulių kraštas: P. Višinskio g. 26, Šiauliai 77155; tel. (41) 591555; fax (41) 524581; e-mail redakcija@skrastas.lt; internet www.skrastas.lt; Dir and Editor-in-Chief VLADAS VERTELIS.

Vakaro žinios (Evening News): Jogailos g. 11/2-11, Vilnius 01116; tel. and fax (5) 261-6875; e-mail vakarozinios@takas.lt; daily; circ. 70,000.

Vakarų ekspresas (Western Express): M. Mažvydo 3, Klaipėda 92131; tel. (46) 411308; fax (46) 402408; e-mail sekretore@ve.lt; internet www.ve.lt; f. 1990; 6 a week; Editor-in-Chief GINTARAS TOMKUS; circ. 16,000–22,000.

Verslo žinios (Business News): J. Jasinskio 16A, Vilnius 01112; tel. (5) 252-6300; fax (5) 252-6313; e-mail info@vz.lt; internet www.vz.lt; f. 1994; 5 a week; Editor LINAS KMIELIAUSKAS; circ. 9,000.

PRINCIPAL PERIODICALS

Artuma (Presence): Rotušės a. 23, Kaunas 44279; tel. and fax (37) 209683; e-mail redakcija@artuma.lt; internet www.artuma.lt; f. 1989 as *Caritas*; name changed as above in 1997; monthly; Catholic family magazine; Editor-in-Chief DARIUS CHMIELIAUSKAS; circ. 12,500.

Kultūros barai (Domains of Culture): Latako g. 3, Vilnius 01125; tel. (5) 262-3861; fax (5) 261-0538; e-mail kulturosbarai@takas.lt; internet www.eurozine.com; f. 1965; monthly; independent cultural magazine; Editor-in-Chief LAIMA KANOPKIENĖ; circ. 2,200.

Laima: J. Jasinskio g. 16, Vilnius 01112; tel. (5) 252-6538; fax (5) 252-6531; e-mail laima@redakcija.lt; internet www.redakcija.lt/zurnalai/laima; f. 1993; monthly; lifestyle and feature magazine for women; Editor-in-Chief GITANA BUKAUSKIENĖ; circ. 30,000.

Liaudies kultūra (Ethnic Culture): Barboros Radvilaitės 8, Vilnius 01124; tel. (5) 261-3412; fax (5) 261-2607; e-mail llkc@llkc.lt; internet www.llkc.lt; f. 1988; 6 a year; Gen. Editor DALIA ANTANINA RASTENIENĖ; circ. 550.

Literatūra ir menas (Literature and Art): Mesiniu 4, Vilnius 01133; tel. (5) 269-1977; fax (5) 212-6556; e-mail lmenas@takas.lt; internet www.culture.lt/lmenas; f. 1946; weekly; publ. by the Lithuanian Writers' Union; Editor-in-Chief KORNELIJUS PLATELIS; circ. 2,000.

Lithuania in the World: J. Basanavičiaus g. 7, Vilnius 01118; tel. (5) 261-4432; fax (5) 212-5560; e-mail info@liw.lt; internet www.liw.lt; f. 1993; 6 a year; in English and Lithuanian; Exec. Editor JOLANTA LAUMENSKAITĖ; circ. 10,000.

Magazyn Wileński (Vilnius Journal): Laisvės pr. 60, Vilnius 05120; tel. (5) 242-7718; fax (5) 242-9065; e-mail magazyn@magwil.lt; internet www.magwil.lt; f. 1990; monthly; political, cultural; in Polish; Editor HELENA OSTROWSKA; circ. 5,000.

Mano Namai: Ozo g. 10A, Vilnius 08200; tel. (5) 247-7714; e-mail dalia@manomai.lt; internet www.mano-namai.lt; household, interiors and food; Editor DALIA DAUGIRDIENĖ.

Metai (Year): K. Sirvydo g. 6, Vilnius 01101; tel. (5) 261-7344; e-mail metai@takas.lt; f. 1991; monthly; journal of the Lithuanian Writers' Union; Editor-in-Chief DANIELIUS MUŠINSKAS; circ. 2,000.

Mokslas ir gyvenimas (Science and Life): Antakalnio g. 36, Vilnius 10305; tel. and fax (5) 234-1572; e-mail mgredacija@takas.lt; internet ausis.gf.vu.lt/mg; f. 1957; monthly; popular and historical science; Editor-in-Chief JUOZAS BALDAUSKAS; circ. 3,500.

Moteris (Woman): Ozo g. 10A, Vilnius 08200; tel. (5) 247-7712; tel. and fax (5) 247-7711; e-mail info@moteris.lt; internet www.moteris.lt; f. 1952; monthly; popular, for women; Editor-in-Chief GRAŽINA MICHNEVIČIŪTĖ; circ. 20,000.

Naujasis Židinys-Aidai (New Hearth–Echoes): Didžioji g. 34, Vilnius 01128; tel. (5) 212-0311; fax (5) 212-2363; e-mail aidai@aidai.lt; internet www.aidai.lt/zidinys; f. 1991; monthly; religion, culture and social affairs; Editor-in-Chief SAULIUS DRAZDAUSKAS; circ. 1,000.

Nemunas: Gedimino g. 45, Kaunas 44239; tel. and fax (37) 322244; e-mail nemunasr@gmail.com; internet test.svs.lt/?Nemunas; f. 1967; weekly since 2004; Thursdays; culture and art; journal of the Lithuanian Writers' Union; Editor-in-Chief VIKTORAS RUDŽIANSKAS; circ. 1,500.

Panelė (Young Miss): Ozo g. 10A, Vilnius 08200; tel. (5) 247-7716; fax (5) 210-2557; e-mail magazine@panele.lt; internet www.panele.lt; f. 1994; monthly; popular, for ages 12–25; Editor-in-Chief JURGA BALTRUKONYTĖ; circ. 66,000.

Psihologija Tau: Trakų g. 8, Vilnius 01132; tel. (5) 262-6763; fax (5) 262-7671; e-mail redakcija@psichologijatau.lt; internet www.psichologijatau.lt; popular psychology; Editor RŪTA CHOMENTAUSKAITĖ.

Septynios meno dienos (7 meno dienos) (Seven Days of Art): Bernardinų g. 10, Vilnius 01124; tel. (5) 261-3039; fax (5) 261-1926; e-mail 7md@takas.lt; internet www.culture.lt/7menodienos; f. 1992; weekly; culture; Editor-in-Chief LINAS VILDŽIŪNAS; circ. 1,500.

Tremtinys (Deportee): Laisvės al. 39, Kaunas 44282; tel. (37) 323204; e-mail tremtinys@erdvas.lt; internet www.lpkts.lt/tremtinys.htm; f. 1988; weekly; publ. of fmr Lithuanian Union of Political Prisoners and Deportees (now part of Homeland Union—Lithuanian Christian Democrats); Editor-in-Chief AUDRONĖ KAMINSKIENĖ; circ. 4,500.

Valstiečių laikraštis (Farmer's Newspaper): Saltoniškių g. 29/Sėlių g. 3, Vilnius 08105; tel. and fax (5) 210-0110; fax (5) 242-1281; e-mail redakcija@valstietis.lt; internet www.valstietis.lt; f. 1940; 2 a week; Editor-in-Chief STASYS JOKŪBAITIS; circ. 68,000.

Vasario 16 (16 February): J. Gruodžio g. 9/404, Kaunas 44293; tel. (37) 225219; f. 1988; fortnightly; journal of Order and Justice Party; Sec. PRIMAS NOREIKA; circ. 1,600.

NEWS AGENCIES

Baltic News Service (BNS): Jogailos g. 9/1, Vilnius 01116; tel. (5) 205-8501; fax (5) 205-8504; e-mail arturas@bns.lt; internet www.bns.lt; f. 1991; Dir and Editor-in-Chief ARTŪRAS RAČAS.

ELTA Lithuanian News Agency (ELTA Lietuvos Naujienų Agentūra): Gedimino pr. 21/2, Vilnius 01103; tel. (5) 262-8864; fax (5) 261-9507; e-mail zinios@elta.lt; internet www.elta.lt; f. 1920; 18.4%

LITHUANIA

owned by Ziniu Partneriai; 39.5% owned by Respublikos Investicija (both cos controlled by Respublika Gp); Dir Grazina Ramanauskaitė-Tiumenevienė.

Publishers

Alma littera: A. Juozapavičiaus 6/2, Vilnius 09310; tel. (5) 263-8877; fax (5) 272-8026; e-mail post@almali.lt; internet www.almali.lt; f. 1990; fiction, children's books, textbooks; Dir-Gen. Arvydas Andrijauskas.

Baltos lankos leidykla (White Meadows Publishing House): Aušros Vartų g. 29/1, Vilnius 01129; tel. (5) 240-8673; fax (5) 240-7446; e-mail leidykla@baltoslankos.lt; internet www.baltoslankos.lt; f. 1992; literature, humanities, social sciences, fiction and textbooks; Dir Saulius Žukas.

Eugrimas: Kalvariju 98/36, Vilnius 08211; tel. and fax (5) 273-3955; e-mail info@eugrimas.lt; internet www.eugrimas.lt; f. 1995; academic and professional literature, incl. economics, business, law and politics; Dir Eugenija Petrulienė.

Katalikų pasaulio leidiniai (Editions of the Catholic World): Pylimo 27/14, Vilnius 01141; tel. (5) 212-2422; fax (5) 212-0375; internet www.katalikuleidiniai.lt; f. 1990; Dir Birutė Bartasūnaite.

Lietuvos rašytoju sąjungos leidykla (Lithuanian Writers' Union Publishers): K. Sirvydo 6, Vilnius 01101; tel. and fax (5) 262-8945; e-mail info@rsleidykla.lt; internet www.rsleidykla.lt; f. 1990; fiction, essays, literary heritage, children's books; Dir Giedre Soriene.

Mintis leidykla (Mintis Publishing House): Z. Sierakausko g. 15, Vilnius 03105; tel. (5) 233-2943; fax (5) 216-3157; e-mail redakcija@mintis.org; internet www.mintis.org; f. 1949; philosophy, politics, history, law, mythology, textbooks, encyclopedias, biographies, fiction; also book distributor, bookshop; Dir Leonardas Armonas.

Mokslo ir enciklopedijų leidybos institutas (Science and Encyclopedia Publishing Institute): L. Asanavičiūtės 23, Vilnius 04315; tel. (5) 245-8526; fax (5) 245-8537; e-mail meli@meli.lt; internet www.meli.lt; f. 1992; encyclopedias, science and reference books, dictionaries, higher education textbooks, books for the general reader; Dir Rimantas Kareckas.

Presvika: Kauno g. 28, Vilnius 03202; tel. (5) 262-3182; fax (5) 262-3110; e-mail presvika@presvika.lt; internet www.presvika.lt; f. 1996; psychological and educational literature, textbooks, fiction; Dir Violeta Bilaišytė.

Šviesa (Light): E. Ožeškienės g. 10, Kaunas 44252; tel. (37) 409126; fax (37) 342032; e-mail mail@sviesa.lt; internet www.sviesa.lt; f. 1945; textbooks and pedagogical literature; Dir Asta Verkienė.

Tyto alba: J. Jasinskio g. 10, Vilnius 01112; tel. (5) 249-7453; fax (5) 298-8602; internet www.tytoalba.lt; f. 1993; contemporary Lithuanian literary fiction and non-fiction, fiction in translation; Dir Lolita Varanavičienė.

UAB Leidykla Vaga (Furrow Publishing House Ltd): Gedimino pr. 50, Vilnius 01110; tel. (5) 249-8121; fax (5) 249-8122; e-mail info@vaga.lt; internet www.vaga.lt; f. 1945 as Lithuanian State Publishing House of Fiction; privatized and restructured in 1994; fiction, non-fiction, art, children's books; Dir Vytas V. Petrošius.

UAB Versus Aureus leidykla: Rūdninkų g. 10, Vilnius 01135; tel. and fax (5) 265-2730; e-mail versus@versus.lt; internet www.versus.lt; f. 2003; fiction, non-fiction and educational literature.

PUBLISHERS' ASSOCIATION

Lietuvos Leidėjų Asociacija (Lithuanian Publishers' Association): A. Jakšto 22–13, Vilnius 01105; tel. and fax (5) 261-7740; e-mail lla@centras.lt; internet www.lla.lt; f. 1989; Pres. Eugenijus Kaziliūnas.

Broadcasting and Communications

TELECOMMUNICATIONS

Regulatory Authority

Communications Regulatory Authority (Ryšių reguliavimo tarnyba): Algirdo 27, Vilnius 03219; tel. (5) 210-5633; fax (5) 216-1564; e-mail rrt@rrt.lt; internet www.rrt.lt; f. 2001; Dir Tomas Barakauskas.

Service Providers

UAB BITĖ Lietuva: Žemaitės 15, Vilnius 03118; tel. (6) 560-0656; fax (6) 990-0111; e-mail info@bite.lt; internet www.bite.lt; mobile telecommunications service provider; 1.8m. subscribers (Dec. 2006); CEO Martin Amtoft-Christensen.

UAB Eurocom: Ozo g. 25, Vilnius 07150; tel. (5) 274-4699; fax (5) 274-4612; e-mail eurocom@eurocom.lt; internet www.eurocom.lt; f. 2001; fixed line and mobile telecommunications service provider; a subsidiary of VP Market; Dir Sediminas Jovaiša.

Omnitel UAB: T. Ševčenkos 25, Vilnius 03503; tel. (698) 63333; fax (5) 274-5574; e-mail info@omnitel.net; internet www.omnitel.lt; f. 1991 as Litcom; owned by Telia Sonera (Sweden); largest mobile GSM communications provider in Lithuania; Pres. Antanas Juozas Zabulis.

UAB Tele2: POB 147, Vilnius 01003; tel. (684) 00212; fax (5) 236-6301; e-mail tele2@tele2.lt; internet www.tele2.lt; f. 1999; owned by Tele2 AB (Sweden); provider of GSM, internet and fixed-line telecommunications services; Chief Exec. Petras Masiulis.

Teo LT AB: Savanorių pr. 28, Vilnius 03116; tel. (5) 262-1511; fax (5) 212-6655; internet www.teo.lt; f. 1992 under the name Lietuvos Telekomas AB; present name adopted 2006; privatized 1998; operates public telecommunications network, repairs telecommunications equipment; monopoly withdrawn in 2003; Chair. Erik Hallberg; Gen. Man. Arūnas Šikšta; 3,200 employees.

BROADCASTING

Regulatory Authority

Lietuvos radijo ir televizijos komisija (Radio and Television Commission of Lithuania): Vytenio g. 6/23, Vilnius 03113; tel. (5) 233-0660; fax (5) 264-7125; e-mail lrtk@rtk.lt; internet www.rtk.lt; f. 1996; licensing and licence compliance; Chair. Jonas Liniauskas.

Radio

Lietuvos radijas ir televizija (LRT) (Lithuanian Radio and Television): S. Konarskio 49, Vilnius 03123; tel. (5) 236-3209; fax (5) 236-3208; e-mail lrt@lrt.lt; internet www.lrt.lt; f. 1926; govt-owned; non-profit public broadcasting co; operates three national radio channels and two national television channels; Chair. of Bd Gediminas Ilgūnas; Dir-Gen. Audrius Siaurusevičius; 650 employees.

Lietuvos radijas (Lithuanian Radio): S. Konarskio 49, Vilnius 03123; tel. (5) 236-3000; fax (5) 213-5333; e-mail rimgel@lrt.lt; internet www.lrt.lt; f. 1926; broadcasts in Lithuanian, Russian, Polish, Yiddish, Belarusian and Ukrainian; Dir Jurgita Litvinienė.

A2 Radijo Stotis: Laisvės pr. 3, Vilnius 04215; tel. (5) 245-4922; e-mail a2@a2.lt; internet www.a2.lt; private, commercial; Dir Vydas Ivanauskas.

UAB Aukštaitijos radijas (AR): Laisvės a. 1, Panevėžys 35175; tel. and fax (45) 596969; e-mail ar@laineta.lt; private, commercial; Dir Algirdas Šatas.

FM 99: Rotušės a. 2, POB 119, Alytus 62141; tel. (315) 76120; fax (315) 74646; e-mail fm99@fm99.lt; internet www.fm99.lt; private, commercial; broadcast by UAB Alytaus radijas; Dir Liudas Ramanauskas.

Kauno fonas 105.4: Savanorių pr. 192–802, Kaunas 44151; tel. (37) 327427; fax (37) 327447; internet www.kf.lt; private, commercial; Dir Udrys Staselka.

UAB Laisvoji banga: Lvovo 25, Vilnius 09320; tel. and fax (5) 233-3121; e-mail info@laisvojibanga.lt; internet www.europeanhitradio.lt; private, commercial; broadcasts news and music; Dir Jūratė Overlingienė.

Laluna: Taikos pr. 81, Klaipėda 94114; tel. (46) 390808; fax (46) 390805; e-mail info@laluna.lt; internet www.laluna.lt; private, commercial; Dir Tadas Žemaitis.

M-1: Laisvės pr. 60, Vilnius 05120; tel. (5) 236-0360; fax (5) 236-0366; e-mail m-1@m-1.fm; internet www.m-1.fm; f. 1989; private, commercial; Gen. Man. Rūta Grušnienė.

Mažeikių aidas (MA): POB 17, Ventos g. 49, Mažeikiai 89103; tel. (443) 65055; fax (443) 65600; e-mail info@mazeikiuaidas.lt; internet www.mazeikiuaidas.lt; f. 1996; private, commercial; Dir Tomas Ruginis.

Pūkas, UAB: Ringuvos g. 61, Kaunas 45242; tel. (37) 342424; fax (37) 342434; e-mail pukas@pukas.lt; internet www.pukas.lt; f. 1991; private, commercial; operates two radio stations and a television station; Dir Kęstutis Pūkas.

Radiocentras, UAB: Laisvės pr. 60, Vilnius 05120; tel. (5) 212-8706; fax (5) 242-9073; e-mail biuras@rc.lt; internet www.rc.lt; f. 1991; private, commercial; Gen. Man. Artūras Mironcikas.

Saulės radijas, UAB: Aušros al. 64, Šiauliai 76235; tel. (41) 525141; fax (41) 424404; e-mail info@saulesradijas.lt; internet www.saulesradijas.lt; private, commercial; Dir Rasa Akučkiene.

Tau: Draugystės g. 19–357, Kaunas 51230; tel. (37) 352790; fax (37) 352128; e-mail info@tau.lt; internet www.tau.lt; private, commercial; Dir Giedrius Gipas.

LITHUANIA   *Directory*

Vsļ Kauno radijas ir televizija: S. Daukanto 28A, Kaunas 44246; tel. (37) 321010; fax (37) 322570; e-mail kaunas@lrtv.lt; Dir P. GARNYS.

Znad Wilii, UAB: Laisvės pr. 60, Vilnius 05120; tel. (5) 249-0870; fax (5) 278-4446; e-mail radio@znadwilii.lt; internet www.znadwilii.lt; f. 1992; private, commercial; Dir-Gen. MIROSLAVAS JUCHNEVIČIUS.

Television

Lietuvos televizija (LTV): S. Konarskio 49, Vilnius 03123; tel. (5) 236-3100; fax (5) 216-3282; e-mail lrt@lrt.lt; internet www.lrt.lt; f. 1957; subsidiary of LRT (see Radio); programmes in Lithuanian, Russian, Polish, Ukrainian and Belarusian; Dir RIMVYDAS PALECKIS.

Aidas, UAB (Echo): Birutės skg. 42, Trakai 21114; tel. (528) 52480; fax (528) 55656; e-mail tvaidas@uab.lt; mainly relays German programmes; private, commercial; Dir ČESLOVAS RULEVIČIUS.

Baltijos televizija (BTV): Laisvės pr. 60, Vilnius 05120; tel. (5) 278-0805; fax (5) 278-0804; internet www.btv.lt; f. 1993; broadcasts own programmes and relays German, Polish and US broadcasts; private, commercial; Dir-Gen. GINTARAS SONGAILA.

KTV plius: Nemuno g. 79, Panevėžys 37355; tel. (45) 514103; fax (45) 443561; e-mail pictura@kateka.lt; internet www.ktvplius.lt; private, commercial; Pres. ROLANDAS MEILIŪNAS.

LNK TV (UAB Laisvas ir nepriklausomas kanalas): Šeškinės g. 20, Vilnius 07156; tel. (5) 212-4061; fax (5) 278-4530; e-mail info@lnk.lt; internet www.lnk.lt; private, commercial; broadcasts TV1; Dir PAULIUS KOVAS.

PAN-TV: Respublikos g. 19–8, Panevėžys 35185; tel. (45) 464267; e-mail pantv@takas.lt; private, commercial; Dir SAULIUS BUKELIS.

Raseiniu TV: Vytauto Vilniaus 1A, Raseiniai 60187; tel. (428) 54433; fax (428) 70422; e-mail office@mirkliai.lt; broadcast by Všļ Raseinių televizijos ir radijo centras; Dir KĘSTUTIS SKAMARAKAS.

Šiaulių TV: Liejyklos g. 10, Šiauliai 78147; tel. and fax (41) 523809; internet www.stv.lt; private; Dir ANDRIUS ŠEDŽIUS.

TV3: Nemenčinės pl. 4, Vilnius 10102; tel. (5) 276-4264; fax (5) 276-4253; e-mail postmaster@tv3.lt; internet www.tv3.lt; broadcasts own programmes (20% of schedule) in Lithuanian and English, and relays international satellite channels; private, commercial; Dir RAMŪNAS ŠAUČIKOVAS.

Finance

(cap. = capital; res = reserves; dep. = deposits; m. = million; brs = branches; amounts in litai)

BANKING
Central Bank

Bank of Lithuania (Lietuvos bankas): Gedimino pr. 6, Vilnius 01103; tel. (5) 268-0029; fax (5) 262-8124; e-mail info@lb.lt; internet www.lb.lt; f. 1922; re-est. 1990; central bank, responsible for bank supervision; cap. 200.0m., res 794.1m., dep. 4,519.6m. (Dec. 2008); Chair. of Bd VITAS VASILIAUSKAS; 2 brs.

Commercial Banks

Bankas Snoras: A. Vivulskio g. 7, Vilnius 03221; tel. (5) 239-2239; fax (5) 232-7300; e-mail info@snoras.com; internet www.snoras.com; f. 1992; cap. 411.9m., res 66.4m., dep. 7,673.4m. (Dec. 2008); Chair. of Supervisory Bd VLADIMIR ANTONOV; Chair. of Management Bd RAIMONDAS BARANAUSKAS.

Citadele Bank AB: K. Kalinausko g. 13, Vilnius 03107; tel. (5) 266-4600; fax (5) 266-4601; e-mail info@parex.lt; internet www.citadele.lt; f. 1996 as Parex Bankas; renamed in 2010; owned by Citadele banka (Latvia); cap. 115.0m., res 0.5m., dep. 445.9m. (June 2007); Chair. and Chief Exec. ALMA VAITKUNSKIENE; 6 brs.

DnB NORD Bankas: J. Basanavičiaus g. 26, Vilnius 03601; tel. (5) 239-3444; fax (5) 213-9057; e-mail info@dnbnord.lt; internet www.dnbnord.lt; f. 1924; registered as AB Lietuvos Žemės Ūkio Bankas in 1993; privatized in March 2002; present name adopted 2006; 93.1% obtained by Bank DnB Nord A/S (Denmark) in Dec. 2005; cap. 591.0m., res 282.5m., dep. 11,694.9m. (Dec. 2008); Chair. of Management Bd, Pres. and CEO WERNER SCHILLI; 77 brs.

Medicinos Bankas (Medical Bank): Pamėnkalnio g. 40, Vilnius 01114; tel. (5) 264-4800; fax (5) 264-4801; e-mail info@medbank.lt; internet www.medbank.lt; f. 1992; cap. 68.8m., res 16.8m., dep. 580.0m. (Dec. 2008); Chair. of Bd KĘSTUTIS OLŠAUSKAS; 7 brs.

SEB Bankas (SEB Bank): Gedimino pr. 12, Vilnius 01103; tel. (5) 268-2800; fax (5) 268-2333; e-mail info@seb.lt; internet www.seb.lt; f. 1990 as Spaudos Bankas; present name adopted 2008; 100% owned by Skandinaviska Enskilda Banken AB (Sweden); cap. 1,034.6m., res 167.4m., dep. 17,560m. (Dec. 2010); Pres. and CEO RAIMONDAS KVEDARAS.

Šiaulių Bankas: Tilžės str. 149, Šiauliai 76348; tel. (41) 595607; fax (41) 430774; e-mail info@sb.lt; internet www.sb.lt; f. 1992; cap. 180.3m., res 51.0m., dep. 1,761.3m. (Dec. 2008); Chair. of Bd ALGIRDAS BUTKUS; 60 brs and client service centres (2007).

Swedbank: Konstitucijos pr. 20A, Vilnius 03502; tel. (5) 268-4444; fax (5) 258-2700; e-mail info@swedbank.lt; internet www.swedbank.lt; f. 1919 as Lietuvos Taupomasis Bankas; renamed Bankas Hansabankas in 2003; present name adopted 2009; 99.5% owned by Swedbank AB (Sweden); cap. 845.9m., res 200.6m., dep. 17,029.1m. (Dec. 2008); Chair. of Bd ANTANAS DANYS.

Ūkio Bankas: Maironio g. 25, Kaunas 44250; tel. (37) 301301; fax (37) 323188; e-mail ub@ub.lt; internet www.ub.lt; f. 1989; cap. 196.7m., res 189.1m., dep. 3,322.4m. (Dec. 2008); Chair. of Bd EDITA KARPAVIČIENE; Chief Exec. GINTARAS UGIANSKIS; 12 brs.

Banking Association

Association of Lithuanian Banks (Lietuvos Bankų Asociacija): Ankštoji g. 5/3, Vilnius 01109; tel. (5) 249-6669; fax (5) 249-6139; e-mail info@lba.lt; internet www.lba.lt; f. 1991; Pres. STASYS KROPAS; 11 mems.

STOCK EXCHANGE

Vilnius Stock Exchange (VSE) (Vilniaus vertybinių popierių birža): Konstitucijos pr. 7, Vilnius 08501; tel. (5) 272-3871; fax (5) 272-4894; e-mail vilnius@nasdaqomx.com; internet www.nasdaqomxbaltic.com; f. 1993; 93.1% owned by the NASDAQ OMX Group (USA); Chair. of Bd ARMINTA SALADŽIENĖ.

INSURANCE
Principal Insurance Companies

Commercial Union Lietuva Gyvybės draudimas: Lvovo g. 25, Vilnius 09320; tel. (5) 269-0169; fax (5) 269-0269; e-mail info@aviva.lt; internet www.commercialunion.lt; f. 2001; owned by Commercial Union Polska—Towarzystwo Ubezpieczeń na Zycie SA (Poland), part of the Aviva Group (United Kingdom); Dir A. UNGULAITIENĖ.

Ergo Lietuva: Geležinio vilko g. 6A, Vilnius 03507; tel. (5) 268-3000; fax (5) 268-3045; e-mail info@ergo.lt; internet www.ergo.lt; f. 1991; owned by Ergo International AG (Germany); formerly Drauda UAB; name changed as above in 2000; in 2002 merged with Preventa; CEO S. JOKUBAITIS.

Lietuvos draudimas AB (Lithuanian Insurance): J. Basanavičiaus g. 12, Vilnius 03600; tel. (5) 243-1167; fax (5) 231-4138; e-mail info@ldr.lt; internet www.ld.lt; f. 1921; privatized in 1999; part of RSA group (United Kingdom); principal non-life insurance co in Lithuania; CEO KĘSTUTIS SERPYTIS.

PZU Lietuva UAB: Konstitucijos pr. 7, Vilnius 09308; tel. (5) 279-0007; fax (5) 279-0019; e-mail info@pzu.lt; internet www.pzu.lt; f. 1993; owned by Powszechny Zaklad Ubezpieczen (PZU) SA (Poland); Chair. BOGDAN BENCZAK.

SEB VB Gyvybės Draudimas UAB: Gedimino pr. 12, Vilnius 01103; tel. (5) 268-1555; fax (5) 268-1556; e-mail draudimas@seb.lt; internet www.seb.lt; f. 1999; owned by SEB Vilniaus bankas AB; Dir B. KAMUNTAVIČIENĖ.

Swedbank gyvybės draudimas AB (Swedbank Life Insurance): Konstitucijos pr. 20A, Vilnius 03502; tel. (5) 268-4444; fax (5) 258-2700; e-mail info@swedbank.lt; internet www.hansadraudimas.lt; f. 1995; owned by Swedbank AS (Sweden); formerly Lietuvos Draudimo gyvybės draudimas, then Hansa gyvybės draudimas; present name adopted 2009; life; Dir CARL ERIC STÅLBERG.

Insurance Association

Association of Lithuanian Insurers: Gedimino pr. 45/11, Vilnius 01109; tel. (5) 231-0381; e-mail asociacija@draudikai.lt; internet www.draudikai.lt; f. 1992; Dir ANDRIUS ROMANOVSKIS.

Supervisory Body

Insurance Supervisory Commission: Ukmergės g. 222, Vilnius 07157; tel. (5) 243-1370; fax (5) 272-3689; e-mail dpk@dpk.lt; internet www.dpk.lt; Chair. MINDAUGAS ŠALČIUS.

Trade and Industry

GOVERNMENT AGENCY

State Property Fund (Valstybės Turto Fondas—VTS): Vilniaus g. 16, Vilnius 01402; tel. (5) 268-4999; fax (5) 268-4997; e-mail info@vtf.lt; internet www.vtf.lt; f. 1995; privatization and management of state-owned and municipal property; Chair. ARNOLDAS BURKOVSKIS; Dir-Gen. JONAS NIAURA.

LITHUANIA

DEVELOPMENT AGENCY

National Regional Development Agency (Nacionalinė Regionų Plėtros Agentūra): Vilniaus g. 88, Šiauliai 76285; tel. (41) 552061; fax (41) 523903; e-mail info@nrda.lt; internet www.nrda.lt; f. 1999 by the Asscn of Lithuanian Chambers of Commerce, Industry and Crafts; Dir VAIDAS KAZAKEVIČIUS.

CHAMBERS OF COMMERCE

Association of Lithuanian Chambers of Commerce, Industry and Crafts (Lietuvos prekybos, pramonės ir amatų rūmų asociacija): J. Tumo-Vaižganto g. 9/1–63A, Vilnius 01108; tel. (5) 261-2102; fax (5) 261-2112; e-mail info@chambers.lt; internet www.chambers.lt; f. 1992; mem. of International Chamber of Commerce and of Asscn of European Chambers of Commerce and Industry; Pres. RIMANTAS STANKEVIČIUS.

Kaunas Chamber of Commerce, Industry and Crafts: K. Donelaičio g. 8, POB 2111, Kaunas 44213; tel. (37) 229212; fax (37) 208330; e-mail chamber@chamber.lt; internet www.chamber.lt; f. 1925; re-est. 1991; br. at Marijampolė; Pres. Prof. M. RONDOMANSKAS.

Klaipėda Chamber of Commerce, Industry and Crafts: Danės g. 17, POB 148, Klaipėda 92117; tel. (46) 390861; fax (46) 410626; e-mail klaipeda@chambers.lt; internet www.kcci.lt; Pres. BENEDIKTAS PETRAUSKA; Gen. Dir VIKTORAS KROLIS; 200 mems.

Panevėžys Chamber of Commerce, Industry and Crafts: Respublikos g. 34, Panevėžys 35173; tel. (45) 463687; fax (45) 500309; e-mail panevezys@chambers.lt; internet www.ccic.lt; f. 1991; Pres. SIGITAS GAILIŪNAS; Gen. Dir VISVALDAS MATKEVIČIUS.

Šiauliai Chamber of Commerce, Industry and Crafts: Vilniaus g. 88, Šiauliai 76285; tel. (41) 523224; fax (41) 523903; e-mail siauliai@chambers.lt; internet www.rumai.lt; f. 1993; Dir-Gen. ALFREDAS JONUŠKA.

Vilnius Chamber of Commerce, Industry and Crafts: Algirdo g. 31, Vilnius 03219; tel. (5) 213-5550; fax (5) 213-5542; e-mail vilnius@cci.lt; internet www.cci.lt; f. 1991; Dir-Gen. BORISAS ZAUBIDOVAS; 480 mems.

INDUSTRIAL ASSOCIATION

Lithuanian Confederation of Industrialists (Lietuvos pramonininkų konfederacija—LPK): A. Vienuolio g. 8, Vilnius 01104; tel. (5) 212-5217; fax (5) 212-5209; e-mail sekretoriatas@lpk.lt; internet www.lpk.lt; f. 1989; Pres. BRONISLOVAS LUBYS.

EMPLOYERS' ORGANIZATION

Lithuanian Business Employers' Confederation (Lietuvos verslo darbdavių konfederacija—LVDK): Algirdo g. 31, Vilnius 03219; tel. (5) 249-8345; fax (5) 249-6448; e-mail info@lvdk.eu; internet www.lvdk.eu; f. 1999; Gen. Dir DANUKAS ARLAUSKAS.

UTILITIES

Energy Agency (Energetikos agentūra): Gedimino pr. 38/Vasario 16-osios g. 2, Vilnius 01104; tel. (5) 261-9225; fax (5) 262-6845; e-mail eainfo@ena.lt; internet www.ena.lt; f. 1993; state enterprise; attached to the Ministry of Energy; Dir MARIJUS FRANCKEVIČIUS.

Electricity

AB Lesto: Žvejų g. 14, Vilnius 09310; tel. (5) 277-7524; fax (5) 277-7514; e-mail info@lesto.lt; internet www.lesto.lt; f. 2010 following the reorganization of Rytų Skirstomieji Tinklai AB and Vakarų Skirstomieji Tinklai AB; distribution network operator; CEO ARVYDAS TARASEVIČIUS.

Lietuvos Energija AB (Lithuanian Power): Žvejų g. 14, Vilnius 09310; tel. (5) 262-6822; fax (5) 212-6736; e-mail info@lietuvosenergija.lt; internet www.lpc.lt; f. 1995; restructured in 2000; 96.5% owned by LEO LT AB; Chair. of Bd HENRIKAS BERNATAVIČIUS; CEO ALOYZAS KORYZNA.

Gas

Lietuvos Dujos AB (Lithuanian Gas): Aguonų g. 24, Vilnius 03212; tel. (5) 236-0209; fax (5) 236-0200; e-mail ld@lietuvosdujos.lt; internet www.dujos.lt; f. 1995; natural gas import, sale and transportation; 17.7% state-owned; 38.9% owned by E.ON Ruhrgas International AG (Germany); 37.1% owned by OAO Gazprom (Russia); Chair. Dr VALERY GOLUBEV; Gen. Man. VIKTORAS VALENTUKEVIČIUS; 1,900 employees.

TRADE UNIONS

Lithuanian Labour Federation (Lietuvos Darbo Federacija): Vytauto g. 14, Vilnius 03106; tel. and fax (5) 231-2029; e-mail ldforg@ldf.lt; internet www.ldf.lt; f. 1919 as a Christian trade union org.; re-est. 1991; 20,000 mems; Chair. VYDAS PUSKEPALIS; Sec.-Gen. JANINA SVEDIENĖ.

Lithuanian Trade Union Confederation (Lietuvos profesinių sąjungų konfederacija—LPSK): J. Jasinskio g. 9/213, Vilnius 01111; tel. (5) 249-6921; fax (5) 249-8078; e-mail lpsk@lpsk.lt; internet www.lpsk.lt; f. 2002 by merger of Lithuanian Union of Trade Unions (LPSS) and Lithuanian Trade Union Centre (LPSC); 26 branch trade unions with 70,000 mems; Pres. ARTŪRAS ČERNIAUSKAS.

Lithuanian Trade Union: Solidarumas (Lietuvos profesinė sąjunga 'Solidarumas'): K. Kalinausko 2, Vilnius; tel. (5) 262-1743; fax (5) 213-3295; e-mail info@lps.lt; internet www.lps.lt; f. 2002; fmrly the Lithuanian Workers' Union: Labora (f. 1989); Pres. ALDONA JAŠINSKIENĖ; 52,000 mems.

Transport

RAILWAYS

In 2008 there were 1,765 km of railway track in use in Lithuania, of which 122 km were electrified. Main lines link Vilnius with Minsk (Belarus), Kaliningrad (Russia) and Warsaw (Poland), in the latter case by way of the Belarusian town of Grodno (Horadnia).

Lithuanian Railways (Lietuvos geležinkeliai): Mindaugo g. 12–14, Vilnius 03603; tel. (5) 269-2038; fax (5) 269-2028; e-mail lgkanc@litrail.lt; internet www.litrail.lt; f. 1991; Dir-Gen. STASYS DAILYDKA; 10,334 employees.

ROADS

In 2007 the total length of the road network was estimated at 80,715 km, 88% of which were paved; the motorway network totalled 309 km.

Lithuanian Road Administration (Lietuvos automobilių kelių direkcija—LAKD): J. Basanavičiaus g. 36/2, Vilnius 03109; tel. (5) 232-9600; fax (5) 232-9609; e-mail lra@lra.lt; internet www.lra.lt; Dir-Gen. VIRGAUDAS PUODŽIUKAS.

SHIPPING

The main port is at Klaipėda. In 2007 there were 441 km of inland navigable waterways.

Port Authority

Klaipėda State Seaport Authority: J. Janonio g. 24, Klaipėda 92251; tel. (46) 499799; fax (46) 499777; e-mail info@port.lt; internet www.port.lt; multi-purpose, deep-water universal port; connects sea, land and rail routes from east and west; Dir-Gen. ALGIRDAS KAMARAUSKAS (acting).

Shipowning Company

Lithuanian Shipping Company (AB Lietuvos Jūrų Laivininkystė): Malunininku g. 3, Klaipėda 92264; tel. (46) 393105; fax (46) 393119; e-mail gp@ljl.lt; internet www.ljl.lt; f. 1969 as LISCO; partially privatized and renamed as above in June 2001; 73.24% state-owned; transportation of cargo; owns 18 vessels; Gen. Dir VYTAUTAS VISMANTAS.

CIVIL AVIATION

There are international airports at Vilnius, Kaunas, Palanga and Šiauliai.

Directorate of Civil Aviation (Oro Navigacija): Rodūnios kelias 2, Vilnius 02188; tel. (5) 273-9102; fax (5) 273-9161; e-mail info@ans.lt; internet www.ans.lt; Dir-Gen. ALGIMANTAS RAŠČIUS.

Small Planet Airlines: Smolensko g. 4, Vilnius 03201; tel. (5) 252-5660; fax (5) 252-5661; e-mail info@smallplanet.aero; internet www.smallplanet.aero; f. 2007 as flyLAL Charters; present name adopted 2010; operates passenger and cargo charter flights; CEO VYTAUTAS KAIKARIS.

Tourism

Tourist attractions in Lithuania include the historic cities of Vilnius, Kaunas, Kėdainiai, Trakai and Klaipėda, coastal resorts, such as Palanga and Kuršių Nerija, and picturesque countryside. Some 752,389 tourists visited the country in 2009; tourist receipts (including passenger transport) totalled US $1,192m. in 2007.

State Dept of Tourism: Švitrigailos 11M, Vilnius 03228; tel. (5) 210-8796; fax (5) 210-8753; e-mail vtd@tourism.lt; internet www.tourism.lt; Dir NIJOLĖ KLIOKIENĖ.

Defence

Until independence, Lithuania had no armed forces separate from those of the USSR. The Department of State Defence (established in April 1990) was reorganized as the Ministry of Defence in October 1991. As assessed at November 2010, Lithuania's armed forces totalled an estimated 10,640, including an army of 8,200 (including 4,700 active reserves), a navy of 410 (including 120 conscripts) and an air force of 980. There was also a paramilitary force of 14,600 (including a border guard of 5,000) and a total of 6,700 reserves. Military service is compulsory and lasts for 12 months. Lithuania became a full member of the North Atlantic Treaty Organization (NATO) on 29 March 2004.

Defence Expenditure: Budgeted at 990m. litai in 2011.

Commander-in-Chief of the Armed Forces: Maj.-Gen. ARVYDAS POCIUS.

Commander of the Land Force: Brig.-Gen. VYTAUTAS JONAS ŽUKAS.

Commander of the Air Force: Brig.-Gen. EDVARDAS MAŽEIKIS.

Commander of the Naval Force: Commdr ARTŪRAS STANKAITIS (acting).

Education

Education, beginning at six years of age, is free and compulsory until the age of 16. Pre-school education is available for children aged between one and six years. Children spend four years at primary school (Grades 1–4), followed by six years at lower secondary school (basic education, Grades 5–10) and two years at upper secondary school or gymnasium (Grades 10–12). Vocational training is available. From 2003 a uniform tuition fee was introduced for students in higher education, although there were exemptions for the highest achievers. In 2007/08 92.8% of children in the relevant age-group were enrolled in primary education, while the comparable rates of enrolment in lower secondary education and in upper secondary education were 94.9% and 78.4%, respectively. In the 2009/10 academic year 488,390 students were enrolled in 1,442 general and vocational schools. In that year there were 23 colleges and 23 universities; total enrolment in institutions of higher education was 201,005. In 1991 the first private schools were opened; by 2007/08 there were 26 private schools, 12 private colleges and seven private universities. Lithuanian is the main language of instruction, although in 2007/08 4.2% of students at general schools were taught in Russian and 3.4% were taught in Polish. Central government expenditure on education in 2007 amounted to 2,027.1m. litai (9.9% of total expenditure).

LUXEMBOURG

Introductory Survey

LOCATION, CLIMATE, LANGUAGE, RELIGION, FLAG, CAPITAL

The Grand Duchy of Luxembourg is a land-locked country in Western Europe. It is bordered by Belgium to the west and north, by Germany to the east and by France to the south. The climate is temperate, with cool summers and mild winters. The average temperature ranges from 1°C (33°F) in January to 18°C (64°F) in July, while annual rainfall averages 782 mm. Luxembourgish (Lëtzebuergesch), a German-Moselle-Frankish dialect, is the spoken language and became the official language in 1984. French is generally used for administrative purposes, while German is the principal written language of commerce and the press. Almost all of the inhabitants profess Christianity: about 87% are Roman Catholics and a small minority are Protestants. The national flag (proportions 3 by 5) consists of three equal horizontal stripes, of red, white and blue. The capital is the city of Luxembourg.

CONTEMPORARY POLITICAL HISTORY

Historical Context

Luxembourg's independence was affirmed in 1839 under the First Treaty of London, at which time it joined the German Customs Union (*Zollverein*), to counter French and Belgian influence. However, to prevent war between Prussia and France over the political status of Luxembourg, its independence and neutrality were reaffirmed under the Second Treaty of London in 1867; Luxembourg remained a member of the German Customs Union until 1919. The King of the Netherlands remained as head of state of Luxembourg until 1890, when the Dutch throne passed to his daughter, while he was succeeded as Grand Duke of Luxembourg by Adolphe I, the last Duke of Nassau, in accordance with the Nassau Family Pact, which favoured male heirs.

Luxembourg was invaded and occupied by Germany during the First and Second World Wars. After the Second World War Luxembourg became a founder member of the UN in 1946, the North Atlantic Treaty Organization (NATO, see p. 368) in 1949, and the European Community (later European Union—EU, see p. 270) in 1957. The Belgo-Luxembourg Economic Union (BLEU) has existed since 1922 (following the signing of a treaty in 1921), except during the period of German occupation in 1940–44. In 1948 the Benelux Economic Union (see p. 445) was inaugurated between Belgium, Luxembourg and the Netherlands, becoming effective in 1960, and establishing the three countries as a single customs area in 1970.

Domestic Political Affairs

Pierre Werner, leader of the Chrëschtlech Sozial Volleksparteï (CSV—Christian Social Party), became Prime Minister in February 1959 and, during 1959–74, led successive coalition governments in which the CSV was the dominant partner, along with either the Demokratesch Partei (DP—Democratic Party) or the Lëtzebuerger Sozialistesch Arbechterpartei (LSAP—Socialist Workers' Party of Luxembourg). However, at a general election in May 1974 the CSV suffered a decrease in popularity, and, for the first time since 1919, entered into opposition. In the following month a centre-left coalition between the DP and the LSAP was formed under the premiership of the leader of the DP, Gaston Thorn. At the next general election, which took place in June 1979, the CSV increased its representation in the Chamber of Deputies (Chambre des Députés), and in July Werner again formed a coalition Government, comprising the CSV and the DP.

At a general election in June 1984 the CSV again secured the largest number of seats in the legislature, but the LSAP substantially increased its representation. A centre-left coalition was formed in July between the CSV and the LSAP, with Jacques Santer of the CSV as Prime Minister. Following the election in June 1989, at which the CSV, the LSAP and the DP each lost three seats, Santer renewed the outgoing coalition. At the next general election, in June 1994, the CSV and the LSAP each lost one representative in the legislature, while the DP gained one seat. The CSV-LSAP coalition was again renewed, with Santer as Prime Minister.

In January 1995 Santer took office as President of the European Commission. He was succeeded as Prime Minister by Jean-Claude Juncker of the CSV, hitherto Minister of the Budget, of Finance and of Labour. The two coalition partners both recorded losses at the general election in June 1999, the CSV winning 19 of the 60 seats and the LSAP 13. The DP increased its representation from 12 to 15 seats, while the conservative Aktiounskomitee fir Demokratie a Rentegerechtegkeet (ADR—Action Committee for Democracy and Pensions Justice) took seven seats (an increase of two). The environmentalist party, Déi Gréng (The Greens), retained its five seats in the legislature. Juncker, who remained as Prime Minister, subsequently formed a new centre-right coalition of the CSV and the DP, which took office in August.

In March 1998 Grand Duke Jean conferred broad constitutional powers upon his eldest son and heir, Prince Henri, permitting him to deputize for the Grand Duke in all official capacities. In October 2000 Grand Duke Jean abdicated and Prince Henri succeeded his father as head of state.

Luxembourg's banking secrecy laws have for many years been a cause of concern. In April 1993 legislation was introduced that permitted the confiscation of deposits in Luxembourg banks accruing from suspected illegal drugs-related activities, and in 1997 the powers of confiscation were extended to include other illegal activities, including arms-smuggling. During 1997 the country's financial sector came under renewed scrutiny when the Belgian authorities conducted an investigation into alleged widespread tax evasion by Belgian citizens and companies based in Luxembourg. The German authorities also launched a similar investigation. Luxembourg was further criticized for refusing, as did Switzerland, to endorse the code of conduct with respect to tax havens drafted by the Organisation for Economic Co-operation and Development (OECD, see p. 376) in April 1998. During 1998 Luxembourg also opposed European Commission proposals for European taxation harmonization, which would oblige Luxembourg to impose tax on non-residents' interest and dividend income for the first time, thereby reducing the attraction of Luxembourg as a financial centre. It was in May 2000, however, that Luxembourg first endorsed OECD proposals aimed at limiting the use of bank secrecy laws for the purpose of tax evasion. In October the Chamber of Deputies approved a relaxation of bank secrecy laws to facilitate co-operation with the US Internal Revenue Service in its attempts to halt tax evasion. Luxembourg was exempted for at least six years from a requirement for EU member states to exchange banking information from 2005 under new EU taxation rules concerning overseas investments agreed in early 2003 (see Economic Affairs).

At the general election held on 13 June 2004 the CSV increased its representation in the legislature from 19 to 24 seats. The LSAP secured 14 seats, while the DP took 10, five fewer than in 1999. Déi Gréng won seven seats and the ADR secured five. A new coalition Government comprising members of the CSV and the LSAP was sworn in on 31 July, again under the leadership of Juncker. Jean Asselborn of the LSAP was appointed as Deputy Prime Minister and Minister of Foreign Affairs and Immigration.

In April 2006 the ADR adopted a new name, Alternativ Demokratesch Reformpartei (Alternative Democratic Reform Party), in an attempt to broaden its appeal. However, the concurrent redesign of the party's logo to incorporate the colours of the national flag provoked criticism that it was adopting a more right-wing, nationalist stance. Several members of the ADR subsequently resigned from the party, including one of its five deputies, who remained in the legislature as an independent; the ADR consequently lost its status as an official parliamentary group.

In January 2008 two former police officers were arrested in connection with a bombing campaign that targeted a number of public buildings in 1985. Later that month both the General Director and the Secretary-General of the police force, Pierre Reuland and Guy Stebens, were suspended from office, following the publication of an open letter by the Attorney-General, Robert Biever, in which he expressed doubts over the credibility of

LUXEMBOURG

public statements made by the two officials regarding the original investigation into the attacks; Reuland and Stebens were dismissed in September.

In February 2008 Luxembourg became the third EU member state (along with Belgium and the Netherlands) to approve legislation decriminalizing euthanasia and assisted suicide, despite opposition from the governing CSV. However, in early December Grand Duke Henri precipitated a constitutional crisis by indicating that he would refuse to ratify the legislation, citing his religious convictions. Despite his own party's opposition to the bill, Juncker criticized the Grand Duke for disregarding the expressed will of parliament and announced a proposal to amend Article 34 of the Constitution, thereby removing the Grand Duke's powers to veto legislation adopted by the legislature. The amendment was approved by the Chamber of Deputies in December and received final approval at a second reading in March 2009. Meanwhile, the legislation decriminalizing euthanasia and assisted suicide was approved at a second reading in the Chamber of Deputies in December 2008 and was promulgated by Grand Duke Henri in March 2009.

At a general election held on 7 June 2009 the CSV increased its representation in the Chamber of Deputies to 26 seats. The LSAP and the DP each lost one seat, taking 13 and nine, respectively, while Déi Gréng's representation was unchanged at seven seats. The ADR won four seats. On 23 July Junker renewed the outgoing CSV-LSAP coalition; Asselborn remained as Deputy Prime Minister and Minister of Foreign Affairs, and most of the other ministers from the previous Government were also retained.

Divisions emerged within the ruling coalition in 2010 over the proposed revision of the wage indexation system, whereby salaries are automatically adjusted according to changes in the cost of living. Fearing that the current system could lead to a loss of economic competitiveness, the CSV Minister of Finance, Luc Frieden, supported by the LSAP Minister of the Economy and External Trade, Jeannot Krecké, advocated the exclusion of energy, alcohol and tobacco prices from the calculation. However, such a reform was strongly opposed by other members of the LSAP and by the trade unions, and appeared to have been abandoned in September, when it was agreed, none the less, that the next index-linked rise in wages would be delayed until October 2011, the last having occurred in July 2010.

Foreign Affairs

As a founder member of the European Community (EC, now European Union—EU, see p. 270), of which the city of Luxembourg is one of the main bases, Luxembourg has played a significant role in progress towards European integration since the Second World War. Luxembourg's commitment to such integration was exemplified by its status as one of the original signatories to the Schengen Agreement (named after the town in Luxembourg where the accord was signed by a number of EC member countries in June 1990), which binds signatories to the abolition of internal border controls.

In December 2000 the Luxembourg Government was prominent during negotiations regarding the Treaty of Nice, which aimed to reform the institutions of the EU in light of its forthcoming enlargements. The terms of the treaty substantially safeguarded Luxembourg's privileged position in the EU: Luxembourg was to continue to have a European Commissioner, to maintain its six seats in the European Parliament and to continue to enjoy a voting weight in the Council of the European Union out of proportion to its size. In July 2001 the Chamber of Deputies ratified the treaty by a large majority. At the same time, Luxembourg continued, much to the frustration of most of its EU partners, to oppose the removal of the Secretariat of the European Parliament from the city of Luxembourg, together with its 1,500 staff, whose continued presence was considered by the Luxembourg Government to be vital to the local economy.

In July 2005 Luxembourg held a national referendum (the first since 1936) on the EU constitutional treaty, which had finally been approved by the EU in mid-2004. Although there were concerns that the proposed constitution was not wholly advantageous for the smaller member states of the EU, the vast majority of political parties in Luxembourg supported the document and Juncker threatened to resign if the electorate rejected the treaty. Opposition to the treaty increased when the French and Dutch, at respective referendums in May and June, voted against its ratification. None the less, the draft treaty was approved by some 56.5% of the Luxembourg electorate. In June 2007, at a summit meeting of EU heads of state and of government in Brussels, a preliminary agreement was reached over a reform treaty to replace the constitutional treaty rejected by French and Dutch voters in 2005. In December 2007 the reform treaty was signed by EU leaders, including Juncker, following a summit meeting in Lisbon, Portugal. The so-called Treaty of Lisbon was ratified by the Chamber of Deputies in May 2008 and entered into force in December 2009, following ratification by all 27 EU member states.

Popular opposition in Luxembourg to a potential US-led military campaign in Iraq to remove the regime of Saddam Hussain culminated in nation-wide demonstrations in February 2003. The Government's opposition to the military intervention (which was undertaken the following month without the support of a UN resolution) adversely affected relations with the USA. Following the swift removal of the Iraqi regime, however, the Luxembourg Government announced the allocation of €3.5m. for the financing of a humanitarian aid programme for Iraq. In March the Chamber of Deputies approved the secondment of 10 officers and men to the International Security Assistance Force in Afghanistan (ISAF) and that of one officer to the EU's peace-keeping mission to the former Yugoslav republic of Macedonia.

In June 2008, at a summit meeting in The Hague, Netherlands, Juncker and his counterparts from Belgium and the Netherlands signed a new Benelux Treaty on political and economic co-operation. The document expanded the scope of the previous treaty, signed in 1958, to provide for greater co-operation between the three Governments on justice and home affairs, as well as customs and cross-border trade. In recognition of this, the official title was to change from the Benelux Economic Union to the Benelux Union. The treaty was ratified by Luxembourg's Chamber of Deputies in May 2009 and by the legislatures of the other two countries and by the parliaments of three of the five Belgian federal units during 2010; it was approved by the parliaments of Belgium's French Community and Walloon Region in April and May 2011, respectively. The treaty was due to enter into effect in July.

CONSTITUTION AND GOVERNMENT

The Constitution dates back to 1868, but in 1919 a constituent assembly introduced some important changes, declaring that the sovereign power resided in the nation, that all secret treaties were denounced and that deputies were to be elected by a list system by means of proportional representation, on the basis of universal adult suffrage. Luxembourg is an hereditary and constitutional monarchy. Legislative power is exercised by the unicameral Chamber of Deputies (Chambre des Députés), with 60 members elected by universal adult suffrage for five years (subject to dissolution). Some legislative functions are also entrusted to the advisory State Council (Conseil d'Etat), with 21 members appointed for life by the Grand Duke, but decisions made by this body can be overruled by the legislature.

Executive power is vested in the Grand Duke, but is normally exercised by the Council of Ministers, led by the President of the Government (Prime Minister). The Grand Duke appoints ministers, but they are responsible to the legislature. Luxembourg is divided into three districts (Luxembourg, Diekirch, Grevenmacher), 12 cantons and 118 municipalities.

REGIONAL AND INTERNATIONAL CO-OPERATION

Luxembourg was a founder member of the European Community, now the European Union (EU, see p. 270), and hosts a number of the EU's institutions. It was also a founder member of the Benelux Economic Union (see p. 445), the Council of Europe (see p. 250) and the Organization for Security and Co-operation in Europe (OSCE, see p. 385).

Luxembourg was a founder member of the UN in 1945. As a contracting party to the General Agreement on Tariffs and Trade, Luxembourg joined the World Trade Organization (WTO, see p. 430) on its establishment in 1995. Luxembourg was also a founder member of the North Atlantic Treaty Organization (NATO, see p. 368) and the Organisation for Economic Co-operation and Development (OECD, see p. 376).

ECONOMIC AFFAIRS

In 2009, according to estimates by the World Bank, Luxembourg's gross national income (GNI), measured at average 2007–09 prices, was US $37,056m., equivalent to $74,430 per head (or $57,640 per head on an international purchasing-power parity basis). During 2000–09, it was estimated, the population increased at an average rate of 1.5% per year, while gross domestic product (GDP) per head grew, in real terms, by an average of 1.4% per year during the same period. Overall GDP

LUXEMBOURG

increased, in real terms, at an average annual rate of 2.9% in 2000–09; according to official figures, GDP declined by 3.6% in 2009, but increased by 3.5% in 2010.

Agriculture (including forestry and fishing) contributed 0.3% of GDP in 2009. In 2008 1.4% of the employed labour force were engaged in the agricultural sector. The principal crops are cereals, potatoes and wine grapes. Livestock-rearing is also of some importance. According to World Bank estimates, agricultural GDP decreased at an average annual rate of 5.1% in 2000–08. Real agricultural GDP declined by 2.9% in 2008.

Industry (including mining, manufacturing, construction and power) provided 13.1% of GDP in 2009, and engaged 21.8% of the employed labour force in 2008. According to World Bank estimates, industrial GDP increased, in real terms, at an average annual rate of 1.8% in 2000–08; it rose by 2.6% in 2007, and by 0.2% in 2008.

Manufacturing activities constitute the most important industrial sector, contributing 6.5% of GDP in 2009 and engaging 10.5% of the employed work-force in 2007. Although the country's deposits of iron ore are no longer exploited, the iron and steel industry remains one of the most important sectors of the Luxembourg economy; metal manufactures accounted for 27.4% of total exports in 2009. The Luxembourg steel industry is dominated by Arcelor Mittal, which was formed from a merger of Arcelor and Mittal Steel in 2006. Machinery and other equipment provided 17.2% of total exports in 2009. Other important branches of manufacturing are basic manufactures and chemicals and related products. Real manufacturing GDP increased by an average of 0.8% per year in 2000–08; it grew by 8.1% in 2007, but declined by 4.2% in 2008.

Construction contributed 13.1% of GDP in 2009 and engaged 11.0% of the employed labour force in 2007. During 2000–08, the sector grew at an average annual rate of 4.0%; growth was 1.6% in 2008.

In 2008 58.7% of net electricity production was thermal, while 27.1% was from hydroelectric installations. Imports of mineral fuels and lubricants comprised 18.0% of the value of total imports in 2009.

The services sector contributed 86.6% of GDP in 2009, and engaged 76.7% of the employed labour force in 2008. Favourable laws governing banking secrecy and taxation encouraged the development of Luxembourg as a major international financial centre. Financial services contributed 26.0% of GDP in 2009. In March 2010 there were 150 banks in Luxembourg, most of which are foreign-owned. In accordance with the demands of the European Commission, however, Luxembourg abolished its preferential tax regime for holding companies from 1 January 2007, although existing companies were permitted to retain their tax benefits until 2010. The replacement regime, the Family Private Assets Management Company, which was aimed at the wealth management sector, was introduced in 2007. Stock exchange activities (notably the Eurobond market and investment portfolio management) are also prominent. From the mid-1990s Luxembourg has had the largest investment fund sector in Europe: in 2005 investment funds accounted for 8% of GDP. In 2007 there were 94 approved insurance companies in Luxembourg, as well as 262 reinsurance companies. According to World Bank estimates, the GDP of the services sector increased, in real terms, at an average annual rate of 4.4% in 2000–08; it rose by 7.6% in 2007, but by only 0.1% in 2008.

In 2009, according to IMF figures, Luxembourg recorded a visible trade deficit of US $4,323m., but there was a surplus of $3,495m. on the current account of the balance of payments.

Other members of the European Union (EU, see p. 270) account for much of Luxembourg's foreign trade. In 2009 the principal source of imports (36.1%) was Belgium; other major providers were Germany (29.6%), France (11.7%) and the Netherlands (6.8%). The principal market for exports in that year was Germany (27.7%); other major purchasers were France (17.3%), Belgium (13.3%) and the Netherlands (5.3%). The principal exports in 2009 were manufactured goods, particularly metal manufactures, and machinery. The principal imports were machinery, transport equipment, manufactured articles, notably metal manufactures, and mineral fuels and lubricants.

In 2010 there was a budgetary deficit of €709,900, equivalent to 1.7% of GDP. Luxembourg's general government gross debt was €7,660.9m. in 2010, equivalent to 18.4% of GDP. The annual rate of inflation averaged 2.2% in 2000–09; consumer prices rose by 2.3% in 2010. The rate of unemployment averaged 6.8% in 2009. In 2009 net cross-border commuters from neighbouring states totalled 136,600, constituting 38.8% of the total employed in Luxembourg.

Luxembourg's economy expanded at an average annual rate of more than 5% during 1985–2000; its success based on its development as an international financial centre, following the decline in the importance of the previously dominant iron and steel industry. The rapid economic expansion of the late 1990s slowed significantly in the early 2000s, but high GDP growth resumed in 2005–07, largely led by the banking and insurance sectors. However, the banking sector was adversely affected by the global financial crisis from mid-2008. The Government acted swiftly to restore confidence in the sector, substantially raising the state deposit guarantee and contributing to efforts to rescue banks threatened by the crisis, including Fortis and Dexia. Luxembourg was well placed to withstand the downturn, owing to its low levels of public debt and strong public finances. Indeed, although the stimulus measures introduced to address the downturn contributed to a worsening of the fiscal situation, at 0.7% of GDP, the general government deficit in 2009 was the lowest in the EU. The deficit widened to 1.7% in 2010, but this was significantly lower than previously projected, owing to higher revenues than anticipated. The Government aimed to return the budget to surplus by 2014. In December 2010 the Chamber of Deputies adopted a range of fiscal measures aimed at reducing the deficit, including the imposition on individuals of a 'crisis contribution' of 0.8%, to be levied on all income. Having contracted by 3.6% in 2009, GDP increased by 3.5% in 2010. None the less, the unemployment rate remained relatively high, at 6.3% in February 2011, compared with 4.0% in June 2008. Moreover, the future profitability of Luxembourg's financial sector was somewhat uncertain, because of the effects of EU integration, including the harmonization of taxation and regulatory structures, which threatened the banking secrecy and tax advantages that made the country attractive to investors. Under EU rules, Luxembourg (along with Austria and Belgium) was allowed to retain banking secrecy until at least 2011, levying a withholding tax on non-residents' savings instead, which rose incrementally from 15% in 2005 to 35% in 2011.

PUBLIC HOLIDAYS

2012: 1 January (New Year's Day), 9 April (Easter Monday), 1 May (Labour Day), 17 May (Ascension Day), 28 May (Whit Monday), 23 June (National Day), 15 August (Assumption), 1 November (All Saints' Day), 25 December (Christmas Day), 26 December (St Stephen's Day).

Statistical Survey

Source (unless otherwise stated): Service Central de la Statistique et des Etudes Economiques (STATEC), Centre Administratif Pierre Werner, 13 rue Erasme, 1468 Luxembourg; tel. 274-84218; fax 46-42-89; e-mail info@statec.etat.lu; internet www.statec.lu.

AREA AND POPULATION

Area: 2,586 sq km (999 sq miles).

Population: 384,634 at census of 1 March 1991; 439,539 (males 216,540, females 222,999) at census of 15 February 2001; 502,066 (males 249,406, females 252,660) official estimate at 1 January 2010.

Density (at 1 January 2010): 194.1 per sq km.

Population by Age and Sex (official estimates at 1 January 2010): *0–14:* 89,111 (males 45,841, females 43,270); *15–64:* 342,909 (males 173,850, females 169,059); *65 and over:* 70,046 (males 29,715, females 40,331); *Total* 502,066 (males 249,406, females 252,660).

Principal Towns (2010): Luxembourg (capital) 90,848; Esch-sur-Alzette 30,147; Differdange 21,530; Dudelange 18,507; Pétange 15,582; Sanem 14,421; Hesperange 13,163.

LUXEMBOURG

Statistical Survey

Births, Marriages and Deaths (2009): Live births 5,638 (birth rate 11.4 per 1,000); Marriages 1,739 (marriage rate 3.5 per 1,000); Deaths 3,657 (death rate 7.4 per 1,000).

Life Expectancy (years at birth, WHO estimates): 80 (males 77; females 83) in 2008. Source: WHO, *World Health Report*.

Immigration and Emigration (2009): Arrivals 15,751; Departures 9,168.

Employment ('000 persons, incl. armed forces, 2007): Agriculture, hunting, forestry and fishing 5.0; Mining and quarrying 0.3; Manufacturing 35.1; Electricity, gas and water supply 1.7; Construction 36.8; Wholesale and retail trade, repair of motor vehicles, motorcycles and personal and household goods 44.2; Hotels and restaurants 15.6; Transport, storage and communications 26.7; Financial intermediation 38.4; Real estate, renting and business activities 54.9; Public administration and defence and compulsory social security 17.4; Education 14.9; Health and social work 25.6; Other community, social and personal service activities 11.8; Private households with employed persons 4.8; *Total employed* 333.2. *2008* ('000): Agriculture and fishing 5.0; Mining and quarrying, manufacturing, and fuel and water 37.7; Construction 38.4; Trade, hotels and restaurants, and trade and communications 89.6; Financial intermediation 41.3; Real estate, renting and business activities 59.5; Other services 77.1; Total employed 348.7; Unemployed 11.0; Total labour force 359.7 (Source ILO). *2009* ('000): Total employed 352.1.

HEALTH AND WELFARE
Key Indicators

Total Fertility Rate (children per woman, 2008): 1.7.

Under-5 Mortality Rate (per 1,000 live births, 2008): 3.

HIV/AIDS (% of persons aged 15–49, 2007): 0.2.

Physicians (per 1,000 head, 2004): 2.7.

Hospital Beds (per 1,000 head, 2004): 6.3.

Health Expenditure (2007): US $ per head (PPP): 5,734.

Health Expenditure (2007): % of GDP: 7.1.

Health Expenditure (2007): public (% of total): 90.9.

Total Carbon Dioxide Emissions ('000 metric tons, 2007): 10,834.4.

Carbon Dioxide Emissions Per head (metric tons, 2007): 22.6.

Human Development Index (2010): ranking: 24.

Human Development Index (2010): value: 0.852.

For sources and definitions, see explanatory note on p. vi.

AGRICULTURE, ETC.

Principal Crops ('000 metric tons unless otherwise indicated, 2009): Wheat 91.0; Rye 7.0; Barley 54.4; Oats 7.2; Triticale (wheat-rye hybrid) 25.4; Potatoes 20.0; Rapeseed 18.1; Mushrooms 5.0 (metric tons); Apples 10.2; Grapes 16.9.

Livestock ('000 head, year ending September 2009): Cattle 196.5; Horses 4.6; Pigs 80.2; Sheep 8.8; Chickens 97.4.

Livestock Products (metric tons, 2009): Cattle meat 15,100 (unofficial figure); Pig meat 10,034; Chicken meat 13,775 (FAO estimate); Milk 283,876.

Forestry ('000 cubic metres, 2009, FAO estimates): *Roundwood Removals:* 273.8 (Sawlogs, veneer logs and logs for sleepers 139.4, Fuel wood 16.5, Pulpwood 97.6, Other 20.3); *Sawnwood Production* (incl. railway sleepers) 129.3 (Coniferous 92.7, Broadleaved 36.5).

Source: FAO.

INDUSTRY

Selected Products ('000 metric tons, 2009, unless otherwise indicated): Crude steel 2,141; Rolled steel products 1,937; Wine ('000 hl) 134.8 (2009/10); Beer ('000 hl) 373.7 (2005); Electric energy (million kWh) 3,557.1 (2008).

FINANCE

Currency and Exchange Rates: 100 cent = 1 euro (€). *Sterling and Dollar Equivalents* (31 December 2010): £1 sterling = 1.172 euros; US $1 = 0.748 euros; €10 = £8.54 = $13.36. *Average Exchange Rate* (euros per US dollar): 0.6827 in 2008; 0.7198 in 2009; 0.7550 in 2010. Note: The national currency was formerly the Luxembourg franc. From the introduction of the euro, with Luxembourg's participation, on 1 January 1999, a fixed exchange rate of €1 = 40.3399 Luxembourg francs was in operation. Euro notes and coins were introduced on 1 January 2002. The euro and local currency circulated alongside each other until 28 February, after which the euro became the sole legal tender.

Central Budget (€ million): *Revenue:* 10,042.2 in 2007; 10,512.0 in 2008; 10,476.1 in 2009. *Expenditure:* 9,710.2 in 2007; 10,597.0 in 2008; 11,478.4 in 2009.

International Reserves (US $ million at 31 December 2009): Gold 79.49; IMF special drawing rights 381.30; Reserve position in IMF 81.67; Foreign exchange 267.54; Total 810.00. Source: IMF, *International Financial Statistics*.

Money Supply (incl. shares, depository corporations, national residency criteria, € million at 31 December 2009): Currency issued 2,053 (Banque centrale du Luxembourg 60,754); Demand deposits 90,247; Other deposits 112,824; Securities other than shares 81,923; Money market fund shares 314,596; Shares and other equity 54,515; Other items (net) –161,192; Total 494,966. Source: IMF, *International Financial Statistics*.

Cost of Living (Consumer Price Index; base: 2005 = 100): All items 105.0 in 2007; 108.6 in 2008; 109.0 in 2009. Source: IMF, *International Financial Statistics*.

Gross Domestic Product (€ million at constant 2000 prices): 29,500.6 in 2007; 29,510.1 in 2008; 28,309.0 in 2009.

Expenditure on the Gross Domestic Product (€ million at current prices, 2009): Final consumption expenditure 19,304.4 (Households 12,222.3, Non-profit institutions serving households 710.9, General government 6,371.2); Gross capital formation 6,226.1; *Total domestic expenditure* 25,530.5; Exports of goods and services 63,773.9; *Less* Imports of goods and services 51,260.3; *GDP in market prices* 38,044.1.

Gross Domestic Product by Economic Activity (€ million at current prices, 2009): Agriculture, hunting, forestry and fishing 103.3; Construction 1,837.6; Other industry 2,674.6; Wholesale and retail trade, repair of motor vehicles, motorcycles and personal and household goods; hotels and restaurants and transport and communications 7,393.3; Financial services, real estate, renting and business activities 16,681.6; Other community, social and personal service activities 5,745.8; *Gross value added in basic prices* 34,436.1; Taxes, less subsidies, on products 3,607.9; *GDP in market prices* 38,044.1.

Balance of Payments (US $ million, 2009): Exports of goods f.o.b. 15,527; Imports of goods f.o.b. –19,850; *Trade balance* –4,323; Exports of services 60,652; Imports of services –35,783; *Balance on goods and services* 20,546; Other income received 149,071; Other income paid –164,879; *Balance on goods, services and income* 4,738; Current transfers received 6,731; Current transfers paid –7,974; *Current balance* 3,495; Capital account (net) –385; Direct investment abroad –223,891; Direct investment from abroad 194,844; Portfolio investment assets –235,811; Portfolio investment liabilities 166,352; Financial derivatives (net) –11,335; Other investment assets 148,016; Other investment liabilities –40,795; Net errors and omissions –44; *Overall balance* 446. Source: IMF, *International Financial Statistics*.

EXTERNAL TRADE

Principal Commodities (€ million, 2009): *Imports:* Food and live animals 1,192.0; Beverages and tobacco 410.3; Crude materials (inedible) except fuels 827.9; Mineral fuels, lubricants, etc. 1,635.3; Chemicals and related products 1,370.7; Metal manufactures 1,232.5; Other basic manufactures 1,083.9; Machinery and other equipment 2,098.9; Transport equipment 1,978.4; Miscellaneous manufactured articles 1,540.8; Total 13,370.7. *Exports:* Food and live animals 593.9; Chemicals and related products 713.3; Metal manufactures 2,513.8; Other basic manufactures 1,517.2; Machinery and other equipment 1,573.1; Transport equipment 837.8; Miscellaneous manufactured articles 970.7; Total (incl. others) 9,162.5.

Principal Trading Partners (€ million, 2009): *Imports:* Belgium 4,829.6; France 1,570.5; Germany 3,955.9; Italy 355.4; Netherlands 912.8; Switzerland 60.3; United Kingdom 238.4; USA 278.5; Total (incl. others) 13,370.7. *Exports:* Austria 143.6; Belgium 1,222.5; France 1,585.2; Germany 2,542.1; Italy 427.7; Netherlands 482.7; Spain 201.9; Sweden 122.9; Switzerland 115.2; United Kingdom 405.1; USA 302.4; Total (incl. others) 9,162.5.

TRANSPORT

Railways (traffic, million, 2008): Passenger-km 316; Freight ton-km (excl. transit traffic) 294.

Road Traffic (motor vehicles in use at 1 January 2010): Cars 331,513; Motorcycles 16,277; Buses and coaches 1,624; Goods vehicles 29,185; Tractors 14,286; Total 392,885.

Shipping: *River Traffic* (Port of Mertert, '000 metric tons, 2008): Goods loaded 207, Goods unloaded 941. *Merchant Fleet* (vessels registered at 31 December 2009): Number of vessels 102; Total displacement 754,158 grt (Source: IHS Fairplay, *World Fleet Statistics*).

Civil Aviation (traffic on scheduled services, 2009): Passengers carried 1,551,315; Freight (metric tons) 628,666.

LUXEMBOURG

TOURISM

Tourist Arrivals (at accommodation establishments): 981,262 in 2007; 938,313 in 2008; 907,531 in 2009.

Arrivals by Country (2009): Belgium 172,829; France 114,271; Germany 118,559; Italy 20,381; Netherlands 189,497; Spain 14,919; United Kingdom 52,542; USA 16,781; Total (incl. others) 907,531.

Tourism Receipts (US $ million, excl. passenger transport): 3,636 in 2006; 4,030 in 2007; 4,488 in 2008. Source: World Tourism Organization.

COMMUNICATIONS MEDIA

Mobile Cellular Telephones: 720,000 in 2009.
Telephones: 263,600 main lines in use in 2009.
Personal Computers: 318,000 (672.8 per 1,000 persons) in 2006.
Internet Users ('000, estimate): 170.5 in 2009.
Broadband Subscribers ('000): 159.4 in 2009.
Daily Newspapers: 6 (2005).
Book Production: 513 titles (1997).
Radio Receivers: 285,000 in use (1997).
Television Receivers: 260,000 in use (2000).

Sources: partly UNESCO, *Statistical Yearbook*; International Telecommunication Union.

EDUCATION

(2008/09 unless otherwise indicated)

Nursery: 864 teachers; 9,966 pupils.
Primary: 3,372 teachers; 32,496 pupils.
Secondary and Technical Secondary: 4,054 teachers; 12,469 pupils (secondary), 24,323 pupils (technical secondary).
University-level: 9,227 students, incl. 6,063 studying abroad (2005/06).
Schools (2004/05): 375 offering a combination of nursery and primary education; 32 secondary (5 private).

Directory

The Government

HEAD OF STATE

Grand Duke: HRH Grand Duke HENRI (succeeded to the throne 7 October 2000).

COUNCIL OF MINISTERS
(May 2011)

A coalition of the Chrëschtlech Sozial Vollekspartei (CSV) and the Lëtzebuerger Sozialistesch Arbechterpartei (LSAP).

Prime Minister and Minister of State and of the Treasury: JEAN-CLAUDE JUNCKER (CSV).
Deputy Prime Minister and Minister of Foreign Affairs: JEAN ASSELBORN (LSAP).
Minister of Family Affairs and Integration and of Co-operation and Humanitarian Action: MARIE-JOSÉE JACOBS (CSV).
Minister of National Education and Vocational Training: MADY DELVAUX-STEHRES (LSAP).
Minister of Finance: LUC FRIEDEN (CSV).
Minister of Justice, of the Civil Service and Administrative Reform, of Higher Education and Research, of Communications and the Media, and of Religious Affairs: FRANÇOIS BILTGEN (CSV).
Minister of the Economy and External Trade: JEANNOT KRECKÉ (LSAP).
Minister of Health and of Social Security: MARS DI BARTOLOMEO (LSAP).
Minister of the Interior and the Greater Region and of Defence: JEAN-MARIE HALSDORF (CSV).
Minister of Sustainable Development and Infrastructure: CLAUDE WISELER (CSV).
Minister of Labour, Employment and Immigration: NICOLAS SCHMIT (LSAP).
Minister of Culture, of Relations with Parliament and of Administrative Simplification in the Prime Minister's Office, and Minister-delegate of the Civil Service and Administrative Reform: OCTAVIE MODERT (CSV).
Minister of Housing and Minister-delegate of Sustainable Development and Infrastructure: MARCO SCHANK (CSV).
Minister of the Middle Classes and Tourism and of Equal Opportunities: FRANÇOISE HETTO-GAASCH (CSV).
Minister of Agriculture, Viticulture and Rural Development and of Sport: ROMAIN SCHNEIDER (LSAP).

MINISTRIES

Office of the Prime Minister: 4 rue de la Congrégation, 1352 Luxembourg; tel. 247-82100; fax 46-17-20; e-mail ministere.etat@me.etat.lu; internet www.gouvernement.lu.

Ministry of Agriculture, Viticulture and Rural Development: 1 rue de la Congrégation, 1352 Luxembourg; tel. 247-82500; fax 46-40-27; e-mail info@ma.public.lu; internet www.ma.public.lu.

Ministry of the Civil Service and Administrative Reform: 63 ave de la Liberté, BP 1807, 1931 Luxembourg; tel. 247-83130; fax 264-83621; e-mail info@mfpra.public.lu; internet www.mfpra.public.lu.

Ministry of Culture: 20 montée de la Pétrusse, 2327 Luxembourg; tel. 247-86619; fax 40-24-27; e-mail info@mcesr.public.lu; internet www.mcesr.public.lu.

Ministry of the Economy and External Trade: 19–21 blvd Royal, 2449 Luxembourg; tel. 247-84137; fax 46-04-48; e-mail info@eco.public.lu; internet www.eco.public.lu.

Ministry of Equal Opportunities: 12–14 ave Emile Reuter, 2921 Luxembourg; tel. 247-85814; fax 24-18-86; e-mail info@mega.public.lu; internet www.mega.public.lu.

Ministry of Family Affairs and Integration: 12–14 ave Emile Reuter, 2919 Luxembourg; tel. 247-86500; fax 247-86570; e-mail info@mfi.public.lu; internet www.mfi.public.lu.

Ministry of Finance: 3 rue de la Congrégation, 1352 Luxembourg; tel. 247-82600; fax 47-52-41; internet www.mf.public.lu.

Ministry of Foreign Affairs: Hôtel St Maximin, 5 rue Notre-Dame, 2240 Luxembourg; tel. 247-82300; fax 22-31-44; e-mail webadmin@mae.etat.lu; internet www.mae.lu.

Ministry of Health: Villa Louvigny, allée Marconi, 2120 Luxembourg; tel. 247-85505; e-mail ministere-sante@ms.etat.lu; internet www.ms.etat.lu.

Ministry of Higher Education and Research: 20 montée de la Pétrusse, 2327 Luxembourg; tel. 247-85206; fax 40-66-98.

Ministry of the Interior and the Greater Region: 19 rue Beaumont, 1219 Luxembourg; tel. 247-84606; fax 22-11-25; e-mail info@miat.public.lu; internet www.miat.public.lu.

Ministry of Justice: Centre Administratif Pierre Werner, 13 rue Erasme, 2934 Luxembourg; tel. 247-84537; fax 26-68-48-61; e-mail info@mj.public.lu; internet www.mj.public.lu.

Ministry of Labour and Employment: 26 rue Zithe, 2939 Luxembourg; tel. 247-86100; fax 24-78-61-08; e-mail info@mte.public.lu; internet www.mte.public.lu.

Ministry of the Middle Classes and Tourism: 6 blvd Royal, 2449 Luxembourg; tel. 247-84715; fax 247-84740; e-mail info@mcm.public.lu; internet www.mcm.public.lu.

Ministry of National Education and Vocational Training: 29 rue Aldringen, 2926 Luxembourg; tel. 247-85100; fax 24-78-51-13; e-mail info@men.public.lu; internet www.men.public.lu.

Ministry of Housing: 6 blvd Royal, 2449 Luxembourg; tel. 247-84812; fax 24-78-48-40; e-mail info@logement.lu; internet www.logement.lu.

Ministry of Social Security: 26 rue Sainte Zithe, 2936 Luxembourg; tel. 24-78-63-11; fax 247-86306; e-mail mss@mss.etat.lu; internet www.mss.public.lu.

Ministry of State: 4 rue de la Congrégation, 1352 Luxembourg; tel. 247-82100; fax 22-29-55; e-mail ministere.etat@me.etat.lu; internet www.etat.lu; (incorporating Ministry of Religious Affairs).

Ministry of Sustainable Development and Infrastructure: 4 blvd F. D. Roosevelt, 2450 Luxembourg; tel. 247-83306; fax 22-31-60.

LUXEMBOURG

Legislature

CHAMBER OF DEPUTIES

Chambre des Députés: Hôtel de la Chambre des Députés, 19 rue du Marché-aux-Herbes, 1728 Luxembourg; tel. 966-1; fax 22-02-301; e-mail info@chd.lu; internet www.chd.lu.
President: LAURENT MOSAR.

General Election, 7 June 2009

Party	% of votes	Seats
Chrëschtlech Sozial Vollekspartei	38.04	26
Lëtzebuerger Sozialistesch Arbechterpartei	21.56	13
Demokratesch Partei	14.98	9
Déi Gréng	11.71	7
Alternativ Demokratesch Reformpartei	8.13	4
Déi Lénk	3.29	1
Kommunistesch Partei Lëtzebuerg	1.47	—
BiergerLeschst	0.81	—
Total	**100.00**	**60**

Advisory Councils

Conseil Economique et Social: Centre Administratif Pierre Werner, 13 rue Erasme, BP 1306, 1468 Luxembourg; tel. 43-58-51; fax 42-27-29; e-mail ces@ces.etat.lu; internet www.ces.etat.lu; f. 1966; consultative body on economics and social affairs; 39 mems; Pres. SERGE ALLEGREZZA; Sec.-Gen. MARIANNE NATI-STOFFEL.

Conseil d'Etat: 5 rue Sigefroi, 2536 Luxembourg; tel. 47-30-71; fax 46-43-22; e-mail info@conseil-etat.public.lu; internet www.conseil-etat.public.lu; 21 mems nominated by the Sovereign; Pres. GEORGES SCHROEDER; Sec.-Gen. MARC BESCH.

Political Organizations

Alternativ Demokratesch Reformpartei (ADR) (Alternative Democratic Reform Party): 4 rue de l'Eau, 1449 Luxembourg; tel. 26-20-37-06; fax 26-20-37-36; e-mail adr@chd.lu; internet www.adr.lu; f. 1987 as Aktiounskomitee 5/6 Pensioun fir jiddfereen (Action Committee 5/6 Pensions for Everyone); name changed to Aktiounskomitee fir Demokratie a Rentegerechtegkeet (Action Committee for Democracy and Pensions Justice) in 1994; present name adopted 2006; conservative; established to campaign for improved pension rights for private sector employees, but subsequently sought to broaden its concerns; Pres. ROBERT (ROBY) MEHLEN.

BiergerLeschst (Citizens' List): BP 269, 4003 Esch-sur-Alzette; internet www.biergerleschst.eu; right-wing, populist, supports increased pension rights; Leaders ALPHONSE (ALY) JAERLING, JEAN ERSFELD.

Chrëschtlech Sozial Vollekspartei (CSV) (Christian Social Party): 4 rue de l'Eau, BP 826, 2018 Luxembourg; tel. 22-57-31-1; fax 47-27-16; e-mail csv@csv.lu; internet www.csv.lu; f. 1914; advocates political stability, sustained economic expansion, ecological and social progress; 9,500 mems; Pres. FRANÇOIS BILTGEN; Sec.-Gen. MARCO SCHANK.

Déi Gréng (The Greens): 1 rue de Fort Elisabeth, 1463 Luxembourg; tel. 27-48-27-1; fax 27-48-27-22; e-mail greng@greng.lu; internet www.greng.lu; f. 1983; fmrly Déi Gréng Alternativ (Green Alternative Party); merged with the Gréng Lëscht Ekologesch Initiativ (Green List Ecological Initiative) in 1995; advocates grass-roots democracy, environmental protection, social concern and increased aid to developing countries; Spokespersons SAM TANSON, CHRISTIAN GOEBEL.

Déi Lénk (The Left): BP 817, 2018 Luxembourg; tel. 26-20-20-72; fax 26-20-20-73; e-mail sekretariat@dei-lenk.lu; internet www.dei-lenk.lu; f. 1999; individual membership; no formal leadership.

Demokratesch Partei (DP) (Democratic Party): 5 rue du St Esprit, BP 510, 2015 Luxembourg; tel. 22-10-21; fax 22-10-13; e-mail secretariat@dp.lu; internet www.dp.lu; liberal; Leader CLAUDE MEISCH; Gen. Sec. FERNAND ETGEN.

Kommunistesch Partei vu Lëtzebuerg (KPL) (Communist Party of Luxembourg): 3 rue Zénon Bernard, 4030 Esch-sur-Alzette; tel. 44-60-66-21; fax 44-60-66-66; e-mail kpl@zlv.lu; internet www.kp-l.org; f. 1921; Pres. ALI RUCKERT.

Lëtzebuerger Sozialistesch Arbechterpartei (LSAP) (Socialist Workers' Party of Luxembourg): 68 rue de Gasperich, 1617 Luxembourg; tel. 45-65-73-1; fax 45-65-75; e-mail info@lsap.lu; internet www.lsap.lu; f. 1902; social democrat; 6,000 mems; Pres. ALEX BODRY; Sec. ROMAIN SCHNEIDER.

Diplomatic Representation

EMBASSIES IN LUXEMBOURG

Austria: 3 rue des Bains, 1212 Luxembourg; tel. 47-11-88; fax 46-39-74; e-mail luxemburg-ob@bmeia.gv.at; internet www.bmeia.gv.at/luxemburg; Ambassador Dr CHRISTINE STIX-HACKL.

Belgium: 4 rue des Girondins, 1626 Luxembourg; tel. 44-27-46-1; fax 45-42-82; e-mail luxembourg@diplobel.fed.be; internet www.diplomatie.be/luxemburg; Ambassador LUC TEIRLINCK.

Cape Verde: 117 val de Ste Croix, 1371 Luxembourg; tel. 26-48-09-48; fax 26-48-09-49; e-mail ambcvlux@pt.lu; Ambassador MARIA MASCARENHAS.

China, People's Republic: 2 rue Van der Meulen, Dommeldange, 2152 Luxembourg; tel. 43-69-91-1; fax 42-24-23; e-mail chianemb_lu@mfa.gov.cn; internet lu.china-embassy.org; Ambassador ZENG XIANQI.

Czech Republic: 2 rond-point Robert Schuman, 2525 Luxembourg; tel. 26-47-78; fax 26-47-78-20; e-mail luxembourg@embassy.mzv.cz; internet www.mzv.cz/luxembourg; Ambassador VÍT KORSELT.

Denmark: 4 rue des Girondins, 1626 Luxembourg; tel. 22-21-22-1; fax 22-21-24; e-mail luxamb@um.dk; internet www.ambluxembourg.um.dk; Ambassador LOUISE BANG JESPERSON.

Finland: 2 rue Heine, 1720 Luxembourg; tel. 49-55-51; fax 49-46-40; e-mail sanomat.lux@formin.fi; internet www.finlande.lu; Ambassador MARJA LEHTO.

France: 8B blvd Joseph II, BP 359, 2013 Luxembourg; tel. 45-72-71; fax 45-72-71-227; e-mail ambassade@ambafrance-lu.org; internet www.ambafrance-lu.org; Ambassador CHARLES-HENRI D'ARAGON.

Germany: 20–22 ave Emile Reuter, BP 95, 2420 Luxembourg; tel. 45-34-45-1; fax 45-56-04; internet www.luxemburg.diplo.de; Ambassador Dr HUBERTUS VON MORR.

Greece: 27 rue Marie-Adélaïde, 2128 Luxembourg; tel. 44-51-93-1; fax 45-01-64; e-mail ambgrec@pt.lu; Ambassador GEORGIOS GABRIELIDIS.

Ireland: Résidence Christina, 2nd Floor, 28 route d'Arlon, 1140 Luxembourg; tel. 45-06-10-1; fax 45-88-20; e-mail luxembourg@dfa.ie; internet www.embassyofireland.lu; Ambassador DIARMUID O'LEARY.

Italy: 5–7 rue Marie-Adélaïde, 2128 Luxembourg; tel. 44-36-44-1; fax 45-55-23; e-mail ambasciata.lussemburgo@esteri.it; internet www.amblussemburgo.esteri.it; Ambassador RAFFAELE DE LUTIO.

Japan: 62 ave de la Faïencerie, BP 92, 2010 Luxembourg; tel. 46-41-51-1; fax 46-41-76; e-mail embjapan@pt.lu; internet www.lu.emb-japan.go.jp; Ambassador TAKASHI SUETSUNA.

Netherlands: 6 rue Ste Zithe, 2763 Luxembourg; tel. 22-75-70; fax 40-30-16; e-mail lux@minbuza.nl; internet www.paysbas.lu; Ambassador EDUARD HOEKS.

Poland: 2 rue de Pulvermühl, 2356 Luxembourg; tel. 26-00-32; fax 26-68-75-54; e-mail ambapol@pt.lu; internet www.luksembourg.polemb.net; Chargé d'affaires a.i. LIDIA RACIBORSKA-FERDJANI.

Portugal: 24 rue Guillaume Schneider, 2522 Luxembourg; tel. 46-61-90-1; fax 46-51-69; e-mail luxemburgo@mne.pt; Ambassador JOSÉ MANUEL DA ENCARNAÇÃO PESSANHA VIEGAS.

Romania: 41 blvd de la Pétrusse, 2320 Luxembourg; tel. 45-51-51; fax 45-51-63; e-mail ambroum@pt.lu; internet luxemburg.mae.ro; Ambassador VLAD TUDOR ALEXANDRESCU.

Russia: Château de Beggen, 1719 Luxembourg; tel. 42-23-33; fax 42-23-34; e-mail ambruslu@pt.lu; internet www.ruslux.mid.ru; Ambassador ALEKSANDR SHULGIN.

Spain: 4–6 blvd Emmanuel Servais, 2535 Luxembourg; tel. 46-02-55; fax 46-12-88; e-mail emb.luxemburgo@mae.es; internet www.maec.es/embajadas/luxemburgo; Ambassador MIGUEL BENZO PEREA.

Switzerland: Immeuble Forum Royal, 25A blvd Royal, 3e étage, 2449 Luxembourg; tel. 22-74-74-1; fax 22-74-74-20; e-mail lux.vertretung@eda.admin.ch; internet www.eda.admin.ch/luxembourg; Ambassador PHILIPPE GUEX.

Turkey: 49 rue Siggy vu Lëtzebuerg, 1933 Luxembourg; tel. 44-32-81; fax 44-32-81-34; e-mail ambtrlux@pt.lu; Ambassador CELALETTIN KART.

United Kingdom: 5 blvd Joseph II, 1840 Luxembourg; tel. 22-98-64; fax 22-98-67; e-mail britemb@internet.lu; internet www.britain.lu; Ambassador PETER BATEMAN.

USA: 22 blvd Emmanuel Servais, 2535 Luxembourg; tel. 46-01-23; fax 46-14-01; internet luxembourg.usembassy.gov; Chargé d'affaires a.i. ARNOLD H. CAMPBELL.

LUXEMBOURG

Judicial System

The lowest courts in Luxembourg are those of the Justices of the Peace, of which there are three, at Luxembourg city, Esch-sur-Alzette and Diekirch. These are competent to deal with civil, commercial and criminal cases of minor importance. Above these are the two District Courts, Luxembourg being divided into the judicial districts of Luxembourg and Diekirch. These are competent to deal with civil, commercial and criminal cases. The Superior Court of Justice includes both a court of appeal, hearing decisions made by District Courts, and the Cour de Cassation. As the judicial system of the Grand Duchy does not employ the jury system, a defendant is acquitted if a minority of the presiding judges find him or her guilty. The highest administrative court is the Comité du Contentieux du Conseil d'Etat. Special tribunals exist to adjudicate upon various matters of social administration such as social insurance. The department of the Procureur Général (Attorney-General) is responsible for the administration of the judiciary and the supervision of judicial police investigations. In July 1996 an amendment to the Constitution introduced a Constitutional Court.

Judges are appointed for life by the Grand Duke, and are not removable except by judicial sentence.

Superior Court of Justice: Cité Judiciaire, Bâtiment CR, 2080 Luxembourg; tel. 47-59-81-1; fax 47-59-81-39-6.

President of the Superior Court of Justice: MARIE-PAULE ENGEL.

Attorney-General: ROBERT BIEVER.

Religion

CHRISTIANITY

The Roman Catholic Church

For ecclesiastical purposes, Luxembourg comprises a single archdiocese, directly responsible to the Holy See. At 31 December 2006 adherents numbered 393,800 (around 86.5% of the total population).

Archbishop of Luxembourg: Most Rev. FERNAND FRANCK, Archevêché, 4 rue Génistre, BP 419, 2014 Luxembourg; tel. 46-20-23; fax 47-53-81; e-mail archeveche@cathol.lu; internet www.cathol.lu.

The Anglican Communion

Within the Church of England, Luxembourg forms part of the diocese of Gibraltar in Europe.

Chaplain: Rev. CHRISTOPHER LYON, 89 rue de Muhlenbach, 2168 Luxembourg; tel. and fax 43-95-93; e-mail chris.lyon@anglican.lu; internet www.anglican.lu; English-speaking church (Anglican Chaplaincy).

Protestant Churches

Protestant Church of Luxembourg: 5 rue de la Congrégation, 1352 Luxembourg; tel. 22-96-70; fax 22-96-70-70; e-mail mail@protestant.lu; internet www.protestant.lu; f. 1818 as Protestant Garnison Church, 1868 as multiconfessional community for the Grand Duchy; there are about 1,500 Evangelicals; Pres. Pastor VOLKER STRAUSS.

Protestant Reformed Church of Luxembourg: 11 rue de la Libération, BP 295, 4210 Esch-sur-Alzette; tel. 54-03-45; fax 54-03-46; e-mail eglrefki@pt.lu; internet www.reformiert.lu; f. 1982; 3,500 mems in 4 parishes (2006); Pastor KARL GEORG MARHOFFER.

ISLAM

Centre Culturel Islamique de Luxembourg: 2 route d'Arlon, 8210 Mamer; tel. 31-00-60; fax 26-31-04-26; e-mail info@islam.lu; internet www.islam.lu; f. 1985; Imam HALIL AHMETSPAHIC.

JUDAISM

Chief Rabbi: JOSEPH SAYAGH, 34 rue Alphouse Munchen, 2172 Luxembourg; tel. 45-23-66; fax 25-04-30.

Consistoire Israélite de Luxembourg (Jewish Community of Luxembourg): 45 ave Monterey, BP 835, 2018 Luxembourg; tel. 45-29-14-20; fax 25-05-30; e-mail info@synagogue.lu; internet www.synagogue.lu; Pres. GUY AACH.

The Press

DAILIES

L'Essentiel: 38 ave Charlotte, 4530 Differdange; tel. 26-58-66-1; fax 26-58-66-628; e-mail denis.berche@lessentiel.lu; internet www.lessentiel.lu; f. 2007; Mon.–Fri.; French; distributed free of charge; publ. by Edita SA; Editor-in-Chief DENIS BERCHE; circ. 57,666 (2007).

Lëtzebuerger Journal: Résidence de Beauvoir, 51 rue de Strasbourg, BP 2101, 1021 Luxembourg; tel. 49-30-33-1; fax 49-20-65; e-mail journal@journal.lu; internet www.journal.lu; f. 1948; organ of the Democratic Party; Editor-in-Chief CLAUDE KARGER.

Luxemburger Wort: 2 rue Christophe Plantin, 2988 Luxembourg; tel. 49-93-1; fax 49-93-384; e-mail wort@wort.lu; internet www.wort.lu; f. 1848; German; Catholic; Christian Democrat; Editor-in-Chief MARC GLESENER; circ. 72,222 (2007).

Le Quotidien: 44 rue du Canal, 4050 Esch-sur-Alzette; tel. 54-71-311; fax 54-71-30; e-mail redaction@lequotidien.lu; internet www.lequotidien.lu; French; circ. 6,818 (2007).

Tageblatt/Zeitung fir Lëtzebuerg: 44 rue du Canal, 4050 Esch-sur-Alzette; tel. 54-71-31-1; fax 54-71-30; e-mail redaktion@tageblatt.lu; internet www.tageblatt.lu; f. 1913; French and German; Editors-in-Chief DANIÈLE FONCK, ALVIN SOLD; circ. 20,046 (2007).

La Voix du Luxembourg: 2 rue Christophe Plantin, 2988 Luxembourg; tel. 49-93-94-00; fax 49-93-773; e-mail voix@voix.lu; internet www.voix.lu; Editor LAURENT MOYSE; circ. 6,573 (2007).

Zeitung vum Lëtzebuerger Vollek: 3 rue Zénon Bernard, 4030 Esch-sur-Alzette; tel. 44-60-66-1; fax 44-60-66-66; e-mail zeiluvol@pt.lu; internet www.zlv.lu; f. 1946; organ of the Communist Party; Editor-in-Chief ALI RUCKERT.

PERIODICALS

Aktuell: 60 blvd Kennedy, BP 149, 4002 Esch-sur-Alzette; tel. 54-05-45-1; fax 54-16-20; e-mail ogbl@ogbl.lu; internet www.ogbl.lu; f. 1979; articles in both French and German; monthly; journal of the Luxembourg General Confederation of Labour; Editor-in-Chief JEAN-CLAUDE REDING; circ. 62,000.

Auto Moto: Inter Editions SA, 7 rue Robert Stumper, 2557 Luxembourg; tel. 49-50-10-1; fax 49-50-11; monthly; motoring; circ. 72,345 (2007).

Carrière: BP 2535, 1025 Luxembourg; tel. and fax 85-89-19; e-mail carrieremag@logic.lu; internet www.logic.lu/carriere; f. 1988; women's interest; French and German; Editor MONIQUE MATHIEU; circ. 8,000.

Contacto: 2 rue Christophe Plantin, 2988 Luxembourg; tel. 49-93-1; fax 49-93-386; e-mail contacto@saint-paul.lu; internet www.jornal-contacto.lu; Portuguese; weekly; Editor-in-Chief JOSÉ CORREIA; circ. 22,800.

Echo des entreprises: 7 rue Alcide de Gasperi, BP 1304, 1013 Luxembourg; tel. 43-53-66-1; fax 43-23-28; e-mail echo@fedil.lu; internet www.fedil.lu/echo; f. 1920; 6 a year; industry, commerce; publ. by FEDIL—Business Federation Luxembourg; Dir NICOLAS SOISSON.

Femmes Magazine: 74 rue Ermesinde, 1469 Luxembourg; tel. 26-45-85-86; fax 26-45-84-94; e-mail redaction@femmesmagazine.lu; internet www.femmesmagazine.lu; 11 a year; women's interest; Dirs MARIA PIETRANGELI, PATRICIA SCIOTTI; circ. 20,128 (2007).

D'Handwierk: 2 circuit de la Foire Internationale, BP 1604, 1016 Luxembourg; tel. 42-45-11-1; fax 42-45-25; e-mail info@fda.lu; internet www.fda.lu; monthly; organ of the Fédération des Artisans and the Chambre des Métiers; Editor CHRISTIAN REUTER.

Horesca: 7 rue Alcide de Gasperi, BP 2524, 1025 Luxembourg; tel. 42-13-55-1; fax 42-13-55-29-9; e-mail horesca@pt.lu; internet www.horesca.lu; monthly; hotel trade, tourism, gastronomy; Editor DAVE GIANNANDREA; circ. 6,000.

Le Jeudi: 44 rue du Canal, 4050 Esch-sur-Alzette; tel. 22-05-50; fax 22-05-44; e-mail redaction@le-jeudi.lu; internet www.lejeudi.lu; f. 1997; weekly; French; Dir DANIÈLE FONCK; circ. 9,965 (2007).

De Konsument: 55 rue des Bruyères, 1274 Howald; tel. 49-60-22-1; fax 49-49-57; e-mail ulc@pt.lu; internet www.ulc.lu; 12 a year; consumer affairs; Man. GUY GOEDERT.

De Lëtzeburger Bauer: 16 blvd d'Avranches, 2980 Luxembourg; tel. 48-81-61-1; fax 40-03-75; e-mail letzeburger.bauer@netline.lu; f. 1944; weekly; journal of Luxembourg farming; circ. 7,500.

D'Lëtzeburger Land: 59 rue Glesener, BP 2083, 1020 Luxembourg; tel. 48-57-57-1; fax 49-63-09; e-mail land@land.lu; internet www.land.lu; f. 1954; weekly (Fri.); political, economic, cultural affairs; Man. Editor ROMAIN HILGERT; circ. 7,500.

Lux-Post: Editions Saphir, 23 rue des Gênets, 1621 Luxembourg; tel. 49-53-63; fax 48-53-70; local news; 4 regional edns; French and German; circ. 135,283 (2007).

Muselzeidung: 30 rue de Trèves, POB 36, 6701 Grevenmacher; tel. 75-87-47; fax 75-84-32; e-mail burton@pt.lu; internet www.muselzeidung.lu; f. 1981; regional magazine; monthly; German; Editor TANIA USELDINGER.

Revue: 2 rue Dicks, BP 2755, 1027 Luxembourg; tel. 49-81-81-1; fax 48-77-22; e-mail revue@revue.lu; internet www.revue.lu; f. 1945; weekly; illustrated; Editor-in-Chief LAURENT GRAAFF; circ. 22,220 (2007).

LUXEMBOURG

Revue Technique Luxembourgeoise: 4 blvd Grande-Duchesse Charlotte, 1330 Luxembourg; tel. 45-13-54; fax 45-09-32; e-mail aliasbl@pt.lu; internet www.aliai.lu; f. 1908; quarterly; technology.

Sauerzeidung: 30 rue de Trèves, BP 36, 6701 Grevenmacher; tel. 75-87-47; fax 75-84-32; e-mail burton@pt.lu; internet www.muselzeidung.lu; f. 1988; regional newspaper; monthly; German; Publr EUGENE BURTON; circ. 10,000.

Soziale Fortschrett/Progrès Social: 11 rue du Commerce, BP 1208, Luxembourg; tel. 49-94-24-1; fax 49-94-24-49; e-mail info@lcgb.lu; internet www.lcgb.lu; f. 1921; monthly; journal of the Confed. of Christian Trade Unions of Luxembourg; Editor DAN SCHANK; circ. 36,000.

Télécran: 2 rue Christophe Plantin, BP 1008, 1010 Luxembourg; tel. 49-93-50-0; fax 49-93-59-0; e-mail telecran@telecran.lu; internet www.telecran.lu; f. 1978; TV and family weekly; illustrated; Editor-in-Chief CLAUDE FRANÇOIS; circ. 36,431 (2007).

Transport: 13 rue du Commerce, BP 2615, 1026 Luxembourg; tel. 22-67-86-1; fax 22-67-09; e-mail syprolux@pt.lu; internet www.fcpt-syprolux.lu; fortnightly; circ. 3,800.

Woxx: 51 ave de la Liberté, 2e étage, BP 684, 2016 Luxembourg; tel. 29-79-99-0; fax 29-79-79; e-mail woxx@woxx.lu; internet www.woxx.lu; f. 1988 as *GréngeSpoun*; weekly; social, ecological, environmental and general issues; circ. 3,000.

NEWS AGENCY

Agence Europe SA: BP 428, 2014 Luxembourg; tel. 22-00-32; fax 46-22-77; e-mail info@agenceurope.eu; internet www.agenceurope.eu; f. 1952.

PRESS ASSOCIATIONS

Association Luxembourgeoise des Editeurs de Journaux: 44 rue du Canal, 4050 Esch-sur-Alzette; tel. 54-71-31; fax 53-05-87; e-mail asold@tageblatt.lu; Pres. ALVIN SOLD.

Association Luxembourgeoise des Journalistes: BP 1732, 1017 Luxembourg; tel. 44-00-44; fax 85-88-40; e-mail rinfalt@tageblatt.lu; Pres. ROGER INFALT.

Publishers

Editions Guy Binsfeld: 14 place du Parc, 2313 Luxembourg; tel. 49-68-68-1; fax 40-76-09; e-mail editions@binsfeld.lu; internet www.editionsguybinsfeld.lu; f. 1979; literature, reference, children's; Dir and Chief Editor ROB KIEFFER.

Editions Mike Koedinger SA: 10 rue des Gaulois, BP 728, 2017 Luxembourg; tel. 29-66-181; fax 29-66-19; e-mail sylvia@mikekoedinger.com; internet www.mikekoedinger.com; trade and customer magazines, business directories, guidebooks; CEO MIKE KOEDINGER.

Editions Phi: Villa Hadir, 51 rue Emile Mark, 4620 Differdange; tel. 44-44-33-1; fax 44-44-33-55-5; e-mail editions.phi@editpress.lu; internet www.phi.lu; f. 1980; literature, art; owned by Editpress SA; Dir CHRISTINE KREMER.

Editions Schortgen: 108 rue d'Alzette, BP 367, 4004 Esch-sur-Alzette; tel. 54-64-87; fax 53-05-34; e-mail editions@schortgen.lu; internet www.editions-schortgen.lu; art, literature, factual, cuisine, comics; Dir JEAN-PAUL SCHORTGEN.

Editpress Luxembourg SA: 44 rue du Canal, BP 147, 4050 Esch-sur-Alzette; tel. 54-71-31-1; fax 54-71-30; e-mail tageblatt@tageblatt.lu; internet www.tageblatt.lu; Dir ALVIN SOLD.

Edouard Kutter: BP 319, 2013 Luxembourg; tel. 22-35-71; fax 47-18-84; e-mail kuttered@pt.lu; internet www.kutter.lu; art, photography, facsimile edns on Luxembourg.

Imprimerie Beffort SA: 7A rue de Bitbourg, 1273 Luxembourg; tel. 25-44-55-1; fax 25-44-19; e-mail jmkerschen@beffort.lu; f. 1869; scientific, economic reviews; Dir JEAN-MARIE KERSCHEN.

Legitech: 10A rue des Mérovingiens, 8070 Bertrange; tel. 26-31-64-1; fax 26-31-64-99; e-mail contact@legitech.lu; internet www.legitech.lu; f. 2006; law and taxation; Dir NICOLAS HENCKES.

Saint-Paul Luxembourg SA: 2 rue Christophe Plantin, 2988 Luxembourg; tel. 49-93-50-0; fax 49-93-38-6; e-mail direction@saint-paul.lu; internet www.saint-paul.lu; f. 1887; Man. Dir PAUL LENERT.

PUBLISHERS' ASSOCIATION

Fédération Luxembourgeoise des Editeurs de Livres: 31 blvd Konrad Adenauer, BP 482, 2014 Luxembourg; tel. 43-94-44; fax 43-94-50; e-mail francoise.schlink@clc.lu; internet www.clc.lu; f. 1991; affiliated to Confédération Luxembourgeoise du Commerce (CLC).

Broadcasting and Communications

TELECOMMUNICATIONS

Regulatory Authority

Institut Luxembourgeois de Régulation (ILR): 45 allée Scheffer, 2520 Luxembourg; tel. 45-88-45-1; fax 45-88-45-88; e-mail info@ilr.lu; internet www.ilr.public.lu; Dir PAUL SCHUH.

Major Service Providers

Cegecom SA: 3 rue Jean Piret, BP 2708, 1027 Luxembourg; tel. 26-49-91; fax 26-49-96-99; e-mail info@cegecom.net; internet www.cegecom.lu; f. 1999; Man. Dirs MICHAEL LEIDINGER, GEORGES MULLER, BERTHOLD WEGMANN.

Entreprise des Postes et Télécommunications (P&TLuxembourg): 8A ave Monterey, 2020 Luxembourg; tel. 47-65-1; fax 47-51-10; e-mail contact@pt.lu; internet www.pt.lu; f. 1992; post, telecommunications and internet service provider; Pres. GASTON REINESCH; CEO MARCEL GROSS.

Luxembourg Online SA: 14 ave du X Septembre, 2550 Luxembourg; tel. 27-99-00-00; fax 27-99-35-55; e-mail administration@internet.lu; internet www.internet.lu; f. 1995; offers fixed-line and mobile telecommunications and broadband internet access; Man. Dir CLAUDE RADOUX.

LUXGSM SA: 90A rue de Strasbourg, 1171 Luxembourg; tel. 24-62-1; fax 24-62-60-00; e-mail communication@luxgsm.lu; internet www.luxgsm.lu; f. 1993; mobile cellular telephone operator; subsidiary of Entreprise des Postes et Télécommunications; Man. Dir MARC ROSENFELD.

Numericable: 283 route d'Arlon, 8011 Strassen; tel. 26-10-23-01; fax 34-93-98; internet www.numericable.lu; fmrly Coditel, name changed 2008; offers digital television, fixed-line telecommunications and broadband internet access; Dir-Gen. PASCAL DORMAL.

Orange SA: BP 53, 8005 Bertrange; e-mail clients@orangeluxembourg.lu; internet www.orange.lu; fmrly called VOXmobile; name changed to present in 2009; mobile cellular and fixed-line telecommunications, broadband internet access; owned by Mobistar (Belgium); Group CEO BENOIT SCHEEN; 80,678 customers.

Tango: 177 route de Luxembourg, BP 32, 8077 Bertrange; tel. 27-77-71-01; fax 27-77-78-88; e-mail info@tango.lu; internet www.tango.lu; f. 1998; fixed and mobile telephony, as well as broadband internet services; fmrly Tele2Tango; acquired by Belgacom SA (Belgium) in 2008; CEO DIDIER ROUMA.

BROADCASTING

Regulatory Authority

Commission Indépendante de la Radiodiffusion: 5 rue Large, 1917 Luxembourg; tel. 47-82-07-5; e-mail isabelle.marinov@smc.etat.lu; Pres. GEORGES SANTER.

Radio

Eldoradio: 45 blvd Pierre Frieden, 1543 Luxembourg; tel. 40-95-09-1; fax 40-95-09-509; e-mail eldoradio@eldoradio.lu; internet www.eldoradio.lu; popular music station; Dir CHRISTOPHE GOOSENS.

Radio 100,7: 45A ave Monterey, BP 1833, 2163 Luxembourg; tel. 44-00-44-1; fax 44-00-44-980; e-mail info@100komma7.lu; internet www.100komma7.lu; f. 1993; non-commercial cultural broadcaster; Dir FERNAND WEIDES.

Radio Ara: 2 rue de la Boucherie, BP 266, 1247 Luxembourg; tel. 22-22-89; fax 22-22-66; e-mail radioara@pt.lu; internet www.ara.lu; f. 1992; music broadcaster; Man. Dir LISA MCLEAN.

Radio DNR: 2 rue Christophe Plantin, 2339 Luxembourg; tel. 40-24-01; fax 40-79-98; e-mail dnr@dnr.lu; internet www.dnr.lu; music broadcaster; Dir JEAN-MARC STURM.

Radio Latina: 3 rue du Fort Bourbon, 1249 Luxembourg; tel. 29-95-96-201; fax 40-24-76; internet www.radiolatina.lu; broadcasts programmes in Portuguese, French, Italian, Spanish and Cape Verdean Créole; Dir LUIS BARREIRA.

Radio LRB: 4 rue Saint Benoît zu Peppeng, BP 8, 3201 Bettembourg; tel. 52-44-88-22; fax 52-44-88-33; e-mail info@lrb.lu; internet www.lrb.lu; popular music; Man. ANDY CRESTO.

RTL Group: 45 blvd Pierre Frieden, 1543 Luxembourg; tel. 24-86-52-00; fax 24-86-51-39; e-mail oliver.herrgesell@rtlgroup.com; internet www.rtlgroup.com; f. 2000 by merger of CLT-UFA and Pearson TV; 91.2% owned by Bertelsmann AG (Germany), 8.8% by private shareholders; 33 radio stations and 40 television channels in 10 countries; CEO GERHARD ZEILER.

RTL Radio Lëtzebuerg: 45 blvd Pierre Frieden, 1543 Luxembourg; tel. 42-14-28-00; fax 42-14-22-737; e-mail news@rtl.lu; internet www.rtl.lu; f. 1959; broadcasts in Lëtzebuergesch; Station Man. FERNAND MATHES; Chief Editor MARC LINSTER.

LUXEMBOURG

Television

RTL Télé Lëtzebuerg: 45 blvd Pierre Frieden, 1543 Luxembourg; tel. 42-14-28-10; fax 42-14-27-43-1; e-mail online@rtl.lu; internet www.rtl.lu; f. 1969; 2 channels: RTL Télé Lëtzebuerg and Den 2. RTL; subsidiary of RTL Group; CEO ALAIN BERWICK; Station Man. STEVE SCHMIT.

Finance

(cap. = capital; res = reserves; dep. = deposits; m. = million; brs = branches; amounts in euros, unless otherwise indicated)

REGULATORY BODY

Commission de Surveillance du Secteur Financier (CSSF): 110 route d'Arlon, 2991 Luxembourg; tel. 26-25-11; fax 26-25-1-601; e-mail direction@cssf.lu; internet www.cssf.lu; f. 1998; supervision of financial sector; Dir-Gen. J. GUILL; Dirs ARTHUR PHILIPPE, SIMONE DELCOURT.

BANKING

In March 2010 there were 150 banks in Luxembourg, most of which were subsidiaries or branches of foreign banks; a selection of the principal banks operating internationally is given below.

Central Bank

Banque centrale du Luxembourg: 2 blvd Royal, 2983 Luxembourg; tel. 47-74-1; fax 47-74-49-10; e-mail info@bcl.lu; internet www.bcl.lu; f. 1998; represents Luxembourg within the European System of Central Banks (ESCB); cap. 25m., res 147m., dep. 46,988m. (Dec. 2008); Pres. YVES MERSCH; Exec. Dirs PIERRE BECK, SERGE KOLB.

Principal Banks

ABN AMRO Bank (Luxembourg) SA: 46 ave J. F. Kennedy, 1855 Luxembourg; tel. 26-07-1; fax 26-07-29-99; internet www.abnamroprivatebanking.com/luxembourg; f. 1991 by merger; cap. 372m., res 63m., dep. 7,390m. (Dec. 2006); Chair. JAN KOOPMAN; Man. Dir TONIKA HIRDMAN.

Banque et Caisse d'Epargne de l'Etat, Luxembourg: 1–2 pl. de Metz, 1930 Luxembourg; tel. 40-15-1; fax 40-15-20-99; e-mail info@bcee.lu; internet www.bcee.lu; f. 1856 as Caisse de l'Epargne de l'Etat du Grand-Duché de Luxembourg; present name adopted 1989; govt-owned; cap. 174m., res 1,717m., dep. 34,442m. (Dec. 2008); Chair. VICTOR ROD; Pres. and CEO JEAN-CLAUDE FINCK; 75 brs.

Banque Degroof Luxembourg SA: 12 rue Eugène Ruppert, 2453 Luxembourg; tel. 45-35-45-1; fax 25-07-21; e-mail investors.relation@degroof.lu; internet www.degroof.be; f. 1987; cap. 37m., res 133m., dep. 2,823m. (Sept. 2008); Chair., Supervisory Cttee ALAIN SIAENS; Chair., Management Cttee REGNIER HAEGELSTEEN.

Banque LBLux SA: 3 rue Jean Monnet, BP 602, 2180 Luxembourg; tel. 42-43-41; fax 42-43-45-09-9; e-mail bank@lblux.lu; internet www.lblux.lu; f. 1973; present name adopted 2002; 75% owned by BayernLB, 25% by Helaba (both Germany); cap. 300m., res 120m., dep. 8,376m. (Dec. 2009); Chair. RUDOLF HANISCH; Man. Dir HENRI STOFFEL.

Banque de Luxembourg SA: 14 blvd Royal, BP 2221, 1022 Luxembourg; tel. 499-24-1; fax 499-24-55-99; e-mail banque.de.luxembourg@bdl.lu; internet www.banquedeluxembourg.com; f. 1920; 71% owned by Crédit Industriel d'Alsace et de Lorraine (France); cap. 104m., res 416m., dep. 16,936m. (Dec. 2009); Pres. ROBERT RECKINGER; Man. Dir PIERRE AHLBORN; 4 brs.

Banque Raiffeisen SC: 46 rue Charles Martel, 2134 Luxembourg; tel. 24-50-1; fax 22-75-41; e-mail direktion@raiffeisen.lu; internet www.raiffeisen.lu; f. 1926 as Caisse Centrale Raiffeisen SC; present name adopted 2001; res 158m., dep. 4,259m., total assets 4,595m. (Dec. 2008); Chair. PAUL LAUTERBOUR; CEO and Gen. Man. ERNEST CRAVATTE.

Banque Safra Luxembourg SA: 10A blvd Joseph II, BP 887, 2018 Luxembourg; tel. 45-47-81-1; fax 45-47-86; internet www.safra.lu; cap. 9m., res 75m., dep. 1,440m. (Dec. 2008); Man. Dir JORGE ALBERTO KININSBERG.

BGL BNP Paribas: 50 ave J. F. Kennedy, 2951 Luxembourg; tel. 42-42-20-00; fax 42-42-25-79; internet www.bgl.lu; f. 1919 as Banque Générale du Luxembourg SA; merged with Fortis Bank Luxembourg SA 2001, restyled Fortis Banque Luxembourg SA in 2005; became part of BNP Paribas in 2009; cap. 699m., res 5,208m., dep. 44,335m. (Dec. 2008); Chair. GASTON REINESCH; Chairs, Management Bd CARLO THILL, ERIC MARTIN; 37 brs.

BHF-BANK International SA: 534 rue de Neudorf, 2220 Luxembourg; tel. 45-76-76-1; fax 45-83-24; e-mail direktion@bhf.lu; f. 1972; present name adopted 2005; subsidiary of BHF-Bank AG (Germany); cap. 26m., res 54m., dep. 3,979m. (Dec. 2008); Mans MONIKA ANELL, THOMAS GRÜNEWALD, STEFAN KRAPF.

BNP Paribas Luxembourg: 10A blvd Royal, 2093 Luxembourg; tel. 46-46-1; fax 46-46-90-00; internet www.bnpparibas.lu; subsidiary of BNP Paribas SA (France); cap. 105m., res 1,214m., dep. 29,286m. (Dec. 2008); Chair. ALAIN PAPIASSE; Man. Dir ERIC MARTIN.

Clearstream Banking SA: 42 ave J. F. Kennedy, 1855 Luxembourg; tel. 243-0; fax 24-33-80-00; e-mail web@clearstream.com; internet www.clearstream.com; f. 1970 as Cedelbank; present name adopted 2000; subsidiary of Deutsche Börse AG; private bank; acts as the central bank's securities depository; total assets 10,600,000m. (Dec. 2007); Chair. RETO FRANCIONI; CEO JEFFREY TESSLER.

Commerzbank International SA (CISAL): 25 rue Edward Steichen, 2540 Luxembourg; tel. 47-79-11-1; fax 47-79-11-270; e-mail info@commerzbank.lu; internet www.commerzbank.lu; f. 1969; cap. 280m., res 154m., dep. 9,776m. (Dec. 2008); Chair. FALK FISCHER; CEO, Luxembourg BERND HOLZENTHAL.

Crédit Agricole Luxembourg: 39 allée Scheffer, BP 1104, 1011 Luxembourg; tel. 24-67-1; fax 24-67-80-00; e-mail marketing@ca-luxembourg.com; internet www.e-private.com; f. 2005; by merger of Crédit Lyonnais Luxembourg and Crédit Agricole Indosuez Luxembourg; merged with Crédit Agricole Luxembourg Bank in 2008; cap. 465m., res 37m., dep. 4,830m. (Dec. 2008); Chair. ALAIN MASSIERA; Dir-Gen. JEAN-FRANÇOIS ABADIE.

Crédit Suisse (Luxembourg) SA: 56 Grand-Rue, BP 40, 2010 Luxembourg; tel. 46-00-11-1; fax 46-32-70; internet www.credit-suisse.com; f. 1974; cap. Swiss francs 43m., res Swiss francs 27m., dep. Swiss francs 5,104m. (Dec. 2006); Chair HANS-ULRICH DOERIG.

Danske Bank International SA: 13 rue Edward Steichen, BP 173, 2011 Luxembourg; tel. 46-12-75-1; fax 47-30-78; e-mail information@danskebank.lu; internet www.danskebank.lu; f. 1976; cap. 91m., res 40m., dep. 4,490m. (Dec. 2008); Chair. NIELS ERIK MOUSTEN; Man. Dir KLAUS MØNSTED PEDERSEN.

DekaBank Deutsche Girozentrale Luxembourg SA: 38 ave J. F. Kennedy, 1855 Luxembourg; tel. 34-09-35; fax 34-09-37; e-mail info@deka.lu; internet www.dekabank.lu; f. 1971 as Deutsche Girozentrale International SA; present name adopted 2002, after merger with DekaBank Luxembourg SA; cap. 50m., res 106m., dep. 10,197m. (Dec. 2008); Chair. OLIVER BEHRENS; Man. Dir RAINER MACH.

Deutsche Bank Luxembourg SA: 2 blvd Konrad Adenauer, 1115 Luxembourg; tel. 42-12-21; fax 42-12-24-49; internet www.db.com/luxembourg; f. 1970 as Deutsche Bank Compagnie Financière Luxembourg; present name adopted 1987; cap. 215m., res 1,657m., dep. 57,960m. (Dec. 2008); Chair. Dr JOSEF ACKERMANN.

Deutsche Postbank International SA: PB Finance Centre, 18–20 Parc d'Activités Sydrall, 5365 Munsbach; tel. 34-95-31-1; fax 34-62-06; e-mail deutsche.postbank@postbank.lu; internet www.postbank.de; f. 1993; cap. 600m., res 137m., dep. 17,987m. (Dec. 2008); Chair. STEFAN JÜTTE; Gen. Mans CHRISTOPH SCHMITZ, JOCHEN BEGAS, TOBIAS GANZÄUER.

Dexia Banque Internationale à Luxembourg SA (Dexia BIL): 69 route d'Esch, 2953 Luxembourg; tel. 45-90-1; fax 45-90-20-10; e-mail contact.lu@dexia.com; internet www.dexia-bil.lu; f. 1856 as Banque Internationale à Luxembourg; present name adopted 2000; 99.9% owned by Dexia SA (Belgium); cap. 141m., res 1,008m., dep. 54,330m. (Dec. 2008); Chair. PIERRE MARIAN; 40 brs.

Dresdner Bank Luxembourg SA: 26 rue de Marché-aux-Herbes, 2097 Luxembourg; tel. 47-60-1; fax 47-60-33-1; e-mail info@dresdner-bank.lu; internet www.dresdner-bank.lu; f. 1967 as Cie Luxembourgeoise de Banque SA; present name adopted 1989; owned by Commerzbank Gruppe (Germany); cap. 125m., res 328m., dep. 9,286m. (Dec. 2008); Chair. HOLGER BOSCHKE; CEO FALK FISCHER; 1 br.

DZ Bank International SA: 4 rue Thomas Edison, BP 661, 1445 Strassen; tel. 44-90-31; fax 44-90-32-00-1; e-mail info@dzi.lu; internet www.dzi.lu; f. 1978 as DG Bank Luxembourg SA; present name adopted 2001, after merger with GZ Bank International SA; 89.7% owned by DZ Bank AG Deutsche Zentral-Genossenschaftsbank; cap. 81m., res 230m., dep. 13,552m. (Dec. 2008); Chair. LARS HILLE; Man. Dir ANDREAS NEUGEBAUER.

EFG Bank (Luxembourg) SA: 14 allée Marconi, 2120 Luxembourg; tel. 26-45-41; fax 26-45-45-00; e-mail infolux@efgbank.com; internet www.efgbank.lu; f. 1986; owned by EFG Eurobank Ergasias (Greece); cap. 20m., dep. 211m. (Dec. 2007); Chair. JEAN PIERRE CUONI; CEO LONNIE HOWELL.

HSBC Private Bank (Luxembourg) SA: 16 blvd d'Avranches, BP 733, 2017 Luxembourg; tel. 47-93-31-1; fax 47-93-31-22-6; e-mail hrlu@hsbcpb.com; internet www.hsbcpb.com; f. 1985; cap. 53m., res 57m., dep. 1,840m. (Dec. 2006); Chair. STEPHEN K. GREEN; CEO CHARLES HALL.

HSBC Trinkaus & Burkhardt (International) SA: 8 rue Lou Hemmer, 1748 Luxembourg; tel. 47-18-47-1; fax 47-18-47-61-3; e-mail contact@hsbctrinkaus.lu; internet www.hsbctrinkaus.lu; f. 1977 as Trinkhaus & Burhardt (International) SA; present name

LUXEMBOURG

adopted 1999; cap. 16m., res 71m., dep. 1,976m. (Dec. 2008); Pres. Dr OLAF HUTH; Man. Dirs HANS-JOACHIM ROSTECK, JÖRG MEIER.

HSH Nordbank Private Banking SA: 2 rue Jean Monnet, BP 612, 2016 Luxembourg; tel. 42-41-21-1; fax 42-41-21-50-9; e-mail info@hsh-nordbank-pb.com; internet www.hsh-nordbank-pb.com; f. 1983; cap. 13m., res 14m., dep. 499m. (Dec. 2008); Chair. BERNHARD VISKER; Man. Dirs JÜRGEN KÜHN, CARSTEN BÄCKER, BERNHARD STAHR.

ING Luxembourg SA: 52 route d'Esch, 2965 Luxembourg; tel. 44-99-11; fax 44-99-12-31; e-mail info@ing.lu; internet www.ing.lu; f. 1960 as Crédit Européen SA; present name adopted 2003; owned by ING Belgium SA/NV; cap. 83m., res 1,274m., dep. 12,162m. (Dec. 2008); Man. Dir RICK VANDENBERGHE; 15 brs.

KBL European Private Bankers SA: 43 blvd Royal, 2955 Luxembourg; tel. 47-97-1; fax 47-97-73-91-2; internet www.kbl.lu; f. 1949; fmrly Kredietbank SA Luxembourgeoise; present name adopted 2008; 99% owned by KBC Bank NV (Belgium); cap. 187m., res 1,106m. (Dec. 2007), dep. 13,323m. (Dec. 2008); Pres. and Gen. Man. ETIENNE VERWILGHEN; 3 brs.

LBBW Luxemburg SA: 10–12 blvd F.D. Roosevelt, BP 84, 2010 Luxembourg; tel. 47-59-21-1; fax 47-59-21-26-9; e-mail info@lbbw.lu; internet www.lbbw.lu; f. 2008, following acquisition of Landesbank Rheinland-Pfalz International by Landesbank Baden-Württemberg (Germany); cap. 615m., res –114m., dep. 11,325m. (Dec. 2008); Man. Dirs MARIE-ANNE VAN DEN BERG, ROBY HAAS.

Norddeutsche Landesbank Luxembourg SA: 26 route d'Arlon, 1140 Luxembourg; tel. 45-22-11-1; fax 45-22-11-30-7; e-mail info@nordlb.lu; internet www.nordlb.lu; f. 1972; cap. 205m., res 469m., dep. 19,528m. (Dec. 2008); Chair, Management Bd HARRY ROSENBAUM.

Nordea Bank SA: 562 rue de Neudorf, BP 562, 2015 Luxembourg; tel. 43-88-71; fax 43-93-76-11; e-mail nordea@nordea.lu; internet www.nordea.lu; f. 1976 as Privatbanken International (Denmark) SA, Luxembourg; changed name to Unibank SA in 1990, present name adopted 2001; cap. 25m., res 46m., dep. 2,831m. (Dec. 2008); Chair. HANS DALBORG; CEO CHRISTIAN CLAUSEN.

Sanpaolo Bank SA: 12 ave de la Liberté, BP 2062, 1020 Luxembourg; tel. 40-37-60-1; fax 40-37-60-35-0; e-mail sanpaolo@sanpaolo.lu; f. 1981 as Sanpaolo-Lariano Bank SA; present name adopted 1995; 99.99% stake owned by Intesa Sanpaolo SpA (Italy); cap. 140m., res 70m., dep. 3,184m. (Dec. 2008); Chair. STEFANO STANGONI.

Skandinaviska Enskilda Banken SA: 6A circuit de la Foire Internationale, BP 487, 2014 Luxembourg; tel. 26-23-1; fax 26-23-20-01; e-mail contact@sebprivatebank.com; internet www.sebgroup.lu; f. 1977; present name adopted 1999; cap. 118m., res 30m., dep. 2,499m. (Dec. 2007); Man. Dir PETER KUBICKI.

Société Européenne de Banque SA: 19–21 blvd du Prince Henri, BP 21, 2010 Luxembourg; tel. 46-14-11; fax 22-37-55; e-mail contact@seb.lu; internet www.seb.lu; f. 1976; cap. 45m., res 321m., dep. 8,385m. (Dec. 2008); subsidiary of Intesa Sanpaolo SpA (Italy); Chair. Prof. ANGELO CALOIA; Man. Dir and CEO MARCO BUS.

Société Générale Bank & Trust: 11 ave Emile Reuter, BP 1271, 2420 Luxembourg; tel. 47-93-11-1; fax 22-88-59; internet www.sgbt.lu; f. 1956 as International and General Finance Trust; present name adopted 1995; cap. 1,179m., res 780m., dep. 35,853m. (Dec. 2008); Chair. PATRICK SUET; CEO FRÉDÉRIC GENET.

UBS (Luxembourg) SA: 33A ave J. F. Kennedy, 1855 Luxembourg; tel. 45-12-11; fax 45-12-12-70-0; internet www.ubs.lu; f. 1998 by merger of Swiss Bank Corporation (Luxembourg) SA and Union de Banques Suisses (Luxembourg) SA; cap. Swiss francs 150m., res Swiss francs 372m., dep. Swiss francs 18,802m. (Dec. 2008); Chair. ARTHUR DECURTINS; Group CEO OSWALD J. GRÜBEL.

UniCredit International Bank (Luxembourg) SA: 8–10 rue Jean Monnet, 2180 Luxembourg; tel. 22-08-42-31-0; fax 46-90-26; e-mail contact@unicreditgroup.lu; internet www.unicreditgroup.eu; merged with Capitalia Luxembourg SA in 2008; owned by Unicredito Italiano SpA; Group CEO ALESSANDRO PROFUMO.

UniCredit Luxembourg SA: 4 rue Alphonse Weicker, 2721 Luxembourg; tel. 42-72-1; fax 42-72-45-00; e-mail contact@hvb.lu; internet www.unicreditbank.lu; f. 1998 by merger of Hypobank International SA and Vereinsbank International SA Luxembourg; fmrly HVB Banque Luxembourg, present name adopted 2009; cap. 238m., res 1,019m., dep. 32,892m. (Dec. 2008); Pres. and Chair. ANDREAS WÖLFER; CEO ANGELO BRIZI.

WestLB International SA: 32–34 blvd Grande-Duchesse Charlotte, BP 420, 2014 Luxembourg; tel. 44-74-11; fax 44-74-12-10; e-mail info@westlb.lu; internet www.westlb.lu; f. 1972; owned by WestLB AG (Germany); cap. 65m., res 220m., dep. 6,042m. (Dec. 2008); Man. Dirs Dr JOHANNES SCHEEL, NORBERT LERSCH, UWE KRÖNERT.

Banking Association

Association des Banques et Banquiers Luxembourg (ABBL): 59 blvd Royal, BP 13, 2449 Luxembourg; tel. 46-36-60-1; fax 46-09-21; e-mail mail@abbl.lu; internet www.abbl.lu; f. 1939; Pres. JEAN MEYER.

STOCK EXCHANGE

Société de la Bourse de Luxembourg SA: 11 ave de la Porte-Neuve, BP 165, 2227 Luxembourg; tel. 47-79-36-1; fax 47-32-98; e-mail info@bourse.lu; internet www.bourse.lu; f. 1928; Chair. RAYMOND KIRSCH; Pres. and CEO MICHEL MAQUIL.

INSURANCE

In 2009 there were 97 approved insurance companies and, in addition, 251 reinsurance companies. A selection of insurance companies is given below:

Aon Luxembourg: 19 rue de Bitbourg, BP 593, 2015 Luxembourg; tel. 31-72-35; fax 31-71-74; e-mail lambert_schroeder@aon.com; internet www.aon.com/luxembourg; f. 1994; insurance and re-insurance broker; subsidiary of Aon Corpn (USA); Pres. and CEO GREGORY C. CASE.

Assurances Mutuelles d'Europe SA (AME Lux): 7 blvd Joseph II, BP 787, 1840 Luxembourg; tel. 47-46-93; fax 47-46-90; e-mail amelife@ame.lu; internet www.ame.lu; f. 1989; Man. Dir ALAIN HAUGLUSTAINE.

AXA Luxembourg: 7 rue de la Chapelle, 1325 Luxembourg; tel. 44-24-24-1; fax 45-57-03; e-mail info@axa.lu; internet www.axa.lu; f. 1977; all branches and life; Dir-Gen. PAUL DE COOMAN.

Fortis Assurances Luxembourg: 16 blvd Royal, 2449 Luxembourg; tel. 24-18-58-1; fax 24-18-58-90-00; e-mail info@fortisinsurance.lu; internet www.fortisinsurance.lu; f. 1996 by merger of AG Luxembourg and CGA Luxembourg; comprises Fortis Luxembourg-VIE SA and Fortis Luxembourg-IARD SA; life and non-life insurance; CEO DIRK BILLEMON.

Groupe Foyer: 12 rue Léon Laval, 2986 Luxembourg; tel. 43-74-37; fax 43-74-32-49-9; e-mail contact@foyer.lu; internet www.foyer.lu; f. 1922; all branches and life; CEO FRANÇOIS TESCH.

La Luxembourgeoise SA d'Assurances: 10 rue Aldringen, 1118 Luxembourg; tel. 47-61-1; fax 47-61-30-0; e-mail groupell@lalux.lu; internet www.lalux.lu; f. 1989; all branches of non-life; Pres. and Dir-Gen. PIT HENTGEN.

West of England Shipowners' Mutual Insurance Asscn (Luxembourg): 33 blvd du Prince Henri, BP 841, 1724 Luxembourg; tel. 47-00-67-1; fax 22-52-53; e-mail carolina.lockwood@westpandi.com; internet www.westpandi.com; f. 1970; marine mutual insurance; Gen. Man. CAROLINA LOCKWOOD.

Insurance Association

Association des Compagnies d'Assurances (ACA): 75 rue de Mamer, BP 29, 8005 Bertrange; tel. 44-21-44-1; fax 44-02-89; e-mail aca@aca.lu; internet www.aca.lu; f. 1956; Pres. PAUL HAMMELMANN; 70 mems.

Trade and Industry

GOVERNMENT AGENCY

Société Nationale de Crédit et d'Investissement (SNCI): 7 rue du Saint Esprit, BP 1207, 1475 Luxembourg; tel. 46-19-71-1; fax 46-19-79; e-mail snci@snci.lu; internet www.snci.lu; f. 1978; cap. €375m., res €185m., dep. €741m., assets €1,036m. (Dec. 2007); SNCI finances participations in certain cos, provides loans for investment and research and devt projects, provides export credit; Pres. GASTON REINESCH; Sec.-Gen. EVA KREMER.

CHAMBER OF COMMERCE

Chambre de Commerce du Grand-Duché de Luxembourg: 7 rue Alcide de Gasperi, 2981 Luxembourg-Kirchberg; tel. 42-39-39-1; fax 43-83-26; e-mail chamcom@cc.lu; internet www.cc.lu; f. 1841; Pres. MICHEL WURTH; 35,000 mems.

INDUSTRIAL AND TRADE ASSOCIATIONS

Centrale Paysanne Luxembourgeoise: BP 48, Agrocenter, 7501 Mersch, Luxembourg; tel. 64-64-48-0; fax 64-64-48-1; e-mail mfiedler@delpa.lu; f. 1945; Pres. MARC FISCH; Sec. LUCIEN HALLER; groups all agricultural organizations.

Chambre d'Agriculture (Landwirtschaftskammer): 261 route d'Arlon, BP 81, 8001 Strassen; tel. 31-38-76; fax 31-38-75; e-mail info@lwk.lu; internet www.lwk.lu; Pres. MARCO GAASCH; Sec.-Gen. POL GANTENBEIN.

Confédération Luxembourgeoise du Commerce (CLC): Bâtiment C, 2e étage, 7 rue Alcide de Gasperi, BP 482, 2014 Luxembourg; tel. 43-94-44; fax 43-94-50; e-mail info@clc.lu; internet www.clc.lu;

LUXEMBOURG

f. 1909; Pres. Michel Rodenbourg; Dir Thierry Nothum; 50,000 individual mems and 10,000 mem. cos.

Fédération des Artisans du Grand-Duché de Luxembourg: 2 circuit de la Foire Internationale, BP 1604, 1016 Luxembourg; tel. 42-45-11-1; fax 42-45-25; e-mail info@fda.lu; internet www.fda.lu; f. 1905; Pres. Norbert Geisen; Dir Romain Schmit; 51 mem. feds.

FEDIL—Business Federation Luxembourg: 7 rue Alcide de Gasperi, BP 1304, 1013 Luxembourg; tel. 43-53-66-1; fax 43-23-28; e-mail fedil@fedil.lu; internet www.fedil.lu; f. 1918; Pres. Robert Dennewald; Dir Nicolas Soisson; c. 450 mems.

UTILITIES

Regulatory Authority

Institut Luxembourgeois de Régulation (ILR): see Broadcasting and Communications.

Electricity and Gas

Enovos International SA: 19–21 blvd Royal, 2449 Luxembourg; tel. 27-37-1; fax 27-37-91-00; internet www.enovos.eu/lu; f. 2009 from merger of Cegedel SA, Soteg SA and Saar Ferngas AG; produces and distributes electricity and gas; fmrly known as Soteg SA; Mems, Exec. Cttee Jean Lucius, Romain Becker, Nestor Didelot.

Creos Luxembourg: 2 rue Thomas Edison, 1445 Strassen; tel. 26-24-1; fax 26-24-51-00; e-mail info@creos.net; internet www.creos-net.lu; f. 1928 as Cegedel SA; renamed in 2009 following merger of Cegedel SA, Soteg SA and Saar Ferngas AG; owns and manages power grids and natural gas pipelines; CEO Romain Becker.

Enovos Luxembourg: 2 rue Thomas Edison, 1445 Luxembourg; tel. 27-37-1; fax 27-37-61-11; internet www.enovos.eu/lu; f. 1928 as Cegedel SA; name changed in 2009 following merger of Cegedel SA, Soteg SA and Saar Ferngas AG; transportation and supply of natural gas and electricity; Chair. Marco Hoffmann; Dir-Gen. Jean Lucius.

Société Electrique de l'Our (SEO): 2 rue Pierre d'Aspelt, BP 37, 2010 Luxembourg; tel. 44-90-21; fax 44-90-28-00; e-mail seo@seo.lu; internet www.seo.lu; f. 1951; electricity production and supply; Pres. Etienne Schneider.

SOTEL Réseau & Cie: 4 rue de Soleuvre, 4321 Esch-sur-Alzette; tel. 55-19-21; fax 57-22-13; f. 2001; distributor of electricity; Man. Dir Nico Wietor.

SUDGAZ SA: 150 rue Jean-Pierre Michels, BP 383, 4004 Esch-sur-Alzette; tel. 55-66-55-1; fax 57-20-44; e-mail contact@sudgaz.lu; internet www.sudgaz.lu; f. 1899; gas distribution co; Pres. Will Hoffmann.

Water

Responsibility for water supply lies with the municipalities. Many municipalities have formed syndicates to manage water supply, the largest of which is listed below.

Distribution d'Eau des Ardennes (DEA): BP 2, 8701 Useldange; tel. 23-64-24-1; fax 23-63-93-55; e-mail dea@dea.lu; internet www.dea.lu; f. 1929; distribution of drinking water in northern Luxembourg; comprises 36 municipalities; Dir Patrick Koster.

TRADE UNIONS

FNCTTFEL—Landesverband der Eisenbahner, Transportarbeiter, Funktionäre und Beamten, Luxemburg (National Union of Luxembourg Railway and Transport Workers and Employees): 63 rue de Bonnevoie, 1260 Luxembourg; tel. 48-70-44-1; fax 48-85-25; e-mail info@landesverband.lu; internet www.landesverband.lu; f. 1909; affiliated to CGT and International Transport Workers' Federation; Pres. Guy Greivelding; 8,000 mems.

Lëtzebuerger Chrëschtleche Gewerkschaftsbond (LCGB) (Confederation of Luxembourg Christian Trade Unions): 11 rue du Commerce, BP 1208, 1012 Luxembourg; tel. 49-94-24-1; fax 49-94-24-49; e-mail info@lcgb.lu; internet www.lcgb.lu; f. 1921; affiliated to ETUC and World Confederation of Labour; Pres. Robert Weber; Gen. Sec. Marc Spautz; 40,000 mems.

Onofhängege Gewerkschaftsbond Lëtzebuerg/Confédération Syndicale Indépendante du Luxembourg (OGB-L) (Luxembourg Independent Confederation of Labour): 60 blvd J. F. Kennedy, BP 149, 4002 Esch-sur-Alzette; tel. 54-05-45-1; fax 54-16-20; e-mail ogbl@ogbl.lu; internet www.ogbl.lu; f. 1916; comprises 15 mem. unions; Pres. Jean-Claude Reding; Sec.-Gen. André Roeltgen; c. 62,000 mems.

Transport

RAILWAYS

At 31 December 2007 there were 275 km of railway track, of which 262 km were electrified. A high-speed link from Luxembourg to Paris, France, opened in June 2007.

Société Nationale des Chemins de Fer Luxembourgeois (CFL): 9 place de la Gare, BP 1803, 1018 Luxembourg; tel. 49-90-0; fax 49-90-44-70; e-mail info@cfl.lu; internet www.cfl.lu; f. 1946; Pres. Jeannot Waringo; Dir-Gen. and CEO Alex Kremer.

ROADS

At 1 January 2008 there were 2,894 km of roads, of which motorways comprised 147 km.

INLAND WATERWAYS AND SHIPPING

Rhine shipping has direct access to the Luxembourg inland port of Mertert as a result of the canalization of the Moselle river. An 'offshore' shipping register was established in 1991.

CIVIL AVIATION

There is an international airport situated at Findel, north-west of the capital.

Luxair SA (Société Luxembourgeoise de Navigation Aérienne): Aéroport de Luxembourg, 2987 Luxembourg; tel. 456-42-55; fax 456-46-05; internet www.luxair.lu; f. 1962; regular services to destinations in Europe and North Africa; Pres. and CEO Adrien Ney.

Cargolux Airlines International SA: Aéroport de Luxembourg, 2990 Luxembourg; tel. 42-11-1; fax 43-54-46; e-mail info@cargolux.com; internet www.cargolux.com; f. 1970; regular international all-freighter services; technological devt; owned by Luxair, a consortium of Luxembourg banks and SAir Logistics (Switzerland); Pres. and CEO Ulrich Ogiermann.

Tourism

Many tourist resorts have developed around the ruins of medieval castles such as Clerf, Esch/Sauer, Vianden and Wiltz. The Benedictine Abbey at Echternach is also much visited. There is a thermal centre at Mondorf-les-Bains, supplied by three mineralized springs. In addition, there are numerous footpaths and hiking trails. The city of Luxembourg, with its many cultural events and historical monuments, is an important centre for congresses. In 2009 there were 907,531 tourist arrivals at hotels and other accommodation establishments. Receipts from tourism totalled US $4,448m. in 2008.

Office National du Tourisme (ONT): 68–70 blvd de la Pétrusse, BP 1001, 1010 Luxembourg; tel. 42-82-82-1; fax 42-82-82-38; e-mail info@ont.lu; internet www.ont.lu; f. 1931; 192 mems; Chair. M. Schank; Dir Robert L. Philippart.

Defence

Luxembourg was a founder member of the North Atlantic Treaty Organization (NATO) in 1949. Compulsory military service was abolished in 1967, but Luxembourg maintains an army of volunteers, totalling 900, and a gendarmerie numbering 612 (as assessed at November 2010). In March 1987 the country became a signatory of the Benelux military convention, together with Belgium and the Netherlands. This aimed at the standardization of training methods and of military equipment in the three countries. In November 2004 Luxembourg committed to contributing troops to one of the 'battlegroups' of the European Union. The EU battlegroups, two of which were to be ready for deployment at any one time, following a rotational schedule, reached full operational capacity from 1 January 2007. Luxembourg participated in a battlegroup with France, Germany and Belgium.

Defence Expenditure: Budget estimated at €200m. for 2011.

Chief of Staff: Gen. Gaston Reinig.

Education

Education in Luxembourg is compulsory from the age of four to 16 years. Pre-primary education begins at the age of four years; the Ministry for Education and Vocational Training has introduced an optional pre-primary level for children at the age of three years. Primary education begins at six years of age and lasts for six years. German is the language of instruction in the first year at primary level. French is added to the programme in the second year, and replaces German as the language of instruction at higher secondary level. In 2007/08 the total enrolment in primary education included 96% of children in the relevant age-group, while the total enrolment in secondary education included 84% of children in the relevant age-group. Total enrolment in pre-primary education in 2007/08 included 86% of children in the relevant age-group.

At the age of 12, pupils can choose between secondary school (*lycée*) and technical education (*lycée technique*). The first year of secondary school is a general orientation course on comprehensive lines, which is then followed by a choice between two sections: the Classical Section, with an emphasis on Latin, and the Modern Section, which stresses English and other modern languages. The completed secondary course lasts seven years, and leads to the *Certificat de Fin d'Etudes Secondaires*, which qualifies for university entrance. The technical education course (six to eight years) leads either to a vocational diploma, a technician's diploma (*diplôme de technicien*) or a technical baccalaureate diploma (*bac technique*) and is devised in three parts: an orientation and observation course; an intermediate course; and an upper course.

The *Centre Universitaire* was established in 1969, offering one- or two-year courses in the humanities, sciences and law and economics, as well as training courses for lawyers and teachers, following which the students generally attend other European universities. The *Institut Supérieur de Technologies* (IST) is an institute for higher education at university level in civil engineering, electrical engineering, applied computer sciences and mechanical engineering. In August 2003 the Government founded the University of Luxembourg through the merger of four major institutions: the University Centre of Luxembourg, *Universitaire de Luxembourg*; the Higher Technological Institute, *Institut Supérieur de Technologie*; the Institute for Higher Studies and Research in Teaching, *Institut Supérieur d'Etudes et de Luxembourg*; and the Institute for Educational and Social Studies, *Institut d'Etudes Educatives et Sociales*. The university operates from three campuses, Kirchberg, Limpertsberg and Walferdange, and offers a full range of degrees and post-graduate qualifications taught in French, German and English. In December 2005 the Government announced that a single site was to be developed at Belval-Ouest, near Esch-sur-Alzette, to accommodate the University of Luxembourg, eventually regrouping the existing, dispersed faculties; the first university buildings at Belval-Ouest were expected to be completed by 2012.

General government expenditure on national education and vocational training in 2008 was €963.6m.

THE FORMER YUGOSLAV REPUBLIC OF MACEDONIA

Introductory Survey

LOCATION, CLIMATE, LANGUAGE, RELIGION, FLAG, CAPITAL

The former Yugoslav republic of Macedonia (FYRM, or, according to its Constitution, the Republic of Macedonia), is situated in south-eastern Europe. The FYRM is a land-locked state and is bounded by Serbia to the north, Kosovo to the north-west, Albania to the west, Greece to the south and Bulgaria to the east. The republic is predominantly mountainous with a continental climate, although the Vardar (Axiós) river valley, which bisects the country from north-west to south-east, across the centre of the republic and into Greece, has a mild Mediterranean climate with an average summertime temperature of 27°C (80°F). The official language of the republic, under the Constitution of November 1991, was originally stipulated as Macedonian, and is most frequently written in the Cyrillic script. It is a South Slavic language most closely related to Bulgarian. Constitutional amendments adopted in November 2001 accorded any minority language, such as Albanian, the status of official language in communities where its speakers constitute 20% of the population. Most of the population is nominally Eastern Orthodox Christian. Most of the ethnic Albanians (officially recorded as 25.2% of the population) are Muslims, as are the majority of the remaining minority groups. The national flag (proportions 1 by 2) comprises, in the centre of a red field, a yellow disc, with eight yellow rays extending to the edges of the flag. The capital is Skopje.

CONTEMPORARY POLITICAL HISTORY

Historical Context

After the First World War, during which Macedonia was occupied by the Bulgarians and the Central Powers of Austria-Hungary and Germany, Vardar Macedonia, the area now known as the former Yugoslav republic of Macedonia (FYRM), became part of the new Kingdom of Serbs, Croats and Slovenes (formally named Yugoslavia in 1929), being widely referred to as 'South Serbia'. In the Second World War, however, the Bulgarian occupation of 1941–44 disillusioned many Yugoslav Macedonians. From 1943 the Partisans of Josip Broz (Tito), the General-Secretary of the Communist Party of Yugoslavia, began to increase their support in the region, and after the war the new Federal People's Republic of Yugoslavia and its communist rulers resolved to include a Macedonian nation as a federal partner. A distinct Macedonian identity was promoted, and a linguistic policy that encouraged the establishment of a Macedonian literary language distinct from Bulgarian increased Macedonian self-awareness.

The presence of a large ethnic Albanian minority in western Macedonia added to Macedonian insecurities. The proximity of the neighbouring Serbian province of Kosovo, which had a majority ethnic Albanian population, and demands, from the late 1960s, for the creation of an Albanian republic within Yugoslavia, alarmed the Macedonian authorities, which became particularly active against Albanian nationalism from 1981. In 1989 the communists amended the republican Constitution to allow for the introduction of a multi-party system; Macedonia was declared to be a nation state of the ethnic Macedonians, and mention of the Albanian and Turkish minorities was excluded.

In November and December 1990 the first multi-party elections to a unicameral Sobranie (Assembly) were held in Macedonia. The Front for Macedonian National Unity, which principally comprised a nationalist party, the Internal Macedonian Revolutionary Organization—Democratic Party for Macedonian National Unity (IMRO—DPMNU), led by Ljubčo Georgievski, and which had previously declared its support for the return of territories within Serbia, alleged irregularities after failing to win any seats at the first round. Following two further rounds of voting, however, the IMRO—DPMNU emerged as the single party with the most seats (37) in the 120-member Sobranie. The League of Communists of Macedonia—Party for Democratic Reform (LCM—PDR, as the League of Communists of Macedonia had renamed itself), led by Petar Gosev, won 31 seats and the two predominantly Albanian parties (the Party for Democratic Prosperity—PDP—and the People's Democratic Party) a total of 25. The republican branch of the federal Alliance of Reform Forces (ARF, subsequently the Liberal Party of Macedonia—LPM) won 19 seats. Following lengthy coalition negotiations, in January 1991 Kiro Gligorov of the LCM—PDR was elected President of the Republic, with Georgievski as Vice-President; Stojan Andov of the ARF was elected President of the Sobranie. The three parties agreed to support a government largely comprising members without political affiliation. In March the Sobranie approved a new administration, headed by Nikola Kljušev. The LCM—PDR was renamed the Social Democratic Alliance of Macedonia (SDAM) in April.

On 25 January 1991 the Sobranie unanimously adopted a motion declaring the republic a sovereign territory. After June declarations of Croatian and Slovenian 'dissociation', Macedonia, wary of the increasing Serbian domination of the remaining federal institutions, declared its neutrality and emphasized its sovereign status. On 8 September a referendum (boycotted by the ethnic Albanian population) approved the sovereignty of Macedonia.

Georgievski resigned the vice-presidency in October 1991, and the IMRO—DPMNU announced that it had joined the opposition, stating that the party had been excluded from the decision-making process. On 17 November the Constitution, which declared the sovereignty of the Republic of Macedonia, was endorsed by 96 of the 120 Assembly members, with opposition from the majority of ethnic Albanian deputies. In January 1992 an unofficial (and illegal) referendum conducted among the ethnic Albanian population reportedly resulted in 99.9% of votes being cast in favour of territorial and political autonomy for the ethnic Albanian population.

The complete withdrawal of federal troops from Macedonia in March 1992, in conjunction with the adoption in April of a new Constitution in Yugoslavia, referring only to Serbia and Montenegro, effectively signalled Yugoslav acceptance of Macedonian secession from the federation.

Domestic Political Affairs

Macedonian affairs were subsequently dominated by the question of wider international recognition. The republic, although no longer part of Yugoslavia, was unable to act as an independent nation in the international community. Bulgaria recognized the state of Macedonia (although not the existence of a distinct Macedonian nationality or language) in January 1992, closely followed by Turkey in February, provoking mass protests in Thessaloníki, the capital of the Greek region of Macedonia. The Greek authorities insisted that 'Macedonia' was a geographical term delineating an area that included a large part of northern Greece, and expressed fears that the republic's independence under the name 'Macedonia' might foster a false claim to future territorial expansion. Greece was instrumental in the formulation of a European Community (EC, now European Union—EU, see p. 270) policy, adopted in early 1992, that the republic should be awarded no formal recognition of independence until stringent constitutional requirements had been fulfilled. In May Gligorov rejected a statement by the EC that it was 'willing to recognize Macedonia as a sovereign and independent state within its existing borders under a name that can be accepted by all concerned'. Negotiations with Greece ended in failure in June. In July, after a motion expressing no confidence in the Government received strong support in the Sobranie (and following large demonstrations against its failure to gain international recognition for an independent Macedonia), the Government resigned. The IMRO—DPMNU failed to form a new alliance, and eventually, in September Branko Crvenkovski, the Chairman of the SDAM, was installed as Prime Minister of a coalition Government.

The adoption of a new flag in August 1992 attracted particular opposition from Greece, which objected to the depiction outside Greece of the 'Vergina Star' (regarded as an ancient Greek symbol of Philip of Macedon and Alexander the Great). As a result of a blockade of petroleum deliveries imposed on Macedonia by Greece, reserves at the Skopje petroleum refinery were exhausted by September. In February 1993 Greece agreed to international arbitration over the issue of Macedonia's name, undertaking to abide by its final outcome. On 8 April the republic was admitted to the UN under the temporary name of 'the former Yugoslav republic of Macedonia', pending settlement of the issue of a permanent name by international mediators. However, Greece continued to assert, and the FYRM to deny, that the use of the 'Vergina Star' emblem and the name 'Macedonia' implied territorial claims on Greek territory, and in October Greece announced its withdrawal from UN-sponsored negotiations on the issue of a permanent name. In January 1994 Greece requested that the other nations of the EU prevail upon the FYRM (which was, by this time, recognized by all the other EU member states) to make concessions concerning its name, flag and Constitution, and threatened to ban trade with the FYRM. From February (by which time Russia and the USA had formally recognized the FYRM) Greece blocked all non-humanitarian shipments to the FYRM through the port of Thessaloníki, and also road and rail transport links with the FYRM. In April the European Commission, which contested that the Greek embargo was in violation of EU trade legislation, initiated legal proceedings against Greece at the Court of Justice of the European Communities. In April 1995, however, the Court issued a preliminary opinion that the embargo was not in breach of Greece's obligations under the Treaty of Rome. Meanwhile, Greece agreed to resume negotiations in April with the FYRM, under the auspices of the UN; in May the Organization for Security and Co-operation in Europe (OSCE, see p. 385) announced that it was to join the mediation efforts. In September an interim accord was signed at the UN headquarters in New York, USA, by the FYRM Minister of Foreign Affairs and his Greek counterpart. The agreement provided for the mutual recognition of existing frontiers and respect for the sovereignty and political independence of each state, and for the free movement of goods and people between the two countries. Greece was to end its trade embargo and veto on the FYRM's entry into international organizations, while the FYRM undertook to abandon its use of the Vergina emblem in any form, and to amend parts of its Constitution that had been regarded by Greece as 'irredentist'. (The issue of a permanent name for the FYRM was to be the subject of further UN-mediated negotiations.) In early October the Sobranie approved a new state flag, depicting an eight-rayed sun in place of the Vergina emblem. The interim accord was ratified by the Sobranie on 9 October, and was formally signed in Skopje by representatives of the FYRM and Greece on 13 October. The border between the two countries was subsequently reopened.

The Albanian Government formally recognized the FYRM in April 1993. However, relations between the FYRM authorities and the minority Albanian population continued to deteriorate. In November several ethnic Albanians were arrested in the western towns of Gostivar and Tetovo, and in Skopje. The Government announced that a conspiracy to form paramilitary groups, with the eventual aim of establishing an Albanian republic in the west of the FYRM, had been discovered. Further arrests followed, and in June 1994 Mithat Emini, the former General Secretary of the PDP, was sentenced to eight years' imprisonment, after being convicted of conspiring to engage in hostile activity; nine others received custodial sentences of between five and eight years. (In February 1995 all the sentences were reduced by two years.)

The PDP split in February 1994, when a faction led by Xheladin Murati (the Deputy President of the Sobranie) and including the party's representatives in the Government and in the legislature, withdrew from the party's congress. The remaining grouping, led by Arben Xhaferi, made more radical demands regarding the status of ethnic Albanians in the FYRM. Organizations representing ethnic Albanians protested that inadequate preparations for a national census, conducted in mid-1994, effectively prevented the full enumeration of the ethnic Albanian community. The sentencing of Emini and his co-defendants prompted ethnic Albanian deputies to boycott the Sobranie in July (although they resumed their seats to defeat a motion, proposed by the IMRO—DPMNU, expressing no confidence in the Government). Murati resigned from the leadership of his PDP faction (and from his role in the Sobranie) later in July, reportedly in protest against the sentences; he was succeeded as party leader by Abdurahman Aliti.

Gligorov, representing the Alliance for Macedonia (a coalition of the SDAM, the LPM and the Socialist Party of Macedonia—SPM), was re-elected to the presidency on 16 October 1994, winning 78.4% of the valid votes cast; his only challenger was Georgievski of the IMRO—DPMNU. A first round of voting to the new Sobranie took place on the same day. The IMRO—DPMNU, which failed to secure any seats, alleged widespread electoral fraud in both elections, and boycotted the second round of legislative voting, which took place on 30 October (a third round was necessary in 10 constituencies on 13 November, owing to irregularities in earlier rounds). The final results confirmed that the Alliance for Macedonia had won the majority of seats in the Sobranie (with the SDAM taking 58 seats, the LPM 29 and the SPM eight). Aliti's 'moderate' PDP, which had been legally recognized as the successor to the original party, secured 10 seats; members of the 'radical' PDP had been obliged to stand as independent candidates (Xhaferi was among the independent candidates to be elected). Gligorov subsequently requested that Crvenkovski form a new government, and the SDAM-led administration, which also included members of the LPM, Aliti's PDP and the SPM, was approved by the Sobranie in December.

Tensions were exacerbated by efforts by the ethnic Albanian community to establish an Albanian-language university in Tetovo. Despite government objections that to establish such an institution would be unconstitutional, the university was formally founded in December 1994. In February 1995 the opening of the university provoked considerable unrest; an ethnic Albanian was killed in clashes with security forces. In July 1996 five of the university's founders, including its rector, received custodial sentences for inciting the riots, prompting protests by ethnic Albanians. (In May 2000 the Sobranie approved legislation granting the university at Tetovo legal status as a private foundation, and in January 2004 further legislation was adopted, transforming it into a state university.)

In October 1995 Gligorov was injured in a car-bomb attack in Skopje; he resumed full presidential duties in January 1996. Meanwhile, divisions had emerged within the governing Alliance for Macedonia, which collapsed in February, prompting the LPM to be excluded from the Government. Andov resigned as President of the Sobranie in early March, stating that Crvenkovski had acted unconstitutionally in expelling the LPM from the Government.

In September 1996, prior to local elections scheduled for 17 November, the Sobranie approved legislation reorganizing the territorial division of the FYRM into 123 municipalities. In October three opposition parties, the IMRO—DPMNU, the PDP and the newly established Movement for All-Macedonian Action—Conservative Party, formed a coalition to contest the elections. Xhaferi's faction, which had been reconstituted as the Party of Democratic Prosperity of Albanians in Macedonia (PDPAM), and the (also ethnic Albanian) National Democratic Party (NDP) agreed to present joint candidates in some constituencies. The SDAM received the greatest number of votes, followed by the coalition led by the IMRO—DPMNU, and the PDP. Observers from the Council of Europe (see p. 250) declared that, overall, the elections had been conducted fairly.

Ethnic Albanian unrest

In January 1997 legislation was adopted to permit Albanian to become a language of instruction at the teacher-training faculty of the university at Skopje, precipitating outrage among ethnic Macedonian students at the faculty. Ethnic tensions were further compounded by the civil conflict in Albania in early 1997. A financial scandal emerged in the FYRM in March, involving the embezzlement of funds invested in 'pyramid' savings schemes. Crvenkovski pledged an investigation to identify those responsible for the losses sustained by large numbers of investors, and several senior officials were subsequently arrested on suspicion of involvement. Although the Government won a vote of confidence in its management of the affair, the LPM deputies withdrew from the parliamentary chamber to register their disapproval of the measures undertaken. In April the Government announced plans to reimburse losses incurred by investors, following the failure of a major savings institution in the south-western town of Bitola; in May the Sobranie approved the replacement of the Governor of the central bank, who was believed to have been involved in the failure of the investment scheme. Following an IMRO—DPMNU demonstration in Skopje to demand the resignation of the Government, a reorganized administration was approved by the Sobranie at the end of May.

THE FORMER YUGOSLAV REPUBLIC OF MACEDONIA

In May 1997 ethnic Albanians in Gostivar took part in protests against a ruling by the Constitutional Court that prohibited the use of the Albanian flag in the FYRM. In June the President of the Constitutional Court issued a statement demanding that the Government enforce the ruling. In early July the Sobranie adopted legislation stipulating that the use of the Albanian flag, and flags of other minority ethnic groups, would only be permitted on national holidays, with the Macedonian flag being displayed at the same time. None the less, the mayors of Gostivar and Tetovo continued to refuse to comply with the order of the Constitutional Court, and government officials forcibly removed Albanian flags that had been displayed at municipal buildings. Ensuing protests in Gostivar resulted in violent clashes between security forces and demonstrators, as a result of which three ethnic Albanians were killed; some 500 protesters were arrested. In September the mayor of Gostivar, Rufi Osmani, received a custodial sentence of some 13 years (reduced to seven years in February 1998), after being convicted on charges of inciting ethnic tension and rebellion, while the Chairman of the municipal council was sentenced to three years' imprisonment for failing to adopt the ruling of the Constitutional Court. In April 1998 the Democratic Party of Albanians (DPA—which had been formed in July 1997 by the amalgamation of the PDPAM and the NDP) announced that it was to withdraw its representatives from all government bodies, in protest against Osmani's imprisonment.

In August 1998 the PDP and the DPA established an alliance to contest forthcoming legislative elections. In early September the IMRO—DPMNU and the newly formed Democratic Alternative (DA) formed an electoral coalition, For Changes. The legislative elections were conducted in two rounds on 18 October and 1 November 1998; the For Changes coalition secured an absolute majority in the Sobranie, with 58 seats, while the SDAM obtained 29 seats, and the alliance of the PDP and the DPA won 24. Owing to irregularities, a further round of voting took place in two electoral districts, at which one seat was won by the For Changes alliance, and the other by the PDP-DPA alliance. Later in November Georgievski was nominated as Prime Minister. The DPA was subsequently invited to join the governing coalition of the IMRO—DPMNU and the DA. In early December a new Government, comprising 14 representatives of the IMRO—DPMNU, eight of the DA and five of the DPA, was formed. At the end of December the Sobranie approved legislation (supported by the new Government) providing for the release of some 8,000 prisoners, among them Osmani. Although Gligorov refused to approve the amnesty in January 1999, in the following month the amnesty legislation was resubmitted to the Sobranie (in accordance with the Constitution) and subsequently adopted.

The first round of the presidential election on 31 October 1999 was contested by six candidates: Tito Petkovski, representing the SDAM, secured 33.2% of the votes cast, and Boris Trajkovski, the IMRO—DPMNU candidate, won 20.6%; Vasil Tupurkovski, the DA leader, took 16.0%, and Muharem Nexipi, the DPA candidate, 14.8%. Since no candidate had secured an outright majority of the votes, Petkovski and Trajkovski progressed to a second round, held on 14 November; Trajkovski was elected to the presidency with 52.8% of the votes cast (after DPA and DA voters transferred support to his candidacy). In late November the Supreme Court upheld a legal appeal by the SDAM against the results, and ruled that a further ballot take place in some western regions. A partial round, affecting about 10% of the total electorate, consequently took place on 5 December. However, the overall results were almost unchanged, with Trajkovski receiving 52.9% of the votes cast. Although the SDAM again claimed that irregularities had taken place, Petkovski finally accepted Trajkovski's election to the presidency. Trajkovski was formally inaugurated as President on 15 December. Following negotiations between the two leaders of the For Changes coalition, Georgievski and Tupurkovski, the IMRO—DPMNU, DA and DPA reached agreement on the formation of a new Government. The coalition administration, which contained seven new ministers (including Tupurkovski, as a Deputy Prime Minister), was formally approved by the Sobranie on 27 December.

In January 2000 the Government announced that amendments to the Constitution, which would allow higher education to be conducted in the language of ethnic minorities, would be submitted for approval by the Sobranie. In April legislation was adopted, obliging the authorities to return property expropriated under the communist regime. In the same month disaffected members of the IMRO—DPMNU, headed by a former Minister of Finance, Boris Zmejkovski, established a breakaway faction, which became known as the IMRO—True Macedonian Reform Option (IMRO—TMRO). In May the SDAM, the Liberal Democratic Party (LDP) and the Democratic League—Liberal Party established an electoral alliance. In July Georgievski reorganized the Government, reducing the number of ministries from 21 to 14. Local government elections took place in two rounds on 10 and 24 September, amid reports of numerous violent incidents. After a further round of voting took place, as a result of electoral irregularities, it was announced at the end of the month that the parties of the governing coalition had secured 75 of the 123 municipalities. Following prolonged dissent between Georgievski and Tupurkovski, the DA withdrew from the coalition Government and from the Sobranie at the end of November. Georgievski subsequently formed a new administration, which, for the first time, included members of the LDP.

In early 2001 ethnic Albanian militants, members of the self-styled National Liberation Army (NLA), began to infiltrate northern parts of the FYRM from Kosovo, clashing with FYRM security forces. In early March NLA forces seized the border village of Tanusevci, north of Skopje, prompting counter-attacks from government troops. The border with Kosovo was officially closed after senior government officials visiting the border region were attacked and temporarily besieged by the NLA. Although the authorities succeeded in regaining control of Tanusevci, in mid-March some 200 NLA forces attempted to occupy Tetovo, precipitating the imposition of curfew regulations in the city. Following an appeal by the Government to the international community for military assistance, the North Atlantic Treaty Organization (NATO, see p. 368) reinforced its military presence at the border with Kosovo to prevent the NLA from receiving supplies from the province. On 21 March the UN Security Council adopted Resolution 1345, condemning the violence by ethnic Albanian nationalists in the FYRM as constituting a threat to the stability of the region. Despite reports that the ethnic Albanian rebels aimed to establish a 'greater Albania' (to include some northern and western regions of the FYRM), the NLA insisted that the conflict had been initiated to put pressure on the FYRM Government to institute constitutional changes guaranteeing equal rights for ethnic Albanians. The prolonged bombardment of rebel positions by government forces resulted in a withdrawal by the NLA from the Tetovo region, and hostilities temporarily subsided in early April. However, at the end of the month eight members of the state security forces were killed in an NLA attack near the border with Kosovo. Their funeral precipitated rioting and attacks by Macedonians on Albanian-owned property in the southern town of Bitola. Government troops subsequently launched an offensive against rebel ethnic Albanian positions near Kumanovo, after two further members of the armed forces were killed.

Meanwhile, in early April 2001, following the temporary suppression of the insurgency, inter-party discussions regarding the ethnic Albanian demands commenced. After signing a Stabilization and Association Agreement with the EU, the Government pledged to initiate political, social and economic reforms by mid-2001. Ethnic Albanian proposals included: the postponement of the national census, due to take place in May, until October, to allow the return of refugees who had fled the conflict; state funding for the university at Tetovo; and the conversion of the state television's third service into an Albanian-language channel. However, the Government continued to oppose principal demands that the Constitution be amended to grant the ethnic Albanian population (hitherto officially categorized as a minority) equal rights with the Macedonian population, and Albanian the status of a second official language.

In early May 2001, following the resumption of intensive hostilities in the north of the country, the Government announced that the declaration of a state of war (which would, subject to the approval of a two-thirds' majority in the Sobranie, allow the authorities to adopt emergency powers and Trajkovski to rule by decree) was under debate. Intensive discussions ensued between the principal political parties, with EU and NATO mediation, and it was agreed that the SDAM, the DPA and the PDP would join a government of national unity, and the parliamentary debate on the declaration of a state of war was suspended. The PDP subsequently demanded that the Government declare a cease-fire in the conflict in the north, as a precondition to the ethnic Albanian party's participation in the new administration. After the government offensive against the rebels was temporarily suspended, the Government of national unity (headed by Georgievski) was approved by the Sobranie on 13 May. NLA leaders stated that the rebel move-

THE FORMER YUGOSLAV REPUBLIC OF MACEDONIA

ment (which still held several villages) would continue hostilities until the Government agreed to enter into negotiations.

The Ohrid Agreement

On 8 June 2001 Trajkovski announced proposals for a comprehensive peace plan, which provided for the proportional representation of ethnic Albanians at all levels of government, the increased official use of the Albanian language, and a partial amnesty for NLA combatants. Despite EU support for the plan, the NLA demanded that the Government end hostilities and enter into negotiations on constitutional reforms, and rebel forces seized the town of Aracinovo, some 6 km east of Skopje. Later in June the Government announced the suspension of its offensive against the NLA, following pressure from international envoys. However, violent protests were staged by Macedonian nationalists at the parliament building in Skopje, in response to the NATO-mediated cease-fire arrangement at Aracinovo, which was perceived to be lenient towards the ethnic Albanian rebels. On 29 June NATO formally approved an operation to deploy a 3,500-member multinational force in the FYRM to assist in the disarmament of the NLA, which was, however, conditional on the imposition of a lasting cease-fire. On 5 July the Government announced that an official cease-fire agreement had been signed by both sides, and negotiations resumed between leaders of the principal Macedonian and ethnic Albanian parties regarding a permanent peace settlement. However, Georgievski and his nationalist cabinet supporters strongly opposed proposals, detailed by the EU and US special envoys, for the extension of the use of the Albanian language, and accused them of bias towards the rebels. The cease-fire collapsed after 17 days, when the NLA launched further attacks on government forces deployed near Tetovo. (By that time some 60,000 ethnic Albanians had fled to Kosovo, while a further 30,000 had become internally displaced.) International diplomatic efforts subsequently intensified, following renewed fears of widespread civil conflict. On 26 July it was announced that an accord had been reached to restore the cease-fire between government forces and the ethnic Albanian rebels, who had agreed to withdraw from newly captured territory near Tetovo. At the end of July further negotiations on the peace proposals, between government and ethnic Albanian representatives, commenced at the western town of Ohrid. Progress in the discussions was reported, following the resolution of the two main issues of contention (the extension of the official use of the Albanian language and the right to proportional representation of the ethnic Albanian community in the security forces). In response to increasing pressure from the EU and the USA, the Government announced a unilateral cease-fire, and on 13 August the Government and ethnic Albanian leaders at Ohrid signed a framework peace agreement, providing for the amendment of the Constitution to grant greater rights to the ethnic Albanian community. On the following day the NLA leader, Ali Ahmeti, agreed that the NLA, numbering an estimated 2,500–3,000, would relinquish its armaments to NATO troops. Following an assessment of the security situation, NATO announced that the cease-fire was generally being observed, and on 22 August the activation order for a NATO mission, Operation Essential Harvest, was released. The force, which finally comprised 4,500 troops (of which the United Kingdom contributed about 1,900), had a mandate to disarm the ethnic Albanian combatants and destroy their weapons within 30 days of its deployment. The Ministry of Internal Affairs claimed the NLA to be in possession of some 85,000 armaments; however, NATO estimated the number of weapons to be collected at 3,000–4,000.

In early September 2001 parliamentary debate on constitutional reform was delayed by mass nationalist protests against the peace plan. Macedonian nationalist parties in the legislature continued to dispute the details of a number of the proposed amendments, while ethnic Albanian representatives insisted that attempts to limit the reforms would provoke renewed conflict. Meanwhile, investigators from the International Criminal Tribunal for the former Yugoslavia (ICTY, see p. 20) at the Hague, Netherlands, had been dispatched to the FYRM to conduct preliminary inquiries into the killing of six ethnic Albanian civilians in the village of Ljuboten in early August; the nationalist Minister of Internal Affairs, Ljube Boškovski, was suspected of responsibility for the operation. On 26 September NATO's 30-day disarmament programme was declared to have been successful, with the collection of some 3,875 armaments. On the same day the establishment of a further, reduced NATO mission, Operation Amber Fox, was authorized. (In response to international pressure, the Government had invited NATO to retain a military presence in the country, despite domestic opposition.) The new mission, comprising 700 troops, together with 300 forces already stationed in the FYRM, was deployed under German leadership, with a three-month renewable mandate to protect EU and OSCE monitors supervising the implementation of the peace agreement. On 27 September Ahmeti announced that the NLA had been formally dissolved, following the completion of the disarmament process. In early October the EU criticized delays in implementing constitutional reforms, after Macedonian parties announced that the legislative process would be suspended pending the release of 14 Macedonian civilians allegedly seized by the NLA earlier that year. Following pressure from Trajkovski, and the international community, which urged acceptance of the plan, discussion on the measures resumed in the Sobranie. Later that month Trajkovski approved plans for the deployment of ethnically mixed security units in regions formerly held by the NLA.

On 16 November 2001, after extensive debate, the Sobranie adopted 15 main amendments to the existing Constitution. The principal reforms were: the revision of the Constitution's preamble to include a reference to members of non-ethnic Macedonian communities as citizens of the country; the introduction in the Sobranie of a 'double majority' system, whereby certain legislation would require the approval of a minority group; the establishment of Albanian as the second official language in districts in which ethnic Albanians accounted for more than 20% of the population; and the right to proportional representation for ethnic Albanians in the Constitutional Court, all areas of government administration and the security forces. The adoption of the reforms was received with approval by the international community. Later in November the SDAM and the LDP withdrew from the coalition Government (which was subsequently reorganized), on the grounds that their participation was no longer necessary.

In early December 2001 NATO extended the mandate of Operation Amber Fox until 26 March 2002, and it was subsequently extended until 26 June. An EU-sponsored international donor conference on economic assistance for the FYRM, originally scheduled to take place in October 2001, was further postponed in December, pending the implementation of additional reforms. In January 2002 new legislation providing for the devolution of greater authority to local government (thereby granting a measure of self-rule to predominantly ethnic Albanian regions) was approved by the Sobranie, and the donor conference duly took place in March. Also in January a Deputy Prime Minister, Dosta Dimovska (who was considered to be a moderate), resigned from the Government, following disagreement with Georgievski over issues relating to the deployment of security units in previously NLA-controlled villages. In February the three principal ethnic Albanian political parties (the DPA, the PDP and the NDP) and the former NLA leadership officially established a co-ordinating council. In March the Sobranie adopted legislation granting immunity from prosecution to several thousand former NLA insurgents (excluding those indictable by the ICTY), in accordance with the peace settlement. In May the mandate of Operation Amber Fox was further extended, to 26 October. In accordance with the peace agreement, the Sobranie was dissolved on 18 July, prior to legislative elections, which were scheduled for 15 September and were to be monitored by the OSCE.

The SDAM administration

In May 2002 Ahmeti established a new political party, the Democratic Union for Integration (DUI), which was believed to comprise mainly former NLA combatants. Later that month two ministers belonging to the IMRO—TMRO resigned from the Government, on the grounds that former NLA members had become dominant within the principal ethnic Albanian parties. In the same month the Sobranie approved legislation whereby Albanian became an official language, in accordance with the Ohrid peace accord. At the end of August ethnic Albanians took hostage five Macedonian civilians at Gostivar; security forces surrounded an ethnic Albanian base and killed two of the kidnappers. None the less, the elections to the legislature took place peacefully on 15 September, attracting commendation from the international community, after OSCE observers declared them to have been conducted democratically. Georgievski's Government was removed from power by a 10-party alliance (led by the SDAM and the LDP), Together for Macedonia, which secured 60 of the 120 seats in the Sobranie. The IMRO—DPMNU won 33 seats and the DUI 16 seats. The Together for Macedonia alliance and the DUI subsequently

THE FORMER YUGOSLAV REPUBLIC OF MACEDONIA

signed an agreement for the establishment of a coalition Government (which was, however, to exclude former NLA combatants). The new administration, comprising members of the SDAM, the LDP and the DUI, and headed by Crvenkovski, was officially approved by the Sobranie on 1 November.

In October 2002 NATO agreed to extend the mandate of Operation Amber Fox until December. On 14 December Operation Amber Fox was succeeded by a 450-member mission, Allied Harmony, with a mandate to protect international monitors and advise FYRM security forces. On 31 March 2003 this contingent was, in turn, replaced by an EU-led mission, Operation Concordia, comprising 350 military personnel from a total of 13 EU member states and 14 non-EU nations. The purpose of the operation, which was deployed at the official request of Trajkovski, was to maintain security in order to facilitate the implementation of the Ohrid peace agreement. Meanwhile, in early 2003 a newly emerged ethnic Albanian extremist group, the Albanian National Army (ANA), threatened to launch a military offensive against the Government. In September, after ethnic Albanian militants clashed with a security patrol at the border with Kosovo, the authorities dispatched security forces to the region in an operation to suppress dissident activity (a measure that was criticized by the DUI).

In May 2003 Nikola Gruevski became the new leader of the IMRO—DPMNU. In November Ljupco Jordanovski of the SDAM was elected as the new President of the Sobranie, replacing Nikola Popovski, who had been appointed as Deputy Prime Minister and Minister of Finance. In December Operation Concordia was replaced by a 200-member EU mission, Operation Proxima, which, in addition to maintaining security and combating organized crime in the country, was to advise the FYRM police forces (the mandate of Operation Proxima expired in December 2005). In early 2004 the Government announced plans to redemarcate municipal boundaries, as part of a process of administrative decentralization included in the provisions of the Ohrid Agreement, although there was widespread popular opposition to the proposals.

On 26 February 2004 President Trajkovski, together with eight government officials, was killed, when an aircraft transporting him to a international investment conference in Bosnia and Herzegovina crashed in a southern, mountainous region of that country. Jordanovski, as speaker of the Sobranie, assumed the presidency in an acting capacity, pending an election, which, under the terms of the Constitution, was to take place within 40 days. At the presidential election, held on 14 April, Crvenkovski, representing the SDAM, won 42.5% of the votes cast; since he failed to secure the 50% of the votes necessary to be elected outright, he progressed to a second round with Saško Kedev, hitherto a parliamentary deputy and a member of the IMRO—DPMNU (who had won 34.1% of the votes). Two former NLA commanders, the DUI Secretary-General, Gzim Ostreni, and Zudi Xhelili of the DPA, also contested the election, obtaining 14.8% and 8.7% of the votes cast, respectively. On 28 April Crvenkovski was elected to the presidency with 62.7% of the votes. Kedev immediately claimed that widespread malpractice had been perpetrated and appealed against the election results, which were, however, described as legitimate by OSCE monitors. Crvenkovski was inaugurated on 12 May.

On 2 June 2004 the Sobranie approved the formation of a coalition administration, with Hari Kostov of the SDAM as Prime Minister, and comprising members of that party, the DUI and the LDP. The only new ministerial appointment was that of Siljan Avramovski as Minister of Internal Affairs, replacing Kostov. In July, after lengthy negotiations and under pressure from the international community, the parties of the governing coalition reached an agreement on the planned redemarcation of the country's municipal boundaries. The total number of administrative districts was to be reduced from 123 to 84, with the ethnic balance of 26 districts becoming predominantly Albanian, and the adoption of Albanian as a second official language in a number of these, including Skopje and Struga. The agreement prompted strong public criticism and protests, which in Struga escalated into violence. On 26 July a large demonstration was staged in Skopje, in protest against the draft agreement on decentralization, which had been submitted for approval to the Sobranie.

On 7 November 2004, following a petition presented by Macedonian nationalist parties, a referendum on the proposed redemarcation of administrative districts was conducted. However, the governing coalition, together with representatives of the international community, urged a boycott and voter par-

Introductory Survey

ticipation in the referendum was estimated at only 26%, thereby invalidating the results and allowing the local government reforms to proceed. In mid-November Kostov tendered his resignation as Prime Minister, claiming that the DUI had obstructed the parliamentary approval of reforms essential to attract foreign investment, and that the DUI Minister of Transport and Communications, in particular, had been involved in corrupt practices. Later that month Crvenkovski nominated Vlado Buckovski, hitherto the Minister of Defence, as Prime Minister. (Buckovski was also elected as Chairman of the SDAM.) On 17 December the Sobranie approved a new Government, formed by Buckovski, who pledged his commitment to the implementation of economic reforms, and again comprising members of the SDAM, the LDP and the DUI. In March 2005 the ICTY issued indictments against Boškovski and a former head of security, John Tarculovski, in connection with the August 2001 killings in Ljuboten.

The first round of local government elections, which were to effect the significant devolution of powers to 84 municipal authorities (including the City of Skopje), took place, with some reported irregularities, on 13 March 2005. A second round of voting for 47 municipalities was conducted on 27 March. After upholding claims of irregularities in the first round, the Supreme Court had ordered polls to be repeated in several constituencies, and an OSCE observer mission announced that the second round of the elections again failed to meet OSCE and Council of Europe standards in some municipalities. The DPA and the PDP, which had urged a boycott of the vote, refused to recognize the results. Supporters of the IMRO—DPMNU staged protests in Ohrid to demand that the second round be repeated in that municipality on grounds of malpractice. On 10 April further ballots were conducted in 19 municipalities and the City of Skopje, where electoral irregularities had occurred. According to official results, 36 of the mayoral contests were won by the Together for Macedonia governing coalition, and 15 by the DUI, with the IMRO—DPMNU securing 21 mayoralties. In mid-July, in accordance with the Ohrid Agreement, the Sobranie adopted legislation enabling any ethnic minority community to display its flag, together with the Macedonian flag, in regions where it constituted at least 50% of the population (in effect, in 19 municipalities, of which 16 were predominantly ethnic Albanian, two ethnic Turkish and one Roma).

In December 2005 the Sobranie approved a series of constitutional amendments providing for extensive reform of the judicial system; the process of ensuring the complete independence of the judiciary, regarded as important to the country's application for EU membership (see below), was to be implemented over several years. In March 2006 the Sobranie adopted a series of amendments to electoral regulations, in preparation for legislative elections. In May the Sobranie abolished custodial sentences for those convicted of press offences.

IMRO—DPMNU *returns to power*

In the legislative elections, held on 5 July 2006, the IMRO—DPMNU secured 32.5% of the votes cast, defeating Prime Minister Buckovski's SDAM, which obtained only 23.3% of the votes. A coalition of the DUI and the PDP secured the majority of ethnic Albanian votes, attracting 12.2% of the total ballot, while Xhaferi's DPA received 7.2% of the votes. Reported electoral irregularities caused the Supreme Court to demand that elections be repeated in eight constituencies, following which the IMRO—DPMNU's number of seats in the Sobranie was increased from 44 to 45. In August Gruevski, the Chairman of the IMRO—DPMNU, was formally appointed as Prime Minister and his Government was approved by the Sobranie a few days later. The new coalition administration comprised 10 members of the IMRO—DPMNU (including Trajko Slaveski as Minister of Finance and Antonio Milososki as Minister of Foreign Affairs), four of the DPA, three of the New Social Democratic Party (formed in the previous year) and one each of the LPM and of the SPM. Ljubiša Georgievski was appointed as President of the Sobranie.

In November 2006 the Sobranie adopted amendments to the FYRM's anti-corruption legislation. In January 2007 the DUI and the PDP announced a boycott of parliamentary proceedings, in protest against their continued exclusion from Gruevski's Government. In February Ahmeti announced two preconditions to the resumption of political dialogue: a reconsideration by the Government of the composition of the Committee for Cross-Community Relations; and a constitutional amendment to ensure fairer representation for ethnic minorities within future governments. In February the Sobranie approved a government reorganization, which included the appointment of Imer Aliu (hitherto Minister of the Environment and Physical Planning) to the position of Deputy Prime Minister, responsible for the implementation of the Ohrid Framework Agreement. In April Boškovski and Tarculovski became the first of those accused of war crimes during the 2001 insurgency to stand trial at the ICTY. At the end of May 2007 the PDP announced that its representatives were to resume participation in the Sobranie, after reaching an agreement with the IMRO—DPMNU permitting it to join the Government; members of the PDP received several state posts. The DUI also officially ended its boycott of the Sobranie, but criticized the PDP's admission to the Government (and subsequently repeatedly withdrew from parliamentary sessions). The return of the PDP and the DUI enabled the Sobranie to adopt, on 5 June, legislation providing for full co-operation with the ICTY by the Government. In December legislation amending the judicial system was approved, as part of the requirements for NATO accession.

In December 2007 Abduraman Memeti of the PDP announced his resignation as Minister of Local Self-Government. In January 2008 the Minister of the Economy, Vera Rafajlovska, also tendered her resignation, citing personal reasons. In March the DPA announced its withdrawal from the Government, in protest against the failure of the IMRO—DPMNU both to recognize the independence of Kosovo (see below), and to provide increased rights for the use of the Albanian language and flag. Later that month, however, it was reported that the DPA had retracted its decision (with only Aliu expected to resign from his post), after reaching an agreement with the IMRO—DPMNU on inter-party co-operation to adopt legislation on the use of language, in accordance with the Constitution and the Ohrid Framework Agreement. Following the failure of negotiations with Greece on the issue of the country's official name, and Greece's consequent decision to veto NATO membership for the FYRM at a summit meeting of the Alliance held on 2 April (see below), the DUI proposed a motion for the dissolution of the Sobranie. The motion received the support of the IMRO—DPMNU, on the grounds that the existing legislature had obstructed reforms, and was approved on 12 April by 70 deputies in the Sobranie, despite opposition from Crvenkovski (with SDAM representatives boycotting the vote). Early legislative elections were scheduled for 1 June.

At the elections on 1 June 2008 voting was disrupted in a number of constituencies by outbreaks of violence between rival ethnic Albanian groups, in which at least one person was killed and several injured. The OSCE consequently assessed that the conduct of the elections failed to meet international standards. Elections were repeated on 15 June in those districts in which disorder had prevented voting from taking place, and in a small number of constituencies a further round of voting was necessary on 29 June. According to official results, a 19-party coalition, led by the IMRO—DPMNU, known as For a Better Macedonia, secured 48.8% of the votes cast and 63 of the 120 seats in the legislature, thereby becoming the first grouping to obtain an absolute majority in the Sobranie. The Sun Coalition for Europe, an eight-party coalition led by the SDAM, was placed second, with 23.7% of votes and 27 seats. The DUI received 18 seats (with 12.8%) and the DPA 11 seats (8.5%). It was subsequently announced that the PDP, which failed to obtain legislative representation, was to merge with the DPA. On 12 July Gruevski announced a new Government, which was approved by the Sobranie on 26 July; the coalition administration principally comprised members of the IMRO—DPMNU and the DUI, while the SPM, the Democratic Party of Turks in Macedonia and the (predominantly Roma) United Party for Emancipation were also represented. In the same month Boškovski was acquitted of all charges at the ICTY, and returned to the FYRM shortly afterwards. (However, Tarculovski was sentenced to 12 years' imprisonment for the August 2001 killings in Ljuboten.)

Gjorge Ivanov is elected President

In January 2009 the Speaker of the Sobranie scheduled the forthcoming presidential and municipal elections for 22 March; it was also announced that the major political parties had agreed that the minimum voter turn-out required for a valid poll be reduced from 50% to 40%. Later in January a convention of the IMRO—DPMNU selected a university professor and non-party member, Gjorge Ivanov, as its presidential candidate, while a former minister, Ljubomir Frčkoski, was nominated by the SDAM. Boškovski also declared his intention to contest the poll as an independent candidate. At the first round of the presidential election, which was contested by seven candidates on 22 March, Ivanov received about 35.1% of votes cast, while Frčkoski won 20.5%, Imer Selmani of New Democracy 15.0% and Boškovski 14.9%. A second round of voting was scheduled for 5 April, concurrently with run-off ballots for the municipal elections. According to official results, Ivanov was elected to the presidency, with some 63.1% of votes cast. Voter turn-out at the presidential poll was recorded at only 42.6% (owing, in part, to a boycott by ethnic Albanian voters), marginally exceeding the minimum rate of participation required for the poll to be valid. At the two rounds of municipal elections, held concurrently, the IMRO—DPMNU-led coalition secured 55 mayoralties, including Skopje; the DUI won 14 and SDAM nine mayoral posts. OSCE and Council of Europe observers declared that the organization of the elections met democratic commitments, but recommended further electoral reforms, including an end to the requirement of the minimum 40% turn-out. Ivanov was inaugurated as President on 12 May.

In late May 2009 Crvenkovski was unanimously elected as Chairman of the SDAM (which position he had previously held, in 1991–2004). At the end of June 2009 the Deputy Prime Minister, responsible for European Integration, Ivica Bocevski, tendered his resignation. In early July, following the dismissal of Trajko Slaveski as Minister of Finance and the resignation of two other ministers, the Sobranie approved a government reorganization. A law professor, Vasko Naumovski, succeeded Bocevski as Deputy Prime Minister, responsible for European Integration. The incumbent Deputy Prime Minister, responsible for Economic Affairs, Zoran Stavreski, became the new Minister of Finance (while remaining a deputy premier), and was replaced in his former position by a business director, Vladimir Peševski. In early August the Chairman of the DPA, Menduh Thaçi, announced a parliamentary boycott by party members, on the grounds that some of the provisions of the Ohrid Framework Agreement were not being observed. In September an encyclopedia published by the Macedonian Academy of Arts and Science (MANU) prompted outrage from Albanian academics and politicians, owing to its reportedly derogatory portrayal of the Albanian community (which included references to ethnic Albanians resident in the territories of the FYRM as 'settlers'). The publication was denounced by the Governments of Albania and Kosovo, while Greece and Bulgaria also objected to its account of Macedonian history. The MANU subsequently suspended distribution of the encyclopedia, and the Academy's editorial board was subsequently replaced and assurances given that the disputed content would be revised. In March 2010 Stavreski survived a parliamentary motion demanding his dismissal proposed by opposition deputies, as a result of the economic deterioration in the previous year.

Recent developments: announcement of early legislative elections

In November 2010 the SDAM renewed demands for early legislative elections, accusing the Government of economic mismanagement and failing to advance EU integration aspirations. In early December an anti-Government demonstration, which received the support of the main opposition parties, was organized by the SDAM in Skopje. In the same month a parliamentary motion submitted by the SDAM in support of the dissolution of the Sobranie was defeated. Later in December the owner of a major independent television channel, A1 TV, Velija Ramkovski, and 16 executives from associated companies were arrested for suspected tax evasion and other corruption offences. In January 2011 employees of A1 TV broadcast news bulletins from street locations outside government offices in Skopje, rather than from their studios, in protest at the freezing of the station's bank accounts by the authorities, claiming that the corruption investigation was politically motivated. Crvenkovski announced the withdrawal of the SDAM from the Sobranie in support of A1 TV; the LDP and other allied parties, and New Democracy joined the boycott, which was condemned by IMRO—DPMNU. In February a court in Skopje ruled in favour of reimposing the freezing of the bank accounts of A1 TV and nine associated companies. In the same month clashes, in which eight people were injured, broke out between ethnic Albanian protesters (who were supported by senior officials from the ethnic Albanian parliamentary parties), expressing opposition to the planned construction of a museum building, with the appearance of a medieval church, within the historic Skopje Fortress and supporters of the project. Later in February the Chairman of the State Election Commission, who was a member of the SDAM, tendered his resignation. Meanwhile, Gruevski indicated that he would consider the organization of early elections; following a meeting with the Prime Minister in March, however, Crvenkovski insisted that the SDAM would stage a boycott of an early poll unless its other demands, including an end to the freezing of A1 TV's accounts, were met. Later that month discussions between government and opposition leaders resulted in a measure of agreement in meeting opposition demands for reforms to electoral regulations. The DPA ended its boycott of the Sobranie in late March in the expectation of early elections (but was only to resume participation in the work of parliamentary commissions relating to electoral legislation). On 30 March Gruevski announced that the IMRO—DPMNU would propose that early legislative elections be scheduled for June, after Crvenkovski withdrew his preconditions and agreed that the SDAM would participate in the poll (although the party's boycott of the Sobranie continued). After the Sobranie had approved amendments to the electoral code and the appointment of a new Chairman of the State Election Commission (again of the SDAM), a motion dissolving the legislature was unanimously adopted on 14 April. On the following day it was confirmed that elections to the Sobranie would take place on 5 June.

Foreign Affairs
Regional relations

Both the September 1995 interim agreement with Greece and the November Dayton peace accord (for further details, see the chapter on Bosnia and Herzegovina) were of great significance for the FYRM, despite the unresolved issue of a permanent name for the country. The FYRM was admitted to the Council of Europe in late September, and to the OSCE in mid-October; in the following month the FYRM joined NATO's 'Partnership for Peace' programme (see p. 371). The agreement with Greece facilitated the establishment of full diplomatic relations with the EU from January 1996, and negotiations subsequently began for a co-operation accord; a declaration on co-operation was, furthermore, signed with the European Free Trade Association (see p. 447) in early April. By the end of 1996 more than 75 countries had recognized the FYRM, with about two-thirds using the country's constitutional name, the Republic of Macedonia.

Regular trade with Greece and Yugoslavia resumed in late 1995, and, under the interim agreement of September (see above), UN-mediated discussions continued between FYRM and Greek officials regarding the issue of a permanent name for the FYRM. By 1999 the FYRM's relations with Greece had improved significantly, and the principal border crossing between the FYRM and Greece was reopened at the end of 2000. Meanwhile, work on the construction of a 214-km pipeline to transport petroleum from the FYRM's capital, Skopje, to Thessaloníki was officially completed in July 2002. Greece strongly opposed a decision by the USA, announced in November 2004, that it would henceforth recognize the FYRM by its constitutional name of 'Republic of Macedonia'. The announcement in December 2006 that the international airport near Skopje was to be renamed after Alexander 'the Great' (considered by Greece to be integral to its cultural heritage) provoked renewed tension. Discussions continued in Ohrid in January 2007; it was reported that the FYRM authorities were only prepared to accept a 'double formula', whereby 'Republic of Macedonia' would be used for international instances and a separate name adopted for bilateral communications with Greece. In October Prime Minister Kostas Karamanlis announced that Greece would veto the FYRM's NATO and EU applications if no resolution was reached on the issue. In March 2008 UN Special Envoy Matthew Nimetz increased pressure on both Governments to reach a compromise resolution prior to a NATO conference on 2–4 April. Demonstrations against changing the country's constitutional name were staged in Skopje, and at the end of March the Greek ambassador formally protested to the Macedonian Government at the public display of posters depicting the Greek flag overprinted with a Nazi swastika. Following the FYRM's failure to receive an invitation to join NATO in April, owing to the continued impasse, the Government pledged to intensify efforts to resolve the dispute, and early legislative elections were subsequently scheduled for June, in the hope that the efficacy of governance would be improved. In November the FYRM Government submitted a legal challenge against Greece to the International Court of Justice (ICJ, see p. 23), claiming that it had violated the terms of the September 1995 interim accord regulating relations between the two countries, which stipulated that Greece would not veto the FYRM's accession to international institutions under that provisional name; a decision on the issue was expected within four years. In October 2009 Prime Minister Gruevski reiterated that any name proposed as a resolution to the dispute would be submitted to a national referendum in the FYRM (despite the opposition of the European Commission). In March 2010 the FYRM Government protested formally to the Greek ambassador against anti-Macedonian slogans used during a military parade in the Greek capital, Athens. In March 2011 proceedings began at the ICJ on the FRYM's appeal against Greece; the Court was expected to issue a ruling later that year.

In late 1992 the UN Security Council approved the deployment of members of the UN Protection Force (UNPROFOR) along the FYRM's border with Yugoslavia and Albania, in an effort to protect the FYRM from any external threat to its security; in March 1995 the operation in the FYRM was renamed the UN Preventive Deployment Force (UNPREDEP). Following a reduction in UNPREDEP's authorized strength by the Security Council, the US contingent of military personnel was placed under direct US administration. In April 1997 the mandate of UNPREDEP was extended to the end of May, in view of the civil disorder in Albania (q.v.); it was further extended in June and December. Following the civil unrest in Albania, a number of border incursions by armed groups of Albanian rebels were reported. In October the Ministers of Defence of the FYRM and Albania signed an agreement providing for increased security along the joint border between the two countries.

In early 1998 increasing clashes were reported in Kosovo between members of the Serbian security forces and the ethnic Albanian KLA. In late July the UN Security Council extended the mandate of UNPREDEP until 28 February 1999 and agreed to increase the size of the contingent from 750 to about 1,100, with the aim of reinforcing border control. In early December 1998, following discussions between President Gligorov and NATO officials, it was announced that a NATO 'extraction force' was to be deployed in the FYRM to effect the evacuation of OSCE monitors in Kosovo in the event of large-scale conflict. Following the commencement by NATO forces of an intensive aerial bombardment of strategic targets in Yugoslavia in late March 1999 (see the chapter on Serbia), by early April some 140,000 refugees had fled to the FYRM. Some 14,000 NATO troops were deployed near the FYRM border with Kosovo, and were involved in assisting the refugees. Owing to concern over internal destabilization, the FYRM authorities repeatedly closed the border with Kosovo to prevent the continued arrival of large numbers of ethnic Albanians, and demanded that the international community fulfil pledges to accept a proportion of the refugees. By late May some 60,000 refugees had been transported from the FYRM for provisional resettlement abroad, while an estimated 250,000 remained in the country. In early June the strength of NATO forces stationed in the FYRM was increased to 16,000. Shortly afterwards the Yugoslav Government accepted a peace plan, which provided for the withdrawal of Serbian forces from Kosovo, the return of ethnic Albanian refugees and the deployment of a NATO-led Kosovo Force (KFOR). NATO troops, which were to be deployed under the KFOR mandate, entered Kosovo from the FYRM. On 20 June NATO announced that the air campaign had officially ended, and large numbers of ethnic Albanian refugees subsequently began to return to the province from the FYRM.

In March 2005 Prime Minister Buckovski urged a resolution on demarcation of the border between the FYRM and Kosovo (contested since a 2001 agreement between the Governments of the FYRM and Serbia and Montenegro, owing to the continued unresolved status of Kosovo). Prolonged negotiations between Kosovan Albanian and Serbian delegations on the final status of Kosovo, which commenced in early 2006, and subsequent deliberations in the UN Security Council failed to result in a resolution. Kosovo's declaration of independence, with the support of many EU member states and the USA, on 17 February 2008 (see the chapter on Kosovo) was celebrated by ethnic Albanians in Skopje. The FYRM Government reacted with caution to the declaration and requested that the new Kosovo authorities rapidly proceed with demarcation of the border between the two countries in order to avert regional instability. In October the FYRM (together with Montenegro) announced the extension of diplomatic recognition to Kosovo, after a motion proposed by the DPA and the DUI was adopted by the Sobranie; the decision was welcomed by the USA and the EU but prompted an official protest from Serbia, which expelled the FYRM and Montenegrin ambassadors to Serbia in reprisal. Diplomatic relations with Kosovo were formally established in October 2009, following the ratification of an agreement on the demarcation of the common border by the legislatures of both countries. Following economic co-operation accords reached between the FYRM and Kosovo in early 2011, the Ministers of the Interior of the two states in April signed an agreement establishing joint border patrols, in an effort to improve security.

Other external relations

The FYRM Government signed a Stabilization and Association Agreement with the EU in April 2001, which came into effect in April 2004. A formal application for membership of the EU was submitted in March 2004. Following the recommendation of the European Commission, the FYRM was officially declared to have candidate status at an EU summit meeting in Brussels, Belgium, in mid-December 2005, prompting public celebrations in Skopje. In October 2007 NATO member states adopted a resolution supporting the accession application of the FYRM (together with those of Albania and Croatia). The Government expressed confidence that an official invitation would be extended at a NATO summit meeting in Bucharest, Romania, on 2–4 April 2008; however, the unresolved dispute with Greece over the issue of the country's permanent name presented a continued obstacle, and, despite intensified diplomatic efforts by the UN special envoy (see above), Greece vetoed the FYRM's application. NATO confirmed that the country had fulfilled other membership prerequisites, and that an invitation would be extended upon the settlement of the issue. In July 2009 the European Commission announced that the FYRM had fulfilled all the requirements for the end of visa restrictions, and at the end of November the abolishment of visas for citizens of the FYRM (and of Montenegro and Serbia) visiting the countries of the Schengen zone was announced, with effect from mid-December. In October the European Commission released a progress report recommending the opening of accession negotiations between the EU and the FYRM; however, Greece continued to impose a veto on the beginning of negotiations, owing to the unresolved name issue. In early December EU foreign ministers postponed a decision on establishing a start date for membership negotiations with the FYRM. In a further generally favourable progress report in November 2010, the European Commission confirmed that the FYRM's unresolved dispute with Greece remained the only main obstacle to the commencement of accession negotiations. In March 2011 the European Parliament adopted a draft resolution urging the opening of EU accession talks with the FYRM.

CONSTITUTION AND GOVERNMENT

According to the 1991 Constitution, which was amended in November 2001, legislative power is vested in the Sobranie (Assembly), with 120 members, elected for a four-year term by universal adult suffrage (85 in single-seat constituencies and 35 members by proportional representation). The President is directly elected for a five-year term, and appoints a Prime Minister to head the Government. The Ministers are elected by the Sobranie. Judicial power is exercised by 27 Courts of First Instance, three Courts of Appeal and the Supreme Court. For the purposes of local government, the FYRM is divided into 84 municipalities.

REGIONAL AND INTERNATIONAL CO-OPERATION

The FYRM is a member of the Council of Europe (see p. 250) the Organization for Security and Co-operation in Europe (OSCE, see p. 385) and the Central European Free Trade Agreement (CEFTA, see p. 446).

The FYRM was admitted to the UN in 1993, provisionally as 'the former Yugoslav Republic of Macedonia', pending settlement of the dispute over its name (see Contemporary Political History). The country became a member of the World Trade Organization (WTO, see p. 430) in 2003.

ECONOMIC AFFAIRS

In 2009, according to World Bank estimates, the FYRM's gross national income (GNI), measured at average 2007–09 prices, was US $8,983m., equivalent to $4,400 per head (or $10,550 per head on an international purchasing-power parity basis). During 2000–09, it was estimated, the population increased by an average of 0.2% per year, while gross domestic product (GDP) per head increased, in real terms, at an average annual rate of 2.1%. Overall GDP increased, in real terms, at an average annual rate of 2.3% in 2000–09; real GDP increased by 4.8% in 2008 but decreased by 0.7% in 2009.

Agriculture (including hunting, forestry and fishing) contributed 11.2% of GDP in 2009 and engaged 19.7% of the employed labour force in 2008. Dairy farming is significant, and the principal agricultural exports are tobacco, vegetables and fruit. The wine industry is of considerable importance, and the FYRM is also a producer of wheat, maize and barley. During 2000–09 the GDP of the agricultural sector declined at an average annual rate of 1.5%, according to the World Bank; real agricultural GDP increased by 6.5% in 2008.

Industry contributed 42.5% of GDP in 2009 and engaged 31.3% of the employed labour force in 2008. During 2000–09, the GDP of the industrial sector increased, in real terms, at an average annual rate of 3.1%, according to the World Bank; real industrial GDP increased by 7.5% in 2009.

Mining contributed 1.2% of GDP in 2009 and engaged 1.1% of the employed labour force in 2008. The only major mining activity is the production of lignite (brown coal), although there are also deposits of iron, zinc, lead, copper, chromium, manganese, antimony, silver, gold and nickel.

The manufacturing sector contributed an estimated 16.2% of GDP in 2009 and engaged 21.2% of the employed labour force in 2008. The GDP of the manufacturing sector increased, in real terms, at an average annual rate of 2.8% in 2000–09, according to the World Bank; real manufacturing GDP increased by 7.5% in 2009.

The construction sector contributed an estimated 5.9% of GDP in 2009 and engaged 6.5% of the employed labour force in 2008. The GDP of the sector increased, in real terms, at an average annual rate of 2.2% in 2000–08; real manufacturing GDP increased by 3.4% in 2007 but decreased by 3.5% in 2008, according to official estimates.

Energy is derived principally from coal and lignite, which provided 77.9% of the electricity generated in 2007. Hydroelectric sources accounted for another 15.0% of production. The first stage of a pipeline from the Bulgarian border to carry natural gas to the FYRM from Russia became operational in 1995. A 214-km pipeline to transport petroleum from the Greek port of Thessaloníki to Skopje was inaugurated in July 2002. Mineral fuels accounted for 17.7% of the value of total imports in 2010.

Services accounted for 46.4% of GDP in 2009, and the sector engaged 49.0% of the employed labour force in 2008. During 2000–09 the GDP of the services sector increased, in real terms, at an average annual rate of 2.0%, according to the World Bank; services GDP increased by 3.2% in 2008 but fell by 5.6% in 2009.

In 2009 the FYRM recorded a visible trade deficit of US $2,156.9m., and there was a deficit of $645.6m. on the current account of the balance of payments. In 2010 the principal source of imports was Germany (accounting for an estimated 11.2% of total imports); other major sources were Russia, Greece, Serbia, Italy, Bulgaria the People's Republic of China and the United Kingdom. The principal market for exports in that year was Germany (accounting for an estimated of 21.0% of all exports); other important purchasers were Bulgaria, Serbia, Greece and Italy. The principal exports in 2010 were basic manufactures (30.0%), miscellaneous manufactured articles, chemicals and related products, food and live animals, inedible crude materials (except fuels), mineral fuels, lubricants, and beverages and tobacco. The main imports in that year were basic manufactures (25.2%), machinery and transport equipment, mineral fuels and lubricants (notably petroleum and petroleum products), chemical products, food and live animals and miscellaneous manufactured articles.

The FYRM recorded an overall budgetary deficit of 11,593m. new denars in 2009. FYRM's general government gross debt was 97.053m. new denars in 2009, equivalent to 23.5% of GDP. At the end of 2008 the FYRM's external debt totalled US $4,678m., of which $1,538m. was public and publicly guaranteed debt. In 2008 the cost of debt-servicing was equivalent to 8.7% of the value of exports of goods and services. The annual rate of inflation averaged 2.4% in 2000–09. Consumer prices increased by 8.4% in 2007 but decreased by 0.8% in 2009. The rate of unemployment was 34.9% in 2007 and 33.8% in 2008.

Economic prospects in the FYRM advanced significantly following the removal, in late 1995, of a Greek embargo on trade, and UN sanctions against Yugoslavia, which had severely disrupted trading links. A subsequent improvement in relations with Greece enabled substantial Greek investment, while in April 2001 a Stabilization and Association Agreement (SAA) was signed with the European Union (EU, see p. 270). Although ethnic hostilities in the north of the FYRM in early 2001 caused a sizeable deterioration of the fiscal position, considerable pledges to support reconstruction ensued from a World Bank- and EU-sponsored donor aid conference in March 2002; a new stand-by credit agreement with the IMF was also signed in 2003. Following progress by the authorities in attracting major investment projects, in mid-2005 the IMF approved a further three-year stand-by arrangement. Notable measures adopted by the Government in 2008 included reducing the corporate tax rate, removing the minimum capital requirement previously applied to new enterprises, increasing pensions (by 13% in January and by some 7% in July, despite the pension system being in deficit), and raising public sector wages. Critical areas of concern remained the widening current account deficit, the need to diversify exports, and the very high rate of unemployment. The FYRM was adversely affected by the international financial crisis from the end of 2008, experiencing a collapse in export demand and a decline in external financing, which resulted in a sharp slowdown in the economy, reduced tax revenues, and a significant loss of central bank foreign exchange reserves. However, numerous measures undertaken by the authorities, including the cancellation of planned spending increases and the issuance of euro-denominated bonds, as well as the FYRM's low reliance on external finance, served to limit the negative impact of the downturn. Following a small economic contraction in 2009, real GDP growth recovered to an estimated 1.2% in 2010, according to the IMF, and the Government was expected largely to achieve its fiscal objectives for that year. In a progress report issued in November 2010, the European Commission stated that the FYRM had continued to meet its obligations under the SAA, particularly in reducing trade restrictions and improving the judicial system, but confirmed that the unresolved dispute with Greece over the country's name remained an obstacle to the opening of accession negotiations. In January 2011 the FYRM became the first IMF member state to be granted a two-year Precautionary Credit Line (PCL) financial arrangement, under which the country was entitled to receive up to €475.6m. Meanwhile, following a parliamentary boycott and persistent demands by opposition parties in early 2011, the Government agreed to organize early legislative elections. In March the FYRM (which had previously declared the intention not to draw on the PCL arrangement) announced that it was to access credit of €220m., citing a change in circumstances as a result of the early elections.

PUBLIC HOLIDAYS

2012: 1 January (New Year), 6–7 January (Orthodox Christmas), 13–16 April (Orthodox Easter), 1 May (Labour Day), 24 May (Day of the Apostles SS Methodius), 2 August (National Day), 18 August* (Small Bayram, end of Ramadan), 8 September (Independence Day), 11 October (Anti-Fascism Day), 23 October (Day of the Macedonian Revolution), 25 October* (Great Bayram, Feast of the Sacrifice), 8 December (St Clement of Ohrid Day).

* These holidays are dependent on the Islamic lunar calendar and may vary by one or two days from the dates given.

Statistical Survey

Source (unless otherwise indicated): State Statistical Office of the Republic of Macedonia, 91000 Skopje, Dame Gruev 4, POB 506; tel. (2) 114904; fax (2) 111336; e-mail info@stat.gov.mk; internet www.stat.gov.mk.

Area and Population

AREA, POPULATION AND DENSITY

Area (sq km)	25,713*
Population (census results)†	
20 June 1994	1,945,932
31 October 2002	
Males	1,015,377
Females	1,007,170
Total	2,022,547
Population (UN estimates at mid-year)‡	
2009	2,042,000
2010	2,043,000
2011	2,044,005
Density (per sq km) at mid-2011	79.5

* 9,928 sq miles.
† Comprising persons with an official place of residence in the country (including those temporarily abroad for less than a year), persons from other countries who have been granted a residence permit in the FYRM and have been present there for at least a year, and foreigners with refugee status; excluding foreign diplomatic and military personnel.
‡ Source: UN, *World Population Prospects: The 2008 Revision*.

2009 (official population estimate at 31 December): 2,052,722.

POPULATION BY AGE AND SEX
(UN estimates at mid-2011)

	Males	Females	Total
0–14	183,275	169,851	353,126
15–64	731,807	711,929	1,443,736
65 and over	105,380	141,763	247,143
Total	1,020,462	1,023,543	2,044,005

Source: UN, *World Population Prospects: The 2008 Revision*.

PRINCIPAL ETHNIC GROUPS
(census of 31 October 2002)

	Number	%
Macedonian	1,297,981	64.2
Albanian	509,083	25.2
Turkish	77,959	3.9
Roma (Gypsy)	53,879	2.7
Serb	35,939	1.8
Muslim	17,018	0.8
Vlach	9,695	0.5
Others	20,993	1.0
Total	2,022,547	100.0

PRINCIPAL TOWNS
(2004, official estimates)*

Skopje (capital)	515,419	Prilep	76,768
Kumanovo	105,484	Struga	63,376
Bitola	95,385	Ohrid	55,749
Tetovo	86,580	Veles	55,108
Gostivar	81,042	Strumica	54,676

* Population by municipality, except for Skopje, which comprises 10 municipalities.

Source: Ministry of Local Self-Government, Skopje.

Mid-2009 (incl. suburbs, UN estimate): Skopje 480,383 (Source: UN, *World Urbanization Prospects: The 2009 Revision*).

THE FORMER YUGOSLAV REPUBLIC OF MACEDONIA

BIRTHS, MARRIAGES AND DEATHS

	Registered live births Number	Rate (per 1,000)	Registered marriages Number	Rate (per 1,000)	Registered deaths Number	Rate (per 1,000)
2002	27,761	13.7	14,522	7.2	17,962	8.9
2003	27,011	13.3	14,402	7.1	18,006	8.9
2004	26,883	13.2	14,073	6.9	18,265	9.0
2005	22,697	11.1	14,500	7.1	18,406	9.0
2006	22,786	11.2	14,908	7.3	18,630	9.1
2007	22,688	11.1	15,490	7.6	19,594	9.6
2008	22,945	11.2	14,695	7.2	18,982	9.3
2009	23,684	11.5	14,923	7.3	19,060	9.3

Life expectancy (years at birth, WHO estimates): 74 (males 72; females 76) in 2008 (Source: WHO, *World Health Statistics*).

ECONOMICALLY ACTIVE POPULATION
(sample surveys, '000 persons aged 15 years and over)

	2006	2007	2008
Agriculture, hunting and forestry	114.5	107.4	119.5
Fishing	0.3	0.3	0.3
Mining and quarrying	3.9	5.1	6.7
Manufacturing	123.1	126.2	129.0
Electricity, gas and water	16.0	15.6	15.5
Construction	43.2	38.0	39.4
Wholesale and retail trade, repair of motor vehicles, motorcycles and articles for personal use and for households	73.0	83.0	86.6
Hotels and restaurants	19.0	17.5	19.1
Transport, storage and communications	30.0	35.5	37.7
Financial intermediation	7.1	9.0	7.7
Real estate, renting and business activities	15.4	15.9	16.3
Public administration and defence, compulsory social security	39.3	41.4	42.2
Education	33.4	34.4	33.6
Health and social work	32.6	32.9	32.9
Other community, social and personal services	18.3	24.7	21.0
Private households with employed persons	0.5	1.4	0.7
Extra-territorial organizations and bodies	1.0	1.9	0.8
Total employed	570.4	590.2	609.0
Unemployed	321.3	316.9	310.4
Total labour force	891.7	907.1	919.4
Males	543.9	548.1	561.7
Females	347.8	359.0	357.7

Source: ILO.

Health and Welfare

KEY INDICATORS

Total fertility rate (children per woman, 2008)	1.4
Under-5 mortality rate (per 1,000 live births, 2008)	11
HIV/AIDS (% of persons aged 15–49, 2007)	<0.1
Physicians (per 1,000 head, 2006)	2.6
Hospital beds (per 1,000 head, 2006)	4.6
Health expenditure (2007): US $ per head (PPP)	669
Health expenditure (2007): % of GDP	7.1
Health expenditure (2007): public (% of total)	65.6
Access to sanitation (% of total population, 2006)	89
Total carbon dioxide emissions ('000 metric tons, 2007)	11,266.8
Carbon dioxide emissions per head (metric tons, 2007)	5.5
Human Development Index (2010): ranking	71
Human Development Index (2010): value	0.701

For sources and definitions, see explanatory note on p. vi.

Agriculture

PRINCIPAL CROPS
('000 metric tons)

	2007	2008	2009
Wheat	218.1	291.7	271.1
Rice, paddy	15.4	16.1	19.9
Barley	106.6	162.8	146.4
Maize	118.4	127.1	154.2
Rye	6.7	9.9	9.1
Potatoes	180.9	191.1	207.2
Sugar beet	7.9	8.0*	8.0*
Beans, dry	7.0*	7.0*	n.a.
Olives*	13.8	13.8	n.a.
Cabbages and other brassicas	86.2	93.9	112.1
Tomatoes	118.0	121.6	145.4
Cucumbers and gherkins	39.2	40.6	41.5
Chillies and peppers, green	140.6	141.7	154.8
Onions, dry	33.5	34.9	41.9
Beans, green	10.9	12.8	12.8
Watermelons	123.8	129.3	123.9
Apples	152.1	174.3	106.4
Peaches and nectarines	10.5	11.3	10.3
Plums and sloes	27.8	32.8	35.6
Grapes	209.7	236.8	253.5
Tobacco, unmanufactured	22.1	17.1	24.1

* FAO estimate(s).

Aggregate production ('000 metric tons, may include official, semi-official or estimated data): Total cereals 468.7 in 2007, 613.0 in 2008, 605.7 in 2009; Total roots and tubers 180.9 in 2007, 191.1 in 2008, 207.2 in 2009; Total vegetables (incl. melons) 580.2 in 2007, 603.7 in 2008, 662.4 in 2009; Total fruits (excl. melons) 429.3 in 2007, 487.1 in 2008, 436.7 in 2009.

Source: FAO.

LIVESTOCK
('000 head, year ending September)

	2007	2008	2009
Horses	31	31	29
Cattle	254	253	253
Pigs	255	247	194
Sheep	818	817	455
Chickens	2,264	2,226	2,172

Source: FAO.

LIVESTOCK PRODUCTS
('000 metric tons)

	2007	2008	2009
Cattle meat	7.1	7.0	7.3
Sheep meat	6.5	5.2	5.2
Pig meat	8.9	8.7	8.3
Chicken meat	3.5	3.0	3.3
Cows' milk	385.3	369.2	342.6
Sheep's milk	36.6	34.3	32.9
Hen eggs*	18.0	15.5	15.4
Honey	0.7	0.8	0.8
Wool, greasy	1.1	1.0	1.0

* Unofficial figures.

Source: FAO.

THE FORMER YUGOSLAV REPUBLIC OF MACEDONIA

Forestry

ROUNDWOOD REMOVALS
('000 cubic metres, excl. bark)

	2007	2008	2009
Sawlogs, veneer logs and logs for sleepers	129	154	84
Other industrial wood	26	39	25
Fuel wood	479	516	530
Total	634	709	639

Source: FAO.

SAWNWOOD PRODUCTION
('000 cubic metres, incl. railway sleepers)

	2007	2008	2009
Coniferous (softwood)	4	—	—
Broadleaved (hardwood)	13	9	2
Total	17	9	2

Source: FAO.

Fishing

(metric tons, live weight)

	2006	2007	2008
Capture	89	122	122
Trouts	1	30	36
Aquaculture	646	1,096	1,331
Common carp	167	206	247
Other freshwater fishes	43	77	130
Trouts	378	758	910
Huchen	3	4	6
Total catch	735	1,218	1,453

Source: FAO.

Mining

('000 metric tons, unless otherwise indicated)

	2007	2008	2009
Lignite	6,569	7,746	7,454
Copper concentrates*	7	8	8
Lead concentrates*	29	34	52
Gypsum	256	242	155
Crude steel	372	252	276

* Figures refer to the metal content of concentrates.

Gold (estimates): 450 kg in 2006–08.
Silver: 10,000 kg in 2003.

Source: US Geological Survey.

Industry

SELECTED PRODUCTS
('000 metric tons, unless otherwise indicated)

	2005	2006	2007
Flour	79	72	64
Refined sugar	37	19	36
Wine ('000 hectolitres)	811	703	911
Beer ('000 hectolitres)	695	670	695
Soft drinks ('000 hectolitres)	1,174	1,311	1,480
Cigarettes (million)	5,763	5,123	5,485
Footwear with leather uppers ('000 pairs)	1,515	1,124	1,563
Motor spirit (petrol)	183	190	180
Naphthas	226	0	0
Gas-diesel (distillate fuel) oil	394	443	424
Residual fuel oils	295	327	402
Cement	887	924	902
Ferro-alloys*	105	104	169
Crude steel*	326	360	372
Lead: refined*	11	32	34
Zinc: refined*	11	20	28
Electric energy (million kWh)	6,945	7,009	6,729

* Data from US Geological Survey.

Source (unless otherwise indicated): UN Industrial Commodity Statistics Database.

Finance

CURRENCY AND EXCHANGE RATES

Monetary Units
100 deni = 1 new Macedonian denar.

Sterling, Dollar and Euro Equivalents (31 December 2010)
£1 sterling = 72.505 new denars;
US $1 = 46.314 new denars;
€1 = 61.885 new denars;
1,000 new denars = £13.79 = $21.59 = €16.16.

Average Exchange Rate (new denars per US $)
2008   41.868
2009   44.101
2010   46.486

BUDGET
(million new denars)*

Revenue	2007	2008†	2009†
Tax revenue	66,734	73,669	88,036
Personal income tax	8,320	8,331	10,126
Profit tax	5,721	5,254	10,241
Value-added tax	31,841	36,305	42,422
Excises	13,200	14,185	15,193
Import duties	5,652	7,420	6,954
Special revenue accounts tax	211	401	558
Social contributions	31,325	33,217	37,931
Pension insurance	20,878	22,526	25,703
Unemployment contributions	1,390	1,457	1,658
Health insurance	9,057	9,234	10,570
Non-tax revenue	15,445	18,763	21,105
Capital revenue	564	695	2,537
Foreign donations	1,819	1,994	2,946
Repayment of loans	20	—	100
Total	116,118	128,739	153,213

THE FORMER YUGOSLAV REPUBLIC OF MACEDONIA

Statistical Survey

Expenditure

Expenditure	2007	2008†	2009†
Current expenditure	105,307	112,846	135,546
Wages, salaries and allowances	24,335	23,204	25,138
Other purchases of goods and services	17,166	18,696	22,690
Transfers	61,053	68,637	84,215
Pensions	28,532	30,798	37,190
Unemployment benefits	1,748	1,733	2,006
Social benefits	4,152	4,140	4,400
Health care	16,032	16,264	19,124
Interest payments	2,753	2,309	3,503
Capital expenditure	14,306	21,435	29,260
Total	**119,615**	**134,281**	**164,806**

* Figures refer to the consolidated accounts of the general Government, comprising the transactions of the central Government and the operations of extrabudgetary funds.
† Projections.

Source: Ministry of Finance, Skopje.

INTERNATIONAL RESERVES
(US $ million at 31 December)

	2007	2008	2009
Gold (national valuation)	182.6	188.8	241.0
IMF special drawing rights	1.5	1.4	91.1
Foreign exchange	2,080.8	1,919.0	1,959.9
Total	**2,264.9**	**2,109.2**	**2,292.0**

Source: IMF, *International Financial Statistics*.

MONEY SUPPLY
(million new denars at 31 December)

	2007	2008	2009
Currency outside depository corporations	17,908	17,600	16,266
Transferable deposits	41,296	52,144	56,444
Other deposits	119,920	128,934	136,913
Broad money	**179,124**	**198,678**	**209,623**

Source: IMF, *International Financial Statistics*.

COST OF LIVING
(Consumer Price Index; base: 2000 = 100)

	2007	2008	2009
Food	109.1	125.8	123.8
Fuel and light	125.0	134.2	142.6
Clothing (incl. footwear)	116.3	118.4	118.4
Housing	127.1	134.8	137.5
All items (incl. others)	**114.8**	**124.4**	**123.4**

Source: ILO.

NATIONAL ACCOUNTS
(million new denars at current prices)

Expenditure on the Gross Domestic Product

	2007	2008	2009
Government final consumption expenditure	62,481	75,088	78,525
Private final consumption expenditure	279,880	330,399	312,022
Changes in inventories*	18,371	24,002	25,230
Gross fixed capital formation	71,557	86,403	81,872
Total domestic expenditure	**432,289**	**515,892**	**497,649**
Exports of goods and services	191,111	209,557	160,264
Less Imports of goods and services	258,410	313,721	248,812
GDP in purchasers' values	**364,989**	**411,728**	**409,100**

* Including statistical discrepancy.

Gross Domestic Product by Economic Activity

	2007	2008	2009
Agriculture, hunting and forestry	33,053	41,267	39,766
Fishing	56	74	79
Mining and quarrying	2,604	4,350	4,137
Manufacturing	64,083	70,634	57,856
Electricity, gas and water supply	9,516	11,159	15,034
Construction	20,835	20,258	21,110
Wholesale and retail trade	47,355	50,270	53,583
Hotels and restaurants	5,565	5,952	5,051
Transport and communications	29,017	33,143	32,234
Financial services	10,619	11,090	10,562
Real estate and business services*	36,890	45,982	44,915
Public administration and defence	22,757	26,677	29,852
Education	11,329	12,467	14,224
Health care and social work	12,304	13,577	15,707
Other community, social and personal services	7,495	10,548	13,200
Sub-total	**313,478**	**357,450**	**357,312**
Value-added tax	46,227	50,449	49,706
Import duties	6,199	6,275	5,229
Less Subsidies on products	915	2,445	3,146
GDP in purchasers' values	**364,989**	**411,728**	**409,100**

* Including imputed rents of owner-occupied dwellings.

BALANCE OF PAYMENTS
(US $ million)

	2007	2008	2009
Exports of goods f.o.b.	3,391.5	3,970.9	2,685.5
Imports of goods f.o.b.	−5,030.0	−6,543.4	−4,842.3
Trade balance	**−1,638.5**	**−2,572.5**	**−2,156.9**
Exports of services	818.4	1,011.7	862.7
Imports of services	−784.0	−1,000.2	−822.6
Balance on goods and services	**−1,604.1**	**−2,561.1**	**−2,116.8**
Other income received	213.1	272.7	178.1
Other income paid	−598.1	−387.4	−306.2
Balance on goods, services and income	**−1,989.2**	**−2,675.8**	**−2,244.8**
Current transfers received	1,480.9	1,525.6	1,672.4
Current transfers paid	−97.5	−70.0	−73.2
Current balance	**−605.7**	**−1,220.1**	**−645.6**
Capital account (net)	4.9	−17.6	28.4
Direct investment abroad	1.1	13.5	−13.1
Direct investment from abroad	699.1	587.0	247.9
Portfolio investment assets	−2.8	−1.1	−51.2
Portfolio investment liabilities	157.9	−71.4	198.8
Other investment assets	−80.9	297.7	−143.6
Other investment liabilities	67.4	360.0	488.2
Net errors and omissions	−42.0	4.8	26.3
Overall balance	**199.0**	**−47.2**	**136.1**

Source: IMF, *International Financial Statistics*.

THE FORMER YUGOSLAV REPUBLIC OF MACEDONIA

External Trade

PRINCIPAL COMMODITIES
(distribution by SITC, US $ million)

Imports c.i.f.	2008	2009	2010
Food and live animals	620.9	560.4	558.1
Meat and meat preparations	139.6	141.2	125.6
Mineral fuels, lubricants, etc.	1,419.3	809.7	966.8
Petroleum, petroleum products, etc.	934.6	621.1	744.8
Electric energy	347.1	120.9	115.7
Chemicals and related products	614.1	568.8	662.6
Basic manufactures	1,862.9	1,201.5	1,374.2
Iron and steel	757.3	301.7	354.6
Machinery and transport equipment	1,442.4	1,209.3	1,090.8
General industrial machinery	206.9	170.9	128.6
Electrical machinery, apparatus, etc. (excl. telecommunications and sound equipment)	197.3	182.7	187.2
Road vehicles and transport equipment	461.9	360.4	391.3
Miscellaneous manufactured articles	451.6	392.9	395.6
Total (incl. others)	6,882.7	5,043.1	5,450.7

Exports f.o.b.	2008	2009	2010
Food and live animals	308.5	283.5	328.7
Vegetables and fruit	165.7	142.5	181.1
Beverages and tobacco	218.8	197.0	202.5
Beverages	95.5	86.0	79.0
Tobacco and tobacco manufactures	123.3	111.0	123.5
Crude materials (inedible) except fuels	272.0	172.9	260.0
Mineral fuels, lubricants, etc.	314.3	202.9	257.4
Petroleum and petroleum products	305.7	191.3	218.1
Chemicals and related products	181.1	172.2	381.8
Basic manufactures	1,602.8	770.9	989.9
Textile yarn, fabrics, etc.	55.9	45.5	56.4
Iron and steel	1,296.5	534.0	777.8
Machinery and transport equipment	186.4	142.7	152.8
Electrical machinery, apparatus, etc. (excl. telecommunications and sound equipment)	89.7	66.2	48.3
Miscellaneous manufactured articles	892.8	740.3	715.1
Clothing and accessories (excl. footwear)	714.7	582.7	562.5
Total (incl. others)	3,990.6	2,691.5	3,301.8

PRINCIPAL TRADING PARTNERS
(US $ million)

Imports c.i.f.	2008	2009	2010
Austria	119.9	100.3	93.7
Bulgaria	327.9	242.6	301.6
China, People's Republic	315.6	289.4	287.4
Croatia	137.8	118.3	113.3
France	124.7	91.4	85.0
Germany	652.9	517.5	610.1
Greece	511.7	439.2	448.6
Italy	390.2	361.7	327.3
Netherlands	94.1	70.4	68.5
Poland	265.3	83.2	69.8
Romania	117.7	107.8	126.2
Russia	932.0	495.0	552.5
Serbia	533.1	397.1	418.4
Slovenia	203.4	190.9	165.1
Spain	55.6	48.3	60.4
Switzerland-Liechtenstein	292.8	123.1	97.5
Turkey	272.1	250.7	260.3
Ukraine	203.0	84.5	116.6
United Kingdom	70.6	62.5	283.6
USA	101.6	110.7	102.4
Total (incl. others)	6,882.7	5,043.1	5,450.7

Exports f.o.b.	2008	2009	2010
Bosnia and Herzegovina	104.8	86.6	84.9
Bulgaria	379.3	217.0	294.0
Croatia	230.5	152.7	123.6
France	24.3	12.6	13.9
Germany	564.9	450.4	692.5
Greece	536.4	290.0	245.1
Italy	321.4	218.0	234.6
Netherlands	70.6	61.5	70.3
Russia	32.7	22.5	26.7
Serbia	934.8	337.6	271.8
Slovenia	65.1	34.3	69.1
Spain	77.0	38.7	73.7
Turkey	31.6	40.8	50.9
United Kingdom	70.1	42.9	59.3
USA	11.2	9.5	14.2
Total (incl. others)	3,990.6	2,691.5	3,301.8

Transport

RAILWAYS
(traffic)

	2006	2007	2008
Passenger journeys ('000)	1,011	1,104	1,448
Passenger-km (million)	105	109	148
Freight carried ('000 metric tons)	3,800	4,686	4,206
Freight ton-km (million)	614	779	743

ROAD TRAFFIC
(motor vehicles in use at 31 December)

	2006	2007	2008
Motorcycles	3,442	4,437	8,626
Passenger cars	242,287	248,774	263,112
Buses	2,220	2,284	2,270
Freight vehicles	13,545	12,981	13,325
Special vehicles	12,169	10,002	11,615
Tractors, working vehicles and trailers	8,622	8,744	9,546

THE FORMER YUGOSLAV REPUBLIC OF MACEDONIA

INLAND WATERS
(lake transport)

	2006	2007	2008
Passengers carried	17,060	46,560	55,460
Passenger-km ('000)	317	1,063	2,560

CIVIL AVIATION
(traffic on scheduled services)

	2004	2005	2006
Kilometres flown (million)	3	3	3
Passengers carried ('000)	211	192	209
Passenger-kilometres (million)	276	249	269
Total ton-kilometres (million)	25	22	24

Source: UN, *Statistical Yearbook*.

Tourism

TOURISTS BY COUNTRY OF ORIGIN*

	2006	2007	2008
Albania	14,402	15,183	14,223
Bosnia and Herzegovina	3,783	4,465	3,799
Bulgaria	15,548	17,284	18,036
Croatia	7,976	11,239	10,821
Germany	7,412	8,410	8,407
Greece	28,868	26,822	18,551
Italy	4,473	4,969	4,910
Netherlands	3,653	3,516	4,634
Serbia and Montenegro	33,032	38,932	35,956
Slovenia	8,156	10,913	11,184
Turkey	7,173	8,495	14,073
United Kingdom	5,219	5,658	6,765
USA	8,073	7,738	7,468
Total (incl. others)	185,185	210,163	213,829

* Figures refer to arrivals from abroad at all accommodation establishments.

Tourism receipts (US $ million, incl. passenger transport): 156 in 2006; 219 in 2007, 262 in 2008.

Source: World Tourism Organization.

Communications Media

	2007	2008	2009
Telephones ('000 main lines in use)	463.6	457.1	437.3
Mobile cellular telephones ('000 subscribers)	1,794.4*	1,967.5	1,943.2
Internet users ('000)†	740.5	939.8	1,057.4
Broadband subscribers ('000)	100.5*	181.0	218.7
Newspapers			
Titles	26	14	14
Circulation ('000 copies)	29,401	8,935	7,131
Magazines			
Titles	177	130	110
Circulation ('000 copies)	13,299	10,586	9,176

* Figure as at June of that year.
† Estimates.

Radio receivers ('000 in use): 410 in 1997.

Television receivers ('000 in use): 570 in 2000.

Book production (titles, including pamphlets): 727 in 2000; 737 in 2001; 1,102 in 2002.

Book production ('000 copies, including pamphlets): 968 in 2000; 1,061 in 2001; 1,899 in 2002.

Personal computers: 749,760 (367.6 per 1,000 persons) in 2007.

Sources: mainly International Telecommunication Union; UNESCO, *Statistical Yearbook*; and UN, *Statistical Yearbook*.

Education

(2008/09, unless otherwise indicated)

	Institutions	Teachers	Students
Primary and lower secondary	1,046	16,462	211,857
Upper secondary	117	7,024	96,311
University level*	29	1,487	44,731
Other higher*	1	32	893

* 2002/03 figures.

Pupil-teacher ratio (primary education, UNESCO estimate): 17.3 in 2007/08 (Source: UNESCO Institute for Statistics).

Adult literacy rate (UNESCO estimates): 97.0% (males 98.6%; females 95.4%) in 2008 (Source: UNESCO Institute for Statistics).

Directory

The Government

HEAD OF STATE

President of the Republic: Dr GJORGE IVANOV (elected 5 April 2009; inaugurated 12 May).

GOVERNMENT
(May 2011)

Comprising representatives of the Internal Macedonian Revolutionary Organization—Democratic Party for Macedonian National Unity (IMRO—DPMNU), the Democratic Union for Integration (DUI), the Socialist Party of Macedonia (SPM), the Democratic Party of Turks in Macedonia (DPTM) and the United Party for Emancipation (UPE).

Prime Minister: NIKOLA GRUEVSKI (IMRO—DPMNU).

Deputy Prime Minister, responsible for Economic Affairs: VLADIMIR PEŠEVSKI (IMRO—DPMNU).

Deputy Prime Minister, responsible for European Integration: VASKO NAUMOVSKI (IMRO—DPMNU).

Deputy Prime Minister and Minister of Finance: ZORAN STAVRESKI (IMRO—DPMNU).

Deputy Prime Minister, responsible for the implementation of the Ohrid Framework Agreement: ABDILAQIM ADEMI (DUI).

Minister of Foreign Affairs: ANTONIO MILOŠOSKI (IMRO—DPMNU).

Minister of Defence: ZORAN KONJANOVSKI (IMRO—DPMNU).

Minister of Internal Affairs: GORDANA JANKULOSKA (IMRO—DPMNU).

Minister of Justice: MIHAJLO MANEVSKI (IMRO—DPMNU).

Minister of the Economy: FATMIR BESIMI (DUI).

Minister of Agriculture, Forestry and Water Resources: LJUPČO DIMOVSKI (SPM).

Minister of Health: BUJAR OSMANI (DUI).

Minister of Education and Science: NIKOLA TODOROV (IMRO—DPMNU).

Minister of the Information Society and Administration: IVO IVANOVSKI (IMRO—DPMNU).

Minister of Local Self-Government: MUSA XHAFERI (DUI).

Minister of Culture: ELIZABETA KANČESKA MILEVSKA (IMRO—DPMNU).

Minister of Transport and Communications: MILE JANAKIESKI (IMRO—DPMNU).

Minister of the Environment and Physical Planning: NEXHATI JAKUPI (DUI).

Minister of Labour and Social Welfare: XHELAL BAJRAMI (DUI).

THE FORMER YUGOSLAV REPUBLIC OF MACEDONIA

Minister without Portfolio: VELE SAMAK (IMRO—DPMNU).
Minister without Portfolio: HADI NEZIR (DPTM).
Minister without Portfolio: NEŽDET MUSTAFA (UPE).

MINISTRIES

Office of the President: 1000 Skopje, Aco Karamanov bb; tel. and fax (2) 3253105; e-mail president@president.gov.mk; internet www.president.gov.mk.

Office of the Prime Minister: 1000 Skopje, Ilindenska bb; tel. (2) 3118022; fax (2) 3112561; e-mail primeminister@primeminister.gov.mk; internet www.vlada.mk.

Ministry of Agriculture, Forestry and Water Resources: 1000 Skopje, Jurij Gagarin 15; tel. and fax (2) 3134477; e-mail irena.ristoska@mzsv.gov.mk; internet www.mzsv.gov.mk.

Ministry of Culture: 1000 Skopje, ul. Gjuro Gjakovik 61; tel. (2) 3240600; fax (2) 3240561; e-mail info@kultura.gov.mk; internet www.kultura.gov.mk.

Ministry of Defence: 1000 Skopje, Orce Nikolov bb; tel. (2) 3282042; fax (2) 3283991; e-mail info@morm.gov.mk; internet www.morm.gov.mk.

Ministry of the Economy: 1000 Skopje, Jurij Gagarin 15; tel. (2) 3093408; fax (2) 3084472; e-mail contact@economy.gov.mk; internet www.economy.gov.mk.

Ministry of Education and Science: 1000 Skopje, Mito Hadzivasilev Jasmin bb; tel. (2) 3117896; fax (2) 3118414; e-mail contact@mon.gov.mk; internet www.mon.gov.mk.

Ministry of the Environment and Physical Planning: 1000 Skopje, Goce Delcev, MRTV Bldg; tel. (2) 3251400; fax (2) 3220165; e-mail info@moepp.gov.mk; internet www.moepp.gov.mk.

Ministry of Finance: 1000 Skopje, Dame Gruev 14; tel. (2) 3117288; fax (2) 3117280; e-mail finance@finance.gov.mk; internet www.finance.gov.mk.

Ministry of Foreign Affairs: 1000 Skopje, Dame Gruev 6; tel. (2) 3110333; fax (2) 3115790; e-mail mailmnr@mfa.gov.mk; internet www.mfa.gov.mk.

Ministry of Health: 1000 Skopje, Vodnjanska bb; tel. (2) 3112500; fax (2) 3113014; internet www.zdravstvo.gov.mk.

Ministry of the Information Society and Administration: 1000 Skopje, Mito Hadzivasilev Jasmin bb; tel. (2) 3200870; fax (2) 3221883; e-mail contact_mis@mis.gov.mk; internet www.mio.gov.mk.

Ministry of Internal Affairs: 1000 Skopje, ul. Dimče Mirčev bb; tel. (2) 3117222; fax (2) 3112468; e-mail kontakt@moi.gov.mk; internet www.mvr.gov.mk.

Ministry of Justice: 1000 Skopje, Dimitrija Čupovski 9; tel. (2) 3117277; fax (2) 3226975; internet www.pravda.gov.mk.

Ministry of Labour and Social Welfare: 1000 Skopje, Dame Gruev 14; tel. (2) 3106212; fax (2) 3220408; e-mail mtsp@mtsp.gov.mk; internet www.mtsp.gov.mk.

Ministry of Local Self-Government: 1000 Skopje, Mito Hadzivasilev Jasmin bb; tel. (2) 3216134; internet www.mls.gov.mk.

Ministry of Transport and Communications: 1000 Skopje, pl. Crvena skopska opština 4; tel. (2) 3145497; fax (2) 3126228; internet www.mtc.gov.mk.

President

Presidential Election, First Ballot, 22 March 2009

Candidate	Votes	% of votes
Gjorge Ivanov (Internal Macedonian Revolutionary Organization—Democratic Party for Macedonian National Unity)	343,374	35.05
Ljubomir Frčkoski (Social Democratic Alliance of Macedonia)	200,316	20.45
Imer Selmani (New Democracy)	146,795	14.98
Ljube Boškovski (Independent)	145,638	14.87
Agron Buxhaku (Democratic Union for Integration)	73,567	7.51
Nano Ružin (Liberal Democratic Party)	39,645	4.05
Mirushe Hoxha (Democratic Party of Albanians)	30,281	3.09
Total	**979,616**	**100.00**

Second Ballot, 5 April 2009

Candidate	Votes	% of votes
Gjorge Ivanov (Internal Macedonian Revolutionary Organization—Democratic Party for Macedonian National Unity)	453,616	63.14
Ljubomir Frčkoski (Social Democratic Alliance of Macedonia)	264,828	36.86
Total	**718,444**	**100.00**

Legislature

Sobranie
(Assembly)

1000 Skopje, 11 Oktomvri bb; tel. (2) 3112255; fax (2) 3237947; e-mail sobranie@sobranie.mk; internet www.sobranie.mk.

President: TRAJKO VELJANOSKI.

General Election, 1 June 2008*

Party	Votes	% of votes	Seats
For a Better Macedonia†	481,602	48.80	63
Sun Coalition for Europe‡	233,362	23.65	27
Democratic Union for Integration	125,997	12.77	18
Democratic Party of Albanians	83,678	8.48	11
Party for a European Future	14,473	1.47	1
Others	47,710	4.83	—
Total	**986,822**	**100.00**	**120**

* Includes the results of voting in six constituencies where voting was repeated on 15 June. A further repeated round of voting was held in a small number of polling stations on 29 June.
† An electoral coalition of 19 parties, led by the Internal Macedonian Revolutionary Organization—Democratic Party for Macedonian National Unity.
‡ An electoral coalition of eight parties, led by the Social Democratic Alliance of Macedonia and the Liberal Democratic Party.

Election Commission

State Election Commission (Drzhavna izborna komisija): 1000 Skopje, Makedonija 19; tel. (2) 3244744; fax (2) 3244745; e-mail izbori@sec.mk; internet www.sec.mk; Chair. BORIS KONDARKO.

Political Organizations

Democratic Party of Albanians (DPA) (Partia Demokratike Shqiptare) (PDSh): Tetovo, Maršal Tito 15/1; tel. and fax (44) 333581; e-mail m.thaci@fountain-pdsh.org; internet www.pdsh.info; f. 1997; officially registered 2002; absorbed the Party for Democratic Prosperity in 2008; Chair. MENDUH THAÇI.

Democratic Party of Serbs in Macedonia (DPSM): Skopje, 27 Mart 11; tel. (2) 3254274; f. 1996; contested 2008 legislative elections as mem. of For a Better Macedonia coalition; Pres. IVAN STOILKOVIĆ.

Democratic Party of Turks in Macedonia (DPTM) (Makedonya Türk Demokratik Partisi): 1000 Skopje, Üsküp, ul. Stiv Naumov bb; tel. and fax (2) 3214053; e-mail info@tdp.org.mk; internet www.tdp.org.mk; contested 2008 legislative elections as mem. of For a Better Macedonia coalition; Pres. Dr KENAN HASIPI.

Democratic Renewal of Macedonia (Demokratska Obnova na Makedonija): 1000 Skopje, ul. Nikola Vapcarov 18/1; tel. and fax (2) 5112900; e-mail dom@dom.org.mk; internet www.dom.org.mk; f. 2006; contested 2008 legislative elections as mem. of For a Better Macedonia coalition; Leader LILJANA POPOVSKA.

Democratic Union for Integration (DUI) (Bashkimi Demokratik për Integrim/Demokratska Unija za Integracija) (BDI): 1200 Tetovo, Rruga 170 Nr 2, Reçicë e Vogël; tel. (4) 4334398; fax (4) 4334397; e-mail bdi@bdi.org.mk; internet www.bdi.org.mk; f. 2002; ethnic Albanian, dominated by fmr mems of rebel National Liberation Army; Chair. ALI AHMETI; Sec.-Gen. GEZIM OSTRENI.

Internal Macedonian Revolutionary Organization—Democratic Party for Macedonian National Unity (IMRO—DPMNU) (Vnatrešno-Makedonska Revolucionerna Organizacija—Demokratska Partija za Makedonsko Nacionalno Edinstvo—VMRO—DPMNE): 1000 Skopje, Makedonija 17A; tel. (2) 3215550; fax (2) 3211586; e-mail info@vmro-dpmne.org.mk; internet www

.vmro-dpmne.org.mk; nationalist; Pres. NIKOLA GRUEVSKI; Sec.-Gen. MARTIN PROTOGJER.

Internal Macedonian Revolutionary Organization—People's Party (IMRO—People's Party) (Vnatrešno Makedonska Revolucionerna Organizacija—Narodna Partija—VMRO—NP): 1000 Skopje, ul. Nikola Vapcarov br. 2; tel. and fax (2) 6131692; e-mail contact@vmro-np.org.mk; internet www.vmro-np.org.mk; f. 2004 by fmr mems of IMRO—DPMNU (q.v.); Chair. MARJAN DODOVSKI.

Liberal Democratic Party (LDP) (Liberalno-Demokratska Partija): 1000 Skopje, Partizanski odredi 89; tel. (2) 3298261; fax (2) 3298268; e-mail contact@ldp.org.mk; internet www.ldp.org.mk; f. 1996; contested 2008 legislative elections as mem. of Sun Coalition for Europe; Chair. JOVAN MANSIJEVSKI; Sec.-Gen. ROZA TOPUZOVA-KAREVSKA.

Liberal Party of Macedonia (LPM) (Liberalna Partija na Makedonija): 1000 Skopje, ul. Vasko Karangeleski bb; tel. (2) 2464955; fax (2) 2464956; e-mail info@lp.org.mk; internet www.lp.org.mk; f. 1990; contested 2008 legislative elections as mem. of Sun Coalition for Europe; centrist, free-market oriented; Pres. IVON VELIČKOVSKI; Sec.-Gen. DUŠKO POPOVSKI.

New Democracy (Demokracia e Re): 1000 Skopje, Khristian Todorovski 94A; tel. (2) 2616220; fax (2) 2616217; e-mail info@demokraciaere.org; internet www.demokraciaere.org; f. 2008 by fmr mems of DPA (q.v.); Pres. IMER SELMANI.

New Social Democratic Party (NSDP) (Nova Socijaldemokratska Partija): 1000 Skopje, Dame Gruev 5; tel. (2) 3238775; fax (2) 3290465; e-mail contact@nsdp.org.mk; internet www.nsdp.org.mk; f. 2005; contested 2008 legislative elections as mem. of Sun Coalition for Europe; Pres. TITO PETKOVSKI.

Social Democratic Alliance of Macedonia (SDAM) (Socijaldemokratski Sojuz na Makedonija—SDSM): 1000 Skopje, Bihakjka 8; tel. (2) 3293100; fax (2) 3293109; e-mail contact@sdsm.org.mk; internet www.sdsm.org.mk; f. 1943; fmrly League of Communists of Macedonia—Party of Democratic Reform; contested 2008 legislative elections as mem. of Sun Coalition for Europe; Chair. BRANKO CRVENKOVSKI; Gen. Sec. ANDREJ PETROV.

Socialist Party of Macedonia (SPM) (Socijalistiska Partija na Makedonija): 1000 Skopje, 11 Oktomvri 17; tel. (2) 3228015; fax (2) 3220025; e-mail contact@spm.org.mk; internet www.spm.org.mk; f. 1990; left-wing; contested 2008 legislative elections as mem. of For a Better Macedonia coalition; Chair. LJUBISAV IVANOV.

United Party for Emancipation (Obedinita Partija za Emancipacija): c/o Sobranie, 1000 Skopje, 11 Oktomvri bb; tel. (2) 3112255 ext. 135; e-mail nezdet.mustafa@gs.gov.mk; f. 2002 by merger of Democratic Progressive Roma Party of Macedonia and First Roma Party of Macedonia; contested 2008 elections as mem. of For a Better Macedonia coalition; Leader NEŽDET MUSTAFA.

Diplomatic Representation

EMBASSIES IN THE FORMER YUGOSLAV REPUBLIC OF MACEDONIA

Albania: 1000 Skopje, Slavej Planina 2; tel. (2) 3246726; fax (2) 3246727; e-mail embassy.skopje@mfa.gov.al; Ambassador ARBEN ÇEJKU.

Austria: 1000 Skopje, Mile Popjordanov 8; tel. (2) 3083400; fax (2) 3083150; e-mail skopje-ob@bmeia.gv.at; internet www.aussenministerium.at/skopje; Ambassador Dr ALOIS KRAUT.

Bosnia and Herzegovina: 1000 Skopje, Mile Pop-Jordanov 56; tel. (2) 3086216; fax (2) 3086221; e-mail emb.bih@neotel.net.mk; internet www.ambasadabih.org.mk; Ambassador MILAN BALABAN.

Bulgaria: 1000 Skopje, Zlatko Shnajder 3; tel. (2) 3229444; fax (2) 3246493; e-mail secretary@bgemb.org.mk; internet www.mfa.bg/skopje; Ambassador RAKOVSKI LASHEV.

China, People's Republic: 1000 Skopje, 474 No 20; tel. (2) 3213163; fax (2) 3122500; e-mail chinaembmk@mfa.gov.cn; internet mk.china-embassy.org; Ambassador DONG CHUNFENG.

Croatia: 1000 Skopje, Mitropolit Teodosij Gologanov 44; tel. (2) 3248170; fax (2) 3246004; e-mail croemb.skopje@mvpei.hr; internet mk.mvp.hr; Ambassador ZLATKO KRAMARIĆ.

Czech Republic: 1000 Skopje, Salvador Aljende 35; tel. (2) 3109805; fax (2) 3178380; e-mail skopje@embassy.mzv.cz; internet www.mzv.cz/skopje; Ambassador JOZEF BRAUN.

France: 1000 Skopje, Salvador Aljende 73; tel. (2) 3244300; fax (2) 3244313; e-mail franamba@mt.net.mk; internet www.ambafrance-mk.org; Ambassador JEAN-CLAUDE SCHLUMBERGER.

Germany: 1000 Skopje, Lerinska 59; tel. (2) 3093900; fax (2) 3093899; e-mail info@skop.auswaertiges-amt.de; internet www.skopje.diplo.de; Ambassador ULRIKE MARIA KNOTZ.

Hungary: 1000 Skopje, Mirka Ginova 27; tel. (2) 3063423; fax (2) 3063070; e-mail mission.skp@kum.hu; internet www.mfa.gov.hu/emb/skopje; Ambassador Dr FERENC KÉKESI.

Iran: 1000 Skopje, Vasil Stefanovski 25; tel. and fax (2) 3217420; e-mail iriemb@t-home.mk; Ambassador (vacant).

Italy: 1000 Skopje, Osma Udarna brig. 22; tel. (2) 3236500; fax (2) 3236505; e-mail segreteria.skopje@esteri.it; internet www.ambskopje.esteri.it; Ambassador FABIO CRISTIANI.

Kosovo: 1000 Skopje, Samoilova 136; tel. (2) 3290320; fax (2) 3290322; Chargé d'affaires a.i. SKENDER DURMISHI.

Montenegro: 1000 Skopje, Vasil Stefanovski 7; tel. (2) 3227277; fax (2) 3227254; e-mail mail@montenegroembassy.org.mk; internet www.montenegroembassy.org.mk; Ambassador DUŠAN MRDOVIĆ.

Netherlands: 1000 Skopje, Leninova 69–71; tel. (2) 3109250; fax (2) 3129309; e-mail sko@minbuza.nl; internet www.nlembassy.org.mk; Ambassador SIMONE FILIPPINI.

Norway: 1000 Skopje, Osma Udarna brig. 2; tel. (2) 3129165; fax (2) 3111138; e-mail embskp@mfa.no; internet www.norway.org.mk; Ambassador KJETIL PAULSEN.

Poland: 1000 Skopje, Djuro Djaković 50; tel. and fax (2) 3119744; e-mail ambasada@skopje.polemb.net; internet www.skopje.polemb.net; Ambassador DARIUSZ KAROL BACHURA.

Romania: 1000 Skopje, Rajko Zinzifov 42; tel. (2) 3228055; fax (2) 3228036; e-mail romanamb@cabletel.net.mk; internet skopje.mae.ro; Ambassador ADRIAN STEFAN CONSTANTINESCU.

Russia: 1000 Skopje, Pirinska 44; tel. (2) 3117160; fax (2) 3117808; e-mail embassy@russia.org.mk; internet www.russia.org.mk; Ambassador OLEG N. SHCHERBAK.

Serbia: 1000 Skopje, Pitu Guli 8; tel. (2) 3129298; fax (2) 3131428; e-mail srbamb@unet.com.mk; internet www.scgembassy.org.mk; Ambassador TOMISLAV ĐURIN.

Slovenia: 1000 Skopje, Vodnjanska 42; tel. (2) 3176663; fax (2) 3176631; e-mail vsk@gov.si; internet www.skopje.embassy.si; Ambassador ALAIN BRIAN BERGANT.

Spain: 1000 Skopje, 27 Mart 7; tel. (2) 3231002; fax (2) 3220612; e-mail ambspanija@mt.net.mk; Ambassador FERNANDO DE GALAINENA RODRIGUEZ.

Sweden: 1000 Skopje, Osma Udarna Brigada 2; tel. (2) 3297880; fax (2) 3112065; e-mail ambassaden.skopje@foreign.ministry.se; internet www.swedenabroad.com/skopje; Ambassador LARS WAHLUND.

Switzerland: 1000 Skopje, Maksim Gorki 19; tel. (2) 3103300; fax (2) 3103301; e-mail vertretung@sko.admin.ch; internet www.eda.admin.ch/skopje; Ambassador STEFANO LAZZAROTTO.

Turkey: 1000 Skopje, Slavej Planina bb; tel. (2) 3113270; fax (2) 3117024; e-mail turkish@on.net.mk; internet skopje.emb.mfa.gov.tr; Ambassador GÜROL SÖKMENSÜER.

Ukraine: 1000 Skopje, Albert Svjcer 7–9; tel. and fax (2) 3178120; e-mail emb_mk@mfa.gov.ua; internet www.mfa.gov.ua/macedonia; Ambassador YURIY O. HONCHARUK.

United Kingdom: 1000 Skopje, Salvador Aljende 73; tel. (2) 3299299; fax (2) 3179726; e-mail britishembassyskopje@fco.gov.uk; internet ukinmacedonia.fco.gov.uk; Ambassador CHRISTOPHER YVON.

USA: 1000 Skopje, Samoilova 21; tel. (2) 3102000; fax (2) 3102499; e-mail embskowebm@t-home.mk; internet skopje.usembassy.gov; Ambassador PHILIP THOMAS REEKER.

Judicial System

The former Yugoslav republic of Macedonia has 27 Courts of First Instance and three Courts of Appeal. The Republican Judicial Council, which comprises seven members elected by the Sobranie for a term of six years, proposes the election or dismissal of judges to the Sobranie. The Constitutional Court, comprising nine judges elected by the Sobranie with a mandate of nine years, is responsible for the protection of constitutional and legal rights, and ensures that there is no conflict in the exercise of legislative, executive and judicial powers. The Supreme Court is the highest court in the country, and guarantees the equal administration of legislation by all courts.

Constitutional Court (Ustaven Sud na Republika Makedonija): 1000 Skopje, 12 Udarna brig. 2; tel. and fax (2) 3163063; e-mail mail@ustavensud.mk; internet www.ustavensud.mk; f. 1964; Pres. BRANKO NAUMOSKI.

Supreme Court: 1000 Skopje, Krste Misirkova bb; tel. (2) 3234064; fax (2) 3237538; Pres. JOVO VANGELOVSKI.

Republican Judicial Council: 1000 Skopje, Veljko Vlahovikj bb; tel. (2) 3218130; fax (2) 3218131; Pres. ALEKSANDRA ZAFIROVSKA.

Office of the Public Prosecutor (Javno Obvinitelstvo na RM): 1000 Skopje, Krste Misirkova bb; tel. (2) 3219850; fax (2) 3219866;

e-mail jorm@jorm.org.mk; internet www.jorm.org.mk; Public Prosecutor Ljupčo Svrgovski.

Religion

Most ethnic Macedonians are adherents of the Eastern Orthodox Church, and since 1967 there has been an autocephalous Macedonian Orthodox Church. However, the Serbian Orthodox Church (of which the Macedonian Church formed a part) does not recognize the autocephalous church, and nor do other Orthodox Churches. There are some adherents of other Orthodox jurisdictions in the country. Those Macedonian (and Bulgarian) Slavs who converted to Islam during the Ottoman era are known as Pomaks or as ethnic Muslims. The substantial Albanian population is mostly Muslim (mainly Sunni, but there are some adherents of a Dervish sect); there are some Catholic Christians (of both Byzantine and Latin rites) and a small Jewish community.

CHRISTIANITY

Macedonian Orthodox Church: 1000 Skopje, Partizanski Odredi 12, POB 69; tel. (2) 3230697; fax (2) 3230685; internet www.mpc.org.mk; Metropolitan See of Ohrid revived in 1958; autocephaly declared 1967; 1.5m. mems; comprises seven bishoprics in Macedonia and three abroad; Head of Church and Archbishop of Ohrid and Macedonia Metropolitan Archbishop of Skopje Stefan Veljanovski.

The Roman Catholic Church

The diocese of Skopje, suffragan to the archdiocese of Vrhbosna (based in Sarajevo, Bosnia and Herzegovina), covers most of the FYRM. The Bishop is also Apostolic Exarch for Catholics of the Byzantine Rite in the FYRM. At 31 December 2008 there were an estimated 15,037 adherents of the Latin Rite in the diocese, and the country had an estimated 15,037 adherents of the Byzantine Rite.

Latin Rite Bishop of Skopje and Apostolic Exarch for the Byzantine Rite Faithful Resident in the former Yugoslav republic of Macedonia: Rt Rev. Kiro Stojanov, 1000 Skopje, Risto Šiškov 31; tel. and fax (2) 3164123; e-mail katbiskupija@mt.net.mk.

ISLAM

Islamic Community of Macedonia (Bashkësia Fetare Islame e Republikës së Maqedonisë): Skopje, Çairska 52; tel. (2) 3117410; fax (2) 3117883; e-mail bim@bim.org.mk; internet www.bim.org.mk; Leader Haji Sulejman Rexhepi.

The Press

In 2002 a total of 39 newspapers and 178 magazines were published in the former Yugoslav republic of Macedonia.

PRINCIPAL DAILY NEWSPAPERS

Denes (Today): 1000 Skopje, M. H. Jasmin 50; tel. (2) 3110239; fax (2) 3110150; e-mail denes@unet.com.mk; Editor Nik Denes.

Dnevnik (Daily): 1000 Skopje, Teodosij Gologanov 28; tel. (2) 3297555; fax (2) 3297554; e-mail dnevnik@dnevnik.com.mk; internet www.dnevnik.com.mk; independent; Editor-in-Chief Sašo Kokalanov.

Nova Makedonija (New Macedonia): 1000 Skopje, Atinska br. 12; tel. and fax (2) 5511711; e-mail nm@novamakedonija.com.mk; internet www.novamakedonija.com.mk; f. 1944; morning; in Macedonian; Dir Ratko Lazarevski; Editor-in-Chief Zoran Andonovskii; circ. 25,000.

Utrinski Vesnik (Morning Herald): 1000 Skopje, ul. Dimitrie Čuposki br. 11/5; tel. (2) 3236900; fax (2) 3236901; e-mail contact@utrinski.com.mk; internet www.utrinski.com.mk; Dir Dr Srgjan Kerim; Editor-in-Chief Nina Nineska-Fidanoska.

Večer (The Evening): 1000 Skopje, Nikola Vapcarov 2; tel. (2) 3219650; fax (2) 3219651; e-mail latas@vecer.com.mk; internet www.vecer.com.mk; f. 1963; evening; Editor-in-Chief Dragan Pavlovikj-Latas; circ. 29,200.

Vest (News): Skopje; internet www.vest.com.mk; popular; Editor-in-Chief Goran Mihailovskii.

PERIODICALS

Delo: 1000 Skopje, Mihail Cokov bb; tel. (2) 3133306; fax (2) 3136477; e-mail delo@unet.com.mk; internet www.delo.com.mk; f. 1993; weekly; nationalist; Editor-in-Chief Vlado Mokrov.

Fokus: Skopje, Železnička 53; tel. (2) 3111327; fax (2) 3111685; weekly; independent; Editor-in-Chief Nikola Mladenov.

Makedonsko Vreme/Macedonian Times: 91000 Skopje, Vasil Gjorgov 39/7; tel. and fax (2) 3121182; e-mail mtimes@unet.com.mk; f. 1994; monthly; politics and current affairs; in Macedonian and English; Editor-in-Chief Jovan Pavlovski.

Puls (Pulse): 1000 Skopje, Mito Hadživasilev bb; tel. (2) 3117124; fax (2) 3118024; internet www.puls.com.mk; weekly; business and technology; Editor-in-Chief Mirče Tomovski.

Roma Times: Skopje; e-mail mail@dostae.net.mk; internet www.dostae.net.mk/mk/press_mk_roma.htm; f. 2001; 3 a week; circ. 3,000.

Sport Magazine: 1000 Skopje, Mito Hadživasilev Jasmin bb; tel. and fax (2) 3116254; e-mail lav@unet.com.mk; f. 1991; weekly; circ. 6,000.

Trudbenik (Worker): 1000 Skopje, Udarna brigada 12; f. 1945; weekly; organ of Macedonian Trade Unions; Editor Simo Ivanovski.

NEWS AGENCIES

Macedonian Information Agency (Makedonska Informativna Agencija—MIA): 1000 Skopje, Bojmija 2; tel. (2) 2461600; fax (2) 2464048; e-mail mia@mia.mk; internet www.mia.mk; f. 1992; news service in Macedonian, Albanian and English; Exec. Dir Ljupčo Jakimoski.

Macedonian Information Centre (Makedonski Informativen Centar—MIC): 1000 Skopje, Naum Naumovski Borce 73; tel. (2) 3117876; e-mail contact@micnews.com.mk; internet www.micnews.com.mk; f. 1992; English; independent; Man. Dragan Antonov.

Makfax: 1000 Skopje, 11 Oktomvri 33a; tel. (2) 3227127; fax (2) 3110125; e-mail makfax@makfax.com.mk; internet www.makfax.com.mk; f. 1992; independent; provides daily regional news service; in Macedonian, Albanian and English; Exec. Dir Davor Pashovski.

PRESS ASSOCIATION

Journalists' Association of Macedonia: 1000 Skopje, Gradskizid 13, POB 498; tel. (2) 3298139; fax (2) 3116447; e-mail znm@on.net.mk; internet www.znm.org.mk; Pres. Naser Selmani.

Publishers

Detska radost/Nova Makedonija (Children's Happiness/New Macedonia) Publishing House: 1000 Skopje, Mito Hadživasilev Jasmin bb; tel. (2) 3213059; fax (2) 3225830; f. 1944; children's books; Dir Kiril Donev.

Kultura: 1000 Skopje, Sv. Kliment Ohridski 68a; tel. (2) 3111332; fax (2) 3228608; e-mail ipkultura@kultura.com.mk; internet www.kultura.com.mk; f. 1945; history, philosophy, art, poetry, children's literature and fiction; in Macedonian; Dir Dimitar Baševski.

Kulturen Život (Cultural Life) Publishing House: 1000 Skopje, Ruzveltova 6; tel. (2) 3239134; f. 1971; Editor Ljubica Arsovska.

Makedonska kniga (Macedonian Book) Publishing House: 1000 Skopje, 11 Oktomvri; tel. (2) 3224055; fax (2) 3236951; f. 1947; arts, non-fiction, novels, children's books; Dir Sande Stojčevski.

Matica Makedonska: 1000 Skopje, ul. Kliment Ohridski 23; tel. (2) 3221138; fax (2) 3229244; f. 1991; Dir Rade Siljan.

Metaforum: 1000 Skopje, Goce Delčev 6; tel. (2) 3114890; fax (2) 3115634; f. 1993; Dir Ružica Bilko.

Misla (Thought) Publishing House: 1000 Skopje, Partizanski odredi 1; tel. (2) 3221844; fax (2) 3118439; f. 1966; modern and classic Macedonian and translated literature; Pres. Zlata Bunteslea.

Naša kniga (Our Book) Publishing House: 1000 Skopje, M. Gorki 21, POB 132; tel. (2) 3228066; fax (2) 3116872; f. 1948; Dir Stojan Lekovski.

Prosvetno delo (Educational) Publishing House: 1000 Skopje, Dimitrija Čuposki 15; tel. (2) 3117255; fax (2) 3225434; f. 1945; works of domestic writers and textbooks in Macedonian for elementary, professional and high schools; fiction and scientific works; Dir Dr Krste Angelovski.

Tabernakul: 1000 Skopje, POB 251, Mihail Cokov bb; tel. (2) 3127073; fax (2) 3115329; e-mail contact@tabernakul.com.mk; internet www.tabernakul.com.mk; f. 1989; religion, history, literature, philosophy, popular science; Dir Cvetan Vraživirski.

Broadcasting and Communications

TELECOMMUNICATIONS

Cosmofon: 1000 Skopje, Orce Nikolov bb; internet www.cosmofon.com.mk; f. 2003; majority share owned by Hellenic Telecommunications Organization (Greece); mobile cellular telecommunications; 140,000 subscribers (June 2004).

THE FORMER YUGOSLAV REPUBLIC OF MACEDONIA

Directory

Makedonski Telekom (MT): 1000 Skopje, Orce Nikolov bb; tel. (2) 3100200; fax (2) 3100300; e-mail kontakt@telekom.mk; internet www.telekom.mk; fmrly Makedonski telekomunikacii; present name adopted 2008; mem. of Deutsche Telekom group (Germany), 34.8% state-owned; CEO Nikolaj J. V. Bekers.

T-Mobile Macedonia: 1000 Skopje, Orce Nikolov bb; tel. (2) 3131131; fax (2) 3201269; e-mail kontakt@t-mobile.com.mk; internet www.t-mobile.com.mk; f. 1996 as Mobimak; present name adopted 2006; mobile cellular telecommunications; CEO Rubin Zareski; 450,000 subscribers (Aug. 2003).

VIP operator DOOEL Skopje: 1000 Skopje, Dimitrie Čupovski 2; tel. (2) 3110077; e-mail kontakt@vipoperator.com.mk; internet www.vipoperator.com.mk; f. 2007; subsidiary of MobilKom (Austria); mobile cellular telecommunications services; Gen. Dir Nikola Ljušev.

BROADCASTING

Radio

Makedonska Radio-Televizija (MRT): 1000 Skopje, Goce Delčev bb; tel. (2) 3236839; fax (2) 3111821; e-mail mkrtvcor@mt.com.mk; internet www.mkrtv.com.mk; f. 1944; fmrly Radiotelevizija Skopje, name changed 1991; three radio channels; broadcasts in Macedonian, Albanian, Turkish, Serbian, Roma and Vlach; Dirs Janez Sajovic, Boris Stavrov; Dir of Radio Grigori Popovski.

Antenna 5 Radio: 1000 Skopje, Tetovska 35; tel. (2) 3111911; fax (2) 3113281; e-mail mail@antenna5.com.mk; internet www.antenna5.com.mk; f. 1994; 12 transmitters broadcast to 90% of the country; Gen. Man. Zoran Petrov.

Television

Makedonska Radio-Televizija (MRT): 1000 Skopje, Goce Delčev bb; tel. (2) 3112200; fax (2) 3111821; e-mail gstosic@unet.com.mk; internet www.mkrtv.com.mk; f. 1964; fmrly Radiotelevizija Skopje, name changed 1991; state broadcasting co; three television services; broadcasts in Macedonian, Albanian, Turkish, Serbian, Roma and Vlach; Dirs Janez Sajovic, Boris Stavrov; Dir of Television Ljubčo Tozija.

A1 TV: 1000 Skopje, Pero Nakov 60; tel. (2) 2550301; fax (2) 2550330; e-mail a1tv@a1.com.mk; internet www.a1.com.mk; Gen. Man. Darko Perusevski.

SITEL Television: 1000 Skopje, Gradski Stadion bb; tel. (2) 3116566; fax (2) 3229799; e-mail sitelvesti@on.net.mk; internet www.sitel.com.mk; Gen. Man. Govan Ivanovski.

Finance

(cap. = capital; res = reserves; dep. = deposits; m. = million; amounts in new Macedonian denars; brs = branches)

BANKS

A programme to privatize the banking sector of the former Yugoslav republic of Macedonia was completed in early 2000. At September 2008 the banking system comprised 18 commercial banks and 11 savings houses; 14 of the banks were majority foreign-owned.

National Bank

National Bank of the Republic of Macedonia (Narodna Banka na Republika Makedonija): 1000 Skopje, POB 401, Kompleks banki bb; tel. (2) 3108203; fax (2) 3124054; e-mail governorsoffice@nbrm.mk; internet www.nbrm.mk; f. 1992; central bank and bank of issue; cap. 1,289.7m., res 10,489.7m., dep. 58,924.1m. (Dec. 2008); Gov. Petar Gošev.

Selected Banks

Alpha Banka a.d. Skopje: 1000 Skopje, Dame Gruev 1, POB 564; tel. (2) 3289427; fax (2) 3116830; e-mail centrala@alphabank.com.mk; internet www.alphabank.com.mk; f. 1993; wholly owned by Alpha Bank AE Athens (Greece); present name adopted 2002; cap. 560.2m., res 1,021.0m., dep. 9,545.0m. (Dec. 2008); Chair. Spyros Filaretos; Gen. Man. Constantinos M. Papachristoforou; 25 brs.

InvestBanka a.d. Skopje: 1000 Skopje, Makedonija 9/11; tel. (2) 3200500; fax (2) 3200515; e-mail contact@investbanka.com.mk; internet www.investbanka.com.mk; f. 1992; 96% owned by Steiermärkische Bank und Sparkassen AG (Austria); cap. 679.1m., res 93.7m., dep. 5,285.8m. (Dec. 2008); Pres. Krstic Srgjan.

Izvozna i Kreditna Banka a.d. (IK Banka—Export and Credit Bank): 1000 Skopje, bul. Mito Hadzivasilev Jasmin bb, POB 421; tel. (2) 3240800; fax (2) 3240833; e-mail ikbanka@ikbanka.com.mk; internet www.ikbanka.com.mk; f. 1993; 66.6% owned by Demir-Halk Bank (Netherlands); cap. 414.1m., res 528.2m., dep. 3,915.9m. (Dec. 2007); Chair. Selcuk Saldirak; Chief Exec. Yucel Inan; 19 brs.

Komercijalna Banka a.d. Skopje: 1000 Skopje, Kej Dimitar Vlahov 4; tel. (2) 3107107; fax (2) 3119627; e-mail contact@kbnet.com.mk; internet www.kb.com.mk; f. 1955 as Komunalna Banka; name changed as above in 1991; cap. 2,014.0m., res 2,871.8m., dep. 47,342.3m. (Dec. 2008); CEO Hari Kostov.

Makedonska Banka za Poddrshka na Razvojot a.d. Skopje (Macedonian Bank for Development Promotion): Skopje, Veljko Vlahovikj 26; tel. (2) 3115844; fax (2) 3239688; e-mail info@mbdp.com.mk; internet www.mbdp.com.mk; f. 1998; cap. 932.4m., res 631.6m., total assets 2,989.9m. (Dec. 2008); CEO Dragan Martinovski.

NLB Tutunska Banka a.d. Skopje: 1000 Skopje, Vodnjanska 1; tel. (2) 3105600; fax (2) 3105681; e-mail tbanka1@tb.com.mk; internet www.tb.com.mk; f. 1985; fmrly Tutunska Banka; present name adopted 2006; cap. 785.6m., res 2,197.2m., dep. 29,531.8m. (Dec. 2007); Pres. Gorgi Jancevski; 32 brs.

Ohridska Banka (Ohrid Bank): 6000 Ohrid, Makedonski Prosvetiteli 19; tel. (46) 206600; fax (46) 254130; e-mail obinfo@ob.com.mk; internet www.ob.com.mk; cap. 979.5m., res 65.6m., dep. 9,306.5m. (Dec. 2007); Pres. Jitka Pantuchkova; 5 brs.

ProCredit Bank Macedonia: 1000 Skopje, Jane Sandanski 109a; tel. (2) 3219900; fax (2) 3219901; e-mail info@procreditbank.com.mk; internet www.procreditbank.com.mk; f. 2003; cap. 613.7m., res 49.0m., dep. 8,518.5m. (Dec. 2009); Chair. Jovanka Popovska.

Stopanska Banka a.d. Bitola: 7000 Bitola, Dobrivoe Radosavljević 21; tel. (47) 207500; fax (47) 207541; e-mail stbbt@stbbt.com.mk; internet www.stbbt.com.mk; f. 1948 as Komunalna Banka Bitola; present name adopted 1995; cap. 1,172.9m., res 268.3m., dep. 4,292.0m. (Dec. 2008); Pres. Blagej Dzalev.

Stopanska Banka a.d. Skopje: 1000 Skopje, 11 Oktomvri 7; tel. (2) 3295295; fax (2) 3114503; e-mail sbank@stb.com.mk; internet www.stb.com.mk; f. 1944; cap. 3,511.2m., res 438.0m., dep. 49,078.8m. (Dec. 2008); 73.0% owned by National Bank of Greece, 10.8% by European Bank for Reconstruction and Development, 10.8% by International Finance Corpn (World Bank); Chair. Ioannis Pechlivanidis; 25 brs.

TTK Banka a.d. Skopje: 1000 Skopje, POB 198, ul. Naroden Front 19a; tel. (2) 3236400; fax (2) 3236444; e-mail ttk@ttk.com.mk; internet www.ttk.com.mk; f. 2001; present name adopted 2006; cap. 907.8m., res 8.8m., dep. 5,109.2m. (Dec. 2008); Pres. Gligorie Gogovski.

UniBanka—Universalna Investiciona Banka a.d. Skopje (Universal Investment Bank): 1000 Skopje, M. Gorki 6; tel. (2) 3111111; fax (2) 3224162; e-mail info@unibank.com.mk; internet www.unibank.com.mk; f. 1993 as Balkanska Banka a.d. Skopje; present name adopted 2004; cap. 546.0m., res 564.9m., dep. 7,217.3m. (Dec. 2008); Pres. Costa Mitrovski.

STOCK EXCHANGE

Macedonian Stock Exchange (Makedonska Berza a.d. Skopje): 1000 Skopje, Orce Nikolov 75; tel. (2) 3122055; fax (2) 3122069; e-mail mse@mse.org.mk; internet www.mse.com.mk; f. 1995; CEO Ivan Steriev.

INSURANCE

In 2008 the insurance system in the FYRM comprised 12 insurance companies, seven insurance brokerage companies and three insurance agencies.

QBE Makedonija: 1000 Skopje, 11 Oktomvri 25; tel. (2) 3115188; fax (2) 3114020; internet www.qbeeurope.com/makedonija; subsidiary of QBE Insurance Group (Australia); stock company for insurance and reinsurance; CEO Frank O'Halloran.

Sava Tabak a.d. Skopje: 1000 Skopje, Treta Makedonska brigada bb; tel. (2) 3105608; fax (3) 3105685; e-mail info@savatabak.com.mk; internet www.savatabak.com.mk; fmrly Tabak Osiguravanje; 66.67% owned by Sava Re (Slovenia).

Trade and Industry

CHAMBER OF COMMERCE

Economic Chamber of Macedonia (Stopanska Komora na Makedonija): 1000 Skopje, Dimitrija Čupovski 13; tel. (2) 3244000; fax (2) 3244088; e-mail ic@ic.mchamber.org.mk; internet www.mchamber.org.mk; f. 1962; Pres. Branko Azeski.

UTILITIES

Electricity

EVN Macedonia: 1000 Skopje, 11 Oktombri 9; tel. (2) 3111077; fax (2) 3227827; e-mail lenche.karpuzovska@evn.com.mk; internet www.evn.com.mk; production and distribution of electric power; 90%

THE FORMER YUGOSLAV REPUBLIC OF MACEDONIA

owned by EVN AG (Austria); fmrly Electric Power Co of Macedonia (Elektrostopanstovo na Makedonija); Chair. GEORG VALDNER.

TRADE UNIONS

Federation of Trade Unions of Macedonia: 1000 Skopje; tel. (2) 3231374; fax (2) 3115787; 18 affiliated unions; Pres. VANCO MURATOVSKI.

Transport

RAILWAYS

In 2002 the rail network totalled 699 km, of which 233 km were electrified. Train services between Skopje and Prishtina, Kosovo, suspended since 1999, were resumed in 2006.

Makedonski Železnici (MZ) (Macedonian Railways): 1000 Skopje, Železnička 50; tel. (2) 3227903; fax (2) 3462330; e-mail muzunova@mz.com.mk; internet www.mz.com.mk; f. 1992; Chair. KOSANA MAZNEVA; Dir-Gen. NIKOLA DIMITROVSKI.

ROADS

The FYRM's road network totalled 12,974 km in 2002, of which about 6,806 km were paved.

CIVIL AVIATION

The FYRM has two international airports, at Ohrid, and the Aleksandar Veliki (Alexander the Great) Airport, near Skopje.

Tourism

Tourist arrivals numbered 213,829 in 2008, when receipts from tourism amounted to US $262m.

Tourist Association of Macedonia: 1000 Skopje, Dame Gruev 28/5; tel. (2) 3290862; e-mail tarm@mt.net.mk.

Defence

As assessed at November 2010, the armed forces of the FYRM totalled 8,000 in active service. Paramilitary forces comprised a police force of 7,600, of whom some 5,000 were armed. There was also a reserve force of 4,850. Conscription was abolished with effect from 2007.

Defence Expenditure: Budgeted at 6,520m. new denars in 2010.

Chief of Staff of the Army: Lt-Gen. MIROSLAV STOJANOVSKI.

Education

Elementary education is free and compulsory for all children between the ages of seven and 15. Various types of secondary school, beginning at 15 and lasting for four years, are available to those who qualify. In 2006/07 some 88.7% of children in the relevant age-group were enrolled in primary education, while the comparable ratio for secondary education was 81.3% in 2004/05. According to the terms of the Constitution, nationals are granted the right to elementary and secondary education in their mother tongue. In 2001/02 Albanian was the language of education in 275 primary schools and 24 secondary schools, Turkish in 55 primary schools and five secondary schools, and Serbian in 13 primary schools. There are universities at Skopje, Bitola and Tetova (the latter of which operates in Albanian). In 2002/03 some 45,624 students were enrolled in higher education. Expenditure on education by the central Government in 2002 was budgeted at 7,591m. new denars (11.4% of total expenditure).

MADAGASCAR

Introductory Survey

LOCATION, CLIMATE, LANGUAGE, RELIGION, FLAG, CAPITAL

The Republic of Madagascar comprises the island of Madagascar, the fourth largest in the world, and several much smaller offshore islands, in the western Indian Ocean, about 500 km (300 miles) east of Mozambique, in southern Africa. The inland climate is temperate; in Antananarivo temperatures are generally between 8°C (48°F) and 27°C (81°F), with cooler, dryer weather between May and October. The coastal region is tropical, with an average daily maximum temperature of 32°C (90°F). The rainy season extends from November to April in the highlands (average annual rainfall is 1,000 mm–1,500 mm) but is more prolonged on the coast, where average annual rainfall can reach 3,500 mm. The official languages are Malagasy and French. Following a referendum held in April 2007, English was adopted as the third official language. Hova and other dialects are also widely spoken. More than 50% of the population follow animist beliefs, while about 41% are Christians and the remainder are Muslims. The national flag (proportions 2 by 3) has a vertical white stripe (one-third of the length) at the hoist and two equal horizontal stripes, of red and green, in the fly. The capital is Antananarivo.

CONTEMPORARY POLITICAL HISTORY

Historical Context

A French possession since 1896, Madagascar became an autonomous state within the French Community in October 1958, as the Malagasy Republic. In May 1959 Philibert Tsiranana, leader of the Parti social démocrate (PSD), was elected President. The country achieved full independence on 26 June 1960. Prior to independence France supported the PSD, which was identified with the majority coastal tribes (côtiers), as an alternative to the more nationalistic highland people, the Merina, who were the traditional ruling group in the island.

After 1967 the economy deteriorated, and there was growing opposition to the Government's alleged authoritarianism and subservience to French interests. In May 1972, following civil unrest, President Tsiranana transferred full powers to the Army Chief of Staff, Gen. Gabriel Ramanantsoa. In October 1973 pro-Government parties secured a decisive victory in legislative elections. A prolonged crisis followed an attempted military coup in December 1974, and in early February 1975 Ramanantsoa transferred power to Col Richard Ratsimandrava, hitherto Minister of the Interior; however, Ratsimandrava was assassinated shortly afterwards. On 12 February Brig.-Gen. Gilles Andriamahazo assumed power and imposed martial law. All political parties were suspended. In June Andriamahazo was succeeded as Head of State by Lt-Commdr (later Adm.) Didier Ratsiraka, a côtier and a former Minister of Foreign Affairs, who became Chairman of the Supreme Revolutionary Council (SRC).

In a referendum in December 1975 more than 94% of voters approved a new Constitution, which provided for radical administrative and agrarian reforms, and the appointment of Ratsiraka as President of the Republic for a term of seven years. The country's name was changed to the Democratic Republic of Madagascar, and a 'Second Republic' was proclaimed. In March 1976 the Avant-garde de la révolution malgache (AREMA—Antoky Ny Revolosiona Malagasy) was founded as the nucleus of the Front national pour la défense de la révolution socialiste malgache (FNDR), the only political organization permitted by the Constitution. Ratsiraka was re-elected to the presidency in 1982 and 1989.

Domestic Political Affairs

In August 1989 Ratsiraka assented to opposition demands for discussions about the future role and structure of the FNDR. In December the National People's Assembly adopted a constitutional amendment abolishing the requirement for political parties to be members of the FNDR (thereby effectively dissolving the FNDR), despite opposition from Mouvement pour le progrès de Madagascar (Mpitolona ho amin'ny Fandrosoan'ny Madagasikara—MFM) deputies.

In March 1990 the Government formally permitted the resumption of multi-party politics. Numerous new organizations emerged, while other parties that had hitherto operated within the FNDR became official opposition movements. Several pro-Government political associations joined AREMA to form a new coalition, the Mouvement militant pour le socialisme malagasy (MMSM). The principal opposition movements included the Union nationale pour le développement et la démocratie (UNDD) and MFM. An informal alliance, the Comité des forces vives—subsequently known as Forces vives (FV, Hery Velona)—was formed by 16 opposition factions, and trade unions and other groups.

In May 1991 legislation providing for extensive constitutional amendments was submitted to the National People's Assembly. Opposition parties criticized the proposals, on the grounds that the revised Constitution would retain references to socialism. In June opposition leaders applied to the Haute Cour Constitutionnelle (High Constitutional Court—HCC) to effect Ratsiraka's removal from office, while the FV organized demonstrations in support of its demands for the resignation of the President and the convening of a national conference to draft a new constitution. Later in June the FV formed a 'parallel' administration, which it termed the 'Provisional Government'.

In July 1991 the FV organized a general strike, warning that it would continue until the Government acceded to its demands for constitutional reform. The FV appointed Jean Rakotoharison, a retired army general, as President of the 'Provisional Government', and Albert Zafy, the leader of the UNDD, as its Prime Minister. However, Manandafy Rakotonirina, the leader of the MFM, rejected the formation of the 'Provisional Government', favouring further negotiations, and withdrew his party from the FV. Members of the 'Provisional Government' subsequently occupied the premises of six official government ministries. Later in July Ratsiraka ordered the detention of several members of the 'Provisional Government' and imposed a state of emergency in Antananarivo. The FV withdrew from negotiations with the MMSM, in protest against the arrests, while the French Government appealed to Ratsiraka to release the opposition leaders. In response to increasing public pressure, Ratsiraka dissolved the Council of Ministers and pledged to organize a constitutional referendum before the end of 1991. Members of the 'Provisional Government' were released from custody, and Ratsiraka repealed legislation that authorized the detention of opponents of the Government.

In August 1991 Ratsiraka appointed Guy Razanamasy, the mayor of Antananarivo, as Prime Minister. Later that month Ratsiraka declared Madagascar to be a federation of six states, with himself as President, and claimed to command the support of five provinces where AREMA continued to hold the majority of seats in regional councils. At the end of August Razanamasy formed an interim Government, which did not include any members of the FV or the MFM.

In October 1991 representatives of the Government, the FV, the MFM, church leaders and the armed forces signed an agreement providing for the suspension of the Constitution and the creation of a transitional Government, which was to remain in office for a maximum period of 18 months, pending presidential and legislative elections. The SRC and the National People's Assembly were to be replaced by interim bodies, respectively the High State Authority for Transition to the Third Republic and the National Committee for Economic and Social Regeneration. On an interim basis, Ratsiraka was to remain as President of the Republic and Razanamasy as Prime Minister. Zafy was designated President of the High State Authority, while Rakotonirina and Pastor Richard Andriamanjato were appointed as joint Presidents of the 131-member National Committee for Economic and Social Regeneration. The power to appoint or to dismiss government ministers, hitherto vested in the President, was granted to Razanamasy. A new constitution was to be submitted to a national referendum by the end of 1991. Zafy subsequently rejected the agreement, on the grounds that Ratsiraka was to retain the nominal post of Commander-in-Chief of the Armed Forces. In November Razanamasy formed a new interim Government, which included three representatives of the MFM and one MMSM member. Francisque Ravony, of the MFM, was appointed to the new post of Deputy Prime Minister. Owing to Zafy's refusal to participate in the Government, 10 portfolios that had been allocated to the FV remained vacant. Later in November, however, Zafy agreed to accept the presidency of the High State Authority.

In December 1991 Razanamasy announced that the formation of the coalition Government had proved unsuccessful, and 11 ministers, including Ravony, resigned. Razanamasy appointed a larger Government of national consensus, in which 14 (of 36) portfolios were allocated to the FV. In January 1992 it was announced that all political factions had now accepted the terms of the October 1991 agreement. The institutions that had been established by the accord were to prepare for the constitutional referendum, now scheduled for June 1992, and for local, presidential and legislative elections, which were to take place by the end of the year. In February the High State Authority for Transition to the Third Republic announced the dissolution of the SRC and the National People's Assembly, in accordance with the October 1991 agreement, and indicated that a new body was to be created to supervise local elections, replacing the existing system of government, based on village assemblies (*fokontany*). However, the MMSM claimed that the High State Authority was not empowered to dissolve the local government structure. The Government subsequently announced that control of local government was to be transferred from elected councils to special delegations, and that security commissions were to be established to organize the *fokontany*.

Establishment of the Third Republic

The draft constitution of the Third Republic, as submitted to the Government in April 1992, envisaged a unitary state and provided for a bicameral legislature, comprising a Senate and a National Assembly. Two-thirds of the members of the Senate were to be selected by an electoral college, with the remaining one-third to be appointed by the President, while the 184-member National Assembly was to be elected by universal suffrage, under a system of proportional representation, for a four-year term. The authority of the President was to be reduced, and executive power was to be vested in the Prime Minister, who was to be appointed by the National Assembly. Ratsiraka reiterated his intention to contest the presidential election and demanded that a draft providing for a federal system of government also be submitted to the forthcoming referendum.

The new Constitution was approved by 72.2% of votes cast in a national referendum in August 1992 and at the presidential election held in November Zafy secured 45.1% of votes cast, while Ratsiraka took 29.2%. At a second round of voting, in February 1993, Zafy secured 66.7% of the votes cast. Zafy's inauguration the following month was accompanied by violent clashes between security forces and federalists in the north. In accordance with the Constitution, Zafy resigned as President of the UNDD at a party congress in May; Emmanuel Rakotovahiny, the Minister of State for Agriculture and Rural Development, was elected as his successor.

Several constituent parties of the FV that had not supported Zafy in the first round of the presidential election subsequently presented independent lists of candidates for the forthcoming legislative elections; the remaining parties in the alliance became known as Forces vives Rasalama (Hery Velona Rasalama—HVR). The elections, to a reduced 138-member National Assembly, took place on 16 June 1993, and were contested by 121 political associations. The HVR secured 46 seats, the MFM 15, and a new alliance of pro-Ratsiraka parties 11 seats. The official results indicated that parties supporting Zafy had won 75 seats in the National Assembly. In August Francisque Ravony was elected Prime Minister and formed a new Council of Ministers. Richard Andriamanjato was elected President of the National Assembly.

In mid-1995 Zafy announced that he was unable to co-operate with Ravony and decreed that a constitutional amendment empowering the President, rather than the National Assembly, to select the Prime Minister be submitted for approval in a national referendum. Ravony indicated that he would resign after the referendum, regardless of the outcome. In August Ravony formed a new Council of Ministers, comprising representatives of the parliamentary majority that had supported him in the previous month. The referendum proceeded in September, at which the constitutional amendment was approved by 63.6% of votes cast. Ravony duly resigned in October, and Zafy appointed Rakotovahiny as Prime Minister.

Dissension emerged between the parties that supported Zafy over the composition of the new Council of Ministers, and in December 1995 associates of Andriamanjato demanded that an alternative cabinet be appointed. In May 1996 a motion of censure against Rakotovahiny's Government was approved by a large majority in the National Assembly. Rakotovahiny submitted his administration's resignation, and Norbert Ratsirahonana, hitherto President of the HCC, was appointed Prime Minister.

Zafy refused to approve the new Government initially proposed by Ratsirahonana, insisting on the inclusion of five UNDD members who had served in the previous Council of Ministers. Ratsirahonana, however, won a vote of confidence in the legislature in July 1996, by associating the vote with legislation providing for the implementation of economic reforms stipulated by the IMF and the World Bank. On 26 July a motion in the National Assembly to remove Zafy from office for numerous contraventions of the Constitution was supported by 99 of 131 votes cast. The HCC endorsed the President's impeachment in September, upholding the majority of the charges against him; Zafy maintained that his impeachment was illegal, but resigned the same day. Ratsirahonana was appointed interim President by the HCC, pending an election; he formed a new interim Government that represented the majority in the National Assembly and excluded members of the UNDD. Zafy announced his intention to contest the forthcoming election, as did Ratsiraka and Ratsirahonana.

In all, 15 candidates stood in the first round of the presidential election, which proceeded peacefully on 3 November 1996; Ratsiraka (with 36.6% of the votes cast) and Zafy (with 23.4%) qualified to contest the second round. The head of Libéralisme économique et action démocratique pour la reconstruction nationale (LEADER/Fanilo), Herizo Razafimahaleo, obtained 15.1%, and Ratsirahonana 10.1%, of the votes. Razafimahaleo urged his supporters to vote for Ratsiraka. None of the unsuccessful candidates chose to support Zafy, who declared his intention, if elected, to retain Ratsirahonana (who had successfully concluded an agreement with the IMF in August) as Prime Minister; Ratsirahonana, however, refused to endorse either candidate. At the second round, which took place on 29 December, Ratsiraka narrowly won, with 50.7% of the valid votes cast, although more than 50% of the registered electorate abstained from voting. Ratsiraka was inaugurated as President on 9 February 1997. He appointed Pascal Rakotomavo (a former Minister of Finance) as Prime Minister. Rakotomavo's Government included Razafimahaleo as Deputy Prime Minister, responsible for Foreign Affairs.

In March 1998 extensive revisions to the Constitution, which provided for a 'federal-style' state, composed of six autonomous provinces, and for an increase in the powers of the President, were narrowly endorsed by 51.0% of votes cast at a referendum.

Elections to an expanded National Assembly took place in May 1998, under a new electoral law. Of the 150 seats, 82 were to be filled from single-member constituencies, with the remaining deputies to be elected by a system of proportional representation in 34 two-member constituencies. Ratsiraka's party, AREMA, performed well in the elections, winning 63 seats, while the pro-presidential LEADER/Fanilo and the Rassemblement pour le socialisme et la démocratie (RPSD) secured 16 and 11 seats, respectively. Ratsirahonana's party, Ny asa vita no ifampitsara (AVI), emerged as the strongest opposition party, with 14 seats, while Zafy's new party—Asa, Faharaminana, Fampandrasoana, Arinda (AFFA)—won six seats; independent candidates took 32 seats. The AVI and 24 independent deputies were subsequently reported to have joined the AREMA majority, leaving the AFFA and the remaining independents as the only significant parliamentary opposition. In July Tantely Andrianarivo, hitherto Deputy Prime Minister, was appointed as Prime Minister, retaining responsibility for finance and the economy. The 31-member Council of Ministers was dominated by AREMA, with the key portfolios largely unchanged; 12 new ministers were appointed.

The first local government elections—communal voting for 20,000 councillors and 1,392 mayors—since the reintroduction of the three-tier system of local government (provinces, regions and communes), under the amended Constitution of 1998, took place on 14 November 1999. The greatest successes were recorded by nominally independent candidates. Most notably, Marc Ravalomanana, the head of the country's largest agro-industrial processor, Tiko, was elected mayor of Antananarivo, while Roland Ratsiraka, a nephew of the President, was elected independent mayor of Toamasina. Provincial elections took place on 3

December 2000 to elect 336 councillors, as a preliminary step to the decentralization of certain powers to six autonomous provinces (legislation on the organization of which had been approved by the National Assembly in August). It was reported that AREMA had secured control of most of the major towns, although the AVI won a majority of seats in Antananarivo.

Disputed presidential election

A presidential election took place on 16 December 2001, contested by six candidates, including Ratsiraka, Zafy, Razafimahaleo and Ravalomanana. According to the official results, Ravalomanana secured 46.2% of the votes cast and Didier Ratsiraka 40.9%, thereby necessitating a second round of voting. However, Ravalomanana's own electoral observers disputed this result, claiming that he had won an outright victory, with 52.2% of the votes, and demanded a public comparison of voting records. The opposition was supported in these demands by international electoral observers. A recount was subsequently conducted, and on 25 January 2002 the HCC endorsed the official results and ruled that a second round of voting should take place within 30 days. Ravalomanana rejected this verdict and appealed for a national strike in protest. Some 500,000 people responded by gathering in Antananarivo; government offices, public utilities and banks ceased operations, and air traffic was suspended. Ravalomanana's supporters also closed the central bank in order to prevent Ratsiraka from withdrawing special funds from the treasury. Strike action continued, in varying forms, for eight weeks.

On 22 February 2002 Ravalomanana accelerated events by unilaterally declaring himself President at a ceremony in Antananarivo attended by 100,000 supporters. The President of the Senate immediately declared Ravalomanana's proclamation to be illegal, and it was widely condemned by the international community. In response, President Ratsiraka declared a three-month 'state of national necessity', according himself broad powers, including the right to adopt laws by decree. On 26 February Ravalomanana named Jacques Sylla, a former Minister of Foreign Affairs under Zafy's presidency, as his Prime Minister. Violent clashes erupted between supporters of Ratsiraka and Ravalomanana in Antananarivo, prompting Ratsiraka to decree martial law and appoint a military governor, Gen. Léon-Claude Raveloarison, in the capital. None the less, Ravalomanana proceeded with the formation of his rival Government in early March, while opposition supporters erected barricades against the army and set fire to the military headquarters; 17 of those appointed to Ravalomanana's administration were successfully installed in government offices, accompanied by large crowds of supporters and unopposed by the military. On the same day the governors of the five remaining provinces of the country declared their allegiance to Ratsiraka, recognizing his hometown, Toamasina (where Ratsiraka and his ministers had relocated) as a temporary 'alternative capital'. A few days later Gen. Ranjeva resigned as Minister of the Armed Forces, shortly after Ravalomanana's rival Government had taken control of his offices in Antananarivo. Gen. Raveloarison resigned as military governor of Antananarivo some three weeks after his appointment, having failed to apply martial law and order troops to end protests, on the grounds that this would have incurred deaths. Later in March 58 of Madagascar's 150 deputies attended a parliamentary session called by Ravalomanana and elected an interim President of the National Assembly.

On 10 April 2002 the Supreme Court ruled that there had been irregularities in the appointment, shortly before the presidential election, of six of the nine judges of the HCC, which had endorsed the official results; one week later the Supreme Court annulled the disputed results and ordered a recount of the votes. On the following day Ratsiraka and Ravalomanana signed a peace accord in Dakar, Senegal, where they had been holding talks under the auspices of the Organization of African Unity (OAU) and the UN, and with mediation by the Presidents of Senegal, Benin, Côte d'Ivoire and Mozambique. Following the completion of the recount, in late April, the HCC ruled that Ravalomanana had secured the presidency, with 51.5% of the votes cast, while Ratsiraka had won 35.9%. Ratsiraka refused to accept the Court's decision. Nevertheless, Ravalomanana was inaugurated as President on 6 May, largely without international recognition, and appointed a new Council of Ministers later that month. Four of the country's six provincial governors, who were loyal to Ratsiraka, subsequently threatened to secede. Heavy fighting ensued, as troops loyal to Ravalomanana conducted a military offensive against areas controlled by Ratsiraka, securing two provincial capitals, Mahajanga and Toliary, in mid-June.

Ravalomanana's presidency

In mid-June 2002 Ravalomanana dissolved the Government that he had formed in May, immediately reappointing Sylla as Prime Minister; however, despite nominating six new members of the Council of Ministers, he failed to appoint a government of national unity. At the end of June the USA recognized Ravalomanana as the legitimate leader of Madagascar; endorsement soon followed from France and, in contravention of the policy of the OAU, Senegal. Meanwhile, the OAU suspended Madagascar from its meetings, pending the staging of free and fair elections leading to the establishment of a legitimate government; this decision was upheld by the African Union (AU, see p. 183), which replaced the OAU in July. In early July Ravalomanana's government troops took control of Antsiranana and Toamasina, and Ratsiraka sought exile in France; this apparent admission of defeat allowed for an international conference to take place in Paris, France, on the donation of aid for the reconstruction of Madagascar. The new Government was in full control of the island by the middle of the month. Ravalomanana replaced the 30 presidentially appointed members of the Senate, with the approval of the HCC, despite the fact that those appointed by Ratsiraka had been appointed for a tenure of six years. In August six of the nine members of the HCC were also replaced.

In mid-October 2002 the National Assembly was dissolved, in preparation for legislative elections, brought forward from May 2003, in response to pressure from aid donors, in order to finalize the legitimacy of Ravalomanana's mandate. At the elections, which took place on 15 December 2002, Ravalomanana's party, Tiako i Madagasikara (TIM—I Love Madagascar), won 104 of the 160 seats and the pro-Ravalomanana Firaisankinam-Pirenena, an alliance of the AVI and elements of the RPSD, secured a further 22 seats; notably, 23 independent deputies were elected, and the formerly incumbent AREMA party won only three seats. In mid-January 2003 a new Government was appointed, which included 10 new ministers and was reduced in overall size from 30 to 20 ministers; the former Minister of Public Works, Jean Lahiniriko, was elected President of the National Assembly. Madagascar's suspension from meetings of the AU—hitherto the only remaining significant authority not to have recognized the new Government—was formally revoked at the organization's General Assembly in July of that year; the legitimacy of the Ravalomanana administration was thus considered finally to have been established. In August former President Ratsiraka was sentenced, in absentia, to 10 years' hard labour for the embezzlement of public funds and declared unfit for public office.

In November 2005 the Minister of the Interior and Administrative Reform, Gen. André Soja, was unexpectedly dismissed, following an alleged attempt on the President's life; he was replaced by Lt-Gen. Charles Rabemananjara. Meanwhile, in October the Government forcibly closed the Fiangonana Protestanta Vaovao eto Madagasikara (FPVM) protestant church, for illegally occupying churches of the Fiangonan' i Jesoa Kristy eto Madagasikara (FJKM), of which President Ravalomanana was a senior official, and posing a threat to public order. Some observers feared a threat to the secular status of the country, with the President declaring that he hoped for a Christian nation. The FPVM challenged the closure, but it was ruled by a civil court that only the President could overturn the decision.

A presidential election was held on 3 December 2006. According to results released by the HCC on 23 December, Ravalomanana secured 54.8% of votes cast in the first-round ballot. His closest rival was Jean Lahiniriko, who took 11.7% of the votes. The poll was generally accepted by independent observers as free and fair. President Ravalomanana was formally sworn in for a second term in office on 19 January 2007 and the following day he appointed Rabemananjara as Prime Minister. The majority of those appointed to the new Government announced later that month were members of the FJKM church, including, most notably, Harison Edmond Randriarimanana, who was appointed to head the newly created Ministry of the Economy, Planning, the Private Sector and Commerce.

At a national referendum conducted on 4 April 2007 75.3% of participants voted in favour of amendments to the Constitution, which included the abolition of autonomous powers for the six provinces. Voter turn-out was reported at just 44%. The new Constitution also adopted English as the country's third official language alongside Malagasy and French and granted extended powers to the President, including the right to legislate by decree in the event of the declaration of a state of emergency.

President Ravalomanana dissolved the National Assembly on 24 July 2007, claiming that its composition was no longer

MADAGASCAR

representative of the recently restructured regional and national administrative order. Elections to the 127-seat legislature (reduced from 160) were held on 23 September, in which the TIM secured 105 seats while independent candidates won 11. However, results in two constituencies were annulled owing to alleged voting irregularities. In October the President of the TIM, Razoharimihaja Solofonantenaina, resigned, citing ill health; Yvan Randriasandratriniony, the Minister of Decentralization and Territorial Development, was selected as his successor. Later that month, in a governmental reorganization, Cécile Manorohanta was appointed Minister of National Defence, while Bakolalao Ramanandraibe Ranaivoharivony was named as Minister of Justice and Keeper of the Seals; Haja Nirina Razafinjatovo became Minister of Finance and the Budget. In early January 2009 Desiré Rasolofomanana was appointed Minister of Internal Security and Gervais Rakotonirina Minister of the Interior.

The Haute autorité de la transition

Relations between President Ravalomanana and the Mayor of Antananarivo and the leader of the Tanora malaGasy Vonona (TGV—Determined Malagasy Youth), Andry Rajoelina, had become strained in December 2008 when Ravalomanana closed Rajoelina's television station after it broadcast a number of anti-Government programmes and an interview with former President Ratsiraka. Against a background of increasing social discontent in the country, this prompted violent protests by several thousand of Rajoelina's supporters who attacked state-owned television and radio stations and began looting businesses. A political impasse developed, with Rajoelina, speaking at an opposition rally in late January 2009, accusing the President of failing in his duties and insisting that he resign. Violence continued to escalate and sizeable areas of the capital were destroyed by fire, resulting in at least 44 deaths. Ravalomanana appealed for Rajoelina's co-operation in order to stabilize the situation; however, in early February Rajoelina, who had been gaining popular support, was dismissed from the mayoralty and replaced by Guy Randrianarisoa, resulting in days of further violent disturbances: some 28 people were killed and more than 200 injured when the security forces fired on demonstrators. Days later the Minister of Defence, Manorohanta, announced her resignation in protest at the actions of the security forces; she was replaced by Vice-Adm. Mamy Ranaivoniarivo. Meanwhile, Rajoelina declared himself President of a Haute autorité de la transition (HAT—High Transitional Authority) and named, among others, Monja Roindefo as Prime Minister and Manantsoa Masimana as Minister of the Interior. The parallel administration was not recognized by the international community but received widespread internal popular support. Nevertheless, the security forces removed a number of Rajoelina's supporters who had attempted to seize four government buildings, including those of the interior and security ministries.

Ravalomanana and Rajoelina held a series of discussions with the aim of finding a resolution to the crisis and on 21 February 2009 agreed a five-point plan, which included steps to end the violence and the inflammatory statements emanating from both parties. However, several days later Rajoelina announced that the talks had failed and urged his supporters to hold daily protests until Ravalomanana agreed to step down. Pressure continued to increase on Ravalomanana and, following a military assault on the presidential residence and the central bank on 16 March and demands from Rajoelina that the President be arrested, he dissolved the Government and resigned, relinquishing power to a military executive committee led by the most senior figure in the armed forces, Vice-Adm. Hyppolite Ramaroson. Later that day the military transferred executive powers to Rajoelina, despite the terms of the Constitution stipulating that the President should be aged 40 years or above; Rajoelina, at 34 years of age, was too young to fulfil this requirement. Although international organizations refused to acknowledge Rajoelina's authority, and what was perceived as a coup received widespread international condemnation, on 18 March the HCC endorsed Rajoelina's assumption of interim power (he was officially sworn in as President on 21 March), and on 19 March he dissolved the National Assembly and the Senate. Rajoelina announced that elections would be held within two years and that a new constitution would be drafted. Both the AU and the Southern African Development Community (SADC) subsequently suspended Madagascar's membership pending a return to constitutional order.

In late March 2009 Rajoelina appointed a 22-member Government, retaining those ministers named in February; other appointments included Col Noël Rakotonandrasana as Minister of the Armed Forces, Benja Joas Razafimahaleo as Minister of Finance and the Budget and Ny Hasina Andriamanjato as Minister of Foreign Affairs. In mid-April Ravalomanana, who had fled to exile in South Africa, named Rakotonirina as his own 'legal' Prime Minister in an attempt to regain his authority and, despite the issuing of a warrant for his arrest, pledged to return to Madagascar. Later in April Rakotonirina was arrested in Antananarivo and charged with threatening the security of the state, illegitimately declaring himself Prime Minister, instigating the destruction of property and the illegal possession of firearms. 'Consensus talks' between representatives of the HAT, Ravalomanana, Zafy and Ratsiraka took place in Anosy, in southern Madagascar, in late May, but ended without progress. In early June Ravalomanana was sentenced *in absentia* to four years in prison and fined US $70m.

Representatives from the UN, the AU, SADC and the Organisation Internationale de la Francophonie were responsible for mediation at a summit meeting held in Maputo, Mozambique, on 5–9 August 2009. Following the successful conclusion of the talks, Ravalomanana, Ratsiraka, Zafy and Rajoelina agreed upon a Transitional Charter (Charte de la transition) that was to remain in place for a maximum duration of 15 months, following which presidential and legislative elections would be held. Furthermore, according to the Charter, which provided for the establishment of a bicameral transitional legislature, a National Union Government of Transition (NUGT) was to be established, comprising a Prime Minister, three Deputy Prime Ministers and 28 ministers. The Prime Minister was to be selected by consensus and officially appointed by Rajoelina, who, in his capacity as President of the Transition, would exercise the functions of Head of State. A new constitution was to be drafted, thus bringing an end to the Third Republic.

However, on 5 September 2009 Rajoelina unilaterally, and in contravention of the Maputo accord, named Roindefo as Prime Minister; he subsequently announced the composition of the NUGT. Both decisions were rejected and condemned by the three former Presidents, who declared their determination to implement a power-sharing deal and that they no longer recognized the authority of Rajoelina. Protests in Antananarivo were violently dispersed by the security forces, and several international organizations, including the AU and SADC, expressed their discontent at the violation of the Maputo power-sharing agreement. Negotiations recommenced and the following month Eugène Regis Mangalaza was chosen by consensus as Prime Minister, although this decision provoked further division as a result of an increase in the powers granted to the premiership under the new accord. Furthermore, Roindefo initially refused to relinquish the post of Prime Minister, claiming that the decision to appoint Mangalaza had not been taken by all four factions.

By November 2009, following further negotiations in Addis Ababa, Ethiopia, a tentative power-sharing agreement (which was to supplement the Maputo accord) had been reached under which executive decisions were to be undertaken jointly by the President and two Vice-Presidents. The agreement also provided for the formation of a 31-member government to be led by a Prime Minister, supported by three Deputy Prime Ministers. The proposed appointment of Emmanuel Rakotovahiny, from Zafy's AFFA, and Fetison Andrianirina of the TIM as Vice-Presidents caused concern when considering the functions of these new posts; however, President Rajoelina reiterated that the two positions would share responsibility for roles that would have been carried out by the previously envisioned single post of Vice-President. In early December Ravalomanana, Ratsiraka and Zafy proceeded with further negotiations in Maputo regarding the composition of the proposed transitional administration, despite Rajoelina's refusal to attend. The three former Presidents subsequently announced that they had concluded arrangements regarding the formation of a new unity government. However, Rajoelina stated that he would no longer participate in power-sharing negotiations, and refused permission for aircraft carrying the three men and their delegations to land in Madagascar. On 18 December Mangalaza was dismissed by Rajoelina, who initially named Manorohanta as his replacement. Nevertheless, that appointment was almost immediately revoked and Col (later Gen.) Albert Camille Vital was installed as Prime Minister.

Despite dissatisfaction among international organizations and his domestic political rivals, Rajoelina continued to reject external mediation attempts and any proposals for a power-sharing government, insisting instead on holding legislative elections in March 2010. In January the AU requested that the elections be postponed; however, it was not until the UN wrote to the NUGT, requesting continued dialogue on the establishment of a power-sharing government, that Rajoelina agreed to postpone the elections, initially until May. In February Andriamanjato, the Deputy Prime Minister, responsible for Foreign Affairs, resigned, citing increasing dissension within the NUGT. Shortly afterwards the AU announced that it would impose sanctions on Madagascar if the resolutions of the Maputo and Addis Ababa power-sharing agreements were not implemented by mid-March. Ramaroson was appointed as Andriamanjato's replacement in late February.

The AU's attempts to persuade Rajoelina to attend further negotiations in Addis Ababa in early March 2010 were unsuccessful, and in mid-March the AU duly imposed sanctions, including the freezing of assets and diplomatic isolation, on 109 individuals, including all members of the NUGT and the HAT. In response, Rajoelina announced that the HAT would seek to charge Ravalomanana with 'corruption, threatening state security and plotting high treason with foreign factions'. Furthermore, Ratsiraka and Zafy would be barred from returning to Madagascar and members of the three former Presidents' political parties would be prevented from leaving the country and have their assets frozen. Meanwhile, in February Rajoelina announced the creation of a committee of inquiry into the violent disturbances of February 2009, which was to be led by Jean de Dieu Maharante, the Minister of Stockbreeding in the NUGT.

Vital dismissed Rakotonandrasana from his position as Minister of the Armed Forces in early April 2010, amid rumours of plans to stage a coup. (Some 19 people, including a number of army officers, were subsequently detained by the authorities.) Later in April senior military officials presented Rajoelina with an ultimatum to find a suitable solution to the country's political crisis by the end of the month. Shortly afterwards Rajoelina pledged to appoint a new unity government and indicated his willingness to engage in further talks with Ravalomanana. Discussions between the two, who were also joined by Zafy and Ratsiraka, commenced in late April in Pretoria, South Africa, but ended inconclusively after two days. On 7 May the army retracted its ultimatum, and on 12 May Rajoelina confirmed that he would not contest a presidential election, which was scheduled to be held on 30 November, following a referendum on constitutional reform on 26 August and legislative elections on 30 September. On 25 May Rajoelina announced the formation of a new 32-member Government; however, the neutrality of the new administration (which included five new members of the military) was immediately questioned by senior opposition figures; the new ministers included Gen. André Lucien Rakotoarimasy as Minister of the Armed Forces and Christine Razanamahasoa as Minister of Justice and Keeper of the Seals. Meanwhile, on 20 May several people were killed in a confrontation between dissident elements of the gendarmerie (with the support of several hundred anti-Government protesters) and forces loyal to Rajoelina, who accused Ravalomanana of instigating the unrest.

Recent developments: constitutional referendum and transitional programme

In late June 2010 the head of the Commission électorale nationale indépendante (CENI) announced that the referendum would be postponed, since the draft constitution had not been finalized. On 11 August, following discussions with about 100 political parties, the Government signed an agreement rescheduling the constitutional referendum for 17 November 2010 and legislative elections for 16 March 2011, to be followed by the first round of a presidential election on 4 May; under the new accord, Rajoelina would continue to hold office as head of the HAT until the inauguration of the next president, while the HAT was to be reconstituted as a transitional parliament. (However, the agreement failed to address several outstanding issues of contention and the political movements of the three former Presidents, Ravalomanana, Ratsiraka and Zafy, which failed to participate in the discussions, denounced what they considered to be the imposition of another unilateral solution.) At the end of August Ravalomanana was sentenced *in absentia* to life imprisonment for the killing of at least 30 people by his presidential guards in February 2009. In September 2010 the Government organized a conference of representatives of political parties and civil society, which was to resolve issues related to the implementation of the August agreement; delegates endorsed a proposal that Rajoelina remain as Head of State but appoint a consensus prime minister who was not from his native region, and also supported the replacement of mayors and regional authorities by provisional bodies. On 7 October the HCC approved a decree by Rajoelina establishing a Parlement de la Transition. Accordingly, on 11 October a 256-member lower parliamentary chamber, the Congrès de la Transition, was installed, with representation assigned according to the arrangement established in the accord reached in August: notably, a gathering of all the political parties and associations that participated in the drafting of the agreement, known as l'Espace de concertation des partis politiques (ESCOPOL), was allocated 62 seats, the TIM 52, the TGV 52 and a grouping of parties supporting Rajoelina, the Union des démocrates et républicains—Fanovana (UDR—Fanovana) 29. On 12 October a 90-member upper chamber, the Conseil Supérieur de la Transition, took office; the deputies included 25 representatives of the UDR—Fanovana, 21 of the TIM, 18 of ESCOPOL and 10 of the TGV.

A draft constitution, which included requirements that presidential candidates be at least 35 years of age (rather than the previous minimum of 40 years) and have lived in Madagascar for at least six months prior to the elections, was submitted to the delayed national referendum on 17 November 2010. On the same day some 20 disaffected senior army officers, led by Rakotonandrasana, staged a coup attempt, announcing from a military barracks near Antananarivo that the Government had been overthrown. However, prominent members of the Government and military announced their support for Rajoelina, and on 21 November troops loyal to the HAT stormed the barracks, arresting a number of the officers for threatening state security. Later that month it was announced that a former International Court of Justice judge, Raymond Ranjeva, had also been detained, owing to his connection with the rebels. Two days after the referendum, the CENI released official results, according to which the new Constitution had been endorsed by about 74.2% of votes cast, with a voter turn-out of 52.6% (after the opposition urged a boycott). On 23 November the HCC upheld the results of the referendum, despite opposition complaints of electoral irregularities. The new Constitution of the Fourth Republic of Madagascar entered into effect on 11 December. Later that month an SADC mission began to mediate a resumption of negotiations between the authorities and the opposition. In January 2011 Ravalomanana submitted a legal complaint to the judicial authorities against the instigators of the effective coup in March 2009.

On 9 March 2011 a new transitional programme proposed by the SADC mediators was signed by eight of the 11 principal political groups, but rejected by the parties of Ravalomanana, Ratsiraka and Zafy, which strenuously opposed the legitimacy conferred on Rajoelina's presidency. Under the new plan, Rajoelina was permitted to remain in office pending elections (for which no dates were specified), and to appoint a consensus Prime Minister proposed by the signatory groups, while the Parlement de la Transition and the CENI were to be expanded. On the following day the Government of Prime Minister Vital resigned; however, on 16 March Rajoelina reappointed Vital as premier, despite the objections of the three main opposition parties that he failed to meet the consensus criteria of the agreement. On 26 March a new, 32-member administration, termed a Government of national unity, was established under the transitional programme; nine former government members retained their posts, among them the ministers responsible for finance and the budget, mining and hydrocarbons, justice, and defence, although members of Ravalomanana's TIM were also included.

Foreign Affairs

Madagascar's foreign policy is officially non-aligned: while it formerly maintained close links with communist countries (particularly the People's Republic of China, the Democratic People's Republic of Korea and the former USSR), the Zafy Government established relations with Israel, South Africa and the Republic of Korea. Relations with France have been affected by disputes over compensation for nationalized French assets and over the continuing French claim to the Iles Glorieuses, north of Madagascar, and three other islets in the Mozambique Channel. In 1980 the UN voted in favour of restoring all the disputed islets to Madagascar. In early 1986 the Government announced the extension of Madagascar's exclusive economic zone to include the Iles Glorieuses and the three islets. In 1997 government announcements regarding future privatization plans in Madagascar prompted renewed appeals from France for compensation for nationalized French assets. In response, the Government allocated some 50,000m. francs MG as initial compensation in

MADAGASCAR

the budget for 1998. In February 2000 it was agreed that the Iles Glorieuses would be co-administered by France, Madagascar and Mauritius, without prejudice to the question of sovereignty. In April 2004, during a state visit to Madagascar by Prime Minister Paul Bérenger of Mauritius, political and economic co-operation agreements between the two countries were signed.

Relations with China were strengthened in January 1999, during a visit by Vice-President Hu Jintao; agreements were signed on the expansion of bilateral economic relations and China's provision of preferential loans to Madagascar. In September 2000 the representative office for Taiwan in Madagascar was closed down, following an official visit by the Malagasy Minister of Foreign Affairs to China. (It was claimed that this was carried out by the Government in support of the 'one China' policy; however, the Taiwanese claimed that the office had never functioned effectively.) Following the suspension of US and European Union donor assistance programmes in Madagascar in response to Andry Rajoelina's assumption of the presidency in March 2009, the transitional Government announced a number of major infrastructure projects in late 2010 that were to be undertaken in collaboration with Chinese companies.

CONSTITUTION AND GOVERNMENT

Under an August 2010 agreement between the Government and about 100 political parties, a Parlement de la Transition, comprising a 256-member lower chamber, the Congrès de la Transition, and a 90-member upper chamber, the Conseil Supérieur de la Transition, was installed in October and was to remain in place pending legislative elections. On 17 November 2010 the Constitution of the Fourth Republic of Madagascar was approved at a national referendum by some 74% of the participating electorate. The President of the Republic is the Head of State and is elected by direct universal suffrage for a five-year mandate, renewable only once. Candidates for the presidency must be at least 35 years of age and have resided in Madagascar for at least six months prior to the date of the submission of candidacies. The President nominates a Prime Minister from the party or group of parties which secures the largest number of seats in the Assemblée nationale. The President also nominates members of the Government, upon the advice of the Prime Minister. Members of the Assemblée nationale are elected by direct universal suffrage for five-year terms. The Constitution also provides for the election of members to the Sénat, each of whom serves a five-year mandate.

REGIONAL AND INTERNATIONAL CO-OPERATION

Madagascar is a member of the Indian Ocean Commission (see p. 448) and of the Common Market for Eastern and Southern Africa (COMESA, see p. 228). In August 2005 Madagascar joined the Southern African Development Community (SADC, see p. 420), although its membership of that organization and of the African Union (see p. 183) was suspended in 2009.

Madagascar became a member of the UN in 1960 and was admitted to the World Trade Organization (WTO, see p. 430) in 1995. Madagascar participates in the Group of 77 (G77, see p. 447) developing countries.

ECONOMIC AFFAIRS

In 2008, according to estimates by the World Bank, Madagascar's gross national income (GNI), measured at average 2006–08 prices, was US $7,932m., equivalent to about $420 per head (or $1,050 per head on an international purchasing-power parity basis). During 2000–09, it was estimated, the population increased at an average annual rate of 2.8%, while gross domestic product (GDP) per head increased, in real terms, by an average of 0.5% per year. Overall GDP increased, in real terms, at an average annual rate of 3.4% in 2000–09; GDP increased by 0.4% in 2009.

In 2009 the agricultural sector (including forestry and fishing) accounted for an estimated 28.5% of GDP according to the African Development Bank (AfDB); the sector employed an estimated 82.0% of the economically active population in 2005 and, according to FAO, engaged 69.6% of the total labour force in mid-2011. Rice, the staple food crop, is produced on some 50% of cultivated land. Since 1972, however, imports of rice have been necessary to supplement domestic production. The most important cash crops are spices (which accounted for an estimated 9.0% of total export revenue in 2009). Following a long drought in 2003, vanilla production was estimated to have halved in that year, leading to a dramatic escalation in world prices and the development of the crop in other countries, as well as an increase in synthetic alternatives; however, prices had declined significantly at the beginning of 2005, having a negative impact on producers. Sugar, coconuts, tropical fruits, sweet potatoes and maize are also cultivated. Cattle-farming is important. Sea fishing by coastal fishermen (particularly for crustaceans) is being expanded, while vessels from the European Union fish for tuna and prawns in Madagascar's exclusive maritime zone, within 200 nautical miles (370 km) of the coast, in return for compensation. According to World Bank figures, agricultural GDP increased by an average of 2.2% per year in 2000–09; the sector's GDP increased by 3.2% in 2009.

Industry (including mining, manufacturing, construction and power) contributed an estimated 14.4% of Madagascar's GDP in 2009, according to the AfDB, and employed 3.4% of the employed labour force in 2005. According to the World Bank, industrial GDP increased at an average annual rate of 4.1% in 2000–09; the sector's GDP increased by 10.4% in 2009.

The mining sector contributed only 0.2% of GDP in 2009, according to the AfDB, and engaged 0.2% of the employed labour force in 2005. However, Madagascar has sizeable deposits of a wide range of minerals, principally chromite (chromium ore), which, with graphite and mica, is exported, together with small quantities of semi-precious stones. A major project to resume the mining of ilmenite (titanium ore) in south-eastern Madagascar, which would generate US $550m. over a 30-year period, received approval from the Government in 2001. Construction of the mining facilities and rehabilitation of a deep-sea multi-purpose port at Ehoala, near Fort Dauphin (Tolagnaro), was completed in early 2009. The facility began ilmenite production operations in January, and was expected to produce 750,000 metric tons per year by 2012. Other potential mineral projects included the exploitation of an estimated 100m. tons of bauxite in the south-east of the country, and of nickel and cobalt deposits in Ambatovy, central Madagascar. The presence of significant grades of the platinum group of metals was confirmed, as well as copper and nickel, in 2004. Renewed interest was also shown in that year in reviving the country's long-inactive uranium mines. An agreement with the People's Republic of China in 2005 for the export of chrome ore held significant potential for the development of that sector. In late 2007 it was announced that a large nickel mining project was to begin production by 2010, with annual output expected to reach 60,000 tons of nickel and 5,600 tons of cobalt. The project was expected to provide employment for some 5,000 workers. In early 2008 a pilot project in the north-west produced the first oil in the country for some 60 years, improving Madagascar's prospects for generating export revenue.

According to the AfDB, manufacturing contributed 18.7% of GDP in 2009 and engaged some 2.8% of the employed labour force in 2005. The petroleum refinery at Toamasina, using imported petroleum, provides a significant share of export revenue. Other important branches of manufacturing are textiles and clothing, food products, beverages and chemical products. The introduction of a new investment code in 1990 and the creation of a number of export-processing zones achieved some success in attracting foreign private investment, particularly in the manufacturing branches of textiles, cement, fertilizers and pharmaceuticals. According to the World Bank, manufacturing GDP increased at an average annual rate of 4.5% in 2000–09; the GDP of the sector increased by 8.2% in 2009.

Construction contributed an estimated 4.2% of Madagascar's GDP in 2009, and employed 0.1% of the employed labour force in 2005.

Energy generation depends on imports of petroleum (which accounted for an estimated 10.1% of the value of total imports in 2009) to fuel thermal installations, although hydroelectric resources have also been developed, and accounted for an estimated 62.0% of electricity production in 2008.

The services sector accounted for an estimated 57.1% of GDP in 2009, according to the AfDB, and engaged some 14.6% of the employed labour force in 2005. An information communication technologies business park was under development in Antananarivo as part of an effort to diversify Madagascar's economic growth. In March 2010 Madagascar was connected to the Eastern Africa Submarine Cable System, a high bandwidth fibre optic cable that links countries on Africa's eastern coast to the rest of the world, and would enable the transfer of data at speeds 40 times faster than the hitherto available dial-up connection. This was expected to allow the development of service outsourcing activities on the island. According to the World Bank, the GDP of

MADAGASCAR

the services sector increased by an average of 4.8% per year in 2000–09; services GDP increased by 8.8% in 2009.

In 2005 Madagascar recorded a visible trade deficit of US $592m., and there was a deficit of $626m. on the current account of the balance of payments. The principal source of imports in 2009 was Thailand (18.3%); other major suppliers were the People's Republic of China, France and Belgium. France was the principal market for exports (accounting for 33.1% of exports in that year); the USA and Germany were also important purchasers. The principal exports in 2009 were clothing, spices and crustaceans; food and live animals constituted 26.0% of the value of total exports. The principal imports in that year were basic manufactures, machinery and transport equipment, mineral fuels and food and live animals.

Madagascar's overall budget deficit for 2007 (excluding grants) was estimated at 1,265,800m. ariary. Madagascar's general government gross debt was 5,669.96m. ariary in 2009, equivalent to 33.7% of GDP. Madagascar's external debt totalled US $2,086m. at the end of 2008, of which $1,722m. was public and publicly guaranteed debt. The cost of debt-servicing in 2005 was estimated to be equivalent to 5.8% of the value of exports of goods, services and income. The annual rate of inflation averaged 10.2% in 2000–10; consumer prices increased by 9.2% in 2010. About 2.8% of the labour force was unemployed in 2005.

Economic activity in Madagascar was impeded by repeated instances of political instability during the 2000s. The economy was severely affected by the suspension of Madagascar's participation in the Southern African Development Community (see p. 420) and the African Union (AU, see p. 183), and of economic co-operation with international financial institutions, following the removal of President Marc Ravalomanana in March 2009. In May the USA and the World Bank suspended Madagascar from the Millennium Challenge Corporation, while in December the former also suspended trade benefits granted to Madagascar under the African Growth and Opportunity Act. The events of 2009–10 appeared likely to reverse much of the progress made by the country with the assistance of the IMF and the World Bank during the mid-2000s when international creditors had restructured the country's significant external debt. In September 2008, following the fourth and fifth reviews under the three-year Poverty Reduction and Growth Facility, the IMF had acknowledged continued progress in meeting the majority of its objectives and had supported the Malagasy authorities' request for increasing the country's quota under the arrangement by 15% to guard against the impact of the global financial crisis and related increases in fuel and food prices. Following his assumption of the presidency in March 2009, Andry Rajoelina froze all mining contracts and announced a review of the sector. In March 2010 the AU imposed sanctions against members of the transitional authorities, following their failure to implement power-sharing arrangements, and in June the European Union suspended for a further year a disbursement of €600m. in budgetary and development aid to Madagascar, owing to the Government's failure to adhere to democratic principles. Despite the negative impact of the political instability on foreign investment, in late 2010 Rajoelina (who had pledged not to contest a presidential election scheduled for May 2011) announced a number of significant infrastructure agreements, principally with China International Fund and China Sonangol. Several large projects, which included the establishment of a national train service and a metropolitan tramway system for Antananarivo, the construction of a new cement factory, and the rehabilitation of the national airline, Air Madagascar, were to be undertaken by the Chinese companies, in exchange for interests in mining natural resources. In early 2011 the World Food Programme reported food shortages affecting some 720,000 people in the south of the country, following successive years of crop failure owing to drought.

PUBLIC HOLIDAYS

2012: 1 January (New Year), 29 March (Martyr's Day, Commemoration of 1947 Rebellion), 9 April (Easter Monday), 1 May (Labour Day), 17 May (Ascension Day), 27 May (Whitsun), 25 May (Organization of African Unity Day), 26 June (Independence Day), 15 August (Assumption), 1 November (All Saints' Day), 25 December (Christmas).

Statistical Survey

Source (unless otherwise stated): Institut National de la Statistique Malagache, BP 485, Anosy Tana, 101 Antananarivo; tel. (20) 2227418; e-mail dridnstat@wanadoo.mg; internet www.instat.mg; Ministry of the Economy and Industry, Bâtiment Commerce, Ambohidahy, 101 Antananarivo; internet www.mepspc.gov.mg.

Area and Population

AREA, POPULATION AND DENSITY

Area (sq km)	587,295*
Population (census results)	
1974–75†	7,603,790
1–19 August 1993	
Males	5,991,171
Females	6,100,986
Total	12,092,157
Population (UN estimates at mid-year)‡	
2009	19,625,029
2010	20,146,442
2011	20,675,002
Density (per sq km) at mid-2011	35.2

* 226,756 sq miles.
† The census took place in three stages: in provincial capitals on 1 December 1974; in Antananarivo and remaining urban areas on 17 February 1975; and in rural areas on 1 June 1975.
‡ Source: UN, *World Population Prospects: The 2008 Revision*.

POPULATION BY AGE AND SEX
(UN estimates at mid-2011)

	Males	Females	Total
0–14	4,367,202	4,332,954	8,700,156
15–64	5,634,619	5,711,983	11,346,602
65 and over	291,962	336,282	628,244
Total	10,293,783	10,381,219	20,675,002

Source: UN, *World Population Prospects: The 2008 Revision*.

PRINCIPAL ETHNIC GROUPS
(estimated population, 1974)

Merina (Hova)	1,993,000	Sakalava	470,156*
Betsimisaraka	1,134,000	Antandroy	412,500
Betsileo	920,600	Antaisaka	406,468*
Tsimihety	558,100		

* 1972 figure.

MADAGASCAR

PRINCIPAL TOWNS
(population at 1993 census)

Antananarivo (capital)	1,103,304	Mahajanga (Majunga)	106,780
Toamasina (Tamatave)	137,782	Toliary (Tuléar)	80,826
Antsirabé	126,062	Antsiranana (Diégo-Suarez)	59,040
Fianarantsoa	109,248		

2001 (estimated population, incl. Renivohitra and Avaradrano): Antananarivo 1,111,132.

Mid-2010 (incl. suburbs, UN estimate): Antananarivo 1,879,013 (Source: UN, *World Urbanization prospects: The 2009 Revision*).

BIRTHS AND DEATHS

	2007	2008	2009
Birth rate (per 1,000)	36.5	35.9	35.3
Death rate (per 1,000)	9.4	9.2	8.9

Source: African Development Bank.

Life expectancy (years at birth, WHO estimates): 60 (males 58; females 61) in 2008 (Source: WHO, *World Health Statistics*).

ECONOMICALLY ACTIVE POPULATION
(labour force survey, '000 persons)

	2005
Agriculture, hunting and forestry	7,745.3
Fishing	99.0
Mining and quarrying	18.8
Manufacturing	267.5
Electricity, gas and water	27.5
Construction	13.0
Wholesale and retail trade; repair of motor vehicles, motor cycles and personal and household goods	470.5
Hotels and restaurants	63.9
Transport, storage and communications	86.3
Financial intermediation	4.1
Public administration and defence; compulsory social security	202.4
Education	44.5
Health and social work	9.9
Other community, social and personal service activities	517.7
Total employed	**9,570.4**
Unemployed	274.3
Total labour force	**9,844.7**
Males	4,942.2
Females	4,902.4

Source: ILO.

Mid-2011 (estimates in '000): Agriculture, etc. 7,268; Total labour force 10,437 (Source: FAO).

Health and Welfare

KEY INDICATORS

Total fertility rate (children per woman, 2008)	4.7
Under-5 mortality rate (per 1,000 live births, 2008)	106
HIV/AIDS (% of persons aged 15–49, 2007)	0.1
Physicians (per 1,000 head, 2004)	0.3
Hospital beds (per 1,000 head, 2005)	0.3
Health expenditure (2007): US $ per head (PPP)	41
Health expenditure (2007): % of GDP	4.1
Health expenditure (2007): public (% of total)	66.2
Access to water (% of persons, 2008)	41
Access to sanitation (% of persons, 2008)	11
Total carbon dioxide emissions ('000 metric tons, 2007)	2,249.7
Carbon dioxide emissions per head (metric tons, 2007)	0.1
Human Development Index (2010): ranking	135
Human Development Index (2010): value	0.435

For sources and definitions, see explanatory note on p. vi.

Agriculture

PRINCIPAL CROPS
('000 metric tons)

	2005	2006	2007*
Rice, paddy	3,393	3,485	3,000
Maize	391	495	370
Potatoes	215	221	225
Sweet potatoes	879	869	890
Cassava (Manioc)	2,964	2,359	2,400
Taro (Cocoyam)*	230	235	240
Sugar cane	2,446	2,691	2,600
Beans, dry	78	88	88
Groundnuts, in shell	61	61	42
Coconuts*	86	90	95
Oil palm fruit*	21	21	21
Tomatoes*	22	22	22
Bananas*	310	315	325
Oranges*	87	88	90
Guavas, mangoes and mangosteens*	210	215	220
Avocados*	23	24	25
Pineapples*	51	52	54
Cashewapple*	68	69	70
Coffee, green	56	62	67
Vanilla	3	3	3
Cinnamon (Canella)*	2	2	2
Cloves*	10	10	10
Sisal*	17	17	17
Tobacco, unmanufactured	2	2*	2*

* FAO estimate(s).

2008: Figures assumed to be unchanged from 2007 (FAO estimates). Note: Data were not available for individual crops in 2009.

Aggregate production ('000 metric tons, may include official, semi-official or estimated data): Total cereals 3,795 in 2005, 3,991 in 2006, 3,382 in 2007–09; Total roots and tubers 4,287 in 2005, 3,683 in 2006, 3,805 in 2007–09; Total vegetables (incl. melons) 344 in 2005, 354 in 2006, 364 in 2007–09; Total fruits (excl. melons) 985 in 2005, 1,007 in 2006, 1,040 in 2007–09.

Source: FAO.

LIVESTOCK
('000 head, year ending September)

	2006	2007*	2008*
Cattle	9,573	9,600	9,700
Pigs	1,300*	1,350	1,360
Sheep	712	715	720
Goats	1,249	1,250	1,260
Chickens*	24,727	25,000	25,500
Ducks*	3,873	3,900	3,900
Geese and guinea fowls*	3,000	3,000	3,000
Turkeys*	2,000	2,000	2,000

* FAO estimate(s).

Note: Data were not available for 2009.

Source: FAO.

LIVESTOCK PRODUCTS
('000 metric tons, FAO estimates)

	2006	2007	2008
Cattle meat	134.3	134.6	150.5
Sheep meat	2.7	2.7	2.8
Goat meat	6.3	6.3	6.4
Pig meat	52.5	54.3	54.6
Chicken meat	36.5	36.6	36.8
Duck meat	11.0	11.0	11.0
Goose meat	12.6	12.6	12.6
Turkey meat	8.4	8.4	8.4
Cows' milk	520	530	530
Hen eggs	14.9	14.9	14.9
Other eggs	4.6	4.6	4.5
Honey	4.0	4.0	4.0

2009: Figures assumed to be unchanged from 2008 (FAO estimates).

Source: FAO.

MADAGASCAR

Forestry

ROUNDWOOD REMOVALS
('000 cubic metres, excl. bark)

	2006	2007	2008
Sawlogs, veneer logs and logs for sleepers*	193	222	267
Pulpwood	23*	22	10
Fuel wood*	13,100	13,100	13,100
Total*	13,316	13,344	13,377

* FAO estimate(s).

2009: Figures assumed to be unchanged from 2008 (FAO estimates).
Source: FAO.

SAWNWOOD PRODUCTION
('000 cubic metres, incl. railway sleepers)

	2006	2007	2008
Coniferous (softwood)	1	2	42
Broadleaved (hardwood)	886*	886*	50
Total	887	888	92

* FAO estimate.

2009: Figures assumed to be unchanged from 2008 (FAO estimates).
Source: FAO.

Fishing

('000 metric tons, live weight)

	2006	2007	2008
Capture*	133.7	147.8	120.5
Cichlids*	23.5	23.4	23.4
Other freshwater fishes*	5.0	4.9	4.9
Narrow-barred Spanish mackerel	12.0	12.0	12.0
Other marine fishes	75.0	82.4	65.3
Shrimps and prawns	9.4	16.6	6.7
Aquaculture*	11.2	11.3	9.6
Giant tiger prawn	8.5	8.5	6.8*
Total catch*	144.9	159.1	130.0

* FAO estimate(s).

Note: Figures exclude aquatic plants ('000 metric tons, capture only): 5.3 in 2006; 3.7 in 2007–08. Also excluded are crocodiles, recorded by number rather than weight, and shells. The number of Nile crocodiles caught was: 6,660 in 2006; 5,550 in 2007; 2,640 in 2008.

Source: FAO.

Mining

(metric tons)

	2006	2007	2008
Chromite*	132,335	122,260	84,000
Salt (marine)†	75,000	75,000	75,000
Graphite (natural)	4,857	5,000†	5,000†
Mica‡	1,071	1,349	1,233

* Figures refer to gross weight. The estimated chromium content is 27%.
† Estimate(s).
‡ Figures refer to exports.
Source: US Geological Survey.

Industry

SELECTED PRODUCTS
(metric tons, unless otherwise indicated)

	1999	2000	2001
Raw sugar	61,370	62,487	67,917
Beer ('000 hectolitres)	610.1	645.5	691.7
Cigarettes	3,839	4,139	4,441
Woven cotton fabrics (million sq metres)	20.4	23.3	29.6
Leather footwear ('000 pairs)	460	570	568
Plastic footwear ('000 pairs)	375	303	291
Paints	1,918	1,487	1,554
Soap	15,884	15,385	15,915
Motor spirit—petrol ('000 cu metres)	98.0	122.6	128.3
Kerosene ('000 cu metres)	65.0	65.2	75.1
Gas-diesel (distillate fuel) oil ('000 cu metres)	119.0	150.4	150.2
Residual fuel oils ('000 cu metres)	198.8	225.7	247.2
Cement	45,701	50,938	51,882
Electric energy (million kWh)*	721.3	779.8	833.9

* Production by the state-owned utility only, excluding electricity generated by industries for their own use.

2002: Raw sugar 35,000 metric tons; Beer 439,000 hectolitres; Woven cotton fabrics 20m. sq metres; Soap 14,100 metric tons; Motor spirit—petrol 112,000 metric tons (estimate); Kerosene 66,000 metric tons (estimate); Gas-diesel (distillate fuel) oil 57,000 metric tons (estimate); Residual fuel oils 77,000 metric tons (estimate); Electric energy 790m. kWh (Source: mainly UN, *Industrial Commodity Statistics Yearbook*).

2003: Raw sugar 35,000 metric tons; Motor spirit—petrol 113,000 metric tons; Kerosene 67,000 metric tons; Gas-diesel (distillate fuel) oil 57,000 metric tons; Residual fuel oils 77,000 metric tons; Electric energy 900m. kWh (Source: mainly UN, *Industrial Commodity Statistics Yearbook*).

2004: Raw sugar 26,000 metric tons; Motor spirit—petrol 113,000 metric tons; Kerosene 67,000 metric tons; Gas-diesel (distillate fuel) oil 57,000 metric tons; Residual fuel oils 77,000 metric tons; Electric energy 990m. kWh (Source: UN, *Industrial Commodity Statistics Yearbook*).

2005: Raw sugar 27,000 metric tons; Motor spirit—petrol 114,000 metric tons; Kerosene 68,000 metric tons; Gas-diesel (distillate fuel) oil 58,000 metric tons; Residual fuel oils 78,000 metric tons; Electric energy 1,035m. kWh (Source: UN, *Industrial Commodity Statistics Yearbook*).

2006: Raw sugar 20,000 metric tons; Electric energy 990m. kWh (estimate) (Source: UN Industrial Commodity Statistics Database).

2007: Raw sugar 20,000 metric tons; Electric energy 935m. kWh (estimate) (Source: UN Industrial Commodity Statistics Database).

Cement ('000 metric tons, estimates): 170 in 2004; 150 in 2005; 150 in 2006; 270 in 2007; 460 in 2008 (estimate) (Source: US Geological Survey).

Finance

CURRENCY AND EXCHANGE RATES

Monetary Units
5 iraimbilanja = 1 ariary.

Sterling, Dollar and Euro Equivalents (31 December 2010)
£1 sterling = 3,359.75 ariary;
US $1 = 2,146.12 ariary;
€1 = 2,867.65 ariary;
100,000 ariary = £2.98 = $4.66 = €3.49.

Average Exchange Rate (ariary per US $)
2008 1,708.4
2009 1,956.2
2010 2,090.0

Note: A new currency, the ariary, was introduced on 31 July 2003 to replace the franc malgache (franc MG). The old currency was to remain legal tender until 30 November. Some figures in this survey are still given in terms of francs MG.

MADAGASCAR

BUDGET
('000 million ariary, central government operations)

Revenue and grants	2005	2006*	2007†
Tax revenue	1,020.0	1,259.2	1,523.8
Non-tax revenue	82.8	80.8	28.3
Grants	579.5	5,580.0	699.3
Total	1,682.3	6,920.0	2,251.4

Expenditure	2005	2006*	2007†
Current expenditure	1,107.2	1,240.6	1,411.1
Budgetary expenditure	1,021.5	1,226.2	1,397.5
Wages and salaries	456.4	596.9	721.0
Other non-interest expenditure	298.5	375.9	455.3
Interest payments	266.6	253.4	221.1
Treasury operations (net)	84.2	12.5	13.7
Counterpart funds-financed operations	1.5	1.9	—
Capital expenditure	1,038.3	1,290.3	1,406.8
Total	2,145.5	2,530.9	2,817.9

* Provisional.
† Forecasts.

2008 ('000 million ariary, projections): *Revenue:* Tax revenue 1,931.5 (Domestic taxes 920.2, Taxes on foreign trade 1,011.4); Other revenue 46.9; Total 1,978.4 (excl. grants 788.0). *Expenditure:* Current expenditure 1,840.7 (Wages and salaries 815.5, Interest payments 139.7, Treasury operations 127.3, Others 758.2); Capital expenditure 1,581.5 (Domestically financed 468.1; Foreign-financed 1,113.5); Total 3,422.3 (Source: IMF, *Republic of Madagascar: Fourth Review Under the Three-Year Arrangement Under the Poverty Reduction and Growth Facility and Request for Waiver of Performance Criteria, Modification of Performance Criteria, and Augmentation of Access—Staff Report; Staff Supplement and Statement; Press Release on the Executive Board Discussion; and Statement by the Executive Director for Republic of Madagascar*—July 2008).

2009 ('000 million ariary, projections): *Revenue:* Tax revenue 2,322.4 (Domestic taxes 1,099.2, Taxes on foreign trade 1,223.2); Other revenue 54.2; Total 2,376.5 (excl. grants 863.1). *Expenditure:* Current expenditure 1,977.5 (Wages and salaries 941.0, Interest payments 157.7, Treasury operations 146.9, Others 732.0); Capital expenditure 1,816.7 (Domestically financed 690.0, Foreign-financed 1,126.7); Total 3,794.2 (Source: IMF, *Republic of Madagascar: Fourth Review Under the Three-Year Arrangement Under the Poverty Reduction and Growth Facility and Request for Waiver of Performance Criteria, Modification of Performance Criteria, and Augmentation of Access—Staff Report; Staff Supplement and Statement; Press Release on the Executive Board Discussion; and Statement by the Executive Director for Republic of Madagascar*—July 2008).

2010 ('000 million ariary, projections): *Revenue:* Tax revenue 2,826.6 (Domestic taxes 1,373.6, Taxes on foreign trade 1,453.0); Other revenue 63.7; Total 2,890.3 (excl. grants 974.6). *Expenditure:* Current expenditure 2,310.9 (Wages and salaries 1,122.8, Interest payments 153.1, Treasury operations 171.9, Others 863.2); Capital expenditure 2,159.8 (Domestically financed 872.9, Foreign-financed 1,286.9); Total 4,470.7 (Source: IMF, *Republic of Madagascar: Fourth Review Under the Three-Year Arrangement Under the Poverty Reduction and Growth Facility and Request for Waiver of Performance Criteria, Modification of Performance Criteria, and Augmentation of Access—Staff Report; Staff Supplement and Statement; Press Release on the Executive Board Discussion; and Statement by the Executive Director for Republic of Madagascar*—July 2008).

INTERNATIONAL RESERVES
(excl. gold, US $ million at 31 December)

	2007	2008	2009
IMF special drawing rights	0.0	0.2	153.2
Foreign exchange	846.6	982.0	982.3
Total	846.7	982.3	1,135.5

2010: IMF special drawing rights 148.6.

Source: IMF, *International Financial Statistics*.

MONEY SUPPLY
('000 million ariary at 31 December)

	2008	2009	2010
Currency outside banks	936.33	1,010.72	1,171.29
Demand deposits at deposit money banks	1,326.55	1,392.18	1,444.17
Total money	2,262.88	2,402.91	2,615.47

Source: IMF, *International Financial Statistics*.

COST OF LIVING
(Consumer Price Index for Malagasy in Antananarivo; base: 2000 = 100)

	2007	2008	2009
Food	202.1	223.2	241.6
Electricity, gas and other fuels	214.9	234.7	n.a.
Clothing*	144.4	157.5	178.2
Rent	289.2	315.2	277.0
All items (incl. others)	202.6	221.4	241.2

* Including household linen.

2010: Food 257.2; All items (incl. others) 263.5.

Source: ILO.

NATIONAL ACCOUNTS
('000 million ariary at current prices)

Expenditure on the Gross Domestic Product

	2007	2008	2009
Government final consumption expenditure	1,372	1,497	1,927
Private final consumption expenditure	10,932	12,834	12,937
Increase in stocks / Gross fixed capital formation	4,456	7,094	5,724
Total domestic expenditure	16,760	21,425	20,588
Exports of goods and services	4,172	4,290	4,786
Less Imports of goods and services	7,164	9,584	8,771
GDP in purchasers' values	13,768	16,131	16,604

Gross Domestic Product by Economic Activity

	2007	2008	2009
Agriculture, hunting, forestry and fishing	3,219	3,596	4,393
Mining and quarrying	16	17	27
Manufacturing	1,877	2,152	1,347
Electricity, gas and water	144	203	191
Construction	547	706	647
Wholesale and retail trade, restaurants and hotels	1,636	1,933	2,060
Transport and communications	2,595	3,162	3,063
Finance, insurance, real estate and business services	2,006	2,341	2,331
Public administration and defence	606	669	1,348
Sub-total	12,646	14,779	15,407
Less Imputed bank service charges	135	193	182
Indirect taxes, less subsidies	1,256	1,545	1,379
GDP in purchasers' values	13,768	16,131	16,604

Source: African Development Bank.

Directory

The Government

HEAD OF STATE

President of the Haute autorité de la transition: ANDRY RAJOELINA (inaugurated 21 March 2009).

GOVERNMENT OF NATIONAL UNITY
(May 2011)

Prime Minister: Gen. ALBERT CAMILLE VITAL.
Minister of State, in charge of the Economy and Industry: PIERROT RAJAONARIVELO.
Minister of State, in charge of Relations with the Institutions: YVES AIMÉ RAKOTOARISOA.
Minister of Sport: JEAN ANDRÉ NDREMANJARY.
Minister of Culture and Heritage: ELISA RAZAFITOMBO ALIBENA.
Minister of Higher Education and Scientific Research: ANTOINE ZAFERA RABESA.
Minister of Foreign Affairs: YVETTE SYLLA.
Minister of Internal Security: DIEUDONNÉ RANAIVOSON.
Minister of Justice and Keeper of the Seals: CHRISTINE RAZANAMAHASOA.
Minister of Transport: BENJAMINA RAMARCEL RAMANANTSOA.
Minister of Defence: Gen. ANDRÉ LUCIEN RAKOTOARIMASY.
Minister of Public Health: Gen. PASCAL JACQUES RAJAONARISON.
Minister of the Civil Service, Labour and Social Legislation: HENRI RASAMOELINA.
Minister of Communication: HARRY LAURENT RAHAJASON.
Minister in charge of the Interior: FLORENT RAKOTOARISOA.
Minister of Energy: ELYSÉ RATSIRAKA.
Minister of Technical Education and Professional Training: GILBERT NGOLO.
Minister of the Environment and Forests: Gen. HERILANTO RAVELOARISON.
Minister of Population and Social Affairs: NADINE RAMAROSON.
Minister of Finance and the Budget: HERY MARTIAL RAJAONARIMAMPIANINA.
Minister of Stockbreeding: BARY RAFATROLAZA.
Minister of Water: JULIEN REBOZA.
Minister of Public Works and Meteorology: ALAIN MANANJARY RAZAFIMBELO.
Minister of Mining and Hydrocarbons: MAMY RATOVOMALALA.
Minister of National Education: JEAN JACQUES RABENIRINA.
Minister of Posts, Telecommunications and New Technologies: NY HASINA ANDRIAMANJATO.
Minister of Fisheries: HERY RAHARISAINA.
Minister of Youth and Leisure: JOHASY ELÉONORE RAHARISOA.
Minister of Land Settlement and Decentralization: HAJO ANDRIANAINARIVELO.
Minister of Trade: RINARISOA IRÈNE EVA RAZAFIMANDIMBY.
Minister of Agriculture: VYVATO RAKOTOVAO.
Minister of Tourism and Crafts: RIANA ANDRIAMANDAVY, VII.
Secretary of State responsible for the Gendarmerie: Gen. RANDRIANAZARY.

MINISTRIES

Office of the President: BP 955, 101 Antananarivo; tel. (20) 2254703; fax (20) 2256252; e-mail communication@presidence.gov.mg; internet www.presidence.gov.mg.

Office of the Prime Minister: BP 248, Palais d'Etat Mahazoarivo, 101 Antananarivo; tel. (20) 2264498; fax (20) 2233116; e-mail stp-ca@primature.gov.mg; internet www.primature.gov.mg.

Ministry of Agriculture: BP 301, Anosy, 101 Antananarivo; tel. (20) 2261002; fax (20) 2264308; e-mail info@agriculture.gov.mg; internet www.agriculture.gov.mg.

Ministry of the Civil Service, Labour and Social Legislation: BP 207, Cité des 67 Hectares, 101 Antananarivo; tel. (20) 2224209; fax (20) 2233856; e-mail ministre@mfptls.gov.mg; internet www.mfptls.gov.mg.

Ministry of Communication: BP 305, 101 Antananarivo.

Ministry of Culture and Heritage: 101 Antananarivo; e-mail ministre@mcp.gov.mg; internet www.mcp.gov.mg.

Ministry of Defence: BP 08, Ampahibe, 101 Antananarivo; tel. (20) 2222211; fax (20) 2235420; e-mail mdn@wanadoo.fr; internet www.defense.gov.mg.

Ministry of the Economy and Industry: Bâtiment Commerce, Ambohidahy, 101 Antananarivo; tel. (20) 2264681; fax (20) 2234530; e-mail sg@mepspc.gov.mg; internet www.mei.gov.mg.

Ministry of Energy: BP 280, rue Farafaty Ampandrianomby, 101 Antananarivo; tel. (20) 2257193; fax (20) 2241776; e-mail bsg_mem@yahoo.fr; internet www.mem.gov.mg.

Ministry of the Environment and Forests: Fernand Kasanga, BP 610 Tsimbazaza, 101 Antananarivo; tel. (20) 2266805; fax (20) 2235410; e-mail sp@meeft.gov.mg; internet www.meeft.gov.mg.

Ministry of Finance and the Budget: BP 61, Antaninarenina, Antananarivo; tel. (20) 2230173; fax (20) 2264680; e-mail mrazanajato@mefb.gov.mg; internet www.mefb.gov.mg.

Ministry of Fisheries: 101 Antananarivo.

Ministry of Foreign Affairs: BP 836, Anosy, 101 Antananarivo; tel. (20) 2221198; fax (20) 2234484; e-mail contact@madagascar-diplomatie.net; internet www.madagascar-diplomatie.net.

Ministry of Higher Education and Scientific Research: 101 Antananarivo; internet www.mesupres.gov.mg.

Ministry of the Interior: BP 833, Anosy, 101 Antananarivo; tel. (20) 2223084; fax (20) 2235579; internet www.mid.gov.mg.

Ministry of Internal Security: BP 23 bis, 101 Antananarivo; tel. (20) 2221029; fax (20) 2231861; internet www.policenationale.gov.mg.

Ministry of Justice: rue Joel Rakotomalala, BP 231, Faravohitra, 101 Antananarivo; tel. (20) 2237684; fax (20) 2264458; e-mail presse.justice@justice.gov.mg; internet www.justice.gov.mg.

Ministry of Land Settlement and Decentralization: Antananarivo; internet www.matd.gov.mg.

Ministry of Mining and Hydrocarbons: BP 280, rue Farafaty Ampandrianomby, 101 Antananarivo; tel. (20) 2257193; fax (20) 2241776; e-mail bsg_mem@yahoo.fr; internet www.mem.gov.mg.

Ministry of National Education: BP 247, Anosy, 101 Antananarivo; tel. (20) 2224308; fax (20) 2223897; e-mail mlraharimalala@yahoo.fr; internet www.education.gov.mg.

Ministry of Population and Social Affairs: 2 rue Razanakombana, Ambohijatovo, 101 Antananarivo; tel. 330968906 (mobile); e-mail hndev@gmail.com; internet www.population.gov.mg.

Ministry of Posts, Telecommunications and New Technologies: pl. de l'Indépendance, Antaninarenina, 101 Antananarivo; tel. (20) 2222902; fax (20) 2234115; internet www.mtpc.gov.mg.

Ministry of Public Health: BP 88, Ambohidahy, 101 Antananarivo; tel. (20) 2263121; e-mail ministre@sante.gov.mg; internet www.sante.gov.mg.

Ministry of Public Works and Meteorology: BP 295, 101 Antananarivo; tel. (20) 2228715; fax (20) 2220890; e-mail secreab@mtpm.gov.mg; internet www.mtpm.gov.mg.

Ministry of Relations with the Institutions: 101 Antananarivo.

Ministry of Sport: Ambohijatovo, pl. Goulette, BP 681, 101 Antananarivo; tel. (20) 2227780; fax (20) 2234275; e-mail mjs_101@yahoo.fr; internet www.mscl.gov.mg.

Ministry of Stockbreeding: 101 Antananarivo.

Ministry of Technical Education and Professional Training: BP 793, 101 Antananarivo.

Ministry of Tourism and Crafts: 101 Antananarivo; e-mail mintour@dts.mg; internet www.mtoura.gov.mg.

Ministry of Trade: 101 Antananarivo; internet www.commerce.gov.mg.

Ministry of Transport: BP 610, rue Fernand Kasanga Tsimbazaza, 101 Antananarivo; tel. (20) 2262816; fax (20) 2235410; internet www.transport.gov.mg.

Ministry of Water: Antananarivo; e-mail dircab@mineau.gov.mg; internet www.mineau.gov.mg.

Ministry of Youth and Leisure: 101 Antananarivo; internet www.mjl.gov.mg.

MADAGASCAR

President and Legislature

PRESIDENT

Presidential Election, 3 December 2006

Candidate	Votes	% of votes
Marc Ravalomanana	2,435,199	54.79
Jean Lahiniriko	517,994	11.65
Iarovana Roland Ratsiraka	450,717	10.14
Herizo J. Razafimahaleo	401,473	9.03
Norbert Lala Ratsirahonana	187,552	4.22
Ny Hasina Andriamanjato	185,624	4.18
Others	266,191	5.99
Total	4,444,750*	100.00

* Excluding 87,196 invalid votes.

LEGISLATURE

On 7 October 2010 the High Constitutional Court approved a decree by President Rajoelina establishing a Parlement de la Transition. Accordingly, on 11 October a 256-member lower parliamentary chamber, the Congrès de la Transition, was installed, with representation assigned according to the arrangement established in the accord reached in August: notably, a gathering of all the political parties and associations that participated in the drafting of the agreement, known as l'Espace de concertation des partis politiques (ESCOPOL), was allocated 62 seats, the TIM 52, the TGV 52 and a grouping of parties supporting Rajoelina, the Union des démocrates et républicains—Fanovana (UDR—Fanovana) 29. On 12 October a 90-member upper chamber, the Conseil Supérieur de la Transition, took office; the deputies included 25 representatives of the UDR—Fanovana, 21 of the TIM, 18 of ESCOPOL and 10 of the TGV.

President of the Congrès de la Transition: ANDRIANANTOANDRO RAHARINAIVO.

President of the Conseil Supérieur de la Transition: Gen. RASOLOSOA DOLIN.

Election Commission

Commission électorale nationale indépendante (CENI): Immeuble Microréalisation, 4 étage, 67 ha, 101 Antananarivo; tel. (20) 2225179; fax (20) 2225881; e-mail ceni@ceni-madagascar.mg; internet www.ceni-madagascar.mg; 19 mems.

Political Organizations

Association pour la renaissance de Madagascar (Andry sy riana enti-manavotra an'i Madigasikara) (AREMA): f. 1975 as Avant-garde de la révolution malgache; adopted present name 1997; party of fmr Pres. Adm. (retd) Ratsiraka (now in exile); control disputed between two factions, headed by Gen. Sec. PIERROT RAJAONARIVELO (in exile), and Asst Gen. Sec. PIERRE RAHARIJAONA.

Comité pour la Réconciliation Nationale (CRN): Villa la Franchise, Lot II-I 160 A, Alarobia, Antananarivo; tel. (20) 2242022; f. 2002 by fmr President Zafy; radical opposition; formed part of the 3FN (Trois Forces Nationales) group of opposition parties, established in Sept. 2005; Leader ALBERT ZAFY.

FAFI-V: f. 2009; Pres. NAIVO NAIVO RAHOLDINA.

Hasin'i Madagasikara: Lot K 7-97 bis IIA Mamory Ivato, BP 682, 101 Antananarivo; tel. 340220665 (mobile); e-mail madahasin@gmail.com; internet hasinimadagasikara.mg; f. 2009; Pres. SARAHA GEORGET RABEHARISOA.

Herim-Bahoaka Mitambatra (HBM) (Union of Popular Forces): formed part of the coalition supporting Marc Ravalomanana prior to the 2006 presidential election; Leader TOVONANAHARY RABETSITONTA.

Libéralisme économique et action démocratique pour la reconstruction nationale (LEADER/Fanilo) (Torch): f. 1993 by Herizo Razafimahaleo; Sec. Gen. MANASSÉ ESOAVELOMANDROSO.

Mouvement pour le progrès de Madagascar (Mpitolona ho amin'ny Fandrosoan'ny Madagasikara) (MFM): 42 & 44 Cité Ampefiloha Bldg, 101 Antananarivo; tel. (20) 2437560; e-mail contact@mfm-madagascar.com; internet www.mfm-madagascar.com; f. 1972 as Mouvement pour le pouvoir prolétarien (MFM); adopted present name in 1990; advocates liberal and market-orientated policies; Leader MANANDAFY RAKOTONIRINA; Sec.-Gen. OLIVIER RAKOTOVAZAHA.

Ny asa vita no ifampitsara (AVI) (People are judged by the work they do): f. 1997 to promote human rights, hard work and devt; Leader NORBERT RATSIRAHONANA.

Directory

Parti socialiste et démocratique pour l'union de Madagascar (PSDUM): f. 2006; Pres. JEAN LAHINIRIKO.

Rassemblement des forces nationales (RFN): f. 2005; a coalition of parties comprising the AKFM, LEADER/Fanilo and Fihavanantsika (led by Pasteur Daniel Rajakoba); formed part of the 3FN (Trois Forces Nationales) group of opposition parties, established in Sept. 2005; Leader Pasteur EDMOND RAZAFIMAHEFA.

Rassemblement pour le socialisme et la démocratie (RPSD): f. 1993 by fmr mems of PSD; also known as Renaissance du parti social-démocratique; Jean-Eugène Voninahitsy formed a breakaway party known as the RPSD Nouveau in 2003; Leader EVARISTE MARSON.

Tanora malaGasy Vonona (TGV) (Determined Malagasy Youth): Antananarivo; internet www.tgvonona.org; f. 2007; Leader ANDRY RAJOELINA.

Tiako i Madagasikara (TIM) (I Love Madagascar): internet www.tim-madagascar.org; f. 2002; supports former Pres. Ravalomanana; Pres. YVAN RANDRIASANDRATRINIONY.

Diplomatic Representation

EMBASSIES IN MADAGASCAR

China, People's Republic: Ancien Hôtel Panorama, BP 1658, 101 Antananarivo; tel. (20) 2240129; fax (20) 2240215; e-mail chinaemb_mg@mfa.gov.cn; internet mg.china-embassy.org; Ambassador WO RUIDI.

Comoros: Antananarivo; tel. (20) 2265819; Ambassador (vacant).

Egypt: Lot MD 378 Ambalatokana Mandrosoa Ivato, BP 4082, 101 Antananarivo; tel. (20) 2245497; fax (20) 2245379; Ambassador MAGID FOAD SALEH FOAD.

France: 3 rue Jean Jaurès, BP 204, 101 Antananarivo; tel. (20) 2239898; fax (20) 2239927; e-mail ambatana@moov.mg; internet www.ambafrance-mada.org; Ambassador JEAN-MARC CHÂTAIGNER.

Germany: 101 rue du Pasteur Rabeony Hans, BP 516, Ambodirotra, 101 Antananarivo; tel. (20) 2223802; fax (20) 2226627; e-mail info@antananarivo.diplo.de; internet www.antananarivo.diplo.de; Ambassador HANS-DIETER STELL.

Holy See: Amboniloha Ivandry, BP 650, 101 Antananarivo; tel. (20) 2242376; fax (20) 2242384; e-mail nuntiusantana@wanadoo.mg; Apostolic Nuncio Most Rev. EUGENE MARTIN NUGENT (Titular Archbishop of Domnach Sechnaill).

India: 4 Làlana Emile Rajaonson, Tsaralalana, BP 1787, 101 Antananarivo; tel. (20) 2223334; fax (20) 2233790; e-mail indembmd@blueline.mg; Ambassador AZAD SINGH TOOR.

Indonesia: 26–28 rue Patrice Lumumba, BP 3969, 101 Antananarivo; tel. (20) 2224915; fax (20) 2232857; Chargé d'affaires a.i. SLAMET SUYATA SASTRAMIHARDZA.

Iran: route Circulaire, Lot II L43 ter, Ankadivato, 101 Antananarivo; tel. (20) 2228639; fax (20) 2222298; Ambassador ABDOL RAHIM HOMATASH.

Japan: 8 rue du Dr Villette, BP 3863, Isoraka, 101 Antananarivo; tel. (20) 2226102; fax (20) 2221769; Ambassador TETSURO KAWAGUCHI.

Korea, Democratic People's Republic: 101 Antananarivo; tel. (20) 2244442; Ambassador RI YONG HAK.

Libya: Lot IIB, 37A route Circulaire Ampandrana-Ouest, 101 Antananarivo; tel. (20) 2221892; Chargé d'affaires a.i. Dr MOHAMED ALI SHARFEDIN AL-FITURI.

Mauritius: Villa David IV, Manakambahiny, 101 Antananarivo; tel. (20) 2221864; fax (20) 2221939; e-mail memad@moov.mg; Ambassador ERNEST GÉRARD LEMAIRE.

Morocco: Bâtiment D1, Rez-de-chaussée, Ankorondrano, BP 12, 104 Antananarivo; tel. (20) 2221347; fax (20) 2221124; e-mail amar_med@hotmail.com; Ambassador MUHAMMAD AMAR.

Norway: Explorer Business Park, Bâtiment 2D, Antananarivo; tel. (20) 2230507; fax (20) 2237799; e-mail emb.antananarivo@mfa.no; internet www.amb-norvege.mg; Ambassador DAG NISSEN.

Russia: BP 4006, Ivandry-Ambohijatovo, 101 Antananarivo; tel. (20) 2242827; fax (20) 2242642; e-mail ambrusmad@blueline.mg; internet www.madagascar.mid.ru; Ambassador VLADIMIR B. GONCHARENKO.

Senegal: Lot 82A, Ter Ambohijanahary Antehiroka, Antananarivo; tel. (20) 2248042; fax (20) 2248032; e-mail ambassene.tana@moov.mg; Ambassador CÉSAR COLY.

South Africa: Lot IVO 68 bis, rue Ravoninahitriniarivo, Ankorondrano, BP 12101-05, 101 Antananarivo; tel. (20) 2243350; fax (20) 2249514; e-mail antananarivo@foreign.gov.za; Ambassador MOKGETHI SAMUEL MONAISA.

Switzerland: Immeuble ARO, Solombavambahoaka, Frantsay 77, BP 118, 101 Antananarivo; tel. (20) 2262997; fax (20) 2228940; e-mail

MADAGASCAR

ant.vertretung@eda.admin.ch; internet www.eda.admin.ch/antananarivo; Ambassador CARLOS ORGA.

Turkey: Hotel Carlton, Chambre no. 1410, rue Pierre Stibbe, BP959 Antananarivo 101; tel. (20) 2226060; fax (20) 2267609; AHMET ENÇ ERCEMUND.

USA: 14–16 rue Rainitovo, Antsahavola, BP 620, 101 Antananarivo; tel. (20) 2221257; fax (20) 2234539; internet www.antananarivo.usembassy.gov; Chargé d'affaires a.i. ERIC W. STROMAYER.

Judicial System

According to the Constitution of the Fourth Republic of Madagascar, endorsed by national referendum on 17 November 2010, justice is administered by the Supreme Court, the High Constitutional Court, the High Court of Justice and any courts of appeal that may be established.

HIGH CONSTITUTIONAL COURT

Haute Cour Constitutionnelle: POB 835, Ambohidahy, 101 Antananarivo; tel. (20) 2266061; e-mail hcc@hcc.gov.mg; internet www.hcc.gov.mg; interprets the Constitution and rules on constitutional issues; nine mems; Pres. JEAN-MICHEL RAJAONARIVONY.

HIGH COURT OF JUSTICE

Haute Cour de Justice: 101 Antananarivo; 9 mems.

SUPREME COURT

Cour Suprême: Palais de Justice, Anosy, 101 Antananarivo; 9 mems; Pres. CLÉMENTINE CÉCILE RAJAONERA DELMOTTE; Attorney-General COLOMBE RAMANANTSOA (acting); Chamber Pres YOLANDE RAMANGASOAVINA, FRANÇOIS RAMANANDRAIBE.

OTHER COURTS

Tribunaux de Première Instance: at Antananarivo, Toamasina, Antsiranana, Mahajanga, Fianarantsoa, Toliary, Antsirabé, Ambatondrazaka, Antalaha, Farafangana and Maintirano; for civil, commercial and social matters, and for registration.

Cours Criminelles Ordinaires: tries crimes of common law; attached to the Cour d'Appel in Antananarivo but may sit in any other large town. There are also 31 Cours Criminelles Spéciales dealing with cases concerning cattle.

Tribunaux Spéciaux Economiques: at Antananarivo, Toamasina, Mahajanga, Fianarantsoa, Antsiranana and Toliary; tries crimes specifically relating to economic matters.

Tribunaux Criminels Spéciaux: judges cases of banditry and looting; 31 courts.

Religion

It is estimated that more than 50% of the population follow traditional animist beliefs, some 41% are Christians (about one-half of whom are Roman Catholics) and some 7% are Muslims.

CHRISTIANITY

Fiombonan'ny Fiangonana Kristiana eto Madagasikara (FFKM)/Conseil Chrétien des Eglises de Madagascar (Christian Council of Churches in Madagascar): Vohipiraisana, Ambohijatovo-Atsimo, BP 798, 101 Antananarivo; tel. (20) 2623433; e-mail ffkmfoibe@gmail.com; f. 1980; four mems and two assoc. mems; Pres. Pastor Dr LALA HAJA RASENDRAHASINA; Gen. Sec. Rev. MAHERY RAKOTONANDRIANINA.

Fiombonan'ny Fiangonana Protestanta eto Madagasikara (FFPM)/Fédération des Eglises Protestantes à Madagascar (Federation of the Protestant Churches in Madagascar): VK 3 Vohipiraisana, Ambohijatovo-Atsimo, BP 4226, 101 Antananarivo; tel. (20) 2415888; e-mail edmrazafi@fuller.edu; f. 1958; two mem. churches; Pres Rev. Dr LALA RASENDRAHASINA; Gen. Sec. Rev. Dr EDMOND RAZAFIMANANTSOA.

The Anglican Communion

Anglicans are adherents of the Church of the Province of the Indian Ocean, comprising seven dioceses (five in Madagascar, one in Mauritius and one in Seychelles). The Archbishop of the Province is the Bishop of Antsiranana. The Church has about 160,000 adherents in Madagascar, including the membership of the Eklesia Episkopaly Malagasy (Malagasy Episcopal Church), founded in 1874.

Bishop of Antananarivo: Rt Rev. SAMOELA JAONA RANARIVELO, Evêché anglican, Lot VK57 ter, Ambohimanoro, 101 Antananarivo; tel. (20) 2220827; fax (20) 2261331; e-mail eemdanta@yahoo.com.

Bishop of Antsiranana: Rt Rev. ROGER CHUNG PO CHEN, Evêché anglican, 4 rue Grandidier, BP 278, 201 Antsiranana; tel. (20) 8222650; e-mail mgrchungpo@blueline.mg; internet www.antsirananadiocese.org.

Bishop of Fianarantsoa: Rt Rev. GILBERT RATELOSON RAKOTONDRAVELO, Evêché anglican, BP 1418, 531 Fianarantsoa.

Bishop of Mahajanga: Rt Rev. JEAN-CLAUDE ANDRIANJAFIMANANA, Evêché anglican, BP 169, 401 Mahajanga; e-mail eemdmaha@dts.mg.

Bishop of Toamasina: Rt Rev. JEAN PAUL SOLO, Evêché anglican, rue James Seth, BP 531, 501 Toamasina; tel. (20) 5332163; fax (20) 5331689.

The Roman Catholic Church

Madagascar comprises five archdioceses and 16 dioceses. About 26% of the total population were Roman Catholics.

Bishops' Conference

Conférence episcopale de Madagascar, 102 bis, rue Cardinal Jerôme Rakotomalala, BP 667, 101 Antananarivo; tel. (20) 2220478; fax (20) 2224854; e-mail ecar@vitelcom.mg.

f. 1969; Pres. Most Rev. FULGENCE RABEMAHAFALY (Archbishop of Fianarantsoa).

Archbishop of Antananarivo: ODON ARSÈNE RAZANAKOLONA, Archevêché, Andohalo, BP 3030, 101 Antananarivo; tel. (20) 2220726; fax (20) 2264181; e-mail didih@simicro.org.

Archbishop of Antsiranana: Most Rev. MICHEL MALO, Archevêché, 5 blvd le Myre de Villers, BP 415, 201 Antsiranana; tel. and fax (82) 21605; e-mail archevediego@blueline.mg.

Archbishop of Fianarantsoa: Most Rev. FULGENCE RABEMAHAFALY, Archevêché, pl. Mgr Givelet, BP 1440, Ecar Ambozontany, 301 Fianarantsoa; tel. (20) 7550027; fax (20) 7551436; e-mail ecardiofianar@mel.moov.mg.

Archbishop of Toamasina: Most Rev. DÉSIRÉ TSARAHAZANA, 11 rue du Commerce, BP 98, 501 Toamasina; tel. (20) 5332128.

Archbishop of Toliary: Most Rev. FULGENCE RABEONY, Archevêché, Maison Saint Jean, BP 30, 601 Toliary; tel. (20) 9442416; e-mail diocese_tulcar@wanadoo.mg.

Other Christian Churches

Fiangonan'i Jesoa Kristy eto Madagasikara/Eglise de Jésus-Christ à Madagascar (FJKM): Lot 11 B18, Tohatohabato Ranavalona 1, Trano 'Ifanomezantsoa', BP 623, 101 Antananarivo; tel. (20) 2228237; fax (20) 2227033; e-mail fjkm@wanadoo.mg; internet foibefjkm.mg; f. 1968; Pres. LALA HAJA RASENDRAHASINA; Gen. Sec. Rev. RÉMY RALIBERA; 2m. mems.

Fiangonana Loterana Malagasy (Malagasy Lutheran Church): BP 1741, 19, rue Jules Pochard, 101 Antananarivo; tel. (20) 2422703; e-mail drmodeste@yahoo.fr; internet www.flm-mada.org; f. 1867; Pres. Rev. Dr ENDOR MODESTE RAKOTO; 3m. mems (2009).

The Press

In December 1990 legislation was adopted guaranteeing the freedom of the press and the right of newspapers to be established without prior authorization.

PRINCIPAL DAILIES

Bulletin de l'Agence Nationale d'Information 'TARATRA' (ANTA): 8/10 Làlana Rainizanabololona, Antanimena, BP 194, 101 Antananarivo; tel. (20) 2234308; e-mail administration@taratramada.com; internet www.taratramada.com; f. 1977; Malagasy; Editor-in-Chief HANITRA RABETOKOTANY.

L'Express de Madagascar: BP 3893, 101 Antananarivo; tel. (20) 2221934; fax (20) 2262894; e-mail lexpress@malagasy.com; internet www.lexpressmada.com; f. 1995; French and Malagasy; Editor-in-Chief SYLVAIN RANJALAHY; circ. 10,000.

Gazetiko: rue Ravoninahitriniarivo, BP 1414 Ankorondrano, 101 Antananarivo; tel. (20) 2269779; fax (20) 2227351; e-mail gazetiko@midi-madagasikara.mg; internet www.gazetiko.mg; Malagasy; circ. 50,000.

La Gazette de la Grande Ile: Lot II, W 23 L Ankorahotra, route de l'Université, BP 8678, Antananarivo; tel. (20) 2261377; fax (20) 2265188; e-mail james@lagazette-dgi.com; internet www.lagazette-dgi.com; French; 24 pages; Pres. JAMES RAMAROSAONA; circ. 15,000–30,000.

Imongo Vaovao: 11K 4 bis Andravoahangy, BP 7014, 101 Antananarivo; tel. (20) 2233110; f. 1955; Malagasy; Dir ANDRÉ RATSIFEHERA; circ. 15,000.

MADAGASCAR

Madagascar Tribune: Immeuble SME, rue Ravoninahitriniarivo, BP 659, Ankorondrano, 101 Antananarivo; tel. (20) 2222635; fax (20) 2222254; e-mail contact@madagascar-tribune.com; internet www.madagascar-tribune.com; f. 1988; independent; French and Malagasy; Editor Rahaga Ramaholimihaso; circ. 12,000.

Maresaka: Cité Logt. 288, Analamahitsy, 101 Antananarivo; tel. (20) 2431665; f. 1953; independent; Malagasy; Editor R. Rabefananina; circ. 5,000.

Midi Madagasikara: Làlana Ravoninahitriniarivo, BP 1414, Ankorondrano, 101 Antananarivo; tel. (20) 2269779; fax (20) 2227351; e-mail contact@midi-madagasikara.mg; internet www.midi-madagasikara.mg; f. 1983; French and Malagasy; Dir-Gen. Juliana Andriambelo Rakotoarivelo; circ. 21,000 (Mon.–Fri.), 35,000 (Sat.).

Les Nouvelles: 8/10, rue Rainizanabololona, BP 194, 101 Antananarivo; tel. (20) 2235433; fax (20) 2229993; e-mail administration@les-nouvelles.com; internet www.les-nouvelles.com; in French and Taratra; f. 2003; Dir-Gen. Naina Andriantsitohaina.

Ny Vaovaontsika: BP 11137, MBS Anosipatrana; tel. (20) 2227717; e-mail nyvaovaontsika@mbs.mg; f. 2004; re-est. as a daily; Malagasy; owned by the Malagasy Broadcasting System; Editor-in-Chief Roland Andriamahenina; circ. 10,000.

Le Quotidien: BP 11 097, 101 Antananarivo; tel. (20) 2227717; fax (20) 2265447; e-mail lequotidien@mbs.mg; internet www.lequotidien.mg; f. 2003; owned by the Tiko Group plc; French.

PRINCIPAL PERIODICALS

Basy Vava: Lot III E 96, Mahamasina Atsimo, 101 Antananarivo; tel. (20) 2220448; f. 1959; daily; Malagasy; Dir Gabriel Ramananjato; circ. 3,000.

Bulletin de la Société du Corps Médical Malgache: Imprimerie Volamahitsy, 101 Antananarivo; Malagasy; monthly; Dir Dr Rakotomalala.

Dans les Médias Demain (DMD): 51 rue Tsiombikibo, BP 1734, Ambatovinaky, 101 Antananarivo; tel. (20) 2241664; fax (20) 2241665; e-mail admin@dmd.mg; f. 1986; independent; economic information and analysis; weekly; Editorial Dir Jean Eric Rakotoarisoa; circ. 4,000.

Feon'ny Mpiasa: Lot M8, Isotry, 101 Antananarivo; trade union affairs; Malagasy; monthly; Dir M. Razakanaivo; circ. 2,000.

Gazetinao: Lot IPA 37, BP 1758, Anosimasina, 101 Antananarivo; tel. (33) 1198161; e-mail mitantanasymitarika@yahoo.fr; f. 1976; French and Malagasy; monthly; religion and culture; Editor-in-Chief David Alden Einsten Rakotomahanina; circ. 3,000.

L'Hebdo: BP 3893, 101 Antananarivo; tel. (20) 2221934; e-mail courrier@hebdomada.com; f. 2005; French and Malagasy; weekly; Editor-in-Chief Nasolo Valiavo Andriamihaja.

Isika Mianakavy: Ambatomena, 301 Fianarantsoa; f. 1958; Roman Catholic; Malagasy; monthly; Dir J. Ranaivomanana; circ. 21,000.

Journal Officiel de la République de Madagascar/Gazetim-Panjakan' Ny Repoblika Malagasy: BP 248, 101 Antananarivo; tel. (20) 2265010; fax (20) 2225319; f. 1883; official announcements; Malagasy and French; weekly; Dir Honorée Elianne Ralalaharison; circ. 1,545.

Journal Scientifique de Madagascar: BP 3855, Antananarivo; f. 1985; Dir Prof. Manambelona; circ. 3,000.

Jureco: BP 6318, Lot IVd 48 bis, rue Razanamaniraka, Behoririka, 101 Antananarivo; tel. (20) 2255271; e-mail jureco@malagasy.com; law and economics; monthly; French; Dir Mboara Andrianarimanana.

Lakroan'i Madagasikara/La Croix de Madagascar: BP 7524, CNPC Antanimena, 101 Antananarivo; tel. (20) 2266128; fax (20) 2224020; e-mail lakroa@moov.mg; internet www.lakroa.mg; f. 1927; Roman Catholic; French and Malagasy; weekly; Dir Fr Vincent Rabemahafaly; circ. 25,000.

La Lettre de Madagascar (LLM): Antananarivo; f. 2003; 2 a month; in French and English; economic; Editor-in-Chief Daniel Lamy.

Mpanolotsaina: BP 623, 101 Antananarivo; tel. (20) 2226845; fax (20) 2226372; e-mail fjkm@wanadoo.mg; religious, educational; Malagasy; quarterly; Dir Raymond Rajoelisol.

New Magazine: BP 7581, Newprint, route des Hydrocarbures, 101 Antananarivo; tel. (20) 2233335; fax (20) 2236471; e-mail newmag@wanadoo.mg; internet www.newmagazine.mg; monthly; in French; Dir Clara Ravoavahy.

Ny Mpamangy-FLM: 9 rue Général Gabriel Ramanantsoa Isoraka, 101 Antananarivo; tel. (20) 2228943; f. 1882; monthly; Dir Lucie Norosoanomenjanahary; circ. 3,000.

Ny Sakaizan'ny Tanora: BP 538, Antsahaminitra, 101 Antananarivo; tel. (20) 2228943; f. 1878; monthly; Editor-in-Chief Elisabeth Rahelinoro; circ. 5,000.

PME Madagascar: rue Hugues Rabesahala, BP 953, Antsakaviro, 101 Antananarivo; tel. (20) 2222536; fax (20) 2234534; f. 1989; French; monthly; economic review; Dir Romain Andrianarisoa; circ. 3,500.

Recherche et Culture: BP 907, 101 Antananarivo; tel. (20) 2226600; f. 1985; publ. by French dept of the University of Antananarivo; 2 a year; Dir Ginette Ramaroson; circ. 1,000.

Revue de l'Océan Indien: Communication et Médias Océan Indien, rue H. Rabesahala, BP 46, Antsakaviro, 101 Antananarivo; tel. (20) 2222536; fax (20) 2234534; e-mail roi@dts.mg; internet www.madatours.com/roi; f. 1980; monthly; French; Dir-Gen. Hery M. A. Ranaivosoa; circ. 5,000.

Sahy: Lot VD 42, Ambanidia, 101 Antananarivo; tel. (20) 2222715; f. 1957; political; Malagasy; weekly; Editor Aline Rakoto; circ. 9,000.

Sosialisma Mpiasa: BP 1128, 101 Antananarivo; tel. (20) 2221989; f. 1979; trade union affairs; Malagasy; monthly; Dir Paul Rabemananjara; circ. 5,000.

Vaovao: BP 271, 101 Antananarivo; tel. (20) 2221193; f. 1985; French and Malagasy; weekly; Dir Marc Rakotonoely; circ. 5,000.

NEWS AGENCIES

Agence Nationale d'Information 'TARATRA' (ANTA): 7 rue Jean Ralaimongo, Ambohiday, BP 386, 101 Antananarivo; tel. and fax (20) 2236047; e-mail taratra.mtpc@mtpc.gov.mg; f. 1977; Man. Dir Joé Anaclet Rakotoarison.

Mada: Villa Joëlle, Lot II J 161 R, Ivandry, 101 Antananarivo; tel. (20) 2242428; e-mail courrier@mada.mg; internet www.mada.mg; f. 2003; independent information agency; Dir Richard Claude Ratovonarivo.

Publishers

Edisiona Salohy: BP 4226, 101 Antananarivo; Dir Mirana Vololoarisoa Randrianarison.

Editions Ambozontany Analamalintsy: BP 7553, 101 Antananarivo; tel. and fax (20) 2243111; e-mail editionsj@moov.mg; f. 1952; religious, educational, historical, cultural and technical textbooks; Dir Fr Guillaume de Saint Pierre Rakotonandratoniarivo.

Foibe Filankevitry Ny Mpampianatra (FOFIPA): BP 202, 101 Antananarivo; tel. (20) 2227500; f. 1971; textbooks; Dir Frère Razafindrakoto.

Imprimerie Nouvelle: PK 2, Andranomahery, route de Majunga, BP 4330, 101 Antananarivo; tel. (20) 2221036; fax (20) 2269225; e-mail nouvelle@wanadoo.mg; Dir Eugène Raharifidy.

Imprimerie Takariva: 4 rue Radley, BP 1029, Antanimena, 101 Antananarivo; tel. (20) 2222128; f. 1933; fiction, languages, school textbooks; Man. Dir Paul Rapatsalahy.

Madagascar Print and Press Co (MADPRINT): rue Rabesahala, Antsakaviro, BP 953, 101 Antananarivo; tel. (20) 2222536; fax (20) 2234534; f. 1969; literary, technical and historical; Dir Georges Ranaivosoa.

Maison d'Edition Protestante Antso: 19 rue Venance Manifatra, Imarivolanitra, BP 660, 101 Antananarivo; tel. (20) 2220886; fax (20) 2226372; e-mail fjkm@dts.mg; f. 1972; religious, school, social, political and general; Dir Hans Andriamampianina.

Nouvelle Société de Presse et d'Edition (NSPE): Immeuble Jeune Afrique, 58 rue Tsiombikibo, BP 1734, Ambatorinaky, 101 Antananarivo; tel. (20) 2227788; fax (20) 2230629.

Office du Livre Malgache: Lot 111 H29, Andrefan' Ambohijanahary, BP 617, 101 Antananarivo; tel. (20) 2224449; f. 1970; children's and general; Sec.-Gen. Juliette Ratsimandrava.

Société Malgache d'Edition (SME): BP 659, Ankorondrano, 101 Antananarivo; tel. (20) 2222635; fax (20) 2222254; e-mail tribune@wanadoo.mg; f. 1943; general fiction, university and secondary textbooks; Dir Rahaga Ramaholimihaso.

Société Nouvelle de l'Imprimerie Centrale (SNIC): Làlana Ravoninahitriniarivo, BP 1414, 101 Antananarivo; tel. (20) 2221118; e-mail mrakotoa@wanadoo.mg; f. 1959; science, school textbooks; Man. Dir Mamy Rakotoarivelo.

Société de Presse et d'Edition de Madagascar: Antananarivo; non-fiction, reference, science, university textbooks; Man. Dir Rajaofera Andriambelo.

Trano Printy Fiangonana Loterana Malagasy (TPFLM): BP 538, 9 rue Général Gabriel Ramanantsoa, 101 Antananarivo; tel. (20) 2224569; fax (20) 2262643; e-mail impluth@yahoo.fr; f. 1877; religious, educational and fiction; Man. Raymond Randrianatoandro.

MADAGASCAR

GOVERNMENT PUBLISHING HOUSE

Imprimerie Nationale: BP 38, 101 Antananarivo; tel. (20) 2223675; e-mail dinm@wanadoo.mg; all official publs; Dir Jean Denis Randrianirina.

Broadcasting and Communications

TELECOMMUNICATIONS

Office Malagasy d'Etudes et de Régulation des Télécommunications (OMERT): BP 99991, route des Hydrocarbures-Alarobia, 101 Antananarivo; tel. (20) 2242119; fax (20) 2321516; e-mail omert@moov.mg; internet www.omert.mg; f. 1997; Gen. Man. Gilbert Andrianirina Rajaonasy.

Airtel Madagascar: Explorer Business Park, Ankorondrano, Antananarivo 101; tel. (33) 1100100; e-mail info.africa@airtel.com; internet africa.airtel.com/madagascar; f. 1997 as Madacom; fmrly Celtel and subsequently Zain Madagascar; name changed as above in 2010; Dir-Gen. Heiko Schlittke.

Orange Madagascar: Antananarivo; internet www.orange.mg; f. 1998; fmrly Antaris, la Société Malgache de Mobiles; name changed as above 2003; mobile telecommunication GSM network provider; market leader; Dir-Gen. Jean-Luc Bohé.

Télécom Malagasy SA (TELMA): BP 763, 101 Antananarivo; tel. (20) 2532705; fax (20) 2253871; e-mail telmacorporate@telma.mg; internet www.telma.mg; 68% owned by Distacom (Hong Kong); owns DTS Wanadoo internet service provider; Chair. David White; Dir-Gen. Patrick Pisal-Hamida.

BROADCASTING

Radio

In 2001 there were an estimated 127 radio stations.

Radio MBS (Malagasy Broadcasting System): BP 11137, Anosipatrana, Antananarivo; tel. (20) 2266702; fax (20) 2268941; e-mail marketing@mbs.mg; internet www.mbs.mg; broadcasts by satellite; Man. Sarah Ravalomanana.

Radio Nationale Malagasy: BP 442, Anosy, 101 Antananarivo; tel. (20) 2221745; fax (20) 2232715; e-mail rnmdir@dts.mg; internet www.rnm.mg; state-controlled; part of the Office de Radiodiffusion et de Télévision de Madagascar (ORTM); broadcasts in French and Malagasy; Dir Johary Ravoajanahary.

Le Messager Radio Evangélique: BP 1374, 101 Antananarivo; tel. (20) 2234495; internet mreradio.com; broadcasts in French, English and Malagasy; Dir Jocelyn Ranjarison.

Radio Antsiva: BP 632, Enceinte STEDIC, Village des Jeux, Zone Industrielle Nord, route des Hydrocarbures, 101 Antananarivo; tel. (20) 2254849; e-mail antsiva@freenet.mg; internet www.antsiva.mg; f. 1994; broadcasts in French and Malagasy.

Radio Don Bosco: Maison Don Bosco, BP 60, 105 Ivato; tel. (20) 2244387; fax (20) 2244511; e-mail rdb@radiodonbosco.org; internet www.radiodonbosco.org; f. 1996; Catholic, educational and cultural; Dir Luca Treglia.

Radio Feon'ny Vahoaka (RFV): 103 Immeuble Ramaroson, 8e étage, 101 Antananarivo; tel. (20) 2233820; broadcasts in French and Malagasy; Dir Alain Ramaroson.

Radio Lazan'iarivo (RLI): Lot V A49, Andafiavaratra, 101 Antananarivo; tel. (20) 2229016; fax (20) 2267559; e-mail rli@simicro.mg; broadcasts in French, English and Malagasy; privately owned; specializes in jazz music; Dir Ihoby Rabarijohn.

Radio Viva: Antananarivo; Owner Andry Rajoelina.

Television

MA TV: BP 1414 Ankorondrano, 101 Antananarivo; tel. (20) 2220897; fax (20) 2234421.

MBS Television (Malagasy Broadcasting System): BP 11137, Anosipatrana, Antananarivo; tel. (20) 2266702; fax (20) 2268941; e-mail journaltv@mbs.mg; internet www.mbs.mg; broadcasts in French and Malagasy.

Radio Télévision Analamanga (RTA): Immeuble Fiaro, 101 Antananarivo; tel. (20) 2224503; e-mail rta@rta.mg; internet www.rta.mg; incl. four provincial radio stations; Dir-Gen. Selven Naidu.

Télévision Nasionale Malgache: BP 1202, Anosy, 101 Antananarivo; tel. (20) 2222381; state-controlled; part of the Office de Radiodiffusion et de Télévision de Madagascar (ORTM); broadcasts in French and Malagasy; Gen. Man. Jphary Ravaojanahary.

Télévision Viva: Antananarivo; Owner Andry Rajoelina.

Finance

(cap. = capital; res = reserves; dep. = deposits; m. = million; brs = branches; amounts in ariary)

BANKING
Central Bank

Banque Centrale de Madagascar: rue de la Révolution Socialiste Malgache, BP 550, 101 Antananarivo; tel. (20) 2221751; fax (20) 2234532; e-mail sbu@bfm.mg; internet www.banque-centrale.mg; f. 1973; bank of issue; cap. 111,000m., res 32,420m., dep. 1,305,852m. (Dec. 2008); Gov. Frédéric Rasamoely; Dir Gen. Christian G. D. Rasolomanana.

Other Banks

Bank of Africa (BOA)—Madagascar: 2 pl. de l'Indépendance, BP 183, 101 Antananarivo; tel. (20) 2239100; fax (20) 2266125; e-mail boa@boa.mg; internet www.boa.mg; f. 1976 as Bankin'ny Tantsaha Mpamokatra; name changed as above 1999; 38.86% owned by Bank of Africa Group (Luxembourg), 10.00% state-owned; commercial bank, specializes in micro-finance; cap. 33,000.0m., res 36,511.4m., dep. 1,048,790.9m. (Dec. 2008); Chair. and Pres. Paul Derreumaux; Gen. Man. Jacques Dilet; 55 brs.

Banque Industrielle et Commerciale de Madagascar (BICM): 2 rue du Dr Raseta Andraharo, BP 889, 101 Antananarivo; tel. (20) 2356568; fax (20) 2356656; e-mail bicm@bicm.mg; internet www.bicm.mg; f. 2002; successor of the Banque Internationale Chine Madagascar, fmrly Compagnie Malgache de Banque; cap. 5,779.2m., dep. 3,680.4m. (Dec. 2007) res −1,804.6m.(Dec. 2005); Pres. Chi Ming Hui; Dir-Gen. Dr Huang Wei Guang.

Banque Malgache de l'Océan Indien (BMOI) (Indian Ocean Malagasy Bank): pl. de l'Indépendance, BP 25 bis, Antaninarenina, 101 Antananarivo; tel. (20) 2238251; fax (20) 2238544; e-mail bmoi.st@bnpparibas.com; internet www.bmoi.mg; f. 1989; 75% owned by BNP Paribas SA (France); cap. and res 40,200.0m., dep. 377,700.0m. (Dec. 2006); Pres. Gaston Ramenason; Dir Jean Luc Razafison; 8 brs.

Banque SBM Madagascar: rue Andrianary Ratianarivo Antsahavola 1, 101 Antananarivo; tel. (20) 2266607; fax (20) 2266608; e-mail bsbmmtana@sbm.intnet.mu; f. 1998; 79.99% owned by SBM Global Investments Ltd (Mauritius), 20.01% owned by Nedbank Africa Investments Ltd (South Africa); cap. 7,404.1m., res 2,363.5m., dep. 92,221.2m. (Dec. 2007); Chair. Chaitlall Gunness; Gen. Man. Krishnadutt Rambojun.

BFV—Société Générale: 14 rue Général Rabehevitra, BP 196, Antananarivo 101; tel. (20) 2220691; fax (20) 2237140; e-mail relation.client@socgen.com; internet www.bfvsg.mg; f. 1977 as Banky Fampandrosoana ny Varotra; changed name in 1998; 70% owned by Société Générale (France), 28.5% state-owned; cap. 14,000.0m., res 48,833.0m., dep. 583,398.8m. (Dec. 2008); Pres. Philippe Lamé; 40 brs.

BNI Madagascar: 74 rue du 26 Juin 1960, BP 174, 101 Antananarivo; tel. (20) 2222800; fax (20) 2233749; e-mail info@bni.mg; internet www.bni.mg; f. 1976 as Bankin 'ny Indostria; 51% owned by IUB Holding (France), 32.58% state-owned; cap. 10,800.0m., res 43,496.2m., dep. 693,056.1m. (Dec. 2007); Pres. and Chair. Evariste Marson; Man. Dir Pascal Fall; 25 brs.

Mauritius Commercial Bank (Madagascar) SA (MCB): 77 rue Solombavambahoaka Frantsay, Antsahavola, BP 197, 101 Antananarivo; tel. (20) 2227262; fax (20) 2228740; e-mail mcb.int@mcbmadagascar.com; internet www.mcbmadagascar.com; f. 1992 as Union Commercial Bank; name changed as above in 2007; 70% owned by Mauritius Commercial Bank Ltd; cap. 17,913.9m., res 6,753.6m., dep. 134,956.2m. (Dec. 2008); Chair. Jean François Desvaux de Marigny; Gen. Man. Marc Marie Joseph de Bollivier; 3 brs.

INSURANCE

ARO (Assurances Réassurances Omnibranches): Antsahavola, BP 42, 101 Antananarivo; tel. (20) 2220154; fax (20) 2234464; e-mail aro1@moov.mg; internet www.aro.mg; state-owned; Dir-Gen. Guy Rolland Rasoanaivo.

ASCOMA Madagascar: 13 rue Patrice Lumumba, BP 673, 101 Antananarivo; tel. (20) 2223162; fax (20) 2222785; e-mail madagascar@ascoma.com; internet www.ascoma.com; f. 1952; Dir Viviane Ramanitra.

Compagnie Malgache d'Assurances et de Réassurances 'Ny Havana': Immeuble 'Ny Havana', Zone des 67 Ha, BP 3881, 101 Antananarivo; tel. (20) 2226760; fax (20) 2224303; e-mail nyhavana@wanadoo.mg; internet nyhavana.net; f. 1968; state-owned; cap. 5,435.6m. (2006); Dir-Gen. Roger Emile Ranaivoson.

Mutuelle d'Assurances Malagasy (MAMA): Lot 1F, 12 bis Ambalavao-Isotry, BP 185, 101 Antananarivo; tel. (20) 2261882; fax (20)

MADAGASCAR

2261883; e-mail assurancemama@moov.mg; f. 1968; Dir SETH AIMÉ RANDRIANARIJAONA.

Trade and Industry

DEVELOPMENT ORGANIZATIONS

Bureau d'Information pour les Entreprises (BIPE): Nouvel Immeuble ARO, Ampefiloha, 101 Antananarivo; tel. (20) 2230512; internet www.bipe.mg; part of the Ministry of the Economy and Industry.

Economic Development Board of Madagascar (EDBM): ave Gabriel Ramanantsoa, Antaninarenina, Antananarivo 101; tel. (20) 2268121; fax (20) 2266105; e-mail edbm@edbm.mg; internet www.edbm.gov.mg; f. 2006; service for the facilitation and promotion of investment in Madagascar; advisory service for starting a business, obtaining visas and land acquisition; Interim CEO ÉRIC RAKOTO ANDRIANTSILAVO.

La maison de l'entreprise: rue Samuel Ramahefy Ambatonakanga, BP 74, 101 Antananarivo; tel. (20) 2225386; fax (20) 2233669; e-mail cite@cite.mg; internet www.cite.mg; f. 1967; supports and promotes Malagasy businesses; Dir-Gen. ISABELLE GACHIE.

Office des Mines Nationales et des Industries Stratégiques (OMNIS): 21 Làlana Razanakombana, BP 1 bis, 101 Antananarivo; tel. (20) 2224283; fax (20) 2222985; e-mail omnissecdg@moov.mg; internet www.omnis-madagascar.mg; f. 1976; promotes the exploration and exploitation of mining resources, in particular oil resources; Dir-Gen. JOELI VALÉRIEN LALAHARISAINA.

Société d'Etude et de Réalisation pour le Développement Industriel (SERDI): BP 3180, 101 Antananarivo; tel. (20) 2225204; fax (20) 2229669; f. 1966; Dir-Gen. RAOILISON RAJAONARY.

CHAMBERS OF COMMERCE

Fédération des Chambres de Commerce, d'Industrie et d'Agriculture de Madagascar: BP 166, 20 rue Henri Razanatseheno, Antaninarenina, Antananarivo 101; tel. (20) 2220211; fax (20) 2220213; e-mail cciaa@tana-cciaa.org; internet www.tana-cciaa.org; 12 mem. chambers; Pres. SIMON RAKOTONDRAHOVA; Chair. HENRI RAZANATSEHENO; Sec.-Gen. HUBERT RATSIANDAVANA.

Chambre de Commerce, d'Industrie, d'Artisanat et d'Agriculture—Antananarivo (CCIAA): BP 166, 20 rue Henri Razanatseheno, Antaninarenina, 101 Antananarivo; tel. (20) 2220211; fax (20) 2220213; e-mail cciaa@tana-cciaa.org; internet cci-tana.org; f. 1993; Pres. BEZO ANDRIANARIVELO RAZAFY.

TRADE ASSOCIATION

Société d'Intérêt National des Produits Agricoles (SINPA): BP 754, rue Fernand-Kasanga, Tsimbazaza, Antananarivo; tel. (20) 2220558; fax (20) 2220665; f. 1973; monopoly purchaser and distributor of agricultural produce; Chair. GUALBERT RAZANAJATOVO; Gen. Man. JEAN CLOVIS RALIJESY.

EMPLOYERS' ORGANIZATIONS

Groupement des Entreprises de Madagascar (GEM): Kianja MDRM sy Tia Tanindrazana, Ambohijatovo, BP 1338, 101 Antananarivo; tel. (20) 2223841; fax (20) 2221965; e-mail gem@iris.mg; internet www.gem-madagascar.com; f. 1975; 16 nat. syndicates and five regional syndicates comprising 1,000 cos and 50 directly affiliated cos; Pres. NAINA ANDRIANTSITOHAINA; Sec.-Gen. ZINAH RASAMUEL RAVALOSON.

Groupement National des Exportateurs de Vanille de Madagascar (GNEV): BP 21, Antalaha; tel. (13) 20714532; fax (13) 20816017; e-mail rama.anta@sat.blueline.mg; 18 mems; Pres. JEAN GEORGES RANDRIAMIHARISOA.

Malagasy Entrepreneurs' Association (FIV.MPA.MA): Lot II, 2e étage, Immeuble Santa, Antaninarenina; tel. (20) 2229292; fax (20) 2229290; e-mail fivmpama@moov.mg; comprises 10 trade assocs, representing 200 mems, and 250 direct business mems; Chair. HERINTSALAMA RAJAONARIVELO.

Syndicat des Industries de Madagascar (SIM): Immeuble Holcim, Lot 1 bis, Tsaralalàna; BP 1695, 101 Antananarivo; tel. (20) 2224007; fax (20) 2222518; e-mail syndusmad@wanadoo.mg; internet www.syndusmad.com; f. 1958; Pres. HERY RANAIVOSOA; 82 mems (2006).

Syndicat des Planteurs de Café: 37 Làlana Razafimahandry, BP 173, 101 Antananarivo.

Syndicat Professionnel des Agents Généraux d'Assurances: Antananarivo; f. 1949; Pres. SOLO RATSIMBAZAFY; Sec. IHANTA RANDRIAMANDRANTO.

Syndicat Professionel des Producteurs d'Extraits Aromatiques, Alimentaires et Medicinaux de Madagascar (SYPEAM): 7 rue Rakotoson Toto Radona, Antsahavola, BP 5038, Antananarivo 101; tel. (20) 2235363; e-mail itd.madagascar@moov.mg.

UTILITIES

Electricity and Water

Office de Regulation de l'Electricité (ORE): rue Tsimanindry, Ambatoroka, Antananarivo; tel. (20) 2264813; fax (20) 2264191; e-mail ore@ore.mg; internet www.ore.mg; f. 2004; Pres. AIMÉE ANDRIANASOLO.

Jiro sy Rano Malagasy (JIRAMA): BP 200, 149 rue Rainandriamampandry, Faravohitra, 101 Antananarivo; tel. (20) 2220031; fax (20) 2233806; e-mail dgjirama@jirama.mg; internet www.jirama.mg; f. 1975; controls production and distribution of electricity and water; managed by local manager; Pres. HAJA RESAMPA; Dir-Gen. RASIDY DÉSIRÉ.

TRADE UNIONS

Cartel National des Organisations Syndicales de Madagascar (CARNOSYMA): BP 1035, 101 Antananarivo.

Confédération des Travailleurs Malagasy Révolutionnaires (FISEMARE): Lot IV N 76-A, Ankadifotsy, BP 1128, Befelatanana-Antananarivo 101; tel. (20) 2221989; fax (20) 2267712; f. 1985; Pres. PAUL RABEMANANJARA.

Confédération des Travailleurs Malgaches (Fivomdronamben'ny Mpiasa Malagasy—FMM): Lot IVM 133 A Antetezanafovoany I, BP 846, 101 Antananarivo; tel. (20) 2224565; e-mail rjeannot2002@yahoo.fr; f. 1957; Sec.-Gen. JEANNOT RAMANARIVO; 30,000 mems.

Fédération des Syndicats des Travailleurs de Madagascar (Firaisan'ny Sendika eran'i Madagaskara—FISEMA): Lot III, rue Pasteur Isotry, BP 172, 101 Antananarivo; e-mail fisema@gmail.co; internet fisema.org; f. 1956; Pres. DESIRÉ RALAMBOTAHINA; Sec.-Gen. M. RAZAKANAIVO; 8 affiliated unions representing 60,000 mems.

Sendika Kristianina Malagasy (SEKRIMA) (Christian Confederation of Malagasy Trade Unions): Soarano, route de Mahajanga, BP 1035, 101 Antananarivo; tel. (20) 2223174; f. 1937; Pres. MARIE RAKOTOANOSY; Gen. Sec. RAYMOND RAKOTOARISAONA; 158 affiliated unions representing 40,000 mems.

Union des Syndicats Autonomes de Madagascar (USAM): Lot III M 33 BC, Andrefan'Ambohijanahary, BP 1038, 101 Antananarivo; tel. and fax (20) 2227485; e-mail usam@moov.mg; f. 1954; Pres. THÉOPHILE JOËL RUFIN RAZAKARIASY; Sec.-Gen. SAMUEL RABEMANANTSOA; 49 affiliated unions representing 30,000 mems.

Transport

RAILWAYS

In 2001 there were 893 km of railway, including four railway lines, all 1-m gauge track. The northern system, which comprised 720 km of track, links the east coast with Antsirabé, in the interior, via Moramanga and Antananarivo, with a branch line from Moramanga to Lake Alaotra, and was privatized in 2001. The southern system, which comprised 163 km of track, links Manakara, on the east coast, with Fianarantsoa.

Réseau National des Chemins de Fer Malagasy (RNCFM): 1 ave de l'Indépendance, BP 259, Soarano, 101 Antananarivo; tel. (20) 2220521; fax (20) 2222288; f. 1909; in the process of transfer to private sector; Administrator DANIEL RAZAFINDRABE.

Fianarantsoa-Côte Est (FCE): FCE Gare, Fianarantsoa; tel. (20) 7551354; e-mail fce@blueline.mg; internet www.fce-madagascar.com; f. 1936; southern network, 163 km.

Madarail: Gare de Soarano, 1 ave de l'Indépendance, BP 1175, 101 Antananarivo; tel. (20) 2234599; fax (20) 2221883; e-mail madarail@wanadoo.mg; internet www.comazar.com/madarail.htm; f. 2001; jt venture, operated by Comazar, South Africa; 45% of Comazar is owned by Sheltam Locomotive and Rail Services, South Africa; 31.6% is owned by Transnet Freight Rail, South Africa; operates the northern network of the Malagasy railway (650 km); Chair. ERIC PEIFFER; Gen. Dir PATRICK CLAES; 878 employees.

ROADS

In 2001 there were an estimated 49,837 km of classified roads; about 11.6% of the road network was paved. In 1987 there were 39,500 km of unclassified roads, used only in favourable weather. A road and motorway redevelopment programme, funded by the World Bank (€300m.) and the European Union (EU—€61m.), began in June 2000. In August 2002 the EU undertook to disburse US $10m. for the reconstruction of 11 bridges destroyed during the political crisis in that year. In 2003 Japan pledged $28m. to build several bridges and a 15-km bypass. The Government planned to have restored and upgraded 14,000 km of highways and 8,000 km of rural roads to an operational status by 2015. In 2005, according to the IMF, 8,982 km of roads had been maintained or rehabilitated.

INLAND WATERWAYS

The Pangalanes canal runs for 600 km near the east coast from Toamasina to Farafangana. In 1990 432 km of the canal between Toamasina and Mananjary were navigable.

SHIPPING

There are 18 ports, the largest being at Toamasina, which handles about 70% of total traffic, and Mahajanga; several of the smaller ports are prone to silting problems. A new deep-sea port was to be constructed at Ehoala, near Fort Dauphin, in order to accommodate the activity of an ilmenite mining development by 2008.

CMA—CGM Madagascar: Village des jeux, Bat. C1 Ankorondrano, BP 12042, 101 Antananarivo; tel. (20) 2235949; fax (20) 2266120; e-mail tnr@cma-cgm.mg; internet www.cma-cgm.com; maritime transport; Gen. Man. JOËL LE JULIEN.

Compagnie Générale Maritime Sud (CGM): BP 1185, Lot II U 31 bis, Ampahibe, 101 Antananarivo; tel. (20) 2220113; fax (20) 2226530.

Compagnie Malgache de Navigation (CMN): rue Rabearivelo, BP 1621, 101 Antananarivo; tel. (20) 2225516; fax (20) 2230358; f. 1960; coasters; 13,784 grt; 97.5% state-owned; privatization pending; Pres. ELINAH BAKOLY RAJAONSON; Dir-Gen. ARISTIDE EMMANUEL.

SCAC-SDV Shipping Madagascar: rue Rabearivelo Antsahavola, BP 514, 102 Antananarivo; tel. (20) 2220631; fax (20) 2247862; operates the harbour in Antananarivo Port.

Société Malgache des Transports Maritimes (SMTM): 6 rue Indira Gandhi, BP 4077, 101 Antananarivo; tel. (20) 2227342; fax (20) 2233327; f. 1963; 59% state-owned; privatization pending; services to Europe; Chair. ALEXIS RAZAFINDRATSIRA; Dir-Gen. JEAN RANJEVA.

CIVIL AVIATION

The Ivato international airport is at Antananarivo, while the airports at Mahajanga, Toamasina and Nossi-Bé can also accommodate large jet aircraft. There are 211 airfields, two-thirds of which are privately owned. In 1996 the Government authorized private French airlines to operate scheduled and charter flights between Madagascar and Western Europe.

Aeromarine: Zone Industrielle FORELLO, Tanjombato, BP 3844, 102 Antananarivo; tel. (20) 2248286; fax (20) 2258026; e-mail aeromarine@blueline.mg; internet www.aeromarine.mg; f. 1991; Dir-Gen. RIAZ BARDAY.

Air Madagascar (Société Nationale Malgache des Transports Aériens): 31 ave de l'Indépendance, Analakely, BP 437, 101 Antananarivo; tel. (20) 2222222; fax (20) 2233760; e-mail commercial@airmadagascar.com; internet www.airmadagascar.com; f. 1962; 90.60% state-owned; 3.17% owned by Air France (France); transfer to the private sector pending; restructured and managed by Lufthansa Consulting since 2002; extensive internal routes connecting all the principal towns; external services to France, Italy, the Comoros, Kenya, Mauritius, Réunion, South Africa and Thailand; Chair. HERINIAINA RAZAFIMAHEFA; Gen. Man. ROLAND RANJATOELINA.

Air Transport et Transit Régional (ATTR): tel. (32) 0518811; fax (32) 3205218; e-mail attr.reservation@blueline.mg; internet www.attrmada.com; f. 2006; private; regular local and regional services; services suspended in 2008; Dir Gen. FRÉDÉRIC RABESAHALA.

Aviation Civile de Madagascar (ACM): 13 rue Fernand Kasanga, BP 4414, 101 Tsimbazaza-Antananarivo; tel. (20) 2222438; fax (20) 2224726; e-mail acm@acm.mg; internet www.acm.mg; f. 2000; Chair. TOKIARITEFY RABESON; Dir-Gen. MAMONJISOA WILFRID RATSIRAHONANA (acting).

Transports et Travaux Aériens de Madagascar (TAM): 17 ave de l'Indépendance, Analakely, Antananarivo; tel. (20) 2222222; fax (20) 2224340; e-mail tamdg@wanadoo.mg; f. 1951; provides airline services; Administrators LALA RAZAFINDRAKOTO, FRANÇOIS DANE.

Tourism

Madagascar's attractions include unspoiled scenery, many unusual varieties of flora and fauna, and the rich cultural diversity of Malagasy life. In 2008 some 375,010 tourists visited Madagascar, the majority were from France (56.0%). Revenue from tourism in 2008 was estimated at US $620m.

Direction d'Appui aux Investissements Publiques: BP 610, rue Fernand Kasanga Tsimbazaza, 101 Antananarivo; tel. (20) 2262816; fax (20) 2235410; e-mail mintourdati@wandaoo.mg; internet www.tourisme.gov.mg.

Office National du Tourisme de Madagascar: 3 rue Elysée Ravelontsalama, Ambatomena, 101 Antananarivo; tel. (20) 2266115; fax (20) 2266098; e-mail ontm@moov.mg; internet www.madagascar-tourisme.com; Pres. JOEL RANDRIAMANDRANTO.

Defence

As assessed at November 2010, total armed forces numbered 13,500 men: army 12,500, navy 500 and air force 500. There is a paramilitary gendarmerie of 8,100.

Defence Expenditure: Budgeted at an estimated 119,000m. ariary in 2010.

Chief of Staff of the Armed Forces: Col ANDRÉ ANDRIARIJAONA.

Education

Education is officially compulsory between six and 13 years of age. Madagascar has both public and private schools, although legislation that was enacted in 1978 envisaged the progressive elimination of private education. Primary education generally begins at the age of six and lasts for five years. Secondary education, beginning at 11 years of age, lasts for a further seven years, comprising a first cycle of four years and a second of three years. According to UNESCO estimates, in 2006/07 primary enrolment included 98% of children in the relevant age-group (male 98%; females 99%), while in 2008/09 secondary enrolment included 26% of children in the relevant age-group (males 26%; females 25%). In 2008/09 68,500 students attended institutions providing tertiary education; there are six universities in Madagascar. In 2008 spending on education represented 13.4% of total budgetary expenditure.

MALAWI

Introductory Survey

LOCATION, CLIMATE, LANGUAGE, RELIGION, FLAG, CAPITAL

The Republic of Malawi is a land-locked country in southern central Africa, with Zambia to the west, Mozambique to the south and east, and Tanzania to the north. Lake Malawi forms most of the eastern boundary. The climate is tropical, but much of the country is sufficiently high above sea-level to modify the heat. Temperatures range from 14°C (57°F) to 18°C (64°F) in mountain areas, but can reach 38°C (100°F) in low-lying regions. There is a rainy season between November and April. The official language is English, although Chichewa is being promoted as the basis for a 'Malawi Language'. Chitumbuka, a national language, and Yao are also widely spoken. More than 70% of the population profess Christianity, while a further 20%, largely Asians, are Muslims. Most of the remaining Malawians follow traditional beliefs, although there is also a Hindu minority. The national flag (proportions 2 by 3) has three equal horizontal stripes, of red, black and green, with a white sun in the centre of the black stripe. The capital is Lilongwe.

CONTEMPORARY POLITICAL HISTORY

Historical Context

Malawi was formerly the British protectorate of Nyasaland. In 1953 it was linked with two other British dependencies, Northern and Southern Rhodesia (now Zambia and Zimbabwe), to form the Federation of Rhodesia and Nyasaland. The Federation was dissolved in December 1963 and Nyasaland gained independence, as Malawi, on 6 July 1964. The country became a republic and a one-party state, with Dr Hastings Kamuzu Banda, the leader of the Malawi Congress Party (MCP), as its first President, on 6 July 1966. Malawi created a major controversy among African states in 1967 by officially recognizing the Republic of South Africa. In 1971 Banda, named Life President in that year, became the first African head of state to visit South Africa. In 1976, however, Malawi recognized the communist-backed Government in Angola in preference to the South African-supported forces. Malawi did not recognize the 'independence' granted by South Africa to four of its African 'homelands'.

Domestic Political Affairs

Until 1993 all Malawian citizens were obliged to be members of the MCP; no political opposition was tolerated, and only candidates who had been approved by Banda were allowed to contest elections to the National Assembly. Frequent reorganizations of the Cabinet effectively prevented the emergence of any political rival to Banda. However, it was reported in 1983 that a conflict had developed between Dick Matenje, the Minister without Portfolio in the Cabinet and Secretary-General of the MCP, and John Tembo, the Governor of the Reserve Bank of Malawi, concerning the eventual succession to Banda. In May the authorities reported that Matenje and three other senior politicians had died in a road accident; Malawian exiles claimed that the four men had been shot while attempting to flee the country.

Opposition to the Government intensified during 1992 and in September opposition activists formed the Alliance for Democracy (AFORD)—a pressure group operating within Malawi, under the chairmanship of Chakufwa Chihana, a prominent trade union leader—which aimed to campaign for democratic political reform. Another opposition grouping, the United Democratic Front (UDF), was formed in October. In that month Banda conceded that a referendum on the introduction of a multi-party system would take place. However, in November the Government banned AFORD. In the following month Chihana was found guilty of sedition and sentenced to two years' hard labour (reduced to nine months in March 1993).

At the referendum on the introduction of a multi-party system, held on 14 June 1993, 63.2% of those who participated (some 63.5% of the electorate) voted for an end to single-party rule. Banda rejected opposition demands for the immediate installation of an interim government of national unity. He agreed, however, to the establishment of a National Executive Council to oversee the transition to a multi-party system and the holding of free elections, and of a National Consultative Council to implement the necessary amendments to the Constitution. Both councils were to include members of the Government and the opposition. Banda announced an amnesty for thousands of political exiles, and stated that a general election would be held, on a multi-party basis, within a year. In late June the Constitution was amended to allow the registration of political parties other than the MCP: by mid-August five organizations, including AFORD and the UDF, had been accorded official status.

In September 1993 Banda carried out an extensive cabinet reshuffle, relinquishing the post of Minister of External Affairs, which he had held since 1964. In October 1993 Banda underwent neurological surgery in South Africa. Interim executive power was assumed by a three-member Presidential Council, chaired by the new Secretary-General of the MCP, Gwandaguluwe Chakuamba. In November a further cabinet reshuffle relieved Banda of all ministerial responsibilities. Later in November the National Assembly approved a Constitutional Amendment Bill, which, inter alia, abolished the institution of life presidency, ended the requirement that election candidates be members of the MCP and repealed the right of the President to nominate members of the legislature exclusively from the MCP.

Having made a rapid and unexpected recovery, Banda resumed full presidential powers in December 1993. Shortly afterwards, in response to increasing pressure from the opposition, the Government amended the Constitution to provide for the appointment of an acting President in the event of the incumbent being incapacitated. In February 1994 the MCP announced that Banda was to be the party's presidential candidate in the forthcoming general election (scheduled for May). Also in February the National Assembly approved an increase in the number of elective seats in the legislature from 141 to 177.

On 16 May 1994 the National Assembly adopted a provisional Constitution, which provided for the appointment of a Constitutional Committee and of a human rights commission, and abolished the system of 'traditional' courts. Malawi's first multi-party parliamentary and presidential elections took place on 17 May. In the presidential election the Secretary-General of the UDF, (Elson) Bakili Muluzi (a former government minister and MCP Secretary-General), took 47.3% of the votes cast, defeating Banda (who won 33.6% of the votes). Eight parties contested the legislative elections: of these, the UDF won 85 seats in the National Assembly, the MCP 56 and AFORD 36. The Constitution was introduced for a one-year period on 18 May; it was to be subject to further review prior to official ratification one year later.

The Muluzi presidency

President Muluzi and his Vice-President, Justin Malewezi, were inaugurated on 21 May 1994. The new UDF-dominated Government proclaimed an amnesty for the country's remaining political prisoners, and commuted all death sentences to terms of life imprisonment. In August it was announced that Banda, while remaining honorary Life President of the MCP, was to retire from active involvement in politics. Chakuamba, as Vice-President of the party, effectively became the leader of the MCP.

In September 1994 a number of AFORD members were appointed to the Government, including Chihana as Second Vice-President and Minister of Irrigation and Water Development. Meanwhile, the creation of the post of Second Vice-President had necessitated a constitutional amendment, and provoked severe criticism from the MCP. In March the National Assembly (in the absence of MCP deputies, who boycotted the vote) approved the retention of the second vice-presidency; the Assembly also endorsed recommendations for the establishment—although not before May 1999—of a second chamber of parliament. The Constitution took effect on 18 May 1995.

In June 1994 Muluzi established an independent commission of inquiry to investigate the deaths of Matenje and his associates in May 1983. In January 1995, in accordance with the findings of the commission, Banda was placed under house arrest and Tembo and two former police officers were detained; the four were charged with murder and conspiracy to murder. A former inspector-general of police was charged later in the month. In April Cecilia Kadzamira, Tembo's niece and the former President's 'Official Hostess', was also charged with conspiracy to murder. The trial opened later that month, but was immediately adjourned, owing to Banda's failure to appear in court (his defence counsel asserted that he was too ill to stand trial) and to the failure of the state prosecution to submit certain evidence to the defence. Hearings resumed, in Banda's absence, in July. In September Tembo and the two former police officers were granted bail, and most restrictions on Banda's movements were ended. The case against Kadzamira was abandoned in December, owing to lack of evidence, and later that month Banda, Tembo and the other defendants were found not guilty of conspiracy to murder and conspiracy to defeat justice. In January 1996 an MCP-owned newspaper printed a statement by Banda in which he admitted that he might unknowingly have been responsible for brutalities perpetrated under his regime and apologized to Malawians for 'pain and suffering' inflicted during his presidency. In November 1997 Banda died in South Africa, where he had been undergoing emergency medical treatment. He was accorded a state funeral, with full military honours

Meanwhile, there were further allegations that the Muluzi administration had been involved in dubious financial transactions. It emerged, in mid-1995, that the President had authorized the payment of some 6.2m. kwacha from the state poverty alleviation account to UDF deputies; there was also evidence of the involvement of government ministers in the smuggling of maize to neighbouring countries. In February 1996 Muluzi announced that an independent Anti-Corruption Bureau (ACB) was to be established to investigate allegations of corruption.

In June 1998 the National Assembly approved legislation providing for the introduction of a single-ballot electoral system to replace the existing multiple-ballot system and for a strengthening of the authority and independence of the Malawi Electoral Commission (MEC). In November legislation was adopted to allow presidential and parliamentary elections to run concurrently (as Muluzi's term was due to end several weeks earlier than that of the National Assembly), and the elections were subsequently scheduled for 18 May 1999. In February the National Assembly adopted a controversial report by the MEC that recommended the creation of a further 72 parliamentary seats, including an additional 42 in the Southern Region, a UDF stronghold. In response to widespread opposition to the proposals, however, only 16 of the 72 seats were approved.

Having been postponed twice, the presidential and legislative elections were held on 15 June 1999. Muluzi was re-elected to the presidency, securing 51.4% of the votes cast, while Chakuamba obtained 43.3%. Turn-out was high, at 93.8%. At the elections to the expanded National Assembly the ruling UDF won 94 seats, while the MCP secured 66 seats, AFORD 29 and independent candidates four. Despite declarations from international observers that the elections were largely free and fair, the MCP-AFORD alliance filed two petitions with the High Court, challenging Muluzi's victory and the results in 16 districts. The opposition alleged irregularities in the voter registration process and claimed that Muluzi's victory was unconstitutional, as he had failed to gain the support of 50% of all registered voters. None the less, Muluzi was inaugurated later in June, and a new Cabinet was appointed. In August the UDF regained a parliamentary majority when the four independent deputies decided to ally themselves with the UDF, of which they had previously been members.

Chakuamba, who had maintained a boycott of the new parliament pending the result of his party's challenge to the outcome of the elections, was suspended from the chamber in June 2000. Tembo assumed the leadership of the opposition and appointed his supporters to prominent posts within the MCP. Chakuamba was reinstated in September, and a dispute between the two factions ensued. In October the opposition's petitions against the election results were dismissed by the High Court.

In January 2001 deputies from the Tembo faction of the MCP ensured the approval by the National Assembly of a UDF proposal to abandon plans (ostensibly for financial reasons) for the creation of a second legislative chamber, the Senate, which would have had powers to impeach the President; AFORD boycotted the vote. In November seven deputies who had joined the opposition National Democratic Alliance (NDA) were excluded from the National Assembly for abandoning the political parties for which they had been elected, an action proscribed by law since May, when the UDF acted to prevent defections to the NDA; Sam Mpasu, the Speaker, defied an order of the High Court restraining him from expelling the deputies.

Proposed legislation to change the Constitution to allow Muluzi to seek a third presidential term failed to gain the requisite two-thirds' majority in July 2002. A further attempt to introduce a constitutional amendment also failed in January 2003, when the bill was withdrawn. The UDF declared that it would hold a referendum on the issue later in the year. However, in March Muluzi declared that he would not seek a third presidential term, and proposed Dr Bingu wa Mutharika, recently appointed Minister of Economic Planning and Development, as his successor, to contest the presidential election scheduled for May 2004. (Mutharika had represented the United Party at the 1999 presidential election, but subsequently defected to the UDF.)

In May 2003 Tembo and Chakuamba were elected, respectively, as President and Vice-President of the MCP. Tembo was subsequently named as the MCP's candidate to contest the 2004 presidential election. Chakuamba resigned from the MCP and formed the Republican Party (RP). On 1 January 2004 Justin Malewezi, Malawi's First Vice-President and Minister responsible for Privatization, resigned from the UDF for 'personal reasons', but did not relinquish his position in the Government, stating that he would remain in office, but on leave, until after the presidential election had taken place. Malewezi subsequently joined the People's Progressive Movement (PPM), an opposition party founded the previous year. Later that month Aleke Banda, who had resigned from the UDF in May 2003, was elected as President of the PPM, while Malewezi was chosen as its Vice-President. Also in January 2004 the PPM, the RP and several other opposition parties announced the formation of the Mgwirizano Coalition to contest the forthcoming presidential election; Chakuamba was elected as the coalition's presidential candidate in February. Malewezi subsequently announced that he would contest the election as an independent. A minor cabinet reorganization was effected in late February, and Muluzi appointed Hetherwick Ntaba, the leader of the New Congress for Democracy (NCD), as Minister of Energy and Mining at the end of March, following the NCD's decision to join the UDF-AFORD electoral alliance.

Mutharika elected President

At the presidential election held on 20 May 2004 Mutharika, representing the ruling UDF, secured 35.9% of the valid votes cast. Tembo, of the MCP, and Chakuamba, representing the Mgwirizano Coalition, took 27.1% and 25.7% of the vote, respectively. Cassim Chilumpha, of the UDF, was elected as Vice-President. At concurrent elections to the National Assembly, however, the MCP emerged as the largest party, winning 56 of the 193 seats in the legislature, while the UDF secured 49 seats and the Mgwirizano Coalition 25; 39 of the remaining seats were taken by independent candidates, while voting in six constituencies was not conducted owing to irregularities. International observers criticized the conduct of the polls and opposition parties disputed the results. Mutharika was sworn in as President on 24 May amid rioting by opposition supporters. The new Cabinet, appointed in June 2004, comprised 21 ministers, compared with 32 under the previous administration. Mutharika, in defiance of critics who believed that he would merely serve to act as Muluzi's 'puppet', pledged to take measures to combat corruption and to effect wide-ranging economic reforms. In October the former Minister of Finance, Friday Jumbe, was arrested in connection with illegal sales of maize during 2001–02 while General Manager of the Agriculture Development and Marketing Corporation; he was subsequently charged with four counts of corruption. Also in October 2004 it was announced that at least 10 former senior ministers were under investigation by the ACB following the disappearance of more than 10,000m. kwacha during the Muluzi presidency.

In February 2005 Mutharika resigned from the leadership of the UDF—of which Muluzi was Chairman—claiming that the party was opposing his campaign against corruption. Prior to the announcement, Mutharika dismissed three members of the Government loyal to Muluzi, including Chihana, who was replaced as Minister of Agriculture, Irrigation and Food Security by Chakuamba. Later that month Mutharika announced his intention to form a new political party, the Democratic Progressive Party (DPP), which was formally registered in March. In May the Minister of Education and Human Resources, Yusuf Mwawa, was arrested on charges of corruption, fraud and misuse of public funds. (In February 2006 Mwawa was sentenced to five years' imprisonment.) In June 2005 the UDF introduced before the National Assembly a motion of impeachment against Mutharika, alleging statutory violations of the Constitution and misuse of public funds.

In October 2005 Muluzi was summoned to appear before the ACB, which was investigating the misappropriation of 1,400m. kwacha in foreign aid during his presidency. It was alleged that much of this money had been diverted to personal bank accounts and had also been used to finance the 2004 presidential campaign. Muluzi was able to obtain an injunction from the High Court, which allowed him to refuse to answer the ACB's questions. However, later that month police and ACB officers raided three properties belonging to Muluzi, confiscating computer equipment and banking documents. In November Vice-President Chilumpha was arrested in connection with the alleged embezzlement of 187m. kwacha during his tenure as Minister of Education. Chilumpha obtained an injunction against criminal proceedings on the grounds that as the incumbent Vice-President he was immune from prosecution.

Meanwhile, following an agreement between the UDF and Tembo, in October 2005 the National Assembly voted in favour of beginning proceedings to impeach Mutharika. Envoys from several donor countries (including the United Kingdom, the USA and South Africa) were signatories to a letter to the opposition requesting that they reconsider their decision in the interests of the country at large. Despite their appeal, Mutharika was summoned to face indictment before the National Assembly later that month. However, the impeachment process was halted by the High Court after concern was expressed over the constitutionality of the process. In December former regional heads of state—Nelson Mandela of South Africa, Joachim Chissano of Mozambique and Sir Ketumile Masire of Botswana—brokered talks between Mutharika, Muluzi and Tembo in an attempt to halt the impeachment proceedings; however, they ended without success. The impeachment motion was eventually withdrawn in January 2006, prompting the resignation of seven UDF members, five of whom subsequently joined the DPP.

In February 2006 it was announced that Mutharika had accepted Chilumpha's 'constructive resignation'. In a letter to Chilumpha, the President asserted that Chilumpha had abandoned his duties as Vice-President, leading the Cabinet to conclude that he had resigned. Chilumpha refuted the allegations made against him—*inter alia*, that he had attended only 16 out of 48 cabinet meetings and had left the country without informing Mutharika—and brought the matter before the High Court on the grounds that his dismissal was unconstitutional: as an elected minister he could only be dismissed by Parliament, not by the President. In March the High Court apparently ordered Chilumpha's full restitution; however, the Supreme Court ruled later that month that although Chilumpha was confirmed in his position as Vice-President, the Government was permitted to strip him of all benefits and entitlements. In April Chilumpha was arrested and charged with treason and conspiring to murder the President. His trial commenced in early 2007 and was ongoing in 2011, having been subject to numerous delays.

A High Court ruling in November 2006 stated that the section of the Constitution that stipulated that the Speaker must declare vacant the parliamentary seat of any member of the legislature wishing to move to a different political party did not breach any other principle of the Constitution. The decision was passed after it was noted that many deputies had realigned themselves with the ruling DPP without first consulting their constituency. The DPP challenged the decision; however, in June 2007 the Supreme Court of Appeal ruled that the Speaker had the authority to expel from the National Assembly any member of that body who switched party allegiances. Opposition deputies insisted upon the expulsions and in July members of the MCP and the UDF refused to participate in discussions regarding the budget for the 2007/08 financial year. In the following month an injunction was granted allowing the opposition to continue their delay of the debate on the budget, although that order was overturned after an appeal by the Attorney-General. In August the debate began without the participation of opposition deputies, and in September the budget was finally approved. A similar dispute arose the following year, delaying the approval of the 2008/09 budget by one month.

In February 2008 President Mutharika carried out a reorganization of the Cabinet, in which the Minister of Defence and the Minister of Health were replaced. Muluzi was nominated in April by the UDF as that party's candidate for the presidential election due to be held concurrently with legislative elections in May 2009; having previously served two terms in office, opponents objected to his candidacy. However, Muluzi's supporters maintained that the Constitution stipulated only that a President may not serve more than two 'consecutive' terms. In March 2009 the MEC ruled that Muluzi was ineligible to contest the election on the grounds that he had already served as President for the maximum period of two five-year terms. Muluzi appealed against the decision, but in May the Constitutional Court rejected his challenge. He subsequently declared his support for Tembo, who had been selected as the presidential candidate for the UDF-MCP-New Republican Party (NRP) alliance.

Meanwhile, reports emerged in May 2008 that eight high-ranking security officials, including former Commander-in-Chief of the Armed Forces Lt-Gen. Joseph Chimbayo, had been arrested following accusations by Mutharika that they had been acting under instruction from Muluzi in an attempt to remove him from office; seven were subsequently released on bail. Later that month Muluzi was questioned by police and placed under house arrest. Muluzi denied the allegations and was later released without charge. In December Chakuamba, the President of the NRP, was arrested for encouraging violence against Mutharika's Lhomwe tribe but was released on bail. In February 2009 Muluzi was again detained on charges of corruption relating to the misappropriation of donor funds during his presidency (see above). He appeared in court in April, but refused to enter a plea. Muluzi's legal representatives maintained that they were in possession of evidence that demonstrated that Mutharika had been responsible for instigating renewed investigation into the case by the ACB. Muluzi's trial commenced in March 2011, after the High Court dismissed an application to halt proceedings on the grounds of the former President's ill health; he denied the corruption charges against him.

Recent developments: Mutharika's second term

In April 2009 Chakuamba announced that the NRP, together with the MCP and the UDF, had formed an alliance to contest the forthcoming presidential and legislative elections. By late April several smaller parties had also indicated their willingness to join the new alliance. Nevertheless, Mutharika won an overwhelming victory in the presidential election, which was held on 19 May, with 64.4% of the votes cast, while the DPP retained control of the National Assembly in the concurrent legislative poll. The DPP won 112 of the 192 available seats (voting in one constituency was postponed owing to the death of a candidate), the MCP took only 27 seats (compared with 56 in the 2004 election) and the UDF, the influence of which was predominantly limited to the south of the country, 18 seats (compared with 49 in 2004). A further 32 seats were secured by independent candidates, many of whom had connections to the DPP. Tembo, who had secured 29.9% of the votes in the presidential election, claimed that there was evidence of electoral fraud; however, the MEC declared the ballot to have been free and fair. In mid-June 2009 President Mutharika announced the formation of a new Government, which included a number of new appointments to key roles. Ken Edward Kandodo was named Minister of Finance, replacing Dr Goodall E. Gondwe, despite the latter's involvement in supporting the country's economic recovery following the global downturn. Prof. Arthur Peter Mutharika, the President's brother, assumed the role of Minister of Justice and Constitutional Affairs, amid widespread reports that he was being prepared to take over the presidency in 2014. In December 2009 Muluzi stepped down as Chairman of the UDF; he was replaced as party leader on an interim basis by Friday Jumbe, who assumed the position of President of the UDF.

After his defeat in the presidential election, in November 2009 Tembo was replaced as the leader of the opposition in the National Assembly by Ephraim Abel Kayembe, also of the MCP, as a result of a vote in which deputies of all parties were permitted to participate. Following complaints by the MCP's National Executive Committee, in May 2010 the High Court invalidated Kayembe's appointment as leader of the opposition on the grounds that he had been elected by the National Assembly rather than by the MCP, in contravention of the Constitution. In accordance with this decision, the MCP promptly elected Tembo as Kayembe's replacement. However, in spite of a subsequent confirmation of the ruling by the Supreme Court, the Speaker of the National Assembly refused to recognize Tembo as the new leader of the opposition. Legal action to resolve the issue was ongoing in 2011.

Malawi's conservative stance on civil liberties came under international scrutiny in May 2010, when a homosexual couple, who had allegedly been forced to endure beatings and intrusive medical examinations while in custody, were convicted of 'gross indecency and unnatural acts' and sentenced to 14 years' imprisonment. Following criticism from Western donor nations and human rights organizations, Mutharika pardoned the two men, and they were released later that month, although the President denied that international pressure had prompted him to take this action.

In August 2010 Mutharika effected a cabinet reorganization. The ministers responsible for health, transport, local government and gender were all dismissed, while Arthur Peter Mutharika was appointed as Minister of Education, Science and Technology; the President controversially allocated his wife, Callista wa Mutharika, responsibility for maternal, infant and child health, although it was later clarified that she would not be a cabinet member, nor receive a ministerial salary. There was speculation that the Minister of Local Government and Rural Development, former finance minister Goodall Gondwe, had been replaced because of the repeated postponement of the local elections—last held in 2000 and due since 2005—ostensibly owing to procedural delays and a lack of progress in the implementation of local government reforms. (The local elections were subsequently rescheduled for April 2011.) However, press reports claimed that the dismissals had been prompted by a dispute within the DPP over who would become the party's presidential candidate in the 2014 election in place of Mutharika, who was constitutionally prohibited from standing for a third term of office. President Mutharika favoured his brother, Arthur Peter Mutharika, and had been manoeuvring against Vice-President Joyce Banda, viewed as a potential rival candidate, in an attempt to secure her expulsion from the DPP. The dismissed ministers had reportedly criticized the President's efforts to remove Banda from the ruling party. Amid rising factionalism within the DPP, in September 2010 the party terminated official ties with its youth wing, the allegedly pro-Banda Progressive Democratic Youth Movement, which subsequently denounced the DPP's 'undemocratic endorsement' of Arthur Peter Mutharika's candidature. Meanwhile, in a further attempt to marginalize Banda, President Mutharika had transferred some of the Vice-President's responsibilities to his wife. In December the DPP finally expelled Banda, accusing her of involvement in 'anti-party activities' and of 'forming parallel structures in the party and Government', although it was widely believed that her expulsion had resulted from her failure to support Arthur Peter Mutharika as the DPP's official presidential candidate. Hundreds of DPP members nation-wide resigned from the party in protest and formed a new grouping, the Friends of Joyce Banda. Despite reported death threats against her, it was anticipated that Vice-President Banda would announce the creation of a new political organization, the People's Party, in March 2011.

In January 2011 the UDF's National Executive Committee elected Dr George Nga Ntafu as party Chairman; however, Jumbe denounced the Committee's action as a 'failed *coup d'état*' and refused to stand down from the interim presidency of the UDF, effectively splitting the party into two factions. Jumbe's faction subsequently elected former Vice-President Chilumpha, who had secured a seat in the National Assembly as an independent in the 2009 elections, as its Chairman. The leadership of the UDF remained in dispute in March 2011, although the party's deputies had expressed their support for Ntafu.

Foreign Affairs
Regional relations
Despite being the only African country to have maintained full diplomatic relations with South Africa during the apartheid era, Malawi joined the Southern African Development Co-ordination Conference (subsequently the Southern African Development Community, see p. 420—SADC), which originally aimed to reduce the dependence of southern African countries on South Africa.

Relations with Mozambique were frequently strained during the early and mid-1980s by the widely held belief that the Banda regime was supporting the Resistência Nacional Moçambicana (Renamo—see the chapter on Mozambique). Following the death of President Machel of Mozambique in an air crash in South Africa in October 1986, the South African Government claimed that documents discovered in the wreckage revealed a plot by Mozambique and Zimbabwe to overthrow the Banda Government. Angry protests from Malawi were answered by denials of the accusations from the Mozambican and Zimbabwean Governments. In December, however, Malawi and Mozambique signed an agreement on defence and security matters, which was believed to include co-operation in eliminating Renamo operations. In July 1988, during an official visit to Malawi, President Chissano of Mozambique stated that he did not believe Malawi to be supporting Renamo. In December of that year Malawi, Mozambique and the office of the UN High Commissioner for Refugees (UNHCR) signed an agreement to promote the voluntary repatriation of an estimated 650,000 Mozambican refugees who had fled into Malawi during the previous two years. However, by mid-1992 the number of Mozambican refugees in Malawi had reportedly reached 1m. Large numbers of refugees returned to Mozambique in 1993–94, but in May 1995 Malawi demanded the repatriation of the remainder—estimated to total some 39,000—stating that food aid and other assistance to those who failed to leave would be reduced. The programme of the Malawi-Mozambique-UNHCR commission officially ended in November: it was estimated that a total of 1m. refugees had been repatriated.

Other external relations
Until early 2008 Malawi was one of a small number of nations that accorded Taiwan recognition as an independent country. In January of that year, however, it was announced that Malawi had withdrawn its support for Taiwan and established diplomatic relations with the People's Republic of China.

CONSTITUTION AND GOVERNMENT
Under the provisions of the Constitution promulgated on 18 May 1995, the Head of State is the President, who is elected by universal adult suffrage, in the context of a multi-party political system, for a term of five years. Executive power is vested in the President, and legislative power in the National Assembly, which has 193 elective seats. Members of the Assembly are elected for five years, by universal adult suffrage, in the context of a multi-party system. Cabinet ministers are appointed by the President. The country is divided into three administrative regions (Northern, Central and Southern), sub-divided into 24 districts.

REGIONAL AND INTERNATIONAL CO-OPERATION
Malawi is a member of the African Union (see p. 183), the Southern African Development Community (SADC, see p. 420) and the Common Market for Eastern and Southern Africa (COMESA, see p. 228). Nine members of COMESA, including Malawi, became inaugural members of the COMESA Free Trade Area in October 2000.

Malawi became a member of the UN in 1964 and was admitted to the World Trade Organization (WTO, see p. 430) in 1995. Malawi participates in the Group of 77 (G77, see p. 447) developing countries. The country also belongs to the International Tea Promotion Association (see p. 444) and to the International Tobacco Growers' Association (see p. 444).

ECONOMIC AFFAIRS
In 2009, according to estimates by the World Bank, Malawi's gross national income (GNI), measured at average 2007–09 prices, was US $4,198m., equivalent to $280 per head (or $760 per head on an international purchasing-power parity basis). During 2000–09, it was estimated, the population increased at an average annual rate of 2.9%, while gross domestic product (GDP) per head increased, in real terms, by an average of 1.3% per year. Overall GDP increased, in real terms, at an average annual rate of 4.2% in 2000–09; real GDP increased by 7.7% in 2009.

Agriculture (including forestry and fishing) contributed 35.9% of GDP in 2009, according to the World Bank, and engaged an estimated 78.7% of the labour force in 2011, according to FAO. The principal cash crops are tobacco (which accounted for 63.9% of total export earnings in 2009), tea and sugar cane. The principal food crops are maize, cassava, potatoes, bananas and groundnuts. Periods of severe drought and flooding have necessitated imports of basic foods in recent years. During 2000–09, according to the World Bank, agricultural GDP increased at an average annual rate of 1.7%; it increased by 8.5% in 2009.

Industry (including manufacturing, mining, construction and power) contributed 20.5% of GDP in 2009, according to the World Bank, and engaged 4.5% of the employed labour force in 1998. During 2000–09 industrial GDP increased by an average of 3.2% per year. Industrial GDP increased by 6.0% in 2008 but by only 0.9% in 2009.

Mining and quarrying contributed 4.6% of GDP in 2007, according to the African Development Bank (AfDB), and engaged less than 0.1% of the employed labour force in 1998. Limestone, coal and gemstones are mined, and there are plans to develop deposits of bauxite, high-calcium marble and graphite. There are also reserves of phosphates, uranium, glass sands, asbestos and vermiculite. Environmental and financial concerns have delayed plans to exploit an estimated 30m. metric tons of bauxite deposits at Mount Mulanje. Uranium mining, which commenced at Kayelekera, in northern Malawi, in 2009, was expected to increase the country's export revenue by some 25%. The GDP of the mining sector increased at an average annual rate of 17.6% in 2002–08, according to official figures; mining GDP increased by 6.8% in 2008.

Manufacturing contributed 14.5% of GDP in 2009, according to the World Bank, and engaged 2.7% of the employed labour force in 1998. During 2000–09 manufacturing GDP increased by an average of 2.4% per year. The GDP of the sector grew by 5.9% in 2009.

Construction contributed 3.9% of GDP in 2007, according to the AfDB, and engaged 1.6% of the employed labour force in 1998. The GDP of the construction sector increased at an average annual rate of 0.7% in 2002–08, according to official figures; construction GDP increased by 8.1% in 2008.

Production of electrical energy is by hydroelectric (principally) and thermal installations. Some 95% of energy for domestic use is derived from hydroelectric power. In October 2000 a hydroelectric power plant, with a generation capacity of 64 MW, was opened at Kapichira; in February 2009 the Government pledged funds amounting to some 2,500m. kwacha for the Kapichira Hydroelectric Power Phase II Project, which would double the capacity of the plant. In 2011 the total generation capacity of Malawi's hydroelectric power plants was 282.5 MW. Meanwhile, a World Bank-supported project was planned to connect Malawi's electricity system to Mozambique's Cahora Bassa hydroelectric power plant, which would increase Malawi's power supply by some 200 MW. Investment in alternative sources of energy, such as solar power, the production of gel fuel from ethanol and coal-mining, was also being encouraged, with the construction of a coal-fired plant to generate 300 MW of electricity under consideration. In January 2001 the Government introduced a campaign to widen access to electricity, especially in rural areas. Imports of mineral fuels and lubricants comprised 10.4% of the value of total imports in 2009.

According to the World Bank, the services sector contributed 43.6% of GDP in 2009, and engaged 11.0% of the employed labour force in 1998. The GDP of the services sector increased by an average of 4.1% per year in 2000–09. Services GDP increased by 6.0% in 2009.

Malawi recorded a visible trade deficit of 74,513.9m. kwacha in 2009, while there was a deficit of 108,179.6m. kwacha on the current account of the balance of payments, according to preliminary figures. In 2009 the principal source of imports was South Africa (34.1%); Mozambique and the People's Republic of China were also notable suppliers. Belgium was the principal market for exports (17.5%) in that year; other important markets were South Africa, Egypt and Mozambique. The principal imports in 2009 were machinery and transport equipment, chemicals and related products, basic manufactures, and mineral fuels and lubricants. The principal exports in that year were tobacco, food and live animals (particularly tea and raw cane sugars), and crude materials (inedible) except fuels.

Preliminary figures indicated that in the financial year ending 30 June 2009 Malawi's overall budget deficit was an estimated 37,250m. kwacha. Malawi's general government gross debt was 303,718m. kwacha in 2009, equivalent to 42.4% of GDP. The country's external debt in 2008 totalled US $963m., of which $839m. was public and publicly guaranteed debt. In 2003 the cost of debt-servicing was equivalent to 9.0% of the value of exports of goods, services and income. The annual rate of inflation averaged 12.5% in 2000–09; consumer prices increased by an average of 8.4% in 2009. Some 1.4m. people were unemployed in 2007.

Malawi's natural impediments to growth (including its land-locked position, the vulnerability of the dominant agricultural sector to drought, and a high rate of population growth) were compounded by the severe mismanagement of economic affairs during the early 2000s. The dispersal of funds under the IMF's Poverty Reduction and Growth Facility (PRGF) was delayed and it was not until August 2005 that approval was finally given for a three-year PRGF programme worth US $55m. In September 2006 the World Bank approved the disbursement of debt relief funds amounting to $646m. under the initiative for heavily indebted poor countries. Amid concern regarding the country's vulnerability to the effects of the global financial crisis, in particular the rising cost of importing fuel and fertilizers, in January 2009 Malawi became the first recipient country of the IMF's new Exogenous Shock Facility, under which a one-year loan of $77.1m. was approved. In the budget statement for 2009/10 it was announced that the agricultural sector would receive the largest allocation of funds, including support for a fertilizer subsidy programme in order to safeguard against a recurrence of the food shortages experienced in the mid-2000s, although spending on irrigation and water development projects was to be reduced; in May 2009, however, the AfDB announced the provision of $47.2m. towards the Malawian national water development programme. In February 2010 a supplementary budget increased total expenditure by 11,500m. kwacha (including 950m. kwacha for the purchase of maize) following depleted crop harvests as a result of unexpectedly dry weather in previous months. Also in February the IMF approved a three-year arrangement for Malawi under its Extended Credit Facility, worth $79.4m., of which the Government had received $21.4m. by the end of the year. Additional funding was provided by the European Union, which released a total of €44m. during 2010 under the Vulnerability-Flex Mechanism to mitigate the negative effects of the international economic crisis on Malawi's economy. Nevertheless, IMF projections of GDP growth of 6.0% in 2010 and 6.3% in 2011, driven by the mining and services sectors, demonstrated that the economy had withstood the impact of the global downturn.

PUBLIC HOLIDAYS

2012: 1 January (New Year's Day), 15 January (John Chilembwe Day), 3 March (Martyrs' Day), 6–9 April (Easter), 1 May (Labour Day), 14 June (Freedom Day), 6 July (Republic Day), 13 October (Mothers' Day), 25–26 December (Christmas).

MALAWI

Statistical Survey

Sources (unless otherwise indicated): National Statistical Office of Malawi, POB 333, Zomba; tel. 1524377; fax 1525130; e-mail enquiries@statistics.gov.mw; internet www.nso.malawi.net; Reserve Bank of Malawi, POB 30063, Capital City, Lilongwe 3; tel. 1770600; fax 1772752; e-mail webmaster@rbm.mw; internet www.rbm.mw.

Area and Population

AREA, POPULATION AND DENSITY

Area (sq km)	
Land	94,276
Inland water	24,208
Total	118,484*
Population (census results)	
1–21 September 1998	9,933,868
8–28 June 2008	
Males	6,358,933
Females	6,718,227
Total	13,077,160
Population (official projections at mid-year)	
2009	13,520,101
2010	13,947,952
2011	14,388,550
Density (per sq km) at mid-2011	152.6†

* 45,747 sq miles.
† Land area only.

POPULATION BY AGE AND SEX
(official projections at mid-2011)

	Males	Females	Total
0–14	3,305,931	3,352,176	6,658,107
15–64	3,504,220	3,730,333	7,234,553
65 and over	218,998	276,892	495,890
Total	7,029,149	7,359,401	14,388,550

REGIONS
(population at census of June 2008)

Region	Area (sq km)*	Population	Density (per sq km)	Regional capital
Southern	31,753	5,858,035	184.5	Blantyre
Central	35,592	5,510,195	154.8	Lilongwe
Northern	26,931	1,708,930	63.5	Mzuzu
Total	94,276	13,077,160	138.7	

* Excluding inland waters, totalling 24,208 sq km.

PRINCIPAL TOWNS
(population at census of June 2008)

Lilongwe (capital)	674,448	Karonga	40,334
Blantyre	661,256	Kasungu	39,640
Mzuzu	133,968	Mangochi	39,575
Zomba	88,314	Salima	27,852

BIRTHS AND DEATHS
(annual averages, UN estimates)

	1995–2000	2000–05	2005–10
Birth rate (per 1,000)	47.0	43.7	40.5
Death rate (per 1,000)	14.8	14.6	12.4

Source: UN, *World Population Prospects: The 2008 Revision*.

2008 (official estimates): Live births 609,487 (birth rate 46.5 per 1,000); deaths 195,014 (death rate 14.9 per 1,000).

Life expectancy (years at birth, WHO estimates): 53 (males 52; females 54) in 2008 (Source: WHO, *World Health Statistics*).

ECONOMICALLY ACTIVE POPULATION*
(persons aged 10 years and over, 1998 census)

	Males	Females	Total
Agriculture, hunting, forestry and fishing	1,683,006	2,082,821	3,765,827
Mining and quarrying	2,206	293	2,499
Manufacturing	94,545	23,938	118,483
Electricity, gas and water	6,656	663	7,319
Construction	70,196	3,206	73,402
Trade, restaurants and hotels	176,466	80,923	257,389
Transport, storage and communications	29,438	3,185	32,623
Financing, insurance, real estate and business services	10,473	3,484	13,957
Public administration	82,973	18,460	101,433
Community, social and personal services	52,980	33,016	85,996
Total employed	2,208,940	2,249,989	4,458,929
Unemployed	34,697	15,664	50,361
Total labour force	2,243,637	2,265,653	4,509,290

* Excluding armed forces.

Mid-2011 (estimates in '000): Agriculture, etc. 5,313; Total labour force 6,755 (Source: FAO).

Health and Welfare

KEY INDICATORS

Total fertility rate (children per woman, 2008)	5.5
Under-5 mortality rate (per 1,000 live births, 2008)	100
HIV/AIDS (% of persons aged 15–49, 2007)	11.9
Physicians (per 1,000 head, 2004)	0.02
Hospital beds (per 1,000 head, 2007)	1.1
Health expenditure (2007): US $ per head (PPP)	50
Health expenditure (2007): % of GDP	9.9
Health expenditure (2007): public (% of total)	59.7
Access to water (% of persons, 2008)	80
Access to sanitation (% of persons, 2008)	56
Total carbon dioxide emissions ('000 metric tons, 2007)	1,055.2
Carbon dioxide emissions per head (metric tons, 2007)	0.1
Human Development Index (2010): ranking	153
Human Development Index (2010): value	0.385

For sources and definitions, see explanatory note on p. vi.

MALAWI

Agriculture

PRINCIPAL CROPS
('000 metric tons)

	2006	2007	2008
Rice, paddy	91.5	113.2	114.9
Maize	2,611.5	3,226.4	2,634.7
Millet	27.0	32.3	31.9
Sorghum	54.3	63.7	62.0
Potatoes	2,309.4	2,858.8	2,993.8
Cassava (Manioc)	2,832.1	3,238.9	3,491.2
Beans, dry	117.3	128.6	124.7
Chick-peas*	35	40	40
Cow peas, dry*	54	55	55
Pigeon peas	131.0	159.4	149.9
Groundnuts, with shell	203.1	261.8	243.2
Cabbages and other brassicas*	58	60	60
Tomatoes*	39	40	40
Onions, dry*	54	56	56
Guavas, mangoes and mangosteens*	66	67	67
Bananas*	380	390	390
Plantains*	320	330	330
Sugar cane*	2,450	2,500	2,500
Coffee, green	2.1	1.4	1.1
Tea	45	48.1	48.1*
Tobacco, unmanufactured	121.6	118.0*	160.2

* FAO estimate(s).

Note: Data for individual crops in 2009 were not available.

Aggregate production ('000 metric tons, may include official, semi-official or estimated data): Total cereals 2,786.3 in 2006, 3,440.1 in 2007, 2,845.8 in 2008–09; Total roots and tubers 5,142.0 in 2006, 6,098.2 in 2007, 6,485.4 in 2008–09; Total vegetables (incl. melons) 336.5 in 2006, 342.6 in 2007–09; Total fruits (excl. melons) 967.4 in 2006, 988.4 in 2007–09.

Source: FAO.

LIVESTOCK
('000 head, year ending September)

	2006	2007	2008
Cattle	799	871	947
Pigs	637	929	1,229
Sheep	175	186	189
Goats	2,301	2,720	3,106
Chickens*	15,200	15,300	15,300

* FAO estimates.

Note: Data for 2009 were not available.

Source: FAO.

LIVESTOCK PRODUCTS
('000 metric tons)

	2007	2008	2009
Cattle meat	26.6	28.8	n.a.
Goat meat	17.1	19.6	19.6*
Pig meat	25.0	34.0	34.0*
Chicken meat*	15.3	15.3	15.3
Cows' milk	29.7	35.5	n.a.
Hen eggs*	19.8	19.8	n.a.

* FAO estimate(s).

Source: FAO.

Forestry

ROUNDWOOD REMOVALS
('000 cubic metres, excluding bark, FAO estimates)

	2007	2008	2009
Sawlogs, veneer logs and logs for sleepers	130	130	130
Other industrial wood	390	390	390
Fuel wood	5,240	5,293	5,348
Total	5,760	5,813	5,868

Source: FAO.

SAWNWOOD PRODUCTION
('000 cubic metres, including railway sleepers)

	1991*	1992†	1993
Coniferous (softwood)	28	28	30
Broadleaved (hardwood)	15	15	15†
Total	43	43	45

* Unofficial figures.
† FAO estimate(s).

1994–2009: Production assumed to be unchanged from 1993 (FAO estimates).

Source: FAO.

Fishing

('000 metric tons, live weight)

	2006	2007	2008
Capture	72.8	66.5	70.0
Cyprinids	4.2	12.6	15.4
Tilapias	9.7	14.3	11.1
Cichlids	50.2	30.4	33.9
Torpedo-shaped catfishes	4.5	5.4	5.3
Other freshwater fishes	4.3	3.9	4.4
Aquaculture	1.5	1.5	1.7
Total catch	74.3	68.0	71.7

Note: Figures exclude aquatic mammals, recorded by number rather than weight. The number of Nile crocodiles caught was: 698 in 2006; 1,287 in 2007; 3,370 in 2008.

Source: FAO.

Mining

('000 metric tons, unless otherwise indicated)

	2006	2007	2008*
Bituminous coal	60.4	58.6	60.0
Lime	21.1	19.0	19.0
Gemstones (kg)	2,171	3,710	3,700
Stone (crushed for aggregate)	192.0	226.4	230.0
Limestone	34.2	42.1	74.0

* Estimates.

Source: US Geological Survey.

MALAWI

Industry

SELECTED PRODUCTS
('000 metric tons, unless otherwise indicated)

	2000	2001	2002
Raw sugar	96	107	260*
Beer ('000 hectolitres)	739	1,033	n.a.
Blankets ('000)	574	281	n.a.
Cement	198	111	174

* Natural sodium carbonate (Na_2Co_3).

2003 ('000 metric tons): Raw sugar (Na_2Co_3) 257; Cement 161 (Source: US Geological Survey).

Electric energy (million kWh): 1,537 in 2005; 1,580 in 2006; 1,637 in 2007.

Raw sugar ('000 metric tons): 265 in 2005; 230 in 2006; 280 in 2007.

Source (unless otherwise indicated): UN Industrial Commodity Statistics Database.

Cement ('000 metric tons, hydraulic): 187.6 in 2006, 185.3 in 2007; 240.0 in 2008 (estimate) (Source: US Geological Survey).

Finance

CURRENCY AND EXCHANGE RATES

Monetary Units
100 tambala = 1 Malawi kwacha (K).

Sterling, Dollar and Euro Equivalents (30 June 2010)
£1 sterling = 226.579 kwacha;
US $1 = 150.801 kwacha;
€1 = 185.048 kwacha;
1,000 Malawi kwacha = £4.41 = $6.63 = €5.40.

Average Exchange Rate (kwacha per US $)
2007   139.957
2008   140.523
2009   141.167

BUDGET
(K million, year ending 30 June)

Revenue	2003/04	2004/05	2005/06*
Tax revenue	27,793.2	43,635.0	55,797.8
Taxes on income and profits	12,706.6	19,854.0	23,973.0
Companies	4,796.6	5,386.0	6,710.3
Individuals	7,910.0	14,468.0	17,263.5
Taxes on goods and services	12,160.4	18,830.0	25,909.8
Surtax	8,630.0	13,739.0	17,796.6
Excise duties	3,530.4	5,091.0	8,113.2
Taxes on international trade	3,766.1	5,952.0	7,374.4
Less Tax refunds	840.0	1,001.0	1,460.2
Non-tax revenue	4,874.0	4,461.0	8,127.0
Departmental receipts	1,173.2	2,447.0	4,595.3
Total	32,667.2	48,096.0	63,924.8

Expenditure	2003/04	2004/05	2005/06*
General public services	21,889.6	22,719.7	35,519.5
General administration	19,445.9	17,581.0	26,997.5
Defence	1,139.1	2,552.6	4,157.3
Public order and safety	1,304.6	2,586.1	4,364.7
Social and community services	12,606.7	17,509.0	24,363.2
Education	6,310.1	8,631.9	9,500.8
Health	3,692.4	5,247.6	11,057.9
Social security and welfare	2,105.7	2,706.4	2,221.3
Housing and community amenities	356.7	395.8	1,325.6
Recreational, cultural and other social services	75.4	76.8	106.2
Broadcasting and publishing	66.4	450.5	151.3
Economic affairs and services	4,799.0	8,721.1	6,927.3
Energy and mining	108.9	105.2	115.4
Agriculture and natural resources	2,482.4	4,345.5	2,837.2
Tourism	150.0	—	—
Physical planning and development	101.6	1,144.3	527.9
Transport and communications	1,496.3	2,048.5	2,299.1
Industry and commerce	210.7	390.0	599.6
Labour relations and employment	231.2	346.5	404.2
Scientific and technological services	—	314.4	144.0
Other economic services	17.9	26.7	—
Unallocable expenditure	1,505.2	677.3	—
Total recurrent expenditure	40,800.5	49,627.0	66,810.0
Debt amortization	18,736.5	18,752.0	17,328.0
Total	59,537.0	68,379.0	84,138.0

* Estimates.

2006/07 (K million, year ending 30 June): *Revenue:* Tax revenue 77,321; Non-tax revenue 6,974; Total 84,295 (excl. grants 63,337). *Expenditure:* Current expenditure 99,464 (Wages and salaries 23,778, Interest payments 16,378, Other 59,307); Development expenditure 53,665; Total 153,128 (excl. net lending 452) (Source: IMF, *Malawi: Request for a One-Year Exogenous Shocks Facility Arrangement - Staff Report; Press Release on the Executive Board Discussion; and Statement by the Executive Director for Malawi*—January 2009).

2007/08 (K million, year ending 30 June, preliminary figures): *Revenue:* Tax revenue 96,387; Non-tax revenue 8,567; Total 104,954 (excl. grants 59,600). *Expenditure:* Current expenditure 115,622 (Wages and salaries 30,018, Interest payments 12,331, Other 73,272); Development expenditure 63,775; Total 179,397 (Source: IMF, *Malawi: Request for a One-Year Exogenous Shocks Facility Arrangement - Staff Report; Press Release on the Executive Board Discussion; and Statement by the Executive Director for Malawi*—January 2009).

2008/09 (K million, year ending 30 June, budgeted figures): *Revenue:* Tax revenue 107,300; Non-tax revenue 10,867; Total 118,167 (excl. grants 89,905). *Expenditure:* Current expenditure 172,306 (Wages and salaries 37,256, Interest payments 16,169, Other 118,881); Development expenditure 57,219; Total 229,525 (Source: IMF, *Malawi: Staff Report for 2009 Article IV Consultation and Request for a Three-Year Arrangement Under the Extended Credit Facility*—March 2010).

2009/10 (K million, year ending 30 June, budgeted figures): *Revenue:* Tax revenue 139,900; Non-tax revenue 23,200; Total 163,100 (excl. grants 81,093). *Expenditure:* Current expenditure 188,182 (Wages and salaries 43,539, Interest payments 19,794, Other 124,849); Development expenditure 66,587; Total 256,769 (incl. net lending 2,000) (Source: IMF, *Malawi: Staff Report for 2009 Article IV Consultation and Request for a Three-Year Arrangement Under the Extended Credit Facility*—March 2010).

2010/11 (K million, year ending 30 June, projected figures): *Revenue:* Tax revenue 169,942; Non-tax revenue 29,384; Total 199,326 (excl. grants 93,520). *Expenditure:* Current expenditure 213,361 (Wages and salaries 51,423, Interest payments 20,705, Other 141,233); Development expenditure 99,421; Total 312,781 (Source: IMF, *Malawi: Staff Report for 2009 Article IV Consultation and Request for a Three-Year Arrangement Under the Extended Credit Facility*—March 2010).

MALAWI

INTERNATIONAL RESERVES
(US $ million at 31 December)

	2007	2008	2009
Gold (national valuation)	0.54	0.54	14.03
IMF special drawing rights	0.03	0.08	1.93
Reserve position in IMF	3.66	3.59	3.80
Foreign exchange	212.92	239.10	143.63
Total	217.15	243.31	163.39

Source: IMF, *International Financial Statistics*.

MONEY SUPPLY
(K million at 31 December)

	2007	2008	2009
Currency outside banks	20,587.5	25,261.3	27,493.1
Demand deposits at commercial banks	30,142.3	45,335.5	54,407.1
Total money (incl. others)	50,729.8	70,596.7	81,900.2

Source: IMF, *International Financial Statistics*.

COST OF LIVING
(Consumer Price Index; base: 2000 = 100)

	2007	2008	2009
Food (incl. beverages)	224.7	240.3	258.0
Clothing (incl. footwear)	221.2	237.6	259.1
Rent	291.4	319.1	328.3
All items (incl. others)	244.1	265.4	287.7

Source: ILO.

NATIONAL ACCOUNTS
(K million at current prices)

Expenditure on the Gross Domestic Product

	2005	2006	2007
Government final consumption expenditure	97,328	164,884	163,227
Private final consumption expenditure	246,623	237,092	317,938
Gross fixed capital formation	31,866	17,356	70,285
Changes in inventories	6,589	7,483	14,735
Total domestic expenditure	382,406	426,815	566,185
Exports of goods and services	68,750	66,148	132,707
Less Imports of goods and services	149,737	175,993	201,800
GDP in purchasers' values	301,420	316,970	497,092

Gross Domestic Product by Economic Activity

	2005	2006	2007
Agriculture, forestry and fishing	137,762	139,648	153,063
Mining and quarrying	11,468	11,827	19,384
Manufacturing	14,017	14,455	23,691
Electricity, gas and water	8,742	7,851	12,868
Construction	9,632	9,902	16,229
Wholesale and retail trade, restaurants and hotels	28,019	27,437	44,967
Transport and communications	15,090	15,917	26,087
Finance, insurance and real estate	27,030	29,145	47,767
Public administration and defence	30,416	29,802	48,843
Other services	17,079	17,319	28,385
GDP at factor cost	299,256	303,305	421,283
Taxes on products	2,164	13,665	75,809
GDP at purchasers' values	301,420	316,970	497,092

Note: Deduction for imputed bank service charge assumed to be distributed at source.

Source: African Development Bank.

BALANCE OF PAYMENTS
(K million)

	2007	2008*	2009*
Exports of goods f.o.b.	99,258.4	120,705.2	131,004.3
Imports of goods f.o.b.	−175,556.6	−188,021.1	−205,518.2
Trade balance	−76,298.2	−67,315.9	−74,513.9
Net services	−32,228.4	−33,579.3	−38,996.5
Balance on goods and services	−108,526.6	−100,895.2	−113,510.4
Net other income	−2,974.3	−2,945.0	−5,407.2
Balance on goods, services and income	−111,500.9	−103,840.2	−118,917.6
Net transfers	10,908.3	11,226.0	10,738.0
Current balance	−100,592.5	−92,614.2	−108,179.6
Government transfers (net)	38,346.6	43,069.1	71,160.2
Government drawings on loans	10,631.9	14,487.5	14,197.0
Public enterprises (net)	1,570.5	1,746.2	1,704.7
Private sector (net)	503.3	518.0	554.2
Short-term capital (net)	83.5	85.9	91.9
Errors and omissions	32,038.2	24,503.6	−906.8
Statistical discrepancy	12,883.7	17,264.8	14,100
Overall balance†	−4,534.8	9,060.9	−7,278.4

* Preliminary figures.
† Excluding debt relief (K million): 155.4 in 2007; n.a. in 2008; n.a. in 2009.

External Trade

PRINCIPAL COMMODITIES
(distribution by SITC, US $ million)

Imports c.i.f.	2007	2008	2009
Food and live animals	80.8	136.7	158.7
Cereals and cereal preparations	47.2	94.1	102.0
Beverages and tobacco	35.8	75.2	62.8
Tobacco and tobacco products	34.3	74.0	58.4
Mineral fuels, lubricants, etc.	190.3	214.8	210.6
Petroleum, petroleum products, etc.	188.6	211.7	208.9
Refined petroleum products	180.5	202.0	198.3
Chemicals and related products	383.4	603.5	464.1
Medicinal and pharmaceutical products	85.8	95.4	114.2
Manufactured fertilizers	188.2	367.1	176.8
Basic manufactures	199.2	271.4	328.9
Paper, paperboard, etc.	28.3	38.4	53.8
Textile yarn, fabrics, etc.	43.7	44.2	46.9
Iron and steel	42.5	66.9	63.2
Machinery and transport equipment	306.6	593.8	529.4
Machinery specialized for particular industries	43.5	238.1	96.6
General industrial machinery, equipment and parts	29.5	41.7	53.1
Office machinery and automatic data-processing equipment	21.3	23.3	32.1
Telecommunications, sound recording and reproducing equipment	25.8	45.8	74.7
Road vehicles	143.2	181.7	191.7
Goods vehicles (lorries and trucks)	31.7	59.6	61.3
Miscellaneous manufactured articles	133.2	228.3	191.0
Total (incl. others)	1,377.8	2,203.7	2,029.0

MALAWI

Statistical Survey

Exports f.o.b.	2007	2008	2009
Food and live animals	268.4	139.2	212.9
Sugar and honey	64.3	53.0	70.3
Raw cane sugars	60.5	50.7	70.2
Coffee, tea, cocoa and spices	61.4	42.5	84.4
Tea	55.4	36.9	78.3
Beverages and tobacco	423.8	593.2	760.5
Tobacco and tobacco products	422.7	590.0	759.5
Unstripped tobacco	336.6	428.2	472.4
Stripped or partly stripped tobacco	86.0	161.7	268.6
Crude materials (inedible) except fuels	83.8	57.2	109.3
Textile fibres	23.9	23.4	30.1
Basic manufactures	10.9	30.9	12.1
Machinery and transport equipment	11.8	15.5	28.1
Miscellaneous manufactured articles	50.2	35.1	53.2
Total (incl. others)	868.6	879.0	1,187.9

Source: UN, *International Trade Statistics Yearbook*.

PRINCIPAL TRADING PARTNERS
(US $ million)

Imports	2007	2008	2009
Belgium	9.2	8.6	6.0
China, People's Repub.	41.3	72.4	119.7
Denmark	32.9	40.8	35.0
France (incl. Monaco)	16.0	16.7	52.2
Germany	25.5	22.4	34.2
Hong Kong	8.0	15.1	23.7
India	69.2	106.8	95.8
Indonesia	9.1	15.1	18.5
Italy	7.1	7.6	10.3
Japan	16.2	32.7	18.0
Kenya	31.3	54.9	39.8
Korea, Repub.	8.7	18.0	18.2
Mozambique	167.8	447.1	259.5
Netherlands	26.4	46.3	18.9
South Africa	401.0	585.2	691.5
Tanzania	82.5	128.6	79.4
United Arab Emirates	96.6	111.0	80.3
United Kingdom	69.2	74.8	85.3
USA	49.5	45.0	52.7
Zambia	32.0	68.5	72.7
Zimbabwe	47.5	38.5	38.2
Total (incl. others)	1,377.8	2,203.7	2,029.0

Exports	2007	2008	2009
Belgium	69.9	114.7	208.3
Denmark	31.8	2.1	5.3
Egypt	20.4	25.3	73.2
France (incl. Monaco)	9.9	8.1	5.3
Germany	50.8	36.7	38.5
India	9.9	2.8	27.4
Kenya	7.1	6.9	13.7
Korea, Repub.	30.7	28.2	10.7
Mozambique	17.3	23.9	64.1
Netherlands	31.5	51.8	52.2
Philippines	1.9	8.4	26.8
Poland	18.9	30.6	15.8
Portugal	28.9	34.0	28.7
Russia	29.8	25.0	36.1
South Africa	128.5	88.7	121.6
Spain	9.2	6.3	7.6
Switzerland (incl. Liechtenstein)	9.2	36.0	52.6
Turkey	17.1	17.3	17.7
United Kingdom	57.0	78.4	50.4
USA	36.3	50.3	48.6
Zambia	18.8	15.4	23.0
Zimbabwe	132.0	22.6	35.8
Total (incl. others)	868.6	879.0	1,187.9

Source: UN, *International Trade Statistics Yearbook*.

Transport

RAILWAYS
(traffic)

	2006	2007	2008
Passengers carried ('000)	449	624	814
Passenger-kilometres ('000)	28,670	43,815	54,336
Net freight ton-kilometres ('000)	46,754	31,982	51,434

ROAD TRAFFIC
(estimates, motor vehicles in use at 31 December)

	1994	1995	1996
Passenger cars	23,520	25,480	27,000
Lorries and vans	26,000	29,000	29,700

2007: Passenger cars 53,300; Lorries and vans 59,800; Buses 6,500; Motorcycles 10,400.

Source: International Road Federation, *World Road Statistics*.

SHIPPING

Inland Waterways
(lake transport)

	2006	2007	2008
Passengers carried ('000)	57	n.a.	69
Passenger-km ('000)	4,582	5,038	6,032
Net freight-ton km	2,132	6,132	4,833

CIVIL AVIATION
(traffic on scheduled services)

	2004	2005	2006
Kilometres flown (million)	5	5	5
Passengers carried ('000)	122	132	146
Passenger-km (million)	167	182	197
Total ton-km (million)	18	20	23

Source: UN, *Statistical Yearbook*.

Tourism

FOREIGN TOURIST ARRIVALS BY COUNTRY OF RESIDENCE

	2006	2007	2008
Mozambique	105,708	111,924	139,296
North America	34,515	45,630	43,085
Southern Africa*	67,957	104,226	106,724
United Kingdom and Ireland	50,842	48,627	50,786
Zambia	47,577	63,581	76,408
Zimbabwe	167,707	171,684	143,363
Total (incl. others)	637,780	734,598	742,457

*Comprising South Africa, Botswana, Lesotho and Swaziland.

Tourism receipts (US $ million, incl. passenger transport): 43 in 2005–06; 48 in 2007.

Source: World Tourism Organization.

MALAWI

Communications Media

	2007	2008	2009
Telephones ('000 main lines in use)	175.2	175.0	175.0
Mobile cellular telephones ('000 subscribers)	1,050.9	1,781.0	2,400.0
Internet users ('000)	139.5	316.1	716.4
Broadband subscribers ('000)	1.6	2.5	3.4

Personal computers: 25,000 (1.8 per 1,000 persons) in 2005.

Radio receivers ('000 in use): 4,929 in 1998.

Television receivers ('000 in use): 40 in 2001.

Book production (first editions only): 120 titles in 1996.

Daily newspapers: 5 in 1998 (estimated average circulation 26,000 copies).

Non-daily newspapers: 4 in 1996 (estimated average circulation 120,000 copies).

Sources: UNESCO Institute for Statistics; UN, *Statistical Yearbook*; International Telecommunication Union.

Education

(2008/09 unless otherwise indicated)

	Institutions	Teachers	Students
Primary	5,461*	34,444*	3,250,111
Secondary	n.a.	22,878*	666,679
Tertiary	6†	861‡	6,458‡

* 2007/08.
† 2003 figure.
‡ 2006/07 figure.

Source: partly UNESCO Institute for Statistics.

Pupil-teacher ratio (primary education, UNESCO estimate): 92.8 in 2007/08 (Source: UNESCO Institute for Statistics).

Adult literacy rate (UNESCO estimates): 72.8% (males 80.2%; females 65.8%) in 2008 (Source: UNESCO Institute for Statistics).

Directory

The Government

HEAD OF STATE

President: Dr BINGU WA MUTHARIKA (took office 24 May 2004; re-elected 19 May 2009).
Vice-President: JOYCE BANDA.

CABINET
(May 2011)

President, Minister of National Defence and Commander-in-Chief of the Malawi Defence Force and Police Service: Dr BINGU WA MUTHARIKA.
Minister of Agriculture and Food Security: Prof. PETER NELSON MWANZA.
Minister of Foreign Affairs: Prof. ETTA ELIZABETH BANDA.
Minister of Finance: KEN EDWARD KANDODO.
Minister of Education, Science and Technology: Prof. ARTHUR PETER MUTHARIKA.
Minister of Development Planning and Co-operation: ABBIE MARAMBIKA SHABA.
Minister of Transport and Public Infrastructure: MOHAMMED SIDIK MIA.
Minister of Justice and Constitutional Affairs: Dr GEORGE THAPATULA CHAPONDA.
Minister of Irrigation and Water Development: RICHIE BISWICK MUHEYA.
Minister of Local Government and Rural Development: ANNA NAMATHANGA KACHIKHO.
Minister of Industry and Trade: EUNICE KAZEMBE.
Minister of Lands, Housing and Urban Development: JOHN BANDE.
Minister of Gender, Child Development and Community Development: THERESA MWALE.
Minister of Tourism, Wildlife and Culture: KEN LIPENGA.
Minister of Labour: YUNUS MUSSA.
Minister of Youth Development and Sports: Dr LUCIOUS GRANDSON KANYUMBA.
Minister of Health: DAVID MPHANDE.
Minister of Home Affairs and Internal Security: AARON SANGALA.
Minister of National Defence: (vacant).
Minister of Information and Civic Education: VUWA SYMON KAUNDA.
Minister of Natural Resources, Energy and the Environment: GRAIN WYSON MALUNGA.
Minister of Persons with Disabilities and the Elderly: RENE BESSIE KACHERE.

There were also 19 Deputy Ministers.

MINISTRIES

Office of the President and Cabinet: Private Bag 301, Capital City, Lilongwe 3; tel. 1789311; fax 1788456; internet www.malawi.gov.mw/opc/opc.htm.

Office of the Vice President: POB 30399, Capital City, Lilongwe; tel. 1788444; fax 1788218; e-mail vicepres@malawi.gov.mw.

Ministry of Agriculture and Food Security: POB 30134, Capital City, Lilongwe 3; tel. 1789033; fax 1789218; e-mail agriculture@agriculture.gov.mw; internet www.malawi.gov.mw/Agriculture/Home%20%20Agriculture.htm.

Ministry of Development Planning and Co-operation: POB 30136, Capital City, Lilongwe 3; tel. 1788390; fax 1788131; e-mail epd@malawi.net; internet www.malawi.gov.mw/Economic%20Planning/Home%20Economic%20Planning.htm.

Ministry of Education, Science and Technology: Private Bag 328, Lilongwe 3; tel. 1789422; fax 1788064; e-mail education@malawi.gov.mw; internet www.malawi.gov.mw/Education/Home%20%20Education.htm.

Ministry of Finance: Capital Hill, POB 30049, Lilongwe 3; tel. 1789355; fax 1789173; internet www.malawi.gov.mw/Finance/Home%20Finance.htm.

Ministry of Foreign Affairs: POB 30315, Lilongwe 3; tel. 1789323; fax 1788482; e-mail foreign@malawi.net; internet www.malawi.gov.mw/Foreign%20Affairs/Home%20ForeignAffairs.htm.

Ministry of Gender, Child Development and Community Development: Private Bag 330, Capital City, Lilongwe 3; tel. 1770411; fax 1770826.

Ministry of Health: POB 30377, Capital City, Lilongwe 3; tel. 1789400; fax 1789431; e-mail doccentre@malawi.net; internet www.malawi.gov.mw/Health/Home%20Health.htm.

Ministry of Home Affairs and Internal Security: Private Bag 331, Lilongwe 3; tel. 1789177; fax 1789509; internet www.malawi.gov.mw/Home%20Affairs/Home%20HomeAffairs.htm; comprises the Immigration Dept, Prison and Police Services.

Ministry of Industry and Trade: POB 30366, Capital City, Lilongwe 3; tel. 1770244; fax 1770680; e-mail minci@malawi.net; internet www.malawi.gov.mw/Trade/Home%20%20Trade.htm.

Ministry of Information and Civic Education: Private Bag 326, Capital City, Lilongwe 3; tel. 1775499; fax 1770650; e-mail psinfo@sdnp.org.mw; internet www.malawi.gov.mw/Information/Home%20Information.htm.

Ministry of Irrigation and Water Development: Tikwere House, Private Bag 390, Capital City, Lilongwe 3; tel. 1770238; fax 1773737; internet www.malawi.gov.mw/water/Home%20%20Water.htm.

Ministry of Justice and Constitutional Affairs: Private Bag 333, Capital City, Lilongwe 3; tel. 1788411; fax 1788332; e-mail justice@malawi.gov.mw; internet www.malawi.gov.mw/Justice/Home%20%20Justice.htm; also comprises the Attorney-General's Chambers and the Directorate of Public Prosecutions.

MALAWI

Ministry of Labour: Private Bag 344, Capital City, Lilongwe 3; tel. 1773277; fax 1773803; e-mail labour@malawi.net; internet www.malawi.gov.mw/Labour/Home%20%20Labour.htm.

Ministry of Lands, Housing and Urban Development: POB 30548, Lilongwe 3; tel. 1774766; fax 1773990.

Ministry of Local Government and Rural Development: POB 30312, Lilongwe 3; tel. 1789388; fax 1788083; internet www.malawi.gov.mw/LocalGovt/Home%20%20LocalGovt.htm.

Ministry of National Defence: Private Bag 339, Lilongwe 3; tel. 1789600; fax 1789176; internet www.malawi.gov.mw/Defence/Home%20Defence.htm.

Ministry of Natural Resources, Energy and the Environment: Private Bag 350, Lilongwe 3; tel. 1789488; fax 1773379; internet www.malawi.gov.mw/natres/natres.htm.

Ministry of Persons with Disabilities and the Elderly: Lilongwe 3.

Ministry of Tourism, Wildlife and Culture: Lilongwe 3; tel. 1772702; fax 1770650; e-mail tourism@malawi.net.

Ministry of Transport and Public Infrastructure: Private Bag 322, Capital City, Lilongwe 3; tel. 1789377; fax 1789328; internet www.malawi.gov.mw/Transport/Home%20Transport.htm.

Ministry of Youth Development and Sports: Lingadzi House, Private Bag 384, Lilongwe 3; tel. 1774999; fax 1771018; e-mail sports@malawi.gov.mw; internet www.malawi.gov.mw/Youth/Home%20%20Youth.htm.

President and Legislature

PRESIDENT

Presidential Election, 19 May 2009

Candidate	Votes	% of votes
Bingu wa Mutharika (DPP)	2,961,099	64.36
John Tembo (MCP)	1,373,459	29.85
Walter Chibambo (PETRA)	35,296	0.77
Others	230,903	5.02
Total	**4,600,757**	**100.00**

NATIONAL ASSEMBLY

National Assembly: Parliament Bldg, Private Bag B362, Lilongwe 3; tel. 1773566; fax 1774196; internet www.malawi.gov.mw/parliament/parliament.htm.

Speaker: Henry Chimunthu Banda.

General Election, 19 May 2009

Party	Seats
Democratic Progressive Party (DPP)	112
Malawi Congress Party (MCP)	27
United Democratic Front (UDF)	18
Alliance for Democracy (AFORD)	1
Malawi Forum for Unity and Development (MAFUNDE)	1
Maravi People's Party (MPP)	1
Independents	32
Total	**192***

*Voting in one constituency did not take place owing to the death of a candidate.

Election Commission

Malawi Electoral Commission (MEC): Development House, Private Bag 113, Blantyre; tel. 1822033; fax 1821846; e-mail ceo@mec.org.mw; internet www.mec.org.mw; f. 1998; Chair. Anastasia Msosa; Chief Elections Officer David Bandawe.

Political Organizations

Alliance for Democracy (AFORD): Private Bag 28, Lilongwe; f. 1992; in March 1993 absorbed membership of fmr Malawi Freedom Movement; Pres. Dindi Gowa Nyasulu.

Congress of Democrats (CODE): Mzuzu; Pres. Ralph Kasambara.

Congress for National Unity (CONU): Lilongwe; f. 1999; Pres. Bishop Daniel Kamfosi Nkhumbwa.

Democratic Progressive Party (DPP): Lilongwe 3; internet dppmw.org; f. 2005 following Bingu wa Mutharika's resignation from the UDF; Leader Dr Bingu wa Mutharika; Sec.-Gen. Binton Kutsaira.

Malawi Congress Party (MCP): Private Bag 388, Lilongwe 3; tel. 999223228; internet www.malawicongressparty.org; f. 1959; sole legal party 1966–93; Pres. John Tembo.

Malawi Democratic Party (MDP): Lilongwe; Pres. (vacant).

Malawi Forum for Unity and Development (MAFUNDE): f. 2002; aims to combat corruption and food shortages; Pres. George Mnesa.

Maravi People's Party (MPP): Lilongwe; Pres. Uladi Mussa; Sec.-Gen. Dr Yusuf Haudi (acting).

Movement for Genuine Democratic Change (MGODE): Plot No. 52, Kanjedza Drive, Mzuzu; f. 2003 by fmr mems of AFORD; Chair. Sam Kandodo Banda (acting); Dir Greene Lulilo Mwamondwe; Sec.-Gen. Rodger Nkwazi.

National Democratic Alliance (NDA): Blantyre; tel. 1842593; f. 2001 by fmr mems of the UDF; officially merged with the UDF in June 2004 but maintained independent structure; Pres. Brown James Mpinganjira; Nat. Chair. James Makhumula Nkhoma.

National Rainbow Coalition (NARC): POB 40508, Kanengo, Lilongwe 4; tel. 1774007; internet www.narcparty.com; f. 2008; Pres. Loveness Gondwe.

National Solidarity Movement: Leader Ngwazi Kazuni Kumwenda.

National Unity Party (NUP): Blantyre; Pres. Harry Chiume; Sec.-Gen. Harry Muyenza.

New Dawn for Africa (NDA): Legends Compound, Blantyre, POB 76, Liwonde; f. 2003; associated with the UDF; Pres. Thom Chiumia; Sec.-Gen. Chikumbutso Mtumodzi.

New Republican Party (NRP): f. 2005; Pres. Gwandaguluwe Chakuamba; Vice-Pres. Ken Zikhale Ng'oma.

People's Progressive Movement (PPM): f. 2003 by fmr mems of the UDF; Pres. Mark Katsonga; Sec.-Gen. Knox Varela.

People's Transformation Party (PETRA): POB 31964, Chichiri, Blantyre 3; tel. 1871577; fax 1871573; e-mail umunthu@sdnp.org.mw; internet www.petra.mw; f. 2002; Pres. Kamuzu Chibambo; Sec.-Gen. Derek Lakudzala.

Republican Party (RP): Lilongwe; Pres. Stanley Masauli.

United Democratic Front (UDF): POB 5446, Limbe; internet www.udf.malawi.net; f. 1992; officially merged with the NDA in June 2004 but maintained independent structure; rival faction led by Cassim Chilumpha and Friday Jumbe; Chair. Dr George Nga Ntafu; Sec.-Gen. Kennedy Makwangwala.

The Movement for the Restoration of Democracy in Malawi (f. 1996) is based in Mozambique and consists of fmr Malawi Young Pioneers; it conducts occasional acts of insurgency.

Diplomatic Representation

EMBASSIES AND HIGH COMMISSIONS IN MALAWI

China, People's Republic: No. 342, Area 43, POB 31799, Lilongwe; tel. 1794751; fax 1794752; e-mail chinaemb_mw@mfa.gov.cn; internet mw.chineseembassy.org/eng; Pan Hejun.

Egypt: 10/247 Tsoka Rd, POB 30451, Lilongwe 3; tel. 1780668; fax 1794660; Ambassador Akram Mohsen Hamdy.

Germany: Convention Dr., POB 30046, Lilongwe 3; tel. 1772555; fax 1770250; e-mail info@lilongwe.diplo.de; internet www.lilongwe.diplo.de; Ambassador Rainer Müller.

Ireland: Arwa House, 3rd Floor, Capital City, Lilongwe; tel. 1776405; e-mail lilongweemdiplomats@dfa.ie; Ambassador Liam MacGabhann.

Japan: Plot No. 14/191, Petroda Glass House, POB 30780, Lilongwe 3; tel. 1770284; fax 1773528; Ambassador Fujio Samukawa.

Mozambique: Area 40/14A, POB 30579, Lilongwe 3; tel. 1774100; fax 1771342; e-mail embamoc.malawi@minec.gov.mz; High Commissioner Pedro João de Azevedo Davane.

South Africa: Kang'ombe House, 3rd Floor, City Centre, POB 30043, Lilongwe 3; tel. 1773722; fax 1772571; e-mail sahc@malawi.net; High Commissioner N. I. Mabude.

Tanzania: POB 922, Capital City, Lilongwe 3; tel. 1770150; fax 1770148; e-mail tanzanianhighcomm@tz.lilongwe.mw; High Commissioner Maj.-Gen. (retd) Makame Rashid.

United Kingdom: British High Commission Bldg, Capital Hill, POB 30042, Lilongwe 3; tel. 1772400; fax 1772657; e-mail bhclilongwe@fco.gov.uk; internet ukinmalawi.fco.gov.uk; High Commissioner Fergus Cochrane-Dyet (expelled April 2011).

MALAWI

USA: Area 40, Plot No. 18, 16 Jomo Kenyatta Rd, POB 30016, Lilongwe 3; tel. 1773166; fax 1770471; e-mail consularlilong@state.gov; internet lilongwe.usembassy.gov; Chargé d'affaires LISA VICKERS.

Zambia: Area 40/2, City Centre, POB 30138, Lilongwe 3; tel. 1772100; fax 1774349; High Commissioner RICHARD KACHINGWE.

Zimbabwe: POB 30187, Lilongwe 3; tel. 1774988; fax 1772382; e-mail zimhighcomllw@malawi.net; Ambassador THANDIWE S. DUMBUTSHENA.

Judicial System

The courts administering justice are the Supreme Court of Appeal, High Court and Magistrates' Courts.

The High Court, which has unlimited jurisdiction in civil and criminal matters, consists of the Chief Justice and five puisne judges. Traditional Courts were abolished under the 1994 Constitution. Appeals from the High Court are heard by the Supreme Court of Appeal in Blantyre.

High Court of Malawi

POB 30244, Chichiri, Blantyre 3; tel. 1670255; fax 1670213; e-mail highcourt@sdnp.org.mw; internet www.judiciary.mw; Registrar H. S. POTANI.

Chief Justice: LOVEMORE MUNLO.

Religion

According to the census of 2008, 82.7% of the population profess Christianity. Islam is practised by about 13.0% of the population.

CHRISTIANITY

Malawi Council of Churches (MCC): POB 30068, Capital City, Lilongwe 3; tel. 1783499; fax 1783106; f. 1939; Chair. Rev. JOSEPH P. BVUMBWE; Gen. Sec. Rev. Dr OSBORNE JODA-MBEWE; 24 mem. churches.

The Anglican Communion

Anglicans are adherents of the Church of the Province of Central Africa, covering Botswana, Malawi, Zambia and Zimbabwe. The Church comprises 15 dioceses, including four in Malawi. There were about 230,000 adherents in Malawi at mid-2000.

Archbishop of the Province of Central Africa and Bishop of Upper Shire: (vacant), Private Bag 1, Chilema, Zomba; tel. and fax 1539203; e-mail dionorth@zamnet.zm.

Bishop of Lake Malawi: (vacant), POB 30349, Capital City, Lilongwe 3; tel. 1797858; fax 1797548; e-mail anglama@eomw.net.

Bishop of Northern Malawi: Rt Rev. CHRISTOPHER JOHN BOYLE, POB 120, Mzuzu; tel. 1331486; fax 1333805; e-mail angdioofnm@sdnp.org.mw.

Bishop of Southern Malawi: Rt Rev. JAMES TENGATENGA, POB 30220, Chichiri, Blantyre 3; tel. 1641218; fax 1641235; e-mail angsoma@sdnp.org.mw; internet www.angsoma.org.mw.

Protestant Churches

At mid-2001 there were an estimated 2.1m. Protestants in Malawi.

Assemblies of God in Malawi: POB 1220, Lilongwe; tel. 1761057; fax 1762056; Pres. LAZARUS CHAKWERA; 639,088 mems in 3,114 churches (2005).

Baptist Convention of Malawi (BACOMA): Lali Lubani Rd, POB 30212, Chichiri, Blantyre 3; tel. 1671170; e-mail bacoma@sdnp.org.mw; 175,000 adherents, 1,375 churches (2007); Gen. Sec. Rev. FLETCHER KAIYA.

Church of Central Africa Presbyterian (CCAP): Blantyre Synod, POB 413, Blantyre; tel. and fax 1633942; e-mail btsynod@malawi.net; internet www.blantyresynod.org; comprises 3 synods in Malawi (Blantyre, Livingstonia and Nkhoma); Co-ordinator Rev. J. J. MPHATSE; Gen. Sec. DANIEL GUNYA; Exec. Dir ROBSON CHITENGO; more than 1m. adherents in Malawi.

Evangelical Association of Malawi: POB 2120, Blantyre; tel. and fax 9936681; Chair. Rev. Dr LAZARUS CHAKWERA; Gen. Sec. FRANCIS MKANDAWIRE.

Evangelical Lutheran Church in Malawi: POB 650, Lutheran Church Centre, Plot 22, Chidzanja Rd, Lilongwe; tel. and fax 1726288; fax 1725910; e-mail elcmwi@elcmw.org; Bishop. Dr JOSEPH P. BVUMBWE; 80,000 mems (2010).

Seventh-day Adventist Church: Robins Rd, Kabula Hill, POB 951, Blantyre; tel. 1620264; fax 1620528; e-mail musda@malawi.net; Pres. SAUSTIN K. MFUNE; Exec. Sec. BAXTER D. CHILUNGA; 200,000 mems.

The African Methodist Episcopal Church, the Churches of Christ, the Free Methodist Church, the New Apostolic Church and the United Evangelical Church in Malawi are also active. At mid-2000 there were an estimated 2m. adherents professing other forms of Christianity.

The Roman Catholic Church

Malawi comprises two archdioceses and five dioceses. There are some 3.9m. adherents of the Roman Catholic Church (equivalent to approximately 23% of the total population).

Episcopal Conference of Malawi

Catholic Secretariat of Malawi, Chimutu Rd, POB 30384, Capital City, Lilongwe 3; tel. 1782066; fax 1782019; e-mail ecm@malawi.net. f. 1969; Sec.-Gen. Rev. GEORGE BULEYA.

Archbishop of Blantyre: Most Rev. TARCISIUS GERVAZIO ZIYAYE, Archbishop House, POB 385, Blantyre; tel. and fax 1637905; e-mail archdblantyre@africa-online.net.

Archbishop of Lilongwe: Most Rev. RÉMI JOSEPH GUSTAVE SAINTE-MARIE, POB 33, Lilongwe; tel. 1754667; fax 1752767.

ISLAM

Muslim Association of Malawi (MAM): POB 497, Blantyre; tel. 1622060; fax 1623581; f. 1946 as the Nyasaland Muslim Asscn; umbrella body for Muslim orgs; provides secular and Islamic education; Sec.-Gen. MOHAMMED IMRAN SHAREEF.

BAHÁ'Í FAITH

National Spiritual Assembly: POB 30922, Lilongwe 3; tel. 1771177; fax 1771713; e-mail bahaimalawi@africa-online.net; f. 1970; mems resident in over 1,200 localities.

The Press

The Chronicle: Private Bag 77, Lilongwe; tel. 1756530; e-mail thechronicle@africa-online.net; f. 1993; publ. by Jamieson Publications; Mon. and Thur.; English; ceased publ. in Dec. 2006; Owner and Editor-in-Chief ROBERT JAMIESON; circ. c. 5,000 (2006).

The Daily Times: Scott Rd, Private Bag 39, Blantyre; tel. 1670115; fax 1671233; e-mail info@bnl.bppmw.com; internet www.dailytimes.bppmw.com; f. 1895; fmrly the *Nyasaland Times*; Mon.–Fri., Sun.; English; publ. by Blantyre Newspapers Ltd (Chayamba Trust); affiliated to the MCP; Editor JAMES MPHANDE; circ. Mon.–Fri. c. 20,000, Sun. c. 40,000 (2006).

The Democratus: Aquarius House, Convention Dr., City Centre, Box 1100, Lilongwe 3; tel. 1770033; internet democratusmalawi.blogspot.com; f. 2004; publ. by Democratus Ltd; Wed. and Sun.; Chair. ZIKHALE NG'OMA.

The Dispatch: The Dispatch Publications Ltd, POB 30353, Capital City, Lilongwe 3; tel. 1751639; fax 9510120; e-mail thedispatchmw@sdnp.org.mw; Thur. and Sun.; Publr and Man. Editor MARTINES NAMINGAH; circ. Thur. 5,000, Sun. 7,000.

The Enquirer: POB 1745, Blantyre; tel. 1670022; e-mail pillycolette@yahoo.co.uk; English and Nyanja; affiliated to the UDF; Owner LUCIOUS CHIKUNI.

The Guardian: Capital City, Private Bag B341, Lilongwe; tel. 1761996; fax 1761996; Man. Editor DUWA MUTHARIKA-MUBAIRA; circ. c. 5,000 (2006).

The Lamp: Montfort Media, POB 280, Balaka, Zomba; tel. 1545267; e-mail montfortmedia@malawi.net; f. 1995; fortnightly; Roman Catholic and ecumenical; Editor Fr GAMBA PIERGIORGIO; circ. 5,500.

Malawi Government Gazette: Government Printer, POB 37, Zomba; tel. 1523155; fax 1522301; f. 1894; weekly.

Malawi News: Scott Rd, Private Bag 39, Blantyre; tel. 1871679; fax 1871233; internet www.malawinews.bppmw.com; f. 1959; weekly; English and Chichewa; publ. by Blantyre Newspapers Ltd (Chayamba Trust); Man. Editor EDWARD CHISAMBO; Editor STEVEN NHLANE, Jr; circ. c. 40,000 (2006).

The Malawi Standard: POB 31781, Blantyre 3; tel. 1674013; e-mail bligomeka@yahoo.co.uk; fortnightly; Editor BRIAN LIGOMEKA.

The Mirror: POB 30721, Blantyre; tel. 1675043; f. 1994; weekly; English and Nyanja; affiliated to the UDF; Owner and Publr BROWN MPINGANJIRA; circ. 10,000.

The Nation: POB 30408, Chichiri, Blantyre 3; tel. 1673611; fax 1674343; e-mail nation@nationmalawi.com; internet www.nationmw.net; f. 1993; daily; publ. by Nation Publs Ltd; weekly edn of *The Weekend Nation* (circ. 30,000); English and Nyanja; Owner ALEKE BANDA; Editor EDWARD CHITSULO; circ. 15,000.

MALAWI

Odini: POB 133, Lilongwe; tel. 1721135; fax 1721141; f. 1949; fortnightly; Chichewa and English; Roman Catholic; Dir P. I. Akomenji; circ. 12,000.

UDF News: POB 3052, Blantyre; tel. 1645314; fax 1645725; e-mail echapusa@yahoo.co.uk; organ of the UDF; fortnightly; English and Nyanja.

Weekly Courier: Lilongwe 3; affiliated to the Democratic Progressive Party; Man. Editor Denis Mzembe; circ. c. 3,000 (2006).

The Weekly News: Dept of Information, POB 494, Blantyre; tel. 1642600; fax 1642364; f. 1996; English and Nyanja; publ. by the Ministry of Information and Civic Education; Editor-in-Chief George Tukhuwa.

There is also an online newspaper, the Nyasa Times (internet www.nyasatimes.com).

PERIODICALS

Boma Lathu: POB 494, Blantyre; tel. 1620266; fax 1620039; f. 1973; quarterly; Chichewa; publ. by the Ministry of Information; circ. 100,000.

Business Monthly: POB 906646, Blantyre 9; tel. 16301114; fax 1620039; f. 1995; English; economic, financial and business news; Editor Anthony Livuza; circ. 10,000.

Fairlane Magazine: POB 1745, Blantyre; tel. 1880205; e-mail fairlane@sndp.org.mw; internet www.fairlanemagazine.com; f. 2006; 6 a year; lifestyle magazine; English and Chichewa; Man. Dir Marie France Chikuni.

Kuunika (The Light): POB 17, Nkhoma, Lilongwe; tel. 1722807; e-mail nkhomasynod@globemw.net; f. 1909; monthly; Chichewa; publ. by the Church of Central Africa (Presbyterian) Nkhoma Synod; Presbyterian; Editor Rev. M. C. Nkhalambayausi; circ. 6,000.

Malawi Medical Journal: College of Medicine and Medical Assen of Malawi, Private Bag 360, Blantyre 3; tel. and fax 1878254; e-mail mmj@medcol.mw; internet www.mmj.medcol.mw; f. 1980; replaced *Medical Quarterly*; quarterly; Chair. Prof. Eric Borgstein; Editor-in-Chief Prof. Malcolm E. Molyneux.

Moni Magazine: POB 5592, Limbe; tel. 1651833; fax 1651171; f. 1964; monthly; Chichewa and English; circ. 40,000.

Moyo Magazine: Health Education Unit, POB 30377, Lilongwe 3; 6 a year; English; publ. by the Ministry of Health; Editor-in-Chief Jonathan Nkhoma.

Pride: POB 51668, Limbe; tel. 1640569; f. 1999; quarterly; Publr John Saini.

This is Malawi: POB 494, Blantyre; tel. 1620266; fax 1620807; f. 1964; monthly; English and Chichewa edns; publ. by the Dept of Information; Editor Anthony Livuza; circ. 12,000.

Together: Montfort Media, POB 280, Balaka, Zomba; tel. 1545267; e-mail together@sdnp.org.mw; f. 1995; quarterly; Roman Catholic and ecumenical, youth; Editor Luigi Gritti; circ. 6,000.

Other publications include *Dzukani, Inspiration* and *Msilikali*.

NEWS AGENCY

Malawi News Agency (MANA): POB 28, Blantyre; tel. 1622122; fax 1634867; f. 1966; Exec. Dir George Thindwa.

Publishers

Christian Literature Association in Malawi (CLAIM): POB 503, Blantyre; tel. 1620839; f. 1968; Chichewa and English; general and religious; Gen. Man. J. T. Matenje.

Likuni Press and Publishing House: POB 133, Lilongwe; tel. 1721388; fax 1721141; f. 1949; English and Chichewa; general and religious.

Macmillan Malawi Ltd: Private Bag 140, Kenyatta Dr., Chitawira, Blantyre; tel. 1676449; fax 1675751; e-mail mayeso@macmillanmw.net; Gen. Man. Hastings Matewere.

Montfort Press and Popular Publications: POB 5592, Limbe; tel. 1651833; fax 1641126; f. 1961; general and religious; Gen. Man. Vales Machila.

GOVERNMENT PUBLISHING HOUSE

Government Press: Government Printer, POB 37, Zomba; tel. 1525515; fax 1525175.

Broadcasting and Communications

TELECOMMUNICATIONS

Regulatory Authority

Malawi Communications Regulatory Authority (MACRA): Salmon Amour Rd, Private Bag 261, Blantyre; tel. 1883611; fax 1883890; e-mail dg-macra@macra.org.mw; internet www.macra.org.mw; f. 1998; Chair. Dr Benson Tembo; Dir-Gen. Charles Nsaliwa.

Service Providers

Airtel Malawi: Mwai House, City Centre, POB 57, Lilongwe; tel. 1774800; fax 1774802; e-mail info.africa@airtel.com; internet africa.airtel.com/malawi; f. 1999; fmrly Zain Malawi, present name adopted in 2010; Man. Dir Saulos Chilima.

Malawi Telecommunications Ltd (MTL): Lamya House, Masauko Chipembere Highway, POB 537, Blantyre; tel. 1870278; fax 1846445; e-mail mtlceo@malawi.net; internet www.mtl.mw; f. 2000 following division of Malawi Posts and Telecommunications Corpn into 2 separate entities; privatized in 2006; 80% owned by Telecom Holdings Ltd, 20% state-owned; CEO Charles Chuka.

Telekom Networks Malawi (TNM): Livingstone Towers, Lower Ground Floor, POB 3039, Blantyre; tel. 1830888; fax 1830092; e-mail customercare@tnm.co.mw; internet www.tnm.co.mw; f. 1995; owned by Malawi Telecommunications Ltd; operates mobile cellular telephone network; CEO Werner Schrijver.

BROADCASTING

Radio

Malawi Broadcasting Corpn: POB 30133, Chichiri, Blantyre 3; tel. 1671222; fax 1671257; e-mail dgmbc@malawi.net; internet www.mbcradios.com; f. 1964; merged with Television Malawi in July 2010; state-run; 2 channels: MBC 1 and Radio 2 (MBC 2); programmes in English, Chichewa, Chitonga, Chitumbuka, Kyangonde, Lomwe, Sena and Yao; Chair. Inkosi ya Makosi Mbelwa IV; Dir.-Gen. Bright Malopa.

Private commercial and religious radio stations include:

African Bible College Radio (Radio ABC): POB 1028, Lilongwe; tel. 1761965; fax 1761602; e-mail radioabc@malawi.net; internet africanbiblecolleges.org; f. 1995; regional Christian religious programming; Station Man. Macleod Munthali.

Calvary Family Radio: POB 30239, Blantyre 3; tel. 1671627; fax 1671642; e-mail calvaryministries@hotmail.com; operated by the Calvary Family Church; religious community radio station.

Capital Radio 102.5 FM: 1st Floor, Kapeni House, cnr of Victoria Ave and Chilembwe Rd, Blantyre; Private Bag 437, Chichiri, Blantyre 3; tel. 1820858; fax 1823382; e-mail stationmanager@capitalradiomalawi.com; internet www.capitalradiomalawi.com; f. 1999; commercial radio station; music and entertainment; Man. Dir and Editor-in-Chief Alaudin Osman.

Channel for All Nations (CAN): POB 1220, Lilongwe; tel. 1761763; fax 1762056; e-mail kawembale@yahoo.com; f. 2004; operated by the Assemblies of God Church; regional Christian religious programming.

Dzimwe Community Radio (DCR): POB 425, Chichiri, Blantyre; tel. 1672288; fax 1624330; e-mail mamwa@yahoo.com; f. 1997; operated by the Malawi Media Women's Asscn; focus on rural women's issues; Station Man. Janet Karim.

Joy FM: Private Bag 17, Limbe, Blantyre; tel. 1638330; fax 1638329; e-mail joyradio@globemalawi.net; commercial radio station; Owner Bakili Muluzi.

MIJ FM: POB 30165, Chichiri, Blantyre 3; tel. 1675087; fax 1675649; e-mail mij@clcom.net; internet www.mij.mw/aboutradio.html; f. 1996; operated by students of the Malawi Institute of Journalism; community radio station; closed by the Govt during May 2004.

Nkhota Kota Community Radio: Nkhota Kota; f. 2003 with assistance from UNESCO; focus on social and devt issues.

Power 101 FM: POB 761, Blantyre; tel. 1844101; fax 1841387; e-mail fm101@malawi.net; f. 1998; commercial radio station; music and entertainment; Dir and Station Man. Oscar Thomson.

Radio Alinafe: Maula Cathedral, POB 631, Lilongwe; tel. 1759971; fax 1752767; e-mail radioalinafe@sdnp.org.mw; f. 2002; Chichewa and English; operated by the Archdiocese of Lilongwe; regional Roman Catholic religious programming; Dir Gabriel Jana; Editor Moses Kaufa.

Radio Islam: PO Box 5400, Limbe; tel. 1641408; e-mail zakaat@globemw.net; f. 2001; operated by the Islamic Zakaat Fund; religious programming; Dir Mahmud Sardar Issa.

Radio Maria Malawi: POB 408, Mangochi; tel. 1599626; fax 1599691; e-mail radiomaria@malawi.net; internet www.radiomaria.mw; f. 2003; operated by Asscn of Radio Maria Malawi as part of the World Family of Radio Maria, Italy; Roman Catholic

MALAWI

religious programming; Chichewa, Chiyao and English; Gen. Man. JOSEPH KIMU; Dir of Programmes HENRY SAINDI.

Radio Tigawane: Bishop's House, POB 252, Mzuzu; tel. 1332271; e-mail tigawane@sndp.org.mw; f. 2005; operated by the Diocese of Mzuzu; regional Roman Catholic religious programming; Tumbuka, Chichewa and English; Project Co-ordinator EUGENE NGOMA.

Star FM: Agma House, 2nd Floor, Maselema, POB 815, Blantyre; tel. 1878522; fax 1878523; e-mail info@starradiomw.com; internet www.starradiomw.com; f. 2006; commercial radio station; Station Man. DENNIS KAUTSI.

Trans World Radio Malawi (TWR): POB 52, Lilongwe; tel. and fax 1751870; e-mail twr@malawi.net; f. 2000; part of Trans World Radio-Africa, South Africa; Christian religious programming; Chair. ISAAC MTAMBO; Nat. Dir VICTOR KAONGA (acting).

Zodiak Broadcasting Station (ZBS): Private Bag 312, Lilongwe 3; tel. 1762557; fax 1762751; internet www.zodiakmalawi.com; f. 2005; operated by Zodiak Broadcasting Services; programmes in Chichewa and English; Man. Dir GOSPEL KAZAKO.

Television

MBC: (see Radio).

Finance

(cap. = capital; res = reserves; dep. = deposits; m. = million; br(s). = branch(es); amounts in kwacha)

BANKING

In 2010 there were 11 commercial banks and three other financial institutions in Malawi.

Central Bank

Reserve Bank of Malawi: Convention Dr., POB 30063, Capital City, Lilongwe 3; tel. 1770600; fax 1772752; e-mail webmaster@rbm.mw; internet www.rbm.mw; f. 1965; bank of issue; cap. 19,484m., res 12,191m., dep. 48,715m. (Dec. 2009); Gov. Dr PERKS LIGOYA; br. in Blantyre.

Commercial Banks

INDEBank Ltd: INDEBank House, Kaohsiong Rd, Top Mandala, POB 358, Blantyre; tel. 1820055; fax 1823353; e-mail enquiriesho@indebank.com; internet www.indebank.com; f. 1972 as Investment and Devt Bank of Malawi Ltd; total assets 2,162.6m. (Dec. 2003); 41.38% owned by Trans-Africa Holdings Ltd, 30% owned by Press Trust, 25.67% owned by ADMARC Investments Holding, 2.95% owned by Employee Ownership Scheme; commercial and devt banking; provides loans to statutory corpns and to private enterprises in the agricultural, industrial, tourism, transport and commercial sectors; Chair. FRANKLIN KENNEDY; Man. Dir and CEO WILLIAM CHATSALA; 6 brs.

Loita Bank Ltd: c/o Fintech (Malawi) Ltd, Peoples Bldg, 1st Floor, Victoria Ave, Private Bag 264, Blantyre; tel. 1822099; fax 1822683; e-mail lib@mw.loita.com; internet www.loita.com; total assets 3,100.3m. (Dec. 2003); 100% owned by Loita Capital Partners Int.; Chair. and CEO N. JUSTIN CHIMYANTA; 2 brs.

National Bank of Malawi: 19 Victoria Ave, POB 945, Blantyre; tel. 1820622; fax 1820321; e-mail chiefexec@natbankmw.com; internet www.natbank.co.mw; f. 1971; 52% owned by Press Corpn Ltd, 25% owned by Old Mutual Group; cap. 466m., res 2,592m., dep. 55,338m. (Dec. 2009); Chair. Dr MATHEWS CHIKAONDA; CEO GEORGE B. PARTRIDGE; 25 service centres.

NBS Bank Ltd: Ginnery Cnr, Chipembere Highway, off Masajico, POB 32251, Chichiri, Blantyre; tel. 1876222; fax 1875041; e-mail nbs@nbsmw.com; internet www.nbsmw.com; f. 2003; 60% owned by NICO, 8% owned by the Nat. Investment Trust; fmrly New Building Society; cap. 246.7m., res 733.7m., dep. 24,317m. (Dec. 2009); Chair. FELIX L. MLUSU; CEO JOHN S. BIZIWICK.

Nedbank (Malawi) Ltd: Development House, cnr Henderson St and Victoria Ave, POB 750, Blantyre; tel. 1620477; fax 1620102; e-mail office@mw.nedcor.com; f. 1999; fmrly Fincom Bank of Malawi Ltd; 68.8% owned by Nedbank Africa Investments Ltd, 28.4% owned by SBM Nedcor Holdings Ltd; total assets 1,426.9m. (Dec. 2003); Chair. C. DREW; Man. Dir PAUL TUBB.

Standard Bank Ltd: Kaomba Centre, cnr Glyn Jones Rd and Victoria Ave, POB 1111, Blantyre; tel. 1820144; fax 1820117; e-mail stanbicmw@standardbank.co.mw; internet www.standardbank.co.mw; f. 1970 as Commercial Bank of Malawi; present name adopted June 2003; 60.18% owned by Stanbic Africa Holdings Ltd, 20.00% owned by Nat. Insurance Co; cap. 213m., res 2,392m., dep. 38,147m. (Dec. 2009); Chair. ALEX CHITSIME; Man. Dir CHARLES MUDIWA; 8 brs.

Development Bank

Opportunity International Bank of Malawi Ltd (OIBM): Opportunity Bank Bldg, POB 1794, Lilongwe; tel. 1758403; fax 1758400; e-mail lilongwe@oibm.mw; internet www.oibm.mw; f. 2003; 63.7% owned by Opportunity Transformation Investments, USA, 25.3% owned by Opportunity Micro Investments (UK) Ltd, United Kingdom, 11% owned by Trust for Transformation; total assets 967.4m. (Dec. 2005); Chair. FRANCIS PELEKAMOYO; CEO RODGER VOORHIES.

Discount Houses

Continental Discount House: Unit House, 5th Floor, Victoria Ave, POB 1444, Blantyre; tel. 1821300; fax 1822826; e-mail info@cdh-malawi.com; internet www.cdh-malawi.com; f. 1998; 84% owned by Trans-Africa Holdings; total assets 6,728.8m. (Dec. 2005); Chair. ROBERT SEKOH ABBEY; Man. Dir and CEO MISHECK ESAU.

First Discount House Ltd: Umoyo House, 1st Floor, 8 Victoria Ave North, POB 512, Blantyre; tel. 1820219; fax 1523044; e-mail fdh@fdh.co.mw; internet www.fdh.co.mw; f. 2000; 40.16% owned by Kingdom Financial Holdings Ltd, 39.84% owned by Thomson F. Mpinganjira Trust, 20% owned by Old Mutual Life Assurance Co (Malawi) Ltd; total assets 5,960.7m. (Dec. 2004); CEO THOMSON F. MPINGANJIRA; Chair. NIGEL M. K. CHAKANIRA.

Merchant Banks

First Merchant Bank Ltd: Livingstone Towers, Glyn Jones Rd, Private Bag 122, Blantyre; tel. 1821955; fax 1821978; e-mail fmb.headoffice@fmbmalawi.com; internet www.fmbmalawi.com; f. 1994; cap. 111.3m., res 2,281.5m., dep. 11,539.5m. (Dec. 2008); 44.9% owned by Zambezi Investments Ltd, 22.5% owned by Simsbury Holdings Ltd, 11.2% owned each by Prime Capital and Credit Ltd, Kenya, and Prime Bank Ltd, Kenya; Chair. RASIKBHAI C. KANTARIA; Man. Dir KASHINATH N. CHATURVEDI; 7 brs.

Leasing and Finance Co of Malawi Ltd: Livingstone Towers, Glyn Jones Rd, POB 1963, Blantyre; tel. 1820233; fax 1820275; f. 1986; subsidiary of First Merchant Bank Ltd since June 2002; total assets 2,087.4m. (Dec. 2006); Chair. HITESH ANADKAT; Gen. Man. MBACHAZWA LUNGU.

Savings Bank

Malawi Savings Bank: Umoyo House, Victoria Ave, POB 521, Blantyre; tel. 1625111; fax 1621929; internet www.msb.mw; f. 1994; 99.9% state-owned; total assets 1,191.7m. (Dec. 2003); Sec.-Treas. P. E. CHILAMBE; Gen. Man. IAN C. BONONGWE.

STOCK EXCHANGE

Malawi Stock Exchange: Old Reserve Bank Bldg, 14 Victoria Ave, Private Bag 270, Blantyre; tel. 1824233; fax 1823636; e-mail mse@mse-mw.com; internet www.mse.co.mw; f. 1996; Chair. KRISHNA SAVJANI; CEO SYMON MSEFULA; 15 cos listed in 2008.

INSURANCE

In 2010 the insurance sector comprised 12 insurance companies and one reinsurance company. Of these, eight companies dealt in non-life insurance.

NICO Holdings Ltd: CHIBISA House, 19 Glyn Jones Rd, POB 501, Blantyre; tel. 1831902; fax 1822364; e-mail info@nicomw.com; internet www.nicomw.com; f. 1970; fmrly National Insurance Co Ltd; transferred to private sector in 1996; incorporates NICO Gen. Insurance Co Ltd, NICO Life Insurance Co Ltd and NICO Technologies Ltd; cap. and res 104.7m. (Sept. 1997); offices at Blantyre, Lilongwe, Mzuzu and Zomba; agencies country-wide; Chair. GEORGE A. JAFFU; CEO and Man. Dir FELIX L. MLUSU.

Old Mutual Malawi: 30 Glyn Jones Rd, Old Mutual Building, POB 393, Blantyre; tel. 1820677; fax 1822649; e-mail info@oldmutual.co.mw; internet www.oldmutualmalawi.com; f. 1845; subsidiary of Old Mutual PLC, United Kingdom; Chair. SIMON ITAYE; Man. Dir CHRIS KAPANGA.

REAL Insurance Co of Malawi Ltd: Hannover House, Independence Dr., POB 442, Blantyre; tel. 1824044; fax 1823862; e-mail blantyre@realinsurance.co.mw; internet www.realinsurance.co.mw; associate of Royal and SunAlliance PLC, United Kingdom; Chair. TOB KANYUKA; CEO SOPHIE W. KARANJA.

United General Insurance Co Ltd (UGI): Michiru House, Victoria Ave, POB 383, Blantyre; tel. 1821770; fax 1821980; e-mail ugi@ugimalawi.com; internet www.ugimalawi.com; f. 1986 as Pearl Assurance Co Ltd; latterly Property and Gen. Insurance Co Ltd; present name adopted following merger with Fide Insurance Co Ltd in July 1998; 74% owned by ZimRE Holdings, Zimbabwe; Chair. ALBERT NDUNA; Man. Dir IAN K. KUMWENDA.

Vanguard Life Assurance Co (Pvt) Ltd: MDC House, 2nd Floor, Glyn Jones Rd, POB 1625, Blantyre; tel. 1823326; fax 1823056;

MALAWI

e-mail vanguard@vanguardlifemw.com; internet www.vanguardlifemw.com; f. 1999; 90% owned by Fidelity Life Assurance Ltd, Zimbabwe; Chair. S. Tembo; Man. Dir George Mazhude.

Trade and Industry

GOVERNMENT AGENCIES

Agricultural Development and Marketing Corpn (ADMARC): POB 5052, Limbe; tel. 1840044; fax 1840486; e-mail admce@admarc.co.mw; internet www.admarc.co.mw; f. 1971; involved in cultivation, processing, marketing and export of grain and other crops; Chair. Ernest Malenga; CEO Dr Charles J. Matabwa.

Malawi Export Promotion Council (MEPC): Kanabar House, 2nd Floor, Victoria Ave, POB 1299, Blantyre; tel. 1820499; fax 1820995; e-mail mepco@malawi.net; internet www.malawiepc.com; f. 1971; promotes and facilitates export and investment, and provides technical assistance and training to exporters; Gen. Man. Lawrence M. Chaluluka.

Malawi Investment Promotion Agency (MIPA): Aquarius House, Private Bag 302, Lilongwe 3; tel. 1770800; fax 1771781; e-mail mipa@mipamw.org; internet www.malawi-invest.net; f. 1993; promotes and facilitates local and foreign investment; CEO James R. Kaphweleza Banda.

Petroleum Control Commission: POB 2827, Blantyre; e-mail sichioko@pccmalawi.com; state-owned; held monopoly on fuel imports until 2000; also serves regulatory role; Chair. Rev. Dr Lazarus Chakwera; Gen. Man. Ishmael Chioko.

Privatisation Commission of Malawi: Livingstone Towers, 2nd Floor, Glyn Jones Rd, POB 937, Blantyre; tel. 1823655; fax 1821248; e-mail info@pcmalawi.org; internet www.pcmalawi.org; f. 1996; has sole authority to oversee divestiture of govt interests in public enterprises; Chair. Alex Chitsime; CEO Jimmy Lipunga; 75 privatizations completed by January 2008.

Tobacco Control Commission: POB 40045, Kanengo, Lilongwe 4; tel. 1712777; fax 1712632; e-mail tcclib@tccmw.com; internet www.tccmw.com; f. 1939; regulates tobacco production and marketing; advises Govt on sale and export of tobacco; Chair. Gamaliel Bandawe; CEO Dr Bruce Munthali; regional offices in Mzuzu and Limbe.

DEVELOPMENT ORGANIZATIONS

Council for Non-Governmental Organizations in Malawi (CONGOMA): Chitawira, Waya Bldg, Makata Rd, Makata Industrial Site, POB 480, Blantyre; tel. 1876409; fax 1876459; internet www.congoma.org; f. 1992; promotes social and economic devt; Chair. Tadeyo Shaba; Exec. Dir Emmanuel Ted Nandolo; 86 mem. orgs (2004).

Small Enterprise Development Organization of Malawi (SEDOM): POB 525, Blantyre; tel. 1622555; fax 1622781; e-mail sedom@sdnp.org.mw; f. 1982; financial services and accommodation for indigenous small- and medium-scale businesses; Chair. Stella Ndau.

CHAMBER OF COMMERCE

Malawi Confederation of Chambers of Commerce and Industry (MCCCI): Masauko Chipembere Highway, Chichiri Trade Fair Grounds, POB 258, Blantyre; tel. 1871988; fax 1871147; e-mail mccci@mccci.org; internet www.mccci.org; f. 1892; promotes trade and encourages competition in the economy; Chair. Matthews J. Chikankheni; CEO Chancellor L. Kaferapanjira; 400 mems.

INDUSTRIAL AND TRADE ASSOCIATIONS

Dwangwa Cane Growers Trust (DCGT): POB 156, Dwangwa; tel. 1295111; fax 1295164; e-mail dcgt@malawi.net; f. 1999; fmrly Smallholder Sugar Authority; CEO Wilfred Chakanika.

National Hawkers and Informal Business Association (NAHIBA): Chichiri Trade Fair, POB 60544, Ndirande, Blantyre; tel. 1945315; fax 1624558; e-mail nazulug@yahoo.com; f. 1995; Exec. Dir Eva Joachim.

Smallholder Coffee Farmers Trust: POB 20133, Luwinga, Mzuzu 2; tel. 1332899; fax 1333902; e-mail mzuzucoffee@malawi.net; f. 1971; successor to the Smallholder Coffee Authority, disbanded in 1999; producers and exporters of Arabica coffee; Gen. Man. Harrison Kalua; 4,000 mems.

Smallholder Tea Co (STECO): POB 135, Mulanje; f. 2002 by merger of Smallholder Tea Authority and Malawi Tea Factory Co Ltd.

Tea Association of Malawi Ltd (TAML): Kidney Crescent Rd, POB 930, Blantyre; tel. 1671182; fax 1671427; e-mail taml@malawi.net; internet www.taml.co.mw; f. 1934; CEO Clement C. Thindwa; 10 mems.

Tobacco Association of Malawi (TAMA): 13/64 Independence Dr., TAMA House, POB 31360, Lilongwe 3; tel. 1773099; fax 1773493; e-mail tama@tamalawi.com; internet www.tamalawi.com; f. 1929; Pres. Rueben Jefred Maigwa; Chief Exec. Felix Mkumba; brs in Mzuzu, Limbe and Chinkhoma; 75,000 mems.

Tobacco Exporters' Association of Malawi Ltd (TEAM): Private Bag 403, Kanengo, Lilongwe 4; tel. 1775839; fax 1774069; f. 1930; Chair. Charles A. M. Graham; Gen. Man. H. M. Mbale; 9 mems.

EMPLOYERS' ORGANIZATIONS

Employers' Consultative Association of Malawi (ECAM): Claim Bldg, Glyn Jones Rd, POB 2134, Blantyre; tel. and fax 1830075; fax 1830075; e-mail ecam@ecammw.com; internet www.ecammw.com; f. 1963; Pres. Dapther Namandwa; Exec. Dir Beyani Munthali (acting); 250 mem. asscns and 6 affiliates representing 80,000 employees.

Master Printers' Association of Malawi: POB 2460, Blantyre; tel. 1632948; fax 1632220; f. 1963; Chair. Paul Frederick; 21 mems.

Motor Traders' Association: POB 311, Blantyre; tel. and fax 1833312; f. 1954; Chair. Jolly Nkhojera; 13 mems (2008).

UTILITY

Electricity

Electricity Supply Corpn of Malawi (ESCOM): ESCOM House, Haile Selassie Rd, POB 2047, Blantyre; tel. and fax 1822000; fax 1822008; e-mail info@escommw.com; internet www.escommw.com; f. 1966; controls electricity generation and distribution; Chair. Thomas Mpinganjira; Acting CEO Arthur Mandambwe.

TRADE UNIONS

According to the Malawi Congress of Trade Unions, in 2005 some 18% of the workforce was unionized.

Congress of Malawi Trade Unions (COMATU): POB 1443, Lilongwe; tel. 1757255; fax 1770885; Pres. Thomas L. Banda; Gen. Sec. Phillmon E. Chimbalu.

Malawi Congress of Trade Unions (MCTU): POB 1271, Lilongwe; tel. 1752162; fax 1820716; e-mail mctusecretariat@mctumw.com; f. 1995 as successor to the Trade Union Congress of Malawi (f. 1964); Pres. Luther Mambala; Sec.-Gen. Robert James D. Mkwezalamba; 113,000 paid-up mems (2008).

Affiliated unions include:

Building Construction, Civil Engineering and Allied Workers' Union (BCCEAWU): c/o MCTU, POB 5094, Limbe; tel. 1620381; fax 1622304; e-mail johnmwafulirwa@yahoo.com; f. 1961; Pres. Lawrence Kafere; Gen. Sec. John O. Mwafulirwa; 6,401 mems (2006).

Commercial Industrial and Allied Workers' Union (CIAWU): c/o MCTU, POB 5094, Limbe; tel. 1820716; fax 1622303; e-mail mareydzinyemba@yahoo.com; Pres. Tryson Kalanda; Gen. Sec. Mary Dzinyemba; 3,075 mems (2006).

Communications Workers' Union of Malawi: Armarsi Odvarji Plaza, 1st Floor, Chipembere Highway, Private Bag 186, Blantyre; tel. and fax 1830830; e-mail cowuma@yahoo.co.uk; f. 1997; Pres. Batwell Kulemero; Gen. Sec. Robert James Daniel Mkwezalamba; 5,340 mems (2009).

Electronic Media Workers' Union: POB 30133, Chichiri, Blantyre 3; tel. 1871343; e-mail mmsowoya@hotmail.com; Pres. Lasten Kunkeyani; Gen. Sec. Malani Msowoya; 243 mems (2006).

ESCOM Staff Union: POB 2047, Blantyre; tel. 1773447; Pres. Oscar Chimwezi; Gen. Sec. Rachel Chasweka; 1,899 mems (2006).

Hotels, Food and Catering Service Union: c/o MCTU 5094, Limbe; tel. 1820314; e-mail hfpcwu@sdnp.org.mw; Pres. Austin Kalimanjira; Gen. Sec. Dorothea Makhasu; 3,565 mems (2006).

Malawi Housing Co-operation Workers' Union: c/o MHC, POB 84, Mzuzu; tel. 1332655; Pres. Grey Sadiki; Gen. Sec. Roosevelt Msiska; 236 mems (2006).

Plantation and Agriculture Workers' Union: POB 181, Lucheza; Pres. Patrick Kadyanji; Gen. Sec. Dennis Banda; 2,086 mems (2006).

Private Schools Employees' Union of Malawi (PSEUM): c/o MCTU, Kepell Compton Cres., Area 3/089, POB 1271, Lilongwe; tel. 1755614; fax 1752162; e-mail hendrixbanda@yahoo.com; Pres. Samuel Njiwa; Gen. Sec. Hendrix S. Banda; 2,670 mems (2008).

Railway Workers' Union of Malawi (Central East African Railway Workers' Union—CEARWU): POB 5393, Limbe; tel. 1640844; e-mail cear@cearcdn.mw; f. 1954; Pres. Dina M'mera; Gen. Sec. Luther Mambala; 485 mems (2006).

Sugar Plantation and Allied Workers' Union (SPAWUM): c/o Illovo Sugar (Malawi) Ltd, Private Bag 50, Blantyre; tel. 1425200;

MALAWI

e-mail spawum@illovo.co.za; Pres. Keeper Gumbo; Gen. Sec. Stephen Mkwapatira; 8,598 mems (2006).

Teachers' Union of Malawi: Aphunzitsi Centre, Private Bag 11, Lilongwe; tel. 1727302; fax 1727302; e-mail tum@sdnp.org.mw; Pres. Chauluka Muwake; Gen. Sec. Denis Kalekeni; 46,207 mems (2006).

Textile, Garment, Leather and Security Services Workers' Union: POB 5094, Limbe; tel. 8345576; e-mail textilegarmentunion@yahoo.com; f. 1995; Gen. Sec. Grace Nyirenda; 8,900 mems (2009).

Tobacco Tenants Workers' Union: POB 477, Nkhotakota; tel. 1292288; e-mail totawum@malawi.net; Pres. Luther Mambala; Gen. Sec. Raphael Sandram; 5,579 mems (2006).

Transport and General Workers' Union: POB 2778, Blantyre; tel. 8877795; fax 1830219; e-mail ronaldmbewe2002@yahoo.com; f. 1945; Pres. Francis Antonio; Gen. Sec. Ronald Mbewe; 3,257 mems (2006).

Water Employees' Trade Union of Malawi (WETUM): c/o Lilongwe Water Board, Madzi House, off Likuni Rd, POB 96, Lilongwe; tel. 1750366; fax 1752294; Pres. Anthony A. Chimphepo; Gen. Sec. Olivia Kunje; 1,195 mems (2006).

Transport

RAILWAYS

The Central East African Railways Co (fmrly Malawi Railways) operates between Nsanje (near the southern border with Mozambique) and Mchinji (near the border with Zambia) via Blantyre, Salima and Lilongwe, and between Nkaya and Nayuchi on the eastern border with Mozambique, covering a total of 797 km. The Central East African Railways Co and Mozambique State Railways connect Malawi with the Mozambican ports of Beira and Nacala. There is a rail/lake interchange station at Chipoka on Lake Malawi, from where vessels operate services to other lake ports in Malawi. The construction of a 27-km railway line linking Mchinji with Chipata, Zambia, was completed in 2010.

Central East African Railways Co Ltd (CEAR): Station Rd, POB 5144, Limbe; tel. 1640844; fax 1643496; f. 1994 as Malawi Railways Ltd; sold to a consortium owned by Mozambique's Empresa Nacional dos Portos e Caminhos de Ferro de Moçambique and the USA's Railroad Development Corpn in mid-1999 and subsequently renamed as above; ceased passenger services in Oct. 2005; Dir Russell Neely.

ROADS

In 2004 Malawi had a total road network of some 15,500 km, of which 3,600 km was paved. In addition, unclassified community roads total an estimated 10,000 km. All main roads, and most secondary roads, are all-weather roads. Major routes link Lilongwe and Blantyre with Harare (Zimbabwe), Lusaka (Zambia) and Mbeya and Dar es Salaam (Tanzania). A 480-km highway along the western shore of Lake Malawi links the remote Northern Region with the Central and Southern Regions. A project to create a new trade route, or 'Northern Corridor', through Tanzania, involving road construction and improvements in Malawi, was completed in 1992.

Department of Road Traffic: c/o Ministry of Transport and Public Infrastructure, Private Bag 257, Capital City, Lilongwe 3; tel. 1756138; fax 1752592; comprises the Nat. Roads Authority.

National Roads Authority: Functional Bldg, off Chilambula Rd, Private Bag B346, Lilongwe 3; tel. 1753699; fax 1750307; e-mail nra@nramw.com; internet www.ra.org.mw; f. 1997; CEO Titus Thyolamwendo.

Road Transport Operators' Association: Chitawira Light Industrial Site, POB 30740, Chichiri, Blantyre 3; tel. 1870422; fax 1871423; e-mail rtoa@sdnp.org.mw; f. 1956; Chair. P. Chakhumbira; Exec. Dir Shadreck Matsimbe; 200 mems (2004).

United Bus Co: POB 176, Blantyre; tel. 888863912; fax 1870038; e-mail ubc@ubcmw.com; internet www.ubcmw.com; f. 2008 by fmr employees of Shire Bus Lines Ltd following its liquidation in 2006; operates local and long-distance bus services between Makata, Blantyre, Malangalanga, Mzimba and Mzuzu and rural areas; services to Harare (Zimbabwe) and Johannesburg (South Africa); Chair. Al-haj Sheik Alidi Likonde.

SHIPPING

There are 23 ports and landing points on Lake Malawi. The four main ports are at Chilumba, Nkhata Bay, Chipoka and Monkey Bay. Ferry services carry around 60,000 passengers annually; the principal cargoes transported are sugar, fertilizer, dried fish and maize. A new landing point at Ngala, near Dwangwa, to carry sugar to Chipoka was inaugurated in 2005. Smaller vessels are registered for other activities including fishing and tourism. Lake Malawi is at the centre of the Mtwara Development Corridor transport initiative agreed between Zambia, Malawi, Tanzania and Mozambique in December 2004.

Department of Marine Services: c/o Department of Transport and Public Works, Private Bag A-81, Lilongwe; tel. 1751531; fax 1756290; e-mail marinedepartment@malawi.net; responsible for vessel safety and control, ports services, and maritime pollution control.

Malawi Lake Services Ltd (MLS): POB 15, Monkey Bay; tel. and fax 1587221; fax 1587309; e-mail ilala@malawi.net; f. 1994; state-owned; operates passenger and freight services to Mozambique, and freight services to Tanzania; Gen. Man. Owen Singini; 9 vessels, incl. 3 passenger and 4 cargo vessels.

CIVIL AVIATION

Kamuzu (formerly Lilongwe) International Airport was opened in 1982. There is also an international airport at Chileka (Blantyre) and domestic airports at Mzuzu and Karonga in the Northern region and at the Club Makokola resort near Mangochi.

Department of Civil Aviation: c/o Ministry of Transport and Public Infrastructure, Private Bag B311, Lilongwe 3; tel. 1770577; fax 1774986; e-mail aviationhq@malawi.net; Dir L. Z. Phesele.

Air Malawi Ltd: 4 Robins Rd, POB 84, Blantyre; tel. 1820811; fax 1820042; e-mail enquiries@airmalawi.com; internet www.airmalawi.com; f. 1967; privatization, begun in 1999, was postponed in 2005; scheduled domestic and regional services; owns 5 subsidiary cos incl. Air Cargo Ltd and Lilongwe Handling Co Ltd; Chair. Patrick Chilambe; CEO Capt. A. B. W. Mchungula.

Tourism

Fine scenery, beaches on Lake Malawi, big game and an excellent climate form the basis of the country's tourist potential. According to official figures, the number of foreign visitor arrivals was 742,457 in 2008. Receipts from tourism totalled US $48m. in 2007.

Department of Tourism: POB 402, Blantyre; tel. 1620300; fax 1620947; f. 1969; responsible for tourism policy; inspects and licenses tourist facilities, sponsors training of hotel staff and publishes tourist literature; Dir of Tourism Services Isaac K. Msiska.

Malawi Tourism Association (MTA): POB 1044, Lilongwe; tel. 1770010; fax 1770131; e-mail mta@malawi.net; internet www.malawi-tourism-association.org.mw; f. 1998; Exec. Dir Sam Botomani.

Defence

As assessed at November 2010, Malawi's defence forces comprised a land army of 5,300, a marine force of 220 and an air force of 200; all form part of the army. There was also a paramilitary police force of 1,500.

Defence Expenditure: Estimated at K7,200m. in 2009.

Commander-in-Chief of the Malawi Defence Force: Dr Bingu wa Mutharika.

Commander of the Malawi Defence Force: Gen. Mark Daiton Chidziko.

Education

Primary education, which is officially compulsory, begins at six years of age and lasts for eight years. Secondary education, which begins at 14 years of age, lasts for four years, comprising two cycles of two years. According to UNESCO, in 2008/09 primary enrolment included 91% of children in the relevant age-group (males 88%; females 93%), while secondary enrolment included 25% of children in the relevant age-group (males 26%; females 24%). A programme to expand education at all levels has been undertaken; however, the introduction of free primary education in September 1994 led to the influx of more than 1m. additional pupils, resulting in severe overcrowding in schools. In January 1996 the International Development Association granted US $22.5m. for the training of 20,000 new teachers, appointed in response to the influx. In 2008 there were some 46,333 primary school teachers, of whom 18,026 were female. In 1997 additional funding was provided by the African Development Bank for the construction of primary and secondary schools. The five constituent colleges of the University of Malawi had a total of 6,454 students in 2008, while 1,428 students were enrolled at Mzuzu University, 358 at the Catholic University and 148 at the University of Livingstonia. Some students attend institutions in the United Kingdom and the USA. A small number of students attended the Marine College at Monkey Bay, established in 1998. Recurrent expenditure on education in 2008/09 was estimated at 21,413m. kwacha (equivalent to 13.7% of total recurrent expenditure).

MALAYSIA

Introductory Survey

LOCATION, CLIMATE, LANGUAGE, RELIGION, FLAG, CAPITAL

The Federation of Malaysia, situated in South-East Asia, consists of 13 states. Eleven of these are in Peninsular Malaysia, in the southern part of the Kra peninsula (with Thailand to the north and the island of Singapore to the south), and two, Sabah and Sarawak, are on the north coast of the island of Borneo, two-thirds of which comprises the Indonesian territory of Kalimantan. Sarawak also borders Brunei, a coastal enclave in the north-east of the state. The climate is tropical, there is rain in all seasons and temperatures are generally between 22°C (72°F) and 33°C (92°F), with little variation throughout the year. The official language is Bahasa Malaysia, based on Malay, but English is also widely used. Chinese, Tamil and Iban are spoken by minorities. Islam is the established religion, practised by about 53% of the population (including virtually all Malays), while about 19%, including most of the Chinese community, follow Buddhism. The Indians are predominantly Hindus. There is a minority of Christians among all races, and traditional beliefs are practised, particularly in Sabah and Sarawak. Malaysia's national flag (proportions 1 by 2) has 14 horizontal stripes, alternating red and white, with a blue rectangular canton, containing a yellow crescent and a 14-pointed yellow star, in the upper hoist. The capital is Kuala Lumpur. A new administrative capital, Putrajaya, has been developed south of Kuala Lumpur.

CONTEMPORARY POLITICAL HISTORY

Historical Context

The 11 states of Malaya, under British protection, were united as the Malayan Union in April 1946 and became the Federation of Malaya in February 1948. An armed communist offensive began in 1948, and was not effectively suppressed until the mid-1950s. After 1960 the remainder of the banned Communist Party of Malaya (CPM) took refuge in southern Thailand. Meanwhile, Malaya was granted independence, within the Commonwealth, on 31 August 1957. Malaysia was established on 16 September 1963, through the union of the independent Federation of Malaya (renamed the States of Malaya), the internally self-governing state of Singapore, and the former British colonies of Sarawak and Sabah (North Borneo). Singapore left the federation in August 1965, reducing the number of Malaysia's component states from 14 to 13. The States of Malaya were designated West Malaysia in 1966 and later styled Peninsular Malaysia.

Domestic Political Affairs

In 1970 serious inter-communal rioting, engendered by Malay resentment of the Chinese community's economic dominance and of certain pro-Chinese electoral results, precipitated the resignation of Tunku Abdul Rahman, who had been Prime Minister of Malaya (and subsequently of Malaysia) since independence. The new Prime Minister, Tun Abdul Razak, widened the government coalition, dominated by the United Malays National Organization (UMNO), to create a national front, Barisan Nasional (BN). The BN originally comprised 10 parties, absorbing most of the former opposition parties. In January 1976 the Prime Minister died and was succeeded by the Deputy Prime Minister, Dato' Hussein bin Onn.

Political stability was subsequently threatened by the resurgence of the communist guerrilla movement, which conducted a series of terrorist attacks in Peninsular Malaysia during 1976–78. However, CPM activity subsequently declined, owing to co-operation between Malaysia and Thailand in military operations along their common border. In 1987, in a Thai-sponsored amnesty, about 700 Malaysian communists surrendered to the Thai authorities. In December 1989, following a year of negotiations with the Thai Government, the remaining 1,188 rebels (including recruits from Thailand and Singapore) agreed to terminate all armed activities. The peace agreements, signed by the leader of the CPM and representatives of the Malaysian and Thai Governments, made provision for the resettlement of the insurgents in either Malaysia or Thailand and their eventual participation in legitimate political activity in Malaysia.

In October 1977 the expulsion of the Chief Minister (Menteri Besar) of the state of Kelantan from the dominant Parti Islam se Malaysia (PAS—Islamic Party of Malaysia) resulted in violent political disturbances in Kelantan and the declaration of a state of emergency by the federal Government. Direct rule was imposed in Kelantan, and the PAS was expelled from the BN coalition in December. In the federal and state elections of July 1978 Hussein consolidated the position of the BN, while the PAS, in opposition, suffered a serious reversal. In 1978, following the federal Government's rejection of proposals for a Chinese university, racial and religious tensions re-emerged.

In July 1981 Hussein was succeeded as Prime Minister by Dato' Seri Dr Mahathir Mohamad, Deputy Prime Minister since 1976. Mahathir called a general election in April 1982; the BN coalition won convincingly in all states and increased its overall strength in the House of Representatives.

A new political party, the Parti Bersatu Sabah (PBS—Sabah United Party), won control of the Sabah State Legislative Assembly at an election in April 1985. The legality of the new PBS administration was challenged by Muslim opponents, and in February 1986 the Chief Minister (Ketua Menteri) called a further election. In the May election the PBS won an increased majority of seats in the Assembly, and in June the BN agreed to admit the PBS into its ruling coalition, together with the United Sabah National Organization (USNO), which had been expelled in 1984.

In February 1986 Mahathir's leadership of the federal Government and of UMNO was challenged when Datuk Musa Hitam, the Deputy Prime Minister, resigned from the Government, owing to 'irreconcilable differences' with Mahathir. However, Musa retained his position as Deputy President of UMNO. During the following months Musa's supporters became increasingly critical of Mahathir. At an early general election in August, the BN coalition took 148 of the 177 seats in an enlarged House of Representatives: UMNO secured 83 seats, while the Malaysian Chinese Association (MCA) won 17. Of the opposition parties, the Democratic Action Party (DAP) won 24 seats, having gained support from ethnic Chinese voters who were disillusioned with the MCA. In concurrent state elections, the BN retained control of all the State Legislative Assemblies in Peninsular Malaysia. Several ministers who had supported Musa were subsequently demoted or removed from the Government.

In early 1987 there was a serious challenge for the presidency of UMNO from Tengku Razaleigh Hamzah, the Minister of Trade and Industry. At the UMNO General Assembly in April, none the less, Mahathir was elected UMNO President for the third time (and thus retained the position of Prime Minister at the head of the BN coalition), albeit with a greatly reduced majority. The General Assembly also narrowly elected Abdul Ghafar Baba (who had replaced Musa as Deputy Prime Minister in February 1986) as UMNO Deputy President. Mahathir subsequently announced the resignation of Razaleigh from his cabinet post.

Criticism of Mahathir's leadership persisted during 1987, both from within UMNO and from other political parties. At the same time, racial tensions intensified in various parts of the country over Chinese-language education, religion and other issues. In October–November, allegedly to prevent violent racially motivated riots between Chinese and Malays over politically sensitive issues, 106 people were detained under the provisions of the Internal Security Act (ISA), which allowed detention without trial on grounds of national security. Those detained included politicians from all parties (most notably the leader of the DAP, Lim Kit Siang), lawyers, journalists and leaders of pressure groups. Three newspapers were closed by the Government, and political rallies were prohibited. In November the Government introduced legislation to impose stringent penalties on editors and publishers disseminating what the Government regarded as 'false' news. From December the Minister of Information was empowered to monitor all radio and television broadcasts, and to revoke the licence of any private broadcasting company not conforming with 'Malaysian values'. By April 1989 all the detainees under the ISA had been released (although often under restrictive conditions).

In February 1988 the High Court gave a ruling on a suit filed by dissatisfied members of UMNO, who claimed that, since some of the delegations taking part in the UMNO elections of April 1987 had not been legally registered, the elections should be declared null and void. On account of the irregularities, the Court ruled that UMNO was an 'unlawful society' and that there had been 'no election at all'. Mahathir maintained that the ruling did not affect the legal status of the Government, and the Head of State, Tunku Mahmood Iskandar, expressed support for Mahathir. Later in February 1988 Mahathir announced that UMNO Baru (New UMNO) had been formed and that members of the original party would have to re-register in order to join. Razaleigh and his supporters were excluded from UMNO Baru (hereafter referred to as UMNO).

Tension between the executive and the judiciary was intensified by Parliament's approval in March 1988 of constitutional amendments limiting the power of the judiciary to interpret laws. The Lord President of the Supreme Court, Tun Mohammed Salleh bin Abas, wrote to the Head of State to complain about government attempts to reduce the independence of the judiciary, and was subsequently dismissed from office. In June 1989 the Government introduced a security law removing the right of persons being detained under provisions of the ISA to have recourse to the courts.

In September 1988 Razaleigh and 12 others followed two earlier dissidents and left the BN to join the opposition in the House of Representatives as independents. They were joined in October by Musa. In December Musa and his supporters drafted a six-point resolution (the Johore Declaration), specifying the terms under which they would consent to join UMNO. These terms were accepted by UMNO in January 1989 but were binding only in the state of Johor. Following the defeat at a by-election in that month of an opposition representative by an MCA candidate with UMNO support, Musa announced his membership of UMNO, prompting a further eight dissident representatives in Johor to join the party.

In March 1989 Razaleigh's movement established an alliance with the fundamentalist PAS. In May Razaleigh's party registered as Semangat '46 (Spirit of 1946, a reference to the year of foundation of the original UMNO). The DAP, whose followers were largely urban Chinese, agreed to co-operate with Semangat '46 and the PAS, but refused to join a formal alliance, owing to their opposition to the PAS's proclaimed policy of forming an Islamic state in Malaysia. In June a former breakaway faction from the PAS, Barisan Jama'ah Islamiah Sa-Malaysia, left the BN coalition to join Semangat '46, the PAS and the Parti Hisbul Muslimin Malaysia in an opposition coalition, Angkatan Perpaduan Ummah (APU—Muslim Unity Movement). APU subsequently won a by-election in Trengganu.

The opposition parties formed an informal electoral alliance, Gagasan Rakyat (People's Might), to contest the general election held in October 1990. (Gagasan Rakyat was formally registered in April 1992, and Razaleigh was elected as Chairman in July.) Prior to the election the PBS withdrew from the BN and aligned itself with the opposition. None the less, the BN controlled 127 of the 180 seats in the enlarged House of Representatives, thus retaining the two-thirds' majority necessary to amend the Constitution. Elections to 11 of the 13 State Legislative Assemblies (excluding Sabah and Sarawak) took place simultaneously. The BN obtained a majority of seats in all states except Kelantan, where APU won every seat in both the federal and state elections.

In November 1990, at a meeting of the UMNO General Assembly, Mahathir and Abdul Ghafar Baba were unanimously re-elected as President and Deputy President of the party. In February 1991 Mahathir appointed Anwar Ibrahim as Minister of Finance and Abdullah Badawi as Minister of Foreign Affairs.

In January 1991 the Chief Minister of Sabah and President of the PBS, Datuk Seri Joseph Pairin Kitingan, was arrested and charged with corruption. It was widely conjectured that his arrest and his press adviser's detention, under the ISA, were politically motivated. In May UMNO secured its first seat in Sabah, in a by-election necessitated by the defection to UMNO of USNO's founder and President, Tun Mustapha Harun. Shortly afterwards Jeffrey Kitingan (the brother of the Chief Minister) was detained under the ISA, accused of plotting Sabah's secession from Malaysia.

In 1992 Mahathir began drafting amendments to the Constitution that reduced the nine hereditary rulers' privileges, an action that was widely suspected to be due, in part, to the Sultan of Kelantan's open support for Razaleigh (a prince of Kelantan) in the 1990 general election. By the end of 1992, after initial resistance, the Sultans had agreed to the amendments with some slight modifications, and they were adopted in March 1993. The changes included ending the Sultans' legal immunity, curtailing their power to pardon the offences of relatives, and allowing parliamentary criticism of their misdeeds.

In October 1993 Mahathir was returned unopposed as President of UMNO. In the following month Anwar, representing the *Malayu baru* (new Malays—younger, urban, mainly professional Malays who had prospered as a result of economic expansion), was elected Deputy President of the party (a particularly significant post as the incumbent was traditionally also accorded the position of Deputy Prime Minister). All three vice-presidential posts were won by Anwar's self-styled 'Vision Team', which comprised Tan Sri Dato' Haji Muhyiddin bin Mohd Yassin (the Chief Minister of Johor), Dato' Sri Mohd Najib bin Tun Haji Abdul Razak (the Minister of Defence) and Tan Sri Dato' Mohammad Haji Mohammad Taib (the Chief Minister of Selangor). Anwar was appointed Deputy Prime Minister in December.

In April 1993 USNO, now led by Tun Mustapha Amirkahar (the son of Tun Mustapha Harun), left the opposition in the Sabah State Legislative Assembly to form a coalition with the ruling PBS. Prior to the announcement six of the 11 elected representatives of USNO joined UMNO. USNO's defection prompted the federal Government successfully to seek the party's deregistration in August, on the grounds that it had breached its own statutes. In the same month Tun Mustapha Harun was appointed to the federal post of Minister of Sabah Affairs.

In January 1994 Pairin Kitingan dissolved the Sabah State Legislative Assembly in preparation for early elections. Shortly afterwards Pairin Kitingan was convicted on charges of corruption by the High Court, but fined less than the minimum RM 2,000 required to disqualify him from office. Although Pairin Kitingan gained popular sympathy owing both to his perceived victimization in the corruption case and to his resistance to federal encroachment on Sabahan authority, a faction emerged in the PBS that favoured more harmonious relations with the federal Government. Former members of the deregistered USNO joined the PBS for the election, and the party also gained the support of Tun Mustapha Harun, who had resigned as Minister of Sabah Affairs and as a member of UMNO in January. (Tun Mustapha Harun died in January 1995.) At the election in February 1994 the PBS won a narrow majority, securing 25 of the 48 elective seats. In March, however, several PBS members defected to the opposition, among them Jeffrey Kitingan, who had been released from detention under the ISA in December 1993. As a result, PBS was stripped of its majority and Pairin Kitingan was replaced as Chief Minister by Tan Sri Sakaran Dandai, a leader of the Sabah wing of UMNO.

In June 1994 the BN coalition agreed to admit two breakaway parties from the PBS, the Parti Demokratik Sabah (Sabah Democratic Party), led by Datuk Bernard Dompok, and the Parti Bersatu Rakyat Sabah (PBRS—United Sabah People's Party), led by Joseph Kurup. In August Dompok was appointed Minister in the Prime Minister's Department, while Jeffrey Kitingan, who had been cleared of corruption in the High Court in June, became Deputy Minister for Housing and Local Government.

Meanwhile, in May 1994 the House of Representatives approved the 1994 Constitution (Amendment) Act, which further restricted the powers of the monarchy and provided for the restructuring of the judiciary. Hitherto, the Yang di-Pertuan Agong (Head of State) had been competent to withhold assent from and return legislation, within 30 days, to Parliament for further consideration. The amendment required the Yang di-Pertuan Agong to give his assent to a bill within 30 days; if he failed to do so, the bill would, none the less, become law. The changes to the judiciary in the amendment included the creation of a Court of Appeal, the restyling of the Supreme Court as the Federal Court and of the Lord President as the Chief Justice.

In the April 1995 general election the BN won an overwhelming majority, taking 162 of the 192 seats in the House of Representatives (with some 64% of the total votes cast). The PBS won eight of Sabah's federal seats, including those held by Jeffrey Kitingan and Dompok. Although this constituted a loss of six seats, it was an indication that, despite the BN's assumption of power at state level through the defection of former PBS members of the legislature, the PBS remained a significant political force in Sabah. The BN also retained control of 10 of the 11 State Legislative Assemblies for which voting took place, in most cases securing a two-thirds' majority. In Kelantan, which remained the only state under opposition control, a coalition of the PAS and Semangat '46 took 35 of the 43 state seats.

Despite his election victory, Mahathir's position appeared vulnerable during the divisional elections of UMNO in 1995. The defeat of several Mahathir supporters was widely attributed to the influence of Anwar's associates, and prompted speculation that Anwar might challenge Mahathir for the leadership. In November, however, UMNO's General Assembly adopted an unprecedented resolution to avoid any contest for the two senior party positions in 1996; Anwar finally declared that he would not challenge Mahathir, and Mahathir for the first time said that he would retire in the near future and again named Anwar as his successor.

Semangat '46 was formally dissolved in October 1996, and its members were admitted to UMNO. At that month's UMNO General Assembly Mahathir and Anwar were, as anticipated, returned unopposed to their posts. In contrast to the 1993 party elections, in which Anwar's supporters had been particularly successful, a large proportion of Mahathir loyalists were now elected. Notably, in the elections for the vice-presidencies, Muhyiddin Yassin, the only member of Anwar's 'Vision Team' who had remained loyal to the Deputy President, was defeated by Abdullah Badawi (the Minister of Foreign Affairs, who had been a vice-president prior to 1993); Najib Razak and Mohammad Taib were re-elected. However, the leadership of the women's wing and the youth wing, both previously held by Mahathir loyalists, were both taken by Anwar supporters. No former member of Semangat '46, including Razaleigh, secured a position on the UMNO Supreme Council.

In October 1996 the PAS announced that it was to abandon its attempt to replace secular criminal laws with *hudud*, the Islamic criminal code, in Kelantan: Mahathir was known to be strongly opposed to such a policy. The PAS won a by-election for the State Legislative Assembly in Kelantan in January 1997. Although the PAS took the seat from Semangat '46 by only a narrow margin, the results were nevertheless indicative of Razaleigh's weakened position in the state.

Mahathir's response to the currency crisis affecting the region in 1997, following Thailand's effective devaluation of the baht in early July, and his criticism of international investors, was widely perceived to have exacerbated Malaysia's economic position. Meanwhile, Anwar benefited politically from the situation, appearing to act responsibly in reassuring investors and rescinding the newly imposed financial restrictions. However, political opponents attempted to undermine Anwar through the circulation of a series of letters accusing him of sexual indiscretions. International criticism of Mahathir's outspokenness prompted popular demonstrations of support for the premier within Malaysia and near unanimous support for a vote of confidence in his leadership, which was held in the House of Representatives during November. In the same month Mahathir announced the formation of an executive authority to address the economic crisis, the National Economic Action Council, which was approved by the Cabinet in January 1998. At the UMNO annual convention in September 1997 Mahathir criticized the increasing tendency of Malaysian Muslims to attach excessive importance to external symbols of Islam (such as beards and headscarves) and warned of the dangers of extremism. Mahathir's speech, which was resented by many Muslims, followed the widely publicized arrest, in June, of three Muslim women for taking part in a beauty contest in Selangor. The arrests prompted debate concerning the position of women in Malaysian society and resulted in demands for the reform of the Islamic Syariah (Shari'a or Shariah) courts; a *fatwa* (religious edict) had the force of law in the state in which it was issued, which arguably violated the liberties of Malaysians as guaranteed under the federal Constitution. In November 10 men were detained under the ISA for disseminating Shi'a Muslim teachings (Malaysian Muslims belong predominantly to the Sunni sect) that were perceived as militant and a threat to national security. Many non-governmental organizations (NGOs) and political parties urged that the detainees be released or allowed to stand trial under the Sedition Act.

The first trials of Anwar Ibrahim

At internal elections for divisional committee members in UMNO, which took place in March 1998, most of Mahathir's supporters retained their positions. However, evidence of a growing division between Mahathir and Anwar became apparent at the UMNO annual party congress held in June, where Dato' Seri Dr Ahmad Zahid bin Hamidi, the head of the youth wing of UMNO and one of Anwar's supporters, made a speech criticizing what he termed the debilitating impact of corruption in the party. Zahid's speech, which was reminiscent of Anwar's recent condemnation of corruption and political restrictions, was perceived as an attack on the party's leadership; Mahathir responded by publishing a list of hundreds of people and companies who had received privatization contracts in recent years, which included close associates of Anwar and members of his family. During the following weeks Mahathir acted to counter the influence of Anwar, promoting allies and dismissing newspaper editors close to Anwar. The resignation in August of the Governor (a close ally of Anwar) and Deputy Governor of the central bank, reportedly owing to a disagreement over policy with Mahathir, served as an indication of the intensification of the rift within the Government. Supporters loyal to the Prime Minister responded to the perceived threat to Mahathir's leadership by circulating a brochure entitled *Fifty Reasons Why Anwar Cannot Become Prime Minister*, in which Anwar was accused of sexual offences and corruption.

Allegations of Anwar's supposed sexual misconduct increased throughout the months following the UMNO congress, and, following Anwar's refusal to resign, culminated in Mahathir's dismissal of Anwar as Deputy Prime Minister and Minister of Finance on 2 September 1998, on the grounds that he was morally unfit to hold office. On the following day Anwar was expelled from UMNO, and affidavits accusing him of sexual impropriety were filed with the High Court. The allegations were denied by Anwar, who asserted that they constituted part of a senior-level political conspiracy to discredit him. Anwar began a tour of the country, drawing extensive support for his calls for the wide-ranging reform of the political system from the many thousands who attended his public appearances. His supporters adopted the slogan *'reformasi'* (reform), which had united the popular forces that ousted President Suharto in Indonesia. In mid-September Anwar's adoptive brother, Sukma Darmawan Samitaat Madja, and a former speech-writer for Anwar, Munawar Ahmad Anees, were each sentenced to six months' imprisonment after they confessed to illegal homosexual activity with Anwar. The following day, at a meeting attended by at least 40,000 people in Kuala Lumpur, Anwar called directly for Mahathir's resignation; he was arrested shortly afterwards and detained under the ISA. A further 17 people, including a number of close associates of Anwar, were also detained under the same act. Anwar's arrest provoked demonstrations of protest, which erupted into violence when demonstrations involving up to 60,000 people were violently dispersed by the security forces; 132 people were arrested.

Following Anwar's arrest, his wife, Wan Azizah Wan Ismail, emerged as the de facto leader of the opposition movement. Despite a restriction order issued against Wan Azizah, barring her from holding rallies at her residence, demonstrations in protest against Anwar's detention were held throughout September 1998; these became the forum for demands for widespread political reform and for the removal of the restrictions on freedom of speech and assembly imposed under the ISA. At a court hearing in Petaling Jaya, Anwar pleaded not guilty to five charges of corruption and five charges of sexual impropriety. Allegations made by Anwar, who appeared in court with visible bruising to his face, that he had been severely beaten while in police custody and had subsequently been denied medical attention for a number of days, provoked expressions of extreme concern from foreign Governments—in particular from the Presidents of the Philippines and Indonesia—and the UN Secretary-General, Kofi Annan. In December the Inspector-General of the Malaysian police force, Tan Sri Abdul Rahim Noor, resigned after an initial inquiry blamed the police for the injuries that Anwar had received. Malaysia's Attorney-General publicly admitted in January 1999 that Anwar had been assaulted by the police while in custody, and a Royal Commission of Inquiry into Anwar's injuries, which was completed in March, found Rahim Noor to be personally responsible for the beating. He was eventually sentenced to two months' imprisonment and fined RM 2,000 after pleading guilty to a charge of assault against Anwar.

Anwar's trial on four charges of corruption (which related to efforts allegedly made by him in 1997 to obtain through the police written denials that he was guilty of sexual misconduct and sodomy) began in November 1998, and in April 1999 Anwar was found guilty on each of the four charges of corruption and a sentence of six years' imprisonment was imposed (under Malaysian law, this would be followed by a five-year period of disqualification from political office). Following the delivery of the verdict, supporters of the former Deputy Prime Minister clashed with security forces outside the court. Violent protests continued for the next three days, resulting in the arrest of 18 demonstrators. Following the trial, three prosecution witnesses who had withdrawn their testimony against Anwar, including his adoptive brother and speech writer, who claimed their confessions had been obtained through police coercion, were charged with perjury. In late April Anwar was further charged with one count of illegal homosexual activity, to which he pleaded not guilty; it was announced that four other similar charges and one additional corruption charge against him had been suspended.

On the first day of Anwar's second trial in early June 1999 the prosecution amended the wording of its charge, changing (for the second time) the month and year in which the alleged crimes were supposedly committed. The trial was adjourned in September; Anwar was sent for medical examination following claims by the defence that he had proven high levels of arsenic in his blood and was possibly the victim of deliberate poisoning. In the same month some 10,000 supporters of Anwar gathered to demonstrate against the Government's treatment of him; following the protests, several of his prominent allies were reported to have been arrested. However, Anwar's trial resumed in late September after medical tests detected no clinical signs of arsenic poisoning. In his testimony in court in October and November, Anwar made potentially damaging allegations of corruption against members of the Government who, he alleged, had conspired to remove him from office. In mid-November the trial was adjourned indefinitely without explanation; supporters of Anwar claimed that the adjournment was a government attempt to silence him in the approach to the general election, which was to be held in late November. The trial resumed on 25 January 2000, but was adjourned again in late February at the request of the defence. In April the Court of Appeal upheld Anwar's conviction on four charges of corruption.

Anwar suffered a further set-back in June 2000, after the Court of Appeal rejected his plea for a stay of proceedings, ordering the trial on charges of sodomy to continue. In July the presiding judge ordered Anwar's defence lawyers to conclude their case, although they protested that they had intended to call further witnesses. The High Court found Anwar guilty of sodomy, sentencing him to a further nine years' imprisonment, thus bringing his term to a total of 15 years. His adoptive brother, Sukma Darmawan, was sentenced to six years' imprisonment and four strokes of the cane for the same offence.

Although Anwar had been effectively removed from public office for 15 years, the affair continued to receive prominence in the media. Anwar was hospitalized in November 2000, suffering from an acute back problem that required surgery and which he claimed had resulted from the beatings that he had received while detained in police custody in 1998. The Government refused a request for Anwar to travel abroad for surgery and in April 2001 issued an ultimatum to Anwar either to accept treatment in a state hospital or return to his cell; he returned to his cell in May. In the same month public prosecutors announced that the remaining charges of corruption and sodomy against him were to be abandoned and, in July, Anwar lodged an appeal against his sodomy conviction. Meanwhile, in June 2001 the contempt verdict against one of Anwar's lawyers was overruled when the High Court concluded that the lawyer had been acting only in the interests of his client. In July 2002 Anwar lost his final appeal against his corruption conviction. In October of the same year Mahathir launched bankruptcy proceedings against Anwar, following his refusal to pay the costs of a defamation lawsuit that he had brought against the Prime Minister in 1999. In April 2003 Anwar's appeal against his final conviction for sodomy was rejected by the Court of Appeal. A few days previously he had completed his sentence for corruption, the last two years of his six-year sentence having been remitted for good behaviour. In September 2004 Anwar was released from prison after his appeal against his conviction for sodomy was upheld by the Federal Court, which deemed the evidence against Anwar unreliable. Although he remained disqualified from holding political office until April 2008, owing to his corruption conviction, Anwar announced his intention to resume his campaign for political reform.

Consolidation of power and suppression of dissent

In January 1999, meanwhile, prior to the closure of the first trial of Anwar, Mahathir effected a major cabinet reorganization, in which Abdullah Badawi was appointed as Deputy Prime Minister and Minister for Home Affairs (a post relinquished by Mahathir) and Daim Zainuddin was allocated the finance portfolio. Also in January 1999 the UMNO Supreme Council announced its decision to postpone for 18 months elections for senior posts within the party, previously scheduled to be held in June, effectively preventing any potential challenge to Mahathir's leadership from within the party. The BN won a significant victory in the elections to the State Legislative Assembly in Sabah on 12–13 March, securing 31 of the 48 seats; however, Mahathir indicated that the result would not induce him to call an early general election. In early April a new opposition party, the Parti Keadilan Nasional (PKN—National Justice Party), was launched by Wan Azizah in anticipation of the general election; the new party reportedly aimed to establish itself as a multi-ethnic and multi-religious party and declared that its first act, should it come to power, would be to seek a royal pardon for Anwar. However, Anwar himself did not join the new party. Despite its stated aspirations to multi-ethnicity, the initial membership of the party appeared to be predominantly Muslim.

In November 1999 the Government unexpectedly announced that a general election was to be held later in the same month. The opposition expressed dissatisfaction at the limited period of time allowed for campaigning. At the election, which was held on 29 November, a decisive victory was won by the governing BN coalition, which gained 148 of a total of 193 seats in the House of Representatives, thereby retaining the two-thirds' majority required to allow the Government to amend the Constitution. The opposition coalition, the Barisan Alternatif (Alternative Front—which had been formed by the PAS, the PKN, the DAP and the Parti Rakyat Malaysia (PRM—Malaysian People's Party) in June 1999 and which subsequently selected Anwar as its prime ministerial candidate) won a total of 42 seats, while the opposition PBS (which remained outside the Barisan Alternatif) secured three seats. Despite the BN's victory, UMNO experienced a significant decline in support among Malay voters (mainly to the PAS, which secured 27 seats) and lost 23 seats, including those of four cabinet ministers. The party also performed poorly in the assembly elections held simultaneously in 11 Malaysian states: the PAS secured control of the state legislature in Trengganu, retained power in Kelantan and made significant gains in Mahathir's home state of Kedah. This erosion of confidence in UMNO was widely believed to be a result of the Government's treatment of Anwar and the concomitant decline of public confidence in the country's institutions, including the police and the judicial system. While there were a number of new appointments to the Cabinet, which was announced in early December, many of the important portfolios remained unchanged. However, in an unexpected development, Mahathir promoted the unelected academic Musa Mohamad, neither an existing government minister nor a member of UMNO, to the influential post of Minister of Education; Musa replaced Najib Razak, who was transferred to the less powerful Ministry of Defence in what was perceived by many as an effective demotion. Also in December Mahathir announced that he intended this (his fifth) term of office to be his last, and for the first time formally identified Abdullah Badawi as his preferred successor. In the same month the Barisan Alternatif nominated Fadzil Nor, President of the PAS, as the new parliamentary leader of the opposition. He replaced Lim Kit Siang, who had lost his seat in the general election and who in early December resigned as the Secretary-General of the DAP; however, Lim remained a prominent figure within the party.

At the UMNO party elections in May 2000 Mahathir and Abdullah Badawi were formally elected President and Deputy President of the party, respectively. In November the Prime Minister appointed Mohamed Dzaiddin Abdullah as the new Chief Justice, in a bid to enhance the credibility of the judiciary, tarnished by the Anwar trials. Later that month UMNO held a special general assembly, at which measures were approved to revitalize the image of the party and to attract more young professionals, including women. However, these developments failed to prevent the opposition PKN from taking a seat from the BN coalition at a by-election in the Lunas constituency of Kedah.

After taking leave in April 2001, the Minister of Finance, Daim Zainuddin, formally resigned from his post in June, following widespread allegations that he had taken advantage of public funds to help business associates, including the heavily indebted Malaysia Airlines and Time dotCom (the telecommunications unit of the Renong Group). Mahathir assumed the finance portfolio on an interim basis.

In January 2000, meanwhile, government suppression of dissent increased significantly. The deputy leader of the DAP and Anwar's legal representative, Karpal Singh, and the Vice-President of the PKN, Marina Yusoff, were charged under the Sedition Act. Mohamad Ezam Mohamad Noor was charged under the Official Secrets Act and subsequently placed on trial. In the same month the editor and the printer of the popular PAS newspaper, *Harakah*, were also charged with sedition in connection with an article concerning the trial of Anwar, and in March the Government ordered that *Harakah* be published just twice a month instead of twice weekly and restricted sales of the publication to members of the PAS only. The group editor-in-chief of the *New Straits Times*, Kadir Jasin, was forced to resign in June over an editorial that questioned the UMNO Supreme Council's rejection of demands that the party's two most senior positions be contested from within the party in the forthcoming UMNO internal elections. In January 2002 public prosecutors abandoned the sedition charges against Karpal Singh without explanation.

The Anwar issue continued to incite public unrest, and in April 2000 a protest to mark the anniversary of Anwar's conviction for corruption was broken up by riot police, 48 PKN activists being arrested. Public criticism of the Government, and subsequent detentions, became more frequent after Anwar's second conviction, as confidence in Mahathir's leadership continued to decline. Mohamad Ezam Mohamad Noor was arrested in March 2001 as a result of allegedly seditious comments, despite already being on trial for releasing a secret report on corruption. A month later he was detained again, along with six other opposition leaders, including the PKN Vice-President, Tian Chua, and the PKN youth Vice-Chairman, N. Gobala Krishnan, under the ISA (which allows for detention without trial for up to two years). The aim of these arrests seemed to be to dissuade protesters from gathering for the second anniversary of Anwar's conviction. The approach proved successful, as only 2,000 demonstrators defied the authorities' ban to attend the peaceful 'Black 14' rally, named after and coinciding with the date of Anwar's first conviction, 14 April. However, the seven detainees were not immediately released after the rally, and three more arrests were made under the ISA. During late April PKN youth leaders Dr Badrul Amin Baharom and Lokman Noor Adam were arrested, as was the human rights activist Badaruddin Ismail, thus bringing the total number of recent detainees under the provisions of the ISA to 10. In August 2002 Mohamad Ezam Mohamad Noor was sentenced to a two-year prison term, having been convicted of 'leaking' state secrets. In June 2003 he was freed on bail, pending an appeal; his conviction was overruled by the High Court in April 2004.

In August 2001 an extraordinary session of the Court of Final Appeal heard arguments against the detention of five people under the ISA. Significantly, the judges ruled that the onus was on the State to produce evidence that those arrested posed a real threat to national security. Meanwhile, Nik Adli Nik Abdul Aziz, son of PAS spiritual leader Datuk Haji Nik Abdul Aziz Nik Mat, was one of 10 men detained under the same Act on suspicion of membership of the Kumpulan Mujahidin Malaysia (KMM), an Islamist fundamentalist group believed to be engaged in a long-term plot to overthrow the Government. Seven of those taken into custody were also members of the PAS. Soon afterwards 25 supporters of Anwar Ibrahim were freed from prison and promptly rearrested on new charges, before being granted bail. In September the Government announced that Nik Adli was to be detained for two years without trial under the provisions of the ISA. Eight of the nine men arrested with him were also imprisoned. Human rights activists accused the Government of exploiting the aftermath of the terrorist attacks on the USA in the same month (see the chapter on the USA) to suppress national opposition groups. Further arrests continued to be made under the ISA.

Meanwhile, in March 2001 Mahathir confirmed that the National Vision Policy (NVP), which had replaced the National Development Plan (NDP) in 2000, was to remain in force until at least 2010. The Prime Minister thus provided for a continuation of the preferential conditions that had been afforded to the Malay majority in the NDP—the precursor to the NDP—the New Economic Policy (NEP)—upon its implementation in 1971; this favourable treatment prevailed specifically within the fields of education and commerce. (In the event, the NVP was abandoned, and the NEP reinstated, in 2006.) In September 2001 the opposition was destabilized by the withdrawal of the DAP from the Barisan Alternatif. The party accused the PAS of alienating Chinese voters through its support for an Islamic state. In the same month an election in Malaysia's largest state, Sarawak, confirmed the strength of the ruling coalition. The BN won 60 out of 62 available seats in the state legislature. The DAP secured one seat; an independent candidate the other. In January 2002 the PBS was formally readmitted to the BN following more than a decade of absence from power. Also in January, at a by-election in the Perlis district of Indera Kayangan, the PKN was heavily defeated by the BN. The PAS accused the Government of using devious methods to exploit popular fear of Islamist militancy in the aftermath of the September terrorist attacks.

On 21 November 2001 the Head of State, Sultan Salahuddin Abdul Aziz Shah Al-Haj ibni al-Marhum Sultan Hisamuddin Alam Shah Al-Haj, died at the age of 75. On 13 December the Raja of Perlis, Tuanku Syed Sirajuddin Syed Putra Jamalullail, was sworn in as the new monarch, following his election by secret ballot from among the remaining eight Malay rulers. The Sultan of Terengganu continued as his deputy.

In December 2001 a court convicted 19 members of the Islamist cult al-Ma'unah of treason for plotting to overthrow the Government. The men had been arrested following the murder of two hostages during a confrontation with security forces after a weapons robbery in July 2000. Ten other cult members had pleaded guilty to lesser charges and received 10-year prison terms. Three of the sect's ringleaders were sentenced to death for their part in the armed rebellion. The remaining men were given life terms. (In November 2003 15 members of the cult, who had played only minor roles in the robbery and who later expressed remorse for their actions, were released, having been held under the ISA.) In January 2002 the Government announced that, with effect from May, students and staff at public universities would be required to sign a pledge declaring allegiance to their king, country and government. Students had played a leading role in the protests that had followed the dismissal of Anwar Ibrahim in 1998.

In June 2002, during a speech to the annual congress of UMNO, Prime Minister Mahathir unexpectedly announced that he intended to resign from the Government with immediate effect. However, he was persuaded to withdraw his resignation shortly afterwards and, following some discussion, it was decided that he would remain in power until October 2003, when he would be succeeded by Abdullah Badawi. During the transition period Abdullah would assume increased responsibility for the running of the Government. Fadzil Nor, President of the PAS, died following complications arising from heart surgery in June 2002; Abdul Hadi Awang assumed the party leadership on an interim basis. In July Abdul Hadi announced the imposition of Islamic law in Terengganu state, of which he was the Chief Minister; however, the Government continued to oppose efforts to enforce the new law code. In the same month, at a by-election to the Kedah seat of Pendang, which had become vacant upon the death of Fadzil Nor, the BN secured a narrow victory.

In October 2002 police arrested five men, believed to be members of the regional Islamist organization Jemaah Islamiah (JI), under the ISA. The arrests brought the total number of ISA detainees to approximately 70. Members of JI were believed to be responsible for the recent terrorist attack on the Indonesian island of Bali (see the chapter on Indonesia), which had resulted in the deaths of 202 people, including many tourists. In November the ISA attracted renewed criticism when a court ordered the release of Nasharuddin Nasir, who had been detained under its provisions since April of that year, on the grounds that no evidence had been provided to substantiate claims that he had engaged in terrorist activities. The Government, in contravention of the judicial order, rearrested him almost immediately after his release. It was announced subsequently that the ISA was to be strengthened in order to prevent further challenges by the courts. Meanwhile, Prime Minister Mahathir announced the appointment of Datuk Dr Jamaluddin Jarjis as Minister of Finance II; Mahathir himself retained the other finance portfolio.

In May 2003 Minister of Transport Ling Liong Sik announced his resignation. In the following month it was revealed that three members of the PKN who had been imprisoned under the ISA for more than two years were to be released. In August the PKN merged with the smaller PRM, forming the Parti Keadilan Rakyat (PKR—People's Justice Party), in advance of the next general election. It was hoped that the merger would strengthen opposition to the BN and promote Anwar's cause. The President of the PKN, Wan Azizah, continued as President of the new party. In September it was announced that nine suspected members of the KMM who had been detained under the ISA in August 2001, including Nik Adli Nik Abdul Aziz, would be imprisoned for a further two years. After more than five years of incarceration without charge, Nik Adli was finally released in October 2006.

The Government of Abdullah Badawi

Prime Minister Mahathir Mohamad formally retired in October 2003, having spent 22 years in power. Abdullah Badawi was then sworn in as Prime Minister, retaining the home affairs portfolio and, in addition, assuming Mahathir's role as Minister of Finance. In November Abdullah was also endorsed as the new Chairman of the BN. Meanwhile, the PAS announced plans to transform Malaysia fully into an Islamic state should it come to power, attracting criticism not only from non-Muslim members of the BN but also from political allies of the PAS, including the PKR. In January 2004 Abdullah effected his first cabinet reorganization, nominating Minister of Defence Najib Razak as Deputy Prime Minister.

In February 2004, as a result of an ongoing anti-corruption campaign initiated by the new Prime Minister, both the Minister of Land and Co-operative Development, Tan Sri Datuk Kasitah bin Gaddam, and the former head of the national steel company Perwaja Steel Bhd, Eric Chia Eng Hock, were arrested and charged with corruption. Kasitah announced his resignation shortly afterwards. However, both men were subsequently acquitted, Chia in June 2007 and Kasitah in August 2009. Meanwhile, a national service programme was introduced in February 2004 with the intention of promoting national unity; conscripts were to perform military service for three months. A Royal Commission of Inquiry into the police force released its final report in May 2005, in which it urged the swift establishment of an Independent Police Complaints and Misconduct Commission, in order to render the police more accountable to the public; the report noted that the incidence of corruption within the police force was higher than in other government agencies. Meanwhile, in early March 2004 it was announced that Parliament was to be dissolved and a general election held later in that month, several months before the constitutional deadline of November. Later in March it was reported that six suspected Indonesian members of JI had been captured in Malaysia and were being held under the ISA, bringing the total number of suspected militants detained under the Act to 96.

On 21 March 2004, following a brief campaign period, elections took place to an enlarged 219-member House of Representatives and to 12 of the 13 State Legislative Assemblies (Sarawak was exempted, having held elections to its legislature in September 2001). The BN secured a commanding victory, winning 198 of the 219 seats in the House of Representatives and taking control of 11 of the 12 State Legislative Assemblies, including that of Terengganu, which had previously been governed by the PAS. The PAS retained control of Kelantan by a narrow margin. The DAP secured 12 seats in the House of Representatives, followed by the PAS, which won seven (compared with 27 at the election of 1999) and the PKR, which retained only one seat, that held by Wan Azizah. Having been sworn in again as head of government, Abdullah Badawi announced a major reorganization of his Cabinet, which was enlarged through the creation of two new ministries—the Ministry of Federal Territories and the Ministry of Natural Resources and the Environment—and the division of three existing ministries, those of Home Affairs, Education and Culture, Arts and Tourism. Najib Razak continued as Deputy Prime Minister and Minister of Defence.

The Prime Minister launched a National Integrity Plan in April 2004, aimed at reducing corruption and abuse of power. In May the Government allowed journalists to visit a detention centre for those held under the ISA, in an attempt to dispel recent allegations, made by the US-based organization Human Rights Watch, that detainees had been tortured. In August the BN succeeded in retaining its seat at a state assembly by-election in Kuala Berang in Terengganu, increasing its majority in the constituency.

Abdullah Badawi's control over UMNO was questioned in September 2004, when three members of his Cabinet failed to secure re-election to the party's Supreme Council at its General Assembly; some observers attributed their defeat to a reaction by party members against the Prime Minister's anti-corruption campaign. None the less, Abdullah and Najib Razak were formally endorsed as the party's President and Deputy President, respectively. UMNO leaders ruled out a return to the party for Anwar Ibrahim, who had been freed from prison earlier in September (see above). At the time, Anwar's release was widely regarded as evidence that the Prime Minister was fulfilling a pledge to respect the independence of the judiciary. In December Anwar launched a nation-wide campaign against the ISA. In August 2005 he was awarded RM 4.5m. in damages by the High Court for the false allegations contained within the pamphlet *Fifty Reasons Why Anwar Ibrahim Cannot Become Prime Minister*, published in 1998. In January 2006 Anwar filed a lawsuit against former Prime Minister Mahathir for falsely having depicted him as a homosexual and causing 'irreparable damage' to his reputation. (In September 2005 Mahathir had controversially told reporters that he had dismissed Anwar in order to avoid the potential appointment of a homosexual Prime Minister.) However, in July 2007 the High Court dismissed the lawsuit, which Mahathir had claimed was a ploy by Anwar to 'rehabilitate himself for high office'.

Meanwhile, in October 2005 Tan Sri Mohamed Isa Abdul Samad resigned from the position of Minister of Federal Territories, having been found guilty by the ruling party of vote-buying and political corruption pertaining to the UMNO party elections of September 2004. The UMNO Supreme Council subsequently rejected Isa's appeal against his three-year suspension from the party.

In November 2005 a new Malaysian coastguard agency was launched, with operations initially focused on the Strait of Melaka, where piracy remained a serious problem. The Government committed to disburse an estimated RM 578m. by the end of 2007 to finance the agency's operations, which were to be expanded gradually to cover Malaysia's other territorial waters. Malaysia, Indonesia and Singapore agreed to improve co-operation in their efforts to protect vessels traversing the busy maritime trade route.

Also in November 2005, Azahari Husin, a notorious Malaysian bomb-maker thought to be responsible for many of JI's operations, was killed in Indonesia during a police operation at a property in Batu, near Malang, East Java. In January 2006 another prominent Malaysian Islamist militant, Noordin Mohammad Top, released a message in which he claimed responsibility for the bombings on the Indonesian island of Bali in 2005 (see the chapter on Indonesia) and declared himself to be the head of a new South-East Asian Islamist militant organization, namely Tanzam Qaedat al Jihad (Organization of the Basis of Jihad). The statement served to remind Malaysia of the threat posed by its own nationals to regional security.

In February 2006 the Prime Minister effected a reorganization of the Cabinet. Datuk Paduka Abdul Kadir Sheikh Fadzir had previously announced his resignation from the position of Minister of Information and was replaced by Datuk Zainuddin Maidin. Other notable changes included the appointment of Datuk Seri Radzi Sheikh as Minister of Home Affairs, in place of Datuk Azmi Khalid, and the appointment of Dato' Haji Zulhasnan Rafique as Minister of Federal Territories. The Sarawak State Legislative Assembly was dissolved in April and an election held in May. The BN won 62 of the 71 seats in the expanded state legislature, while the DAP took six seats and the remaining three were divided among the PKR, the Sarawak National Party and an independent candidate.

Relations with Singapore became a source of internal disharmony in April 2006 when Abdullah Badawi suspended the construction of a bridge designed to replace the Johor Strait causeway to Singapore. It was hoped that the new bridge would reduce congestion on the route and allow the passage of ships through the waterway. Singapore had expressed uncertainty about the plan on financial and environmental grounds but, in the absence of a bilateral consensus, construction work on the Malaysian half of the bridge had nevertheless begun in January. The incident provoked a harsh reaction from former Prime Minister Mahathir, who was outspoken in his criticism of what he regarded as a 'surrender (of) sovereignty' to Singapore. In June the rupture in relations deepened when the former leader, who remained powerful in many quarters, appeared to question his own choice of successor, and expressed disapproval at the Prime Minister's reluctance to complete certain projects started in the Mahathir era. The UMNO Supreme Council responded by voicing its support for Abdullah, both as Prime Minister and UMNO President. Mahathir continued his apparent campaign against Abdullah and his administration in the months that followed, warning in August that he had evidence to substantiate his accusations of government corruption. In September Mahathir was unable to secure election as a delegate to the annual UMNO assembly scheduled for November, amid speculation that he had intended to use the meeting to renew his offensive against the Government of Abdullah.

Sultan Tuanku Mizan Zainal Abidin ibni al-Marhum Sultan Mahmud, the Sultan of Terengganu, was sworn in as the country's Yang di-Pertuan Agong on 13 December 2006 and was enthroned on 26 April 2007.

Several corruption scandals, involving senior officials, emerged in early 2007. In March it was revealed that the Anti-Corruption Agency (ACA) was investigating allegations that the Deputy Minister of Internal Security, Datuk Mohd Johari Baharum, had accepted more than RM 5m. in bribes in return for the release of three men suspected of being involved in organized crime. Moreover, the Director-General of the ACA, Datuk Seri Zulkipli Mat Noor, had himself been accused by a former colleague of illicit self-enrichment. The Prime Minister's Office announced at the end of March that Zulkipli's contract, which had just expired, would not be renewed. However, in July the Attorney-General halted investigations into the activities of Zulkipli and Johari owing to a lack of evidence. Meanwhile, the position of the Deputy Prime Minister and Minister of Defence, Najib Razak, was undermined by opposition attempts to link him to a murder that his political adviser, Abdul Razak Baginda, was charged with abetting. In April Najib denied having any connection to the killing or to the victim, Altantuya Shaariibuu, a Mongolian translator who had been involved in a relationship with Abdul Razak, whom she had allegedly been blackmailing prior to her death in 2006. (Abdul Razak was subsequently acquitted of Shaariibuu's murder, of which two members of a special police unit were convicted in April 2009; both were sentenced to death.)

A state assembly by-election held in Ijok, in Selangor, in April 2007 marked the return to active politics of Anwar Ibrahim, who campaigned vigorously on behalf of the PKR candidate. Nonetheless, the ruling BN retained the seat with an increased majority. Anwar declared his intention to contest the presidency of the PKR at its annual conference in May, despite being barred from holding public office until April 2008, but at a very late stage withdrew his candidacy, amid some internal dissent over his decision to stand; Wan Azizah was consequently re-elected unopposed. Anwar's renewed prominence was not welcomed by all members of the PKR and prompted the resignation from the party of a number of senior members. Meanwhile, Abdullah Badawi's announcement that civil servants would receive pay rises of up to 35% (the first increase in 15 years) prompted speculation that the Prime Minister intended to call an early general election.

In mid-November 2007 police used tear gas and water cannons to disperse up to 30,000 protesters who were marching in Kuala Lumpur to campaign for electoral reform. The demonstration, which had been declared illegal, was organized by the Gabungan Pilihanraya Bersih dan Adil (Bersih—the Coalition for Clean and Fair Elections), comprising a number of opposition parties, including the DAP, the PAS and the PKR, and civil society organizations. Bersih's main demands were equal access to the state-controlled media for all parties, a complete revision of the electoral register, the use of indelible ink to prevent multiple voting, and the abolition of postal voting except for diplomats and overseas voters. A second banned demonstration, involving at least 8,000 ethnic Indians, took place outside the British High Commission in Kuala Lumpur later that month, ending in violence, as police clashed with the protesters. The rally was organized by the Hindu Rights Action Force (Hindraf, a coalition of some 30 Hindu NGOs) to highlight perceived discrimination against Indians in Malaysia (who accounted for some 7% of the population) and, more specifically, in support of a lawsuit, filed in the British courts in August, demanding that the British Government pay reparations to the descendants of Indians transported to Malaysia as indentured labourers during the 19th century. In December five Hindraf members were detained under the ISA on the grounds that their actions had threatened national security.

The Minister of Health, Datuk Seri Chua Soi Lek, resigned in January 2008 after admitting his involvement in a sexual scandal; he was replaced by Dato' Seri Ong Ka Ting. In February Abdullah Badawi announced the dissolution of Parliament, and a general election was called for 8 March, more than one year earlier than the constitutional deadline. The Prime Minister gave no explanation for his decision, which observers attributed to a desire to secure a renewed mandate in advance of a widely anticipated deterioration in economic conditions. The timing of the election also ensured the exclusion of Anwar Ibrahim, whose disqualification from seeking public office was not due to expire until a month later. Also in February, several hundred ethnic Indians participated in another banned demonstration organized by Hindraf in Kuala Lumpur to protest against the alleged marginalization of the Indian minority group.

On 8 March 2008 the BN sustained heavy losses in elections to an enlarged House of Representatives and to 12 of the 13 State Legislative Assemblies (Sarawak having conducted elections to its legislature in May 2006). The ruling coalition failed to retain its two-thirds' majority in the House of Representatives, taking only 140 of the 222 seats, and lost control of the Legislative Assemblies of Kedah, Penang, Perak and Selangor. Of the opposition parties, which had pledged not to present candidates against each other, the PKR made the most significant gains in the House of Representatives, winning a total of 31 seats (compared with only one in 2004), while the DAP and the PAS both increased their representation by 16 seats, to 28 seats and 23 seats, respectively. The PAS also strengthened its majority in the Kelantan state legislature. The BN's poor performance was attributed to public discontent with renewed ethnic tensions and rising inflation, as well as concern about crime levels and corruption. Having dismissed demands for his resignation, including from within UMNO, Abdullah Badawi reorganized his Cabinet 10 days after the election. The Prime Minister retained the finance portfolio, while Najib Razak remained Deputy Prime Minister and Minister of Defence, but most other portfolios were affected by the reallocations. The most notable departure from the Government was perhaps that of Dato' Seri Paduka Rafidah binti Aziz, who had served as Minister of International Trade and Industry since 1987, but had been criticized in 2006 over procedures for the import of foreign vehicles; she was replaced by Muhyiddin Yassin, hitherto Minister of Agriculture and Agro-Based Industry. Rais Yatim assumed responsibility for the foreign affairs portfolio. Other new appointees included Datuk Mohd Zaid bin Ibrahim, a former lawyer and member of UMNO, who had previously been critical of the Government, as a Minister in the Prime Minister's Department. Zaid was charged with reforming the judiciary, which had been damaged during the second half of 2007 by allegations of corruption in the appointment process for judges.

In May 2008 Anwar Ibrahim was accused of sodomy by a party aide, Mohd Saiful Bukhari Azlan; the allegations against him were similar to those made 10 years previously. At the end of June, fearing for his safety, Anwar sought temporary refuge at the Turkish embassy in Kuala Lumpur. He was arrested in July and questioned by the police, before being released on the following day. The Kuala Lumpur Sessions Court formally charged Anwar with sodomy in August, but released him on bail pending a further hearing. In November the Kuala Lumpur Sessions Court ruled against a decision by the Attorney-General to transfer the trial to the High Court. In July, meanwhile, Wan Azizah vacated the seat that she had occupied in the House of Representatives since her husband's conviction in 1999, thus enabling Anwar to stand as a candidate at the ensuing by-election for the seat that he had previously held. Polling took place in August, when Anwar secured victory by a large majority. As the de facto leader of the opposition, he subsequently gained the support of the PAS.

In October 2008 Abdullah Badawi announced his intention to vacate the presidency of UMNO and to resign as Prime Minister in early 2009, having been placed under increasing pressure to depart, owing to the recent electoral losses of the BN and to his perceived failure effectively to address the issue of corruption. Furthermore, the first ever parliamentary motion of no confidence against a Malaysian Prime Minister had been drafted in June 2008, only to be withdrawn on a technicality. In September Abdullah had transferred the finance portfolio to Najib Razak, his designated successor, in exchange for that of defence.

The editor of online newspaper *Malaysia Today*, Raja Petra Kamaruddin, was arrested under the ISA in September 2008 on the grounds that he had published articles provoking racial tension. Later in that month Raja Petra received a two-year detention order on charges of insulting Islam, but this was overruled in November when the High Court found that the Government had acted beyond its legal powers in issuing such an order. Raja Petra also implicated Najib Razak and his wife in the murder of the Mongolian translator Altantuya Shaariibuu.

Datuk Mohd Zaid bin Ibrahim resigned from his position in the Prime Minister's Department in mid-September 2008. In a letter submitted to the Prime Minister, Zaid expressed frustration at the pace of legal reforms and criticized the use of the ISA to imprison three dissidents earlier in the month. (Following his resignation, Zaid cautioned against the appointment of Najib

Razak as Prime Minister on account of his alleged links to the killing of Shaariibuu; Zaid was subsequently suspended from UMNO, before joining the PKR in June 2009.) Other cabinet ministers were also reported to have questioned the authorities' increasing recourse to the ISA. In December 2008 a Singaporean newspaper reported that it had been informed of the unannounced release of more than a dozen Islamist militants closely linked to JI, who had been also been imprisoned under the ISA. The Malaysian Government appeared to defend the release of the prisoners on the grounds that they had been rehabilitated.

In March 2009 Gobind Singh Deo, a member of the DAP, was banned from Parliament for one year after accusing Najib Razak of involvement in the murder of Shaariibuu. Gobind's exclusion from the House of Representatives prompted opposition members to abandon the parliamentary session, protesting that Gobind had not been given an opportunity to defend his statement. Gobind's father, DAP Chairman Karpal Singh, who was also an eminent lawyer and was representing the murdered woman's family, was charged with sedition, allegedly having insulted the Sultan of Perak. Karpal accused the Government of using the Sedition Act as a 'political weapon against its political opponents'. Two opposition newspapers, the PAS's *Harakah* and the PKR's *Suara Keadilan*, were banned from publishing for three months by the Government in March 2009, shortly before the appointment of Najib Razak as Prime Minister and the holding of three by-elections in April (only one of which was won by the BN). Earlier in March riot police in Kuala Lumpur used tear gas to disperse thousands of demonstrators, who were protesting against the use of English as a medium of instruction in mathematics and science classes. More than 100 protesters were reported to have been detained.

Meanwhile, in February 2009 the BN regained control of Perak state after three PKR members of the State Legislative Assembly defected to the BN. The Sultan of Perak confirmed the BN's majority in the state legislature and deposed the Chief Minister, Mohammad Nizar Jamaluddin, appointing a BN member, Datuk Zambry Abdul Kadir, in his place. The formation of a new Government was strongly contested by the PKR, which argued that the transition was unconstitutional; the opposition therefore demanded the holding of state elections. Following a series of protests and parliamentary manoeuvres to obstruct the new Government, PKR legislators were prevented by the police from entering the assembly building. The case was referred to the High Court; however, prior to the Court's ruling, and amid protests and the arrest of dozens of protesters and opposition members, the BN Government forcibly removed the Assembly's Speaker and took control of the state legislature. The next session of the Assembly was then officially opened by the son of the Sultan of Perak. Four days later, in mid-May, the High Court ruled that the opposition was the lawful Government of Perak and that Nizar Jamaluddin was the rightful Chief Minister; on the following day, however, Zambry was reinstated, pending an appeal. In late May the Court of Appeal overruled the High Court's decision and declared that Zambry was in fact the rightful Chief Minister. The Federal Court, Malaysia's highest judicial body, unanimously ruled in February 2010 that the Court of Appeal had been right to rescind the High Court's verdict and reaffirmed Zambry's validity as Chief Minister.

Recent developments: the Government of Najib Razak

Having officially resigned as UMNO President at the party's annual congress in March 2009, Abdullah Badawi formally submitted his resignation as Prime Minister on 2 April; Najib Razak, who had replaced Abdullah as party leader, was inaugurated as Prime Minister on the following day. In a demonstration of support, Mahathir rejoined UMNO on 4 April, having resigned from the party in May 2008 insisting that he would not return until Abdullah had resigned; however, he had previously described Najib as 'incompetent' and it remained to be seen whether his return to UMNO would be a unifying, or a destructive, influence. Najib announced the composition of his Cabinet on 9 April: eight ministers from the outgoing administration were dismissed, including Minister of Home Affairs Syed Hamid Albar, who was replaced by Hishammuddin Hussein, hitherto the Minister of Education; the education portfolio was assumed by Muhyiddin Yassin, hitherto the Minister of International Trade and Industry, who was concurrently promoted to the position of Deputy Prime Minister; other notable appointments included that of Ahmad Zahid Hamidi as Minister of Defence and that of Datuk Anifah bin Haji Aman as Minister of Foreign Affairs.

In his inaugural address on 3 April 2009, the new Prime Minister, who retained the finance portfolio, pledged to make use of the ISA in a more appropriate way and to release a group of 13 detainees held under its provisions; Najib also rescinded the suspensions of *Harakah* and *Suara Keadilan*, and pledged to address the problems encountered by minority communities, notably the grievances of Malaysia's ethnic Indians. In May the 13 detainees were duly released without having been formally charged; among them were members of Hindraf who had been detained since organizing the anti-Government protests of 2007. At the end of June 2009 Najib announced that the Government was to abandon certain aspects of the NEP, which had guided government policy since 1971; non-Malay business people and investors welcomed Najib's proposals, as a result of which, *inter alia*, the majority of public companies would no longer be required to reserve 30% of their shares for ethnic Malays.

In mid-April 2009, despite the seemingly conciliatory tone struck by Najib Razak upon his assumption of the premiership, a new law enhancing the powers of the police to ban demonstrations deemed a threat to public order was approved by the legislature. The new law was denounced by the opposition as a further erosion of human rights. In July P. Uthayakumar, one of the 13 detainees released in May, registered a new, Indian-based political party: the stated aim of the Human Rights Party (HRP) was to 'politically empower and liberate the Indians from the clutches of especially UMNO's tyranny through legal, constitutional and democratic means'. In advance of an official visit to Kuala Lumpur by the Indian Prime Minister, Manmohan Singh, in October 2010, the HRP, claiming to have had 'no positive response' from the Malaysian Government since the party's inception, appealed to Singh to represent the interests of Malaysian Indians and to press Najib on the issue of 'serious human rights violations' perpetrated against the ethnic minority group.

Meanwhile, the death in July 2009 of Teoh Beng Hock, a journalist and political aide to Ean Yong Hian Wah—a member of the Selangor State Legislative Assembly—caused a public outcry; on the previous day Teoh had been questioned by the Malaysian Anti-Corruption Commission (MACC—formerly the ACA) in connection with corruption allegations against Ean Yong. The Malaysian authorities claimed that Teoh had committed suicide, but others contended that he had died from injuries sustained during his interrogation, highlighting the harsh methods employed by the MACC. During a mass demonstration in Kuala Lumpur in August, when an estimated 20,000 citizens gathered to protest against the ISA, some protesters took the opportunity to decry the authorities' perceived ill-treatment of Teoh, as well as of Anwar Ibrahim. Riot police resorted to the use of tear gas and water cannons to disperse the protesters, and more than 600 people were reported to have been arrested. An inquest into Teoh's death commenced later that month, and in October a Thai pathology expert testified that it was 'an 80% probability' that Teoh's death had been a case of homicide; as a result of this testimony, Teoh's body was exhumed and a second autopsy was conducted. In January 2011 the coroner recorded an open verdict, declaring that there was insufficient evidence to determine how Teoh had died; although suicide was ruled out as a possible cause of death, the coroner also noted the absence of 'evidence of third-party involvement'. The verdict was strongly condemned by Teoh's supporters and the political opposition, who contended that evidence had been suppressed during the 17-month inquest in order to protect the reputation of the authorities. The Attorney-General filed an application to the High Court seeking a review of the open verdict. In an apparent attempt to appease critics, Najib announced that a Royal Commission of Inquiry was to be held into the MACC's interrogation procedures. However, the Inquiry's remit was widely denounced as being too limited in its scope, prompting some to question the sincerity of the Government's pursuit of the carriage of justice. Following much criticism, Najib agreed in late January to widen the scope of the Inquiry to include an investigation into the specific circumstances surrounding Teoh's death. The five-member Commission of Inquiry, which was to be headed by Federal Court judge Tan Sri James Foong, was scheduled to commence its work in mid-February, and its final report was due to be submitted to the Yang di-Pertuan Agong in mid-April.

The second trial of Anwar Ibrahim on sodomy charges, which had finally commenced in February 2010, was beset by numerous delays and adjournments, and the proceedings continued in early 2011. Anwar continued to dismiss the allegations against him as a political conspiracy contrived by the Government in order to end his career, while his supporters noted that the claims had been announced shortly after the PKS had made significant gains in the 2008 legislative elections; however, the Government vehemently denied any wrongdoing. The lead defence counsel for Anwar, DAP Chairman Karpal Singh, drew attention to numerous apparent discrepancies in the prosecution's case and in the testimony of a number of its witnesses, including that of the claimant, Mohd Saiful Bukhari Azlan. An appeal by Anwar in August 2010 for the charges against him to be withdrawn, owing to allegations that a female member of the prosecution team was involved in a romantic relationship with Saiful (which, Anwar argued, constituted evidence of a conspiracy against him) was rejected later that month by the presiding High Court judge, Datuk Mohad Zabidin Mohd Diah. While acknowledging the apparent veracity of the allegations, Zabidin ruled that the association between the prosecutor and Saiful had not compromised the integrity of the trial, which was therefore to continue. In response, Anwar stated that their association, together with Zabidin's ruling, merely supported his contention that the trial was politically motivated and 'a farce'. Two attempts by Singh to force the removal of Zabidin proved unsuccessful: in February 2010, following Zabidin's refusal to censure the newspaper *Utusan Malaysia* for its allegedly biased coverage of the court proceedings, which, Singh argued, demonstrated the judge's own lack of objectivity in the case; and in December, on the grounds that Zabidin had allegedly intimidated Singh during the previous court session. On the latter occasion Singh formally protested against Zabidin's refusal to step down, but this was rejected by the Court of Appeal in January 2011; the court was scheduled to be reconvened in mid-February. Meanwhile, in March 2010 the Federal Court ruled that Mahathir's dismissal of Anwar as Deputy Prime Minister and Minister of Finance in September 1998 (see The first trials of Anwar Ibrahim) had been constitutional and valid.

In December 2010 the House of Representatives voted to suspend Anwar Ibrahim for a period of six months, following a parliamentary disciplinary inquiry in response to claims made by Anwar earlier in the year that a government campaign to promote racial unity under the banner of '1Malaysia' had been inspired by the 'One Israel' electoral campaign of former Israeli Prime Minister Ehud Barak in 1999. Anwar was deemed to have misled legislators on the issue, which was a source of considerable embarrassment to the Government. (Muslim-majority Malaysia had no diplomatic relations with Israel and was a staunch proponent of an independent Palestinian state.) Three of Anwar's parliamentary allies, among them Karpal Singh, were also suspended for a six-month period having been cited for contempt, owing to their criticism of the disciplinary action against Anwar. Opposition legislators responded angrily to the four suspensions, as a result of which the opposition constituted less than one-third of parliamentary members, with many deputies walking out of the parliamentary session in protest. With an early election expected by many observers to be called by Najib Razak in 2011, speculation abounded that the action against Anwar and his allies, while not precluding their participation in any poll, was intended to discredit the opposition with a view to bolstering support for the UMNO-led governing coalition.

Meanwhile, a minor cabinet reorganization announced by Najib Razak in early June 2010 was widely interpreted as an attempt to regain support for the governing coalition among Malaysia's ethnic Chinese and Indian communities: the representation of both ethnic minority groups within the Cabinet was increased as a result of the changes. The most senior portfolios were unaffected by the reorganization; however, notable changes included the departure from the Cabinet of former MCA President Ong Tee Keat, hitherto Minister of Transport, who was replaced by MCA Secretary-General Dato' Seri Kong Cho Ha, and the appointment of Dato' Chor Chee Heung as Minister of Housing and Local Government. The governing coalition's efforts to boost its support among Malaysia's ethnic minorities were widely believed to have helped it to secure victory in two by-elections held in November, following the death of the two incumbent legislators.

Meanwhile, restrictions on the media appeared to increase during the course of 2010. In June the Government banned the publication of *1Funny Malaysia*, a book of satirical political cartoons, which the Government claimed posed a threat to national security. In July the PKR's *Suara Keadilan* and the PAS's *Harakah* were again the target of government action, together with *The Rocket* (the official publication of the DAP), prompting renewed speculation that the Government was attempting to silence its critics and intimidate the opposition. In early July the Government declined to renew the publishing permit of *Suara Keadilan*, after the newspaper was alleged to have disseminated 'false information that could incite public unrest', following the publication of an article in which it had been claimed that the Federal Land Development Authority was in dire financial straits. The Minister of Home Affairs, Dato' Seri Hishammuddin bin Tun Hussein, insisted that there was no political agenda relating to the decision, claiming that the publication's permit had not been renewed exclusively as a result of the 'defamatory' article. Following the decision of *Suara Keadilan* to continue publishing in spite of the non-renewal of its permit, the Government threatened the publication with legal action and announced that its permit would be suspended indefinitely. The renewal of the permit of *Harakah* was initially withheld in mid-July owing to 'technical reasons', including the sale of copies to non-PAS members and a delay in submitting issues of the newspaper for the approval of the Ministry of Home Affairs; a new licence was granted later in July, but *Harakah* was permitted to continue publishing only under stringent restrictions, and the newspaper was henceforth to be sold only from the PAS's headquarters. Meanwhile, *The Rocket* received a demand from the Ministry of Home Affairs in mid-July to explain its continued publication after the expiry of its permit; according to a DAP spokesperson, an application to renew the permit had been submitted prior to its expiry but had seemingly been ignored by the Ministry of Home Affairs. The publication's permit was eventually renewed by the Ministry in mid-August. In late July Human Rights Watch appealed to the Government to repeal the 1984 Printing Presses and Publications Act, which effectively granted the Ministry of Home Affairs the right of censorship over all publication content within Malaysia, highlighting Najib Razak's own pledge made in 2009 to ensure that the media was empowered responsibly to 'report what they see without fear of consequence'. The permit of *Suara Keadilan* remained suspended at early 2011.

In February 2011 a PKR state legislator, Shuhaimi Shafiei, was charged with sedition after posting a comment on his website in December 2010 that was deemed to be critical of the Sultan of Selangor. Shuhaimi denied any wrongdoing, claiming that he was a victim of political manipulation, as part of a wider effort by the governing coalition to discredit the opposition prior to elections. A preliminary hearing was postponed to late April 2011; if convicted, Shuhaimi would be forced to forfeit his seat in the Selangor state legislature and be barred from standing for political office for five years.

Religious Tensions

The right to religious freedom, as prescribed by Article 11 of the Malaysian Constitution, and the country's multi-faith status were prominent issues during the early 21st century, with ongoing debates about religious conversion laws, the jurisdiction of Islamic and civil courts, and punishments for apostasy. In January 2005, at a night-club in Kuala Lumpur, about 100 Muslims, including many women, were detained on charges of public indecency and other 'anti-Islamic' crimes. Amid the ensuing public outcry, the legitimacy of these arrests was questioned, as the application of Islamic law in federal territories was restricted to marriage and related matters. The Government subsequently instructed the Federal Territories Islamic Department to abandon the charges. However, such police operations against night-clubs and hotels continued to be reported, with hundreds of Muslims arrested during 2005–11 for *khalwat*, an offence defined as unmarried men and women meeting 'in close proximity . . . in any secluded place or in a house or room under circumstances which may give rise to suspicion that they were engaged in immoral acts', and which carried a maximum penalty of two years' imprisonment and a fine of RM 3,000. In April 2010 a university student died in a fall from the fifth floor of an apartment building after reportedly attempting to evade arrest during a search by the authorities for those committing *khalwat*. A Syariah High Court judge and a female associate were charged with *khalwat* in January 2011.

In February 2006, meanwhile, the Malaysian Government suspended indefinitely the licence of the *Sarawak Tribune*, in response to the newspaper's decision to reprint controversial cartoons depicting the Prophet Muhammad, which had first been published in a Danish newspaper and had provoked outrage in the international Muslim community. This was the first time in almost two decades that the licence of a Malaysian publication had been revoked, and the episode renewed concerns about the status of religious freedom and freedom of expression. The licences of *Guang Ming Daily* and *Berita Petang Sarawak* were also revoked, for a two-week period, after they too reprinted the cartoons.

In May 2007 the Federal Court rejected an appeal by a convert from Islam to Christianity to have the word 'Islam' removed from the religion section of her identity card, ruling that Syariah courts held jurisdiction in this area. Observers noted that the judgment effectively made it impossible to renounce Islam legally, given that apostasy was a criminal offence under Islamic law, and renewed the debate about the constitutionally enshrined right to religious freedom. This was perhaps the most high profile of a number of similar cases that were provoking religious tension in Malaysia. In August the Government suspended publication of the Tamil-language newspaper *Makkal Osai* for one month, after the newspaper published an image of Jesus Christ apparently smoking a cigarette and drinking alcohol. In December controversy arose over the use of the word 'Allah' by non-Muslims, when a Roman Catholic weekly newspaper, *The Herald*, encountered difficulties in renewing its publishing permit because its Malay-language section employed the word 'Allah' when referring to the Christian God, which the Government argued might confuse Muslims. (It was alleged by some Muslim groups that the Christian Church using a word so closely associated with Islam was a ploy to convert Muslims to Christianity, a transition that remained illegal in Malaysia.) The newspaper's permit was eventually renewed on the condition that it adhere to a government ban on non-Muslims using the word 'Allah'. *The Herald* filed for a judicial review, insisting that it had used the word 'Allah' to refer to the Christian God for decades and had a constitutional right to do so. In December 2009 the High Court ruled in favour of *The Herald*, reversing the government ban on the use of the word by non-Muslims on the grounds that it was 'unconstitutional'; shortly afterwards the Government announced that it intended to appeal against the decision. The ruling resulted in an intensification of Muslim–Christian tensions in Malaysia, provoking a series of violent attacks on churches, mosques and a Sikh temple in early 2010. In August two men were convicted of arson, having been found to have set alight a church in Kuala Lumpur in January; they were sentenced to five years' imprisonment. In January Mahathir was forced to deny allegations that he was trying to arouse 'anti-Christian' sentiments, following public comments in which the former Prime Minister had claimed that there was strong evidence to suggest that the terrorist attacks carried out against the USA in September 2001 had been 'staged' by elements within that country to provide perceived legitimacy for the mounting of attacks on Muslim states.

Meanwhile, in April 2009, shortly after the inauguration of Najib Razak as Prime Minister, the Government outlawed the religious conversion of children without the prior consent of both parents. The ban followed several controversial cases in which children had been converted to Islam following a divorce, despite vehement objections from the non-Muslim parent. (Such conversions had been aided by rulings issued by Syariah courts.) The Government's decision, in July 2010, to appoint female judges to Syariah courts for the first time was described by Najib as a serious attempt 'to enhance justice in cases involving families and women's rights'. However, while welcoming the appointment of the two female judges as a positive development, a senior figure within the influential Sisters in Islam group, which sought to promote Muslim women's rights, appealed for more far-reaching reform.

Muslim-Hindu relations were strained in August 2009 when a group of Muslims paraded the severed head of a cow through the streets of Shah Alam, Selangor, in protest against proposals to erect a Hindu temple in the vicinity; the group was accused of promoting hostility towards the minority Hindu population, to whom the cow is a sacred animal. Twelve men were charged with illegal assembly, six of whom were also charged with sedition. In July 2010 all 12 were convicted of illegal assembly and each was ordered to pay a fine of RM 1,500, while two of the men, purported to be the ringleaders of the group, were also convicted of sedition; the other four defendants answering sedition charges were discharged by the court

Foreign Affairs

Malaysia's foreign policy has been dominated by its membership of the Association of Southeast Asian Nations (ASEAN, see p. 206), which was founded in 1967. In February 2008 Malaysia ratified the new ASEAN Charter, codifying the principles and purposes of the Association, which had been signed in November 2007 at the 13th summit meeting in Singapore. Prime Minister Mahathir Mohamad was instrumental in bringing Myanmar into ASEAN in 1997 under the Policy of Constructive Engagement. Malaysia has been involved with Brunei, Viet Nam, the People's Republic of China, the Philippines and Taiwan in disputed sovereignty claims over the Spratly Islands in the South China Sea. In November 2002 the ASEAN member states approved a non-legally binding Code of Conduct for the islands; the agreement was also sanctioned by China. Proposals to formulate a binding Code of Conduct were espoused in October 2010, and discussions to this end were ongoing at early 2011.

Relations with South-East Asian countries

Relations with Singapore have traditionally been characterized by mistrust since the city-state left the Federation of Malaya in 1965. Resentment increased as Singapore advanced more swiftly than Malaysia economically, creating a certain acrimonious competition between the two countries. However, as Malaysia also developed, bilateral relations became more cordial, and co-operation increased. Relations were threatened from early 2002, however, as tensions arose over the renegotiation of a 1961 agreement by which Malaysia supplied Singapore with water. Negotiations took place in July and October 2002 in an attempt to resolve the problems arising from the water dispute, but without success. In February 2003 Prime Minister Mahathir stated that, while Malaysia would cease to supply Singapore with untreated water in 2011, it would continue to supply filtered water, at a reasonable price, for as long as necessary. Following the retirement of Mahathir in October 2003, bilateral relations showed signs of improvement under new Prime Minister Abdullah Badawi. In January 2004 Abdullah and his Singaporean counterpart, Goh Chok Tong, exchanged visits and discussed the tensions in the relationship. In October, on his first official visit to Malaysia, the new Prime Minister of Singapore, Lee Hsien Loong, announced that his predecessor, Goh, now Senior Minister in the Prime Minister's Office, would lead his country's efforts to resolve outstanding bilateral issues. Abdullah and Goh held talks in Kuala Lumpur in December; issues discussed included the dispute over the sale of water to Singapore and the use of Malaysian airspace by Singapore's air force. In January 2005 Malaysia and Singapore appeared to have resolved a dispute over the latter's land reclamation project in the Straits of Johor, which separate the two countries; Malaysia accepted that the reclamation work could proceed, while Singapore agreed to co-operate with Malaysia to ensure navigational safety and environmental protection of the waterway. In 2006, however, relations became strained over the Johor Strait bridge dispute (see Domestic Political Affairs), and deteriorated further in September, when Singapore's Minister Mentor and former Prime Minister, Lee Kuan Yew, remarked that Malaysia's Chinese minority was being systematically marginalized because of its success. Lee later apologized to Abdullah for causing him 'discomfort' and stated that he did not want to interfere in Malaysian politics. Prime Minister Lee Hsien Loong visited Malaysia in May 2007 for two days of informal talks with Abdullah. The most significant outcome of the discussions was a decision to form a joint ministerial committee to oversee collaboration on Malaysia's plan to establish an economic development zone in southern Johor, to be known as the Iskandar Development Region, with both leaders agreeing that outstanding issues of dispute, such as water sales to Singapore and the suspended construction of the Johor Strait bridge, should not be allowed to impede bilateral co-operation in other areas. A long-standing dispute between Malaysia and Singapore over their conflicting claims to the island of Batu Puteh (Pedra Branca) was finally concluded in May 2008 when the International Court of Justice (ICJ, see p. 23)—to which the dispute had been referred as per an agreement signed by the two countries in February 2003—ruled in favour of Singapore. During a meeting between Prime Ministers Najib Razak and Lee Hsien Loong in May 2010, the two leaders affirmed their commitment to enhancing bilateral co-operation, and agreed to the joint development of a rapid transit system between Johor Bahru and Singapore. In September the premiers finalized a land swap agreement, which provided for the exchange of six Singaporean land parcels for six pieces of Malaysian land, in a deal hailed by Najib as 'mutually beneficial'.

In January 1993 Gen. Fidel Ramos visited Malaysia, the first Philippine President to do so since 1968, owing to strained relations over the Philippines' claim to Sabah; Mahathir and Ramos agreed to establish a joint commission to address bilateral problems. In February 1994 Mahathir made the first official visit by a Malaysian head of government to the Philippines. Bilateral relations were strained in 1998 when the new Philippine President, Joseph Estrada, publicly criticized the arrest in September of former Malaysian Deputy Prime Minister and Minister of Finance Anwar Ibrahim (see Domestic Political Affairs). Although the controversy surrounding Anwar's treatment receded as an international issue in 1999, bilateral relations were adversely affected by President Estrada's granting of an audience to Anwar's wife when she visited the Philippines in April. Relations with the Philippines were further strained in April 2000, when Muslim separatists from the southern Philippines abducted a group of tourists from the Malaysian resort of Sipadan, off the coast of Sabah. Following a similar kidnapping incident in September, the Malaysian Government dispatched an additional 600 troops to the region. (In August 2008 Malaysia extended the deployment of its troops for a further three months. At the end of their mandate in November all Malaysian troops were withdrawn, despite a request from the Philippine Government for them to remain.) Bilateral relations were threatened in November 2001 when the Malaysian authorities arrested the fugitive Philippine rebel leader Nur Misuari on charges of attempting to enter Malaysia illegally. After much indecision, he was finally deported in January 2002 to stand trial in the Philippine capital, Manila. In March 2009 the Philippine President, Gloria Arroyo, met with Prime Minister Abdullah Badawi to request further assistance in peace talks with the rebel Moro Islamic Liberation Front (MILF—see the chapter on The Philippines). Bilateral relations were threatened by the abduction of two Malaysian labourers in Sabah by a group of unidentified Philippine assailants in February 2010. However, the safe return of the pair was secured in December, and was hailed by the Malaysian embassy in Manila as a 'reflection of the close co-operation' between the two countries' respective police forces.

While generally remaining cordial, relations with Indonesia have suffered numerous set-backs in recent years. The flow of illegal Indonesia immigrants into Malaysia, which wide-ranging amendments to Malaysia's Immigration Act in October 1996 failed to halt, was blamed for rising social tensions. Bilateral relations were tested in late 1998 when, like his Philippine counterpart, Indonesian President Bucharuddin Jusuf (B. J.) Habibie publicly denounced the Malaysian Government for its treatment of Anwar Ibrahim. However, relations improved during the presidency of Abdurrahman Wahid, who visited Kuala Lumpur immediately after his election in October 1999. President Wahid's successor, Megawati Sukarnoputri, visited Malaysia in August 2001. In the same year the Government of Malaysia announced that it would deport 10,000 illegal Indonesian immigrants each month in an attempt to tighten controls on foreign labour in the country. Following rioting by Indonesian labourers, in January 2001 a temporary ban was imposed on new workers arriving from Indonesia. The Indonesian Government issued a formal apology for its workers.

In May 2002 Malaysia, Indonesia and the Philippines signed an anti-terrorism pact enabling them to exchange intelligence and to launch joint police operations; Thailand and Cambodia acceded to the pact later in the year. In August the implementation of new legislation requiring that all illegal immigrants leave Malaysia or risk penalties strained relations with both the Philippines and Indonesia, as the majority of the workers affected were citizens of those countries. In September the Malaysian Government announced a temporary halt to deportations, owing to diplomatic pressure, exacerbated by public protests in Indonesia and the Philippines over the apparently inhumane nature of the expulsions. In December the ICJ ruled that Malaysia would be awarded sovereignty of Sipadan and Ligitan, two small islands off the coast of Borneo, thereby bringing an end to a protracted dispute between Malaysia and Indonesia over conflicting claims to the islands. In early 2004, however, the Indonesian Government urged a global boycott of Malaysian timber, following the release of a report alleging that protected trees from Indonesia were being smuggled across the border, 'laundered' and re-exported. In July Malaysia and Indonesia, together with Singapore, commenced co-ordinated patrols of the Strait of Melaka between Malaysia and Indonesia, in an attempt to curb piracy.

At the end of October 2004 a 17-day amnesty began for illegal migrant workers to leave Malaysia voluntarily without penalty. Thousands of Indonesians had fled to Malaysia since the Indonesian authorities had commenced military operations against separatists in the province of Aceh in May 2003. In November 2004 Malaysia agreed to extend the amnesty until the end of the year; the amnesty was subsequently further extended following a request from President Susilo Bambang Yudhoyono of Indonesia. It was reported that around 380,000 of an estimated 1.2m. illegal foreign workers had left Malaysia by the end of January 2005. In February, following talks with President Yudhoyono in Kuala Lumpur, the Malaysian Prime Minister announced that the amnesty would expire at the end of the month, and in March the forced repatriation of illegal immigrants recommenced. Human rights organizations, including Amnesty International, expressed serious misgivings about the standard of training and supervision given to officers of the Malaysian Immigration Department, amid allegations of widespread physical abuse of immigrants. In July 2006 it was estimated by the Minister of Home Affairs, Radzi Sheikh, that approximately 500,000 illegal immigrants were still living in Malaysia. In October 2007 a temporary ban was imposed on Malaysian employers recruiting new workers from Bangladesh, following a series of cases of ill-treatment of migrants, including the abandonment of several thousand at Kuala Lumpur airport. In January 2008 it was reported that the Malaysian Government aimed to reduce the number of foreign workers in the country from some 2.3m. to 1.5m. by 2015, by introducing stricter regulations on their employment. In early 2009 the Government announced the cancellation of work permits for nearly 100,000 Indonesian and 55,000 Bangladeshi migrant workers. Yudhoyono travelled to Kuala Lumpur in November, during which visit both he and Prime Minister Najib Razak pledged to improve relations and to strengthen bilateral co-operation. In February 2010 it was reported that Malaysia and Indonesia were close to concluding a comprehensive agreement intended better to protect Indonesian migrant workers in Malaysia from abuse by their employers. During 2010 the Malaysian authorities reported the arrest of several alleged militants with purported links to Indonesia, including that in October of Fadli Sadama, who was alleged to be a member of Jemaah Ansharut Tauhid (JAT—a new terrorist network thought to have been established by Amar Usman, alias Dulmatin, a senior JI leader suspected of involvement in the 2002 Bali bombings—see the chapter on Indonesia).

Relations with Thailand deteriorated in February 1996, owing to Malaysia's construction of a 27-km wall along the border with Thailand, intended to deter illegal immigration from that country. However, in January 1997 the two countries agreed to co-operate in preventing Bangladeshi migrant workers from entering Malaysia and in expediting the return of illegal Thai workers from Malaysia. The arrest in January 1998 of three Thai Muslim separatists by the Malaysian authorities and their deportation to Thailand demonstrated continued co-operation between the two countries, since Malaysia was often regarded as a place of sanctuary for Muslim separatists in southern Thailand. Relations between Malaysia and Thailand were further enhanced in April, when the two countries signed an agreement to share equally the natural gas produced in an offshore area to which both countries had made territorial claims. However, the Thai Minister of Foreign Affairs, Surin Pitsuwan, was among a number of international political figures who expressed concern at the arrest and detention of Anwar Ibrahim in September. In April 2001 the Thai Prime Minister, Thaksin Shinawatra, made his first official visit to the country on a trip intended to enhance co-operation. Bilateral talks were also held in January 2002 in an attempt to resolve problems arising from a planned project to build a gas pipeline between the two countries. In January 2004 new Prime Minister Abdullah Badawi visited Thailand for security discussions, following several attacks believed to have been perpetrated by separatists in southern Thailand close to the joint border. The two countries agreed to co-operate in efforts to bring an end to the violence and began joint border patrols. Amid continuing unrest on the Thai side of the border, Thaksin visited Malaysia in mid-April for further security talks with Abdullah. In late April Malaysia increased its border security after militants launched a series of attacks on police posts in southern Thailand; the attacks were violently suppressed by the Thai security forces. (Parts of the border were subsequently fenced off, in an attempt to prevent the cross-border transit of those thought to be responsible for the ongoing violence.) Security at the border was heightened again in October following renewed clashes in southern Thailand between government troops and Muslim protesters in which 85 people died, many of whom suffocated after being forced into army trucks. Hundreds of Malaysians demonstrated outside the Thai embassy in Kuala Lumpur in protest against the deaths. Bilateral relations were further strained in December, when the Thai Government claimed to have photographic evidence that militants in southern Thailand had received training in the Malaysian state of Kelantan. In

MALAYSIA

January 2005 the Malaysian authorities arrested Abdul Rahman Ahmad, whom Thailand held responsible for organizing the separatist violence in the south. A diplomatic dispute arose between the two countries in October, concerning the fate of 131 Muslim villagers who had fled from the violence-stricken province of Narathiwat, in southern Thailand, to neighbouring Malaysia. The Malaysian authorities insisted that they would not sanction the return of the asylum-seekers to Thailand unless they received a guarantee of their safety from the Thai authorities. One of the villagers, suspected of involvement in a raid on a Thai military camp in January 2004, was subsequently relinquished to the Thai authorities, while the other 130 refugees remained in a Malaysian detention centre in Terengganu. Discussions aimed at resolving the dispute were held in November 2005 between former Prime Minister Mahathir and Thaksin; negotiations were also held between Thaksin and Abdullah in the same month, during the course of the APEC summit meeting in Busan, the Republic of Korea. The ongoing dispute took relations between the two countries to their lowest point in recent years. In February 2006 the Thai Government indicated that it was prepared to cease its attempts to repatriate the villagers and was to allow them to remain in Malaysia. There was some improvement in bilateral relations from October, when Gen. Surayud Chulanont was appointed as Thai Prime Minister following a coup in which Thaksin was ousted from power. Surayud visited Malaysia later that month, holding talks with Abdullah on the ongoing insurgency in Thailand's southern provinces. An official visit to Thailand by Abdullah in February 2007 was reciprocated by Surayud in August. In December Abdullah and Surayud officially opened a new bridge across the Golok River, linking Kelantan to Narathiwat, as part of efforts to improve the economy of the border region and, as a consequence, reduce violence. In July 2008 the Malaysian Minister of Foreign Affairs, Rais Yatim, undertook a three-day visit to Thailand for discussions with the Thai Deputy Prime Minister, Somchai Wongsawat. Rais Yatim discussed the political situation in Thailand and pledged that Malaysia would continue to assist the Thai Government in resolving the ongoing violence in the country's Muslim-dominated southern provinces. In June 2010 the two countries announced plans to foster closer co-ordination in anti-narcotics operations. In November a Thai woman was sentenced to death after being convicted of drugs-trafficking by Malaysia's High Court. The woman was found to have ingested a large amount of cocaine, which she had smuggled into the country from Argentina, prior to being apprehended by the Malaysian authorities in July.

Malaysia played an integral role in bringing together the Myanma military junta and opposition leader Aung San Suu Kyi for negotiations in late 2000, although it was thought that financial considerations might have been significant, with a promise of direct investment in Myanmar by Malaysia's national petroleum corporation, PETRONAS, in return for a semblance of progress on the part of the junta. Mahathir's visit to Myanmar in January 2001 confirmed Malaysia's interest in Myanmar, a possible alternative source of natural gas. In September 2001 the Myanma leader, Gen. Than Shwe, paid an official visit to Malaysia during which a number of bilateral agreements were signed. In August 2002 Mahathir visited Myanmar again; during his visit he met with Suu Kyi and, it was thought, attempted to encourage the junta to engage in further dialogue with the opposition. In March 2006 the Malaysian Minister of Foreign Affairs, Syed Hamid Albar, was denied access to Suu Kyi on a visit to Myanmar as an ASEAN envoy to assess the country's progress towards political reform. Albar, who had held a meeting with Lt-Gen. Soe Win, the Myanma Prime Minister, was initially positive about the visit. However, ASEAN's forbearance with regard to the military regime of Myanmar seemed to be decreasing in July when Albar implied that the Association's development was being impeded by Myanmar, claiming that ASEAN could no longer defend the country as Myanmar was 'not making an attempt to co-operate or help itself'. A Malaysian business delegation to Myanmar in December 2010, led by the Malaysia External Trade Development Corporation, identified numerous new opportunities in Myanmar's rapidly developing oil and gas sector, including the expansion of existing oil and gas infrastructure, and engineering, logistics and marine services.

Other regional relations

Malaysia's relations with the People's Republic of China remained extremely cordial, with Malaysia frequently offering public support to China, particularly in response to US criticism. The year 2004 was designated Malaysia-China Friendship Year, to mark the 30th anniversary of the establishment of bilateral relations. The importance of these relations was demonstrated in May 2009 when Najib Razak travelled to China in his first official visit to a non-ASEAN country since being inaugurated as Prime Minister in the previous month. The implementation in January 2010 of a free trade agreement between ASEAN and China was expected further to deepen Malaysia's growing economic dependence on the People's Republic.

Malaysia forged closer links with Japan in December 2005 with the signing of a bilateral free trade agreement, which entered into force in July 2006. Under the terms of the accord, the two countries were to eliminate tariffs on all industrial goods and on most agricultural, forestry and fishery products within a 10-year period. The agreement also covered protection of intellectual property rights, investment rules, competition policies, business facilitation and personnel training. In keeping with the spirit of invigorated relations, the Emperor and Empress of Japan paid a state visit to Malaysia in June 2006, their first official trip to the country since 1991, and Japanese Prime Minister Shinzo Abe visited Malaysia in August 2007, marking the 50th anniversary of the establishment of diplomatic relations between the two countries. Malaysian Prime Minister Najib Razak made his first official visit to Japan in April 2010, whereupon he met with his Japanese counterpart, Yukio Hatoyama; the two leaders pledged further to strengthen co-operation, including practical measures towards the realization of the concept of an East Asian Community.

Mahathir's proposal to establish an East Asian Economic Caucus (EAEC), a trade group intended to exclude the USA, met with considerable resistance from the US Government (which continued to promote the US-dominated Asia-Pacific Economic Co-operation forum—APEC, see p. 197) and Australia. In July 1993 ASEAN agreed, despite the continuing reluctance of Japan to participate, that the EAEC should operate as an East Asian interest group within APEC. In November 1999 (although Mahathir was absent owing to the Malaysian general election) the third informal summit meeting of the 10 ASEAN countries and the People's Republic of China, Japan and the Republic of Korea (collectively known as 'ASEAN + 3') took place. At the meeting it was agreed to strengthen present economic co-operation with the distant aim of forming an East Asian bloc with a common market and monetary union. This ambition was brought closer in April 2001 when, at a meeting of the ASEAN + 3 group, plans were agreed for a network of currency 'swap' arrangements to prevent a repetition of the regional financial crisis of 1997. At the annual ASEAN summit meeting held in Laos in November 2004 it was agreed to transform the ASEAN + 3 summit meeting, which was first held in 1997, into the East Asia Summit, with the long-term objective of establishing an East Asian Community. In December 2005 Kuala Lumpur hosted the inaugural East Asia Summit, held during the course of the ASEAN summit meeting. At the first East Asia Summit, which was chaired by the Malaysian Prime Minister, representatives from the participating nations held discussions on a wide range of issues, including international terrorism, maritime security, the threat of avian influenza ('bird flu'), trade and development, and the promotion of human rights and democracy. It was agreed that the Summit should convene annually. The fifth Summit, held in Hanoi, Viet Nam, in October 2010, was attended by US Secretary of State Hillary Clinton and the Russian Minister of Foreign Affairs, Sergei Lavrov, who had been invited to participate as observers; the USA and Russia were both formally invited to join the Summit as full members from the sixth meeting, which was due to be held in Indonesia in late 2011.

Meanwhile, in 1999 Mahathir objected to Australia's leadership of the UN-mandated peace-keeping mission in East Timor (now Timor-Leste, following the territory's accession to independence in May 2002), the UN Transitional Administration in East Timor (UNTAET), claiming that an ASEAN-led mission would be more appropriate. However, other ASEAN members were reluctant to assume responsibility for the peace-keeping body and Australia and East Timor both objected to the notion of Malaysia leading transitional arrangements, owing to its close relations with Indonesia. Only after the intervention of the UN Secretary-General did Malaysia finally contribute limited personnel to UNTAET. In February 2001 Malaysia announced that it would open a liaison office in Dili, East Timor, which became an embassy upon the territory's accession to independence.

Malaysia's relations with Australia, which were frequently strained under Mahathir, appeared to improve following the succession of Abdullah Badawi to the premiership in October 2003. In June 2004, during a visit to Malaysia by the Australian Minister for Foreign Affairs, Alexander Downer, agreement was reached to hold formal annual talks between the two countries' foreign ministers and separate regular consultations between senior security officials. At the same time Prime Minister Abdullah accepted an invitation to make a state visit to Australia. This took place in April 2005 and was the first by a Malaysian leader in more than 20 years. However, the Malaysian Government had dismissed a plan announced by the Australian Prime Minister, John Howard, in September 2004 to establish specialist counter-terrorist centres in South-East Asia and Australia, complaining that it had not been consulted about the proposal. None the less, formal negotiations on a free trade agreement between Malaysia and Australia commenced in mid-2005. In July 2008 Australian Prime Minister Kevin Rudd embarked upon a one-day visit to Malaysia, where he had discussions with Abdullah. The two Prime Ministers agreed to implement an education programme to train teachers in Afghanistan, as part of a new initiative to enhance the regional forces' peace-keeping capacity in that country. The two leaders also agreed to strengthen diplomatic links through regular meetings. Relations were hindered in February 2010 when more than 50 Australian legislators lodged a protest against the second sodomy trial of Anwar Ibrahim, which had commenced earlier in the month (see Domestic Political Affairs); in a formal statement, the legislators indirectly suggested that the trial was politically motivated and urged that it be abandoned. A few days later hundreds of pro-Government demonstrators gathered outside the Australian high commission in Kuala Lumpur to decry the notion that the Government would resort to any such political machinations, and to protest against what they claimed constituted Australian interference in the internal affairs of Malaysia. Following the conclusion in October 2010 of an eighth round of negotiations between Malaysian and Australian officials, both sides stated that they expected a bilateral free trade agreement to be signed in mid-2011.

Other external relations

In July 1997 Mahathir (who was often regarded as the international spokesperson for developing countries) indicated that he might submit a proposal to the UN to review its 1948 Universal Declaration of Human Rights, with regard to the specific priorities of less-developed countries. While this sentiment was supported by many Asian countries, the USA reacted angrily to any suggestion of compromise on the issue of human rights. Relations with the USA were also strained by the involvement of PETRONAS in a consortium that signed an agreement during September 1997 to invest in Iran, in contravention of US sanctions against Iran. In October Mahathir paid a formal visit to Cuba, the first such visit by a Malaysian leader, and urged Malaysian firms to invest in the country, in defiance of US legislation that threatened reprisals against firms conducting business with Cuba. Relations with the USA deteriorated further in the same month following Mahathir's suggestion that the economic crisis in the South-East Asian region was due to hostile Jewish currency speculation aimed at preventing progress among Muslim nations. A resolution tabled by 34 members of the US Congress calling for the retraction of the remarks or Mahathir's resignation was condemned by Mahathir and the Malaysian press. Bilateral relations were further strained in 1998 following US condemnation of the detention and treatment of the former Deputy Prime Minister and Minister of Finance, Anwar Ibrahim; the Malaysian Government was particularly angered by a speech delivered at the APEC summit meeting in Kuala Lumpur in November by the US Vice-President, Albert Gore, in which Gore expressed support for the movement for political reform in Malaysia. During a speech to UMNO members in June 1999, Mahathir criticized the influence on the country of non-Malaysians (and, in particular, ethnic Europeans), who Mahathir claimed were attempting to 're-colonize' Malaysia. Relations with the USA were improved following a visit by Adm. Dennis Blair, the Commander-in-Chief of the US Pacific Command, to Kuala Lumpur in January 2001. At his meeting with Mahathir, the first between the Prime Minister and a US Pacific commander, the two countries agreed to extend military co-operation, although the new US President, George W. Bush, insisted that any further improvement in relations would depend on better treatment for Anwar Ibrahim and other detained members of the Malaysian opposition.

However, in September 2001 relations with the USA were greatly strengthened when Mahathir acted quickly to condemn the terrorist attacks on the US mainland for which the al-Qa'ida network claimed responsibility. However, during a meeting with President Bush at an APEC summit meeting in Shanghai, China, in October, Mahathir refused to lend his Government's support to the US-led retaliatory attacks on Afghanistan that had begun earlier that month, voicing concern at the large numbers of civilian casualties resulting from the raids. At a meeting of ASEAN leaders in November, Malaysia agreed to co-operate with other member nations in the fight against terrorism. In January 2002 the USA congratulated the Malaysian Government on its demonstration of support for the international coalition against terrorism, following the detention of at least 15 suspected terrorists. However, it demanded assurances that the suspects would receive a fair trial under the ISA. In November Malaysia and the USA co-established the Southeast Asia Regional Centre for Counter-Terrorism; based in Kuala Lumpur, the Centre officially opened in July 2003.

While Prime Minister Mahathir made clear his opposition to the US-led campaign to remove the regime of Saddam Hussain in Iraq in 2003, relations with the USA remained generally stable, owing largely to the Government's ongoing operation against suspected domestic terrorists, which was in line with the global anti-terrorism campaign being pursued by the Bush Administration. However, in October 2003, at a summit meeting of the Organization of the Islamic Conference (OIC, see p. 400) held in Putrajaya, Mahathir attracted criticism from the USA, Israel and several European countries when he attacked what he described as Jewish subjugation of Islamic countries during his opening address to the meeting. The Government later issued an apology for the comments. In early 2004 relations with the USA were threatened when new Prime Minister Abdullah Badawi accused the USA of using unreliable intelligence to implicate Malaysia in a global nuclear smuggling network. (The US Government had alleged that a company owned by Abdullah's son had supplied components to the network.) In May the USA welcomed the arrest, under the ISA, of Buhary Syed Abu Tahir, a Sri Lankan businessman resident in Malaysia, for his alleged involvement in the network. In 2006 Malaysia and the USA began negotiations on the establishment of a free trade agreement, which drew opposition from several quarters in Malaysia, including farmers and trade unions fearful of the potential impact of US competition on local livelihoods, as well as from US politicians who disapproved of Malaysia's gas agreement with Iran. However, negotiations proved problematic and were suspended on several occasions, latterly by Malaysia in January 2009 in protest against the USA's support for the Israeli military offensive in the Gaza Strip (see the respective chapters on Israel and the Palestinian Autonomous Areas). In December the Administration of US President Barack Obama announced that it was to prioritize negotiations on the establishment of a regional Asia-Pacific trade pact, prompting the suggestion that plans for a US-Malaysian free trade agreement had been abandoned altogether. Relations were further impeded in January 2010 by comments made by Mahathir claiming that the terrorist attacks of September 2001 had been 'staged' (see Religious Tensions). However, bilateral relations were improved by a visit to Washington, DC, in April 2010 by Prime Minister Najib Razak, who described his visit as 'most fruitful'. During separate visits to Malaysia in November, US Secretary of State Clinton and Secretary of Defence Robert Gates spoke highly of the US-Malaysian relationship, commending the performance of the Malaysian Government and praising the South-East Asian country as a vital regional and global influence. The absence of comment by either Clinton or Gates on the allegations that the criminal charges against Anwar Ibrahim were politically motivated, together with Clinton's refusal to meet with Anwar during her visit, prompted some observers to suggest that the US Administration was compromising its position on human rights in order to preserve cordial relations with the UMNO-led coalition Government; local media reports speculated that this apparent pandering to the Malaysian Government was a reflection of US efforts to counter China's increasing regional prominence.

In June 1997 the inauguration took place of a group that aimed to foster economic co-operation among Muslim developing countries, the Developing-Eight (D-8), comprising Malaysia, Bangladesh, Egypt, Indonesia, Iran, Nigeria, Pakistan and Turkey. Malaysia continued to express its close relationship with Arab countries after it denounced US and British air strikes against Iraq in February 2001, while demanding the removal of UN sanctions. It was hoped that a D-8 agreement on preferential tariffs signed in May 2006 would further strengthen economic relations between the group's members. In November 2007, furthermore, Malaysia and Pakistan signed a bilateral free trade agreement, which entered into force in January 2008.

In December 2006 Prime Minister Abdullah Badawi visited Venezuela; discussions with President Hugo Chávez resulted in initial agreements in the areas of trade and energy co-operation. In July 2007 the inaugural 'Venezuela Week' was hosted in Kuala Lumpur; the event, organized by the Venezuelan embassy and subsequently held annually, was intended to bolster cultural understanding between the two countries. Negotiations on the establishment of a Malaysian-Chilean free trade agreement (Malaysia's first such arrangement with a Latin American country) were concluded in November 2010. The agreement, which was restricted to trade in goods and economic co-operation, was scheduled to take effect in mid-2011; both countries pledged their commitment to working towards a comprehensive agreement that would include services and investment.

CONSTITUTION AND GOVERNMENT

Malaysia is a federation of 13 states. The capital, Kuala Lumpur, is a separate Federal Territory, as is the island of Labuan and the newly developed administrative capital of Putrajaya. The Head of State, or Supreme Head of Malaysia, is a monarch (Yang di-Pertuan Agong), elected for a five-year term (with a Deputy Head of State) by and from the hereditary rulers of nine of the states. The monarch acts on the advice of Parliament and the Cabinet. Parliament consists of the Dewan Negara (Senate) and the Dewan Rakyat (House of Representatives). The Senate has 70 members, including 44 appointed by the Head of State, four of whom are from the Federal Territories, and 26 elected members, two chosen by each of the 13 State Legislative Assemblies. The House of Representatives consists of 222 members (increased from 219 at the March 2008 general election), elected for five years by universal adult suffrage: 165 from Peninsular Malaysia (including 11 from Kuala Lumpur and one from Putrajaya), 31 from Sarawak and 26 from Sabah (including one from Labuan). The Head of State appoints the Prime Minister and, on the latter's recommendation, other ministers. The Cabinet is responsible to Parliament. The country is divided into 137 administrative districts.

REGIONAL AND INTERNATIONAL CO-OPERATION

Malaysia is a member of the Association of Southeast Asian Nations (ASEAN, see p. 206), the Asia-Pacific Economic Co-operation (APEC, see p. 197) forum, the Asian Development Bank (ADB, see p. 202), the UN's Economic and Social Commission for Asia and the Pacific (ESCAP, see p. 37), and the Colombo Plan (see p. 446), which promotes economic and social development in Asia and the Pacific.

Malaysia became a member of the UN in 1957. As a contracting party to the General Agreement on Tariffs and Trade (GATT), Malaysia joined the World Trade Organization (WTO, see p. 430) upon its establishment in 1995. Malaysia participates in the Organization of the Islamic Conference (OIC, see p. 400), the Group of 77 (G77, see p. 447) developing countries and the Developing Eight (D-8, see p. 446). The country is a member of the Non-aligned Movement (see p. 461) and of the International Labour Organization (ILO, see p. 138). Malaysia also participates in the Five-Power Defence Arrangements with Australia, New Zealand, Singapore and the United Kingdom.

ECONOMIC AFFAIRS

In 2009, according to estimates by the World Bank, Malaysia's gross national income (GNI), measured at average 2007–09 prices, was US $198,650m., equivalent to $7,230 per head (or $13,530 per head on an international purchasing-power parity basis). During 2000–09, it was estimated, the population increased at an annual average of 1.9%, while gross domestic product (GDP) per head increased, in real terms, by an average of 2.4% per year. Overall GDP increased, in real terms, at an average annual rate of 4.3% in 2000–09. According to the Asian Development Bank (ADB), GDP contracted by 1.7% in 2009 but expanded by 7.2% in 2010.

Agriculture (including forestry and fishing) contributed 10.4% of GDP in 2010. The sector engaged 13.5% of the employed labour force in 2009. Malaysia is one of the world's leading producers of palm oil, exports of which contributed 6.6% of the value of total merchandise exports in 2009. Other important crops include rice, rubber, cocoa, coconuts, bananas, tea and pineapples. During 2000–09, according to estimated figures from the Asian Development Bank (ADB), agricultural GDP increased, in real terms, at an average annual rate of 3.0%. According to the ADB, agricultural GDP increased by 0.4% in 2009 and by 1.7% in 2010.

Industry (including mining, manufacturing, construction and utilities) contributed 44.1% of GDP in 2010. The sector engaged 27.0% of the employed labour force in 2009. During 2000–09, according to figures from the ADB, industrial GDP increased, in real terms, at an average annual rate of 2.3%. According to the ADB, industrial GDP contracted by 7.1% in 2009, expanding by 8.6% in 2010.

Mining contributed 12.8% of GDP in 2010. However, it engaged only 0.6% of the employed labour force in 2009. At the end of 2009 estimated proven gas reserves stood at 2,381,000m. cu m, and petroleum reserves at 5,520m. barrels. Petroleum production in 2009 averaged 740,000 barrels per day, sufficient to maintain production at that year's level for more than 20 years. In 2009 exports of liquefied natural gas accounted for 5.6% of total export revenue, while crude petroleum and condensates provided 4.5% of export earnings. Malaysia is one of the world's leading producers of tin. Bauxite, iron, gold and coal are also mined. The GDP of the mining sector increased at an average annual rate of 0.8% in 2000–09, according to ADB figures. Mining GDP contracted by 2.4% in 2008 and by 3.8% in 2009.

Manufacturing (the largest export sector) contributed 25.6% of GDP in 2010, and engaged 16.6% of the employed labour force in 2009. The most important branches of manufacturing include electrical machinery and appliances, food products, metals and metal products, non-electrical machinery, transport equipment, rubber and plastic products, chemical products, wood products and furniture. According to figures from the ADB, during 2000–09 manufacturing GDP increased, in real terms, at an average annual rate of 2.6%. Manufacturing GDP increased by 1.3% in 2008 but contracted by 9.3% in 2009.

Construction contributed 3.2% of GDP in 2010; 9.3% of the employed labour force were engaged in the sector in 2009. According to figures from the ADB, the GDP of the sector grew by 4.2% in 2008 and by 5.8% in 2009.

Energy is derived principally from Malaysia's own reserves of hydrocarbons. The country's dependence on petroleum as a source of electric energy declined from 55.9% in 1990 to 2.0% in 2007. The share contributed by natural gas reached 62.0% in 2007, while hydropower and coal accounted for 6.4% and 29.5%, respectively, of the country's electricity output. Production of electricity reached 106,943m. kWh in 2009. Imports of fuel accounted for 8.3% of total import costs in 2009.

Services contributed 45.5% of GDP in 2010. The sector engaged 59.5% of the employed labour force in 2009. Tourism makes a major contribution to the economy. Revenue from this source reached an estimated RM 56,500m. in 2010, in which year tourist arrivals rose to a record 24.6m. In 2010 the financial sub-sector contributed 8.4% of GDP. The GDP of the services sector increased by an average of 6.2% per year in 2000–09, according to ADB data. The sector's GDP grew by 2.6% in 2009 and by 6.8% in 2010.

In 2009 Malaysia recorded a visible trade surplus of US $40,253m., with a surplus of $31,801m. on the current account of the balance of payments. In 2009 the principal sources of imports were the People's Republic of China (which provided 13.9% of the total), Japan (12.5%), the USA and Singapore. Other important suppliers included Thailand and Indonesia. The principal market for exports (accounting for 14.0%) was Singapore; other significant purchasers were China (12.2%), the USA, Japan, Thailand and India. The principal imports in 2009 were intermediate goods (which provided 68.4% of the total), parts and accessories of capital goods and miscellaneous industrial supplies, as well as capital goods and consumption goods. The principal exports were electrical machinery and parts (particularly electronic components and semiconductors), palm oil, chemicals and liquefied natural gas.

The 2009 budget envisaged total spending of RM 157,067m. (including net development expenditure of RM 48,997m.). Revenue reached an estimated RM 158,639m. The Government hoped to reduce the budgetary deficit from the equivalent of 7.0% of GDP in 2009 to 5.6% in 2010. In comparison with the previous year, in 2010 operating expenditure was projected to be reduced by 13.7%, to total RM 138,300m. Malaysia's general government gross debt was RM 376,387m. in 2009, equivalent to 55.4% of GDP. According to the ADB, at the end of 2010 Malaysia's external debt totalled US $73,391m. The cost of debt-servicing in 2009 was equivalent to 6.8% of the value of exports of goods and services. The annual rate of inflation

MALAYSIA

averaged 2.3% in 2000–09. Consumer prices were reported to have increased by 1.7% in 2010. The rate of unemployment was estimated at 3.4% of the total labour force in 2010.

The global recession of 2008/09 seriously affected Malaysia's export trade and led to a sharp decline in investment inflows. In November 2008 a programme of economic stimulus, envisaging expenditure of RM 7,000m., was implemented. In March 2009 additional stimulus measures, with projected spending of RM 60,000m., were announced. Foreign direct investment in Malaysia was estimated to have increased from US $1,430m. in 2009 to $8,584m. in 2010. The Government's budget for 2011 placed further emphasis on the importance of public-private partnerships in infrastructure projects. The continued development of Islamic finance was envisaged, and under the 2011 budget the tax obligations of issuers of Islamic financial instruments were to be reduced. Although the economy contracted in 2009 as a whole, GDP expanded in the final quarter of the year. As the economies of Malaysia's major trading partners recovered (the deceleration in the Chinese economy notwithstanding), as commodity prices strengthened and as private consumption increased, GDP expanded more strongly than anticipated in 2010. Following this robust recovery, the ADB envisaged more moderate GDP growth in 2011, of 5.3%. An important objective of the Ninth Malaysia Plan (2006–10) was the eradication of poverty, the incidence of which was reduced from 5.7% in 2005 to 3.8% in 2009. The Government's New Economic Model, announced in March 2010, envisaged various reforms, including the transfer of state-owned companies to private ownership and a reappraisal of the system of government subsidies. The Tenth Malaysia Plan, encompassing the period 2011–15, envisioned an annual GDP growth rate of 6%, with the services and manufacturing sectors at the forefront of this expansion. The agricultural sector was to be revitalized, with a greater emphasis on higher value added. An ambitious objective of the Plan was to raise private sector investment inflows by 13.8% annually, while the Government aimed to reduce its fiscal deficit from 5.3% of GDP in 2010 to less than 3.0% by 2015. Development expenditure under the 2011–15 plan was projected at RM 230,000m. The expansion of basic facilities in rural areas was one of the Government's priorities.

PUBLIC HOLIDAYS

Each state has its own public holidays, and the following federal holidays are also observed:

2012 (provisional): 23–24 January* (Chinese New Year), 4 February† (Mouloud, Prophet Muhammad's Birthday), 1 May (for Labour Day), 17 May (Vesak Day), 5 June (for Official Birthday of HM the Yang di-Pertuan Agong), 18–19 August† (Hari Raya Puasa, end of Ramadan), 31 August (National Day), 25 October† (Hari Raya Haji, Feast of the Sacrifice), 13 November‡ (Deepavali), 14 November† (Muharram, Islamic New Year), 25 December (Christmas Day).

* The first two days of the first moon of the lunar calendar.
† These holidays are dependent on the Islamic lunar calendar and may vary by one or two days from the dates given.
‡ Except Labuan and Sarawak.

Statistical Survey

Sources (unless otherwise stated): Department of Statistics, Blok C6, Parcel C, Pusat Pentadbiran Kerajaan Persekutuan, 62514 Putrajaya; tel. (3) 88857000; fax (3) 88889248; e-mail jpbpo@stats.gov.my; internet www.statistics.gov.my; Bank Negara Malaysia (Central Bank of Malaysia), Jalan Dato' Onn, POB 10922, 50929 Kuala Lumpur; tel. (3) 26988044; fax (3) 26912990; e-mail info@bnm.gov.my; internet www.bnm.gov.my; Departments of Statistics, Kuching and Kota Kinabalu.

Note: Unless otherwise indicated, statistics refer to all states of Malaysia.

Area and Population

AREA, POPULATION AND DENSITY

Area (sq km)	
Peninsular Malaysia	132,631
Sabah (incl. Labuan)	73,722
Sarawak	124,450
Total	330,803*
Population (census results)	
5–20 July 2000†	23,274,690
6 July 2010 (preliminary)	
Males	14,112,667
Females	13,453,154
Total	27,565,821
Density (per sq km) at July 2010 census	83.3

* 127,724 sq miles.
† Including adjustment of 4.6% for underenumeration, enumerated total was 22,198,276.

POPULATION BY AGE AND SEX
('000, official estimates at mid-2009)

	Males	Females	Total
0–14	4,647.0	4,367.7	9,014.7
15–64	9,157.6	8,848.4	18,005.8
65 and over	602.7	683.5	1,286.2
Total	14,407.2	13,899.4	28,306.7

Note: Estimates not adjusted to take account of preliminary results of 2010 census; totals may not be equal to the sum of components, owing to rounding.

PRINCIPAL ETHNIC GROUPS
(at census of August 1991)*

	Peninsular Malaysia	Sabah†	Sarawak	Total
Malays and other indigenous groups	8,433,826	1,003,540	1,209,118	10,646,484
Chinese	4,250,969	218,233	475,752	4,944,954
Indians	1,380,048	9,310	4,608	1,393,966
Others	410,544	167,790	10,541	588,875
Non-Malaysians	322,229	464,786	18,361	805,376
Total	14,797,616	1,863,659	1,718,380	18,379,655

* Including adjustment for underenumeration.
† Including the Federal Territory of Labuan.

Mid-2009 ('000 persons): Malays 14,409.9; Other indigenous groups 3,128.4; Chinese 6,437.7; Indian 1,939.2; Others 340.5; Non-Malaysians 2,051.0; Total 28,306.7.

MALAYSIA

ADMINISTRATIVE DIVISIONS
(population at 2010 census, preliminary results)

	Area (sq km)	Population ('000)	Density (per sq km)	Capital
States				
Johor (Johore)	19,210	3,233.4	168	Johor Bahru
Kedah	9,500	1,890.1	199	Alor Star
Kelantan	15,099	1,460.0	97	Kota Bharu
Melaka (Malacca)	1,664	788.7	474	Melaka
Negeri Sembilan (Negri Sembilan)	6,686	997.1	149	Seremban
Pahang	36,137	1,443.4	40	Kuantan
Perak	21,035	2,258.4	107	Ipoh
Perlis	821	227.0	277	Kangar
Pulau Pinang (Penang)	1,048	1,520.1	1,451	George Town
Sabah	73,631	3,120.0	42	Kota Kinabalu
Sarawak	124,450	2,420.0	19	Kuching
Selangor	8,104	5,411.3	668	Shah Alam
Terengganu (Trengganu)	13,035	1,015.8	78	Kuala Terengganu
Federal Territories				
Kuala Lumpur	243	1,627.2	6,696	—
Labuan	91	85.3	937	—
Putrajaya	49	68.0	1,387	—
Total	330,803	27,565.8	83	

PRINCIPAL TOWNS
(population at 2000 census)

Kuala Lumpur (capital)	1,305,792	Sabang Jaya	447,183
Johor Bahru	642,944	Shah Alam	314,440
Kelang (Klang)	626,699	Kota Kinabalu	306,920
Ipoh	536,832	Seremban	290,709
Petaling Jaya	432,619	Kuantan	288,727
Kuching	422,240	Sandakan	276,791

2010 census (preliminary): Kuala Lumpur 1,627,172.

BIRTHS AND DEATHS*

	Registered live births		Registered deaths	
	Number	Rate (per 1,000)	Number	Rate (per 1,000)
2004	477,800	19.1	112,700	4.5
2005	469,200	18.5	113,700	4.5
2006*	465,100	18.1	115,100	4.5
2007*	472,000	18.1	118,200	4.5
2008*†	470,900	17.8	123,300	4.7
2009*†	471,600	17.6	121,800	4.5

* Figures are rounded to nearest 100.
† Preliminary estimates.

Life expectancy (years at birth, official estimates, 2009): Males 72.0; females 76.8.

ECONOMICALLY ACTIVE POPULATION*
(sample surveys, ISIC major divisions, '000 persons aged 15 to 64 years)

	2007	2008	2009
Agriculture, hunting and forestry	1,437.3	1,365.6	1,349.6
Fishing	120.9	122.1	121.5
Mining and quarrying	39.4	54.5	62.7
Manufacturing	1,977.3	1,944.7	1,807.1
Electricity, gas and water	60.8	60.5	58.1
Construction	922.5	998.0	1,015.9
Wholesale and retail trade; repair of motor vehicles, motorcycles and personal and household goods	1,712.1	1,729.4	1,831.8
Hotels and restaurants	760.7	783.6	800.5
Transport, storage and communications	538.2	583.4	592.0
Financial intermediation	282.2	276.0	271.5
Real estate, renting and business activities	558.1	553.2	601.9

—continued	2007	2008	2009
Public administration and defence; compulsory social security	716.1	751.1	813.9
Education	632.7	656.5	731.4
Health and social work	238.9	252.6	271.7
Other community, social and personal service activities	266.5	274.2	303.3
Private households with employed persons	272.7	253.0	262.5
Extra-territorial organizations and bodies	1.7	1.1	1.7
Total employed	10,538.1	10,659.6	10,897.3
Unemployed	351.4	368.5	418.0
Total labour force	10,889.5	11,028.1	11,315.3
Males	6,963.5	7,074.6	7,218.1
Females	3,926.0	3,953.5	4,097.2

* Excluding members of the armed forces.

Health and Welfare

KEY INDICATORS

Total fertility rate (children per woman, 2008)	2.6
Under-5 mortality rate (per 1,000 live births, 2008)	6
HIV/AIDS (% of persons aged 15–49, 2007)	0.5
Physicians (per 1,000 head, 2002)	0.7
Hospital beds (per 1,000 head, 2006)	1.9
Health expenditure (2007): US $ per head (PPP)	604
Health expenditure (2007): % of GDP	4.4
Health expenditure (2007): public (% of total)	44.4
Access to sanitation (% of persons, 2008)	96
Total carbon dioxide emissions ('000 metric tons, 2007)	194,316.6
Carbon dioxide emissions per head (metric tons, 2007)	7.3
Human Development Index (2010): ranking	57
Human Development Index (2010): value	0.744

For sources and definitions, see explanatory note on p. vi.

Agriculture

PRINCIPAL CROPS
('000 metric tons)

	2007	2008	2009
Rice, paddy	2,375	2,353	2,510
Maize	32	33	35
Sweet potatoes	30	18	19
Cassava (Manioc)	430*	430*	n.a.
Sugar cane	560	694	700*
Coconuts	503	455	460
Oil palm fruit	79,100*	83,000*	n.a.
Cabbages	66	73	n.a.
Tomatoes	73	76	n.a.
Cucumbers and gherkins	56	58	n.a.
Watermelons	157	166	n.a.
Bananas*	530	600	625
Pineapples	316	385	400
Papayas	72*	72*	n.a.
Coffee, green	31	29	n.a.
Cocoa beans	35	28	18
Pepper	20	25	23
Natural rubber	1,200	1,072	857

* FAO estimate(s).

Aggregate production ('000 metric tons, may include official, semi-official or estimated data): Total cereals 2,407 in 2007, 2,386 in 2008, 2,545 in 2009; Total oilcrops 17,819 in 2007, 19,990 in 2008, 19,752 in 2009; Total vegetables (incl. melons) 617 in 2007, 637 in 2008, 637 in 2009; Total fruits (excl. melons) 1,306 in 2007, 1,443 in 2008, 1,482 in 2009.

Source: FAO.

MALAYSIA

LIVESTOCK
('000 head, year ending September)

	2006	2007	2008
Cattle	774	785	790*
Buffaloes	131	130*	131*
Goats	286	285*	285*
Sheep	112	115*	115*
Pigs	2,092	2,866	1,861
Chickens*	187,000	190,000	190,000
Ducks*	46,000	47,000	47,000

* FAO estimate(s).
Source: FAO.

LIVESTOCK PRODUCTS
('000 metric tons)

	2006	2007	2008
Cattle meat*	22.0	22.3	22.5
Buffalo meat*	4.5	4.5	4.7
Pig meat	216.8	200.1	195.1
Chicken meat	922.0†	931.0†	931.0*
Duck meat*	108.0	111.0	111.0
Cows' milk*	38.7	39.3	39.3
Buffaloes' milk	7.5	7.5	7.9
Hen eggs*	453.0	465.0	465.0
Other poultry eggs*	11.0	11.0	11.0

* FAO estimate(s).
† Unofficial figure.
2009 (FAO estimates): Cattle meat 22.5; Buffalo meat 4.7; Pig meat 199.1; Buffaloes' milk 7.9.
Source: FAO.

Forestry

ROUNDWOOD REMOVALS
('000 cubic metres, excl. bark)

	2007	2008	2009
Sawlogs, veneer logs and logs for sleepers	23,522	21,244	18,713
Pulpwood	703	703	703
Other industrial roundwood	769	798	710
Fuel wood	2,959	2,908	2,858
Total	27,953	25,653	22,984

Source: FAO.

SAWNWOOD PRODUCTION
('000 cubic metres, incl. railway sleepers)

	2007	2008	2009
Total (all broadleaved)	5,084	4,486	3,875

Source: FAO.

Fishing

('000 metric tons, live weight)

	2006	2007	2008
Capture	1,286.5	1,385.7	1,395.9
Indian scad	99.1	90.0	96.9
Kawakawa	25.3	24.0	30.3
Indian mackerels	117.5	156.7	169.5
Squids	60.5	59.7	56.3
Aquaculture	168.3	178.2	243.1
Blood cockle	45.7	49.6	61.1
Total catch	1,454.8	1,563.9	1,639.0

Note: Figures exclude crocodiles, recorded by number rather than by weight. The number of estuarine crocodiles caught was: 1,790 in 2006; 540 in 2007; 1,043 in 2008. Also excluded are shells and corals. Catches of turban shells (metric tons, FAO estimates) were: 80 in 2006; 80 in 2007; 80 in 2008. Catches of hard corals (metric tons, FAO estimates) were: 4,000 in 2006; 4,000 in 2007; 4,000 in 2008.
Source: FAO.

Mining

PRODUCTION
(metric tons unless otherwise indicated)

	2007	2008	2009
Tin-in-concentrates	2,264	2,607	2,412
Bauxite	156,785	275,069	263,432
Iron ore*	800,895	981,932	1,470,186
Kaolin	498,639	419,157	463,736
Gold (kg)	2,916	2,490	2,794
Hard coal	1,053,879	1,151,024	2,116,374†
Ilmenite*‡	60,250	36,779	15,983
Crude petroleum ('000 barrels)	249,190	251,811	240,843
Natural gas (net production, million cu ft)	2,147,805	2,154,853	2,068,548
Zirconium*§	7,393	984	1,145

* Figures refer to the gross weight of ores and concentrates.
† Preliminary figure.
‡ Concentrate from amang retreatment plants.
§ Source: US Geological Survey.

Industry

SELECTED PRODUCTS
('000 metric tons, unless otherwise indicated)

	2007	2008	2009
Canned fish, frozen shrimps/prawns	45.5	45.8	47.7
Palm oil (crude)	15,823	17,734	n.a.
Refined sugar	1,597.6	1,519.0	1,488.8
Soft drinks ('000 litres)	2,138.4	2,069.4	1,667.0
Cigarettes (metric tons)	23,723	23,004	20,892
Woven cotton fabrics (million metres)	157.1	200.7	166.3
Veneer sheets ('000 cu metres)	1,175.7	948.1	753.5
Plywood ('000 cu metres)	4,943.2	4,557.8	3,655.2
Kerosene and jet fuel	3,306.9	3,940.4	3,402.8
Liquefied petroleum gas	3,807.3	3,625.6	3,265.3
Inner tubes and tyres ('000)	34,379	35,532	27,647
Rubber gloves (million pairs)	21,118.9	22,585.6	23,132.7
Earthen brick and cement roofing tiles (million)	1,055.3	1,129.7	311.6
Cement	21,909	19,629	19,457

MALAYSIA

—continued

	2007	2008	2009
Iron and steel bars and rods	2,837.6	2,368.3	1,890.7
Television receivers ('000)	6,027.7	5,732.4	6,361.8
Radio receivers ('000)	46,253	61,539	58,410
Semiconductors (million)	22,192	20,520	14,885
Electronic transistors (million)	30,888	31,346	29,271
Integrated circuits (million)	33,558	30,752	23,279
Passenger motor cars ('000)*	333.7	419.6	409.4
Commercial vehicles ('000)*	79.6	85.2	67.6
Motorcycles and scooters ('000)	470.1	550.3	514.5
Electric energy (million kWh)†	104,950	106,357	106,943

* Vehicles assembled from imported parts.
† Source: Asian Development Bank.

Tin (smelter production of primary metal, metric tons): 25,471 in 2007; 31,691 in 2008; 36,407 in 2009 (Source: US Geological Survey).

Finance

CURRENCY AND EXCHANGE RATES

Monetary Units
100 sen = 1 ringgit Malaysia (RM—also formerly Malaysian dollar).

Sterling, US Dollar and Euro Equivalents (31 December 2010)
£1 sterling = RM 4.8272;
US $1 = RM 3.0835;
€1 = RM 4.1202;
RM 100 = £20.72 = US $32.43 = €24.27.

Average Exchange Rate (ringgit Malaysia per US $)
2008   3.336
2009   3.525
2010   3.221

FEDERAL BUDGET
(RM million)

Revenue	2007	2008	2009
Tax revenue	95,168	112,897	106,504
Taxes on income and profits	69,396	82,138	78,375
Companies (excl. petroleum)	32,149	37,741	30,199
Individuals	11,661	14,966	15,590
Petroleum	20,453	24,191	27,231
Export duties	2,322	2,779	1,152
Import duties	2,424	2,635	2,114
Excises on goods	8,990	10,682	10,068
Sales tax	6,642	8,374	8,603
Service tax	3,013	3,345	3,344
Others	2,380	2,944	2,847
Other revenue	44,717	46,896	52,135
Total	139,885	159,793	158,639

Expenditure	2007	2008	2009
Emoluments	32,587	41,011	42,778
Pensions and gratuities	8,251	10,022	10,146
Debt service charges	12,911	12,797	14,222
Domestic	11,485	11,642	13,312
External	1,426	1,155	909
Supplies and services	23,622	25,197	26,372
Subsidies	10,481	29,867	18,624
Asset acquisition	2,532	2,835	2,582
Other grants and transfers	31,501	30,922	41,658
Other expenditure	1,197	849	685
Total	123,084	153,499	157,067

FEDERAL DEVELOPMENT EXPENDITURE
(RM million)

	2007	2008	2009
Defence and security	5,702	5,779	3,956
Social services	12,893	13,717	17,388
Education	6,271	7,892	10,827
Health	1,496	1,652	2,575
Housing	2,947	1,780	1,395
Economic services	20,116	21,353	26,440
Agriculture and rural development	3,842	4,184	5,508
Public utilities	2,358	2,795	2,899
Trade and industry	4,904	4,581	4,916
Transport	8,500	9,212	9,450
General administration	1,853	1,998	1,731
Sub-total	40,564	42,847	49,515
Less Loan recoveries	3,105	959	519
Total	37,460	41,889	48,997

INTERNATIONAL RESERVES
(US $ million at 31 December)

	2008	2009	2010
Gold (national valuation)	379	1,281	1,641
IMF special drawing rights	226	2,124	2,088
Reserve position in IMF	317	442	471
Foreign exchange	90,605	92,865	102,298
Total	91,527	96,712	106,498

Source: IMF, *International Financial Statistics*.

MONEY SUPPLY
(RM million at 31 December)

	2007	2008	2009
Currency outside depository corporations	36,246	40,431	43,438
Transferable deposits	138,059	150,840	170,431
Other deposits	610,161	681,907	749,555
Securities other than shares	48,556	47,606	28,628
Broad money	833,022	920,784	992,052

Source: IMF, *International Financial Statistics*.

COST OF LIVING
(Consumer Price Index; base 2005 = 100)

	2008	2009	2010
Food and non-alcoholic beverages	115.9	120.7	101.4
Alcoholic beverages and tobacco	123.6	131.2	104.6
Clothing and footwear	96.8	95.9	98.8
Rent and other housing costs, heating and lighting	104.4	105.9	100.8
Furniture, domestic appliances, tools and maintenance	105.3	108.4	100.0
Medical care	106.0	108.4	100.8
Transport	123.6	112.0	102.9
Communications	96.8	96.3	100.0
Education	105.8	108.3	100.4
All items (incl. others)	111.4	112.1	101.2

MALAYSIA

NATIONAL ACCOUNTS
(RM million at current prices)

Expenditure on the Gross Domestic Product

	2008	2009	2010
Government final consumption expenditure	92,531	95,918	97,131
Private final consumption expenditure	334,712	338,894	368,275
Changes in inventories	−1,685	−38,358	8,887
Gross fixed capital formation	144,634	136,824	154,237
Total domestic expenditure	570,192	533,278	628,530
Exports of goods and services	765,370	655,336	744,497
Less Imports of goods and services	594,655	508,927	607,061
GDP in purchasers' values	740,907	679,687	765,966
GDP at constant 2000 prices	530,181	521,095	558,382

Gross Domestic Product by Economic Activity

	2008	2009	2010
Agriculture, forestry and fishing	75,611	64,716	81,100
Mining and quarrying	123,978	87,534	100,140
Manufacturing	194,652	173,230	200,010
Electricity, gas and water	16,910	17,709	19,127
Construction	20,606	22,425	24,773
Trade	82,691	81,122	90,211
Restaurants and hotels	16,218	17,092	18,253
Transport and storage	24,641	23,752	25,609
Communications	21,205	22,433	24,679
Finance and insurance	59,418	61,650	65,360
Real estate and business services	29,917	31,301	34,560
Government services	53,987	55,096	58,758
Other services	33,223	35,367	37,421
Sub-total	753,057	693,427	780,001
Import duties	7,436	6,968	7,648
Less Financial intermediation services indirectly measured	19,587	20,708	21,683
GDP in purchasers' values	740,907	679,687	765,966

BALANCE OF PAYMENTS
(US $ million)

	2007	2008	2009
Exports of goods f.o.b.	176,220	199,733	157,655
Imports of goods f.o.b.	−138,493	−148,472	−117,402
Trade balance	37,727	51,261	40,253
Exports of services	29,462	30,321	28,769
Imports of services	−28,668	−30,270	−27,472
Balance on goods and services	38,520	51,313	41,551
Other income received	11,380	12,081	11,213
Other income paid	−15,462	−19,218	−15,382
Balance on goods, services and income	34,438	44,176	37,381
Current transfers received	391	419	1,077
Current transfers paid	−5,059	−5,681	−6,657
Current balance	29,770	38,914	31,801
Capital account (net)	−54	187	−45
Direct investment abroad	−11,334	−15,203	−8,014
Direct investment from abroad	8,590	7,376	1,387
Portfolio investment assets	−3,932	−2,878	−6,339
Portfolio investment liabilities	9,320	−21,083	6,048
Financial derivatives assets	198	−1,165	32
Financial derivatives liabilities	−246	506	651
Other investment assets	−17,400	3,826	−17,667
Other investment liabilities	3,427	−5,352	1,263
Net errors and omissions	−5,195	−8,578	−5,199
Overall balance	13,144	−3,450	3,918

Source: IMF, *International Financial Statistics*.

External Trade

PRINCIPAL COMMODITIES
(RM million)

Imports c.i.f.	2007	2008	2009
Capital goods*	69,996	69,913	65,769
Intermediate goods	358,506	379,136	297,340
Miscellaneous industrial supplies, processed	110,718	120,230	94,001
Parts and accessories of capital goods (excl. transportation equipment)	172,667	164,120	132,962
Consumption goods	28,888	32,304	31,427
Total (incl. others)†	502,045	521,611	434,940

Exports f.o.b.	2007	2008	2009
Palm oil	32,027	45,955	36,365
Crude petroleum and condensates	31,882	43,040	24,873
Liquefied natural gas	26,936	40,732	31,195
Semi-conductors	96,653	89,819	92,972
Electronic components	117,051	106,114	86,115
Consumer electrical products	16,461	21,388	18,794
Industrial and commercial electrical products	29,696	31,088	23,986
Electrical industrial machinery and equipment	24,297	25,382	21,905
Chemicals and chemical products	37,159	40,926	34,146
Metal manufactures	26,372	29,257	22,644
Total (incl. others)	604,300	663,494	553,295

* Figures net of re-exports.
† Including re-exports.

2010 (provisional): Total imports 529,195; total exports 639,428.

PRINCIPAL TRADING PARTNERS
(RM million)

Imports c.i.f.	2007	2008	2009
Australia	10,205	11,765	9,485
China, People's Republic	64,903	66,882	60,660
France	7,717	7,554	7,059
Germany	23,423	22,471	18,417
Hong Kong	14,676	13,659	10,812
India	7,067	10,302	7,869
Indonesia	21,379	24,185	23,030
Japan	65,539	65,126	54,288
Korea, Republic	24,933	24,226	20,125
Philippines	9,775	6,942	4,008
Singapore	57,955	57,326	48,115
Taiwan	28,712	25,094	18,467
Thailand	27,006	29,275	26,308
United Kingdom	7,266	7,654	5,999
USA	54,688	56,454	48,635
Total (incl. others)	502,045	521,611	434,940

Exports f.o.b.	2007	2008	2009
Australia	20,400	24,404	19,999
China, People's Republic	53,035	63,210	67,241
France	7,352	6,361	5,450
Germany	14,832	15,361	14,830
Hong Kong	27,970	28,317	28,845
India	20,204	24,732	16,998
Indonesia	17,749	20,736	17,294
Japan	55,241	71,800	54,424
Korea, Republic	23,032	25,887	21,100
Netherlands	23,599	23,443	18,421
Philippines	8,739	9,760	6,962
Singapore	88,508	97,784	77,195
Taiwan	16,462	16,233	14,431
Thailand	29,984	31,735	29,853
United Kingdom	9,899	9,488	7,082
USA	94,519	82,728	60,584
Total (incl. others)	604,300	663,494	553,295

2010 (provisional): Total imports 529,195; total exports 639,428.

MALAYSIA

Transport

RAILWAYS
(traffic, Peninsular Malaysia only)

	2002	2003	2004
Passenger-km (million)	1,138	1,031	1,152
Freight ton-km (million)	1,073	887	1,017

Source: UN, *Statistical Yearbook*.

ROAD TRAFFIC
(registered motor vehicles at 31 December)

	2001	2002	2003
Passenger cars	4,624,557	5,069,412	5,499,707
Buses and coaches	49,771	51,158	52,846
Lorries and vans	689,668	713,148	1,101,737
Road tractors	329,198	345,604	n.a.
Motorcycles and mopeds	5,609,351	5,842,617	6,164,958

2006: Passenger cars 7,024,043; Buses and coaches 59,991; Lorries and vans 836,579; Motorcycles and mopeds 7,458,128.

2008: Passenger cars 8,056,999; Buses and coaches 64,050; Lorries and vans 909,243; Motorcycles and mopeds 8,487,451.

Source: IRF, *World Road Statistics*.

SHIPPING
Merchant Fleet
(registered at 31 December)

	2007	2008	2009
Number of vessels	1,151	1,238	1,344
Total displacement ('000 grt)	6,974.6	7,078.2	7,717.8

Source: IHSFairplay, *World Fleet Statistics*.

Sea-borne Freight Traffic*
(Peninsular Malaysia, international and coastwise, '000 metric tons)

	2006	2007	2008
Goods loaded	90,755	96,972	103,669
Goods unloaded	105,355	117,086	125,885

* Including transshipments.

Source: UN, *Monthly Bulletin of Statistics*.

CIVIL AVIATION
(traffic on scheduled services)

	2004	2005	2006
Kilometres flown (million)	278	291	291
Passengers carried ('000)	19,227	20,369	21,009
Passenger-km (million)	44,642	49,578	47,442
Total ton-km (million)	6,672	7,103	6,971

Source: UN, *Statistical Yearbook*.

Tourism

TOURIST ARRIVALS BY COUNTRY OF RESIDENCE*

	2007	2008	2009
Brunei	1,172,154	1,085,115	1,061,357
China, People's Republic (incl. Hong Kong and Macao)	783,788	949,864	1,019,756
Indonesia	1,804,535	2,428,605	2,405,360
Japan	367,567	433,462	395,746
Singapore	10,492,692	11,003,492	12,733,082
Thailand	1,625,698	1,493,789	1,449,262
Total (incl. others)	20,972,822	22,052,488	23,646,191

* Including Singapore residents crossing the frontier by road through the Johore Causeway.

Source: Malaysia Tourism Promotion Board.

Tourism receipts (US $ million, excl. passenger transport): 10,427 in 2006; 14,053 in 2007; 15,293 in 2008 (Source: World Tourism Organization).

Communications Media

	2007	2008	2009
Telephones ('000 main lines in use)	4,350.0	4,292.0	4,312.0
Mobile cellular telephones ('000 subscribers)	23,347.0	27,713.0	30,144.0
Internet users ('000)	14,791.5	15,074.0	15,354.5
Broadband subscribers ('000)	1,025.0	1,718.0	1,671.8

Personal computers: 6,040,000 (231.5 per 1,000 persons) in 2006.

Radio receivers ('000 in use, 1997): 9,100.

Television receivers ('000 in use, 2001): 4,773.

Book production (incl. pamphlets, 1999): 5,084 titles (29,040,000 copies in 1996).

Daily newspapers (2004): 35 (average circulation 2,753,000 copies).

Non-daily newspapers (1997): 3 (average circulation 312,000 copies).

Periodicals (1992): 25 titles (average circulation 996,000 copies).

Sources: International Telecommunication Union; UNESCO, *Statistical Yearbook*; UN, *Statistical Yearbook*.

Education

(at 30 June 2008 unless otherwise indicated)

	Institutions	Teachers	Students
Primary	7,644	210,912	3,154,090
Secondary	2,181	159,019	2,310,660
Regular	1,845	139 740	2,126,146
Fully residential	54	3 368	33,289
Technical	90	7 713	69,006
Religious	55	3 306	38,865
Special	4	190	773
Special Model	11	879	10,437*
Sports	2	174	912†
Tertiary‡	48	14,960	210,724
Universities	9	7,823	97,103
Teacher training	31	3,220	46,019
MARA Institute of Technology	1	2,574	42,174

* 2004 figure.
† 2003 figure.
‡ 1995 figures.

Source: Ministry of Education, Putrajaya.

Teachers (2006/07): Pre-primary 27,389; Primary 205,772; Secondary 166,940(; Tertiary 42,355 (Source: UNESCO Institute for Statistics).

Students (2006/07): Pre-primary 654,150; Primary 3,103,579; Secondary 2,499,165; Tertiary 805,136 (Source: UNESCO Institute for Statistics).

Pupil-teacher ratio (primary education, UNESCO estimate): 15.1 in 2006/07 (Source: UNESCO Institute for Statistics).

Adult literacy rate (UNESCO estimates): 92.1% (males 94.3%; females 89.8%) in 2008 (Source: UNESCO Institute for Statistics).

MALAYSIA

Directory

The Government

SUPREME HEAD OF STATE

HM Yang di-Pertuan Agong: HRH Sultan Tuanku Mizan Zainal Abidin ibni al-Marhum Sultan Mahmud (Sultan of Terengganu) (took office 13 December 2006).

Deputy Supreme Head of State

Timbalan Yang di-Pertuan Agong: HRH Tuanku Haji Abdul Halim Mu'adzam Shah ibni al-Marhum Sultan Badlishah (Sultan of Kedah).

CABINET
(May 2011)

The Government is formed by the Barisan Nasional (National Front), led by the United Malays National Organization (UMNO).

Prime Minister and Minister of Finance: Dato' Sri Mohd Najib bin Tun Haji Abdul Razak.
Deputy Prime Minister and Minister of Education: Tan Sri Dato' Haji Muhyiddin bin Mohd Yassin.
Minister of Foreign Affairs: Datuk Anifah bin Haji Aman.
Minister of Home Affairs: Dato' Seri Hishammuddin bin Tun Hussein.
Minister of Defence: Dato' Seri Dr Ahmad Zahid bin Hamidi.
Minister of International Trade and Industry: Dato' Mustapa bin Mohamed.
Minister of Domestic Trade, Co-operatives and Consumerism: Dato' Sri Ismail Sabri bin Yaakob.
Minister of Transport: Datuk Seri Kong Cho Ha.
Minister of Energy, Green Technology and Water: Datuk Peter Chin Fah Kui.
Minister of Works: Dato' Shaziman bin Abu Mansor.
Minister of Higher Education: Dato' Seri Mohamed Khaled bin Nordin.
Minister of Information, Communications and Culture: Dato' Seri Dr Rais Yatim.
Minister of Human Resources: Datuk Dr S. Subramaniam.
Minister of Natural Resources and the Environment: Datuk Douglas Uggah Embas.
Minister of Plantation Industries and Commodities: Tan Sri Bernard Giluk Dompok.
Minister of Tourism: Dato' Sri Dr Ng Yen Yen.
Minister of Science, Technology and Innovation: Datuk Dr Maximus Johnity Ongkili.
Minister of Health: Dato' Sri Liow Tiong Lai.
Minister of Agriculture and Agro-Based Industry: Dato' Haji Noh bin Omar.
Minister of Rural and Regional Development: Dato' Seri Haji Mohd Shafie bin Haji Apdal.
Minister of Federal Territories and Urban Well-being: Dato' Raja Nong Chik bin Dato' Raja Zainal Abidin.
Minister of Women, Family and Community Development: Dato' Sri Shahrizat Abdul Jalil.
Minister of Finance II: Dato' Seri Haji Ahmad Husni bin Mohamad Hanadzlah.
Minister of Housing and Local Government: Dato' Chor Chee Heung.
Minister of Youth and Sports: Dato' Ahmad Shabery Cheek.
Ministers in the Prime Minister's Department: Tan Sri Dr Koh Tsu Koon, Dato' Seri Mohamed Nazri bin Abdul Aziz, Maj.-Gen. Dato' Jamil Khir bin Baharum, Tan Sri Nor Mohamed bin Yakcop, Dato' Sri Idris Jala.

MINISTRIES

Prime Minister's Office (Jabatan Perdana Menteri): Federal Government Administration Center, Bangunan Perdana Putra, 62502 Putrajaya; tel. (3) 88888000; fax (3) 88883444; e-mail fuad@pmo.gov.my; internet www.pmo.gov.my.

Ministry of Agriculture and Agro-Based Industry: Wisma Tani, 28 Persiaran Perdana, Presint 4, Pusat Pentadbiran Kerajaan Persekutuan, 62624 Putrajaya; tel. (3) 88701000; fax (3) 88886020; e-mail pro@moa.gov.my; internet www.moa.gov.my.

Ministry of Defence (Kementerian Pertahanan): Wisma Pertahanan, Jalan Padang Tembak, 50634 Kuala Lumpur; tel. (3) 26921333; fax (3) 26914163; e-mail szy.ppm@mod.gov.my; internet www.mod.gov.my.

Ministry of Domestic Trade, Co-operatives and Consumerism (Kementerian Perdagangan Dalam Negeri, Koperasi Dan Kepenggunaan): 13 Persianan Perdana, Presint 2, Pusat Pentadbiran Kerajaan Persekutuan, 62623 Putrajaya; tel. (3) 88825500; fax (3) 88825762; e-mail aduan@kpdnkk.gov.my; internet www.kpdnkk.gov.my.

Ministry of Education (Kementerian Pendidikan): Blok E8, Parcel E, Pusat Pentadbiran Kerajaan Persekutuan, 62604 Putrajaya; tel. (3) 88846000; fax (3) 88895235; e-mail kpkpm@moe.gov.my; internet www.moe.gov.my.

Ministry of Energy, Green Technology and Water (Kementerian Tenaga, Teknologi Hijau dan Air): Blok E4–5, Parcel E, Pusat Pentadbiran Kerajaan Persekutuan, 62668 Putrajaya; tel. (3) 88836000; fax (3) 88893712; e-mail webmaster@kettha.gov.my; internet www.kettha.gov.my.

Ministry of Federal Territories and Urban Well-being (Kementerian Wilayah Persekutuan Dan Kesejahteraan Bandar): Aras G-4, Blok 2, Menara PJH, Presint 2, 62100 Putrajaya; tel. (3) 88897888; fax (3) 88880375; e-mail zainor@kwp.gov.my; internet www.kwp.gov.my.

Ministry of Finance (Kementerian Kewangan): Kompleks Kementerian Kewangan, 5 Persiaran Perdana, Presint 2, Pusat Pentadbiran Kerajaan Persekutuan, 62592 Putrajaya; tel. (3) 88823000; fax (3) 88823893; e-mail shafei@treasury.gov.my; internet www.treasury.gov.my.

Ministry of Foreign Affairs (Kementerian Luar Negeri): Wisma Putra, 1 Jalan Wisma Putra, Presint 2, 62602 Putrajaya; tel. (3) 88874000; fax (3) 88891717; e-mail webmaster@kln.gov.my; internet www.kln.gov.my.

Ministry of Health (Kementerian Kesihatan): Blok E1, E6–7 & E10, Parcel E, Pusat Pentadbiran Kerajaan Persekutuan, 62590 Putrajaya; tel. (3) 88833888; fax (3) 26985964; e-mail kkm@moh.gov.my; internet www.moh.gov.my.

Ministry of Higher Education (Kementerian Pengajian Tinggi): Blok E3, Parcel E, Pusat Perbadanan Kerajaan Persekutuan, 62505 Putrajaya; tel. (3) 88835000; fax (3) 88893921; e-mail minister@mohe.gov.my; internet www.portal.mohe.gov.my.

Ministry of Home Affairs (Kementerian Hal Ehwal Dalam Negeri): Blok D1–2, Parcel D, Pusat Pentadbiran Kerajaan Persekutuan, 62546 Putrajaya; tel. (3) 88868000; fax (3) 88891613; e-mail menteri@moha.gov.my; internet www.moha.gov.my.

Ministry of Housing and Local Government (Kementerian Perumahan dan Kerajaan Tempatan): Aras 1–7, Blok K, Pusat Bandar Damansara, 50782 Kuala Lumpur; tel. (3) 20947033; fax (3) 20949720; e-mail pro@kpkt.gov.my; internet www.kpkt.gov.my.

Ministry of Human Resources (Kementerian Sumber Manusia): Tingkat 6–9, Blok D3, Parcel D, Pusat Pentadbiran Kerajaan Persekutuan, 62530 Putrajaya; tel. (3) 88865000; fax (3) 88892381; e-mail ksm1@mohr.gov.my; internet www.mohr.gov.my.

Ministry of Information, Communications and Culture (Kementerian Penerangan Komunikasi Dan Kebudayaan): Tingkat 5, Wisma TV, Angkasapuri, Bukit Putra, 50610 Kuala Lumpur; tel. (3) 22825333; fax (3) 22848115; e-mail azmi@kpkk.gov.my; internet www.kpkk.gov.my.

Ministry of International Trade and Industry (Kementerian Perdagangan Antarabangsa dan Industri): Blok 10, Kompleks Pejabat Kerajaan, Jalan Duta, 50622 Kuala Lumpur; tel. (3) 62033022; fax (3) 62012337; e-mail webmiti@miti.gov.my; internet www.miti.gov.my.

Ministry of Natural Resources and the Environment (Kementerian Sumber Asli dan Alam Sekitar): Wisma Sumber Asli, 25 Persiaran Perdana, Presint 4, Pusat Pentadbiran Kerajaan Persekutuan, 62574 Putrajaya; tel. (3) 88861111; fax (3) 88892672; e-mail james@nre.gov.my; internet www.nre.gov.my.

Ministry of Plantation Industries and Commodities (Kementerian Perusahaan Perladangan dan Komoditi): Aras 6–13, 15 Persiaran Perdana, Presint 2, Pusat Pentadbiran Kerajaan Persekutuan, 62654 Putrajaya; tel. (3) 88803300; fax (3) 88803441; e-mail aduan@kppk.gov.my; internet www.kppk.gov.my.

Ministry of Rural and Regional Development (Kementerian Kemajuan Luar Bandar dan Wilayah): Aras 4–9, Blok D9, Parcel D, Pusat Pentadbiran Kerajaan Persekutuan, 62606 Putrajaya; tel. (3) 88863500; fax (3) 88892104; e-mail sitisarah@rurallink.gov.my; internet www.rurallink.gov.my.

Ministry of Science, Technology and Innovation: Aras 1–7, Blok C4–5, Parcel C, Pusat Pentadbiran Kerajaan Persekutuan,

MALAYSIA

62662 Putrajaya; tel. (3) 88858000; fax (3) 88889070; e-mail info@mosti.gov.my; internet www.mosti.gov.my.

Ministry of Tourism (Kementerian Pelancongan): Tingkat 17, Menara Dato' Onn, Pusat Dagangan Dunia Putra, 45 Jalan Tun Ismail, 50695 Kuala Lumpur; tel. (3) 26937111; fax (3) 26941146; e-mail info@motour.gov.my; internet www.motour.gov.my.

Ministry of Transport (Kementerian Pengangkutan): Aras 4–7, Blok D5, Parcel D, Pusat Pentadbiran Kerajaan Persekutuan, 62616 Putrajaya; tel. (3) 88866000; fax (3) 88891569; e-mail woon@mot.gov.my; internet www.mot.gov.my.

Ministry of Women, Family and Community Development (Kementerian Pembangunan Wanita, Keluarga dan Masyarakat): Aras 1–6, Blok E, Kompleks Petabat Kerajaan Bukit Perdana, Jalan Dato' Onn, 50515 Kuala Lumpur; tel. (3) 26930095; fax (3) 26934982; e-mail info@kpwkm.gov.my; internet www.kpwkm.gov.my.

Ministry of Works (Kementerian Kerja Raya): Tingkat 6, Blok B, Kompleks Kerja Raya, Jalan Sultan Salahuddin, 50580 Kuala Lumpur; tel. (3) 27111100; fax (3) 27111590; e-mail pro@kkr.gov.my; internet www.kkr.gov.my.

Ministry of Youth and Sports (Kementerian Belia dan Sukan): Aras 17, Menara KBS, 27 Persiaran Perdana, Presint 4, Pusat Pentadbiran Kerajaan Persekutuan, 62570 Putrajaya; tel. (3) 88713333; fax (3) 88888770; e-mail hanizan@kbs.gov.my; internet www.kbs.gov.my.

Legislature

PARLIAMENT

Dewan Negara
(Senate)

The Senate has 70 members, of whom 26 are elected. Each State Legislative Assembly elects two members. The Supreme Head of State appoints the remaining 44 members, including four from the three Federal Territories.

President: Dato' WONG FOON MENG.

Dewan Rakyat
(House of Representatives)

The House of Representatives has a total of 222 members: 165 from Peninsular Malaysia (including 11 from Kuala Lumpur and one from the Federal Territory of Putrajaya), 31 from Sarawak and 26 from Sabah (including one from the Federal Territory of Labuan).

Speaker: Tan Sri PANDIKAR AMIN MULIA.
Deputy Speakers: Datuk RONALD KIANDEE, Datuk Dr WAN JUNAIDI TUANKU JAAFAR.

General Election, 8 March 2008

Party	Seats
Barisan Nasional (National Front)	140
United Malays National Organization	79
Malaysian Chinese Association	15
Parti Pesaka Bumiputera Bersatu	14
Parti Rakyat Sarawak	6
Sarawak United People's Party	6
Sabah Progressive Democratic Party	4
United Kadazan People's Organization	3
Sarawak Progressive Party	3
Malaysian Indian Congress	3
Parti Bersatu Sabah	3
Parti Gerakan Rakyat Malaysia	2
Parti Bersatu Rakyat Sabah	1
Liberal Democratic Party	1
Parti Keadilan Rakyat	31
Democratic Action Party	28
Parti Islam se Malaysia	23
Total	**222**

The States

JOHOR
(Capital: Johor Bahru)

Sultan: HRH Tuanku IBRAHIM ISMAIL IBNI AL-MARHUM Sultan ISKANDER.
Menteri Besar: Datuk Haji ABDUL GHANI OTHMAN.
State Legislative Assembly: internet www.johor.gov.my; 56 seats: Barisan Nasional 50; Democratic Action Party 4; Parti Islam se Malaysia 2; elected March 2008.

KEDAH
(Capital: Alor Star)

Sultan: HRH Tuanku Haji ABDUL HALIM MU'ADZAM SHAH IBNI AL-MARHUM Sultan BADLISHAH.
Menteri Besar: AZIZAN ABDUL RAZAK.
State Legislative Assembly: internet www.kedah.gov.my; 36 seats: Parti Islam se Malaysia 16; Barisan Nasional 14; Parti Keadilan Rakyat 4; Democratic Action Party 1; Independent 1; elected March 2008.

KELANTAN
(Capital: Kota Bharu)

Sultan: HRH Sultan MUHAMMAD V PETRA.
Menteri Besar: Tuan Guru Haji Nik ABDUL AZIZ BIN Nik MAT.
State Legislative Assembly: internet www.kelantan.gov.my; 45 seats: Parti Islam se Malaysia 38; Barisan Nasional 6; Parti Keadilan Rakyat 1; elected March 2008.

MELAKA (MALACCA)
(Capital: Melaka)

Yang di-Pertua Negeri: Tan Sri KHALIL YAAKOB.
Ketua Menteri: Datuk WIRA MOHAMED ALI RUSTAM.
State Legislative Assembly: internet www.melaka.gov.my; 28 seats: Barisan Nasional 23; Democratic Action Party 5; elected March 2008.

NEGERI SEMBILAN
(Capital: Seremban)

Yang di-Pertuan Besar: Tuanku MUKHRIZ IBNI AL-MARHUM Tuanku MUNAWIR.
Menteri Besar: Datuk MOHAMAD HASAN.
State Legislative Assembly: 36 seats: Barisan Nasional 21; Democratic Action Party 10; Parti Keadilan Rakyat 4; Parti Islam se Malaysia 1; elected March 2008.

PAHANG
(Capital: Kuantan)

Sultan: HRH Haji AHMAD SHAH AL-MUSTA'IN BILLAH IBNI AL-MARHUM Sultan ABU BAKAR RI'AYATUDDIN AL-MU'ADZAM SHAH.
Menteri Besar: Dato' ADNAN BIN YAAKOB.
State Legislative Assembly: Unit Pengurusan Teknologi Maklumat, Pejabat Setiausaha Kerajaan, Negeri Pahang, Tingkat 6, Wisma Sri Pahang, 25503 Kuantan, Pahang Darul Makmur; tel. (9) 5129425; fax (9) 5163490; internet www.pahang.gov.my; 42 seats: Barisan Nasional 37; Democratic Action Party 2; Parti Islam se Malaysia 2; Independent 1; elected March 2008.

PERAK
(Capital: Ipoh)

Note: the federal Government took direct control of the state legislature in May 2009, and the ruling coalition installed its own Speaker in the Perak legislature (see Contemporary Political Affairs).

Sultan: HRH Sultan Tuanku AZLAN MUHIBUDDIN SHAH IBNI AL-MARHUM Sultan YUSUF IZUDDIN GHAFARULLAH SHAH.
Menteri Besar: Datuk ZAMBRY ABDUL KADIR.
State Legislative Assembly: Pejabat Setiausaha Kerajaan Negeri Perak, Bangunan Perak Darul Ridzuan, Bahagian Majlis, Jalan Panglima Bukit Gantang Wahab, 30000 Ipoh; tel. (5) 2531957; fax (5) 2414869; e-mail prosuk@perak.gov.my; internet www.perak.gov.my; 59 seats: Barisan Nasional 28; Democratic Action Party 18; Parti Keadilan Rakyat 7; Parti Islam se Malaysia 6; elected March 2008.

PERLIS
(Capital: Kangar)

Raja: HM Tuanku SYED SIRAJUDDIN IBNI AL-MARHUM SYED PUTRA JAMALULLAIL.
Menteri Besar: Datuk Dr MOHAMMAD ISA SABU.
State Legislative Assembly: e-mail sukpls@perlis.gov.my; internet www.perlis.gov.my/webperlis/welcome.html; 15 seats: Barisan Nasional 14; Parti Islam se Malaysia 1; elected March 2008.

PULAU PINANG (PENANG)
(Capital: George Town)

Yang di-Pertua Negeri: HE Datuk ABDUL RAHMAN Haji ABBAS.
Ketua Menteri: LIM GUAN ENG.
State Legislative Assembly: 40 seats: Democratic Action Party 19; Barisan Nasional 11; Parti Keadilan Rakyat 9; Parti Islam se Malaysia 1; elected March 2008.

MALAYSIA

SABAH
(Capital: Kota Kinabalu)

Yang di-Pertua Negeri: HE Datuk JUHAR MAHIRUDDIN.
Ketua Menteri: Datuk Seri MUSA AMAN.
State Legislative Assembly: Dewan Undangan Negeri Sabah, Aras 4, Bangunan Dewan Undangan Negeri Sabah, Peti Surat 11247, 88813 Kota Kinabalu; tel. (88) 427533; fax (88) 427333; e-mail pejduns@sabah.gov.my; internet www.sabah.gov.my; 60 seats: Barisan Nasional 59; Democratic Action Party 1; elected March 2008.

SARAWAK
(Capital: Kuching)

Yang di-Pertua Negeri: HE Tun Datuk Patinggi Abang Haji MUHAMMED SALAHUDDIN.
Ketua Menteri: Datuk Patinggi Tan Sri Haji ABDUL TAIB BIN MAHMUD.
State Legislative Assembly: Bangunan Dewan Undangan Negeri, Petra Jaya, 93502 Kuching, Sarawak; tel. (82) 441955; fax (82) 440628; e-mail abangof@sarawaknet.gov.my; internet www.dun.sarawak.gov.my; f. 1867; 71 seats: Barisan Nasional 55; Democratic Action Party 12; Parti Keadilan Rakyat 3; Independent 1; elected April 2011.

SELANGOR
(Capital: Shah Alam)

Sultan: Tuanku IDRIS SHARAFUDDIN ALHAJ SHAH.
Menteri Besar: Tan Sri Dato' ABDUL KHALID BIN IBRAHIM.
State Legislative Assembly: internet www.selangor.gov.my; 56 seats: Barisan Nasional 20; Parti Keadilan Rakyat 15; Democratic Action Party 13; Parti Islam se Malaysia 8; elected March 2008.

TERENGGANU
(Capital: Kuala Terengganu)

Yang Di-Pertuan Muda (Regent): Tuanku MUHAMMAD ISMAIL Sultan MIZAN ZAINAL ABIDIN.
Menteri Besar: Datuk AHMAD SAID.
State Legislative Assembly: internet www.terengganu.gov.my; 32 seats: Barisan Nasional 24; Parti Islam se Malaysia 8; elected March 2008.

Election Commission

Suruhanjaya Pilihan Raya (SPR): Aras 4–5, Blok C7, Parcel C, Pusat Pentadbiran Kerajaan Persekutuan, 62690 Putrajaya; tel. (3) 88856500; fax (3) 88889117; e-mail spr@spr.gov.my; internet www.spr.gov.my; f. 1957; Chair. Tan Sri Dato' Seri ABD AL-AZIZ BIN MUHAMMAD YUSOF.

Political Organizations

Barisan Nasional (BN) (National Front): Suites 1–2, Tingkat 8, Menara Dato' Onn, Pusat Dagangan Dunia Putra, Jalan Tun Ismail, 50480 Kuala Lumpur; tel. (3) 26920384; fax (3) 26934743; e-mail info@bn.org.my; f. 1973; the governing multiracial coalition of 14 parties; Chair. Dato' Sri MOHD NAJIB BIN Tun Haji ABDUL RAZAK; Sec.-Gen. Datuk Sri Tengku ADNAN Tengku MANSOR; comprises:

Liberal Democratic Party: Tingkat 1, Unit 33, Karamunsing Warehouse, POB 16033, 88868 Kota Kinabalu, Sabah; tel. (88) 218587; fax (88) 240598; e-mail ldpkk@tm.net.my; internet ldp.org.my; f. 1989; Chinese-dominated; Pres. Datuk LIEW VUI KEONG; Sec.-Gen. TEO CHEE KANG.

Malaysian Chinese Association (MCA): Wisma MCA, Tingkat 8, 163 Jalan Ampang, POB 10626, 50450 Kuala Lumpur; tel. (3) 21618044; fax (3) 21619772; e-mail info@mca.org.my; internet www.mca.org.my; f. 1949; 900,000 mems; Pres. Datuk Seri Dr CHUA SOI LEK; Sec.-Gen. Dato' Seri KONG CHO HA.

Malaysian Indian Congress (MIC): Menara Manickavasagam, 6th Floor, 1 Jalan Rahmat, 50350 Kuala Lumpur; tel. (3) 40424377; fax (3) 40427236; e-mail michq@mic.org.my; internet www.mic.org.my; f. 1946; 401,000 mems (1992); Pres. Datuk G. PALANIVEL; Sec.-Gen. Dr S. MURUGESAN.

Parti Bersatu Rakyat Sabah (PBRS) (United Sabah People's Party): POB 20148, Luyang, Kota Kinabalu, 88761 Sabah; tel. and fax (88) 269282; f. 1994; breakaway faction of the PBS; mostly Christian Kadazans; Leader Datuk JOSEPH KURUP.

Parti Bersatu Sabah (PBS) (Sabah United Party): Blok M, Lot 4, Tingkat 2–3, Donggongon New Township, 89500 Penampang,

Directory

Sabah; tel. (88) 702111; fax (88) 718067; e-mail pbshq@pbs-sabah.org; internet www.pbs-sabah.org; f. 1985; left the BN in 1990; rejoined in Jan. 2002; multiracial party; Pres. Datuk Seri JOSEPH PAIRIN KITINGAN; Sec.-Gen. HENRYNUS AMIN.

Parti Gerakan Rakyat Malaysia (GERAKAN) (Malaysian People's Movement): Tingkat 5, Menara PGRM, 8 Jalan Pudu Ulu, Cheras, 56100 Kuala Lumpur; tel. (3) 92876868; fax (3) 92878866; e-mail gerakan@gerakan.org.my; internet www.gerakan.org.my; f. 1968; 300,000 mems; Pres. Tan Sri KOH TSU KOON; Sec.-Gen. TENG CHANG YEOW.

Parti Pesaka Bumiputera Bersatu (PBB) (United Traditional Bumiputra Party): Lot 401, Jalan Bako, POB 1053, 93722 Kuching, Sarawak; tel. (82) 448299; fax (82) 448294; e-mail pbb1@bumiputerasarawak.org.my; internet www.bumiputerasarawak.org.my; f. 1983; Pres. Tan Sri Datuk Patinggi Amar Haji ABDUL TAIB MAHMUD; Dep. Pres. Datuk ALFRED JABU AK NUMPANG.

Parti Progresif Penduduk Malaysia (PPP) (People's Progressive Party): 74 Jalan Rotan, Kampung Attap, 50460 Kuala Lumpur; tel. (3) 22738199; fax (3) 22736199; e-mail ppporg@ppp.org.my; internet www.ppp.org.my; f. 1953; est. as Perak Progressive Party; joined the BN in 1972; Pres. Datuk M. KAYVEAS.

Parti Rakyat Sarawak (PRS) (Sarawak People's Party): Sarawak; f. 2003; reported to be considering merger with the SPDP; Pres. Datuk Sri Dr JAMES MASING; Sec.-Gen. Datuk WILFRED NISSOM.

Sabah Progressive Party (SAPP) (Parti Maju Sabah): Lot 23, 2nd Floor, Bornion Centre, 88300 Kota Kinabalu, Sabah; tel. (88) 242107; fax (88) 249188; e-mail sappkk@streamyx.com; internet www.sapp.org.my; f. 1994; non-racial; Pres. Datuk YONG TECK LEE; Sec.-Gen. Datuk RICHARD YONG WE KONG.

Sarawak Progressive Democratic Party (SPDP): Lot 4319–4320, Jalan Stapok, Sungai Maong, 93250 Kuching, Sarawak; tel. (82) 311180; fax (82) 311190; f. 2003; est. by breakaway faction of Sarawak Nat. Party; reported to be considering merger with the PRS; Pres. Datuk WILLIAM MAWAN ANAK IKOM; Sec.-Gen. NELSON BALANG RINING.

Sarawak United People's Party (SUPP): 7 Jalan Tan Sri Ong Kee Hui, POB 454, 93710 Kuching, Sarawak; tel. (82) 246999; fax (82) 256510; e-mail supphq@gmail.com; internet www.supp.org.my; f. 1959; Sarawak Chinese minority party; Pres. Tan Sri Dr CHEN KANG NAM; Sec.-Gen. SHEN YOSHITERU.

United Kadazan People's Organization (UPKO) (United Pasokmomogun Kadazandusun Murut Organization): Penampang Lot 9 & 10, New World Commercial Centre, Tingkat 2–3, Peti Surat 420, 89507 Penampang, Sabah; tel. (88) 718182; fax (88) 718180; e-mail upkohq@gmail.com; internet www.upko.org.my; f. 1994; est. as Parti Demokratik Sabah (PDS—Sabah Democratic Party) after collapse of PBS Govt by fmr PBS leaders; represents mostly Kadazandusun, Rungus and Murut communities; Pres. Tan Sri BERNARD GILUK DOMPOK; Sec.-Gen. Datuk WILFRED M. TANGAU.

United Malays National Organization (Pertubuhan Kebangsaan Melayu Bersatu—UMNO Baru) (New UMNO): Menara Dato' Onn, 38th Floor, Jalan Tun Ismail, 50480 Kuala Lumpur; tel. (3) 40429511; fax (3) 40412358; e-mail email@umno.net.my; internet www.umno-online.com; f. 1988; replaced the original UMNO (f. 1946), which had been declared an illegal org., owing to the participation of unregistered brs in party elections in April 1987; Supreme Council of 45 mems; 2.5m. mems; Pres. Dato' Sri MOHD NAJIB BIN Tun Haji ABDUL RAZAK; Sec.-Gen. Datuk Seri Tengku ADNAN Tengku MANSOR.

Barisan Alternatif (Alternative Front): Kuala Lumpur; f. 1999; est. to contest 1999 general election; opposition electoral alliance originally comprising the PAS, the DAP, the PKN and the PRM; the DAP left in 2001; the PKN and the PRM merged in 2003 to form the PKR.

Barisan Jama'ah Islamiah Sa-Malaysia (Berjasa) (Pan-Malaysian Islamic Front): Kelantan; f. 1977; pro-Islamic; 50,000 mems; Pres. Dato' Haji WAN HASHIM BIN Haji WAN ACHMED; Sec.-Gen. MAHMUD ZUHDI BIN Haji ABDUL MAJID.

Bersatu Rakyat Jelata Sabah (Berjaya) (Sabah People's Union): Natikar Bldg, 1st Floor, POB 2130, Kota Kinabalu, Sabah; f. 1975; 400,000 mems; Pres. Haji MOHAMMED NOOR MANSOOR.

Democratic Action Party (DAP): 24 Jalan 20/9, 46300 Petaling Jaya, Selangor; tel. (3) 79578022; fax (3) 79575718; e-mail dap@dapmalaysia.org; internet www.dapmalaysia.org; f. 1966; main opposition party; advocates multiracial society based on democratic socialism; 12,000 mems; Chair. KARPAL SINGH; Sec.-Gen. LIM GUAN ENG.

Human Rights Party (HRP): 6 Jalan Abdullah, off Jalan Bangsar, 59000 Kuala Lumpur; tel. (3) 22825241; fax (3) 22825245; e-mail info@humanrightspartymalaysia.com; internet www.humanrightspartymalaysia.com; f. 2009; Sec.-Gen. P. UTHAYAKUMAR.

MALAYSIA

Kongres Indian Muslim Malaysia (KIMMA): Kuala Lumpur; tel. (3) 2324759; f. 1977; aims to unite Malaysian Indian Muslims politically; 25,000 mems; Pres. SAMMY VELLU; Sec.-Gen. MOHAMMED ALI BIN Haji NAINA MOHAMMED.

Malaysia Makkal Sakti Party (MMSP): Shah Alam, Selangor; f. 2009; est. by fmr mems of the Hindu Rights Action Force; represents ethnic Indians in Malaysia; Founder R. S. THANENTHIRAN; Pres. KANNAN RAMASAMY.

Pakatan Rakyat (People's Alliance): f. 2008; est. following the legislative election; opposition alliance of the PKR, the DAP and PAS.

Parti Hisbul Muslimin Malaysia (Hamim) (Islamic Front of Malaysia): Kota Bharu, Kelantan; f. 1983; est. as an alternative party to PAS; Pres. Datuk ASRI MUDA.

Parti Ikatan Masyarakat Islam (Islamic Alliance Party): Terengganu.

Parti Islam se Malaysia (PAS) (Islamic Party of Malaysia): 318A Jalan Raja Laut, 50350 Kuala Lumpur; tel. (3) 26925000; fax (3) 26938399; e-mail editor@parti-pas.org; internet www.pas.org.my; f. 1951; seeks to establish an Islamic state; 700,000 mems; Pres. Dato' Seri ABDUL HADI AWANG; Sec.-Gen. Dato' Haji MUSTAFA ALI.

Parti Keadilan Rakyat (PKR) (People's Justice Party): A1-09, 1 Merchant Sq., 1 Jalan Tropicana Selatan, 47410 Petaling Jaya; tel. (3) 78850530; fax (3) 78850531; e-mail contact@partikeadilanrakyat .org; internet www.keadilanrakyat.org; f. 2003; est. following merger of Parti Keadilan Nasional and Parti Rakyat Malaysia; comprises supporters of Anwar Ibrahim; Pres. Datin Seri Dr WAN AZIZAH WAN ISMAIL; Sec.-Gen. SAIFUDDIN NASUTION ISMAIL.

Parti Kesejahteraan Insan Tanah Air (KITA) (Malaysian People's Welfare Party): B-2-19, Merchant Sq., Jalan Tropicana Selatan 1, PJU 3, 47410 Petaling Jaya, Selangor; tel. (3) 78850023; fax (3) 78850027; e-mail info@partikita.com; internet www.partikita.com; f. 1995; fmrly Angkatan Keadilan Insan Malaysia (AKIM); relaunched as above in 2010; Pres. Datuk ZAID IBRAHIM.

Persatuan Rakyat Malaysia Sarawak (PERMAS) (Malaysian Sarawak Party): Kuching, Sarawak; f. 1987; est. by fmr mems of PBB; Leader Haji BUJANG ULIS.

Sabah Chinese Consolidated Party (SCCP): POB 704, Kota Kinabalu, Sabah; f. 1964; 14,000 mems; Pres. JOHNNY SOON; Sec.-Gen. CHAN TET ON.

Sabah Chinese Party (PCS): Kota Kinabalu, Sabah; f. 1986; Pres. FRANCIS LEONG.

Sarawak National Party (SNAP): 304–305 Bangunan Mei Jun, 1 Jalan Rubber, POB 2960, 93758 Kuching, Sarawak; tel. (82) 254244; fax (82) 253562; internet sarawak-national-party.blogspot.com; f. 1961; deregistered Nov. 2002, but deregistration deferred indefinitely in April 2003 following appeal; Pres. EDWIN DUNDANG BUGAK; Sec.-Gen. STANLEY JUGOL.

Setia (Sabah People's United Democratic Party): Sabah; f. 1994.

Diplomatic Representation

EMBASSIES AND HIGH COMMISSIONS IN MALAYSIA

Afghanistan: 2nd Floor, Wisma Chinese Chamber, 258 Jalan Ampang, 50450 Kuala Lumpur; tel. (3) 42569400; fax (3) 42566400; e-mail consular@afghanembassykl.org; internet www .afghanembassykl.org; Ambassador MOHAMMAD YUNOS FARMAN.

Albania: UBN Tower 10, 31st Floor, Jalan P. Ramlee, 50250 Kuala Lumpur; tel. (3) 20788690; fax (3) 20702285; e-mail embassy .kualalumpur@mfa.gov.al; Chargé d'affaires a.i. DILAVER QESJA.

Algeria: 5 Jalan Mesra, off Jalan Damai, 55000 Kuala Lumpur; tel. (3) 21488159; fax (3) 21488154; e-mail dz@algerianembassy.org.my; internet www.algerianembassy.org.my; Ambassador ABDELMALEK BOUHEDDOU.

Argentina: Suite 16-03, 16th Floor, Menara Keck Seng, 203 Jalan Bukit Bintang, 55100 Kuala Lumpur; tel. (3) 21441451; fax (3) 21441428; e-mail emsia@pd.jaring.my; Ambassador MARÍA ISABEL RENDON.

Australia: 6 Jalan Yap Kwan Seng, 50450 Kuala Lumpur; tel. (3) 21465555; fax (3) 21415773; e-mail public-affairs-klpr@dfat.gov.au; internet www.australia.org.my; High Commissioner MILES KUPA.

Austria: Suite 10.01–02, Tingkat 10, Wisma Goldhill 67, Jalan Raja Chulan, 50200 Kuala Lumpur; tel. (3) 20570020; fax (3) 23817168; e-mail kuala-lumpur-ob@bmeia.gv.at; internet www.bmeia.gv.at/ kualalumpur; Ambassador ANDREA WICKE.

Azerbaijan: 2nd Floor, Wisma Chinese Chamber, 258 Jalan Ampang, 50450 Kuala Lumpur; tel. (3) 42526800; fax (3) 42571800; e-mail kualalumpur@mission.mfa.gov.az; internet www .azembassy.com.my; Ambassador TAHIR KARIMOV.

Bangladesh: Blok 1, Lorong Damai 7, Jalan Damai, 55000 Kuala Lumpur; tel. (3) 21487940; fax (3) 21413381; e-mail bddoot@ streamyx.com; internet www.bangladesh-highcomkl.com; High Commissioner ATIQUR RAHMAN.

Belgium: Suite 10-02, 10th Floor, Menara Tan & Tan, 207 Jalan Tun Razak, 50400 Kuala Lumpur; tel. (3) 21620025; fax (3) 21620023; e-mail kualalumpur@diplobel.fed.be; internet www.diplomatie.be/ kualalumpur; Ambassador MARC MULLIE.

Bosnia and Herzegovina: JKR 854, Jalan Bellamy, 50460 Kuala Lumpur; tel. (3) 21440353; fax (3) 21426025; e-mail embbhkl@tm.net .my; Ambassador ENSAR EMINOVIĆ.

Brazil: Suite 20-01, 20th Floor, Menara Tan & Tan, 207 Jalan Tun Razak, 50400 Kuala Lumpur; tel. (3) 21711420; fax (3) 21711427; e-mail embassy@brazilembassy.org.my; internet www .brazilembassy.org.my; Ambassador SÉRGIO DE SOUZA ARRUDA.

Brunei: Suite 19-01, 19th Floor, Menara Tan & Tan, 207 Jalan Tun Razak, 50400 Kuala Lumpur; tel. (3) 21612800; fax (3) 21631302; e-mail bhckl@brucomkul.com.my; High Commissioner Dato' Paduka Haji ISHAAQ BIN Haji ABDULLAH.

Cambodia: 46 Jalan U Thant, 55000 Kuala Lumpur; tel. (3) 42571150; fax (3) 42571157; e-mail reckl@tm.net.my; Ambassador HRH Samdech Preah ANOCH NORODOM ARUNRASMY.

Canada: 17th Floor, Menara Tan & Tan, 207 Jalan Tun Razak, 50400 Kuala Lumpur; tel. (3) 27183333; fax (3) 27183399; e-mail klmpr@international.gc.ca; internet www.canadainternational.gc .ca/malaysia-malaisie; High Commissioner RANDOLPH MANK.

Chile: 8th Floor, West Block, Wisma Selangor Dredging, 142C Jalan Ampang, Peti Surat 27, 50450 Kuala Lumpur; tel. (3) 21616203; fax (3) 21622219; e-mail eochile@embassyofchile.org.my; internet chileabroad.gov.cl/malasia; Ambassador JOSÉ MANUEL OVALLE BRAVO.

China, People's Republic: 229 Jalan Ampang, 50450 Kuala Lumpur; tel. (3) 21428495; fax (3) 21414552; e-mail cn@tm.net.my; internet my.china-embassy.org/eng; Ambassador CHAI XI.

Colombia: UOA Centre, Tingkat 28, 19 Jalan Pinang, 50450 Kuala Lumpur; tel. (3) 21645488; fax (3) 21645487; e-mail ekualalumpur@ cancilleria.gov.co; internet www.ecolombia.com.my; Ambassador SILVIA CASTAÑO DE GONZÁLEZ.

Croatia: 3 Jalan Menkuang, off Jalan Ru Ampang, 55000 Kuala Lumpur; tel. (3) 42535340; fax (3) 42535217; e-mail croemb .kuala-lumpur@mvpei.hr; Ambassador ZELJKO BOSNJAK.

Cuba: No. 18, 2 Jalan Kent, off Jalan Maktab, 54000 Kuala Lumpur; tel. (3) 26911066; fax (3) 26911141; e-mail admin@cubemb.com.my; internet www.cubaemb.com.my; Ambassador CARLOS A. AMORES.

Czech Republic: 32 Jalan Mesra, off Jalan Damai, 55000 Kuala Lumpur; tel. (3) 21427185; fax (3) 21412727; e-mail kualalumpur@ embassy.mzv.cz; internet www.mzv.cz/kualalumpur; Ambassador JAN FŮRY.

Denmark: Wisma Denmark, 22nd Floor, 86 Jalan Ampang, 50450 Kuala Lumpur; tel. (3) 20322001; fax (3) 20322012; e-mail kulamb@ um.dk; internet www.ambkualalumpur.um.dk; Ambassador SVEND WAEVER.

Ecuador: 10th Floor, West Block, Wisma Selangor Dredging, 142C Jalan Ampang, 50450 Kuala Lumpur; tel. (3) 21635078; fax (3) 21635096; e-mail embecua@po.jaring.my; Ambassador LOURDES PUMA PUMA.

Egypt: 12 Jalan Rhu, off Jalan Ampang, 55000 Kuala Lumpur; tel. (3) 42568184; fax (3) 42573515; e-mail egyembkl@tm.net.my; Ambassador MOHAMED SAAD IBRAHIM EBEID.

Fiji: Menara Chan, Tingkat 2, 138 Jalan Ampang, 50450 Kuala Lumpur; tel. (3) 27323335; fax (3) 27327555; e-mail fhckl@pd.jaring .my; internet www.fijibulamaleya.org.my; High Commissioner SULIASI LUTUBULA.

Finland: Wisma Chinese Chamber, 5th Floor, 258 Jalan Ampang, 50450 Kuala Lumpur; tel. (3) 42577746; fax (3) 42577793; e-mail sanomat.kul@formin.fi; internet www.finland.org.my; Ambassador TAPIO SAARELA.

France: 192–196 Jalan Ampang, 50450 Kuala Lumpur; tel. (3) 20535500; fax (3) 20535501; e-mail ambassade.kuala -lumpur-amba@diplomatie.gouv.fr; internet www.ambafrance -my.org; Ambassador MARC BARÉTY.

Germany: 26th Floor, Menara Tan & Tan, 207 Jalan Tun Razak, 50400 Kuala Lumpur; tel. (3) 21709666; fax (3) 21619800; e-mail info@kuala-lumpur.diplo.de; internet www.kuala-lumpur.diplo.de; Ambassador GÜNTER GRUBER.

Ghana: 14 Ampang Hilir, off Jalan Ampang, 55000 Kuala Lumpur; tel. (3) 42526995; fax (3) 42578698; e-mail ghcomkl@tm.net.my; High Commissioner DAN K. ABODAKPI.

Guinea: 5 Jalan Kedondong, off Jalan Ampang Hilir, 55000 Kuala Lumpur; tel. (3) 42576500; fax (3) 42511500; e-mail mwcnakry@ sotelgui.net.gn; Ambassador MOHAMED SAMPIL.

MALAYSIA

Hungary: Menara Tan & Tan, 10th Floor, Suite 10-04, Jalan Tun Razak, 50400 Kuala Lumpur; tel. (3) 21637914; fax (3) 21637918; e-mail mission.kul@kum.hu; Ambassador TAMÁS TÓTH.

India: 2 Jalan Taman Duta, off Jalan Duta, 50480 Kuala Lumpur; tel. (3) 20933510; fax (3) 20933507; e-mail cons@indianhighcommission.com.my; internet www.indianhighcommission.com.my; High Commissioner VIJAY K. GOKHALE.

Indonesia: 233 Jalan Tun Razak, POB 10889, 50400 Kuala Lumpur; tel. (3) 21164000; fax (3) 21423878; e-mail info@kbrikualalumpur.org; internet www.kbrikualalumpur.org; Ambassador DA'I BACHTIAR.

Iran: 1 Lorong U Thant Satu, off Jalan U Thant, 55000 Kuala Lumpur; tel. (3) 42514824; fax (3) 42521563; e-mail ir_emb@tm.net.my; internet www.iranembassy.com.my; Ambassador MOHAMMAD MEHDI ZAHEDI.

Iraq: 2 Jalan Langgak Golf, off Jalan Tun Razak, 55000 Kuala Lumpur; tel. (3) 21480555; fax (3) 21414331; e-mail quaemb@iraqmofamail.net; Ambassador AMAL MUSSA HUSSAIN ALI AL-RUBAYE.

Ireland: Ireland House, The Amp Walk, 218 Jalan Ampang, POB 10372, 50450 Kuala Lumpur; tel. (3) 21612963; fax (3) 21613427; e-mail info@ireland-embassy.com.my; internet www.ireland-embassy.com.my; Ambassador DECLAN KELLY.

Italy: 99 Jalan U Thant, 55000 Kuala Lumpur; tel. (3) 42565122; fax (3) 42573199; e-mail ambasciata.kualalumpur@esteri.it; internet www.ambkualalumpur.esteri.it; Ambassador FOLCO DE LUCA GABRIELLI.

Japan: 11 Pesiaran Stonor, off Jalan Tun Razak, 50450 Kuala Lumpur; tel. (3) 21772600; fax (3) 21672314; internet www.my.emb-japan.go.jp; Ambassador MASAHIKO HORIE.

Jordan: 2 Jalan Kedondong, off Jalan Ampang Hilir, 55000 Kuala Lumpur; tel. (3) 42521268; fax (3) 42528610; e-mail general@jordanembassy.org.my; internet www.jordanembassy.org.my; Ambassador MAHER LUKASHA.

Kazakhstan: 115 Jalan Ampang Hilir, 55000 Kuala Lumpur; tel. (3) 42522999; fax (3) 42523999; e-mail kuala-lumpur@kazembassy.org.my; internet www.kazembassy.org.my; Ambassador BEIBUT ATAMKULOV YERBOLAT NAZARBAYEV.

Kenya: 8 Jalan Taman U Thant, 55000 Kuala Lumpur; tel. (3) 21461163; fax (3) 21451087; e-mail admin@kenyahighcom.org.my; internet www.kenyahighcom.org.my; High Commissioner SAMORI AN'GWA OKWIYA.

Korea, Democratic People's Republic: 4 Jalan Persiaran Madge, off Jalan U Thant, 55000 Kuala Lumpur; tel. (3) 42569913; fax (3) 42569933; e-mail dprkorea@streamyx.com; Ambassador JANG YONG CHOL.

Korea, Republic: Lot 9 and 11, Jalan Nipah, off Jalan Ampang, 55000 Kuala Lumpur; tel. (3) 42512356; fax (3) 42521425; e-mail korem-my@mofat.go.kr; internet mys.mofat.go.kr/eng/index.jsp; Ambassador LEE YONG-JOON.

Kuwait: 229 Jalan Tun Razak, 50400 Kuala Lumpur; tel. (3) 21410033; fax (3) 21456121; e-mail kuwait@streamyx.com; Ambassador MONTHER BADER SULAIMAN AL-EISSA.

Kyrgyzstan: 10th Floor, Wisma Sin Heap Lee, 346 Jalan Tun Razak, 50400 Kuala Lumpur; tel. (3) 21632010; fax (3) 21632024; e-mail embassy@kyrgyzembassy.org.my; internet www.kyrgyzembassy.org.my; Ambassador Dr BAKIR UULU TURSUNBAY.

Laos: 12A Persiaran Madge, off Jalan Ampang Hilir, 55000 Kuala Lumpur; tel. (3) 42511118; e-mail embassylao-kualalumpur@hotmail.com; Ambassador Dr BOUNTHEUANG MOUNLASY.

Lebanon: 56 Jalan Ampang Hilir, 55000 Kuala Lumpur; tel. (3) 42516690; fax (3) 42603426; Ambassador KHALED AL-KILANI.

Libya: 6 Jalan Madge, off Jalan U Thant, 55000 Kuala Lumpur; tel. (3) 21411293; fax (3) 21413549; Ambassador ABUBAKAR ALMABROUK AL-MANSOURI.

Luxembourg: Menara Keck Seng Bldg, 16th Floor, 203 Jalan Bukit Bintang, 55100 Kuala Lumpur; tel. (3) 21433134; fax (3) 21433157; e-mail emluxem@po.jaring.my; Chargé d'affaires CHARLES SCHMIT.

Maldives: Suite 07-01, Menara See Hoy Chan, 374 Jalan Tun Razak, 50400 Kuala Lumpur; tel. (3) 21637244; fax (3) 21647244; e-mail mail@maldives.org.my; internet www.maldives.org.my; High Commissioner MOHAMED ZAKI.

Mauritius: 17th Floor, West Block, Wisma Selangor Dredging, Jalan Ampang, 50450 Kuala Lumpur; tel. (3) 21411870; e-mail maurhckl@streamyx.com; Chargé d'affaires a.i. D. P. GOKULSING.

Mexico: Suite 22-05, 22nd Floor, Menara Tan & Tan, 207 Jalan Tun Razak, 50400 Kuala Lumpur; tel. (3) 21646362; fax (3) 21640964; e-mail embamex@mexico.org.my; internet portal.sre.gob.mx/malasia; Ambassador JORGE ALBERTO LOZOYA LEGORRETA.

Morocco: Unit 9, 3rd Floor, East Block, Wisma Selangor Dredging, 142B Jalan Ampang, 50450 Kuala Lumpur; tel. (3) 21610701; fax (3) 21623081; e-mail moremb@streamyx.com; Ambassador AHMED AMAZIANE.

Myanmar: 8C Jalan Ampang Hilir, 55000 Kuala Lumpur; tel. (3) 42516355; fax (3) 42513855; e-mail mekl@tm.net.my; Ambassador TIN LATT.

Namibia: Suite 15-01, Tingkat 15, Menara HLA, 3 Jalan Kia Peng, 50450 Kuala Lumpur; tel. (3) 21433593; e-mail namhckl@streamyx.com; High Commissioner TJI-TJAI UANIVI.

Nepal: Suite 13A-01, 13th Floor, Wisma MCA, 163 Jalan Ampang, 50450 Kuala Lumpur; tel. (3) 21645934; fax (3) 21648659; e-mail info@nepalembassy.com.my; internet www.nepalembassy.com.my; Ambassador RISHI RAJ ADHIKARI.

Netherlands: The Amp Walk, 7th Floor, South Block, 218 Jalan Ampang, POB 10543, 50450 Kuala Lumpur; tel. (3) 21686200; fax (3) 21686240; e-mail kll@minbuza.nl; internet www.netherlands.org.my; Ambassador PAUL BEKKERS.

New Zealand: Menara IMC, 21st Floor, 8 Jalan Sultan Ismail, 50250 Kuala Lumpur; tel. (3) 20782533; fax (3) 20780387; e-mail nzhckl@streamyx.com; internet www.nzembassy.com/malaysia; High Commissioner DAVID PINE.

Nigeria: 85 Jalan Ampang Hilir, 55000 Kuala Lumpur; tel. (3) 42517843; fax (3) 42524302; e-mail info@nigeria.org.my; internet www.nigeria.org.my; High Commissioner PETER ANEGBEH.

Norway: Suite CD, 53rd Floor, Empire Tower, Jalan Tun Razak, 50400 Kuala Lumpur; tel. (3) 21750300; fax (3) 21750308; e-mail emb.kualalumpur@mfa.no; internet www.norway.org.my; Ambassador ARILD BRAASTAD.

Oman: 109 Jalan U Thant, 55000 Kuala Lumpur; tel. (3) 42577378; fax (3) 42571400; e-mail omanemb@po.jaring.my; Ambassador AFLAH BIN SULEIMAN AL-TAEI.

Pakistan: 132 Jalan Ampang, 50450 Kuala Lumpur; tel. (3) 21618877; fax (3) 21645958; e-mail pahickl@gmail.com; internet www.pahickl.com; High Commissioner MASOOD KHALID.

Papua New Guinea: 11 Lingkungan U Thant, off Jalan U Thant, 55000 Kuala Lumpur; tel. (3) 42575405; fax (3) 42576203; High Commissioner VEALI VAGI.

Peru: Wisma Selangor Dredging, 6th Floor, South Block, 142A Jalan Ampang, 50450 Kuala Lumpur; tel. (3) 21633034; fax (3) 21633039; e-mail embperu@streamyx.com; Ambassador WILLIAM BELEVAN MCBRIDE.

Philippines: 1 Changkat Kia Peng, 50450 Kuala Lumpur; tel. (3) 21484233; fax (3) 21483576; e-mail consular@philembassykl.org.my; internet www.philembassykl.org.my; Ambassador VICTORIANO M. LECAROS.

Poland: POB 10052, 50704 Kuala Lumpur; tel. (3) 21610780; fax (3) 21649924; e-mail kualalumpur.amb.sekretariat@msz.gov.pl; internet www.kualalumpur.polemb.net; Ambassador ADAM JELONEK.

Qatar: 113 Jalan Ampang Hilir, POB 13118, 55000 Kuala Lumpur; tel. (3) 42565552; fax (3) 42565553; e-mail qekl113@streamyx.com; Chargé d'affaires a.i. RASHID MAIRZA AL-MULLA.

Romania: 114 Jalan Damai, off Jalan Ampang, 55000 Kuala Lumpur; tel. (3) 21423172; fax (3) 21448713; e-mail roemb@streamyx.com; internet kualalumpur.mae.ro; Ambassador PETRU PETRA.

Russia: 263 Jalan Ampang, 50450 Kuala Lumpur; tel. (3) 42567252; fax (3) 42576091; e-mail rusembmalaysia@yandex.ru; internet www.malaysia.mid.ru; Ambassador LYUDMILA GEORGIEVNA VOROBYEVA.

Saudi Arabia: Wisma Chinese Chamber, Tingkat 4, 258 Jalan Ampang, 50450 Kuala Lumpur; tel. (3) 42579433; fax (3) 42578751; e-mail saembssy@tm.net.my; Ambassador MOHAMMED REDA HUSSEIN ABU AL-HAMAYEL.

Senegal: 9 Lorong U Thant, off Jalan U Thant, 55000 Kuala Lumpur; tel. (3) 42567343; fax (3) 42563205; e-mail senamb_mal@yahoo.fr; Ambassador BABACAR DIOP.

Singapore: 209 Jalan Tun Razak, 50400 Kuala Lumpur; tel. (3) 21616277; fax (3) 21616343; e-mail singhc_kul@sgmfa.gov.sg; internet www.mfa.gov.sg/kl; High Commissioner T. JASUDASEN.

Slovakia: 11 Jalan U Thant, 55000 Kuala Lumpur; tel. (3) 21150016; fax (3) 21150018; e-mail emb.kualalumpur@mzv.sk; internet www.mzv.sk/kualalumpur; Ambassador MILAN LAJČIAK.

South Africa: Menara HLA, Suite 22-01, 3 Jalan Kia Peng, 50450 Kuala Lumpur; tel. (3) 21702400; fax (3) 21688591; e-mail sahcadm@streamyx.com; High Commissioner THAMSANQA DENNIS MSELEKU.

Spain: 200 Jalan Ampang, 50450 Kuala Lumpur; tel. (3) 21484868; fax (3) 21424582; e-mail emb.kualalumpur@maec.es; internet www.maec.es/embajadas/kualalumpur; Ambassador JOSÉ RAMÓN BARAÑANO FERNÁNDEZ.

Sri Lanka: 12 Jalan Keranji Dua, off Jalan Kedondong, Ampang Hilir, 55000 Kuala Lumpur; tel. (3) 42568987; fax (3) 42532497;

MALAYSIA

e-mail slhicom@streamyx.com; internet www.slhc.com.my; High Commissioner D. D. RANASINGHE.

Sudan: 2A Persiaran Ampang, off Jalan Ru, 55000 Kuala Lumpur; tel. (3) 42569104; fax (3) 42568107; e-mail assalam12@hotmail.com; Ambassador ABDEL RAHMAN HAMZAH ELRAYA.

Swaziland: Suite 22-03 & 22-03A, Menara Citibank, 165 Jalan Ampang, 50450 Kuala Lumpur; tel. (3) 21632511; fax (3) 21633326; e-mail swdkl_2@streamyx.com; High Commissioner MPUMELELO J. N. HLOPE.

Switzerland: 16 Persiaran Madge, 55000 Kuala Lumpur; tel. (3) 21480622; fax (3) 21480935; e-mail kua.vertretung@eda.admin.ch; internet www.eda.admin.ch/kualalumpur; Ambassador Dr ROLF LENZ.

Syria: 93 Jalan U Thant, 55000 Kuala Lumpur; tel. (3) 42516349; fax (3) 42516363; e-mail enquiry@syrianembassy.com.my; internet www.syrianembassy.com.my; Ambassador (vacant).

Thailand: 206 Jalan Ampang, 50450 Kuala Lumpur; tel. (3) 21488222; fax (3) 21486527; e-mail thaikula@mfa.go.th; internet www.mfa.go.th/web/1830.php?depcode=23000100; Ambassador THANA DUANGRATANA.

Timor-Leste: 62 Jalan Ampang Hilir, 55000 Kuala Lumpur; tel. (3) 42562046; fax (3) 42562016; e-mail embaixada_tl_kl@yahoo.com; Ambassador JUVÉNCIO DE JESUS MARTINS.

Turkey: 118 Jalan U Thant, 55000 Kuala Lumpur; tel. (3) 42572225; fax (3) 42572227; e-mail embassy.kualalumpur@mfa.gov.tr; internet www.kualalumpur.be.mfa.gov.tr; Ambassador SERAP ATAAY.

Ukraine: Suite 22-02, 22nd Floor, Menara Tan & Tan, 207 Jalan Tun Razak, 50400 Kuala Lumpur; tel. (3) 21669552; fax (3) 21664371; e-mail emb_my@mfa.gov.ua; internet www.mfa.gov.ua/malaysia; Ambassador IHOR V. HUMENNYI.

United Arab Emirates: 1 Gerbang Ampang Hilir, off Persiaran Ampang Hilir, 55000 Kuala Lumpur; tel. (3) 42535221; fax (3) 42535220; e-mail uaemal@tm.net.my; Ambassador MUHAMMAD REDA HUSSEIN ABU AL-HAMAYEL.

United Kingdom: 185 Jalan Ampang, 50450 Kuala Lumpur; tel. (3) 21702200; fax (3) 21702370; e-mail political.kualalumpur@fco.gov.uk; internet ukinmalaysia.fco.gov.uk; High Commissioner SIMON FEATHERSTONE.

USA: 376 Jalan Tun Razak, POB 10035, 50400 Kuala Lumpur; tel. (3) 21685000; fax (3) 21485801; e-mail klconsular@state.gov; internet malaysia.usembassy.gov; Ambassador PAUL W. JONES.

Uruguay: 6th Floor, UBN Tower, 10 Jalan P. Ramlee, 50250 Kuala Lumpur; tel. (3) 20313669; fax (3) 20315669; e-mail urukuala@streamyx.com; Ambassador PABLO SADER.

Uzbekistan: Wisma Chinese Chamber, 2nd Floor, 258 Jalan Ampang, 50450 Kuala Lumpur; tel. (3) 42532406; fax (3) 42535406; e-mail uzbekemb@streamyx.com; internet www.malaysia.mfa.uz; Ambassador SHUKUR SABITOV.

Venezuela: Suite 20-05, 20th Floor, Menara Tan & Tan, 207 Jalan Tun Razak, 50400 Kuala Lumpur; tel. (3) 21633444; fax (3) 21636819; e-mail info@venezuela.org.my; internet www.venezuela.org.my; Ambassador MANUEL ANTONIO GUZMÁN HERNÁNDEZ.

Viet Nam: 4 Jalan Persiaran Stonor, 50450 Kuala Lumpur; tel. (3) 21484036; fax (3) 21483270; e-mail daisevn@putra.net.my; internet www.mofa.gov.vn/vnemb.my; Ambassador HOANG TRONG LAP.

Yemen: 7 Jalan Kedondong, off Jalan Ampang Hilir, 55000 Kuala Lumpur; tel. (3) 42511793; fax (3) 42511794; e-mail secretary@yemenembassykl.com; internet yemenembassykl.com; Ambassador Dr ABDULLA MOHAMED ALI AL-MONTSER.

Zimbabwe: 124 Jalan Sembilan, Taman Ampang Utama, 68000 Ampang, Selangor Darul Ehsan; tel. (3) 42516779; fax (3) 42517252; e-mail zhck@tm.net.my; Ambassador LUCAS PANDE TAVAYA.

Judicial System

The two High Courts, one in Peninsular Malaysia and the other in Sabah and Sarawak, have original, appellate and revisional jurisdiction as the federal law provides. Above these two High Courts is the Court of Appeal, which was established in 1994 as an intermediary court between the Federal Court (formerly the Supreme Court) and the High Court. When appeals to the Privy Council in the United Kingdom were abolished in 1985 the former Supreme Court became the final court of appeal. Therefore, at that stage only one appeal was available to a party aggrieved by the decision of the High Court; hence, the establishment of the Court of Appeal. The Federal Court has, to the exclusion of any other court, jurisdiction in any dispute between states or between the Federation and any state; it also has special jurisdiction as to the interpretation of the Constitution. The Federal Court is headed by the Chief Justice (formerly the Lord President); the other members of the Federal Court are the President of the Court of Appeal, the two Chief Judges of the High Courts and the Federal Court Judges. Members of the Court of Appeal are the President and the Court of Appeal judges, and members of the High Courts are the two Chief Judges and their respective High Court judges. All judges are appointed by the Yang di-Pertuan Agong on the advice of the Prime Minister, after consulting the Conference of Rulers. In 1993 a Special Court was established to hear cases brought by or against the Yang di-Pertuan Agong or a Ruler of State (Sultans).

The Sessions Courts, which are situated in the principal urban and rural centres, are presided over by a Sessions Judge, who is a member of the Judicial and Legal Service of the Federation and is a qualified barrister or a Bachelor of Law from any of the recognized universities. The criminal jurisdiction of the Sessions Courts covers the less serious indictable offences, excluding those that carry the death penalty. Civil jurisdiction of a Sessions Court is up to RM 250,000. The Sessions Judges are appointed by the Yang di-Pertuan Agong.

The Magistrates' Courts are also found in the main urban and rural centres and have both civil and criminal jurisdiction, although of a more restricted nature than that of the Sessions Courts. The Magistrates consist of officers from the Judicial and Legal Service of the Federation. They are appointed by the State Authority in which they officiate on the recommendation of the Chief Judge.

There are also Syariah (*Shari'a*) courts for rulings under Islamic law. In July 1996 the Cabinet announced that the Syariah courts were to be restructured with the appointment of a Syariah Chief Judge and four Court of Appeal justices, whose rulings would set precedents for the whole country.

Prior to February 1995 trials in the High Courts for murder and kidnapping were heard with jury and assessors, respectively. The amendment to the Criminal Procedure Code abolished both the jury and the assessors systems, and all criminal trials in the High Courts are now heard by a judge sitting alone. In 1988 an amendment to the Constitution empowered any federal lawyer to confer with the Attorney-General to determine the courts in which any proceedings, excluding those before a Syariah court, a native court or a court martial, be instituted, or to which such proceedings be transferred.

Chief Justice of the Federal Court: Tan Sri Dato' ZAKI BIN TUN AZMI, Palace of Justice, Presint 3, 62506 Putrajaya; tel. (3) 88803500; fax (3) 88803507; e-mail cj@kehakiman.gov.my; internet www.kehakiman.gov.my.

President of the Court of Appeal: Tan Sri Dato' ALAUDDIN BIN MOHD SHERIFF; tel. (3) 88803566; fax (3) 88803596; e-mail alauddin@kehakiman.gov.my.

Chief Judge of the High Court in Peninsular Malaysia: Tan Sri ARIFIN BIN ZAKARIA; tel. (3) 88803552; fax (3) 88803556; e-mail cjm@kehakiman.gov.my.

Chief Judge of the High Court in Sabah and Sarawak: Tan Sri Datuk Seri RICHARD MALANJUM, High Court, Jalan Gersik, 93050 Sarawak.

Attorney-General: Tan Sri ABDUL GANI PATAIL.

Religion

Islam is the established religion. While freedom of religious practice is enshrined in the Constitution, Malaysia's parallel Islamic judicial system holds great sway over the Muslim majority on religious issues. In May 2005 21 members of the controversial sect known as 'Sky Kingdom' were arrested for propagating 'devious' teachings said to humiliate Islam. Almost all ethnic Malays are Muslims, representing 60.4% of the total population in 2000. In that year 19.2% of the population followed Buddhism, 9.1% Christianity and 6.3% Hinduism.

Malaysian Consultative Council of Buddhism, Christianity, Hinduism, Sikhism and Taoism (MCCBCHST): 8 Jalan Duku, off Jalan Kasipillai, 51200 Kuala Lumpur; tel. (3) 40414669; fax (3) 40444304; f. 1981; a non-Muslim group.

ISLAM

President of the Majlis Islam: Datuk Haji MOHD FAUZI BIN Haji ABDUL HAMID (Kuching, Sarawak).

Istitut Kefahaman Islam Malaysia (IKIM) (Institute of Islamic Understanding Malaysia): 2 Langgak Tunku, off Jalan Duta, 50480 Kuala Lumpur; tel. (3) 62010889; fax (3) 62014189; internet www.ikim.gov.my.

Jabatan Kemajuan Islam Malaysia (JAKIM) (Department of Islamic Development Malaysia): Aras 4–9, Blok D7, Pusat Pentadbiran Kerajaan Persekutuan, 62519 Putrajaya; tel. (3) 88864000; e-mail faizal@islam.gov.my; internet www.islam.gov.my.

BUDDHISM

Malaysian Buddhist Association (MBA): MBA Bldg, 182 Jalan Burmah, 10050 Pinang; tel. (4) 2262690; fax (4) 2263024; e-mail mba

MALAYSIA

Directory

.hq@streamyx.com; internet www.malaysianbuddhistassociation.org; f. 1959; the national body for Chinese and English-speaking monks and nuns and temples from the Mahayana, Theravada and Vajrayana tradition; 13 state brs and 33 other brs nation-wide; 30,000 mems; Pres. Ven. SECK JIT HENG.

Buddhist Missionary Society Malaysia (BMSM): 123 Jalan Berhala, off Jalan Tun Sambanthan, 50470 Kuala Lumpur; tel. (3) 22730150; fax (3) 22740245; e-mail president@bmsm.org.my; internet www.bmsm.org.my; f. 1962 as Buddhist Missionary Society; Pres. ANG CHOO HONG.

Buddhist Tzu-Chi Merit Society (Malaysia): 316 Jalan Macalister, 10450 Pulau Pinang; tel. (4) 2281013; fax (2) 2261013; e-mail info@tzuchi.org.my; internet www.tzuchi.org.my.

Malaysian Fo Kuang Buddhist Association: 2 Jalan SS3/33, Taman University, 47300 Petaling Jaya, Selangor; tel. (3) 78776512; fax (3) 78776511; e-mail myfoguang@yahoo.com.

Sasana Abhiwurdhi Wardhana Society: 123 Jalan Berhala, off Jalan Tun Sambanthan, 50490 Kuala Lumpur; f. 1894; the national body for Sri Lankan Buddhists belonging to the Theravada tradition.

Young Buddhist Association of Malaysia (YBAM): 9 Jalan SS25/24, 47301 Petaling Jaya, Selangor; tel. (3) 78049154; fax (3) 78049021; e-mail ybam@streamyx.com; internet www.ybam.org.my; f. 1970; Pres. ONG SEE YEW.

CHRISTIANITY

Majlis Gereja-Gereja Malaysia (Council of Churches of Malaysia): 10 Jalan 11/9, 46200 Petaling Jaya, Selangor; tel. (3) 75967092; fax (3) 79560353; e-mail cchurchm@streamyx.org; internet www.ccmalaysia.org; f. 1947; 18 mem. churches; 10 assoc. mems; Pres. Rev. Dr THOMAS PHILIPS (Mar Thoma Syrian Church); Gen. Sec. Rev. Dr HERMEN SHASTRI.

The Anglican Communion

Malaysia comprises three Anglican dioceses, within the Church of the Province of South East Asia.

Primate: Most Rev. Dr JOHN CHEW (Bishop of Singapore).

Bishop of Kuching: Rt Rev. BOLLY ANAK LAPOK, The House of the Epiphany, POB 347, 93704 Kuching, Sarawak; tel. (82) 240187; fax (82) 426488; e-mail bishopk@streamyx.com; has jurisdiction over Sarawak, Brunei and part of Indonesian Kalimantan (Borneo).

Bishop of Sabah: Most Rev. ALBERT VUN CHEONG FUI, Rumah Bishop, Jalan Tangki, POB 10811, 88809 Kota Kinabalu, Sabah; tel. (88) 247008; fax (88) 245942; e-mail dosabah@streamyx.com.

Bishop of West Malaysia: Rt. Rev. NG MOON HING, Bishop's House, 16 Jalan Pudu Lama, 50200 Kuala Lumpur; tel. (3) 20312728; fax (3) 20313213; e-mail anglican@streamyx.com; internet www.anglicanwestmalaysia.org.my.

The Baptist Church

Malaysia Baptist Convention: 2 Jalan Dispensary 2/38, 46000 Petaling Jaya, Selangor; tel. (3) 77823564; fax (3) 77833603; e-mail mbcpj@tm.net.my; internet www.mbc.org.my; Chair. Rev. BERNARD ANG; Gen. Sec. Rev. RONNIE CHIU.

The Methodist Church

Methodist Church in Malaysia: 69 Jalan 5/31, 46000 Petaling Jaya, Selangor; tel. (3) 79541811; fax (3) 79541787; e-mail info@methodistchurch.org.my; internet www.methodistchurch.org.my; f. 1885; 164,400 mems; Bishop Dr HWA YUNG.

The Presbyterian Church

Presbyterian Church in Malaysia: Joyful Grace Church, Jalan Alsagoff, 82000 Pontian, Johor; tel. (7) 711390; fax (7) 324384; e-mail office@gpm.org.my; internet www.gpm.org.m; Moderator Rev. CHUA HUA PENG.

The Roman Catholic Church

Malaysia comprises three archdioceses and six dioceses. At 31 December 2007 approximately 3.0% of the population were adherents.

Catholic Bishops' Conference of Malaysia, Singapore and Brunei

Xavier Hall, 133 Jalan Gasing, 46000 Petaling Jaya, Selangor Darul Ehsan; tel. and fax (3) 79581371; e-mail cbcmsb@pc.jaring.my; Pres. Most Rev. MURPHY NICHOLAS XAVIER PAKIAM (Archbishop of Kuala Lumpur).

Archbishop of Kota Kinabalu: Most Rev. JOHN LEE HIONG FUN-YIT HAW, Archbishop's House, POB 10289, 88803, Kota Kinabalu, Sabah; tel. (88) 712297; fax (88) 711954.

Archbishop of Kuala Lumpur: Most Rev. MURPHY NICHOLAS XAVIER PAKIAM, Archbishop's House, 528 Jalan Bukit Nanas, 50250 Kuala Lumpur; tel. (3) 20788828; fax (3) 20313815; e-mail mpakiam@pd.jaring.my.

Archbishop of Kuching: Most Rev. JOHN HA TIONG HOCK, Archbishop's Office, 118 Jalan Tun Abang Haji Openg, POB 940, 93718 Kuching, Sarawak; tel. (82) 242634; fax (82) 425724; e-mail abcofku@pd.jaring.my.

BAHÁ'Í FAITH

Spiritual Assembly of the Bahá'ís of Malaysia: 4 Lorong Titiwangsa 5, off Jalan Pahang, 53200 Kuala Lumpur; tel. (3) 79819059; fax (3) 79819073; e-mail nsa-sec@bahai.org.my; internet www.bahai.org.my; f. 1964; mems resident in 800 localities.

The Press

PENINSULAR MALAYSIA DAILIES

English Language

Business Times: Balai Berita 31, Jalan Riong, 59100 Kuala Lumpur; tel. (3) 22822628; fax (3) 22825424; e-mail support@nstp.com.my; internet www.btimes.com.my; f. 1976; morning; Editor SHAHRIMAN JOHARI; circ. 15,000.

The Edge: 1 Menara KLK, Level 3, Jalan PJU 7/6, Mutiara Damansara, 47810 Petaling Jaya, Selangor; tel. (3) 77218000; fax (3) 77218010; e-mail info@bizedge.com; internet www.theedgedaily.com; f. 1996; weekly, with daily internet edition; business and investment news; Editor AU FOONG YEE; circ. 22,821.

Malay Mail: Lot 2A, Jalan 13/2, 46200 Petaling Jaya, Selangor; tel. (3) 79472288; fax (3) 79472323; e-mail mmnews@mmail.com.my; internet www.mmail.com.my; f. 1896; afternoon; Editor-in-Chief YUSHAIMI YAHAYA; circ. 75,000.

Malaysiakini: 48 Jalan Kemuja, Bangsar Utama, 59000 Kuala Lumpur; tel. (3) 22835567; fax (3) 22892579; e-mail enquiries@malaysiakini.com; internet www.malaysiakini.com; f. 1999; Malaysia's first online newspaper; English and Malay; Editor STEVEN GAN.

New Straits Times: Balai Berita 31, Jalan Riong, 59100 Kuala Lumpur; tel. (3) 22823322; fax (3) 22821434; e-mail news@nstp.com.my; internet www.nst.com.my; f. 1845; morning; Group Editor-in-Chief Dato' SYED NADZRI SYED HARUN; circ. 107,513.

The Star: 15 Jalan 16/11, 46350 Petaling Jaya, POB 12474, Selangor Darul Ehsan; tel. (3) 79671388; fax (3) 79550439; e-mail msd@thestar.com.my; internet www.thestar.com.my; f. 1971; morning; Group Chief Editor Datuk WONG CHUN WAI; circ. 302,658.

The Sun: Sun Media Corpn Sdn Bhd, 4th Floor, Lot 6, Jalan 51/217, Section 51, 46050 Petaling Jaya, Selangor Darul Ehsan; tel. (3) 77846688; fax (3) 77835871; e-mail info@thesundaily.com; internet www.thesundaily.com; f. 1993; free tabloid newspaper in print and online formats; Man. Editor CHONG CHENG HAI; circ. 300,587.

Chinese Language

Chung Kuo Pao (China Press): 80 Jalan Riong, off Jalan Bangsar, 59100 Kuala Lumpur; tel. (3) 22896363; fax (3) 22827125; e-mail enews@chinapress.com.my; internet www.chinapress.com.my; f. 1946; Editor POON CHAU HUAY; Gen. Man. NG BENG LYE; circ. 161,794.

Guang Ming Daily: 19 Jalan Semangat, 46200 Petaling Jaya, Selangor; tel. (3) 79658888; fax (3) 79658477; e-mail gmkl@mail.guangming.com.my; internet www.guangming.com.my; Editor-in-Chief YE NING; circ. 94,287.

Kwong Wah Yit Poh: 19 Jalan Presgrave, 11300 Pinang; tel. (4) 2612312; fax (4) 2628540; e-mail editor@kwongwah.com.my; internet www.kwongwah.com.my; f. 1910; morning; Chief Editor HU JINCHANG; circ. 100,000.

Nanyang Siang Pau (Malaysia): 1st Floor, 1 Jalan SS7/2, 47301 Petaling Jaya, Selangor; tel. (3) 78726888; fax (3) 78726800; e-mail editor@nanyang.com.my; internet www.nanyang.com.my; f. 1923; morning and evening; Editor-in-Chief CHONG CHOONG NAM; circ. 180,000 (daily), 220,000 (Sunday).

Sin Chew Jit Poh (Malaysia): 19 Jalan Semangat, POB 367, Jalan Sultan, 46200 Petaling Jaya, Selangor; tel. (3) 79658888; fax (3) 79556881; e-mail editorial@sinchew.com.my; internet www.sinchew-i.com; f. 1929; morning; Group Editor-in-chief SIEW NYOKE CHOW; circ. 440,002 (daily), 230,000 (Sunday).

Malay Language

Berita Harian: Balai Berita, 31 Jalan Riong, 59100 Kuala Lumpur; tel. (3) 22822323; fax (3) 20567081; e-mail bhnews@bharian.com.my; internet www.bharian.com.my; f. 1957; morning; Group Editor Datuk MIOR KAMARUL SHAHID; circ. 166,400.

MALAYSIA

Mingguan Perdana: 48 Jalan Siput Akek, Taman Billion, Kuala Lumpur; tel. (3) 619133; Group Chief Editor KHALID JAFRI.

Utusan Malaysia: 46M Jalan Lima, off Jalan Chan Sow Lin, 55200 Kuala Lumpur; tel. (3) 92217055; fax (3) 92227876; e-mail corpcomm@utusan.com.my; internet www.utusan.com.my; Editor ABDUL AZIZ ISHAK; circ. 171,582.

Watan: 23-1 Jalan 9A/55A, Taman Setiawangsa, 54200 Kuala Lumpur; tel. (3) 4523040; fax (3) 4523043; circ. 80,000.

Tamil Language

Makkal Osai: 11B Jalan Murai Dua, Batu Kompleks, off Jalan Ipoh, 52000 Kuala Lumpur; tel. (3) 62512251; fax (3) 62535981; f. 1990; est. as a Sunday newspaper after *Tamil Osai* ceased publication; publ. daily since Dec. 2005; Gen. Man. S. M. PERIASAMY; circ. 52,000 (daily), 95,000 (Sunday).

Malaysia Nanban: 544-3 Batu Complex, off Jalan Ipoh, Batu 3 1/4, 51200 Kuala Lumpur; e-mail news@nanban.com.my; internet www.nanban2u.com; tel. (3) 62515981; fax (3) 62591617; circ. 45,000; Editor M. MALAYANDY.

Tamil Nesan: 23, Jalan SBC 5, Taman Sri Batu Caves, 68100 Batu Caves, Selangor Darul Ehsaan; tel. (3) 61841818; fax (3) 61871818; e-mail mytamilnesan@yahoo.com; internet www.tamilnesan.com.my; f. 1924; morning; Editor-in-Chief PADMANATHAN; circ. 35,000 (daily), 60,000 (Sunday).

SUNDAY NEWSPAPERS
English Language

New Sunday Times: Balai Berita 31, Jalan Riong, 59100 Kuala Lumpur; tel. (3) 2822328; fax (3) 2824482; e-mail news@nstp.com.my; f. 1931; morning; Group Editor Datuk HISHAMUDDIN AUN; circ. 191,562.

Sunday Mail: Balai Berita 31, Jalan Riong, 59100 Kuala Lumpur; tel. (3) 2822328; fax (3) 2824482; e-mail smail@nstp.com.my; f. 1896; morning; Editor JOACHIM S. P. NG; circ. 75,641.

Sunday Star: 13 Jalan 13/6, 46200 Petaling Jaya, POB 12474, Selangor Darul Ehsan; tel. (3) 7581188; fax (3) 7551280; f. 1971; Editor DAVID YEOH; circ. 232,790.

Malay Language

Berita Minggu: Balai Berita 31, Jalan Riong, 59100 Kuala Lumpur; tel. (3) 22822323; fax (3) 20567082; e-mail bhnews@bharian.com.my; f. 1957; morning; Group Editor Datuk MIOR KAMARUL SHAHID; circ. 421,127.

Metro Ahad: Balai Berita 31, Jalan Riong, 59100 Kuala Lumpur; tel. (3) 22822328; fax (3) 22821482; e-mail metahad@nstp.com.my; internet www.nstp.com.my/Corporate/nstp/products/productMetroAhd.htm; f. 1995; morning; circ. 136,974.

Mingguan Malaysia: 11A The Right Angle, Jalan 14/22, 46100 Petaling Jaya; tel. (3) 7563355; fax (3) 7577755; f. 1964; Editor MOHD HASSAN MOHD NOOR; circ. 543,232.

PENINSULAR MALAYSIA PERIODICALS
English Language

Her World: Lot 7, Jalan Bersatu 13/4, Section 13, 46200 Petaling Jaya, Selangor Darul Ehsan; tel. (3) 79527000; fax (3) 79600148; e-mail herworld@bluinc.com.my; internet www.herworld.com.my; monthly; Editor ALICE CHEE LAN NEO; circ. 35,000.

The Herald: Archdiocesan Pastoral Centre, 5 Jalan Robertson, 50150 Kuala Lumpur; tel. (3) 20268290; e-mail editor@herald.com.my; internet www.heraldmalaysia.com; weekly; Catholic; Publr Rev. Tan Sri MURPHY PAKIAM; Editor Fr ANDREW LAWRENCE; circ. 14,000.

Malaysia Warta Kerajaan Seri Paduka Baginda (HM Government Gazette): Percetakan Nasional Malaysia Berhad, Jalan Chan Sow Lin, 50554 Kuala Lumpur; tel. (3) 92212022; fax (3) 92220690; e-mail pnmb@po.jaring.my; fortnightly.

Malaysian Agricultural Journal: Ministry of Agriculture and Agro-based Industry, Publications Unit, Wisma Tani, Jalan Sultan Salahuddin, 50624 Kuala Lumpur; tel. (3) 2982011; fax (3) 2913758; f. 1901; 2 a year.

Malaysian Forester: Forestry Department Headquarters, Jalan Sultan Salahuddin, 50660 Kuala Lumpur; tel. (3) 26988244; fax (3) 26925657; e-mail skthai@forestry.gov.my; f. 1931; quarterly; Editor THAI SEE KIAM.

The Planter: Wisma ISP, 29 & 31–33 Jalan Taman U Thant, POB 10262, 50708 Kuala Lumpur; tel. (3) 21425561; fax (3) 21426898; e-mail isphq@tm.net.my; internet www.isp.org.my; f. 1919; publ. by Isp Management (M); monthly; Editor AZIZAN ABDULLAH; circ. 4,000.

The Rocket: 24 Jalan 20/9, 46300 Petaling Jaya, Selangor; tel. (3) 79578022; fax (3) 79575718; e-mail rocket@dapmalaysia.org; internet daprocket.com; monthly; official newsletter of Democratic Action Party; also published in Chinese and Malay; Editor TONY PUA.

Young Generation: 11A The Right Angle, Jalan 14/22, 46100 Petaling Jaya, Selangor; tel. (3) 7563355; fax (3) 7577755; monthly; circ. 50,000.

Chinese Language

Mister Weekly: 2A Jalan 19/1, 46300 Petaling Jaya, Selangor; tel. (3) 7562400; fax (3) 7553826; f. 1976; weekly; Editor WONG AH TAI; circ. 25,000.

Mun Sang Poh: 472 Jalan Pasir Puteh, 31650 Ipoh; tel. (5) 3212919; fax (5) 3214006; bi-weekly; circ. 77,958.

New Life Post: 80M Jalan SS21/39, Damansara Utama, 47400 Petaling Jaya, Selangor; tel. (3) 7571833; fax (3) 7181809; f. 1972; bi-weekly; Editor LOW BENG CHEE; circ. 231,000.

New Tide Magazine: Nanyang Siang Pau Bldg, 2nd Floor, Jalan 7/2, 47301 Petaling Jaya, Selangor; tel. (3) 76202118; fax (3) 76202131; e-mail newtidemag@hotmail.com; f. 1974; monthly; Editor NELLIE OOI; circ. 39,000.

Malay Language

Dewan Masyarakat: Dewan Bahasa dan Pustaka, Jalan Wisma Putra, POB 10803, 50926 Kuala Lumpur; tel. (3) 2481011; fax (3) 2484211; f. 1963; monthly; current affairs; Editor ZULKIFLI SALLEH; circ. 48,500.

Dewan Pelajar: Dewan Bahasa dan Pustaka, Jalan Wisma Putra, POB 10803, 50926 Kuala Lumpur; tel. (3) 2481011; fax (3) 2484211; f. 1967; monthly; children's; Editor ZALEHA HASHIM; circ. 100,000.

Dewan Siswa: POB 10803, 50926 Kuala Lumpur; tel. (3) 2481011; fax (3) 2484208; monthly; circ. 140,000.

Gila-Gila: 38-1, Jalan Bangsar Utama Satu, Bangsar Utama, 59000 Kuala Lumpur; tel. (3) 22824970; fax (3) 22824967; fortnightly; circ. 70,000.

Harakah: 5 Jalan, 65C, Off Jalan Pahang Barat, Pekeliling Business Center, 53000 Kuala Lumpur; tel. (3) 40212009; fax (3) 40212029; e-mail harakahenglish@yahoo.com; internet www.beritaharakah.com; two a week; f. 1980; organ of the PAS; Editor ZULKIFLI SULONG.

Jelita: Berita Publishing Sdn Bhd, 16–20 Jalan 4/109E, Desa Business Park, Taman Desa, off Jalan Klang Lama, 58100 Kuala Lumpur; tel. (3) 76208171; fax (3) 76208026; e-mail jelita@beritapub.com.my; internet www.beritapublishing.com.my; monthly; fashion and beauty magazine; Editor SARIMAH HUSIN; circ. 133,727.

Mangga: 11A The Right Angle, Jalan 14/22, 46100 Petaling Jaya, Selangor; tel. (3) 7563355; fax (3) 7577755; monthly; circ. 56,609.

Mastika: Utusan Karya Sdn Bhd, Lot 6, Jalan P/10, Seksyen 10, 43650 Bandar Baru Bangi, Selangor Darul Ehsan; tel. (3) 8926-2999; fax (3) 8925-9277; f. 1941; monthly; illustrated magazine; Editor SAHIDAN JAAFAR; circ. 350,000.

Utusan Radio dan TV: 11A The Right Angle, Jalan 14/22, 46100 Petaling Jaya, Selangor; tel. (3) 7563355; fax (3) 7577755; fortnightly; Editor NORSHAH TAMBY; circ. 115,000.

Wanita: 11A The Right Angle, Jalan 14/22, 46100 Petaling Jaya, Selangor; tel. (3) 7563355; fax (3) 7577755; monthly; women; Editor Nik RAHIMAH HASSAN; circ. 28,651.

Punjabi Language

Navjiwan Punjabi News: 52 Jalan 8/18, Jalan Toman, 46050 Petaling Jaya, Selangor; tel. (3) 7565725; f. 1950; weekly; Assoc. Editor TARA SINGH; circ. 9,000.

SABAH DAILIES

Api Siang Pau (Kota Kinabalu Commercial Press): 24 Lorong Dewan, POB 170, Kota Kinabalu; f. 1954; morning; Chinese; Editor Datuk LO KWOCK CHUEN; circ. 3,000.

Borneo Post (Nountan Press Sdn Bhd): 1 Jalan Bakau, 1st Floor, off Jalan Gaya, 88999 Kota Kinabulu; tel. (88) 238001; fax (88) 238002; internet www.theborneopost.com; English; Chief Editor JIMMY ADIT; circ. 22,533.

Daily Express: News House, 16 Jalan Pasar Baru, POB 10139, 88801 Kota Kinabalu; tel. (88) 256422; fax (88) 238611; e-mail forum@dailyexpress.com.my; internet www.dailyexpress.com.my; f. 1963; morning; English, Bahasa Malaysia and Kadazan; Editor-in-Chief SARDATHISA JAMES; circ. 28,555.

Hwa Chiaw Jit Pao (Overseas Chinese Daily News): News House, 16 Jalan Pasar Baru, POB 10139, 88801 Kota Kinabalu; tel. (88) 256422; fax (88) 238611; e-mail sph@dailyexpress.com.my; internet www.ocdn.com.my; f. 1936; morning; Chinese; Editor HII YUK SENG; circ. 16,489.

MALAYSIA

Merdeka Daily News: Lot 56, BDC Estate, Mile 1½ North Road, POB 332, 90703 Sandakan; tel. (89) 214517; fax (89) 275537; e-mail merkk@tm.net.my; f. 1968; morning; Chinese; Editor-in-Chief FUNG KON SHING; circ. 8,000.

New Sabah Times: Jalan Pusat Pembangunan Masyarakat, off Jalan Mat Salleh, 88100 Kota Kinabalu; tel. (88) 230055; fax (88) 231155; e-mail chng.boonheng@newsabahtimes.com.my; internet www.newsabahtimes.com.my; English, Malay and Kadazan; Editor-in-Chief CHENG BOON HENG; circ. 22,525.

Syarikat Sabah Times: Kota Kinabalu; tel. (88) 52217; f. 1952; English, Malay and Kadazan; circ. 25,000.

Tawau Jih Pao: POB 464, 1072 Jalan Kuhara, Tawau; tel. (89) 72576; Chinese; Editor-in-Chief STEPHEN LAI KIM YEAN.

SARAWAK DAILIES

Berita Petang Sarawak: Lot 8322, Lorong 7, Jalan Tun Abdul Razak, 93450 Kuching; POB 1315, 93726 Kuching; tel. (82) 480771; fax (82) 489006; f. 1972; evening; Chinese; Chief Editor HWANG YU CHAI; circ. 12,000.

Borneo Post: 40 Jalan Tuanku Osman, POB 20, 96000 Sibu; tel. (84) 332055; fax (84) 321255; internet www.borneopost.com.my; morning; English; Man. Dir LAU HUI SIONG; Editor NGUOI HOW YIENG; circ. 60,000.

International Times: Lot 2215, Jalan Bengkel, Pending Industrial Estate, POB 1158, 93724 Kuching; tel. (82) 482215; fax (82) 480996; e-mail news@intimes.com; internet www.intimes.com.my; f. 1968; morning; Chinese; Editor LEE FOOK ONN; circ. 24,292.

Malaysia Daily News: 7 Island Rd, POB 237, 96009 Sibu; tel. (84) 330211; tel. (84) 320540; f. 1968; morning; Chinese; Editor WONG SENG KWONG; circ. 22,735.

Sarawak Tribune and Sunday Tribune: Lot 231, Jalan Abell Utara, 93100 Kuching; tel. (82) 424411; fax (82) 415024; e-mail st@tru.my; internet tribune.my; f. 1945; English; licence suspended in Feb. 2006; reappeared in May 2010 as New Sarawak Tribune; Editor (vacant); circ. 29,598.

See Hua Daily News: 40 Jalan Tuanku Osman, POB 20, 96000 Sibu; tel. (84) 332055; fax (84) 321255; f. 1952; morning; Chinese; Man. Editor LAU HUI SIONG; circ. 80,000.

United Daily News: tel. (84) 219251; fax (84) 215037; internet www.eunited.com.my; f. 2004 following merger between Chinese Daily News and Miri Daily News; morning; Chinese; Man. Editor CHRISTINE LIU QING; circ. 35,000.

SARAWAK PERIODICALS

Pedoman Rakyat: Malaysian Information Dept, Mosque Rd, 93612 Kuching; tel. (82) 240141; f. 1956; monthly; Malay; Editor SAIT BIN Haji YAMAN; circ. 30,000.

Pemberita: Malaysian Information Services, Mosque Rd, 93612 Kuching; tel. (82) 247231; internet www.penerangan.gov.my; f. 1950; every 2 months; Iban; Editor PHILIP NYARU BUNDAK; circ. 20,000.

Sarawak Gazette: Sarawak Museum, Jalan Tun Abang Haji Openg, 93566 Kuching; tel. (82) 244232; fax (82) 246680; e-mail museum@po.jaring.my; f. 1870; 2 a year; English; Chief Editor Datu Haji SALLEH SULAIMAN.

Utusan Sarawak: Lot 231, Jalan Nipah, off Jalan Abell Utara, POB 138, 93100 Kuching; tel. (82) 424411; fax (82) 415024; internet www.utusansarawak.com.my; f. 1949; Malay; Editor Haji ABDUL AZIZ Haji MALIM; circ. 32,292.

NEWS AGENCY

Bernama (Malaysian National News Agency): Wisma Bernama, 28 Jalan 1/65A, off Jalan Tun Razak, POB 10024, 50400 Kuala Lumpur; tel. (3) 26939933; fax (3) 26913972; e-mail helpdesk@bernama.com; internet www.bernama.com; f. 1968; general and foreign news, economic features and photo services, public relations wire, screen information and data services, stock market on-line equities service, real-time commodity and monetary information services; daily output in Malay and English; in June 1990 Bernama was given the exclusive right to receive and distribute news in Malaysia; Editor-in-Chief Datuk YONG SOO HEONG.

PRESS ASSOCIATION

Magazine Publishers' Association of Malaysia (MPA): 3-3, Jalan 11/48A, Sentul Blvd, 51000 Kuala Lumpur; tel. (3) 40430500; fax (3) 40437648; e-mail jameselva@brandequity.com.my; internet www.mpamalaysia.org; 16 mems; Chair. ADI SATRIA AHMAD.

Persatuan Penerbit-Penerbit Akhbar Malaysia (Malaysian Newspaper Publishers' Asscn): Unit 706, Blok B, Phileo Damansara 1, 9 Jalan 16/11, off Jalan Damansara, 46350 Petaling Jaya; tel. (3) 76608535; fax (3) 76608532; e-mail mnpa@macomm.com.my; Chair. MOHD NASIR ALI.

Publishers

JOHOR

Penerbitan Pelangi Sdn Bhd: 66 Jalan Pingai, Taman Pelangi, 80400 Johor Bahru; tel. (7) 89269553; fax (7) 3329201; e-mail info@pelangibooks.com; internet www.pelangibooks.com; f. 1979; children's books, guidebooks and reference; Man. Dir SAMUEL SUM KOWN CHEEK.

Textbooks Malaysia Sdn Bhd: 49 Jalan Tengku Ahmad, POB 30, 85000 Segamat, Johor; tel. (7) 9318323; fax (7) 9313323; school textbooks, children's fiction, guidebooks and reference; Man. Dir FREDDIE KHOO.

KUALA LUMPUR

Arus Intelek Sdn Bhd: Plaza Mont Kiara, Suite E-06-06, Mont Kiara, 50480 Kuala Lumpur; tel. (3) 62011558; fax (3) 62018698; e-mail afusint@streamyx.com; Man. Datin AZIZAH MOKHZANI.

Berita Publishing Sdn Bhd: 16–20 Jalan 4/109E, Desa Business Park, Taman Desa, off Jalan Klang Lama, 58100 Kuala Lumpur; tel. (3) 76208111; fax (3) 76208018; e-mail mbeditor@beritapub.com; internet www.beritapublishing.com.my; education, business, fiction, cookery; Chair. A. KADIR JASIN.

Dewan Bahasa dan Pustaka (DBP) (Institute of Language and Literature): Jalan Dewan Bahasa, 50460 Kuala Lumpur; tel. (3) 21481011; fax (3) 21447248; internet www.dbp.gov.my; f. 1956; textbooks, magazines and general; Chair. Dato' JOHAN JAAFFAR.

Jabatan Penerbitan Universiti Malaya (University of Malaya Press): University of Malaya, Lembah Pantai, 50603 Kuala Lumpur; tel. (3) 79574361; fax (3) 79574473; e-mail terbit@um.edu.my; internet umweb.um.edu.my/umpress; f. 1954; general fiction, literature, economics, history, medicine, politics, science, social science, law, Islam, engineering, dictionaries; Man. ABDUL MANAF SAAD.

Malaya Press Sdn Bhd: Kuala Lumpur; tel. (3) 5754650; fax (3) 5751464; f. 1958; education; Man. Dir LAI WING CHUN.

Pustaka Antara Sdn Bhd: Lot UG 07 and 09, Upper Ground Floor, Kompleks Wilayah, 2 Jalan Munshi Abdullah, 50100 Kuala Lumpur; tel. (3) 26980044; fax (3) 26917997; e-mail pantara4@streamyx.com; textbooks, children's, languages, fiction; Man. Dir Datin HAPSAH BINTI MUHAMAD NOR.

Utusan Publications and Distributors Sdn Bhd: 1 and 3 Jalan 3/91A, Taman Shamelin Perkasa, Cheras, 56100 Kuala Lumpur; tel. (3) 92856577; fax (3) 92856341; e-mail rose@utusan.com.my; f. 1976; school textbooks, children's, languages, fiction, general; Exec. Dir ROSELINA JOHARI.

NEGERI SEMBILAN

Bharathi Press: 166 Taman AST, POB 74, 70700 Seremban, Negeri Sembilan Darul Khusus; tel. (6) 7622911; f. 1939; Mans M. SUBRAMANIA BHARATHI, BHARATHI THASAN.

PULAU PINANG

Syarikat United Book Sdn Bhd: 187–189 Lebuh Carnarvon, 10100 Pulau Pinang; tel. (4) 2626891; fax (4) 2626892; textbooks, children's, reference, fiction, guidebooks; Man. Dir CHEW SING GUAN.

SELANGOR

Federal Publications Sdn Bhd: Lot 46, Subang Hi-Tech Industrial Park, Batu Tiga, 40000 Shah Alam, Selangor; tel. (3) 56286888; fax (3) 56364620; e-mail fpsb@tpg.com.my; f. 1957; computer, children's magazines; Gen. Man. STEPHEN K. S. LIM.

FEP International Sdn Bhd: 6 Jalan SS 4C/5, POB 1091, 47301 Petaling Jaya, Selangor; tel. (3) 7036150; fax (3) 7036989; f. 1969; children's, languages, fiction, dictionaries, textbooks and reference; Man. Dir LIM MOK HAI.

International Law Book Services: 10 Jalan PJU 8/5G, Perdana Business Centre, Bandar Damansara Perdana, 47820 Petaling Jaya, Selangor Darul Ehsan; tel. (3) 77274121; fax (3) 77273884; e-mail gbc@pc.jaring.my; internet www.malaysialawbooks.com; CEO Dr SYED IBRAHIM.

Mahir Publications Sdn Bhd: 39 Jalan Nilam 1/2, Subang Sq., Subang Hi-Tech Industrial Park, Batu Tiga, 40000 Shah Alam, Selangor; tel. (3) 7379044; fax (3) 7379043; e-mail mahirpub@tm.net.my; Gen. Man. ZAINORA BINTI MUHAMAD.

Minerva Publications (NS) Sdn Bhd: 51 Jalan SG 3/1, Tan Sri Gombak, Batu Caves, 68100 Selangor; tel. (3) 61882876; fax (3) 61883876; e-mail minerva@streamyx.com; f. 1974; general, chil-

MALAYSIA

dren's, reference, medical, law; Dir and Chief Editor Sujaudeen; Man. Dir Thanjudeen.

Pearson Education Malaysia Sdn Bhd: Lot 2, Jalan 215, off Jalan Templer, 46050 Petaling Jaya, Selangor; tel. (3) 78012000; fax (3) 77818005; e-mail inquiry@pearsoned.com.my; internet www.pearsoned.com.my; textbooks, mathematics, physics, science, general, educational materials; Dir Wong Wee Woon; Man. Wong Mei Mei.

Pelanduk Publications (M) Sdn Bhd: 12 Jalan SS 13/3e, Subang Jaya Industrial Estate, 47500 Subang Jaya, Selangor; tel. (3) 56386885; fax (3) 56386575; e-mail pelpub@tm.net.my; internet www.pelanduk.com; f. 1984; politics, history, anthropology, religion, education, language, economics, business and management, culture, self-improvement, women's studies, law; Man. Jackson Tan.

Penerbit Fajar Bakti Sdn Bhd: 4 Jalan U1/15, Sekseyen U1, Hicom-Glenmarie Industrial Park, 40150 Shah Alam, Selangor; tel. (3) 7047011; fax (3) 7047024; e-mail edes@pfb.po.my; school, college and university textbooks, children's, fiction, general; Man. Dir Edda de Silva.

Penerbit Pan Earth Sdn Bhd: 11 Jalan SS 26/6, Taman Mayang Jaya, 47301 Petaling Jaya, Selangor; tel. (3) 7031258; fax (3) 7031262; Man. Stephen Cheng.

Penerbit Universiti Kebangsaan Malaysia: Universiti Kebangsaan Malaysia, 43600 UKM, Selangor; tel. (3) 8292840; fax (3) 8254375; e-mail penerbit@ukm.my; internet www.ukm.my/penerbit; Head Kamaruddin M. Said.

Pustaka Delta Pelajaran Sdn Bhd: Wisma Delta, Lot 18, Jalan 51A/22A, 46100 Petaling Jaya, Selangor; tel. (3) 7570000; fax (3) 7576688; economics, language, environment, geography, geology, history, religion, science; Man. Dir Lim Kim Wah.

Pustaka Sistem Pelajaran Sdn Bhd: Lot 17–22 and 17–23, Jalan Satu, Bersatu Industrial Park, Cheras Jaya, 43200 Cheras, Selangor; tel. (3) 9047558; fax (3) 9047573; Man. T. Thiru.

Sasbadi Sdn Bhd: Lot 12, Jalan Teknologi 3/4, Taman Sains Selangor 1, Kota Damansara, 47810 Petaling Jaya, Selangor; tel. (3) 61451188; fax (3) 61569080; e-mail enquiry@sasbadi.com; internet www.sasbadi.com; Man. Dir Law King Hui.

SNP Panpac (Malaysia) Sdn Bhd: Lot 3, Jalan Saham 23/3, Kawasan MIEL Phase 8, Section 23, 40300 Shah Alam, Selangor Darul Ehsan; tel. (3) 55481088; fax (3) 55481080; e-mail eastview@snpo.com.my; f. 1980; fmrly SNP Eastview Publs Sdn Bhd; school textbooks, children's, fiction, reference, general; Dir Chia Yan Heng.

Times Educational Co Sdn Bhd: 22 Jalan 19/3, 46300 Petaling Jaya, Selangor; tel. (3) 79571766; fax (3) 79573607; e-mail presco@po.jaring.my; general and reference; Man. Foong Chui Lin.

GOVERNMENT PUBLISHING HOUSE

Percetakan Nasional Malaysia Bhd (Malaysia National Printing Ltd): Jalan Chan Sow Lin, 50554 Kuala Lumpur; tel. (3) 2212022; fax (3) 2220690; fmrly the Nat. Printing Dept; incorporated as a co under govt control in Jan. 1993.

PUBLISHERS' ASSOCIATION

Malaysian Book Publishers Association: 7-6, Block E2, 42A Jalan PJU, Dataran Prima, 47301 Petaling Jaya, Selangor; tel. (3) 78805840; fax (3) 78805841; e-mail info@mabopa.com.my; internet www.mabopa.com.my; f. 1968; Pres. Law King Hui; 171 mems.

Broadcasting and Communications

TELECOMMUNICATIONS

Jabatan Telekomunikasi Malaysia (JTM) (Department of Telecommunications): c/o Ministry of Energy, Green Technology and Water, Blok E4–5, Parcel E, Pusat Pentadbiran Kerajaan Persekutuan, 62668 Putrajaya; tel. (3) 88836000; fax (3) 88893712; e-mail webmaster@kttha.gov.my; internet www.jtm.gov.my; regulatory body for telecommunications industry.

Celcom (Malaysia) Sdn Bhd: Menara Celcom, 82 Jalan Raja Muda Abdul Aziz, 50300 Kuala Lumpur; tel. (3) 26883939; fax (3) 36308889; e-mail careline@celcom.com.my; internet www.celcom.com.my; f. 1988; private co licensed to operate mobile cellular telephone service; merged with TM Cellular Sdn Bhd in 2003; Chair. Dato' Sri Jamaludin Ibrahim; CEO Dato' Sri Mohammed Shazalli Ramly.

DiGi Telecommunications Sdn Bhd: D'House, Lot 10, Jalan Delima 1/1, Subang Hi-Tech Industrial Park, 40000 Shah Alam, Selangor; tel. (3) 57211800; fax (3) 57210238; internet www.digi.com.my; private co licensed to operate mobile telephone service; Chair. Sigve Brekke; CEO Henrik Clausen.

Maxis Communications Bhd: Menara Maxis, Aras 18, Kuala Lumpur City Centre, off Jalan Ampang, 50088 Kuala Lumpur; tel. (3) 23307000; fax (3) 23300008; internet www.maxis.com.my; f. 1995; provides mobile, fixed-line and multimedia services; approx. 11.4m. subscribers in 2009; Chair. Tan Sri Dato' Seri Arshad bin Tun Uda; CEO Sandip Das.

Technology Resources Industries Bhd (TRI): Menara TR, 23rd Floor, 161b Jalan Ampang, 50450 Kuala Lumpur; tel. (3) 2619555; fax (3) 2632018; operates mobile cellular telephone service; Chair. and Chief Exec. Tan Sri Dato' Tajudin Ramli.

Telekom Malaysia Bhd: Tingkat 51, North Wing, Menara Telekom, off Jalan Pantai Baru, 50672 Kuala Lumpur; tel. (3) 22401221; fax (3) 22832415; e-mail help@tm.com.my; internet www.tm.com.my; f. 1984; public listed co responsible for operation of basic telecommunications services; 74% govt-owned; 4.22m. fixed lines (95% of total); Chair. Datuk Dr Halim Shafie; Chief Exec. Dato' Sri Mohd Isa Zamzamzairant.

Time dotCom Bhd: 14 Jalan Majistret, U1/26 Hicom Glenmarie Industrial Park, 40150 Shah Alam, Selangor; tel. (3) 50326000; fax (3) 50326010; e-mail customerservice@time.com.my; internet www.time.com.my; f. 1996; est. as Time Telecommunications Holdings Bhd; name changed as above in Jan. 2000; state-controlled co licensed to operate trunk network and mobile cellular telephone service; Chair. Abdul Kadir Mohamed Kassim; CEO Afzal Abdul Rahim.

BROADCASTING

Regulatory Authority

Under the Broadcasting Act (approved in December 1987), the Government is empowered to control and monitor all radio and television broadcasting, and to revoke the licence of any private company violating the Act by broadcasting material 'conflicting with Malaysian values'.

Radio Televisyen Malaysia (RTM): Dept of Broadcasting, Tingkat 2, Wisma TV, Angkasapuri, 50614 Kuala Lumpur; tel. (3) 22887200; e-mail halimaton@rtm.gov.my; fax (3) 22825103; internet www.rtm.gov.my; f. 1946; television introduced 1963; supervises radio and television broadcasting; Dir-Gen. Norhyati Ismail.

Radio

Radio Malaysia: Radio Televisyen Malaysia (see Regulatory Authority), POB 11272, 50740 Kuala Lumpur; tel. (3) 2823991; fax (3) 2825859; f. 1946; domestic service; operates six networks; broadcasts in Bahasa Malaysia, English, Chinese (Mandarin and other dialects), Tamil and Aborigine (Temiar and Semai dialects); Dir of Radio Madzhi Johari.

Radio Televisyen Malaysia—Sabah: Jalan Tuaran, 88614 Kota Kinabalu; tel. (88) 213444; fax (88) 223493; f. 1955; television introduced 1971; a dept of RTM; broadcasts programmes on over two networks for 280 hours a week in Bahasa Malaysia, English, Chinese (two dialects), Kadazan, Murut, Dusun and Bajau; Dir of Broadcasting Jumat Engson.

Radio Televisyen Malaysia—Sarawak: Broadcasting House, Jalan P. Ramlee, 93614 Kuching; tel. (82) 248422; fax (82) 241914; e-mail pvgrtmsw@tm.net.my; f. 1954; a dept of RTM; broadcasts 441 hours per week in Bahasa Malaysia, English, Chinese, Iban, Bidayuh, Melanau, Kayan/Kenyah; Dir of Broadcasting Norhyati Ismail.

Airtime Management and Programming Sdn Bhd (AMP): All Asia Broadcast Centre, Technology Park, Lebuhraya Puchong, Simpang Besi, Bukit Jalil, 57000 Kuala Lumpur; tel. (3) 9543-8888; fax (3) 9543-3888; internet ampradio.my; f. 1997; operates nine stations: Era, Hitz, Lite FM, Mix FM, MY FM, Sinar FM, THR Gegar, THR Raaga and X FM; broadcasts in Chinese, English, Malay and Tamil; Exec. Dir Dato' Borhanuddin Osman.

Media Prima Bhd: 3 Persiaran Bandar Utama, 47800 Petaling Jaya, Selangor; tel. (3) 77266333; fax (3) 77103876; e-mail communications@mediaprima.com.my; internet www.mediaprima.com.my; owns and operates three networks: Fly FM, Hot FM and One FM; Chair. Datuk Johan Jaaffar; CEO Ahmad Izham Omar.

Rediffusion Sdn Bhd: Rediffusion House, 17 Jalan Pahang, 53000 Kuala Lumpur; tel. (3) 4424544; fax (3) 4424614; f. 1949; two programmes; 44,720 subscribers in Kuala Lumpur; 11,405 subscribers in Pinang; 6,006 subscribers in Province Wellesley; 20,471 subscribers in Ipoh; Gen. Man. Rosni B. Rahmat.

Suara Islam (Voice of Islam): Islamic Affairs Division, Prime Minister's Department, Blok Utama, Tingkat 1–5, Pusat Pentadbiran Kerajaan Persekutuan, 62502 Putrajaya; f. 1995; Asia-Pacific region; broadcasts in Bahasa Malaysia on Islam.

Suara Malaysia (Voice of Malaysia): Wisma Radio, Tingkat 3, South Wing, Angkasapuri, 50740 Kuala Lumpur; tel. (3) 22887826; fax (3) 22847594; e-mail suaramalaysia@rtm.gov.my; internet www.vom.com.my; f. 1963; overseas service in Bahasa Malaysia, Arabic, Myanmar (Burmese), English, Bahasa Indonesia,

MALAYSIA

Chinese (Mandarin/Cantonese), Tagalog and Thai; Controller of Overseas Service STEPHEN SIPAUN.

Television

Radio Televisyen Malaysia—Sabah: see Radio.

Radio Televisyen Malaysia—Sarawak: see Radio.

Televisyen Malaysia: Radio Televisyen Malaysia (see Regulatory Authority); f. 1963; operates two national networks, TV1 and TV2; Controller of Programmes ISMAIL MOHAMED JAH.

Measat Broadcast Network Systems Sdn Bhd: All Asia Broadcast Centre, Technology Park Malaysia, Lebuhraya Puchong, Simpang Besi, Bukit Jalil, 57000 Kuala Lumpur; tel. (3) 95434129; fax (3) 95437333; e-mail custcare@astro.com.my; internet www.astro.com.my; nation-wide subscription service; Malaysia's first satellite, Measat 1, was launched in Jan. 1996; a second satellite was launched in Oct. 1996; Chair. Haji BADRI Haji MASRI.

Media Prima Bhd: see Radio; operates four stations: Metropolitan Television Sdn Bhd (8TV); Sistem Televisyen Malaysia Bhd (TV3); ntv7; and TV9.

Under a regulatory framework devised by the Government, a ban on privately owned satellite dishes was ended in 1996.

Finance

(cap. = capital; auth. = authorized; res = reserves; dep. = deposits; m. = million; brs = branches; amounts in ringgit Malaysia)

BANKING

Following a series of mergers, 10 domestic banking groups and about 30 banks were operating in 2008. In February 2004 53 banks held 'offshore' licences in Labuan.

Central Bank

Bank Negara Malaysia: Jalan Dato' Onn, POB 10922, 50929 Kuala Lumpur; tel. (3) 26988044; fax (3) 26912990; e-mail bnmtelelink@bnm.gov.my; internet www.bnm.gov.my; f. 1959; bank of issue; financial regulatory authority; cap. 100.0m., res 47,992.6m., dep. 234,804.5m. (Dec. 2009); Gov. Tan Sri Dato' Sri Dr ZETI AKHTAR AZIZ; 6 brs.

Regulatory Authority

Labuan Offshore Financial Services Authority (LOFSA): Main Office Tower, Tingkat 17, Financial Park Labuan, Jalan Merdeka, 87000 Labuan; tel. (87) 591200; fax (87) 413328; e-mail communication@lofsa.gov.my; internet www.labuanfsa.gov.my; regulatory body for Int. Offshore Financial Centre of Labuan est. in Oct. 1990; chaired by Gov. of Bank Negara Malaysia; Dir-Gen. Dato' AZIZAN ABDUL RAHMAN.

Commercial Banks

Peninsular Malaysia

Affin Bank Bhd: Menara AFFIN, 17th Floor, 80 Jalan Raja Chulan, 50200 Kuala Lumpur; tel. (3) 20559000; fax (3) 20261415; e-mail head.ccd@affinbank.com.my; internet www.affinbank.com.my; f. 1975; est. as Perwira Habib Bank Malaysia Bhd; name changed to Perwira Affin Bank Bhd in 1994; present name adopted upon merger with BSN Commercial Bank (Malaysia) Bhd in 2001; cap. 1,439.2m., res 1,371.4m., dep. 26,430.5m. (Dec. 2009); Chair. Gen. Tan Sri Dato' Seri ISMAIL Haji OMAR; Pres. and CEO Dato' ZULKIFLEE ABBAS BIN ABDUL HAMID; 106 brs.

Alliance Bank Malaysia Bhd: Menara Multi-Purpose, 3rd Floor, Capital Sq., 8 Jalan Munshi Abdullah, 50100 Kuala Lumpur; tel. (3) 26944888; fax (3) 26946200; e-mail info@alliancebg.com.my; internet www.alliancebank.com.my; f. 1982 as Malaysian French Bank Bhd; name changed to Multi-Purpose Bank Bhd 1996; name changed as above Jan. 2001, following acquisition of six merger partners; cap. 600.5m., res 1,215.3m., dep. 22,828.4m. (March 2010); Chair. Dato' THOMAS MUN LUNG LEE; CEO SEOW WAH; 79 brs.

AmBank Bhd: 22nd Floor, Bangunan AmBank Group, 55 Jalan Raja Chulan, 50200 Kuala Lumpur; tel. (3) 20362633; fax (3) 20321914; e-mail ir@ambankgroup.com; internet www.ambankgroup.com; f. 1969; wholly owned subsidiary of AMMB Holdings Bhd; fmrly Arab-Malaysian Bank Bhd; name changed as above 2002; cap. 670.3m., res 20,942.4m., dep. 61,916.4m. (March 2009); Chair. Tan Sri AZMAN HASHIM; Man. Dir CHEA TEK KUANG.

Bangkok Bank Bhd (Thailand): 105 Jalan Tun H. S. Lee, 50000 Kuala Lumpur; tel. (3) 21737200; fax (3) 21737300; e-mail bbb@bangkokbank.com; internet www.bangkokbank.com; f. 1958; cap. 265.0m., res 115.6m., dep. 1,670,5m. (Dec. 2009); Chair. CHATRI SOPHONPANICH; CEO ROBERT LOKE TAN CHENG; 4 brs.

Bank of America Malaysia Bhd: Wisma Goldhill, Jalan Raja Chulan, 50200 Kuala Lumpur; tel. (3) 20321133; fax (3) 20319087; internet www.bankofamerica.com/my; cap. 135.8m., res 318.5m., dep. 1,005.2m. (Dec. 2009); Chair. KRISTJAN DRAKE.

Bank of Nova Scotia Bhd: Menara Boustead, 69 Jalan Raja Chulan, 50200 Kuala Lumpur; tel. (3) 21410766; fax (3) 21412160; e-mail bns.kualalumpur@scotiabank.com; internet www.scotiabank.com.my; f. 1973; cap. 122.3m., res 426.4m., dep. 2,106.8m. (Oct. 2009); Man. Dir RASOOL KHAN.

Bank of Tokyo-Mitsubishi UFJ (Malaysia) Bhd (Japan): Tingkat 9–11, Menara IMC, 8 Jalan Sultan Ismail, 50250 Kuala Lumpur; tel. (3) 20348000; fax (3) 20788870; e-mail edpbtm@tm.net.my; f. 1996; est. following merger of Bank of Tokyo and Mitsubishi Bank; fmrly known as Bank of Tokyo-Mitsubishi; present name adopted following merger with UFJ; cap. 200m., res 1,056m., dep. 5,094m. (Dec. 2009); Chair. TETSUO TANAKA; Pres. and CEO HAJIME WASHIZU.

CIMB Bank Bhd: Bangunan CIMB, 5th Floor, Jalan Semantan Damansara Heights, 50490 Kuala Lumpur; tel. (3) 20930379; fax (3) 20939688; internet www.cimbbank.com.my; f. 1999; est. as Bumiputra Commerce Bank Bhd, following merger of Bank Bumiputra Malaysia Bhd with Bank of Commerce Bhd; name changed as above 2006; cap. 3,794.2m., res 10,834.2m., dep. 138,170.5m. (Dec. 2009); Chair. Tan Sri Dato' MOHAMED NOR YUSOF; Group CEO Dato' MOHAMED NAZIR ABDUL RAZAK ALI; 230 brs.

Citibank Bhd (USA): 165 Jalan Ampang, POB 11725, 50450 Kuala Lumpur; tel. (3) 23830000; fax (3) 23836666; internet www.citibank.com.my; f. 1959; cap. 121.7m., res 3,153.6m., dep. 33,572m. (Dec. 2009); Country Officer AJAY BANGA; 3 brs.

Deutsche Bank (Malaysia) Bhd (Germany): 18–20 Menara IMC, 8 Jalan Sultan Ismail, 50250 Kuala Lumpur; tel. (3) 20536788; fax (3) 20319822; internet www.db.com/malaysia; f. 1994; cap. 173.5m., res 1,016m., dep. 8,249m. (Dec. 2009); Man. Dir RAYMOND YEOH.

EON Bank Bhd: Menara EON Bank, 12th Floor, 288 Jalan Raja Laut, 50350 Kuala Lumpur; tel. (3) 26941188; fax (3) 26949588; e-mail caf@eonbank.com.my; internet www.eonbank.com.my; f. 1963; fmrly Kong Ming Bank Bhd; merged with Oriental Bank Bhd 2001; cap. 1,329.8m., res 2,328.3m., dep. 34,412.4m. (Dec. 2009); Chair. GOOI HOE SOON; CEO and Exec. Dir MICHAEL LOR CHEE LENG; 95 brs.

Hong Leong Bank Bhd: Wisma Hong Leong, Tingkat 8, 18 Jalan Perak, 50450 Kuala Lumpur; tel. (3) 21648228; fax (3) 21642503; internet www.hlb.com.my; f. 1905; fmrly MUI Bank Bhd; merged with Wah Tat Bank Bhd in 2001; cap. 1,580.1m., res 4,235m., dep. 67,315m. (June 2010); Chair. Tan Sri QUEK LENG CHAN; Man. Dir YVONNE CHIA; 187 local brs, 2 overseas brs.

HSBC Bank Malaysia Bhd (Hong Kong): 2 Leboh Ampang, POB 10244, 50100 Kuala Lumpur; tel. (3) 20753000; fax (3) 20701146; internet www.hsbc.com.my; f. 1860; fmrly Hongkong Bank Malaysia Bhd; adopted present name in 1999; cap. 114.5m., res 3,689m., dep. 45,232.3m. (Dec. 2009); Chair. PETER WONG TUN SHUN; CEO MAKHTAR HUSSAIN.

Malayan Banking Bhd (Maybank): Menara Maybank, 14th Floor, 100 Jalan Tun Perak, 50050 Kuala Lumpur; tel. (3) 20708833; fax (3) 20702611; e-mail publicaffairs@maybank.com.my; internet www.maybank2u.com.my; f. 1960; acquired Pacific Bank Bhd Jan. 2001; merged with PhileoAllied Bank (Malaysia) Bhd March 2001; cap. 7,078m., res 18,178.8m., dep. 202,500m. (June 2010); Chair. Tan Sri Dato' MEGAT ZAHARUDDIN MEGAT MOHAMED NOR; Pres. and CEO Dato' Sri ABDUL WAHID OMAR; 327 domestic brs, 30 overseas brs.

OCBC Bank (Malaysia) Bhd: Menara OCBC, 18 Jalan Tun Perak, 50050 Kuala Lumpur; tel. (3) 83175000; fax (3) 26984363; internet www.ocbc.com.my; f. 1932; cap. 291.5m., res 3,370m., dep. 43,089.6m. (Dec. 2009); Group Chair. Tan Sri Dato' NASRUDDIN BIN BAHARI; CEO JEFFREY CHEW SUN TEONG; 25 brs.

Public Bank Bhd: Menara Public Bank, 146 Jalan Ampang, 50450 Kuala Lumpur; tel. (3) 21638888; fax (3) 21639917; e-mail pbbcosec@publicbank.com.my; internet www.publicbank.com.my; f. 1965; merged with Hock Hua Bank Bhd March 2001; cap. 3,532m., res 6,910.2m., dep. 157,027.5m. (Dec. 2009); Chair. Tan Sri Dato' Dr TEH HONG PIOW; Man. Dir Tan Sri Dato' Sri TAY AH LEK; 241 domestic brs, 3 overseas brs.

RHB Bank Bhd: Towers Two and Three, Menara AA, 426 Jalan Tun Razak, 50400 Kuala Lumpur; tel. (3) 92878888; fax (3) 92879000; e-mail md_ceo@rhbbank.com.my; internet www.rhbbank.com.my; f. 1997; est. by merger between Development & Commercial Bank Bhd and Kwong Yik Bank Bhd; acquired Sime Bank Bhd 1999; merged with Bank Utama (Malaysia) Bhd 2003; cap. 3,915m., res 3,862m., dep. 81,033.4m. (Dec. 2009); Chair. (non-exec.) Tan Sri AZLAN ZAINOL; Man. Dir Dato' TAJUDDIN ATAN; 148 brs.

The Royal Bank of Scotland Bhd: Menara Maxis, Level 1, Kuala Lumpur City Centre, 50088 Kuala Lumpur; tel. (3) 21609828; fax (3) 21609905; e-mail my.customer.care@rbs.com; internet www.rbs.my;

MALAYSIA

f. 1888; cap. 203m., res 374.2m., dep. 5,536m. (Dec. 2009); Man. Dir Harry Naysmith.

Standard Chartered Bank Malaysia Bhd: Menara Standard Chartered, Level 16, 30 Jalan Sultan Ismail, 50250 Kuala Lumpur; tel. (3) 21177777; fax (3) 27116006; internet www.standardchartered.com.my; 31 brs.

United Overseas Bank (Malaysia) Bhd: Menara UOB, Tingkat 2, Jalan Raja Laut, POB 11212, 50738 Kuala Lumpur; tel. (3) 26924511; fax (3) 26940617; e-mail uob121@uob.com.my; internet www.uob.com.my; f. 1920; merged with Chung Khiaw Bank (Malaysia) Bhd in 1997 and with Overseas Union Bank (Malaysia) Bhd in 2002; cap. 470m., res 2,996.7m., dep. 38,381.5m. (Dec. 2009); Chair. Wee Cho Yaw; CEO Chan Kok Seong; 37 brs.

Merchant Banks

Affin Merchant Bank Bhd: Menara Boustead, 27th Floor, 69 Jalan Raja Chulan, POB 11424, 50744 Kuala Lumpur; tel. (3) 21423700; fax (3) 21423799; e-mail enquiry@affinmerchantbank.com.my; internet www.affininvestmentbank.com.my; f. 1970; est. as Permata Chartered Merchant Bank Bhd; present name adopted 2001; cap. 222.2m., res 329.2m., dep. 2,856.4m. (Dec. 2009); Chair. Tan Sri Yaacob bin Mohamed Zain; Man. Dir Datin Maimoonah Hussain.

Alliance Investment Bank Bhd (AIB): Menara Multi-Purpose, 19th Floor, Capital Sq., 8 Jalan Munshi Abdullah, 50100 Kuala Lumpur; tel. (3) 26927788; fax (3) 26928787; e-mail eallianceshare@allianceinvestment.com.my; internet www.allianceinvestmentbank.com.my; f. 1974; est. as Amanah-Chase Merchant Bank Bhd; name changed to Alliance Merchant Bank Bhd in 2001, following merger with Bumiputra Merchant Bankers Bhd; name changed as above in 2006, following merger with Kuala Lumpur City Securities (KLCS); cap. 365.0m., res 117.7m., dep. 1,670m. (March 2010); Chair. Dato' Thomas Mun Lung Lee; CEO Rafidz Rasiddi.

AmInvestment Bank Bhd: 22nd Floor, Bangunan AmBank Group, 55 Jalan Raja Chulan, 50200 Kuala Lumpur; tel. (3) 20362633; fax (3) 20782842; e-mail customercare@ambg.com.my; internet www.ambg.com.my; f. 1975; fmrly Arab-Malaysian Merchant Bank Bhd; later known as AmMerchant Bank Bhd; name changed as above 2006; cap. 200m., res 203.1m., dep. 623,513m. (March 2010); Chair. Tan Sri Dato' Azman Hashim; Group Man. Dir Cheah Tek Kuang; 5 brs.

CIMB Investment Bank Bhd: Bangunan CIMB, 10th Floor, Jalan Semantan, Damansara Heights, 50490 Kuala Lumpur; tel. (3) 20848888; fax (3) 20848885; e-mail info@cimb.com.my; internet www.cimbbank.com.my; f. 1974; fmrly Commerce Int. Merchant Bankers Bhd; present name adopted 2006; cap. 100m., res 301.7m., dep. 5,916.6m. (Dec. 2009); Chair. Tan Sri Dato' Mohamed Nor Yusof.

Maybank Investment Bank Berhad: Menara Maybank, 33rd Floor, 100 Jalan Tun Perak, 50050 Kuala Lumpur; tel. (3) 20591888; fax (3) 20784194; e-mail enquiries@maybank-ib.com; internet www.maybank-ib.com; f. 1973; cap. 50.1m., res 338.3m. (June 2010), dep. 4,095.3m. (June 2009); Chair. Tan Sri Dato' Megat Zaharuddin Megat Mohamed Nor; CEO Tengku Dato' Zafrul Tengku Abdul Aziz; 2 brs.

MIDF Amanah Investment Bank Bhd: Menara MIDF, Level 21, 82 Jalan Raja Chulan, 50200 Kuala Lumpur; tel. (3) 21738888; fax (3) 21738877; e-mail inquiry-feedback@midf.com.my; internet www.midf.com.my; f. 1975; est. as Utama Wardley Bhd; name changed to Utama Merchant Bank Bhd in 1996; present name adopted 2006; cap. 156.5m., res 577.6m., dep. 3,693.2m. (Dec. 2009); Chair. Tan Sri Dato' Mahmood bin Taib; Group CEO Datuk Mohamed Najib Haji Abdullah; 1 br.

MIMB Investment Bank Bhd: Menara EON Bank, 21st Floor, 288 Jalan Raja Laut, 50350 Kuala Lumpur; tel. (3) 26910200; fax (3) 26985388; internet www.mimb.com.my; f. 1970; fmrly Malaysian Int. Merchant Bankers Bhd; wholly owned subsidiary of EON Bank Bhd; cap. 75m., res 176m., dep. 155.3m. (Dec. 2009); Chair. Gooi Hoe Soon; 2 brs.

Public Islamic Bank Bhd: Menara Public Bank, 27th Floor, 146 Jalan Ampang, 50450 Kuala Lumpur; tel. (3) 21766341; fax (3) 21639917; e-mail islamicbkg@publicislamicbank.com.my; internet www.publicislamicbank.com.my; f. 1973; est. as Asian Int. Merchant Bankers Bhd; became Sime Merchant Bankers Bhd 1996; present name adopted 2008; cap. 170.2m., res 1,335.6m., dep. 21,124.8m. (Dec. 2009); Chair. Tan Sri Dato' Sri Dr Teh Hong Piow; CEO Abu Hassan Assari bin Ibrahim.

RHB Investment Bank Bhd: Tower Three, 9th Floor, RHB Centre, 426 Jalan Tun Razak, 50400 Kuala Lumpur; tel. (3) 92805475; fax (3) 27118501; e-mail publicaffairs@rhb.com.my; internet www.rhb.com.my; f. 1974; fmrly RHB Sakura Merchant Bankers Bhd; present name adopted 2006; cap. 263.6m., res 479m., dep. 4,340m. (Dec. 2009); Chair. Patrick Chin Yoke Chung; CEO Sharifatul Hanizah Said Ali.

Co-operative Bank

Bank Kerjasama Rakyat Malaysia Berhad: Bangunan Bank Rakyat, Jalan Tangsi, Peti Surat 11024, 50732 Kuala Lumpur; tel. (3) 26129600; fax (3) 26129636; internet www.bankrakyat.com.my; f. 1954; 83,095 mems. of which 823 were co-operatives (Dec. 1996); Chair. Tan Sri Dato' Dr Syed Jalaludin Syed Salim; Man. Dir Datuk Kamaruzaman Che Mat; 67 brs.

Development Banks

Bank Pembangunan Malaysia Bhd: Menara Bank Pembangunan, 1016 Jalan Sultan Ismail, 50250 Kuala Lumpur; tel. (3) 26113888; fax (3) 26985701; e-mail feedback@bpmb.com.my; internet www.bpmb.com.my; f. 1973; govt-owned; fmrly Bank Pembangunana & Infrastruktur Malaysia Bhd; present name adopted upon merger with Bank Industri & Teknologi Malaysia Bhd in 2005; specializes in infrastructure, maritime and high-technology sectors; cap. 3,078.7m., res 4,051.8m., dep. 8,233m. (Dec. 2009); Chair. Datuk Abdul Samad Alias; Pres. Dato' Zafer Hashim; 15 brs.

Bank Perusahaan Kecil & Sederhana Malaysia Bhd (SME Bank): Menara SME Bank, Jalan Sultan Ismail, Peti Surat 12352, 50774 Kuala Lumpur; tel. (3) 26152020; fax (3) 26928520; e-mail enq_y@smebank.com.my; internet www.smebank.com.my; f. 2005; wholly owned subsidiary of Bank Pembangunan Malaysia Bhd; provides both financial and non-financial assistance to SMEs; cap. 1,350.0m., res −225.2m., dep. 2,033.5m. (Dec. 2009); Chair. Dato' Gumuri Hussain; Man. Dir Datuk Mohd Radzif Mohd Yunus.

Sabah Development Bank Bhd: SDB Tower, Wisma Tun Fuad Stephens, km 2.4, Jalan Tuaran, POB 12172, 88824 Kota Kinabalu, Sabah; tel. (88) 232177; fax (88) 261852; e-mail info@sabahdevbank.com; internet www.sabahdevbank.com; f. 1977; wholly owned by Sabah state govt; cap. 430.0m., res 121.8m., dep. 1,335.8m. (Dec. 2009); Chair. Peter Siau Wui Kee; Man. Dir and CEO Datuk Peter Lim Siong Eng.

Islamic Banks

Affin Islamic Bank Bhd: Menara Affin, 17th Floor, 80 Jalan Raja Chulan, 50200 Kuala Lumpur; tel. (3) 20559000; fax (3) 20261415; e-mail yourvoice@affinbank.com.my; f. 2006; cap. 260m., res 138m., dep. 5,865.7m. (Dec. 2009); CEO Kamarul Ariffin Mohd Jamil.

AmIslamic Bank Bhd: Bangunan AmBank Group, 22nd Floor, 55 Jalan Raja Chulan, 50200 Kuala Lumpur; tel. (3) 20362633; fax (3) 20321914; e-mail ir@ambankgroup.com; internet www.ambankgroup.com; f. 1994; wholly owned subsidiary of AmBank Bhd; cap. 403m., res 880.5m., dep. 12,214.5m. (March 2009); CEO Datuk Mahdi Morad.

Bank Islam Malaysia Bhd: Darul Takaful, 11th Floor, Jalan Sultan Ismail, 50734 Kuala Lumpur; tel. (3) 26935566; fax (3) 26949077; e-mail communications@bankislam.com.my; internet www.bankislam.com.my; f. 1983; cap. 1,725.4m., res −206m., dep. 25,509m. (June 2009); Chair. Dato' Zamani Abdul Ghani; Man. Dir Dato' Sri Zukri Samat; 90 brs.

Bank Muamalat Malaysia Bhd: Menara Bumiputra, 5th Floor, 21 Jalan Melaka, 50100 Kuala Lumpur; tel. (3) 26988787; fax (3) 20325997; e-mail webmaster@muamalat.com.my; internet www.muamalat.com.my; f. 1999; cap. 1,000m., res 318.4m., dep. 15,036.4m. (March 2010); Chair. Tan Sri Dato' Dr Mohd Munir Abdul Majid; CEO Dato' Haji Mohd Redza Shah Abdul Wahid; 40 brs.

OCBC Al-Amin Bank Bhd: 25th Floor, Wisma Lee Rubber, 1 Jelan Melaka, 50100 Kuala Lumpur; tel. (3) 83149090; fax (3) 20260825; subsidiary of OCBC Bank Bhd; cap. 65m., res 145.2m., dep. 4,299.5m. (Dec. 2009); CEO Syed Abdull Aziz Syed Kechik.

'Offshore' Banks

AmInternational (L) Ltd: Main Office Tower, Blok 4, Tingkat 12B, Financial Park Labuan, Jalan Merdeka, 87000 Labuan; tel. (87) 413133; fax (87) 425211; e-mail felix-leong@ambankgroup.com.my; internet www.ambankgroup.com; f. 1995; Head of Br. Iskandar Mohamed Hafidz.

AmInvestment Bank Bhd, Labuan Branch: Main Office Tower, Blok 4, Tingkat 12B, Financial Park Labuan, Jalan Merdeka, 87000 Labuan; tel. (87) 417891; fax (87) 417898; Man. Dir Cheah Tek Kuang.

Bank of America, Labuan Branch: Main Office Tower, Tingkat 10, Financial Park Labuan, Jalan Merdeka, 87000 Labuan; tel. (87) 411778; fax (87) 424778; Gen. Man. Pengiran Nur Farhah Ooi Abdullah.

The Bank of East Asia Ltd, Labuan Branch: Main Office Tower, Tingkat 10C, Financial Park Labuan, Jalan Merdeka, 87000 Labuan; tel. (87) 451145; fax (87) 451148; e-mail arraisag@hkbea.com; Gen. Man. Alvin Arrais.

MALAYSIA

Directory

Bank Islam Malaysia Bhd: Main Office Tower, Tingkat 15A, Financial Park, Jalan Merdeka, 87000 Labuan; tel. (87) 451802; fax (87) 451800; e-mail engkuafandi@bankislam.com.my; Branch Man. ENGKU AFANDI TAIB.

Bank of Nova Scotia, Labuan Branch: Main Office Tower, Tingkat 10C, Financial Park Labuan, Jalan Merdeka, 87000 Labuan; tel. (87) 451101; fax (87) 451099; Man. NAVEEN CHANDER.

Bank of Tokyo-Mitsubishi UFJ Ltd, Labuan Branch: Main Office Tower, Tingkat 12A, Financial Park Labuan, Jalan Merdeka, 87000 Labuan; tel. (87) 410487; fax (87) 410476; e-mail pulaubtm@tm.net.my; Gen. Man. WATURU TANAKA.

Barclays Bank PLC: Main Office Tower, Tingkat 5A, Financial Park Labuan, Jalan Merdeka, 87000 Labuan; tel. (87) 425571; fax (87) 425575; e-mail barclay@tm.net.my; Man. MIAW SIAW LOONG.

Bayerische Landesbank Girozentrale, Labuan Branch: Office Tower, Blok 4, Tingkat 14C, Financial Park Labuan, Jalan Merdeka, 87000 Labuan; tel. (87) 422170; fax (87) 422175; e-mail blblab@tm.net.my; Exec. Vice-Pres., CEO and Gen. Man. LOUISE PAUL.

BNP Paribas, Labuan Branch: Main Office Tower, Tingkat 9E, Financial Park Labuan, Jalan Merdeka, 87000 Labuan; tel. (87) 422328; fax (87) 419328; e-mail krishna.chetti@asia.bnpparibas.com; internet www.bnpparibas.com.my; Head KRISHNA CHETTI.

Cathay United Bank, Labuan Branch: Main Office Tower, Tingkat 3C, Financial Park Labuan, Jalan Merdeka, 87000 Labuan; tel. (87) 452168; fax (87) 453678; Gen. Man. YEH PIN HUNG.

CIMB Bank (L) Ltd: Main Office Tower, Tingkat 14B, Financial Park Labuan, Jalan Merdeka, 87000 Labuan; tel. (87) 410302; fax (87) 410313; e-mail bumitrst@tm.net.my; Gen. Man. JEMIMA HAZIZ.

Citibank Malaysia (L) Ltd: Main Office Tower, Tingkat 11F, Financial Park Labuan, Jalan Merdeka, 87000 Labuan; tel. (87) 421181; fax (87) 419671; Gen. Man. CLARA LIM AI CHENG.

City Credit Investment Bank Ltd: Main Office Tower, Tingkat 11-D1, Financial Park Labuan, Jalan Merdeka, 87000 Labuan; tel. (87) 582368; fax (87) 582308; e-mail info@ccibl.net; internet www.citycreditinvestmentbank.com; Chair. Tan Sri Dato' HANAFIAH HUSSAIN.

Commercial IBT Bank, Labuan Branch: Tingkat 2, Wisma Lucas Kong, Jalan Merdeka, 87000 Labuan; tel. (87) 411868; fax (87) 416818; e-mail info@cibtbank.com; internet www.cibtbank.com; Pres. Dir Dr ADRIAN ONG CHEE BENG.

Crédit Agricole CIB, Labuan Branch: Main Office Tower, Tingkat 6th Floor B, Financial Park Labuan, Jalan Merdeka, 87000 Labuan; tel. (87) 408331; fax (87) 408335; e-mail hoimeng.chew@ca-cib.com; fmrly known as Crédit Agricole Indosuez, Calyon; Gen. Man. HOI MENG CHEW.

Crédit Industriel et Commercial: Main Office Tower, Tingkat 11C, Financial Park Labuan, Jalan Merdeka, 87000 Labuan; tel. (87) 452008; fax (87) 452009; Gen. Man. YEOW TIANG HUI.

Crédit Suisse AG, Labuan Branch: Main Office Tower, Tingkat 10B, Financial Park Labuan, Jalan Merdeka, 87000 Labuan; tel. (87) 425381; fax (87) 425384; investment banking; Gen. Man. RUDOLF ZAUGG.

Deutsche Bank, Labuan Branch: Main Office Tower, Tingkat 9-G2, Financial Park Labuan, Jalan Merdeka, 87000 Labuan; tel. (87) 439811; fax (87) 439866; internet www.db.com/malaysia; Man. Dir KUAH HUN LIANG.

Development Bank of Singapore (DBS Bank) Ltd, Labuan Branch: Main Office Tower, Tingkat 10A, Financial Park Labuan, Jalan Merdeka, 87000 Labuan; tel. (87) 595500; fax (87) 423376; internet www.dbs.com/my; Gen. Man. JEFFRY LING.

ECM Libra Investment Bank Ltd: Main Office Tower, Tingkat 3-I1, Financial Park Complex, Jalan Merdeka, 87000 Labuan; tel. (87) 408525; fax (87) 408527.

Hongkong & Shanghai Banking Corporation, Offshore Banking Unit: Main Office Tower, Tingkat 11D, Financial Park Labuan, Jalan Merdeka, 87000 Labuan; tel. (87) 417168; fax (87) 417169; Man. PREM KUMAR.

ING Bank NV: Main Office Tower, Tingkat 8B, Financial Park Labuan, Jalan Merdeka, 87000 Labuan; tel. (87) 425733; fax (87) 425734; Gen. Man. MILLY TAN.

J. P. Morgan Chase Bank, Labuan Branch: Main Office Tower, Tingkat 5F, Financial Park Labuan, Jalan Merdeka, 87000 Labuan; tel. (87) 424384; fax (87) 424390; e-mail fauziah.hisham@chase.com; Gen. Man. LEONG KET TI.

J. P. Morgan Malaysia Ltd: Main Office Tower, Tingkat 5, Unit 5F, Financial Park Labuan, Jalan Merdeka, 87000 Labuan; tel. (87) 459000; fax (87) 451328; Gen. Man. LEONG KET TI.

Macquarie Bank Ltd, Labuan Branch: Main Office Tower, Tingkat 3A, Financial Park Labuan, Jalan Merdeka, 87000 Labuan; tel. (87) 583080; fax (87) 583088; Division Dir DARREN WOODWARD.

Maybank International (L) Ltd: Main Office Tower, Tingkat 16B, Financial Park Labuan, Jalan Merdeka, 87000 Labuan; tel. (87) 414406; fax (87) 414806; e-mail millmit@streamyx.com; Chair. Dato' JOHAN ARIFFIN.

Mizuho Corporate Bank Ltd, Labuan Branch: Main Office Tower, Tingkat 9B-C, Financial Park Labuan, Jalan Merdeka, 87000 Labuan; tel. (87) 417766; fax (87) 419766; Gen. Man. ISAKU TANIMURA.

National Australia Bank, Labuan Branch: Main Office Tower, Tingkat 12C, Financial Park Complex, Jalan Merdeka, 87008 Labuan; tel. (87) 426386; fax (87) 428387; e-mail natausm@po.jaring.my; Gen. Man. LIONEL LIM.

Natixis: Main Office Tower, Tingkat 9G, Financial Park Labuan, Jalan Merdeka, 87000 Labuan; tel. (87) 582009; fax (87) 583009; e-mail rizal.abdullah@ap.natixis.com; fmrly Natexis Banque Populaires; Gen. Man. RIZAL ABDULLAH.

OSK Investment Bank (Labuan) Ltd: Lot 3B, Tingkat 5, Wisma Lazenda, Jalan Kemajuan, Labuan; tel. (87) 581885; fax (87) 582885; CEO CHEN HOCK.

Oversea-Chinese Banking Corporation Ltd, Labuan Branch: Main Office Tower, Tingkat 8C, Financial Park Labuan, Jalan Merdeka, 87000 Labuan; tel. (87) 423381; fax (87) 423390; Gen. Man. BERNARD FERNANDO.

Public Bank (L) Ltd: Bangunan Lucas Kong, 5 Jalan Merdeka, 87007 Labuan; tel. (87) 414201; fax (87) 412388; Man. ALEXANDER WONG.

RHB Bank (L) Ltd: Main Office Tower, Tingkat 15B, Financial Park Labuan, Jalan Merdeka, 87000 Labuan; tel. (87) 417480; fax (87) 417484; e-mail rhbl@streamyx.com; Gen. Man. TOH AY LENG.

RUSD Investment Bank Inc: Lot 17, Jalan Kemajuan, 87000 Labuan; tel. (87) 452100; fax (87) 453100; e-mail info@rusdbank.com; internet www.rusdbank.com; Chair. Dr SALEH J. MALAIKAH; Man. Dir NASEERUDDIN A. KHAN.

Société Générale, Labuan Branch: Main Office Tower, Tingkat 11B, Financial Park Labuan, Jalan Merdeka, 87000 Labuan; tel. (87) 421676; fax (87) 421669; Gen. Man. RAMZAN ABU TAHIR.

Standard Chartered Bank Offshore Labuan: Main Office Tower, Tingkat 10F, Financial Park Labuan, Jalan Merdeka, 87000 Labuan; tel. (87) 417200; fax (87) 417202; Gen. Man. EDWARD NG.

Sumitomo Mitsui Banking Corpn, Labuan Branch: Main Office Tower, Tingkat 12B-C, Financial Park Labuan, Jalan Merdeka, 87000 Labuan; tel. (87) 410955; fax (87) 410959; Gen. Man. JUNICHI IKENO.

UBS AG, Labuan Branch: Main Office Tower, Tingkat 4-A1, Financial Park Labuan, Jalan Merdeka, 87000 Labuan; tel. (87) 421743; fax (87) 421746; Man. ZELIE HO SWEE LUM.

United Overseas Bank Ltd, Labuan Branch: Main Office Tower, Tingkat 6A, Financial Park Labuan, Jalan Merdeka, 87000 Labuan; tel. (87) 424388; fax (87) 424389; Gen. Man. HO FONG KUN.

Banking Associations

Association of Banks in Malaysia (ABM): UBN Tower, 34th Floor, 10 Jalan P. Ramlee, 50250 Kuala Lumpur; tel. (3) 20788041; fax (3) 20788004; e-mail banks@abm.org.my; internet www.abm.org.my; f. 1973; Chair. Dato' Sri ABDUL WAHID OMAR; Exec. Dir CHUAH MEI LIN.

Institute of Bankers Malaysia: Wisma IBI, 5 Jalan Semantan, Damansara Heights, 50490 Kuala Lumpur; tel. (3) 20956833; fax (3) 20952322; e-mail ibbm@ibbm.org.my; internet www.ibbm.org.my; f. 1977; professional and educational body for the banking and finance industry; Chair. Tan Sri Dato' AZMAN HASHIM.

Malayan Commercial Banks' Association: POB 12001, 50764 Kuala Lumpur; tel. (3) 2983991.

Persatuan Institusi Perbankan Tanpa Faedah Malaysia (Association of Islamic Banking Institutions Malaysia—AIBIM): Menara Tun Razak, Tingkat 23, Jalan Raja Laut, 50350 Kuala Lumpur; tel. (3) 26948002; fax (3) 26948012; e-mail admin@aibim.com; internet www.aibim.com; f. 1995; Pres. Dato' MOHAMED REDZA SHAH ABDUL WAHID; Exec. Dir MOHAMED SHAMSUDIN.

STOCK EXCHANGE

Bursa Malaysia: Tingkat 10, Exchange Sq., Bukit Kewangan, 50200 Kuala Lumpur; tel. (3) 20347000; fax (3) 20264122; e-mail customerservice@bursamalaysia.com; internet www.bursamalaysia.com; f. 1973; fmrly Kuala Lumpur Stock Exchange (KLSE); present name adopted 2004; merged with Malaysian Exchange of Securities Dealing and Automated Quotation Bhd (MESDAQ) in March 2002; authorized in 1988 the ownership of up to 49% of Malaysian stockbroking cos by foreign interests; 988 listed cos (Jan. 2008); Chair. TUN MOHAMED DZAIDDIN Haji ABDULLAH; CEO Dato' TAJUDDIN ATAN.

MALAYSIA

Regulatory Authority

Securities Commission (SC): 3 Persiaran Bukit Kiara, Bukit Kiara, 50490 Kuala Lumpur; tel. (3) 62048777; fax (3) 62015078; e-mail cau@seccom.com.my; internet www.sc.com.my; f. 1993; Chair. Tan Sri ZARINAH ANWAR.

INSURANCE

From 1988 onwards, all insurance companies were placed under the authority of the Central Bank, Bank Negara Malaysia. In 1997 there were 69 insurance companies operating in Malaysia, including nine reinsurance companies, 11 composite, 40 general and life and two takaful (compliant with Islamic law) insurance companies.

Principal Insurance Companies

Allianz General Insurance Malaysia Bhd: Plaza Sentral, Suite 3A, Level 15, Blok 3A, Jalan Stesen Sentral 5, 50470 Kuala Lumpur; tel. (3) 22641188; fax (3) 22641199; e-mail partner@allianz.com.my; internet www.allianz.com.my/general; f. 2001; Chair. Tan Sri RAZALI ISMAIL; CEO ZAKRI KHIR.

Allianz Life Insurance Malaysia Bhd: Plaza Sentral, Suite 3A, Level 15, Blok 3A, Jalan Stesen Sentral 5, 50470 Kuala Lumpur; tel. (3) 22641188; fax (3) 22641199; e-mail partner@allianz.com.my; internet www.allianz.com.my; fmrly MBA Life Assurance Sdn Bhd; CEO JENS REISCH.

Commerce Life Assurance Bhd: 338 Jalan Tunku Abdul Rahman, 50100 Kuala Lumpur; tel. (3) 26123600; fax (3) 26987035; f. 1992; est. as AMAL Assurance Bhd; present name adopted 1999.

Great Eastern Life Assurance (Malaysia) Bhd: Menara Great Eastern, 303 Jalan Ampang, 50450 Kuala Lumpur; tel. (3) 42598888; fax (3) 42598000; e-mail wecare@lifeisgreat.com.my; internet www.lifeisgreat.com.my; CEO KOH YAW HUI.

Hong Leong Assurance Sdn Bhd: Petaling Jaya City Development 15A, Menara B, Level 3, Jalan 219, 46100 Selangor; tel. (3) 76501818; fax (3) 76501991; e-mail corpcomm@hla.hongleong.com.my; internet www.hla.com.my; Chair. Tan Sri QUEK LENG CHAN; Man. Dir and CEO LOH GUAT LAN.

ING Insurance Bhd: Menara ING, 84 Jalan Raja Chulan, POB 10846, 50927 Kuala Lumpur; tel. (3) 21617255; fax (3) 27110175; internet www.ing.com.my; f. 1987; fmrly Aetna Universal Insurance Bhd; Chair. Tengku ABDULLAH IBNI AL-MARHUM Sultan ABU BAKAR.

Jerneh Insurance Corpn Sdn Bhd: Wisma Jerneh, 12th Floor, 38 Jalan Sultan Ismail, POB 12420, 50788 Kuala Lumpur; tel. (3) 21163300; fax (3) 21426672; e-mail slim@jerneh.com.my; internet www.jerneh.com.my; f. 1970; general; CEO LIM SUN.

Etiqa Insurance Bhd: Level 12B, Academy Etiqa, 23 Jalan Melaka, 50100 Kuala Lumpur; tel. (3) 26125301; fax (3) 26125068; internet www.etiqa.com.my; life and general; fmrly Malaysia National Insurance Sdn Bhd, name changed as above after merger with Etiqa in 2007; Chair. Dato' MOHAMAD SALLEH Haji HARUN.

Manulife Insurance (Malaysia) Bhd: Menara Manulife RB, 12th Floor, 6 Jalan Gelenggang, Damansara Heights, 50490 Kuala Lumpur; tel. (3) 20948055; fax (3) 20935487; internet www.manulife.com.my; f. 1963; life and non-life insurance; fmrly British American Life and General Insurance Bhd; name then changed to John Hancock Life Insurance (Malaysia) Bhd; present name adopted 2005, following 2004 merger between John Hancock Financial Services, Inc and Manulife Financial Corpn; Chair. Tan Sri Dato' MOHAMED SHERIFF BIN MOHAMED KASSIM.

Mayban Assurance Bhd: Mayban Assurance Tower, Level 15, Dataran Maybank, 1 Jalan Maarof, 59000 Kuala Lumpur; tel. (3) 22972888; fax (3) 22972828; e-mail mayassur@tm.net.my; internet www.maybank2u.com.my; Chair. Dato' JOHAN ARIFFIN.

MBf Insurans Sdn Bhd: Plaza MBf, 5th Floor, Jalan Ampang, POB 10345, 50710 Kuala Lumpur; tel. and fax (3) 2613466; Man. MARC HOOI TUCK KOK.

MCIS Zürich Insurance Bhd: Wisma MCIS Zurich, Jalan Barat, 46200 Petaling Jaya, Selangor; tel. (3) 79552577; fax (3) 79571562; e-mail info@mciszurich.com.my; internet www.mciszurich.com.my; f. 1954; Chair. Dato' BALARAM PETHA NAIDU.

Multi-Purpose Insurans Bhd: Menara Multi-Purpose, 8th Floor, Capital Sq., 8 Jalan Munshi Abdullah, 50100 Kuala Lumpur; tel. (3) 20349888; fax (3) 26945758; e-mail generalenquiries@mpib.com.my; internet www.mpib.com.my; fmrly Kompas Insurans Bhd; Chair. YAHYA BIN AWANG.

Oriental Capital Assurance Bhd: 36 Jalan Ampang, 50450 Kuala Lumpur; tel. (3) 20702828; fax (3) 20724150; e-mail oricap@oricap.com.my; internet www.oricap.com.my; f. 2002; est. by merger of Capital Insurance Bhd and United Oriental Assurance Sdn Bhd; Chair. Dato' VIJAYA KUMAR CHORNALINGAM; CEO LAI POONG SHEN.

Overseas Assurance Corpn (Malaysia) Bhd: Menara Great Eastern, Level 18, 303 Jalan Ampang, 50450 Kuala Lumpur; tel. (3) 42597888; fax (3) 48132737; e-mail enquiry@oac.com.my; internet www.oac.com.my; Chair. FANG AI LIAN.

Progressive Insurance Sdn Bhd: Plaza Berjaya, Menara BGI, 7th, 9th and 10th Floors, 12 Jalan Imbi, 55100 Kuala Lumpur; tel. (3) 21188000; fax (3) 21188101; e-mail progressive@progressiveinsurance.com.my; internet www.progressiveinsurance.com.my; Chair. Datuk DATU HARUN bin DATU MANSOR.

RHB Insurance Bhd: Tower 1, 8th Floor, RHB Centre, Jalan Tun Razak, 50400 Kuala Lumpur; tel. (3) 92812731; fax (3) 92812729; e-mail rhbi_general@rhbinsurance.com.my; Chair. Haji KHAIRUDDIN BIN AHMAD.

Uni.Asia General Insurance Bhd: Menara Uni.Asia, 10th Floor, 1008 Jalan Sultan Ismail, 50250 Kuala Lumpur; tel. (3) 2938111; fax (3) 26932893; e-mail callcentre@uniasiageneral.com.my; internet www.uniasiageneral.com.my; f. 1931; fmrly South-East Asia Insurance Bhd; Chair. DAVID CHAN MUN WAI.

Trade and Industry

GOVERNMENT AGENCIES

Danamodal Nasional Bhd (Danamodal): 10th Floor, Bangunan Sime Bank, Jalan Sultan Sulaiman, 50000 Kuala Lumpur; tel. (3) 20312255; fax (3) 20310786; e-mail info@danamodal.com.my; f. 1998; est. to recapitalize banks and restructure financial institutions, incl. arranging mergers and consolidations; Chair. Raja Datuk ARSHAD Raja Tun UDA; Man. Dir MARIANUS VONG SHIN TZOI.

Federal Agricultural Marketing Authority (FAMA): Bangunan FAMA Point, Lot 17304, Jalan Persiaran 1, Bandar Baru Selayang, 68100 Batu Caves, Selangor; tel. (3) 61262020; fax (3) 61383650; e-mail fama@fama.gov.my; internet www.fama.gov.my; f. 1965; est. to supervise, co-ordinate and improve marketing of agricultural produce, and to seek and promote new markets and outlets for agricultural produce; Chair. Dato' Paduka Haji BADRUDDIN BIN AMIRULDIN; Dir-Gen. Haji AHMAD B. ISHAK.

Federal Land Development Authority (FELDA): Wisma FELDA, Jalan Perumahan Gurney, 54000 Kuala Lumpur; tel. (3) 26172617; fax (3) 26920087; e-mail upd@felda.net.my; internet www.felda.net.my; f. 1956; govt statutory body formed to develop land into agricultural smallholdings to eradicate rural poverty; involved in rubber, oil palm and sugar-cane cultivation; Chair. Tan Sri MOHD ISA ABDUL SAMAD; Dir-Gen. Dato' AHMAD TARMIZI ALIAS.

Khazanah Nasional: Petronas Twin Towers, Tower 2, Tingkat 33, 50088 Kuala Lumpur; tel. (3) 20340000; fax (3) 20340300; e-mail info@khazanah.com.my; internet www.khazanah.com.my; f. 1994; state-controlled investment co; assumed responsibility for certain assets fmrly under control of the Ministry of Finance; holds 40% of Telekom Malaysia Bhd, 40% of Tenaga Nasional Bhd, 6.6% of HICOM Bhd and 17.8% of Proton; Chair. Dato' Sri MOHD NAJIB BIN Haji ABDUL RAZAK; Man. Dir Tan Sri Dato' AZMAN BIN Haji MOKHTAR.

Malaysia External Trade Development Corpn (MATRADE): Menara MATRADE, Jalan Khidmat Usaha, off Jalan Duta, 50480 Kuala Lumpur; tel. (3) 62077077; fax (3) 62037253; e-mail info@matrade.gov.my; internet www.matrade.gov.my; f. 1993; responsible for external trade devt and promotion; Chair. Dato' MAH SIEW KEONG.

Malaysian Institute of Economic Research: Podium City Point, Level 2, Kompleks Dayabumi, Jalan Sultan Hishamuddin, 50050 Kuala Lumpur; tel. (3) 22725897; fax (3) 22730197; e-mail zakariah@mier.po.my; internet www.mier.org.my; f. 1986; Chair. Tan Sri Dato' MOHAMED SHERIFF MOHAMED KASSIM; Exec. Dir Dr ZAKARIAH ABDUL RASHID.

Malaysian Palm Oil Board (MPOB): 6 Persiaran Institusi, Bandar Baru Bangi, 43000 Kajang, Selangor; tel. (3) 87694400; fax (3) 89259446; e-mail webmaster@mpob.gov.my; internet www.mpob.gov.my; f. 2000; est. by merger of Palm Oil Registration and Licensing Authority and Palm Oil Research Institute of Malaysia; Chair. Dato' Seri SHAHRIR BIN ABDUL SAMAD.

Malaysian Timber Industry Board (Lembaga Perindustrian Kayu Malaysia): 13–17 Menara PGRM, 8 Jalan Pudu Ulu, 56100 Cheras, Kuala Lumpur; tel. (3) 92822235; fax (3) 92851477; e-mail info@mtib.gov.my; internet www.mtib.gov.my; f. 1973; promotes and regulates the export of timber and timber products from Malaysia; Chair. Datuk WILFRED MADIUS TANGAU; Dir-Gen. Dr JALALUDDIN BIN HARUN.

Muda Agricultural Development Authority (MADA): MADA HQ, Ampang Jajar, 05990 Alor Setar, Kedah; tel. (4) 7728255; fax (4) 7722667; e-mail promada@mada.gov.my; internet www.mada.gov.my; Chair. Dato' Seri MAHDZIR BIN KHALID; Gen. Man. Dato' Haji ABDUL RAHIM BIN SALEH.

National Economic Action Council: NEAC-MTEN, Prime Minister's Office, Menara Usahawan, Blok Utama, Tingkat 5, 18 Per-

MALAYSIA

Directory

siaran Perdana, Pusat Pentadbiran Kerajaan Persekutuan, 62652 Putrajaya; tel. (3) 88886513; fax (3) 88882902; e-mail feedback@neac.gov.my; internet www.neac.gov.my; Chair. Tan Sri AMIRSHAM AZIZ.

National Information Technology Council (NITC): c/o The Ministry of Science, Technology and Innovationi, Aras 1-7, Blok C4–5, Kompleks C, Pusat Pentadbiran Kerajaan Persekutuan, 62662 Putrajaya; tel. (3) 88858000; fax (3) 88884328; internet www.nitc.my; Sec. Datuk Tengku Dr MOHD AZZMAN SHARIFFADEEN.

National Timber Certification Council: C-8-5, Megan Ave II, 12 Jalan Yap Kwan Seng, 50450 Kuala Lumpur; tel. (3) 21612298; fax (3) 21612293; e-mail info@mtcc.com.my; internet www.mtcc.com.my; Chair. Dato' Dr FREEZAILAH CHE YEOM.

Perbadanan Nasional Bhd (PERNAS): Menara Dato' Onn, Level 9B, 45 Jalan Tun Ismail, 50480 Kuala Lumpur; tel. (3) 26986670; fax (3) 26986617; e-mail enquiries@pns.com.my; internet www.pns.com.my; f. 1969; govt-sponsored; promotes trade, banking, property and plantation development, construction, mineral exploration, steel manufacturing, inland container transportation, mining, insurance, industrial development, engineering services, telecommunication equipment, hotels and shipping; cap. p.u. RM 116.25m.; 10 wholly owned subsidiaries, over 60 jointly owned subsidiaries and 18 assoc. cos; Chair. Datuk IDRIS BIN HASHIM; Man. Dir Tuan Syed KAMARULZAMAN BIN Syed ZAINOL KHODKI SHAHABUDIN.

DEVELOPMENT ORGANIZATIONS

Fisheries Development Authority of Malaysia: Plaza Utama Alam Mesra, Kota Kinabalu, Sabah; tel. (3) 26177000; fax (3) 26911931; e-mail info@lkim.gov.my; internet lkim.gov.my; Chair. Dato' Haji JIDIN BIN MOHD SHAFEE; Dir-Gen. Dato' Haji KHAZIN BIN MOHD HAMZAH.

Johor Corporation: Level 2, Persada Johor, Jalan Abdullah Ibrahim, 80000 Johor Bahru; tel. (7) 2232692; fax (7) 2233175; e-mail pdnjohor@jcorp.com.my; internet www.jcorp.com.my; devt agency of the Johor state govt; Chair. Dato' Haji ABDUL GHANI BIN OTHMAN; Chief Exec. Haji KAMARUZZAMAN BIN ABU KASSIM.

Kumpulan FIMA Bhd (Food Industries of Malaysia): Plaza Damansara, Blok C, Tingkat 4, Suite 4.1, 45 Jalan Medan Setia 1, Bukit Damansara, 50490 Kuala Lumpur; tel. (3) 20921211; fax (3) 20925923; e-mail enquiry@fima.com.my; internet www.fima.com.my; f. 1972; fmrly govt corpn; transferred to private sector in 1991; promotes food and related industry through investment on its own or by co-ventures with local or foreign entrepreneurs; oil palm, cocoa and fruit plantation developments; manufacturing and packaging, trading, supermarkets and restaurants; Chair. MUHAMMAD RADZI BIN Haji MANSOR; Man. Dir Encik ROSLAN BIN HAMIR; 1,189 employees.

Majlis Amanah Rakyat (MARA) (Trust Council for the People): Bangunan Medan MARA, 25th Floor, Jalan Raja Laut, 50609 Kuala Lumpur; tel. (3) 26915111; fax (3) 26913620; e-mail webmaster@mara.gov.my; internet www.mara.gov.my; f. 1966; est. to promote, stimulate, facilitate and undertake economic and social development, and to participate in industrial and commercial undertakings and jt ventures; Dir-Gen. IBRAHIM BIN AHMAD.

Malaysian Agricultural Research and Development Institute (MARDI): POB 12301, General Post Office, 50774 Kuala Lumpur; tel. (3) 89437111; fax (3) 89483664; e-mail enquiry@mardi.gov.my; internet www.mardi.gov.my; f. 1969; research and development in food and tropical agriculture; Dir-Gen. Datuk Dr ABD. SHUKOR BIN ABD. RAHMAN.

Malaysian Industrial Development Authority (MIDA): Plaza Sentral, Block 4, 5 Jalan Stesen Sentral, 50470 Kuala Lumpur; tel. (3) 22673633; fax (3) 22747970; e-mail corporate@mida.gov.my; internet www.mida.gov.my; f. 1967; Chair. Tan Sri Dr SULAIMAN MAHBOOB; Dir-Gen. Datuk JALILAH BABA.

Malaysian Industrial Development Finance Bhd (MIDF): Level 21, Menara MIDF, 82 Jalan Raja Chulan, 50200 Kuala Lumpur; tel. (3) 21738888; fax (3) 21738877; e-mail inquiry-feedback@midf.com.my; internet www.midf.com.my; f. 1960 by the Govt; banks, insurance cos, industrial financing, advisory services, project development, merchant and commercial banking services; Chair. Tan Sri Dato' MAHMOOD BIN TAIB; Man. Dir Datuk MOHAMED NAJIB Haji ABDULLAH.

Malaysian Pepper Board: Lot 115, Jalan Utama, 93916 Kuching, Sarawak; tel. (82) 331811; fax (82) 336877; e-mail info@mpb.gov.my; internet www.mpb.gov.my; f. 2007; est. to replace the Pepper Marketing Bd; responsible for the statutory grading of all Sarawak pepper for export, licensing of pepper dealers and exporters, trading and the development and promotion of pepper grading, storage and processing facilities. Chair. Datuk ALEXANDER NANTA LINGGI; Dir-Gen. GRUNSIN AYOM.

Pinang Development Corporation: 1 Pesiaran Mahsuri, Bandar Bayan Baru, 11909 Bayan Lepas, Pinang; tel. (4) 6340111; fax (4) 6432405; e-mail enquiry@pdc.gov.my; internet www.pdc.gov.my;

f. 1969; development agency of the Pinang state government; Gen. Man. Dato' ROSLI JAAFAR.

Sarawak Economic Development Corpn: Menara SEDC, 6th–11th Floors, Sarawak Plaza, Jalan Tunku Abdul Rahman, 93100 Kuching; tel. (82) 416777; fax (82) 424330; e-mail ssedc@po.jaring.my; internet www.sedc.com.my; f. 1972; statutory org. responsible for commercial and industrial development in Sarawak either solely or jtly with foreign and local entrepreneurs; responsible for the development of tourism infrastructure; Chair. Datuk Haji TALIB ZULPILIP.

Selangor State Development Corporation (PKNS): Level 2, Menara HPAIC, Laman Seri Business Park, Seksyen 13, 40100 Shah Alam, Selangor; tel. (3) 55201234; fax (3) 55102149; e-mail wazir@pkns.gov.my; internet www.pkns.gov.my; f. 1964; partially govt-owned; Gen. Man. OTHMAN BIN Haji OMAR.

CHAMBERS OF COMMERCE

Associated Chinese Chambers of Commerce and Industry of Malaysia: Wisma Chinese Chamber, 6th Floor, 258 Jalan Ampang, 50450 Kuala Lumpur; tel. (3) 42603090; fax (3) 42603080; e-mail acccim@acccim.org.my; internet www.acccim.org.my; Pres. Tan Sri WILLIAM CHENG; Sec.-Gen. Datuk DAVID CHUA.

Malay Chamber of Commerce Malaysia: 29 & 31 Jalan Lawan Pedang, 13/27 Shah Alam, 40100 Selangor; tel. (3) 55199110; fax (3) 55120801; e-mail info@dpmmns.com.my; internet www.dpmms.com.my; f. 1957; fmrly Associated Malay Chambers of Commerce of Malaya; present name adopted 1992; Pres. Tan Sri ROZALI ISMAIL BIN; Sec.-Gen. ZAKI SAID.

Malaysian Associated Indian Chambers of Commerce and Industry: Megan Ave II, Blok B, 9th Floor, Unit 1, 12 Jalan Yap Kwan Seng, 50450 Kuala Lumpur; tel. (3) 21712616; fax (3) 21711195; e-mail info@maicci.org.my; internet www.maicci.org.my; f. 1950; Pres. Datuk K. K ESWARAN; 8 brs.

Malaysian International Chamber of Commerce and Industry (MICCI) (Dewan Perniagaan dan Perindustrian Antarabangsa Malaysia): C-8-8, Plaza Mont' Kiara, 2 Jalan Kiara, 50480 Kuala Lumpur; tel. (3) 62017708; fax (3) 62017705; e-mail micci@micci.com; internet www.micci.com; f. 1837; brs in Pinang, Perak, Johor, Melaka and Sabah; 1,000 corp. mems; Pres. CHARLES IRELAND; Exec. Dir STEWART J. FORBES.

National Chamber of Commerce and Industry of Malaysia: Menara MATRADE, Level 3, West Wing, Jalan Khidmat Usaha, off Jalan Duta, 50480 Kuala Lumpur; tel. (3) 62049811; fax (3) 62049711; e-mail enquiry@nccim.org.my; internet www.nccim.org.my; f. 1962; Pres. Tuan Syed ALI MOHAMED ALATTAS; Hon. Sec.-Gen. Dato' Syed HUSSEIN AL-HABSHEE.

Sabah Bumiputera Chamber of Commerce (SBCC): Lot 119, 4th Floor, SBCC Bldg, Locked Bag 154, Jalan Gaya, 88999 Kota Kinabalu; tel. (88) 222442; fax (88) 223454; f. 1972; Pres. Datuk Haji AHMAD ALIP LOPE ABDUL AZIZ; Sec.-Gen. JURIL Haji SUDIN.

Sabah United Chinese Chambers of Commerce (SUCCC): POB 12176, 88824 Kota Kinabalu; tel. (88) 225460; fax (88) 218185; e-mail succc01@tm.net.my; internet www.succc.org; f. 1955; Pres. Datuk Seri Panglima SARI NUAR.

Sarawak Chamber of Commerce and Industry (SCCI): DUBS Commercial Centre, 2nd Floor, Lot 376, Seksyen 54, Jalan Petanak, 93100 Kuching; tel. (82) 237148; fax (82) 237186; e-mail scci@cdc.net.my; internet www.scci.org.my; f. 1950; Chair. Datuk Abang Haji ABDUL KARIM Tun Abang Haji OPENG.

INDUSTRIAL AND TRADE ASSOCIATIONS

Federation of Malaysian Manufacturers: Wisma FMM, 3 Persiaran Dagang, PJU 9 Bandar Sri Damansara, 52200 Kuala Lumpur; tel. (3) 62761211; fax (3) 62741266; e-mail webmaster@fmm.org.my; internet www.fmm.org.my; f. 1968; offers guidance and advice relating to trade and industry; presents problems and concerns to the Govt; 2,117 mems (Jan. 2005); Pres. Tan Sri Datuk MUSTAFA MANSUR; CEO LEE CHENG SUAN.

Federation of Rubber Trade Associations of Malaysia: 138 Jalan Bandar, 50000 Kuala Lumpur; tel. (3) 2384006.

Malayan Agricultural Producers' Association: Plaza Ampang City, 16G-L, Jalan Ampang, 50734 Kuala Lumpur; tel. (3) 2545253; fax (3) 2413158; e-mail mapa@myjaring.net; internet www.mapa.net.my; f. 1997; 406 mem. estates and 108 factories/mills; Pres. Tan Sri Dato' Dr MOHD NOOR BIN ISMAIL; Dir MOHAMAD BIN AUDONG.

Malaysian Automotive Association: F-1-47, Blok F, Jalan PJU 1A/3, 2 Taipan Damansara, Parcel 1, Ara Damansara, 47301 Petaling Jaya, Selangor Darul Ehsan; tel. (3) 78439947; fax (3) 78430847; e-mail secretariat@maa.org.my; internet www.maa.org.my; f. 1960 as Fed. of Malaya Motor Traders' Asscn; renamed following merger with Malaysian Motor Vehicle Assemblers' Asscn in 2000; Pres. Datuk AISHAH AHMAD; Sec.-Gen. GOH CHENG MENG.

MALAYSIA

Malaysian Iron and Steel Industry Federation: 28E–30E, Tingkat 5, Blok 2, Worldwide Business Park, Jalan Tinju 13/50, Seksyen 13, Shah Alam, 40675 Selangor; tel. (3) 55133970; fax (3) 55133891; e-mail enquiry@misif.org.my; internet www.misif.org.my; Pres. CHOW CHONG LONG; 150 mems.

Malaysian Palm Oil Association (MPOA): Bangunan Getah Asli I, 12th Floor, 148 Jalan Ampang, 50450 Kuala Lumpur; tel. (3) 27105680; fax (3) 27105679; e-mail mpoa@mpoa.org.my; internet www.mpoa.org.my; f. 1999; est. as result of rationalization of plantation industry; secr. for producers of palm oil; Chair. Dato' AZHAR ABDUL HAMID.

Malaysian Pineapple Industry Board: Wisma Nanas, 5 Jalan Padi Mahsuri, Bandar Baru UDA, 81200 Johor Bahru; tel. (7) 2361211; fax (7) 2365694; e-mail umum@mpib.gov.my; internet www.mpib.gov.my; Dir-Gen. Haji SAHDAN BIN SALIM.

Malaysian Rubber Board: POB 10150, 50908 Kuala Lumpur; tel. (3) 92062000; fax (3) 21634492; e-mail general@lgm.gov.my; internet www.lgm.gov.my; f. 1998; implements policies and development programmes to ensure the viability of the Malaysian rubber industry; regulates the industry (in particular, the packing, grading, shipping and export of rubber); Dir-Gen. Dr SALMIAH AHMAD.

Malaysian Rubber Products Manufacturers' Association: 1 Jalan USJ 11/1J, Subang Jaya, 47620 Petaling Jaya, Selangor; tel. (3) 56316150; fax (3) 56316152; e-mail mrpma@po.jaring.my; f. 1952; Pres. Tan Sri Datuk ARSHAD AYUB; 144 mems.

Malaysian Timber Certification Council (MTCC): C-8-5, Megan Ave II, 12 Jalan Yap Kwan Seng, 50450 Kuala Lumpur; tel. (3) 21612298; fax (3) 21612293; e-mail info@mtcc.com.my; internet www.mtcc.com.my; f. 1999; operates a voluntary national timber certification scheme to encourage sustainable forest management; Chair. Dato' Dr FREEZAILAH CHE YEOM.

Malaysian Wood Industries Association: Menara PGRM, 18th Floor, 8 Jalan Pudu Ulu, Cheras, 55100 Kuala Lumpur; tel. (3) 92811999; fax (3) 92828999; e-mail mwia@tm.net.my; internet www.mtc.com.my; f. 1957; CEO CHEA KAM HUAN.

National Tobacco Board Malaysia (Ibu Pejabat Lembaga Tembakau Negara): Kubang Kerian, POB 198, 15720 Kota Bharu, Kelantan; tel. (9) 7652212; fax (9) 7655640; e-mail ltnm@ltn.gov.my; internet www.ltn.gov.my; Dir-Gen. TEO HUI BEK.

Northern Malaya Rubber Millers and Packers Association: 22 Pitt St, 3rd Floor, Suites 301–303, 10200 Pinang; tel. (4) 620037; f. 1919; 153 mems; Pres. HWANG SING LUE; Hon. Sec. LEE SENG KEOK.

Palm Oil Refiners' Association of Malaysia (PORAM): 801 C/802A Blok B, Executive Suites, Kelana Business Centre, 97 Jalan SS7/2, 47301 Kelana Jaya, Selangor; tel. (3) 74920006; fax (3) 74920128; e-mail info@poram.org.my; internet www.poram.org.my; f. 1975; est. to promote the palm oil refining industry; Chair. MOHD ZAIN ISMAIL; CEO MOHD JAAFAR AHMAD; 90 mems.

Rubber Industry Smallholders Development Authority (RISDA): Bangunan RISDA, km 7, Jalan Ampang, Karung Berkunci 11067, 50990 Kuala Lumpur; tel. (3) 4564022; fax (3) 42576726; e-mail webmaster@risda.gov.my; internet www.risda.gov.my; Chair. Tan Sri RAHIM TAMBY CHIK; Dir-Gen. Datuk MOHD IZAT HASAN.

Tin Industry Research and Development Board: West Block, 8th Floor, Wisma Selangor Dredging, Jalan Ampang, POB 12560, 50782 Kuala Lumpur; tel. (3) 21616171; fax (3) 21616179; e-mail mcom@mcom.com.my; Chair. MOHAMED AJIB ANUAR; Sec. MUHAMAD NOR MUHAMAD.

EMPLOYERS' ORGANIZATIONS

Malaysian Employers' Federation: 3A06–3A07, Blok A, Pusat Dagangan Phileo Damansara II, 15 Jalan 16/11, off Jalan Damansara, 46350 Petaling Jaya, Selangor; tel. (3) 79557778; fax (3) 79556808; e-mail mef-hq@mef.org.my; internet www.mef.org.my; f. 1959; Pres. Dato' AZMAN SHAH Dato' Seri HARUN; Exec. Dir Haji SHAMSUDDIN BARDAN; private sector org. incorporating 13 employer orgs and 4,611 individual enterprises, incl.:

  Association of Insurance Employers: c/o Royal Insurance (M) Sdn Bhd, Menara Boustead, 5th Floor, 69 Jalan Raja Chulan, 50200 Kuala Lumpur; tel. (3) 2410233; fax (3) 2442762; Pres. NG KIM HOONG.

  Commercial Employers' Association of Peninsular Malaysia: c/o The East Asiatic Co (M) Bhd, 1 Jalan 205, 46050 Petaling Jaya, Selangor; tel. (3) 7913322; fax (3) 7913561; Pres. HAMZAH Haji GHULAM.

  Malaysian Chamber of Mines: West Block, Wisma Selangor Dredging, 8th Floor, 142C Jalan Ampang, 50450 Kuala Lumpur; tel. (3) 21616171; fax (3) 21616179; e-mail mcom@mcom.com.my; internet www.mcom.com.my; f. 1914; promotes and protects interests of Malaysian mining industry; Pres. MOHAMED AJIB ANUAR; Exec. Dir MUHAMAD NOR MUHAMAD; 100 mems.

Malaysian Textile Manufacturers' Association: C-9-4, Megan Ave 1, 189 Jalan Tun Razak, 50400 Kuala Lumpur; tel. (3) 21621454; fax (3) 21625148; e-mail info@mtma.org.my; internet www.fashion-asia.com; Pres. J. C. SURESH; CEO ANDREW HONG; 100 mems.

Pan Malaysian Bus Operators' Association: 88 Jalan Sultan Idris Shah, 30300 Ipoh, Perak; tel. (5) 2549421; fax (5) 2550858; Sec. TEOH EWE HUN.

Sabah Employers' Consultative Association: Dewan SECA, No. 4, Block A, 1st Floor, Bandar Ramai-Ramai, 90000 Sandakan, Sabah; tel. and fax (89) 272846; Chair. LING AH HONG.

Stevedore Employers' Association: 5 Pengkalan Weld, POB 288, 10300 Pinang; tel. (4) 2615091; Pres. ABDUL RAHMAN MAIDIN.

UTILITIES

Energy Commission of Malaysia: 12 Jalan Tun Hussein, Precinct 2, 62100 Putrajaya; tel. (3) 88708500; fax (3) 88888637; e-mail fauzih@st.gov.my; internet www.st.gov.my; f. 2002; regulatory body supervising electricity and gas supply; Chair. Tan Sri Datuk Dr AHMAD TAJUDDIN ALI; CEO Ir AHMAD FAUZI BIN HASAN.

Electricity

Tenaga Nasional Bhd: 129 Jalan Bangsar, POB 11003, 50732 Kuala Lumpur; tel. (3) 2825566; fax (3) 22833686; e-mail webadmin@tnb.com.my; internet www.tnb.com.my; f. 1990; est. through corporatization and privatization of Nat. Electricity Bd; 53% govt-controlled; generation, transmission and distribution of electricity in Peninsular Malaysia; generating capacity of 7,621 MW (63% of total power generation); also purchases power from 12 licensed independent power producers; Chair. Tan Sri Dato' Amar LEO MOGGIE; Pres. and CEO Dato' Che KHALIB BIN MOHAMAD NOH.

Sabah Electricity Supply Board (SESB): Wisma SESB, Jalan Tunku Abdul Rahman, 88673 Kota Kinabalu; tel. (88) 282500; fax (88) 282314; e-mail webmaster@sesb.com.my; internet www.sesb.com.my; generation, transmission and distribution of electricity in Sabah; Man. Dir Ir BAHARIN BIN DIN.

Syarikat Sesco Bhd (SESCO): POB 149, 93700 Kuching, Sarawak; tel. (82) 441188; fax (82) 444433; e-mail public_enquiry@sesoc.com.my; internet www.sesco.com.my; fmrly Sarawak Electricity Supply Corpn; generation, transmission and distribution of electricity in Sarawak; Chair. Datuk ABDUL HAMED SEPAWI.

Gas

Gas Malaysia Sdn Bhd: 5 Jalan Serendah 26/17, Seksyen 26, Peti Surat 7901, 40732 Shah Alam, Selangor Darul Ehsan; tel. (3) 51923000; e-mail ccu@gasmalaysia.com; internet www.gasmalaysia.com; f. 1992; Chair. Tan Sri Datuk Dr HAMZAH BAKAR; CEO MUHAMAD NOOR HAMID.

Water

Under the federal Constitution, water supply is the responsibility of the state Governments. In 1998, owing to water shortages, the National Water Resources Council was established to co-ordinate management of water resources at national level. Malaysia's sewerage system is operated by Indah Water Konsortium, owned by Prime Utilities.

National Water Resources Council: c/o Ministry of Works, Jalan Sultan Salahuddin, 50580 Kuala Lumpur; tel. (3) 2919011; fax (3) 2986612; f. 1998; co-ordinates management of water resources at national level through co-operation with state water boards; chaired by the Prime Minister.

Regulatory Authorities

Johor State Regulatory Body: c/o Pejabat Setiausaha Kerajaan Negeri Johor, Aras 1, Bangunan Sultan Ibrahim, Jalan Bukit Timbalan, 80000 Johor Bahru; tel. (7) 223850; Dir Haji OMAR BIN AWAB.

Kelantan Water Department: Tingkat Bawah, Blok 6, Kota Darul Naim, 15503 Kota Bharu, Kelantan; tel. (9) 7475240; fax (9) 7475220; e-mail jank@kelantan.gov.my; internet www.jank.kelantan.gov.my; Dir Tengku ADLI BIN Tengku ABDULLAH.

Water Supply Authorities

Kedah Public Works Department: Bangunan Sultan Abdul Halim, Jalan Sultan Badlishah, 05582 Alor Setar, Kedah; tel. (4) 7334041; fax (4) 7341616; internet kedah.jkr.gov.my; Dir Ir ROSLAND BIN GHANI.

Kelantan Water Sdn Bhd: Bangunan Perbadanan Menteri Besar Kelantan, Lot 2 & 257, Jalan Kuala Krai, 15050 Kota Bharu, Kelantan; tel. (9) 7437777; fax (9) 7472030; internet www.airkelantan.com.my; Dir PETER NEW BERKLEY.

MALAYSIA

Directory

Kuching Water Board: Jalan Batu Lintang, 93200 Kuching, Sarawak; tel. (82) 240371; fax (82) 244546; e-mail juliab@kwb.gov.my; internet www.kwb.gov.my; Chair. Dato' Sri AHMAD TARMIZI BIN HAJI SULAIMAN; Gen. Man. PAUL CHAN PHOO THIEN (acting).

Labuan Public Works Department: Jalan Kg. Jawa, POB 2, 87008 Labuan; tel. (87) 414040; fax (87) 412370; Dir Ir ZULKIFLY BIN MADON.

LAKU Management Sdn Bhd: Menara Soon Hup, 6th Floor, Lot 907, Jalan Merbau, 98000 Miri; tel. (85) 442000; fax (85) 442005; e-mail laku@lakumyy.po.my; internet www.lakumanagement.com.my; f. 1995; serves Miri, Limbang and Bintulu; Chair. HUBERT THIAN CHONG HUI; CEO WONG TIONG KAI.

Melaka Water Corpn: Tingkat Bawah, 1st & 10th–13th Floors, Graha Maju, Jalan Graha Maju, 75300 Melaka; tel. (6) 2821700; fax (6) 2837266; e-mail baharam@pamwtr.gov.my; Dir Ir Haji BAHARAM BIN HAJI MOHAMAD.

Negeri Sembilan Water Department: Wisma Negeri, 70990 Seremban; tel. (6) 7610505; fax (6) 7617841; Dir Ir ZULKIFLI IBRAHIM.

Pahang Water Supply Department (Jabatan Bekalan Air Pahang): Kompleks JBA, Bandar Indera Mahkota, 25200 Kuantan, Pahang; tel. (9) 5712222; fax (9) 5712221; e-mail p-jba@pahang.gov.my; internet jba.pahang.gov.my; Dir Ir Haji ISMAIL BIN HAJI MAT NOOR.

Perak Water Board: Jalan St John, Peti Surat 589, 30760 Ipoh, Perak; tel. (5) 2551155; fax (5) 2556397; internet www.lap.com.my; Dir Dato' Ir MOHD YUSOF MOHD ISA.

Pinang Water Supply Corpn: Menara KOMTAR, Level 32, Jalan Pinang, 10000 Pinang; tel. (4) 2634200; fax (4) 2613581; e-mail customer@pba.com.my; internet www.pba.com.my; f. 1973; Gen. Man. Ir JASENI BIN MAIDINSA.

Sabah State Water Department: Wisma MUIS, Blok A, Tingkat 6, Beg Berkunci 210, 88825 Kota Kinabalu; tel. (88) 232364; fax (88) 232396; e-mail jans.hq@sabah.gov.my; internet www.sabah.gov.my/air; Man. MOHAMAD TAHIR BIN MOHAMAD TALIB.

SAJ Holdings Sdn Bhd: Bangunan Ibu Pejabat SAJ Holdings, Jalan Garuda, Larkin, POB 262, 80350 Johor Bahru; tel. (7) 2244040; fax (7) 2241990; e-mail support@saj.com.my; internet www.saj.com.my; f. 1999; Exec. Chair. Tan Sri Dato' Paduka Dr SALEHUDDIN MOHAMED.

Sarawak Public Works Department: Wisma Seberkas, Jalan Tun Haji Openg, 93582 Kuching; tel. (82) 203100; fax (82) 429679; internet www.jkr.sarawak.gov.my; Dir Dato' Ir HUBERT THIAN CHONG HUI.

Selangor Water Supply Co: POB 5001, Jalan Pantai Baru, 59990 Kuala Lumpur; tel. (3) 2826244; fax (3) 22955168; e-mail puspel@syabas.com.my; internet www.syabas.com.my; f. 1972; CEO Dato' RUSLAN HASSAN.

Sibu Water Board: Km 5, Jalan Salim, POB 405, 96007 Sibu, Sarawak; tel. (84) 211001; fax (84) 211543; e-mail swbs@swb.gov.my; internet www.swb.gov.my; Gen. Man. DANIEL WONG PARK ING.

Terengganu Water Department: Wisma Negeri, Tingkat 3, Jalan Pejabat, 20200 Kuala Terengganu; tel. (9) 6222444; fax (9) 6221510; Dir Ir Haji WAN NGAH BIN WAN.

TRADE UNIONS

Congress of Unions of Employees in the Public Administrative and Civil Services (CUEPACS): Wisma CUEPACS, 34A, Jalan Gajah, off Jalan Yew, Pudu 55100, Kuala Lumpur; tel. (3) 9285-6110; fax (3) 9285-9457; mems: 100 public sector unions; Pres. Haji OMAR BIN Haji OSMAN; Sec.-Gen. LOK YIM PHENG.

Malaysian Trades Union Congress (MTUC): Wisma MTUC, 10-5, Jalan USJ 9/5T, 47620 Subang Jaya, Selangor; POB 3073, 46000 Petaling Jaya, Selangor; tel. (3) 80242953; fax (3) 80243225; e-mail mtuc@tm.net.my; internet www.mtuc.org.my; f. 1949; 247 affiliated unions, representing approx. 500,000 workers; Pres. MOHD KHALID ATAN; Sec.-Gen. ABDUL HALIM MANSOR.

Principal affiliated unions:

All Malayan Estates Staff Union: 29-3, Jalan USJ 1/1A, 47620 Subang Jaya; tel. (3) 80249533; fax (3) 80247822; e-mail amesu@streamyx.com; internet amesu.org; 2,654 mems; Pres. JEYA PASKAR; Gen. Sec. JEY KUMAR.

Amalgamated Union of Employees in Government Clerical and Allied Services: 32A Jalan Gajah, off Jalan Yew, Pudu 55100 Kuala Lumpur; tel. (3) 92859513; fax (3) 92838632; e-mail auegcas@tm.net.my; internet www.auegcas.org.my; 6,703 mems; Pres. IBRAHIM BIN ABDUL WAHAB; Gen. Sec. MOHAMED IBRAHIM BIN ABDUL WAHAB.

Chemical Workers' Union: 35B Jalan SS15/4B, Subang Jaya, 47500 Petaling Jaya, Selangor; 1,886 mems; Pres. RUSIAN HITAM; Gen. Sec. JOHN MATHEWS.

Electricity Industry Workers' Union: 55-2 Jalan SS15/8A, Subang Jaya, 47500 Petaling Jaya, Selangor; tel. (3) 7335243; 22,000 mems; Pres. ABDUL RASHID; Gen. Sec. P. ARUNASALAM.

Federation of Unions in the Textile, Garment and Leather Industry: c/o Selangor Textile and Garment Manufacturing Employees Union, 9D Jalan Travers, 50470 Kuala Lumpur; tel. (3) 2742578; f. 1989; four affiliates; Pres. ABDUL RAZAK HAMID; Gen. Sec. ABU BAKAR IBRAHIM.

Harbour Workers' Union, Port Klang: 106 Persiaran Raja Muda Musa, Port Klang; 2,426 mems; Pres. MOHAMED SHARIFF BIN YAMIN; Gen. Sec. MOHAMED HAYAT BIN AWANG.

Kesatuan Pekerja-Pekerja FELDA: 2 Jalan Maktab Enam, Melalui Jalan Perumahan Gurney, 54000 Kuala Lumpur; tel. (3) 26929972; fax (3) 26913409; 2,900 mems; Pres. INDERA PUTRA Haji ISMAIL; Gen. Sec. MOHAMAD BIN ABDUL RAHMAN.

Kesatuan Pekerja-Pekerja Perusahaan Membuat Tekstil dan Pakaian Pulau Pinang dan Seberang Prai: 23 Lorong Talang Satu, Prai Gardens, 13600 Prai; tel. (4) 301397; 3,900 mems; Pres. ABDUL RAZAK HAMID; Gen. Sec. KENNETH STEPHEN PERKINS.

Kesatuan Pekerja Tenaga Nasional Bhd: 30 Jalan Liku Bangsar, POB 10400, 59100 Kuala Lumpur; tel. (3) 2745657; 10,456 mems; Pres. MOHAMED ABU BAKAR; Gen. Sec. IDRIS BIN ISMAIL.

Malayan Technical Services Union: 3A Jalan Menteri, off Jalan Cochrane, 55100 Kuala Lumpur; tel. (3) 92851778; fax (3) 92811875; e-mail info@mtsu.org.my; internet www.mtsu.org.my; 6,000 mems; Pres. SHUHAIMI OTHMAN; Gen. Sec. SAMUEL DEVADASAN.

Malaysian Rubber Board Staff Union: POB 10150, 50908 Kuala Lumpur; tel. (3) 42565102; 850 mems; Pres. HASNAH GANI; Gen. Sec. SUBRAMANIAM SINNASAMY.

Metal Industry Employees' Union: Metalworkers' House, 5 Lorong Utara Kecil, 46200 Petaling Jaya, Selangor; tel. (3) 79567214; fax (3) 79550854; e-mail mieum@tm.net.my; 15,491 mems; Pres. SAMUSUDDIN USOP; Gen. Sec. JACOB ENGKATESU.

National Union of Bank Employees (NUBE): 12 NUBE House, 3rd Floor, Jalan Tun Sambanthan 3, Brickfield, 50470 Kuala Lumpur; tel. (3) 22749800; fax (3) 22601800; e-mail nube_hq@streamyx.com; internet www.nube.org.my; f. 1958; 30,000 mems; Gen. Sec. JOSEPH SOLOMON.

National Union of Commercial Workers: Bangunan NUCW, 98A–D Jalan Masjid India, 50100 Kuala Lumpur; POB 12059, 50780 Kuala Lumpur; tel. (3) 26927385; fax (3) 26925930; f. 1959; 11,937 mems; Pres. TAIB SHARIF; Gen. Sec. C. KRISHNAN.

National Union of Plantation Workers: 428A–B Jalan 5/46, Gasing Indah, POB 73, 46700 Petaling Jaya, Selangor; tel. (3) 77877622; fax (3) 77815321; e-mail nupw@tm.net.my; f. 1946; 29,251 mems; Pres. NADARAJA ANAK laki KUMARAN; Gen. Sec. Dato' G. SANKARAN.

National Union of PWD Employees: 32B Jalan Gajah, off Jalan Yew, 55100 Kuala Lumpur; tel. (3) 9850149; 5,869 mems; Pres. KULOP IBRAHIM; Gen. Sec. S. SANTHANASAMY.

National Union of Telecoms Employees: Wisma NUTE, 17A Jalan Bangsar, 59200 Kuala Lumpur; tel. (3) 2821599; fax (3) 2821015; 15,874 mems; Pres. MOHAMED SHAFIE B. P. MAMMAL; Gen. Sec. MOHD JAFAR BIN ABDUL MAJID.

Non-Metallic Mineral Products Manufacturing Employees' Union: 99A Jalan SS14/1, Subang Jaya, 47500 Petaling Jaya, Selangor; tel. (3) 56339006; fax (3) 56333863; e-mail nonmet@tm.net.my; 10,000 mems; Pres. ABDULLAH ABU BAKAR; Sec. S. SOMAHSUNDRAM.

Railwaymen's Union of Malaya: Bangunan Tong Nam, 1st Floor, Jalan Tun Sambathan (Travers), 50470 Kuala Lumpur; tel. (3) 2741107; fax (3) 2731805; 5,500 mems; Pres. ABDUL RAZAK MOHD HASSAN; Gen. Sec. S. VEERASINGAM.

Technical Services Union—Tenaga Nasional Bhd: Bangunan Keselamatan, POB 11003, Bangsar, Kuala Lumpur; tel. (3) 2823581; 3,690 mems; Pres. RAMLY YATIM; Gen. Sec. CLIFFORD SEN.

Timber Employees' Union: 10 Jalan AU5C/14, Ampang, Ulu Kelang, Selangor; 7,174 mems; Pres. ABDULLAH METON; Gen. Sec. MINHAT SULAIMAN.

Transport Workers' Union: 21 Jalan Barat, Petaling Jaya, 46200 Selangor; tel. (3) 7566567; 10,447 mems; Pres. NORASHIKIN; Gen. Sec. ZAINAL RAMPAK.

Independent Federations and Unions

Kongres Kesatuan Guru-Guru Dalam Perkhidmatan Pelajaran (Congress of Unions of Employees in the Teaching Services): Johor; seven affiliates; Pres. RAMLI BIN MOHD JOHAN; Sec.-Gen. KASSIM BIN Haji HARON.

Malaysian Medical Association: MMA House, 4th Floor, 124 Jalan Pahang, 53000 Kuala Lumpur; tel. (3) 40411375; fax (3) 40418187; e-mail info@mma.org.my; internet www.mma.org.my; f. 1959; 10 affiliates; Pres. Dr DAVID QUEK KWANG LENG.

MALAYSIA

National Union of Journalists: 30B Jalan Padang Belia, 50470 Kuala Lumpur; tel. (3) 2742867; fax (3) 2744776; f. 1962; 1,700 mems; Gen. Sec. ONN EE SENG.

National Union of Newspaper Workers: 11A–B Jalan 20/14, Paramount Garden, 46300 Petaling Jaya, Selangor; tel. (3) 78768118; fax (3) 78751490; e-mail nunwl@streamyx.com; f. 1967; 3,000 mems; Pres. RAHIM OMAR; Gen. Sec. R. CHANDRASEKARAN.

Sabah

Sabah Banking Employees' Union: POB 11649, 88818 Kota Kinabalu; tel. (88) 213830; fax (88) 260860; e-mail sbeu2004@streamyx.com; internet www.sbeu.org; 729 mems; Pres. MARGARET CHIN SAT PENG; Gen. Sec. CATHERINE JIKUNAN.

Sabah Civil Service Union: Kota Kinabalu; f. 1952; 1,356 mems; Pres. J. K. K. VOON; Sec. STEPHEN WONG.

Sabah Commercial Employees' Union: Sinsuran Shopping Complex, Lot 3, Block N, 2nd Floor, POB 10357, 88803 Kota Kinabalu; tel. (88) 225971; fax (88) 213815; e-mail sceu-kk@tm.net.my; f. 1957; 980 mems; Pres. CRISPINA FIDELIS; Gen. Sec. REBECCA CHIN.

Sabah Medical Services Union: POB 11257, 88813 Kota Kinabalu; tel. (88) 242126; fax (88) 242127; e-mail smsu65@hotmail.com; 4,000 mems; Pres. KATHY LO NYUK CHIN; Gen. Sec. LAURENCE VUN.

Sabah Petroleum Industry Workers' Union: POB 1087, Kota Kinabalu; tel. (88) 720737; e-mail victorsyb@yahoo.com; internet www.sabah.org.my/spiwu; f. 1966; 168 mems; Pres. PETER LEE YUN LOONG; Gen. Sec. DANY SIBATU.

Sabah Teachers' Union: POB 10912, 88810 Kota Kinabalu; tel. (88) 420034; fax (88) 431633; f. 1962; 3,001 mems; Pres. KWAN PING SIN; Sec.-Gen. PATRICK Y. C. CHOK.

Sarawak

Kepak Sarawak (Kesatuan Pegawai-Pegawai Bank, Sarawak): POB 62, Bukit Permata, 93100 Kuching, Sarawak; tel. (19) 8549372; e-mail kepaksar@tm.net.my; bank officers' union; 1,430 mems; Gen. Sec. DOMINIC CH'NG YUNG TED.

Sarawak Commercial Employees' Union: POB 807, Kuching; 1,636 mems; Gen. Sec. SONG SWEE LIAP.

Sarawak Teachers' Union: Wisma STU, Lot 10964–10966, Jalan Song, 93350 Kuching; tel. (82) 575120; fax (82) 574120; e-mail thomas@stu.org.my; internet stu.org.my; f. 1965; 17,000 mems; Pres. WILLIAM GHANI BINA; Sec.-Gen. THOMAS HUO KOK SEN.

Transport

RAILWAYS

Peninsular Malaysia

The state-owned Malayan Railways had a total length of 1,672 km in Peninsular Malaysia in 1996. The main railway line follows the west coast and extends 782 km from Singapore, south of Peninsular Malaysia, to Butterworth (opposite Pinang Island) in the north. From Bukit Mertajam, close to Butterworth, the Kedah line runs north to the Thai border at Padang Besar where connection is made with the State Railway of Thailand. The East Coast Line, 526 km long, runs from Gemas to Tumpat (in Kelantan). A 21-km branch line from Pasir Mas (27 km south of Tumpat) connects with the State Railway of Thailand at the border station of Sungei Golok. Branch lines serve railway-operated ports at Port Dickson and Telok Anson as well as Port Klang and Jurong (Singapore). Malaysia's first Light Rail Transit (LRT) system was opened in the Kuala Lumpur area in 1996. A second line began operating within the same system in 1998; a second LRT system, comprising one line, also commenced operations in that year. An express rail link connecting central Kuala Lumpur and the new Kuala Lumpur International Airport (KLIA) opened in 2001.

Keretapi Tanah Melayu Bhd (KTMB) (Malayan Railways): KTMB Corporate Headquarters, Jalan Sultan Hishamuddin, 50621 Kuala Lumpur; tel. (3) 22631111; fax (3) 27105706; e-mail callcenter@ktmb.com.my; internet www.ktmb.com.my; f. 1885; incd as a co under govt control in 1992; privatized in 1997; managed by the consortium Marak Unggal (Renong, DRB and Bolton); Chair. Dato' Sri MOHD ZIN BIN MOHAMED.

Sabah

Sabah State Railway: Karung Berkunci 2047, 88999 Kota Kinabalu; tel. (88) 254611; fax (88) 236395; e-mail webmaster.jkns@sabah.gov.my; internet www.sabah.gov.my/railway; 134 track-km of 1-m gauge (2008); goods and passenger services from Tanjong Aru to Tenom, serving part of the west coast and the interior; diesel trains are used; Gen. Man. Ir BENNY WANG.

ROADS

Peninsular Malaysia

Peninsular Malaysia's road system is extensive, in contrast to those of Sabah and Sarawak. In 2004 the road network in Malaysia totalled an estimated 109,333 km, of which 1,821 km were motorways and 16,275 km were highways.

Sabah

Jabatan Kerja Raya Sabah (Sabah Public Works Department): Jalan Sembulan, Locked Bag 2032, 88582 Kota Kinabalu, Sabah; tel. (88) 244333; fax (88) 237234; e-mail jkrweb@sabah.gov.my; internet www.jkr.sabah.gov.my; f. 1881; implements and maintains public infrastructures such as roads, bridges, buildings and sewerage systems throughout Sabah; maintains a road network totalling 15,756.6 km, of which 5,686.5 km are sealed roads; Dir JOHN ANTHONY.

Sarawak

Jabatan Kerja Raya Sarawak (Sarawak Public Works Department): Tingkat 11–18, Wisma Saberkas, Jalan Tun Abang Haji Openg, 93582 Kuching, Sarawak; tel. (82) 203100; fax (82) 429679; e-mail limkh@sarawaknet.gov.my; internet www.jkr.sarawak.gov.my; implements and maintains public infrastructures in Sarawak; road network totalling 10,979 km, of which 3,986 km are sealed roads; Dir HUBERT THIAN CHONG HUI.

SHIPPING

The ports in Malaysia are classified as federal ports, under the jurisdiction of the federal Ministry of Transport, or state ports, responsible to the state ministries of Sabah and Sarawak.

Peninsular Malaysia

The federal ports in Peninsular Malaysia are Klang (the principal port), Pinang, Johor and Kuantan.

Johor Port Authority: 6A1–8A1 Pusat Perdagangan Pasir Gudang, Jalan Bandar, 81700 Pasir Gudang, Johor; tel. (7) 2534000; fax (7) 2517684; e-mail admin@lpj.gov.my; internet www.lpj.gov.my; f. 1976; Gen. Man. Nik AZIZ BIN HUSSAIN.

Johor Port Bhd: POB 151, Wisma Kontena, 81707 Pasir Gudang, Johor; tel. (7) 2535888; fax (7) 2510980; e-mail jpb@johorport.com.my; internet www.johorport.com.my; Chair. Datuk MOHD SIDIK BIN SHAIK OSMAN.

Klang Port Authority: POB 202, Jalan Pelabuhan, 42005 Port Klang, Selangor; tel. (3) 31688211; fax (3) 31689177; e-mail onestopagency@pka.gov.my; internet www.pka.gov.my; f. 1963; Gen. Man. LIM THEAN SHIANG.

Kuantan Port Authority: Tanjung Gelang, POB 161, 25720 Kuantan, Pahang; tel. (9) 5858000; fax (9) 5833866; e-mail lpktn@lpktn.gov.my; internet www.lpktn.gov.my; f. 1974; Gen. Man. Dato' KHAIRUL ANUAR BIN ABDUL RAHMAN.

Penang Port Commission: 3A–6 Sri Weld Bldg, Weld Quay, 10300 Penang; tel. (4) 2633211; fax (4) 2626211; e-mail sppp@penangport.gov.my; internet www.penangport.gov.my; f. 1956; Gen. Man. NOOR ARIF BIN YUSOFF.

Sabah

The main ports, which are administered by the Sabah Ports Authority, are Kota Kinabalu, Sandakan, Tawau, Lahad Datu, Kudat, Semporna and Kunak. Many international shipping lines serve Sabah. Local services are operated by smaller vessels.

Sabah Ports Authority: Bangunan SPA, Jalan Tun Fuad, Tanjung Lipat, Locked Bag 2005, 88617 Kota Kinabalu, Sabah; tel. (88) 538400; fax (88) 223036; e-mail sabport@tm.net.my; internet www.lpps.sabah.gov.my; f. 1968; Gen. Man. Eng. MAYONG OMAR.

Sarawak

There are four port authorities in Sarawak: Kuching, Rajang, Miri and Bintulu. Kuching, Rajang and Miri are state ports, while Bintulu is a federal port. Kuching port serves the southern region of Sarawak, Rajang port the central region, and Miri port the northern region.

Kuching Port Authority: Jalan Pelabuhan, Pending, POB 530, 93450 Kuching, Sarawak; tel. (82) 482144; fax (82) 481696; e-mail hq@kuport.com.my; internet www.kpa.gov.my; f. 1961; Gen. Man. LIU MOI FONG.

Rajang Port Authority: Jalan Pulau, 96000 Sibu, Sarawak; tel. (84) 319004; fax (84) 318754; e-mail rpa@rajangport.gov.my; internet www.rajangport.gov.my; f. 1970; Gen. Man. HELEN LIM HUI SHYAN.

Principal Shipping Companies

Malaysia Shipping Corpn Sdn Bhd: Office Tower, Plaza Berjaya, Suite 14C, 14th Floor, 12 Jalan Imbi, 55100 Kuala Lumpur; tel. (3) 21418788; fax (3) 21429214; Chair. Y. C. CHANG.

MALAYSIA

Directory

Malaysian International Shipping Corpn Bhd (National Shipping Line of Malaysia): Menara Dayabumi, Level 25, Jalan Sultan Hishamuddin, 50050 Kuala Lumpur; tel. (3) 22738088; fax (3) 22736602; e-mail caffairs@miscbhd.com; internet www.misc.com.my; f. 1968; regular services between South-East Asia, South Asia, Australia, Japan and Europe; also operates chartering, tanker, haulage and warehousing and agency services; majority stake owned by Petroliam Nasional Bhd (PETRONAS); Chair. Dato' SHAMSUL AZHAR BIN ABBAS; Pres. and CEO Datuk NASARUDIN BIN MOHD IDRIS.

Perbadanan Nasional Shipping Line Bhd (PNSL): Kuala Lumpur; tel. (3) 2932211; fax (3) 2930493; f. 1982; specializes in bulk cargoes; a wholly owned subsidiary of Konsortium Logistik Bhd; Chair. Tunku Dato' SHAHRIMAN BIN Tunku SULAIMAN; Exec. Dep. Chair. Dato' SULAIMAN ABDULLAH.

Persha Shipping Agencies Sdn Bhd: Bangunan Mayban Trust, Penthouse Suite, Jalan Pinang, 10200 Pinang; tel. (4) 2612400; fax (4) 2623122; Man. Dir MOHD NOOR MOHD KAMALUDIN.

Syarikat Perkapalan Kris Sdn Bhd (The Kris Shipping Co Ltd): POB 8428, 46789 Petaling Jaya, Selangor; tel. (3) 7046477; fax (3) 7048007; domestic services; Chair. Dato' Seri Syed NAHAR SHAHABUDIN; Gen. Man. ROHANY TALIB.

Trans-Asia Shipping Corpn Sdn Bhd: Lot 1A, Persiaran Jubli Perak, Jalan 22/1, Seksyen 22, 40300 Shah Alam, Selangor; tel. (3) 51018888; fax (3) 55488288; e-mail kytan@tasco.com.my; internet www.tasco.com.my; f. 1974; Man. Dir LEE CHECK POH.

CIVIL AVIATION

The new Kuala Lumpur International Airport (KLIA), situated in Sepang, Selangor (50 km south of Kuala Lumpur) began operations in June 1998, with an initial capacity of 25m.–30m. passengers a year, which was projected to rise to 45m. by 2020. An express rail link between central Kuala Lumpur and KLIA opened in early 2001. There are regional airports at Kota Kinabalu, Pinang, Johor Bahru, Kuching and Pulau Langkawi. In addition, there are airports catering for domestic services at Alor Star, Ipoh, Kota Bharu, Kuala Terengganu, Kuantan and Melaka in Peninsular Malaysia, Sibu, Bintulu and Miri in Sarawak, and Sandakan, Tawau, Lahad Datu and Labuan in Sabah. There are also numerous smaller airstrips.

Department of Civil Aviation (Jabatan Penerbangan Awam Malaysia): 27 Persiaran Perdana, Aras 1–4, Blok Podium, 62618 Putrajaya; tel. (3) 88714000; fax (3) 88901640; e-mail webmaster@dca.gov.my; internet www.dca.gov.my; Dir-Gen. Dato' AZHARUDDIN ABDUL RAHMAN.

AirAsia Sdn Bhd: LCC Terminal Jalan KLIA S3, Southern Support Zone, KLIA, 64000 Sepang, Selangor; tel. (3) 86604333; fax (3) 87751100; e-mail tellus@airasia.com; internet www.airasia.com; f. 1993; 85% owned by HICOM; low-cost national carrier with licence to operate domestic, regional and international flights; Chair. ABDUL AZIZ BIN ABU BAKAR; CEO TONY FERNANDES.

Berjaya Air Sdn Bhd: POB 7591, 40720 Shah Alam, Selangor; tel. (3) 78427300; fax (3) 78427330; e-mail admin@berjaya-air.com; internet www.berjaya-air.com; f. 1989; scheduled and charter domestic services; Pres. Tan Sri Dato' Seri VINCENT TAN CHEE YIOUN.

Firefly: Sultan Abdul Aziz Shah Airport, Admin Bldg 1, 3rd Floor, Kompleks A, 47200 Subang, Selangor; e-mail contactus@fireflyz.com.my; internet www.fireflyz.com.my; f. 2007; wholly owned by Malaysia Airlines; low-cost domestic and regional flights; Man. Dir EDDY LEONG.

Malaysia Airlines: Bangunan Pentadbiran 1, Tingkat 3, MAS Kompleks A, Sultan Abdul Aziz Shah Airport, 47200 Subang, Selangor; tel. (3) 78404550; fax (3) 78463932; e-mail tanwf@malaysiaairlines.com.my; internet www.malaysiaairlines.com.my; f. 1971; est. as the Malaysian successor to Malaysia Singapore Airlines (MSA); known as Malaysian Airline System (MAS) until Oct. 1987; 114 international routes and 118 domestic routes; Chair. Tan Sri Dr MOHAMED MUNIR BIN ABDUL MAJID; Man. Dir and CEO Tengku Dato' AZMIL ZAHRUDDIN.

Transmile Air Sdn Bhd: Cargo Kompleks, Sultan Abdul Aziz Shah Airport, 47200 Subang, Selangor; tel. (3) 78849898; fax (3) 78849899; e-mail info@transmile.com; internet www.transmile.com; f. 1992; scheduled and charter regional and domestic services for passengers and cargo; Chair. Tan Sri A. RAZAK BIN RAMLI.

Tourism

Malaysia has a rapidly growing tourist industry, and tourism is an important source of foreign-exchange earnings. In 2010 a record 24.6m. tourists visited Malaysia, while receipts from tourism were estimated to total RM $56,500m. Singapore is the main source of visitors, followed by Indonesia and Thailand. Health tourism has significantly expanded in recent years; in 2008 some 370,000 foreign patients sought medical treatment at the 35 participating private hospitals in Malaysia.

Malaysia Tourism Promotion Board (Tourism Malaysia): Menara Dato' Onn, Tingkat 17, Putra World Trade Centre, 45 Jalan Tun Ismail, 50480 Kuala Lumpur; tel. (3) 26158188; fax (3) 26935884; e-mail enquiries@tourism.gov.my; internet www.tourismmalaysia.gov.my; f. 1972; est. to co-ordinate and promote activities relating to tourism in Malaysia; Dir-Gen. AZIZAN NOORDIN (acting); Chair. Datuk Dr VICTOR WEE.

Sabah Tourist Association: POB 12181, 88824 Kota Kinabalu, Sabah; tel. and fax (88) 486089; e-mail secretariat@sta.my; internet www.sta.my; f. 1963; independent promotional org.; Chair. LEN PONG LIEW.

Sabah Tourism Board: Mail Bag 112, 88993 Kota Kinabalu, Sabah; tel. (88) 212121; fax (88) 212075; e-mail info@sabahtourism.com; internet www.sabahtourism.com; f. 1976; parastatal promotion org.; Chair. Datuk Seri Tengku ZAINAL ADLIN Tengku MAHAMOOD.

Sarawak Tourism Board: Levels 6 and 7, Bangunan Yayasan Sarawak, Jalan Masjid, 93400 Kuching; tel. (82) 423600; fax (82) 416700; e-mail stb@sarawaktourism.com; internet www.sarawaktourism.com; f. 1995; CEO Datuk RASHID KHAN.

Defence

As assessed at November 2010, the total strength of the armed forces was 109,000; army 80,000 (although this was to be reduced to 60,000–70,000), navy 14,000, air force 15,000; military service is voluntary. Paramilitary forces included the Police-General Operations Force of 18,000 and the People's Volunteer Corps of 240,000. Malaysia is a participant in the Five-Power Defence Arrangements with Singapore, Australia, New Zealand and the United Kingdom.

Defence Expenditure: RM 9,100m. budgeted for 2010.

Chief of the Defence Forces: Gen. Tan Sri Dato' Seri AZIZAN ARIFFIN.

Chief of Army: Gen. Dato' Sri MUHAMMAD ZULKIFELI BIN ZIN.

Chief of Navy Staff: Adm. Tan Sri Dato' Sri ABDUL AZIZ JAAFAR.

Chief of Air Force Staff: Gen. Dato' Seri RODZALI BIN DAUD.

Education

Under the Malaysian education system, free schooling is provided at government-assisted schools for children between the ages of six and 18. There are also private schools, which receive no government financial aid. Education is compulsory for 11 years between the ages of six and 16 years. The Federal Government's development expenditure on education was budgeted at RM 10,827m. in 2009 (21.9% of projected expenditure). Scholarships are awarded at all levels and there are many scholarship-holders studying at universities and other institutes of higher education at home and abroad.

PRIMARY EDUCATION

The national language, Bahasa Malaysia, is the main medium of instruction, although English, Chinese and Tamil are also used. Two-thirds of the total primary school enrolment is in National Schools where Malay is used and the remainder in National-Type Primary Schools where Tamil or Chinese is used. A place in primary school is now assured to every child from the age of six onwards, and parents are free to choose the language of instruction. In 2008 some 3,154,090 students were enrolled in primary education. In 2006/07 the total enrolment at primary level included 96% of all children in the relevant age-group. The primary school course lasts for six years.

SECONDARY EDUCATION

Bahasa Malaysia is the main medium of instruction in secondary schools, while English is taught as a second language and Chinese and Tamil are taught as pupils' own languages. Private Chinese secondary schools are also in operation. Secondary education lasts for seven years, comprising a first cycle of three years and a second of four. In 2008 there were 2,310,660 students enrolled in secondary education. In 2006/07 the total enrolment at the secondary level included 68% of students in the relevant age-group.

HIGHER EDUCATION

In 2008 there were 20 government-funded universities and 33 private universities. In 1995 there were 210,724 students enrolled in tertiary education. In 2002 enrolment at the tertiary level was equivalent to 28% (males 25%, females 31%) of those in the relevant age-group. Malaysia's universities adhere to a quota system (55% of entrants should be Malays and 45% non-Malays), which, in practice, makes it considerably more difficult for non-Malays to gain a place at university. The Government has attempted to encourage foreign universities to establish campuses in Malaysia to improve standards and reduce the cost of sending Malaysian students abroad to study.

THE MALDIVES

Introductory Survey

LOCATION, CLIMATE, LANGUAGE, RELIGION, FLAG, CAPITAL

The Republic of Maldives (commonly referred to as 'the Maldives') is in southern Asia. The country, lying about 675 km (420 miles) south-west of Sri Lanka, consists of 1,192 small coral islands (of which 197 are inhabited), grouped in 26 natural atolls (but divided, for administrative purposes, into 20 atolls), in the Indian Ocean. The climate is warm and humid. The annual average temperature is 27°C (80°F), with little daily or seasonal variation, while annual rainfall is generally between 2,540 mm and 3,800 mm (100 ins to 150 ins). The national language is Dhivehi (Maldivian), which is related to Sinhala. Islam is the state religion, and most Maldivians are Sunni Muslims. The national flag (proportions 2 by 3) is red, with a green rectangle, containing a white crescent, in the centre. The capital is Malé.

CONTEMPORARY POLITICAL HISTORY

Historical Context

The Maldives, called the Maldive Islands until April 1969, formerly had an elected Sultan as head of state. The islands were placed under British protection, with internal self-government, in 1887. They became a republic in January 1953, but the sultanate was restored in February 1954. In 1956 the Maldivian and British Governments agreed to the establishment of a Royal Air Force staging post on Gan, an island in the southernmost atoll, Addu. The Maldives became fully independent, outside the Commonwealth, on 26 July 1965. Following a referendum, the country became a republic again in November 1968, with Amir Ibrahim Nasir, Prime Minister since 1957, as President. A new Constitution, promulgated in 1968, vested considerable powers in the President, including the right to appoint and dismiss the Prime Minister and the Cabinet of Ministers. In 1975 the British Government decided to close the airbase on Gan and completed the withdrawal of its forces the following year.

Domestic Political Affairs

President Gayoom in power (1978–2009)

In March 1975, following rumours of a coup conspiracy, President Nasir dismissed the Prime Minister, Ahmed Zaki, and the premiership was abolished. Unexpectedly, President Nasir announced that he would not seek re-election at the end of his second term in 1978. To succeed him, the Majlis (legislature) chose Maumoon Abdul Gayoom, Minister of Transport under Nasir, who was approved by referendum in July 1978 and took office in November. President Gayoom announced that his main priority would be the development of the poor rural regions, while in foreign affairs the existing policy of non-alignment would be continued.

Ex-President Nasir left the country after his resignation, but the authorities subsequently sought his return to the Maldives, where he was required to answer charges of misappropriating government funds. In 1980 President Gayoom confirmed reports of an attempted coup against the Government and implicated Nasir in the alleged plot. Nasir was to stand trial, in his absence, on these and other charges. In April 1981 Ahmed Naseem, former Deputy Minister of Fisheries and brother-in-law of Nasir, was sentenced to life imprisonment for plotting to overthrow President Gayoom. Nasir himself denied any involvement in the coup, and attempts to extradite him from Singapore were unsuccessful. (In July 1990, however, President Gayoom officially pardoned Nasir *in absentia*, in recognition of the role that he had played in winning national independence.) In September 1983 Gayoom was re-elected as President, for a further five years, by a national referendum (with 95.6% of the popular vote). In September 1988 he was again re-elected unopposed, for a third five-year term, obtaining a record 96.4% of the popular vote.

Another attempt to depose President Gayoom took place in November 1988, when a sea-borne mercenary force, which was composed of around 80 alleged Sri Lankan Tamil separatists (led by a disaffected Maldivian businessman, Abdullah Luthufi), landed in Malé and endeavoured to seize control of important government installations. At the request of President Gayoom, however, the Indian Government dispatched an emergency contingent of 1,600 troops, which rapidly and successfully suppressed the attempted coup. Nineteen people were reported to have been killed in the fighting. In September 1989 the President commuted to life imprisonment the death sentences imposed on 12 Sri Lankans and four Maldivians who had taken part in the aborted coup.

In February 1990, despite alleged opposition from powerful members of the privileged élite, President Gayoom announced that, as part of proposals for a broad new policy of liberalization and democratic reform, he was planning to introduce legislation enabling him to distribute powers, currently enjoyed by the President alone, amongst other official bodies. A further sign of growing democratization in the Maldives was the holding of discussions by the President's Consultative Council, in early 1990, concerning freedom of speech (particularly in the local press). In April, however, it became apparent that some Maldivians opposed political change when three pro-reform members of the Majlis received anonymous death threats. A few months later, following the emergence of several politically outspoken magazines, including *Sangu* (The Conchshell), there was an abrupt reversal of the Government's policy regarding the liberalization of the press. All publications not sanctioned by the Government were banned, and a number of leading writers and publishers were arrested.

As part of a major cabinet reorganization in May 1990, President Gayoom dismissed the Minister of State for Defence and National Security, Ilyas Ibrahim (who also held the Trade and Industries portfolio and headed the State Trading Corporation), following the latter's abrupt and unannounced departure from the country. The Government later disclosed that Ibrahim (Gayoom's brother-in-law) was to have appeared before a presidential special commission investigating alleged embezzlement and misappropriation of government funds. On his return to the Maldives in August, Ibrahim was placed under house arrest. In March 1991, however, the special commission concluded that there was no evidence of involvement, either direct or indirect, by Ibrahim in the alleged financial misdeeds; in the same month the President appointed Ibrahim as Minister of Atolls Administration. In April the President established an anti-corruption board, which was to investigate allegations of corruption, bribery, fraud, misappropriation of government funds and property, and misuse of government office.

In early August 1993, a few weeks before the Majlis vote on the presidential candidate, Gayoom was informed that Ibrahim, whose position as Minister of Atolls Administration had afforded him the opportunity to build a political base outside Malé (where he already enjoyed considerable popularity), was seeking the presidency and attempting to inveigle members of the Majlis (at that time, the Majlis nominated and elected by secret ballot a single candidate, who was presented to the country in a referendum). In the Majlis vote held in late August, the incumbent President, who had previously been unanimously nominated for the presidency by the legislature, obtained 28 votes, against 18 for his brother-in-law. For his allegedly unconstitutional behaviour, however, Ibrahim was charged with attempting to 'influence the members of the Majlis' and he promptly left the country once again. Ibrahim was subsequently tried *in absentia* and sentenced to 15 years' imprisonment. (Ibrahim returned to the Maldives in 1996 when he was placed under house arrest; this restriction was lifted in 1997.) In October 1993 Gayoom's re-election as President for a further five years was endorsed by a national referendum, in which he obtained 92.8% of the popular vote.

In November 1994 President Gayoom outlined various measures intended to strengthen the political system and to advance the process of democratization. These included the granting of greater autonomy and responsibilities to the Cabinet of Ministers, the introduction of regulations governing the conduct of civil servants (in order to increase their accountability), the introduction of democratic elections to island development committees and atoll committees, and the establishment of a Law Commission to enact reforms to the judicial system.

In November 1996 President Gayoom effected an extensive cabinet reshuffle and a reorganization of government bodies, including the establishment of a Supreme Council for Islamic Affairs, which was to be under direct presidential control and was to advise the Government on matters relating to Islam. In early 1997 Gayoom announced that the Citizens' Special Majlis (which was established in 1980 with the specific task of amending the Constitution) had resolved to complete its revision during that year and to implement the amended version of the Constitution by 1 January 1998. The Citizens' Special Majlis finished its 17-year-long task in early November 1997. The revised Constitution was ratified by the President on 27 November and came into effect, as planned, on 1 January 1998. Under the new 156-article Constitution, a formal, multi-candidate contest was permitted for the legislature's nomination for the presidency; no restriction was placed on the number of terms a president might serve; for administrative purposes, the number of atolls was increased from 19 to 20; the Majlis, which was henceforth known as the People's Majlis, was enlarged from 48 to 50 seats; and the Citizens' Special Majlis was renamed the People's Special Majlis.

In September 1998 five individuals declared their candidacy for the presidency; the People's Majlis unanimously voted by secret ballot for the incumbent President Gayoom to go forward to the national referendum. In the referendum, which was held in mid-October, Gayoom was re-elected as President for a fifth term in office, obtaining 90.9% of the popular vote.

In November 1999 elections for 42 members of the 50-seat People's Majlis were conducted (on a non-partisan basis). As part of a government initiative to promote the advancement of women in public life, President Gayoom appointed a woman as the new Island Chief of Himmafushi in June 2001. In December a woman was appointed as Atoll Chief of Vaavu Atoll (the first woman to be assigned a senior executive position of responsibility for an atoll).

Meanwhile, in early 2001 an attempt by 42 prominent Maldivians, including members of the People's Majlis, former cabinet ministers and business executives, to register the newly formed Maldivian Democratic Party (MDP) was blocked by the People's Majlis on the grounds that the existence of political parties would encourage divisions among the public and, therefore, be counter-productive. It was believed by some, however, that President Gayoom had enforced the decision and, in doing so, had acted unconstitutionally.

In July 2002 three journalists were charged with defamation and inciting violence, and were sentenced to life imprisonment for writing articles criticizing the President and the Government. In July a Maldivian businessman was sentenced to life imprisonment for publishing an article via the internet urging that the Government be overthrown. Later that month the human rights group Amnesty International issued a report citing frequent cases of arbitrary detentions, unfair trials and long-term imprisonment and torture of political opponents in the Maldives. The Maldivian authorities strongly rejected the allegations.

In September 2003 detainees at the prison on Maafushi Island near Malé held protests in response to the death of a fellow prisoner. Reports of the violent suppression of the rioting by the country's National Security Service (NSS), and the death of another detainee, prompted major anti-Government protests in the capital, the first ever during President Gayoom's tenure. Large numbers of alleged demonstrators were arrested, and a state of emergency was declared in Malé and its neighbouring islands. Gayoom appealed for calm and announced an investigation into the deaths of the prisoners (the subsequent demise of another two detainees brought the number of deaths to four). Eleven members of the NSS were arrested for their alleged involvement in the over-zealous curbing of the riots, and the Deputy Chief of the NSS and National Police Commissioner, Brig. Adam Zahir, was removed from office (he was reinstated in mid-February 2004, after the inquiry cleared him of any misconduct). In December 2003 a Human Rights Commission was established in Malé. At the end of that month a report by the presidential commission investigating the deaths of the prisoners in September was submitted to Gayoom. The President subsequently stated that the security personnel implicated in the prisoners' deaths had acted illegally and would be prosecuted. He also announced that a programme of penal reform was under way.

Meanwhile, on 25 September 2003 Gayoom was re-elected unanimously by secret ballot in the People's Majlis for a sixth presidential term, defeating three other candidates. His re-election was ratified at a public referendum on 17 October, when he secured 90.3% of the votes cast. One day after the beginning of his new term in office President Gayoom effected a cabinet reorganization, in which the Attorney-General, Dr Mohamed Munavvar, and the Minister of Planning and National Development, Ibrahim Hussain Zaki, were dismissed. Gayoom gave no reason for the dismissals, although it was alleged that the two had been removed for supporting reformers attempting to register a political party. In the same month a group of political activists established the MDP in exile in Sri Lanka, in response to the rise in discontent with the Maldives Government. In February 2004 members of the MDP claimed that more than 15 of the party's supporters had been arrested in Malé in an attempt to disrupt a planned protest march; however, the Government asserted that the raids were aimed at criminal offenders and that only eight people had been detained.

In May 2004 the election, by universal suffrage, of a People's Special Majlis, which was empowered to amend the Constitution, took place. Voters chose 42 members from 121 independent candidates. The President appointed an additional eight people to serve on the council; the People's Special Majlis also included members of the People's Majlis and the Cabinet of Ministers. Gayoom invited members of the public to send him proposals for constitutional reform and in early June the President himself proposed a number of radical constitutional reforms. The People's Special Majlis convened in July to discuss the proposals.

In August 2004 President Gayoom declared an indefinite state of emergency after a pro-democracy protest in the capital became violent. Four police officers were reportedly stabbed and about 185 people, including former Attorney-General Dr Mohamed Munavvar and members of the People's Special Majlis, were arrested during the protests. The Government claimed that the demonstration had been a coup attempt, a charge denied by the opposition MDP, whose exiled founding leader, Mohamed Latheef, accused Gayoom's administration of 'ruthlessly suppressing dissent'. The Government invited a European Union (EU) fact-finding team to Malé. The EU envoys, however, were denied access to the detainees and expressed concern about the continuing detention without charge of the alleged protesters and the ongoing emergency measures. In October the state of emergency was revoked and in December President Gayoom announced that all charges of treason and public order offences against those taken into custody following the August protest were to be suspended.

On 26 December 2004 a tsunami generated by a massive earthquake in the Indian Ocean, off the coast of Indonesia, devastated many of the low-lying Maldive islands. While the resultant death toll was not as high as might have been expected, several of the islands were rendered uninhabitable and an estimated 15,000 people were left homeless by the disaster. The economic consequences of the catastrophe on the Maldives were extensive, owing in large part to the significant contribution made by the tourism industry to the economy.

On 22 January 2005 a total of 149 independent candidates contested elections to the People's Majlis. Candidates supported by the MDP reportedly won 18 of the 42 elective legislative seats. However, the Government stated that only 12 opposition candidates had been successful, claiming that the results were a sign of widespread popular support for its reform policies. In June the People's Majlis unanimously approved a constitutional amendment permitting the registration of political parties in the Maldives, reversing its 2001 decision opposing the establishment of a multi-party democracy. The MDP was subsequently officially registered in the Maldives as a political party, together with several others, including the Dhivehi Rayyithunge Party (DRP—Maldivian People's Party), established by President Gayoom.

In August 2005 a protest took place in Malé demanding the release of all political prisoners. Shortly afterwards the Chairman of the MDP, Mohamed Nasheed, was arrested, prompting several days of unrest in the capital and on various other atolls. Nasheed was subsequently charged with terrorism and attempting to perpetrate anti-Government actions; his trial began in October.

In a significant development towards the further democratization of the Maldives, from June 2006 representatives of the Government and the MDP conducted informal talks at the British High Commission in Colombo, Sri Lanka. These negotiations resulted in what subsequently became known as the Westminster House Agreement. The reported terms of the agreement included the release of a number of opposition detainees and the advancement of constitutional reform, on the part of the Government, in return for MDP assurances that the party would curb public demonstrations and renounce violent protest. Mohamed Nasheed was released in September, although the charges against him were not withdrawn.

In November 2006 more than 100 members of the MDP were arrested in the run-up to a planned demonstration to demand the swifter implementation of reforms; the rally was cancelled by the MDP amid fears for the welfare of protesters. Officials alleged that the MDP had organized the rally as an attempt to overthrow the Government, and that, if held, it would have posed a threat to public safety. In a subsequent report Amnesty International expressed concern at reports of 'repressive measures' being used by government officials. These allegations were vehemently denied by the Government, but they prompted widespread calls for the urgent introduction of a reform programme to prevent the arbitrary detention, mistreatment and torture of dissidents.

Meanwhile, in early 2006 meetings of the People's Special Majlis, which had been established in mid-2004 to draw up and implement constitutional amendments, were obstructed by President Gayoom's refusal to permit the removal of presidential appointees from the body. The MDP condemned the continued presence of representatives who had not been elected, stressing that they should be withdrawn in advance of the redrafting of the Constitution. In February 2006 the MDP boycotted the opening of the People's Majlis in protest at the President's alleged obstruction of the constitutional amendment process. A Police Integrity Commission was established in August, and in November the Human Rights Commission was reconstituted as legally autonomous; however, the introduction of new regulations on press freedom and access to information was delayed indefinitely by the Government in January 2007. A referendum to determine whether to adopt a presidential or parliamentary system of government, which was originally scheduled to be held in September 2006, was postponed owing to disagreements between the Government and the opposition.

In January 2007 Latheef ended three years of voluntary exile in Sri Lanka with his return to the Maldives. In February a demonstration organized by the MDP in protest at police violence against civilians reportedly attracted an estimated 1,000 participants. In April the discovery in Malé harbour of the corpse of a man who was alleged to have died in police custody prompted further demonstrations and numerous arrests. In the same month the Minister of Higher Education, Employment and Social Security, Abdullah Yameen, resigned amid rumours of discord within the Cabinet of Ministers. Yameen also stood down as a member of the DRP, and was reported to be planning the creation of a new political party (he founded the People's Alliance (PA) in 2008).

The death of an inmate of Maafushi prison in the Kaafu atoll in unclear circumstances during a prison revolt in June 2007 precipitated a hunger strike by hundreds of the deceased's fellow prisoners and public outrage at the regulation and conditions of the prison. There was speculation that the subsequent cabinet reorganization was related to the crisis. Further cabinet changes took place in August, when Minister of Justice Mohamed Jameel Ahmed and Attorney-General Hassan Saeed resigned, reportedly over their concerns regarding impediments and delays to the programme of democratic reforms. Minister of Foreign Affairs Dr Ahmed Shaheed resigned later in the month. The three dissident former government members subsequently launched a new body entitled the New Maldives Movement (NMM) and encouraged the formation of a united front of pro-democracy groups. In early January 2008 the official newspaper of the governing DRP, *Hamaroalhi Daily News*, accused the NMM of fostering terrorism. Later in the month the Government declared that the movement had not sought official registration and was therefore illegal. Consequently the NMM was banned by the Government, which granted a licence to two members of the DRP to operate an NGO under the name of the New Maldives Movement. Meanwhile, a press freedom bill was approved by the People's Majlis in August 2007, despite criticism that it fell short of international standards.

The potential threat of terrorism to the Maldives came to the fore when a bomb exploded in Malé on 29 September 2007, injuring 12 foreign tourists. The explosion—the first recorded terrorist attack to take place in the Maldives—was widely believed to have been perpetrated by Islamist extremists. In December three Maldivian men were each sentenced to 15 years in prison for their part in the incident, which they confessed to having planned as a deliberate attack on the country's vital tourism industry. In an attempt to combat the perceived threat of growing Islamic fundamentalism and to protect the lucrative tourism sector, the Government introduced a number of measures, including arresting suspected extremists, banning the wearing of the full veil in public, advocating the promotion of moderate Islamic views in schools and colleges, forbidding the convention of unlicensed Muslim prayer groups, and banning foreign Islamic clerics from visiting the islands unless they had been explicitly invited by the authorities. While visiting an atoll in the far north of the island chain in January 2008, President Gayoom himself escaped unhurt after an attempted knife attack by a 20-year-old Maldivian man. The Government claimed that the President's political rivals were the most likely organizers of the apparent assassination attempt, rather than Islamist extremists, as some early reports had suggested.

Democratization and a new Constitution

The results of a referendum on the system of government, which took place on 18 August 2007, indicated popular support for retaining the presidential system, with a reported 62% of those who participated in favour. In late June 2008 the People's Special Majlis approved final amendments to the draft Constitution, which was then passed to the Cabinet of Ministers and the President in turn. The new Constitution was ratified by the President on 7 August; major points included the direct election of the President (and his declared Vice-President) and the restriction of presidential terms of office to two (whether consecutive or not); the removal of the gender bar on the presidency; the election, rather than presidential appointment, of the Speaker and Deputy Speaker of the People's Majlis; the establishment of a Supreme Court as the highest judicial authority; and the granting to citizens the right to hold peaceful demonstrations. The People's Special Majlis and Judicial Advisory Council were duly dissolved, while the Speaker of the People's Majlis was replaced by an elected incumbent. Meanwhile, the Cabinet of Ministers was in a state of flux as numerous ministers resigned for constitutional and other reasons. By early September a total of 12 political parties had registered in the Maldives. In that month the Election Commissioner, who had been assigned the post by President Gayoom, was replaced by a new five-member Elections Commission, which was nominated and appointed by the People's Majlis.

Mohamed Nasheed elected President

The first multi-party presidential election in the Maldives was held on 8 October 2008. Despite opposition to Gayoom standing for a seventh presidential term, the DRP argued that the new two-term limit did not exclude him from contesting what would be the first election under the new Constitution. Five other candidates contested the presidency, including former political prisoner and leader of the MDP, Mohamed Nasheed. Gayoom secured 40.3% of the votes, Nasheed won 24.9%, Hassan Saeed, who was running as an independent candidate, secured 16.7%, and he was closely followed by Qasim Ibrahim of the Jumhooree Party (JP—Republican Party), with 15.2% of the votes. It was reported that 85.5% of the electorate participated in the poll. As no candidate secured more than 50% of the ballot in the first round of voting, the two leading candidates contested a second round on 28 October. In an historic victory, Nasheed secured the presidency, with 53.7% of the votes, and was consequently inaugurated on 11 November. On the same day the country's first elected Vice-President, Dr. Mohamed Waheed Hassan Manik of the National Unity Party (NUP—Gaumee Itthihaad), was also sworn in. The new President appointed a coalition Cabinet of Ministers, comprising members of the MDP, the NUP, the JP, the Social Liberal Party (SLP) and the Adhaalath Party (Justice Party). On appointing his new Government, Nasheed carried out a significant reorganization of the ministries, including the establishment of a Ministry of Islamic Affairs, which replaced the Supreme Council for Islamic Affairs that had operated under President Gayoom since 1996. In addition, President Nasheed appointed eight new members of the People's Majlis to replace the eight appointees of former President Gayoom to ensure that the Government had a working majority. One of Nasheed's first acts as new Head of State was to request the resignation of the National Police Commissioner, Adam Zahir, who had long been held personally accountable for various human rights abuses on the part of the police, including torture and custodial deaths. In December Nasheed's Cabinet suffered its first real set-back when the Minister of Home Affairs, Qasim Ibrahim, who was also the leader of the JP, resigned. Ibrahim claimed that his resignation had been prompted by the Government's unwillingness to allocate funds to prison reform, but several sources alleged that his departure came as a result of criticism of his heavy-handed response to a strike by employees at a tourist resort (the police reportedly used electric batons and pepper spray against the striking staff). In mid-February 2009 the President's Special Advisor, Dr. Hassan Saeed, resigned from his post; earlier that month he had formed a new political party entitled the Dhivehi Qaumee Party (DQP—Maldivian National Party).

In February 2009 the People's Majlis passed two electoral bills, paving the way for the holding of the Maldives' first multi-party legislative election. One of the two bills was the Parliamentary Constituencies Bill, according to which the population of each administrative atoll would determine how many electoral constituencies would be created, and two members of parliament would be elected for every 5,000 residents registered in each constituency. A total of 77 seats were contested in the election, which was held on 9 May, and, according to preliminary results, the DRP won the highest number of seats (28), while the MDP gained 25 seats. Although independent candidates took 13 seats, the predominance of the leading parties in the voting illustrated the population's willing adoption of a party political system.

In May 2009 a special presidential commission was established to investigate the alleged embezzlement of state funds and resources by the former administration. In August controversial decentralization bill was presented to the People's Majlis (as part of the process of devolution, the Ministry of Atolls Development had already been closed down by the President and its responsibilities divided between numerous smaller regional offices). The bill, the main proposal of which was the division of the existing 21 administrative districts into seven provinces—each headed by a provincial state minister (appointed by the President) and a council—was opposed by the DRP and the PA on the grounds that it was unconstitutional, would create additional bureaucracy and posed a threat to representative democracy and the unitary state. A revised Decentralization Act was presented to the Majlis in March 2010, which recognized the creation of the seven provinces, but not as administrative units, retained the existing 21 administrative districts and the atoll and island chiefs, and provided for the election of island, atoll and city councils. The act was approved by the legislature at the end of April and ratified by President Nasheed in mid-May. In October the Government issued a finalized list of administrative divisions, including 184 islands, 19 atolls and two designated cities—Malé and Addu City (formerly Addu atoll). Meanwhile, in April Maumoon Abdul Gayoom was replaced as leader of the DRP by Ahmed Thasmeen Ali.

Recent developments: political deadlock

The country was faced with a political crisis on 29 June 2010 when the entire Cabinet of Ministers resigned en masse following threats by the opposition to introduce a parliamentary vote of no confidence against each minister; however, Nasheed and his Vice-President remained in their posts. The Government claimed that it had become impossible to work effectively with the opposition-controlled People's Majlis and that the constant use of blocking tactics by the opposition parties had made the country virtually ungovernable. On the same day two leading opposition figures, Abdullah Yameen of the PA and Qasim Ibrahim of the JP, were placed under house arrest and accused of bribing fellow parliamentarians and conspiring to overthrow the Government; both of the politicians claimed that their arrests were unconstitutional and vehemently denied the accusations. On 7 July, with the political situation in turmoil and the rift between the Government and the opposition appearing deadlocked, President Mahinda Rajapakse of Sri Lanka arrived in the Maldives, at the request of Nasheed, to act as a mediator in talks between the two sides. Later that day President Nasheed reappointed the Cabinet of Ministers (with one change of portfolio), but there were doubts whether all the reinstated ministers would be approved by the People's Majlis (as required by the Constitution). On 9 July Ahmed Nazim, the Deputy Speaker of the People's Majlis and parliamentary group leader of the PA, was arrested and charged with bribery and conspiring to assault political opponents.

Despite the reinstatement of the Cabinet of Ministers and the release from house arrest of Yameen and Ibrahim, the political impasse between the Government and the opposition persisted, with the latter refusing to recognize the legitimacy of Nasheed's administration. The rising tension led to violent protests being staged in Malé by both sides, once again placing the country's vital tourism industry under threat. In early August 2010 the constitutional crisis escalated when the People's Majlis voted against legitimizing a number of interim state institutions, including the Supreme Court, the Civil Service Commission and the Human Rights Commission (according to the Constitution, the two-year transition period of these bodies expired on 7 August). In protest at the opposition's continuing intransigence, the Attorney-General, Husnu Suood, resigned. However, a few days later the power struggle over the judiciary was resolved when the People's Majlis unanimously voted to appoint a permanent Supreme Court and Chief Justice (as nominated by the President). None the less, the deadlock over the official recognition of the Cabinet continued, with the opposition insisting that the ministers be endorsed on an individual basis and Nasheed claiming that the approval procedure should be carried out on a 'ceremonial' and collective basis. On 22 November the People's Majlis voted not to endorse seven of the cabinet ministers appointed by the President and demanded that they resign immediately. Despite protests by the MDP that the legislature's action was unconstitutional, on 9 December the Supreme Court ruled that the rejected ministers (including Dr Ahmed Ali Sawad, who had been nominated as the new Attorney-General in August) should not remain in office: they all resigned two days later. Nasheed subsequently carried out an extensive cabinet reorganization, including the appointment of two of the rejected ministers as advisors, and, in defiance of the judicial ruling, reappointed Sawad as Attorney-General on 13 December. On 21 March 2011 the People's Majlis endorsed the appointments of a further four ministers, but again refused to approve the nomination of Sawad. Later that day the President installed Abdulla Muiz as the new Attorney-General and Ahmed Naseem as the new Minister of Foreign Affairs; in early April Ahmed Inaz was appointed Minister of Finance and Treasury.

Meanwhile, in February 2011 multi-party local council elections were held in the Maldives for the first time: the MDP performed strongly in the city councils, while the DRP won the majority of seats in the atoll and island councils.

In the first few months of 2011 serious rifts within the DRP came increasingly to the fore as Gayoom continued to criticize the leadership of his successor, Ahmed Thasmeen Ali, accusing him of 'dictatorial' behaviour; by the end of March the DRP had effectively split into two opposing factions led by Thasmeen and Gayoom. In February a report published in an Indian magazine alleged that during his presidency Gayoom and his half-brother Abdullah Yameen had been involved in an international fraud (worth around US $800m.) involving the illegal sale of petroleum to the military junta in Myanmar. In early April the People's Majlis was instructed to investigate the allegations.

At the end of April anti-government protestors staged a series of large demonstrations in Malé provoked by rising commodity prices, which had been exacerbated by a recent devaluation of the Maldivian currency, the rufiyaa, against the US dollar. Several hundred protestors were arrested and dozens injured in clashes with riot police during the demonstrations, which continued for eight days in the capital. The Government rejected allegations by the opposition that the police had used excessive force and that journalists had been obstructed in their efforts to report on the unrest.

Environmental Concerns

Environmental issues have become increasingly important in Maldivian politics, particularly given the fact that around 80% of the islands are no more than one metre above sea level and are thus extremely vulnerable to climate change. In November 1989 the Maldives hosted an international conference with delegates from other small island nations, to discuss the threat posed to low-lying island countries by the predicted rise in sea-level caused by heating of the earth's atmosphere as a result of pollution (the 'greenhouse effect'). In June 1990 an Environmental Research Unit, which was to operate under the Ministry of Planning and the Environment, was established in the Maldives. The Maldives reiterated its serious concern with regard to problems of world-wide environmental pollution when it hosted the 13th conference of the UN's Intergovernmental Panel on Climate Change (IPCC, see p. 70) in September 1997. In September 1999 a special session of the UN General Assembly was convened in New York to address the specific problems faced by the 43-member Alliance of Small Island States (see p. 459) (including the Maldives), notably climate change, rising sea levels and globalization. The Maldives Government expressed its grave disappointment and concern at the USA's decision in April 2001 to reject the Kyoto Protocol to the UN's Framework Convention on Climate Change. A large part of the international community adopted the protocol in July after many of the

THE MALDIVES

emissions targets had been reduced. In March 2002 the Maldives, Kiribati and Tuvalu announced their decision to take legal action against the USA for refusing to sign the Kyoto Protocol and thus threatening the very survival of the low-lying island states. At the World Summit on Sustainable Development held in September in Johannesburg, South Africa, President Gayoom warned the international community that low-lying islands were at greater risk than ever before. He demanded urgent action, including the universal ratification and implementation of the Kyoto Protocol, to prevent a global environmental catastrophe. In July 2008 a meeting of experts and environment ministers from the Maldives and other member countries of the South Asian Association for Regional Co-operation (SAARC) finalized a five-year plan of action, with funding expected to be provided by development partners, to combat the adverse effects of climate change in the region. On assuming the presidency in November, Mohamed Nasheed immediately announced government plans to use some of the revenue from the tourism sector to establish a sovereign wealth fund to finance a long-term plan to purchase land abroad should the relocation of the Maldivian population become necessary owing to rising sea levels. In March 2009 President Nasheed announced plans to make the Maldives the world's first 'carbon neutral' state (i.e. a zero net contributor to greenhouse gas emissions) within 10 years by switching to using only renewable energy sources such as wind, wave and solar power, and through carbon offsetting. It was estimated that the ambitious plan would cost the country around US $110m. per year throughout the following decade and Nasheed expressed his hopes that it would serve as a blueprint to other nations considering adopting such measures.

CONSTITUTION AND GOVERNMENT

On 7 August 2008 the President ratified a new 301-article Constitution, which replaced the 1998 Constitution and which introduced a directly elected presidency and a democratic system of multi-party legislative elections. Legislative authority is vested in the People's Majlis. The People's Majlis shall consist of 77 members elected from Malé and the 20 administrative atolls for five years by universal adult suffrage. Executive power is vested in the President, who is elected directly by the people, with more than 50% of the vote, for a period of five years. The President (who is not permitted to serve for more than two terms) governs with the assistance of an appointed Cabinet of Ministers (including a Vice-President), which is responsible to the People's Majlis. The country has 21 administrative divisions (19 atolls, the capital, Malé, and Addu City), which are grouped into seven provinces.

REGIONAL AND INTERNATIONAL CO-OPERATION

The Maldives is a founder member of the South Asian Association for Regional Co-operation (SAARC, see p. 417), which was formally constituted in December 1985, and the country became a full member of the Commonwealth in June 1985. In early 2011 the Maldives had a total of 12 resident overseas diplomatic missions and had established diplomatic relations with 158 countries.

Having joined the UN in 1965, the Maldives is a member of the UN Economic and Social Commission for Asia and the Pacific (ESCAP, see p. 37). As a contracting party to the General Agreement on Tariffs and Trade (GATT), the Maldives became a member of the World Trade Organization (WTO, see p. 430) on its establishment in 1995.

ECONOMIC AFFAIRS

In 2009, according to estimates by the World Bank, the Maldives' gross national income (GNI), measured at average 2007–09 prices, was US $1,197m., equivalent to $3,870 per head (or $5,230 per head on an international purchasing-power parity basis). During 2000–09, it was estimated, the population increased at an average annual rate of 1.4%, while gross domestic product (GDP) per head grew, in real terms, by an average of 5.0% per year over the same period. Overall GDP increased, in real terms, at an average annual rate of 6.5% in 2000–09. According to the Asian Development Bank (ADB), GDP declined by 4.6% in 2005 following the devastating tsunami of December 2004; however, subsequent reconstruction efforts contributed to impressive growth, of 18.0%, in 2006, 7.2% in 2007 and 6.2% in 2008; GDP declined by 2.3% in 2009, but grew by 4.8% in 2010.

Agriculture and fishing contributed an estimated 5.2% of GDP (the primary fishing sector alone accounted for 3.2%) in 2010. About 12.0% of the total working population were employed in the sector (more than 7% in fishing) at the March 2006 census. In 2009 revenue from exports of marine products totalled 958.4m. rufiyaa, thus accounting for 97.7% of total export earnings. Small quantities of various fruits, vegetables and cereals are produced, but virtually all of the principal staple foods have to be imported. As a result of salt-water intrusion caused by the December 2004 tsunami, a significant amount of cultivable land was ruined. The dominant agricultural activity (not including fishing) in the Maldives is coconut production. The GDP of the agriculture and fisheries sector decreased, in real terms, at an average annual rate of 0.4% in 2001–10. According to official figures, real agricultural GDP declined by 5.1% (7.6% for the fisheries sector alone) in 2008, by 7.9% in 2009, and by 3.2% in 2010.

Industry (including mining, manufacturing, construction and utilities) contributed an estimated 16.3% of GDP in 2010, and employed 25.4% of the working population at the March 2006 census. Sectoral GDP increased, in real terms, at an average annual rate of 6.3% in 2001–10. Industrial GDP grew by 8.2% in 2008, decreased by 11.0% in 2009, but grew by 2.3% in 2010.

Mining and quarrying (mostly for coral and sand) contributed 0.5% of GDP in 2010, and employed 0.3% of the working population at the March 2006 census. No reserves of petroleum or natural gas have, as yet, been discovered in Maldivian waters. Mining GDP increased, in real terms, at an average annual rate of 2.6% in 2001–10. The GDP of the mining sector grew by 2.1% in 2008, fell by 3.7% in 2009, but grew by 0.3% in 2010.

The manufacturing sector contributed 6.5% of GDP in 2010, and employed 18.3% of the working population at the March 2006 census. There are only a small number of 'modern' manufacturing enterprises in the Maldives, including fish-canning, garment-making and soft-drink bottling. Although cottage industries (such as the weaving of coir yarn and boat-building) employ nearly one-quarter of the total labour force, there is little scope for expansion, owing to the limited size of the domestic market. Because of its lack of manufacturing industries, the Maldives has to import most essential consumer and capital goods. From the late 1980s traditional handicrafts, such as lacquer work and shell craft, revived as a result of the expansion of the tourism sector. Manufacturing GDP increased, in real terms, at an average annual rate of 3.1% in 2001–10. Real manufacturing GDP rose by 2.8% in 2008, fell by 4.0% in 2009, but rose by 1.3% in 2010.

Construction contributed 4.7% of GDP in 2010, and employed 5.6% of the working population at the March 2006 census. Construction GDP increased, in real terms, at an average annual rate of 9.2% in 2001–10. The GDP of the construction sector grew by 16.3% in 2008, but experienced a substantial decline, of 29.2%, in 2009. The sector registered a moderate growth of 2.6% in 2010.

Energy is derived principally from petroleum, and imports of mineral fuels and oils comprised 22.6% of the cost of imports in 2008. Owing to a surge in commercial activities and a significant increase in construction projects in Malé, demand for electricity in the capital grew rapidly in the late 1980s and early 1990s. Accordingly, plans were formulated in late 1991 to augment the generating capacity of the power station in Malé and to improve the distribution network. In 2004–07 the fourth phase of the Malé power project, further to increase the capital's power supply, was undertaken. Meanwhile, in December 2001 the ADB agreed to provide a loan to improve the supply of electricity to some 40 outer islands. By 2004 a total of 21 inhabited islands had been provided with electricity. In 2006 the ADB supplied another loan, of US $8m., to enable the electrification of those outer islands not included in the first project.

Following the decline of the shipping industry in the 1980s, tourism gained in importance as an economic sector, and by 1989 it had overtaken the fishing industry as the Maldives' largest source of foreign exchange. The tourism sector recovered well and surprisingly swiftly from the devastating effects of the tsunami that struck the Indian Ocean at the end of 2004; by the end of 2005 all of the resorts affected by the disaster had reopened. Tourist arrivals reached their highest level in 2010, rising by 20.7%, compared with the previous year, to reach 791,917; revenue increased by 17.4% to total US $714.0m. in that year. The GDP of the tourism sector increased, in real terms, at an average annual rate of 3.1% in 2000–09. The services sector as a whole contributed 78.5% of GDP in 2010, and employed 62.7% of labour force at the March 2006 census. The GDP of the services sector increased, in real terms, by an average of 6.3% per year in 2001–10. Sectoral GDP grew by 6.7% in 2008, by 0.3% in 2009 and by 5.9% in 2010.

In 2009 the Maldives recorded a visible trade deficit of an estimated US $682.2m. and there was a deficit of approximately

THE MALDIVES

$402.9m. on the current account of the balance of payments. In 2009 the principal source of imports was Singapore (accounting for 21.4% of the total); other major sources were the United Arab Emirates, India, Malaysia, Sri Lanka and Thailand. In 2009 the principal market for exports was Thailand (accounting for 20.7% of the total); other major purchasers were Sri Lanka, France and the United Kingdom. The principal exports were marine products (tuna being the largest export commodity). The principal imports were mineral products, machinery and mechanical appliances, prepared foodstuffs, beverages, spirits and vinegar, and vegetable products.

In the aftermath of the December 2004 tsunami, the Maldives received a significant amount of international aid, in the form of both grants and concessional loans, principally from the UN, the ADB, the World Bank and Japan (which has traditionally been the Maldives' largest aid donor). According to government figures, foreign financing rose by 36.7% in 2009, compared with the previous year, to reach an estimated 1,739.4m. rufiyaa. In 2009, in terms of central government finance, there was an estimated fiscal deficit of 4,923.6m. rufiyaa. The Maldives' total external debt was US $987.0m. at the end of 2008, of which $499.0m. was public and publicly guaranteed debt. According to the ADB, total external debt had risen to $943m. by the end of 2010. In 2009 the cost of debt-servicing was equivalent to 5.5% of revenue from exports of goods and services. According to the ILO, during 2000–09 the average annual rate of inflation was 3.6%. Owing to a sharp rise in global commodity prices (notably petroleum and food), consumer prices rose substantially, by 12.3%, in 2008; in 2009 and 2010 consumer prices increased by 4.0% and 4.5%, respectively. According to the March 2006 census, 14.4% of the total labour force was unemployed at that time (compared with around 2% in 2000).

The economic consequences of the Indian Ocean tsunami of December 2004, which resulted in widespread destruction of infrastructure and housing on the Maldives, were severe; GDP in 2005 contracted by 4.6% and the cost of reconstruction was estimated at US $375m., the equivalent of approximately 50% of annual GDP. Substantial loss of revenue in conjunction with the increasing levels of capital expenditure that were required to proceed with reconstruction projects placed considerable pressure on the budget (despite high inflows of aid from international donors) and the budgetary deficit grew by 19.5% in 2005, by 14.2% in 2006 and by 16.6% in 2007. However, the tourism sector recovered well from 2007, indicating that it remained the most dynamic subdivision of the economy; a total of 35 new holiday resorts were opened in 2007 (a further 50 were scheduled to be opened during 2010–12). Nevertheless, the tsunami disaster highlighted the vulnerability of the economy to external events, both economic and environmental, and vividly illustrated the fact that the long-term prosperity of the Maldives required sustained growth and diversification of activities. Partly as a result of the ongoing global financial crisis GDP growth contracted by 2.3% in 2009, compared with positive growth of 6.2% in 2008. In December 2009 the IMF provided the Maldives with a standby loan of $92.5m. to help the islands in their recovery from the adverse effects of the global economic crisis. However, in November 2010 the IMF announced its decision to delay the disbursement of the third tranche of the loan citing the Maldives' lack of progress in lowering public-sector wages, and delays in the introduction of new taxes. Although the Maldivian economy recovered well in 2010, with GDP growth of 4.8% fuelled by a very strong performance in the tourism sector (with a notable rise in the numbers of visitors from the more affluent countries in Asia such as India and China), the IMF expressed concern over the islands' persistently large public and fiscal deficits. In January 2011 the Maldives' socio-economic progress was illustrated by the change in its UN-designated status from that of 'least developed country' to 'middle income country'. However, this graduation in status was not universally welcomed, since it meant that the Maldives (despite the continuing vulnerability of its economy to external shocks) would lose special trade preferences and aid. In the same month a new tax on all tourism-related services was introduced in the Maldives, which was expected to be vital in helping to reduce the fiscal deficit (which was estimated to have narrowed to 16.4% of GDP in 2010 from 30.9% in 2009).

PUBLIC HOLIDAYS

2012: 24 January* (National Day), 4 February* (Birth of the Prophet Muhammad), 24 February (Day Maldives Embraced Islam), 19 July* (Ramadan begins), 26 July (Independence Day), 18 August* (Id al-Fitr, end of Ramadan), 25 October* (Id al-Adha, feast of the Sacrifice), 3 November (Victory Day), 11 November (Republic Day), 14 November* (Islamic New Year).

* These holidays are dependent on the Islamic lunar calendar and may vary by one or two days from the dates given.

Statistical Survey

Source (unless otherwise stated): Ministry of Planning and National Development, Ghaazee Bldg, 4th Floor, Ameer Ahmed Magu, Malé 20-05; tel. 3322919; fax 3327351; internet www.planning.gov.mv.

AREA AND POPULATION

Area: 298 sq km (115 sq miles).

Population: 270,101 at census of 31 March–7 April 2000; 298,968 (males 151,459, females 147,509) at census of 21–28 March 2006. *Mid-2011* (official estimate): 325,135 (males 164,349, females 160,786).

Density (official estimate, mid-2011): 1,091.1 per sq km.

Population by Age and Sex (official estimates at mid-2011): *0–14:* 87,635 (males 44,809, females 42,826); *15–64:* 221,572 (males 110,935, females 110,637); *65 and over:* 15,928 (males 8,605, females 7,323); *Total* 325,135 (males 164,349, females 160,786).

Administrative Divisions (population, 2006 census): *Capital City:* Malé 103,693. *Atolls:* North Thiladhunmathi 13,495; South Thiladhunmathi 16,237; North Miladhunmadulu 11,940; South Miladhunmadulu 10,015; North Maalhosmadulu 14,756; South Maalhosmadulu 9,578; Faadhippolhu 9,190; Malé 15,441; North Ari 5,776; South Ari 8,379; Felidhe 1,606; Mulakatholhu 4,710; North Nilandhe 3,765; South Nilandhe 4,967; Kolhumadulu 8,493; Hadhdhunmathi 11,990; North Huvadhu 8,262; South Huvadhu 11,013; Gnaviyani 7,636; Addu 18,026.

Births, Marriages and Deaths (2009): Registered live births 7,336 (birth rate 22.6 per 1,000); Marriages 6,569 (marriage rate 20.2 per 1,000); Registered deaths 1,158 (death rate 3.6 per 1,000).

Life Expectancy (years at birth, WHO estimates): 74 (males 73; females 75) in 2008. Source: WHO, *World Health Statistics*.

Economically Active Population (persons aged 12 years and over, census of March 2006): Agriculture, hunting and forestry 4,236; Fishing 8,388; Mining and quarrying 339; Manufacturing 19,259; Electricity, gas and water 1,229; Construction 5,930; Wholesale and retail trade and repairs 11,711; Restaurants and hotels 12,090; Transport, storage and communications 7,098; Financing, insurance, real estate and business services 1,738; Public administration and defence 15,949; Education 9,872; Health and social work 4,182; Other community, social and personal service activities 3,248; Extra-territorial organizations and bodies 216; Activities not adequately defined 4,746; *Total employed* 110,231 (males 69,701, females 40,530); Unemployed 18,605; *Total labour force* 128,836. *Mid-2011* (estimates in '000): Agriculture, etc. 22; Total labour force 155 (Source: FAO).

HEALTH AND WELFARE

Key Indicators

Total Fertility Rate (children per woman, 2008): 2.0.

Under-5 Mortality Rate (per 1,000 live births, 2008): 28.

HIV/AIDS (% of persons aged 15–49, 2007): <0.1.

Physicians (per 1,000 head, 2004): 0.92.

Hospital Beds (per 1,000 head, 2003): 2.26.

Health Expenditure (2007): US $ per head (PPP): 514.

Health Expenditure (2007): % of GDP: 9.8.

Health Expenditure (2007): public (% of total): 65.4.

Access to Water (% of persons, 2008): 91.

THE MALDIVES

Access to Sanitation (% of persons, 2008): 98.
Total Carbon Dioxide Emissions ('000 metric tons, 2007): 897.7.
Carbon Dioxide Emissions Per Head (metric tons, 2007): 3.0.
Human Development Index (2010): ranking: 107.
Human Development Index (2010): value: 0.602.

For sources and definitions, see explanatory note on p. vi.

AGRICULTURE, ETC.

Principal Crops (production in long-term leased islands*, metric tons, 2007 unless otherwise indicated): Coconuts 94.4; Tender coconuts 116.2; Aubergines 31.7; Cucumbers 48.6; Pumpkins 48.4; Bitter gourds 4.4 (2006); Ridged peppers 63.6; Papayas 631.1; Watermelons 395.7; Bananas 499. *2009:* Bananas 4,340 (unofficial figure); Coconuts 271; Papayas 1,228. (Source: FAO).
* Comprising the atolls of North Thiladhunmathi, South Thiladhunmathi, North Miladhunmadulu, South Ari, Mulakatholhu, North Nilandhe, Kolhumadulu and Hadhdhunmathi.

Sea Fishing ('000 metric tons, 2008): Total catch 133.1 (Skipjack tuna—Oceanic skipjack 87.3; Yellowfin tuna 21.6). Source: FAO.

INDUSTRY

Selected Products (metric tons, 2008): Frozen fish 49,351.76 (Skipjack 41,319.81); Salted or dried fish 5,981.79; Canned fish 1,940.21.
Electric Energy (million kWh): 269.8 in 2007; 204.1 in 2008; 288.4 in 2009.

FINANCE

Currency and Exchange Rates: 100 laari (larees) = 1 rufiyaa (Maldivian rupee). *Sterling, Dollar and Euro Equivalents* (31 December 2010): £1 sterling = 20.038 rufiyaa; US $1 = 12.800 rufiyaa; €1 = 17.103 rufiyaa; 1,000 rufiyaa = £49.90 = $78.13 = €58.47. *Exchange Rate* (rufiyaa per US dollar): since July 2001 the mid-point rate of exchange has been fixed at US $1 = 12.80 rufiyaa.

Budget (central government finance, million rufiyaa, 2009): *Revenue:* Tax revenue 2,653.9 (Import duty 1,790.0); Other current revenue 2,690.9 (Resort lease rents 992.6); Capital revenue 10.6; Grants 602.4; Total 5,957.8. *Expenditure:* General administration of public services 2,279.1; Defence 635.5; Public order and internal security 1,114.4; Environmental protection 115.3; Education 2,066.5; Health 845.2; Social security and welfare 772.9; Community programmes 1,181.2; Economic services 1,600.3 (Agriculture and fishing 79.3, Trade and industry 622.3, Electricity, gas and water 234.4, Transport and communications 511.9, Tourism 152.4); Interest on public debt 339.9; Net lending –68.9; Total 10,881.4 (Current 7,942.4, Capital and net lending 2,939.0).

International Reserves (excl. gold, US $ million at 31 December 2010): IMF special drawing rights 11.75; Reserve position in IMF 2.39; Foreign exchange 335.96; Total 350.10. Source: IMF, *International Financial Statistics.*

Money Supply (million rufiyaa at 31 December 2010): Currency outside depository corporations 1,571.05; Transferable deposits 10,941.25; Other deposits 3,348.03; Broad money 15,860.33. Source: IMF, *International Financial Statistics.*

Cost of Living (Consumer Price Index; base: 2005 = 100): All items 111.1 in 2007; 124.7 in 2008; 129.7 in 2009. Source: IMF, *International Financial Statistics.*

Gross Value Added in Basic Prices (million rufiyaa at constant 1995 prices, 2010, estimates): Agriculture 211.6; Fishing and fisheries 352.5; Coral and sand mining 52.7; Manufacturing 703.0; Electricity and water supply 515.7; Construction 509.6; Wholesale and retail trade 410.9; Transport and communications 2,163.1; Finance, real estate and business services 1,201.9; Tourism 3,127.8; Public administration 1,909.9; Education, health and social service 163.5; *Sub-total* 11,322.2; Financial intermediation services indirectly measured –423.6; *Gross value added in basic prices* 10,898.6.

Balance of Payments (US $ million, 2009): Exports of goods f.o.b. 169.0; Imports of goods f.o.b. –851.3; *Trade balance* –682.2; Exports of services 659.8; Imports of services –284.6; *Balance on goods and services* –307.1; Other income received 5.0; Other income paid –49.3; *Balance on goods, services and income* –351.4; Current transfers received 64.1; Current transfers paid –115.6; *Current balance* –402.9; Direct investment from abroad 112.3; Other investment assets –11.2; Other investment liabilities 259.7; Net errors and omissions 57.4; *Overall balance* 15.3. Source: IMF, *International Financial Statistics.*

EXTERNAL TRADE

Principal Commodities (million rufiyaa, 2009, unless otherwise indicated): *Imports c.i.f.:* Live animals and animal products 687.1; Vegetable products 967.9; Prepared foodstuffs, beverages, spirits and vinegar 1,045.2; Mineral products 2,949.5; Intermediate and capital goods 6,718.9 (Plastics and rubber and articles thereof 369.3; Wood, articles of wood, wood charcoal, cork and articles and pulp of wood 684.4; Construction materials 282.0; Base metal and articles of base metal 595.2; Machinery and mechanical appliances 2,232.1; Textiles 340.1; Chemicals and chemical products 675.3; Transport equipment and parts 646.0; Miscellaneous manufactured goods 475.6); Total (incl. others) 12,368.5. *Exports:* Marine products 958.4 (Fresh, chilled or frozen tuna 651.8); Other products (mostly clothing and waste and scrap of alloy steel) 22.9; Total 981.3. *Re-exports:* (US $ million, 2010) 125.9.

Principal Trading Partners (million rufiyaa, 2009): *Imports:* Australia 341.1; China, People's Republic 328.2; France 196.5; Germany 243.5; India 1,497.1; Japan 162.2; Malaysia 811.1; Singapore 2,648.9; Sri Lanka 804.4; Thailand 620.3; United Arab Emirates 1,944.4; United Kingdom 134.2; USA 311.3; Total (incl. others) 12,368.5. *Exports:* France 110.3; Germany 33.9; Japan 39.0; Sri Lanka 167.8; Thailand 203.6; United Kingdom 98.1; Total (incl. others) 981.3.

TRANSPORT

Road Traffic (motor vehicles in use at 31 December 2007): Passenger cars 3,063; Buses and coaches 74; Lorries and vans 2,867; Motorcycles and mopeds 26,777. Source: IRF, *World Road Statistics.*

Merchant Shipping Fleet (displacement, '000 gross registered tons at 31 December): 125.5 in 2007; 144.1 in 2008; 141.1 in 2009. Source: IHS Fairplay, *World Fleet Statistics.*

International Shipping (freight traffic, '000 metric tons, 1990): Goods loaded 27; Goods unloaded 78. Source: UN, *Monthly Bulletin of Statistics.*

Civil Aviation (traffic at Malé International Airport, 2009): *International Flights:* Arrivals 831,924; Departures 845,399. *Domestic Flights:* Arrivals 408,603; Departures 414,514.

TOURISM

Tourist Arrivals: 683,012 in 2008; 655,852 in 2009; 791,917 in 2010.

Foreign Visitors by Country of Nationality (2010): China, People's Republic 118,961; France 54,789; Germany 77,108; Italy 89,596; Japan 38,791; Korea, Republic 24,808; Russia 49,111; Switzerland 27,766; United Kingdom 114,158; Total (incl. others) 791,917.

Tourism Receipts (US $ million): 696.3 in 2008; 608.3 in 2009; 714 in 2010.

COMMUNICATIONS MEDIA

Radio Receivers (July 2000): 29,724 registered.
Television Receivers (July 2000): 10,701 registered.
Telephones (main lines in use): 33,100 in 2007; 46,900 in 2008; 49,000 in 2009.
Mobile Cellular Telephones: 313,500 in 2007; 435,600 in 2008; 457,800 in 2009.
Personal Computers: 60,000 (202.4 per 1,000 persons) in 2006.
Internet Users (estimates): 49,000 in 2007; 70,700 in 2008; 86,400 in 2009.
Broadband Subscribers: 10,400 in 2007; 15,700 in 2008; 17,800 in 2009.

Sources: Telecommunications Authority of Maldives, Malé; International Telecommunication Union.

EDUCATION

Schools (2009): 375 (government 218, community 64, private 93). Source: Ministry of Education.

Teachers (2009): Pre-primary 851; Primary 3,524; Lower secondary 3,114; Upper secondary 318. Source: Ministry of Education.

Pupils (2009): Pre-primary 16,126 (males 8,168, females 7,958); Primary 44,530 (males 23,125, females 21,405); Lower secondary 26,120 (males 13,053, females 13,067); Upper secondary 2,920 (males 1,463, females 1,457); Special needs 145 (males 82, females 63). Source: Ministry of Education.

Maldives College of Higher Education: Academic staff 138 (2003); Students 4,388 (2007). Source: Maldives College of Higher Education.

Pupil-Teacher Ratio (primary education, UNESCO estimate): 12.7 in 2008/09 (Source: UNESCO Institute for Statistics).

Adult Literacy Rate (UNESCO estimates): 98.4% (males 98.4%; females 98.4%) in 2006 (Source: UNESCO Institute for Statistics).

Directory

The Government

HEAD OF STATE

President: MOHAMED NASHEED (took office 11 November 2008).

THE CABINET OF MINISTERS
(May 2011)

A coalition of the Maldivian Democratic Party (MDP), the Social Liberal Party (SLP), the National Unity Party (NUP, Gaumee Itthihaad), and the Adhaalath Party (AP, Justice Party).

Vice-President: Dr MOHAMED WAHEED HASSAN MANIK (NUP).
Minister of Economic Development: MAHMOOD RAZEE (MDP).
Minister of Home Affairs: HASSAN AFEEF (MDP).
Minister of Foreign Affairs: AHMED NASEEM (MDP).
Minister of Finance and Treasury: AHMED INAZ (MDP).
Minister of Housing and Environment: MOHAMED ASLAM (MDP).
Minister of Health and Family, and Acting Minister of Fisheries and Agriculture: Dr AMINATH JAMEEL (MDP).
Minister of Education: SHIFA MOHAMED (MDP).
Minister of Transport and Communication: MOHAMED ADIL SALEEM (MDP).
Minister of Tourism, Arts and Culture: Dr MARIYAM ZULFA (MDP).
Minister of Human Resources, Youth and Sports: HASSAN LATHEEF (SLP).
Minister of Islamic Affairs: Dr ABDUL MAJEED ABDUL BARI (AP).
Attorney-General: ABDULLA MUIZ.

MINISTRIES

President's Office: Boduthakurufaanu Magu, Malé 20-05; tel. 3320701; fax 3325500; e-mail info@presidencymaldives.gov.mv; internet www.presidencymaldives.gov.mv.

Attorney-General's Office: Huravee Bldg, 3rd Floor, Ameer Ahmed Magu, Malé 20-05; tel. 3323809; fax 3314109; e-mail it@agoffice.gov.mv; internet www.agoffice.gov.mv.

Ministry of Defence and National Security: Ameer Ahmed Magu, Malé 20-126; tel. 3322607; fax 3332689; e-mail admin@defence.gov.mv; internet www.defence.gov.mv.

Ministry of Economic Development: Ghaazee Bldg, Ameer Ahmed Magu, Malé 20-125; tel. 3323668; fax 3323840; e-mail info@trade.gov.mv; internet www.trade.gov.mv.

Ministry of Education: Boduthakurufaanu Magu, Malé 20-05; tel. and fax 3333234; e-mail media@moe.gov.mv; internet www.moe.gov.mv.

Ministry of Finance and Treasury: Ameenee Magu, Malé 20-379; tel. 3328790; fax 3324432; e-mail admin@finance.gov.mv; internet www.finance.gov.mv.

Ministry of Fisheries and Agriculture: Ghaazee Bldg, Ground Floor, Ameer Ahmed Magu, Malé 20-05; tel. 3322625; fax 3326558; e-mail it@fishagri.gov.mv; internet www.fishagri.gov.mv.

Ministry of Foreign Affairs: Boduthakurufaanu Magu, Malé 20-077; tel. 3323400; fax 3323841; e-mail admin@foreign.gov.mv; internet www.foreign.gov.mv.

Ministry of Health and Family: Ameenee Magu, Malé 20-379; tel. 3328887; fax 3328889; e-mail admin@health.gov.mv; internet www.health.gov.mv.

Ministry of Home Affairs: Huravee Bldg, 3rd Floor, Ameer Ahmed Magu, Malé 20-05; tel. 3323820; fax 3324739; e-mail minhah@dhivenhinet.net.mv; internet www.homeaffairs.gov.mv.

Ministry of Housing and Environment: Ameenee Magu, Malé 20-392; tel. 3004300; fax 3004301; e-mail secretariat@environment.gov.mv; internet www.environment.gov.mv.

Ministry of Human Resources, Youth and Sports: Haveeree Hingun, Malé 20-125; tel. 3347300; fax 3347490; e-mail admin@employment.gov.mv; internet www.employment.gov.mv.

Ministry of Islamic Affairs: POB 20103, Malé; tel. 3352671; fax 3323103; internet www.islamicaffairs.gov.mv.

Department of Justice: Justice Bldg, Orchid Magu, Malé 20-212; tel. 3322303; fax 3325447; e-mail admin@justice.gov.mv; internet www.justice.gov.mv.

Ministry of Tourism, Arts and Culture: Ghazee Bldg, 1st Floor, Ameer Ahmed Magu, Malé 20-05; tel. 3323224; fax 3322512; e-mail info@maldivestourism.gov.mv; internet www.tourism.gov.mv.

Ministry of Transport and Communication: 7th Floor, PA Complex, Hilaalee Magu, Malé 20–307; tel. 3324992; fax 3323039; e-mail civav@aviainfo.gov.mv; internet www.aviainfo.gov.mv.

President and Legislature

PRESIDENT

Presidential Election, First Ballot, 8 October 2008

Candidates	Votes	% of votes
Maumoon Abdul Gayoom (Dhivehi Rayyithunge Party)	71,731	40.3
Mohamed Nasheed (Maldivian Democratic Party)	44,293	24.9
Hassan Saeed (Independent)	29,633	16.7
Qasim Ibrahim (Jumhooree Party)	27,056	15.2
Umar Naseer (Islamic Democratic Party)	2,472	1.4
Ibrahim Ismail (Social Liberal Party)	1,382	0.8
Invalid or blank votes	1,235	0.7
Total	**177,802**	**100.0**

Presidential Election, Second Ballot, 28 October 2008

Candidates	Votes	% of votes
Mohamed Nasheed (Maldivian Democratic Party)	97,222	53.7
Maumoon Abdul Gayoom (Dhivehi Rayyithunge Party)	82,121	45.3
Other (invalid)	1,861	1.0
Total	**181,204**	**100.0**

LEGISLATURE

People's Majlis

The People's Majlis (People's Council) comprises members elected by the people of Malé and each of the 20 atolls (for a five-year term).

Speaker: ABDULLA SHAHID.
Deputy Speaker: AHMED NAZIM.

Election, 9 May 2009

Party	Seats
Dhivehi Rayyithunge Party	28
Maldivian Democratic Party	25
Independents	13
People's Alliance	7
Dhivehi Qaumee Party	2
Jumhooree Party	1
Vacant	1
Total	**77**

Elections Commission

Elections Commission of Maldives: PA Complex, 3rd Floor, Hilaalee Magu, Malé; tel. 3324426; fax 3323997; e-mail info@elections.gov.mv; internet www.elections.gov.mv; f. 1998; five-mem. independent body nominated and appointed by People's Majlis; Pres. MOHAMED IBRAHIM; Vice-Pres. AHMED SHAHID; Commrs MOHAMED MAHIR, FUAD THAUFEEQ; Sec.-Gen. IBRAHIM SHAREEF.

Political Organizations

Adhaalath Party (Justice Party): Malé; tel. and fax 3342676; internet www.adhaalath.org.mv; f. 2005; Islamic; Leader Sheikh HUSSAIN RASHEED AHMED.

Dhivehi Qaumee Party (DQP) (Maldivian National Party): M. Maahi, 2nd Floor, Malé; tel. 3304548; fax 3343844; e-mail sitee@qaumee.org.mv; internet qaumee.org.mv; f. 2009; Leader Dr HASSAN SAEED; Dep. Leader Dr MOHAMED JAMEEL AHMED; Gen. Sec. ABDULLA AMEEN.

Dhivehi Rayyithunge Party (DRP) (Maldivian People's Party): Sinamalé 3 Galolhu, Malé; tel. 3320456; fax 3344774; e-mail info@

drp.org.mv; internet drp.org.mv; f. 2005; Pres. AHMED THASNEEM ALI; Vice-Pres. ALI WAHEED; Sec.-Gen. Dr ABDULLAH MAUSOOM; 38,149 mems (June 2010); in early 2011 supporters of the founder of the DRP, former President of the Maldives Maumoon Abdul Gayoom, split from the party and formed the Zaeem–DRP (Z–DRP) faction (Sec.-Gen. YUMNA MAUMOON); in May 2011 the Z–DRP announced its intention to field a separate candidate in the 2013 presidential election.

Islamic Democratic Party: Malé; tel. 3326962; fax 3327385; e-mail info@idp.org.mv; internet www.idp.org.mv; f. 2005; Pres. UMAR NASEER; Dep. Leader MOHAMED HASSAN MANIK.

Jumhooree Party (JP) (Republican Party): M. Chan'beyleege, 4th Floor, Malé; tel. 3309595; fax 3306699; internet www.jumhooreeparty.org.mv; Leader QASIM IBRAHIM.

Maldivian Democratic Party (MDP): H. Sharasha, 2nd Floor, Sosun Magu, Malé 20-059; tel. 3340044; fax 3322960; e-mail secretariat@mdp.org.mv; internet www.mdp.org.mv; f. 2001; fmrly based in Colombo, Sri Lanka; official registration in Maldives permitted June 2005; Chair. MARIYA AHMED DIDI; Vice-Pres. and Acting Pres. IBRAHIM HUSSAIN ZAKI; Sec.-Gen. HASSAN SHAH.

Maldivian Labour Party (MLP): Malé; f. 2008; established as Poverty Alleviation Party; renamed as above 2009; Pres. AHMED SALEEM (acting).

Maldivian National Congress (MNC): G. Blue Lagoon, 1st Floor, Faashanakilege Magu, Malé; tel. 3316944; fax 3348988; e-mail secretariat@mnc.org.mv; internet www.mnc.org.mv; f. 2007; Leader (vacant).

Maldivian Social Democratic Party: Malé; f. 2006; Leader IBRAHIM MANIK.

National Unity Party (NUP) (Gaumee Itthihaad): 1st Floor, Jawahiru Vadhee, Orchid Magu, Malé; tel. 3304002; fax 3308036; internet www.gip.org.mv; f. 2008; Chair. Dr MOHAMED WAHEED HASSAN MANIK.

People's Alliance (PA): Malé; f. 2008; Founder and Leader ABDULLAH YAMEEN; Sec.-Gen. AHMED MUSTHAFA (acting).

People's Party: Malé.

Social Liberal Party (SLP): Malé; f. 2008; est. as breakaway faction of the Maldivian Democratic Party; Leader MAZLAN RASHEED; Dep. Leader HASSAN LATHEEF.

Diplomatic Representation

HIGH COMMISSIONS IN THE MALDIVES

Bangladesh: M. Kurinbee Lodge, 5th Floor, Izzudheen Magu, Malé; tel. 3315541; fax 3315543; e-mail bdootmal@dhivehinet.net.mv; High Commissioner Rear Adm. A. S. M. A. AWAL.

India: H. Athireege-Aage, Ameeru Ahmed Magu, Malé; tel. 3323015; fax 3324778; e-mail maldives_hc_india@hotmail.com; internet www.hcimaldives.com; High Commissioner Dr D. M. MULAY.

Pakistan: G. Helengely, Lily Magu, Malé; tel. 3323005; fax 3321832; e-mail parepmale@hotmail.com; internet mofa.gov.pk/maldives; High Commissioner AKHTAR ALI SULEHRI.

Sri Lanka: 1st Floor, H. Haifa Bldg, Bodufungadu Magu, Malé; tel. 3322845; fax 3321652; e-mail highcom@dhivehinet.net.mv; internet www.slhcmaldives.com; High Commissioner DICKSON SARATHCHANDRA DELA BANDARA.

Judicial System

The administration of justice is undertaken in accordance with Islamic (*Shari'a*) law. In 1980 the Maldives High Court was established. There are four courts in Malé, and one island court in every inhabited island.

In January 1999 the Government declared that the island court of each atoll capital would thenceforth oversee the administration of justice in that atoll. At the same time it was announced that arrangements were being made to appoint a senior magistrate in each atoll capital.

According to the provisions of the new Constitution, which was enacted in August 2008, a Supreme Court—the highest authority for the administration of justice in the Maldives—was to be formed. In the following month the President appointed five judges to the interim Supreme Court after consultation with the newly established Judicial Service Commission and confirmation of the appointments by a two-thirds' majority of the People's Majlis. With the establishment of the Supreme Court, there was to be no further recourse of appeal from the High Court to the President. The interim Supreme Court was to function until a new Chief Justice and judges to the Supreme Court were appointed by the President after the election of a new People's Majlis in May 2009. The Maldives' first Prosecutor-General was appointed by the President in early September 2008, following approval by the People's Majlis.

Prosecutor-General: AHMED MUIZZU.

SUPREME COURT

Chief Justice: AHMED FAIZ HUSSAIN.

Religion

Islam is the state religion, and the majority of Maldivians are Sunni Muslims.

In November 2008 a Ministry of Islamic Affairs was established to replace the Supreme Council for Islamic Affairs, which had been founded in 1996 to authorize state policies with regard to Islam and to advise the Government on Islamic affairs.

The Press

DAILIES

Aafathis Daily News: Silver Cloud, Maafannu, Malé 20-02; tel. 3318609; fax 3312425; e-mail aafathis@dhivehinet.net.mv; internet www.aafathisnews.com.mv; f. 1979; Dhivehi and English; Editor ABDULLAH NAEEM IBRAHIM; circ. 3,000.

Dhives: Malé; e-mail editor@dhives.com; f. 2009; organ of the Dhivehi Rayyithunge Party; Editor AHMED NIHAN.

Haama Daily: Ma. Night Rose, Dhilbahaaru Magu, POB 20232, Malé; tel. 3340077; fax 3343726; e-mail haama@haamadaily.com; internet www.haamadaily.com; Dhivehi and English; Chair. QASIM IBRAHIM.

Haveeru Daily: Ameenee Magu, POB 20103, Malé; tel. 3325671; fax 3323103; e-mail haveeru@haveeru.com.mv; internet www.haveeru.com.mv; f. 1979; Dhivehi and English; Chair. MOHAMED ZAHIR HUSSAIN; Editor ALI RAFEEQ; circ. 4,500.

Jazeera Daily: M. Zenthuram, Izzudheen Magu, Malé; tel. 3343738; fax 3343736; e-mail info@jazeera.com.mv; internet www.jazeera.com.mv.

Miadhu News: G. Maple Leaf, Ameenee Magu, Malé; tel. 3320700; fax 3320500; e-mail admin@miadhu.com.mv; internet www.miadhu.com; Chair. MOHAMED NABEEL; Editor ABDUL LATHEEF.

Minivan News: Malé; tel. 3334888; e-mail editorial@minivannews.com; internet www.minivannews.com; f. 2005; independent; English-language newspaper; Editor J. J. ROBINSON.

Raajje Daily: Malé; e-mail info@raajje.mv; f. 2008; independent; predominantly Dhivehi with English section; Editor HASSAN SAEED.

Sangu Daily: G. Aabin, Dhonadharaadhahigun, Malé; tel. 3300065; fax 3300064; e-mail sangu@sangudaily.com; Editor IKRAM ABDUL LATHEEF.

PERIODICALS

Adduvas: Malé; f. 2000; weekly; news, entertainment, health issues and social affairs; Editor AISHATH VELEZINEE.

Dhivehingetharika (Maldivian Heritage): National Centre for Linguistic and Historical Research, Soasun Magu, Malé 20-05; tel. 3323206; fax 3326796; e-mail nclhr@dhivehinet.net.mv; internet www.qaumiyyath.gov.mv; f. 1998; Dhivehi; Maldivian archaeology, history and language.

The Evening Weekly: Ameenee Magu, POB 20103, Malé; tel. 3325671; fax 3323103; e-mail info@eveningweekly.com.mv; internet www.haveeru.com.mv; weekly; English; owned by the Haveeru news group; Chair. MOHAMED ZAHIR HUSSAIN.

Faiythoora: National Centre for Linguistic and Historical Research, Soasun Magu, Malé 20-05; tel. 3323206; fax 3326796; e-mail nclhr@dhivehinet.net.mv; internet www.qaumiyyath.gov.mv; f. 1979; monthly magazine; Dhivehi; Maldivian history, culture and language; Editor Uz ABDULLA HAMEED; circ. 800.

Furadhaana: Dept of Information, Ministry of Tourism, Arts and Culture, Ghazee Bldg, 1st Floor, Ameer Ahmed Magu, Malé 20-05; tel. 3334333; fax 3334334; e-mail informat@dhivehinet.net.mv; internet www.maldivesinfo.gov.mv; f. 1990; monthly; Dhivehi; Editor IBRAHIM MANIK; circ. 1,000.

Hidhaayathuge Magu (The Road to Steadfastness): Malé; f. 2008; weekly; Dhivehi; religious; publ. by the Ministry of Islamic Affairs.

Huvaas Magazine: Ameenee Magu, POB 20103, Malé; tel. 3325671; fax 3323103; e-mail huvaas@haveeru.com.mv; internet www.haveeru.com.mv/huvaas; f. 2001; fortnightly; Chair. Dr MOHAMED ZAHIR HUSSAIN.

THE MALDIVES

Jamaathuge Khabaru (Community News): Centre for Continuing Education, Salahudeen Bldg, Malé 20-04; tel. 3328772; fax 3322223; monthly; Dhivehi; Editor AHMED ZAHIR; circ. 1,500.

Maldives News Bulletin: Maldives News Bureau, Department of Information, Ministry of Tourism, Arts and Culture, Ghazee Bldg, 1st Floor, Ameer Ahmed Magu, Malé 20-05; tel. 3334333; fax 3334334; e-mail informat@dhivehinet.net.mv; internet www.maldivesinfo.gov.mv; f. 1980; weekly; English; online only since Feb. 2008.

Marine Research Centre Bulletin: Marine Research Centre, Ministry of Fisheries and Agriculture, H. White Waves, Malé 20-025; tel. 3322328; fax 3322509; e-mail info@mrc.gov.mv; internet www.mrc.gov.mv; f. 1984; biannual; fisheries and marine research; Exec. Dir Dr MOHAMED SHIHAM ADAM.

Our Environment: Forum of Writers on the Environment, c/o Ministry of Economic Development, Ghaazee Bldg, Ameer Ahmed Magu, Malé 20-05; tel. 3324861; fax 3327351; f. 1990; monthly; Dhivehi; Editor FAROUQ AHMED.

Rasain: Ministry of Fisheries and Agriculture, Ghaazee Bldg, Ameer Ahmed Magu, Malé 20-05; tel. 3322625; fax 3326558; e-mail fishagri@dhivehinet.net.mv; f. 1980; annual; fisheries devt.

NEWS AGENCIES

Haveeru News Service (HNS): POB 20103, Malé; tel. 3325671; fax 3323103; e-mail haveeru@haveeru.com.mv; internet www.haveeru.com.mv; f. 1979; Chair. Dr MOHAMED ZAHIR HUSSAIN; Man. Editor AHMED ZAHIR.

Maldives News Bureau (MNB): Department of Information, Ministry of Tourism, Arts and Culture, Ghazee Bldg, 1st Floor, Ameer Ahmed Magu, Malé 20-05; tel. 3334333; fax 3334334; e-mail informat@dhivehinet.net.mv; internet www.maldivesinfo.gov.mv.

Publishers

Corona Press: Feeroaz Magu, Maafannu, Malé; tel. 3310052; fax 3314741.

Cypea Printers: 25 Boduthakurufaanu Magu, Malé; tel. 3333883; fax 3323523; e-mail cyprea@dhivehinet.net.mv; f. 1984 as Cyprea Printers; Man. Dir ABDULLA SAEED.

Loamaafaanu Print: Alkariyya Bldg, Ground Floor, Ameenee Magu, Malé 20-354; tel. 3317209; fax 3313815; e-mail haveeru@netlink.net.mv.

Novelty Printers and Publishers: M. Vaarey Villa, Izzudhdheen Magu, Malé 20-317; tel. 3318844; fax 3327039; e-mail novelty@dhivehinet.net.mv; f. 1965; general and reference books; Man. Dir ASAD ALI.

Ummeedhee Press: M. Aasthaanaa Javaahirumagu, Malé 20-02; tel. 3325110; fax 3326412; e-mail ummpress@dhivehinet.net.mv; f. 1986; printing and publishing; Principal Officers ABDUL SHAKOOR ALI, MOHAMED SHAKOOR.

Broadcasting and Communications

TELECOMMUNICATIONS

Telecommunications Authority of Maldives: Telecom Bldg, Husnuheena Magu, Malé 20-04; tel. 3323344; fax 3320000; e-mail secretariat@tam.gov.mv; internet www.tam.gov.mv; f. 2003; regulatory authority; Chair. Dr HASSAN HAMEED; CEO MOHAMED AMIR.

Dhivehi Raajjeyge Gulhun Ltd (Dhiraagu): 19 Medhuziyaaraiy Magu, POB 2082, Malé 20-03; tel. 3322802; fax 3322800; e-mail 123@dhiraagu.com.mv; internet www.dhiraagu.com.mv; f. 1988; jtly owned by the Maldivian Govt (55%) and Cable and Wireless PLC (United Kingdom—45%); operates all nat. and int. telecommunications services in the Maldives (incl. internet service—Dhivehinet); CEO ISMAIL RASHEED.

Wataniya Telecom Maldives Pvt Ltd: 2nd Floor, Urban Development Bldg, Hulhumalé; tel. 9621111; fax 3350519; e-mail media@wataniya-maldives.com; internet www.wataniya.mv; f. 2005; provides advanced cellular mobile telephone services throughout the Maldives; Chair. SOLAH FAHUD SULTAN; CEO IBRAHIM HALEEL.

WARF Telecom International (Pvt) Ltd: Hulhumalé; f. 2005 by jt venture of Wataniya Telecom Maldives, Reliance Communications (India), and Focus Infocomm to lay fibre-optic cable between Hulhumalé and mainland India; owned by Wataniya Telecom Maldives (65%), Reliance Communications Ltd (20%) and Focus Infocomm (15%); awarded 15-year operating licence in March 2007; CEO AHMAD HALEEM.

BROADCASTING

Maldives National Broadcasting Corpn Ltd (MNBC): Malé; internet www.mnbc.com.mv; f. 2009; Chair. MOHAMED 'MADULU' WAHEED; manages Television Maldives, Youth TV, Voice of Maldives and Raajje FM.

Radio

From May 2007 the Maldives Government permitted private broadcasting under its 'Roadmap for the Reform Agenda' programme. Five national radio stations and a number of small local operators secured terrestrial broadcasting rights. The first private radio station commenced broadcasting operations in July.

Capital Radio: 03 Marvel, Roashanee Magu, Malé 20-05; tel. 3310214; fax 3310213; e-mail info@capital956.fm; internet www.capital956live.com; f. 2007; operated by Asna Maldives Pte Ltd; broadcasts BBC news bulletins, music, current affairs and analysis programmes; Man. Dir MOHAMED NASHEED.

DhiFM 95.2: Malé; e-mail admin@dhifm.com; internet www.dhifm.fm; f. 2007; operated by Maldives Media Co Pvt; broadcasts news, music and general interest programmes in Dhivehi and English; operates 24-hour nation-wide service; Chief Exec. Dir IBRAHIM KHALEEL; Editorial Dir MASOOD ALI.

HFM 92.6: Ma. Thimarafusheege, 8th Floor, Dhilbahaaru Magu, POB 20231, Malé; tel. 3301171; fax 3301170; e-mail info@hfm.com.mv; internet www.hfm.com.mv; f. 2008; operated by Haveeru Media Group; broadcasts 24 hrs daily.

Radio Atoll: Ma. Eastern Lagoon, POB 20193, Malé 20; tel. 3349696; fax 3319600; e-mail info@radioatoll.com; internet www.radioatoll.com; broadcasts current affairs, entertainment and general interest programmes.

Voice of Maldives (VOM) (Dhivehi Raajjeyge Adu): Voice of Maldives Bldg, Maafaanu, Malé; tel. 3314515; fax 3317273; e-mail gs@vom.gov.mv; internet www.vom.gov.mv; radio broadcasting began in 1962 under name of Malé Radio; name changed as above in 1980; operates one channel for religious broadcasts and another for music and current affairs; home service in Dhivehi and English; began broadcasting 24 hrs daily from Jan. 2005; Dir-Gen. BADRU NASEER.

Television

Under the Maldivian Government's 'Roadmap for the Reform Agenda', licences for the establishment of national television stations were made available to private bidders in May 2007.

Atoll Television: Ma. Eastern Lagoon, Dhilkushaa Goalhi, Malé; tel. and fax 3349600; e-mail fazeel@radioatoll.com; f. 2007; operated by Atoll Investment Pvt Ltd.

DhiTV: Champa Bldg, Daisy Magu, Galolhu, Malé 20-02; tel. 3304555; fax 3307666; e-mail info@dhitv.com.mv; internet www.dhitv.com.mv; f. 2008; pvt cable television channel; Chief Exec. YOOSUF NAWAAL FIRAG.

Future Television: Malé; f. 2008; broadcasts for 12 hrs daily in Dhivehi; Man. Dir MOHAMED FAYAZ.

Television Maldives: Buruzu Magu, Malé 20-144; tel. 3342200; fax 3325083; e-mail comments@tvm.gov.mv; internet www.tvm.gov.mv; television broadcasting began in 1978; two channels: TVM broadcasts for an average of 18 hrs daily and TVM Plus (f. 1994) broadcasts for 10 hrs daily; covers a 40-km radius around Malé; Exec. Dir HUSSAIN MOHAMED.

Finance

(cap. = capital; res = reserves; dep. = deposits; m. = million; brs = branches; amounts in rufiyaas unless otherwise stated)

BANKING

Central Bank

Maldives Monetary Authority (MMA): Boduthakurufaanu Magu, Malé 20182; tel. 3312343; fax 3323862; e-mail mail@mma.gov.mv; internet www.mma.gov.mv; f. 1981; bank of issue; supervises and regulates commercial bank and foreign exchange dealings, and advises the Govt on banking and monetary matters; cap. 1m., res 5,525m., dep. 20m. (Dec. 2009); Gov. and Chair. FAZEEL NAJEEB.

Commercial Bank

Bank of Maldives PLC: 11 Boduthakurufaanu Magu, Malé 20094; tel. 3322948; fax 3328233; e-mail info@bml.com.mv; internet www.bankofmaldives.com.mv; f. 1982; 75% state-owned; cap. 269m., res 1,070m., dep. 7,826m. (Dec. 2009); Chair. (vacant); CEO PETER HORTON; 25 brs.

THE MALDIVES

DEVELOPMENT FINANCE ORGANIZATION

Housing Development Finance Corpn Plc: 4th Floor, H. Milani, Sosun Magu, Malé; tel. 3338810; fax 3315138; e-mail info@hdfc.com.mv; internet www.hdfc.com.mv; f. 2004 to provide public housing loans; partially privatized in 2008; 49% of shares held by Govt; Chair. RENU SUD KARNAD; Man. Dir Dr A. D. PRIYANKA BADDEVITHANA.

INSURANCE

Allied Insurance Co of the Maldives (Pte) Ltd: 2nd Floor, Fen Bldg, Ameenee Magu, Machchangolhi Malé 20375; tel. 3341001; fax 3325035; e-mail info@alliedmaldives.net; internet www.alliedmaldives.com; f. 1985; all classes of non-life insurance; operated by State Trading Organization (see below); Chair. AHMED MAZIN; Man. Dir ABDUL WAHID THOWFEEQ.

Trade and Industry

GOVERNMENT AGENCIES

Invest Maldives: Ministry of Economic Development, 1st Floor, Malé 20-05; tel. 3324767; fax 3322528; e-mail info@investmaldives.org; internet www.investmaldives.org; govt agency est. to promote, regulate and license foreign investment; under admin of Ministry of Economic Development; Dir-Gen. AHMED NASEEM.

Maldives Privatization Committee: Malé; Chair. MAHMOOD RAZEE.

CHAMBER OF COMMERCE AND INDUSTRY

Maldives National Chamber of Commerce and Industry (MNCCI): G. Viyafaari Hiya, Ameenee Magu, Malé 20-04; tel. 3326634; fax 3310233; e-mail mncci@dhivehinet.net.mv; internet www.mncci.com.mv; f. 1978; merged with Maldivian Traders' Asscn in 2000; Pres. IBRAHIM JIHAD.

INDUSTRIAL AND TRADE ASSOCIATIONS

Maldives Association of Construction Industry (MACI): PA Complex, Ground Floor, Hilaalee Magu, Malé; tel. 3318660; fax 3318796; e-mail maci@dhivehinet.net.mv; internet www.maci.org.mv; f. 2001; Pres. MOHAMED ALI JANAH; Treas. AHMED ABDULLA.

Sri Lanka Trade Centre: Girithereyege Bldg, 3rd Floor, Hithaffinivaa Magu, Malé; tel. 3315183; fax 3315184; e-mail dirsltc@avasmail.com.mv; f. 1993 to facilitate and promote trade, tourism, investment and services between Sri Lanka and the Maldives; Dir M. I. SUFIYAN.

State Trading Organization PLC (STO): STO Bldg, Boduthakurufaanu Magu, Maafaanu, Malé 20-345; tel. 3344333; fax 3344334; e-mail info@stomaldives.net; internet www.stomaldives.com; f. 1964 as Athirimaafannuge Trading Account, renamed as above in 1976; became a PLC in 2001; state-controlled commercial org.; under administration of independent Board of Directors; imports and distributes staple foods, fuels, pharmaceuticals and general consumer items; acts as purchaser for govt requirements; undertakes long-term devt projects; Chair. FAROOQ UMAR; Man. Dir SHAHID ALI.

UTILITIES

Electricity

Maldives Energy Authority: 4th Floor, Fen Bldg, Ameenee Magu, Malé 20-156; tel. 3331695; fax 3331043; e-mail mea@meew.gov.mv; f. 2006 to replace Maldives Electricity Bureau; under administration of Ministry of Housing and Environment; regulatory authority; Dir-Gen. ABDULLA WAHID.

State Electric Co (STELCO) Ltd: Ameenee Magu, Malé; tel. 3320982; fax 3327036; e-mail admin@stelco.com.mv; internet www.stelco.com.mv; f. 1997 to replace Maldives Electricity Board; under administration of Ministry of Economic Development; provides electricity, consultancy services, electrical spare parts service, etc.; operates 28 power stations; installed capacity 57,134.8 kW (2007); Chair. HASSAN ZAHIR; 650 employees (2006).

Gas

Maldive Gas Pvt Ltd: H. Maizan, 1st Floor, Sosun Magu, Malé; tel. 3335614; fax 3335615; e-mail info@maldivegas.com; internet www.maldivegas.com; f. 1999 as a jt venture between State Trading Organization and Champa Gas and Oil Co; Chair. HAMDHY AGEEL.

Water

Malé Water and Sewerage Co Pvt Ltd: Ameenee Magu, Machangolhi, POB 2148, Malé 20375; tel. 3323209; fax 3324306; e-mail mwsc@dhivehinet.net.mv; internet www.mwsc.com.mv; f. 1995; 76% govt-owned; produces c. 8,500 metric tons of fresh, desalinated water daily, using 7 plants; provides water and sewerage services to the islands of Malé, Hulhumalé and Villingili; provides water services to the islands of Maafushi and L. Gan; Chair. AHMED MANSOOR; Man. Dir MOHAMED AHMED DIDI.

TRADE UNIONS

The 2008 Constitution provides for a minimum wage and grants employees the right to form trade unions and to organize strikes. A number of workers' associations have been established, notably in the tourism and education sectors, although by mid-2011 there were still no trade unions in operation.

Transport

Maldives Transport and Contracting Co Ltd (MTCC): MTCC Bldg, 5th Floor, Boduthakurufaanu Magu, POB 263, Malé 20-181; tel. 3326822; fax 3323221; e-mail info@mtcc.com.mv; internet www.mtcc.com.mv; f. 1980; 60% state-owned, 40% privately owned; marine transport, civil and technical contracting, harbour devt, shipping agents for general cargo, passenger liners and oil tankers; Chair. HUSSAIN HILMY; Man. Dir MOHAMED NASEEM IBRAHIM.

SHIPPING

Vessels operate from the Maldives to Sri Lanka and Singapore at frequent intervals, also calling at points in India, Pakistan, Myanmar (formerly Burma), Malaysia, Bangladesh, Thailand, Indonesia and the Middle East. In December 2005 the merchant shipping fleet of the Maldives numbered 70 vessels, with a combined aggregate displacement of 87,402 grt; by 31 December 2009 the displacement had increased to 141,100 grt. Smaller vessels provide services between the islands on an irregular basis. Malé is the only port handling international traffic. Ambitious government-led plans for the construction of 60 new harbours and a transshipment port in the north of the country were under development from 2006.

Maldives Ports Limited: Boduthakurufaanu Magu, Maafaanu, Malé 20-250; tel. 3329339; fax 3325293; e-mail info@port.com.mv; internet www.port.com.mv; f. 2008; replaced the former Maldives Port Authority (f. 1986); operates Malé Port and serves as the national port authority; govt-owned; Chair. HUSSAIN NIZAR; Gen. Man. MOHAMED HASHIM.

Island Enterprises Pvt Ltd: H. Green, 3rd Floor, Majeedee Magu, POB 2169, Malé 20-070; tel. 3323531; fax 3325645; e-mail info@ielmaldives.com; internet www.ielmaldives.com; f. 1978; fleet of eight vessels; exporters of frozen fish, owners of processing plant, shipping agents, chandlers, cruising agents, surveyors and repairs; Exec. Dir IBRAHIM WASEEM.

   Precision Marine Pvt Ltd: H. Orchidmaage, Ground Floor, Malé; tel. 3315663; fax 3315107; e-mail info@pmlboatyard.com.mv; internet www.pmlboatyard.com.mv; f. 1990; mfrs and repairers of fibreglass boats, launches, yachts, marine sports equipment, etc.; Man. Dir OMAR MANIKU.

Maldives National Shipping Ltd: Ship Plaza, 2nd Floor, 1/6 Orchid Magu, POB 2022, Malé 20-02; tel. 3323871; fax 3324323; e-mail male@maldiveshipping.com.mv; internet www.maldiveshipping.com; f. 1948; 100% state-owned; fleet of 3 container vessels; br. in Singapore; Chair. AIMON JAMEEL.

Matrana Enterprises (Pvt) Ltd: 79 Majeedhee Magu, Malé; tel. 3331166; fax 3322832; e-mail webmaster@matrana.org; Sr Exec. MOHAMED ABDULLA.

Villa Shipping and Trading Co (Pvt) Ltd: Villa Bldg, POB 2073, Malé 20-02; tel. 3325195; fax 3325177; e-mail info@villa.com.mv; internet www.villa.com.mv; operates five tourist resorts and owns a trading operation supported by a fleet of eight cargo vessels and tankers; Man. Dir QASIM IBRAHIM.

CIVIL AVIATION

The existing airport on Hululé Island near Malé, which was first opened in 1966, was expanded and improved to international standards with financial assistance from abroad and, as Malé International Airport, was officially opened in 1981. Further expansion was completed in 2006, including the construction of the world's largest water aerodrome. In June 2010 the Government transferred Malé International Airport to private ownership under a 25-year agreement with an Indian company.

   In addition, there are four domestic airports covering different regions of the country. These are located on Gan Island, Addu atoll, on Kadhdhoo Island, Hadhdhummathi atoll, on Hanimaadhoo Island, South Thiladhummathi atoll, and on Kaadedhdhoo Island, South Huvadhu atoll. Facilities at Gan Airport have been upgraded with a view to the introduction of international services. In early 2011 a joint venture agreement on the management and development of Gan International Airport was signed between the State

Trading Organization, Maldives Airports Co Ltd and Gan Airport Co Ltd. In early 2011 construction work was under way on three further domestic airports at Thimarafushi (Thaa atoll), Dharavandhoo (Baa atoll) and Fuvahmulah. In early 1995 there were 10 helipads in use in the Maldives.

Maldives Airport Co Ltd (MACL): Malé International Airport, Hululé 22-000; tel. 3338800; fax 3331515; e-mail info@maclnet.net; internet www.airports.com.mv; f. 2000; 100% govt-owned; under admin. of Ministry of Civil Aviation and Communication; serviced by 13 charter airlines and 12 scheduled carriers; Chair. of Bd IBRAHIM SALEEM; Man. Dir MOHAMED IBRAHIM.

Island Aviation Services Ltd: 26 Ameer Ahmed Magu, Malé; tel. 3335566; fax 3314806; e-mail info@island.com.mv; internet www.island.com.mv; f. 2000; 100% govt-owned; operates domestic flights; commenced flights to Sri Lanka in Jan. 2008; Chair. MOHAMED UMAR MANIK; Man. Dir BANDHU IBRAHIM SALEEM.

Maldivian Air Taxi: Malé International Airport, POB 2023, Malé; tel. 3315201; fax 3315203; e-mail info@maldivianairtaxi.com; internet www.maldivianairtaxi.com; f. 1993; seaplane services between Malé and outer islands; operates 24 aircraft; Chair. LARS ERIK NIELSEN; Gen. Man. A. U. M. FAWZY.

Trans Maldivian Airways (Pvt) Ltd: Malé International Airport, POB 2079, Malé; tel. 3348400; fax 3348409; e-mail mail@tma.com.mv; internet www.tma.com.mv; f. 1989 as Hummingbird Island Airways Pvt Ltd; name changed as above in 2000; operates 35 aircraft; Man. Dir EDWARD ALSFORD.

Tourism

The tourism industry brings considerable foreign exchange to the Maldives. The islands' attractions include white sandy beaches, excellent diving conditions and multi-coloured coral formations. At the end of 2008 there were 94 island resorts in operation, providing some 19,704 hotel beds; a further 2,094 hotel beds were available on live-aboard safari vessels, 1,110 beds in hotels and 400 beds in guest houses. In 2010 a record number of visitor arrivals was achieved, at 791,917, and receipts from tourism (in US dollar terms) rose by 17.4% compared with the previous year, to reach an estimated US $714m.

Maldives Association of Tourism Industry (MATI): Gadhamoo Bldg, 3rd Floor, Boduthakurufaanu Magu, POB 2056, Malé; tel. 3326640; fax 3326641; e-mail mati@dhivehinet.net.mv; internet www.matimaldives.com; f. 1984; promotes and develops tourism; Chair. MOHAMED UMAR MANIKU; Sec.-Gen. SIM I. MOHAMED.

Maldives Tourism Development Corpn Plc (MTDC): 1st Floor, G. Fathuruvehi, Buruzu Magu, Malé 20–123; tel. 3347766; fax 3347733; e-mail info@mtdc.com.mv; internet www.mtdc.com.mv; Chair. IBRAHIM SALEEM; Man. Dir and CEO MOHAMED MIHAD.

Maldives Tourism Promotion Board: H. Aage, 3rd Floor, 12 Boduthakurufaanu Magu, Malé 20-05; tel. 3323228; fax 3323229; e-mail mtpb@visitmaldives.com; internet www.visitmaldives.com; f. 1998; Dir Dr ABDULLA MAUSOOM.

Lets Go Maldives Pvt Ltd: Lets Go Tower, 1st Floor, Haveeree Hingun, Malé 20-320; tel. 3347755; fax 3307755; e-mail info@letsgomaldives.com; internet www.letsgomaldives.com; f. 2006; tourism agency incl. port handling and aviation services; Man. Dir MOHAMED RIYAZ.

Defence

There is no army, navy or air force. A voluntary National Security Service, which was founded in 1892 and renamed the Maldives National Defence Force in 2006, undertakes paramilitary security duties (including coast-guard duties) and comprises some 2,000 members. The first female recruits were sworn into the former National Security Service in 1989.

Defence Budget: Totalled 635.5m. rufiyaa (5.8% of total expenditure) in 2009.

Commander-in-Chief of the Maldives National Defence Force: Pres. MOHAMED NASHEED.

Chief of Staff of the Maldives National Defence Force: Maj.-Gen. MOOSA ALI JALEEL.

Education

Until the late 1970s, education was centred largely on the capital, Malé. In 1976 the 16 schools in existence were all in Malé and catered mainly for children of primary school age. In 1977 the Government established a teacher-training institute (which had produced more than 400 qualified teachers by the end of 1986). UNICEF, in particular, has contributed to provincial development, and in 1978 the first primary school outside Malé opened, on Baa atoll. The construction of the first secondary school outside Malé was completed, on Addu atoll, in 1992. By early 2005 there were 22 schools in Malé and 312 schools in the rest of the Maldives, and by 2009 there were a total of 375 schools throughout the islands.

Education is not compulsory. There are three types of formal education: traditional Koranic schools (*Makthab*), Dhivehi-medium primary schools (*Madhrasa*) and English-medium primary and secondary schools. Primary education begins at six years of age and lasts for five years. Secondary education, beginning at the age of 11, lasts for up to seven years, comprising a first cycle of five years and a second of two years. In 2007/08 enrolment at primary schools included 96% of children in the relevant age-group; the ratio for secondary enrolment of pupils in the relevant age-group was an estimated 69% in the same year.

In 1989 the Government established a National Council on Education, under the chairmanship of the President, to oversee the development of education in the Maldives. There is a full-time vocational training centre, a teacher-training institute, an Institute of Hotel and Catering Services, an Institute of Management and Administration, a Science Education Centre, a Centre for Social Education, an Institute of Health Sciences, an Institute for Islamic Studies and a Centre for Continuing Education. The Maldives Institute of Technical Education, which was completed in 1996, was expected to help to alleviate the problem of the lack of local skilled labour. The Maldives College of Higher Education (MCHE), which was established to provide a uniform framework and policies for post-secondary education institutes, was opened in 1998. Following the passage of a National University Act in December 2010, the MCHE was redesignated as the country's first university: the Maldives National University (www.mnu.edu.mv) was inaugurated in February 2011.

Budgetary expenditure on education by the central Government in 2009 was 2,066.5m. rufiyaa, representing 19.0% of total spending.

MALI

Introductory Survey

LOCATION, CLIMATE, LANGUAGE, RELIGION, FLAG, CAPITAL

The Republic of Mali is a land-locked country in West Africa, with Algeria to the north, Mauritania and Senegal to the west, Guinea and Côte d'Ivoire to the south, and Burkina Faso and Niger to the east. The climate is hot throughout the country. The northern region of Mali is part of the Sahara, an arid desert. It is wetter in the south, where the rainy season is from June to October. Temperatures in Bamako are generally between 16°C (61°F) and 39°C (103°F). The official language is French but a number of other languages, including Bambara, Fulfulde, Sonrai, Tamashek, Soninke and Dogon, are widely spoken. It is estimated that about 80% of the population are Muslims and 18% follow traditional animist beliefs; under 2% are Christians. The national flag (proportions 2 by 3) has three equal vertical stripes, of green, gold and red. The capital is Bamako.

CONTEMPORARY POLITICAL HISTORY

Historical Context

Mali, as the former French West African colony of Soudan, merged in April 1959 with Senegal to form the Federation of Mali, which became independent on 20 June 1960. Senegal seceded two months later, and the remnant of the Federation was proclaimed the Republic of Mali on 22 September. Its first President was Modibo Keita, the leader of the Union soudanaise—Rassemblement démocratique africain (US—RDA), who pursued authoritarian socialist policies. Following a series of purges of US—RDA and public officials, Keita was overthrown in November 1968 by a group of junior army officers, who assumed power as the Comité militaire pour la libération nationale (CMLN). The Constitution was abrogated, and all political activity was banned. Lt (later Gen.) Moussa Traoré became Head of State and President of the CMLN.

A draft Constitution, providing for the establishment of a one-party state at the end of a five-year transitional period of military rule, was approved by a national referendum in June 1974. Keita died in custody in 1977, prompting anti-Government demonstrations. The single political party, the Union démocratique du peuple malien (UDPM), was officially constituted in March 1979, and presidential and legislative elections took place in June. Traoré, the sole candidate for the presidency, was elected for a five-year term; a single list of UDPM candidates for the 82-member Assemblée nationale was elected for a four-year term. Traoré and the UPDM were re-elected at all subsequent elections.

Domestic Political Affairs

Mali's first cohesive opposition movements began to emerge in 1990, among them the Comité national d'initiative démocratique (CNID) and the Alliance pour la démocratie au Mali (ADEMA), which together organized mass pro-democracy demonstrations in December. The security forces harshly repressed violent pro-democracy demonstrations in Bamako in March 1991: official figures later revealed that 106 people were killed, and 708 injured, in three days of unrest. On 26 March it was announced that Traoré had been arrested. A military Conseil national de réconciliation (CNR), led by Lt-Col (later Gen.) Amadou Toumani Touré, the commander of the army's parachute regiment, assumed power, and the Constitution and its institutions were abrogated. The CNR was succeeded by a 25-member Comité de transition pour le salut du peuple (CTSP), chaired by Touré. It was announced that a national conference would be convened, and that the armed forces would relinquish power to democratic institutions in January 1992. Soumana Sacko (who had briefly been Minister of Finance and Trade in 1987) returned to Mali from the Central African Republic to head a transitional, civilian-dominated government.

The transitional regime affirmed its commitment to the economic adjustment efforts of recent years, and undertook the reform of Malian political life. Among those arrested in subsequent months were Gen. Sékou Ly, Brig.-Gen. Mamadou Coulibaly (respectively, Minister of the Interior and Basic Development and Minister of Defence at the time of the violently repressed demonstrations in early 1991) and the former army Chief of Staff, Ousmane Coulibaly. In July 1991 an amnesty for most political prisoners detained under Traoré was proclaimed, and provision made for the legalization of political parties. The CNID was registered as the Congrès national d'initiative démocratique, and ADEMA adopted the additional title of Parti panafricain pour la liberté, la solidarité et la justice. Pre-independence parties, banned for many years, re-emerged, most notably the US—RDA.

The National Conference began in July 1991. Over a period of two weeks its 1,800 delegates adopted a draft Constitution, an electoral code and a charter governing the activities of political parties. In November the period of transition to democratic rule was extended until March 1992. The delay was attributed principally to the CTSP's desire to conclude a peace agreement with Tuareg rebels in the north of the country (see below). The draft Constitution was submitted to a national referendum on 12 January 1992, when it was endorsed by 99.8% of those who voted (about 43% of the registered electorate).

At municipal elections, held on 19 January 1992, ADEMA enjoyed the greatest success, winning 214 of 751 seats. At the elections to the Assemblée nationale, on 23 February and 8 March, ADEMA won 76 of the 129 seats, the CNID took nine seats, and the US—RDA eight. The date for the transition to civilian rule was again postponed, and the first round of the presidential election eventually proceeded on 12 April, contested by nine candidates. The leader of ADEMA, Alpha Oumar Konaré, won the largest share of the votes cast (some 45%). He and his nearest rival, Tiéoulé Mamadou Konaté (of the US—RDA), proceeded to a second round, on 26 April, at which Konaré secured 69% of the votes. Overall, only about 20% of the electorate were reported to have voted in the presidential election; a similar turn-out was reported in the legislative polls. Konaré was inaugurated as President on 8 June. He appointed Younoussi Touré (hitherto the national director of the Banque centrale des états de l'Afrique de l'ouest) as Prime Minister. Touré's first Council of Ministers was dominated by members of ADEMA, although a small number of portfolios were allocated to representatives of the US—RDA and of the Parti pour la démocratie et le progrès (PDP).

The trial of Traoré and his associates began in November 1992. In February 1993 Traoré, Ly, Mamadou Coulibaly and Ousmane Coulibaly were sentenced to death, having been convicted, inter alia, of premeditated murder at the time of the March 1991 unrest. The Supreme Court rejected appeal proceedings in May 1993; however, Konaré subsequently indicated that no death penalty would be exacted under his presidency. Charges remained against Traoré, his wife and several others in connection with the 'economic crimes' of the former administration.

Touré resigned in April 1993, following violent disturbances in Bamako, involving students and school pupils disaffected by the adverse effects of economic austerity measures. The new Prime Minister, Abdoulaye Sekou Sow (hitherto Minister of State, responsible for Defence, and who was not a member of any political party), implemented an extensive reorganization of the Government. The Council of Ministers remained dominated by ADEMA, but also included representatives of other parties, including the CNID. Following the resignation of ADEMA's Vice-President, Mohamed Lamine Traoré, from a senior government post, a major reorganization of the Council of Ministers was effected in November.

Meanwhile, a programme of austerity measures, announced in September 1993, provoked considerable political controversy and failed to prevent the suspension of assistance by the IMF and the World Bank. The 50% devaluation of the CFA franc, in January 1994, exacerbated differences regarding economic policy within the Government. Sow resigned in February, and was replaced by Ibrahim Boubacar Keïta, a member of ADEMA's 'radical' wing, which was opposed to Sow's economic policies. The withdrawal from the coalition of the CNID and the Rassemblement pour la démocratie et le progrès (RDP) prompted the appointment of a new Government, again dominated by ADEMA; the PDP in turn withdrew.

Following the election of Keïta as President of ADEMA in September 1994, Mohamed Lamine Traoré and other prominent figures resigned from the party and subsequently formed the Mouvement pour l'indépendance, la renaissance et l'intégration africaine (MIRIA). In January 1995 a party established by supporters of the UDPM, the Mouvement patriotique pour le renouveau (MPR), was granted official status. In October the Parti pour la renaissance nationale (PARENA), comprising several leading members of the CNID, who alleged excessive dominance by the party Chairman, Mountaga Tall, was registered. PARENA and ADEMA established a political alliance in February 1996, and PARENA's leaders, Yoro Diakité and Tiébilé Dramé, were appointed to the Government in July.

The 1997 elections

In early 1997 the first round of elections to the enlarged (147-seat) Assemblée nationale was postponed from 9 March until 13 April. As early results indicated that ADEMA was the only party to have won seats outright at this round, the main opposition parties denounced the results as fraudulent and announced their intention to withdraw from the second round. The opposition parties also withdrew their candidates from the forthcoming presidential and municipal elections. On 24 April the Constitutional Court invalidated the results of the first round of voting, citing irregularities in the conduct of the poll.

The presidential election was postponed, by one week, until 11 May 1997. Konaré stated that he did not wish to be the sole candidate and appealed to the opposition to participate. In early May the leader of the Parti pour l'unité, la démocratie et le progrès, Mamadou Maribatou Diaby, announced that he was prepared to contest the presidency. According to the final results, Konaré was re-elected to the presidency, securing 95.9% of the valid votes cast. Members of the radical opposition, which had campaigned for a boycott by voters, stated that the low rate of participation (28.4% of the registered electorate) effectively invalidated Konaré's victory. At the end of the month the municipal elections were postponed indefinitely. Violent protests occurred in Bamako in June, as Konaré was sworn in for a second term of office and the first round of the legislative elections (due on 6 July) was postponed by two weeks.

A small number of opposition parties announced their intention to present candidates for the Assemblée nationale, but the radical collective, known as the Collectif des partis politiques de l'opposition (COPPO), at this time numbering 18 parties of varying political tendencies, reiterated its refusal to re-enter the electoral process. Violent disturbances, in which two deaths were reported, preceded the first round of voting on 20 July 1997, which was contested by 17 parties (including five 'moderate' opposition parties) and a number of independent candidates. COPPO again asserted that its appeal for a boycott had been heeded, and that the low rate of participation by voters (at about 12% of the registered electorate in Bamako, and 22% outside the capital) would render the new parliament illegitimate. A second round of voting was necessary for eight seats on 3 August. The final results allocated 130 of the 147 seats to ADEMA, eight to PARENA, four to the Convention démocratique et sociale (CDS), three to the Union pour la démocratie et le développement (UDD) and two to the PDP.

In September 1997 Konaré held a meeting with some 20 opposition leaders, including representatives of COPPO, at which he presented proposals for a broadly based coalition government. A new Council of Ministers, under Keïta, was appointed in mid-September. The new administration included, in addition to members of ADEMA and its allies, a small number of representatives of the moderate opposition parties (among them the UDD and PDP). Further measures intended to promote national reconciliation were implemented, and in December Konaré commuted some 21 death sentences, including those imposed on ex-President Traoré and his associates, to terms of life imprisonment. Although several parties had withdrawn from COPPO, little progress was made towards a full political reconciliation.

In October 1998 the trial for 'economic crimes' began in Bamako of ex-President Traoré, his wife Mariam, her brother, Abraham Douah Cissoko (the former head of customs), a former Minister of Finance and Trade, Tiénan Coulibaly, and the former representative in France of the Banque de Développement du Mali, Moussa Koné. In January 1999 Traoré, his wife and brother-in-law were sentenced to death, having been convicted of 'economic crimes' to the value of some US $350,000 (the original charges had cited embezzled funds amounting to $4m.). Coulibaly and Koné were acquitted. In September Konaré commuted the death sentences to terms of life imprisonment.

In February 2000 Keïta submitted his Government's resignation. An extensively reorganized Council of Ministers was subsequently appointed. The new Prime Minister, Mandé Sidibé, was widely regarded as a supporter of economic reform. In June Choguel Kokala Maïga, the leader of the MPR, was among opposition leaders who announced their intention to participate fully in the presidential and parliamentary elections to be held in 2002, stating that conditions for electoral fairness and transparency seemed likely to be achieved.

Constitutional amendments

In July 2000 the Assemblée nationale approved legislation providing for state funding of political parties. The Assemblée also adopted a revision of the Constitution proposed by Konaré, according to which some 50 articles of the 1992 document would be amended, subject to approval by referendum. Notably, people of dual nationality were to be permitted to contest presidential elections, while the Supreme Court was to be abolished. Also in July COPPO, which now comprised 15 parties and was led by Almamy Sylla of the RDP, announced that it would henceforth participate in the electoral process.

Keïta resigned from the leadership of ADEMA in October 2000, following the announcement that his opponents within the party had succeeded in calling an extraordinary congress of the party, to be held in late November. At the congress, several new members were appointed to ADEMA's executive committee, and Dioncounda Traoré was elected as the new Chairman of the party. A minor ministerial reshuffle was effected in June 2001. In July a new party led by Keïta, the Rassemblement pour le Mali (RPM), was officially registered.

In November 2001 Konaré indefinitely postponed a referendum, which had been due to take place in December, on the constitutional amendments adopted by the legislature in July 2000, following pressure from opposition parties and the judiciary. In January 2002 Soumaïla Cissé was elected as ADEMA's candidate for the forthcoming presidential election. In March Modibo Keïta, hitherto Secretary-General at the presidency, was appointed as Prime Minister, following Sidibé's resignation to contest the presidency as an independent candidate. In early April 16 opposition parties, including the CNID, the RPM and the MPR, formed an electoral alliance, Espoir 2002, agreeing to support a single opposition candidate (generally expected to be Ibrahim Boubacar Keïta, who was to contest the election on behalf of the RPM) in the event of a second round of voting. Meanwhile, an alliance of 23 political parties, including MIRIA, PARENA and the US—RDA, declared their support for the candidacy of Gen. (retd) Amadou Toumani Touré.

At the first round of the presidential election, which was held on 28 April 2002, contested by 24 candidates, Touré secured the largest share of the votes cast, with 28.7%, followed by Cissé, with 21.3%, and Keïta, with 21.0%. As no candidate had secured an overall majority, Touré and Cissé progressed to a second round of voting, held on 12 May. Touré was elected to the presidency, with 65.0% of the votes cast, having obtained the support of more than 40 parties, including those of Espoir 2002. The electoral process was marred by allegations of fraud and incompetence, which led the Constitutional Court to annul 25% of the votes cast in the first ballot. None the less, international observers described the elections as generally free, fair and open. Touré was inaugurated as President on 8 June, and subsequently formed an interim Government, comprising 21 ministers. The new Prime Minister and Minister of African Integration, Ahmed Mohamed Ag Hamani, was regarded as a technocrat; in addition to having previously held various ministerial posts under Traoré, he had, more recently, served as ambassador to Belgium and to Morocco and as High Commissioner of the Organisation pour la mise en valeur du fleuve Sénégal (see p. 447). President Touré emphasized that he was not affiliated to any particular political party, and would be prepared to govern with any future parliamentary majority.

The elections to the Assemblée nationale in July 2002 further demonstrated the lack of any one dominant political grouping in Mali, while the rate of participation, at 25.7% nation-wide, in the second round, was low. The first round of polls was largely inconclusive and, as a result of various irregularities in the conduct of the elections, several thousand votes were invalidated; following the publication, in early August, of the results by the Constitutional Court, the RPM emerged as the single largest party, with 46 of the 147 seats (although 20 of its seats had been

MALI

won in local electoral alliances with other parties of the Espoir 2002 grouping), while other parties of Espoir 2002 obtained a further 21 seats, giving a total of 67 to allies of the RPM. ADEMA secured 45 seats, while the pro-ADEMA Alliance pour la République et la démocratie won an additional six seats, giving a total of 51. The CNID received 13 seats, while parties belonging to an informal alliance supportive of President Touré, the Convergence pour l'alternance et le changement (ACC), including PARENA and the US—RDA, won a total of 10 seats. The Constitutional Court declared void the results of voting in eight constituencies in Sikasso, in the south, and Tin-Essako, in the north, owing to administrative flaws; by-elections were held in October. In early September 19 deputies, comprising those of the ACC parties, several independent deputies and other declared supporters of Touré, formed a grouping within the legislature, with the declared intention of forming a stable presidential majority. Later in the month Ibrahim Boubacar Keïta was elected President of the Assemblée nationale.

In mid-October 2002 Touré announced the formation of a Government of National Unity. Although many of the principal posts remained unchanged from the interim administration appointed in June, one notable appointment was that of Bassari Touré, a former official of the World Bank, as Minister of the Economy and Finance, who was expected to institute an expedited process of reform. Meanwhile, ADEMA increased its representation in the Assemblée nationale to 53 deputies, becoming the largest party grouping, following its victory in by-elections in all eight constituencies where elections were re-run on 20 October. A minor government reorganization was announced in November.

In late April 2004 Ag Hamani tendered his resignation as Prime Minister, apparently in response to a request by President Touré. A new administration, headed by Prime Minister Ousmane Issoufi Maïga, hitherto Minister of Equipment and Transport (and not affiliated to any political party), was formed in early May. Moctar Ouane was appointed Minister of Foreign Affairs and International Co-operation, and Aboubacar Traoré became Minister of the Economy and Finance. ADEMA was the most successful party at municipal elections held on 23 May (postponed from the previous month), winning 28% of the seats contested, followed by the Union pour la République et la démocratie (URD), which secured 14%, and the RPM, with 13%; the rate of participation by the electorate was relatively high, at 43.6%. ADEMA and the RPM subsequently formed an alliance, which, with ADEMA holding 44 seats and the RPM 35, gave the new grouping a majority in the 147-seat Assemblée nationale (although still short of the two-thirds' majority needed to enact a motion of no confidence against the head of the Government).

From mid-2004 there was considerable speculation regarding potential realignments of political organizations ahead of the presidential and legislative elections due in 2007. In February and March 2005 the President held a series of consultations with the leaders of various political organizations. However, there were signs that the political consensus that had existed since Touré's election in 2002 was likely to come to an end before the elections, as parties began to distance themselves from the President. In November 2005 the RPM announced that it would henceforth oppose the Government, stating that it had been increasingly marginalized within the ruling coalition. In February 2006 the executive committee of ADEMA announced that the party would support the candidacy of Touré at the presidential election due in April 2007 and that it would not, consequently, present its own candidate in the election.

Recent developments: Touré's second term

The presidential election was duly held on 29 April 2007, at which 36.2% of the registered electorate participated. Touré received 71.20% of the total votes cast, securing a second, and final, five-year term while avoiding a second round of voting. His closest rival was Keïta, who received 19.15% of the votes cast. Although a number of opposition candidates challenged the results, alleging that Touré had used public funds to finance his campaign and had manipulated the lists of voters, most independent observers believed the election to have been conducted fairly.

The legislative elections took place on 1 and 22 July 2007. According to official results, ADEMA secured 51 seats, while the URD took 34 seats and the RPM 11. Turn-out was, however, low at 12%, rising to 33% in rural areas. In total, parties supporting President Touré won 113 seats in the Assemblée nationale. In early September Dioncounda Traoré was elected President of that body.

On 27 September 2007 Prime Minister Maïga tendered his resignation and that of his Government. The following day President Touré named Modibo Sidibé, hitherto Secretary-General of the Presidency, as Maïga's successor. Sidibé announced a new Council of Ministers in early October; the most notable appointments were Gen. Sadio Gassama as Minister of Internal Security and Civil Protection, and a Tuareg, Mohammed El Moctar, as Minister of Culture. Ouane retained the foreign affairs portfolio and Gen. Kafougouna Koné was reappointed to head the Ministry of Territorial Administration and Local Communities. In April 2008 Ahmadou Abdoulaye Diallo replaced Bâ Fatoumata Nènè Sy as Minister of Economy, Industry and Commerce, while in October Mamadou Igor Diarra was appointed Minister of Energy and Water following the resignation of Ahmed Sow. Further ministerial changes were effected in April 2009, including the appointment of Sanoussi Touré as Minister of the Economy and Finance.

In July 2010, after its congress in Bamako, the pro-Government Mouvement citoyen, launched a new political party, the Parti pour le développement économique et la solidarité (PDES), in a move largely regarded as an attempt to consolidate President Touré's influence and to counter the dominance of ADEMA ahead of the elections due to be held in 2012. Touré, who had already confirmed that he had no intention of seeking to amend the Constitution in order to be able to contest a third term of office, expressed his support for the PDES and its members, several of whom were government ministers; the Minister of Equipment and Transport, Hamed Diane Séméga, who had been designated President of the new party, was reported to be among the most likely potential presidential candidates in the 2012 ballot.

The Minister of Health, Oumar Ibrahima Touré, was dismissed from the Government in December 2010, and a number of officials from the Ministry of Health were detained, after an investigation revealed that resources granted to Mali by the Global Fund to Fight AIDS, Tuberculosis and Malaria had been misappropriated. Badara Aliou Macalou, the Minister of Malians Abroad and African Integration, was allocated additional responsibility for the health portfolio.

On 3 April 2011 President Touré announced the appointment of Mariam Kaïdama Sidibé Cissé as Prime Minister, following the resignation of Sidibé in late March, and on 6 April a new Government was installed.

Tuareg Issues

A predominant concern in the first half of the 1990s was the rebellion in the north of Mali, which began as large numbers of Tuareg nomads, who had migrated to Algeria and Libya at times of drought, began to return to West Africa (see also the chapter on Niger). A Tuareg attack in June 1990 on Menaka (near the border with Niger) precipitated a state of emergency in the Gao and Tombouctou regions, and the armed forces began a campaign against the nomads. A peace accord signed in January 1991 in Tamanrasset, Algeria, by representatives of the Traoré Government and delegates from two Tuareg groups, the Mouvement populaire de l'Azaouad (MPA) and the Front islamique-arabe de l'Azaouad (FIAA), failed to provide a lasting solution to the conflict. Following the overthrow of the Traoré regime, the transitional administration affirmed its commitment to the Tamanrasset accord, and Tuareg groups were represented in the CTSP. However, unrest continued. At the time of the National Conference it was reported that at least 150 members of the armed forces had been killed since 1990; meanwhile, thousands of Tuaregs, Moors and Bella (the descendants of the Tuaregs' black slaves, some of whom remained with the nomads) had fled to neighbouring countries.

In February 1992, following negotiations between representatives of the Malian Government and of the Mouvements et fronts unifiés de l'Azaouad (MFUA), comprising the MPA, the FIAA and the Armée révolutionnaire de l'Azaouad (ARLA), with Algerian mediation, a truce entered into force, and a commission of inquiry was inaugurated to examine acts of violence perpetrated and losses suffered during the conflict; the more militant Front populaire de libération de l'Azaouad (FPLA) was not reported to have attended the talks. Following further discussions, the Malian authorities and the MFUA signed a draft 'National Pact' in April: joint patrols were duly established, and in November President Konaré visited the north to inaugurate new administrative structures. In February 1993 the Malian Government and the MFUA signed an accord facilitating the integration of an initial 600 Tuaregs into the national army. In May it was announced that the office of the UN High Commissioner for Refugees (UNHCR) was to oversee a two-year voluntary repatriation programme, whereby 12,000 refugees would be resettled from southern Algeria to Mali by the end of 1993. However, the assassination, in February 1994, of the MPA's military leader—now, in accordance with the Pact, a senior officer in the Malian army—resulted in several weeks of clashes between the MPA and the ARLA, which was blamed for his death.

In May 1994 the Malian authorities and Tuareg leaders reached agreement regarding the integration of 1,500 former rebels into the Malian army and of a further 4,860 Tuaregs into civilian sectors. The success of the agreement was, however, undermined by an intensification of disorder in northern Mali. Meanwhile, a Songhaï-dominated black resistance movement, the Mouvement patriotique malien Ganda Koy ('Masters of the Land'), emerged, amid rumours of official complicity in its offensives against the Tuaregs. In June one of the leaders of the FIAA died during clashes with members of the armed forces. Meeting in Tamanrasset shortly afterwards, the Malian authorities and the MFUA endorsed a reinforcement of the army presence in areas affected by the violence, and agreed procedures for the more effective integration of Tuareg fighters. Despite a serious escalation of violence in July, the ministers responsible for foreign affairs of Mali, Algeria, Burkina Faso, Libya, Mauritania and Niger met in Bamako in August to discuss the Tuareg issue, and a new agreement for the voluntary repatriation from Algeria of Malian refugees was reached. Although MFUA leaders welcomed the agreement, pledged the reconciliation of the Tuareg movements, and reiterated their commitment to the National Pact, sporadic hostilities continued.

In October 1994 both the Government and the MFUA appealed for an end to the violence, following an attack on Gao (for which the FIAA claimed responsibility) and retaliatory action, as a result of which 66 deaths were officially reported. A new Minister of the Armed Forces and Veterans was appointed shortly afterwards, and the authorities subsequently appeared to adopt a less conciliatory approach to the dissident rebel groups, with the FIAA becoming increasingly marginalized in the peace process. Further discussions involving Tuareg groups, Ganda Koy and representatives of local communities resulted in the signing, in April 1995, of an agreement providing for co-operation in resolving hitherto contentious issues. In June the FIAA announced an end to its armed struggle, and expressed its willingness to join national reconciliation efforts. A programme for the encampment of former rebels, in preparation for their eventual integration into the national army or civilian structures, began in November and ended in February 1996, by which time some 3,000 MFUA fighters and Ganda Koy militiamen had registered and surrendered their weapons. The MFUA and Ganda Koy subsequently issued a joint statement affirming their adherence to Mali's Constitution, national unity and territorial integrity, urging the full implementation of the National Pact and associated accords and proclaiming the 'irreversible dissolution' of their respective movements.

In September 1997 the graduation of MFUA and Ganda Koy contingents in the gendarmerie was reported as marking the accomplishment of the integration of all fighters within the national armed and security forces. In October the former FPLA leader, Rhissa Ag Sidi Mohamed, who had not previously been regarded as a party to the peace process, returned to Mali and expressed willingness to join efforts to consolidate peace and promote the development of the north. None the less, the Ministers of Justice and of the Armed Forces and Veterans expressed concern that the continued proliferation of weapons, as well as the inadequacy of military and administrative structures in the north, could result in renewed clashes. In November 2000 it was reported that Malian government forces had been dispatched to end widespread banditry by an armed group, led by Ibrahim Bahanga, a former Tuareg rebel, in the Kidal area, near to the border with Algeria. In September 2001 Bahanga reportedly announced that his forces were to cease hostilities, following talks with a state official.

Tensions arose again in May 2006 when Tuareg rebels launched an attack on the town of Kidal in the north-east of Mali. Two military bases were seized, as were two radio stations and a further military base south of Kidal, and it was reported that two government soldiers were shot and killed during army attempts to regain control of the installations. Military reinforcements were deployed to the region; however, the rebel group had taken much of the army's ammunition and weaponry and withdrawn to an area close to the Niger border, from where they demanded the commencement of negotiations with the Government over the conditions in which the Tuaregs had been forced to live since their integration into the armed forces. At a meeting between the Malian Government and the Tuareg group in June, mediated by Algerian officials, corruption and fraud were also cited among the reasons for the May attack. However, discussions were positive, including proposals for greater autonomy in the administration of the mountainous region of Kidal. In July a peace deal was signed in Algiers, Algeria, which included agreement on an investment programme for the region and the reintegration of rebels into the armed forces. There was some criticism of the Government for its relenting attitude towards the insurgents, but President Touré reiterated his determination to find a peaceful resolution to the conflict. A further reconciliation agreement was signed on 23 February 2007 between the Malian Government and the Tuareg rebels, stipulating guidelines for the implementation of the agreement signed in July the previous year. The accord also outlined the establishment of special security units in the Kidal region, and measures for facilitating the reintegration of the Tuaregs into Malian society. In August several attacks on military personnel by Tuareg rebels were reported to have occurred near to the border with Niger. The main Tuareg group insisted that it was continuing to uphold the reconciliation agreement; however, a splinter group announced that it had formed an alliance with Tuareg militia in Niger, who had launched an offensive against the Niger Government. Following talks between the Tuareg rebels and the Malian Government in September, hostages taken in the attacks were released. Nevertheless, later that month a US aircraft carrying aid supplies into Mali came under fire from Tuareg troops, which prompted President Touré to demand the holding of an urgent conference on peace and security in the region.

In April 2008 a new agreement, brokered by Libyan authorities, was signed by the Malian Government and a Tuareg rebel group led by Bahanga, styled the Alliance tuareg Nord-Mali pour le changement (ATNMC); the accord committed both parties to reducing the number of troops stationed in the Kidal area. In addition, Libya pledged its support to the development of the region, which was believed to be one of the underlying causes of tension in the area. However, fighting subsequently intensified and in May it was reported that 27 soldiers and rebels had been killed in an attack on a military base in Abebara, north of Kidal. Despite President Touré reiterating his commitment to restoring peace to the region and to adhering to the terms of recent peace agreements, he maintained that he would not negotiate with individual Tuareg groups. Nevertheless, meeting in Algiers in July, the Government and the leaders of a group believed to be allied to the ATNMC, the Alliance démocratique du 23 mai pour le changement (ADC), reached an agreement on peace and security, and in September the rebels released 44 government soldiers who had been held hostage in the north of the country (although a number remained in captivity). Despite the establishment in November of the first joint special unit comprising rebel fighters and Malian soldiers, raising hopes for continued progress towards peace, further unrest was reported the following month in which nine soldiers were killed. None the less, in January 2009 the ADC in Kidal released the last remaining Malian hostages following a period in which the Government used increased force to seize ammunition and weapons. It was later announced that three Tuareg factions, including the ADC, had united and agreed to rejoin peace negotiations. The Malian military then claimed in February that it had taken the last of the ATNMC positions (that organization was believed by this stage to number only some 165 members) and that Bahanga and an unknown number of fighters had crossed the border into Algeria. Later that month it was reported that he had been granted refuge in Libya, while some 500 members of the ADC surrendered their weapons and agreed to join the peace process.

In November 2010 it was reported that a group of Tuareg, Arab and Songhaï youths from northern Mali had formed the Mouvement national de l'Azaouad with the aim of restoring 'usurped historic rights' to local people who, they claimed, had not been consulted by the Government before it signed a number of agreements with companies in the area.

Foreign Affairs

The presence of large numbers of refugees from the conflict in northern Mali dominated Mali's relations with its neighbours during the 1990s, and even after the completion of the process of repatriation in mid-1998 (and the conclusion of a UNHCR pro-

MALI

gramme in June 1999) the north of the country remained vulnerable to cross-border banditry. In December 1998 Mali and Senegal agreed to improve border security, and in February 1999 Mali and Algeria agreed to revive their joint border committee to promote development and stability in the region. In March Konaré visited Mauritania to discuss border stability; however, in June a dispute over watering rights escalated into an armed conflict between neighbouring Malian and Mauritanian communities, in which 13 people were killed. The two Governments responded to the disturbances by increasing border controls and by sending a joint delegation to the villages involved. In August, at a meeting in Dakar, Senegal, the Malian, Mauritanian and Senegalese ministers responsible for the interior agreed to establish an operational unit drawn from the police forces of the three countries in order to ensure security in the area of their joint border. Bilateral relations between Mali and Mauritania were further strengthened by a military co-operation agreement regarding border security signed by the countries' respective Presidents in January 2005.

Concerns about insecurity in the region re-emerged in mid-2003, following reports, in July, that some 15 German, Swiss and Dutch tourists, said to have been kidnapped in February by Islamist militants allegedly associated with the Groupe salafiste pour la prédication et le combat (GSPC) in southern Algeria, had been smuggled into Mali. Following negotiations with the kidnappers, conducted by a former rebel Tuareg leader, Iyad Ag Agaly, 14 hostages were released in August (the remaining hostage had reportedly died earlier from heat-stroke). In March 2004 Mali announced that it was to increase anti-terrorism co-operation with the authorities in Algeria, Chad and Niger. In November 2007 the Presidents of Mali and Algeria agreed to establish a joint border patrol.

In February 2009 Al-Qa'ida in the Islamic Maghreb (AQIM, as the GSPC had been restyled), an Islamist militant group largely operating in southern Algeria and northern Mali, claimed responsibility for the kidnapping of four European tourists the previous month and of two diplomats in December 2008. The diplomats and two of the tourists were released in April 2009, and in June a 2,000-strong Malian force, supported by Algerian troops and aircraft, launched an attack on an AQIM base in northern Mali. During the offensive it was reported that 26 Islamist militants were killed and several more detained; 10 Malian soldiers were also killed in the fighting. The Swiss hostage was released in July; however, it was reported that, owing to the British Government's refusal to release a detained radical Jordanian cleric or to pay a ransom, the British hostage had been killed in late May. In August the Tuareg, Moor and Songhaï groups took part in a reconciliation ceremony, the first of its kind in 10 years, pledging to establish permanent structures for intra-group dialogue and to co-operate in supporting the Government to address the increasing AQIM threat. The movement had in recent years been relocating a number of its bases from Algeria towards Mali and Niger, causing disagreements between those countries and international observers over appropriate measures to counter the threat. The US authorities appeared keen to maintain a military presence in the region, while Algeria stated that it preferred to limit US and European support to the provision of technology and information. In September delegates from Mali, Mauritania, Niger and Algeria met to discuss a new anti-terror plan and agreed to allow military co-operation in the fight against terrorism in the region. In response to the kidnapping of the four European citizens in early 2009 and the seizure in Mauritania (and subsequent transfer to Mali) of three Spanish and two Italian tourists later that year, in January 2010 Mali and Mauritania announced plans to further strengthen security co-operation. The following month, however, relations with neighbouring countries became strained after Mali released four Islamist militants, detained in April 2009 on weapons charges, in exchange for the release of a French citizen taken hostage in November. Both Algeria and Mauritania subsequently withdrew their ambassadors from Bamako, claiming that Mali's decision to release the terrorists was an infringement of the agreement on security co-operation reached at the September regional summit. One of the Spanish hostages was released in March, followed by the other two in August; it was reported that the Spanish Government had paid a ransom to secure the release of the prisoners, although the Spanish authorities denied that any fee had been paid. The two Italian hostages were released in April. Meanwhile, in mid-March foreign ministers from seven Saharan states, including Mali, Mauritania and Algeria, meeting in Algiers agreed that they would commence the sharing of operational information and co-ordinate their actions against AQIM in an attempt to 'collectively confront the threat of terrorism'.

In February 1999 some 488 Malian troops joined the Economic Community of West African States (ECOWAS, see p. 261) Cease-fire Monitoring Group forces in Sierra Leone, although the Malian authorities emphasized that these troops would take on a purely peace-keeping role. However, following widespread demands in Mali for a withdrawal, during August the majority of the force departed Sierra Leone; it was later announced that seven Malian soldiers had been killed and 10 seriously injured while serving in Sierra Leone. As Chairman of ECOWAS, in March 2001 Konaré hosted a mini-summit, attended by the leaders of the three countries of the Mano River Union (see p. 448), Sierra Leone, Liberia and Guinea, in Bamako on the subject of the peace process in Sierra Leone. Konaré sought to emphasize the role of Mali in ECOWAS, and in November 2000 a 120-member ECOWAS parliament, which was to promote regional co-operation, was inaugurated in Bamako.

Mali has in recent years forged closer relations with Libya, and was a founder member of the Community of Sahel-Saharan States (see p. 446), established in Tripoli, Libya, in 1997.

CONSTITUTION AND GOVERNMENT

The Constitution of the Third Republic, which was approved in a national referendum on 12 January 1992, provides for the separation of the powers of the executive, legislative and judicial organs of state. Executive power is vested in the President of the Republic, who is elected for five years by universal suffrage. The President appoints a Prime Minister, who, in turn, appoints a Council of Ministers. Legislative power is vested in the 147-seat unicameral Assemblée nationale, elected for five years by universal suffrage. Elections take place in the context of a multi-party political system.

Mali has eight administrative regions, each presided over by a governor, and a district government in Bamako. Following a significant revision of local government structures in 1999, and a further minor revision in 2001, the number of elected mayors across Mali increased from 19 to 703.

REGIONAL AND INTERNATIONAL CO-OPERATION

Mali is a member of the African Union (see p. 183), the Economic Community of West African States (ECOWAS, see p. 257), the West African organs of the Franc Zone (see p. 332), the African Groundnut Council (see p. 442), the Niger Basin Authority (see p. 448) and the Organisation pour la mise en valeur du fleuve Sénégal (OMVS, see p. 447).

Mali became a member of the UN in 1960 and was admitted to the World Trade Organization (WTO, see p. 430) in 1995. Mali participates in the Group of 77 (G77, see p. 447) developing countries.

ECONOMIC AFFAIRS

In 2009, according to estimates by the World Bank, Mali's gross national income (GNI), measured at average 2007–09 prices, was US $8,862m., equivalent to $680 per head (or $1,190 on an international purchasing-power parity basis). During 2000–09, it was estimated, the population increased at an average annual rate of 2.4%, while gross domestic product (GDP) per head increased, in real terms, by an average of 3.1% per year. Overall GDP increased, in real terms, at an average annual rate of 5.6% in 2000–09. According to the World Bank, real GDP increased by 4.3% in 2009.

Agriculture (including livestock-rearing, forestry and fishing) contributed 40.0% of GDP in 2009, according to the African Development Bank (AfDB). According to FAO, some 74.2% of the labour force were estimated to be employed in the sector in mid-2011. Mali is among Africa's foremost producers and exporters of cotton (exports of which contributed an estimated 10.6% of the value of total exports in 2008). According to the IMF, cotton production increased from 202,397 metric tons in 2008 to 236,000 tons in 2009. Sheanuts (karité nuts), groundnuts, vegetables and mangoes are also cultivated for export. A government project introduced in 2006 to support diversification in the agricultural sector has had considerable success, resulting, for example, in a 135% increase in the value of mango exports between 2005 and 2009. The principal subsistence crops are millet, rice, sorghum and maize. Cereal imports remain necessary in most years. The livestock-rearing and fishing sectors make an important contribution to the domestic food supply and (in the case of the former) to export revenue, providing 7.0% of total exports in 2009, according to the AfDB, although both are highly vulnerable to drought. According to the World Bank, agricultural GDP increased by an average of 4.9% per year in 2000–07. The sector grew by 13.2% in 2008 and by 5.7% in 2009, according to the AfDB.

Industry (including mining, manufacturing, construction and power) contributed 20.1% of GDP in 2009, according to the AfDB. It engaged 16.5% of the employed labour force in 2004. According to the World Bank, industrial GDP increased at an average annual rate of 6.0% in 2000–07. It increased by 3.7% in 2007.

Mining contributed 6.7% of GDP in 2009, according to the AfDB. It engaged 0.5% of the employed labour force in 2004. The importance of the sector has increased with the successful exploitation of the country's gold reserves: exports of gold contributed an estimated 74.9% of the value of total exports in 2008. Output of gold increased significantly in the second half of the 1990s, as new mining facilities commenced operations, and by 2001 Mali had become the third largest gold producer in Africa. Gold production declined by an estimated 16.5% in 2010, according to the IMF, owing to a delay in the opening of a new mine, but was forecast to rise sharply in 2011, before contracting gradually from 2013 as mines near the end of their reserves. Two new open-pit mines, at Yalea and Loulo, operated by Randgold Resources (of South Africa), commenced operations in late 2005; underground development began at Loulo in 2010 and was expected to produce 1.2m. oz of gold by 2014. Salt, diamonds, marble and phosphate rock are also mined. The future exploitation of deposits of iron ore and uranium is envisaged. According to the IMF, the GDP of the mining sector increased at an average annual rate of 46.8% in 1996–2002; according to the AfDB, mining GDP declined by 0.6% in 2009.

The manufacturing sector contributed 5.7% of GDP in 2009, according to the AfDB. It engaged 11.5% of the employed labour force in 2004. The main area of activity is agro-industrial (chiefly the processing of cotton, sugar and rice). Brewing and tobacco industries are represented, and some construction materials are produced for the domestic market. According to the World Bank, manufacturing GDP increased at an average annual rate of 3.6% in 2000–07. According to the AfDB, the GDP of the sector declined by 14.4% in 2008, but increased by 4.4% in 2009.

According to the AfDB, construction contributed 5.6% of GDP in 2009, while it engaged 4.3% of the employed labour force in 2004. The sector grew by 6.0% in 2009.

Mali began to receive power supplies from the Manantali hydroelectric project (constructed and operated under the auspices of the Organisation pour la mise en valeur du fleuve Sénégal—OMVS) from December 2001, and there were also plans to link the Malian network with those of Côte d'Ivoire, Burkina Faso and Ghana. An agreement on energy supply was also reached with Algeria in February 1998. Imports of petroleum, petroleum products and related materials comprised an estimated 21.1% of the value of merchandise imports in 2008.

The services sector contributed 39.9% of GDP in 2009, according to the AfDB. It engaged 41.9% of the employed labour force in 2004. According to the World Bank, the GDP of the services sector increased at an average annual rate of 6.3% in 2000–07. Services GDP increased by 7.6% in 2007.

In 2008 Mali recorded a visible trade deficit of US $638.7m., and there was a deficit of $1,066.4m. on the current account of the balance of payments. In 2008 the principal sources of imports were Senegal (which supplied 17.2% of total imports), France, Côte d'Ivoire, the People's Republic of China and the USA. The largest market for exports in that year was South Africa, which accounted for 72.5% of total exports, followed by Senegal (6.8%). The principal exports in 2008 were gold, cotton, and food and live animals. The principal imports in that year were machinery and transport equipment, petroleum, petroleum products and related materials, manufactured goods, chemicals and related products, and food and live animals.

In 2009, according to IMF estimates, Mali recorded an overall budget deficit of 178,900m. francs CFA, equivalent to 4.2% of GDP. Mali's general government gross debt was 1,012,830m. francs CFA in 2009, equivalent to 23.9% of GDP. Mali's total external debt was US $2,190m. at the end of 2008, of which $2,150m. was public and publicly guaranteed debt. In 2007 the cost of debt-servicing was equivalent to 2.9% of the value of exports of goods, services and income. The annual rate of inflation averaged 2.9% in 2000–09. Consumer prices increased by 2.2% in 2009. An estimated 8.8% of the labour force were unemployed in 2004.

Mali's economic development is hindered by its vulnerability to drought, its dependence on imports and its narrow range of exports. The country also lacks facilities for the processing of its important cotton crop; it was reported in 2002 that only 1% of Mali's cotton crop was processed in the country. In the first half of the 2000s the cotton sector underwent restructuring, with the partial transfer to private ownership of the cotton-ginning company, the Compagnie Malienne pour le Développement des Textiles; the full privatization of the company was expected to be completed in 2011. Recent emphasis in economic policy has been placed on food security, agricultural productivity and water management. A number of projects were being undertaken in 2010 to broaden the country's exports and increase rural farming income. In particular, a six-year Fostering Agricultural Productivity Project, costing some US $152m. and funded largely by the World Bank's International Development Association and by the International Fund for Agricultural Development, was initiated in that year, while the AfDB was providing financing for a public-private venture, involving the South African company Illovo Sugar, for the development of a 14,000-ha irrigated sugar cane plantation and a processing plant in Markala, in the central Ségou region. In January 2011 the IMF completed its fifth review of Mali's performance under a programme supported by the Extended Credit Facility, which released a further $3.1m. in assistance (bringing total disbursements to some $40.5m.), and extended the three-year arrangement by six months, to the end of 2011. The Fund noted that the impact of the global recession on Mali had been only limited, owing to buoyant international prices for gold and revenue from the privatization of the state telecommunications provider, but advocated further diversification of the economy to reduce reliance on gold exports. Steady economic growth and a low inflation rate were maintained in 2010; the outlook for 2011 was generally positive, with gold prices forecast to rise further, accompanied by a projected increase in gold production from some 46 metric tons in 2010 to 56 tons in 2011.

PUBLIC HOLIDAYS

2012: 1 January (New Year's Day), 20 January (Armed Forces Day), 4 February* (Mouloud, Birth of the Prophet), 11 March* (Baptism of the Prophet), 25 March (Commemoration of the overthrow of Moussa Traoré), 9 April (Easter Monday), 1 May (Labour Day), 25 May (Africa Day, anniversary of the OAU's foundation), 16 August* (Korité, end of Ramadan), 22 September (Independence Day), 26 October* (Tabaski, Feast of the Sacrifice), 25 December (Christmas Day).

* These holidays are determined by the Islamic lunar calendar and may vary by one or two days from the dates given.

Statistical Survey

Source (unless otherwise stated): Direction Nationale de la Statistique et de l'Informatique, rue Archinard, porte 233, BP 12, Bamako; tel. 2022-2455; fax 2022-7145; e-mail cnpe.mali@afribonemali.net; internet www.dnsi.gov.ml.

Area and Population

AREA, POPULATION AND DENSITY

Area (sq km)	1,240,192*
Population (census results)†	
1–30 April 1987	7,696,348
17 April 1998	
Males	4,847,436
Females	4,943,056
Total	9,790,492
Population (UN estimates at mid-year)‡	
2009	13,010,000
2010	13,323,000
2011	13,644,326
Density (per sq km) at mid-2011	11.0

* 478,841 sq miles.
† Figures are provisional and refer to the *de jure* population.
‡ Source: UN, *World Population Prospects: The 2008 Revision*.

POPULATION BY AGE AND SEX
(UN estimates at mid-2011)

	Males	Females	Total
0–14	3,034,617	2,971,946	6,006,563
15–64	3,565,583	3,763,520	7,329,103
65 and over	140,309	168,351	308,660
Total	6,740,509	6,903,817	13,644,326

Source: UN, *World Population Prospects: The 2008 Revision*.

Ethnic Groups (percentage of total, 1995): Bambara 36.5; Peul 13.9; Sénoufo 9.0; Soninké 8.8; Dogon 8.0; Songhaï 7.2; Malinké 6.6; Diola 2.9; Bobo and Oulé 2.4; Tuareg 1.7; Moor 1.2; Others 1.8 (Source: La Francophonie).

ADMINISTRATIVE DIVISIONS
(*de jure* population at 1998 census, provisional figures)

District			
Bamako	1,016,167	Mopti	1,475,274
Regions		Kayes	1,372,019
Sikasso	1,780,042	Tombouctou	461,956
Ségou	1,679,201	Gao	397,516
Koulikoro	1,565,838	Kidal	42,479

PRINCIPAL TOWNS*
(*de jure* population at 1998 census, provisional figures)

Bamako (capital)	1,016,167	Koutiala	74,153
Sikasso	113,813	Kayes	67,262
Ségou	90,898	Gao	54,903
Mopti	79,840	Kati	49,756

* With the exception of Bamako, figures refer to the population of communes (municipalities).

Mid-2010 ('000, incl. suburbs, UN estimate): Bamako 1,698,520 (Source: UN, *World Urbanization Prospects: The 2009 Revision*).

BIRTHS AND DEATHS
(annual averages, UN estimates)

	1995–2000	2000–05	2005–10
Birth rate (per 1,000)	44.1	43.3	42.8
Death rate (per 1,000)	19.1	17.4	15.9

Source: UN, *World Population Prospects: The 2008 Revision*.

Life expectancy (years at birth, WHO estimates): 49 (males 48; females 50) in 2008 (Source: WHO, *World Health Statistics*).

ECONOMICALLY ACTIVE POPULATION
('000 persons, 2004, estimates)

	Males	Females	Total
Agriculture, hunting and forestry	657.7	291.7	949.4
Fishing	33.3	2.0	35.2
Mining	8.4	3.0	11.4
Manufacturing	136.1	136.4	272.5
Electricity, gas and water	5.1	—	5.1
Construction	97.5	4.7	102.1
Wholesale and retail trade; repair of motor vehicles, motorcycles and personal household goods	266.1	402.1	668.1
Hotels and restaurants	1.4	6.3	7.6
Transport, storage and communications	51.8	3.5	55.3
Financial intermediation	4.4	—	4.4
Real estate	3.5	0.6	4.0
Public administration	33.3	6.6	39.9
Education	35.6	18.3	53.9
Health and social work	11.4	9.5	20.9
Other social services	42.6	97.5	140.1
Total employed	1,388.3	982.5	2,370.8
Unemployed	107.0	120.5	227.4
Total labour force	1,495.3	1,103.0	2,598.2

Source: ILO.

Mid-2011 (estimates in '000): Agriculture, etc. 2,681; Total labour force 3,611 (Source: FAO).

Health and Welfare

KEY INDICATORS

Total fertility rate (children per woman, 2008)	5.5
Under-5 mortality rate (per 1,000 live births, 2008)	194
HIV/AIDS (% of persons aged 15–49, 2007)	1.5
Physicians (per 1,000 head, 2004)	0.08
Hospital beds (per 1,000 head, 2005)	0.30
Health expenditure (2007): US $ per head (PPP)	67
Health expenditure (2007): % of GDP	5.7
Health expenditure (2007): public (% of total)	51.4
Access to water (% of persons, 2008)	56
Access to sanitation (% of persons, 2008)	36
Total carbon dioxide emissions ('000 metric tons, 2007)	578.9
Carbon dioxide emissions per head (metric tons, 2007)	<0.1
Human Development Index (2010): ranking	160
Human Development Index (2010): value	0.309

For sources and definitions, see explanatory note on p. vi.

MALI

Agriculture

PRINCIPAL CROPS
('000 metric tons)

	2007	2008	2009
Rice, paddy	1,082.4	1,624.2	1,950.8
Maize	689.9	695.1	1,477.0
Millet	1,175.1	1,413.9	1,390.4
Sorghum	900.8	1,027.2	1,465.6
Fonio	28.7	41.3	35.5
Sweet potatoes	283.0	290.0*	n.a.
Cassava (Manioc)	96.1	100.0*	n.a.
Yams	85.3	90.0*	n.a.
Sugar cane	341.8	350.0*	n.a.
Groundnuts, with shell	324.2	325.0*	334.7
Karité nuts (Sheanuts)	182.2	190.0*	n.a.
Cottonseed†	151.0	116.0	150.0
Tomatoes	173.8	175.0*	n.a.
Onions, dry	37.0	38.0*	n.a.
Guavas, mangoes and mangosteens	69.3	70.0*	n.a.
Cotton (lint)*	75.0	54.0	72.0

* FAO estimate(s).
† Unofficial figures.

Aggregate production ('000 metric tons, may include official, semi-official or estimated data): Total cereals 3,885.6 in 2007, 4,814.9 in 2008, 6,334.6 in 2009; Total pulses 77.5 in 2007, 106.3 in 2008, 130.9 in 2009; Total roots and tubers 578.9 in 2007, 600.0 in 2008–09; Total vegetables (incl. melons) 792.7 in 2007, 795.9 in 2008–09; Total fruits (excl. melons) 388.5 in 2007, 394.1 in 2008–09.

Source: FAO.

LIVESTOCK
('000 head, year ending September)

	2006	2007	2008*
Cattle	7,431	7,843	8,278
Sheep	8,240	8,871	9,500
Goats	9,207	9,667*	10,150
Pigs	105	71	75*
Horses	93	101*	111
Asses	1,480	1,617*	1,767*
Camels	837	960*	1,100*
Chickens*	32,000	33,000	34,000

* FAO estimate(s).

2009 (FAO estimate): Horses 111.

Source: FAO.

LIVESTOCK PRODUCTS
('000 metric tons, FAO estimates)

	2007	2008	2009
Cattle meat	112.3	129.1	n.a.
Sheep meat	37.7	41.6	n.a.
Goat meat	40.2	42.6	n.a.
Chicken meat	38.3	39.4	39.4
Game meat	18.5	18.5	n.a.
Pig meat	2.3	2.4	2.4
Cows' milk	269.0	284.0	284.0
Sheep's milk	133.1	142.5	142.5
Goats' milk	203.0	213.2	213.2
Camels' milk	112.3	128.7	128.7

Source: FAO.

Forestry

ROUNDWOOD REMOVALS
('000 cubic metres, excl. bark, FAO estimates)

	2007	2008	2009
Sawlogs, veneer logs and logs for sleepers	4	4	4
Other industrial wood	409	409	409
Fuel wood	5,143	5,203	5,264
Total	5,556	5,616	5,677

Source: FAO.

SAWNWOOD PRODUCTION
('000 cubic metres, incl. railway sleepers)

	1987	1988	1989
Total (all broadleaved)	11	13	13*

* FAO estimate.

1990–2009: Production assumed to be unchanged from 1989 (FAO estimates).

Source: FAO.

Fishing

('000 metric tons, live weight)

	2006*	2007	2008
Capture	100.0	100.0	100.0*
Nile tilapia	30.0	30.0	30.0
Elephantsnout fishes	7.0	7.0	7.0
Characins	5.0	5.0	5.0
Black catfishes	4.0	4.0	4.0
North African catfish	25.0	25.0	25.0
Nile perch	6.0	6.0	6.0*
Other freshwater fishes	23.0	23.0	23.0
Aquaculture	1.0	0.6	0.8
Total catch	101.0	100.6	100.8*

* FAO estimate(s).

Source: FAO.

Mining

(metric tons unless otherwise indicated)

	2007	2008	2009*
Gold (kg)	43,850	41,160	42,364
Salt*	6,000	6,000	6,000
Semi-precious stones	10,000*	10,000*	10,000

* Estimated figure(s).

Source: US Geological Survey.

MALI

Industry

SELECTED PRODUCTS
('000 metric tons unless otherwise indicated)

	2005	2006	2007
Raw sugar	34	34	34
Fish (dried, salted or in brine); smoked fish and edible fish meal	14.2	5.7	8.8
Cigarettes (million)	330.4	625.8	546.8
Electric energy (million kWh)	475	489	495

Cement: 10,000 metric tons in 2000 (Source: US Geological Survey).
Source: mainly UN Industrial Commodity Statistics Database.

Finance

CURRENCY AND EXCHANGE RATES

Monetary Units
100 centimes = 1 franc de la Communauté financière africaine (CFA).

Sterling, Dollar and Euro Equivalents (31 December 2010)
£1 sterling = 768.523 francs CFA;
US $1 = 490.912 francs CFA;
€1 = 655.957 francs CFA;
10,000 francs CFA = £13.01 = $20.37 = €15.24.

Average Exchange Rate (francs CFA per US $)
2008   447.81
2009   472.19
2010   495.28

Note: An exchange rate of 1 French franc = 50 francs CFA, established in 1948, remained in force until January 1994, when the CFA franc was devalued by 50%, with the exchange rate adjusted to 1 French franc = 100 francs CFA. This relationship to French currency remained in effect with the introduction of the euro on 1 January 1999. From that date, accordingly, a fixed exchange rate of €1 = 655.957 francs CFA has been in operation.

BUDGET
('000 million francs CFA)*

Revenue†	2008	2009‡	2010§
Budgetary revenue	540.6	653.2	709.0
Tax revenue	519.4	624.3	677.1
Non-tax revenue	21.2	28.9	31.9
Special funds and annexed budgets	66.7	71.8	71.5
Total	607.3	725.0	780.5

Expenditure‖	2008	2009‡	2010§
Budgetary expenditure	753.9	1,004.4	1,010.7
Current expenditure	459.1	549.0	611.8
Wages and salaries	186.0	213.5	235.7
Interest payments (scheduled)	14.1	15.7	22.7
Other current expenditure	259.0	319.8	353.4
Capital expenditure	294.9	455.4	398.9
Externally financed	172.8	303.2	223.9
Special funds and annexed budgets	66.7	71.8	71.5
Total	820.6	1,076.2	1,082.2

* Figures represent a consolidation of the central government budget, special funds and annexed budgets.
† Excluding grants received ('000 million francs CFA): 134.2 in 2008; 193.9 in 2009 (estimate); 165.0 in 2010 (projected).
‡ Estimates.
§ Projected.
‖ Excluding net lending ('000 million francs CFA): –7.6 in 2008; 21.6 in 2009 (estimate); 27.4 in 2010 (projected).

Source: IMF, *Mali—Fifth Review Under the Three-Year Arrangement Under the Extended Credit Facility and Request for Extension of the Arrangement and Rephasing of Disbursement—Staff Report; Joint IDA/IMF Debt Sustainability Analysis; Informational Annex; Staff Statement; Statement by the Executive Director for Mali; and Press Release on the Executive Board Discussion* (February 2011).

INTERNATIONAL RESERVES
(excl. gold, US $ million at 31 December)

	2007	2008	2009
IMF special drawing rights	0.1	0.1	115.0
Reserve position in IMF	15.1	14.9	15.5
Foreign exchange	1,071.9	1,056.5	1,473.9
Total	1,087.1	1,071.5	1,604.4

Source: IMF, *International Financial Statistics*.

MONEY SUPPLY
('000 million francs CFA at 31 December)

	2007	2008	2009
Currency outside banks	327.5	318.3	304.6
Demand deposits	376.2	416.2	495.5
Total money (incl. others)	704.2	734.9	800.5

Source: IMF, *International Financial Statistics*.

COST OF LIVING
(Consumer Price Index for Bamako: base: 2000 = 100)

	2007	2008	2009
Food, beverages and tobacco	117.3	132.6	136.6
Clothing	97.3	105.9	108.7
Housing, water, electricity and gas	112.3	118.2	118.4
All items (incl. others)	115.7	126.3	129.1

Source: ILO.

NATIONAL ACCOUNTS
(million francs CFA at current prices)

Expenditure on the Gross Domestic Product

	2007	2008	2009
Government final consumption expenditure	596,809	687,739	744,554
Private final consumption expenditure	2,215,069	2,495,017	2,659,812
Changes in inventories	73,983	74,696	103,397
Gross fixed capital formation	664,444	715,794	804,881
Total domestic expenditure	3,550,305	3,973,246	4,312,644
Exports of goods and services	995,871	896,284	950,666
Less Imports of goods and services	1,121,641	956,760	1,082,324
GDP in purchasers' values	3,424,535	3,912,771	4,180,987

Gross Domestic Product by Economic Activity

	2007	2008	2009
Agriculture, hunting, forestry and fishing	1,114,794	1,412,222	1,521,949
Mining and quarrying	229,100	242,315	256,732
Manufacturing	235,544	207,245	215,134
Electricity, gas and water	66,150	74,662	81,693
Construction	168,543	190,569	212,104
Wholesale and retail trade, restaurants and hotels	490,458	559,657	602,415
Transport and communications	191,699	220,806	235,163
Finance, insurance, real estate and other business services	26,770	29,730	29,397
Public administration and defence	332,440	359,435	377,651
Other services	236,551	262,788	273,325
Sub-total	3,092,049	3,559,429	3,805,563
Less Imputed bank service charges	12,711	14,723	15,056
Indirect taxes, less subsidies	345,199	368,065	390,480
GDP in purchasers' values	3,424,535	3,912,771	4,180,987

Source: African Development Bank.

MALI

Statistical Survey

BALANCE OF PAYMENTS
(US $ million)

	2006	2007	2008
Exports of goods f.o.b.	1,550.4	1,556.3	2,097.2
Imports of goods f.o.b.	–1,475.4	–1,846.0	–2,735.9
Trade balance	75.0	–289.7	–638.7
Exports of services	313.3	376.7	454.3
Imports of services	–674.5	–776.6	–1,024.3
Balance on goods and services	–286.2	–689.6	–1,208.7
Other income received	69.0	71.5	101.6
Other income paid	–326.5	–362.9	–414.2
Balance on goods, services and income	–543.7	–981.1	–1,521.3
Current transfers received	380.9	482.8	554.0
Current transfers paid	–55.8	–82.9	–99.2
Current balance	–218.6	–581.1	–1,066.4
Capital account (net)	140.6	301.8	328.8
Direct investment abroad	–1.2	–7.3	–0.6
Direct investment from abroad	83.4	72.8	180.3
Portfolio investment assets	–6.9	–31.0	–117.9
Portfolio investment liabilities	–4.2	–15.5	22.6
Financial derivatives assets	—	–0.1	3.6
Other investment assets	–209.3	–68.4	205.5
Other investment liabilities	–1,771.9	279.1	326.7
Net errors and omissions	–46.8	30.1	34.0
Overall balance	–2,035.0	–19.7	–83.4

Source: IMF, *International Financial Statistics*.

External Trade

PRINCIPAL COMMODITIES
(distribution by SITC, US $ million)

Imports c.i.f.	2006	2007	2008
Food and live animals	257.0	252.2	320.1
Cereals and cereal preparations	112.4	91.3	117.9
Mineral fuels, lubricants, etc.	435.7	484.9	713.2
Petroleum, petroleum products and related materials	430.8	478.4	704.4
Chemicals and related products	252.9	338.9	471.6
Medicinal and pharmaceutical products	67.3	140.2	136.2
Manufactured goods	312.2	399.7	683.1
Iron and steel	68.9	89.0	142.5
Machinery and transport equipment	407.9	534.5	860.2
Road vehicles	142.0	158.9	220.5
Miscellaneous manufactured articles	76.3	83.1	162.7
Total (incl. others)*	1,819.8	2,184.8	3,338.9

Exports f.o.b.	2006	2007	2008
Food and live animals	79.4	93.7	127.7
Crude materials, inedible, excluding fuels	260.5	207.4	213.1
Cotton	254.1	198.7	203.1
Machinery and transport equipment	19.4	27.3	58.5
Road vehicles	6.6	5.1	21.7
Gold, non-monetary, unwrought, in powder or semi-manufactured	1,131.8	1,082.5	1,437.1
Total (incl. others)	1,526.1	1,440.6	1,918.3

* Including commodities and transactions not classified according to kind (US $ million): 448.3 in 2006; 492.2 in 2007; 734.0 in 2008.

Source: UN, *International Trade Statistics Yearbook*.

SELECTED TRADING PARTNERS
(US $ million)

Imports c.i.f.	2006	2007	2008
Belgium	44.6	67.2	86.4
Benin	163.8	97.5	74.6
Brazil	37.8	36.4	58.8
Burkina Faso	17.1	35.8	5.3
China, People's Repub.	111.9	130.0	342.1
Côte d'Ivoire	197.6	277.0	346.9
France (incl. Monaco)	277.3	325.9	464.8
Germany	53.3	52.3	81.3
Ghana	46.1	65.3	55.7
India	39.7	78.3	66.1
Italy	21.8	21.4	36.9
Japan	48.2	41.1	91.9
Netherlands	15.4	15.8	23.2
Senegal	220.6	432.2	575.7
South Africa	67.8	79.5	151.2
Thailand	16.0	11.2	39.5
Togo	90.2	87.3	45.1
Ukraine	34.5	12.1	37.4
United Arab Emirates	17.6	14.6	40.0
USA	91.7	81.6	221.4
Total (incl. others)	1,819.8	2,184.8	3,338.9

Exports f.o.b.	2006	2007	2008
Bangladesh	12.4	11.8	5.2
Belgium	4.7	30.4	6.4
Burkina Faso	12.0	10.9	18.5
China, People's Repub.	94.5	32.1	35.4
Côte d'Ivoire	18.8	36.0	49.1
France (incl. Monaco)	16.6	12.6	24.2
Germany	4.2	2.9	7.8
Guinea	10.2	11.3	11.8
Indonesia	20.6	25.7	11.8
Pakistan	2.8	30.1	16.5
Senegal	40.6	61.1	131.1
South Africa	1,084.0	966.0	1,390.1
Switzerland-Liechtenstein	22.6	65.6	49.0
Thailand	26.2	27.0	27.2
United Kingdom	19.6	26.5	1.3
Viet Nam	34.6	23.5	21.7
Total (incl. others)	1,526.1	1,440.6	1,918.3

Source: UN, *International Trade Statistics Yearbook*.

Transport

RAILWAYS
(traffic)

	1999	2000	2001
Passengers ('000)	778.7	682.3	649.0
Freight carried ('000 metric tons)	535	438	358

Passenger-km (million): 210 in 1999.

Freight ton-km (million): 241 in 1999.

ROAD TRAFFIC
(motor vehicles in use, estimates)

	1994	1995	1996
Passenger cars	24,250	24,750	26,190
Lorries and vans	16,000	17,100	18,240

2007 (motor vehicles in use): Passenger cars 86,967; Vans and lorries 26,759; Motorcycles and mopeds 10,035.

Source: IRF, *World Road Statistics*.

MALI

CIVIL AVIATION
(traffic on scheduled services)*

	1999	2000	2001
Kilometres flown (million)	3	3	1
Passengers carried ('000)	84	77	46
Passenger-km (million)	235	216	130
Total ton-km (million)	36	32	19

* Including an apportionment of the traffic of Air Afrique.

Source: UN, *Statistical Yearbook*.

Tourism

FOREIGN VISITORS BY NATIONALITY*

	2006	2007	2008
Austria	977	988	2,638
Belgium, Luxembourg and the Netherlands	9,258	10,280	8,166
Canada	4,285	5,076	6,940
France	42,661	57,682	41,778
Germany	6,623	6,962	9,033
Italy	8,615	9,272	8,269
Japan	1,636	1,416	4,672
Middle Eastern states	1,128	1,190	4,176
Scandinavian states	2,015	1,436	3,883
Spain	7,787	7,792	10,164
Switzerland	2,066	2,480	5,037
United Kingdom	5,006	5,224	5,357
USA	14,222	12,488	12,579
West African states	18,902	18,914	15,276
Total (incl. others)	152,660	164,124	189,511

* Arrivals at hotels and similar establishments.

Receipts from tourism (US $ million, incl. passenger transport): 149.2 in 2005; 175.4 in 2006; 227.0 in 2007.

Source: World Tourism Organization.

Communications Media

	2007	2008	2009
Telephones ('000 main lines in use)	80.0	81.1	84.8
Mobile cellular telephones ('000 subscribers)	2,530.9	3,439.0	4,445.5
Internet users ('000)	100.5	199.5	249.8
Broadband subscribers ('000)	3.2	2.7	2.1

Personal computers 100,000 (8.1 per 1,000 persons) in 2007.

Source: International Telecommunication Union.

Television receivers ('000 in use): 160 in 2000 (Source: UNESCO, *Statistical Yearbook*).

Radio receivers ('000 in use): 570 in 1997 (Source: UNESCO, *Statistical Yearbook*).

Daily newspapers (national estimates): 3 (total circulation 12,350 copies) in 1997; 3 (total circulation 12,600) in 1998; 9 in 2004 (Source: UNESCO Institute for Statistics).

Book production: 14 titles (28,000 copies) in 1995 (first editions only, excluding pamphlets); 33 in 1998 (Sources: UNESCO, *Statistical Yearbook*, UNESCO Institute for Statistics).

Education

(2007/08 unless otherwise indicated)

	Institutions*	Teachers	Males	Females	Total
Pre-primary	212	1,637	30.7	30.8	61.5
Primary	2,871	35,442	1,005.6	817.4	1,823.0
Secondary	n.a.	25,990	375.5	236.5	612.0
Tertiary	n.a.	1,112†	46.7	21.1	67.8

Students ('000)

* 1998/99 figures.
† 2004/05 figure.

Source: mainly UNESCO Institute for Statistics.

2005/06: *Pre-primary*: 412 institutions; 1,510 teachers; 51,071 students; *Primary and Secondary (lower)*: 8,079 institutions; 39,109 teachers; 1,990,765 students (1,137,787 males, 852,978 females); *Secondary (higher)*: 121 institutions; 1,904 teachers; 47,279 students (31,724 males, 15,555 females—estimates); *Secondary (technical and vocational)*: 119 institutions; 41,137 students; *Secondary (teacher training)*: 10,467 students (Source: Office of the Secretary-General of the Government, Bamako).

Pupil-teacher ratio (primary education, UNESCO estimate): 50.1 in 2008/09 (Source: UNESCO Institute for Statistics).

Adult literacy rate (UNESCO estimates): 26.2% (males 34.9%; females 18.2%) in 2006 (Source: UNESCO Institute for Statistics).

Directory

The Government

HEAD OF STATE

President: Gen. (retd) AMADOU TOUMANI TOURÉ (took office 8 June 2002; re-elected 29 April 2007).

COUNCIL OF MINISTERS
(May 2011)

Prime Minister: MARIAM KAÏDAMA SIDIBÉ CISSÉ.
Minister of the Environment and Sanitation: TIÉMOKO SANGARE.
Minister of Labour and Civil Service: ABDOUL WAHAB BERTHÉ.
Minister of Equipment and Transport: HAMED DIANE SÉMÉGA.
Minister of Territorial Administration and Local Communities: Gen. KAFOUGOUNA KONÉ.
Minister of Stockbreeding and Fisheries: Dr BOKARY TRETA.
Minister of Foreign Affairs and International Co-operation: SOUMEYLOU BOUBEYE MAIGA.
Minister of Health: MADELEINE DIALLO BÂ.
Minister of Employment and Professional Training: MODIBO KADJOKÉ.
Minister of Crafts and Tourism: N'DIAYE BA.
Minister of Defence and Veterans: NATIÉ PLÉAH.
Minister of Internal Security and Civil Protection: Gen. SADIO GASSAMA.
Minister of Agriculture: AGATHANE AG ALASSANE.
Minister of Education, Literacy and the National Languages: SALIKOU SANOGO.
Minister of Justice, Keeper of the Seals: MAHARAFA TRAORÉ.
Minister of the Economy and Finance: LASSINE BOUARÉ.
Minister of Industry, Investment and Commerce: SANGARÉ NIAMOTO BÂ.
Minister of Youth and Sports: DJIGUIBA KEÏTA.
Minister of Higher Education and Scientific Research: SIBY GINETTE BELLEGARDE.

MALI

Minister of Housing, Town Planning and Land Affairs: YACOUBA DIALLO.
Minister of Culture: HAMANE NIANG.
Minister of State Reform: DABA DIAWARA.
Minister of Mining: AMADOU CISSÉ.
Minister of Energy and Water: HABIB OUANE.
Minister of Posts and New Technologies: MODIBO IBRAHIM TOURÉ.
Minister of Relations with the Institutions: ABDOULAYE SALL.
Minister of Malians Abroad and African Integration: BADARA ALIOU MACALOU.
Minister of Communication and Government Spokesperson: SIDIKI N'FÀ KONATÉ.
Minister of Social Development, Solidarity and the Elderly: HAROUNA CISSÉ.
Minister for the Promotion of Women, Children and the Family: Dr MARIAM KONARÉ KALAPO.
Minister-delegate at the Office of the Prime Minister, responsible for the Integrated Development of the Office du Niger Zone: ABOU SOW.
Minister-delegate at the Ministry of the Economy, responsible for the Budget: SAMBOU WAGUÉ.
Minister-delegate at the Ministry of Territorial Administration and Local Communities, responsible for Decentralization: DAVID SAGARA.

MINISTRIES

Office of the President: BP 1463, Koulouba, Bamako; tel. 2022-2572; fax 2023-0026; internet www.koulouba.pr.ml.
Office of the Prime Minister: Quartier du Fleuve, BP 790, Bamako; tel. 2022-4310; fax 2023-9595; e-mail ecrireaupm@primature.gov.ml; internet www.primature.gov.ml.
Office of the Secretary-General of the Government: BP 14, Koulouba, Bamako; tel. 2022-2552; fax 2022-7050; e-mail sgg@sgg.gov.ml; internet www.sgg.gov.ml.
Ministry of Agriculture: BP 1676, Bamako; tel. 2022-2785; e-mail ministere@ma.gov.ml; internet www.maliagriculture.org.
Ministry of Communication and New Information Technologies: ave de l'Yser, Quartier du Fleuve, BP 116, Bamako; tel. and fax 2022-2054.
Ministry of Crafts and Tourism: Badalabougou, Semagesco, BP 2211, Bamako; tel. 2029-6450; fax 2029-3917; e-mail malitourisme@afribone.net.ml; internet www.malitourisme.com.
Ministry of Culture: rue 321, Porte 287, BP 4075, Bamako; tel. 2023-2640; fax 2023-2646; e-mail info@culture.gov.ml; internet www.maliculture.net.
Ministry of Defence and Veterans: route de Koulouba, BP 2083, Bamako; tel. 2022-5021; fax 2023-2318.
Ministry of the Economy and Finance: Bamako; internet www.finances.gov.ml.
Ministry of Education, Literacy and the National Languages: Bamako.
Ministry of Employment and Professional Training: Bamako; tel. 2022-3431.
Ministry of Energy and Water: Bamako.
Ministry of the Environment and Sanitation: Bamako; tel. 2023-0539.
Ministry of Equipment and Transport: Bamako; tel. 2022-3937.
Ministry of Foreign Affairs and International Co-operation: Koulouba, Bamako; tel. 2022-8314; fax 2022-5226.
Ministry of Health: BP 232, Koulouba, Bamako; tel. 2022-5302; fax 2023-0203.
Ministry of Higher Education and Scientific Research: BP 71, Bamako; tel. 2022-5780; fax 2022-2126; e-mail info@education.gov.ml; internet www.education.gov.ml.
Ministry of Housing, Town Planning and Land Affairs: Bamako; tel. 2023-0539; internet www.mlafu.gov.ml.
Ministry of Industry, Investment and Commerce: BP 234, Koulouba, Bamako; tel. 2022-5156; fax 2022-0192.
Ministry of Internal Security and Civil Protection: BP E 4771, Bamako; tel. 2022-0082.
Ministry of Justice: Quartier du Fleuve, BP 97, Bamako; tel. 2022-2642; fax 2023-0063; e-mail ucprodej@afribone.net.ml; internet www.justicemali.org.
Ministry of Labour, Civil Service and State Reform: Bamako; tel. 2022-3180.
Ministry of Malians Abroad and African Integration: Cité du Niger, route de l'Hotel Mandé, Bamako; tel. 2021-8148; fax 2021-2505; e-mail maliensdelexterieur@yahoo.fr; internet www.maliensdelexterieur.gov.ml.
Ministry of Mining: BP 238, Bamako; tel. 2022-4184; fax 2022-2160.
Ministry for the Promotion of Women, Children and the Family: porte G9, rue 109, Badalabougou, BP 2688, Bamako; tel. 2022-6659; fax 2023-6660; e-mail mpfef@cefib.com; internet www.mpfef.gov.ml.
Ministry of Social Development, Solidarity and the Elderly: Bamako; tel. 2023-2301.
Ministry of Stockbreeding and Fisheries: Bamako; tel. 2023-3696.
Ministry of Territorial Administration and Local Communities: face Direction de la RCFM, BP 78, Bamako; tel. 2022-4212; fax 2023-0247; internet www.matcl.gov.ml.
Ministry of Youth and Sports: route de Koulouba, BP 91, Bamako; tel. 2022-3153; fax 2023-9067; e-mail mjsports@mjsports.gov.ml; internet www.mjsports.gov.ml.

President and Legislature

PRESIDENT

Presidential Election, 29 April 2007

Candidate	Votes	% of votes
Gen. (retd) Amadou Toumani Touré (Independent)	1,612,912	71.20
Ibrahim Boubacar Keïta (RPM)	433,897	19.15
Tiébilé Dramé (PARENA)	68,956	3.04
Oumar Mariko (SADI)	61,670	2.72
Others	88,048	3.89
Total	**2,265,483**	**100.00**

LEGISLATURE

Assemblée nationale
BP 284, Bamako; tel. 2021-5724; fax 2021-0374; e-mail mamou@blonba.malinet.ml.

President: DIONCOUNDA TRAORÉ.

General Election, 1 and 22 July 2007

Party	Seats
Alliance pour la démocratie au Mali—Parti pan-africain pour la liberté, la solidarité et la justice (ADEMA)	51
Union pour la République et la démocratie (URD)	34
Rassemblement pour le Mali (RPM)	11
Mouvement patriotique pour le renouveau (MPR)	8
Congrès national d'initiative démocratique—Faso Yiriwa Ton (CNID)	7
Parti pour la renaissance nationale (PARENA)	4
Parti de la solidarité africaine pour la démocratie et l'indépendance (SADI)	4
Union pour la démocratie et le développement (UDD)	3
Bloc des alternances pour le renouveau, l'intégration et la coopération africaine (BARICA)	2
Mouvement pour l'indépendance, la renaissance et l'intégration africaine (MIRIA)	2
Parti de la solidarité et du progrès (PSP)	2
Bloc pour la démocratie et l'intégration africaine—Faso Jigi (BDIA)	1
Parti citoyen pour le renouveau (PCR)	1
Rassemblement national pour la démocratie (RND)	1
Union soudanaise—Rassemblement démocratique africain (US—RDA)	1
Independents	15
Total	**147**

Election Commission

Commission électorale nationale indépendante (CENI): Bamako; Pres. FODIÉ TOURÉ.

MALI

Advisory Councils

Economic, Social and Cultural Council: BP E15, Koulouba, Bamako; tel. 2022-4368; fax 2022-8452; e-mail cesc@cefib.com; internet www.cesc.org.ml; f. 1987; Pres. JEAMILLE BITTAR.

High Council of Communities: Bamako; compulsorily advises the Govt on issues relating to local and regional devt; comprises national councillors, elected indirectly for a term of five years; Pres. OUMAROU AG MOHAMED IBRAHIM HAÏDARA.

Political Organizations

In 2007 there were 94 political parties officially registered in Mali, the most active of which included:

Alliance pour la démocratie au Mali—Parti pan-africain pour la liberté, la solidarité et la justice (ADEMA): rue Fankélé, porte 145, BP 1791, Bamako-Coura; tel. 2022-0368; internet www.adema-pasj.org; f. 1990 as Alliance pour la démocratie au Mali; Pres. DIONCOUNDA TRAORÉ; Sec.-Gen. MARIMATIA DIARRA.

Bloc des alternances pour le renouveau, l'intégration et la coopération africaine (BARICA): Bamako.

Bloc pour la démocratie et l'intégration africaine—Faso Jigi (BDIA): Bolibana, rue 376, porte 83, BP E 2833, Bamako-Coura; tel. 2023-8202; f. 1993; liberal, democratic; Leader SOULEYMANE MAKAMBA DOUMBIA.

Congrès national d'initiative démocratique—Faso Yiriwa Ton (CNID): rue 426, porte 58, Niarela, BP 2572, Bamako; tel. 2021-4275; fax 2022-8321; e-mail mc_tall@hotmail.com; f. 1991; Chair. Me MOUNTAGA TALL; Sec.-Gen. Dr AMADOU SY.

Convention démocratique et sociale (CDS): Ouolofobougou-Bolibana, rue 417, porte 46, Bamako; tel. 2029-2625; f. 1996; Chair. MAMADOU BAKARY SANGARÉ.

Convention parti du peuple (COPP): Korofina nord, BP 9012, Bamako; fax 2021-3591; e-mail lawyergakou@datatech.toolnet.org; f. 1996; Pres. Me MAMADOU GACKOU.

Mouvement patriotique pour le renouveau (MPR): Quinzambougou, BP E 1108, Bamako; tel. 2021-5546; fax 2021-5543; f. 1995; Pres. Dr CHOGUEL KOKALA MAÏGA.

Mouvement pour l'indépendance, la renaissance et l'intégration africaine (MIRIA): Dravéla, Bolibana, rue 417, porte 66, Bamako; tel. 2029-2981; fax 2029-2979; e-mail miria12002@yahoo.fr; f. 1994 following split in ADEMA; Pres. MAMADOU KASSA TRAORÉ.

Parti citoyen pour le renouveau (PCR): Niaréla II, rue 428, porte 592, Bamako; tel. 6672-0988; internet pcrmali.net; f. 2005; supports administration of Pres. Touré; Pres. OUSMANE BEN FANA TRAORÉ.

Parti de la solidarité africaine pour la démocratie et l'indépendance (SADI): Djélibougou, rue 246, porte 559, BP 3140, Bamako; tel. 2024-1004; f. 2002; Leader CHEICK OUMAR SISSOKO.

Parti de la solidarité et du progrès (PSP): rue 552, porte 255, Quinzambougou, Bamako; tel. 2021-9960; f. 1945; Pres. OUMAR HAMMADOUN DICKO.

Parti pour la démocratie et le progrès/Parti socialiste (PDP/PS): Korofina sud, rue 96, porte 437, Bamako; tel. 2024-1675; fax 2020-2314; f. 1991; Leader FRANÇOIS KABORÉ.

Parti pour la démocratie et le renouveau—Dounkafa Ton (PDR): Bamako; f. 1998; Pres. ADAMA KONÉ; Leader KALILOU SAMAKE.

Parti pour le développement économique et la solidarité (PDES): Bamako; internet www.pdesmali.net; f. 2010; Pres. HAMED DIANE SÉMÉGA.

Parti pour la renaissance nationale (PARENA): rue Soundiata, porte 1397, BP E 2235, Ouolofobougou, Bamako; tel. 2023-4954; fax 2022-2908; e-mail info@parena.org.ml; internet www.parena.org.ml; f. 1995 following split in CNID; Pres. TIÉBILÉ DRAMÉ; Sec.-Gen. AMIDOU DIABATE.

Parti pour l'indépendance, la démocratie et la solidarité (PIDS): Hippodrome, rue 250, porte 1183, BP E 1515, Bamako; tel. 2077-4575; f. 2001 by dissidents from US—RDA; Pres. DABA DIAWARA.

Rassemblement malien pour le travail (RAMAT): Marché, Hippodrome, rue 224, porte 1393, BP E 2281, Bamako; tel. 6674-4603; f. 1991; Leader ABDOULAYE MACKO.

Rassemblement national pour la démocratie (RND): Niaréla, route Sotuba, porte 1892, Hamdallaye, Bamako; tel. 2029-1849; fax 2029-0939; f. 1997 by 'moderate' breakaway group from RDP; Pres. ABDOULAYE GARBA TAPO.

Rassemblement pour la démocratie et le progrès (RDP): Niarela, rue 485, porte 11, BP 2110, Bamako; tel. 2021-3092; fax 2024-6795; f. 1991; Sec.-Gen. IBRAHIM DIAKITE (acting).

Rassemblement pour le Mali (RPM): Hippodrome, rue 232, porte 130, BP 9057, Bamako; tel. 2021-1433; fax 2021-1336; e-mail siegerpmbko@yahoo.fr; internet www.rpm.org.ml; f. 2001; Pres. IBRAHIM BOUBACAR KEÏTA; Sec.-Gen. Dr BOCARY TRETA.

Union des forces démocratiques pour le progrès—Sama-ton (UFDP): Quartier Mali, BP E 37, Bamako; tel. 2023-1766; f. 1991; mem. of informal alliance supportive of Pres. Touré, the Convergence pour l'alternance et le changement (ACC), during 2002 legislative elections; Sec.-Gen. Col YOUSSOUF TRAORÉ.

Union pour la démocratie et le développement (UDD): ave OUA, porte 3626, Sogoniko, BP 2969, Bamako; tel. 2020-3971; f. 1991 by supporters of ex-Pres. Traoré; Leader Me HASSANE BARRY.

Union pour la République et la démocratie (URD): Niaréla, rue 268, porte 41, Bamako; tel. 2021-8642; e-mail contact@urd-mali.net; internet www.urd-mali.net; f. 2003 by fmr mems of ADEMA (q.v.) allied to 2002 presidential candidate Soumaïla Cissé; Pres. YOUNOUSSI TOURÉ.

Union soudanaise—Rassemblement démocratique africain (US—RDA): Hippodrome, porte 41, BP E 1413, Bamako; tel. and fax 2021-4522; f. 1946; sole party 1960–68, banned 1968–1991; 'moderate' faction split from party in 1998; Leader Dr BADARA ALIOU MACALOU.

Diplomatic Representation

EMBASSIES IN MALI

Algeria: Daoudabougou, BP 02, Bamako; tel. 2020-5176; fax 2022-9374; Ambassador NOUREDDINE AYADI.

Burkina Faso: ACI-2000, Commune III, BP 9022, Bamako; tel. 2023-3171; fax 2021-9266; e-mail ambafaso@experco.net; Ambassador Prof. SANNÉ MOHAMED TOPAN.

Canada: route de Koulikoro, Immeuble Séméga, Hippodrome, BP 198, Bamako; tel. 2021-2236; fax 2021-4362; e-mail bmako@international.gc.ca; internet www.bamako.gc.ca; Ambassador VIRGINIE SAINT-LOUIS.

China, People's Republic: route de Koulikoro, Hippodrome, BP 112, Bamako; tel. 2021-3597; fax 2022-3443; e-mail chinaemb_ml@mfa.gov.cn; internet ml.china-embassy.org/fra; Ambassador CAO ZHONGMING.

Côte d'Ivoire: square Patrice Lumumba, Immeuble CNAR, 3e étage, BP E 3644, Bamako; tel. 2022-0389; fax 2022-1376; Ambassador AHIPEAUD GUEBO EMMANUEL.

Cuba: porte 31, rue 328, Niarela, Bamako; tel. 2021-0289; fax 2021-0293; e-mail emcuba.mali@orangemali.net; internet emba.cubaminrex.cu/malifr; Ambassador SIDENIO ACOSTA ADAY.

Denmark: Immeuble UATT, Quartier du Fleuve, BP E 1733, Bamako; tel. 2023-0377; fax 2023-0194; e-mail bkoamb@um.dk; Ambassador TINA ANBAEK.

Egypt: Badalabougou-est, BP 44, Bamako; tel. 2022-3565; fax 2022-0891; e-mail mostafa@datatech.net.ml; Ambassador HAMED AHMED CHOUKRY HAMED.

France: square Patrice Lumumba, BP 17, Bamako; tel. 4497-5757; fax 2022-3136; e-mail ambassade@france-mali.org.ml; internet www.ambafrance-ml.org; Ambassador CHRISTIAN ROUYER.

Germany: Badalabougou-est, rue 14, porte 330, BP 100, Bamako; tel. 2070-0770; fax 2022-9650; e-mail allemagne@orangemali.net; internet www.bamako.diplo.de; Ambassador KARL FLITTNER.

Ghana: BP 3161, Bamako; Ambassador DONALD ADABERE ADABRE.

Guinea: Immeuble Saybou Maïga, Quartier du Fleuve, BP 118, Bamako; tel. 2022-3007; fax 2021-0806; Ambassador OUSMANE KONATÉ.

India: 101 ave de l'OUA, Badalabougou Est, Bamako; tel. 2023-5420; fax 2023-5417; e-mail hoc.bamako@mea.gov.in; f. 2009; Ambassador K. J. FRANCIS.

Iran: ave al-Quds, Hippodrome, BP 2136, Bamako; tel. 2021-7638; fax 2021-0731; Chargé d'affaires ABOLMOUHSEN SHARIF MOHAMMADI.

Korea, Democratic People's Republic: Bamako; Ambassador KIM PONG HUI.

Libya: Badalabougou-ouest, face Palais de la Culture, BP 1670, Bamako; tel. 2022-3496; fax 2022-6697; Ambassador Dr ALI MUHAMMAD ALMAGOURI.

Mauritania: route de Koulikoro, Hippodrome, BP 135, Bamako; tel. 2021-4815; fax 2022-4908; e-mail ambarimbko@yahoo.fr; Ambassador SIDI MOHAMED OULD HANANA.

Morocco: Badalabougou-est, rue 25, porte 80, BP 2013, Bamako; tel. 2022-2123; fax 2022-7787; e-mail sifamali@afribone.net.ml; Ambassador MOULAY DRISS FADHILL.

MALI — *Directory*

Netherlands: rue 437, BP 2220, Hippodrome, Bamako; tel. 2021-5611; fax 2021-3617; e-mail bam@minbuza.nl; internet www.mfa.nl/bam; Ambassador ELLEN VAN DER LAAN.

Nigeria: Badalabougou-est, BP 57, Bamako; tel. 2021-5328; fax 2022-3974; e-mail ngrbko@malinet.ml; Ambassador MOHAMMED SANI KANGIWA.

Russia: BP 300, Niarela, Bamako; tel. 2021-5592; fax 2021-9926; e-mail ambrusse_mali@orangemali.net; Ambassador ALEXEY G. DOULIAN.

Saudi Arabia: Villa Bal Harbour, 28 Cité du Niger, BP 81, Bamako; tel. 2021-2528; fax 2021-5064; e-mail mlemb@mofa.gov.sa; Ambassador NAHID BIN ABDULRAHMAN AL-HARBI.

Senegal: porte 341, rue 287, angle ave Nelson Mandela, BP 42, Bamako; tel. 2021-0859; fax 2016-9268; Ambassador MANKEUR NDIAYE.

South Africa: bât. Diarra, Hamdallaye, ACI-2000, BP 2015, Bamako; tel. 2029-2925; fax 2029-2926; e-mail bamako@foreign.gov.za; Ambassador R. W. MOKOU.

Spain: porte 81, rue 13, Badalabougou-est, BP 3230, Bamako; tel. 2023-6527; fax 2023-6524; e-mail emb.bamako@maec.es; Ambassador Dr LOURDES MELÉNDEZ GARCÍA.

Tunisia: Quartier du Fleuve, Bamako; tel. 2023-2891; fax 2022-1755; Ambassador MOHAMED NACEUR QORT.

USA: ACI 2000, rue 243, porte 297, Bamako; tel. 2070-2300; fax 2070-2479; e-mail webmaster@usa.org.ml; internet mali.usembassy.gov; Ambassador GILLIAN ARLETTE MILOVANOVIC.

Judicial System

The 1992 Constitution guarantees the independence of the judiciary.

High Court of Justice: Bamako; competent to try the President of the Republic and ministers of the Government for high treason and for crimes committed in the course of their duties, and their accomplices in any case where state security is threatened; mems designated by the mems of the Assemblée nationale, and renewed annually.

Supreme Court: BP 7, Bamako; tel. 2022-2406; e-mail csupreme@afribone.net.ml; f. 1969; comprises judicial, administrative and auditing sections; judicial section comprises five chambers, administrative section comprises two chambers, auditing section comprises three chambers; Pres. DIALLO KAÏTA KAYENTAO; Sec.-Gen. ALKAÏDY SANIBIÉ TOURÉ.

President of the Bar: Me MAGATTÉ SÈYE.

Constitutional Court: BP E 213, Bamako; tel. 2022-5609; fax 2023-4241; e-mail tawatybouba@yahoo.fr; f. 1994; Pres. AMADI TAMBA CAMARA; Sec.-Gen. BOUBACAR TAWATY.

There are three Courts of Appeal, seven Tribunaux de première instance (Magistrates' Courts) and also courts for labour disputes.

Religion

According to the UN Development Programme's *Human Development Report*, around 80% of the population are Muslims, while 18% follow traditional animist beliefs and under 2% are Christians.

ISLAM

Association Malienne pour l'Unité et le Progrès de l'Islam (AMUPI): Bamako; state-endorsed Islamic governing body.

Chief Mosque: pl. de la République, Bagadadji, Bamako; tel. 2021-2190.

Haut Conseil Islamique: Bamako; f. 2002; responsible for management of relations between the Muslim communities and the State; Pres. MAHMOUD DICKO.

CHRISTIANITY

The Roman Catholic Church

Mali comprises one archdiocese and five dioceses. Approximately 2% of the total population practices Roman Catholicism.

Bishops' Conference

Conférence Episcopale du Mali, Archevêché, BP 298, Bamako; tel. 2222-5499; fax 2222-5214; e-mail cemali@afribone.net.ml. f. 1973; Pres. Most Rev. JEAN-GABRIEL DIARRA (Bishop of San).

Archbishop of Bamako: JEAN ZERBO, Archevêché, BP 298, Bamako; tel. 2222-5842; fax 2222-7850; e-mail mgrjeanzerbo@afribonemali.net.

Other Christian Churches

There are several Protestant mission centres, mainly administered by US societies.

BAHÁ'Í FAITH

National Spiritual Assembly: BP 1657, Bamako; e-mail ntirandaz@aol.com.

The Press

The 1992 Constitution guarantees the freedom of the press. In 2000 there were six daily newspapers, 18 weekly or twice-weekly publications and six-monthly or twice-monthly publications.

DAILY NEWSPAPERS

Les Echos: Hamdallaye, ave Cheick Zayed, porte 2694, BP 2043, Bamako; tel. 2029-6289; fax 2026-7639; e-mail lesechos@jamana.org; internet www.jamana.org/lesechos; f. 1989; daily; publ. by Jamana cultural co-operative; circ. 30,000; Dir ALEXIS KALAMBRY; Editor-in-Chief ABOUBACAR SALIPH DIARRA.

L'Essor: square Patrice Lumumba, BP 141, Bamako; tel. 2022-3683; fax 2022-4774; e-mail info@essor.gov.ml; internet www.essor.gov.ml; f. 1949; daily; pro-Govt newspaper; Editor SOULEYMANE DRABO; circ. 3,500.

Info Matin: rue 56/350, Bamako Coura, BP E 4020, Bamako; tel. 2023-8209; fax 2023-8227; e-mail redaction@info-matin.com; internet www.info-matin.com; independent; Dir SAMBI TOURÉ; Editor-in-Chief MOHAMED SACKO.

Le Républicain: 116 rue 400, Dravéla-Bolibana, BP 1484, Bamako; tel. 2029-0900; fax 2029-0933; internet www.lerepublicain.net.ml; f. 1992; independent; Dir SALIF KONÉ.

PERIODICALS

26 Mars: Badalabougou-Sema Gesco, Lot S13, BP MA 174, Bamako; tel. 2029-0459; f. 1998; weekly; independent; Dir BOUBACAR SANGARÉ.

L'Aurore: Niarela 298, rue 438, BP 3150, Bamako; tel. and fax 2021-6922; e-mail aurore@timbagga.com.ml; f. 1990; 2 a week; independent; Dir KARAMOKO N'DIAYE.

Le Canard Déchaîné: Immeuble Koumara, bloc 104, Centre Commercial, Bamako; tel. 7621-2686; fax 2022-86-86; e-mail maison.presse@afribone.net.ml; weekly; satirical; Dir OUMAR BABI; circ. 3,000 (2006).

Le Carrefour: ave Cheick Zayed, Hamdallaye, Bamako; tel. 2023-9808; e-mail journalcarrefour@yahoo.fr; f. 1997; Dir MAHAMANE IMRANE COULIBALY.

Citoyen: Bamako; f. 1992; fortnightly; independent.

Le Continent: AA 16, Banankabougou, BP E 4338, Bamako; tel. and fax 2029-5739; e-mail le_continent@yahoo.fr; f. 2000; weekly; Dir IBRAHIMA TRAORÉ.

Le Courrier: 230 ave Cheick Zayed, Lafiabougou Marché, BP 1258, Bamako; tel. and fax 2029-1862; e-mail journalcourrier@webmails.com; f. 1996; weekly; Dir SADOU A. YATTARA; also *Le Courrier Magazine*, monthly.

L'Indépendant: Immeuble ABK, Hamdallaye ACI, BP E 1040, Bamako; tel. and fax 2023-2727; e-mail independant@cefib.com; 2 a week; Dir SAOUTI HAÏDARA.

L'Inspecteur: Immeuble Nimagala, bloc 262, BP E 4534, Bamako; tel. 6672-4711; e-mail inspecteurmali@yahoo.fr; f. 1992; weekly; Dir ALY DIARRA.

Jamana—Revue Culturelle Malienne: BP 2043, Bamako; BP E 1040; e-mail infos@jamana.org; f. 1983; quarterly; organ of Jamana cultural co-operative.

Journal Officiel de la République du Mali: Koulouba, BP 14, Bamako; tel. 2022-5986; fax 2022-7050; official gazette.

Kabaaru: Village Kibaru, Bozola, BP 24, Bamako; f. 1983; state-owned; monthly; Fulbé (Peul) language; rural interest; Editor BARRY BELCO MOUSSA; circ. 3,000.

Kibaru: Village Kibaru, Bozola, BP 1463, Bamako; f. 1972; monthly; state-owned; Bambara and three other languages; rural interest; Editor NIANZÉ SAMAKÉ; circ. 5,000.

Liberté: Immeuble Sanago, Hamdallaye Marché, BP E 24, Bamako; tel. 2028-1898; e-mail ladji.guindo@cefib.com; f. 1999; weekly; Dir ABDOULAYE LADJI GUINDO.

Le Malien: rue 497, porte 277, Badialan III, BP E 1558, Bamako; tel. 2023-5729; fax 2029-1339; e-mail lemalien2000@yahoo.fr; f. 1993; weekly; Dir SIDI KEITA.

Match: 97 rue 498, Lafiabougou, BP E 3776, Bamako; tel. 2029-1882; e-mail bcissouma@yahoo.fr; f. 1997; 2 a month; sports; Dir BABA CISSOUMA.

MALI

Musow: BP E 449, Bamako; tel. 2028-0000; fax 2028-0001; e-mail musow@musow.com; internet www.musow.com; women's interest.

Nyéléni Magazine: Niarela 298, rue 348, BP 13150, Bamako; tel. 2029-2401; f. 1991; monthly; women's interest; Dir MAÏMOUNA TRAORÉ.

L'Observateur: Galérie Djigué, rue du 18 juin, BP E 1002, Bamako; tel. and fax 2023-0689; e-mail belcotamboura@hotmail.com; f. 1992; 2 a week; Dir BELCO TAMBOURA.

Le Reflet: Immeuble Kanadjigui, route de Koulikoro, Boulkassoumbougou, BP E 1688, Bamako; tel. 2024-3952; fax 2023-2308; e-mail lereflet@afribone.malinet.ml; weekly; fmrly *Le Carcan*; present name adopted Jan. 2001; Dir ABDOUL KARIM DRAMÉ.

Royal Sports: BP 98, Sikasso; tel. 6672-4988; weekly; also *Tatou Sports*, publ. monthly; Pres. and Dir-Gen. ALY TOURÉ.

Le Scorpion: 230 ave Cheick Zayed, Lafiabougou Marché, BP 1258, Bamako; tel. and fax 2029-1862; f. 1991; weekly; Dir MAHAMANE HAMÈYE CISSÉ.

Le Tambour: rue 497, porte 295, Badialan III, BP E 289, Bamako; tel. and fax 2022-7568; e-mail tambourj@yahoo.fr; f. 1994; 2 a week; Dir YÉRO DIALLO.

NEWS AGENCY

Agence Malienne de Presse et Publicité (AMAP): square Patrice Lumumba, BP 141, Bamako; tel. 2022-3683; fax 2022-4774; e-mail amap@afribone.net.ml; f. 1977; Dir SOULEYMANE DRABO.

PRESS ASSOCIATIONS

Association des Editeurs de la Presse Privée (ASSEP): BP E 1002, Bamako; tel. 6671-3133; e-mail belcotamboura@hotmail.com; Pres. BELCO TAMBOURA.

Association des Femmes de la Presse Privée: porte 474, rue 428, BP E 731, Bamako; tel. 2021-2912; Pres. FANTA DIALLO.

Association des Journalistes Professionels des Médias Privés du Mali (AJPM): BP E 2456, Bamako; tel. 2022-1915; fax 2023-5478; Pres. MOMADOU FOFANA.

Association des Professionnelles Africaines de la Communication (APAC MALI): porte 474, rue 428, BP E 731, Bamako; tel. 2021-2912; Pres. MASSIRÉ YATTASSAYE.

Maison de la Presse de Mali: 17 rue 619, Darsalam, BP E 2456, Bamako; tel. 2022-1915; fax 2023-5478; e-mail maison.presse@afribone.net.ml; internet www.mediamali.org; independent media asscn; Pres. SADOU A. YATTARA.

Union Interprofessionnelle des Journalistes et de la Presse de Langue Française (UIJPLF): rue 42, Hamdallaye Marché, BP 1258, Bamako; tel. 2029-9835; Pres. MAHAMANE HAMÈYE CISSÉ.

Union Nationale des Journalistes Maliens (UNAJOM): BP 1300, Bamako; tel. 2022-1915; fax 2023-5478; e-mail ibrafam@yahoo.fr; Pres. IBRAHIM FAMAKAN COULIBALY.

Publishers

EDIM SA: ave Kassé Keïta, BP 21, Bamako; tel. 2022-4041; fax 2029-3001; e-mail edim@afribone.net.ml; f. 1972 as Editions Imprimeries du Mali; general fiction and non-fiction, textbooks; Chair. and Man. Dir ALOU TOMOTA.

Editions Donniya: Cité du Niger, BP 1273, Bamako; tel. 2021-4646; fax 2021-9031; e-mail imprimcolor@cefib.com; internet www.imprimcolor.cefib.com; f. 1996; general fiction, history, reference and children's books in French and Bambara.

Le Figuier: 151 rue 56, Semal, BP 2605, Bamako; tel. and fax 2023-3211; e-mail lefiguier@afribone.net.ml; f. 1997; fiction and non-fiction.

Editions Jamana: BP 2043, Bamako; tel. 2029-6289; fax 2029-7639; e-mail jamana@timbagga.com.ml; internet www.jamana.org; f. 1988; literary fiction, poetry, reference; Dir BA MAÏRA SOW.

Editions Teriya: BP 1677, Bamako; tel. 2024-1142; theatre, literary fiction; Dir GAOUSSOU DIAWARA.

Broadcasting and Communications

TELECOMMUNICATIONS

Regulatory Authority

Comité de Régulation des Télécommunications (CRT): ACI 2000 Hamdallaye, rue 390, porte 1849, BP 2206, Bamako; tel. 2023-1490; fax 2023-1494; e-mail crtmali@crt.ml; internet www.crt-mali.org; f. 1999; Dir Dr CHOGUEL K. MAÏGA.

Service Providers

Orange Mali SA: Immeuble Orange Mali ACI-2000, BP E 3991, Bamako; tel. 4499-9000; fax 4499-9001; e-mail orange@orangemali.com; internet www.orangemali.com; f. 2003 as Ikatel; repackaged under brand name Orange in 2007; fixed-line and mobile cellular telecommunications; jtly owned by France Télécom and Société Nationale des Télécommunications du Sénégal; Dir-Gen. ALIOUME N'DIAYE; 100,000 subscribers (2003).

Société des Télécommunications du Mali—Malitel (SOTELMA): route de Koulikoro, Hippodrome, BP 740, Bamako; tel. 2021-5280; fax 2021-3022; e-mail segal@sotelma.ml; internet www.sotelma.ml; f. 1990; 51% owned by Itissalat al-Maghrib—Maroc Télécom (Morocco), 20% state-owned; operates fixed-line telephone services, also mobile and cellular telecommunications in Bamako, Kayes, Mopti, Ségou and Sikasso; 90,000 fixed lines and 480,000 subscribers to mobile cellular telecommunications services (2007); Dir-Gen. NOREDDINE BOUMZEBRA.

BROADCASTING

Radio

Office de Radiodiffusion-Télévision Malienne (ORTM): 287 rue de la Marne, BP 171, Bamako; tel. 2021-2019; fax 2021-4205; e-mail ortm@ortm.ml; internet www.ortm.ml; Dir-Gen. SIDIKI KONATÉ; Dir of Radio OUMAR TOURÉ.

Radio Mali–Chaîne Nationale: BP 171, Bamako; tel. 2021-2019; fax 2021-4205; e-mail ortm@spider.toolnet.org; f. 1957; state-owned; radio programmes in French, Bambara, Peul, Sarakolé, Tamashek, Sonrai, Moorish, Wolof, English.

Chaîne 2: Bamako; f. 1993; radio broadcasts to Bamako.

In late 2003 there were an estimated 130 community, commercial and religious radio stations broadcasting in Mali.

Fréquence 3: Bamako; f. 1992; commercial.

Radio Balanzan: BP 419, Ségou; tel. 2132-0288; commercial.

Radio Bamakan: Marché de Médine, BP E 100, Bamako; tel. and fax 2021-2760; e-mail radio.bamakan@ifrance.com; internet bamakan.net; f. 1991; community station; 104 hours of FM broadcasts weekly; Man. MODIBO DIALLO.

Radio Espoir—La Voix du Salut: Sogoniko, rue 130, porte 71, BP E 1399, Bamako; tel. 2020-6708; e-mail accm@mali.maf.net; f. 1998; broadcasts 16 hours of radio programming daily on topics including Christianity, devt and culture; Dir DAOUDA COULIBALY.

Radio Foko de Ségou Jamana: BP 2043, Bamako; tel. 2132-0048; fax 2022-7639; e-mail radiofoko@cefib.com.

Radio Guintan: Magnambougou, BP 2546, Bamako; tel. 2020-0938; f. 1994; community radio station; Dir RAMATA DIA.

Radio Jamana: BP 2043, Bamako; tel. 2029-6289; fax 2029-7639; e-mail radio@jamana.org; internet www.jamana.org.

Radio Kayira: Djélibougou Doumanzana, BP 3140, Bamako; tel. 2024-8782; fax 2022-7568; internet www.kayira.org; f. 1992; community station; Dir OUMAR MARIKO.

Radio Klédu: Cité du Niger, BP 2322, Bamako; tel. 2021-0018; e-mail rkledudirect@cefib.com; internet www.kleducommunication.com; f. 1992; commercial; Dir-Gen. JACQUES DEZ.

Radio Liberté: BP 5015, Bamako; tel. 2023-0581; f. 1991; commercial station broadcasting 24 hours daily; Dir ALMANY TOURÉ.

Radio Patriote: Korofina-Sud, BP E 1406, Bamako; tel. 2024-2292; f. 1995; commercial station; Dir MOUSSA KEÏTA.

Radio Rurale: Plateau, BP 94, Kayes; tel. 2153-1476; e-mail rrk@afribone.net.ml; f. 1988; community stations established by the Agence de coopération culturelle et technique (ACTT); transmitters in Niono, Kadiolo, Bandiagara and Kidal; Dir FILY KEÏTA.

Radio Sahel: BP 394, Kayes; tel. 2152-2187; f. 1991; commercial; Dir ALMAMY S. TOURÉ.

Radio Tabalé: Bamako-Coura, BP 697, Bamako; tel. and fax 2022-7870; internet www.radiotabale.org; f. 1992; independent public-service station; broadcasting 57 hours weekly; Dir TIÉMOKO KONÉ.

La Voix du Coran et du Hadit: Grande Mosquée, BP 2531, Bamako; tel. 2021-6344; f. 1993; Islamic station broadcasting on FM in Bamako; Dir El Hadj MAHMOUD DICKO.

Radio Wassoulou: BP 24, Yanfolila; tel. 2165-1097; internet wassoulou.radio.org.ml; commercial.

Radio France International, the Voix de l'Islam and the Gabonese-based Africa No. 1 began FM broadcasts in Mali in 1993; broadcasts by Voice of America and the World Service of the British Broadcasting Corpn are also transmitted via private radio stations.

Television

Office de Radiodiffusion-Télévision Malienne (ORTM): see Radio; Dir of Television BALY IDRISSA SISSOKO.

MALI

Multicanal SA: Quinzambougou, BP E 1506, Bamako; tel. 2021-4964; e-mail sandrine@multi-canal.com; internet www.multi-canal.com; private subscription broadcaster; relays international broadcasts; Pres. ISMAÏLA SIDIBÉ; Dir-Gen. MOHAMED KEITA.

TV Klédu: 600 ave Modibo Keïta, BP E 1172, Bamako; tel. 2023-9000; fax 2023-7050; e-mail info@tvkledu.com; private cable TV operator; relays international broadcasts; Pres. MAMADOU COULIBALY.

Finance

(cap. = capital; res = reserves; dep. = deposits; m. = million; br(s). = branch(es); amounts in francs CFA)

BANKING

In 2009 there were 13 banks and four other financial institutions in Mali.

Central Bank

Banque centrale des états de l'Afrique de l'ouest (BCEAO): ave Moussa Travele, BP 206, Bamako; tel. 2022-2541; fax 2022-4786; internet www.bceao.int; f. 1962; HQ in Dakar, Senegal; bank of issue for the mem. states of Union économique et monétaire ouest-africaine (UEMOA, comprising Benin, Burkina Faso, Côte d'Ivoire, Guinea-Bissau, Mali, Niger, Senegal and Togo); cap. 134,120m., res 1,474,195m., dep. 2,124,051m. (Dec. 2009); Interim Gov. JEAN-BAPTISTE MARIE PASCAL COMPAORÉ; Dir in Mali IDRISSA TRAORÉ; brs at Mopti and Sikasso.

Commercial Banks

Bank of Africa—Mali (BOA—MALI): 418 ave de la Marné, Bozola, BP 2249, Bamako; tel. 2070-0500; fax 2070-0560; e-mail information@boamali.net; internet www.boamali.com; f. 1983; cap. 5,500.0m., res 5,818.0m., dep. 139,178.2m. (Dec. 2009); Pres. BOUREIMA SYLLA; Dir-Gen. MAMADOU SENE; 18 brs.

Banque Commerciale du Sahel (BCS-SA): ave Bozola 127, BP 2372, Bamako; tel. 2021-0535; fax 2021-1660; e-mail dg@bcss.mali.com; f. 1980; fmrly Banque Arabe Libyo-Malienne pour le Commerce Extérieur et le Développement; 96.61% owned by Libyan-Arab Foreign Bank; cap. 7,500m., res 1,046m., total assets. 37,953m. (Dec. 2006); Pres. KABA DIAMINATOU DIALLO; Dir-Gen. IBRAHIM ABOUJAFAR SWEAI; 1 br.

Banque de l'Habitat du Mali (BHM): ACI 2000, ave Kwamé N'Krumah, BP 2614, Bamako; tel. 2022-9190; fax 2022-9350; e-mail bhm@bhm-sa.com; internet www.bhm-sa.com; f. 1990; present name adopted 1996; 25.8% owned by Institut National de Prévoyance Social; cap. and res 5,414.7m., total assets 98,237.5m. (Dec. 2003); Pres. and Dir-Gen. MODIBO CISSÉ; 5 brs.

Banque Internationale pour le Commerce et l'Industrie au Mali (BICI–Mali): blvd du 22 octobre 1946, Quartier du Fleuve, BP 72, Bamako; tel. 2070-0700; fax 2023-3373; e-mail bicim-dg@africa.bnpparibas.com; f. 1998; 85% owned by BNP Paribas BDDI Participations (France); cap. and res 3,678m., total assets 40,076m. (Dec. 2003); Pres. and Dir-Gen. PIERRE BEREGOVOY; 1 br.

Banque Internationale pour le Mali (BIM): ave de l'Indépendance, BP 15, Bamako; tel. 2022-5066; fax 2022-4566; e-mail bim@bim.com.ml; internet www.bim.com.ml; f. 1980; present name adopted 1995; 51% owned by Attijariwafa Bank Group (Morocco), 10.5% state-owned; cap. 4,254m., dep. 120,250m., total assets 131,159m. (Dec. 2006); Pres. and Dir-Gen. MOHAMMED KRISNI; 14 brs.

Ecobank Mali: Immeuble Amadou Sow, pl. de la Nation, Quartier du Fleuve, BP E 1272, Bamako; tel. 2070–0600; fax 2023-3305; e-mail ecobankml@ecobank.com; internet www.ecobank.com; f. 1998; 49.5% owned by Ecobank Transnational Inc., 17.8% by Ecobank Bénin, 14.9% by Ecobank Togo, 9.9% by Ecobank Burkina; cap. and res 2,973.9m., total assets 46,222.7m. (Dec. 2003); Pres. SAMBA DIALLO; Dir-Gen. BINTA N'DOYE TOURÉ; 2 brs.

Development Banks

Banque de Développement du Mali (BDM-SA): ave Modibo Keïta, Quartier du Fleuve, BP 94, Bamako; tel. 2022-2050; fax 2022-5085; e-mail info@bdm-sa.com; internet www.bdm-sa.com; f. 1968; absorbed Banque Malienne de Crédit et de Dépôts in 2001; 27.38% owned by Banque Marocaine du Commerce Extérieur (Morocco), 19.58% state-owned, 15.96% by BCEAO, 15.96% by Banque ouest-africaine de développement; cap. and res 15,658m., total assets 276,148m. (Dec. 2002); Pres. and Dir-Gen. ABDOULAYE DAFFÉ; 14 brs.

Banque Malienne de Solidarité (BMS): ave du Fleuve, Immeuble Dette Publique, 2e étage, BP 1280, Bamako; tel. and fax 2023-5034; e-mail bms-sa@bms-sa.com; f. 2002; cap. 2.4m.; Dir BABALI BAH; 1 br.

Banque Nationale de Développement Agricole—Mali (BNDA—Mali): Immeuble BNDA, blvd du Mali, ACI 2000, BP 2424, Bamako; tel. 2029-6464; fax 2029-2575; e-mail bnda@bndamali.com; internet www.bndamali.com; f. 1981; 36.5% state-owned, 22.8% owned by Agence française de développement (France), 21.4% owned by Deutsche Entwicklungsgesellschaft (Germany), 19.4% owned by BCEAO; cap. 12,096.2m., res 2,059.0m., dep. 125,447.5m. (Dec. 2008); Chair., Pres. and Gen. Man. MOUSSA ALASSAME DIALLO; 22 brs.

Financial Institutions

Direction Générale de la Dette Publique: Immeuble ex-Caisse Autonome d'Amortissement, Quartier du Fleuve, BP 1617, Bamako; tel. 2022-2935; fax 2022-0793; management of the public debt; Dir NAMALA KONÉ.

Equibail Mali: rue 376, porte 1319, Niarela, BP E 566, Bamako; tel. 2021-3777; fax 2021-3778; e-mail equip.ma@bkofafrica.com; f. 1999; 50.2% owned by African Financial Holding, 17.5% by Bank of Africa—Benin; cap. 300m. (Dec. 2002); Mems of Administrative Council RAMATOULAYE TRAORÉ, PAUL DERREUMAUX, LÉON NAKA.

Société Malienne de Financement (SOMAFI): Immeuble Air Afrique, blvd du 22 octobre 1946, BP E 3643, Bamako; tel. 2022-1866; fax 2022-1869; e-mail somafi@malinet.ml; f. 1997; cap. and res 96.9m., total assets 3,844.9m. (Dec. 2002); Man. Dir ERIC LECLÈRE.

STOCK EXCHANGE

Bourse Régionale des Valeurs Mobilières (BRVM): Chambre de Commerce et de l'Industrie du Mali, pl. de la Liberté, BP E 1398, Bamako; tel. 2023-2354; fax 2023-2359; e-mail abocoum@brvm.org; f. 1998; nat. branch of BRVM (regional stock exchange based in Abidjan, Côte d'Ivoire, serving the mem. states of UEMOA); Man. AMADOU DJÉRI BOCOUM.

INSURANCE

Allianz Mali: ave de la Nation, BP E4447, Bamako; tel. 2022-4165; fax 2023-0034; e-mail allianz.mali@allianz-ml.com; internet www.allianz-africa.com/mali/index.php; Dir-Gen. OLIVIER PICARD.

Assurances Lafia: Immeuble Assurances Lafia SA, Hamdallaye ACI 2000, ave du Mali, BP 1542, Bamako; tel. 2029-0940; fax 2029-5223; e-mail info@assurancelafia.com; internet www.assurancelafia.com; f. 1983; cap. 1,000m.; Dir-Gen. AMINATA DEMBÉLÉ CISSÉ; 17 brs.

Caisse Nationale d'Assurance et de Réassurance du Mali (CNAR): BP 568, square Patrice Lumumba, Bamako; tel. 2021-3117; fax 2021-2369; f. 1969; state-owned; cap. 50m.; Dir-Gen. F. KEITA; 10 brs.

Colina Mali SA: ave Modibo Keita, BP E 154, Bamako; tel. 2022-5775; fax 2023-2423; e-mail mali@groupecolina.com; internet www.groupecolina.com/fr/ml; f. 1990; cap. 1,000m.; Dir-Gen. MARCUS K. LABAN.

Compagnie d'Assurance Privée—La Soutra: BP 52, Bamako; tel. 2022-3681; fax 2022-5523; f. 1979; cap. 150m.; Chair. AMADOU NIONO.

Compagnie d'Assurance et de Réassurance de Mali: BP 1822, Bamako; tel. 2022-6029.

Compagnie d'Assurance et de Réassurance Sabu Nyuman: rue 350, porte 129, Bamako-Coura, BP 1822, Bamako; tel. 2022-6029; fax 2022-5750; e-mail assur.sn@malinet.ml; f. 1984; cap. 250m.; Pres. MOMADOU SANOGO; Dir-Gen. YAYA DIARRA.

Gras Savoye Mali: Immeuble SOGEFIH, 3ème etage, Quartier du Fleuve, ave Moussa Travele, BP E 5691, Bamako; tel. 2022-6469; fax 2022-6470; e-mail grassavoyemali@ml.grassavoye.com; affiliated to Gras Savoye (France); Man. FAYEZ SAMB.

Nouvelle Alliance d'Assurance (NALLIAS): BP 12671, Bamako; tel. 2022-2244; fax 2022-9422; e-mail contact@nalliasmali.com; f. 2007; Dir-Gen. CHEIKNA DIAWARA.

Nouvelle Société Interafricaine d'Assurance (NSIA Mali): Immeuble du Patronat, derrière le Gouvernorat, ACI 2000, Bamako; tel. 2023-2440; fax 2023-2441; f. 2009; Dir-Gen. GEORGES ALAIN N'GORAN; also (NSIA Vie Mali) ; Dir-Gen. KODJO SALAMI WOROU.

Société Nouvelle d'Assurance—Vie (SONA—VIE): Immeuble Sonavie, ACI 2000, BP E 2217, Bamako; tel. 2029-5400; fax 2029-5501; e-mail sonavie@cefib.com; internet www.sonavie.com; f. 1996; Dir-Gen. MAMADOU TOURÉ.

Trade and Industry

GOVERNMENT AGENCIES

Agence Nationale pour l'Emploi (ANPE): BP 211, Bamako; tel. 2022-3187; fax 2023-2624; e-mail anpe@anpe-mali.org; internet www.anpe-mali.org; f. 2001; Dir-Gen. Prof. MAKAN MOUSSA SISSOKO.

MALI

Agence pour la Promotion des Investissements au Mali (API-Mali): Quartier du fleuve, BP 1980, Bamako; tel. 2022-9525; fax 2022-9527; e-mail contact@apimali.gov.ml; internet www.apimali.gov.ml; f. 2005; CEO Mansour Haïdara.

Direction Nationale des Affaires Economiques (DNAE): BP 210, Bamako; tel. 2022-2314; fax 2022-2256; involved in economic and social affairs.

Direction Nationale des Travaux Publics (DNTP): ave de la Liberté, BP 1758, Bamako; tel. and fax 2022-2902; administers public works.

Guichet Unique–Direction Nationale des Industries: rue Titi Niare, Quinzambougou, BP 96, Bamako; tel. and fax 2022-3166.

Office National des Produits Pétroliers (ONAP): Quartier du Fleuve, rue 315, porte 141, BP 2070, Bamako; tel. 2022-2827; fax 2022-4483; e-mail onapmali@afribone.net.ml; internet www.onapmali.com; Dir-Gen. Tapa Nouga Nadio.

Office du Niger: BP 106, Ségou; tel. 2132-0292; fax 2132-0143; e-mail on@office-du-niger.org.ml; internet www.office-du-niger.org.ml; f. 1932; taken over from the French authorities in 1958; restructured in mid-1990s; cap. 7,139m. francs CFA; principally involved in cultivation of food crops, particularly rice; the Office du Niger zone is the western region of the Central Niger Delta; Pres. and Dir-Gen. Seydou Idrissa Traoré.

Office des Produits Agricoles du Mali (OPAM): BP 132, Bamako; tel. 2022-3755; fax 2021-0406; e-mail opam@cefib.com; f. 1965; state-owned; manages National (Cereals) Security Stock, administers food aid, responsible for sales of cereals and distribution to deficit areas; cap. 5,800m. francs CFA; Pres. and Dir-Gen. Youssouf Mahamane Touré.

DEVELOPMENT ORGANIZATIONS

Agence Française de Développement (AFD): Quinzambougou, route de Sotuba, BP 32, Bamako; tel. 2021-2842; fax 2021-8646; e-mail afdbamako@ml.groupe-afd.org; internet www.afd.fr; Country Dir Hervé Bougault.

Agence pour le Développement du Nord-Mali (ADN): Gao; f. 2005 to replace l'Autorité pour le Développement Intégré du Nord-Mali (ADIN); govt agency with financial autonomy; promotes devt of regions of Tombouctou, Gao and Kidal; br. in Bamako.

Office de Développement Intégré du Mali-Ouest (ODIMO): square Patrice Lumumba, Bamako; tel. 2022-5759; f. 1991 to succeed Office de Développement Intégré des Productions Arachidières et Céréalières; devt of diversified forms of agricultural production; Man. Dir Zana Sanogo.

Service de Coopération et d'Action Culturelle: square Patrice Lumumba, BP 84, Bamako; tel. 2021-8338; fax 2021-8339; administers bilateral aid from France; Dir Bertrand Commelin.

CHAMBER OF COMMERCE

Chambre de Commerce et d'Industrie du Mali (CCIM): pl. de la Liberté, BP 46, Bamako; tel. 2022-5036; fax 2022-2120; e-mail ccim@cimali.org; internet www.ccimmali.org; f. 1906; Pres. Jeamille Bittar; Sec.-Gen. Daba Traoré.

EMPLOYERS' ASSOCIATIONS

Association Malienne des Exportateurs de Légumes (AMELEF): Bamako; tel. 7608-9048; fax 2029-2836; f. 1984; Pres. Bakary Yaffa; Sec.-Gen. Birama Traoré.

Association Malienne des Exportateurs de Ressources Animales (AMERA): Bamako; tel. 2022-5683; f. 1985; Pres. Ambarké Yermangore; Admin. Sec. Ali Hacko.

Fédération Nationale des Employeurs du Mali (FNEM): route de Sotuba, BP 2445, Bamako; tel. 2021-6311; fax 2021-9077; e-mail fnem@spider.toolnet; f. 1980; Pres. Moussa Mary Balla Coulibaly; Permanent Sec. Lassina Traoré.

UTILITIES

Electricity

Energie du Mali (EdM): square Patrice Lumumba, BP 69, Bamako; tel. 2022-3020; fax 2022-8430; e-mail sekou.edm@cefib.com; internet www.edm-sa.com.ml; f. 1960; 66% state-owned, 34% owned by Industrial Promotion Services (West-Africa); planning, construction and operation of power-sector facilities; cap. 7,880m. francs CFA; Pres. Ousmane Issoufi Maïga; Dir-Gen. Sékou Alpha Djitèye.

Enertech GSA: marché de Lafiabougou, BP 1949, Bamako; tel. 2022-3763; fax 2022-5136; f. 1994; cap. 20m. francs CFA; solar energy producer; Dir Moctar Diakité.

Société de Gestion de l'Energie de Manantali (SOGEM): Parcelle 2501, ACI 2000, BP E 4015, Bamako; tel. 2023-3286; fax 2023-8350; generates and distributes electricity from the Manantali hydro-electric project, under the auspices of the Organisation pour la mise en valeur du fleuve Sénégal; Dir-Gen. Saloum Cissé.

Gas

Maligaz: route de Sotuba, BP 5, Bamako; tel. 2022-2394; gas distribution.

Water

Société Malienne de Gestion de l'Eau Potable (SOMAGEP): Bamako; f. 2010; responsible for the operation of public drinking water supplies; Pres. Boubacar Kané.

Société Malienne du Patrimoine de l'Eau Potable (SOMAPEP): Bamako; f. 2010; responsible for the management and development of infrastructure for supplying drinking water; Pres. Adama Tiémoko Diarra.

TRADE UNION FEDERATION

Union nationale des travailleurs du Mali (UNTM): Bourse du Travail, blvd de l'Indépendance, BP 169, Bamako; tel. 2022-3699; fax 2023-5945; f. 1963; 13 nat. and 8 regional unions, and 52 local orgs; Sec.-Gen. Siaka Diakité.

There are, in addition, several non-affiliated trade unions.

Transport

RAILWAYS

Mali's only railway runs from Koulikoro, via Bamako, to the Senegal border. The line continues to Dakar, Senegal, a total distance of 1,286 km, of which 729 km is in Mali. The track is in very poor condition, and is frequently closed during the rainy season. In 1995 the Governments of Mali and Senegal agreed to establish a joint company to operate the Bamako–Dakar line, and the line passed fully into private ownership in 2003. Some 358,000 metric tons of freight were handled on the Malian railway in 2001. Plans exist for the construction of a new rail line linking Bamako with Kouroussa and Kankan, in Guinea.

Transrail SA: Immeuble la Roseraie, 310 ave de la liberté, BP 4150, Bamako; tel. 2022-5967; fax 2022-5433; e-mail ericpeiffer@transrailsa.com; f. 2003 on transfer to private management of fmr Régie du Chemin de Fer du Mali; jt venture of Canac (Canada) and Getma (France); Dir-Gen. Eric Peiffer.

ROADS

The Malian road network in 2004 comprised 18,709 km, of which about 3,370 km were paved. A bituminized road between Bamako and Abidjan (Côte d'Ivoire) provides Mali's main economic link to the coast; construction of a road linking Bamako and Dakar (Senegal) is to be financed by the European Development Fund. The African Development Bank also awarded a US $31.66m. loan to fund the Kankan–Kouremale–Bamako road between Mali and Guinea. A road across the Sahara to link Mali with Algeria is also planned.

Compagnie Malienne de Transports Routiers (CMTR): BP 208, Bamako; tel. 2022-3364; f. 1970; state-owned; Man. Dir Mamadou Touré.

INLAND WATERWAYS

The River Niger is navigable in parts of its course through Mali (1,693 km) during the rainy season from July to late December. The River Senegal was, until the early 1990s, navigable from Kayes to Saint-Louis (Senegal) only between August and November, but its navigability was expected to improve following the inauguration, in 1992, of the Manantali dam, and the completion of works to deepen the river-bed.

Compagnie Malienne de Navigation (COMANAV): BP 10, Koulikoro; tel. 2026-2094; fax 2026-2009; f. 1968; 100% state-owned; river transport; Pres. and Dir-Gen. Dembélé Goundo Diallo.

Conseil Malien des Chargeurs (CMC): Dar-salam, BP E 4031, Bamako; tel. 2023-0486; fax 2023-0489; e-mail contact@cmchargeurs.com; internet www.cmchargeurs.com; f. 1999; Pres. Ousmane Babalaye Daou.

Société Navale Malienne (SONAM): Bamako-Coura, BP 2581, Bamako; tel. 2021-6066; fax 2022-6066; f. 1981; transferred to private ownership in 1986; Chair. Alioune Keïta.

Société Ouest-Africaine d'Entreprise Maritime (SOAEM): rue Mohamed V, BP 2428, Bamako; tel. 2022-5832; fax 2022-4024; maritime transport co.

CIVIL AVIATION

The principal airport is at Bamako-Senou. The other major airports are at Bourem, Gao, Goundam, Kayes, Kita, Mopti, Nioro, Ségou,

Tessalit and Tombouctou. There are about 40 small airfields. Mali's airports are being modernized with external financial assistance. In early 2005 the Malian Government announced the creation of a new national airline, in partnership with the Aga Khan Fund for Economic Development and Industrial Promotion Services.

Agence Nationale de l'Aéronautique Civile (ANAC): Ministère de l'Equipement et des Transports, BP 227, Bamako; tel. 2029-5524; fax 2029-6177; e-mail anacmali@hotmail.com; internet www.anac-mali.org; f. 2005 to replace Direction Nationale de l'Aéronautique Civile (f. 1990); Dir-Gen. TÉNÉ SANOGO ISSABRE.

Air Affaires Mali: BP E 3759, Badalabougou, Bamako; tel. 2022-6136.

Air Mali: Immeuble Tomota, ave Cheick Zayed, BP E 2286, Bamako; tel. 2022-2424; fax 2022-7111; e-mail dc.cam@cam-mali.org; internet www.camaero.com; f. 2005; 51% owned by Fonds Aga Khan pour le Développement Economique (AKAFED), 20% state-owned; domestic and international flights; Dir-Gen. ABDERRAHMANE BERTHÉ.

STA Trans African Airlines: Quartier du Fleuve, BP 775, Bamako; tel. 2022-4444; fax 2021-0981; internet www.sta-airlines.com; f. 1984 as Société des Transports Aériens; privately owned; local, regional and international services; Man. Dir MELHEM ELIE SABBAGUE.

Tourism

Mali's rich cultural heritage is promoted as a tourist attraction. In 1999 the Government launched a three-year cultural and tourism development programme centred on Tombouctou, Gao and Kidal. In 2008 189,511 tourists visited Mali, while receipts from tourism totalled some US $227m. in 2007.

Ministry of Crafts and Tourism: see section on The Government.

Defence

As assessed at November 2010, the active Malian army numbered some 7,350 men. Paramilitary forces numbered 4,800 and there was an inactive militia of 3,000 men. Military service is by selective conscription and lasts for two years.

Defence Expenditure: Estimated at 103,000m. francs CFA in 2009.

Chief of Staff of the Armed Forces: Gen. GABRIEL POUDIOUGOU.

Chief of Staff of the Air Force: Col MAMADOU TOGOLO.

Chief of Staff of the Land Army: Col MAMADOU ADAMA DIALLO.

Chief of Staff of the National Guard: Col BROULAYE KONÉ.

Education

Education is provided free of charge and is officially compulsory for nine years between seven and 16 years of age. Primary education begins at the age of seven and lasts for six years. Secondary education, from 13 years of age, lasts for a further six years, generally comprising two cycles of three years. The rate of school enrolment in Mali is among the lowest in the world. According to UNESCO, in 2008/09 primary enrolment included 73% of children in the appropriate age-group (males 79%; females 66%), while secondary enrolment included only 30% of those in the appropriate age-group (males 37%; females 23%). Tertiary education facilities include the national university, developed in the mid-1990s. In 2007/08 there were some 67,800 students enrolled in tertiary education. Hitherto many students have received higher education abroad, mainly in France and Senegal. In 2005 spending on education represented 14.8% of total budgetary expenditure.

MALTA

Introductory Survey

LOCATION, CLIMATE, LANGUAGE, RELIGION, FLAG, CAPITAL

The Republic of Malta is in southern Europe. The country comprises an archipelago in the central Mediterranean Sea, consisting of the inhabited islands of Malta, Gozo and Comino, and the uninhabited islets of Cominotto, Filfla and St Paul's. The main island, Malta, lies 93 km (58 miles) south of the Italian island of Sicily and 288 km (179 miles) east of the Tunisian coast, the nearest point on the North African mainland. The climate is warm, with average temperatures of 22.6°C (72.7°F) in summer and 13.7°C (56.6°F) in winter. Average annual rainfall is 578 mm (22.8 ins). Maltese and English are the official languages, although Italian is widely spoken. About 95% of the inhabitants are Christians adhering to the Roman Catholic Church, the country's established religion. The national flag (proportions 2 by 3) consists of two equal vertical stripes, white at the hoist and red at the fly, with a representation of the George Cross, edged with red, in the upper hoist. The capital is Valletta, on the island of Malta.

CONTEMPORARY POLITICAL HISTORY

Historical Context

Malta, which had been a Crown Colony of the United Kingdom since 1814, became an independent sovereign state, within the Commonwealth, in September 1964. The Government, led by Dr Giorgio Borg-Olivier of the Nationalist Party (Partit Nazzjonalista—PN), negotiated defence and financial aid agreements, effective over a 10-year period, with the United Kingdom.

In June 1971 the Malta Labour Party (MLP), led by Dom Mintoff, assumed power after winning a general election. Pursuing a policy of non-alignment, the Government concluded agreements for cultural, economic and commercial co-operation with Italy, Libya, Tunisia, the USSR, several East European countries, the USA, the People's Republic of China and others. The MLP Government abrogated the 1964 Mutual Defence and Assistance Agreement with the United Kingdom. This agreement was replaced in 1972 by a new seven-year agreement, under which Malta was to receive substantially increased rental payments for the use of military facilities by the United Kingdom and other members of the North Atlantic Treaty Organization (NATO, see p. 368). British troops were finally withdrawn in March 1979.

Domestic Political Affairs

Malta became a republic in December 1974. The MLP retained power at general elections held in September 1976 and in December 1981, when it secured a majority of three seats in the 65-seat House of Representatives, although obtaining only 49.1% of the votes cast. The PN, which had received 50.9% of the votes cast, contested the result, refused to take its seats in the legislature and organized a campaign of civil disobedience. In March 1983 the PN terminated its legislative boycott, but immediately withdrew again, in protest against a government resolution to loosen ties with the European Community (EC, now the European Union—EU, see p. 270). Although Mintoff promised constitutional amendments and weekly consultations with the opposition, these arrangements collapsed in June, when the MLP blamed the PN for a bomb attack on government offices. In November a police raid on the PN headquarters was alleged to have discovered a cache of arms and ammunition.

In June 1983 the House of Representatives approved controversial legislation, under which about 75% of church property was to be expropriated to provide finance for a programme of universal free education and the abolition of fee-paying church schools. Opponents of the measure denounced it as both unconstitutional and a violation of religious liberty, and in September 1984 the courts disallowed the legislation. In April 1984 the House of Representatives approved legislation forbidding any school to accept fees (including voluntary gifts and donations). The Roman Catholic Archbishop of Malta rejected the government conditions and ordered the closure of all church schools, in response to growing tensions and public unrest. An agreement was finally reached in November, when the schools were re-opened.

Mintoff retired in December 1984 and was replaced as Prime Minister by the new leader of the MLP, Dr Carmelo Mifsud Bonnici. In April 1985 the Government reached agreement with the Roman Catholic Church, providing for the phased introduction of free education in church secondary schools, and guaranteeing the autonomy of church schools. However, in July 1988 the enforced introduction of new licensing procedures for church schools led to demands by the Roman Catholic Church that the state should reduce its supervisory powers over church education.

At a general election held in May 1987 the PN obtained 50.9% of the votes cast, but won only 31 of the 65 seats in the House of Representatives, while the MLP, with 48.9% of the votes cast, won the remaining 34 seats. However, in accordance with a constitutional amendment that had been adopted in January (see Constitution and Government), the PN was allocated four additional seats, giving it a majority of one in the legislature, thus ending the MLP's 16-year tenure in office. The leader of the PN, Dr Eddie Fenech Adami, became Prime Minister. The PN secured an increased majority of three seats over the MLP at a general election held in February 1992. This result was widely interpreted as an endorsement of the PN's pro-EC policies.

Application for EU membership

On becoming Prime Minister in May 1987, Fenech Adami declared that the Government, while retaining Malta's policy of non-alignment, would seek closer relations with the USA and other Western countries, and would apply for full membership of the EC. A formal application for full membership of the EC was submitted by the Maltese Government in July 1990. In June 1993 the European Commission recommended that, subject to the Government of Malta's satisfying the Commission's requirements for regulatory reforms in financial services, competition and consumer protection, favourable consideration should be given to the future accession of Malta to the EU (as the EC had become in 1992).

Domestic opposition to Maltese accession to the EU had been led by the MLP, on the grounds that EU agricultural policies would increase the cost of living, and that integration into the EU would conflict with the Republic's traditional neutrality in its foreign relations. In September 1996 the PN Government, seeking to confirm its mandate to pursue the goal of full membership of the EU, called a general election for the following month. Although the PN contested the election on its record of economic success, the Government's introduction of value-added tax (VAT), as a precondition of Malta's admission to the EU, had proved unpopular with the electorate, and its proposed abolition by the MLP (which would concurrently disqualify Malta from EU membership) was widely regarded as the decisive factor in the election. With a participation rate of 97.1% of eligible voters, the MLP won 50.7% of the votes cast, compared with 47.8% for the PN. The MLP obtained 31 seats in the House of Representatives, while the PN received 34. (As the MLP actually won three seats less than the PN in the election, four seats were added to its final total, giving it a one-seat majority in the legislature.) Dr Alfred Sant, the leader of the MLP, formed a new Government with the declared intention of replacing the existing association agreement, signed in 1970, with new arrangements providing for an eventual free trade zone between Malta and the EU.

In February 1997 the Government announced the initiation of a 'national discussion' of proposals to legalize divorce. However, the imposition of tax increases and levies on public utilities substantially diminished the Government's popularity. Sant called a general election for September, three years earlier than constitutionally required, at which the PN, led by Fenech Adami, obtained a five-seat majority. Immediately following the election, Fenech Adami reactivated Malta's application for full membership of the EU. In December 1999 the European Commission agreed that accession negotiations could recommence in February 2000. In November of that year the Commission published a report which stated that Malta was among the best-equipped economically of those countries seeking to join the EU. Further action was required in Malta to reduce state aid (notably the politically sensitive LM 15m. annual subsidy to the island's dry docks), to implement privatization plans and to strengthen tax and customs administrations.

Talks over EU accession were formally concluded on 13 December 2002 in Copenhagen, Denmark. Malta had obtained 77 exemptions in the discussions, aimed largely at protecting its industrial and agricultural sectors, but also including cultural issues, such as the right to maintain the ban on divorce. A non-binding referendum was called for 8 March 2003 to determine whether the country would join the EU. Support for membership of the EU was led by the ruling PN and opposition to it by the MLP. Following an acrimonious campaign, 53.6% of valid votes cast were in favour of EU membership.

In accordance with the Constitution, Fenech Adami called a general election for 12 April to confirm the referendum result, four days before the proposed signing of the EU accession treaty by 10 applicant countries, including Malta. At the election the PN won an absolute majority of 35 seats with 51.8% of the votes, while the MLP won 30 seats (47.5%). Fenech Adami was sworn in as Prime Minister on 14 April and signed the EU accession treaty in Athens, Greece, on 16 April. The House of Representatives eventually ratified the treaty on 14 July by 34 votes to 25 (with six members boycotting the vote). Malta thus became a full member of the EU on 1 May 2004.

Developments since EU accession

Following the MLP's defeat at the 2003 general election, the party leadership decided to accept the majority public opinion in favour of accession to the EU and work within the reality of EU membership. This decision proved divisive, and was resisted by a faction of the MLP led by Mifsud Bonnici. However, delegates at a subsequent party conference agreed that the MLP would not withdraw Malta from the EU if the party came to power. Moreover, it was agreed that the incumbent Government would henceforth be able to rely on the MLP's support in its efforts to defend Malta's influence within the EU, particularly with regard to negotiations relating to the draft EU constitutional treaty. In January 2004 the Minister of Foreign Affairs, Dr Joe Borg, was named as Malta's first member of the European Commission.

In February 2004 Fenech Adami announced his intention to retire as leader of the PN and as Prime Minister. At a party conference later in February the Deputy Prime Minister and Minister for Social Policy, Dr Lawrence Gonzi, was elected as the PN's new leader. On his assumption of the premiership in March, Gonzi stated that his main priorities in the post would be full participation in the EU, the creation of jobs and the improvement of the economy. When naming his Cabinet, Gonzi assumed responsibility for the finance portfolio and appointed his former rival for the party leadership, John Dalli, as Minister of Foreign Affairs. Later in March Fenech Adami was elected President by the House of Representatives, by 33 votes to 29, following his nomination by Gonzi. His appointment was controversial, as party leaders had not traditionally stood for the post, and it was bitterly opposed by the MLP. Fenech Adami was sworn in as President in April.

In July 2004 Dalli resigned his post as Minister of Foreign Affairs, claiming he was unable to continue amid attacks from 'different sides', which was thought to be a reference to criticism from within the PN. There were also allegations, which Dalli denied, of irregularities involving a large shipping deal and the handling of ministry travel expenses. He was replaced by his junior minister, Michael Frendo.

On 8 March 2008 Malta held its first general election since joining the EU. The Prime Minister, Gonzi, emphasized the economic achievements of the PN, while the MLP leader, Sant, campaigned on an anti-corruption platform, with pledges for greater transparency in government. The PN emerged victorious with 49.3% of the votes cast, while the MLP won 48.8% but secured the majority of parliamentary seats (34 seats, compared with 31 for the PN); 93.3% of the electorate voted. Consequently, the PN was assigned four additional seats to ensure that it had a parliamentary majority. Following the results of the election, Sant immediately resigned as MLP leader. After his re-election as Prime Minister, Gonzi announced the composition of the new Cabinet, which comprised eight ministers (compared with 12 in the previous administration) and six parliamentary secretaries. The Minister for Gozo, Giovanna Debono, was the only member of the outgoing Cabinet to retain the same portfolio. Dr Tonio Borg remained as Deputy Prime Minister but was allocated the foreign affairs portfolio in place of justice and home affairs, while the former parliamentary secretaries, Dr Tonio Fenech and Dr Carmelo Mifsud Bonnici, were appointed Minister for Finance, the Economy and Investment and Minister for Justice and Home Affairs, respectively. Dalli was reappointed to the Cabinet as Minister for Social Policy.

In June 2008 Dr Joseph Muscat was elected Leader of the MLP. However, as a member of the European Parliament, Muscat was unable officially to assume the role of leader of the opposition until September, when he was co-opted to the House of Representatives. Following his election as MLP Leader, Muscat indicated his intention to rejuvenate the party's image and to reform its internal structures. At a special party conference held in November, delegates approved a programme of reforms, most notably including changing the party's official title to Partit Laburista (PL) and dispensing with its historic emblem, the flaming torch.

On 1 April 2009 Dr George Abela of the PL (Muscat's main rival in the party leadership election) was unanimously elected President by the House of Representatives, having been nominated by Gonzi, in accordance with an agreement reached by the two main parties earlier that year. It was the first time that a Prime Minister had proposed a member of an opposing party for the role of President. Abela was duly sworn in on 4 April.

In November 2009 Gonzi nominated Dalli to assume Malta's seat on the European Commission. Dalli duly relinquished his ministerial post in February 2010, shortly before he was due to begin his new role. No new figures were appointed in the ensuing government reshuffle: Joe Cassar, who had hitherto sat in the Cabinet as a parliamentary secretary, assumed much of Dalli's portfolio as Minister for Health, the Elderly and Community Care, while Dolores Cristina was given responsibility for family affairs in addition to her existing education portfolio. Minor changes to the attributions of other ministers and parliamentary secretaries were also effected.

In July 2010 a private member's bill proposing the legalization of divorce in Malta (for many years previously a matter of controversy) was introduced in the House of Representatives by a member of the PN, apparently without the prior knowledge of the party leadership. An amended version of the bill was presented in December. Support for the legalization was expressed by some members of both the main parties, but opposition appeared to be more widespread among members of the PN. In February 2011 the PL proposed that a consultative referendum on divorce should take place before any parliamentary debate on the subject, while senior members of the PN recommended that a referendum should only be conducted if and when the divorce law had been approved by the legislature. A parliamentary debate on the conducting of a referendum began in late February. A motion proposing a referendum on divorce received parliamentary approval in March after Gonzi, although personally expressing his opposition to divorce, allowed representatives of the PN a free vote. The referendum, which was to take place on 28 May and was not legally binding, was to pose the question of whether a no-fault divorce should be permitted after four years of marital separation.

Immigration Issues

Following its accession to the EU in 2004, illegal immigration became an increasing problem for Malta, partly owing to its proximity to North Africa. According to the Office of the UN High Commissioner for Refugees (UNHCR, see p. 71), of all EU states Malta received the second largest number of asylum seekers per 1,000 inhabitants in 2005 (after Cyprus). Given Malta's extremely high population density the European Commission supported the Government's request in July 2005 that a proportion of the migrants arriving there be transferred to other EU states. Malta received offers of assistance from the Czech Republic, Ireland, the Netherlands and the United Kingdom. An investigation was launched in September to determine whether the recent influx of illegal immigrants was the result of human trafficking. In October the House of Representatives adopted amendments to refugee legislation aimed at facilitating the repatriation of failed asylum seekers. In December a first group of migrants granted refugee status was transferred to the Netherlands. Malta also sought an agreement with Libya on the repatriation of illegal immigrants to that country. In February 2006 immigrants housed in detention centres across Malta protested, claiming that they were poorly fed and kept in unsanitary conditions. Malta had been criticized by UNHCR over its treatment of asylum seekers in January 2005.

MALTA

In July 2006 Malta refused permission to a vessel transporting a group of 51 illegal migrants, originating mainly from sub-Saharan Africa, to enter the port of Valletta. The Government insisted that, as the vessel was Spanish-owned and had been rescued in Libyan waters, Malta would not accept responsibility for it, nor for its passengers. However, Spain also refused to accept responsibility for the migrants and the ship remained at sea for some eight days, during which discussions were held between the Maltese and Spanish Governments, and the Vice-President of the European Commission, responsible for Justice, Freedom and Security, Franco Frattini. Under the resulting agreement, Malta allowed the passengers to disembark at Valletta and accepted eight migrants, while Spain accepted 18; the remainder were transferred to Libya, Italy and Andorra. Later that month the EU announced its intention to deploy a police force to patrol the borders of member countries experiencing problems with illegal immigration, which would include a maritime patrol in the Mediterranean Sea between Malta and North Africa. None the less, in May 2007 there were several incidents in which the Maltese authorities refused to take responsibility for migrants arriving by sea from Africa, usually setting off from Libya, including a case in which 27 African migrants were left in the water for several days by a Maltese vessel, until they were rescued by the Italian navy. In June Frattini accused the Maltese Government of failing to meet its international responsibilities to save lives at sea. The Government insisted that Malta could not accept responsibility for all illegal immigrants rescued in the Mediterranean, particularly if they were in international and third country search and rescue areas. It proposed the creation of a system of shared responsibility for rescued migrants between EU member states on a quota basis. Although Frattini acknowledged Malta's predicament, immediate EU assistance was limited to the provision of an improved marine patrol force in the waters surrounding Malta, Sicily and Libya.

In March 2009 Malta and Libya signed a memorandum of understanding on search and rescue, in order to enhance co-operation between the two countries. In the same month the Maltese Government offered to deploy Maltese military personnel to assist in planned joint patrols of Libyan waters by Italian and Libyan forces, which were intended to curtail the illegal transportation of migrants across the Mediterranean. The patrols commenced in May. Meanwhile, in February Malta, together with Cyprus, Greece and Italy, submitted proposals to the European Commission intended to strengthen co-operation between member states on immigration and asylum policy, including the establishment of a European Asylum Support Office (EASO). The proposals were adopted at an EU summit in June, and the EASO, was formally established in Valletta in 2010. In March of that year Malta disputed new EU rules which stipulated that migrants intercepted by naval patrols in the Mediterranean should be landed in the country whose personnel were leading the patrol in question: the Maltese Government argued that such a policy would only encourage illegal migration, and that, since Maltese officers led many such patrols, Malta would therefore be obliged to receive a larger number of migrants than would otherwise have been the case. In February 2011, following the popular protests in Tunisia and Egypt that led to the resignation of their respective heads of state, and escalating civil unrest in Libya, Malta was among six Mediterranean EU states to request the establishment by the EU of a 'burden-sharing mechanism' and an emergency fund, in anticipation of a massive influx of asylum seekers, particularly from Libya in the event of civil war occurring in that country. In the same month Malta accepted requests from several countries to provide a transit point for many of the thousands of expatriate workers who were being evacuated from Libya by air and sea.

Other Foreign Affairs

In November 2005 Malta hosted the Commonwealth Heads of Government Meeting, at which leaders discussed improving co-operation in development, mass migration and combating terrorism. The British Prime Minister, Tony Blair, attended the meeting and later held talks with Gonzi on a number of issues, including illegal immigration. It was the first visit to Malta by a British Prime Minister in some 60 years.

In July 2005 Malta extended its maritime jurisdiction and established exclusive fisheries zones in response to similar measures adopted by Libya and Tunisia. Malta also requested permission from Libya for 15 vessels to operate within its unilaterally declared fisheries conservation zone at any one time during the year. In early 2006 Malta and Libya discussed reviving their 1984 co-operation agreement and agreed to consider a number of options with regard to petroleum, not limited to exploration; in March 2008 Libya warned a Canadian petroleum company not to begin operations in an area of the seabed that Malta had licensed the company to explore, but which was claimed by Libya. The disputed delineation of areas of the continental shelf apportioned to Malta and Libya respectively was still under discussion in early February 2011, when the Maltese Prime Minister, Lawrence Gonzi, paid a visit to Libya. In February 2006, meanwhile, Malta and Tunisia signed an agreement on joint petroleum exploration and exploitation in zones of the continental shelf located between the two countries. In January 2011 Malta made a formal protest to Italy, after the Italian Government offered licences for petroleum exploration in a contested area of the continental shelf.

The widespread anti-Government unrest that occurred in North Africa and the Middle East during early 2011 was a source of grave concern to Malta, not only because of the increase in the number of migrants seeking asylum, but also because of the possible effect of regional instability on Malta's economy, with investment and tourism likely to be adversely affected.

CONSTITUTION AND GOVERNMENT

Under the 1974 Constitution, legislative power is held by the unicameral House of Representatives, whose 65 members are elected by universal adult suffrage for five years (subject to dissolution) on the basis of proportional representation. The Constitution was amended in January 1987 to ensure that a party that received more than 50% of the total votes cast in a general election would obtain a majority of seats in the legislature (by the allocation—if necessary—of additional seats to that party). The President is the constitutional Head of State, elected for a five-year term by the House of Representatives, and executive power is exercised by the Cabinet. The President appoints the Prime Minister and, on the latter's recommendation, other Ministers. The Cabinet is responsible to the House of Representatives.

REGIONAL AND INTERNATIONAL CO-OPERATION

Malta is a member of the European Union (EU, see p. 270) and uses the single currency, the euro. It is also a member of the Council of Europe (see p. 250) and the Organization for Security and Co-operation in Europe (OSCE, see p. 385) and of the Commonwealth (see p. 230).

Malta joined the UN following independence in 1964. As a contracting party to the General Agreement on Tariffs and Trade, Malta joined the World Trade Organization (WTO, see p. 430) on its establishment in 1995. Malta participates in the 'Partnership for Peace' programme of the North Atlantic Treaty Organization (NATO, see p. 368).

ECONOMIC AFFAIRS

In 2007, according to estimates by the World Bank, Malta's gross national income (GNI), measured at average 2005–07 prices, was US $6,826m., equivalent to $16,690 per head (or $22,640 per head on an international purchasing-power parity basis). During 2000–09, it was estimated, the population increased at an average annual rate of 0.7%, while gross domestic product (GDP) per head increased, in real terms, at an average annual rate of 0.9% during 2000–07. Overall GDP increased, in real terms, at an average annual rate of 1.6% in 2000–07. According to the IMF, GDP contracted by 1.9% in 2009.

Agriculture (including hunting, forestry and fishing) contributed 1.9% of GDP in 2009 and engaged 1.6% of the working population in August 2010. The principal export crop is potatoes. Tomatoes and other vegetables, cereals (principally wheat and barley) and fruit are also cultivated. Livestock and livestock products are also important, and efforts are being made to develop the fishing industry. According to FAO figures, Malta's agricultural production increased at an average rate of 0.7% per year in 1995–2004. Output increased by 4.4% in 2004.

Industry (including mining, manufacturing, construction and power) provided 19.2% of GDP in 2009 and engaged 24.7% of the employed labour force in August 2010. According to the IMF, industrial production increased at an average rate of 3.4% per year in 1995–2004; it rose by 3.8% in 2003, but declined by 1.2% in 2004.

Mining and quarrying contributed 0.3% of GDP in 2009 and engaged 0.3% of the employed labour force in August 2010. The principal activities are stone- and sand-quarrying. There are

MALTA

reserves of petroleum in Maltese offshore waters, and petroleum and gas exploration is proceeding.

Manufacturing contributed 13.4% of GDP in 2009 and engaged 14.3% of the working population in August 2010. Based on the gross value of output, the principal branches of manufacturing, excluding ship-repairing, in 2007 were electrical and optical equipment (accounting for around 27.3% of the total), chemicals, chemical products and man-made fibres (15.3%) and food products and beverages (13.7%).

Construction contributed 3.4% of GDP in 2009 and engaged 8.3% of the employed labour force in August 2010.

Energy is derived principally from imports of crude petroleum (the majority of which is purchased, at preferential rates, from Libya) and coal. Imports of mineral fuels comprised a provisional 12.1% of the value of total imports in 2010.

Services provided 78.9% of GDP in 2009 and engaged 73.7% of the employed labour force in August 2010. Tourism is a major source of foreign exchange earnings. In 2009 Malta received 1,182,490 foreign visitors, and revenue from the sector reached US $1,215m. in 2008. In August 2010 6.7% of the employed labour force were engaged in employment in the hotels and restaurants sub-sector.

In 2009 Malta recorded a visible trade deficit of US $1,211m., and there was a deficit of $491m. on the current account of the balance of payments. In 2010, according to provisional figures, the principal source of imports (accounting for a provisional 25.2% of the total value) was Italy (including San Marino); other major suppliers were the United Kingdom and Germany. Germany was the principal market for exports (taking 12.2% of the total value); other significant purchasers of exports were Singapore, France, the USA and the United Kingdom. The principal domestic exports in 2010 were machinery and transport equipment, accounting for 51.7% of the total, and miscellaneous manufactured articles. The principal imports were machinery and transport equipment, accounting for 45.2% of the total, miscellaneous manufactured articles and semi-manufactures.

In 2009 Malta recorded an estimated budget deficit of €161.6m., equivalent to 2.8% of GDP. Malta's general government gross debt was €3,886.9m. in 2009, equivalent to 67.6% of GDP. According to the International Labour Organization (ILO), the annual rate of inflation averaged 2.4% in 2000–09; consumer prices increased by 1.4% in 2010. In 2009 the unemployment rate averaged 6.9%.

Following the closure, in 1979, of the British military base and naval docks, on which Malta's economy had been largely dependent, successive governments pursued a policy of restructuring and diversification. The domestic market is limited, owing to the small population. There are few natural resources, and almost all raw materials have to be imported. Malta's development has therefore been based on the promotion of the island as an international financial centre and on manufacturing for export (notably in non-traditional fields, such as electronics, information technology and pharmaceuticals), together with the continuing development of tourism. From 2004 Malta's membership of the European Union (EU, see p. 270) entailed a commitment on the part of the Government to reduce Malta's budgetary deficit to below 3.0% of GDP in order to comply with the convergence criteria for participation in Economic and Monetary Union (EMU). Through the implementation of strict monetary policies, institutional reform and a privatization programme, Malta reduced its deficit from more than 10% of GDP in 2003 to 1.8% in 2007. Malta adopted the euro as its currency in January 2008. Along with other European countries, Malta was affected by the global economic downturn of 2008–09, although its banking sector remained relatively unharmed by the financial crisis that had its origin in the USA. Income from both exports and tourism declined sharply, owing to a decline in demand, particularly from France and the United Kingdom. The budget deficit increased to 4.5% of GDP in 2008, but declined again to 3.8% in 2009, primarily as a result of increased revenue from taxation, including that paid by international companies registered in Malta. According to the IMF, GDP declined, in real terms, by 1.9% in 2009, but increased by an estimated 3.1% in 2010. Manufacturing output and tourism both recovered in 2010, although investment, particularly in the construction industry, remained at a comparatively low level. Unemployment declined in that year, at a faster rate than in any other EU member state. The IMF forecast that continuing GDP growth of 2.0% would be achieved in 2011.

PUBLIC HOLIDAYS

2012: 1 January (New Year's Day), 10 February (St Paul's Shipwreck), 19 March (St Joseph), 31 March (Freedom Day), 6 April (Good Friday), 1 May (St Joseph the Worker), 7 June (Memorial of the 1919 Riot), 29 June (St Peter and St Paul), 15 August (Assumption), 8 September (Our Lady of Victories), 21 September (Independence Day), 8 December (Immaculate Conception), 13 December (Republic Day), 25 December (Christmas Day).

Statistical Survey

Source (unless otherwise stated): National Statistics Office, Lascaris, Valletta VLT 1921; tel. 21223221; fax 21249841; e-mail nso@magnet.mt; internet www.nso.gov.mt.

AREA AND POPULATION

Area: 316 sq km (122 sq miles).

Population: 404,962 (males 200,819, females 204,143) at census of 27 November 2005 (figures refer to *de jure* population). *2009* (estimated population at 31 December): 412,970 (males 205,419, females 207,551).

Density (at 31 December 2009): 1,306.9 per sq km.

Population by Age and Sex (official estimates at 31 December 2009): *0–14:* 64,566 (males 33,161, females 31,405); *15–64:* 287,309 (males 146,175, females 141,134); *65 and over:* 61,095 (males 26,083, females 35,012); *Total* 412,970 (males 205,419, females 207,551).

Principal Towns (total population at 31 December 2009): Birkirkara 22,492; Mosta 19,155; Qormi 16,730; Żabbar 14,981; San Pawl Il-Baħar 14,481; Sliema 13,508; San Gwann 13,103; Valletta (capital) 6,221.

Births, Marriages and Deaths (2009): Registered live births 4,143 (birth rate 10.0 per 1,000); Marriages 2,353 (marriage rate 5.7 per 1,000); Registered deaths 3,221 (death rate 7.8 per 1,000).

Life Expectancy (years at birth, WHO estimates): 80 (males 78; females 82) in 2008. Source: WHO, *World Health Statistics*.

Migration (2004, unless otherwise indicated): Emigrants 70 (all to United Kingdom); Returning emigrants 459; Non-Maltese nationals settling in the islands 533 (in 2002). *2005:* Total emigrants 70.

Economically Active Population (persons in full-time employment, labour force survey, August 2010): Agriculture and hunting 1,787; Fishing 490; Mining and quarrying 389; Manufacturing 20,842; Electricity, gas and water supply 2,686; Construction 12,161; Wholesale and retail trade and repair of motor vehicles, motorcycles and personal and household goods 22,266; Hotels and restaurants 9,791; Transport, storage and communications 11,409; Financial intermediation 5,795; Real estate, renting and business activities 15,990; Public administration and defence and compulsory social security 10,771; Education 12,675; Health and social work 10,602; Other community, social and personal service activities 8,292; Private households with employed persons 2; Extra-territorial organizations and bodies 167; *Total employed* 146,115 (males 97,857, females 48,258); Registered unemployed 6,589; *Total labour force* 152,704. Note: figures exclude apprentices, trainees and students engaged in holiday work (649 in August 2010).

HEALTH AND WELFARE

Key Indicators

Total Fertility Rate (children per woman, 2008): 1.3.

Under-5 Mortality Rate (per 1,000 live births, 2008): 7.

HIV/AIDS (% of persons aged 15–49, 2007): 0.1.

Physicians (per 1,000 head, 2006): 3.9.

Hospital Beds (per 1,000 head, 2006): 8.

Health Expenditure (2007): US $ per head (PPP): 4,053.

Health Expenditure (2007): % of GDP: 7.5.

MALTA

Health Expenditure (2007): public (% of total): 77.5.
Human Development Index (2010): ranking: 33.
Human Development Index (2010): value: 0.815.
Total Carbon Dioxide Emissions ('000 metric tons, 2007): 2,722.4.
Carbon Dioxide Emissions Per Head (metric tons, 2007): 6.7.

For sources and definitions, see explanatory note on p. vi.

AGRICULTURE, ETC.

Principal Crops ('000 metric tons, 2009): Wheat 9.5*; Barley 1.6*; Potatoes 10.1; Cabbages and other brassicas 3.1*; Tomatoes 11.6; Cauliflowers and broccoli 5.4; Pumpkins, squash and gourds 1.5; Onions, dry 7.6; Garlic 0.7; Broad beans, dry 0.8*; Melons 3.9; Citrus fruit 2.8*; Grapes 4.8.
*FAO estimate.

Livestock ('000 head, year ending September 2009): Cattle 17.8; Pigs 65.5; Sheep 12.8; Goats 6.4; Chickens 500*; Horses 1.1*.
*FAO estimate.

Livestock Products ('000 metric tons, 2009): Cattle meat 1.5; Pig meat 7.4; Rabbit meat 1.8*; Chicken meat 4.7; Cows' milk 39.5; Sheep's milk 1.8; Hen eggs 7.0.
*FAO estimate.

Fishing (metric tons, live weight, 2008): Capture 1,279 (Atlantic bluefin tuna 296; Common dolphinfish 237; Swordfish 260); Aquaculture 1,692 (European sea bass 97; Gilthead sea bream 1,574); *Total catch* 2,971.

Source: FAO.

INDUSTRY

Production ('000 metric tons, 2001, unless otherwise indicated): Limestone flux and calcareous stones 2,000 (Limestone only); Cigarettes (1992, million) 1,475; Washing powders and detergents 9.7; Quicklime (1992, incl. other types of lime) 5; Tankers, launched (1996, number, completions) 5; Other seagoing merchant vessels launched (number, 2002) 1 (5 grt); Electricity (2007, million kWh, by public utilities) 2,296 (Source: UN, *Industrial Commodity Statistics Yearbook* and Database).

FINANCE

Currency and Exchange Rates: 100 cent = 1 euro (€). *Sterling and Dollar Equivalents* (31 December 2010): £1 sterling = 1.1716 euros; US $1 = 0.7484 euros; €10 = £8.54 = $13.36. *Average Exchange Rate* (euros per US dollar): 0.6827 in 2008; 0.7198 in 2009; 0.7550 in 2010. Note: The national currency was formerly the Maltese lira (LM; plural liri). Malta adopted the euro on 1 January 2008 at a fixed exchange rate of €1 = LM 0.429300. The euro and local currency circulated alongside each other until 31 January, after which the euro became the sole legal tender.

Budget (€ million, consolidated fund, 2009): *Revenue:* Income tax 739.4; Customs and excise 174.4; Licences and fines 236.2; Value-added tax 454.0; Social security 526.1; Grants 72.9; Other recurrent revenue 167.8; Non-recurrent revenue 458.6; Total 2,829.4. *Expenditure:* Recurrent expenditure 2,204.4 (Personal emoluments 543.8; Programmes and initiatives 1,381.3); Public debt servicing 192.0; Capital expenditure 271.3; Total 2,667.8.

International Reserves (US $ million at 31 December 2009): Gold (national valuation) 6.5; IMF special drawing rights 150.5; Reserve position in IMF 51.9; Foreign exchange 329.7; Total 538.6. Source: IMF, *International Financial Statistics*.

Money Supply (incl. shares, depository corporations, national residence criteria, € million at 31 December 2009): Currency issued 711 (Central Bank of Malta 806); Demand deposits 3,634; Other deposits 4,883; Securities other than shares 250; Shares and other equity 4,793; Other items (net) −218; Total 14,053. Source: IMF, *International Financial Statistics*.

Cost of Living (Consumer Price Index; base: 2005 = 100): All items 104.1 in 2007; 108.5 in 2008; 110.8 in 2009. Source: IMF, *International Financial Statistics*.

Gross Domestic Product (€ million at constant 2000 prices, provisional): 4,339.4 in 2006; 4,523.1 in 2007; 4,638.3 in 2008. Source: IMF, *International Financial Statistics*.

National Income and Product (€ million at current prices, 2009): Compensation of employees 2,516.5; Gross operating surplus and mixed income 2,433.4; *Gross domestic product at factor cost* 4,949.9; Taxes on production and imports 833.8; *Less* Subsidies 63.4; *GDP in purchasers' values* 5,720.3.

Expenditure on Gross Domestic Product (€ million at current prices, 2009): Final consumption expenditure 4,921.4 (General government 1,246.2, Households 3,586.0, Non-profit institutes serving households 89.2); Gross capital formation 700.4 (Gross fixed capital formation 813.9, Changes in inventories −99.9, Acquisitions, less disposals, of valuables −13.6); *Total domestic expenditure* 5,621.8; Exports of goods and services 4,159.0; *Less* Imports of goods and services 4,060.5; *GDP in purchasers' values* 5,720.3.

Gross Domestic Product by Economic Activity (€ million at current prices, 2009): Agriculture, hunting and forestry 77.2; Fishing 16.0; Mining and quarrying 16.3; Manufacturing 662.4; Electricity, gas and water supply 98.0; Construction 170.0; Wholesale and retail trade, repair of motor vehicles, motorcycles and household goods 524.8; Hotels and restaurants 227.1; Transport, storage and communications 429.6; Financial intermediation 296.4; Real estate, renting and business activities 898.8; Public administration and defence, compulsory social security 349.1; Education 298.5; Health and social work 334.4; Other community, social and personal services 536.2; Private households with employed persons 7.5; *Gross value added at basic prices* 4,942.2; Indirect taxes 798.2; *Less* Subsidies 20.2; *GDP in purchasers' values* 5,720.3. Note: Financial services indirectly measured assumed to be distributed at origin.

Balance of Payments (US $ million, 2009): Exports of goods f.o.b. 2,383; Imports of goods f.o.b. −3,594; *Trade balance* −1,211; Exports of services 3,407; Imports of services −2,144; *Balance on goods and services* 51; Other income received 2,295; Other income paid −2,812; *Balance on goods, services and income* −465; Current transfers received 1,435; Current transfers paid −1,461; *Current balance* −491; Capital account (net) 103; Direct investment abroad −114; Direct investment from abroad 882; Portfolio investment assets −2,741; Portfolio investment liabilities −40; Financial derivatives assets −3; Financial derivatives liabilities −85; Other investment assets 5,067; Other investment liabilities −2,688; Net errors and omissions 241; *Overall balance* 130. Source: IMF, *International Financial Statistics*.

EXTERNAL TRADE

Principal Commodities (€ million, 2010, provisional): *Imports:* Food 375.1; Beverages and tobacco 60.2; Animal and vegetable oils and fats 6.9; Crude materials (inedible) except fuels 30.6; Mineral fuels, lubricants, etc. 443.5; Chemicals 357.3; Manufactured goods 373.9; Semi-manufactures 319.7; Machinery and transport equipment 1,652.8; Miscellaneous transactions 39.2; Total 3,659.1. *Exports:* Food 135.4; Beverages and tobacco 22.3; Crude materials (inedible) except fuels 13.7; Mineral fuels, lubricants, etc. 173.4; Chemicals 268.1; Manufactured goods 324.9; Semi-manufactures 123.0; Machinery and transport equipment 1,145.5; Miscellaneous transactions 9.5; Total 2,215.8.

Principal Trading Partners (€ million, 2010, provisional): *Imports:* European Union 2,349.5 (France—incl. Monaco 293.5; Germany 258.5; Italy—incl. San Marino 923.1; United Kingdom 314.2); Other Europe 274.9; Africa 107.5; Americas 276.5 (USA 92.3); Asia 568.6 (China, People's Republic 117.8; Singapore 127.4); Australasia 80.1; Total 3,659.1 (incl. ships' and aircraft stores and bunkers 2.0). *Exports:* European Union 961.4 (France—incl. Monaco 220.3; Germany 270.1; Italy—incl. San Marino 133.2; United Kingdom 125.3); Other Europe 50.1; Africa 154.3; Americas 228.8 (USA 196.1); Asia 686.5 (Japan 104.3; Singapore 229.4); Australasia 11.2; Total 2,215.8 (incl. ships' and aircraft stores and bunkers 123.5).

TRANSPORT

Road Traffic (motor vehicles in use, December 2009): Private cars 227,264; Commercial vehicles 47,212; Minibuses 451; Coaches and buses 735; Motorcycles 14,380; Total (incl. others) 297,776.

Shipping: *Merchant Fleet* (31 December 2009): Vessels 1,613; Total displacement 35,036,988 grt (Source: IHS Fairplay, *World Fleet Statistics*). *International Freight Traffic* ('000 metric tons, 2007): Goods loaded 410.2; Goods unloaded 1,669.2.

Civil Aviation (traffic on scheduled services, 2006): Kilometres flown (million) 25; Passengers carried ('000) 1,495; Passenger-km (million) 2,476; Total ton-km (million) 233. Source: UN, *Statistical Yearbook*. 2009: Passenger movements on scheduled services 2,605,177; Total cargo handled (metric tons) 16,080.8.

TOURISM

Tourist Arrivals (based on departures by air and sea): 1,243,510 in 2007; 1,290,856 in 2008; 1,182,490 in 2009.

Arrivals by Country of Origin (based on departures by air and sea, 2009): France 71,930; Germany 127,373; Italy 161,737; Libya 14,281; Netherlands 33,419; United Kingdom 398,472; Total (incl. others) 1,182,490.

Tourism Receipts (US $ million, incl. passenger transport): 966 in 2006; 1,142 in 2007; 1,215 in 2008.

Source: partly World Tourism Organization.

MALTA

COMMUNICATIONS MEDIA

Radio Receivers (1997): 255,000 in use*.
Television Receivers (1999): 212,000 in use*.
Telephones (main lines, 2009): 244,900 in use†.
Mobile Cellular Telephones (2009): 422,100 subscribers†.
Personal Computers (2005): 126,000 in use†.
Internet Users (2009): 240,600†.
Broadband Subscribers (2009): 105,800†.
Book Production (1998): 237 titles*.
Daily Newspapers (1999): 4 titles (combined average circulation 54,000 copies per issue).
Non-daily Newspapers (1999): 10 titles.
Other Periodicals (1992): 359 titles*.

* Source: UN, *Statistical Yearbook*.
† Source: International Telecommunication Union.

EDUCATION

Pre-primary (2007/08 unless otherwise stated): 131 schools (1999/2000); 657 teachers; 8,391 students. Source: UNESCO.
Primary (2007/08 unless otherwise stated): 126 schools (1999/2000); 2,546 teachers; 26,771 students. Source: UNESCO.
Secondary (2007/08 unless otherwise stated): *General:* 75 schools (1999/2000); 4,373 teachers; 31,512 students. *Vocational:* 23 schools (1999/2000); 364 teachers; 5,735 students. *Junior College* (1995/96): 1 school; 1,800 students. Source: UNESCO, partly *Statistical Yearbook*.
Universities, etc. (2007/08 unless otherwise stated): 968 teachers (2004/05); 9,472 students. Source: UNESCO.
Pupil-teacher Ratio (primary education, UNESCO estimate): 10.5 in 2007/08. Source: UNESCO Institute for Statistics.
Adult Literacy Rate (UNESCO estimates): 92.4% (males 91.2%; females 93.5%) in 2005. Source: UNESCO Institute for Statistics.

Directory

The Government

HEAD OF STATE

President: Dr GEORGE ABELA (took office 4 April 2009).

THE CABINET
(May 2011)

The Government is formed by the Partit Nazzjonalista (PN—Nationalist Party).

Prime Minister: Dr LAWRENCE GONZI.
Deputy Prime Minister and Minister of Foreign Affairs: Dr TONIO BORG.
Minister for Gozo: GIOVANNA DEBONO.
Minister for Infrastructure, Transport and Communications: Dr AUSTIN GATT.
Minister for Resources and Rural Affairs: GEORGE PULLICINO.
Minister for Education, Employment and the Family: DOLORES CRISTINA.
Minister of Finance, the Economy and Investment: Dr TONIO FENECH.
Minister for Justice and Home Affairs: Dr CARMELO MIFSUD BONNICI.
Minister for Health, the Elderly and Community Care: Dr JOE CASSAR.

PARLIAMENTARY SECRETARIES (ATTACHED TO MINISTRIES)

Parliamentary Secretary for Consumers, Fair Competition, Local Councils and Public Dialogue in the Office of the Prime Minister: Dr CHRIS SAID.
Parliamentary Secretary for Tourism, the Environment and Culture in the Office of the Prime Minister: Dr MARIO DE MARCO.
Parliamentary Secretary for Youth and Sport in the Ministry of Education, Employment and the Family: CLYDE PULI.
Parliamentary Secretary for Small Business and Land in the Ministry of Finance, the Economy and Investment: Dr JASON AZZOPARDI.
Parliamentary Secretary for the Elderly and Community Care in the Ministry for Health, the Elderly and Community Care: MARIO GALEA.

MINISTRIES

Office of the President: The Palace, Valletta VLT 1190; tel. 21221221; fax 21241241; e-mail president@gov.mt; internet www.president.gov.mt.
Office of the Prime Minister: Auberge de Castille, Valletta VLT 2000; tel. 22001400; fax 22001467; e-mail lawrence.gonzi@gov.mt; internet www.opm.gov.mt.
Ministry of Education, Employment and the Family: Palazzo Ferreria, 310 Republic St, Valletta VLT 1110; tel. 25903100; fax 25903216; e-mail info.mfss@gov.mt; internet www.msp.gov.mt.
Ministry of Finance, the Economy and Investment: Maison Demandols, South St, Valletta VLT 1102; tel. 25998244; fax 25998311; e-mail info.mfin@gov.mt; internet www.mfin.gov.mt.
Ministry of Foreign Affairs: Palazzo Parisio, Merchants St, Valletta VLT 1171; tel. 21242191; fax 21236604; e-mail info.mfa@gov.mt; internet www.mfa.gov.mt.
Ministry for Gozo: St Francis Sq., Victoria VCT 1335, Gozo; tel. 21561482; fax 21559360; e-mail webmaster.mog@gov.mt; internet www.gozo.gov.mt.
Ministry of Health, the Elderly and Community Care: Palazzo Castellania, 15 Merchants St, Valletta VLT 2000; tel. 21224071; fax 22992655; e-mail info.moh@gov.mt; internet www.sahha.gov.mt.
Ministry for Infrastructure, Transport and Communications: 168 Strait St, Valletta VLT 1433; tel. 21226808; fax 21250700; e-mail mitc@gov.mt; internet www.mitc.gov.mt.
Ministry for Justice and Home Affairs: Auberge d'Aragon, Independence Sq., Valletta VLT 2000; tel. 22957000; fax 22957348; e-mail customercare.mjha@gov.mt; internet www.mjha.gov.mt.
Ministry for Resources and Rural Affairs: Francesco Buonamici St, Floriana FRN 1700; tel. 22952000; fax 22952212; e-mail info.mrra@gov.mt; internet www.mrra.gov.mt.

Legislature

House of Representatives

The Palace, Valletta VLT 1190; tel. 25596000; fax 25596314; e-mail parliament@gov.mt; internet www.parliament.gov.mt.

Speaker: Dr MICHAEL FRENDO.

General Election, 8 March 2008

Party	Votes	% of votes	Seats
Partit Nazzjonalista (Nationalist Party)	143,468	49.34	35
Partit Laburista (Malta Labour Party)	141,888	48.79	34
Alternattiva Demokratika—The Green Party	3,810	1.31	—
Azzjoni Nazzjonali (National Action)	1,461	0.50	—
Others	172	0.06	—
Total	290,799	100.00	69

Election Commission

Electoral Commission: Electoral Office, Evans Bldg, St Elmo Pl., Valletta VLT 2000; tel. 21221994; fax 21248457; e-mail electoral.office@gov.mt; internet www.electoral.gov.mt; independent; Chair. and Chief Electoral Commr SAVIOUR GAUCI; Sec. JOE CALLEJA.

MALTA

Political Organizations

Alternattiva Demokratika—The Green Party (AD): POB 38, Marsa MTP 1001; tel. 99894962; e-mail info@alternattiva.org.mt; internet www.alternattiva.org.mt; f. 1989; emphasizes social and environmental issues; Chair. MICHAEL BRIGUGLIO; Sec.-Gen. RALPH CASSAR.

Partit Laburista (PL) (Labour Party): National Labour Centre, Mile End Rd, Hamrun HMR 1717; tel. 21249900; fax 21244204; e-mail mlp@mlp.org.mt; internet www.mlp.org.mt; f. 1921; fmrly known as the Malta Labour Party; adopted current name in 2008; democratic socialist; Leader Dr JOSEPH MUSCAT; Pres. STEFAN ZRINZO AZZOPARDI.

Partit Nazzjonalista (PN) (Nationalist Party): Herbert Ganado St, Pietà PTA 1541; tel. 21243641; fax 21243640; e-mail admin@pn.org.mt; internet www.pn.org.mt; f. 1880; Christian democratic; Leader Dr LAWRENCE GONZI; Sec.-Gen. PAUL BORG OLIVIER.

Diplomatic Representation

EMBASSIES AND HIGH COMMISSIONS IN MALTA

Australia: Villa Fiorentina, Ta'Xbiex Terrace, Ta'Xbiex XBX 1034; tel. 21338201; fax 21344059; e-mail aushicom@onvol.net; internet www.malta.embassy.gov.au; High Commr ANNE MARIE QUINANE.

Austria: Whitehall Mansions, 3rd Floor, Ta'Xbiex Seafront, Ta'Xbiex XBX 1026; tel. 23279000; fax 21317430; e-mail valletta-ob@bmeia.gv.at; internet www.aussenministerium.at/botschaft/valletta.html; Ambassador Dr CAROLINE GUDENUS.

Belgium: Europa Centre, 8–9 John Lopez St, Floriana FLN 1400; tel. 21228214; fax 21243246; e-mail valletta@diplobel.fed.be; internet www.diplomatie.be/valletta; Ambassador JEAN-FRANÇOIS DELAHAUT.

China, People's Republic: Karmnu Court, Lapsi St, St Julian's STJ 1264; tel. 21384889; fax 21344730; e-mail chinaemb_mt@mfa.gov.cn; internet mt.chineseembassy.org; Ambassador ZHANG KEYUAN.

Egypt: Villa Mon Rêve, 10 Sir Temi Zammit St, Ta'Xbiex XBX 1013; tel. 21314158; fax 21319230; e-mail embegmlt@onvol.net; Ambassador ABD AL-MAWGOUD ELHABASHY.

France: POB 408, Valletta VLT 1000; 130 Melita St, Valletta VLT 1000; tel. 22480600; fax 22480626; e-mail ambafrance@maltanet.net; internet www.ambafrance-mt.org; Ambassador DANIEL RONDEAU.

Germany: 'Il-Piazzetta', Entrance B, 1st Floor, Tower Rd, Sliema SLM 1605; POB 48, Marsa MRS 1000; tel. 22604000; fax 22604115; e-mail info@valletta.diplo.de; internet www.valletta.diplo.de; Ambassador BERND BRAUN.

Greece: Villino Fondgalland, 6 Ir-Rampa, Ta'Xbiex XBX 1035; tel. 21320889; fax 21320788; e-mail gremb.val@mfa.gr; Ambassador ALEXANDROS RALLIS.

Holy See: Apostolic Nunciature, V20/22 Pietru Caxaru St, Tal-Virtù, Rabat RBT 2604; tel. 21453422; fax 21453423; e-mail nuntius@onvol.net; Apostolic Nuncio Most Rev. TOMMASO CAPUTO (Titular Archbishop of Otricoli).

Ireland: Whitehall Mansions, Ta'Xbiex Seafront, Ta'Xbiex XBX 1026; tel. 21334744; fax 21334755; e-mail vallettaembassy@dfa.ie; internet www.embassyofireland.org.mt; Ambassador PAT HENNESSY (resident in Rome, Italy).

Italy: 5 Vilhena St, Floriana FRN 1040; tel. 21233157; fax 21239217; e-mail ambasciata.lavalletta@esteri.it; internet www.amblavalletta.esteri.it; Ambassador EFISIO LUIGI MARRAS.

Libya: Dar Jamahiriya, Triq I-Imdina St, Balzan BZN 9033; tel. 21486347; fax 21483939; e-mail libyanpeople@waldonet.net.mt; Ambassador Dr SAADUN ISMAIL SUAYEH.

Netherlands: Whitehall Mansions, 3rd Floor, Ta'Xbiex Seafront, Ta'Xbiex XBX 1026; tel. 21313980; fax 21313990; e-mail val@minbuza.nl; internet www.mfa.nl/val; Ambassador ROBERT JAN GABRIËLSE.

Portugal: Whitehall Mansions, 3rd Floor, Ta'Xbiex Seafront, Ta'Xbiex XBX 1026; tel. 21322924; fax 21322927; e-mail info@embportmalta.com; internet www.embportmalta.com; Ambassador ANTÓNIO JOSÉ DA CÂMARA RAMALHO ORTIGÃO.

Russia: Ariel House, 25 Anthony Schembri St, Kappara, San Ġwann SGN 08; tel. 21371905; fax 21372131; e-mail rusemb@onvol.net; internet www.malta.mid.ru; Ambassador BORIS YU. MARCHUK.

Spain: Whitehall Mansions, Ta'Xbiex Seafront, Ta'Xbiex XBX 1026; tel. 21317365; fax 21317362; e-mail emb.valletta@mae.es; internet www.maec.es/embajadas/lavalletta; Ambassador MARÍA ISABEL VICANDI.

Tunisia: Valletta Rd, Attard ATD 9052; tel. 21417070; fax 21413414; e-mail at.lavalette@maltanet.net; internet www.atunisie-mt.org; Ambassador ABDERRAHMANE BELHAJ.

Turkey: 35 Sir Luigi Preziosi Sq., Floriana FRN 1154; tel. 21223424; fax 21224308; e-mail valetta.be@mfa.gov.tr; Ambassador ISMAIL ETHEM TOKDEMIR.

United Kingdom: Whitehall Mansions, Ta'Xbiex Seafront, Ta'Xbiex XBX 1026; tel. 23230000; fax 23232216; e-mail bhcvalletta@fco.gov.uk; internet ukinmalta.fco.gov.uk; High Commr LOUISE STANTON.

USA: Development House, 3rd Floor, St Anne St, Floriana FRN 9010; tel. 25614000; fax 21243229; e-mail usembmalta@state.gov; internet malta.usembassy.gov; Ambassador DOUGLAS W. KMIEC.

Judicial System

The legal system consists of enactments of the Parliament of Malta, and those of the British Parliament not repealed or replaced by enactments of the Maltese legislature. Maltese Civil Law derives largely from Roman Law, while British Law has significantly influenced Maltese public law.

The Constitutional Court, composed of three judges, is appellate in cases involving alleged violations of human rights, the interpretation of the Constitution and the invalidity of laws. It has jurisdiction to decide questions as to membership of the House of Representatives and any reference made to it relating to voting for election of members of the House of Representatives.

The Court of Appeal is composed of three judges, when it hears appeals from the judgments of the Civil Court, and of one judge, when it hears appeals from the Court of Magistrates in its civil jurisdiction. An appeal also lies to the Court of Appeal from the decisions of a number of administrative tribunals, mostly on points of law.

The Court of Criminal Appeal consists of three judges and hears appeals from persons convicted by the Criminal Court. A person convicted on indictment may appeal against his conviction in all cases or against the sentence passed on his conviction, unless the sentence is one fixed by law. An appeal can never result in a sentence of greater severity. An accused person may also appeal against a verdict of not guilty on the grounds of insanity. In certain cases the court may also order a retrial. The Attorney-General, who is the prosecutor before the Criminal Court, cannot appeal from a verdict of acquittal or, in certain cases, against the sentence passed. This court, when formed of one judge, hears appeals from judgments delivered by the Court of Magistrates in its criminal jurisdiction.

The Criminal Court is formed by one judge, who sits with a jury of nine persons to try, on indictment, offences exceeding the competence of the Court of Magistrates. This court may, in certain exceptional cases, sit without a jury.

The Civil Court is divided into three sections. The First Hall takes cognisance of all causes of a civil and a commercial nature, exceeding the jurisdiction of the Courts of Magistrates. The Voluntary Jurisdiction Section (formerly the Second Hall) is assigned all matters of a civil nature, such as authority to proceed the tutorship of minors, adoption, the interdiction and incapacitation of persons, the opening of successions and the confirmation of testamentary executors. The Family Section is assigned matters of a civil nature regulated by titles I, II and IV of the First Book of the Civil Code; the Maintenance Orders (Facilities for Enforcement) Ordinance; the Maintenance Ordinance (Reciprocal Enforcement) Act; the Marriage Act and the Child Abduction and Child Custody Act. One judge presides in all three sections.

The Magistrates' Court, which is composed of one magistrate, exercises both a civil and a criminal jurisdiction. The Court of Magistrates, in civil matters, has an inferior jurisdiction of first instance, limited to claims exceeding €3,494.06 (LM 1,500) but not exceeding €11,646.87 (LM 5,000). In criminal matters, the court has a two-fold jurisdiction, namely, as a court of criminal judicature for the trial of offences which fall within its jurisdiction, and as a court of inquiry in respect of offences which fall within the jurisdiction of a higher tribunal.

The Court of Magistrates for Gozo, in civil matters, has a two-fold jurisdiction—an inferior jurisdiction comparable to that exercised by its counterpart court in Malta, and a superior jurisdiction, both civil and commercial, in respect of causes which in Malta are cognisable by the First Hall of the Civil Court. Within the limits of its territorial jurisdiction, this court has also the powers of a court of voluntary jurisdiction.

The Small Claims Tribunal is presided over by an adjudicator who decides cases on principles of equity, according to law. Adjudicators are appointed from among advocates for a term of five years, and decide cases brought before them without delay. The aim is to have claims not exceeding the sum of LM 1,500 decided summarily. Sittings of this Tribunal are held in Malta or Gozo. An appeal

MALTA

Directory

from the decision of the Tribunal lies to the Court of Appeal on specific cases listed in the Act establishing the Tribunal.

The Juvenile Court consists of a Magistrate, as Chairman, and two members. Sittings are held in Santa Venera. The court hears charges against, and holds other proceedings relating to, minors under the age of 16 years, and may also issue Care Orders in their regard. Given the confidential nature of such sittings, attendance to hearings is restricted to persons mentioned in the law establishing the court.

Chief Justice and President of the Court of Appeal and the Constitutional Court: Dr SILVIO CAMILLERI.

Judges: CARMEL A. AGIUS, JOSEPH A. FILLETTI, ALBERTO J. MAGRI, GEOFFREY VALENZIA, GIANNINO CARUANA DEMAJO, GINO CAMILLERI, CARMELO FARRUGIA SACCO, RAYMOND PACE, DAVID P. SCICLUNA, JOSEPH R. MICALLEF, TONIO MALLIA, NOEL CUSCHIERI, JOSEPH AZZOPARDI, ABIGAIL LOFARO, ANNA FELICE, JOSEPH ZAMMIT MCKEON, MICHAEL MALLIA, LAWRENCE QUINTANO, MARK CHETCUTI.

Attorney-General: Dr PETER GRECH.

Religion

CHRISTIANITY

The Roman Catholic Church

Malta comprises one archdiocese and one diocese. The Constitution enshrines Roman Catholicism as the state religion. Adherents comprise an estimated 95% of the population.

Bishops' Conference

Conferenza Episcopale Maltese, Archbishop's Curia, St Calcedonius Sq., Floriana FRN 1535; tel. 25906403; fax 21226457; e-mail joe.magro@maltadiocese.org; internet www.maltadiocese.org.

f. 1971; Pres. Most Rev. PAUL CREMONA (Archbishop of Malta); Sec. Rev. JOE MAGRO.

Archbishop of Malta: Most Rev. PAUL CREMONA, Archbishop's Curia, St Calcedonius Sq., Floriana FRN 1535; POB 29, Valletta; tel. 21235350; fax 21223307; e-mail info@maltadiocese.org.mt.

Bishop of Gozo: Rt Rev. MARIO GRECH, Chancery Office, POB 1, Republic St, Victoria VCT 1000, Gozo; tel. 21556661; fax 21551278; e-mail info@gozodiocese.org; internet gozodiocese.org.

The Anglican Communion

Malta forms part of the Diocese in Europe.

Church of England: Pro-Cathedral of St Paul, Independence Sq., Valletta VLT 1535; tel. 21225714; fax 21225867; e-mail anglican@onvol.net; internet www.anglicanmalta.org; Senior Chaplain and Chancellor of the Pro-Cathedral Rev. Canon SIMON GODFREY.

Other Christian Churches

In 2004 there were approximately 680 Jehovah's Witnesses and 148 members of the Church of Jesus Christ of Latter-day Saints (Mormons). The Bible Baptist Church had 30 members and the Fellowship of Evangelical Churches had about 100 affiliates.

OTHER RELIGIONS

There is one Muslim mosque and a Muslim primary school. There are an estimated 3,000 Muslims in the country. There is one Jewish congregation. Zen Buddhism and the Bahá'í Faith have about 30 members each.

The Press

DAILY NEWSPAPERS

The Malta Independent: Standard House, Birkirkara Hill, St Julian's STJ 1149; tel. 21345888; fax 21344860; e-mail scalleja@independent.com.mt; internet www.independent.com.mt; English; Editor STEPHEN CALLEJA.

In-Nazzjon (The Nation): Herbert Ganado St, POB 37, Pietà PTA 1450; tel. 21243641; fax 21243640; e-mail alex.attard@media.link.com.mt; internet www.mument.com.mt; f. 1970; Maltese; affiliated to Partit Nazzjonalista; Editor ALEX ATTARD.

L-orizzont (The Horizon): Union Print Co, A-41 Industrial Estate, Valletta Rd, Marsa MRS 3000; tel. 21244557; fax 21238484; e-mail info@unionprint.com.mt; internet www.l-orizzont.com; f. 1962; Maltese; organ of the General Workers' Union; Editor JOSEF CARUANA; circ. 20,000 (2008).

The Times: Allied Newspapers Ltd, 341 St Paul St, Valletta VLT 1211; tel. 25594100; fax 25594116; e-mail daily@timesofmalta.com; internet www.timesofmalta.com; f. 1935; English; Editor RAY BUGEJA.

OTHER NEWSPAPERS

Business Today: Vjal ir-Rihan, San Gwann SGN 9020; tel. 21382741; fax 21385075; internet www.businesstoday.com.mt; Wed.; Man. Editor SAVIOUR BALZAN.

Il-Gensillum (The People Today): Media Centre, National Rd, Blata il-Bajda HMR 1640; tel. 25699119; fax 25699151; e-mail gens@mediacentre.org.mt; internet www.mediacentre.org.mt; f. 2004 to succeed *Il-Gens* (The People); Maltese; Roman Catholic; Editor Rev. JOHN AVELLINO; circ. 13,000 (2008).

Illum (Today): MediaToday Co Ltd, Vjal ir-Rihan, San Gwann SGN 9016; tel. 21382741; fax 21385075; e-mail illum@mediatoday.com.mt; internet www.illum.com.mt; weekly; Maltese; Editor JULIA FARRUGIA.

KullHadd: Centru Nazzjonali Laburista, Mile End Rd, Hamrun HMR 1717; tel. 21225312; fax 21238252; e-mail felix@kullhadd.com; internet www.kullhadd.com; f. 1993; organ of Partit Laburista; Maltese; Editor FELIX AGIUS.

Lehen is-Sewwa: Catholic Institute, Floriana FRN 1441; tel. and fax 21225847; e-mail lehenissewwa@vol.net.mt; f. 1928; Roman Catholic; Editor Rev. JOHN CIARLÓ; circ. 10,000 (2008).

The Malta Business Weekly: Standard House, Birkirkara Hill, St Julian's STJ 1149; tel. 21345888; fax 21344860; e-mail csultana@independent.com.mt; internet www.independent.com.mt; f. 1994; English; Editor CHRISTOPHER SULTANA.

The Malta Independent on Sunday: Standard House, Birkirkara Hill, St Julian's STJ 1149; tel. 21345888; fax 21344884; e-mail ngrima@independent.com.mt; internet www.independent.com.mt; English; Editor NOEL GRIMA.

MaltaToday: MediaToday Co Ltd, Vjal ir-Rihan, San Gwann SGN 9016; tel. 21382741; fax 21385075; e-mail maltatoday@mediatoday.com.mt; internet www.maltatoday.com.mt; f. 1998; Wed. and Sun.; English; Editor MATTHEW VELLA.

Il-Mument (The Moment): Herbert Ganado St, POB 37, Pietà PTA 1450; tel. 21243641; fax 21243640; e-mail mument@media.link.com.mt; internet www.mument.com.mt; f. 1972; Maltese; affiliated to Partit Nazzjonalista; Editor VICTOR CAMILLERI.

The Sunday Times: Allied Newspapers Ltd, POB 328, Valletta VLT 1211; tel. 25594500; fax 25594510; e-mail sunday@timesofmalta.com; internet www.timesofmalta.com; f. 1922; English; Editor STEVE MALLIA; circ. 40,000 (2008).

It-Torca (The Torch): Union Press, A 41, Marsa Industrial Estate, Marsa MRS 3000; tel. 21244557; fax 21238484; e-mail info@unionprint.com.mt; internet www.it-torca.com; f. 1944; Maltese; organ of the General Workers' Union; Editor ALEKS FARRUGIA.

SELECTED PERIODICALS

Commercial Courier: Malta Chamber of Commerce, Enterprise and Industry, Exchange Bldgs, Republic St, Valletta VLT 1117; tel. 21233873; fax 21245223; e-mail info@maltachamber.org.mt; internet www.chamber.org.mt; bi-monthly; Editor KEVIN J. BORG.

The Employer: Malta Employers' Asscn, 35/1 South St, Valletta VLT 1100; tel. 21222992; fax 21230227; e-mail admin@maltaemployers.com; internet www.maltaemployers.com; quarterly; Editor JOSEPH FARRUGIA.

Malta Government Gazette: Department of Information, 3 Castille Pl., Valletta VLT 2000; tel. 22001700; fax 22001775; e-mail info.doi@gov.mt; internet www.doi.gov.mt; f. 1813; official notices; Maltese and English; 2 a week.

Malta In Figures: National Statistics Office, Lascaris, Valletta VLT 2000; tel. 25997000; fax 25997205; e-mail nso@gov.mt; internet www.nso.gov.mt; official statistics; annual.

Malta This Month: Advantage Advertising Ltd, 118 St John's St, Valletta VLT 1169; tel. 21249924; fax 21249927; e-mail advantage@onvol.net; publ. by Air Malta; monthly; Editor PETER DARMANIN.

The Retailer: Association of General Retailers and Traders, Exchange Bldgs, Republic St, Valletta VLT 1117; tel. 21230459; fax 21246925; internet www.grtu.eu; monthly; publ. by Malta Chamber of Small and Medium-sized Enterprises; Editor VINCENT FARRUGIA.

The Teacher: Teachers' Institute, 213 Republic St, Valletta VLT 1118; tel. 21237815; fax 21244074; e-mail info@mut.org.mt; internet www.mut.org.mt; f. 1919; journal of the Malta Union of Teachers; 2 a year; Editor FRANKLIN BARBARA.

Xpress: Alternattiva Demokratika, POB 38, Marsa MTP 1001; e-mail info@alternattiva.org.mt; publ. of the Alternattiva Demokratika—The Green Party; Maltese; monthly; Editor NEIL SPITERI.

Publishers

Malta University Publishers: Old University Building, St. Paul St, Valletta VLT 1216; tel. 21248218; fax 21230551; e-mail info@

MALTA

maltauniversitybooks.com; internet www.maltauniversitybooks.com; f. 1995; owned by University of Malta; Maltese folklore, history, law, bibliography and language; COO BRIAN GRIMA.

Merlin Library Ltd: Mountbatten St, Blata l-Bajda HMR 08; tel. 21234438; fax 21221135; e-mail mail@merlinlibrary.com; internet www.merlinlibrary.com; f. 1996; dictionaries, educational, fiction and children's books; Dir CHRISTOPHER GRUPPETTA.

Publishers Enterprises Group (PEG) Ltd: PEG Bldg, UB7 Industrial Estate, San Gwann SGN 3000; tel. 21440083; fax 21488908; e-mail contact@peg.com.mt; internet www.peg.com.mt; f. 1983; educational, children's, cookery, technical, tourism, leisure; Man. Dir EMANUEL DEBATTISTA.

Broadcasting and Communications

TELECOMMUNICATIONS

Regulatory Authority

Malta Communications Authority (MCA): Pinto Wharf, Valletta Waterfront, Floriana FRN 1913; tel. 21336840; fax 21336846; e-mail info@mca.org.mt; internet www.mca.org.mt; national agency responsible for regulating telecommunications; f. 2001; Exec. Chair. and Dir-Gen. PHILIP MICALLEF.

Service Providers

GO PLC: Spencer Hill, POB 40, Marsa MRS 1001; tel. 21210210; fax 25945895; e-mail info@go.com.mt; internet www.go.com.mt; f. 1975; fmrly Maltacom PLC; restyled 2007; mobile cellular and fixed-line telecommunications, broadband internet access, digital television services; 60% owned by TECOM Investments and the Dubai Investment Group, both mems of Dubai Holding; Chair. DEEPAK PADMANABHAN; CEO DAVID KAY.

   GO Mobile: Fra Diego St, Marsa MRS 1501; tel. 21246200; fax 21234314; internet www.go.com.mt/gomobile.

Melita PLC: Gasan Centre, Mriehel Bypass, Mriehel BKR 3000; tel. 21490006; fax 22745050; e-mail info@melitaplc.com; internet www.melita.com; f. 1992; offers mobile and fixed-line telecommunications services, and broadband internet access; also digital television services; CEO ANDREI TORRIANI.

Vodafone Malta: Vodafone House, Msida Rd, Birkirkara BKR 9024; tel. 21482820; fax 92111369; e-mail customerservice.malta@vodafone.com; internet www.vodafone.com.mt; mobile telecommunications and broadband internet services; CEO INAKI BERROETA.

BROADCASTING

Regulatory Authority

Broadcasting Authority, Malta: 7 Mile End Rd, Hamrun HMR 1719; tel. 21247908; fax 21240855; e-mail info@ba-malta.org; internet www.ba-malta.org; f. 1961; statutory body responsible for the supervision and regulation of radio and television broadcasting; Chair. ANTHONY J. TABONE; CEO PIERRE CASSAR.

Radio and Television

Digital terrestrial television was introduced on 1 February 2011; analogue transmission was scheduled to end on 1 June.

Bay Radio: Eden Pl., St George's Bay, St Julian's STJ 3310; tel. 23710800; fax 23710845; e-mail 897@bay.com.mt; internet www.bay.com.mt; Station Man. SIMON LUMSDEN.

Calypso Radio 101.8 FM: Calypso Media Communications, 28, New St in Valletta Rd, Luqa; tel. 21578022; fax 21578026; e-mail info@calypsoradio.com; internet www.calypsoradio.com; Station Man. FRANK CAMILLERI.

Campus FM: Old Humanities Bldg, University of Malta, Msida MSD 06; tel. 21333313; fax 21314485; e-mail campusfm@um.edu.mt; internet campusfm.um.edu.mt; Man. Rev. JOSEPH BORG.

Education 22: Mile End St, Hamrun HMR 1716; tel. 21239274; fax 21240701; e-mail info@e22.com.mt; internet www.e22.com.mt; f. 1996; educational television channel.

Media.link Communications Co Ltd: Dar Centrali, Herbert Ganado St, Pietà PTA 1450; tel. 21243641; fax 21243640; e-mail antona@vol.net.mt.

   Net TV: Dar Centrali, Herbert Ganado St, Pietà PTA 1450; tel. 21243641; fax 21226645.

   Radio 101: Independence Point, Herbert Ganado St, Pietà PTA 1450; tel. 21241164; fax 21564111; e-mail news@media.link.com.mt; internet www.radio101.com.mt.

ONE Productions Ltd: A28B, Industrial Estate, Marsa MRS 3000; tel. 25682568; fax 25682309; e-mail info@one.com.mt; internet www.one.com.mt; f. 1999; owned by Partit Laburista; Exec. Chair JASON MICALLEF.

   One Television: A28B Industrial Estate, Marsa MRS 3000; tel. 25682568; fax 21231472; e-mail ruth.vella@one.com.mt; broadcasts 126 hours weekly; Dir of Television RUTH VELLA.

   Super One Radio: A28B, Industrial Estate, Marsa MRS 3000; tel. 25682600; fax 21231472; e-mail ray.azzopardi@one.com.mt; broadcasts 24 hours daily; Senior Man. RAY AZZOPARDI.

Public Broadcasting Services Ltd (PBS): 75 St Luke's Rd, Gwardamangia PTA 1025; tel. 21225051; fax 21244601; e-mail info@pbs.com.mt; internet www.pbs.com.mt; f. 1991; govt-owned; operates national radio and television services: Radju Malta, Radju Parlament, Ten Sixty Six, Magic 91.7 and Television Malta; Chair. JOSEPH MIZZI; CEO ANTON ATTARD.

Radju Marija: Kunvent Patrijiet Dumnikani, Misrah San Duminku, Rabat RBT 06; tel. 21453105; fax 21453103; e-mail info.mal@radiomaria.org; internet www.radjumarija.org.

RTK Radio: Media Centre, National Rd, Blata il-Bajda HMR 1640; tel. 25699150; fax 25699151; e-mail rtknews@rtk.org.mt; internet www.rtk.org.mt; f. 1992; radio station of the Catholic Church of Malta; Chair. FRANCO AZZOPARDI; CEO MICHAEL FRANCALANZA.

Smash TV and Radio: Smash Communications, Thistle Lane, Paola PLA 19; tel. 21667777; fax 21697830; f. 1992; Man. Dir JOSEPH BALDACCHINO.

XFM 100.2 FM: 24, A. Cuschieri St, Fleur-de-Lys, Birkirkara BKR 4916; tel. 21378165; fax 21378167; e-mail news@xfmmalta.com; internet www.xfmmalta.com; f. 2003; programmes in Maltese and English; music; Station Man. DAVID AZZOPARDI.

Finance

(cap. = capital; res = reserves; dep. = deposits; m. = million; brs = branches; amounts in euros, unless otherwise indicated)

REGULATORY AUTHORITY

Malta Financial Services Authority: Notabile Rd, Attard BKR 3000; tel. 21441155; fax 21441188; e-mail communications@mfsa.com.mt; internet www.mfsa.com.mt; f. 2002; supervises the financial services sector, incl. banking, insurance and investments; regulates activities of Malta Stock Exchange; houses Malta's Companies Registry; Chair. Prof. JOSEPH V. BANNISTER.

BANKING

Central Bank

Central Bank of Malta: Pjazza Kastilja, Valletta VLT 1060; tel. 25500000; fax 25502500; e-mail info@centralbankmalta.org; internet www.centralbankmalta.org; f. 1968; govt-owned; cap. and res 240m. (Dec 2009), dep. 964m. (Dec. 2008); Gov. MICHAEL C. BONELLO.

Commercial Banks

APS Bank Ltd: APS House, 24 St Anne Sq., Floriana FRN 9020; tel. 21226644; fax 21226202; e-mail headoffice@apsbank.com.mt; internet www.apsbank.com.mt; f. 1910; cap. 16m., res 10m., dep. 653m. (Dec. 2009); Chair. Prof. EMMANUEL P. DELIA; CEO EDWARD CACHIA; 6 brs.

Banif Bank (Malta) PLC: Level 2, 203 Rue D'Argens, Gzira GZR 1368; tel. 22601000; fax 21312000; e-mail customercare@banif.com.mt; internet www.banif.com.mt; f. 2008; owned by Grupo Banif (Portugal); Chair. JOSEPH SAMMUT; CEO JOAQUIM SILVA PINTO; 5 brs.

Bank of Valletta PLC: BOV Centre, Cannon Rd. St Venera SVR 9030; tel. 21312020; fax 22753730; e-mail customercare@bov.com; internet www.bov.com; f. 1974; merged with Valletta Investment Bank Ltd in Oct. 2000; cap. 200m., res 25m., dep. 5,533m. (Sept. 2010); Chair. RODERICK CHALMERS; CEO TONIO DEPASQUALE; 41 brs.

HSBC Bank Malta PLC: 233 Republic St, Valletta VLT 1116; tel. 23802380; fax 23804923; e-mail infomalta@hsbc.com; internet www.hsbc.com.mt; f. 1975 as Mid-Med Bank; 70.03% owned by HSBC Europe BV; dep. 4,266m., total assets 5,118m. (Dec. 2009); CEO ALAN RICHARDS; 43 brs.

Lombard Bank Malta PLC: Lombard House, 67 Republic St, Valletta VLT 1117; tel. 25581100; fax 25581150; e-mail mail@lombardmalta.com; internet www.lombardmalta.com; f. 1969; cap. 9m., res 17m., dep. 444m. (Dec. 2008); Chair. CHRISTIAN LEMMERICH; Dir and CEO JOSEPH SAID; 6 brs.

Volksbank Malta Ltd: 53 Dingli St, Sliema SLM 09; tel. 27777777; fax 21336090; e-mail info@volksbank.com.mt; f. 1995 as an 'offshore' bank; licensed to operate as a commercial bank in 2002; Chair. WINSTON V. ZAHRA; Man. Dir HERBERT SKOK.

Principal 'Offshore' Bank

FIMBank PLC: Plaza Commercial Centre, 7th Floor, Bisazza St, Sliema SLM 1640; tel. 21322100; fax 21322122; e-mail info@fimbank

.com; internet www.fimbank.com; f. 1994 as First International Merchant Bank PLC; cap. US $67m., dep. US $466m., total assets US $586m. (Dec. 2008); Chair. NAJEEB H. M. AS-SALEH; Pres. MARGRITH LÜTSCHG-EMMENEGGER.

Bankers' Association

Malta Bankers' Association: 48/2 Birkirkara Rd, Attard ATD 1210; tel. 21412210; fax 21424580; e-mail info@maltabankers.org; internet www.maltabankers.org; f. 1962; Chair. VICTOR RIZZO GIUSTI; Sec.-Gen. JAMES BONELLO; 24 mems.

STOCK EXCHANGE

Malta Stock Exchange: Garrison Chapel, Castille Pl., Valletta VLT 1063; tel. 21244051; fax 25696316; e-mail borza@borzamalta.com.mt; internet www.borzamalta.com.mt; f. 1992; Chair. Dr ARTHUR GALEA SALOMONE; Chief Exec. MARK A. GUILLAUMIER.

INSURANCE

Aon—Mediterranean Insurance Brokers (Malta) Ltd: 53 Mediterranean Bldg, Abate Rigord St, Ta'Xbiex XBX 1122; tel. 23433234; fax 21341597; e-mail info@mib.com.mt; internet www.mib.com.mt; f. 1976; Man. Dir JOSEPH CUTAJAR.

Middle Sea Insurance PLC: Middle Sea House, Floriana FRN 1442; tel. 21246262; fax 21248195; e-mail middlesea@middlesea.com; internet www.middlesea.com; f. 1981; Exec. Chair. MARIO C. GRECH.

Numerous foreign insurance companies, principally British, Canadian and Italian, are represented in Malta by local agents.

Insurance Association

Malta Insurance Association: 43A/2, St Paul's Bldgs, West St, Valletta VLT 1532; tel. 21232640; fax 21248388; e-mail mia@maltainsurance.org; internet www.maltainsurance.org; Pres. ALBERT P. MAMO; 22 mem. cos (2009).

Trade and Industry

GOVERNMENT AGENCIES

Malta Enterprise: Enterprise Centre, Industrial Estate, San Gwann SGN 3000; tel. 25420000; fax 25423401; e-mail info@maltaenterprise.com; internet www.maltaenterprise.com; f. 2004; Exec. Chair. ALAN CAMILLERI.

Malta Investment Management Co Ltd (MIMCOL): Enterprise Centre, San Gwann Industrial Estate, San Gwann SGN 3000; tel. 21497970; fax 21499568; e-mail info@mimcol.com; internet www.mimcol.com; f. 1988; manages govt investments in domestic commercial enterprises and encourages their transfer to private sector ownership; Chair. JOHN IVAN FALZON; CEO MARIO MIZZI.

EMPLOYERS' ORGANIZATIONS

The Malta Chamber of Commerce, Enterprise and Industry: Exchange Bldgs, Republic St, Valletta VLT 1117; tel. 21233873; fax 21245223; e-mail info@maltachamber.org.mt; internet www.maltachamber.org.mt; f. 2008 by merger of Malta Chamber of Commerce and Enterprise with Malta Federation of Industry; Pres. HELGA ELLUL; 1,200 mems.

Malta Employers' Association: 35/1 South St, Valletta VLT 1100; tel. 21222992; fax 21230227; e-mail admin@maltaemployers.com; internet www.maltaemployers.com; f. 1965; Pres. JOSHUA ZAMMIT; Dir-Gen. JOSEPH FARRUGIA.

UTILITIES

Malta Resources Authority: Millennia, 2nd Floor, Aldo Moro Rd, Marsa MRS 9065; tel. 21220619; fax 22955200; e-mail enquiry@mra.org.mt; internet www.mra.org.mt; set up by the Maltese Parliament through the Malta Resources Authority Act of 2000; regulates water and energy utilities; Chair. Dr REUBEN BALZAN; CEO ANTHONY RIZZO.

Electricity and Gas

Easygas (Malta) Ltd: Malta; licensed supplier of LPG gas.

Enemalta Corporation: Church Wharf, Marsa HMR 01; tel. 21224600; fax 21246637; e-mail info.emc@enemalta.com.mt; internet www.enemalta.com.mt; f. 1977; state-owned energy corpn responsible for generating and distributing electricity and storing liquefied petroleum gas for the distributors; Acting Chair. WILLIAM SPITERI BAILEY; CEO Ing. KARL V. A. CAMILLERI.

Liquigas Malta Limited: Freeport Centre, Kalafrana, B'Buga BBG 3011; tel. 21651661; fax 22486060; e-mail info@liquigasmalta.com; internet www.liquigasmalta.com; jt venture of Liquigas S.p.A (Italy) and Multigas Limited (Malta); responsible for providing LPG gas; CEO ROBERTO CAPELLUTO.

Water

Water Services Corporation: Qormi Rd, Luqa LQA 9043; tel. 22445566; fax 22443900; e-mail customercare@wsc.com.mt; internet www.wsc.com.mt; f. 1992; govt corpn responsible for the production and distribution of drinking water and the local sewerage system; Chair. MICHAEL FALZON; CEO MARC MUSCAT.

TRADE UNIONS

Confederation of Malta Trade Unions (CMTU): 9C Mikiel Anton Vassalli St, Valletta VLT 1310; tel. 21237313; fax 21250146; e-mail info@cmtu.org.mt; internet www.cmtu.org.mt; f. 1958; affiliated to the World Confed. of Labour, to the Commonwealth Trade Union Council and to the ETUC; Pres. WILLIAM PORTELLI; Gen. Sec. CHARLES MAGRO.

The principal affiliated unions include:

General Retailers & Traders Union (GRTU) (Asscn of General Retailers and Traders): Exchange Bldgs, Republic St, Valletta VLT 1117; tel. 21232881; fax 21246925; e-mail info@grtu.org.mt; internet www.grtu.org.mt; f. 1948; Pres. PAUL ABELA; Dir-Gen. VINCENT FARRUGIA; 7,000 mems.

Union Haddiema Maghqudin (UHM) (Malta Workers' Union): 'Dar Reggie Miller', St Thomas St, Floriana FLN 1123; tel. 21220847; fax 21246091; e-mail info@uhm.org.mt; internet www.uhm.org.mt; f. 1966; also affiliated to Malta Confed. of Women's Org, to the National Council of Women, to the National Youth Council and to the Malta Council of the European Movement; Pres. GAETANO TANTI; Sec.-Gen. GETJU VELLA.

Malta Union of Teachers: Teachers' Institute, 213 Republic St, Valletta VLT 1118; tel. 21237815; fax 21244074; e-mail info@mut.org.mt; internet www.mut.org.mt; f. 1919; Pres. JOHN BENCINI; Gen. Sec. FRANKLIN BARBARA.

The General Workers' Union (GWU): Workers' Memorial Bldg, South St, Valletta VLT 1100; tel. 25679200; e-mail info@gwu.org.mt; internet www.gwu.org.mt; f. 1943; affiliated to the ITUC, the ETUC, and other European federations; Pres. VICTOR CARACHI; Gen. Sec. TONY ZARB.

Transport

REGULATORY BODIES

Malta Transport Authority: Sa Maison Rd, Floriana FRN 1613; tel. 25608000; fax 21255740; e-mail info@maltatransport.com; internet www.maltatransport.com; regulatory body for all land transport in Malta; Chair. SIMON VELLA.

RAILWAYS

There are no railways in Malta.

ROADS

In 2008 there were 3,096 km of roads, of which about 87.5% of roads were paved. Bus services serve all parts of the main island and most parts of Gozo.

Roads Department: Cannon Rd, St Venera SVR 9030; tel. 21483609; fax 21243753; e-mail carmel.zammit@magnet.mt; Chair. C. DEMICOLI; CEO M. FALZON.

SHIPPING

Malta's national shipping register is open to ships of all countries. At 31 December 2009 Malta's merchant fleet comprised 1,613 vessels, with a total displacement of 35.0m. grt. The island's dry dock facilities are also an important source of revenue.

Malta Maritime Authority: Maritime Trade Centre, Xatt l-Ghassara ta' l-Gheneb, Marsa MRS 1912; tel. 21222203; fax 21250365; e-mail info@mma.gov.mt; internet www.mma.gov.mt; f. 1991; govt agency supervising the administration and operation of ports and yachting centres, and of vessel registrations under the Maltese flag; Chair. MARK PORTELLI; CEO Dr STANLEY PORTELLI.

Bianchi & Co (1916) Ltd: Palazzo Marina, 143 St Christopher St, Valletta VLT 1465; tel. 21232241; fax 21232991; e-mail info@bianchi.com.mt; Man. Dir R. BIANCHI.

Cassar & Cooper Ltd: Valletta Bldgs, 54 South St, POB 311, Valletta VLT 1103; tel. 25584000; fax 21237864; e-mail info@cassar-cooper.com; internet www.cassar-cooper.com; cargo shipping; also ship agency; Dir MICHAEL COOPER.

Gollcher Group: 19 Saint Zachary St, POB 268, Valletta VLT 1133; tel. 25691100; fax 21234195; e-mail contact@gollcher.com; internet www.gollcher.com; f. 1854; Dir MARK GOLLCHER.

MALTA

Malta Freeport Terminals Ltd: Freeport Centre, Port of Marsaxlokk, Kalafrana BBG 3011; tel. 21650200; fax 22251900; e-mail marketing@maltafreeport.com.mt; internet www.maltafreeport.com.mt; f. 1988; 2 container terminals; also operates petroleum products terminal and general warehousing facilities; Man. Dir UWE MALEZKI.

Malta Motorways of the Sea Ltd: 21–22 St Barbara Bastion, Valletta VLT 1961; tel. 21251564; fax 21226876; e-mail info@mmos.com.mt; internet www.mmos.com.mt; f. 2005; owned by Grimaldi Group (Italy); operates ro-ro and passenger ferry services between Malta, Italy (including Sicily) and Libya; Man. Dir ERNEST SULLIVAN; Gen. Man. JOE BUGEJA.

Medserv PLC: Malta Freeport, Port of Marsaxlokk, Birzebbugia BBG 3011; tel. 22202302; fax 22202328; e-mail info@medservmalta.com; internet www.medservmalta.com; logistic and supply base for petroleum and gas extraction industry; Dirs ANTHONY S. DIACONO, ANTHONY J. DUNCAN; Gen. Man. GODWIN BORG.

Mifsud Brothers Ltd: 26 South St, Valletta VLT 1102; tel. 21232157; fax 21221331; e-mail info@mbl.com.mt; internet www.mbl.com.mt; f. 1860; shipping and travel agents; Man. Dir IVAN MIFSUD.

SMS Shipping: 131 East St, Valletta VLT 1252; tel. 21233127; fax 21234180; e-mail ship@sms.com.mt; internet www.sms.com.mt; ship and forwarding agency; also ship supplies and bunkering; subsidiary of SMS Group Ltd; Exec. Man. PAUL SAVONA.

Sullivan Shipping Agencies Ltd: Exchange Bldgs, Republic St, Valletta VLT 1117; tel. 21245127; fax 21233417; e-mail info@sullivanshipping.com.mt; internet www.sullivanshipping.com.mt; Chair. and CEO JOHN E. SULLIVAN.

Thomas Smith & Co Ltd: 12 St Christopher St, Valletta VLT 1468; tel. 22058000; fax 22058199; e-mail info@tcsmith.com; internet www.tcsmith.com; Man. Dir JOE GERADA.

Virtu Ferries Ltd: Ta' Xbiex Terrace, Ta'Xbiex XBX 1034; tel. 23491000; fax 21314533; e-mail info@virtuferries.com; internet www.virtuferries.com; f. 1945; Malta–Sicily (Italy) express passenger ferry service.

CIVIL AVIATION

Malta International Airport is situated at Gudja (8 km from Valletta).

Air Malta PLC: Vjal l'Avjazzjoni, Luqa LQA 9023; tel. 21690890; fax 21692861; e-mail info@airmalta.com.mt; internet www.airmalta.com; f. 1973; national airline with a 96.4% state shareholding; scheduled passenger and cargo services to mainland Europe, the United Kingdom, North Africa and the Middle East; charter services to the United Kingdom and mainland Europe; Chair. SONNY PORTELLI; CEO PETER DAVIES.

Tourism

Malta offers climatic, scenic and historical attractions, including fine beaches. Tourism forms a major sector of Malta's economy, generating foreign exchange earnings of US $1,215m. in 2008. Tourist arrivals totalled 1,290,856 in 2008 and 1,182,490 in 2009.

Malta Tourism Authority (MTA): Auberge d'Italie, Merchants St, Valletta VLT 1170; tel. 22915000; fax 22915394; e-mail info@visitmalta.com; internet www.mta.com.mt; Chair. LOUIS FARRUGIA; CEO JOSEF FORMOSA GAUCI.

Defence

As assessed at November 2010, the armed forces of Malta comprised a regular army of 1,954. There was also a reserve of 167. Military service is voluntary.

Defence Expenditure: €5,935m. in 2009 (2.1% of total expenditure).

Commander of the Armed Forces: Brig. MARTIN G. XUEREB.

Education

The Ministry of Education, Employment and the Family is responsible for providing all levels of education. From the age of two years and nine months until the age of four years, children study in kindergarten centres, although it is not compulsory. Provision is free in all government schools and church schools. Education is free and compulsory between the ages of five and 16 years. In 2006/07 enrolment at pre-primary level included 86% of children in the relevant age-group. Primary education begins at five years of age and lasts for six years. In 2006/07 enrolment at primary level included 91% of children in the relevant age-group. Secondary education, beginning at 11 years of age, lasts for a maximum of seven years, but this period is extended in the case of technology and vocational courses. Enrolment at secondary level in 2006/07 included 82% of children in the relevant age-group. After completing five years of secondary-level education, students with the necessary qualifications may opt to follow a higher academic, technical or vocational course. The junior college, administrated by the University of Malta, is attended by students aged between 16 and 18 years. It prepares students specifically for a university course by providing them with a Matriculation Certificate after successful completion of a two-year course. About 30% of the student population attend schools administered by the Roman Catholic Church, from kindergarten to higher secondary level. The Government subsidizes the provision of free education for students in church schools. Higher education is available at the University of Malta. There are also a number of technical institutes, specialist schools and an extended skills training scheme for trade-school graduates. There were 9,472 students enrolled in higher education in 2007/08. The Government also provides adult education courses. General government expenditure on education totalled €321.7m. (12.74% of total expenditure) in 2009.

THE MARSHALL ISLANDS

Introductory Survey

LOCATION, CLIMATE, LANGUAGE, RELIGION, FLAG, CAPITAL

The Republic of the Marshall Islands consists of two groups of islands, the Ratak ('sunrise') and Ralik ('sunset') chains, comprising 29 atolls (some 1,225 islets) and five islands, and covering about 180 sq km (70 sq miles) of land. The territory lies within the area of the Pacific Ocean known as Micronesia (which includes Kiribati, Tuvalu and other territories). The islands lie about 3,200 km (2,000 miles) south-west of Hawaii and about 2,100 km (1,300 miles) south-east of Guam. Rainfall decreases from south to north, with January, February and March being the driest months, although seasonal variations in rainfall and temperature are generally small. The native population comprises various ethno-linguistic groups, but English is widely understood. The principal religion is Christianity. The national flag (proportions 100 by 190) is dark blue, with a representation of a white star (with 20 short and four long rays) in the upper hoist; superimposed across the field are two progressively wider stripes (orange above white), running from near the lower hoist corner to near the upper fly corner. The capital is the Delap-Uliga-Darrit Municipality, on Majuro Atoll.

CONTEMPORARY POLITICAL HISTORY

Historical Context

The first European contact with the Marshall and Caroline Islands was by Spanish expeditions in the 16th century, including those led by Alvaro de Saavedra and Fernão de Magalhães (Ferdinand Magellan), the Portuguese navigator. The islands received their name from the British explorer, John Marshall, who visited them at the end of the 18th century. Spanish sovereignty over the Marshall Islands was recognized in 1886 by the Papal Bull of Pope Leo XIII, which also gave Germany trading rights there (German trading companies had been active in the islands from the 1850s). In 1899 Germany bought from Spain the Caroline Islands and the Northern Mariana Islands (except Guam, which had been ceded to the USA after the Spanish–American War of 1898). In 1914, at the beginning of the First World War, Japan occupied the islands, and received a mandate for its administration from the League of Nations in 1920. After the capture of the islands by US military forces in 1944 and 1945, most of the Japanese settlers were repatriated, and in 1947 the UN established the Trust Territory of the Pacific Islands (comprising the Caroline Islands, the Marshall Islands and the Northern Mariana Islands), to allow the USA to administer the region. The territory was governed by the US Navy from 1947 until 1951, when control passed to a civil administration—although the Northern Mariana Islands remained under military control until 1962.

From 1965 onwards there were increasing demands for local autonomy. In that year the Congress of Micronesia was formed; in 1967 a commission was established to examine the future political status of the islands. In 1970 it declared Micronesians' rights to sovereignty over their own lands, of self-determination, to their own constitution and to revoke any form of free association with the USA. In 1977, after eight years of negotiations, US President Jimmy Carter announced that his Administration intended to adopt measures to terminate the trusteeship agreement by 1981.

On 9 January 1978 the Marianas District achieved separate status as the Commonwealth of the Northern Mariana Islands (q.v.), but remained legally a part of the Trusteeship until 1986. The Marshall Islands District drafted its own Constitution, which came into effect on 1 May 1979, and the four districts of Yap, Truk (now Chuuk), Ponape (now Pohnpei) and Kosrae ratified a new Constitution, to become the Federated States of Micronesia (q.v.), on 10 May 1979. In the Palau District a referendum in July 1979 approved a proposed local constitution, which took effect on 1 January 1981, when the district became the Republic of Palau (q.v.).

Having signed a Compact of Free Association with the Republic of Palau in August 1982, the USA reached agreement with the Marshall Islands on land use in October of that year. The trusteeship of the islands was due to end after the principle and terms of the Compacts had been approved by the respective peoples and legislatures of the new countries, by the US Congress and by the UN Security Council. Under the Compacts, the four countries (including the Northern Mariana Islands) would be independent of each other and would manage their internal and foreign affairs separately, while the USA would be responsible for defence and security. Moreover, Marshallese citizens were granted the right to live and work in the USA. In June 1983 the final draft of the Compact of Free Association with the USA was signed by the Marshall Islands. The Compacts with the Federated States of Micronesia and the Marshall Islands were approved in plebiscites in June and September 1983, respectively. The Congress of the Federated States of Micronesia ratified the country's decision in September. Under the Compact with the Marshall Islands, the USA was to retain its military bases in the Marshall Islands for at least 15 years and, over the same period, was to provide annual aid of US $30m.

Domestic Political Affairs

The Compact between the Marshall Islands and the USA took effect on 21 October 1986, following its approval by the islands' Government. In November US President Ronald Reagan issued a proclamation formally ending US administration of Micronesia. The first President of the Republic of the Marshall Islands was Iroijlaplap (Paramount Chief) Amata Kabua, who was re-elected in 1984, 1988, 1992 and 1995. In December 1990 the UN Security Council finally ratified the termination of the trusteeship agreement; the Marshall Islands became a member of the UN in 1991. Prior to their scheduled expiry in 2001, the terms of Compact were extended for a further two-year period, pending negotiation of new arrangements (see below).

The Marshall Islands' atolls of Bikini and Enewetak were used by the USA for experiments with nuclear weapons: Bikini in 1946–58 and Enewetak in 1948–58. A total of 67 such tests were carried out during this period. The native inhabitants of Enewetak were evacuated before tests began, and were allowed to return to the atoll in 1980, after much of the contaminated area had supposedly been rendered safe. The inhabitants of Bikini Atoll campaigned for similar treatment, and in 1985 the US Administration agreed to decontaminate Bikini Atoll over a period of 10–15 years. In 1985 the entire population of Rongelap Atoll, which had been engulfed by radioactive fall-out from the tests at Bikini in 1954, was forced to resettle on Mejato Atoll, after surveys suggested that levels of radiation at Rongelap remained dangerous. In April 2001, following the adoption by the USA of a new standard of radioactivity considered to be acceptable, some six times lower than the previous level, the Tribunal announced that Ailuk Atoll was to be evacuated and environmental studies conducted.

Under the terms of the Compact, the US Government consented to establish a US $150m. Nuclear Claims Fund to settle claims against the USA resulting from nuclear testing in the Marshall Islands during the 1940s and 1950s. Accordingly, the Marshall Islands Nuclear Claims Tribunal was established in 1988, with jurisdiction to 'render final determination upon all claims past, present and future, of the Government, citizens and nationals of the Marshall Islands' in respect of the nuclear testing programme. A compensation programme was implemented in 1991 for personal injuries deemed to have resulted from the testing programme. Following an approach defined in legislation adopted by the US Congress in 1990, which established a 'presumptive' programme of compensation for specified diseases contracted by US civilian and military personnel who had been physically present in what was termed the 'affected area' during periods of atmospheric testing in Nevada, the Marshall Islands Nuclear Claims Tribunal initially identified 25 diseases for which credible evidence demonstrated a significant statistical relationship between exposure to radiation and subsequent development of a disease; in response to the findings of later studies, the Tribunal's list had by 2003 been extended to include 11 further conditions. Compensation awards totalling $83m. had by the end of 2003 been made to, or on behalf of, 1,865 individuals who had contracted one or more of these conditions. Additionally, an award of some $578m. had been ordered in May 2000 in respect of a class action brought by the people of Enewetak for loss of and damage to property; and an award of $563m. had been made in March 2002 in settlement of a class action brought by the peoples of Bikini Atoll; settlements of similar class actions by the peoples of Rongelap and Utrik Atolls were being finalized, while a new class action had been submitted by the people of Ailuk Atoll. However, only $45.8m. had been made available for actual payment of awards decided by the Tribunal; furthermore, less than $6m. remained of the original value of the Fund. In view of the inadequacy of the Fund to meet the compensation awards made by the Tribunal, in September 2000 the Marshall Islands Government formally petitioned the US Congress for a renegotiation of the settlement agreed under the Compact; the basis of the petition, which sought additional compensation amounting to some $3,000m., was an article of the agreement providing for what were termed 'Changed Circumstances'. In August 2004 the Tribunal declared a deadline for islanders' compensation claims of the end of that month (subsequently extended to 31 December). The reason given for the deadline was that the Tribunal's funds had diminished to some $5m., a level that not only jeopardized future compensation payments but also the very existence of the Tribunal itself.

In January 2005, following the publication of a report by the US Department of State's Bureau of East Asian and Pacific Affairs, the Administration of George W. Bush recommended that Congress reject the Marshall Islands' request for additional compensation payments, citing a lack of a scientific or legal basis for the request. In February delegates from Bikini, Rongelap, Enewetak and Utrik met in the US city of Seattle with officials of the US Senate Committee on Energy and Natural Resources in preparation for a congressional hearing on the Marshall Islands' request for additional payments. At the hearing, held in May, the Bush Administration's rejection of the appeal was reiterated, although several committee members expressed support for further consideration of the matter. At a Small Islands Summit meeting held in October in the Papua New Guinean capital of Port Moresby, the Marshall Islands' delegation reiterated its demand for a further US $3,000m. in compensation from the US Government. In April 2006 it was announced that the people of Bikini were suing the US Government in the Court of Federal Claims for $561m. as compensation or damages: the original award of $563m. minus the actual payment of $2.3m. The Marshall Islands Government expressed its support for the action. In April 2007 the Marshall Islands Nuclear Claims Tribunal ruled that claimants of Rongelap should receive $1,000m. in compensation; at the same time, however, the funds available to the Tribunal had decreased to just $1m. In August the Court of Federal Claims dismissed the lawsuit submitted against the US Government on the basis that it had been submitted after the expiry of a six-year statute of limitations for the filing of such claims. The lawyer representing the people of Bikini then took the case to the US Court of Appeals for the Federal Circuit, arguing that the Fifth Amendment forbade the acquisition of private property without compensation. In February 2009, however, the Court of Appeals upheld the judgment dismissing the claim. The US Supreme Court upheld the decision of the Court of Appeals in April 2010. Meanwhile, in March 2009, following confirmation by France that further consideration was to be given to compensation claims by those affected by its nuclear tests, the Marshall Islands renewed its request for additional compensation from the US Government. An amended version of a US Senate bill first proposed in September 2007, which had sought additional compensation for inhabitants of Bikini, Enewetak, Rongelap and Utrik, was introduced to the upper congressional chamber in mid-February 2011; the bill was subsequently referred to the Senate Committee on Energy and Natural Resources.

In January 1994, meanwhile, several senior members of the Marshall Islands' legislature, the Nitijela, demanded that the US authorities release detailed information on the effects of its nuclear-testing programme in the islands. In July documentation released by the US Department of Energy gave conclusive evidence that Marshall Islanders had been deliberately exposed to high levels of radiation in order that its effects on their health could be studied by US medical researchers. Further evidence emerged during 1995 that the USA had withheld the medical records of islanders involved in radiation experiments (which included tritium and chromium-51 injections and genetic and bone-marrow transplant experiments).

Despite the publication of a study conducted by US scientists (in 1992) into contamination levels on Bikini Atoll, which suggested that radiation levels there remained dangerous, in February 1997 a group of Bikini Islanders returned for the first time since 1946 to assist in the rehabilitation of the atoll for resettlement. The operation was to involve the removal of radioactive topsoil (although the matter of its disposal presented a serious problem) and the saturation of the remaining soil with potassium, which was believed to inhibit the absorption of radioactive material by root crops. In early 1999 the Nuclear Claims Tribunal demanded the adoption of US Environmental Protection Agency standards in the rehabilitation of contaminated islands, claiming that Marshall Islanders deserved to receive the same treatment as US citizens would in similar circumstances. The US Department of Energy, however, expressed strong resistance to the suggestion. In February 2001 a report published by an eminent Japanese scientist stated that radiation levels on Rongelap Island, according to research conducted in 1999, had now declined to such a level that human habitation of the island was again possible. In early 2004 the Marshall Islands protested that a reduction, decided upon by the US Department of Energy without consultation with Island representatives, of some US $740,000 in congressional funding allocated to nuclear test-related studies would result in the closure of a centre on Bikini Atoll used to support scientific studies at the former test site. A UN General Assembly committee adopted a resolution in April 2010 undertaking to produce by the end of 2011 a comprehensive report examining the effects of the USA's nuclear-testing programme in the Marshall Islands.

Another atoll in the Marshall Islands, Kwajalein, has been used since 1947 as a target for the testing of missiles fired from California, USA. The Compact as ratified in 1986 committed the US Government to provide an estimated US $170m. in rent over a period of 30 years for land used as the site of a missile-tracking station, and a further $80m. for development projects. The inhabitants of Kwajalein Atoll were concentrated on the small island of Ebeye, adjacent to the US base on Kwajalein Island, before a new programme of weapons-testing began in 1961. Consequent overcrowding reportedly led to numerous social problems on Ebeye. In 1989 the Marshall Islands Government agreed that the USA could lease a further four islands in the atoll, for five years, for the purpose of military tests. A further lease agreement was signed in 1995 for the use of Biken Island (in Aur Atoll) and Wake Island in the missile-testing programme. The issue of the Kwajalein lease proved to be one of the most controversial aspects of the renegotiated terms of the Compact, as signed in 2003 (see below). In January 2003 it was announced that the Marshall Islands Government and the USA had reached agreement on new terms extending the lease of the Kwajalein site, previously scheduled to end in 2016, until 2066 (with the USA retaining the right to extend the lease by a further 20 years). The renegotiated terms envisaged that payments for use of the site would be increased from $13.5m. annually to $16.9m. (including continued provision of $1.9m. annually in social funding for the residents of Ebeye), with a further increase, to more than $19.9m. per year, to enter into effect from 2014. However, Kwajalein landowners, who deemed the new terms unacceptable, asserted that the new arrangement was invalid, since they had not consented, as constitutionally required, to its terms. The landowners refused to accept the agreement.

Following the legislative election of November 1995, at which eight incumbent members of the 33-seat Nitijela were defeated, President Kabua was re-elected for a fifth term. Upon his death in December 1996, Iroijlaplap Imata Kabua, a cousin of the late President, was elected to succeed him in January 1997.

In 1996 the Nitijela approved legislation allowing for the introduction of gambling in the islands, in order to provide an additional source of revenue. However, income earned from the venture did not fulfil expectations. Moreover, a vociferous campaign by local church leaders to revoke the legislation led to fierce debate in the Nitijela in early 1998. In April the Nitijela voted to repeal the law legalizing gambling: several influential politicians (including Imata Kabua) known to have major gambling interests were disqualified from voting. A second bill containing further measures to ensure the prohibition of all gambling activity in the islands was narrowly approved. Three ministers who had supported the anti-gambling legislation were dismissed in a cabinet reorganization in August. In the following month one of the dismissed ministers proposed a motion of no confidence in Kabua. The President and his supporters boycotted subsequent sessions of the Nitijela, thereby rendering the legislature inquorate and effectively precluding the vote, as well as delaying the approval of the budget for the impending financial year. Despite opposition claims that Kabua's continued absence from the Nitijela violated the terms of the Constitution, the motion of no confidence in Kabua was eventually defeated by a margin of one vote in October.

At the legislative election of November 1999 the opposition United Democratic Party (UDP) secured a convincing victory over the incumbent administration, winning 18 of the 33 seats in the Nitijela. Five senior members of the outgoing Government were defeated, including the Ministers of Finance and of Foreign Affairs and Trade—both of whom had played a prominent role in the establishment of diplomatic relations with Taiwan in 1998 (see below). The former Nitijela Speaker, Kessai Note, was elected President on 3 January 2000 (the islands' first non-traditional leader to assume the post). The UDP Chairman, Litokwa Tomeing, became Speaker of the legislature. Note subsequently appointed a 10-member Cabinet, and reiterated his administration's intention to pursue anti-corruption policies. In May a task-force was established by the Government for the purposes of investigating misconduct and corruption.

In November 2000 it was reported that finance officials had discovered that Imata Kabua had used funds granted to the Marshall Islands under the terms of the Compact of Free Association to pay off a personal loan, although the former President denied any wrongdoing. In January 2001 Imata Kabua and former ministers in his Government, including the former Minister of Education, Justin deBrum, presented a no confidence motion against President Note to the Nitijela. Although it was suggested that the vote had been intended to delay the publication of a report into mismanagement and corruption on the part of the former Government, deBrum stated that the motion resulted from a number of failings by the Note Government, including its unwillingness to renegotiate land rental payments with the USA for the use of the military base on Kwajalein Atoll. However, the Government was successful in defeating the vote by a margin of 19 to 14.

In September 2000 the Nitijela approved legislation to ensure the closer regulation of the banking and financial sector. In May of that year the Group of Seven industrialized nations (G7) had expressed its view that the Marshall Islands had become a significant centre for the laundering of money generated by international criminal activity, and in June the Marshall Islands was one of more than 30 countries and territories criticized by the Organisation for Economic Co-operation and Development (OECD, see p. 376) for the provision of inappropriate 'offshore' financial establishments. OECD threatened to implement sanctions against 'unco-operative tax havens' unless reforms were introduced before July 2001. The Marshall Islands remained on the OECD list of unco-operative tax havens until 2007. In October 2002, meanwhile, following a commendation from the IMF on a series of new measures to combat fraud, including specific legislation and the establishment of a Domestic Financial Intelligence Unit, the Financial Action Task Force on Money Laundering (see p. 451) removed the Marshall Islands from its list of countries judged to be unhelpful in the combating of international financial crime.

Negotiations began between the US and Marshall Islands Governments in July 2001 to renew the provisions of the Compact of Free Association ratified in 1986, which was due to expire at the end of September 2001. A two-year extension was permitted while negotiations were under way, during which time annual assistance to the Marshall Islands was to increase by some US $5.5m. An agreement was originally scheduled for early 2002 in order to allow adequate time for the US Congress to review it and to approve the requisite legislation (by 1 October 2003), but the procedure was postponed until early May 2002 after the Marshall Islands Government submitted a proposal seeking financing of more than $1,000m. over 15 years. The Government had also objected to being allocated 25%–30% less in US grant assistance per caput than that apportioned to the Federated States of Micronesia since the year 2000. In a further attempt to increase the national income, the Government sought to raise significantly the level of taxes levied on the Kwajalein base (see above). In early November 2002 the USA and the Marshall Islands announced a programme of direct funding of $822m., to be disbursed over 20 years, in addition to the expansion of many US government services in the islands. It was envisaged that the Marshall Islands would receive some $30.5m. a year; furthermore, a trust fund would be established, to which the USA would contribute $7m. annually in order to provide a means of income after the termination of direct US assistance in 2023. The amended Compact of Free Association was signed by the Governments of the Marshall Islands and the USA in May 2003. Under the new Compact, Marshall Islanders would for the first time require passports in order to enter the USA. They would, however, retain the right to enter the USA to live, work and study, and would no longer be required to obtain work authorization documentation before taking up employment in the USA. Other than the issue of the Kwajalein lease, a principal obstacle to the negotiation of Compact amendments had been that of immigration: the USA, increasingly preoccupied by issues of homeland security, had been notably concerned to prevent future sales of Marshallese passports (although this controversial programme had officially been suspended in 1997). Final terms, including the restoration of some rights of access to US health care and education programmes, were approved by the US Congress in November 2003, and ratified by President George W. Bush in December.

At a legislative election held on 17 November 2003 the UDP returned 20 Senators to the 33-member Nitijela. The opposition grouping Ailin Kein Ad (Our Islands), which had campaigned against the terms of the renewed Compact and which received particularly strong support from Marshall Islanders resident in the USA, secured 10 seats (the re-election of the incumbent Ailin Kein Ad Senator for Ailinglaplap Atoll was decided following a recount of votes conducted in late January 2004). Note was re-elected for a second presidential term in a vote held in the Nitijela on 4 January 2004, defeating Justin deBrum, the candidate of Ailin Kein Ad, by 20 votes to nine. He and his new Cabinet were sworn in on 12 January.

A legislative election was held on 19 November 2007. There were complaints in Majuro, where several polling stations failed to open at the appointed time; irregularities in the counting procedure were subsequently criticized. The level of participation was relatively low, at approximately 50%. According to unofficial results published in December, neither the incumbent UDP nor the opposition Ailin Kein Ad had succeeded in securing the requisite majority of 17 or more seats; both parties contested the results. While the UDP claimed that it should remain in power, Ailin Kein Ad—which had gained former Speaker and UDP leader Litokwa Tomeing as a member prior to the election—maintained that, with the support of independent candidates, its United People's Party coalition would be able to defeat the UDP. Recounts in two constituencies and negotiations between the parties and independent candidates followed. The United People's Party coalition prevailed in January 2008, when the Nitijela elected Tomeing as the country's President by 18 votes (to 15 for the incumbent President Kessai Note), and Jurelang Zedkaia as Speaker by the same margin. Tomeing's new Cabinet included Christopher Loeak in the position of Minister in Assistance to the President and Tony deBrum as Minister of Foreign Affairs.

In February 2008 President Tomeing established a commission of inquiry into the organizational failures of the 2007 election. The commission published its findings in August 2008; the election failures were attributed to the former Minister of Internal Affairs, Rien Morris, and to the Public Service Commission. It was concluded that Morris had unconstitutionally interfered in the election process by appointing Carl Alik as the Chief Electoral Officer against the wishes of the Public Service Commission. The commission of inquiry made numerous recommendations, which included the establishment of an election commission of five independent members, who would be responsible for the appointment of the Chief Electoral Officer.

In April 2008 the Attorney-General, Posesi Bloomfield, resigned in order to pursue studies overseas. He was replaced by Filimon Manoni, who had served as chairman of the commission of inquiry into the election of 2007.

Recent developments: President Tomeing's removal and corruption allegations

In October 2008 the opposition UDP tabled a no-confidence motion against President Litokwa Tomeing, citing the Government's alleged failures in negotiations with the USA (notably with regard to the financing of health care for islanders affected by the nuclear tests between 1946 and 1958—see above) and its refusal to proceed with an elementary school project in Majuro. However, the motion was withdrawn after the opposition conceded that it had been unable to secure the requisite support of at least 17 of the 33 members of the Nitijela.

Tony deBrum was dismissed as Minister of Foreign Affairs in February 2009, following his public criticism of President Tome-

THE MARSHALL ISLANDS

ing's administration. DeBrum had been particularly critical of the President's perceived failure to provide sufficient support to landowners in their attempts to secure an increase in the rents payable to them by the USA for the use of the military base at Kwajalein Atoll (see above). John Silk was subsequently appointed as deBrum's replacement.

In April 2009 the Ailin Kein Ad and the United People's Party coalition presented a motion of no confidence against President Tomeing, which was defeated by 18 ballots to 14, after UDP members of the Nitijela voted in Tomeing's favour. Following the defeat of the motion, President Tomeing announced a cabinet reorganization in which several ministers were dismissed, including Christopher Loeak, who was replaced as Minister in Assistance to the President by Ruben Zackhras. All of the incoming ministers were members of the opposition UDP.

President Tomeing was finally ousted from power when a third motion of no confidence was submitted against him in October 2009. In the first successful vote of no confidence in the history of the Marshall Islands, the motion was carried by 17 ballots to 15. A few days later an election was conducted by the Nitijela to appoint Tomeing's replacement; Jurelang Zedkaia, hitherto Speaker of the Nitijela, emerged victorious, defeating former President Kessai Note by 17 votes to 15. Zedkaia was formally sworn in as the new President in early November; during the inauguration ceremony, Zedkaia pledged to put an end to the factionalism that had characterized the Nitijela since the 2007 elections, as well as to improve the quality of services in the fields of health, education and in the outer islands. With the exception of the Minister of Justice, David Kramer, who resigned and was replaced by Brenson Wase, Zedkaia retained all the members of his predecessor's Cabinet. Alvin Jacklick was elected as the new Speaker of the Nitijela in mid-November. In January 2010, at the first session of the Nitijela since his appointment, Jacklick undertook to implement reforms intended to reduce spending and to improve the quality of legislation and service to the public.

In late 2010 allegations emerged of widespread government fraud, with two criminal cases filed against the Ministry of Finance and the Ministry of Health in December. On the opening day of the new parliamentary session in early January 2011, President Zedkaia pledged to ensure that those persons found to have been complicit in any wrongdoing would be prosecuted 'to the fullest extent of the law'. By the end of January three employees at the Ministry of Finance and two at the Ministry of Health had been suspended in relation to the allegations. Officials at the Ministry of Education were reported also to have been incriminated by the findings of the police investigation, which remained ongoing at mid-2011, and which was reported to have uncovered evidence of fraud and theft within government departments dating back as far as 2006. According to local media reports, in mid-January 2011 the US embassy in Majuro had formally notified the Marshall Islands Government of its 'interest' in the situation and requested additional information on the ongoing investigation.

Environmental Concerns

In 1989 a UN report on the greenhouse effect (heating of the earth's atmosphere) predicted a possible resultant rise in sea-level of some 3.7 m by 2030, which would completely submerge the Marshall Islands. In early 2002 the Intergovernmental Panel on Climate Change (IPCC) projected that during the 21st century global sea-level rises would submerge over 80% of Majuro Atoll. The islands appeared to be increasingly vulnerable to adverse weather conditions, as exemplified in December 2008 when a state of emergency was declared owing to widespread flooding that followed unusually high tides; hundreds of people were displaced and considerable damage was caused to property. In his opening address to mark the new parliamentary session in January 2011, President Jurelang Zedkaia identified climate change as 'the single most serious threat' to the Marshall Islands.

The Marshall Islands Government caused regional environmental concerns with regard to the possible establishment of large-scale facilities for the storage of nuclear waste. Criticism by the US Government of the plans, announced in 1994, was strongly denounced by the Marshall Islands authorities, which claimed that the project constituted the only opportunity for the country to generate sufficient income for the rehabilitation of contaminated islands and the provision of treatment for illnesses caused by the US nuclear-test programme. In mid-1997 President Imata Kabua announced the indefinite suspension of the project (despite the initiation of a feasibility study into the development of a nuclear-waste storage facility). The Government nevertheless approved plans for a new feasibility study on the subject in April 1998.

Regional Affairs

In February 2010 the leaders of eight western Pacific island states—the Marshall Islands, together with Kiribati, Micronesia, Nauru, Palau, Papua New Guinea, Solomon Islands and Tuvalu—convened in Koror, Palau, for the first Presidential Summit of the Parties to the Nauru Agreement (PNA), a multilateral organization established in 1982 with the aim of protecting the western Pacific region's tuna industry and improving the quality of its tuna fisheries through sustainable management and innovation. At the Summit, the member states signed the 'Koror Declaration', which provided for the implementation of a ban on tuna-fishing in an area in the Pacific Ocean encompassing some 4.5m. sq km. In October the PNA voted to expand the area in which fishing was prohibited, and to implement further restrictions on tuna-fishing in the wider region, including enhanced observer monitoring of licensed fishing vessels, with effect from 1 January 2011. It was estimated that about one-quarter of the global tuna catch was caught in the waters of the eight PNA members.

The Marshall Islands established full diplomatic relations with Taiwan in November 1998. The action was immediately condemned by the People's Republic of China, which in December severed diplomatic relations with the islands, closing its embassy in Majuro and suspending all intergovernmental agreements. The Note administration, which took office in January 2000, emphasized its commitment to the maintenance of diplomatic relations with Taiwan. In February 2001 a proposed visit by a flotilla of Taiwanese naval vessels to the Marshall Islands was vetoed by the USA, on the grounds that the defence protocol of the Compact of Free Association prohibited such a visit. In August 2004 the Chinese Vice-Minister of Foreign Affairs, Zhou Wenzhong, expressed his country's willingness to restore normal relations, on condition that the Marshall Islands withdraw its diplomatic recognition of Taiwan. In April 2005 it was alleged that members of the ruling UDP had accepted bribes from Chinese officials hoping to expedite a return to normal diplomatic relations and the end of Marshallese recognition of Taiwan; the Government denied the allegations. Meanwhile, in September 2004 it was announced that Taiwan was to contribute more than US $40m. over a 20-year period to the Marshall Islands trust fund established in May. In June 2006 a delegation of Marshall Islands parliamentary representatives paid a visit to the mainland Chinese capital of Beijing, at the invitation of the National People's Congress, causing consternation among some government officials over the effect on the Marshall Islands' relations with Taiwan (which in April had been bolstered by President Note's third trip to Taipei, where he met Taiwanese President Chen Shui-bian for discussions). The leader of the delegation, Vice-Speaker of the Nitijela Ruben Zackhras, insisted that the Marshall Islands was simply responding to an invitation, while the Ministry of Foreign Affairs reaffirmed the country's commitment to Taiwan. In January 2008 the newly elected President, Litokwa Tomeing, who had previously expressed support for alignment with China, nevertheless confirmed that strong links with Taiwan would continue, and reinforced this position during a visit by the Taiwanese Vice-President, Annette Lu, in late January. The Minister of Foreign Affairs, Tony deBrum, visited Taiwan in February; his visit was followed by that of President Tomeing in March.

Relations with Taiwan were further strengthened in March 2010 when Taiwanese President Ma Ying-jeou visited the Marshall Islands during a week-long tour of South Pacific allies; the theme of Ma's visit to the Marshall Islands was medical health. In late June–early July of that year Jurelang Zedkaia made his first official visit to Taiwan since assuming the presidency in November 2009. During his six-day visit Zedkaia met with President Ma, whereupon the two leaders acclaimed the positive results of recent medical co-operation and pledged further to enhance bilateral co-operation in a number of areas, including the fisheries industry, education, and arts and culture. President Ma also expressed his gratitude to the Marshall Islands for advocating more meaningful Taiwanese participation within the international community. During 2010 Taiwan had pledged to donate about US $10m., to be disbursed in quarterly payments of around $2.5m., to the Marshall Islands, as in previous years. The funding was intended to support the welfare of the local population through various government projects in the fields of, *inter alia*, construction, education, finance and transport. However, in January 2011 it was announced that the disbursement of the

THE MARSHALL ISLANDS

proportion of the fourth quarterly payment intended for development projects in the Marshall Islands, which amounted to some $1.5m., was not to be completed until a progress report detailing the results generated by the third-quarter funds had been submitted by the Marshall Islands Government. With Taiwanese funding accounting for almost 8% of total annual budgetary spending in the Marshall Islands, it was feared that Taiwan's imposition of more stringent accountability requirements for funding would hinder bilateral relations. The overdue payment was released by Taiwan in late March.

The Marshall Islands Government has consistently supported Japan at the International Whaling Commission, voting in favour of commercial whaling, and also in the country's attempt to secure a permanent seat on the UN Security Council. By 2008 Japan was reported to be the third largest donor of aid to the Marshall Islands (after the USA and Taiwan). In April of that year President Tomeing undertook an official visit to Japan, where he had discussions with Prime Minister Yasuo Fukuda. Climate change and rising sea levels were among the topics discussed. In December it was announced that Japan was to provide a grant of US $2.2m. to support the islands' energy sector. Following a covert investigation conducted by a British newspaper, *The Sunday Times*, it was claimed in June 2010 that the Marshall Islands' vote in favour of commercial whaling, together with those of Kiribati, St Kitts and Nevis, Grenada, Côte d'Ivoire and Guinea, had been secured as a result of Japanese bribery that was purported to include offers of additional aid donations, cash incentives and the funding of delegations' visits to whaling meetings. In an exchange between a Marshall Islands Marine Resources Authority official, Doreen deBrum, and an undercover reporter, deBrum was alleged to have stated: 'We support Japan because of what they give us'. DeBrum subsequently denied the allegations, while Japanese officials insisted that the issue of whaling played no part in Japan's aid programme. (In July 2001 the then head of the Japanese Fisheries Agency, Maseyuku Komatsu, had stated publicly that Japan used overseas aid as a tool with which to secure support for its position on whaling; however, this was swiftly denied in a formal statement issued by the Ministry.)

CONSTITUTION AND GOVERNMENT

The Constitution of the Republic of the Marshall Islands, which took effect on 1 May 1979, provides for a parliamentary form of government, with legislative authority vested in the 33-member Nitijela. The Nitijela (members of which are elected, by popular vote, for a four-year term) elects the President of the Marshall Islands (also a four-year mandate) from among its own members. Under the terms of the Compact of Free Association, the Republic of the Marshall Islands is a sovereign, self-governing state. The first Compact was finalized by the Governments of the Marshall Islands and the USA on 25 June 1983, and was effectively ratified by the US Congress on 14 January 1986. A revised Compact was signed by the Governments of the two countries on 1 May 2003; it was ratified by the US Congress in November 2003, and signed by US President George W. Bush in December of that year. Amendments to the Compact were signed in May 2004.

Local governmental units are the municipalities and villages. Elected Magistrates and Councils govern the municipalities. Village government is largely traditional.

REGIONAL AND INTERNATIONAL CO-OPERATION

The Marshall Islands is a member of the Pacific Community (see p. 410), the Pacific Islands Forum (see p. 413), the South Pacific Regional Trade and Economic Co-operation Agreement (SPARTECA, see p. 414), the UN's Economic and Social Commission for Asia and the Pacific (ESCAP, see p. 37) and the Asian Development Bank (ADB, see p. 202). The Marshall Islands hosts the secretariat of the Parties to the Nauru Agreement, a multilateral organization charged with protecting the tuna industry in the western Pacific region.

The Marshall Islands became a member of the UN in 1991, and participates in the Group of 77 (G77, see p. 447) developing countries.

ECONOMIC AFFAIRS

In 2009, according to estimates by the World Bank, the Marshall Islands' gross national income (GNI), measured at average 2007–09 prices, was US $187m., equivalent to $3,060 per head. During 2000–09, it was estimated, the population increased at an average annual rate of 2.0%; gross domestic product (GDP) per head declined, in real terms, at an average rate of 0.1% per year over the same period. According to figures from the UN, overall GDP increased, in real terms, at an estimated average annual rate of 2.6% in 2000–09; real GDP increased by 1.4% in 2008 and remained constant in 2009.

Agriculture is mainly on a subsistence level. The sector (including fishing and livestock-rearing) contributed an estimated 10.0% of GDP in 2009, according to UN estimates. According to FAO, the sector engaged 7,000 people (mainly in subsistence fishing) in mid-2011. Fishing engaged 5.1% of those employed in the private sector in 2006/07. The principal crops are coconuts, cassava and sweet potatoes. Copra production increased from 4,646 short tons in 2006 to an estimated 6,053 tons in 2007. Reports suggested that in 2007/08 the amount of copra processed exceeded 7,000 tons for only the third time since records began in 1951, assisted by improved shipping services and higher global prices for the commodity. In 2006/07 exports of coconut oil and copra cake accounted for 10.3% of the total value of exports. The fishing sector incorporates a commercial tuna-fishing industry, including a transshipment base on Majuro. A new tuna-processing plant, employing more than 600 local workers and built by a Chinese company, had become fully operational by 2009. The sale of fishing licences is an important source of revenue and earned the islands an estimated US $1.4m. in 2006/07. According to UN estimates, agricultural GDP increased by an annual average of 2.5% during 2000–09; the sector's GDP increased, in real terms, by 0.8% in 2008 and by 0.1% in 2009.

Industrial activities (including mining, manufacturing, construction and utilities) engaged 18.9% of the employed labour force in 1999, and contributed an estimated 19.2% of GDP in 2009 according to UN estimates. Construction and manufacturing employed 8.3% of private-sector wage-earners in 2006/07. The islands have few mineral resources, although there are high-grade phosphate deposits on Ailinglaplap Atoll. The industrial sector's GDP increased, in real terms, by an annual average of 2.5% during 2000–09; industrial GDP expanded by 0.8% in 2008 and by 0.1% in 2009.

Manufacturing activity, which provided 4.4% of GDP in 2009, according to UN estimates, consists mainly of the processing of coconuts (to produce copra and coconut oil) and other agricultural products, and of fish (see above). According to the IMF, manufacturing engaged 1.1% of those employed in the private sector in 2006/07. Manufacturing GDP increased, in real terms, by an annual average of 1.9% during 2000–09; the sector's GDP increased by 0.9% in 2008 and by 0.2% in 2009.

The construction sector contributed 11.4% of GDP in 2009, according to UN estimates. According to IMF figures, the sector engaged 14.2% of the employed population in the private sector in 2006/07. Construction GDP increased, in real terms, at an average annual rate of 2.7% during 2000–09; the sector's GDP increased 0.9% in 2008 and remained constant in 2009.

The islands are heavily reliant on imported diesel fuel for energy supplies. Severe difficulties in financing purchases of fuel led to the declaration of a state of economic emergency in 2008 (see below). A rapid energy assessment, funded by the Asian Development Bank (ADB), made numerous recommendations for greater energy efficiency in the islands. The wider use of alternative sources of energy, such as solar power, was under consideration.

The services sector (comprising trade, transport, storage, communications and other activities) engaged 59.8% of the employed labour force in 1999, and, according to UN estimates, provided an estimated 70.7% of GDP in 2009. The international shipping registry experienced considerable expansion following political unrest in Panama in 1989, and subsequently continued to expand (largely as a result of US, Japanese and South Korean ships' reflagging in the islands). The number of vessels registered rose from 853 in December 2005 to 1,376 at the end of 2009. Tourist receipts reached US $4.5m. in 2007 but declined to $3.0m in 2008. In comparison with the previous year, the number of tourist arrivals was reported to have declined by 7% in 2010, to 4,563 visitors. Services GDP increased, in real terms, at an average annual rate of 2.4% during 2000–09; the sector's GDP expanded by 1.1% in 2008 but declined in 2009 by 0.1%.

In 2008/09 the Marshall Islands recorded an estimated trade deficit of US $71.0m., while there was a deficit of $12.1m. on the current account of the balance of payments. According to the ADB, there was a current account deficit equivalent to 10.5% of GDP in 2009/10. The only significant domestic exports in 2006/07 were coconut products. Re-exports of diesel fuel totalled $13.3m. in 2005, their value greatly exceeding that of domestic exports.

THE MARSHALL ISLANDS

The principal imports in 2000 included mineral fuels and lubricants (which accounted for 37.3% of total expenditure on merchandise imports), food and live animals, and machinery and transport equipment. In 2006 the principal sources of imports were the USA (which provided 45.8% of total imports), Australia (8.4%) and Japan (8.1%). In 2000 the USA was also the principal export destination (purchasing 57.1% of total exports).

Financial assistance from the USA, in accordance with the terms stipulated in the Compact of Free Association, contributes a large part of the islands' revenue. Grants and military payments from the USA for use of the missile-testing site on Kwajalein, along with trust fund contributions, provide most government revenue. In 2011/12 the USA was to provide US $67.1m. in Compact funding to the Marshall Islands. Considerable support has also been provided by Taiwan since the late 1990s (see Contemporary Political History). The 2008/09 budget provided for expenditure of US $104.0m., including grants of $67.1m., while revenue totalled $103.7m. A budget surplus equivalent to 0.3% of GDP was reported in 2009/10, in comparison with a deficit of 1.8% in the previous year. The islands' external debt totalled $96m. in 2008/09. In that year the cost of debt-servicing was estimated to be the equivalent of 22.7% of revenue from the export of goods and services. Annual inflation in Majuro averaged 3.8% in 2000–08. According to the ADB, consumer prices increased by 14.7% in 2008, but rose by only 0.5% in 2009 and 1.0% in 2010. The ADB estimated that 30.9% of the work-force were unemployed in 2008. The rate of youth unemployment was estimated at 60% in 2006.

The amended Compact of Free Association, signed by the Governments of the Marshall Islands and the USA in 2003 (see Contemporary Political History), planned for the gradual decrease in grant assistance over a 20-year period. The Marshallese Government declared a state of economic emergency in July 2008, following sharp increases in the costs of essential imports of fuel and foodstuffs. Serious concerns with regard to the Marshall Islands' fiscal management re-emerged in late 2010. As a major investigation into allegations of fraud progressed, in February 2011 the USA threatened to suspend its funding. Meanwhile, Taiwan planned to transfer a total of US $1m. to the Government's trust fund each year until 2009 and thereafter, until 2023, an annual sum of $2.4m. In early 2011, however, in the first such occurrence, Taiwan's release of a quarterly payment was postponed for more than two months, pending the Marshall Islands' provision of a report complying with accountability requirements in relation to the previous quarter's expenditure (see Contemporary Political History). Foreign direct investment decreased from an estimated $6m. in 2008 to $3m. in 2009. Air Marshall Islands continued to operate at a substantial loss, the shortcomings of the state-owned domestic carrier having been cited as a factor in the closure in 2008 of a major scuba diving operation on Bikini Atoll. It was reported that in comparison with the previous year visitor arrivals from Japan declined by 38% in 2010, while arrivals from the USA decreased by 22%; however, the number of Taiwanese visitors increased by an estimated 58%. Rising international prices for copra and coconut oil resulted in an increase in export earnings from these sources in 2010. Tax collection in the islands was also reported to have improved. Following two consecutive years of contraction, in the 12 months to September 2010 GDP expanded by 0.5%, according to the ADB, which anticipated further growth, of 1.0%, in 2010/11. However, by early 2011 inflationary pressures were again in evidence, largely owing to steep rises in the costs of imports of fuel and other commodities.

PUBLIC HOLIDAYS

2012: 2 January (for New Year's Day), 1 March (Nuclear Victims' Remembrance Day), 6 April (Good Friday), 1 May (Constitution Day), 6 July (Fishermen's Day), 7 September (Dri-Jerbal), 28 September (Manit—Culture Day), 16 November (for Presidents' Day), 7 December (Kamolol—Gospel Day), 25 December (Christmas Day).

Statistical Survey

Source (unless otherwise indicated): Economic Policy, Planning and Statistics Office (EPPSO), Office of the President, POB 2, Majuro, MH 96960; tel. (625) 3802; fax (625) 3805; e-mail planning@ntamar.net; internet www.spc.int/prism/country/mh/stats.

AREA AND POPULATION

Area: 181.4 sq km (70.0 sq miles) (land only); two island groups, the Ratak Chain (88.1 sq km) and the Ralik Chain (93.3 sq km).

Population: 43,380 at census of 13 November 1988; 50,840 (males 26,026, females 24,814) at census of 1 June 1999. *By Island Group* (1999): Ratak Chain 30,925 (Majuro Atoll 23,676); Ralik Chain 19,915 (Kwajalein Atoll 10,902). *Mid-2011* (Secretariat of the Pacific Community estimate): 54,999 (Source: Pacific Regional Information System).

Density (mid-2011, land area only): 303.2 per sq km.

Population by Age and Sex (Secretariat of the Pacific Community estimates at mid-2011): *0–14:* 22,877 (males 11,820, females 11,057); *15–64:* 30,823 (males 15,809, females 15,014); *65 and over:* 1,299 (males 599, females 700); *Total* 54,999 (males 28,228, females 26,771) (Source: Pacific Regional Information System).

Principal Towns (population of urban places, 1999 census): Ebeye 9,345; Darrit (Djarrot) 7,103; Delap 6,339; Rairok 3,846; Laura 2,256; Uliga 2,044. Note: The country's capital is the combined municipality of Delap-Uliga-Darrit.

Births and Deaths (2006): Registered live births 1,576; Registered deaths 318. Note: Registered live births exclude US military personnel, their dependants and contract employees (Source: UN, *Population and Vital Statistics Report*). *2010* (Secretariat of the Pacific Community estimates): Birth rate 31.1 per 1,000; death rate 5.8 per 1,000 (Source: Pacific Regional Information System).

Life Expectancy (years at birth, WHO estimates): 59 (males 58; females 60) in 2008. Source: WHO, *World Health Statistics*.

Economically Active Population (persons aged 15 years and over, 1999 census): Agriculture and fishery 2,114; Manufacturing 761; Electricity, gas and water 258; Construction 848; Wholesale and retail trade 788; Transport, storage and communications 763; Finance, insurance, real estate and business services 559; Community, social and personal services 3,803; *Sub-total* 9,894; Activities not reported 247; *Total employed* 10,141 (males 7,008, females 3,133); Unemployed 4,536 (males 2,671, females 1,865); *Total labour force* 14,677 (males 9,679, females 4,998). *2006/07* (private sector only): Fishing 281; Manufacturing 60; Construction 782; Wholesale and retail trade 1,791; Total employed (incl. others) 5,491 (Source: IMF, *Republic of the Marshall Islands: Selected Issues and Statistical Appendix*—June 2008). *Mid-2011* (estimates): Agriculture, etc. 7,000; Total labour force 31,000 (Source: FAO).

HEALTH AND WELFARE

Key Indicators

Total Fertility Rate (children per woman, 2008): 3.7.
Under-5 Mortality Rate (per 1,000 live births, 2008): 36.
Physicians (per 1,000 head, 2000): 0.5.
Hospital Beds (per 1,000 head, 1999): 2.1.
Health Expenditure (2007): US $ per head (PPP): 357.
Health Expenditure (2007): % of GDP: 14.7.
Health Expenditure (2007): public (% of total): 97.4.
Access to Water (% of persons, 2008): 94.
Access to Sanitation (% of persons, 2008): 73.
Total Carbon Dioxide Emissions ('000 metric tons, 2007): 98.9.
Carbon Dioxide Emissions Per Head (metric tons, 2007): 1.7.

For sources and definitions, see explanatory note on p. vi.

AGRICULTURE, ETC.

Principal Crop ('000 metric tons, 2008, FAO estimate): Coconuts 27.5. Note: No data were available for 2009.

Livestock ('000 head, year ending September 2003): Pigs 12.9; Poultry 86.0.

THE MARSHALL ISLANDS

Fishing ('000 metric tons, live weight, 2008): Bigeye tuna 2.1; Skipjack tuna 27.1; Yellowfin tuna 4.2; Total catch (incl. others) 35.4.
Source: FAO.

INDUSTRY

Electric Energy (million kWh, Majuro only): 81.0 in 2004; 81.3 in 2005; 78.0 in 2006. Source: Asian Development Bank.

FINANCE

Currency and Exchange Rates: United States currency is used: 100 cents = 1 United States dollar (US $). *Sterling and Euro Equivalents* (31 December 2010): £1 sterling = US $1.5655; €1 = US $1.3362; US $100 = £63.88 = €74.84.

Budget (US $ million, year ending 30 September 2009, estimates): *Revenue:* Recurrent 36.6 (Tax 23.1, Non-tax 13.5); Grants 67.1; Total 103.7. *Expenditure:* Recurrent 83.0; Capital (incl. net lending) 21.0; Total 104.0. Source: IMF, *Republic of the Marshall Islands: 2009 Article IV Consultation—Staff Report; a Public Information Notice; and a Statement by the Executive Director of the Republic of Marshall Islands on the Executive Board Discussion* (February 2010).

Cost of Living (Consumer Price Index for Majuro, average of quarterly figures; base: Jan.–March 2003 = 100): All items 112.4 in 2006; 115.8 in 2007; 136.2 in 2008.

Gross Domestic Product (US $ million at constant 2005 prices): 142.4 in 2007; 144.5 in 2008; 144.5 in 2009. Source: UN National Accounts Main Aggregates Database.

Expenditure on the Gross Domestic Product (US $ million at current prices, 2009): Government final consumption expenditure 92.4; Private final consumption expenditure 155.5; Gross capital formation 96.9; *Total domestic expenditure* 344.8; Exports of goods and services 21.2; *Less* Imports of goods and services 195.3; *GDP in purchasers' values* 170.7. Source: UN National Accounts Main Aggregates Database.

Gross Domestic Product by Economic Activity (US $ million at current prices, 2009): Agriculture, hunting, forestry and fishing 16.5; Mining, electricity, gas and water 5.7; Manufacturing 7.2; Construction 18.7; Trade, restaurants and hotels 28.8; Transport, storage and communications 8.8; Other activities 78.9; *Sub-total* 164.7; Net of indirect taxes 6.0 (obtained as a residual); *GDP in purchasers' values* 170.7. Source: UN National Accounts Main Aggregates Database.

Balance of Payments (US $ million, year ending 30 September 2009, estimates): Merchandise exports f.o.b. 14.0; Merchandise imports c.i.f. −85.0; *Trade balance* −71.0; Services (net) −31.7; *Balance on goods and services* −102.7; Other income 30.5; *Balance on goods, services and income* −72.2; Private unrequited transfers (net) 60.1; *Current balance* −12.1. Source: IMF, *Republic of the Marshall Islands: 2009 Article IV Consultation—Staff Report; a Public Information Notice; and a Statement by the Executive Director of the Republic of Marshall Islands on the Executive Board Discussion* (February 2010).

EXTERNAL TRADE

Principal Commodities (US $ million): *Imports* (2000, estimates): Food and live animals 5.0; Beverages and tobacco 6.0; Crude materials, inedible, except fuels 2.6; Mineral fuels, lubricants and related materials 20.4; Animal and vegetable oils and fats 2.4; Chemicals 0.1; Basic manufactures 3.0; Machinery and transport equipment 8.2; Miscellaneous manufactured articles 1.4; Goods not classified by kind 5.8; Total 54.7. *Exports* (year ending September 2007): Coconut oil (crude) 2.0; Copra cake 0.1; Total (incl. others) 20.3. Sources: Asian Development Bank and IMF, *Republic of the Marshall Islands: Selected Issues and Statistical Appendix* (June 2008).

Principal Trading Partners (US $ million): *Imports* (2006): Australia 5.7; Hong Kong 1.2; Japan 5.5; New Zealand 2.2; USA 31.0; Total (incl. others) 67.7 (Source: Asian Development Bank). *Exports* (2000, estimates): USA 5.2; Total (incl. others) 9.1.

TRANSPORT

Road Traffic (vehicles registered, 1999): Trucks 64; Pick-ups 587; Sedans 1,404; Jeeps 79; Buses 75; Vans 66; Scooters 47; Other motor vehicles 253.

Shipping: *Merchant Fleet* (at 31 December 2009): Vessels 1,376; Displacement ('000 grt) 49,088.3 (Source: IHS Fairplay, *World Fleet Statistics*). *International Sea-borne Freight Traffic** (estimates, '000 metric tons, 1990): Goods loaded 29; Goods unloaded 123 (Source: UN, *Monthly Bulletin of Statistics*).
* Including the Northern Mariana Islands, the Federated States of Micronesia and Palau.

Civil Aviation (traffic on scheduled services, 2006): Kilometres flown 1 million; Passengers carried 30,000; Passenger-km 42 million; Total ton-km 4 million. Source: UN, *Statistical Yearbook*.

TOURISM

Tourist Arrivals: 5,780 in 2006; 7,200 in 2007; 6,022 in 2008.

Arrivals by Country (2008): Japan 1,501; Other Asia 2,535; USA 1,563; Total (incl. others) 6,022.

Tourism Receipts (US $ million, incl. passenger transport): 6.6 in 2006; 4.5 in 2007; 3.0 in 2008.

Source: World Tourism Organization.

COMMUNICATIONS MEDIA

Telephones (main lines in use, estimate): 4,400 in 2009*.

Mobile Cellular Telephones (subscriptions, estimate): 3,000 in 2009*.

Personal Computers: 5,000 in 2005*.

Internet Users: 2,200 in 2009*.

Non-daily Newspaper: 1 (average circulation 3,000 copies) in 2004†.

* Source: International Telecommunication Union.
† Source: UNESCO, *Statistical Yearbook*.

EDUCATION

Pre-primary (2008/09 unless otherwise indicated): 126 teachers (2002/03); 1,524 pupils enrolled.

Primary (2008/09 unless otherwise indicated): 103 schools (1998); 526 teachers (2002/03, estimate); 8,398 pupils enrolled.

Secondary (2008/09 unless otherwise indicated): 16 schools (1998); 387 teachers (2002/03, estimate); 5,229 pupils enrolled.

Higher (2002/03 unless otherwise indicated): 1 college (1994); 49 teachers (estimate); 919 students enrolled (estimate).

Pupil-teacher Ratio (primary education, UNESCO estimate): 14.5 in 2002/03.

Source: UNESCO Institute for Statistics.

Directory

The Government

HEAD OF STATE

President: JURELANG ZEDKAIA (took office 26 October 2009; inaugurated 2 November 2009).

CABINET
(May 2011)

Minister in Assistance to the President: RUBEN ZACKHRAS.
Minister of Education: NIDEL LORAK.
Minister of Finance: JACK ADING.
Minister of Transportation and Communication: KENNETH KEDI.
Minister of Health: AMENTA MATTHEW.
Minister of Public Works: MAYNARD ALFRED.
Minister of Internal Affairs: NORMAN MATTHEW.
Minister of Justice: BRENSON S. WASE.
Minister of Resources and Development: MATTLAN ZACKHRAS.
Minister of Foreign Affairs: JOHN SILK.

MINISTRIES

Office of the President: Govt of the Republic of the Marshall Islands, POB 2, Majuro, MH 96960; tel. (625) 3445; fax (625) 4021; e-mail pressoff@ntamar.net; internet www.rmigovernment.org.

THE MARSHALL ISLANDS

Ministry of Education: POB 3, Majuro, MH 96960; tel. (625) 5262; fax (625) 3861; e-mail rmimoe@rmimoe.net; internet www.rmimoe.net.
Ministry of Finance: POB P, Majuro, MH 96960; tel. (625) 3320; fax (625) 3607; e-mail secfin@ntamar.net.
Ministry of Foreign Affairs: POB 1349, Majuro, MH 96960; tel. (625) 3181; fax (625) 4979; e-mail mofasec@ntamar.net.
Ministry of Health: POB 16, Majuro, MH 96960; tel. (625) 3355; fax (625) 3432; e-mail jusmohe@ntamar.net.
Ministry of Internal Affairs: POB 18, Majuro, MH 96960; tel. (625) 8240; fax (625) 5353; e-mail rmihpo@ntamar.net.
Ministry of Justice: c/o Office of the Attorney-General, Majuro, MH 96960; tel. (625) 3244; fax (625) 5218; e-mail agoffice@ntamar.net.
Ministry of Public Works: POB 1727, Majuro, MH 96960; tel. (625) 8911; fax (625) 3005; e-mail secpw@ntamar.net.
Ministry of Resources and Development: POB 1727, Majuro, MH 96960; tel. (625) 3206; fax (625) 7471; e-mail rndsec@ntamar.net; internet rmirnd.net.
Ministry of Transportation and Communication: POB 1079, Majuro, MH 96960; tel. (625) 8869; fax (625) 3486; e-mail rmimotc@ntamar.net.

STATE TRIBUNAL

Nuclear Claims Tribunal: POB 702, Majuro, MH 96960; tel. (625) 3396; fax (625) 3389; e-mail nctmaj@ntamar.net; internet www.nuclearclaimstribunal.com; f. 1988; authorized under Section 177 of the first Compact of Free Association between the Govt of the Marshall Islands and the Govt of the USA to decide all claims arising from the nuclear-testing programme conducted by the USA in the Marshall Islands in 1946–58; Chair. GREGORY DANZ; Defender of the Fund PHILIP A. OKNEY; Public Advocate BILL GRAHAM.

Legislature

THE NITIJELA

The Nitijela (lower house) consists of 33 elected Senators. Following the national election held on 19 November 2007, the Ailin Kein Ad (Our Islands) party, supported by independent candidates, was able to secure a parliamentary majority.
Speaker: ALVIN JACKLICK.

THE COUNCIL OF IROIJ

The Council of Iroij is the upper house of the bicameral legislature, comprising 12 tribal chiefs who advise the Presidential Cabinet and review legislation affecting customary law, land tenure or any traditional practice.
Chairman: Iroij KOTAK LOEAK.

Election Commission

Electoral Commission: POB 18, Majuro, MH 96900; Chief Electoral Officer CARL ALIK.

Political Organizations

Ailin Kein Ad (Our Islands): Majuro; f. 2002; formed United People's Party coalition following 2007 elections; Chair. CHRISTOPHER LOEAK.
United Democratic Party: Majuro; Chair. RUBEN ZACKHRAS; Pres. KESSAI NOTE.

Diplomatic Representation

EMBASSIES IN THE MARSHALL ISLANDS

Japan: A1 Lojkar Village, POB 300, Majuro, MH 96960; tel. (247) 7463; e-mail royoji@ntamar.net; Ambassador SHOJI SATO.
Taiwan (Republic of China): A5–6 Lojkar Village, Long Island, POB 1229, Majuro, MH 96960; tel. (247) 4141; fax (247) 4143; e-mail eoroc@ntamar.net; Ambassador GEORGE T. K. LI.
USA: POB 1379, Majuro, MH 96960; tel. (247) 4011; fax (247) 4012; e-mail publicmajuro@state.gov; internet majuro.usembassy.gov; Ambassador MARTHA CAMPBELL.

Judicial System

The judicial system consists of the Supreme Court and the High Court, which preside over District and Community Courts, and the Traditional Rights Court.
Supreme Court of the Republic of the Marshall Islands: POB 378, Majuro, MH 96960; tel. (625) 3201; fax (625) 3323; e-mail jutrep@ntamar.com; internet www.rmicourts.org; Chief Justice DANIEL N. CADRA.
High Court of the Republic of the Marshall Islands: Majuro; e-mail judrep@ntamar.net; Chief Justice CARL B. INGRAM.
District Court of the Republic of the Marshall Islands: Majuro, MH 96960; tel. (625) 3201; fax (625) 3323; Presiding Judge MILTON ZACKIOS.
Traditional Rights Court of the Marshall Islands: Majuro, MH 96960; customary law only; Chief Judge WALTER K. ELBON.

Religion

The population is predominantly Christian, mainly belonging to the Protestant United Church of Christ. The Roman Catholic Church, Assembly of God, Bukot Nan Jesus, Seventh-day Adventists, the Church of Jesus Christ of Latter-day Saints (Mormons), the Full Gospel and the Bahá'í Faith are also represented.

CHRISTIANITY

The Roman Catholic Church

The Apostolic Prefecture of the Marshall Islands included 5,020 adherents at 31 December 2007.
Prefect Apostolic of the Marshall Islands: Rev. Fr RAYMUNDO SABIO, POB 8, Majuro, MH 96960; tel. (625) 8307; fax (625) 6507; e-mail diocesemarshalls@yahoo.com.

Protestant Churches

The Marshall Islands come under the auspices of the United Church Board for World Ministries (475 Riverside Drive, New York, NY 10115, USA); Sec. for Latin America, Caribbean and Oceania Dr PATRICIA RUMER.

BAHÁ'Í FAITH

National Spiritual Assembly: POB 1017, Majuro, MH 96960; tel. (247) 3512; fax (247) 7180; e-mail nsamarshallislands@yahoo.com; internet www.mh.bahai.org; mems resident in 50 localities; Sec. Dr IRENE J. TAAFAKI.

The Press

Kwajalein Hourglass: POB 23, Kwajalein, MH 96555; tel. (355) 3539; e-mail jbennett@kls.usaka.smdc.army.mil; f. 1954; 2 a week; Editor JIM BENNETT; circ. 2,300.
Marshall Islands Gazette: monthly; govt publ.
Marshall Islands Journal: POB 14, Majuro, MH 96960; tel. (625) 8143; fax (625) 3136; e-mail journal@ntamar.net; internet www.marshallislandsjournal.com; f. 1970; weekly; Editor GIFF JOHNSON; circ. 3,700.

Broadcasting and Communications

TELECOMMUNICATIONS

National Telecommunications Authority (NTA): POB 1169, Majuro, MH 96960; tel. (625) 3676; fax (625) 3952; e-mail info@ntamar.net; internet www.ntamar.net; privatized in 1991; sole provider of local and long-distance tel. services and internet communications in the Marshall Islands; Chair. ALEX BING; Pres. and CEO ANTHONY M. MULLER.

BROADCASTING

Radio

Marshall Islands Broadcasting Co: POB 19, Majuro, MH 96960; tel. (625) 3250; fax (625) 3505; Chief Information Officer PETER FUCHS.
Radio Marshalls V7AB: POB 3250, Majuro, MH 96960; tel. (625) 8411; fax (625) 5353; govt-owned; commercial; programmes in English and Marshallese; Station Man. ANTARI ELBON.
Other radio stations include Micronesia Heatwave and V7AA.

Television

Marshalls Broadcasting Co Television: POB 19, Majuro, MH 96960; tel. (625) 3413; Chief Information Officer PETER FUCHS.

The US Department of Defense operates the American Forces Radio and Television Service for the Bucholz Army Airfield on Kwajalein Atoll.

Finance

(cap. = capital; res = reserves; dep. = deposits; amounts in US dollars)

BANKING

Bank of Guam (USA): POB C, Majuro, MH 96960; tel. (625) 3322; fax (625) 3444; Man. ROMY A. ANGEL; brs in Ebeye, Kwajalein and Majuro.

Bank of the Marshall Islands: POB J, Majuro, MH 96960; tel. (625) 3636; fax (625) 3661; e-mail bankmar@ntamar.net; internet www.bomi.biz; f. 1982; 40% govt-owned; cap. 2.1m., res.20m., dep. 39.2m. (Dec. 2009); Chair. GRANT LABAUN; Pres. and Gen. Man. PATRICK CHEN; brs in Majuro, Kwajalein, Ebeye and Santo.

Marshall Islands Development Bank: POB 1048, Majuro, MH 96960; tel. (625) 3230; fax (625) 3309; e-mail rmimidb@ntamar.net; f. 1989; lending suspended in 2003; Man. Dir AMON TIBON.

INSURANCE

Majuro Insurance Company: POB 60, Majuro, MH 96960; tel. (625) 8885; fax (625) 8188; Man. LUCY RUBEN.

Marshalls Insurance Agency: POB 113, Majuro, MH 96960; tel. (625) 3366; fax (625) 3189; Man. TOM LIKOVICH.

Moylan's Insurance Underwriters (Marshall) Inc: POB 727, Majuro, MH 96960; tel. (625) 3220; fax (625) 3361; e-mail marshalls@moylans.net; internet www.moylansinsurance.com; Founder, Chair. and Pres. KURT S. MOYLAN; Br. Man. STEVE PHILLIP.

Trade and Industry

DEVELOPMENT ORGANIZATIONS AND STATE AUTHORITIES

Marshall Islands Development Authority: POB 1185, Majuro, MH 96960; tel. (625) 3417; fax (625) 3158; Gen. Man. DAVID KABUA.

Marshall Islands Environmental Protection Authority (RMIEPA): POB 1322, Majuro, MH 96960; tel. (625) 3035; fax (625) 5202; e-mail eparmi@ntamar.net; internet www.rmiepa.org; Gen. Man. DEBORAH BARKER-MANASE.

Marshall Islands Marine Resources Authority (MIMRA): POB 860, Majuro, MH 96960; tel. (625) 8262; fax (625) 5447; e-mail kiko@mimra.com; internet www.mimra.com; specializes in farming techniques and research and devt; Exec. Dir GLEN JOSEPH.

Tobolar Copra Processing Authority: POB G, Majuro, MH 96960; tel. (625) 3116; fax (625) 7206; e-mail wpcandilas@ntamar.net; Plant Man. WILFREDO CANDILAS.

CHAMBER OF COMMERCE

Marshall Islands Chamber of Commerce: POB 1226, Majuro, MH 96960; tel. (625) 3177; fax (625) 2500; e-mail commerce@ntamar.net; internet marshallislandschamber.net; fmrly known as Majuro Chamber of Commerce; Pres. STEVE PHILLIPS; Sec. JIM McLEAN.

UTILITIES

Electricity

Marshalls Energy Company: POB 1439, Majuro, MH 96960; tel. (625) 3827; fax (625) 3397; e-mail meccorp@ntamar.net; internet www.mecrmi.net; Gen. Man. DAVID PAUL.

Kwajalein Atoll Joint Utility Resource (KAJUR): POB 5819, Ebeye Island, Kwajalein, MH 96970; tel. (329) 3799; fax (329) 3722; Man. WESLEY LEMARI.

Water

Majuro Water and Sewage Services: POB 1751, Majuro, MH 96960; tel. (625) 8934; fax (625) 3837; Man. TERRY MELLAN.

CO-OPERATIVES

These include the Ebeye Co-op, Farmers' Market Co-operative, Kwajalein Employees' Credit Union, Marshall Is Credit Union, Marshall Is Fishermen's Co-operative, and the Marshall Is Handicraft Co-operative.

Transport

ROADS

Tarmac and concrete roads are found in the more important islands. In 1996 there were 152 km of paved roads in the Marshall Islands, mostly on Majuro and Ebeye. Other islands have stone and coral-surfaced roads and tracks. A road improvement programme was completed in 1999.

SHIPPING

The Marshall Islands operates an 'offshore' shipping register. At the end of 2009 the merchant fleet comprised 1,376 vessels, with a combined displacement of some 49.3m. grt.

Vessel Registry:

International Registries Inc: 11495 Commerce Park Drive, Reston, VA 20191-1506, USA; tel. (703) 620-4880; fax (703) 476-8522; e-mail info@register-iri.com; internet www.register-iri.com; Pres. WILLIAM R. GALLAGHER.

The Trust Company of the Marshall Islands Inc: Trust Company Complex, Ajeltake Island, POB 1405, Majuro, MH 96960; tel. (247) 3018; fax (247) 3017; e-mail tcmi@ntamar.net; Pres. GUY EDISON CLAY MAITLAND.

Marshall Islands Ports Authority (MIPA): Majuro; tel. 625-8269; fax 625-4269; internet rmipa-aip.org; responsible for seaports and airports; Dir JACK CHONG GUM.

CIVIL AVIATION

Air Marshall Islands (AMI): POB 1319, Majuro, MH 96960; tel. (625) 3731; fax (625) 3730; e-mail amisales@ntamar.net; internet www.airmarshallislands.com; f. 1980; internal services for the Marshall Islands; also charter, air ambulance and maritime surveillance operations; agency for Aloha airlines; Chair. KUNIO LAMARI.

Continental Airlines Micronesia: POB 156, Majuro; tel. (625) 3209; fax (625) 3730; e-mail cmimaj@ntamar.net; international flights between Majuro, the Federated States of Micronesia, Guam and Honolulu; also internal services between Majuro and Kwajalein; based in Hagåtña, Guam; Man. LEO SION.

Tourism

The islands' attractions include excellent opportunities for diving, game-fishing and the exploration of sites and relics of Second World War battles. Bikini Atoll was listed by UNESCO as a World Heritage site in 2010. The Marshall Islands Visitor Authority has implemented a short-term tourism development programme focusing on special-interest tourism markets. In the longer term, the Visitor Authority planned to promote the development of small-island resorts throughout the country. Tourism receipts totalled US $3.0m. in 2008. In 2010 there were an estimated 4,563 tourist arrivals. The leading sources of visitors include the USA and Japan.

Marshall Islands Visitor Authority: POB 5, Majuro, MH 96960; tel. (625) 6482; fax (625) 6771; e-mail tourism@ntamar.net; internet www.visitmarshallislands.com; f. 1997; Gen. Man. DOLORES DE-BRUM-KATTIL.

Defence

Defence is the responsibility of the USA, which maintains a military presence on Kwajalein Atoll. The US Pacific Command is based in Hawaii.

Education

There is a school system, based on that of the USA, operated by the state. However, the development of secondary facilities has been constrained by the limitations of resources. In 1998 there were 103 primary schools, with a total enrolment of 12,421 pupils, but only 16 secondary schools, with a total of 2,667 pupils enrolled. In 2008/09 there were an estimated 8,398 pupils enrolled in primary schools and an estimated 5,229 pupils enrolled in secondary schools. In 2006/07 enrolment at pre-primary schools included 9.3% of pupils in the relevant age-group; enrolment at primary schools included 66.3% of the relevant age-group, and the comparable figure for secondary schools included 44.9% of pupils. The College of the Marshall Islands, which became independent from the College of Micronesia in 1993, is based on Majuro; in 2002/03 there were 919 students enrolled at the College. The Fisheries and Nautical Center offers vocational courses for Marshall islanders seeking employment in the fishing industry or on passenger liners, cargo ships and tankers. In the proposed budget for 2008/09, education was allocated some US $21m.

MAURITANIA

Introductory Survey

LOCATION, CLIMATE, LANGUAGE, RELIGION, FLAG, CAPITAL

The Islamic Republic of Mauritania lies in north-west Africa, with the Atlantic Ocean to the west, Algeria and the disputed territory of Western Sahara (occupied by Morocco) to the north, Mali to the east and south, and Senegal to the south. The climate is hot and dry, particularly in the north, which is mainly desert. Average annual rainfall in the capital in the 1990s was 131 mm (5.1 ins). The 1991 Constitution designates Arabic (which is spoken by the Moorish majority) as the official language, and Arabic, Poular, Wolof and Solinke as the national languages. The black population in the south is largely French-speaking, and French is widely used in commercial and business circles. Islam is the state religion, and the inhabitants are almost all Muslims. The national flag (proportions 2 by 3) comprises a green field, bearing, on the vertical median, a yellow five-pointed star between the upward-pointing horns of a yellow crescent. The capital is Nouakchott.

CONTEMPORARY POLITICAL HISTORY

Historical Context

Mauritania, formerly part of French West Africa, achieved full independence on 28 November 1960 (having become a self-governing member of the French Community two years earlier). Moktar Ould Daddah, leader of the Mauritanian Assembly Party (MAP) and Prime Minister since June 1959, became Head of State, and was elected President in August 1961. All parties subsequently merged with the MAP to form the Mauritanian People's Party (MPP), with Ould Daddah as Secretary-General, and Mauritania became a one-party state in 1964. In 1973 Mauritania joined the League of Arab States (see p. 361), and withdrew from the Franc Zone in the following year.

Under a tripartite agreement of November 1975, Spain ceded Spanish (now Western) Sahara to Mauritania and Morocco, to be apportioned between them. The agreement took effect in February 1976, when Mauritania occupied the southern portion of the territory. Fighting ensued between Moroccan and Mauritanian troops and the guerrilla forces of the Frente Popular para la Liberación de Saguia el-Hamra y Río de Oro (the Polisario Front), which sought independence for Western Sahara. Attacks within Mauritania by Polisario forces proved highly damaging to the economy, and, following the removal of Ould Daddah in a bloodless military coup in July 1978, Mauritania renounced its territorial claims in Western Sahara. A peace treaty was signed with Polisario in August 1979 and Morocco announced its annexation of the entire territory.

Domestic Political Affairs

In December 1984, while the Head of State, Lt-Col Mohamed Khouna Ould Haidalla, was temporarily absent from the country, the Prime Minister and Minister of Defence, Lt-Col (later Col) Maaouiya Ould Sid'Ahmed Taya, assumed the presidency in a bloodless coup. Ould Haidalla was detained upon his return to Mauritania, but was released, with five of his associates, in December 1988.

At a national referendum on 12 July 1991, a draft Constitution, which accorded extensive powers to the presidency and provided for the introduction of a multi-party political system, was supported by 97.9% of those who voted (85.3% of the registered electorate), according to official reports. Meanwhile, legislation permitting the registration of political parties was promulgated: among the first organizations to be accorded official status was the Democratic and Social Republican Party (DSRP), which was closely linked with Taya.

Taya was elected President on 17 January 1992, with 62.7% of the votes cast, defeating three other candidates; his nearest rival was Ahmed Ould Daddah, with 32.8%. The rate of voter participation was 51.7%. In legislative elections, which were held on 6 and 13 March, Taya's party took 67 of the 79 seats in the National Assembly, and he was inaugurated as President on 18 April.

In January 1996 Taya appointed Cheikh el Avia Ould Mohamed Khouna as Prime Minister, to head a new Council of Ministers. At legislative elections held on 11 and 18 October the DSRP won 71 of the 79 seats in the National Assembly. The Rally for Democracy and Unity (RDU), closely allied with the administration, also secured a seat. Action for Change (AC), which sought to represent the interests of Harratin (mainly dark-skinned Moors who had formerly been slaves), was the only opposition party to obtain representation in the Assembly; six independent candidates also secured election.

In January 1997 several opposition leaders, including Messaoud Ould Boulkheir, the AC Chairman, were arrested on charges of maintaining 'suspicious relations' with Libya. Although Ould Boulkheir and several others had been freed by February, five other opposition activists received prison sentences for conspiring to break the law; in April four of the five convicted were acquitted on appeal. In February five prominent opposition parties, including the AC and the Union of Democratic Forces—New Era (UDF—NE), formed a coalition, the Forum of Opposition Parties (FOP).

At the presidential election, held on 12 December 1997, Taya was returned to office with 90.9% of the valid votes cast; his nearest rival, Mohamed Lemine Ch'Bih Ould Cheikh Melainine, won 7.0% of the vote. Opposition parties alleged that there had been widespread electoral fraud and disputed the official rate of voter participation, of 73.8%. Taya subsequently appointed Mohamed Lemine Ould Guig, a university academic, as Prime Minister, and a new Council of Ministers was installed. In November 1998 Khouna was again appointed Prime Minister.

Meanwhile, in March 1998 internal divisions in the UDF—NE resulted in a split in the party into two rival factions, led by Ahmed Ould Daddah and Moustapha Ould Bedreddine. In November the Government banned the pro-Iraqi Baathist National Vanguard Party (Taliaa), a constituent member of the FOP, following its criticism of the Mauritanian Government's decision to establish full diplomatic relations with Israel in the previous month.

From October 2000, following the onset of the second *intifada* (uprising) in the Palestinian Autonomous Areas, the Mauritanian Government experienced increasing pressure from opposition groups, including the UDF—NE, to break off diplomatic relations with Israel. In October several pro-Palestinian demonstrations in Nouakchott and Nouadhibou led to violent anti-Israeli protests. Arrests of members of clandestine Islamist groups and of UDF—NE activists were reported. In late October the Council of Ministers officially dissolved the UDF—NE, on the grounds that the party had incited violence and sought to damage Mauritanian national interests. Ould Daddah refused to recognize the dissolution of the party, and the UDF—NE's partners in the FOP condemned the Government's action as unconstitutional. Meanwhile, the faction of the UDF—NE led by Moustapha Ould Bedreddine, which remained authorized, restyled itself as the Union of Progressive Forces (UPF).

Some 15 political parties contested legislative and municipal elections held on 19 and 26 October 2001, at which an electoral turn-out of some 55% was reported. The DSRP won 64 of the 81 seats in the enlarged National Assembly, and the RDU and the Union for Democracy and Progress (UDP), which were now both allied with the ruling party, each secured three seats. The AC was the most successful of the opposition parties, winning four seats, while the UPF and the newly formed Rally of Democratic Forces (RDF), which replaced the banned UDF—NE, also each took three seats, and the Popular Front (PF) secured the remaining seat. In November President Taya reappointed Khouna as Prime Minister, and a reshuffled Council of Ministers was appointed.

In January 2002 Ould Daddah was elected President of the RDF; four former vice-presidents of the UDF—NE were also appointed to the 12-member executive committee of the RDF. In that month the Government officially dissolved the AC, on the grounds that the party promoted racism and extremism. At partial senatorial elections, held in April, the RDF won one seat, the first time that part of the radical opposition had secured representation in the Senate, in which the DSRP enjoyed a large majority. In August the Convention for Change (CC), an organization including many former members of the AC, and led by Ould Boulkheir, was denied the right to register as a political party.

In October 2002 the UPF announced that it was to organize a series of meetings intended to promote a 'national dialogue' between the authorities and the opposition parties. However, later that month seven other opposition parties, including the CC (which remained banned), the PF and the RDF, formed a new grouping, the United Opposition Framework (UOF), which also stated as its purpose the co-ordination of dialogue between the opposition and the Government pertaining to democratic reform; the UPF was, notably, excluded from the UOF. Consequently, the initial meeting was postponed indefinitely, and, expressing discontent at the situation, in mid-November the UPF announced its withdrawal from the National Assembly. As a result of the departure of the three UPF deputies from the Assembly, the group of opposition deputies was dissolved, as it was now reduced to eight members, fewer than the 10 required for the formation of a parliamentary group.

In March 2003 US-led military action in Iraq, aimed at ousting the Baathist regime of Saddam Hussain, prompted protests in Mauritania, with widespread demonstrations held to demand that the Government break off diplomatic relations with the two principal nations involved in the conflict, the United Kingdom and the USA, and also with Israel. As opposition to the Government's broadly pro-US stance intensified in early May, police raided the headquarters of a tolerated—although not officially authorized—Baathist party, the National Renaissance Party (NRP—Nouhoudh). Three leaders of the NRP were arrested on unspecified charges; 13 other Baathists were also arrested over a period of four days. (Ten of those arrested were later charged with attempting to re-establish Taliaa.)

Opposition to Taya

In early May 2003 Taya effected a minor government reorganization: the appointment of Lembrabott Ould Mohamed Lemine as Minister of Culture and Islamic Affairs was regarded as an attempt to reduce tensions between the Government and Islamic communities. However, at the end of May the publication of a pro-Islamist weekly journal, *Ar-Rayah*, was suspended, and nine Baathists were convicted by a Nouakchott court of engaging in illegal political activity. In early June four Islamic cultural associations were closed down, and, according to opposition reports, more than 100 alleged Islamists were detained, 36 of whom were charged with plotting against the constitutional order.

The tensions that had been escalating throughout the first half of 2003 culminated in an attempted *coup d'état*, which commenced on 8 June. Exchanges of fire were reported near the presidential palace and at other strategic locations in Nouakchott. According to official reports, 15 people (including six civilians) died in ensuing clashes between the insurgents and the security forces, including the Chief of Staff of the Armed Forces, Col Mohamed Lamine Ould Ndiayane, with a further 68 people injured. Government forces regained control of the city on 9 June. Although the exact identity and motives of the rebels were unclear, Taya subsequently stated that Islamists had been responsible for the rebellion. (Other sources claimed that the attempted coup had been prompted by tribal rivalries.)

In the days following the restoration of order at least 12 alleged rebel leaders were arrested, while more than 30 detained Islamists, who had been freed during the disorder, were reported to have surrendered themselves to the authorities. In July 2003 another suspected coup leader, Lt Didi Ould M'Hamed, who had fled to Senegal, was extradited to Mauritania; it was subsequently announced that he would face a civil trial.

In early July 2003 Taya appointed a new Prime Minister: Sghaïr Ould M'Barek, a Harratin, was regarded as a close ally of the President. A new Government was subsequently formed. Further arrests of Islamists were reported throughout the month. In early August more than 80 members of the military who had been arrested following the attempted coup were released, although many more remained in detention. Some 41 Islamists had also been released from detention by the end of the month, although others continued to face charges. In September it was announced that some 30 members of the military, including 20 senior officers, were to be tried in connection with the coup attempt.

In October 2003 the Constitutional Council approved the nominations of six candidates, including Taya, Ould Daddah, Ould Boulkheir and former President Ould Haidalla, for the forthcoming presidential election. Ould Haidalla was widely regarded as the most credible challenger to Taya, but only secured 18.7% of the votes cast, and Taya was re-elected with 66.7%. Some 60.8% of the electorate participated in the election. Opposition candidates accused the Government of perpetrating fraud at the election, which international observers had not been permitted to monitor.

In August 2004 some 31 army officers were arrested after the security forces discovered a plot to overthrow Taya. The Mauritanian authorities accused the Governments of Libya and Burkina Faso of providing assistance to the alleged conspirators; however, both states strongly denied the allegations. In September the Government announced that it had averted another attempted coup, seizing a large quantity of weapons and making a number of arrests; among those detained was Capt. Abderahmane Ould Mini, who, it was reported, had also participated in the failed coup in June 2003.

The trial of more than 190 soldiers and civilians accused of participation in the attempted coup in June 2003 and in subsequent conspiracies to overthrow the Head of State commenced in November 2004. The defendants included the alleged leaders of the group, Saleh Ould Hnana, Ould Mini and Mohammed Ould Sheikhna, the latter being one of 19 people tried *in absentia* (also among this number was Sidi Mohamed Mustapha Ould Limam Chavi, an adviser to Burkinabè President Blaise Compaoré); the civilians on trial, meanwhile, included opposition leaders Ould Haidalla, Ould Daddah and Cheikh Ould Horma. Ould Hnana and Ould Mini pleaded guilty to the charge of conspiring to overthrow President Taya, while the remaining accused military personnel entered pleas of not guilty. In February 2005 Ould Hnana, Ould Mini, Ould Sheikhna and a fourth officer, Capt. Mohammed Ould Salek, were sentenced to life imprisonment with hard labour, while 79 others received lesser jail sentences; Ould Haidalla, Ould Daddah and Ould Horma were among the 111 acquitted. Following his release, Ould Daddah urged the Government to initiate dialogue with the opposition.

Some 15 soldiers were killed, and a further 17 injured, in an attack in June 2005 by some 150 assailants on a military post at Lemgheity, in north-eastern Mauritania, for which an Algerian radical Islamist militant group, the Groupe salafiste pour la prédication et le combat (GSPC), subsequently claimed responsibility. Later in June it was reported that the existence of a radical Islamist group based in Mauritania with links to the GSPC, the Mauritanian Group for Preaching and Jihad, had been uncovered, as had details of proposed targets of attack in the country. At the end of the month the Senate adopted legislation aimed at countering terrorism and money-laundering. In May 2007 the trial of 25 suspected Islamist militants commenced in Nouakchott; several of the accused were being tried *in absentia*. Some of the defendants were charged in connection with the attack in Lemgheity, while others were accused of having received training from the GSPC (which had reportedly restyled itself as the al-Qa'ida Organization in the Islamic Maghreb—AQIM). In early June 24 of the defendants were acquitted owing to lack of evidence, and one defendant, who had escaped from prison in April 2006, was sentenced, *in absentia*, to two years' imprisonment for falsifying identity papers. The trial of a second group of 14 alleged militants began in late June 2007. Three were charged with participating in the attack at Lemgheity, while 11 were charged with having links to the GSPC.

The Military Council for Justice and Democracy

Meanwhile, on 3 August 2005, while President Taya was absent from Mauritania, attending the funeral of the late King Fahd ibn Abd al-Aziz as-Sa'ud of Saudi Arabia, a group of army officers seized control of state broadcasting services and the presidential palace in a bloodless coup. A 16-member Military Council for Justice and Democracy (MCJD) under the leadership of Col Ely Ould Mohamed Vall, hitherto the Director of National Security, who had been regarded as a close ally of Taya, announced that it had assumed power. The Council stated that it would preside over the country for a transitional period of up to two years, at the end of which democratic elections, in which members of the MCJD and the Government would be prohibited from participating, would be held; although the National Assembly elected in 2001 was dissolved, the 1991 Constitution and most of its institutions (including the Constitutional Council and judicial bodies) were to be retained, as supplemented and amended by the charter of the MCJD. Taya was prevented from re-entering the country and was flown initially to Niamey, Niger; he subsequently took up residence in The Gambia.

MAURITANIA

On 7 August 2005 Vall appointed Sidi Mohamed Ould Boubacar, hitherto Ambassador to France, as Prime Minister, a position that he had previously held in 1992–96; a new, civilian, Government was named on 10 August, and Vall announced the intention of holding a constitutional referendum within one year. None of the ministers in the outgoing Government were reappointed, although, notably, Ahmed Ould Sid'Ahmed, who, in his former capacity as Minister of Foreign Affairs and Co-operation, had been largely responsible for Mauritania's rapprochement with Israel in 1999, was reappointed to that position. In the immediate aftermath of the coup, which was initially widely condemned internationally, the African Union (AU, see p. 183) announced the suspension of Mauritania's membership. However, the overthrow of Taya's regime was reported to have widespread domestic support. In mid-August a delegation from the AU met members of the MCJD, subsequently announcing the willingness of the Union to co-operate with the new leadership of Mauritania, although the country was to remain suspended from the organization pending democratic elections, in accordance with the Constitutive Act of the AU.

In early September 2005 the new administration announced that it was to offer a general amnesty for political prisoners; 32 such detainees, principally from among those imprisoned in February 2005 for their role in attempted coups in 2003 and 2004, were among the first to benefit from the amnesty. However, some Islamist detainees were not freed, prompting 19 such prisoners to commence a hunger strike later in September 2005 demanding their release. In mid-October, moreover, the authorities refused to recognize a recently formed Islamist political party, the Party for Democratic Convergence, on the grounds that its programme violated Mauritanian law. Indeed, Ould Vall announced that no Islamist party would be legalized.

In November 2005 the MCJD issued a timetable for the transition to democratic rule: a constitutional referendum was to be held in June 2006, followed by elections to municipal councils and to the National Assembly in November, elections to the Senate in January 2007 and, finally, a presidential election in March. A 15-member National Independent Electoral Commission was inaugurated at the end of November 2005. Meanwhile, the former ruling DSRP, which had changed its name to the Republican Party for Democracy and Renewal (RPDR), elected Ethmane Ould Cheikh Ebi el Maali, hitherto Ambassador to Kuwait, as its new President.

In March 2006 the MCJD approved proposals presented by the transitional Government on constitutional amendments to be put to a national referendum on 25 June. The principal changes envisaged included: limiting the presidential term of office to five years, renewable only once; stipulating a maximum age of 75 years for presidential candidates; and prohibiting the President from holding any other official post, particularly the leadership of a political party. The proposed reforms were generally supported by most major political parties, including the RPDR. In May the European Union (EU, see p. 270) announced the resumption of co-operation with Mauritania, which had been suspended following the coup in August 2005.

The constitutional referendum was held, as scheduled, on 25 June 2006. Several days earlier five associates of former President Taya had been arrested on suspicion of planning to sabotage the plebiscite, while a coalition of four parties critical of the Vall administration, the Bloc of Parties for Change, encouraged their supporters to boycott the referendum. None the less, observers from the AU and the Arab League declared their satisfaction with the conduct of the poll. According to official results, 96.9% of the valid votes cast were in favour of the amendments to the Constitution and a turn-out of 76.5% of the registered electorate was recorded. In late June 10 political parties, including the RDF, the PF, the Popular Progressive Alliance (PPA) and the Rally for Mauritania (RPM—Temam), announced the formation of the Coalition of Forces for Democratic Change (CFDC) to contest the forthcoming legislative and local elections.

Democratic elections

At the legislative elections, which were held as scheduled on 19 November and 3 December 2006, the RDF took 15 seats, the UPF eight, the RPDR seven and the PPA five, while the Centrist Reformists and the Mauritanian Party for Union and Change—Hatem both secured four seats; 41 seats were taken by independent candidates. Indirect elections to the Senate took place on 21 January and 4 February 2007 at which independent candidates secured 34 of the 56 seats, while representatives of the CFDC took 15.

The presidential election took place as scheduled over two rounds on 11 and 25 March 2007. At the first round, which was contested by 20 candidates, Sidi Mohamed Ould Cheikh Abdellahi took 24.8% of votes cast, while Ould Daddah won 20.7%, Zeine Ould Zeidane 15.3% and Ould Boulkheir 9.8%. The rate of voter participation was recorded at 70.1%. Abdellahi and Ould Daddah thus proceeded to the second round, at which Abdellahi (a government minister under both Moktar Ould Daddah and Taya) was elected President, having secured 52.9% of the valid votes cast. Some 67.5% of the electorate participated in the second round. Ould Boubacar submitted the resignation of his Government on 31 March, although the administration was to remain in office in a 'caretaker' capacity pending the inauguration of the new President, scheduled for 19 April. Abdellahi was duly inaugurated on that date, assuming executive powers in place of the MCJD, which was disbanded, and on the following day he appointed Zeidane as Prime Minister. Later in April a new Government, mainly comprising technocrats with no previous ministerial experience, was installed. The elections were largely deemed to have been fair and democratic and on 10 April Mauritania was readmitted to the AU. In June President Abdellahi effected a minor ministerial reorganization.

In late December 2007 four French tourists were shot dead by a group of gunmen near the town of Aleg, in the south-west of Mauritania, in what was initially believed to be a robbery. However, the Government later attributed the killings to Islamist militants, and in January 2008 two Mauritanian men with previous convictions for training with the GSPC and having links to al-Qa'ida, were arrested in Guinea-Bissau in connection with the incident. According to the Guinea-Bissau police, both detainees admitted to the killings and they were handed over to the Mauritanian authorities. In April one of the suspects, Sidi Ould Sidna, escaped from police custody in Nouakchott, although he was later recaptured, and on 10 April the alleged leader of the group, Marouf Ould Haiba, was arrested; in the same month a police officer and an Islamist militant were killed in a shoot-out in the capital. In May Ould Sidna and Ould Haiba were charged for their role in the murder of the French tourists, along with 28 other suspected Islamist militants who faced various charges. In September 12 Mauritanian soldiers who were abducted and later found dead, were believed to have been victims of an attack by al-Qa'ida militants. Ould Sidna, Ould Haiba and Mohammed Ould Chabarnou were sentenced to death in May 2010, having been convicted of the murder of the French tourists.

Meanwhile, in May 2008 Zeidane was dismissed as Prime Minister and replaced by Yahya Ould Ahmed el Waghef, leader of the National Party for Democracy and Development (NPDD). A 31-member Council of Ministers was named, and later approved by Abdellahi, which included members of the opposition UPF and the National Rally for Reform and Development. However, on 1 July a motion of no confidence was submitted by 39 legislators from the NPDD, and the Government resigned on 3 July. Abdellahi initially threatened to dissolve the legislature, but then accepted the Government's resignation and invited el Waghef to form a new Council of Ministers, which was appointed on 10 July and included 14 new members.

Military coup

On 6 August 2008 President Abdellahi announced the dismissal of four senior military officials, including Gen. Mohamed Ould Abdel Aziz, the Presidential Chief of Staff. Later that day Ould Abdel Aziz led a bloodless military coup to overthrow Abdellahi and declared himself President of a new interim executive, the High Council of State (HCS), which included two other generals—Mohamed Ould Cheik Mohamed Ahmed and Felix Negre—and eight colonels. Prime Minister el Waghef was also removed from office and detained along with Abdellahi, although the former Prime Minister was released later in August, while Abdellahi remained under house arrest until December. There was little opposition to the coup: less than 100 demonstrators took to the streets of Nouakchott on 7 August and these were quickly dispersed by the security forces, while 107 of the 146 members of the National Assembly declared their support for the new regime. Ould Abdel Aziz claimed that a presidential election would be held 'as soon as possible'. (A timetable was eventually announced which established the election date as 6 June 2009.) The HCS issued a constitutional ordinance, which stated that it would exercise the powers of the President as defined by the Constitution, and granted Ould Abdel Aziz the power to appoint a prime minister, military officials and civil servants. On 14 August 2008 Ould Abdel Aziz named Moulaye Ould Mohamed

MAURITANIA

Laghdaf, hitherto Mauritania's Ambassador to Belgium and the EU, as the new Prime Minister, and in early September a new Government was formed which featured a number of ministers from the previous administration. The coup received widespread international condemnation and on 9 August the AU announced Mauritania's suspension from the organization, pending the restoration of democratic government.

In April 2009 Ould Abdel Aziz resigned his position as head of the HCS, in order to contest the presidential election. He was also elected as Chairman of a new political party, the Union for the Republic (UR), which had been formed in March. A spokesman for the National Front for the Defence of Democracy (NFDD), a coalition of political parties opposed to the coup, denounced the planned election, claiming it was a means of legitimizing military rule; in May the NFDD and RDF held a joint demonstration in Nouakchott, in which several thousand people protested against the proposed election.

Meanwhile, in early February 2009 the AU's Peace and Security Council imposed further sanctions, including travel restrictions and a freezing of funds, on some 60 Mauritanian nationals, including five members of the HCS, seven government ministers and 10 parliamentary deputies, and called on AU member states to contribute to efforts to restore political order in Mauritania. However, the Chairman of the AU Assembly, Libyan Revolutionary Leader Col Muammar al-Qaddafi, endorsed the electoral timetable set by the HCS for the presidential election (which had been rejected by the opposition and numerous international bodies), while visiting Mauritania in March. Several members of the opposition walked out of the National Assembly during an address by Qaddafi, accusing him of supporting the military junta.

The Senegalese Government hosted negotiations between representatives of the HCS, the NFDD and the RDF in May 2009, and early the following month all parties agreed upon a resolution to the ongoing political crisis. This provided for the formal resignation of Ould Cheikh Abdellahi (which took place on 27 June), the formation of a transitional unity government and the postponement of the presidential election until 18 July. Furthermore, el Waghef was to be released from custody. Thus on 27 June the HCS was restyled the Superior Council of National Defence (SCND) and it was announced that Ba Mamadou dit M'Baré, the President of the Senate who had replaced Ould Abdel Aziz as President of the HCS in April, would act as interim President of the SCND until the presidential election. The new Government, which was also installed on 27 June, was headed by Ould Mohamed Laghdaf. In early July the AU removed the sanctions imposed in February and restored Mauritania's membership of the organization.

Recent developments: Ould Abdel Aziz elected President

The presidential election, contested by 10 candidates, was duly held on 18 July 2009, and, according to provisional figures released by the Ministry of the Interior the following day, Ould Abdel Aziz received 52.6% of the valid votes cast. His closest challenger, Messaoud Ould Boulkheir, representing the NFDD, secured 16.3%, while Ahmed Ould Daddah—the candidate of the RDF—was placed third, with 13.7%. Some 64.6% of the registered electorate participated in the ballot. Several of Ould Abdel Aziz's challengers alleged that electoral fraud had been perpetrated, and the President of the National Independent Electoral Commission resigned from his position, citing doubts regarding the 'reliability' of the poll. None the less, Ould Abdel Aziz's victory was confirmed later in July by the Constitutional Council, which rejected formal challenges from Ould Boulkheir, Ould Daddah and Col Ely Ould Mohamed Vall (who had contested the election as an independent, receiving 3.8% of the votes). Ould Abdel Aziz was sworn in as President on 5 August. He reappointed Ould Mohamed Laghdaf to the premiership on 11 August and a new Government was installed; Hamadi Ould Hamadi assumed the national defence portfolio, while Kane Ousmane became Minister of Finance and Mohamed Ould Boilil was appointed Minister of the Interior and Decentralization. The new Council of Ministers also included the first female Minister of Foreign Affairs and Co-operation, Naha Mint Mouknass.

In his inaugural address, President Ould Abdel Aziz stated his intention to combat corruption and terrorism and its causes, while also pledging to implement reform within the armed forces. At partial elections to the Senate, held on 8 and 15 November 2009, the UR secured 13 of the 17 seats contested. In January 2010 Ould Mohamed Laghdaf confirmed the imminent restructuring of the army and the security forces, and also announced that deputies had approved amendments to anti-terrorism legislation that granted police increased powers of search and detention. At the end of March Ould Abdel Aziz effected a reorganization of the Government, appointing, most notably, new ministers of justice, of finance and of petroleum and energy. The trial of former Prime Minister Ould Ahmed el Waghef, on charges related to the alleged purchase of spoiled foodstuffs for an emergency aid programme, was adjourned in July. In the same month Mohamed Mahmoud Ould Mohamed Lemine was elected Chairman of the UR at its first congress in Nouakchott. In November Ould Abdel Aziz issued a decree ordering the pardon and release from prison of at least 117 convicted criminals, including 17 Islamist militants. In December the NPDD announced its support for the ruling UR. In the same month eight opposition parties, including the RDF and the UPF, established a new coalition, the Co-ordination of the Democratic Opposition. A government reorganization was effected in March 2011. Mint Mouknass was replaced as Minister of Foreign Affairs and Co-operation by Hamadi Ould Hamadi, hitherto Minister of National Defence, who was, in turn, succeeded by Ahmedou Ould Idey Ould Mohamed Radhi, formerly Minister-delegate to the Minister of State for National Education, in charge of Primary Education.

Foreign Affairs
Regional relations

A long-standing border dispute with Senegal was exacerbated by the deaths, in April 1989, of two Senegalese farmers, who had been involved in a dispute regarding grazing rights with Mauritanian livestock-breeders. Mauritanian nationals resident in Senegal were attacked, and their businesses (primarily those of the retail trade) looted, while Senegalese nationals in Mauritania and black Mauritanians suffered similar aggression. By early May it was believed that several hundred people, mostly Senegalese, had been killed. Operations to repatriate nationals of both countries commenced, with international assistance. Amid allegations that the Mauritanian authorities had begun to instigate expulsions of the indigenous black population to Senegal or to Mali, a prominent human rights organization, Amnesty International, expressed concern at the reported violation of black Mauritanians' rights. Mauritania and Senegal suspended diplomatic relations in August 1989, and sporadic outbreaks of violence were reported later that year. In late 1990 the Senegalese Government denied accusations made by the Mauritanian authorities that it was implicated in an alleged attempt to overthrow Taya. In December the arrests of large numbers of black Mauritanians were reported. In early 1991 Mauritanian naval vessels were reported to have opened fire on Senegalese fishing boats, apparently in Senegal's territorial waters; in March several deaths were reported to have resulted from a military engagement on Senegalese territory, following an incursion by Senegalese troops into Mauritania.

Following renewed diplomatic activity, diplomatic relations with Senegal were resumed in April 1992, and the process of reopening the border began in May. However, Mauritanian refugees in Senegal insisted that, as long as the Taya Government refused to recognize their national identity (*mauritanité*) and land and property rights, they would not return to Mauritania. In June 2000 relations between Mauritania and Senegal deteriorated after Mauritania accused the new Senegalese administration of relaunching an irrigation project, which involved the use of joint waters from the Senegal river, in contravention of the Organisation pour la mise en valeur du fleuve Sénégal project (see p. 449). The dispute escalated when the Mauritanian authorities requested that all of its citizens living in Senegal return home and issued the estimated 100,000 Senegalese nationals living in Mauritania with a 15-day deadline by which to leave the country. In mid-June, following mediation by King Muhammad VI of Morocco and the Presidents of The Gambia and Mali, the Mauritanian Minister of the Interior announced that the decision to expel Senegalese citizens had been withdrawn and that Mauritanians living in Senegal could remain there. President Abdoulaye Wade of Senegal visited Mauritania later that month and announced that the irrigation project had been abandoned. By late 2000 the number of Mauritanian refugees in Senegal had declined to 19,800 (compared with 65,500 in mid-1995). In April 2001 President Taya's presence as guest of honour at a ceremony in Dakar to commemorate the 41st anniversary of the independence of Senegal demonstrated an improvement in relations between

MAURITANIA

the countries. At the end of 2007 some 19,503 Mauritanian refugees still remained in Senegal, according to provisional figures. In January 2008 about 100 Mauritanian refugees returned from Senegal, following the conclusion of a repatriation agreement between the Senegalese and the Mauritanian authorities, which envisaged the eventual resettlement of all remaining Mauritanian refugees in Senegal.

Diplomatic relations between Mauritania and Morocco were severed in 1981, following accusations, denied by both countries, of involvement in mutual destabilization attempts. In 1983 Mauritania sought to improve relations between the Maghreb countries (Algeria, Morocco, Mauritania, Tunisia and Libya) and was a signatory of the Maghreb Fraternity and Co-operation Treaty, drafted by Algeria and Tunisia. Relations with Morocco again deteriorated from February 1984, when Mauritania announced its recognition of the Sahrawi Arab Democratic Republic (the Western Saharan state proclaimed by Polisario in 1976), although Taya restored diplomatic relations with Morocco in April 1985. In February 1989 Mauritania was a founder member, with Algeria, Libya, Morocco and Tunisia, of the Union of the Arab Maghreb (UMA, see p. 450), although relations with Libya were reported to have deteriorated from the mid-1990s; Libya was a particularly vehement critic of Mauritania's decision to establish and maintain full diplomatic relations with Israel (see Other external relations). Diplomatic relations with Libya, severed in 1995, were none the less restored in 1997. In September 2001 King Muhammad VI of Morocco paid a three-day official visit to Mauritania, aimed at improving bilateral relations between the two countries. In March 2004 President Taya led an official delegation to Morocco, and again met with King Muhammad. King Muhammad returned to Mauritania in March 2005 as part of a tour of West Africa. There was speculation that, during his visits to both Mauritania and Burkina Faso, the King had attempted to mediate informally between the two countries' Presidents (whose relations remained strained following Mauritania's accusation that Burkina Faso and Libya had supported an attempt to overthrow Taya), but without apparent success.

Relations with both Libya and Burkina Faso were severely strained in the wake of allegations by the Mauritanian Government that those two countries had provided support to rebel elements in the Mauritanian military, accused of participating in the failed coup of June 2003 and of subsequently conspiring to overthrow President Taya (see Opposition to Taya). It was alleged that Ould Hnana and Ould Sheikhna, who were held responsible by the Mauritanian authorities of leading the 2003 coup, had been granted refuge in Burkina Faso and received weapons, money and training, while the Libyan Government was accused of supplying the rebels with weapons, vehicles and other equipment. Libya and Burkina Faso, meanwhile, strenuously denied the accusations. In March 2005 a ministerial commission appointed by the UMA to investigate the Mauritanian allegations against Libya concluded that Qaddafi had 'no connection' to the events in Mauritania, which it described as a 'purely Mauritanian affair'.

In September 2009 delegates from Mali, Mauritania, Niger and Algeria met to discuss a new anti-terror plan and agreed to allow military co-operation in the fight against terrorism in their border regions. In response to the kidnapping of four European citizens by al-Qa'ida in the Islamic Maghreb (AQIM, as the GSPC had been restyled) in early 2009, and the seizure in Mauritania (and subsequent transfer to Mali) of three Spanish aid workers and two Italian tourists later that year, in January 2010 Mali and Mauritania announced plans to strengthen security co-operation further. The following month, however, bilateral relations became strained after the Malian Government approved the release of four Islamist militia (including one Mauritanian citizen), detained in April 2009 on weapons charges, in exchange for the freeing of a French citizen taken hostage in November. Both Algeria and Mauritania subsequently withdrew their ambassadors from Bamako, claiming that Mali's decision to release the terrorists was an infringement of the agreement on security co-operation reached at the September regional summit. In March 2010 foreign ministers from seven Saharan states, including Mauritania, Mali and Algeria, meeting in Algiers agreed that they would commence the sharing of operational information and co-operate their actions against AQIM in an attempt to 'collectively confront the threat of terrorism'. Meanwhile, in February an alleged Mauritanian terrorist, Oumar Ould Sid'Ahmed (also known as 'Sahraoui'), who was believed to have been involved in the seizure of the Spanish and Italian citizens in late 2009, was extradited from Mali to Mauritania; in the following month he and six others were charged with kidnapping offences. In July 2010 Ould Sid'Ahmed was sentenced to 12 years' imprisonment and a fine of UM 5m. for kidnapping the Spanish aid workers (who were released by AQIM in March and August). In September Mauritania's Ambassador to Mali returned to his post. Shortly afterwards Mauritanian military forces, in co-operation with the Malian Government, launched a series of ground and air attacks against suspected AQIM militants in northern Mali. Following the adoption of a law on terrorism in July, which granted AQIM members who surrendered to the authorities special conditions, five young AQIM militants surrendered to the Mauritanian army in November.

Other external relations

In November 1995 Mauritania signed an agreement to recognize and establish relations with Israel. In October 1998 Mauritania's Minister of Foreign Affairs and Co-operation visited Israel, where he held talks with the Prime Minister, Binyamin Netanyahu. The Arab League strongly criticized the visit, claiming that it contravened the League's resolutions on the suspension of the normalization of relations with Israel, and threatened to impose sanctions on Mauritania. Widespread controversy was provoked both domestically, and in Arab countries, by the establishment of full diplomatic relations between Mauritania and Israel in October 1999. (Of Arab countries, only Egypt and Jordan had taken such a step, under the terms of their respective peace treaties with Israel.) Following the resumption of the Palestinian uprising in September 2000, the Mauritanian Government came under renewed pressure to suspend diplomatic relations with Israel. A visit by the Mauritanian Minister of Foreign Affairs and Co-operation, Dah Ould Abdi, to Israel in May 2001, when he met Israeli Prime Minister Ariel Sharon and President Moshe Katsav, and entered into negotiations with the Minister of Foreign Affairs, Shimon Peres, provoked further controversy, particularly as a result of an appeal by the Arab League, issued earlier that month, for all member countries to cease political contacts with Israel. A further meeting between Peres, Taya and Ould Abdi, in Nouakchott, in October 2002, provoked further controversy. A visit to Mauritania by the Israeli Deputy Prime Minister and Minister of Foreign Affairs, Silvan Shalom, in early May 2005 was preceded, and followed, by the detention of several Islamists, although the Government denied that the arrests were linked to Shalom's presence. His visit prompted a number of anti-Israeli protests in Nouakchott. Although some concern was initially expressed, following the coup of August 2005, that diplomatic relations between the two countries might be terminated, the appointment, later in the month, of Ahmed Ould Sid'Ahmed as Minister of Foreign Affairs and Co-operation (who had held that position when Mauritania re-established full diplomatic relations with Israel in 1999) appeared to indicate that the new regime intended to maintain amicable relations with Israel. In April 2007 newly elected President Abdellahi appealed for a public debate on the future of Mauritania's diplomatic ties with Israel. The Israeli embassy in Nouakchott was attacked in February 2008 by gunmen who opened fire and injured three people. Nevertheless, relations did not seriously deteriorate until after the assumption of power in Mauritania by the HCS. In January 2009 Mauritania recalled its ambassador from Israel and suspended diplomatic relations in response to the Israeli invasion of the Gaza Strip in December 2008; in March 2009 it was reported that the Israeli embassy in Nouakchott had been closed down and the ambassador ordered to leave the country. The Mauritanian Minister of Foreign Affairs and Co-operation announced the 'complete and definitive' abrogation of diplomatic relations with Israel in March 2010.

CONSTITUTION AND GOVERNMENT

Under the provisions of the Constitution adopted in July 1991 and amended in June 2006, the Head of State is the President, who is elected, by universal adult suffrage, for a term of five years, renewable only once. Legislative power is vested in the National Assembly, which is elected by universal suffrage for a period of five years, and in the Senate, which is elected by municipal leaders for a six-year term, one-third of its membership being renewed every two years. All elections are conducted in the context of a multi-party political system. The President of the Republic appoints the Prime Minister and, on the recommendation of the latter, the members of the Council of Ministers.

For the purpose of local administration, Mauritania is divided into 13 wilayat (regions), comprising a total of 53 moughataa (counties), which are subdivided into 216 communes (districts).

REGIONAL AND INTERNATIONAL CO-OPERATION

Mauritania is a member of the African Union (see p. 183), of the Organisation pour la mise en valeur du fleuve Sénégal (see p. 449) and of the Union of the Arab Maghreb (see p. 450). Mauritania withdrew from the Economic Community of West African States (see p. 257), with effect from 31 December 2000, owing to decisions adopted by the organization at its summit in December 1999, including the integration of the armed forces of member states and the removal of internal border controls and tariffs.

Mauritania became a member of the UN in 1961 and was admitted to the World Trade Organization (WTO, see p. 430) in 1995. Mauritania participates in the Group of 77 (G77, see p. 447) developing countries.

ECONOMIC AFFAIRS

In 2009, according to estimates by the World Bank, Mauritania's gross national income (GNI), measured at average 2007–09 prices, was US $3,159m., equivalent to $960 per head (or $1,960 on an international purchasing-power parity basis). During 2000–09, it was estimated, the population increased at an average annual rate of 2.6%, while gross domestic product (GDP) per head increased, in real terms, by an average of 1.3% per year. According to the World Bank, overall GDP increased, in real terms, at an average annual rate of 4.0% in 2000–09; GDP increased by 3.7% in 2008, but declined by 1.1% in 2009.

Agriculture (including forestry and fishing) contributed 12.7% of GDP in 2009, according to the African Development Bank (AfDB). In 2011, according to FAO estimates, about 50.0% of the labour force were employed in the sector. Owing to the unsuitability of much of the land for crop cultivation, output of staple foods (millet, sorghum, rice and pulses) is insufficient for the country's needs. Livestock-rearing is the principal occupation of the rural population. Fishing, which in 2007 provided 18.3% of export earnings, supplies 5%–10% of annual GDP and a sizeable proportion of budgetary revenue, and also makes a significant contribution to domestic food requirements. During 2000–07, according to the World Bank, agricultural GDP increased by an average of 0.5% per year; the sector's GDP increased by 1.9% in 2007.

Industry (including mining, manufacturing, construction and power) provided 46.8% of GDP in 2009, according to the AfDB, and engaged 9.1% of the economically active population in 2000. During 2000–07 industrial GDP increased at an average annual rate of 3.4%; it increased by 1.9% in 2007.

Mining contributed 21.6% of GDP in 2009, according to the AfDB, and engaged 5.1% of the economically active population in 2000. The principal activity in this sector is the extraction of iron ore, exports of which contributed 41.3% of total merchandise export earnings in 2007. Gypsum, salt, gold and copper are also mined. Other exploitable mineral resources include diamonds, phosphates, sulphur, peat, manganese and uranium. In October 1999 highly valuable blue granite deposits were discovered in the north of the country. Many international companies were involved in offshore petroleum exploration in Mauritania in the early 2000s, with reserves at the offshore Shafr el Khanjar and Chinguetti fields estimated at 450m.–1,000m. barrels; production commenced at Chinguetti in February 2006. According to the IMF, the GDP of the mining sector increased by an average of 8.9% per year in 1996–2005. The sector's GDP increased by an estimated 0.6% in 2005.

The manufacturing sector contributed 18.6% of GDP in 2009, according to the AfDB, and engaged 1.0% of the economically active population in 2000. Fish processing (which contributed 3.9% of GDP in 2002) is the most important activity. The processing of minerals (including imported petroleum) is also of some significance. According to the World Bank, manufacturing GDP declined at an average annual rate of 2.7% in 2000–07; however, it increased by 11.6% in 2006 and by 1.9% in 2007.

Construction contributed 6.6% of GDP in 2009, according to the AfDB, and engaged 2.6% of the economically active population in 2000.

Mauritania began to utilize electricity generated at hydroelectric installations constructed under the auspices of the Organisation pour la mise en valeur du fleuve Sénégal (OMVS) in late 2002, thus reducing the country's dependence on power generated at thermal stations. Imports of petroleum products comprised 30.6% of the total value of merchandise imports in 2007.

The services sector contributed 40.5% of GDP in 2009, according to the AfDB, and engaged 38.1% of the economically active population in 2000. The combined GDP of the services sector increased at an average rate of 7.0% per year during 2000–07. Services GDP rose by 1.9% in 2007.

In 2008 Mauritania's visible trade surplus was projected at US $207.4m.; however, there was a projected deficit of an estimated $227.1m. on the current account of the balance of payments. In 2007 the principal source of imports (15.8%) was France; other major suppliers were Brazil and the People's Republic of China. The principal markets for exports (excluding exports of petroleum, gold and copper) in that year were France (18.3%), Spain, Italy, Germany, Japan, Belgium and China. The principal exports in 2007 were iron ore, petroleum and fish. The principal imports in that year were petroleum products, food products, construction materials, and road vehicles and parts.

Mauritania's overall budget deficit for 2010 was projected at UM 53,400m. The country's general government gross debt was UM 816,916m. in 2009, equivalent to 103.0% of GDP. Total external debt in 2008 was US $1,960m., of which $1,643m. was public and publicly guaranteed debt. In 1998 the cost of debt-servicing was equivalent to 14.2% of the value of exports of goods, services and income. The annual rate of inflation averaged 6.4% in 2000–09; consumer prices increased by an average of 2.2% in 2009. The overall rate of unemployment in 2000 was 28.9%.

The exploitation, from the mid-2000s, of previously untapped petroleum reserves, principally at offshore locations, was expected to have a significant impact on Mauritania's economy, and in particular on export revenues, which had hitherto been largely dependent on fishing and on the extraction of iron ore. The first major offshore field, at Chinguetti, began production, operated by Woodside Petroleum (of Australia), in 2006; the rise in international petroleum prices was expected to result in increased revenue from that sector and further potential for growth was represented by ongoing onshore petroleum and natural gas drilling operations. In recent years government revenue has also been bolstered by the sale of fishing licences to foreign fleets. Following the election of Gen. Mohamed Ould Abdel Aziz to the presidency in July 2009, in December the European Union restored diplomatic relations with Mauritania and resumed its aid programmes, which had been suspended after the coup of 2008. Co-operation with the IMF was also reinstated and a three-year Extended Credit Facility (ECF) agreement, aimed at addressing corruption and poverty and at reviving development initiatives, was approved in March 2010. The rapid rise in the cost of foodstuffs—Mauritania is obliged to import more than 70% of its staple food requirements—precipitated unrest in the late 2000s and exacerbated the already precarious food security situation. Although a food security agreement was signed with Italy in December 2009, which included €4.5m. of funding towards the stabilization of food production and supply, there remained concerns regarding the adverse effect of poor harvests. In November 2010 the IMF completed its first review of Mauritania's economic performance under the programme supported by the ECF arrangement and approved a further disbursement of US $17m. Following a recession in 2009, precipitated by the international financial crisis, the Fund noted indications of strong economic recovery, supported by a resurgence in prices for the country's main exports. The Government was to continue efforts to improve tax and customs administration, to accelerate public service reform to contain the wage bill and to restrain other expenditure. In late 2010 France agreed to provide €3m. to support Mauritania's state budget.

PUBLIC HOLIDAYS

2012: 1 January (New Year's Day), 4 February* (Mouloud, Birth of Muhammad), 1 May (Labour Day), 25 May (African Liberation Day, anniversary of the OAU's foundation), 16 June* (Leilat al-Meiraj, Ascension of Muhammad), 10 July (Armed Forces Day), 18 August* (Korité—Id al-Fitr, end of Ramadan), 26 October* (Tabaski—Id al-Adha, Feast of the Sacrifice), 15 November* (Islamic New Year), 28 November (Independence Day).

* These holidays are determined by the Islamic lunar calendar and may vary by one or two days from the dates given.

MAURITANIA

Statistical Survey

Source (unless otherwise stated): Office National de la Statistique, BP 240, Nouakchott; tel. 45-25-28-80; fax 45-25-51-70; e-mail webmaster@ons.mr; internet www.ons.mr.

Area and Population

AREA, POPULATION AND DENSITY

Area (sq km)	1,030,700*
Population (census results)	
5–20 April 1988	1,864,236†
1–15 November 2000‡	
Males	1,241,712
Females	1,266,447
Total	2,508,159
Population (official estimates)	
2009	3,456,430
2010	3,340,623
2011	3,440,053
Density (per sq km) at mid-2011	3.3

* 397,950 sq miles.
† Including an estimate of 224,095 for the nomad population.
‡ Figures include nomads, totalling 128,163 (males 66,007; females 62,156), enumerated during 10 March–20 April 2001.

Ethnic Groups (percentage of total, 1995): Moor 81.5; Wolof 6.8; Toucouleur 5.3; Sarakholé 2.8; Peul 1.1; Others 2.5 (Source: La Francophonie).

POPULATION BY AGE AND SEX
(UN estimates at mid-2011)

	Males	Females	Total
0–14	689,668	650,833	1,340,501
15–64	1,017,598	989,768	2,007,366
65 and over	37,621	54,565	92,186
Total	1,744,887	1,695,166	3,440,053

Source: UN, *World Population Prospects: The 2008 Revision*.

REGIONS
(census of November 2000)

Region	Area ('000 sq km)	Population*	Chief town
Hodh Ech Chargui	183	281,600	Néma
Hodh el Gharbi	53	212,156	Aïoun el Atrous
Assaba	37	242,265	Kiffa
Gorgol	14	242,711	Kaédi
Brakna	33	247,006	Aleg
Trarza	68	268,220	Rosso
Adrar	215	69,542	Atâr
Dakhlet-Nouadhibou	22	79,516	Nouadhibou
Tagant	95	76,620	Tidjikja
Guidimagha	10	177,707	Sélibaby
Tiris Zemmour	253	41,121	Zouïrât
Inchiri	47	11,500	Akjoujt
Nouakchott (district)	1	558,195	Nouakchott
Total	1,030	2,508,159	

* Including nomad population, enumerated during 10 March–20 April 2001.

PRINCIPAL TOWNS
(population at census of 2000*)

Nouakchott (capital)	558,195	Kiffa	32,716
Nouadhibou	72,337	Bougadoum	29,045
Rosso	48,922	Atâr	24,021
Boghé	37,531	Boutilimit	22,257
Adel Bagrou	36,007	Theiekane	22,041
Kaédi	34,227	Ghabou	21,700
Zouïrât	33,929	Mal	20,488

* With the exception of Nouakchott, figures refer to the population of communes (municipalities), and include nomads.

Mid-2009 (incl. suburbs, UN estimate): Nouakchott 708,789 (Source: UN, *World Urbanization Prospects: The 2009 Revision*).

BIRTHS AND DEATHS
(annual averages, UN estimates)

	1995–2000	2000–05	2005–10
Birth rate (per 1,000)	37.4	35.8	33.8
Death rate (per 1,000)	10.8	10.6	10.5

Source: UN, *World Population Prospects: The 2008 Revision*.

Life expectancy (years at birth, WHO estimates): 58 (males 56; females 59) in 2008 (Source: WHO, *World Health Statistics*).

ECONOMICALLY ACTIVE POPULATION
(census of 2000, persons aged 10 years and over, including nomads)

	Males	Females	Total
Agriculture, hunting, forestry and fishing	219,771	94,535	314,306
Mining and quarrying	5,520	249	5,769
Manufacturing	18,301	11,855	30,156
Electricity, gas and water	2,655	182	2,837
Construction	15,251	311	15,562
Trade, restaurants and hotels	83,733	24,799	108,532
Transport, storage and communications	17,225	691	17,916
Financing, insurance, real estate and business services	1,557	454	2,011
Community, social and personal services	72,137	26,583	98,720
Other and unspecified	33,350	22,608	55,958
Total	469,500	182,267	651,767

Mid-2011 (estimates in '000): Agriculture, etc. 741; Total labour force 1,481 (Source FAO).

Health and Welfare

KEY INDICATORS

Total fertility rate (children per woman, 2008)	4.5
Under-5 mortality rate (per 1,000 live births, 2008)	118
HIV/AIDS (% of persons aged 15–49, 2007)	0.8
Physicians (per 1,000 head, 2004)	0.11
Hospital beds (per 1,000 head, 2006)	0.40
Health expenditure (2007): US $ per head (PPP)	47
Health expenditure (2007): % of GDP	2.4
Health expenditure (2007): public (% of total)	65.3
Access to water (% of persons, 2008)	49
Access to sanitation (% of persons, 2008)	26
Total carbon dioxide emissions ('000 metric tons, 2007)	1,949.2
Carbon dioxide emissions per head (metric tons, 2007)	0.6
Human Development Index (2010): ranking	136
Human Development Index (2010): value	0.433

For sources and definitions, see explanatory note on p. vi.

MAURITANIA

Agriculture

PRINCIPAL CROPS
('000 metric tons)

	2007	2008	2009
Rice, paddy	82.2	82.2	99.3*
Maize	17.0	15.5	12.5*
Sorghum	80.0	85.6	90.3*
Millet	1.6	2.3	5.0*
Peas, dry	10.0	10.0	n.a.
Cow peas, dry	8.0	8.0	n.a.
Beans, dry	9.9*	9.9*	10.0†
Dates	20.0	19.2	20.0†

* Unofficial figure.
† FAO estimate.

Aggregate production ('000 metric tons, may include official, semi-official or estimated data): Total cereals 183 in 2007, 191 in 2008, 212 in 2009; Total pulses 45 in 2007–09; Total roots and tubers 7 in 2007–09; Total vegetables (incl. melons) 4 in 2007–09; Total fruits (excl. melons) 23 in 2007, 22 in 2008, 23 in 2009.

Source: FAO.

LIVESTOCK
('000 head, year ending September)

	2007	2008	2009
Cattle	1,700	1,628	1,700
Goats	5,600	5,600	5,600*
Sheep	8,850†	8,850*	n.a.
Asses*	160	160	160
Horses	20*	20*	n.a.
Camels	1,494	1,495	1,600*
Chickens*	4,300	4,300	4,300

* FAO estimate(s).
† Unofficial figure.
Source: FAO.

LIVESTOCK PRODUCTS
('000 metric tons, FAO estimates)

	2004	2005	2006
Goat meat	14.6	14.6	14.6
Camel meat	23.5	24.0	22.5
Chicken meat	4.4	4.4	4.5
Camel milk	26.3	26.3	26.3
Cows' milk	122.5	124.3	126.0
Sheep's milk	97.9	97.9	97.9
Goats' milk	110.7	100.7	111.2
Hen eggs	5.3	5.3	5.4

2007–09: Figures assumed to be unchanged from 2006 (FAO estimates).
Source: FAO.

Forestry

ROUNDWOOD REMOVALS
('000 cubic metres, excl. bark, FAO estimates)

	2007	2008	2009
Sawlogs, veneer logs and logs for sleepers	1	1	1
Other industrial wood	2	2	2
Fuel wood	1,704	1,747	1,791
Total	1,707	1,750	1,794

Source: FAO.

Fishing
('000 metric tons, live weight)

	2006	2007	2008
Freshwater fishes*	15.0	15.0	15.0
Sardinellas	14.6	28.8	21.8
European pilchard (sardine)	9.1	22.3	15.3
European anchovy	16.3	17.7	12.6
Jack and horse mackerels	28.2	24.8	34.2
Chub mackerel	2.9	7.6	6.3
Octopuses	12.1	11.5	7.6
Total catch (incl. others)*	165.3	223.2	195.3

* FAO estimates.
Source: FAO.

Mining
('000 metric tons)

	2007	2008	2009
Gypsum	49.2	44.4	36.9
Iron ore: gross weight	11,817	10,950	10,275
Iron ore: metal content*	7,680	7,120	6,680

* Estimates.
Source: US Geological Survey.

Industry

SELECTED PRODUCTS
('000 metric tons unless otherwise indicated)

	2007	2008	2009
Cement*	410	322	340
Crude steel*	5	5	5
Electric energy (million kWh)	415.3	477.0	n.a.

* Data from US Geological Survey.

Finance

CURRENCY AND EXCHANGE RATES

Monetary Units
5 khoums = 1 ouguiya (UM).

Sterling, Dollar and Euro Equivalents (31 March 2010)
£1 sterling = 401.172 ouguiyas;
US $1 = 264.800 ouguiyas;
€1 = 356.924 ouguiyas;
1,000 ouguiyas = £2.49 = $3.78 = €2.80.

Average Exchange Rate (ouguiyas per US $)
2007 258.587
2008 238.203
2009 262.366

MAURITANIA

BUDGET
('000 million ouguiyas)

Revenue*	2003	2004	2005†
Tax revenue	44.9	59.2	76.0
Taxes on income and profits	12.0	16.3	26.6
Tax on business profits	6.6	9.3	15.7
Tax on wages and salaries	4.8	6.3	9.9
Taxes on goods and services	24.7	30.8	36.2
Value-added tax	16.6	21.8	26.7
Turnover taxes	3.3	2.7	2.8
Tax on petroleum products	2.4	2.8	2.5
Other excises	1.6	2.7	3.3
Taxes on international trade	7.3	11.1	10.8
Other current revenue	42.9	47.4	38.8
Fishing royalties and penalties	32.6	36.6	35.3
Revenue from public enterprises	2.1	4.2	0.6
Capital revenue	16.1	11.3	6.2
Other revenue (incl. special accounts)	8.3	6.6	2.8
Total	**103.9**	**117.9**	**121.0**

Expenditure‡	2003	2004	2005†
Current expenditure	105.0	96.7	126.7
Wages and salaries	16.0	17.2	22.4
Goods and services	35.3	36.9	60.6
Transfers and subsidies	26.3	9.6	8.7
Military expenditure	16.4	18.6	17.7
Interest on public debt	9.3	11.9	16.1
Capital expenditure	44.0	43.1	36.7
Domestically financed	25.4	24.6	21.4
Financed from abroad	18.6	18.5	15.2
Unidentified	9.2	9.6	0.0
Total	**158.1**	**149.3**	**163.4**

* Excluding grants received ('000 million ouguiyas): 15.7 in 2003; 12.5 in 2004; 10.3 (preliminary) in 2005.
† Preliminary figures.
‡ Excluding restructuring and net lending ('000 million ouguiyas): 1.4 in 2003; 0.2 in 2004; 2.9 in 2005 (preliminary).

Source: IMF, *Islamic Republic of Mauritania: Statistical Appendix* (July 2006).

2005 ('000 million ouguiyas, revised estimates): Total revenue 131.3; Total expenditure 166.1.

2006 ('000 million ouguiyas, preliminary figures): Total revenue 406.0; Total expenditure 206.4 (Source: IMF, *Islamic Republic of Mauritania: 2008 Article IV Consultation and Third Review Under the Three-Year Arrangement Under the Poverty Reduction and Growth Facility—Staff Report; Staff Supplement; Public Information Notice and Press Release on the Executive Board Discussion; and Statement by the Executive Director for the Islamic Republic of Mauritania*—July 2008).

2007 ('000 million ouguiyas): Total revenue 185.4; Total expenditure 217.3 (Source: IMF, *Islamic Republic of Mauritania: 2009 Article IV Consultation and Request for a Three- Year Arrangement Under the Extended Credit Facility—Staff Report; Public Information Notice and Press Release on the Executive Board Discussion; and Statement by the Executive Director for the Islamic Republic of Mauritania*—April 2010).

2008 ('000 million ouguiyas, estimates): Total revenue 189.0; Total expenditure 262.0 (Source: IMF, *Islamic Republic of Mauritania: 2009 Article IV Consultation and Request for a Three- Year Arrangement Under the Extended Credit Facility—Staff Report; Public Information Notice and Press Release on the Executive Board Discussion; and Statement by the Executive Director for the Islamic Republic of Mauritania*—April 2010).

2009 ('000 million ouguiyas, estimates): Total revenue 188.5; Total expenditure 242.9 (Source: IMF, *Islamic Republic of Mauritania: 2009 Article IV Consultation and Request for a Three- Year Arrangement Under the Extended Credit Facility—Staff Report; Public Information Notice and Press Release on the Executive Board Discussion; and Statement by the Executive Director for the Islamic Republic of Mauritania*—April 2010).

2010 ('000 million ouguiyas, projections): Total revenue 231.0; Total expenditure 284.4 (Source: IMF, *Islamic Republic of Mauritania: 2009 Article IV Consultation and Request for a Three- Year Arrangement Under the Extended Credit Facility—Staff Report; Public Information Notice and Press Release on the Executive Board Discussion; and Statement by the Executive Director for the Islamic Republic of Mauritania*—April 2010).

INTERNATIONAL RESERVES
(US $ million at 31 December)

	2007	2008	2009
Gold*	9.5	9.9	12.6
IMF special drawing rights	0.1	0.1	0.2
Foreign exchange	197.8	188.5	225.2
Total	**207.4**	**198.5**	**238.0**

*Valued at market-related prices.

Source: IMF, *International Financial Statistics*.

MONEY SUPPLY
(million ouguiyas at 31 December)

	2007	2008	2009
Currency outside banks	68,924	69,988	82,226
Demand deposits at deposit money banks	102,133	133,068	148,967
Total money (incl. others)	**171,057**	**203,056**	**232,111**

Source: IMF, *International Financial Statistics*.

COST OF LIVING
(Consumer Price Index; base: 2000 = 100)

	2006	2007	2008
Food (incl. beverages)	157.3	173.9	190.6
Clothing (incl. footwear)	143.5	149.7	152.5
Rent	145.1	157.3	169.6
All items (incl. others)	**147.9**	**158.7**	**170.4**

Source: ILO.

All items (Consumer Price Index; base: 2005 = 100): 113.9 in 2007; 122.3 in 2008; 125.0 in 2009 (Source: IMF, *International Financial Statistics*).

NATIONAL ACCOUNTS
(million ouguiyas at current prices)

Expenditure on the Gross Domestic Product

	2007	2008	2009
Government final consumption expenditure	159,082	193,423	205,835
Private final consumption expenditure	597,069	533,301	674,036
Gross fixed capital formation	162,321	223,294	287,097
Changes in stocks	1,640	2,255	2,900
Total domestic expenditure	**920,112**	**952,273**	**1,169,868**
Exports of goods and services	399,724	574,491	559,863
Less Imports of goods and services	529,998	621,949	703,234
GDP in purchasers' values	**789,838**	**904,815**	**1,026,496**

Gross Domestic Product by Economic Activity

	2007	2008	2009
Agriculture, hunting, forestry and fishing	100,759	102,286	116,960
Mining and quarrying	133,862	211,782	199,539
Manufacturing	117,500	124,166	171,110
Construction	49,871	51,806	61,153
Wholesale and retail trade, restaurants and hotels	86,649	88,260	102,550
Transport and communications	35,348	37,588	43,629
Finance, insurance, real estate and business and other services	81,990	86,457	99,325
Public administration and defence	106,625	110,001	127,480
Sub-total	**712,604**	**812,346**	**921,745**
Indirect taxes, less subsidies	77,234	92,470	104,751
GDP in purchasers' values	**789,838**	**904,815**	**1,026,496**

Note: Deduction for imputed bank service charge assumed to be distributed at origin.

Source: African Development Bank.

MAURITANIA

BALANCE OF PAYMENTS
(US $ million)

	2006*	2007†	2008‡
Exports of goods f.o.b.	1,366.6	1,454.4	2,006.7
Imports of goods f.o.b.	−1,167.0	−1,431.5	−1,799.2
Trade balance	199.6	22.9	207.4
Exports of services	86.7	84.2	116.9
Imports of services	−406.3	−511.8	−639.8
Balance on goods and services	−120.0	−404.7	−315.5
Other income received	119.0	140.9	145.4
Other income paid	−193.3	−201.7	−282.1
Balance on goods, services and income	−194.3	−465.5	−452.2
Private unrequited transfers (net)	66.5	70.2	75.6
Official transfers	92.1	74.0	149.5
Current balance	−35.6	−321.3	−227.1
Capital account (net)	1,107.2	50.8	1,117.2
Direct investment (net)	154.6	138.3	103.2
Official medium- and long-term loans	−835.7	79.3	260.7
Other capital	−168.3	48.0	−218.1
Net errors and omissions	60.2	20.8	0
Overall balance	282.3	15.8	1,035.9

* Preliminary figures.
† Estimated figures.
‡ Projected estimates.

Source: IMF, *Islamic Republic of Mauritania: 2008 Article IV Consultation and Third Review Under the Three-Year Arrangement Under the Poverty Reduction and Growth Facility—Staff Report; Staff Supplement; Public Information Notice and Press Release on the Executive Board Discussion; and Statement by the Executive Director for the Islamic Republic of Mauritania* (July 2008).

External Trade

PRINCIPAL COMMODITIES
('000 million ouguiyas)

Imports	2005	2006	2007
Food products	32.2	65.0	84.0
Cosmetic chemical products	4.1	6.1	6.2
Petroleum products	35.9	77.8	113.3
Construction materials	17.6	24.3	31.3
Road vehicles and parts	11.6	20.1	26.0
Various equipment and appliances	231.7	52.5	68.1
Total (incl. others)	356.7	292.4	369.8

Exports	2005	2006	2007
Iron ore	101.3	122.2	144.4
Fish	46.4	46.0	64.0
Petroleum	n.a.	170.5	87.5
Total (incl. others)	147.7	340.6	349.9

PRINCIPAL TRADING PARTNERS
(US $ million)

Imports c.i.f.	2005	2006	2007
Belgium	9.9	14.0	16.7
Brazil	8.5	17.1	22.2
China, People's Republic	7.6	16.4	21.8
Côte d'Ivoire	0.6	1.5	6.3
France	36.7	43.7	58.6
Germany	8.5	12.1	14.4
Greece	2.3	4.2	5.7
Italy	1.8	6.8	16.5
Japan	6.4	10.3	12.5
Malaysia	1.0	2.6	5.1
Morocco	1.6	2.8	5.7
Netherlands	2.4	6.2	5.7
Singapore	1.4	1.6	6.3
Spain	6.0	9.7	14.0
United Arab Emirates	3.0	4.8	7.8
United Kingdom	83.6	3.5	15.4
USA	28.7	15.9	16.6
Total (incl. others)	357.1	292.4	369.8

Exports c.i.f.*	2005	2006	2007
Belgium	20.3	21.9	19.1
China, People's Republic	2.2	3.2	17.6
Finland	1.0	n.a.	3.4
France	25.9	29.3	38.1
Germany	21.5	23.2	25.9
Italy	24.0	31.8	27.1
Japan	20.4	21.2	20.7
Russia	n.a.	1.4	5.0
Spain	15.8	19.7	30.9
United Kingdom	1.9	3.2	8.1
Total (incl. others)	147.7	168.2	208.5

* Excluding exports of petroleum, gold and copper.

Transport

RAILWAYS

1984: Passengers carried 19,353; Passenger-km 7m.; Freight carried 9.1m. metric tons; Freight ton-km 6,142m.

Freight ton-km (million, estimates): 6,720 in 1991; 6,810 in 1992; 6,890 in 1993 (figures for 1988–93 are) (Source: UN Economic Commission for Africa, *African Statistical Yearbook*).

ROAD TRAFFIC
(motor vehicles registered)

	2004	2005	2006
Passenger cars	6,033	6,040	6,182
Government vehicles	251	317	369
Specialist vehicles	413	542	504

SHIPPING

Merchant Fleet
(registered at 31 December)

	2007	2008	2009
Number of vessels	152	155	155
Total displacement ('000 grt)	51.5	52.0	52.0

Source: IHS Fairplay, *World Fleet Statistics*.

International Sea-borne Freight Traffic
(Port of Nouakchott, '000 metric tons)

	2005	2006	2007
Goods loaded	113.2	80.4	250.8
Goods unloaded	1,712.9	1,696.6	2,045.1

Source: Port Autonome de Nouakchott.

MAURITANIA

CIVIL AVIATION
(traffic on scheduled services)*

	2004	2005	2006
Kilometres flown (million)	1	1	1
Passengers carried ('000)	128	139	149
Passenger-km (million)	56	60	65
Total ton-km (million)	5	6	6

* Including an apportionment of the traffic of Air Afrique.

Source: UN, *Statistical Yearbook*.

Tourism

Tourist arrivals (estimates, '000): 24 in 1999.

Receipts from tourism (US $ million, excl. passenger transport): 28 in 1999 (Source: World Tourism Organization).

Communications Media

	2007	2008	2009
Telephones ('000 main lines in use)	40.3	76.4	74.5
Mobile cellular telephones ('000 subscribers)	1,414.0	2,092.0	2,182.2
Internet users ('000)	45	60	75
Broadband subscribers	4,000	5,900	9,000

Personal computers: 139,000 (45.4 per 1,000) in 2006.

Television receivers ('000 in use): 247 in 1999.

Radio receivers ('000 in use): 570 in 1997.

Daily newspapers: Estimated average circulation ('000 copies) 12 in 1996; 3 in 2004.

Sources: UNESCO, *Statistical Yearbook*; UN, *Statistical Yearbook*; International Telecommunication Union.

Education
(2008/09 unless otherwise indicated)

			Students		
	Institutions	Teachers	Males	Females	Total
Pre-primary	n.a.	251*	n.a.	n.a.	4,856*
Primary	2,676†	13,131‡	254,281‡	258,717‡	512,998‡
Secondary	n.a.	4,154	54,054	45,204	99,258
Tertiary	4§	353‖	n.a.	n.a.	11,794

* 2004/05.
† 1998/99.
‡ 2009/10.
§ 1995/96.
‖ 2005/06.

Pupil-teacher ratio (primary education, UNESCO estimate): 39.1 in 2008/09.

Adult literacy rate (UNESCO estimates): 56.8% (males 64.1%; females 49.5%) in 2008.

Sources: mainly UNESCO Institute for Statistics and Ministry of National Education, Nouakchott.

Directory

While no longer an official language, French is still widely used in Mauritania, especially in the commercial sector. Many organizations are therefore listed under their French names, by which they are generally known.

The Government

HEAD OF STATE

President: MOHAMED OULD ABDEL AZIZ (inaugurated 5 August 2009).

COUNCIL OF MINISTERS
(May 2011)

Prime Minister: MOULAYE OULD MOHAMED LAGHDAF.

Minister, Secretary-General to the President of the Republic: ADAMA SY.

Minister of State for National Education, Higher Education and Scientific Research: AHMED OULD BAHYA.

Minister of Justice: ABIDINE OULD EL KHAIRE.

Minister of Foreign Affairs and Co-operation: HAMADI OULD BABA OULD HAMADI.

Minister of National Defence: AHMEDOU OULD IDEY OULD MOHAMED RADHI.

Minister of the Interior and Decentralization: MOHAMED OULD BOILIL.

Minister of Economic Affairs and Development: SIDI OULD TAH.

Minister of Finance: THIAM DIOMBAR.

Minister of Islamic Affairs and Original Education: AHMED OULD NEINI.

Minister of the Civil Service and the Modernization of the Administration: MATY MINT HAMADY.

Minister of Health: BA HOUSSEINOU HAMADY.

Minister of Petroleum, Energy and Mines: TALEB OULD ABDI VALL.

Minister of Fisheries and the Maritime Economy: GHDAFNA OULD EYIH.

Minister of Trade, Industry, Crafts and Tourism: BAMBA OULD DARAMANE.

Minister of Housing, Urban Development and Land Settlement: ISMAIL OULD BEDDE OULD CHEIKH SIDIYA.

Minister of Rural Development: BRAHIM OULD M'BARECK OULD MOHAMED EL MOCTAR.

Minister of Equipment and Transport: YAHYA OULD HADEMINE.

Minister of Water Resources and Sanitation: MOHAMED LEMINE OULD ABOYE.

Minister of Culture, Youth and Sports: CISSÉ MINT CHEIKH OULD BOYDE.

Minister of Communication and Relations with Parliament: HAMDY OULD MAHJOUB.

Minister of Social Affairs, Childhood and Families: MOULATY MINT EL MOCTAR.

Minister-delegate to the Prime Minister, in charge of the Environment and Sustainable Development: AMEDI CAMARA.

Minister-delegate to the Minister of State for National Education, in charge of Primary Education: HAMED HAMOUNY.

Minister-delegate to the Minister of State for National Education, in charge of Secondary Education: OUMAR OULD MATALLA.

MAURITANIA

Minister-delegate to the Minister of State for National Education, in charge of Employment, Vocational Training and New Technologies: MOHAMED OULD KHOUNA.
Secretary-General of the Government: MOHAMED OULD MOHAMEDOU.

MINISTRIES

Office of the President: BP 184, Nouakchott; tel. and fax 45-25-26-36.
Office of the Prime Minister: BP 237, Nouakchott; tel. 45-25-33-37.
Ministry of Capital Works and Transport: BP 237, Nouakchott; tel. 45-25-33-37.
Ministry of the Civil Service and the Modernization of the Administration: BP 193, Nouakchott; tel. and fax 45-25-84-10.
Ministry of Communication: Nouakchott.
Ministry of Culture, Youth and Sports: BP 223, Nouakchott; tel. 45-25-11-30.
Ministry of Economic Affairs and Development: 303 Ilot C, BP 5150, Nouakchott; tel. 45-25-16-12; fax 45-25-51-10; e-mail nfomaed@mauritania.mr; internet www.economie.gov.mr.
Ministry of Finance: BP 181, Nouakchott; tel. 45-25-20-20; internet www.finances.gov.mr.
Ministry of Fisheries and the Maritime Economy: BP 137, Nouakchott; tel. 45-25-46-07; fax 45-25-31-46; e-mail ministre@mpem.mr; internet www.mpem.mr.
Ministry of Foreign Affairs and Co-operation: BP 230, Nouakchott; tel. 45-25-26-82; fax 45-25-28-60.
Ministry of Health and Social Affairs: BP 177, Nouakchott; tel. 45-25-20-52; fax 45-25-22-68; internet www.sante.gov.mr.
Ministry of Higher Education and Scientific Research: Nouakchott.
Ministry of the Interior and Decentralization: BP 195, Nouakchott; tel. 45-25-36-61; fax 45-25-36-40; e-mail paddec@mauritania.mr; internet www.interieur.gov.mr.
Ministry of Islamic Affairs and Original Education: Nouakchott; internet www.affairesislamiques.gov.mr.
Ministry of Justice: BP 350, Nouakchott; tel. 45-25-10-83; fax 45-25-70-02.
Ministry of National Education: BP 387, Nouakchott; tel. 45-25-12-37; fax 45-25-12-22.
Ministry of Petroleum, Energy and Mines: Nouakchott; tel. 45-25-71-40.
Ministry of Rural Development and the Environment: BP 366, Nouakchott; tel. 45-25-15-00; fax 45-25-74-75; internet www.agriculture.gov.mr.
Ministry of Trade, Industry, Crafts and Tourism: BP 182, Nouakchott; tel. 45-25-35-72; fax 45-25-76-71.
Ministry of Water Resources and Sanitation: BP 4913, Nouakchott; tel. 45-25-71-44; fax 45-29-42-87; e-mail saadouebih@yahoo.fr.
Office of the Secretary-General of the Government: BP 184, Nouakchott.

President and Legislature

PRESIDENT

Presidential Election, 18 July 2009, provisional results

Candidate	Votes	% of votes
Mohamed Ould Abdel Aziz	409,100	52.64
Messaoud Ould Boulkheir	126,782	16.31
Ahmed Ould Mohameden Ould Daddah	106,263	13.67
Mohamed Jemil Ould Brahim Ould Mansour	37,059	4.77
Ibrahima Moktar Sarr	35,709	4.60
Ely Ould Mohamed Vall Ould Eleya	29,681	3.82
Kane Hamidou Baba	11,568	1.49
Saleh Ould Mohamedou Ould Hanena	10,219	1.32
Hamady Ould Abdallahi Meymou	8,936	1.15
Sghair Ould M'Bareck	1,788	0.23
Total	**777,105**	**100.00**

Al-Jamiya al-Wataniyah
(National Assembly)

ave de l'Indépendance, BP 185, Nouakchott; tel. 45-25-11-30; fax 45-25-70-78; internet www.mauritania.mr/assemblee.
President: MESSOUD OULD BOULKHEIR.

General Election, 19 November and 3 December 2006

Party	Constituency seats	National list seats	Total seats
Rally of Democratic Forces	12	3	15
Union of Progressive Forces	7	1	8
Republican Party for Democracy and Renewal	5	2	7
Popular Progressive Alliance	4	1	5
Centrist Reformists	2	2	4
Mauritanian Party for Union and Change—Hatem	3	1	4
Union for Democracy and Progress	2	1	3
Rally for Democracy and Unity	2	1	3
Democratic Renewal	1	1	2
Alternative	1	—	1
Union of the Democratic Centre	1	—	1
Popular Front	—	1	1
Independents	41	—	41
Total	**81**	**14**	**95**

Majlis ash-Shuyukh
(Senate)

ave de l'Indépendance, BP 5838, Nouakchott; tel. 45-25-68-77; fax 45-25-73-73; internet www.senat.mr.
President: BÂ MAMADOU DIT M'BARÉ.

The total number of seats in the Senate is 56 with three seats reserved for representatives of the Mauritanian diaspora. After elections held on 21 January and 4 February 2007, the strength of the parties was as follows:

Party	Seats
Independents	34
Coalition of Forces for Democratic Change	15
Republican Party for Democracy and Renewal	3
Total*	**52**

*The result from one constituency was annulled by the Constitutional Council and the remaining three reserved seats were yet to be allocated.

Elections to renew 17 seats were held on 8 and 15 November 2009, at which the Union for the Republic secured 13 seats, the Union for Democracy and Progress and the National Rally for Reform and Development (Tawassoul) one seat each and independent candidates won two seats.

Election Commission

National Independent Electoral Commission: Nouakchott; 15 mems; Pres. (vacant).

Advisory Council

Economic and Social Council: Nouakchott.

Political Organizations

Alliance for Justice and Democracy (AJD): Nouakchott; Leader CISSÉ AMADOU CHIEKHOU.

Alternative (Al-Badil): Nouakchott; f. 2006; mem. of Co-ordination of the Democratic Opposition coalition, formed in 2010; Leader MOHAMED YEHDHIH OULD MOKTAR EL HASSEN.

Centrist Reformists: Nouakchott; f. 2006; mem. of Coalition of Forces for Democratic Change, formed in advance of legislative and local elections in 2006; moderate Islamist grouping.

Democratic Renewal: Nouakchott; f. 2005; mem. of Coalition of Forces for Democratic Change, formed in advance of legislative and local elections in 2006; Pres. MOUSTAPHA OULD ABEIDERRAHMANE.

Mauritanian African Liberation Forces—Renovation (MALF—Renovation): Nouakchott; tel. 22-28-77-40 (mobile); internet www.flam-renovation.org; f. 2006 in split from clandestine, exiled, Mauritanian African Liberation Forces; represents interests of Afro- (Black) Mauritanians; mem. of Coalition of Forces for Democratic Change, formed in advance of legislative and local elections in 2006; Leader MAMADOU BOCAR BÂ.

MAURITANIA

Mauritanian Labour Party: Nouakchott; f. 2001; Leader MOHAMED EL HAFEDH OULD DENNA.

Mauritanian Party for the Defence of the Environment (MPDE—The Greens): Nouakchott; internet pmde.hautetfort .com; ecologist; mem. of Bloc of Parties for Change, formed in advance of legislative and local elections in 2006; Pres. MOHAMED OULD SIDI OULD DELLAHI.

Mauritanian Party for Renewal and Agreement: Nouakchott; f. 2001; Leader MOULAY EL-HASSEN OULD JIYID.

Mauritanian Party for Union and Change—Hatem: Nouakchott; f. 2005 by leadership of the fmr prohibited Knights of Change militia and reformist elements of the fmr ruling Democratic and Social Republican Party; mem. of Coalition of Forces for Democratic Change, formed in advance of legislative and local elections in 2006; Pres. SALEH OULD HNANA; Sec.-Gen. ABDERAHMANE OULD MINI.

Mauritanian People's Rally Party (MPRP): Nouakchott; f. 2009 by parliamentary deputies in support of ruling military junta; Leader Dr LOULEID OULD WEDAD.

National Party for Democracy and Development (NPDD): Nouakchott; Leader YAHYA OULD EL WAGHEF.

National Rally for Reform and Development (NRRD) (Tawassoul): f. 2007; Islamist; Leader MOHAMED JEMIL OULD MANSOUR.

Party for Liberty, Equality and Justice (PLEJ): Nouakchott; internet www.plej.biz; mem. of Bloc of Parties for Change, formed in advance of legislative and local elections in 2006; mem. of Co-ordination of the Democratic Opposition coalition, formed in 2010; Pres. MAMADOU ALASSANE BÂ.

Popular Front (PF): Nouakchott; f. 1998; social-liberal; mem. of Coalition of Forces for Democratic Change, formed in advance of legislative and local elections in 2006; Leader MOHAMED LEMINE CH'BIH OULD CHEIKH MELAININE.

Popular Progressive Alliance (PPA): Nouakchott; internet www .app.mr; f. 1991; mem. of Coalition of Forces for Democratic Change, formed in advance of legislative and local elections in 2006; mem. of Co-ordination of the Democratic Opposition coalition, formed in 2010; Pres. MESSAOUD OULD BOULKHAR.

Rally for Democracy and Unity (RDU): Nouakchott; f. 1991; supported regime of fmr Pres. Taya; Chair. AHMED OULD SIDI BABA.

Rally of Democratic Forces (RDF): Ilot K, 120, BP 4986, Nouakchott; tel. 45-25-67-46; fax 45-25-65-70; e-mail info@rfd-mauritanie .org; internet www.rfd-mauritanie.org; f. 2001; mem. of Coalition of Forces for Democratic Change, formed in advance of legislative and local elections in 2006; mem. of Co-ordination of the Democratic Opposition coalition, formed in 2010; Pres. AHMED OULD DADDAH.

Republican Party for Democracy and Renewal (RPDR): ZRB, Tevragh Zeina, Nouakchott; tel. 45-29-18-36; fax 45-29-18-00; e-mail info@prdr.mr; internet www.prdr.mr; f. 2006 to replace Democratic and Social Republican Party, the fmr ruling party, prior to *coup d'état* of August 2005; Leader SIDI MOHAMED OULD MED VALL DIT GHRINY.

Reward (Sawab): Nouakchott; f. 2004; social democratic; Chair. of Central Council MOHAMED MAHMOUD OULD GHOULMA; Pres. Dr CHEIKH OULD SIDI OULD HANENA.

Union for Democracy and Progress (UDP): Ilot V, 70, Tevragh Zeina, BP 816, Nouakchott; tel. 45-25-52-89; fax 45-25-29-95; f. 1993; Pres. NAHA HAMDI MINT.

Union of the Democratic Centre (UDC): Nouakchott; f. 2005 by fmr mems of the Democratic and Social Republican Party, the fmr ruling party; Pres. CHEIKH SID'AHMED OULD BABA.

Union of Democratic Youth (UDY): f. 2008; promotes patriotism and moderate Islamic values, opposes extremism; Pres. JEDDOU OULD AHMAD.

Union of Progressive Forces (UPF) (Ittihad Quwa al-Taqaddum): Nouakchott; e-mail ufpweb2@yahoo.fr; internet www.ufpweb .org; tel. 45-29-32-66; fax 45-24-35-86; e-mail infos@ufpweb.org; f. 2000; mem. of Coalition of Forces for Democratic Change, formed in advance of legislative and local elections in 2006; mem. of Co-ordination of the Democratic Opposition coalition, formed in 2010; Pres. MOHAMED OULD MAOULOUD; Sec.-Gen. MOHAMED EL MOUSTAPHA OULD BEDREDDINE.

Union for the Republic (UR): Nouakchott; f. 2009; Chair. MOHAMED MAHMOUD OULD MOHAMED LEMINE.

Unauthorized, but influential, is the Islamic **Ummah Party** (the Constitution prohibits the operation of religious political organizations), founded in 1991 and led by Imam SIDI YAHYA, and the Baathist **National Vanguard Party (Taliaa)**, which was officially dissolved by the Government in 1999 and is led by AHMEDOU OULD BABANA. The clandestine **Mauritanian African Liberation Forces (MALF)** was founded in 1983 in Senegal to represent Afro-Mauritanians (Point d'ébullition, BP 5811, Dakar-Fann, Senegal; tel. +221 822-80-77; e-mail ba_demba@yahoo.fr; internet members.lycos.co.uk/ flamnet; Pres. SAMBA THIAM); a faction broke away from this organization and returned to Mauritania in early 2006, forming the Mauritanian African Liberation Forces—Renovation. A further group based in exile is the **Arab-African Salvation Front against Slavery, Racism and Tribalism—AASF** (e-mail faas@caramail .com; internet membres.lycos.fr/faas). In August 2007 a further 18 new parties were registered: included were an Islamist party, the **National Rally for Reform and Development**, and two parties led by women, the **National Party for Development**, led by SAHLA BINT AHMAD ZAYID, and the **Mauritanian Hope Party**, led by TAHI BINT LAHBIB.

Diplomatic Representation

EMBASSIES IN MAURITANIA

Algeria: Ilot A, Tevragh Zeina, BP 625, Nouakchott; tel. 45-25-35-69; fax 45-25-47-77; Ambassador ZAHANI ABDEL HAMID.

China, People's Republic: rue 42-133, Tevragh Zeina, BP 257, Nouakchott; tel. 45-25-20-70; fax 45-25-24-62; e-mail chinaemb_mr@ mfa.gov.cn; internet mr.china-embassy.org; Ambassador CHEN GONGLAI.

Congo, Democratic Republic: Tevragh Zeina, BP 5714, Nouakchott; tel. 45-25-46-12; fax 45-25-50-53; e-mail ambardc.rim@ caramail.com; Chargé d'affaires a.i. TSHIBASU MFUAD.

Egypt: Villa 468, Tevragh Zeina, BP 176, Nouakchott; tel. 45-25-21-92; fax 45-25-33-84; Ambassador Dr YOUSSOUF AHMED CHARGHAOUI.

France: rue Ahmed Ould Hamed, Tevragh Zeina, BP 231, Nouakchott; tel. 45-29-96-99; fax 45-29-69-38; e-mail ambafrance .nouakchott-amba@diplomatie.gouv.fr; internet www .france-mauritanie.mr; Ambassador MICHEL VENDEPOORTER.

Germany: Tevragh Zeina, BP 372, Nouakchott; tel. 45-25-17-29; fax 45-25-17-22; e-mail info@nouakchott.diplo.de; internet www .nouakchott.diplo.de; Ambassador DIETMAR BLAAS.

Iraq: Tevragh Zeina, Nord Villa 399, Nouakchott; tel. 45-24-32-52; fax 45-24-32-51; e-mail nokemb@iraqmfamail.com; Ambassador AHMED NAEEF RASHID AL-DULAIMI.

Japan: Hotel al-Khaima, 10 rue Mamadou Konate, BP 5219, Nouakchott; tel. 45-25-09-77; fax 45-25-09-76; Ambassador HIROSHI AZUMA.

Korea, Democratic People's Republic: Nouakchott; Ambassador (vacant).

Kuwait: Tevragh Zeina, BP 345, Nouakchott; tel. 45-25-33-05; fax 45-25-41-45; Ambassador ADNAN ABDELLAH AL-AHMED.

Libya: BP 673, Nouakchott; tel. 45-25-52-02; fax 45-25-50-53; Chargé d'affaires ISSA ALI EL-VENAS.

Mali: Tevragh Zeina, BP 5371, Nouakchott; tel. 45-25-40-81; fax 45-25-40-83; e-mail ambmali@hotmail.com; Ambassador ETHMANE KONÉ.

Morocco: 569 ave de Gaulle, Tevragh Zeina, BP 621, Nouakchott; tel. 45-25-14-11; fax 45-29-72-80; e-mail sifmankttt@mauritel.mr; Ambassador ABDERRAHMANE BENOMAR.

Nigeria: Ilot P9, BP 367, Nouakchott; tel. 45-25-23-04; fax 45-25-23-14; Ambassador Alhaji BALA MOHAMED SANI.

Qatar: BP 609, Nouakchott; tel. 45-25-23-99; fax 45-25-68-87; e-mail nouakchoti@mofa.gov.qa; Ambassador MOHAMMED KURDI TALEB AL-MERRI.

Russia: rue Abu Bakr, BP 221, Nouakchott; tel. 45-25-19-73; fax 45-25-52-96; e-mail ambruss@opt.mr; Ambassador VLADIMIR BAYBAKOV.

Saudi Arabia: Las Balmas, Zinat, BP 498, Nouakchott; tel. 45-25-26-33; fax 45-25-29-49; e-mail mremb@mofa.gov.sa; Ambassador SAOUD BEN ABDEL AZIZ EL-JABIRI.

Senegal: Villa 500, Tevragh Zeina, BP 2511, Nouakchott; tel. 45-25-72-90; fax 45-25-72-91; Ambassador MAHMOUDOU CHEIKH KANE.

South Africa: Hotel Tfeila, Mezzanine Floor, Salon el-Waha, ave Charles de Gaulle, BP 2006, Nouakchott; tel. 45-24-55-90; fax 45-24-55-91; e-mail nouakchott@foreign.gov.za; Ambassador JOHANNES JACOBUS SPIES.

Spain: BP 232, Nouakchott; tel. 45-25-20-80; fax 45-25-40-88; e-mail emb.nouakchott@mae.es; Ambassador ALONSO DEZCALLAR Y MAZARREDO.

Syria: Tevragh Zeina, BP 288, Nouakchott; tel. 45-25-27-54; fax 45-25-45-00; Ambassador SAID EL-BENI.

Tunisia: BP 631, Nouakchott; tel. 45-25-28-71; fax 45-25-18-27; Ambassador CHAFIK HAJJI.

United Arab Emirates: Tafarugh Zeena Quarter, ZRA 742 bis, Nouakchott; tel. 45-25-10-98; fax 45-25-09-92; e-mail embeau@ mauritel.mr; Ambassador ABDULLAH MOHAMMED AT-TAKAWI.

USA: rue Abdallaye, BP 222, Nouakchott; tel. 45-25-26-60; fax 45-25-15-92; e-mail tayebho@state.gov; internet mauritania.usembassy .gov; Ambassador JO ELLEN POWELL.

MAURITANIA

Yemen: Tevragh Zeina, BP 4689, Nouakchott; tel. 45-25-55-91; fax 45-25-56-39; Ambassador Mohamed Ali Yahya Shiban.

Judicial System

The Code of Law was promulgated in 1961 and subsequently modified to incorporate Islamic institutions and practices. The main courts comprise three courts of appeal, 10 regional tribunals, two labour tribunals and 53 departmental civil courts. A revenue court has jurisdiction in financial matters. The members of the High Court of Justice are elected by the National Assembly and the Senate.

Shari'a (Islamic) law was introduced in February 1980. A special Islamic court was established in March of that year, presided over by a magistrate of Islamic law, assisted by two counsellors and two *ulemas* (Muslim jurists and interpreters of the Koran). A five-member High Council of Islam, appointed by the President, advises upon the conformity of national legislation to religious precepts, at the request of the President.

Audit Court (Cour des Comptes): Nouakchott; audits all govt institutions; Pres. Sow Adama Samba.

Constitutional Council: f. 1992; includes six mems, three nominated by the Head of State and three designated by the Presidents of the Senate and National Assembly; Pres. Sghair Ould M'Barek; Sec.-Gen. Sy Adama.

High Council of Islam (al-Majlis al-Islamiya al-A'la'): Nouakchott; f. 1992; Pres. Mahfoudh Ould Lemrabott.

High Court of Justice: Nouakchott; f. 1961; comprises an equal number of appointees elected from their membership by the National Assembly and the Senate, following each partial or general renewal of those legislative bodies; competent to try the President of the Republic in case of high treason, and the Prime Minister and members of the Government in case of conspiracy against the State.

Supreme Court: BP 201, Palais de Justice, Nouakchott; tel. and fax 45-25-67-40; f. 1961; comprises an administrative chamber, two civil and social chambers, a commercial chamber and a criminal chamber; Pres. Seyid Ould Ghailany.

Religion

ISLAM

Islam is the official religion, and the population are almost entirely Muslims of the Malekite rite. The major religious groups are the Tijaniya and the Qadiriya. Chinguetti, in the region of Adrar, is the seventh Holy Place in Islam. A High Council of Islam supervises the conformity of legislation to Muslim orthodoxy.

CHRISTIANITY

Roman Catholic Church

Mauritania comprises the single diocese of Nouakchott, directly responsible to the Holy See. The Bishop participates in the Bishops' Conference of Senegal, Mauritania, Cape Verde and Guinea-Bissau, based in Dakar, Senegal. There were an estimated 4,500 adherents, mainly non-nationals, in the country.

Bishop of Nouakchott: Most Rev. Martin Albert Happe, Evêché, BP 5377, Nouakchott; tel. 45-25-04-27; fax 45-25-37-51; e-mail mgrmartinhappe@yahoo.fr.

The Press

Of some 400 journals officially registered in Mauritania in 2004, some 30 were regular, widely available publications, of which the following were among the most important:

Al-Akhbar: BP 5346, Nouakchott; tel. 45-25-08-94; fax 45-25-37-57; e-mail fr.redaction@alakhbar.info; internet fr.alakhbar.info; f. 1995; weekly; Arabic.

Biladi: BP 1122, Nouakchott; tel. and fax 45-24-02-75; e-mail bbiladi@gmail.com; internet www.rmibiladi.com; French; Dir of Publication Moussa Ould Hamed.

Al-Qalam/Le Calame: BP 1059, Nouakchott; tel. 45-24-08-29; fax 45-24-08-30; e-mail calame@compunet.mr; internet www.lecalame.mr; f. 1994; weekly; Arabic and French; independent; Editors-in-Chief Riyad Ould Ahmed el-Hadi (Arabic edn), Ahmed Cheikh (French edn).

Châab: BP 371, Nouakchott; tel. 45-25-29-40; fax 45-25-85-47; e-mail chaabrim@gmail.com; internet www.ami.mr/chaab; f. 1975; daily; Arabic; also publ. in French *Horizons*; publ. by Agence Mauritanienne de l'Information; Dir-Gen. Mohamed el-Hafed Ould Maham.

Challenge: BP 1346, Nouakchott; tel. and fax 45-29-22-46; e-mail challengehebdo@yahoo.fr; internet www.challenge-mr.com; weekly.

Ech-tary: BP 1059, Nouakchott; tel. 45-25-50-65; e-mail info@echtary.net; internet www.echtary.net; fortnightly; Arabic; satirical.

Essirage Hebdo: Nouakchott; tel. 22-01-09-82; e-mail wadiaa@maktoob.com; internet www.essirage.net; weekly.

L'Essor: BP 5310, Nouakchott; tel. 36-30-21-68 (mobile); fax 45-25-88-90; e-mail sidiel2000@yahoo.fr; monthly; the environment and the economy; Dir Sidi el-Moctar Cheïguer; circ. 2,500.

L'Eveil-Hebdo: BP 587, Nouakchott; tel. 45-25-67-14; fax 45-25-87-54; e-mail symoudou@yahoo.fr; f. 1991; weekly; independent; Dir of Publication Sy Mamadou.

Journal Officel: BP 188, Nouakchott; tel. 45-25-33-37; fax 45-25-34-74; fortnightly.

Maghreb Hebdo: BP 5266, Nouakchott; tel. 45-25-98-10; fax 45-25-98-11; f. 1994; weekly; Dir Khattri Ould Diè.

Mauritanies1: Nouakchott; e-mail contact@mauritanies1.com; internet www.mauritanies1.com; monthly.

Al-Mourabit: Nouakchott; tel. 45-24-95-35; e-mail brahimbakar@almourabit.mr; internet www.almourabit.mr; weekly; French; Editor-in-Chief Brahim Ould Bakar Ould Sneiba.

Nouakchott-Info: Immeuble Abbas, Tevragh Zeina, BP 1905, Nouakchott; tel. 45-25-02-71; fax 45-25-54-84; e-mail aboulmaaly@yahoo.com; internet www.ani.mr; f. 1995; daily; independent; Arabic and French; Dir of Publication and Editor-in-Chief Mohamed Mahmoud Aboul Maaly.

Points Chauds: Ilot L prés de la garde Nationale (face de Mauritanie couleur), Nouakchott; tel. 45-25-06-04; fax 45-29-37-97; e-mail info@pointschauds.info; internet www.pointschauds.info; Editor-in-Chief Moulay Ahmed.

Le Quotidien de Nouakchott: BP 1153 Nouakchott; tel. 45-24-53-74; e-mail khalioubi@yahoo.fr; internet www.quotidien-nouakchott.com; French; Editor-in-Chief Khalilou Diagana.

Ar-Rayah (The Banner): Nouakchott; e-mail team@rayah.info; internet www.rayah.info; f. 1997; independent; weekly; pro-Islamist; Editor Ahmed Ould Wediaa.

Tahalil Hebdo: BP 5205, Nouakchott; tel. 45-24-18-00; fax 45-25-80-87; e-mail contact@journaltahalil.com; internet www.journaltahalil.com; weekly; French.

La Tribune: BP 6227, Nouakchott; tel. 46-46-18-82 (mobile); e-mail contact@la-tribune.info; internet www.la-tribune.info; weekly; French; Editor-in-Chief Kissima Tocka Diagana.

NEWS AGENCY

Agence Mauritanienne de l'Information (AMI): BP 371, Nouakchott; tel. 45-25-29-40; fax 45-25-45-87; e-mail ami@mauritania.mr; internet www.ami.mr; fmrly Agence Mauritanienne de Presse; state-controlled; news and information services in Arabic and French; Man. Dir Yarba Ould Sghair.

Publishers

Imprimerie Commerciale et Administrative de Mauritanie: BP 164, Nouakchott; textbooks, educational.

Imprimerie Nationale: BP 618, Nouakchott; tel. 45-25-44-38; fax 45-25-44-37; f. 1978; state-owned; Pres. Rachid Ould Saleh; Man. Dir Issimou Mahjoub.

GOVERNMENT PUBLISHING HOUSE

Société Nationale d'Impression: BP 618, Nouakchott; Pres. Moustapha Saleck Ould Ahmed Brihim.

Broadcasting and Communications

TELECOMMUNICATIONS

Autorité de Régulation: 428 rue 23023 Ksar, BP 4908, Nouakchott; tel. 45-29-12-70; fax 45-29-12-79; e-mail webmaster@are.mr; internet www.are.mr; f. 1999; Pres. Mohamed Salem Ould Lekhal.

Chinguitel: Carrefour Cité SMAR, Nouakchott; tel. 22000291; internet www.chinguitel.mr; provides mobile cellular, fixed-line and internet services; Dir-Gen. Abderrahmane Ousmane.

Mauritel: BP 7000, Nouakchott; tel. 45-25-23-40; fax 45-25-17-00; e-mail webmaster@mauritel.mr; internet www.mauritel.mr; fmrly Société Mauritanienne des Télécommunications; 46% state-owned, 34% owned by Maroc Télécom (Morocco), 20% owned by Abdallahi Ould Noueigued group; Dir-Gen. Lhoussaine Oussalah.

MAURITANIA

El-Jawal Mauritel Mobiles: ave du Roi Fayçal, BP 5920, Nouakchott; tel. 45-29-80-80; fax 45-29-81-81; e-mail mminfos@mauritel.mr; internet www.eljawal.mr; f. 2000; operates a mobile cellular telephone network (El-Jawal) in Nouakchott and more than 27 other locations and three highways nation-wide; more than 350,000 subscribers (2005).

Société Mauritano-Tunisienne de Télécommunications (Mattel): 441 ave Charles de Gaulle, Tevragh-Zeina, BP 3668, Nouakchott; tel. 45-29-53-54; fax 45-29-81-03; e-mail mattel@mattel.mr; internet www.mattel.mr; f. 2000; privately owned Mauritanian-Tunisian co; operates mobile cellular communications network in Nouakchott and more than 10 other locations nation-wide; Dir-Gen. MOHAMMED HADJ KHALIFA.

BROADCASTING
Radio

Radio de Mauritanie (RM): ave Gamal Abdel Nasser, BP 200, Nouakchott; tel. and fax 45-25-21-64; e-mail rm@radiomauritanie.com; f. 1958; state-controlled; five transmitters; radio broadcasts in Arabic, French, Sarakolé, Toucouleur and Wolof; Dir SID BRAHIM OULD HAMDINOU.

Television

Télévision de Mauritanie (TVM): BP 5522, Nouakchott; tel. 45-25-40-67; fax 45-25-40-69; e-mail dgtvm@tvmsat.mr; internet www.tvm.mr; f. 1982; Dir-Gen. DIEH OULD SIDATY.

Finance

(cap. = capital; res = reserves; dep. = deposits; m. = million; br(s).= branch(es); amounts in ouguiyas)

BANKING

In 2010 there were 10 commercial banks, two other financial institutions and some 80 microfinance institutions operating in Mauritania.

Central Bank

Banque Centrale de Mauritanie (BCM): ave de l'Indépendance, BP 623, Nouakchott; tel. 45-25-22-06; fax 45-25-27-59; e-mail info@bcm.mr; internet www.bcm.mr; f. 1973; bank of issue; cap. 200m., res 2,869.7m., dep. 96,225.3m. (2009); Gov. SID'AHMED OULD RAISS; 4 brs.

Commercial Banks

Attijari Bank Mauritanie: 91/92 rue Mamadou Konaté, Nouakchott; tel. 45-29-63-74; fax 45-29-64-40; cap. 3,398m. (Dec. 2010).

Banque El Amana (BEA): Rue Mamadou Konaté BP 5559, Nouakchott; tel. 45-25-59-53; fax 45-25-34-95; e-mail info@bea.mr; internet www.bea.mr; f. 1996; 72% privately owned, 27% owned by Société Nationale Industrielle et Minière; cap. 4,790.3m. (March 2011); CEO AHMED SALEM BOUNA MOKHTAR; Gen. Man. AHMED SALEM ELY EL KORY.

Banque pour le Commerce et l'Industrie (BCI): ave Gemal Abdel Nasser, BP 5050, Nouakchott; tel. 45-29-28-76; fax 45-29-28-77; e-mail bci@bci-banque.com; internet www.bci-banque.com; f. 1999; privately owned; cap. 4,000m. (Dec. 2010); Pres. and Dir-Gen. ISSELMOU OULD DIDI OULD TAJEDINE; 11 brs.

Banque pour le Commerce et l'Investissement en Mauritanie (Bacim-Bank): P54, ave du Général Charles de Gaulle 20, rue 42-060, BP 1268, Nouakchott; tel. 45-29-19-00; fax 45-29-13-60; e-mail bacim-bank@mauritel.mr; internet www.bacim.mr; f. 2002; privately owned; cap. 1,500m. (Dec. 2005); Dir-Gen. HENRI CHAINTREUIL; 6 brs.

Banque Mauritanienne pour le Commerce International (BMCI): Immeuble Afarco, ave Nasser, BP 622, Nouakchott; tel. 45-25-28-26; fax 45-25-20-45; e-mail info@bmci.mr; internet www.bmci.mr; f. 1974; 95.82% owned by Group Abbas; cap. 4,000m., res 3,402m., dep. 31,005m. (Dec. 2006); Pres. and Dir-Gen. MOULAY SIDI OULD HACEN OULD ABASS; 18 brs.

Banque Nationale de Mauritanie (BNM): ave Gamal Abdel Nasser, BP 614, Nouakchott; tel. 45-25-26-02; fax 45-25-33-97; e-mail bnm10@bnm.mr; internet www.bnm.mr; f. 1989; privately owned; res 977m., dep. 20,659m. (Dec. 2003); cap. 6,000m. (Dec. 2005); Pres. and Dir-Gen. MOHAMED OULD NOUEIGUED; 10 brs.

Chinguitty Bank: ave Gamal Abdel Nasser, BP 626, Nouakchott; tel. 45-25-21-73; fax 45-25-33-82; e-mail chinguittybank@mauritel.mr; f. 1972; 51% owned by Libyan Arab Foreign Bank, 49% state-owned; cap. and res 4,002.9m., total assets 11,428.7m. (Dec. 2007); Pres. MOHAMED OULD DIDI; Gen. Man. YOUNIS TAHER AS-SOUDI; 2 brs.

Générale de Banque de Mauritanie pour l'Investissement et le Commerce SA (GBM): ave de l'Indépendance, BP 5558, Nouakchott; tel. 45-25-36-36; fax 45-25-46-47; e-mail gbm@gbm.mr.com; f. 1995; 70% privately owned; cap. 7,200m., res 14,037.6m., dep. 15,142.5m. (Dec. 2006); Pres. and Dir-Gen. MOHAMED HMAYEN OULD BOUAMATOU; 1 br.

Société Générale Mauritanie (SGM): ave Charles de Gaulle, BP 5085, Nouakchott; tel. 45-29-70-00; fax 45-24-53-00; internet www.sgm.mr; f. 2005; present name adopted 2007; cap. 4,000m. (Jan. 2006); Pres. and Dir-Gen. JEAN-PHILLIPE EQUILBECQ; 1 br.

Islamic Bank

Banque al-Wava Mauritanienne Islamique (BAMIS): 758, rue 22–018, ave du Roi Fayçal, BP 650, Nouakchott; tel. 45-25-14-24; fax 45-25-16-21; e-mail bamis@bamis.mr; internet www.bamis.mr; f. 1985; fmrly Banque al-Baraka Mauritanienne Islamique; majority share privately owned; cap. 2,000m., res 2,821m., dep. 13,778m. (Dec. 2005); Pres. MOHAMED ABDELLAHI OULD ABDELLAHI; Dir-Gen. MOHAMED ABDELLAHI OULD SIDI; Exec. Dir MOHAMED OULD TAYA; 2 brs.

INSURANCE

In 2008 there were eight insurance companies in Mauritania.

Assurances Générales de Mauritanie: BP 2141, ave de Gaulle, TZA Ilot A 667, Nouakchott; tel. 45-29-29-00; fax 45-29-29-11; Man. MOULAYE ELY BOUAMATOU.

Compagnie Nationale d'Assurance et de Réassurance (NASR): 12 ave Nasser, BP 163, Nouakchott; tel. 45-25-26-50; fax 45-25-18-18; e-mail nasr@nasr.mr; internet www.nasr.mr; f. 1994; state-owned; Pres. MOHAMED ABDALLAHI OULD SIDI; Dir-Gen. AHMED OULD SIDI BABA.

Mauritanienne d'Assurances et de Réassurances (MAR): Nouakchott; tel. 45-24-12-18; e-mail mar@mar-assur.mr; internet www.mar-assur.mr; f. 2002.

Société Anonyme d'Assurance et de Réassurance (SAAR): ave J. F. Kennedy, Immeuble El-Mamy, BP 2841, Nouakchott; tel. 45-25-30-56; fax 45-25-25-36; e-mail saar@infotel.mr; f. 1999; Pres. and Dir-Gen. AHMED BEZEID OULD MED LEMINE.

TAAMIN: BP 5164, Nouakchott; tel. 45-29-40-00; fax 45-29-40-02; e-mail info@assurancestaamin.com; internet www.assurancestaamin.com; Pres. and Dir-Gen. MOULAYE EL HASSEN OULD MOCTAR EL HASSEN.

Trade and Industry

DEVELOPMENT ORGANIZATIONS

Agence Française de Développement (AFD): rue Mamadou Kouaté prolongée, BP 5211, Nouakchott; tel. 45-25-25-25; fax 45-25-49-10; e-mail afdnouakchott@groupe-afd.org; internet www.afd.fr; Country Dir DIDIER GREBERT.

Service de Coopération et d'Action Culturelle: BP 203, Nouakchott; tel. 45-25-21-21; fax 45-25-20-50; e-mail mcap.coop.france@opt.mr; administers bilateral aid from France; Dir FRANÇOISE GIANVITI.

Société Nationale pour le Développement Rural (SONADER): BP 321, Nouakchott; tel. 45-21-18-00; fax 45-25-32-86; e-mail sonader@toptechnology.mr; f. 1975; Dir-Gen. MOHAMED OULD AHMAHOULLAH.

CHAMBER OF COMMERCE

Chambre de Commerce, d'Industrie et d'Agriculture de Mauritanie: BP 215, Nouakchott; tel. 45-25-22-14; fax 45-25-38-95; internet www.chambredecommerce.mr; f. 1954; Pres. MOHAMEDOU OULD MOHAMED MAHMOUD; Dir ABDEL AZIZ WANE.

EMPLOYERS' ORGANIZATION

Union Nationale du Patronat Mauritanien (UNPM): 824 ave de Roi Fayçal, Ksar, BP 383, Nouakchott; tel. 45-25-33-01; fax 45-25-91-08; e-mail germe@opt.mr; f. 1960; professional asscn for all employers active in Mauritania; Pres. AHMED BABA OULD AZIZI; Sec.-Gen. SEYID OULD ABDALLAHI.

UTILITIES
Electricity

Société Mauritanienne d'Electricité (SOMELEC): BP 355, Nouakchott; tel. 45-25-23-08; fax 45-25-39-95; e-mail dahane@somelec.mr; internet www.somelec.mr; f. 2001; state-owned; transfer to majority private sector ownership proposed; production and distribution of electricity; Dir-Gen. TALEB OULD ABDI VALL.

MAURITANIA

Gas

Société Mauritanienne de Gaz (SOMAGAZ): POB 5089, Nouakchott; tel. 45-24-28-58; fax 45-25-18-71; e-mail somagaz@somagaz.com; internet www.somagaz.com; f. 1987; production and distribution of butane gas; Dir-Gen. ABDALLAHI OULD BENANE.

Water

Société Nationale d'Eau (SNDE): 106 ave 42-096, Tevragh Zeina, BP 796, Nouakchott; tel. 45-25-52-73; fax 45-25-19-52; e-mail mfoudail@infotel.mr; f. 2001; Dir-Gen. CHEIKH ABDALLAH OULD HOUEIBIB.

TRADE UNIONS

Confédération Générale des Travailleurs de Mauritanie: BP 6164, Nouakchott; tel. 45-25-60-24; fax 45-25-80-57; e-mail admin@cgtm.org; internet cgtm.org; f. 1992; obtained official recognition in 1994; Sec.-Gen. ABDALLAHI OULD MOHAMED.

Confédération Libre des Travailleurs de Mauritanie: BP 6902, Nouakchott; fax 45-25-23-16; f. 1995; Sec.-Gen. SAMORY OULD BÉYE.

Confédération Nationale des Travailleurs de Mauritanie (CNTM): Nouakchott; tel. 45-00-17-01; fax 45-24-35-80; e-mail contact@cntm-rim.org; internet www.cntm-rim.org; Sec.-Gen. MOHAMED AHMED OULD SALECK.

Union des Travailleurs de Mauritanie (UTM): Bourse du Travail, BP 630, Nouakchott; f. 1961; Sec.-Gen. ABDERAHMANE OULD BOUBOU; 45,000 mems.

Transport

RAILWAYS

A 704-km railway connects the iron-ore deposits at Zouérate with Nouadhibou; a 40-km extension services the reserves at El Rhein, and a 30-km extension those at M'Haoudat. Motive power is diesel-electric. The Société Nationale Industrielle et Minière (SNIM) operates one of the longest (2.4 km) and heaviest (22,000 metric tons) trains in the world.

SNIM—Direction du Chemin de Fer et du Port: BP 42, Nouadhibou; tel. 45-74-51-74; fax 45-74-53-96; e-mail m.khalifa.beyah@zrt.snim.com; internet www.snim.com; f. 1963; Gen. Man. MOHAMED EL-MOCTAR OULD TALEB.

ROADS

In 2006 there were about 11,066 km of roads and tracks, of which only 2,966 km were paved. The 1,100-km Trans-Mauritania highway, completed in 1985, links Nouakchott with Néma in the east of the country. Plans exist for the construction of a 7,400-km highway, linking Nouakchott with the Libyan port of Tubruq (Tobruk). In August 1999 the Islamic Development Bank granted Mauritania a loan worth US $9.4m. to help finance the rebuilding of the Chouk–Kiffa road. The construction of a 470-km highway between Nouakchott and Nouadhibou was completed in 2004.

Société Mauritanienne des Transports (SOMATRA): Nouakchott; tel. 45-25-29-53; f. 1975; Pres. CHEIKH MALAININE ROBERT; Dir-Gen. MAMADOU SOULEYMANE KANE.

INLAND WATERWAYS

The River Senegal is navigable in the wet season by small coastal vessels as far as Kayes (Mali) and by river vessels as far as Kaédi; in the dry season as far as Rosso and Boghé, respectively. The major river ports are at Rosso, Kaédi and Gouraye.

SHIPPING

The principal port, at Point-Central, 10 km south of Nouadhibou, is almost wholly occupied with mineral exports. There is also a commercial and fishing port at Nouadhibou. The deep-water Port de l'Amitié at Nouakchott, built and maintained with assistance from the People's Republic of China, was inaugurated in 1986, and has a total capacity of about 1.5m. tons annually. In 2009 Mauritania's merchant fleet consisted of 155 vessels and had a total displacement of some 52,000 grt.

Mauritanienne de Transport Maritime: Nouakchott; tel. 45-25-44-79; fax 45-25-44-76; e-mail mtm@mtm.mr; internet www.mtm.mr; Pres. and Dir-Gen. A. KADER KAMIL.

Port Autonome de Nouadhibou: BP 236, Nouadhibou; tel. 45-74-51-36; fax 45-74-51-36; e-mail contact@pan.mr; internet www.portndb.com; f. 1973; state-owned; Pres. BAL MOHAMED EL HABIB; Dir-Gen. MOHAMED ABDERRAHMANE BRAHIM.

Port Autonome de Nouakchott (Port de l'Amitié): BP 5103, El Mina, Nouakchott; tel. 45-25-38-59; fax 45-25-16-15; e-mail info@panpa.mr; internet www.panpa.mr; f. 1986; deep-water port; Dir-Gen. AHMEDOU OULD HAMED.

Shipping Companies

Cie Mauritanienne de Navigation Maritime (COMAUNAM): 119 ave Nasser, BP 799, Nouakchott; tel. 45-25-36-34; fax 45-25-25-04; f. 1973; 51% state-owned, 49% owned by Govt of Algeria; nat. shipping co; forwarding agent, stevedoring; Chair. MOHAND TIGHILT; Dir-Gen. KAMIL ABDELKADER.

Société d'Acconage et de Manutention en Mauritanie (SAMMA): BP 258, Nouadhibou; tel. 45-74-52-63; fax 45-74-52-37; e-mail didi.samma@snim.com; internet www.samma.mr; f. 1960; freight and handling, shipping agent, forwarding agent, stevedoring; Man. Dir DIDI OULD BIHA.

Société Générale de Consignation et d'Entreprises Maritimes (SOGECO): 1765 rue 22-002, Commune du Ksar, BP 351, Nouakchott; tel. 45-25-22-02; fax 45-25-39-03; e-mail sogeco@sogeco.sa.mr; internet www.sogecosa.com; f. 1973; shipping agent, forwarding, stevedoring; Man. Dir SID'AHMED OULD ABEIDNA.

Société Mauritanienne pour la Pêche et la Navigation (SMPN): BP 40254, Nouakchott; tel. 45-25-36-38; fax 45-25-37-87; e-mail smpn@toptechnology.mr; Dir-Gen. ABDALLAHI OULD ISMAIL.

VOTRA: route de l'Aéroport, BP 454, Nouakchott; tel. 45-25-24-10; fax 45-25-31-41; e-mail info@votra.net; internet www.votra.net; Dir-Gen. MOHAMED MAHMOUD OULD MAYE.

CIVIL AVIATION

There are international airports at Nouakchott, Nouadhibou and Néma, and 23 smaller airstrips.

Mauritania Airlines International: Nouakchott; f. 2010; expected to commence operations in 2011.

Tourism

Mauritania's principal tourist attractions are its historical sites, several of which have been listed by UNESCO under its World Heritage Programme, and its game reserves and national parks. Some 24,000 tourists visited Mauritania in 1999. Receipts from tourism in that year totalled an estimated US $28m.

Office National du Tourisme: BP 2884, Nouakchott; tel. 45-29-03-44; fax 45-29-05-28; e-mail ont@tourisme-mauritanie.com; f. 2002; Dir KHADIJÉTOU MINT BOUBOU.

SOMASERT: BP 42, Nouadhibou; tel. 45-74-29-91; fax 45-74-90-43; e-mail somasert@snim.com; internet www.somasert.com; f. 1987; subsidiary of SNIM; responsible for promoting tourism, managing hotels and organizing tours; Dir-Gen. SAAD CHEIK SAAD BOUH.

Defence

As assessed at November 2010, the total armed forces numbered an estimated 15,870 men: army 15,000, navy about 620, air force 250. Full-time membership of paramilitary forces totalled about 5,000. Military service is by authorized conscription, and lasts for two years.

Defence Expenditure: Estimated at UM 30,100m. in 2009.

Chief of Staff of the Armed Forces: Gen. MOHAMED OULD CHEIKH MOHAMED AHMED.

Chief of Staff of the Navy: Col CHEIKH OULD BAYE.

Chief of Staff of the National Gendarmerie: Col N'DIAGA DIENG.

Education

Primary education, which is officially compulsory, begins at six years of age and lasts for six years. In 2008/09 total enrolment at primary schools included 76% of children in the relevant age-group (74% of boys; 79% of girls), according to UNESCO estimates. Secondary education begins at 12 years of age and lasts for six years, comprising two cycles of three years each. Total enrolment at public secondary schools in 2006/07 included only 16% of children in the appropriate age-group (17% of boys; 15% of girls), according to UNESCO estimates. In 2008/09 a total of 11,794 students were enrolled at Mauritania's higher education institutions (including the Université de Nouakchott, which was opened in 1983). In 2005 spending on education represented 8.3% of total budgetary expenditure.

MAURITIUS

Introductory Survey

LOCATION, CLIMATE, LANGUAGE, RELIGION, FLAG, CAPITAL

The Republic of Mauritius lies in the Indian Ocean. The principal island, from which the country takes its name, lies about 800 km (500 miles) east of Madagascar. The other main islands are Rodrigues, the Agalega Islands and the Cargados Carajos Shoals (St Brandon Islands). The climate is maritime sub-tropical and generally humid. The average annual temperature is 23°C (73°F) at sea-level, falling to 19°C (66°F) at an altitude of 600 m (about 2,000 ft). Average annual rainfall varies from 890 mm (35 ins) at sea-level to 5,080 mm (200 ins) on the highest parts. Tropical cyclones, which may be severe, occur between September and May. Most of the population are of Indian descent. The most widely spoken languages in 2000 were Creole (38.6%) and Bhojpuri (30.6%). English is the country's official language, and Creole (derived from French) the lingua franca. The principal religious group are Hindus, who comprise more than 50% of the population. About 30% are Christians and 17% are Muslims. The national flag (proportions 2 by 3) has four equal horizontal stripes, of red, blue, yellow and green. The capital is Port Louis.

CONTEMPORARY POLITICAL HISTORY

Historical Context

The islands of Mauritius and Rodrigues, formerly French possessions, passed into British control in 1810. Subsequent settlement came mainly from East Africa and India, and the European population has remained largely French-speaking.

A ministerial form of government was introduced in 1957. The first elections under universal adult suffrage, held in 1959, were won by the Mauritius Labour Party (MLP), led by Dr (later Sir) Seewoosagur Ramgoolam. Mauritius became independent, within the Commonwealth, on 12 March 1968, with Ramgoolam as Prime Minister.

In November 1965 the United Kingdom transferred the Chagos Archipelago (including the atoll of Diego Garcia), a Mauritian dependency about 2,000 km (1,250 miles) north-east of the main island, to the newly created British Indian Ocean Territory (BIOT, q.v.). Mauritius has subsequently campaigned for the return of the islands, which have been developed as a major US military base. Mauritius also claims sovereignty of the French-held island of Tromelin, about 550 km (340 miles) to the north-west.

Domestic Political Affairs

During the 1970s political opposition to successive coalition governments formed by Ramgoolam was led by a radical left-wing group, the Mouvement militant mauricien (MMM), founded by Paul Bérenger. Although the MMM became the largest single party in the Legislative Assembly following a general election in December 1976, Ramgoolam was able to form a new coalition Government with the support of the Parti mauricien social démocrate (PMSD). However, social unrest and rising unemployment undermined popular support for the Government, and at a general election in June 1982 the MMM, in alliance with the Parti socialiste mauricien (PSM), won all 60 contested seats on the main island. Anerood (later Sir Anerood) Jugnauth, the leader of the MMM, became Prime Minister, and Bérenger Minister of Finance.

The MMM/PSM coalition collapsed in March 1983, when Bérenger and his supporters resigned, following differences concerning economic policy. Jugnauth formed a new Government and a new party, the Mouvement socialiste militant (MSM), which subsequently merged with the PSM. A general election took place in August, at which an electoral alliance of the MSM, the MLP and the PMSD, led by Sir Gaëtan Duval, gained a legislative majority. Jugnauth formed a new coalition Government, in which Duval became Deputy Prime Minister. The MLP, however, withdrew from the coalition in February 1984.

Following a general election in August 1987, the MSM again formed an electoral alliance with the PMSD and the MLP; the three parties obtained 39 of the 62 elective seats. Bérenger, who failed to secure a seat, transferred his functions as leader of the opposition in the Legislative Assembly to Dr Paramhansa Nababsingh (while Bérenger himself replaced Nababsingh as Secretary-General of the MMM). A new coalition, led by Jugnauth, took office in September, and the Government subsequently announced plans to make Mauritius a republic within the Commonwealth. In August 1988, following a disagreement over employment policies, the PMSD withdrew from the coalition.

In July 1990 the MSM and the MMM agreed to form an alliance to contest the next general election, and to promote constitutional measures allowing Mauritius to become a republic within the Commonwealth. This proposal, however, was jointly opposed by the MLP and the PMSD, prompting Jugnauth to dismiss the MLP leader, Sir Satcam Boolell, from the Government, together with two dissident ministers from the MSM. A further three ministers representing the MLP resigned, leaving only one MLP member in the Government. Boolell subsequently relinquished the leadership of the MLP to Dr Navinchandra Ramgoolam (the son of the late Sir Seewoosagur Ramgoolam). In September Jugnauth formed a new coalition Government.

At a general election, which took place on 15 September, an alliance of the MSM, the MMM and the small Mouvement des travaillistes démocrates (MTD) won 57 of the 62 directly elected seats, while the MLP/PMSD alliance obtained three seats. The two remaining seats were secured by the Organisation du peuple rodriguais (OPR). Four 'additional' seats were subsequently allocated to members of the MLP/PMSD alliance. Jugnauth formed a new government coalition, to which nine representatives of the MMM (including Bérenger, who became Minister of External Affairs) and one representative of the MTD were appointed.

In December 1991 the Legislative Assembly approved the constitutional framework for the country's transition to a republic within the Commonwealth. Following the proclamation of the Republic of Mauritius on 12 March 1992, the Legislative Assembly was redesignated as the National Assembly, and the incumbent Governor-General, Sir Veerasamy Ringadoo, became interim President. Later in March the Government announced its choice of Cassam Uteem, the Minister of Industry and Industrial Technology and a member of the MMM, to assume the presidency in June. Uteem was duly elected President by the National Assembly; Sir Rabindrah Ghurburrun, a member of the MMM, took office as Vice-President.

The removal of Bérenger from the Council of Ministers in August 1993, on the grounds that he had repeatedly criticized government policy, precipitated a serious crisis within the MMM, the political bureau of which decided that the other nine members of the party who held ministerial portfolios should remain in the coalition Government. Led by Nababsingh, the Deputy Prime Minister, and Jean-Claude de l'Estrac, the Minister of Industry and Industrial Technology, supporters of the pro-coalition faction announced in October 1993 that Bérenger had been suspended as Secretary-General of the MMM. Bérenger and his supporters responded by expelling 11 MMM officials from the party, and seeking a legal ban on Nababsingh and de l'Estrac from using the party name. The split in the MMM led in November to a government reorganization, in which the remaining two MMM ministers supporting Bérenger were replaced by members of the party's pro-coalition faction.

Nababsingh and the dissident faction of the MMM, having lost Bérenger's legal challenge for the use of the party name, formed a new party, the Renouveau militant mauricien (RMM), which formally commenced political activity in June 1994. In the same month Jugnauth declared that the Government, which retained a cohesive parliamentary majority, would remain in office to the conclusion of its mandate in September 1996.

During the course of a parliamentary debate in November 1994 Bérenger and de l'Estrac accepted a mutual challenge to resign their seats in the National Assembly and to contest by-elections. In the following month the MSM indicated that it would not oppose RMM candidates in the two polls. In January 1995, however, Jugnauth unsuccessfully sought to undermine the MLP/MMM alliance by offering electoral support to the MLP.

The by-elections, held in February, were both won by MLP/MMM candidates, and Bérenger was returned to the National Assembly. Following these results, Jugnauth opened political negotiations with the PMSD, the leader of which, Charles Gaëtan Xavier-Luc Duval (the son of Sir Gaëtan Duval), entered the coalition as Minister of Industry and Industrial Technology and Minister of Tourism. The post of Attorney-General and Minister of Justice was also allocated to the PMSD, and Sir Gaëtan Duval agreed to act as an economic adviser to the Prime Minister. As a result, however, of widespread opposition within the PMSD to participation in the coalition, Xavier-Luc Duval left the Government in October, and Sir Gaëtan Duval subsequently resumed the leadership of the party. The Minister for Rodrigues, representing the OPR, also left the Government.

The 1995 general election

In November 1995 the Government was defeated in a parliamentary vote, requiring a two-thirds' majority, to introduce a constitutional requirement for instruction in oriental languages to be provided in primary schools. Jugnauth dissolved the National Assembly, and at the subsequent general election in December the MLP/MMM alliance won a decisive victory: of the 62 elected seats, the MLP secured 35 seats, the MMM obtained 25 seats and the OPR two seats. Under constitutional arrangements providing representation for unsuccessful candidates attracting the largest number of votes, Sir Gaëtan Duval re-entered the National Assembly, together with two members of the Mouvement rodriguais (MR) and one representative of Hizbullah, an Islamist fundamentalist group. Ramgoolam became Prime Minister of the new MLP/MMM coalition, with Bérenger as Deputy Prime Minister with responsibility for foreign and regional relations. Sir Gaëtan Duval died in May 1996 and was succeeded in the National Assembly and as leader of the PMSD by his brother, Hervé Duval, although Xavier-Luc Duval continued to command a significant following within the party.

Serious divisions began to emerge within the coalition Government in late 1996, when differences were reported between Ramgoolam and Bérenger over the allocation of ministerial responsibilities and the perception by the MMM of delays in the implementation of social and economic reforms. Bérenger's criticism of the coalition's performance intensified in the following months, and culminated in June in his dismissal from the Government and the consequent withdrawal of the MMM from the coalition. Following unsuccessful efforts by Ramgoolam to draw the PMSD into a new administration, an MLP Council of Ministers was formed by Ramgoolam, who additionally assumed Bérenger's former responsibilities for foreign affairs. Ramgoolam emphasized his determination to remain in office for the full legislative term to December 2000. On 28 June 1997 the National Assembly re-elected Cassam Uteem to a second five-year term as President. A prominent supporter of the MLP, Angidi Verriah Chettiar, was elected Vice-President.

Following the dissolution of the MLP/MMM alliance, Bérenger sought to assume the leadership of a consolidated political opposition to the Government. In August 1997 two small parties, the Mouvement Militant Socialiste Mauricien (MMSM) and the Rassemblement pour la réforme (RPR), agreed to support Bérenger in this aim. The alliance was extended to include a breakaway faction of the PMSD, known as the 'Vrais bleus', under the leadership of Hervé Duval, who had been replaced as party leader by Xavier-Luc Duval, an opponent of co-operation with the MMM.

In April 1998 the MMM, the MMSM, the RPR and the 'Vrais bleus' formed an electoral coalition, the Alliance nationale, to contest a by-election for a vacant seat in the National Assembly. The seat, which was retained by the MLP, had also been sought by Jugnauth on behalf of the MSM, which remained unrepresented in the National Assembly. Jugnauth, seeking to revitalize his party's prospects in preparation for the next general election (which was constitutionally required to take place by December 2000), subsequently entered negotiations with Bérenger for an electoral alliance, and in December 1998 both parties agreed terms for a joint list of candidates.

The MLP announced in mid-1999 its endorsement of the candidature of Xavier-Luc Duval for a legislative by-election to be held in September. Xavier-Luc Duval, after obtaining the vacant seat, joined the Government as Minister of Industry, Commerce, Corporate Affairs and Financial Services, following an extensive government reorganization completed at the end of the month. The selection in October of Pravind Jugnauth, the son of Sir Aneerood Jugnauth, as Deputy Leader of the MSM gave rise to speculation that Sir Aneerood was contemplating retirement from politics and intended his son to be his successor.

In August 2000 the MSM/MMM formed an alliance, in advance of the imminent general election, on the basis that Jugnauth would lead as Prime Minister for three years in the event of victory, before assuming the more honorary role of President, thus allowing Bérenger to become Prime Minister for the remaining two years.

The premiership of Aneerood Jugnauth

A general election was held on 11 September 2000, with 81% of the 790,000 registered electors casting their ballots. The MSM/MMM alliance achieved an overwhelming victory, winning 54 of the 62 directly elected seats in the National Assembly, while the MLP/PMSD alliance gained only six seats and the OPR two seats. As agreed, Sir Aneerood Jugnauth became Prime Minister again, while Paul Bérenger was appointed Deputy Prime Minister and Minister of Finance. A new Council of Ministers was appointed one week later.

In November 2000 the British High Court of Justice ruled that the eviction of several thousand inhabitants of the Chagos Archipelago between 1967 and 1973, to allow the construction of a US military base on the atoll of Diego Garcia, had been unlawful, and overturned a 1971 ordinance preventing the islanders from returning to the Archipelago. (The majority of the displaced islanders had been resettled in Mauritius, which had administered the Chagos Archipelago until its transfer to BIOT in 1965.) Following the ruling, the Mauritian Government declared its right to sovereignty over the islands to be indisputable and sought international recognition as such. Jugnauth stated that he would be prepared to negotiate with the USA over the continued presence of the military base. The United Kingdom responded that it would return the islands if, as had been maintained for many years, the USA was prepared to move out of the base on Diego Garcia. India declared its support for the Mauritian Government's claim to sovereignty, as part of the close relationship being encouraged between the two countries.

In November 2001 exiled Chagos islanders demonstrated outside the British High Commission in Port Louis, in support of their demands for compensation from the British Government. In February 2002 legislation allowing the displaced islanders to apply for British citizenship received royal assent in the United Kingdom. At that time the British Government was also examining the feasibility of a return to the Chagos Archipelago for the islanders, who continued to seek compensation.

In January 2002 a commission on constitutional and electoral reform presented its proposals at a series of public forums, before submitting them to the Government for consideration. Recommendations included the introduction of a system of proportional representation in legislative elections and a reinforcement of presidential powers. In mid-February controversial legislation on the prevention of terrorism was finally promulgated by the Chief Justice of the Supreme Court, Arianga Pillay, acting as interim President, following the resignations of both President Uteem and his successor, Vice-President Chettiar, over the issue. The legislation had been rejected by opposition parties and proved unpopular with many sections of society for arrogating excessive powers to the authorities and infringing on citizens' rights. On 25 February Karl Offman was elected as President by an extraordinary session of the National Assembly, which was boycotted by opposition deputies. Although formally elected for five years, Offman was to relinquish the presidency to Jugnauth in October 2003; in preparation for this, in April 2003 Jugnauth announced his resignation from the leadership of the MSM, to be succeeded by his son, Pravind.

In August 2003, in preparation for the transfer of governing roles, a constitutional amendment was approved by the National Assembly to increase the powers of the President, giving the incumbent the right to refuse a request from the Prime Minister to dissolve the legislature following a vote of no confidence. As agreed, on 1 October Offman resigned as President and was replaced, in an acting capacity, by the Vice-President, Raouf Bundhun, pending the election by the National Assembly of Sir Aneerood Jugnauth as his successor one week later. Jugnauth had resigned as Prime Minister on 30 September and was immediately replaced by Paul Bérenger, who appointed a new Council of Ministers. During his first months in office Bérenger conducted a premiership active in international diplomacy, visiting two of the country's principal trading partners, India and France, and signing co-operation agreements with Madagascar. In early 2004 he also renewed the campaign to reclaim sovereignty of the Chagos Archipelago from the United Kingdom, on

MAURITIUS

the basis that international law does not allow the dismemberment of a country before independence, and of Tromelin from France. It was established in 2004 that Mauritius had the right to pursue the case of the Chagos islands at the International Court of Justice, in spite of British objections on the basis of restrictions imposed by membership of the Commonwealth.

In early February 2005 the Minister of Public Infrastructure, Land Transport and Shipping, Anil Bachoo, resigned, to be replaced by Govindranath Gunness; the Minister of Local Government and Solid Waste Management, Mookhesswur Choonee, also left office the following week and was succeeded by Prithvirajsing Roopun. The two erstwhile ministers formed a new opposition party the following month, the Mouvement sociale démocrate (MSD), having also resigned from the MSM alleging poor leadership of that party by Pravind Jugnauth. Bachoo and Choonee reportedly disapproved of an apparent pre-electoral agreement between the parties of the ruling coalition, whereby, should they successfully be re-elected to office, Bérenger would relinquish the premiership in mid-term in favour of Pravind Jugnauth, just as the incumbent President (Pravind Jugnauth's father) had in September 2003. The MSD announced the formation of an electoral alliance with the MLP, known as the Social Alliance, thus creating a credible rival political force to the governing parties for the forthcoming legislative elections.

Navinchandra Ramgoolam becomes Prime Minister

At the elections, which were held on 3 July 2005, the Social Alliance bloc defeated the incumbent coalition, winning 38 of the 62 directly elected mandates. The MSM/MMM alliance took 22 seats while the OPR secured two. The rate of voter participation was 81.5%. Ramgoolam was appointed as Prime Minister and a new 19-member Council of Ministers was sworn into office later that month. Following the elections, the PMSD withdrew from the opposition alliance in which it had participated with the MSM and MMM. Tensions between the politically opposed premier and President initially proved somewhat obstructive to the functioning of the Government; however, they subsequently eased.

The Social Alliance Government continued with efforts to regain sovereignty over the Chagos Archipelago. A group of 102 Chagossians was permitted to visit the Archipelago in late March 2006 principally in order to visit the graves of relatives. In May the British High Court of Justice overturned the Orders in Council issued by the British Government under the royal prerogative in June 2004, ruling them to be unlawful, and confirmed the right of the islanders to return to the Archipelago without any conditions. In February 2007 the British Government commenced proceedings in the Court of Appeal to overturn the May 2006 ruling. However, in May 2007 that court confirmed that the residents of the Chagos Archipelago had been unlawfully removed and upheld the displaced islanders' immediate right to return. In November the House of Lords granted the British Government the right to appeal against the Court of Appeal's decision, on the condition that the Chagossians' costs were met by the British Government. In November 2008 the House of Lords ruled in favour of the British Government, thus denying the Chagossians the right to return, citing as its main reason the fact that the United Kingdom would have been obliged to meet the costs of economic, social and educational advancement of the residents. Having exhausted the appeals process in the United Kingdom, the Chagossians announced that they would take their case to the European Court of Human Rights (ECHR). It was estimated that only approximately 500 of the 2,000 Chagossians deported during the 1960s and 1970s were still alive.

In April 2010 the British Government announced that it had designated the Chagos archipelago a marine protection area (MPA), within which all fishing and other activities were to be prohibited. The conservation area, covering some 544,000 sq km, was to be patrolled by a ship vested with the powers to arrest fleets caught fishing illegally, to impose fines of up to £100,000 and to confiscate boats and fishing equipment. These plans were expected to have an impact on the Chagossians' hearing at the ECHR as the ban on fishing would remove the legal means by which they could sustain their standard of living. In December the Mauritian Government announced that it had taken a case against the United Kingdom to the UN International Tribunal for the Law of the Sea on the grounds that the MPA was not compatible with the UN Convention on the Law of the Sea. Furthermore, the Chagossians also appealed for a judicial review of the decision to create the MPA, although this was not to take place until after the ECHR had delivered its verdict.

Meanwhile, in April 2006 the opposition was further weakened when the MSM/MMM alliance collapsed following weeks of increasing tension between Pravind Jugnauth and Bérenger, and the PMSD announced that it was joining the government coalition. The MSM withdrew its support from Bérenger as official leader of the opposition, and he was succeeded by Nando Bodha, the Secretary-General of the MSM and a close ally of Pravind Jugnauth (who had failed to retain his seat in the legislature in July 2005), since the MSM held 11 seats in the National Assembly to the MMM's 10. Bodha's nomination was rejected by Ashock Jugnauth, a senior member of the MSM (and uncle of Pravind), who resigned from the party and established a new opposition party, the Union nationale. In August 2007 Chettiar resumed the position of Vice-President, replacing Bundhun. In September Bodha resigned as leader of the opposition and in October Bérenger once again assumed the role. Prime Minister Ramgoolam dismissed Minister of Foreign Affairs, International Trade and Co-operation Madan Murlidhar Dulloo in March 2008, assuming responsibility for that portfolio himself in an acting capacity.

Ramgoolam carried out a further reorganization of the Government in mid-September 2008, appointing four new ministers, including Jean François Chaumiere as Minister of Labour, Industrial Relations and Employment. Anil Bachoo was reinstated as Minister of Public Infrastructure, Land Transport and Shipping, and Arvin Boolell, hitherto in charge of international trade, was awarded the post of Minister of Foreign Affairs, Regional Integration and International Trade. On 19 September the National Assembly unanimously re-elected Anerood Jugnauth as President for a second five-year term, and on the following day legislation was approved that allowed for two ministers to hold the title of Vice-Prime Minister: these positions were awarded to Xavier-Luc Duval and Dr Rama Sithanen, with the former also retaining the tourism, leisure and external communications portfolio, while Sithanen retained the finance and economic empowerment portfolio. (The position of Deputy Prime Minister remained the second most senior post in the Council of Ministers—Ahmed Rashid Beebeejaun was appointed to this office and also assumed responsibility for the renewable energy and public utilities portfolio.) In January 2010 Hervé Aimé was appointed Minister of Local Government, Rodrigues and Outer Islands, following the sudden death of James Burty David the previous month.

Meanwhile, in February 2009 the Truth and Justice Commission Act came into force, providing for the establishment of a five-member commission, which would conduct inquiries into slavery and indentured labour in Mauritius during the colonial period; the commission was to be chaired by Professor Robert Shell, a South African national.

Recent developments: the 2010 legislative elections

In late March 2010 Ramgoolam announced the dissolution of the National Assembly in advance of legislative elections, which were scheduled to take place on 5 May. A total of 65 parties and alliances registered to contest the elections, most notably the Alliance de l'avenir, comprising the MLP, the PMSD and the MSM, and the Alliance du coeur, formed by the MMM, the Union nationale and the Mouvement mauricien social démocrate. In the event the Alliance de l'avenir secured 41 of the 62 directly elected seats and was awarded four additional seats. The Alliance du coeur took 18 directly elected seats and two additional seats, while the remaining directly elected seats were won by the MR (two) and the Front solidarité mauricienne (one). A further additional seat was allocated to the OPR, although the eighth seat remained vacant. The rate of voter participation was reported at some 78%. On 11 May Ramgoolam appointed a new Government (featuring 13 new ministers), in which he also assumed responsibility for the defence, home affairs and external communications portfolio. Beebeejaun was reappointed Deputy Prime Minister, while Xavier-Luc Duval became Vice-Prime Minister and Minister of Social Integration and Economic Empowerment, and Pravind Jugnauth became Vice-Prime Minister and Minister of Finance and Economic Development. Following the death of Chettiar in September, Monique Ohsan-Bellepeau of the MLP was elected Vice-President by the National Assembly in November (becoming the first woman to hold the vice-presidential office).

CONSTITUTION AND GOVERNMENT

Constitutional amendments, which were approved by the Legislative Assembly (henceforth known as the National Assembly) in December 1991 and came into effect on 12 March 1992, provided for the establishment of a republic. The constitutional Head of State is the President of the Republic, who is elected by a simple majority of the National Assembly for a five-year term of office. Legislative power is vested in the unicameral National Assembly, which comprises the Speaker, 62 members elected by universal adult suffrage for a term of five years, up to eight 'additional' members (unsuccessful candidates who receive the largest number of votes at a legislative election, to whom seats are allocated by the Electoral Supervisory Commission to ensure a balance in representation of the different ethnic groups), and the Attorney-General (if not an elected member). Executive power is vested in the Prime Minister, who is appointed by the President and is the member of the National Assembly best able to command a majority in the Assembly. The President appoints other ministers, on the recommendation of the Prime Minister.

REGIONAL AND INTERNATIONAL CO-OPERATION

Mauritius is a member of the Common Market for Eastern and Southern Africa (COMESA, see p. 228), the Southern African Development Community (SADC, see p. 420) and the Indian Ocean Commission (IOC, see p. 448), which aims to promote regional economic co-operation. Mauritius was among the founder members of the Indian Ocean Rim Association for Regional Co-operation (IOR—ARC, see p. 448) in 1997.

Mauritius became a member of the UN in 1968. As a contracting party to the General Agreement on Tariffs and Trade, Mauritius joined the World Trade Organization (WTO, see p. 430) on its establishment in 1995. Mauritius participates in the Group of 77 (G77, see p. 447) developing countries.

ECONOMIC AFFAIRS

In 2009, according to estimates by the World Bank, Mauritius' gross national income (GNI), measured at average 2007–09 prices, was US $9,236m., equivalent to $7,240 per head (or $13,270 per head on an international purchasing-power parity basis). During 2000–09, it was estimated, the population increased at an average annual rate of 0.8%, while gross domestic product (GDP) per head increased, in real terms, by an average of 2.7% per year. Overall GDP increased, in real terms, at an average annual rate of 3.5% in 2000–09; growth in 2009 was 2.1%.

Agriculture (including hunting, forestry and fishing) contributed an estimated 3.6% of GDP in 2010 and engaged 8.5% of the employed labour force in 2009. The principal cash crops are sugar cane (which contributed 1.1% of GDP in 2010), tea and tobacco. Food crops include potatoes tomatoes and bananas. Chicken farming is also practised. During 2000–09, according to the World Bank, the GDP of the agricultural sector showed no growth; however, it grew by 7.2% in 2009.

Industry (including mining, manufacturing, construction and utilities) contributed an estimated 27.2% of GDP in 2010 and engaged 31.4% of the employed labour force in 2009. During 2000–09, according to the World Bank, industrial GDP increased, in real terms, at an average annual rate of 1.9%; it increased by 0.8% in 2009. Mining is negligible, accounting for less than 0.1% of employment in 2009 and less than 0.1% of GDP in 2010.

Manufacturing contributed an estimated 18.3% of GDP in 2010 and engaged 21.2% of the employed labour force in 2009. The principal branches of manufacturing are clothing and food products, mainly sugar. Clothing (excluding footwear) provided 41.9% of export earnings in 2009, according to official figures. Factories in the Export Processing Zone (EPZ) import raw materials to produce goods for the export market. Clothing and apparel firms accounted for 75.8% of total EPZ employment in September 2005. Other important products include fish preparations, textiles, and precious stones. Export receipts from EPZ products provisionally represented 46.1% of total export earnings (and 16.6% of import earnings) in 2005. During 2000–09, according to the World Bank, the GDP of the manufacturing sector increased, in real terms, at an average annual rate of 0.7%; manufacturing GDP increased by 0.1% in 2009.

Construction contributed an estimated 6.9% of GDP in 2010 and engaged 9.6% of the employed labour force in 2009.

Electric energy is derived principally from thermal (oil-fired) and hydroelectric power stations. Bagasse (a by-product of sugar cane) is also used as fuel for generating electricity, and in 2006 it accounted for 19.0% of electricity produced (93% of indigenous production; 20% of electricity was produced locally). Imports of mineral fuels comprised 19.2% of the value of merchandise imports in 2009. Thermal energy accounted for 96.7% of electricity generated in 2006.

The services sector contributed an estimated 69.3% of GDP in 2010 and engaged 60.1% of the employed labour force in 2009. Tourism is the third most important source of revenue, after manufacturing and agriculture. The number of foreign tourist arrivals increased to 934,827 in 2010 from 422,000 in 1995. Gross receipts from tourism were estimated to total Rs 39,456m. in 2010. An 'offshore' banking sector and a stock exchange have operated since 1989. According to the World Bank, the real GDP of the services sector increased at an average annual rate of 5.5% in 2000–09; growth in 2009 was 3.2%.

In 2009 Mauritius recorded a visible trade deficit of US $1,556.9m., and there was a deficit of $674.5m. on the current account of the balance of payments. In 2010 the principal source of imports (22.3%) was India; other major suppliers were the People's Republic of China, South Africa and France. The principal market for exports in that year (21.7%) was the United Kingdom; other significant purchasers were France, the USA, Italy, South Africa, Madagascar and Spain. The principal exports (excluding re-exports) in 2010 were miscellaneous manufactured articles, food and live animals, and basic manufactures. The principal imports in that year were machinery and transport equipment, mineral fuels and lubricants, basic manufactures, food and live animals, and chemicals.

In 2007/08 there was an estimated budgetary deficit of Rs 9,331.4m. (equivalent to 3.5% of GDP). Mauritius' external debt totalled US $626m. at the end of 2008, of which $577m. was public and publicly guaranteed debt. In that year the cost of debt-servicing was equivalent to 2.8% of the value of exports of goods, services and income. The annual rate of inflation averaged 5.9% in 1996–2006. Consumer prices increased by an average of 2.9% in 2010. About 7.1% of the labour force were unemployed in 2009.

From the 1980s the Mauritius Government pursued a successful policy of economic diversification away from its traditional dependence on sugar production, encouraging labour-intensive manufacturing (particularly of clothing) in the EPZ, and implemented extensive reforms with IMF support. The geographical location of Mauritius, as well as a number of incentive measures implemented by the Government, has contributed to its successful establishment as an international financial centre. By the late 1990s the island had become a significant provider of 'offshore' banking and investment services for a number of South Asian countries (particularly India), as well as for members of SADC. Mauritius has also been promoted as a future hub of information and communications technology, with the aim of encouraging the next stage of economic development and transferring the emphasis towards services. In September 2009 Mauritius, along with four other African countries, signed an interim Economic Partnership Agreement with the European Union (EU, see p. 270). This agreement would allow immediate access to European markets while implementing measures to open gradually their domestic markets to the EU over the course of five years. In November it was announced that a Law of Foundation was to be introduced to support the Mauritius International Finance Centre and to encourage greater foreign direct investment. In late 2009 development began on a Chinese special economic zone, the Jin Fei Trade and Economic Cooperation Zone, near Port Louis; it was envisaged that the project, which was expected to be completed in 2016, would generate export earnings equivalent to US $220m. annually. Although the banking sector in Mauritius remained relatively unaffected by the global financial crisis, with financial institutions reporting no serious capitalization or liquidity issues, weaker external demand for textiles and tourism and a decline in foreign investment nevertheless had a negative impact on the country's economy, resulting in a fall in GDP growth, to about 2%, in 2009. In August 2010 the Government announced a stimulus programme of Rs 12,000m., which was designed to assist businesses affected by the financial crisis in Europe, develop tourism markets in India and the People's Republic of China, and support the sugar sector. In September the Monetary Policy Committee of the Bank of Mauritius reduced the repo rate of the bank from 5.75% to 4.75%, in a further loosening of monetary policy; the measure was expected to lower costs to businesses and enable them to restructure, and also to bring interest rates in keeping with those of the country's main trading partners. An IMF mission in early 2011 reported indications that Mauritius had recovered well from the economic crisis and that, following measures implemented by the authorities in 2008–10, including fiscal stimuli, GDP growth had increased to about 4% in 2010, with a further rise anticipated in 2011.

MAURITIUS

PUBLIC HOLIDAYS

2012: 1–2 January (New Year), 23 January (Chinese New Year), 1 February (Abolition of Slavery Commemoration), 20 February (Maha Shivaratree), 12 March (National Day), 23 March (Ougadi), 1 May (Labour Day), 15 August (Assumption), 18 August* (Id al-Fitr, end of Ramadan), 19 September (Ganesh Chathurti), 2 November (Arrival of Indentured Labourers), 13 November (Diwali), 25 December (Christmas Day).

Thaipoosam Cavadee is also celebrated in late January or early February. However, the exact date is dependent on the appearance of a full moon.

* This holiday is dependent on the Islamic lunar calendar and may vary by one or two days from the date given.

Statistical Survey

Source (unless otherwise stated): Central Statistics Office, LIC Bldg, President John F. Kennedy St, Port Louis; tel. 212-2316; fax 211-4150; e-mail cso@mail.gov.mu; internet statsmauritius.gov.mu.

Area and Population

AREA, POPULATION AND DENSITY

Area (sq km)	2,040*
Population (census results)	
1 July 1990	1,058,942†
2 July 2000‡	
Males	583,949
Females	595,188
Total	1,179,137
Population (official estimates at 31 December)	
2008	1,272,031
2009	1,277,851
2010	1,283,415
Density (per sq km) at 31 December 2010	629.1

* 788 sq miles.
† Including an adjustment of 2,115 for underenumeration.
‡ Excluding an adjustment for underenumeration.

POPULATION BY AGE AND SEX
(official estimates at 1 July 2010)

	Males	Females	Total
0–14	140,467	136,264	276,731
15–64	453,009	458,310	911,319
65 and over	38,216	54,658	92,874
Total	631,692	649,232	1,280,924

Note: Estimates exclude data for Agalega and St Brandon.

ISLANDS

		Population	
	Area (sq km)	2000 census	Official estimates 31 December 2010
Mauritius	1,865	1,143,069	1,245,289
Rodrigues	104	35,779	37,837
Other islands	71	289	289

Ethnic Groups: Island of Mauritius, mid-1982: 664,480 Indo-Mauritians (507,985 Hindus, 156,495 Muslims), 264,537 general population (incl. Creole and Franco-Mauritian communities), 20,669 Chinese.

LANGUAGE GROUPS
(census of 2 July 2000)*

Arabic	806	Marathi	16,587
Bhojpuri	361,250	Tamil	44,731
Chinese	16,972	Telegu	18,802
Creole	454,763	Urdu	34,120
English	1,075	Other languages	169,619
French	21,171	Not stated	3,170
Hindi	35,782	**Total**	1,178,848

* Figures refer to the languages of cultural origin of the population of the islands of Mauritius and Rodrigues only. The data exclude an adjustment for underenumeration.

POPULATION BY DISTRICT
(official estimates at 1 July 2009)

Black River	74,572	Port Louis	129,449
Flacq	139,064	Riv du Rempart	108,363
Grand Port	114,889	Rodrigues	37,749
Moka	80 958	Savanne	70,328
Pamplemousses	136,664		
Plaine Wilhems	382,996	**Total**	1,275,032

PRINCIPAL TOWNS
(official estimates at 1 July 2009)

Port Louis (capital)	148,928	Curepipe	84,239
Beau Bassin/Rose Hill	110,337	Quatre Bornes	81,409
Vacoas/Phoenix	107,678		

BIRTHS, MARRIAGES AND DEATHS*

	Registered live births		Registered marriages		Registered deaths	
	Number	Rate (per 1,000)	Number	Rate (per 1,000)	Number	Rate (per 1,000)
2003	19,343	15.8	10,812	8.8	8,520	7.0
2004	19,230	15.5	11,385	9.2	8,475	6.8
2005	18,829	15.1	11,294	n.a.	8,648	7.0
2006	17,605	14.1	11,471	9.1	9,162	7.3
2007	17,034	13.5	11,547	9.1	8,498	6.7
2008	16,372	12.9	11,197	8.8	9,004	7.1
2009	15,344	12.0	10,619	n.a.	9,224	7.2
2010†	15,005	11.7	10,555	n.a.	9,131	7.1

* Figures refer to the islands of Mauritius and Rodrigues only. The data are tabulated by year of registration, rather than by year of occurrence.
† Provisional.

Life expectancy (years at birth, WHO estimates): 73 (males 69; females 77) in 2008 (Source: WHO, *World Health Statistics*).

ECONOMICALLY ACTIVE POPULATION
('000 persons aged 16 years and over, incl. foreign workers)

	2007	2008	2009*
Agriculture, forestry and fishing	47.2	46.2	46.2
Sugar cane	17.7	16.0	15.5
Mining and quarrying	0.2	0.2	0.2
Manufacturing	123.0	123.3	115.8
Electricity, gas and water	3.0	3.1	3.1
Construction	49.5	51.5	52.4
Wholesale and retail trade, repair of motor vehicles and household goods	78.4	81.5	85.1
Hotels and restaurants	32.0	36.3	35.8
Transport, storage and communications	37.4	39.0	40.0
Financial intermediation	10.5	11.9	12.6

MAURITIUS

—continued	2007	2008	2009*
Real estate, renting and business activities	24.7	28.4	31.4
Public administration and defence; compulsory social security	39.1	39.6	39.4
Education	28.8	29.4	30.1
Health and social work	15.5	16.4	16.7
Other services	34.4	36.2	37.0
Total employed	523.7	543.0	545.8
Males	347.1	355.7	355.3
Females	176.6	187.3	190.5
Unemployed	46.8	40.4	41.5
Total labour force	570.5	583.4	587.3

* Provisional.

Health and Welfare

KEY INDICATORS

Total fertility rate (children per woman, 2008)	1.8
Under-5 mortality rate (per 1,000 live births, 2008)	16
HIV/AIDS (% of persons aged 15–49, 2007)	1.7
Physicians (per 1,000 head, 2004)	1.1
Hospital beds (per 1,000 head, 2006)	3.0
Health expenditure (2007): US $ per head (PPP)	502
Health expenditure (2007): % of GDP	4.2
Health expenditure (2007): public (% of total)	49.0
Access to water (% of persons, 2008)	99
Access to sanitation (% of persons, 2008)	91
Total carbon dioxide emissions ('000 metric tons, 2007)	3,883.8
Carbon dioxide emissions per head (metric tons, 2007)	3.1
Human Development Index (2010): ranking	72
Human Development Index (2010): value	0.701

For sources and definitions, see explanatory note on p. vi.

Agriculture

PRINCIPAL CROPS
('000 metric tons)

	2007	2008	2009
Potatoes	15.4	14.9	19.8
Sugar cane	4,235.8	4,533.0	4,669.4
Coconuts*	3.6	3.7	n.a.
Cabbages and other brassicas	4.4	3.7	4.6
Lettuce and chicory	1.1	0.9	0.9
Tomatoes	11.1	11.5	12.6
Cauliflowers and broccoli	1.6	1.2	1.7
Pumpkins, squash and gourds	14.9	13.8	17.1
Cucumbers and gherkins	8.8	8.7	11.1
Aubergines (Eggplants)	2.8	1.8	2.8
Onions, dry	6.2	5.6	4.9
Carrots and turnips	4.8	4.7	7.4
Bananas	9.0	10.5	10.9
Pineapples	6.4	6.4	8.9
Tea	1.6	1.7	1.5
Tobacco, unmanufactured	0.3	0.3	0.3

* FAO estimates.

Aggregate production ('000 metric tons, may include official, semi-official or estimated data): Total cereals 1.0 in 2007, 0.8 in 2008, 0.8 in 2009; Total roots and tubers 16.8 in 2007, 16.3 in 2008, 21.5 in 2009; Total vegetables (incl. melons) 65.5 in 2007, 59.0 in 2008, 71.7 in 2009; Total fruits (excl. melons) 19.3 in 2007, 20.8 in 2008, 23.7 in 2009.

Source: FAO.

LIVESTOCK
('000 head, year ending September)

	2007	2008	2009
Cattle	72	73	72
Pigs	17	13	14
Sheep*	11	11	12
Goats	25	26	26
Chickens*	12,750	13,500	13,650

* FAO estimates.
Source: FAO.

LIVESTOCK PRODUCTS
('000 metric tons)

	2007	2008	2009
Cattle meat	2	2	2
Chicken meat	40	42	44
Cows' milk	4	3	4
Hen eggs	12	11	10

Source: FAO.

Forestry

ROUNDWOOD REMOVALS
('000 cubic metres, excl. bark)

	2007	2008	2009
Sawlogs, veneer logs and logs for sleepers*	6	6	6
Other industrial wood	3	3*	3*
Fuel wood*	7	7	6
Total*	16	16	15

* FAO estimate(s).
Source: FAO.

SAWNWOOD PRODUCTION
('000 cubic metres, incl. railway sleepers)

	2006	2007	2008*
Coniferous (softwood)	3.5	2.7	2.7
Broadleaved (hardwood)	0.5	0.3	0.3
Total	4.0	3.0	3.0

* FAO estimates.
2009: Production assumed to be unchanged from 2008 (FAO estimates).
Source: FAO.

Fishing

(metric tons, live weight)

	2006	2007	2008
Capture	8,681*	8,087	6,152
Groupers and seabasses	44	924	556
Snappers and jobfishes	1,674	816	404
Emperors (Scavengers)	2,969	2,962	3,022
Goatfishes	204	138	100
Spinefeet (Rabbitfishes)	90	200	111
Swordfish	705	512	9
Tuna-like fishes	706	164	200
Octopuses	84	68	92
Aquaculture	443	175	246
Red drum	416	155	175
Total catch	9,124*	8,262	6,398

* Estimate.

Note: Figures exclude aquatic animals, recorded by number rather than weight. The number of Nile crocodiles captured was: 180 in 2007.

Source: FAO.

MAURITIUS

Industry

SELECTED PRODUCTS
('000 metric tons, unless otherwise indicated)

	2007	2008	2009*
Fish	48.6	85.5	65.7
Frozen	3.6	3.1	3.3
Canned	44.3	78.8	61.7
Raw sugar	436.0	452.1	467.2
Molasses	130.9	167.9	145.7
Beer and stout ('000 hectolitres)	337.7	360.8	351.7
Cigarettes (million)	620	6	n.a.
Iron bars and steel tubes	n.a.	19.0	31.0
Fertilizers	n.a.	4.0	4.4
Electric energy (million kWh)	2,465	2,557	2,577

* Provisional.

Finance

CURRENCY AND EXCHANGE RATES

Monetary Units
100 cents = 1 Mauritian rupee.

Sterling, Dollar and Euro Equivalents (31 December 2010)
£1 sterling = 47.58 rupees;
US $1 = 30.39 rupees;
€1 = 40.61 rupees;
1,000 Mauritian rupees = £21.02 = $32.90 = €24.63.

Average Exchange Rate (Mauritian rupees per US $)
2008 28.453
2009 31.960
2010 30.784

BUDGET
(million rupees, year ending 30 June)

Revenue*

	2005/06	2006/07	2007/08
Current revenue	38,508.7	41,818.2	52,744.3
Tax revenue	35,381.5	38,185.9	47,831.4
Taxes on income, profits and capital gains	7,468.9	7,607.6	10,558.2
Individual income tax	2,767.9	2,332.3	3,405.7
Corporate tax	4,701.0	5,275.3	6,236.4
Taxes on property	1,939.5	2,798.5	4,003.0
Domestic taxes on goods and services	18,762.0	21,403.6	26,477.4
Excise duties	2,467.8	2,998.9	4,198.0
Value-added tax	13,709.5	15,468.1	18,542.0
Taxes on international trade	7,195.4	6,299.2	6,646.2
Other tax revenue	15.7	77.0	146.6
Non-tax revenue	3,127.2	3,632.3	4,912.9
Property income	1,804.8	2,179.5	3,406.0
Other non-tax revenue	1,322.4	1,452.8	1,506.9
Capital revenue	221.7	28.7	23.2
Total	38,730.4	41,846.9	52,767.5

EXPENSE/OUTLAYS

Expense by economic type	2005/06	2006/07	2007/08
Current expenditure	41,915.3	44,122.2	48,423.3
Wages and salaries	12,298.7	12,263.4	12,700.0
Other purchases of goods and services	4,593.6	4,111.8	4,269.4
Interest payments	7,354.7	8,882.5	10,675.2
Subsidies and other current transfers	17,668.3	18,864.5	20,778.7
Transfer to non-profit institutions and households	14,130.9	15,775.8	17,373.1
Capital expenditure	6,959.9	7,110.9	11,682.3
Acquisition of fixed capital assets	5,159.2	4,608.7	8,105.1
Capital transfers	1,653.0	2,348.5	3,307.5
Total	48,875.2	51,233.1	60,105.6

Outlays by function of government	2005/06	2006/07	2007/08
General government services	7,419.0	7,499.6	7,812.6
General public services	3,439.3	3,438.3	3,610.3
Defence	345.4	334.5	} 4,202.3
Public order and safety	3,634.3	3,726.8	
Community and social services	21,110.7	22,514.5	24,394.0
Education	6,127.7	6,387.4	6,845.6
Health	4,049.0	4,240.1	4,468.6
Social security and welfare	9,578.8	10,595.9	11,606.5
Housing and community amenities	869.6	821.0	979.7
Recreational, cultural and religious services	485.6	470.1	493.6
Economic services	3,884.8	3,067.1	3,276.1
Agriculture, forestry, fishing and hunting	1,187.6	1,193.0	1,279.1
Transportation and communications	822.3	982.2	1,060.7
Other current expenditure	9,500.8	11,041.0	12,940.6
Public debt interest	7,354.7	8,882.5	10,675.2
Capital expenditure	6,959.9	7,110.9	11,682.3
Total expenditure	48,875.2	51,233.1	60,105.6

* Excluding grants received (million rupees): 489.2 in 2005/06; 321.9 in 2006/07; 454.1 in 2007/08.

INTERNATIONAL RESERVES
(US $ million at 31 December)

	2008	2009	2010
Gold (market prices)	42.7	124.9	159.6
IMF special drawing rights	29.0	156.7	153.7
Reserve position in IMF	20.3	20.6	34.0
Foreign exchange	1,693.4	2,001.5	2,254.2
Total	1,785.4	2,303.7	2,601.5

Source: IMF, *International Financial Statistics*.

MONEY SUPPLY
(million rupees at 31 December)

	2008	2009	2010
Currency outside depository corporations	16,156.1	17,152.6	18,975.0
Transferable deposits	59,434.2	70,923.4	70,035.5
Other deposits	197,188.4	207,632.2	227,244.8
Securities other than shares	1,535.0	772.2	2,868.9
Broad money	274,313.7	296,480.4	319,124.2

Source: IMF, *International Financial Statistics*.

MAURITIUS

Statistical Survey

COST OF LIVING
(Consumer Price Index; base: July 2001–June 2002 = 100)

	2004	2005	2006
Food and non-alcoholic beverages	112.5	119.1	131.0
Alcoholic beverages and tobacco	119.8	127.0	143.6
Clothing and footwear	105.0	106.3	113.4
Housing, fuel and electricity	107.1	110.8	123.6
Household operations	107.6	112.8	120.3
All items (incl. others)	112.1	117.6	128.1

All items (Consumer Price Index; base: July 2006–June 2007 = 100): 103.8 in 2007; 113.9 in 2008; 116.8 in 2009; 120.2 in 2010.

NATIONAL ACCOUNTS
(million rupees in current prices, revised estimates)

National Income and Product

	2008	2009	2010
Compensation of employees	91,705	97,324	102,537
Operating surplus			
Consumption of fixed capital	148,976	152,613	160,991
Gross domestic product (GDP) at factor cost	240,681	249,937	263,528
Taxes on production and imports			
Less Subsidies	33,635	32,968	36,439
GDP in purchasers' values	274,316	282,905	299,967
Primary incomes received from abroad			
Less Primary incomes paid abroad	2,073	−1,291	3,656
Gross national income	276,389	281,614	303,623
Current transfers from abroad			
Less Current transfers paid abroad	6,409	6,909	5,630
Gross national disposable income	282,798	288,523	309,253

Expenditure on the Gross Domestic Product

	2008	2009	2010
Private final consumption expenditure	200,760	208,858	220,305
Government final consumption expenditure	34,789	39,729	41,625
Gross fixed capital formation	67,529	74,430	74,395
Increase in stocks	7,352	−13,658	−1,702
Total domestic expenditure	310,430	309,359	334,623
Exports of goods and services	145,204	138,168	156,255
Less Imports of goods and services	181,319	164,622	190,912
GDP in purchasers' values	274,316	282,905	299,967

Gross Domestic Product by Economic Activity

	2008	2009	2010
Agriculture, hunting, forestry, and fishing	9,942	9,800	9,469
Sugar cane	4,230	3,489	2,863
Mining and quarrying	108	101	107
Manufacturing	47,128	48,078	48,586
Electricity, gas and water	4,590	5,498	5,401
Construction	16,473	17,486	18,231
Wholesale and retail trade, repair of motor vehicles and personal goods	29,028	28,800	31,398
Hotels and restaurants	19,170	16,754	18,514
Transport, storage and communications	23,922	24,194	25,361
Financial intermediation	23,909	25,411	26,578
Real estate, renting and business activities	27,258	29,849	32,777
Public administration and defence; compulsory social security	13,780	15,322	16,159
Education	10,273	11,080	11,686
Health and social work	7,729	8,936	9,694
Other services	9,805	10,857	12,050
Gross value added in basic prices	243,115	252,166	266,011
Taxes, less subsidies, on products	31,201	30,739	33,956
GDP in market prices	274,316	282,905	299,967

BALANCE OF PAYMENTS
(US $ million)

	2007	2008	2009
Exports of goods f.o.b.	2,237.9	2,383.9	1,942.0
Imports of goods f.o.b.	−3,655.7	−4,386.0	−3,498.8
Trade balance	−1,417.8	−2,002.1	−1,556.9
Exports of services	2,205.2	2,543.9	2,238.9
Imports of services	−1,569.4	−1,919.9	−1,607.4
Balance on goods and services	−782.0	−1,378.1	−925.3
Other income received	816.4	819.9	428.0
Other income paid	−593.3	−641.7	−401.0
Balance on goods, services and income	−558.9	−1,200.0	−898.3
Current transfers received	250.1	411.2	413.1
Current transfers paid	−125.2	−187.0	−189.4
Current balance	−433.9	−975.8	−674.5
Capital account (net)	−1.6	−1.4	−1.4
Direct investment abroad	−59.6	−52.4	−37.8
Direct investment from abroad	340.8	377.7	256.7
Portfolio investment assets	−95.3	−92.9	−50.2
Portfolio investment liabilities	153.7	−76.8	−33.8
Other investment assets	−2,972.8	631.8	−357.7
Other investment liabilities	3,128.2	155.7	948.9
Net errors and omissions	376.6	211.9	334.6
Overall balance	436.0	177.9	384.7

Source: IMF, *International Financial Statistics*.

MAURITIUS

External Trade

PRINCIPAL COMMODITIES
(million rupees)

Imports c.i.f.	2008	2009	2010*
Food and live animals	23,817	22,051	24,606
Fish and fish preparations	8,474	7,055	7,810
Mineral fuels, lubricants, etc.	28,352	18,557	25,929
Refined petroleum products	24,042	15,293	21,449
Chemicals	10,417	10,711	12,465
Basic manufactures	25,033	21,452	25,091
Textile yarn, fabrics, etc.	2,476	2,012	2,496
Cotton fabrics	2,241	1,965	2,160
Machinery and transport equipment	25,930	27,689	27,451
Machinery specialized for particular industries	2,604	2,614	2,441
General industrial machinery, equipment and parts	3,848	4,704	4,178
Telecommunications and sound equipment	4,901	3,483	4,357
Other electrical machinery, apparatus, etc.	4,062	3,853	4,256
Road motor vehicles	6,057	5,446	6,794
Miscellaneous manufactured articles	10,804	11,028	12,188
Total (incl. others)	132,165	118,444	135,393

Exports f.o.b.†	2008	2009	2010*
Food and live animals	18,451	18,593	20,856
Basic manufactures	5,255	5,106	5,834
Chemicals and related products	1,765	1,957	2,204
Machinery and transport equipment	3,727	1,285	1,678
Miscellaneous manufactured articles	28,109	27,709	29,474
Total (incl. others)	59,015	56,162	61,997

* Provisional.
† Excluding stores and bunkers for ships and aircraft (million rupees): 8,955 in 2008; 5,519 in 2009; 6,869 in 2010 (provisional).

PRINCIPAL TRADING PARTNERS
(million rupees)*

Imports c.i.f.	2008	2009	2010†
Argentina	2,121	1,772	1,907
Australia	3,201	3,344	4,224
Belgium	1,649	1,703	1,237
China, People's Repub.	15,288	14,903	18,027
Denmark	310	352	1,114
Finland	617	235	172
France	10,159	13,812	10,992
Germany	2,966	3,123	3,230
Hong Kong	535	535	533
Hungary	625	249	295
India	31,699	22,336	30,239
Indonesia	3,077	2,987	2,995
Italy	3,269	2,727	2,979
Japan	5,221	3,823	4,517
Korea, Repub.	2,155	1,440	1,648
Madagascar	657	543	568
Malaysia	3,422	3,417	3,474
Pakistan	1,497	964	1,316
Saudi Arabia	637	85	151
Singapore	1,098	993	1,044
South Africa	10,723	10,236	11,393
Spain	3,759	2,800	3,653
Switzerland	1,452	1,107	1,366
Thailand	3,122	3,120	3,080
United Arab Emirates	576	803	1,164
United Kingdom	2,996	2,925	2,980
USA	2,990	2,576	3,420
Total (incl. others)	132,165	118,444	135,394

Exports f.o.b.	2008	2009	2010†
Belgium	1,945	1,454	1,324
France	7,915	9,317	10,376
Germany	1,695	1,327	1,186
Italy	2,686	3,090	4,390
Madagascar	3,451	3,587	3,529
Netherlands	801	830	840
Portugal	731	1,400	313
Réunion	2,022	2,321	1,978
South Africa	2,146	2,553	3,613
Spain	1,902	2,549	4,052
Switzerland	933	758	1,028
United Arab Emirates	1,820	184	448
United Kingdom	20,134	15,280	13,542
USA	3,926	4,624	6,229
Total (incl. others)	59,015	56,162	61,997

* Imports by country of origin; exports by country of destination (including re-exports, excluding ships' stores and bunkers).
† Provisional.

Transport

ROAD TRAFFIC
(motor vehicles registered at 31 December)

	2008	2009	2010
Private vehicles:			
Cars	155,528	165,036	175,634
Motorcycles and mopeds	147,988	152,935	159,329
Commercial vehicles:			
Buses	2,762	2,803	2,845
Taxis	6,941	6,941	6,924
Lorries and trucks	12,726	12,950	13,186

SHIPPING

Merchant Fleet
(registered at 31 December)

	2007	2008	2009
Number of vessels	43	47	50
Total displacement ('000 grt)	39.7	41.1	66.2

Source: IHS Fairplay, *World Fleet Statistics*.

Sea-borne Freight Traffic
('000 metric tons)

	2007	2008	2009
Goods unloaded	5,062	5,140	4,761
Goods loaded*	1,165	1,155	1,117

* Excluding ships' bunkers.

CIVIL AVIATION
(traffic)

	2007	2008	2009
Aircraft landings	8,543	9,384	9,824
Freight unloaded (metric tons)	22,663	22,152	20,400
Freight loaded (metric tons)	24,894	24,522	21,924

MAURITIUS

Tourism

FOREIGN TOURIST ARRIVALS

Country of residence	2008	2009	2010*
France	260,054	275,599	302,185
Germany	61,484	51,279	52,886
India	43,911	39,252	49,779
Italy	66,432	56,736	56,540
Réunion	96,174	104,946	114,914
South Africa	84,448	74,176	81,458
Switzerland	16,037	15,349	18,577
United Kingdom	107,919	101,996	97,548
Total (incl. others)	930,456	871,356	934,827

* Provisional.

Tourism earnings (gross, million rupees): 41,213 in 2008; 35,693 in 2009; 39,456 in 2010 (provisional).

Communications Media

	2007	2008	2009
Telephones ('000 main lines in use)	360.8	363.5	375.2
Mobile cellular telephones ('000 subscribers)	928.6	1,033.3	1,086.7
Internet users ('000)	257	279.1	290
Broadband subscribers ('000)	61.5	40.4	91.5
Television sets licensed ('000)	289.9	318.0	315.0
Daily newspapers	8	8	8*
Non-daily newspapers	39	49	54*

* Provisional.

Personal computers: 220,000 (45.4 per 1,000 persons) in 2006.

1996: Book production: titles 80, copies ('000) 163.

Sources: partly UNESCO, *Statistical Yearbook*; UN, *Statistical Yearbook*; International Telecommunication Union.

Education

(March 2010)

	Institutions	Teachers	Students*
Pre-primary	1,042	2,538	35,139
Primary	305	5,472	117,432
Secondary	182	7,695	115,003
Technical and vocational	124	628	7,442

* By enrolment.

Pupil-teacher ratio (primary education, UNESCO estimate): 21.6 in 2008/09 (Source: UNESCO Institute for Statistics).

Adult literacy rate (UNESCO estimates): 87.5% (males 90.4%; females 84.8%) in 2008 (Source: UNESCO Institute for Statistics).

Directory

The Government

HEAD OF STATE

President: Sir ANEROOD JUGNAUTH (took office 7 October 2003; re-elected by vote of the National Assembly 19 September 2008).
Vice-President: MONIQUE OHSAN-BELLEPEAU.

COUNCIL OF MINISTERS
(May 2011)

Prime Minister, Minister of Defence, Home Affairs and External Communications: Dr NAVINCHANDRA RAMGOOLAM.
Deputy Prime Minister and Minister of Energy and Public Utilities: Dr AHMED RASHID BEEBEEJAUN.
Vice-Prime Minister and Minister of Social Integration and Economic Empowerment: CHARLES GAËTAN XAVIER-LUC DUVAL.
Vice-Prime Minister and Minister of Finance and Economic Development: Dr PRAVIND KUMAR JUGNAUTH.
Minister of Public Infrastructure, the National Development Unit, Land Transport and Shipping: ANIL KUMAR BACHOO.
Minister of Foreign Affairs, Regional Integration and International Trade: Dr ARVIN BOOLELL.
Minister of Housing and Lands: ABU TWALIB KASENALLY.
Minister of Gender Equality, Child Development and Family Welfare: SHEILABAI BAPPOO.
Minister of Tourism and Leisure: NANDCOOMAR BODHA.
Minister of Education and Human Resources: Dr VASANT KUMAR BUNWAREE.
Minister of Agro-industry, Food Production and Security: SATYA VEYASH FAUGOO.
Minister of Industry and Commerce: SHOWKUTALLY SOODHUN.
Minister of the Environment and Sustainable Development: DEVANAND VIRAHSAWMY.
Minister of Tertiary Education, Science, Research and Technology: Dr RAJESHWAR JEETAH.
Minister of Youth and Sports: SATYAPRAKASH RITOO.
Minister of Social Security, National Solidarity and Reform Institutions: LEELA DEVI DOOKUN-LUCHOOMUN.
Minister of Local Government and Outer Islands: LOUIS HERVÉ AIMÉ.
Minister of Health and Quality of Life: SANTI BAI HANOOMANJEE.
Minister of Arts and Culture: MOOKHESSWUR CHOONEE.
Minister of Information and Communication Technology: TASSARAJEN PILLAY CHEDUMBRUM.
Minister of Fisheries and Rodrigues: LOUIS JOSEPH VON-MALLY.
Minister of Civil Service and Administrative Reforms: ASHIT KUMAR GUNGAH.
Minister of Labour, Industrial Relations and Employment: SHAKEEL AHMED YOUSUF ABDUL RAZACK MOHAMED.
Attorney-General: YATINDRA NATH VARMA.
Minister of Business, Enterprise, Co-operatives and Consumer Protection: JOHN MICHAËL TZOUN SAO YEUNG SIK YUEN.

MINISTRIES

Office of the President: State House, Le Réduit, Port Louis; tel. 454-3021; fax 464-5370; e-mail president@mail.gov.mu; internet www.gov.mu/portal/site/president.

Office of the Prime Minister: New Treasury Bldg, Intendance St, Port Louis; tel. 207-9595; fax 208-8619; e-mail primeminister@mail.gov.mu; internet www.gov.mu/portal/site/pmsite.

Ministry of Agro-industry and Food Production and Security: Renganaden Seeneevassen Bldg, 8th and 9th Floor, cnr Jules Koenig and Maillard Sts, Port Louis; tel. 212-2335; fax 212-4427; e-mail moa-headoffice@mail.gov.mu; internet www.gov.mu/portal/site/moa.

MAURITIUS

Ministry of Arts and Culture: Renganaden Seeneevassen Bldg, 7th Floor, cnr Pope Hennessy and Maillard Sts, Port Louis; tel. 212-2112; fax 210-0681; e-mail moac@mail.gov.mu; internet www.gov.mu/portal/site/mac.

Ministry of Business, Enterprise and Co-operatives: Air Mauritius Centre, 8th Floor, John F. Kennedy St, Port Louis; tel. 210-3774; fax 201-3289; e-mail Mincom@intnet.mu; internet www.gov.mu/portal/site/commercesite.

Ministry of the Civil Service and Administrative Reforms: New Government Centre, 7th Floor, Port Louis; tel. 201-2886; fax 212-9528; e-mail civser@mail.gov.mu; internet www.gov.mu/portal/site/mcsasite.

Ministry of Consumer Protection and the Citizens' Charter: LIC Centre, 3rd Floor, John F. Kennedy St, Port Louis; tel. 208-4812; fax 211-5701; e-mail mcpcc@mail.gov.mu; internet www.gov.mu/portal/site/consumer.

Ministry of Defence, Home Affairs and External Communications: New Government Centre, 4th Floor, Port Louis; tel. 201-2409; fax 212-9393; e-mail pmo@mail.gov.mu; internet pmo.gov.mu/dha.

Ministry of Education and Human Resources: IVTB House, Pont Fer, Phoenix; tel. 697-7862; fax 698-3601; e-mail moeps@mail.gov.mu; internet www.gov.mu/portal/site/education.

Ministry of Energy and Public Utilities: Air Mauritius Centre, 10th Floor, John F. Kennedy St, Port Louis; tel. 211-0049; fax 208-6497; e-mail mpu@mail.gov.mu; internet www.gov.mu/portal/site/mpusite.

Ministry of the Environment and Sustainable Development: Ken Lee Tower, cnr Barracks and St Georges Sts, Port Louis; tel. 203-6200; fax 212-8324; e-mail menv@mail.gov.mu; internet www.gov.mu/portal/site/menvsite.

Ministry of Finance and Economic Development: Government House, Ground Floor, Port Louis; tel. 201-1146; fax 211-0096; e-mail mof@mail.gov.mu; internet www.gov.mu/portal/site/MOFSite.

Ministry of Foreign Affairs, Regional Integration and International Trade: Newton Tower, 9th–11th Floors, Sir William Newton St, Port Louis; tel. 201-1648; fax 208-8087; e-mail mfa@mail.gov.mu; internet www.gov.mu/portal/site/mfasite.

Ministry of Gender Equality, Child Development and Family Welfare: CSK Bldg, cnr Remy Ollier and Emmanuel Anquetil Sts, Port Louis; tel. 206-3700; fax 240-7717; e-mail mfwcd@mail.gov.mu; internet www.gov.mu/portal/site/women-site.

Ministry of Health and Quality of Life: 5th Floor, Emmanuel Anquetil Bldg, Sir Seewoosagur Ramgoolam St, Port Louis; tel. 201-2175; fax 208-7222; e-mail moh@mail.gov.mu; internet www.gov.mu/portal/site/mohsite.

Ministry of Housing and Lands: Moorgate House, Port Louis; tel. 212-6022; fax 212-7482; internet www.gov.mu/portal/site/housing.

Ministry of Industry and Commerce: Air Mauritius Centre, 7th Floor, John F. Kennedy St, Port Louis; tel. 210-7100; fax 211-0855; e-mail mind@mail.gov.mu; internet www.gov.mu/portal/site/industry-site.

Ministry of Information and Communication Technology: Air Mauritius Centre, 9th Floor, John F. Kennedy St, Port Louis; tel. 210-0201; fax 212-1673; e-mail mict@mail.gov.mu; internet www.gov.mu/portal/site/telcomit.

Ministry of Labour, Industrial Relations and Employment: Victoria House, cnr St Louis and Barracks Sts, Port Louis; tel. 207-2600; fax 212-3070; e-mail mol@mail.gov.mu; internet www.gov.mu/portal/site/laboursite.

Ministry of Local Government and Outer Islands: Emmanuel Anquetil Bldg, 3rd Floor, cnr Sir Seewoosagur Ramgoolam and Jules Koenig Sts, Port Louis; tel. 201-2155; fax 208-9729; e-mail mlg@mail.gov.mu; internet www.gov.mu/portal/site/mlge.

Ministry of Public Infrastructure, the National Development Unit, Land Transport and Shipping: Moorgate House, 9th Floor, Sir William Newton St, Port Louis; tel. 208-0281; fax 208-7149; e-mail mpi@mail.gov.mu; internet www.gov.mu/portal/site/mpisite.

Ministry of Social Integration and Economic Empowerment: Port Louis.

Ministry of Social Security, National Solidarity and Reform Institutions: Renganaden Seeneevassen Bldg, 13th Floor, cnr Jules Koenig and Maillard Sts, Port Louis; tel. 207-0625; fax 212-8190; e-mail mss@mail.gov.mu; internet www.gov.mu/portal/site/ssnssite.

Ministry of Tertiary Education, Science, Research and Technology: Port Louis.

Ministry of Tourism and Leisure: Air Mauritius Centre, 5th Floor, John F. Kennedy St, Port Louis; tel. 211-7930; fax 208-6776; e-mail mtou@mail.gov.mu; internet www.gov.mu/portal/site/tourist.

Ministry of Youth and Sports: Emmanuel Anquetil Bldg, 3rd Floor, Sir Seewoosagur Ramgoolam St, Port Louis; tel. 201-2543; fax 211-2986; e-mail mys@mail.gov.mu; internet www.gov.mu/portal/site/sportsSite.

Legislature

National Assembly

Port Louis; tel. 201-1414; fax 212-8364; e-mail themace@intnet.mu; internet mauritiusassembly.gov.mu.

Speaker: KAILASH PURRYAG.

General Election, 5 May 2010

Party	Directly elected	Additional*	Total
Alliance de l'avenir†	41	4	45
Alliance du coeur‡	18	2	20
Mouvement rodriguais (MR)	2	—	2
Front solidarité mauricienne (FSM)	1	—	1
Organisation du peuple rodriguais (OPR)	—	1	1
Total	**62**	**7**	**69**

* Awarded to those among the unsuccessful candidates who attracted the largest number of votes, in order to ensure that a balance of ethnic groups is represented in the Assembly.
† Alliance comprising the Mauritius Labour Party, the Parti mauricien social démocrate and the Mouvement socialiste militant.
‡ Alliance comprising the Mouvement militant mauricien, the Union nationale and the Mouvement mauricien social démocrate.

Election Commission

Electoral Commissioner's Office (ECO): 4th Floor, Max City Bldg, cnr Louis Pasteur and Remy Ollier Sts, Port Louis; tel. 241-7000; fax 241-0967; e-mail elec@mail.gov.mu; internet electoral.gov.mu; under the aegis of the Prime Minister's Office; Commissioner appointed by the Judicial and Legal Service Commission; Electoral Commissioner M. I. ABDOOL RAHMAN.

Political Organizations

Forum des citoyens libres (FCL): Leader GEORGES AH-YAN.

Front solidarité mauricienne (FSM): Leader CEHL MEEAH.

Mauritius Labour Party (MLP) (Parti Travailliste): 7 Guy Rozemont Sq., Port Louis; tel. 212-6691; fax 210-0189; e-mail info@labourparty.mu; internet www.labourparty.mu; f. 1936; formed part of the Alliance de l'avenir for the 2010 elections; Leader Dr NAVINCHANDRA RAMGOOLAM; Pres. MONIQUE OHSAN-BELLEPEAU; Sec.-Gen. DEVENAND VIRAHSAWMY.

Mouvement mauricien social démocrate (MMSD): Morcellement Piat, Forest-Side, POB 1, Port Louis; tel. 670-4000; fax 670-1111; e-mail mmsd@orange.mu; internet www.mmsd.mu; f. 2009; formed part of the Alliance du coeur for the 2010 elections; Leader ERIC GUIMBEAU.

Mouvement militant mauricien (MMM): 21 Poudrière St, Port Louis; tel. 212-6553; fax 208-9939; internet www.lemmm.org; f. 1969; socialist; formed part of the Alliance du coeur for the 2010 elections; Pres. SAM LAUTHAN; Leader PAUL BÉRENGER; Secs-Gen. STEVEN OBEEGADOO, RAJESH BHAGWAN.

Mouvement rodriguais (MR): Port Mathurin, Rodrigues; tel. 831-1876 (Port Mathurin); tel. and fax 831-2648 (Port Louis); e-mail nvmally@intnet.mu; f. 1992; represents the interests of Rodrigues; Leader LOUIS JOSEPH (NICHOLAS) VON-MALLY.

Mouvement sociale démocrate (MSD) (Social Democratic Movement): Port Louis; f. 2005; Leader ANIL BACHOO.

Mouvement socialiste militant (MSM): Sun Trust Bldg, 1st Floor, 31 Edith Cavell St, Port Louis; tel. 212-8787; fax 212-9334; e-mail info@msmparty.org; internet www.msmparty.org; f. 1983 by fmr mems of the MMM; formed part of the Alliance de l'avenir for the 2010 elections; Leader Dr PRAVIND KUMAR JUGNAUTH; Pres. JOE LESJONGARD; Sec.-Gen. NANDO BODHA.

Organisation du peuple rodriguais (OPR): Mont Lubin, Rodrigues; represents the interests of Rodrigues; f. 1976; Leader LOUIS SERGE CLAIR.

Parti mauricien social démocrate (PMSD): Melville, Grand Gaube; internet www.pmsd.mu; centre-right; formed part of the

MAURITIUS

Alliance de l'avenir for the 2010 elections; Leader CHARLES GAËTAN XAVIER-LUC DUVAL; Sec.-Gen. RAMA VALAYDEN.

Union nationale (Mauritian National Union): Port Louis; f. 2006; formed part of the Alliance du coeur for the 2010 elections; Chair. ASHOCK JUGNAUTH.

Some of the blocs and parties that participated in the 2010 elections include **Les verts fraternels/The Greens** (Leader SYLVIO MICHEL), the **Parti du peuple mauricien (PPM)**, the **Rezistans ek Alternativ** (Secretary ASHOK SUBRON), **Lalit** (lalitmauritius.com) and the **Tamil Council**.

Diplomatic Representation

EMBASSIES AND HIGH COMMISSIONS IN MAURITIUS

Australia: Rogers House, 2nd Floor, John F. Kennedy St, POB 541, Port Louis; tel. 202-0160; fax 208-8878; e-mail ahc.portlouis@dfat .gov.au; internet www.mauritius.embassy.gov.au; High Commissioner SANDRA VEGTING.

China, People's Republic: Royal Rd, Belle Rose, Rose Hill; tel. 454-9111; fax 464-6012; e-mail chinaemb_mu@mfa.gov.cn; internet www .ambchine.mu; Ambassador BIAN YANHUA.

Egypt: Sun Trust Bldg, 2nd floor, Edith Cavell St, Port Louis; tel. 213-1765; fax 213-1768; Ambassador ABD-AL HAMEED AHMAD MARZOUK.

France: 14 St George St, Port Louis; tel. 202-0100; fax 202-0110; e-mail ambafr.port-louis@hotmail.fr; internet www.ambafrance-mu .org; Ambassador JACQUES MAILLARD.

India: LIC Centre, 6th Floor, John F. Kennedy St, POB 162, Port Louis; tel. 208-8891; fax 208-6859; e-mail hicom.ss@intnet.mu; internet indiahighcom.intnet.mu; High Commissioner MADHUSUDAN GANAPATHI.

Madagascar: Guiot Pasceau St, Floreal, POB 3, Port Louis; tel. 686-5015; fax 686-7040; e-mail madmail@intnet.mu; Ambassador (vacant).

Pakistan: 9A Queen Mary Ave, Floreal, Port Louis; tel. 698-8501; fax 698-8405; e-mail pareportlouis@hotmail.com; High Commissioner (vacant).

Russia: Queen Mary Ave, POB 10, Floreal, Port Louis; tel. 696-1545; fax 696-5027; e-mail rusemb.mu@intnet.mu; Ambassador OLGA IVANOVA.

South Africa: BAI Bldg, 4th Floor, 25 Pope Hennessy St, POB 908, Port Louis; tel. 212-6925; fax 212-6936; e-mail sahc@intnet.mu; High Commissioner MADUMANE M. MATABANE.

United Kingdom: Les Cascades Bldg, 7th Floor, Edith Cavell St, POB 1063, Port Louis; tel. 202-9400; fax 202-9408; e-mail bhc@intnet .mu; High Commissioner NICK LEAKE.

USA: Rogers House, 4th Floor, John F. Kennedy St, POB 544, Port Louis; tel. 202-4400; fax 208-9534; e-mail usembass@intnet.mu; internet mauritius.usembassy.gov; Ambassador MARY JO WILLS.

Judicial System

The laws of Mauritius are derived both from the French Code Napoléon and from English Law. The Judicial Department consists of the Supreme Court, presided over by the Chief Justice and such number of Puisne Judges as may be prescribed by Parliament (currently nine), who are also Judges of the Court of Criminal Appeal and the Court of Civil Appeal. These courts hear appeals from the Intermediate Court, the Industrial Court and 10 District Courts (including that of Rodrigues). The Industrial Court has special jurisdiction to protect the constitutional rights of the citizen. There is a right of appeal in certain cases from the Supreme Court to the Judicial Committee of the Privy Council in the United Kingdom.

Supreme Court: Jules Koenig St, Port Louis; tel. 212-0275; fax 212-9946; internet supremecourt.intnet.mu.

Chief Justice: YEUNG KAM JOHN YEUNG SIK YUEN.

Senior Puisne Judge: KESHOE PARSAD MATADEEN.

Religion

Hindus are estimated to comprise more than 50% of the population, with Christians accounting for some 30% and Muslims 17%. There is also a small Buddhist community.

CHRISTIANITY

The Anglican Communion

Anglicans in Mauritius are within the Church of the Province of the Indian Ocean, comprising seven dioceses (five in Madagascar, one in Mauritius and one in Seychelles). The Archbishop of the Province is the Bishop of Antananarivo, Madagascar.

Bishop of Mauritius (also Archbishop of the Province of the Indian Ocean): Most Rev. GERALD JAMES (IAN) ERNEST, Bishop's House, Phoenix; tel. 686-5158; fax 697-1096; e-mail dioang@intnet .mu.

The Presbyterian Church of Mauritius

Minister: Pasteur ANDRÉ DE RÉLAND, cnr Farquhar and Royal Rds, Coignet, Rose Hill; tel. 464-5265; fax 395-2068; e-mail embrau@bow .intnet.mu; f. 1814.

The Roman Catholic Church

Mauritius comprises a single diocese, directly responsible to the Holy See, and an apostolic vicariate on Rodrigues. Some 26% of the total population are Roman Catholics.

Bishop of Port Louis: Rt Rev. MAURICE PIAT, Evêché, 13 Mgr Gonin St, Port Louis; tel. 208-3068; fax 208-6607; e-mail eveche@intnet.mu.

BAHÁ'Í FAITH

National Spiritual Assembly: Port Louis; tel. 212-2179; mems resident in 190 localities.

ISLAM

World Islamic Mission (Mauritius): Shah Noorani Centre, Old Moka Rd, Bell Village, Port Louis; tel. 211-1092; fax 210-9445; e-mail wim@wimmauritius.org; internet www.wimmauritius.org; f. 1975; Gen. Sec. HAMADE AUBDOOLLAH.

The Press

DAILIES

China Times: 24 Emmanuel Anquetil St, POB 325, Port Louis; tel. 240-3067; f. 1953; Chinese; Editor-in-Chief LONG SIONG AH KENG; circ. 3,000.

Chinese Daily News: 32 Rémy Ollier St, POB 316, Port Louis; tel. 240-0472; f. 1932; Chinese; Editor-in-Chief WONG YUEN MOY; circ. 5,000.

L'Express: 3 rue des Oursins, Riche-Terre, Baie du Tombeau, POB 247, Port Louis; tel. 206-8200; fax 247-1010; internet www.lexpress .mu; f. 1963; owned by La Sentinelle Ltd; English and French; Dir of Publication ARIANE CAVALOT DE L'ESTRAC; Editor-in-Chief RAJ MEETARBHAN; circ. 35,000.

The Independent Daily: Port Louis; internet theindependent.mu.

Le Matinal: AAPCA House, 6 La Poudrière St, Port Louis; tel. 207-0909; fax 213-4069; e-mail editorial@lematinal.com; internet www .lematinal.com; f. 2003; in French and English; owned by AAPCA (Mauritius) Ltd; CEO (vacant).

Le Mauricien: 8 St George St, POB 7, Port Louis; tel. 208-3251; fax 208-7059; e-mail redaction@lemauricien.com; internet www .lemauricien.com; f. 1907; English and French; Dir of Publication JACQUES RIVET; Editor-in-Chief GAËTAN SÉNÈQUE; circ. 35,000.

Le Quotidien: Pearl House, 4th Floor, 16 Sir Virgile Naz St, Port Louis; tel. 208-2631; fax 211-7479; e-mail quotidien@bow.intnet.mu; f. 1996; English and French; Dirs JACQUES DAVID, PATRICK MICHEL; circ. 30,000.

Le Socialiste: Manilall Bldg, 3rd Floor, Brabant St, Port Louis; tel. 208-8003; fax 211-3890; English and French; Editor-in-Chief VEDI BALLAH; circ. 7,000.

WEEKLIES AND FORTNIGHTLIES

5-Plus Dimanche: 3 Brown Sequard St, Port Louis; tel. 213-5500; fax 213-5551; e-mail comments@5plusltd.com; internet www .5plusltd.com; f. 1994; English and French; Editor-in-Chief FINLAY SALESSE; circ. 30,000.

5-Plus Magazine: 3 Brown Sequard St, Port Louis; tel. 213-5500; fax 213-5551; e-mail comments@5plusltd.com; f. 1990; English and French; Editor-in-Chief PIERRE BENOÎT; circ. 10,000.

Bollywood Massala: Le Défi Bldg, Royal Rd, Port Louis; tel. 211-8131; fax 213-0959; e-mail ledefi.plus@intnet.mu; internet www .defimedia.info.

Business Magazine: TN Tower, 2nd Floor, 13 St George St, Port Louis; tel. 211-3048; fax 211-1926; e-mail businessmag@intnet.mu; internet www.businessmag.mu; f. 1992; owned by Business

MAURITIUS

Publications Ltd; English and French; Editor-in-Chief LINDSAY RIVIÈRE; circ. 7,500.

Le Défi-Plus: Le Défi Bldg, Royal Rd, Port Louis; tel. 211-8131; fax 213-0959; e-mail ledefi.plus@intnet.mu; internet www.defimedia.info; Saturdays; Dir of Publication ESHAN KHODABUX.

L'Hèbdo: Le Défi Bldg, Royal Rd, Port Louis; tel. 211-8131; fax 213-0959; e-mail ledefi.plus@intnet.mu; internet www.defimedia.info.

Impact News: 10 Dr Yves Cantin St, Port Louis; tel. 211-5284; fax 211-7821; e-mail farhadr@wanadoo.mu; internet www.impactnews.info; English and French; Editor-in-Chief FARHAD RAMJAUN.

Lalit de Klas: 153B Royal Rd, G.R.N.W., Port Louis; tel. 208-2132; e-mail lalitmail@intnet.mu; internet www.lalitmauritius.org; English, French and Mauritian Creole; Editor RADA KISTNASAMY.

Mauritius Times: 23 Bourbon St, Port Louis; tel. and fax 212-313; e-mail mtimes@intnet.mu; internet www.mauritiustimes.com; f. 1954; English and French; Editor-in-Chief MADHUKAR RAMLALLAH; circ. 15,000.

News on Sunday: Dr Eugen Laurent St, POB 230, Port Louis; tel. 211-5902; fax 211-7302; e-mail newsonsunday@news.intnet.mu; f. 1996; owned by Le Défi Group; weekly; in English; Editor NAGUIB LALLMAHOMED; circ. 10,000.

Le Nouveau Militant: 21 Poudrière St, Port Louis; tel. 212-6553; fax 208-2291; f. 1979; publ. by the Mouvement militant mauricien; English and French; Editor-in-Chief J. RAUMIAH.

Le Rodriguais: Saint Gabriel, Rodrigues; tel. 831-1613; fax 831-1484; f. 1989; Creole, English and French; Editor JACQUES EDOUARD; circ. 2,000.

Samedi Plus: Port Louis; Editor-in-Chief DHARMANAND DOOHARIKA.

Star: 38 Labourdonnais St, Port Louis; tel. 212-2736; fax 211-7781; e-mail starpress@intnet.mu; internet www.mauriweb.com/star/; English and French; Editor-in-Chief REZA ISSACK.

Sunday: Port Louis; tel. 208-9516; fax 208-7059; f. 1966; English and French; Editor-in-Chief SUBASH GOBIN.

Turf Magazine: 8 George St, POB 7, Port Louis; tel. 207-8200; fax 208-7059; e-mail bdlm@intnet.mu; internet www.lemauricien.com/turfmag; owned by Le Mauricien Ltd.

La Vie Catholique: 28 Nicolay Rd, Port Louis; tel. 242-0975; fax 242-3114; e-mail viecatho@intnet.mu; internet www.laviecatholique.com; f. 1930; weekly; English, French and Creole; Editor-in-Chief DANIÈLE BABOORAM; circ. 8,000.

Week-End: 8 St George St, POB 7, Port Louis; tel. 207-8200; fax 208-3248; e-mail redaction@lemauricien.com; internet www.lemauricien.com/weekend; f. 1966; owned by Le Mauricien Ltd; French and English; Editor JOSIE LEBRASSE; circ. 80,000.

Week-End Scope: 8 St George St, POB 7, Port Louis; tel. 207-8200; fax 208-7059; e-mail wes@lemauricien.com; internet www.lemauricien.com/wes; f. 1989; owned by Le Mauricien Ltd; English and French; Editor-in-Chief JACQUES ACHILLE.

OTHER SELECTED PERIODICALS

CCI–INFO: 3 Royal St, Port Louis; tel. 208-3301; fax 208-0076; e-mail mcci@intnet.mu; internet www.mcci.org; English and French; f. 1995; quarterly; publ. of the Mauritius Chamber of Commerce and Industry.

Ciné Star Magazine: 64 Sir Seewoosagur Ramgoolam St, Port Louis; tel. 240-1447; English and French; Editor-in-Chief ABDOOL RAWOOF SOOBRATTY.

Education News: Edith Cavell St, Port Louis; tel. 212-1303; English and French; monthly; Editor-in-Chief GIAN AUBEELUCK.

Le Message de L'Ahmadiyyat: c/o Ahmadiyya Muslim Asscn, POB 6, Rose Hill; tel. 464-1747; fax 454-2223; e-mail darussalaam@intnet.mu; French; monthly; Editor-in-Chief MOHAMMAD AMEEN JOWAHIR; circ. 3,000.

Le Progrès Islamique: 51B Solferino St, Rose Hill; tel. 467-1697; fax 467-1696; f. 1948; English and French; monthly; Editor DEVINA SOOKIA.

La Voix d'Islam: Parisot Rd, Mesnil, Phoenix; f. 1951; English and French; monthly.

Publishers

Business Publications Ltd: TN Tower, 2nd Floor, St George St, Port Louis; tel. 211-3048; fax 211-1926; internet www.businessmag.mu; f. 1993; English and French; Dir LYNDSAY RIVIÈRE.

Editions du Dattier: 82 Goyavier Ave, Quatre Bornes; tel. 466-4854; fax 446-3105; e-mail dattier@intnet.mu; English and French; Dir JEAN-PHILIPPE LAGESSE.

Editions de l'Océan Indien: Stanley, Rose Hill; tel. 464-6761; fax 464-3445; e-mail eoibooks@intnet.mu; internet www.eoi-info.com;

f. 1977; general, textbooks, dictionaries, literature; English, French and Asian languages; Gen. Man. DEVANAND DEWKURUN.

Editions Le Printemps: 4 Club Rd, Vacoas; tel. 696-1017; fax 686-7302; e-mail elp@bow.intnet.mu; Man. Dir A. I. SULLIMAN.

Editions Vizavi: 9 St George St, Port Louis; tel. 211-3047; e-mail vizavi@intnet.mu; Dir PASCALE SIEW.

Broadcasting and Communications

TELECOMMUNICATIONS

Information and Communication Technologies Authority (ICTA): The Celicourt, 12th Floor, 6 Sir Celicourt Antelme St, Port Louis; tel. 211-5333; fax 211-9444; e-mail icta@intnet.mu; internet www.icta.mu; f. 1999; regulatory authority; Chair. TRILOK DWARKA.

Mauritius Telecom Ltd: Telecom Tower, Edith Cavell St, Port Louis; tel. 203-7000; fax 208-1070; e-mail ceo@mauritiustelecom.com.mu; internet www.mauritiustelecom.com; f. 1992; 60% owned by Govt of Mauritius, State Bank of Mauritius and National Pensions Fund, 40% owned by France Télécom through RIMCOM; privatized in 2000; provides all telecommunications services, including internet and digital mobile cellular services; Chair. APPALSAMY (DASS) THOMAS; CEO SARAT DUTT LALLAH.

Cellplus Mobile Communications Ltd: Telecom Tower, 9th Floor, Edith Cavell St, Port Louis; tel. 203-7500; fax 211-6996; e-mail cellplus@intnet.mu; internet www.orange.mu/mobile; f. 1996; introduced the first GSM cellular network in Mauritius and recently in Rodrigues (Cell-Oh); a wholly owned subsidiary of Mauritius Telecom.

Emtel: 11–12 Ebene Cyber City, Ebene; tel. 454-5400; fax 454-1010; e-mail emtel@emtelnet.com; internet www.emtel-ltd.com; f. 1989; CEO SHYAM ROY.

Outremer Télécom Maurice: POB 113, Hassamal Bldg, Rémono St, Rose Hill; tel. 401-9400; fax 401-9422; e-mail info@outremer-telecom.mu; internet www.outremer-telecom.mu; Man. Dir MICHEL RIGOT.

BROADCASTING

In 1997 the Supreme Court invalidated the broadcasting monopoly held by the Mauritius Broadcasting Corporation.

Independent Broadcasting Authority: The Celicourt, 2nd Floor, 6 Sir Celicourt Antelme St, Port Louis; tel. 213-3890; fax 213-3894; e-mail iba@intnet.mu; internet iba.gov.mu; Dir DULLIPARSAD SURAJ BALI.

Radio

Mauritius Broadcasting Corpn: 1 Royal Rd, Moka; tel. 402-8000; fax 433-3330; e-mail customercare@mbc.intnet.mu; internet www.mbcradio.tv; f. 1964; parastatal organization operating eight national radio services and nine television channels; Chair. CLAUDE NARAIN; Dir-Gen. DHANJAY CALLIKAN.

Radio One: 3 Brown Sequard St, Port Louis; tel. 211-4555; fax 211-4142; e-mail sales@r1.mu; internet www.r1.mu; f. 2002; owned by Sentinelle media group; news and entertainment; Dir-Gen. NICOLAS ADELSON.

Radio Plus: 4B Labourdonnais St, Port-Louis; tel. 208-6002; fax 212-0042; e-mail radioplus@intnet.mu; internet www.radioplus.mu.

Top FM: The Peninsula, Caudan Bldg, 7th Floor, 2A Falcon St, Caudan, Port Louis; tel. 213-2121; fax 213-2222; e-mail topfm@intnet.mu; internet www.topfmradio.com; f. 2003; part of the International Broadcasting Group, in partnership with the Sunrise Group; Chair. BALKRISHNA KAUNHYE.

Television

Independent television stations were to commence broadcasting from 2002, as part of the liberalization of the sector.

Mauritius Broadcasting Corpn: see Radio.

Finance

(cap. = capital; res = reserves; dep. = deposits; m. = million; brs = branches; amounts in Mauritian rupees, unless otherwise stated)

BANKING

Central Bank

In 2010 there were 19 commercial banks and 11 non-bank deposit-taking institutions in Mauritius. The first Islamic bank of Mauritius, Century Banking Corpn Ltd, started its operation in 2011.

MAURITIUS

Bank of Mauritius: Sir William Newton St, POB 29, Port Louis; tel. 202-3800; fax 208-9204; e-mail governor.office@bom.intnet.mu; internet bom.intnet.mu; f. 1966; bank of issue; cap. 1,000.0m., res 19,158.8m., dep. 27,353.7m. (June 2010); Gov. RUNDHEERSING BHEENICK.

Principal Commercial Banks

ABC Banking Corpn Ltd: 7 Duke of Edinburgh Ave, Place d'Armes, Port Louis; tel. 206-8000; fax 208-0088; internet www.abcbanking.mu; f. 2010; Chair. Prof. DONALD AH CHUEN; CEO MOHAMED KHALIL ALKHUSHAIRI.

AfrAsia Bank Ltd: Bowen Square, 10 Dr Ferriere St, Port Louis; tel. 208-5500; fax 213-8850; e-mail afrasia@afrasiabank.com; internet www.afrasiabank.com; f. 2007; Chair. ARNAUD LAGESSE; CEO JAMES BENOIT.

Bank of Baroda: 32 Sir William Newton St, POB 553, Port Louis; tel. 208-1504; fax 208-3892; e-mail info@bankofbaroda-mu.com; internet www.bankofbaroda-mu.com; f. 1962; total assets 2,655,000m. (June 2007); Vice-Pres. (Mauritius Operations) S. K. CHAWLA; 7 brs.

Bank One Ltd: 16 Sir William Newton St, POB 485, Port Louis; tel. 202-9200; fax 210-4712; e-mail info@firstcitybank-mauritius.com; internet www.bankone.mu; f. 1991 as the Delphis Bank Ltd; merged with Union International Bank in 1997; private bank; taken over by consortium in 2002; name changed as above in 2008; 50% owned by Investments & Mortgages Bank Ltd (Kenya), 50% by Ciel Investments Ltd; cap. 491.4m., res 142.1m., dep. 9,481.3m. (Dec. 2009); Chair. SARIT SHAH; CEO RAJ DUSSOYE.

Barclays Bank PLC, Mauritius: Harbour Front Bldg, 8th Floor, John F. Kennedy St, POB 284, Port Louis; tel. 402-1000; fax 467-0618; e-mail barclays.mauritius@barclays.com; f. 1919; absorbed Banque Nationale de Paris Intercontinentale in 2002; cap. 100.0m., res 616.1m., dep. 6,886.7m. (Dec. 2001); Man. Dir RAVIN DAJEE; 16 brs.

Bramer Banking Corpn Ltd: 26 Bourbon St, Port Louis; tel. 208-8826; fax 213-4792; internet www.bramerbank.mu; f. 1989; present name adopted 2008; owned by British American Investment Group (BAI); cap. 200.0m., res 39.9m., dep. 4,301.8m. (Dec. 2009); Chair. HASSAM A. M. VAYID; 16 brs.

Deutsche Bank Mauritius Ltd: 4th Floor, Barkly Wharf East, Le Caudan Waterfront, POB 615, Port Louis; tel. 202-7878; fax 202-7898; internet www.db.com/mauritius.

Habib Bank Ltd: 30 Louis Pasteur St, Port Louis; tel. 217-7600; fax 216-3829; e-mail habib@intnet.mu; f. 1964; 2 brs.

Hongkong and Shanghai Banking Corpn Ltd (HSBC): HSBC Centre, 5th Floor, 18 Cyber City, Ebene, Port Louis; tel. 403-0701; fax 403-8300; e-mail hsbcmauritius@hsbc.co.mu; internet www.hsbc.co.mu; f. 1916; CEO SANDEEP UPPAL; Man. Dir JAMES BOUCHER.

Investec Bank (Mauritius) Ltd: 7th Floor, Dias Pier Bldg, Le Caudan Waterfront, Port Louis; tel. 207-4000; fax 207-4003; internet www.investec.com; f. 1997; Chair. HUGH S. HERMAN; CEO CRAIG C. MCKENZIE.

Mauritius Commercial Bank Ltd: MCB Centre, 9–15 Sir William Newton St, POB 52, Port Louis; tel. 202-5000; fax 208-7054; e-mail mcb@mcb.co.mu; internet www.mcb.mu; f. 1838; cap. 2,554.9m., res 3,990.0m., dep. 132,569.1m. (June 2010); Pres. GERARD J. HARDY; CEO PIERRE-GUY NOEL; 42 brs.

Mauritius Post and Co-operative Bank Ltd: 1 Sir William Newton St, Port Louis; tel. 207-9999; fax 208-7270; e-mail mpcb@mpcb.mu; internet www.mpcb.mu; f. 2003; 44.3% owned by The Mauritius Post Ltd, 35.7% state owned, 10% owned by the Sugar Investment Trust; cap. 384.0m., res 119.4m., dep. 7,131.9m. (Dec. 2009); CEO RAJIV KUMAR BEEHARRY; Gen. Man. PAVADAY THONDRAYON.

P. T. Bank Internasional Indonesia (Mauritius): 5th Floor, Barkly Wharf, Caudan Waterfront, Port Louis; tel. 210-6365; fax 210-5458; e-mail biimrt@intnet.mu; internet bii.intnet.mu; f. 1998; CEO SARAH JANE KATE NIRSIMLOO.

SBI Mauritius: 34 Sir William Newton St, POB 863, Port Louis; tel. 208-0121; fax 208-0039; e-mail info@sbimauritius.com; internet www.sbimauritius.com; f. 1978 as Indian Ocean International Bank Ltd; merged with SBI International in 2008 and renamed as above; cap. 48.6m., res 62.0m., dep. 438.4m. (March 2009); Chair. PRATIP CHAUDHURI; Man. Dir and CEO V. SRINIVASAN; 12 brs.

Standard Chartered Bank (Mauritius) Ltd: Ebene House, 2nd Floor, 33 Cyber City, Ebene; tel. 466-5000; fax 466-5161; e-mail info.scbm@sc.com; internet www.standardchartered.com/mu; wholly owned subsidiary of Standard Chartered Bank PLC; 'offshore' banking unit.

State Bank of Mauritius Ltd: State Bank Tower, 1 Queen Elizabeth II Ave, POB 152, Port Louis; tel. 202-1111; fax 202-1234; e-mail sbm@sbm.intnet.mu; internet www.sbmonline.com; f. 1973; cap. 303.7m., res 2,975.1m., dep. 61,252.9m. (June 2010); Chair. MUNI KRISHNA REDDY; CEO GAUTAM VIR; 43 brs.

Development Bank

Development Bank of Mauritius Ltd: rue La Chaussée, POB 157, Port Louis; tel. 203-3600; fax 208-8498; e-mail dbm@intnet.mu; internet www.dbm.mu; f. 1964; name changed as above in 1991; 85% govt-owned; cap. 225m., res 1,646.5m., dep. 4,155.9m. (June 2009); Chair. ERIC N. G. PING CHEUN; Man. Dir IQBAL CARRIM (acting); 6 brs.

Principal 'Offshore' Banks

Banque des Mascareignes Ltd: 1 Cathedral Sq., Level 8, 16 Jules Koenig St, POB 43, Port Louis; tel. and fax 213-1675; e-mail serviceclient@bm.mu; internet www.banquedesmascareignes.mu; f. 2004; name changed as above 2005; 69.5% owned by Financière Océor (France), 27.7% owned by Banque de la Réunion; cap. 838.7m., res 115.1m., dep. 9,304.4m. (Dec. 2009); Chair. BERNARD BOBROWSKI; CEO NELLY JIRARI.

Bank of Baroda, Barclays Bank PLC, AfrAsia Bank Ltd, PT Bank International Indonesia, Investec Bank (Mauritius), Standard Chartered Bank (Mauritius) and HSBC Bank PLC also operate 'offshore' banking units.

Islamic Bank

Century Banking Corpn Ltd : 4th Floor, Barkly Wharf, Le Caudan Waterfront, Port Louis; f. 2010; Pres. HESHAM SHOKRY.

Banking Organization

Mauritius Bankers Association (MBA): Level 15, Newton Tower, Sir William Newton St, Port Louis; tel. 213-2390; fax 213-0968; e-mail mba@mba.mu; internet www.mba.mu; f. 1967; Chair. RAVIN DAJEE; CEO AISHA C. TIMOL; 18 mems.

STOCK EXCHANGE

Financial Services Commission: FSC House, 54 Cyber City, Ebene; tel. 403-7000; fax 467-7172; e-mail fscmauritius@intnet.mu; internet www.fscmauritius.org; f. 2001; regulatory authority for securities, insurance and global business activities; Chair. SAID LALLOO; Chief Exec. (vacant).

Stock Exchange of Mauritius Ltd: 1 Cathedral Sq. Bldg, 4th Floor, 16 Jules Koenig St, Port Louis; tel. 212-9541; fax 208-8409; e-mail stockex@sem.intnet.mu; internet www.stockexchangeofmauritius.com; f. 1989; 11 mems; Chair. GAETAN LAN HUN KUEN; CEO SUNIL BENIMADHU.

INSURANCE

Albatross Insurance Co Ltd: 22 St George St, POB 116, Port Louis; tel. 207-9007; fax 208-4800; e-mail headoffice@albatross-insurance.com; internet www.albatross-insurance.com; f. 1975; Chair. VAUGHAN HEBERDEN.

Anglo-Mauritius Assurance Society Ltd: Swan Group Centre, 10 Intendance St, POB 837, Port Louis; tel. 202-8600; fax 208-8956; e-mail anglo@intnet.mu; internet www.anglo.mu; f. 1951; Chair. CYRIL MAYER; CEO LOUIS RIVALLAND.

BAI Co (Mauritius) Ltd: BAI Centre, 217 Royal Rd, Curepipe; tel. 602-3000; fax 670-3384; e-mail bai@bai.intnet.mu; internet www.bai.mu; f. 1988 as British American Insurance Co (Mauritius) Ltd; renamed as above in 2010; Pres. and CEO RISHI SOOKDAWOOR.

Indian Ocean General Assurance Ltd: 35 Corderie St, POB 865, Port Louis; tel. 212-4125; fax 212-5850; e-mail info@iogaltd.com; internet iogaltd.com; f. 1971; total assets 221m. (June 2007); Gen. Man. R. L. MATHUR.

Jubilee Insurance (Mauritius) Ltd: Cathedral Sq., Pope Hennessy St, Port Louis; tel. 210-3678; fax 212-7970; e-mail sarah.hossen@jubileemauritius.com; f. 1998; Admin. Officer SARAH HOSSEN.

Lamco International Insurance Ltd: Lamco Bldg, 12 Barracks St, Port Louis; tel. 212-4494; fax 208-0612; e-mail lamco@intnet.mu; internet www.lamcoinsurance.com; f. 1978; Chair. ABOO BAKAR YACOOB ATCHIA; Gen. Man. NAJEEB C. ADIA.

Life Insurance Corpn of India: LIC Centre, John F. Kennedy St, POB 310, Port Louis; tel. 212-5316; fax 208-6392; e-mail liccmm@intnet.mu; f. 1956; Chief Man. NAVIN PRAKASH SINHA.

Mauritian Eagle Insurance Co Ltd: 1st Floor, IBL House, Caudan Waterfront, POB 854, Port Louis; tel. 203-2200; fax 203-2299; e-mail caudan@mauritianeagle.com; internet www.mauritianeagle.com; f. 1973; Chair. PATRICE D'HOTMAN DE VILLIERS; Man. Dir ERIC A. VENPIN.

Mauritius Union Assurance Co Ltd: 4 Léoville L'Homme St, POB 233, Port Louis; tel. 207-5500; fax 212-2962; e-mail info@mauritiusunion.com; internet www.mauritiusuniongroup.com;

MAURITIUS

f. 1948; Chair. DOMINIQUE GALEA; Group Man. Dir KRIS LUTCHMENARRAIDOO.

Mauritius Union General Insurance: 4 Léoville L'Homme St, Port Louis; tel. 207-5500; fax 212-2962; internet www.mauritiusunion.com.

The New India Assurance Co Ltd: Bank of Baroda Bldg, 3rd Floor, 15 Sir William Newton St, POB 398, Port Louis; tel. 208-1442; fax 208-2160; e-mail niasurance@intnet.mu; internet www.niacl.com; f. 1935; general insurance; Chief Man. S. VAIDESWARAN.

Phoenix Insurance (Mauritius) Co Ltd: 36 Sir William Newton St, POB 852, Port Louis; tel. 208-0056; fax 213-3882; e-mail tilakf@intnet.mu; f. 1977; CEO TILAK FERNANDO (acting).

Rainbow Insurance Co Ltd: 23 Edith Cavell St, POB 389, Port Louis; tel. 202-8800; fax 208-8750; e-mail raininsu@intnet.mu; internet www.rainbowinsurance.mu; f. 1976; Chair. B. GOKULSING; Gen. Man. PRAVIN RAMBURN.

State Insurance Co of Mauritius Ltd (SICOM): SICOM Bldg, Sir Célicourt Antelme St, Port Louis; tel. 203-8400; fax 208-7662; e-mail email@sicom.intnet.mu; internet www.sicom.mu; f. 1975; Man. Dir K. G. BHOOJEDHUR-OBEEGADOO.

Sun Insurance Co Ltd: 2 St George St, Port Louis; tel. 208-0769; fax 208-2052; e-mail suninsco@intnet.mu; f. 1981; Chair. Sir KAILASH RAMDANEE; Man. Dir A. MUSBALLY.

Swan Insurance Co Ltd: Swan Group Centre, 10 Intendance St, POB 364, Port Louis; tel. 207-3500; fax 208-6898; e-mail swan@intnet.mu; f. 1955; Chair. J. M. ANTOINE HAREL; CEO LOUIS RIVALLAND.

L. and H. Vigier de Latour Ltd: Les Jamalacs Bldg, Old Council St, Port Louis; tel. 212-2034; fax 212-6056; Chair. and Man. Dir L. J. D. HENRI VIGIER DE LATOUR.

Trade and Industry

GOVERNMENT AGENCIES

Agricultural Marketing Board (AMB): Dr G. Leclézio Ave, Moka; tel. 433-4025; fax 433-4837; e-mail agbd@intnet.mu; internet amb.intnet.mu; f. 1964; operates under the aegis of the Ministry of Agro-industry and Food Security; markets certain locally produced and imported food products (such as potatoes, onions, garlic, spices and seeds); provides storage facilities to importers and exporters; Gen. Man. PARMANAND RAMNAWAZ.

Mauritius Meat Authority: Abattoir Rd, Roche Bois, POB 612, Port Louis; tel. 242-5884; fax 217-1077; e-mail mauritiusmeat@intnet.mu; f. 1974; licensing authority; controls and regulates sale of meat and meat products; also purchases and imports livestock and markets meat products; Gen. Man. A. BALGOBIN.

Mauritius Sugar Authority: Ken Lee Bldg, 2nd Floor, Edith Cavell St, Port Louis; tel. 208-7466; fax 208-7470; e-mail msa@intnet.mu; regulatory body for the sugar industry; Chair. S. HANOOMANJEE; Exec. Dir Dr G. RAJPATI.

Mauritius Tea Board: Wooton St, Curepipe Rd, Curepipe; POB 28, Eau Coulée; tel. 675-3497; fax 676-1445; e-mail teaboard@intnet.mu; internet www.gov.mu/portal/site/teaboard; f. 1975; regulates and controls the activities of the tea industry; Gen. Man. A. SEEPERGAUTH.

Mauritius Tobacco Board: Plaine Lauzun, Port Louis; tel. 212-2323; fax 208-6426; e-mail tobacco@intnet.mu; internet tobaccoboard.intnet.mu; Gen. Man. HEMRAJSINGH RAMAHOTAR.

DEVELOPMENT ORGANIZATIONS

Board of Investment—Mauritius (BOI): Cathedral Sq. Bldg 1, 10th Floor, 16 Jules Koenig St, Port Louis; tel. 211-4190; fax 208-2924; e-mail invest@boi.intnet.mu; internet www.boimauritius.com; f. 2001 to promote international investment, business and services; Chair. of Bd MAURICE LAM; Gen. Man. RAJU JADDOO.

Enterprise Mauritius: 7th Floor, Saint James Court, Saint Denis St, Port Louis; tel. 212-9760; fax 212-9767; e-mail info@em.intnet.mu; internet www.enterprisemauritius.biz; f. 2004 from parts of the Mauritius Industrial Development Authority, the Export Processing Zones Development Authority and the Sub-contracting and Partnership Exchange—Mauritius; comprises a Corporate Services Unit, a Strategic Direction Unit, a Business Development Unit, a Client-Services Unit and a Special Support Unit (est. from the former Clothing and Textile Centre); Chair. AMÉDÉE DARGA; CEO PRAKESH BEEHARRY.

Joint Economic Council (JEC): Plantation House, 3rd Floor, pl. d'Armes, Port Louis; tel. 211-2980; fax 211-3141; e-mail jec@intnet.mu; internet www.jec-mauritius.org; f. 1970; the co-ordinating body of the private sector of Mauritius, including the main business orgs of the country; Pres. GÉRARD GARRIOCH; Dir RAJ MAKOOND.

Mauritius Freeport Authority (MFA): Level 10, 1 Cathedral Sq. Bldg 16, Jules Koeing St, Port Louis; tel. 203-3800; fax 208-2924; e-mail contact@investmauritius.com; internet www.efreeport.com; f. 1990; Man. NANDA NARRAINEN.

National Productivity and Competitiveness Council (NPCC): 4th Floor, Alexander House, Cyber City, Reduit; tel. 467-7700; fax 467-3838; e-mail natpro@intnet.mu; internet www.npccmauritius.com; f. 2000; represents the Govt, the private sector and trade unions; Exec. Dir Dr KRISHNALALL COONJAN.

Small Enterprises and Handicraft Development Authority (SEHDA): Industrial Zone, Coromandel; tel. 233-0500; fax 233-5545; e-mail sehda@intnet.mu; internet www.sehda.org; f. 2006 following the merger of the Small and Medium Industries Development Organization and the National Handicraft Promotion Agency; provides support to potential and existing small entrepreneurs; Man. Dir VIJAY RAMGOOLAM.

State Investment Corpn Ltd (SIC): Air Mauritius Centre, 15th Floor, John F. Kennedy St, Port Louis; tel. 202-8900; fax 208-8948; e-mail contactsic@stateinvestment.com; internet www.stateinvestment.com; f. 1984; provides support for new investment and transfer of technology, in agriculture, industry and tourism; Man. Dir IQBAL MALLAM-HASHAM; Chair. RAJ RINGADOO.

CHAMBERS OF COMMERCE

Chinese Chamber of Commerce: Suite 206, Jade Court, Jummah Mosque St, Port Louis; tel. and fax 242-0156; e-mail admin@cccmauritius.org; f. 1908; Pres. ANNABELLE KOK SHUN.

Mauritius Chamber of Commerce and Industry: 3 Royal St, Port Louis; tel. 208-3301; fax 208-0076; e-mail mcci@intnet.mu; internet www.mcci.org; f. 1850; 400 mems; Pres. MARDAY VENKATASAMY; Sec.-Gen. MAHMOOD CHEEROO.

INDUSTRIAL ASSOCIATIONS

Association of Mauritian Manufacturers (AMM): c/o The Mauritius Chamber of Commerce and Industry, 3 Royal St, Port Louis; tel. 208-3301; fax 208-0076; e-mail mcci@intnet.mu; f. 1995; Pres. PATRICK RIVALLAND.

Mauritius Export Processing Zone Association (MEPZA): Unicorn House, 6th Floor, 5 Royal St, Port Louis; tel. 208-5216; fax 212-1853; f. 1976; consultative and advisory body; Chair. LOUIS LAI FAT FUR.

Mauritius Sugar Producers' Association (MSPA): Plantation House, 2nd Floor, Edinburgh Ave, Port Louis; tel. 212-0295; fax 212-5727; e-mail mspa@mspa.intnet.mu; f. 1947; Chair. JACQUES MARRIER D'UNIENVILLE; Dir JEAN LI YUEN FONG.

EMPLOYERS' ORGANIZATION

Mauritius Employers' Federation: MEF-MCCI Bldg, Ebene Cyber City, Ebene; tel. 466-3600; fax 465-8200; e-mail mef@intnet.mu; internet www.mef-online.org; f. 1962; Chair. ANWAR JOONAS; Dir Dr AZAD JEETUN.

UTILITIES

Electricity

Central Electricity Board: Royal Rd, POB 40, Curepipe; tel. 601-1100; fax 675-7958; e-mail ceb@intnet.mu; internet cebweb.intnet.mu; f. 1952; state-operated; Chair. PATRICK ASSIRVADEN; Gen. Man. C. DABEEDIN.

Water

Central Water Authority: Royal Rd, St Paul, Phoenix; tel. 601-5000; fax 686-6264; e-mail cwa@intnet.mu; corporate body; scheduled for privatization; f. 1973; Gen. Man. H. K. BOOLUCK; Chair. Prof. ANWAR HUSSEIN SUBRATTY.

Waste Water Management Authority: Sir Celicourt Antelme St, Port Louis; tel. 206-3000; fax 211-7007; e-mail wma@intnet.mu; internet wma.gov.mu; f. 2000; Chair. KHUSHAL LOBINE; Gen. Man. ROBIN SOONARANE.

TRADE UNIONS

Federations

Federation of Civil Service and Other Unions (FCSOU): Jade Court, Rm 308, 3rd Floor, 33 Jummah Mosque St, Port Louis; tel. 216-1977; fax 216-1475; e-mail f.c.s.u@intnet.mu; internet www.fcsu.org; f. 1957; 72 affiliated unions with 30,000 mems (2006); Pres. TOOLSYRAJ BENYDIN; Sec. AWADHKOOMARSINGH BALLUCK.

General Workers' Federation: 7 Impasse Ruisseau des Creoles, Port Louis; tel. 213-1771; Pres. SERGE JAUFFRET; Sec.-Gen. DEVIANAND NARRAIN.

MAURITIUS

Directory

Mauritius Labour Congress (MLC): 8 Louis Victor de la Faye St, Port Louis; tel. 212-4343; fax 208-8945; e-mail mlcongress@intnet.mu; f. 1963; 55 affiliated unions with 70,000 mems (1992); Pres. Nurdeo Luchmun Roy; Gen. Sec. Jugdish Lollbeeharry.

Mauritius Trade Union Congress (MTUC): Emmanuel Anquetil Labour Centre, James Smith St, Port Louis; tel. 210-8567; internet www.mtucmauritius.org; f. 1946; Pres. Dewan Quedou.

Trade Union Trust Fund: Richard House, 2nd Floor, cnr Jummah Mosque and Remy Ollier Sts, Port Louis; tel. and fax 217-2073; internet www.gov.mu/portal/site/tradeuniontf; f. 1997 to receive and manage funds and other property obtained from the Govt and other sources; to promote workers' education and provide assistance to workers' orgs; Chair. Radhakrisna Sadien.

Principal Unions

Government Servants' Association: 107A Royal Rd, Beau Bassin; tel. 464-4242; fax 465-3220; e-mail gsa@intnet.mu; internet www.gsa.mauritius.org; f. 1945; Pres. Radhakrisna Sadien; Sec.-Gen. Poonit Ramjug.

Government Teachers' Union: 3 Mgr Gonin St, POB 1111, Port Louis; tel. 208-0047; fax 208-4943; f. 1945; Pres. Jugduth Seegum; Sec. Mohammad Saleem Choolun; 4,550 mems (2005).

Nursing Association: 159 Royal Rd, Beau Bassin; tel. and fax 464-5850; e-mail nur.ass@intnet.mu; f. 1955; Pres. Cassam Kureeman; Sec.-Gen. Francis Supparayen.

Organization of Artisans' Unity: 42 Sir William Newton St, Port Louis; tel. and fax 212-4557; f. 1973; Pres. Auguste Follet; Sec. Roy Ramchurn; 2,874 mems (1994).

Plantation Workers' Union: 8 Louis Victor de la Faye St, Port Louis; tel. 212-1735; f. 1955; Pres. N. L. Roy; Sec. Gopal Bhujan; 13,726 mems (1990).

Port Louis Harbour and Docks Workers' Union: Port Louis; tel. 208-2276; Pres. José François; Sec.-Gen. Gerard Bertrand.

Sugar Industry Staff Employees' Association: 1 Rémy Ollier St, Port Louis; tel. 212-1947; f. 1947; Chair. T. Bellerose; Sec.-Gen. G. Chung Kwan Fang; 1,450 mems (1997).

Textile, Clothes and Other Manufactures Workers' Union: Thomy d'Arifat St, Curepipe; tel. 676-5280; Pres. Padmatee Teeluck; Sec.-Gen. Désiré Guildaree.

Union of Bus Industry Workers: Port Louis; tel. 212-3338; f. 1970; Pres. M. Babooa; Sec.-Gen. F. Auchoybur.

Union of Employees of the Ministry of Agriculture and other Ministries: 28 Hennessy Ave, Quatre-Bornes; tel. 465-1935; e-mail bruno5@intnet.mu; f. 1989; Sec. Bruneau Dorasami; 2,500 mems (Dec. 2003).

Union of Labourers of the Sugar and Tea Industry: Royal Rd, Curepipe; f. 1969; Sec. P. Ramchurn.

Transport

RAILWAYS

There are no operational railways in Mauritius.

ROADS

In 2009 there were 2,028 km of paved roads, of which 75 km were motorways, 950 km were other main roads, and 592 km were secondary roads. An urban highway links the motorways approaching Port Louis. A motorway connects Port Louis with Plaisance airport.

SHIPPING

Mauritius is served by numerous foreign shipping lines. In 1990 Port Louis was established as a free port to expedite the development of Mauritius as an entrepôt centre. At 31 December 2009 Mauritius had a merchant fleet of 50 vessels, with a combined displacement of 66,200 grt.

Mauritius Ports Authority: H. Ramnarain Bldg, Mer Rouge, Port Louis; tel. 206-5400; fax 240-0856; e-mail info@mauport.com; internet www.mauport.com; f. 1976; Chair. D. Appadu; Dir-Gen. Shekur Suntah.

Ireland Blyth Ltd: IBL House, Caudan, Port Louis; tel. 203-2000; fax 203-2001; e-mail iblinfo@iblgroup.com; internet www.iblgroup.com; Chair. Thierry Lagesse; CEO Patrice d'Hotman de Villiers; 2 vessels.

Mauritius Freeport Development Co Ltd: Freeport Zone 5, Mer Rouge; tel. 206-2000; fax 206-2025; e-mail info@mfd.mu; internet www.mfd.mu; f. 1997; manages and operates Freeport Zone 5, more than 40,000 sq m of storage facility; facilities include dry warehouses, cold warehouses, processing and transformation units, open storage container parks and a container freight station; largest logistics centre in the Indian Ocean region; Chair. René Leclézio; CEO Dominique De Froberville.

Mauritius Shipping Corpn Ltd: St James Court, Suite 417/418, St Denis St, Port Louis; tel. 208-5900; fax 210-5176; internet www.mauritiusshipping.mu; f. 1985; state-owned; operates two passenger-cargo vessels between Mauritius, Rodrigues, Réunion and Madagascar; Man. Dir Capt. J. Patrick Rault.

Société Mauricienne de Navigation Ltée: 1 rue de la Reine, POB 53, Port Louis; tel. 208-3241; fax 208-8931; Man. Dir Capt. François de Gersigny.

CIVIL AVIATION

Sir Seewoosagur Ramgoolam International Airport is at Plaisance, 4 km from Mahébourg. From 2006 air routes with France and the United Kingdom were liberalized, allowing new carriers to operate on the routes.

Civil Aviation Department: Sir Seewoosagur Ramgoolam International Airport, Plaine Magnien; tel. 603-2000; fax 637-3164; e-mail civil-aviation@mail.gov.mu; internet civil-aviation.gov.mu; overseen by the Prime Minister's Office (External Communications Division); Dir Anand Gungah.

Air Mauritius: Air Mauritius Centre, John F. Kennedy St, POB 441, Port Louis; tel. 207-7070; fax 208-8331; e-mail contact@airmauritius.com; internet www.airmauritius.com; f. 1967; 51% state-owned; services to 28 destinations in Europe, Asia, Australia and Africa; Chair. Rajkamal Taposeea; CEO Soobhiraj Bungsraz.

Tourism

Tourists are attracted to Mauritius by its scenery and beaches, the pleasant climate and the blend of cultures. Accommodation capacity totalled 21,072 beds in 2005. The number of visitors increased from 300,670 in 1990 to 934,827 in 2010, when the greatest numbers of visitors were from France (32.3%), Réunion (12.3%) and the United Kingdom (10.4%). Gross revenue from tourism in 2010 was estimated at MRs 39,456m. The Government sought to increase the volume of tourists visiting the country (to some 2m. people by 2015) by improving the jetty facilities in the port in order to welcome cruise ships and by liberalizing air transit rules.

Mauritius Tourism Promotion Authority: Victoria House, 4th and 5th Floor, St Louis St, Port Louis; tel. 210-1545; fax 212-5142; e-mail mtpa@intnet.mu; internet www.tourism-mauritius.mu; Chair. Robert Desvaux.

Tourism Authority (TA): Victoria House, 1st and 2nd Floor, St Louis St, Port Louis; tel. 213-1738; fax 213-1745; e-mail tourism.authority@intnet.mu; f. 2003; parastatal; issues licences for and monitors compliance of the regulation of the tourism industry; Dir Ashvin Gokhool.

Defence

The country has no standing defence forces, although as assessed at November 2010 paramilitary forces were estimated to number 2,000, comprising a special 1,500-strong mobile police unit, to ensure internal security, and a coast-guard of 500.

Defence Expenditure: Budgeted at Rs 1,240m. in 2009.

Education

Education is officially compulsory for seven years between the ages of five and 12. Primary education begins at five years of age and lasts for six years. Secondary education, beginning at the age of 11, lasts for up to seven years, comprising a first cycle of three years and a second of four years. At March 2005 up to 77% of pre-primary schools were privately run institutions. Primary and secondary education are available free of charge and became compulsory in 2005. According to UNESCO estimates, in 2008/09 enrolment at primary schools included 94% of pupils in the relevant age-group (males 93%; females 95%), while the comparable ratio for secondary schools in 2004/05 was 81% (males 79%; females 80%). The education system provides for instruction in seven Asian languages (71% of primary school children and 30% of secondary school children were studying at least one of these in 2005). The Government exercises indirect control of the large private sector in secondary education (in 2005 only 70 of 188 schools were state administered). The University of Mauritius had 7,531 students in 2006/07 (34.3% of whom were part-time students); in addition, many students receive further education abroad. Of total expenditure by the central Government in 2007/08, Rs 6,973.8m. (11.7%) was for education.

MEXICO

Introductory Survey

LOCATION, CLIMATE, LANGUAGE, RELIGION, FLAG, CAPITAL

The United Mexican States is bordered to the north by the USA, and to the south by Guatemala and Belize. The Gulf of Mexico and the Caribbean Sea lie to the east, and the Pacific Ocean and Gulf of California to the west. The climate varies with altitude. The tropical southern region and the coastal lowlands are hot and wet, with an average annual temperature of 18°C (64°F), while the highlands of the central plateau are temperate. Much of the north and west is arid desert. In Mexico City, which lies at about 2,250 m (nearly 7,400 ft) above sea-level, temperatures are generally between 5°C (42°F) and 25°C (78°F). The country's highest recorded temperature is 58°C (136°F). The principal language is Spanish, spoken by more than 90% of the population, while about 8% speak indigenous languages, of which Náhuatl is the most widely spoken. Almost all of Mexico's inhabitants profess Christianity, and about 85% are adherents of the Roman Catholic Church. The national flag (proportions 4 by 7) has three equal vertical stripes from hoist to fly, of green, white and red, with the state emblem (a brown eagle, holding a snake in its beak, on a green cactus, with a wreath of oak and laurel beneath) in the centre of the white stripe. The capital is Mexico City.

CONTEMPORARY POLITICAL HISTORY

Historical Context

Conquered by Hernán Cortés in the 16th century, Mexico was ruled by Spain until the wars of independence of 1810–21. After the war of 1846, Mexico ceded about one-half of its territory to the USA. Attempts at political and social reform by the anti-clerical Benito Juárez precipitated civil war in 1857–60, and the repudiation of Mexico's external debts by Juárez in 1860 led to war with the United Kingdom, the USA and France. The Austrian Archduke Maximilian, whom France tried to install as Emperor of Mexico, was executed, on the orders of Juárez, in 1867. Order was restored during the dictatorship of Porfirio Díaz, which lasted from 1876 until the Revolution of 1910. The Constitution of 1917 embodied the aims of the Revolution by revising land ownership, drafting a labour code and curtailing the power of the Roman Catholic Church. From 1929–2000 the country was dominated by the Partido Revolucionario Institucional (PRI), for much of that time in an effective one-party system, although a democratic form of election was maintained. However, allegations of widespread electoral malpractice persistently arose in connection with PRI victories.

Domestic Political Affairs

In a presidential election held in July 1976 the PRI candidate, José López Portillo, was elected with almost 95% of the votes cast. In 1977 López Portillo initiated reforms to increase minority party representation in the legislature and to widen democratic participation. The high level of political participation in the presidential election of July 1982 was without precedent, with left-wing groups taking part for the first time; however, the PRI's candidate, Miguel de la Madrid Hurtado, was successful. The concurrent elections to the Cámara Federal de Diputados (Federal Chamber of Deputies) resulted in another overwhelming victory for the PRI. On taking office in December, the new President embarked on a programme of major economic reform, giving precedence to the repayment of Mexico's debts, a policy that imposed severe financial constraints upon the middle and lower classes, leading to growing disaffection among traditional PRI supporters. The opposition Partido Acción Nacional (PAN) made important gains at municipal elections in two state capitals in mid-1983. The PRI's effective response ensured success at the remaining elections, but provoked opposition allegations of electoral fraud. At gubernatorial and congressional elections in July 1985, the PRI secured all seven of the available state governorships and 288 of the 300 directly elective seats in the Cámara Federal de Diputados.

The formation of a six-party left-wing alliance, the Partido Mexicano Socialista (PMS), in 1987 and, in particular, the emergence of a dissident faction, the Corriente Democrática (CD), within the PRI in 1986 were disturbing political developments for the ruling party. In early 1988 the CD and four left-wing parties (including the PMS coalition) formed an electoral alliance, the Frente Democrático Nacional (FDN), headed by CD leader Cuauhtémoc Cárdenas Solórzano. The legitimacy of the PRI victory at the presidential and congressional elections, conducted in July, was fiercely challenged by the opposition, following a delay in the publication of the results and reports of widespread electoral fraud. For the first time ever, the opposition secured seats in the Senado (Senate), while the PRI suffered defeats in the Distrito Federal and at least three other states.

In August 1988 the new Congreso de la Unión (Congress) was installed and immediately assumed the function of an electoral college, in order to investigate the claims of both sides. In September the allocation of 200 seats in the Cámara Federal de Diputados by proportional representation afforded the PRI a congressional majority and effective control of the electoral college. Opposition members withdrew from the Cámara in protest at the PRI's obstruction of the investigation, enabling the ruling party to ratify Carlos Salinas de Gortari as the new President. The results, although widely regarded as having been manipulated by the PRI, revealed a considerable erosion in support for the party.

Agreements on rescheduling Mexico's vast foreign debts were reached with the 'Paris Club' of official creditors in 1989, and with some 450 commercial banks in early 1990. In January 1989 a Pact for Economic Stability and Growth was implemented, with the agreement of employers' organizations and trade unions, and was subsequently extended until the end of 1994. None the less, the country experienced severe labour unrest in 1989 in support of greater pay increases and in protest at the Government's divestment programme.

During 1989 political opposition to the PRI was strengthened by success in gubernatorial and municipal elections. In October proposed constitutional amendments were approved with the unexpected support of the PAN. A 'governability clause', whereby an absolute majority of seats in the Cámara Federal de Diputados would be awarded to the leading party, should it receive at least 35% of the votes at a general election, was criticized by the Partido de la Revolución Democrática (PRD), the successor party to the FDN.

In June 1990, in response to continuing allegations of federal police complicity in abuses of human rights, President Salinas announced the creation of a national commission for human rights. In October the Government proposed legislation transferring responsibility for the interrogation of suspected criminals from the federal judicial police to the public magistrate's office. The proposed legislation also sought to undermine the validity of confession alone (often allegedly extracted under torture) as sufficient grounds for conviction.

In July 1991 the Federal Electoral Code was approved by the Cámara Federal de Diputados with support from all represented parties, except the PRD. The legislation contained provisions for the compilation of a new electoral roll, the issue of more detailed identification cards for voters, the modification of the Instituto Federal Electoral (IFE—Federal Electoral Institute), and the creation of a Tribunal Federal Electoral (Federal Electoral Tribunal, which, in 1996, became the Tribunal Electoral del Poder Judicial de la Federación).

The PRI continued to secure disputed electoral success at municipal and state level in 1991. At mid-term congressional elections in August, the party won almost all of the 300 directly elective seats in the Cámara Federal de Diputados (plus 30 of the 200 seats awarded by proportional representation) and 31 of the 32 contested seats in the Senado. The return to the level of support that the PRI had enjoyed prior to the 1988 elections was largely attributed to the success of the Government's programme of economic reform.

PRI victories at gubernatorial and legislative elections in several states during 1993 were denounced by the opposition as fraudulent. In September the Congreso approved electoral reforms that included restrictions on party funding and measures to increase the representation of minority parties in the legislature.

The Zedillo presidency, 1994–2000

In March 1994 Luis Donaldo Colosio, the PRI's presidential candidate, was assassinated at a campaign rally. Mario Aburto Martínez, arrested at the scene of the murder, was later identified as the apparently motiveless assassin. However, speculation that Colosio had been the victim of a conspiracy within the PRI establishment increased following the arrest, in connection with the incident, of a number of party members associated with police and intelligence agencies. The PRI subsequently named Ernesto Zedillo Ponce de León, a former cabinet minister who had most recently been acting as Colosio's campaign manager, as the party's presidential candidate. Zedillo was elected President on 21 August, with 49% of the votes, ahead of the PAN candidate, Diego Fernández de Cevallos (26%), and the PRD candidate, Cuauhtémoc Cárdenas (17%). The PRI also achieved considerable success at the concurrent congressional elections. However, numerous incidents of electoral malpractice were reported.

The report of a special investigation into Colosio's murder, published in July 1994, concluded that Aburto Martínez had acted alone in the assassination, reversing the findings of a preliminary investigation, which had suggested the existence of a number of conspirators. Nevertheless, speculation that Colosio had been the first victim of a politically motivated campaign of violence, conducted by a cabal of senior PRI traditionalists in order to check the advance of the party's reformist wing, intensified following the murder, in September, of the PRI Secretary-General, José Francisco Ruiz Massieu. In February 1995 a report issued by the Attorney-General was highly critical of all previous investigations of the Colosio assassination, concluding that the assassination had involved at least two gunmen. Meanwhile, in November 1994 Ruiz Massieu's brother, Mario, resigned his post as Deputy Attorney-General, claiming that senior PRI officials, including the party's President and Secretary-General, had impeded his investigation into his brother's death, in an attempt to protect the identities of those responsible for the assassination. In February 1995 Raúl Salinas de Gortari, brother of former President Salinas, was arrested on charges of complicity in Ruiz Massieu's murder, and in April several new conspirators, including five state Governors, were implicated. In October two men were each sentenced to 18 years' imprisonment for the murder of the PRI Secretary-General. In October 1996 the case against Raúl Salinas was prejudiced further by the discovery of a body buried in the grounds of his property in Mexico City.

In March 1995, following the arrest of his brother, former President Salinas began a public campaign to discredit the new administration and to defend himself from accusations of responsibility for the country's economic crisis and from allegations that he had obstructed attempts to bring to justice those responsible for Colosio's death. Raúl Salinas was convicted of murder and, in January 1999, sentenced to 50 years' imprisonment (later reduced to almost 28 years); in August 2002 he was additionally charged with the embezzlement of up to 209m. new pesos from a secret presidential fund under his brother's control. In September 1999 Mario Ruiz Massieu committed suicide in the USA while awaiting trial on charges of laundering money gained from drugs-trafficking; he left a note repeating his earlier accusations against the PRI and blaming Zedillo and other senior officials for his own death and the assassination of Colosio.

In July 1996 the PRI, the PAN, the PRD and the Partido del Trabajo (PT, a labour party) reached consensus on reforms that would include introducing a directly elected governor of the Distrito Federal, increasing and regulating public financing for political parties, employing proportional representation in elections to the Senado, granting a right of vote to Mexican citizens resident abroad, and allowing the IFE greater independence. The reforms received congressional approval in August. However, in November, in apparent response to their diminishing share of the vote in recent municipal elections, PRI traditionalists secured the adoption by the Cámara Federal de Diputados of a series of amendments to the electoral reform bill, increasing public funding in 1997 for political parties by some 476%, pronouncing that to exceed campaign finance limits would no longer be a criminal or electoral offence, expanding the Government's access to the media, and restricting the right of opposition parties to form coalitions.

Meanwhile, in May 1996 President Zedillo dismissed Mexico City's chief of police following public outcry at the violent tactics employed by his officers to disperse a group of striking teachers in the capital. In the following months hundreds of police employees throughout the country were dismissed for incompetence or corruption, while army officers were increasingly appointed to positions within the police force. In March 1997 some 2,500 members of Mexico City's police force were replaced by army personnel, and in October an élite police unit was disbanded after accusations that as many as 35 of its members were implicated in the torture and murder of three youths in September. Several officers at the anti-abduction unit in the state of Morelos were also accused of torture and murder in early 1998, precipitating the resignation of the state's PRI Governor in May.

At elections held in July 1997 for all 500 seats in the Cámara Federal de Diputados, the PRI lost its overall majority for the first time, while the PRD and the PAN made substantial gains. At concurrent elections held for one-quarter of the seats in the Senado, the PRI retained its overall majority, albeit significantly reduced, while the PAN and the PRD increased their representation. An informal congressional alliance between the PAN, the PRD, the Partido Verde Ecologista de México (PVEM) and the PT meant that opposition parties were able to take control of important legislative committees. The election of Cárdenas, the PRD candidate, as Head of Government of the Distrito Federal was particularly significant. The electoral defeats suffered by the PRI exacerbated tensions within the party, and several party members defected to the PRD.

The Fox presidency, 2000–06

A presidential election was held on 2 July 2000. The PRI's candidate was the former Secretary of the Interior, Francisco Labastida Ochoa, while the former Governor of Guanajuato state, Vicente Fox Quesada, represented a PAN-PVEM alliance known as the Alianza por el Cambio (AC), and Cárdenas was once again the PRD's nominee (officially he stood for the PRD-dominated Alianza por México—AM). Fox secured 43% of the votes cast, while Labastida attracted 37% and Cárdenas 17%. Fox was thus elected President, ending the PRI's 71-year hegemony in Mexican government. In the concurrent elections to the Congreso, the AC secured 223 of the 500 seats, compared with 209 won by the PRI and 68 by the AM. The PRI remained the largest grouping in the Senado, however, with 60 seats. Fox took office as President on 1 December, stating that his priorities were a reduction in poverty, improved relations with the USA, and peace and reconciliation within Mexico.

In January 2002 the Government announced that an investigation was to be held into allegations that the state petroleum company, Petróleos Mexicanos (PEMEX), had covertly funded Labastida's presidential election campaign. A former director of PEMEX, Manuel Gómez-Peralta, was detained in connection with the allegations in May, and a former PEMEX President, Rogelio Montemayor, was arrested in Houston, TX, USA, in October. In that month opposition parties demanded that President Fox allow the reopening of investigations into allegations that the PAN organization Amigos de Fox, responsible for Fox's presidential campaign, had received substantial illegal foreign funding. In October 2003 the IFE fined both the PAN and the PVEM for receiving illegal campaign funding from Amigos de Fox.

In November 2003 the Supreme Court ruled that prosecution for murder could proceed even in cases where no body had been found. The ruling enabled prosecutions to proceed for human rights abuses committed during the 'guerra sucia' ('dirty war') of the late 1970s; in February 2004 Miguel Nazar Haro, former director of the covert Dirección General de Seguridad, was arrested in connection with the disappearance of left-wing activist Jesús Piedra Ibarra in 1975. In mid-2004 the Supreme Court made a further ruling that cases concerning disappearance could be brought in connection with the suppression of dissent in the 1970s and 1980s. Meanwhile, a special prosecutor, Ignacio Carrillo, was appointed to investigate the role of, among others, former President Luis Echeverría in the 'guerra sucia'; however, Carrillo's request that Echeverría be arrested was rejected. In February 2005 the Supreme Court ruled that the Vienna Convention on genocide, which came into force in 2002, could not be applied retrospectively, while in July 2005 the case against Echeverría was dismissed on the grounds that there was no evidence of genocide. This dismissal, however, was itself overruled on appeal in November 2006, thereby reopening the possibility of a prosecution.

In December 2003 118 PRI deputies voted to replace Elba Esther Gordillo Morales, the party's Secretary-General, as leader of the PRI legislative bloc. Gordillo initially refused to accept her dismissal and continued to rely on the support of 104

PRI deputies. It was widely believed that the underlying reason for the split was a feud between Gordillo and party President Roberto Madrazo Pintado over who would secure the PRI nomination for the presidential election due in 2006.

In March 2004 a scandal emerged surrounding the PRD Head of Government of the Distrito Federal, Andrés Manuel López Obrador, a likely candidate in the 2006 presidential election. A videotape appeared to show López Obrador's finance chief, Gustavo Ponce Meléndez, gambling large amounts at a casino in the USA (Ponce was arrested in October 2004). A further video recording came to light that apparently showed the Head of Government's former private secretary accepting money from a prominent Argentine businessman, Carlos Ahumada, who was accused of corruption. López Obrador denied any knowledge of either incident and claimed that a 'dirty tricks' campaign was being waged against him. In June the Attorney-General's office announced that it was to prosecute López Obrador and a formal request was made to the Congreso to rescind his immunity from prosecution. In an indication of his popularity in Mexico City, however, in August thousands of supporters attended a march against the move to impeach him. In April 2005 the Cámara Federal de Diputados voted to remove López Obrador's immunity. Later in April as many as 1.2m. people participated in a demonstration in Mexico City in support of their mayor, who returned to his post the following day. The federal Attorney-General was subsequently dismissed; this was widely interpreted as an admission by the Government that its plan to prevent López Obrador from contesting the forthcoming presidential election had failed (people facing criminal charges were prohibited from running for office); indeed, in May the new Attorney-General dismissed all charges against López Obrador and in July he secured the PRD's presidential nomination.

Discord continued within the PRI during 2005 between the supporters of Gordillo and Madrazo in their respective campaigns to secure the party's nomination for the presidential election. In January Gordillo and the powerful teachers' union, the Sindicato Nacional de Trabajadores de la Educación, of which she was President, launched the Nueva Alianza (NA) in order to consolidate support for her candidacy. In August a third faction, Unidad Democrática, more commonly known as Todos Unidos Contra Madrazo (TUCOM—Everyone United against Madrazo), elected Arturo Montiel, the outgoing Governor of the Estado de México, as its nominee for the PRI's presidential candidate. However, in October, following allegations of corruption regarding his use of public money during his time as Governor, Montiel withdrew from the primary contest. It was widely assumed that Madrazo had been behind the allegations. A series of defections in late 2005 by prominent members of the PRI opposed to Madrazo further highlighted the divisions within the party. None the less, in November Madrazo won an overwhelming victory in the election for the PRI's presidential nomination.

Meanwhile, in October 2005 the former Secretary of Energy, Felipe Calderón Hinojosa, from the traditional, clericist wing of the PAN, unexpectedly won that party's 2006 presidential nomination, defeating Santiago Creel Miranda, who had enjoyed the support of President Fox. In December the PRI and the PVEM announced an alliance, Alianza por México, to contest the 2006 elections. The PRD and two smaller left-wing parties, Convergencia and the PT, also formed an alliance, Por el Bien de Todos (For the Good of Everyone), which later became the Frente Amplio Progresista (FAP).

The Calderón presidency, 2006–

At the presidential election, held on 2 July 2006, the PAN's Calderón secured an extremely narrow margin of victory, of just 0.6% (243,934 votes out of almost 42m. cast), over López Obrador. According to official results, Calderón polled 35.9% of the total votes cast, compared with López Obrador's 35.3%. Madrazo, the PRI nominee, trailed in third place with 22.2%, an historic low for the party. López Obrador did not accept the results, alleging that electoral irregularities, combined with the narrow margin of defeat, undermined their legitimacy. Calderón was inaugurated as President on 1 December in a ceremony notable for its lack of celebration and ostentation. A week earlier López Obrador had held a ceremony in Mexico City's main square, declaring himself to be Mexico's legitimate President in front of a large crowd.

Results of elections to the Congreso, also held on 2 July 2006, were evenly distributed among the three leading parties, ensuring that the new President would face a legislature dominated by the opposition. The PAN secured 206 of the 500 seats in the Cámara Federal de Diputados, with the PRD-led Por el Bien de Todos alliance winning 158 seats and the PRI's Alianza por México garnering 123 seats. In the 128-seat Senado, the PAN won 52 seats, the Alianza por México 39 seats and Por el Bien de Todos 36 seats. Political obstacles in the Congreso threatened to undermine the new Government's ability to introduce reforms to the state sector, just as they had during President Fox's administration.

One of the first major challenges that the new Government faced was the increasing unrest in Oaxaca. In June 2006 some 70,000 teachers had begun industrial action in support of salary increases. This had been accompanied by demonstrations, which became violent when police and protesters clashed, leaving around 100 people injured. Indigenous Indian rights activists and local farmers' co-operatives joined the protests. In September five protesters were shot dead by police, and a further three protesters were shot dead in the following month. President-elect Calderón dispatched 5,000 security personnel supported by armoured trucks and helicopters to retake control of the centre of the city. More that 150 people were subsequently arrested for their part in the protests, and many more were injured during violent confrontations. In total, 14 people were killed during the disturbances. A series of bomb explosions in Mexico City in November, which caused severe damage to property, were reportedly in response to 'repression in Oaxaca'; although no particular group claimed responsibility for the attacks, the Ejército Popular Revolucionario (EPR), a left-wing guerrilla group hitherto active only in the southern states, was believed to have been linked to them. The EPR did claim responsibility for a series of bomb attacks affecting petroleum and gas pipelines belonging to PEMEX in central Mexico in July, as well as another similar series of explosions in September, both of which caused severe disruption to major industries.

A law to reform the electoral system by reducing the influence of money in elections was approved with the votes of all three main parties in the Senado in September 2007 and entered into law in November. The provisions of the reform, *inter alia*, reduced from 270m. new pesos to 40m. new pesos the amount that a party could spend on an election campaign, granted each party a limited amount of publicity in the broadcast media and prohibited the diffusion of propaganda that denigrated parties or candidates; the latter provision was in response to the negative campaign conducted by opponents of López Obrador that had preceded the 2006 presidential election.

Rapidly declining oil production, apparently owing to a lack of investment in exploration and refineries, led the PAN to propose energy reforms in early 2008 aimed at liberalizing the oil sector and allowing PEMEX to form alliances with foreign companies. The reforms were strongly opposed by the PRD, and facilitated the political revival of López Obrador, who led the protests, arguing that any private investment in PEMEX would threaten national sovereignty. However, the Congreso approved the energy reforms in October.

Meanwhile, in March 2008 an election to choose the President of the PRD highlighted the divisions in the party between a faction that supported López Obrador's continued claim to the presidency and refused to deal with what it considered to be an illegitimate Government, and those who favoured a more pragmatic approach. Preliminary indications suggested that Alejandro Encinas, representing the pro-López Obrador faction, had defeated the moderate candidate, Jesús Ortega Martínez; however, counting of ballots was suspended in several states following allegations of irregularities by both sides. In November the Tribunal Electoral del Poder Judicial de la Federación (TEPJF) ruled that Ortega was the rightful winner of the March election, provoking further tensions within the party. The result led to López Obrador threatening to split away from the PRD in December.

An outbreak of the A(H1N1) strain of the influenza virus (commonly known as 'swine flu') in Mexico in April 2009 led to fears of a global pandemic. In an attempt to contain the spread of the virus, Calderón ordered the closure of schools, universities, government offices, factories, restaurants and markets across the country. The Government's decisive response to the crisis appeared to have had some success in controlling the spread of the disease within Mexico.

Recent developments: mid-term and gubernatorial elections

At the mid-term congressional elections on 5 July 2009, the PAN suffered a major defeat, securing only 143 seats in the Cámara Federal de Diputados (compared with its previous 206 seats), while the PRI won 237 seats (compared with its previous total of

108). The PVEM won a total of 22 seats, which, owing to the party's allegiance to the PRI, gave the PRI the necessary representation to have an absolute majority in the lower house. Participation in the election was low, estimated at some 44% of eligible voters. The PAN also suffered electoral losses in many of the state and municipal elections that took place concurrently. The scale of its defeat prompted the resignation of the President of the PAN, Germán Martínez Cazares. He was replaced by José César Nava Vázquez.

Gubernatorial, state and municipal elections took place in 12 states on 4 July 2010. The PRI retained six of the state governorships and secured control of an additional three (in Aguascalientes, Tlaxcala and Zacatecas), but lost the other three contested (in Oaxaca, Puebla and Sinaloa) to 'anti-PRI' alliances led by the PAN and the PRD. The apparent success of the PAN-PRD alliances in restraining the growth in support for the PRI prompted speculation that the two parties might field a joint candidate in the 2012 presidential election, although there were doubts that either party would be willing to cede the position to the other. Meanwhile, six days before polling, the PRI candidate for the governorship of Tamaulipas, Rodolfo Torre Cantú, was assassinated, the killing being attributed to members of a drugs gang; his brother, Egidio Torre Cantú, was selected as the party's new candidate and retained the state governorship for the PRI. A minor government reorganization was effected in mid-July. The Secretary of the Interior, Fernando Gómez-Mont Urueta, who had resigned from the PAN in February, after expressing his opposition to the party's decision to form electoral alliances with the PRD, was replaced by José Francisco Blake Mora, while Bruno Ferrari García de Alba succeeded Gerardo Ruiz Mateos as Secretary of the Economy, following the latter's appointment as the President's Chief of Staff.

The three main parties elected new leaders in late 2010 and early 2011: Gustavo Enrique Madero Muñoz, a senator from Chihuahua and the candidate preferred by Calderón, became President of the PAN in December 2010; Humberto Moreira Valdés, hitherto Governor of Coahuila, was chosen as President of the PRI in January 2011; and in March the PRD elected Jesús Zambrano Grijalva, who came from the same moderate faction of the party as his predecessor, Ortega, and supported the electoral alliances with the PAN, as its President. Meanwhile, in December 2010 the Cámara Federal de Diputados voted to remove the immunity from prosecution of one of its members, Julio César Godoy Toscano of the PRD, who was charged with having links to organized crime and money-laundering.

In mid-January 2011 President Calderón appointed Dionisio Pérez-Jácome Friscione and José Antonio Meade Kuribreña, both hitherto undersecretaries in the Secretariat of State for Finance and Public Credit, as Secretary of Communications and Transport and Secretary of Energy, respectively. Juan Molinar Horcasitas, the outgoing Secretary of Communications and Transport, was allocated a post within the National Executive Committee of the PAN, while Georgina Kessel Martínez, formerly responsible for energy, became Director-General of the state-owned Banco Nacional de Obras y Servicios Públicos. The PRD retained the governorship of Guerrero at an election later that month, but lost the governorship of Baja California Sur to the PAN in February, having been weakened by continuing internal divisions. Also in February clashes broke out in Oaxaca between police and teachers who were protesting against an announcement by Calderón, during a visit to the city, that private school fees were to become tax deductible; further demonstrations by teachers took place in March.

Human Rights and the Illegal Drugs Trade

Mexico's poor human rights record was highlighted in late 2001 by the assassination in October of a leading civil liberties lawyer, Digna Ochoa, and by the publication, in December, of an Amnesty International report alleging that Mexican security forces were involved in widespread human rights violations. In response, President Fox announced an official inquiry into the 'disappearance' of 532 people detained by security forces in the 1970s and 1980s. In February 2002 Fox ordered the immediate release of Gen. José Francisco Gallardo, who had been sentenced to 28 years' imprisonment in 1993 after being convicted of misappropriating military property. Human rights groups and supporters of Gallardo had maintained that the charges were fabricated and that he had been incarcerated after demanding a reform of the military justice system. However, in August 2003 Amnesty International published a report that accused the Government of inefficiency and negligence in investigating the rape and murder of an estimated 307 women (and the disappearance of a further 500) in Ciudad Juárez over the previous 10 years. In 2004 some 130 government officials were investigated for negligence in the ongoing murder investigations. In mid-2004 a further Amnesty International report asserted that widespread abuse of human rights persisted. The report alleged that the police and military routinely abused peasants, and that torture was commonly used by police and in the justice system. According to official figures, 531 kidnappings occurred in Mexico in 2003; however, other sources estimated that the real figure was 3,000. In December 2004 President Fox announced a National Plan for Human Rights, aimed at eliminating torture and abuse. A report commissioned by Fox in 2002, which was published in November 2006, acknowledged government responsibility in the massacres, torture and 'disappearances' of the 1970s. In March 2007 the investigating magistrate ordered the murder case of Digna Ochoa to be reopened.

An anti-narcotics effort by the Fox administration led to an increased number of arrests in 2002–04, including those of the leaders of the Tijuana and Golfo cocaine cartels. However, the anti-drugs programme was itself the subject of an anti-corruption drive in 2002, leading to a number of specialized army units being dismantled. Meanwhile, in November the investigation into the 'guerra sucia' of the late 1970s resulted in the convictions of Brig.-Gen. Mario Acosta and Gen. Francisco Quirós on charges of protecting the operations of the Juárez cartel; they also faced charges over the disappearance of 143 activists. Despite efforts by President Fox to address the crime problem, drugs-related crime continued to escalate as the amount of narcotics crossing the Mexican–US border increased. It appeared that an internecine war between the Tijuana, Golfo and Sinaloa cartels was taking place in the north of Mexico. During 2005 more than 180 people were killed in Nuevo Laredo, Tamaulipas, in what appeared to be an ongoing conflict between two drugs cartels. In November Ricardo García Urquiza, alleged to be the leader of the Juárez cartel, was arrested in Mexico City.

Upon his election in mid-2006, President Calderón announced that law enforcement would form one of his priorities in office. A major offensive was subsequently launched in December against the activities of the drugs cartels in Michoacán state with the deployment of 7,000 troops and federal police officers. A second major operation was launched in Tijuana, Baja California, in early January 2007, while later in the same month some 9,000 troops were sent into the states of Sinaloa, Durango and Chihuahua. Meanwhile, Calderón was highly commended by the US authorities for his decision in January to allow the extradition of 15 drugs-trafficking suspects to the USA. The extradition of the individuals (who included the head of the Golfo cartel and senior figures from the Sinaloa and Tijuana cartels) represented a significant change in policy from previous administrations, which had refused to allow extradition until suspects had faced a Mexican court. By mid-May the army and federal police had been deployed in a law-enforcement role in 10 states. Although these offensives against organized crime appeared to have little immediate impact (according to official figures, at least 2,500 people were killed by gangsters in 2007, compared with 2,350 in 2006), the Government emphasized that its strategy would take several years to accomplish. In January 2008 the arrest, in Culiacán, Sinaloa, of Alfredo Beltrán Leyva, a senior leader of the Sinaloa cartel, was one of a number of important successes in the offensive. The arrest, however, provoked further battles between rival factions of the Sinaloa-based Arellano Félix cartel, one loyal to Beltrán Leyva and the other to the notorious drugs-trafficker Joaquín Guzmán ('El Chapo'). Drugs-related violence escalated in 2008, with a reported 6,844 killings, more than twice the murder toll of the previous year. As previously, the violence was particularly, but not exclusively, concentrated in the states of Baja California, Chihuahua and Sinaloa, with 12 decapitated bodies also discovered in Yucatán in August, and a further dozen found in Chilpancingo, Guerrero, in December.

Confronted by widespread insecurity about the increasing crime rate, Calderón held a summit in August 2008, during which state governors, congressmen and other representatives agreed on a three-year plan to introduce 75 anti-crime measures, including the construction of maximum-security gaols and a national database to track mobile telephone usage. The high-profile kidnap and murder of Fernando Martí, the 14-year-old son of a well-known businessman, incited Calderón to toughen sentences for kidnappers and to launch a new anti-kidnap squad. Nevertheless, the Government failed to inspire confidence about the security situation in many Mexicans. In late August more than 200,000 people filled the capital's main square in a night-time demonstration to denounce not only murders, kidnappings and drugs-trafficking, but also alleged police and government complicity and corruption. The arrest of one of the Arellano Félix brothers, Eduardo, in October, was followed by the revelation that two senior officials in the government unit for the investigation of organized crime, the Subprocuraduría de Investigación Especializada en Delincuencia Organizada (SIEDO), were in the pay of the Beltrán Leyva cartel. The SIEDO's reputation was damaged further in November when its former head, Noé Ramírez, was accused of having accepted US $450,000 from the Sinaloa cartel in exchange for supplying information about police investigations.

Despite the deployment of some 40,000 troops in the war against drugs, army incursions into the problem areas had little impact and tended to exacerbate violence; one confrontation between the army and gang members in a border town of Chihuahua in February 2009 resulted in 21 deaths. The armed forces launched a renewed campaign against drugs gangs in Ciudad Juárez in March, sending 7,000 troops and police into the city. Persistent fears about the role of corrupt officials continued to hamper the war against the drugs cartels. In May a judge, 10 mayors and 17 other senior officials from Michoacán state were arrested and charged with drugs-related offences. Moreover, in July 29 state police officers were arrested in connection with the massacre of 12 federal agents whose bodies were dumped by a road in Michoacán in that month. A further 5,500 additional security personnel were deployed in the state in response to increasing violence in the area. Many observers, however, accused the Government of provoking more violence between rival drugs gangs by bringing extra troops into the area, citing the ever increasing murder toll as evidence of the policy's failure.

Ongoing violence in the country was brought to international attention in March 2010. First, 13 people were killed in Acapulco, a southern Mexican beach resort popular with US tourists. Some of the decapitated victims' bodies were dumped in scenic areas frequented by tourists. Second, three people associated with the US consulate in Ciudad Juárez (two of whom were US citizens) were murdered, provoking expressions of outrage from the US authorities. President Calderón urged the US Government to increase its assistance to Mexico in tackling the drugs cartels, describing the task as a shared responsibility. According to an official government report leaked to a newspaper in April, 22,743 people had been killed in drugs-related violence in Mexico since Calderón took office in 2006, with the number of deaths rising steadily each year. Chihuahua was identified as the most violent state, followed by Sinaloa, Guerrero, Baja California and Michoacán. The security situation continued to deteriorate throughout 2010, amid signs that the violence was spreading to states that had previously been less affected, such as Tamaulipas and Nuevo León. In July the director of a prison in Durango was arrested and accused of allowing prisoners to carry out contract killings at night, using prison weapons and vehicles, for gangs involved in organized crime; the prisoners were alleged to have perpetrated three massacres in the city of Torreón. The murders, in August and September, of four mayors (bringing the total number of mayors killed that year to 10) followed that of the PRI candidate for the governorship of Tamaulipas in June. In August the bodies of 72 migrants from various Central and South American countries were discovered in Tamaulipas; the massacre was attributed to members of the Zetas gang and prompted the resignation of the head of the National Institute of Migration. Meanwhile, the Mexican authorities were making some progress in their pursuit of a list of 37 gang members, with the arrest in mid-2010 of Edgar Valdéz Villarreal and Sergio Villarreal Barragán, leaders of rival factions of the Beltrán Leyva cartel (which was no longer aligned with the Sinaloa cartel and had been riven by infighting). However, the detention of cartel leaders did not lead to a reduction in the violence, and in October, in addition to numerous killings, including those of at least nine police officers, 22 Mexican tourists were kidnapped in Acapulco. In January 2011 Flavio Méndez Santiago, a suspected founder member of the Zetas gang, was detained, becoming the 20th of the 37 suspected drugs gangsters being sought to be either captured or killed; two others, Ezequiel Cárdenas Guillén of the Gulf cartel and Nazario Moreno González of the Familia cartel (based in Michoacán), had been killed in gun battles with the security forces in the previous two months.

The Government released official statistics on drugs-related killings for the first time in January 2011: the number of deaths rose to 15,273 in 2010 from 9,614 in 2009 (6,837 in 2008 and 2,826 in 2007). Of the total of 34,612 deaths that had been recorded since 1 December 2006, when President Calderón took office, 89% were the result of inter-cartel conflict. In late January 2011, in response to escalating violence in Nuevo León, particularly around its capital, Monterrey (where more than 120 people, including 20 police officers, had reportedly been killed that month), the Government deployed troops to conduct joint patrols with police officers in the state. According to unofficial figures, drugs-related killings in Nuevo León had increased from some 99 in 2009 to 610 in 2010. In early March 2011 a municipal government official in Ciudad Juárez, where more than 3,100 people had been killed in 2010, announced that the closure of more than 2,000 of the city's streets had been authorized, with security guards posted to monitor gates erected to prevent the entrance of non-residents. A series of marches held in some 20 cities and towns nation-wide in April 2011 in protest against drugs-related violence coincided with the discovery in San Fernando, Tamaulipas, of eight mass graves, containing a total of 59 bodies, by police investigating the alleged abduction of bus passengers some two weeks earlier; a further 29 bodies were found in six graves in the following days.

Zapatista Insurgency

On 1 January 1994 armed Indian groups numbering 1,000–3,000 took control of four municipalities of the southern state of Chiapas. The rebels issued the Declaration of the Lacandona Jungle, identifying themselves as the Ejército Zapatista de Liberación Nacional—EZLN (after Emiliano Zapata, who championed the land rights of Mexican peasants during the 1910–17 Revolution), and detailed a series of demands for economic and social change in the region, culminating in a declaration of war against the Government and a statement of intent to depose the 'dictator', President Salinas. A charismatic rebel spokesman, identified as 'subcomandante Marcos' (later tentatively identified as Rafael Sebastián Guillén Vicente, a former professor at the Universidad Autónoma Metropolitana), stated that the insurgency had been timed to coincide with the implementation of the North American Free Trade Agreement (NAFTA), which the rebels considered to be the latest in a series of segregative government initiatives adopted at the expense of indigenous groups. Negotiations between the Zapatistas and government representatives concluded with the publication of a document detailing 34 demands of the EZLN, and the Government's response to them. A preliminary accord was reached following the Government's broad acceptance of many of the rebels' stipulations, including an acceleration of the wide-ranging anti-poverty programme in the region, the incorporation of traditional Indian structures of justice and political organization, and a commitment from the Government to investigate the impact of NAFTA and recent land reform legislation on Indian communities. Official figures suggested that 100–150 guerrillas, soldiers and civilians had been killed during the conflict, while the Roman Catholic Church estimated that there had been as many as 400 casualties. In June the EZLN announced that the Government's peace proposal had been rejected by an overwhelming majority of the movement's supporters. However, a similar majority had rejected the resumption of hostilities with the security forces, and had endorsed the extension of the cease-fire pending renewed bilateral discussions. Tensions, however, continued over the following years, with attempts to reach an accord between the Zapatistas and the Government proving unsuccessful. In February 1996 the EZLN and the Government signed an agreement guaranteeing the cultural, linguistic and local government rights of indigenous groups. However, the EZLN withdrew from negotiations in September on the grounds that the agreement had not been implemented. In September 1997 several thousand Zapatistas and their sympathizers staged a peaceful demonstration in Mexico City, during which the EZLN inaugurated the Frente Zapatista de Liberación Nacional, a political movement that embodied the Zapatistas' ideology. In December there was widespread disquiet at the killing of 45 Indians in a church in the village of Acteal, in the municipality of Chenalhó, Chiapas. Emilio Chuayffet, the Secretary of the Interior, and Julio César Ruiz Ferro, the Governor of Chiapas, were forced to resign, following criticism of their roles in the events leading to the Acteal massacre. In April 1998 Gen. Julio César Santiago Díaz, who had been acting chief of staff of Chiapas state police at the time of the massacre, was arrested and charged with failing to intervene to prevent the bloodshed. In September 1999 Jacinto Arias, mayor of Chenalhó at the time of the massacre, was convicted on charges of supplying the weapons used in the massacre and sentenced to 35 years' imprisonment. In November 2002 18 people were each sentenced

MEXICO

to 36 years' imprisonment for their involvement in the deaths as part of a paramilitary group with links to the PRI; they joined 70 others previously convicted.

In February 2001 subcomandante Marcos and other Zapatista leaders began a tour of Mexico, which culminated in Mexico City in early March, where a rally in the capital's main square, attended by an estimated 150,000 people, was held in support of congressional approval of the proposed indigenous rights legislation. Following a congressional vote, four EZLN leaders were permitted to address both legislative chambers, and, in March, the EZLN announced that formal dialogue with the Government would recommence. Subcomandante Marcos successfully negotiated the dismantling of the remaining three garrisons in Chiapas, and in April the Congreso approved amendments to six articles of the Constitution, which recognized and guaranteed indigenous political, legal, social and economic rights, and prohibited discrimination against Indians based on race and tribal affiliation. However, the legislation fell short of granting indigenous peoples the right to autonomy over land and natural resources; in response, the EZLN suspended all contact with the Government. In August 2003 the EZLN declared that 30 municipalities in Chiapas, hitherto under Zapatista control, were to be granted autonomy. 'Councils of Good Government' (Juntas de Buen Gobierno) would oversee the transition from military to civilian control in these areas. The transformation of the EZLN into a political force was underlined in August 2005, when subcomandante Marcos announced his plans to create a left-wing alliance of peasants' organizations. In early 2006 the Zapatistas began an alternative presidential election campaign, although it failed to gather significant support.

Foreign Affairs

Relations with the USA

Mexico's foreign policy has been determined largely by relations with the USA. The rapid expansion of petroleum production from the mid-1970s gave Mexico a new independence, empowering it to favour the left-wing regimes in Cuba and Nicaragua, opposed by the USA, during the 1980s. In February 1985 relations between Mexico and the USA deteriorated following the murder of an agent of the US Drug Enforcement Administration (DEA) by Mexican drugs-traffickers. The situation worsened in April 1990, when a Mexican physician was abducted, in Mexico, by agents employed by the DEA, and transported to the USA to be arrested on charges relating to the murder. Meanwhile, relations between Mexico and the USA remained tense, largely because of disagreement over the problem of illegal immigration from Mexico into the USA and Mexico's failure to take effective action against the illegal drugs trade. This situation improved following the deportation to the USA in 1996 of Juan García Abrego, the alleged head of the Golfo drugs cartel, and in the following year the USA 'certified' Mexico as a country co-operating in its campaign against drugs-trafficking. Bilateral relations were strained in May 1998, when a major US counter-narcotics operation was conducted in Mexico, without Mexican authorization. None the less, additional co-operation agreements were signed by the two countries in early 1999, and Mexico continued to be 'certified' by the USA. Although President Fox advocated abolition of the certification practice, it was reaffirmed in 2001.

NAFTA, comprising Mexico, the USA and Canada, took effect from 1 January 1994. Among the Agreement's provisions were the gradual reduction of tariffs on 50% of products over a period of 10–15 years (some 57% of tariffs on agricultural trade between the USA and Mexico were removed immediately), and the establishment, by Mexico and the USA, of a North American Development Bank (NADBank) charged with the funding of initiatives for the rehabilitation of the two countries' common border. From January 2003 tariffs on a number of agricultural products were reduced or removed entirely, provoking widespread discontent among Mexico's 25m.-strong rural community. In particular, they pointed to the greater subsidies received by US farmers and to a poor transport infrastructure, which resulted in higher costs. Following the collapse, in September 2003, of the fifth Ministerial Conference of the World Trade Organization (WTO) in Cancún, Mexico joined the group of developing countries led by Brazil that opposed US-European Union (EU, see p. 270) subsidies of agricultural products. At a summit meeting in March 2005 between President Fox, US President George W. Bush and Canadian Prime Minister Paul Martin, the three leaders announced an accord to increase regional co-operation on economic and security issues.

Introductory Survey

The Fox Government sought to persuade the US Administration of George W. Bush, which took office in 2001, to adopt a more liberal position on Mexican immigrants to the USA. However, progress on immigration policy was suspended following the terrorist attacks in the USA on 11 September 2001, and proposals to tighten security on the US–Mexican border were approved by the US Congress in 2002. In March of that year, nevertheless, following a summit meeting in Monterrey, the two Presidents announced a 'smart border' partnership agreement, intended to facilitate the legal entry of Mexican people and goods into the USA while, at the same time, securing the frontier against possible acts of terrorism. In September, however, Fox requested that the emphasis in US-Mexican relations be shifted back to bilateral issues, which had been neglected in favour of border security. In the same month Mexico unilaterally withdrew from the Inter-American Treaty of Reciprocal Assistance (the Rio Treaty), the defence pact linking Mexico to the USA, resulting in a downturn in relations with the USA.

In March 2003, with Mexican public opinion strongly against armed intervention to remove the regime of Saddam Hussain in Iraq, President Fox risked a deterioration of relations with both the USA and Spain by stating his opposition to war. His stance was all the more significant owing to Mexico's place as one of the 10 non-permanent members of the UN Security Council. In January 2004 the announcement of a revised US immigration initiative, which offered significantly less to Mexican immigrants in the USA than had been hoped, was met with disappointment by the Mexican Government, which had hoped to increase freedom of movement between the two countries. In the same month US officials began managing the security arrangements for US-bound flights leaving Mexico City's airport.

Throughout 2005 tensions remained high between Mexico and the USA over border security, specifically regarding illegal immigration from Mexico to the USA, and also escalating drugs-related violence in Mexico (see Human Rights and the Illegal Drugs Trade). However, in October a Mexican-US joint effort to reduce lawlessness in the border area was announced: a bilateral agreement was signed in March 2006. None the less, the Mexican Government expressed strong opposition to the USA's Secure Border Initiative (SBI), which was announced in late 2005 and envisaged the construction of security fences along some 1,130 km of the most accessible sections of the border in order to deter illegal immigrants. By September 2006, despite the objections of the Mexican authorities, the proposal, involving the construction of a triple barrier, monitored by look-out towers, sensors and cameras, had been approved by the US Congress. The Mexican Government appealed direct to President Bush to veto the bill, claiming that it would harm bilateral relations and be contrary to the spirit of co-operation necessary in guaranteeing the security of the common border. Various indigenous groups with territories that straddled the border also expressed concern at the proposal. Other commentators speculated on the possibility that, by forcing Mexicans to take more dangerous routes into US territory, there would be an increase in the death rate of migrants. By early 2010 some 1,035 km of the border fencing had been constructed. However, in January 2011 the US Secretary of Homeland Security, Janet Napolitano, announced the cancellation of SBInet, the part of the project involving the erection of sensors and cameras, which had encountered a series of technical difficulties and had been criticized by observers on both sides of the border for the way in which it had been implemented. Napolitano stated that henceforth existing surveillance technologies would be used to monitor the border. In August 2010 US President Barack Obama had enacted legislation providing for the deployment of an additional 1,500 agents to patrol the US–Mexican border, as well as unmanned surveillance drones.

US-Mexican relations had deteriorated somewhat following Calderón's accession to the presidency in 2007, as a result not only of the USA's continued uncompromising stance on border security but also of Mexico's improved relations with Cuba and Venezuela (see Other external relations). None the less, as a result of negotiations between Presidents Bush and Calderón in March in Mérida, Yucatán, in October Bush promised the Mexican Government some US $500m. per year in order to combat drugs-related crime. The Mérida Initiative, as it became known, was signed into law in July 2008. In March 2009, however, the US Senate voted to reduce the Mérida Initiative budget to $300m. None the less, the new US Administration of President Obama pledged to increase border security and assist Mexico in fighting the drugs cartels, including increasing the presence of its own border officials and contributing $700m. for helicopters and law enforcement equipment. The move reflected concerns that drugs-related violence was increasingly affecting US border towns. President Calderón addressed the US Congress during a state visit in May 2010, notably urging legislators to introduce measures to restrict the flow of weapons from the USA to drugs gangs in Mexico.

US-Mexican relations were further strained in September 2010, when US Secretary of State, Hillary Clinton, likened organized crime in Mexico to an insurgency, comparing the situation with that experienced in Colombia some 20 years earlier, when insurgents and drugs cartels controlled large parts of Colombian territory, and making reference to a number of car bombs that had recently been planted. The Mexican Government rejected the comparison with Colombia and the suggestion that it was combating an insurgency, insisting that the drugs-traffickers were not politically motivated. The killing, in February 2011, of a US immigration and customs enforcement agents in the state of San Luis Potosí, allegedly by members of the Zetas drugs gang, was strongly condemned by the US authorities, which subsequently announced that they would seek the extradition of suspects who had been detained in Mexico in connection with the murder. Tensions arose between Calderón and US officials that month, after the President claimed, in a newspaper interview, that there was lack of co-ordination between US security agencies and accused the US ambassador to Mexico, Carlos Pascual, of distorting the security situation in Mexico. Calderón's comments followed the publication of leaked diplomatic cables in which Pascual had questioned the abilities of Mexico's intelligence and security services. Pascual resigned as ambassador in March. Meanwhile, revelations that the US Bureau of Alcohol, Tobacco, Firearms and Explosives, an agency of the Department of Justice, had allowed thousands of weapons to be smuggled into Mexico from the USA, under an operation apparently intended to monitor the movement of arms from US smugglers to Mexican drugs-traffickers, provoked outrage in Mexico.

Other external relations

In April 2004 Mexico's relations with Cuba were strained after Mexico voted in favour of a UN motion to censure Cuba for human rights abuses. In May the Cuban leader, Fidel Castro Ruz, criticized Mexico's stance and accused the Fox Government of interference in the island's affairs. In response, President Fox expelled the Cuban ambassador from the country and recalled the Mexican ambassador in Cuba; the ambassadors returned to their posts in July. Under President Calderón Mexico effected a rapprochement towards Cuba, and in June 2007 Mexico voted in favour of a UN Human Rights Council resolution to end UN scrutiny of human rights in Cuba. In late 2005 Mexico and Venezuela recalled their respective ambassadors, after left-wing President Lt-Col (retd) Hugo Chávez Frías of Venezuela criticized President Fox for being subservient to the USA. Full diplomatic relations between the two countries were restored in August 2007.

In January 1991 a preliminary free trade agreement was signed with Honduras, Guatemala, El Salvador, Nicaragua and Costa Rica, in order to facilitate the negotiation of bilateral agreements between Mexico and each of the five countries, leading to free trade in an increasing range of products over a six-year period. During the 1990s Mexico concluded agreements for greater economic co-operation and increased bilateral trade with Colombia and Venezuela (as the Group of Three, see p. 447), and with Bolivia, Costa Rica and the EU. A free trade accord with Nicaragua came into force in 1998; a similar accord with Chile was signed in that year and came into force in 1999. A further trade agreement with Guatemala, Honduras and El Salvador (the Northern Triangle) was concluded in 2000. In March Mexico and the EU signed a free trade agreement, the first to be signed between the EU and a Latin American country. The accord provided for the gradual elimination of tariffs on industrial and agricultural products, the progressive liberalization of trade in services, and preferential access to public procurement; it also obliged the signatories to respect democratic principles and human rights. In October 2003 Mexico signed an Organization of American States agreement on regional security, which was also aimed at increasing co-operation on social and environmental issues. In April 2004 the Secretary of Foreign Affairs, Luis Ernesto Derbez, announced Mexico's aim of becoming a full member of the Southern Common Market (Mercado Común del Sur—Mercosur, see p. 425), and in late 2004 he declared Mexico's intention of seeking permanent representation on the UN Security Council.

CONSTITUTION AND GOVERNMENT

The present Mexican Constitution was proclaimed on 5 February 1917, at the end of the Revolution, which began in 1910, against the regime of Porfirio Díaz. Its provisions regarding religion, education, and the ownership and exploitation of mineral wealth reflect the long revolutionary struggle against the concentration of power in the hands of the Roman Catholic Church and the large landowners, and the struggle that culminated, in the 1930s, in the expropriation of the properties of the foreign petroleum companies. It has been amended from time to time.

Mexico is a federal republic comprising 31 states and a Distrito Federal (Federal District, comprising the capital). Under the 1917 Constitution, legislative power is vested in the bicameral Congreso de la Unión (Congress), elected by universal adult suffrage. The Senado (Senate) has 128 members (four from each state and the Distrito Federal), serving a six-year term. The Cámara Federal de Diputados (Federal Chamber of Deputies), directly elected for three years, has 500 seats, of which 300 are filled from single-member constituencies. The remaining 200 seats, allocated so as to achieve proportional representation, are filled from parties' lists of candidates. Executive power is held by the President, directly elected for six years at the same time as the Senado. He governs with the assistance of an appointed Cabinet. Each state has its own constitution and is administered by a Governor (elected for six years) and an elected Chamber of Deputies. The Distrito Federal is administered by a Head of Government.

REGIONAL AND INTERNATIONAL CO-OPERATION

Mexico is a signatory nation to the North American Free Trade Agreement (NAFTA, see p. 367). The country is a member of the Inter-American Development Bank (IDB, see p. 333), and of the Latin American Integration Association (ALADI, see p. 359).

Mexico became a member of the UN in 1945. As a contracting party to the General Agreement on Tariffs and Trade, Mexico joined the World Trade Organization (see p. 430) on its establishment in 1995. Mexico was admitted to the Asia-Pacific Economic Co-operation group (APEC, see p. 197) in 1993, and joined the Organisation for Economic Co-operation and Development (OECD, see p. 376) in 1994. The country is a member of the Group of 15 (G15, see p. 447) and of the Group of 20 (G20, see p. 451).

ECONOMIC AFFAIRS

In 2009, according to estimates by the World Bank, Mexico's gross national income (GNI), measured at average 2007–09 prices, was US $958,759m., equivalent to $8,920 per head (or $14,110 per head on an international purchasing-power parity basis). During 2000–09, it was estimated, while the population increased at an average annual rate of 1.0%, while gross domestic product (GDP) per head increased, in real terms, by an average of 0.3% per year. Overall GDP increased, in real terms, at an average annual rate of 1.3% in 2000–09; GDP increased by 1.5% in 2008, but declined by 6.0% in 2009.

Agriculture (including forestry and fishing) contributed 3.9% of GDP in 2009 and engaged 13.4% of the employed labour force in 2010. The staple food crops are maize, wheat, sorghum, barley, rice, beans and potatoes. The principal cash crops are coffee, cotton, sugar cane, and fruit and vegetables (particularly tomatoes). Livestock-raising and fisheries are also important. During 2000–09, according to World Bank estimates, agricultural GDP increased at an average annual rate of 2.1%; agricultural GDP increased by 1.1% in 2009. The reduction and eventual removal of import tariffs proposed under the North American Free Trade Agreement (NAFTA) was a significant blow to Mexico's agriculture sector, which had lower subsidies and higher overhead costs than in the USA.

Industry (including mining, manufacturing, construction and power) engaged 24.1% of the employed labour force in 2010 and provided 33.1% of GDP in 2009. According to the World Bank, during 2000–09 industrial GDP increased by an average of 0.2% per year; industrial GDP increased by 0.5% in 2008, but decreased by 8.0% in 2009.

Mining contributed 7.8% of GDP in 2009, and, together with electricity production and distribution, engaged 0.7% of the employed labour force in 2010. During 2000–07 the GDP of the mining sector increased by an average of 1.9% per year; mining GDP increased by 0.2% in 2007. Mexico has large reserves of petroleum and natural gas (mineral products accounted for an estimated 13.9% of total export earnings in 2009). Zinc, salt, silver, copper, celestite and fluorite are also major mineral exports. In addition, mercury, bismuth, antimony, cadmium, manganese and phosphates are mined, and there are significant reserves of uranium.

Manufacturing provided 17.1% of GDP in 2009 and engaged 15.6% of the employed labour force in 2010. According to the World Bank, manufacturing GDP decreased at an average annual rate of 0.2% in 2000–09; the sector's GDP increased by only 0.2% in 2008, and decreased by 11.0% in 2009. The *maquila* sector (where intermediate materials produced on US territory are processed or assembled on the Mexican side of the border) grew in importance from the 1990s. By December 2000 Mexico had 3,703 *maquila* export plants, providing an estimated 1.3m. jobs and making a significant contribution to the manufacturing sector; however, the sector suffered a downturn in the early 2000s, and the number of plants fell to an estimated 2,860 in 2005. *Maquila* exports were valued at an estimated 214,430.2m. new pesos in 2006, equivalent to 45% of total revenue from manufacturing exports. In 2005 an estimated 1.2m. people were employed in the *maquila* sector.

Construction engaged 7.8% of the employed labour force in 2010 and provided 7.1% of GDP in 2009.

Energy is derived principally from hydrocarbons, coal and hydroelectric power. In 2007, according to the World Bank, some 20.3% of total output of electricity production was derived from petroleum, 48.8% came from natural gas, 12.3% was generated from coal-powered plants and 10.6% came from hydroelectric plants. In 2004 the IMF recommended that Mexico further open its energy sector to private investment. In 2009, according to Petróleos Mexicanos, oil production was an estimated 2.6m. barrels per day, representing a 6.8% decline on average output compared with the previous year. However, production of natural gas was estimated to have increased by 12.4% in 2008, reaching 6,919m. cu ft per day. In 2009 mineral imports were estimated at 7.1% of total merchandise imports, while exports of petroleum accounted for an estimated 13.9% of the total export value in the same year. Plans to construct a US $10m. oil refinery were announced in 2009, a move expected to lessen Mexico's reliance on imports of refined petroleum products.

The services sector contributed 62.9% of GDP in 2009 and engaged 62.5% of the employed labour force in 2010. According to World Bank figures, the GDP of the sector increased by an average of 1.4% per year in 2000–09; the sector experienced growth of 1.9% in 2008, but it declined by 9.4% in 2009. Tourism is one of Mexico's principal sources of foreign exchange. In that year there were an estimated 21.5m. foreign visitors to Mexico (mostly from the USA and Canada). Revenue from the sector totalled US $10,817m. in 2008.

In 2009 Mexico recorded a visible trade deficit of an estimated US $4,602m., and there was a deficit of $5,734m. on the current account of the balance of payments. In 2010 the principal source of imports (48.1%) was the USA, which was also the principal market for exports (80.0%). The principal exports in 2009 were mechanical and electrical appliances, mineral products and transport equipment; the same categories also represented the principal imports.

In 2010 there was an estimated budgetary deficit of 358,044m. new pesos. In the previous year the deficit totalled 262,063m. new pesos, equivalent to 2.2% of GDP. Mexico's general government gross debt was 5,312,140m. new pesos in 2009, equivalent to 44.9% of GDP. Mexico's external debt totalled US $203,983.7m. at the end of 2008, of which $113,955m. was public and publicly guaranteed debt. In that year the cost of debt-servicing was equivalent to 12.1% of the value of exports of goods, services and income. The average annual rate of inflation was 4.7% in 2000–09. Consumer prices increased by an average of 5.3% in 2009. An estimated 5.6% of the total labour force were unemployed in 2010. In 2009 remittances from Mexicans living abroad totalled an estimated $21,200m., a 15.5% decline on 2008, mainly owing to the global economic downturn. It was estimated that remittances were Mexico's second largest source of foreign income, after petroleum exports.

A slowdown occurred in the Mexican economy in the early 2000s, caused by the sluggish performance of Mexico's largest trading partner, the USA, particularly in the *maquila* sector. A deceleration in US economic growth, which began in 2007, deteriorated in 2008, and, with the onset of the global banking crisis in September, the strength of Mexico's economic links with the USA were revealed. The recall of investment and the serious depreciation of the peso created problems in the financial and business sectors. The central bank attempted to counter depreciation through a large-scale purchase of Mexican pesos, a measure that drew on a significant portion of the country's international reserves. Elsewhere, inflows of remittances declined, owing to rising unemployment in the US construction sector, which had engaged a large section of the migrant labour force. The official rate of unemployment increased for the first time in four years in September 2008, reaching a peak of 6.0% a year later; it remained relatively high in February 2011, at 5.3%. Foreign demand declined rapidly in late 2008 and 2009, leading to further contraction in the manufacturing sector (particularly the *maquila* industries), which relied heavily on exports to the USA. In response to the economic conditions, President Calderón introduced a 60,000m.-peso stimulus package in January 2009, which included measures to create employment, freeze the price of oil and reduce the price of gas. Despite these measures, GDP contracted by 6.0% in GDP in 2009. An increase in GDP of an estimated 5.5% in 2010 largely reflected an improvement in global economic conditions, with exports and inflows of remittances rising strongly. However, although the economy expanded in all four quarters of the year, the rate of year-on-year growth slowed from 7.7% in the second quarter to 5.3% in the third and to 4.6% in the fourth. The budget for 2011 forecast a deceleration in GDP growth in that year, to 3.9%. Meanwhile, there was concern that the upsurge in drugs-related violence, predominantly in the northern states (see Contemporary Political History), would deter foreign investors.

PUBLIC HOLIDAYS

2012: 1 January (New Year's Day), 6 February (Constitution Day), 19 March (Birthday of Benito Juárez), 5 April (Maundy Thursday)*, 6 April (Good Friday)*, 1 May (Labour Day), 5 May (Anniversary of the Battle of Puebla)*, 16 September (Independence Day), 2 November (All Souls' Day)*, 19 November (Anniversary of the Revolution), 12 December (Day of Our Lady of Guadalupe)*, 25 December (Christmas).

* Widely celebrated unofficial holidays.

MEXICO

Statistical Survey

Sources (unless otherwise stated): Instituto Nacional de Estadística, Geografía e Informática (INEGI), Edif. Sede, Avda Patriotismo 711, Torre A, 10°, Col. San Juan Mixcoac, Del. Benito Juárez, 03730 México, DF; tel. (55) 5278-1000 (ext. 1282); fax (55) 5278-1000 (ext. 1523); e-mail comunicacionsocial@inegi.org.mx; internet www.inegi.org.mx; Banco de México, Avda 5 de Mayo 1, Col. Centro, Del. Cuauhtémoc, 06059 México, DF; tel. (55) 5237-2000; fax (55) 5237-2370; internet www.banxico.org.mx.

Area and Population

AREA, POPULATION AND DENSITY

Area (sq km)
- Continental 1,959,248
- Islands 5,127
- Total 1,964,375*

Population (census and by-census results)
- 29 October 2005 103,263,388
- 12 June 2010
  - Males 54,855,231
  - Females 57,481,307
  - Total 112,336,538
- Density (per sq km) at census of June 2010 . . . 57.2

*758,449 sq miles.

POPULATION BY AGE AND SEX
(census of June 2010)

	Males	Females	Total
0–14	16,498,731	16,017,065	32,515,796
15–64	34,453,410	37,031,013	71,484,423
65 and over	3,202,871	3,736,042	6,938,913
Total*	54,855,231	57,481,307	112,336,538

*Including 1,397,406 persons (males 700,219, females 697,187) of unspecified age.

ADMINISTRATIVE DIVISIONS
(at census of June 2010)

States	Area (sq km)*	Population	Density (per sq km)	Capital
Aguascalientes (Ags)	5,623	1,184,996	210.7	Aguascalientes
Baja California (BC)	71,540	3,155,070	44.1	Mexicali
Baja California Sur (BCS)	73,937	637,026	8.6	La Paz
Campeche (Camp.)	57,718	822,441	14.2	Campeche
Chiapas (Chis)	73,680	4,796,580	65.1	Tuxtla Gutiérrez
Chihuahua (Chih.)	247,490	3,406,465	13.8	Chihuahua
Coahuila (de Zaragoza) (Coah.)	151,447	2,748,391	18.1	Saltillo
Colima (Col.)	5,629	650,555	115.6	Colima
Distrito Federal (DF)	1,485	8,851,080	5,960.3	Mexico City
Durango (Dgo)	123,364	1,632,934	13.2	Victoria de Durango
Guanajuato (Gto)	30,617	5,486,372	179.2	Guanajuato
Guerrero (Gro)	63,618	3,388,768	53.3	Chilpancingo de los Bravos
Hidalgo (Hgo)	20,855	2,665,018	127.8	Pachuca de Soto
Jalisco (Jal.)	78,624	7,350,682	93.5	Guadalajara
México (Méx.)	22,332	15,175,862	679.6	Toluca de Lerdo
Michoacán (de Ocampo) (Mich.)	58,672	4,351,037	74.2	Morelia
Morelos (Mor.)	4,894	1,777,227	363.1	Cuernavaca
Nayarit (Nay.)	27,861	1,084,979	38.9	Tepic
Nuevo León (NL)	64,206	4,653,458	72.5	Monterrey
Oaxaca (Oax.)	93,348	3,801,962	40.7	Oaxaca de Juárez
Puebla (Pue.)	34,246	5,779,829	168.8	Heroica Puebla de Zaragoza
Querétaro (de Arteaga) (Qro)	11,659	1,827,937	156.8	Querétaro
Quintana Roo (Q.Roo)	42,544	1,325,578	31.2	Ciudad Chetumal
San Luis Potosí (SLP)	61,165	2,585,518	42.3	San Luis Potosí
Sinaloa (Sin.)	57,334	2,767,761	48.3	Culiacán Rosales
Sonora (Son.)	179,527	2,662,480	14.8	Hermosillo
Tabasco (Tab.)	24,747	2,238,603	90.5	Villahermosa
Tamaulipas (Tamps)	80,155	3,268,554	40.8	Ciudad Victoria
Tlaxcala (Tlax.)	3,988	1,169,936	293.4	Tlaxcala de Xicohténcatl
Veracruz-Llave (Ver.)	71,856	7,643,194	106.4	Jalapa Enríquez
Yucatán (Yuc.)	39,675	1,955,577	49.3	Mérida
Zacatecas (Zac.)	75,412	1,490,668	19.8	Zacatecas
Total	1,959,248	112,336,538	57.3	—

*Excluding islands.

PRINCIPAL TOWNS
(population at census of June 2010)

Ciudad de México (Mexico City, capital)	8,851,080	Tlalnepantla de Baz (Tlalnepantla)	664,225
Ecatepec de Morelos (Ecatepec)	1,656,107	Benito Juárez (Cancún)	661,176
Tijuana	1,559,683	Torreón	639,629
Heroica Puebla de Zaragoza (Puebla)	1,539,819	Santa María Chimalhuacán (Chimalhuacán)	614,453
Guadalajara	1,495,189	Reynosa	608,891
León	1,436,480	Tlaquepaque	608,114
Ciudad Juárez	1,332,131	Victoria de Durango (Durango)	582,267
Zapopan	1,243,756	Tuxtla Gutiérrez	553,374
Monterrey	1,135,550	Veracruz Llave (Veracruz)	552,156
Nezahualcóyotl	1,110,565	Irapuato	529,440
Mexicali	936,826	Tultitlán	524,074
Culiacán Rosales (Culiacán)	858,638	Cuautitlán Izcalli	511,675
Naucalpan de Juárez (Naucalpan)	833,779	Atizapán de Zaragoza	489,937
Mérida	830,732	Matamoros	489,193
Toluca de Lerdo (Toluca)	819,561	Tonalá	478,689
Chihuahua	819,543	Iztapaluca	467,361
Querétaro	801,940	Ensenada	466,814
Aguascalientes	797,010	Jalapa Enríquez (Xalapa)	457,928
Acapulco de Juárez (Acapulco)	789,971	San Nicolás de los Garzas	443,273
Hermosillo	784,342	Mazatlán	438,434
San Luis Potosí	772,604	Nuevo Laredo	384,033
Morelia	729,279	Cuernavaca	365,168
Saltillo	725,123	Valle de Chalco (Xico)	357,645
Guadalupe	678,006		

3088

MEXICO

BIRTHS, MARRIAGES AND DEATHS

	Registered live births Number	Rate (per 1,000)	Registered marriages Number	Rate (per 1,000)	Registered deaths Number	Rate (per 1,000)
2001	2,767,610	22.9	665,434	6.7	443,127	4.8
2002	2,699,084	21.7	616,654	6.1	459,687	4.8
2003	2,655,894	20.6	584,142	5.7	472,140	4.8
2004	2,625,056	19.8	600,563	5.8	473,417	4.8
2005	2,567,906	19.3	595,713	5.7	495,240	4.8
2006	2,505,939	19.0	586,978	5.6	494,471	4.8
2007	2,655,083	18.6	595,209	5.6	514,420	4.9
2008	2,636,110	18.3	589,352	5.5	539,530	5.1

2009 (official projections): Crude birth rate 18.0 per 1,000; crude death rate per 4.9 1,000.

2010 (official projections): Crude birth rate 17.8 per 1,000; crude death rate 5.0 per 1,000.

Life expectancy (years at birth, UN estimates): 76 (males 73; females 78) in 2008 (Source: WHO, *World Health Statistics*).

ECONOMICALLY ACTIVE POPULATION
(sample surveys, '000 persons aged 14 years and over, July–September)

	2008	2009	2010
Agriculture, hunting, forestry and fishing	5,909.1	5,989.6	5,903.3
Mining, quarrying and electricity	383.9	418.5	319.7
Manufacturing	6,891.4	6,531.7	6,914.3
Construction	3,628.1	3,412.1	3,430.1
Trade	8,639.1	8,713.6	8,908.3
Hotels and restaurants	2,795.7	2,822.1	2,944.3
Transport and communications	2,204.5	2,258.7	2,183.6
Finance and business services	2,767.4	2,869.4	2,908.7
Social services	3,474.7	3,696.9	3,746.4
Other services	4,424.7	4,673.0	4,651.5
Public sector	2,179.1	2,248.5	2,272.4
Sub-total	43,297.8	43,634.1	44,182.6
Activities not adequately defined	327.9	283.1	298.0
Total employed	43,625.7	43,917.3	44,480.6
Unemployed	1,909.7	2,925.0	2,651.0
Total labour force	45,535.4	46,842.3	47,131.6
Males	28,532.9	28,907.9	29,308.6
Females	17,002.5	17,934.4	17,823.0

Health and Welfare

KEY INDICATORS

Total fertility rate (children per woman, 2008)	2.2
Under-5 mortality rate (per 1,000 live births, 2008)	17
HIV/AIDS (% of persons aged 15–49, 2007)	0.3
Physicians (per 1,000 head, 2002)	1.5
Hospital beds (per 1,000 head, 2004)	1.0
Health expenditure (2007): US $ per head (PPP)	819
Health expenditure (2007): % of GDP	5.9
Health expenditure (2007): public (% of total)	45.4
Access to water (% of persons, 2008)	94
Access to sanitation (% of persons, 2008)	85
Total carbon dioxide emissions ('000 metric tons, 2007)	471,073.2
Carbon dioxide emissions per head (metric tons, 2007)	4.5
Human Development Index (2010): ranking	56
Human Development Index (2010): value	0.750

For sources and definitions, see explanatory note on p. vi.

Agriculture

PRINCIPAL CROPS
('000 metric tons)

	2006	2007	2008
Wheat	3,378	3,515	4,019
Rice, paddy	337	295	224
Barley	869	653	811
Maize	21,893	23,513	24,320
Oats	152	125	148
Sorghum	5,519	6,203	6,611
Potatoes	1,523	1,751	1,670
Sugar cane	50,676	52,089	51,107
Beans, dry	1,386	994	1,123
Chick peas	163	148	165
Soybeans (Soya beans)	81	88	153
Groundnuts, with shell	68	83	81
Coconuts*	1,132	1,167	1,246
Safflower seed	74	113	96
Cabbages	211	219	215
Lettuce and chicory	274	286	285
Tomatoes	2,899	3,150	2,937
Cauliflower and broccoli	305	326	371
Pumpkins, squash and gourds	547	517	486
Cucumbers and gherkins	496	490	475
Chillies and peppers, green*	1,681	1,890	2,055
Onions, dry	1,238	1,387	1,252
Carrots and turnips	382	404	386
Bananas	2,196	1,965	2,159
Oranges	4,157	4,249	4,307
Tangerines, mandarins, clementines and satsumas	350	469	469*
Lemons and limes	1,867	1,936	2,224
Grapefruit and pomelos	387	313	395
Apples	602	505	525
Peaches and nectarines	222	192	202
Strawberries	192	176	207
Grapes	244	356	307
Watermelons	977	1,059	1,200
Cantaloupes and other melons	570	543	582
Guavas, mangoes and mangosteens	2,046	1,911	1,855
Avocados	1,134	1,143	1,125
Pineapples	634	671	686
Papayas	799	919	638
Coffee, green	280	269	266
Cocoa beans	38	30	28
Tobacco, unmanufactured	19	13	11

* FAO estimate(s).

2009: Wheat 4,148; Rice, paddy 262; Barley 746 (unofficial figure); Maize 20,203; Oats 135; Sorghum 6,175; Beans, dry 1,051; Soybeans (Soya beans) 121.

Aggregate production ('000 metric tons, may include official, semi-official or estimated data): Total cereals 32,154.7 in 2006, 34,311.1 in 2007, 36,141.2 in 2008, 31,676.0 in 2009; Total fruits (excl. melons) 15,776.5 in 2006, 15,825.5 in 2007, 16,122.2 in 2008, 16,122.2 in 2009; Total vegetables (incl. melons) 11,451.8 in 2006, 12,121.1 in 2007, 12,100.9 in 2008, 12,100.9 in 2009.

Source: FAO.

LIVESTOCK
('000 head, year ending September)

	2006	2007	2008
Horses*	6,300	6,350	6,350
Asses*	3,260	3,260	3,260
Mules*	3,280	3,280	3,280
Cattle	31,163	31,950*	32,565*
Pigs	15,257	15,500*	16,100*
Sheep	7,287	7,500*	7,825*
Goats	8,890	8,900*	8,831*
Chickens	481,421	487,250	496,674
Ducks*	8,150	8,200	8,200
Turkeys	4,587	4,300	4,500

* FAO estimate(s).

2009 (FAO estimates): Chickens 506,000; Pigs 16,100.

Source: FAO.

MEXICO

LIVESTOCK PRODUCTS
('000 metric tons)

	2006	2007	2008
Cattle meat	1,613	1,635	1,667
Sheep meat	48	49	51
Goat meat	43	43	43
Pig meat	1,109	1,152	1,161
Horse meat*	79	79	79
Chicken meat	2,464	2,542	2,581
Cows' milk	10,089	10,346	10,766
Goats' milk	164	167	165
Hen eggs	2,290	2,291	2,337
Honey	56	55	55

* FAO estimates.

2009 (FAO estimates): Pig meat 1,163; Chicken meat 2,600.

Source: FAO.

Forestry

ROUNDWOOD REMOVALS
('000 cubic metres, excl. bark)

	2007	2008	2009
Sawlogs, veneer logs and logs for sleepers	5,210	5,308	5,308
Pulpwood	882	932	932
Other industrial wood	214	185	185
Fuel wood*	38,600	38,676	38,752
Total	44,906	45,101	45,177

* FAO estimates.

Source: FAO.

SAWNWOOD PRODUCTION
('000 cubic metres, incl. railway sleepers)

	2006	2007	2008
Coniferous (softwood)	2,324	2,366	2,409
Broadleaved (hardwood)	326	321	405
Total	2,650	2,687	2,814

2009: Production assumed to be unchanged from 2008 (FAO estimates).
Source: FAO.

Fishing
('000 metric tons, live weight)

	2006	2007	2008
Capture	1,357.4	1,483.7*	1,588.9*
Tilapias	66.3	78.2	69.0
California pilchard (sardine)	268.9	324.7*	386.0*
Yellowfin tuna	77.8	65.6	83.3
American cupped oyster	42.9	43.8	33.3
Jumbo flying squid	65.6	57.6	84.4
Aquaculture	154.5	128.4*	151.1*
Whiteleg shrimp	112.5	111.8	130.2
Total catch	1,511.8	1,612.1*	1,739.9*

* FAO estimate.

Note: Figures exclude aquatic plants ('000 metric tons, capture only): 4.5 in 2006; 5.1 in 2007; 4.9 in 2008. Also excluded are aquatic mammals and crocodiles (recorded by number rather than by weight), shells and corals. The number of gray whales caught was 1 in 2006. The number of bottlenose dolphins caught was 1 in 2007; 9 in 2008. The number of Morelet's crocodiles caught was: 158 in 2006; 11 in 2007; n.a. in 2008. The catch of marine shells and corals (metric tons) was: 578 in 2006; 581 in 2007 (FAO estimate); 581 in 2008 (FAO estimate).

Source: FAO.

Mining
(metric tons, unless otherwise indicated)

	2006	2007	2008
Antimony*	778	414	380
Arsenic*	1,595	513	—
Barytes	199,605	185,921	140,066
Bismuth*	1,186	1,170	1,132
Cadmium*	1,399	1,605	1,550
Celestite	128,321	96,902	29,621
Coal	10,882,685	11,886,757	10,402,658
Coke	1,569,561	1,536,325	1,547,391
Copper*	327,536	335,502	268,620
Crude petroleum ('000 barrels per day)†	3,256	3,076	2,792
Diatomite	62,948	82,519	128,536
Dolomite	1,282,590	1,123,225	1,233,993
Feldspar	459,209	438,696	445,519
Flourite	936,433	933,361	1,057,649
Gas (million cu ft per day)*	5,356	6,058	6,919
Gold (kg)*	35,899	39,355	50,365
Graphite	11,773	9,900	7,229
Gypsum	5,950,794	5,963,715	5,135,151
Iron*	6,589,586	7,323,121	7,725,959
Kaolin	18,852	86,784	85,092
Lead*	120,450	89,838	100,725
Manganese*	124,417	152,446	169,908
Molybdenum*	2,519	6,491	7,812
Salt	7,987,318	8,032,273	8,808,714
Silica	2,661,770	2,950,438	2,779,075
Silver*	2,413,147	2,351,570	2,668,028
Sulphur	1,076,391	1,029,736	1,040,546
Wollastonite	44,280	50,809	46,844
Zinc*	432,347	426,509	397,306

2009: Crude petroleum ('000 barrels per day) 2,601.
* Figures for metallic minerals refer to metal content of ores.
† Source: Petróleos Mexicanos, México, DF.

Industry

SELECTED PRODUCTS
('000 metric tons, unless otherwise indicated)

	2005	2006	2007
Wheat flour	2,646	2,689	2,679
Maize (corn) flour	1,617	1,656	1,685
Raw sugar	3,257	3,016	3,200
Beer ('000 hectolitres)	72,030	78,040	80,510
Soft drinks ('000 hectolitres)	141,451	144,608	151,581
Cigarettes (million units)	41,439	44,295	39,763
Cotton yarn (pure and mixed)	44	44	45
Tyres ('000 units)*	11,650	10,825	10,233
Cement	37,452	40,362	41,213
Non-electric, cooking or heating appliances—household ('000 units)	3,962	4,093	4,278
Refrigerators—household ('000 units)	2,844	3,043	2,650
Washing machines—household ('000 units)	988	1,042	962
Lorries, buses, tractors, etc. ('000 units)	501	561	556
Passenger cars ('000 units)	1,128	1,430	1,501
Electric energy (million kWh)	234,895	249,648	257,455

* Tyres for road motor vehicles.

Source: UN Industrial Commodity Statistics Database.

2008 (million kWh, preliminary): Electric energy 192,407.

Finance

CURRENCY AND EXCHANGE RATES

Monetary Units
100 centavos = 1 Mexican nuevo peso.

Sterling, Dollar and Euro Equivalents (31 December 2010)
£1 sterling = 19.345 nuevos pesos;
US $1 = 12.357 nuevos pesos;
€1 = 16.512 nuevos pesos;
1,000 Mexican nuevos pesos = £51.69 = $80.93 = €60.56.

Average Exchange Rate (nuevos pesos per US $)
2008   11.130
2009   13.514
2010   12.636

Note: Figures are given in terms of the nuevo (new) peso, introduced on 1 January 1993 and equivalent to 1,000 former pesos.

BUDGET*
(million new pesos)

Revenue	2008	2009	2010
Taxation	994,552.3	1,129,552.6	1,260,458.7
Income taxes	562,222.3	534,198.6	626,546.1
Value-added tax	457,248.3	407,795.1	504,433.6
Excise tax	−168,325.2	50,567.4	4,452.7
Import duties	35,783.1	30,196.4	24,515.1
Other revenue	1,055,384.0	870,895.5	819,605.6
Total revenue	2,049,936.3	2,000,448.1	2,080,064.3

Expenditure	2008	2009	2010
Programmable expenditure	1,607,040.7	1,639,602.7	1,762,925.3
Current expenditure	284,843.0	345,275.5	365,441.2
Wages and salaries	181,455.6	205,441.7	217,425.7
Acquisitions	17,181.7	17,945.4	18,840.0
Other current expenditure	86,205.6	121,888.4	129,175.5
Capital expenditure	170,490.1	101,524.5	113,050.1
Transfers	1,151,707.6	1,192,802.7	1,284,434.0
Non-programmable expenditure	638,661.1	622,908.7	675,182.9
Interest and fees	200,121.7	231,265.4	216,270.7
Revenue sharing	423,454.9	375,717.3	437,334.5
Total expenditure	2,245,701.8	2,262,511.4	2,438,108.2

* Figures refer to the consolidated accounts of the central Government, including government agencies and the national social security system. The budgets of state and local governments are excluded.

INTERNATIONAL RESERVES
(excl. gold, US $ million at 31 December)

	2007	2008	2009
IMF special drawing rights	466	519	4,525
Reserve position in the Fund	334	613	961
Foreign exchange	86,309	93,994	94,103
Total	87,109	95,126	99,589

Source: IMF, *International Financial Statistics*.

MONEY SUPPLY
(million new pesos at 31 December)

	2007	2008	2009
Currency outside depository corporations	429,854	494,345	536,824
Transferable deposits	695,346	755,947	1,079,230
Other deposits	1,830,063	1,996,329	1,999,716
Securities other than shares	33,971	8,624	14,513
Broad money	2,989,234	3,255,245	3,630,283

Source: IMF, *International Financial Statistics*.

COST OF LIVING
(Consumer Price Index; base: 2000 = 100)

	2006	2007	2008
Food, beverages and tobacco	134.1	142.6	154.1
Clothing and footwear	113.5	115.0	117.0
Electricity, gas and other fuel	173.1	178.2	190.7
Rent	133.2	137.2	141.4
All items (incl. others)	131.8	137.0	144.0

2009: Food, beverages and tobacco 167.5; All items (incl. others) 151.6.
Source: ILO.

NATIONAL ACCOUNTS
('000 million new pesos at current prices)
Expenditure on the Gross Domestic Product

	2007	2008	2009
Government final consumption expenditure	1,182.26	1,307.01	1,423.30
Private final consumption expenditure	7,315.47	7,856.38	7,825.59
Increase in stocks	579.05	584.59	246.29
Gross fixed capital formation	2,392.89	2,696.32	2,562.89
Total domestic expenditure	11,469.67	12,444.30	12,058.07
Exports of goods and services	3,161.64	3,416.59	3,295.58
Less Imports of goods and services	3,340.55	3,688.58	3,465.61
GDP in purchasers' values	11,290.75	12,172.31	11,888.05
GDP at constant 2003 prices	8,818.62	8,953.33	8,415.52

Source: IMF, *International Financial Statistics*.

Gross Domestic Product by Economic Activity
(million new pesos at current prices, preliminary)
Source: IMF, *International Financial Statistics*.

	2007	2008	2009
Agriculture, forestry and fishing	396,414.4	432,861.3	457,013.0
Mining and quarrying	978,958.1	1,197,580.5	905,336.1
Manufacturing	2,004,409.8	2,110,408.4	1,992,708.5
Construction	771,252.8	867,150.8	822,686.1
Electricity, gas and water	164,499.8	183,979.9	137,569.7
Trade	1,689,131.9	1,869,119.2	1,743,273.0
Restaurants and hotels	264,714.5	274,045.9	263,474.7
Transport, storage and communications	1,093,528.3	1,146,151.2	1,155,202.7
Finance, insurance, real estate and business services	2,177,656.0	2,353,080.7	2,380,390.8
Public administration	416,499.1	459,814.5	504,471.8
Community, social and personal services	349,885.6	377,467.5	395,443.9
Education	514,912.0	559,565.6	593,156.3
Other activities	266,279.3	278,990.9	289,207.3
Sub-total	11,088,141.6	12,110,216.4	11,639,933.9
Less Financial intermediation services indirectly measured	203,673.4	219,081.6	215,089.9
GDP at factor cost	10,884,468.2	11,891,134.8	11,424,844.0
Indirect taxes, *less* subsidies	436,368.1	308,997.5	504,673.4
GDP in purchasers' values	11,320,836.4	12,200,132.0	11,929,517.3

BALANCE OF PAYMENTS
(US $ million)

	2007	2008	2009
Exports of goods f.o.b.	271,875	291,343	229,783
Imports of goods f.o.b.	−281,949	−308,603	−234,385
Trade balance	−10,074	−17,261	−4,602
Exports of services	17,609	18,480	15,423
Imports of services	−24,064	−25,235	−23,212
Balance on goods and services	−16,529	−24,016	−12,390
Other income received	7,621	7,114	4,683
Other income paid	−26,180	−24,781	−19,481
Balance on goods, services and income	−35,088	−41,684	−27,188

MEXICO

—continued

	2007	2008	2009
Current transfers received	26,508	25,575	21,515
Current transfers paid	−108	−128	−60
Current balance	−8,687	−16,237	−5,734
Direct investment abroad	−8,256	−1,157	−7,598
Direct investment from abroad	28,707	24,297	13,978
Portfolio investment assets	−4,730	−5,255	−6,176
Portfolio investment liabilities	13,347	4,841	15,253
Other investment assets	−17,046	−2,668	−4,789
Other investment liabilities	9,062	5,616	10,417
Net errors and omissions	−2,146	−1,707	−9,662
Overall balance	10,250	7,731	5,690

Source: IMF, *International Financial Statistics*.

External Trade

PRINCIPAL COMMODITIES
(distribution by HS, US $ million)

Imports f.o.b.	2007	2008	2009
Live animals and products thereof	5,159.1	5,486.7	4,342.5
Vegetable products	7,580.6	10,078.9	7,449.1
Animal and vegetable oils and fats	1,064.5	1,518.3	1,073.6
Prepared food, beverages, spirits and tobacco	5,147.7	5,600.5	5,105.5
Mineral products	20,990.9	31,070.1	16,558.5
Chemicals and related industries	20,873.4	23,903.6	19,786.6
Plastics, rubber and articles thereof	20,136.2	20,238.8	15,817.4
Raw hides, skins, leather and furs	1,308.9	1,268.4	856.2
Wood, charcoal, cork, straw, etc.	1,517.2	1,509.0	1,022.6
Paper-making material; paper and paperboard and articles thereof	6,485.7	6,700.8	5,474.4
Textiles and textile articles	8,678.0	8,512.9	6,718.6
Footwear, headgear, umbrellas, etc.	643.3	729.4	601.8
Articles of stone, plaster, cement, asbestos, etc.; glass and glassware	2,425.7	2,153.5	1,596.6
Pearls, precious stones and metals and articles thereof; imitation jewellery and coins	1,226.6	1,127.6	881.7
Base metals and articles thereof	24,714.0	26,888.2	18,235.9
Machinery and mechanical appliances; electrical equipment, parts and accessories	102,372.2	110,245.2	91,881.9
Vehicles, aircraft, vessels and associated transport equipment	28,569.8	27,842.8	19,078.4
Optical, photographic, measuring, precision and medical apparatus; clocks and watches; musical instruments	13,060.1	12,785.7	8,827.9
Arms and ammunitions, parts and accessories	47.0	52.7	60.9
Miscellaneous manufactured articles	6,022.5	6,215.7	4,540.7
Works of art, collectors' pieces, antiques	19.7	13.8	12.3
Total (incl. others)	281,949.0	308,603.3	234,385.0

Exports f.o.b.	2007	2008	2009
Live animals and products thereof	1,751.7	1,701.4	1,726.3
Vegetable products	6,557.1	7,296.2	7,033.6
Animal and vegetable oils and fats	115.8	184.8	127.2
Prepared food, beverages, spirits and tobacco	6,303.1	7,100.9	7,137.0
Mineral products	44,419.1	52,211.4	32,021.1
Chemicals and related industries	7,819.8	8,752.2	7,805.9
Plastics, rubber and articles thereof	6,716.0	6,839.2	5,780.0
Raw hides, skins, leather and furs	565.9	514.5	414.9
Wood, charcoal, cork, straw, etc.	434.6	394.5	303.5
Paper-making material; paper and paperboard and articles thereof	1,920.8	1,944.8	1,665.7
Textiles and textile articles	7,318.2	6,862.5	5,664.6
Footwear, headgear, umbrellas, etc.	394.6	386.4	367.9

Exports f.o.b.—continued	2007	2008	2009
Articles of stone, plaster, cement, asbestos, etc.; glass and glassware	2,848.9	2,895.9	2,342.8
Pearls, precious stones and metals and articles thereof; imitation jewellery and coins	3,824.9	5,262.7	6,198.1
Base metals and articles thereof	15,073.5	16,162.8	10,640.5
Machinery and mechanical appliances; electrical equipment, parts and accessories	104,177.6	108,888.7	89,361.7
Vehicles, aircraft, vessels and associated transport equipment	43,933.2	45,022.8	34,835.5
Optical, photographic, measuring, precision and medical apparatus; clocks and watches; musical instruments	8,936.5	9,513.4	8,694.6
Arms and ammunitions, parts and accessories	17.6	20.8	22.4
Miscellaneous manufactured articles	8,060.7	8,078.3	6,344.7
Works of art, collectors' pieces, antiques	8.2	8.1	7.5
Total (incl. others)	271,875.3	291,342.6	229,783.0

Note: The *maquila* sector is responsible for a large percentage of both merchandise imports and exports, but official figures on the value of the sector were last published in 2006, when imports were valued at US $86,527.3m. (equivalent to some 34% of total imports) and exports were valued at $111,823.8m. (almost 45% of total exports).

PRINCIPAL TRADING PARTNERS*
(US $ million)

Imports c.i.f.	2008	2009	2010
Argentina	1,436.4	1,144.6	1,092.8
Brazil	5,182.7	3,495.3	4,327.5
Canada	9,442.5	7,303.7	8,607.5
Chile	2,592.3	1,650.6	1,952.3
China, People's Republic	34,690.3	32,529.0	45,607.6
France	3,511.0	2,502.5	3,024.4
Germany	12,605.7	9,727.3	11,076.8
Italy	5,219.3	3,146.7	3,996.9
Japan	16,282.5	11,397.1	15,014.7
Korea, Republic	13,548.1	10,958.7	12,776.6
Malaysia	4,659.2	4,035.5	5,276.2
Netherlands	4,183.6	2,170.9	2,810.8
Philippines	1,238.4	1,069.7	1,545.5
Singapore	1,697.7	1,377.8	1,456.5
Spain	4,055.8	3,004.0	3,232.3
Switzerland	1,412.9	1,208.0	n.a.
Taiwan	6,658.5	4,592.1	5,620.7
Thailand	2,207.9	1,983.2	2,697.9
United Kingdom	2,595.5	1,837.8	2,005.0
USA	151,334.6	112,433.8	145,007.4
Total (incl. others)	308,644.7	234,385.0	301,481.8

Exports f.o.b.	2008	2009	2010
Aruba	1,494.6	104.0	n.a.
Canada	7,102.4	8,244.3	10,683.7
China, People's Republic	2,044.8	2,207.8	4,195.9
Colombia	3,032.4	2,490.5	3,757.0
Germany	5,008.2	3,210.2	3,571.9
Japan	2,064.0	1,600.6	1,923.2
Spain	4,232.9	2,507.8	3,830.9
United Kingdom	1,749.3	1,243.1	1,733.7
USA	233,522.7	185,180.6	238,559.2
Venezuela	2,310.3	1,417.7	1,563.9
Total (incl. others)	291,342.6	229,783.0	298,361.2

* Imports by country of origin; exports by country of destination.

Transport

RAILWAYS
(traffic)

	2007	2008	2009*
Passengers carried ('000)†	288	8,915	28,001
Passenger-kilometres (million)	84	178	n.a.
Freight carried ('000 tons)	99,845	99,692	90,321
Freight ton-kilometres (million)	77,169	74,582	69,185

*Preliminary.
† From 2008 data include passengers carried on Linea 1 of the Ferrocarril Subourbano de la Zona Metropolitana del Valle de México.
Source: Dirección General de Planeación, Secretaría de Comunicaciones y Transportes.

ROAD TRAFFIC
('000 vehicles in use at 31 December, estimates)

	2006	2007	2008
Passenger cars	15,313	17,533	19,248
Lorries and vans	7,563	7,870	8,453
Buses and coaches	284	283	334
Motorcycles and mopeds	706	869	1,079

Source: IRF, *World Road Statistics*.

SHIPPING

Merchant Fleet
(registered at 31 December)

	2007	2008	2009
Number of vessels	780	799	834
Total displacement ('000 grt)	1,217.0	1,278.9	1,383.5

Source: IHS Fairplay, *World Fleet Statistics*.

Sea-borne Shipping
(domestic and international freight traffic, '000 metric tons)

	2006	2007	2008
Goods loaded	181,234	169,870	163,643
Goods unloaded	106,197	103,065	101,594

Source: Coordinación General de Puertos y Marina Mercante.

CIVIL AVIATION
(traffic on scheduled services)

	2006	2007	2008
Passengers carried ('000)	45,406	52,217	53,293
Freight carried ('000 tons)	544	572	525

Source: Dirección General de Planeación, Secretaría de Comunicaciones y Transportes.

Tourism

VISITOR ARRIVALS BY COUNTRY OF ORIGIN
(including cross-border visitors)

	2006	2007	2008
Argentina	84,583	112,165	126,685
Brazil	31,890	57,834	76,739
Canada	785,457	952,810	1,144,650
Chile	41,230	54,259	60,024
Colombia	35,955	59,066	67,644
France	173,184	191,855	208,635
Germany	135,251	151,969	158,276
Guatemala	31,444	37,012	52,051
Italy	163,289	166,729	168,078
Japan	68,981	71,857	69,946
Korea, Republic	30,742	37,631	35,851
Netherlands	70,202	73,034	76,252
Spain	261,458	280,089	285,454
United Kingdom	260,146	286,411	312,829
USA	17,512,050	17,248,429	18,034,158
Venezuela	38,015	62,532	82,721
Total (incl. others)	21,352,605	21,369,721	22,637,405

2009: Total arrivals 21.5m.

Tourism receipts (excluding excursionists, US $ million): 9,559 in 2006; 10,340 in 2007; 10,817 in 2008.

Source: mainly World Tourism Organization.

Communications Media

	2007	2008	2009
Telephones ('000 main lines in use)	19,997.9	20,491.4	19,333.1
Mobile cellular telephones ('000 subscribers)	66,559.5	75,303.5	83,527.9
Internet users ('000)	23,862.1	25,619.1	31,019.6
Broadband subscribers ('000)	4,473.7	7,489.5	9,651.7*

*Preliminary figure.

Personal computers: 15,000,000 (143.9 per 1,000 persons) in 2006.

Radio receivers ('000 in use): 31,000 in 1997.

Television receivers ('000 in use): 28,000 in 2000.

Daily newspapers (2002): Number 300; Average circulation 9,251,000 in 2000.

Non-daily newspapers (2002): Number 11; Average circulation 614,000 in 2000.

Books published (titles): 15,542 in 2002.

Sources: partly International Telecommunication Union; UNESCO Institute for Statistics; UNESCO, *Statistical Yearbook*; UN, *Statistical Yearbook*.

Education

(2008/09, preliminary)

	Institutions	Teachers	Students ('000)
Pre-primary	89,395	218,206	4,634.4
Primary	98,575	568,751	14,815.7
Secondary (incl. technical)	34,380	369,548	6,153.5
Intermediate: professional/technical	1,426	28,962	367.0
Intermediate: Baccalaureate	12,677	243,855	3,556.9
Higher (incl. post-graduate)	5,560	291,268	2,705.2

Pupil-teacher ratio (primary education, UNESCO estimate): 28.0 in 2007/08 (Source: UNESCO Institute for Statistics).

Adult literacy rate (UNESCO estimates): 92.9% (males 94.6%; females 91.5%) in 2008 (Source: UNESCO Institute for Statistics).

MEXICO

Directory

The Government

HEAD OF STATE

President: Felipe Calderón Hinojosa (took office 1 December 2006).

CABINET
(May 2011)

The Government is formed by the Partido de Acción Nacional.

Secretary of the Interior: José Francisco Blake Mora.
Secretary of Foreign Affairs: Patricia Espinosa Cantellano.
Secretary of Finance and Public Credit: Ernesto Cordero Arroyo.
Secretary of National Defence: Gen. Guillermo Galván Galván.
Secretary of the Navy: Adm. Mariano Francisco Saynez Mendoza.
Secretary of the Economy: Bruno Ferrari García de Alba.
Secretary of Social Development: Heriberto Félix Guerra.
Secretary of Public Security: Genaro García Luna.
Secretary of Public Function: Salvador Vega Casillas.
Secretary of Communications and Transport: Dionisio Pérez-Jácome Friscione.
Secretary of Labour and Social Welfare: Javier Lozano Alarcón.
Secretary of the Environment and Natural Resources: Juan Rafael Elvira Quesada.
Secretary of Energy: José Antonio Meade Kuribreña.
Secretary of Agriculture, Livestock, Rural Development, Fisheries and Food: Francisco Javier Mayorga Castañeda.
Secretary of Public Education: Alonso Lujambio Irazábal.
Secretary of Health: José Angel Córdova Villalobos.
Secretary of Tourism: Gloria Guevara Manzo.
Secretary of Agrarian Reform: Abelardo Escobar Prieto.
Procurator-General: Marisela Morales Ibáñez.

SECRETARIATS OF STATE

Office of the President: Los Pinos, Col. San Miguel Chapultepec, 11850 México, DF; tel. (55) 5093-5300; fax (55) 5277-2376; e-mail felipe.calderon@presidencia.gob.mx; internet www.presidencia.gob.mx.

Secretariat of State for Agrarian Reform: Avda Heroica Escuela Naval Militar 669, Col. Presidentes Ejidales, 2a Sección, Del. Coyoacán, 04470 México, DF; tel. (55) 5624-0000; fax (55) 5695-6368; e-mail sra@sra.gob.mx; internet www.sra.gob.mx.

Secretariat of State for Agriculture, Livestock, Rural Development, Fisheries and Food: Avda Municipio Libre 377, Col. Santa Cruz Atoyac, Del. Benito Juárez, 03310 México, DF; tel. (55) 3871-1000; fax (55) 9183-1018; e-mail contacto@sagarpa.gob.mx; internet www.sagarpa.gob.mx.

Secretariat of State for Communications and Transport: Avda Xola y Universidad, Col. Narvarte, Del. Benito Juárez, 03020 México, DF; tel. (55) 5723-9300; fax (55) 5530-0093; e-mail webmaster@sct.gob.mx; internet www.sct.gob.mx.

Secretariat of State for the Economy: Alfonso Reyes 30, Col. Hipódromo Condesa, 06140 México, DF; tel. (55) 5729-9100; fax (55) 5729-9320; e-mail primercontacto@economia.gob.mx; internet www.economia.gob.mx.

Secretariat of State for Energy: Insurgentes Sur 890, 17°, Col. del Valle, Del. Benito Juárez, 03100 México, DF; tel. (55) 5000-6000; fax (55) 5000-6222; e-mail calidad@energia.gob.mx; internet www.energia.gob.mx.

Secretariat of State for the Environment and Natural Resources: Blvd Adolfo Ruíz Cortines 4209, Col. Jardines en la Montaña, Del. Tlalpan, 14210 México, DF; tel. (55) 5628-0600; fax (55) 5628-0643; e-mail contactodgeia@semarnat.gob.mx; internet www.semarnat.gob.mx.

Secretariat of State for Finance and Public Credit: Palacio Nacional, Plaza de la Constitución, Col. Centro, Del. Cuauhtémoc, 06000 México, DF; tel. (55) 9158-2000; fax (55) 9158-1142; e-mail secretario@hacienda.gob.mx; internet www.hacienda.gob.mx.

Secretariat of State for Foreign Affairs: Avda Juárez 20, Col. Centro, Del. Cuauhtémoc, 06010 México, DF; tel. (55) 3686-5100; fax (55) 3686-5582; e-mail comentario@sre.gob.mx; internet www.sre.gob.mx.

Secretariat of State for Health: Lieja 7, 1°, Col. Juárez, Del. Cuauhtémoc, 06600 México, DF; tel. (55) 5286-2383; fax (55) 5553-7917; e-mail portalesweb@salud.gob.mx; internet www.salud.gob.mx.

Secretariat of State for the Interior: Abraham González 48, Col. Juárez, Del. Cuauhtémoc, 06600 México, DF; tel. (55) 5728-7400; fax (55) 5728-7300; e-mail contacto@segob.gob.mx; internet www.gobernacion.gob.mx.

Secretariat of State for Labour and Social Welfare: Periférico Sur 4271, Col. Fuentes del Pedregal, Del. Tlalpan, 14149 México, DF; tel. (55) 3000-2100; fax (55) 5645-5594; e-mail correo@stps.gob.mx; internet www.stps.gob.mx.

Secretariat of State for National Defence: Blvd Manuel Avila Camacho, esq. Avda Industria Militar, 3°, Col. Lomas de Sotelo, Del. Miguel Hidalgo, 11640 México, DF; tel. (55) 2122-8800; fax (55) 5395-2935; e-mail ggalvang@mail.sedena.gob.mx; internet www.sedena.gob.mx.

Secretariat of State for the Navy: Eje 2 oriente, Tramo Heroica, Escuela Naval Militar 861, Col. Los Cipreses, Del. Coyoacán, 04830 México, DF; tel. (55) 5624-6500; e-mail srio@semar.gob.mx; internet www.semar.gob.mx.

Secretariat of State for Public Education: Argentina 28, Centro Histórico, 06029 México, DF; tel. (55) 3601-1000; fax (55) 5329-6873; e-mail educa@sep.gob.mx; internet www.sep.gob.mx.

Secretariat of State for Public Function: Insurgentes Sur 1735, 10°, Col. Guadalupe Inn, Del. Alvaro Obregón, 01020 México, DF; tel. (55) 2000-3000; e-mail contactociudadano@funcionpublica.gob.mx; internet www.funcionpublica.gob.mx.

Secretariat of State for Public Security: Avda Constituyentes 947, Ex Hacienda de Belem, Del. Alvaro Obregón, 01110 México, DF; tel. (55) 1103-6000; e-mail enlace@ssp.gob.mx; internet www.ssp.gob.mx.

Secretariat of State for Social Development: Avda Paseo de la Reforma 116, Col. Juárez, Del. Cuauhtémoc, 06600 México, DF; tel. (55) 5328-5000; e-mail contacto@sedesol.gob.mx; internet www.sedesol.gob.mx.

Secretariat of State for Tourism: Avda Presidente Masaryk 172, Col. Chapultepec Morales, Del. Miguel Hidalgo, 11587 México, DF; tel. (55) 3002-6300; fax (55) 1036-0789; e-mail atencion@sectur.gob.mx; internet www.sectur.gob.mx.

Office of the Procurator-General: Avda Paseo de la Reforma 211–213, Col. Cuauhtémoc, Del. Cuauhtémoc, 06500 México, DF; tel. (55) 5346-0000; fax (55) 5346-0908; e-mail ofproc@pgr.gob.mx; internet www.pgr.gob.mx.

State Governors
(April 2011)

Aguascalientes: Carlos Lozano (PRI).
Baja California: José Guadalupe Osuna Millán (PAN).
Baja California Sur: Narciso Agúndez Montaño (PRD), Marcos Covarrubias Villaseñor (elect—PAN).
Campeche: Fernando Ortega Bernés (PRI).
Chiapas: Juan José Sabines Guerrero (PRD).
Chihuahua: César Horatio Duarte Jáquez (PRI).
Coahuila (de Zaragoza): Jorge Juan Torres López (acting—PRI).
Colima: Mario Anguiano Moreno (PRI).
Durango: Jorge Herrera Caldera (PRI).
Guanajuato: Juan Manuel Oliva Ramírez (PAN).
Guerrero: Carlos Zeferino Torreblanca Galindo (PRD), Angel Heladio Aguirre Rivero (elect—PRD).
Hidalgo: Francisco Olvera (PRI).
Jalisco: Emilio González Márquez (PAN).
México: Enrique Peña Nieto (PRI).
Michoacán (de Ocampo): Leonel Godoy Rangel (PRD).
Morelos: Marco Antonio Adame Castillo (PAN).
Nayarit: Ney González Sánchez (PRI).
Nuevo León: Rodrigo Medina de la Cruz (PRI).
Oaxaca: Gabino Cué Monteagudo (Convergencia).
Puebla: Rafael Moreno Valle (PAN).
Querétaro (de Arteaga): José Calzada Rovirosa (PRI).
Quintana Roo: Roberto Borge (PRI).
San Luis Potosí: Fernando Toranzo Fernández (PRI).

MEXICO

Sinaloa: Mario López Valdez (PAN).
Sonora: Guillermo Padrés Elías (PAN).
Tabasco: Andrés Rafael Granier Melo (PRI).
Tamaulipas: Egidio Torre Cantú (PRI).
Tlaxcala: Mariano González Zarur (PRI).
Veracruz-Llave: Javier Duarte de Ochoa (PRI).
Yucatán: Ivonne Ortega Pacheco (PRI).
Zacatecas: Miguel Alonso Reyes (PRI).
Head of Government of the Distrito Federal: Marcelo Luis Ebrard Casaubón (PRD).

President and Legislature

PRESIDENT

Election, 2 July 2006

Candidate	Number of votes	% of votes
Felipe Calderón Hinojosa (PAN)	14,916,927	35.89
Andrés Manuel López Obrador (Por el Bien de Todos*)	14,683,096	35.33
Roberto Madrazo Pintado (Alianza por México†)	9,237,000	22.23
Patricia Mercado Castro (PASC‡)	1,124,280	2.71
Roberto Campa Cifrián (Nueva Alianza)	397,550	0.96
Total§	41,557,430	100.00

* An alliance of the PRD, the PT and Convergencia.
† An alliance of the PRI and the PVEM.
‡ The Partido Alternativa Socialdemócrata y Campesina, subsequently renamed the Partido Socialdemócrata.
§ Including 900,373 invalid votes and 298,204 votes for unregistered candidates.

CONGRESO DE LA UNIÓN

Senado

Senate: Xicoténcatl 9, Centro Histórico, 06010 México, DF; tel. (55) 5130-2200; internet www.senado.gob.mx.

President: Manlio Fabio Beltrones Rivera (PRI).

Elections, 2 July 2006

Party	Seats
Partido Acción Nacional (PAN)	52
Partido Revolucionario Institucional (PRI)*	33
Partido de la Revolución Democrática (PRD)†	29
Partido Verde Ecologista de México (PVEM)*	6
Convergencia†	5
Partido del Trabajo (PT)†	2
Nueva Alianza	1
Total	128

* Part of the Alianza por México.
† Part of the Por el Bien de Todos alliance.

Cámara Federal de Diputados

Federal Chamber of Deputies: Avda Congreso de la Unión 66, Col. El Parque, Del. Venustiano Carranza, 15969 México, DF; tel. (55) 5628-1300; internet www.diputados.gob.mx.

President: Jorge Carlos Ramírez Marín (PRI).

Elections, 5 July 2009

Party	Seats
Partido Revolucionario Institucional (PRI)*	237
Partido Acción Nacional (PAN)	143
Partido de la Revolución Democrática (PRD)†	71
Partido Verde Ecologista de México (PVEM)*	22
Partido del Trabajo (PT)†	13
Nueva Alianza	8
Convergencia†	6
Total	500

* Part of the Alianza por México.
† Part of the Por el Bien de Todos alliance.

Election Commission

Instituto Federal Electoral (IFE): Viaducto Tlalpan 100, Col. Arenal Tepepan, Del. Tlalpan, 14610 México, DF; e-mail info@ife.org.mx; internet www.ife.org.mx; f. 1990; independent; Pres. Leonardo Valdés Zurita; Sec. Edmundo Jacobo Molina.

Political Organizations

To retain legal political registration, parties must secure at least 1.5% of total votes at two consecutive federal elections. Following the 2009 mid-term elections eight national political parties were registered.

Convergencia: Louisiana 113, Col. Nápoles, esq. Nueva York, Del. Benito Juárez, 03810 México, DF; tel. (55) 1167-6767; e-mail gestionsocial@convergencia.org.mx; internet www.convergencia.org.mx; f. 1995 as Convergencia por la Democracia; part of the Por el Bien de Todos alliance formed to contest 2006 presidential election, later renamed the Frente Amplio Progresista; Pres. Luis Walton Arburto; Sec.-Gen. Armando López Velarde Campa.

Nueva Alianza: Durango 199, Col. Roma, Del. Cuauhtémoc, 06700 México, DF; tel. (55) 3685-8485; fax (55) 3685-8455; e-mail contacto@nueva-alianza.org.mx; internet www.nueva-alianza.org.mx; f. 2005 by dissident faction of the PRI; includes mems of the Sindicato Nacional de Trabajadores de la Educación (SNTE, see Trade Unions) and supporters of Elba Esther Gordillo Morales; Pres. Jorge Kahwagi Macari; Sec.-Gen. Fermín Trujillo Fuentes.

Partido Acción Nacional (PAN): Avda Coyoacán 1546, Col. del Valle, Del. Benito Juárez, 03100 México, DF; tel. (55) 5200-4000; e-mail correo@cen.pan.org.mx; internet www.pan.org.mx; f. 1939; democratic party; 150,000 mems; Pres. Gustavo Enrique Madero Muñoz; Sec.-Gen. Cecilia Romero Castillo.

Partido Popular Socialista (PPS): Avda Alvaro Obregón 185, Col. Roma, Del. Cuauhtémoc, 06797 México, DF; tel. (55) 5208-5063; fax (55) 2454-6593; e-mail info@partidopopularsocialista.org.mx; internet www.partidopopularsocialista.org.mx; f. 1948; Marxist-Leninist, Lombardist; Sec.-Gen. Jesús Antonio Carlos Hernández; Org. Sec. Héctor Marín Rebollo.

Partido de la Revolución Democrática (PRD): Avda Benjamín Franklin 84, Col. Escandón, Del. Miguel Hidalgo, 11800 México, DF; tel. (55) 1085-8000; fax (55) 1085-8144; e-mail comunicacion@prd.org.mx; internet www.prd.org.mx; f. 1989; centre-left; leading mem. of the Por el Bien de Todos alliance formed to contest 2006 presidential election, later renamed the Frente Amplio Progresista; factions include Izquierda Unida (radical faction supporting Andrés Manuel López Obrador's claim to the presidency) and Nueva Izquierda (moderate); Pres. Jesús Zambrano Grijalva; Sec.-Gen. Dolores Padierna Luna.

Partido Revolucionario Institucional (PRI): Edif. 2, Insurgentes Norte 59, Col. Buenavista, Del. Cuauhtémoc, 06359 México, DF; tel. (55) 5729-9600; internet www.pri.org.mx; f. 1929 as the Partido Nacional Revolucionario; regarded as the natural successor to the victorious parties of the revolutionary period; broadly based and centrist; formed Alianza por México alliance with PVEM to contest 2006 presidential election; Pres. Humberto Moreira Valdés; Sec.-Gen. Cristina Díaz; groups within the PRI include: the Corriente Crítica Progresista, the Corriente Crítica del Partido, the Corriente Constitucionalista Democratizadora, Corriente Nuevo PRI XIV Asamblea, Democracia 2000, México Nuevo and Galileo.

Partido del Trabajo (PT): Avda Cuauhtémoc 47, Col. Roma Norte, Del. Miguel Hidalgo, 06700 México, DF; tel. and fax (55) 5525-2727; internet www.partidodeltrabajo.org.mx; f. 1990; labour party; part of the Por el Bien de Todos alliance formed to contest 2006 presidential election, later renamed the Frente Amplio Progresista; Leader Alberto Anaya Gutiérrez.

Partido Verde Ecologista de México (PVEM): Loma Bonita 18, Col. Lomas Altas, Del. Miguel Hidalgo, 11950 México, DF; tel. and fax (55) 5257-0188; internet www.partidoverde.org.mx; f. 1987; ecologist party; formed Alianza por México alliance with PRI to contest 2006 presidential election; Pres. Jorge Emilio González Martínez; Sec.-Gen. Marco Antonio de la Mora Torreblanca.

The following parties are not officially registered but continue to be politically active:

Fuerza Ciudadana: Rochester 94, Col. Nápoles, 03810 México, DF; tel. (55) 5534-4628; e-mail info@fuerzaciudadana.org.mx; internet www.fuerzaciudadana.org.mx; f. 2002; citizens' asscn; Pres. Jorge Alcocer Villanueva; Sec. Alberto Consejo Vargas.

Partido Democrático Popular Revolucionario: f. 1996; political grouping representing the causes of 14 armed peasant orgs, including the EPR and the PROCUP.

Partido Revolucionario Obrerista y Clandestino de Unión Popular (PROCUP): peasant org.

MEXICO

Partido Socialdemócrata (PSD): Tejocotes 164, Col. Tlacoquemécatl del Valle, Del. Benito Juárez, 03200 México, DF; tel. (55) 5488-1520; fax (55) 5488-1598; internet www.psd.org.mx; f. 2005 as Partido Alternativa Socialdemócrata y Campesina; adopted current name 2008; progressive and peasants' rights; lost political registration following 2009 mid-term elections; Pres. JORGE CARLOS DÍAZ CUEVOS.

Illegal organizations active in Mexico include the following:

Ejército Popular Revolucionario (EPR): e-mail pdprepr@hotmail.com; f. 1994; left-wing guerrilla group active mainly in southern states, linked to the Partido Democrático Popular Revolucionario (q.v.).

Ejército Revolucionario Popular Insurgente (ERPI): f. 1996; left-wing guerrilla group active in Guerrero, Morelos and Oaxaca; Leader JACOBO SILVA NOGALES.

Ejército Zapatista de Liberación Nacional (EZLN): e-mail laotra@ezln.org.mx; internet www.ezln.org.mx; f. 1993; left-wing guerrilla group active in the Chiapas region; Leader 'Subcomandante MARCOS'.

Frente Democrático Oriental de México Emiliano Zapata (FDOMEZ): peasant org.

Other armed groups include the Tendencia Democrática Revolucionaria-Ejército del Pueblo and the Comando Popular Revolucionario—La Patria es Primero.

Diplomatic Representation

EMBASSIES IN MEXICO

Algeria: Sierra Madre 540, Col. Lomas de Chapultepec, Del. Miguel Hidalgo, 11000 México, DF; tel. (55) 5520-6950; fax (55) 5540-7579; e-mail embajadadeargelia@yahoo.com.mx; Ambassador ABDELHAMID ABROUS.

Angola: Gaspar de Zúñiga 226, Col. Lomas de Chapultepec, Sección Virreyes, Del. Miguel Hidalgo, 11000 México, DF; tel. (55) 5202-4421; fax (55) 5540-5928; e-mail info@embangolamex.org; Ambassador JOSÉ JAIME FURTADO GONÇALVEZ.

Argentina: Avda Palmas 910, Col. Lomas de Chapultepec, Del. Miguel Hidalgo, 11000 México, DF; tel. (55) 5520-9430; fax (55) 5540-5011; e-mail embajadaargentina@prodigy.net.mx; Ambassador PATRICIA VACA NARVAJA.

Australia: Rubén Darío 55, Col. Polanco, Del. Miguel Hidalgo, 11580 México, DF; tel. (55) 1101-2200; fax (55) 1101-2201; e-mail embaustmex@yahoo.com.mx; internet www.mexico.embassy.gov.au; Ambassador KATRINA ANNE COOPER.

Austria: Sierra Tarahumara 420, Col. Lomas de Chapultepec, Del. Miguel Hidalgo, 11000 México, DF; tel. (55) 5251-0806; fax (55) 5245-0198; e-mail mexiko-ob@bmaa.gv.at; internet www.embajadadeaustria.com.mx; Ambassador ALFRED LANGLE.

Azerbaijan: Avda Virreyes 1015, Col. Lomas de Chapultepec, Del. Miguel Hidalgo, 11000 México, DF; tel. (55) 5540-4109; fax (55) 5540-1366; Ambassador ILGAR MUKHTAROV.

Belgium: Alfredo Musset 41, Col. Polanco, Del. Miguel Hidalgo, 11550 México, DF; tel. (55) 5280-0758; fax (55) 5280-0208; e-mail mexico@diplobel.org; internet www.diplomatie.be/mexico; Ambassador BOUDEWIJN E. G. DEREYMAEKAR.

Belize: Bernardo de Gálvez 215, Col. Lomas de Chapultepec, Del. Miguel Hidalgo, 11000 México, DF; tel. (55) 5520-1274; fax (55) 5520-6089; e-mail embelize@prodigy.net.mx; Ambassador ROSENDO URBINA.

Bolivia: Goethe 104, Col. Anzures, Del. Miguel Hidalgo, 11590 México, DF; tel. and fax (55) 5255-3620; e-mail embajada@embol.org.mx; internet www.embol.org.mx; Ambassador JORGE MANSILLA TORRES.

Brazil: Lope de Armendáriz 130, Col. Lomas Virreyes, Del. Miguel Hidalgo, 11000 México, DF; tel. (55) 5201-4531; fax (55) 5520-4929; e-mail embrasil@brasil.org.mx; internet www.brasil.org.mx; Ambassador SERGIO AGOSTO DE ABREU E LIMA FLORENCIO SOBRINHO.

Bulgaria: Paseo de la Reforma 1990, Col. Lomas de Chapultepec, Del. Miguel Hidalgo, 11000 México, DF; tel. (55) 5596-3283; fax (55) 5596-1012; e-mail ebulgaria@yahoo.com; Ambassador SERGEY PENCHEV MICHEV.

Canada: Schiller 529, Col. Polanco, Del. Miguel Hidalgo, 11560 México, DF; tel. (55) 5724-7900; fax (55) 5724-7980; e-mail mxico@international.gc.ca; internet www.canadainternational.gc.ca/mexico-mexique; Ambassador GUILLERMO E. RISHCHYNSKI.

Chile: Andrés Bello 10, 18°, Col. Polanco, Del. Miguel Hidalgo, 11560 México, DF; tel. (55) 5280-9681; fax (55) 5280-9703; e-mail echilmex@prodigy.net.mx; internet www.embajadadechile.com.mx; Ambassador GERMÁN GUERRERO PAVEZ.

China, People's Republic: Avda San Jerónimo 217B, Del. Alvaro Obregón, 01090 México, DF; tel. (55) 5616-0609; fax (55) 5616-0460; e-mail embchina@data.net.mx; internet www.embajadachina.org.mx; Ambassador ZENG GANG.

Colombia: Paseo de la Reforma 379, 5°, Col. Cuauhtémoc, Del. Cuauhtémoc, 06500 México, DF; tel. (55) 5525-0277; fax (55) 5208-2876; e-mail emcol@colombiaenmexico.org; internet www.embajadaenmexico.gob.co; Ambassador JOSÉ GABRIEL ORTIZ ROBLEDO.

Costa Rica: Río Po 113, Col. Cuauhtémoc, Del. Cuauhtémoc, 06500 México, DF; tel. (55) 5525-7764; fax (55) 5511-9240; e-mail embajada@embajada.decostaricaenmexico.org; internet www.embajada.decostaricaenmexico.org; Ambassador GABRIELA JIMÉNEZ CRUZ.

Côte d'Ivoire: Tennyson 67, Col. Polanco, Del. Miguel Hidalgo, 11560 México, DF; tel. 5280-8573; fax 5282-2954; Ambassador ANNE GNAHOURET TATRET.

Cuba: Presidente Masaryk 554, Col. Polanco, Del. Miguel Hidalgo, 11560 México, DF; tel. (55) 5280-8039; fax (55) 5280-0839; e-mail embajada@embacuba.com.mx; internet www.embacuba.com.mx; Ambassador MANUEL FRANCISCO AGUILERA DE LA PÁZ.

Cyprus: Sierra Gorda 370, Col. Lomas de Chapultepec, Del. Miguel Hidalgo, 11000 México, DF; tel. (55) 5202-7600; fax (55) 5520-2693; e-mail chipre@att.net.mx; Ambassador VASILIOS PHILIPPOU.

Czech Republic: Cuvier 22, esq. Kepler, Col. Nueva Anzures, Del. Miguel Hidalgo, 11590 México, DF; tel. (55) 5531-2777; fax (55) 5531-1837; e-mail mexico@embassy.mzv.cz; internet www.mzv.cz/mexico; Ambassador JIŘÍ HAVLÍK.

Denmark: Tres Picos 43, Col. Chapultepec Morales, Del. Miguel Hidalgo, 11580 México, DF; tel. (55) 5255-3405; fax (55) 5545-5797; e-mail mexamb@um.dk; internet www.ambmexicocity.um.dk; Ambassador SUSANNE RUMOHR HÆKKERUP.

Dominican Republic: Prado Sur 755 (entre Monte Blanco y Monte Everest), Col. Lomas de Chapultepec, Del. Miguel Hidalgo, 11000 México, DF; tel. (55) 5540-3841; fax (55) 5520-0779; e-mail embajada@embadom.org.mx; internet www.embadom.org.mx; Ambassador FERNANDO ANTONIO PÉREZ MEMÉN.

Ecuador: Tennyson 217, Col. Polanco, Del. Miguel Hidalgo, 11560 México, DF; tel. (55) 5545-3141; fax (55) 5254-2442; e-mail mecuamex@prodigy.net.mx; Ambassador GALO GALARZA DÁVILA.

Egypt: Alejandro Dumas 131, Col. Polanco, Del. Miguel Hidalgo, 11560 México, DF; tel. (55) 5281-0823; fax (55) 5282-1294; e-mail embofegypt@prodigy.net.mx; Ambassador IBRAHIM AHDY KHAIRAT.

El Salvador: Temístocles 88, Col. Polanco, Del. Miguel Hidalgo, 11560 México, DF; tel. (55) 5281-5725; fax (55) 5280-0657; e-mail embesmex@webtelmex.net.mx; Ambassador HUGO ROBERTO CARRILLO CORLETO.

Finland: Monte Pelvoux 111, 4°, Col. Lomas de Chapultepec, Del. Miguel Hidalgo, 11000 México, DF; tel. (55) 5540-6036; fax (55) 5540-0114; e-mail finmex@prodigy.net.mx; internet www.finlandia.org.mx; Ambassador ULLA MARIANNA VAISTO.

France: Campos Elíseos 339, Col. Polanco, Del. Miguel Hidalgo, 11560 México, DF; tel. (55) 9171-9893; fax (55) 9171-9703; e-mail prensa@ambafrance-mx.org; internet www.ambafrance-mx.org; Ambassador DANIEL PARFAIT.

Germany: Horacio 1506, Col. Los Morales, Del. Miguel Hidalgo, 11530 México, DF; tel. (55) 5283-2200; fax (55) 5281-2588; e-mail info@mexi.diplo.de; internet www.mexiko.diplo.de; Ambassador EDMUND DUCKWITZ.

Greece: Sierra Gorda 505, Col. Lomas de Chapultepec, Del. Miguel Hidalgo, 11010 México, DF; tel. (55) 5520-2070; fax (55) 5202-4080; e-mail grem.mex@mfa.gr; Ambassador VASSILIS KARANTONIS.

Guatemala: Explanada 1025, Col. Lomas de Chapultepec, Del. Miguel Hidalgo, 11000 México, DF; tel. (55) 5540-7520; fax (55) 5202-1142; e-mail embaguatemx@minex.gob.gt; Ambassador RITA JOSÉFINA CLAVERIE DE SCIOLLI.

Haiti: Presa Don Martín 53, Col. Irrigación, Del. Miguel Hidalgo, 11500 México, DF; tel. (55) 5557-2065; fax (55) 5395-1654; e-mail ambadh@mail.internet.com.mx; Ambassador ROBERT MANUEL.

Holy See: Juan Pablo II 118, Col. Guadalupe Inn, Del. Alvaro Obregón, 01020 México, DF; tel. (55) 5663-3999; fax (55) 5663-5308; Apostolic Nuncio Most Rev. CHRISTOPHE PIERRE (Titular Archbishop of Gunela).

Honduras: Alfonso Reyes 220, Col. Condesa, Del. Cuauhtémoc, 06170 México, DF; tel. (55) 5211-5747; fax (55) 5211-5425; e-mail emhonmex@prodigy.net.mx; Ambassador JOSÉ MARIANO CASTILLO MERCADO.

Hungary: Paseo de las Palmas 2005, Col. Lomas de Chapultepec, Del. Miguel Hidalgo, 11000 México, DF; tel. (55) 5596-0523; fax (55) 5596-2378; internet www.mfa.gov.hu/kulkepviselet/MX/hu; Ambassador TEREZ DÖRÖMBÖZI DE DEHELAN.

MEXICO

India: Musset 325, Col. Polanco, Del. Miguel Hidalgo, 11550 México, DF; tel. (55) 5531-1050; fax (55) 5254-2349; e-mail indembmx@prodigy.net.mx; internet www.indembassy.org; Ambassador DINESH KUMAR JAIN.

Indonesia: Julio Verne 27, Col. Polanco, Del. Miguel Hidalgo, 11560 México, DF; tel. (55) 5280-6363; fax (55) 5280-7062; e-mail kbrimex@prodigy.net.mx; Ambassador HAMDANI DJAFAR.

Iran: Paseo de la Reforma 2350, Col. Lomas Altas, Del. Miguel Hidalgo, 11950 México, DF; tel. (55) 9172-2691; fax (55) 9172-2694; e-mail iranembmex@hotmail.com; Ambassador MOHAMMAD HASSAN GHADIRI ABYANEH.

Iraq: Paseo de la Reforma 1875, Col. Lomas de Chapultepec, Del. Miguel Hidalgo, 11000 México, DF; tel. (55) 5596-0933; fax (55) 5596-0254; e-mail mxcemb@iraqfamail.com; Chargé d'affaires a.i. SALIH MAROUF MIRANI.

Ireland: Cerrada Blvd Manuel Avila Camacho 76, 3°, Col. Lomas de Chapultepec, Del. Miguel Hidalgo, 11000 México, DF; tel. (55) 5520-5803; fax (55) 5520-5892; e-mail emexicoembassy@dfa.ie; internet www.irishembassy.com.mx; Ambassador EAMONN HICKEY.

Israel: Sierra Madre 215, Col. Lomas de Chapultepec, Del. Miguel Hidalgo, 11000 México, DF; tel. (55) 5201-1500; fax (55) 5201-1555; e-mail ambassadorsec@mexico.mfa.gov.il; internet mexico-city.mfa.gov.il; Ambassador RODICA RADIAN-GORDON.

Italy: Paseo de las Palmas 1994, Col. Lomas de Chapultepec, Del. Miguel Hidalgo, 11000 México, DF; tel. (55) 5596-3655; fax (55) 5596-2472; e-mail segreteria.messico@esteri.it; internet www.ambcittadelmessico.esteri.it; Ambassador ROBERTO SPINELLI.

Jamaica: Schiller 326, 8°, Col. Chapultepec Morales, Del. Miguel Hidalgo, 11570 México, DF; tel. (55) 5250-6804; fax (55) 5250-6160; e-mail embajadadejamaica@prodigy.net.mx; Ambassador DELROSE MONTAGUE.

Japan: Paseo de la Reforma 395, Apdo 5-101, Col. Cuauhtémoc, Del. Cuauhtémoc, 06500 México, DF; tel. (55) 5211-0028; fax (55) 5207-7743; e-mail embjapmx@mail.internet.com.mx; internet www.mx.emb-japan.go.jp; Ambassador MASAAKI ONO.

Korea, Democratic People's Republic: Calle Halley 12, Col. Anzures, Del. Miguel Hidalgo, 11590 México, DF; tel. (55) 5250-0263; fax (55) 5545-8775; e-mail dpkoreaemb@prodigy.net.mx; Ambassador AN KUN SONG.

Korea, Republic: Lope de Armendáriz 110, Col. Lomas Virreyes, Del. Miguel Hidalgo, 11000 México, DF; tel. (55) 5202-9866; fax (55) 5540-7446; e-mail coremex@prodigy.net.mx; internet mex.mofat.go.kr; Ambassador CHO WHAN-BOK.

Lebanon: Julio Verne 8, Col. Polanco, Del. Miguel Hidalgo, 11560 México, DF; tel. (55) 5280-5614; fax (55) 5280-8870; e-mail embalibano@embajadadelibano.org.mx; internet www.embajadadelibano.org.mx; Ambassador NOUHAD MAHMOUD.

Libya: Horacio 1003, Col. Polanco, Del. Miguel Hidalgo, 11550 México, DF; tel. (55) 5545-5725; fax (55) 5545-5677; e-mail libia.mexico@yahoo.com; Chargé d'affaires a.i. KHALID A. A. DAHAN.

Malaysia: Sierra Nevada 435, Col. Lomas de Chapultepec, Del. Miguel Hidalgo, 11000 México, DF; tel. (55) 5282-5166; fax (55) 5282-4910; e-mail mwmexico@prodigy.net.mx; Chargé d'affaires a.i. HARRIS BIN ALWI.

Morocco: Paseo de las Palmas 2020, Col. Lomas de Chapultepec, Del. Miguel Hidalgo, 11000 México, DF; tel. (55) 5245-1786; fax (55) 5245-1791; e-mail sifamex@infosel.net.mx; internet www.marruecos.org.mx; Ambassador MAHMOUD RMIKI.

Netherlands: Edif. Calakmul, 7°, Avda Vasco de Quiroga 3000, Col. Santa Fe, Del. Alvaro Obregón, 01210 México, DF; tel. (55) 5258-9921; fax (55) 5258-8138; e-mail mex-info@minbuza.nl; internet www.paisesbajos.com.mx; Ambassador CORA MINDERHOUD.

New Zealand: Edif. Corporativo Polanco, 4°, Jaime Balmes 8, Col. Los Morales Polanco, Del. Miguel Hidalgo, 11510 México, DF; tel. (55) 5283-9460; fax (55) 5283-9480; e-mail kiwimexico@prodigy.net.mx; internet www.nzembassy.com/mexico; Ambassador CHRISTINE BOGLE.

Nicaragua: Prado Norte 470, Col. Lomas de Chapultepec, Del. Miguel Hidalgo, 11000 México, DF; tel. (55) 5540-5625; fax (55) 5520-6961; e-mail embanic@prodigy.net.mx; Ambassador HORACIO BRENES ICABALCETA.

Nigeria: Paseo de las Palmas 1880, Col. Lomas de Chapultepec, Del. Miguel Hidalgo, 11000 México, DF; tel. (55) 5245-1487; fax (55) 5245-0105; e-mail nigembmx@att.net.mx; Ambassador LAWRENCE NWANCHO NWURUKU.

Norway: Avda de los Virreyes 1460, Col. Lomas Virreyes, Del. Miguel Hidalgo, 11000 México, DF; tel. (55) 5540-3486; fax (55) 5202-3019; e-mail emb.mexico@mfa.no; internet www.noruega.org.mx; Ambassador ARNE AASHEIM.

Pakistan: Hegel 512, Col. Chapultepec Morales, Del. Miguel Hidalgo, 11570 México, DF; tel. (55) 5203-3636; fax (55) 5203-9907; e-mail parepmex@hotmail.com; Ambassador RAJA ALI EJAZ.

Panama: Sócrates 339, Col. Polanco, Del. Miguel Hidalgo, 11560 México, DF; tel. (55) 5280-7857; fax (55) 5280-7586; e-mail informes@embpanamamexico.com; internet www.embpanamamexico.com; Ambassador FRANCISCO TROYA AGUIRRE.

Paraguay: Homero 415, 1°, esq. Hegel, Col. Polanco, Del. Miguel Hidalgo, 11570 México, DF; tel. (55) 5545-0405; fax (55) 5531-9905; e-mail embapar@prodigy.net.mx; Ambassador CARLOS HERIBERTO RIVEROS SALCEDO.

Peru: Paseo de la Reforma 2601, Col. Lomas Reforma, Del. Miguel Hidalgo, 11000 México, DF; tel. (55) 1105-2270; fax (55) 1105-2279; e-mail embaperu@prodigy.net.mx; Ambassador LUIS ALVARADO CONTRERAS.

Philippines: Río Rhin 56, Cuauhtémoc, Del. Cuauhtémoc, 06500 México, DF; tel. (55) 5202-8456; fax (55) 5202-8403; e-mail ambamexi@yahoo.com.mx; Ambassador FRANCISCO ORTIGAS MIRANDA.

Poland: Cracovia 40, Col. San Angel, Del. Alvaro Obregón, 01000 México, DF; tel. (55) 5481-2051; fax (55) 5481-2056; e-mail embajadadepolonia@prodigy.net.mx; internet www.meksyk.polemb.net; Ambassador ANNA ELZBIETA NIEWIADOMSKA.

Portugal: Avda Alpes 1370, Lomas de Chapultepec, Del. Miguel Hidalgo, 11000 México, DF; tel. (55) 5520-7897; fax (55) 5520-4688; e-mail embpomex@prodigy.net.mx; internet embpomex.wordpress.com; Ambassador JOÃO JOSÉ GOMES CAETANO DA SILVA.

Romania: Sófocles 311, Col. Polanco, Del. Miguel Hidalgo, 11560 México, DF; tel. (55) 5280-0197; fax (55) 5280-0343; e-mail secretariat@rumania.org.mx; internet www.rumania.org.mx; Ambassador MANUELA VULPE.

Russia: José Vasconcelos 204, Col. Hipódromo Condesa, Del. Cuauhtémoc, 06140 México, DF; tel. (55) 5273-1305; fax (55) 5273-1545; e-mail embrumex@hotmail.com; internet www.embrumex.com.mx; Ambassador VALERY I. MOROZOV.

Saudi Arabia: Paseo de las Palmas 2075, Col. Lomas de Chapultepec, Del. Miguel Hidalgo, 11000 México, DF; tel. (55) 5596-0173; fax (55) 5020-3160; e-mail saudiemb@prodigy.net.mx; Ambassador HUSSEIN MOHAMMAD ABDULFATAH AL-ASSIRI.

Serbia: Montañas Rocallosas Oeste 515, Col. Lomas de Chapultepec, Del. Miguel Hidalgo, 11000 México, DF; tel. (55) 5520-0524; fax (55) 5520-9927; e-mail embajadaserbia@alestra.net.mx; Ambassador ZORAN STANOJEVIĆ.

Slovakia: Julio Verne 35, Col. Polanco, Del. Miguel Hidalgo, 11560 México, DF; tel. (55) 5280-6669; fax (55) 5280-6294; e-mail eslovaquia@prodigy.net.mx; Ambassador JOZEF ADAMEC.

South Africa: Edif. Forum, 9°, Andrés Bello 10, Col. Polanco, Del. Miguel Hidalgo, 11560 México, DF; tel. (55) 1100-4970; fax (55) 5282-9259; e-mail safrica@prodigy.net.mx; Ambassador MPHAKAMA NYANGWENI MBETE.

Spain: Galileo 114, esq. Horacio, Col. Polanco, Del. Miguel Hidalgo, 11550 México, DF; tel. (55) 5282-2271; fax (55) 5282-1520; e-mail embaes@prodigy.net.mx; internet www.mae.es/embajadas/mexico; Ambassador MANUEL ALABART FERNANDEZ-CAVADA.

Sweden: Paseo de las Palmas 1375, Col. Lomas de Chapultepec, Del. Miguel Hidalgo, 11000 México, DF; tel. (55) 9178-5010; fax (55) 5540-3253; e-mail suecia@prodigy.net.mx; internet www.suecia.com.mx; Ambassador ANNA LINDSTEDT.

Switzerland: Paseo de las Palmas 405, 11°, Torre Óptima, Col. Lomas de Chapultepec, Del. Miguel Hidalgo, 11000 México, DF; tel. (55) 9178-4370; fax (55) 5520-8685; e-mail vertretung@mex.rep.admin.ch; internet www.eda.admin.ch/mexico; Ambassador RUDOLF KNOBLAUCH.

Thailand: Paseo de las Palmas 1610, Col. Lomas de Chapultepec, Del. Miguel Hidalgo, 11000 México, DF; tel. (55) 5540-4551; fax (55) 5540-4817; e-mail thaimex@prodigy.net.mx; internet www.thaiembmexico.co.nr; Ambassador SUVAT CHIRAPANT.

Turkey: Monte Líbano 885, Col. Lomas de Chapultepec, Del. Miguel Hidalgo, 11000 México, DF; tel. (55) 5282-4277; fax (55) 5282-4894; e-mail turkishembassy@hotmail.com; internet www.turkembmex.org; Ambassador ALEV KILIC.

Ukraine: Paseo de la Reforma 730, Col. Lomas de Chapultepec, Del. Miguel Hidalgo, 11000 México, DF; tel. (55) 5282-4085; fax (55) 5282-4768; e-mail ucraniaemb@prodigy.net.mx; Ambassador OLEKSIY V. BRANASHKO.

United Kingdom: Río Lerma 71, Col. Cuauhtémoc, Del. Cuauhtémoc, 06500 México, DF; tel. (55) 5242-8500; fax (55) 5242-8517; e-mail ukinmex@att.net.mx; internet www.embajadabritanica.com.mx; Ambassador JUDITH ANNE MACGREGOR.

USA: Paseo de la Reforma 305, Del. Cuauhtémoc, 06500 México, DF; tel. (55) 5080-2000; fax (55) 5080-2005; internet mexico.usembassy.gov; Ambassador (vacant).

Uruguay: Hegel 149, 1°, Col. Chapultepec Morales, Del. Miguel Hidalgo, 11560 México, DF; tel. (55) 5531-0880; fax (55) 5545-3342;

MEXICO

e-mail uruguaymex@prodigy.net.mx; Ambassador JOSÉ RODOLFO CAMAROSANO BERSANI.

Venezuela: Schiller 326, Col. Chapultepec Morales, Del. Miguel Hidalgo, 11570 México, DF; tel. (55) 5203-4233; fax (55) 5254-1457; e-mail venezmex@prodigy.net.mx; Ambassador TRINO ALCIDES DÍAZ.

Viet Nam: Sierra Ventana 255, Col. Lomas de Chapultepec, Del. Miguel Hidalgo, 11000 México, DF; tel. (55) 5540-1632; fax (55) 5540-1612; e-mail vietnam.mx@mofa.gov.vn; internet www.vietnamembassy-mexico.org/vi; Ambassador PHAM VAN QUE.

Judicial System

The principle of the separation of the judiciary from the legislative and executive powers is embodied in the 1917 Constitution. The judicial system is divided into two areas: the federal, dealing with federal law, and the local, dealing only with state law within each state.

The federal judicial system has both ordinary and constitutional jurisdiction, and judicial power is exercised by the Supreme Court of Justice, the Electoral Court, Collegiate and Unitary Circuit Courts and District Courts. The Supreme Court comprises two separate chambers: Civil and Criminal Affairs, and Administrative and Labour Affairs. The Federal Judicature Council is responsible for the administration, surveillance and discipline of the federal judiciary, except for the Supreme Court of Justice.

In 2006 there were 172 Collegiate Circuit Courts (Tribunales Colegiados), 62 Unitary Circuit Courts (Tribunales Unitarios) and 285 District Courts (Juzgados de Distrito). Mexico is divided into 29 judicial circuits. The Circuit Courts may be collegiate, when dealing with the *derecho de amparo* (protection of constitutional rights of an individual), or unitary, when dealing with appeal cases. The Collegiate Circuit Courts comprise three magistrates with residence in the cities of México, Toluca, Naucalpan, Guadalajara, Monterrey, Hermosillo, Puebla, Boca del Río, Xalapa, Torreón, Saltillo, San Luis Potosí, Villahermosa, Morelia, Mazatlán, Oaxaca, Mérida, Mexicali, Guanajuato, León, Chihuahua, Ciudad Juárez, Cuernavaca, Ciudad Victoria, Ciudad Reynosa, Tuxtla Gutiérrez, Tapachula, Acapulco, Chilpancingo, Querétaro, Zacatecas, Aguascalientes, Tepic, Durango, La Paz, Cancún, Tlaxcala and Pachuca. The Unitary Circuit Courts comprise one magistrate with residence mostly in the same cities as given above.

SUPREME COURT OF JUSTICE

Suprema Corte de Justicia de la Nación: Pino Suárez 2, Col. Centro, 06065 México, DF; tel. (55) 5522-0096; fax (55) 5522-0152; e-mail administrator@mail.scjn.gob.mx; internet www.scjn.gob.mx.
Chief Justice: GUILLERMO I. ORTÍZ MAYAGOITIA.

First Chamber—Civil and Criminal Affairs
President: SERGIO ARMANDO VALLS HERNÁNDEZ.

Second Chamber—Administrative and Labour Affairs
President: JOSÉ FERNANDO FRANCO GONZÁLEZ SALAS.

ELECTORAL TRIBUNAL OF THE FEDERAL JUDICIARY

Tribunal Electoral del Poder Jucicial de la Federación (TEPJF): Carlota Amero 5000, Col. Culhuacán, Del. Coyoacán, 04480 México, DF; tel. (55) 5728-2300; fax (55) 5728-2400; e-mail unidad.enlace@te.gob.mx; internet www.te.gob.mx; Pres. MARÍA DEL CARMEN ALANIS FIGUEROA.

Religion

CHRISTIANITY

The Roman Catholic Church

The prevailing religion is Roman Catholicism, but the Church, disestablished in 1857, was for many years, under the Constitution of 1917, subject to state control. A constitutional amendment, promulgated in January 1992, officially removed all restrictions on the Church. For ecclesiastical purposes, Mexico comprises 18 archdioceses, 68 dioceses, five territorial prelatures and two eparchies (both directly subject to the Holy See). According to the latest available census figures (2000), some 88% of the population are Roman Catholics.

Bishops' Conference

Conferencia del Episcopado Mexicano (CEM), Edif. S. S. Juan Pablo II, Prolongación Ministerios 26, Col. Tepeyac Insurgentes, Apdo 118-055, 07020 México, DF; tel. (55) 5781-8462; fax (55) 5577-5489; e-mail segcem@cem.org.mx; internet www.cem.org.mx; Pres. CARLOS AGUIAR RETES (Archbishop of Tlalnepantla); Sec.-Gen. JOSÉ LEOPOLDO GONZÁLEZ GONZÁLEZ.

Archbishop of Acapulco: CARLOS GARFIAS MERLOS, Arzobispado, Quebrada 16, Apdo 201, Centro, 39300 Acapulco, Gro; tel. and fax (744) 482-0763; e-mail arzobispadoaca@aca.cableonline.com.mx; internet www.arquidiocesisacapulco.org.mx.

Archbishop of Antequera, Oaxaca: JOSÉ LUIS CHÁVEZ BOTELLO, García Virgil 600, Anexos de Catedral, Col. Centro, 68000 Oaxaca, Oax.; tel. (951) 516-4822; fax (951) 514-1348; e-mail arzobispadooaxaca@hotmail.com; internet arquidiocesisoaxaca.org.mx.

Archbishop of Chihuahua: CONSTANCIO MIRANDA WECKMANN, Arzobispado, Avda Cuauhtémoc 1828, Apdo 7, Col. Cuauhtémoc, 31020 Chihuahua, Chih.; tel. (614) 410-3202; fax (614) 410-5621; e-mail ferar@megalink.com.mx; internet www.arquichi.org.mx.

Archbishop of Durango: HÉCTOR GONZÁLEZ MARTÍNEZ, Arzobispado, 20 de Noviembre 306, Poniente Centro, 34000 Durango, Dgo; tel. (618) 811-4242; fax (618) 812-8881; e-mail arqdgo@prodigy.net.mx.

Archbishop of Guadalajara: Cardinal JUAN SANDOVAL IÑIGUEZ, Arzobispado, Liceo 17, Apdo 1-331, Col. Centro, 44100 Guadalajara, Jal.; tel. (33) 3614-5504; fax (33) 3658-2300; e-mail arzgdl@arquinet.com.mx; internet www.arquidiocesisgdl.org.mx.

Archbishop of Hermosillo: JOSÉ ULISES MACÍAS SALCEDO, Arzobispado, Dr Paliza y Ocampo, Ala Sur de la Catedral, Col. Centenario, 83260 Hermosillo, Son.; tel. (662) 213-2138; fax (662) 213-1327; e-mail arzohmo@hotmail.com; internet www.iglesiahermosillo.com.mx.

Archbishop of Jalapa: HIPÓLITO REYES LARIOS, Arzobispado, Avda Manuel Avila Camacho 73, Apdo 359, Col. Centro, 91000 Jalapa, Ver.; tel. (228) 812-0579; fax (228) 817-5578; e-mail arzobispadoalxal@prodigy.net.mx.

Archbishop of León: JOSÉ GUADALUPE MARTÍN RÁBAGO, Arzobispado, Pedro Moreno 312, Apdo 108, 37000 León, Gto; tel. (477) 713-2747; fax (477) 713-1286; e-mail canciller@arquidiocesisleon.org.mx; internet www.arquidiocesisdeleon.org.mx.

Archbishop of Mexico City: Cardinal NORBERTO RIVERA CARRERA, Curia del Arzobispado de México, Durango 90, 5°, Col. Roma, Apdo 24433, 06700 México, DF; tel. (55) 5208-3200; fax (55) 5208-5350; e-mail arzobisp@arquidiocesismexico.org.mx; internet www.arzobispadomexico.org.mx.

Archbishop of Monterrey: Cardinal FRANCISCO ROBLES ORTEGA, Zuazua 1100 Sur con Ocampo Centro, Apdo 7, 64000 Monterrey, NL; tel. (81) 1158-2450; fax (81) 1158-2488; e-mail cancilleria@arquidiocesismty.org; internet www.arquidiocesismty.org.mx.

Archbishop of Morelia: ALBERTO SUÁREZ INDA, Arzobispado, Costado Catedral, Frente Avda Madero, Apdo 17, 58000 Morelia, Mich.; tel. (443) 313-2493; fax (443) 312-0919; e-mail asuarexi@prodigy.net.mx; internet www.arquimorelia.org.mx.

Archbishop of Puebla de los Angeles: VÍCTOR SÁNCHEZ ESPINOSA, Avda 2 Sur 305, Apdo 235, Col. Centro, 72000 Puebla, Pue.; tel. (222) 232-4591; fax (222) 246-2277; e-mail rhuesca@mail.cem.org.mx.

Archbishop of San Luis Potosí: LUIS MORALES REYES, Arzobispado, Francisco Madero 300, Apdo 1, Col. Centro, 78000 San Luis Potosí, SLP; tel. (444) 812-4555; fax (444) 812-7979; e-mail arqsanluis@iglesiapotosina.org; internet www.iglesiapotosina.org.

Archbishop of Tijuana: RAFAEL ROMO MUÑOZ, Arzobispado, Calle Décima y Avda Ocampo 8525, Apdo 226, 22000 Tijuana, BC; tel. (664) 684-8411; fax (664) 684-7683; internet www.iglesiatijuana.org.

Archbishop of Tlalnepantla: CARLOS AGUIAR RETES, Arzobispado, Avda Juárez 42, Apdo 268, Col. Centro, 54000 Tlalnepantla, Méx.; tel. (55) 5565-3944; fax (55) 5565-2751; e-mail curia@arqtlalnepantla.org; internet www.arqtlalnepantla.org.

Archbishop of Tulancingo: DOMINGO DÍAZ MARTÍNEZ, Arzobispado, Plaza de la Constitución, Apdo 14, 43600 Tulancingo, Hgo; e-mail sgamitra@netpac.net.mx.

Archbishop of Tuxtla Gutiérrez: ROGELIO CABRERA LÓPEZ, Uruguay 500A, Col. El Retiro, Apdo 365, 29040 Tuxtla Gutiérrez, Chis; e-mail casaepiscopal@prodigy.net.mx.

Archbishop of Yucatán: EMILIO CARLOS BERLIE BELAUNZARÁN, Arzobispado, Calle 58 501, Col. Centro, 97000 Mérida, Yuc.; tel. (999) 924-7777; fax (999) 923-7983; e-mail aryu@prodigy.net.mx; internet www.arquidiocesisdeyucatan.org.

The Anglican Communion

Mexico is divided into five dioceses, which form the Province of the Anglican Church in Mexico, established in 1995.

Bishop of Cuernavaca: RAMIRO DELGADO VERA, Minerva 1, Col. Delicias, 62431 Cuernavaca, Mor.; tel. and fax (777) 315-2870; e-mail adoc@cableonline.com.mx; internet www.cuernavaca-anglican.org.

MEXICO

Bishop of Mexico City and Primate of the Anglican Church in Mexico: CARLOS TOUCHÉ PORTER, La Otra Banda 40, Avda San Jerónimo 117, Col. San Ángel, 01000 México, DF; tel. and fax (55) 5616-2205; e-mail contacto@iglesiaanglicanademexico.org; internet www.iglesiaanglicanademexico.org.

Bishop of Northern Mexico: MARCELINO RIVERA DELGADO, Simón Bolívar 2005 Nte, Col. Mitras Centro, 64460 Monterrey, NL; tel. (81) 8333-0922; fax (81) 8348-7362; e-mail diocesisdelnorte@att.net.mx.

Bishop of South-Eastern Mexico: BENITO JUÁREZ MARTÍNEZ, Avda de las Américas 73, Col. Aguacatl, 91130 Jalapa, Ver.; tel. and fax (228) 814-6951; e-mail dioste99@aol.com.

Bishop of Western Mexico: LINO RODRÍGUEZ-AMARO, Francisco Javier Gamboa 255, Col. Barrera, 45150 Guadalajara, Jal.; tel. (33) 3615-5070; fax (33) 3615-4413; e-mail iamoccidente@prodigy.net.mx; internet www.iamoccidente.org.mx.

Protestant Churches

According to the 2002 census, some 5% of the population are Protestant or Evangelical Christians.

Iglesia Luterana Mexicana: POB 1-1034, 44101 Guadalajara, Jal.; tel. (33) 3639-7253; e-mail dtrejocoria@hotmail.com; f. 1951; Pres. DANIEL TREJO CORIA; 1,500 mems.

Iglesia Metodista de México, Asociación Religiosa: Miravelle 209, Col. Albert, 03570 México, DF; tel. (55) 5539-3674; e-mail prenapro@iglesia-metodista.org.mx; internet www.iglesia-metodista.org.mx; f. 1930; 55,000 mems; Pres. Rev. MOISÉS VALDERRAMA GÓMEZ; 370 congregations; comprises six episcopal areas.

National Baptist Convention of Mexico: Tlalpan 1035- A, Col. Américas Unidas, 03610 México, DF; tel. (55) 5539-7720; fax (55) 5539-2302; e-mail comunicacion@cnbm.org.mx; internet www.cnbm.org.mx; f. 1903; Pres. Rev. JOSÉ TRINIDAD BONILLA MORALES.

BAHÁ'Í FAITH

National Spiritual Assembly of the Bahá'ís of Mexico: Emerson 421, Col. Chapultepec Morales, 11570 México, DF; tel. (55) 5545-2155; fax (55) 5255-5972; e-mail info@bahaimexico.org; internet www.bahaimexico.org; mems resident in 978 localities.

JUDAISM

According to the 2000 census, the Jewish community numbers 45,260 (less than 1% of the population).

Comité Central de la Comunidad Judía de México: Cofre de Perote 115, Lomas Barrilaco, 11010 México, DF; tel. (55) 5520-9393; fax (55) 5540-3050; e-mail comitecentral@prodigy.net.mx; internet www.tribuna.org.mx; f. 1938; Pres. RAFAEL ZAGA.

The Press

DAILY NEWSPAPERS

México, DF

La Afición: Ignacio Mariscal 23, Apdo 64 bis, Col. Tabacalera, 06030 México, DF; tel. (55) 5546-4780; fax (55) 5546-5852; internet www.laaficion.com; f. 1930; sport; Pres. FRANCISCO A. GONZÁLEZ; circ. 85,000.

La Crónica de Hoy: Londres 36, Col. Juárez, 06600 México, DF; tel. and fax (52) 5512-3429; e-mail suscripciones@cronica.com.mx; internet www.cronica.com.mx; Pres. JORGE KAHWAGI GASTINE; Editorial Dir PABLO HIRIART LE BERT.

Cuestión: Laguna de Mayrán 410, Col. Anáhuac, 11320 México, DF; tel. (55) 5260-0499; fax (55) 5260-3645; internet www.cuestion.com.mx; f. 1980; midday; Dir-Gen. Lic. ALBERTO GONZÁLEZ PARRA; circ. 48,000.

Diario de México: Chimalpopoca 38, Col. Obrera, 06800 México, DF; tel. (55) 5442-6501; fax (55) 5588-4289; e-mail redaccion@diariodemexico.com.mx; internet www.diariodemexico.com.mx; f. 1949; morning; Dir-Gen. FEDERICO BRACAMONTES BAZ; Editorial Dir ABEL MAGAÑA CAMPUZANO; circ. 76,000.

El Economista: Avda Coyoacán 515, Col. del Valle, 03100 México, DF; tel. (55) 5326-5454; fax (55) 5687-3821; e-mail jppadilla@eleconomista.com.mx; internet www.economista.com.mx; f. 1988; financial; Pres. JOSÉ GÓMEZ CAÑIBE; Editor-in-Chief DAVID CUEN; circ. 37,448.

Esto: Guillermo Prieto 7, 1°, Col. San Rafael, Del. Cuauhtémoc, 06470 México, DF; tel. and fax (55) 5566-1511; e-mail esto@oem.com.mx; internet www.esto.com.mx; f. 1941; published by Organización Editorial Mexicana; morning; sport; Dir MARIO VÁZQUEX RAÑA; circ. 400,000, Mondays 450,000.

Excélsior: Paseo de la Reforma 18 y Bucareli 1, Apdo 120 bis, Col. Centro, 06600 México, DF; tel. (55) 5705-4444; fax (55) 5566-0223; e-mail foro@excelsior.com.mx; internet www.excelsior.com.mx; f. 1917; morning; independent; Pres. OLEGARIO VÁZQUEX RAÑA; Dir ERNESTO RIVERA AGUILAR; circ. 200,000.

El Financiero: Lago Bolsena 176, Col. Anáhuac entre Lago Peypus y Lago Onega, 11320 México, DF; tel. (55) 5227-7600; fax (55) 5254-6427; internet www.elfinanciero.com.mx; f. 1981; financial; Dir-Gen. PILAR ESTANDÍA DE CÁRDENAS; circ. 119,000.

El Heraldo de México: Dr Lucio, esq. Dr Velasco, Col. Doctores, 06720 México, DF; tel. (55) 5578-7022; fax (55) 5578-9824; e-mail heraldo@iwm.com.mx; internet www.heraldo.com.mx; f. 1965; morning; Dir-Gen. GABRIEL ALARCÓN VELÁZQUEZ; circ. 209,600.

La Jornada: Avda Cuauhtémoc 1236, Col. Santa Cruz Atoyac, Del. Benito Juárez, 03310 México, DF; tel. (55) 9183-0300; internet www.jornada.unam.mx; f. 1984; morning; Dir-Gen. CARMEN LIRA SAADE; Gen. Man. JORGE MARTÍNEZ JIMÉNEZ; circ. 86,275.

Milenio Diario: México, DF; internet www.milenio.com; publishes Mexico City and regional edns, and a weekly news magazine, *Milenio Semanal*; Pres. FRANCISCO A. GONZÁLEZ; Dir-Gen. FRANCISCO D. GONZÁLEZ A.

Novedades: Balderas 87, esq. Morelos, Col. Centro, 06040 México, DF; tel. (55) 5518-5481; fax (55) 5521-4505; internet www.novedades.com.mx; f. 1936; morning; independent; Pres. and Editor-in-Chief ROMULO O'FARRILL, Jr; Vice-Pres. JOSÉ ANTONIO O'FARRILL AVILA; circ. 42,990, Sundays 43,536.

Ovaciones: Lago Zirahuén 279, 20°, Col. Anáhuac, 11320 México, DF; tel. (55) 5328-0700; fax (55) 5260-2219; e-mail ovaciones@ova.com.mx; internet www.ovaciones.com; f. 1947; morning and evening editions; Pres. and Dir-Gen. MAURICIO VÁZQUEZ RAMOS; circ. 130,000; evening circ. 100,000.

La Prensa: Basilio Vadillo 40, Col. Tabacalera, 06030 México, DF; tel. (55) 5228-9977; fax (55) 5521-8209; e-mail bmedina@la-prensa.com.mx; internet www.la-prensa.com.mx; f. 1928; published by Organización Editorial Mexicana; morning; Pres. and Dir-Gen. MARIO VÁZQUEZ RAÑA; Dir MAURICIO ORTEGA CAMBEROS; circ. 270,000.

Reforma: Avda México Coyoacán 40, Col. Santa Cruz Atoyac, 03310 México, DF; tel. (55) 5628-7100; fax (55) 5628-7188; internet www.reforma.com; f. 1993; morning; Pres. and Dir-Gen. ALEJANDRO JUNCO DE LA VEGA ELIZONDO; circ. 94,000.

El Sol de México: Guillermo Prieto 7, 20°, Col. San Rafael, 06470 México, DF; tel. (55) 5566-1511; fax (55) 5535-5500; e-mail enlinea@elsoldemexico.com.mx; internet www.elsoldemexico.com.mx; f. 1965; published by Organización Editorial Mexicana; morning and midday; Pres. and Dir-Gen. MARIO VÁZQUEZ RAÑA; Man. EDGAR FIERRO GRANADOS; circ. 76,000.

El Universal: Bucareli 8, Apdo 909, Col. Centro, Del. Cuauhtémoc, 06040 México, DF; tel. (55) 5709-1313; fax (55) 5510-1269; e-mail rdirgral@eluniversal.com.mx; internet www.eluniversal.com.mx; f. 1916; morning; independent; centre-left; Pres. JUAN FRANCISCO EALY ORTIZ; Dir-Gen. JUAN FRANCISCO EALY, Jr; circ. 165,629, Sundays 181,615.

Unomásuno: Gabino Barreda 86, Col. San Rafael, México, DF; tel. (55) 1055-5500; fax (55) 5598-8821; e-mail cduran@servidor.unam.mx; internet www.unomasuno.com.mx; f. 1977; morning; left-wing; Pres. NAIM LIBIEN KAUI; Dir JOSÉ LUIS ROJAS RAMÍREZ; circ. 40,000.

PROVINCIAL DAILY NEWSPAPERS

Baja California

El Sol de Tijuana: Rufino Tamayo 4, Zona del Río, 22320 Tijuana, BC; tel. (664) 634-3232; fax (664) 634-2234; e-mail soltij@oem.com.mx; internet www.oem.com.mx/elsoldetijuana; f. 1989; published by Organización Editorial Mexicana; morning; Gen. Man. MARIO VALDÉS HERNÁNDEZ; Dir MIGUEL ANGEL TORRES PONCE; circ. 50,000.

La Voz de la Frontera: Avda Madero 1545, Col. Nueva, Apdo 946, 21100 Mexicali, BC; tel. (686) 562-4545; fax (686) 562-6912; e-mail ramondiaz@lavozdelafrontera.com.mx; internet www.oem.com.mx/lavozdelafrontera; f. 1964; morning; published by Organización Editorial Mexicana; Dir FELIPE DE JESÚS LÓPEZ RODRÍGUEZ; Gen. Man. Lic. MARIO VALDÉS HERNÁNDEZ; circ. 65,000.

Chihuahua

El Diario: Publicaciones Paso del Norte, Avda Paseo Triunfo de la República 2505, Zona Pronaf, 32310 Ciudad Juárez, Chih.; tel. (656) 629-6900; internet www.diario.com.mx; f. 1976; Pres. OSVALDO RODRÍGUEZ BORUNDA.

El Heraldo de Chihuahua: Avda Universidad 2507, Apdo 1515, 31240 Chihuahua, Chih.; tel. (614) 432-3800; fax (614) 413-5625; e-mail elheraldo@buzon.online.com.mx; internet www.oem.com.mx/elheraldodechihuahua; f. 1927; published by Organización Editorial Mexicana; morning; Dir Lic. JAVIER H. CONTRERAS; circ. 27,520, Sundays 31,223.

El Mexicano de Ciudad Juárez: Ciudad Juárez, Chih.; e-mail director@pesquisasenlinea.org; f. 1959; published by Organización

MEXICO

Editorial Mexicana; morning; Dir RAFAEL NAVARRO; Editor-in-Chief JAIME NÚÑEZ; circ. 80,000.

Coahuila

El Siglo de Torreón: Avda Matamoros 1056 Pte, Col. Centro, 27000 Torreón, Coah.; tel. (871) 759-1200; e-mail internet@elsiglodetorreon.com.mx; internet www.elsiglodetorreon.com.mx; f. 1922; morning; Pres. OLGA DE JUAMBELZ Y HORCASITAS; Dir-Gen. ANTONIO IRAZOQUI Y DE JUAMBELZ; circ. 38,611, Sundays 38,526.

Vanguardia: Blvd Venustiano Carranza 1918, esq. con Chiapas, República Oriente, 25280 Saltillo, Coah.; tel. (844) 450-1000; e-mail hola@vanguardia.com.mx; internet www.vanguardia.com.mx; Dir-Gen. DIANA MARÍA GALINDO DE CASTILLA.

Colima

Diario de Colima: Avda 20 de Noviembre 380, 28060 Colima, Col.; tel. (312) 312-5688; internet www.diariodecolima.com; f. 1953; Dir-Gen. HÉCTOR SÁNCHEZ DE LA MADRID; Man. Dir ENRIQUE ZÁRATE CANSECO.

Guanajuato

Correo de Guanajuato: Carreterra Guanajuato—Juventino Rosas Km 9.5, 36260 Guanajuato, Gto; tel. (477) 733-1253; fax (477) 733-0057; e-mail correo@correo-gto.com.mx; internet www.correo-gto.com.mx; Dir-Gen. ARNALDO CUÉLLAR.

El Sol de Salamanca: Faro de Oro 800, 36700 Salamanca, Gto; tel. (464) 647-0144; e-mail aherrera@elsoldeirapuato.com.mx; internet www.elsoldesalamanca.com.mx; published by Organización Editorial Mexicana; Dir-Gen. ALEJANDRO HERRERA SÁNCHEZ.

Jalisco

El Informador: Independencia 300, Apdo 3 bis, 44100 Guadalajara, Jal.; tel. (33) 3678-7700; e-mail webmanager@informador.com.mx; internet www.informador.com.mx; f. 1917; morning; Editor JORGE ÁLVAREZ DEL CASTILLO; circ. 50,000.

El Occidental: Calzada Independencia Sur 324, Apdo 1-699, 44100 Guadalajara, Jal.; tel. (33) 3613-0690; fax (33) 3613-6796; e-mail silvia@eloccidental.com.mx; internet www.eloccidental.com.mx; f. 1942; published by Organización Editorial Mexicana; morning; Pres. and Dir-Gen. MARIO VÁSQUEZ RAÑA; Dir JAVIER VALLE CHÁVEZ; circ. 49,400.

México

ABC: Avda Hidalgo Oriente 1339, Centro Comercial, Col. Ferrocarriles Nacionales, 50070 Toluca, Méx.; tel. (722) 217-9880; fax (722) 217-8402; e-mail miled1@mail.miled.com; internet www.miled.com; f. 1984; morning; Pres. and Editor MILED LIBIEN KAUI; circ. 65,000.

Diario de Toluca: Allende Sur 209, 50000 Toluca, Méx.; tel. (722) 215-9105; fax (722) 214-1523; f. 1980; also publishes *Siete Días* and *El Noticiero*; morning; Pres. ANUAR MACCISE DIB; circ. 22,200.

El Heraldo de Toluca: Salvador Díaz Mirón 700, Col. Sánchez Colín, 50150 Toluca, Méx.; tel. (722) 217-3542; fax (722) 212-2535; e-mail editotol@prodigy.net.mx; internet www.heraldotoluca.com; f. 1955; morning; Editor ALBERTO BARRAZA SÁNCHEZ; circ. 90,000.

El Sol de Toluca: Santos Degollado 105, Apdo 54, Col. Centro, 50050 Toluca, Méx.; tel. (722) 214-7077; fax (722) 215-2564; internet www.oem.com.mx/elsoldetoluca; f. 1947; published by Organización Editorial Mexicana; morning; Dir RAFAEL VILCHIS GIL DE ARÉVALO; circ. 42,000.

Michoacán

La Voz de Michoacán: Blvd del Periodismo 1270, Col. Arriaga Rivera, Apdo 121, 58190 Morelia, Mich.; tel. (443) 327-3712; fax (443) 327-3728; e-mail jcgonzalez@voznet.com.mx; internet www.vozdemichoacan.com.mx; f. 1948; morning; Dir-Gen. MIGUEL MEDINA ROBLES; circ. 50,000.

Morelos

El Diario de Morelos: Morelos Sur 132, Col. Las Palmas, 62050 Cuernavaca, Mor.; tel. and fax (777) 362-0220; e-mail redaccion@diariodemorelos.com; internet www.diariodemorelos.com; f. 1978; morning; Propr Grupo BRACA de Comunicación; CEO and Editor-in-Chief MIGUEL BRACAMONTES; circ. 35,000.

Nayarit

Meridiano de Nayarit: Independencia 335, Fracc. Las Aves, Tepic, Nay.; tel. (311) 210-3211; e-mail ventas@meridiano.com.mx; internet meridiano.nayaritpuntocom.com; f. 1942; morning; Dir Dr DAVID ALFARO; circ. 60,000.

Nuevo León

ABC: Platón Sánchez Sur 411, 64000 Monterrey, NL; tel. (81) 8344-2510; fax (81) 8344-5990; f. 1985; morning; Dir-Gen. GONZALO ESTRADO TORRES; circ. 40,000, Sundays 45,000.

El Norte: Washington 629 Oeste, Apdo 186, 64000 Monterrey, NL; tel. (81) 8150-8100; fax (81) 8343-2476; internet www.elnorte.com.mx; f. 1938; morning; Man. Dir ALEJANDRO JUNCO DE LA VEGA; circ. 133,872, Sundays 154,951.

El Porvenir: Galeana Sur 344, Apdo 218, 64000 Monterrey, NL; tel. (81) 8345-4080; fax (81) 8345-7795; internet www.elporvenir.com.mx; f. 1919; morning; Dir-Gen. JOSÉ GERARDO CANTÚ ESCALANTE; circ. 75,000.

Oaxaca

El Imparcial: Armenta y López 312, Apdo 322, 68000 Oaxaca, Oax.; tel. (951) 516-2812; fax (951) 514-7020; e-mail subdireccion@imparcialenlinea.com; internet www.imparoax.com.mx; f. 1951; morning; Dir-Gen. BENJAMÍN FERNÁNDEZ PICHARDO; circ. 17,000, Sundays 20,000.

Puebla

La Opinión: 3 Oriente 1207, Barrio del Analco, 238 Puebla, Pue.; tel. (222) 246-4358; fax (222) 232-7772; internet www.opinion.com.mx; f. 1924; morning; Dir-Gen. OSCAR LÓPEZ MORALES; circ. 40,000.

El Sol de Puebla: Avda 3 Oriente 201, Col. Centro, 72000 Puebla, Pue.; tel. (222) 514-3300; fax (222) 246-0869; e-mail elsoldepuebla@elsoldepuebla.com.mx; internet www.oem.com.mx/elsoldepuebla; f. 1944; published by Organización Editorial Mexicana; morning; Dir SERAFÍN SALAZAR ARELLANO; circ. 67,000.

San Luis Potosí

El Heraldo: Villerías 305, 78000 San Luis Potosí, SLP; tel. (444) 812-3312; fax (444) 812-2081; e-mail redaccion@elheraldoslp.com.mx; internet www.elheraldoslp.com.mx; f. 1954; morning; Dir-Gen. ALEJANDRO VILLASANA MENA; circ. 60,620.

Pulso: Galeana 485, Centro, 78000 San Luis Potosí, SLP; tel. (444) 812-7575; fax (444) 812-3525; internet www.pulsoslp.com.mx; morning; Dir-Gen. PABLO VALLADARES GARCÍA; circ. 60,000.

El Sol de San Luis: Avda Universidad 565, Apdo 342, 78000 San Luis Potosí, SLP; tel. and fax (444) 812-4412; internet www.oem.com.mx/elsoldesanluis; f. 1952; published by Organización Editorial Mexicana; morning; Dir JOSÉ ANGEL MARTÍNEZ LIMÓN; circ. 60,000.

Sinaloa

El Debate de Culiacán: Madero 556 Pte, 80000 Culiacán, Sin.; tel. (667) 716-6353; fax (667) 715-7131; e-mail andrea.miranda@lai.com.mx; internet www.debate.com.mx; f. 1972; morning; Dir ROSARIO I. OROPEZA; circ. 23,603, Sundays 23,838.

Noroeste Culiacán: Grupo Periódicos Noroeste, Angel Flores 282 Oeste, Apdo 90, 80000 Culiacán, Sin.; tel. (667) 759-8100; fax (667) 712-8006; e-mail direccion@noroeste.com.mx; internet www.noroeste.com.mx; f. 1973; morning; Dir-Gen. BEATRIZ BECERRA GONZÁLEZ; Editor RODOLFO DIAZ; circ. 35,000.

El Sol de Sinaloa: Blvd G. Leyva Lozano y Corona 320, Apdo 412, 80000 Culiacán, Sin.; tel. (667) 713-1621; fax (667) 713-1800; internet www.elsoldesinaloa.com.mx; f. 1956; published by Organización Editorial Mexicana; morning; Dir JORGE LUIS TÉLLEZ SALAZAR; circ. 30,000.

Sonora

Expreso: Blvd Abelardo L Rodirquez 16, Col. San Benito, 83190 Hermosillo, Son.; tel. (662) 108-3000; fax (662) 108-3006; e-mail romandia@expreso.com.mx; internet www.expreso.com.mx; f. 2005; Dir-Gen. LUIS ROMANDIA; circ. 17,000, Sundays 18,000.

El Imparcial: Sufragio Efectivo y Mina 71, Col. Centro, Apdo 66, 83000 Hermosillo, Son.; tel. (662) 259-4700; fax (662) 217-4483; e-mail lector@elimparcial.com; internet www.elimparcial.com; f. 1937; morning; Pres. and Dir-Gen. JUAN F. HEALY; circ. 32,083, Sundays 32,444.

Tabasco

Tabasco Hoy: Avda de los Ríos 206, Col. Tabasco 2000, 86035 Villahermosa, Tab.; tel. (993) 316-2135; internet www.tabascohoy.com.mx; f. 1987; morning; Dir-Gen. MIGUEL CANTÓN ZETINA; circ. 50,000.

Tamaulipas

El Bravo: Morelos y Primera 129, Apdo 483, 87300 Matamoros, Tamps; tel. (871) 816-0100; fax (871) 816-2007; e-mail comenta@elbravo.com.mx; f. 1951; morning; Pres. and Dir-Gen. JOSÉ CARRETERO BALBOA; circ. 60,000.

MEXICO

El Diario de Nuevo Laredo: González 2409, Apdo 101, 88000 Nuevo Laredo, Tamps; tel. (867) 711-5500; fax (867) 712-8221; internet www.diario.net; f. 1948; morning; Editor RUPERTO VILLARREAL MONTEMAYOR; circ. 68,130, Sundays 73,495.

Expresión: Calle 3 y Novedades 3, Col. Periodistas, 87457 Matamoros, Tamps; tel. (868) 817-9555; fax (868) 817-3307; e-mail xpresion@prodigy.net.mx; morning; Dir-Gen. MIGUEL GARAY AVILA; circ. 50,000.

El Mañana: Juárez y Perú, Col. Juárez, Nuevo Laredo, Tamps; tel. (867) 711-9900; fax (867) 715-0405; e-mail mauricio.deleon@elmanana.com.mx; internet www.elmanana.com.mx; f. 1932; morning; Pres. NINFA DEÁNDAR MARTÍNEZ; Editor HERIBERTO CANTÚ DEÁNDAR; circ. 16,473, Sundays 20,957.

El Mañana de Reynosa: Calle Matías Canales 504, Apdo 14, Col. Ribereña, 88620 Ciudad Reynosa, Tamps; tel. (899) 921-9950; fax (899) 924-9348; internet www.elmananarey.com.mx; f. 1949; morning; Chief Editors HERIBERTO DEÁNDAR ROBINSON, HILDEBRANDO DEÁNDAR AYALA; circ. 52,000.

Prensa de Reynosa: Matamoros y González Ortega, Zona Centro, 88500 Reynosa, Tamps; tel. (899) 922-0299; fax (899) 922-2412; e-mail prensa_88500@yahoo.com; internet www.prensadereynosa.com; f. 1963; morning; Dir-Gen. FÉLIX GARZA ELIZONDO; circ. 60,000.

El Sol de Tampico: Altamira 311 Pte, Apdo 434, 89000 Tampico, Tamps; tel. (833) 212-1067; fax (833) 212-6821; internet www.oem.com.mx/elsoldetampico; f. 1950; published by Organización Editorial Mexicana; morning; Dir-Gen. RUBÉN DÍAZ DE LA GARZA; circ. 77,000.

Veracruz

Diario del Istmo: Avda Hidalgo 1115, Col. Centro, 96400 Coatzacoalcos, Ver.; tel. (921) 211-8000; e-mail info@istmo.com.mx; internet www.diariodelistmo.com; f. 1979; morning; Dir-Gen. HÉCTOR ROBLES BARAJAS; circ. 64,600.

El Dictamen: 16 de Septiembre y Arista, 91700 Veracruz, Ver.; tel. (229) 931-1745; fax (229) 931-5804; e-mail dovali@hotmail.com; internet www.eldictamen.com.mx; f. 1898; morning; Pres. BERTHA ROSALIA MALPICA DE AHUED; circ. 25,000, Sundays 28,000.

La Opinión: Poza Rica de Hidalgo, Ver.; e-mail publicidad@laopinion.com.mx; internet www.laopinion.com.mx; Dir ABEL ANDRADE LICONA.

Yucatán

Diario de Yucatán: Calle 60 521, 97000 Mérida, Yuc.; tel. (999) 942-2222; fax (999) 942-2204; internet www.yucatan.com.mx; f. 1925; morning; Dir-Gen. CARLOS R. MENÉNDEZ NAVARRETE; circ. 54,639, Sundays 65,399.

Por Esto!: Calle 60, No 576 entre 73 y 71, 97000 Mérida, Yuc.; tel. (999) 24-7613; fax (999) 28-6514; e-mail redaccion@poresto.net; internet www.poresto.net; f. 1991; morning; Dir-Gen. MARIO RENATO MENÉNDEZ RODRÍGUEZ; circ. 26,985, Sundays 28,727.

Zacatecas

Imagen: Calzada Revolución 24, Col. Tierra y Libertad, 98600 Guadalupe, Zac.; tel. and fax (492) 923-8898; e-mail buzon@imagenzac.com.mx; internet www.imagenzac.com.mx; Dir-Gen. EUGENIO MERCADO.

SELECTED WEEKLY NEWSPAPERS

El Heraldo Bajio: Hermanos Aldama 222, Apdo 299, Zona Centro, 37000 León, Gto; tel. (477) 719-8800; e-mail heraldo@el-heraldo-bajio.com.mx; internet www.el-heraldo-bajio.com.mx; f. 1957; Pres. and Dir-Gen. MAURICIO BERCÚN LÓPEZ; circ. 85,000.

Segundamano: Insurgentes Sur 619, Col. Nápoles, Del. Benito Juárez, 03810 México, DF; tel. (55) 5350-7070; e-mail soporte@segundamano.com.mx; internet www.segundamano.com.mx; f. 1986; Dir-Gen. LUIS MAGAÑA MAGAÑA; circ. 105,000.

Zeta: Avda las Américas 4633, Fraccionamiento El Paraíso, Tijuana, BC; tel. (664) 681-6913; fax (664) 621-0065; e-mail Asistente@zetatijuana.com; internet www.zetatijuana.com; f. 1980; news magazine; Editor ADELA NAVARRO.

SELECTED PERIODICALS

Boletín Industrial: Luis Khune 55-B, Col. Las Águilas, 01710 México, DF; tel. (55) 5337-2200; fax (55) 5337-2230; e-mail hvalades@boletinindustrial.com; internet www.boletinindustrial.com; f. 1983; publ. by Editorial Nova SA de CV; monthly; Pres. HUMBERTO VALADÉS; circ. 37,200.

Casas & Gente: Amsterdam 112, Col. Hipódromo Condesa, 06100 México, DF; tel. (55) 5286-7794; fax (55) 5211-7112; e-mail informac@casasgente.com; internet www.casasgente.com; 10 a year; interior design; Dir-Gen. IGNACIO DÍAZ SÁNCHEZ.

Contenido: Darwin 101, Col. Anzures, 11590 México, DF; tel. (55) 5531-3162; fax (55) 5545-7478; e-mail contenido@contenido.com.mx; internet www.contenido.com.mx; f. 1963; monthly; popular appeal; Editor-in-Chief MARIANA CHAVEZ RODRÍGUEZ; circ. 124,190.

Cosmopolitan México: Vasco de Quiroga 2000, Col. Santa Fe, Del. Alvaro Obregón, 01210 México, DF; tel. (55) 5261-2600; fax (55) 5261-2704; internet www2.esmas.com/cosmopolitan; f. 1973; fortnightly; women's magazine; Dir SARA MARÍA CASTANY; circ. 300,000.

Expansión: Avda Constituyentes 956, Col. Lomas Altas, 11950 México, DF; tel. and fax (55) 9177-4100; e-mail quien@expansion.com.mx; internet www.expansion.com.mx; fortnightly; business and financial; Editor ARMANDO TALAMANTES.

Fama: Avda Eugenio Garza Sada 2245 Sur, Col. Roma, Apdo 3128, 64700 Monterrey, NL; tel. (81) 8359-2525; internet www.revistafama.com; fortnightly; show business; Pres. JESÚS D. GONZÁLEZ; Dir RAÚL MARTÍNEZ; circ. 350,000.

Gaceta Médica de México: Academia Nacional de Medicina, Unidad de Congresos del Centro Médico Nacional Siglo XXI, Bloque B, Avda Cuauhtémoc 330, Col. Doctores, 06725 México, DF; tel. (55) 5578-2044; fax (55) 5578-4271; internet www.medigraphic.com; f. 1864; every 2 months; journal of the Academia Nacional de Medicina de México; Editor ALFREDO ULLOA AGUIRRE; circ. 20,000.

Kena Mensual: Río Balsas 101, Col. Cuauhtémoc, 06500 México, DF; tel. (55) 5442-9600; e-mail corporativo@grupoarmonia.com.mx; f. 1977; fortnightly; women's interest; Editor GINA URETA; circ. 100,000.

Letras Libres: Chilaque 9, Col. San Diego Churubusco, 04120 México, DF; tel. (55) 9183-7800; fax (55) 9183-7836; e-mail revista@letraslibres.infonegocio.com; internet www.letraslibres.com; monthly; culture; Dir ENRIQUE KRAUZE.

Manufactura: Avda Constituyentes 956, esq. Rosaleda, Col. Lomas Altas, 11950 México, DF; tel. (55) 9177-4369; e-mail valcantara@expansion.com.mx; internet www.manufacturaweb.com; f. 1994; monthly; industrial; Dir-Gen. DAVID LUNA ARELLANO; circ. 25,000.

Marie Claire: Editorial Televisa, SA de CV, Avda Vasco de Quiroga 2000, Edif. E, 3°, Col. Santa Fe, 01210 México, DF; tel. (55) 5261-2622; fax (55) 5261-2733; e-mail mmartinezgom@editorial.televisa.com.mx; internet www.esmas.com/editorialtelevisa; f. 1990; monthly; women's interest; Editor MÓNICA MARTÍNEZ GÓMEZ; circ. 145,000.

Mecánica Popular (Popular Mechanics en Español): Vasco de Quiroga 2000, Col. Santa Fe, Del. Alvaro Obregón, 01210 México, DF; tel. (55) 5447-4711; fax (55) 5261-2705; internet www.mimecanicapopular.com; f. 1947; monthly; crafts and home improvements; Dir ANDRÉS JORGE; circ. 55,000.

Men's Health: Vasco de Quiroga 2000, Col. Santa Fe, Del. Alvaro Obregón, 01210 México, DF; tel. (55) 5261-2645; fax (55) 5261-2733; internet www.menshealth.com.mx; f. 1994; monthly; health; Editor JUAN ANTONIO SEMPERE; circ. 130,000.

Muy Interesante: Vasco de Quiroga 2000, Col. Santa Fe, Del. Alvaro Obregón, 01210 México, DF; tel. (55) 5261-2600; fax (55) 5261-2707; e-mail gsifuentesm@editorial.televisa.com.mx; internet www.esmas.com/editorialtelevisa; f. 1984; monthly; publ. by Editorial Televisa; scientific devt; Dir FRANCISCO VILLASEÑOR; circ. 250,000.

Negocios y Bancos: Bolívar 8-103, Apdo 1907, Col. Centro, 06000 México, DF; tel. (55) 5510-1884; fax (55) 5512-9411; e-mail nego_bancos@mexico.com; f. 1951; fortnightly; business, economics; Dir ALFREDO FARRUGIA REED; circ. 10,000.

Proceso: Fresas 7, Col. del Valle, 03100 México, DF; tel. (55) 5636-2028; e-mail buzon@proceso.com.mx; internet www.proceso.com.mx; f. 1976; weekly; news analysis; Dir RAFAEL RODRÍGUEZ CASTAÑEDA; circ. 98,784.

Quién: Avda Constituyentes 956, Col. Lomas Altas, CP 11950, México, DF; tel. (55) 9177-4100; e-mail quien@expansion.com.mx; internet www.quien.com; fortnightly; celebrity news, TV, radio, films; Editor BLANCA GÓMEZ MORERA.

La Revista Peninsular: Calle 35, 489 x 52 y 54, Zona Centro, Mérida, Yuc.; tel. and fax (999) 926-3014; e-mail direccion@larevista.com.mx; internet www.larevista.com.mx; f. 1988; weekly; news and politics; Dir-Gen. RODRIGO MENÉNDEZ CÁMARA.

Selecciones del Reader's Digest: Avda Prolongación Paseo de la Reforma 1236, 10°, Col. Santa Fe, Del. Alvaro Obregón, 05348 México, DF; tel. (55) 5351-2200; internet www.selecciones.com.mx; f. 1940; monthly; Editor AUDÓN CORIA; circ. 611,660.

Siempre!: Vallarta 20, Col. Tabacalera, 06030 México, DF; tel. and fax (55) 5566-1804; e-mail suscripciones@siempre.com.mx; internet www.siempre.com.mx; f. 1953; weekly; left of centre; Dir Lic. BEATRIZ PAGÉS REBOLLAR DE NIETO; circ. 100,000.

Tele-Guía: Vasco de Quiroga 2000, Col. Santa Fe, Del. Alvaro Obregón, 01210 México, DF; tel. (55) 5261-2600; fax (55) 5261-

MEXICO

2704; internet www.esmas.com/editorialtelevisa; f. 1952; weekly; television guide; Editor María Eugenia Hernández; circ. 375,000.

Tiempo Libre: Holbein 75 bis, Col. Nochebuena Mixcoac, Del. Benito Juárez, 03720 México, DF; tel. (55) 5611-2884; fax (55) 5611-3982; e-mail buzon@tiempolibre.com.mx; internet www.tiempolibre.com.mx; f. 1980; weekly; entertainment guide; Dir Juan Alberto Becerra; Editor Alicia Labra Gómez; circ. 95,000.

Tú: Vasco de Quiroga 2000, Col. Santa Fe, Del. Alvaro Obregón, 01210 México, DF; tel. (55) 5261-2600; fax (55) 5261-2730; internet www.esmas.com/editorialtelevisa; f. 1980; monthly; teenage; Editor María Antonieta Salamanca; circ. 250,000.

TV y Novelas: Vasco de Quiroga 2000, Col. Santa Fe, Del. Alvaro Obregón, 01210 México, DF; tel. (55) 5261-2600; fax (55) 5261-2704; f. 1982; weekly; television guide and short stories; Dir Jesús Gallegos; circ. 460,000.

Ultima Moda: Morelos 16, 6°, Col. Centro, 06040 México, DF; tel. (55) 5518-5481; fax (55) 5512-8902; e-mail revista_ultimamoda@yahoo.com.mx; f. 1966; monthly; fashion; Pres. Romulo O'Farrill, Jr; Gen. Man. Lic. Samuel Podolsky Rapoport; circ. 110,548.

Vanidades: Vasco de Quiroga 2000, Col. Santa Fe, Del. Alvaro Obregón, 01210 México, DF; tel. (55) 5261-2600; fax (55) 5261-2704; e-mail vanidades@editorialtelevisa.com; internet www.esmas.com/vanidades; f. 1961; fortnightly; women's magazine; Dir Jaqueline Blanco; circ. 290,000.

Vogue (México): Condé Nast México, México, DF; tel. (55) 5095-8076; fax (55) 5245-7109; f. 1999; monthly; women's fashion; circ. 208,180.

ASSOCIATIONS

Asociación Nacional de Periodistas y Comunicadores, A.C.: Luis G. Obregón 17, Of. 209, Col. Centro, 06020 México, DF; tel. (55) 5341-1523; Pres. Moisés Huerta.

Federación de Asociaciones de Periodistas Mexicanos (Fapermex): Humboldt 5, Col. Centro, 06030 México, DF; tel. (55) 5510-2679; e-mail fapermexmail@gmail.com; internet www.fapermex.com; Pres. Roberto Piñón Olivas; 88 mem. asscns; c. 9,000 mems.

Federación Latinoamericana de Periodistas (FELAP): Nuevo Leon 144, 1°, Col. Hipódromo Condesa, 06170 México, DF; tel. (55) 5286-6055; fax (55) 5286-6085; internet www.ciap-felap.org; Pres. Juan Carlos Camaño; Sec.-Gen. José Rafael Vargas.

Fraternidad de Reporteros de México (FREMAC): Avda Juárez 88, Col. Centro, Del. Cuauhtémoc, México, DF; e-mail info@fremac.org.mx; internet www.fremac.org.mx; f. 1995; Sec.-Gen. Marcela Yarce Viveros.

NEWS AGENCIES

Agencia de Información Integral Periodística (AIIP): Tabasco 263, Col. Roma, Del. Cuauhtémoc, 06700 México, DF; tel. and fax (55) 5440-5284; e-mail aiipmx@aiip.com.mx; internet www.aiip.com.mx; f. 1987; Dir-Gen. Miguel Herrera López.

Agencia Mexicana de Información (AMI): Avda Cuauhtémoc 16, Col. Doctores, 06720 México, DF; tel. (55) 5761-9933; e-mail info@red-ami.com; internet www.ami.com.mx; f. 1971; Dir-Gen. José Luis Becerra López; Gen. Man. Eva Vázquez López.

Notimex, SA de CV: Morena 110, 3°, Col. del Valle, 03100 México, DF; tel. (55) 5420-1163; fax (55) 5420-1188; e-mail ventas@notimex.com.mx; internet www.notimex.com.mx; f. 1968; services to press, radio and television in Mexico and throughout the world; Dir-Gen. Sergio Uzeta Murcio.

Publishers

MÉXICO, DF

Alfaomega Grupo Editor, SA de CV: Pitágoras 1139, Col. Del Valle, Del. Benito Juárez, 03100 México, DF; tel. (55) 5575-5022; fax (55) 5575-2420; e-mail atencioncliente@alfaomega.com.mx; internet www.alfaomega.com.mx; engineering, management, technology and computing; Dir Alberto Umaña Carrizosa.

Arbol Editorial, SA de CV: Avda Cuauhtémoc 1430, Col. Santa Cruz Atoyac, Del. Benito Juárez, 03310 México, DF; tel. (55) 5605-7677; fax (55) 5605-7600; e-mail editorialpax@maxis.com; internet www.arboleditorial.com.mx; f. 1979; health, philosophy, theatre; Man. Dir Gerardo Gally Teomonford.

Artes de México y del Mundo, SA de CV: Córdoba 69, Col. Roma, 06700 México, DF; tel. (55) 5525-5905; fax (55) 5525-5925; e-mail artesdemexico@artesdemexico.com; internet www.artesdemexico.com; f. 1988; art, design, poetry; Dir-Gen. Alberto Ruy Sánchez Lacy.

Cengage Learning Editores, SA. de CV: Avda Santa Fe 505, 12°, Col. Cruz Manca, Del. Cuajimalpa, 05349 México, DF; tel. (55) 1500-6000; fax (55) 1500-6019; e-mail clientes.ca@cengage.com; internet www.cengage.com.mx; educational; Country Man. Pedro Turbay Garrido.

Cidcli, SC (Centro de Información y Desarrollo de la Comunicación y la Literatura Infantiles): Avda México 145-601, Col. Coyoacán, 04100 México, DF; tel. (55) 5659-7524; fax (55) 5659-3186; e-mail elisa@cidcli.com.mx; internet www.cidcli.com.mx; f. 1980; children's literature; Dir Patricia van Rhijn Armida.

Círculo Editorial Azteca, SA: Calle de la Luna 225–227, Col. Guerrero, 06300 México, DF; tel. (55) 5526-1157; fax (55) 5526-2557; e-mail info@circuloeditorialazteca.com.mx; internet www.circuloeditorialazteca.com.mx; f. 1956; part of Grupo Salinas; religion, literature and technical; Man. Dir Josefina Larragoiti.

Ediciones B México, SA de CV: Bradley 52, Anzures, Del. Miguel Hidalgo, 11590 México, DF; tel. (55) 1101-0660; fax (55) 5254-0569; e-mail info@edicionesb.com; internet www.edicionesb.mx; general fiction; Dir Carlos Graef Sánchez.

Ediciones Era, SA de CV: Calle del Trabajo 31, Col. La Fama, Tlalpan, 14269 México, DF; tel. (55) 5528-1221; fax (55) 5606-2904; e-mail info@edicionesera.com.mx; internet www.edicionesera.com.mx; f. 1960; general and social science, art and literature; Gen. Man. Nieves Espresate Xirau.

Ediciones Larousse, SA de CV: Londres 247, Col. Juárez, Del. Cuauhtémoc, 06600 México, DF; tel. (55) 1102-1300; fax (55) 5208-6225; e-mail larousse@larousse.com.mx; internet www.larousse.com.mx; f. 1965; Dir-Gen. Gerardo Guillermo Guerrero Ibarra.

Editorial Avante, SA de CV: Luis G. Obregón 9, 1°, Apdo 45-796, Col. Centro, 06020 México, DF; tel. (55) 5510-8804; fax (55) 5521-5245; e-mail didactips@editorialavante.com.mx; internet www.editorialavante.com.mx; f. 1948; educational, drama, linguistics; Man. Dir Lic. Mario Alberto Hinojosa Saenz.

Editorial Everest Mexicana, SA: Calzada Ermita Iztapalapa 1681, Col. Barrio San Miguel del Iztapalapa, Apdo 55-570, 09360 México, DF; tel. (55) 5685-3704; fax (55) 5685-3433; e-mail editevem@prodigy.net.mx; f. 1980; general textbooks; Dir José Luis Huidobro León.

Editorial Fondo de Cultura Económica, SA de CV: Carretera Picacho-Ajusco 227, Col. Bosques del Pedregal, Tlalpan, 14200 México, DF; tel. (55) 5227-4672; fax (55) 5227-4659; e-mail director.general@fondodeculturaeconomica.com; internet www.fondodeculturaeconomica.com; f. 1934; economics, history, philosophy, children's books, science, politics, psychology, sociology, literature; Dir Joaquín Díez-Canedo Flores.

Editorial Herder: Tehuantepec 50, esq. con Ures, Col. Roma Sur, Del. Cuauhtemoc, 06760 México, DF; tel. (55) 5523-0105; fax (55) 5669-2387; e-mail herder@herder.com.mx; internet www.herder.com.mx; social sciences; Dir Jan-Cornelius Schulz Sawade.

Editorial Iztaccíhuatl, SA de CV: Miguel E. Schultz, No 21 y 25, Col. San Rafael, 06470 México, DF; tel. (55) 5705-0938; fax (55) 5535-2321; e-mail iztagerencia@editorializtaccihuatl.com.mx; internet www.editorializtaccihuatl.com.mx; Dir Nora María Vieyra Sicilia.

Editorial Jus, SA de CV: Donceles 66, Centro Histórico, México, DF; tel. (55) 9150-1400; fax (55) 5529-0951; e-mail aramos@jus.com.mx; internet www.jus.com.mx; f. 1938; history of Mexico, law, philosophy, economy, religion; Dir Felipe Garrido.

Editorial Lectorum, SA de CV: Calle Centeno 79-A, Col. Granjas Esmeralda, México, DF; tel. (55) 5581-3202; fax (55) 5646-6892; e-mail direccion@lectorum.com.mx; internet www.lectorum.com.mx; humanities, literature and sciences; Dir-Gen. Porfirio Rom Lizarraga.

Editorial Limusa, SA de CV: Balderas 95, 1°, Col. Centro, Del. Cuauhtémoc, 06040 México, DF; tel. (55) 5130-0700; fax (55) 5510-9415; e-mail limusa@noriegaeditores.com; internet www.noriega.com.mx; f. 1962; part of Grupo Noriega Editores; science, technical, textbooks; Dir-Gen. Carlos Bernardo Noriega Arias.

Editorial Orión: Calle Sierra Mojada 325, Lomas de Chapultepec, 11000 México, DF; tel. (55) 5520-0224; f. 1942; archaeology, philosophy, psychology, literature, fiction; Man. Dir Silvia Hernández Baltazar.

Editorial Planeta Mexicana, SA de CV: Avda Presidente Masarik 111, 2°, Col. Chapultepec Morales, Del. Miguel Hidalgo, 11570 México, DF; tel. (55) 3000-6200; fax 3000-6257; e-mail rrodriguez@planeta.com.mx; internet www.editorialplaneta.com.mx; general literature, non-fiction; part of Grupo Planeta (Spain); Grupo Planeta incorporates Destino, Editorial Diana, Editorial Joaquín Mortiz, Emecé, Espasa Calpe, Lunwerg Editores, Martínez Roca, Seix Barral, Temas de Hoy and Timun Mas; Man. Dir Jose Calafell.

Editorial Porrúa Hnos, SA: Argentina 15, 5°, Col. Centro, 06020 México, DF; tel. (55) 5704-7500; fax (55) 5704-7502; e-mail editorial@porrua.com; internet www.porrua.com; f. 1944; general literature; Dir José Antonio Pérez-Porrúa Suárez.

MEXICO

Editorial Progreso, SA de CV: Sabino 275, Col. Santa María la Ribera, Del. Cuauhtémoc, 06400 México, DF; tel. (55) 1946-0620; fax (55) 1946-0649; e-mail dirgeneral@editorialprogreso.com.mx; internet www.progresoeditorial.com.mx; educational; Dir JOAQUÍN FLORES SEGURA.

Editorial Serpentina, SA de CV: Santa Margarita 430, Col. Del Valle, 03100 Mexico, DF; tel. (55) 5559-8338; fax (55) 5575-8362; e-mail editorial@editorialserpentina.com; internet www.editorialserpentina.com; f. 2004; cultural, adolescent and children's literature; Dir ALEJANDRA CANALES UCHA.

Editorial Trillas, SA: Avda Río Churubusco 385 Pte, Col. Xoco, Apdo 10534, 03330 México, DF; tel. (55) 5688-4233; fax (55) 5604-1364; e-mail fernando@trillas.com.mx; internet www.etrillas.com.mx; f. 1954; science, technical, textbooks, children's books; Man. Dir FERNANDO TRILLAS SALAZAR.

Fernández Editores, SA de CV: Eje 1 Pte México-Coyoacán 321, Col. Xoco, 03330 México, DF; tel. (55) 5090-7700; fax (55) 5688-9173; e-mail sfernandez@feduca.com.mx; internet www.fernandezeditores.com.mx; f. 1943; children's literature, textbooks, educational toys; Man. Dir SOFÍA FERNÁNDEZ PEÑA.

Grupo Editorial Patria, SA de CV: Renacimiento 180, Col. San Juan Tlihuaca, Del. Azcapotzalco, 02400 México, DF; tel. (55) 5354-9100; fax (55) 5354-9109; e-mail info@editorialpatria.com.mx; internet www.editorialpatria.com.mx; f. 1933; fiction, general trade, children's books; Pres. CARLOS FRIGOLET LERMA.

McGraw-Hill Interamericana de México, SA de CV: Torre A, 17°, Paseo de la Reforma 1015, Col. Santa Fé, 01376 México, DF; tel. (55) 1500-5000; fax 1500-5159; e-mail adriana_velazquez@mcgraw-hill.com; internet www.mcgraw-hill.com.mx; education, business, science; Man. Dir ANDRÉS RODRÍGUEZ.

Medios Publicitarios Mexicanos, SA de CV: Eugenia 811, Eje 5 Sur, Col. del Valle, 03100 México, DF; tel. (55) 5523-3342; fax (55) 5523-3379; e-mail editorial@mpm.com.mx; internet www.mpm.com.mx; f. 1958; advertising media rates and data; Gen. Man. FERNANDO VILLAMIL ÁVILA.

Ocean Sur Editorial México, SA de CV: 2ª Cerrada de Corola 17, Col. El Reloj, Del. Coyoacán, 04640 México, DF; tel. (55) 5421-4165; fax (55) 5553-5512; e-mail mexico@oceansur.com; internet www.oceansur.com; iberoamerican cultural literature; Dir MIGUEL ÁNGEL AGUILAR.

Petra Ediciones, SA de CV: Calle El Carmen 268, Col. Camino Real, 45040 México, DF; tel. (55) 3629-0832; fax (55) 3629-3376; e-mail petra@petraediciones.com; internet www.petraediciones.com; art, literature, photography and theatre; Dir MARÍA ESPERANZA ESPINOSA BARRAGÁN.

Random House Mondadori, SA de CV: Homero 544, Col. Chapultepec Morales, 11570, México, DF; tel. (55) 3067-8400; e-mail rbanchik@rhmx.com.mx; internet www.randomhousemondadori.com.mx; f. 1954; owned by Mondadori (Italy); general fiction, history, sciences, philosophy, children's books; Man. Dir ROBERTO BANCHIK.

Reverté Ediciones, SA de CV: Río Pánuco 141A, Col. Cuauhtémoc, 06500 México, DF; tel. (55) 5533-5658; fax (55) 5514-6799; e-mail reverte@reverte.com; internet www.reverte.com; f. 1955; science, technical, architecture; Man. Dir RAMÓN REVERTÉ MASCÓ.

Siglo XXI Editores, SA de CV: Avda Cerro del Agua 248, Col. Romero de Terreros, Del. Coyoacán, 04310 México, DF; tel. (55) 5658-7999; fax (55) 5658-7588; e-mail informes@sigloxxieditores.com.mx; internet www.sigloxxieditores.com.mx; f. 1966; art, economics, education, history, social sciences, literature, philology and linguistics, philosophy and political science; Dir-Gen. Dr JAIME LABASTIDA OCHOA; Gen. Man. JOSÉ MARÍA CASTRO MUSSOT.

Universidad Nacional Autónoma de México: Dirección General de Publicaciones y Fomento Editorial, Avda del Imán 5, Ciudad Universitaria, 04510 México, DF; tel. (55) 5622-6572; e-mail corbolgg@libros.unam.mx; internet www.unam.mx; f. 1935; publications in all fields; Dir-Gen. JULIA TAGÜEÑA PARGA.

ESTADO DE MÉXICO

Editorial Gustavo Gili de México, SA: Valle de Bravo 21, Naucalpan, 53050 Méx.; tel. (55) 5560-6011; fax (55) 5360-1453; e-mail info@ggili.com.mx; internet www.ggili.com.mx; f. 1902 in Spain; architecture, design, fashion, art and photography; Dir CARLOS LERMA.

Pearson Educación de México, SA de CV: Atlacomulco 500, 4°, Industrial Atoto, Naucalpan de Juárez, 53519 Méx.; tel. (55) 5387-0700; fax (55) 5358-0808; e-mail alma.vallejo@pearsoned.com; internet www.pearsoneducacion.net; f. 1984; educational books under the imprints Addison-Wesley, Prentice Hall, Allyn and Bacon, Longman and Scott Foresman; Pres. STEVE MARBAN; Dir JAIME ANDRÉS EDUARDO VALENZUELA SOLAR.

ASSOCIATIONS

Cámara Nacional de la Industria Editorial Mexicana: Holanda 13, Col. San Diego Churubusco, Del. Coyoacán, 04120 México, DF; tel. (55) 5688-2011; fax (55) 5604-3147; e-mail contacto@caniem.com; internet www.caniem.com; f. 1964; Pres. VÍCTORICO ALBORES SANTIAGO; Dir-Gen. CARLOS M. ESPINO GAYTÁN.

Centro Mexicano de Protección y Fomento de los Derechos de Autor, SGC: Avda Cuauhtémoc 1486, Despacho 601- A, Col. Santa Cruz Atoyac, Del. Benito Juárez, 03310 México, DF; tel. (55) 5601-3528; fax (55) 5604-9856; e-mail info@cempro.com.mx; internet www.cempro.com.mx; f. 1998; manages intellectual property rights of authors and publrs; Pres. JULIO SANZ; Dir-Gen. VALERIA LEILANI SÁNCHEZ AGUIÑAGA.

Broadcasting and Communications

TELECOMMUNICATIONS

Regulatory Authorities

Comisión Federal de Telecomunicaciones (Cofetel): Bosque de Radiatas 44, 4°, Col. Bosques de las Lomas, Del. Cuajimalpa, 05120 México, DF; tel. and fax (55) 5015-4000; e-mail nuevaimagen@cft.gob.mx; internet www.cofetel.gob.mx; Pres. MONY DE SWANN ADDATI.

Dirección General de Política de Telecomunicaciones y de Radiodifusión: Centro Nacional SCT, Cuerpo C, 1°, Avda Xola y Universidad s/n, Col. Narvarte, Del. Benito Juárez, 03020 México, DF; tel. (55) 5723-9369; fax (55) 5723-9300; e-mail hector.olavarria@sct.gob.mx; internet www.sct.gob.mx; part of Secretariat of State for Communications and Transport; Dir HECTOR OLAVARRÍA TAPIA.

Principal Operators

Alestra: Optima II, Paseo de las Palmas 275, 8°, Col. Lomas de Chapultepec, 11000 México, DF; tel. (55) 8503-5000; internet www.alestra.com.mx; 49% owned by AT&T; Chair. ARMANDO GARZA SADA; Dir-Gen. ROLANDO ZUBIRÁN SHETLER.

América Móvil, SA de CV: Edif. Telcel 2, Lago Alberto 366, Col. Anáhuac, 11320 México, DF; tel. (55) 2581-4449; fax (55) 2581-3948; e-mail daniela.lacuna@americamovil.com; internet www.americamovil.com; f. 2000 as a spin off from Telmex; subsidiaries operate mobile telephone services in 18 countries in the Americas; Chair. PATRICK SLIM DOMIT; CEO DANIEL HAJJ ABOUMRAD.

Telcel: internet www.telcel.com; f. 1978, present name adopted 1989; subsidiary of above, providing mobile services in Mexico; COO PATRICIA RAQUEL HEVIA COTO.

AT&T México: Montes Urales 470, Col. Lomas de Chapultepec, 11000 México, DF; internet www.att.com; Pres. (México) MICHAEL BOWLING.

Axtel: Blvd Díaz Ordáz Km 3.33, Zona Industrial, 66215 San Pedro Garza García, NL; tel. (81) 8114-0000; e-mail contacto@axtel.com.mx; internet www.axtel.com.mx; f. 1993; fixed-line operator; Chair. and CEO TOMÁS MILMO SANTOS.

Grupo Iusacell, SA de CV: Montes Urales No 460, Col. Lomas de Chapultepec, Del. Miguel Hidalgo, 11000 México, DF; tel. (55) 5109-0611; e-mail ateclientes@iusacell.com.mx; internet www.iusacell.com.mx; f. 1992; merger with Unefon announced in 2006; operates mobile cellular telephone network; 74% owned by Móvil Access; Pres. RICARDO BENJAMÍN SALINAS PLIEGO.

Maxcom Telecomunicaciones, SAB de CV: Guillermo González Camarena 2000, Col. Centro Ciudad Santa Fe, Del. Álvaro Obregón, 01210 México, DF; tel. (55) 5147-1111; internet www.maxcom.com; f. 1996; fixed-line operator; Chair. and Exec. Pres. EDUARDO ARROYO; CEO SALVADOR ALVAREZ.

Telecomunicaciones de México (TELECOMM): Torre Central de Telecomunicaciones, Eje Central Lázaro Cárdenas 567, 11°, Ala Norte, Col. Narvarte, Del. Benito Juárez, 03020 México, DF; tel. (55) 5090-1166; fax (55) 1035-2408; e-mail muycerca@telecomm.net.mx; internet www.telecomm.net.mx; govt-owned; Dir-Gen. JAVIER LIZARRAGA GALINDO.

Telefónica México (Movistar México): Prolongación Paseo de la Reforma 1200, Lote B-2, Col. Santa Fe, Cruz Manca, 05348 México, DF; tel. (55) 1616-5000; e-mail francisco.caballero@telefonica.com; internet www.telefonica.com.mx; f. 1924 (in Spain); owned by Telefónica, SA (Spain); fixed, mobile and broadband services; operates telephone service Telefónica Móviles México (movistar), call centre co Atento, and research and devt co Telefónica I+D; Pres. FRANCISCO GIL DÍAZ; Dir FRANCISCO DE ASIS CABALLERO FERNÁNDEZ.

Teléfonos de México, SA de CV (Telmex): Parque Vía 190, Col. Cuauhtémoc, 06599 México, DF; tel. (55) 5222-1212; fax (55) 5545-5500; e-mail ri@telmex.com; internet www.telmex.com.mx; majority-owned by Carso Global Telecom; Pres. CARLOS SLIM DOMIT; Dir-Gen. HÉCTOR SLIM SEADE.

MEXICO

Unefon: Periférico Sur 4119, Col. Fuentes del Pedregal, 14141 México, DF; tel. (55) 8582-5000; e-mail ainfante@unefon.com.mx; internet www.unefon.com.mx; mobile operator; a merger with Grupo Iusacell was announced in Sept. 2006; Pres. RICARDO SALINAS.

BROADCASTING

Regulatory Authority

Dirección General de Sistemas de Radio y Televisión (DGSRT): Roma 41, Col. Juaréz, Del. Cuauhtémoc, 06600 México, DF; tel. (55) 5140-8000; fax (55) 5530-4315; e-mail buzonrtc@segob.gob.mx; internet www.rtc.gob.mx; f. 1977; Dir-Gen. ALVARO LUIS LOZANO GONZÁLEZ.

Radio

There were 1,423 radio stations in Mexico in 2004. Among the most important commercial networks are:

ABC Radio ((XEABC)): Basilio Badillo 29,Col. Tabacalera, Del. Cuauhtémoc, 06030 México, DF; tel. (55) 3640-5210; fax (55) 3640-5277; e-mail rita@abcradio.com.mx; internet www.oem.com.mx/abcradio; Pres. JAVIER MEDINA; Gen. Man. JOSÉ ANTONIO MARTÍNEZ RAMÍREZ.

Corporación Mexicana de Radiodifusión (CMR): Calle Tetitla 23, esq. Calle Coapa, Col. Toriello Guerra, Del. Tlalpan, 14050 México, DF; tel. (55) 5424-6380; fax (55) 5666-5422; e-mail comentarios@cmr.com.mx; internet www.cmr.com.mx; f. 1962; Pres. ENRIQUE BERNAL SERVÍN; Dir-Gen. OSCAR BELTRÁN MARTÍNEZ DE CASTRO.

El Universal Radio: Bucareli 8, Col. Centro, Del. Cuauhtémoc, 06040 México, DF; tel. (55) 5709-1313; e-mail radio@eluniversal.com.mx; internet www.eluniversalradio.com.mx; Man. ROGELIO ARIAS DÍAZ DE LEÓN.

Firme, SA (Funcionamiento Íntegro de Radiodifusoras Mexicanas Enlazadas, SA): Ejercito Nacional 552, Col. Polanco Reforma, 11550 México, DF; tel. (55) 5250-7788; fax (55) 5250-7906; e-mail radiodifusion@firmesa.com.mx; internet www.firmesa.com.mx; f. 1972; Dir-Gen. LUIS IGNACIO SANTIBÁÑEZ FLORES.

Grupo Acir, SA: Monte Pirineos 770, Col. Lomas de Chapultepec, Del. Miguel Hidalgo, 11000 México, DF; tel. (55) 5201-1700; fax (55) 5201-1771; e-mail servicio@grupoacir.com.mx; internet www.grupoacir.com.mx; f. 1965; comprises 140 stations; Exec. Pres. FRANCISCO IBARRA LÓPEZ.

Grupo Imagen Radio: Mariano Escobedo 700, Col Anzures, 11590 México, DF; tel. (55) 5089-9000; fax (55) 5089-9139; e-mail rfml@imagen.com.mx; internet www.imagen.com.mx; Pres. OLEGARIO VÁZQUEZ ALDIR; Dir-Gen. JOSÉ RAÚL MOLINA VARELA.

Grupo Radio Capital: Montes Urales 425, Col. Lomas de Chapultepec, 1000 México, DF; tel. (55) 3099-3000; fax (55) 5202-3370; internet gruporadiocapital.com.mx; f. 1968; operates 12 radio stations; Dir-Gen. LUÍS MACCISE URIBE.

Grupo Radio Centro, SA de CV: Constituyentes 1154, Col. Lomas Atlas, Del. Miguel Hidalgo, 11950 México, DF; tel. (55) 5728-4800; fax (55) 5728-4900; e-mail rcentro@grc.com.mx; internet radiocentro.com.mx; f. 1965; comprises 100 radio stations; Pres. FRANCISCO AGUIRRE GÓMEZ; Dir-Gen. CARLOS AGUIRRE GÓMEZ.

Grupo Radio Digital: Avda Chapultepec 473, 7°, Col. Juárez, Del. Cuahutémoc, 06600 México, DF; tel. (55) 5211-1734; fax (55) 5211-7534; e-mail info@gruporadiodigital.com.mx; internet www.gruporadiodigital.com.mx; operates eight radio stations in four provinces; Dir-Gen. SIMÓN VALANCI BUZALI; Gen. Man. LOURDES SOUSA SMITH.

Grupo Siete Comunicación: Montecito 38, 31°, Of. 33, Col. Nápoles, Del. Benito Juárez, 03810 México, DF; tel. (55) 9000-0787; fax (55) 9000-0747; e-mail jch@gruposiete.com.mx; internet www.gruposiete.com.mx; f. 1997; Pres. Lic. FRANCISCO JAVIER SÁNCHEZ CAMPUZANO; Dir-Gen. PEDRO MOGOYÁN SOLANO.

Instituto Mexicano de la Radio (IMER): Mayorazgo 83, 2°, Col. Xoco, Del. Benito Juárez, 03330 México, DF; tel. (55) 5628-1704; fax (55) 5628-1738; e-mail general@imer.com.mx; internet www.imer.com.mx; f. 1983; Dir-Gen. ANA CECILIA TERRAZAS VALDÉS.

MVS Radio: Mariano Escobedo 532, Col. Anzures, 11590 México, DF; tel. (55) 5203-4574; fax (55) 5255-1425; e-mail eahumada@mvs.com; internet www.mvsradio.com; f. 1968; operates four stations, EXA FM, La Mejor FM, FM Globo and Noticias MVS; Pres. ALEJANDRO VARGAS GUJARDO.

Núcleo Radio Mil (NRM): Prolongación Paseo de la Reforma 115, Col. Paseo de las Lomas, Santa Fe, 01330 México, DF; tel. (55) 5258-1200; e-mail radiomil@rnm.com.mx; internet www.nrm.com.mx; f. 1942; comprises seven radio stations; Pres. and Dir-Gen. EDILBERTO HUESCA PERROTÍN.

Radio Cadena Nacional, SA (RCN): Lago Victoria 78, Col. Granada, 11520 México, DF; tel. (55) 5250-0324; fax (55) 2624-0052; e-mail rcnmex@prodigy.net.mx; internet www.rcn.com.mx; f. 1948; Pres. SERGIO FAJARDO ORTIZ; Gen. Man. GUADALUPE CAMPUZANO.

Radio Educación: Angel Urraza 622, Col. del Valle, 03100 México, DF; tel. (55) 4155-1050; e-mail direccion@radioeducacion.edu.mx; internet www.radioeducacion.edu.mx; f. 1968; Dir-Gen. ANTONIO TENORIO MUÑOZ COTA.

Radio Fórmula, SA: Privada de Horacio 10, Col. Polanco, 11560 México, DF; tel. (55) 5282-1016; e-mail jcoello@grupoformula.com.mx; internet www.radioformula.com.mx; f. 1968 as Radio Distrito Federal; Pres. ROGERIO AZCARRAGA MADERO.

Radio Universidad Nacional Autónoma de México: Adolfo Prieto 133, Col. del Valle, Del. Benito Juárez, 03100 México, DF; tel. (55) 5536-8989; fax (55) 5687-3989; e-mail contacto@radiounam.unam.mx; internet www.radiounam.unam.mx; Dir-Gen. FERNANDO CHAMIZO GUERRERO.

Radiodifusoras Asociadas, SA de CV (RASA): Durango 341, 2°, Col. Roma, 06700 México, DF; tel. (55) 5286-1222; fax (55) 5211-6159; e-mail rasa@rasa.com.mx; internet www.rasa.com.mx; f. 1956; Exec. Pres. JOSÉ LARIS RODRÍGUEZ; Dir-Gen. SARA LARIS RODRÍGUEZ.

Radiópolis, SA de CV: Tlalpan 3000, Col. Espartaco, Del. Coyoacán, 04870 México, DF; tel. (55) 5327-2000; fax (55) 5679-9710; e-mail rrodriguezg@televisa.com.mx; owned by Grupo Televisa and Grupo Prisa; owns 5 radio stations; affiliated to Radiorama, SA de CV (q.v.) in 2004; Dir-Gen. RAÚL RODRÍGUEZ GONZÁLEZ.

Radiorama, SA de CV: Reforma 2620, 2°, Col. Lomas Altas, Del. Miguel Hidalgo, 11950 México, DF; tel. (55) 1105-0000; fax (55) 1105-0002; e-mail grupo@radiorama.com.mx; internet www.radiorama.com.mx; Pres. JAVIER PÉREZ DE ANDA.

Sociedad Mexicana de Radio, SA de CV (SOMER): Paseo de la Reforma 115, 4°, Col. Lomas, Santa Fé, 01330 México, DF; tel. (55) 9177-6660; fax (55) 9177-6677; e-mail somer@somer.com.mx; internet www.somer.com.mx; Dir-Gen. HUMBERTO HUESCA BUSTAMENTE.

Radio Insurgente, the underground radio station of the Ejército Zapatista de Liberación Nacional (EZLN—Zapatistas), is broadcast from south-eastern Mexico. Programmes can be found on www.radioinsurgente.org.

Television

There were 658 television stations in 2004. Among the most important are:

Canal 22: Edif. Pedro Infante, Atletas 2, Col. Country Club, Del. Coyoacán, 04220 México, DF; tel. (55) 2122-9680; fax (55) 5549-1647; e-mail correo@canal22.org.mx; internet www.canal22.org.mx; f. 1993; part of Consejo Nacional para la Cultura y las Artes of the govt; Dir-Gen. IRMA PÍA GONZÁLEZ LUNA CORVERA.

MVS (Multivisión): Blvd Manuel Ávila Camacho 147, Col. Chapultepec Morales, 11510 México, DF; tel. (55) 5283-4300; fax (55) 5283-4314; e-mail jvargas@mvs.com; internet www.mvs.com; subscriber-funded; Pres. JOAQUÍN VARGAS GUAJARDO; Vice-Pres. ERNESTO VARGAS.

Once TV: Carpio 475, Col. Casco de Santo Tomás, 11340 México, DF; tel. (55) 5166-4000; fax (55) 5396-8001; e-mail info@oncetvmexico.ipn.mx; internet www.oncetv.ipn.mx; f. 1959; Dir RAFAEL LUGO SÁNCHEZ.

Tele Cadena Mexicana, SA: Avda Chapultepec 18, 06724 México, DF; tel. (55) 5535-1679; commercial, comprises about 80 stations; Dir JORGE ARMANDO PIÑA MEDINA.

Televisa, SA de CV: Edif. Televicentro, 8°, Avda Chapultepec 28, Col. Doctores, 06724 México, DF; tel. (55) 5709-3333; fax (55) 5709-3021; e-mail imagencorporativa2@televisa.com.mx; internet www.televisa.com; f. 1973; commercial; began broadcasts to Europe via satellite in Dec. 1988 through its subsidiary, Galavisión; 406 affiliated stations; Chair. and CEO EMILIO AZCÁRRAGA JEAN.

Televisión Azteca, SA de CV: Anillo Periférico Sur 4121, Col. Fuentes del Pedregal, 14141 México, DF; tel. (55) 5447-8844; fax (55) 5645-4258; e-mail contacto@tvazteca.com; internet www.tvazteca.com; f. 1992; assumed responsibility for fmr state-owned channels 7 and 13; Pres. RICARDO B. SALINAS PLIEGO; Dir-Gen. MARIO SAN ROMÁN.

Televisión de la República Mexicana: Mina 24, Col. Guerrero, México, DF; tel. (55) 5510-8590; cultural; Dir EDUARDO LIZALDE.

Association

Cámara Nacional de la Industria de Radio y Televisión (CIRT): Avda Horacio 1013, Col. Polanco Reforma, Del. Miguel Hidalgo, 11550 México, DF; tel. (55) 5726-9909; fax (55) 5545-6767; e-mail cirt@cirt.com.mx; internet www.cirt.com.mx; f. 1942; Pres. TRISTÁN CANALES NAJJAR; Dir-Gen. MÓNICA ASPE BERNAL.

MEXICO

Finance

(cap. = capital; res = reserves; dep. = deposits; m. = million; brs = branches; amounts in new pesos unless otherwise stated)

BANKING

The Mexican banking system comprises the Banco de México (the central bank of issue), multiple or commercial banking institutions and development banking institutions. Banking activity is regulated by the Federal Government.

Commercial banking institutions are constituted as *Sociedades Anónimas*, with wholly private social capital. Development banking institutions exist as *Sociedades Nacionales de Crédito*; participation in their capital is exclusive to the Federal Government, notwithstanding the possibility of accepting limited amounts of private capital.

All private banks were nationalized in 1982. By 1992, however, the banking system had been completely returned to the private sector. Legislation removing all restrictions on foreign ownership of banks received congressional approval in 1999.

Supervisory Authority

Comisión Nacional Bancaria y de Valores (CNBV) (National Banking and Securities Commission): Avda Insurgentes Sur 1971, Torre Norte, Sur y III, Col. Guadalupe Inn, Del. Alvaro Obregón, 01020 México, DF; tel. and fax (55) 1454-6000; e-mail info@cnbv.gob.mx; internet www.cnbv.gob.mx; f. 1924; govt commission controlling all credit institutions in Mexico; Pres. GUILLERMO ENRIQUE BABATZ TORRES.

Central Bank

Banco de México (BANXICO): Avda 5 de Mayo 2, Col. Centro, Del. Cuauhtémoc, 06059 México, DF; tel. (55) 5237-2000; fax (55) 5237-2070; e-mail comsoc@banxico.org.mx; internet www.banxico.org.mx; f. 1925; currency issuing authority; became autonomous on 1 April 1994; cap. 6.3m., res -77.2m., dep. 704.9m. (Dec. 2007); Gov. AGUSTÍN CARSTENS CARSTENS; Dir-Gen. DAVID AARON MARGOLÍN SCHABES; 6 brs.

Commercial Banks

Banco del Bajío, SA: Avda Manuel J. Clouthier 508, Col. Jardines del Campestre, 37128 León, Gto; tel. (477) 710-4600; fax (477) 710-4693; e-mail internacional@bancobajio.com.mx; internet www.bancobajio.com.mx; f. 1994; cap. 2,141m., res 5,195m., dep. 55,895m. (Dec. 2008); Pres. SALVADOR OÑATE.

Banco Mercantil del Norte, SA (BANORTE): Avda Revolución 3000, Col. Primavera, 64830 Monterrey, NL; tel. (81) 3319-7200; fax (81) 3319-5216; internet www.banorte.com; f. 1899; merged with Banco Regional del Norte in 1985; cap. 13,409.0m., res 17,379.0m., dep. 308,198.0m. (Dec. 2008); Chair. ROBERTO GONZÁLEZ BARRERA; Dir-Gen. ALEJANDRO VALENZUELA; 457 brs.

Banco Nacional de México, SA (Banamex): Avda Isabel la Católica 44, 06089 México, DF; tel. (55) 5720-7091; fax (55) 5920-7323; e-mail prensa@banamex.com; internet www.banamex.com; f. 1884; transferred to private ownership in 1991; merged with Citibank México, SA in 2001; cap. 30,248.0m., res 53,010.0m., dep. 400,191.0m. (Dec. 2007); CEO MANUEL MEDINA MORA; 1,260 brs.

Banca Santander, SA: Mod 401, 4°, Prolongación Paseo de la Reforma 500, Col. Lomas de Santa Fe, Del. Alvaro Obregon, 01219 México, DF; tel. (55) 5261-1543; fax (55) 5261-5549; internet www.santander.com.mx; f. 1864 as Banco Serfin; acquired by Banco Santander Central Hispano (Spain) in Dec. 2000; adopted current name 2006; cap. 11,091.0m., res 49,053.0m., dep. 407,119.0m. (Dec. 2008); Exec. Pres. and Dir-Gen. MARCOS MARTÍNEZ GAVICA; 554 brs.

BBVA Bancomer, SA: Centro Bancomer, Avda Universidad 1200, Col. Xoco, 03339 México, DF; tel. (55) 5621-3434; fax (55) 5621-3230; internet www.bancomer.com.mx; f. 2000 by merger of Bancomer (f. 1864) and Mexican operations of Banco Bilbao Vizcaya Argentaria (Spain); privatized in 2002; cap. 21,430.0m., res 40,754.0m., dep. 1,009,367.0m. (Dec. 2008); Pres. IGNACIO DESCHAMPS GONZÁLEZ.

HSBC México: Paseo de la Reforma 156, Col. Juárez, Del. Cuauhtémoc, 06600 México, DF; tel. (55) 5721-2222; fax (55) 5721-2393; internet www.hsbc.com.mx; f. 1941; bought by HSBC (United Kingdom) in 2002; name changed from Banco Internacional, SA (BITAL) in 2004; cap. 4,271.6m., res 22,040.6m., dep. 359,574.3m. (Dec. 2008); Dir-Gen. LUIS JAVIER PEÑA KEGEL; 1,400 brs.

Scotiabank Inverlat, SA: Blvd Miguel Avila Camacho 1, 18°, Col. Lomas de Chapultepec, Del. Miguel Hidalgo, 11009 México, DF; tel. (55) 5728-1000; fax (55) 5229-2019; internet www.scotiabankinverlat.com; f. 1977 as Multibanco Comermex, SA; changed name to Banco Inverlat, SA in 1995; 55% holding acquired by Scotiabank Group (Canada) and adopted current name 2001; cap. 7,451.0m., surplus and res 14,833.0m., dep. 121,321.0m. (Dec. 2008); Pres. PETER C. CARDINAL; 476 brs.

Directory

Development Banks

Banco Nacional de Comercio Exterior, SNC (BANCOMEXT): Periférico Sur 4333, Col. Jardines en la Montaña, Del. Tlalpan, 14210 México, DF; tel. (55) 5449-9100; fax (55) 5652-9342; e-mail bancomext@bancomext.gob.mx; internet www.bancomext.com; f. 1937; cap. 15,040.0m., res -6,471.0m., dep. 77,920.0m. (Dec. 2008); Dir-Gen. HÉCTOR RANGEL DOMENE.

Banco Nacional del Ejército, Fuerza Aérea y Armada, SNC (BANJERCITO): Avda Industria Militar 1055, Col. Lomas de Sotelo, Del. Miguel Hidalgo, 11200 México, DF; tel. and fax (55) 5626-0500; e-mail info@banjercito.com.mx; internet www.banjercito.com.mx; f. 1947; Dir-Gen. Gen. FERNANDO MILLÁN VILLEGAS.

Banco Nacional de Obras y Servicios Públicos, SNC (BANOBRAS): Avda Javier Barros Sierra 515, Col. Lomas de Santa Fe, Del. Álvaro Obregón, 01219 México, DF; tel. (55) 5270-1552; fax (55) 5270-1564; internet www.banobras.gob.mx; f. 1933; govt-owned; cap. 11,765.0m., res 1,963.0m., dep. 123,406.0m. (Dec. 2008); Dir-Gen. GEORGINA KESSEL MARTÍNEZ.

Compartamos Banco: Insurgentes Sur 552, Col. Escandón, 11800 México, DF; tel. (55) 5276-7250; fax (55) 5276-7299; e-mail servicioalcliente@compartamos.com; internet www.compartamos.com; f. 1990; Dir-Gen. FERNANDO ALVAREZ TOCA.

Financiera Rural: Agrarismo 227, Col. Escandón, Del. Miguel Hidalgo, CP 11800, México, DF; tel. (55) 5230-1600; internet www.financierarural.gob.mx; f. 2004; state-run devt bank, concerned with agricultural, forestry and fishing sectors; Dir-Gen. ENRIQUE DE LA MADRID CORDERO.

Nacional Financiera, SNC (NAFIN): Insurgentes Sur 1971, Torre IV, 13°, Col. Guadalupe Inn, 01020 México, DF; tel. (55) 5325-6700; fax (55) 5661-8418; e-mail info@nafin.gob.mx; internet www.nafin.com; f. 1934; cap. 7,952.0m., res 4,222.0m., dep. 148,386.0m. (Dec. 2008); Dir-Gen. HÉCTOR RANGEL DOMENE; 32 brs.

BANKERS' ASSOCIATION

Asociación de Bancos de México: 16 de Setiembre 27, 3°, Col. Centro Histórico, 06000 México, DF; tel. (55) 5722-4300; internet www.abm.org.mx; f. 1928; Pres. IGNACIO DESCHAMPS GONZÁLEZ; Dir-Gen. JUAN CARLOS JIMÉNEZ ROJAS; 52 mems.

STOCK EXCHANGE

Bolsa Mexicana de Valores, SA de CV: Paseo de la Reforma 255, Col. Cuauhtémoc, 06500 México, DF; tel. (55) 5726-6000; fax (55) 5726-6836; e-mail cinforma@bmv.com.mx; internet www.bmv.com.mx; f. 1894; Pres. and CEO LUIS TÉLLEZ KUENZLER.

INSURANCE

México, DF

ACE Seguros: Bosques de Alisos, 47A, 1°, Col. Bosques de las Lomas, Del. Cuajimalpa, 05120 México, DF; tel. (5) 5258-5800; fax (5) 5258-5899; e-mail info@acelatinamerica.com; internet www.acelatinamericaRoot/Mexico/; f. 1990; fmrly Seguros Cigna; Pres. and Gen. Man. ROBERTO FLORES.

Aseguradora Cuauhtémoc, SA: Manuel Avila Camacho 164, 11570 México, DF; tel. (55) 5250-9800; fax (55) 5540-3204; f. 1944; general; Exec. Pres. JUAN B. RIVEROLL; Dir-Gen. JAVIER COMPEÁN AMEZCUA.

Grupo Nacional Provincial, SAB: Avda Cerro de las Torres 395, Col. Campestre Churubusco, Del. Coyoacán, 04200 México, DF; tel. (55) 5227-3999; internet www.gnp.com.mx; f. 1936; member of Grupo BAL; general; Chair. ALBERTO BAILLÈRES; CEO ALEJANDRO BAILLÈRES.

ING Mexico: Avda Paseo de la Reforma 222, 4°, 5° y 6°, Col. Juárez 06600, México, DF; tel. (55) 5169-2500; internet www.ing.com.mx; f. 1936 as La Comercial; acquired by ING Group in 2000; life, etc.; CEO JAN HOMMEN.

MetLife: Blvd Manuel Avila Camacho 32, SKY 14–20 y PH, Col. Lomas de Chapultepec, Del. Miguel Hidalgo, 11000 México, DF; tel. (55) 5328-7000; e-mail contacto@metlife.com.mx; internet www.metlife.com.mx; f. 1931 as Aseguradora Hidalgo, acquired by MetLife Inc in 2002; life; CEO ALBERTO VILAR.

Pan American de México, Cía de Seguros, SA: Reforma 355, 8°, Cuauhtémoc, 06500 México, DF; tel. (55) 5525-7024; f. 1940; Pres. Lic. JESS N. DALTON; Dir-Gen. GILBERTO ESCOBEDA PAZ.

Royal & SunAlliance Mexico: Blvd Adolfo López Mateos 2448, Col. Altavista, 01060 México, DF; tel. (55) 5723-7999; fax (55) 5723-7941; e-mail direccion.general@mx.rsagroup.com; internet www.royalsun.com.mx; f. 1941; acquired Seguros BBV-Probursa in 2001; general, except life; Chair. JOHN NAPIER.

Seguros Azteca, SA: Insurgentes Sur 3579, Tlalpan La Joya, 14000 México, DF; tel. (55) 1720-9854; e-mail infoseguros@segurosazteca

MEXICO

.com.mx; internet www.segurosazteca.com.mx; f. 1933, renamed as above in 2003; general including life; Dir-Gen. ALFREDO HONSBERG.

Seguros Banamex, SA: Venustiano Carranza 63, Col. Centro Histórico, Del. Cuauhtémoc, 06000 México, DF; tel. (55) 1226-8100; e-mail sbainternet@banamex.com; internet www.segurosbanamex.com; f. 1994; life, accident and health; Dir-Gen. DANIEL GARDUÑO GUTIÉRREZ.

Seguros La República, SA: Paseo de la Reforma 383, México, DF; f. 1966; general; 43% owned by Commercial Union (United Kingdom); Pres. LUCIANO ARECHEDERRA QUINTANA; Gen. Man. JUAN ANTONIO DE ARRIETA MENDIZÁBAL.

Seguros Monterrey New York Life: Presidente Mazaryk 8, Bosques de Chapultepec, Del. Miguel Hidalgo, México, DF; tel. (55) 5326-9000; fax (55) 5536-9610; e-mail clientes@monterrey-newyorklife.com.mx; internet www.monterrey-newyorklife.com.mx; f. 1940 as Monterrey Cía de Seguros; acquired by New York Life in 2000; casualty, life, etc.; Dir-Gen. MARIO VELA BERRONDO.

Insurance Association

Asociación Mexicana de Instituciones de Seguros, AC (AMIS): Francisco I Madero 21, Col. Tlacopac, San Angel, 01040 México, DF; tel. (55) 5480-0646; fax (55) 5662-8036; e-mail amis@mail.internet.com.mx; internet www.amis.com.mx; f. 1946; all insurance cos operating in Mexico are mems; Pres. JUAN IGNACIO GIL ANTÓN; Dir-Gen. RECAREDO ARIAS JIMÉNEZ.

Trade and Industry

GOVERNMENT AGENCIES

Comisión Federal de Protección Contra Riesgos Sanitarios (COFEPRIS): Monterrey 33, esq. Oaxaca, Col. Roma, Del. Cuauhtémoc, 06700 México, DF; tel. (55) 5080-5200; fax (55) 5207-5521; e-mail mdiosdado@salud.gob.mx; internet www.cofepris.gob.mx; f. 2003; pharmaceutical regulatory authority; Sec.-Gen. (vacant).

Comisión Nacional Forestal (CONAFOR): Carretera a Nogales s/n, esq. Periférico Poniente 5360, 5°, San Juan de Ocotán, 45019 Zapopan, Jal.; tel. (33) 3777-7000; fax (33) 3777-7012; e-mail conafor@conafor.gob.mx; internet www.conafor.gob.mx; f. 2001; Dir-Gen. JUAN MANUEL TORRES ROJO.

Comisión Nacional de Inversiones Extranjeras (CNIE): Dirección General de Inversión Extranjera, Insurgentes Sur 1940, 8°, Col. Florida, 01030 México, DF; tel. (55) 5229-6100; fax (55) 5229-6507; e-mail gcanales@economia.gob.mx; f. 1973; govt commission to co-ordinate foreign investment; Exec. Sec. GREGORIO MANUEL CANALES RAMÍREZ.

Comisión Nacional de los Salarios Mínimos (CNSM): Avda Cuauhtémoc 14, 2°, Col. Doctores, Del. Cuauhtémoc, 06720 México 7, DF; tel. (55) 5998-3800; fax (55) 5578-5775; e-mail cnsm1@conasami.gob.mx; internet www.conasami.gob.mx; f. 1962, in accordance with Section VI of Article 123 of the Constitution; national commission on minimum salaries; Pres. Lic. BASILIO GONZÁLEZ NÚÑEZ.

Instituto Nacional de Investigaciones Nucleares (ININ): Centro Nuclear de México, Carretera México–Toluca Km 36.5, La Marquesa, 52750 Ocoyoacac, Méx.; tel. (55) 5329-7200; fax (55) 5329-7296; e-mail hernan.rico@inin.gob.mx; internet www.inin.mx; f. 1979 to plan research and devt of nuclear science and technology; also researches the peaceful uses of nuclear energy, for the social, scientific and technological devt of the country; administers the Secondary Standard Dosimetry Laboratory and the Nuclear Information and Documentation Centre, which serves Mexico's entire scientific community; operates a tissue culture laboratory for medical treatment; the 1-MW research reactor, which came into operation in 1967, supplies part of Mexico's requirements for radioactive isotopes; also operates a 12-MV Tandem van de Graaff; Mexico has two nuclear reactors, each with a generating capacity of 654 MW; the first, at Laguna Verde, became operational in 1989 and is administered by the Comisión Federal de Electricidad (CFE); Dir-Gen. RAÚL ORTÍZ MAGAÑA.

Instituto Nacional de Pesca (INAPESCA) (National Fishery Institute): Pitágoras 1320, Col. Santa Cruz Atoyac, Del. Benito Juárez, 03310 México, DF; tel. (55) 3871-9517; fax (55) 5604-9169; e-mail gerardo.garcia@inapesca.sagarpa.gob.mx; internet www.inapesca.gob.mx; f. 1962; Dir MIGUEL ANGEL CISNEROS MATA.

Procuraduría Federal del Consumidor (Profeco): Avda José Vasconcelos 208, Col. Condesa, Del. Cuauhtémoc, 06140 México, DF; tel. (55) 5625-6700; internet www.profeco.gob.mx; f. 1975; consumer protection; Procurator ANTONIO MORALES DE LA PEÑA.

Servicio Geológico Mexicano (SGM): Blvd Felipe Angeles, Carretera México–Pachuca, Km 93.50-4, Col. Venta Prieta, 42080 Pachuca de Soto, Hgo; tel. (771) 711-4266; fax (771) 711-4204; e-mail gintproc@sgm.gob.mx; internet www.coremisgm.gob.mx; f. 1957; govt agency for the devt of mineral resources; Dir-Gen. RAFAEL ALEXANDRI RIONDA.

DEVELOPMENT ORGANIZATIONS

Centro de Investigación para el Desarollo, AC (CIDAC) (Centre of Research for Development): Jaime Balmes 11, Edif. D, 2°, Col. Los Morales Polanco, 11510 México, DF; tel. (55) 5985-1010; fax (55) 5985-1030; e-mail info@cidac.org.mx; internet www.cidac.org; f. 1984; researches economic and political devt; Pres. LUIS RUBIO.

Comisión Nacional de las Zonas Aridas (CONAZA): Blvd Isidro López Zertuche 2513, Col. Las Maestros, 25260 Saltillo, Coah.; tel. and fax (844) 450-5200; e-mail contacto@conaza.gob.mx; internet www.conaza.gob.mx; f. 1970; commission to co-ordinate the devt and use of arid areas; Dir-Gen. LUIS CARLOS FIERRO GARCÍA.

Fideicomiso de Fomento Mineiro (FIFOMI): Puente de Tecamachalco 26, 2°, Col. Lomas de Chapultepec, Del. Miguel Hidalgo, 11000 México, DF; tel. (55) 5249-9500; e-mail pguerra@fifomi.gob.mx; internet www.fifomi.gob.mx; trust for the devt of the mineral industries; Dir-Gen. ALBERTO ORTIZ TRILLO.

Fideicomisos Instituídos en Relación con la Agricultura (FIRA): Km 8, Antigua Carretera Pátzcuaro 8555, 58341 Morelia, Mich.; tel. (443) 322-2399; fax (443) 327-6338; e-mail webmaster@correo.fira.gob.mx; internet www.fira.gob.mx; a group of devt funds to aid agricultural financing, under the Banco de México, comprising Fondo de Garantía y Fomento para la Agricultura, Ganadería y Avicultura (FOGAGA); Fondo Especial para Financiamientos Agropecuarios (FEFA); Fondo Especial de Asistencia Técnica y Garantía para Créditos Agropecuarios (FEGA); Fondo de Garantía y Fomento para las Actividades Pesqueras (FOPESCA); Dir RODRIGO SÁNCHEZ MÚJICA.

Fondo de Operación y Financiamiento Bancario a la Vivienda (FOVI): Ejército Nacional 180, Col. Anzures, 11590 México, DF; tel. (55) 5263-4500; fax (55) 5263-4541; e-mail jmartinez@fovi.gob.mx; internet www.fovi.gob.mx; f. 1963 to promote the construction of low-cost housing through savings and credit schemes; devt fund under the Banco de México; Dir-Gen. MANUEL ZEPEDA PAYERAS.

Instituto Mexicano del Petróleo (IMP): Eje Central Lázaro Cárdenas 152, Col. San Bartolo Atepehuacan, Del. Gustavo A. Madero, 07730 México, DF; tel. (55) 9175-6000; fax (55) 9175-8000; e-mail gdgarcia@imp.mx; internet www.imp.mx; f. 1965 to foster devt of the petroleum, chemical and petrochemical industries; Dir JOSÉ ENRIQUE VILLA RIVERA.

CHAMBERS OF COMMERCE

Chambers of Commerce exist in the chief town of each state as well as in the larger centres of commercial activity. There are also other international Chambers of Commerce.

American Chamber of Commerce of Mexico (Amcham): Lucerna 78, Col. Juárez, 06600 México, DF; tel. (55) 5141-3800; fax (55) 5141-3833; e-mail amchammx@amcham.com.mx; internet www.amcham.com.mx; f. 1917; brs in Guadalajara and Monterrey; Exec. Vice-Pres. and Dir-Gen. GUILLERMO WOLF.

Cámara de Comercio, Servicios y Turismo Ciudad de México (CANACO) (Chamber of Commerce, Services and Tourism of Mexico City): Paseo de la Reforma 42, 3°, Col. Centro, Apdo 32005, Del. Cuauhtémoc, 06048 México, DF; tel. (55) 3685-2269; fax (55) 5592-2279; e-mail sos@ccmexico.com.mx; internet www.ccmexico.com.mx; f. 1874; 50,000 mems; Pres. ARTURO MENDICUTI NARRO; Dir-Gen. RICARDO CASADO GUZMÁN.

Cámara Nacional de la Industria de Transformación (CANACINTRA): Avda San Antonio 256, Col. Ampliación Nápoles, Del. Benito Juárez, 06849 México, DF; tel. (55) 5482-3000; fax 5598-8044; e-mail direcciongeneral@canacintra.org.mx; internet www.canacintra.org.mx; represents majority of smaller manufacturing businesses; Pres. SERGIO ENRIQUE CERVANTES RODILES.

Confederación de Cámaras Nacionales de Comercio, Servicios y Turismo (CONCANACO-SERVYTUR) (Confederation of National Chambers of Commerce, Services and Tourism): Balderas 144, 3°, Col. Centro, 06070 México, DF; tel. (55) 5722-9300; e-mail comentarios@concanacored.com; internet www.concanaco.com.mx; f. 1917; Pres. JORGE E. DÁVILA FLORES; Dir-Gen. EDUARDO GARCÍA VILLASEÑOR; comprises 283 regional Chambers.

CHAMBERS OF INDUSTRY

The 47 national chambers, 15 regional chambers, 3 general chambers and 42 associations, many of which are located in the Federal District, are representative of the major industries of the country.

Central Confederation

Confederación de Cámaras Industriales de los Estados Unidos Mexicanos (CONCAMIN) (Confed. of Industrial Chambers):

MEXICO

Manuel María Contreras 133, 4°, Col. Cuauhtémoc, Del. Cuauhtémoc, 06500 México, DF; tel. (55) 5140-7800; fax (55) 5140-7831; e-mail webmaster@concamin.org.mx; internet www.concamin.org.mx; f. 1918; represents and promotes the activities of the entire industrial sector; Pres. ISMAEL PLASCENCIA NÚÑEZ; Dir-Gen. FRANCISCO JAVIER JIMÉNEZ ROJAS; 108 mem. orgs.

INDUSTRIAL AND TRADE ASSOCIATIONS

Asociación Nacional de Importadores y Exportadores de la República Mexicana (ANIERM) (National Association of Importers and Exporters): Monterrey 130, Col. Roma, Del. Cuauhtémoc, 06700 México, DF; tel. (55) 5584-9522; fax (55) 5584-5317; e-mail anierm@anierm.org.mx; internet www.anierm.org.mx; f. 1944; Pres. JOSÉ OTHÓN RAMÍREZ GUTTIÉREZ; Exec. Vice-Pres. HUMBERTO SIMONEEN ARDILA.

Asociación Nacional de la Industria Química (ANIQ): Angel Urraza 505, Col. del Valle, 03100 México, DF; tel. (55) 5230-5100; internet www.aniq.org.mx; f. 1959; chemicals asscn; Dir-Gen. MIGUEL BENEDETTO; c. 200 mem. cos.

Comisión Nacional de Seguridad Nuclear y Salvaguardias (CNSNS): Dr José María Barragán 779, Col. Narvarte, Del. Benito Juárez, 03020 México, DF; tel. (55) 5095-3200; fax (55) 5095-3295; e-mail swaller@cnsns.gob.mx; internet www.cnsns.gob.mx; f. 1979; nuclear regulatory agency; Dir-Gen. JUAN EIBENSCHUTZ HARTMAN.

Comisión Petroquímica Mexicana: México, DF; promotes the devt of the petrochemical industry; Tech. Sec. Ing. JUAN ANTONIO BARGÉS MESTRES.

Consejo Mexicano de Asuntos Internacionales (COMEXI): Oficina 502, Torre Magnum, Sierra Mojada 620, Col. Lomas de Chapultepec, 11000 México, DF; tel. (55) 5202-3776; e-mail info@consejomexicano.org; internet www.consejomexicano.org; Pres. FERNANDO SOLANA.

Consejo Mexicano del Café (CMCAFE): José María Ibarrarán 84, 1°, Col. San José Insurgentes, Del. Benito Juárez, 03900 México, DF; tel. and fax (55) 5611-9075; e-mail cmc@sagar.gob.mx; f. 1993; devt of coffee sector; Pres. JAVIER USABIAGA.

Consejo Mexicano de Comercio Exterior (COMCE): Lancaster 15, 2° y 3°, Col. Juárez, 06600 México, DF; tel. (52) 5231-7100; fax (55) 5321-7109; e-mail direccion@comce.org.mx; internet www.comce.org.mx; f. 1999 to promote international trade; Pres. VALENTÍN DIEZ MORODO.

Consejo Nacional de la Industria Maquiladora y Manufacturera de Exportación (CNIME): Ejército Nacional 418, 12°, Of. 1204, Col. Chapultepec Morales, Del. Miguel Hidalgo, 11570 México, DF; tel. (55) 2282-9900; fax (55) 2282-9902; e-mail dirgral@cnimme.org.mx; internet www.cnimme.org.mx; f. 1975; Pres. LUIS AGUIRRE; Dir-Gen. CARLOS PALENCIA.

Instituto Nacional de Investigaciones Forestales y Agropecuarios (INIFAP) (National Forestry and Agricultural Research Institute): Avda Progreso No 5, Col. Barrio de Santa Catarina, Del. Coyoacán, 04010 México, DF; tel. (55) 3871-8700; e-mail brajcich.pedro@inifap.gob.mx; internet www.inifap.gob.mx; f. 1985; conducts research into plant genetics, management of species and conservation; Dir-Gen. PEDRO BRAJCICH GALLEGOS.

EMPLOYERS' ORGANIZATIONS

Consejo Coordinador Empresarial (CCE): Lancaster 15, Col. Juárez, 06600 México, DF; tel. (55) 5229-1100; fax (55) 5592-3857; e-mail sistemas@cce.org.mx; internet www.cce.org.mx; f. 1976; coordinating body of private sector; Pres. ARMANDO PAREDES ARROYO; Dir-Gen. LUIS MIGUEL PANDO.

Consejo Mexicano de Hombres de Negocios (CMHN): México, DF; f. 1963; represents leading businesspeople; affiliated to CCE; Pres. CLAUDIO GONZÁLEZ LAPORTE.

STATE HYDROCARBONS COMPANY

Petróleos Mexicanos (PEMEX): Avda Marina Nacional 329, Col. Huasteca, 11311 México, DF; tel. (55) 1944-2500; fax (55) 5531-6354; e-mail petroleosmexicanos@pemex.com; internet www.pemex.com; f. 1938; govt agency for the exploitation of Mexico's petroleum and natural gas resources; Dir-Gen. JUAN JOSÉ SUÁREZ COPPEL; 106,900 employees.

UTILITIES

Regulatory Authorities

Comisión Nacional del Agua (CONAGUA): Avda Insurgentes Sur 2416, Col. Copilco el Bajo, Del. Coyoacán, 04340 México, DF; tel. (55) 5174-4000; fax (55) 5550-6721; e-mail direccion@cna.gob.mx; internet www.cna.gob.mx; commission to administer national water resources; Dir-Gen. JOSÉ LUIS LUEGE TAMARGO.

Comisión Reguladora de Energía (CRE): Avda Horacio 1750, Col. Los Morales Polanco, Del. Miguel Hidalgo, 11510 México, DF; tel. (55) 5283-1500; e-mail calidad@cre.gob.mx; internet www.cre.gob.mx; f. 1994; commission to control energy policy and planning; Pres. FRANCISCO XAVIER SALAZAR DIEZ DE SOLLANO; Exec. Sec. CARLOS HANS VALADEZ MARTÍNEZ.

Secretariat of State for Energy: see section on The Government (Secretariats of State).

Electricity

Comisión Federal de Electricidad (CFE): Avda Reforma 64, Col. Juárez México, México, DF; tel. (55) 5229-4400; fax (55) 5553-5321; e-mail servicioalcliente@cfe.gob.mx; internet www.cfe.gob.mx; state-owned power utility; Dir-Gen. ALFREDO ELÍAS AYUB.

Gas

Gas Natural México (GNM): Jaime Blames 8-703, Col. Los Morales Polanco, 11510 México, DF; e-mail sugerencias@gnm.com.mx; internet www.gasnaturalmexico.com.mx; f. 1994 in Mexico; distributes natural gas in the states of Tamaulipas, Aguascalientes, Coahuila, San Luis Potosí, Guanajuato, Nuevo León and México and in the Distrito Federal; subsidiary of Gas Natural (Spain); Pres. ANGEL LARRAGA.

Petróleos Mexicanos (PEMEX): see State Hydrocarbons Company; distributes natural gas.

TRADE UNIONS

Confederación Regional Obrera Mexicana (CROM) (Regional Confederation of Mexican Workers): República de Cuba 60, México, DF; f. 1918; Sec.-Gen. IGNACIO CUAUHTÉMOC PALETA; 120,000 mems, 900 affiliated syndicates.

Confederación Revolucionaria de Obreros y Campesinos de México (CROC) (Revolutionary Confederation of Workers and Farmers): Hamburgo 250, Col. Juárez, Del. Cuauhtémoc, 06600 México, DF; tel. (55) 5208-5449; e-mail crocmodel@hotmail.com; internet www.croc.org.mx; f. 1952; Sec.-Gen. ISIAS GONZÁLEZ CUEVAS; 4.5m. mems in 32 state federations and 17 national unions.

Confederación Revolucionaria de Trabajadores (CRT) (Revolutionary Confederation of Workers): Dr Jiménez 218, Col. Doctores, México, DF; f. 1954; Sec.-Gen. MARIO SUÁREZ GARCÍA; 10,000 mems; 10 federations and 192 syndicates.

Confederación de Trabajadores de México (CTM) (Confederation of Mexican Workers): Vallarta 8, Col. Tabacalera, Del. Cuauhtémoc, 06030 México, DF; tel. (55) 5141-1730; e-mail ctmorganizacion@prodigy.net.mx; internet ctmorganizacion.org.mx; f. 1936; admitted to ICFTU; Sec.-Gen. JOAQUÍN GAMBOA; 5.5m. mems.

Congreso del Trabajo (CT): Avda Ricardo Flores Magón 44, Col. Guerrero, 06300 México 37, DF; tel. (55) 5583-3817; internet www.congresodeltrabajo.org.mx; f. 1966; trade union congress comprising trade union federations, confederations, etc.; Pres. JOAQUÍN GAMBOA PASCOE.

Federación Nacional de Sindicatos Independientes (National Federation of Independent Trade Unions): Isaac Garza 311 Oeste, 64000 Monterrey, NL; tel. (81) 8375-6677; e-mail fnsi@prodigy.net.mx; internet www.fnsi.org.mx/esp; f. 1936; Sec.-Gen. JACINTO PADILLA VALDEZ; 230,000 mems.

Federación Obrera de Organizaciones Femeniles (FOOF) (Workers' Federation of Women's Organizations): Vallarta 8, México, DF; f. 1950; women workers' union within CTM; Sec.-Gen. HILDA ANDERSON NEVÁREZ; 400,000 mems.

Federación de Sindicatos de Trabajadores al Servicio del Estado (FSTSE) (Federation of Unions of Government Workers): Gómez Farías 40, Col. San Rafael, 06470 México, DF; internet www.fstse.com; f. 1938; Sec.-Gen. JOEL AYALA ALMEIDA; 2.5m. mems; 80 unions.

Frente Unida Sindical por la Defensa de los Trabajadores y la Constitución (United Union Front in Defence of the Workers and the Constitution): f. 1990 by more than 120 trade orgs to support the implementation of workers' constitutional rights.

Unión General de Obreros y Campesinos de México, Jacinto López (UGOCM-JL) (General Union of Workers and Farmers of Mexico, Jacinto López): José María Marroquí 8, 2°, 06050 México, DF; tel. (55) 5518-3015; f. 1949; admitted to WFTU/CSTAL; Sec.-Gen. JOSÉ LUIS GONZÁLEZ AGUILERA; 7,500 mems, over 2,500 syndicates.

Unión Nacional de Trabajadores (UNT) (National Union of Workers): Villalongen 50, Col. Cuauhtémoc, México, DF; tel. (55) 5140-1425; fax (55) 5703-2583; e-mail secretariageneral@strm.org.mx; internet www.unt.org.mx; f. 1998; Sec.-Gen. FRANCISCO HERNÁNDEZ JUÁREZ.

A number of major unions are non-affiliated, including:

Federación Democrática de Sindicatos de Servidores Públicos (Fedessp) (Democratic Federation of Public Servants): Vallarta 321, frente al Hotel Corinto, Col. Tabacalera, 06030 México, DF; tel. (55) 5546-2755; e-mail ser60gluz@hotmail.com; internet www.fedessp.org; f. 2005; Nat. Sec. JUAN MANUEL ESPINOZA ZAVALA.

Frente Auténtico de los Trabajadores (FAT): Godard 20, Col. Guadalupe Victoria, México, DF; tel. (55) 5556-9314; fax (55) 5556-9316; e-mail contactanos@fat.org.mx; internet www.fatmexico.org.

Sindicato Independiente de Trabajadores de la Educación de México (SITEM): México, DF; f. 2011; teachers' union; Sec.-Gen. JUAN CARLOS VILLANUEVA.

Sindicato Nacional de Trabajadores de la Educación (SNTE) (Education Workers): Venezuela 44, Col. Centro, México, DF; tel. (55) 5702-0005; fax (55) 5702-6303; e-mail info@snte.org.mx; internet www.snte.org.mx; f. 1943; Pres. ELBA ESTHER GORDILLO MORALES; Sec.-Gen. RAFAEL OCHOA GUZMÁN; 1.4m. mems.

Coordinadora Nacional de Trabajadores de la Educación (CNTE): dissident faction; Leader TEODORO PALOMINO.

Sindicato Nacional de Trabajadores Mineros, Metalúrgicos y Similares de la República Mexicana (SNTMM) (Mine, Metallurgical and Related Workers): Avda Dr Vertiz 668, Col. Narvarte, 03020 México, DF; tel. (55) 5519-5690; f. 1933; Sec.-Gen. NAPOLEÓN GÓMEZ URRUTIA; 86,000 mems.

Sindicato de Trabajadores Ferrocarrileros de la República Mexicana (STFRM) (Railway Workers): Avda Ricardo Flores Magón 206, Col. Guerrero, México 3, DF; tel. (55) 5597-1133; e-mail secretarianacional@stfrm.org; internet www.stfrm.org; f. 1933; Sec.-Gen. VÍCTOR F. FLORES MORALES; 100,000 mems.

Sindicato de Trabajadores Petroleros de la República Mexicana (STPRM) (Union of Workers): Zaragoza 15, Col. Guerrero, 06300 México, DF; tel. (55) 5546-0912; e-mail contacto@stprmsec40.org; internet stprmsec40.org; close links with PEMEX; Sec.-Gen. ANGEL MENDOZA FLORES; 110,000 mems; includes:

Movimiento Nacional Petrolero: reformist faction; Leader HEBRAÍCAZ VÁSQUEZ.

Sindicato Unico de Trabajadores Electricistas de la República Mexicana (SUTERM) (Electricity Workers): Río Guadalquivir 106, Col. Cuauhtémoc, 06500 México, DF; tel. (55) 5207-0578; internet www.suterm.org.mx; Sec.-Gen. VICTOR FUENTES DEL VILLAR.

Sindicato Unico de Trabajadores de la Industria Nuclear (SUTIN) (Nuclear Industry Workers): Viaducto Río Becerra 139, Col. Nápoles, 03810 México, DF; tel. (55) 5523-8048; fax (55) 5687-6353; e-mail exterior@sutin.org.mx; internet www.sutin.org.mx; Sec.-Gen. ARTURO DELFÍN LOYA.

Unión Obrera Independiente (UOI) (Independent Workers' Union): non-aligned.

The major agricultural unions are:

Confederación Nacional Campesina (CNC) (National Peasant Confederation): Mariano Azuela 121, Col. Santa María de la Ribera, México, DF; tel. (55) 5547-8042; internet www.cnc.org.mx; Sec.-Gen. CRUZ LOPEZ AGUILAR.

Confederación Nacional de Organizaciones Ganaderas (National Confederation of Stockbreeding Organizations): Calzada Mariano Escobedo 714, Col. Anzures, México, DF; tel. (55) 5203-3506; e-mail teresa.hernandez@cnog.com.mx; internet www.cnog.com.mx; Pres. OSWALDO CHÁZARO MONTALVO; 300,000 mems.

Consejo Agrarista Mexicano (Mexican Agrarian Council): 09760 Iztapalapa, México, DF; Sec.-Gen. HUMBERTO SERRANO.

Unión Nacional de Trabajadores Agriculturas (UNTA) (National Union of Agricultural Workers).

Transport

Road transport accounts for about 98% of all public passenger traffic and for about 80% of freight traffic. Mexico's terrain is difficult for overland travel. As a result, there has been an expansion of air transport, and there were 61 international and national airports in 2009. In 2002 plans to build a new airport in the capital were postponed after conflict over the proposed site. International flights are provided by a large number of national and foreign airlines. Mexico has 140 seaports, 29 river docks and a further 29 lake shelters. More than 85% of Mexico's foreign trade is conducted through maritime transport. In the 1980s the Government developed the main industrial ports of Tampico, Coatzacoalcos, Lázaro Cárdenas, Altamira, Laguna de Ostión and Salina Cruz in an attempt to redirect growth and to facilitate exports. The port at Dos Bocas, on the Gulf of Mexico, was one of the largest in Latin America when it opened in 1999. A 300-km railway link across the isthmus of Tehuantepec connects the Caribbean port of Coatzacoalcos with the Pacific port of Salina Cruz.

Secretariat of State for Communications and Transport: see section on The Government (Secretariats of State).

Caminos y Puentes Federales (CAPUFE): Calzada de los Reyes 24, Col. Tetela del Monte, 62130 Cuernavaca, Mor.; tel. (55) 5200-2000; e-mail contacto@capufe.gob.mx; internet www.capufe.gob.mx; Dir-Gen. TARCISIO RODRÍGUEZ MARTÍNEZ.

RAILWAYS

In 2009 there were 26,717 km of main line track. In 2007 the railway system carried 288,000 passengers and 70,010m. freight ton-km. Ferrocarriles Nacionales de México (FNM), government-owned since 1937, was liquidated in 2001 following a process of restructuring and privatization. A suburban train system for the Valle de México began operations in 2008. In that year plans were under way for the construction of a high-speed rail link between Mexico City and Guadalajara, and a new line from Manzanillo, Aguascalientes, to Mexico City.

Ferrocarril Mexicano, SA de CV (Ferromex): Bosque de Ciruelos 99, Col. Bosques de la Loma, 11700 México, DF; tel. (55) 5246-3700; e-mail webmaster@ferromex.com.mx; internet www.ferromex.com.mx; 50-year concession awarded to Grupo Ferroviario Mexicano, SA, (GFM) commencing in 1998; owned by Grupo México, SA de CV; 8,500 km of track and Mexico's largest rail fleet; links from Mexico City to Guadalajara, Hermosillo, Monterrey, Chihuahua and Pacific ports; Exec. Pres. ALFREDO CASAR PÉREZ; Dir-Gen. ROGELIO VÉLEZ LÓPEZ DE LA CERDA.

Ferrocarril del Sureste (Ferrosur): Bosque de Ciruelos 180, 1°, Col. Bosques de las Lomas, 11700 México, DF; tel. (55) 5387-6500; e-mail magarcia@ferrosur.com.mx; internet www.ferrosur.com.mx; 50-year concession awarded to Grupo Tribasa in 1998; 66.7% sold to Empresas Frisco, SA de CV, in 1999, owned by Grupos Carso, SA de CV; Dir MIGUEL ANGEL GARCÍA.

Kansas City Southern de México (KCSM): Avda Manuel L. Barragán 4850, Col. Hidalgo, 64420 Monterrey, NL; tel. (81) 8305-7800; fax (81) 8305-7766; e-mail werdman@kcsouthern.com; internet www.kcsouthern.com; fmrly Ferrocarril del Noreste; 4,242 km of line, linking Mexico City with the ports of Lázaro Cárdenas, Veracruz, Tampico/Altamira and north-east Mexico; Chair. MICHAEL R. HAVERTY; Pres. and CEO DAVID L. STARLING.

Servicio de Transportes Eléctricos del Distrito Federal (STE): Avda Municipio Libre 402, 3°, Col. San Andrés Tetepilco, Del. Iztapalapa, 09440 Mexico, DF; tel. (55) 2595-0000; fax (55) 5672-4758; e-mail sugiere@ste.df.gob.mx; internet www.ste.df.gob.mx; suburban tram route with 17 stops upgraded to light rail standard to act as a feeder to the metro; also operates bus and trolleybus networks; Pres. MARCELO LUIS EBRARD CASAUBÓN (Head of Govt of the Distrito Federal); Dir-Gen. RUFINO H. LEÓN TOVAR.

Sistema de Transporte Colectivo (Metro) (STC): Delicias 67, 06070 México, DF; tel. (55) 5709-1133; fax (55) 5512-3601; internet www.metro.df.gob.mx; f. 1967; the first stage of a combined underground and surface railway system in Mexico City was opened in 1969; 10 lines, covering 158 km, were operating, in 1998, and five new lines, bringing the total distance to 315 km, are to be completed by 2010; the system is wholly state-owned and the fares are partially subsidized; Dir-Gen. FRANCISCO BOJÓRQUEZ HERNÁNDEZ.

ROADS

In 2009 there were 366,341 km of roads, of which 36.3% were paved. Long-distance buses form one of the principal methods of transport in Mexico, and there are some 600 lines operating services throughout the country. In 2010 the Inter-American Development Bank (IDB) approved an amount of $2.6m. for the Pacific Corridor project (Corredor Pacifico), a highway system connecting Mexico with Panama.

Dirección General de Autotransporte Federal: Calzada de las Bombas 411, 11°, Col. Los Girasoles, Del. Coyoacán, 04920 México, DF; tel. (55) 5677-3561; internet dgaf.sct.gob.mx; co-ordinates long-distance bus services; Dir Dr MIGUEL HERBERTO ELIZALDE LIZARRAGA.

SHIPPING

At the end of 2009 Mexico's registered merchant fleet numbered 834 vessels, with a total displacement of 1,383,500 grt. The Government operates the facilities of seaports.

Coordinación General de Puertos y Marina Mercante (CGPMM): Avda Nuevo León 210, Col. Hipódromo, 06100 México, DF; tel. (55) 5723-9300; fax (55) 5265-3108; e-mail egarciai@sct.gob.mx; internet cgpmm.sct.gob.mx; Co-ordinator ALEJANDRO CHACÓN DOMÍNGUEZ; Dir-Gen. de Puertos ALEJANDRO HERNÁNDEZ CERVANTES; Dir-Gen. de Marina Mercante MARCO ANTONIO VINAZA MARTÍNEZ.

Port of Acapulco: Puertos Mexicanos, Malecón Fiscal s/n, Acapulco, Gro; Harbour Master Capt. RENÉ F. NOVALES BETANZOS.

Port of Coatzacoalcos: Administración Portuaria Integral de Coatzacoalcos, SA de CV, Interior Recinto Portuario s/n, Coatzacoalcos, 96400 Ver.; tel. (921) 211-0270; fax (921) 211-0272; e-mail dirgral@puertocoatzacoalcos.com.mx; internet www.apicoatza.com; Dir-Gen. Ing. GILBERTO RÍOS RUÍZ.

MEXICO

Port of Dos Bocas: Administración Portuaria Integral de Dos Bocas, SA de CV, Carretera Federal Puerto Ceiba–Paraíso 414, Col. Quintín Arzuz, 86600 Paraíso, Tab.; tel. (933) 333-2744; e-mail ventanilla@puertodosbocas.com.mx; internet www.puertodosbocas.com; Dir-Gen. ROBERTO DE LA GARZA LICÓN.

Port of Manzanillo: Administración Portuaria Integral de Manzanillo, SA de CV, Avda Tte Azueta 9, Col. Burócrata, 28250 Manzanillo, Col.; tel. and fax (314) 331-1400; e-mail gcomercial@puertomanzanillo.com.mx; internet www.puertomanzanillo.com.mx; Dir-Gen. ENRIQUE MICHEL RUIZ.

Port of Tampico: Administración Portuaria Integral de Tampico, SA de CV, Edif. API de Tampico, Zona Centro, 89000 Tampico, Tamps; tel. (833) 241-1400; fax (833) 212-5744; e-mail contacto@puertodetampico.com.mx; internet www.puertodetampico.com.mx; Gen. Dir MANUEL FLORES GUERRA.

Port of Veracruz: Administración Porturia Integral de Veracruz, SA de CV, Avda Marina Mercante 210, 7°, Col. Centro, 91700 Veracruz, Ver.; tel. (229) 932-2170; fax (229) 932-3040; e-mail mespinosa@puertodeveracruz.com; internet www.puertodeveracruz.com.mx; privatized in 1994; Dir-Gen. JUAN IGNACIO FERNÁNDEZ CARBAJAL.

Transportación Marítima Mexicana, SA de CV (TMM): Avda de la Cúspide 4755, Col. Parque del Pedregal, Del. Tlalpan, 14010 México, DF; tel. (55) 5629-8866; fax (55) 5629-8899; e-mail grupotmm@tmm.com.mx; internet www.tmm.com.mx; f. 1955; cargo services to Europe, the Mediterranean, Scandinavia, the USA, South and Central America, the Caribbean and the Far East; Pres. JOSÉ F. SERRANO SEGOVIA; Sec. IGNACIO RODRÍGUEZ PULLEN.

CIVIL AVIATION

There were 61 international airports in Mexico in 2009. Of these, México, Cancún, Guadalajara, Monterrey and Tijuana registered the highest number of operations.

Aeropuertos y Servicios Auxiliares (ASA): Edif. B, Avda 602 161, Col. San Juan de Aragón, Del. Venustiano Carranza, 15620 México, DF; tel. (55) 5133-1000; fax (55) 5133-2985; e-mail quejasydenuncias@asa.gob.mx; internet www.asa.gob.mx; f. 1965; oversees airport management and devt; Gen. Man. GILBERTO LÓPEZ MEYER.

Dirección General de Aeronáutica Civil (DGAC): Avda Providencia No 807, 6°, Col. Del Valle, 03100 México, DF; tel. (55) 5523-6642; fax (55) 5523-7207; e-mail hgonzalw@sct.gob.m; internet dgac.sct.gob.mx; subdivision of Secretariat of State for Communications and Transport; regulates civil aviation; Dir-Gen. HECTOR GONZALEZ WEEKS.

Aerocalifornia: Aquiles Serdán 1955, 23000 La Paz, BCS; e-mail aeroll@aerocalifornia.uabcs.mx; f. 1960; services suspended in 2006 over safety concerns; regional carrier with scheduled passenger and cargo services in Mexico and the USA; Chair. PAUL A. ARECHIGA.

Aeromar, Transportes Aeromar: Hotel María Isabel Sheraton, Paseo de la Reforma 325, Local 10, México, DF; tel. (55) 5514-2248; e-mail web.aeromar@aeromar.com.mx; internet www.aeromar.com.mx; f. 1987; scheduled domestic passenger and cargo services; Dir-Gen. AMILIN DEBET.

Aeromexpress Cargo: Avda Texococo s/n, esq. Avda Tahel, Col. Peñón de los Baños, 15520 México, DF; tel. (55) 5133-0203; internet www.aeromexpress.com.mx; owned by state holding co Consorcio Aeroméxico, SA; cargo airline; Commercial Dir ULISES CRUZ GARZA.

Aerovías de México (Aeroméxico): Paseo de la Reforma 445, 3°, Torre B, Col. Cuauhtémoc, 06500 México, DF; tel. (55) 5133-4000; fax (55) 5133-4619; internet www.aeromexico.com; f. 1934 as Aeronaves de México, nationalized 1959; sold by state holding co Consorcio Aeroméxico, SA, to private investors in 2007; services between most principal cities of Mexico and the USA, Chile, Brazil, Peru, France and Spain; Pres. JOSÉ LUIS BARRAZA; Dir-Gen. ANDRÉS CONESA LABASTIDA.

Aviacsa: Aeropuerto Internacional, Zona C, Hangar 1, Col. Aviación General, 15520 México, DF; tel. (55) 5716-9005; fax (55) 5758-3823; internet www.aviacsa.com; f. 1990; operates internal flights, and flights to the USA; Dir-Gen. ANDRÉS FABRE.

Click Mexicana: Avda Xola 535, Col. del Valle, 03100 México, DF; tel. (55) 5284-3132; e-mail servicio.cliente@clickmx.com; internet www.clickmx.com; f. 2005; owned by Mexicana; fmrly known as Aerocaribe; budget airline operating internal flights; CEO ISAAC VOLIN BOLOK.

Interjet (ABC Aerolíneas, SA de CV): Aeropuerto Internacional de Toluca, Toluca, Méx.; tel. (55) 1102-5555; e-mail atencionaclientes@interjet.com.mx; internet www.interjet.com.mx; f. 2005; budget airline operating internal flights; Pres. MIGUEL ALEMÁN MAGNANI.

Mexicana (Compañía Mexicana de Aviación, SA de CV): Avda Xola 535, Col. del Valle, 03100 México, DF; tel. (55) 5448-3000; fax (55) 5448-3129; e-mail dirgenmx@mexicana.com.mx; internet www.mexicana.com; f. 1921; fmrly state-owned; sold to Grupo Posadas in 2005; international services between Mexico City and the USA, Central America and the Caribbean; domestic services; CEO MANUEL BORJA CHICO.

Volaris: Aeropuerto Internacional de la Ciudad de Toluca, 50500 Toluca, Méx.; tel. (55) 1102-8000; e-mail comentarios@volaris.com.mx; internet www.volaris.com.mx; f. 2006; operated by Vuela Compañía de Aviación; budget airline operating internal flights; Pres. GILBERTO PÉREZALONSO CIFUENTES; Dir-Gen. ENRIQUE BELTRANENA.

Tourism

Tourism remains one of Mexico's principal sources of foreign exchange. Mexico received 21.5m. foreign visitors in 2009, and receipts from tourism in 2008 were US $10,817m. More than 90% of visitors come from the USA and Canada. The country is famous for volcanoes, coastal scenery and the great Sierra Nevada (Sierra Madre) mountain range. The relics of the Mayan and Aztec civilizations and of Spanish Colonial Mexico are of historic and artistic interest. Zihuatanejo, on the Pacific coast, and Cancún, on the Caribbean, were developed as tourist resorts by the Government.

Secretariat of State for Tourism: see section on The Government (Secretariats of State).

Asociación Mexicana de Agencias de Viajes (AMAV): Guanajuato 128, México, DF; tel. (55) 5584-9300; e-mail amavcun@prodigy.net.mx; internet www.amavnacional.com; f. 1945; asscn of travel agencies; Pres. JORGE HERNÁNDEZ DELGADO.

Fondo Nacional de Fomento al Turismo (FONATUR): Tecoyotitla 100, Col. Florida, 01030 México, DF; tel. (55) 5090-4200; fax (55) 5090-4469; e-mail jrbusquets@fonatur.gob.mx; internet www.fonatur.gob.mx; f. 1956 to finance and promote the devt of tourism; Dir-Gen. MIGUEL GÓMEZ-MONT URUETA.

Defence

As assessed at November 2010, Mexico's regular armed forces numbered 280,250: army 212,000, navy 56,500 (including naval air force—1,250—and marines—19,533) and air force 11,750. There were also 87,344 reserves. Paramilitary forces numbered 51,500, comprising a federal preventive police force of 29,000, a federal ministerial police force of 4,500 and a rural defence militia numbering 18,000. Military service, on a part-time basis, is by a lottery and lasts for one year.

Defence Budget: 58,400m. new pesos in 2010.

Chief of Staff of National Defence: Gen. LUIS ARTURO OLIVER CEN.

Superintendant and Comptroller of the Army and Air Force: Gen. ROBERTO MIRANDA SÁNCHEZ.

Commander of the Air Force: Gen. LEONARDO GONZÁLEZ GARCÍA.

Chief of Staff of the Navy: Adm. JOSÉ SANTIAGO VALDÉS ÁLVAREZ.

Education

State education in Mexico is free and compulsory at primary and secondary level. Primary education lasts for six years between the ages of six and 11. Secondary education lasts for up to six years. Children aged four years and over may attend nursery school. In 2008 enrolment at primary schools included 98% of pupils in the relevant age-group, while in the same year enrolment at secondary schools included 72% of pupils in the relevant age-group. In 2008/09 nursery schools numbered 89,395 and there were 98,575 primary schools. There were 34,380 secondary schools in the same year, attended, in 2008/09, by 6.2m. pupils. In spite of the existence of more than 80 indigenous languages in Mexico, there were few bilingual secondary schools. In 2008/09 there were an estimated 5,560 institutes of higher education, attended, in 2008/09, by some 2.7m. students. Federal expenditure on education in 2010 was an estimated 211,186.2m. new pesos.

THE FEDERATED STATES OF MICRONESIA

Introductory Survey

LOCATION, CLIMATE, LANGUAGE, RELIGION, FLAG, CAPITAL

The Federated States of Micronesia forms (with Palau, q.v.) the archipelago of the Caroline Islands, about 800 km east of the Philippines. The Federated States of Micronesia comprises 607 islands and includes (from west to east) the states of Yap, Chuuk (formerly Truk), Pohnpei (formerly Ponape) and Kosrae. The islands are subject to heavy rainfall, although precipitation decreases from east to west. January, February and March are the driest months, although seasonal variations in rainfall and temperature are generally small. Average annual temperature is 27°C (81°F). The native population consists of various ethno-linguistic groups, but English is widely understood. The principal religion is Christianity, much of the population being Roman Catholic. The national flag (proportions 10 by 19) consists of four five-pointed white stars, arranged as a circle, situated centrally on a light blue field. The capital is Palikir, on Pohnpei.

CONTEMPORARY POLITICAL HISTORY

Historical Context

The Federated States of Micronesia was formerly part of the US-administered Trust Territory of the Pacific Islands (for history up to 1965, see the chapter on the Marshall Islands).

From 1965 there were increasing demands for local autonomy within the Trust Territory of the Pacific Islands. In that year the Congress of Micronesia was formed, and in 1967 a commission was established to examine the future political status of the islands. In 1970 it declared Micronesians' rights to sovereignty over their own lands, to self-determination, to devise their own constitution and to revoke any form of free association with the USA. In May 1977, after eight years of negotiations, US President Jimmy Carter announced that his administration intended to adopt measures to terminate the trusteeship agreement by 1981. Until 1979 the four districts of Yap, Truk (Chuuk since 1990), Ponape (Pohnpei since 1984) and Kosrae were governed by a local Administrator, appointed by the President of the USA. However, on 10 May 1979 the four districts ratified a new Constitution to become the Federated States of Micronesia. The Constitution was promulgated in 1980.

The USA signed the Compact of Free Association with the Republic of Palau in August 1982, and with the Marshall Islands and the Federated States of Micronesia in October. Under the Compacts, the four countries (including the Northern Mariana Islands) became independent of each other and took charge of both their internal and foreign affairs separately, while the USA remained responsible for defence and security. The Compact was approved by plebiscite in the Federated States of Micronesia in June 1983, and was ratified by the islands' Congress in September.

Domestic Political Affairs

In May 1986 the UN Trusteeship Council endorsed the US Government's request for the termination of the existing trusteeship agreement with the islands. US administration of the Federated States of Micronesia was formally ended in November of that year. The UN Security Council ratified the termination of the trusteeship agreement in December 1990. Ponape was renamed Pohnpei in November 1984, when its Constitution came into effect. Truk was renamed Chuuk in January 1990, when its new Constitution was proposed (being later adopted). The Federated States of Micronesia was admitted to the UN in September 1991.

The incumbent President (since 1987), John Haglelgam, was replaced by Bailey Olter, a former Vice-President, in May 1991. At congressional elections in March 1995 Olter was re-elected to the Pohnpei Senator-at-Large seat (each of the four Micronesian states choosing a Senator-at-Large to serve a four-year term). In May Olter was re-elected to the presidency unopposed. Similarly, Jacob Nena was re-elected as Vice-President. Allegations that financial mismanagement by the Governor of Chuuk, Sasao Gouland, had resulted in state debts of some US $20m. led to his resignation in June 1996, in order to avoid impeachment proceedings. In July Olter suffered a stroke. Jacob Nena served as acting President during Olter's absence from office, and in May 1997 was sworn in as President of the country. (Olter died in February 1999.)

Congressional elections took place in March 1997 for the 10 Senators elected on a two-yearly basis, at which all of the incumbents were returned to office. A referendum held concurrently on a proposed amendment to the Constitution (which envisaged increasing the allocation of national revenue to the state legislatures from 50% to 80% of the total budget) was approved in Chuuk and Yap, but rejected in Pohnpei and Kosrae.

In February 1998 Congress approved proposals to restructure and reorganize the Cabinet. Several ministerial portfolios were consequently merged or abolished, with the aim of reducing government expenditure. Congressional elections took place on 2 March 1999, at which President Nena was re-elected to the Kosrae Senator-at-Large seat and Vice-President Leo Falcam to the Pohnpei Senator-at-Large seat. On 11 May Congress elected Falcam as President and the Chuuk Senator-at-Large, Redley Killion, as Vice-President.

A first round of renegotiations of the Compact of Free Association (certain terms of which were due to expire in 2001) was completed in late 1999. The USA and the Federated States of Micronesia pledged to maintain defence and security relations. It was also agreed that the USA would continue to provide economic aid to the islands and assist in the development of the private sector, as well as in promoting greater economic self-sufficiency. In July 2001 the USA offered annual assistance of US $61m. and a trust fund of $13m., and expressed concern that the $2,600m. it had given to Micronesia and the Marshall Islands since 1986 had been mismanaged. The Compact's funding terms for Micronesia were originally due to expire on 3 November 2001, but negotiations regarding a new Compact were not completed by this time. Funding was, nevertheless, continued at the Compact's 15-year average level while negotiations remained in progress. Following a proposal by the USA in April 2002 to extend economic assistance for a period of 20 years, a new draft funding structure was agreed, and in March the US budget projections for 2004 granted Micronesian citizens access to private health care resources in the USA as part of the Federated States' continued entitlement to US federal programmes. On 1 May 2003 the amended Compact of Free Association was signed by representatives of the two countries in Pohnpei. The revised Compact envisaged direct annual grants of $76.2m. in 2004, in addition to a further $16m. annually, which was to be paid into a trust fund for Micronesia. From 2007 direct grants were to decrease by some $800,000, with this amount being transferred to the trust fund. (The total amount to be paid prior to the expected termination of US assistance in 2023 amounted, in 2004 terms, to some $1,760m.) Furthermore, the Micronesian Government also undertook to provide frequent, strictly monitored audit information on all US funding in order to ensure greater accountability. In October 2003 final agreement was reached on some outstanding security and immigration issues, and the US Congress approved the amended Compact in November. President George W. Bush signed the pact in December, and representatives of both Governments signed a document of implementation in June 2004.

Nevertheless, there remained widespread concern in the Federated States of Micronesia that the new Compact represented a substantial overall reduction in annual income over the long term. Moreover, the formula for the distribution of Compact funds to each of Micronesia's states and the removal of certain US subsidies remained the subject of considerable controversy. In August representatives of Micronesia and the USA met to review the management of Compact funds in the first session of the Joint Economic Management Committee. In August 2008

THE FEDERATED STATES OF MICRONESIA

these concerns were renewed when the US Department of the Interior partly suspended Compact funding for the state of Chuuk, citing financial management problems that needed to be resolved before the funds could be approved. In March 2008 the US Office of Insular Affairs had confirmed that in 2008/09 the sum of almost $20.3m. was to be allocated to the country's trust fund, in addition to the annual operating grants.

In September 2002 unrest occurred on the Faichuk islands, part of Chuuk, where the Faichuk Commission for Statehood continued its campaign to secede from Chuuk and gain equal status within the Federation. The secessionists believed that independence would bring more goods, services, medical treatment and capital improvement projects. Local dissatisfaction worsened in September, following allegations of electoral manipulation against the village mayor of Udot island, with a large crowd appearing to support attempts by local security forces to prevent the mayor's arrest. In March 2005 Congressman Twiter Aritos introduced to the national Congress legislation to grant Faichuk the status of the Federation's fifth state.

Also in September 2002 a referendum was held on a number of proposed amendments to the Constitution. The prospective changes included a provision for the direct election of presidential candidates, the extension of the right of islanders to hold dual citizenship and changes to the distribution formula for Compact of Free Association funds. However, the measures did not receive the required three-quarters' majority of votes and were thus rejected.

At the congressional elections of 6 March 2003 President Leo Falcam unexpectedly failed to achieve re-election to a further four-year term as Senator-at-Large for Pohnpei. In May Congress appointed the Senator-at-Large for Yap, Joseph J. Urusemal, to the presidency. The elections were the subject of some controversy, as it appeared that elected officials had disbursed a portion of the 2002 US funding for Micronesia in order to enhance their electoral prospects. The alleged misallocation of funds was reportedly a significant factor in the worsening fiscal positions of Chuuk, Pohnpei and Kosrae. Moreover, perceptions of official accountability continued to deteriorate in 2003; in November three serving Congressmen were indicted for their role in an alleged fraud involving some US $1.2m. in public funds. In January 2004 the national Congress approved a resolution to dismiss the judge assigned to the case. President Urusemal lodged a petition against the dismissal on the grounds that it infringed the constitutionally guaranteed separation of powers. In August the Supreme Court ruled in favour of the petition and overturned the judge's dismissal. Also in January 2004, members of the national Congress attempted to introduce legislation effectively absolving public officials from corruption allegations relating to Compact of Free Association funds. The proposals aroused widespread public hostility, and several representatives of state legislatures threatened to secede from the federation unless the measure were withdrawn. In March the so-called 'amnesty bill' was returned to a congressional sub-committee for further discussion; however, at mid-2011 no subsequent developments had been reported.

At congressional elections held on 7 March 2005 all but one of the four incumbent Senators-at-Large were re-elected, with results from Chuuk awaiting confirmation in early April. On the following day eight of the 10 incumbent Senators with two-year mandates were re-elected in separate polls. (Results from Chuuk were annulled, owing to alleged voting irregularities, and in late April a new round of voting was held in this state, at which, amid further allegations of electoral malpractice, Peter S. Sitan was elected.) Concurrent with the second round of congressional elections, a referendum was held over three proposed amendments to the Constitution, including the question of whether each state should recognize and uphold the laws and judicial rulings of other states, and whether to allow dual citizenship. Although a majority of voters favoured the proposed amendments, these could not be implemented because the majority of 75% or more of the votes, as required by the Constitution, had not been obtained.

In April 2006 the national Congress filed a lawsuit against President Urusemal in protest at his use of the presidential veto against certain items of proposed legislation. In June the Supreme Court approved the Department of Justice's decision, on behalf of the President, to dismiss the lawsuit, on the basis that the judicial system was not authorized to examine the reasons for a presidential veto. Urusemal had argued that these bills were unconstitutional because relevant first and second readings had been held on the same day; he later urged the Congress to resubmit them.

Recent developments

At congressional elections held on 6 March 2007 for all 14 seats of the chamber, the incumbent Senators-at-Large for Kosrae, Pohnpei and Yap were re-elected, while Immanuel Mori defeated Vice-President Redley Killion to become Senator-at-Large for Chuuk. On 11 May 2007, in a congressional vote, Mori was elected President of the Federated States of Micronesia, taking office on the same day; Alik L. Alik of Kosrae succeeded Redley Killion as Vice-President. 'Special' congressional elections were conducted in July to fill the seats vacated by Mori and Alik. In a protracted confirmation process, members of Mori's Government were individually nominated and sworn in during the latter half of 2007 and early 2008. A reorganization of ministries was also instigated, including the creation of a Department of Education.

In March 2008 Senator Roosevelt D. Kansou of Chuuk was found guilty of conspiracy and was consequently removed from his seat in Congress. In May a special congressional election was held to determine Kansou's successor. The election was won by Tesime Kofot, who took up the seat in September.

On 3 March 2009 elections were conducted for 10 of the 14 seats in the national Congress. Elections were also held to determine the Governor and Lieutenant-Governor of Chuuk. After initial results failed to provide a clear winner, a second round of polling was held in April when the incumbent Governor of Chuuk, Wesley Simina, and Lieutenant-Governor Johnson Elimo were both re-elected. In October a special congressional election was held to select a new Senator-at-Large for Pohnpei, following the death in June of the incumbent, Resio S. Moses; Peter M. Christian was elected with 44% of the votes cast, and was inaugurated in December.

Alongside gubernatorial and municipal elections held in Yap in November 2010, at which the incumbent Governor and Lieutenant-Governor—Sebastian Anefal and Anthony Tareg, respectively—were both re-elected, a referendum on a proposed amendment to the state Constitution was held. The amendment, which proposed the introduction to Yap's Constitution of a new section granting the state legislature the power to present for a popular vote, at a future election, the question of whether Yap should review its political status as a state, was approved by a sizeable majority.

On 8 March 2011 a total of 23 candidates contested the elections for all 14 seats in the national Congress. President Mori retained his seat as Chuuk's Senator-at-Large for a further four-year term. Vice-President Alik was also re-elected to his seat, as were six other incumbent Senators. On 11 May, following its re-election of Isaac Figir as Speaker at its first session, the newly installed Congress then proceeded to choose the country's President and Vice-President from among the four Senators-at-Large. President Mori was re-elected unopposed, and Vice-President Alik was also appointed to serve a further four-year term.

Environmental Concerns and Human Development

Periodic extreme weather formations have caused loss of life and severe damage to crops, property and infrastructure in Micronesia. Following a severe typhoon in December 2002, President George W. Bush of the USA declared Micronesia a federal disaster area and ordered emergency US funding and resources to be allocated to the relief effort. A further typhoon that struck Yap in April 2004 left 1,200 people homeless; the US Government offered to assume 75% of the cost of the recovery effort.

In late 2000 marine biologists issued a warning regarding the erosion of the islands' coastlines, caused by the destruction of the coral reefs by pollution, overfishing and increasing sea temperatures. Furthermore, in late 2003 concerns over environmental pollution increased, owing to the environmental damage caused by former US and Japanese military equipment submerged in Micronesian waters.

In September 2003 President Joseph Urusemal urged the UN General Assembly to work towards halting climate change and its consequent effects on sea-levels and weather patterns. In March 2008 the Federated States of Micronesia's Permanent Representative to the UN, Masao Nakayama, attended a US congressional hearing on the subject of the environment; Nakayama argued that climate change was directly affecting Micronesia and urged the USA to take action to alleviate the problem. In October 2009, at the invitation of the President of the European Commission, José Manuel Barroso, President Immanuel Mori addressed European and other world leaders on the

THE FEDERATED STATES OF MICRONESIA

issue of climate change at the European Development Days conference, held in the Swedish capital, Stockholm. Declaring that Micronesia was at 'the front line of a global crisis that threatens not only our water supplies, our agricultural productivity and our ocean resources, but also our very existence', Mori appealed to developed nations to establish and contribute to an Adaptation Fund in order to assist poorer nations in their efforts to mitigate and adapt to the effects of climate change.

At a conference held in Geneva, Switzerland in June 2010 of Parties to the Montreal Protocol on Substances that Deplete the Ozone Layer—a multilateral treaty implemented in 1989 with the objective of phasing out the production of substances believed to be responsible for ozone depletion—the head of the Micronesian delegation emphasized the importance of taking 'urgent action' more effectively to control the release into the atmosphere of hydrofluorocarbons (HFCs—substances introduced to replace the use of ozone-depleting gases, some of which are believed nevertheless to contribute to climate change). At the annual UN Climate Change Conference held in the Mexican resort of Cancún in November–December 2010, Micronesia resubmitted a proposal that it had made in the previous year urging governments to take immediate action on the 50% of global warming thought to be caused by gases other than carbon dioxide, including methane and some HFCs. Micronesia also proposed transferring control of HFC emissions, currently under the remit of the Kyoto Protocol, to the Montreal Protocol, a strategy also propounded by the USA, Canada and Mexico in a separate, though similar, North American proposal.

The *Human Development Report 2010*, published by the UN Development Programme in November of that year, included the Federated States of Micronesia in its Human Development Index for the first time. Micronesia was ranked 103rd out of 169 countries, its overall score falling below both the regional and global average. Life expectancy at birth was estimated at 69.0, while the under-five mortality rate stood at 39 per 1,000 live births.

Regional Affairs

In February 2003 Pohnpei hosted the first Summit of Micronesian Leaders. At the second summit, held in Koror, Palau, in March 2004, President Joseph Urusemal and the leaders of Palau, the Northern Mariana Islands and Guam undertook to increase co-operation among the Pacific island states in the areas of tourism and the environment. Further co-operation in the fields of health, the economy and labour were discussed at a summit meeting in late 2007. At a summit meeting convened in Garapan, in the Northern Mariana Islands, in June 2010, Pacific leaders pledged their commitment to the fostering of closer co-operation in addressing, *inter alia*, climate change, the high cost of health care and rising fuel prices.

In July 2006 the Chinese Minister of Foreign Affairs, Li Zhaoxing, became the most senior official of the People's Republic of China ever to visit the Federated States of Micronesia, meeting President Urusemal and Sebastian Anefal, then the Secretary of the Department of Foreign Affairs. In September residences built by the Chinese for the Micronesian President, Vice-President, Speaker of Congress and Chief Justice were presented to the Government at a ceremony that highlighted the strong links between the two countries. Bilateral relations were further bolstered by the opening of a Micronesian embassy in Beijing in May 2007; Micronesia's first resident ambassador in Beijing, Akillino Susaia, took up the post in April 2010 (previously the embassy had been under the remit of the Micronesian ambassador to Japan). Meanwhile, Vice-President Alik made a six-day official visit to Beijing, at the invitation of his Chinese counterpart, Xi Jinping, in July 2009, during which he thanked China for its ongoing support of Micronesian development; affirmed the island state's continued adherence to the 'one China' policy; and pledged further to increase bilateral co-operation. Alik returned to the Chinese capital in November to mark the 20th anniversary of the formal establishment of diplomatic relations between Micronesia and China. In May 2010 President Immanuel Mori met with Chinese President Hu Jintao in the Chinese city of Shanghai. Hu appealed for greater co-operation in the fields of new energy, infrastructure, construction and the fisheries industry, as well as an intensification of cultural, educational and tourism exchanges. Hu also pledged a continuation of Chinese offers of economic and technological aid to the Federated States of Micronesia and of encouragement and support to Chinese businesses looking to invest in the island state. Mori expressed his gratitude for Chinese economic support, notably in the areas of health and education, and reiterated Micronesia's continued adherence to the 'one China' policy.

In the early years of the 21st century, Japan was the second largest donor to the Federated States of Micronesia, behind only the USA. Bilateral relations were further enhanced in June 2008 when the Japanese embassy in Kolonia welcomed its first resident ambassador, Shoji Sato. President Mori made an official visit to Japan in November to mark the 20th anniversary of the establishment of diplomatic relations between the two states. During another visit to Japan, in November 2010, Mori expressed gratitude for Japanese economic co-operation and assistance in Micronesia, which, the President stated, had made a significant contribution to Micronesian 'nation-building efforts', while Japanese Prime Minister Naoto Kan thanked Micronesia for its support of Japan's bid to secure a permanent seat on the UN Security Council. During his visit, Mori also met with the Japanese Minister for Foreign Affairs, Seiji Maehara, who confirmed Japan's commitment further to stimulate the Micronesian economy by means of enhanced bilateral co-operation in a number of fields, including tourism and the fisheries industry.

CONSTITUTION AND GOVERNMENT

On 10 May 1979 the locally drafted Constitution of the Federated States of Micronesia, incorporating the four states of Kosrae, Yap, Ponape (later Pohnpei) and Truk (later Chuuk), became effective. The federal legislature, the Congress, comprises 14 members (Senators). The four states each elect one Senator-at-Large, for a four-year term. The remaining 10 Senators are elected for two-year terms: their seats are distributed in proportion to the population of each state. Each of the four states also has its own Constitution, Governor and legislature. The federal President and Vice-President are elected by the Congress from among the four Senators-at-Large; the offices rotate among the four states. (By-elections are then held for the seats to which the President and Vice-President had been elected.) In November 1986 the Compact of Free Association was signed by the Governments of the Federated States of Micronesia and the USA. Certain of its terms, due to expire in 2001, were renegotiated in late 1999, and an amended Compact was signed by the Governments of both countries on 1 May 2003. By the terms of the Compact, the Federated States of Micronesia is a sovereign, self-governing state.

Local government units are the municipalities and villages. Elected Magistrates and Councils govern the municipalities. Village government is largely traditional.

REGIONAL AND INTERNATIONAL CO-OPERATION

The Federated States of Micronesia is a member of the Pacific Community (see p. 410), the Pacific Islands Forum (see p. 413), the South Pacific Regional Trade and Economic Co-operation Agreement (SPARTECA, see p. 414), the UN's Economic and Social Commission for Asia and the Pacific (ESCAP, see p. 37) and the Asian Development Bank (ADB, see p. 202). The Federated States of Micronesia hosts the Tuna Commission, a multilateral agency to manage migratory fish stocks in the central and western Pacific region.

The Federated States of Micronesia became a member of the UN in 1991, and participates in the Group of 77 (G77, see p. 447) developing countries.

ECONOMIC AFFAIRS

In 2009, according to estimates by the World Bank, gross national income (GNI) in the Federated States of Micronesia, measured at average 2007–09 prices, was US $246m., equivalent to $2,220 per head (or $2,810 per head on an international purchasing-power parity basis). During 2000–09, it was estimated, the population increased at an average annual rate of 0.4%, while gross domestic product (GDP) per head decreased, in real terms, by an average of 2.2% per year. According to figures from the UN, overall GDP decreased, in real terms, at an estimated average annual rate of 0.3% in 2000–09; real GDP decreased by 3.5% in 2008 and by 0.9% in 2009.

Agriculture is mainly on a subsistence level, although its importance is diminishing. The principal crops are coconuts, bananas, betel nuts, cassava and sweet potatoes. White peppercorns are produced on Pohnpei. The sector (including forestry and fishing) contributed an estimated 19.1% of GDP in 2009. Agriculture engaged about 21.8% of the total labour force in mid-2011, according to FAO estimates. In the year to September 2005 fishing access fees, mainly from Japanese fleets, totalled

THE FEDERATED STATES OF MICRONESIA

US $13.3m. (some 25% of total government current revenue). Exports of fish are a major source of revenue. The islands' tuna-processing facilities were being upgraded in 2009/10, funded with Chinese assistance. According to UN estimates, agricultural GDP decreased, in real terms, at an average annual rate of 0.3% during 2000–09; the GDP of the agricultural sector contracted by 3.5% in 2008 and by 0.9% in 2009.

Industry (including mining, manufacturing, utilities and construction) provided an estimated 4.0% of GDP in 2009. There is little manufacturing, other than the production of buttons using trochus shells, and the mining sector is negligible. According to UN estimates, industrial GDP decreased, in real terms, at an average annual rate of 0.3% during 2000–09; the sector's GDP contracted by 3.5% in 2008 and by 0.9% in 2009.

According to UN figures, manufacturing contributed just 1.4% of GDP in 2009. Manufacturing GDP decreased, in real terms, at an average annual rate of 0.3% during 2000–09; the sector's GDP contracted by 3.5% in 2008 and by 0.9% in 2009.

Construction contributed only 1.0% of GDP in 2009, according to UN estimates. The sector's GDP was estimated to have decreased, in real terms, at an average annual rate of 0.3% during 2000–09; construction GDP contracted by 3.5% in 2008 and by 0.9% in 2009.

The islands are heavily dependent on imported fuels. Purchases of mineral products accounted for 23.6% of the costs of total imports in 2008. In April 2009 a new bio-gas project was initiated in Pohnpei, the first of four schemes financed by the Chinese province of Zhejiang.

The services sector provided 76.9% of GDP in 2009, according to UN estimates. A total of 14,788 people were employed in services in 2006/07, equivalent to some 90% of total employment in the formal sector. Tourism is an important industry, with receipts for 2005 totalling some US $17m. The number of tourist arrivals increased from 21,146 in 2007 to 25,627 in 2008. Remittances from overseas emigrants are a significant source of income support. The GDP of the services sector decreased, in real terms, at an average annual rate of 0.3% during 2000–09; the sector's GDP contracted by 3.5% in 2008 and by 0.9% in 2009.

In the financial year ending September 2006 there was a visible trade deficit of an estimated US $128.9m., with a deficit of $38.4m. on the current account of the balance of payments. The principal sources of imports in 2007 were the USA (which supplied 41.2% of the total), Guam (14.4%) and Japan (8.5%). Guam was the principal market for exports in 2007, purchasing 22.5% of the total, while the USA accounted for 17.2%. The principal imports in 2007 were mineral products (22.1% of the total), prepared foodstuffs, beverages and tobacco (17.1%) and machinery, mechanical appliances and electrical equipment (14.4%). Fish is the major export commodity; marine products accounted for 76.0% of total exports in 2007. Other exports in that year included betel nuts and kava.

The budget deficit was estimated to be the equivalent of 0.7% of GDP in 2009/10. The budget for 2010/11 projected expenditure of US $39.0m. The Federated States of Micronesia relies heavily on financial assistance, particularly from the USA, with funding made available under the Compact of Free Association (see Contemporary Political History). In 2011/12 the USA was to provide a total of $105.5m. in Compact funding to Micronesia. Bilateral grants have been provided by Japan, a major donor, and the People's Republic of China. At the end of the 2009/10 financial year, according to the Asian Development Bank (ADB), the islands' total external debt stood at $68m. In 2008/09 the cost of debt-servicing was equivalent to 6.2% of the value of exports of goods and services. The annual rate of inflation averaged 3.2% in 2000–09. According to the ADB, the inflation rate decreased from an annual average of 7.7% in 2009 to 3.5% in 2010. Some 22% of the labour force were unemployed at the 2000 census.

Constraints upon the islands' economic development have included their remote location and the high rate of emigration. It was hoped that Micronesia would be in a position to achieve financial self-sufficiency by 2023, upon the expiry of the Compact of Free Association (see Contemporary Political History). However, concerns continued with regard to the lack of progress in restructuring the economy in preparation for the impact of the withdrawal of direct US aid. Under the amended Compact, instead of general budgetary grants, US aid was to be targeted mainly towards specific projects. Also, aid was to be conditional upon the efficiency of its management and use, and was to be reviewed annually. Meanwhile, the trust fund established to support the Micronesian economy in the longer term remained vulnerable to the volatility of international financial markets. Although inflationary pressures eased significantly in 2010, there was renewed pressure on consumer prices in early 2011; this was largely due to increases in the costs of imports of essential commodities, particularly fuel and foodstuffs. Remittances from emigrant workers were sustained in 2010. The number of tourist arrivals increased in the 12 months to September 2009, and receipts from tourism were reported to have improved in the following year. The extension of the runway at Pohnpei airport, to accommodate larger aircraft, was scheduled for completion in mid-2011. Along with improved flight connections, it was envisaged that the upgrading of the airport would bring major benefits to the tourism sector. The National Trade Policy for the Federated States of Micronesia, endorsed by Congress in February 2011, was regarded as an historic advance for the country's strategy. In addition to emphasis on the importance of trade agreements, the objectives of the policy included: the creation of conditions conducive to investment and private sector development; the addressing of supply constraints and the issue of non-tariff barriers; the encouragement of import substitution; and the promotion of exports of value added goods and services. Following several consecutive years of decline, the ADB estimated that Micronesia's GDP grew by 0.5% in both 2008/09 and 2009/10; expansion of 1.0% was forecast for 2010/11.

PUBLIC HOLIDAYS

2012 (provisional): 2 January (for New Year's Day), 30 March (for Micronesian Culture and Traditions Day), 6 April (Good Friday, Pohnpei only), 11 May (for Constitution Day), 24 October (United Nations Day), 2 November (for Independence Day), 12 November (Veterans of Foreign Wars Day), 22 November (Thanksgiving, Chuuk only), 25 December (Christmas Day).

Statistical Survey

Source (unless otherwise indicated): Statistics Unit, Office of Statistics, Budget and Economic Management, Overseas Development Assistance and Compact Management (SBOC), POB PS-12, Palikir, Pohnpei, FM 96941; tel. 320-2820; fax 320-5854; e-mail fsmstat@sboc.fm; internet www.sboc.fm/index.php.

AREA AND POPULATION

Area: 700.8 sq km (270.6 sq miles): Chuuk (Truk, 294 islands) 127.4 sq km; Kosrae (5 islands) 109.6 sq km; Pohnpei (Ponape, 163 islands) 345.2 sq km; Yap (145 islands) 118.6 sq km.

Population: 107,008 at census of 1 April 2000; 102,624 (males 52,055, females 50,569) at census of 4 April 2010. *By State* (2010): Chuuk 48,651; Kosrae 6,616; Pohnpei 35,981; Yap 11,376.

Density (at 2010 census): 146.4 per sq km.

Population by Age and Sex (at 2010 census): *0–14:* 36,650 (males 18,788, females 17,862); *15–64:* 62,558 (males 31,851, females 30,707); *65 and over:* 3,416 (males 1,416, females 2,000); *Total* 102,624 (males 52,055, females 50,569).

Principal Towns (population of municipalities at 2000 census): Weno (Moen) 13,802; Palikir (capital) 6,444; Nett 6,158; Kitti 6,007. Source: Thomas Brinkhoff, *City Population* (internet: www.citypopulation.de).

Births and Deaths (2003, official estimates): Registered live births 2,568 (birth rate 23.9 per 1,000); Deaths 442 (death rate 4.1 per 1,000). *2006:* Registered live births 2,147. *2005–10* (annual averages, UN estimates): Birth rate 21.9 per 1,000; Death rate 5.1 per 1,000 (Source: UN, *World Population Prospects: The 2008 Revision*).

Life Expectancy (years at birth, WHO estimates): 69 (males 68; females 70) in 2008. Source: WHO, *World Health Statistics*.

Economically Active Population (persons aged 15 years and over, 2000 census): Agriculture, forestry and fishing 15,216; *Total*

THE FEDERATED STATES OF MICRONESIA

employed (incl. others) 29,175 (males 16,957, females 12,218); Unemployed 8,239 (males 4,419, females 3,820); *Total labour force* 37,414 (males 21,376, females 16,038). *Mid-2011* (estimates in '000): Agriculture, etc. 12; Total labour force 55 (Source: FAO).

HEALTH AND WELFARE
Key Indicators

Total Fertility Rate (children per woman, 2008): 3.6.

Under-5 Mortality Rate (per 1,000 live births, 2008): 39.

Physicians (per 1,000 head, 2003): 0.6.

Hospital Beds (per 1,000 head, 2006): 3.3.

Health Expenditure (2007): US $ per head (PPP): 373.

Health Expenditure (2007): % of GDP: 13.2.

Health Expenditure (2007): public (% of total): 95.8.

For sources and definitions, see explanatory note on p. vi.

AGRICULTURE, ETC.

Principal Crops ('000 metric tons, 2008, FAO estimates): Coconuts 41; Cassava 12; Sweet potatoes 3; Vegetables 3; Bananas 2. Note: Data were not available for 2009.

Livestock ('000 head, year ending September 2008, FAO estimates): Pigs 33; Cattle 14; Goats 4; Chickens 190. Note: Data were not available for 2009.

Livestock Products (metric tons, 2009, FAO estimates): Cattle meat 258; Pig meat 876; Chicken meat 140; Hen eggs 184.

Fishing ('000 metric tons, live weight, 2008): Skipjack tuna 15.9; Yellowfin tuna 2.2; Bigeye tuna 1.3; Total catch (incl. others) 21.7 (FAO estimate).

Source: FAO.

FINANCE

Currency and Exchange Rates: United States currency is used: 100 cents = 1 United States dollar (US $). *Sterling and Euro Equivalents* (31 December 2010): £1 sterling = US $1.5655; €1 = US $1.3362; US $100 = £63.88 = €74.84.

Budget (US $ million, year ending 30 September 2008): *Revenue:* Current 55.4 (Tax 29.3, Non-tax 26.1); Grants 94.3; Total 149.8. *Expenditure:* Current 141.6; Capital 12.6; Total 154.2. Note: Figures represent a consolidation of the accounts of the national Government and the four state governments.

International Reserves (US $ '000 at 31 December 2009): IMF special drawing rights 9,721; Reserve position in IMF 0; Foreign exchange 45,997; *Total* 55,718. Source: IMF, *International Financial Statistics*.

Money Supply (US $ '000 at 31 December 2009): Demand deposits at banking institutions 29,021. Source: IMF, *International Financial Statistics*.

Cost of Living (Consumer Price Index, average of quarterly figures; base: April–June 2008 = 100): All items 91.5 in 2006; 94.9 in 2007; 101.3 in 2008.

Gross Domestic Product (US $ million at constant 2005 prices): 239.2 in 2007; 232.2 in 2008; 229.9 in 2009. Source: UN National Accounts Main Aggregates Database.

Expenditure on the Gross Domestic Product (US $ million at current prices, 2009): Government final consumption expenditure 140.1; Private final consumption expenditure 201.7; Gross fixed capital formation 85.3; Changes in inventories 5.4; *Total domestic expenditure* 432.5; Exports of goods and services 46.5; *Less* Imports of goods and services 209.5; *GDP in purchasers' values* 269.6. Source: UN National Accounts Main Aggregates Database.

Gross Domestic Product by Economic Activity (US $ million at current prices, 2009): Agriculture, hunting, forestry and fishing 48.5; Mining, electricity, gas and water 3.8; Manufacturing 3.6; Construction 2.7; Trade, restaurants and hotels 60.9; Transport, storage and communications 11.9; Other activities 122.5; *Sub-total* 253.7; Net of indirect taxes 15.9 (obtained as a residual); *GDP in purchasers' values* 269.6. Source: UN National Accounts Main Aggregates Database.

Balance of Payments (US $ million, year ending 30 September 2006, estimates): Merchandise exports f.o.b. 17.0; Merchandise imports f.o.b. −145.9; *Trade balance* −128.9; Exports of services 20.1; Imports of services −57.5; *Balance on goods and services* −166.2; Other income received 20.5; Other income paid −5.3; *Balance on goods, services and income* −151.0; Private unrequited transfers (net) 5.3; Official unrequited transfers (net) 107.3; *Current balance* −38.4; Capital account (net) 12.0; Other long-term capital (net) 1.9; Other short-term capital (net) 0.8; *Overall balance* (incl. errors and omissions) −23.6.

EXTERNAL TRADE

Principal Commodities (US $ '000, 2007): *Imports c.i.f.:* Mineral products 31,476; Prepared foodstuffs, beverages and tobacco 24,390; Machinery, mechanical appliances and electrical equipment 20,553; Vegetable products 8,538; Animals and animal products 8,755; Transportation equipment 8,480; Chemicals 7,660; Base metals and articles thereof 6,216; Total (incl. others) 142,658. *Exports f.o.b.:* Marine products 12,301; Betel nuts 2,224; Citrus 416; Kava 2,224; Total (incl. others) 16,190.

Principal Trading Partners (US $ '000, 2007): *Imports*: Australia 5,844; China, People's Republic 5,444; Guam 20,512; Hong Kong 8,955; Japan 12,067; Korea, Republic 5,820; Philippines 5,083; Singapore 12,413; USA 58,785; Total (incl. others) 142,658. *Exports*: Guam 3,641; Japan 660; USA (mainland only) 2,790; Total (incl. others) 16,190.

TRANSPORT

Shipping: *Merchant Fleet* (registered at 31 December 2009): Vessels 28; Total displacement ('000 grt) 11.8. Source: IHS Fairplay, *World Fleet Statistics*.

TOURISM

Foreign Tourist Arrivals: 19,136 in 2006; 21,146 in 2007; 25,627 in 2008.

Tourist Arrivals by Country or Region of Residence (2008): Europe 2,788; Japan 2,949; Philippines 2,168; Other Asia 4,121; USA 8,732; Total (incl. others) 25,627.

Tourism Receipts (US $ million, incl. passenger transport): 16.5 in 2004; 17.1 in 2005; 18.3 in 2006.

Source: World Tourism Organization.

COMMUNICATIONS MEDIA

Telephones (main lines in use, 2009): 8,700.

Mobile Cellular Telephones (2009): 38,000 subscribers.

Internet Users (2009): 17,000.

Broadband Subscribers (2009): 100.

Personal Computers: 6,000 (54.8 per 1,000 persons) in 2005.

Radio Receivers (1996): 22,000 in use.

Television Receivers (1996): 19,800 in use.

Source: partly International Telecommunication Union.

EDUCATION

Primary (2006/07, unless otherwise indicated): 174 schools (1995); 1,113 teachers; 18,512 pupils (Sources: UN, *Statistical Yearbook for Asia and the Pacific* and UNESCO Institute for Statistics).

Secondary (2006/07, unless otherwise indicated): 24 schools (1995); 829 teachers; 14,742 pupils (Sources: UN, *Statistical Yearbook for Asia and the Pacific* and UNESCO Institute for Statistics).

Tertiary (1998/99): 1,510 students (Sources: UN, *Statistical Yearbook for Asia and the Pacific* and UNESCO Institute for Statistics).

Pupil-teacher Ratio (primary education, UNESCO estimate): 16.6 in 2006/07 (Source: UNESCO Institute for Statistics).

Adult Literacy Rate (population aged 10 years and over, 2000 census): 92.4% (males 92.9%; females 91.9%).

Directory

The Government

HEAD OF STATE

President: IMMANUEL (MANNY) MORI (took office 11 May 2007; re-elected 11 May 2011).
Vice-President: ALIK L. ALIK.

CABINET
(May 2011)

Secretary of the Department of Finance and Administration: FINLEY S. PERMAN.
Secretary of the Department of Foreign Affairs: LORIN S. ROBERT.
Secretary of the Department of Resources and Development: PETER M. CHRISTIAN.
Secretary of the Department of Health and Social Affairs: Dr VITA AKAPITO SKILLING.
Secretary of the Department of Justice: MAKETO ROBERT.
Secretary of the Department of Transportation, Communication and Infrastructure: FRANCIS I. ITIMAI.
Secretary of the Department of Education: CASIANO SHONIBER.
Public Defender: JULIUS JOEY SAPELALUT.
Postmaster-General: Rev. MIDION G. NETH.

GOVERNMENT OFFICES

Office of the President: POB PS-53, Palikir, Pohnpei, FM 96941; tel. 320-2228; fax 320-2785; e-mail ppetrus@mail.fm; internet www.fsmpio.fm.
Department of Education: POB PS-87, Palikir, Pohnpei, FM 96941; tel. 320-2643; fax 320-5500.
Department of Finance and Administration: POB PS-158, Palikir, Pohnpei, FM 96941; tel. 320-2640; fax 320-2380; e-mail fsmsofa@mail.fm.
Department of Foreign Affairs: POB PS-123, Palikir, Pohnpei, FM 96941; tel. 320-2641; fax 320-2933; e-mail foreignaffairs@mail.fm; internet www.fsmgov.org/ovmis.html.
Department of Health and Social Affairs: POB PS-70, Palikir, Pohnpei, FM 96941; tel. 320-2872; fax 320-5263; e-mail fsmhealth@mail.fm.
Department of Justice: POB PS-105, Palikir, Pohnpei, FM 96941; tel. 320-2644; fax 320-2234; e-mail pdochuuk@mail.fm.
Department of Resources and Development: POB PS-12, Palikir, Pohnpei, FM 96941; tel. 320-2648; fax 320-5854; e-mail fsmrd@dea.fm; internet www.fsminvest.fm.
Department of Transportation, Communication and Infrastructure: POB PS-2, Palikir, Pohnpei, FM 96941; tel. 320-2865; fax 320-5853; e-mail transcom@mail.fm; internet www.ict.fm.
Office of the Public Auditor: POB PS-05, Palikir, Pohnpei, FM 96941; tel. 320-2863; fax 320-5482; e-mail hhainrick@fsmopa.fm; internet www.fsmopa.fm.
Office of the Public Defender: POB PS-174, Palikir, Pohnpei, FM 96941; tel. 320-2648; fax 320-5775.
Public Information Office: POB PS-34, Palikir, Pohnpei, FM 96941; tel. 320-2548; fax 320-4356; e-mail fsmpio@mail.fm.

Legislature

CONGRESS OF THE FEDERATED STATES OF MICRONESIA

The Congress comprises 14 members (Senators): four Senators-at-Large (one for each of the four states), who are elected for a four-year term; and 10 Senators who serve a two-year term. The most recent election was held on 8 March 2011. There are no formal political parties.

Speaker: ISAAC V. FIGIR.

STATE LEGISLATURES

Chuuk State Legislature: POB 189, Weno, Chuuk, FM 96942; tel. 330-2234; fax 330-2233; Senate of 10 mems and House of Representatives of 28 mems elected for four years; Gov. WESLEY W. SIMINA.
Kosrae State Legislature: POB 187, Tofol, Kosrae, FM 96944; tel. 370-3002; fax 370-3162; e-mail kosraelc@mail.fm; unicameral body of 14 mems serving for four years; Gov. ROBERT J. WEILBACHER.
Pohnpei State Legislature: POB 114, Kolonia, Pohnpei, FM 96941; tel. 320-2753; fax 320-2754; e-mail legislature@mail.fm; internet www.fm/pohnpeileg; 27 representatives elected for four years (terms staggered); Gov. JOHN EHSA.
Yap State Legislature: POB 39, Colonia, Yap, FM 96943; tel. 350-2108; fax 350-4113; 10 mems, six elected from the Yap Islands proper and four elected from the Outer Islands of Ulithi and Woleai, for a four-year term; Gov. SEBASTIAN L. ANEFAL.

Election Commission

National Election Commission: POB 1685, Kolonia, Pohnpei 96941; tel. 320-4283; fax 320-7805; e-mail ned@mail.fm; Dir Rev. KIMEUO KIMIUO.

Political Organizations

There are no formal political parties in the Federated States of Micronesia.

Diplomatic Representation

EMBASSIES IN THE FEDERATED STATES OF MICRONESIA

Australia: POB S, Kolonia, Pohnpei, FM 96941; tel. 320-5448; fax 320-5449; e-mail australia@mail.fm; internet www.australianembassy.fm; Ambassador MARTIN QUINN.
China, People's Republic: POB 1530, Kolonia, Pohnpei, FM 96941; tel. 320-5575; fax 320-5578; e-mail chinaemb@mail.fm; internet fm.chineseembassy.org/eng; Ambassador ZHANG WEIDONG.
Japan: Pami Bldg, 3rd Floor, POB 1837, Kolonia, Pohnpei, FM 96941; tel. 320-5465; fax 320-5470; internet www.micronesia.emb-japan.go.jp; Ambassador EIICHI SUZUKI.
USA: POB 1286, Kolonia, Pohnpei, FM 96941; tel. 320-2187; fax 320-2186; e-mail usembassy@mail.fm; internet kolonia.usembassy.gov; Ambassador PETER ALAN PRAHAR.

Judicial System

Supreme Court of the Federated States of Micronesia: POB PS-J, Palikir Station, Pohnpei, FM 96941; tel. 320-2357; fax 320-2756; e-mail fsmsupcourt@mail.fm; internet www.fsmlaw.org; Chief Justice MARTIN G. YINUG.

State Courts and Appellate Courts have been established in Yap, Chuuk, Kosrae and Pohnpei.

Religion

The population is predominantly Christian, mainly Roman Catholic. The Assembly of God, Jehovah's Witnesses, Seventh-day Adventists, the Church of Jesus Christ of Latter-day Saints (Mormons), the United Church of Christ, Baptists and the Bahá'í Faith are also represented.

CHRISTIANITY

The Roman Catholic Church

The Federated States of Micronesia forms a part of the diocese of the Caroline Islands, suffragan to the archdiocese of Agaña (Guam). The Bishop participates in the Catholic Bishops' Conference of the Pacific, based in Fiji. At 31 December 2007 there were 79,199 adherents in the diocese.

Bishop of the Caroline Islands: Most Rev. AMANDO SAMO, Bishop's House, POB 939, Weno, Chuuk, FM 96942; tel. 330-2399; fax 330-4585; e-mail diocese@mail.fm; internet www.dioceseofthecarolines.org.

Other Churches

Calvary Baptist Church: Kolonia, Pohnpei, POB 2179, FM 96941; tel. 320-2830; fax 320-3887; e-mail cca_pohnpei@yahoo.com; Pastor ISAMO WELLES.

THE FEDERATED STATES OF MICRONESIA

Liebenzell Mission: Rev. Seigbert Betz, POB 9, Weno, Chuuk, FM 96942; tel. 330-3869; e-mail missions@liebenzellusa.org; internet www.liebenzellusa.org.

Truth Independent Baptist Church: Kolonia, Pohnpei, POB 65, FM 96941; tel. 320-3643; fax 320-6769; Pastor RICARDO P. VERACRUZ.

United Church of Christ in Pohnpei: Kolonia, Pohnpei, POB 864, FM 96941; tel. 320-2271; fax 320-4404; Pres. BERNELL EDWARD.

The Press

Da Rohng: Jano News Service, POB 510, Kolonia, Pohnpei FM 96941; tel. 320-6494; fax 320-4200; e-mail darohng2005@yahoo.com; Editor MARTIN JANO.

The Island Tribune: Pohnpei, FM 96941; f. 1997; fortnightly.

Kaselehlie Press: POB 2222, Pohnpei, FM 96941; tel. 320-6547; fax 320-6571; e-mail kpress@mail.fm; internet www.kpress.info; f. 2001; fortnightly; Man. Editor BILL JAYNES.

Micronesian Alliance: POB 543, Tofol, Kosrae, FM 96944; tel. 370-6131; e-mail equatormedia@yahoo.com.

Broadcasting and Communications

TELECOMMUNICATIONS

FSM Telecommunication Corporation: POB 1210, Kolonia, Pohnpei, FM 96941; tel. 320-2740; fax 320-2745; e-mail customerservice@telecom.fm; internet www.fm; provides domestic and international services; Pres. and CEO JOHN D. SOHL.

BROADCASTING

Radio

Federated States of Micronesia Public Information Office: POB PS-34, Palikir, Pohnpei, FM 96941; tel. 320-2548; fax 320-4356; e-mail fsmpio@mail.fm; internet www.fsmpio.fm/pio.htm; govt-operated; four regional stations, each broadcasting 18 hours daily; Information Officer PATRICK BLANK.

Station V6AH: POB 1086, Kolonia, Pohnpei, FM 96941; programmes in English and Pohnpeian; Man. WEIDEN MANUEL.

Station V6AI: POB 117, Colonia, Yap, FM 96943; tel. 350-2174; fax 350-4426; programmes in English, Yapese, Ulithian and Satawalese; Man. SEBASTIAN F. TAMAGKEN.

Station V6AJ: POB 147, Tofol, Kosrae, FM 96944; tel. 370-3040; fax 370-3880; e-mail kosraebroadcast@yahoo.com; programmes in English and Kosraean; Man. MCDONALD ITTU.

Station V6AK: Wenn, Chuuk, FM 96942; tel. 330-2596; programmes in Chuukese and English; Man. JOE COMMOR.

WSZA Yap: Dept of Youth and Civic Affairs, POB 30, Colonia, Yap 96943; tel. 350-2174; Media Dir PETER GARAMFEL.

WSZD Pohnpei: POB 1086, Kolonia, Pohnpei 96941; tel. 320-2296; programmes in English and Pohnpeian; Man. FRANCIS ZARRED.

Television

Island Cable TV—Pohnpei: POB 1628, Pohnpei, FM 96941; tel. 320-2671; fax 320-2444; e-mail ictv@mail.fm; f. 1991; Gen. Man. DAVID O. CLIFFE.

TV Station Chuuk (TTTK): Wenn, Chuuk, FM 96942; tel. 330-4475; commercial.

TV Station Pohnpei (KPON): Central Micronesia Communications, POB 460, Kolonia, Pohnpei, FM 96941; f. 1977; commercial; Tech. Dir DAVID CLIFFE.

TV Station Yap (WAAB): Colonia, Yap, FM 96943; tel. 350-2160; fax 350-4113; govt-owned; Man. LOU DEFNGIN.

Finance

BANKING

Regulatory Authority

Federated States of Micronesia Banking and Insurance Board: POB 1887, Kolonia, Pohnpei, FM 96941; tel. 320-2015; fax 320-5433; e-mail fmbb@mail.fm; f. 1980; Chair. ALEXANDER NARRUHN; Commissioner WILSON F. WAGUK.

Banks are also supervised by the US Federal Deposit Insurance Corporation.

Commercial Banks

Bank of the Federated States of Micronesia: POB 98, Kolonia, Pohnpei, FM 96941; tel. 320-2838; fax 320-5359; cap. US $4.6m., dep. US $74.8m. (Dec. 2010); brs in Kosrae, Yap, Pohnpei and Chuuk.

Bank of Guam (USA): POB 367, Kolonia, Pohnpei, FM 96941; tel. 320-2550; fax 320-2562; e-mail bogpohn@mail.fm; internet www.bankofguam.com; Br. Mans JOANNE H. AKINAGA, VIDA B. RICAFRENTE; brs in Chuuk and Pohnpei.

Yap Credit Union: POB 610, Colonia, Yap; tel. 350-2142.

Development Bank

Federated States of Micronesia Development Bank: POB M, Kolonia, Pohnpei, FM 96941; tel. 320-2840; fax 320-2842; e-mail info@fsmdb.fm; internet www.fsmdb.fm/index; f. 1979; total assets US $35.6m. (2007); Chair. IHLEN JOSEPH; Pres. ANNA MENDIOLA; 4 brs. Banking services for the rest of the islands are available in Guam, Hawaii and on the US mainland.

INSURANCE

Actouka Executive Insurance: POB 55, Kolonia, Pohnpei; tel. 320-5331; fax 320-2331; e-mail mlamar@mail.fm.

Caroline Insurance Underwriters: POB 37, Chuuk; tel. 330-2705; fax 330-2207.

FSM Insurance Group: Kosrae; tel. 370-3788; fax 370-2120.

Islands Insurance: POB K, Kolonia, Pohnpei; tel. 320-3422.

Moylan's Insurance Underwriters: POB 1448, Kolonia, Pohnpei, FM 96941; tel. 320-2118; fax 320-2519; e-mail pohnpei@moylans.net; Pres. and Gen. Man. MELNER ISAAC.

Oceania Insurance Co: POB 1202, Weno, Chuuk, FM 96942; tel. 330-3036; fax 330-3764; e-mail oceanpac@mail.fm; also owns and manages Pacific Basin Insurance; Region Man. ERICSON MARAR.

Pacific Islands Insurance Underwriters: POB 386, Colonia, Yap; tel. 350-2340; fax 350-2341.

Transpacific Insurance: POB 510, Kolonia, Pohnpei; tel. 320-5525; fax 320-5524.

Yap Insurance Agency: POB 386, Colonia, Yap; tel. 350-2340; fax 350-2341; e-mail tachelioyap@mail.fm.

Trade and Industry

GOVERNMENT AGENCIES

Coconut Development Authority: POB 297, Kolonia, Pohnpei, FM 96941; tel. 320-2892; fax 320-5383; e-mail fsmcda@mail.fm; f. 1981; responsible for all purchasing, processing and exporting of copra and copra by-products in the islands; Gen. Man. NAMIO NANPEI.

FSM National Fisheries Corporation: POB R, Kolonia, Pohnpei, FM 96941; tel. 320-2529; fax 320-2239; e-mail nfcairfreight@mail.fm; internet www.fsmgov.org/nfc; f. 1984; established in 1990, with the Economic Devt Authority and an Australian co, the Caroline Fishing Corpn (three vessels); promotes fisheries development; Pres. NICK SOLOMON.

National Oceanic Resource Management Authority (NORMA): POB PS-122, Palikir, Pohnpei, FM 96941; tel. 320-2700; fax 320-2383; e-mail info@norma.fm; internet norma.fm; fmrly Micronesian Fisheries Authority; name changed 2002; responsible for conservation, management and development of tuna resources and for issue of fishing licences; Exec. Dir PATRICK MACKENZIE; Deputy Dir EUGENE PANGELINAN.

Office of Compact Management: 253 Palikir Station, Pohnpei FM 96941; tel. 320-8375; fax 320-8377; Exec. Dir EHPEL ILON.

Pohnpei Economic Development Authority: POB 738, Kolonia, Pohnpei, FM 96941; tel. 320-2298; fax 320-2775; e-mail eda@mail.fm; chaired by the President of the Federated States of Micronesia; Exec. Dir SHELTEN NETH.

CHAMBERS OF COMMERCE

Chuuk Chamber of Commerce: POB 700, Weno, Chuuk, FM 96941; tel. 330-2318; fax 330-2314; e-mail larry.bruton@mail.fm; Pres. WILLIAM STINNETT.

Kosrae Chamber of Commerce: POB 877, Tofol, Kosrae, FM 96944; tel. 370-3483; e-mail info@kosraechamberofcommerce.org; internet www.kosraechamberofcommerce.org; Chair. WITSON PHILLIP.

Pohnpei Chamber of Commerce: POB 405, Kolonia, Pohnpei, FM 96941; tel. 320-2452; fax 320-5277; e-mail amc@mail.fm; Pres. LEON SENDA.

Yap Chamber of Commerce: Colonia, Yap, FM 96943; tel. 350-2298; Pres. PHILLIP RANGANBAY.

UTILITIES

Chuuk Public Works (CPW): POB 248, Weno, Chuuk, FM 96942; tel. 330-2242; fax 320-4815.

Kosrae Utility Authority: POB 277, Tofol, Kosrae, FM 96944; tel. 370-3799; fax 370-3798; e-mail info@kosraepower.com; internet kosraepower.com; corporatized in 1994; Gen. Man. FRED N. SKILLING.

Pohnpei Utilities Corporation: POB C, Kolonia, Pohnpei, FM 96941; tel. 320-2374; fax 320-2422; e-mail info@puc.fm; internet www.puc.fm; f. 1992; provides electricity, water and sewerage services; Gen. Man. FELICIANO PERMAN.

Yap State Public Service Corpn (YSPSC): POB 621, Colonia, Yap, FM 96943; tel. 350-2175; fax 350-2331; f. 1996; provides electricity, water and sewerage services; Gen. Man. FAUSTINO R. YANGMOG.

CO-OPERATIVES

Chuuk: Chuuk Co-operative, Faichuk Cacao and Copra Co-operative Asscn, Pis Fishermen's Co-operative, Fefan Women's Co-operative.

Pohnpei: Pohnpei Federation of Co-operative Asscns (POB 100, Pohnpei, FM 96941), Kapingamarangi Copra Producers' Asscn, Kitti Minimum Co-operative Asscn, Kolonia Consumers' and Producers' Co-operative Asscn, Kosrae Island Co-operative Asscn, Metalanim Copra Co-operative Asscn, Mokil Island Co-operative Asscn, Ngatik Island Co-operative Asscn, Nukuoro Island Co-operative Asscn, PICS Co-operative Asscn, Pingelap Consumers' Co-operative Asscn, Pohnpei Fishermen's Co-operative, Pohnpei Handicraft Co-operative, Uh Soumwet Co-operative Asscn.

Yap Co-operative Association Inc: POB 159, Colonia, Yap, FM 96943; tel. 350-2209; fax 350-4114; e-mail yca@mail.fm; internet yapcoop.com; f. 1952; Pres. FAUSTINO YANGMOG; Gen. Man. TONY GANNGIYAN; 1,832 mems.

Transport

ROADS

In 2000 the Federated States of Micronesia had a total road network of 240 km. Tarmac and concrete roads are found in the more important islands. Other islands have stone- and coral-surfaced roads and tracks.

SHIPPING

Pohnpei, Chuuk, Yap and Kosrae have deep-draught harbours for commercial shipping. The ports provide warehousing and transshipment facilities.

Caroline Fisheries Corporation (CFC): POB 7, Kolonia, Pohnpei, FM 96941; tel. 320-3926; fax 320-4733; e-mail cfc@mail.fm; Gen. Man. MILAN KAMBER.

Pacific Shipping Agency: POB 154, Lelu, Kosrae FM 96944; tel. 370-3956; fax 370-3750; e-mail KosraeAce@mail.fm; f. 1990; Gen. Man. SMITH SIGRAH.

Pohnpei Transfer & Storage, Inc: POB 340, Kolonia, Pohnpei FM 96941; tel. 320-2552; fax 320-2389; e-mail fsmlinejv@mail.fm; Gen. Man. JOE VITT.

Truk Transportation Company (TRANSCO): POB 99, Weno, Chuuk FM 96942; tel. 330-2143; fax 330-2726; e-mail transco@mail.fm; f. 1964; Pres. MYRON HASHIGUCHI; Gen. Man. GIDEON BISALEN.

Waab Transportation Company: POB 177, Colonia, Yap FM 96943; tel. 350-2301; fax 350-4110; e-mail waabtrans@mail.fm; agents for PM & O Lines (USA); Man. LOUIS GAW.

CIVIL AVIATION

The Federated States of Micronesia is served by Continental Micronesia, Our Airline (formerly Air Nauru) and Continental Airlines (USA). Pacific Missionary Aviation, based in Pohnpei and Yap, provides domestic air services. There are international airports on Pohnpei, Chuuk, Yap and Kosrae, and airstrips on the outer islands of Onoun and Ta in Chuuk. The extension of the runway at Pohnpei airport, to accommodate larger aircraft, was scheduled for completion in 2011.

Tourism

The tourist industry is a significant source of revenue, although it has been hampered by the lack of infrastructure. Visitor attractions include excellent conditions for scuba-diving (notably in Chuuk Lagoon), Second World War battle sites and relics (many underwater) and the ancient ruined city of Nan Madol on Pohnpei. The number of tourist arrivals was estimated to total 25,627 in 2008. Tourist receipts totalled an estimated US $18.3m. in 2006.

Federated States of Micronesia Visitors Board: National Government, PO Box PS-12, Palikir, Pohnpei, FM 96941; tel. 320-5133; fax 320-3251; e-mail fsminfo@visit-fsm.org; internet www.visit-micronesia.fm.

Chuuk Visitors Bureau: POB FQ, Weno, Chuuk, FM 96942; tel. 330-4133; fax 330-4194; e-mail cvb@mail.fm.

Kosrae Visitors Bureau: POB 659, Tofol, Kosrae, FM 96944; tel. 370-2228; fax 370-3000; e-mail kosrae@mail.fm; internet www.kosrae.com.

Pohnpei Department of Tourism and Parks: POB 66, Kolonia, Pohnpei, FM 96941; tel. 320-2421; fax 320-6019; e-mail tourismparks@mail.fm; Deputy Chief BUMIO SILBANUZ.

Pohnpei Visitors Bureau: POB 1949, Kolonia, Pohnpei, FM 96941; tel. 320-4851; fax 320-4868; e-mail pohnpeiVB@mail.fm; internet www.visit-pohnpei.fm.

Yap Visitors Bureau: POB 988, Colonia, Yap, FM 96943; tel. 350-2298; fax 350-7015; e-mail yvb@mail.fm; internet www.visityap.com; Chair. ALPHONSO GANANG; Gen. Man. LAURENCE KENBAROY.

Defence

Defence and security are the responsibility of the USA. The US Pacific Command is based in Hawaii.

Education

Primary education, which begins at six years of age and lasts for eight years, is compulsory. Secondary education, beginning at 14 years of age, comprises two cycles, each of two years. The education system is based on the US pattern of eight years' attendance at an elementary school and four years' enrolment at a high school. The Micronesia Maritime and Fisheries Academy, which was opened in Yap in 1990, provides education and training in fisheries technology at secondary and tertiary levels. The College of Micronesia offers two- and three-year programmes leading to a degree qualification. In 2006/07 there were 18,512 pupils enrolled in primary education and 14,742 pupils enrolled in secondary education. In 2005/06 approximately 2,283 pupils were studying at college level.

MOLDOVA

Introductory Survey

LOCATION, CLIMATE, LANGUAGE, RELIGION, FLAG, CAPITAL

The Republic of Moldova is a small, landlocked country situated in south-eastern Europe. The republic is bounded to the north, east and south by Ukraine. To the west it borders Romania. The climate is favourable for agriculture, with long, warm summers and relatively mild winters. Average temperatures in Chișinău range from 21°C (70°F) in July to −4°C (24°F) in January. The 1994 Constitution describes the official language as Moldovan, a Romance language that is widely considered to be identical to Romanian. Most of the inhabitants of Moldova profess Orthodox Christianity. The national flag (proportions 1 by 2) consists of three equal vertical stripes, of light blue, yellow and red; the yellow stripe has at its centre the arms of Moldova (a shield bearing a stylized bull's head in yellow, set between an eight-pointed yellow star, a five-petalled yellow flower, and a yellow crescent, the shield being set on the breast of an eagle, in gold and red, which holds a green olive branch in its dexter talons, a yellow sceptre in its sinister talons, and a yellow cross in its beak). The capital is Chișinău.

CONTEMPORARY POLITICAL HISTORY

Historical Context

The area of the present-day Republic of Moldova corresponds to only part of the medieval principality of Moldova (Moldavia), which emerged as an important regional power in the 15th century. In the following century the principality came under Turkish Ottoman (Osmanlı) domination. Following a period of conflict between the Ottoman and Russian Empires, Moldova was divided into two parts in 1812: the eastern territory of Bessarabia, situated between the Prut and Dniester (Dnestr or Nistru) rivers—which roughly corresponds to the modern Republic of Moldova—was ceded to Russia, while the Ottomans retained control of western Moldova. A Romanian nationalist movement evolved in western Moldova and the neighbouring region of Wallachia during the 19th century, culminating in the proclamation of a Romanian state in 1877. In June 1918, after the collapse of the Russian Empire, Bessarabia was proclaimed an independent republic, although in November it voted to become part of Romania. This union was recognized in the Treaty of Paris (1920). However, the USSR (established in 1922) refused to recognize Romania's claims to the territory, and in October 1924 formed a Moldovan Autonomous Soviet Socialist Republic (ASSR) on the eastern side of the Dniester, within the Ukrainian Soviet Socialist Republic (SSR). In June 1940 Romania was forced to cede Bessarabia and northern Bucovina to the USSR, under the terms of the Treaty of Non-Aggression, concluded with Nazi Germany in August 1939. Northern Bucovina, southern Bessarabia and the Kotovsk-Balța region of the Moldovan ASSR were incorporated into the Ukrainian SSR. The remaining parts of the Moldovan ASSR and of Bessarabia were merged to form the Moldovan SSR, which formally joined the USSR on 2 August 1940.

Between July 1941 and August 1944 the Moldovan SSR was reunited with Romania. However, the Soviet Army reannexed the region in 1944, and the Moldovan SSR was re-established. Soviet policy in Moldova concentrated on isolating the region from its historical links with Romania: cross-border traffic virtually ceased, the Cyrillic script was imposed on the Romanian language (which was referred to as Moldovan) and Russian and Ukrainian immigration was encouraged. In the 1950s thousands of ethnic Romanians were deported to Central Asia.

Domestic Political Affairs

In May 1989 a number of independent cultural and political groups, which were denied legal status, allied to form the Popular Front (PF). In June some 70,000 people attended a protest demonstration, organized by the PF, on the anniversary of the Soviet annexation of Bessarabia in 1940. In August 1989 mass demonstrations were convened in the capital, Chișinău, in support of proposals by the Moldovan Supreme Soviet (Supreme Council—legislature) to declare Romanian the official language of the republic. Following protests by non ethnic-Romanians, the proposals were amended: legislation was enacted providing for Russian to be retained as a language of inter-ethnic communication, but the official language was to be Romanian, written in the Latin script. Following disturbances in Chișinău, during the celebrations of the anniversary of the Bolshevik Revolution on 7 November, the First Secretary of the ruling Communist Party of Moldova (CPM), Semion Grossu, was dismissed. He was replaced by Petru Lucinschi.

The increasing influence of the Romanian-speaking population was strongly opposed by other inhabitants of the republic (who, at the 1989 census, comprised some 35% of the total population). In the areas east of the Dniester, Transnistria or Pridnestrovie, where Russians and Ukrainians predominated (and which had mostly constituted the Moldovan ASSR in 1924–40), the local authorities refused to implement the language law. Opposition to growing Moldovan nationalism was led by the Unity Movement dominated by leading CPM members, and the Slav-dominated United Work Collectives. Both organizations had links with Gagauz People, the most prominent of the political groups representing the 150,000-strong Gagauz minority (a Turkic, Orthodox Christian people, resident mostly in southern regions of Moldova). In January 1990 a referendum took place in the eastern town of Tiraspol, in which the predominantly Russian-speaking population voted to seek greater autonomy for Transnistria.

None of the independent political groups was officially allowed to endorse candidates in elections to the Moldovan Supreme Soviet in February 1990. About 80% of the 380 deputies elected were members of the CPM, but many were also sympathetic to the aims of the PF. The new Supreme Soviet convened in April, whereupon Mircea Snegur, a CPM member supported by the PF, was elected Chairman. In the following month the Government resigned after losing a vote of no confidence. A new Council of Ministers, chaired by an economist, Mircea Druc, implemented far-reaching political changes, revoking the CPM's constitutional right to power. On 23 June the Supreme Soviet adopted a declaration of sovereignty asserting the supremacy of Moldova's Constitution and law. The Supreme Soviet also declared the 1940 Soviet annexation of Bessarabia to have been illegal. In September Snegur was elected to the newly instituted post of President of the Republic.

The actions of the increasingly radical Romanian majority in the legislature provoked further anxiety among the country's minority ethnic groups. In August 1990 a separate 'Gagauz SSR' was proclaimed in the southern region around Comrat (Komrat), and in September east-bank Slavs proclaimed their secession from Moldova and the establishment of the 'Transdnestrian SSR', with its self-styled capital at Tiraspol (this territory contained much of Moldova's industry, as well as three of the republic's five largest cities). Both declarations were immediately annulled by the Moldovan Supreme Soviet. In October Moldovan nationalists sought to thwart elections to a Gagauz Supreme Soviet by sending some 50,000 armed volunteers to the area. Violence was prevented only by the dispatch of Soviet troops to the region. The new Gagauz Supreme Soviet convened in Comrat and elected Stepan Topal as its President. Inter-ethnic violence occurred east of the Dniester in November, when elections were announced to a Transnistrian Supreme Soviet. Negotiations in Moscow, the Russian and Soviet capital, involving the Moldovan Government, the east-bank Slavs and the Gagauz, failed to resolve the crisis, but the elections proceeded without further violence.

In mid-December 1990 around 800,000 people, attending a 'Grand National Assembly', voted to reject any new union treaty (which was being negotiated by other Soviet republics), and in February 1991 the Moldovan Supreme Soviet resolved not to participate in the all-Union referendum on the future of the USSR. Despite the official boycott, in March some 650,000 people (mostly ethnic Russians, Ukrainians and Gagauz) did take part, voting almost unanimously for the preservation of the USSR. Nevertheless, the ethnic-Romanian-dominated Government and legislature continued the process of de facto secession. In

May the designation 'Soviet Socialist' was removed from the republic's name and the Supreme Soviet was renamed Parlamentul (the Parliament). In the same month, following a vote of no confidence by the legislature, Druc was removed as Prime Minister.

Independence

Following the attempted coup by conservative communists in Moscow in August 1991, the commanders of the USSR's South-Western Military District sought to impose a state of emergency in Moldova. However, the republican leadership immediately announced its support for the Russian President, Boris Yeltsin, in his opposition to the coup. On 27 August, after the coup had collapsed, Moldova proclaimed its independence. In September President Snegur ordered the creation of national armed forces, and assumed control of the republican KGB (state security service), transforming it into a Ministry of National Security, while the CPM was proscribed.

At the election to the republican presidency on 8 December 1991, Snegur, the sole candidate, received 98.2% of the votes cast. On 21 December Moldova was among the 11 signatories to the Almaty (Alma-Ata) Declaration establishing the Commonwealth of Independent States (CIS, see p. 238). Moldovan affairs during the first half of 1992 were dominated by the armed conflict in Transnistria (see below) and by the question of possible unification with Romania, strongly advocated by the ruling PF (which in February was re-formed as the Christian Democratic Popular Front—CDPF). A National Council for Reintegration had been established in December 1991, comprising legislators from both Moldova and Romania who were committed to the idea of a unified Romanian state. Within Moldova, however, popular support for unification remained insubstantial. In June 1992 the CDPF-dominated Government announced its resignation. Andrei Sangheli was appointed Prime Minister, and a new Government 'of national accord' was formed, led by the Agrarian Democratic Party (ADP), which largely comprised members of the former communist leadership. The CDPF became the main opposition party. The ADP declared its commitment to consolidating Moldovan statehood, rejecting any future union with Romania. These policies were strongly supported by President Snegur, who in January 1993 proposed that the issue be resolved in a referendum. This proposal was narrowly rejected by Parlamentul, but the ensuing political crisis led to several resignations, including that of the legislative Chairman, Alexandru Moșanu, who was replaced by Lucinschi.

During 1993 the ADP made substantial progress with the drafting of a new constitution, which was to be ratified following the election of a new parliament. The draft Constitution provided, inter alia, for a reduced, 104-member legislature. Moldova's first multi-party elections were held on 27 February 1994, with the participation of more than 73% of the electorate. In Transnistria the local leadership did not open polling stations, although residents were able to vote on the west bank of the Dniester. In all, 13 parties and blocs contested the elections. The ADP obtained an overall majority in Parlamentul (56 seats). The successor party to the CPM, the Socialist Party (SP), in alliance with the Unity Movement, won 28 seats. Two pro-unification groups shared the remaining 20 seats: the Peasants' Party of Moldova/Congress of Intelligentsia alliance (11) and the CDPF (nine). In a referendum held on 6 March, more than 95% of the votes cast by 75% of the electorate were in favour of continued independence. A new Council of Ministers led by Sangheli, solely comprising members of the ADP, was appointed in April. In May the CPM was permitted to re-form, as the Party of Communists of the Republic of Moldova (PCRM).

The new Constitution, adopted by Parlamentul in July 1994, entered into force in August. As well as establishing the country's permanent neutrality, the Constitution provided for a 'special autonomous status' for Transnistria and Gagauz-Yeri (Gagauzia, the Gagauz-majority areas) within Moldova. The state language was specified as Moldovan (rather than Romanian). In June, following the rejection by the ADP and its allies in Parlamentul of the proposal that the state language be constitutionally described as Romanian, Snegur resigned his membership of the ADP (which he had joined in 1994) and in August 1995 established the Party of Rebirth and Conciliation (PRC), with the support of several disaffected ADP deputies. In February 1996 Parlamentul again rejected the proposed redesignation of the state language as Romanian.

At the presidential election, held on 17 November 1996, Snegur received the largest share of the votes cast (39%) of any of the nine candidates; his failure to win an absolute majority necessitated a second round of voting, in which his opponent was Lucinschi, now supported by the ADP. In the second round of polling, held on 1 December, Lucinschi emerged as the winner, with 54% of the votes cast. The authorities in Transnistria again boycotted the poll, and there were reports that residents were prevented from leaving the region to vote. Lucinschi was inaugurated as President on 15 January 1997, and a new Government was announced later that month, headed by Ion Ciubuc, a non-party economist. In March the leader of the ADP, Dumitru Moțpan, was elected as Chairman of Parlamentul.

Parliamentary elections took place on 22 March 1998. In an apparent rejection of Lucinschi's economic reform programme, the elections were won by the PCRM, led by Vladimir Voronin, which took 30.1% of the votes cast (40 seats). The Democratic Convention of Moldova (CDM), an alliance led by Snegur, won 19.2% (26 seats), while the Movement for a Democratic and Prosperous Moldova (MDPM) received 18.2% (24 seats) and the Moldovan Party of Democratic Forces 8.8% (11 seats). The ADP failed to secure the 4% of the votes required for representation. The elections were again boycotted in Transnistria, but voters were permitted to cross the Dniester to vote.

At the first session of the new legislature, convened in April 1998, Dumitru Diacov was elected Chairman. The Government resigned shortly afterwards. Since none of the political parties had secured an overall parliamentary majority, the new Government, appointed in May (with Ciubuc retaining his post as Prime Minister), comprised members of the Alliance for Democracy and Reforms coalition led within Parlamentul by Snegur, including members of the MDPM, the CDM and the Moldovan Party of Democratic Forces.

Ciubuc resigned as Prime Minister in February 1999. Snegur resigned as parliamentary leader of the government coalition one day later, after his nominee for the premiership was rejected. Lucinschi then nominated the Mayor of Chișinău, Serafim Urechean, as Prime Minister. He was, however, unable to obtain the support of the parliamentary majority. Consequently, Lucinschi nominated Ion Sturza, the Deputy Prime Minister and Minister of the Economy and Reforms, as premier. Although Parlamentul twice failed to endorse his proposed government, Lucinschi nominated Sturza a third time. Confronted with a choice between acceptance or the constitutional requirement to hold an early general election, Parlamentul narrowly approved Sturza's Government in March.

Local elections were held on 23 May 1999, after which the country was reorganized into nine provinces and two autonomous entities (Gagauz-Yeri and Transnistria). A referendum held on the same day, approving increased presidential powers, was invalidated by the low rate of electoral participation, and was subsequently ruled to have been illegal, as it had not been announced and organized by Parlamentul.

In October 1999 the creation of a new, independent political bloc, principally comprising members of the MDPM, weakened the Government's support in Parlamentul. In November Sturza lost a vote of confidence in the legislature, after the defeat of legislation on the privatization of the wine and tobacco industries; the IMF and the World Bank subsequently suspended credits to Moldova (the bill was finally approved in October 2000). Following the failure of two candidates for the premiership (including Voronin) to secure the necessary support in the legislature, the President's nomination of Dumitru Braghiș, hitherto Deputy Minister of the Economy and Reform, as Prime Minister was approved in December.

In July 2000 Parlamentul voted in favour of amending the Constitution to permit the legislature to elect the Head of State. Parlamentul swiftly overturned President Lucinschi's decision to veto the proposed amendment, which duly took effect. In October Parlamentul announced that a presidential election would be contested within the legislature in December.

Neither of the two candidates in the presidential election—Voronin, for the PCRM, and Pavel Barbalat, the Chairman of the Constitutional Court, who had been proposed by a coalition of the Democratic Party of Moldova (PDM, as the MDPM had been renamed in April), the CDM, the Christian Democratic People's Party (PPCD, formerly the CDPF) and the Moldovan Party of Democratic Forces—obtained the requisite number of votes to secure an overall victory after three rounds of voting. The PDM, the CDM, the PPCD and the Moldovan Party of Democratic Forces boycotted a fourth round of voting on 21 December 2000, thereby permitting the President to dissolve the legislature and schedule early parliamentary elections.

MOLDOVA

Communists return to power

At the legislative elections, held on 25 February 2001, the PCRM won an overall majority in Parlamentul, securing 49.9% of the votes cast and 71 seats. The Braghiș Alliance, formed by the incumbent Prime Minister, obtained 19 seats, while the PPCD obtained 11 seats. The elections were described as free and fair by observers from the Organization for Security and Co-operation in Europe (OSCE, see p. 385). The rate of voter participation was some 70%. In the presidential election, which took place on 4 April, Voronin secured 71 votes, Braghiș obtained 15 and another communist candidate, Valerian Cristea, won three; the 11 PPCD deputies abstained from voting. Following his inauguration as President on 7 April, Voronin nominated Vasile Tarlev, a former businessman without party affiliation, as premier.

Proposals by the Minister of Education, Ilie Vancea, for the introduction of the compulsory teaching of Russian language and history to the national curriculum from 2002, were confirmed in December 2001. A demonstration, organized by the PPCD and involving an estimated 3,000 people, took place in Chișinău in January 2002 to protest against these measures; protests continued throughout the month. In late January the Ministry of Justice suspended the PPCD from participation in political activities for one month, preventing it from organizing further protests. However, in February, following intervention by the Council of Europe, the PPCD's suspension was annulled in order to allow the party to campaign for local elections, due to be held in April. In mid-February, however, the Constitutional Court ruled that the scheduling of early local elections for April was unconstitutional.

Meanwhile, in February 2002 the Deputy Prime Minister and Minister of the Economy, Andrei Cucu, and the reformist Minister of Finance, Mihai Manole, the only two non-PCRM members of the Council of Ministers, tendered their resignations. Following further protests against the proposed educational reforms, Vancea announced that the proposed legislation would be retracted; he was dismissed on 26 February. On the following day Vasile Draganel resigned as Minister of the Interior, amid reports that he had been unwilling to dispel protesters by force. Draganel was replaced by Gheorghe Papuc, a long-serving member of the security forces. Despite a ruling by the Supreme Court declaring the ongoing protests to be illegal, in February 2002 demonstrators began to protest outside the headquarters of the national television company against state censorship and misinformation. In March the Deputy Chairman of the PPCD, Vlad Cubreacov, who had been involved in organizing the anti-Government protests, was declared missing; thousands of demonstrators subsequently gathered to protest against Cubreacov's disappearance. In May Cubreacov was discovered alive, although his kidnappers remained unidentified.

Local elections took place on 25 May and 8 June 2003, in which the PCRM won the majority of seats, followed by the newly formed Our Moldova alliance, comprising the Alliance of Independents of Moldova, the National Liberal Party and the Social Democratic Alliance of Moldova. Following the elections, new legislation on administrative reform, approved by the Government in January, came into effect, according to which the provinces and autonomous regions introduced in 1999 were replaced with 33 districts and two municipalities. In July 2003 the parties of the Our Moldova bloc formally merged, together with the Popular Democratic Party of Moldova, to form the Our Moldova Alliance (AMN), led by Braghiș, Urechean and Veaceslav Untilă.

Thousands of protesters took part in opposition demonstrations in November 2003, against the Government's initial support for a Russian proposal for the federalization of Moldova (see below). The proposals, rejected in late November, had envisaged the installation of a popularly elected president and a new, bicameral legislature, with a planned upper house to comprise nine representatives of Transnistria, four of Gagauz-Yeri and 13 of the remainder of Moldova; Transnistria and Gagauz-Yeri were to have been represented at federal level by deputy prime ministers. New legislation, approved on 19 December, which sought to promote the use of Russian as a language of inter-ethnic communication (as it had also been designated in the USSR), while retaining Moldovan as an official language, was a further cause of demonstrations.

In February 2004 Andrei Strătan replaced Nicolae Dudău as Minister of Foreign Affairs. Also in February Parlamentul withdrew the immunity from prosecution of the Chairman, Iurie Roșca, and two other deputies of the PPCD, to permit their prosecution on charges of organizing and participating in unauthorized protests. From April the PDM and the Social Liberal Party agreed to co-operate with the AMN, forming the Democratic Moldova bloc, in preparation for parliamentary elections due to be held in 2005. In October the Minister of Defence, Victor Gaicuc, was dismissed from office following the theft of substantial quantities of military ordnance from army depots. In December Strătan was appointed as Deputy Prime Minister, retaining the foreign affairs portfolio.

In the legislative elections, held on 6 March 2005, the PCRM won 46.0% of the votes cast and 56 seats, the Democratic Moldova bloc 28.5% (34 seats) and the PPCD 9.1% (11 seats). Although the PCRM held a majority of seats in Parlamentul, it did not hold the quorum of 61 necessary for the election of a president. At the inaugural session of Parlamentul, the PDM withdrew from the Democratic Moldova bloc, forming its own eight-member faction, and three members of the Social Liberal Party subsequently also left the bloc, which was renamed the AMN faction in the legislature. Despite declarations that opposition deputies would boycott the presidential vote, in the event only the AMN did so. The election was held on 4 April, contested by the incumbent, Voronin, and another PCRM-nominated candidate, Gheorghe Duca. Voronin secured 75 of the 101 votes available (some 95 legislators were present); Duca received only one vote. Voronin was inaugurated as President on 7 April, and on 19 April Parlamentul approved a new Government, again led by Tarlev and retaining many members of the previous Council of Ministers.

In October 2005 members of the PCRM voted in Parlamentul to remove the parliamentary immunity of Urechean and two other deputies, following allegations of abuse of office. In the same month Mihai Pop was appointed Minister of Finance, in succession to Zinaida Grecianîi, who became First Deputy Prime Minister. In November Braghiș left the AMN, of which Urechean remained the sole leader, to form the Party of Social Democracy of Moldova. In January 2006 a former Minister of Defence, Valeriu Pasat, was sentenced to 10 years' imprisonment, after being convicted of defrauding the state when selling redundant fighter aircraft to the USA in 1997. In February 2006 Pasat was indicted on further, unrelated charges of having organized protests during the 2005 legislative elections in an attempt to overthrow Voronin and of conspiring to murder PPCD leader Roșca. (However, in July 2007 Pasat was released by the Court of Appeal and in July 2009 all remaining charges against him were withdrawn.)

In September 2006 Voronin replaced the Minister of Justice, appointing the hitherto government representative to the European Court of Human Rights to the post. In June 2007 local elections were conducted throughout Moldova; voter turnout was recorded at 52.3% nation-wide and about 37.2% in Chișinău. Although the PCRM was the most successful party overall, both nationally and in Chișinău, Dorin Chrtoaca of the Liberal Party (PL) was elected Mayor of the capital. In the same month Voronin dismissed the Minister of Defence, Valeriu Plesca, after a civilian was killed when journalists were permitted to participate in a military training exercise. In July he was replaced by Vitalie Vrabie, hitherto Deputy Prime Minister and Minister of Local Public Administration.

In January 2008 Voronin appointed a prominent member of the PCRM, Victor Stepaniuc, as a Deputy Prime Minister. On 19 March Tarlev and his Government resigned. Voronin subsequently nominated Grecianîi to the premiership. On 31 March Parlamentul voted to approve a new Government by 56 votes, with opposition deputies abstaining from voting; Igor Dodon, the Minister of Economy and Trade, succeeded Grecianîi as First Deputy Prime Minister. In October the hitherto Minister of Internal Affairs, Valentin Mejinschi, became Deputy Prime Minister, while Gheorghe Papuc was reappointed to the internal affairs ministry. In the same month Tarlev was elected Chairman of the Centrist Union of Moldova (UCM).

The April and July 2009 legislative elections

Elections to Parlamentul on 5 April 2009 resulted in a majority for the PCRM, which (according to preliminary results) secured about 49.5% of votes cast, while the PL won 13.1%, the Liberal Democratic Party of Moldova (PLDM) obtained 12.4% and the AMN received 9.8% of the votes cast. Despite a positive assessment of the conduct of the elections by the OSCE and other international observers, protests at alleged electoral malpractice, involving some 20,000, began on 6 April, apparently having been organized spontaneously through a micro-blogging website. On the following day anti-Government demonstrations degenerated into violent rioting, which included attacks on parliamentary and presidential buildings. The protests were suppressed by police, after clashes and the arrest of some 200 demonstrators. Voronin accused the Romanian Government of organizing a coup attempt (since many of the protesters had exhibited pro-Romanian sentiments), and immediately expelled the Romanian ambassador and recalled the Moldovan envoy in Bucharest, the Romanian capital; a number of Romanian journalists were also refused entry into the country (as a result of the introduction of visa requirements). Romania denied the allegations of involvement and demanded that the European Union (EU, see p. 270) investigate alleged abuses by the Moldovan authorities. Russia declared support for the Moldovan authorities and strongly condemned the protests. On 12 April the Constitutional Court officials ordered a recount of the preliminary results, following a request by Voronin. Human rights groups corroborated claims that demonstrators in custody were subjected to assaults and other ill treatment by police, and it was reported that at least three protesters had died following the arrests. The EU Special Representative to Moldova, Kalman Mizsei, undertook the mediation of negotiations with opposition leaders; in mid-April Voronin announced an amnesty for all suspects in detention or under investigation for involvement in the riots, excepting those with criminal records, although the Prosecutor-General's Office subsequently announced that 20 protesters had been officially charged in connection with the disturbances. On 20 April the Electoral Commission announced that the recount had not resulted in a significant change to the official results of the poll: the PCRM had secured 60 seats in Parlamentul (one fewer than the number required to elect a President), while the PL and PLDM had each received 15 seats, and the AMN 11 seats. (None of the further eight parties, that, together with independent candidates, contested the elections, achieved the requisite 6% of votes cast to obtain representation.) On 23 April the Constitutional Court endorsed the election results, following an appeal against them, submitted by the PL, the PLDM and the AMN, based on alleged evidence of electoral malpractice. The PCRM subsequently nominated Voronin as its candidate for Chairman of Parlamentul; he was elected to the post on 12 May. On the following day the PCRM declared that it would present Grecianîi as its candidate to succeed Voronin as President.

In mid-May 2009 it was announced that Grecianîi and a further candidate nominated by the PCRM, Stanislav Gropa, were to contest an election for the presidential office within Parlamentul on 20 May. The deputies of the PL, the PLDM and the AMN boycotted the election, and although all 60 PCRM deputies voted for the candidacy of Grecianîi, this was insufficient for her election to be constitutionally valid. A second ballot, held on 3 June, was again boycotted by the three opposition parties and was therefore similarly inconclusive. On 10 June Parlamentul approved an acting Council of Ministers, headed by Grecianîi, the composition of which remained largely unchanged. Meanwhile, the PCRM suffered a reverse when a senior figure in the party, and Voronin's predecessor as Chairman of Parlamentul, Marian Lupu, announced his departure from the party, citing its lack of support for his reform efforts. Lupu joined the PDM (which, having obtained just under 3% of the votes cast at the elections in April, had failed to obtain legislative representation) later in the month, becoming its Chairman. In early June, in anticipation that fresh legislative elections would prove necessary before a President could be elected, Parlamentul approved several amendments to the electoral code, reducing the threshold for securing parliamentary representation from 6% of the votes cast to 5%, the minimum voter turn-out required to validate elections from 50% of the electorate plus one vote to 33% plus one vote, and removing the minimum turn-out requirement for repeated elections. The opposition boycotted the vote on these reforms, which were broadly welcomed by the Parliamentary Assembly of the Council of Europe. On 15 June Voronin issued a decree dissolving Parlamentul, with effect from the following day, scheduling new parliamentary elections for 29 July. On 16 June, seemingly in an attempt to attract opposition support towards the PCRM, Voronin appointed Roşca (whose PPCD had narrowly failed to obtain legislative representation) as a Deputy Prime Minister. On 22 June Voronin visited Moscow, where he met both Russian President Dmitrii Medvedev and Chairman of the Government Vladimir Putin and secured a loan of some US $500m.

Although the PCRM lost its majority at the elections to Parlamentul conducted on 29 July 2009, it remained the largest party in the legislature, securing 44.7% of the votes cast and 48 of the 101 seats. The PLDM increased its share of the votes cast to 16.6%, receiving 18 seats; the PL obtained 14.7% and 15 seats. Following the defection to the party of Lupu, the PDM increased its support substantially, obtaining 12.5% of the votes cast and 13 seats, while support for the AMN decreased somewhat, to 7.4% and seven seats. (The PPCD again failed to gain legislative representation, and its support declined to only 1.9% of those who voted.) A turn-out of 58.8% was recorded. OSCE observers reported that there was some evidence of voter intimidation and media bias, but concluded that major electoral fraud did not occur. On 8 August the PLDM, the PL, the PDM and the AMN announced the formation of a coalition, the Alliance for European Integration (AIE), with the intention of establishing a reformist government that would be committed to seeking eventual EU membership for Moldova. With a combined total of 53 seats in Parlamentul, the Alliance would require the support of at least eight PCRM deputies to secure the election of its presidential candidate. On 28 August Mihai Ghimpu, the Chairman of the PL, was elected as the parliamentary Chairman, having obtained the support of all 53 AIE deputies. (The PCRM deputies boycotted the vote.) On 9 September Grecianîi resigned as Prime Minister, thereby effectively acknowledging that the PCRM Government did not have the support of the new legislature, although her resignation was formally attributed to the incompatability between serving as premier while simultaneously holding a parliamentary mandate. On 11 September Voronin resigned as President of the Republic; Ghimpu, as Chairman of Parlamentul, succeeded Voronin in an acting capacity, in accordance with constitutional requirements. On 17 September Ghimpu signed a decree nominating Vladimir Filat, the President of the PLDM, as Prime Minister. He also abolished the visa requirements imposed in April on Romanians entering the country. On 25 September Filat's Council of Ministers assumed office. In total, seven posts (including that of Prime Minister) were allocated to the PLDM, five to the PL and four to each of the PDM and the AMN, while each of the four coalition parties provided one Deputy Prime Minister. Lupu was nominated as the candidate of the governing AIE coalition in the forthcoming presidential election. Numerous new appointments were made to various state posts during October–November, including that of the Prosecutor-General and Chief of General Staff and Commander of the National Army (the latter in an acting capacity, after the resignation of the incumbent officeholder). In November Tarlev resigned from the leadership and membership of the UCM.

Constitutional impasse

Two attempts by the new legislature to elect a President, on 10 November and 7 December 2009, failed. On both occasions the PCRM boycotted the vote, and all 53 deputies from the AIE voted in support of Lupu's candidacy, eight too few for the election to be validated. Consequently, in accordance with constitutional norms, the legislature was to be dissolved, and further elections held. However, constitutional law dictated that a sitting of Parlamentul could not be dissolved less than one year after the most recent legislative dissolution. In an attempt to resolve this contradiction, in December the Constitutional Court requested that the Venice Commission of the Council of Europe provide its legal opinion on the state of affairs. At the end of the month the President of the state-controlled national television and radio broadcaster, Teleradio Moldova, Valentin Todercan, was dismissed, having been criticized for failing to guarantee political balance in broadcasts. In January 2010 a left-wing and pro-Russian faction of the PCRM, including five legislative deputies, announced the formation of a new party, United Moldova (MU), under the leadership of Vladimir Ţurcan, a former Minister of Internal Affairs and ambassador to Russia; much of the remaining membership of the UCM joined MU in the same month. In late February the state announced that it was to reacquire, on a temporary basis, two prominent newspapers, the Moldovan/Romanian-language *Moldova Suverană* and the Russian-language *Nezavisimaya Moldova*, which had been transferred from state ownership by apparently irregular means in the mid-2000s.

In early March 2010 Parlamentul voted to approve a motion presented by the PLDM for the dismissal of Ion Muruianu as President of the Supreme Court of Justice, after he had referred to journalists as 'rabid dogs' that constituted a threat to social order and after he was responsible for the loss of various documents concerned with cases at the European Court of Human Rights. In mid-March the Venice Commission provided its legal opinion on the constitutional impasse, stating that the demand that Parlamentul be dissolved no more than once a year should take precedence over the requirement that parliamentary dissolution take place when the election of a President by a three-fifths' legislative majority has proved impossible on two successive occasions. The Commission also recommended that Moldova adopt constitutional reforms in order to prevent any recurrence of the constitutional impasse that had been made evident by the inability to elect a President. On 16 March the Constitutional Court confirmed that Parlamentul could only be dissolved after 16 June (one year after its previous dissolution). Ghimpu, as acting President, stated that he would not permit the dissolution of Parlamentul until the constitutional provisions on electing the head of state had been amended. The PCRM criticized this decision, announcing that it would seek to organize a referendum of no confidence in the Government. At the end of April the Constitutional Court ruled that the dismissal of Muruianu as President of the Supreme Court of Justice had been unconstitutional; he was subsequently reappointed to his former position.

Meanwhile, rival political factions developed alternative proposals for constitutional reform that would permit the election of a President. In late April 2010 the Constitutional Court ruled that proposals for constitutional amendments presented by the PCRM, providing for a gradual reduction of the number of deputies required to approve the appointment of a President, could be presented, after a period of six months, for legislative consideration. In early May the Court issued a similar ruling with regard to proposals prepared by the AIE, in accordance with which the President would be elected by direct popular vote, and could be dismissed with the approval of two-thirds of legislative deputies. The approval of either set of constitutional amendments would require the support of 67 of the 101 members of Parlamentul to take effect. On 18 June Parlamentul approved a number of amendments to the electoral code, which had been proposed by the AIE: the number of deputies required for a quorum was reduced from 52 to 51 (in response to the parliamentary boycott by the PCRM); the minimum requirement for a party to secure parliamentary representation was reduced from 5% to 4%, and from 3% to 2% for independent candidates; the period for arranging a referendum before or after elections was lowered from 120 to 60 days; and the minimum required rate of participation in the referendum was reduced from 60% to 33% of the electorate.

Recent developments: further legislative elections

On 7 July 2010 Parlamentul approved the scheduling of a referendum, to be held on 5 September, on a new constitutional text, based on the reforms presented by the AIE, including provisions for direct presidential elections. Although 87.8% of the votes in the referendum were in support of the proposals, the rate of participation, at 30.3%, was insufficient for the reforms to be approved. The low rate of turn-out followed demands that the plebiscite be boycotted by numerous opposition parties, notably the PCRM. On 28 September, in accordance with a Constitutional Court ruling, Ghimpu announced the dissolution of Parlamentul, with effect from the following day, and scheduled legislative elections for 28 November. It was subsequently announced that the parties of the AIE would contest the election separately, and that an attempt to elect a President within Parlamentul would take place after a new legislative session had been convened.

The legislative elections on 28 November 2010 were contested by a total of 20 political parties, including the PCRM. According to the final results, which were announced by the Central Electoral Commission on 6 December, neither the PCRM nor the parties of the AIE together had secured the 61 legislative seats required to elect a new President. The PCRM again won the largest share of votes cast, with 39.3%, obtaining a reduced representation of 42 seats, followed by the PLDM, with 29.4% of votes and 32 seats (compared with 14 seats previously), the PDM, with 12.7% and 15 seats, and the PL, with 10% and 12 seats. Voter turnout of 63.4% was recorded. Although the PCRM claimed electoral violations had occurred, observers from the OSCE and the Council of Europe stated that the conduct of the elections had met most democratic commitments. On 30 December, following lengthy negotiations, a reconstituted AIE coalition in the new Parlamentul elected Lupu as its Chairman, and consequently as acting President, with 57 votes (the PCRM boycotting the session). On 14 January 2011 the formation of a new AIE coalition Government, again under the premiership of Filat, was approved in Parlamentul, with the PCRM boycotting the vote. Nevertheless, the ruling coalition's lack of the parliamentary majority required to elect a President or revise the Constitution presented a continued cause of concern. In February 2011, in response to a request for clarification presented by a group of PCRM deputies, the Constitutional Court ruled that, as a period of more than two months had passed since the expiry of the mandate of an elected President, Parlamentul had the right to decide when a presidential election should be held. By April no such date had been set. In that month the PDLM absorbed the AMN.

Transnistria

Following the proclamation of secession by Slavs resident on the east bank of the Dniester in September 1990, relations with the Moldovan Government remained tense. Armed conflict broke out in December 1991, as the leadership of the self-proclaimed Transnistrian Republic, opposed to the Moldovan Government's objective of reunification with Romania, launched a campaign to gain control of the territories on the east bank, with the ultimate aim of unity with Russia. Over six months of military conflict ensued, as Moldovan government troops were dispatched to combat the local Slav militia. The situation was complicated by the presence (and involvement in support of the east-bank Slavs) of the former Soviet 14th Army, which was still stationed in the region and jurisdiction over which had been transferred to Russia. Although peace negotiations were held at regular intervals, with the participation of Moldova, Russia, Ukraine and Romania, none of the agreed cease-fires was observed. By June 1992 some 700 people were believed to have been killed in the conflict, with an estimated 50,000 people forced to take refuge in Ukraine. On 21 July, however, a peace agreement was finally negotiated by President Snegur of Moldova and his Russian counterpart, Boris Yeltsin, whereby Transnistria was to be accorded 'special status' within Moldova (the terms of which were to be formulated later). Later in July Russian, Moldovan and Transnistrian peace-keeping troops were deployed in the region to monitor the cease-fire.

Transnistria continued to demand full statehood, and in January 1994 the Moldovan Government accepted proposals by the Conference on Security and Co-operation in Europe (CSCE—later OSCE) for greater autonomy for Transnistria, within a Moldovan confederation. The Transnistrian leadership expressed approval of the proposals, and the result of the Moldovan parliamentary elections of the following month further enhanced the prospects for a settlement. In April President Snegur and the Transnistrian leader, Igor Smirnov, pledged their commitment to holding negotiations for a peaceful resolution of the conflict, based on the CSCE recommendations.

In July 1994, following the adoption of the new Moldovan Constitution, which provided for a 'special autonomous status' for Transnistria, negotiations commenced on the details of the region's future status within Moldova. Progress was obstructed by disagreement over the future of the 15,000-strong 14th Army, the continued presence of which was demanded by the Transnistrian leadership as a guarantor of security. In October, however, the Moldovan and Russian Governments reached an agreement, under which Russia was gradually to withdraw the 14th Army, whereupon Transnistria's negotiated 'special autonomous status' would take effect. A referendum (declared illegal by President Snegur) was held in Transnistria in March 1995, in which some 91% of participants voted against the withdrawal of the 14th Army. In December two further referendums were held in Transnistria: 82.7% of the electorate endorsed a new constitution that proclaimed the region's independence, while 89.7% voted for Transnistria to join the CIS as a sovereign state. In February 1996, however, the CIS rejected admittance for Transnistria on such terms.

In July 1996 the executive and legislative authorities of Moldova and Transnistria initialled a memorandum, on normalizing relations. Smirnov was re-elected as President of Transnistria in December. In May 1997 the memorandum was signed in Moscow by the new Moldovan President, Lucinschi, and Smirnov, with Russia and Ukraine acting as guarantors of the document. Representatives of Moldova and Transnistria, meeting in Moscow in October, subsequently reached agreement on a number of 'confidence-building measures'. On 20 March 1998 a further agreement (the Odesa Accords) was signed by Lucinschi, Smirnov, Russian premier Viktor Chernomyrdin and President Leonid Kuchma of Ukraine, which envisaged a reduction in Moldovan and Transnistrian peace-keeping forces, while Russian troops were to remain in Transnistria until a final political settlement was reached. In June Russian and Moldovan delegations to the joint commission monitoring the Odesa Accords agreed proposals for the composition of peace-keeping forces in the security zone, and Moldova's peace-keeping troops were gradually reduced in number. In late May 1999 Transnistria was formally designated an autonomous entity. In July a further joint declaration on the normalization of relations between Moldova and Transnistria was signed; however, Smirnov declared that differences remained.

In June 2000 the 'Transnistrian Supreme Soviet' was converted to a unicameral legislature, and in July Smirnov introduced a form of presidential rule. The Moldovan President elected in April 2001, Vladimir Voronin, declared the pursuit of a final political settlement for Transnistria to be a priority. Relations with the Transnistrian authorities deteriorated in September, following the Moldova Government's introduction of new customs procedures, in accordance with World Trade Organization (WTO, see p. 430) requirements, leading to Transnistria alleging that Moldova was attempting to impose an 'economic blockade' on the region. Smirnov was re-elected to a second presidential term in December, although the election was recognized by neither Moldova nor the international community. In December 2002 the OSCE extended a deadline agreed in 1999 for the removal of Russian forces from Moldova by a further year, until December 2003.

In July 2002 mediators from Russia, Ukraine and the OSCE submitted a new draft agreement (the 'Kyiv agreement'), according to which Moldova would become a federal state, in which the autonomous territories would maintain their own legislatures and constitutions, although Smirnov continued to insist upon recognition of Transnistrian independence. On 27 February 2003 the EU and the USA, and subsequently other countries, imposed a travel ban on those Transnistrian officials considered to be 'primarily responsible for a lack of co-operation in promoting a political settlement'. In November the Russian President, Vladimir Putin, announced new proposals for a settlement. Drafted by the deputy head of the Russian presidential administration, Dmitrii Kozak, the plan envisaged the establishment of an 'asymmetrical federation', comprising Moldova and Transnistria, with unified defence, customs and finance systems. The leaders of both Transnistria and Moldova initially responded positively to the proposals, but Voronin withdrew his support later in the month. Although new proposals for the establishment of a federal Moldovan state were submitted to OSCE mediators in February 2004, they failed to satisfy both the Moldovan and Transnistrian parties. In mid-2004 controversy arose over the closure by the Transnistrian authorities of Moldovan-language schools teaching a Moldovan syllabus, in the Latin script. The Moldovan Government responded by withdrawing from the OSCE-mediated negotiation process and imposing economic sanctions on Transnistria, which retaliated in kind. The EU, the USA and other international parties condemned the closure of the schools and added a further 10 Transnistrian officials to the list of those prohibited from travelling to their countries, and a case was submitted to the European Court of Human Rights.

In December 2004, at an OSCE meeting held in Sofia, Bulgaria, the Russian delegation obstructed the adoption of a final statement containing a reference to the Russian commitment to withdraw troops and ammunition from Moldova. Russian representatives also refused to sign a Moldovan-drafted Declaration of Stability and Security, which proposed the inclusion of the EU and the USA in talks for the resolution of the Transnistrian conflict.

In April 2005 President Viktor Yushchenko of Ukraine presented a plan for the resolution of the Transnistrian conflict during a summit meeting in Chișinău. The plan envisaged that Transnistria would be awarded 'special status', as an autonomous entity within Moldova, and would be permitted to participate in foreign-policy decisions affecting its interests. In June Parlamentul endorsed the Yushchenko Plan, while noting that it made no mention of either the withdrawal of Russian troops or the establishment of border controls along the Transnistrian–Ukrainian border. In July Moldova removed the trade sanctions imposed against Transnistria in the previous year. In September all five parties to the negotiations on the status of Transnistria agreed to invite the EU and the USA (but not Romania) to participate in the process as observers; however, subsequent negotiations failed to record any substantive progress. Legislative elections (recognized by neither Moldova nor the international community) were held in Transnistria in December, at which the reformist Renewal bloc won the most seats in the region's Supreme Soviet.

At the end of November 2005 the EU launched a mission to help secure the Transnistrian–Ukrainian border, following appeals from Presidents Voronin and Yushchenko. At the end of December the Prime Ministers of Moldova and Ukraine signed a joint declaration on external trade, whereby Ukraine agreed not to recognize Transnistria's customs regime and to deal only in goods processed through the Moldovan customs system, in an attempt to combat smuggling. The new measures came into force in March 2006. In response, the Transnistrian authorities withdrew from the internationally mediated negotiations and introduced legislation banning all foreign-financed non-governmental organizations. In late March Russia suspended the import of Moldovan wine and other agricultural products, ostensibly owing to hygiene concerns. In early 2007 the Russian authorities announced that the import of fruit and vegetables from Moldova had resumed. In October the Russian Government announced that Moldovan wineries that had passed safety assessments were permitted to resume exports to Russia.

Following the initiation in February 2006 of formal negotiations to determine the final status of the Serbian UN-administered province of Kosovo (see the chapter on Kosovo), Transnistrian officials declared their intention to schedule a referendum on future relations with Moldova. On 17 September the Transnistrian authorities conducted an internationally unrecognized referendum on the territory's independence and potential options for eventual integration with Russia, at which some 97% voted for a continuation of de facto independence from Moldova and an agreement of eventual unification with Russia, while some 95% voted against the territory being ruled as part of Moldova. On 10 December a presidential election in Transnistria (again unrecognized by the international community) was won by Smirnov, with 82.4% of votes cast. Some 65.4% of registered voters participated in the election. Shortly after Kosovo's unilateral declaration of independence on 17 February 2008, Transnistria requested that the Russian legislature, the UN and other organizations recognize its independence. In March, following strong indications that Russia was not prepared to recognize Transnistria, Smirnov announced that he was willing to enter into discussions with the Moldovan Government. In April he and Voronin met for the first time since 2001 in Tighina (Bender), located on the west bank of the Dniester but nonetheless controlled by the Transnistrian authorities; the discussions that followed between Moldovan and Transnistrian delegations in Odesa, Ukraine, were regarded as preparatory to the resumption of official negotiations on a political resolution of the status of Transnistria.

In February 2009 the Russian Minister of Foreign Affairs, Sergei Lavrov, made an official visit to Moldova, preparatory to a meeting between Voronin and Smirnov, which was convened, under the aegis of Russian President Dmitrii Medvedev, in Moscow on 18 March. On that occasion the three leaders signed a Russian-drafted declaration providing for the conversion of the existing peace-keeping force in Transnistria into an OSCE-supervised operation (with the implication that the Moldovan Government would abandon demands for the withdrawal of Russian troops); the leaders expressed the intention to continue direct contacts but reiterated commitments to return to the '5 + 2' negotiating format (comprising Moldova, Transnistria, Russia, Ukraine and the OSCE, together with the USA and the EU). However, Voronin subsequently accused the Transnistrian authorities of failing to respect their obligations to continue dialogue and abandoned a planned meeting with Smirnov in Tiraspol on 25 March. On 8 July Yevgenii Shevchuk announced his resignation as President of the Transnistrian Supreme Soviet, citing 'deep disagreements' with Smirnov. The deputy leader of the Renewal parliamentary faction, Anatolii Kaminskii, was elected to the post unopposed later in the month. In December 2010 a Moldovan journalist, who had been arrested in April, was sentenced to 15 years' imprisonment by a court in Tiraspol, on charges of espionage for the Moldovan authorities. Internationally unrecognized legislative elections took place in Transnistria on 12 December; it was reported that the Renewal bloc had won 25 of the 43 seats in the Supreme Soviet, with about 42% of the electorate participating. Also in December, a court in Tiraspol sentenced a journalist of a Russian news agency, Ernest Vardanean, to 15 years' imprisonment, after he had been found guilty of espionage. Vardanean denied the Transnistrian authorities' allegations that he was spying for the Moldovan secret services, and the case attracted international attention and criticism from the Moldovan authorities. In early May 2011, after receiving a written appeal from Vardanean, Smirnov

MOLDOVA

signed a pardon permitting Vardanean's release from custody. Meanwhile, following the installation of a new reformist Government in January 2011, an OSCE initiative for the resumption of negotiations on the status of Transnistria began, with the support of the Russian Minister of Foreign Affairs, Sergei Lavrov (reportedly in exchange for the prospect of increased Russian involvement in EU security decision-making). However, at unofficial consultations in Vienna, Austria, in April, the Transnistrian delegation rejected the envisaged return to the '5 + 2' format, and continued to present a series of preconditions to negotiations.

Gagauz-Yeri

During the Transnistrian conflict in 1991–92, the situation in Gagauz-Yeri (which, unlike Transnistria, constitutes several non-contiguous territories) remained peaceful, although the region continued to demand full statehood. The 1994 Moldovan Constitution provides for a 'special autonomous status' for Gagauz-Yeri, as for Transnistria, and negotiations duly commenced on the details of this status. Agreement was quickly reached between the Government and the Gagauz authorities, and in December Parlamentul adopted legislation on the status of Gagauz-Yeri. The regions of southern Moldova populated by the Gagauz were to enjoy broad self-administrative powers, and Gagauz was to be one of three official languages (with Moldovan and Russian). Legislative power was to be vested in a regional assembly, and a directly elected başkan (governor) was to hold a quasi-presidential position. The law entered into force in February 1995, and in March a local referendum was held to determine which settlements would form part of the region. Elections to the 35-seat Halk Toplusu (Popular Assembly) took place in May–June. Concurrent elections held to the post of Başkan were won by Gheorghe Tabunscic, the First Secretary of the branch of the PCRM in the principal Gagauz-inhabited city, Comrat. Under the new Constitution, Tabunscic, as Gagauz leader, became a member of the Council of Ministers of Moldova. In May 1999 Gagauz-Yeri, like Transnistria, was designated an autonomous entity within Moldova. Elections to the Halk Toplusu and to the post of Başkan were held in late August. Following a second round of voting in September, Dumitru Croitor was elected as Başkan, with 61.5% of the votes cast. In mid-February 2002 the Halk Toplusu adopted a vote of no confidence in Croitor, and scheduled a referendum in the hope of securing his dismissal. On 24 February, the date that the referendum was scheduled to take place, the regional security forces reportedly seized the offices of the regional electoral commission, declaring its mandate to have expired and the plebiscite to be illegal. President Voronin subsequently visited the region and demanded the resignations of both Croitor and the Chairman of the Halk Toplusu. Croitor finally resigned at the end of June. At a second round of voting in an election held on 11 October, Tabunscic regained the post of Başkan. On 25 July 2003 Parlamentul officially recognized the autonomous status of Gagauz-Yeri through an amendment to the national Constitution, which awarded the Halk Toplusu the right to self-determination and to propose its own legislation. Legislative elections were held in the region in November–December, in which the PCRM and independent candidates each won almost one-half of the seats contested. On 17 December 2006 an independent candidate, Mihail Formuzal, was elected Başkan at a second round of voting. Further elections to the Halk Toplusu took place in March 2008, with voter turnout estimated at 60.5%. A coalition formed by the PCRM with independent candidates commanded the greatest parliamentary representation, with 14 seats, while supporters of Formuzal won eight seats. Following prolonged disagreement between the factions in the Halk Toplusu over the election of a Chairman, at the end of July an independent deputy and prominent journalist, Ana Harlamenco, was elected unanimously to the post. On 22 September the Halk Toplusu narrowly approved a resolution formally recognizing the separatist regions of Abkhazia and South Ossetia as independent from Georgia, following Russian recognition of those territories as independent states, and declaring support for Russia's military action in Georgia in August (see the chapter on Georgia).

Foreign Affairs

Regional relations

Owing to the changing domestic situation, Moldova's membership of the CIS was equivocal until early 1994. In August 1993 Parlamentul failed by four votes to ratify the Almaty Declaration, largely owing to the influence of deputies favouring unification with Romania. However, in September President Snegur signed a treaty to join the new CIS economic union. Following Moldova's parliamentary elections of February 1994 and the referendum in March, which strongly endorsed continued independence, Parlamentul reversed its earlier decision, and in April it finally ratified membership of the CIS.

The communist Government elected in 2001 initially undertook a policy of rapprochement with Russia, and in December Parlamentul ratified a treaty on friendship and co-operation, which had been signed by the two countries' respective Presidents in the previous month. The treaty was ratified by the Russian Gosudarstvennaya Duma (State Duma) in April 2002. However, in 2004 relations deteriorated, largely owing to developments associated with Transnistria (see above). From the beginning of 2006 Russia attempted to increase two-fold the price charged to Moldova for supplies of natural gas (from US $80 to $160 per 1,000 cu m). Gas supplies from Russia temporarily ceased in January, after Moldova refused to sign a new contract with the Russian state-controlled gas supplier, Gazprom. In mid-January a compromise agreement was reached, covering the first three months of the year; in return for agreeing to relinquish the Transnistrian assets of the joint-venture company MoldovaGaz to Gazprom (which already held a majority stake in the company), Moldova was be charged $110 per 1,000 cu m for its gas supplies from Russia. Leading officials of MoldovaGaz and Gazprom signed a five-year agreement, providing for staged increases in the price of gas supplied to Moldova, while the Moldovan Government was to transfer control of its gas distribution system to Gazprom. Relations with Russia became strained after the reformist Government of the AIE assumed office in September 2009. In June 2010 Russia again suspended imports of Moldovan wine on grounds of poor quality; the Moldovan Government claimed that the decision was in reprisal for a decree issued by acting President Ghimpu designating 28 June as the 'Day of Soviet Occupation'. Prior to further legislative elections in November, PDM leader Lupu (who subsequently became acting President) signed a political partnership agreement with the ruling United Russia in Moscow, reportedly without informing the other parties of the AIE. In early 2011 Gazprom increased the price of gas supplied to Moldova by about 12% (in accordance with the existing agreement); it was reported the Russian Government had offered gas price discounts to Moldova, in exchange for military basing rights.

In November 2004 Moldova condemned suspected electoral malpractice in Ukraine during the presidential election there and subsequently established cordial relations with the new administration of President Viktor Yushchenko in Ukraine. Moldova had also established good relations with the new, western-orientated Government in Georgia, under President Mikheil Saakashvili, who was inaugurated in early 2004. In December 2005 Moldova attended a meeting in Kyiv, Ukraine, to launch the new Community of Democratic Choice, originally conceived by Ukraine and Georgia. The nine-member alliance aimed to remove divisions and resolve conflicts in the Baltic, Black Sea and Caspian regions. In May 2006 the leaders of Georgia, Ukraine, Azerbaijan and Moldova met in Kyiv, Ukraine, to revive the regional GUAM organization, renaming it the Organization for Democracy and Economic Development—GUAM.

Relations with Romania were subject to tensions. A basic political treaty, in preparation for six years, was agreed in May 1999 and initialled in April 2000; however, it was not signed, and in late 2003 the Romanian Prime Minister, Adrian Năstase, indicated that the country no longer considered the treaty to be relevant to the political situation. In February 2000 many Moldovans applied to obtain Romanian citizenship as formal negotiations on Romania's accession to the EU commenced. The Romanian Government subsequently introduced measures to simplify the application process, angering the Moldovan authorities, since the Moldovan Constitution prohibited dual citizenship. The situation was resolved when President Lucinschi drafted a new law, allowing Moldovans to hold dual citizenship with Israel, Romania and Russia, which was enacted in August. In March 2002 a Romanian diplomat was expelled from Moldova, after having reportedly met organizers of opposition protests; Romania responded by expelling a Moldovan diplomat. From April 2003 ministerial co-operation between Moldova and Romania was resumed, together with preliminary negotiations regarding a border agreement; it was confirmed

MOLDOVA

Introductory Survey

that Romania would not require Moldovan citizens to possess entry visas to that country prior to Romania's eventual accession to the EU. None the less, in October Moldova appealed to the Council of Europe for assistance with its deteriorating relations with Romania, after that country failed to sign a bilateral treaty confirming Moldova's borders. In January 2005 the new President of Romania, Traian Băsescu, visited Moldova and declared his support for the country's desire to achieve eventual membership of the EU, which had begun to formulate an official policy towards Moldova. In March 2007 Moldova strongly criticized Romania for granting Romanian citizenship to large numbers of Moldovans (with an estimated 800,000 applications pending), on the grounds that the policy undermined Moldova's statehood. Romania's accession to full EU membership, which took effect in January 2007, resulted in Moldovan citizens being required to possess entry visas to enter that country; in protest at this, the Moldovan authorities reversed a decision to allow Romania to open two new consulates in the country. In December Moldova expelled two Romanian diplomats, who had allegedly supplied funds to opposition newspapers, for activities 'incompatible with their status'. The civil disturbances following legislative elections in early April 2009 (see above) prompted a number of retaliatory measures from the Moldovan Government, which accused Romania of organizing a coup attempt: the expulsion of the Romanian ambassador, the recall of the Moldovan envoy in Bucharest and the immediate introduction of visa requirements for Romanians entering the country. The Romanian President, Traian Băsescu, subsequently pledged that the Romanian Government would expedite the process of granting Romanian citizenship to Moldovans, claiming that some 1m. applications had been received. In late April it was reported that the Moldovan authorities had refused to accredit a new Romanian ambassador. The visa requirements for Romanian citizens wishing to visit Moldova were rescinded in September by the reformist Government led by Vladimir Filat.

In March 2010 Moldova and Romania signed an agreement providing for co-operation in the development of the Moldovan military air force. In July acting President Ghimpu appointed a Romanian political analyst, Dan Dungaciu (who had been granted Moldovan citizenship), as Moldova's presidential adviser on European integration. On 8 November Prime Minister Filat and the Romanian Minister of Foreign Affairs, on the occasion of a regional summit meeting in Bucharest, signed the bilateral treaty confirming the border between the two states and providing for closer co-operation.

Other external relations

Following the approval of the European Commission's Eastern Partnership initiative (which provided the framework for a closer relationship between the EU and Armenia, Azerbaijan, Belarus, Georgia, Moldova and Ukraine), at an EU summit meeting in March 2009, the acting Prime Minister of the Czech Republic, Mirek Topolánek, in his capacity as President of the EU Council, visited Moldova in late April. During a meeting with the outgoing Moldovan President, Vladimir Voronin, Topolánek extended officially an invitation to the Moldovan authorities for an Eastern Partnership summit meeting (which was scheduled to take place in early May). Topolánek also met principal opposition leaders, who presented alleged evidence to support their claims of electoral malpractice at the legislative elections held earlier in the month; he subsequently announced that he had recommended the establishment of a committee, comprising representatives of the European Commission and opposition parties, to investigate the violence. In early May Moldova was included in the EU's Eastern Partnership programme, which was officially inaugurated at a summit in Prague, Czech Republic, and envisaged enhanced free trade and visa arrangements. However, President Voronin chose not to attend the summit, Moldova instead being represented by the Deputy Prime Minister and Minister of Foreign Affairs and European Integration, Andrei Strătan. In March 2011, following the installation of a new AIE coalition Government, US Vice-President Joe Biden made an official visit to Chişinău (becoming the most senior US official to visit the country), where he met government leaders and declared US support for their political and economic reform efforts.

CONSTITUTION AND GOVERNMENT

Under the Constitution of 1994, as subsequently amended, supreme legislative power is held by the unicameral Parlamentul (Parliament), which is directly elected every four years. Parlamentul comprises 101 members. The President is Head of State and holds executive power in conjunction with the Council of Ministers, led by the Prime Minister. The President is elected by the legislature for a four-year term. Judicial power is exercised by the Supreme Court of Justice, the Court of Appeal, tribunals and courts of law. Judges sitting in the courts of law and the Supreme Court of Justice are appointed by the President following proposals by the Higher Magistrates' Council. The country is divided into 33 districts (rayons), two municipalities, and two autonomous entities—Gagauz-Yeri and Transnistria (the latter of which remained outside government control in mid-2011).

REGIONAL AND INTERNATIONAL CO-OPERATION

Moldova is a member of the Commonwealth of Independent States (CIS, see p. 238), the Council of Europe (see p. 250), the Organization for Security and Co-operation in Europe (OSCE, see p. 385) and the Organization of the Black Sea Economic Co-operation (see p. 398).

Moldova joined the UN in 1992 and became a member of the World Trade Organization (see p. 430) in 2001.

ECONOMIC AFFAIRS

In 2009, according to estimates by the World Bank, Moldova's gross national income (GNI), measured at average 2007–09 prices, was US $5,653m., equivalent to $1,590 per head (or $3,060 per head on an international purchasing-power parity basis). During 2000–09, it was estimated, the population decreased at an average annual rate of 1.4%, while gross domestic product (GDP) per head increased, in real terms, at an average annual rate of 5.1%. Overall GDP increased, in real terms, at an average annual rate of 4.9% in 2000–09; GDP increased by 7.8% in 2008, but decreased by 6.5% in 2009.

As a result of its extremely fertile land and temperate climate, Moldova's economy is dominated by agriculture and related industries. Some 85% of the country's terrain is cultivated. In 2010 agriculture (including hunting, forestry and fishing) contributed 14.3% of GDP, according to preliminary figures. In 2008 the sector provided 31.1% of employment. Principal crops include wine grapes and other fruit, tobacco, vegetables and grain. The wine industry has traditionally occupied a central role in the economy. The private ownership of land was legalized in 1991, although the sale of agricultural land was not permitted until 2001. In 2004 some 73.1% of agricultural land was privately owned and the private sector accounted for some 99% of production. According to the World Bank, the GDP of the agricultural sector, in real terms, remained constant during 2000–09. Agricultural GDP declined, in real terms, by 35.0% in 2008 but increased by only 2.0% in 2009, according to World Bank estimates.

In 2010 industry (including mining, manufacturing, power and construction) contributed 19.7% of GDP, according to preliminary data. The sector provided 19.7% of employment in 2008. In 2000–09, according to the World Bank, industrial GDP decreased at an average rate of 1.5% per year. Industrial GDP decreased by 0.5% in 2008 but fell by a massive 25.0% in 2009.

Mining and quarrying contributed 0.4% of GDP in 2010, according to preliminary figures, and employed just 0.3% of the working population in 2008. Moldova has extremely limited mineral resources. Activity is focused primarily on the extraction and processing of industrial minerals such as gypsum, limestone, sand and gravel. Deposits of petroleum and natural gas were discovered in southern Moldova in the early 1990s; total reserves of natural gas have been estimated at 22,000m. cu m.

The manufacturing sector contributed 12.7% of GDP in 2010, according to preliminary figures, and provided 10.9% of employment in 2008. The sector is dominated by food-processing, wine and tobacco production, machine-building and metal-working, and light industry. According to the World Bank, manufacturing GDP increased, in real terms, by an annual average of 0.7% in 2000–09. Manufacturing GDP grew by 0.6% in 2008, but fell drastically by 25.0% in 2009.

Construction contributed 3.8% of GDP in 2010, according to preliminary figures, and engaged 6.6% of the employed labour force in 2008.

Moldova relies heavily on imported energy—primarily natural gas and petroleum products—from Russia, Romania and Ukraine (such imports accounted for 76.7% of consumption in 2004). In the mid-2000s Moldova announced its intention to diversify its gas suppliers, and to increase domestic energy production substantially; domestic production represented 23.3% of consumption in 2004. A large proportion of natural

MOLDOVA

gas imports supply the Moldoveneasca power station, located in Transnistria, which contributes much of the country's electricity-generating capacity. The growing importance of natural gas to the generation of electricity has been paralleled by the rapid decline, from the mid-1990s, in the importance of coal-fired power sources; whereas in 1995 some 31.5% of electricity generated in Moldova was of coal origin, by 2004 the contribution of coal to electricity generation was negligible. In February 2005 an Azerbaijani company purchased the unfinished Giurgiulesti petroleum terminal in southern Moldova; the terminal commenced operations in September 2007. Natural gas accounted for 98.2% of electricity production in 2007, when hydroelectric power accounted for 0.9%. Petroleum products comprised 21.5% of the value of total merchandise imports in 2009, according to the World Bank.

Services accounted for 65.9% of GDP in 2010, according to preliminary figures, and the sector provided 49.3% of total employment in 2008. The GDP of the services sector increased, in real terms, at an annual average rate of 8.1% in 2000–09. Services GDP remained constant in 2008, but decreased by 4.5% in 2009.

In 2009 Moldova recorded a visible trade deficit of US $1,944.2m., while there was a deficit of $534.0m. on the current account of the balance of payments. In 2009 the principal source of imports was Ukraine (accounting for 14.0% of the value of total imports). Other major suppliers were Russia, Romania, Germany, the People's Republic of China, Italy, and Turkey. The main market for exports in that year was Russia (accounting for 22.3% of the value of total exports). Other important purchasers were Romania, Italy, Ukraine, Belarus, and Germany. In 2009 the principal imports were mineral products, machinery and mechanical appliances, chemicals and related products, foodstuffs, beverages and tobacco, textiles and textile articles, plastics, rubber and articles thereof, and base metals. The main exports in that year were foodstuffs, beverages and tobacco, vegetable products, textiles, and machinery and mechanical appliances.

In 2010, according to IMF projections, the consolidated state budget recorded a deficit of an estimated 5,943m. Moldovan lei (equivalent to 8.3% of GDP). Moldova's general government gross debt was 16,548m. Moldovan lei in 2009, equivalent to 27.6% of GDP. At the end of 2008 Moldova's total external debt totalled US $3,787m., of which $792m. was public and publicly guaranteed debt. In that year the cost of debt-servicing was equivalent to 11.3% of the value of exports of goods, services and income. Consumer prices decreased at an annual average rate of 0.2% during 2001–10. The average rate of inflation was 7.4% in 2010. The average rate of unemployment was 3.9% in 2008.

Although the economy recorded continued growth from 2000, by the mid-2000s Moldova was the poorest country in Europe, and remittances from Moldovan workers abroad accounted for some 30% of GDP in 2005, with emigration a particular cause of concern. In 2006 agreement was reached with the IMF on a three-year Poverty Reduction and Growth Facility (PRGF) arrangement amounting to some US $167m. In the second half of the 2000s the reorganization of the taxation system and a programme of privatization were undertaken, in an effort to improve public finances and attract additional investment, although the energy sector remained substantially unreformed. The European Union's Eastern Partnership programme, launched in May 2009, envisaged the release of aid and the gradual creation of a free trade zone for Moldova and five other former Soviet states. The global economic crisis had a severe impact upon the Moldovan economy in that year, as export trade, foreign investment and remittances from abroad all declined markedly. The reformist Government that assumed power in September undertook to remove numerous external trade restrictions, and also to rationalize the operations of the civil service. In January 2010 the IMF announced that it had approved the release of funds worth $574.4m. over a period of three years, under its Extended Credit Facility (the successor to the PRGF) and Extended Fund Facility. The organization of further legislative elections in November 2010 failed to resolve conclusively the protracted political crisis (see Contemporary Political History). Following the installation of a renewed coalition Government in early 2011, the US Administration pledged continued financial assistance to Moldova. After the sharp economic contraction in 2009, GDP growth had resumed, and by early 2011 the IMF considered that GDP had recovered to its pre-crisis level. In April the IMF completed a second favourable review of Moldova's economic performance under its programme (despite delays in meeting some criteria, owing to the repeated eand technical difficulties).

PUBLIC HOLIDAYS

2012: 1 January (New Year's Day), 7–8 January (Russian Orthodox Christmas), 8 March (International Women's Day), 15–16 April (Orthodox Easter), 23 April ('Paştele Blajinilor', Parents' Day), 1 May (Labour Day), 9 May (Victory and Commemoration Day), 27 August (Independence Day), 31 August ('Limbă Noastră', National Language Day), 24–25 December (Romanian Orthodox Christmas).

Statistical Survey

Principal sources (unless otherwise indicated): State Department for Statistics and Sociology, 2028 Chişinău, şos. Hînceşti 53D; tel. (22) 73-37-74; fax (22) 22-61-46; e-mail dass@statistica.md; internet www.statistica.md.

Note: Most of the figures from 1993 onwards exclude the Transnistria (Pridnestrovie) region, which remained outside central government control.

Area and Population

AREA, POPULATION AND DENSITY

Area (sq km)	33,800*
Population (census results)†	
12 January 1989	4,335,360
5–12 October 2004	
Males	1,627,689
Females	1,755,643
Total	3,383,332
Population (official estimates at 1 January)‡	
2009	3,567,512
2010	3,563,695
2011	3,560,400§
Density (per sq km) at January 2011‡	105.3

* 13,050 sq miles.
† Figures refer to the *de jure* population. The *de facto* total at the 1989 census was 4,337,592 (males 2,058,160, females 2,279,432).
‡ Excluding Transnistria.
§ Rounded figure.

POPULATION BY AGE AND SEX
(official estimates at 1 January 2010)

	Males	Females	Total
0–14	305,712	289,784	595,496
15–64	1,272,508	1,334,890	2,607,398
65 and over	135,267	225,534	360,801
Total	1,713,487	1,850,208	3,563,695

MOLDOVA

POPULATION BY ETHNIC GROUP*
(permanent inhabitants, 2004 census)

	Number	%
Moldovan	2,564,849	75.8
Ukrainian	282,406	8.4
Russian	201,218	5.9
Gagauz	147,500	4.4
Romanian	73,276	2.2
Bulgarian	65,662	1.9
Others and unknown	48,421	1.4
Total	3,383,332	100.0

* According to official declaration of nationality.

ADMINISTRATIVE DIVISIONS
('000, official estimates of population at 1 January 2011)

Districts (raione)

Anenii Noi	83.1	Nisporeni		66.8
Basarabeasca	29.2	Ocnița		56.1
Briceni	75.3	Orhei		125.9
Cahul	124.8	Rezina		52.6
Cantemir	62.8	Rîșcani		70.0
Călărași	78.8	Sîngerei		93.4
Căușeni	92.3	Soroca		100.4
Cimișlia	61.7	Strășeni		91.3
Criuleni	73.1	Șoldănești		43.3
Dondușeni	45.1	Ștefan Vodă		71.9
Drochia	90.1	Taraclia		44.2
Dubăsari	35.2	Telenești		74.2
Edineț	82.9	Ungheni		117.4
Fălești	92.6	*Municipalities*		
Florești	90.0	Bălți		148.9
Glodeni	61.9	Chișinău		789.5
		Autonomous		
Hîncești	122.0	*Territory*		
Ialoveni	99.1	Gagauz-Yeri		160.7
Leova	53.8	**Total**		3,560.4

Population of Transnistria (Pridnestrovie) (estimated figure obtained as residual from total country population estimates at 1 January 2003): 601,088.

PRINCIPAL TOWNS
(population at census of 5–12 October 2004)

Chișinău (capital)	589,455	Soroca	28,362
Bălți	122,669	Orhei	25,641
Cahul	35,488	Comrat	23,327
Ungheni	32,530	Ceadîr-Lunga	19,401

Population at 1 January 2011 (official estimates): Chișinău 664,700, Bălți 144,000, Cahul 41,000, Ungheni 38,100, Soroca 37,400, Orhei 33,500, Comrat 25,300, Ceadîr-Lunga 22,800.

Principal Towns within Transnistria (estimated population at Moldovan census of 1 January 1996): Tiraspol 187,000; Tighina (Bender) 128,000; Râbnita (Rybnitsa) 62,900.

IMMIGRATION AND EMIGRATION

	2007	2008	2009
Immigrants	2,070	2,749	2,010
Emigrants	7,172	6,988	6,663

BIRTHS, MARRIAGES AND DEATHS

	Registered live births		Registered marriages		Registered deaths	
	Number	Rate (per 1,000)	Number	Rate (per 1,000)	Number	Rate (per 1,000)
2002	35,705	9.9	21,685	6.0	41,852	11.6
2003	36,471	10.1	24,961	6.9	43,079	11.9
2004	38,272	10.6	25,164	7.0	41,668	11.6
2005	37,695	10.5	27,187	7.6	44,689	12.4
2006	37,587	10.5	27,128	7.6	43,137	12.0
2007	37,973	10.6	29,213	8.2	43,050	12.0
2008	39,018	10.9	26,666	7.5	41,948	11.8
2009	40,803	11.4	26,781	7.5	42,139	11.8

Life expectancy (years at birth, WHO estimates): 69 (males 65; females 73) in 2008 (Source: WHO, *World Health Statistics*).

ECONOMICALLY ACTIVE POPULATION
(labour force survey, '000 persons aged 15 years and over)

	2006	2007	2008
Agriculture, hunting and forestry	421.6	407.8	387.4
Fishing	0.8	0.8	1.2
Mining and quarrying	3.4	3.7	3.8
Manufacturing	134.5	128.5	136.2
Electricity, gas and water supply	23.5	25.9	23.3
Construction	67.3	75.7	82.8
Wholesale and retail trade; repair of motor vehicles, motorcycles and personal and household goods	174.1	176.4	187.6
Hotels and restaurants	21.8	21.5	21.2
Transport, storage and communications	65.3	68.7	70.8
Financial intermediation	15.0	15.5	17.0
Real estate, renting and business activities	31.0	28.9	30.4
Public administration and defence; compulsory social security	71.9	66.3	68.1
Education	120.4	116.8	112.0
Health and social work	64.3	67.4	68.1
Other community, social and personal service activities	36.5	37.1	35.7
Private households with employed persons	4.7	5.3	4.5
Extra-territorial organizations and bodies	1.1	0.9	0.9
Total employed	1,257.3	1,247.2	1,251.0
Unemployed	99.9	66.7	51.7
Total labour force	1,357.2	1,313.9	1,320.8
Males	690.3	663.0	658.8
Females	666.9	650.8	644.1

Source: ILO.

Health and Welfare

KEY INDICATORS

Total fertility rate (children per woman, 2008)	1.5
Under-5 mortality rate (per 1,000 live births, 2008)	17
HIV/AIDS (% of persons aged 15–49, 2007)	0.4
Physicians (per 1,000 head, 2006)	2.7
Hospital beds (per 1,000 head, 2006)	6.3
Health expenditure (2007): US $ per head (PPP)	281
Health expenditure (2007): % of GDP	10.3
Health expenditure (2007): public (% of total)	50.8
Access to water (% of persons, 2008)	90
Access to sanitation (% of persons, 2008)	79
Total carbon dioxide emissions ('000 metric tons, 2007)	4,700.9
Carbon dioxide emissions per head (metric tons, 2007)	1.3
Human Development Index (2010): ranking	99
Human Development Index (2010): value	0.623

For sources and definitions, see explanatory note on p. vi.

MOLDOVA

Agriculture

PRINCIPAL CROPS
('000 metric tons)

	2007	2008	2009
Wheat	406.5	1,286.3	735.0
Barley	115.0	353.1	245.0*
Maize	362.7	1,478.6	1,140.0
Potatoes	199.4	271.0	261.0
Sugar beet	612.3	960.7	336.0
Beans, dry	4.8	16.3	11.0*
Peas, dry	8.0	18.2	13.0*
Sunflower seed	155.5	371.9	284.0
Cabbages and other brassicas	27.2	61.3	50.0*
Tomatoes	46.6	83.8	68.0*
Cucumbers and gherkins	15.9	22.8	19.0*
Chillies and peppers, green	16.5	15.8	13.0*
Aubergines (Eggplants)	4.8	4.7	4.0*
Onions, dry	24.7	48.5	40.0*
Carrots and turnips	13.9	18.6	15.0*
Watermelons	39.4	67.2	70.0†
Apples	218.2	255.1	213.0*
Plums and sloes	14.0	56.2	46.0*
Grapes	598.0	635.5	682.0
Tobacco, unmanufactured	3.6	3.9	4.2

* Unofficial figure.
† FAO estimate.

Aggregate production ('000 metric tons, may include official, semi-official or estimated data): Total cereals 887.1 in 2007, 3,132.3 in 2008, 2,130.8 in 2009; Total vegetables (incl. melons) 263.2 in 2007, 446.3 in 2008, 380.5 in 2009; Total fruits (excl. melons) 865.0 in 2007, 992.3 in 2008, 975.9 in 2009.

Source: FAO.

LIVESTOCK
('000 head at 1 January)

	2007	2008	2009
Horses	66.8	58.4	56.0
Cattle	299.1	231.7	218.0
Pigs	531.8	298.7	284.0
Sheep	835.1	753.9	766.0*
Goats	111.9	99.3	100.0*
Chickens*	22,400	17,050	18,220

* Unofficial figure(s).
Source: FAO.

LIVESTOCK PRODUCTS
('000 metric tons)

	2007	2008	2009*
Cattle meat	15.2	10.6	12.0
Sheep meat	2.3	2.2	3.0
Pig meat	58.9	35.1	41.0
Chicken meat	31.8	29.6	35.0
Cows' milk	571.4	510.5	540.2
Sheep's milk	20.7	21.6	22.8
Goats' milk	11.8	11.2	12.0
Hen eggs*	39.3	31.4	36.0
Honey	2.3†	3.0	n.a.
Wool, greasy	2.1	2.0	n.a.

* Unofficial figures.
† FAO estimate.
Source: FAO.

Forestry

ROUNDWOOD REMOVALS
('000 cubic metres, excl. bark)

	2005*	2006	2007
Sawlogs, veneer logs and logs for sleepers	19	27	26
Other industrial wood	75	18	17
Fuel wood	94	334	309
Total	188	379	352

* FAO estimates.
2008–09: Production assumed to be unchanged from 2007 (FAO estimates).
Source: FAO.

SAWNWOOD PRODUCTION
('000 cubic metres, incl. railway sleepers)

	2005*	2006	2007
Coniferous (softwood)	—	14	16
Broadleaved (hardwood)	31	17	18
Total	31	31	34

* FAO estimates.
2008–09: Production assumed to be unchanged from 2007 (FAO estimates).
Source: FAO.

Fishing

(metric tons, live weight)

	2006	2007	2008
Capture	612	1,160	1,407
Common carp	239	538	580
Crucian carp	186	265	420
Aquaculture*	5,000	4,700	4,700
Common carp*	1,860	1,750	1,750
Silver carp*	3,110	2,920	2,920
Total catch*	5,612	5,860	6,107

* FAO estimates.
Source: FAO.

Mining

('000 cu m)

	2006	2007	2008
Limestone	293.6	311.9	n.a.
Gypsum	726	846	701
Sand and gravel	2,324.4	2,685.5	2,846.8

2009 ('000 cu m): Sand and gravel 1,905.4.

Peat ('000 metric tons, estimated production): 475 in 2005–08 (Source: US Geological Survey).

MOLDOVA

Industry

SELECTED PRODUCTS
('000 metric tons unless otherwise indicated)

	2007	2008	2009
Fruit and vegetable preserves	94.0	98.1	58.1
Flour	113.3	122.6	113.2
Raw sugar	74.0	134.0	42.4
Wine ('000 hectolitres)	1,230	1,540	1,190
Mineral water ('000 hectolitres)	1,290	1,230	1,130
Soft drinks ('000 hectolitres)	940	770	600
Cigars and cigarettes (million)	4,975	n.a.	n.a.
Carpets and rugs ('000 sq m)	5,246	n.a.	n.a.
Footwear ('000 pairs, excl. rubber)	3,796	3,832	2,050
Glasses and bottles (million)	302.7	284.7	201.3
Plaster	311,900	n.a.	n.a.
Electric energy (million kWh)	1,100	1,097	1,028

Cement ('000 metric tons): 837.0 in 2006; 800.0 in 2007 (estimate); 750.0 in 2008 (estimate) (Source: US Geological Survey).

Finance

CURRENCY AND EXCHANGE RATES

Monetary Units
100 bani (singular: ban) = 1 Moldovan leu (plural: lei).

Sterling, Dollar and Euro Equivalents (31 December 2010)
£1 sterling = 19.027 lei;
US $1 = 12.154 lei;
€1 = 16.240 lei;
1,000 Moldovan lei = £52.56 = $82.28 = €61.58.

Average Exchange Rate (Moldovan lei per US$)
2008 10.392
2009 11.110
2010 12.369

Note: The Moldovan leu was introduced (except in Transnistria) on 29 November 1993, replacing the Moldovan rouble at a rate of 1 leu = 1,000 roubles. The Moldovan rouble had been introduced in June 1992, as a temporary coupon currency, and was initially at par with the Russian (formerly Soviet) rouble.

STATE BUDGET
(million lei)*

Revenue†	2009	2010‡	2011‡
Tax revenue	19,325	20,448	22,581
Taxes on profits	443	216	316
Taxes on personal incomes	1,465	1,493	1,631
Value-added tax	7,596	8,188	9,132
Excises	1,540	1,995	2,018
Taxes on international trade	905	964	1,070
Social Fund contributions	5,587	5,731	6,325
Health Fund contributions	1,377	1,449	1,583
Other taxes	414	411	506
Non-tax revenue	1,035	1,121	1,141
Total	20,360	21,569	23,722

Expenditure§	2009	2010‡	2011‡
Current expenditure	24,367	25,725	25,855
Wages	7,000	7,531	7,531
Goods and services	6,067	6,290	6,236
Health insurance fund	3,071	3,376	3,597
Interest payments	843	808	914
Transfers	10,156	10,676	10,757
Other current expenditure	302	420	417
Capital expenditure	3,004	3,940	4,855
Total	27,371	29,665	30,710

* Figures refer to a consolidation of the operations of central (republican) and local governments, including the Social Fund.
† Excluding grants received (million lei): 1,288 in 2009; 2,067 in 2010 (budget programme); 1,704 in 2011 (budget programme).
‡ Budget programme.
§ Excluding net lending (million lei): −28 in 2009; −86 in 2010 (budget programme); −78 in 2011 (budget programme).

Source: IMF, *Republic of Moldova: 2010 Article IV Consultation and Staff Report for the 2010 Article IV Consultation, First Reviews Under the Extended Arrangement and Under the Three-Year Arrangement Under the Extended Credit Facility, and Request for Modification of a Performance Criterion—Staff Report; Staff Statement and Supplement; Public Information Notice and Press Release on the Executive Board Discussion; and Statement by the Executive Director for the Republic of Moldova* (July 2010).

INTERNATIONAL RESERVES
(excluding gold, US $ million at 31 December)

	2008	2009	2010
IMF special drawing rights	0.15	3.57	0.35
Reserve position in IMF	0.01	0.01	0.01
Foreign exchange	1,672.25	1,476.68	1,717.33
Total	1,672.41	1,480.27	1,717.69

Source: IMF, *International Financial Statistics*.

MONEY SUPPLY
(million lei at 31 December)

	2008	2009	2010
Currency outside depository corporations	7,578.66	8,848.98	10,107.57
Transferable deposits	5,981.66	7,157.21	8,533.62
Other deposits	18,103.58	16,676.94	18,408.85
Securities other than shares	16.86	1.34	1.28
Broad money	31,680.77	32,684.46	37,051.32

Source: IMF, *International Financial Statistics*.

COST OF LIVING
(Consumer Price Index; base: previous year = 100)

	2008	2009	2010
Food and beverages	106.5	96.2	107.1
Other consumer goods	102.1	102.5	107.7
Services	117.4	102.2	109.7
All items (incl. others)	112.7	100.0	107.4

MOLDOVA

NATIONAL ACCOUNTS
(million lei at current prices, excl. Transnistria)

Expenditure on the Gross Domestic Product

	2008	2009	2010*
Final consumption expenditure	71,451.4	68,574.1	82,611.3
Households	57,804.4	53,352.6	65,649.3
Non-profit institutions serving households	13,646.9	15,221.5	16,962.0
Gross capital formation	24,683.0	13,984.7	16,996.7
Gross fixed capital formation / Acquisitions, less disposals, of valuables	21,391.4	13,655.0	16,305.6
Changes in inventories	3,291.6	329.7	691.1
Total domestic expenditure	96,134.4	82,558.8	99,608.0
Exports of goods and services	25,684.0	22,281.8	28,447.6
Less Imports of goods and services	58,896.8	44,410.6	56,206.3
GDP in market prices	62,921.5	60,429.8	71,849.2

Gross Domestic Product by Economic Activity

	2008	2009	2010*
Agriculture, hunting, forestry and fishing	5,544.0	5,134.5	8,582.1
Mining and quarrying	315.1	241.2	259.8
Manufacturing	7,093.9	6,390.8	7,622.3
Electricity, gas and water supply	1,328.1	1,398.8	1,637.9
Construction	3,115.0	2,108.7	2,300.0
Wholesale and retail trade; repair of motor vehicles, motorcycles and personal and household goods	8,148.6	7,954.1	9,252.7
Hotels and restaurants	845.1	809.7	936.1
Transport, storage and communications	7,601.1	7,226.0	8,216.0
Financial intermediation	3,781.2	3,850.9	4,188.6
Real estate, renting and business activities	5,189.9	5,183.9	5,821.8
Public administration and defence; compulsory social security	2,642.0	2,857.0	2,674.7
Education	3,523.3	4,250.4	4,832.4
Health and social work	2,379.5	2,685.4	2,997.3
Other community, social and personal services	1,575.7	1,702.6	2,061.3
Sub-total	53,082.7	51,794.0	61,383.0
Less Financial intermediation services indirectly measured	1,309.1	984.8	1,488.3
Gross value added in basic prices	51,773.6	50,809.2	59,894.5
Taxes, *less* subsidies, on products and imports	11,148.0	9,620.6	11,954.7
GDP in market prices	62,921.5	60,429.8	71,849.2

* Preliminary figures.

BALANCE OF PAYMENTS
(US $ million)

	2007	2008	2009
Exports of goods f.o.b.	1,373.3	1,646.0	1,331.6
Imports of goods f.o.b.	−3,671.4	−4,869.1	−3,275.8
Trade balance	−2,298.1	−3,223.2	−1,944.2
Exports of services	625.5	837.3	668.9
Imports of services	−650.1	−838.6	−712.9
Balance on goods and services	−2,322.7	−3,224.5	−1,988.2
Other income received	710.1	905.0	590.0
Other income paid	−293.7	−306.4	−287.1
Balance on goods, services and income	−1,906.3	−2,625.9	−1,685.2
Current transfers received	1,245.1	1,688.4	1,254.6
Current transfers paid	−65.1	−111.5	−103.4
Current balance	−726.3	−1,049.1	−534.0

—continued	2007	2008	2009
Capital account (net)	−8.0	−14.6	−17.5
Direct investment abroad	−17.4	−16.1	−6.8
Direct investment from abroad	533.6	712.8	127.8
Portfolio investment assets	−0.1	—	−0.3
Portfolio investment liabilities	−4.4	6.4	−5.6
Financial derivatives assets	−0.5	−0.1	−0.1
Financial derivatives liabilities	0.1	1.0	0.4
Other investment assets	35.3	52.1	−210.6
Other investment liabilities	457.1	518.0	184.3
Net errors and omissions	117.3	84.8	57.7
Overall balance	386.7	295.3	−404.5

Source: IMF, *International Financial Statistics*.

External Trade

PRINCIPAL COMMODITIES
(distribution by Harmonized System, US $ million)

Imports c.i.f.	2007	2008	2009
Vegetable products	150.4	166.8	132.6
Foodstuffs, beverages and tobacco	237.9	343.4	289.7
Mineral products	788.4	1,126.0	718.2
Mineral fuels, mineral oils and related materials	774.8	1,104.6	702.5
Chemicals and related products	317.7	416.8	365.9
Pharmaceutical products	114.2	151.4	172.2
Plastics, rubber and articles thereof	224.9	276.8	186.5
Plastics	178.3	213.5	144.6
Textiles and textile articles	249.6	285.4	244.4
Base metals and articles of base metals	336.7	372.5	183.8
Articles of iron or steel	112.7	147.0	73.5
Machinery and mechanical appliances	544.6	765.5	467.5
Apparatus such as nuclear reactors, boilers, machinery and mechanical appliances, and parts thereof	324.5	427.6	200.3
Electrical machinery and equipment and parts thereof; sound recorders and reproducers, television image and sound recorders and reproducers, and parts and accessories thereof	220.1	337.9	267.2
Vehicles and associated transport equipment	286.1	390.6	157.3
Vehicles other than railway or tramway rolling stock, and parts and accessories thereof	274.6	377.9	151.8
Total (incl. others)	3,689.5	4,898.8	3,278.3

Exports f.o.b.	2007	2008	2009
Vegetable products	162.9	210.1	268.4
Edible fruit	92.9	85.4	125.4
Cereals	17.2	50.3	70.9
Oil seeds and oleaginous fruits, etc	47.2	68.2	65.8
Animal or vegetable fats	55.3	62.9	50.7
Foodstuffs, beverages and tobacco	276.0	311.9	281.0
Preparations of vegetables or fruits	79.5	51.4	50.1
Beverages, spirits and vinegar	135.5	195.9	159.5
Mineral products	57.1	63.5	14.4
Salt; sulphur; earths and stone; plastering materials, lime and cement	52.5	60.4	8.9

MOLDOVA

Exports f.o.b.—continued	2007	2008	2009
Articles of stone, plaster, cement, ceramic or glass	51.3	52.5	25.8
Textiles and textile articles	276.3	313.9	257.8
Articles of apparel and clothing accessories, not knitted	141.5	156.6	127.4
Base metals and articles of base metals	110.5	119.1	29.4
Iron and steel	38.5	51.2	2.2
Machinery and mechanical appliances	90.7	167.5	139.3
Apparatus such as nuclear reactors, boilers, machinery and mechanical appliances, and parts thereof	51.7	50.8	32.1
Electrical machinery and equipment and parts thereof; sound recorders and reproducers, television image and sound recorders and reproducers, and parts and accessories thereof	39.0	116.7	107.1
Miscellaneous manufactured items	44.8	59.8	38.8
Furniture; bedding, mattresses, mattress supports, cushions and similar stuffed furnishings; lamps and lighting fittings, not elsewhere specified or included; illuminated signs, illuminated nameplates etc.; prefabricated buildings	35.4	48.8	28.5
Total (incl. others)	1,341.7	1,591.2	1,287.5

2010 (provisional): Total imports 3,855.3; Total exports 1,541.5.

PRINCIPAL TRADING PARTNERS
(US $ million)

Imports c.i.f.	2007	2008	2009
Austria	37.3	74.6	55.2
Belarus	118.7	199.1	137.4
Belgium	37.6	33.9	22.2
Bulgaria	50.4	45.1	40.8
China, People's Repub.	202.9	325.5	246.5
Czech Republic	43.6	57.5	37.6
France	94.8	103.4	61.3
Germany	319.3	364.5	252.3
Hungary	46.4	69.2	52.2
Italy	269.3	306.2	231.5
Japan	43.9	83.6	31.6
Korea, Republic	38.7	42.7	17.7
Netherlands	41.2	49.5	32.4
Poland	89.1	121.3	87.6
Romania	449.0	590.8	311.7
Russia	498.6	666.1	373.2
Turkey	166.8	231.9	172.4
Ukraine	687.0	839.0	458.8
United Kingdom	38.2	61.7	50.5
USA	46.8	93.3	45.0
Total (incl. others)	3,689.5	4,898.8	3,278.3

Exports f.o.b.	2007	2008	2009
Austria	30.8	12.5	7.8
Belarus	82.0	92.8	80.7
Belgium	11.2	9.7	5.6
Bulgaria	27.3	22.3	13.9
France	24.8	21.4	22.2
Germany	86.3	63.8	75.5
Hungary	5.1	18.5	13.2
Italy	140.2	167.1	135.7
Kazakhstan	45.5	44.5	26.5
Netherlands	14.4	13.2	10.9
Poland	48.3	56.1	33.7
Romania	211.2	335.8	239.7
Russia	232.7	318.4	286.5
Slovakia	8.9	7.6	6.7
Switzerland	22.6	39.7	21.7
Turkey	32.1	33.4	33.1
Ukraine	167.9	142.8	81.3
United Kingdom	34.1	52.3	60.3
USA	15.2	15.1	12.2
Total (incl. others)	1,341.7	1,591.2	1,287.5

2010 (provisional): Total imports 3,855.3; Total exports 1,541,5.

Transport

RAILWAYS
(traffic)

	2008	2009	2010*
Passenger journeys (million)	5.8	5.2	5.0
Passenger-km (million)	486	423	399
Freight transported (million metric tons)	11.0	4.4	3.9
Freight ton-km (million)	2,873	1,058	958

* Provisional data.

ROAD TRAFFIC
(motor vehicles in use)

	2007	2008	2009
Passenger cars	338,944	366,351	386,365
Buses and minibuses	21,095	21,491	21,346
Lorries and vans	94,828	115,967	120,174

INLAND WATERWAYS
(traffic)

	2008	2009	2010*
Passenger journeys (million)	0.1	0.1	0.1
Passenger-km (million)	0.2	0.2	0.2
Freight transported ('000 metric tons)	202.0	182.0	127.2
Freight ton-km (million)	0.8	0.6	0.4

* Provisional data.

MOLDOVA

CIVIL AVIATION
(traffic)

	2008	2009	2010*
Passengers carried ('000)	473.9	459.5	649.2
Passenger-km (million)	637	604	751
Freight transported ('000 metric tons)	0.83	0.83	1.30
Freight ton-km (million)	1.2	1.1	1.7

* Provisional figures.

Tourism

FOREIGN VISITOR ARRIVALS
(incl. excursionists)

Country of origin	2008	2009	2010
Belarus	145	176	105
Bulgaria	46	380	324
France	174	196	283
Germany	502	460	482
Italy	440	258	474
Netherlands	125	154	311
Romania	1,070	765	1,698
Russia	1,793	1,713	1,327
Turkey	461	1,002	526
Ukraine	1,542	979	730
United Kingdom	430	744	405
USA	239	194	451
Total (incl. others)	8,710	9,189	8,956

Receipts from tourism (US $ million, incl. passenger transport): 148 in 2006; 225 in 2007; 289 in 2008 (Source: World Tourism Organization).

Communications Media

	2007	2008	2009
Telephones ('000 main lines in use)	1,079.9	1,114.6	1,138.7
Mobile cellular telephones ('000 subscribers)	1,882.8	2,423.4	2,784.8
Internet users ('000)	750.0	850.0	1,333.3
Broadband subscribers ('000)	47.2	115.1	187.0

Television receivers ('000 in use): 1,300 in 2000.

Radio receivers ('000 in use): 3,220 in 1997.

Personal computers: 423,950 (114.3 per 1,000 persons) in 2006.

Book production (including pamphlets): 921 titles (2,779,000 copies) in 1996.

Daily newspapers: 6 in 2000 (average circulation 261,000 in 1996).

Non-daily newspapers: 170 in 2000 (estimated average circulation 1,350,000 in 1996).

Other periodicals: 76 (average circulation 196,000) in 1994.

Sources: UNESCO, *Statistical Yearbook*; International Telecommunication Union.

Education

(2009/10)

	Institutions	Teachers	Students
Pre-primary	1,362	11,696	1,26,000*
Primary and Secondary: general	1,512	37,000*	415,500*
Secondary: vocational	75	2,234	22,161
Higher: colleges	47	2,502	32,249
Higher: universities	33	6,413	109,892

* Rounded figure.

Pupil-teacher ratio (primary education, UNESCO estimate): 15.7 in 2008/09 (Source: UNESCO Institute for Statistics).

Adult literacy rate (UNESCO estimates): 98.3% (males 99.0%; females 97.8%) in 2008 (Source: UNESCO Institute for Statistics).

Directory

The Government

HEAD OF STATE

President: MARIAN LUPU (acting).

COUNCIL OF MINISTERS
(May 2011)

A coalition, principally comprising representatives of the Liberal Democratic Party of Moldova (PLDM), the Liberal Party (PL) and the Democratic Party of Moldova (PDM).

Prime Minister: VLADIMIR FILAT (PLDM).
Deputy Prime Minister and Minister of Foreign Affairs and European Integration: IURIE LEANCĂ (PLDM).
Deputy Prime Minister: MIHAI MOLDOVANU (PL).
Deputy Prime Minister and Minister of the Economy: VALERIU LAZĂR (PDM).
Deputy Prime Minister: EUGEN CARPOV (Independent).
Minister of Agriculture and the Food Industry: VASILE BUMACOV (PLDM).
Minister of Regional Development and Construction: MARCEL RĂDUCAN (PDM).
Minister of Finance: VEACESLAV NEGRUȚA (PLDM).
Minister of Information and Communications Technologies: PAVEL FILIP (PDM).
Minister of Transport and Road Infrastructure: ANATOLIE ȘALARU (PL).
Minister of the Environment: GHEORGHE ȘALARU (PL).
Minister of Education: MIHAI ȘLEAHTIȚCHI (PLDM).
Minister of Health: ANDREI USATÎI (PLDM).
Minister of Labour, Social Protection and the Family: VALENTINA BULIGA (PDM).
Minister of Culture: BORIS FOCȘA (PDM).
Minister of Justice: ALEXANDRU TĂNASE (PLDM).
Minister of Internal Affairs: ALEXEI ROIBU (PLDM).
Minister of Defence: VITALIE MARINUȚA (PL).
Minister of Youth and Sport: ION CEBANU (PL).

Note: the President of the Moldovan Academy of Sciences, GHEORGHE DUCA, and the Bașkan (Governor) of the Autonomous Territory of Gagauz-Yeri (Gagauzia), MIHAIL FORMUZAL, are also members of the Government.

MINISTRIES

Office of the President: 2073 Chișinău, bd. Ștefan cel Mare 154; tel. (22) 25-02-44; internet www.president.md.

Office of the Council of Ministers: 2033 Chișinău, Piața Marii Adunări Naționale 1; tel. (22) 25-01-01; fax (22) 24-26-96; e-mail petitii@gov.md; internet www.gov.md.

Ministry of Agriculture and the Food Industry: 2012 Chișinău, bd. Ștefan cel Mare 162; tel. (22) 23-34-27; fax (22) 21-02-04; e-mail adm_maia@moldova.md; internet www.maia.gov.md.

Ministry of Culture: 2033 Chișinău, Piața Marii Adunări Naționale 1, Of. 326; tel. (22) 22-76-20; fax (22) 23-23-88; e-mail office@mc.gov.md; internet www.mc.gov.md.

MOLDOVA

Ministry of Defence: 2021 Chişinău, şos. Hînceşti 84; tel. (22) 25-22-22; fax (22) 25-24-00; e-mail ministru@army.md; internet www.army.md.

Ministry of the Economy: 2033 Chişinău, Piaţa Marii Adunări Naţionale 1; tel. (22) 23-74-48; fax (22) 23-40-64; e-mail mineconcom@mec.gov.md; internet www.mec.gov.md.

Ministry of Education: 2033 Chişinău, Piaţa Marii Adunări Naţionale 1; tel. (22) 23-33-48; fax (22) 23-35-15; e-mail consilier@edu.md; internet www.edu.md.

Ministry of the Environment: 2005 Chişinău, str. Cosmonauţilor 9; tel. (22) 20-45-07; fax (22) 22-68-58; e-mail egreta@mediu.gov.md; internet www.mediu.gov.md.

Ministry of Finance: 2005 Chişinău, str. Cosmonauţilor 7; tel. (22) 22-66-29; fax (22) 24-00-55; e-mail cancelaria@minfin.moldova.md; internet www.minfin.md.

Ministry of Foreign Affairs and European Integration: 2012 Chişinău, str. 31 August 80; tel. (22) 57-82-07; fax (22) 23-23-02; e-mail secdep@mfa.md; internet www.mfa.gov.md.

Ministry of Health: 2009 Chişinău, str. Vasile Alecsandri 2; tel. (22) 72-99-07; fax (22) 73-87-81; e-mail office@ms.gov.md; internet www.ms.md.

Ministry of Information and Communications Technologies: 2012 Chişinău, bd. Ştefan cel Mare şi Sfînt 134; tel. and fax (22) 23-84-76; e-mail mtic@mtic.gov.md; internet www.mtic.gov.md.

Ministry of Internal Affairs: 2012 Chişinău, bd. Ştefan cel Mare 75; tel. (22) 25-53-46; e-mail mai@mai.md; internet www.mai.md.

Ministry of Justice: 2012 Chişinău, str. 31 August 1989 82; tel. (22) 23-33-40; fax (22) 23-47-97; e-mail secretariat@justice.gov.md; internet www.justice.gov.md.

Ministry of Labour, Social Protection and the Family: 2009 Chişinău, str. Vasile Alecsandri 1; tel. (22) 26-93-01; fax (22) 26-93-10; e-mail secretariat@mmpsf.gov.md; internet www.mpsfc.gov.md.

Ministry of Regional Development and Construction: 2005 Chişinău, str Cosmonauţilor 9; tel. (22) 20-45-69; fax (22) 22-07-48; e-mail mcdr@mcdr.gov.md; internet www.mcdt.gov.md.

Ministry of Transport and Road Infrastructure: 2004 Chişinău, bd. Ştefan cel Mare 162; tel. (22) 82-07-13; e-mail resurse.umane@mtid.gov.md; internet www.mtid.gov.md.

Ministry of Youth and Sport: 2004 Chişinău, bd. Ştefan cel Mare 162; tel. and fax (22) 82-08-61; e-mail minister@mts.gov.md; internet www.mts.gov.md.

President

Following legislative elections on 5 April 2009, after which the outgoing President VLADIMIR VORONIN was elected as Chairman of Parlamentul (the Parliament), two attempts by the legislature to elect a new president, on 20 May and 3 June, failed; consequently, on 15 June Parlamentul was dissolved by presidential decree, and fresh legislative elections were held on 29 July. Voronin resigned as President of the Republic, which position he had continued to hold in an acting capacity, on 11 September; he was succeeded, also in an acting capacity, by the Chairman of the recently elected Parlamentul, MIHAI GHIMPU, pending the election by legislative deputies of a new President. Two attempts by the new legislature to elect a President, on 10 November and 7 December, also failed. Following the failure, in a referendum held on 5 September 2010, to approve proposed constitutional amendments that would facilitate the direct election of the President, Paralamentul was again dissolved, and fresh elections to the legislature were held on 28 November. On 30 December the new Chairman of Parlamentul, MARIAN LUPU, became acting President. As the results of these elections were also inconclusive, it appeared that would again prove impossible to elect a President. In February 2011 the Constitutional Court ruled that, as a period of more than two months had passed since the expiry of the mandate of an elected President, Parlamentul had the right to decide when a presidential election should be held. By April no such date had been set.

Legislature

Parlamentul
(The Parliament)

2073 Chişinău, bd. Ştefan cel Mare 105; tel. (22) 23-33-52; fax (22) 23-30-12; e-mail info@parlament.md; internet www.parlament.md.

Chairman: MARIAN LUPU.

General Election, 28 November 2010

Parties and alliances	Votes	%	Seats
Party of Communists of the Republic of Moldova	676,671	39.32	42
Liberal Democratic Party of Moldova	506,365	29.42	32
Democratic Party of Moldova	218,847	12.72	15
Liberal Party	171,434	9.96	12
Our Moldova Alliance	35,282	2.05	—
European Action Movement	21,105	1.23	—
Humanist Party of Moldova	15,456	0.90	—
National Liberal Party	10,923	0.63	—
Social Democratic Party	10,161	0.59	—
Christian Democratic People's Party	9,046	0.53	—
Others	45,657	2.65	—
Total	**1,720,947**	**100.00**	**101**

Election Commission

Comisia Electorală Centrală a Republicii Moldova (Central Electoral Commission of the Republic of Moldova): 2012 Chişinău, str. Vasile Alecsandri 119; tel. (22) 25-14-51; fax (22) 23-40-47; e-mail info@cec.md; internet www.cec.md; Pres. Dr IURIE CIOCAN.

Political Organizations

In January 2009 28 political parties were registered with the Ministry of Justice; the following were among the most important of those registered in early 2011.

Christian Democratic People's Party (PPCD) (Partidul Popular Creştin Democrat): 2009 Chişinău, str. N. Iorga 5; tel. and fax (22) 23-33-56; e-mail echipa@ppcd.md; internet www.ppcd.md; f. 1989 as the People's Front of Moldova, renamed 1992, and as above 1999; advocates Moldova's entry into the EU and NATO; Chair. IURIE ROŞCA.

Democratic Party of Moldova (PDM) (Partidul Democrat din Moldova): 2001 Chişinău, str. Tighina 32; tel. (22) 27-82-29; fax (22) 27-82-30; e-mail pdm@mtc.md; internet www.pdm.md; f. 1997; centrist; fmrly Movement for a Democratic and Prosperous Moldova, name changed in April 2000; contested 2005 legislative elections as mem. of the Democratic Moldova bloc; merged with Social Liberal Party in Feb. 2008; Chair. MARIAN LUPU.

European Action Movement (Mişcarea Acţiunea Europeană—MAE): 2012 Chişinău, str. Bucureşti 88; tel. (22) 92-99-66; e-mail office@ae.md; internet ae.md; f. 2006; supports closer integration of Moldova with the European Union; Leader VEACESLAV UNTILĂ.

Green Alliance Ecological Party of Moldova (Alianţa Verde—PEM–AVE): 2009 Chişinău, str. Kogalniceanu, 54; f. 1992; Chair. VLADIMIR BRAGA.

Humanist Party of Moldova (Partidul Umanist din Moldova—PUM): 2011 Chişinău, or. Codru, Str. Sf. Gheorghe 12; tel. (22) 23-41-51; e-mail presa.pasat@gmail.com; internet www.pum.md; f. 2005; Christian humanist party, associated with the Moldovan Orthodox Church; Pres. VALERIU PASAT.

Liberal Democratic Party of Moldova (PLDM) (Partidul Liberal Democrat din Moldova): 2012 Chişinău, str. Bucureşti 88; tel. (22) 81-51-54; fax (22) 81-51-63; e-mail info@pldm.md; internet www.pldm.md; f. 2007; absorbed Our Moldova Alliance Apr. 2011; Pres. VLADIMIR FILAT.

Liberal Party (PL) (Partidul Liberal): Chişinău, str. Bucureşti 87; tel. (22) 23-26-89; fax (22) 22-80-97; e-mail liberal@pl.md; internet www.pl.md; f. 1993 as Party of Reform; renamed as above 2005; Chair. MIHAI GHIMPU; 12,000 mems.

National Liberal Party (Partidul Naţional Liberal—PNL): 2069 Chişinău, Calea Ieşilor 6; tel. (22) 21-18-18; fax (22) 21-16-77; e-mail contacts@pnl.md; internet www.pnl.md; f. 2007; right-of-centre liberal party; Pres. VITALIA PAVLICENCO.

Party of Communists of the Republic of Moldova (PCRM) (Partidul Comuniştilor din Republica Moldova): 2012 Chişinău, str. N. Iorga 11; tel. (22) 23-46-14; fax (22) 23-36-73; e-mail ccpcrm@gmail.com; internet www.pcrm.md; fmrly the Communist Party of Moldova (banned Aug. 1991); revived as above April 1994; First Sec. VLADIMIR VORONIN.

Social Democratic Party (PSD) (Partidul Social Democrat): 2012 Chişinău, str. 31 August 1989 101/1; tel. and fax (22) 22-10-20; fax (22) 22-78-78; e-mail info@psdm.md; internet www.psdm.md; f. 1990; merged with Party of Social Democracy in Dec. 2007; Pres. VICTOR ŞELIN.

MOLDOVA

United Moldova Party (MU) (Partidul Moldova Unită): 2069 Chişinău, Calea Ieşilor 14/2; tel. (22) 26-81-10; fax (22) 74-68-20; e-mail mail@moldovaunita.md; internet www.moldovaunita.md; f. 2010 by fmr members of Communist Party of Republic of Moldova and fmr Centrist Union of Moldova; leftist, supportive of closer relations with Russia; Leader VLADIMIR ŢURCAN.

Parties and organizations in Transnistria include: **Renewal** (Obnovleniye), led by YEVGENII SHEVCHUK; **Transnistrian Communist Party (PKP)** (Pridnestrovskaya Kommunisticheskaya Partiya), led by OLEG KHORZHAN; **Patriotic Party of Transnistria (PPP)** (Patrioticheskaya Partiya Pridnestroviya), led by OLEG SMIRNOV; and **Republic** (Respublica), led by YURII SUKHOV.

Parties and organizations in Gagauz-Yeri include: **Fatherland** (Vatan), led by ANDREI CHESHMEJI; **Gagauz People** (Gagauz Halky), led by KONSTANTIN TAUSHANDJI; and **People's Republican Party** (Respublika Halk Partiyası), led by, among others, MIHAIL FORMUZAL.

Diplomatic Representation

EMBASSIES IN MOLDOVA

Azerbaijan: 2012 Chişinău, str. Kogelnichanu 64; tel. (22) 23-22-77; fax (22) 22-75-58; e-mail chisinau@mission.mfa.gov.az; internet www.azembassy.md; Ambassador NAMIK ALIYEV.

Belarus: 2009 Chişinău, str. Mateevici 83/1; tel. (22) 60-29-80; fax (22) 23-83-00; e-mail moldova@belembassy.org; internet www.belembassy.org/moldova; Ambassador VYACHESLAV A. OSIPENKO.

Bulgaria: 2012 Chişinău, str. Bucureşti 92; tel. (22) 23-79-83; fax (22) 23-79-78; e-mail ambasada-bulgara@mtc.md; internet www.mfa.government.bg/bg/52/; Ambassador GEORGI PANAYOTOV.

China, People's Republic: 2004 Chişinău, str. Mitropolit Dosoftei 124; tel. (22) 21-07-12; fax (22) 29-59-60; e-mail chinaemb@mtc.md; internet md.chineseembassy.org; Ambassador FANG LI.

Czech Republic: 2005 Chişinău, str. Moara Roşie 23; tel. (22) 20-99-42; fax (22) 29-64-37; e-mail chisinau@embassy.mzv.cz; internet www.mzv.cz/chisinau; Ambassador JAROMÍR KVAPIL.

France: 2009 Chişinău, str. V. Pîrcălab 6; tel. (22) 20-04-00; fax (22) 20-04-01; e-mail infos.chisinau-amba@diplomatie.gouv.fr; internet www.ambafrance.md; Ambassador PIERRE ANDRIEU.

Germany: 2012 Chişinău, str. Maria Cibotari 35; tel. (22) 20-06-00; fax (22) 23-46-80; e-mail info@chisinau.diplo.de; internet www.chisinau.diplo.de; Ambassador BERTHOLD JOHANNES.

Hungary: 2004 Chişinău, bd. Ştefan cel Mare 131; tel. (22) 22-34-04; fax (22) 22-45-13; e-mail mission.kiv@kum.hu; internet www.mfa.gov.hu/emb/chisinau; Ambassador GYÖRGY VARGA.

Israel: 2001 Chişinău, str. Tighina 12; tel. (22) 54-42-84; Ambassador OREN DAVID (resident in Jerusalem, Israel).

Lithuania: 2001 Chişinău, str. I. Valilenco 24/1; tel. (22) 54-31-94; fax (22) 23-42-87; e-mail amb.md@urm.lt; internet md.mfa.lt; Ambassador VIOLETA MOTULAITĖ.

Poland: 2019 Chişinău, str. Grenoble 126 A; tel. (22) 28-59-50; fax (22) 28-90-00; e-mail kiszyniow.amb.sekretariat@msz.gov.pl; internet www.kiszyniow.polemb.net; Ambassador BOGUMIŁ LUFT.

Romania: 2001 Chişinău, str. Bucureşti 66/1; tel. (22) 21-30-37; fax (22) 22-81-29; e-mail secretariat@ambasadaromaniei.md; internet chisinau.mae.ro; Ambassador MARIUS LAZURCA.

Russia: 2004 Chişinău, bd. Ştefan cel Mare 153; tel. (22) 23-49-43; fax (22) 23-51-07; e-mail domino@mtc.md; internet www.moldova.mid.ru; Ambassador VALERII I. KUZMIN.

Sweden: 2004 Chişinău, str. Toma Ciorba 12; tel. and fax (22) 26-73-20; e-mail ambassaden.chisinau@sida.se; internet www.swedenabroad.com/Chisinau; Ambassador INGRID TERSMAN.

Turkey: Chişinău, str. Valeriau Cupcea 60; tel. (22) 50-91-00; fax (22) 22-55-28; e-mail turkemb.kishinev@mfa.gov.tr; internet www.chisinau.emb.mfa.gov.tr; Ambassador AHMET FERIT ÜLKER.

Ukraine: 2008 Chişinău, bd. Vasile Lupu 17; tel. (22) 58-21-51; fax (22) 58-51-08; e-mail ambasua@starnet.md; internet www.mfa.gov.ua/moldova; Ambassador SERHIY I. PYROZHKOV.

United Kingdom: 2012 Chişinău, str. N. Iorga 18; tel. (22) 22-59-02; fax (22) 25-18-59; e-mail enquiries.chisinau@fco.gov.uk; internet ukinmoldova.fco.gov.uk; Ambassador KEITH SHANNON.

USA: 2009 Chişinău, str. Mateevici 103; tel. (22) 40-83-00; fax (22) 23-30-44; e-mail irechisinau@state.gov; internet moldova.usembassy.gov; Ambassador ASIF J. CHAUDHRY.

Directory

Judicial System

Supreme Court of Justice of the Republic of Moldova (Curtea Supremă de Justiţie a Republicii Moldova): 2009 Chişinău, str. M. Kogălniceanu 70; tel. and fax (22) 22-31-69; internet www.csj.md; comprises penal, economic, and civil and administrative chambers; Pres. ION MURUIANU.

Constitutional Court of the Republic of Moldova (Curtea Constitutionala a Republicii Moldova): 2004 Chişinău, str. A. Lapuşneanu 28; tel. (22) 25-37-08; fax (22) 25-37-46; e-mail curtea@constcourt.md; internet www.constcourt.md; f. 1994; Chair. DUMITRU PULBERE.

Prosecutor-General: VALERIU ZUBCO, 2005 Chişinău, str. Mitropolit Bănulescu-Bodoni 26; tel. (22) 22-50-75; fax (22) 21-20-32; internet www.procuratura.md.

Religion

The majority of the inhabitants of Moldova profess Christianity, the largest denomination being the Eastern Orthodox Church. The Gagauz, of Turkic descent, are also adherents of Orthodox Christianity.

CHRISTIANITY

Eastern Orthodox Church

In December 1992 the Patriarch of Moscow and All Russia issued a decree altering the status of the Eparchy of Chişinău and Moldova to that of a Metropolitan See, which later became known as the Moldovan Orthodox Church (distinct from the Metropolitanate of Moldova and Bucovina of the Romanian Orthodox Church). In 2002 the Government permitted the registration of an Autonomous Metropolitate of Bessarabia. The recognition of the church, an exarchate of the Romanian Orthodox Church, was confirmed by the Supreme Court in late 2004. In late 2007 the Romanian Orthodox Church announced that three dioceses in Moldova, which had been abolished in 1944 following the Soviet occupation of the territory, were to be reactivated.

Metropolitanate of Bessarabia, Archbishop of Chişinău: 2004 Chişinău, str. 31 August 161; e-mail gbadea2006@yahoo.com; internet www.mitropoliabasarabiei.ro; Metropolitan of Bessarabia PETRU (PĂDURARU).

Moldovan Orthodox Church (Moscow Patriarchate): 2004 Chişinău, str. Bucureşti 119; tel. (22) 23-78-78; e-mail sec@mitropolia.md; internet www.mitropolia.md; 1,520 parishes (2004); Metropolitan of Chişinău and all-Moldova VLADIMIR (CANTAREAN).

Roman Catholic Church

In October 2001 the diocese of Chişinău, covering the whole country, was established. At 31 December 2007 there were an estimated 20,000 Catholics in the Republic of Moldova.

Bishop of Chişinău: Rt Rev. ANTON COŞA, 2012 Chişinău, str. Mitropolit Dosoftei 85; tel. (22) 22-34-70; fax (22) 22-52-10; e-mail episcopia@starnet.md.

The Press

The publications listed below are in Moldovan, except where otherwise indicated.

PRINCIPAL NEWSPAPERS

Analytique Moldpresa: 2200 Chişinău, str. 31 August 85; tel. (22) 22-19-20; fax (22) 22-67-04; e-mail analytique@analytique.md; internet www.analytique.md; f. 2006; weekly; in Russian; Chief Editor NATALIA UZUN; circ. 8,000 (2008).

Argumenty i Fakty v Moldove (Arguments and Facts in Moldova): 2000 Chişinău, str. Armenească 55/101; tel. (22) 27-89-28; fax (22) 54-65-80; e-mail info@aif.md; internet www.aif.md; f. 1978; Moldovan version of *Argumenty i Fakty* (Russia); in Russian; weekly; Chief Editor YEVGENIYA ANOKHINA; circ. 25,000 (2008).

Curierul Agricol (The Agricultural Courier): 2012 Chişinău, str. Puşkin 22/214; tel. (22) 23-39-64; fax (22) 23-43-93; e-mail curier06@mail.md; f. 2006; weekly; Chief Editor DUMITRU ŢIRA; circ. 4,000 (2008).

Curierul Economic (The Economic Courier): 2005 Chişinău, str. Bănulescu Bodoni 61/103; tel. (22) 40-28-33; fax (22) 24-52-57; e-mail curierul@ase.md; internet www.curier.ase.md; f. 1999; weekly; Dir TATIANA ROŞCA; circ. 4,000 (2008).

Ekonomicheskoye Obozreniye (Economic Review): 2000 Chişinău, str. S. Lazo 40; tel. (22) 88-77-77; fax (22) 88-77-89; e-mail

MOLDOVA

Directory

red@logos.press.md; internet logos.press.md; f. 1990; weekly; in Russian; Chief Editor SERGEI MIŞIN; circ. 9,500 (2008).

Flux Continu: 2004 Chişinău, str. N. Iorga 8; tel. (22) 23-50-91; fax (22) 23-74-75; e-mail ap@flux.md; internet www.flux.md; f. 1995; 5 a week; Chief Editor SERGIU PRAPORŞCIC; circ. 35,000 (Fri.), 3,000 (Mon.–Thur.) (2008).

Glasul Naţiunii (The Voice of the Nation): 2001 Chişinău, str. 31 August 15; tel. (22) 54-27-82; fax (22) 54-31-37; e-mail glasul_natiunii@yahoo.com; f. 1989 as Glasul; 4 a week; culture, arts, literature, sport, politics; circ. 10,000 (2008).

Jurnal de Chişinău (Chişinău Journal): 2012 Chişinău, str. Vlaicu Pârcălab 63/3; tel. (22) 23-83-31; fax (22) 23-42-30; e-mail cotidian@jurnal.md; internet www.jurnal.md; f. 1999; 3 a week; Chief Editor RODICA MAHU; circ. 26,000 (2008).

Kishinevskii Obozrevatel (Chişinău Correspondent): Chişinău, str. B. Pirkalab 45/405; tel. and fax (22) 21-02-27; e-mail red@ko.md; internet www.ko.md; weekly; in Russian; Chief Editor IRINA ASTAKHOVA.

Kishinevskiye Novosti (Chişinău News): 2012 Chişinău, str. Puşkin 22; tel. and fax (22) 23-39-18; e-mail kn@kn.md; internet www.kn.md; f. 1991; weekly; in Russian; Chief Editor SERGHEI DROBOT; circ. 9,000 (2008).

Kommersant Plus (Businessman Plus): 2012 Chişinău, str. Puşkin 22/601; tel. and fax (22) 23-36-94; e-mail inform@commert.press.md; internet www.km.press.md; weekly; in Russian; politics and economics, incl. coverage of Gagauz-Yeri and Transnistria; Chief Editor ARTEM VARENIŢA; circ. 11,000 (2008).

Komsomolskaya Pravda v Moldove (Young Communist League Truth in Moldova): 2012 Chişinău, str. Vlaicu Pîrcălab 45; tel. (22) 22-45-12; fax (22) 22-12-74; e-mail kp@kp.md; internet www.kp.md; f. 1996; daily; in Russian; Moldovan edition of *Komsomolskaya Pravda* (Russia); Editor-in-Chief V. N. SUNGORKIN; circ. 9,000 (2008).

Moldavskiye Vedomosti (Moldovan Gazette): 2012 Chişinău, str. Vlaicu Pîrcălab 63; tel. and fax (22) 23-86-18; e-mail editor@vedomosti.md; internet vedomosti.md; f. 1995; 2 a week; in Russian; Editor-in-Chief NATALIYA UZUN; circ. 9,000 (2010).

Moldova Suverană (Sovereign Moldova): 2012 Chişinău, str. Puşkin 22, 3rd Floor; tel. and fax (22) 23-35-38; e-mail cotidian@moldova-suverana.md; internet www.moldova-suverana.md; f. 2005; daily; state-owned; Editor ION BERLINSKI; circ. 20,000 (per week).

Nezavisimaya Moldova (Independent Moldova): 2012 Chişinău, str. Puşkin 22; tel. (22) 23-36-08; fax (22) 23-31-41; e-mail mail@nm.md; internet www.nm.md; f. 2005; state-owned; daily; in Russian; Chief Editor IURII TIŞCENCO; circ. 92,700 (per month).

Timpul de Dimineaţa (The Morning Times): 2005 Chişinău, bd. Grigore Vieru 22/2; tel. (22) 22-56-70; e-mail secretariat@timpul.md; internet www.timpul.md; f. 2001; daily; Dir CONSTANTIN TANASE; Chief Editor SORINA ŞTEFÎRŢĂ; circ. 46,750 (2008).

Unimedia: 2012 Chişinău, str. Petru Movilă 23/1; tel. and fax (22) 23-54-75; e-mail info@unimedia.md; internet www.unimedia.md; f. 2005; online only.

Vremya (Time): 2000 Chişinău, str. Ştefan cel Mare 13; tel. (22) 54-44-46; e-mail nata@vremea.md; f. 1998; daily; in Russian; Chief Editor EVGHENII PASCARI; circ. 8,800 (2008).

Gagauz-Yeri

Stolitsa Komrat (Capital City Comrat): 3805 Comrat, str. Tretiakov 36; tel. (298) 2-42-61; e-mail capitala@mail.ru; f. 2005; in Russian and Gagauz; Chief Editor ANA HARLAMENKO; circ. 8,000 (2008).

Vesti Gagauzii (Gagauz-Yeri News): 3800 Comrat, str. Lenin 200; tel. (298) 2-28-93; e-mail vesti@mtc-co.md; f. 1996; weekly; in Russian and Gagauz; publ. by the Halk Toplusu (People's Assembly) of Gagauz-Yeri; politics, culture, language; Chief Editor DMITRII MARINOV; circ. 4,500 (2008).

Transnistria

Dnestrovskaya Pravda (Dnestr Truth): 3300 Tiraspol, str. 25 Octombrie 101/236–237; tel. and fax (533) 9-46-86; e-mail tiraspol@dn_prav.mldnet.com; internet www.tiraspol.tripod.com; f. 1941; 3 a week; in Russian; Editor TATYANA M. RUDENKO; circ. 1,300 (2008).

Gomin (The Echo): Rîbniţa, str. Kirov, 130; tel. (555) 3-08-61; fax (555) 4-26-27; e-mail gomin130@mail.ru; f. 1996; weekly; in Ukrainian; Chief Editor DMITRII CERNEGA; circ. 2,460 (2008).

Pridnestrovye (Transnistria): 3300 Tiraspol, str. Lunacearski 13; tel. (533) 9-30-24; fax (533) 7-47-00; e-mail pridnestr@idknet.com; internet www.pridnestrovie-daily.net; f. 1994; 5 a week; in Russian; politics, economics, culture; Chief Editor VLADIMIR MASLENIKOV; circ. 4,241 (2008).

PRINCIPAL PERIODICALS

Alunelul (Little Hazelnut Tree): 2612 Chişinău, str. Puşkin 22; tel. (22) 22-26-41; f. 1982; for children aged 5–10 years; 10 a year; Chief Editor ŞTEFAN MELNIC; circ. 20,000 (2008).

Aquarelle: 2012 Chişinău, str. Puşkin 47/1A/3; tel. and fax (22) 22-07-73; e-mail aquarelle@aquarelle.md; internet www.aquarelle.md; f. 2003; in Russian; monthly; general women's interest; Chief Editor ANGELA SÎRBU; circ. 3,500 (2008).

Chipăruş Plus (Sharp Peppercorn): 2000 Chişinău, str. Ion Creangă 66/45; tel. and fax (22) 74-48-82; e-mail chiparusplus@yahoo.com; f. 2007; monthly; satirical; Dir MARGARETA CHIŢCATÎI; circ. 10,000 (2008).

Curierul Ortodox (The Orthodox Courier): 2060 Chişinău, bd. Traian 3, Biserica Sfîntul Dumitru; tel. (22) 77-25-33; e-mail fustei_nicolae@yahoo.com; internet curierulortodox.info; f. 1995; monthly; publ. of the Orthodox Church in the Republic of Moldova (Moscow Patriarchate); Chief Editor NICOLAE FUŞTEI; circ. 1,200 (2008).

Democraţia (Democracy): 2012 Chişinău, str. Puşkin 22/518; tel. (22) 24-32-53; fax (22) 24-35-85; e-mail democratiasaptaminal@yahoo.com; f. 2001; monthly; economics, politics, sport; Editor-in-Chief CORNEL CIUREA; circ. 11,000 (2008).

Florile Dalbe (The White Flowers): 2012 Chişinău, str. Puşkin 22; tel. and fax (22) 23-37-78; e-mail florile_d@mtc.md; f. 1941; weekly; education; Dir ION ANTON; circ. 15,000 (2008).

Legea şi Viaţa (The Law and Life): 2012 Chişinău, str. Puşkin 22/512; tel. and fax (22) 23-37-90; e-mail legea@molddata.md; f. 1990; monthly; in Moldovan and Russian; Chief Editor LEONTIE ARSENE; circ. 5,000 (2008).

Moldova (Moldova): 2012 Chişinău, str. Puşkin 22/539; tel. (22) 23-31-46; fax (22) 23-74-63; e-mail revistamoldova@list.ru; internet www.revista.md; f. 2004; monthly; in Moldovan, Russian and English; the arts; Editor NICOLAE ROŞCA; circ. 3,000 (2008).

Natura (Nature): 2004 Chişinău, str. S. Lazo 13; tel. and fax (22) 23-71-49; e-mail natura@natura.md; internet www.natura.md; f. 1990; monthly; nature and the environment; Chief Editor BORIS VIERU; circ. 7,800 (2008).

Noi (Us): 2012 Chişinău, str. Puşkin 22; tel. (22) 23-31-91; e-mail revistanoi@mail.md; f. 1935; for adolescents; Chief Editor VALERIU VOLONTIR; circ. 5,000 (2008).

Okhotnik i rybalov v Moldove (The Hunter and Fisherman in Moldova): 2005 Chişinău, str. Şipotelor 2; tel. (22) 24-20-27; fax (22) 24-32-43; e-mail ooirm@mail.ru; internet www.oxoma.md; f. 2006; monthly; in Russian; hunting, shooting, fishing; Chief Editor SERGEI YAVTUSHENKO; circ. 2,000 (2010).

Omnibus: 2000 Chişinău, str. V. Alecsandri 35A; tel. (22) 73-39-72; e-mail omnibus@hotbox.ru; f. 1993; in Russian; agriculture; Chief Editor MIHAIL BEREZICOV; circ. 5,500 (2008).

Profit/ Banky i Finansy (Profit/ Banks and Finance): 2014 Chişinău, str. Kogălniceanu 76; tel. (22) 23-49-30; fax (22) 23-49-33; e-mail office@profit.md; internet www.profit.md; f. 1995; monthly; in Romanian, Russian and English; economics and finance; Dir ALEXANDER TANAS; total circ. 4,800 (2009).

Puls (Pulse): 2001 Chişinău, str. Dosoftei 118; tel. (22) 83-81-86; fax (22) 29-59-54; e-mail red@puls.md; internet www.puls.md; f. 2004; monthly; in Russian; politics and economics; Chief Editor DMITRII KAVRUK; circ. 5,000 (2008).

Săptămína (The Week): 2012 Chişinău, str. 31 August 107; tel. (22) 22-62-51; fax (22) 22-44-61; e-mail saptamin@mdl.net; internet www.saptamina.md; f. 1992; weekly; politics, economics, social and cultural affairs; Chief Editor VIOREL MIHAIL; circ. 12,722 (2008).

Siesta: 2000 Chişinău, str. Kogălniceanu 88; tel. (22) 20-79-31; fax (22) 28-87-73; e-mail info@siesta.md; internet www.siesta.md; f. 2003; monthly; in Russian, Moldovan and English; coverage of cultural events in Chişinău; Chief Editor VLADIMIR GLADUN; circ. 6,000 (2008).

VIP Magazin (VIP Magazine): 2012 Chişinău, str. Puşkin 22/42-84-32; tel. (22) 23-31-64; fax (22) 23-40-01; e-mail vip_magazin@mld.net; internet www.vipmagazin.md; f. 2002; monthly; politics, business, entertainment; Chief Editor SERGIU GAVRILIŢĂ; circ. 3,500 (2010).

Transnistria

Obnovleniye (Renewal): 3300 Tiraspol, str. 25 Octombrie 118; tel. (533) 5-25-55; internet www.obnovlenie.info; f. 2000; monthly; in Russian; politics and economics; circ. 80,000 (2008); Chair. ANATOLII V. KAMINSKII.

Partner (Partner): 3300 Tiraspol, ul. Lenina 48; tel. (533) 9-64-80; e-mail makireeva@yandex.ru; internet www.tiraspol.ru/partner; f. 2004; monthly; in Russian; publ. by the Chamber of Trade and Industry of the 'Transnistrian Moldovan Republic'; Chief Editor MARINA KIREYEVA; circ. 999 (2008).

MOLDOVA

NEWS AGENCIES

Infotag News Agency: 2014 Chişinău, str. Kogâlniceanu 76; tel. (22) 23-49-31; fax (22) 23-49-33; e-mail office@infotag.md; internet www.infotag.md; f. 1993; Dir ALEXANDRU TANAS.

State Information Agency—Moldpres: 2012 Chişinău, str. Puşkin 22; tel. (22) 23-23-72; fax (22) 23-26-98; e-mail inform@moldpres.md; internet www.moldpres.md; f. 1940 as ATEM, reorganized 1990 and 1994; Dir VALERIU RENITA.

Transnistria

Olvia-Press: 3300 Tiraspol, str. Pravda 31; tel. (3022) 8-24-97; fax (3022) 8-20-04; e-mail olvia@idknet.com; internet www.olvia.idknet.com; f. 1992; sole press agency of the 'Transnistrian Moldovan Republic'; reports political, economic and cultural developments in the region; Editor-in-Chief OLEG A. YELKOV.

PRESS ASSOCIATIONS

Association of Independent Press (API): 2012 Chişinău, str. Bucuresti 77; tel. (22) 22-09-96; fax (22) 20-36-86; e-mail api@api.md; internet www.api.md; f. 1997; Pres. SLAVA PERUNOV; Exec. Dir PETRU MACOVEI.

Independent Journalism Centre (IJC): 2012 Chişinău, str. Sciusev 53; tel. (22) 21-36-52; fax (22) 22-66-81; e-mail editor@ijc.md; internet www.ijc.md; f. 1994; non-governmental org.

Publishers

Editura Cartea Moldovei: 2004 Chişinău, bd. Ştefan cel Mare 180; tel. and fax (22) 29-59-35; f. 1977; fiction, non-fiction, poetry, art books; Dir RAISA SUVEICĂ.

Editura Hyperion: 2004 Chişinău, bd. Ştefan cel Mare 180; tel. (22) 24-40-22; f. 1976; fiction, literature, arts; Dir VALERIU MATEI.

Editura Lumina (Light): 2004 Chişinău, bd. Ştefan cel Mare 180; tel. (22) 29-58-67; f. 1966; educational textbooks; Dir VICTOR STRATAN; Editor-in-Chief ANATOL MALEV.

Editura Ştiinţa (Science): 2028 Chişinău, str. Academiei 3; tel. (22) 73-96-16; fax (22) 73-96-27; e-mail prini@stiinta.asm.md; f. 1959; textbooks, encyclopedias, dictionaries, children's books and fiction in various languages; Dir GHEORGHE PRINI.

Technica-Info: 2004 Chişinău, bd. Ştefan cel Mare 168; tel. and fax (22) 44-13-00; e-mail almar@mail.utm.md; internet www.utm.md; f. 1993; technology; educational textbooks; Dir ALEXANDRU MARIN.

Univers Pedagogic: 2020 Chişinău, str. Socoleni 16/1, Centrul Ştiinţific; tel. (22) 24-32-79; e-mail univers_ped@yahoo.com; f. 1991; part of Ministry of Education; textbooks, guide books, children's literature; Dir I. SCUTELNICIUC.

Broadcasting and Communications

TELECOMMUNICATIONS

Regulatory Authority

National Regulatory Agency in Electronic Communications and Information Technology (ANRCETI) (Agenţia Naţională pentru Reglementare în Comunicaţii Electronice şi Tehnologia Informatiei): 2012 Chişinău, bd. Ştefan cel Mare 134; tel. (22) 25-13-17; fax (22) 22-28-85; e-mail office@anrceti.md; internet www.anrceti.md; f. 2000; Dir SERGIU SITNIC.

Service Providers

Eventis: 2008 Chişinău, str. Ghioceilor 1; tel. (22) 30-05-67; fax (22) 71-95-85; internet www.eventis.md; f. 2007; 51% owned by Eventis Telecom Holdings (Cyprus); mobile cellular telecommunications; Man. Dir IURIE CEBAN.

Moldcell: 2060 Chişinău, str. Belgrad 3; tel. (22) 20-62-06; fax (22) 20-62-07; e-mail moldcell@moldcell.md; internet www.moldcell.md; f. 1999; mobile telecommunications; owned by Fintur Holdings b.v. (Netherlands).

Moldtelecom: 2001 Chişinău, bd. Ştefan cel Mare 10; tel. (22) 57-01-01; fax (22) 57-01-11; e-mail office@moldtelecom.md; internet www.moldtelecom.md; f. 1993; telephone communication and internet service provider; scheduled for partial privatization; Gen. Dir STELA SÇOLA.

Orange Moldova: 2071 Chişinău, str. Alba-Iulia 75; tel. (22) 57-50-10; e-mail orange@orange.md; internet www.orange.md; f. 1998 as Voxtel SA; present name adopted 2007; mobile cellular telecommunications; 56.7% owned by France Telecom Mobiles (France), 33.4% by MMT-BIS; Dir-Gen. BRUNO DUTOIT.

Unité: 2001 Chişinău, bd. Ştefan cel Mare 10; e-mail marketing@unite.md; internet www.unite.md; f. 2007; mobile cellular communications; 100% owned by Moldtelecom.

BROADCASTING

Regulatory Authorities

National Radio Frequencies Centre (Centrul National pentru Frecvente Radio): 2021 Chişinău, str. Drumul Viilor 28/2; tel. (22) 73-53-64; fax (22) 73-39-41; e-mail cnfr@cnfr.md; internet www.mdi.gov.md/main_gis_md; f. 1993; responsible for frequency allocations and monitoring, certification of post and communications equipment and services; Gen. Dir TEODOR CICLICCI.

Radio and Television Co-ordinating Council (Consiliul Coordonator al Audiovizualului): 2012 Chişinău, str. Mihai Eminescu 28; tel. (22) 27-74-70; fax (22) 27-74-71; e-mail office@cca.md; internet www.cca.md; f. 1995; state owned; regulatory and licensing body; Pres. GHEORGHE ION GORINCIOI.

Radio

Radio Moldova: 2028 Chişinău, str. Miorita 1; tel. and fax (22) 72-33-47; e-mail a.dorogan@yahoo.fr; internet www.trm.md; f. 1930; subsidiary of Teleradio Moldova (q.v.); broadcasts in Romanian, Russian, Ukrainian, Gagauz and Yiddish; Dir-Gen. ALEXANDRU DOROGAN.

Radio Vocea Basarabiei (Radio Voice of Bessarabia): 2012 Chişinău, str. Puşkin 20A; tel. (22) 84-41-61; e-mail vinzari@voceabasarabiei.net; internet www.voceabasarabiei.net; f. 2000; Dir VEACESLAV TIBULEAC.

Television

Teleradio Moldova: 2028 Chişinău, str. Miorita 1; tel. (22) 72-10-77; fax (22) 72-33-52; e-mail international@trm.md; internet www.trm.md; f. 1958; state-owned; Pres. CONSTANTIN MARIN; Exec. Dir (TV) ANGELA SIRBU.

Finance

(cap. = capital; res = reserves; dep. = deposits; m. = million; brs = branches; amounts in Moldovan lei, unless otherwise stated)

BANKING

The National Bank of Moldova, established in 1991, is independent of the Government (but responsible to Parlamentul) and has the power to regulate monetary policy and the financial system. At February 2010 there were 15 authorized commercial banks in operation (with total assets amounting to 39,548m. lei).

Central Bank

National Bank of Moldova (Banca Naţională a Moldovei): 2005 Chişinău, bd. Grigore Vieru 7; tel. (22) 40-90-06; fax (22) 22-05-91; e-mail official@bnm.org; internet www.bnm.org; f. 1991; cap. 288.9m., res −957.7m., dep. 9,899.4m. (Dec. 2008); Gov. DORIN DRĂGUŢANU.

Commercial Banks

Banca de Economii a Moldovei: 2012 Chişinău, str. Columna 115; tel. (22) 21-80-05; fax (22) 21-80-06; e-mail bem@bem.md; internet www.bem.md; f. 1992; cap. 29.3m., res 18.8m., dep. 2,641.5m. (Dec. 2008); Pres. GRIGORE GACIKEVICI; 37 brs.

Banca de Finanţe şi Comerţ (FinComBank SA—Finance and Trade Bank JSC): 2012 Chişinău, str. Puşkin 26; tel. (22) 26-99-00; fax (22) 23-73-08; e-mail fincom@fincombank.com; internet www.fincombank.com; f. 1993; cap. 179.7m., dep. 854.7m., total assets 1,229.8m. (June 2007); Chair. OLEG VORONIN; 13 brs.

Banca Socială: 2005 Chişinău, str. Bănulescu-Bodoni 61; tel. (22) 22-14-94; fax (22) 22-42-30; e-mail office@socbank.md; internet www.socbank.md; f. 1991; jt-stock commercial bank; cap. 65.0m., res 68.9m., dep. 1,411.8m. (Dec. 2008); Chair. VLADIMIR SUETNOV; Pres. VALENTIN CUNEV; 20 brs.

Energbank: 2012 Chişinău, str. Vasile Alecsandri 78; tel. (22) 54-43-77; fax (22) 27-98-55; e-mail office@energbank.com; internet www.energbank.com; f. 1997; cap. 80m., dep. 681m., total assets 1,237m. (June 2008); Chair. IURII VASILACHI; 68 brs.

EuroCreditBank: 2001 Chişinău, str. Ismail 33; tel. (22) 50-02-00; fax (22) 54-88-27; e-mail telebank@ecb.md; internet www.telebank.md; f. 1992; jt-stock co; commercial investment bank; cap. 108.0m., res 10.3m., dep. 57.8m. (Dec. 2007); dep. 64.0m. (June 2008); Pres. AURELIU CINCILEI; 3 brs.

Eximbank: 2004 Chişinău, bd. Ştefan cel Mare şi Sfânt 171/1; tel. (22) 30-11-02; fax (22) 60-16-11; e-mail info@eximbank.com; internet

MOLDOVA

Directory

www.eximbank.com; f. 1994; total assets 3,717.3m. (Dec. 2008); Gen. Dir MARCEL CHIRCĂ.

Mobiasbanca: 2012 Chişinău, bd. Ştefan cel Mare şi Sfânt 81A; tel. and fax (22) 54-19-74; e-mail office@mobiasbanca.md; internet www.mobiasbanca.md; f. 1990; 67.9% owned by Société Générale (France); acquired Bancoop in 2001; commercial bank; cap. 100.0m., res 162.0m., dep. 1,969.0m. (Dec. 2008); Chair. of Bd JEAN-FRANÇOIS MYARD; 11 brs.

Moldova Agroindbank: 2006 Chişinău, str. Cosmonauţilor 9; tel. (22) 85-65-65; fax (22) 22-80-58; e-mail aib@maib.md; internet www.maib.md; f. 1991; joint-stock commercial bank; cap. 194.7m., res 172.4m., dep. 5,556.7m. (Dec. 2008); Chair. of Bd VICTOR MICULEŢ; Chair. NATALIA VRABIE; 45 brs.

Unibank: 2012 Chişinău, str. Mitropolit G. Bănulescu-Bodoni 45; tel. (22) 25-38-01; fax (22) 22-05-30; e-mail welcome@unibank.md; internet www.unibank.md; f. 1993; jt-stock commercial bank; cap. 186.1m., res 24.6m., dep. 232.2m. (Jan. 2008); Pres. DUMITRU TUGULSCHI; 5 brs.

Universalbank: 2004 Chişinău, bd. Ştefan cel Mare 180; tel. (22) 26-97-00; fax (22) 26-96-99; e-mail office@mail.universalbank.md; internet www.universalbank.md; f. 1994; cap. 86.8m., res 10.0m., dep. 56.7m. (Dec. 2008); Chair. of Bd OKSANA DEMIDEVSCHI (acting); 7 brs.

Victoriabank: 2004 Chişinău, str. 31 August 1989 141; tel. (22) 57-61-00; fax (22) 23-45-33; e-mail office@victoriabank.md; internet www.victoriabank.md; f. 1990; cap. 32.0m., res 14.3m., dep. 4,520.4m. (Dec. 2008); Pres. NATALIA POLITOV-CANGAS; 55 brs.

STOCK EXCHANGE

Moldovan Stock Exchange (Bursa de Valori a Moldovei SA): 2001 Chişinău, bd. Ştefan cel Mare 73; tel. (22) 27-75-94; fax (22) 27-73-56; e-mail postmaster@moldse.md; internet www.moldse.md; f. 1994; Chair. SERGIU CEBOTARI.

INSURANCE

In March 2010 there were 24 insurance companies operating in Moldova.

Acord Grup: 2038 Chişinău, str. Trandafirilor 7/2; tel. (22) 57-98-79; fax (22) 53-88-33; e-mail office@acordgrup.md; f. 2002; Dir VLADIMIR DOBRÎNIN.

Alianţa Modocoop: 2001 Chişinău, bd. Ştefan cel Mare 67; tel. and fax (22) 27-21-63; f. 2001; life and non-life; Dir NICOLAE RODEANU.

Artas: 2009 Chişinău, str. Puşkin 4; tel. (22) 22-84-74; fax (22) 22-96-49; e-mail asigurari.artas@gmail.com; internet www.artas.md; f. 1993; non-life; Dir EUGENIA GOHBERG.

Asito: 2005 Chişinău, str. Bănulescu-Bodoni 57/1; tel. (22) 22-62-12; fax (22) 22-11-79; e-mail asito@asito.md; internet www.asito.md; f. 1991; 48.3% owned by Moldova Investment Group (United Kingdom); fmrly QBE Asito; Gen. Man. EUGEN ŞLOPAC.

Asterra Grup: 2005 Chişinău, O. Goga 26; tel. (22) 21-17-58; fax (22) 21-17-59; internet www.asterra.md; life and non-life; Dir ANATOLII BANTAŞ.

Donaris Group: 2012 Chişinău, str. 31 August 1989, 108/1; tel. (22) 26-57-10; fax (22) 27-83-94; e-mail d.gherasim@dg.md; internet www.donaris.md; life and non-life, insurance and reinsurance; Dir DINU GHERASIM.

Galas: 2012 Chişinău, str. Diordiţa 2; tel. (22) 21-34-50; fax (22) 22-39-54; e-mail galas@dnt.md; internet www.galas.md; Dir VERA VIERU.

Garantie: 2005 Chişinău, str. Puşkin 47/1; tel. (22) 27-00-50; fax (22) 27-00-55; e-mail office@garantie.md; internet www.garantie.md; f. 1993; life and non-life; Pres. ALEXEI TOPOROV.

Grawe Carat Asigurări: 2012 Chişinău, str. Alexandru cel Bun 51; tel. (22) 27-93-32; fax (22) 27-93-56; e-mail office@grawe.md; internet www.grawe.md; f. 1972; life and non-life; Dir PETER KASYK.

Klassika Asigurări: 2001 Chişinău, str. Tighina 12; tel. (22) 85-09-50; fax (22) 22-32-43; e-mail office@klassikaasig.md; internet www.klassikaasig.md; f. ; life and non-life; Dir NIKOLAI DIYAKONU.

Moldasig: 2009 Chişinău, str. M. Eminescu 2; tel. (22) 23-81-61; fax (22) 23-83-46; e-mail moldasig@dnt.md; internet www.moldasig.md; f. 2002; 51% owned by Banca de Economii SA, 25% owned by Calea Ferată din Moldova, 24% owned by Poşta Moldovei; Gen. Dir VITALI I. BODYA.

Moldcargo: 2012 Chişinău, str. V. Alecsandri 97; tel. (22) 24-55-67; fax (22) 23-36-70; e-mail office@moldcargo.md; internet www.moldcargo.md; f. 1999; life and non-life; Pres. VLADIMIR FLOREA.

Sigur-Asigur: 2009 Chişinău, str. M. Kogălniceanu 73/2; tel. (22) 25-60-00; fax (22) 27-82-62; e-mail info@sigur-asigur.md; internet www.sigur-asigur.md; f. 2003; life and non-life; Dir SERGIU CERTAN.

Victoria Asigurări: 2005 Chişinău, str. Romană 8; tel. (22) 22-83-50; fax (22) 22-83-52; e-mail office@victoria-asiguari.md; internet www.victoria-asigurari.md; fmrly Orateh, name changed as above in October 2006; life and non-life; Dir.-Gen. OCTAVIAN LUNGU.

Regulatory Commission

National Commission for the Financial Market (Comisia Naţională a Pieţei Financiare): 2012 Chişinău, str. Stefan cel Mare, 77; tel. (22) 22-76-95; fax (22) 22-38-77; e-mail cnpf@cnpf.md; internet www.cnpf.md; f. 2007; regulates non-banking financial market; Chair. MIHAIL CIBOTARU.

Trade and Industry

GOVERNMENT AGENCIES

State Department for Privatization (Departamentul Privatizarii al Republicii Moldova): 2012 Chişinău, str. Puşkin 26; tel. (22) 23-43-50; fax (22) 23-43-36; e-mail dep.priv@moldtelecom.md; Dir-Gen. ALEKSANDR BANNICOV.

Moldovan Investment and Export Promotion Organization (MEPO) (Organizaţia de Atragere a Investiţiilor şi Promovare a Exportului din Moldova): 2009 Chişinău, str. Mateevici 65; tel. (22) 27-36-54; fax (22) 22-43-10; e-mail office@miepo.md; internet www.miepo.md; f. 1999; assists enterprises in increasing exports and improving business environment; Exec. Dir ANDREI TIMUS.

CHAMBERS OF COMMERCE

Chamber of Commerce and Industry of the Republic of Moldova (Camera de Comerţ şi Industrie a Republicii Moldova): 2012 Chişinău, str. Ştefan cel Mare 151; tel. (22) 23-53-32; fax (22) 23-13-91; e-mail camera@chamber.md; internet www.chamber.md; f. 1991; brs in Bălţi, Cahul, Ceadir-Lunga (Gagauz-Yeri), Edineţ, Lapusna, Orhei, Soroca, Tighina (Bendery), Ungheni; 16 sub-brs; Pres. GHEORGHE CUCU.

Chamber of Commerce and Industry of the 'Transnistrian Moldovan Republic' (Pridnestrovie) (TPP PMR): 3300 Tiraspol, ul. Lenina 48; tel. (533) 5-07-03; fax (533) 9-42-03; e-mail tpp@tiraspol.ru; internet www.tiraspol.ru; f. 1996; non-commercial patnership; brs in Tighina (Bender), Râbniţa and Dubăsari; Pres. VASILY KOZHAN.

UTILITIES

Regulatory Authority

National Energy Regulatory Agency (ANRE): 2012 Chişinău, str. Columna 90; tel. (22) 54-13-84; fax (22) 22-46-98; e-mail anre@anre.md; internet www.anre.md; f. 1997; autonomous public institution; Dir ANATOL BURLACOB; Gen. Dir NICOLAE TRIBOI.

Electricity

The sector comprises one transmission company, five distribution companies and four power generation plants.

MoldElectrica IS: 2012 Chişinău, str. V. Alecsandri 78; tel. (22) 22-22-70; fax (22) 25-31-42; e-mail disp@moldelectrica.md; internet www.moldelectrica.md; f. 2000 to assume the transmission and distribution functions of Moldtranselectro; Dir MARC RÎMIŞ.

Red Union Fenosa: 2024 Chişinău, str. A. Doga 4; tel. (22) 43-16-55; fax (22) 43-16-75; e-mail info@ufmoldova.com; internet www.ufmoldova.com; privatized in 2000; wholly owned by Unión Eléctrica Fenosa (Spain); distribution co supplying electricity to Chişinău; Pres. RADU SILVIA.

Gas

MoldovaGaz SA: 2005 Chişinău, str. Albişoara 38; tel. (22) 57-80-02; fax (22) 22-00-02; e-mail office@moldovagaz.md; internet www.moldovagaz.md; f. 1999; national gas pipeline and distribution networks; comprises 2 transmission companies and 18 distribution companies; 64% owned by Gazprom (Russia), 35% owned by Govt of Moldova; Pres. ALEKSANDR GUSEV.

TRADE UNIONS

Confederation of Trade Unions of the Republic of Moldova (Confederaţia Sindecatelor din Republica Moldova): 2012 Chişinău, str. 31 August 129; tel. (22) 26-65-02; fax (22) 23-45-08; e-mail office@cnsm.md; internet www.cnsm.md; f. 1990; Pres. OLEG BUDZA.

Transport

RAILWAYS

Calea Ferată din Moldova: 2012 Chişinău, str. Vlaicu Pîrcălab 48; tel. (22) 25-44-08; fax (22) 22-13-80; internet www.railway.md; f. 1992; total network 1,075 km; Dir-Gen. MIRON GAGAUZ.

ROADS

In 2000 Moldova's network of roads totalled 12,691 km (86.1% of which was hard-surfaced), including 3,328 km of main roads.

INLAND WATERWAYS

In 1997 the total length of navigable waterways in Moldova was 424 km. The main river ports are located within the separatist territory of Transnistria, at Tighina (Bender) and at Râbniţa.

CIVIL AVIATION

Moldova has four civilian airports, in Chişinău, Tiraspol, Bălţi and Mărculeşti.

Civil Aviation Administration (Administraţia de stat a Aviaţiei Civile): 2026 Chişinău, Aeroportul Chişinău; tel. (22) 52-40-64; fax (22) 52-91-18; e-mail info@caa.md; internet www.caa.md; f. 1993; Dir-Gen. VALENTIN VIZANT.

Air Moldova (Compania Aeriana Moldova): 2026 Chişinău, bd. Dacia 80/2, Aeroportul Chişinău; tel. (22) 52-55-02; fax (22) 52-60-09; e-mail info@airmoldova.md; internet www.airmoldova.md; f. 1993; wholly state-owned; scheduled and charter passenger and cargo flights to destinations in Europe and the CIS; Dir-Gen. VASILE BOTNARI.

Moldavian Airlines: 2026 Chişinău, Aeroportul Chişinău; tel. (22) 52-93-56; fax (22) 52-50-64; e-mail sales@mdv.md; internet www.mdv.md; f. 1994; scheduled flights to Budapest (Hungary), İstanbul (Turkey) and Timisoara (Romania); also charter passenger and cargo flights; Pres. and Chief Exec. NICOLAE PETROV.

Tourism

There were 8,956 tourist arrivals, including excursionists, in 2010; receipts from tourism (including passenger transport) totalled US $289m. in 2008.

Department of Tourism Development: 2004 Chişinău, bd. Ştefan cel Mare şi Sfânt 180, bir. 901; tel. (22) 21-07-74; fax (22) 23-26-26; e-mail dept@turism.md; internet www.turism.md.

Defence

Following independence from the USSR, the Moldovan Government initiated the creation of national armed forces. As assessed at November 2010, these numbered 5,354, with an army of 3,231, an air force of 826 and a logistic support force of 1,297. In addition, there were 57,971 reserves. Paramilitary forces attached to the Ministry of Internal Affairs number 2,379, including 900 riot police. The term of conscription is 12 months.

Under an agreement concluded in late 1994, the former Soviet 14th Army (under Russian jurisdiction) was to have been withdrawn from Transnistria within three years, but in March 1998 it was announced that Russian forces would remain in Transnistria until a political settlement for the region was reached. Despite subsequent agreements providing for a withdrawal, some 1,500 Russian troops (including 355 peace-keeping troops) remained in Transnistria at November 2010. There were also 12 OSCE troops and 10 Ukrainian military observers in Moldova at that time.

In early 1994 Moldova joined the North Atlantic Treaty Organization's (NATO) 'Partnership for Peace' programme, although the country's Constitution guarantees a neutral status.

Defence Expenditure: Budgeted at 205m. lei in 2010.

Chief of General Staff and Commander of the National Army: Col IURIE DOMINIC.

Education

Primary education begins at seven years of age and lasts for four years. Secondary education lasts for a maximum of seven years, comprising a first cycle of five years and a second of two years. In 2006/07 estimated total enrolment at primary schools included 88% of children in the relevant age-group, while the comparable figure for secondary schools was 81%. In 2007/08 79.8% of those enrolled in primary and secondary schools were taught in Moldovan and 20.0% in Russian. In 2009/10 some 415,500 students were enrolled at Moldova's 1,512 primary and secondary schools, while 142,141 students were enrolled at one of the 80 higher education institutions. In 2010 general government expenditure on education amounted to 4,832.4m. lei, according to preliminary figures (equivalent to 7.9% of total general spending).

MONACO

Introductory Survey

LOCATION, CLIMATE, LANGUAGE, RELIGION, FLAG

The Principality of Monaco lies in Western Europe. The country is a small enclave in south-eastern France, about 15 km east of Nice. It has a coastline on the Mediterranean Sea but is otherwise surrounded by French territory. The climate is Mediterranean, with warm summers and very mild winters. The official language is French, but Monégasque (a mixture of the French Provençal and Italian Ligurian dialects), Italian and English are also spoken. Most of the population profess Christianity, with about 91% belonging to the Roman Catholic Church. The national flag (proportions 4 by 5) has two equal horizontal stripes, of red and white. The state flag (proportions 4 by 5) displays the princely arms of Monaco (a white shield, held by two monks and superimposed on a pavilion of ermine) on a white background.

CONTEMPORARY POLITICAL HISTORY

Historical Context

The Principality of Monaco is an hereditary monarchy, which has been ruled by the Grimaldi dynasty since 1297. It was abolished during the French Revolution but re-established in 1814. In 1861 Monaco became an independent state under the protection of France. The first Constitution, promulgated in January 1911, vested legislative power jointly in the Prince and a 12-member Conseil national (National Council), selected for a term of five years by a panel comprising nine delegates of the municipality and 21 members elected by universal suffrage. Agreements in 1918 and 1919 between France and Monaco provided that, should the reigning prince die without leaving a male heir, Monaco would become an autonomous state under French sovereignty. Prince Louis II, the ruler of Monaco since 1922, died in May 1949, and was succeeded by his grandson, Prince Rainier III. A new Constitution, introduced in December 1962, abolished the principle of the divine right of the ruler and stipulated that the Conseil national (enlarged to 18 members) was to be elected by universal adult suffrage.

Domestic Political Affairs

Supporters of Prince Rainier, grouped in the Union nationale et démocratique (UND), dominated at five-yearly elections in 1963–88, on all but two occasions taking all 18 seats on the Conseil national. A UND list of candidates was not formed for the 1993 general election, although a list headed by Jean-Louis Campora (the President of the Principality's football team, AS Monaco) secured 15 seats. At legislative elections in February 1998 the UND list, now headed by Campora, secured all 18 seats.

In March 2002 the electoral law was amended, and in April the Conseil national approved a number of significant constitutional amendments. Both measures were in part intended to expedite Monaco's application for full membership of the Council of Europe (see p. 250), which had been submitted in October 1998. The age of majority was lowered from 21 years to 18 years, and several executive powers of the Prince were transferred to the Conseil national, the size of which was to be increased to 24 members following the elections in 2003. Additionally, the law of succession was modified, to permit succession through the female line.

In late 2002 discontent was reported at a proposal, supported by Campora, to sell AS Monaco to a Russian investment company based in the Principality, Fedcominvest. Following allegations that Fedcominvest was involved in money-laundering, Prince Rainier, who, on behalf of the Principality, retained ultimate control over the club, prohibited the sale. The ensuing scandal appeared to be a significant factor in appreciably reducing support for Campora's UND at the legislative elections, held on 9 February 2003, when the UND secured only three seats on the enlarged Conseil national; the remaining 21 seats were awarded to the list of the Union pour Monaco (UpM), a coalition mainly comprising members of the Union pour la principauté (UP) and the Union nationale pour l'avenir de Monaco (UNAM) and led by a former member of the UND, Stéphane Valeri.

In April 2004 the Parliamentary Assembly of the Council of Europe ruled that further reforms were required before Monaco could be considered for full membership; among the principal requirements were the extension of eligibility for several senior government positions, including the Minister of State (who, under the terms of a 1930 treaty, was required to be a French civil servant), to Monégasque citizens, and an enhancement of fiscal regulation. Following the decision of the Joint Committee of the Council of Europe (comprising representatives of the Parliamentary Assembly and the Committee of Ministers) that talks between France and Monaco had demonstrated significant progress towards the eventual reform of the 1930 convention, Monaco was admitted as the 46th member of the Council of Europe in October. A convention on administrative co-operation between France and Monaco was duly signed in November 2005, allowing Monégasque citizens to be appointed to senior government positions, subject to consultation with the French authorities. Agreements on financial regulation and judicial co-operation were signed concurrently.

On 6 April 2005 Prince Rainier died at the age of 81. He was succeeded by his son, Prince Albert II, who had acted as Regent of the Principality since 31 March. In July, several days before his formal inauguration as Head of State, it was confirmed that Prince Albert, who was unmarried and had no legal heir, had fathered a child in 2003. It was announced, however, that the Prince's son would neither bear the name Grimaldi nor be eligible to inherit the throne. (In June 2006 Prince Albert formally acknowledged paternity of a second child, who also would not take the family name or be eligible to inherit the throne.) Albert II was formally enthroned as the Ruling Prince in November 2005. In June 2010 it was announced that Prince Albert would marry Charlene Wittstock; the civil wedding was to take place on 1 July 2011 and the religious ceremony on 2 July.

At legislative elections held on 3 February 2008, the UpM retained its 21 seats in the Conseil national. The remaining three seats were won by the Rassemblement et Enjeux pour Monaco list.

In December 2008 Prince Albert announced that a plan to extend the Principality (by some 5%) into the sea, by creating an artificial peninsula, had been abandoned due to funding constraints as a result of the international financial crisis and unresolved environmental concerns.

A minor reorganization of the Council of Government took place in March 2009. Sophie Thevenoux, hitherto Director General of the Department of Finance and the Economy, replaced Gilles Tonelli as Government Councillor for Finance and the Economy, while Tonelli returned to his previous portfolio of facilities, the environment and urban planning. In January 2010 Stéphane Valeri, the President of the Conseil national, replaced Jean-Jacques Campana as Government Councillor for Social Affairs and Health. Jean-François Robillon was subsequently elected to the presidency of the Conseil national. In April divisions within the UpM prompted the withdrawal from the coalition of the UNAM, which held four seats in the legislature.

In March 2010 Michel Roger, a French civil servant, replaced Jean-Paul Proust as Minister of State; Prince Albert had declined to exercise his new authority, under the Franco-Monégasque treaty of 2005, to appoint a Monégasque citizen to the post. A reorganization of the Council of Government was effected in January 2011. José Badia, hitherto ambassador to Belgium, was appointed as Government Councillor for External Relations, succeeding Franck Biancheri, while Marco Piccinini and Marie-Pierre Gramaglia replaced Thevenoux and Tonelli, respectively, who were both assigned new ambassadorial roles working with the Minister of State to enhance bilateral relations with certain countries.

Foreign Affairs

Monaco participates in the work of a number of international organizations, becoming a member of the UN in 1993 and the Council of Europe in 2004 (see above). In October 2002 Monaco and France signed a treaty of friendship and co-operation to replace the Franco-Monégasque Treaty of 1918. Under its terms,

MONACO

France guaranteed Monaco's full sovereignty and territorial integrity and recognized the law of succession as established by the recent constitutional amendments; the possibility that France might assume sovereignty over Monaco in the event of the throne becoming vacant was thus eliminated. In addition, the treaty provided for the establishment of diplomatic-level relations between the two states, while Monaco agreed to conduct its foreign relations in accordance with France's fundamental interests. In February 2006 France upgraded the status of its diplomatic representation in Monaco from consular to ambassadorial level in accordance with the treaty, becoming the first country to operate an embassy in the Principality. Italy also opened an embassy in Monaco later in the year.

Controversy surrounding the use of Monaco's financial sector for the transfer of funds derived from criminal activities intensified in 1998 with the culmination of an investigation into the deposit of US $5.5m. in cash, suspected of originating from the illegal drugs trade, at a bank in Monaco in 1995. The affair led to a crisis in relations between France and the Principality, with the French Government overruling Prince Rainier by refusing to extend the mandate of Monaco's Chief Prosecutor, whom it suspected of not conducting a sufficiently thorough investigation of the scandal. Following further criticisms of Monégasque banking practice in a report by the Organisation for Economic Co-operation and Development (OECD, see p. 376) in 2000, the French Government recommended a rapid revision of the bilateral treaties between Monaco and France, proposing that Monégasque institutions be brought into greater conformity with French excise, fiscal and banking regulations. In a list published in April 2002, OECD defined Monaco as an 'unco-operative tax haven'; in early 2009 Monaco was removed from the list (see Economic Affairs). In December 2004 the EU signed an agreement with Monaco on the taxation of savings income. Under the agreement, savings income, in the form of interest payments made in Monaco to residents of the EU, was to be subject to a withholding tax from 1 July 2005. Monaco also agreed to exchange information on request with EU member states in criminal or civil cases of tax fraud or comparable offences.

CONSTITUTION AND GOVERNMENT

Under the Constitution of 17 December 1962, as amended on 2 April 2002, legislative power is vested jointly in the Prince, an hereditary ruler, and the 24-member Conseil national (National Council), which is elected by universal adult suffrage, partly under a system of proportional representation, for a term of five years. The electorate comprises only Monégasque citizens aged 18 years or over. Executive power is exercised, under the authority of the Prince, by the five-member Council of Government, headed by the Minister of State (a Monégasque or French civil servant appointed by the Prince after consultation with the French Government). The Prince represents the Principality in its relations with foreign powers, and signs and ratifies treaties. For the purposes of local administration there is, additionally, a consultative Conseil communal (Municipal Council), comprising 15 members elected for a term of four years, headed by a mayor.

REGIONAL AND INTERNATIONAL CO-OPERATION

Monaco is a member of the Council of Europe (see p. 250) and the Organization for Security and Co-operation in Europe (OSCE, see p. 385). By virtue of its customs union and open border with France, it forms part of the customs territory of the European Union (EU, see p. 270) and participates in the EU's Schengen Agreement on border controls; it also uses the euro as its currency. Monaco joined the UN in 1993.

ECONOMIC AFFAIRS

In 2001, according to World Bank estimates, Monaco's gross national income (GNI), measured at average 1999–2001 prices, was equivalent to approximately US $24,700 per head. In 2000, according to World Bank estimates, GNI, measured at average 1998–2000 prices, was equivalent to approximately $25,200 per head, or approximately $25,700 on an international purchasing-power parity basis. According to UN estimates, Monaco's gross domestic product (GDP) was $847m. in 1995 (equivalent to $26,470 per head). The annual rate of population increase averaged 0.3% in 2003–08. Monaco has the highest population density of all the independent states in the world. During 2005–08 GDP increased, in real terms, at an average annual rate of 6.7%. GDP grew by 14.6% in 2007, but by only 0.4% in 2008.

There is no agricultural land in Monaco. In 1990 a Belgian enterprise established an offshore fish farm for sea bass and sea bream. In 2009 there were just 41 private sector employees working in the primary sector.

Industry (including construction and public works) contributed 10.3% of the Principality's turnover in 2008. The sector engaged 15.8% of those employed in the private sector in 2009. Industry is mainly light in Monaco. The principal sectors are chemicals, pharmaceuticals and cosmetics (which together accounted for 41.7% of all industrial turnover in 2006), plastics (30.7%), electrical and electronic goods (9.7%), machine goods and paper and textile production.

Service industries represent the most significant sector of the economy in Monaco, contributing 89.7% of total turnover in 2008, and providing employment to 84.1% of those working in the private sector in 2009. Banking and finance accounted for more than 24.6% of the services sector and employed some 1,400 people in the late 1990s. At the end of 2006 the total value of deposits in Monaco's private banking sector was estimated at €23,450m. Trade accounted for 31.9% of national turnover in 2009, while banking and financial activities accounted for 15.8%.

Tourism is also an important source of income; it engaged some 20% of the employed labour force in the late 1990s, while the hotel business alone contributed 3.1% of the Principality's total turnover in 2008, and (together with restaurants and associated activities) engaged 16.5% of those employed in the private sector in 2007. In 2009 some 264,540 tourists (excluding excursionists) visited Monaco, compared with 323,705 in 2008. The greatest number of visitors (excluding excursionists) in 2009 were from France (21.4%), Italy (20.0%), the United Kingdom (11.7%) and the USA (7.1%).

Monaco's external trade is included in the figures for France. Excluding trade within the association with France, in 2009 Monaco's principal merchandise imports were consumer goods and semi-finished non-metallic goods. The most significant exports were semi-finished non-metallic goods, consumer goods and processed agricultural manufactures. Excluding France, the most important source of imports in 2009 was Italy (30.5% of the total value), followed by the People's Republic of China and the United Kingdom. Germany was the most important market for exports (excluding France), contributing 20.1% of total export earnings. Spain, Italy and the United Kingdom were also important markets for exports.

In 2009 there was a budgetary deficit of €71.8m.; expenditure amounted to €837.7m. Value-added tax (VAT) contributes about one-half of total government revenue.

Monaco is a prosperous state, which attracts wealthy residents through its tax regime; there is no income or inheritance tax and business rates are favourable. Monaco is largely dependent on imports from France, owing to its lack of natural resources. The economy is reliant on migrant workers (many of whom remain resident in France and Italy). Following the establishment of a casino in the 1860s, tourism became the dominant sector in the economy. In particular, the Principality has sought to establish itself as a major centre of the conference industry. An 18.3% decline in tourist arrivals in 2009 was attributed to recessionary conditions in the countries that provide the majority of Monaco's visitors, although the sector began to recover in 2010, as the global economic outlook improved. From the 1980s the industry and real estate sectors expanded, as a series of land reclamation projects increased Monaco's area by 20%. A number of foreign companies and banks are registered in Monaco in order to take advantage of the low rates of taxation on company profits. In March 2009 Monaco announced that it would adopt Organisation for Economic Co-operation and Development (OECD, see p. 376) standards on transparency and information exchange with regards to bank data, in an effort to combat tax evasion. Consequently, in May Monaco was removed from the OECD list of 'unco-operative tax havens'.

PUBLIC HOLIDAYS

2012: 1 January (New Year's Day), 27 January (St Devota's Day), 9 April (Easter Monday), 1 May (Labour Day), 17 May (Ascension Day), 28 May (Whit Monday), 15 August (Assumption), 1 November (All Saints' Day), 19 November (National Day/Fête du Prince), 8 December (Immaculate Conception), 25–26 December (Christmas).

MONACO

Statistical Survey

Source (unless otherwise stated): Direction de l'expansion économique, Division des statistiques et des études économiques, 9 rue du Gabian, MC 98000; tel. 93-15-41-59; fax 93-15-87-59.

AREA AND POPULATION

Area: 2.02 sq km.

Population: 32,020 at census of July 2000; 31,109 (males 15,076, females 15,914) at census of June–July 2008. Note: Total includes 119 persons with gender not declared. *2009* (official estimate at 31 December): 35,646 (includes adjustment for census underenumeration).

Density (at 31 December 2009): 18,280 per sq km.

Population by Age and Sex (at 2008 census): *0–14:* 3,965 (males 2,010, females 1,955); *15–64:* 19,063 (males 9,502, females 9,561); *65 and over:* 7,366 (males 3,276, females 4,090); *Total* 31,109 (males 15,076, females 15,914). Note: Total includes 715 persons of unknown age-group, and 119 persons with gender not declared.

Population by Nationality (at 2008 census): French 8,785; Monégasque 6,687; Italian 5,778; Other 9,859.

Districts (population at 2008 census): Monte-Carlo 14,586; La Condamine 11,946; Fontvieille 3,602; Monaco-Ville 975.

Births, Marriages and Deaths (2009 unless otherwise indicated): Live births 1,008; Marriages 171 (2004); Deaths 554.

Life expectancy (years at birth, WHO estimates): 82 (males 78; females 85) in 2008. Source: WHO, *World Health Statistics*.

Employment (private sector only, December 2009): Agriculture, hunting, forestry and fishing 41; Mining and quarrying 2; Manufacturing 3,201; Construction 3,867; Electricity and gas 165; Services 38,380 (Hotels, restaurants 4,084; Real estate, renting and business services 11,321); *Total* 45,656.

HEALTH AND WELFARE
Key Indicators

Total Fertility Rate (children per woman, 2008): 1.5.

Under-5 Mortality Rate (per 1,000 live births, 2008): 4.

Physicians (per 1,000 head, 1995): 5.80.

Hospital Beds (per 1,000 head, 1995): 19.6.

Health Expenditure (2007): US $ per head (PPP): 2,139.

Health Expenditure (2007): % of GDP: 4.0.

Health Expenditure (2007): public (% of total): 74.8.

For sources and definitions, see explanatory note on p. vi.

FINANCE

Currency and Exchange Rates: French currency: 100 cent = 1 euro (€). *Sterling and Dollar Equivalents* (31 December 2010): £1 sterling = 1.172 euros; US $1 = 0.748 euros; £1 = £8.54 = $13.36. *Average Exchange Rate* (euros per US dollar): 0.6827 in 2008; 0.7198 in 2009; 0.7550 in 2010. Note: The local currency was formerly the French franc, although some Monégasque currency, at par with the French franc, also circulated. From the introduction of the euro, with French participation, on 1 January 1999, a fixed exchange rate of €1 = 6.55957 French francs was in operation. Euro notes and coins were introduced on 1 January 2002. The euro and local currency circulated alongside each other until 17 February, after which the euro became the sole legal tender.

Budget (€ million, 2009): Revenue 744.2; Expenditure 805.5 (Current expenditure 613.4, Capital expenditure 192.1).

Turnover of the Principality (official figures, private sector only, € million, 2009): Industry 839.6; Public works and real estate 828.2; Hotel business 455.4; Banking and finance 2,058.3; Wholesale and retail trade 5,661.4; Transport 283.5; Other activities 3,033.3; *Total* 13,159.7.

Gross Domestic Product (€ million at constant 2000 prices): 3,772.8 in 2007; 3,785.0 in 2008; 3,355.2 in 2009.

National Income and Product (€ million at current prices, 2008): Compensation of employees 2,153.6; Gross operating surplus 1,993.3; Taxes, less subsidies, on production 345.9; *Gross domestic product* 4,492.7.

Gross Domestic Product by Economic Activity (€ million at constant 2000 prices, 2009): Industry 376.7; Finance 517.1; Other services 2,461.3; *Total* 3,355.2.

EXTERNAL TRADE

Note: Monaco's imports and exports are included in the figures for France, and separate figures for Monaco's trade with France are not included here.

Principal Commodities (€ million, 2009): *Imports:* 436.7 (Jewellery and musical instruments 63.7; Plastic products 57.8; Road vehicles and trailers 41.4; Ships and boats 38.7; Clothing 28.5). *Exports:* 509.9 (Soaps, cleaning products and perfumes 108.0; Ships and boats 49.5; Plastic products 45.3; Automobiles 31.5; Pharmaceutical products and preparations 23.3).

Principal Trading Partners (€ million, 2009): *Imports:* Austria 7.0; Belgium 40.5; Canada 5.3; China, People's Republic 45.2; Estonia 17.1; Germany 24.1; Italy 133.3; Japan 5.4; Madagascar 8.1; Netherlands 4.4; Russia 5.8; Spain 11.6; Switzerland 13.5; Tunisia 18.9; United Kingdom 42.8; USA 14.5; Viet Nam 6.0; Total (incl. others) 436.7. *Exports:* Algeria 6.6; Belgium 12.1; Brazil 7.2; China, People's Republic 18.6; Côte d'Ivoire 6.8; Gabon 10.4; Germany 102.6; Italy 55.4; Poland 12.5; Portugal 18.2; Spain 55.7; Switzerland 14.3; Tunisia 17.3; United Kingdom 33.0; USA 13.5; Total (incl. others) 509.9.

TRANSPORT

Road Traffic (vehicles in use at 31 December 2008): Passenger cars 23,938; Buses and coaches 90; Lorries and vans 4,208; Motorcycles and mopeds 8,368. Source: IRF, *World Road Statistics*.

TOURISM

Tourist Arrivals (excluding excursionists): 323,705 in 2008; 264,540 in 2009; 279,166 in 2010. Figures refer to arrivals of foreign visitors at hotels and similar establishments.

Tourist Arrivals by Country (2009): France 56,685; Germany 11,587; Italy 52,951; Japan 5,124; Russia 13,795; Spain 5,990; Switzerland 7,870; United Kingdom 31,067; USA 18,987; Total (incl. others) 264,540.

COMMUNICATIONS MEDIA

Radio Receivers (1997): 34,000 in use.

Television Receivers (1997): 25,000 in use.

Daily Newspapers (2004): 1 title (estimated circulation 8,000 copies).

Non-daily Newspapers (2004): 2 titles (estimated circulation 5,500 copies).

Telephones (2009): 35,400 main lines in use.

Book production (1999): 72 titles.

Mobile Cellular Telephones (2009): 23,000 subscribers.

Internet Users (2009): 23,000.

Broadband Subscribers (2009): 15,000 (Sources: mostly International Telecommunication Union; UN, *Statistical Yearbook*; UNESCO Institute for Statistics).

EDUCATION

(2008/09 unless otherwise indicated)

Pre-primary: 40 teachers (33 public, 7 private) (2004/05); 890 pupils (714 public, 176 private).

Elementary: 133 teachers (108 public, 25 private) (2004/05); 1,837 pupils (1,417 public, 420 private).

Secondary: 519 teachers (2007/08); 2,440 pupils (2,373 public, 67 private).

Note: Educational establishments in Monaco in 2004/05 comprised the following: three public pre-primary schools; four primary schools (three public, one private), which integrate pre-primary and elementary age-groups; one public elementary school; three public secondary schools, comprising one lower secondary school, one general upper secondary school, and one vocational secondary school; and one private school integrating primary and secondary age-groups. There was also one private higher educational establishment, the International University of Monaco, a business school where instruction is conducted in English.

Source: Direction de l'éducation nationale, de la jeunesse et des sports.

Directory

The Government

HEAD OF STATE

Ruling Prince: HSH Prince ALBERT II (succeeded 6 April 2005).

COUNCIL OF GOVERNMENT
(May 2011)

Minister of State: MICHEL ROGER.
Government Councillor for Finance and the Economy: MARCO PICCININI.
Government Councillor for the Interior: PAUL MASSERON.
Government Councillor for Facilities, the Environment and Urban Planning: MARIE-PIERRE GRAMAGLIA.
Government Councillor for Social Affairs and Health: STÉPHANE VALERI.
Minister Plenipotentiary, Government Councillor for External Relations and International Economic and Financial Affairs: JOSÉ BADIA.

MINISTRY OF STATE AND DEPARTMENTS

Ministry of State: place de la Visitation, MC 98000; tel. 98-98-80-00; fax 98-98-82-17; e-mail sgme@gouv.mc; internet www.gouv.mc.
Department of Facilities, the Environment and Urban Planning: Ministère d'Etat, place de la Visitation, MC 98000; tel. 98-98-81-92.
Department of External Relations: Ministère d'Etat, place de la Visitation, BP 522, MC 98000 Cedex; tel. 98-98-89-04; fax 98-98-85-54; e-mail relext@gouv.mc; internet www.diplomatie.gouv.mc.
Department of Finance and the Economy: Ministère d'Etat, place de la Visitation, MC 98000; tel. 98-98-82-56.
Department of the Interior: Ministère d'Etat, place de la Visitation, MC 98000; tel. 98-98-84-56; fax 93-50-82-45.
Department of Social Affairs and Health: Ministère d'Etat, place de la Visitation, MC 98000; tel. 98-98-19-19; fax 98-98-19-99; e-mail afss@gouv.mc.

Legislature

Conseil national

12 rue Col Bellando de Castro, MC 98000; tel. 93-30-41-15; fax 93-25-31-90; e-mail vviora@conseil-national.mc; internet www.conseilnational.mc.
President: JEAN-FRANÇOIS ROBILLON.
Vice-President: FABRICE NOTARI.

Election, 3 February 2008

	% of votes	Seats
Union pour Monaco (Union for Monaco)	52.20	21
Rassemblement et Enjeux pour Monaco (Rally and Issues for Monaco)	40.49	3
Monaco Ensemble (Monaco Together)	7.31	—
Total	100.00	24

Advisory Councils

Conseil d'Etat: Palais de Justice, Monte-Carlo; advises on proposed laws or ordinances submitted for its approval by the Ruling Prince or by the Government, or on any other matter; 12 mems, appointed by the Ruling Prince, following the advice of the Minister of State and the Director of Judicial Services; Pres. PHILIPPE NARMINO; Sec. BRIGITTE GRINDA-GAMBARINI.

Conseil de la Couronne: Monte-Carlo; f. 1942; advises the Ruling Prince on matters of state, and must be consulted by the Ruling Prince prior to the implementation of certain constitutional matters, including the signature or ratification of treaties, the dissolution of the Conseil national, questions of naturalization or reintegration, the issuing of pardons or amnesties; 7 mems, appointed for renewable terms of 3 years; Pres. and 3 mems are appointed by free choice of the Ruling Prince, the remaining 3 mems are nominated by the Ruling Prince on the recommendation of the Conseil national; all mems must hold Monégasque nationality; Pres. CHARLES BALLERIO; Sec. RICHARD MILANESIO.

Conseil économique et social: Centre Administratif, 8 rue Louis-Notari, MC 98000; tel. 97-97-77-91; fax 93-50-05-96; f. 1945; advises on economic matters; 36 mems, appointed for a term of 3 years; 12 mems directly appointed by Govt, 12 appointed by Govt from list prepared by Union des Syndicats de Monaco, 12 appointed by Govt from list prepared by the Fédération Patronale Monégasque; the Ruling Prince appoints Pres. and 2 Vice-Pres from among the mems; Pres. ANDRÉ GARINO; Vice-Pres ANDRÉ THIBAULT, JACQUES WOLZOK.

Political Organizations

There were traditionally no political parties as such in Monaco; instead, candidates were generally grouped into lists to contest elections to the Conseil national. However, since 2003 political groupings have begun to establish a more permanent presence. The following groups were among those contesting the February 2008 election to the Conseil national:

Rassemblement et Enjeux pour Monaco (REM) (Rally and Issues for Monaco): 1 rue de Vedel, MC 98000; tel. 92-16-20-13; fax 93-25-20-09; e-mail info@rassemblement-enjeux.org; internet www.rassemblement-enjeux.org; coalition comprising members of the Rassemblement pour Monaco and Valeurs et Enjeux; Pres. LAURENT NOUVIAN.

Union Nationale pour l'Avenir de Monaco (UNAM) (National Union for the Future of Monaco): Monaco; mem. of Union pour Monaco; Pres. ERIC GUAZZONE.

Union pour Monaco (UPM) (Union for Monaco): 11 rue du Gabian, MC 98000 Monaco; internet www.unionpourmonaco.com; coalition comprising members of the Union pour la Principauté and the Union Nationale pour l'Avenir de Monaco; Pres. STÉPHANE VALERI.

Diplomatic Representation

In February 2006 France opened an embassy in Monaco, becoming the first country to institute ambassadorial-level diplomatic relations with the Principality. Italy opened an embassy in Monaco later in the year. By January 2011 ambassadors from 65 countries were accredited to Monaco; most were resident in France, Spain or Belgium.

France: Le Roc fleuri, 1 rue du Tenao, BP 45, MC 98006 Cedex; tel. 92-16-54-60; fax 92-16-54-64; e-mail courrier@ambafrance-mc.org; internet www.ambafrance-mc.org; Ambassador ODILE REMIK ADIM.

Italy: L'Annonciade, 17 ave de l'Annonciade, MC 98000; tel. 93-50-22-71; fax 93-50-06-89; e-mail ambasciata.montecarlo@esteri.it; internet www.ambprincipatomonaco.esteri.it; Ambassador ANTONIO MORABITO.

Judicial System

The organization of the legal system is similar to that of France. There is one Justice of the Peace, a Tribunal de Première Instance (Tribunal of First Instance), a Cour d'Appel (Court of Appeal), a Cour de Révision (High Court of Appeal), a Tribunal Criminel (Criminal Tribunal) and finally the Tribunal Suprême (Supreme Tribunal), which deals with infringements of the rights and liberties provided by the Constitution, and also with legal actions aiming at the annulment of administrative decisions for abusive exercise of power.

Palais de Justice

5 rue Col Bellando de Castro, MC 98000; tel. 98-98-88-11; fax 98-98-85-89.
Director of Judicial Services: PHILIPPE NARMINO.
President of the Supreme Tribunal: HUBERT CHARLES.
President of the Court of Revision: JEAN APOLLIS.
First President of the Court of Appeal: ROBERT CORDAS.
President of the Tribunal of First Instance: BRIGITTE GRINDA-GAMBARINI.
Attorney-General: JEAN-PIERRE DRÉNO.

MONACO

Directory

Religion

CHRISTIANITY

The Roman Catholic Church

Monaco comprises a single archdiocese, directly responsible to the Holy See. At 31 December 2006 there were an estimated 29,000 adherents in the Principality, representing about 90.6% of the total population.

Archbishop of Monaco: Most Rev. BERNARD BARSI, Archevêché, 1 rue de l'Abbaye, BP 517, MC 98015 Cedex; tel. 93-30-77-86; fax 92-16-39-31; e-mail info@eglise-catholique.mc; internet www.eglise-catholique.mc.

The Anglican Communion

Within the Church of England, Monaco forms part of the diocese of Gibraltar in Europe.

Chaplain: Fr WALTER H. RAYMOND, St Paul's Church House, 22 ave de Grande Bretagne, Monte-Carlo, MC 98000; tel. 93-30-71-06; fax 93-30-50-39; e-mail chaplain@stpaulsmonaco.com; internet www.stpaulsmonaco.com.

The Principality also has two Protestant churches and a synagogue.

The Press

La Gazette de Monaco: 1 ave Princesse Alice, MC 98000; tel. 97-97-61-22; fax 93-50-68-27; e-mail lagazette@aip.mc; internet www.lagazettedemonaco.com; f. 1976; monthly; regional information; Dir-Gen. MAX POGGI; Editor-in-Chief NOËLLE BINE-MULLER; circ. 10,000.

Journal de Monaco: Ministère d'Etat, place de la Visitation, BP 522, MC 98015; tel. 98-98-80-00; fax 93-15-82-17; e-mail journaldemonaco@gouv.mc; internet www.gouv.mc/DataWeb/jourmon.nsf; f. 1858; edited at the Ministry of State; official weekly; contains texts of laws and decrees; Editor ROBERT COLLE.

Monaco Actualité: 2 rue du Gabian, MC 98000; tel. 92-05-75-36; fax 92-05-75-34; e-mail actualite@monaco.mc; Dir-Gen. MAURICE RICCOBONO; circ. 15,000.

Monaco Hebdo: 27 blvd d'Italie, MC 98000; tel. 93-50-56-52; fax 93-50-19-22; e-mail monacohebdo@free.fr; internet monacohebdo.free.fr; Man. Editor ROBERTO TESTA.

Monte-Carlo Méditerranée: 46, blvd des Moulins, 98000 Monaco; tel. and fax 93-25-10-00; Dir-Gen. GÉRARD COMMAN; Editor-in-Chief CAROLE CHABRIER.

French newspapers are widely read, and a special Monaco edition of the daily *Nice-Matin* is published in Nice, France.

NEWS AGENCY

Monte-Carlo Press: Le Beverly Palace, 13 blvd de Belgique, MC 98000; tel. 97-70-74-24; e-mail mcpress@mcpress.mc; internet www.mcpress.mc; f. 1987.

Publishers

Editions Alphée: 28 rue Comte Félix Gastaldi, BP 524, MC 98015; tel. 93-30-40-06; fax 97-70-37-00; e-mail contact@editions-alphee.com; internet www.editions-alphee.com; f. 1972; spirituality, personal devt; Dir JEAN-PAUL BERTRAND.

Editions EGC: 9 ave Albert II, BP 438, MC 98011 Cedex; e-mail multiprint@multiprintmc.com; economics, history, literature; Gen. Man. GÉRARD COMMAN.

Editions Victor Gadoury: 57 rue Grimaldi, MC 98000; tel. 93-25-12-96; fax 93-50-13-39; e-mail contact@gadoury.com; internet www.gadoury.com; f. 1967; numismatics.

Marsu Productions: 9 ave des Castelans, MC 98000; tel. 92-05-61-11; fax 92-05-76-60; e-mail contact@marsupilami.com; internet www.marsupilami.com; comic strips, children's entertainment.

Editions de l'Oiseau-Lyre SAM: Les Remparts, BP 515, MC 98015 Cedex; tel. 93-30-09-44; fax 93-30-19-15; e-mail oiseaulyre@monaco.mc; internet www.oiseaulyre.com; f. 1932; owned by The Lyrebird Trust; classical music publishers; Pres. and Man. Dir KENNETH GILBERT.

Editions Regain S.N.C. Boy et Cie: Monte-Carlo; tel. 93-50-62-04; f. 1946; fiction, essays, autobiography, travel, religion, philosophy, poetry; Dir-Gen. MICHÈLE G. BOY.

Editions du Rocher: 28 rue Comte Félix Gastaldi, BP 521, MC 98015; tel. 99-99-67-17; fax 99-99-67-18; internet www.editionsdurocher.fr; f. 1943; fiction, history, sciences; Pres. ERNESTO ROSSI DI MONTELERA; Man. Dirs MARC LARIVÉ, SERGE BÉRARD; Dir-Gen. PATRICK MAHÉ.

Editions André Sauret SAM: Monte-Carlo; tel. 93-50-67-94; fax 93-30-71-04; art, fiction; Dir RAYMOND LEVY.

Broadcasting and Communications

TELECOMMUNICATIONS

Direction du Controle des Concessions et des Télécommunications: 23 ave Albert II, MC 98000; tel. 98-98-88-00; fax 97-98-56-57; e-mail nic@nic.mc; internet www.nic.mc; Dir MARIE-PIERRE GRAMAGLIA.

Monaco Telecom: 25 blvd de Suisse, BP 14, MC 98000 Cedex; tel. 99-66-63-00; fax 99-66-63-01; e-mail communication@monaco-telecom.mc; internet www.monaco-telecom.mc; f. 1997; 49% owned by Cable & Wireless (United Kingdom), 45% by the Société Nationale de Financement (wholly owned by Govt of Monaco), 6% by the Compagnie Monégasque de Banque; incorporates the wholly owned subsidiaries Monaco Telecom International, Société Monégasque de Services de Telecoms (SMST), Société Monégasque de Télédistribution (SMT) and Divona; Pres. ETIENNE FRANZI; Dir-Gen. MARTIN PERONNET.

BROADCASTING

Radio

Monte-Carlo Doualiya: 1 ave Henri Dunant, MC 98000; internet www.mc-doualiya.com; fmr subsidiary of RMC, transferred to Radio-France Internationale in 1996; in French and Arabic; Pres. ANTOINE SCHWARZ; Dep. Man. Dir PHILIPPE BEAUVILLARD.

Radio Monaco: 7 rue du Gabian, MC 98000; tel. 702707; e-mail info@radio-monaco.com; internet www.radio-monaco.com; Dir-Gen. GILDO PASTOR.

Riviera Radio: 10 quai Antoine 1er, MC 98000; tel. 97-97-94-94; fax 97-97-94-95; e-mail info@rivieraradio.mc; internet www.rivieraradio.mc; owned by Morris Communications Co (USA); broadcasts in English; Man. Dir PAUL KAVANAGH.

Trans World Radio SC: c/o Courtin Global Assistance, BP 349, MC 98007; tel. 97-77-70-04; fax 92-05-92-32; e-mail cdetwiler@twr.org; internet www.twr.org; f. 1955; Evangelical Christian broadcaster; Pres. LAUREN LIBBY.

Television

Monaco was scheduled to end analogue broadcasting in November 2011.

TMC Monte-Carlo: 6 bis Antoine 1er, MC 98000; tel. 92-16-54-80; fax 92-16-54-81; internet www.tmc.tv; f. 1954; Dir-Gen. CAROLINE GOT.

TVI Monte-Carlo: 8 quai Antoine 1er, MC 98000; tel. 92-16-88-20; fax 93-25-46-39; e-mail tvimc@frateschi.mc; programmes in Italian; CEO LUIGI FRATESCHI.

Société Spéciale d'Entreprises Télé Monte-Carlo: 16 blvd Princesse Charlotte, BP 279, MC 98090; tel. 93-50-59-40; fax 93-25-01-09; f. 1954; Pres. JEAN-LOUIS MÉDECIN.

Finance

(cap. = capital, res = reserves, dep. = deposits, m. = million, br(s) = branch(es), amounts in euros)

BANKING

In 2009 a total of 39 banks, including major British, French, Italian and US banks, were represented in the Principality.

Banque de Gestion Edmond de Rothschild: BP 317, Les Terrasses, 2 ave de Monte-Carlo, MC 98000; tel. 93-10-47-47; fax 93-25-75-57; e-mail bger@lcf-rothschild.mc; internet www.lcf-rothschild.com; f. 1986; present name adopted 1993; cap. 12.0m., res 21.0m., dep. 633.7m. (Dec. 2008); Chair. LEONARDO P. A. POGGI; Gen. Man. GIAMPAOLO BERNINI.

Banque J. Safra (Monaco): La Belle Epoque, 15–17 bis ave d'Ostende, MC 98000; tel. 93-10-66-55; fax 93-50-60-71; internet www.safra.com; f. 1994 as Banque du Gothard (Monaco); present name adopted 2006; 100% owned by Banque Jacob Safra (Switzerland); cap. 40.0m., res 7.4m., dep. 1,304.4m. (Dec. 2008); Pres. JOSEPH SAFRA; Gen. Man. YVES BRACCALENTI.

BNP Paribas Private Bank Monaco: 15–17 ave d'Ostende, MC 98000; tel. 93-15-68-00; fax 93-15-68-01; e-mail wealthmanagement.monaco@bnpparibas.com; internet www.privatebank.bnpparibas.mc; f. 2003 by merger of United European Bank—Monaco and BNP Paribas Private Bank Monaco; acquired Société Monégasque de

MONACO

Banque Privée and Bank Von Ernst (Monaco) 2005; private banking; cap. 13.0m. (April 2007); Dir-Gen. ERIC GEORGES.

Compagnie Monégasque de Banque: 23 ave de la Costa, BP 149, MC 98007; tel. 93-15-77-77; fax 93-25-08-69; e-mail cmb@cmb.mc; internet www.cmb.mc; f. 1976; 100% owned by Mediobanca—Banca di Credito Finanziario SpA (Italy); cap. 111.1m., res 234.8m., dep. 2,569.0m. (Dec. 2008); Chair. ETIENNE FRANZI; Vice Chair. ALDO CIVASCHI; 2 brs.

Crédit Foncier de Monaco (CFM Monaco): 11 blvd Albert 1er, BP 499, MC 98012 Cedex; tel. 93-10-20-00; fax 93-10-23-50; internet www.cfm.mc; f. 1922; 77.1% owned by Calyon (France); cap. 35.0m., res 140.9m., dep. 3,924.5m. (Dec. 2008); Chair. YVES BARSALOU; CEO GILLES MARTINENGO.

Crédit Suisse (Monaco): 27 ave de la Costa, BP 155, MC 98003; tel. 93-15-27-27; fax 93-25-27-99; e-mail alain.ucari@credit-suisse.com; f. 1987; cap. 12.0m., res 14.4m., dep. 1,336.6m. (Dec. 2007); Chair. FRANCO MULLER; Man ALAIN UCARI.

EFG Eurofinancière d'Investissements SAM: Villa Les Aigles, 15 ave d'Ostende, MC 98000; tel. 93-15-11-11; fax 93-15-11-12; e-mail enquiries_mco@efgbank.com; internet www.efggroup.com; f. 1990; merged with Banque Monegasque de Gestion SA in 2007; owned by EFG Bank (Switzerland); private banking; cap. 16.0m., res 3.3m., dep. 341.4m. (Dec. 2005); Dir-Gen. GEORGE CATSIAPIS.

HSBC Private Bank (Monaco): 17 ave d'Ostende, MC 98000; tel. 93-15-25-25; fax 93-15-25-00; internet www.hsbcprivatebank.com; f. 1997 as Republic National Bank of New York (Monaco) SA; present name adopted 2004; owned by HSBC Private Banking Holdings (Suisse) SA (Switzerland); private banking; cap. 151.0m., dep. 5,442.4m., total assets 5,795.9m. (Dec. 2008); Chief Exec. and Dir-Gen. GÉRARD COHEN.

KBL Monaco Private Bankers: 8 ave de Grande Bretagne, BP 262, MC 98005; tel. 92-16-55-55; fax 92-16-55-99; internet www.europeanprivatebankers.com; f. 1996; owned by KBL European Private Bankers S.A; cap. 8.5m., res 2.8m., dep. 411.1m.; Chair. JEAN-PAUL LOOS; Man. Dir STEPHEN BARBALACO.

UBS (Monaco) S.A.: 2 ave de Grande Bretagne, BP 189, MC 98007; tel. 93-15-58-15; fax 93-15-58-00; e-mail antonio.mancino@ubs.com; internet www.ubs.com/monaco; f. 1956; present name adopted 1998; owned by UBS AG (Switzerland); cap. 9.2m., res 28.7m., dep. 2,279.4m. (Dec. 2007); Chair. NIKLAUS PFAU; CEO PETER CONRAD.

INSURANCE

Assurances J.P. et C. Sassi AXA: Le Suffren, 7 rue Suffren-Reymond, BP 25, MC 98001; tel. 93-30-45-88; fax 93-25-86-07; e-mail agence.sassi@axa.fr; f. 1968; Dir JEAN-PIERRE SASSI.

The Eric Blair Network: 11 ave. St Michael, 98000 Monaco; tel. 93-50-99-66; fax 97-70-72-00; e-mail eric@insure.monaco.mc; internet www.ericblairnet.com; Chief Exec. ERIC BLAIR.

Gramaglia Assurances: 9 ave Princesse Alice, BP 153, MC 98003 Cedex; tel. 92-16-59-00; fax 92-16-59-16; e-mail assur@gramaglia.mc; internet www.gramaglia.mc; Dir ANTOINE GRAMAGLIA.

Monaco Insurance Services: 9 rue de Millo, MC 98000; tel. 97-97-39-39; fax 93-25-74-37; e-mail maoun@monaco377.com; Dir PIERRE AOUN.

Mourenon et Giannotti: 22 blvd Princesse Charlotte, MC 98000; tel. 97-97-08-88; fax 97-97-08-80; f. 1975; Dirs JEAN-PHILIPPE MOURENON, JOSÉ GIANNOTTI.

Silvain Assurances: 33 blvd Princesse Charlotte, BP 267, MC 98005; tel. 93-25-54-45; fax 93-50-39-05; Dir FRANÇOIS SILVAIN.

Société Française de Recours Cie d'Assurances: 28 blvd Princesse Charlotte, MC 98000; tel. 93-50-52-63; fax 93-50-54-49; Dir FLORIANO CONTE.

Trade and Industry

GOVERNMENT AGENCIES

Direction de l'Environnement: 3 ave de Fontvieille, MC 98013; tel. 98-98-80-00; fax 92-05-28-91; e-mail environnement@gouv.mc; Dir CYRIL GOMEZ.

Direction de l'Expansion Economique: 9 rue du Gabian, MC 98000; tel. 98-98-88-12; fax 92-05-75-20; e-mail expansion@gouv.mc; comprises 5 divisions: General Administration; Economic Development; Economic and Financial Enquiries; Intellectual Property; and Statistics and Economic Studies; Dir CATHERINE ORECCHIA-MATTHYSSENS.

Direction de la Prospective, de l'Urbanisme et de la Mobilité: 23 ave Albert II, MC 98000; tel. 98-98-22-99; fax 98-98-88-02; e-mail prospective@gouv.mc; Dir JEAN-MICHEL MANZONE.

Direction des Services Fiscaux: 'Le Panorama', 57 rue Grimaldi, BP 475, MC 98000; tel. 98-98-80-00; fax 93-15-81-55; Dir ANTOINE DINKEL.

CHAMBER OF COMMERCE

Jeune Chambre Economique de Monaco: 1 ave des Castelans, MC 98000; tel. 92-05-20-19; fax 92-05-31-29; e-mail jcemonaco@jcemonaco.mc; internet www.jcemonaco.mc; f. 1963; 102 mems; Pres. KEVIN HIN.

EMPLOYERS' ASSOCIATION

Fédération Patronale Monégasque (FPM) (Employers' Fed. of Monaco): 'Le Coronado', 20 ave de Fontvieille, MC 98000; tel. 92-05-38-92; fax 92-05-20-04; e-mail info@federation-patronale.mc; internet www.federation-patronale.mc; f. 1944; Pres. PHILIPPE ORTELLI; Sec.-Gen. CORINNE BERTANI; 25 mem. orgs, with 1,200 individual mems.

UTILITIES

Electricity and Gas

Société Monégasque de l'Electricité et du Gaz (SMEG): 10 ave de Fontvieille, BP 633, MC 98013 Cedex; tel. 92-05-05-00; fax 92-05-05-92; e-mail smeg@smeg.mc; internet www.smeg.mc; f. 1890; 64% owned by GDF SUEZ (France); 20% owned by the Govt of Monaco; Dir-Gen. GUY MAGNAN.

Water

Société Monégasque des Eaux (SME): 5 ave de Fontvieille, MC 98000; tel. 97-98-51-00; fax 92-05-23-83; e-mail sme@sme.mc; internet www.sme.mc; f. 1983; Pres. STÉPHANE GIACCARDI.

TRADE UNION FEDERATION

Union des Syndicats de Monaco (USM): 28 blvd Rainier III, BP 113, MC 98000; tel. 93-30-19-30; fax 93-25-06-73; e-mail usm@usm.mc; internet www.usm.mc; f. 1944; Sec.-Gen. ANGÈLE BRAQUETTI; 41 mem. unions.

Transport

RAILWAYS

The 1.7 km of railway track in Monaco, running from France to Monte-Carlo, is operated by the French state railway, the Société Nationale des Chemins de fer Français (SNCF). As part of the Government's policy of land reclamation, an underground railway station was opened in 1999.

ROADS

In 2007 there were an estimated 50 km of major roads in the Principality.

SHIPPING

Direction des Affaires Maritimes: quai Jean-Charles Rey, BP 468, MC 98012 Cedex; tel. 98-98-86-78; fax 98-98-37-15; e-mail marine@gouv.mc; Dir JEAN-LOUIS BISSUEL.

Société d'Exploitation des Ports de Monaco (SEPM): 6 quai Antoine 1er, BP 453, MC 98011 Cedex; tel. 97-77-30-00; fax 97-77-30-01; e-mail info@ports-monaco.com; internet www.ports-monaco.com; f. 2002; state-owned; responsible for management and devt of the 2 principal ports in Monaco, at La Condamine (Port Hercule) and Fontvieille; Pres. ALECO KEUSSEOGLOU; Gen. Man. GIANBATTISTA BOREA D'OLMO.

Shipping Companies

d'Amico Dry Ltd: 20 blvd de Suisse, MC 98000 Cedex; tel. 93-10-57-20; fax 93-10-56-07; e-mail info@damicoship.com; internet www.cogema-sam.com; owned by d'Amico Società di Navigazione SpA (Italy); Group CEO CESARE D'AMICO.

MC Shipping Inc.: Gildo Pastor Center, 7 rue du Gabian, MC 98000; tel. 97-97-49-90; fax 97-97-49-99; e-mail operations@mcshipping.com; internet www.mcshipping.com; f. 1989; Chair. of Bd CHARLES LONGBOTTOM; Pres. and CEO ANTONY CRAWFORD.

Société Anonyme Monégasque d'Administration Maritime et Aérienne (SAMAMA): Villa Saint Jean, 3 ruelle Saint Jean, MC 98000; tel. 99-99-51-00; fax 99-99-51-09; e-mail general@samama-monaco.com; f. 1975; Pres. FRANK O. WALTERS; Dir-Gen. J.F. MEGGINSON.

MONACO

CIVIL AVIATION

There is a helicopter shuttle service between the international airport at Nice, France, and Monaco's heliport at Fontvieille.

Héli Air Monaco SAM: Héliport de Monaco, MC 98000; tel. 92-05-00-56; fax 92-05-00-51; e-mail helico@heliairmonaco.com; internet www.heliairmonaco.com; Pres. JACQUES CROVETTO.

Tourism

Tourists are attracted to Monaco by the Mediterranean climate, dramatic scenery and numerous entertainment facilities, including a casino. In 2010 279,166 tourists (excluding excursionists) visited Monaco.

Direction du Tourisme et des Congrès: 2A blvd des Moulins, MC 98030 Cedex; tel. 92-16-61-16; fax 92-16-60-00; e-mail dtc@gouv.mc; internet www.visitmonaco.com; Dir-Gen. of Tourism MICHEL BOUQUIER.

Société des Bains de Mer (SBM): place du Casino, BP 139, MC 98000; tel. 92-16-25-25; fax 92-16-26-26; e-mail resort@sbm.mc; internet www.montecarloresort.com; f. 1863; corpn in which the Govt holds a 69.5% interest; controls the entertainment facilities of Monaco, including the casino and numerous hotels, clubs, restaurants and sporting facilities; Chair. JEAN-LUC BIAMONTI; Gen. Man. BERNARD LAMBERT.

Defence

France is responsible for the Principality's defence.

Education

Education follows the French system. Compulsory education lasts for 10 years for children aged six to 16 years. Primary education begins at six years of age and lasts for five years. Secondary education begins at 11 years of age and lasts for seven years. In 2004 expenditure on education was equivalent to 4.4% of GDP.

MONGOLIA

Introductory Survey

LOCATION, CLIMATE, LANGUAGE, RELIGION, FLAG, CAPITAL

Mongolia is a land-locked country in central Asia, with the Russian Federation to the north and the People's Republic of China to the south, east and west. The climate is dry, with generally mild summers but very cold winters. Temperatures in Ulan Bator (traditional spelling; Ulaanbaatar in transcription from Mongolian Cyrillic) range between −32°C (−26°F) and 22°C (71°F). The principal language is Khalkha Mongolian. Kazakh is spoken in the province of Bayan-Ölgii. There is no state religion, but Buddhist Lamaism is being encouraged once again. The national flag (proportions 1 by 2) has three equal vertical stripes, of red, blue and red, with the 'soyombo' symbol (a combination of abstract devices) in gold on the red stripe at the hoist. The capital is Ulan Bator (Ulaanbaatar).

CONTEMPORARY POLITICAL HISTORY

Historical Context

The country was formerly the Manchu province of Outer Mongolia. In 1911, following the republican revolution in China, Mongolian princes declared the province's independence. With support from Tsarist Russia, Outer Mongolia gained autonomy, as a feudal Buddhist monarchy, but Russia accepted Chinese suzerainty over the province in 1915. Following the Russian revolution of 1917, China began to re-establish control in Mongolia in 1919. In 1920 Mongol nationalists appealed to the new Soviet regime for assistance, and in March 1921 they met on Soviet territory to found the Mongolian People's Party (renamed the Mongolian People's Revolutionary Party—MPRP—in 1924) and established a Provisional People's Government. After nationalist forces, with Soviet help, drove anti-Bolshevik troops from the Mongolian capital, the People's Government was proclaimed on 11 July 1921. Soviet Russia recognized the People's Government in November of that year. In November 1924, after the death of Bogd Khan (King) Javzandamba Khutagt VIII, the Mongolian People's Republic was proclaimed.

The Mongolian People's Republic became increasingly dependent on the USSR's support. The Government conducted campaigns to collectivize the economy and to destroy the power of the nobility and Buddhist priests. In 1932 an armed uprising was suppressed with Soviet assistance. Following his reorganization of the MPRP and army leadership in 1936–39, power was held by Marshal Khorloogiin Choibalsan as Prime Minister and MPRP leader. The dictatorship of Choibalsan closely followed the model of the regime of Stalin (Iosif Dzhugashvili, 1924–53) in the USSR. The thousands of victims included eminent politicians, military officers, religious leaders and intellectuals. In 1939 a Japanese invasion from Manchuria was repelled by Soviet and Mongolian forces at Khalkhyn Gol (Nomonhan). In accordance with the Yalta agreement to preserve the status quo in Mongolia, war was declared on Japan in August 1945, four days before the Japanese surrender, and northern China was invaded. In a Mongolian plebiscite in October, it was reported that 100% of the votes were cast in favour of independence, and this was recognized by China in January 1946.

Domestic Political Affairs

Choibalsan died in January 1952 and was succeeded as Prime Minister by Yumjaagiin Tsedenbal, who had been the MPRP's First Secretary since 1940. Dashiin Damba was appointed First Secretary of the MPRP in April 1954. In 1955 India became the first non-communist country to recognize Mongolia. Tsedenbal replaced Damba as First Secretary of the MPRP in November 1958, and a new Constitution was adopted in July 1960.

Jamsrangiin Sambuu, Head of State since July 1954, died in May 1972. He was replaced in June 1974 by Tsedenbal, who remained First Secretary of the MPRP (restyled General Secretary in 1981) but relinquished the post of Chairman of the Council of Ministers to Jambyn Batmönkh. In August 1984 Tsedenbal was removed from the party leadership and state presidency, apparently owing to ill health, and Batmönkh replaced him as General Secretary of the MPRP. In December Batmönkh also became Head of State, while Dumaagiin Sodnom, hitherto a Deputy Chairman of the Council of Ministers and the Chairman of the State Planning Commission, was appointed Chairman of the Council of Ministers.

By the end of 1988 the MPRP Political Bureau was obliged to admit that economic renewal was not succeeding because of the need for social reforms. Batmönkh advocated greater openness and offered the prospect of multi-candidate elections. Between December 1989 and March 1990 there was a great increase in public political activity, as several newly formed opposition movements organized a series of peaceful demonstrations in Ulan Bator, demanding political and economic reforms. The most prominent of the new opposition groups was the Mongolian Democratic Union (MDU), founded in December 1989. In January 1990 dialogue was initiated between MPRP officials and representatives of the MDU, including its chief co-ordinator, Sanjaasürengiin Zorig (a university lecturer). The emergence of further opposition groups, together with escalating public demonstrations (involving as many as 20,000 people), led to a crisis of confidence within the MPRP. At a party plenum in mid-March Batmönkh announced the resignation of the entire Political Bureau as well as of the Secretariat of the Central Committee. Gombojavyn Ochirbat, a former head of the Ideological Department of the Central Committee and a former Chairman of the Central Council of Mongolian Trade Unions, was elected the new General Secretary of the party, replacing Batmönkh. A new five-member Political Bureau was formed. The plenum voted to expel the former MPRP General Secretary, Yumjaagiin Tsedenbal, from the party and to rehabilitate several prominent officials who had been removed by Tsedenbal in the 1960s.

At a session of the People's Great Khural (legislature), held shortly after the MPRP plenum, Punsalmaagiin Ochirbat, hitherto the Minister of Foreign Economic Relations and Supply, was elected Chairman of the Presidium (Head of State), replacing Batmönkh, and other senior positions in the Presidium were reallocated. Dumaagiin Sodnom was dismissed from his post as Chairman of the Council of Ministers and was replaced by Sharavyn Gungaadorj, a Deputy Chairman and Minister of Agriculture and the Food Industry. The Khural also adopted amendments to the Constitution, including the deletion of references to the MPRP as the 'guiding force' in Mongolian society. It also approved a new electoral law, with early legislative elections scheduled for mid-1990. Meanwhile, all limits on personal livestock holdings were removed, and new regulations were introduced to encourage foreign investment in Mongolia. However, in late March 1990 an estimated 13,000 disenchanted citizens demonstrated in Ulan Bator to demand the dissolution of the Khural. Opposition leaders demanded the introduction of a multi-party electoral law.

In April 1990 the MPRP held an extraordinary congress, at which more than three-quarters of the membership of the Central Committee was renewed. General Secretary Gombojavyn Ochirbat was elected to the restyled post of Chairman of the party. The Political Bureau was renamed the Presidium, and a new, four-member Secretariat of the Central Committee was appointed. In May the People's Great Khural adopted a law on political parties, which legalized the new 'informal' parties through official registration, and also adopted further amendments to the Constitution, introducing a presidential system with a standing legislature, the State Little Khural, which was to be elected by proportional representation of parties.

At the July 1990 legislative election and consequent re-elections, 430 deputies were elected to serve a five-year term: 357 from the MPRP (in some instances unopposed), 16 from the Mongolian Democratic Party (MDP, the political wing of the MDU), 19 shared among the Mongolian Revolutionary Youth League, the Mongolian National Progress Party (MNPP), and the Mongolian Social-Democratic Party (MSDP), and 39 without party affiliation. Under constitutional amendments adopted in May, the People's Great Khural was required to convene at least four times in the five years of its term.

In September 1990 the People's Great Khural elected Punsalmaagiin Ochirbat to be the country's first President, with a five-year term of office; the post of Chairman of the Presidium was abolished. Dashiin Byambasüren was appointed Prime Minister (equivalent to the former post of Chairman of the Council of Ministers) and began consultations on the formation of a multiparty government. The newly restyled Cabinet was elected by the State Little Khural in September and October. Under the amended Constitution, the President, Vice-President and ministers were not permitted to remain concurrently deputies of the People's Great Khural; therefore, re-elections of deputies to the legislature were held in November.

The 20th Congress of the MPRP, held in February 1991, elected a new 99-member Central Committee, which, in turn, appointed a new Presidium. The Central Committee also elected a new Chairman, Büdragchaagiin Dash-Yondon, the Chairman of the Ulan Bator City Party Committee, who had become a member of the Presidium in November 1990.

A new Constitution was adopted by the Great Khural in January 1992. It provided for a unicameral Mongolian Great Khural, comprising 76 members, to replace the People's Great Khural, following elections to be held in June. (The State Little Khural was abolished.) The country's official name was changed from the Mongolian People's Republic to Mongolia, and the communist gold star was removed from the national flag.

The elections to the Mongolian Great Khural of June 1992 were contested by the MPRP, an alliance of the MDP, the MNPP and the United Party (UP), the MSDP, and six other parties and another alliance. A total of 293 candidates stood for 76 seats in 26 constituencies, comprising the 18 *aimag* (provinces), the towns of Darkhan and Erdenet, and the six constituencies of Ulan Bator City. A total of 95.6% of the electorate participated in the elections. Candidates were elected by a simple majority, provided that they obtained the support of at least 50% of the electorate in their constituency. The MPRP candidates received some 57% of the total votes, while the candidates of the other parties (excluding independents) achieved a combined total of 40%. However, the outcome of the election was disproportionate, with the MPRP winning 70 seats (71 including a pro-MPRP independent). The remaining seats were taken by the MDP (two, including an independent), the MSDP, MNPP and UP (one each).

The first session of the Mongolian Great Khural opened in July 1992 with the election of officers, the nomination of Puntsagiin Jasrai (who had served as a Deputy Chairman of the Council of Ministers in the late 1980s) to the post of Prime Minister, and the approval of his Cabinet. Natsagiin Bagabandi, a Vice-Chairman of the MPRP Central Committee, was elected Chairman of the Great Khural (Speaker). Jambyn Gombojav (Chairman of the People's Great Khural from late 1990 to late 1991) was elected Vice-Chairman of the new Khural. Meanwhile, a National Security Council was established, with the country's President as its Chairman, and the Prime Minister and Chairman of the Great Khural as its members.

In October 1992 the MDP, MNPP, UP and the Mongolian Renewal Party amalgamated to form the Mongolian National Democratic Party (MNDP), with a General Council headed by the MNPP leader, Davaadorjiin Ganbold, and including Sanjaasürengiin Zorig and other prominent opposition politicians. In the same month the MPRP Central Committee was renamed the MPRP Little Khural, and its membership was increased to 169 (and subsequently to 198). The Presidium was replaced by a nine-member party Leadership Council, headed by Büdragchaagiin Dash-Yondon as its General Secretary.

The Great Khural adopted a Presidential Election Law in March 1993, and direct elections to the presidency were scheduled for June. Lodongiin Tüdev, a member of the party Leadership Council and Editor-in-Chief of the MPRP organ, *Ünen*, was chosen as the MPRP's candidate, while President Ochirbat was nominated by a coalition of the MNDP and the MSDP. The result of the election was a convincing victory for Ochirbat, who received 57.8% of the votes cast, compared with 38.7% for Tüdev.

In early 1996 the MPRP forced through the Great Khural the passage of amendments that increased the number of constituencies from 26 to 76, making them all single-seat constituencies, while preserving the majority vote system. To be declared elected, a candidate was required to have received only 25% of the constituency votes. In response, opposition parties formed an election coalition, the Democratic Alliance, which received support from the Mongolian Green Party and the MDU.

The end of MPRP rule

At the legislative election, held at the end of June 1996, a resounding victory was achieved by the Democratic Alliance, which won 50 of the 76 seats in the Great Khural, receiving some 46.7% of the total votes cast. The MPRP took only 25 seats (40.6%), while one seat was won by a candidate of the United Heritage Party (UHP). Electoral turn-out was 92.2%. At the legislature's inaugural session in mid-July the leader of the MSDP, Radnaasümbereliin Gonchigdorj, was elected to the post of Chairman of the Great Khural. Mendsaikhany Enkhsaikhan, the leader of the Democratic Alliance and the group's choice for Prime Minister, was nominated by President Ochirbat and voted into office. Following the rejection of MPRP demands concerning the allocation of positions in the Great Khural, MPRP members organized a three-day boycott of the legislature, leaving it inquorate and unable to function. After the boycott ended, the leader of the MNDP, Tsakhiagiin Elbegdorj, was elected Vice-Chairman of the Great Khural; a new Government was formed at the end of July.

Following their election defeat, and amid growing evidence of a rift between supporters of tradition and advocates of the reform process, in July 1996 the MPRP Little Khural elected a new Leadership Council and General Secretary of the party, Nambaryn Enkhbayar. Indications of a division in the party increased in February 1997, when the leaders of the MPRP sought to enforce their uncompromising policies on the party congress. Several prominent dissenting members resigned from the party, and Natsagiin Bagabandi, who had been Chairman of the Great Khural in 1992–96, was elected Chairman of the party.

With a date in May 1997 set for the presidential election, the MNDP and the MSDP proposed a joint candidate for the post of President—the incumbent, Ochirbat. The MPRP nominated the party Chairman, Bagabandi, while the UHP adopted Jambyn Gombojav, a former Vice-Chairman of the Great Khural. The election was won convincingly by Bagabandi, with some 60.8% of the total votes cast. In a severe set-back to the democratic movement, Ochirbat received only 29.8%, a reflection of popular dissatisfaction at the rigorous economic reform policies implemented by the ruling Democratic Alliance. Gombojav obtained 6.6% of the votes. Following Bagabandi's success in the presidential election, Enkhbayar was elected Chairman of the MPRP in his place. In August he won a by-election for Bagabandi's former seat in the Great Khural.

In April 1998 the Democratic Alliance decided that, henceforth, the Cabinet was to comprise members of the Great Khural, headed by the leader of the Alliance. Tsakhiagiin Elbegdorj, leader of the MNDP, was thus appointed Prime Minister, and a new Cabinet was formed in May. The Government became embroiled in a dispute over the amalgamation of the state-owned Reconstruction Bank, declared bankrupt after over-extending its credit, with the private Golomt Bank. Amid accusations that Democratic Alliance leaders had obtained loans from the bank shortly before its failure, the MPRP effected a boycott of the Great Khural. The party rejected the Government's reinstatement of Reconstruction Bank and returned to the Great Khural in late July to pursue a motion of no confidence in the Government. The vote was carried by 42 votes to 33, with the support of 15 members of the Democratic Alliance.

In August 1998 the Democratic Alliance nominated as its candidate for Prime Minister Davaadorjiin Ganbold, Chairman of the Economic Standing Committee of the Great Khural (who had been chief Deputy Prime Minister in 1990–92 and President of the MNDP in 1992–96). President Bagabandi rejected Ganbold's nomination, on the grounds of his failure to act to resolve the bank merger crisis in his capacity as Chairman of the Committee. Ganbold was nominated a second time, and again rejected by Bagabandi, who proposed Great Khural member Dogsomyn Ganbold. The Democratic Alliance persisted, and by the end of the month Davaadorjiin Ganbold had been nominated and rejected five times. The Democratic Alliance then proposed Rinchinnyamyn Amarjargal, acting Minister of External Relations and a member of the MNDP General Council. President Bagabandi accepted the nomination, but it was rejected by one vote in the Great Khural in September. Two other candidates were subsequently rejected by Bagabandi.

Bagabandi subsequently named six more prime ministerial candidates of his own, including Dogsomyn Ganbold and the Mayor of Ulan Bator, Janlavyn Narantsatsralt. The Democratic Alliance disregarded the presidential list and for the sixth time nominated Davaadorjiin Ganbold. Although the nomination was supported by all 48 Democratic Alliance members of the Great Khural, Bagabandi once again rejected him. The political crisis was then deepened by a new Constitutional Court ruling that members of the Great Khural could not serve concurrently in the Government. In late 1998 the Democratic Alliance finally nominated Bagabandi's candidate, Narantsatsralt, who was appointed Prime Minister in December. The formation of his Government was completed in January 1999.

Narantsatsralt's Government remained in power for just over six months. In July 1999 the Prime Minister was challenged in the Great Khural over a letter that he had written in January to Yurii Maslyukov, First Deputy Chairman of the Russian Government, in which he seemingly acknowledged Russia's right to privatize its share in the Erdenet copper-mining joint venture without reference to Mongolia. Unable to offer a satisfactory explanation, in late July Narantsatsralt lost a vote of confidence, in which MSDP members of the Great Khural voted with the opposition MPRP. The Democratic Alliance nominated Rinchinnyamyn Amarjargal for the post of Prime Minister, but the proposal was immediately challenged by Bagabandi. The President insisted that, following the Constitutional Court ruling of late 1998, he could consider Amarjargal's suitability for nomination in the Great Khural only after the candidate had resigned from his seat. After several days of arguments, representatives of the Democratic Alliance and the President adopted a formula that allowed the Great Khural's approval of the prime ministerial nomination and the nominee's resignation of his Great Khural seat to take place simultaneously. Amarjargal was elected Prime Minister at the end of July. The ministers of Narantsatsralt's Government remained in office in an acting capacity until early September, when all but one (the Minister of Law) were reappointed. The formation of the Government was completed in late October with the appointment of Dashpuntsagiin Ganbold as Minister of Law. In November 1999 Amarjargal assumed the presidency of the MNDP, replacing Narantsatsralt.

The 1992 Constitution was amended for the first time in December 1999 by a Great Khural decree supported by all three parliamentary parties, which simplified the procedure for the appointment of the Prime Minister and allowed members of the Great Khural to serve as government ministers while retaining their seats in the legislature. An attempt by the President to veto the decree was defeated by the Great Khural in January 2000, but the Constitutional Court ruled in March that the decree had been illegal. When the Great Khural opened its spring session in April, members rejected the ruling and refused to discuss it. The Constitutional Court's demand for a statement on the issue was disregarded by the Great Khural.

As the legislative election approached, a breakaway grouping of the MNDP re-established the Mongolian Democratic Party, and a faction of the MSDP founded the Mongolian New Social Democratic Party. Sanjaasürengiin Oyuun (the sister of Sanjaasürengiin Zorig, former Minister of Infrastructure Development and founder of the Mongolian Democratic Movement, who had been murdered in October 1998) established the Civil Courage Party (CCP). The CCP (or Irgenii Zorig Nam, subsequently also known as Citizens' Will) drew away from the MNDP several more members of the Great Khural, and formed an electoral alliance with the Mongolian Green Party. The MNDP, unable to reconstitute the previously successful Democratic Alliance with the MSDP, therefore formed a new Democratic Alliance with the Mongolian Believers' Democratic Party.

The MPRP's return to power

At the election, held in early July 2000, three coalitions and 13 parties were represented by a total of 603 candidates, including 27 independents. The MPRP won 72 of the 76 seats in the Great Khural. Prime Minister Rinchinnyamyn Amarjargal and his entire Cabinet lost their seats. The MPRP received 50.2% of the votes cast. The level of participation was 82.4% of the electorate. The MPRP's main support lay in rural constituencies, where it was widely seen as willing and able to halt the economic and social stagnation of the countryside. The Democratic Alliance won 13% of the votes cast, while the Mongolian Democratic New Socialist Party (MDNSP, which had amalgamated with the Mongolian Workers' Party in 1999) received 10.7% of the votes; each of them won one seat. The MSDP received 8.9% of the votes cast but won no seats.

When the legislature opened, Lkhamsürengiin Enebish, the MPRP General Secretary, was elected Chairman of the Great Khural. However, the nomination of the MPRP Chairman, Nambaryn Enkhbayar, for the post of Prime Minister was rejected by President Bagabandi, on the grounds that priority be given to the constitutional amendments. After a week of discussions a compromise was reached whereby Enkhbayar's nomination was presented to the Great Khural, while the amendments remained in force pending a Great Khural debate and a full nine-member session of the Constitutional Court. In July 2000 the Great Khural approved Enkhbayar's appointment as Prime Minister by 67 MPRP members' votes to three. Enkhbayar's Cabinet was approved in August.

At a conference in early December 2000 five parties—the MNDP, the MSDP, the Mongolian Democratic Party, the Mongolian Believers' Democratic Party and the Democratic Renewal Party—decided to dissolve themselves and form a new Democratic Party (DP). Dambyn Dorligjav, a former Minister of Defence and director of the Erdenet copper enterprise, was elected Chairman, while Janlavyn Narantsatsralt and the former Minister of the Environment, Sonomtserengiin Mendsaikhan, were elected as Vice-Chairmen. The party's National Advisory Committee was formed in February 2001, comprising two members from each of the Great Khural's 76 constituencies.

In mid-December 2000 the Great Khural readopted, unchanged and for immediate implementation, the decree of December 1999 amending the 1992 Constitution. The President's veto of the decree was rejected. However, the Constitutional Court was unable to meet in full session because the election of replacements for time-expired members was delayed in the Great Khural. President Bagabandi finally approved the amendments in May 2001.

In February 2001 the 23rd Congress of the ruling MPRP re-elected Prime Minister Nambaryn Enkhbayar as its Chairman, approved the establishment of a new Little Khural of 244 members and enlarged the party Leadership Council from 11 to 15 members. At the end of September Lkhamsürengiin Enebish, Chairman of the Great Khural and recently re-elected as General Secretary of the MPRP, died; he was succeeded in the latter post by Doloonjingiin Idevkhten and as Chairman of the Great Khural by Sanjbegziin Tömör-Ochir, MPRP Secretary.

At the presidential election of May 2001, the incumbent Natsagiin Bagabandi, the MPRP candidate, was re-elected, having received nearly 58.0% of the votes cast. Radnaasümbereliin Gonchigdorj of the DP won 36.6% of votes; Luvsandambyn Dashnyam, candidate of the CCP received 3.54%.

In March 2002 Sanjaasürengiin Oyuun's CCP merged with Bazarsadyn Jargalsaikhan's Mongolian Republican Party (MRP) to form the Civil Courage Republican Party, under Oyuun's leadership. However, in June 2003 Jargalsaikhan withdrew from the merger after disagreement about the formation of a coalition with the DP. Attempts in December to oust Oyuun from the party leadership failed, and in March 2004 she agreed to join the Motherland Democracy (MD) coalition comprising Erdenebat's MDNSP and the DP.

In June 2002 the Great Khural approved the Law on Land and the Law on Land Privatization. Although less than 1% of the country's total territory was to be available for privatization, the laws generated much controversy. From November farmers took part in several demonstrations in Ulan Bator. The demonstrators, led by DP leader Erdeniin Bat-Üül, protested that the poor would be denied land by the 'oligarchy'. The privatization law duly entered into force in May 2003.

In May 2003 Lamjavyn Gündalai, a DP member of the Great Khural who had condemned the imprisonment of journalists and criticized the land privatization programme, alleged that the Minister of Justice and Home Affairs, Tsendiin Nyamdorj, had links with the special services of a foreign country. In July Gündalai was removed from an aircraft at Ulan Bator airport, while en route to a conference in Singapore, and arrested for 'violation of the border'. This provoked an uproar regarding the breaching of Gündalai's parliamentary immunity. In late July, on the same day as a newspaper published extracts from the material relating to the allegations against Nyamdorj, Gündalai was released, and in August the charges against him were abandoned. In October Gündalai succeeded, for a third time, in disrupting the opening session of the Great Khural, and the Prime Minister was once again unable to deliver his address.

The National Human Rights Commission's 2003 annual report was highly critical of bureaucracy, corruption and cronyism, and the police were accused of numerous cases of brutality. The National Human Rights Programme was adopted in December of that year. Also in 2003, Damirangiin Enkhbat, who had been suspected of the murder of Sanjaasürengiin Zorig in 1998 and had since been resident in France, was reported to have been abducted by Mongolian secret agents and subsequently imprisoned in Mongolia. In early 2004 reports from the human rights organization Amnesty International suggested that Enkhbat had been tortured during interrogation. In June 2005 the UN's Special Rapporteur charged with investigating such allegations, Manfred Nowak, carried out a prison inspection and met Enkhbat and his lawyer. Nowak's report, which was published in December but did not appear in the Mongolian press until a year later, condemned torture in Mongolian prisons and criticized the provisions of the Law on State Secrets for preventing dissemination of information about death sentences. (Enkhbat was released from prison in February 2006 on the grounds of ill health, and subsequently died.)

Meanwhile, campaigning began for the next election to the Mongolian Great Khural, which was scheduled for mid-2004. The new General Election Committee (GEC) incorporated many MPRP nominees. The opposition MD election pact, formed by Mendsaikhany Enkhsaikhan's DP and Badarchiin Erdenebat's MDNSP, was joined by Sanjaasürengiin Oyuun's Civil Courage Republican Party, minus the followers of Bazarsadyn Jargalsaikhan, who left to re-establish the Republican Party. After the registration of participating political parties and coalitions, the GEC examined the official lists, rejecting all Mongolian Youth Party candidates. Before polling day three candidates withdrew, leaving the final number at 241: 76 each for the MPRP and the MD coalition, 33 for the Republican Party, 23 for the National Solidarity Party, nine for the Mongolian Traditional United Party (also known as the United Heritage Party), five for the Mongolian Green Party, four for the Liberal Party and 15 independents.

The initial results of the election of 27 June 2004 (compiled as percentages of the total ballot in each constituency) left the political scene in disarray: the MPRP and the MD coalition had each won about one-half of the seats, leaving neither with the necessary majority of 39 (one-half of the Great Khural seats plus one seat). The three independents elected, although all DP members, were discounted. The Republican Party won one seat. The rate of participation was 82.2% of registered voters. In 25 constituencies there was a straight contest between the MPRP and the MD coalition. Amid mutual accusations of bribery and fraud in several constituencies, efforts to form a government became embroiled in disputes at the GEC and the recently established City Administrative Court.

The GEC submitted the results in 74 of the 76 constituencies to President Bagabandi in early July 2004, at the first session of the newly elected Great Khural, which was boycotted by the MPRP. The MD members were not allowed to take the oath. Meeting separately, 70 of the MPRP members elected in 2000 filed a lawsuit against the President on the grounds that he had contravened the Constitution and allowed the Great Khural to meet without a quorum (57 members being present) before the final session of the outgoing Great Khural had taken place. The closing session of the previous legislature was held in late July 2004. Among other decisions, it released the Great Khural's Deputy Chairman Jamsrangiin Byambadorj (who had lost his parliamentary seat in the recent election) to take up a vacant seat in the Constitutional Court and accused the President of acting unconstitutionally in convening the first session of the incoming legislature. All these decisions were vetoed by President Bagabandi in late July as unconstitutional. (Byambadorj was elected a member, then the Chairman, of the Constitutional Court in January 2005.)

Postponed after another MPRP boycott, the first plenary session of the new Great Khural was held in late July 2004, when 74 members were sworn in. Following several weeks of discussions, at the end of August former Prime Minister Nambaryn Enkhbayar of the MPRP was appointed Chairman of the Great Khural, and Tsakhiagiin Elbegdorj of the MD coalition became Prime Minister. Although the newly elected members of the Mongolian Great Khural agreed on the formation, chairmanship and membership of the Khural's standing committees and sub-committees, discussion of the basic principles for the establishment of a coalition government were protracted. In late September the new Cabinet was appointed. The deputy ministers, one-half nominated by the MD coalition and one-half by the MPRP, were appointed in November and December respectively.

The National Human Rights Commission's annual report for 2004 noted the need for the rights of vulnerable groups and the human rights activities of legal organizations to remain the 'centre of attention'. The report noted that torture and severe punishment were still common activities and that many police officers equated punishment with physical torture. Furthermore, the report stated that effective measures were not being taken to address these issues and that the provisions of the UN Convention against Torture and other Cruel, Inhuman or Degrading Treatment or Punishment, which Mongolia signed in 2000, were not widely known.

Coalition government

At the end of December 2004 Radnaasümbereliin Gonchigdorj took the chairmanship of the DP at a meeting of the executive of its National Consultative Committee and installed his supporters in other senior posts. His predecessor, Mendsaikhany Enkhsaikhan, appeared to retain the support of the DP's National Assembly. Although a court ruled that the leadership change was contrary to the party's regulations, it declined to intervene. Badarchiin Erdenebat, the Minister of Defence and leader of the MDNSP, then withdrew from the MD coalition, which collapsed. The Civil Courage Republican Party leader, Sanjaasürengiin Oyuun, was obliged to relinquish her post of Deputy Chairwoman of the Great Khural in January 2005. Prime Minister Elbegdorj took over the defence portfolio from Erdenebat in February, and a new Minister of Defence, Tserenkhüügiin Sharavdorj, was appointed in March. The MD coalition's parliamentary group in the Great Khural disbanded, and many DP members, including Gonchigdorj (but not Enkhsaikhan), joined the Khural's MPRP group members to form a parliamentary 'combined group', of which Gonchigdorj was elected Deputy Chairman. Meanwhile, Doloonjingiin Idevkhten was replaced as General Secretary of the MPRP by Sanjaagiin (Sanjiin) Bayar, the Mongolian ambassador to Russia. In February Jügderdemidiin Gürragchaa (MPRP) and in September Zandaakhüügiin Enkhbold (MD) were declared the winners in the two constituencies where the results of the 2004 election to the Great Khural election had been contested. Gürragchaa was duly sworn in, but Enkhbold had already accepted the post of Chairman of the State Property Committee in December 2004.

In March 2005, in the fourth demonstration in Ulan Bator since January by the Healthy Society Citizens' Movement, protesters demanded the resignations of the Great Khural Chairman and MPRP leader, Nambaryn Enkhbayar, of Prime Minister Elbegdorj and of the DP rebels in the Great Khural who had joined the MPRP's parliamentary group. Four of the five parliamentary political parties presented candidates for the forthcoming presidential election, scheduled for late May. The candidates were Nambaryn Enkhbayar (of the MPRP), Bazarsadyn Jargalsaikhan (Republican Party), Badarchiin Erdenebat (Motherland Party, as the MDNSP had recently been renamed) and Mendsaikhany Enkhsaikhan (DP). The election, held on 22 May, was won by Enkhbayar, who secured more than 53% of the votes cast.

Enkhbayar's victory led to personnel changes in the MPRP and in the Great Khural. At the MPRP's congress in June 2005 the Mayor of Ulan Bator, Miyeegombyn Enkhbold, was chosen to replace Enkhbayar as the new party Chairman. The party Leadership Council was enlarged to 21 members: nine re-elected (with four failing to secure re-election) and 10 new members, including Party Secretary Yondongiin Otgonbayar, the Ministers of Foreign Affairs, of Food and Agriculture, and of Health, and six MPRP Great Khural members. Two vacancies were held open, including one for a new head of the Presidential Secretariat. Enkhbayar was inaugurated as President of Mongolia on 24 June. At the beginning of July the Great Khural elected the Minister of Justice and Home Affairs, Tsendiin Nyamdorj (of the MPRP), to replace Enkhbayar as Chairman of the Great Khural.

After an attempt by the MPRP to force the Prime Minister to resign, including the expulsion of DP members from the 'combined' MPRP parliamentary group (the 'group of 62'), and shortly before the closing of its spring 2005 session, the Great Khural voted in favour of the formation of a DP parliamentary group, which 25 party members (headed by Gonchigdorj) joined. The by-election in Enkhbayar's former constituency was to be held at the end of August. The MPRP chose its Chairman, Miyeegombyn Enkhbold, as its candidate, and the DP nominated Prime Minister Tsakhiagiin Elbegdorj. However, Elbegdorj's nomination was withdrawn at the beginning of August, a coalition accord having been signed by the DP and the MPRP. The by-election was subsequently won by Miyeegombyn Enkhbold.

In January 2006 a Motherland Party deputy defected to the MPRP, thereby giving the latter its 38th seat in the Great Khural. Following demands by the MPRP for Prime Minister Elbegdorj's resignation, the 10 MPRP ministers in his Cabinet resigned and the 'grand coalition' Government was voted out of office. Miyeegombyn Enkhbold, MPRP Chairman and Mayor of Ulan Bator, was elected Prime Minister. He formed a new 'national solidarity' Government that included the Motherland and Republican Party leaders Erdenebat and Jargalsaikhan, ex-DP member Gündalai, who had recently established a new party, the Party of the People, and three DP members—Enkhsaikhan,

MONGOLIA

Narantsatsralt and Sonompil—who were subsequently expelled from the remnant DP, now excluded from the MPRP's new coalition.

Following his appointment in January 2006 to the post of Deputy Prime Minister, Mendsaikhany Enkhsaikhan and his supporters began forming a new party, which was named the National New Party at its first congress in May. After the death of legislator Onomoogiin Enkhsaikhan in March, the resultant by-election was delayed (possibly unconstitutionally) until early September, when it was won by the Minister of Education, Culture and Science, Ölziisaikhany Enkhtüvshin (MPRP).

Meanwhile, the high levels of corruption in Mongolia had become a major concern among international partners. Furthermore, the political upheaval of early 2006 delayed a decision on amendments to the 1997 Minerals Law, introduced at the end of December 2005, which caused disquiet among foreign investors in Mongolia's mining industry. Amid much public debate about the merits of state control of the country's resources and various protests, the Great Khural discussed the amendments, consolidated them in committee and finally adopted a new redaction of the 1997 law in July 2006. According to initial reports of the text prior to publication, mining licences were to be granted only to companies, not to individuals; foreign and domestic investors in mining were to be taxed at the same rate; stability agreements were to be replaced by investment contracts; and local people in proposed mining areas would be granted greater rights with regard to decisions on exploitation licences. Also, the Government would have the right to acquire up to 50% of the resources of deposits discovered with the help of state funds and to control up to 34% of resources obtained from privately funded deposits. Royalties were to be raised from 2.5% to 5.0%, severe penalties were envisaged for serious environmental damage and the size of foreign work-forces would be limited to 10%.

In October 2006 a parliamentary motion of no confidence was submitted against the Government: Enkhbold was accused of misconduct in relation to land sales during his tenure of the post of Mayor of Ulan Bator, while the Government was criticized for alleged incompetence and its failure to improve the living standards of the population. However, the motion failed to garner sufficient votes to succeed.

Meanwhile, in preparation for the legislative election of mid-2008, the Great Khural approved amendments to the electoral law, restoring 26 large multi-candidate constituencies (similar to those prevailing at the time of the 1992 legislative election) and introducing a quota for female members.

In early 2007 it emerged that Tsendiin Nyamdorj, the Chairman of the Great Khural, had re-edited legislation, including the Election Law and the Minerals Law, after the final texts had been approved by the Great Khural. Following a Constitutional Court ruling that his actions were unconstitutional, Nyamdorj was obliged to resign from his post in June. He was replaced by the Deputy Chairman, Danzangiin Lündeejantsan.

At the MPRP's 25th Congress in October 2007, delegates expressed their dissatisfaction with Miyeegombyn Enkhbold's performance by voting to remove him from the chairmanship of the party, in favour of General Secretary Sanjaagiin Bayar. The members of a new 255-member MPRP Little Khural and 23-member Leadership Council were later announced; in total, 13 of the 19 Leadership Council members elected in 2005 were replaced and three were re-elected. Former MPRP secretary Yondongiin Otgonbayar was elected General Secretary and six new secretaries were approved, including Enkhbold and Nyamdorj. For the first time, intra-party political movements and factions were represented by three Leadership Council members; also of note was the inclusion of four women, one of them a Mongolian Kazakh.

An important consequence of these events was Enkhbold's resignation as Prime Minister in early November 2007, thus allowing Sanjaagiin Bayar's election to the position later in the month. Bayar's first acts included the appointment of Ravdangiin Bold, ambassador to the USA, to the post of head of the Main Directorate of Intelligence and the dismissal of the ministers responsible for disaster reduction and professional inspection, their portfolios passing to the new Deputy Prime Minister, Enkhbold. After the signing of co-operation agreements with the CCP and the National New Party, Bayar formed a new Cabinet in December. Among three female appointees was CCP leader Sanjaasürengiin Oyuun, who assumed the role of Minister of Foreign Affairs. Meanwhile, the Mayor and Governor of Ulan Bator, Tsogtyn Batbayar, was replaced by Tüdeviin Bilegt, head of the Presidential Secretariat.

Janlavyn Narantsatsralt, Minister of Construction and Urban Development and former Prime Minister, was killed in a car accident in November 2007. He was replaced by Tserendashiin Tsolmon, who also became Chairman of the National New Party in February 2008. In the same month a new political organization was registered, the Mongolian Democratic Movement Party.

In preparation for the next election, in December 2007 the electoral law was amended to dispense with the requirement for a 30% quota of female members in the legislature. President Enkhbayar unsuccessfully attempted to veto the Great Khural's revision of the law. A total of 356 candidates were registered to contest the legislative election, which was held on 29 June 2008. The level of participation in the polls was reported to be 74.3%. Amid allegations of widespread irregularities, the Chairman of the DP, Tsakhiagiin Elbegdorj, demanded that the votes be recounted. The Citizens' Alliance (CA, a grouping that represented the Citizens' Movement Party, the Mongolian Green Party and the MSDP) accused both the MPRP and the DP of malpractice. Following the publication of provisional results awarding a narrow parliamentary majority to the MPRP, thousands of demonstrators took to the streets of Ulan Bator to protest against the perceived electoral fraud. Several people were killed in the rioting that ensued, mostly from gunshot wounds, and hundreds were injured. About 700 demonstrators were reported to have been detained. The headquarters of the MPRP were damaged by arson, and the GEC building was also attacked. On 1 July a state of emergency was declared, which remained in place for four days.

It was reported in mid-July 2008 that the GEC had allocated 39 seats in the Great Khural to the MPRP, 25 to the DP, one to the CCP and one to an independent candidate. The winners of 10 of the 76 seats were yet to be declared. Nevertheless, the legislature was instructed by President Enkhbayar to convene its first session. The session duly opened but was swiftly abandoned by DP members, who refused to be inaugurated pending the announcement of the final election results. The withdrawal of the DP from the proceedings thus removed the quorum required for the registration of legislators. Futhermore, the DP demanded an investigation into the conduct of the election by the Chairman of the GEC, Bataagiin Battulga. After several unsuccessful attempts, the Great Khural finally convened at the end of August, with the participation of the DP and with 67 legislators in attendance. Damdingiin Demberel of the MPRP was appointed as the chamber's Chairman.

On 11 September 2008 the Great Khural re-elected Sanjaagiin Bayar as Prime Minister. Negotiations between the MPRP and the DP, which had encompassed the contentious issue of the development of the country's mineral resources, resulted in an agreement on the formation of a coalition Government, whereby 60% of the ministerial positions were to be allocated to the MPRP and 40% to the DP. Norovyn Altankhuyag, who in late August had replaced Elbegdorj as Chairman of the DP following the latter's resignation, became First Deputy Prime Minister. Miyeegombyn Enkhbold of the MPRP was appointed as Deputy Prime Minister. Sükhbaataryn Batbold (MPRP) was allocated responsibility for external relations, formerly the portfolio of foreign affairs, which had been modified to incorporate economic matters. The Ministry of Trade and Industry was abolished and a new Ministry of Mining and Energy was established.

As the GEC continued its investigations into the disputed results in six constituencies, the DP resumed its boycott of the Great Khural. In early 2009 the election results for four seats in a constituency in Ulan Bator remained outstanding. When these results were eventually declared, the MPRP held a total of 45 seats in the Great Khural and the DP 27; one seat was occupied by a representative of the CCP, one by a member of the Mongolian Green Party and another by an independent parliamentarian. Meanwhile, the winner of one seat had been imprisoned, pending an investigation into charges of fraud, allegedly committed during his tenure of a previous post.

Recent developments: the presidential election of 2009 and other events

At the presidential election held on 24 May 2009 the incumbent Head of State, Nambaryn Enkhbayar of the MPRP, was defeated by Tsakhiagiin Elbegdorj, the former Prime Minister and candidate of the Democratic Party, whose campaign had focused on the issues of corruption and the need for a more equitable distribution of the country's mineral wealth. Elbegdorj, who had served as Prime Minister in 1998 and again in 2004–06, received 51.2% of the votes cast. His candidacy was supported by

MONGOLIA

the Mongolian Green Party and the Civil Courage Party. The level of voter participation reached 73.6% of the registered electorate. Enkhbayar swiftly conceded defeat, and in a smooth transition Elbegdorj was inaugurated for a four-year term on 18 June.

In October 2009 Prime Minister Sanjaagiin Bayar resigned owing to ill health and was replaced by Sükhbaataryn Batbold, hitherto the Minister of External Relations. In the following month Gombojavyn Zandanshatar was allocated the portfolio of external relations, and Chimediin Khürelbaatar, also of the MPRP, was appointed to head the Government Affairs Directorate. Batbold replaced Bayar as Chairman of the MPRP in April 2010.

One of Bayar's last official duties, in October 2009, was to attend the signing of a highly significant agreement with representatives of international mining companies for the development of the Oyuutolgoi copper and gold deposits. The exploitation of these resources, located in the Gobi region and to be developed in collaboration with Canadian and Australian interests, was expected to transform the Mongolian economy (see Economic Affairs)

Mongolia experienced its most severe winter conditions for several decades in 2009/10. The exceptionally low temperatures and persistent snowfalls resulted in the loss of millions of livestock and extreme hardship for many Mongolians. In February 2010, in return for payments to herders, the UN Development Programme initiated a scheme for the collection of animal carcasses, the accumulation of which posed a serious health risk upon the return of milder weather. Humanitarian assistance was provided by the International Committee of the Red Cross, which in March launched a global appeal for emergency funding, and by other relief agencies.

In April 2010 about 5,000 demonstators rallied in Ulan Bator to protest against the inequalities in Mongolian society arising from the perceived inequitable distribution of the benefits of the country's substantial mineral wealth. The protesters demanded the dissolution of the Great Khural and the release of government aid to impoverished Mongolians, upon whom the unusually harsh winter conditions had had a serious impact.

In a development that was welcomed by human rights groups, in January 2010 the President announced that there was to be a moratorium on the implementation of the death penalty. It was hoped that the formal abolition of the death penalty would follow, although many opposition members of the Great Khural were reported to favour its retention.

In early November 2010 the delegates attending the MPRP's 26th party congress in Ulan Bator voted to change the name of the party back to the Mongolian People's Party (MPP—as it had been called from its foundation in 1921 until 1925, when, under Soviet influence, the word 'revolutionary' had been added). Prime Minister Batbold claimed that the word 'revolutionary' had confrontational connotations that were no longer appropriate for the more pragmatic environment of modern-day Mongolia. It was reported that all but eight of the 801 delegates at the congress voted for the party's change of name; former President Nambaryn Enkhbayar was one of the few who voted against the measure. Also during the congress, Batbold was elected to retain the post of party Chairman, securing 657 votes against the 116 votes received by Ulziisaikhan Enkhtuvshin, the Chairman of the Standing Committee of the Great Khural. A few days after the conclusion of the party congress, the Supreme Court officially approved the registration of the change of name of the MPRP. At the first conference of the renamed party, the Leadership Council was enlarged from 21 to 31 members. In early January 2011 Enkhbayar was elected as leader of a new Mongolian People's Revolutionary Party formed by those who had rejected the change in the party's name in November 2010. In March 2011 this breakaway faction, which claimed to have around 20,000 members, was reported to be seeking official registration as the MPRP. However, the MPP asserted that the usage of its former nomenclature would be illegal.

Foreign Affairs

Following its admission to the UN in 1961, Mongolia was accorded diplomatic recognition by the United Kingdom (in 1963) and other Western European states, as well as by many developing countries. By January 1987, when Mongolia was finally granted diplomatic recognition by the USA, it maintained diplomatic relations with more than 100 states.

Regional Relations

Relations with the People's Republic of China were good until the onset of the Sino-Soviet dispute in the 1960s. In 1986, however, Sino-Mongolian relations improved significantly when the Chinese Vice-Minister of Foreign Affairs visited Ulan Bator, and the two countries signed agreements on consular relations and trade. In June 1987 a delegation from the Chinese National People's Congress visited Ulan Bator. A treaty concerning the resolution of border disputes was subsequently initialled by representatives of the two Governments.

A new Treaty of Friendship and Co-operation was concluded during a visit to Ulan Bator by Chinese Premier Li Peng in April 1994. Mongolia continued to protest in 1995 at the series of nuclear tests being carried out in the Xinjiang region of China. Mongolian human rights groups and the Ulan Bator press supported protests in Inner Mongolia against the arrest by the Chinese authorities of human rights activists in December. Prime Minister Jasrai's official visit to China in March 1996, focusing on trade and co-operation, appeared unaffected by these events. Relations with China were further consolidated in 1997 by the visits to Ulan Bator of Qiao Shi, the Chairman of the National People's Congress Standing Committee, in April, and of Qian Qichen, the Chinese Deputy Premier and Minister of Foreign Affairs, in August.

In July 1999 Chinese President Jiang Zemin undertook a state visit to Mongolia to promote bilateral relations and in November Prime Minister Amarjargal reciprocated by visiting China. In June 2003 Chinese President Hu Jintao visited Ulan Bator for discussions with President Bagabandi and Prime Minister Enkhbayar. China granted Mongolia 50m. yuan for the purposes of building a road across the border from Zamyn-Üüd to Erlian.

President Bagabandi paid a state visit to China in July 2004, visiting Hainan and the Special Administrative Region of Macao, and discussing economic co-operation with President Hu Jintao. In August 2006 the Dalai Lama undertook his seventh visit to Mongolia, at the invitation of local Buddhists, and presided over religious ceremonies in Ulan Bator. In November Miyeegombyn Enkhbold signed a trade and economic co-operation agreement with China, during his first official visit to Beijing since becoming Prime Minister in January; he also visited Urumqi, in the Xinjiang region. In April 2008 President Enkhbayar travelled to China to attend the Bo'ao Forum for Asia, at which he had discussions with President Hu Jintao. In March 2010, in response to the plight of residents of south-western Mongolia affected by severe weather conditions, China donated a consignment of flour and rice. President Elbegdorj embarked upon a six-day state visit to China at the end of April, hoping to strengthen bilateral co-operation in areas such as the formulation of measures to combat desertification. In the same month Prime Minister Batbold attended the Bo'ao conference in China, and in June of that year the Chinese Premier, Wen Jiabao, paid an official visit to Mongolia (the first by a Chinese premier for 16 years), during which the two sides signed an intergovernmental border regime agreement (renewing an accord of 1998). In addition, the two countries agreed to enhance bilateral co-operation in areas such as energy, trade and environmental protection, and Premier Wen proposed the arrangement of an early date for a feasibility study of the establishment of a Sino-Mongolian free trade area.

In July 1999 Prime Minister Keizo Obuchi of Japan made an official visit to Mongolia. In February 2001 Prime Minister Nambaryn Enkhbayar embarked upon his first visit to a foreign country, travelling to Japan, where he was received by Emperor Akihito and participated in talks with Japanese Prime Minister Yoshio Mori. In August 2004 the Japanese Minister of Foreign Affairs, Yoriko Kawaguchi, visited Mongolia. Kawaguchi engaged in discussions with Prime Minister Tsakhiagiin Elbegdorj and President Natsagiin Bagabandi. The discussions included the promotion of democratization in Mongolia. In July 2006 Mongolia received Japanese Prime Minister Junichiro Koizumi, who discussed joint efforts to develop energy resources in Mongolia, as well as issues relating to the Democratic People's Republic of Korea (North Korea). In February 2007 President Enkhbayar visited Japan and signed a joint agreement with Japanese Prime Minister Shinzo Abe pledging to expand bilateral relations, including plans to utilize mineral resources in Mongolia. The two leaders agreed to co-operate in resolving tensions caused by the North Korean nuclear dispute and to collaborate in Japan's quest to attain a permanent seat on the UN Security Council. During a visit to the Japanese capital of Tokyo in July 2009, Prime Minister Bayar had discussions with his counterpart, Taro Aso, during which Bayar expressed his desire for much closer relations with Japan. In November 2010, during a state visit by President Elbegdorj to Japan, the two countries signed a Mongolia-Japan Joint Declaration aimed at strengthening strategic relations.

In May 1999 Mongolia received South Korean President Kim Dae-Jung, marking the first such visit by a Korean head of state. Following talks with the Mongolian Minister of Defence, Sharavdorj Tuvdendorj, President Kim obtained the Mongolian Government's support for his policy of political engagement with the North Korean regime. In November Mongolian Prime Minister Amarjargal made a reciprocal visit to the Republic of Korea and engaged in discussions to improve bilateral relations. In May 2006 the South Korean President, Roh Moo-Hyun, undertook a state visit to Mongolia, where he discussed a range of issues with President Enkhbayar, including trade and environmental co-operation. President Enkhbayar expressed support for South Korean involvement in the six-party talks aimed at resolving the North Korean nuclear issue (see the chapter on the Democratic People's Republic of Korea). In March 2011 Prime Minister Batbold paid an official visit to South Korea, during which the two sides held talks on co-operation in the development of coal and other mineral resources in Mongolia.

In November 1999 Prime Minister Amarjargal visited the North Korean capital of Pyongang and exchanged views with Premier Hong Song Nam on the development of bilateral relations. Prime Minister Amarjargal also met with, Kim Yong Nam, President of the Presidium of the North Korean Supreme People's Assembly. President Bagabandi visited Pyongyang in December 2005 to promote joint co-operation. In July 2007 Mongolia received Kim Yong Nam, and a bilateral agreement to co-operate in the areas of public health, medical science and marine transport was signed. In November 2010 the close nature of relations between Mongolia and North Korea was revealed following the online release by WikiLeaks, an organization publishing leaked private and classified content, of a series of US diplomatic cables; in one such communiqué a Mongolian diplomat divulged that during a meeting between Mongolian and North Korean officials in August 2009 a North Korean government minister had proposed that Mongolia host disarmament talks between the USA and North Korea.

Other external relations

For many years foreign affairs were dominated by Mongolia's relations with the Soviet Union. Following the dissolution of the USSR in 1991, co-operation with Russia, the largest of the successor states, continued. During an official visit to Russia in January 1993, President Ochirbat and the Russian President, Boris Yeltsin, issued a joint statement expressing regret at the execution and imprisonment of Mongolian citizens in the USSR during the Stalinist period. Ochirbat and Yeltsin also signed a new 20-year Mongolian-Russian Treaty of Friendship and Co-operation to replace the defunct Mongolian-Soviet treaty of 1986. A similar treaty had been signed with Ukraine in November 1992, during the official visit to Mongolia by Ukrainian President Leonid Kravchuk. In November 2000 the Russian President, Vladimir Putin, made a brief stop in Ulan Bator en route to a conference in Brunei, thus becoming the most senior Russian or Soviet visitor to Mongolia since 1974. Presidents Bagabandi and Putin issued a joint declaration on bilateral co-operation and the protection of each other's national interests. Russia affirmed its commitment to guaranteeing Mongolia's security in connection with its nuclear weapons-free status. Russian Prime Minister Mikhail Kasyanov undertook an official visit to Mongolia in late March 2002 to discuss economic and military co-operation, and also the issue of Mongolia's outstanding debt of 11,400m. transferable roubles that the Russian Government claimed it was owed for Soviet aid granted during 1947–91; the Mongolian Government referred to this as the 'big debt'. The two countries had been unable to agree terms for the previous 10 years. Mongolia disagreed with Russia's position that the debt should be paid in full at par value with the US dollar, and there was also Mongolian opposition pressure to offset the cost of damage done to the environment by Soviet military activity.

When the two Prime Ministers met in the Russian capital of Moscow in July 2003, a new five-year agreement on the operation of the Erdenet copper enterprise was reached, preserving Mongolia's 51% ownership of stock. Russia agreed that Mongolia had already repaid the cost of building the Erdenet plant. Otherwise, Mongolia's main concern was to reduce Russian taxes on imports of Mongolian goods. At the end of December Russia announced that it had received Mongolia's payment in settlement of the 'big debt'. Russia had waived 98% of the total debt and accepted US $250m. Prime Minister Nambaryn Enkhbayar celebrated a political and diplomatic victory for the MPRP Government, but the details of the settlement remained unclear. DP leader and former Prime Minister Enkhsaikhan pointed out that, under the Constitution, international agreements required approval by the Great Khural.

In July 2006 Russian Prime Minister Mikhail Fradkov visited Mongolia and participated in discussions with Mongolian Prime Minister Enkhbold concerning investment in the Mongolian mining sector. In December President Enkhbayar toured the Republics of Buryatiya and Kalmykiya, before flying to Moscow for the first state visit by a Mongolian president in 13 years. Following a meeting with President Putin, a treaty on the border regime was signed, as were trade and economic agreements. In April 2008 Prime Minister Sanjaagiin Bayar visited Russia for discussions with Vladimir Putin, who had since become the country's Prime Minister. In the following month President Enkhbayar also visited Moscow, where he had a meeting with President Dimitrii Medvedev.

Prime Minister Bayar revisited Moscow in March 2009, when the Russian Government announced the offer of a loan of US $300m. to support the Mongolian agricultural sector. The proposed financing was linked to Mongolia's purchase of Russian equipment and other agricultural supplies. President Medvedev's visit to Mongolia in August resulted in the signing of various agreements relating to mining ventures and providing for greater Russian participation in the management of railway operations in Mongolia. The question of the settlement of Mongolia's long-standing debt to Russia was also raised, when Medvedev stated that issues remained unresolved. Mongolia's strengthening links with Russia were underlined in early 2011 by the Mongolian Government's approval of plans to construct a 1,500-km rail link to the north-east of the country where it was to connect with the Russian Trans-Siberian network.

In March 2000 Prime Minister Amarjargal paid an official visit to the United Kingdom. In November 2004 Great Khural Chairman Nambaryn Enkhbayar was received by Queen Elizabeth during a visit to the United Kingdom. In April 2007 President Enkhbayar, as he had since become, revisited the United Kingdom, and had discussions with Prime Minister Tony Blair. However, diplomatic relations between Mongolia and the United Kingdom came under considerable pressure in September 2010 when the former head of Mongolia's counter-terrorism unit and the chief executive of the country's National Security Council, Bat Khurts, was arrested (at the request of the German authorities) on his arrival in London for his alleged involvement in the kidnapping and rendition of a Mongolian refugee, Damirangiin Enkhbat, from France in 2003. The Mongolian authorities expressed their disapproval of the apparent circumstances of Khurt's arrest (he had reportedly been invited to conduct high-level talks with the British Government on intelligence co-operation) and demanded his release from prison. Prime Minister Batbold's abrupt cancellation of a planned visit to the United Kingdom in November 2010 and the recall of the British ambassador from Ulan Bator were both widely believed to be directly connected to the diplomatic dispute. In February 2011 the British judiciary ruled that Khurt could be extradited on a European arrest warrant to Germany to stand trial.

Nambaryn Enkhbayar's first overseas trip as Prime Minister was to the World Economic Forum in Davos, Switzerland, in January 2001. Enkhbayar's first official foreign tour after his inauguration as President of Mongolia was in July 2005 to Astana, the capital of Kazakhstan, where he attended a meeting of the Shanghai Co-operation Organization with Russian President Vladimir Putin, Chinese President Hu Jintao and other leaders (Mongolia had been granted observer status). In August 2007 President Enkhbayar returned to Astana for a further summit meeting of the Shanghai Co-operation Organization.

During an official visit to the USA in November 2001, Prime Minister Enkhbayar addressed the UN General Assembly in New York; he also had a meeting with President George W. Bush. Enkhbayar reaffirmed his country's strategic partnership with the USA and urged greater US investment in Mongolia. Having condemned the attacks of 11 September against the USA, he informed President Bush of Mongolia's readiness to allow the use of its air space to help combat terrorism. The Secretary-General of the UN, Kofi Annan, paid a brief visit to Mongolia in October 2002. Following the US military intervention in Iraq in March 2003, soldiers of the Mongolian army's élite battalion were sent to Iraq for tours of duty with the Polish contingent stationed to

MONGOLIA

Introductory Survey

the north of Baghdad. (The Mongolian deployment remained in Iraq until September 2008.)

In July 2004 President Bagabandi visited the USA, where he met President George W. Bush and signed a Trade and Investment Framework Agreement. In the following month US Assistant Secretary of State James Kelly visited Ulan Bator. The US Secretary of Defense, Donald Rumsfeld, visited Ulan Bator briefly in October 2005. Rumsfeld stated that the USA was willing to help Mongolia enhance its peace-keeping capabilities. In 2005 the USA provided Mongolia with US $18m. in military assistance, including regular training exchanges and peace-keeping exercises.

On the first visit to Mongolia by an incumbent US President, in November 2005 George W. Bush spent four hours in Ulan Bator where he had discussions with President Enkhbayar. A joint statement noted that President Bush welcomed Mongolia's progress towards becoming a mature and stable democracy and the country's development of a free market economy, led by the private sector. The two Presidents also emphasized their commitment to combating terrorism.

In February 2006, following a closed meeting in Ulan Bator with foreign donors (the World Bank, the Asian Development Bank, the IMF, the UN, Japan, the USA and Germany), which urged greater accountability, the US Administration issued a statement noting that the US Agency for International Development had found that corruption in Mongolia was increasing at all levels. Mongolia was to be required to draw up lists of specific actions to combat corruption and to detail all the changes needed within existing law in order that it might comply with the UN Convention Against Corruption (UNCAC). A new Anti-Corruption Law was adopted by the Mongolian legislature in July.

In 2004 Mongolia was deemed eligible for development assistance under the US-funded Millennium Challenge Compact. In October 2007 President Enkhbayar visited the USA, meeting the UN Secretary-General and President George W. Bush; Enkhbayar and Bush signed a Millennium Challenge contract, which pledged US $285m. in funds for Mongolia. In June 2009 the Minister of External Relations, Sükhbaataryn Batbold, travelled to Washington, DC, where he met US Secretary of State Hillary Clinton for discussions on the issue of the financing pledged by the Millennium Challenge; Russia had objected to an allocation to the development of the Mongolian railway network.

In October 2004 President Bagabandi embarked upon a state visit to Canada for a meeting with Prime Minister Paul Martin. The two leaders agreed that regular bilateral meetings would be held henceforth. In January 2008 the Canadian Minister of International Trade, David Emerson, visited Mongolia to discuss the development of bilateral trade and investment, especially in Mongolia's mining sector. Later that year Canada's first resident ambassador in Ulan Bator assumed office.

During a visit to Mongolia in July 2009 UN Secretary-General Ban Ki-Moon expressed his gratitude for the country's contribution to peace-keeping operations, which had included deployments in Iraq. Issues under discussion included that of climate change. Nearly 30 Mongolians had died in recent flash flooding, reported to be the most serious for several decades. Emergency funding to restore supplies of safe drinking water and sewerage services to the Ulan Bator area was disbursed by the World Health Organization. In an address to the UN General Assembly in September, President Elbegdorj reiterated Mongolia's concerns regarding the phenomenon of climate change, which was believed to be contributing to the country's increasing desertification.

CONSTITUTION AND GOVERNMENT

Supreme legislative power is vested in the 76-member Mongolian Great Khural (Assembly), elected by universal adult suffrage for four years. The Great Khural recognizes the President on his election and appoints the Prime Minister and members of the Cabinet, which is the highest executive body. The President, who is directly elected for a term of four years, is Head of State and Commander-in-Chief of the Armed Forces. A revision to the electoral law, adopted in December 2005, provided for the replacement of the 76 single-seat constituencies with 26 multi-seat constituencies, with effect from the 2008 election.

Mongolia is divided into 21 provinces (*aimag*) and one municipality (Ulan Bator), with appointed governors and elected local assemblies. However, plans to reduce the number of *aimag* to four (the original pre-revolutionary divisions) and to develop the town of Kharkhorin (the ancient Karakorum) as the future capital were under consideration.

REGIONAL AND INTERNATIONAL CO-OPERATION

Mongolia is a member of the Asian Development Bank (ADB, see p. 202), of the Association of Southeast Asian Nations (ASEAN) Regional Forum (ARF, see p. 209) and of the UN's Economic and Social Commission for Asia and the Pacific (ESCAP, see p. 37).

Mongolia became a member of the UN in 1961. It was admitted to the World Trade Organization (WTO, see p. 430) in 1997. Mongolia is also a member of the European Bank for Reconstruction and Development (EBRD, see p. 265), and Mongolbank, the country's central bank, has joined the Bank for International Settlements (see p. 216). Mongolia also participates in the Group of 77 (G77, see p. 447).

ECONOMIC AFFAIRS

In 2009, according to estimates by the World Bank, Mongolia's gross national income (GNI), measured at average 2007–09 prices, was US $4,361m., equivalent to $1,630 per head (or $3,330 per head on an international purchasing-power parity basis). During 2000–09, it was estimated, the population increased at an average annual rate of 1.2%, while gross domestic product (GDP) per head increased, in real terms, at an average of 5.1% per year. Overall GDP increased, in real terms, at an average annual rate of 6.5% in 2000–09. According to Asian Development Bank (ADB) estimates, real GDP grew by 8.9% in 2008 but declined by 1.3% in 2009, before increasing, once again, by 6.1% in 2010.

Agriculture (including forestry and fishing) contributed 22.9% of GDP in 2009. The sector engaged 34.7% of the employed labour force in that year. Animal herding is the main economic activity and is practised throughout the country. Most livestock is privately owned. Following exceptionally severe weather, livestock numbers (sheep, goats, horses, cattle and camels) declined sharply in 2002, to fewer than 23.7m., before steadily recovering to exceed 44m. by the end of 2009. However, the summer drought of 2009 was followed by unusually low winter temperatures, as a result of which a total of 8.2m. livestock were reported to have died by May 2010; more than half of these losses were goats. By the end of 2010 livestock numbers had dwindled once again, to 32.5m. The principal crops are wheat, potatoes and vegetables. Production of cereals rose from 114,800 metric tons in 2007 to 391,700 tons in 2009, but declined again in 2010, to 355,100 tons. During 2000–08, according to figures from the World Bank, the GDP of the agricultural sector increased, in real terms, at an average annual rate of 3.1%. According to the ADB, agricultural GDP increased by an estimated 3.6% in 2009, but a huge decline, of 16.8%, was recorded in 2010.

Industry (comprising mining, manufacturing, construction and utilities) provided 31.8% of GDP in 2009 and the sector (excluding printing and publishing) engaged 15.6% of the employed labour force in the same year. According to the World Bank, during 2000–08 industrial GDP increased, in real terms, at an average rate of 6.8% per year. According to the ADB, the industrial sector's GDP declined by 0.4% in 2009, but increased by 7.7% in 2010.

Mining contributed 23.8% of GDP in 2009, and some 13,700 workers were engaged in the sector in January 2007. Mongolia has significant, largely unexplored, mineral resources and is a leading producer and exporter of copper, gold, molybdenum and fluorspar concentrates. In 2008 the value of exports of copper concentrate was estimated at US $835.7m., but this declined to just $501.9m. in 2009. In addition to the major copper-molybdenum works at Erdenet, a Mongolian-Russian joint venture, the sites of other mineral deposits are being developed in collaboration with various foreign enterprises, notably the Oyuutolgoi copper and gold deposits (see Contemporary Political History). Production at Oyuutolgoi was scheduled to commence in 2013. The Tavantolgoi coalfield, reported to be among the largest unexploited deposits in the world, was also expected to be opened to foreign investment. Meanwhile, gold production declined from some 22,600 kg in 2006 to 9,803 kg in 2009. Output of coal rose from 8.1m. metric tons in 2006 to 14.4m. tons in 2009. Other mineral resources include tungsten, tin, uranium and lead. Mongolia's production of crude petroleum has increased rapidly, from 366,800 barrels in 2006 to 1,870,000 barrels in 2009. According to the ADB, the GDP of the mining sector expanded at an average annual rate of 8.1% in 2003–09; the sector's GDP decreased, in real terms, by 2.9% in 2008, but increased by 3.7% in 2009.

The manufacturing sector accounted for 4.5% of GDP in 2009. Manufacturing industries are based largely on the products of the agricultural and animal husbandry sector. The principal branches of manufacturing include food products, beverages, textiles and garments. Mongolia is one of the world's foremost producers of cashmere, and the country also manufactures garments, leather goods and carpets. According to figures from the World Bank, manufacturing GDP increased by an annual average of 11.3% in 2000–08. The sector's GDP contracted substantially in 2005, but significant growth was recorded in 2007 and 2008, before a contraction of 11.1% in 2009, according to ADB data.

Construction accounted for just 0.9% of GDP in 2009, and the sector engaged 4.9% of the employed population in that year. According to figures from the ADB, the sector's GDP decreased by an annual average of 9.5% in 2003–09. Real growth of 8.6% was recorded in 2007, but the sector's GDP declined, in real terms, by 12.8% in 2008 and by a massive 48.9% in 2009.

Energy is derived principally from thermal power stations, fuelled by coal. Most provincial centres have thermal power stations or diesel generators, while minor rural centres generally rely on small diesel generators. In more isolated areas wood, roots, bushes and dried animal dung are used for domestic fuel. Mongolia imports from Russia electricity and petroleum products, including liquid petroleum gas. In 2008 the cost of Mongolia's imports of fuels and lubricants rose to US $919.0m., thus accounting for 28.3% of the total cost of merchandise imports, but this share decreased to 25.5% in 2009, when the total cost of these imports declined to $544.4m.

The services sector contributed 45.4% of GDP in 2009 and engaged 49.8% of the employed labour force in the same year. During 2000–08, according to figures from the World Bank, the GDP of the sector increased, in real terms, by an average of 9.9% annually. According to the ADB, the GDP of the services sector increased by 16.6% in 2008, but real growth in the sector was just 0.8% in 2009 and 4.6% in 2010. Receipts from tourism were estimated to have reached US $222.4m. in 2010. The number of visitor arrivals increased from 446,446 in 2008 to 557,414 in 2010, when about 35% of visitors came from the People's Republic of China.

According to IMF figures, Mongolia's visible trade deficit was US $188.8m. in 2009, and there was a deficit of $341.8m. on the current account of the balance of payments. In 2009 the principal source of imports was Russia, supplying 36.2% of the total, followed by China, the Republic of Korea and the USA. China was the principal market for exports, purchasing 63.9% of the total. Other important purchasers were Canada and the United Kingdom. The principal imports in 2009 were machinery and vehicles (32.3% of the total value of imports), followed by fuels and lubricants, manufactured goods, food and live animals and chemical products. The leading export was raw materials (53.3% of the total value of exports), and specifically copper concentrate. Other significant exports included fuels and lubricants and gold.

In 2009 there was a budget deficit of 328,600m. tögrög, and the ADB estimated that the deficit was equivalent to 5.0% of GDP in that year. The draft budget for 2010 projected a deficit of 282,600m. tögrög. Mongolia's total external debt was US $1,721m. at the end of 2008, of which $1,653m. was public and publicly guaranteed debt. In 2006 the cost of debt-servicing was equivalent to 2.1% of the value of exports of goods, services and income. According to figures from the IMF, the annual rate of inflation averaged 8.6% during 2000–09. Consumer prices rose by 6.3% in 2009 and by 10.2% in 2010. The number of registered unemployed persons increased slightly, from 38,100 in 2009 to 38,300 in 2010. However, the number of unregistered unemployed persons was believed to be far greater. The ADB estimated the rate of unemployment at 5.0% of the (registered) labour force in 2010.

The international financial crisis that began in the latter part of 2008 had major repercussions for the Mongolian mining sector. The reduction in the value of the country's exports, notably copper, as well as a substantial decrease in cashmere prices, had a serious impact. However, in a major advance for the Mongolian economy, in October 2009 the Government concluded an agreement with foreign mining interests for the development of the Oyuutolgoi copper and gold deposits. New banking legislation was introduced in February 2010 aimed at improving the regulation and supervision of the country's banks. Meanwhile, the agricultural sector was seriously affected by drought in 2009, which was followed by exceptionally cold weather in early 2010, resulting in major losses (about one-quarter of Mongolian livestock perished). Nevertheless, in 2010 the economy recovered strongly from the contraction of the previous year, with GDP recording growth of more than 6% and a sharp rebound in the value of exports. The recovery was due mainly to an increase in international prices of minerals, to high levels of investment in the mining sector (total foreign direct investment in Mongolia rose from $570m. in 2009 to $1,635m. in 2010) and to a robust economic revival in China. The rate of growth of GDP was projected by the ADB to continue accelerating, to reach 10% in 2011. However, the rapid rise in fiscal expenditure in 2010 led to an increase in the rate of inflation to double-digit levels. The Government, aware of the risks implicit in its highly expansionary fiscal policies, introduced a number of measures aimed at fostering budgetary discipline and avoiding the insecurities inherent in mineral-based economies. Among these was the establishment of a fiscal stability fund to be used during periods of economic downturn. Other ongoing concerns of the Government included the need to promote economic diversification (to avoid over-reliance on the mining sector) and the persistent levels of poverty (around one-third of the population still lived below the poverty line). In November 2010 the international mining industry was surprised by a decision made on the part of the Mongolian Government to suspend about 250 gold mining licences, citing 'environmental concerns'.

PUBLIC HOLIDAYS

2012: 1 January (New Year), 22–23 February (Tsagaan Sar, lunar new year), 8 March (International Women's Day), 1 June (Children's Day), 11–13 July (Naadam, national sports festival), 26 November (Republic Day).

MONGOLIA

Statistical Survey

Unless otherwise indicated, revised by Alan J. K. Sanders

Area and Population

AREA, POPULATION AND DENSITY

Area (sq km)	1,564,116*
Population (census results)	
5 January 2000	2,373,493
19 November 2010 (provisional)	2,650,673
Population (official estimates at 31 December)†	
2007	2,635,200
2008	2,683,500
2009	2,735,800
Density (per sq km) at 2010 census	1.7

* 603,909 sq miles.
† Estimates not adjusted to take account of preliminary results of 2010 census.

POPULATION BY AGE AND SEX
(UN estimates at mid-2011)

	Males	Females	Total
0–14	350,208	338,392	688,600
15–64	952,026	978,888	1,930,914
65 and over	48,156	64,029	112,185
Total	1,350,390	1,381,309	2,731,699

Note: Data not adjusted to take account of the provisional results of the 2010 census.

Source: UN, *World Population Prospects: The 2008 Revision*.

Population by Age ('000, official estimates at 31 December 2009): *0–14*: 755.5; *15–64*: 1,869.3; *65 and over*: 111.0; *Total* 2,735.8.

Note: Data not adjusted to take account of the provisional results of the 2010 census.

ADMINISTRATIVE DIVISIONS
(official population estimates at 31 December 2009)

Province (Aimag)	Area ('000 sq km)	Estimated population ('000)	Provincial centre
Arkhangai	55.3	92.5	Tsetserleg
Bayankhongor	116.0	85.4	Bayankhongor
Bayan-Ölgii	45.7	101.9	Ölgii
Bulgan	48.7	62.3	Bulgan
Darkhan-Uul	3.3	90.0	Darkhan
Dornod (Eastern)	123.6	73.6	Choibalsan
Dornogobi (East Gobi)	109.5	58.3	Sainshand
Dundgobi (Central Gobi)	74.7	47.7	Mandalgobi
Gobi-Altai	141.4	59.4	Altai
Gobi-Sümber	5.5	13.3	Choir
Khentii	80.3	71.5	Öndörkhaan
Khovd	76.1	88.5	Khovd
Khövsgöl	100.6	124.1	Mörön
Orkhon	0.8	83.1	Erdenet
Ömnögobi (South Gobi)	165.4	49.3	Dalanzadgad
Övörkhangai	62.9	117.5	Arvaikheer
Selenge	41.2	103.5	Sükhbaatar
Sükhbaatar	82.3	55.0	Baruun Urt
Töv (Central)	74.0	88.5	Zuun mod
Ulan Bator (Ulaanbaatar)*	4.7	1,112.3	(capital city)
Uvs	69.6	78.8	Ulaangom
Zavkhan	82.5	79.3	Uliastai
Total	1,564.1	2,735.8	

* Ulan Bator, including Nalaikh, and Bagakhangai and Baganuur districts beyond the urban boundary, has special status as the capital city.

ETHNIC GROUPS
(January 2000 census)

	Number	%
Khalh (Khalkha)	1,934,700	81.5
Kazakh (Khasag)	103,000	4.3
Dörvöd (Durbet)	66,700	2.8
Bayad (Bayat)	50,800	2.1
Buryat (Buriat)	40,600	1.7
Dariganga	31,900	1.3
Zakhchin	29,800	1.3
Uriankhai	25,200	1.1
Other ethnic groups	82,600	3.5
Foreign citizens	8,100	0.3
Total	2,373,500	100.0

PRINCIPAL TOWNS
(estimated population at December)

Ulan Bator (capital) 1,161,800*   Erdenet 74,300†

* 2010.
† 2007.

BIRTHS, MARRIAGES AND DEATHS

	Registered births		Registered marriages*		Registered deaths	
	Number	Rate (per 1,000)	Number	Rate (per 1,000)	Number	Rate (per 1,000)
2002	46,922	19.1	13,514	9.2	15,857	6.4
2003	45,723	18.4	14,572	9.6	16,006	6.4
2004	45,501	18.1	11,242	7.2	16,404	6.5
2005	45,326	17.8	14,993	9.3	16,480	6.5
2006	49,092	19.0	48,996	19.0	16,682	6.5
2007	56,636	21.7	40,965	15.7	16,259	6.2
2008	63,768	24.0	32,982	12.4	15,413	5.8
2009	69,167	25.5	34,071	12.6	16,911	6.2

* Persons aged 18 years and over.

2010: Registered births 65,900.

Life expectancy (years at birth): 67.23 (males 63.69; females 70.98) in 2008 (Source: *Mongolian Statistical Yearbook*).

EMPLOYMENT
('000 employees at 31 December)

	2007	2008	2009
Agriculture, forestry and fishing	385.6	377.6	348.8
Industry*	123.1	124.1	107.0
Construction	60.0	66.8	49.6
Transport and communications	44.1	46.3	78.9
Trade	162.2	169.7	160.3
Public administration	48.5	50.9	56.1
Education			
Science, research and development	64.8	66.2	74.9
Health	40.2	42.3	35.7
Total (incl. others)	1,024.1	1,041.7	1,006.3

* Comprising manufacturing (except printing and publishing), mining and quarrying, electricity and water.

Source: *Mongolian Statistical Yearbook*.

Mongolians working abroad ('000 in 2009, official estimates): 182.5 (Kazakhstan 90.0; Republic of Korea 31.0) (Source: Montsame—Mongolian News Agency).

Registered unemployed ('000 at 31 December): 32.9 in 2006; 29.9 in 2007; 29.6 in 2008; 38.1 in 2009; 38.3 in 2010 (Sources: Asian Development Bank; Mongolian Statistical Office).

Total unemployed ('000 in 2009): 131.6 (Ulan Bator 54.2) (Source: *Mongolian Statistical Yearbook*).

MONGOLIA

Health and Welfare

KEY INDICATORS

Total fertility rate (children per woman, 2008)	2.0
Under-5 mortality rate (per 1,000 live births, 2008)	41
HIV/AIDS (% of persons aged 15–49, 2007)	0.1
Physicians (per 1,000 head, 2002)	2.6
Hospital beds (per 1,000 head, 2006)	6.4
Health expenditure (2007): US $ per head (PPP)	138
Health expenditure (2007): % of GDP	4.3
Health expenditure (2007): public (% of total)	81.7
Access to water (% of persons, 2008)	76
Access to sanitation (% of persons, 2008)	50
Total carbon dioxide emissions ('000 metric tons, 2007)	10,574.3
Carbon dioxide emissions per head (metric tons, 2007)	4.0
Human Development Index (2010): ranking	100
Human Development Index (2010): value	0.622

For sources and definitions, see explanatory note on p. vi.

Agriculture

PRINCIPAL CROPS
(metric tons)

	2008	2009	2010
Cereals*	212,894	391,659	355,100
Potatoes	134,773	151,211	168,100
Other vegetables	78,553	77,976	82,300
Hay	1,030,900	912,300	1,132,300

* Mostly wheat, but also small quantities of barley and oats.

LIVESTOCK
(at December census)

	2008	2009	2010
Sheep	18,362,300	19,274,700	14,480,400
Goats	19,969,400	19,651,500	13,883,200
Horses	2,186,900	2,221,300	1,920,300
Cattle	2,503,400	2,599,300	2,176,000
Camels	266,400	277,100	269,600
Pigs	29,285	25,808	n.a.
Poultry	259,900	399,400	n.a.

LIVESTOCK PRODUCTS
('000 metric tons, unless otherwise indicated)

	2007	2008	2009
Meat	191.2	223.1	264.4
Beef	46.8	54.2	56.2
Mutton and goat meat	102.8	122.0	162.3
Sheep's wool	18.2	20.8	22.4
Cashmere	4.9	5.9	6.4
Hides and skins ('000)	7,218.4	9,762.4	12,722.8
Milk	465.6	457.4	493.7
Eggs (million)	46.2	47.9	47.9

Source: *Mongolian Statistical Yearbook*.

Forestry

ROUNDWOOD REMOVALS
('000 cubic metres)

	2006	2007	2008
Total	574.8	580.5	612.0

Source: *Mongolian Statistical Yearbook*.

SAWNWOOD PRODUCTION
('000 cubic metres, incl. railway sleepers)

	2007	2008	2009
Total	27.7	34.1	28.8

Source: *Mongolian Statistical Yearbook*.

Fishing

(metric tons, live weight)

	2006	2007	2008
Total catch (freshwater fishes)	289	185	88

Source: FAO.

Mining

(metric tons, unless otherwise indicated)

	2007	2008	2009
Salt	4	115	5
Coal ('000 metric tons)	9,238	10,072	14,442
Fluorspar concentrate	131,800	142,900	115,300
Copper concentrate*	371,900	362,300	370,900
Molybdenum concentrate*	4,209	4,042	5,125
Zinc concentrate*	154,700	143,600	141,500
Iron ore	265,100	1,387,400	1,379,000
Gold (kilograms)	17,472	15,184	9,803
Crude petroleum (barrels)	850,200	1,174,200	1,870,000

* Figures refer to the gross weight of concentrates. Copper concentrate has an estimated copper content of 35%, while the metal content of molybdenum concentrate is 47% and that of zinc is 50%.

Source: *Mongolian Statistical Yearbook*.

Industry

SELECTED PRODUCTS

	2007	2008	2009
Flour ('000 metric tons)	70.8	62.0	105.3
Bread ('000 metric tons)	20.4	25.8	23.5
Confectionery ('000 metric tons)	13.0	13.2	12.8
Sheep's guts ('000 bunches)	644.3	641.1	1,057.1
Vodka and wine ('000 litres)	12,591.3	15,277.4	17,410.9
Beer ('000 litres)	18,377.7	19,891.1	32,445.1
Soft drinks ('000 litres)	69,732.1	85,975.8	86,967.9
Cashmere (combed) (metric tons)	1,554.7	1,723.8	1,586.7
Wool, scoured (metric tons)	1,700.0	1,800.0	1,300.0
Felt ('000 metres)	87.8	86.5	128.7
Camelhair blankets ('000 metres)	37.7	35.0	36.9
Spun thread (metric tons)	32.8	28.1	56.4
Knitwear ('000 garments)	4,220.1	2,148.2	639.2
Trousers ('000)	4,523.4	1,996.5	163.2
Shirts ('000)	4,375.4	678.7	0.6
Carpets ('000 sq metres)	658.1	856.5	542.2
Leather footwear ('000)	21.4	5.5	5.3
Felt footwear ('000 pairs)	9.3	6.3	13.0
Surgical syringes (million)	12.6	10.9	10.3
Bricks (million)	20.8	28.9	18.0
Lime ('000 metric tons)	43.3	54.8	43.1
Cement ('000 metric tons)	179.8	269.3	234.8
Copper (metric tons)	3,006.5	2,586.6	2,470.1
Copper wire (metric tons)	294.8	705.8	298.5
Electricity (million kWh)	3,700.7	4,000.6	4,038.8

Source: *Mongolian Statistical Yearbook*.

MONGOLIA

Finance

CURRENCY AND EXCHANGE RATES

Monetary Units
100 möngö = 1 tögrög (tughrik).

Sterling, Dollar and Euro Equivalents (31 December 2010)
£1 sterling = 1,967.0 tögrög;
US $1 = 1,256.5 tögrög;
€1 = 1,678.9 tögrög;
10,000 tögrög = £5.08 = $7.96 = €5.96.

Average Exchange Rate (tögrög per US $)
2008 1,165.74
2009 1,437.80
2010 1,358.93

BUDGET
(million tögrög)

Revenue	2007	2008	2009
Tax revenue	1,502,309.9	1,890,896.6	1,615,251.2
Income tax	648,514.4	754,839.9	520,006.4
Excise duty	133,757.8	178,466.9	166,753.0
Taxes on goods and services	411,776.7	562,018.1	508,656.9
Value-added tax	265,051.2	368,049.5	325,804.7
Other current revenue	353,653.7	260,153.2	350,259.1
Social insurance	160,522.8	229,353.2	257,339.2
Grants and transfers	22,004.1	16,118.6	24,517.3
Other revenue	2,521.2	3,201.6	2,958.2
Total	**1,880,488.9**	**2,170,370.0**	**1,992,985.8**

Expenditure	2007	2008	2009
Current expenditure	1,367,668.0	1,761,190.6	1,792,065.7
Goods and services	672,733.0	1,054,940.6	969,549.4
Wages and salaries	296,289.9	544,450.3	578,871.7
Interest payments	18,575.5	19,949.0	28,965.6
Subsidies and transfers	676,359.5	686,301.5	793,550.8
Capital expenditure	299,498.3	624,389.8	457,923.9
Foreign financed	23,316.0	20,182.5	26,360.7
Lending (net)	80,144.2	81,194.0	71,610.0
Total	**1,747,310.5**	**2,466,774.4**	**2,321,599.6**

Source: *Mongolian Statistical Yearbook*.

2010 (million tögrög, revised forecasts): Total revenue 2,140,492.5; total expenditure 2,423,103.4 (Source: *Töriin Medeelel*).

2011 (million tögrög, forecasts): Total revenue 2,492,330.3; total expenditure 2,782,697.5 (Source: *Töriin Medeelel*).

INTERNATIONAL RESERVES
(US $ million at 31 December)

	2008	2009	2010
Gold (national valuation)	95.91	32.83	91.56
IMF special drawing rights	0.06	76.42	72.73
Reserve position in IMF	0.21	0.21	0.21
Foreign exchange	561.21	1,217.84	2,123.76
Total	**657.39**	**1,327.3**	**2,288.3**

Source: IMF, *International Financial Statistics*.

MONEY SUPPLY
(million tögrög at 31 December)

	2008	2009	2010
Currency outside depository corporations	328,779	284,994	388,203
Transferable deposits	601,736	738,245	1,535,555
Other deposits	1,292,521	1,810,362	2,728,573
Securities other than shares	47,021	46,432	27,651
Broad money	**2,270,056**	**2,880,034**	**4,679,981**

Source: IMF, *International Financial Statistics*.

COST OF LIVING
(Consumer Price Index at December; base: December 2005 = 100)

	2007	2008	2009
Foods	134.0	166.1	166.9
Clothing and footwear	113.1	131.7	146.0
Rent and utilities	123.6	151.5	152.5
All items (incl. others)	125.0	152.6	159.1

Source: *Mongolian Statistical Yearbook*.

All items (Consumer Price Index; base: 2005 = 100): 143.3 in 2008; 152.3 in 2009; 167.8 in 2010 (Source: IMF, *International Financial Statistics*).

NATIONAL ACCOUNTS

Expenditure on the Gross Domestic Product
('000 million tögrög at current prices)

	2007	2008	2009
Government final consumption expenditure	598.6	929.7	848.5
Private final consumption expenditure	2,291.6	3,007.0	3,011.6
Increase in stocks	147.0	732.7	732.7
Gross fixed capital formation	1,703.8	2,407.6	2,234.2
Total domestic expenditure	**4,741.0**	**7,077.0**	**6,827.0**
Exports of goods and services	2,954.9	3,507.1	3,381.3
Less Imports of goods and services	2,888.0	4,447.2	3,792.5
Statistical discrepancy*	−208.3	−117.0	−360.1
GDP in purchasers' values	**4,599.5**	**6,019.8**	**6,055.8**
GDP at constant 2005 prices	**3,325.9**	**3,622.7**	**3,564.3**

* Referring to the difference between the sum of the expenditure components and official estimates of GDP, compiled from the production approach.

Source: Asian Development Bank.

Gross Domestic Product by Economic Activity
(million tögrög at current prices)

	2007	2008	2009
Agriculture	943,077.7	1,297,677.3	1,284,787.1
Fishing	73.2	17.5	17.5
Mining	1,337,457.3	1,325,975.8	1,337,983.7
Manufacturing	184,466.7	257,774.4	254,301.8
Electricity, heating and water supply	102,278.6	129,805.7	144,222.6
Construction	78,600.8	89,945.7	49,439.2
Trade	321,313.6	472,493.4	363,255.6
Hotels and restaurants	29,117.6	38,978.6	34,903.2
Transport and communications	438,741.1	567,942.0	644,602.6
Financial intermediation	150,575.2	208,196.9	179,285.3
Real estate, renting and other business activities	257,671.8	479,122.9	543,472.4
Public administration, defence and social security	144,469.2	252,316.4	270,066.1
Education, health and other services	291,111.1	462,933.4	513,737.6
Sub-total	**4,278,953.9**	**5,583,180.0**	**5,620,074.7**
Less Financial intermediation services indirectly measured	171,278.1	236,158.7	155,906.3
Gross value added in basic prices	**4,107,675.8**	**5,347,021.3**	**5,464,168.4**
Taxes, less subsidies, on products	491,866.0	672,817.0	591,625.9
GDP in market prices	**4,599,541.5**	**6,019,838.1**	**6,055,794.3**

Source: *Mongolian Statistical Yearbook*.

MONGOLIA

BALANCE OF PAYMENTS
(US $ million)

	2007	2008	2009
Exports of goods	1,950.7	2,529.1	1,885.4
Imports of goods	−2,003.1	−3,156.3	−2,074.2
Trade balance	−52.4	−627.2	−188.8
Exports of services	581.8	499.4	414.5
Imports of services	−472.4	−610.2	−557.8
Balance on goods and services	57.0	−738.0	−332.0
Other income received	53.5	16.5	24.3
Other income paid	−151.0	−189.3	−219.8
Balance on goods, services and income	−40.5	−910.8	−527.4
Current transfers received	303.8	378.4	260.3
Current transfers paid	−91.5	−157.7	−74.6
Current balance	171.8	−690.1	−341.8
Capital account (net)	—	84.1	160.5
Direct investment abroad	−12.8	−6.2	−53.8
Direct investment from abroad	372.8	844.7	623.6
Portfolio investment assets	−1.2	−51.2	−138.8
Portfolio investment liabilities	76.0	14.8	56.7
Other investment assets	−207.8	64.5	−144.8
Other investment liabilities	49.0	281.2	265.6
Net errors and omissions	−158.7	−774.7	127.6
Overall balance	289.1	−233.1	554.7

Source: IMF, *International Financial Statistics*.

External Trade

PRINCIPAL COMMODITIES
(US $ million, distribution by SITC)

Imports c.i.f.	2007	2008	2009
Food and live animals	208.3	344.0	240.4
Raw materials	14.3	14.9	15.6
Fuels and lubricants	634.8	919.0	544.4
Chemical products	118.3	172.3	143.1
Manufactured goods, classified chiefly by material	325.3	485.2	321.7
Machinery and vehicles	613.1	1,060.5	689.7
Miscellaneous manufactured articles	93.5	156.8	114.5
Total (incl. others)	2,061.8	3,244.5	2,137.7

Exports f.o.b.	2007	2008	2009
Food and live animals	33.6	27.1	42.7
Raw materials	1,366.9	1,435.6	1,005.4
Copper concentrate	811.5	835.7	501.9
Fuels and lubricants	88.9	297.4	437.5
Chemical products	2.0	34.2	1.0
Manufactured goods, classified chiefly by material	84.1	67.4	46.3
Machinery and vehicles	21.6	34.9	23.7
Miscellaneous manufactured articles	114.7	37.5	19.1
Gold, unwrought or in semi-manufactured forms	234.9	599.9	308.5
Total (incl. others)	1,947.5	2,534.5	1,885.4

2010: Total imports 3,277.9; Total exports 2,899.2.

Source: *Mongolian Statistical Yearbook*.

PRINCIPAL TRADING PARTNERS
(US $ million)

Imports c.i.f.	2007	2008	2009
China, People's Republic	674.3	898.7	538.6
Germany	76.5	92.6	70.3
Japan	140.2	238.5	97.0
Korea, Republic	119.6	194.8	155.1
Russia	745.0	1,242.3	772.8
USA	58.6	84.1	103.7
Total (incl. others)	2,170.1	3,244.5	2,137.7

Exports f.o.b.	2007	2008	2009
Canada	178.6	174.6	147.5
China, People's Republic	1,413.0	1,635.9	1,393.9
Italy	56.7	42.2	31.4
Luxembourg	3.7	162.0	46.2
Russia	58.5	86.3	68.2
United Kingdom	22.1	165.8	126.9
Total (incl. others)	1,949.2	2,534.5	1,885.4

2010: Total imports 3,277.9; Total exports 2,899.2.

Source: *Mongolian Statistical Yearbook*.

Transport

FREIGHT CARRIED
('000 metric tons)

	2007	2008	2009
Rail	14,072.6	14,646.9	14,171.5
Road	9,207.1	9,255.7	10,563.8
Air	1.9	1.8	1.4
Total (incl. other)	23,281.6	23,904.4	24,736.7

2010: Total freight carried 29,400,000 metric tons.

Source: Mongolian Statistical Office.

PASSENGERS CARRIED
(million)

	2007	2008	2009
Rail	4.5	4.3	3.1
Road	205.0	226.9	229.0
Air*	0.4	0.4	0.3
Total	209.9	231.6	232.4

* MIAT only.

2010: Total passengers carried 250,700,000.

Source: Mongolian Statistical Office.

RAILWAYS
(traffic)

	2007	2008	2009
Passengers carried ('000)	4,473.9	4,300.0	3,100.0
Freight carried ('000 metric tons)	14,072.6	14,646.9	14,171.5
Freight ton-km (million)	8,360.7	8,261.4	7,852.1

Source: Mongolian Statistical Office.

ROAD TRAFFIC
(motor vehicles in use)

	2007	2008	2009
Passenger cars	110,150	127,538	153,906
Buses and coaches	13,038	15,780	16,136
Lorries, special vehicles and tankers	38,801	47,141	54,026

Source: Mongolian Statistical Office.

MONGOLIA

CIVIL AVIATION
(traffic on scheduled services)

	2007	2008	2009
Passengers carried ('000)	388.3	365.5	309.1
International passengers ('000)	266.1	262.8	235.7
Freight carried (tons)	1,887.2	1,847.0	1,369.3

Source: Mongolian Statistical Office.

Tourism

FOREIGN ARRIVALS BY NATIONALITY

Country	2008	2009	2010
China, People's Republic	196,832	229,451	193,370
France	6,688	6,706	8,050
Germany	8,027	6,867	8,093
Japan	14,939	11,401	14,369
Korea, Republic	43,396	38,273	42,231
Russia	109,975	108,105	121,647
United Kingdom	6,781	5,872	5,983
USA	12,474	11,344	12,589
Total (incl. others)	446,446	492,836	557,414

Source: *Mongolian Statistical Yearbook*.

Tourism receipts (US $ million): 213.3 in 2009; 222.4 in 2010 (Source: Ministry of Environment and Tourism, Ulan Bator).

Communications Media

	2007	2008	2009
Television receivers ('000 in use)	400.1	454.0	489.5
Cable television subscribers ('000)	89.7	101.3	112.9
Telephones ('000 main lines in use)	149.6	151.6	142.9
Mobile cellular telephones ('000 subscribers)	1,175.1	1,745.9	2,208.7
Internet users ('000)	30.0	42.0	45.0
Personal computers ('000 in use)	119.5	150.9	189.5
Books (million printers' sheets)	27.7	42.1	49.7
Newspapers (million printers' sheets)	45.5	64.8	37.5

2010 ('000): Internet users 48.4.

Book production (1994): 128 titles; 640,000 copies.

Newspapers (titles): 170 in 2004 (daily 6, non-daily 164).

Periodicals (titles): 60 in 2004.

Sources: mainly *Mongolian Statistical Yearbook*.

Education
(2009/10)

	Institutions	Teachers	Students ('000)
General education schools:			
Primary (grades 1–3)	69		274.0
Incomplete secondary (grades 4–9)	157	26,100	178.7
Complete secondary (grades 10–11)	529		69.4
Vocational schools			
State-owned	44	2,000	33.4
Private	19		11.3
Universities			
State-owned	10		74.3
Private	4	7,200	14.7
Other higher education			
State-owned	32		26.3
Private	96		49.1

Note: In addition, 700 students were studying abroad through inter-governmental agreements.

Pre-school institutions (2009/10): 810 kindergartens, with 4,500 teachers, attended by 105,100 infants.

Source: *Mongolian Statistical Yearbook*.

2009/10 (official estimates): Student enrolment at all education establishments 736,800; student enrolment abroad 9,550 (Sources: Montsame (Mongolian News Agency) and *Mongolian Statistical Yearbook*).

Pupil-teacher ratio (primary education, UNESCO estimate): 30.4 in 2008/09 (Source: UNESCO Institute for Statistics).

Adult literacy rate (UNESCO estimates): 97.3% (males 96.7%; females 97.8%) in 2008 (Source: UNESCO Institute for Statistics).

Directory

The Government

PRESIDENCY

President and Commander-in-Chief of the Armed Forces: TSAKHIAGIIN ELBEGDORJ (elected 24 May 2009; inaugurated 18 June 2009).

Head of Presidential Secretariat: DASHJAMTSYN BATTULGA.

NATIONAL SECURITY COUNCIL

The President heads the National Security Council; the Prime Minister and the Chairman of the Mongolian Great Khural are its members. The Secretary is the President's national security adviser.

Chairman: TSAKHIAGIIN ELBEGDORJ.

Secretary: TSAGAANDARIIN ENKHTÜVSHIN.

Members: DAMDINGIIN DEMBEREL, SÜKHBAATARYN BATBOLD.

CABINET
(May 2011)

The coalition Government comprises members of the Mongolian People's Party (MPP, formerly the Mongolian People's Revolutionary Party) and the Democratic Party (DP).

Prime Minister: SÜKHBAATARYN BATBOLD (MPP).

Chief Deputy Prime Minister: NOROVYN ALTANKHUYAG (DP).

Deputy Prime Minister: MIYEEGOMBYN ENKHBOLD (MPP).

General Ministries

Minister of External Relations: GOMBOJAVYN ZANDANSHATAR (MPP).

Minister of Finance: SANGAJAVYN BAYARTSOGT (DP).

Minister of Justice and Home Affairs: TSENDIIN NYAMDORJ (MPP).

Sectoral Ministries

Minister of Defence: LUVSANVANDANGIIN BOLD (DP).

Minister of Education, Culture and Science: YONDONGIIN OTGONBAYAR (MPP).

MONGOLIA

Minister of Environment and Tourism: LÜIMEDIIN GANSÜKH (DP).
Minister of Food, Agriculture and Light Industry: TÜNJINGIIN BADAMJUNAI (MPP).
Minister of Health: SAMBUUGIIN LAMBAA (DP).
Minister of Mineral Resources, Fuel and Power: DASHDORJIIN ZORIGT (MPP).
Minister of Roads, Transport, Construction and Urban Development: KHALTMAAGIIN BATTULGA (DP).
Minister of Social Welfare and Labour: TÖGSJARGALYN GANDI (MPP).
Head of Government Affairs Directorate: CHIMEDIIN KHÜREL-BAATAR (MPP).

MINISTRIES AND GOVERNMENT DEPARTMENTS

All Ministries and Government Departments are in Ulan Bator.
Prime Minister's Office: State Palace, Sükhbaataryn Talbai 1, Ulan Bator; tel. (11) 322356; fax (11) 328329; internet www.pmis.gov.mn.
Ministry of Defence: Government Bldg 7, Dandaryn Gudamj 51, Bayanzürkh District, Ulan Bator; tel. (11) 458495; fax (11) 451727; e-mail mdef@mdef.pmis.gov.mn; internet www.mdef.pmis.gov.mn.
Ministry of Education, Culture and Science: Government Bldg 3, Baga Toiruu 44, Sükhbaatar District, Ulan Bator; tel. (11) 262480; fax (11) 323158; e-mail mecs@mecs.gov.mn; internet www.mecs.gov.mn.
Ministry of Environment and Tourism: Government Bldg 2, Negdesen Ündesnii Gudamj 5/2, Ulan Bator; tel. (11) 266171; fax (11) 321402; internet www.mne.mn.
Ministry of External Relations: Enkh Taivny Örgön Chölöö 7A, Sükhbaatar District, Ulan Bator; tel. (11) 262788; fax (11) 322127; e-mail mongmer@magicnet.mn; internet www.mfat.gov.mn.
Ministry of Finance: Government Bldg 2, Negdsen Ündestnii Gudamj 5/1, Chingeltei District, Ulan Bator; tel. and fax (11) 264891; internet www.mof.gov.mn.
Ministry of Food, Agriculture and Light Industry: Government Bldg 9, Enkh Taivny Örgön Chölöö 16A, Bayanzürkh District, Ulan Bator; tel. (11) 262376; fax (11) 453121; e-mail mofa@mofa.gov.mn; internet www.mofa.gov.mn.
Ministry of Health: Government Bldg 8, Olimpiin Gudamj 2, Sükhbaatar District, Ulan Bator; tel. (51) 263913; fax (11) 320916; e-mail admin@moh.mn; internet www.moh.mn.
Ministry of Justice and Home Affairs: Government Bldg 5, Khudaldaany Gudamj 6/1, Chingeltei District, Ulan Bator; tel. (11) 267014; fax (11) 325225; e-mail admin@mojha.gov.mn; internet www.mojha.gov.mn.
Ministry of Mineral Resources, Fuel and Power: Government Bldg 2, Negdsen Ündestnii Gudamj 5/1, Chingeltei District, Ulan Bator; tel. (11) 261511; fax (11) 318169; e-mail info@mmre.energy.mn; internet www.mmre.energy.mn.
Ministry of Roads, Transport, Construction and Urban Development: Government Bldg 2, Negdsen Ündestnii Gudamj 5/2, Chingeltei District, Ulan Bator; tel. (11) 310597; fax (11) 310612; e-mail info@mrtcud.mn; internet www.mrtcud.gov.mn.
Ministry of Social Welfare and Labour: Government Bldg 2, Negdsen Ündestnii Gudamj 5/1, Chingeltei District, Ulan Bator; tel. (11) 264918; fax (11) 328634; e-mail mswl@mongolnet.mn; internet www.mswl.gov.mn.
Government Affairs Directorate (Cabinet Secretariat): State Palace, Sükhbaataryn Talbai 1, Ulan Bator; tel. and fax (11) 310011; internet www.pmis.gov.mn/cabinet.

President and Legislature

PRESIDENT

Office of the President: State Palace, Sükhbaataryn Talbai, Ulan Bator; fax (11) 311121; internet www.president.mn.

Election, 24 May 2009

Candidate	Votes	%
Tsakhiagiin Elbegdorj (Democratic Party)	562,718	51.21
Nambaryn Enkhbayar (MPRP)	520,948	47.41

MONGOLIAN GREAT KHURAL

Under the fourth Constitution, which came into force in February 1992, the single-chamber Mongolian Great Khural is the State's supreme legislative body. With 76 members elected for a four-year term, the Great Khural must meet for at least 50 working days in every six months. Its Chairman may act as President of Mongolia when the President is indisposed.; State Palace, Sükhbaataryn Talbai, Ulan Bator; e-mail secretariat@parliament.mn; internet www.parliament.mn

Chairman (Speaker): DAMDINGIIN DEMBEREL.
Vice-Chairmen: GAVAAGIIN BATKHÜÜ, NYAMAAGIIN ENKHBOLD.

General Election, 29 June 2008

Party	Seats
Mongolian People's Revolutionary Party (MPRP)	45
Democratic Party (DP)	28
Civil Courage Party (CCP)	1
Mongolian Green Party	1
Independent	1
Total	**76**

Election Commission

General Election Committee: Government Bldg 11, Sambuugiin Gudamj 11, Ulan Bator 38; tel. (11) 263383; fax (11) 326975; e-mail gecm@mongol.net; internet www.gec.gov.mn; f. 1992; Chair. NAMS-RAIJAVYN LUVSANJAV.

Political Organizations

Citizens' Movement Party: Rm 304, National Information and Technology Park, Baga Toiruu 49, Sükhbaatar District, Ulan Bator; tel. (11) 321900; f. 2007; 815 mems; Chair. NYAMAAGIIN DAVAA.
Civil Courage-Green Party (CC-GP): amalgamation of parties begun in March 2011; see Civil Courage Party and Mongolian Green Party; Chair. DANGAASÜRENGIIN ENKHBAT; Deputy Chair. SANJAASÜR-ENGIIN OYUUN.
Civil Courage Party (CCP): Civil Courage Party Management Office, Baga Toiruu 24/2, Chingeltei District, Ulan Bator (POB 46/253); tel. 99098741; fax (11) 319009; e-mail oyun@mail.parl.gov.mn; internet www.izn.mn; f. 1994; merged with Mongolian National Solidarity Party in April 2008; also known as Citizens' Will; 35,000 mems (2008); Chair. SANJAASÜRENGIIN OYUUN; Sec.-Gen. MÖNKHCHU-LUUNY ZORIGT.
Democratic Party (DP): Central Post, POB 578, Sükhbaatar District, Ulan Bator; tel. (11) 322755; fax (11) 323755; e-mail international@demparty.mn; internet www.demparty.mn; f. 2000; est. by amalgamation of the Mongolian National Democratic Party, Mongolian Social-Democratic Party, Mongolian Democratic Party, Mongolian Democratic Renewal Party and the Mongolian Believers' Democratic Party; Mongolian Social-Democratic Party re-est. as independent party in 2004; c. 150,000 mems. (2008); Chair. NOROV ALTANKHUYAG; Sec.-Gen. DONDOGDORJ ERDENEBAT.
Development Programme Party: Rm 2, Poverty Reduction Programme Foundation Bldg, 14th Sub-District, Sükhbaatar District, Ulan Bator; tel. 96019222; f. 2007; 933 mems (2008); Chair. N. ZUUNNAST.
Freedom Implementer Party: Varyeta Centre, 1st Sub-District, Bayangol District, Ulan Bator (POB 48/117); tel. 88113439; fax (11) 327899; e-mail freedom_ofmn@yahoo.com; 1,600 mems; f. 2006; Chair. SHOOVDORYN TÖMÖRSÜKH.
Mongolian Democratic Movement Party: Rm 306, Ikh Surguuliin Gudamj 3/2, 6th Sub-District, Sükhbaatar District, Ulan Bator (POB 20A/158); tel. 99009093; f. 2008; 850 mems (2008); Chair. T. OYUUNA; Sec.-Gen. M. GANZORIG.
Mongolian Green Party: Internom Block B, Amaryn Gudamj 2, Sükhbaatar District, Ulan Bator; tel. 314560; e-mail info@greenparty.mn; internet www.greenparty.mn; f. 1990; political wing of Alliance of Greens; majority of mems joined Civil Courage-Green Partyin 2011; Co-Chair. O. BUM-YALAGCH.
Mongolian Liberal Party: Ulan Bator Higher School of Intellect, 4th Sub-District, Chingeltei District, Ulan Bator (POB 23/320); tel. 99852957; fax (11) 328198; f. 1999 as Mongolian Civil Democratic New Liberal Party, renamed 2004; ruling body Little Khural of 90 mems with Leadership Council of nine; 1,300 mems (2008); Chair. L. ALTANCHIMEG.
Mongolian People's Party (MPP): Baga Toiruu 37/1, Ulan Bator; tel. and fax (6) 5007805; e-mail contact@mprp.mn; f. 1921; est. as Mongolian People's Party; renamed as Mongolian People's Revolutionary Party (MPRP) in 1925; reorganized in the 1990s; reverted to Mongolian People's Party in Nov. 2010; 163,805 mems (2011); ruling body Party Baga Khural (310 mems at Nov. 2010), which elects the

MONGOLIA

Leadership (Steering) Council (31 mems); Chair. SÜKHBAATARYN BATBOLD; Gen. Sec. UKHNAAGIIN KHÜRELSÜKH.

Mongolian People's Revolutionary Party: Ulan Bator; f. 2011; breakaway faction of the Mongolian People's Party; seeking official registration as MPRP, April 2011; 20,000 mems; Chair. NAMBARYN ENKHBAYAR; Dep. Chair. TSENDIIN SHINEBEYAR.

Mongolian Social-Democratic Party (MSDP): Room 12, No. 5 Bldg, 1st Sub-District, Sükhbaatar District, Ulan Bator (CPOB 680); tel. 99114273; fax (11) 323828; f. 1990; merged in Dec. 2000 to form part of Democratic Party; refounded Jan. 2005; c. 3,000 mems (2008); Chair. ARYAAGIIN GANBAATAR; Gen. Sec. LOSOLYN BYAMBAJARGAL.

Mongolian Traditional United Party (MTUP): Room 3, Mika Hotel, Elchingiin Gudamj, 1st Sub-District, Sükhbaatar District, Ulan Bator (POB 44/5240); tel. (11) 327690; fax (11) 310133; also known as the United Heritage (conservative) Party; f. 1994; est. as an amalgamation of the United Private Owners' Party and the Independence Party; 1,503 mems (2008); ruling body General Political Council; Chair. BATDELGERIIN BATBOLD.

Motherland Party: Motherland Party Central Bldg, Jukovyn Örgön Chölöö 7a, Ulan Bator (POB 49/404); tel. 90150268; fax (11) 453178; internet www.mongol.net/mdnsp; f. 1998; amalgamated with Mongolian Workers' Party 1999; fmrly Mongolian Democratic New Socialist Party, name changed as above in 2005; reported to be disbanding in 2009; c. 160,000 mems (2008); Chair. BADARCHIIN ERDENEBAT.

National New Party: No. 2 Bldg, Enkh Taivny Örgön Chölöö 12, 1st Sub-District, Sükhbaatar District, Ulan Bator; tel. (11) 260535; fax (11) 312596; f. 2006; formed after a split in the leadership of the Democratic Party upon the formation of the national solidarity government; 2,400 mems (2008); Chair. TSERENDASHIIN TSOLMON.

Republican Party (RP): Rm 106, Buyan Holding Co Bldg, 3rd Sub-District, Bayangol District, Ulan Bator; tel. (11) 344844; fax (11) 344843; f. 2004; 50,000 mems (2008); Chair. BAZARSADYN JARGALSAIKHAN; Sec.-Gen. S. BAYARMANLAI.

Diplomatic Representation

EMBASSIES IN MONGOLIA

Bulgaria: Olimpiin Gudamj 8, Ulan Bator (CPOB 702); tel. (11) 322841; fax (11) 324841; e-mail posolstvobg@magicnet.mn; Ambassador (vacant).

Canada: Central Tower, 6th Floor, Sükhbaataryn Talbai 2, Sükhbaatar District, Ulan Bator (CPOB 1028); tel. (11) 328285; fax (11) 328289; e-mail ulaan@international.gc.ca; internet www.mongolia.gc.ca; Ambassador GREGORY GOLDHAWK.

China, People's Republic: Zaluuchuudyn Örgön Chölöö 5, Ulan Bator (CPOB 672); tel. (11) 320955; fax (11) 311943; internet mn.chineseembassy.org; Ambassador WANG XIAOLONG.

Cuba: Negdsen Ündestnii Gudamj 18, Ulan Bator (CPOB 710); tel. (11) 323778; fax (11) 327709; Ambassador MARÍA ORTENSIA FEBLES MIRABAL.

Czech Republic: Olimpiin Gudamj 12, Ulan Bator (CPOB 665); tel. (11) 321886; fax (11) 323791; e-mail czechemb@magicnet.mn; internet www.mzv.cz/ulaanbaatar; Ambassador VÁCLAV JÍLEK.

France: Enkh Taivny Örgön Chölöö 3, Chingeltei District, Ulan Bator (CPOB 687); tel. (11) 324519; fax (11) 319176; e-mail contact@ambafrance-mn.org; internet www.ambafrance-mn.org; Ambassador JEAN-PAUL DUMONT.

Germany: Negdsen Ündestnii Gudamj 7, Ulan Bator (CPOB 708); tel. (11) 323325; fax (11) 323905; internet www.ulan-bator.diplo.de; Ambassador PIUS A. FISCHER.

India: Zaluuchuudyn Örgön Chölöö 10, Ulan Bator (CPOB 691); tel. (11) 329522; fax (11) 329532; e-mail indembmongolia@magicnet.mn; Ambassador SATBIR SINGH.

Japan: Olimpiin Gudamj 8, Ulan Bator (CPOB 1011); tel. (11) 320777; fax (11) 313332; e-mail eojmongol@magicnet.mn; internet www.eojmongolia.mn; Ambassador TAKUO KIDOKORO.

Kazakhstan: Diplomatic Corps Bldg 95, Apartment 2–11, Chingeltei District, Ulan Bator (CPOB 291); tel. (11) 312240; fax (11) 312204; e-mail kzemby@mbox.mn; Ambassador ORMAN NURBAYEV.

Korea, Democratic People's Republic: Khuvisgalchdyn Gudamj, Ulan Bator (CPOB 1015); tel. (11) 326153; fax (11) 330529; Ambassador RI CHOL GWANG.

Korea, Republic: Olimpiin Gudamj 10, Ulan Bator (CPOB 1039); tel. (11) 321548; fax (11) 311157; Ambassador CHEUNG IL.

Laos: Ikh Toiruu 59, Ulan Bator (CPOB 1030); tel. (11) 326440; fax (11) 321048; e-mail emblao@magicnet.mn; Ambassador PENG INTHARATH.

Poland: Diplomatic Corps Bldg 95, Apartment 66, Ulan Bator (CPOB 1049); tel. (11) 320641; fax (11) 320576; e-mail polkonsulat@magicnet.mn; Ambassador TADEUSZ CHOMICKI.

Russia: Enkh Taivny Gudamj 6-A, Ulan Bator (CPOB 661); tel. (11) 327191; fax (11) 327018; Ambassador VIKTOR V. SAMOILENKO.

Turkey: Enkh Taivny Örgön Chölöö 5, Ulan Bator (CPOB 1009); tel. (11) 311200; fax (11) 313992; Ambassador AHMET ASIM ARAR.

United Kingdom: Enkh Taivny Gudamj 30, Ulan Bator 13 (CPOB 703); tel. (11) 458133; fax (11) 458036; Ambassador THORHILDA MARY VIVIA ABBOTT-WATT.

USA: Ikh Toiruu 59/1, Ulan Bator (CPOB 1021); tel. (11) 329095; fax (11) 320776; e-mail cons@usembassy.mn; internet mongolia.usembassy.gov; Ambassador JONATHAN S. ADDLETON.

Viet Nam: Enkh Taivny Örgön Chölöö 47, Ulan Bator (CPOB 670); tel. (11) 458917; fax (11) 458923; Ambassador HOANG TUAN THINH.

Judicial System

Under the fourth Constitution, judicial independence is protected by the General Council of Courts, consisting of the Chief Justice (Chairman of the Supreme Court), the Procurator General, the Minister of Justice and Home Affairs and others. Members of the Supreme Court are nominated by the Council and appointed (or rejected) by the President. The Chief Justice is chosen from among the members of the Supreme Court and approved by the President for a six-year term. Routine civil, criminal and administrative cases are handled by 30 rural district and inter-district courts and eight urban district courts. There are 22 appellate courts at provincial and capital city level. Some legal cases are required by law to be dealt with by the Supreme Court, appellate courts or special courts (military, railway, etc.). The Procurator General and his deputies, who play an investigatory role, are nominated by the President and approved by the Great Khural for six-year terms.

Chief Justice: TSEVEGMIDIIN ZORIG.

Procurator General: DAMBYN DORLIGJAV.

Religion

The 1992 Constitution maintains the separation of Church and State. The Law on State-Church Relations (of November 1993) sought to make Buddhism the predominant religion and restricted the dissemination of beliefs other than Buddhism, Islam and shamanism. During the early years of communist rule Mongolia's traditional Mahayana Buddhism was virtually destroyed. In the early 1990s some 2,000 lamas (monks) established small communities at the sites of 120 former monasteries, temples and religious schools, some of which were being restored. The Kazakhs of western Mongolia are nominally Sunni Muslims. Mosques, also destroyed in the 1930s or closed subsequently, are only now being rebuilt or reopened. Traces of shamanism from the pre-Buddhist period still survive. In recent years there has been an increase in Christian missionary activity in Mongolia.

BUDDHISM

At the end of 2009 there were 113 Buddhist temples and monasteries in Mongolia, including 31 in Ulan Bator, with 1,593 lamas, 2,479 employees and 839 students in religious schools. It is estimated that about 70% of the adult population (975,600) are Buddhists, that is, some 39% of the total population.

Living Buddha: The Ninth Javzandamba Khutagt (Ninth Bogd), Jambalnamdolchoijinjaltsan.

Asian Buddhist Conference For Peace: Gandan, Ulan Bator (CPOB 38); tel. and fax (11) 360069; e-mail blgn_abcp@yahoo.com; Sec.-Gen. Dr T. BULGAN.

Gandantegchinlen Monastery: Zanabazaryn Gudamj, Bayangol District, Ulan Bator; tel. (11) 360354; Centre of Mongolian Buddhists; Khamba Lama (Abbot) DEMBERELIIN CHOIJAMTS.

'Good Merit' Buddhist Society: Ulan Bator; Pres. Lama A. ERDENEBAT.

Karmapa Monastery: Khamba Lama (Abbot) DAVAASAMBUUGIIN TAIVANSAIKHAN.

Pethub Buddhist Institute: Ikh Toiruu, Chingeltei District, Ulan Bator (POB 38/105); tel. (11) 321867; fax (11) 320676; e-mail pethubmongolia@magicnet.mn; internet www.pethubmonastery.com; f. 2001 by Ven. Kushok Bakula Rinpoche (Indian Ambassador to Mongolia 1990–2000).

MONGOLIA

CHRISTIANITY

At the end of 2009 there were 110 Christian congregations in Mongolia, including 84 in Ulan Bator, with 147 priests and ministers, 612 employees and 237 students attending Christian studies.

Roman Catholic Church

The Church is represented in Mongolia by a single mission. At December 2007, according to Vatican sources, there were 417 Catholics in the country.

Catholic Mission: 18th Sub-District, Bayanzürkh District, Ulan Bator (CPOB 694); tel. (11) 458825; fax (11) 458027; e-mail info@ccmvatican.mn; internet www.ccmvatican.mn; f. 1992; Apostolic Prefect Bishop WENCESLAO PADILLA.

Protestant Church

Association of Mongolian Protestants: f. 1990; Pastor M. BOLDBAATAR.

Mongolian Evangelical Alliance: Jijig Ür Bldg, 3rd Sub-District, Bayanzürkh District, Ulan Bator; tel. 70152040 (mobile); e-mail mea@magicnet.mn; internet www.mea.mn; f. 1998; a branch of the World Evangelical Alliance.

Other Christian Churches

Church of Jesus Christ of Latter-Day Saints (Mormon): Khudaldaany Gudamj, Chingeltei District, Ulan Bator; tel. (11) 312761.

Jesus Reigns Assembly: Ulan Bator; Pastor D. NARANMANDAKH.

Russian Orthodox Church: Holy Trinity Church, Jukovyn Gudamj 55, Bayanzürkh District, Ulan Bator; tel. 99256732; fax 11454425; e-mail fateraleksei@hotmail.com; internet www.pravoslavie.mn; opened in 1864, closed in 1927; services recommenced 1997 for Russian community; new Holy Trinity Church consecrated in June 2009; Head Father ALEKSEI TRUBACH.

Seventh-day Adventist Church: 5th Sub-District, Bayangol District, Ulan Bator; tel. (11) 688031; fax (11) 688032.

ISLAM

At the end of 2009 there were five Muslim congregations, all but one (in Ulan Bator) in western Mongolia, with 14 clergy, 24 employees and 365 students. A mosque was due to be built in Ulan Bator. It is assumed that the majority of Mongolia's ethnic Kazakh population (numbering 103,000 at the January 2000 census) are Muslim. It was stated in March 2005 that Mongolia had 32 mosques in Bayan-Ölgii and Khovd provinces and in the towns of Darkhan and Nalaikh.

Chief Imam (Ölgii): KH. BATYRBEK.

Imam of Gümyr shrine (Ölgii): DÖITENGIIN SHERKHAN.

Association of Mongolian Muslim Societies: f. 2009; Exec. Dir KH. BATYRBEK.

BAHÁ'Í FAITH

Bahá'í Society: Ulan Bator; tel. (11) 321867; f. 1989; Leader A. ARIUNAA.

SHAMANISM

Darkhad Shamanic Study Centre: Ulan Bator; Leader CH. TSERENBAAVAI.

Tengeriin Süld Shamanic Union: Ulan Bator; Pres. CH. CHINBAT.

The Press

PRINCIPAL NATIONAL NEWSPAPERS

State-owned publications in Mongolia were denationalized with effect from 1 January 1999, although full privatization could not proceed immediately. The number of newspapers published annually decreased from 134.1m. copies in 1990 to 18.5m. copies in 2003. As of January 2010, Mongolia had 139 newspapers and periodicals. A total of 31 provincial and town newspapers were published 36 times a year, with four appearing 48 times a year.

Ardchilal (Democracy): Democracy Palace, 11th Sub-District, Sükhbaatar District, Ulan Bator; tel. 70110187; 260 a year; Editor-in-Chief KH. ÖLZIIBAYAR.

Ardyn Erkh (People's Power): Movie Factory, Gudamj 78, Bayanzurkh District, Ulan Bator; tel. and fax (11) 434635; e-mail info@news.mn; f. 2004; original title ceased publication in 1999 (see *Ödriin Sonin*, below); subsequently assumed by new publr; 256 a year; Exec. Dir BAYARMAGNAIN TEMÜÜLEN; Dep. Dir NARANTUYA DANGAASUREN.

Mongolyn Medee (Mongolian News): Jigjidjavyn Gudamj 6-1, Chingeltei District, Ulan Bator; tel. (11) 322005; fax (11) 311215; e-mail news-of-mon@mongolnet.mn; 256 a year; Editor-in-Chief YO. GERELCHULUUN; circ. 2,900.

Mongolyn Ünen (Mongolian Truth): Baga Toiruu 11, Ulan Bator; tel. (11) 321287; fax (11) 323223; e-mail unen@mongol.net; internet www.unen.imedia.mn; f. 1920; publ. 1925–2010 by MPRP as Ünen; 256 a year; Editor-in-Chief TSERENSODNOMYN GANBAT; circ. 8,330.

Montsame-giin Medee (Montsame News): Montsame News Agency, Jigjidjavyn Gudamj 8, Ulan Bator (CPOB 1514); tel. (11) 321324; e-mail localnews@montsame.mn; internet www.montsame.mn; daily news digest primarily for govt depts; 248 a year; Editor B. NOMINCHIMED.

Ödriin Sonin (Daily News): Ödriin Sonin Bldg, Ikh Toiruu 20, Sükhbaatar District, Ulan Bator; tel. 99030027; fax (11) 353897; internet www.dailynews.mn; f. 1924; restored 1990; fmrly Ardyn Erkh, Ardyn Ündesnii Erkh, Ündesnii Erkh and Ödriin Toli; 312 a year; Editor-in-Chief JAMBALYN MYAGMARSÜREN; circ. 14,200.

Öglöönii Sonin (Morning News): No. 1 Bldg, 4th Sub-District, Chingeltei District, Ulan Bator (POB 46/411); tel. (11) 319386; fax (11) 315695; e-mail ugluuniisonin@yahoo.com; 252 a year; Editor-in-Chief O. MÖNKH-ERDENE.

Önöödör (Today): Mongol News Co Bldg, Juulchny Gudamj 40, Ulan Bator; tel. (11) 330797; fax (11) 330798; e-mail mntoday@mobinet.mn; internet www.mongolnews.mn; f. 1996; 300 a year; Editor-in-Chief B. NANDINTÜSHIG; circ. 5,500.

Ulaanbaatar Taims (Ulan Bator Times): Apt 5, Bldg 30, Baga Toiruu, 8th Sub-District, Sükhbaatar District, Ulan Bator; tel. (11) 322215; e-mail ubtimes1@yahoo.com; internet www.ubtimes.mn; f. 1929; est. as Ulaanbaatar Khotyn Medee; renamed Ulaanbaataryn Medee in 1955, Ulaanbaatar Taims in 1990, and Ulaanbaatar Taims in 1999; publ. by Ulan Bator City Govt; 252 a year; Editor-in-Chief J. SARUULBAYAN; circ. 2,000.

Ündesnii Shuudan (National Post): fmr Ardyn Erkh Bldg, Ikh Toiruu, Ulan Bator; tel. (11) 354632; fax (11) 354631; e-mail zuuniishuudan@yahoo.com; 312 a year; Editor-in-Chief BAASANJAVYN GANBOLD.

Zuuny Medee (Century's News): Amaryn Gudamj 1, Ulan Bator; tel. (11) 313499; fax (11) 321279; e-mail zuuniimedee@yahoo.com; internet www.zuuniimedee.mn; f. 1991; previously titled Zasgiin Gazryn Medee; 312 a year; Editor-in-Chief DEMCHIGJAVYN OTGONBAYAR; circ 8,000.

OTHER NEWSPAPERS AND PERIODICALS

4 dekh Zasaglal (Fourth Estate): Mongol Sonin Co, Gazar Holding Bldg, Variete Centre, Ulan Bator (POB 46A/81); tel. 99188125; e-mail dorovdekhzasaglal@yahoo.com; 36 a year; Editor A. ENKHBAYAR.

81-r Suvag (Channel 81): Söüliin Gudamj, Bayangol District, Ulan Bator (POB 46A/81); tel. 96003992; fax (11) 460718; publishes views of the Mongolian Newspaper Asscn; 36 a year; Editor-in-Chief T. TSOGT-ERDENE.

Altangadas (Pole Star): AG Töv, Söüliin Gudamj, Bayanzürkh District, Ulan Bator (CPOB 430); tel. (11) 319411; fax (11) 319414; e-mail info@altangadas.mn; internet www.altangadas.mn; monthly political magazine; Editor NOROVYN ALTANKHUYAG.

Anagaakh Arga Bilig (The Healthy Way of Yin and Yang): Ulan Bator (CPOB 1053); tel. (11) 321367; e-mail arslny7144@magicnet.mn; 24 a year; Editor YA. ARSLAN.

Bagsh (Teacher): Rm 106, Teachers' College, Ulan Bator; tel. 99183398; f. 1989; est. by Ministry of Education; 24 a year.

Biznesiin Medee (Business News): Democratic Party Bldg, Sükhbaatar District, Ulan Bator (POB 20/335); tel. (11) 350541; fax (11) 350548; e-mail info@businessnews.mn; 36 a year; Editor-in-Chief S. KHÜREL.

Bolson Yavdal (Events): Söüliin Gudamj, Sükhbaatar District, Ulan Bator (POB 36/346); e-mail bolsonyavdal@yahoo.com; 36 a year; Editor T. SANGAA.

Business Times: Chamber of Commerce and Industry, Government Bldg 11, Rm 712, Erkh Chölöönii Talbai, Ulan Bator; tel. and fax (11) 325374; e-mail marketing@mongolchamber.mn; 36 a year; Editor BATSÜKHIIN SARANTUYAA.

Deed Shüükhiin Medeelel (Supreme Court Information): Mongolian Supreme Court, Ulan Bator; quarterly journal.

Deedsiin Amidral (Elite's Life): Bldg 4, Rm 514, A. Amaryn Gudamj, Ulan Bator (CPOB 356); tel. 91189699; fax (11) 323847; e-mail deedsiinamidral@mongol.mn; 36 a year; Editor-in-Chief B. OTGONBAYAR.

Deedsiin Khüreelen (Elite's Forum): Ulan Bator (CPOB 1114); tel. and fax (11) 450602; e-mail deed_huree@yahoo.com; 48 a year; Publr M. SÜKHBAATAR; Editor KH. UYANGA; circ. 12,000.

Ekh Orny Manaa (Guard of the Motherland): Main Directorate of Border Defence, Ulan Bator; internet bpo.gov.mn; 36 a year.

Emiin Medeelel (Medicine Information): National Health Development Centre, Ministry of Health, Ulan Bator; tel. (11) 321485; fax

MONGOLIA

(11) 320633; e-mail zorig@nchd.mn; bimonthly magazine published by the National Health Development Centre; Editor T. ZORIG.

Erüül Mend (Health): Super Zuun Co, Ulan Bator (POB 20/412); tel. 99192239; fax (11) 321278; e-mail dr_jargal_d@yahoo.com; publ. by Ministry of Health; monthly; Editor D. JARGALSAIKHAN; circ. 5,600.

Khani (Spouse): National Agricultural Co-operative Members' Association Bldg, Rm 201, Enkh Taivny Gudamj 18A, Bayanzürkh District, Ulan Bator (POB 49/600); tel. (11) 460698; fax (11) 458550; e-mail khani_sonin@yahoo.com; women and family issues; 32 a year; Editor-in-Chief DEMBERELIIN BATSÜKH; circ. 64,920.

Khiimori (Wind-Horse): Ödriin Sonin Bldg, Ikh Toiruu 20, Sükhbaatar District, Ulan Bator; tel. (11) 354565; monthly; Editor-in-Chief A. ERDENETUYAA.

Khödölmör (Labour): Sükhbaataryn Talbai 3, Ulan Bator; tel. (11) 323026; f. 1928; publ. by Confederation of Mongolian Trade Unions; 48 a year; Editor-in-Chief TSOODOLYN KHULAN; circ. 64,920.

Khökh Tolbo (Blue Spot): Mon-Azi Co Bldg, Ulan Bator (POB 24/306); tel. (11) 313405; fax (11) 312794; 36 a year; Publr BATYN ERDENEBAATAR; Editor-in-Chief E. ENKHTSOLMON; circ. 3,500.

Khöröngiin Zakh Zeel (Capital Market): Mongolian Stock Exchange, Sükhbaataryn Talbai 2, Ulan Bator; tel. (11) 313511; fax (11) 325170; e-mail info@mse.mn; monthly; Editor (vacant).

Khuuli Züin Medee (Legal News): Ministry of Justice and Home Affairs, Ulan Bator; f. 1990; 24 a year; publ. by National Legal Institute.

Khuviin Soyol (Personal Culture): Rm 2, Block 39, behind No. 5 School, Baga Toiruu, Ulan Bator (CPOB 1254); 24 a year; Editor BEKHBAZARYN BEKHSÜREN.

Khümüün Bichig (People and Script): Montsame News Agency, Jigjidjavyn Gudamj 8, Ulan Bator (CPOB 1514); tel. (11) 329486; fax (11) 327857; e-mail khumuun@montsame.mn; current affairs in Mongolian classical script; 48 a year; Editor T. GALDAN; circ. 15,000.

Khümüüs (People): Central Palace of Culture, Ulan Bator (POB 46/411); 48 a year; Editor O. MÖNKH-ERDENE.

Khümüüsiin Amidral (People's Lives): Central Palace of Culture, Ulan Bator (POB 46/411); 48 a year; Editor B. AMGALAN.

Mash Nuuts (Top Secret): Mongol Shaazan Bldg, Ulan Bator (POB 49/113); tel. (11) 328675; fax (11) 330690; e-mail tsecret@mongolnet.mn; 32 a year; Editor-in-Chief ONONGIIN CHINZORIG.

Mongoljin Goo (Mongolian Beauty): Mongolian Women's Federation, Ulan Bator (POB 44/717); tel. (11) 320790; fax (11) 367406; e-mail monwofed@magicnet.mn; f. 1990; monthly; Editor J. ERDENECHIMEG; circ. 3,000.

Mongolyn Anagaakh Ukhaan (Mongolian Medicine): Ulan Bator (CPOB 696); tel. (11) 112306; fax (11) 451807; e-mail nymadawa@hotmail.com; publ. by Scientific Society of Mongolian Physicians and Mongolian Academy of Sciences; 6 a year; Editor-in-Chief Prof. PAGVAJAVYN NYAMDAVAA.

Mongolyn Khödöö (Mongolian Countryside): Agricultural University, Zaisan, Ulan Bator; tel. (11) 345211; e-mail haaint@magicnet.mn; publ. by Mongolian State University of Agriculture and Academy of Agricultural Sciences; 36 a year; Editor-in-Chief Prof. BEGZIIN DORJ.

Mongolyn Neg Ödör (One Day of Mongolia): Bldg 31, Bayanzürkh District, Ulan Bator (POB 44/764); tel. (11) 450103; fax (11) 460718; e-mail oneday@mongolmedia.com; 48 a year; Editor-in-Chief SH. OTGONSETSEG.

Myangany Zuuch (Millennium Messenger): Mönkh Press Co, West side of Choijin Lama Temple, Sükbaataar District, Ulan Bator (POB 46/390); tel. and fax (11) 319745; e-mail monkh@mobinet.mn; 36 a year; Deputy Editor G. ENKHJARGAL.

Niigmiin Toli (Mirror of Society): Chingeltei District, Ulan Bator; tel. (11) 314571; e-mail niigmiintoli@nml.mn; 312 a year.

Notstoi Medee (Important News): Maximus Press Co, Ulan Bator (POB 20/359); tel. (11) 316953; 36 a year; Editor B. GALSANSÜKH.

Nyam Garig (Sunday): Mongol News Co Bldg, Juulchny Gudamj, Ulan Bator; tel. (11) 330797; fax (11) 330798; e-mail weekend@mongolnews.mn; weekly supplement of Önöödör; Editor-in-Chief B. BOLDKHÜÜ.

Onigoo (Jokes): Konsulyn Gudamj 5-13, Bayanzürkh District, Ulan Bator (POB Sky Post 46/50); tel. 70150001; e-mail onigoosonin@yahoo.com; 16 a year; Editor S. SARANCHIMEG.

Sankhüügiin Medee (Financial News): Ulan Bator; 36 a year; Editor L. DONDOG.

Serüüleg (Alarm Clock): Business Plaza Bldg 2, Enkh Taivny Örgön Chölöö, Ulan Bator (CPOB 1094); tel. (11) 455570; fax (11) 459182; e-mail a.tsaschikher@yahoo.com; 48 a year; Editor-in-Chief BAYANMÖNKHIIN TSOOJCHULUUNTSETSEG; circ. 28,600.

Setgüülch (Journalist): Ulan Bator (POB 46/600); tel. (11) 325388; fax (11) 313912; f. 1982; publ. by Union of Journalists; journalism,

politics, literature, art, economy; quarterly; Editor TSENDIIN ENKHBAT.

Shar Sonin (Yellow Newspaper): Ulan Bator (POB 46A/225); tel. (11) 313984; e-mail thesharsonin@yahoo.com; 36 a year; Editor B. NAMUUN.

Shine Erkh Chölöö (New Freedom): Ödriin Sonin Bldg, Ikh Toiruu, Ulan Bator (CPOB 2590); tel. and fax 70137010; e-mail erkhcholoo2007@yahoo.com; monthly; social and political affairs; Editor-in-Chief TS. OYUUNCHIMEG.

Shine Yörtönts (New World): Empathy Centre, Baga Toiruu, 6th Sub-District, Ulan Bator; tel. (11) 313019; fax (11) 324657; quarterly; popular science magazine; Editor B. SARNAI.

Shinjlekh Ukhaany Akademiin Medee (Academy of Sciences News): Yörönkhii Said Amaryn Gudamj 1, Ulan Bator; tel. (11) 265163; fax (11) 261993; e-mail mas@mas.ac.mn; internet www.mas.ac.mn; f. 1961; publ. by Academy of Sciences; quarterly; Editor-in-Chief DÜGERIIN REGDEL.

Shuurkhai Zar (Quick Advertisement): Ulan Bator Bank Bldg, Rm 104, 1st Floor, Ulan Bator (POB 46A/151); tel. (11) 313778; e-mail shirevger@mobinet.mn; 96 a year; Editor E. TSEYENKHORLOO.

Solongo (Rainbow): Baruunselbe Service Centre, Ulan Bator (POB 23/628); tel. 99860276; f. 1992; monthly; Deputy Editor-in-Chief T. BAYANJARGAL.

Soyombo: Ministry of Defence, Ulan Bator; tel. 91177221; f. 1924; est. as Ardyn Tsereg (People's Soldier); renamed Ekh Orny Tölöö (For the Motherland), then Ulaan Od (Red Star); weekly; Dep. Editor-in-Chief Lt-Col G. NYAMDORJ.

Strategi Sudlal (Strategic Studies): Institute of Strategic Studies, National Security Council, Ulan Bator (CPOB 870); tel. (11) 260710; fax (11) 324055; f. 1991; 4 a year; Editor BEGZIIN DAVAADORJ.

Tavan Tsagarig (Five Rings): National Olympic Committee, Ikh Toiruu 20, Ulan Bator; tel. (11) 70111095; fax (11) 343541; e-mail noc@olympic.mn; internet www.mongolnews.mn/tavantsagarig; f. 1995; 100 a year; Editor-in-Chief TSAGAANBAATARYN BYAMBAA.

Tengerleg Khümüüs (Heavenly People): Soyombo Press Co, Partizany Gudamj 17, Sükbaatar District, Ulan Bator (POB 44/716); tel. (11) 325250; fax (11) 330383; 36 a year; Dir-Gen. D. AMBARBAYASGALAN; Editor P. JARGALSAIKHAN.

Tonshuul (Woodpecker): Enkh Taivny Örgön Chölöö 4, Rm 148, Bayanzürkh District (CPOB 322), Ulan Bator; tel. 99118668; fax (11) 459265; e-mail ariun_tonshuul@yahoo.com; fortnightly magazine of cartoons, humour and satire; Editor TS. ARIUNAA.

Töriin Medeelel (State Information): Secretariat of the Mongolian Great Khural, Government Palace, Ulan Bator; tel. (11) 265958; fax (11) 322866; e-mail turiin_medeelel@parliament.mn; internet www.parl.gov.mn; f. 1990; presidential and governmental decrees, state laws; 48 a year; circ. 5,000.

Tsonkh (Window): Chingisiin Örgön Chölöö 1, Ulan Bator (CPOB 1085); tel. (11) 310717; publ. by the Democratic Party's Political Department; 6 a year.

Tsog (Ember): Mongolian Union of Writers, Ulan Bator; literary; quarterly.

Uls Töriin Sonin (Political Newspaper): Delta Centre, Juulchny Gudamj, Chingeltei District, Ulan Bator (POB 46/796); tel. 99095040; fax (11) 312608; f. 2005 following closure of the Mongol Times; 48 a year; Editor GANTÖMÖRIIN UYANGA.

Utga Zokhiol Urlag (Literature and Art): Mongolian Union of Writers, Sükhbaataryn Gudamj 11, Ulan Bator (POB 46A/555); tel. (11) 318035; fax (11) 320817; e-mail info@utgazokhiol.mn; f. 1955; 36 a year; Editor JAMSRANGIIN BAYARJARGAL; circ. 3,000.

Üg (The Word): Bldg 86, Chingeltei District, Ulan Bator; tel. 55152675; fax (11) 329795; e-mail ugsonin@mol.mn; journal of the Mongolian Social-Democratic Party (from 2005); Editor-in-Chief ARYAAGIIN GANBAATAR.

Zar Medee (Advertisement News): Bldg 20, 4th Sub-District, Juulchny Gudamj, Chingeltei District, Ulan Bator; tel. 70110008; fax 70110009; e-mail advertisement-news@yahoo.com; personal and company adverts; 100 a year; Editor D. BAYASGALAN.

Zindaa (Ranking): Rm 305, fmr Ardyn Erkh Bldg, Sükhbaatar District, Ulan Bator; tel. (11) 354545; fax (11) 354555; wrestling news; 36 a year; Editor-in-Chief KH. MANDAKHBAYAR.

FOREIGN LANGUAGE PUBLICATIONS

Inspiring Mongolia: Mongolian National Chamber of Commerce and Industry, Mahatma Gandhi Gudamj, 1st Sub-District, Khan-Uul District, Ulan Bator; tel. (11) 312501; fax (11) 324620; e-mail marketing@mongolchamber.mn; internet www.mongolchamber.mn; magazine in English, publ. twice a year; Editor-in-Chief SAMBUUGIIN DEMBEREL.

MONGOLIA

Menggu Xiaoxi Bao (News of Mongolia): Montsame News Agency, Ulan Bator (CPOB 1514); tel. (11) 320077; e-mail mgxxbao@chinggis.com; f. 1929; weekly; in Chinese; Sec. P. Oyuuntsetseg.

The Mongol Messenger: Montsame News Agency, Jigjidjavyn Gudamj 8, Ulan Bator (CPOB 1514); tel. (11) 266740; fax (11) 325512; e-mail monmessenger@magicnet.mn; f. 1991; weekly newspaper in English; owned by Montsame national news agency; Editor-in-Chief Borkhondoin Indra; circ. 2,000.

Mongolian Magazine: Interpress Publishers, Ulan Bator; f. 2004; English-language monthly illustrated magazine about Mongolian history, culture, nature, life and customs.

Mongolia This Week: Ulan Bator; tel. and fax (11) 318339; e-mail mongoliathisweek@mobinet.mn; weekly in English, online daily; Editor-in-Chief D. Narantuyaa; English Editor Eric Mustafa.

Mongolia Today: Montsame News Agency, Jigjidjavyn Gudamj 8, Ulan Bator (CPOB 1514); quarterly; in English; Editor-in-Chief G. Pürevsambuu.

Mongoliya Segodnya (Mongolia Today): Zoos Goyol Co Bldg, Chingeltei District, Ulan Bator (POB 46/609); tel. and fax (11) 324141; weekly; in Russian; Editor-in-Chief Dünger-Yaichiliin Solongo.

Mongoru Tsushin (Mongolia News): Montsame News Agency, Jigjidjavyn Gudamj 8, Ulan Bator (CPOB 1514); weekly; in Japanese.

Montsame Daily News: Montsame News Agency, Jigjidjavyn Gudamj 8, Ulan Bator (CPOB 1514); tel. (11) 314574; fax (11) 327857; e-mail montsame@magicnet.mn; daily English news digest for embassies, etc.; Editor-in-Chief Bayanbatyn Bayasgalan.

Novosti Mongolii (News of Mongolia): Montsame News Agency, Jigjidjavyn Gudamj 8, Ulan Bator (CPOB 1514); tel. (11) 310157; fax (11) 327857; e-mail novosty_mongolii@yahoo.co.uk; f. 1942; weekly; in Russian; Editor-in-Chief Dügersürengiin Ariunbold.

The UB Post: Mongol News Co, Juulchny Gudamj, Ulan Bator; tel. (11) 70111095; fax (11) 330798; e-mail ubpost@mongolnews.mn; internet ubpost.mongolnews.mn; f. 1996; 100 a year; in English; Editor-in-Chief Choimboroljavyn Sumyaabazar; circ. 4,000.

NEWS AGENCIES

Montsame (Mongol Tsakhilgaan Medeenii Agentlag) (Mongolian News Agency): Jigjidjavyn Gudamj 8, Ulan Bator (CPOB 1514); tel. (11) 266904; fax (11) 327857; e-mail montsame@magicnet.mn; internet www.montsame.mn; f. 1921; govt-controlled; Gen. Dir Tugalkhüügiin Baasansüren; Editor-in-Chief B. Nominchimed.

Mongolyn Medee (Mongolian News): Public Radio and Television, Khuvisgalyn Zam, Ulan Bator; Dir Ts. Sükhbaatar.

PRESS ASSOCIATIONS

Daily Newspaper Association: c/o Önöödör, Mongol News Co, Juulchny Gudamj, Ulan Bator; f. 2006; Pres. B. Temüülen.

Mongolian Newspaper Association: Ulan Bator; Pres. Radnaagiin Khadbaatar.

Press Institute: Ulan Bator; internet www.pressinst.org.mn; f. 1995; Dir M. Mönkhmandakh.

Publishers

The ending of the state monopoly has led to the establishment of several small commercial publishers, including Shuvuun Saaral (Ministry of Defence), Mongol Khevlel and Soyombo Co, Mongolpress (Montsame), Erdem (Academy of Sciences), Süülenkhüü children's publishers, Sudaryn Chuulgan, Interpress, Sükhbaatar Co, Öngöt Khevlel, Admon, Ödsar, Khee Khas Co, etc.

Admon Co: Amaryn Gudamj 2, Sükhbaatar District, Ulan Bator (CPOB 92); tel. (11) 329253; fax (11) 327251; e-mail admon@magicnet.mn; Dir R. Enkhbat.

Chölööt Khevlel San (Free Press Foundation): Ikh Toiruu 11B, Ulan Bator (POB 20/357); tel. (11) 350016; e-mail mpfnph@magicnet.mn; f. 1996; the country's largest printer of newspapers and the biggest pre-press service provider; Man. Dir Baastyn Galsandorj.

Darkhan Sergelen Co: Naadamchdyn Gudamj, Darkhan; tel. (37) 23049; fax (37) 24741; internet www.munkhiin-useg.mn.

Khevleliin Khüreelen (Press Institute NGO): Ikh Toiruu 11, Sükhbaatar District, Ulan Bator; tel. and fax (11) 350012; e-mail ts_byambaa12@yahoo.com; internet www.owc.org.mn/press institute; Chair. Ts. Enkhbat.

Mongol News Group: Mongol News Group Bldg, Juulchny Gudamj, Ulan Bator; tel. (11) 330797; fax (11) 330798; e-mail mntoday@mobinet.mn; f. 1996; owns newspapers *MN-Önöödör*, *Tavan Tsagarig*, *Nyam Garig* and *The UB Post*, TV Channel 25 and ABM Co printers; Pres. B. Nandintüshig.

Mönkhiin Üseg Group: Teeverchdiin Gudamj, Songinokhairkhan District, Ulan Bator; tel. (11) 320807; fax (11) 321318; e-mail munuseg@mbox.mn; internet www.munkhiin-useg.mn; Chair. G. Batmönkh.

Novum Co: Migma Bldg, Ulan Bator; tel. (11) 319140; fax (11) 319319; e-mail print@mynovum.com; internet www.mynovum.com.

Öngöt Khevlel Co: Amaryn Gudamj 2, Sükhbaatar District, Ulan Bator; tel. (11) 323121; fax (11) 329519; e-mail ungut_khevlel@mongolnet.mn.

Soyombo Printing Co: Natsagdorjiin Gudamj, Sükhbaatar District, Ulan Bator; tel. (11) 325052.

Sükhbaatarprint Co: Amaryn Gudamj 2, Sükhbaatar District, Ulan Bator; tel. and fax (11) 320504; e-mail sukhprint@magicnet.mn.

Zurag Züi Co (Cartography): Ikh Toiruu 15, Ulan Bator; tel. (11) 322164; e-mail cart@magicnet.mn; publisher and retailer of maps and atlases.

PUBLISHERS' ASSOCIATIONS

Local Press and Information Association: Ulan Bator; f. 2006; Pres. S. Sharavdorj.

Mongolian Book Publishers' Association: Ulan Bator; Exec. Dir S. Tserendorj.

Mongolian Free Press Publishers' Association: Ulan Bator (POB 24/306); tel. and fax (11) 313405; Pres. Batyn Erdenebaatar.

Broadcasting and Communications

TELECOMMUNICATIONS

Digital exchanges have been installed in Ulan Bator, Darkhan, Erdenet, Sükhbaatar, Bulgan and Arvaikheer, while radio relay lines have been digitalized between: Ulan Bator–Darkhan–Sükhbaatar; Ulan Bator–Darkhan–Erdenet; and Dashinchilen–Arvaikheer. Mobile telephone companies operate in Ulan Bator and other central towns, in addition to Arvaikheer, Sainshand and Zamyn-Üüd. By May 2005 a total of 1,776 km of fibre optic cable had been installed in Mongolia, with plans to lay another 1,400 km by the end of the year. The Ulan Bator–Bulgan cable was under construction.

Bodicom: Ulan Bator; tel. (11) 325144; fax (11) 318486; e-mail bodicom@mongolnet.mn.

Datacom: Rm 112, Mongolian Technology National Park, Baga Toiruu, Sükhbaatar District, Ulan Bator; tel. (11) 327309; fax (11) 320210; e-mail billing@datacom.mn; internet www.datacom.mn; service provider for MagicNet connection to internet; Dir Dangaasürengiin Enkhbat.

G-Mobile: Gem International Co, 1st Sub-District, Chingeltei District, Ulan Bator; tel. (11) 333636; e-mail info@g-mobile.mn; internet www.g-mobile.mn; Dir-Gen. Ts. Tserenpuntsag.

Incomnet: Enkh Taivny Örgön Chölöö, Bayanzürkh District, Ulan Bator (CPOB 582); tel. and fax (11) 480808; e-mail info@incomnet.mn; internet www.incomnet.mn; internet service provider, cable TV, satellite communications; Gen. Dir S. Ganbataar.

MagicNet Co: Rm 222, Ground Floor, Science and Technology Information Centre, Ulan Bator; tel. (11) 312061; fax (11) 311496; e-mail info@magicnet.mn; internet www.magicnet.mn; internet service provider.

MCSCom: MCS Plaza, 3rd Floor, Baga Toiruu 49, Ulan Bator; tel. (11) 327854; fax (11) 311323; e-mail sales@mcscom.mn; internet www.mcscom.mn; internet service provider.

Medeelel Kholboo: Central Post Office Bldg, Sükhbaataryn Talbai 1, Chingeltei District, Ulan Bator; tel. and fax 70112519; internet www.icnc.mn; installation of digital radio relays and fibre optic cables for communications and internet, television and radio.

Micom: Central Post Office Bldg, Sükhbaataryn Talbai 1, Chingeltei District, Ulan Bator (CPOB 1124); tel. (11) 313229; fax (11) 322473; e-mail info@micom.mng.mn; internet www.micom.mn; Dir Ch. Narantungalag.

MobiCom: Sambuugiin Gudamj 47, Chingeltei District, Ulan Bator; fax (11) 310411; e-mail feedback@mobicom.mn; internet www.mobicom.mn; mobile telephone service provider; Exec. Dir Fumiaki Shiga; Dir-Gen. D. Bolor.

Moncom: Ulan Bator (POB 51/207); tel. (11) 329409; e-mail ch.enkhmend@hotmail.com; pager services.

Mongolia Telecom: Central Post Office Bldg, Sükhbaataryn Talbai 1, Ulan Bator (CPOB 1166); tel. (11) 320597; fax (11) 325412; e-mail mt@mtcone.net; internet www.mongol.net; 54.6% state-owned, 40.0% owned by Korea Telecom; Pres. and CEO Oonoigiin Shaaluu; Exec. Dir O. Batchuluun.

MonSat: New Horizon Bldg, Olimpiin Gudamj 6, 1st Sub-District, Sükhbaatar District, Ulan Bator; tel. (11) 323705; fax (11) 312699;

MONGOLIA

e-mail monsat@mcs.mn; internet www.monsat.mcs.mn; satellite communications, mobile telephone and internet services.

Newcom LLC: Enkh Taivny Örgön Chölöö 3/1, Bayanzürkh District, Ulan Bator; tel. (11) 313183; fax (11) 318521; e-mail secretary@newcom.mn; internet www.newcom.mn; Chair. Ts. BOLDBAATAR; Exec. Dir B. BYAMBASAIKHAN.

Newtel Co: TEDY Centre, Sambuugiin Gudamj 18, Chingeltei District, Ulan Bator (CPOB 425); tel. and fax (11) 311581; e-mail marketing@ntc.mn; internet www.ntc.mn; Exec. Dir D. BOLOR.

Orbitnet: New Horizon Bldg, Olimpiin Gudamj 6, Sükhbaatar District, Ulan Bator; tel. (11) 323705; fax (11) 312699; e-mail orbitnet@mcs.mn; internet www.orbitnet.mcs.mn.

Railcom: Mongolian Railways (MTZ), Teeverchdiin Gudamj, 3rd Sub-District, Bayangol District, Ulan Bator (CPOB 376); tel. (11) 252525; e-mail info@railcom.mn; internet www.railcom.mn; telephone, TV and internet service provider.

Skynetcom: 1st Sub-District, Chingeltei District, Ulan Bator; tel. (11) 318840; fax (11) 318841; e-mail info@skynetcom.mn; internet www.skynetcom.mn; mobile telephone service provider.

Skytel: Skytel Plaza Centre, Chingisiin Örgön Chölöö 9, Ulan Bator; tel. (11) 319191; fax (11) 318487; e-mail skytel_comment@yahoo.com; internet www.skytel.mn; mobile telephone and voice mail service provider; Mongolia-Republic of Korea jt venture; Dir-Gen. R. GANBOLD; Marketing Man. G. TÜVSHINTÖGS.

Ulusnet: TEDY Centre, Sambuugiin Gudamj 18, Chingeltei District, Ulan Bator; tel. (11) 321434; fax (11) 322686; e-mail service@ulusnet.mn; internet www.ulusnet.mn; Mongolia's first Wimax service provider.

Unitel: Central Tower, Sükhbaataryn Talbai 2, Sükhbaatar District, Ulan Bator; tel. (11) 328888; fax (11) 330708; e-mail info@unitel.mn; internet www.unitel.mn; f. 2005 by MBSB Telecom, Uangel Corpn (Republic of Korea) and Dream Choice Co (Canada); mobile telephone service provider; Dir-Gen. B. BILGÜÜN.

Univision: Unitel Corpn, Ulan Bator; tel. 77118811; internet www.univision.mn; HD cable TV, internet, mobile telephone service provider; CEO N. NARANBAT.

BROADCASTING

A 1,900-km radio relay line from Ulan Bator to Altai and Ölgii provides direct-dialling telephone links as well as television services for western Mongolia. New radio relay lines have been built from Ulan Bator to Choibalsan, and from Ulan Bator to Sükhbaatar and Sainshand. Most of the population is in the zone of television reception, following the inauguration of relays via satellites operated by the International Telecommunications Satellite Organization (INTELSAT). In 2004 Mongolia had 30 radio stations and 35 television stations.

In 2009 Mongolia had 373 television transmitters and relay stations. However, over 54,600 households continued to receive radio broadcasts by the old wired networks.

All provincial centres receive two channels of Mongolian national television, and all district centres can receive television. At the beginning of 2005 the first legislative measures were taken to end state control, with the approval of the Law on Public Broadcasting, the provisions of which entered into force on 1 July 2005, creating an independent public service broadcaster to be known as Public Radio and Television. Also in 2005 it was planned to extend television coverage (UBS, TV-5, TV-9 and Channel 25) to outlying areas of Ulan Bator, including Partizan, Songino and Gachuurt, by installing additional local transmitters. In 2009 Mongolia's first internet television station, Mongol TV, was launched.

Public Radio and Television (ONRT): Khuvisgalyn Zam 3, Bayangol District, Ulan Bator; f. 2006; replaced the govt-run Directorate of Radio and Television Affairs; Chair. of National Council KHAIDAVYN CHILAAJAV; Dir-Gen. MYANGANBUUGIIN NARANBAATAR; Editor-in-Chief DEMBERELIIN ERDENETSETSEG.

Radio

Mongolian National Public Radio (Mongolradio): Khuvisgalyn Zam 3, Bayangol District, Ulan Bator; tel. (11) 323096; f. 1934; operates for 17 hours daily on three long-wave and one medium-wave frequency, and VHF; programmes in Mongolian (two); part of Public Radio and Television; Dir B. PÜREVDASH; Dep. Dir B. KHANDDOLGOR.

Voice of Mongolia: Ulan Bator (CPOB 365); e-mail densmaa9@yahoo.com; internet www.vom.mn; external service of Mongolradio; broadcasts in Russian, Chinese, English and Japanese on short wave; Dir B. NARANTUYAA.

AE and JAAG Co: Amryn Gudamj 2, Ulan Bator (POB 20/126); tel. (11) 352463; fax (11) 326545; e-mail aejaag@magicnet.mn; f. 1996; broadcasts for 4.5–5 hours daily; CEO Z. ALTAI.

FM 96.3 Avtoradio: Ulan Bator.

FM 98.9 Hi Fi (Hit First): Khair Tokhoi Co Bldg, Chingisiin Örgön Chölöö 10/1, Ulan Bator; tel. and fax (11) 330989; e-mail hifi@hi-fi.mn; internet www.hi-fi.mn.

FM 99.3 Ineemseglel (Smile): Central Palace of Culture, Sükhbaatar District, Ulan Bator; tel. 99147994; fax (11) 319789; Dir KH. IKHBAYAR.

FM 100.1 Kiss: Ulan Bator; tel. (11) 312234.

FM 100.5 Minii Mongol (My Mongolia): Central Palace of Culture, Sükhbaatar District, Ulan Bator; tel. (11) 323599.

FM 100.9 Khökh Tenger (Blue Sky Radio): Mongolian National Television Bldg, Chingeltei District, Ulan Bator; tel. (11) 320522; broadcasts for 12 hours Mon. to Sat. and shorter hours on Sun; short-wave transmitter on 4,850 kHz; Dir L. AMARZAYAA.

FM 101.7 Niisleliin Radio: Narny Titem, 5th Sub-District, Chingeltei District, Ulan Bator; tel. 70110981; fax (11) 322472; Dir U. BULGAN.

FM 102.1 Ekh Oron (Homeland): Central Palace of Culture, Sükhbaatar District, Ulan Bator; tel. (11) 327383; fax (11) 322472; operated by the Open Information Foundation.

FM 103.1: Ulan Bator; BBC World Service Relay.

FM 103.6 Dotno (Inside): Amaryn Gudamj, Sükhbaatar District, Ulan Bator; tel. 70110632; TV-9's radio station; Dir M. BAYANZUL.

FM 104 Life: Alaska Centre, 13th Sub-District, Bayanzürkh District, Ulan Bator; tel. (11) 463782.

FM 104.5 Ger Büliin Radio (Family Radio): Mamba Datsan, Bayanzürkh District, Ulan Bator; tel. (11) 461045; fax (11) 452987.

FM 105 Tany Derged (Near You): Central Palace of Culture, Sükhbaatar District, Ulan Bator; tel. (11) 319789.

FM 105.5 Info Radio: Russian Foundation, Od Plaza, Sükhbaatar District, Ulan Bator; tel. (11) 319492; fax (11) 313687; internet www.inforadio.mn; Dir B. TÜVSHINTÖGS.

FM 106.6: Democratic Party Bldg, Chingisiin Örgön Chölöö, Ulan Bator; tel. (11) 329353; Voice of America news and information in Mongolian, English lessons and music.

FM 107.5 Shine Dolgion (New Wave): Namyanjügiin Gudamj 40, Bayanzürkh District, Ulan Bator; tel. and fax (11) 452444; e-mail info@fm1075.mn; internet www.fm1075.mn; relays of Voice of America broadcasts in English and Russian, entertainment programmes; Dir TS. ARIUNAA.

There are seven long- and short-wave radio transmitters and 49 FM stations in 23 towns.

Television

Mongolian Television Association: Ulan Bator; mems: BTV, Channel 25, Eagle, Education, NTV, SBN, TM, TV5, TV8, TV9 and UBS.

Mongolian National Public Television (MNTV): Mongolian National Television, Khuvisgalyn Zam 3, Bayangol District, Ulan Bator (CPOB 365); tel. (11) 327214; fax (11) 328939; e-mail mrtv@magicnet.mn; f. 1967; daily 16-hour transmissions, except Mon; short news bulletins in English Mon., Wed. and Fri; part of Public Radio and Television; Dir TSAGAANY OYUUNDARI.

Bolovsrol (Education) TV Channel: Bayangol District, Behind Mongolian National Public TV Bldg, Ulan Bator; tel. (11) 300722; fax (11) 300710; e-mail develop@edutv.mn; f. 2005; broadcasts 20–22 hours a day; Gen. Dir NATSAGDORJIIN SANJ.

C-1: Supermarket No. 1, Tömörchnii Gudamj, Chingeltei District, Ulan Bator; tel. (11) 312126; fax (11) 313651; f. 2006; daily 17-hour transmissions; news link with Reuters; Dir BEN MOYLE.

Channel 25: Mongol News Bldg, Juulchny Gudamj, Chingeltei District, Ulan Bator; tel. (11) 321989; daily 18-hour transmissions; Dir ZORIGIIN ALTAI; Gen. Man. AYUUSHIIN AVIRMED.

Eagle Broadcasting Co: Erkhüüd Centre, Lkhagvasürengiin Gudamj, Ulan Bator; tel. (11) 463088; fax (11) 463087; internet www.eagle-tv.mn; f. 1994; several news bulletins a day; Christian message; commenced operations in 1996; broadcasts restarted 2005 after two years off air; Pres. THOMAS TERRY; Dir BALJINNYAMYN BAYARSAIKHAN.

Khiimori Co: Bldg 3A, No. 2 Combined Clinical General Hospital, Ulan Bator; tel. (11) 458531; fax (11) 458569; f. 1995; cable TV service provider.

New TV (NTV): Media Group Co Bldg, Chingisiin Örgön Chölöö 14, Khan-Uul District, Ulan Bator; tel. 77117777; fax 77110002; internet www.ntv.mn; Dir M. ULAMBADRAKH.

Sansar KATV: Sansar Bldg, Enkh Taivny Örgön Chölöö, 3rd Sub-District, Chingeltei District, Ulan Bator; tel. (11) 313752; fax (11) 313770; e-mail sansarll@magicnet.mn.

SBN (Supervision Broadcasting Network): Khuvisgalchdyn Gudamj, Bayangol District, Ulan Bator; tel. (11) 301641; fax (11) 301643; Exec. Dir B. BAT-ORGIL.

MONGOLIA

Supervision KATV: No. 3 Bldg, Enkh Taivny Örgön Chölöö, 3rd Sub-District, Bayanzürkh District, Ulan Bator; tel. (11) 455082; fax (11) 320396; internet www.supervision.mn.

TV-5: Sapporo Centre, 1st Sub-District, Songinokhairkhan District; tel. (11) 680327; fax (11) 680326; e-mail feedback@tv5.mn; internet www.tv5.mn; daily 18-hour transmissions; Editor-in-Chief E. DAGIIMAA.

TV-8: Amaryn Gudamj, 8th Sub-District, Sükhbataar District, Ulan Bator; tel. (11) 315680; fax (11) 318006; Dep. Dir A. TSASCHIKHER.

TV-9: Media Holding Co, TV9 Television Bldg, Ulan Bator; tel. 70110628; fax (11) 70110631; e-mail programm@tv9.mn; internet www.tv9.mn; f. 2003; 24-hour broadcaster; Dir Ts. ENKHBAT.

UBS (Ulaanbaatar Broadcasting System): Khasbaatar Gudamj 47, Bayangol District,Ulan Bator; tel. (11) 301973; fax (11) 368108; e-mail ext_affairs@ubs.mn; internet www.ubs.mn; f. 1992; fmrly state-owned; privatized in 2005; three channels; Dir-Gen. LKHAGVA-DORJIIN BALKHJAV.

Cable television companies (29 in total) operate in 19 towns. There are local television stations in Ulan Bator (three), Darkhan, Sükhbaatar and Baganuur. Chinese, Kazakh, Russian, German and French television services are among those that can also be received.

Finance

(cap. = capital; res = reserves; dep. = deposits; m. = million; brs = branches; amounts in tögrög, unless otherwise stated)

BANKING

Before 1990 the State Bank was the only bank in Mongolia, responsible for issuing currency, controlling foreign exchange and allocating credit. With the inauguration of market reforms in Mongolia in the early 1990s, the central and commercial functions of the State Bank were transferred to the newly created specialized commercial banks: the Bank of Capital Investment and Technological Innovation and the State Bank International. In May 1991 the State Bank became an independent central bank, and the operation of private, commercial banks was permitted. In November 1996 amendments were made to banking legislation to improve the regulation and supervision of commercial banks, and two major insolvent banks were liquidated. Restructuring of the banking sector subsequently continued.

Central Bank

Bank of Mongolia (Mongolbank): Baga Toiruu 9, Ulan Bator; tel. (11) 310413; fax (11) 311471; e-mail ad@mongolbank.mn; internet www.mongolbank.mn; f. 1924; est. as the State Bank of the Mongolian People's Republic; cap. 5,000m., res 103,504m., dep. 2,369,433m. (Dec. 2009); Pres. LKHNAASÜRENGIIN PÜREVDORJ; Chief Vice-Pres. BOLDYN JAVKHLAN.

Other Banks

Capital Bank: Sambuugiin Gudamj 43, Chingeltei District, Ulan Bator; tel. (11) 315500; fax (11) 310833; e-mail info@capitalbank.mn; internet www.capitalbank.mn; cap. 8,007m., res 16.5m., dep. 66,751.1m. (Dec. 2009); f. 1990; 99% owned by Bishrelt Holding Co; CEO AGVAANJAMBYN ARIUNBOLD; Dep. CEO S. ALTANGEREL; 24 brs.

Capitron Bank: Capitron Bank Bldg, Usny Gudamj 4, Sükhbaatar District, Ulan Bator; tel. (11) 328373; fax (11) 328372; e-mail info@capitronbank.mn; internet www.capitronbank.mn; f. 2001; cap. 8,000.5m., res 333m., dep. 58,530.3m. (Dec. 2009); 49% owned by B. Medree, 46% by P. Mönkhsaikhan; CEO MÖNKHSAIKHAN PUREVJAV.

Chinggis Khaan Bank: New Century Plaza, Chingisiin Örgön Chölöö 15, Sükhbaatar District, Ulan Bator (POB 28/418); tel. (11) 318367; fax (11) 318373; e-mail bank@ckbank.mn; internet www.ckbank.mn; f. 2001; est. by Millennium Securities Management Ltd and Coral Sea Holdings Ltd (British Virgin Islands); cap. 39,373m., dep. 98,820m. (Dec. 2009); Chair. SERGEI GROMOV; CEO (vacant).

Credit Bank: Sükhbaataryn Talbai 20A, Sükhbaatar District, Ulan Bator; tel. (11) 319038; fax (11) 321897; e-mail info@creditbank.mn; internet www.creditbank.mn; f. 1997; owned by Basic Element Finance Ltd, Cyprus; cap. 8,090m., res 20,594m., dep. 12,363m. (July 2006); Propr OLEG DERIPASKA; Exec. Dir B. TSENGEL.

Erel Bank: Chingisiin Örgön Chölöö, Khan-Uul District, Ulan Bator; tel. and fax (11) 344550; fax (11) 343387; e-mail info@erelbank.mn; internet www.erelbank.mn; f. 1997; cap. 4,000m., res 45.9m., dep. 3,163.4m. (Dec. 2005); Owner BADARCHIIN ERDENEBAT; CEO GOMBOJAVYN DORJ.

Golomt Bank of Mongolia: Golomt Bank Central Bldg, Sükhbaataryn Talbai, Ulan Bator; tel. (11) 311530; fax (11) 311958; e-mail mail@golomtbank.com; internet www.golomtbank.com; f. 1995; est. by Mongolian-Portuguese IBH Bodi International Co Ltd; cap. 21,934.1m., res −25.9m., dep. 848,564m. (Dec. 2009); Chair. DANZANDORJIIN BAYASGALAN; Exec. Dir L. BADAMTSETSEG; 14 brs.

Khadgalamjiin Bank (Savings Bank): Kholboochdyn Gudamj 4, Chingeltei District, Ulan Bator; tel. (11) 310103; fax (11) 327467; e-mail contact@savingsbank.mn; internet www.savingsbank.mn; f. 1996; est. as Ardyn Bank; owned by MD Securities Co, a consortium of Chinggis Khaan Bank, Mongol Daatgal Consortium and Bratsk People's Bank (Russian Federation); took over Mongol Shuudan Bank (Post Bank) 2010; cap. 8,031.0m., res 2,544.5m., dep. 65,986.0m. (Dec. 2007); Chair. SH. BATKHÜÜ; Exec. Dir O. KHÜRELBAATAR; 60 brs.

Khan Bank (KhAAN or Agricultural Bank): Söüliin Gudamj 25, Sükhbaatar District, Ulan Bator (POB 44/192); tel. (11) 332333; fax (11) 70117023; e-mail info@khanbank.com; internet www.khanbank.com; f. 1991; purchased by H and S Securities (Japan) in Feb. 2003; cap. 12,994m., res 14,591.7m., dep. 869,790m. (Dec. 2009); owned by Itochu Corpn and Tavan Bogd Group; Chair. HIDEO SAWADA; CEO SIMON MORRIS; Dep. Exec. Dir R. MÖNKHTUYAA; 380 brs.

National Investment Bank: City Plaza Bldg, Söüliin Gudamj 6 Sükhbaatar District, Ulan Bator; tel. (11) 321995; fax (11) 330913; 55% owned by D. Dagvadorj, 22% by UB Diversified Ltd, and 22% by Firebird Funds; f. 2006; Dir DOLGORSÜRENGIIN SUMYAABAZAR.

State Bank (Töriin Bank): Baga Toiruu 7/1, 1st Sub-District, Chingeltei District, Ulan Bator; fax (11) 330595; e-mail contact@statebank.mn; internet www.statebank.mn; f. 1999; cap. 14,666.7m., res 11,971m., dep. 159,806m. (Dec. 2008); fmrly Zoos Bank; name changed as above when nationalized in 2009; Exec. Dir J. OTGONBILEG.

Trade and Development Bank of Mongolia (Khudaldaa Khögjliin Bank): Cnr of Juulchny Gudamj 7 and Baga Toiruu 12, Ulan Bator; tel. (11) 312362; fax (11) 327028; e-mail hqbranch@tdbm.mn; internet www.tdbm.mn; f. 1991; carries out Mongolbank's foreign operations; cap. 6,610.1m., res 14,619.2m., dep. 670,631.5m. (Dec. 2009); 76% equity bought by Banca Commerciale (Lugano) and Gerald Metals (Stanford, CT), May 2002; Chair. D. ERDENEBILEG; Pres. RANDOLPH KOPPA; CEO BALBARYN MEDREE.

Transport and Development Bank (Trans Bank): Juulchny Gudamj, 1st Sub-District, Chingeltei District, Ulan Bator; tel. and fax 70110206 (mobile); e-mail info@transbank.mn; internet www.transbank.mn; owned by Russian interests; Propr D. ENKHTUYAA; CEO A. E. NOVOZHILOV; Chair. DANZANBALJIRYN ENKHTAIVAN.

Ulaanbaatar City Bank: Sükhbaataryn Gudamj 16, Ulan Bator (POB 46/370); tel. (11) 319041; fax (11) 330508; e-mail info@ubcbank.mn; internet www.ubcbank.mn; f. 1998; est. by Capital City with assistance from the Bank of Taipei (Taiwan); cap. 5,349m., dep. 50,064m. (June 2005); Propr L. ERDENEBILEG; CEO A. ENKHMEND.

XacBank: Yörönkhii Said Amaryn Gudamj, Sükhbaatar District, Ulan Bator (POB 46/721); tel. (11) 318185; fax (11) 328701; e-mail bank@xacbank.mn; internet www.xacbank.org; f. 2001; cap. 13,290.6m., res 13,605.4m., dep. 148,804.1m. (Dec. 2009); owned by Mercy Corps; Chair. CHULUUNY GANBOLD; Exec. Dir DÜGERSÜRENGIIN BAT-OCHIR.

Bankers' Association

Mongolian Bankers' Association: Chingisiin Örgön Chölöö 17, Sükhbaatar District, Ulan Bator (CPOB 101); tel. (11) 314105; fax (11) 314104; e-mail monba@mongolnet.mn; internet www.mba.mn; f. 2000; Pres. BALBARYN MEDREE; Exec. Dir ZUUNAIN SHAGDARSÜREN.

STOCK EXCHANGE

Stock Exchange: Sükhbaataryn Talbai 2, Ulan Bator; tel. (11) 313511; fax (11) 325170; e-mail info@mse.mn; internet www.mse.mn; f. 1991; Exec. Dir KH. ALTAI (acting).

INSURANCE

Ard Daatgal: Tavan Bogd Plaza, Amaryn Gudamj 8, Ulan Bator; tel. (11) 331185; fax (11) 330083; est. with Omni Whittington Guernsey.

Bodi Daatgal Co: Bodi Tower, Jigjidjavyn Gudamj, Ulan Bator; tel. (11) 323444; fax (11) 326535; e-mail bodi@bodiinsurance.mn; internet www.bodiinsurance.mn; Dir L. BOLDKHUYAG.

Ganzam Insurance: Mongolian Railways (MTZ), Zamchdyn Gudamj, Ulan Bator; tel. and fax (11) 242643.

MIG Daatgal: MIG Bldg, 1st Sub-District, Chingeltei District, Ulan Bator; tel. (11) 330130; fax (11) 330131; e-mail mig@magicnet.mn; internet www.mig.mn; f. 1997; privately owned; Pres. and CEO JANDAVYN BAT-ORSHIKH.

Mongol Daatgal: Enkh Taivny Örgön Chölöö 13, Ulan Bator; tel. (11) 313615; fax (11) 310347; e-mail insurance@mongoldaatgal.mn; internet www.mongoldaatgal.mn; f. 1934; sold Dec. 2003 to consortium formed by Angara-SKB and Chinggis Khan Bank; Chair. BADARCHIIN ENKHBAT; CEO. T. BATZÜL.

MONGOLIA

Directory

National Life Daatgal: Financial Service Corpn, Ambassador Bldg, Enkh Taivny Örgön Chölöö 17A/5, 1st Sub-District, Sükhbaatar District, Ulan Bator (POB 48/35); tel. 70110784; fax 70110781; e-mail national.life@fscomongolia.mn; internet www.fscomongolia.mn; Exec. Dir B. BATBAYAR.

Nomin Daatgal: State Department Store, Enkh Taivny Örgön Chölöö, Ulan Bator; tel. (11) 330023; fax (11) 325528; e-mail insurance@nomin.net; internet www.insurance.nomin.net.

Ochir Undraa Daatgal: Söüliin Gudamj 15/2, 4th Sub-District, Sükhbaatar District, Ulan Bator (POB 44/398); tel. (11) 324248; fax (11) 326466; e-mail insurance@ochir-undraa.com; internet www.ochir-undraa.com.

Tüshig Daatgal Co: Zoos Bank Bldg, Baga Toiruu, Chingeltei District, Ulan Bator; tel. (11) 316119; fax (11) 330578; e-mail insurance@tushigdaatgal.mn; internet www.tushigdaatgal.mn; Exec. Dir M. JALAVDORJ.

UB Daatgal Co: Baga Toiruu 37B, Sükbataar District, Ulan Bator (POB 46/385); tel. (11) 324828; fax (11) 322362; e-mail sanal_huselt@ubdaatgal.mn; internet www.ubdaatgal.mn.

INSURERS' ASSOCIATION

Mongolian Insurers' Association: Ulan Bator; Pres. G. KHONGOR.

Trade and Industry

GOVERNMENT AGENCIES

Energy Directorate: Ulan Bator; f. 2008; subordinate to Minister of Mineral Resources, Fuel and Power; Head TSENDSÜRENGIIN BAYARBAATAR.

Foreign Capital Investment Directorate: Ulan Bator; f. 2008; subordinate to Minister of External Relations; Head BAASANKHÜÜGIIN GANZORIG.

Mineral Resources Directorate: Government Bldg 12, Barilgachdyn Talbai 3, Chingeltei District, Ulan Bator; tel. (11) 263701; fax (11) 310370; internet mram.gov.mn; f. 2008; subordinate to Minister of Mineral Resources, Fuel and Power; Head DORJPÜREVIIN BATKHUYAG.

Nuclear Energy Directorate: Ulan Bator; f. 2008; subordinate to Prime Minister; Head SODNOMYN ENKHBAT.

Petroleum Directorate: Ulan Bator; f. 2008; subordinate to Minister of Mineral Resources, Fuel and Power; Head DASHZEVEGIIN AMARSAIKHAN.

Small and Medium Enterprise Directorate: Ulan Bator; f. 2008; subordinate to Minister of Food, Agriculture and Light Industry; Head TS. NYAM-OSOR.

DEVELOPMENT ORGANIZATIONS

Agricultural Equipment, Science and Technology Production Association: Ulan Bator; devt of farm machinery, including biogas plants; Exec. Dir J. TÜMEN.

Economics and Market Research Centre: Government Bldg 1, J. Sambuugiin Gudamj 11, Ulan Bator; tel. (11) 324258; fax (11) 324620; e-mail emrc@mongolchamber.mn; internet www.mongolchamber.mn; Dir J. BOZKHÜÜKHEN.

Mongolian Business Development Agency: Yörönkhii Said Amaryn Gudamj, Ulan Bator (CPOB 458); tel. (11) 311094; fax (11) 311092; internet www.mbda-mongolia.org; f. 1994; Gen. Man. D. BAYARBAT.

Mongolian Development Research Centre: Rm 50, Baga Toiruu 13, Chingeltei District, Ulan Bator (POB 20A/63); tel. and fax (11) 315686; internet www.mdrc.mn; f. 1998; Chair. TSEDENDAMBYN BATBAYAR.

National Centre for Renewable Energy: Ulan Bator; Dir N. ENEBISH.

CHAMBERS OF COMMERCE

Mongolian Franchising Council of the Mongolian National Chamber of Commerce and Industry: MNCCI Bldg, Makhatma Gandiin Gudamj, Khan-Uul District, Ulan Bator; tel. (11) 327176; fax (11) 324620; e-mail munkhnast@mongolchamber.mn; internet www.mongolchamber.mn; Chair. DEMBEREL SAMBUU.

Mongolian National Chamber of Commerce and Industry: Makhatma Gandiin Gudamj 11, 1st Sub-District, Khan-Uul District, Ulan Bator 38; tel. (11) 327176; fax (11) 324620; e-mail chamber@mongolchamber.mn; internet www.mongolchamber.mn; f. 1960; responsible for establishing economic and trading relations, contacts between trade and industrial organizations, both at home and abroad, and for generating foreign trade; organizes commodity inspection, press information, and international exhibitions and fairs at home and abroad; registration of trademarks and patents; issues certificates of origin and of quality; Chair. SAMBUUGIIN DEMBEREL.

INDUSTRIAL AND TRADE ASSOCIATIONS

Association of Exporters of Livestock, Raw Materials and Semi-Processed Products: Ulan Bator; Exec. Dir B. TÖRMÖNKH.

Association of Mongolian Sewn Goods and Knitwear Products Manufacturers: Ulan Bator; Pres. N. DASH-ÖLZII.

Building Materials Industry Association: Ulan Bator; Exec. Dir O. LKHAGVADORJ.

Financial Market Association: Ulan Bator; Pres. Ö. GANZORIG.

Funeral Services Association: Ulan Bator; f. 2008; Pres. G. IDERMAA.

Grain Producers' Association: Ulan Bator; Pres. TSEVEENJAVYN ÖÖLD.

Mongolian Air Traffic Controllers' Association: National Air Traffic Services, Chinggis Khaan International Airport, Buyant-Ukhaa, Ulan Bator; tel. (11) 282008; fax (11) 282108; e-mail monatca@mcaa.gov.mn.

Mongolian Association of Container and Packaging Makers and Users: Ulan Bator; Pres. DEMBERELIIN OTGONBAATAR.

Mongolian Builders' Association: Block 3, Urt Tsagaan, Chingeltei District, Ulan Bator; tel. 99112636; fax (11) 318685; Pres. MÖNKHBAYARYN BATBAATAR.

Mongolian Coal Association: Ulan Bator; tel. and fax (11) 328582; e-mail coalasso@yahoo.com; Exec. Dir T. NARAN.

Mongolian Entrepreneurs' Association: Ulan Bator; Chair. B. GARMAASÜREN.

Mongolian Exporters' Association: Ulan Bator; Exec. Dir D. GALSANDORJ.

Mongolian Farmers' and Flour Producers' Association: Agro-Pro Business Centre, 19th Sub-District, Bayangol District, Ulan Bator; tel. (11) 300114; fax (11) 362875; e-mail agropro@magicnet.mn; f. 1997; research and quality inspection services in domestic farming and flour industry; Pres. SHARAVYN GUNGAADORJ.

Mongolian Felt Producers' Association: Ulan Bator; Vice-Pres. G. ALZAKHGÜI.

Mongolian Food Producers' Association: Ulan Bator; Pres. L. DAMDINSÜREN.

Mongolian Foodstuffs Traders' Association: Ulan Bator; Exec. Dir KH. GIIMAA.

Mongolian Industrial Geologists' Association: Ulan Bator; Pres. D. BAT-ERDENE.

Mongolian Institute of Internal Auditors: Ulan Bator; tel. (11) 312773; e-mail miia@bizcon.mn; internet www.bizcon.mn/miia; Pres. L. OTGONBAYAR.

Mongolian International Financial Market Association: Ulan Bator; Pres. Ö GANZORIG.

Mongolian Marketing Association: Ulan Bator; tel. 99096400 (mobile); fax 70113756; e-mail bold_dag@yahoo.com; Pres. B. DAVAASÜREN; Exec. Dir D. BOLD.

Mongolian Meat Association: Ulan Bator; Pres. SH. BATKHÜÜ.

Mongolian Metallurgists' Association: School of Technology, Darkhan-Uul Province; tel. (37) 24723; Pres. TS. MÖNKHJARGAL.

Mongolian Mining Engineers' Association: Ulan Bator; Pres. KH. VLADIMIR.

Mongolian Motor Transporters' United Association: Ulan Bator; f. 1996; est. as Mongolian National Society of Motor Transport Owners, amalgamated 2005 with the Mongoltrans Transporters' Asscn; 39 mem. businesses and orgs incl. the Private Bus Owners' Asscn, Taxi Owners' Asscn and Large & Small Bus Asscn; Pres. GAVAAGIIN BATKHÜÜ.

Mongolian National Construction Association: Ulan Bator; Exec. Dir D. TSEND.

Mongolian National Industrialists' Association: Ulan Bator; Pres. NAMJAAGIIN DASHZEVEG.

Mongolian National Mining Association: 501 Geosan Company Bldg, Ikh Surguuliin Gudamj 8, Ulan Bator; tel. (11) 314877; fax (11) 330032; e-mail info@miningmongolia.mn; internet www.miningmongolia.mn; f. 1994; provides legal protection and represents views of mining interests in govt policy and devt of mineral sector; Pres. DAMJINY DAMBA; Exec. Dir NAMGARYN ALGAA.

Mongolian Pig Farmers' Association: Ulan Bator; Exec. Dir M. ZOLZAYAA.

Mongolian Power Engineers' Association: Ulan Bator; Pres. R. GANJUUR.

Mongolian PR Association: Ulan Bator; Chair. D. BOLDKHUYAG.

MONGOLIA

Mongolian Printing Works Association: Ulan Bator; Pres. E. Myagmarpürev.

Mongolian Skins and Hides Production Association: Ulan Bator; Pres. B. Enkh-Amgalan.

Mongolian Surveyors' Association: Ulan Bator; Pres. D. Dondov.

Mongolian Timber Industry Association: Mon-Frukt Co, 1st Sub-District, Bayangol District, Ulan Bator (POB 36/51); tel. 91111191; fax (11) 343145; e-mail tsogoots@gmail.com.

Mongolian Wool and Cashmere Federation: Khan-Uul District, Ulan Bator; tel. (11) 341871; fax (11) 342814; Pres. D. Gankhuyag; Vice-Pres. G. Yondonsambuu.

National Information and Communications Association: Ulan Bator; Pres. D. Bolor.

Petroleum Gas Association: Ulan Bator; f. 2005; Pres. Sharavyn Gungaadorj.

Pharmacology Organizations United Association: Ulan Bator; Pres. B. Tuyaa.

EMPLOYERS' ORGANIZATIONS

Employers' and Owners' United Association: Rm 401, 4th Floor, Mongolian Youth Association 'B' Bldg, Ulan Bator; tel. (11) 326513; Exec. Dir B. Sembeejav.

Federation of National Small and Medium Enterprise Managers: Ulan Bator; Exec. Dir P. Altan-Erdene.

Federation of Professional Business Women of Mongolia: Ulan Bator; tel. and fax (11) 315638; e-mail mbpw@mongolnet.mn; f. 1992; provides education, training, and opportunities for women to achieve economic independence; Pres. Ochirbatyn Zayaa; 7,000 mems, 14 brs.

Forestry and Timber Production Managers' Association: Ulan Bator; tel. (11) 341310; e-mail info@fmwa.mn; internet fmwa .mn; f. 2010; Head D. Baasanbyamba.

Immovable Property (Real Estate) Business Managers' Association: Ulan Bator; Pres. J. Byambadorj.

Mongolian Employers' Federation: Baga Toiruu 44a, Ulan Bator 48; tel. and fax (11) 325635; e-mail monef@magicnet.mn; internet www.monef.mn; f. 1990; fmrly Private Industry Owners' Association; 8,100 mems; Pres. Kh. Ganbaatar.

Mongolian Food Trade Managers' Association: Ulan Bator; Dir D. Namsrai.

Mongolian Gas Managers' Association: Ulan Bator; Chair. N. Baatarjav.

Mongolian Management Association: 102 and 202, Bldg B, The Academy of Management, Chingisiin Örgön Chölöö, Khan Uul District, Ulan Bator; tel. (11) 341570; e-mail info@mamo.mn; internet www.eng.mamo.mn; Pres. Dagvadorjiin Tserendorj.

Private Business Owners' Association: Tsatsral Mon Bldg, 1st Sub-District, Songinokhairkhan District, Ulan Bator; tel. (11) 682905; Pres. T. Nyamdorj.

Private Employers' Association: Ulan Bator; Pres. O. Natsagdorj.

Refuse Disposal Business Managers' Association: Ulan Bator; Chair. Sh. Baasanjav.

Scrap Business Managers' Association: Ulan Bator; Dir S. Altantsetseg.

Securities Exchange Managers' Association: Ulan Bator; Exec. Dir L. Tseveenravdan.

Small and Medium Business Directors' United Association: Ulan Bator; Pres. P. Altan-Erdene.

UTILITIES

Electricity

Darkhan-Selenge TsTS Co: Darkhan; management of electric power network in northern Mongolia; Exec. Dir Ch. Enkhbold.

Dulaan Tsakhilgaan Stants-IV Co: 20th Sub-District, Bayangol District, Ulan Bator; tel. (11) 631768; Mongolia's biggest power station; Exec. Dir B. Tseveen.

Ulaanbaatar Power Distribution Network: Chingisiin Örgön Chölöö 45, Ulan Bator; tel. (11) 341674; fax (11) 343061; e-mail info@ ubedn.mn; internet www.ubedn.mn; Exec. Dir Dashjamtsyn Battulga.

Water

Dulaany Süljee Co: Ulan Bator; tel. (11) 343047; e-mail engineer@ dhc.mn; internet www.dhc.mn; supervision of hot water district heating network in Ulan Bator; Exec. Dir D. Byamba-Ochir.

USAG: Khökh Tengeriin Gudamj 5, Ulan Bator; tel. (11) 455055; fax (11) 450120; e-mail usag@magicnet.mn; supervision of water supply network in Ulan Bator; Chair. Osoryn Erdenebaatar.

IMPORT AND EXPORT ORGANIZATIONS

Agrotekhimpeks: Ulan Bator; imports agricultural machinery and implements, seed, fertilizer, veterinary medicines and irrigation equipment.

Altjin: Ulan Bator; company imports and distributes oil and oil products; manages distilleries; fmrly part of APU; Dir G. Altan.

Arisimpex: Ulan Bator; tel. (11) 343007; fax (11) 343008; exports hides and skins, fur and leather goods; imports machinery, chemicals and accessories for leather, fur and shoe industries; Pres. A. Tserenbaljid.

Avtoimpeks: Ulan Bator; f. 1934; state-owned; international trader in motor vehicles; Exec. Dir S. Chuluunbat.

Barter and Border: Khuvisgalchdyn Gudamj, Ulan Bator; tel. (11) 324848; barter and border trade operations.

Khorshoololimpeks: Tolgoit, Ulan Bator (CPOB 262); tel. (11) 332926; fax (11) 331128; f. 1964; exports skins, hides, wool and furs, handicrafts and finished products; imports equipment and materials for housing, and for clothing and leather goods; Dir L. Ölziibuyan.

Kompleksimport: Enkh Taivny Gudamj 7, Ulan Bator; tel. and fax (11) 688948; f. 1963; imports consumer goods, foodstuffs, sets of equipment and turnkey projects; training of Mongolians abroad; state-owned pending planned privatization; cap. 3,500m. tögrög.

Makhimpeks: 4th Sub-District, Songinokhairkhan District, Ulan Bator; tel. (11) 632471; fax (11) 632517; f. 1946; abattoir, meat processing, canning, meat imports and exports; 51% share privatized in 1999; cap. 7,800m. tögrög; Exec. Dir G. Büdragchaa.

Materialimpex: Teeverchdiin Gudamj 2b, Bayangol District, Ulan Bator; tel. (11) 363803; fax (11) 367904; e-mail matimpex@mongolnet .mn; internet www.materialimpex.com; f. 1957; exports cashmere, wool products, animal skins; imports glass, roofing material, dyes, sanitary ware, metals and metalware, wallpaper, bitumen, wall and floor tiles; partially privatized Feb. 1999, but most shares still state-owned; Gen. Dir B. Zorig; 126 employees.

Medimpex International: Khan Holdings Bldg, Olimpiin Gudamj, 1st Sub-District, Sükhbaatar District, Ulan Bator; tel. (11) 310429; fax (11) 318254; e-mail medimpex@mcs.mn; internet www .medimpex.mcs.mn.

Metallimpeks (Metalimpex): Ulan Bator; tel. (11) 331154; Dir D. Ganbat.

Monfa Trade: Monfarma Trade Co, Bldg 69, First 40,000, 4th Sub-District, Sükhbaatar District, Ulan Bator; tel. and fax (11) 324420; e-mail monfatrade@mongol.net; procurement and distribution of pharmaceuticals.

Mongoleksport Co Ltd: Government Bldg 7, 8th Fl., Erkh Chölöönii Talbai, Ulan Bator; tel. (11) 329234; fax (11) 327884; exports wool, hair, cashmere, mining products, antlers, skins and hides; Dir-Gen. D. Chimeddambaa.

Mongolemimpex: Teeverchdiin Gudamj 39, Ulan Bator; tel. (11) 322695; fax (11) 323877; e-mail info@meic.mn; internet www.meic .mn; f. 1923; procurement and distribution to hospitals and pharmacies of drugs and surgical appliances; Dir-Gen. Batbayaryn Bolormaa.

Mongolimpeks: Khuvisgalchdyn Örgön Chölöö, Ulan Bator; tel. (11) 326081; exports cashmere, camels' wool, hair, fur, casings, powdered blood and horn, antlers, wheat gluten, alcoholic drinks, cashmere and camels' wool knitwear, blankets, copper concentrate, souvenirs, stamps and coins; imports light and mining industry machinery, scientific instruments, chemicals, pharmaceuticals and consumer goods; state-owned; Dir-Gen. Dorjpalamyn Dökhömbayar.

Monnis International: Monnis Tower, Chingisiin Örgön Chölöö 15, Ulan Bator; tel. (11) 311687; fax (11) 323248; e-mail info@monnis .com; internet www.monnis.com; f. 1998; est. as distributor for Nissan Motor Co Ltd; other commercial interests incl. geology, mining, energy, construction, freight forwarding, foreign trade, communications, banking and aviation; CEO B. Chuluunbaatar; 700 employees, 8 subsidiaries.

Monnoos: Ulan Bator (POB 36/450); tel. (11) 343201; fax (11) 342591; e-mail monnoos@mongolnet.mn; wool trade enterprise; Dir Sanjinjin Bat-Oyuun.

Monos Cosmetics: Monos Group, Bldg 25, 2nd 40,000, 2nd Sub-District, Chingeltei Division, Ulan Bator; tel. and fax (11) 633257; e-mail cosmetics@monos.mn; internet www.monoscosmetics.mn; f. 1990; production, export and import of cosmetics; Chair. and CEO Baldandorjiin Erdenekhishig; Exec. Dir Kh. Solongo; 90 employees.

Monos Pharm Trade: Monos Group, Namyanjügiin Gudamj 23, 18th Sub-District, Bayanzürkh District, Ulan Bator; tel. and fax (11) 450054; fax (11) 463158; internet www.monos.mn; f. 1990; production, export and import of medicine, medical equipment and health food; Dir-Gen. Luvsangiin Erdenechimeg; 280 employees.

MONGOLIA

NIK (Neft Import Kontsern): Petrovis Co Bldg, Yörönkhii Said Amaryn Gudamj, Sükhbaatar District, Ulan Bator; tel. (11) 321277; fax (11) 327001; e-mail nic@nic.com.mn; internet www.nic.com.mn; Exec. Dir S. SÜKHBAATAR.

Noosimpeks: Ulan Bator; tel. (11) 341577; exports scoured sheep's wool, yarn, carpets, fabrics, blankets, mohair and felt boots; imports machinery and chemicals for wool industry.

Nüürs: Ulan Bator; tel. (11) 327428; exports and imports in coal-mining field; Man. D. DÜGERJAV.

Packaging: Tolgoit, Ulan Bator; tel. (11) 31053; exports raw materials of agricultural origin, sawn timber, consumer goods, unused spare parts and equipment, and non-ferrous scrap; imports machinery and materials for packaging industry, and consumer goods.

Petrovis: Petrovis Co Bldg, Yörönkhii Said Amaryn Gudamj 7, Sükhbaatar District, Ulan Bator; tel. (11) 327051; fax (11) 327288; e-mail info@petrovis.mn; internet www.petrovis.mn; oil products importer and distributor; in Feb. 2004 acquired the 80% state-owned shares in the country's biggest distributor NIK (Neft Import Kontsern) for US $8.5m; Exec. Dir D. ENKHCHIMEG.

Raznoimpeks: 3rd Sub-District, Bayangol District, Ulan Bator; tel. (11) 329465; fax (11) 329901; f. 1933; exports wool, cashmere, hides, canned meat, powdered bone, alcoholic drinks, macaroni and confectionery; imports cotton and woollen fabrics, silk, knitwear, shoes, fresh and canned fruit, vegetables, tea, milk powder, acids, paints, safety equipment, protective clothing, printing and packaging paper; state-owned pending planned privatization; cap. 6,100m. tögrög; Exec. Dir Ts. BAT-ENKH.

Tekhnikimport: Ulan Bator; tel. (11) 685149; imports machinery, instruments and spare parts for light, food, wood, building, power and mining industries, road-building and communications; state-owned; Dir-Gen. D. GANTSETSEG.

Tüshig Trade Co Ltd: Enkh Taivny Örgön Chölöö, Ulan Bator (POB 44/481); tel. (11) 314062; fax (11) 314052; exports sheep and camel wool, and cashmere goods; imports machinery for small enterprises, foodstuffs and consumer goods; Dir-Gen. D. GANBAATAR.

Whole Sale: Songinokhairkhan District, Ulan Bator; tel. 99112100; fax (11) 632119; e-mail boch30@mobinet.mn; f. 1952; wholesale trader; privately owned; Dir-Gen. OCHBADRAKHYN BALJINNYAM.

YuniGaz: Petrovis Co Bldg, Yörönkhii Said Amaryn Gudamj 8, Sükhbaatar District, Ulan Bator; tel. (11) 314018; fax (11) 327253; e-mail info@unigas.mn; internet www.unigas.mn; petrol, diesel and LPG distributor; Dir-Gen. B. TÜMENTSOGT.

CO-OPERATIVES

Association of Private Herders' Co-operatives: Ulan Bator (POB 21/787); tel. (11) 633601; fax (11) 325935; e-mail mongolherder@magicnet.mn; f. 1991; Pres. R. ERDENE; Exec. Dir Ts. MYAGMAR-OCHIR.

Central Association of Consumer Co-operatives: Ulan Bator; tel. and fax (11) 329025; f. 1990; wholesale and retail trade; exports animal raw materials; imports foodstuffs and consumer goods; Chair. G. MYANGANBAYAR.

Mongolian Association of Production Co-operatives: Urt Tsagaan, Khudaldaany Gudamj 12, Chingeltei District, Ulan Bator; tel. (11) 310956; e-mail cumic@mol.mn.

Mongolian Association of Savings and Credit Co-operatives: Bldg 2, State Property Committee, Chingeltei District, Ulan Bator; tel. (11) 313665; Pres. SH. GOOKHÜÜ.

Mongolian Co-operatives Development Centre: Ulan Bator; Dir DANZANGIIN RADNAARAGCHAA.

National Association of Mongolian Agricultural Co-operative Members: Enkh Taivny Örgön Chölöö, 18A/1, Ulan Bator; tel. (11) 453535; fax (11) 458899; e-mail info@namac.mn; internet www.namac.mn; f. 1992; Pres. NADMIDYN BAYARTSAIKHAN.

Union of Mongolian Production and Services Co-operatives: Bldg 16, 2nd 40,000, 3rd Sub-District, Chingeltei District, Ulan Bator (POB 46/470); tel. (11) 327583; fax (11) 328446; e-mail umpscoop@hotmail.com; f. 1990; Pres. SAMDANY ENKHTUYAA.

TRADE UNIONS

Confederation of Mongolian Trade Unions: Sükhbaataryn Talbai 3, Ulan Bator; tel. (11) 327253; fax (11) 322128; e-mail mpcd@cmtu.mn; internet www.cmtu.mn; brs throughout the country; Chair. SAINKHÜÜGIIN GANBAATAR; Sec.-Gen. M. GANAA.

Mongolian United Confederation of Journalists: Ulan Bator; Pres. T. BAASANSÜREN.

Transport

MTT (Mongol Transport Team): MTT Bldg, 5th Sub-District, Bayangol District, Ulan Bator; tel. (11) 689000; fax (11) 684953; e-mail mtt@mtteam.mn; internet www.mtteam.mn; international freight forwarding by air, sea, rail and road; offices in Beijing, Berlin, Moscow and Prague.

Tuushin Co Ltd: Tuushin Bldg, Yörönkhii Said Amaryn Gudamj, Sükhbaatar District, Ulan Bator; tel. (11) 312092; fax (11) 325570; e-mail tuushin@magicnet.mn; internet www.tuushin.mn; f. 1990; international freight forwarders; transport and forwarding policy and services, warehousing, customs agent; tourism; offices in Beijing, Moscow and Prague; Dir-Gen. N. ZORIGT.

RAILWAYS

Railway Authority of Mongolia: Chinggis Ave, Sükhbaatar District, Ulan Bator; tel. 976243404; fax 976243405; e-mail osorjamaa.e@railway.gov.mn; internet www.railway.gov.mn; Chair. TÖGSÖÖGIIN BATBOLD.

Mongolyn Tömör Zam (Mongolian Railways): Ulan Bator; f. 2009; state-owned limited co, est. by Erdenes Mongol and Russian Railways (50% each) to modernize Ulan Bator Railway.

Ulan Bator Railway: Söüliin Gudamj 42, Bayangol District, Ulan Bator (CPOB 376); tel. and fax (21) 243012; internet www.ubtz.mn; f. 1949; jt-stock co (equal shares) with Russia; Dir TUVDENGIIN OCHIRKHÜÜ; Chairs O. N. MOROZOV, AMARJARGALYN GANSÜKH.

External Lines: from the Russian frontier at Naushki/Sükhbaatar (connecting with the Trans-Siberian Railway) to Ulan Bator and on to the Chinese frontier at Zamyn-Üüd/Erenhot, connecting with Beijing (total length 1,110 km).

Branches: from Darkhan to Sharyn Gol coalfield (length 63 km); branch from Salkhit near Darkhan, westwards to Erdenet (Erdenetiin-ovoo open-cast copper mine) in Bulgan Province (164 km); from Bagakhangai to Baganuur coal-mine, south-east of Ulan Bator (96 km); from Khar Airag to Bor-Öndör fluorspar mines (60 km); from Sainshand to Züünbayan oilfield (63 km).

Planned railway construction 2011–13: broad-gauge lines (1,040 km) from Tavantolgoi coal mine to Züünbayan, and from Sainshand to Baruun-Urt and Choibalsan (existing link with the Trans-Siberian); standard-gauge line (80 km) from Oyuutolgoi copper mine to Gants Mod on the Chinese border.

Eastern Railway, linking Mongolia with the Trans-Siberian and Chita via Borzya; from the Russian frontier at Solovyevsk to Choibalsan (238 km), with branch from Chingis Dalan to Mardai uranium mine near Dashbalbar (110 km), possibly inactive.

IFFC (International Freight-forwarding Centre of Mongolian Railways): Mongolian Railway Headquarters, Zamchdyn Gudamj 1, Bayangol District, Ulan Bator (CPOB 376); tel. (11) 312509; fax (11) 313165; e-mail iffc@railcom.mn; internet www.iffc.mn; international freight forwarding.

ROADS

Mongolia divides its road system into state-grade and country-grade roads. State-grade roads (of which there were 11,000 km in 2005) run from Ulan Bator to provincial centres and from provincial centres to the border. Country-grade roads account for the remaining roads, but they are mostly rough cross-country tracks. The total length of hard-surfaced roads reached 2,600 km in 2007. To mark the millennium, the Government announced its decision to construct a new east–west road, linking the Chinese and Russian border regions via Ulan Bator. In 2011 some sections of the Millennium Road were to be realigned to avoid areas of permafrost.

Motor Roads Directorate: Ulan Bator; govt agency; Dir B. ENKHTÖR.

Motor Transport Directorate: Ulan Bator; govt agency; Dir B. TSENGEL.

SHIPPING

In 2003 the Government opened a shipping register. By May 2010 more than 1,700 vessels had been registered, with a tonnage exceeding 5m. g.r.t.

Maritime Administration: Ulan Bator; state-owned co, operating until 2010 with Singapore-based Maritime Chain as its agent; Dir DAMDINGIIN GALSANDONDOG.

CIVIL AVIATION

Civil aviation in Mongolia, including the provision of air traffic control and airport management, is the responsibility of the Main Directorate of Civil Aviation, which provides air traffic and airport management services. It also supervises the Mongolian national airline (MIAT) and smaller operators such as Khangarid and Tengeriin Ulaach, which operate local flights. Aeroflot (Russia) and Air

MONGOLIA

China operate flights to Ulan Bator (Chinggis Khaan International Airport). Mongolia has 14 airfields with surfaced runways, and 31 with dirt strips.

Ulan Bator's new international airport, with a 3,600m runway, is under construction at Khöshigiin Khöndii, south of the capital; it will have a 37-km motorway link. Due to enter into service in 2015, the airport will have twice the capacity of Chinggis Khaan (Buyant-Ukhaa) airport, where high ground limits the use of the runway to arrivals and departures from and to the north.

Main Directorate of Civil Aviation: Chinggis Khaan International Airport, Buyant-Ukhaa, Ulan Bator; tel. (11) 282051; fax (11) 313151; e-mail webmaster@mcaa.gov.mn; internet www.mcaa.gov.mn; Dir-Gen. SANJAAJAVYN BATMÖNKH.

A-Jet Aviation: Olimpiin Gudamj, 1st Sub-District, Sükhbaatar District, Ulan Bator (POB 46/202); tel. (11) 318480; fax (11) 319780; e-mail aviation@ajet.mn; internet www.aviation.ajet.mn; f. 2000; fmrly Central Mongolia Airways; 3 Mi-8 helicopters for tourist travel, aerial surveys and photography; Exec. Dir NYAMBARYN LKHAMJAV.

Aero Mongolia Co Ltd: Chinggis Khaan International Airport, Buyant-Ukhaa, Ulan Bator (POB 34/105); tel. (11) 379616; fax (11) 379943; e-mail management@aeromongolia.mn; internet www.aeromongolia.mn; f. 2001; began operations June 2003; scheduled international flights to Irkutsk, Russia, and Hohhot, China, and scheduled internal flights to five provincial centres and Juulchin's South Gobi tourist camp by Fokker-50 aircraft; twice-weekly flights by Fokker-100 to the Republic of Korea inaugurated in Feb. 2006; Dir B. JARGALSAIKHAN.

Blue Sky Aviation: Door 2, Apt S-61, 1st Sub-District, Sükhbaatar District, Ulan Bator; tel. (11) 312085; fax (11) 322857; e-mail bsa@maf-europe.org; internet www.blueskyaviation.mn; jt venture of Mission Aviation Fellowship and Exodus International; operates charter flights and medical emergency services; f. 1999; Dir TOM MASON; Operations Man. BATSUURIIN BAYARJIN.

Eznis (Easiness) Airways: Naiman Zokhis Bldg, Söüliin Gudamj, Sükhbaatar District, Ulan Bator; tel. (11) 313689; fax (11) 314258; internet www.eznis.com; f. 2006; operates two SAAB 340B aircraft on internal routes; twice-weekly flights to Hailar (northern China) inaugurated in July 2009, operating via Choibalsan from Sept. 2009; CEO SUKHBAATAR MUNKHSUKH.

Khangarid: Room 210, MPRP Bldg, Baga Toiruu 37/1, Ulan Bator; tel. (11) 320138; fax (11) 311333; e-mail hangard_air_co@magicnet.mn; domestic and international passenger and freight services; Dir L. SERGELEN.

Mongolian Civil Air Transport (MIAT): MIAT Bldg, Chinggis Khaan International Airport, Buyant-Ukhaa, Khan-Uul District, Ulan Bator; tel. (11) 379935; fax (11) 379919; e-mail contact@miat.com; internet www.miat.com; f. 1956; scheduled services to Moscow, Beijing, Seoul, Osaka, Berlin and Tokyo; internal flights to Mörön and Khovd resumed with Boeing aircraft in July 2009; Chair. D. MAKHBAL; Exec. Dir TS. ORKHON.

MIAT Cargo: Gobi 44 Bldg, 5th Sub-District, Sükhbaatar District, Ulan Bator; tel. (11) 313389; fax (11) 313809; e-mail horol@magicnet.mn.

Tengeriin Ulaach (Sky Horse Aviation): Chinggis Khaan International Airport, Buyant-Ukhaa, Khan-Uul District, Ulan Bator (POB 34/17); tel. (11) 282023; fax (11) 379765; e-mail skyhorsenew@mbox.mn; internal helicopter transport for tourists and business passengers; Dir L. TÖMÖR.

Trans-Ölgii: Ölgii, Bayan-Ölgii Province; f. 2006; operates one leased An-24 on Ölgii–Ulan Bator route twice a week.

Tourism

The country's main attractions are its scenery, wildlife and historical relics. A foreign tourist service bureau was established in 1954, but the tourism sector remained undeveloped. At March 2008 there were 248 tour operators, 326 hotels (with 8,000 beds) and 30 tourist camps (with 6,400 beds). Of the 30 or more hotels in Ulan Bator, all but four are relatively small, and in the peak summer season there is a shortage of rooms. The outlying tourist centres (Terelj, South Gobi, Öndör-Dov and Khujirt) have basic facilities. Total tourist arrivals rose from 492,836 in 2009 to 557,414 in 2010, when Chinese and Russian tourists were again most numerous. Tourism revenue reached US $222m. in 2010.

Juulchin World Tours Corporation: Jamyan Günii Gudamj 5/3, Ulan Bator; tel. (11) 319401; fax (11) 319402; e-mail info@juulchinworld.com; internet www.juulchinworld.com; f. 1954; offices in Berlin, Fairfax, VA and Tokyo; tours, trekking, safaris, jeep tours,

Directory

expeditions; Pres. SHAGDARSÜRENGIIN NERGÜI; Gen. Man. D. BATNASAN.

Mongolian Adventure Tourism Association: Ulan Bator; Pres. B. JIYAANDORJ.

Mongolian Tourism Association: Rm 318, Building of the Mongolian Trade Unions Confederation, Sükhbaataryn Talbai, Ulan Bator; tel. (11) 323026; fax (11) 327820; e-mail info@travelmongolia.org; internet www.travelmongolia.org; internet www.mnto.org; Pres. BAYARSAIKHANY TSEVELMAA; Vice-Pres. N. ERDENEBAT.

Defence

As assessed at November 2010, according to the International Institute for Strategic Studies, Mongolia's defence forces numbered 10,000, comprising an army of 8,900 (of whom 3,300 were thought to be conscripts), 800 air defence personnel and 300 construction troops. There was a paramilitary force of about 7,200, comprising 1,200 internal security troops and 6,000 border guards under the Ministry of Justice and Home Affairs. Each year a small quota of men can purchase exemption from conscription. In 2010 a total of 1,709 men paid 2.3m. tögrög each. Army reserves numbered an estimated 137,000. Military service is for 12 months (for males aged 18–25 years), but only about 40% of conscripts are found fit for service. There are financial inducements for regular service soldiers, especially those in the best trained and equipped 'élite' battalions, some of whom have served with coalition forces in Iraq and on UN peacekeeping operations elsewhere.

Mongolia has restarted annual military exercises with the Russian army, during which its Soviet-made equipment is serviced and updated. In 2010 Russia was reported to be supplying small numbers of BTR-80 personnel carriers and T-72 tanks, Mi-24M attack helicopters, MiG-29 fighters and missiles.

Defence Expenditure: Defence spending for 2011 was projected at 103,060m. tögrög (some 3.7% of total planned government expenditure in that year).

Chief of Staff of the Mongolian Armed Forces: Maj.-Gen. TSERENDEJIDIIN BYAMBAJAV.

Deputy Chief of Staff, Commander General Purpose Troops: Brig.-Gen. RADNAABAZARYN SÜKHBAT.

Deputy Chief of Staff, Director of Peacekeeping: Brig.-Gen. B. BAYARMAGNAI.

Commander of Air Defence Troops: Brig.-Gen. TOJOONY DASHDELEG.

Education

General education is state-administered. Eleven-year education is compulsory, and 12-year education is being introduced. In the 2009/10 school year there were an esimated 522,100 pupils receiving general education, and teaching staff totalled 26,100. The 44 state and 19 private vocational schools, with a total of 44,700 students in 2009/10, train personnel for the service industries, including electricians, drivers and machine operators.

The Mongolian State University has three faculties (biology; chemistry; geography and geology) and nine schools (including foreign languages, mathematics, computer science, law, economics and social sciences). The School of Foreign Service provides diplomatic training. A total of 89,000 students were enrolled at the 10 state and four private universities in 2009/10.

In 2009/10 there were 32 state-owned and 96 private institutes of other higher education; 26,300 students were enrolled at the state institutes and 49,100 at the private institutes of higher education, excluding those studying in Russia, Germany, Turkey, the USA and elsewhere. The student enrolment abroad was estimated at 9,550 in 2009/10.

In July 2010 the Government approved a project for reform of higher education during 2010–12, which included structural change such as the consolidation of some colleges and institutes (e.g. the merger of Ulaanbaatar University and the Higher School of Trade and Industry with the Mongolian State University) and an improved admissions policy in order to raise teaching and research standards to international levels.

The state budget allocation to the Ministry of Education, Culture and Science for 2011 was 655,318.8m. tögrög (23.5% of planned budgetary expenditure).

MONTENEGRO

Introductory Survey

LOCATION, CLIMATE, LANGUAGE, RELIGION, FLAG, CAPITAL

Montenegro is situated in the central Balkan peninsula, in south-eastern Europe. Montenegro has frontiers with Bosnia and Herzegovina to the west and north-west, Serbia to the north, Kosovo to the east, and Albania to the south-east, and a short frontier with Croatia in the south-west. There is a western coastline along the Adriatic Sea (part of the Mediterranean). Montenegro has a rugged mountainous terrain, being dominated by the Black Mountains (Crna Gora), from which the country takes its name. The climate is Mediterranean near the coast, and continental inland. Mountainous areas have a colder climate with heavy snowfall in winter. Average temperatures range from between −7°C (19.4°F) and 23°C (73.4°F) inland, and between 11°C (51.8°F) and 28°C (84.2°F) on the coast. Montenegro's mountainous regions receive some of the highest amounts of rainfall in Europe. The 2007 Constitution describes the principal language as Montenegrin, with the Cyrillic and Latin alphabets of equal status. Serbian, Bosnian, and Croatian (all of which, in common with Montenegrin, were formerly described as variants of Serbo-Croat) and Albanian are also in official use. The principal religion is Orthodox Christianity, and there are significant Roman Catholic and Muslim communities. The national flag (proportions 1 by 2) is red, with a golden coat of arms depicting a double-headed eagle. Podgorica is the capital of Montenegro. The historical capital is Cetinje.

CONTEMPORARY POLITICAL HISTORY

Historical Context

After the Second World War, Montenegro became one of the six constituent republics of the federal Yugoslavia established by the Communist Party of Yugoslavia (later the League of Communists of Yugoslavia—LCY) under Josip Broz (Tito). Montenegrins were strongly represented among the ranks of the LCY and of the Yugoslav People's Army. Montenegro generally supported the Serbian reassertion of dominance within Yugoslavia after the death of Tito in the 1980s. Institutionally, this was helped by the installation of a new party leadership in the republic, following demonstrations during 1988 in favour of the Serbian leader, Slobodan Milošević. Subsequent reforms transformed the Skupština Crne Gore (Assembly of Montenegro) into a unicameral body of 125 members and replaced Montenegro's collective Presidency with a directly elected state President. The elections, in December 1990, represented a victory for the ruling League of Communists of Montenegro (subsequently renamed the Democratic Party of Socialists of Montenegro—DPS), which secured 83 seats in the new legislature, while its presidential candidate, Momir Bulatović, became President, after a second round of voting. In February 1991 Bulatović invited one of his party colleagues, Milo Đukanović, to head the republican Government. The third member of the new Montenegrin leadership was Svetozar Marović, the chairman of the Skupština.

The onset of armed conflict in Yugoslavia prompted Montenegro to adopt a pragmatic response to the disintegration of the federation. Although Montenegro adopted a declaration of state sovereignty on 18 October 1991 and a new Constitution in November, it remained committed to the federation with Serbia, confirming this conclusively in a referendum in March 1992. The two republics announced a new federal Constitution, creating the Federal Republic of Yugoslavia (FRY), which came into effect on 27 April, and which was a continuation of the old state, but effectively acknowledged the secession of the other four federal units. A new Montenegrin Constitution was introduced on 12 October and, early in 1993, the disposition of power was confirmed by the re-election of Bulatović as State President and the continuation of Đukanović as premier. Meanwhile, another Montenegrin, Radoje Kontić, became the federal Prime Minister.

Relations between Montenegro and Serbia deteriorated from the mid-1990s, particularly as a result of perceived Serbian encroachments on Montenegrin autonomy, in particular the attempts of Serbian leader Milošević to disassemble separate republican defence and foreign policy structures. Montenegro also wished to obtain international aid, which entailed its pursuit of a distinct foreign policy, often at variance with that of the federal authorities, while Montenegrin economic policy was also more supportive of a free market than that of Serbia. Increasingly, however, the principal division in Montenegrin politics became between the republican presidency and premiership. Bulatović became more and more identified by his support for Milošević. In February 1997, conversely, Đukanović publicly declared Milošević unfit to hold public office, and in March he resisted the demands of Bulatović that he dismiss all anti-Milošević ministers in the Montenegrin Government. The ruling DPS (which again won Montenegrin legislative elections in November 1996) split into two factions during 1997, as a result of Bulatović's support for the Serbian leader (who became the federal Yugoslav President in July). In July supporters of Đukanović within the DPS voted to remove Bulatović from the party leadership. Bulatović and Đukanović became the leading candidates in the Montenegrin presidential election of October. Đukanović won the second round of voting, with 50.8% of the votes cast.

Đukanović was inaugurated as the President of Montenegro in January 1998, amid violent protests from supporters of Bulatović (who refused to accept the result as legitimate). A compromise agreement on early legislative elections in May was reached, pending which a transitional Government, led by the Đukanović faction of the DPS, was formed in February. Bulatović's faction refused to participate and renamed itself the Socialist People's Party of Montenegro (SPPM). In the elections, held in May, the DPS won an outright majority, and a coalition Government, led by Filip Vujanović, was formed in July. Montenegro had become increasingly suspicious of Serbia's intentions, particularly with the appointment of Bulatović as federal Prime Minister in May. Bulatović proceeded to purge many Montenegrin officials from federal institutions. Montenegro refused to acknowledge the administration of Bulatović, suspending all links with the federal Government in August.

Domestic Political Affairs

Relations between the federal Yugoslav partners continued to deteriorate during 1999. Escalating civil conflict in the Serbian province of Kosovo, a majority of the population of which comprised ethnic Albanians, led to aerial bombardment of Yugoslavia by forces of the North Atlantic Treaty Organization (NATO, see p. 368) in March–June. Despite suffering damage during the NATO offensive, Montenegro continued to distance itself from Serbian military action; in March Montenegro refused to recognize the state of war declared by the federal Government at the commencement of the NATO bombardment, and in April Đukanović refused to place Montenegrin security forces under federal military command, as ordered by President Milošević.

In the aftermath of the open conflict in Kosovo, the Yugoslav federation became increasingly unstable. The Government of Montenegro proposed the replacement of the federal system with an association of two states, threatening a referendum on full independence if Milošević did not agree; in October 1999 the Skupština enacted a citizenship law, which was viewed as progress towards such an arrangement. Economically, Montenegro attempted to separate itself from the isolated Serbian economy; in November Montenegro replaced the depreciating Yugoslav dinar with the German Deutsche Mark as its official currency (the federal Constitutional Court declared the measure illegal in January 2000, to little effect). Serbia confirmed the economic rupture by imposing a partial blockade and then, in January 2000, introduced a ban on the export of foodstuffs to Montenegro, followed by a full economic embargo in March. While most of the Montenegrin Government preferred a looser confederation with Serbia, fears of Milošević increasing his political influence or of Serbian military action (such as the federal army's seizure of control over Montenegro's main airport in December 1999) further escalated tensions.

Partial municipal elections in Montenegro in mid-2000 indicated the divided state of public opinion. In Podgorica, the DPS-led ruling coalition commanded an overall majority, but the

MONTENEGRO

Bulatović-led alliance remained robust, while the pro-independence Liberal Alliance of Montenegro (LAM) did not perform strongly. Attempts to reform federal institutions so as to weaken the influence of Montenegro in the federation were viewed with alarm, and the Skupština voted against the proposals in July. However, the anti-Milošević stance of Đukanović became less significant following the change of regime in Serbia in October (the ruling Montenegrin coalition having boycotted the federal polls of the previous month), which included Bulatović's resignation as federal Prime Minister. Đukanović began to advocate full independence for Montenegro, urging a referendum on the issue. This prompted the pro-federation People's Party of Montenegro to withdraw from the ruling republican coalition, precipitating legislative elections in April 2001. The DPS-led coalition won 36 of the 77 seats, the SPPM-led alliance 33 and the LAM six. Vujanović was reappointed as premier. Meanwhile, negotiations about a new form of federal association were ongoing, and, from November, were mediated by the European Union (EU, see p. 270). The federal and republican leaderships signed a framework agreement on confederation on 14 March 2002, providing for the maintenance of separate economies and state structures by each of Serbia and Montenegro, which would be united by a shared presidency and legislature in charge of foreign and defence policies. Crucially, Montenegro had the right to refer the issue of independence to a referendum after three years. Later in March the LAM resigned from the Government in protest at the agreement. The Skupština approved the accord on 9 April; however, Vujanović's inability to form a new coalition administration caused him to dissolve the legislature in July and schedule further elections, in the hope of obtaining a more substantial parliamentary majority.

On 20 October 2002 the DPS-led, pro-independence ruling coalition, the Democratic List for a European Montenegro, won 39 of the 75 seats in the republican legislature. Together for Changes, which had opposed looser union with Serbia and was led by the SPPM (under a new leadership), retained 30 seats. Vujanović, who continued to act as premier until a new coalition was formed, was elected Speaker of the Skupština on 5 November. Vujanović became acting President of the Republic of Montenegro 20 days later, when Đukanović resigned so that he could be nominated to form a government. A dispute over the allocation of ministerial portfolios with the DPS's ally, the Social Democratic Party of Montenegro (SDP), delayed the formalization of the coalition, but the new Government headed by Đukanović was finally approved by the legislature on 8 January 2003. Meanwhile, both the SPPM and the pro-independence LAM had organized a boycott of the presidential election, held on 22 December 2002, which was consequently won by Vujanović, with 83.7% of the votes cast, but with those votes amounting to less than the one-half of the total electorate legally required to validate the result. Vujanović won 82.0% of votes in the repeated poll held on 9 February 2003, but this poll, too, was declared invalid, as only 47% of the electorate participated, prompting the Skupština to abolish the regulation on participation in advance of a further attempt to elect a President. Vujanović was duly elected President on 11 May, with 62.9% of the votes cast (about 48% of the electorate participated). His nearest rival was Miodrag Živković of the LAM, who received 30.7%. Upon his election, Vujanović pledged to schedule a referendum on independence for Montenegro after a period of three years.

Meanwhile, on 29 January 2003 the Skupština approved the new arrangements for confederation with Serbia. On 4 February the federal parliament formally adopted a Constitutional Charter, thereby transforming Yugoslavia into the State Union of Serbia and Montenegro. A Skupština, President (former Montenegrin parliamentary Speaker and DPS leader, Marović) and Prime Minister of the State Union were elected in late February and March. In July the Skupština adopted a new Montenegrin flag and anthem, and declared 13 July (the anniversary of the 1878 recognition of Montenegrin independence by the Congress of Berlin and of the 1941 start of a popular revolt against the occupying Axis powers) a national holiday.

Politicians in Serbia and Montenegro agreed that the EU should set the conditions for and supervise the conduct of any referendum on Montenegrin independence. In February 2006, amid much controversy, the EU announced that any proposal of Montenegrin independence would require the approval of 55% of those voting (with a minimum rate of participation of 50% of the registered electorate), in order to secure international recognition. The Government, which favoured a simple majority, reluctantly agreed to the conditions. Legislation providing for a referendum to be held on 21 May was duly enacted on 1 March. In April the Government formally presented to the Serbian Government a guarantee of equal status for Serbian citizens within Montenegro in the event of independence.

Independence

Two days after the referendum of 21 May 2006, the electoral authorities declared Montenegro to have voted in favour of independence. With a participation rate of over 86%, some 55.5% of votes cast at the referendum were in favour of independence and 44.5% against, thereby narrowly fulfilling the EU criteria. The EU and other international organizations declared the vote to have been free and fair. The Skupština duly declared Montenegro independent on 3 June. Serbia, which declared itself to be the successor state to the State Union of Serbia and Montenegro on 5 June, officially recognized Montenegro's independence in mid-June and established diplomatic relations one week later. Montenegro was admitted to the Organization for Security and Co-operation in Europe (see p. 385) on 22 June and to the UN on 28 June, acceding to the Geneva Conventions on 2 August. A new Ministry of Defence formally assumed responsibility for all military units of the Union on Montenegrin territory, while in July agreement was reached on the division of the financial rights and obligations of the former State Union (Montenegro was to receive 5.9% of the convertible currency and gold reserves of Serbia and Montenegro). On 11 July President Vujanović announced that legislative and local elections had been scheduled for September.

The legislative elections on 10 September 2006 were won outright, by the ruling coalition of the DPS and the SDP, which secured 41 of the 81 seats in an expanded Skupština. The SPPM-led alliance only obtained 11 seats (eight for the SPPM itself), being displaced as the largest opposition grouping by the Serbian List, led by Andrija Mandić of the Serb People's Party of Montenegro, which took 12 seats. A new, pro-European party, the Movement for Changes, also obtained 11 seats. The Liberal Party of Montenegro (the successor organization to the LAM, which split in 2004), in alliance with the Bosniak Party of Montenegro, secured three seats. In October 2006 Đukanović announced that he would not seek to continue his premiership, as he wished to develop his business interests. (He had been accused of involvement with organized crime, and was under investigation by the Italian authorities, mainly in connection with large-scale illicit tobacco trade in the Balkans.) The Minister of Justice, Željko Šturanović, became the agreed Prime Minister-designate. The appointment of a new Government, headed by Šturanović, was duly approved by the new Skupština on 10 November. The legislature was subsequently also to act as a constituent assembly and to debate a new constitution.

The Government declared its aspirations to join NATO and the EU. (In July 2006 the EU had agreed to adapt negotiations on a Stabilization and Association Agreement—SAA—that had commenced with the former State Union to the new situation of two independent states.) On 14 December Montenegro (together with Serbia, and Bosnia and Herzegovina) was admitted to NATO's 'Partnership for Peace' (see p. 371) programme. On 18 January 2007 Montenegro officially became a member of the World Bank, also joining the IMF and the other associated institutions. Montenegro initialled the SAA with the EU on 15 March. (The adoption of a new constitution in accordance with EU standards was required for the official signing of the SAA and its ratification by EU member states.) On 11 May Montenegro was admitted to the Council of Europe (see p. 250).

After prolonged acrimonious debate (particularly in the areas of state symbols, and the designation of the official language and religious communities), a new Constitution was finally approved by 55 of the 76 deputies present in the Skupština on 19 October 2007, narrowly achieving the requisite two-thirds' majority of votes; the Constitution was officially promulgated on 22 October. Serbian parties denounced the new Constitution (which described the main official language as Montenegrin, in place of Serbian), and the Serbian List issued a declaration repudiating its ratification. The adoption of the Constitution allowed the official signature of the SAA at a meeting of EU foreign ministers in the same month.

In mid-January 2008 the parliamentary Speaker announced that the forthcoming presidential election would take place on 6 April. On 31 January Šturanović resigned as Prime Minister, on grounds of ill health. On 29 February the appointment of Đukanović as premier and of his Government (which remained unchanged from the previous administration) was narrowly approved, with 41 votes cast, in the Skupština. (Although the

MONTENEGRO

Introductory Survey

Italian investigation into organized crime allegations continued, Đukanović's immunity from prosecution was restored by his return to office.)

Vujanović's re-election to the presidency on 6 April 2008, with 51.9% of the votes cast, further consolidated the strength of the DPS. Mandić won 19.6% of the votes, while the reformist leader of the Movement for Changes, Nebojša Medojević, obtained 16.7%; and Srđan Milić of the SPPM received 11.9%. The rate of voter participation was estimated at about 69% (considerably higher than in 2003). Vujanović was inaugurated for a second term on 21 May. In October the Montenegrin Government's recognition of Kosovo as a sovereign state prompted pro-Serbian opposition parties (which demanded that a referendum be organized on the issue) to organize a protest in Podgorica. On 15 December 2008 Montenegro submitted an official application for EU membership (see Foreign Affairs).

The 2009 legislative elections

In January 2009 the governing coalition (which had already agreed that legislative elections, due in 2010, be brought forward to September 2009) submitted a proposal to the Skupština that the elections take place that March in order to allow the administration a stronger mandate to fulfil Montenegro's commitments in the EU integration process. On 26 January the Skupština voted in favour of ending its mandate to allow an early poll; on the following day Vujanović announced that the legislative elections would be conducted on 29 March. Later in January Mandić merged his Serb People's Party of Montenegro with the People's Socialist Party to form a new party, New Serbian Democracy, and initiated discussions with the SPPM in an effort to form a broad alliance against Đukanović's ruling coalition. (However, in the event, the SPPM contested the elections separately.)

The elections to the Skupština on 29 March 2009 were contested by a total of 16 parties and alliances; Đukanović's For a European Montenegro coalition secured a decisive victory, with 51.9% of the votes cast and 48 seats in the chamber, while the SPPM won 16.8% of the votes and 16 seats, New Serbian Democracy 9.2% of the votes and eight seats, and the Movement for Changes 6.0% of the votes and five seats. Four other groups each obtained one seat. A participation rate of about 66.2% of the electorate was recorded. The EU Commissioner for Enlargement, Olli Rehn, praised the democratic organization of the poll, but urged the Government to reform electoral legislation. The President of the SDP, Ranko Krivokapić, was re-elected parliamentary Speaker in early May. Following endorsement of his premiership, a new Government, formed by Đukanović, was approved in the Skupština Crne Gore in early June; the six new ministers included former President of the State Union of Serbia and Montenegro Svetozar Marović, who became a Deputy Prime Minister. In December Đukanović confirmed that he planned to relinquish his office before the end of the Government's mandate.

In March 2010 Vujanović announced that local elections would be conducted to 14 municipal councils on 23 May, despite opposition demands for a later date. A motion of no confidence in the Government, proposed by the Movement for Changes, on the grounds that it had failed to combat corruption and organized crime, and to address the economic situation effectively, was defeated in the Skupština on 13 April. At the local elections on 23 May, the DPS won a majority in seven of the contested 14 municipal councils, and was to form a coalition, mostly with the SDP, in five others, including in Podgorica; an SPPM-led opposition alliance secured control of two councils.

Recent developments: new Government

In October 2010 the mandate of the Governor of the Central Bank, Ljubiša Krgović, was ended, after he criticized the provision of state assistance for the loss-making Prva Banka, in which the brother of Prime Minister Đukanović held a majority share; the Skupština approved Vujanović's nomination of Radoje Žugić (hitherto Director of the Pension and Disability Insurance Fund) to replace Krgović. On 21 December Đukanović tendered his resignation as premier (but was to remain DPS Chairman); Deputy Prime Minister and Minister of Finance Igor Lukšić was nominated by the DPS as his successor. On the same day Marović also resigned his government post, following the initiation of an investigation into the illegal construction of a tourist complex on the Zavala peninsula in Budva. Later in December the Mayor of Budva municipality, Rajko Kuljaca, his deputy Dragan Marović (who was the brother of former Deputy Prime Minister Marović) and eight other officials were arrested on suspicion of abuse of office in connection with the investigation. On 29 December the Skupština endorsed the nomination of Lukšić and the establishment of a new Government (comprising the same coalition parties as previously) under his premiership. Milorad Katnić replaced Lukšić as Minister of Finance in the new administration. In March 2011 small anti-Government demonstrations, organized through social networking internet sites, were staged in central Podgorica, in protest at the economic situation and the perceived failure of the authorities to combat organized crime. Also in March Kuljaca, Dragan Marović and nine other suspects were formally charged with abuse of office.

Foreign Affairs

Regional relations

In March 2008 Prime Minister Đukanović and his Croatian counterpart, meeting in Zagreb, declared that the question of the demarcation of the maritime boundary between the two countries around the Prevlaka peninsula, near the Croatian town of Dubrovnik, (which was regulated by a 2002 interim agreement) would be referred to the International Court of Justice at The Hague, the Netherlands. In October 2008 Montenegro (together with the FYRM) announced official recognition of Kosovo as a sovereign state, following its declaration of independence on 17 February; the decision was welcomed by the USA and the EU, while Serbia expressed outrage and expelled the Montenegrin ambassador in reprisal. In May 2009 President Vujanović visited the Serbian capital, Belgrade, in an effort to improve bilateral relations; Serbian President Boris Tadić made a reciprocal visit to Montenegro in June. In October Serbia finally accepted the Montenegrin Government's nomination of a new ambassador. In January 2010 Serbia recalled its ambassador, in protest at Montenegro's decision to establish diplomatic relations with Kosovo; the Serbian ambassador returned to Podgorica in February.

Other external relations

Following independence in June 2006, Montenegro's admission to international organizations proceeded rapidly (see Domestic Political Affairs). At a NATO summit meeting, held in Bucharest, Romania, in April 2008, Montenegro (together with Bosnia and Herzegovina) was invited to enter into an intensified dialogue towards membership. (According to a subsequent opinion poll, however, only around one-quarter of Montenegrins supported NATO membership for the country.) In April 2009 the EU Council of Ministers approved consideration of Montenegro's EU membership application (which was submitted in December 2008); EU officials emphasized that further reforms of the state administration and judiciary, and the instigation of further sustained measures against corruption and organized crime, were necessary before the opening of accession negotiations could be agreed. (It was reported that several EU member states, notably the Netherlands, opposed a rapid decision to grant Montenegro EU candidate status.) At the end of November 2009 it was announced that Montenegro (together with Serbia and the former Yugoslav republic of Macedonia—FYRM) had met EU requirements for the abolition of visa requirements, which were thereby removed from the citizens of these countries with effect from late December. Also in December Montenegro was granted a NATO Membership Action Plan. The Stabilization and Association Agreement that Montenegro signed with the EU in October 2007 (see above) entered into effect on 1 May 2010, following its ratification by all member states. In November the European Commission issued a report recommending that Montenegro be accorded the status of an official candidate, although further progress on strengthening the rule of law and curbing organized crime was deemed necessary. On 17 December the European Council accordingly granted Montenegro candidate status for EU membership. In March 2011 the European Parliament adopted a resolution commending Montenegro's progress towards EU integration, but also urging continuing reform efforts.

CONSTITUTION AND GOVERNMENT

Montenegro became independent of the former State Union of Serbia and Montenegro on 3 June 2006, following a national referendum held on 21 May. The Constitution of Montenegro was adopted by the legislature on 19 October 2007 and was officially promulgated on 22 October. Legislative power is vested in the 81-member Skupština Crne Gore (Assembly of Montenegro), which is directly elected for a period of four years. Executive power is vested in the Government and judicial power in the courts of law. The President is directly elected for a term of five years, and is restricted to two terms in office. Constitutionality and legality are protected by the Constitutional Court. The President nominates the Prime Minister for approval by the Skupština. The Prime Minister proposes the composition of the Government to the Skupština. The Supreme Court is the highest court in Montenegro. For administrative purposes, Montenegro is divided into 21 municipalities.

REGIONAL AND INTERNATIONAL CO-OPERATION

Montenegro is a member of the Organization for Security and Co-operation in Europe (OSCE, see p. 385), the Council of Europe (see p. 250), and the Central European Free Trade Agreement (CEFTA, see p. 446).

Montenegro joined the UN on 28 June 2006.

ECONOMIC AFFAIRS

In 2009, according to estimates by the World Bank, Montenegro's gross national income (GNI), measured at average 2007–09 prices, was US $4,089m., equivalent to $6,550 per head (or $13,130 per head on an international purchasing-power parity basis). During 2000–09, it was estimated, the population decreased at an average annual rate of 0.6%, while gross domestic product (GDP) per head increased, in real terms, by an average of 4.2% per year during 2000–09. Overall GDP increased, in real terms, at an average annual rate of 3.6% in 2000–09; real GDP increased by 6.9% in 2008, but declined by 7.0% in 2009.

Agriculture (including hunting, forestry and fishing) contributed 10.0% of GDP in 2009, and the sector engaged 1.6% of the employed labour force in that year. The principal crops are potatoes, maize and wheat. The cultivation of fruit (particularly grapes, plums, oranges and tangerines) and vegetables is also important. According to the World Bank, agricultural output increased by an annual average of 0.8% during 2000–09; output increased by 11.1% in 2009.

Industry (including mining, manufacturing, construction and power) contributed 20.1% of GDP in 2009, and the sector engaged 23.2% of the employed labour force in that year. According to the World Bank, industrial production increased by an annual average of 0.4% during 2000–09; sectoral output increased by 3.3% in 2008, but decreased by 15.0% in 2009.

The mining and quarrying sector contributed 0.8% of GDP and engaged 1.8% of the employed labour force in 2009. The principal minerals extracted are lignite, red bauxite and sea salt. Production in the sector declined by an annual average rate of 2.0% during 2002–06. Output decreased by 62.9% in 2009.

The manufacturing sector contributed 5.9% of GDP in 2009, and the sector engaged 12.5% of the employed labour force in that year. In 2005 the principal branches of manufacturing were metals, building materials, chemicals, woodworking, and food and tobacco products. Production in the sector decreased by 1.4% during 2000–09, according to the World Bank; output decreased by 20.3% in 2009.

The construction sector contributed 6.5% of GDP and engaged 5.7% of the employed labour force in 2009. Real GDP of the sector decreased by 19.2% in 2009.

Energy in Montenegro is derived principally from hydroelectric power (which provided about 65.2% of total electricity generated in 2005) and thermoelectric power (34.8%). Imports of mineral fuels accounted for only 12.6% of the value of total imports in 2009.

Services contributed 69.9% of GDP in 2009, and the sector engaged 75.2% of the employed labour force in the same year. Total foreign tourist arrivals increased from 1,031,212 in 2008 to 1,044,014 in 2009, but decreased to 990,168 in 2010. According to the World Bank, services GDP increased by an annual rate of 5.0% during 2000–09; the sector grew by 7.3% in 2008, but declined by the same amount in 2009.

In 2009 Montenegro recorded a trade deficit of €1,371.7m., and there was a deficit of €896.3m. on the current account of the balance of payments. In 2009 the principal source of imports was Serbia (27.0%); other major sources were Germany, Italy and Greece. Serbia was also the principal market for exports in that year (contributing 27.9% of the total exports); other important purchasers were Greece, Italy and Slovenia. The principal imports in 2009 were machinery and transport equipment, food and live animals, basic manufactures, and mineral fuels and lubricants. The main exports in that year were basic manufactures.

In 2007, according to preliminary figures, the overall budgetary surplus was €29m., which was equivalent to 1.0% of GDP. Montenegro's general government gross debt was €1,140m. in 2009, equivalent to 38.2% of GDP. The total external debt of the country was US $1,490.1m. in 2008, of which $879.0m. was public and publicly guaranteed debt. Consumer prices increased by 3.4% in 2009 but declined by 2.8% in 2010. The rate of unemployment was 14.0% in 2009.

In November 2006 the EU issued a progress report on Montenegro's first months of independence, which emphasized the need for economic reform to combat a continuing over-reliance on certain sectors of the economy, high unemployment and regulatory obstacles. Agreements on bilateral economic relations were signed with neighbouring and other European countries. High levels of growth followed, based largely on capital growth and massive inflows of foreign direct investment (FDI), particularly in the tourism, banking and construction sectors, while unemployment was reduced from 19.7% in 2005 to 10.7% in 2008. Montenegro signed a Stabilization and Association Agreement (SAA) with the EU in October 2007. An Interim Agreement on trade and trade-related issues entered into force on 1 January 2008, pending ratification of the SAA, and Montenegro from 2007 received pre-accession financial assistance from the EU. Montenegro submitted an application to the World Trade Organization (WTO, see p. 430) while it formed part of the State Union of Serbia and Montenegro, in February 2005, and membership negotiations began in October. Montenegro submitted its application for EU membership in December 2008. The onset of the international economic crisis in late 2008 caused a dramatic fall in FDI and the consequent suspension of many construction projects in the country. The country's competitiveness was, moreover, eroded as a result of steep wage increases. Following a sharp contraction in GDP in 2009, a gradual economic recovery, with a stabilization of the financial situation, during 2010 resulted in a resumption of positive growth at a low level. The SAA entered into effect on 1 May 2010. In December Montenegro was officially granted candidate status for EU membership; the Government immediately announced the adoption of a plan to meet EU criteria, particularly with regard to measures to combat endemic corruption and organized crime. In early 2011 continued poor economic conditions contributed to social discontent and the organization of anti-Government demonstrations.

PUBLIC HOLIDAYS

2012: 1–2 January (New Year), 7–8 January (Orthodox Christmas), 13–16 April (Orthodox Easter), 1–2 May (Labour Day), 21 May (Independence Day), 13 July (National Day).

Statistical Survey

Source: Statistical Office of Montenegro, 81000 Podgorica, IV Proleterske 2; tel. (20) 241206; fax (20) 241270; e-mail statistika@cg.yu; internet www.monstat.org.

AREA AND POPULATION

Area: 13,812 sq km (5,333 sq miles). *By Municipality* (sq km): Andrijevica 283; Bar 598; Berane 717; Bijelo Polje 924; Budva 122; Cetinje 910; Danilovgrad 501; Herceg Novi 235; Kolašin 897; Kotor 335; Mojkovac 367; Nikšić 2,065; Plav 486; Pljevlja 1,346; Plužine 854; Podgorica 1,441; Rožaje 432; Šavnik 553; Tivat 46; Ulcinj 255; Žabljak 445.

Population: 620,145 (males 305,225, females 314,920) at census of 31 October 2003. *Mid-2009* (official estimate) 631,536. *Mid-2011* (UN estimate) 626,067 (Source: UN, *World Population Prospects: The 2008 Revision*.

Density (at mid-2011): 45.3 per sq km.

Population by Age and Sex (UN estimates at mid-2011): *0–14:* 119,197 (males 61,767, females 57,430); *15–64:* 426,283 (males 212,103, females 214,180); *65 and over:* 80,587 (males 34,117, females 46,470); *Total* 626,067 (males 307,987, females 318,080) (Source: UN, *World Population Prospects: The 2008 Revision*).

MONTENEGRO

Statistical Survey

Population by Municipality (official estimates at mid-2009): Andrijevica 5,447; Bar 42,784; Berane 34,767; Bijelo Polje 49,548; Budva 17,333; Cetinje 17,617; Danilovgrad 16,659; Herceg Novi 33,225; Kolašin 9,159; Kotor 22,726; Mojkovac 9,412; Nikšić 75,329; Plav 13,899; Pljevlja 33,957; Plužine 3,789; Podgorica 180,810; Rožaje 23,791; Savnik 2,566; Tivat 13,762; Ulcinj 20,972; Žabljak 3,984; Total 631,536.

Ethnicity (population as declared at 2003 census): Montenegrin 267,669; Serb 198,414; Bosniak 48,184; Albanian 31,163; Muslim 24,625; Croat 6,811.

Principal Towns (population in '000, official estimates on 1 January 2009): Podgorica 181; Nikšić 75; Bijelo Polje 50; Bar 43; Berane 35; Rožaje 24.

Births, Marriages and Deaths (2009): Live births 8,642 (birth rate 13.7 per 1,000); Marriages 3,829 (marriage rate 6.1 per 1,000); Deaths 5,862 (death rate 9.3 per 1,000).

Life Expectancy (WHO estimates, years at birth): 74 (males 72; females 76) in 2008 (Source: WHO, *World Health Statistics*).

Economically Active Population (persons aged 15 years and over, annual averages, 2009): Agriculture, hunting, forestry and fishing 2,819; Mining and quarrying 3,178; Manufacturing 21,824; Electricity, gas and water supply 5,456; Construction 9,997; Wholesale and retail trade, repair of motor vehicles, motorcycles, and personal and household goods 36,117; Hotels and restaurants 16,678; Transport, storage and communications 13,858; Financial intermediation 3,748; Real estate, renting and business activities 7,356; Public administration and defence, and compulsory social security 18,860; Education 12,992; Health and social work 12,238; Other community, social and personal service activities 9,031; *Total employed* 174,152; Unemployed 28,387; *Total labour force* 202,539.

HEALTH AND WELFARE
Key Indicators

Total Fertility Rate (children per woman, 2008): 1.6.

Under-5 Mortality Rate (per 1,000 live births, 2008): 9.

Physicians (per 1,000 head, 2006): 2.0.

Hospital Beds (per 1,000 head, 2006): 4.1.

Health Expenditure (2007): US $ per head (PPP): 1,107.

Health Expenditure (2007): % of GDP: 8.9.

Health Expenditure (2007): public (% of total): 57.2.

Access to Water (% of persons, 2008): 98.

Access to Sanitation (% of persons, 2008): 92.

Human Development Index (2010): ranking: 49.

Human Development Index (2010): value: 0.769.

AGRICULTURE, ETC.

Principal Crops (metric tons, 2008 unless otherwise indicated, FAO estimates): Wheat 2,500 (2009); Maize 6,937; Barley 1,200; Potatoes 110,000; Tobacco 358; Plums 6,076; Olives 1,211; Oranges and tangerines 5,239; Grapes 35,402. Source: FAO.

Livestock ('000 head, 2008 unless otherwise indicated): Cattle 109.3; Horses 5.5; Pigs 10.5 (2009, FAO estimate); Sheep 222.2; Poultry 510 (2009, FAO estimate). Source: FAO.

Livestock Products (metric tons, 2008 unless otherwise indicated, FAO estimates): Cattle meat 4,991; Pig meat 2,400 (2009); Sheep meat 674; Milk 169; Eggs 2,730; Honey 485. Source: FAO.

Forestry ('000 cu m, 2009 unless otherwise indicated): *Timber Removals:* 444.4 (Broadleaved 216.6, Coniferous 227.8); *Assortments* (2008 figures): 485.0 (Broadleaved 201.9, Coniferous 283.1).

Fishing (metric tons, 2009): Total catch 1,660 (marine 773, freshwater 887).

MINING

Selected Products ('000 metric tons, 2009): Lignite 957.0; Red bauxite 45.8; Sea salt 17.0.

INDUSTRY

Selected Products ('000 metric tons unless otherwise indicated, 2009): Wheat flour 38.1; Wines ('000 hl) 105.9; Beer ('000 hl) 456.9; Spruce and fir lumber ('000 cu m) 44.7; Oxygen, nitrogen and acetylene 3.3; Cut marble panels ('000 sq m) 40.8; Steel ingots 13.8; Steel castings 76.6; Aluminium oxide 58.5; Aluminium ingots 64.0; Electric energy (kWh) 2,759.8m.

FINANCE

Currency and Exchange Rates: 100 cent = 1 euro (€). *Sterling and Dollar Equivalents* (31 December 2010): £1 sterling = 1.172 euros; US $1 = 0.748 euros; €10 = £8.54 = $13.36. *Average Exchange Rate* (euros per US dollar): 0.6827 in 2008; 0.7198 in 2009; 0.7550 in 2010.

Budget (€ million, 2007, preliminary): Total current revenues 785.4 (Taxes 708.0, Duties 18.4, Reimbursements 22.9, Other current revenues 36.1); Property disbursements 5.4; Loan repayment revenues and assets from the previous year 5.5; Grants and loans 2.5; *Total revenue* 798.8; Total expenses 605.6 (Gross wages and salaries 192.9, Other personal income and fringe benefits 17.2, Expenditure for materials and services 75.4, Maintenance 20.6, Interest rates 25.1, Leasing 4.9, Subventions 13.1, Transfers to individuals and institutions 128.6, Social protection transfers 44.7, Other current expenses 5.7, Capital expenses 77.4); Total loans and loan repayments 153.4; Total reserves 10.8; *Total expenditure* 769.8. Source: Central Bank of Montenegro.

International Reserves (US $ million at 31 December 2010; excl. gold): IMF special drawing rights 40.29; Reserve position in IMF 10.17; Foreign exchange 505.70; *Total* 556.16. Source: IMF, *International Financial Statistics*.

Money Supply (€ million at 31 December 2010): Demand deposits at banking institutions 586.0. Source: IMF, *International Financial Statistics*.

Cost of Living (Consumer Price Index; base: 2008 = 100): All items 93.1 in 2007; 103.4 in 2009; 100.5 in 2010.

Expenditure on the Gross Domestic Product (€ million at current prices, 2009): Government final consumption expenditure 661.4; Private final consumption expenditure 2,503.7; Gross fixed capital formation 797.6; Changes in inventories 10.9; *Total domestic expenditure* 3,973.6; Exports of goods and services 957.5; *Less* Imports of goods and services 1,950.1; *GDP in purchasers' values* 2,981.0.

Gross Domestic Product by Economic Activity (€ million at current prices, 2009): Agriculture, hunting, forestry and fishing 246.8; Mining and quarrying 19.7; Manufacturing 145.8; Electricity, gas and water supply 169.5; Construction 161.5; Wholesale and retail trade, repair of motor vehicles, motorcycles, and personal and household goods 357.1; Hotels and restaurants 152.1; Transport, storage and communications 283.8; Financial intermediation 120.8; Real estate, renting and business activities 250.7; Public administration and defence; compulsory social security 254.8; Education 125.4; Health and social work 118.4; Other community, social and personal service activities 66.1; *Sub-total* 2,472.5; Taxes, less subsidies, on products 508.4; *GDP in purchasers' values* 2,981.0.

Balance of Payments (€ million, 2009): Exports of goods 296.3; Imports of goods –1,668.0; *Trade balance* –1,371.7; Exports of services 680.5; Imports of services –295.9; *Balance on goods and services* –987.1; Other income received 162.8; Other income paid –157.4; *Balance on goods, services and income* –981.7; Current transfers received 117.7; Current transfers paid –32.3; *Current balance* –896.3; Capital account (net) 2.0; Direct investments (net) 919.0; Portfolio investments (net) –41.9; Other investments (net) –266.3; Net errors and omissions 368.2; *Overall balance* 84.7. Source: Central Bank of Montenegro.

EXTERNAL TRADE

Principal Commodities (excluding trade with Serbia, € million, 2009): *Imports:* Food and live animals 312.8; Mineral fuels, lubricants, etc. 208.1; Chemical products 167.9; Basic manufactures 274.8; Machinery and transport equipment 357.7; Total (incl. others) 1,654.2. *Exports:* Crude materials (except fuels) 25.1; Basic manufactures 153.7; Machinery and transport equipment 27.7; Miscellaneous manufactured articles 9.5; Total (incl. others) 277.0.

Principal Trading Partners (€ million, 2009): *Imports:* Austria 47.4; Brazil 30.3; China, People's Republic 90.3; Croatia 80.9; Germany 111.1; Greece 99.6; Italy 106.2; Russia 24.7; Serbia 446.1; Switzerland 54.7; Total (incl. others) 1,654.2. *Exports:* Bosnia and Herzegovina 17.8; Greece 47.8; Italy 32.9; Serbia 77.3; Slovenia 24.3; Total (incl. others) 277.0.

TRANSPORT

Road Transport (2009): 178,919 passenger cars in use.

Railways (traffic, 2009): Passengers carried ('000) 852; Passenger-km ('000) 99,200; Freight carried ('000 metric tons) 854; Total ton-km ('000) 100,546.

Shipping (freight handled, '000 metric tons, 2008): Goods loaded 613.7 Goods unloaded 829.5.

Civil Aviation (2009): Passenger movements 956,405; Freight carried 1,478 metric tons.

MONTENEGRO

TOURISM

Total Foreign Tourist Arrivals: 1,031,212 in 2008; 1,044,014 in 2009; 990,168 in 2010.
Overnight Stays by Nationality (foreign tourists, 2010): Albania 181,178; Bosnia and Herzegovina 722,927; Czech Republic 160,438; France 225,316; Germany 144,835; Italy 191,816; Russia 1,210,347; Serbia 2,050,354; Slovenia 96,935; USA 25,103; Total (incl. others) 6,772,721.

COMMUNICATIONS MEDIA

Telephones (main lines in use, 2009): 166,805.
Mobile Cellular Telephones (subscribers, 2009): 1,573,151.

EDUCATION

Pre-primary (2009/10): Schools 90; Pupils 12,728; Teaching staff 1,326.
Primary (2008/09 unless otherwise indicated): Schools 442; Pupils 72,993 (2009/10); Teaching staff 5,039.
Secondary (2008/09 unless otherwise indicated): Schools 47; Students 31,643 (2009/10); Teaching staff 2,243.
Higher (incl. faculties, art academies and private institutions, 2008/09 unless otherwise indicated): Schools 38; Students 21,199 (2009/10); Teaching staff 1,405.
Adult Literacy Rate: 97.65% (males 99.63; females 95.70) at 2003 census.

Directory

The Government

HEAD OF STATE

President: FILIP VUJANOVIĆ (elected 11 May 2003; took office 13 June 2003; re-elected 6 April 2008).

COUNCIL OF MINISTERS
(May 2011)

The Government comprises members of the Democratic Party of Socialists of Montenegro (DPS), the Social Democratic Party of Montenegro (SDP), the Democratic Union of Albanians (DUA) and the Bosniak Party (BP).

Prime Minister: IGOR LUKŠIĆ (DPS).
Deputy Prime Minister, responsible for the Political System, Internal and Foreign Affairs, and Minister of Justice: DUŠKO MARKOVIĆ (DPS).
Deputy Prime Minister, responsible for Economic Policy and the Financial System, and Minister of the Information Society and Telecommunications: VUJICA LAZOVIĆ (SDP).
General Secretary of the Government: ŽARKO ŠTURANOVIĆ.
Minister of Foreign Affairs and European Integration: MILAN ROĆEN (DPS).
Minister of Internal Affairs: IVAN BRAJOVIĆ (SDP).
Minister of Finance: MILORAD KATNIĆ (DPS).
Minister of Defence: BORO VUČINIĆ (DPS).
Minister of the Economy: VLADIMIR KAVARIĆ (DPS).
Minister of Transport and Maritime Affairs: ANDRIJA LOMPAR (SDP).
Minister of Sustainable Development and Tourism: PREDRAG SEKULIĆ (DPS).
Minister of Agriculture and Rural Development: TARZAN MILOŠEVIĆ (DPS).
Minister of Education and Sports: SLAVOLJUB STJEPOVIĆ (DPS).
Minister of Science: SANJA VLAHOVIĆ (DPS).
Minister of Labour and Social Welfare: SUAD NUMANOVIĆ (DPS).
Minister of Health: MIODRAG RADUNOVIĆ (DPS).
Minister of Culture: BRANISLAV MIĆUNOVIĆ (DPS).
Minister for Human and Minority Rights: FERHAT DINOŠA (DUA).
Minister without Portfolio: RAFET HUSOVIĆ (BP).

MINISTRIES

Office of the President: 81000 Podgorica, Sveti Petra Cetinjskog 3; tel. (20) 241410; fax (20) 245849; e-mail filip.vujanovic@predsjednik.me; internet www.predsjednik.me.
Office of the Prime Minister: 81000 Podgorica, Jovana Tomaševića bb; tel. (20) 242530; fax (20) 242329; e-mail vojin.vlahovic@gov.me; internet www.gov.me.
Ministry of Agriculture and Rural Development: 81000 Podgorica, Rimski trg 46, Poslovni centar Vektra; tel. (20) 482109; fax (20) 234306; internet www.minpolj.gov.me.
Ministry of Culture: 81000 Podgorica, Vuka Karadžića 3; tel. (20) 231561; fax (20) 231540; e-mail kabinet.kultura@gov.me; internet www.ministarstvokulture.gov.me.
Ministry of Defence: 81000 Podgorica, Jovana Tomaševića 29; tel. (20) 224042; fax (20) 224702; e-mail kabinet@mod.co.me; internet www.gov.me/odbrana.
Ministry of the Economy: 81000 Podgorica, Rimski trg 46; tel. (20) 482163; fax (20) 234027; e-mail irena.soc@gov.me; internet www.minekon.gov.me.
Ministry of Education and Sports: 81000 Podgorica, Vaka Đurovića bb; tel. (20) 410100; fax (20) 410101; e-mail mpin@gov.me; internet www.mpin.gov.me.
Ministry of Finance: 81000 Podgorica, Stanka Dragojevića 2; tel. (20) 242835; fax (20) 224450; e-mail mf@gov.me; internet www.mf.gov.me.
Ministry of Foreign Affairs and European Integration: 81000 Podgorica, Stanka Dragojevića 2; tel. (20) 246357; fax (20) 224670; e-mail milan.rocen@gov.me; internet www.mip.gov.me.
Ministry of Health: 81000 Podgorica, Rimski trg 46; tel. (20) 242276; fax (20) 242762; e-mail mzdravlja@gov.me; internet www.mzdravlja.gov.me.
Ministry for Human and Minority Rights: 81000 Podgorica, Cetinjski put bb; tel. (20) 482126; fax (20) 234198; e-mail sahmanovic@hotmail.com; internet www.minmanj.gov.me.
Ministry of the Information Society and Telecommunications: 81000 Podgorica, Rimski trg 45; tel. (20) 241412; fax (20) 241790; e-mail mid@gov.me; internet www.mid.gov.me.
Ministry of Internal Affairs: 81000 Podgorica, bul. Svetog Petra Cetinjskog 22; tel. (20) 241590; fax (20) 246779; e-mail mup.kabinet@t-com.me; internet www.mup.gov.me.
Ministry of Justice: 81000 Podgorica, Vuka Karadžića 3; tel. (20) 407501; fax (20) 407515; e-mail minpravde@gov.me; internet www.pravda.gov.me.
Ministry of Labour and Social Welfare: 81000 Podgorica, Rimski trg 46; tel. (20) 482148; fax (20) 234227; e-mail sandra.krivokapic@gov.me; internet www.gov.me/minradiss.
Ministry of Science: Podgorica.
Ministry of Sustainable Development and Tourism: 81000 Podgorica, Rimski trg 46; tel. (20) 482329; fax (20) 234168; e-mail zeljka.radak@gov.me; internet www.mte.gov.me.
Ministry of Transport and Maritime Affairs: 81000 Podgorica, Rimski trg 46; tel. (20) 482156; fax (20) 234342; e-mail jelena.kaludjerovic@gov.me; internet www.minsaob.gov.me.

President

Presidential Election, 6 April 2008

Candidate	Votes	%
Filip Vujanović (Democratic Party of Socialists of Montenegro)	171,118	51.89
Andrija Mandić (Serb People's Party of Montenegro)	64,473	19.55
Nebojša Medojević (Movement for Changes)	54,874	16.64
Srđan Milić (Socialist People's Party of Montenegro)	39,316	11.92
Total	**329,781**	**100.00**

MONTENEGRO

Legislature

**Skupština Crne Gore
(Assembly of Montenegro)**
81000 Podgorica, bul. Svetog Petra Cetinjskog 10; tel. (20) 241083; fax (20) 242192; e-mail ranko.krivokapic@skupstina.me; internet www.skupstina.me.
Speaker: RANKO KRIVOKAPIĆ.

Election, 29 March 2009

Party	Votes	%	Seats
Coalition for a European Montenegro*	168,290	51.94	48
Socialist People's Party of Montenegro	54,545	16.84	16
New Serbian Democracy	29,885	9.22	8
Movement for Changes	19,546	6.03	5
Democratic Union of Albanians	4,747	1.47	1
New Democratic Power	2,939	0.91	1
Democratic League of Montenegro-Albanian Alternative coalition	2,898	0.89	1
Albanian Coalition—Perspective	2,619	0.81	1
Others	38,521	11.89	—
Total	323,990	100.00	81

*Comprising the Democratic Party of Socialists of Montenegro, the Social Democratic Party of Montenegro, the Croatian Civic Initiative and the Bosniak Party.

Political Organizations

Albanian Alternative (Albanska alternativa): c/o Skupština Crne Gore, 81000 Podgorica, bul. Svetog Petra Cetinjskog 10; tel. (20) 404565; e-mail press@skupstina.me; Pres. GJERGJ CAMAJ.

Albanian Coalition—Perspective (Albanska Koalicija—Perspektiva): c/o Skupština Crne Gore, 81000 Podgorica, bul. Svetog Petra Cetinjskog 10; tel. (20) 404565; e-mail press@skupstina.me; Pres. AMIR HOLAJ.

Bosniak Party (BP) (Bošnjačka Stranka): 84310 Rožaje; tel. (51) 270164; fax (51) 270165; e-mail info@bosnjackastranka.org; internet www.bosnjackastranka.org; f. 2006; Pres. RAFET HUSOVIĆ.

Croatian Civic Initiative (Hrvatska građanska inicijativa—HGI): 85320 Tivat; tel. (32) 660345; fax (32) 660348; e-mail hgicg@t-com.me; internet www.hgi.co.me; f. 2003; joined Democratic Party of Socialists of Montenegro coalition 2006; Pres. MARIJA VUČINOVIĆ.

Democratic Centre of Montenegro (Demokratski Centar Crne Gore): 81000 Podgorica, Hercegovačka 13; tel. (20) 101011; e-mail dcinfo@dccg.me; internet www.dccg.me; f. 2009; Pres. Dr GORAN BATRIĆEVIĆ.

Democratic League of Montenegro (Demokratski Savez Crne Gore): 81000 Podgorica; f. 1990; ethnic Albanian party; Leader MEHMET BARHDI.

Democratic Party of Socialists of Montenegro (DPS) (Demokratska Partija Socijalista Crne Gore): 81000 Podgorica, Jovana Tomaševića bb; tel. (20) 243952; fax (20) 243347; e-mail office@dps.me; internet www.dps.me; fmrly League of Communists of Montenegro in 1991; Chair. MILO ĐUKANOVIĆ.

Democratic Serbian Party of Montenegro (DSP) (Demokratska Srpska Stranka Crne Gore—DSS): 81000 Podgorica; f. 2003; centre-right; Leader RANKO KADIĆ.

Democratic Union of Albanians (DUA) (Demokratska Unija Albanaca): c/o Skupština Crne Gore, 81000 Podgorica, bul. Svetog Petra Cetinjskog 10; tel. (20) 404565; e-mail press@skupstina.me; Leader FERHAT DINOŠA.

Liberal Party of Montenegro (LPM) (Liberalna Partija Crne Gore—LPCG): 81000 Podgorica, Vardarska 12; tel. (20) 500884; e-mail info@lpcg.org; internet www.lpcg.org; f. 2004; Pres. ANDRIJA POPOVIĆ.

Movement for Changes (MFC) (Pokret za Promjene—PZP): 81000 Podgorica, Dalmatinska 130 D; tel. and fax (20) 269337; e-mail gzp@t-com.me; internet www.promjene.org; f. 2002 as non-governmental org.; became political party in 2006; supports European integration; Pres. NEBOJŠA MEDOJEVIĆ.

New Democratic Power (Nova Demokratska Snaga—FORCA): 85360 Ulcinj, Skenderbeu; tel. (30) 401760; fax (30) 401761; internet www.forca.me; f. 2005; principally ethnic Albanian party; Chair. NAZIF CUNGU.

New Serbian Democracy (Nova Srpska Demokratija—NOVA): 81000 Podgorica, Vojislava Grujića 4; tel. (20) 651903; fax (20) 652147; e-mail centar@nova.org.me; internet www.nova.org.me; f. 2009 by merger of Serb People's Party with People's Socialist Party and other small groups; Pres. ANDRIJA MANDIĆ.

People's Party (PP) (Narodna Stranka): 81000 Podgorica, Vasa Raickovića bb; tel. (20) 238715; fax (20) 238717; e-mail narodna@t-com.me; internet www.narodnastranka.com; conservative; supports close relations with Serbia; Chair. PREDRAG POPOVIĆ.

Social Democratic Party of Montenegro (SDP) (Socijaldemokratska Partija Crne Gore): 81000 Podgorica, Jovana Tomaševića bb; tel. (20) 248648; fax (20) 612133; e-mail sdp@sdp.co.me; internet www.sdp.co.me; Pres. RANKO KRIVOKAPIĆ.

Socialist People's Party of Montenegro (SPPM) (Socijalistička Narodna Partija Crne Gore—SNP): 81000 Podgorica, Vaka Đurovića 5; tel. (20) 272421; fax (20) 272420; e-mail snp@t-com.me; internet www.snp.co.me; Pres. SRĐAN MILIĆ.

Diplomatic Representation

Albania: 81000 Podgorica, Zmaj Jovina 30, Stari Aerodrom; tel. (20) 652796; fax (20) 652798; e-mail embassy.potgorica@mfa.gov.al; Ambassador TONIN BECI.

Austria: 81000 Podgorica, Kralja Nikole 104; tel. (20) 601580; fax (20) 624344; e-mail podgorica-ob@bmaa.gv.at; Ambassador MARTIN PAMMER.

Bosnia and Herzegovina: 81000 Podgorica, Atinska 58; tel. (20) 618105; fax (20) 618016; e-mail amb.podgorica@mvp.gov.ba; Ambassador BRANIMIR JUKIĆ.

Bulgaria: 81000 Podgorica, Vukice Mitrovića 10; tel. (20) 655009; fax (20) 655008; e-mail bg.embassy.me@abv.bg; internet www.mfa.bg/podgorica; Ambassador MAYA N. DOBREVA.

China, People's Republic: 81000 Podgorica, Radosava Burića 4A; tel. and fax (20) 609275; e-mail chinaemb_me@mfa.gov.cn; Ambassador ZHI SHAOLIN.

Croatia: 81000 Podgorica, Vladimira Ćetkovića 2; tel. (20) 269760; fax (20) 269810; e-mail croemb.podgorica@mvpei.hr; Ambassador PETAR TURČINOVIĆ.

France: 81000 Podgorica, Atinska 35; tel. (20) 665348; fax (20) 655643; e-mail ambafrance@ambafrance.co.me; internet www.ambafrance-me.org; Ambassador DOMINIQUE RGAZUY.

Germany: 81000 Podgorica, Hercegovačka 10; tel. and fax (20) 667285; internet www.podgorica.diplo.de; Ambassador PETER PLATTE.

Greece: 81000 Podgorica, Atinska 4C; tel. (20) 655544; fax (20) 655543; e-mail gremb.pod@mfa.gr; Ambassador EMMANUEL PAPADOGIORGAKIS.

Hungary: 81000 Podgorica, Kralja Nikole 104; tel. (20) 602910; fax (20) 625243; e-mail mission.pdg@kum.hu; internet www.mfa.gov.hu/emb/podgorica; Ambassador TIBOR CSÁSZÁR.

Italy: 81000 Podgorica, Džordža Vašingtona 83; tel. (20) 234661; fax (20) 234663; e-mail segreteria.podgorica@esteri.it; internet www.ambpodgorica.esteri.it; Ambassador SERGIO BARBANTI.

Macedonia, former Yugoslav republic: 81000 Podgorica, Hercegovačka 49/3; tel. (20) 667415; fax (20) 667205; e-mail podgorica@mfa.gov.mk; Ambassador ALEKSANDAR VASILEVSKI.

Poland: 20000 Podgorica, Kozaračka 79; tel. (20) 608320; fax (20) 658581; e-mail podgorica.amb.sekretariat@msz.gov.pl; internet www.podgorica.polemb.net; Chargé d'affaires a.i. JAROSŁAW LINDENBERG.

Romania: 81000 Podgorica, Vukice Mitrovića 40; tel. (20) 618040; fax (20) 655081; e-mail ambs.romania.mne@t-com.me; Ambassador MIHAIL FLOROVICI.

Russia: 81000 Podgorica, Veliše Mugoše 1; tel. (20) 272460; fax (20) 272315; e-mail info@ambrus.me; internet www.ambrus.me; Ambassador ALEKSEI NESTERENKO.

Serbia: 81000 Podgorica, Hercegovačka 18; tel. (20) 667305; fax (20) 664301; e-mail embassy.podgorica@mfa.rs; Ambassador ZORAN LUTOVAC.

Slovenia: 81000 Podgorica, Atinska 41; tel. (20) 618150; fax (20) 655671; e-mail kpg@gov.si; internet podgorica.embassy.si; Ambassador JERNEJ VIDETIČ.

Turkey: 81000 Podgorica, Radosava Burica bb; tel. (20) 445700; fax (20) 445777; e-mail embassy.podgorica@mfa.gov.tr; Ambassador EMINE BIRGEN KEŞOĞLU.

Ukraine: 81000 Podgorica, ul. Serdara Jola Piletica 15; tel. (20) 227521; fax (20) 227181; e-mail emb_me@mfa.gov.ua; internet www.mfa.gov.ua/montenegro; Ambassador OKSANA SLYUSARENKO.

United Arab Emirates: 81000 Podgorica, bul. Svetog Petra Cetinjskog 147; tel. (20) 411411; fax (20) 411402; e-mail montenegro@mofa.gov.ae; Ambassador HAFSA ABDULLAH MUHAMMAD SHARIF AL-ULAMA.

United Kingdom: 81000 Podgorica, Ulcinjska 8, Gorica C; tel. (20) 618010; fax (20) 618020; e-mail podgorica@fco.gov.uk; internet ukinmontenegro.fco.gov.uk; Ambassador CATHERINE KNIGHT-SANDS.

MONTENEGRO

USA: 81000 Podgorica, Ljubljanska bb; tel. (20) 410500; fax (20) 241358; e-mail Podgoricaacs@state.gov; internet podgorica.usembassy.gov; Ambassador SUE KATHRINE BROWN.

Judicial System

Constitutional Court (Ustavni Sud Crne Gore): 81000 Podgorica, Njegoševa 2; tel. and fax (20) 665410; e-mail ustavni.sud@ustavnisud.me; internet www.ustavnisudcg.co.me; comprises a President and five judges; Pres. Dr MILAN MARKOVIĆ.

Supreme Court (Vrhovni Sud Crne Gore): 81000 Podgorica, Njegoševa 10; tel. (20) 665390; fax (20) 665405; e-mail vrhsud@t-com.me; internet www.vrhsudcg.gov.me; comprises a President and 17 judges; incorporates criminal, civil and administrative divisions; Pres. VESNA MEDENICA.

Office of the Supreme State Prosecutor (Vrhovni državni tužilac): 81000 Podgorica, Slobode 20; tel. and fax (20) 230624; internet www.tuzilastvocg.co.me; Public Prosecutor RANKA ČARAPIĆ.

Religion

CHRISTIANITY

The Eastern Orthodox Church

Montenegrin Orthodox Church (Crnogorska Pravoslavna Crkva): 81250 Cetinje, Gruda bb; tel. and fax (41) 31310; e-mail crkva@moc-cpc.org; internet www.moc-cpc.org; autocephalous until 1920, when it was dissolved and annexed to the Serbian Orthodox Church; restored 1993; Archbishop of Cetinje and Metropolitan of Montenegro MIHAILO (DEDEIĆ).

Orthodox Metropolitanate of Montenegro and the Littoral—Serbian Orthodox Church (Pravoslavna Mitropolitija Crnogorsko Primorska—Srpska Pravoslavna Crkva): 81250 Cetinje; e-mail euo@mitropolija.me; internet www.mitropolija.me; Metropolitan of Montenegro and the Littoral AMFILOHIJE (RADOVIĆ).

The Roman Catholic Church

At 31 December 2008 there were an estimated 12,475 adherents in the archdiocese of Bar (which is directly answerable to the Holy See) and an estimated 10,000 adherents in the Diocese of Kotor (which is suffragan to the archdiocese of Split-Makarska, based in Croatia). There is also an Apostolic Exarchate for adherents of the Byzantine Rite in Serbia and Montenegro, based in Belgrade, Serbia.

Archbishop of Bar: Most Rev. ZEF GASHI, 85000 Bar, Popovići 98; tel. (30) 344236; fax (30) 344233.

Bishop of Kotor: Most Rev. ILIJA JANJIĆ, 85330 Kotor, Stari grad 336; tel. (32) 322315; fax (32) 322175.

ISLAM

Almost 20% of the population of Montenegro profess Islam, many being ethnic Slav Muslims (Bosniaks) of the Sandžak region (which was partitioned between Montenegro and Serbia in 1913).

The Press

PRINCIPAL DAILIES

Dan (The Day): 81000 Podgorica, 13 Jula 10; tel. (20) 481520; fax (20) 481522; e-mail dan@t-com.me; internet www.dan.co.me; f. 1999; Chief Editor MLADEN MILUTINOVIĆ.

Pobjeda (Victory): 81000 Podgorica, bul. Revolucije 15, POB 101; tel. (20) 244474; fax (20) 202455; e-mail urednik@pobjeda.co.me; internet www.pobjeda.co.me; f. 1944; morning; Editor-in-Chief SRĐAN KUSOVAC; circ. 18,000 (2003).

Republika (The Republic): 81000 Podgorica, trg Republike bb; tel. (20) 215260; fax (20) 215270; Editor-in-Chief VELIZAR BRAJOVIĆ.

Vijesti (The News): 81000 Podgorica, bul. Revolucije 9; tel. (20) 406901; fax (20) 242306; e-mail mihailo.jovovic@vijesti.me; internet www.vijesti.me; f. 1997; Editor-in-Chief MIHAILO JOVOVIĆ.

PERIODICALS

Koha Javore: 81000 Podgorica, bul. Revolucije 9; tel. (20) 247799; fax (20) 247674; e-mail kohajavore@t-com.me; internet www.kohajavore.co.me; weekly; f. 2002; science and culture; in Albanian; Editor-in-Chief ALI SALAJ.

Monitor: 81000 Podgorica, Vuka Karadžića 11; tel. (20) 231955; fax (20) 231944; e-mail monitor@t-com.me; internet www.monitor.co.me; f. 1990; weekly; independent; politics, general; Editor-in-Chief ESAD KOČAN.

NEWS AGENCY

Montenegrin News Agency (MINA): Podgorica; tel. (81) 264363; e-mail mnnews@mnnews.net; internet www.mnnews.net; f. 2002; commercial; Montenegrin, Albanian and English; Exec. Dir JAŠA JOVIĆEVIĆ.

PRESS ASSOCIATION

Asscn of Journalists of Montenegro (UNCG) (Udruženja novinara Crne Gore): 81000 Podgorica; Pres VLATKO VUJOVIĆ.

Publishers

Obod: 81250 Cetinje, Njegoševa 3; tel. (41) 21331; fax (41) 21953; general literature; Dir VASKO JANKOVIĆ.

Pobjeda (Victory) Publishing House: 81000 Podgorica, Južni bul. bb; tel. (20) 44433; f. 1974; poetry, fiction, lexicography and scientific works.

Broadcasting and Communications

TELECOMMUNICATIONS

Regulatory Agency

Agency for Electronic Communications and Postal Services (Agencija za elektronske komunikacije i poštansku djelatnost—EKIP): 81000 Podgorica, bul. Revolucije 1; tel. (20) 246786; fax (20) 241805; e-mail ekip@ekip.me; internet www.ekip.me; f. 2001 as Agency for Telecommunications; renamed as above in 2008; independent regulatory body; Exec. Dir ZORAN SEKULIĆ.

Service Providers

Crnogorski Telekom: 81000 Podgorica, Moskovska 29; tel. (20) 433433; fax (20) 432400; e-mail office@telekom.me; internet www.telekom.me; 76.53% owned by Magyar Telekom (Hungary); Chair. of Bd of Dirs BENCE MAKAI.

m:tel: 81000 Podgorica, Kralja Nikole 27A; internet www.mtel-cg.com; f. 2007; owned by Telekom Srbija (Serbia) and Ogalar (Netherlands); mobile cellular telecommunications services; Chair. of Bd of Dirs BRANKO RADUJKO.

Promonte: 81000 Podgorica, bul. Džordža Vašingtona 83; tel. (20) 235000; fax (20) 235035; e-mail info@promonte.com; internet www.promonte.com; f. 1996; 100% owned by Telenor (Norway); mobile cellular telecommunications services; Gen. Dir KARE GUSTAD.

T-Mobile Crna Gora: 81000 Podgorica, bul. Svetog Petra Cetinjskog bb; tel. (20) 400801; fax (20) 225752; e-mail office@monetcg.com; internet www.t-mobileme; f. 2000; fmrly Monet; present name adopted 2006; subsidiary of Crnogorski Telekom; mobile cellular telecommunications services.

BROADCASTING

Regulatory Agency

Montenegro Broadcasting Agency (Agencija za radio-diffuziu Crne Gore): 81000 Podgorica, bul. Svetog Petra Cetinjskog 9; fax (20) 201440; internet www.ardcg.org; CEO ABAZ BELI DŽAFIĆ.

Television and Radio

Radiotelevizija Crne Gore (Radio and Television of Montenegro): 81000 Podgorica, Cetinjski put bb; tel. (20) 225602; fax (20) 225108; internet www.rtcg.org; f. 1944 (radio) and 1971 (television); two terrestrial television channels and one satellite channel; two radio channels; Dir-Gen. RADOVAN MILJANIĆ; Dir of Television VELJO JAUKOVIĆ; Dir of Radio BUDIMIR RAIČEVIĆ.

Radio D: 81000 Podgorica, 13 Jula bb; tel. (20) 238909; internet www.radioddplus.com; f. 2000; independent; also Radio D Plus; Chief Editor DRAGANA KUKRIĆ.

RTV Corona: 85000 Bar, Jovana Tomaševica, Poslovni centar G-9; tel. (30) 317727; e-mail mcorona@t-com.me; f. 2000; comprises Radio Corona (founded 2000) and TV Corona (founded 2008); information and entertainment programming; Exec. Dir DRAGAN DESPOTOVIĆ.

TV Vijesti: 81000 Podgorica, Trg Republike bb; tel. (20) 404601; fax (20) 232065; e-mail tvvijesti@t-com.me; f. 2007; broadcasts 24 hours a day; information, news, politics, economics, culture, entertainment, sport; Exec. Dir SLAVOLJUB SCEKIC.

MONTENEGRO

Finance

(cap. = capital; res = reserves; dep. = deposits; m. = million; amounts in euros; br. = branch)

BANKING

Central Bank

The Central Bank of Montenegro was established in 2001.

Central Bank of Montenegro (Centralna Banka Crne Gore—CBCG): 81000 Podgorica, bul. Petra Cetinjskog 6; tel. and fax (20) 403105; e-mail pristup.informacijama@cb-cg.org; internet www.cb-mn.org; f. 2001; cap. 2.5m., res 41.9m., dep. 438.9m. (Dec. 2007); Gov. Radoje Žugić.

Selected Banks

In 2008 some 11 banks were operating in Montenegro, seven of which were foreign-owned.

Crnogorska komercijalna banka a.d. Podgorica (CKB): 81000 Podgorica, Moskovska bb; tel. (20) 404232; fax (20) 235757; e-mail info@ckb.me; internet www.ckb.me; f. 1997; 100% owned by National Savings and Commercial Bank—OTP Bank (Hungary); cap. 46.8m., res 0.9m., dep. 793.5m. (Dec. 2008); Pres. József Windheim; 40 brs.

Erste Bank a.d. Podgorica: 81000 Podgorica, Marka Miljanova 46; tel. (20) 440440; fax (20) 440432; e-mail info@erstebank.me; internet www.erstebank.me; f. 2002; fmrly Opportunity Bank; present name adopted 2009; subsidiary of Erste Bank der Oesterreichischen Sparkassen AG (Austria); cap. 5.3m., res 3.1m., dep. 90.5m. (Dec. 2008); Chief Exec. Aleksa Lukić.

NLB Montenegrobanka a.d. Podgorica: 81000 Podgorica, Dragojevića 46; tel. (20) 402000; fax (20) 402212; e-mail info@montenegro-banka.com; internet www.montenegrobanka.com; f. 1905; fmrly MNB Crnogorska banka—Banque de Montenegro; present name adopted Jan. 2010; 86.97% owned by Nova Ljubljanska Banka d.d. (Slovenia); cap. 8.1m., res 10.2m., dep. 322.4m. (Dec. 2008); Pres. Matej Narat; CEO Crtomir Mesarić.

STOCK EXCHANGES

Montenegro Stock Exchange (Montenegroberza): 81000 Podgorica, Moskovska 77; tel. and fax (20) 228502; e-mail mberza@t-com.me; internet www.montenegroberza.com; f. 1993; CEO Dejana Šuškavčević.

New Securities Exchange of Montenegro (NEX): 81000 Podgorica, Miljana Vukova bb; tel. (20) 230690; fax (20) 230640; e-mail info@nexmontenegro.com; internet www.nexmontenegro.com; f. 2001; Pres. Saša Popović; Exec. Dir Mila Redžepagić.

INSURANCE

Lovćen Osiguranje a.d. Podgorica (Lovćen Insurance Co Podgorica): 81000 Podgorica, ul. Slobode 13 A; tel. (20) 404400; fax (20) 665281; e-mail lovosig@co.me; internet www.lovcenosiguranje.co.me; majority stake owned by Zavarovalnica Triglav d.d. (Slovenia); insurance and reinsurance; Exec. Dir Purić Radenko.

Sava Montenegro Osiguranje: 81000 Podgorica, Rimski trg 70, PC 'Kruševac'; tel. (20) 234008; fax (20) 234407; e-mail info@sava.co.me; internet www.sava.co.me; wholly owned by Sava Re (Slovenia); fmrly Montenegro Osiguranje; life and non-life, insurance and reinsurance; Chief Exec. Nebojša Šćekić.

Swiss Osiguranje a.d. Podgorica (Swiss Insurance Co Podgorica): 81000 Podgorica, Novaka Miloševa 6/II; tel. (20) 230734; e-mail info@swiss-osiguranje.com; internet www.swiss-osiguranje.com/swiss; fmrly Agroosiguranje a.d. Podgorica; life and non-life, insurance and reinsurance; Exec. Dir Dragan Ivanović.

Trade and Industry

CHAMBER OF COMMERCE

Chamber of Commerce of Montenegro (Privredna Komora Crne Gore): 81000 Podgorica, Novaka Miloševa 29; tel. (20) 230545; fax (20) 230493; e-mail predsjednik@pkcg.org; internet www.pkcg.org; Pres. Velimir Mijusković.

UTILITIES

Electricity

Elektroprivreda Crne Gore a.d. Nikšić (EPCG) (Montenegro Electricity Co): 81400 Nikšić, Vuka Karadžića 2; tel. (40) 204137; fax (40) 214329; e-mail milvujacic@epcg.co.me; internet www.epcg.co.me; production, transmission and distribution of electric power; Exec. Dir Enrico Malerba.

Transport

RAILWAYS

Željeznica Crne Gore: 81000 Podgorica, trg Goolootočkih žrtava 13; tel. (20) 441302; fax (20) 633957; internet www.zcg-prevoz.me; 60.1% state-owned; Chair. of Bd of Dirs Ranko Medenića; Gen. Man. Rešad Nuhodžić.

SHIPPING

The principal coastal outlet is the port of Bar, which is linked to the Italian ports of Ancona and Bari by a regular ferry service.

Port of Bar (Luka Bar): 85000 Bar, Luka Bar; tel. (30) 312409; fax (30) 312409; e-mail lukabar@t-com.me; internet www.lukabar.me; f. 1906; Chair. of Bd Prof. Dr Predrag Ivanović.

CIVIL AVIATION

Montenegro Airlines: 81000 Podgorica, Beogradska 10; tel. (20) 405501; fax (20) 405548; internet www.montenegroairlines.com; f. 1994; operations commenced 1997; direct flights between Podgorica and Tivat (Montenegro), Belgrade and Niš (Serbia), Frankfurt (Germany), Ljubljana (Slovenia), Paris (France), Rome (Italy), Vienna (Austria), and Zurich (Switzerland); Pres. Zoran Durišić; CEO Petar Glomazić.

Tourism

There were 990,168 tourist arrivals in 2010.

National Tourism Organization of Montenegro: 81000 Podgorica, Omladinskih brigada 7; tel. (20) 230959; fax (20) 230979; e-mail info@visit-montenegro.com; internet www.visit-montenegro.com; Man. Dir Predrag Jelušić.

Defence

Following Montenegro's declaration of independence on 3 June 2006, the Montenegrin Government established a Ministry of Defence and revoked compulsory military service. In December Montenegro was admitted to the 'Partnership for Peace' programme of the North Atlantic Treaty Organization (NATO). As assessed at November 2010, Montenegro's total armed forces numbered 3,127, comprising an army of an estimated 2,500, a navy of 401 and an air force of 226. There was, in addition, a paramilitary force of an estimated 10,100, comprising 6,000 Ministry of Internal Affairs personnel and 4,100 members of special police units.

Defence Expenditure: Budgeted at €27m. in 2010.

Chief of Staff: Vice-Adm. Dragan Samardžić.

Education

Elementary education is free and compulsory for all children between the ages of seven and 15. Higher education is offered at the University of Montenegro, Podgorica, which was established in 1974, and at post-secondary schools. Some 21,199 students were enrolled in higher education in 2009/10.

MOROCCO

Introductory Survey

LOCATION, CLIMATE, LANGUAGE, RELIGION, FLAG, CAPITAL

The Kingdom of Morocco is situated in the extreme north-west of Africa. It has a long coastline on the shores of the Atlantic Ocean and, east of the Strait of Gibraltar, on the Mediterranean Sea, facing southern Spain. Morocco's eastern frontier is with Algeria, while to the south lies the disputed territory of Western Sahara (under Moroccan occupation), which has a lengthy Atlantic coastline and borders Mauritania to the east and south. The Spanish External Territories, Ceuta and Melilla, lie within Moroccan territory on the Mediterranean coast. Morocco's climate is semi-tropical. It is warm and sunny on the coast, while the plains of the interior are intensely hot in summer. Average temperatures are 27°C (81°F) in summer and 7°C (45°F) in winter for Rabat, and 38°C (101°F) and 4°C (40°F), respectively, for Marrakesh. The rainy season in the north is from November to April. The official language is Arabic, but a large minority speak Berber. Spanish is widely spoken in the northern regions, and French in the rest of Morocco. The established religion is Islam, and most of the country's inhabitants are Muslims. There are small minorities of Christians and Jews. The national flag (proportions 2 by 3) is red, with a green pentagram (intersecting lines in the form of a five-pointed star), known as 'Solomon's Seal', in the centre. The capital is Rabat.

CONTEMPORARY POLITICAL HISTORY

Historical Context

In 1912, under the terms of the Treaty of Fez, most of Morocco became a French protectorate, while a smaller Spanish protectorate was instituted in the north and far south of the country. Spain also retained control of Spanish Sahara (now Western Sahara), and Tangier became an international zone in 1923. A nationalist movement developed in Morocco during the 1930s and 1940s, led by the Istiqlal (Independence) grouping, and on 2 March 1956 the French protectorate achieved independence as the Sultanate of Morocco. Sultan Muhammad V, who had reigned since 1927 (although he had been temporarily removed from office by the French authorities between 1953 and 1955), became the first Head of State. The northern zone of the Spanish protectorate joined the new state in April 1956, and Tangier's international status was abolished in October. The southern zone of the Spanish protectorate was ceded to Morocco in 1958, but no agreement was reached on the enclaves of Ceuta and Melilla, in the north, the Ifni region in the south, or the Saharan territories to the south of Morocco, which all remained under Spanish control. The Sultan was restyled King of Morocco in August 1957, and became Prime Minister in May 1960. He died in February 1961, and was succeeded by his son, Moulay Hassan, who took the title of Hassan II.

Elections to Morocco's first House of Representatives took place in May 1963, and six months later King Hassan relinquished the post of Prime Minister. In June 1965, however, increasing political fragmentation prompted Hassan to declare a 'state of exception', and to resume full legislative and executive powers. The emergency provisions remained in force until July 1970, when a new Constitution was approved. Elections in the following month resulted in a pro-Government majority in the new Majlis al-Nuab (Chamber of Representatives).

Domestic Political Affairs

In July 1971 an attempted *coup d'état* was suppressed by forces loyal to the King. Among those subsequently arrested were numerous members of the left-wing Union nationale des forces populaires (UNFP), five of whom were sentenced to death. Although a revised Constitution was approved in March 1972 by popular referendum, a general election did not take place until June 1977. Two-thirds of the deputies in the Chamber of Representatives were directly elected, the remainder being elected by local government councils, professional associations and labour organizations. Supporters of the King's policies won a majority of seats in the new legislature. A Government of national unity was formed, including opposition representatives from Istiqlal and the Mouvement populaire (MP) in addition to the pro-monarchist independents.

In October 1981, when it was announced that the term of office of the Chamber of Representatives was to be extended from four to six years, all 14 deputies belonging to the Union socialiste des forces populaires (USFP) withdrew from the assembly. Elections to the legislature were postponed and an interim Government of national unity was appointed, headed by Muhammad Karim Lamrani (Prime Minister in 1971–72). The new Government included members of the six main political parties: Istiqlal, the MP, the Parti national démocrate (PND), the Rassemblement national des indépendants (RNI), the Union constitutionnelle (UC) and the USFP. The postponed legislative elections took place in September and October 1984. Despite significant gains by the USFP, the Chamber of Representatives was again dominated by the centre-right parties. A new Cabinet, appointed in April 1985, included members of the MP, the PND, the RNI and the UC. Lamrani resigned in September 1986, on the grounds of ill health, and was replaced by Azzeddine Laraki.

King Hassan announced in March 1992 that the Constitution was to be revised and submitted for approval in a national referendum, in preparation for legislative elections (which had been postponed since 1990, pending settlement of the Western Sahara dispute). The King indicated in July that the elections would take place in November, and that voting would be extended to include Western Sahara—irrespective of the UN's progress in organizing a referendum on the territory's status (see below). In August the King dissolved the Government, and named Lamrani as Prime Minister in an interim, non-partisan Government. According to official results, the revised Constitution was overwhelmingly endorsed by 99.96% of voters in the national referendum, which was held in September. Under the terms of the new Constitution, the King would retain strong executive powers, including the right to appoint the Prime Minister, although government members would henceforth be nominated by the premier. The Government would be required to reflect the composition of the Chamber of Representatives, and was obliged to submit its legislative programme for the Chamber's approval; new legislation would be promulgated one month after having been endorsed by parliament, regardless of whether royal assent had been received. Provision was also made for the establishment of a Constitutional Council and of an Economic and Social Council, and guarantees of human rights were enshrined in the document.

Legislative elections eventually took place on 25 June 1993. Parties of the Bloc démocratique (also known as the Koutla démocratique)—grouping Istiqlal, the USFP, the Parti du progrès et du socialisme (PPS), the Organisation de l'action démocratique et populaire (OADP) and the UNFP—won a combined total of 99 of the 222 directly elective seats in the enlarged chamber. The MP won 33 seats, the RNI 28 and the UC 27. The indirect election (by an electoral college) of the remaining 111 members of the Chamber, which followed on 17 September, was less favourable to the Bloc démocratique, which won only 21 further seats. Of the 333 seats in the Chamber, the USFP now controlled 56, the UC 54, Istiqlal 52, the MP 51 and the RNI 41. In November the King reappointed Lamrani as premier.

In May 1994 Hassan replaced Lamrani with Abdellatif Filali, who retained his post as Minister of State for Foreign Affairs and Co-operation when a new Government was formed. In July the King appealed to all political parties to participate in a government of national unity, and in October he announced his intention to select a premier from the ranks of the opposition. However, negotiations on the formation of a coalition government failed, apparently owing to the Bloc démocratique's refusal to join an administration in which Driss Basri (a long-serving government member and close associate of the King) remained as Minister of the Interior and Information, and in January 1995 Hassan instructed Filali to form a new cabinet.

Muhammad Basri, a prominent opposition figure (sentenced to death *in absentia* in 1974) and founder member of both the UNFP and the USFP, returned to Morocco from France in June 1995, after 28 years in exile. It was widely believed that his rehabilitation had been precipitated by the royal amnesty of July 1994 and by the return to Morocco (also from France) in May 1995 of the First Secretary of the USFP, Abd al-Rahman el-Youssoufi. Despite King Hassan's assertion that there were no longer any political detainees in Morocco, a report published by the Association marocaine des droits humains (AMDH) in February 1996 claimed that 58 political prisoners (primarily radical Islamists, supporters of independence for Western Sahara and left-wing activists) remained in detention.

In August 1996 the King presented further constitutional amendments, including the creation of an indirectly elected second parliamentary assembly, the Majlis al-Mustasharin (Chamber of Advisers), and the introduction of direct elections for all members of the Chamber of Representatives. Most political parties supported the reforms; however, an appeal by the OADP leadership for a boycott of a planned referendum on the amendments led to a split in the party and the subsequent creation of the Parti socialiste démocratique (PSD). According to official results of the referendum, held in September, the reforms were approved by 99.6% of voters. Legislation regarding the new bicameral parliament was promulgated in August 1997: the Chamber of Representatives was to comprise 325 members, directly elected for a five-year term; the 270 members of the Chamber of Advisers would be indirectly elected, for a nine-year term, by local councils (which would choose 162 members), chambers of commerce (81) and trade unions (27).

At elections to the Chamber of Representatives held on 14 November 1997, the Bloc démocratique won a combined total of 102 seats (of which the USFP took 57 and Istiqlal 32); the centre-right Entente nationale took 100 (50 secured by the UC and 40 by the MP), and centrist parties 97 (including 46 obtained by the RNI). The Mouvement populaire constitutionnel et démocratique (MPCD), which earlier in the year had formally absorbed members of the Islamist Al Islah wa Attajdid, won nine seats, securing parliamentary representation for the first time. (In October 1998 the MPCD changed its name to the Parti de la justice et du développement—PJD.) At indirect elections to the Chamber of Advisers, which followed on 5 December, centrist parties won 90 of the seats (42 secured by the RNI and 33 by the Mouvement démocratique et social), the Entente nationale 76 (28 obtained by the UC and 27 by the MP) and the Bloc démocratique 44 (21 won by Istiqlal). In February 1998 the King appointed el-Youssoufi as the new Prime Minister; this was the first time since independence that a socialist had been appointed to the Moroccan premiership.

The accession of King Muhammad VI

King Hassan died on 23 July 1999, after several years of ill health. His eldest son, Crown Prince Sidi Muhammad, succeeded as King Muhammad VI. At the end of July the new King decreed an amnesty whereby some 8,000 prisoners were freed and more than 38,000 had their sentences reduced. In August the King ordered the creation within the Conseil Consultatif des Droits de l'Homme (CCDH)—established by King Hassan in April 1990—of an independent commission to determine levels of compensation for families of missing political activists and for those subjected to arbitrary detention. In April 1999 the CCDH had announced that it had been agreed to compensate the families of 112 people who were now officially acknowledged as having 'disappeared' between 1960 and 1990. However, independent Moroccan human rights organizations asserted that the number of missing people amounted to almost 600. In November 1999 King Muhammad approved the return to Morocco of the family of former opposition activist and UNFP leader Mehdi Ben Barka, who had been abducted and apparently murdered in Paris, France, in 1965.

Meanwhile, in November 1999 King Muhammad dismissed the long-serving Minister of State for the Interior, Driss Basri, apparently in response to the violent suppression of protests in Western Sahara in September (see Western Sahara). The new Minister of the Interior, Ahmed Midaoui (a former Director of National Security), immediately pledged to work towards the strengthening of democracy and the reconciliation of the administration and the people of Morocco. Victims of repression and their families, together with left-wing political parties and non-governmental organizations, subsequently formed a 'Justice and Trust' organization, which aimed to investigate human rights abuses in Morocco since independence. In April 2000 the Government commenced payments, reportedly totalling 40m. dirhams, in respect of the cases of an initial 40 victims of arbitrary detention, from the fund established in the previous year.

In September 2000 King Muhammad appointed Driss Jettou, a former Minister of Finance and Industry, as Minister of the Interior. (Ahmed Midaoui became an adviser to the King.) In October Muhammad established a royal institute charged with preserving the language and culture of the country's Berber population; the institute would also work towards integrating the Berber language into the education system.

In June 2001 the Moroccan authorities granted Jean-Baptiste Parlos, the French judge leading the inquiry into the disappearance of Mehdi Ben Barka (see above), permission to visit Morocco as part of his investigation. Later that month Ahmed Boukhari, a former member of the Moroccan special services, alleged in a newspaper article that Ben Barka had been kidnapped in Paris by French police officers in the employ of the Moroccan secret service and had been tortured to death by Morocco's then Minister of the Interior, Gen. Muhammad Oufkir. In July Boukhari received a summons to appear before the French investigation into Ben Barka's disappearance; however, the Moroccan authorities refused to grant Boukhari a passport, and in the following month he was arrested on charges of financial irregularity. Boukhari's detention was condemned by human rights organizations, which claimed that the Moroccan Government was attempting to prevent Boukhari from testifying at the Parlos inquiry. In December 2002 the Moroccan authorities announced that they would co-operate fully with the French investigation into the Ben Barka affair, and in January 2003 a French judge travelled to Rabat where he interviewed Boukhari about the disappearance of Ben Barka. In October 2007 a French magistrate issued arrest warrants for five Moroccan officials suspected of involvement in the case. However, the release of the warrants was delayed until 1 October 2009, and the following day it was announced by the French Ministry of Justice and Freedoms that the release was to be suspended to allow the French authorities to obtain more details on the suspects as required by the International Criminal Police Commission (Interpol).

Meanwhile, el-Youssoufi stated in January 2002 that he would stand down as Prime Minister after the forthcoming legislative elections, but would remain as First Secretary of the USFP. In March the Government agreed a number of changes to the electoral system, including the introduction of proportional representation and the guarantee that at least 10% of the 325 seats in the lower house would be reserved for women. At the general election, which took place on 27 September, the USFP won the largest number of seats, although its representation in the Chamber of Representatives was reduced from 57 to 50 seats. Istiqlal increased its parliamentary representation to 48 members, while the PJD took 42 seats, the RNI 41, the MP 27, the Mouvement national populaire (MNP) 18 and the UC 16. The rate of voter participation was recorded at just 51.6% of the electorate. In October King Muhammad appointed Jettou as the new Prime Minister, and a new Government was announced in the following month. Despite securing the third highest number of seats in the Chamber of Representatives, the PJD was not allocated any ministerial portfolios. The new Cabinet comprised members of the USFP, Istiqlal, the RNI, the MNP, the MP and the PPS, as well as a number of non-affiliated technocrats—one of whom, Al Mustapha Sahel, replaced Jettou as Minister of the Interior. Three women were appointed to the Government. In early May 2003 King Muhammad marked the occasion of the birth of a son and heir to the throne, Prince Moulay Hassan, by ordering the release of an estimated 9,000 prisoners and reducing the gaol terms of a further 38,000.

Suicide attacks in Casablanca

In mid-May 2003 45 people died and more than 100 others were injured in a series of suicide bomb attacks in central Casablanca, which targeted the Belgian consulate, a Spanish restaurant and a Jewish cultural centre. Among those killed were reported to be 12 suicide bombers, and two other suspected attackers were detained by the security forces along with some 30 others thought to have been involved in the bombings. The Moroccan authorities believed that the bombers were linked to a small Moroccan-based militant Islamist group, al-Assirat al-Moustaquim (Righteous Path), but that the attacks had been orchestrated by an international terrorist network operating in Europe, possibly the al-Qa'ida organization of the Saudi Arabian-born Islamist Osama bin Laden. In late May the suspected co-ordinator of the attacks, who had been arrested in Fez, died in police custody as a result of ill health. Later in May stricter anti-terrorism measures were approved by the legislature, including an increase in the number of offences punishable by the death sentence.

In mid-July 2003 10 of the alleged 31 members of the radical Islamist group Salafia Jihadia, who had been arrested during police operations against Islamist networks in 2002, were sentenced to death by a court in Casablanca, having been convicted of murder and attempted murder. The remainder of the accused received lengthy prison terms. Later in July 2003 it was announced that more than 700 people would be tried in connection with the bomb attacks; 52 defendants subsequently appeared before Casablanca's criminal court. In August four men, including the two suspected surviving suicide bombers, received death sentences for their roles in the violence; 39 others were sentenced to life imprisonment for plotting further attacks in Agadir, Marrakesh and Essaouira. In February 2005 10 men were imprisoned for eight years for membership of Salafia Jihadia, and in July two members of Salafia Jihadia were sentenced to death, having been convicted of the murders in Casablanca of five people, including an official of the Ministry of the Interior. In April 2008 nine of the men convicted for their links to the suicide bombings in Casablanca escaped from prison in Kénitra, north of Rabat. Seven of the fugitives were reportedly serving life sentences, while the other two were serving terms of 20 years.

Despite the clampdown on Islamist activity following the Casablanca bombings, King Muhammad continued to pursue his policies of reform and modernization of Moroccan society, including provision for the teaching of the Berber language in schools. In October 2003 the King announced major revisions to the *mudawana* (family code), which he claimed would promote female equality and protect children's rights. The reforms (originally outlined in 2000) would raise the legal age of marriage for women from 15 to 18 and simplify the procedure for women seeking a divorce from their husband. Although polygamy was not to be outlawed under the new legislation, women would be able to prevent their husbands from taking a second wife and would also be provided with equal authority and property rights within the marriage. In January 2004 the changes to the *mudawana* were approved by the legislature.

In February 2006 King Muhammad appointed Chakib Benmoussa, a non-affiliate, as Minister of the Interior to replace Sahel, who became Morocco's ambassador to the UN. In May–June the police arrested more than 500 members of Al-Adl wal-Ihsan, an unauthorized but generally tolerated Islamist movement, after unconfirmed reports that it was planning an uprising; most of those detained were quickly released. Al-Adl wal-Ihsan had launched an 'open doors' campaign earlier in 2006 to disseminate information among the general public and recruit new members outside its traditional areas of support such as mosques and universities. Indications of a possible threat from militant Islamism surfaced in August, when 56 members of a group called Ansar al-Mahdi were arrested on suspicion of planning a campaign of violence against the monarchy. Among those detained were several members of the police and armed forces as well as three women, two of whom were married to pilots of the national airline, Royal Air Maroc. In January 2008 the leader of Ansar al-Mahdi, Hassan Khattab, was sentenced to 25 years in prison, while 49 other members of the group were given prison terms of between two and 20 years, having been convicted of various crimes including plotting to attack government buildings and stealing funds to enable them to pursue militant activities.

In March 2007 a suicide bomb attack at an internet café in Casablanca resulted in three people being injured. In April, during a police operation in the city in connection with the recent bombing, three suspected Islamist militants detonated explosive belts and a fourth was shot dead by police as he attempted to do so. Four days later two suicide bombers targeted the US consulate and a US cultural centre in the city. The series of attacks coincided with two large explosions in Algiers, Algeria, that were claimed by al-Qa'ida Organization in the Land of the Islamic Maghreb (AQIM, formerly the Groupe salafiste pour la prédication et le combat—see the chapter on Algeria). Although an internet statement purporting to be from al-Qa'ida claimed responsibility for the explosions in Casablanca, Moroccan police insisted that they were the work of a group with no links to external organizations. In October 2008 more than 40 people received prison sentences, ranging from two to 30 years, for their involvement in the Casablanca bombings. Meanwhile, in February 2008 32 members of the small Islamist party al-Badil al-Hadari (Alternative Civilization)—including its Secretary-General, Mustapha Moatassim—were arrested in Morocco on suspicion of being involved in plans to carry out politically motivated attacks. The party was subsequently banned by the Moroccan authorities following the discovery of weapons and allegations of links with international terrorist networks, including al-Qa'ida in Afghanistan. By February 2008 Moroccan police claimed to have dismantled at least 50 terrorist cells and to have made nearly 3,000 arrests since the Casablanca suicide bombings in 2003. Extensive anti-terrorism operations continued, with 32 people being imprisoned in October 2008, charged with recruiting militants to fight in Iraq. In April 2009 43 people were convicted on charges of belonging to terrorist organizations, including AQIM; 29 received prison sentences of between two and 20 years; the remainder were fined. A further 24 terror suspects were apprehended in September when the Moroccan authorities carried out a series of arrests across the country, claiming to have dismantled a terrorist recruiting network with links to al-Qa'ida-affiliated organizations in Iraq, Somalia and Afghanistan.

At the general election held on 7 September 2007, Istiqlal won a majority of seats (52) in the Chamber of Representatives. The PJD came in second place with 46 seats, followed by the MP (which had merged with the MNP and the Union démocratique in 2006) with 41, and the RNI with 39. The USFP, which previously held the majority of seats in the legislature, only managed to secure 38 seats. Voter turn-out for the election was at a record low of 37% of eligible participants. On 19 September Abbas el-Fassi, the leader of Istiqlal and Minister of State in the outgoing administration, was appointed as the new Prime Minister by King Muhammad. In October a new Government made up of a coalition of four parties (Istiqlal, the RNI, the USFP and the PPS), along with several independent ministers, was sworn into office. Former Minister of Industry Salaheddine Mezouar was named as Minister of the Economy and Finance, and the Deputy Minister of Foreign Affairs and Co-operation, Taieb Fassi Fihri, was promoted to head the foreign affairs portfolio. The new Cabinet included seven women (two of these becoming deputy ministers).

The formation of the Parti de l'authenticité et de la modernité

A new political organization, the Parti de l'authenticité et de la modernité (PAM), was founded in August 2008 by Fouad Ali el-Himma, a former Deputy Minister of the Interior and a close ally of King Muhammad. A number of existing parties, including the Parti Al Ahd, the Parti de l'environnement et du développement and the PND, joined the new grouping. (However, differences quickly emerged within the broad coalition and the former leaders of those parties left the PAM to re-form their previous organizations in 2008–09.) In January 2009, following the announcement that municipal elections would be held in June, a new quota reserving 2,822 seats (some 12% of the total) for female candidates was introduced. The initiative followed a year-long campaign, supported by female members of parliament and various non-governmental organizations, demanding a quota of one-third of seats for women candidates. In the previous municipal elections in 2003 women candidates had won just 127 seats.

In May 2009 the PAM announced that it was to withdraw its support from the governing coalition and align itself with the opposition, allowing itself to present itself as a viable alternative, despite its close links to the King. Indeed, at the municipal elections in June the PAM won the largest share of the votes cast, with 21.7%, replacing Istiqlal as the major party at municipal level and representing a major upset for the governing coalition. Istiqlal secured 19.1% of the votes cast, while the RNI obtained 14.8% and the USFP 11.6%. Despite its success at the 2007 legislative elections, the PJD secured only 5.5% of the vote; it was claimed by the party following the elections that alleged vote-buying by its rivals had contributed to its poor result. Turn-out was registered at 52.4% of the electorate. In late June 2010 Abdelilah Benkirane was elected as Secretary-General of the PJD; he succeeded Saâdeddine Othmani, who had been blamed by many party members for its recent electoral failure.

King Muhammad effected a government reorganization in early January 2010. Notable among the changes were the replacement of Chakib Benmoussa as Minister of the Interior with Taïb Cherkaoui (hitherto First President of the Supreme Court), and the appointment of Muhammad Naciri as Minister of Justice. The reorganization followed the announcement by the King of a plan to devolve certain powers from central government to local councils. The programme, under the supervision of a newly created Advisory Commission on Regionalization, aimed to provide regional authorities with greater powers to determine

MOROCCO

their own development plans; it was ongoing in early 2011. Meanwhile, in late February 2010 King Muhammad appointed Mustapha Farès as the new First President of the Supreme Court. In April Abdelwahed Radi, the First Secretary of the USFP, was elected as President of the Chamber of Representatives. In December Abdellatif Loudiyi was named as the new Minister-delegate in charge of National Defence, following the death of the previous incumbent, Abderrahmane Sbaï, in October.

It was reported in April 2010 that 24 suspected AQIM militants had been detained by the Moroccan authorities on suspicion on planning terrorist attacks against foreign nationals in Morocco. The security forces claimed to have uncovered details of several other terrorist cells during 2010–11: these included the apparent discovery, in June 2010, of a Palestinian-led network, which was plotting to attack Jewish institutions in the kingdom, and the dismantling, in January 2011, of a cell apparently linked to AQIM training camps in Algeria and Mali, which was plotting suicide and car bomb attacks against Moroccan security targets. Some 27 alleged Islamist militants from the cell were detained and significant numbers of weapons were reportedly discovered by the Moroccan authorities.

Recent developments: King Muhammad announces political and economic reforms

In February 2011 a series of street protests were held in Rabat and a number of other cities by thousands of Moroccans seeking improved living conditions, an end to state corruption, and reform of the country's political system, in particular reduced powers for the monarch. Some youths set fire to themselves, in imitation of an act of self-immolation by a Tunisian in December 2010, which had sparked a wave of unrest across the Middle East and North Africa. The largest pro-reform demonstrations, held in around 20 Moroccan cities on 20 February 2011, were attended by various groups, including left-wing activists, students and Islamists; the protesters thus came to be known as the February 20 Movement. Five people were reported to have died in a fire started by rioters in al-Hoceima, while the security forces made a total of 120 arrests. On 21 February King Muhammad inaugurated a new Conseil économique et social (CES—the provision for which had been enshrined in the 1992 Constitution), under the chairmanship of former Minister of the Interior Benmoussa. The CES was to formulate a new social chapter and to advise the Government on a wide range of socio-economic issues, such as the demands of the labour market (see Economic Affairs). On 9 March King Muhammad delivered a speech to the nation in which he pledged to implement a far-reaching review of the Constitution and to carry out other political reforms such as introducing an independent judiciary, strengthening the role of parliament, allowing for the leader of the party with the largest representation in the Chamber of Representatives to form a government, and implementing the plan to devolve certain powers to Morocco's regional authorities. On 14 March a new consultative committee—to include representatives of political parties, civil society organizations and trade unions—was appointed and requested to issue its proposals on possible constitutional amendments by June. The King promised to allow the electorate to vote on any constitutional changes in a national referendum.

Meanwhile, on 3 March 2011 the Moroccan authorities had granted increased powers to the Advisory Council on Human Rights, which was renamed the National Human Rights Council and was to monitor the country's human rights situation and investigate alleged violations. Largely peaceful rallies in support of political, social and economic reforms continued during March and April in several cities, including Rabat, Casablanca and Marrakesh. Meanwhile, from mid-March many Islamists being held in Moroccan prisons on terrorism-related charges staged hunger strikes in protest against what they deemed to be their unfair detention, leading the Ministry of Justice to initiate a dialogue with representatives of the prisoners in order to address their grievances. In early April the US Department of State's 2010 report on Morocco commended the country's leadership for its considerable achievements in having improved female representation in local government and for efforts to improve the country's human rights situation. French officials also praised King Muhammad for the reforms he had announced in March 2011. However, these favourable assessments contrasted sharply with those of the US-based Human Rights Watch, which, in its World Report published in January 2011, described certain aspects of Morocco's human rights record in 2010 as 'decidedly poor'; the organization was particularly critical of the lack of press freedom, and the treatment both of suspected Islamist militants being held in Moroccan gaols and of the population in the disputed region of Western Sahara.

Western Sahara

Following the cession of the Spanish enclave of Ifni to Morocco in 1969, political opinion in Morocco was united in opposing the continued occupation by Spain of areas considered to be historically parts of Moroccan territory: namely Spanish Sahara and Spanish North Africa (q.v.)—a number of small enclaves on Morocco's Mediterranean coast. A campaign to annex Spanish Sahara, initiated in 1974, received active support from all Moroccan political parties. In October 1975 King Hassan ordered a 'Green March' by more than 300,000 unarmed Moroccans to occupy the territory. The marchers were stopped by the Spanish authorities when they had barely crossed the border, but in November Spain agreed to cede the territory to Morocco and Mauritania, to be apportioned equally between them. Spain formally relinquished sovereignty of Spanish Sahara in February 1976. Moroccan troops moved into the territory to confront a guerrilla uprising led by the Frente Popular para la Liberación de Saguia el-Hamra y Río de Oro (the Polisario Front), a national liberation movement supported by Algeria and (later) Libya, which aimed to achieve an independent Western Saharan state. On 27 February the Polisario Front declared the 'Sahrawi Arab Democratic Republic' (SADR), and shortly afterwards established a 'Government-in-exile' in Algeria. In protest, Morocco severed diplomatic relations with Algeria.

Moroccan troops inflicted heavy casualties on the insurgents, and ensured the security of Western Sahara's main population centres, but they failed to prevent constant infiltration, harassment and sabotage by Polisario forces. Moreover, Polisario had considerable success against Mauritanian troops, and in August 1979 Mauritania renounced its claim to Saharan territory and signed a peace treaty with the Polisario Front. Morocco immediately asserted its claim to the whole of Western Sahara and annexed the region.

In July 1980 the SADR applied to join the Organization of African Unity (OAU, now African Union—AU, see p. 183) as a sovereign state. Although 26 of the 50 members then recognized the Polisario Front as the rightful government of Western Sahara, Morocco insisted that a two-thirds' majority was needed to confer membership. Morocco rejected an OAU proposal for a cease-fire and a referendum on the territory, and in 1981 heavy fighting resumed in the region. The SADR was accepted as the OAU's 51st member in early 1982, but a threat by 18 members to leave the organization in protest necessitated a compromise whereby the SADR, while remaining a member, agreed not to attend OAU meetings. In late 1984 a SADR delegation did attend a summit meeting of the OAU with little opposition from other states, causing Morocco to resign from the organization. Meanwhile, decisive victories for Polisario in Western Sahara proved impossible, as Morocco constructed a 2,500-km defensive wall of sand, equipped with electronic detectors, to surround the territory.

In October 1985 Morocco announced a unilateral cease-fire in Western Sahara, and invited the UN to supervise a referendum to be held there the following January. A series of indirect talks between the two sides in 1986–87 failed to achieve a solution, and in January 1988 Polisario forces renewed their offensive against Moroccan positions in Western Sahara. In August, however, it was announced that the Polisario Front and Morocco had provisionally accepted a peace plan proposed by the UN Secretary-General, Javier Pérez de Cuéllar, which envisaged the conclusion of a formal cease-fire, a reduction in Moroccan military forces in Western Sahara and the withdrawal of Polisario forces to their bases, to be followed by a referendum on self-determination in Western Sahara. A list of eligible voters was to be based on the Spanish census of 1974. A meeting in Marrakesh in January 1989 between King Hassan and officials of the Polisario Front and the SADR—the first direct contact for 13 years—was apparently limited to exchanges of goodwill, but was followed, in February, by the announcement of a unilateral cease-fire by Polisario. In September, however, Hassan rejected the possibility of official negotiations with the SADR, and, later that month, Polisario renewed its military attacks on Moroccan positions.

UN Security Council Resolution No. 690 of April 1991 established a peace-keeping force, the UN Mission for the Referendum in Western Sahara (MINURSO, see p. 90), which was to implement the 1988 plan for a referendum on self-determination. In

June 1991 Polisario agreed to a formal cease-fire, with effect from 6 September, from which date the 2,000-strong MINURSO delegation would undertake its duties in the region. Reports in September suggested that some 30,000 people had entered Western Sahara from Morocco, prompting claims that the Moroccan authorities were attempting to alter the region's demography in advance of the referendum. It was also reported that more than 170,000 Sahrawis who had fled the region since 1976 were being repatriated in order that they might participate in the referendum. By November 1991 only 200 MINURSO personnel had been deployed in Western Sahara, and the peace process was undermined further by Morocco's failure to withdraw any of its forces from the region (under the terms of the cease-fire agreement, Morocco was to have withdrawn one-half of its 130,000 troops from Western Sahara by mid-September). In May 1992 Pérez de Cuéllar's successor as UN Secretary-General, Dr Boutros Boutros-Ghali, announced that Morocco and Polisario representatives were to begin indirect talks under his auspices. In the same month, however, Morocco appeared to prejudge the result of the proposed referendum by including the population of Western Sahara in the voting lists for its own regional and local elections. In June the SADR Government, which by this time was recognized by 75 countries, appealed to the international community and the UN to condemn alleged Moroccan violations of the cease-fire and to exert pressure for the implementation of the UN peace plan.

In July 1993 the first direct negotiations took place between the Moroccan Government and Polisario, although little progress was achieved. In April 1994 Polisario accepted the UN programme for the registration of voters. However, the work of a UN voter identification commission, which had been due to commence in June, was delayed by the Moroccan Government's objection to the inclusion of OAU observers in the process. In mid-1995 Polisario withdrew from the voter identification process, in protest against the severity of sentences placed upon pro-independence Sahrawi protesters by the Moroccan authorities and against alleged Moroccan violations of the cease-fire. In September the SADR announced the formation of a new 14-member Government, headed by Mahfoud Ali Beïba, and in October the first elected Sahrawi National Assembly was inaugurated at a refugee camp in Tindouf, Algeria.

The UN Security Council voted periodically to extend MINURSO's mandate on a short-term basis; however, in May 1996 it was announced that the mission's personnel was to be reduced by 20%. Also that month the Security Council voted to suspend the registration of voters in Western Sahara until 'convincing proof' was offered by the Moroccan Government and the Sahrawi leadership that they would not further obstruct preparations for the referendum.

In March 1997 the new UN Secretary-General, Kofi Annan, appointed James Baker (a former US Secretary of State) as his Personal Envoy for Western Sahara. In June Baker mediated in talks in Portugal between representatives of Morocco and the SADR. By September 1998 a total of 147,350 voters had been identified since the commencement of the process of identification in August 1994, but the issue of the disputed tribes remained unresolved. In June 1998, meanwhile, as Morocco intensified its efforts to rejoin the OAU, several member states debated the expulsion from the organization of the SADR; only a minority of OAU member countries continued to recognize its independent status.

During talks with Moroccan and SADR officials in November 1998, the UN Secretary-General warned that the UN would withdraw from Western Sahara if the two parties failed to show political will towards resolving the conflict. Annan presented proposals regarding the disputed tribes, the publication of a list of voters not contested by either party, and the repatriation of refugees under the auspices of the UN High Commissioner for Refugees. Although the proposals were accepted by Polisario, the Moroccan authorities expressed reservations. Morocco delayed the signing of a technical agreement with the UN until February 1999: Algeria and Mauritania had signed similar accords with the UN in November 1998. In July 1999 MINURSO published a list of 84,251 people provisionally entitled to vote in the referendum, which was scheduled to be held on 31 July 2000.

In February 1999, meanwhile, the SADR announced the formation of a new Government, led by Beïba's predecessor, Bouchraya Hammoudi Bayoune. In September the Polisario Front congress re-elected the President of the SADR, Muhammad Abd al-Aziz, as Secretary-General of the organization. In October a delegation comprising several ministers of the Moroccan Government was dispatched to el-Aaiún (the principal city in Western Sahara, also known as Laâyoune) for consultations with the Sahrawi population at the behest of King Muhammad—who had in September established a royal commission to monitor affairs in Western Sahara.

In response to indications by UN officials in November 1999 that the referendum was likely to be subject to a further postponement, Polisario stated that it could not rule out a return to an armed struggle. Nevertheless, in late November Polisario released 191 Moroccan prisoners. In December the mandate of MINURSO was once again extended to enable it to complete its work on the identification of possible voters in the referendum. In January 2000 it was announced that 86,381 out of a total of 198,481 people identified in Western Sahara would be eligible to vote in the referendum. In February, however, Annan postponed the referendum indefinitely, and warned, furthermore, of the possibility that it might never take place, owing to the persistent differences regarding criteria for eligibility to vote. By March the number of appeals lodged by those deemed ineligible to vote exceeded 130,000, and Abd al-Aziz reiterated the threat of the resumption of armed hostilities if Morocco continued to obstruct the UN peace plan.

In May 2000 Baker chaired further direct talks between representatives of Morocco and Polisario in London, United Kingdom; however, the meeting failed to make any substantive progress. In October Annan urged Morocco partially to devolve authority in Western Sahara, stating that if no such concessions were granted, the UN would reactivate plans to hold a referendum in the territory. In February 2001 Annan announced that if Morocco failed to offer or support some devolution of governmental authority, MINURSO would be directed to begin the process of hearing appeals regarding eligibility to vote in the referendum.

In June 2001 the UN Security Council unanimously approved a compromise resolution (No. 1359), formulated by Baker, which encouraged Polisario and Morocco to discuss an autonomy plan for Western Sahara without abandoning the delayed referendum. Under the terms of the autonomy proposal, the inhabitants of Western Sahara would have the right to elect their own legislative and executive bodies and have control over most areas of local government for a period of at least five years, during which Morocco would retain control over defence and foreign affairs. A referendum on the final status of the territory would take place within this five-year period. In August Baker hosted talks in Wyoming, USA, attended by representatives from Polisario, Mauritania and Algeria; however, Polisario subsequently accused the UN of ceding to Moroccan pressure and in September Polisario announced its formal rejection of Baker's proposal. In the following month King Muhammad visited Western Sahara for the first time since his accession to the throne, and in November he granted an amnesty to 56 prisoners in Western Sahara.

Following exploratory negotiations held between Baker and government officials in Mauritania and Algeria, as well as with Abd al-Aziz and King Muhammad, in May 2003 Annan formally released details of a new peace plan aimed at ending the Western Sahara dispute. The new plan, known as 'Baker Plan II', proposed immediate self-government for Western Sahara for a period of four to five years, after which time a referendum would be held in order to give all bona fide residents the opportunity to decide the long-term future of the territory. The Security Council approved Annan's proposals in June. At the end of that month Polisario, under strong pressure from Algeria, accepted the Baker plan as a basis for negotiation. Morocco, however, refused to accept any 'imposed decision' on Western Sahara. On 31 July the UN Security Council unanimously adopted Resolution 1495, which supported Baker Plan II and called on parties and states of the region to co-operate fully with the Secretary-General and his Personal Envoy in working towards its implementation. (However, following strong opposition from France, the resolution did not demand that Morocco and Polisario comply with the plan.) It also called on Polisario to release without further delay all remaining Moroccan prisoners of war, and for both sides to co-operate with the International Committee of the Red Cross to resolve the fate of persons unaccounted for since the beginning of the conflict. Polisario released 243 Moroccan prisoners of war in September, 300 in November, and a further 100 in February 2004.

In late April 2004 the UN Security Council unanimously adopted Resolution 1541, which urged the two sides to accept the UN plan to grant Western Sahara immediate self-government and which extended MINURSO's mandate until October. (The Security Council continued thereafter to extend MINURSO's mandate at regular intervals.) Morocco, however, continued to reject this proposal, maintaining that it could not accept a plan for a referendum that included independence as an option, and remained insistent on granting the territory 'autonomy within the framework of Moroccan sovereignty'. In June 2004 James Baker resigned as Annan's Personal Envoy for Western Sahara; at the request of Annan, he was replaced by Alvaro de Soto, a former Peruvian diplomat who had hitherto been the Secretary-General's Special Representative for the region. In September de Soto commenced talks with the Moroccan authorities and Polisario to attempt to resolve the impasse, and a resolution (No. 1570) adopted by the Security Council in October calling for an advancement towards a political solution was welcomed by the Moroccan authorities. In early 2005 de Soto left his role of Special Representative and immediately assumed the position of UN Special Co-ordinator for the Middle East Peace Process. In July Annan appointed Peter van Walsum of the Netherlands as his new Personal Envoy for Western Sahara, and in August it was announced that Francesco Bastagli of Italy would replace de Soto as Special Representative of the Secretary-General and MINURSO Chief of Mission. Later that month Polisario released the remaining 408 Moroccan prisoners of war, some of whom had been held in Tindouf for more than 20 years, one month after Abd al-Aziz had urged Morocco to release 150 Sahrawis he claimed were still in detention. In a televised address to mark the 30th anniversary of the Green March, King Muhammad announced his intention to consult with Morocco's political parties on the issue of autonomy for Western Sahara 'within the sovereignty of the kingdom'. However, Polisario immediately rejected the plan and stated that a referendum was the only viable solution.

In March 2006 King Muhammad visited Western Sahara for the third time since his accession to the throne in 1999, and royal pardons were granted to 216 Sahrawi prisoners. (In April the King ordered the release of all the remaining 48 Sahrawi prisoners held by Morocco.) During the visit Muhammad also announced the appointment of a revised Royal Advisory Council for Saharan Affairs (CORCAS), a body that had been originally established in 1981 by King Hassan II. The 140 newly appointed members were to assist with the formulation of draft proposals for Sahrawi autonomy. In mid-April 2006 Annan submitted a report to the UN Security Council in which he noted the demise of Baker Plan II, which had not been mentioned in any of the relevant Security Council resolutions since Morocco rejected the proposal in 2004, and called on all parties in the dispute, including Algeria, to engage in direct negotiations without preconditions in order to reach a consensual solution to the impasse. In February 2007 the new UN Secretary-General, Ban Ki-Moon, appointed Julian Harston of the United Kingdom as his Special Representative.

The 'Moroccan initiative for negotiating an autonomy statute for the Sahara region' was finally presented to the UN Security Council in April 2007. It proposed the granting of extensive legislative, executive and judicial autonomy to the region, with Morocco retaining sovereignty and control of borders, as well as responsibility for national security, and foreign and religious affairs, among other areas. The plan was rejected by Polisario, which described it as 'null and void' and on the same day offered the UN a rival plan for a referendum with three options—full independence, autonomy within Morocco or full integration—including proposals for a special political and economic relationship with Morocco in the event of a vote for independence. On 30 April the Security Council unanimously adopted Resolution 1754, which described Morocco's plan as 'serious and credible', while also noting the Polisario proposal, and again called on both sides to enter into direct negotiations without preconditions under the aegis of the Secretary-General. UN-mediated talks between Morocco and Polisario (attended by representatives of Algeria and Mauritania) were duly held in June and August in Manhasset, New York, USA. Two further rounds of negotiations were held in January and March 2008. While the talks failed to achieve any significant progress, Moroccan officials and Polisario agreed to consider relaxing restrictions on people travelling by road to visit families in the disputed territory. A further resolution (No. 1813), adopted by the Security Council on 30 April, emphasized the legitimacy of the Moroccan autonomy proposal.

A renewed UN effort to facilitate another round of peace talks began in January 2009 with the appointment of Christopher Ross, a former US diplomat, as Personal Envoy to the Secretary-General for Western Sahara. In April the Security Council approved Resolution 1871, which reiterated the principles of the preceding resolution and extended MINURSO's mandate for a further year. In July Ban Ki-Moon appointed Hany Abdel-Aziz of Egypt as Special Representative, replacing Harston, who had relinquished the role in February. Informal talks took place between representatives of Polisario and the Moroccan Government in Vienna, Austria, in August. However, tensions arose in October when seven Sahrawi human rights activists were arrested in Casablanca and charged with making contact with parties hostile to Morocco after they had visited Sahrawi refugee camps in Tindouf. In November a prominent Sahrawi activist, Aminatou Haidar, was expelled from Morocco and stranded at Lanzarote Airport in the Canary Islands, Spain, having refused to declare Moroccan nationality upon returning to Western Sahara from the USA. Haidar began a 32-day hunger strike before the Moroccan authorities reversed their decision and allowed her to return to el-Aaiún. Further informal discussions between the two parties were held, under UN auspices, in Armonk, New York, in February 2010; however, the talks, which reportedly included ways of resolving the issue of alleged human rights violations by both Morocco and Polisario, ended without agreement.

On 30 April 2010 the UN Security Council approved Resolution 1920, which extended MINURSO's mandate until 30 April 2011; Polisario complained that the resolution failed to address its ongoing concerns about Moroccan human rights abuses. In May 2010 Polisario officials announced that they were suspending contact with MINURSO, owing to its failure to implement the referendum on self-determination, and accused the UN mission of supporting Morocco's occupation of Western Sahara. By contrast, the Moroccan Minister of Foreign Affairs and Co-operation, Taieb Fassi Fihri, expressed his satisfaction that the UN continued to place the focus of the bilateral negotiations on Morocco's autonomy proposal. Another round of informal talks (with Algerian and Mauritanian participation) was held in Manhasset in early November. Despite a negative assessment of the talks by Polisario representatives, there had reportedly been agreement on the convening of future talks and on ways to resume confidence-building measures. Meanwhile, violent demonstrations occurred in el-Aaiún, after Moroccan security forces forcibly entered a camp close to the city, where a large group of displaced Sahrawis had for several weeks been protesting against social and economic conditions in the territory. Moroccan officials stated that 12 people (10 of whom were security officials) had died in the clashes at the camp, while Polisario claimed that at least 36 Sahrawis had been killed. A sixth round of UN-sponsored informal talks took place in Valletta, Malta, in March 2011. In mid-April a draft resolution calling on both parties to respect human rights and extending MINURSO's mandate was circulated to members of the Security Council, following the publication of the Secretary-General's report at the beginning of that month.

Foreign Affairs

Regional relations

Relations with other North African states, which had been strained due to the situation in Western Sahara, improved significantly in the late 1980s. Morocco re-established diplomatic relations with Mauritania in April 1985 (they had been suspended in 1981) and with Algeria in May 1988. In February 1989 North African heads of state, meeting in Marrakesh, signed a treaty establishing the Union du Maghreb arabe (UMA—Union of the Arab Maghreb, see p. 450). The new body, grouping Morocco, Algeria, Libya, Mauritania and Tunisia, aimed to promote trade by allowing the free movement of goods, services and workers. However, there were political disagreements particularly concerning Algeria's continued support for the Polisario Front, and over Moroccan condemnation of Iraq's invasion of Kuwait in August 1990. In early 1993 the five UMA members decided that there should be a 'pause' in the development of a closer union; of 15 conventions signed since the inauguration of the UMA, none had as yet been fully applied. However, the organization continued to hold meetings on an annual basis. In December 1995 King Hassan expressed disapproval at Algeria's continued support for the independence of Western Sahara, and demanded that UMA activities be suspended.

In March 1999 President Zine al-Abidine Ben Ali of Tunisia made his first official visit to Morocco, during which he pledged to improve bilateral relations and to reactivate the UMA. At bilateral meetings during 2000 with other Maghreb heads of state King Muhammad also pledged to take measures to revive the UMA. A summit meeting of ministers responsible for foreign affairs of the five UMA states proceeded in the Algerian capital in March 2001. However, the meeting, which was to have made preparations for the first summit meeting of UMA heads of state since 1995, quickly broke down following disagreements between Moroccan and Algerian representatives. Libya assumed the chairmanship of the UMA in December 2003, and Libyan leader Col Muammar al-Qaddafi subsequently pledged to host a summit meeting of the UMA heads of state in Tripoli, Libya, in May 2005. However, a statement of renewed support for the Polisario Front by the Algerian President, Abdelaziz Bouteflika, provoked a fresh dispute between Morocco and Algeria days before the meeting was due to begin and King Muhammad declined to attend. Despite the ongoing failure to convene an official UMA summit, a meeting was held in Tangiers in April 2008 to celebrate the 50th anniversary of the first proposal of a union of Arab states in the Maghreb. This was attended by both Prime Minister Abbas el-Fassi and the Prime Minister of Algeria, Abdelaziz Belkhadem, along with delegates from the three other UMA member states. In spite of a dispute between Belkhadem and the Minister of State and leader of the Moroccan USFP, Muhammad el-Yazghi, over the situation in Western Sahara, the meeting ended amicably, with renewed appeals for regional co-operation. A year later ministers responsible for foreign affairs from the UMA member states met again in Tripoli, where they reiterated their commitment to improving regional political and economic co-operation.

The Western Sahara issue remained a source of tension between Morocco and Algeria, but in mid-1998 the Moroccan authorities indicated their desire to normalize relations with Algeria and to reopen the common border. In September 1999, however, President Bouteflika claimed that radical Islamist rebels were launching attacks on Algeria from Morocco, and accused Morocco of ignoring the increasing trade in illicit drugs between the two countries. Bouteflika also criticized Morocco for negotiating a separate trade agreement with the European Union (EU, see p. 270), claiming that this was not in the interests of the UMA. None the less, both Morocco and Algeria subsequently reiterated their commitment to reviving the activities of the UMA.

Although relations remained generally co-operative, Bouteflika was vocal in opposing the UN proposals for Western Sahara in mid-2001, which he claimed favoured Morocco. In February 2002, furthermore, Morocco asserted that Algerian support for the partition of Western Sahara risked destabilizing the region; for its part, Algeria accused Morocco of blocking a UN-sponsored solution to the Western Sahara issue. During a visit to Algiers by the Moroccan Minister of Foreign Affairs and Co-operation in June 2003, it was agreed to establish three bilateral commissions to consider political, economic and social matters. Following talks in July 2004 between the Moroccan Minister of the Interior, Al Mustapha Sahel, and his Algerian counterpart, Noureddine Yazid Zerhouni, the two countries signalled their desire to improve diplomatic relations. In May 2005, however, Bouteflika issued a statement renewing Algeria's support for the Polisario Front, and in October allegations by Polisario that Morocco had abandoned African migrants in the Western Saharan desert further increased tensions between the two countries. Prime Minister Jettou accused Algeria of instigating the allegations, and claimed that Algeria had exacerbated the problem by allowing some illegal immigrants to establish camps close to their joint border. In April 2009, at the Tripoli meeting of UMA ministers of foreign affairs, the Moroccan Minister of Foreign Affairs and Co-operation, Taieb Fassi Fihri, declared his country's readiness to renew bilateral relations with Algeria. In early July 2010 King Muhammad sent a senior Moroccan delegation, including Fihri, to the Algerian capital to express his nation's condolences following the death of President Bouteflika's brother; he also pledged to seek 'reconciliation and solidarity' between the two neighbours.

Tensions arose briefly between Libya and Morocco in September 2009 when the Polisario leader, Muhammad Abd al-Aziz, attended the 40th anniversary celebrations of the coup in which Libyan leader Col Muammar al-Qaddafi came to power, prompting Morocco to withdraw its representatives. However, a statement issued by the Libyan authorities, which insisted that the Polisario representatives had not been invited to the celebrations and were merely in Libya to attend the AU summit held in Tripoli in August, appeared to have relieved the situation. Following a meeting of the Moroccan-Libyan High Joint Commission in Rabat in October, representatives of the two countries signed agreements aimed at consolidating co-operation in areas such as tourism, industry and trade.

From the late 1990s Morocco was actively involved in wider regional integration efforts, as a member of the Community of Sahel-Saharan States (CEN-SAD, see p. 446), and also through bilateral and multilateral free trade arrangements; in May 2001, notably, the Governments of Morocco, Iraq, Jordan and Tunisia agreed, at a meeting in Agadir, to establish a free trade zone.

In September 1994 Morocco became only the second Arab country (after Egypt) to establish direct links with Israel; liaison offices were subsequently opened in Rabat and Tel-Aviv. In March 1997, however, in condemnation of recent Israeli settlement policy, ministers of foreign affairs of the League of Arab States (Arab League, see p. 361) recommended a number of sanctions against Israel, including the closure of representative missions. In January 2000 Morocco and Israel agreed in principle to upgrade diplomatic relations to ambassadorial level, although no indication was given as to when embassies would be established. In October, however, as the crisis in Israeli–Palestinian relations deepened, Morocco announced that it had closed down Israel's liaison office in Rabat and its own representative office in Tel-Aviv. There was widespread outrage in Morocco in response to the Israeli military offensive in Palestinian-controlled areas of the West Bank from March 2002. Public demonstrations also took place in January 2009 in response to the military campaign launched by Israel against Islamic Resistance Movement (Hamas) targets in the Gaza Strip in December 2008.

Other external relations

Morocco has generally maintained close relations with France. However, the French Government expressed considerable concern following the imposition of death sentences on three defendants in January 1995, all of whom had been resident in France prior to their arrest. As the development of a Maghreb union slowed, Morocco attempted to improve relations with the EU, which had been critical of Morocco's human rights record. In February 1996, after two years of negotiations, Morocco signed an association agreement with the EU, which provided for greater political and economic co-operation, financial aid, and the eventual establishment of a free trade zone. In March 2000 King Muhammad attended talks with President Jacques Chirac in France, during which he expressed his hope that Morocco would be accorded partnership status with the EU and, ultimately, full membership of the union.

In 2007 Nicolas Sarkozy proposed the idea of a Mediterranean Union as part of his election campaign for the French presidency. Envisaged as an international body capable of fostering economic, political and cultural links between Mediterranean states, the initiative was described by Sarkozy as building upon the Barcelona Process launched by Euro-Mediterranean foreign ministers in November 1995. By the beginning of 2008 the project had been modified to encompass not just those nations bordering the Mediterranean Sea, but all EU member states, and had been renamed the Union for the Mediterranean. However, King Muhammad was not among the many heads of state of the 43 EU and Mediterranean member nations in attendance at the official inauguration of the union in Paris in July 2008; his absence was officially attributed to scheduling problems, rather than to any political or diplomatic concerns. (Morocco was represented by the King's brother, Prince Moulay Rachid.) Meanwhile, in April 2008 Morocco and France signed a number of agreements aimed at consolidating their economic and social co-operation. The agreements were a result of decisions reached during the ninth Franco-Moroccan intergovernmental seminar in October 2007, during a visit by President Sarkozy to Morocco. A further 11 co-operation accords were signed in July 2010, including an agreement concerning French assistance to Morocco in the field of nuclear energy. The French Government also pledged €600m. in financial aid to Morocco for 2010–12 to assist the authorities with their ongoing reform programme.

Morocco was accorded 'advanced status' relations with the EU in October 2008. The new status, which was the culmination of more than eight years of negotiations, was expected to enable Morocco to attract more European investment and financial aid, as well as allowing for Moroccan participation in some EU agencies and committees. Morocco was the first Maghreb country to attain such a relationship with the EU, and the development was widely regarded as signifying European recognition of Morocco's programme of social and political reforms. Of the countries in the Middle East and North Africa, Morocco is the second largest recipient (after the Palestinian Autonomous Areas) of EU financial assistance, with €580m. of funds being pledged for the 2011–13 period.

In February 1995, following the approval by the Spanish parliament of statutes of autonomy for the enclaves of Ceuta and Melilla, Morocco intensified its diplomatic campaign to obtain sovereignty over the territories. In January 1998 the two countries established a joint commission to examine security issues including illegal immigration (to Spain) and drugs-trafficking. In August 1999 Prime Minister el-Youssoufi urged a review of the statutes of Ceuta and Melilla; however, Spain asserted that no Moroccan sovereignty claims with regard to this issue would be considered. The Spanish premier, José María Aznar, visited Morocco in May 2000, and in September, during King Muhammad's first visit to Spain since his accession, two economic co-operation agreements were signed. Nevertheless, relations remained strained owing to lack of progress in negotiations with the EU regarding a new fisheries accord and attacks by Spanish fishermen on lorries carrying Moroccan products through Spanish ports.

In July 2001, in an attempt to limit the increasing number of Moroccans entering Spain illegally, the two countries signed an agreement that would allow as many as 20,000 Moroccans to enter Spain each year in search of employment. In September, however, Spain refuted allegations made by King Muhammad that Spanish criminal associations were responsible for the large increase in numbers of Moroccan economic migrants attempting illegally to cross the Straits of Gibraltar, asserting that collusion between Moroccan police and the smugglers was ongoing. Later that month Morocco recalled its ambassador from Spain. Moroccan–Spanish relations were further strained in July 2002, when a small detachment of Moroccan troops occupied the uninhabited rocky islet of Perejil (known as Leila to Morocco), west of the Spanish enclave of Ceuta and close to the Moroccan coastline. Morocco claimed that it was establishing a surveillance post on the island as part of its campaign against illegal emigration and drugs-smuggling. However, Spain insisted that there had been an agreement since 1990 that neither country would occupy Perejil, and, with the support of the EU and North Atlantic Treaty Organisation (NATO, see p. 368), demanded the immediate evacuation of Moroccan troops from the island. A few days later Spain's ambassador to Morocco was recalled, and Spanish special forces intervened and forcibly removed Moroccan troops from Perejil. Following mediation by the US Secretary of State, Colin Powell, Spanish forces withdrew from the island. Talks held later in July 2002 in Rabat between the Spanish Minister of Foreign Affairs, Ana Palacio, and her Moroccan counterpart, Muhammad Benaïssa, resulted in an accord whereby both states agreed to return to the *status quo ante*. In January 2003 King Muhammad temporarily allowed Spanish boats to fish in Moroccan waters, and in the following month the two countries agreed to the return of their respective ambassadors. In December Morocco and Spain announced plans to construct a 39-km underwater rail tunnel between the two countries; by late 2010 the feasibility study for the project—the completion date of which was 2025—had been concluded.

In March 2004 a series of bomb attacks on commuter trains in the Spanish capital, Madrid, killed 191 people. A number of Moroccans from the Groupe islamique combattant marocain (GICM), who had also been linked with the Casablanca bombings of 2003, were among a group of suspected militant Islamists detained by the Spanish authorities in connection with the attacks, and in December 2004 a Moroccan man, Hassan al-Haski, was charged with having planned the bombings. (Al-Haski was sentenced to 14 years' imprisonment in Spain for his involvement in the Madrid bombings, and, following his extradition to Morocco in 2008, was also convicted of involvement in the Casablanca bombings and sentenced to 10 years' imprisonment.) The Moroccan authorities were quick to show their commitment to fighting terrorism, and in April 2004, following an official visit to Morocco by the new Spanish Prime Minister, José Luis Rodríguez Zapatero, the two countries announced renewed diplomatic ties. In May the two Governments revealed plans to establish a joint task force to tackle terrorism and organized crime. However, during June–July 2005 six delegations of Spanish politicians and journalists, seeking to conduct investigations following demonstrations in Western Sahara, were accused by Morocco of supporting Sahrawi independence and were refused permission to enter the disputed territory (see above).

In September–October 2005 at least 11 African migrants were reported to have died while attempting to enter Ceuta and Melilla illegally. Four were shot dead by Moroccan troops as the migrants scaled fences constructed to protect the borders between Morocco and the Spanish enclaves. The Spanish Government urged its Moroccan counterpart to increase its efforts to prevent illegal border crossings but later ended the practice of returning unsuccessful migrants to Morocco, amid claims by human rights organizations that migrants had been taken to the southern Moroccan desert and abandoned by the authorities. In January 2006 Zapatero visited Ceuta and Melilla, the first visit by an incumbent Spanish premier for 25 years. At a summit meeting held between Spain and Morocco in March 2007 and attended by Zapatero, the two countries reached an agreement on the prevention of unaccompanied child migrants. Zapatero also welcomed Morocco's plan for autonomy in Western Sahara (see above) as a means to the opening of dialogue within the framework of the UN, while maintaining that Spain was committed to a consensual solution to the issue that respected the principles laid down by the UN. However, diplomatic relations between Morocco and Spain deteriorated in November, when it was announced that King Juan Carlos of Spain would pay his first royal visit to Ceuta and Melilla. The trip provoked criticism from the Moroccan Government, and the country recalled its ambassador to Spain, Omar Azziman, in protest. Azziman returned to his post in January 2008. Bilateral relations improved markedly in late 2008, and Prime Ministers Zapatero and el-Fassi attended a summit meeting in Madrid in December. Talks at the summit encompassed bilateral relations, immigration, the issue of Western Sahara, and economic and security co-operation. A Spanish investment fund of more than €520m. for infrastructure projects in Morocco was subsequently announced. In January 2009 agreements between the two countries on increased co-operation in security and law-enforcement were finalized. The first EU-Morocco summit (a product of Morocco's 'advanced status' relations with the EU since 2008) was hosted by Spain during its presidency of the EU in March 2010. The summit ended with the signing of a joint declaration and an operational agenda aimed at developing Morocco's already close relationship with the EU. In mid-August there were renewed difficulties between Spain and Morocco, after Moroccan demonstrators blockaded the country's border crossing with Melilla to assert their claims of sovereignty over the enclave. The protest followed official complaints by the Moroccan authorities that its citizens who entered the two Spanish enclaves on a daily basis had suffered mistreatment at the hands of the Spanish police.

The Moroccan Government was swift to condemn the September 2001 attacks on New York and Washington, DC, USA, for which the al-Qa'ida network was believed to be responsible. In June 2002 the Moroccan authorities announced that they had arrested three Saudi nationals who were alleged to be members of an Islamist cell linked to al-Qa'ida that was preparing terrorist attacks on US and British warships in the Strait of Gibraltar. Seven Moroccans, including two of the suspects' wives, had also been arrested for allegedly acting as couriers between the Saudis in Morocco and al-Qa'ida, which had provided them with funds and logistical support. In February 2003 the three Saudis were sentenced to 10 years' imprisonment by a court in Casablanca; six of the Moroccans received sentences ranging from four months to one year for their roles in the plot. Also in February a Moroccan student, Mounir al-Motassadek, who was alleged to have been a member of the cell that had planned and executed the September 2001 attacks, was convicted by a court in Hamburg, Germany, of belonging to a terrorist group and of aiding and abetting the murder of 3,066 people. He was sentenced to 15 years' imprisonment. In March 2004 al-Motassadek's conviction was quashed by the German Federal Criminal Court, and he was released from detention in April. A retrial began in August, and al-Motassadek was acquitted in August 2005 of involvement in the September 2001 attacks; he was nevertheless convicted of belonging to a terrorist organization and sentenced to seven years' imprisonment. In November 2006 the German Federal Court of Justice overturned al-Motassadek's acquittal on charges of accessory to murder, and he was again sentenced to 15 years' imprisonment in January 2007. A final appeal was rejected by the Federal Court of Justice in May.

In June 2004 Morocco became only the second Arab country (after Jordan in 2001) to sign a free trade agreement with the USA. Both the Moroccan Chamber of Representatives and Chamber of Advisers ratified the accord in January 2005.

MOROCCO

Morocco's relations with Iran deteriorated in February 2009, following a speech by Ali Akbar Nateq Nouri, a senior political figure in Iran, in which he described Bahrain as a former province of Iran. The remark, which was interpreted by many as an attack on Bahrain's sovereignty, provoked vociferous condemnation from numerous regional and international leaders, including King Muhammad. According to the Moroccan Government, its chargé d'affaires in Tehran was the only diplomatic representative to be summoned by the Iranian authorities to explain their country's response to the incident. The Moroccan representative was recalled from Iran in late February, and in early March the Ministry of Foreign Affairs and Co-operation announced the suspension of diplomatic relations with Iran. The Ministry also accused Iran of interfering in the religious unity of Morocco through its promotion of Shi'a Islam in the mainly Sunni country. Bilateral relations had not been re-established by early May 2011.

CONSTITUTION AND GOVERNMENT

The 1992 Constitution (amended by referendum in 1996) provides for a modified constitutional monarchy, with a hereditary King as Head of State. Legislative power is vested in the Majlis al-Nuab (Chamber of Representatives), with 325 members directly elected, on the basis of universal adult suffrage, for five years, and in the Majlis al-Mustasharin (Chamber of Advisers), with 270 members chosen by electoral colleges (representing mainly local councils, with the remainder selected from professional associations and trade unions) for a nine-year term. Executive power is vested in the King, who appoints (and may dismiss) the Prime Minister and (on the latter's recommendation) other members of the Cabinet. The King may also dissolve the legislature. In March 2011 the Consultative Committee for the Revision of the Constitution was sworn in by King Muhammad VI; the committee comprised politicians, civil society activists and trade union leaders, and was expected to propose amendments to the Constitution later that year (see Contemporary Political History).

REGIONAL AND INTERNATIONAL CO-OPERATION

Morocco is a founder member of the Union du Maghreb arabe (UMA—Union of the Arab Maghreb, see p. 450). The permanent headquarters of the organization are located in the Moroccan capital, Rabat. The country also participates in the League of Arab States (Arab League, see p. 361) and the Community of Sahel-Saharan States (CEN-SAD, see p. 446).

Morocco became a member of the UN in November 1956, having gained independence in March of that year. As a contracting party to the General Agreement on Trade and Tariffs, Morocco joined the World Trade Organization (WTO, see p. 430) on its establishment in 1995. The country also adheres to the Organization of the Islamic Conference (OIC, see p. 400).

ECONOMIC AFFAIRS

In 2009, according to estimates by the World Bank, Morocco's gross national income (GNI), measured at average 2007–09 prices, was US $90,685m., equivalent to $2,790 per head (or $4,450 per head on an international purchasing-power parity basis). During 2000–09, it was estimated, the population increased at an average annual rate of 1.2%, while gross domestic product (GDP) per head increased, in real terms, by an average of 3.8% per year. Overall GDP increased, in real terms, at an average annual rate of 5.1% in 2000–09; it increased by 5.0% in 2009.

Agriculture (including forestry and fishing) contributed 16.4% of GDP in 2009, and engaged 40.9% of the employed labour force in 2008. The principal crops are cereals (mainly wheat and barley), potatoes, sugar beet and sugar cane, tomatoes, melons, and citrus fruit. Almost all of Morocco's meat requirements are produced within the country. The sale of licences to foreign fishing fleets is an important source of revenue. According to provisional figures, seafoods and seafood products accounted for 8.2% of total exports in 2009. According to the World Bank, during 2000–09 agricultural GDP increased at an average annual rate of 8.2%; after a prolonged period of drought in 2007, sectoral GDP grew by 16.4% in 2008 and by a further 27.0% in 2009.

Industry (including mining, manufacturing, construction and power) provided 28.5% of GDP in 2009, and engaged 21.7% of the employed labour force in 2008. According to the World Bank, during 2000–09 industrial GDP increased by an average of 3.5% per year; sectoral GDP grew by 2.6% in 2008, but declined by 2.7% in 2009.

Mining and quarrying contributed 2.6% of GDP in 2009, and the sector engaged 0.5% of the employed labour force in 2007. The major mineral exports are phosphate rock and phosphoric acid, which together earned 11.8% of export revenues in 2009, according to provisional figures. Morocco is the world's largest exporter of phosphate rock. Petroleum exploration activity was revived at the end of the 1990s, and the discovery of major oil and natural gas reserves in the Talsinnt region of eastern Morocco was announced in August 2000. Coal, salt, iron ore, barytes, lead, copper, zinc, silver, gold and manganese are mined. Deposits of nickel, cobalt and bauxite have been discovered. During 1990–2002 mining GDP increased at an average annual rate of 1.3%. According to official estimates, mining GDP increased by 1.8% in 2006.

Manufacturing, together with oil-refining, contributed 16.1% of GDP in 2009. The manufacturing sector engaged 11.8% of the employed labour force in 2007. The most important branches, measured by gross value of output, are oil-refining and energy products, food-processing, textiles, and chemicals. According to provisional figures, manufactured garments accounted for 15.9% of export revenues in 2009. According to the World Bank, during 2000–09 manufacturing GDP increased at an average annual rate of 2.7%; the sector's GDP expanded by 2.1% in 2008, but decreased by 2.6% in 2009.

Construction contributed 7.0% of GDP in 2009. The sector engaged 8.9% of the employed labour force in 2008.

In 2007 electric energy was derived principally from coal (57.1%), petroleum (22.3%), natural gas (13.6%) and hydroelectric power stations (5.8%). Facilities for generating wind power have also been developed, while plans to harness solar energy were announced in 2009 (see below). According to provisional figures, imports of energy and lubricants comprised an estimated 20.4% of the value of total merchandise imports in 2009.

The services sector contributed an estimated 55.1% of GDP in 2009, and engaged 37.4% of the employed labour force in 2008. The tourism industry is generally a major source of revenue, and tourist arrivals totalled some 9.2m. in 2010. The GDP of the services sector increased by an average of 4.8% per year during 2000–09, and by 2.0% in 2009.

In 2009 Morocco recorded a visible trade deficit of US $16,363m., and there was a deficit of $5,362m. on the current account of the balance of payments. According to preliminary figures, in 2009 the principal source of imports was France (which provided 15.7% of merchandise imports); other major suppliers in that year included Spain, the People's Republic of China, the USA, Italy and Germany. France was also the principal market for exports (24.5%) in 2009; Spain and India were important purchasers of Moroccan exports. The principal exports in 2009 were finished consumer products (notably manufactured garments and hosiery), semi-finished products (including phosphoric acid and electronic components), and foodstuffs, beverages and tobacco (particularly seafoods and seafood products). The principal imports in that year were finished capital goods, fuel and energy products (notably crude petroleum), and finished and semi-finished products.

In 2009, according to preliminary figures, Morocco recorded an overall budget deficit of 19,400m. dirhams. The country's general government gross debt was 351,209m. dirhams in 2009, equivalent to 47.7% of GDP. Morocco's total external debt in 2008 was US $20,825m., of which $16,538m. was public and publicly guaranteed debt. The cost of debt-servicing in that year was equivalent to 10.3% of exports of goods, services and income. The annual rate of inflation averaged 2.0% in 2000–08; consumer prices increased by an average of 3.7% in 2008, and by 1.0% in 2009. According to official figures, some 9.1% of the labour force were unemployed in 2010, representing no change from the previous year.

Despite a decline in GDP growth in 2007, reflecting low levels of agricultural production as a result of drought, Morocco has generally seen strong and sustained growth since the mid-2000s. A recovery in the agricultural sector in 2008, in conjunction with the strong performance of the construction and services industries, and high levels of private sector activity, resulted in an overall growth rate of close to 6%. While Morocco was affected in 2009 by the global economic slowdown, which gathered pace from mid-2008, its effect was limited to tourism, exports and foreign direct investment, owing to the country's limited exposure to global financial markets, strong public spending and an excellent cereal harvest. An increase of 30.6% in agricultural output

MOROCCO

Statistical Survey

contributed to overall GDP growth of 5.0% in 2009; growth was estimated at 3.2% in 2010. However, the persistent high unemployment, especially among the young, and related low literacy rates were emphasized as areas of particular concern by the IMF in both its 2008 and 2009 assessments. Indeed, a principal demand of demonstrators who organized mass street protests from February 2011 was a reduction in the level of unemployment; in that month King Muhammad created a long-awaited Economic and Social Council, one of the principal tasks of which was to examine the issues of graduate unemployment and training. It was hoped that 150,000 new jobs could be created during 2011. The authorities also agreed to increase subsidies on some basic commodities to ease concerns about rising prices. The Government's 'Vision 2010' strategy, launched in 2001, succeeded in raising the number of tourist visitors to Morocco from 4.4m. in that year to 9.2m. in 2010, just below the strategy's target of 10m. According to a new 10-year development plan for the tourism industry, announced in November 2010, 177,000m. dirhams would be invested in order to double the number of visitors and create some 147,000 new jobs. Several major projects aimed at improving the country's transport infrastructure were under way in 2011. Morocco is heavily reliant on imports of fossil fuels and electricity to meet its energy demands owing to a lack of petroleum or natural gas reserves. Confronted with fluctuating international energy prices in the 2000s, the authorities made increased efforts to diversify the country's electricity generation and exploit its own natural resources. In November 2009 the Government detailed a US $9,000m. project to develop five solar power plants. The project was due for completion by 2020 and was expected to have a capacity of 2,000 MW, equivalent to some 38% of Morocco's installed energy capacity. In June 2010 a $300m. wind farm was opened near Tangier, having been part-funded by the EU; the new facility—the largest in Africa—had a production capacity of 140 MW.

PUBLIC HOLIDAYS

2012: 1 January (New Year), 11 January (Independence Manifesto), 4 February* (Mouloud, Birth of the Prophet), 1 May (Labour Day), 30 July (Festival of the Throne, anniversary of King Muhammad's accession), 14 August (Oued el-Dahab Day, anniversary of the 1979 annexation), 18 August* (Eid el-Seghir—Id al-Fitr, end of Ramadan), 20 August (The King and People's Revolution), 21 August (Festival of Youth—King Muhammad's Birthday), 25 October* (Eid el-Kebir—Id al-Adha, Feast of the Sacrifice), 6 November (Anniversary of the Green March), 14 November* (Muharram, Islamic New Year), 18 November (Independence Day).

*These holidays are dependent on the Islamic lunar calendar and may vary by one or two days from the dates given.

Statistical Survey

Sources (unless otherwise stated): Haut Commissariat au Plan, Direction de la Statistique, rue Muhammad Belhassan el-Ouazzani, BP 178, Rabat 10001; tel. (53) 7773606; fax (53) 7773217; e-mail statguichet@statistic.gov.ma; internet www.hcp.ma; Bank Al-Maghrib, 277 ave Muhammad V, BP 445, Rabat; tel. (53) 7702626; fax (53) 7706667; e-mail webmaster@bkam.ma; internet www.bkam.ma.

Note: Unless otherwise indicated, the data exclude Western (formerly Spanish) Sahara, a disputed territory under Moroccan occupation.

Area and Population

AREA, POPULATION AND DENSITY

Area (sq km)	710,850*
Population (census results)†	
2 September 1994	
Males	12,944,517
Females	13,074,763
Total	26,019,280
2 September 2004	29,891,708
Population (UN estimates at mid-year)‡	
2009	31,992,593
2010	32,381,283
2011	32,770,852
Density (per sq km) at mid-2011	46.1

* 274,461 sq miles. This area includes the disputed territory of Western Sahara, which covers 252,120 sq km (97,344 sq miles).
† Including Western Sahara, with an estimated population of 417,000 at the 2004 census.
‡ Source: UN, *World Population Prospects: The 2008 Revision*.

POPULATION BY AGE AND SEX
(UN estimates at mid-2011)

	Males	Females	Total
0–14	4,619,549	4,465,322	9,084,871
15–64	10,657,648	11,242,588	21,900,236
65 and over	805,744	980,001	1,785,745
Total	16,082,941	16,687,911	32,770,852

Source: UN, *World Population Prospects: The 2008 Revision*.

REGIONS
(population at 2004 census)

	Population
Oued el-Dahab Lagouira*	99,367
El-Aaiún Boujdour*	256,152
Guelmim el-Semara†	462,410
Souss Massa-Draa	3,113,653
Gharb Chrarda Beni-Hsen	1,859,540
Chaouia Ouardigha	1,655,660
Marrakech Tensift al-Haou	3,102,652
Oriental	1,918,094
Grand Casablanca	3,631,061
Rabat Salé Zemmour Zaer	2,366,494
Doukkala Abda	1,984,039
Tadla Azilal	1,450,519
Meknès Tafilalet	2,141,527
Fès Boulemane	1,573,055
Taza al-Hoceima Taounate	1,807,113
Tanger Tétouan	2,470,372
Total	29,891,708

* Regions situated in Western Sahara.
† Region partly situated in Western Sahara.

MOROCCO

PRINCIPAL TOWNS
(population at 2004 census)

Casablanca	2,933,684	Tétouan	320,539
Rabat (capital)*	1,622,860	Safi	284,750
Fès (Fez)	946,815	Mohammedia	188,619
Marrakech (Marrakesh)	823,154	El-Aaiún†	183,691
Agadir	678,596	Khouribga	166,397
Tanger (Tangier)	669,685	Beni-Mellal	163,286
Meknès	536,232	El-Jadida	144,440
Oujda	400,738	Taza	139,686
Kénitra	359,142		

* Including Salé and Temara.
† Town situated in Western Sahara.

Source: Thomas Brinkhoff, *City Population* (internet www.citypopulation.de).

Mid-2010 (incl. suburbs, UN estimates): Casablanca 3,283,605; Rabat 1,802,331; Fès 1,065,496; Marrakech 928,019; Tanger (Tangier) 787,504; Agadir 783,210 (Source: UN, *World Urbanization Prospects: The 2009 Revision*).

BIRTHS AND DEATHS
(annual averages, UN estimates)

	1995–2000	2000–05	2005–10
Birth rate (per 1,000)	23.4	20.9	20.5
Death rate (per 1,000)	6.4	6.0	5.8

Source: UN, *World Population Prospects: The 2008 Revision*.

Life expectancy (years at birth, WHO estimates): 72 (males 70; females 75) in 2008 (Source: WHO, *World Health Statistics*).

ECONOMICALLY ACTIVE POPULATION
(sample surveys, '000 persons aged 15 years and over)

	2005	2006	2007
Agriculture, hunting, forestry and fishing	4,505.2	4,303.3	4,235.1
Mining and quarrying	41.8	39.9	48.4
Manufacturing	1,153.9	1,142.0	1,191.3
Electricity, gas and water	31.7	42.8	39.4
Construction	705.4	789.6	838.9
Wholesale and retail trade; repairs; hotels and restaurants	1,656.9	1,602.3	1,637.0
Transport, storage and communications	380.3	394.7	401.9
General administration and community services	1,301.4	1,449.5	1,478.7
Financial intermediation, real estate and business services	130.2	152.4	171.9
Sub-total	9,906.8	9,916.6	10,042.5
Activities not adequately defined	6.5	11.1	13.7
Total employed	9,913.3	9,927.7	10,056.2
Unemployed	1,226.4	1,062.5	1,088.9
Total labour force	11,139.7	10,990.2	11,145.1

2008: Agriculture, hunting, forestry and fishing 4,168.2; Mining, manufacturing and utilities 1,307.3; Construction 903.8; Wholesale, retail trade, and hotels and restaurants 1,456.9; Transport, storage and communications 451.1; Other services 1,883.7; *Sub-total* 10,171.0; Activities not adequately defined 18.3; *Total employed* 10,189.3; Unemployed 1,077.8; *Total labour force* 11,267.1.

Source: ILO.

Health and Welfare

KEY INDICATORS

Total fertility rate (children per woman, 2008)	2.4
Under-5 mortality rate (per 1,000 live births, 2008)	36
HIV/AIDS (% of persons aged 15–49, 2007)	0.1
Physicians (per 1,000 head, 2004)	0.51
Hospital beds (per 1,000 head, 2004)	0.90
Health expenditure (2007): US $ per head (PPP)	202
Health expenditure (2007): % of GDP	5.0
Health expenditure (2007): public (% of total)	33.8
Access to water (% of persons, 2008)	81
Access to sanitation (% of persons, 2008)	69
Total carbon dioxide emissions ('000 metric tons, 2007)	46,367.9
Carbon dioxide emissions per head (metric tons, 2007)	1.5
Human Development Index (2010): ranking	114
Human Development Index (2010): value	0.567

For sources and definitions, see explanatory note on p. vi.

Agriculture

PRINCIPAL CROPS
('000 metric tons)

	2006	2007	2008
Wheat	6,327	1,583	3,769
Rice, paddy	34	33	45
Barley	2,535	763	1,353
Maize	297	95	121
Potatoes	1,569	1,437	1,537
Sugar cane	997	934	913
Sugar beet	2,252	2,484	2,926
Broad beans, dry	180	70	109
Peas, dry	24	12	16
Chick peas	66	33	38
Lentils	34	9	9
Almonds, with shell	83	81	87
Groundnuts, with shell	38	50	41
Olives	631	659*	765
Sunflower seed	28	33	32
Cabbages and other brassicas	44	30	35
Artichokes	55	52	60
Tomatoes	1,245	1,237	1,312
Cauliflowers and broccoli	73	57	52
Pumpkins, squash and gourds	169	170*	234
Cucumbers and gherkins	70	75	89
Aubergines (Eggplants)	57	34	35
Chillies and peppers, green	236	214	232
Onions, dry	882	700	662
Peas, green	147	121	117
String beans	163	187	182
Carrots and turnips	299	300*	281
Carobs*	25	25	25
Watermelons	712	704	651
Cantaloupes and other melons	648	734	737
Figs	77	62	70
Grapes	363	324	291
Dates	45	74	73
Apples	374	427	404
Pears	35	44	38
Quinces	28	35	33

MOROCCO

—continued	2006	2007	2008
Peaches and nectarines	72	77	75
Plums and sloes	80	79	66
Strawberries	112	100*	130
Oranges	788	750*	750*
Tangerines, mandarins, clementines and satsumas	454	450*	450*
Apricots	129	105	113
Bananas	203	202	215
Anise, badian, fennel and coriander*	23	23	23

* FAO estimate(s).

2009 ('000 metric tons, FAO estimates): Olives 770; Sunflower seed 35; Cabbages and other brassicas 35; Tomatoes 1,300; Cauliflowers and broccoli 52; Cucumbers and gherkins 90; Aubergines (Eggplants) 35; Onions, dry 650; Peas, green 118; Carrots and turnips 280; Watermelons 650; Figs 70; Grapes 300; Dates 72; Apples 400; Strawberries 130; Oranges 780; Tangerines, mandarins, clementines and satsumas 450; Bananas 220.

Aggregate production ('000 metric tons, may include official, semi-official or estimated data): Total cereals 2,505 in 2007, 5,331 in 2008, 5,331 in 2009; Total pulses 171 in 2007, 228 in 2008, 228 in 2009; Total roots and tubers 1,446 in 2007, 1,548 in 2008, 1,548 in 2009; Total vegetables (incl. melons) 5,224 in 2007, 5,302 in 2008, 5,271 in 2009; Total fruits (excl. melons) 2,914 in 2007, 2,871 in 2008, 2,881 in 2009.

Source: FAO.

LIVESTOCK

('000 head, year ending September)

	2007	2008	2009
Cattle	2,781	2,814	2,861
Sheep	16,894	17,078	17,476
Goats	5,284	5,118	5,251
Camels*	40	45	50
Horses	152	162	153
Asses	990	968	967
Mules	514	515	505
Chickens*	150,000	160,000	165,000

* FAO estimates.
Source: FAO.

LIVESTOCK PRODUCTS

('000 metric tons)

	2007	2008	2009*
Cattle meat	169	172	163
Sheep meat	120	120	120
Goat meat	22	22	23
Chicken meat	380	440	450
Cows' milk	1,600	1,700	1,700
Sheep's milk*	27	27	n.a.
Goats' milk*	34	34	n.a.
Hen eggs*	244	244	244
Honey	3	4	4
Wool, greasy*	40	40	n.a.

* FAO estimates.
Source: FAO.

Forestry

ROUNDWOOD REMOVALS
('000 cubic metres, excl. bark)

	2007	2008	2009
Sawlogs, veneer logs and logs for sleepers	238	184	190
Pulpwood	377	393	305
Fuel wood	425	339	266
Total	1,040	916	761

Source: FAO.

SAWNWOOD PRODUCTION
('000 cubic metres, incl. railway sleepers)

	1987*	1988	1989
Coniferous (softwood)	40	26*	43*
Broadleaved (hardwood)	40	27	40
Total	80	53	83

* FAO estimate(s).

1990–2009: Production assumed to be unchanged from 1989 (FAO estimates).

Source: FAO.

Fishing

('000 metric tons, live weight)

	2006	2007	2008
Capture	876.8	879.3	995.8
European pilchard (sardine)	542.0	519.3	647.0
Chub mackerel	72.0	104.9	106.5
Jack and horse mackerels	34.0	29.0	26.3
Octopuses	43.7	33.5	56.4
Aquaculture	1.2	1.6	1.4*
Total catch (incl. others)	878.0	880.9	997.2*

* FAO estimate.

Note: Figures exclude aquatic plants ('000 metric tons, all capture): 14.9 in 2006; 12.4 in 2007; 9.0 in 2008. Also excluded are corals (metric tons, all capture): 3.6 in 2006; 3.5 in 2007; 3.7 in 2008.

Source: FAO.

MOROCCO

Mining

('000 metric tons)

	2007	2008	2009*
Crude petroleum	11.1	9.0	n.a.
Iron ore†	48.0	22.9	30.5
Copper concentrates†	19.9	21.1	42.1
Lead concentrates†	60.0	47.8	49.0
Manganese ore†	41.6	102.3	51.8
Zinc concentrates†	108.7	161.5	88.4
Phosphate rock‡	27,834.0	24,861.0	18,307.0
Fluorspar (acid grade)	78.8	56.7	72.1
Barytes	664.7	725.1	586.9
Salt (unrefined)	215.8	219.2	310.4
Bentonite	136.1	50.1	84.1

* Preliminary.
† Figures refer to the gross weight of ores and concentrates.
‡ Including production in Western Sahara.

Source: Ministère de l'Energie, des Mines, de l'Eau et de l'Environnement.

Industry

SELECTED PRODUCTS
('000 metric tons, unless otherwise indicated)

	2005	2006	2007
Wine*	38	36	35†
Olive oil (crude)	50	75	75
Motor spirit—petrol	372	373	365
Naphthas	650	530	596
Kerosene	2	3	—
Distillate fuel oils	2,295	2,033	1,996
Residual fuel oils	2,545	2,265	2,269
Jet fuel	264	236	292
Petroleum bitumen—asphalt	198	213	257
Liquefied petroleum gas ('000 barrels)‡	2,435	2,500†	2,500†
Cement	10,289	11,357	12,787
Carpets and rugs ('000 sq m)	313	315	226
Electric energy (million kWh)	22,456	23,192	22,858

* Source: FAO.
† Estimated figure.
‡ Source: US Geological Survey.

Source: partly UN Industrial Commodity Statistics Database.

2008 ('000 metric tons, unless otherwise indicated): Wine 35 (FAO estimate); Liquefied petroleum gas ('000 barrels) 2,500 (Sources: FAO; US Geological Survey).

2009 ('000 barrels): Liquefied petroleum gas 2,500 (Sources: US Geological Survey).

Finance

CURRENCY AND EXCHANGE RATES

Monetary Units:
100 centimes (santimat) = 1 Moroccan dirham.

Sterling, Dollar and Euro Equivalents (30 November 2010):
£1 sterling = 13.279 dirhams;
US $1 = 8.552 dirhams;
€1 = 11.115 dirhams;
100 Moroccan dirhams = £7.53 = $11.69 = €9.00.

Average Exchange Rate (dirhams per US $):
2007 8.192
2008 7.750
2009 8.057

GENERAL BUDGET
('000 million dirhams)*

Revenue†	2007	2008‡	2009§
Tax revenue	153.3	187.5	170.1
Direct taxes	60.3	81.6	72.9
Indirect taxes	67.1	80.0	73.8
Import taxes	14.4	14.3	11.1
Other tax revenues	11.5	11.7	12.3
Non-tax revenue	15.3	15.5	16.3
Total	**168.7**	**203.0**	**186.5**

Expenditure‖	2007	2008‡	2009§
Current	133.9	155.8	150.0
Wages	65.7	70	76.5
Food and petroleum subsidies	16.4	31.5	12.0
Food subsidies	−7.6	5.8	0.9
Petroleum subsidies	24.0	25.7	11.1
Other	32.6	36.2	43.1
Interest	19.3	18.2	18.4
Capital	26.3	35.9	41.1
Road fund	1.9	2.3	2.2
Transfers to local government&para	14.9	18.4	16.6
Total	**177.0**	**212.4**	**209.9**

* Excluding grants ('000 million dirhams): 2.8 in 2007; 9.6 in 2008 (preliminary figure); 4.0 in 2009 (budget projection), GSM revenues and receipts from privatization ('000 million dirhams): 6.1 in 2007; 0.0 in 2008 (preliminary figure); 0.0 in 2009 (budget projection), and net transactions associated with the Hassan II Fund ('000 million dirhams): 1.3 in 2007; 1.3 in 2008 (preliminary figure); 2.3 in 2009 (budget projection).
† Includes tariffs destined for food subsidies and road fund revenues.
‡ Preliminary figures.
§ Projections.
‖ Excluding net lending ('000 million dirhams): 0.0 in 2007; 0.0 in 2008 (preliminary figure); 0.0 in 2009 (budget projection).
&para Equivalent to 30% of value-added tax revenue.

Source: IMF, *Morocco: 2009 Article IV Consultation—Staff Report; Public Information Notice on the Executive Board Discussion; and Statement by the Executive Director for Morocco* (March 2010).

INTERNATIONAL RESERVES
(US $ million at 31 December)

	2007	2008	2009
Gold (national valuation)	593	613	783
IMF special drawing rights	32	19	763
Reserve position in IMF	111	109	110
Foreign exchange	23,980	21,976	21,924
Total	**24,716**	**22,717**	**23,580**

Source: IMF, *International Financial Statistics*.

MONEY SUPPLY
(million dirhams at 31 December)

	2007	2008	2009
Currency outside depository corporations	120,045	128,091	136,664
Transferable deposits	308,914	324,533	341,668
Other deposits	228,405	289,989	301,016
Securities other than shares	5,614	6,512	13,526
Broad money	**662,979**	**749,124**	**792,875**

Source: IMF, *International Financial Statistics*.

MOROCCO

COST OF LIVING
(Consumer Price Index for urban areas; base: 2006 = 100)

	2007	2008	2009
Food and non-alcoholic beverages	104.6	112.3	113.3
Alcoholic beverages and tobacco	102.1	104.6	108.2
Clothing	101.0	102.8	103.8
Shelter	102.1	103.0	103.8
Household equipment	101.9	103.4	105.4
All items (incl. others)	102.5	106.3	107.4

NATIONAL ACCOUNTS
(million dirhams at current prices)

Expenditure on the Gross Domestic Product

	2007	2008	2009
Government final consumption expenditure	112,234	118,132	132,277
Private final consumption expenditure	360,008	400,395	419,392
Change in inventories	7,614	35,095	38,783
Gross fixed capital formation	192,573	227,465	226,054
Total domestic expenditure	672,429	781,087	816,506
Exports of goods and services	220,302	258,165	210,459
Less Imports of goods and services	276,477	350,409	290,759
GDP in purchasers' values	616,254	688,843	736,206

Gross Domestic Product by Economic Activity

	2007	2008	2009
Agriculture, hunting and forestry	68,716	82,969	100,890
Fishing and aquaculture	6,212	7,721	6,293
Mining and quarrying	13,155	45,121	16,925
Manufacturing	82,074	86,996	104,004
Oil refining and energy products	841	963	1,084
Electricity and water	15,749	16,123	18,953
Construction	37,233	38,663	45,776
Commerce	65,058	70,597	72,054
Hotels and restaurants	16,294	16,278	16,775
Transport	23,264	23,897	25,795
Post and communications	19,887	21,365	22,097
Public administration and social security	51,910	54,000	58,860
Other services	145,300	154,939	164,959
Sub-total	545,693	619,632	654,465
Taxes, less subsidies, on imports	70,561	69,211	81,741
GDP in purchasers' values	616,254	688,843	736,206

BALANCE OF PAYMENTS
(US $ million)

	2007	2008	2009
Exports of goods f.o.b.	15,146	20,330	14,044
Imports of goods f.o.b.	−29,316	−39,827	−30,408
Trade balance	−14,170	−19,497	−16,363
Exports of services	12,165	13,416	12,336
Imports of services	−5,416	−6,694	−6,899
Balance on goods and services	−7,421	−12,775	−10,927
Other income received	961	1,059	925
Other income paid	−1,365	−1,581	−2,421
Balance on goods, services and income	−7,825	−13,297	−12,422
Current transfers received	7,786	7,849	7,278
Current transfers paid	−185	−211	−218
Current balance	−224	−5,659	−5,362
Capital account (net)	−3	−2	—
Direct investment abroad	−632	−316	−479
Direct investment from abroad	2,807	2,466	1,970
Portfolio investment assets	−16	−257	−12
Portfolio investment liabilities	−64	148	−4
Other investment assets	−1,617	−413	−56
Other investment liabilities	−1,195	−1,257	63
Net errors and omissions	105	−414	−523
Overall balance	−840	−5,704	−4,404

Source: IMF, *International Financial Statistics*.

External Trade

PRINCIPAL COMMODITIES
(million dirhams)

Imports c.i.f.	2007	2008	2009*
Foodstuffs, beverages and tobacco	26,726	31,864	24,253
Wheat	9,407	12,428	5,483
Energy and lubricants	53,988	72,715	54,172
Crude petroleum	26,250	30,683	17,166
Crude products	15,847	26,685	13,623
Semi-finished products	59,782	69,489	53,637
Chemical products	10,010	12,221	9,825
Finished capital goods	55,819	71,657	66,770
Finished consumer products	48,906	53,525	52,681
Pharmaceutical products	2,936	3,283	4,069
Textile and cotton fabrics	7,732	7,191	6,237
Total (incl. others)	259,747	326,042	265,188

Exports f.o.b.	2007	2008*	2009*
Foodstuffs, beverages and tobacco	24,162	26,198	23,940
Crustaceans and molluscs	5,165	5,537	4,340
Prepared and preserved fish	3,899	4,524	4,842
Energy and lubricants	2,803	3,351	2,268
Crude mineral products	10,240	21,387	7,992
Phosphates	6,086	17,684	5,163
Semi-finished products	33,937	53,172	30,190
Phosphoric acid	9,069	22,831	8,042
Natural and chemical fertilizers	7,182	10,946	5,632
Finished industrial capital goods	14,040	15,508	12,219
Electric wire and cable	8,206	8,886	5,175
Finished consumer products	36,060	33,593	32,670
Manufactured garments	20,474	18,924	17,752
Hosiery	7,882	6,659	6,460
Total (incl. others)	123,941	155,740	111,967

* Provisional figures.

MOROCCO

PRINCIPAL TRADING PARTNERS
(million dirhams)*

Imports c.i.f.	2007	2008	2009
Algeria	6,793	7,559	5,636
Belgium-Luxembourg	4,683	5,137	4,183
Brazil	4,534	5,511	6,048
Canada	2,097	2,720	3,191
China, People's Republic	15,146	18,538	20,712
France	41,607	48,950	41,584
Germany	12,900	15,201	14,409
India	2,566	2,722	3,211
Italy	16,695	21,742	17,298
Japan	4,281	5,726	4,042
Netherlands	8,252	6,860	6,343
Spain	29,084	36,447	31,968
United Kingdom	7,109	9,035	5,123
USA	15,442	16,624	18,850
Total (incl. others)	259,747	326,042	265,188

Exports f.o.b.	2007	2008	2009
Belgium-Luxembourg	3,032	5,184	2,010
Brazil	4,247	7,538	2,395
France	35,054	31,384	27,464
Germany	3,705	4,036	3,469
India	4,853	10,520	5,950
Italy	6,480	7,261	5,190
Japan	1,313	1,781	1,303
Netherlands	2,587	3,659	3,011
Spain	25,559	27,862	23,710
United Kingdom	6,388	5,350	3,672
USA	2,994	6,085	3,673
Total (incl. others)	123,941	155,740	111,967

* Imports by country of production; exports by country of last consignment.

Transport

RAILWAYS
(traffic)*

	2002	2003	2004
Passengers carried ('000)	14,685	16,516	18,543
Passenger-km (million)	2,145	2,374	2,645
Freight ('000 metric tons)	29,945	30,552	32,901
Freight ton-km (million)	4,974	5,146	5,563

* Figures refer to principal railways only.

2007: Passengers carried ('000) 26,116; Passenger-km (million) 3,659; Freight ('000 metric tons) 36,088; Freight ton-km (million) 5,837.

2008: Passengers carried ('000) 27,527; Passenger-km (million) 3,836 (provisional); Freight ('000 metric tons) 31,703; Freight ton-km (million) 4,985 (provisional).

2009 (provisional): Passengers carried ('000) 29,600; Freight ('000 metric tons) 25,000.

ROAD TRAFFIC
('000 motor vehicles in use at 31 December)

	1999	2000	2001
Passenger cars	1,161.9	1,211.1	1,253.0
Commercial vehicles	400.3	415.7	431.0

Motorcycles and scooters: 20,388 in 2000; 20,569 in 2001.

Passenger cars: 1,326,108 in 2003.

2007: Passenger cars 1,644,523; Buses and coaches 22,841; Vans and lorries 525,334; Motorcycles and mopeds 22,841.

Sources: IRF, *World Road Statistics*; UN, *Statistical Yearbook*.

SHIPPING
Merchant Fleet
(registered at 31 December)

	2007	2008	2009
Number of vessels	517	509	512
Total displacement ('000 grt)	489.6	494.5	470.6

Source: IHS Fairplay, *World Fleet Statistics*.

International Sea-borne Freight Traffic
('000 metric tons)

	2002	2003	2004*
Goods loaded	24,891	24,355	27,355
Goods unloaded	32,097	31,785	34,149

* Provisional figures.

2007 ('000 metric tons): Goods loaded 31,136; Goods unloaded 41,697.

2008 ('000 metric tons, provisional): Goods loaded 26,158; Goods unloaded 41,557.

CIVIL AVIATION
(traffic on scheduled services)

	2004	2005	2006
Kilometres flown (million)	70	76	96
Passengers carried ('000)	3,004	3,493	4,150
Passenger-km (million)	5,551	6,434	8,086
Total ton-km (million)	642	714	768

Source: UN, *Statistical Yearbook*.

Tourism

FOREIGN TOURIST ARRIVALS*

Country of nationality	2007	2008	2009
France	1,605,503	1,707,055	1,699,201
Germany	159,844	179,037	174,384
Italy	160,047	163,315	177,915
Spain	540,186	595,279	642,817
United Kingdom	338,304	274,762	252,945
Other European countries	188,727	205,746	209,153
Maghreb countries	122,750	135,820	135,766
USA	109,079	110,778	121,144
Total (incl. others)	4,030,898	4,211,855	4,292,958

* Excluding Moroccans resident abroad (3,376,719 in 2007; 3,666,784 in 2008; 4,048,279 in 2009).

Cruise-ship passengers: 293,333 in 2007; 329,920 in 2008; 319,353 in 2009.

Receipts from tourism (US $ million, incl. passenger transport): 6,900 in 2006; 8,307 in 2007; 8,885 in 2008 (Source: World Tourism Organization).

Communications Media

	2007	2008	2009
Telephones ('000 main lines in use)	2,393.8	2,991.2	3,516.3
Mobile cellular telephones ('000 subscribers)	20,029.3	22,815.7	25,310.8
Internet users ('000)	6,713.2	10,461.5	13,212.9
Broadband subscribers ('000)	477.4	483.9	475.8

1997: Radio receivers ('000 in use) 6,640; Facsimile machines (number in use) 18,000 (estimate).

1999: Book production (titles) 386.

2000: Television receivers ('000 in use) 4,700; Daily newspapers 23 (average circulation 846,000 copies); Other newspapers 507 (average circulation 4,108,000 copies); Periodicals 364 (average circulation 4,956,000 copies).

2004: Daily newspapers 24 (average circulation 350,000 copies in 2003); Other newspapers 594.

Personal computers: 1,800,000 (57.0 per 1,000 persons) in 2008.

Sources: UNESCO, *Statistical Yearbook*; UN, *Statistical Yearbook*; and International Telecommunication Union.

Education

(2007/08 unless otherwise indicated)

	Institutions	Teachers	Males	Females	Total
Pre-primary	33,577*	36,833	391,122	278,243	669,365
Primary	6,565†	146,187	2,067,742	1,810,898	3,878,640
public	5,940†	n.a.	1,884,457	1,647,604	3,532,061
private	625†	n.a.	183,285	163,294	346,579
Secondary (public and private)	1,664†	100,367‡	1,184,132§	989,322§	2,173,454§
Tertiary	68*	19,103	211,456	189,637	401,093

* 1997/98 figure.
† 1999/2000 figure.
‡ 2003/04 figure.
§ 2006/07 figure.

Pupils/Students (2008/09): Primary 3,863,838 (public 3,492,312, private 371,526); Secondary 2,232,289 (public 2,103,768, private 128,521).

Teachers: Primary 144,722 in 2008/09.
Source: Ministry of National Education, Higher Education, Staff Training and Scientific Research; UNESCO Institute for Statistics.

Pupil-teacher ratio (primary education, UNESCO estimate): 26.6 in 2008/09 (Source: UNESCO Institute for Statistics).

Adult literacy rate (UNESCO estimates): 56.4% (males 69.4%; females 44.1%) in 2008 (Source: UNESCO Institute for Statistics).

Directory

The Government

HEAD OF STATE

Monarch: HM King MUHAMMAD VI (acceded 23 July 1999).

CABINET
(May 2011)

A coalition of Istiqlal, the Union socialiste des forces populaires (USFP), the Rassemblement national des indépendants (RNI), the Mouvement Populaire (MP), the Parti du progrès et du socialisme (PPS) and independents (Ind.).

Prime Minister: ABBAS EL-FASSI (Istiqlal).

Ministers of State: MUHAMMAD EL-YAZGHI (USFP), MOHAND LAENSER (MP).

Minister of Justice: MUHAMMAD NACIRI (Ind.).

Minister of the Interior: TAÏB CHERKAOUI (Ind.).

Minister of Foreign Affairs and Co-operation: TAIEB FASSI FIHRI (Ind.).

Minister of Habous (Religious Endowments) and Islamic Affairs: AHMED TOUFIQ (Ind.).

Secretary-General of the Government: DRISS DAHAK (Ind.).

Minister in charge of Relations with Parliament: DRISS LACHGUER (USFP).

Minister of the Economy and Finance: SALAHEDDINE MEZOUAR (RNI).

Minister of Agriculture and Fisheries: AZIZ AKHENOUCH (RNI).

Minister of Employment and Vocational Training: JAMAL AGHMANI (USFP).

Minister of National Education, Higher Education, Staff Training and Scientific Research: AHMED AKHCHICHINE (Ind.).

Minister of Culture: BENSALEM HIMMICH (USFP).

Minister of Tourism and Handicrafts: YASSIR ZNAGUI (Ind.).

Minister of Equipment and Transport: KARIM GHELLAB (Istiqlal).

Minister of Housing, Town Planning and Development: AHMED TAOUFIQ HEJIRA (Istiqlal).

Minister of Industry, Trade and New Technologies: AHMED REDA CHAMI (USFP).

Minister of Health: YASMINA BADDOU (Istiqlal).

Minister of Youth and Sports: MONCEF BELKHAYAT (Ind.).

Minister of Energy, Mining, Water and the Environment: AMINA BENKHADRA (RNI).

Minister of Communication and Government Spokesperson: KHALID NACIRI (PPS).

Minister of Foreign Trade: ABDELLATIF MAÂZOUZ (Istiqlal).

Minister of Social Development, the Family and Solidarity: NOUZHA SKALLI (PPS).

Minister-delegate to the Prime Minister, in charge of Economic and General Affairs: NIZAR BARAKA (Istiqlal).

Minister-delegate to the Prime Minister, in charge of National Defence: ABDELLATIF LOUDIYI (Ind.).

Minister-delegate to the Prime Minister, in charge of the Modernization of the Public Sector: MUHAMMAD SAÂD ALAMI (Istiqlal).

Minister-delegate to the Prime Minister, in charge of Moroccans Resident Abroad: MUHAMMAD AMEUR (USFP).

There are also seven Secretaries of State.

MINISTRIES

Office of the Prime Minister: Palais Royal, Touarga, Rabat; tel. (53) 7219400; fax (53) 7768656; e-mail courrier@pm.gov.ma; internet www.pm.gov.ma.

Ministry of Agriculture and Fisheries: Quartier Administratif, pl. Abdellah Chefchaouni, BP 607, Rabat; tel. (53) 7760933; fax (53) 7776411; e-mail info@mardrpm.gov.ma; internet www.madrpm.gov.ma.

Ministry of Communication: ave Allal el-Fassi, Madinat al-Irfane Souissi, 10000 Rabat; tel. (53) 7128167; fax (53) 7680178; e-mail ministre@mincom.gov.ma; internet www.mincom.gov.ma.

Ministry of Culture: 1 rue Ghandi, Rabat; tel. (53) 7209494; fax (53) 7209400; e-mail webmaster@minculture.gov.ma; internet www.minculture.gov.ma.

Ministry of the Economy and Finance: blvd Muhammad V, Quartier Administratif, Chellah, Rabat; tel. (53) 7677501; fax (53) 7677527; e-mail internet@finances.gov.ma; internet www.finances.gov.ma.

Ministry of Employment and Vocational Training: ave Muhammad V, Hassan, BP 5015, Rabat; tel. (53) 7760521; fax (53) 7750192; e-mail communication@emploi.gov.ma; internet www.emploi.gov.ma.

Ministry of Energy, Mining, Water and the Environment: rue Abou Marouane Essaadi, BP 6208, Agdal, Rabat; tel. (53) 7688857; fax (53) 7688863; e-mail dsi@mem.gov.ma; internet www.mem.gov.ma.

MOROCCO

Ministry of Equipment and Transport: Quartier Administratif, Chellah, Rabat; tel. (53) 7684151; fax (53) 7764825; internet www.mtpnet.gov.ma.

Ministry of Foreign Affairs and Co-operation: ave Franklin Roosevelt, Rabat; tel. (53) 7761583; fax (53) 7765508; e-mail mail@maec.gov.ma; internet www.maec.gov.ma.

Ministry of Foreign Trade: 63 ave Moulay Youssef, Rabat; tel. (53) 7706321; fax (53) 7703231; e-mail ministere@mce.gov.ma; internet www.mce.gov.ma.

Ministry of Habous (Religious Endowments) and Islamic Affairs: al-Mechouar Essaid, Rabat; tel. (53) 7766801; fax (53) 7666037; e-mail infos@islam-maroc.ma; internet www.habous.gov.ma.

Ministry of Health: 335 blvd Muhammad V, Rabat; tel. (53) 7764019; fax (53) 7768401; internet srvweb.sante.gov.ma.

Ministry of Housing, Town Planning and Development: rues al-Jouaze and al-Joumaize, Hay Riad, Secteur 16, 10000 Rabat; tel. (53) 7577000; fax (53) 7577373; e-mail zerrad@mhuae.gov.ma; internet www.mhuae.gov.ma.

Ministry of Industry, Trade and New Technologies: 1 ave el-Hassan, Rabat; tel. (53) 7268600; fax (53) 7766265; e-mail webmaster@technologies.gov.ma; internet www.technologies.gov.ma.

Ministry of the Interior: Quartier Administratif, Chellah, Rabat; tel. (53) 7761868; fax (53) 7762056.

Ministry of Justice: pl. Mamounia, Rabat; tel. (53) 7732941; fax (53) 7730772; e-mail kourout@justice.gov.ma; internet www.justice.gov.ma.

Ministry of the Modernization of the Public Sector: Quartier Administratif, rue Ahmed Cherkaoui, Agdal, BP 1076, Rabat; tel. (53) 7773106; fax (53) 7778438; e-mail info@mmsp.gov.ma; internet www.mmsp.gov.ma.

Ministry of National Education, Higher Education, Training and Scientific Research: Bab Rouah, Rabat; tel. (53) 7771822; fax (53) 7771874; e-mail divcom@men.gov.ma; internet www.men.gov.ma.

Ministry in charge of Relations with Parliament: Nouveau Quartier Administratif, Agdal, Rabat; tel. (53) 7775170; fax (53) 7777719; e-mail mirepa@mcrp.gov.ma; internet www.mcrp.gov.ma.

Ministry of Social Development, the Family and Solidarity: 47 ave ibn Sina, Agdal, Rabat; tel. (53) 7684060; fax (53) 7671967; e-mail mdsfs@mdsfs.ma; internet www.social.gov.ma.

Ministry of Youth and Sports: blvd ibn Sina, Rabat; tel. (53) 7680028; fax (53) 7680145; e-mail masterweb@mjs.gov.ma.

Legislature

Majlis al-Nuab
(Chamber of Representatives)

POB 431, Rabat; tel. (53) 7760960; fax (53) 7767726; e-mail parlement@parlement.ma; internet www.parlement.ma.

President: ABDELWAHED RADI.

General Election, 7 September 2007

Party	Votes	% of votes	Seats
Istiqlal	494,256	10.7	52
Parti de la justice et du développement (PJD)	503,396	10.9	46
Mouvement populaire (MP)	426,849	9.3	41
Rassemblement national des indépendants (RNI)	447,244	9.7	39
Union socialiste des forces populaires (USFP)	408,945	8.9	38
Union constitutionnelle (UC)	335,116	7.3	27
Parti du progrès et du socialisme (PPS)	248,103	5.4	17
Parti national démocrate (PND)/Parti Al Ahd	253,816	5.5	14
Front des forces démocratiques (FFD)	207,982	4.5	9
Mouvement démocratique et social (MDS)	168,960	3.7	9
Parti de l'avant-garde démocratique socialiste (PADS)/Congrès national ittihadi (CNI)/Parti socialiste unifié (PSU)	123,897	2.7	6
Parti travailliste (PT)	140,224	3.0	5
Parti de l'environnement et du développement (PED)	131,524	2.9	5
Parti du renouveau et de l'équité (PRE)	83,516	1.8	4
Other parties	552,301	12.0	8
Independents	81,364	1.8	5
Total	**4,607,493***	**100.0***	**325†**

* Excluding votes for the seats reserved for women (see below).

† 30 of the 325 seats were reserved for women. Of these, the PJD and Istiqlal each won six seats; the RNI, the MP and the USFP all secured five; and the PPS received three.

Majlis al-Mustasharin
(Chamber of Advisers)

POB 432, Rabat; tel. (53) 7218304; fax (53) 7733192; e-mail info@conseiller.ma; internet www.conseiller.ma.

President: MUHAMMAD CHEIKH BIADILLAH.

Election, 5 December 1997*

	Seats
Rassemblement national des indépendants (RNI)	42
Mouvement démocratique et social (MDS)	33
Union constitutionnelle (UC)	28
Mouvement populaire (MP)	27
Parti national démocrate (PND)	21
Istiqlal	21
Union socialiste des forces populaires (USFP)	16
Mouvement national populaire (MNP)	15
Parti de l'action (PA)	13
Front des forces démocratiques (FFD)	12
Parti du progrès et du socialisme (PPS)	7
Parti social et démocratique (PSD)	4
Parti démocratique et de l'indépendance (PDI)	4
Trade unions	
Confédération Démocratique du Travail (CDT)	11
Union Marocaine du Travail (UMT)	8
Union Générale des Travailleurs du Maroc (UGTM)	3
Others	5
Total	**270**

* Of the Chamber of Advisers' 270 members, 162 were elected by local councils, 81 by chambers of commerce and 27 by trade unions.

Political Organizations

Congrès national ittihadi (CNI): 209 blvd Strasbourg, Résidence C, 2ème étage, Casablanca; tel. and fax (52) 2447664; e-mail onittihadi@caramail.com; f. 2001 by dissident mems of USFP; Sec.-Gen. ABDESSALAM ELAZIZ.

Front des forces démocratiques (FFD): 13 ave Tariq ibn Ziad, Hassan, Rabat; tel. (53) 7661625; fax (53) 7660621; e-mail forces@menara.ma; internet www.ffd.ma; f. 1997 after split from PPS; Sec.-Gen. THAMI EL-KHYARI.

Istiqlal (Independence): 4 ave Ibn Toumert, Bab el-Had, 50020 Rabat; tel. (53) 7730951; fax (53) 7725417; e-mail p.istiqlal2009@hotmail.com; internet www.partistiqlal.org; f. 1944; aims to raise living standards and to confer equal rights on all; emphasizes the Moroccan claim to Western Sahara; Sec.-Gen. ABBAS EL-FASSI.

Mouvement démocratique et social (MDS): 4 ave Imam Malik, route des Zaërs, Rabat; tel. (57) 7631552; fax (53) 7658253; f. 1996 as Mouvement national démocratique et social after split from Mouvement national populaire (MNP); adopted current name in Nov. 1996; Leader MAHMOUD ARCHANE.

Mouvement populaire (MP): 66 rue Patrice Lumumba, Rabat; tel. (53) 7766431; fax (53) 7767537; e-mail parti_mp@hotmail.fr; internet www.harakamp.org; f. 1958; merged with the MNP and Union démocratique in 2006; liberal; Sec.-Gen. MOHAND LAENSER.

Parti de l'action (PA): 113 ave Allal Ben Abdallah, Rabat; tel. (53) 7206661; f. 1974; advocates democracy and progress; Sec.-Gen. MUHAMMAD EL-IDRISSI.

Parti Al Ahd Démocratique: 14 rue Idriss al-Akbar, rue Tafraout, Hassan, Rabat; tel. (53) 7204816; fax (53) 7204786; e-mail alhakika@iam.net.ma; f. 2002; Chair. NAJIB EL-OUAZZANI.

Parti de l'authenticité et de la modernité (PAM): internet www.pam.ma; f. 2008; Founder FOUAD ALI EL-HIMMA; Sec.-Gen. MUHAMMAD CHEIKH BIADILLAH.

MOROCCO

Parti de l'avant-garde démocratique socialiste (PADS): BP 2091, 54 ave de la Résistance Océan, Rabat; tel. (53) 7200559; fax (53) 7708491; e-mail pads1@caramail.com; an offshoot of USFP; legalized in April 1992; Sec.-Gen. AHMAD BENJELLOUN.

Parti démocrate national (PDN): f. May 2009 by fmr members of Parti national démocrate, following that party's merger into the PAM; Sec.-Gen. ABDULLAH KADIRI.

Parti démocratique et de l'indépendance (PDI): 9 Lalla Yakout, rue Araar, Apt 11, 2ème étage, blvd d'Anfa, Casablanca; tel. (52) 2200949; fax (52) 2200928; f. 1946; Sec.-Gen. ABDELWAHID MAÂCH.

Parti de l'environnement et du développement durable (PEDD): 3 rue Azilal, Hassan, Rabat; tel. and fax (53) 7670620; e-mail pedmaroc@menara.ma; internet www.pedmaroc.ma; f. 2002 as Parti de l'environnement et du développement; merged with PAM in 2008; relaunched as above in 2009; environmentalist; Sec.-Gen. AHMAD AL-ALAMI.

Parti des forces citoyennes (PFC): 353 blvd Muhammad V, 9ème étage, Casablanca; tel. (52) 2400608; fax (52) 2400613; e-mail citoyennes@menara.ma; f. 2001; Sec.-Gen. ABDERRAHIM LAHJOUJI.

Parti de la justice et du développement (PJD): ave Abdelwahed Elmorakechi, rue Elyafrani, 4 les Orangers, Rabat; tel. (53) 7208862; fax (53) 7208854; e-mail info@pjd.ma; internet www.pjd.ma; f. 1967 as Mouvement populaire constitutionnel et démocratique; breakaway party from MP; formally absorbed mems of the Islamic asscn Al Islah wa Attajdid in June 1996; adopted current name in Oct. 1998; Sec.-Gen. ABDELILAH BENKIRANE.

Parti marocain libéral (PML): 114 ave Allal Ben Abdellah, 2ème étage, Rabat; tel. (53) 7733670; fax (53) 7733611; e-mail pml@menara.ma; f. 2002; Nat. Co-ordinator MUHAMMAD ZIANE.

Parti du progrès et du socialisme (PPS): 29 ave John Kennedy, Youssoufia, Rabat; tel. (53) 7759464; fax (53) 7759476; e-mail sg@pps.maroc.org; internet www.ppsmaroc.com; f. 1974; successor to Parti communiste marocain (banned in 1952) and Parti de la libération et du socialisme (banned in 1969); left-wing; advocates modernization, social progress, nationalization and democracy; 35,000 mems; Sec.-Gen. NABIL BENABDELLAH.

Parti de la réforme et du développement (PRD): 34 ave Pasteur, Rabat; tel. and fax (53) 7703801; f. 2001 by fmr mems of RNI; Leader ABDERRAHMAN EL-KOUHEN.

Parti de la renaissance et de la vertu: Bouznika; f. 2005; national democratic party based on the principles of Islam; Sec.-Gen. MUHAMMAD KHALIDI.

Parti du renouveau et de l'équité (PRE): 16 rue Sebou, Apt 5, Agdal, Rabat; tel. (53) 7777266; fax (53) 7777452; f. 2002; Pres. CHAKIR ACHEHBAR.

Parti socialiste unifié (PSU): 9 rue d'Agadir, Immeuble Maréchal Ameziane, Casablanca; tel. (52) 2485902; fax (52) 2278442; e-mail psumaroc@yahoo.fr; internet psu.apinc.org; f. 2005 by merger of Parti de la gauche socialiste unifieé and Fidélité à la démocratie; Sec.-Gen. MUHAMMAD MOUJAHID.

Parti travailliste (PT): 9 rue Ksar Essouk, Hassan, Rabat; f. 2005; centre-left; Sec.-Gen. ABDELKRIM BENATIQ.

Rassemblement national des indépendants (RNI): 6 rue Laos, ave Hassan II, Rabat; tel. (53) 7721420; fax (53) 7733824; internet www.rni.ma; f. 1978 from the pro-Govt independents' group that then formed the majority in the Chamber of Representatives; Pres. SALAHEDDINE MEZOUAR.

Union constitutionnelle (UC): 158 ave des Forces Armées Royales, Casablanca; tel. (52) 2441144; fax (52) 2441141; e-mail union_constit@menara.ma; f. 1983; 51-mem. Political Bureau; Sec.-Gen. MUHAMMAD ABIED.

Union Marocaine pour la démocratie (UMD): Rabat; f. 2006; Sec.-Gen. ABDELLAH AZMANI.

Union socialiste des forces populaires (USFP): 9 ave al-Araâr, Hay Riad, Rabat; tel. (53) 7565511; fax (53) 7565510; e-mail usfp@usfp.ma; internet www.usfp.ma; f. 1959 as Union nationale des forces populaires (UNFP); became USFP in 1974 after UNFP split into two separate entities; merged with Parti socialiste démocratique in 2005; democratic socialist and progressive party; 160,000 mems; First Sec. ABDELWAHED RADI.

The following movement is not authorized as a political party by the Government, but is generally tolerated:

Al-Adl wal-Ihsan (Justice and Charity): internet www.aljamaa.net; advocates an Islamic state based on *Shari'a* law; rejects violence; Leader ABDESSALAM YASSINE.

The following group is active in the disputed territory of Western Sahara:

Frente Popular para la Liberación de Saguia el-Hamra y Río de Oro (Frente Polisario) (Polisario Front): BP 10, el-Mouradia, Algiers, Algeria; fax (2) 747206; e-mail dgmae@mail.wissal.dz; f. 1973 to gain independence for Western Sahara, first from Spain and then Morocco and Mauritania; signed peace treaty with Mauritanian Govt in 1979; supported by Algerian Govt; in February 1976 proclaimed the Sahrawi Arab Democratic Republic (SADR); admitted as the 51st mem. of the OAU in Feb. 1982 and currently recognized by more than 75 countries world-wide; its main organs are a 33-mem. Nat. Secretariat, a 101-mem. Sahrawi Nat. Assembly (Parliament) and a 13-mem. Govt; Sec.-Gen. of the Polisario Front and Pres. of the SADR MUHAMMAD ABD AL-AZIZ; Prime Minister of the SADR ABDELKADER TALEB OUMAR.

Diplomatic Representation

EMBASSIES IN MOROCCO

Algeria: 46–48 blvd Tariq ibn Ziad, BP 448, 10001 Rabat; tel. (53) 7661574; fax (53) 7762237; Ambassador AHMED BEN YAMINA.

Angola: km 5, 53 Ahmed Rifaï, BP 1318, Souissi, Rabat; tel. (53) 7659239; fax (53) 7659238; e-mail amb.angola@menara.ma; Ambassador Dr LUIS JOSÉ DE ALMEIDA.

Argentina: 4 ave Mehdi Ben Barka, Souissi, 10000 Rabat; tel. (53) 7755120; fax (53) 7755410; e-mail emarr@mrecic.gov.ar; Ambassador JOSÉ PEDRO PICO.

Austria: 2 rue Tiddas, BP 135, 10000 Rabat; tel. (53) 7761698; fax (53) 7765425; e-mail rabat-ob@bmeia.gv.at; Ambassador Dr GEORG MAUTNER-MARKHOF.

Azerbaijan: rue 3 Abu Hanifa, Aqdal, Rabat; tel. (53) 7671915; fax (53) 7671918; e-mail azembma@menara.ma; Ambassador SABIR AGHABAYOV.

Bahrain: rue Béni Hassan, km 6.5, route des Zaërs, Villa 318, POB 1470, Souissi, Rabat; tel. (53) 7633500; fax (53) 7630732; e-mail rabat.mission@mofa.gov.bh; Ambassador KHALID BIN SALMAN AL KHALIFA.

Bangladesh: 25 ave Tarek ibn Ziad, BP 1468, Rabat; tel. (53) 7766731; fax (53) 7766729; e-mail bdoot@mtds.com; Ambassador MOSUD MANNAN.

Belgium: 6 ave de Muhammad el-Fassi, Tour Hassan, Rabat; tel. (53) 7268060; fax (53) 7767003; e-mail rabat@diplobel.fed.be; internet www.diplomatie.be/rabat; Ambassador JEAN-LUC BODSON.

Benin: 30 ave Mehdi Ben Barka, BP 5187, Souissi, 10105 Rabat; tel. (53) 7754158; fax (53) 7754156; e-mail benin@menara.ma; Ambassador BIO TORO OROUGUIWA.

Brazil: 10 ave el-Jacaranda, Secteur 2, Hay Riad, 10000 Rabat; tel. (53) 7714663; fax (53) 7714808; e-mail ambassadedubresil@menara.ma; internet www.ambassadedubresil.org; Ambassador VIRGÍLIO MORETZSOHN DE ANDRADE.

Bulgaria: 4 ave Ahmed el-Yazidi, BP 1301, 10000 Rabat; tel. (53) 7765477; fax (53) 7763201; e-mail bulemrab@yahoo.com; internet www.mfa.bg; Ambassador KATIA PETROVA TODOROVA.

Burkina Faso: 7 rue al-Bouziri, BP 6484, Agdal, 10101 Rabat; tel. (53) 7675512; fax (53) 7675517; e-mail ambfrba@smirt.net.ma; Ambassador Brig.-Gen. IBRAHIM TRAORÉ.

Cameroon: 20 rue du Rif, BP 1790, Souissi, Rabat; tel. (53) 7758818; fax (53) 7750540; e-mail ambacam@iam.net.com; Ambassador MOUHAMADOU YOUSSIFOU.

Canada: 13 bis rue Jaâfar al-Sadik, BP 709, Agdal, Rabat; tel. (53) 7687400; fax (53) 7687430; e-mail rabat@international.gc.ca; internet www.morocco.gc.ca; Ambassador CHRISTOPHER WILKIE.

Central African Republic: Villa No 4, ave Souss, Cité Saâda, Quartier Administratif, BP 770, Agdal, 10000 Rabat; tel. (53) 7631654; fax (53) 7631655; e-mail centrafricaine@iam.net.ma; Ambassador ISMAÏLA NIMAGA.

Chile: 35 ave Ahmed Balafrej, Souissi, Rabat; tel. (53) 7636065; fax (53) 7636067; e-mail embachilema@menara.ma; Ambassador CARLOS CHARME SILVA.

China, People's Republic: 16 ave Ahmed Balafrej, 10000 Rabat; tel. (53) 7754056; fax (53) 7757519; e-mail chinaemb_ma@mfa.gov.cn; internet ma.china-embassy.org; Ambassador XU JINGHU.

Congo, Democratic Republic: 34 ave de la Victoire, BP 553, 10000 Rabat; tel. (53) 7262280; fax (53)7207407; Chargé d'affaires a.i. WAWA BAMIALY.

Congo, Republic: 197 ave Général Abdendi Britel, Souissi II, Rabat; tel. (53) 7659966; fax (53) 7659959; Ambassador JEAN-MARIE EWENGUE.

Côte d'Ivoire: 21 rue de Tiddas, BP 192, 10001 Rabat; tel. (53) 7763151; fax (53) 7762792; e-mail ambcim@clam.net.ma.

Croatia: 73 rue Marnissa, Souissi, Rabat; tel. (53) 7638824; fax (53) 7638827; e-mail croemb.rabat@mvpei.hr; Ambassador DARKO BEKIĆ.

Czech Republic: Villa Merzaa, km 4.5, route des Zaërs, BP 410, Zankat Aït Melloul, Souissi, 10200 Rabat; tel. (53) 7755421; fax (53) 7754393; e-mail rabat@embassy.mzv.cz; internet www.mzv.cz/rabat; Ambassador TOMÁŠ BURIL.

MOROCCO

Denmark: 14 rue Tiddas angle rue Roudana, 10020 Rabat; tel. (53) 7665020; fax (53) 7665021; e-mail rbaamb@um.dk; internet www.rabat.um.dk; Ambassador Lars Vissing.

Dominican Republic: 3 ave Mehdi Ben Barka, 10000 Rabat; tel. (53) 7715905; fax (53) 7715957; Ambassador Francisco A. Caraballo.

Egypt: 31 rue al-Jazair, 10000 Rabat; tel. (53) 7731833; fax (53) 7706821; e-mail embegypt@mtds.com; internet www.mfa.gov.eg/Missions/morocco/rabat/embassy/fr-FR; Ambassador Abu Bakr Hefni.

Equatorial Guinea: ave President Roosevelt, angle rue d'Agadir 9, Rabat; tel. and fax (53) 7769454; Ambassador Juan Ndong Nguema Mbengono.

Finland: 145 rue Soufiane Ben Wahb, BP 590, 10002 Rabat; tel. (53) 7658775; fax (53) 7658904; e-mail sanomat.rab@formin.fi; internet www.finlande.ma; Ambassador Antti Rytövuori (resident in Lisbon, Portugal).

France: 3 rue Sahnoun, BP 602, Rabat; tel. (53) 7689700; fax (53) 7689701; internet www.ambafrance-ma.org; Ambassador Bruno Joubert.

Gabon: km 3.5, route des Zaêrs, BP 1239, 10100 Rabat; tel. (53) 7751950; fax (53) 7757550; Ambassador François Banga Eboumi.

The Gambia: 27 ave Lotissement Mouline II, Muhammad VI, Souissi, 10000 Rabat; tel. (53) 7638045; fax (53) 7752908; Ambassador Ousman Badjie.

Germany: 7 Zankat Madnine, BP 235, 10000 Rabat; tel. (53) 7218600; fax (53) 706851; e-mail info@rabat.diplo.de; internet www.rabat.diplo.de; Ambassador Ulf-Dieter Klemm.

Ghana: 27 rue Ghomara, La Pinede, Souissi, Rabat; tel. (53) 7757620; fax (35) 7757630; Ambassador Clifford Akotey.

Greece: km 5, route des Zaêrs, Villa Chems, Souissi, 10000 Rabat; tel. (53) 7638964; fax (53) 7638990; e-mail gremb.rab@mfa.gr; Ambassador Panagiotis Stournaras.

Guinea: 15 rue Hamzah, Agdal, 10000 Rabat; tel. and fax (53) 7674148; fax (53) 7675070; e-mail ambaguirabat@gmail.com; Ambassador Mamadouba Diabate.

Holy See: rue Béni M'tir, BP 1303, Souissi, Rabat (Apostolic Nunciature); tel. (53) 7772277; fax (53) 7756213; e-mail nuntius@iam.net.ma; Apostolic Nuncio Most Rev. Antonio Sozzo (Titular Archbishop of Concordia).

Hungary: route des Zaêrs, 17 Zankat Aït Melloul, BP 5026, Souissi, Rabat; tel. (53) 7750757; fax (53) 7754123; e-mail rba.missions@kum.hu; internet www.mfa.gov.hu/emb/rabat; Ambassador Csaba László Pap.

India: 13 ave de Michlifen, Agdal, 10000 Rabat; tel. (53) 7671339; fax (53) 7671269; e-mail india@maghrebnet.net.ma; internet www.indianembassymorocco.com; Ambassador B. B. Tyagi.

Indonesia: 63 rue Béni Boufrah, km 5.9, route des Zaêrs, BP 576, 10105 Rabat; tel. (53) 7757860; fax (53) 7757859; e-mail kbrirabat@iam.net.ma; internet www.indonesie.ma; Ambassador Tosari Widjaja.

Iran: ave Imam Malik, BP 490, 10001 Rabat; tel. (53) 7752167; fax (53) 7659118; e-mail iranembassy@iam.net.ma; Ambassador (vacant).

Iraq: 39 blvd Mehdi Ben Barka, 10100 Rabat; tel. (53) 7754466; fax (53) 7759749; e-mail rbtemb@iraqmofamail.net; Ambassador Hazem Ahmed Mahmoud al-Yousofi.

Italy: 2 rue Idriss al-Azhar, BP 111, 10001 Rabat; tel. (53) 7219730; fax (53) 7706882; e-mail ambassade.rabat@esteri.it; internet www.ambrabat.esteri.it; Ambassador Piergiorgio Cherubini.

Japan: 39 ave Ahmed Balafrej, Souissi, 10100 Rabat; tel. (53) 7631782; fax (53) 7750078; e-mail amb-japon@fusion.net.ma; internet www.ma.emb-japan.go.jp; Ambassador Toshinori Yanagiya.

Jordan: 65 Villa Wafaa Lodgement Militaire, Souissi II, Rabat; tel. (53) 7751125; fax (53) 7758722; e-mail jo.am@iam.net.ma; Ambassador Faisal al-Shoubaki.

Korea, Republic: 41 ave Mehdi Ben Barka, Souissi, 10100 Rabat; tel. (53) 7756791; fax (53) 7750189; e-mail morocco@mofat.go.kr; internet mar.mofat.go.kr; Ambassador Choi Jai-Chul.

Kuwait: km 4.3, route des Zaêrs, BP 11, 10001 Rabat; tel. (53) 7631111; fax (53) 7753591; e-mail alrabat@mofa.gov.kw; Ambassador Shamlan Abd al-Aziz al-Roumi.

Lebanon: 19 ave Abd al-Karim Ben Jalloun, 10000 Rabat; tel. (53) 7760728; fax (53) 7766667; Ambassador Mustapha Hassan Mustapha.

Liberia: Lot 7, Napabia, rue Ouled Frej, Souissi, Rabat; tel. (53) 7638426; fax (53) 7638426; Chargé d'affaires Morieba K. Sanoe.

Libya: km 5.5, route de Zaêrs, ave Imam Malek, Souissi, Rabat; tel. (53) 7631871; fax (53) 7631877; Ambassador (vacant).

Malaysia: 17 ave Bir Kacem, Souissi, Rabat; tel. (53) 7658324; fax (53) 7658363; e-mail malrabat@kln.gov.my; internet www.kln.gov.my/perwakilan/rabat; Ambassador (vacant).

Mali: 7 rue Thami Lamdaouar, Souissi, Rabat; tel. (53) 7759121; fax (53) 7754742; Ambassador Toumani Djimé Diallo.

Mauritania: 6 rue Thami Lamdouar, BP 207, Souissi, 10000 Rabat; tel. (53) 7656678; fax (53) 7656680; e-mail ambarim_rabat@menara.ma; internet www.ambarimrabat.ma; Ambassador Mohamed Ould Tolba.

Mexico: 6 rue Kadi Mohamed Brebri, BP 1789, Souissi, 10100 Rabat; tel. (53) 7631969; fax (53) 7631971; e-mail embamexmar@smirt.net.ma; Ambassador Porfirio Thierry Muñoz-Ledo Chevannier.

Netherlands: 40 rue de Tunis, BP 329, Hassan, 10001 Rabat; tel. (53) 7219605; fax (53) 7219666; e-mail rab@minbuza.nl; internet www.mfa.nl/rab; Ambassador A. H. F. van Aggelen.

Niger: 14 bis, rue Jabal al-Ayachi, Agdal, Rabat; tel. (53) 7674615; fax (53) 7674629; Ambassador Garba Seyni.

Nigeria: 70 ave Omar ibn al-Khattab, BP 347, Agdal, Rabat; tel. (53) 7671857; fax (53) 7672739; e-mail nigerianrabat@menara.ma; Ambassador Alhaji Abubakar Shehu Wurno.

Norway: 9 rue Khénifra, BP 757, Agdal, 10006 Rabat; tel. (53) 7764084; fax (53) 7764088; e-mail emb.rabat@mfa.no; internet www.norvege.ma; Ambassador Fred Harald Nomme.

Oman: 21 rue Hamza, Agdal, 10000 Rabat; tel. (53) 7673788; fax (53) 7674567; Ambassador Mousa Hamdan Mousa al-Taei.

Pakistan: 37 ave Ahmed Balafrej, Souissi, Rabat; tel. (53) 7631192; fax (53) 7631243; e-mail pareprabat@menara.ma; internet www.mofa.gov.pk/morocco/mission.aspx; Ambassador Rizwan-ul-Haq Mahmood.

Peru: 16 rue d'Ifrane, 10000 Rabat; tel. (53) 7723236; fax (53) 7702803; e-mail leprurabat@menara.ma; Ambassador Luis Manuel Márcovich Monasi.

Poland: 23 rue Oqbah, Agdal, BP 425, 10000 Rabat; tel. (53) 7771173; fax (53) 7775320; e-mail apologne@menara.ma; internet www.rabat.polemb.net; Ambassador Witold Spirydowicz.

Portugal: 5 rue Thami Lamdouar, Souissi, 10100 Rabat; tel. (53) 7756446; fax (53) 7756445; e-mail ambassade.portugal@menara.ma; Ambassador João Rosa La.

Qatar: 4 ave Tarik ibn Ziad, BP 1220, 10001 Rabat; tel. (53) 7765681; fax (53) 7765774; e-mail rabat@mofa.gov.qa; Ambassador Saqr Mubarak al-Mansouri.

Romania: 10 rue d'Ouezzane, Hassan, 10000 Rabat; tel. (53) 7724694; fax (53) 7700196; e-mail amb.roumanie@menara.ma; internet rabat.mae.ro; Ambassador Vasile Popovici.

Russia: km 4, route des Zaêrs, 10100 Rabat; tel. (53) 7753509; fax (53) 7753590; e-mail ambrus@iam.net.ma; Ambassador Boris Bolotin.

Saudi Arabia: 322 ave Imam Malik, km 6, route des Zaêrs, Rabat; tel. (53) 657789; fax (53) 7768587; e-mail ambassd@goodinfo.net.ma; Ambassador Dr Muhammad Abd al-Rahman ibn Abd al-Aziz Bachar.

Senegal: 17 rue Cadi Ben Hamadi Senhaji, Souissi, BP 365, 10000 Rabat; tel. (53) 7754171; fax (53) 7754149; e-mail ambassene@iam.net.ma; Ambassador Amadou Habibou Ndiaye.

Serbia: BP 5014, 23 ave Mehdi Ben Barka, Souissi, 10105 Rabat; tel. (53) 7752201; fax (53) 7753258; e-mail sermont@menara.ma; Ambassador Stanislav Stakic.

South Africa: 34 rue Saâdiens, Rabat; tel. (53) 7706760; fax (53) 7724550; e-mail selekan@foreign.gov.za; Chargé d'affaires N. K. M. Seleka.

Spain: 3 rue Aïn Khalouiya, km 5.3, route des Zaêrs, Souissi, 10000 Rabat; tel. (53) 7633900; fax (53) 7630600; e-mail emb.rabat@maec.es; internet www.maec.es/subwebs/embajadas/rabat; Ambassador Alberto José Navarro González.

Sudan: 5 ave Ghomara, Souissi, 10000 Rabat; tel. (53) 7752863; fax (53) 7752865; e-mail soudanirab@maghrebnet.net.ma; Ambassador Tayeb Ali Ahmed.

Sweden: 159 ave John Kennedy, BP 428, Souissi, 10001 Rabat; tel. (53) 7633210; fax (53) 7758048; e-mail ambassaden.rabat@foreign.ministry.se; internet www.swedenabroad.com/rabat; Chargé d'affaires a.i. Margareta Kristianson.

Switzerland: sq. de Berkane, BP 169, 10020 Rabat; tel. (53) 7268030; fax (53) 7268040; e-mail rab.vertretung@eda.admin.ch; internet www.eda.admin.ch/rabat; Ambassador Louis Bertrand.

Syria: km 5.2, route des Zaêrs, BP 5158, Souissi, Rabat; tel. (53) 7755551; fax (53) 7757522; Ambassador Nabih Ismail.

Thailand: 33 ave Lalla Meriem, Souissi, BP 10000, Rabat; tel. (53) 7634603; fax (53) 7634607; e-mail thaima@menara.ma; Ambassador Kundalee Prachimdhit.

Tunisia: 6 ave de Fès et 1 rue d'Ifrane, 10000 Rabat; tel. (53) 7730636; fax (53) 7730637; Ambassador Sadok Korbi.

MOROCCO

Turkey: 7 ave Abdelkrim Benjelloun, 10000 Rabat; tel. (53) 7661522; fax (53) 7660476; e-mail amb-tur-rabat@menara.ma; internet rabat.emb.mfa.gov.tr; Ambassador TUNÇ UGDÜL.

Ukraine: rue Mouaouya Ben Houdaig, Villa 212, Cité OLM, Souissi II, Rabat; tel. (53) 7657840; fax (53) 7754679; e-mail emb_ma@mfa.gov.ua; internet www.mfa.gov.ua/morocco; Chargé d'affaires a.i. TATIANA NEDYALKOVA.

United Arab Emirates: 11 ave des Alaouines, 10000 Rabat; tel. (53) 7702085; fax (53) 7724145; e-mail eua@menara.ma; Ambassador AL-ASRI SAID AHMAD AL-DAHIRI.

United Kingdom: 28 ave S. A. R. Sidi Muhammad, Souissi, Rabat; tel. (53) 7633333; fax (53) 7758709; e-mail generalenquiries.rabat@fco.gov.uk; internet ukinmorocco.fco.gov.uk; Ambassador TIMOTHY MORRIS.

USA: 2 ave de Muhammad el-Fassi, Rabat; tel. (53) 7762265; fax (53) 7765661; e-mail ircrabat@usembassy.ma; internet rabat.usembassy.gov; Ambassador SAMUEL L. KAPLAN.

Venezuela: 58 Lot OLM, Villa Yasmine, rue Capitaine Abdeslam el-Moudden el-Alami, Souissi, Rabat; tel. (53) 7650315; fax (53) 7650372; e-mail emvenez@menara.ma; Ambassador LUISA REBECA SÁNCHEZ BELLO.

Yemen: ave Imam Malek, Rabat; tel. (53) 7631220; fax (53) 7674769; e-mail info@yemenembassyrabat.com; Ambassador AHMAD A. AL-BASHA.

Judicial System

SUPREME COURT

Al-Majlis al-Aala

Hay Riad, Ave al-Nakhil, Rabat; tel. (53) 7714931; fax (53) 7715106; e-mail coursupreme@coursupreme.ma; internet www.coursupreme.ma.

Responsible for the interpretation of the law and regulates the jurisprudence of the courts and tribunals of the Kingdom. The Supreme Court sits at Rabat and is divided into six Chambers.

First President: MUSTAPHA FARÈS.

Attorney-General: MUSTAPHA MEDDAH.

The 21 Courts of Appeal hear appeals from lower courts and also comprise a criminal division.

The 65 Courts of First Instance pass judgment on offences punishable by up to five years' imprisonment. These courts also pass judgment, without possibility of appeal, in personal and civil cases involving up to 3,000 dirhams.

The Communal and District Courts are composed of one judge, who is assisted by a clerk or secretary, and hear only civil and criminal cases.

The seven Administrative Courts pass judgment, subject to appeal before the Supreme Court pending the establishment of administrative appeal courts, on litigation with government departments.

The nine Commercial Courts pass judgment, without the possibility of appeal, on all commercial litigations involving up to 9,000 dirhams. They also pass judgment on claims involving more than 9,000 dirhams, which can be appealed against in the commercial appeal courts.

The Permanent Royal Armed Forces' Court tries offences committed by the armed forces and military officers.

Religion

ISLAM

About 99% of Moroccans are Muslims (of whom about 90% are of the Sunni sect), and Islam is the state religion.

CHRISTIANITY

There are about 69,000 Christians, mostly Roman Catholics.

The Roman Catholic Church

Morocco (excluding the disputed territory of Western Sahara) comprises two archdioceses, directly responsible to the Holy See. At 31 December 2007 there were an estimated 27,129 adherents in the country, representing less than 0.1% of the population. The Moroccan archbishops participate in the Conférence Episcopale Régionale du Nord de l'Afrique (f. 1985).

Bishops' Conference: Conférence Episcopale Régionale du Nord de l'Afrique, 1 rue Hadj Muhammad Riffaï, BP 258, 10001 Rabat; tel. (53) 7709239; fax (53) 7706282; e-mail archev.rabat@wanadoo.net.ma; f. 1985; Pres. Most Rev. VINCENT LANDEL (Archbishop of Rabat).

Archbishop of Rabat: Most Rev. VINCENT LANDEL, Archevêché, 1 rue Hadj Muhammad Riffaï, BP 258, 10001 Rabat; tel. (53) 7709239; fax (53) 7706282; e-mail landel@wanadoo.net.ma.

Archbishop of Tangier: Most Rev. SANTIAGO AGRELO MARTÍNEZ, Archevêché, 55 rue Sidi Bouabid, BP 2116, 9000 Tangier; tel. (53) 9932762; fax (53) 9949117; e-mail agrelomar@hotmail.com.

Western Sahara comprises a single Apostolic Prefecture, with an estimated 80 Catholics (2007).

Prefect Apostolic of Western Sahara: Fr ACACIO VALBUENA RODRÍGUEZ, Misión Católica, BP 31, 70001 el-Aaiún; e-mail omisahara@menara.ma.

The Anglican Communion

Within the Church of England, Morocco forms part of the diocese of Gibraltar in Europe. There are Anglican churches in Casablanca and Tangier.

Protestant Church

Evangelical Church: 33 rue d'Azilal, 20000 Casablanca; tel. (52) 2302151; fax (52) 2444768; e-mail eeam@lesblancs.com; f. 1920; established in eight towns; Pres. Pastor JEAN-LUC BLANC; 1,000 mems.

JUDAISM

It is estimated that there are fewer than 7,000 Jews in Morocco, of whom approximately 5,000 reside in Casablanca, with smaller communities in Rabat and other cities.

Conseil des Communautés Israélites du Maroc: 52 Béni Snassen, Souissi, Rabat; tel. (52) 222861; fax (52) 266953; Pres. SERGE BERDUGO.

The Press

DAILIES

Casablanca

Al-Ahdath al-Maghribia (Moroccan Events): 5 rue Saint-Emilion, Casablanca; tel. (52) 2443038; fax (52) 2442976; e-mail elberini@ahdath.info; f. 1998; Arabic; Dir MUHAMMAD EL-BERINI; circ. 19,811 (2008/09).

Assabah (The Morning): Groupe Ecomedia, 70 blvd al-Massira al-Khadra, Casablanca; tel. (52) 2953660; fax (52) 2364358; e-mail assabahcasa@leconomiste.com; internet www.assabah.press.ma; f. 2000; Arabic; sister publication of l'Economiste; Pres. ABDELMOUNAÏM DILAMI; Dir-Gen. KHALID BELYAZID; circ. 71,935 (2008/09).

Assahra al-Maghribia: 17 rue Othman Ben Affan, Casablanca; tel. (52) 2489120; fax (52) 2203935; e-mail web.master@almaghribia.ma; internet www.almaghribia.ma; f. 1989; Arabic; Dir AHMED NACHATTI.

Aujourd'hui le Maroc: 213 Rond-Point d'Europe, 20490 Casablanca; tel. (52) 2262674; fax (52) 2262443; e-mail alm@aujourdhui.ma; internet www.aujourdhui.ma; f. 2001; French; Dir KHALIL HACHIMI IDRISSI; Editor-in-Chief OMAR DAHBI; circ. 5,435 (2008/09).

Al-Bayane (The Manifesto): 119 blvd Emile Zola, 8ème étage, BP 13152, Casablanca; tel. (52) 2307882; fax (52) 2308080; internet www.casanet.net.ma/albayane; f. 1971; Arabic and French; organ of the Parti du progrès et du socialisme; Dir ALLAL EL-MALEH; Editor AHMED ZAKI; circ. 2,364 (2008/09).

L'Economiste: Groupe Ecomedia, 70 blvd al-Massira al-Khadra, Casablanca; tel. (52) 2953600; fax (52) 2365926; e-mail info@leconomiste.com; internet www.leconomiste.com; f. 1991; French; Pres. ABDELMOUNAÏM DILAMI; Dir-Gen. KHALID BELYAZID; Editor-in-Chief NADIA SALAH; circ. 19,937 (2008/09).

Al-Ittihad al-Ichtiraki (Socialist Unity): 33 rue Amir Abdelkader, BP 2165, Casablanca; tel. (52) 2407385; fax (52) 2619405; e-mail ail@menara.ma; internet www.alittihad.press.ma; Arabic; f. 1983; organ of the Union socialiste des forces populaires; Dir ABD AL-HADI DATE; Editor MUSTAPHA LAÁRAKI; circ. 9,513 (2008).

Libération: 33 rue Amir Abdelkader, BP 2165, Casablanca; tel. (52) 2619400; fax (52) 2620972; e-mail liberation@usfp.ma; internet www.liberation.press.ma; f. 1964; French; organ of the Union socialiste des forces populaires; Dir ABDELHADI KHAÏRAT; circ. 2,719 (2008).

Al-Massae (The Evening): 10 ave des Forces Armées Royales, 2ème étage, Casablanca; tel. (52) 2275918; fax (52) 2275597; e-mail contact@almassae.press.ma; internet www.almassae.press.ma; f. 2006; Arabic; independent; Dir RACHID NINI; circ. 113,849 (2008/09).

Le Matin du Sahara et du Maghreb: 17 rue Othman Ben Affane, Casablanca; tel. (52) 2489100; fax (52) 2203048; e-mail m.jouahri@lematin.ma; internet www.lematin.ma; f. 1971; French; royalist; Dir-Gen. MUHAMMAD JOUAHRI; Editor-in-Chief ABDELHADI GADI; circ. 24,816 (2008/09).

MOROCCO

Rissalat al-Oumma (The Message of the Nation): 152 ave des Forces Armées Royales, BP 20005, Casablanca; tel. (52) 2901925; fax (52) 2901926; Arabic; weekly edn in French; organ of the Union constitutionnelle; Dir MUHAMMAD TAMALDOU.

Rabat

Al-Alam (The Flag): ave Hassan II, Lot Vita, BP 141, Rabat; tel. (53) 7294832; fax (53) 7291784; e-mail alalam@alalam.ma; internet www.alalam.ma; f. 1946; Arabic; literary supplement on Saturdays; organ of the Istiqlal party; Dir ABD AL-JABBAR SUHEIMAT; Editor in Chief HASSAN ABDELKHALEK; circ. 10,274 (2008/09).

Annahar Al Maghribia (The Moroccan Day): 12 pl. des Alaouites, 2ème étage, Rabat; tel. (53) 7737568; fax (53) 7737547; e-mail annaharalmaghribia@menara.ma; internet www.annahar.ma; Arabic; Dir and Editor-in-Chief ABDELKRIM BADI; circ. 6,953 (2008).

Attajdid (Reform): 3 blvd al-Moukawama, BP 9173, Rabat; tel. (53) 7705854; fax (53) 7705852; e-mail attajdid@attajdid.ma; internet www.attajdid.ma; f. 1999; Arabic; associated with the Parti de la justice et du développement; Dir ABDELILLAH BENKIRANE; circ. 2,903 (2008/09).

Al-Haraka (Progress): 66 rue Patrice Lumumba, BP 1317, Rabat; tel. (53) 7768667; fax (53) 7767537; e-mail harakamp@menara.ma; internet www.harakamp.ma; Arabic; organ of the Mouvement populaire; Dir ALI ALAOUI; circ. 1,002 (2008).

L'Opinion: ave Hassan II, Lot Vita, Rabat; tel. (53) 7293002; fax (53) 7292639; e-mail lopinion@lopinion.ma; internet www.lopinion.ma; f. 1962; French; organ of Istiqlal; Dir MUHAMMAD IDRISSI KAÏTOUNI; Editor-in-Chief JAMAL HAJJAM; circ. 18,347 (2008/09).

SELECTED PERIODICALS

Casablanca

actuel: 1 blvd Abdellatif Ben Kaddour, 20050 Casablanca; tel. (52) 2951815; fax (52) 2951814; e-mail courrier@actuel.ma; internet www.actuel.ma; f. 2009; weekly; French; publ. by Logique Presse; Dir and Editor HENRI LOIZEAU.

Al-Ayam (The Days): Espace Paquet, 508 rue Muhammad Smiha, Casablanca; tel. (52) 2442694; fax (52) 2441173; e-mail alayams75@yahoo.fr; f. 2001; Arabic; weekly; Editor NOUREDDINE MIFTAH; circ. 22,163 (2008).

CGEM Infos: 23 blvd Muhammad Abdou, Palmiers, 20340 Casablanca; tel. (52) 2997000; fax (52) 2983971; e-mail cgeminfos@cgem.ma; internet www.cgeminfos.ma; weekly; French; organ of the Confédération Générale des Entreprises du Maroc; Dir MOULAY HAFID ELALAMY; Editor-in-Chief MUSTAPHA MOULAY.

Challenge Hebdo: 58 ave des Forces Armées Royales, Tour des Habous, 13ème étage, Casablanca; tel. (52) 2548150; fax (52) 2318094; e-mail redaction@challengehebdo.com; internet www.challengehebdo.com; weekly; French; business; Dir ADIL LAHLOU; Editor-in-Chief KHALID TRITKI; circ. 8,410 (2008/09).

Construire: 744 rue Boukrâa (angle rue Ouled Said), Résidence Hanane Jassim I, Bourgogne, Casablanca; tel. (52) 2220271; fax (52) 2273627; e-mail nlleconstruire@yahoo.fr; internet www.nouvelleconstruire.com; f. 1940; weekly; French; building and architecture magazine; Dir ABDELKRIM TALAL.

Femmes du Maroc: Immeuble Zénith I, Lot Attaoufik, route de Nouaceur, Sidi Maârouf, Casablanca; tel. (52) 2973949; fax (52) 2973929; internet www.femmesdumaroc.com; monthly; French; lifestyle magazine for women; Dir AÏCHA ZAÏMI SAKHRI; Editor-in-Chief GÉRALDINE DULAT; circ. 12,029 (2008/09).

La Gazette du Maroc: ave des Forces Armées Royales, Tour des Habous, 13ème étage, Casablanca; tel. (52) 2548150; fax (52) 2318094; e-mail info@lagazettedumaroc.com; internet www.lagazettedumaroc.com; weekly; French; Dir KAMAL LAHLOU; Editor-in-Chief ABD AL-LATIF EL-AZIZI; circ. 8,969 (2008).

Le Journal Hebdomadaire: 61 ave des Forces Armées Royales, BP 20000, Casablanca; tel. (52) 2546670; fax (52) 2446185; e-mail courrier@lejournal-press.com; internet www.lejournal-press.com; weekly; French; news, politics, economics; Dir ALI AMAR; Editor-in-Chief ABOUBAKR JAMAÏ; circ. 11,895 (2008/09).

Maroc Hebdo International: 4 rue des Flamants, Casablanca; tel. (52) 2238176; fax (52) 2981346; e-mail mhi@maroc-hebdo.press.ma; internet www.maroc-hebdo.com; f. 1991; weekly; French; Editor-in-Chief MUHAMMAD SELHAMI; circ. 10,510 (2008).

Nissae min al-Maghrib (Women of Morocco): Immeuble Zénith I, Lot Attaoufik, route de Nouaceur, Sidi Maârouf, Casablanca; tel. (52) 2973949; fax (52) 2973929; e-mail y.guennoun@akwagroup.com; internet www.nissaa.com; monthly; Arabic edn of *Femmes du Maroc*; Editor-in-Chief KHADIJA SABIL; circ. 30,703 (2008/09).

La Nouvelle Tribune: 320 blvd Zerktouni, angle rue Bouardel, Casablanca; tel. (52) 2424670; fax (52) 2200031; e-mail courrier@lanouvelletribune.com; internet www.lanouvelletribune.com; f. 1996; weekly (Thur.); French; Dir FAHD YATA; circ. 6,741 (2007).

Parade: Immeuble Zénith I, Lot Attaoufik, route de Nouaceur, Sidi Maârouf, Casablanca; tel. (52) 2973949; fax (52) 2973929; e-mail y.guennoun@akwagroup.com; monthly; French; Editor-in-Chief MARIA DAIF; circ. 4,716 (2006).

Perspectives du Maghreb: 8 blvd Yacoub el Mansour, 31 Maârif, Casablanca; tel. (52) 2257844; fax (52) 2257738; e-mail popmedia@menara.ma; f. 2005; monthly; French; circ. 6,531 (2007).

La Quinzaine du Maroc: 53 rue el-Bakri, Casablanca; tel. (52) 2440033; fax (52) 2440426; e-mail mauro@editionsmauro.ma; internet www.quinzainedumaroc.com; f. 1951; fortnightly; English and French; visitors' guide; Dir HUBERT MAURO.

Le Reporter: 1 Sahat al-Istiqlal, 2ème étage, 20000 Casablanca; tel. (52) 2541103; fax (52) 2541105; e-mail redaction@lereporter.ma; internet www.lereporter.ma; f. 1998; weekly; French; Dir BAHIA AMRANI.

TelQuel: 28 ave des Forces Armées Royales, Casablanca; tel. (52) 2220951; fax (52) 2220563; e-mail courrier@telquel.info; internet www.telquel-online.com; f. 2001; weekly; French; Dir AHMED BENCHEMSI; Editor-in-Chief KARIM BOUKHARI; circ. 23,172 (2008/09).

Version Homme: ave des Forces Armées Royales, Tour des Habous, 13ème étage, Casablanca; tel. (52) 2450089; fax (52) 2442213; e-mail redaction@versionhomme.com; internet www.versionhomme.com; monthly; lifestyle magazine for men; Dir ADIL LAHLOU; circ. 6,051 (2008/09).

La Vie éco: 5 blvd Abdallah Ben Yacine, 20300 Casablanca; tel. (52) 2450555; fax (52) 2304542; e-mail vieeco@marocnet.net.ma; internet www.lavieeco.com; f. 1921; weekly; French; economics; Dir FADEL AGOUMI; Editor-in-Chief SAÂD BEN MANSOUR; circ. 16,426 (2008/09).

La Vie Touristique Africaine: 17 rue El Houcine Ben Ali, Casablanca; tel. (52) 2227643; fax (52) 2275319; e-mail vietouristique@wanadoo.net.ma; internet www.vietouristique.com; fortnightly; French; tourist information; Dir AHMED ZEGHARI.

Al-Watan al-An (The Nation Now): 33 rue Muhammad Bahi, Casablanca; tel. (52) 2251295; fax (52) 2251325; e-mail alwatanpress@menara.ma; internet www.alwatan.press.ma; weekly; Arabic; news; Editor ABDERRAHIM ARIRI; circ. 5,982 (2008).

Rabat

Al-Alam al-Amazighi: Éditions Amazigh, 5 rue Dakar, BP 477, Rabat; tel. 66-1767073 (mobile); fax (53) 7727283; e-mail lemondeamazigh@hotmail.com; weekly; Berber.

Asdae (Echoes): 30 ave Okba, Rabat; tel. (53) 7773706; e-mail asdae@menara.ma; internet www.asdae.com; weekly; Arabic; Dir and Editor-in-Chief EL-HASSAN ARBAI; circ. 1,415 (2008/09).

Da'ouat al-Haqq (Call of the Truth): al-Michwar al-Said, Rabat; tel. (53) 7766851; e-mail direction_haq@habous.gov.ma; internet www.daouatalhaq.ma; publ. by Ministry of Habous (Religious Endowments) and Islamic Affairs; f. 1957; monthly; Arabic.

Al-Mountakhab (The Team): 42 bis rue de Madagascar, Rabat; tel. (53) 7201774; fax (53) 7201776; e-mail contact@almountakhab.com; internet www.almountakhab.com; f. 1986; fortnightly; Arabic; sport; Dir MUSTAFA BADRI; Editor-in-Chief BADREDDINE IDRISSI; circ. 25,137 (2008/09).

Al-Tadamoun (Solidarity): Apt 1, Immeuble 6, rue Aguensous, ave Hassan II, Les Orangers, BP 1740, Rabat; tel. (53) 7730961; fax (53) 7738851; e-mail amdh1@mtds.com; internet www.amdh.org.ma; monthly; Arabic; organ of the Association marocaine des droits humains; Dir ABD AL-MAJID SEMLALI EL-HASANI.

Tangier

Achamal 2000: 137 blvd Prince Héritier, 1, Tangier; tel. (53) 9940391; fax (53) 9944216; e-mail ashamal@menara.ma; weekly; Arabic; Editor-in-Chief KHALID MECHBAL; circ. 7,912 (2008/09).

Le Journal de Tanger: 7 bis, rue Omar Ben Abdelaziz, Tangier; tel. (53) 9943008; fax (53) 9945709; e-mail direct@lejournaldetanger.com; internet www.lejournaldetanger.com; f. 1904; weekly; French, English, Spanish and Arabic; Dir ABDELHAK BAKHAT; Editor-in-Chief MUHAMMAD ABOUABDILLAH; circ. 8,776 (2008/09).

NEWS AGENCY

Maghreb Arabe Presse (MAP): 122 ave Allal Ben Abdallah, BP 1049, 10000 Rabat; tel. (53) 7279464; fax (53) 7279465; e-mail mapweb@map.co.ma; internet www.map.ma; f. 1959; Arabic, French, English and Spanish; state-owned; Dir-Gen. ALI BOUZERDA.

PRESS ASSOCIATIONS

Fédération Marocaine des Editeurs de Journaux (FMEJ): Groupe Ecomedia, 70 blvd al-Massira al-Khadra, Casablanca; tel. (52) 2953600; fax (52) 2365926; f. 2005; Pres. ABDELMOUNAIM DILAMI.

Organisme de Justification de la Diffusion (OJD Maroc): 4 rue des Flamants, Casablanca; tel. (52) 2238176; fax (52) 2981346; e-mail

MOROCCO   *Directory*

asmae@maroc-hebdo.press.ma; internet www.ojd.ma; f. 2004; compiles circ. statistics; Pres. AISSAM FATHYA; Dir ASMAE HASSANI.

Publishers

Afrique Orient: 159 bis blvd Yacoub el-Mansour, Casablanca; tel. (52) 2259813; fax (52) 2440080; f. 1983; sociology, philosophy and translations; Dir MUSTAPHA CHAJII.

Belvisi: 17 rue Abbas Ibnou Farnass, BP 8044, Casablanca; tel. (52) 2250973; fax (52) 2986258; f. 1986.

Dar el-Kitab: place de la Mosquée, Quartier des Habous, BP 4018, Casablanca; tel. (52) 2305419; fax (52) 3026630; f. 1948; Arabic and French; philosophy, history, Africana, general and social science; state-controlled; Dir BOUTALEB ABDOU ABD AL-HAY; Gen. Man. KHADIJA EL-KASSIMI.

Editions Le Fennec: 89B blvd d'Anfa, 14ème étage, Casablanca; tel. (52) 2209314; fax (52) 2277702; e-mail info@lefennec.com; internet www.lefennec.com; f. 1987; fiction, social sciences; Dir LAYLA B. CHAOUNI.

Editions La Porte: 281 blvd Muhammad V, BP 331, Rabat; tel. (53) 7709958; fax (53) 7706476; e-mail la_porte@meganet.net.ma; law, guides, economics, educational books.

Les Editions Maghrébines: Quartier Industriel, blvd E, N 15, Sin Sebaâ, Casablanca; tel. (52) 2351797; fax (52) 2357892; f. 1962; general non-fiction.

Les Editions Toubkal: Immeuble I. G. A, pl. de la Gare Voyageurs, Bélvèdere, 20300 Casablanca; tel. and fax (52) 22342323; e-mail contact@toubkal.ma; internet www.toubkal.ma; f. 1985; economy, history, social sciences, literature, educational books; Dir ABDELJALIL NADEM.

Malika Editions: 60 blvd Yacoub el-Mansour, 20100 Casablanca; tel. (52) 2235688; fax (52) 2251651; e-mail edmalika@connectcom.net.ma; internet www.malikaedition.com; art publications.

Tarik Editions: 321 route el-Jadida, 20000 Casablanca; tel. (52) 2259007; fax (52) 2232550; e-mail tarik.editions@wanadoo.net.ma; f. 2000; history and social sciences; Dir BICHR BENNANI.

Yomad: rue Boronia, secteur 17, Hay Riad, Rabat; tel. (53) 7717590; fax (53) 7717589; e-mail yomadeditions@yahoo.com; f. 1998; children's literature; Dir NADIA EL-SALMI.

GOVERNMENT PUBLISHING HOUSE

Imprimerie Officielle: ave Yacoub el-Mansour, Rabat-Chellah; tel. (53) 7765024; fax (53) 7765179.

Broadcasting and Communications

TELECOMMUNICATIONS

Regulatory Authority

Agence Nationale de Réglementation des Télécommunications (ANRT): Centre d'Affaires, blvd al-Riad, BP 2939, Hay Riad, 10100 Rabat; tel. (53) 7718400; fax (53) 7203862; e-mail com@anrt.ma; internet www.anrt.ma; f. 1998; Dir-Gen. AZDIR EL-MOUNTASSIR BILLAH.

Principal Operators

inwi: Lot la Colline II, Sidi Maârouf, 20190 Casablanca; tel. (5) 2900000; internet www.inwi.ma; f. 2009 as Wana following award of third GSM licence; mobile telephone and internet services launched Feb. 2010; Dir-Gen. FRÉDÉRIC DEBORD.

Itissalat al-Maghrib—Maroc Télécom: ave Annakhil Hay Riad, Rabat; tel. (53) 7719000; fax (53) 7714860; e-mail webmaster@iam.ma; internet www.iam.ma; f. 1998; privatized in 2004; Vivendi SA (France) holds a 53% stake; Chair. ABDESLAM AHIZOUNE.

Méditel: Twin Centre, angle blvd Zerktouni et blvd Massira al-Khadra, Casablanca; e-mail hassan.bouchachia@meditel.ma; internet www.meditel.ma; f. 1999; in Aug. 2009 Caisse de Dépôt et de Gestion (CDG) and FinanceCom purchased a 64.4% stake previously held by Spain's Telefónica SA and Portugal Telecom; provides national mobile telecommunications services; Dir-Gen. MUHAMMAD EL-MANDJRA; Chair. OTHMAN BENJELLOUN; 8.63m. subscribers (June 2009).

BROADCASTING

Morocco can receive broadcasts from Spanish radio stations, and the main Spanish television channels can also be received in northern Morocco.

Radio

Radio Casablanca: c/o Loukt s.a.r.l, BP 16011, Casa Principal, 20001 Casablanca; e-mail i-rc@maroc.net; internet www.maroc.net/rc; f. 1996; Gen. Man. AMINE ZARY.

Radio Méditerranée Internationale: 3 rue M'sallah, BP 2055, 9000 Tangier; tel. (53) 9936363; fax (53) 9935755; e-mail medi1@medi1.com; internet www.medi1.com; Arabic and French; Man. Dir PIERRE CASALTA.

Voice of America Radio Station in Tangier: c/o US Consulate-General, chemin des Amoureux, Tangier.

Television

Société Nationale de Radiodiffusion et de Télévision: 1 rue el-Brihi, BP 1042, 1000 Rabat; tel. (53) 7685100; fax (53) 7733733; internet www.snrt.ma; govt station; transmission commenced 1962; 45 hours weekly; French and Arabic; carries commercial advertising; Dir-Gen. and Dir Television FAIÇAL LARAICHI.

SOREAD 2M: Société d'études et de réalisations audiovisuelles, km 7.3, route de Rabat, Aïn-Sebaâ, Casablanca; tel. (52) 2667373; fax (52) 2677856; e-mail portail@tv2m.co.ma; internet www.2m.tv; f. 1988; transmission commenced 1989; public television channel; owned by Moroccan Govt (72%) and by private national foreign concerns; broadcasting in French and Arabic; Man. Dir SAMI EL-JAI.

Finance

(cap. = capital; res = reserves; dep. = deposits; m. = million; br(s) = branch(es); amounts in dirhams)

BANKING

Central Bank

Bank Al-Maghrib: 277 ave Muhammad V, BP 445, Rabat; tel. (53) 7702626; fax (53) 7706667; e-mail webmaster@bkam.ma; internet www.bkam.ma; f. 1959 as Banque du Maroc; name changed as above in 1987; bank of issue; cap. 500m., res 5,033m., dep. 47,366m. (Dec. 2009); Gov. ABDELLATIF JOUAHRI; Gen. Man. ABDELLATIF FAOUZI; 20 brs.

Other Banks

Attijariwafa Bank: 2 blvd Moulay Youssef, BP 11141, 20000 Casablanca; tel. (52) 2298888; fax (52) 2294125; e-mail contact@attijariwafa.com; internet www.attijariwafabank.com; f. 2004 by merger between Banque Commerciale du Maroc SA and Wafabank; 33.2% owned by Groupe ONA, 14.6% by Grupo Santander (Spain); cap. 1,929m., res 13,258m., dep. 180,360m. (Dec. 2009); Chair. and CEO MUHAMMAD EL-KETTANI.

Banque Centrale Populaire (Crédit Populaire du Maroc): 101 blvd Muhammad Zerktouni, BP 10622, 21100 Casablanca; tel. (52) 2202533; fax (52) 2229699; e-mail bcp@banquepopulairemorocco.ma; internet www.cpm.co.ma; f. 1961; 51% state-owned, 49% privately owned; merged with Société Marocaine de Dépôt et Crédit in 2003; cap. 2,679m., res 13,645m., dep. 169,479m. (Dec. 2009); Pres. and Gen. Man. NOUREDDINE OMARY; 530 brs.

Banque Marocaine du Commerce Extérieur SA (BMCE): 140 ave Hassan II, BP 13425, 20000 Casablanca; tel. (52) 2200325; fax (52) 2200512; e-mail communicationfinanciere@bmcebank.co.ma; internet www.bmcebank.ma; f. 1959; transferred to majority private ownership in 1995; cap. and res 5,754m., dep. 144,281m. (Dec. 2009); Pres. and CEO OTHMAN BENJELLOUN; 310 domestic brs and 3 brs abroad.

Banque Marocaine pour le Commerce et l'Industrie SA (BMCI): 26 pl. des Nations Unies, BP 15573, Casablanca; tel. (52) 22461000; fax (52) 22299406; e-mail adiba.lahbabi@africa.bnpparibas.com; internet www.bmcinet.com; f. 1964; 65.05% owned by BNP Paribas (France); cap. 1,327.9m., res 4,759.0m., dep. 49,104.1m. (Dec. 2009); Chair. MOURAD CHERIF; 260 brs.

Citibank-Maghreb: Zénith Millenium, Immeuble 1, Lot Attaoufik, Sidi Maârouf, BP 13362, Casablanca; tel. (52) 2489600; fax (52) 2974197; f. 1967; cap. and res 194.0m., total assets 1,211.0m. (Dec. 2003); Pres. NUHAD SALIBA; 2 brs.

Crédit Agricole du Maroc SA: 29 rue Abou Faris al-Marini, BP 49, 10000 Rabat; tel. (53) 7208219; fax (53) 7445063; e-mail m_kettani@creditagricole.ma; internet www.creditagricole.ma; f. 1961 as Caisse Nationale de Crédit Agricole; became a limited co and adopted present name in 2003; 78% owned by Ministry of the Economy and Finance; cap. 2,820m., res −1,197m., dep. 60,843m. (Dec. 2009); Chair. TARIQ SIJILMASSI.

Crédit Immobilier et Hôtelier: 187 ave Hassan II, Casablanca; tel. (52) 2479000; fax (52) 2479363; e-mail info-client@cih.co.ma; internet www.cih.co.ma; f. 1920; transferred to majority private

MOROCCO

ownership in 1995; cap. 2,280m., res 297m., dep. 23,026m. (Dec. 2009); Pres. and CEO AHMAD RAHHOU; 91 brs.

Crédit du Maroc SA: 48–58 blvd Muhammad V, BP 13579, 20000 Casablanca; tel. (52) 2477477; fax (52) 2477127; e-mail mohammadine.menjra@ca-cdm.ma; internet www.cdm.co.ma; f. 1963 as Crédit Lyonnais Maroc; name changed as above in 1966; 52.6% owned by Crédit Agricole (France); cap. 1,897m., res 366m., dep. 37,658m. (Dec. 2009); Chair. PIERRE-LOUIS BOISSIERE; 264 domestic brs, 1 br. abroad.

Société Générale Marocaine de Banques SA: 55 blvd Abdelmoumen, BP 13090, 21100 Casablanca; tel. (52) 2438888; fax (52) 2234931; e-mail contact@sgmaroc.com; internet www.sgmaroc.com; f. 1962; cap. 2,050m., res 2,742m., dep. 54,937m. (Dec. 2009); Pres. ABDELAZIZ TAZI; 300 brs.

STOCK EXCHANGE

Bourse de Casablanca: angle ave des Forces Armées Royales et rue Muhammad Errachid, Casablanca; tel. (52) 2452626; fax (52) 2452625; e-mail contact@casablanca-bourse.com; internet www.casablanca-bourse.com; f. 1929; Chair. AOMAR YIDAR; CEO K. HAJJI.

INSURANCE

Assurances Al-Amane: 122 ave Hassan II, 20000 Casablanca; tel. (52) 2267272; fax (52) 2265664; f. 1975; cap. 120m.; Pres. and Dir-Gen. MUHAMMAD BOUGHALEB.

Atlanta Assurances: 181 blvd d'Anfa, BP 13685, 20001 Casablanca; tel. (52) 2957676; fax (52) 2369812; e-mail info@atlanta.ma; internet www.atlanta.ma; f. 1947; cap. 591.6m.; Dir-Gen. MUHAMMAD HASSAN BENSALAH.

AXA Assurance Maroc: 120–122 ave Hassan II, 20000 Casablanca; tel. (52) 2889292; fax (52) 2889189; e-mail communication@axa.ma; internet www.axa.ma; cap. 900m.; Dir-Gen. DANIEL ANTUNÈS.

CNIA Saada Assurance: 216 blvd Muhammad Zerktouni, 20000 Casablanca; tel. (52) 2474040; fax (52) 2206081; internet www.cniasaada.ma; f. 2009 by merger of CNIA Assurance and Es-Saada; 53% owned by Groupe Saham; Pres. and Dir-Gen. MOULAY HAFID ELALAMY.

Compagnie d'Assurances et de Réassurances SANAD: 181 blvd d'Anfa, Tours Balzac, Casablanca; tel. (52) 2957878; fax (52) 2360406; e-mail webmaster@sanad.ma; internet www.sanad.ma; f. 1946; cap. 125m.; Chair. MUHAMMAD HASSAN BENSALAH; Dir-Gen. ABDELTIF TAHIRI.

La Marocaine Vie: 37 blvd Moulay Youssef, Casablanca; tel. (52) 2206320; fax (52) 2297307; f. 1978; 83% owned by Société Générale Marocaine de Banques SA; Pres. MARC DUVAL; Gen. Man. KARIM MOULTAKI.

Mutuelle Centrale Marocaine d'Assurances (MCMA): 16 rue Abou Inane, BP 27, Rabat; tel. (53) 7767800; fax (53) 7766440; f. 1968; part of the MAMDA-MCMA group; CEO HICHAM BELMRAH.

Mutuelle d'Assurances des Transporteurs Unis (MATU): 215 blvd Muhammad Zerktouni, Casablanca; tel. (52) 2954500; fax (52) 2367721; e-mail info@matu.ma; Pres. HADJ OMAR BENNOUNA; Dir-Gen. AHMAD MAZOUZ.

RMA Watanya: 83 ave des Forces Armées Royales, 20000 Casablanca; tel. (52) 2312163; fax (52) 2313137; e-mail contact@rmawatanya.com; internet www.rmawatanya.com; f. 2005 by merger of Al-Wataniya and La Royale Marocaine d'Assurances; cap. 1,774m.; Pres. OTHMAN BENJELLOUN.

Société Centrale de Réassurance (SCR): Tour Atlas, pl. Zallaqa, BP 13183, Casablanca; tel. (52) 2460400; fax (52) 2460460; e-mail scr@scrmaroc.com; internet www.scrmaroc.com; f. 1960; cap. 30m.; Chair. AHMAD ZINOUN; Man. Dir MUHAMMAD LARBI NALI.

Société Marocaine d'Assurance à l'Exportation (SMAEX): 24 rue Ali Abderrazak, BP 15953, Casablanca; tel. (52) 2982000; fax (52) 2252070; e-mail smaex@smaex.com; internet www.smaex.com; f. 1988; insurance for exporters in the public and private sectors; assistance for export promotion; Pres. and Dir-Gen. NEZHA LAHRICHI; Asst Dir-Gen. ABDERRAZZAK M'HAIMDAT.

WAFA Assurance: 1–3 blvd Abd al-Moumen, BP 13420, 20001 Casablanca; tel. (52) 2224575; fax (52) 2209103; e-mail webmaster@wafaassurance.com; internet www.attijariwafabank.com; subsidiary of Attijariwafa Bank; Pres. ABDELAZIZ ALAMI; CEO MUHAMMAD EL-KETTANI.

Zurich Assurances Maroc: 166 angle Zerktouni et rue Hafid Ibrahim, 20000 Casablanca; tel. (52) 22499808; fax (52) 22491733; e-mail customerservice@zurich.com; f. 1954; cap. 90m.; all kinds of insurance; Pres. and Dir-Gen. BERTO FISLER.

Insurance Association

Fédération Marocaine des Sociétés d'Assurances et de Réassurances: 154 blvd d'Anfa, Casablanca; tel. (52) 2391850; fax (52) 2391854; e-mail contact@fmsar.ma; internet www.fmsar.org.ma; f. 1958; 15 mem. cos; Pres. MUSTAPHA BAKHOURY.

Trade and Industry

GOVERNMENT AGENCIES

Agence National pour la Promotion de Petite et Moyenne Entreprise (ANPME): 10 rue Gandhi, BP 211, 10001 Rabat; tel. (53) 7708460; fax (53) 7707695; e-mail info@anpme.ma; internet www.anpme.ma; f. 1973 as the Office pour le Développement Industriel; name changed as above in 2002; state agency to develop industry; Dir-Gen. LATIFA ECHIHABI.

Centre Marocain de Promotion des Exportations (CMPE): 23 rue Ibnou Majed el-Bahar, BP 10937, 20000 Casablanca; tel. (52) 2302210; fax (52) 2301793; e-mail info@marocexport.ma; internet www.cmpe.org.ma; f. 1980; state org. for promotion of exports; Man. Dir SAAD BEN ABDALLAH.

Direction des Entreprises Publiques et de la Privatisation (DEPP): rue Haj Ahmed Cherkaoui, Quartier Administratif, Agdal, Rabat; tel. (53) 7689303; fax (53) 7689347; e-mail talbi@depp.finances.gov.ma; part of the Ministry of the Economy and Finance; in charge of regulation, restructuring and privatization of state enterprises; Dir ABDELAZIZ TALBI.

Office National des Hydrocarbures et des Mines (ONHYM): 5 ave Moulay Hassan, BP 99, 10050 Rabat; tel. (53) 7239898; fax (53) 7709411; e-mail presse@onhym.com; internet www.onhym.com; f. 2003 to succeed Bureau de Recherches et de Participations Minières and Office National de Recherches et d'Exploitations Pétrolières; state agency conducting exploration, valorization and exploitation of hydrocarbons and mineral resources; Dir-Gen. AMINA BENKHADRA.

Société de Gestion des Terres Agricoles (SOGETA): 35 rue Daïet-Erroumi, BP 731, Agdal, Rabat; tel. (53) 7772778; fax (53) 7772765; f. 1973; oversees use of agricultural land; Man. Dir BACHIR SAOUD.

DEVELOPMENT ORGANIZATIONS

Caisse de Dépôt et de Gestion: pl. Moulay el-Hassan, BP 408, 10001 Rabat; tel. (53) 7669000; fax (53) 7763849; e-mail cdg@cdg.ma; internet www.cdg.ma; f. 1959; finances small-scale projects; Dir-Gen. ANASS ALAMI; Sec.-Gen. SAÏD LAFTIT.

Caisse Marocaine des Marchés (Marketing Fund): Résidence el-Manar, 52 blvd Abdelmoumen, 20100 Casablanca; tel. (52) 22984444; fax (52) 22994438; e-mail elkaoumi@cmm.ma; internet www.cmm.ma; f. 1950; cap. 70m. dirhams; Dir-Gen. (vacant).

Société de Développement Agricole (SODEA): ave Hadj Ahmed Cherkaoui, BP 6280, Rabat; tel. (53) 7677953; fax (53) 7771514; internet www.sodea.com; f. 1972; state agricultural devt org.; Man. Dir AHMED HAJJAJI.

Société Nationale d'Investissement (SNI): 60 rue d'Alger, BP 38, 20000 Casablanca; tel. (52) 2224102; fax (52) 2484303; f. 1966; transferred to majority private ownership in 1994; cap. 10,900m. dirhams; Pres. HASSAN BOUHEMOU; Sec.-Gen. SAÂD BENDIDI.

CHAMBERS OF COMMERCE

Fédération des Chambres Marocaines de Commerce, d'Industrie et de Services (FCMCIS): 6 rue Erfoud, BP 218, Hassan, Rabat; tel. (53) 7767078; fax (53) 7767896; e-mail fcmcis@menara.ma; internet www.fcmcis.ma; f. 1962; groups the 28 Chambers of Commerce and Industry; Pres. DRISS HOUAT; Dir-Gen. MUHAMMAD LARBI EL-HARRAS.

Chambre de Commerce, d'Industrie et de Services de la Wilaya de Rabat-Salé: 1 rue Gandhi, BP 131, Rabat; tel. (53) 7706444; fax (53) 7706768; e-mail info@rabat.cci.ma; internet www.ccirabat.ma; Pres. OMAR DERRAJI.

Chambre de Commerce, d'Industrie et de Services de la Wilaya du Grand Casablanca: 98 blvd Muhammad V, BP 423, Casablanca; tel. (52) 2264327; fax (52) 2268436; e-mail ccisc@ccisc.gov.ma; internet www.ccisc.gov.ma; Pres. HASSAN BERKANI.

INDUSTRIAL AND TRADE ASSOCIATIONS

Office National Interprofessionnel des Céréales et des Légumineuses (ONICL): 3 ave Moulay Hassan, BP 154, Rabat; tel. (53) 7217300; fax (53) 7709627; e-mail directeur@onicl.org.ma; internet www.onicl.org.ma; f. 1937; Dir-Gen. ABDELLATIF GUEDIRA.

Office National des Pêches: 15 rue Lieutenant Mahroud, BP 16243, 20300 Casablanca; tel. (52) 2242084; fax (52) 2242305; e-mail onp@onp.co.ma; internet www.onp.co.ma; f. 1969; state fishing org.; Man. Dir MAJID KAISSAR EL-GHAIB.

MOROCCO

EMPLOYERS' ORGANIZATIONS

Association Marocaine des Exportateurs (ASMEX): 36B blvd Anfa, Casablanca; tel. (52) 2261033; fax (52) 2484191; e-mail asmex@asmex.org; internet www.asmex.org; f. 1982; Pres. ABDEL-LATIF BEN MADANI.

Association Marocaine des Industries du Textile et de l'Habillement (AMITH): 92 blvd Moulay Rachid, Casablanca; tel. (52) 2942086; fax (52) 2940587; e-mail amith@amith.org.ma; internet www.textile.ma; f. 1960; 850 mems; textile, knitwear and ready-made garment mfrs; Pres. MUSTAPHA SAJID; Dir-Gen. MUHAMMAD TAZI.

Association des Producteurs d'Agrumes du Maroc (ASPAM): 283 blvd Zerktouni, Casablanca; tel. (52) 2363946; fax (52) 2364041; e-mail aspam@menara.ma; f. 1958; links Moroccan citrus growers; has its own processing plants; Pres. HASSAN LYOUSSI.

Association Professionnelle des Agents Maritimes, Consignataires de Navires, et Courtiers d'Affrètement du Maroc (APRAM): 219 blvd des Forces Armées Royales, 5ème étage, 20000 Casablanca; tel. (52) 2541112; fax (52) 2541415; e-mail apram@wanadoopro.ma; internet www.apram.ma; f. 1999; 37 mems; Pres. ABDELAZIZ MANTRACH.

Association Professionnelle des Cimentiers (APC): Villa APC, Lot Allaymoune 1, 476 Hay Almatar, Casablanca; tel. (52) 2936660; fax (52) 2904491; e-mail apc@menara.ma; internet www.apc.ma; 4 mems; cement mfrs; Pres. JEAN-MARIE SCHMITZ.

Confédération Générale des Entreprises du Maroc (CGEM): 23 blvd Muhammad Abdou, Quartier Palmiers, 20100 Casablanca; tel. (52) 2997000; fax (52) 2983971; e-mail cgem@cgem.ma; internet www.cgem.ma; 25 affiliated feds; Pres. MUHAMMAD HOURANI.

UTILITIES

Electricity and Water

Office National de l'Eau Potable (ONEP): Station de Traitement ONEP, ave Muhammad Belhassan El Ouazzani, BP 10002 Rabat-Chellah, Rabat; tel. (53) 7759600; fax (53) 7759106; e-mail onepbo@onep.ma; internet www.onep.org.ma; f. 1972; responsible for drinking-water supply; Dir-Gen. ALI FASSI FIHRI.

Office National de l'Electricité (ONE): 65 rue Othman Ben Affan, BP 13498, 20001 Casablanca; tel. (52) 2668080; fax (52) 2220038; e-mail offelec@one.org.ma; internet www.one.org.ma; f. 1963; state electricity authority; Dir-Gen. ALI FASSI FIHRI.

Gas

Afriquia Gaz: 139 blvd Moulay Ismail, Aïn Sebaâ, 20700 Casablanca; tel. (52) 22639600; fax (52) 22639666; e-mail r.idrissi@akwagroup.com; internet www.afriquiagaz.com; f. 1992; Morocco's leading gas distributor; Pres. ALI WAKRIM; Dir-Gen. TAWFIK HAMOUMI.

TRADE UNIONS

Confédération Démocratique du Travail (CDT): 64 rue al-Mourtada, Quartier Palmier, BP 13576, Casablanca; tel. (52) 2994470; fax (52) 2994473; e-mail cdtmaroc@cdt.ma; internet www.cdt.ma; f. 1978; Sec.-Gen. NOUBIR EL-AMAOUI.

Fédération Démocratique du Travail (FDT): 12 rue Muhammad Diouri, Sidi Belyoute, Casablanca; tel. (52) 2446362; fax (52) 2446365; e-mail fdt@menara.ma; internet www.fdt.ma; f. 2003 by fmr mems of CDT associated with USFP; Sec.-Gen. ABDERRAHMANE AL-AZZOUZI.

Union Générale des Travailleurs du Maroc (UGTM): 9 rue du Rif, blvd Muhammad VI, Casablanca; tel. (52) 2281788; fax (52) 2282144; e-mail info@ugtm.ma; internet www.ugtm.ma; f. 1960; associated with Istiqlal; supported by unions not affiliated to UMT; Sec.-Gen. HAMID CHABAT.

Union Marocaine du Travail (UMT): Bourse du Travail, 232 ave des Forces Armées Royales, 20000 Casablanca; tel. (52) 2302292; fax (52) 2307854; f. 1955; left-wing; most unions are affiliated; Sec. MAHJOUB BENSEDDIQ.

Union Nationale du Travail du Maroc (UNTM): 352 ave Muhammad V, Immeuble Saâda, Rabat; tel. (53) 7793196; fax (53) 7263546; f. 1976; Islamist, associated with the PJD; Sec.-Gen. MUHAMMAD YATIM.

Transport

Société Nationale des Transports et de la Logistique (SNTL): rue al-Fadila, Quartier Industriel, BP 114, Chellah, Rabat; tel. (53) 7289300; fax (53) 7797850; e-mail ahachemi@sntl.ma; internet www.sntl.ma; f. 1958; Dir-Gen. OUSSAMA LOUDGHIRI.

RAILWAYS

In 2005 there were 1,907 km of railways, of which 418 km were double track; 1,022 km of lines were electrified and diesel locomotives were used on the rest. In 2010 the network carried some 31m. passengers and 36m. metric tons of freight (incl. phosphates). All services are nationalized. Plans for a four-line, 76-km tram system in Casablanca were approved in 2008; Line One, comprising 50 stations on a 29-km route, was scheduled for completion by late 2012. Meanwhile, a feasibility study into plans for a 39-km railway tunnel under the Strait of Gibraltar linking Morocco and Spain commenced in 2007; however, by early 2011 the project had yet to be formally approved. In December 2010 Morocco and France signed an agreement whereby France would provide rolling stock and equipment for the first African high-speed train link; the new line was scheduled to run between Casablanca and Tangier by the end of 2015, and subsequently to be extended to other major Moroccan cities.

Office National des Chemins de Fer (ONCF): 8 bis rue Abderrahmane el-Ghafiki, Rabat-Agdal; tel. (53) 7774747; fax (53) 7774480; e-mail ketary@oncf.ma; internet www.oncf.ma; f. 1963; administers all Morocco's railways; Dir-Gen. MUHAMMAD RABIE KHLIE.

ROADS

In 2008 there were 58,256 km of classified roads, of which 67.8% were paved. The motorway network covered 866 km in that year.

Autoroutes du Maroc (ADM): Hay Riad, Rabat; tel. (53) 7711056; fax (53) 7711059; e-mail naitbrahim.ismail@adm.co.ma; internet www.adm.co.ma; responsible for the construction and upkeep of Morocco's motorway network.

Compagnie de Transports au Maroc (CTM—SA): km 13.5, autoroute Casablanca–Rabat, Casablanca; tel. (52) 2762100; fax (52) 2765428; internet www.ctm.ma; f. 1919; 18 agencies nationwide; privatized in 1993, with 40% of shares reserved for Moroccan citizens; Pres. and Dir-Gen. MUHAMMAD BOUDA.

SHIPPING

According to provisional official figures, Morocco's ports handled 67.7m. metric tons of goods in 2008. The most important ports, in terms of the volume of goods handled, are Casablanca, Jorf Lasfar, Safi and Mohammedia. Tangier is the principal port for passenger services. The first phase of a new container port, Tangier-Med, which had an initial annual capacity of 3.5m. containers, became operational in 2007. Construction work on a second phase began in 2009, which was expected to increase capacity to 8.5m. containers per year on its completion in 2015. At 31 December 2009 Morocco's merchant fleet consisted of 512 vessels, with a combined displacement of 470,600 grt.

Port Authorities

Agence Nationale des Ports (ANP): f. 2006, following division of Office d'Exploitation des Ports; regulator of port activity; also responsible for development and maintenance of port facilities; Dir-Gen. MUHAMMAD JAMAL BENJELLOUN.

Société d'Exploitation des Ports (Marsa Maroc): 175 blvd Zerktouni, 20100 Casablanca; tel. (52) 2258258; fax (52) 2995217; internet www.sodep.co.ma; f. 2006, following division of Office d'Exploitation des Ports; responsible for management of port terminals and quayside facilities; Pres. MUHAMMAD ABDELJALIL.

Principal Shipping Companies

Agence Med SARL: 3 rue ibn Rochd, 90000 Tangier; tel. (53) 9935875; fax (53) 9933239; e-mail agencemed@menara.ma; f. 1904; owned by the Bland Group; also at Agadir, Casablanca, Jorf Lasfar, Nador and Safi; Operations Man. MUHAMMAD CHATT.

Compagnie Chérifienne d'Armement: 5 blvd Abdallah Ben Yacine, 21700 Casablanca; tel. (52) 2309455; fax (52) 2301186; f. 1929; regular services to Europe; Man. Dir MAX KADOCH.

Compagnie Marocaine d'Agences Maritimes (COMARINE): 45 ave des Forces Armées Royales, BP 60, 20000 Casablanca; tel. (52) 2548510; fax (52) 2548570; e-mail comarine@comarine.co.ma.

Compagnie Marocaine de Navigation (COMANAV): 7 blvd de la Résistance, BP 628, Casablanca 20300; tel. (52) 2303012; fax (52) 2302006; e-mail comanav@comanav.co.ma; internet www.comanav.ma; f. 1946 as Cie Franco-Chérifienne de Navigation; name changed as above in 1959; privatization pending; regular services to European, Middle Eastern and West African ports; tramping; Pres. and Dir-Gen. TOUFIQ IBRAHIMI; Sec.-Gen. MEHDI BELGHITI; 12 agencies.

Intercona: 6 rue Méditérranée, Edifici Coficom, Tangier 90000; tel. (53) 9945907; fax (53) 9945909; e-mail intercona-sa@menara.ma; f. 1943; shipping agent; Pres. VICENTE JORRO.

Limadet-ferry: 3 rue ibn Rochd, Tangier; tel. (53) 933639; fax (53) 937173; e-mail headoffice@limadet.com; f. 1966; daily services

MOROCCO

between Algeciras (Spain) and Tangier; Dir-Gen. RACHID BEN MANSOUR.

Société Marocaine de Navigation Atlas: 81 ave Houmane el-Fatouaki, 21000 Casablanca; tel. (52) 2224190; fax (52) 2200164; e-mail atlas@marbar.co.ma; f. 1976; Chair. HASSAN CHAMI; Man. Dir MUHAMMAD SLAOUI.

Voyages Paquet: 65 ave des Forces Armées Royales, 20000 Casablanca; tel. (52) 2761941; fax (52) 2442108; f. 1970; Pres. MUHAMMAD ELOUALI ELALAMI; Dir-Gen. NAÏMA BAKALI ELOUALI ELALAMI.

CIVIL AVIATION

The main international airports are at Casablanca (King Muhammad V), Rabat, Tangier, Marrakesh, Agadir Inezgane, Fez, Oujda, al-Hocima, el-Aaiún, Ouarzazate, Agadir al-Massira and Nador. The completion of a second runway at King Muhammad V airport was followed by the inauguration, in September 2007, of a second terminal, which increased the airport's annual passenger capacity from 5m. to 11m. Plans were under way in 2011 to increase the capacity at Marrakesh International airport from 4.5m. passengers a year to 10m. by 2013.

Atlas Blue: Aéroport Marrakesh Ménara, BP 440, Medina, Marrakesh; fax (52) 44424222; e-mail contact@atlas-blue.com; internet www.atlas-blue.com; f. 2004; wholly owned by Royal Air Maroc; low-cost airline; domestic flights and services to six European countries; Chair. ZOUHAIR MUHAMMAD EL-AOUFIR.

Jet4you: 4 Lot la Colline, Sidi Maarouf, 20190 Casablanca; fax (52) 2584228; internet www.jet4you.com; f. 2006; wholly owned by TUI Travel PLC (United Kingdom); low-cost airline; services to destinations in 5 European countries; CEO JAWAD ZIYAT.

Office National des Aéroports: Siège Social Nouasseur, BP 8101, Casablanca; tel. (52) 2539040; fax (52) 2539901; e-mail onda@onda.ma; internet www.onda.ma; f. 1990; Dir-Gen. MUHAMMAD NOURI.

Regional Air Lines: Aéroport de Muhammad V, BP 83, 20240 Casablanca; tel. (52) 2538020; fax (52) 2538411; e-mail customer-service@regionalmaroc.com; internet www.regionalmaroc.com; f. 1997; privately owned; domestic flights and services to southern Spain, Portugal and the Canary Islands; Pres. MUHAMMAD HASSAN BENSALAH; CEO HICHAM NECHAD.

Royal Air Maroc (RAM): Aéroport de Casablanca-Anfa; tel. (52) 2912000; fax (52) 2912087; e-mail callcenter@royalairmaroc.com; internet www.royalairmaroc.com; f. 1953; 94.4% state-owned; scheduled for partial privatization; domestic flights and services to Western Europe, Scandinavia, the Americas, North and West Africa, the Middle East; Chair. and CEO DRISS BENHIMA.

Tourism

Tourism is Morocco's second main source of convertible currency. The country's tourist attractions include its sunny climate, ancient sites (notably the cities of Fez, Marrakesh, Meknès and Rabat) and spectacular scenery. There are popular holiday resorts on the Atlantic and Mediterranean coasts. In 2009 foreign tourist arrivals totalled 4.29m., compared with 1.63m. in 1996. Tourism receipts, including passenger transport, were estimated at US $8,885m. in 2008.

Office National Marocain du Tourisme: angle rue Oued el-Makhazine et rue Zalaga, BP 19, Agdal, Rabat; tel. (53) 7674013; fax (53) 7674015; e-mail contact@onmt.org.ma; internet www.tourisme-marocain.com/onmt; f. 1918; Dir-Gen. FATHIA BENNIS.

Defence

Commander-in-Chief of the Armed Forces: HM King MUHAMMAD VI.
Estimated Defence Budget (2010): 26,900m. dirhams.
Military Service: 18 months.
Total Armed Forces (as assessed at November 2010): 195,800 (army 175,000—including some 100,000 conscripts; navy 7,800; air force 13,000). Paramilitary forces: royal guard 20,000; auxiliary force 30,000. Reserves: 150,000.

Education

Since independence in 1956, Morocco has tried to resolve a number of educational problems: a youthful and fast-growing population, an urgent need for skilled workers and executives, a great diversity of teaching methods between French, Spanish, Muslim and Moroccan government schools (syllabuses have been standardized since 1967), and, above all, a high degree of adult illiteracy. In recent years increasing attention has been given to education for girls. There are now a number of mixed and girls' schools, notably in urban areas.

In 2008/09 there were an estimated 3,863,838 pupils in primary schools (including those in private schools). A decree of November 1963 made education compulsory for children between the ages of seven and 13 years, and this has now been applied in most urban areas; from September 2002 children were to be educated from six years of age. In 2008/09, according to UNESCO estimates, enrolment at primary level included 90% of the relevant age-group. Instruction is given in Arabic for the first two years and in Arabic and French for the next four years, with English as the first additional language. Teaching in the principal Berber language, Tamazight, began in primary schools in the 2003/04 academic year.

Secondary education, beginning at the age of 13, lasts for up to six years (comprising two cycles of three years), and in 2008/09 provided for an estimated 2,232,289 pupils. In 1988 the secondary school graduation examination, the *baccalauréat*, was replaced by a system of continuous assessment. Secondary enrolment in 2003/04 included an estimated 35% of the relevant age-group. Under the 2009 budget, expenditure on education by the central Government was projected at 47,269m. dirhams (21.7% of total spending).

There are eight universities in Morocco, including the Islamic University of al-Quarawiyin at Fez (founded in 859), the Muhammad V University at Rabat (opened in 1957), and an English-language university, inaugurated at Ifrane in 1995. In addition, there are institutes of higher education in business studies, agriculture, mining, law, and statistics and advanced economics. In 2007/08 there were some 401,093 students enrolled in tertiary education.

MOZAMBIQUE

Introductory Survey

LOCATION, CLIMATE, LANGUAGE, RELIGION, FLAG, CAPITAL

The Republic of Mozambique lies on the east coast of Africa, bordered to the north by Tanzania, to the west by Malawi, Zambia and Zimbabwe, and to the south by South Africa and Swaziland. The country has a coastline of about 2,470 km (1,535 miles) on the shores of the Indian Ocean, and is separated from Madagascar, to the east, by the Mozambique Channel. Except in a few upland areas, the climate varies from tropical to sub-tropical. Rainfall is irregular, but the rainy season is usually from November to March, when average temperatures in Maputo are between 26°C (79°F) and 30°C (86°F). In the cooler dry season, in June and July, the average temperatures are 18°C (64°F) to 20°C (68°F). Portuguese is the official language, while there are 39 indigenous languages, the most widely spoken being Makhuwa, Tsonga, Sema and Lomwe. Many of the inhabitants follow traditional beliefs. There are about 5m. Christians, the majority of whom are Roman Catholics, and 4m. Muslims. The national flag (proportions 2 by 3) has three equal horizontal stripes, of green, black and yellow, separated by narrow white stripes. At the hoist is a red triangle containing a five-pointed yellow star, on which are superimposed an open book, a hoe and a rifle. The capital is Maputo (formerly Lourenço Marques).

CONTEMPORARY POLITICAL HISTORY

Historical Context

Mozambique became a Portuguese colony in the 19th century and an overseas province in 1951. Nationalist groups began to form in the 1960s. The Frente de Libertação de Moçambique (Frelimo—Mozambique Liberation Front) was formed in 1962 and launched a military campaign for independence in 1964. After the coup in Portugal (q.v.) in April 1974, negotiations between Frelimo and the new Portuguese Government resulted in a period of rule in Mozambique by a transitional Government, followed by full independence on 25 June 1975. The leader of Frelimo, Samora Machel, became the first President of Mozambique. Between September and December 1977 elections took place to local, district and provincial assemblies and, at national level, to the Assembleia Popular (People's Assembly).

In March 1976 Mozambique closed its border with Rhodesia (now Zimbabwe) and applied economic sanctions against that country. Mozambique was the principal base for Rhodesian nationalist guerrillas, and consequently suffered considerable devastation as a result of offensives launched by Rhodesian government forces against guerrilla camps. The border was reopened in January 1980.

After Zimbabwean independence in April 1980, South Africa adopted Rhodesia's role as supporter of the Mozambican opposition guerrilla group, Resistência Nacional Moçambicana (Renamo), also known as the Movimento Nacional da Resistência de Moçambique. The activities of Renamo subsequently increased, causing persistent disruption to road, rail and petroleum pipeline links from Mozambican ports, which were vital to the economic independence of southern African nations from South Africa. In March 1984 Mozambique and South Africa signed a formal joint non-aggression pact, the Nkomati Accord, whereby each Government undertook to prevent opposition forces on its territory from launching attacks against the other, and a Joint Security Commission was established. The Accord effectively implied that South Africa would withdraw its covert support for Renamo in return for a guarantee by Mozambique that it would prevent any further use of its territory by the then banned African National Congress of South Africa (ANC). However, following an intensification of Renamo activity, in 1985 the Frelimo Government appealed to foreign powers for increased military assistance, and in June it was agreed that Zimbabwe would augment its military presence in Mozambique. A major military offensive against Renamo in July resulted in the capture, in August, of the rebels' national operational command centre. Mozambique subsequently alleged that South Africa had repeatedly violated the Nkomati Accord by providing material support for the rebels. The Joint Security Commission ceased to meet in 1985.

President Machel died in an air crash in South Africa in October 1986. The causes of the incident were unclear, and the Mozambican Ministry of Information declared that it did not exclude the possibility of South African sabotage. (In May 1998 it was announced that South Africa's Truth and Reconciliation Commission—TRC—was to examine evidence relating to the crash. The TRC's final report stated that the evidence was inconclusive, but a number of questions merited further investigation and in early 2006 the South African Government announced that it was to reopen the inquiry into Machel's death.) In November 1986 the Central Committee of Frelimo appointed Joaquim Alberto Chissano, hitherto Minister for Foreign Affairs, as President. At a Frelimo congress in July 1989, the party's exclusively Marxist-Leninist orientation was renounced, and party membership was opened to Mozambicans from all sectors of society.

Meanwhile, in June 1988 Mozambique, South Africa and Portugal signed an agreement to rehabilitate the Cahora Bassa hydroelectric plant in Mozambique. In May Mozambican and South African officials had agreed to reactivate the Nkomati Accord and to re-establish the Joint Security Commission; subsequently a joint commission for co-operation and development was established.

Domestic Political Affairs

The introduction, on 30 November 1990, of a new Mozambican Constitution, formally ended Frelimo's single-party rule and committed the State to political pluralism and a free-market economy; it also enshrined private property rights and guarantees of press freedom. The official name of the country was changed from the People's Republic of Mozambique to the Republic of Mozambique. Renamo refused to recognize the new Constitution, declaring that it had been drafted without democratic consultation. The President was henceforth to be elected by direct universal suffrage, and the legislature was renamed the Assembleia da República (Assembly of the Republic). A new law concerning the formation, structure and function of political parties came into effect in February 1991. In accordance with the Constitution, Renamo would not be recognized as a legitimate political party until it had renounced violence completely.

In October 1991 Renamo and the Government signed a protocol agreeing fundamental principles and containing a set of mutual guarantees as a basis for a peace accord. Throughout the discussions (held in Rome, Italy) Renamo continued guerrilla attacks, many of which were launched (despite the Nkomati Accord) from South Africa. Under the terms of the protocol, Renamo effectively recognized the legitimacy of the Government and agreed to enter the multi-party political framework. In return, the Government pledged not to legislate on any of the points under negotiation until a general peace accord had been signed. In November a second protocol was signed by both parties, enabling Renamo to begin functioning as a political party immediately after the signing of a general peace accord.

In March 1992 a third protocol was signed establishing the principles for the country's future electoral system. Under its terms, the elections, to be held under a system of proportional representation, were to be supervised by international observers. An electoral commission was to be established, with one-third of its members to be appointed by Renamo. On 7 August, following three days of discussions in Rome, Chissano and the Renamo leader, Afonso Macacho Marceta Dhlakama, signed a joint declaration committing the two sides to a total cease-fire by 1 October, as part of an Acordo Geral de Paz (AGP—General Peace Agreement). In September Chissano and Dhlakama met in Gaborone, Botswana, to attempt to resolve the deadlocked military and security issues. Chissano offered to establish an independent commission to monitor and guarantee the impartiality of the Serviço de Informação e Segurança do Estado (SISE—State Information and Security Service). In addition, the figure of 30,000 was agreed upon as the number of troops to comprise the joint national defence force.

The AGP was finally signed on 4 October 1992. Under the terms of the agreement, a general cease-fire was to come into force immediately after ratification of the treaty by the legislature. Both the Renamo troops and the government forces were to withdraw to assembly points within seven days of ratification. The new national defence force, the Forças Armadas de Defesa de Moçambique (FADM), would then be created, drawing on equal numbers from each side, with the remaining troops surrendering their weapons to a UN peace-keeping force within six months. A Cease-fire Commission, incorporating representatives from the Government, Renamo and the UN, was to be established to assume responsibility for supervising the implementation of the truce regulations. Overall political control of the peace process was to be vested in a Comissão de Supervisão e Controle (CSC—Supervision and Control Commission), comprising representatives of the Government, Renamo and the UN. In addition, Chissano was to appoint a Comissão Nacional de Informação (COMINFO—National Information Commission), with responsibilities including supervision of the SISE. Presidential and legislative elections were to take place, under UN supervision, one year after the signing of the AGP, provided that it had been fully implemented and the demobilization process completed. The AGP was duly ratified by the Assembleia da República and came into force on 15 October. On that day UN observers arrived in Maputo to supervise the first phase of the cease-fire. However, shortly afterwards the Government accused Renamo of systematically violating the accord. Dhlakama subsequently claimed that Renamo's actions had been defensive manoeuvres and, in turn, accused government forces of violating the accord by advancing into Renamo territory.

In November 1992, owing to considerable delays in the formation of the various peace commissions envisaged in the AGP, the timetable for the cease-fire operations was redrafted. In December the UN Security Council finally approved a plan for the establishment of the UN Operation in Mozambique (ONUMOZ), providing for the deployment of some 7,500 troops, police and civilian observers to oversee the process of demobilization and formation of the FADM, and to supervise the forthcoming elections. However, there were continued delays in the deployment of ONUMOZ. In March the peace process was effectively halted when Renamo withdrew from the CSC and the Cease-fire Commission, protesting that proper provisions had not been made to accommodate its officials. In April Dhlakama announced that his forces would begin to report to assembly points only when Renamo received US $15m. to finance its transition into a political party. Meanwhile, the first UN troops became operational on 1 April.

In June 1993 Renamo rejoined the CSC. The commission subsequently agreed to a formal postponement of the election date to October 1994. A meeting in Maputo of international aid donors, also in June 1993, produced promises of additional support for the peace process, bringing the total pledged by donors to US $520m., including support for the repatriation of 1.5m. refugees from neighbouring countries, the resettlement of 4m.–5m. displaced people and the reintegration of some 80,000 former combatants into civilian life. The UN also agreed to establish a trust fund of $10m. to finance Renamo's transformation into a political party, with the disbursement of funds dependent on UN approval. In November 1993 the UN Security Council renewed the mandate of ONUMOZ for a further six months. In addition, it acceded to the joint request by the Government and Renamo for a UN police corps. In the same month consensus was finally reached on the text of the electoral law, which was promulgated at the end of December. At a meeting of the CSC in mid-November an agreement was signed providing for the confinement of troops, to be concluded by the end of the year.

In February 1994 the UN Security Council announced that, in response to demands made by Renamo, it would be increasing the membership of the UN police corps monitoring the confinement areas from 128 to 1,144. By the end of February only 50% of troops had entered designated assembly points, and none had officially been demobilized. In March, in an effort to expedite the confinement process, the Government announced that it was to commence the unilateral demobilization of its troops. Renamo began the demobilization of its troops shortly afterwards. In April Lt-Gen. Lagos Lidimo, the nominee of the Government, and the former Renamo guerrilla commander, Lt-Gen. Mateus Ngonhamo, were inaugurated as the high command of the FADM. In the same month Chissano issued a decree scheduling the presidential and legislative elections for October, and in May the UN Security Council renewed the mandate of ONUMOZ for the final period, ending on 15 November.

On 16 August 1994, in accordance with the provisions of the AGP, the government Forças Armadas de Moçambique were formally dissolved and their assets transferred to the FADM, which was inaugurated as the country's official armed forces on the same day. In December the Cease-fire Commission issued its final report, according to which ONUMOZ had registered a combined total of 91,691 government and Renamo troops during the confinement process, of whom 11,579 had enlisted in the FADM (compared with the 30,000 envisaged in the AGP).

The 1994 elections

In August 1994 Renamo formally registered as a political party. In the same month the Partido Liberal e Democrático de Moçambique, the Partido Nacional Democrático and the Partido Nacional de Moçambique formed an electoral coalition, the União Democrática (UD). The presidential and legislative elections took place on 27–29 October. In the presidential election Chissano secured an outright majority (53.3%) of the votes. His closest rival was Dhlakama, who received 33.7% of the votes. In the legislative elections Frelimo also secured an overall majority, winning 129 of the 250 seats in the Assembleia da República; Renamo obtained 112 seats, and the UD the remaining nine. Later in November the UN Security Council extended the mandate of ONUMOZ until the end of January 1995. Chissano was inaugurated as President on 9 December 1994, and the new Government, in which all portfolios were assigned to members of Frelimo, was sworn in on 23 December.

By the end of March 1995 only a small unit of ONUMOZ officials remained in the country. In February 1996 the Government proposed that municipal elections, which the Constitution stipulated must be conducted no later than October 1996, be held in 1997. Delays in the election process had resulted from a dispute between the opposition, which demanded local elections throughout Mozambique, and the Government, which sought to hold elections only in those areas that had attained municipal status. In October 1996 the Assembleia da República approved a constitutional amendment differentiating between municipalities and administrative posts. In August 1997 the Government postponed the elections until 1998, owing to delays in the disbursement by international donors of funding for the voter registration process. In April Renamo was among 16 opposition parties that officially withdrew from the elections, alleging that the voter registration process had been fraudulent. Renamo subsequently campaigned vigorously to dissuade the electorate from participating in the ballot. At the elections, which took place on 30 June, Frelimo won control of all the municipal authorities contested, its main competition coming from independent candidates. The voter turn-out was only 14.6%, prompting Renamo to demand the annulment of the elections.

Presidential and legislative elections took place on 3–5 December 1999. In the presidential contest, Chissano defeated Dhlakama (his sole challenger), taking 52.3% of the valid votes cast. Frelimo secured 133 of the 250 seats in the Assembleia da República; Renamo—União Eleitoral, a Renamo-led coalition of 11 opposition parties, obtained the remaining seats, although Renamo rejected the outcome, claiming that the vote had been fraudulent. On 15 January 2000 Chissano was sworn in for a further five-year presidential term.

In December 2000 Dhlakama and President Chissano held talks in an attempt to resolve the growing tension between their two parties. Dhlakama stated that he was prepared to accept the results of the 1999 elections, while Chissano pledged to consult Renamo about future state appointments. However, comments by Dhlakama, accusing Frelimo of violence and intimidation towards Renamo, subsequently jeopardized the future of talks between the two parties. In a second meeting between the two leaders in January 2001 it was agreed that a number of working groups (including groups on defence and security, constitutional and parliamentary affairs, and the media) would be established in February. At a further meeting, in March, Chissano referred Dhlakama's demand for the appointment of Renamo state governors to the Assembleia da República, whose Frelimo representatives were strongly opposed to accommodating Renamo demands. In protest, Dhlakama ceased negotiations in April.

President Chissano announced in May 2001 that he would not stand for re-election on the expiry of his term in 2004. At the long-postponed Renamo congress, held in October 2001, Dhlakama was re-elected party President; Joaquim Vaz was elected

Secretary-General. The holding of a party congress by Renamo for the first time since the end of the civil war, as well as the establishment of a 10-member Political Committee, were regarded as confirmation of the movement's decision to establish itself as a full political party, and to decentralize the party leadership and structure.

In June 2002, at the party's eighth congress, Frelimo elected Armando Guebuza as its Secretary-General, and thus also its candidate for the 2004 presidential election. During July Renamo's attempt to establish itself as a legitimate opposition party was threatened after Dhlakama dismissed Vaz as Secretary-General, assuming the position himself, and dissolved the party's Political Committee. In October Renamo announced its intention to contest municipal elections (due in 2003) alone, rather than in coalition, while in November 2002 the party regained some stability with the appointment of Viana Magalhaes as Secretary-General.

In February 2003, in response to Renamo's decision to run alone in the municipal elections, 10 opposition parties announced the formation of a new coalition, the União Eleitoral, led by Raul Domingos, formerly a senior member of Renamo. In October Domingos founded his own party, the Partido para a Paz, Democracia e Desenvolvimento. From mid-2003 divisions became apparent within Frelimo between supporters of its presidential candidate, Guebuza, and Chissano loyalists. The Conselho Constitucional (CC—Constitutional Council), which was to supervise elections and determine the constitutionality of new legislation, was inaugurated in early November. Municipal elections were held on 19 November. Despite allegations by Renamo of irregularities, the elections proceeded smoothly, and their conduct was later commended by an observer mission from the European Union (EU, see p. 270), although voter turn-out, at 24.2%, was low. Frelimo won a majority in 29 municipalities, while Renamo won a majority in four, including Beira. The results were verified by the CC in January 2004.

Luísa Dias Diogo was appointed as Prime Minister in February 2004, to replace Mocumbi, who resigned the premiership to take up an executive post in an EU-sponsored initiative specializing in clinical research. Diogo retained the responsibilities of Minister of Planning and Finance.

In November 2004 the Assembleia da República approved changes to the Constitution, which were to take effect on the day following the declaration of the results of the forthcoming presidential and legislative elections. Notably, the President would no longer be afforded immunity from prosecution and a Conselho de Estado (Council of State) was to be created, which would act as an advisory body to the President. It was also envisaged that elections to provincial assemblies, which were to mirror in structure those to the Assembleia, would take place in 2008. Voter registration for the provincial elections began in September 2007; however, the process was hampered by severe flooding that affected the country in January 2008. The Assembleia subsequently enforced its right to extraordinary powers of amendment to the Constitution and altered the date for the holding of provincial elections to 2009; having been amended in 2004, under normal circumstances the Constitution should not have undergone further review for at least five years.

Guebuza elected to the presidency

The presidential and legislative elections took place as scheduled on 1–2 December 2004, and proceeded without notable incident, although 37 voting stations did not open, reportedly owing to bad weather. For the first time Mozambicans living abroad were able to vote. Although national and international observers stated that the elections had been generally free and fair, they did express concern at the lack of access that they had been granted to the counting process and about the low rate of voter participation, which was recorded at just 36.3%. Renamo, later joined by other opposition parties, announced that it would not recognize the results, owing to alleged irregularities produced by the computer system used to tabulate the votes and demanded that the elections be re-run. Official results, which were released on 21 December, revealed that Guebuza had won 63.7% of the votes cast at the presidential election, while Dhlakama took 31.7% and Domingos 2.7%; the two other candidates each received less than 1% of the vote. In the legislative elections, Frelimo secured 160 of the available 250 seats, while Renamo took 90 seats (a significant decline compared with the 117 seats it had won in the 1999 elections). No other party achieved the minimum of 5% of total votes cast required to secure parliamentary representation. Protests lodged by Renamo with the Comissão Nacional de Eleições (CNE—National Elections Commission) and the CC were rejected in January 2005, and Renamo announced that it would accept the election results and participate in the new legislature.

The new Assembleia da República was inaugurated on 31 January 2005, and Eduardo Mulémbue was re-elected to the post of Chairman. Guebuza was sworn in as President on 2 February and in his inauguration speech pledged to promote rural development and to take measures to combat corruption and poverty. The new Government, featuring a number of new appointees, was announced the following day. Diogo retained her position as Prime Minister; however, in a reorganization of ministerial functions, Manuel Chang became Minister of Finance, while Aiuba Cuereneia headed the newly created Ministry of Planning and Development. In March Chissano resigned as President of Frelimo and was replaced by Guebuza.

Meanwhile, in February 2005 it was reported that members of Dhlakama's guard, protesting against the non-payment of wages and poor living conditions, had taken five Renamo officials hostage. The following month the Government announced plans to integrate the guards (estimated to number 100–150), who had been maintained by Dhlakama as his personal defence force following the end of the civil war in 1992, into the state security forces; however, such attempts were consistently stalled by Dhlakama. In September 2005 conflict between Frelimo and Renamo supporters led to the deaths of 12 people in Mocímboa da Praia, in Cabo Delgado province, following a disputed by-election earlier in the year.

In November 2005 the Assembleia da República adopted legislation providing for the formation of the Conselho de Estado, as envisaged in changes to the Constitution approved in late 2004. Members of the Conselho, including Dhlakama, were subsequently appointed by Guebuza and the Assembleia da República, and took office in December 2005.

In December 2006 the Assembleia da República approved amendments to the electoral legislation. Among the changes were provisions for the restructuring of the CNE, which had been reduced in size to 13 members. Five members were henceforth to be nominated by the Assembleia in proportion to the number of seats held by each political party, while the remaining eight members were to be nominated by legally constituted civil society bodies. A 14th member was to be appointed by the Government, but would not have the right to vote. Also approved was a requirement that the electorate re-register every five years and the abolition of the 5% 'barrier clause', whereby only parties that won at least 5% of votes cast had secured representation in the Assembleia.

In March 2007 an explosion at a munitions storage facility in a residential area of Maputo resulted in the deaths of more than 100 people and left over 500 others injured. A commission of inquiry was established in April to investigate the incident. The Government admitted that it had been storing equipment since the end of the civil war and weapons experts were later deployed to dispose of obsolete military equipment. In June a munitions expert from South Africa was killed in an explosion while assisting with the destruction of unexploded missiles. Following a further explosion in October, the Government agreed to relocate weapons stores away from residential areas.

In early 2008 severe flooding devastated parts of Mozambique, causing 25 deaths, destroying an estimated 117,000 ha of crops, and displacing 95,000 people. A further 200,000 were displaced, and 10 people were killed, by Cyclone Jokwe in March. In July the Government established a new relief agency, the Gabinete de Coordenação da Reconstrução, with responsibility for the resettlement of those displaced by natural disasters.

In late March 2008 Minister of National Defence Gen. (retd) Tobias Joaquim Dai was dismissed and replaced by Filipe Nhussi, hitherto a senior official at the Empresa Nacional dos Portos e Caminhos de Ferro de Moçambique; no official reason was given for the change, although Dai had been severely criticized for the military's negligence with regard to the 2007 armaments explosions. Earlier that month President Guebuza had effected a minor reorganization of the Council of Ministers.

In September 2008 Guebuza was elected unopposed as Frelimo's candidate for the 2009 presidential election. The party secured a resounding victory in municipal elections in November 2008, winning a majority in 42 of the 43 municipal assemblies, while Renamo lost four of the five municipalities it had gained in the elections in 2003. International observers stated that, despite some minor problems, the elections had been conducted in a transparent and fair manner.

Meanwhile, in February 2008 riots broke out in Maputo, as people took to the streets in protest against rising fuel prices and government plans to increase fares on public transport. Some 12 people were killed and hundreds more injured when the police opened fire on the demonstration. The Government subsequently reduced fuel costs for privately operated taxis and minibuses, and cancelled the increase in transport fares. Human rights organization Amnesty International accused the police of acting with impunity and excessive violence in response to rising crime rates. In March 2009 it was reported that three senior police officers had been arrested after 13 prisoners died of asphyxiation while in police detention. According to a local human rights agency, more than 40 detainees were held in a cell with a capacity for just 10 people. The dead were among those arrested in connection with the murders of two Red Cross workers, who had been killed in the village of Quinga, in Nampula province. (Locals believed that they had deliberately contaminated a well with cholera when they had, in fact, been administering chlorine with which to decontaminate it.) According to the Red Cross, there were over 12,000 cases of cholera recorded between January and March 2009, resulting in 157 deaths.

Recent developments: the 2009 elections

In April 2009 the Assembleia da República adopted electoral legislation under which the presidential, legislative and provincial elections would henceforth be held on the same ballot, and later that month President Guebuza confirmed that the elections would take place concurrently on 28 October. At the presidential election, Guebuza secured an overwhelming victory, taking 75.0% of the valid votes cast. His nearest challenger, Dhlakama, won 16.4%, while Daviz Simango of the newly founded Movimento Democrático de Moçambique (MDM) took 8.6%. Members of the opposition alleged that the vote was compromised by fraudulent activity; however, in late December the CC upheld the results initially declared by the CNE on 11 November. The CC acknowledged that certain irregularities had taken place, notably the deliberate invalidation of votes by polling station staff, but that such incidents had not been on a sufficient scale to alter the election results. The CC also confirmed that Guebuza's Frelimo party had increased its majority in the legislature, winning 74.5% of the votes cast and 191 of the 250 seats. Renamo took 17.7% and 51 seats. The MDM was the only other party to gain representation in the Assembleia da República, securing eight seats. Frelimo was also declared to have won 704 of the 812 provincial assembly seats, thus consolidating its power at all three levels.

Guebuza was inaugurated for a second term as President on 14 January 2010, appointing a new Government five days later. Aires Bonifácio Ali was selected as the new Prime Minister, vacating his former position as Minister of Education and Culture. This portfolio was divided between two ministers: Zeferino de Alexandre Martins became Minister of Education, while Armando Artur João assumed responsibility for culture. The key portfolios within the new administration were little altered from the outgoing Government. In late January Veronica Macamo was elected as the first female Chairperson of the Assembleia da República. A Renamo boycott of the legislature, in protest against the conduct of the 2009 elections, was inconsistently observed by the party's 51 deputies and ended fairly rapidly. Meanwhile, legislation on the Assembleia decreed that only parties with at least 11 deputies could form an official parliamentary group, meaning that the MDM, with just eight deputies, was not authorized to participate fully in the legislature. With Frelimo support, however, this legislation was amended in April 2010, and the MDM was officially designated as the third parliamentary group in the Assembleia in May.

Antonio Munguambe, Minister of Transport and Communications in Guebuza's Council of Ministers during 2005–08, was sentenced to 20 years' imprisonment in February 2010 for his involvement in the embezzlement of some US $1.7m. from the state-owned airport management body, Aeroportos de Moçambique (ADM). Two senior ADM officials also received prison sentences, one of 20 years and the other of 22 years. Munguambe was the first former or serving government minister to have been imprisoned since the country gained its independence in 1975.

Violent demonstrations in protest against rising prices, particularly the cost of bread and other essential foodstuffs, erupted in Maputo, Matola, Chimoio and Beira during early September 2010. The Government had just implemented an increase in electricity and water rates, while a global decline in wheat production, combined with the country's depreciating currency, had made wheat imports (upon which Mozambique is heavily dependent) less affordable, resulting in higher bread prices. Protesters erected barricades and clashed with police officers, and widespread looting was reported. The police, who claimed that the protest action was illegal since a permit had not been procured, fired tear gas and live ammunition at the demonstrators, causing the deaths of 13 people and more than 600 injuries. Military units were subsequently deployed to reinforce police patrols and dismantle the roadblocks, and more than 400 protesters were arrested. The authorities also allegedly disrupted mobile telephone text-messaging services, which had reportedly been the main method used by the demonstrators to organize the protests. In response to the unrest, the Government announced on 7 September that it would subsidize bread prices, reduce the duties payable on certain imported foodstuffs, lower electricity and water tariffs, and freeze the salaries of senior officials in the Government and public bodies. Although these measures pacified the protesters, they were financially unsustainable and hence only a temporary solution to the long-standing problems of poverty and unemployment.

Guebuza effected a reorganization of the Council of Ministers in October 2010. Soares Nhaca, the Minister of Agriculture, was replaced by hitherto Minister of the Interior José Condungua Pacheco, who had been widely criticized for supporting the repressive measures employed by the police in response to the food riots. Alberto Mondlane was assigned the interior portfolio, while Alexandre Manguele and Armando Inroga were appointed as Minister of Health and Minister of Industry and Trade, respectively.

In December 2010 the Assembleia da República approved the establishment of a commission to draft unspecified modifications to the Constitution. Amid suspicions that the Frelimo-dominated commission would propose the removal of presidential term limits, thereby allowing Guebuza to contest a third term in office, Renamo announced in January 2011 that it was boycotting the body. Frelimo officials maintained that the aim of the commission was merely to 'consolidate' the Constitution and rejected claims that it would alter the term-limit clauses. (Guebuza had frequently stated that he would not seek re-election.)

Foreign Affairs

After independence, Mozambique developed strong international links with the USSR and other countries of the communist bloc, and with neighbouring African states: it is a member of the Southern African Development Community (SADC, see p. 420), founded in 1979, as the Southern African Development Co-ordination Conference, then with the aim of reducing the region's economic dependence on South Africa, principally by developing trade routes through Mozambique. In December 1996 Mozambique, Malawi, Zambia and Zimbabwe (also SADC members) formally agreed to establish the Beira Development Corridor as a trading route avoiding South Africa's ports. In 1993 full diplomatic relations were established with South Africa. In July 1994 Mozambique and South Africa established a new Joint Defence and Security Commission, replacing the Joint Security Commission originally established in 1984.

During 1995 the activities, principally in the border province of Manica, of a group of mainly Zimbabwean dissidents, known as Chimwenje, came under increasing scrutiny. The group, which was alleged to have links with Renamo, was believed to be preparing for military incursions into Zimbabwe, where it sought the overthrow of President Robert Mugabe. In early 1996 the Chissano Government announced its intention to expel the dissidents from Mozambique. In June, following a series of armed attacks on both sides of the Mozambique–Zimbabwe border, which were believed to have been perpetrated by Chimwenje, the Governments of Mozambique and Zimbabwe agreed to combine and intensify efforts to combat the activities of the dissidents. The group was suppressed in late 1996. During late 2002 and early 2003 Mozambique resettled a number of white Zimbabwean farmers whose land had been appropriated by the Mugabe regime.

After stepping down as President following the election of December 2004, Chissano increasingly took on an international role. In mid-2005, as the UN Secretary-General's special envoy, he monitored the presidential election in Guinea-Bissau, while in August he was appointed mediator for the African Union (see p. 183) in Zimbabwe. In December 2006 Chissano became the UN Secretary-General's special envoy to northern Uganda, and he subsequently engaged in mediation efforts between the Ugandan Government and the rebel Lord's Resistance Army. Having completed his mission in Uganda, Chissano, representing SADC, began moderating talks between the various factions involved in the presidential crisis in Madagascar during July 2009.

Following widespread xenophobic violence in South African townships in May 2008, at least 23 Mozambicans were believed to have been killed and around 40,000 were forced to return home. Refugee camps were established on the common border and near Maputo to deal with the influx of refugees.

Relations between Mozambique and land-locked Malawi were strained during late 2010, after the Malawian Government opened a port at Nsanje on the Shire river in October, in an attempt to create a new trade route to the Indian Ocean via the Zambezi river (which passes through Mozambique). The Mozambican authorities seized a barge that was making the inaugural journey to Nsanje, claiming that permission had not been granted for the vessel to travel through Mozambique's waters, and rejected requests from the Malawian Government for its release. Guebuza insisted that a number of technical studies had to be completed before expanded commercial shipping activities on the Zambezi river would be authorized. However, commentators suspected that the Mozambican Government's actions were mainly motivated by concerns that the new trade route would be financially detrimental to Mozambique's coastal ports.

CONSTITUTION AND GOVERNMENT

The Constitution of 30 November 1990 (amended in 1996 and 2004) provides for a multi-party political system. Legislative power is vested in the Assembleia da República, with 250 members, who are elected for a five-year term. Members are elected by universal, direct adult suffrage in a secret ballot, according to a system of proportional representation. The President of the Republic, who is Head of State, is directly elected for a five-year term; the President holds executive power and governs with the assistance of an appointed Council of Ministers. A Council of State advises the President, who, however, has no obligation to follow its advice. Judicial functions are exercised through the Supreme Court and other courts provided for in the law on the judiciary, which also subordinates them to the Assembleia da República. Judges are independent, subject only to the law. Provincial governors, appointed by the President, have overall responsibility for the functions of government within each of the 11 provinces. For the purposes of local government, Mozambique is divided into 33 municipalities.

REGIONAL AND INTERNATIONAL CO-OPERATION

Mozambique is a member of the African Union (see p. 183) and of the Southern African Development Community (SADC, see p. 420).

Mozambique became a member of the UN in 1975 and was admitted to the World Trade Organization (WTO, see p. 430) in 1995. Mozambique participates in the Group of 77 (G77, see p. 447) developing countries. Mozambique was admitted, by special dispensation, as a full member of the Commonwealth (see p. 230) in 1995 and became an observer member of the Organisation Internationale de la Francophonie (see p. 462) in 2006.

ECONOMIC AFFAIRS

In 2009, according to estimates by the World Bank, Mozambique's gross national income (GNI), measured at average 2007–09 prices, was US $9,962m., equivalent to $440 per head (or $880 per head on an international purchasing-power parity basis). During 2000–09, it was estimated, the population increased at an average annual rate of 2.6%, while gross domestic product (GDP) per head increased, in real terms, by an average of 5.3% per year. Overall GDP increased, in real terms, at an average annual rate of 8.0% in 2000–09; growth in 2009 was 6.3%.

Agriculture (including forestry and fishing) contributed 28.8% of GDP in 2009. In mid-2011 the sector employed an estimated 80.3% of the economically active population, according to FAO. Fishing is a significant export activity: fish, crustaceans and molluscs accounted for 3.0% of total export earnings in 2009. The principal cash crops are fruit and nuts, cotton, sugar cane and copra. After production of cashews fell sharply in the 1990s, the Government attempted to increase revenue from the crop by promoting production and improving processing facilities. The main subsistence crop is cassava. During 2000–09, according to the World Bank, agricultural GDP increased by an average of 8.0% per year; growth in 2009 was 6.7%.

Industry (including mining, manufacturing, construction and power) provided 23.0% of GDP in 2009, and employed 5.6% of the economically active population in 1997. According to the World Bank, during 2000–09 industrial GDP increased at an average annual rate of 9.4%; the sector grew by 1.8% in 2009.

Mining contributed 1.4% of GDP in 2009, and employed 0.5% of the economically active population in 1997. Only coal, bauxite, marble, gold and salt are exploited in significant quantities, although gravel and crushed rocks are also mined. In November 2004 the Companhia Vale do Rio Doce (Brazil) was granted a coal-mining concession in Moatize; production was expected to begin in 2011, with forecast annual production of 11m. metric tons. There are reserves of other minerals, including high-grade iron ore, precious and semi-precious stones, and natural gas. Plans began in 1994 to exploit natural gas reserves at Pande, in the province of Inhambane, which were estimated at 55,000m. cu m. A South African company, SASOL Ltd, was granted a 25-year concession to develop gasfields at Pande and Temane (also in Inhambane province); it was anticipated that the Government would receive revenues of some US $900m. from the project, and the construction of a pipeline to transport the gas to South Africa was completed in early 2004. A gas-processing centre opened in Temane in early 2004. In 1999 the largest reserve of titanium in the world (estimated at 100m. tons) was discovered in the district of Chibuto, in the province of Gaza; the Government was seeking a new company to explore the titanium-bearing heavy sands at Chibuto in early 2011, having revoked the licence of the previous concessionaire, after it concluded that the potential value that could be obtained from the deposit was inadequate to justify its development. Meanwhile, the British company Pan African Resources plc was investigating the viability of developing a new gold mine in Manica province. Preliminary estimates suggested that production could amount to 2,600 kg per year. According to official figures, mining GDP increased at an average annual rate of 19.4% in 2003–09; growth in 2009 was 2.7%.

Manufacturing contributed 13.9% of GDP in 2009, and employed 3.0% of the economically active population in 1997. A large aluminium smelter, Mozal, was opened in 2000 and expanded in 2003, with the completion of Mozal 2, which doubled capacity, to some 506,000 metric tons of aluminium ingots per year. Aluminium production was valued at 19,067,000m. meticais in 2003, equivalent to 16.8% of GDP. Aluminium accounted for 54.7% of total export earnings in 2008, but earnings declined sharply in 2009 owing to low international prices, weak demand resulting from the global economic downturn and electricity shortages; prices recovered strongly in 2010. During 2000–09, according to the World Bank, manufacturing GDP increased at an average annual rate of 8.8%; manufacturing GDP increased by 2.9% in 2008, but declined by 2.5% in 2009.

Construction contributed 3.0% of GDP in 2009, and employed 0.8% of the economically active population according to the census of 1980. According to official figures, construction GDP increased at an average annual rate of 7.6% in 2003–09. Growth in 2009 was 5.8%.

Electrical energy is derived principally from hydroelectric power, which provided some 99.9% of total electricity production in 2007. Mozambique's important Cahora Bassa hydroelectric plant on the Zambezi river supplies electricity to South Africa and Zimbabwe. By 2004 an extended power supply from Cahora Bassa to Zambézia, Manica and Sofala was in operation. In early 2011 an environmental impact study for the construction of a hydroelectric dam at Mepanda Uncua, some 70 km downstream of Cahora Bassa, was under way. It was envisaged that power from the Mepanda Uncua plant, which would have an initial generating capacity of 1,500 MW (to be expanded to 2,500 MW in a second phase), would also be exported to South Africa. Mozambique currently imports all of its petroleum requirements. Imports of mineral fuels and lubricants comprised 15.5% of the value of total imports in 2009.

The services sector contributed 48.2% of GDP in 2009, and engaged 12.3% of the economically active population in 1997. By the end of the 1990s tourism was the fastest growing sector of the economy. It was hoped that the formal opening, in April 2002, of the Great Limpopo Transfrontier Park, comprising South Africa's Kruger National Park, Zimbabwe's Gonarezhou National Park and Mozambique's Limpopo National Park, would attract additional tourists. In 2008 some 2.6m. tourists visited Mozambique, compared with about 711,000 in 2004, and receipts from tourism totalled US $213m. The GDP of the services sector increased by an average of 7.3% per year in 2000–09, according to the World Bank; services GDP increased by 5.5% in 2009.

In 2009 Mozambique recorded a trade deficit of US $1,390.5m., and there was a deficit of $1,171.3m. on the current account of the balance of payments. In 2009 the principal source of imports was

MOZAMBIQUE

South Africa (35.4%), other major suppliers were the Netherlands and India. In 2009 the Netherlands was the principal market for exports (receiving 41.6%); South Africa was the other significant purchaser. The principal exports in 2009 were electrical energy and tobacco. (However, aluminium is generally the most significant export.) The principal imports in 2009 were mineral fuels and lubricants (particularly petroleum oils), road vehicles, nuclear reactors, boilers and machinery, and cereals.

In 2009 there was an overall budgetary deficit of 14,670m. meticais, equivalent to 5.4% of GDP. Mozambique's general government gross debt was 77,159m. meticais in 2009, equivalent to 29.3% of GDP. Total external debt was US $3,432m. in 2008, of which $2,788m. was public and publicly guaranteed debt. In that year the cost of debt-servicing was equivalent to 1.2% of the value of exports of goods, services and income. The average annual rate of inflation was 8.7% in 2005–09; consumer prices increased by an average of 3.3% in 2009, according to the IMF. An unemployment rate of 18.7% was recorded in 2004/05.

During the 1990s Mozambique's economy was one of the fastest growing in the world and in the early 2000s a significant amount of the country's foreign debt was deferred and subsequently cancelled; most notably, as a result of the successful implementation of economic reforms, in December 2005 the IMF cancelled Mozambique's outstanding debt to the Fund, worth an estimated US $153m. The country possesses considerable mineral resources, including aluminium, natural gas, petroleum (of which large-scale exploration was expected to ensue following the allocation of concessions to foreign companies) and coal (reserves of which were estimated at 10,000m. metric tons). Mozambique is, however, prone to natural disasters, and floods in early 2008 exacerbated the increasingly precarious food security situation, destroying more than 117,000 ha of crops. Local shortages, coupled with rising food prices on international markets, left thousands of Mozambicans unable to provide sufficiently for themselves. In 2008 the authorities introduced a three-year agricultural campaign as part of a 'green revolution' strategy, which aimed to guarantee food security. However, following a prolonged period of drought, further flooding occurred during March 2010 and February 2011 in southern and central regions, causing extensive crop damage. It was estimated in March 2010 that more than 450,000 people would require food aid over the following year. Meanwhile, Mozambique's economy withstood the turmoil caused by the global financial crisis, and real GDP grew by 6.3% in 2009. Nevertheless, exports and levels of investment decreased sharply in that year, although the Government's finances were bolstered in June by the IMF's approval of a one-year arrangement worth $176m., under its Exogenous Shocks Facility. The Fund projected GDP growth of 7.2% in 2010 and 7.5% in 2011, driven by rising demand for the country's commodities, prices for which increased throughout 2010. However, an upsurge in the cost of foodstuffs and fuel, caused by global food supply disruptions, rising international demand for oil and Mozambique's weakening currency, led to violent demonstrations in September 2010, prompting the Government to subsidize bread prices, lower import duties and reduce utility tariffs. Despite these measures, annual inflation reached 17.4% in December.

PUBLIC HOLIDAYS

2012: 1 January (New Year's Day), 3 February (Heroes' Day, anniversary of the assassination of Eduardo Mondlane), 7 April (Day of the Mozambican Woman), 1 May (Workers' Day), 25 June (Independence Day), 7 September (Victory Day—anniversary of the end of the Armed Struggle), 25 September (Anniversary of the launching of the Armed Struggle for National Liberation, and Day of the Armed Forces of Mozambique), 4 October (Peace and National Reconciliation Day), 25 December (National Family Day).

Statistical Survey

Source (unless otherwise stated): Instituto Nacional de Estatística, Comissão Nacional do Plano, Av. Ahmed Sekou Touré 21, CP 493, Maputo; tel. 21491054; fax 21490384; e-mail webmaster@ine.gov.mz; internet www.ine.gov.mz.

Area and Population

AREA, POPULATION AND DENSITY

Area (sq km)	799,380*
Land	786,380
Inland waters	13,000
Population (census results)	
1 August 1997	15,278,334
1 August 2007	
Males	9,734,678
Females	10,491,618
Total	20,226,296
Population (UN estimates at mid-year)†	
2009	22,894,291
2010	23,405,670
2011	23,916,413
Density (per sq km) at mid-2011	29.9

* 308,641 sq miles.
† Source: UN, *World Population Prospects: The 2008 Revision*.

POPULATION BY AGE AND SEX
(UN estimates at mid-2011)

	Males	Females	Total
0–14	5,249,462	5,208,254	10,457,716
15–64	6,077,978	6,587,788	12,665,766
65 and over	336,871	456,060	792,931
Total	11,664,311	12,252,102	23,916,413

Source: UN, *World Population Prospects: The 2008 Revision*.

PROVINCES
(at census of 1 August 2007)

Province	Area (sq km)	Population	Density (per sq km)
Cabo Delgado	82,625	1,605,649	19.4
Gaza	75,709	1,226,272	16.2
Inhambane	68,615	1,252,479	18.3
Manica	61,661	1,412,029	22.9
City of Maputo	300	1,094,315	3,647.7
Maputo Province	26,058	1,205,553	46.3
Nampula	81,606	3,985,285	48.8
Niassa	129,056	1,169,837	9.1
Sofala	68,018	1,642,636	24.2
Tete	100,724	1,783,967	17.7
Zambézia	105,008	3,848,274	36.6
Total	**799,380**	**20,226,296**	**25.3**

PRINCIPAL TOWNS
(at 2007 census, preliminary)

Maputo (capital)	1,099,102	Nacala-Porto	207,894
Matola	675,422	Quelimane	192,876
Nampula	477,900	Tete	152,909
Beira	436,240	Xai-Xai	116,343
Chimoio	238,976		

Mid-2010 (incl. suburbs, UN estimates): Maputo 1,654,700; Matola 793,486 (Source: UN, *World Urbanization Prospects: The 2009 Revision*).

MOZAMBIQUE

BIRTHS AND DEATHS

	2007	2008	2009
Crude birth rate (per 1,000)	40.1	39.2	38.3
Crude death rate (per 1,000)	16.2	15.9	15.7

Source: African Development Bank.

Life expectancy (years at birth, WHO estimates): 51 (males 51; females 51) in 2008 (Source: WHO, *World Health Statistics*).

ECONOMICALLY ACTIVE POPULATION
(persons aged 12 years and over, 1980 census)

	Males	Females	Total
Agriculture, forestry, hunting and fishing	1,887,779	2,867,052	4,754,831
Mining and quarrying	} 323,730	23,064	346,794
Manufacturing			
Construction	41,611	510	42,121
Commerce	90,654	21,590	112,244
Transport, storage and communications	74,817	2,208	77,025
Other services*	203,629	39,820	243,449
Total employed	2,622,220	2,954,244	5,576,464
Unemployed	75,505	19,321	94,826
Total labour force	2,697,725	2,973,565	5,671,290

* Including electricity, gas and water.

Source: ILO, *Yearbook of Labour Statistics*.

1997 (percentage distribution of economically active population at census of 1 August): Agriculture, forestry and hunting: 91.3% of females, 69.6% of males; Mining: 0.0% of females, 1.0% of males; Manufacturing: 0.8% of females, 5.5% of males; Energy: 0.0% of females, 0.3% of males; Construction: 0.3% of females, 3.9% of males; Transport and communications: 0.1% of females, 2.3% of males; Commerce and finance: 4.3% of females, 9.7% of males; Services: 2.2% of females, 3.4% of males; Unknown: 0.9% of females, 1.4% of males.

Mid-2011 ('000 persons, estimates): Agriculture, etc. 8,848; Total labour force 11,025 (Source: FAO).

Health and Welfare

KEY INDICATORS

Total fertility rate (children per woman, 2008)	5.1
Under-5 mortality rate (per 1,000 live births, 2008)	130
HIV/AIDS (% of persons aged 15–49, 2007)	12.5
Physicians (per 1,000 head, 2004)	0.03
Hospital beds (per 1,000 head, 2006)	0.8
Health expenditure (2007): US $ per head (PPP)	39
Health expenditure (2007): % of GDP	4.9
Health expenditure (2007): public (% of total)	71.8
Access to water (% of persons, 2008)	47
Access to sanitation (% of persons, 2008)	17
Total carbon dioxide emissions ('000 metric tons, 2007)	2,597.8
Carbon dioxide emissions per head (metric tons, 2007)	0.1
Human Development Index (2010): ranking	165
Human Development Index (2010): value	0.284

For sources and definitions, see explanatory note on p. vi.

Agriculture

PRINCIPAL CROPS
('000 metric tons)

	2006	2007	2008
Rice, paddy	99	105	102
Maize	1,418	1,152	1,285
Millet	23	25	24
Sorghum	205	170	187
Potatoes*	80	80	80
Sweet potatoes*	66	67	67
Cassava (Manioc)	6,765	5,039	5,039*
Cashew nuts, with shell*	63	74	85
Groundnuts, with shell	86	103	94
Coconuts*	290	265	265
Sunflower seed	4	6	5
Tomatoes*	9	9	9
Bananas*	90	90	90
Oranges*	14	14	14
Grapefruits and pomelos*	13	13	13
Guavas, mangoes and mangosteens*	24	24	24
Pineapples*	13	13	13
Papayas*	41	41	41
Tobacco, unmanufactured	95	34	64

* FAO estimate(s).

2009: Sunflower seed 7 (FAO estimate). Note: Data for other individual crops in 2009 were not available.

Aggregate production ('000 metric tons, may include official, semi-official or estimated data): Total cereals 1,747 in 2006, 1,454 in 2007, 1,601 in 2008–09; Total roots and tubers 7,685 in 2006, 6,020 in 2007, 6,035 in 2008–09; Total vegetables (incl. melons) 117 in 2006–09; Total fruits (excl. melons) 334 in 2006, 336 in 2007, 339 in 2008–09.

Source: FAO.

LIVESTOCK
('000 head, year ending September)

	2006	2007	2008
Asses*	45	45	45
Cattle	1,055	1,426	1,240
Pigs	1,183	1,350	1,266
Sheep	145	219	182
Goats	4,255	4,395	4,325
Chickens	18,100	17,800	18,000*

* Estimate(s).

Source: FAO.

LIVESTOCK PRODUCTS
('000 metric tons, FAO estimates)

	2006	2007	2008
Cattle meat	16	22	19
Goat meat	21	22	21
Pig meat	85	97	91
Chicken meat	22	22	22
Cows' milk	68	66	66
Goats' milk	9	9	8
Hen eggs	14	14	14

2009 (FAO estimates): Figures assumed to be unchanged from 2008.

Source: FAO.

MOZAMBIQUE

Forestry

ROUNDWOOD REMOVALS
('000 cubic metres, excl. bark)

	2003	2004	2005
Sawlogs, veneer logs and logs for sleepers	128	123	113
Other industrial wood	1,191	1,191	1,191
Fuel wood	16,724	16,724	16,724
Total	18,043	18,038	18,028

2006–09: Figures assumed to be unchanged from 2005 (FAO estimates).
Source: FAO.

SAWNWOOD PRODUCTION
('000 cubic metres, incl. railway sleepers)

	2005	2006	2007
Total	38	43	57

2008–09: Production assumed to be unchanged from 2007 (FAO estimates).
Source: FAO.

Fishing

(metric tons, live weight)

	2006	2007	2008
Dagaas	16,017	8,882	10,055
Penaeus shrimps	8,760	7,884	7,482
Knife shrimp	1,803	1,366	1,448
Marine fishes	61,775	55,042	78,457
Total catch (incl. others)	101,899*	92,270	119,645

* FAO estimate.

Note: Figures exclude crocodiles, recorded by number rather than by weight. The number of Nile crocodiles caught was: 2,021 in 2006; 179 in 2007; 566 in 2008.
Source: FAO.

Mining

('000 metric tons, unless otherwise indicated)

	2007	2008	2009
Bauxite	8.7	5.4	3.6
Coal	23.6	37.7	25.9
Gold (kilograms)*	97	298	511
Quartz (metric tons)	216.7	157.3	140.6
Gravel and crushed rock ('000 cubic metres)	1,171.0	115.5	1,200.0†
Marble (slab) ('000 square metres)	16.6	7.9	2.5
Salt (marine)†	110	110	110
Natural gas (million cu m)	2,751	3,069	2,803

* Figures exclude unreported gold production; total gold output is estimated at 600 kg–900 kg per year.
† Estimate(s).
Source: US Geological Survey.

Industry

SELECTED PRODUCTS
('000 metric tons unless otherwise indicated)

	2005	2006	2007
Wheat flour	204	193	182
Raw sugar	164	172	183
Groundnut oil ('000 metric tons)*	14.4	11.8	10.1
Beer ('000 hl)	1,412	n.a.	n.a.
Soft drinks ('000 hl)	1,149	1,170	1,170
Cigarettes (metric tons)	1,735	2,543	2,571
Footwear (excl. rubber, '000 pairs)	37	37	40
Cement	564	774	771
Electric energy (million kWh)	13,285	14,737	16,076

* FAO estimates.

2008–09 ('000 metric tons, FAO estimate): Groundnut oil 8.5.
Sources: FAO; UN Industrial Commodity Statistics Database.

Finance

CURRENCY AND EXCHANGE RATES

Monetary Units
100 centavos = 1 metical (plural: meticais).

Sterling, Dollar and Euro Equivalents (30 November 2010)
£1 sterling = 54.94 meticais;
US $1 = 35.38 meticais;
€1 = 46.00 meticais;
1,000 meticais = £18.20 = $28.26 = €21.75.

Average Exchange Rate (meticais per US $)
2007   25.84
2008   24.30
2009   27.52

Note: Between April 1992 and October 2000 the market exchange rate was the rate at which commercial banks purchased from and sold to the public. Since October 2000 it has been the weighted average of buying and selling rates of all transactions of commercial banks and stock exchanges with the public. A devaluation of the metical, with 1 new currency unit becoming equivalent to 1,000 of the former currency, was implemented on 1 July 2006.

BUDGET
('000 million meticais)

Revenue*	2008	2009†	2010†
Taxation	34.02	37.21	49.91
Taxes on income and profits	11.72	12.35	17.50
Domestic taxes on goods and services	18.05	20.18	27.00
Taxes on international trade	3.59	3.85	4.36
Other taxes	0.65	0.83	1.05
Non-tax revenue	4.25	5.34	6.56
Total	38.27	42.55	56.47

Expenditure‡	2008	2009†	2010†
Current expenditure	37.63	45.90	52.85
Compensation of employees	19.27	23.62	27.60
Goods and services	9.71	10.55	11.99
Interest on public debt	1.26	1.39	1.73
Transfer payments	7.40	10.34	11.50
Capital expenditure	27.74	30.46	42.64
Total	65.37	76.36	95.49

* Excluding grants received ('000 million meticais): 22.64 in 2008; 24.16 in 2009 (programmed figure); 26.85 in 2010 (programmed figure).
† Programmed figures.
‡ Excluding net lending ('000 million meticais): 1.48 in 2008; 1.63 in 2009 (programmed figure); 2.38 in 2010 (programmed figure).

Source: IMF, *Mozambique: Sixth Review Under the Policy Support Instrument, Second Review Under the Arrangement Under the Exogenous Shocks Facility, and Request for a Three-Year Policy Support Instrument—Staff Report; Staff Supplement; Press Release on the Executive Board Discussion; and Statement by the Executive Director for Mozambique*. (June 2010).

MOZAMBIQUE

Statistical Survey

INTERNATIONAL RESERVES
(US $ million at 31 December)

	2007	2008	2009
IMF special drawing rights	0.18	0.10	170.34
Reserve position in IMF	0.01	0.01	0.01
Foreign exchange	1,444.50	1,577.62	1,928.91
Total	1,444.69	1,577.73	2,099.27

Source: IMF, *International Financial Statistics*.

MONEY SUPPLY
('000 million meticais at 31 December)

	2007	2008	2009
Currency outside depository corporations	8,950.4	9,586.7	13,053.6
Transferable deposits	37,414.0	44,280.8	60,847.7
Other deposits	18,620.3	26,652.4	33,173.7
Securities other than shares	2,114.7	203.8	—
Broad money	67,099.4	80,723.7	107,075.0

Source: IMF, *International Financial Statistics*.

COST OF LIVING
(Consumer Price Index; base: 1998 = 100)

	2002	2003	2004
Food, beverages and tobacco	151	175	187
Clothing and footwear	126	122	125
Firewood and furniture	190	215	263
Health	119	133	134
Transportation and communications	205	232	234
Education, recreation and culture	145	150	151
Other goods and services	136	154	159
All items	157	179	195

Source: IMF, *Republic of Mozambique: Selected Issues and Statistical Appendix* (August 2005).

All items (Consumer Price Index; base: 2005 = 100): 122.5 in 2007; 135.1 in 2008; 139.5 in 2009 (Source: IMF, *International Financial Statistics*).

NATIONAL ACCOUNTS
('000 million meticais at current prices)

Expenditure on the Gross Domestic Product

	2007	2008	2009
Government final consumption expenditure	24,738	29,691	34,368
Private final consumption expenditure	166,398	192,513	214,369
Change in stocks	−1,721	2,677	−4,164
Gross fixed capital formation	33,504	39,614	43,959
Total domestic expenditure	222,920	264,495	288,532
Exports of goods and services	64,146	72,638	73,799
Less Imports of goods and services	79,423	96,775	96,119
GDP in purchasers' values	207,644	240,358	266,213
GDP at constant 2003 prices	151,300	161,635	171,873

Gross Domestic Product by Economic Activity

	2007	2008	2009
Agriculture, livestock and forestry	49,431	60,109	67,425
Fishing	3,398	4,259	4,227
Mining	2,967	3,318	3,566
Manufacturing	29,370	33,610	34,449
Electricity and water	11,065	10,044	11,586
Construction	5,936	6,860	7,533
Wholesale and retail trade; repairs	28,970	33,457	37,735
Restaurants and hotels	3,081	3,781	3,904
Transport and communications	19,011	22,180	24,913
Financial services	9,088	9,522	10,508
Real estate and business services	12,225	13,495	14,254

—*continued*	2007	2008	2009
Public administration and defence	7,350	8,519	9,848
Education	7,789	9,320	10,888
Health	3,025	3,514	4,015
Other services	3,280	3,677	3,874
Sub-total	195,987	225,665	248,725
Less Financial services indirectly measured	5,335	5,688	6,403
Gross value added in basic prices	190,652	219,977	242,322
Taxes on products	16,991	20,380	23,891
Less Subsidies on products			
GDP in market prices	207,644	240,358	266,213

BALANCE OF PAYMENTS
(US $ million)

	2007	2008	2009
Exports of goods f.o.b.	2,412.1	2,653.3	1,852.6
Imports of goods f.o.b.	−2,811.1	−3,643.4	−3,243.1
Trade balance	−399.0	−990.2	−1,390.5
Exports of services	458.7	555.0	611.7
Imports of services	−855.6	−965.3	−1,062.0
Balance on goods and services	−795.8	−1,400.5	−1,840.8
Other income received	193.6	167.1	164.3
Other income paid	−785.2	−798.5	−259.3
Balance on goods, services and income	−1,387.5	−2,031.9	−1,935.7
Current transfers received	667.6	977.5	931.7
Current transfers paid	−65.4	−125.1	−167.2
Current balance	−785.3	−1,179.4	−1,171.3
Capital account (net)	415.1	419.9	422.3
Direct investment abroad	0.3	—	−2.8
Direct investment from abroad	427.4	591.6	881.2
Portfolio investment assets	−3.5	−8.4	4.4
Portfolio investment liabilities	0.3	0.5	—
Financial derivatives (net)	−16.0	—	—
Other investment assets	−411.5	−80.7	−150.8
Other investment liabilities	445.7	269.7	280.8
Errors and omissions (net)	64.5	107.3	−68.9
Overall balance	137.1	120.6	195.0

Source: IMF, *International Financial Statistics*.

External Trade

PRINCIPAL COMMODITIES
(US $ million)

Imports c.i.f.	2007	2008	2009
Cereals	181.5	244.2	275.6
Rice	116.7	114.5	152.3
Vegetables, fruits and food preparations	119.0	10.5	14.5
Tomatoes, prepared or preserved	66.2	0.5	0.7
Cucumbers, gherkins and onions preserved by vinegar	44.9	0.0	0.0
Mineral fuels, lubricants, etc.	496.7	811.4	582.8
Petroleum oils	360.2	650.8	411.5
Iron and steel and products thereof	91.8	87.7	104.9
Nuclear reactors, boilers, machinery, etc.	250.3	313.4	397.7
Electrical and electronic equipment	178.7	218.7	191.8
Road vehicles	292.4	413.9	452.6
Trucks and motor vehicles for transport of goods	120.9	168.9	180.9
Total (incl. others)	3,049.7	4,007.8	3,764.2

MOZAMBIQUE

Exports f.o.b.	2007	2008	2009
Fish, crustaceans, molluscs and preparations thereof	70.1	75.7	65.4
Crustaceans	65.8	68.7	60.3
Tobacco and manufactured tobacco substitutes	51.8	195.0	180.6
Tobacco, unmanufactured	50.5	193.0	179.3
Mineral fuels, lubricants, etc.	373.4	287.7	374.2
Electrical energy	225.2	226.4	274.4
Aluminium and articles thereof	1,517.4	1,452.5	0.4
Nuclear reactors, boilers, machinery, etc.	40.5	53.1	78.6
Total (incl. others)	2,412.1	2,653.3	2,147.2

Source: Trade Map-Trade Competitiveness Map, International Trade Centre, www.intracen.org/marketanalysis.

PRINCIPAL TRADING PARTNERS
(US $ million)

Imports c.i.f.	2007	2008	2009
Argentina	33.3	41.2	26.6
Bahrain	0.6	269.7	14.9
China, People's Republic	103.2	156.1	173.1
Germany	34.1	64.7	66.4
India	131.8	144.4	244.7
Indonesia	36.3	38.9	16.0
Italy	25.5	31.1	56.9
Japan	94.0	127.8	141.6
Malaysia	15.6	52.1	46.3
Netherlands	447.9	698.0	488.2
Pakistan	41.6	38.1	55.1
Portugal	103.6	115.8	142.0
Saudi Arabia	23.8	3.9	49.3
Singapore	7.4	10.2	67.2
South Africa	970.8	1,164.9	1,333.8
Spain	13.0	44.6	24.7
Taiwan	3.3	117.6	7.2
Thailand	55.6	87.0	127.6
United Arab Emirates	99.5	103.6	75.6
United Kingdom	16.7	52.0	28.4
USA	80.8	160.4	134.8
Yemen	34.6	0.3	0.7
Total (incl. others)	3,049.7	4,007.8	3,764.2

Exports f.o.b.	2007	2008	2009
China, People's Republic	44.0	51.6	74.5
Germany	9.0	24.7	24.8
India	15.9	28.4	56.5
Malawi	17.4	46.8	46.7
Netherlands	10.5	1,476.4	893.9
Poland	4.4	17.8	24.3
Portugal	39.9	26.4	32.2
Russia	5.1	24.0	29.5
Singapore	1.3	1.9	28.4
South Africa	429.3	265.5	460.3
Spain	33.8	51.0	31.4
United Kingdom	24.7	10.2	28.7
USA	2.2	18.2	41.4
Zimbabwe	73.3	81.3	73.8
Total (incl. others)	2,412.1	2,653.3	2,147.2

Source: Trade Map-Trade Competitiveness Map, International Trade Centre, www.intracen.org/marketanalysis.

Transport

RAILWAYS
(traffic)

	2007	2008
Passenger-km (million)	319.6	130.5
Freight ton-km (million)	736.3	667.1

ROAD TRAFFIC
(motor vehicles in use)

	2007	2008
Light vehicles	152,536	159,238
Heavy vehicles	56,010	77,395
Trailers	4,681	6,511
Tractors	2,484	8,737
Motorbikes	38,364	38,726
Total	254,075	290,607

SHIPPING
Merchant Fleet
(registered at 31 December)

	2007	2008	2009
Number of vessels	129	130	129
Total displacement ('000 grt)	37.9	38.2	41.3

Source: IHS Fairplay, *World Fleet Statistics*.

Freight Handled
('000 metric tons)

	2001	2002	2003
Goods loaded and unloaded	7,423	8,201	8,421

International Sea-borne Freight Traffic
('000 metric tons)

	2001	2002	2003
Goods loaded	2,962	2,780	2,982
Goods unloaded	3,144	4,062	3,837

CIVIL AVIATION
(traffic on scheduled services)

	2007	2008
Kilometres flown (million)	8.1	11.5
Passenger-km (million)	440.2	505.0

Tourism

TOURIST ARRIVALS BY COUNTRY OF RESIDENCE

Country	2006	2007	2008
Malawi	115,405	118,820	72,807
Portugal	18,324	24,585	49,116
South Africa	351,307	398,668	1,084,572
Swaziland	27,372	29,093	174,648
United Kingdom	10,319	13,537	36,262
USA	9,039	12,319	32,436
Zimbabwe	101,487	101,895	811,241
Total (incl. others)	1,095,000	1,259,000	2,617,424

Tourism receipts (US $ million, incl. passenger transport): 145 in 2006; 182 in 2007; 213 in 2008.

Source: World Tourism Organization.

MOZAMBIQUE

Communications Media

	2007	2008	2009
Telephones ('000 main lines in use)	78.0	78.3	82.4
Mobile cellular telephones ('000 subscribers)	3,079.8	4,405.0	5,970.8
Internet users ('000)	200	350	614
Broadband subscribers ('000)	5.7	10.2	12.5

2004: Daily newspapers 19 (average circulation 54,900); Non-daily newspapers 50 (estimated average circulation 210,250).

Periodicals: 32 (average circulation 83,000) in 1998.

Television receivers ('000 in use): 230 in 2001.

Radio receivers ('000 in use): 730 in 1997.

Personal computers: 282,590 (13.6 per 1,000 persons) in 2005.

Sources: International Telecommunication Union; UN, *Statistical Yearbook*; UNESCO Institute for Statistics.

Education

(2005, unless otherwise indicated)

	Institutions	Teachers	Students
Pre-primary*†	5,689	28,705	1,745,049
Primary‡			
First level	8,696	45,887	3,393,677
Second level	1,320	11,011	452,888
Secondary§			
First level	156	210,128	5,004
Second level	35	25,737	861
Technical	41	1,028	21,752
Teacher training‖	18	n.a.	9,314

* Public education only.
† 1997 figures.
‡ Primary education is divided into two cycles of five years followed by two years.
§ Secondary education is divided into two cycles of three years.
‖ 2002 figures.

Source: mainly Ministry of Education.

Students (2008/09 unless otherwise indicated): Primary 5,076,283; Secondary 595,555; Tertiary 28,298 (2004/05) (Source: UNESCO Institute for Statistics).

Teachers (2008/09 unless otherwise indicated): Primary 82,753; Secondary 15,730; Tertiary 3,009 (2004/05) (Source: UNESCO Institute for Statistics).

Pupil-teacher ratio (primary education, UNESCO estimate): 61.3 in 2008/09 (Source: UNESCO Institute for Statistics).

Adult literacy rate (UNESCO estimates): 54.0% (males 69.5%; females 40.1%) in 2008 (Source: UNESCO Institute for Statistics).

Directory

The Government

HEAD OF STATE

President of the Republic and Commander-in-Chief of the Armed Forces: ARMANDO EMÍLIO GUEBUZA (took office 2 February 2005; re-elected 28 October 2009).

COUNCIL OF MINISTERS
(May 2011)

Prime Minister: AIRES BONIFÁCIO ALI.
Minister of the Interior: ALBERTO MONDLANE.
Minister of Finance: MANUEL CHANG.
Minister of Planning and Development: AIÚBA CUERENEIA.
Minister of Foreign Affairs and Co-operation: OLDEMIRO JÚLIO MARQUES BALOI.
Minister of National Defence: FILIPE JACINTO NHUSSI.
Minister of Justice: MARIA BENVINDA LEVI.
Minister of Environmental Co-ordination: ALCINDA ANTÓNIO DE ABREU.
Minister of Agriculture: JOSÉ CONDUNGUA PACHECO.
Minister of Health: ALEXANDRE MANGUELE.
Minister of Industry and Trade: ARMANDO INROGA.
Minister of Science and Technology: VENÂNCIO SIMÃO MASSINGUE.
Minister of Labour: MARIA HELENA TAÍPO.
Minister of Transport and Communications: PAULO FRANCISCO ZUCULA.
Minister of Public Works and Housing: CADMIEL FILIANE MUTHEMBA.
Minister of Public Service: VITÓRIA DIAS DIOGO.
Minister of Tourism: FERNANDO SUMBANA JÚNIOR.
Minister of State Administration: CARMELITA RITA NAMASHULUA.
Minister of Mineral Resources: ESPERANÇA LAURINDA FRANCISCO NHIUANE BIAS.
Minister of Energy: SALVADOR NAMBURETE.
Minister of Veterans' Affairs: MATEUS ÓSCAR KIDA.
Minister of Education: ZEFERINO DE ALEXANDRE MARTINS.
Minister of Culture: ARMANDO ARTUR JOÃO.
Minister of Fisheries: VICTOR MANUEL BORGES.
Minister of Women's Affairs and Social Welfare Co-ordination: IOLANDA MARIA PEDRO CAMPOS CINTURA.
Minister of Youth and Sport: PEDRITO FULEDA CAETANO.
Minister of Presidential Affairs: ANTÓNIO CORREIA FERNANDES SUMBANA.
Minister in the Presidency with responsibility for Social Affairs: FELICIANO SALOMÃO GUNDANA.
Minister in the Presidency with responsibility for Parliamentary, Municipal and Provincial Assembly Affairs: ADELAIDE ANCHIA AMURANE.

There were also 23 Deputy Ministers.

MINISTRIES

Office of the President: Av. Julius Nyerere 1780, Maputo; tel. 21491121; fax 21492065; e-mail gabimprensa@teldata.mz; internet www.presidencia.gov.mz.

Office of the Prime Minister: Praça da Marinha Popular, Maputo; tel. 21426861; fax 21426881; internet www.portaldogoverno.gov.mz.

Ministry of Agriculture: Praça dos Heróis Moçambicanos, CP 1406, Maputo; tel. 21460011; fax 21460055; internet www.minag.gov.mz.

Ministry of Culture: Maputo.

Ministry of Education: Av. 24 de Julho 167, CP 34, Maputo; tel. 21492006; fax 21492196; internet www.mec.gov.mz.

Ministry of Energy: Av. 25 de Setembro, 1218 3° andar, CP 1831, Maputo; tel. 21303265; fax 21313971; e-mail asi@me.gov.mz; internet www.me.gov.mz.

Ministry of Environmental Co-ordination: Rua Kassoende 167, Maputo; tel. 21492403; e-mail jwkacha@virconn.com; internet www.micoa.gov.mz.

Ministry of Finance: Praça da Marinha Popular, CP 272, Maputo; tel. 21315000; fax 21306261.

Ministry of Fisheries: Rua Consiglieri Pedroso 347, CP 1723, Maputo; tel. 21431266; fax 21425087; internet www.mozpesca.gov.mz.

MOZAMBIQUE

Ministry of Foreign Affairs and Co-operation: Av. 10 de Novembro, 620–640, Maputo; tel. 21327000; fax 21327020; e-mail minec@minec.gov.mz; internet www.minec.gov.mz.

Ministry of Health: Avs Eduardo Mondlane e Salvador Allende 1008, CP 264, Maputo; tel. 21427131; fax 21427133; e-mail mdgedge@dnsdee.misau.gov.mz; internet www.misau.gov.mz.

Ministry of Industry and Trade: Praça 25 de Junho 300, CP 1831, Maputo; tel. 21352600; fax 214262301; e-mail infomic@mic.gov.mz; internet www.mic.gov.mz.

Ministry of the Interior: Av. Olof Palme 46/48, CP 290, Maputo; tel. 21303510; fax 21420084.

Ministry of Justice: Av. Julius Nyerere 33, Maputo; tel. 21491613; fax 21494264.

Ministry of Labour: Av. 24 de Julho 2351, CP 281, Maputo; tel. 21428301; fax 21421881; internet www.mitrab.gov.mz.

Ministry of Mineral Resources: Av. Fernão de Magalhães 34, 1° andar, CP 294, Maputo; tel. 21314843; fax 320618; e-mail msithole.mirem@tvcabo.co.mz; internet www.mirem.gov.mz.

Ministry of National Defence: Av. Mártires de Mueda 280, CP 3216, Maputo; tel. 21492081; fax 21491619.

Ministry of Planning and Development: Av. Ahmed Sekou Touré 21, CP 4087, Maputo; tel. 21490006; fax 21495477; internet www.mpd.gov.mz.

Ministry of Public Service: Av. Julius Nyerere 3, CP 1225, Maputo; tel. 21485558; fax 21485683; internet www.mfp.gov.mz.

Ministry of Public Works and Housing: Av. Karl Marx 606, CP 268, Maputo; tel. 21430028; fax 21421369; internet www.moph.gov.mz.

Ministry of Science and Technology: Av. Patrice Lumumba 770, Maputo; tel. 21352800; fax 21352860; e-mail secretariado@mct.gov.mz; internet www.mct.gov.mz.

Ministry of State Administration: Rua da Rádio Moçambique 112, CP 4116, Maputo; tel. 21426666; fax 21428565; internet www.mae.gov.mz.

Ministry of Tourism: Av. 25 de Setembro 1018, CP 4101, Maputo; tel. 21306210; fax 21306212; internet www.mitur.gov.mz.

Ministry of Transport and Communications: Av. Mártires de Inhaminga 336, CP 276, Maputo; tel. 21430152; fax 21431028; internet www.mtc.gov.mz.

Ministry of Veterans' Affairs: Rua General Pereira d'Eça 35, CP 3697, Maputo; tel. 21490601.

Ministry of Women's Affairs and Social Welfare Co-ordination: Rua de Tchamba 86, CP 516, Maputo; tel. 21490921; fax 21492757; internet www.mmas.gov.mz.

Ministry of Youth and Sport: Av. 25 de Setembro 529, CP 2080, Maputo; tel. 21312172; fax 21300040; e-mail mjd@tvcabo.co.mz; internet www.mjd.gov.mz.

PROVINCIAL GOVERNORS
(May 2011)

Cabo Delgado Province: ELISEU JOAQUIM MACHAVA.
Gaza Province: RAIMUNDO MAICO DIOMBA.
Inhambane Province: AGOSTINHO ABACAR TRINTA.
Manica Province: ANA COMOANA SOFALA.
Maputo Province: MARIA ELIAS JONAS.
Nampula Province: FELISMINO ERNESTO TOCOLI.
Niassa Province: DAVID NGOANE MARIZANE.
Sofala Province: CARVALHO MUARIA.
Tete Province: ALBERTO CLEMENTINO ANTÓNIO VAQUINA.
Zambézia Province: FRANCISCO ITAE MEQUE.
City of Maputo: LUCÍLIA JOSÉ MANUEL NOTA HAMA.

President and Legislature

PRESIDENT
Presidential Election, 28 October 2009

Candidate	Votes	% of votes
Armando Guebuza (Frelimo)	2,974,627	75.01
Afonso Macacho Marceta Dhlakama (Renamo)	650,679	16.41
Daviz Simango (MDM)	340,579	8.59
Total*	3,965,885	100.00

* Excluding 175,553 invalid votes and 264,655 blank votes.

LEGISLATURE

Assembleia da República: CP 1516, Maputo; tel. 21400826; fax 21400711; e-mail cdi@sortmoz.com.
Chair.: VERONICA MACAMO.

General Election, 28 October 2009

Party	Votes	% of votes	Seats
Frente de Libertação de Moçambique (Frelimo)	2,907,335	74.66	191
Resistência Nacional Moçambicana (Renamo)	688,782	17.69	51
Movimento Democrático de Moçambique (MDM)	152,836	3.93	8
Partido de Liberdade e Desenvolvimento (PLD)	26,929	0.69	—
Partido para a Paz, Democracia e Desenvolvimento (PDD)	22,410	0.58	—
Partido os Verdes de Moçambique (PVM)	19,577	0.50	—
Others	75,989	1.95	—
Total*	3,893,858	100.00	250

* Excluding 143,893 invalid votes and 349,499 blank votes.

Election Commission

Comissão Nacional de Eleições (CNE): Maputo; internet www.stae.org.mz; f. 1997; 13 mems; Pres. JOÃO LEOPOLDO DA COSTA.

Political Organizations

The following political organizations were successful in gaining approval from the Comissão Nacional de Eleições to contest the November 2009 legislative and presidential elections.

Aliança Democrática de Antigos Combatentes para o Desenvolvimento (ADACD): Maputo; f. 2009; coalition comprising the Partido do Progresso do Povo de Moçambique (PPPM), the Partido Socialisa de Moçambique (PSM), the Partido do Congresso Democrático (PACODE) and the Partido da União para a Reconciliação (PUR).

Aliança Independente de Moçambique (ALIMO): f. 1998; Leader KHALID HUSSEIN SIDAT.

Coligação União Eleitoral (UE): f. 1999.

  Partido Ecologista de Moçambique (PEMO): Maputo.

  Partido de Unidade Nacional (PUN): TV Sado 9, Maputo; tel. 21419204; Pres. HIPOLITO COUTO.

Frente de Libertação de Moçambique (Frelimo): Rua Pereira do Lago 10, Bairro de Sommerschield, Maputo; tel. 21490181; fax 21490008; e-mail info@frelimo.org.mz; internet www.frelimo.org.mz; f. 1962 by merger of three nationalist parties; reorg. 1977 as a 'Marxist-Leninist vanguard movement'; in 1989 abandoned its exclusive Marxist-Leninist orientation; Pres. ARMANDO EMÍLIO GUEBUZA.

Movimento Democrático de Moçambique (MDM): Maputo; f. 2009; Pres. DAVIZ SIMANGO; Sec.-Gen. ISMAEL MUSSA.

Movimento Patriótico para Democracia (MPD): f. 2009; Leader MATIAS DIANHANE BANZE.

Partido Ecologista—Movimento da Terra (ECOLOGISTA—MT): Leader JOÃO PEDRO MASSANGO.

Partido Humanitário de Moçambique (Pahumo): Nampula; f. 2010 by fmr mems of the Frente de Libertação de Moçambique (Frelimo), Resistência Nacional Moçambicana (Renamo) and Partido para a Paz, Democracia e Desenvolvimento (PDD); Pres. CORNÉLIO QUIVELA; Sec.-Gen. JOSÉ LOPES.

Partido de Liberdade e Desenvolvimento (PLD): f. 2009; Pres. CAETANO SABILE.

Partido Nacional dos Operários e Camponeses (PANAOC): f. 1998; Leader ARMANDO GIL SUEIA.

Partido para a Paz, Democracia e Desenvolvimento (PDD): Av. Amilcar Cabral 570, Maputo; tel. 21486759; fax 21486765; e-mail pdd@tvcabo.co.mz; internet www.pdd.org.mz; f. 2003; liberal; Leader RAÚL DOMINGOS.

Partido Popular Democrático (PPD): f. 2004; Leader MARCIANO FIJAMA.

Partido de Reconciliação Democrática Social (PRDS): f. 1998; Leader ARMANDO GIL SUEIA.

MOZAMBIQUE

Partido de Reconciliação Nacional (PARENA): Maputo; f. 2004; Leader ANDRÉ BALATE.

Partido de Solidariedade e Liberdade (PAZS): f. 2004; Leader CARLOS INÁCIO COELHO.

Partido Trabalhista (PT): f. 1993; Pres. MIGUEL MABOTE; Sec.-Gen. LUÍS MUCHANGA.

Partido os Verdes de Moçambique (PVM): f. 1997; Leader BRUNO SAPEMBA.

Resistência Nacional Moçambicana (Renamo): Av. Julius Nyerere 2541, Maputo; tel. 21493107; internet www.renamo.org.mz; also known as Movimento Nacional da Resistência de Moçambique (MNR); f. 1976; fmr guerrilla group, in conflict with the Govt between 1976 and Oct. 1992; obtained legal status in 1994; Pres. AFONSO MACACHO MARCETA DHLAKAMA; Sec.-Gen. OSSUFO MOMADE.

União dos Democratas de Moçambique—Partido Popular (UDM—PP): f. 2009; Leader JOSÉ RICARDO VIANA.

União Nacional de Moçambique (UNAMO): f. 1987; breakaway faction of Renamo; social democratic; obtained legal status 1992; Pres. CARLOS ALEXANDRE DOS REIS.

União para a Mudança (UM): f. 1993; Leader FRANCISCO MAINDANE MUARIVA.

Diplomatic Representation

EMBASSIES AND HIGH COMMISSIONS IN MOZAMBIQUE

Algeria: Rua de Mukumbura 121–125, CP 1709, Maputo; tel. 21492070; fax 21490582; e-mail ambalgmaputo@tvcabo.co.mz; Ambassador AHMED LAKHDAR TAZIR.

Angola: Av. Kenneth Kaunda 783, CP 2954, Maputo; tel. 21493139; fax 21493930; Ambassador JOÃO GARCIA BIRES.

Brazil: Av. Kenneth Kaunda 296, CP 1167, Sommerschield, Maputo; tel. 21484800; fax 21484806; e-mail ebrasil@teledata.mz; internet www.ebrasil.co.mz; Ambassador ANTONIO JOSÉ MARIA DE SOUZA E SILVA.

China, People's Republic: Av. Julius Nyerere 3142, CP 4668, Maputo; tel. 21491560; fax 21491196; e-mail chinaemb_mz@mfa.gov.cn; Ambassador HUANG SONGFU.

Congo, Democratic Republic: Av. Kenneth Kaunda 127, CP 2407, Maputo; tel. 21497154; fax 21494929; Ambassador ANTOINE KOLA MASALA NE BEBY.

Congo, Republic: Av. Kenneth Kaunda 783, CP 4743, Maputo; tel. 21490142; Chargé d'affaires a.i. MONSEGNO BASHA OSHEFWA.

Cuba: Av. Kenneth Kaunda 492, CP 387, Maputo; tel. 21492444; fax 21491905; e-mail embacuba.mozambique@tvcabo.co.mz; internet emba.cubaminrex.cu/mozambique; Ambassador RAFAEL ARÍSTIDES JIMENO LÓPEZ.

Denmark: Av. Julius Nyerere 1162, CP 4588, Maputo; tel. 21480000; fax 21480010; e-mail mpmamb@um.dk; internet www.ambmaputo.um.dk; Ambassador JOHNNY FLENTØ.

Egypt: Av. Mao Tse Tung 851, CP 4662, Maputo; tel. 21491118; fax 21491489; e-mail egypt@tvcabo.co.mz; Ambassador ABDEL KADER TANTAWY ES-SAYED.

Finland: Av. Julius Nyerere 1128, CP 1663, Maputo; tel. 21482400; fax 21491662; e-mail sanomat.map@formin.fi; internet www.finland.org.mz; Ambassador KARI ALANKO.

France: Av. Julius Nyerere 2361, CP 4781, Maputo; tel. 21484600; fax 21491727; e-mail ambafrancemz@tvcabo.co.mz; internet www.ambafrance-mz.org; Ambassador CHRISTIAN DAZIANO.

Germany: Rua Damião de Góis 506, CP 1595, Maputo; tel. 21482700; fax 21492888; e-mail info@maputo.diplo.de; internet www.maputo.diplo.de; Ambassador ULRICH KLOECKNER.

Holy See: Av. Kwame Nkrumah 224, CP 2738, Maputo; tel. 21491144; fax 21492217; Apostolic Nuncio Most Rev. ANTONIO ARCARI (Titular Archbishop of Caeciri).

Iceland: Av. Zimbabwe 1694, Maputo; tel. 21483509; fax 21483511; e-mail mozambique@iceida.is; internet www.iceland.org/mo; Chargé d'affaires MARGRÉT EINARSDÓTTIR.

India: Av. Kenneth Kaunda 167, CP 4751, Maputo; tel. 21492437; fax 21492364; e-mail hicomind@tvcabo.co.mz; internet www.hicomind-maputo.org; High Commissioner ASHOK KUMAR AMROHI.

Ireland: Av. Julius Nyerere 3332, Maputo; tel. 21491440; fax 21493023; e-mail maputoembassy@dfa.ie; Ambassador RUAIRÍ DE BURCA.

Italy: Av. Kenneth Kaunda 387, CP 976, Maputo; tel. 21492229; fax 21490503; e-mail ambasciata.maputo@esteri.it; internet www.ambmaputo.esteri.it; Ambassador CARLO LO CASCIO.

Japan: Av. Julius Nyerere 2832, CP 2494, Maputo; tel. 21499819; fax 21498957; internet www.mz.emb-japan.go.jp; Ambassador SUSUMU SEGAWA.

Korea, Democratic People's Republic: Rua da Kaswende 167, Maputo; tel. 21491482; Ambassador PAK KUN GWANG.

Malawi: Av. Kenneth Kaunda 75, CP 4148, Maputo; tel. 21492676; fax 21490224; High Commissioner MARTIN O. KANSICHI.

Mauritius: Rua Dom Carlos 42, Av. de Zimbabwe, Sommerschield, Maputo; tel. 21494624; fax 21494729; e-mail maputo@mail.gov.mu; High Commissioner ALAIN LARIDON.

Netherlands: Av. Kwame Nkrumah 324, CP 1163, Maputo; tel. 21484200; fax 21484248; e-mail map@minbuza.nl; internet www.hollandinmozambique.org; Ambassador FRANS BIJVOET.

Nigeria: Av. Kenneth Kaunda 821, CP 4693, Maputo; tel. and fax 21490991; High Commissioner ALBERT G. PIUS OMOTAIO.

Norway: Av. Julius Nyerere 1162, CP 828, Maputo; tel. 21480100; fax 21480107; e-mail emb.maputo@mfa.no; internet www.norway.org.mz; Ambassador TOVE BRUVIK WESTBERG.

Portugal: Av. Julius Nyerere 720, CP 4696, Maputo; tel. 21490316; fax 21491172; e-mail embaixada@embpormaputo.org.mz; Ambassador MÁRIO GODINHO DE MATOS.

Russia: Av. Vladimir I. Lénine 2445, CP 4666, Maputo; tel. 21417372; fax 21417515; e-mail embrus@tvcabo.co.mz; internet www.mozambique.mid.ru; Ambassador IGOR V. POPOV.

South Africa: Av. Eduardo Mondlane 41, CP 1120, Maputo; tel. 21243000; fax 21493029; e-mail ritterb@dirco.gov.za; High Commissioner D. MOOPELOA.

Spain: Rua Damião de Góis 347, CP 1331, Maputo; tel. 21492048; fax 21494769; e-mail emb.maputo@mae.es; Ambassador EDUARDO LÓPEZ BUSQUETS.

Swaziland: Av. Kwame Nkrumah, CP 4711, Maputo; tel. 21491601; fax 21492117; High Commissioner Prince TSHEKEDI.

Sweden: Av. Julius Nyerere 1128, CP 338, Maputo; tel. 21480300; fax 21480390; e-mail ambassaden.maputo@foreign.ministry.se; internet www.swedenabroad.se/maputo; Ambassador TORVALD AKESSON.

Switzerland: Av. Ahmed Sekou Touré 637, CP 135, Maputo; tel. 21315275; fax 21315276; e-mail map.vertretung@eda.admin.ch; internet www.eda.admin.ch/maputo; Ambassador THERESA ADAM.

Tanzania: Ujamaa House, Av. dos Mártires da Machava 852, CP 4515, Maputo; tel. 21490110; fax 21494782; e-mail ujamaa@zebra.eum.mz; High Commissioner ISSA MOHAMED ISSA.

Timor-Leste: Av. do Zimbabwe 1586, Maputo; tel. 21493644; fax 21493544; e-mail embrdtl@tvcabo.co.mz; Ambassador MARINA RIBEIRO ALKATIRI.

United Kingdom: Av. Vladimir I. Lénine 310, CP 55, Maputo; tel. 21356000; fax 21356060; e-mail bhcgeneral@gmail.com; internet ukinmozambique.fco.gov.uk; High Commissioner ANTHONY SHAUN CLEARY.

USA: Av. Kenneth Kaunda 193, CP 783, Maputo; tel. 21492797; fax 21490114; e-mail maputoirc@state.gov; internet maputo.usembassy.gov; Ambassador LESLIE V. ROWE.

Zambia: Av. Kenneth Kaunda 1286, CP 4655, Maputo; tel. 21492452; fax 21491893; e-mail zhcmmap@zebra.uem.mz; High Commissioner SIMON GABRIEL MWILA.

Zimbabwe: Av. Kenneth Kaunda 816, CP 743, Maputo; tel. 21490404; fax 21492237; e-mail maro@isl.co.mz; Ambassador AGRIPA MUTAMBARA.

Judicial System

The Constitution of November 1990 provides for a Supreme Court and other judicial courts, an Administrative Court, courts-martial, customs courts, maritime courts and labour courts. The Supreme Court consists of professional judges, appointed by the President of the Republic, and judges elected by the Assembleia da República. It acts in sections, as a trial court of primary and appellate jurisdiction, and in plenary session, as a court of final appeal. The Administrative Court controls the legality of administrative acts and supervises public expenditure.

President of the Supreme Court: OSIAS PONDJA.

Attorney-General: AUGUSTO PAULINO.

Conselho Constitucional: Rua Mateus S. Muthemba 493, CP 2372, Maputo; tel. 21487431; fax 21487432; e-mail correiocc@cconstitucional.org.mz; internet www.cconstitucional.org.mz; f. 1990; Pres. LUÍS MONDLANE.

Tribunal Administrativo: Rua Mateus S. Muthemba 65, CP 254, Maputo; tel. 21490170; fax 21498890; e-mail ta@ta.gov.mz; internet www.ta.gov.mz; Pres. MACHATINE PAULO MARRENGANE MUNGUAMBE.

MOZAMBIQUE

Religion

There are an estimated 5m. Christians and 4m. Muslims, as well as small Hindu, Jewish and Bahá'í communities. In 2004 over 100 religious groups were officially registered.

CHRISTIANITY

There are many Christian organizations registered in Mozambique.

Conselho Cristão de Moçambique (CCM) (Christian Council of Mozambique): Av. Agostinho Neto 1584, CP 108, Maputo; tel. 21322836; fax 21321968; f. 1948; 22 mems; Pres. Rt Rev. ARÃO MATSOLO; Gen. Sec. Rev. DINIS MATSOLO.

The Roman Catholic Church

Mozambique comprises three archdioceses and nine dioceses. The number of adherents represented some 22% of the total population.

Bishops' Conference

Conferência Episcopal de Moçambique (CEM), Secretariado Geral da CEM, Av. Paulo Samuel Kankhomba 188/RC, CP 286, Maputo; tel. 21490766; fax 21492174.

f. 1982; Pres. Most Rev. TOMÉ MAKHWELIHA (Archbishop of Nampula).

Archbishop of Beira: Most Rev. JAIME PEDRO GONÇALVES, Cúria Arquiepiscopal, Rua Correia de Brito 613, CP 544, Beira; tel. 23322313; fax 23327639; e-mail arquidbeira@teledata.mz.

Archbishop of Maputo: Most Rev. FRANCISCO CHIMOIO, Paço Arquiepiscopal, Avda Eduardo Mondlane 1448, CP 258, Maputo; tel. 21326240; fax 21321873.

Archbishop of Nampula: Most Rev. TOMÉ MAKHWELIHA, Paço Arquiepiscopal, CP 84, 70100 Nampula; tel. 26213024; fax 26214194; e-mail arquidiocesenpl@teledata.mz.

The Anglican Communion

Anglicans in Mozambique are adherents of the Anglican Church of Southern Africa (formerly the Church of the Province of Southern Africa). There are two dioceses in Mozambique. The Metropolitan of the Province is the Archbishop of Cape Town, South Africa.

Bishop of Lebombo: Rt Rev. DINIS SALOMÃO SENGULANE, CP 120, Maputo; tel. 21734364; fax 21401093; e-mail bispo_sengulane@virconn.com.

Bishop of Niassa: Rev. MARK VAN KOEVERING, CP 264, Lichinga, Niassa; tel. 27112735; fax 27112336; e-mail bishop.niassa@gmail.com.

Other Churches

Baptist Convention of Mozambique: Av. Maguiguane 386, CP 852, Maputo; tel. 2126852; Pres. Rev. BENTO BARTOLOMEU MATUSSE; 78 churches, 25,000 adherents.

The Church of Jesus Christ of the Latter-Day Saints: Maputo; 9 congregations, 1,975 mems.

Evangelical Lutheran Church in Mozambique: Av Kim II Song 520, CP 1488, Sommerschield, Maputo; tel. 212489200; fax 212489201; e-mail mabasso.ielm@tvcabo.co.mz; Sen. Pastor JOSE MABASSO; 12,606 mems (2010).

Free Methodist Church: Pres. Rev. FRANISSE SANDO MUVILE; 214 churches, 21,231 mems.

Igreja Congregational Unida de Moçambique: Rua 4 Bairro 25 de Junho, CP 930, Maputo; tel. 21475820; Pres., Sec. of the Synod A. A. LITSURE.

Igreja Maná: Rua Francisco Orlando Magumbwe 528, Maputo; tel. 21491760; fax 21490896; e-mail adm_mocambique@igrejamana.com; Bishop DOMINGOS COSTA.

Igreja Reformada em Moçambique (IRM) (Reformed Church in Mozambique): CP 3, Vila Ulongue, Anogonia-Tete; f. 1908; Gen. Sec. Rev. SAMUEL M. BESSITALA; 60,000 mems.

Presbyterian Church of Mozambique: Av. Ahmed Sekou Touré 1822, CP 21, Maputo; tel. 21421790; fax 21428623; e-mail ipmoc@zebra.uem.mz; f. 1887; 100,000 adherents; Pres. of Synodal Council Rev. ORIENTE SIBANE.

Seventh-Day Adventist Church: Av. Maguiguana 300, CP 1468, Maputo; tel. and fax 21427200; e-mail victormiconde@teledata.co.mz; 937 churches, 186,724 mems (2004).

Other denominations active in Mozambique include the Church of Christ, the Church of the Nazarene, the Greek Orthodox Church, the United Methodist Church of Mozambique, the Wesleyan Methodist Church, the Zion Christian Church, and Jehovah's Witnesses.

ISLAM

Comunidade Mahometana: Av. Albert Luthuli 291, Maputo; tel. 21425181; fax 21300880; internet www.paginaislamica.8m.com/pg1.htm; Pres. MOMAD BACHIR SULEMAN.

Congresso Islâmico de Moçambique (Islamic Congress of Mozambique): represents Sunni Muslims; Chair. ASSANE ISMAEL MAQBUL.

Conselho Islâmico de Moçambique (Islamic Council of Mozambique): Leader Sheikh AMINUDDIN MOHAMAD.

The Press

DAILIES

Correio da Manha: Av. Filipe Samuel Magaia 528, CP 1756, Maputo; tel. 21305322; fax 21305321; e-mail refi@virconn.com; f. 1997; published by Sojornal, Lda; also publishes weekly Correio Semanal; Dir REFINALDO CHILENGUE.

Diário de Moçambique: Av. 25 de Setembro 1509, 2° andar, CP 2491, Beira; tel. and fax 23427312; f. 1981; under state management since 1991; Dir EZEQUIEL AMBRÓSIO; Editor FARUCO SADIQUE; circ. 5,000 (2003).

Expresso da Tarde: Av. Patrice Lumumba 511, 1° andar, Maputo; tel. 21314912; subscription only; distribution by fax; Dir SALVADOR RAIMUNDO HONWANA.

Mediafax: Av. Amílcar Cabral 1049, CP 73, Maputo; tel. 21301737; fax 21302402; e-mail mediafax@tvcabo.co.mz; f. 1992 by co-operative of independent journalists Mediacoop; news-sheet by subscription only, distribution by fax and internet; Editor BENEDITO NGOMANE.

Notícias de Moçambique: Rua Joaquim Lapa 55, CP 327, Maputo; tel. 21420119; fax 21420575; f. 1926; morning; f. 1906; under state management since 1991; Dir BERNARDO MAVANGA; Editor HILÁRIO COSSA; circ. 12,793 (2003).

Further newspapers available solely in e-mail or fax format include Diário de Notícias and Matinal.

WEEKLIES

Campeão: Av. 24 de Julho 3706, CP 2610, Maputo; tel. and fax 21401810; sports newspaper; Dir RENATO CALDÉIRA; Editor ALEXANDRE ZANDAMELA.

Correio Semanal: Av. Filipe Samuel Magaia 528, CP 1756, Maputo; tel. 21305322; fax 21305312; Dir REFINALDO CHILENGUE.

Desafio: Rua Joaquim Lapa 55, Maputo; tel. 21305437; fax 21305431; Dir ALMIRO SANTOS; Editor BOAVIDA FUNJUA; circ. 3,890 (2003).

Domingo: Rua Joaquim Lapa 55, CP 327, Maputo; tel. 21431026; fax 21431027; f. 1981; Sun.; Dir JORGE MATINE; circ. 15,000 (2007).

Fim de Semana: Rua da Resistência 1642, 1° andar, Maputo; tel. and fax 21417012; e-mail fimdomes@tvcabo.co.mz; internet www.fimdesemana.co.mz; f. 1997; independent.

Savana: Av. Amílcar Cabral 1049, CP 73, Maputo; tel. 21301737; fax 21302402; e-mail savana@mediacoop.co.mz; internet www.savana.co.mz; f. 1994; owned by mediacoop, SA; CEO FERNANDO LIMA; Publr KOK NAM; Editor FERNANDO GONÇALVES; circ. 15,000 (2009).

Tempo: Av. Ahmed Sekou Touré 1078, CP 2917, Maputo; tel. 21426191; f. 1970; magazine; under state management since 1991; Dir ROBERTO UAENE; Editor ARLINDO LANGA; circ. 40,000.

Zambeze: Rua José Sidumo, Maputo; tel. 21302019; Dir ANGELO MUNGUAMBE; circ. 2,000 (2003).

PERIODICALS

Agora: Afrisurvey, Lda, Rua General Pereira d'Eça 200, 1° andar, CP 1335, Maputo; tel. 21494147; fax 21494204; internet www.agora.co.mz; f. 2000; monthly; economics, politics, society; Pres. MARIA DE LOURDES TORCATO; Dir JOVITO NUNES; Editor-in-Chief ERCÍLIA SANTOS; circ. 5,000.

Agricultura: Instituto Nacional de Investigação Agronómica, CP 3658, Maputo; tel. 2130091; f. 1982; quarterly; publ. by Centro de Documentação de Agricultura, Silvicultura, Pecuária e Pescas.

Aro: Av. 24 de Julho 1420, CP 4187, Maputo; f. 1995; monthly; Dir POLICARTO TAMELE; Editor BRUNO MACAME, Jr.

Arquivo Histórico: Av. Filipe Samuel Magaia 715, CP 2033, Maputo; tel. 21421177; fax 21423428; f. 1934; Editor JOEL DAS NEVES TEMBE.

Boletim da República: Av. Vladimir I. Lénine, CP 275, Maputo; govt and official notices; publ. by Imprensa Nacional da Moçambique.

Moçambique–Novos Tempos: Av. Ahmed Sekou Touré 657, Maputo; tel. 21493564; fax 21493590; f. 1992; Dir J. MASCARENHAS.

Mozambiquefile: c/o AIM, Rua da Radio Moçambique, CP 896, Maputo; tel. 21313225; fax 21313196; e-mail aim@aim.org.mz; internet www.sortmoz.com/aimnews; monthly; Dir GUSTAVO MAVIZ; Editor PAUL FAUVET.

MOZAMBIQUE

Mozambique Inview: c/o Mediacoop, Av. Amílcar Cabral 1049, CP 73, Maputo; tel. 21430722; fax 21302402; e-mail inview@mediacoop.co.mz; internet www.mediacoop.odline.com; f. 1994; 2 a month; economic bulletin in English; Editor FRANCES CHRISTIE.

Portos e Caminhos de Ferro: CP 276, Maputo; English and Portuguese; ports and railways; quarterly.

Revista Maderazinco: CP 477, Maputo; tel. 823004770; e-mail maderazinco@yahoo.com; internet www.tropical.maderazinco.co.mz; f. 2002; quarterly; literature; Editor ROGÉRIO MANJATE.

Revista Médica de Moçambique: Instituto Nacional de Saúde, Ministério da Saúde e Faculdade de Medicina, Universidade Eduardo Mondlane, CP 264, Maputo; tel. 21420368; fax 21431103; e-mail mdgedge@malarins.uem.mz; f. 1982; 4 a year; medical journal; Editor MARTINHO DGEDGE.

NEWS AGENCY

Agência de Informação de Moçambique (AIM): Rua da Rádio Moçambique, CP 896, Maputo; tel. 21313225; fax 21313196; e-mail aim@aim.org.mz; internet www.sortmoz.com/aimnews; f. 1975; daily reports in Portuguese and English; Dir GUSTAVO LISSETIANE MAVIE.

Publishers

Arquivo Histórico de Moçambique (AHM): Av. Filipe Samuel Magaia 715, CP 2033, Maputo; tel. 21421177; fax 21423428; internet www.ahm.uem.mz; Dir JOEL DAS NEVES TEMBE.

Central Impressora: c/o Ministério da Saúde, Avs Eduardo Mondlane e Salvador Allende 1008, CP 264, Maputo; tel. 21427131; fax 21427133; owned by the Ministry of Health.

Centro de Estudos Africanos: Universidade Eduardo Mondlane, CP 1993, Maputo; tel. 21490828; fax 21491896; f. 1976; social and political science, regional history, economics; Dir Col SERGIO VIEIRA.

Editora Minerva Central: Rua Consiglieri Pedroso 84, CP 212, Maputo; tel. 2122092; f. 1908; stationers and printers, educational, technical and medical textbooks; Man. Dir J. F. CARVALHO.

Editorial Ndjira, Lda: Av. Ho Chi Minh 85, Maputo; tel. 21300180; fax 21308745; f. 1996.

Empresa Moderna, Lda: Av. 25 de Setembro, CP 473, Maputo; tel. 21424594; f. 1937; fiction, history, textbooks; Man. Dir LOUIS GALLOTI.

Fundo Bibliográfico de Língua Portuguesa: Av. 25 de Setembro 1230, 7° andar, Maputo; tel. 21429531; fax 21429530; e-mail palop@zebra.uem.mz; f. 1990; state owned; Pres. LOURENÇO ROSÁRIO.

Imprensa Universitária: Universidade Eduardo Mondlane, Praça 19 de Maio, Maputo; internet www.uem.mz/imprensa_universitaris; university press.

Instituto Nacional do Livro e do Disco: Av. 24 de Julho 1921, CP 4030, Maputo; tel. 21434870; govt publishing and purchasing agency; Dir ARMÉNIO CORREIA.

Moçambique Editora: Rua Armando Tivane 1430, Bairro de Polana, Maputo; tel. 21495017; fax 21499071; e-mail info@me.co.mz; internet www.me.co.mz; f. 1996; educational textbooks, dictionaries.

Plural Editores: Av. 24 de Julho 414, Maputo; tel. 21486828; fax 21486829; e-mail plural@pluraleditores.co.mz; internet www.pluraleditores.co.mz; f. 2003; educational textbooks; part of the Porto Editora Group.

GOVERNMENT PUBLISHING HOUSE

Imprensa Nacional de Moçambique: Rua da Imprensa, CP 275, Maputo; tel. 21427021; fax 21424858; internet www.imprensanac.gov.mz; part of Ministry of State Administration; Dir VENÂNCIO T. MANJATE.

Broadcasting and Communications

TELECOMMUNICATIONS

Regulatory Authority

Instituto Nacional das Comunicações de Moçambique (INCM): Av. Eduardo Mondlane 123–127, CP 848, Maputo; tel. 21490131; fax 21494435; e-mail info@incm.gov.mz; internet www.incm.gov.mz; regulates post and telecommunications systems; Pres. ISIDORO PEDRO DA SILVA.

Major Telecommunications Companies

TDM's monopoly on the provision of fixed-line services was ended in December 2007, although it remained the sole fixed-line operator at early 2011.

Telecomunicações de Moçambique, SARL (TDM): Rua da Sé 2, CP 25, Maputo; tel. 21431921; fax 21431944; e-mail scatdm@tdm.mz; internet www.tdm.mz; f. 1993; Chair. JOAQUIM RIBEIRO PEREIRA DE CARVALHO; Man. Dir MAMUDO IBRAIMO.

Moçambique Celular (mCel): Rua Belmiro Obadias Muianga 384, CP 1483, Maputo; tel. 21351100; fax 21351117; internet www.mcel.co.mz; f. 1997 as a subsidiary of TDM; separated from TDM in 2003; mobile cellular telephone provider; Pres. SALVADOR ADRIANO.

Vodacom Moçambique (VM): Time Square Complex, Bloco 3, Av. 25 de Setembro, Maputo; tel. 840900000; fax 840901775; e-mail yumna.bhikha@vm.co.mz; internet www.vm.co.mz; f. 2002; mobile cellular telephone provider; owned by Vodacom Group (South Africa) and local shareholders; Chair. SALIMO ABDULA; Man. Dir JOSÉ DOS SANTOS.

BROADCASTING

Radio

Rádio Encontro: Av. Francisco Manyanga, CP 366, Nampula; tel. 26215588; fax 26215878; e-mail radioencontro@teledata.mz.

Rádio Feba Moçambique: Av. Julius Nyerere 441A, CP 1648, Maputo; tel. 21440002; fax 21440009; e-mail febamoz@org.ue.mz; internet febamoz.go.co.mz.

Rádio Maria: Rua Igreja 156A, Machava Sede, Matola, Maputo; tel. 21750505; fax 21752124; e-mail info.moz@radiomaria.org; internet www.radiomaria.org.mz; f. 1995; evangelical radio broadcasts; Dir Fr JOÃO CARLOS H. NUNES.

Rádio Miramar: Rede de Comunicação, Av. Julius Nyerere 1555, Maputo; tel. 21486311; fax 21486813; e-mail jose.guerra@tvcabo.co.mz; owned by Brazilian religious sect, the Universal Church of the Kingdom of God.

Rádio Moçambique: Rua da Rádio 2, CP 2000, Maputo; tel. 21431687; fax 21321816; e-mail sepca_mz@yahoo.com.br; internet www.rm.co.mz; f. 1975; programmes in Portuguese, English and vernacular languages; Chair. RICARDO MADAUANE MALATE.

Rádio Terra Verde: Av. Eduardo Mondlane 2623, 5 andar, Maputo; tel. and fax 21302083; fmrly Voz da Renamo; owned by former rebel movement Renamo; transmitters in Maputo and Gorongosa, Sofala province.

Rádio Trans Mundial Moçambique: Av. Eduardo Mondlane 2998, CP 1526, Maputo; tel. 21440003; fax 21440004; e-mail rtransmundial@isl.co.mz.

Television

Rádio Televisão Klint (RTK): Av. Agostinho Neto 946, Maputo; tel. 21422956; fax 21493306; Dir CARLOS KLINT.

RTP África: Rua Pero de Anaia 248, Maputo; tel. (21) 497344; fax (21) 487347; e-mail rtp.a.moc@teledata.mz.

Televisão Miramar: Rua Pereira Lago 221, Maputo; tel. 21486311; fax 21486813; owned by Brazilian religious sect, the Igrega Universal do Reino de Deus (Universal Church of the Kingdom of God).

Televisão de Moçambique, EP (TVM): Av. 25 de Setembro 154, CP 2675, Maputo; tel. 21308117; fax 21308122; e-mail tvm@tvm.co.mz; internet www.tvm.co.mz; f. 1981; Pres. of Administrative Council ARMINDO CHAVANA.

TV Cabo Moçambique: Av. dos Presidentes 68, CP 1750, Maputo; tel. 21480550; fax 21480501; e-mail tvcabo@tvcabo.co.mz; internet www.tvcabo.co.mz; cable television and internet services in Maputo.

Finance

(cap. = capital; res = reserves; dep. = deposits; m. = million; brs = branches; amounts in meticais, unless otherwise stated)

BANKING

In 2009 there were 14 banks and three microfinance institutions in Mozambique.

Central Bank

Banco de Moçambique: Av. 25 de Setembro 1695, CP 423, Maputo; tel. 21354600; fax 21323247; e-mail gpi@bancomoc.mz; internet www.bancomoc.mz; f. 1975; bank of issue; cap. 248.9m., res 845.2m., dep. 43,260.2m. (Dec. 2009); Gov. ERNESTO GOUVEIA GOVE; 4 brs.

National Banks

Banco de Desenvolvimento e de Comércio de Moçambique, SARL (BDCM): Av. 25 de Setembro 420, 1° andar, sala 8, Maputo; tel. 21313040; fax 21313047; f. 2000; 42% owned by Montepio Geral (Portugal).

Banco Mercantil e de Investimento, SARL (BMI): Av. 24 de Julho 3549, Maputo; tel. 21407979; fax 21408887.

MOZAMBIQUE

Banco Nacional de Investimentos (BNI): Maputo; f. 2010; 49.5% owned by the Govt of Mozambique, 49.5% owned by the Govt of Portugal, 1% owned by Banco Comercial e de Investimentos, SARL; cap. US $500,000m.; Exec. Dir ADRIANO MALEIANE.

Banco Terra: Av. Samora Machel 341 R/C, CP 69, Maputo; tel. 21359300; fax 21316120; internet www.bancoterra.co.mz; f. 2008; provides access to a full range of financial services to the rural and peri urban population in Mozambique; cap. 185m., dep. 100.3m. (Dec. 2007); 30.7% owned by Rabobank (Netherlands); Pres. H. MERTENS; CEO KARL MOURSOND.

Barclays Bank Mozambique SA: Av. 25 de Setembro 1184, CP 757, Maputo; tel. 21351700; fax 21323470; internet www.bancoaustral.co.mz; f. 1995 as Banco Popular de Desenvolvimento (BPD); name changed to Banco Austral SARL in 1998; name changed as above in 2007; 80% owned by Amalgamated Banks of South Africa, 20% owned by União, Sociedade e Participacões, SARL, which represents employees of the bank; cap. 315m., res 311.7m., dep. 5,347.5m. (Dec. 2008); Chair. CASIMIRO FRANCISCO; Man. Dir PAUL NICE; 58 brs and agencies.

BCI Fomento (BCI) (Banco Comercial e de Investimentos, SARL): Edif. John Orr's, Av. 25 de Setembro 1465, CP 4745, Maputo; tel. 21353700; fax 21309831; e-mail bci@bci.co.mz; internet www.bci.co.mz; f. 1996; renamed as above following 2003 merger between Banco Comercial e de Investimentos and Banco de Fomento; 42% owned by Caixa Geral de Depósitos (Portugal), 30% Banco Português de Investimento; cap. 319.8m., res 516.7m., dep. 11,996.4m. (Dec. 2006); Chair. ABDUL MAGID OSMAN; 68 brs.

ICB-Banco Internacional de Comércio, SARL: Av. 25 de Setembro 1915, Maputo; tel. 21311111; fax 21314797; e-mail icbm@icbank-mz.com; internet www.icbank-mz.com; f. 1998; cap. and res 44,923,748m., total assets 164,773,569m. (Dec. 2003); Chair. JOSEPHINE SIVARETNAM; CEO LEE SANG HUAT; 4 brs.

Millennium bim: Av. 25 de Setembro 1800, CP 865, Maputo; tel. 21354496; fax 21354415; e-mail scheman@millenniumbim.co.mz; internet www.millenniumbim.co.mz; f. 1995; name changed from Banco Internacional de Moçambique in 2005; 66.7% owned by Banco Comercial Português, 17.4% by the state; cap. 741.0m., res 2,291.0m., dep. 29,744.7m. (Dec. 2008); Pres. MÁRIO FERNANDES DA GRAÇA MACHUNGO; CEO JOÃO FILIPE DE FIGUEIREDO JÚNIOR; 86 brs.

Moza Banco: Av. Kwame Nkrumah 97, CP 1012, Maputo; tel. 21480800; fax 21480801; e-mail info@mozabanco.co.mz; internet www.mozabanco.co.mz; f. 2008; cap. US $15m.; Chair. PRAKASH RATILAL.

Novo Banco, SARL: Av. do Trabalho 750, Maputo; tel. and fax 21407705; f. 2000; cap. and res 51,995m., total assets 108,847m. (Dec. 2003).

Standard Bank, SARL (Moçambique): Praça 25 de Junho 1, CP 2086, Maputo; tel. 21352500; fax 21426967; e-mail camal.daude@standardbank.co.mz; internet www.standardbank.co.mz; f. 1966 as Banco Standard Totta de Mozambique; 96.0% owned by Stanbic Africa Holdings, UK; cap. 174.0m., res 430.6m., dep. 14,362.1m. (Dec. 2007); Man. Dir ANTONIO COUTINHO; 24 brs.

Foreign Banks

African Banking Corporation (Moçambique), SA: ABC House, Av. Julius Nyerere 99, Polana, CP 1445, Maputo; tel. 21482100; fax 21487474; e-mail abcmoz@africanbankingcorp.com; internet www.africanbankingcorp.com; f. 1999; 100% owned by African Banking Corpn Holdings Ltd (Botswana); fmrly BNP Nedbank (Moçambique), SARL; changed name as above after acquisition in 2002; cap. 148m., res 101m., dep. 3,598.9m. (Dec. 2009); Chair. BENJAMIM ALFREDO; Man. Dir JOSEPH SIBANDA; 2 brs.

African Banking Corporation Leasing, SARL: Rua da Imprensa 256, 7° andar, CP 4447, Maputo; tel. 21300451; fax 21431290; e-mail ulcmoz@mail.tropical.co.mz; 66% owned by African Banking Corpn Holdings Ltd (Botswana); fmrly ULC (Moçambique); changed name as above in 2002; total assets US $1.8m. (Dec. 1998); Chair. ANTÓNIO BRANCO; Gen. Man. VICTOR VISEU.

Mauritius Commercial Bank (Moçambique) SA: Av. Friedrich Engels 400, Maputo; tel. 21481900; fax 21498675; e-mail contact@mcbmozambique.com; internet www.mcbmozambique.com; f. 1999; name changed as above in June 2007; 81% owned by Mauritius Commercial Bank Group; total assets US $46,777m. (Dec. 2006); Chair. PIERRE GUY NOEL; Gen. Man. PETER HIGGINS.

DEVELOPMENT FUND

Fundo de Desenvolvimento Agrário: Rua Joaquim Lapa 192, 2° andar, Maputo; tel. 21302814; fax 21430044; e-mail antonio.andre@ffa.org.mz; f. 2006 to provide credit for small farmers and rural co-operatives; promotes agricultural and rural devt; Sec. ANTÓNIO ANDRÉ.

STOCK EXCHANGE

Bolsa de Valores de Moçambique: Av. 25 de Setembro 1230, Prédio 33, 5° andar, Maputo; tel. 21308826; fax 21310559; e-mail bvm@bvm.co.mz; internet www.bolsadevalores.co.mz; Chair. Dr JUSSUB NURMAMAD.

INSURANCE

In December 1991 the Assembleia da República approved legislation terminating the state monopoly of insurance and reinsurance activities. In 2005 five insurance companies were operating in Mozambique.

Companhia de Seguros de Moçambique, IMPAR: Rua da Imprensa 625, Prédio 33, Maputo; tel. 21429695; fax 21430640; f. 1992; Pres. INOCÊNCIO A. MATAVEL; Gen. Man. MANUEL BALANCHO.

Empresa Moçambicana de Seguros, EE (EMOSE): Av. 25 de Setembro 1383, CP 1165, Maputo; tel. 21356300; fax 21424526; e-mail comercial@emose.co.mz; internet www.emose.co.mz; f. 1977 as state insurance monopoly; took over business of 24 fmr cos; 80% govt-owned, 20% private; cap. 150m.; Chair. VENÂNCIO MONDLANE.

Seguradora Internacional de Moçambique: Av. 25 Setembro 1800, Maputo; tel. 21430959; fax 21430241; e-mail simseg@zebra.uem.mz; Pres. MÁRIO FERNANDES DA GRAÇA MACHUNGO.

Trade and Industry

GOVERNMENT AGENCIES

Centro de Promoção de Investimentos (CPI) (Investment Promotion Centre): Rua da Imprensa 332, CP 4635, Maputo; tel. 21313295; fax 21313325; e-mail cpi@cpi.co.mz; internet www.cpi.co.mz; f. 1987; encourages domestic and foreign investment and IT ventures with foreign firms; evaluates and negotiates investment proposals; Dir LOURENÇO SAMBO.

Instituto do Algodão de Moçambique (IAM): Av. Eduardo Mondlane 2221, 1° andar, CP 806, Maputo; tel. 21424264; fax 21430679; e-mail iampab@zebra.uem.mz; internet www.iam.gov.mz; responsible for promotion and devt of the cotton industry; Dir NORBERTO MALAMBE.

Instituto do Fomento do Cajú (INCAJU): Maputo; internet incaju.gov.mz; national cashew institute; Dir FILOMENA MAIOPUE.

Instituto Nacional de Açúcar (INA): Rua da Gávea 33, CP 1772, Maputo; tel. 21326550; fax 21427436; e-mail gpsca.ina@tvcabo.co.mz; Chair. ARNALDO RIBEIRO.

Instituto Nacional de Petróleo (INP): Av. Fernão de Magalhães 34, 1°/2°andar, CP 4724, Maputo; tel. 21320935; fax 21320932; e-mail info@inp.gov.mz; internet www.inp.gov.mz; f. 2005; regulates energy sector; Pres. ARSÉNIO MABOTE.

Instituto para a Promoção de Exportações (IPEX): Av. 25 de Setembro 1008, 2° andar, CP 4487, Maputo; tel. 21307257; fax 21307256; e-mail ipex@tvcabo.co.mz; internet www.ipex.gov.mz; f. 1990 to promote and co-ordinate national exports abroad; Pres. Dr JOÃO MACARINGUE.

Unidade Técnica para a Reestruturação de Empresas (UTRE): Rua da Imprensa 256, 7° andar, CP 4350, Maputo; tel. 21426514; fax 21421541; implements restructuring of state enterprises; Dir MOMADE JUMAS.

CHAMBERS OF COMMERCE

Câmara de Comércio de Moçambique (CCM): Rua Mateus Sansão Muthemba 452, CP 1836, Maputo; tel. 21491970; fax 21490428; e-mail ccm@tvcabo.co.mz; internet www.ccmoz.org.mz; f. 1980; Pres. JOÃO AMÉRICO MPFUMO; Sec.-Gen. MANUEL NOTIÇO.

Mozambique-USA Chamber of Commerce: Rua Matheus Sansão Muthemba 452, Maputo; tel. 21492904; fax 21492739; e-mail ccmusa@tvcabo.co.mz; internet www.ccmusa.co.mz; f. 1993; Sec. PETER MUCHIRI.

South Africa-Mozambique Chamber of Commerce (SAMOZACC): e-mail info@samozacc.co.za; internet www.samozacc.co.za; f. 2005; Chair. (Mozambique) ANTÓNIO MATOS.

TRADE ASSOCIATIONS

Associação das Indústrias do Cajú (AICAJU): Maputo; cashew processing industry asscn; Chair. CARLOS COSTA; 12 mem. cos.

Confederação das Associações Económicas de Moçambique (CTA): Rua de Castanheda, CP 2975, Maputo; tel. 21491914; fax 21493094; internet www.cta.org.mz; Pres. SALIMO ABDULA; Exec. Dir SÉRGIO CHITARÁ; 58 mem. cos.

MOZAMBIQUE   *Directory*

STATE INDUSTRIAL ENTERPRISES

Empresa Nacional de Hidrocarbonetos de Moçambique (ENH): Av. Fernão de Magalhães 34, CP 4787, Maputo; tel. 21429456; fax 21421608; controls concessions for petroleum exploration and production; Dir MÁRIO MARQUES.

Petróleos de Moçambique (PETROMOC): Praça dos Trabalhadores 9, CP 417, Maputo; tel. 21427191; fax 21430181; internet www.petromoc.co.mz; f. 1977 to take over the Sonarep oil refinery and its associated distribution co; formerly Empresa Nacional de Petróleos de Moçambique; state directorate for liquid fuels within Mozambique, incl. petroleum products passing through Mozambique to inland countries; CEO JOSÉ MATEUS MUÁRIA KATHUPA.

UTILITIES

Electricity

Electricidade de Moçambique (EDM): Av. Agostinho Neto 70, CP 2447, Maputo; tel. 21490636; fax 21491048; e-mail ligacaoexpresso@edm.co.mz; internet www.edm.co.mz; f. 1977; 100% state-owned; production and distribution of electric energy; in 2004 plans were announced to extend EDM grid to entire country by 2020, at an estimated cost of US $700m.; Pres. MANUEL JOÃO CUAMBE; Dir PASCOAL BACELA; 2,700 employees.

Companhia de Transmissão de Moçambique, SARL (MOTRACO) (Mozambique Transmission Co): Prédio JAT, 4° andar, Av. 25 de Setembro 420, Maputo; tel. 21313427; fax 21313447; e-mail asimao@motraco.co.mz; internet www.motraco.co.mz; f. 1998; jt venture between power utilities of Mozambique, South Africa and Swaziland; electricity distribution; Gen. Man. FRANCIS MASAWI.

Water

Direcção Nacional de Águas: Av. 25 de Setembro 942, 9° andar, CP 1611, Maputo; tel. 21420469; fax 21421403; e-mail watco@zebra.uem.mz; internet www.dnaguas.gov.mz; Dir AMÉRICO MUIANGA.

TRADE UNIONS

Freedom to form trade unions, and the right to strike, are guaranteed under the 1990 Constitution.

Confederação de Sindicatos Livres e Independentes de Moçambique (CONSILMO): Sec.-Gen. JEREMIAS TIMANE.

Organização dos Trabalhadores de Moçambique—Central Sindical (OTM—CS) (Mozambique Workers' Organization—Trade Union Headquarters): Rua Manuel António de Sousa 36, Maputo; tel. 21426786; fax 21421671; internet www.otm.org.mz; f. 1983; Pres. CARLOS MUCAREIA; Sec.-Gen. ALEXANDRE MUNGUAMBE; 15 affiliated unions with over 94,000 mems including:

Sindicato Nacional dos Empregadores Bancários (SNEB): Av. Fernão de Magalhães 785, 1° andar, CP 1230, Maputo; tel. 21428627; fax 21303274; e-mail snebmoz@tvcabo.co.mz; internet www.snebmoz.co.mz; f. 1992; Sec.-Gen. ROLANDO LOPES NGULUBE.

Sindicato Nacional da Função Pública (SINAFP): Av. Ho Chi Min 365, Maputo; Sec.-Gen. LEONEL COANA.

Sindicato Nacional dos Profissionais da Estiva e Ofícios Correlativos (SINPEOC): Av. Paulo Samuel Kakhomba 1568, Maputo; tel. and fax 21309535; Sec.-Gen. BENTO MADALA MAUNGUE.

Sindicato Nacional dos Trabalhadores Agro-Pecuários e Florestais (SINTAF): Av. 25 de Setembro 1676, 1° andar, CP 4202, Maputo; tel. 21306284; f. 1987; Sec.-Gen. EUSÉBIO LUÍS CHIVULELE.

Sindicato Nacional dos Trabalhadores da Aviação Civil, Correios e Comunicações (SINTAC): Av. 25 de Setembro 1509, 2° andar, Porta 5, Maputo; tel. 21309574; e-mail sintacnacional@tdm.co.mz; Sec.-Gen. ARMANDO MAZOIO.

Sindicato Nacional dos Trabalhadores do Comércio, Seguros e Serviços (SINECOSSE): Av. Ho Chi Minh 365, 1° andar, CP 2142, Maputo; tel. 21428561; Sec.-Gen. AMÓS JÚNIOR MATSINHE.

Sindicato Nacional dos Trabalhadores da Indústria do Açúcar (SINTIA): Av. das FPLM 1912, Maputo; tel. 21461772; fax 21461975; f. 1989; Sec.-Gen. ALEXANDRE CÂNDIDO MUNGUAMBE.

Sindicato Nacional dos Trabalhadores da Indústria Alimentar e Bebidas (SINTIAB): Av. Eduardo Mondlane 1267, CP 394, Maputo; tel. 21324709; fax 21324123; f. 1986; Gen. Sec. SAMUEL FENIAS MATSINHE.

Sindicato Nacional dos Trabalhadores da Indústria de Cajú (SINTIC): Rua do Jardim 574, 4° andar, Maputo; tel. 21477732; Sec.-Gen. BOAVENTURA MONDLANE.

Sindicato Nacional dos Trabalhadores da Indústria Metalúrgica, Metalomecânica e Energia (SINTIME): Av. Samora Machel 30, 6°, Maputo; Sec.-Gen. MATEUS MUIANGA.

Sindicato Nacional dos Trabalhadores da Indústria Química e Afins (SINTIQUIAF): Av. Olof Palme 255, CP 4439, Maputo; tel. 21320288; fax 21321096; e-mail sintiquigra@tvcabo.co.mz; f. 2008 by merger of SINTEVEC and SINTIQUIGRA; clothing, leather and footwear workers' union; Sec.-Gen. JÉSSICA GUNE.

Sindicato Nacional dos Trabalhadores da Marinha Mercante e Pesca (SINTMAP): Rua Joaquim Lapa 22, 5° andar, No. 6, Maputo; tel. 21305593; Sec.-Gen. DANIEL MANUEL NGOQUE.

Sindicato Nacional dos Trabalhadores dos Portos e Caminhos de Ferro (SINPOCAF): Av. Guerra Popular, esquina Av. 25 de Setembro, CP 2158, Maputo; tel. 21403912; fax 21303839; Sec.-Gen. SAMUEL ALFREDO CHEUANE.

Sindicato Nacional de Jornalistas (SNJ): Av. 24 de Julho 231, Maputo; tel. 21492031; fax 823015912; f. 1978; Sec.-Gen. EDUARDO CONSTANTINO.

Transport

Improvements to the transport infrastructure since the signing of the Acordo Geral de Paz (General Peace Agreement) in 1992 have focused on the development of 'transport corridors', which include both rail and road links and promote industrial development in their environs. The Beira Corridor, with rail and road links and a petroleum pipeline, runs from Manica, on the Zimbabwean border, to the Mozambican port of Beira, while the Limpopo Corridor joins southern Zimbabwe and Maputo. Both corridors form a vital outlet for the land-locked southern African countries, particularly Zimbabwe. The Maputo Corridor links Ressano Garcia in South Africa to the port at Maputo, and the Nacala Corridor runs from Malawi to the port of Nacala. Two further corridors were planned: the Mtwara Development Corridor was to link Mozambique, Malawi, Tanzania and Zambia, while the Zambezi Corridor was to link Zambézia province with Malawi.

RAILWAYS

In 2003 the total length of track was 3,114 km, of which 2,072 km was operational. There are both internal routes and rail links between Mozambican ports and South Africa, Swaziland, Zimbabwe and Malawi. During the hostilities many lines and services were disrupted. Improvement work on most of the principal railway lines began in the early 1980s. In the early 2000s work commenced on upgrading the railway system and private companies were granted non-permanent concessions to upgrade and run the railways. In 2009 plans were announced for the construction of a line connecting Moatize with the Malawian railway south of Blantyre. There were also plans for a line to connect Mutarara with Malema. Reconstruction of the 670-km Sena railway line linking Beira with Moatize was expected to be completed in 2011.

Beira Railway Co: Dondo; f. 2004; 51% owned by Rites & Ircon (India), 49% owned by CFM; rehabilitating and managing Sena and Zimbabwe railway lines.

Portos e Caminhos de Ferro de Moçambique (CFM): Praça dos Trabalhadores, CP 2158, Maputo; tel. 21327173; fax 21427746; e-mail cfmnet@cfmnet.co.mz; internet www.cfmnet.co.mz; fmrly Empresa Nacional dos Portos e Caminhos de Ferro de Moçambique; privatized and restructured in 2002; Chair. ROSÁRIO MUALEIA; comprises four separate systems linking Mozambican ports with the country's hinterland, and with other southern African countries, including South Africa, Swaziland, Zimbabwe and Malawi:

CFM—Centro (CFM—C): Largo dos CFM, CP 236, Beira; tel. 23321000; fax 23329290; lines totalling 994 km linking Beira with Zimbabwe and Malawi, as well as link to Moatize (undergoing rehabilitation); Exec. Dir JOAQUIM VERÍSSIMO.

CFM—Norte: Av. do Trabalho, CP 16, Nampula; tel. 26214320; fax 26212034; lines totalling 872 km, including link between port of Nacala with Malawi; management concession awarded to Nacala Corridor Development Co (a consortium 67% owned by South African, Portuguese and US cos) in January 2000; Dir of Railways MANUEL MANICA.

CFM—Sul: Praça dos Trabalhadores, CP 2158, Maputo; tel. and fax 21430894; lines totalling 1,070 km linking Maputo with South Africa, Swaziland and Zimbabwe, as well as Inhambane–Inharrime and Xai-Xai systems; Exec. Dir JOAQUIM ZUCULE.

CFM—Zambézia: CP 73, Quelimane; tel. 24212502; fax 24213123; 145-km line linking Quelimane and Mocuba; Dir ORLANDO J. JAIME.

ROADS

In 2006 there were an estimated 17,805 km of roads in Mozambique, of which 5,083 km were paved. Under its Road Sector Strategic Plan for 2007–11, the Administraçao Nacional de Estradas pledged to

MOZAMBIQUE

improve or redevelop 5,590 km of roads in 40 separate projects at a cost of some US $786m.

Administração Nacional de Estradas (ANE): Av. de Moçambique 1225, CP 1294, Maputo; tel. 21475157; fax 21475290; internet www.ane.gov.mz; f. 1999 to replace the Direcção Nacional de Estradas e Pontes; implements government road policy through the Direcção de Estradas Nacionais (DEN) and the Direcção de Estradas Regionais (DER); Pres. Eng. CARLOS FRAGOSO; Dir-Gen. PAULO ELIAS.

SHIPPING

Mozambique has three main sea ports, at Nacala, Beira and Maputo, while inland shipping on Lake Niassa and the river system was underdeveloped. At December 2009 Mozambique's registered merchant fleet consisted of 129 vessels, totalling 41,300 grt.

Portos e Caminhos de Ferro de Moçambique (CFM-EP): Praça dos Trabalhadores, CP 2159, Maputo; tel. 21427173; fax 21427746; e-mail cfmnet@cfmnet.co.mz; internet www.cfmnet.co.mz; fmrly Empresa Nacional dos Portos e Caminhos de Ferro de Moçambique; privatized and restructured in 2002; Chair. ROSARIO MUALEIA; Port Dir CFM-Sul Dr JOAQUIM ZUCULE; Port Dir CFM-Norte FRANCO CATUTULA; Port Dir CFM-Centro Dr JOAQUIM VERÍSSIMO.

Agência Nacional de Frete e Navegação (ANFRENA): Rua Consiglieri Pedroso 396, CP 492, Maputo; tel. 21427064; fax 21427822; Dir FERDINAND WILSON.

Empresa Moçambicana de Cargas, SARL (MOCARGO): Rua Consiglieri Pedroso 430, 1°–4° andares, CP 888, Maputo; tel. 21428318; fax 21302067; e-mail msamaral@mocargo.com; internet www.mocargo.co.mz; f. 1982; shipping, chartering and road transport; Man. Dir MANUEL DE SOUSA AMARAL.

Manica Freight Services, SARL: Praça dos Trabalhadores 51, CP 557, Maputo; tel. 21356500; fax 21431084; e-mail fdimande@manica.co.mz; internet www.manica.co.mz; international shipping agents; Man. Dir AHMAD Y. CHOTHIA.

Maputo Port Development Co, SARL (MPDC): Port Director's Building, Porto de Maputo, CP 2841, Maputo; tel. 21313920; fax 21313921; e-mail info@portmaputo.com; internet www.portmaputo.com; f. 2002; private sector international consortium with concession (awarded 2003) to develop and run port of Maputo until 2018; Pres. RONNIE HOLTSHAUSEN; CEO JORGE FERRAZ.

Mozline, SARL: Av. Karl Marx 478, 2° andar, Maputo; tel. 21303078; fax 21303073; e-mail mozline1@virconn.com; shipping and road freight services.

Navique, SARL: Av. Mártires de Inhaminga 125, CP 145, Maputo; tel. 21312705; fax 21426310; e-mail smazoi@navique.co.mz; internet www.navique.com; f. 1985; Chair. J. A. CARVALHO; Man. Dir PEDRO VIRTUOSO.

CIVIL AVIATION

In 2010 there were five international airports.

Instituto de Aviação Civil de Moçambique (IACM): Maputo; civil aviation institute; Dir ANÍBAL SAMUEL.

Air Corridor, SARL: Av. Eduardo Mondlane 945, Nampula; tel. 26213333; fax 26213355; e-mail fagadit@aircorridor.com.mz; internet www.aircorridor.co.mz; f. 2004; domestic carrier and cargo transport; Chair. MOMADE AQUI RAJAHUSSEN; Commercial Dir FARUK ALY GADIT.

Linhas Aéreas de Moçambique, SARL (LAM): Aeroporto Internacional de Maputo, CP 2060, Maputo; tel. 21465137; fax 21422936; e-mail jrviegas@lam.co.mz; internet www.lam.co.mz; f. 1980; 80% state-owned; operates domestic services and international services to South Africa, Tanzania, Mayotte, Zimbabwe and Portugal; Pres. JOSÉ RICARDO ZUZARTE VIEGAS.

Sociedade de Transportes Aéreos/Sociedade de Transporte e Trabalho Aéreo, SARL (STA/TTA): Rua da Tchamba 405, CP 665, Maputo; tel. 21491765; fax 21491763; e-mail sta.tta@sta.co.mz; internet www.sta.co.mz; f. 1991; domestic airline and aircraft charter transport services; acquired Empresa Nacional de Transporte e Trabalho Aéreo in 1997; Chair. ROGÉRIO WALTER CARREIRA; Man. Dir JOSÉ CARVALHEIRA.

Other airlines operating in Mozambique include Serviço Aéreo Regional, South African Airlines, Moçambique Expresso, SA—Airlink International, Transairways (owned by LAM) and TAP Air Portugal.

Tourism

Tourism, formerly a significant source of foreign exchange, ceased completely following independence, and was resumed on a limited scale in 1980. There were 1,000 visitors in 1981 (compared with 292,000 in 1972 and 69,000 in 1974). With the successful conduct of multi-party elections in 1994 and the prospect of continued peace, there was considerable scope for development of this sector. By the late 1990s tourism was the fastest growing sector of the Mozambique economy, and in 2000 it was announced that a comprehensive tourism development plan was to be devised, assisted by funding from the European Union. In 2005 there were 5,030 hotels in Mozambique. The opening of the Great Limpopo Transfrontier Park, linking territories in Mozambique with South Africa and Zimbabwe, was expected to attract additional tourists. Further national parks were planned. There were 2.6m. foreign tourist arrivals in 2008 and tourism receipts in that year totalled US $213m.

Fundo Nacional do Turismo: Av. 25 de Setembro 1203, CP 4758, Maputo; tel. 21307320; fax 21307324; internet www.futur.org.mz; f. 1993; hotels and tourism; CEO Dr ZACARIAS SUMBANA.

Defence

As assessed at November 2010, total active armed forces were estimated at 11,200 (army 10,000, navy 200, air force 1,000).

Defence Expenditure: Budgeted at an estimated 2,020,000m. meticais in 2009.

Commander-in-Chief of the Armed Forces: Pres. ARMANDO EMÍLIO GUEBUZA.

Chief of General Staff: Brig. PAULO MACARINGUE.

Deputy Chief of General Staff: Gen. OLIMPIO CAMBONA.

Education

Education is officially compulsory for seven years from the age of six. Primary schooling begins at six years of age and lasts for seven years. It is divided into two cycles, of five and two years. Secondary schooling, from 13 years of age, lasts for six years and comprises two cycles, each lasting three years. According to UNESCO estimates, in 2008/09 82% of children in the relevant age-group were enrolled at primary schools (males 84%; females 80%), while secondary enrolment included only 9% of children in the relevant age-group (males 9%; females 9%). There were 28,298 students in tertiary education in 2004/05. Two privately owned higher education institutions, the Catholic University and the Higher Polytechnic Institute, were inaugurated in 1996. In 2003 it was announced that education would no longer take place solely in Portuguese, but also in some Mozambican dialects. In 2005 an estimated 5,000 new teachers were to be recruited. In 2006 some US $39m. was granted by international donors to develop educational resources. Education was allocated 20.2% of total current expenditure in that year.

MYANMAR

Introductory Survey

LOCATION, CLIMATE, LANGUAGE, RELIGION, FLAG, CAPITAL

The Republic of the Union of Myanmar (Pyidaungsu Thammada Myanmar Naingngandaw—formerly Burma) lies in the north-west region of South-East Asia, between the Tibetan plateau and the Malay peninsula. The country is bordered by Bangladesh and India to the north-west, by the People's Republic of China and Laos to the north-east and by Thailand to the south-east. The climate is tropical, with an average temperature of 27°C (80°F) and monsoon rains from May to October. Average annual rainfall is between 2,500 mm and 5,000 mm in the coastal and mountainous regions of the north and east, but reaches a maximum of only 1,000 mm in the lowlands of the interior. Temperatures in Yangon (Rangoon) are generally between 18°C (65°F) and 36°C (97°F). The official language is Myanmar (Burmese), and there are also a number of tribal languages. About 87% of the population are Buddhists. There are animist, Muslim, Hindu and Christian minorities. A new national flag (proportions 2 by 3), which was officially introduced in October 2010, consists of three equal horizontal stripes, of yellow, green and red, with a large, five-pointed white star in the centre. In 2006 the functions of the capital city were transferred from Yangon to the new administrative centre of Nay Pyi Taw.

CONTEMPORARY POLITICAL HISTORY

Historical Context

Burma (now Myanmar) was annexed to British India during the 19th century, and became a separate British dependency, with a limited measure of self-government, in 1937. Japanese forces invaded and occupied the country in 1942, and Japan granted nominal independence under a Government of anti-British nationalists. The Burmese nationalists later turned against Japan and aided Allied forces to reoccupy the country in 1945. They formed a resistance movement, the Anti-Fascist People's Freedom League (AFPFL), led by Gen. Aung San, which became the main political force after the defeat of Japan. Aung San was assassinated in July 1947 and was succeeded by U Nu. On 4 January 1948 the Union of Burma became independent, outside the Commonwealth, with U Nu as the first Prime Minister.

Domestic Political Affairs

During the first decade of independence Burma was a parliamentary democracy, and the Government successfully resisted revolts by communists and other insurgent groups. In 1958 the ruling AFPFL split into two wings, the 'Clean' AFPFL and the 'Stable' AFPFL, and U Nu invited the Army Chief of Staff, Gen. Ne Win, to head a caretaker Government. Elections to the Chamber of Deputies in February 1960 gave an overwhelming majority to U Nu, leading the 'Clean' AFPFL (which was renamed the Union Party in March), and he resumed office in April. Despite its popularity, the U Nu administration proved ineffective, and in March 1962 Gen. Ne Win staged a coup to depose U Nu (who was subsequently detained until 1966). The new Revolutionary Council suspended the Constitution and instituted authoritarian control through the government-sponsored Burma Socialist Programme Party (BSPP). All other political parties were outlawed in March 1964.

During the next decade a more centralized system of government was created, in an attempt to win popular support and to nationalize important sectors of the economy. A new Constitution, aiming to transform Burma into a democratic socialist state, was approved in a national referendum in December 1973. The Constitution of the renamed Socialist Republic of the Union of Burma, which came into force in January 1974, confirmed the BSPP as the sole authorized political party, and provided for the establishment of new organs of state. Elections to a legislative People's Assembly took place in January 1974, and in March the Revolutionary Council was dissolved. Ne Win (who, together with other senior army officers, had become a civilian in 1972) was elected President by the newly created State Council. However, Burma's economic problems increased, and in 1974 there were riots over food shortages and social injustices. Student demonstrations took place in 1976, as social problems increased. Following an attempted coup by members of the armed forces in July, the BSPP adopted a new economic programme in 1977 in an effort to quell unrest.

An election in January 1978 gave Ne Win a mandate to rule for a further four years, and in March he was re-elected Chairman of the State Council. In May 1980 a general amnesty was declared for political dissidents, including exiles (as a result of which U Nu, who had been living abroad since 1969, returned to Burma). Gen. San Yu, formerly the Army Chief of Staff, was elected Chairman of the State Council in November 1981. In August 1985 Ne Win was re-elected Chairman of the BSPP. Elections for a new People's Assembly were held in November.

In August 1987, owing to the country's increasing economic problems, an unprecedented extraordinary meeting, comprising the BSPP Central Committee, the organs of the State Council and other state bodies, was convened. Ne Win proposed a review of the policies of the past 25 years. In September the announcement of the withdrawal from circulation of high-denomination banknotes, coupled with rice shortages, provoked student riots (the first civil disturbances since 1976). Owing to continued economic deprivation, further student unrest in Rangoon (now Yangon) in March 1988 culminated in major protests, which were violently suppressed by riot police under the direct command of Sein Lwin, the BSPP Joint General Secretary. Further demonstrations started in June. The Government's response was again extremely brutal, and many demonstrators were killed. In July vain attempts were made to counter the growing unpopularity of the Government, including the removal from office of the Minister of Home and Religious Affairs and the head of the People's Police Force in Rangoon. (The Prime Minister, also, was subsequently dismissed.) Finally, at an extraordinary meeting of the BSPP Congress, Ne Win resigned as party Chairman and asked the Congress to approve the holding of a national referendum on the issue of a multi-party political system. The Congress rejected the referendum proposal and the resignation of four other senior members of the BSPP, including that of Sein Lwin, but accepted the resignation of San Yu, the BSPP Vice-Chairman.

The subsequent election of Sein Lwin to the chairmanship of the BSPP, and his appointment as Chairman of the State Council and as state President, provoked further student-led riots. In August 198 martial law was imposed on Rangoon, and thousands of unarmed demonstrators were reportedly massacred by the armed forces throughout the country. Sein Lwin was forced to resign after only 17 days in office. He was replaced by the more moderate Dr Maung Maung, hitherto the Attorney-General, whose response to the continued rioting was conciliatory. Martial law was revoked; Brig.-Gen. Aung Gyi (formerly a close colleague of Ne Win, now an outspoken critic of the regime), who had been detained under Sein Lwin, was released; and permission was given for the formation of the All Burma Students' Union. However, demonstrations continued, and by September students and Buddhist monks had assumed control of the municipal government of many towns. In that month U Nu requested foreign support for his formation of an 'alternative government'. The emerging opposition leaders, Aung Gyi, Aung San Suu Kyi (daughter of Gen. Aung San) and Gen. (retd) Tin Oo (a former Chief of Staff and Minister of Defence), then formed the National United Front for Democracy, which was subsequently renamed the League for Democracy and later the National League for Democracy (NLD).

At an emergency meeting of the BSPP Congress in September 1988 it was decided that free elections would be held within three months and that members of the armed forces, police and civil service could no longer be affiliated to a political party. Now distanced from the BSPP, the armed forces, led by Gen. (later Senior Gen.) Saw Maung, seized power on 18 September, ostensibly to maintain order until multi-party elections could be arranged. A State Law and Order Restoration Council (SLORC) was formed, all state organs (including the People's Assembly, the State Council and the Council of Ministers) were abolished, demonstrations were banned and a night-time curfew was

MYANMAR

imposed nation-wide. Despite these measures, opposition movements demonstrated in favour of an interim civilian government, and it was estimated that more than 1,000 demonstrators were killed in the first few days following the coup. The SLORC announced the formation of a nine-member Government, with Saw Maung as Minister of Defence and of Foreign Affairs and subsequently also Prime Minister. Although ostensibly in retirement, it was widely believed that Ne Win retained a controlling influence over the new leaders. The new Government changed the official name of the country to the Union of Burma (as it had been before 1973). The law maintaining the BSPP as the sole party was abrogated, and new parties were encouraged to register for the forthcoming elections. The BSPP registered as the National Unity Party (NUP). In December 1988, owing to disagreements with Suu Kyi, Aung Gyi was expelled from the NLD after he had founded the Union National Democracy Party. Tin Oo was elected as the new NLD Chairman. U Nu returned to prominence as the leader of a new party, the League for Democracy and Peace (LDP), and also commanded the support of the new Democracy Party.

From October 1988 to January 1989 Suu Kyi campaigned in townships and rural areas across the nation, and elicited much popular support, despite martial law regulations banning public gatherings of five or more people. In March 1989 there were anti-Government demonstrations in many cities, in protest at the increasing harassment of Suu Kyi and the arrest of many NLD supporters and activists. In July Suu Kyi cancelled a rally to commemorate the anniversary of the assassination of her father, owing to the threat of government violence; two days later, both she and Tin Oo were placed under house arrest.

In May 1989 electoral legislation was ratified, providing for multi-party elections to be held on 27 May 1990. In June 1989 the SLORC changed the official name of the country to the Union of Myanmar (Pyidaungsu Myanmar Naingngandaw), on the grounds that the previous title conveyed the impression that the population consisted solely of ethnic Burmans. The transliteration to the Roman alphabet of many other place names was changed, to correspond more closely with pronunciation.

In December 1989 Tin Oo of the NLD was sentenced by a military tribunal to three years' imprisonment, with hard labour, for his part in the anti-Government uprising in 1988. U Nu was disqualified from contesting the forthcoming general election, owing to his refusal to dissolve the 'alternative government' that he had proclaimed in September 1988. In January 1990 U Nu and 13 members of the 'alternative government' were placed under house arrest. Five members subsequently resigned and were released. Later in January Suu Kyi was barred from contesting the election, owing to her 'entitlement to the privileges of a foreigner' (a reference to her marriage to a British citizen) and her alleged involvement with insurgents.

Martial law was revoked in eight townships in November 1989, and in a further 10 in February 1990. It was reported that during 1989 tens of thousands of residents had been forcibly evicted from densely populated areas in major cities, where anti-Government demonstrations had received much support, and resettled in rural areas. In January and April 1989 Amnesty International, the human rights organization, published information regarding violations of rights in Myanmar, including the torture and summary execution of dissident students. This was followed by criticism from the UN.

In May 1990 93 parties presented a total of 2,296 candidates to contest 492 seats at the general election for the new assembly; there were also 87 independent candidates. The voting was reported to be free and orderly. The NLD received 59.9% of the total votes and won 396 of the 485 seats that were, in the event, contested; the NUP obtained 21.2% of the votes, but won only 10 seats. The NLD demanded the immediate opening of negotiations with the SLORC, and progress towards popular rule. However, the SLORC announced that the election had been intended to provide not a legislature but a Constituent Assembly. The resulting draft constitution would require endorsement by referendum and subsequent approval by the SLORC. In July the SLORC announced Order 1/90, stating that the SLORC would continue as the de facto Government until a new constitution was drafted. Elected members of the NLD responded (independently of their leadership) with the 'Gandhi Hall Declaration', urging that an assembly of all elected representatives be convened by September.

In September 1990 the SLORC arrested six members of the NLD, including the acting Chairman, Kyi Maung, and acting Secretary-General, Chit Hlaing, on charges of passing state secrets to unauthorized persons. Kyi Maung was replaced as acting NLD Chairman by Aung Shwe. Influential monks agreed to support the proposed declaration of a provisional government in Mandalay, but the plan was abandoned after government troops surrounded monasteries. The SLORC subsequently ordered the dissolution of all Buddhist organizations involved in anti-Government activities (all except nine sects) and empowered military commanders to impose death sentences on rebellious monks. More than 50 senior members of the NLD were arrested, and members of all political parties were required to endorse Order 1/90: in acquiescing, the NLD effectively nullified its demand for an immediate transfer of power.

In December 1990 a group of candidates who had been elected to the Constituent Assembly fled to Manerplaw, on the Thai border, and announced a 'parallel government', the National Coalition Government of the Union of Burma (NCGUB), with the support of the Democratic Alliance of Burma (DAB), a broadly based organization uniting ethnic rebel forces with student dissidents and monks. The self-styled Prime Minister of the NCGUB was Sein Win, the leader of the Party for National Democracy (PND) and a cousin of Suu Kyi. The NLD leadership expelled members who had taken part in the formation of the 'parallel government', despite broad support within the NLD. The SLORC subsequently deregistered the PND, the LDP and two other parties and annulled the elected status of the eight members of the NCGUB. In April 1991 Gen. (later Senior Gen. or Field Marshal) Than Shwe, the Vice-Chairman of the SLORC and the Deputy Chief of Staff of the armed forces, officially announced that the SLORC would not transfer power to the Constituent Assembly, as the political parties involved were 'subversive' and 'unfit to rule'. In response to continued pressure from the SLORC, the NLD carried out a complete reorganization of the party's Central Executive Committee, replacing Suu Kyi as General Secretary with the previously unknown U Lwin, and Tin Oo with the former acting Chairman, Aung Shwe.

In July 1991 the SLORC retroactively amended electoral legislation adopted in May 1989, extending the grounds on which representatives of the Assembly could be disqualified or debarred from contesting future elections to include convictions for breaches of law and order. More than 80 elected representatives had already died, been imprisoned or been forced into exile since the election in May 1990. In September 1991 Ohn Gyaw was appointed Minister of Foreign Affairs in place of Saw Maung, becoming the first civilian in the Cabinet.

In October 1991 Suu Kyi was awarded the Nobel Peace Prize. In December Sein Win attended the presentation of the award to Suu Kyi's family in Norway. In Myanmar students who staged demonstrations (the first since 1989) to coincide with the ceremony were dispersed by security forces. It was subsequently announced that Suu Kyi had been expelled from the NLD. In January 1992 Tin Oo's expulsion from the NLD was announced.

Three additional members were appointed to the SLORC in January 1992, and the Cabinet was expanded to include seven new ministers, four of whom were civilians. The changes, together with a reorganization of senior ministers in February, were widely perceived to benefit the Chief of Military Intelligence, Maj.-Gen. (later Lt-Gen.) Khin Nyunt (First Secretary of the SLORC). Khin Nyunt was widely regarded as the most powerful member of the SLORC, owing to Ne Win's continued patronage. Divisions within the ruling junta between Khin Nyunt and the more senior officers were becoming increasingly evident. In March Than Shwe replaced Saw Maung as Minister of Defence, and in April Saw Maung retired as Chairman of the SLORC and Prime Minister for reasons of ill health. Than Shwe was subsequently appointed to both these posts. The SLORC promptly ordered the release of several political prisoners, including U Nu, and announced that Suu Kyi could receive a visit from her family. In June the first meeting took place between members of the SLORC and opposition representatives from the remaining 10 legal parties, in preparation for the holding of a national convention to draft a new constitution.

In January 1993 the National Convention finally assembled, but was adjourned several times during the year, owing to the objections of the opposition members to SLORC demands for a leading role in government for the armed forces. The SLORC reacted to what it regarded as opposition intransigence by suspending any conciliatory gestures (which had included the revocation of two martial law decrees and amnesties for a total of 534 political prisoners), and many arrests were reported. Towards the end of the year the Chairman of the National Convention's Convening Committee, Aung Toe (the Chief Justice), announced (seemingly without grounds) that a consensus existed in favour of the SLORC's demands, which comprised: the inclusion, in both the lower and upper chambers of a proposed parliament, of military personnel (to be appointed by the Commander-in-Chief of the Armed Forces); the election of the President by an electoral college; the independent self-administration of the armed forces; and the right of the Commander-in-Chief to exercise state power in an emergency (effectively granting legitimate status to a future coup).

In September 1993 an alternative mass movement to the NUP (which had lost credibility through its election defeat) was formed to establish a civilian front through which the armed forces could exercise control. The Union Solidarity and Development Association (USDA), the aims of which were indistinguishable from those of the SLORC, was not officially registered as a political party, thus enabling civil servants to join the organization, with the incentive of considerable privileges.

In January 1994 the National Convention reconvened, and in April it was adjourned, having adopted guidelines for three significant chapters of the future Constitution. The changes envisaged Myanmar being renamed the Republic of the Union of Myanmar, comprising seven states (associated with some of the country's minority ethnic groups) and seven divisions in central and southern Myanmar (largely representing the areas populated by the ethnic Bamars—Burmans). The Republic would be headed by an executive President, elected by the legislature for five years; proposals for the disqualification of any candidate with a foreign spouse or children would prevent Suu Kyi from entering any future presidential election. Reconvening in September, the Convention again stressed that the central role of the military (as 'permanent representatives of the people') be enshrined in the new Constitution. It was proposed that legislative power be shared between a bicameral Pyidaungsu Hluttaw (Union Parliament) and divisional and state assemblies, all of which were to include representatives of the military. The Pyidaungsu Hluttaw was to comprise the Pyithu Hluttaw (House of Representatives) and the Amyotha Hluttaw (House of Nationalities): the former would comprise 330 elected deputies and 110 members of the armed forces, and would be elected for five years. The latter would be composed of equal numbers of representatives from the proposed seven regions and seven states of the Republic, as well as members of the military, and was to comprise a maximum of 224 deputies. A general election was scheduled for September 1997 (but never held). The session of the National Convention was adjourned in April 1995.

In September 1994, following mediation by a senior Buddhist monk, Suu Kyi was permitted to leave her home to meet Than Shwe and Khin Nyunt. In October Suu Kyi held a second meeting with senior SLORC members. In November it was reported that Suu Kyi had met other detained members of the NLD, including Tin Oo. In January 1995 the SLORC announced that Suu Kyi would be freed only when the new Constitution had been completed; Suu Kyi simultaneously rejected suggestions that she might reach a compromise with the SLORC on the terms for her release. In February leading members of the SLORC held talks in Yangon with an envoy of the UN Secretary-General. In March the Government released 31 political prisoners, including Tin Oo and Kyi Maung.

In July 1995 Suu Kyi was unexpectedly granted an unconditional release from house arrest, whereupon she made a conciliatory speech, urging negotiations with the SLORC and a spirit of compromise. Suu Kyi swiftly reconciled the early leaders of the NLD with the new leadership, which had compromised with the SLORC. Hundreds of supporters gathered daily to hear Suu Kyi speak outside her house in Yangon. Suu Kyi was reinstated as General Secretary of the NLD in October, in a reorganization of the party's executive committee; Tin Oo and Kyi Maung were named Vice-Chairmen. Aung Shwe, who had led the 'legal' NLD and represented the party at the National Convention, was retained as party Chairman. Meanwhile, in August Win Htein, Suu Kyi's personal assistant, was arrested and sentenced to seven years' imprisonment (subsequently doubled) for allegedly conspiring with groups in India to destabilize the country.

In November 1995 the National Convention reconvened. The NLD attended the opening session, but later withdrew when the SLORC ignored its requests to expand the Convention to make it truly representative. (Suu Kyi was, of course, not a member of the National Convention.) Denouncing the Convention as illegitimate and undemocratic, the NLD for the first time appealed for international support for its cause. The SLORC, which had already begun to imprison NLD supporters for petty crimes, reacted strongly to the NLD boycott, officially expelling the party from the Convention.

In May 1996 more than 260 members of the NLD (mostly delegates elected to the Constituent Assembly in 1990) were arrested prior to the party's first congress. The majority were detained for the duration of the congress, which only 18 NLD members were able to attend. The congress resolved to draft an alternative constitution. In June the SLORC intensified its action against the NLD with an order banning any organization that held illegal gatherings or obstructed the drafting of the new Constitution by the National Convention; members of a proscribed party could be liable to between five and 20 years' imprisonment. In September police erected road-blocks around Suu Kyi's house, and again detained NLD activists, in order to prevent the holding of a further congress. Suu Kyi's telephone line was disconnected, and she was unable to deliver her regular weekend speech for the first time since her release from house arrest. From October the road-block was resumed each week with the purpose of preventing access to Suu Kyi's speech. The SLORC recommenced talks with NLD officials later that month, but relations quickly deteriorated following an attack on vehicles in which Suu Kyi and other NLD leaders were travelling.

In October 1996 student action in Yangon, in protest against the detention and brutal treatment of fellow students, prompted further repression and numerous arrests (among those detained was Kyi Maung). This was followed in early December by the largest pro-democracy demonstration since 1988, involving more than 2,000 students. The gathering was dispersed peacefully, although some 600 demonstrators were temporarily detained. Smaller student demonstrations continued sporadically until mid-December, when Suu Kyi was briefly confined to her home, and tanks were deployed in Yangon; university establishments were closed indefinitely. At the end of December 1996 some 50 members of the Communist Party of Burma (CPB) and of the NLD were arrested in connection with the protests. In January 1997 14 people, including at least five NLD members, were convicted of involvement in the unrest and sentenced to seven years' imprisonment.

In January 1997 Suu Kyi was allowed to deliver her weekly speech for the first time in three months. However, the SLORC imposed new restrictions on media access to Suu Kyi, and barricades remained outside her home. In March there were further arrests of NLD members, together with an increased army presence in several towns. Also in March a series of attacks on Muslim targets by Buddhist monks took place across the country. The attacks were rumoured to have been perpetrated by opponents within the regime of Myanmar's bid to join the Association of Southeast Asian Nations (ASEAN, see p. 206), in an attempt to alienate its Muslim-dominated countries.

In April 1997 a bomb attack at the home of the Second Secretary of the SLORC, Lt-Gen. Tin Oo (as distinct from Tin Oo of the NLD), resulted in the death of his daughter. The Government attributed the bombing to anti-Government groups based in Japan. The attack was rumoured to be related to a power struggle between Khin Nyunt, who was increasingly regarded as a moderate, and the more conservative Commander-in-Chief of the Army and Vice-Chairman of the SLORC, Gen. Maung Aye, who commanded the support of Tin Oo. The detention of NLD members increased during 1997, while government propaganda vilifying the opposition grew ever more frequent and Suu Kyi's freedom of movement and association remained restricted. In July, however, Khin Nyunt invited the NLD Chairman, Aung Shwe, to a meeting, which constituted the first senior-level contact between the SLORC and the NLD since the release of Suu Kyi from house arrest in July 1995. The SLORC granted permission for an NLD congress to be held in September 1997.

The State Peace and Development Council

On 15 November 1997 the ruling junta unexpectedly announced the dissolution of the SLORC and its replacement with the State Peace and Development Council (SPDC). The 19-member SPDC comprised exclusively military personnel; younger regional military commanders were included (largely, it appeared, to prevent them from developing local power bases), while the four most senior members of the SLORC retained their positions at the head of the new junta: Than Shwe was appointed Chairman, Maung Aye Vice-Chairman, Khin Nyunt First Secretary and Tin Oo Second Secretary. A number of former members of the SLORC were ostensibly promoted to an 'Advisory Group', which was subsequently abolished; five members of this group, who had also held positions in the Cabinet, were placed under house arrest in December, pending investigations into allegations of corruption. The SPDC immediately implemented a reorganization of the Cabinet. The new 40-member Cabinet included 25 former ministers, but, in contrast to the SLORC (the members of which had virtually all held cabinet portfolios), only one member of the SPDC, Than Shwe, was appointed to serve concurrently as a cabinet minister. Several supporters of Maung Aye were removed from power. In December the SPDC announced a further cabinet reorganization and the appointment of a new Chairman (the Minister of Hotels and Tourism, Maj.-Gen. Saw Lwin) and Vice-Chairmen of the National Convention Convening Commission; however, the Convention, which had adjourned in March 1996, remained in recess.

Harassment and persecution of members of the NLD and other opposition movements continued. In March 1998 40 people were arrested on charges of complicity in a conspiracy allegedly led by the exiled All-Burma Students Democratic Front (ABSDF, an armed movement formed in 1988 by students within the DAB, which had officially renounced its armed struggle in 1997) to assassinate leaders of the military junta and initiate terrorist attacks on government offices and foreign embassies. The ABSDF, which rejected the allegations, was accused of complicity with the NLD. Six of the accused were sentenced to death at the end of April 1998. However, the SPDC unexpectedly authorized an NLD party congress, attended by 400 delegates, at the end of May to celebrate the eighth anniversary of the general election. In June the NLD demanded that the SPDC reconvene the Pyithu Hluttaw, in accordance with the results of the 1990 election, by 21 August. Some 40 elected NLD representatives were detained at the end of June, and others were forced to sign pledges restricting their freedom of movement. In July the SPDC ordered NLD elected representatives to report to their local police station twice a day and confined them to their townships. Suu Kyi attempted to visit NLD members outside the city, but was repeatedly obstructed by road-blocks. She was forcibly returned to her home by security personnel after a six-day protest in her car in July, following government refusals to comply with her demands for the release of detained opposition members and the commencement of substantive dialogue with the NLD. In a further incident, in August, Suu Kyi was returned to her home by ambulance after spending 13 days in her car.

Shortly before the NLD's prescribed deadline of 21 August 1998 for convening the Pyithu Hluttaw, the SPDC published an official rejection of the NLD's demands. The NLD responded by declaring its intention unilaterally to convene a 'People's Parliament', which would include elected representatives of all the ethnic minority groups. Student demonstrations took place in Yangon (for the first time since December 1996), in support of the NLD's demands. In September 1998 thousands of students staged anti-Government demonstrations, which were dispersed by security forces. Arrests of opposition activists increased dramatically, and by early September 193 elected NLD members of the Pyithu Hluttaw and hundreds of party supporters had been detained. In the same month a 10-member Representative Committee, led by Suu Kyi and Aung Shwe, was established by the NLD to act on behalf of the 'People's Parliament' until a legislature could be convened under the 1990 election law. The Committee asserted that no laws enacted by the military junta over the previous 10 years had legal authority, and also demanded the immediate and unconditional release of all political prisoners. Four parties representing Shan, Mon, Arakanese and Zomi ethnic groups expressed their support for the 'People's Parliament', together with the ABSDF. Also in September 1998, 15 senior military officers were reportedly arrested for allegedly planning to meet with Suu Kyi, and a number of large pro-Government rallies were held in Yangon. The NLD condemned the alleged use of coercion, intimidation and threats by government military intelligence units to secure the involuntary resignations of vast numbers of NLD members and the closure of a number of regional party headquarters. Following the death in custody in October of one of its members, the NLD formally denounced the junta's treatment of detained opposition party members in a letter to Than Shwe. (In August of the same year an elected representative of the NLD, Saw Win, had died in prison while serving an 11-year term of imprisonment, the third NLD member of the Pyithu Hluttaw to die in custody.) In October UN Assistant Secretary-General Alvaro de Soto met with SPDC leaders and also with Suu Kyi during a visit to Myanmar. He reportedly offered large-scale financial and humanitarian aid to the junta in exchange for the initiation of substantive dialogue with the NLD. During October and November about 300 opposition members were released by the Government; however, a further 500 were believed to remain in detention.

In March 1999, despite requests from several foreign Governments, the ruling junta refused to grant a visa to Suu Kyi's terminally ill husband, Michael Aris. The junta instead encouraged Suu Kyi to visit Aris in the United Kingdom; however, Suu Kyi declined to leave Myanmar for fear that she would not be allowed to return. Following Aris's death later that month, more than 1,000 supporters of Suu Kyi were permitted to attend a Buddhist ceremony at her home to mark her husband's demise.

In April 1999 the UN adopted a unanimous resolution deploring the escalation in the persecution of the democratic opposition in Myanmar. Nevertheless, the harassment and intimidation of NLD members continued, with the resignations from the party of nearly 300 members reported in July; further resignations were reported in November and in January 2000. In December 1999 it was reported that an elected representative of the People's Assembly, Maung Maung Myint, had been forced to resign by the ruling SPDC. The lack of political progress by the NLD in 1999 led to the formation of a breakaway faction of the party by a prominent party member, Than Tun, who was subsequently expelled from the NLD.

In August 1999 a series of protests was staged by opposition supporters to mark the anniversary of the massacre of thousands of pro-democracy demonstrators by the military Government in 1988. In October 1999 the Supreme Court rejected a claim by the NLD that its activities had been 'continuously disrupted, prevented and destroyed' and that hundreds of its members had been illegally detained. In April 2000 Suu Kyi alleged that more than 40 youth members of the NLD had been arrested by the SPDC for their involvement in party activities.

In August 2000 Suu Kyi and 14 NLD colleagues attempted to visit members of the party in Kunyangon, a town just outside Yangon. The group was stopped by a military road-block, but refused to return home. A nine-day confrontation finally ended with Suu Kyi and the NLD members being forcibly returned to Yangon. Suu Kyi and eight others were kept under house arrest for the next two weeks. In September the SPDC ordered a raid on the NLD headquarters, and detained a number of other party leaders in their homes. Undeterred, the NLD announced that it was to draft a new constitution for the country, an act declared illegal in 1996 and punishable by 20 years' imprisonment. Later in the month Suu Kyi attempted to leave Yangon again, this time by train to Mandalay, only to be told that all trains were full. The NLD leader was once again returned home and placed under house arrest, while NLD Vice-Chairman Tin Oo and eight other party workers were taken to a government 'guest house'. Pressure on the NLD increased in October 2000, when a deadline for an eviction order for the party to vacate its premises expired.

Despite the sustained suppression of the opposition party, the SPDC's treatment of its political rivals became markedly more liberal from mid-2000. In July the SPDC reportedly allowed 60,000 university students to resume their education. However, the undergraduate universities were relocated in the suburbs, in order to avoid demonstrations in the city centres that might draw in other civilians. Razali Ismail, a Malaysian diplomat newly appointed as the UN Secretary-General's Special Envoy to Myanmar, was allowed access to Suu Kyi during a four-day visit in October 2000, and in the same month James Mawdsley, a British human rights activist sentenced to 17 years' imprisonment in Myanmar in September 1999, was released.

Conciliation between the SPDC and the NLD was confirmed in January 2001, when it was announced that the two parties had been holding secret talks since the previous October, the first senior-level discussions between the opponents since 1994. Lt-Gen. Khin Nyunt met with Suu Kyi several times. Some analysts feared that the resumption of discussions was merely a ploy by the Government to attract foreign investment, a view supported by the initial lack of progress.

In a further placatory gesture in January 2001, the SPDC ordered the media to stop the regular acrimonious attacks on Suu Kyi and the NLD. At the end of January the SPDC released NLD Vice-Chairman Tin Oo and 84 other party supporters, who had been detained since Suu Kyi's attempted train journey in September 2000. A few days later a delegation of the European Union (EU, see p. 270) was permitted to meet with Suu Kyi, as was the UN Special Rapporteur on the situation of human rights in Myanmar, Dr Paulo Sérgio Pinheiro, in April 2001.

A bomb explosion in May 2001 reportedly killed 12 people and injured eight others in a market in Mandalay. In the same month it was reported that religious riots in Toungoo, Bago Division,

MYANMAR

Introductory Survey

had led to the deaths of 24 Buddhist monks. The disturbances spread to other towns, prompting allegations that the SPDC had instigated the riots in an attempt to divert public attention from political and economic problems.

In February 2001 SPRC Second Secretary Lt-Gen. Tin Oo, the Council's fourth most powerful member, was killed in a helicopter crash, amid rumours of assassination; Tin Oo had survived two previous attempts on his life. In November SPDC Third Secretary Lt-Gen. Win Myint and Deputy Prime Minister Tin Hla were dismissed. Both had expressed only muted support for the ongoing talks with Suu Kyi, and it was hoped that their replacement would facilitate the attainment of a political settlement. Two days later the SPDC announced that five government ministers were to retire, including Deputy Prime Ministers Rear-Adm. Maung Maung Khin and Lt-Gen. Tin Tun. Meanwhile, in mid-2001, as discussions continued, the Government ordered the release of a number of NLD members from prison and permitted the reopening of the NLD headquarters and several branch offices in Yangon. In August the release of NLD Chairman Aung Shwe and Vice-Chairman Tin Oo was hailed as an indication of progress. Shortly afterwards Razali Ismail held further talks with Suu Kyi during a visit to Yangon. Ismail revisited the country in November, and expressed satisfaction with the progress that had been made.

In January 2002 it was reported that Suu Kyi had met privately with Gen. Than Shwe for the first time since 1994, raising hopes that the two sides might be close to reaching a breakthrough. However, in February 2002 international pressure on the SPDC to release all remaining political prisoners (an estimated 1,500, according to Amnesty International) and begin a more substantive dialogue with the NLD increased, prompted by the release of a critical report by the US Government. The Myanma Government responded by releasing five further detainees and expressing its confidence that a successful conclusion to the negotiation process was imminent.

In March 2002 the son-in-law and three grandsons of Ne Win were arrested on charges of plotting to overthrow the Government. It was alleged that they had intended to abduct three government leaders and force them to form a figurehead government under Ne Win's influence. Four senior military officials—the Commander-in-Chief of the Air Force, Maj.-Gen. Myint Swe, the Chief of Police, Maj.-Gen. Soe Win, and two regional commanders—were dismissed and questioned in connection with the attempted coup. Ne Win and his daughter, Sandar Win, were placed under house arrest. Despite suspicions that the coup allegations were linked to internal conflicts within the military, owing to the insubstantial nature of the evidence gathered to support the charges, in September Ne Win's four relatives were convicted of high treason and sentenced to death. They entered appeals against the sentences. In December Ne Win himself died while under house arrest.

In May 2002 Suu Kyi was released from house arrest. The SPDC stated that her release was unconditional and that it would not attempt to impose any restrictions upon her travel. Suu Kyi travelled to Mandalay without incident in June. In August Razali Ismail returned to the country with the intention of promoting further political dialogue between the NLD and the SPDC, but made little progress. Meanwhile, Suu Kyi challenged the SPDC to prove its commitment to the achievement of democracy by ordering the release of all political prisoners. In the following month a delegation from the EU visited Myanmar and met with Suu Kyi, but failed to secure a meeting with any members of the SPDC. In November the junta announced the release of 115 prisoners, the largest number to date.

In early 2003 representatives from Amnesty International were permitted to enter Myanmar for the first time and to hold talks with Suu Kyi. Following the visit, the human rights organization condemned Myanmar's judicial system. Meanwhile, 12 political activists in the country were arrested on suspicion of planning anti-Government activities. In February it was reported that Suu Kyi wanted economic sanctions to be maintained against the Myanma Government until it began a meaningful dialogue with the opposition. In the same month it was announced that Lt-Gen. Soe Win would assume the previously vacant post of Second Secretary of the SPDC. Meanwhile, the Minister of Health, Maj.-Gen. Ket Sein, and the Minister of Finance and Revenue, Khin Maung Thein, were permitted to retire. They were replaced, respectively, by Dr Kyaw Myint and Maj.-Gen. Hla Tun. In the following month Paulo Sérgio Pinheiro restated a UN demand that the junta release all remaining political prisoners, estimated to number 1,200, and enter into serious dialogue with the opposition. Later in March a bomb exploded in Yangon, killing one person, during celebrations to commemorate Armed Forces Day. An unexploded bomb was also discovered near the US embassy on the same day.

In April 2003 Suu Kyi issued a rare public criticism of the SPDC for refusing to enter into any substantive dialogue with the opposition. In May 10 members of the NLD were imprisoned on charges that they had organized public protests and participated in clandestine activities. Later in May the political situation deteriorated further when violent confrontations occurred in the northern town of Ye-u, between government supporters and opposition members travelling with an entourage conveying Suu Kyi. While the SPDC insisted that the violence had been provoked by the opposition, it was subsequently reported that Suu Kyi and her supporters had been ambushed and attacked by pro-Government forces. Around 80 members of the entourage were thought to have died. On the following day it was reported that Suu Kyi had been taken into 'protective custody' by the SPDC; meanwhile, the headquarters of the NLD, together with NLD offices across the country, were closed down, 17 other members of the NLD were also detained, and all universities under the control of the Ministry of Education were shut indefinitely. Razali Ismail proceeded with a planned visit to Myanmar in June, when he was permitted to meet with Suu Kyi. The junta's detention of Suu Kyi prompted widespread international criticism. At a meeting of ASEAN ministers of foreign affairs held in mid-June the organization departed from its traditional policy of non-interference in the affairs of other member states, urging Suu Kyi's release and a peaceful transition to democratic practices. Later in June, following the failure of its appeal to the SPDC for the release of Suu Kyi, the country's largest aid donor, Japan, suspended all economic aid to Myanmar. In July the Government announced that it had freed 91 of the NLD activists detained after the violence of May and permitted a delegation from the International Committee of the Red Cross (ICRC) to visit Suu Kyi; the delegates subsequently confirmed that she was in good health.

In July 2003 it was reported that three cabinet ministers, including Minister of Industry (No. 1) Aung Thaung, had been dismissed. In August a major reorganization of the Government was announced, in which the former First Secretary of the SPDC, Lt-Gen. Khin Nyunt, replaced Senior-Gen. Than Shwe as Prime Minister. However, Than Shwe remained Chairman of the SPCD and retained the defence portfolio. Lt-Gen. Soe Win became First Secretary and was replaced as Second Secretary by Lt-Gen. Thein Sein. Khin Nyunt subsequently announced that the Government intended to reconvene the National Convention, which had been in recess since 1996.

In September 2003 it was announced that Suu Kyi had returned to her home and was being held under house arrest, having undergone major surgery in hospital. A visit to Myanmar by Razali Ismail in the following month failed to secure her release or to end the political deadlock. Paulo Sérgio Pinheiro returned to the country in October. In November five members of the NLD's Central Executive Committee, who had been held in connection with the violence in May, were released. In December nine people were sentenced to death, having been convicted of high treason; they were among 12 people arrested in July for allegedly plotting to overthrow the ruling junta. (Four of the nine people subsequently had their sentences commuted to two years' imprisonment on appeal, and that of another was reduced to five years' imprisonment, while the remaining four were to serve sentences of life imprisonment.) In January 2004 the release of a further 26 members of the NLD was announced; in February NLD Vice-Chairman Tin Oo was placed under house arrest, having been imprisoned since May 2003. Also in January 2004, following a meeting with government officials, representatives from 25 ethnic groups and alliances rejected the proposed 'road map' to democracy outlined by the Prime Minister in August 2003 and reiterated demands for the Government to begin talks with the opposition. However, following a visit to Myanmar in March 2004, Razali Ismail expressed confidence that the SPDC would adhere to the 'road map'. In April the SPDC released the NLD's Chairman, Aung Shwe, and its Secretary, U Lwin, who had both been under house arrest since May 2003, and allowed the party's headquarters to reopen.

The National Convention was reconvened in May 2004, despite a boycott by some ethnic minority groups and the NLD, which demanded that the SPDC release Suu Kyi and Tin Oo from house arrest and reopen the party's branch offices. More than 1,000 delegates attended the opening session, which was chaired by SPDC Second Secretary Lt-Gen. Thein Sein. It was stressed that the Convention was to be a continuation of the discussions held between 1993 and 1996, at which a number of constitutional provisions had already been drafted. Strict regulations governing the conduct of the delegates were imposed by the SPDC. The Convention was adjourned in July 2004. In August courts in Yangon and Mandalay refused to accept petitions from the NLD for the release of Suu Kyi and Tin Oo, and for the reopening of the party's branch offices. Shortly afterwards the UN Secretary-General, Kofi Annan, urged the Myanma Government to free Suu Kyi and to hold substantive talks with the NLD and other political parties, noting that the National Convention would otherwise lack credibility. Meanwhile, Razali Ismail had been unable to return to Myanmar since his visit in March, as the authorities had rejected his requests for a visa. In September four members of the NLD were reportedly convicted of threatening national security and were sentenced to seven years' imprisonment.

In September 2004 the civilian Minister of Foreign Affairs, Win Aung, and his deputy, Khin Maung Win, were replaced by senior military officers, Maj.-Gen. Nyan Win and Col Maung Myint, respectively. Amid reports of a power struggle within the SPDC, Khin Nyunt was removed from the premiership and from his position as Chief of Military Intelligence in October, and was placed under house arrest, apparently owing to his alleged involvement in corruption related to smuggling by military intelligence staff. Lt-Gen. Soe Win was appointed as Prime Minister, while Lt-Gen. Thein Sein replaced Soe Win as First Secretary of the SPDC. The National Intelligence Bureau was abolished, and associates of Khin Nyunt, including several relatives and many military intelligence officers, were subsequently arrested. In November it was reported that three senior military intelligence officers had been convicted of corruption charges and sentenced to 22 years' imprisonment, and that 12 senior judicial officials, who were either linked to Khin Nyunt or had resisted the removal of those loyal to the former Prime Minister, had been dismissed. Meanwhile, in early November the SPDC announced that the Minister of Home Affairs, Col Tin Hlaing, the Minister of Science and Technology and of Labour, Tin Win, and four deputy ministers had been permitted to retire. It was reported that Tin Hlaing, an ally of Khin Nyunt, had also been placed under house arrest.

In late November 2004 the SPDC ordered the release of 9,248 prisoners who, it claimed, had been wrongly imprisoned owing to improper conduct by the dissolved National Intelligence Bureau. However, according to the opposition, the mass amnesty included only 43 of an estimated 1,300 political prisoners held by the authorities. In mid-December the SPDC freed a further 5,070 prisoners, 11 of whom were reported to be political prisoners, including the Chairman of the Democracy Party, Thu Wai. However, a number of NLD members were arrested in the same month for allegedly inciting public unrest. In January 2005 widespread rumours of a gun battle involving Maung Aye, Than Shwe, Soe Win and their aides, which were prompted by the unexplained death of Maung Aye's personal assistant, Lt-Col Bo Win Tun, appeared to be unfounded, although speculation about tension within the leadership continued. In the same month it was reported that four associates of Khin Nyunt who had been arrested in October 2004 had died in detention, while the closed trials of some 300 others on corruption charges had commenced in a prison in Yangon. The National Convention resumed in February 2005, again without the participation of the NLD and several ethnic minority groups, amid criticism from the EU, the UN and the USA. Meanwhile, the detention under house arrest of both Suu Kyi and Tin Oo was extended for a further year.

In July 2005 it was announced at the ASEAN Ministerial Meeting held in Laos that Myanmar would not assume the chair of ASEAN in 2006, as scheduled. Myanmar had recently come under increasing pressure from the international community, and in particular from the other member states of ASEAN, to forgo its turn to assume the rotating chair in order to enable the Myanma Government instead to focus its attention on addressing the country's human rights situation. Also in July 2005 Khin Nyunt was convicted on eight charges, including corruption and bribery, and was given a suspended prison sentence of 44 years; his two sons were also convicted and sentenced to prison terms. In the same month the Government authorized the release of dozens of political prisoners; however, in September Paulo Sérgio Pinheiro stated in an address to the UN General Assembly that approximately 1,100 dissidents remained in detention in Myanmar. Pinheiro's report was based on information derived from various independent sources, as Pinheiro himself had been repeatedly refused entry to Myanmar since November 2003. In August 2005 UN Special Envoy to Myanmar Ali Alatas had been allowed to visit the country, the first special envoy to be granted entry since Razali Ismail in March 2004.

Meanwhile, in August 2005 the World Food Programme (WFP) published a report stating that one-third of young children in Myanmar were malnourished; in some border areas afflicted by fighting between rival ethnic rebel groups, the figure was believed to be as high as 60%. The report also noted with concern the high number of Myanma children who received little or no formal education. In September Amnesty International released a report detailing the 'unacceptable' use by the military of tens of thousands of ethnic minority citizens to carry out forced labour; the report also drew attention to the military's use of physical abuse against such labourers.

In November 2005 the Government announced that it had initiated the first phase of a relocation of the country's administrative capital from Yangon to Pyinmana, a sparsely populated mountainous region about 400 km (nearly 250 miles) to the north of Yangon. Minister of Information Brig.-Gen. Kyaw Hsan announced that the decision to move to Pyinmana had been made owing to its central location and resultant ease of access to and from other parts of the country. The new administrative centre was officially named Nay Pyi Taw in March 2006. Also in November 2005 the NLD announced that Suu Kyi's detention under house arrest had again been extended for a further year.

Having being refused access to the country for almost two years, Razali Ismail resigned as the UN Secretary-General's Special Envoy to Myanmar in January 2006, and urged ASEAN to adopt a more forceful role in exerting pressure for democratic reform in Myanmar. Earlier in that month the US-based organization Human Rights Watch had dismissed the junta's pledges of democratic reform as 'empty rhetoric'. In late January the SPDC adjourned a session of the National Convention, with a view to reconvening towards the end of 2006. In April former Minister of Foreign Affairs Win Aung was convicted on corruption and bribery charges, and sentenced to seven years' imprisonment. Meanwhile, in February the detention under house arrest of Tin Oo was again extended by a further year. In May UN envoy Ibrahim Gambari was permitted to enter the country, whereupon he held discussions with Than Shwe and briefly met with Suu Kyi. Following his visit, Gambari concluded that SPDC leaders seemed willing to strengthen links with the international community. Later in the month UN Secretary-General Kofi Annan urged Than Shwe to free Suu Kyi; on the following day, however, her term of house arrest was extended for a further year. In September the UN Security Council reviewed the human rights situation in Myanmar for the first time. Gambari paid a second visit to Myanmar in November and was again allowed to hold a brief meeting with Suu Kyi, who, according to Gambari, welcomed discourse between the UN and the Government of Myanmar. In January 2007 a draft resolution urging the Myanma Government to release all political prisoners and end its violation of human rights was submitted to the UN Security Council, sponsored by the USA and the United Kingdom. However, the resolution was defeated when, in an unusual development, both the People's Republic of China and Russia, two of the five permanent members of the Security Council, exercised their right of veto.

Meanwhile, in April 2006 the ABSDF, the Federation of Trade Unions—Burma (FTUB), the NCGUB and the National League for Democracy—Liberated Area (NLD—LA) were denounced as terrorist organizations by the Government, in relation to a series of bomb attacks and attempted bombings in 2000–06. Several minor cabinet changes were implemented in May 2006 and in June a Supreme Court judge and several deputy ministers were reported to have retired, prompting speculation that they had been dismissed. The National Convention reconvened in October. The admission of the foreign press to the proceedings represented progress to some observers, but the absence of the NLD and the relatively small number of delegates from other political parties did not bode well for democratic reform. In January 2007 it was reported that the SPDC had released 2,831 prisoners in an amnesty to mark Independence Day, although only 30 were political prisoners. The detention under house arrest of Tin Oo was extended for a further year in February, as was that of Suu Kyi in May, despite ongoing international pressure for their release. More than 50 people were arrested in mid-May while attending prayer vigils in support of Suu Kyi; most of the detainees had been freed by the end of June.

MYANMAR

In May 2007 Lt-Gen. Thein Sein, the First Secretary of the SPDC, assumed the role of Prime Minister in an acting capacity, amid conjecture about Lt-Gen. Soe Win's health. The final session of the National Convention commenced in July and was formally closed in September. Thein Sein announced that the Convention had adopted detailed principles for a new constitution; a 54-member commission, chaired by Chief Justice Aung Toe, was appointed by the SPDC in October to draft the new Constitution and commenced work in December without the participation of the opposition.

The protests of September 2007 and subsequent events

Substantial unexpected increases in fuel prices in August 2007 provoked a series of anti-Government protests in Yangon and other towns. More than 60 demonstrators had been arrested by the end of the month; those detained included leaders of the '88 Generation' students' group who had participated in the 1988 pro-democracy uprising. The protests escalated in September 2007 with the involvement of Buddhist monks. During two days of demonstrations in Pakokku, in central Myanmar, monks held some 20 government officials captive for several hours after the security forces had forcibly dispersed some 300–400 monks, detaining around 10 and injuring several. The Alliance of All Burmese Buddhist Monks, a previously unknown group, made a series of demands to the SPDC—an apology for the force used in Pakokku, a reduction in commodity and fuel prices, the release of all political prisoners and those detained for participating in the recent protests, and the initiation of a dialogue with pro-democracy forces—threatening to withdraw all religious services from the authorities if they did not comply by 17 September. The SPDC accused the NLD and 'external groups' of instigating the unrest. Some of the marches were allowed to proceed peacefully, but tear gas was used to disperse a rally of some 1,000 monks and other citizens in the western town of Sittwe. Meanwhile, with the monks' demands unfulfilled, daily marches commenced in Yangon. The Alliance of All Burmese Buddhist Monks issued a statement describing the military Government as 'the enemy of the people' and pledging to continue protesting until the Government was removed from office. On the sixth consecutive day of demonstrations in Yangon, Suu Kyi made a brief public appearance when the monks were permitted to pass her residence. On the same day up to 10,000 monks were reported to have marched in Mandalay. Around 150 Buddhist nuns joined some 5,000 monks in Yangon, and a mass protest in the capital was attended by an estimated 50,000–100,000 monks and civilians, including NLD leaders, while demonstrations also took place in more than 20 other towns.

The SPDC imposed a night-time curfew in Yangon and Mandalay, banned gatherings of more than five people and deployed armed troops on the streets. Up to 10,000 monks and other protesters defied government warnings to halt the marches, troops fired live ammunition, reportedly killing five people. Some 200 monks were later reported to have been detained in overnight operations against several monasteries, during which many were allegedly beaten. Two NLD members were also arrested. The UN Security Council expressed concern at the situation in an emergency meeting, but China, Myanmar's closest ally, rejected a US proposal to consider the imposition of sanctions against the Myanma authorities. Anti-Government protests continued in late September 2007, but were violently suppressed. The Government claimed that 10 people had died in the violence (later increasing this figure to 15), but diplomats and witnesses reported that the death toll was much higher, with some estimating that up to 200 had been killed. By the end of the month the uprising had been largely quashed, with many monks in detention. During October the security forces continued to arrest those suspected of involvement in the street protests, and reports emerged of ill-treatment in detention centres, including claims that an NLD member had died as a result of being tortured in custody. In mid-October the authorities announced that 2,927 protesters (including 596 monks) had been arrested since 26 September, 2,459 of whom had been released after pledging not to participate in further demonstrations. However, other estimates suggested that some 6,000 people had been detained, including 2,400 monks. (In December the UN Special Rapporteur on the situation of human rights in Myanmar, Paulo Sérgio Pinheiro, reported that at least 31 people had died and that 3,000–4,000 people had been arrested in September and October, 500–1,000 of whom were still in detention; according to the security forces, only 80 people, including 21 monks, remained in custody at this time.) Meanwhile, the curfew in Yangon and Mandalay was removed. At the end of October more than 100 monks marched through Pakokku, their progress unimpeded by the security forces.

UN envoy Ibrahim Gambari visited Myanmar in late September 2007, initially holding discussions with acting Prime Minister Thein Sein and other government ministers, as well as with Suu Kyi, and in early October he was finally permitted to meet Than Shwe and Maung Aye. The SPDC agreed to Gambari's recommendation that a government official be appointed to enter into dialogue with Suu Kyi, assigning this role (Minister of Relations with Aung San Suu Kyi) to the Deputy Minister of Labour, Aung Kyi. In mid-October the UN Security Council unanimously adopted a statement deploring the use of violence against peaceful demonstrators, calling for the early release of all political prisoners and remaining detainees.

Thein Sein was formally appointed Prime Minister in October 2007, following Soe Win's death earlier in that month, and was replaced as First Secretary of the SPDC by Lt-Gen. Thiha Thura Tin Aung Myint Oo. At the same time Aung Kyi was promoted to the position of Minister of Labour, while retaining responsibility for liaising with Suu Kyi. On the following day Aung Kyi and Suu Kyi held their first talks.

In early November 2007 the Myanma Government announced the expulsion of Charles Petrie, the most senior UN official resident in the country. Petrie had recently publicly linked the pro-democracy protests to economic hardship and a 'deteriorating humanitarian situation'. Shortly afterwards Gambari arrived for a further visit, during which he held discussions with Thein Sein and Suu Kyi, although not with Than Shwe. It was reported by the Myanma state media that the SPDC had rejected an offer by Gambari to mediate in the dialogue between Suu Kyi and Aung Kyi. However, following the visit, Gambari issued a statement on behalf of Suu Kyi, in which she declared her willingness to co-operate with the SPDC 'in the interest of the nation'. A second meeting subsequently took place between Aung Kyi and Suu Kyi, who was also permitted to meet other members of the NLD for the first time in more than three years. In mid-November the UN Secretary-General, Ban Ki-Moon, urged the SPDC to conduct a 'meaningful and substantive dialogue' with the opposition, amid widespread scepticism regarding the junta's commitment to genuine dialogue aimed at democratic reform. In December the Government announced that it had granted amnesty to 8,585 prisoners since mid-November to mark the conclusion of the National Convention, although it was reported that only 10 were political detainees. Suu Kyi held two rounds of talks with Aung Kyi in January 2008, and was also permitted to meet NLD colleagues again at the end of the month, after which the party announced that its General Secretary was not satisfied with the progress of the dialogues. Meanwhile, in mid-January the UN Security Council expressed regret at the slow rate of progress towards meeting the objectives outlined in its statement of October 2007 (i.e. the release of political prisoners and dialogue with Suu Kyi), and urged Myanmar to allow another visit by Gambari. In late January 2008 Amnesty International claimed that 96 pro-democracy activists had been arrested since November 2007, increasing the total number in detention to 1,850, of whom 700 were accused of participating in the August and September protests. A few days later 10 activists, including Min Ko Naing and Ko Ko Gyi of the '88 Generation' students' group, were reportedly charged with making illegal statements.

In February 2008 the SPDC unexpectedly announced that a constitutional referendum would be held in May, followed by multi-party elections in 2010. Chief Justice Aung Toe subsequently confirmed that his commission had completed the draft constitution. The NLD expressed surprise that elections had been planned before the results of the constitutional referendum were known. A few days later the detention under house arrest of Tin Oo was again extended by a further year; Suu Kyi's house arrest was similarly extended in May. Ibrahim Gambari returned to Myanmar in March, meeting Suu Kyi and several government officials, the most senior of whom was the Minister of Information, Brig.-Gen. Kyaw Hsan. However, no apparent progress was made during the visit, with the Government rejecting Gambari's proposal that independent observers be allowed to monitor the forthcoming referendum and refusing to consider amending the draft constitution to allow Suu Kyi to contest elections. Suu Kyi reportedly refused to meet with Gambari during the envoy's visit to Myanmar in August, arousing speculation about her dissatisfaction with the pace of developments. The newly appointed UN Special Rapporteur on the situation of human rights in Myanmar, Tomás Ojea Quintana, also paid a visit in that month. In his subsequent report, Ojea Quintana recommended the implementation of four major elements of reform prior to the holding of an election: the revision of domestic legislation governing fundamental rights; the release of all political prisoners (who were estimated to total more than 2,000); reform of the military; and the transition to a fully independent judiciary.

In early May 2008 the devastating Cyclone Nargis struck southern Myanmar. Yangon and four other regions, including the Ayeyarwady (Irrawaddy) Delta, were declared disaster areas. The Government's restrictions on international aid efforts exacerbated the difficulties confronting the survivors, many of whom had no access to clean drinking water, food or shelter. Although some provisions supplied by the UN and foreign donors were eventually allowed into the country, the Government continued to refuse entry to foreign aid workers. In mid-May Ban Ki-Moon stated that the Government's reaction to the disaster had been 'unacceptably slow'. By late June the official death toll had risen to more than 84,500. However, the ICRC had suggested that the number of fatalities might be as high as 128,000, while the UN estimated that 2.5m. people had been affected by the cyclone.

Meanwhile, the text of the draft constitution went on sale at government bookshops in April 2008. The draft included the changing of the country's official name to the 'Republic of the Union of Myanmar'. Also reportedly enshrined in the draft was the ultimate establishment of a multi-party democracy. Nevertheless, as proposed in the 1994 sessions of the National Convention, legislative power was to be vested in a bicameral Pyidaungsu Hluttaw, comprising the Pyithu Hluttaw (lower house) and the Amyotha Hluttaw (upper house), with 25% of the seats to be allocated to representatives of the military nominated by the Commander-in-Chief of the Armed Forces. Furthermore, the Commander-in-Chief of the Armed Forces was to designate the government ministers responsible for defence, security, home affairs and border affairs, and was to assume executive, legislative and judicial power in the event of a state of emergency being declared, while Suu Kyi's marriage to a foreign citizen would disqualify her from contesting elections. Despite the widespread destruction caused by Cyclone Nargis, which prompted the Government to postpone the constitutional referendum in the affected regions, the poll proceeded as scheduled in other areas on 10 May. Reporters without Borders, an international group campaigning for press freedom, claimed that debate on the referendum had been subject to severe restrictions. According to official reports, turn-out was high, at 99%, with 92.4% of voters endorsing the new Constitution, thereby completing the ratification process; observers remained sceptical.

In June 2008 reorganizations took place within the Cabinet and the military. Vice-Adm. Soe Thein, hitherto Commander-in-Chief of the Navy, was appointed Minister of Industry (No. 2), while the ministerial duties of Maj.-Gen. Maung Maung Swe were expanded to include a new post-cyclone management and resettlement portfolio. Five senior-level generals reportedly retired. The Minister of Immigration and Population, Maj.-Gen. Saw Lwin, and the Minister of Construction, Maj.-Gen. Saw Tun, were reported to have resigned in early 2009. The Minister of Home Affairs, Maj.-Gen. Maung Oo, was said to have assumed responsibility for the former portfolio, while the latter was transferred to the Minister of Electric Power (No. 2), Maj.-Gen. Khin Maung Myint, although official confirmation of the reorganization was not forthcoming.

On the 20th anniversary of the 1988 pro-democracy uprising, several protesters were arrested in Taunggok in August 2008. Tensions rose in Yangon and surrounding areas as the anniversary of the September 2007 protests approached, with bomb explosions resulting in several fatalities in September 2008; large numbers of dissidents were thought to remain in custody. Also in September, the junta announced a large-scale amnesty involving as many as 9,000 detainees. Among those released was Win Tin, a senior political activist and founding member of the NLD who had been imprisoned for 19 years; however, in October Ohn Kyaing, another veteran NLD member, was detained. This was followed by the culmination of dozens of trials that had begun in July, with the sentencing of more than 100 activists and dissidents in November. Many defendants received substantial prison terms, some as long as 65 years, which were criticized as being unduly harsh. Those convicted included senior members of the '88 Generation', the NLD and monks' groups who were accused of involvement in the September 2007 uprising. In discussions with Ibrahim Gambari in Yangon in February 2009, Suu Kyi reportedly criticized the trial process and suggested that a visit by the UN Secretary-General should be conditional upon the freeing of political prisoners.

In May 2009, shortly before her term of house arrest was due to expire, Suu Kyi was taken to Insein Prison, following an unauthorized visit to her home by an uninvited US citizen, John Yettaw, who had gained access by swimming across the adjacent lake. She was tried on charges of violating the conditions of her house arrest, and in August was convicted and sentenced to three years' imprisonment with hard labour, although this was commuted to 18 months' house arrest. ASEAN expressed disappointment at the verdict, which was widely criticized by the international community. Yettaw, meanwhile, was sentenced to seven years' imprisonment, including four years' hard labour; however, he was subsequently released and allowed to return to the USA, following negotiations between Than Shwe and US Senator Jim Webb—the first time that a senior US official had been allowed to meet with the reclusive Myanma leader. Webb was also granted rare access to Suu Kyi, whose supporters claimed that the incident had been exploited by the military junta as a pretext for further prolonging the opposition leader's detention. In December it was announced that the Supreme Court had agreed to hear an appeal filed by Suu Kyi. During the court proceedings Suu Kyi's lawyers argued that the latest extension to her house arrest was unlawful since it was based on provisions from the 1974 Constitution, which was no longer in effect. However, in February 2010 the Supreme Court rejected Suu Kyi's appeal, ruling that the 1974 Constitution could still be cited as it had not officially been abandoned. Suu Kyi lodged a final appeal against her detention, which was heard by the Special Appellate Bench in October 2010; however, in November the five-judge panel dismissed the appeal, upholding the original verdict. Meanwhile, Tin Oo was finally released from house arrest in February 2010; upon his release, the NLD Vice-Chairman pledged to continue to strive for democracy.

The 2010 legislative election

In March 2010 the junta approved new electoral laws, details of which were released gradually in state media, in advance of the legislative elections that the Government repeatedly offered assurances would, as previously pledged, be held before the end of the year. *Inter alia*, the new laws prohibited anyone with a criminal conviction from belonging to a political party, a rule that was widely interpreted as being intended to force the NLD to expel Suu Kyi from its ranks; Suu Kyi was already barred from standing for political office by the new Constitution. The junta formally annulled the NLD's victory in the 1990 general election, stating that the result was invalid since the poll had been conducted under legislation repealed by the newly enacted laws.

Divisions emerged within the NLD regarding whether the party should expel Suu Kyi, Tin Oo and other members with criminal convictions in order to be able to contest the elections. Several prominent NLD members, including Win Tin, pledged to resign if the majority of the party decided to proceed with registration, while others contended that the NLD's absence from the election would effectively lead to a one-party political system in which the policies of the military junta would remain unchecked. According to her lawyer, Suu Kyi herself was vehemently opposed to NLD registration under what she denounced as 'such an unjust and one-sidedly drawn-up state constitution' but would none the less allow the party to arrive at its collective decision. At the end of March 2010 the NLD announced that it would not be registering for the election, a decision that served severely to compromise the credibility of the poll from the perspective of the international community. In a parade to commemorate Armed Forces' Day in the same month, Than Shwe promised that elections would be free and fair, but warned external powers to 'stay away' and issued the unequivocal statement that 'the nation will be strong only when the armed forces are strong'. In April about 20 senior members of the ruling junta, including Prime Minister Thein Sein, resigned from their military positions in what was widely interpreted as a move to circumvent the restriction, to 25% of the total, of the number of legislative seats that were to be allocated to representatives of the military in the forthcoming elections. Thein Sein applied to register a new political party, the Union Solidarity and Development Party (USDP), which was headed by the premier.

In mid-July 2010 it was announced that the USDA, the mass movement formed in September 1993 to establish a civilian front through which the armed forces could exercise control, had disbanded and that its assets had been transferred to the USDP, prompting widespread criticism from critics of the Government, who argued that the assets belonged to the State and that their transfer to the USDP thus afforded the party an unfair advantage. Suu Kyi's former assistant, Win Htein, was released from prison, having served his sentence of 14 years' imprisonment for conspiracy to destabilize the country. (Win Htein had been briefly released in September 2008 as part of the amnesty announced in that month by the junta, but he had been re-arrested and reimprisoned on the following day, after criticizing the new Constitution approved in May 2008 during an interview broadcast by a dissident radio station, the Democratic Voice of Burma.)

A date for the election was finally announced by the junta in mid-August 2010: the first legislative poll in 20 years was to be held on 7 November, one week prior to the scheduled expiry of the detention under house arrest of Suu Kyi. In mid-September the Union Election Commission (UEC—created in March and chaired by a retired army major-general, Thein Soe) announced that 37 parties had successfully registered to participate in the forthcoming election. Not unexpectedly, the USDP was among those approved, as were the NUP (which had contested the 1990 election) and the National Democratic Force (a splinter group established in April by a group of 25 former NLD members who did wish to participate in the election and chaired by Than Nyein); many of the remainder were small, ethnic-based parties that were contesting a limited number of regional seats. The UEC also announced the formal dissolution of 10 parties, five of which had been dissolved owing to non-registration, including the NLD (the first public confirmation of its suspected dissolution), the Shan Nationalities League for Democracy, which had also performed well in the 1990 election, and the Union Pa-O National Organization; the remaining five (predominantly ethnic-based) parties were disbanded owing to their alleged non-compliance with regulations governing the registration of candidates. UN Secretary-General Ban Ki-Moon expressed concern at this development. The application of the Kachin State Progressive Party (KSPP) to register for the polls was rejected by the UEC on the grounds that the KSPP was allegedly affiliated to the Kachin Independence Organization (KIO—see Insurgency and Dissidence), and the applications of 14 KSPP members who had applied to contest the elections as individuals were also rejected. Also in mid-September the UEC announced the cancellation of voting in about 300 villages across five states, which were deemed to be 'troubled', claiming that voting in those areas would not be free or fair; at least 1.5m. people were thus excluded from voting, leading to speculation that the SPDC was endeavouring to disenfranchise Myanmar's ethnic population.

The official electoral campaign period began on 25 September 2010. However, strict campaigning guidelines were issued to all registered parties, which were each granted 15 minutes of broadcasting time in which to make known their electoral platforms on state television and radio (although full scripts were required to be submitted to the UEC for prior approval). In mid-October the SPDC announced the introduction of a new national flag and anthem, and changed the country's official name from the Union of Myanmar to the Republic of the Union of Myanmar, in accordance with the provisions of the 2008 Constitution.

The elections to both chambers of the Pyidaungsu Hluttaw, and to 14 state and regional assemblies, were held, as scheduled, on 7 November 2010. A total of 3,069 candidates from the 27 registered parties contested more than 1,100 seats. There were widespread allegations of voting irregularities committed by supporters of the USDP, including the use of fraudulent electoral rolls, vote-buying, voter intimidation and the manipulation of ballots cast in advance of the polls by Myanma nationals living abroad. The UEC claimed that 21.9m. voters had turned out to cast their ballots, out of a total of just over 29m. registered voters (representing some 76% of the electorate); however, many independent sources suggested that the actual figure was considerably lower than this, with some claiming a turn-out of only 30%. According to official results released by the UEC via state radio on 17 November, the USDP secured 259 seats of the 330 contested seats in the 440-member Pyithu Hluttaw; the USDP's closest rival, the Shan Nationalities Democratic Party (SNDP), won just 18, while the NUP garnered 12, the Rakhine Nationalities Development Party (RNDP) nine and the National Democratic Force won eight. Other, mostly ethnic-based, parties collectively accounted for a further 19 seats, with one seat won by an independent; the four remaining seats were unfilled at this time. There was a similar pattern evident in the electoral results for the Amyotha Hluttaw, as well as for the seven state and seven regional assemblies. In the Amyotha Hluttaw, in which 168 seats were contested, the USDP was declared to have won 129 seats; the RNDP took seven and the NUP five, while the National Democratic Force, the All Mon Region Democracy Party (AMRDP) and the Chin Progressive Party each won four seats, and the SNDP and the Phalon-Sawaw Democratic Party attained three seats each. In total, the USDP took 882 of the 1,154 contested seats, while the second-placed NUP won 63. The National Democratic Force was placed joint sixth overall—tied with the AMRDP—with just 16 seats, and Chairman Than Nyein announced that the party intended formally to challenge the results, stating that the election had been 'absolutely not free and fair'. However, many losing opposition candidates claimed subsequently that the UEC-sanctioned procedures to file a challenge against the results, including the stipulated payment of 1m. kyats (about US $1,000) for each individual challenge, were designed to confuse and discourage would-be complainants.

Meanwhile, in early October 2010 it was announced that Suu Kyi had lodged a formal appeal at the Supreme Court against the formal dissolution of the NLD. On 13 November, two days after her (largely symbolic) final appeal against her detention under house arrest had been rejected, Suu Kyi was finally released, her latest detention order having expired. Thousands of supporters gathered outside the NLD party headquarters in Yangon to hear Suu Kyi's first public address since her release. At a press conference, which foreign journalists were allowed to attend, Suu Kyi questioned the legitimacy of the recent elections. Later in November the Supreme Court was reported to have refused to hear Suu Kyi's appeal against the dissolution of the NLD.

Recent developments: the appointment of President Thein Sein

In mid-January 2011 Gen. Than Shwe appointed 110 military representatives to the Pyithu Hluttaw, 56 to the Amyotha Hluttaw and 222 to the state and regional assemblies, in accordance with the constitutional quotas. On 31 January 2011 Myanmar's new bicameral Pyidaungsu Hluttaw convened for the first time. The opening of the initial session marked the formal implementation of the new Constitution, and the formal completion of the transfer of power from the military junta to an elected parliament and a President, to be selected by the Pyidaungsu Hluttaw. According to new legislation announced by state media in November 2010, legislators' conduct during parliamentary sessions was to be governed by strict regulations: freedom of speech was to be allowed, with the exception of words deemed to represent a risk to 'national security and unity'; protests within parliament were to be punishable by up to two years' imprisonment. During the first parliamentary session Thura Shwe Man, formerly army chief of staff, was elected Speaker of the Pyithu Hluttaw, while Khin Aung Myint, a former Minister of Culture, was elected Speaker of the Amyotha Hluttaw. USDP members were elected Speaker and Deputy Speaker in all 14 of the state and regional assemblies.

On 1 February 2011 the Pyidaungsu Hluttaw nominated five legislators for three vice-presidential positions; the three candidates selected would become presidential candidates. Among the five nominees were the outgoing Prime Minister, Thein Sein, and former First Secretary of the SPDC Lt-Gen. Tin Aung Myint Oo; the remaining three nominees were members of ethnic minorities, which was widely interpreted as a conciliatory gesture on the part of the USDP legislators, amid increased tensions in the ethnic border areas in the aftermath of the elections (see Insurgency and Dissidence). The announcement of the five nominees prompted much speculation regarding the future role of Than Shwe, who many observers had expected to be named President. However, few anticipated that the outgoing leader would entirely relinquish his power. On 3 February the Pyithu Hluttaw voted for Thein Sein as its presidential candidate, while the Amyotha Hluttaw elected Dr Sai Mauk Kham, a little-known USDP member of the Shan ethnic minority group; Tin Aung Myint Oo, as the vice-presidential nominee of the military representatives in parliament, was automatically approved as the military's presidential candidate. Thein Sein was elected President of Myanmar on 4 February 2011, garnering 408 votes; Tin Aung Myint Oo, who won 171 votes, and Sai Mauk Kham, with 75 votes, were confirmed as Vice-Presidents. In the following week Thein Sein submitted the names of 30 nominees for cabinet positions, all of which were approved by the Pyidaungsu Hluttaw; the list was dominated by former military officers who had retired in order to contest the 2010 legislative elections, including about a dozen who had been ministers in the outgoing Cabinet. However, it was not immediately clear which

MYANMAR

ministers had been assigned to which portfolios. On the day after the list of cabinet ministers was approved, Than Shwe urged the Myanma population to protect the country's nascent 'democracy system', and warned against any disruption.

On 30 March 2011 Thein Sein was finally inaugurated as the country's President, and the SPDC was dissolved. Than Shwe was replaced as Commander-in-Chief of the Defence Services by Gen. Min Aung Hlaing. The incoming Cabinet comprised 30 members. The defence portfolio was allocated to Maj.-Gen. Hla Min and that of home affairs to Lt-Gen. Ko Ko. Wunna Maung Lwin was appointed as Minister of Foreign Affairs, while Maj.-Gen. Thein Htay became Minister of Border Affairs and Myanma Industrial Development.

Meanwhile, in its annual report published in January 2011, Human Rights Watch claimed that the human rights situation in Myanmar had remained 'dire' throughout 2010. According to the organization's report, more than 2,100 political prisoners were still incarcerated in Myanmar, while the army was responsible for 'ongoing abuses against civilians in conflict areas, including widespread forced labor, extrajudicial killings, and forced expulsion of the population'. In a report published in the same month, another US-based group, Physicians for Human Rights, claimed to have documented widespread abuses against Myanmar's Chin ethnic minority group, allegedly perpetrated by the Myanma army. The report purported to include evidence of at least eight violations that the group argued could form the basis for charges of crimes against humanity to be brought against the Myanma army at the International Criminal Court in the Netherlands. Meanwhile, in early November 2010 new legislation was introduced that would allow the Government to draft men (between the ages of 18 and 45) and women (between the ages of 18 and 35) into the armed forces for a two-year period, or for five years during times of 'national crisis'. Anyone failing to report for military service would be liable to receive three years' imprisonment and/or a large fine.

Insurgency and Dissidence

After Burma gained independence in 1948, various groups conducted armed insurgency campaigns against government forces. The most effective of the ethnic-based insurgency groups was the Karen (Kayin) National Union (KNU), founded in 1948, which led a protracted campaign for the establishment of an independent state for the Karen ethnic group (restyled Kayin in the transliteration changes of 1989), partly through the activities of its military wing, the Karen (Kayin) National Liberation Army (KNLA). The KNU was a member of the National Democratic Front (NDF), an organization that at one time comprised 11 ethnic minority groups—including Kachin, Karenni (Kayinni), Mon, Shan, Pa-O, Palaung, Wa, Arakanese (Rakhine) and Lahu parties—formed in 1975 (by five groups, originally) with the aim of making Burma a federal union and opposing both the Government and, initially, the CPB. The CPB was one of the most well-organized insurgent movements, in military terms, and gained control of significant areas in northern Burma. By May 1986 the various minority groups in the NDF had agreed to relinquish their individual demands for autonomy, in favour of a unified demand for a federal system of government. At the same time, the CPB withdrew its demand for a 'one-party' government and entered into an alliance with the NDF. At the second NDF Congress in June 1987, various leadership changes removed all KNU representatives from senior NDF positions. The new NDF leaders advocated the establishment of autonomous, ethnic-based states within a Burmese union.

The insurgent groups were sympathetic to anti-Government movements in the major cities. Continued attacks throughout 1988 engaged government forces in the border areas, leaving fewer of them to impose order in the towns. In September the Karen announced plans to co-operate with protesting students and Buddhist monks to work towards the achievement of democracy. After the armed forces seized power, insurgents intensified operations, aided by at least 3,000 students whom the Karen rebels agreed to train and arm. In November 22 anti-Government groups, led by members of the NDF, formed the DAB. The KNU leader, Gen. Bo Mya, was elected President.

In April 1989 dissatisfaction with the CPB leadership led to a mutiny by Wa tribespeople, who constituted roughly 80%–90% of the CPB's membership. Rebellious Wa soldiers captured the CPB headquarters, and the party's leaders were forced into exile in the People's Republic of China. The leaders of the mutiny subsequently accepted SLORC proposals for the former forces of the CPB army to become government-controlled militia forces in exchange for supplies of rice, financial support and development aid. The former CPB troops agreed to use their main forces against the 25,000-strong rebel separatist Mong Tai (Shan State) Army (formerly the Shan United Army), whose leader, Khun Sa, controlled much of the drug trade in the 'Golden Triangle', the world's major opium-producing area, where the borders of Myanmar, Laos and Thailand meet. The SLORC also approached members of the NDF, and was successful in securing agreements with the Shan State Progressive Party in September 1989, and with the Pa-O National Organization and the Palaung State Liberation Organization in March and May 1991, respectively. At the third NDF Congress in July, these three movements were expelled, reducing the NDF's membership to eight organizations; Nai Shwe Kyin was elected as its new President.

In December 1988, following a visit by the Thai Prime Minister, the SLORC granted licences to Thai business interests to exploit raw materials in Burma, in return for much-needed foreign exchange. Although there was no announcement of any official Thai-Burmese agreement, subsequent offensives by government forces against rebel groups achieved unprecedented success, with troops frequently attacking insurgent bases from Thai territory. By January 1990 eight KNU bases along the Thai border had been captured. In that month the armed forces launched an offensive against Mon separatists. In February they succeeded in capturing Three Pagodas Pass, a principal 'black market' trade route between Thailand and Myanmar, and the headquarters of the New Mon State Party.

Intense fighting between government and rebel forces continued as the KNLA advanced into the lower central Ayeyarwady Delta in late 1991. This potentially diversionary tactic failed to prevent a concerted attempt by government troops to seize control of the KNU and DAB headquarters, which was also the seat of the NCGUB. However, despite the use of sophisticated weaponry purchased from China, government troops failed to capture the camp at Manerplaw. In March 1992 the Thai Government fulfilled prior threats of strong retaliation, forcing hundreds of Myanma troops out of entrenched positions taken up in order to attack the KNU headquarters from the rear. In April the SLORC officially suspended its offensive against the KNU, 'in the interests of national unity'. In October, however, government troops resumed hostilities, making several incursions into Thai territory. In December the Thai and Myanma Governments agreed to 'relocate' the Myanma armed forces, and in February 1993 they resolved to demarcate their common border.

In February and March 1993 the KIO attended peace talks with the Government in the Kachin state capital of Myitkyina. The SLORC was anxious to reach a deal with the Kachins, as the NCGUB would be severely weakened by the loss of their support (although a de facto national cease-fire had been in effect since October 1992). The KIO appeared to have signed a peace agreement in April 1993 but, owing to its attempts to persuade other members of the DAB to enter discussions with the SLORC, the cease-fire was not announced until October. The agreement was ratified in Yangon in February 1994. The KIO was suspended from the DAB in October 1993 for negotiating separately with the SLORC, and the DAB reiterated its conditions for discussions with the SLORC in a series of open letters. Its stipulations included: the recognition of the DAB as a single negotiating body (the SLORC insisted on meeting each ethnic group separately); the location of the negotiating process in a neutral country; an immediate end to the forcible mass relocation of villagers; a new body to draft a constitution; and the release of all political detainees, beginning with Aung San Suu Kyi. However, under Thai pressure, the DAB policy of negotiating as a front was unofficially abandoned subsequently.

In May 1994 the Karenni (Kayinni) National People's Liberation Front concluded a cease-fire agreement with the SLORC, reportedly the 11th insurgent group to do so. This was followed in July by the declaration of a cease-fire by the Kayan New Land Party, and in October by the declaration of a cease-fire by the Shan State Nationalities Liberation Organization. In December government forces launched a new offensive against the KNU, recapturing its headquarters at Manerplaw in January 1995 (and forcing many hundreds of KNU fighters across the border into Thailand). The virtual defeat of the KNU forces was attributed to their reportedly severe lack of ammunition and funds and also to the recent defection from the Christian-led KNU of a mainly Buddhist faction, which established itself as the Democratic Karen (Kayin) Buddhist Army (DKBA). The DKBA, which had comprised about 10% of the strength of the KNLA, allegedly supported the government forces in their offensive. In February

1995 the Myanma army captured the KNU's last stronghold, and in the following month Bo Mya resigned as the Commander-in-Chief of the KNLA (although he remained the leader of the KNU). In March the KNU declared a unilateral cease-fire, with the aim of initiating negotiations with the SLORC. Earlier in the month the Karenni (Kayinni) National Progress Party (KNPP) reportedly became the 14th ethnic insurgent group to abandon its armed struggle against the SLORC. This agreement collapsed in June, however, as government troops entered areas designated in the accord to be under KNPP control. In August 5,000 troops were dispatched to suppress the KNPP rebellion. Clashes continued throughout the year, and in January 1996 government forces captured a major Kayinni stronghold. However, the KNPP continued fighting, with support from the ABSDF.

In January 1997 the DKBA, allegedly supported by government forces, attacked Kayin refugee camps in Thailand. The KNU claimed that requests in late January for further peace negotiations were rejected by the SLORC, which then initiated a new offensive against the KNU. The ensuing fighting between the KNU and government forces, together with the forcible relocation of Kayin away from KNU bases in Myanmar during 1997, forced many Kayin across the border into Thailand. The Thai armed forces denied collusion with the Myanma troops in the process of forced repatriations of Kayin refugees, who were believed to number more than 100,000 in mid-1997. In March 1998 the DKBA, supported by government troops, launched two further attacks on Kayin refugee camps in Thailand, prompting a retaliatory attack by the KNU on DKBA forces. In April 1999 the KNU issued a statement confirming the deaths of seven members of a group of 13 government officials whom they had abducted in February; the remaining six were said to have been released unharmed.

In January 2000 Bo Mya resigned as KNU Chairman owing to ailing health, and was replaced by the former General Secretary of the organization, Saw Ba Thin; Bo Mya assumed the vice-chairmanship. Following his appointment as leader, Ba Thin announced that, while the KNU intended to continue its struggle against the ruling SPDC, the movement was prepared to negotiate a political settlement with the military regime. Initial but inconclusive round of talks between the KNU and the SPDC were held in February, followed by further discussions in March. However, in late 2000 the Government began to use 'scorched-earth' tactics to deprive the KNU of its support base, displacing up to 30,000 people in eastern Myanmar.

In January 2001 Johnny and Luther Htoo, teenage leaders of the Kayin rebel group God's Army, surrendered with 12 of their followers to the Thai authorities. While much smaller than the KNU or the KNLA, God's Army had gained international notoriety owing to the leadership of the twin boys, thought to be aged 13 or 14. Two of the 12 members who surrendered were believed to have been involved in a raid on a Thai village that had left six civilians dead in December 2000.

In April 2003 the KNU claimed responsibility for a series of explosions that had destroyed sections of a gas pipeline in Kayin State over the previous two months, declaring that they had intended to draw the attention of the international community to the human rights abuses being perpetrated by government troops in the area. Several bombings along the border with Thailand in the following month were also attributed to the KNU. In January 2004 Bo Mya and other KNU officials held talks with government representatives in Yangon, which resulted in the conclusion of an informal cease-fire arrangement between the two sides. Bo Mya had previously made any peace agreement conditional both on the release of Suu Kyi and other NLD detainees and on the Government's adherence to UN resolutions delineating a return to democracy for the country. At further talks, held in Mawlamyine (Moulmein) in February, the KNU and the Government discussed the demarcation of KNU territory, the relocation of the armed forces and the resettlement of some 200,000 internally displaced civilians in Kayin State. However, despite the informal cease-fire, sporadic fighting continued between government troops and the KNLA. Further negotiations in Yangon in October were curtailed at the Government's request following the dismissal of Prime Minister Khin Nyunt. Bo Mya retired as Vice-Chairman of the KNU in December because of ill health; he was replaced by Gen. Tamalabaw. In January 2005 10 government troops were reportedly killed in clashes with the KNU after attacking one of the group's bases near the border with Thailand. Later in that month the KNU demanded a resumption of the peace talks, which remained stalled. In the mean time, government forces were reported to have launched an offensive against a KNPP stronghold in Yamu, again close to the Thai border. Further government offensives in Kayin State in early 2006 were reported to have forced an estimated 15,000 Kayin people to flee from the violence. Bo Mya died in a Thai hospital in December 2006. In February 2007 a relatively small breakaway faction of the KNU led by Htain Maung negotiated a peace agreement with the Government, but the goals of the KNU itself were said to be unaffected. In April it was reported that DKBA and government forces had captured four KNU bases near the Thai border. In June 27 people were killed in two separate ambushes on buses in Kayah and Kayin States; the KNU and the KNPP claimed responsibility for the attacks, but insisted that the victims were armed troops and not civilians. Three people were killed in four minor bomb explosions in January 2008, which the authorities attributed to the KNU and other ethnic insurgent groups. A series of bombings in 2009 was also attributed to the KNU. Meanwhile, in February 2008 the General Secretary of the KNU, Pado Mahn Sha, was killed by two unknown gunmen at his home in the Thai border town of Mae Sot; it was speculated that the DKBA was responsible for the assassination. The Chairman of the KNU, Saw Ba Thin, died in May; in October Vice-Chairman Gen. Tamalabaw was appointed as his replacement, while Tamalabaw's daughter, Zipporah Sein, succeeded Mahn Sha as General Secretary.

Following the referendum in 2008 in favour of the new Constitution (see Domestic Political Affairs), the SPDC requested that all ethnic minority groups form political parties to enable their participation in the legislative elections scheduled for 2010. However, many were reluctant to do so owing to the reservation of one-quarter of seats in the national and local legislatures for members of the national army. In April 2009 the SPDC demanded that all ethnic cease-fire groups transform into new 'Border Guard Force' (BGF) battalions, which were to include a unit of 30 government soldiers and one government officer. Although most of the cease-fire groups initially resisted the order, some—including the DKBA—were gradually coerced into acquiescing. The introduction of the BGFs was widely regarded as an attempt to reduce the risk of ethnic uprisings prior to the 2010 elections. The forthcoming polls were a divisive subject among the ethnic-based groups: some were adamantly opposed to any participation, which, they argued, would lend a false impression of legitimacy to the proceedings, while others contended that a refusal to participate would ensure their total exclusion from the legislative process.

As the elections approached, with the SPDC's rejection of a number of ethnic parties and individual candidates, along with its apparent endeavours to disenfranchise a large number of ethnic voters (see Domestic Political Affairs), tensions in the ethnic border areas intensified. In October 2010 the Kachin Independence Army (KIA—the military wing of the KIO, which continued to refuse to become a BGF) was reported to be engaged in a tense confrontation with government troops, following the arrest of three of its members; meanwhile, members of the Shan State Army (SSA) were reported to have been attacked by government forces in several separate incidents. At the beginning of November six ethnic groups were reported to have reached an agreement to join forces in the event of a government attack; a spokesperson for the KIO contested that the ethnic groups had 'no real option but to unite, politically and militarily'. (Many observers feared that in the aftermath of the election the Government might attempt to target those groups that had not agreed to become BGFs.) Heavy fighting broke out in Myawaddy on 8 November, immediately following the legislative election, after a breakaway faction of the DKBA—led by Na Kham Mwe and comprising those opposed to the DKBA leadership's decision to agree to become a BGF—seized control of government buildings in the Kayin town, where they encountered armed opposition from government troops. At least three civilians were killed during the clashes, and an estimated 20,000 Kayin were reported to have fled into neighbouring Thailand to escape the violence. Government troops regained control of Myawaddy a few days later, and issued an ultimatum to the renegade faction, threatening to annihilate it if it did not surrender its weapons and agree to become a BFG by the end of December. However, sporadic fighting continued. In mid-November the DKBA faction and the KNLA agreed to unite in their common pursuit of autonomy, and in December the ABSDF also pledged its support to the DKBA; the Chairman of the ABSDF, Than Khe, professed his willingness to co-operate with any groups that had 'the basic principle of restoring democracy and the federal union to Burma and freeing the people from dictatorship'. Intermittent violent clashes in

Kayin State and other border areas continued into early 2011, intensifying fears of a possible outbreak of a full-scale ethnic conflict.

Meanwhile, in December 1993 the SLORC initiated a major offensive against Khun Sa's Mong Tai Army encampments on the Thai border. During that month Khun Sa convened a Shan 'parliament' in his base of Homong, which was attended by hundreds of delegates. This was followed, in May 1994, by Khun Sa's declaration of an independent Shan State, of which he declared himself 'President'. In the same month fighting intensified between government forces and the Mong Tai Army near the Thai border, with heavy losses reported on both sides. However, Khun Sa claimed that his army retained control of two-thirds of the Shan State. In July he was reported to have offered to end opium cultivation and to surrender to the government forces, in exchange for their withdrawal from the Shan State and a guarantee of Shan independence. In March 1995 government forces launched an intensive campaign, lasting several months, against the Mong Tai Army. In August a faction calling itself the Shan State National Army broke away from the Mong Tai Army, accusing Khun Sa of using Shan nationalism as a 'front' for drugs-trafficking. Khun Sa subsequently offered to relinquish areas under his control to an international force that could ensure the safety of the Shan while eradicating illicit drugs. Khun Sa's position was considerably weakened in September, as improving relations between Thailand and Myanmar led to a Thai pledge to close the common border, thus obstructing his supply routes, and cease-fires with neighbouring ethnic groups allowed the Government to deploy troops in hitherto inaccessible areas. Certain ethnic groups, notably the Wa, were also actively engaged in fighting the Mong Tai Army to gain control of the opium trade. In November Khun Sa announced his retirement from all political and military positions, citing his betrayal by the breakaway group. In January 1996 government troops entered Homong without resistance, and thousands of his former supporters surrendered. Although no formal agreement with the SLORC was announced, it was widely believed that Khun Sa had previously negotiated a settlement with the authorities since he was not detained and it was officially announced that he would not be extradited to the USA on drugs-trafficking charges. (Khun Sa was, moreover, later accorded the status of an honoured elder. He died in Yangon in October 2007.) The Mong Tai Army was subsequently transformed into a militia volunteer unit under the command of the armed forces.

Between November 1996 and February 1997 there were reports of clashes between the Shan United Revolutionary Party (a faction of the Mong Tai Army that had not surrendered in January 1996) and government forces. In September 1997 the alliance between three of the major Shan groups who continued their resistance—including the Shan State National Army (SSNA), remnants of the Mong Tai Army, and the Shan State Peace-keeping Council (SSPC) and its military wing, the SSA—was formalized, and the groups joined together in an enlarged SSA. In November it was reported that Shan separatist groups had launched a further offensive against government troops. In May 1999 it was reported that at least 300,000 Shan had been forced from their villages into resettlement camps by government troops. Clashes between SSA units and government forces were reported in December. In March 2000, following the group's announcement that it wished to seek a peaceful settlement with the ruling junta, the SSA issued a statement outlining cease-fire terms. It was later claimed by the SSA that these terms had been misinterpreted by the Government. In May several senior army officers died in an SSA ambush. In the following month more than 60 Shan and hill tribespeople, who had been forcibly relocated and had then attempted to return to their village, were reportedly killed by the Myanma military in a retaliatory attack. In similar incidents in the region in June, as many as 50 other villagers were believed to have been murdered. In 2001 the Government launched several offensives against SSA border camps, causing hundreds more Shan to flee the area. In September the leader of the SSA, Col Yodsuek, stated that the group would be willing to enter into peace talks with the SPDC.

In late 1996 Gen. Maung Aye ordered that the forces of the United Wa State Army (UWSA—who reached an accommodation with the SLORC in 1989) should withdraw from its principal base or surrender to the Government by the end of 1997. As the deadline approached, tension between the two sides increased until the UWSA was given permission to remain at the base for a further year. In January 2000 it was reported that the SPDC was to launch an operation to relocate 50,000 people from UWSA-controlled opium-growing areas, with the alleged intention of eradicating the production of drugs in the areas by 2005. The relocation programme began to cause ethnic tension in early 2001, as the Shan complained that the Wa tribespeople were occupying land that they had previously owned. It was also claimed that the Wa were still growing opium, in spite of the fact that the scheme had been introduced supposedly to prevent heroin production. In February the office of the UN High Commissioner for Refugees (UNHCR) investigated reports that 300,000 Shan had fled to Thailand owing to the Wa influx.

In late 1989 the SLORC began resettling Bamar (Burman) Buddhists in the predominantly Muslim areas of Arakan (renamed Rakhine), displacing the local Rohingya Muslims. In April 1991 Rohingya refugees were forced over the border into Bangladesh, as a result of the brutal operations of the Myanma armed forces, including the destruction of villages, widespread killings and pillaging. The Rohingyas had been similarly persecuted in 1976–78, when more than 200,000 of them had sought refuge in Bangladesh. The Rohingyas had finally been repatriated, only to lose their citizenship following the introduction of new nationality legislation in 1982. In November 1991 the SLORC pledged to repatriate genuine Myanma citizens, but claimed that many of the refugees were illegal Bengali immigrants. In April 1992 the Myanma and Bangladeshi Governments signed an agreement providing for the repatriation of those Rohingya refugees in possession of official documentation. However, the repatriation programme was delayed, owing to the continuing flow of refugees to Bangladesh (reaching an estimated 270,000 by the end of June). The first Rohingya refugees were returned to Myanmar in September, without the supervision of UNHCR. Despite demonstrations by Rohingyas in Bangladesh against forced repatriation, refugees continued to be returned to Myanmar. The SLORC's agreement, in November 1993, to allow UNHCR access to repatriated Rohingyas was expected to accelerate the programme. In April 1994 guerrillas of the Rohingya Solidarity Organization carried out attacks in the Maungdaw area of Rakhine. By May 1995 more than 216,000 refugees had been repatriated. In July 1999, however, about 20,000 Rohingya refugees remained in camps in Bangladesh, despite the expiry of the official deadline for their repatriation in August 1997.

In April 2000 the International Federation of Human Rights Leagues (FIDH) issued a report condemning the treatment of Rohingya Muslims by the Myanma Government, including forced labour, punitive taxes and extrajudicial killings. The FIDH claimed that the Myanma regime was attempting to force the exodus of Rohingyas from their native Rakhine and criticized UNHCR for its effective complicity with the regime in designating the more recent refugees as economic migrants. In February 2001 violence between Buddhist and Muslim communities in the state capital, Sittwe, was reported to have resulted in at least 12 deaths, prompting the Government to regulate further the movement of Rohingya and other Muslims in and out of Rakhine. In 2003 UNHCR assisted more than 3,000 refugees to return to Myanmar from Bangladesh, following the removal of technical restrictions on their repatriation. In February 2009, during a visit to Bangladesh, the US Assistant Secretary of State urged Myanmar to halt the mistreatment of the Rohingyas. In December it was announced that Myanmar had agreed to repatriate about 9,000 Rohingyas living in Bangladeshi camps following a meeting between the two countries' respective ministers responsible for foreign affairs. Nevertheless, at early 2011 an estimated 28,000 Rohingyas were reported to be living in official refugee camps in Bangladesh, many of whom appeared to be unwilling to return to Myanmar. In addition, it was estimated that some 200,000 Rohingyas were residing in Bangladesh without refugee status. In January the US-based Human Rights Watch urged Thailand to allow the UNHCR unhindered access to a group of 158 Rohingya asylum-seekers who had fled to Thailand from Myanmar earlier in the month, as well as a further 53 Rohingya asylum-seekers detained in Thailand since 2009.

Foreign Affairs

Regional relations

The People's Republic of China restored diplomatic relations with Burma in 1978. From 1988, as Burma's international isolation deepened, China assumed an increasingly important role. It became Myanmar's principal aid donor, supplier of weapons and source of consumer goods. In May 1997 an agreement was reached to establish a trade route through Myanmar to

MYANMAR

provide the Chinese province of Yunnan with access to the Indian Ocean. In the same year the Chinese Government signed a 30-year agreement with Myanmar that allowed for more than 200 Chinese fishing boats to operate in Myanma waters; the agreement was widely perceived as an indication of increasing Chinese influence in Myanmar. In December 2001 the Chinese President, Jiang Zemin, travelled to Myanmar, becoming the first Chinese head of state to visit the country since 1985. Before his arrival the Government announced that it had ordered the release of more than 200 Chinese prisoners as a gesture of goodwill. Following successful discussions, the two Governments signed a series of bilateral agreements intended to enhance co-operative ties. It was reported that China had offered Myanmar US $100m. in aid and investment, although this was thought to be linked to Chinese demands that the ruling junta increase its efforts to eradicate the drug trade between the two countries. Relations between the two countries were further strengthened in March 2004, during a visit to Yangon by Chinese Vice-Premier Wu Yi, by the signing of 24 agreements on economic and technical co-operation. During a visit to Nay Pyi Taw in December 2009, whereupon he met with SPDC Vice-Chairman Maung Aye, Chinese Vice-President Xi Jinping presented a four-point proposal intended further to bolster bilateral relations, which comprised maintaining senior-level contact, deepening reciprocal co-operation, safeguarding the peace and prosperity of their common border area, and strengthening co-ordination on regional and international affairs. Relations were further enhanced by the signing of a series of co-operation agreements between the two countries during a visit to Myanmar in June 2010 by Chinese Premier Wen Jiabao; the accords were reported to pertain to energy and development aid, among other fields. During a reciprocal visit to China by Than Shwe in September, a spokesperson for the Chinese Ministry of Foreign Affairs stressed that the forthcoming legislative elections in Myanmar were an internal matter for that country, but expressed China's hope that the international community would seek constructive engagement with Myanmar. However, one of a series of US diplomatic cables released at the end of 2010 by WikiLeaks, an organization publishing leaked private and classified content, revealed that the Chinese Government was becoming increasingly frustrated with the 'footdragging' of Than Shwe and the general recalcitrance of the Myanma Government. Ongoing unrest in the Myanma ethnic border areas close to China was a further source of tensions between the two countries in 2010–11. Some 5,000 Chinese troops were deployed to the border in mid-2010.

During the 1990s Japan and the member states of ASEAN were anxious to halt Myanmar's excessive dependence on China for aid and trade. Myanmar, in its turn, applied to join ASEAN (which maintained a policy of 'constructive engagement' in relation to Myanmar) in an attempt to end its isolation, accelerate economic growth and gain protection from Western criticism of its internal affairs. In July 1996 Myanmar was granted observer status, and in July 1997 the country was admitted as a full member of the organization. In May 1996 Myanmar joined the ASEAN Regional Forum (ARF, see p. 209) and in May 2000 the country hosted a senior-level meeting of the economic ministers of the ASEAN member countries; the meeting, which was also attended by ministers from China, Japan and the Republic of Korea, attracted strong criticism from the NLD. Myanmar enjoyed particularly cordial relations with Indonesia, and the military regime aspired to Indonesia's internationally accepted political system, in which the dominant role of the armed forces was enshrined in the Constitution. ASEAN links were strengthened by official visits from Cambodian Prime Minister Hun Sen in February 2000, from Vietnamese Minister of Foreign Affairs Nguyen Dy Nien in October and from the Malaysian Prime Minister, Dr Mahathir Mohamad (who had been influential in gaining entry for Myanmar into ASEAN), in January 2001 and again in August 2002. In March 2006 the Malaysian Minister of Foreign Affairs, Syed Hamid Albar, was denied a meeting with Aung San Suu Kyi by the military junta. Albar, acting as an ASEAN envoy to assess the progress of political reform, had held a meeting with Lt-Gen. Soe Win, the Myanma Prime Minister, and was initially positive about the visit. However, he claimed in July that ASEAN's development was being impeded by Myanmar, and that ASEAN could no longer defend Myanmar as it was 'not making an attempt to co-operate or help itself'.

In September 2007, in a rare departure from the Association's policy of non-interference in member states' internal affairs, ASEAN ministers responsible for foreign affairs, meeting in New York, USA, issued a statement in which they declared that they had expressed their 'revulsion' to their Myanma counterpart over reports that anti-Government protests (see Domestic Political Affairs) were being suppressed violently, and had urged the Myanma Government to resume efforts at national reconciliation and release all political detainees. ASEAN came under pressure to take action against Myanmar in advance of its summit meeting in November, at which member states signed a new charter committing themselves, *inter alia*, to strengthening democracy and promoting and protecting human rights, with the US Senate notably approving a resolution urging ASEAN to suspend Myanmar. However, ASEAN's Secretary-General rejected this suggestion, deeming it confrontational, and the Myanma Government also succeeded in forcing the cancellation of a planned address by UN envoy Ibrahim Gambari. None the less, the President of the Philippines warned that her country's legislature was unlikely to ratify the new ASEAN charter unless Myanmar agreed to release Suu Kyi. However, by the end of October 2008 all 10 member nations had ratified the new charter, despite the continued detention of Suu Kyi. Thailand, in its capacity as ASEAN chair in 2009, issued a statement expressing 'deep disappointment' at the latest extension of Suu Kyi's house arrest in August 2009; the statement reiterated previous requests for her immediate release, as well as that of all other political prisoners in Myanmar, in advance of the legislative elections due to be held in 2010.

In July 2010 the Secretary-General of ASEAN, Surin Pitsuwan, stated that ASEAN ministers responsible for foreign affairs had given their Myanma counterpart an 'earful' with regard to the elections, stressing that the polls must be 'free, fair and inclusive'. At the ASEAN summit held in Hanoi, Viet Nam, in October, there was much criticism of the forthcoming polls. The Philippine delegation was particularly vehement in its censure, communicating President Benigno Aquino's view that the forthcoming elections would be 'a farce to democratic values'. The Philippine Secretary of Foreign Affairs gave a speech in which he exhorted all members of ASEAN firmly to urge the Government of Myanmar to implement its own 'road map' to democracy. He also urged the immediate and unconditional release of all political prisoners, including Suu Kyi, and the all-inclusive participation of all parties and sectors of the population in the elections. However, ASEAN's response to the elections was rather less outspoken, with Viet Nam, in its capacity as ASEAN chair in 2010, hailing the polls as 'a significant step forward'. Furthermore, in January 2011 ASEAN urged the USA and other Western nations to remove economic sanctions against Myanmar, following the elections and the release from house arrest of Suu Kyi in November 2010, stating that the sanctions were impeding the country's development, and appealing for 'open and conducive dialogue' in and with Myanmar in order to ensure further progress towards democracy in that country.

Meanwhile, following the release of Suu Kyi from house arrest in July 1995, Japan resumed substantial economic aid to Myanmar, which had been halted in 1988. In November 1999 the Japanese Prime Minister met with Than Shwe during an ASEAN summit meeting in the Philippine capital, Manila; the meeting was the first between the leader of a major world power and a senior member of the military Government since the junta's suppression of the democratic opposition in 1988. In April 2001 Japan accelerated its policy of engagement, promising a US $28m. aid programme intended to facilitate the upgrading of a hydroelectric power plant in Kayah. The renewal of aid to the country was widely perceived to be a political gesture intended to reward the SPDC for its efforts to reach a settlement with the NLD. The international community criticized Japan's decision to resume aid as being premature in the light of Myanmar's failure to end forced labour and other human rights abuses in the country. In June 2003, following the junta's reimprisonment of Suu Kyi in May of that year, the Japanese Government suspended all economic aid to Myanmar. However, in early 2004 it was announced that Japan was to resume aid once again, having been satisfied that the release of some political prisoners by the SPDC constituted adequate progress towards democracy in the country. Tension arose between Japan and Myanmar in September 2007, when a Japanese journalist was killed during the violent suppression of anti-Government protests in Yangon. After evidence emerged that suggested that the journalist might have been deliberately targeted by the security forces, the Japanese Deputy Minister of Foreign Affairs visited Myanmar to investigate the incident. In the following month Japan cancelled some $4.7m. in funding for an educational centre at

Yangon University, as Myanmar continued to maintain that the journalist had been accidentally shot.

In the late 1990s relations between Myanmar and Thailand were rather less cordial than previously, with the Thai Government advocating a more limited 'flexible engagement' with Myanmar, in place of the ASEAN policy of 'constructive engagement' formerly endorsed by the country. Bilateral relations were placed under some strain in late 1999 when a group of armed Myanma student activists, styled the Vigorous Burmese Student Warriors, seized control of the Myanma embassy in Bangkok in early October, demanding the release of all political prisoners in Myanmar and the opening of a dialogue between the military Government and the opposition. All 89 hostages were released by the activists within 24 hours, in exchange for the Thai Government's provision of helicopter transport to the Thai–Myanma border. The Thai Government's release of the perpetrators angered the ruling junta in Myanmar, and Myanmar closed its border with Thailand immediately after the incident. The border was re-opened to commerce in late November, although relations between the two countries remained strained. In January 2000 Thai troops shot dead 10 armed Myanma rebels who had taken control of a hospital in Ratchaburi, holding hundreds of people hostage. The rebels, who were reported by some sources to be linked to the Kayin insurgent group God's Army, had issued several demands, including that the shelling of their base on the Thai–Myanma border by the Thai military be halted, that co-operation between the Thai and Myanma armies against the Kayin should cease, and that Kayin tribespeople be allowed to seek refuge in Thailand. The Thai Government denied reports that the perpetrators had been summarily executed after handing over their weapons.

Tension was heightened in November 2000 as 2,000 Myanma troops were deployed along the Thai–Myanma border, in preparation for an offensive against the KNU. In January 2001 it was reported that a Thai F-16 fighter aircraft had intruded into Myanma airspace, prompting the Government to announce the building of air defence systems along the border. Another border transgression occurred in February, when five Myanma soldiers were arrested by the Thai Border Patrol Police (BPP). The soldiers claimed that they were searching for food, whereas the BPP believed them to be gathering intelligence on Thai positions. On the previous day an offensive had been launched against the KNU, involving 300 Myanma troops, of whom five were killed. In mid-February there was a major incursion into Thai territory by some 200 Myanma troops, in pursuit of 100 SSA rebels. The troops clashed with Thai soldiers and occupied a hill that was within Thai territory for two days. At least two Thai villagers were killed, and officially 14 Myanma soldiers and two civilians also died. A cease-fire was signed, but this did not prevent Myanmar from ordering all SPDC troops on the border to be placed on full combat-ready status. By the end of February Thailand had detained 40 Myanma nationals for spying, according to Myanma figures, while the SPDC accused Thailand of providing support to the SSA.

In May 2001 the Thai Government lodged a formal protest over an incident in which members of the DKBA had allegedly attacked a military unit situated in a Thai border village, causing the deaths of three civilians. A further protest was made several days later when the UWSA captured a hill believed to lie within Thai territory; the hill was later recaptured by Thai troops. In response, the Myanma Government demanded the withdrawal of Thai troops from 35 border outposts and claimed that the Thai army had launched air strikes into its territory, an accusation denied by the Thai authorities. Several senior-level bilateral visits between June and September achieved scant tangible progress. In January 2002 a joint Thai-Myanma commission (meeting for the first time since 1999) agreed to establish a task force to assist in the repatriation of illegal workers. In February 2002 the Thai Minister of Foreign Affairs, Surakiart Sathirathai, visited Yangon. During his stay both countries agreed to co-operate in controlling the cross-border drugs trade.

In mid-2002 relations with Thailand deteriorated sharply when fighting broke out on the border between government troops, allied with the UWSA, and the SSA. It was alleged that Thai troops had fired shells into Myanmar, in the belief that the fighting had encroached upon Thai territory. In response, the Myanma Government again accused Thailand of providing support to the SSA. The border was closed shortly afterwards, as border incursions continued, but reopened in October. Following the adoption of a policy of 'soft engagement' by the Thai Government, in early 2003 the two countries signed an unprecedented agreement pledging that future military exercises would be conducted at a suitable distance from the border.

In December 2003 Thailand hosted an international forum, the 'Bangkok Process', at which the Myanma Minister of Foreign Affairs, Win Aung, presented the 'road map' on democratic reform (see Domestic Political Affairs) to government representatives from 10 other Asian and European countries. A second round of talks in the 'Bangkok Process', scheduled for April 2004, was postponed indefinitely at Myanmar's request. Prime Minister Khin Nyunt visited Thailand in June, and discussed various economic, development and border issues with Prime Minister Thaksin Shinawatra. In December Thaksin paid a visit to Myanmar, his first since the ousting of Khin Nyunt, and held talks with the new Prime Minister, Lt-Gen. Soe Win. In January 2005 Thailand increased security along the border with Myanmar, amid renewed concerns that fighting between Myanma troops and KNPP rebels might encroach upon Thai territory. In April Thailand again intensified border security owing to renewed fighting between the UWSA and the SSA close to Thai territory. In December the Thai Government announced that it was not prepared to host the delayed second meeting of the 'Bangkok Process' since Myanmar had not kept it sufficiently informed of its progress towards democracy. A second 'Friendship Bridge' linking the two countries opened in January 2006. In January 2009 UNHCR reported that around 110,000 Myanma refugees remained resident in nine camps in Thailand, while a total of 20,878 had been resettled in third countries between January 2005 and December 2007, more than one-half having been accepted by the USA. In early 2009 it was alleged that groups of Myanma and Bangladeshi asylum-seekers, attempting to reach Thailand, had been intercepted by Thai security forces and left at sea in boats without engines. A decision by the Myanmar junta in July 2010 to close a border crossing at Myawaddy, adjacent to the Thai border town of Mae Sot, was a source of considerable irritation to the Thai Government; the closure of the crossing was estimated to be costing Thailand nearly US $3m. daily in lost trade. The escalation of tensions in Myanmar's ethnic border areas in the immediate aftermath of the November legislative elections (see Insurgency and Dissidence) was reported to have forced more than 20,000 Myanma people to flee into Thailand to escape the violence. Three Thai nationals were injured when mortar and grenade attacks strayed across the Myanma–Thai border during fighting between the DBKA and Myanma government troops, causing Mae Sot to be evacuated. Thai Prime Minister Abhisit Vejjajiva announced the deployment of additional troops to the area in order to reinforce border security, and offered assurances that Kayin and other Myanma refugees into Thailand would be treated humanely. In early December the Myanma and Thai Ministers of Foreign Affairs met in the Myanma border town of Tachilek, reportedly to discuss the possible reopening of the border crossing at Myawaddy. In an unexpected development a few days later, the Three Pagodas Pass border crossing was reopened after a three-year closure,. In January 2011 Myanmar eased border control restrictions between Myawaddy and Mae Sot, allowing the transit of goods via cross-border trading ports to resume. Cross-border trade was briefly suspended again in early February, following two bomb explosions in neighbouring Myawaddy on the Myanma side of the border, which were reported to have killed three people and injured six others. However, normal service was reported to have resumed later that month, although the land border crossing between Myawaddy and Mae Sot remained closed at the beginning of March.

In October 2002 the Australian Minister for Foreign Affairs, Alexander Downer, arrived in Myanmar; he was the most senior Australian politician to have visited the country for 20 years. During his stay he met with senior members of the SPDC and with Suu Kyi. Following his departure, Suu Kyi reportedly claimed that she would prefer Australia to lend its support to the international sanctions against the country rather than attempt to engage with its leaders. In October 2007 the Australian Government imposed financial sanctions on more than 400 Myanma leaders and associates.

In April 2007 Myanmar and the Democratic People's Republic of Korea (North Korea) agreed to restore diplomatic relations, which had been severed in 1983 after the latter was held responsible for a bomb attack in Yangon during a visit by the President of the Republic of Korea (South Korea). It was speculated that North Korea hoped to gain access to Myanmar's energy resources, while Myanmar would benefit from North Korean military co-operation. In late 2010 the USA was revealed to be

MYANMAR

extremely concerned by, and to be actively investigating, rumours of a secret Myanma nuclear weapons programme allegedly being developed with North Korean assistance (see Other external relations).

Other external relations

In July 1996, as repression increased, Aung San Suu Kyi for the first time urged the imposition of international economic sanctions against Myanmar. From March 1997 the EU withdrew Myanmar's special trading status, in response to concerns over Myanmar's human rights record; two scheduled meetings between the EU and ASEAN, due to take place in late 1997 and early 1999 respectively, were cancelled by the EU, owing to its objection to the representation of Myanmar at the talks. However, an agreement was subsequently reached by the two sides to allow Myanmar to take a 'passive role' in the Joint Co-operation Committee meeting between the EU and ASEAN. The SPDC became more open to the development of external relations when it allowed an EU delegation to visit Myanmar and hold talks with Suu Kyi in January 2001. Despite this, the EU extended its sanctions against Myanmar for a further six months in April. However, in October the EU announced that it had decided to ease its sanctions. After Razali Ismail's fourth visit to Myanmar in November 2001, plans for a US $16m. HIV/AIDS prevention programme were mooted. Several countries, particularly Japan, as well as the EU, indicated that they would be willing to support a carefully monitored international aid programme. In January 2003 the Myanma Deputy Minister of Foreign Affairs, Khin Maung Win, was permitted to attend an EU-ASEAN summit meeting for the first time since Myanmar's suspension from the meetings in 1997. However, in April 2003 the EU elected to extend its sanctions against the country and to increase the list of SPDC officials subject to visa sanctions and freezing of their assets. These sanctions were subsequently renewed annually.

Relations between the EU and ASEAN were strained by pressure from some EU member states to exclude ASEAN's three newest members (Cambodia, Laos and Myanmar) from an Asia-Europe Meeting of heads of government (ASEM) in Viet Nam in October 2004. The EU initially insisted that the SPDC should release Suu Kyi from house arrest and commit to a number of other reforms before Myanmar be allowed to attend. However, ASEAN responded that if its new members were not allowed to participate, then the EU's 10 new members should also be excluded. The result was that Myanmar was represented at the summit meeting by a more junior-level delegation, led by the newly appointed Minister of Foreign Affairs, Maj.-Gen. Nyan Win. Two days after the ASEM summit EU ministers responsible for foreign affairs implemented an earlier threat to broaden sanctions against Myanmar if the country did not make progress towards democratization in time for the meeting. The ministers agreed to widen the list of Myanma officials subject to visa sanctions and to co-ordinate international bans on investment in the country (although France secured an exclusion from such a ban for European countries that had already invested in Myanmar). In November 2007, in response to the use of force to quell anti-Government protests in Myanmar in September, the EU formally increased the number of officials subject to visa sanctions and asset freezing, expanded the scope of an investment ban on state-owned enterprises and imposed a new ban on some Myanma exports, including timber, metals and gemstones.

In September 1999, meanwhile, a diplomatic dispute began between Myanmar and the United Kingdom after British consular staff were refused permission to visit two Britons in detention in Myanmar for their separate involvement in pro-democracy protest action. One of the two Britons was released in November. The second detainee, who had received a prison sentence of 17 years for entering the country illegally and carrying pro-democracy leaflets, was released in October 2000, following international pressure; he claimed to have been beaten heavily while in captivity. In December 2009 British Prime Minister Gordon Brown wrote a personal letter to Suu Kyi pledging the full support of the British Government to her cause and that of the Myanma people; the letter also urged the junta to ensure the freeness and fairness of the forthcoming elections. In March 2010 the United Kingdom was reported to be in support of a recommendation made by the UN Special Rapporteur on the situation of human rights in Myanmar that the International Criminal Court open an investigation into war crimes and crimes against humanity allegedly perpetrated by the military junta.

In May 1997 the USA imposed trade sanctions in protest at persistent and large-scale repression by the SLORC. The sanctions prohibited further investment in Myanmar, but did not affect existing US interests in the country. During 1997–98 the USA denounced Myanmar for its poor human rights record, its lack of progress towards democracy and its treatment of Suu Kyi, and also demanded the release of hundreds of political prisoners. In March 1999 US Secretary of State Madeleine Albright publicly criticized the regime for taking insufficient action to combat the production of and trade in narcotics within Myanmar. The USA showed its support for the SPDC-NLD talks with a visit by a senior Department of State official to Suu Kyi in February 2001. Nevertheless, the US Government renewed its sanctions later in the year. In December pro-democracy activists in Myanmar accused the USA of neglecting their cause after a reappraisal of its foreign policy in the wake of the terrorist attacks on the country in September (see the chapter on the USA). They claimed that the US Government had moderated its criticism of the military junta because it suspected that the international terrorist network al-Qa'ida had a presence in Myanmar. In February 2002 a report issued by the US Government offered the prospect of an easing of sanctions, but only if the junta released all remaining political prisoners and made further tangible progress towards democracy. However, following the detention of Suu Kyi in May 2003, in July US President George W. Bush approved the Burmese Freedom and Democracy Act, already approved by Congress, banning all imports from Myanmar for three years and extending visa sanctions already imposed on SPDC officials. The USA extended economic sanctions against Myanmar for another year in May 2004 and again in subsequent years. In August 2006 President Bush renewed the Burmese Freedom and Democracy Act of 2003 for a further three years, following its approval by Congress. In September 2007 the US Department of State expanded its visa ban to more than 35 additional government and military officials; a further 14 senior officials were also designated subject to freezing of their assets. In October Bush announced the imposition of stricter controls on imports from Myanmar, as well as sanctions affecting the property interests of senior Myanma leaders. In May 2008, furthermore, the US Treasury was ordered to freeze the assets of state-owned companies in Myanmar. Meanwhile, in April the US Senate approved legislation to award the Congressional Gold Medal to Suu Kyi.

The inauguration of Barack Obama as US President in January 2009 was expected by many to herald a new era in Myanmar's relations with the USA. However, although the Obama Administration adopted a policy of 'pragmatic engagement' with those countries with which the USA did not have cordial relations (rather than the policy of isolation to which the Bush Administration had adhered), the new Government stressed that sanctions would remain in place until tangible progress towards democratic change had been achieved by Myanmar. In July Obama renewed the Burmese Freedom and Democracy Act of 2003 for a further three years, following its approval by the US Congress. In November 2009 President Obama attended the ASEAN-US Leaders' Meeting, hosted by Singapore, at which Prime Minister Thein Sein was also present, demonstrating the Obama Administration's stated commitment to re-engaging with Myanmar; previously the USA had boycotted those meetings with ASEAN at which Myanma officials were present. Obama's spokesperson, Robert Gibbs, stated that during the meeting Obama had raised the issue of Suu Kyi's continued detention and urged her release; it was unclear what, if any, response he had received. Following Obama's inauguration, the military junta appeared more amenable to requests from US officials to meet with Suu Kyi and vice versa. As well as Senator Jim Webb, who met with Suu Kyi after securing the release of John Yettaw in August 2009 (see Domestic Political Affairs), several Western diplomats were allowed to meet with the opposition leader in October. Suu Kyi had written to Than Shwe to request the meeting, stating that she wished to establish what sanctions against Myanmar were in place; the meeting was arranged within one week. Furthermore, the US Assistant Secretary of State for East Asian and Pacific Affairs, Kurt Campbell, was allowed to meet with Suu Kyi when he led a fact-finding mission to Myanmar in November; during his visit, Campbell also met with senior members of the military leadership. In January 2010 Campbell expressed frustration at the lack of reciprocal effort that he argued was being made by the junta in response to US efforts aimed at facilitating the holding of direct talks with Myanma officials. Furthermore, Campbell stated that the USA was 'very disappointed and concerned' by the electoral legislation enacted by the junta in March (see Domestic Political

Affairs), which he described as a 'set-back' for US-Myanma relations, as well as for political dialogue within Myanmar. US economic sanctions against Myanmar were extended for a further year in July. In December Joseph Yun, the US Deputy Assistant Secretary for East Asian and Pacific Affairs, visited Yangon, whereupon he met with Suu Kyi, following her release from house arrest in the previous month. Suu Kyi subsequently confirmed that the two had discussed, *inter alia*, the issue of economic sanctions against Myanmar. While welcoming the renewed US engagement with Myanmar, she cautioned against 'rose-tinted glasses', stressing that much progress needed to be made by the Government with regard to human rights issues. During his stay in Myanmar, Yun also met with government officials, including the Minister of Foreign Affairs, Maj.-Gen. Nyan Win; following the meeting, the US embassy in Yangon released a statement declaring that the Obama Administration 'remains open to direct dialogue to make meaningful progress on our core concerns including improving human rights and release of political prisoners'. However, one of the leaked US diplomatic cables published at the end of 2010 by WikiLeaks revealed that the US Government was deeply concerned by persistent rumours that Myanmar was developing a covert nuclear weapons programme in remote locations with North Korean assistance, based on satellite images and other evidence. Myanmar and North Korea both denied the claims.

In November 1998 the SPDC strongly denied claims made by the UN that the Myanma Government was responsible for the widespread abuse of human rights within the country. However, a report published in August by the International Labour Organization (ILO), following an investigation into the alleged use of forced labour and the suppression of trade unions in Myanmar, found the use of forced labour to be 'pervasive' throughout the whole country, and accused the military regime of using beatings, torture, rape and murder in the exaction of its forced labour policy, constituting a 'gross denial of human rights'. In June 1999 a resolution condemning Myanmar for its widespread use of forced labour was adopted by the member countries of the ILO, and the country was barred from participating in any ILO activities. (In the same month the ruling junta was accused by Amnesty International of perpetrating widespread abuses against ethnic minority groups.) Following the failure of the ruling junta to carry out the recommendations made by the ILO Commission of Inquiry in 1998 after the organization's initial investigation, in March 2000 the governing body of the ILO recommended that at its meeting in June the International Labour Conference take action to secure compliance by the junta with the ILO's recommendations. In a statement issued in late March, the SPDC categorically rejected the governing body's decision and recommendations. Despite the Government's assurance in November that it would accept ILO monitors to verify the cessation of forced labour practices, the UN labour body voted to proceed with sanctions against Myanmar. This was the first time such action, the strongest available to the ILO, had been undertaken in the organization's 81-year history. The ILO subsequently requested its members to review their relations with Myanmar and to adopt sanctions. China, India, Malaysia and Russia voted against the action.

In September 2001 an ILO contingent arrived in Myanmar for a three-week visit intended to ascertain whether the military junta had honoured its promise to bring about the abolition of forced labour. In November the ILO issued a report concluding that, while some progress had been made, the practice was still endemic in many parts of the country. It recommended that a permanent ILO presence be established in Myanmar to monitor continued efforts to end forced labour therein; discussions as to how this could be implemented headed the agenda during a further visit by the ILO in February 2002. However, the ILO delegation was not permitted to see Suu Kyi during its visit and, upon departure, the head of the delegation expressed disappointment at the lack of co-operation it had received from the Myanma authorities. Despite this, in March the ILO agreed to establish a liaison office in the country and, in October, an ILO mission visited the country to assist further in the development of good labour practices. In early 2004, following a visit by an ILO envoy, the SPDC agreed to allow ILO representatives to work freely towards the elimination of forced labour practices in the country. At the ILO's annual International Labour Conference in June, it was reported that the use of forced labour remained widespread in Myanmar, particularly on local infrastructure projects and by the army, although there had been some improvement since the 1990s, with forced labour no longer routinely used on national infrastructure projects. In February 2007 the ILO announced that the Myanma authorities had tentatively agreed to allow investigations into submitted forced labour cases without negative repercussions for alleged victims. However, in June 2009 the ILO denounced the Myanma Government's actions to end forced labour thus far as 'totally inadequate', and insisted that it must amend the new Constitution to include an explicit ban on forced labour and must be committed to punishing those found to be employing forced labour.

In November 2000 the UN Special Rapporteur on the situation of human rights in Myanmar, Rajsoomer Lallah, resigned from his position, citing lack of financial and administrative assistance. Lallah had previously produced a damning report of Myanmar's human rights situation, but had not been granted a visa throughout his four-year term. His successor, Dr Paulo Sérgio Pinheiro, was able to visit Myanmar in April 2001, within six months of taking office. He returned for a further visit in October, but was criticized by the NLD for his failure to spend enough time consulting with local communities. In February 2002 Pinheiro visited the country for a third time and held further discussions with senior members of the SPDC and with Suu Kyi and other political prisoners. The Government released 11 political prisoners during his stay and, upon leaving, he declared his visit to have been a success. In October Pinheiro travelled to the country again; during his time there he investigated allegations, made by several human rights groups, that members of the Myanma armed forces routinely raped ethnic women along the border with Thailand. He also met with Suu Kyi. In March 2003 he paid a further visit to the country but curtailed his stay, having discovered a hidden microphone in a room where he was interviewing NLD prisoners. He later urged the SPDC to release all remaining political prisoners and enter into a serious dialogue with the opposition.

In the first half of 2004 Pinheiro was twice denied entry to Myanmar, and in June he described the ongoing National Convention as a 'meaningless and undemocratic exercise'. In October 2007 the UN Human Rights Council adopted a resolution deploring the violent repression of peaceful demonstrations in the previous month and calling for the release of peaceful protesters and all other political detainees. In November, during his first visit to Myanmar since 2003, Pinheiro held talks with government ministers and several prominent political prisoners, although he was not permitted to meet Suu Kyi. Following his visit, Pinheiro stated that the Myanma authorities had admitted that 15 people had been killed during the suppression of the anti-Government protests in September 2007 (five more than previously acknowledged), and in the following month he reported that his investigations indicated that at least a further 16 people had died, that 500–1,000 people were still being detained by the authorities (far more than claimed by the Government) and that 74 people were missing. Pinheiro also reported that the ill-treatment of detainees and the poor conditions in which they were being held had resulted in several deaths in custody. Tomás Ojea Quintana, who replaced Pinheiro at the end of the latter's mandate in April 2008, undertook two trips to Myanmar in August 2008 and February 2009, respectively (see Domestic Political Affairs), and made a third in February 2010, meeting with both government and opposition officials. However, requests to meet with Than Shwe and Suu Kyi were not granted. In a report presented to the UN Human Rights Council following his third visit to Myanmar, Ojea Quintana spoke of 'a pattern of gross and systematic violation of human rights', which, he argued, appeared to be 'the result of a state policy, originating from decisions by authorities in the executive, military and judiciary at all levels'; he also recommended the establishment of a UN commission of inquiry to address the question of international crimes allegedly committed by the junta. The recommendation subsequently gained the support of, *inter alia*, the USA, the United Kingdom, Australia and Canada, but was opposed by China. Meanwhile, in March UN Secretary-General Ban Ki-Moon urged the Myanma Government to create suitable conditions for credible, inclusive elections, which would necessitate the release of political prisoners, including Suu Kyi; he also admitted to frustration at the 'disappointing' progress achieved as a result of UN engagement with the junta, and described the junta's efforts to ensure free and fair elections thus far as 'frustrating'. Shortly after the elections in November, Ibrahim Gambari's replacement as UN Special Envoy to Myanmar, Vijay Nambiar, visited the country, where he met with senior government officials in the outgoing junta, and insisted that they address the widespread criticism and concerns about the polls, contending that this was essential if a 'credible transition' to democratic rule were to be effected; Nambiar also urged the release of all political prisoners in Myanmar. Following the legislature's election of Thein Sein as President in February 2011, Ban Ki-Moon expressed his hope that it would lead to the formation of 'a more inclusive civilian government that is broadly representative of all parties relevant to national reconciliation and more responsive to the aspirations of the people of Myanmar'.

In May 1999 the ICRC, which had withdrawn from Myanmar in 1995 but reopened its office there in October 1998, regained permission from the ruling junta to visit a limited number of prisons in the country. Despite having been initially critical of the ICRC for reaching an agreement with the SPDC, Suu Kyi was reported subsequently to have expressed her support for the Committee's work with political prisoners. The ICRC sent a delegation to the country in July 2003, in order to ascertain that Suu Kyi was in good health following her recent imprisonment by the SPDC. In June 2007, in an unusual departure from its policy of neutrality, the ICRC issued a statement severely criticizing the Myanma authorities, claiming that human rights violations in Myanmar were causing 'immense suffering'.

Despite the killing of three Indian soldiers in a clash with Myanma troops in October 2000, relations between the two countries subsequently improved. Gen. Maung Aye paid a seven-day visit to India in November, meeting both the country's President and the Prime Minister. In February 2001 India's Minister of External Affairs, Jaswant Singh, visited Myanmar, the first Indian cabinet minister to do so since the SLORC's assumption of power in 1988. While there, Singh officially opened the Tamu–Kalewa highway, a road built by India at a cost of US $22m. in order to increase bilateral trade with Myanmar. In January 2003 Minister of Foreign Affairs Win Aung paid a visit to India, during which he met with the Prime Minister and several cabinet ministers. The two Governments agreed to hold regular consultations and to co-operate in counter-terrorism activities. In October 2004 the Chairman of the SPDC, Than Shwe, paid the first visit to India by a Myanma head of state in 24 years, agreeing to further bilateral co-operation at meetings with the Indian President and Prime Minister. Following discussions between the two countries' respective Ministers of Home Affairs in October 2005, Myanmar and India agreed to a policy of joint interrogation of persons arrested for militant activities and on charges of smuggling drugs or weapons. In March 2006 President Aavul Pakkiri Jainulabidin Abdul Kalam visited Yangon, the first ever state visit to Myanmar by an Indian President. In September senior officials of the Myanma and Indian Ministries of Home Affairs signed an agreement to increase security co-operation. Than Shwe visited India for a second time in July 2010, whereupon he met with Indian President Pratibha Patil and Prime Minister Dr Manmohan Singh; during his visit the two countries signed five bilateral agreements intended to enhance co-operation in the fields of energy, anti-terrorism measures and defence, as well as boosting co-operation in efforts to combat transnational drugs-trafficking, money-laundering and weapons-smuggling.

A protocol agreement signed between Myanmar and Russia in 1999 provided for the holding of regular consultation meetings between the two countries' respective ministers responsible for foreign affairs, to facilitate co-operation on regional and international issues; the most recent such meeting was held in Moscow in October 2009. Meanwhile, in May 2007 it was announced that Russia was to assist with the construction of a 10-MW nuclear research reactor in Myanmar; an earlier agreement (concluded in 2002) had reportedly not been implemented because of Russian concerns that payment would not be made. The two countries were reported in December 2009 to have signed a US $570m. agreement whereby Russia would provide Myanmar with 20 fighter aircraft.

CONSTITUTION AND GOVERNMENT

A new Constitution was approved in a national referendum in May 2008 and entered into force on 31 January 2011. Multi-party elections, the first for more than 20 years, were held in November 2010; 25% of seats in the bicameral national legislature, which was to be responsible for choosing the country's President, were reserved for representatives of the military. Following the inauguration in March 2011 of the new President, the State Peace and Development Council (SPDC), which had been established by the ruling military junta in November 1997, was dissolved. The incoming Cabinet comprised 30 members and was dominated by former military officers.

REGIONAL AND INTERNATIONAL CO-OPERATION

Myanmar is a member of the Association of Southeast Asian Nations (ASEAN, see p. 206), the Asian Development Bank (ADB, see p. 202), the UN's Economic and Social Commission for Asia and the Pacific (ESCAP, see p. 37) and the Colombo Plan (see p. 446).

Myanmar became a member of the UN in 1948. As a contracting party to the General Agreement on Tariffs and Trade, Myanmar joined the World Trade Organization (WTO, see p. 430) on its establishment in 1995. Myanmar participates in the Group of 77 (G77, see p. 447) developing countries and the Non-aligned Movement (see p. 461), and is a member of the International Labour Organization (ILO, see p. 138).

ECONOMIC AFFAIRS

In 1986, according to estimates by the World Bank, Myanmar's gross national income (GNI), measured at average 1984–86 prices, was US $7,450m., equivalent to $200 per head. In 2000–09, it was estimated, the population increased at an average annual rate of 0.8%. Gross domestic product (GDP) per head increased, in real terms, by an average of 8.6% per year, while over the same period overall GDP increased by an annual average of 10.8%, according to the IMF. Real GDP expanded by 3.6% in 2008 and by 4.9% in 2009.

According to figures from the Asian Development Bank (ADB), agriculture (including forestry and fishing) contributed an estimated 38.2% of GDP in 2008/09. The sector was projected to engage 66.8% of the employed labour force at mid-2011, according to FAO. Rice is the staple crop, and production reached an estimated 30.5m. metric tons in 2008. In 2009/10 pulses and beans accounted for an estimated 12.3% of total exports. Other crops include sugar cane, maize, groundnuts, sesame seed, plantains and rubber. The fishing sector is also important. The total catch reached an estimated 3.2m. metric tons in 2008. Sales of teak and other hardwood provided an estimated 6.5% of total export revenue in 2009/10. Myanmar remained one of the world's largest sources of illicit opium. After several consecutive years of decline, the area under opium poppy cultivation reportedly began to rise in 2007. According to a survey conducted by the UN Office on Drugs and Crime (UNODC, see p. 83), the area under poppy cultivation expanded by an estimated 20% in 2010 to reach 38,100 ha. The potential production of dry opium was thought likely to have increased from 330 metric tons in 2009 to 580 tons in 2010. According to figures from the ADB, following yearly growth rates that in 2000–05 ranged between 6.0% (recorded in 2002) and a high point of 12.1% (2005), the real GDP of the agricultural sector increased at an average annual rate of 6.3% in 2006–09. Having reportedly expanded by 5.6% in 2008, agricultural GDP increased by a further 5.4% in 2009.

Industry (including mining, manufacturing, construction and utilities) provided an estimated 24.4% of GDP in 2008/09, according to the ADB. The industrial sector engaged 22.0% of the employed labour force (excluding activities not adequately defined) in 2005. According to the ADB, during 2000–05 yearly GDP growth rates ranged between 19.9% (in 2005) and 35.0% (2002). Between 2006 and 2009 industrial GDP increased at an average annual rate of 18.4%. The GDP of the industrial sector reportedly expanded by 18.0% in 2008 and by 17.6% in 2009.

Mining and quarrying was estimated to have contributed less than 1.0% of GDP in 2008/09. The sector engaged 0.7% of the employed labour force in 1997/98. Significant new onshore and offshore discoveries of natural gas and petroleum resulted from exploration and production-sharing agreements with foreign companies, the first of which was signed in 1989. In 2005, however, the Government announced that henceforth all onshore oil and gas blocks would be operated exclusively by a state enterprise. Other important minerals that are commercially exploited include tin, copper, coal, lead, jade, gemstones, silver and gold; some of Myanmar's potentially lucrative mineral resources remain largely unexploited. According to figures from the ADB, the GDP of the mining sector increased at an average annual rate of 10.7% between 2006 and 2009, rising by 12.0% in the latter year.

Manufacturing contributed an estimated 18.2% of GDP in 2008/09, and the sector engaged 9.1% of the employed labour force in 1998. The most important branches are food- and beverage-processing, the production of industrial raw materials (cement, plywood and fertilizers), petroleum refining and textiles. Revenue from garment exports rose from 1,554.6m. kyats in 2007/08 to an estimated 1,593.9m. kyats in 2008/09, equivalent to 4.3% of total exports in the latter year. The real GDP of the manufacturing sector expanded, according to figures from the ADB, at an average annual rate of 19.5% between 2006 and 2009, increasing by 19.0% in 2009.

Construction provided 4.5% of GDP in 2008/09, according to the ADB. The sector engaged only 2.2% of the employed labour force (excluding activities not adequately defined) in 1998. Between 2006 and 2009, according to figures from the ADB, construction GDP increased at an average annual rate of 16.3%. According to ADB data, the sector's GDP was estimated to have grown by 13.8% in 2009.

Energy is derived principally from hydroelectric power, which in 2006 contributed 53.9% of total electricity production; natural gas, which accounted for 40.2%; and petroleum, 5.8%. China has provided assistance in the development of hydropower resources. Imports of mineral oils accounted for around 12.8% of total imports in 2008/09.

The services sector contributed 37.4% of GDP in 2008/09, according to the ADB, and engaged 25.1% of the employed labour force in 1997/98. Tourism revenue is an important source of foreign exchange. However, revenue from this sector declined from US $85m. in 2005 to $59m. in 2006. The number of tourist arrivals decreased from 248,076 in 2007 to 193,319 in 2008. In 2000–05, according to the ADB, the sector's yearly rates of GDP growth ranged between 12.9% (in 2001) and 14.8% (2002). The GDP growth rate of the services sector averaged 12.2% annually in 2006–09. GDP growth in the sector was reported to have reached 11.6% in 2008 and 11.9% in 2009.

In 2006 Myanmar recorded a visible trade surplus of US $2,211.3m., and there was a surplus of $802.0m. on the current account of the balance of payments. In 2009/10 the principal sources of imports were the People's Republic of China (which supplied 30.0% of the total), Singapore (28.9%) and Thailand; other major suppliers were Malaysia and Indonesia. The principal market for exports (42.2%) was Thailand; other significant purchasers were India, Hong Kong, Singapore and China. The principal imports in 2009/10 were machinery and transport equipment, refined mineral oils, and base metals and manufactures. The principal exports in that year included gas (which accounted for 38.4% of total export earnings), dried pulses, teak and other hardwoods and also garments.

In the financial year ending 31 March 2006 there was an estimated budgetary deficit of 189,251m. kyats (excluding the capital account). The budget deficit was estimated by the ADB to have increased from the equivalent of 3.4% of GDP in 2008 to 3.7% in 2009. Myanmar's general government gross debt was 16,356.08m. kyats in 2009, equivalent to 50.8% of GDP. The external debt at the end of 2008 totalled US $7,210m., of which $5,413m. was public and publicly guaranteed debt; in 2006 the cost of servicing external debt was equivalent to 2.5% of exports of goods and services. The annual rate of inflation averaged 25.4% in 2000–08. According to the ADB, the rate of inflation decreased from 8.2% in 2009 to 7.3% in 2010. The rate of unemployment in 2008 was estimated by the ADB at 4.0% of the labour force.

Weaknesses in data, compounded by the vast disparity between the official and market values of the country's currency, have impeded accurate assessments of Myanmar's economy. Following a devastating cyclone in May 2008, an economic recovery plan was drafted for the period 2009–11; the projected budget of US $690m. was to be largely financed by international donors. Steep increases in consumer prices were recorded in 2007–08. Although consumer prices declined substantially during 2009, inflationary pressures were reported to be rising once again in the latter part of 2010. The transfer of various state assets to the private sector was reportedly under consideration in 2010. The value of exports of natural gas rose by 22% in the year to March 2010, and the hydrocarbons sector subsequently benefited from stronger international prices for the commodity. The limitations of Myanmar's banking system and also of its financial markets continued to deter some foreign investors. None the less, foreign direct investment remained relatively stable in 2010, and in early 2011 it was reported that the oil sector had received $8,000m. from Chinese investors. As part of a 10-year programme to develop a major maritime hub and industrial estate in the coastal town of Dawei, in early 2011 plans for the establishment of special economic zones within Myanmar were announced. In view of the success of similar schemes elsewhere in South-East Asia, the Government hoped to attract greater foreign investment to these new zones by means of tax incentives. To be developed in collaboration with Italian and Thai interests, the infrastructure project at Dawei was reported to require total investment of $58,000m. Although official statistics continued to indicate strong economic growth, other sources suggested that progress was more modest. The ADB estimated GDP growth at 7.2% in the year to March 2010, forecasting that GDP would expand by 5.5% in 2010/11, The Bank highlighted the need for the implementation of a more coherent reform strategy. The disparity between the official and the market exchange rates for the country's currency remained a major issue. The ADB also noted the inadequacy of living standards and the continuing shortage of credit facilities for agricultural producers.

PUBLIC HOLIDAYS

2012: 4 January (Independence Day), 13 February (for Union Day), 2 March (Peasants' Day, anniversary of the 1962 coup), March* (Full Moon of Tabaung), 27 March (Armed Forces' Day), 13–15 April* (Maha Thingyan—Water Festival), April* (Myanma New Year), May* (Full Moon of Kason), 1 May (Workers' Day), 2 July* (Full Moon of Waso and beginning of Buddhist Lent), 19 July (Martyrs' Day), 29 October* (Full Moon of Thadingyut and end of Buddhist Lent), 4 November* (Tazaungdaing Festival), 8 December* (National Day), 19 December* (Kayin New Year), 25 December (Christmas Day).

* A number of holidays depend on lunar sightings.

MYANMAR

Statistical Survey

Source (unless otherwise stated): Central Statistical Organization, Ministry of National Planning and Economic Development, Building 32, Nay Pyi Taw; tel. (67) 406325; fax (67) 407265; e-mail cso.stat@mptmail.net.mm; internet www.csostat.gov.mm.

Area and Population

AREA, POPULATION AND DENSITY

Area (sq km)	676,552*
Population (census results)	
31 March 1973	28,885,867
31 March 1983†	
Males	17,507,837
Females	17,798,352
Total	35,306,189
Population (UN estimates at mid-year)‡	
2009	50,019,774
2010	50,495,672
2011	50,992,357
Density (per sq km) at mid-2011	75.4

* 261,218 sq miles.
† Figures exclude adjustment for underenumeration. Also excluded are 7,716 Myanma citizens (males 5,704, females 2,012) abroad.
‡ Source: UN, *World Population Prospects: The 2008 Revision*.

POPULATION BY AGE AND SEX
(UN estimates at mid-2011)

	Males	Females	Total
0–14	6,746,599	6,683,989	13,430,588
15–64	16,886,788	17,856,725	34,743,513
65 and over	1,259,529	1,558,727	2,818,256
Total	24,892,916	26,099,441	50,992,357

Source: UN, *World Population Prospects: The 2008 Revision*.

PRINCIPAL TOWNS
(population at census of 31 March 1983)

Yangon (Rangoon)	2,513,023	Pathein (Bassein)	144,096
Mandalay	532,949	Taunggyi	108,231
Mawlamyine (Moulmein)	219,961	Sittwe (Akyab)	107,621
Bago (Pegu)	150,528	Manywa	106,843

Source: UN, *Demographic Yearbook*.

Mid-2010 (incl. suburbs, UN estimates): Yangon 4,349,604; Mandalay 1,034,167; Nay Pyi Taw 1,024,162 (Source: UN, *World Urbanization Prospects: The 2009 Revision*).

BIRTHS AND DEATHS
(annual averages, UN estimates)

	1995–2000	2000–05	2005–10
Birth rate (per 1,000)	22.2	21.5	20.7
Death rate (per 1,000)	10.1	10.0	9.9

Source: UN, *World Population Prospects: The 2008 Revision*.

Life expectancy (years at birth, WHO estimates): 54 (males 53; females 56) in 2008 (Source: WHO, *World Health Statistics*).

ECONOMICALLY ACTIVE POPULATION*
('000 persons, official estimates)

	1997	1998
Agriculture, hunting, forestry and fishing	11,381	11,507
Mining and quarrying	132	121
Manufacturing	1,573	1,666
Electricity, gas and water	21	48
Construction	378	400
Trade, restaurants and hotels	1,746	1,781
Transport, storage and communications	470	495
Financing, insurance, real estate and business services	577	597
Community, social and personal services†	1,686	1,744
Total employed	**17,964**	**18,359**
Unemployed‡	535	452
Total labour force	**18,499**	**18,811**

* Excludes members of the armed forces.
† Includes activities not adequately defined.
‡ Persons aged 18 years and over.

Unemployed ('000 persons aged 18 years and over): 183.4 in 2006; 118.7 in 2007; 137.8 in 2008 (Source: ILO).

Mid-2011 ('000 persons, estimates): Agriculture, etc. 19,997; Total labour force 29,952 (Source: FAO).

Health and Welfare

KEY INDICATORS

Total fertility rate (children per woman, 2008)	2.3
Under-5 mortality rate (per 1,000 live births, 2008)	122
HIV/AIDS (% of persons aged 15–49, 2007)	0.7
Physicians (per 1,000 head, 2004)	0.4
Hospital beds (per 1,000 head, 2000)	0.7
Health expenditure (2007): US $ per head (PPP)	21
Health expenditure (2007): % of GDP	1.9
Health expenditure (2007): public (% of total)	11.7
Access to water (% of persons, 2008)	71
Access to sanitation (% of persons, 2008)	81
Total carbon dioxide emissions ('000 metric tons, 2007)	13,179.4
Carbon dioxide emissions per head (metric tons, 2007)	0.3
Human Development Index (2010): ranking	132
Human Development Index (2010): value	0.451

For sources and definitions, see explanatory note on p. vi.

Agriculture

PRINCIPAL CROPS
('000 metric tons)

	2006	2007	2008
Wheat	142	158	158*
Rice, paddy	30,924	31,450	30,500†
Maize	1,032	1,114	1,114*
Millet	163†	166†	166*
Potatoes	449	471	471*
Sweet potatoes*	56	57	57
Cassava (Manioc)*	207	211	211
Sugar cane*	7,100	7,000	7,000
Beans, dry	2,502	2,500*	2,500*
Peas, dry*	38	40	40
Chick peas	260	260*	260*
Cow peas, dry	149	150*	150*
Pigeon peas	600	600*	600*
Arecanuts*	59	60	60
Soybeans (Soya beans)	186	185†	192†
Groundnuts, with shell	1,023*	1,000†	1,000*

MYANMAR

—continued

	2006	2007	2008
Coconuts*	365	370	370
Sunflower seed†	350	350	350
Sesame seed	439	590†	620†
Onions, dry*	735	740	740
Garlic	146	147*	147*
Plantains*	625	630	630
Tea	26†	27*	27*
Jute*	30	30	30
Tobacco, unmanufactured*	35	36	36
Natural rubber*	43	45	45

* FAO estimate(s).
† Unofficial figure(s).

2009: Soybeans (Soya beans) 200 (unofficial figure); Sunflower seed 350 (unofficial estimate). Note: Other data for individual crops in 2009 were not available.

Aggregate production ('000 metric tons, may include official, semi-official or estimated data): Total cereals 32,274 in 2006, 32,900 in 2007, 31,950 in 2008–09; Total roots and tubers 712 in 2006, 739 in 2007–09; Total vegetables (incl. melons) 4,031 in 2006, 4,087 in 2007–09; Total fruits (excl. melons) 1,825 in 2006, 1,880 in 2007–09.

Source: FAO.

LIVESTOCK
('000 head, year ending September)

	2006	2007	2008
Horses*	135	140	140
Cattle	12,364	12,634	12,929
Buffaloes	2,770	2,842	2,924
Pigs	6,293	7,007	7,677
Sheep	567	497	525
Goats	2,024	2,376	2,624
Chickens	93,737	107,771	107,771*
Ducks	10,098	11,144	11,144*
Geese*	680	685	685

* FAO estimate(s).

2009 (FAO estimates): Sheep 535; Goats 2,750.

Source: FAO.

LIVESTOCK PRODUCTS
('000 metric tons)

	2007	2008	2009*
Cattle meat	130.2	139.6	114.0
Buffalo meat	29.3	31.6	39.8
Goat meat	22.0	23.7	24.0
Pig meat	410.7	463.1	450.0
Chicken meat	726.5	726.5*	n.a.
Cows' milk	980.3	980.3*	n.a.
Buffaloes' milk	220.5	220.5*	n.a.
Goats' milk*	12.0	13.0	13.0
Hen eggs	231.5	231.5*	n.a.
Other poultry eggs*	16.0	16.0	n.a.

* FAO estimate(s).

Source: FAO.

Forestry

ROUNDWOOD REMOVALS
('000 cubic metres, excl. bark)

	2003	2004	2005
Sawlogs, veneer logs and logs for sleepers	2,885	2,816	2,849
Other industrial wood	1,353	1,380	1,413
Fuel wood	37,954	37,560	38,286
Total	42,191	41,756	42,548

2006–09: Figures assumed to be unchanged from 2005 (FAO estimates).

Source: FAO.

SAWNWOOD PRODUCTION
('000 cubic metres, incl. railway sleepers)

	2004	2005	2006
Coniferous (softwood)*	77	61	80
Broadleaved (hardwood)	1,056	1,530	1,530†
Total†	1,133	1,591	1,610

* Unofficial figures.
† FAO estimate(s).

2007–09: Production assumed to be unchanged from 2006 (FAO estimates).

Source: FAO.

Fishing
('000 metric tons, live weight)

	2006	2007	2008
Capture*	2,006.8	2,235.6	2,493.8
Freshwater fishes	631.1	717.6	814.7
Marine fishes	1,345.4	1,485.7	1,643.6
Aquaculture	575.0*	604.7*	674.8
Common carp	15.8*	16.7*	18.6
Roho labeo	368.0*	389.3*	433.1
Total catch*	2,581.8	2,840.2	3,168.5

* FAO estimate(s).

Source: FAO.

Mining
(metric tons unless otherwise indicated)

	2006	2007	2008
Coal and lignite	331,445	283,703	249,442
Crude petroleum ('000 barrels)	7,675	7,625	7,242
Natural gas (million cu m)*	12,501	13,315	12,445
Copper ore†	19,500	15,100	6,900
Lead ore†‡	2,000	2,000	3,600
Zinc ore†	46	10	20
Tin concentrates†	566	499	499
Silver ore (kilograms)†	684	218	0
Gold ore (kilograms)†§‡	100	100	100
Feldspar‡§	10,000	10,000	10,000
Barite (Barytes)	2,930	6,813	5,679
Salt (unrefined, excl. brine)‡	35,000	35,000	35,000
Gypsum (crude)	68,651	75,116	82,224
Rubies, sapphires and spinel ('000 metric carats)§	3,017	2,847	3,570
Jade	20,647	20,003	30,896

* Marketed production.
† Figures refer to the metal content of ores and concentrates (including mixed concentrates).
‡ Estimated production.
§ Twelve months beginning 1 April of year stated.

Source: US Geological Survey.

MYANMAR

Industry

SELECTED PRODUCTS OF STATE-OWNED ENTERPRISES
('000 metric tons unless otherwise indicated)

	2007/08	2008/09	2009/10
Sugar	25.5	28.4	20.3
Beer ('000 gallons)	1,653.5	1,514.4	441.2
Cigarettes (million)	3,037.6	2,351.8	n.a.
Cotton fabrics ('000 yards)	15.5	19.1	20.0
Cotton yarn ('000 lbs)	16.6	13.9	15.1
Plywood ('000 sq ft)	157.4	135.6	160.2
Fertilizers	110.0	106.1	69.8
Diesel oil ('000 gallons)	55,802	50,582	32,843
Furnace oil ('000 gallons)	15,962	17,078	14,243
Liquefied petroleum gas ('000 gallons)	3,573	3,566	3,199
Motor spirit (petrol, '000 gallons)	109,940	103,854	112,615
Cement	611.4	690.8	628.2
Paper	14.9	19.9	13.3
Soap	76.8	76.9	67.4
Electric energy (million kWh)	6,398.0	6,621.8*	5,850.1*

* Provisional figure.

Finance

CURRENCY AND EXCHANGE RATES

Monetary Units
100 pyas = 1 kyat.

Sterling, Dollar and Euro Equivalents (29 October 2010)
£1 sterling = 8.619 kyats;
US $1 = 5.413 kyats;
€1 = 7.501 kyats;
100 kyats = £11.60 = $18.47 = €13.33.

Average Exchange Rate (kyats per US $)
2007   5.560
2008   5.388
2009   5.519

Note: Since January 1975 the value of the kyat has been linked to the IMF's special drawing right (SDR). Since May 1977 the official exchange rate has been fixed at a mid-point of SDR 1 = 8.5085 kyats. On 1 June 1996 a new customs valuation exchange rate of US $1 = 100 kyats was introduced. In September 2001 the free market exchange rate was $1 = 450 kyats.

CENTRAL GOVERNMENT BUDGET
(million kyats, year ending 31 March, excl. capital account)

Current revenue and grants	2003/04	2004/05	2005/06
Tax revenue	170,569	297,104	476,945
Taxes on income, profits and capital gains	91,860	138,866	206,676
Domestic taxes on goods and services	74,107	136,626	251,821
General sales, turnover or value-added tax	58,214	112,543	225,121
Taxes on international trade and transactions	4,602	21,613	18,448
Other revenue	213,542	290,190	342,273
Grants	111	171	316
Total	384,222	587,465	819,534

Current expenditure	2003/04	2004/05	2005/06
General public services, incl. public order	114,195	206,848	354,848
Defence	172,633	173,558	197,792
Education	71,665	101,936	68,676
Health	18,808	26,545	21,963
Social security and welfare	7,865	9,933	8,406
Recreational, cultural and religious affairs	4,112	5,863	4,511
Economic affairs and services	194,354	234,513	346,361
Agriculture, forestry, fishing and hunting	61,056	71,028	93,300
Transportation	119,190	131,839	198,261
Housing and community amenities	7,397	8,622	6,228
Total	591,029	767,818	1,008,785

Source: IMF, *Government Finance Statistics Yearbook*.

INTERNATIONAL RESERVES
(US $ million at 31 December)

	2004	2005	2006
Gold (national valuation)	12.6	11.6	12.2
IMF special drawing rights	0.0	0.2	0.2
Foreign exchange	672.1	770.5	1,235.4
Total	684.7	782.3	1,247.8

IMF special drawing rights: 0.4 in 2007; 0.1 in 2008; 113.3 in 2009.

Source: IMF, *International Financial Statistics*.

MONEY SUPPLY
(million kyats at 31 December)

	2007	2008	2009
Currency outside banks	2,696,621	2,922,503	3,568,431
Demand deposits at deposit money banks	520,490	513,776	690,219
Total money (incl. others)	3,217,307	3,436,519	4,259,827

Source: IMF, *International Financial Statistics*.

COST OF LIVING
(Consumer Price Index; base: 2000 = 100)

	2006	2007	2008
Food (incl. beverages)	365.7	493.9	638.3
Fuel and light	370.0	491.7	561.9
Clothing (incl. footwear)	337.6	462.9	583.4
Rent	388.8	518.7	658.6
All items (incl. others)	356.5	481.3	610.3

Source: ILO.

NATIONAL ACCOUNTS
(million kyats at current prices, year ending 31 March)

Expenditure on the Gross Domestic Product

	2005/06	2006/07	2007/08
Final consumption expenditure	10,682,305	14,291,377	19,861,427
Increase in stocks	57,041	23,996	43,470
Gross fixed capital formation	1,563,754	2,282,421	3,390,475
Total domestic expenditure	12,303,100	16,597,794	23,295,372
Exports of goods and services	19,803	29,295	33,995
Less Imports of goods and services	11,514	16,835	18,419
Statistical discrepancy	−24,623	242,504	25,165
GDP in purchasers' values	12,286,765	16,852,758	23,336,113
GDP at constant 2005/06 prices	12,286,765	13,893,395	15,559,413

MYANMAR

Gross Domestic Product by Economic Activity

	2007/08	2008/09	2009/10
Agriculture, hunting, forestry and fishing	10,109,849	11,773,735	12,888,806
Mining and quarrying	205,344	254,408	328,488
Manufacturing	3,473,910	4,917,322	6,135,357
Electricity, gas and water	189,790	212,414	251,102
Construction	893,654	1,236,065	1,518,309
Wholesale and retail trade	4,915,159	6,175,063	6,890,046
Transport, storage and communications	2,781,665	3,731,536	4,567,731
Finance	16,948	20,938	22,575
Government services	371,290	399,679	548,674
Other services	378,504	506,375	609,840
GDP in purchasers' values	23,336,113	29,227,535	33,760,928

Source: Asian Development Bank.

BALANCE OF PAYMENTS
(US $ million)

	2004	2005	2006
Exports of goods f.o.b.	2,926.6	3,787.8	4,554.7
Imports of goods f.o.b.	−1,998.7	−1,759.4	−2,343.4
Trade balance	927.9	2,028.4	2,211.3
Exports of services	254.7	259.1	279.5
Imports of services	−459.6	−502.0	−562.9
Balance on goods and services	723.0	1,785.5	1,928.0
Other income received	40.4	55.5	97.8
Other income paid	−785.8	−1,427.3	−1,346.2
Balance on goods, services and income	−22.4	413.8	679.6
Current transfers received	160.6	197.8	161.4
Current transfers paid	−26.7	−23.8	−39.0
Current balance	111.5	587.7	802.0
Direct investment from abroad	213.5	237.2	278.6
Other investment liabilities	−88.3	−71.1	−25.6
Net errors and omissions	−142.7	−610.3	−632.1
Overall balance	94.0	143.6	422.9

Source: IMF, *International Financial Statistics*.

2007 (US $ million): Exports of goods 6,279.3; Imports of goods −3,027.0; *Trade balance* 3,252.3; Services and other income (net) −1,605.2; *Balance on goods, services and income* 1,647.1; Current transfers received 233.2; Current transfers paid −27.3; *Current balance* 1,853.0 (Source: Asian Development Bank).

2008 (US $ million): Exports of goods 6,915.6; Imports of goods −3,887.8; *Trade balance* 3,027.8; Services and other income (net) −1,946.1; *Balance on goods, services and income* 1,081.7; Current transfers received 340.6; Current transfers paid −53.2; *Current balance* 1,369.1 (Source: Asian Development Bank).

2009 (US $ million): Exports of goods 6,673.1; Imports of goods −3,951.4; *Trade balance* 2,721.7; Services and other income (net) −2,254.1; *Balance on goods, services and income* 467.6; Current transfers received 326.0; Current transfers paid −64.0; *Current balance* 729.6 (Source: Asian Development Bank).

External Trade

PRINCIPAL COMMODITIES
(distribution by SITC, million kyats, year ending 31 March)

Imports c.i.f.	2007/08	2008/09	2009/10
Edible vegetable oil and other hydrogenated oils	1,057.7	1,610.0	975.9
Pharmaceutical products	635.6	679.0	797.7
Base metals and manufactures	1,206.2	1,818.3	1,992.9
Machinery and transport equipment	4,161.7	7,240.2	4,908.2
Electrical machinery and apparatus	861.1	948.6	977.1
Paper, paperboard and manufactures	292.3	391.7	318.1
Refined mineral oils	2,034.0	3,192.2	3,674.3
Fabric of artificial materials and synthetics	1,168.5	817.4	780.2
Plastic	857.0	908.8	859.2
Total (incl. others)	18,418.9	24,873.8	22,837.4

Exports f.o.b.	2007/08	2008/09	2009/10
Dried beans, peas, etc. (shelled)	3,462.5	4,068.8	5,062.9
Fresh and dried prawns	556.3	472.1	346.2
Fish and fish products	1,059.4	972.3	1,053.3
Teak	1,540.0	1,146.3	1,171.7
Other hardwood	1,423.8	1,065.7	1,518.9
Base metals and ores	474.8	176.5	182.7
Gas	13,937.9	12,995.7	15,853.8
Garments	1,554.6	1,593.9	1,543.7
Total (incl. others)	35,296.8	37,027.8	41,289.1

PRINCIPAL TRADING PARTNERS
(million kyats, year ending 31 March)

Imports	2007/08	2008/09	2009/10
China, People's Republic	5,472.5	6,578.1	6,854.9
Hong Kong	115.6	177.7	59.8
India	849.7	796.8	1,058.5
Indonesia	1,244.9	1,139.5	760.4
Japan	1,335.0	908.4	1,412.4
Korea, Republic	590.8	1,027.3	1,221.5
Malaysia	635.8	1,972.1	871.3
Singapore	4,489.8	5,712.7	6,593.0
Thailand	2,101.7	2,150.7	2,069.6
Total (incl. others)	18,418.9	24,873.8	22,837.4

Exports	2007/08	2008/09	2009/10
China, People's Republic	3,832.7	3,352.3	3,359.0
Hong Kong	3,573.0	3,611.0	5,162.9
India	4,005.9	4,387.8	5,512.9
Indonesia	477.0	155.1	205.3
Japan	1,021.3	1,005.8	966.1
Malaysia	652.6	1,716.0	832.2
Singapore	2,210.1	4,638.4	3,690.9
Thailand	15,530.0	14,340.6	17,431.0
United Kingdom	316.5	284.4	202.6
Total (incl. others)	35,296.8	37,027.8	41,289.1

Transport

RAILWAYS
(traffic, million)

	2007/08	2008/09	2009/10
Passenger-miles	3,378	3,405	3,338
Freight ton-miles	535	581	658

MYANMAR

ROAD TRAFFIC
(registered motor vehicles at 31 March)

	2007/08	2008/09	2009/10
Passenger cars	222,661	239,895	254,797
Trucks	57,211	58,857	61,132
Buses	19,291	19,683	19,807
Motorcycles	658,997	1,612,423	1,749,083
Others	74,682	68,102	62,585
Total	1,032,842	1,998,960	2,147,404

INLAND WATERWAYS
(traffic by state-owned vessels)

	2007/08	2008/09	2009/10
Passenger-miles (million)	721	783	820
Freight ton-miles (million)	582	639	687

SHIPPING
Merchant Fleet
(registered at 31 December)

	2007	2008	2009
Number of vessels	118	115	117
Displacement ('000 grt)	203.2	165.6	182.5

Source: IHS Fairplay, *World Fleet Statistics*.

International Sea-borne Traffic
('000 metric tons)

	2007/08	2008/09	2009/10
Goods loaded	1,951	2,955	4,539
Goods unloaded	4,252	4,123	6,883

CIVIL AVIATION
(traffic on scheduled services)

	2004	2005	2006
Kilometres flown (million)	19	20	22
Passengers carried ('000)	1,392	1,504	1,621
Passenger-km (million)	1,339	1,448	1,559
Total ton-km (million)	122	132	142

Source: UN, *Statistical Yearbook*.

Passenger-miles (million): 75.3 in 2006/07; 77.6 in 2007/08; 81.9 in 2008/09; 71.9 in 2009/10.

Tourism

TOURIST ARRIVALS BY COUNTRY OF NATIONALITY

	2006	2007	2008
Australia	6,583	6,761	5,374
China, People's Republic	24,893	29,551	30,792
France	15,498	15,521	8,217
Germany	18,003	15,432	8,947
India	7,540	7,675	7,173
Italy	10,774	10,130	3,030
Japan	18,945	15,623	10,881
Korea, Republic	18,265	13,821	12,369
Malaysia	9,588	8,693	8,268
Singapore	10,952	9,310	8,599
Taiwan	15,827	13,707	11,472
Thailand	30,400	35,002	27,311
United Kingdom	7,465	6,356	5,397
USA	18,052	14,862	13,195
Total (incl. others)	263,514	248,076	193,319

Tourism receipts (US $ million, incl. passenger transport): 97 in 2004; 85 in 2005; 59 in 2006.

Source: World Tourism Organization.

Communications Media

	2007	2008	2009
Telephones ('000 main lines in use)	464.1	504.4	552.3
Mobile cellular telephones ('000 subscribers)	247.6	367.4	502.0
Internet users ('000)	106.7	108.9	110.0
Broadband subscribers ('000)	6.5	10.0	15.0

Personal computers: 450,000 (9.2 per 1,000 persons) in 2006.
Book production (1999): 227 titles.
Newspapers (1998): 4 dailies (average circulation 400,000).
Radio receivers ('000 in use): 3,157 in 1999.
Television receivers ('000 in use): 344.3 in 2000.
Sources: International Telecommunication Union; UNESCO, *Statistical Yearbook*; UN, *Statistical Yearbook*.

Education

(1994/95, provisional)

	Institutions	Teachers	Students
Primary schools*	35,856	169,748	5,711,202
Middle schools	2,058	53,859	1,390,065
High schools	858	18,045	389,438
Vocational schools	86	1,847	21,343
Teacher training	17	615	4,031
Higher education	45	6,246	247,348
Universities	6	2,901	62,098

* Excluding 1,152 monastic primary schools with an enrolment of 45,360.

2001/02 (provisional): *Primary:* Institutions 36,010; Teachers 143,490; Students ('000) 4,793.5. *General secondary:* Institutions 2,110; Teachers 53,896; Students ('000) 1,600.9. *Tertiary:* Institutions 958; Teachers 15,947; Students ('000) 587.3 (Source: UN, *Statistical Yearbook for Asia and the Pacific*).

2006/07: *Pre-primary:* Teachers 5,279; Students 98,545. *Primary:* Teachers 172,209; Students 5,013,582. *General secondary:* Teachers 81,943; Students 2,686,198. *Tertiary:* Teachers 10,669; Students 507,660 (Source: UNESCO Institute for Statistics).

2007/08: *Pre-primary:* Teachers 6,390; Students 112,268. *Primary:* Teachers 177,331; Students 5,109,630. *General secondary:* Teachers 82,001; Students 2,828,868. *Tertiary:* Students 507,660 (Source: UNESCO Institute for Statistics).

Pupil-teacher ratio (primary education, UNESCO estimate): 28.8 in 2007/08 (Source: UNESCO Institute for Statistics).

Adult literacy rate (UNESCO estimates): 91.9% (males 94.7%; females 89.2%) in 2008 (Source: UNESCO Institute for Statistics).

MYANMAR

Directory

The Government

HEAD OF STATE

President: Thein Sein (took office 30 March 2011).
Vice-Presidents: Tin Aung Myint Oo, Dr Sai Mauk Kham.

CABINET
(May 2011)

Minister of Defence: Maj.-Gen. Hla Min.
Minister of Home Affairs: Lt-Gen. Ko Ko.
Minister of Border Affairs and Myanma Industrial Development: Maj.-Gen. Thein Htay.
Minister of Foreign Affairs: Wunna Maung Lwin.
Minister of Information and Culture: Kyaw Hsan.
Minister of Agriculture and Irrigation: Myint Hlaing.
Minister of Forestry: Win Tun.
Minister of Finance and Revenue: Hla Tun.
Minister of Construction: Khin Maung Myint.
Minister of National Planning and Economic Development and of Livestock and Fisheries: Tin Naing Thein.
Minister of Commerce: Win Myint.
Minister of Posts and Telecommunications: Thein Tun.
Minister of Labour and of Social Welfare, Relief and Resettlement: Aung Kyi.
Minister of Mines: Thein Htike.
Minister of Co-operatives: Ohn Myint.
Minister of Transportation: Nyan Tun Aung.
Minister of Hotels and Tourism and of Sports: Tint San.
Minister of Industry (No. 1): Kyaw Swar Khine.
Minister of Industry (No. 2): Soe Thein.
Minister of Rail Transportation: Aung Min.
Minister of Energy: Than Htay.
Minister of Electric Power (No. 1): Zaw Min.
Minister of Electric Power (No. 2): Khin Maung Soe.
Minister of Education: Dr Mya Aye.
Minister of Health: Dr Pe Thet Khin.
Minister of Religious Affairs: Thura Myint Maung.
Minister of Science and Technology: Aye Myint.
Minister of Immigration and Manpower: Khin Yi.
Ministers of President Office: Thein Nyunt, Soe Maung.

MINISTRIES

Ministry of President Office: Nay Pyi Taw.
Ministry of Agriculture and Irrigation: Bldg 15, Nay Pyi Taw; tel. (67) 410004; fax (67) 140130; e-mail dap.moai@myanmar.com.mm; internet www.moai.gov.mm.
Ministry of Border Affairs: Bldg 14, Nay Pyi Taw; tel. (67) 409022; e-mail pbanrda@mptmail.net.mm; internet www.myanmar.gov.mm/PBNRDA/index.htm.
Ministry of Commerce: Bldg 3, Nay Pyi Taw; tel. (67) 408002; fax (67) 408004; e-mail moc@commerce.gov.mm; internet www.commerce.gov.mm.
Ministry of Construction: Bldg 11, Nay Pyi Taw; tel. (67) 407073; fax (67) 407181; e-mail pwscon@constuction.gov.mm; internet www.construction.gov.mm.
Ministry of Co-operatives: Bldg 16, Nay Pyi Taw; tel. (67) 410032; fax (67) 410036; e-mail mcop@mptmail.net.mm; internet www.myancoop.gov.mm.
Ministry of Culture: Bldg 35, Nay Pyi Taw; tel. (67) 408023.
Ministry of Defence: Bldg 20, Nay Pyi Taw.
Ministry of Education: Bldg 13, Nay Pyi Taw; tel. (67) 407131; internet www.myanmar-education.edu.mm.
Ministry of Electric Power (No. 1): Bldg 38, Nay Pyi Taw; tel. (67) 411083.
Ministry of Electric Power (No. 2): Bldg 27, Nay Pyi Taw.
Ministry of Energy: Bldg 6, Nay Pyi Taw; tel. (67) 411046; fax (67) 411114; e-mail myanmoe@mptmail.net.mm; internet www.energy.gov.mm.
Ministry of Finance and Revenue: Bldg 26, Nay Pyi Taw; tel. (67) 410046; internet www.myanmar.com/finance.
Ministry of Foreign Affairs: Bldg 9, Nay Pyi Taw; tel. (67) 412359; e-mail mofa.aung@mptmail.net.mm; internet www.mofa.gov.mm.
Ministry of Forestry: Bldg 28, Nay Pyi Taw; tel. (67) 405004.
Ministry of Health: Bldg 4, Nay Pyi Taw; tel. (67) 411358; internet www.moh.gov.mm.
Ministry of Home Affairs: Bldg 10, Nay Pyi Taw; tel. (67) 412079; internet www.myanmar.gov.mm/ministry/home/default.htm.
Ministry of Hotels and Tourism: Bldg 33, Nay Pyi Taw; tel. (67) 406056; fax (67) 406057; e-mail dg.dht@mptmail.net.mm; internet www.myanmartourism.org.
Ministry of Immigration and Manpower: Bldg 23, Nay Pyi Taw; tel. (67) 404026.
Ministry of Industry (No. 1): Bldg 37, Nay Pyi Taw; tel. (67) 408063; fax (67) 408080; e-mail moi1@myanmar.com.mm; internet www.industry1myanmar.com.
Ministry of Industry (No. 2): Bldg 30, Nay Pyi Taw; tel. (67) 405042; e-mail dmip@mptmail.net.mm; internet www.industry2.gov.mm.
Ministry of Information: Bldg 7, Nay Pyi Taw; tel. (67) 412321.
Ministry of Labour: Bldg 51, Nay Pyi Taw; tel. (67) 404339; e-mail mol@mptmail.net.mm; internet www.mol.gov.mm.
Ministry of Livestock and Fisheries: Bldg 36, Nay Pyi Taw; tel. (67) 408045; e-mail dolf@mptmail.net.mm.
Ministry of Mines: Bldg 19, Nay Pyi Taw; tel. (67) 409001; internet www.energy.gov.mm/MOM_1.htm.
Ministry of Myanma Industrial Development: Nay Pyi Taw.
Ministry of National Planning and Economic Development: Bldg 1, Nay Pyi Taw; tel. (67) 407023; fax (67) 407004; e-mail ministry.nped@mptmail.net.mm; internet www.mnped.gov.mm.
Ministry of Posts and Telecommunications: Bldg 2, Nay Pyi Taw; tel. (67) 407037; internet www.mcpt.gov.mm.
Ministry of Rail Transportation: Bldg 29, Nay Pyi Taw; tel. (67) 405034.
Ministry of Religious Affairs: Bldg 31, Nay Pyi Taw; tel. (67) 406008; internet www.mora.gov.mm.
Ministry of Science and Technology: Bldg 21, Nay Pyi Taw; tel. (67) 404004; fax (67) 404011; internet www.most.gov.mm.
Ministry of Social Welfare, Relief and Resettlement: Bldg 23, Nay Pyi Taw; tel. (67) 404021; e-mail social-wel-myan@mptmail.net.mm; internet www.myanmar.gov.mm/ministry/MSWRR/index.html.
Ministry of Sports: Bldg 31, Nay Pyi Taw; tel. (67) 406028; e-mail MOCYGN.MYA@mptmail.net.mm; internet www.mosports.gov.mm.
Ministry of Transportation: Bldg 5, Nay Pyi Taw; tel. (67) 411033; fax (67) 411420; e-mail dept.transport@mptmail.net.mm; internet www.mot.gov.mm.

Legislature

PYIDAUNGSU HLUTTAW (UNION ASSEMBLY)

The 2008 Constitution provided for the establishment of a bicameral Pyidaungsu Hluttaw (Union Assembly), comprising the Pyithu Hluttaw, with 440 seats, and the Amyotha Hluttaw (National Assembly), with 224 seats. In both chambers 25% of seats were reserved for appointed representatives of the armed forces. On 7 November 2010, for the first time in more than 20 years, multi-party elections to both chambers of the Pyidaungsu Hluttaw, and to 14 state and regional assemblies, were held.

Amyotha Hluttaw (National Assembly)

The Amyotha Hluttaw comprises 168 civilian representatives (12 from each of the seven states and seven regions) and 56 military representatives, who are appointed by the Commander-in-Chief of the Defence Services.

Speaker: Khin Aung Myint.

MYANMAR

Pyithu Hluttaw (People's Assembly)

Speaker: SHWE MANN.

General Election, 7 November 2010 (provisional results)

Party	Seats
Union Solidarity and Development Party	259
Shan Nationalities Democratic Party	18
National Democratic Force	12
National Unity Party	12
Rakhine Nationalities Development Party	9
All Mon Region Democracy Party	3
Pa-O National Organization	3
Chin National Party	2
Chin Progressive Party	2
Phalon-Sawaw Democratic Party	2
Wa Democratic Party	2
Others	6
Appointed members*	110
Total	**440**

* Military representatives appointed by the Commander-in-Chief of the Defence Services.

Election Commission

Union Election Commission (UEC): Nay Pyi Taw; f. 2010; Chair. Lt-Gen. (retd) TIN AYE; Sec. WIN KO.

Political Organizations

By September 2010 37 parties had successfully registered to participate in the legislative elections of 7 November; these included:

All Mon Region Democracy Party: Lot 7, Holdings Kha 23, 20th St, Myinethaya Ward, Mawlamyine, Mon State; f. 2010; sole party registered for 2010 election representing the Mon ethnic group; advocates democracy and a free-market economy; Chair. NAI NGWE THEIN.

Chin National Party: 277 BPI Rd, West Gyogon Ward, Insein Township, Yangon; tel. (1) 5030870; f. 2010; Chair. PU ZOZAM.

Chin Progressive Party: Room 22, Bldg 2, Pyi Yeik Mon Housing Estate, Narnattaw Rd, Ward 8, Kamayut Township, Yangon; f. 2010; promotes equal rights and economic opportunities for Chin people; Pres. PU NOTHANKAP.

Democratic Party: 6 Kwat Thit St, Yegyaw, Pazundaung Township, Yangon; f. 1988; re-formed 2010; Leader THU WAI.

88 Generation Students and Youth Organization: Room 301, Bldg F, Pearl Condominium, Kaba Aye Pagoda Rd, Bahan, Yangon; f. 2010; Leader YE HTUN.

Kayin People's Party (KPP): 51 Tawwin Rd, Ward 3, Shwe Pyi Tha, Yangon; f. 2001; Leader SIMON THA; Chair. TUN AUNG MYINT.

Lahu National Development Party: 43 Fourth Lane, Parami Rd, Ward 1, Lashio, Shan State; f. 1988; deregistered 1994; reregistered 2010; Leader DANIEL AUNG.

Mro (or) Khami National Solidarity Organization (MKNSO): 202 Sartaik Rd, Pyitawtha Ward, Kyauktaw, Rakhine State; f. 1988; Chair. and Leader SAN THA AUNG.

National Democratic Force: Room 103, Bldg 3, Dagonlwin Rd, Mittanyunt Ward, Tamwy, Yangon; f. 2010; est. by fmr mems of the National League for Democracy; Chair. Dr THAN NYEIN; Co-Chair. KHIN MAUNG SWE.

National Political Alliance League: 49 16th St, Lanmadaw Township, Yangon; f. 2010; membership includes breakaway factions from the National League for Democracy; Leader OHN LWIN; Chair. TIN TUN MAUNG.

National Unity Party (NUP): 24 Aung Zeya St, Shwe Taung Gyar Ward 1, Bahan, Yangon; tel. (1) 278180; f. 1962; est. as the Burma Socialist Programme Party; sole legal political party until Sept. 1988, when present name was adopted; 15-mem. cen. exec. cttee and 280-mem. cen. cttee; Leader TUN YI; Sec.-Gen. THAN TIN.

Modern People's Party: Fifth Fl., 255 Bogyoke Aung San Rd, between 39th and 40th Sts, Ward 8, Kyauktada, Yangon; f. 2010; fmrly the New Era People's Party; Leader TUN AUNG KYAW.

Pa-O National Organization: 18 West Circular Rd, Zaypaing Ward, Taunggyi, Shan State; signed a cease-fire agreement with the military junta in April 1991; controls Special Region 6 in southern Shan State; 1,235 mems; Patron AUNG KHAM HTI; Chair. KHUN SAN LWIN; military wing: Pa-O National Army.

Peace and Diversity Party (PDP): 2/2/232 Mahawgani Rd, Htaukkyant, Mingaladon Township, Yangon; tel. 98610719 (mobile); f. 2010; Leader NYO MIN LWIN; Gen. Sec. NAY MYO WAI.

Phalon-Sawaw Democratic Party: Ward 7, Hpa-an Township, Karen State; f. 2010; represents the Karen ethnic group; Chair. KHIN KYAW OO.

Rakhine Nationalities Development Party: Khaung Laung Kyaung Rd, Lanmadaw (South) Ward, Sittwe Township, Rakhine State; f. 2010; Chair. Dr AYE MAUNG.

Shan Nationalities Democratic Party (SNDP): 9 Thitsar Uyin Housing, Thitsar Rd, Ward 8, South Okkalapa, Yangon; tel. (9) 5018229; f. 2010; also known as the White Tiger Party; won a total of 57 parliamentary seats in the 2010 national and regional elections; Chair. SAI AIK PAUNG; Vice-Chair. SAI SAUNG SI.

Taaung (Palaung) National Party: 110 Bogyoke Aung San Rd, Mingala Ward, Namhsan Township, Shan State; f. 2010; 3,300 mems; Gen. Sec. MAI OHN KHAING.

Union Democratic Party: 123 U Chit Maung Rd, North-West Saya San Ward, Bahan, Yangon; f. 2010; following a merger between the Public Democracy Party and the Union Democracy Alliance Party; espouses support for democracy, human rights and national reconciliation; Chair. THEIN HTAY.

Union of Myanmar Federation of National Politics (UMFNP): Bldg F, Rm 301, Pearl Condominium, Kabaraye Rd, Bahan Township, Yangon; tel. (1) 556554; f. 2010; broadly pro-govt group; Leader AYE LWIN.

Union Solidarity and Development Party (USDP): Plot 5, cnr of Yazathingaha Rd and C Rd, Dekkhinathiri Township, Nay Pyi Taw; f. 2010; est. as successor to the Union Solidarity and Development Asscn (USDA—formed in 1993 as civil society group intrinsically linked to the military regime); Leader THEIN SEIN; Chair. AUNG THAUNG.

Wa Democratic Party: tel. 4/7 Hsenwi Rd, Ward 8, Lashio, Shan State; f. 2010.

Wunthanu NLD: NanU Lwin Village, Pathein Gyi, Mandalay; f. 2010; Leader YE MIN.

Deregistered parties include:

Democratic Party for a New Society (DPNS): based in Thailand; e-mail hq@dpns.org; internet www.dpns.org; f. 1988; 8-mem. cen. exec. cttee; Chair. AUNG MOE ZAW; Gen. Sec. KHIN MAUNG TINT.

Kachin State Progressive Party (KSPP): Myothit Quarter, Myitkyina; f. 2009; 150-mem. cen. cttee; registration for 2010 elections withdrawn due to alleged links with the Kachin Independence Organisation; Leader Dr MANAN TUJA.

National League for Democracy (NLD): 97B West Shwegondine Rd, Bahan Township, Yangon; e-mail info@nldla.net; internet www.nldla.net; f. 1988; est. as Nat. United Front for Democracy; name subsequently changed to League for Democracy; above name adopted 1988; cen. exec. cttee of 20 mems; cen. cttee of 108 mems; Gen. Sec. AUNG SAN SUU KYI; Chair. AUNG SHWE; Vice-Chair. TIN OO.

Union Karen (Kayin) League: Saw Toe Lane, Yangon; Leaders SAW MAUNG CHAW, SAW THAN AUNG.

Union Pa-O National Organization: f. 1988; Leader KHUN SEIN WIN HLA.

United Nationalities League for Democracy: Yangon; an alliance of parties representing non-Bamar nationalities; won a combined total of 65 seats at the 1990 election.

Wa National Development Party: Lashio, Shan; dissolved following failure to register for 2010 elections; Chair. LOAP PAUNG; Leader SAW PHILIP SAM.

The following groups are, or have been, in armed conflict with the Government:

Chin National Front: internet www.chinland.org; f. 1988; forces trained by Kachin Independence Army 1989–91; first party congress 1993; carried out an active bombing campaign in 1996–97, mainly in Chin State; joined the Democratic Alliance of Burma (1988), the National Democratic Front (1989) and the Chin National Council (2006); Leader ZING CUNG; military wing: Chin National Army (Leader Col RAL HNIN).

Communist Party of Burma (CPB): internet www.cpburma.org; f. 1939; reorg. 1946; operated clandestinely after 1948; participated after 1986 in jt military operations with sections of the NDF; in 1989 internal dissent resulted in the rebellion of about 80% of CPB members, mostly Wa hill tribesmen and Kokang Chinese; the CPB's military efficacy was thus completely destroyed; leadership exiled in the People's Republic of China; Sec.-Gen. KYIN MAUNG.

Democratic Alliance of Burma (DAB): Manerplaw; f. 1988; formed by members of the NDF to incorporate dissident students, monks and expatriates; Pres. Maj.-Gen. BO MYA; Gen. Sec. TIN MAUNG WIN; remaining organizations include:

MYANMAR

All-Burma Student Democratic Front (ABSDF): Dagwin; e-mail absdfhq@csloxinfo.com; internet www.absdf8888.org; f. 1988; in 1990 split into two factions, under Moe Thi Zun and Naing Aung; the two factions reunited in 1993; Chair. Than Khe; Sec.-Gen. Myo Win.

Karen (Kayin) National Union (KNU): f. 1948; Chair. Gen. Tamala Baw; Vice-Chair. David Takapaw; Gen. Sec. Zipporah Sein; military wing: Karen (Kayin) National Liberation Army (KNLA); c. 6,000 troops; Chief of Staff Mu Tu.

Karenni (Kayinni) National Progressive Party: agreement with the SLORC signed in March 1995 but subsequently collapsed; resumed fighting in June 1996; Chair. Gen. Aung Than Lay; military wing: Karenni (Kayinni) Revolutionary Army.

National Democratic Front (NDF): POB 101, Mae Sot, Tak 63110, Thailand; e-mail ndf.burma@gmail.com; f. 1975; alliance of eight ethnic resistance groups incl. KNU, CNF, NMSP, PSLF; aims to establish a federal union based on national self-determination; Chair., Cen. Exec. Cttee David Takapaw.

Palaung State Liberation Front (PSLF): POB 368, Chiang Mai 50000, Thailand; e-mail palaungpslf@gmail.com; f. 1992; est. by mems of Palaung State Liberation Organization opposed to 1991 cease-fire agreement; Sec.-Gen. Mai Aik Phone.

Shan State Army (SSA): formed in 1964, the original SSA was engaged in an armed rebellion against the military regime until the signing of a cease-fire agreement in 1989; elements led by Sao Sai Lek rejected the cease-fire and came to be known as the **Shan State Army—South (SSA—S)**; following the dissolution of the separatist Mong Tai Army (MTA), in 1997 the SSA—S formed an alliance with the Shan State National Army (Leader Karn Yord), the Shan United Revolutionary Army and other MTA remnants; operates five bases close to the Thai–Myanma border; Leader Col Yawd Serk; political wing: **Restoration Council of Shan State** (300 mems; cen. cttee of 21 elected mems).

Most of the following groups signed cease-fire agreements, or reached other means of accommodation, with the ruling military junta (the date given in parentheses indicates the month in which agreement with the junta was concluded. In April 2009 the junta declared that all ethnic cease-fire groups would have to transform into new 'Border Guard Force' (BGF) battalions, including a component of 30 soldiers and one officer from the Myanmar Armed Forces; however, many groups resisted the order.

Democratic Karen (Kayin) Buddhist Organization: Manerplaw; breakaway group from the Karen (Kayin) National Union; military wing: Democratic Karen (Kayin) Buddhist Army; transformed into a BGF in August 2010; however, a breakaway faction rejected the agreement and resumed fighting in November; Leader Thuzana.

Kachin Defence Army: (Jan. 1991); fmrly the 4th Brigade of the Kachin Independence Army; adopted BGF status in Jan 2010; Leader Mahtu Naw.

Kachin Independence Organization (KIO): (Feb. 1994); based in Laiza, Kachin State; rejected the junta's BGF proposal; Chair. Lanyaw Zawng Hra; military wing: Kachin Independence Army (10,000 regular troops, 10,000 reserves).

Karenni (Kayinni) National People's Liberation Front: (May 1994); transformed into a BGF in Nov. 2009; Leader Tun Kyaw.

Kayan National Guard: (Feb. 1992); breakaway faction from the KNLP.

Kayan New Land Party (KNLP): (July 1994); rejected the junta's BGF proposal; Leader Shwe Aye.

Myanmar National Democratic Alliance Army (MNDAA): (March 1989); est. by fmr mems of the CPB; based in Kokang region of northern Shan State; forcibly removed from its cease-fire zone by government forces in late 2009; Leader Peng Jia Xiang.

National Democratic Alliance Army (NDAA): (June 1989); est. by splinter group of the CPB; based in eastern Shan State; Leader Sai Leun.

New Democratic Army—Kachin (NDA—K): (Dec. 1989); est. by fmr officers of the KIO; adopted BGF status in Nov. 2009; Leader Zahkung Ting Ying.

New Mon State Party (NMSP): POB 1 Sangkhlaburi, Kanchanaburi 71240, Thailand; e-mail nmsp2006@yahoo.com; internet www.nmsp.info; f. 1958; (cease-fire agreement, June 1995); Chair. Nai Htaw Mon; military wing: Mon National Liberation Army.

Palaung State Liberation Organization: (April 1991); military wing: Palaung State Liberation Army; 7,000–8,000 men.

Shan State Army—North (SSA—N): Sept. 1989; faction of the original SSA that complied with 1989 ceasefire agreement; Chair. Maj.-Gen. Loimao.

Shan State Nationalities People's Liberation Organization: (Oct. 1994); Chair. Tha Kalei.

United Wa State Party: (May 1989); fmrly part of the CPB; rejected the junta's BGF proposal; seeks the establishment of an autonomous Wa state; military wing: United Wa State Army (20,000–30,000 men); Leaders Chao Ngi Lai, Pao Yu Chang.

Since 1991 the National Coalition Government of the Union of Burma, constituted by representatives elected in the general election of 1990, has served as a government-in-exile:

National Coalition Government of the Union of Burma (NCGUB): POB 693, Rockville, MD 20848, USA; tel. (202) 705-6262; e-mail ncgub@ncgub.net; internet www.ncgub.net; Prime Minister Dr Sein Win.

Diplomatic Representation

EMBASSIES IN MYANMAR

Australia: 88 Strand Rd, Yangon; tel. (1) 251810; fax (1) 246159; e-mail austembassy.rangoon@dfat.gov.au; internet www.burma.embassy.gov.au; Ambassador Bronte Moules.

Bangladesh: 11B Than Lwin Rd, Yangon; tel. (1) 515275; fax (1) 515273; e-mail bdootygn@mptmail.net.mm; Ambassador Maj.-Gen. Anup Kumar Chakma.

Brunei: 317–319 U Wisara Rd, Sanchaung Township, Yangon; tel. (1) 524285; fax (1) 512854; e-mail myangon.myanmar@mfa.gov.bn; Ambassador Dato' Paduka Haji Abdul Hamid bin Haji Muhammad Yassin.

Cambodia: 34 Kaba Aye Pagoda Rd, Bahan Township, Yangon; tel. (1) 549609; fax (1) 541462; e-mail recyangon@myanmar.com.mm; Ambassador Chhong Toeun.

China, People's Republic: 1 Pyidaungsu Yeiktha Rd, Yangon; tel. (1) 221281; fax (1) 227019; e-mail chinaemb_mm@mfa.gov.cn; internet mm.china-embassy.org; Ambassador Li Junhua.

Egypt: 81 Pyidaungsu Yeiktha Rd, Yangon; tel. (1) 222886; fax (1) 222865; Ambassador Youssef Kamal Boutros Hanna.

France: 102 Pyidaungsu Yeiktha Rd, POB 858, Yangon; tel. (1) 212523; fax (1) 212527; e-mail ambafrance.rangoun@diplomatie.gouv.fr; internet www.ambafrance-mm.org; Ambassador Jean-Pierre Lafosse.

Germany: 9 Bogyoke Aung San Museum Rd, POB 12, Yangon; tel. (1) 548951; fax (1) 548899; e-mail info@rangun.diplo.de; internet www.rangun.diplo.de; Ambassador Julius Georg Luy.

India: 545–547 Merchant St, POB 751, Yangon; tel. (1) 243972; fax (1) 254086; e-mail indiaembassy@mptmail.net.mm; internet www.indiaembassy.net.mm; Ambassador Aloke Sen.

Indonesia: 100 Pyidaungsu Yeiktha Rd, POB 1401, Yangon; tel. (1) 254465; fax (1) 254468; e-mail kbriygn@indonesia.com.mm; internet www.deplu.go.id/yangon; Ambassador Sebastianus Sumarsono.

Israel: 15 Khabaung Rd, Hlaing Township, Yangon; tel. (1) 515115; fax (1) 515116; e-mail info@yangon.mfa.gov.il; internet yangon.mfa.gov.il; Ambassador Yaron Mayer.

Italy: 3 Inya Myaing Rd, POB 866, Golden Valley, Bahan Township, Yangon 11201; tel. (1) 527100; fax (1) 514565; e-mail ambyang.mail@esteri.it; internet www.ambyangon.esteri.it; Ambassador Giuseppe Cinti.

Japan: 100 Natmauk Rd, POB 841, Bahan Township, Yangon 11021; tel. (1) 549644; fax (1) 549643; e-mail jembassy@baganmail.net.mm; internet www.mm.emb-japan.go.jp; Ambassador Takashi Saito.

Korea, Republic: 97 University Ave, Bahan Township, POB 1408, Yangon; tel. (1) 515190; fax (1) 513286; e-mail myanmar@mofat.go.kr; internet mmr.mofat.go.kr; Ambassador Park Gi-Jong.

Laos: A1 Diplomatic Quarters, Franser Rd, Yangon; tel. (1) 222482; fax (1) 227446; Ambassador Kouily Souphaket.

Malaysia: 82 Pyidaungsu Yeiktha Rd, Dagon Township, Yangon; tel. (1) 220249; fax (1) 221840; e-mail malyangon@kln.gov.my; internet www.kln.gov.my/web/mmr_yangon; Ambassador Datuk Mazlan Muhammad.

Nepal: 16 Natmauk Yeiktha Rd, POB 84, Tamwe, Yangon; tel. (1) 545880; fax (1) 549803; e-mail nepemb@mptmail.net.mm; Ambassador Gunalaxmi Sharma Biswakarma.

Pakistan: A4 Diplomatic Quarters, Pyay Rd, Dagon Township, POB 581, Yangon; tel. (1) 222881; fax (1) 221147; e-mail pakistan@myanmar.com.mm; internet www.mofa.gov.pk/myanmar; Ambassador Qazi M. Khalilullah.

Philippines: 50 Saya San Rd, Bahan Township, Yangon; tel. (1) 558149; fax (1) 558154; e-mail yangonpe@mptmail.net.mm; Ambassador Maria Hellen M. Barber.

Russia: 38 Sagawa Rd, Dagon Township, Yangon; tel. (1) 241955; fax (1) 241953; e-mail rusinmyan@mptmail.net.mm; internet www.rusembmyanmar.org; Ambassador Mikhail M. Mgeladze.

MYANMAR

Serbia: 114A Inya Rd, Kamayut Township, POB 943, Yangon; tel. (1) 515282; fax (1) 504274; e-mail serbemb@yangon.net.mn; Chargé d'affaires a.i. NINO MALJEVIĆ.

Singapore: 238 Dhamazedi Rd, Bahan Township, Yangon; tel. (1) 559001; fax (1) 559002; e-mail singemb_ygn@sgmfa.gov.sg; internet www.mfa.gov.sg/yangon; Ambassador ROBERT CHUA.

Sri Lanka: 34 Taw Win Rd, POB 1150, Yangon; tel. (1) 222812; fax (1) 221509; e-mail srilankaemb@myanmar.com.mm; internet www.srilankaembassy.net.mm; Chargé d'affaires a.i. NIRMALA PARANAVITANA.

Thailand: 94 Pyay Rd, Dagon Township, Yangon; tel. (1) 222784; fax (1) 221713; e-mail thaiygn@mfa.go.th; internet www.thaiembassy.org/yangon; Ambassador BANSARN BUNNAG.

United Kingdom: 80 Strand Rd, Kyauktada Township, POB 638, Yangon; tel. (1) 380322; fax (1) 370866; e-mail BE.Rangoon@fco.gov.uk; internet ukinburma.fco.gov.uk; Ambassador ANDREW HEYN.

USA: 110 University Ave, Kamayut Township, Yangon; tel. (1) 536509; fax (1) 511069; e-mail consularrangoon@state.gov; internet burma.usembassy.gov; Chargé d'affaires LARRY M. DINGER.

Viet Nam: 70–72 Than Lwin Rd, Bahan Township, Yangon; tel. (1) 511305; fax (1) 514897; e-mail vnembmyr@cybertech.net.mm; internet www.vietnamembassy-myanmar.org; Ambassador CHU CONG PHUNG.

Judicial System

Chief Justice of the Supreme Court: TUN TUN OO, Bldg 24, Nay Pyi Taw; tel. (67) 404140.

Attorney-General: Dr TUN SHIN.

Religion

Freedom of religious belief and practice is guaranteed. In 1992 an estimated 87.2% of the population were Buddhists, 5.6% Christians, 3.6% Muslims, 1.0% Hindus and 2.6% animists or adherents of other religions.

BUDDHISM

State Sangha Maha Nayaka Committee: c/o Dept of Promotion and Propagation of the Sasana, Kaba Aye Pagoda Precinct, Mayangone Township, Yangon; tel. (1) 660759.

CHRISTIANITY

Myanmar Naing-ngan Khrityan Athin-dawmyar Kaung-si (Myanmar Council of Churches): 601 Pyay Rd, University PO, Kamayut, Yangon 11041; tel. (1) 537957; fax (1) 296848; e-mail oikoumedia@gmail.com; internet mcc-mm.org; f. 1914; est. as Burma Representative Council of Mission; reconstituted as Burma Council of Churches in 1974; 13 mem. nat. churches, 9 mem. nat. Christian orgs; Pres. Rev. SAW MAR GAY GYI; Gen. Sec. Rt Rev. SMITH N. ZA THAWNG.

The Roman Catholic Church

Myanmar comprises three archdioceses and 11 dioceses. At 31 December 2007 an estimated 1.2% of the total population were adherents.

Catholic Bishops' Conference of Myanmar
292 Pyay Rd, POB 1080, Sanchaung PO, Yangon 11111; tel. (1) 525868; fax (1) 527198; e-mail clspcbcm@mptmail.net.mm.
f. 1982; Pres. Most Rev. PAUL ZINGTUNG GRAWNG (Archbishop of Mandalay).

Archbishop of Mandalay: Most Rev. PAUL ZINGHTUNG GRAWNG, Archbishop's House, 81st and 25th St, Mandalay 06011; tel. (2) 33916; e-mail paulgrawng@mandalay.net.mm.

Archbishop of Taunggyi: Most Rev. MATTHIAS U SHWE, Archbishop's Office, Bayint Naung Rd, Taunggyi 06011; tel. (81) 21689; fax (81) 22164; e-mail ushwe1@gmail.com.

Archbishop of Yangon: Most Rev. CHARLES MAUNG BO, Archbishop's House, 289 Theinbyu Rd, Botahtaung PO, Yangon 11161; tel. (1) 392517; fax (1) 379059; e-mail archdygn@myanmar.com.mm.

The Anglican Communion

Anglicans are adherents of the Church of the Province of Myanmar, comprising six dioceses. The Province was formed in February 1970, and contained an estimated 45,000 adherents in 1985.

Archbishop of Myanmar and Bishop of Yangon: Most Rev. STEPHEN THAN MYINT OO, Bishopscourt, 140 Pyidaungsu Yeiktha Rd, Dagon PO, Yangon 11191; tel. (1) 285379; fax (1) 251405.

Protestant Churches

Lutheran Bethlehem Church: 181–183 Theinbyu St, Mingala Taung Nyunt PO, POB 773, Yangon 11221; tel. (1) 246585; Pres. Rev. JENSON RAJAN ANDREWS.

Myanmar Baptist Convention: 143 Minye Kyawswa Rd, POB 506, Yangon; tel. (1) 223231; fax (1) 221465; e-mail mbc@mptmail.net.mm; f. 1865; est. as Burma Baptist Missionary Convention; present name adopted 1954; 650,293 mems (2003); Pres. Rev. Dr HONOR NYO; Gen. Sec. Rev. K. D. TU LOM.

Myanmar Methodist Church: 47 Baho Rd, Thazin Lane, Ah Lone Township 65, Alanpya Pagoda Rd, Dagon, Yangon; Pres. Bishop ZOTHAN MAWIA.

Presbyterian Church of Myanmar: Synod Office, Falam, Chin State; 22,000 mems; Pres. Rev. SUN KANGLO.

Other denominations active in Myanmar include the Lisu Christian Church and the Salvation Army.

The Press

DAILIES

Botahtaung (The Vanguard): 22–30 Strand Rd, Botahtaung PO, POB 539, Yangon; tel. (1) 274310; Myanmar.

Guardian: 392–396 Merchant St, Botahtaung PO, POB 1522, Yangon; tel. (1) 270150; English.

Kyahmon (The Mirror): 77 52nd St, Dazundaung PO, POB 819, Yangon; tel. (1) 282777; internet www.myanmar.com/newspaper/kyaymon/index.html; Myanmar.

Myanmar Ahlin (New Light of Myanmar): 58 Komin Kochin Rd, Bahan PO, POB 21, Yangon; tel. (1) 544309; internet www.myanmar.com/newspaper/myanmarahlin/index.html; f. 1963; fmrly Loktha Pyithu Nezin (Working People's Daily); organ of the SPDC; morning; Myanmar; Chief Editor WIN TIN; circ. 400,000.

New Light of Myanmar: 22–30 Strand Rd, Yangon; tel. (1) 297028; e-mail webmaster@myanmar.com; internet www.myanmar.com/newspaper/nlm/index.html; f. 1963; fmrly Working People's Daily; organ of the SPDC; morning; English; Chief Editor KYAW MIN; circ. 14,000.

PERIODICALS

A Hla Thit (New Beauty): 46 90th St, Yangon; tel. (1) 287106; international news.

Dana Business Magazine: 72 8th St, Lanmadaw Township, Yangon; tel. and fax (1) 224010; e-mail dana@mptmail.net.mm; economic; Editor-in-Chief WILLIAM CHEN.

Do Kyaung Tha: Myawaddy Press, 184 32nd St, Yangon; tel. (1) 274655; f. 1965; monthly; Myanmar and English; circ. 17,000.

Gita Padetha: Yangon; journal of Myanma Music Council; circ. 10,000.

Guardian Magazine: 392–396 Merchant St, Botahtaung PO, POB 1522, Yangon; tel. (1) 296510; f. 1953; nationalized 1964; monthly; English; literary; circ. 11,600.

Kyee Pwar Yay (Prosperity): 296 Bo Sun Pat St, Yangon; tel. (1) 278100; economic; Editor-in-Chief MYAT KHINE.

Moethaukpan (Aurora): Myawaddy Press, 184 32nd St, Yangon; tel. (1) 274655; f. 1980; monthly; Myanmar and English; circ. 27,500.

Myanma Dana (Myanmar's Economy): 210A 36th St, Kyauktada Post Office, Yangon; tel. (1) 284660; economic; Editor-in-Chief THIHA SAW.

Myanmar Morning Post: Yangon; f. 1998; weekly; Chinese; news; circ. 5,000.

Myanmar Times & Business Review: 379–383 Bo Aung Kyaw St, Kyauktada Township, Yangon; tel. (1) 392928; fax (1) 254158; e-mail management@myanmartimes.com.mm; internet www.mmtimes.com; f. 2000; CEO Dr TIN TUN OO ; Man. Dir BILL CLOUGH (acting).

Myawaddy Journal: Myawaddy Press, 184 32nd St, Yangon; tel. (1) 274655; f. 1989; fortnightly; news; circ. 8,700.

Myawaddy Magazine: Myawaddy Press, 184 32nd St, Yangon; tel. (1) 274655; f. 1952; monthly; literary magazine; circ. 4,200.

Ngwetaryi Magazine: Myawaddy Press, 184 32nd St, Yangon; tel. (1) 274655; f. 1961; monthly; cultural; circ. 3,400.

Pyinnya Lawka Journal: 529 Merchant St, Yangon; tel. (1) 283611; publ. by Sarpay Beikman Management Board; quarterly; circ. 18,000.

Shwe Thwe: 529 Merchant St, Yangon; tel. (1) 283611; weekly; bilingual children's journal; publ. by Sarpay Beikman Management Board; circ. 100,000.

MYANMAR

Taw Win Journal (Royal Journal): 149 37th St, Yangon; news; Editor-in-Chief SOE THEIN.
Teza: Myawaddy Press, 184 32nd St, Yangon; tel. (1) 274655; f. 1965; monthly; English and Myanmar; pictorial publ. for children; circ. 29,500.
Thwe Thauk Magazine: Myawaddy Press, 184 32nd St, Yangon; f. 1946; monthly; literary.
Ya Nant Thit (New Fragrance): 186 39th St, Yangon; tel. (1) 276799; international news; Editor-in-Chief CHIT WIN MG.

NEWS AGENCY

Myanmar News Agency (MNA): 212 Theinbyu Rd, Botahtaung, Yangon; tel. (1) 270893; f. 1963; govt-controlled; Chief Editors ZAW MIN THEIN (domestic section), KYAW MIN (external section).

Publishers

Hanthawaddy Press: 157 Bo Aung Kyaw St, Yangon; f. 1889; textbooks, multilingual dictionaries; Man. Editor ZAW WIN.
Knowledge Publishing House: 130 Bo Gyoke Aung San St, Yegyaw, Yangon; art, education, religion, politics and social sciences.
Kyipwaye Press: 84th St, Letsaigan, Mandalay; tel. (2) 21003; arts, travel, religion, fiction and children's.
Myawaddy Press: 184 32nd St, Yangon; tel. (1) 276889; journals and magazines; CEO THEIN SEIN.
Sarpay Beikman Management Board: 529 Merchant St, Yangon; tel. (1) 283611; f. 1947; encyclopaedias, literature, fine arts and general; also magazines and translations; Chair. AUNG HTAY.
Shumawa Press: 146 West Wing, Bogyoke Aung San Market, Yangon; mechanical engineering.
Shwepyidan: 12A Haiaban, Yegwaw Quarter, Yangon; politics, religion, law.
Smart and Mookerdum: 221 Sule Pagoda Rd, Yangon; arts, cookery, popular science.
Thu Dhama Wadi Press: 55–56 Maung Khine St, POB 419, Yangon; f. 1903; religious; Propr TIN HTOO; Man. PAN MAUNG.

GOVERNMENT PUBLISHING HOUSE

Printing and Publishing Enterprise: 365–367 Bo Aung Kyaw St, Kyauktada Township, Yangon; tel. (1) 294645; f. 1880; est. as Govt Printing Office; Man. Dir AUNG NYEIN.

PUBLISHERS' ASSOCIATION

Myanma Publishers' Union: 146 Bogyoke Market, Yangon.

Broadcasting and Communications

TELECOMMUNICATIONS

Posts and Telecommunications Department: Blk 68, Ayeyar Wun Rd, South Dagon Township, Yangon; tel. (1) 591388; fax (1) 591383; e-mail dg.ptd@mptmail.net.mm; internet www.mcpt.gov.mm/ptd/index.htm; regulatory authority responsible for supervising radio communication, telephone, telegraph and post operations; Dir-Gen. TIN HTWE.
Myanma Posts and Telecommunications (MPT): No. 2 Office Bldg, Special Development Zone, Nay Pwi Taw; tel. (1) 407333; fax (1) 407008; internet www.mpt.net.mm; fmrly the Posts and Telecommunications Corpn; Man. Dir THAR OO.

BROADCASTING
Radio

Myanma TV and Radio Department (MTRD): 426 Pyay Rd, Kamayut 11041, Yangon; tel. (1) 531850; fax (1) 530211; f. 1946; broadcasts in Bamar, Arakanese (Rakhine), Shan, Karen (Kayin), Kachin, Kayah, Chin, Mon and English; Dir-Gen. KHIN MAUNG HTAY; Dir of Radio Broadcasting KO KO HTWAY.

Television

Myanma TV and Radio Department (MTRD): 426 Pyay Rd, Kamayut 11041, Yangon; tel. (1) 535553; fax (1) 525428; f. 1946; colour television transmissions began in 1980; Dir-Gen. KHIN MAUNG HTAY; Dir of Television Broadcasting MYINT OO.
TV Myawaddy: Hmawbi, Hmawbi Township, Yangon; tel. (1) 620270; f. 1995; military broadcasting station transmitting public information, education and entertainment programmes via satellite.

In 2005 the Democratic Voice of Burma (DVB) began broadcasting Myanmar language news and educational programmes via satellite from Norway.

Finance

(cap. = capital; res = reserves; dep. = deposits; m. = million; brs = branches; amounts in kyats unless otherwise stated)

BANKING
Central Bank

Central Bank of Myanmar: 26A Settmu Rd, POB 184, Yankin Township, Yangon; tel. (1) 543751; fax (1) 543743; e-mail mofr_it_center@mptmail.net.mm; f. 1947; est. as People's Bank of the Union of Burma; present name adopted 1990; bank of issue; cap. 350m., dep. 13,545m.; Gov. THAN NYEIN; 37 brs.

State Banks

Myanma Economic Bank (MEB): Bldg 34, Nay Pyi Taw; tel. (67) 410449; fax (67) 410331; e-mail mebhoadmin@mpt.net.mm; internet www.mebank.com.mm; f. 1975; provides domestic banking network throughout the country; Man. Dir MYAT MAW.
Myanma Foreign Trade Bank: 80–86 Maha Bandoola Garden St, POB 203, Kyauktada Township, Yangon; tel. (1) 284911; fax (1) 289585; e-mail mftb-hoygn@mptmail-net.mm; f. 1976; handles all foreign exchange and international banking transactions; Chair. and Man. Dir THAN YE; Man. and Sec. HTIN KYAW THEIN.

Development Banks

Myanma Agricultural Development Bank (MADB): 1–7 cnr Latha St and Kanna Rd, Yangon; tel. (1) 226734; f. 1953; est. as State Agricultural Bank; reconstituted as Myanma Agricultural and Rural Devt Bank 1990, and as above 1996; state-owned; Man. Dir CHIT SWE.
Myanma Investment and Commercial Bank (MICB): 170–176 Bo Aung Kyaw St, Botahtaung Township, Yangon; tel. (1) 256871; fax (1) 250518; e-mail micb.hoygn@mptmail.net.mm; f. 1989; state-owned; cap. 940m., res 890,75m., dep. 25,040m. (March 2007); Chair. and Man. Dir MYA THAN; 1 br.

Private Banks

In mid-2010 it was reported that four additional licences had been issued to private domestic banks.

Asian Yangon Bank Ltd: 319–321 Maha Bandoola St, Botahtaung Township, Yangon; tel. (1) 245825; fax (1) 245865; f. 1994; est. as Asian Yangon Int. Bank Ltd; name changed as above in 2000; Gen. Man. MYO MYINT.
Co-operative Bank Ltd: 334–336, cnr of Strand Rd & 23rd St, Latha Township, Yangon; tel. (1) 372641; fax (1) 240147; e-mail cbbank@mptmail.net.mm; internet www.cbbank.com.mm; f. 1992; Chair. KHIN MAUNG AYE; Gen. Man. NYUNT HLAING; 18 brs.
First Private Bank Ltd (FPB): 619–621, cnr of Merchant St & Bo Soon Pat St, Pabedan Township, Yangon; tel. (1) 251750; fax (1) 242320; e-mail fpb.hq@mptmail.net.mm; internet www.fpbbank-myanmar.com; f. 1992; est. as the first publicly subscribed bank; fmrly Commercial and Devt Bank Ltd; provides loans to private business and small-scale industrial sectors; cap. 5,000m. (March 2008); Chair. Dr SEIN MAUNG; 16 brs.
Innwa Bank Ltd: 554–556 Merchant St, cnr of 35th & 36th Sts, Kyauktada Township, Yangon; tel. (1) 254642; fax (1) 254431; f. 1997; Gen. Man. YIN SEIN.
Kanbawza Bank Ltd: 615/1 Pyay Rd, Kamayut Township, Yangon; tel. (1) 538075; fax (1) 538069; e-mail kbzinfo@kbzbank.asia; internet www.kbzbank.asia; f. 1994; Chair. AUNG KO WIN; 30 brs.
Myanma Citizens Bank Ltd (MCB): 383 Maha Bandoola St, Kyauktada Township, Yangon; tel. (1) 379176; fax (1) 245932; e-mail mcbankygn@mptmail.net.mm; f. 1991; Chair. HLA TIN; Man. Dir AUNG THIN WIN.
Myanma Oriental Bank Ltd (MOB): 166–168 Pansodan St, Kyauktada Township, Yangon; tel. (1) 246594; fax (1) 253217; e-mail mobl.ygn@mptmail.net.mm; f. 1993; Chair. MYAT KYAW; Man. Dir and CEO WIN MYINT.
Myanmar Industrial Development Bank Ltd: 26–42 Pansodan St, Kyauktada Township, Yangon; tel. (1) 249536; fax (1) 249529; f. 1996; cap. US $335m.
Myawaddy Bank Ltd: 24–26 Sule Pagoda Rd, Kyauktada Township, Yangon; tel. (1) 283665; fax (1) 250093; e-mail mwdbankygn@mtpt400.stems.com; f. 1993; Gen. Mans TUN KYI, MYA MIN.
Tun Foundation Bank Ltd: 165–167 Bo Aung Kyaw St, Yangon; tel. (1) 240710; e-mail tfbbank@mptmail.net.mm; f. 1997; Chair. THEIN TUN.

MYANMAR   *Directory*

Yadanabon Bank Ltd: 58A 26th St, cnr of 84th & 85th Sts, Aung Myay Thar Zan Township, Mandalay; tel. (2) 23577; f. 1992.

Yangon City Bank Ltd: 12–18 Sepin St, Kyauktada Township, Yangon; tel. (1) 289256; fax (1) 289231; f. 1993; auth. cap. 500m.; 100% owned by Yangon City Devt Cttee; Chair. Col MYINT AUNG.

Yoma Bank Ltd: 1 Kungyan St, Mingala Taung Nyunt Township, Yangon; tel. (1) 242138; fax (1) 246548; f. 1993; Chair. SERGE PUN.

Foreign Banks

By November 2003 18 foreign banks had opened representative offices in Yangon.

STOCK EXCHANGE

Myanmar Securities Exchange Centre: 1st Floor, 21–25 Sule Pagoda Rd, Yangon; tel. (1) 283984; f. 1996; jt venture between MEB and Japan's Daiwa Institute of Research; Man. Dir EIJI SUZUKI.

INSURANCE

At the end of November 2003 there were three representative offices of foreign insurance companies in Myanmar.

Myanma Insurance: 627–635 Merchant St, Yangon; tel. (1) 252373; fax (1) 250275; e-mail myansure@mptmail.net.com; internet www.soft-comm.com/myanma_insurance/index.html; f. 1976; govt-controlled; Man. Dir Col THEIN LWIN.

Trade and Industry

GOVERNMENT AGENCIES

Inspection and Agency Services: 383 Maha Bandoola St, Yangon; tel. (1) 284821; fax (1) 284823; promotes business with foreign cos on behalf of state-owned enterprises; Man. Dir OHN KHIN.

Myanmar Economic Corpn (MEC): 74–76 Shwedagon Pagoda Rd, Dagon Township, Yangon; tel. (1) 254738; (retd) Brig.-Gen. Thura MYINT THIEN.

Myanmar Investment Commission (MIC): Ministry of National Planning and Economic Development, Bldg 32, Nay Pyi Taw; tel. (67) 406334; fax (67) 406333; f. 1994; Chair. MAUNG MAUNG THEIN.

Union of Myanmar Economic Holdings: 72–74 Shwadagon Pagoda Rd, Yangon; tel. (1) 78905; f. 1990; public holding co; auth. cap. 10,000m. kyats; 40% of share capital subscribed by the Ministry of Defence and 60% by members of the armed forces.

CHAMBER OF COMMERCE

Union of Myanmar Federation of Chambers of Commerce and Industry (UMFCCI): 29 Min Ye Kyawswa Rd, Lanmadaw Township, Yangon; tel. (1) 214344; fax (1) 214484; e-mail umcci@mptmail.net.mm; internet www.umfcci.com.mm; f. 1919; est. as Burmese Chamber of Commerce; present name adopted 1999; Pres. WIN MYINT; Gen. Sec. SEIN WIN HLAING.

INDUSTRIAL AND TRADE ASSOCIATIONS

Myanmar Aquaculture and Fisheries Association: 74–86 Bo Sun Pat St, Pabedan Township, Yangon; tel. (1) 243150; fax (1) 248177.

Myanmar Computer Industry Association: Myanmar Info-Tech, Main Bldg, Hlaing University Campus, Hlaing Township, Yangon; tel. (1) 652238; e-mail mcia@mail4u.com.mm; internet www.mcia.org.mm; Pres. WAH WAH HTUN.

Myanmar Construction Entrepreneurs' Association: Thanthumar Rd, cnr Thuwunna Rd, Thingankyun Township, Yangon; tel. (1) 579547; fax (1) 575947.

Myanmar Edible Oil Dealers' Association: 81–82 Kantgaw St, Bayint Naung Warehouse, Mayangon Township, Yangon; tel. (1) 680910; Chair. KO KO GYI.

Myanmar Engineers' Association: Bldg 6, Rm 5, MICT Park, Hlaing Township, Yangon; tel. (1) 652294.

Myanmar Fisheries Federation (MFF): cnr Bayint Naung Rd and Say War Sat Yone St, West Gyo Gone, Insein Township, Yangon; tel. (1) 683652; fax (1) 683662; e-mail fish-fed@mff.com.mm; internet www.fishfedmyanmar.com; six mem. asscns; Pres. HTAY MYINT.

Myanmar Forest Products and Timber Merchants' Association: 29 Min Ye Kyaw Swa St, Lanmadaw Township, Yangon; tel. (1) 214838; e-mail mfptma@mptmail.net.mm; internet www.myanmartimberassociation.org; f. 1993; Chair. SEIN LWIN; Sec.-Gen. NAY HTUN MIN.

Myanmar Garment Manufacturers' Association (MGMA): J V-2 Bldg, between Lanthit St and Wardan St, Seikkan Township, Yangon; tel. (1) 220879; fax (1) 222706; Chair. MYINT SOE.

Myanmar Industries Association: 504–506 Merchant St, Kyauktada Township, Yangon; tel. and fax (1) 241919; f. 1993; Chair. PAW HEIN.

Myanmar Livestock Federation: Livestock Breeding and Veterinary Department Compound, Insein Rd, Insein Township, Yangon; tel. (1) 640820; fax (1) 225955.

Myanmar Rice and Paddy Wholesalers' Association: 504–506 Merchant St, Kyauktada Township, Yangon; tel. (1) 241920.

Myanmar Rice Industry Association: f. 2010; est. to co-ordinate the rice industry, promote private investment and develop the export potential of the sector; provides low-interest loans and improved seeds, fertilizers and technology; 40 exec. mems; Chair. CHIT KHAING.

Myanmar Rice Millers' Association: 69 Theinbyu St, Botahtaung Township, Yangon; tel. (1) 296284; Pres. TIN WIN.

Myanmar Women Entrepreneurs' Association: 288–290 Shwedagon Pagoda Rd, Dagon Township, Yangon; tel. (1) 254400; fax (1) 254566; e-mail mwea2008@gmail.com; internet www.mweamm.org; f. 1995; Pres. YI YI MYINT (acting).

UTILITIES

Electricity

Myanma Electric Power Enterprise (MEPE): 197–199 Lower Kyimyindine Rd, Yangon; tel. (1) 220918; fax (1) 221006; e-mail mepe@mptmail.net.mm; Man. Dir ZAW WIN.

Water

Mandalay City Development Committee (Water and Sanitation Dept): cnr of 26th and 72nd Sts, Mandalay; tel. (2) 36173; f. 1992; Head of Water and Sanitation Dept TUN KYI.

Water Resources Utilization Department (WRUD): Ministry of Agriculture and Irrigation, Office 50, Nay Pyi Taw; tel. (67) 431291; internet wrud15.com; f. 1995; Dir.-Gen. KYI HTUT WIN.

Yangon City Development Committee (Water and Sanitation Dept): City Hall, cnr of Maha Bandoola Rd and Sule Pagoda Rd, Kyauktada Township, Yangon; tel. (1) 248112; fax (1) 246016; e-mail priycdc@mptmail.net.mm; internet www.yangoncity.com.mm/ycdc/index.asp; f. 1992; Head of Water and Sanitation Dept ZAW WIN.

CO-OPERATIVES

In 2003, according to official reports, there were 18,041 co-operative societies.

Central Co-operative Society Ltd: Saya San Plaza, Cnr Saya Rd and New University Ave, Bahan Township, Yangon; tel. (1) 557640; fax (1) 553894; e-mail ccsencoop@gmail.com; internet www.ccsmyanmar.com; Chair. KHIN MAUNG AYE.

Co-operative Department: Ministry of Co-operatives, Bldg 16, Nay Pyi Taw; tel. (1) 410339; fax (1) 410024; e-mail coopdeptdg@mptmail.net.mm; internet www.myancoop.gov.mm/co-department.htm; Dir-Gen. MAUNG HTI.

WORKERS' AND PEASANTS' COUNCILS

Peasants' Asiayone (Organization): Yangon; tel. (1) 82819; f. 1977; Chair. Brig.-Gen. THAN NYUNT; Sec. SAN TUN.

Workers' Unity Organization: Central Organizing Committee, 61 Thein Byu St, Yangon; tel. (1) 284043; f. 1968; workers' representative org.; Chair. OHN KYAW; Sec. NYUNT THEIN.

Transport

All railways, domestic air services, passenger and freight road transport services, and inland water facilities are owned and operated by state-controlled enterprises.

RAILWAYS

The railway network comprised 3,955 km of track in 1996/97, most of which was single track.

Myanma Railways: 361 Theinbyu Rd, Botataung Township, Yangon; tel. (1) 298585; fax (1) 284220; f. 1877; govt-operated; Man. Dir MIN SWE; Gen. Man. HLA YI.

ROADS

In 2005 the total length of the road network in Myanmar was an estimated 27,000 km.

Road Transportation Department: 375 Bogyoke Aung San St, Yangon; tel. (1) 284426; fax (1) 289716; f. 1963; controls passenger and freight road transport; Man. Dir OHN MYINT.

INLAND WATERWAYS

The principal artery of traffic is the River Ayeyarwady (Irrawaddy), which is navigable as far as Bhamo, about 1,450 km inland, while parts of the Thanlwin and Chindwinn rivers are also navigable.

Inland Water Transport: 50 Pansodan St, Kyauktada Township, Yangon; tel. (1) 380753; fax (1) 380752; e-mail iwtnpt@mpt.net.mm; internet www.iwt-myanmar.com; f. 1865; govt-owned; operates cargo and passenger services throughout Myanmar with a fleet of 476 vessels; Man. Dir SOE TINT.

SHIPPING

Yangon is the chief port. Vessels with a displacement of up to 15,000 grt can be accommodated. In December 2009 the Myanma merchant fleet comprised 117 vessels, with a total displacement of 182,500 grt.

Myanmar Port Authority: 10 Pansodan St, POB 1, Yangon; tel. (1) 382722; fax (1) 295134; e-mail mpa@mptmail.net.mm; internet www.myanmaportauthority.com; f. 1880; general port and harbour duties; Man. Dir HTIEN HTAY; Gen. Man. HLAING SOON.

Myanma Five Star Line: 132–136 Theinbyu Rd, POB 1221, Yangon; tel. (1) 295279; fax (1) 297669; e-mail mfslhq@mptmail.net.mm; internet www.mfsl-shipping.com; f. 1959; cargo services to the Far East and Australia; Man. Dir MAUNG MAUNG NYEIN; Gen. Man. WIN PE; fleet of 26 coastal and ocean-going vessels.

CIVIL AVIATION

Mingaladon Airport, near Yangon, is equipped to international standards. Mandalay International Airport was inaugurated in September 2000. In 2002 plans for the construction of a third international airport, to serve Nay Pyi Taw, were approved.

Department of Civil Aviation: Yangon International Airport, Yangon 11021; tel. (1) 533000; fax (1) 533016; e-mail dgdca@dca.gov.mm; internet www.dca.gov.mm; Dir-Gen. TIN NAING TUN.

Air Bagan Ltd: 56 Shwe Taung Gyar St, Bahan Township, Yangon; tel. (1) 514861; fax (1) 515102; e-mail info@airbagan.com.mm; internet www.airbagan.com; f. 2004; domestic services to 17 destinations; Chair. TAY ZA; Man. Dir HTOO THET HTWE.

Air Mandalay: 146 Dhammazedi Rd, Bahan Township, Yangon; tel. (1) 501520; fax (1) 525937; e-mail info@airmandalay.com; internet www.airmandalay.com; f. 1994; jt venture between Air Mandalay Holding and Myanma Airways; operates domestic services and regional services to Thailand and Cambodia; Chair. Dr TUN CHIN; Man. Dir ERIC KANG TIAN LYE.

Myanmar Airways (MA): 104 Kanna Rd, Yangon; tel. (1) 284566; fax (1) 89583; e-mail 8mpr@maiair.com.mm; internet www.mot.gov.mm/ma/index.html; f. 1993; govt-controlled; internal network operates services to 21 airports; Man. Dir TIN MAUNG TUN.

Myanmar Airways International (MAI): 08-02 Sakura Tower, 339 Bogyoke Aung San Rd, Yangon; tel. (1) 255260; fax (1) 255305; e-mail management@maiair.com; internet www.maiair.com; f. 1993; govt-owned; est. by Myanmar Airways in jt venture with Singapore's Highsonic Enterprises to provide international services; operates services to Bangkok, Dhaka, Hong Kong, Kuala Lumpur and Singapore; Man. Dir AUNG GYI.

United Myanmar Air: Summit Parkview Hotel, Yangon; internet www.unitedmyanmar.com; f. 2003; jt venture between Myanmar Airways and Sunshine Strategic Investments Holdings of Hong Kong; international services to Bangkok, Hong Kong, Kuala Lumpur and Singapore; CEO EDWARD TAN.

Yangon Airways: MMB Tower, 5th Floor, 166 Upper Pansodan Rd, Mingalar Taungnyunt Township, Yangon; tel. (1) 383100; fax (1) 383109; e-mail cmya@mmb.com.mm; internet www.yangonair.com; f. 1996; domestic services to 13 destinations; Man. Dir AIK HAUK.

Tourism

Yangon, Mandalay, Taunggyi and Pagan possess outstanding palaces, Buddhist temples and shrines. In 2008 there were 193,319 foreign tourist arrivals. Revenue from tourism (including passenger transport) totalled an estimated US $59m. in 2006.

Myanmar Hotels and Tourism Services: 77–91 Sule Pagoda Rd, Yangon 11141; tel. (1) 282013; fax (1) 254417; e-mail mtt.mht@mptmail.net.mm; govt-controlled; manages all hotels, tourist offices, tourist dept stores and duty-free shops; Gen. Man. TIN HTAY.

Myanmar Tourism Promotion Board: Business Centre, 3rd Floor, 223 Signal Pagoda Rd, Yangon; tel. (1) 242828; fax (1) 242800; e-mail mtpb@mptmail.net.mm; internet www.myanmar-tourism.com; Chair. AUNG MYAT KYAW.

Myanmar Travels and Tours: 118–120 Mahabandoola St, Kyauktada Township, Yangon; tel. (1) 371286; fax (1) 254417; e-mail mtt.mht@mptmail.net.mm; internet www.myanmartravelsandtours.com; f. 1964; govt tour operator and travel agent; handles all travel arrangements for groups and individuals; Gen. Man. HTAY AUNG.

Union of Myanmar Travel Association (UMTA): Bldg 69, Yuzana Condo Tower, 6th Floor, Unit 609B, cnr Shwegonedaing Rd and Kabaraye Pagoda Rd, Bahan Township, Yangon; tel. (1) 559673; fax (1) 545707; e-mail UMTA@mptmail.net.mm; internet www.umtanet.org; f. 2002; organizes private travel agencies and tour operators; Chair. MAUNG MAUNG SWE; Sec. HPONE THANT.

Defence

As assessed at November 2010, the total strength of the armed forces was an estimated 406,000 (army 375,000, navy 16,000, air force 15,000). Military service is voluntary. Paramilitary forces include a people's police force (72,000 men) and a people's militia (35,000 men).

Defence Expenditure: estimated at US $1,900m. for 2009.

Commander-in-Chief of the Defence Services: Gen. MIN AUNG HLAING.

Commander-in-Chief of the Army: Gen. MIN AUNG HLAING.

Commander-in-Chief of the Navy: Vice-Adm. NYAN TUN.

Commander-in-Chief of the Air Force: Maj.-Gen. MYAT HEIN.

Education

The organization and administration of education is the responsibility of the Ministry of Education. Pre-school education begins at four years of age. Primary education, which is compulsory, lasts for five years between the ages of five and 10. Secondary education, beginning at 10 years of age, comprises a first cycle of four years and a second of two years. In 2007/08 enrolment at primary and secondary schools was equivalent to 82% of children in the relevant age-groups.

In 2001/02 there were 958 tertiary-level institutions, at which an estimated 587,300 students were enrolled. According to provisional estimates, 507,660 students were enrolled in tertiary-level institutions in 2007/08.

In 2005/06 government expenditure on education was 68,676m. kyats (6.8% of total spending).

NAMIBIA

Introductory Survey

LOCATION, CLIMATE, LANGUAGE, RELIGION, FLAG, CAPITAL

The Republic of Namibia (formerly known as South West Africa) lies in south-western Africa, with South Africa to the south and south-east, Botswana to the east and Angola to the north. The country has a long coastline on the Atlantic Ocean. The narrow Caprivi Strip, between Angola and Botswana in the north-east, extends Namibia to the Zambezi river, giving it a border with Zambia. The climate is generally hot, although coastal areas have relatively mild temperatures. Most of the country is subject to drought and unreliable rainfall. The average annual rainfall varies from about 50 mm (2 ins) on the coast to 550 mm (22 ins) in the north. The arid Namib Desert stretches along the west coast, while the easternmost area is part of the Kalahari Desert. The official language is English; however, most of the African ethnic groups have their own languages. At the 2001 census the most widely spoken African languages were Oshiwambo (used in 48% of households), Nama/Damara (11%), Rukavango (10%) and Otjiherero (8%). In addition, Afrikaans is spoken (11%) and German is also used. About 90% of the population are Christians. The national flag (proportions 2 by 3) comprises a blue triangle in the upper hoist corner, bearing a yellow sun (a blue-bordered disc, surrounded by 12 triangular rays), separated from a green triangle in the lower fly corner by a white-bordered, broad red stripe. The capital is Windhoek.

CONTEMPORARY POLITICAL HISTORY

Historical Context

South West Africa became a German possession in 1884. The territory excluded the port of Walvis Bay and 12 small offshore islands, previously annexed by the United Kingdom and subsequently incorporated into South Africa. During the First World War South African forces occupied South West Africa in 1914, and in 1915 Germany surrendered the territory. In 1920 the League of Nations entrusted South Africa with a mandate to administer South West Africa. In 1925 South Africa granted a Constitution giving limited self-government to European (white) inhabitants only. No trusteeship agreement was concluded with the UN after the Second World War, and in 1946 the UN refused South Africa's request for permission to annex South West Africa. In 1949 the territory's European voters were granted representation in the South African Parliament. The following year the International Court of Justice (ICJ, see p. 23) issued a ruling that the area should remain under international mandate and that South Africa should submit it to UN control. South Africa refused to comply with this judgment. In October 1966 South Africa's security and apartheid laws were extended to South West Africa, retrospective to 1950.

Opposition within South West Africa to South African rule led to the establishment of two African nationalist organizations, the South West Africa People's Organisation (SWAPO—founded in 1957 as the Ovamboland People's Congress) and the South West African National Union (SWANU—formed in 1959). During 1966 SWAPO's military wing, the People's Liberation Army of Namibia (PLAN), launched an armed struggle for the liberation of the territory. PLAN operated from bases in Angola and Zambia, and was controlled by the external wing of SWAPO (led by Sam Nujoma—the organization's President from 1959). SWAPO also had a legal wing, which was tolerated in South West Africa.

South Africa was consistently criticized at the UN over its extension of apartheid to the territory. The UN General Assembly voted to terminate South Africa's mandate in October 1966, established a UN Council for South West Africa in May 1967, and changed the name of the territory to Namibia in June 1968. In 1971 the ICJ ruled that South Africa's presence was illegal. In 1973 the UN General Assembly recognized SWAPO as 'the authentic representative of the Namibian people', and appointed a UN Commissioner for Namibia to undertake 'executive and administrative tasks'.

A multiracial constitutional conference on the territory's future, organized by the all-white South West Africa Legislative Assembly, was convened in Windhoek in September 1975, attended by representatives of the territory's 11 main ethnic groups. However, neither the UN nor the Organization of African Unity (OAU, now the African Union, see p. 183) recognized this so-called Turnhalle Conference, owing to its ethnic and non-democratic basis. In 1976 and 1977 proposals for procedures whereby Namibia was to achieve independence and formulate a constitution were made by the Turnhalle Conference, but rejected by SWAPO, the UN and the OAU. In September 1977 South Africa appointed an Administrator-General to govern the territory. In November the Turnhalle Conference was dissolved, and the Democratic Turnhalle Alliance (DTA), a coalition of conservative political groups representing the ethnic groups involved in the Turnhalle Conference, was formed.

In early 1978 talks were held between South Africa, SWAPO and a 'contact group' comprising Canada, France, the Federal Republic of Germany, the United Kingdom and the USA. In September the contact group's proposals for a Namibian settlement, including the holding of UN-supervised elections, were conditionally accepted by both South Africa and SWAPO and were incorporated in UN Security Council Resolution 435. However, South Africa continued to implement its own internal solution for Namibia with an election for a Constituent Assembly in December. The election was contested by five parties, but boycotted notably by SWAPO. Of the 50 seats in the Assembly, 41 were won by the DTA. In May 1979 South Africa unilaterally established a legislative National Assembly, without executive powers, from the existing Constituent Assembly.

All-party negotiations, held under UN auspices in Geneva, Switzerland, in January 1981, failed in their aim of arranging a cease-fire and eventual UN-supervised elections. Later in 1981 the contact group attempted to secure support for a three-phase independence plan. However, South Africa's insistence (supported by the USA) that any withdrawal of South African forces must be linked to the withdrawal of Cuban troops from Angola was rejected by Angola and the UN. Meanwhile, the Ministerial Council, formed in 1980 and chaired by Dirk Mudge (also Chairman of the DTA), assumed much of the Administrator-General's executive power in September 1981. However, the Ministerial Council was dissolved in January 1983, when, after several months of disagreement with the South African Government regarding the future role of the DTA in the territory, Mudge resigned as Council Chairman. South Africa disbanded the National Assembly and resumed direct rule of Namibia, with Willem van Niekerk as Administrator-General.

The Multi-Party Conference (MPC) was established in November 1983, grouping, initially, seven internal political parties. Boycotted by SWAPO, it appeared to be promoted by South Africa as a means of settling the independence issue outside the framework of Resolution 435, and of reducing SWAPO's dominance in any future post-independence government for Namibia. None the less, South Africa continued to negotiate on the independence issue with SWAPO and Angola. In February 1984 South Africa and Angola agreed to a cease-fire on the Angola–Namibia border, and set up a joint commission to monitor the withdrawal of all South African troops from Angola. Angola undertook to ensure that neither Cuban nor SWAPO forces would move into the areas vacated by the South African troops. Discussions on the independence issue in mid-1984, involving van Niekerk, SWAPO and the MPC, ended inconclusively, as did negotiations in 1984–86 between the South African Government and the US Assistant Secretary of State for African Affairs.

In April 1985 the South African Government accepted a proposal by the MPC for a 'Transitional Government of National Unity' (TGNU) in Namibia. This was formally established in Windhoek in June, although the arrangement was condemned in advance by the contact group and was declared 'null and void' by the UN Secretary-General. The TGNU consisted of an executive Cabinet, drawn from a National Assembly of 62 members who were appointed from among the parties constituting the MPC. Its establishment was accompanied by the proclamation of a 'bill of rights', drafted by the MPC, which prohibited racial discrimination. A Constitutional Council was also established to prepare a constitution for an independent Namibia. The South African Government retained responsibility for foreign affairs, defence and internal security, and all legislation was to be subject to approval by the Administrator-General. Louis Pienaar replaced van Niekerk in this post in July.

During 1987, following the liberalization of labour laws and the legalization of trade unions for black workers in 1986, the trade union movement became increasingly active. In mid-1987 the Constitutional Council published a draft document; however, South Africa indicated that it could not accept the lack of a guarantee of minority rights in the proposal. In March 1988 the Namibian Supreme Court declared the 'AG8' law of 1980 (providing for the election of 'second-tier' legislative assemblies and for the administration of education and health facilities on an ethnic, rather than a geographical, basis) to be in conflict with the 1985 'bill of rights'.

Both Angola and Cuba were reported in January 1988 to have accepted, in principle, the US demand for a complete withdrawal of Cuban troops from Angola, but they reiterated that this would be conditional on the cessation of South African support for the insurgent União Nacional para a Independência Total de Angola (UNITA). In July Angola, Cuba and South Africa reached agreement on 14 'essential principles' for a peaceful settlement, and in August it was agreed that the implementation of Resolution 435 would begin on 1 November. However, it was not until December that Angola, Cuba and South Africa signed a formal treaty designating 1 April 1989 as the implementation date for Resolution 435 and establishing a joint commission to monitor the treaty's implementation. (A further agreement was signed by Angola and Cuba, requiring the evacuation of all Cuban troops from Angola by July 1991.) A Constituent Assembly was to be elected in Namibia on 1 November 1989. South African forces in Namibia were to be confined to their bases, and their numbers reduced to 1,500 by July 1989; all South African troops were to have been withdrawn from Namibia one week after the November election. SWAPO forces were to be confined to bases in Angola in April, before being disarmed and repatriated. A multinational military observer force, the UN Transition Assistance Group (UNTAG), was to monitor the South African withdrawal, and civilian administrators and an international police force were to supervise the election. At the end of February the TGNU was formally disbanded, and on 1 March the National Assembly voted to dissolve itself: until independence the territory was governed by the Administrator-General, in consultation with a Special Representative of the UN Secretary-General, Martti Ahtisaari. Pienaar and Ahtisaari were to be jointly responsible for arranging the November election.

Implementation of Resolution 435 was disrupted by large-scale movements, from April 1989, of SWAPO guerrillas into Namibia from Angola, as a result of which the South African security forces, with the consent of the UN, suspended the cease-fire. About 280 SWAPO troops were reported to have been killed in the subsequent conflict. Following negotiations by the joint monitoring commission, conditions were arranged for an evacuation of the SWAPO forces to Angola, and in May the commission certified the cease-fire to be once more in force. In June most racially discriminatory legislation was repealed, and an amnesty was granted to Namibian refugees and exiles: by late September nearly 42,000 people, including Nujoma, had returned to Namibia. Meanwhile, South Africa completed its troop reduction ahead of schedule.

Voting proceeded peacefully on 7–11 November 1989, with the participation of more than 95% of the electorate. SWAPO received 57.3% of all votes cast and won 41 of the Constituent Assembly's 72 seats, while the DTA, with 28.6% of the votes, secured 21 seats. (In 1991 the South African Government admitted that it had contributed funds to the electoral campaigns of the DTA and several other political parties opposed to SWAPO.) Following the election, South Africa's remaining troops were evacuated from Namibia, while SWAPO's bases in Angola were decommissioned. The SWAPO Government subsequently reached an agreement with South Africa that no legal action would be taken for atrocities committed by either side. The agreement also precluded the establishment of a truth and reconciliation commission.

In February 1990 the Constituent Assembly adopted a draft Constitution, providing for a multi-party democracy based on universal adult suffrage. Later in the month the Constituent Assembly elected Nujoma as Namibia's first President. On 21 March Namibia finally achieved independence; the Constituent Assembly was redesignated the National Assembly, and Nujoma assumed executive power. A Cabinet, headed by the Constituent Assembly Chairman, Hage Geingob (a long-serving SWAPO activist), was also sworn in.

Domestic Political Affairs

Following Namibia's independence, the port of Walvis Bay, its surrounding territory of 1,124 sq km and the 12 offshore Penguin Islands remained under South African jurisdiction. In September 1991 the Namibian and South African Governments agreed to administer the disputed territories jointly, pending a final settlement on sovereignty, and in August 1992 the two countries announced the forthcoming establishment of a joint administration authority. In August 1993, however, South Africa's multi-party constitutional negotiating committee instructed the Government to prepare legislation for the transfer of sovereignty over Walvis Bay to Namibia. Accordingly, negotiations between Namibia and South Africa resulted in bilateral agreements regarding the future of South African interests in the Walvis Bay area. Namibia formally took control of Walvis Bay and its islands from 1 March 1994.

Namibia's first post-independence presidential and legislative elections in December 1994 resulted in overwhelming victories for Nujoma and SWAPO. Nujoma was elected for a second term as President, securing 76.3% of the votes cast, while SWAPO secured 53 of the elective seats in the National Assembly, with 73.9% of the valid votes cast. The DTA won 15 seats (with 20.8% of the votes), and the United Democratic Front (UDF) two. The remaining two seats were won by the Democratic Coalition of Namibia (an alliance of the National Patriotic Front and the German Union) and the Monitor Action Group (MAG).

At the SWAPO Congress in May 1997 Nujoma was re-elected unopposed as party President. Among the resolutions endorsed by the Congress was a proposal that Nujoma should seek re-election for a third term as national President. It was agreed that the Constitution, which stipulated that a President may serve no more than two consecutive terms, could be exceptionally amended to allow Nujoma to seek a further mandate, since the incumbent had initially been appointed by the Constituent Assembly, and had only once been elected President on a popular mandate. In August 1998 a senior SWAPO official, Ben Ulenga, resigned as Namibia's High Commissioner to the United Kingdom, in protest at the proposed arrangement to allow Nujoma to seek a renewed mandate. The exceptional constitutional amendment was approved by the requisite two-thirds' majority in the National Assembly in October and by the National Council in November. In March 1999 it was reported that Ulenga was to establish a new political party, the Congress of Democrats (CoD), with a view to contesting the elections due later in the year.

In August 1998 the DTA's executive announced the suspension of Mishake Muyongo as party President, and dissociated the party from Muyongo's overt support for the secession of the Caprivi Strip—a narrow area of land extending in the north-east, between Angola and Botswana, as far as the Zambezi river (Namibia's border with Zambia). In November it emerged that Muyongo, leading the so-called Caprivi Liberation Movement (CLM), was among more than 100 people who, apparently armed, had crossed into Botswana in October, and who were now seeking asylum in that country. The Namibian Government stated that it had discovered plans for a secessionist rebellion, led by Muyongo and a chief of the Mafwe tribe, Boniface Mamili, in Caprivi. Representatives of the office of the UN High Commissioner for Refugees (UNHCR) subsequently advised the Botswana authorities that the secessionists' fears of persecution, should they be returned to Namibia, were 'plausible'. In subsequent weeks many more people crossed into Botswana, claiming to be fleeing harassment and persecution by the Namibian security forces: among those who left the country were many San, who were not believed to be associated with the secessionist movement. During a visit to Botswana in March 1999 Nujoma reached an agreement with President Festus Mogae of that country, whereby the separatist leaders (whose extradition had hitherto been sought by Namibia in order that they could be tried on terrorist charges) would be accorded refugee status, on condition that they be resettled in a third country. Muyongo and Mamili were subsequently granted asylum in Denmark. The agreement also provided for the return to Namibia, under the auspices of UNHCR and without fear of prosecution or persecution, of the estimated 2,500 refugees who had crossed into Botswana since late 1998.

A period of apparent calm in the Caprivi region ended abruptly in early August 1999 with an armed attack by members of an organization styling itself the Caprivi Liberation Army (CLA), who targeted a military base at Mpacha airport and the police headquarters and offices of the Namibian Broadcasting Corporation in the regional capital, Katima Mulilo. At least eight members of the Namibian security forces and five CLA fighters were killed during the attack and its suppression. Nujoma responded by declaring a state of emergency in the region. While there was support within Namibia for the declaration, the CoD, as well as church leaders and human rights organizations, expressed concern at evidence of the ill-treatment of detainees. Several members of the Government were subsequently reported to have admitted that 'mistakes' were made in the aftermath of the attack; however, the army Chief of Staff maintained that the decisive response of the forces under his command had been justified. Visiting Katima Mulilo in late August, Nujoma announced an end to the state of emergency, although army and police reinforcements were to remain in Caprivi. Initially, 12 alleged rebels were remanded on charges of high treason, murder, public violence and illegal possession of firearms; the prosecution asserted that 17 known leaders of the CLA remained at large. Meanwhile, a further 47 suspects were charged with aiding and abetting the rebels. Repatriations of refugees from Botswana were halted following the attack on Katima Mulilo. In September 2001, in response to a request from the Namibian Government, the Gaborone Magistrates' Court in Botswana ordered the extradition of a group of suspected Caprivi separatists who were wanted to stand trial for high treason in connection with the attack on Katima Mulilo. The Namibian Government was also seeking to extradite Muyongo from Denmark to answer similar charges. In October 2003, after numerous delays, the trial commenced of 121 Namibians charged with offences related to the attack on Katima Mulilo. In February 2004 the trial judge ruled that 13 of the defendants were 'irregularly before the court', as a result of a process of 'disguised extradition' whereby they had been removed from Zambia and Botswana, and ordered their release. It was reported that the 13 defendants thus acquitted had been immediately rearrested on their release. In August 2007 10 individuals were convicted in relation to the rebellion and sentenced to up to 32 years' imprisonment. The trial of the remaining defendants was ongoing in early 2011, marking almost 12 years since the suspects had been detained.

Meanwhile, presidential and legislative elections, which were held on 30 November and 1 December 1999, resulted in an overwhelming victory for Nujoma and SWAPO, with Ulenga and the CoD apparently winning support at the expense of the DTA. In the presidential election Nujoma was returned for a third (and final) term of office, with 76.8% of the votes cast, while Ulenga took 10.5% and Katuutire Kaura (Muyongo's successor as President of the DTA) 9.6%. SWAPO won 55 of the elective seats in the National Assembly, with 76.1% of the votes cast (thus ensuring that it retained the two-thirds' majority required to amend the Constitution); the CoD and the DTA each won seven seats (taking, respectively, 9.9% and 9.5% of the total votes cast).

In August 2002 Nujoma reorganized his Cabinet; Theo-Ben Gurirab was appointed Prime Minister, replacing Geingob. Hidipo Hamutenya became Minister of Foreign Affairs, Information and Broadcasting, but was dismissed without explanation in May 2004: many observers regarded the decision as part of a plan by the President to manoeuvre his own choice of successor, the Minister of Lands, Resettlement and Rehabilitation, Hifikepunye Pohamba, into a stronger position. Pohamba was duly selected as SWAPO's presidential candidate later that month.

The Pohamba presidency

At national elections held on 15–16 November 2004 Pohamba was elected President with, according to official results, 76.4% of the votes cast; his nearest rival, Ulenga, secured 7.3%. SWAPO also recorded a decisive victory in the elections to the National Assembly, retaining 55 of the 72 seats with 76.1% of the national vote. The CoD increased its share of the vote but won only five seats, compared with seven in the 1999 elections. The DTA took four seats, the UDF three and the MAG one seat, while two newly reactivated parties, the National Unity Democratic Organization (NUDO) and the Republican Party (RP), won three seats and one seat, respectively. The Electoral Commission of Namibia (ECN) recorded voter turn-out at 85%. (Following claims of electoral irregularities by members of the opposition, a recount was held in March 2005: with the exception of the CoD, all parties received fewer votes, although the overall allocation of seats remained the same.)

Nujoma stood down as President on 21 March 2005, but remained leader of SWAPO. Following his inauguration as President that day, Pohamba announced his Cabinet, which included six new appointees. The former Minister of Higher Education, Training and Employment Creation, Nahas Angula, and the former Minister of Health and Social Services, Dr Libertina Amathila, were appointed as Prime Minister and Deputy Prime Minister, respectively. The overall structure of the ministries was reorganized and several were renamed to reflect their changed remits.

Meanwhile, in April 2001 the Government announced that it had allocated N $100m. to acquire land for redistribution on a voluntary basis over a five-year period. At that time approximately 4,000 (mainly white-owned) farms occupied 52% of the total land area, while the Government had acquired only some 6% of the land required for resettlement. In October 2002 the Government announced that it was considering the seizure of white-owned farms for redistribution to the landless black population, and criticized white farmers for taking advantage of the voluntary basis for land redistribution by charging excessively high prices for their land. In March 2004 the Government estimated that it would cost more than US $150m. over a five-year period to redistribute some 9m. ha of land among an estimated 243,000 applicants. (It was reported that land prices had increased three-fold between 1990 and 2005.) By September 2004 the Government had bought just over 140 farms at a cost of N $131m.—under the 'willing buyer, willing seller' scheme—and resettled 9,156 people. The expropriation of the first white-owned commercial farm was carried out in November 2005; a further 19 farms were listed for expropriation under compulsory purchase orders. However, an independent report, issued by the Legal Assistance Centre, criticized the government programme, concluding that the resettlement targets were 'logistically impossible' and 'economically unrealistic'.

In December 2005 the National Assembly approved legislation granting former President Nujoma the title of 'Founding Father'. Pohamba was elected as SWAPO leader in November 2007, following Nujoma's retirement. In the same month a new political party, the Rally for Democracy and Progress (RDP), was registered under the leadership of two former cabinet ministers and members of SWAPO. Jesaya Nyamu, who was named as acting Chairman of the party, had been Minister of Trade and Industry until 2004 and Hidipo Hamutenya, acting President of the RDP, was formerly Minister of Foreign Affairs.

A state of emergency was declared by President Pohamba in March 2008, after widespread flooding in central and northern regions of the country killed 42 people and displaced thousands more. In March 2009 Pohamba again declared a state of emergency, when severe flooding affected northern Namibia, killing at least 92 people and displacing hundreds of thousands.

Meanwhile, in April 2008 President Pohamba announced a major reorganization of the Cabinet. The most notable appointment was that of former Prime Minister Geingob to the post of Minister of Trade and Industry.

In May 2008 workers at the Skorpion Zinc Mine in southern Namibia commenced industrial action following a wage dispute. The strike lasted for 19 days before a 12% pay increase was agreed. There was further industrial action in September, when more than 1,900 workers at TransNamib Holdings, a transport services company, went on strike, paralysing the country's rail network. The strike, which lasted for seven days, was estimated by the Government to have cost the Namibian economy some N $180m.

Recent developments: the 2009 elections

Presidential and legislative elections were held concurrently on 27–28 November 2009. In the former poll Pohamba was overwhelmingly re-elected to serve a second presidential term, securing 76.4% of the valid votes cast, according to results released by the ECN in early December. Of his 11 challengers, only Hamutenya, representing the RDP, took more than 4% of the vote, winning 11.1%. SWAPO retained its majority in the National Assembly, taking 54 of the 72 seats in the legislative elections, with 75.3% of the national vote. The RDP won eight seats, while the DTA, NUDO and the UDF all secured two seats. Several African election observer missions declared the polls to have been transparent, free and fair; however, eight of the opposition parties that contested the elections criticized the delay in vote counting and the release of the results, and alleged that numerous irregularities had taken place during the voting process. In March 2010 the Namibian High Court dismissed, owing to 'technical' reasons, a challenge to the results brought by a number of the defeated parties. In response to this ruling, the opposition parties appealed to the Supreme Court, while the RDP, RP and DTA announced a boycott of the National Assembly.

In late March 2010 President Pohamba announced the formation of a new Government, again headed by Prime Minister Angula. Dr Marco Hausiku, hitherto Minister of Foreign Affairs, became Deputy Prime Minister in place of Amathila, while Utoni Nujoma—the son of Sam Nujoma—was among five new ministers appointed to the Cabinet, assuming responsibility for the foreign affairs portfolio. In September the Supreme Court overruled the High Court's earlier judgment and declared that the opposition challenge to the 2009 election results was valid, prompting the RDP and the RP to end their six-month boycott of the National Assembly. (The DTA had ended its boycott in June 2010.) However, after hearing their case, in February 2011 the High Court ruled against the opposition parties, concluding that there was insufficient evidence to support their claims of electoral misconduct. Shortly afterwards the opposition grouping announced its intention to appeal once again to the Supreme Court.

Meanwhile, leaked documents emerged in mid-2010 relating to the Development Capital Portfolio (DCP), an investment arm of the Government Institutions Pension Fund (GIPF) that had ceased operating in 2002 after suffering huge financial losses due to the collapse of a number of companies to which the GIPF had lent large sums of DCP funds. Among the files was a previously unpublished audit report produced by the country's financial regulator, the Namibia Financial Institutions Supervisory Authority (NAMFISA), which in 2006 had conducted an independent investigation into the DCP's losses. The report described the DCP as being 'deeply flawed' and criticized the weak regulations governing the allocation of DCP funding, while media reports alleged that most of the businessmen awarded DCP loans had close ties with the Government or with senior members of the GIPF. NAMFISA had recommended an overhaul of the GIPF, including the removal of senior management, and that measures be taken to recover the lost money from the receivers of the loans; however, the report's recipient, Prime Minister Angula, had failed to act on this guidance. The Government was criticized by trade unions and opposition parties for failing to bring to account those responsible for the DCP's losses, which amounted to over N $650m. according to NAMFISA, and there was widespread outrage among the general public. In response, in October 2010 the Government initiated another audit into the DCP's finances and suspended the DCP's successor scheme, the Unlisted Investment Policy. The results of the second audit, presented to the President in February 2011, corroborated the findings from NAMFISA's earlier investigation, and the reform of the GIPF and the introduction of new lending regulations were recommended. Following a protest march in the capital by hundreds of government workers, Pohamba announced that those who had borrowed DCP funds would be pursued for repayment under threat of prosecution, although he seemed reluctant to hold high-ranking GIPF members responsible for the scandal.

After the failure of negotiations on the formation of an opposition electoral alliance, the RDP merged with the RP in October 2010 (retaining the former's name) in an attempt to present SWAPO with a more robust challenge in the local and regional elections scheduled for the following month. Nevertheless, the elections, held on 26–27 November, resulted in another convincing victory for SWAPO, which secured the overwhelming majority of local and regional council seats. The rate of participation by the electorate, at 39%, was the lowest on record. Shortly before the elections the SWAPO-dominated National Assembly had approved controversial legislation granting the President the power to appoint regional governors, who had hitherto been elected by the regional councillors. Opposition parties had strongly criticized the bill, arguing that it would weaken democracy and that it contradicted the Government's declared adherence to decentralization. The Government, however, claimed that the new law would enhance national unity and deter potential tribal conflict, while providing governors with a direct channel of communication to the central authorities. In December Pohamba duly appointed the 13 regional governors, all of whom were SWAPO members.

Foreign Affairs
Regional relations

Following independence, Namibia became a member of the UN, the Commonwealth, the OAU and the Southern African Development Co-ordination Conference—now the Southern African Development Community (SADC, see p. 420). Despite expressed concerns at South African dominance of the regional economy, the Nujoma regime forged close links with post-apartheid South Africa, and in 1994 SWAPO contributed funds to the electoral campaigns of the African National Congress of South Africa and the Pan-Africanist Congress. In February 1997 legislation providing for the cancellation of Namibia's debt (now amounting to N $1,200m.) was formally approved by the South African Parliament. In August 2001 the foreign ministers of Namibia and South Africa held talks regarding their 400-km border; Namibia claimed its southern border extended to the middle of the Orange river, while South Africa claimed that its territory stretched to the northern bank. (When South Africa's borders were reassessed in 1994, following its first democratic elections, the Surveyors-General of both Namibia and South Africa had agreed to place the border in the middle of the river, but the agreement was never signed.) The confusion over the location of the border has led to differences over mineral and fishing rights in the river, as well as grazing rights on its islands.

In March 1993 UNITA alleged that members of the Namibia Defence Force (NDF) had crossed the border into southern Angola to assist Angolan government forces in offensives against UNITA, and subsequently claimed that some 2,000 Cuban troops had landed at Namibia's southern port of Lüderitz, from where they had been transferred to Angola to assist government forces. The Namibian authorities denied any involvement in the Angolan conflict, however. A 550-km stretch of the Okavango river border was closed from September 1994, following the deaths of three Namibians in an attack attributed by the Namibian authorities to UNITA. In September 1995 the Namibian Government announced the formation of a border control unit to assist police and NDF troops deployed along the Okavango. In November the two countries' defence and security commission agreed new measures aimed at facilitating the work of border patrols. Namibia subsequently announced that the Government was to contribute 200 NDF troops to the UN peace-keeping mission in Angola.

Following the attack on Katima Mulilo by Caprivi separatists in August 1999, the Namibian Government alleged that UNITA was lending military and logistical support to the CLA. (The CLA was also reported to be linked with the separatist Barotse Patriotic Front in Zambia, and the Namibian authorities alleged that the CLA had received training on Zambian territory.) There was considerable speculation that not only was Caprivi an important supply route for UNITA, but also that the Angolan rebel movement was attempting to divert resources of the Namibian armed forces away from the conflict in the Democratic Republic of the Congo (DRC, q.v.).

Tensions in the region of the Namibia–Angola border escalated from late 1999, after the two countries began joint patrols targeting UNITA, and the Namibian Government authorized the Angolan armed forces to launch attacks against UNITA from Namibian territory. In February 2000 it was announced that Nujoma and President José Eduardo dos Santos of Angola had agreed to implement measures to restore security in the border region; by June, when a curfew was imposed on the northeastern border with Angola, more than 50 Namibians had been killed in cross-border raids by the Angolan rebels. Continuing conflict in southern Angola resulted in a large number of refugees entering Namibia (some 6,000 arrived from Angola between November 1999 and August 2000, although increased border security subsequently reduced the flow). In March 2001 President Nujoma ordered a further reinforcement of the Namibian military presence in Caprivi. In October UNITA rebels were reported to have destroyed an electricity substation in the Kavango region, and in November a group of unidentified gunmen killed four people in western Caprivi before escaping to Angola.

In April 2002 the Namibian Government welcomed the signing of a formal cease-fire agreement by the Angolan Government and UNITA. Some stability was restored in the Kavango and Caprivi regions in mid-2002, and in August a number of Angolan refugees were repatriated; the majority of them, estimated at around 20,000, were due to return home in mid-2003, under the auspices of UNHCR. In February 2005 Namibia and Angola reached agreement on a maritime border; negotiations had begun in 1993 but were not formalized until 2003 when a joint commission for delimitation and demarcation was established. In September 2008 Namibia's National Society for Human Rights (NSHR) reported that it had discovered what were believed to be unmarked mass graves near the border with Angola. The organization claimed that it had 'reasonable cause' to believe the remains it had discovered belonged to victims of the Namibian security forces, who were killed between 1994 and 2003. According to the NSHR, in 1994 the Namibian authorities ordered that all illegal immigrants be cleared from the northern border area, some of whom were accused of being members of UNITA. This allegedly resulted in systematic attacks on local people, who were subject to summary executions and 'forced disappearances': the Namibian Government, however, strongly denied these claims.

In February 1995 it was announced that Namibia and Botswana were to refer a dispute regarding the demarcation of their joint border on the Chobe river (specifically, the issue of the sovereignty of the small, uninhabited island of Kasikili-Sedudu) for adjudication by the ICJ. The dispute was formally submitted to the Court in mid-1996. The ICJ ruled in December 1999 that the island formed part of the territory of Botswana; the judgment further ruled that nationals of (and vessels flying the flags of) Botswana and Namibia should enjoy equal treatment in the two channels around the island. In January 1998 the two countries' Joint Commission on Defence and Security held an emergency meeting, following allegations by Namibia that troops from Botswana had taken control of a further island in disputed border territory—Situngu Island in the Caprivi Strip. The Joint Commission agreed to expedite the establishment of a Joint Technical Commission for the demarcation of the border. Relations were complicated by the issue of Caprivi secessionism (see above). Situngu is claimed as Mafwe land; furthermore, Namibia's representative in discussions regarding the island, said to be a member of the secessionist movement, was reported to have fled to Angola. In 2003 Botswana and Namibia accepted the demarcation by a joint commission of their joint border along the Kwando, Linyanti and Chobe rivers.

From August 1998 Namibia, which was participating in regional efforts to resolve the conflict in the DRC, supported a Zimbabwean-led initiative by members of SADC (notably excluding South Africa) for military intervention in support of the regime of President Laurent-Désiré Kabila; as many as 2,000 Namibian troops were subsequently dispatched to the DRC, provoking vociferous criticism by opponents of Nujoma. Namibia's continuing military commitments in the DRC following the failure of the 1999 Lusaka accord (to which Namibia was a signatory), together with the need for additional army resources in north-east Namibia as a result of the Caprivi rebellion and the intensification of operations against UNITA (see above), necessitated the allocation of an additional N $173m. to defence in the 1999/2000 supplementary budget.

President Laurent-Désiré Kabila was assassinated in January 2001, and was succeeded by his son, Maj.-Gen. Joseph Kabila. Efforts to resolve the conflict in the DRC were accelerated, and in February proposals for the withdrawal of troops involved in the regional military intervention, including the estimated 2,000 Namibians, were approved by the participating countries, under the aegis of the UN Security Council. In March it was announced that Namibian forces would remain in the DRC until the specified date for withdrawal in May. All but an estimated 150 Namibian troops eventually withdrew from the DRC in September, although other foreign forces were still deployed in large numbers; at least 30 Namibian troops were reported to have been killed in three years of service. All Namibian troops had been withdrawn by the end of 2002.

Other external relations

Germany has been a major aid donor to Namibia since independence, and relations are generally close. In September 1995, none the less, during a visit by the German Chancellor, Helmut Kohl, some 300 members of the Herero ethnic group staged a demonstration outside the German embassy in Windhoek to demand compensation for suffering inflicted on the Herero under German rule. In June 2001 the Herero filed a lawsuit in Washington, DC, USA, against three German companies (Deutsche Bank AG, Woermann Line and Terex Corporation), claiming US $2,000m. in reparation for the alleged exploitation and eventual extermination of some 65,000 Herero in 1904–07; a second lawsuit, for a further US $2,000m., was filed against the German Government in September 2001. The case against Terex Corporation was subsequently withdrawn, after the company claimed that it was under different management at the time of the atrocities. In October 2003 it was reported that the Federal Court in Washington, DC, had ruled that it did not have jurisdiction over the Herero case, and that the Herero were consequently considering filing a lawsuit in New York. In January 2004, at a commemoration of the Herero uprising against German rule in 1904, the Government of Germany expressed its regret for the extermination of Herero, but declared itself unwilling to pay compensation to descendants of the victims. During a visit to Namibia in August 2004 the German Minister of Economic Co-operation and Development, Heidemarie Wieczorek-Zeul, apologized to the Herero community for the atrocities carried out during 1904–07. During a visit to Germany in December 2005 President Pohamba rejected an offer of reparations valued at N $160m. Bilateral consultations took place in May 2006 and included a German proposal to invest N $150m., over a 10-year period, in regions inhabited by descendants of populations that had suffered during the colonial occupation. The money would be made available in addition to existing aid commitments, which were reported to amount to some €11m. per year. However, the German Government denied that the additional money was intended as war reparations. Germany has also provided Namibia with military assistance in the form of training and equipment donation. In September 2008 it was reported that the German Advisory Group in Namibia had supplied the Namibian Defence Force with an Integrated Logistics System, completing a N $16.5m. project to establish a communications network linking all military bases in the country.

CONSTITUTION AND GOVERNMENT

On 21 March 1990 Namibia became independent, and the Constitution took effect. Executive authority is held by the President, who is the Head of State. According to the Constitution, the President shall be directly elected by universal adult suffrage for a term of five years, and permitted to hold office for a maximum of two terms. (In late 1998 legislation was approved whereby the Constitution was to be exceptionally amended to allow the incumbent President to seek a third term of office.) Legislative power is vested in the National Assembly, comprising 72 members directly elected by universal adult suffrage and as many as six non-voting members nominated by the President. The National Assembly has a maximum term of five years. An advisory National Council, comprising two representatives from each of the country's 13 Regional Councils, elected for a six-year period, operates as the second chamber of parliament. Each region has its own Governor.

REGIONAL AND INTERNATIONAL CO-OPERATION

Namibia is a member of the African Union (see p. 183), of the Common Market for Eastern and Southern Africa (see p. 228), of the Southern African Development Community (see p. 420), and of the Southern African Customs Union (with Botswana, Lesotho, South Africa and Swaziland); and is also a signatory to the Cotonou Agreement with the European Union.

Namibia became a member of the UN in 1990. As a contracting party to the General Agreement on Tariffs and Trade, Namibia joined the World Trade Organization (WTO, see p. 430) on its establishment in 1995. Namibia participates in the Group of 77 (G77, see p. 447) developing countries.

ECONOMIC AFFAIRS

In 2009, according to estimates by the World Bank, Namibia's gross national income (GNI), measured at average 2007–09 prices, was US $9,323m., equivalent to US $4,290 per head (or US $6,410 per head on an international purchasing-power parity basis). During 2000–09, it was estimated, the population increased at an average annual rate of 2.0%, while gross domestic product (GDP) per head increased, in real terms, by an average of 2.6% per year. Overall GDP increased, in real terms, at an average annual rate of 4.6% in 2000–09. According to the Bank of Namibia, real GDP increased by 4.3% in 2008, but declined by 0.7% in 2009.

Agriculture (including hunting, forestry and fishing) contributed 9.3% of GDP in 2009, according to the Bank of Namibia. An estimated 32.8% of the labour force were employed in the sector in 2011, according to FAO. The principal agricultural activity is beef production; the production of karakul sheepskins is also important. In addition, sealing and ostrich farming are practised on a commercial basis. The main subsistence crops are root crops, millet and maize, although Namibia remains highly dependent on imports of basic foods, especially in drought years. Plantations of seedless grapes were developed on the banks of the Orange river in the late 1990s, and projected growth in production was expected to increase significantly their contribution to export revenue. In recent years Namibia's traditionally rich fisheries have suffered a reverse, and in February 2006 fishing quotas were further lowered and a five-year moratorium was declared on new fishing rights. Nevertheless, exports of fish and fish products provided 11.2% of total export earnings in 2008. Legislation aimed at developing aquaculture was adopted in 2003 and a number of fish farms were established. Agricultural GDP decreased at an average annual rate of 3.5% in 2005–09; it increased by 0.4% in 2008, but declined by 4.1% in 2009.

Industry (including mining, manufacturing, construction and power) contributed 31.9% of GDP in 2009, and engaged 14.8% of the employed labour force in 2004. During 2005–09 industrial GDP increased by an average of 2.2% per year. Industrial GDP grew by 2.2% in 2008, but declined by 11.9% in 2009.

Mining and quarrying contributed 10.7% of GDP in 2009, and engaged 2.0% of the employed labour force in 2004. Namibia has rich deposits of many minerals, and is among the world's leading producers of gem diamonds (some 98% of diamonds mined in Namibia are of gem quality). Diamond-mining contributed 36.3% of the sector's GDP in 2009, and diamonds are the principal mineral export, accounting for 16.5% of export earnings in 2008. Total production was 2.4m. carats in 2008, but declined to an estimated 1.2m. carats in 2009, before recovering to some extent in 2010. In July 2004 the Israeli company Lev Leviev Diamonds established a diamond-cutting and -polishing factory in Windhoek, the first in Namibia and the largest of its kind in Africa. Copper production, which ceased in 1998, following the liquidation of the Tsumeb Corporation, resumed at the former Tsumeb sites in September 2000, but was suspended again in late 2008 owing to declining international prices. The smelter at Tsumeb, operated by Ongopolo, continued operations, however, processing imported ore. The Skorpion zinc mine and refinery near Rosh Pinah, opened in 2003 by Anglo American plc and owned since November 2010 by Vedanta Resources plc, produces around 150,000 metric tons of zinc per year. Despite health and environmental concerns, a new uranium mine began production at Langer Heinrich in 2007; Namibia was the fourth largest uranium producer in the world in 2009. In addition, lead, gold, salt, fluorspar, marble and semi-precious stones are extracted, and there are also considerable deposits of hydrocarbons, lithium, manganese, tungsten, cadmium and vanadium. Furthermore, Namibia is believed to have substantial reserves of coal, iron ore and platinum. Mining GDP decreased at an average annual rate of 9.0% in 2005–09; the sector's GDP declined by 2.9% in 2008 and by 45.0% in 2009.

Manufacturing contributed 14.5% of GDP in 2009, and engaged 6.2% of the employed labour force in 2004. The sector has hitherto remained underdeveloped, largely owing to Namibia's economic dependence on South Africa. The principal manufacturing activities are the processing of fish and minerals for export; brewing, meat-processing and the production of chemicals are also significant. Manufacturing GDP increased by an average of 4.9% per year in 2005–09; the sector's GDP increased by 2.1% in 2008 and by 6.5% in 2009.

Construction contributed 4.0% of GDP in 2009, and engaged 5.1% of the employed labour force in 2004. During 2005–09 construction GDP increased by an average of 13.8% per year. Construction GDP grew by 15.1% in 2008, but declined by 7.3% in 2009.

In 2007 92.3% of Namibia's electricity production was derived from hydroelectric power. There is a hydroelectric station at Ruacana, on the Cunene river at the border with Angola, and a second hydroelectric power station was planned at Divundu on the Okavango river. Final agreement was reached on developing the Kudu offshore gasfield in early 2006. An 800-MW 'gas-to-power' plant would supply the domestic market and the surplus would be exported to South Africa under an agreement with that country's Electricity Supply Commission. However, the project subsequently suffered repeated delays. The construction of another 400-MW gas-fired plant, at Walvis Bay, was also envisaged. Imports of mineral fuels and lubricants accounted for 13.6% of the value of total merchandise imports in 2008. South Africa supplies all of Namibia's petroleum requirements.

The services sector contributed 58.8% of GDP in 2009. Tourism is expanding rapidly, and has been the focus of a major privatization initiative. The acquisition of Walvis Bay in March 1994, and subsequent establishment there of a free-trade zone, was expected to enhance Namibia's status as an entrepôt for regional trade. By March 2004 it was estimated that the free-trade zone had attracted some N $80m. of direct foreign investment. In 2006 the Government remained the largest employer in Namibia, accounting for some 70,000 jobs. The GDP of the services sector increased at an average annual rate of 5.8% in 2005–09. Services GDP increased by 5.8% in 2008 and by 4.4% in 2009.

In 2009 Namibia recorded a visible trade deficit of US $983.5m., and there was a deficit of US $161.0m. on the current account of the balance of payments. South Africa was the dominant source of imports in 2008, providing 67.8% of the total, followed by the United Kingdom (8.0%). In that year South Africa was also the principal market for Namibian exports (31.8%), followed by the United Kingdom, Angola, Canada, the USA and Spain. The principal exports were printed matter, diamonds, uranium and thorium ores and concentrates, and fresh or frozen fish. The principal import groups in that year included machinery and transport equipment (notably road vehicles), basic manufactures, mineral fuels and lubricants, chemicals and related products, and food and live animals.

In the financial year ending 31 March 2010 Namibia recorded an estimated overall budget deficit of N $2,721.1m., equivalent to 3.3% of GDP. Namibia's general government gross debt was N $12,477m. in 2009, equivalent to 15.3% of GDP. In 1997 South Africa officially cancelled the external public debt inherited by Namibia at independence. Namibia's external debt was estimated at US $716m. in 2003. The annual rate of inflation averaged 6.3% in 2001–10; consumer prices increased by 4.4% in 2010. According to the 2001 census, some 31% of the labour force were unemployed.

Namibia's potential for economic prosperity remains high, given its abundant mineral reserves and well-developed infrastructure, both of which were enhanced in 1994 by the acquisition of sovereignty over Walvis Bay and of important diamond-mining rights. The mining of offshore diamond deposits is of increasing importance, the leading diamond producer being Namdeb (a joint venture between the Government and De Beers). However, Namibia's economic progress continues to be largely influenced by its dependence on South Africa. (The Namibian dollar, introduced in 1993, is at par with the rand.) The 1995 Export Processing Zones Act aimed to industrialize the economy, which was dominated by primary sector industries, and the Government hoped that the Namibia Diamond Trading Company (established in January 2007) would stimulate production in the country's diamond-cutting industry. However, external demand and diamond output slowed in 2009. Adverse market conditions, resulting from the global financial crisis, also impeded other areas of Namibia's minerals sector in 2008–09, as rapidly declining prices diminished profit margins. Copper production was suspended in late 2008, a decision that led to significant job losses, but several uranium-mining projects were established in 2009, with the potential to create some 5,000 new jobs and make Namibia the world's third largest supplier of uranium by 2015. GDP contracted by 0.7% in 2009, but overall the impact of the downturn was not as severe as had been previously feared, in part because of the Government's expansionary spending policies. The continuation of this counter-cyclical strategy during 2010, combined with renewed international demand and prices for diamonds and uranium, led to a revival in economic activity. The Bank of Namibia estimated that GDP expanded by 4.6% in 2010, driven by a sharp recovery in the mining sector (particularly the diamond industry), and forecast growth of 4.1% in 2011. However, the recent increases in government expenditure had resulted in a fiscal deficit, and the Government recognized that stimulus measures would have to be reduced from 2011. Nevertheless, the medium-term outlook remained favourable owing to the recovery in international commodity markets and the expected commencement of production at several major uranium-mining operations during 2011–14.

PUBLIC HOLIDAYS

2012: 1 January (New Year's Day), 21 March (Independence Day), 6–9 April (Easter), 1 May (Workers' Day), 4 May (Cassinga Day), 17 May (Ascension Day), 25 May (Africa Day, anniversary of the OAU's foundation), 26 August (Heroes' Day), 10 December (Human Rights Day), 25–26 December (Christmas), 26 December (Family Day).

NAMIBIA

Statistical Survey

Source (unless otherwise indicated): Central Bureau of Statistics, National Planning Commission, Government Office Park, Block D2, Luther St, Windhoek; PMB 13356, Windhoek; tel. (61) 2834056; fax (61) 237620; e-mail info@npc.gov.na; internet www.npc.gov.na.

Area and Population

AREA, POPULATION AND DENSITY*

Area (sq km)	824,292†
Population (census results)	
21 October 1991	1,409,920
28 August 2001	
Males	936,718
Females	890,136
Total	1,826,854
Population (UN estimates at mid-year)‡	
2009	2,171,140
2010	2,212,037
2011	2,252,411
Density (per sq km) at mid-2011	2.7

* Including data for Walvis Bay, sovereignty over which was transferred from South Africa to Namibia with effect from March 1994. Walvis Bay has an area of 1,124 sq km (434 sq miles) and had a population of 22,999 in 1991.
† 318,261 sq miles.
‡ Source: UN, *World Population Prospects: The 2008 Revision*.

POPULATION BY AGE AND SEX
('000 persons, UN estimates at mid-2011)

	Males	Females	Total
0–14	406,880	402,595	809,475
15–64	669,454	689,485	1,358,939
65 and over	35,790	48,207	83,997
Total	1,112,124	1,140,287	2,252,411

Source: UN, *World Population Prospects: The 2008 Revision*.

ETHNIC GROUPS
(population, 1988 estimates)

Ovambo	623,000	Caprivian	47,000
Kavango	117,000	Bushmen	36,000
Damara	94,000	Baster	31,000
Herero	94,000	Tswana	7,000
White	80,000	Others	12,000
Nama	60,000	**Total**	1,252,000
Coloured	51,000		

PRINCIPAL TOWNS
(population at 2001 census)

Windhoek	233,529	Rehoboth	21,300
Rundu	44,413	Otjiwarongo	19,614
Walvis Bay	42,015	Keetmanshoop	15,543
Oshakati	28,255	Gobabis	13,856
Katima Mulilo	22,694	Tsumeb	13,108

Mid-2009 (including suburbs, UN estimate): Windhoek (capital) 341,722 (Source: UN, *World Urbanization Prospects: The 2009 Revision*).

BIRTHS AND DEATHS
(annual averages, UN estimates)

	1995–2000	2000–05	2005–10
Birth rate (per 1,000)	32.7	30.0	27.8
Death rate (per 1,000)	8.3	10.5	8.5

Source: UN, *World Population Prospects: The 2008 Revision*.

Life expectancy (WHO estimates, years at birth): 63 (males 61; females 66) in 2008 (Source: WHO, *World Health Statistics*).

EMPLOYMENT
(persons aged 15 to 69 years, 2004 labour force survey)

	Males	Females	Total
Agriculture, hunting and forestry	64,991	37,645	102,636
Fishing	7,933	4,787	12,720
Mining and quarrying	5,909	1,653	7,562
Manufacturing	12,082	11,673	23,755
Electricity, gas and water	5,031	1,120	6,151
Construction	18,296	1,309	19,605
Wholesale and retail trade, repair of motor vehicles, motorcycles and personal and household goods	27,004	26,891	53,895
Restaurants and hotels	5,889	7,243	13,132
Transport, storage and communications	12,744	3,117	15,861
Financial intermediation	3,506	4,076	7,582
Real estate, renting and business activities	5,280	4,095	9,375
Public administration and defence; compulsory social security	20,216	10,469	30,685
Education	12,313	18,855	31,168
Health and social work	3,533	10,477	14,010
Other community, social and personal services	7,480	5,152	12,632
Private households with employed persons	4,067	20,014	24,081
Extra-territorial organizations and bodies	72	—	72
Sub-total	216,346	168,576	384,922
Not classifiable by economic activity	305	102	407
Total employed	216,651	168,678	385,329

Source: ILO.

Mid-2011 ('000 persons, FAO estimates): Agriculture, etc. 260; Total labour force 793 (Source: FAO).

Health and Welfare

KEY INDICATORS

Total fertility rate (children per woman, 2008)	3.4
Under-5 mortality rate (per 1,000 live births, 2008)	42
HIV/AIDS (% of persons aged 15–49, 2007)	15.3
Physicians (per 1,000 head, 2004)	0.3
Hospital beds (per 1,000 head, 2006)	3.3
Health expenditure (2007): US $ per head (PPP)	467
Health expenditure (2007): % of GDP	7.6
Health expenditure (2007): public (% of total)	42.1
Access to water (% of persons, 2008)	92
Access to sanitation (% of persons, 2008)	33
Total carbon dioxide emissions ('000 metric tons, 2007)	3,033.8
Carbon dioxide emissions per head (metric tons, 2007)	1.5
Human Development Index (2010): ranking	105
Human Development Index (2010): value	0.606

For sources and definitions, see explanatory note on p. vi.

NAMIBIA

Agriculture

PRINCIPAL CROPS
('000 metric tons)

	2005	2006	2007*
Wheat	11.0	12.9	13.0
Maize	40.7	60.9	40.0
Millet	47.9	59.0*	60.0
Sorghum	6.5*	6.0*	6.0
Grapes	15.5*	18.2*	18.0

* FAO estimate(s).

2008: Production assumed to be unchanged from 2007 (FAO estimates).

Note: No data were available for individual crops in 2009.

Aggregate production ('000 metric tons, may include official, semi-official or estimated data): Total cereals 106.1 in 2005, 138.7 in 2006, 119.0 in 2007–09; Total roots and tubers 315.0 in 2005, 320.0 in 2006, 320.0 in 2007–09; Total vegetables (incl. melons) 15.4 in 2005, 14.9 in 2006, 14.9 in 2007–09; Total fruits (excl. melons) 30.0 in 2005, 32.7 in 2006, 32.5 in 2007–09.

Source: FAO.

LIVESTOCK
('000 head, year ending September)

	2005	2006	2007*
Horses	47.4	46.2	50.0
Asses	140.3	140.0*	140.0
Cattle	3,133.9	2,384.0	2,500.0
Sheep	2,663.8	2,660.3	2,700.0
Goats	2,043.5	2,061.4	2,100.0
Pigs	31.0	33.0	35.0
Chickens	4,700*	4,800*	4,900

* FAO estimate(s).

2008–09: Figures assumed to be unchanged from 2007 (FAO estimates).

Source: FAO.

LIVESTOCK PRODUCTS
('000 metric tons)

	2006	2007	2008
Cattle meat	36.2	38.6*	38.6*
Sheep meat*	10.6	12.1	12.1
Chicken meat*	9.7	9.8	9.8
Cows' milk*	133	138	138
Hen eggs*	3.1	3.2	3.2
Wool, greasy*	2.1	2.1	2.1

* FAO estimate(s).

2009 (FAO estimates): Chicken meat 10.0; Hen eggs 3.2.

Source: FAO.

Forestry

Separate figures are not yet available. Data for Namibia are included in those for South Africa.

Fishing

('000 metric tons, live weight)*

	2006	2007	2008
Capture	509.6†	413.3	372.8†
Cape hakes (Stokvisse)	135.9	125.5	126.3
Kingklip	4.7	5.3	3.7
Devil anglerfish	9.8	n.a.	8.6
Southern African pilchard	2.3	23.5	20.7
Cape horse mackerel (Maasbanker)	307.9	201.7	192.7
Aquaculture†	0.0	0.0	0.0
Total catch†	509.6	413.4	372.9

* Figures include quantities caught by licensed foreign vessels in Namibian waters and processed in Lüderitz and Walvis Bay. The data exclude aquatic mammals (whales, seals, etc.). The number of South African fur seals caught was: 83,045 in 2006; 34,728 in 2007. The number of Nile crocodiles caught was: 305 in 2006.
† FAO estimate(s).

Source: FAO.

Mining

(metric tons, unless otherwise indicated)

	2007	2008	2009*
Copper ore†	6,580	7,471	n.a.
Lead concentrates†	10,543	14,062	20,000
Zinc concentrates†	46,335	38,319	47,000
Silver ore (kilograms)†	30,000*	30,000*	30,000
Uranium oxide	3,680	4,838	5,375
Gold ore (kilograms)†	2,496	2,126	2,022
Fluorspar (Fluorite)‡	118,766	118,263	80,857
Salt (unrefined)	810,942	732,000	781,800
Diamonds ('000 metric carats)	2,266	2,435	1,192

* Estimate(s).
† Figures refer to the metal content of ores and concentrates.
‡ Figures (on a wet-weight basis) refer to acid-grade material.

Source: US Geological Survey.

Industry

SELECTED PRODUCTS
(metric tons)

	2005	2006	2007
Unrefined (blister) copper (unwrought)	23,551	21,918	20,600*
Electrical energy (million kWh)	1,585	1,491	1,694

* Estimate.

2008 (estimate): Unrefined (blister) copper (unwrought) 16,271.

2009 (estimate): Unrefined (blister) copper (unwrought) 21,543.

Sources: US Geological Survey; UN Industrial Commodity Statistics Database.

NAMIBIA

Finance

CURRENCY AND EXCHANGE RATES

Monetary Units
100 cents = 1 Namibian dollar (N $).

Sterling, US Dollar and Euro Equivalents (31 December 2010)
£1 sterling = N $10.382;
US $1 = N $6.632;
€1 = N $8.861;
N $100 = £9.63 = US $15.10 = €11.30.

Average Exchange Rate (N $ per US $)
2008   8.2612
2009   8.4737
2010   7.3212

Note: The Namibian dollar was introduced in September 1993, replacing (at par) the South African rand. The rand remained legal tender in Namibia.

CENTRAL GOVERNMENT BUDGET
(N $ million, year ending 31 March)

Revenue*	2007/08	2008/09	2009/10†
Taxation	19,183.1	21,224.1	21,099.0
Taxes on income and profits	6,729.7	8,069.7	7,499.0
Taxes on property	148.9	171.1	183.0
Domestic taxes on goods and services	4,081.5	4,339.0	4,680.0
Taxes on international trade and transactions	8,085.1	8,502.1	8,585.0
Other taxes	137.9	142.2	152.0
Non-tax revenue	1,427.5	2,139.7	1,325.9
Entrepreneurial and property income	917.4	1,583.9	731.0
Fines and forfeitures	25.2	36.1	32.0
Administrative fees and charges	468.8	502.8	536.0
Return on capital from lending and equity	16.1	16.9	26.9
Total	20,610.6	23,363.9	22,424.9

Expenditure	2007/08	2008/09	2009/10†
Current expenditure	12,587.1	16,955.9	19,320.2
Personnel expenditure	6,183.2	7,559.9	8,899.5
Expenditure on goods and other services	2,208.0	3,529.0	4,256.1
Interest payments	1,477.7	1,366.1	1,352.0
Subsidies and other current transfers	2,718.2	4,501.0	4,812.6
Capital expenditure	2,143.5	4,989.9	5,608.9
Capital investment	1,462.5	2,931.4	4,206.0
Capital transfers	247.1	769.0	932.9
Total lending and equity participation	433.9	1,289.5	470.0
Statistical discrepancy	—	—	492.9
Total	14,730.6	21,945.8	25,422.0

* Excluding grants received from abroad (N $ million): 78.0 in 2007/08; 82.9 in 2008/09; 276.0 in 2009/10 (estimate).
† Estimates.

Source: Bank of Namibia, *Annual Report 2009*.

INTERNATIONAL RESERVES
(excluding gold, US $ million at 31 December)

	2007	2008	2009
IMF special drawing rights	0.03	0.03	204.44
Reserve position in IMF	0.12	0.12	0.12
Foreign exchange	895.87	1,292.80	1,846.37
Total	896.02	1,292.95	2,050.93

Source: IMF, *International Financial Statistics*.

MONEY SUPPLY
(N $ million at 31 December)

	2007	2008	2009
Currency outside depository corporations	820.3	1,140.4	1,156.7
Transferable deposits	13,815.7	17,430.1	19,739.9
Other deposits	10,166.1	10,666.4	10,067.7
Securities other than shares	6.0	3.9	3.9
Broad money	24,808.2	29,240.8	30,968.2

Source: IMF, *International Financial Statistics*.

COST OF LIVING
(Consumer Price Index; base: December 2001 = 100)

	2008	2009	2010
Food and non-alcoholic beverages	174.0	192.6	198.9
Alcoholic beverages and tobacco	166.4	187.2	205.8
Clothing and footwear	112.9	122.6	126.7
Housing, fuel and power	138.1	148.8	157.4
Health	117.9	124.5	130.4
Transport	171.1	181.2	192.0
Communications	116.2	123.5	125.1
Recreation and culture	127.0	139.4	144.0
Education	168.7	174.6	183.8
All items (incl. others)	152.0	165.4	172.7

NATIONAL ACCOUNTS
(N $ million at current prices)

National Income and Product

	2007	2008	2009
Compensation of employees	24,835	28,545	31,676
Operating surplus	25,328	30,973	29,524
Domestic factor incomes	50,163	59,518	61,200
Consumption of fixed capital	7,251	8,885	10,178
Gross domestic product (GDP) at factor cost	57,414	68,403	71,378
Taxes, less subsidies, on production and imports	4,666	5,598	6,434
GDP in purchasers' values	62,080	74,000	77,812
Primary income received from abroad	1,449	1,870	1,752
Less Primary income paid abroad	2,693	3,666	2,336
Gross national income	60,836	72,203	77,228
Less Consumption of fixed capital	7,251	8,870	10,142
National income in market prices	53,585	63,333	67,086
Other current transfers from abroad	7,421	9,762	11,245
Less Other current transfers paid abroad	369	484	632
National disposable income	60,637	72,612	77,700

Expenditure on the Gross Domestic Product

	2007	2008	2009
Government final consumption expenditure	12,834	15,158	18,951
Private final consumption expenditure	35,636	40,939	45,714
Change in stocks	32	1,794	1,871
Gross fixed capital formation	14,696	18,815	19,351
Total domestic expenditure	63,198	76,706	85,887
Exports of goods and services	31,496	38,777	34,581
Less Imports of goods and services	32,310	39,080	41,488
Statistical discrepancy	−304	−2,402	−1,169
GDP in purchasers' values	62,080	74,000	77,812
GDP in constant 2004 prices	49,371	51,475	51,106

NAMIBIA

Gross Domestic Product by Economic Activity

	2007	2008	2009
Agriculture and forestry	3,045	3,976	3,931
Fishing	2,330	2,411	2,775
Mining and quarrying	6,816	11,772	7,744
Diamond mining	3,535	5,500	2,812
Manufacturing	9,774	9,404	10,489
Electricity and water	1,562	1,663	1,934
Construction	2,286	3,013	2,922
Wholesale and retail trade, repairs, etc.	6,769	7,682	8,610
Hotels and restaurants	1,115	1,283	1,486
Transport, storage and communications	2,955	3,400	3,717
Financial intermediation	2,534	2,879	3,294
Real estate and business services	4,990	5,415	5,987
Public administration and defence	5,157	6,219	8,088
Education	4,570	5,222	5,850
Health	1,859	2,244	2,482
Community, social and personal services	1,979	2,184	2,419
Private households with employed person	424	492	559
Sub-total	58,165	69,259	72,287
Less Financial services indirectly measured	750	855	909
GDP at basic prices	57,414	68,403	71,378
Taxes, less subsidies, on products	4,666	5,598	6,434
GDP in purchasers' values	62,080	74,000	77,812

Source: Bank of Namibia, *Quarterly Bulletin*.

BALANCE OF PAYMENTS
(US $ million)

	2007	2008	2009
Exports of goods f.o.b.	2,921.6	3,116.4	3,535.3
Imports of goods f.o.b.	−3,101.6	−3,833.2	−4,518.8
Trade balance	−180.0	−716.9	−983.5
Exports of services	598.6	554.7	521.5
Imports of services	−513.6	−588.7	−609.0
Balance on goods and services	−95.0	−750.9	−1,071.0
Other income received	273.2	303.1	339.3
Other income paid	−431.5	−457.6	−409.3
Balance on goods, services and income	−253.3	−905.4	−1,141.0
Current transfers received	998.3	1,009.3	1,063.9
Current transfers paid	−52.3	−59.0	−83.8
Current balance	692.6	44.9	−161.0
Capital account (net)	83.4	77.2	79.3
Direct investment abroad	−2.7	−6.2	3.0
Direct investment from abroad	169.9	409.0	490.2
Portfolio investment assets	−1,482.9	−1,023.4	−533.2
Portfolio investment liabilities	4.5	3.9	−58.7
Other investment assets	136.2	−111.8	−401.1
Other investment liabilities	−292.0	−169.5	−172.1
Net errors and omissions	490.5	676.1	173.7
Overall balance	−200.5	−99.9	−579.8

Source: IMF, *International Financial Statistics*.

External Trade

PRINCIPAL COMMODITIES
(US $ million)

Imports c.i.f.	2006	2007	2008
Food and live animals	335.7	502.8	506.1
Mineral fuels and lubricants	86.7	416.4	637.7
Petroleum and petroleum products	83.1	399.4	610.0
Chemicals and related products	294.4	368.4	510.7
Basic manufactures	472.3	671.1	876.5
Non-metallic mineral manufactures	80.7	133.2	254.6
Metal products	152.6	247.5	267.2
Machinery and transport equipment	1,082.0	1,383.5	1,456.5
Machinery specialized for particular industries	135.0	167.2	225.4
General industrial machinery, equipment and parts	106.2	119.6	167.6
Telecommunications and sound equipment	104.4	111.2	108.8
Telecommunications equipment, parts and accessories	80.4	80.3	77.1
Electrical machinery, apparatus, etc.	124.8	143.1	156.6
Road vehicles	413.4	485.2	597.5
Passenger motor vehicles (excl. buses)	243.7	286.9	287.1
Other transport equipment	92.4	169.0	38.0
Miscellaneous manufactured articles	366.7	513.4	477.5
Clothing and accessories	86.8	130.6	115.8
Total (incl. others)	2,798.5	4,026.0	4,688.6

Exports f.o.b.	2006	2007	2008
Food and live animals	746.2	807.9	852.5
Fish, shellfish and preparations thereof	434.7	458.9	527.7
Fresh or frozen fish	415.4	431.7	493.2
Beverages and tobacco	111.9	137.7	195.8
Beverages	107.1	135.6	149.6
Alcoholic beverages	100.7	126.4	136.7
Beer made from malt	85.4	110.5	114.8
Crude materials (inedible) except fuels	336.1	647.9	1,042.5
Metal ores and scrap	188.6	474.5	840.0
Ores and concentrates of uranium and thorium	163.0	350.3	741.7
Basic manufactures	1,516.8	1,556.5	1,314.7
Non-metallic mineral manufactures	911.7	723.0	798.8
Pearl, precious and semi-precious stones	900.8	705.0	780.6
Diamonds	900.4	704.6	780.0
Machinery and transport equipment	121.0	280.3	288.6
Miscellaneous manufactured articles	362.0	422.1	890.7
Printed matter	292.7	357.0	807.3
Total (incl. others)	3,375.9	4,040.3	4,729.3

Source: UN, *International Trade Statistics Yearbook*.

PRINCIPAL TRADING PARTNERS
(US $ million)

Imports c.i.f.	2006	2007	2008
China, People's Repub.	96.8	101.5	153.3
Germany	62.4	83.9	96.6
South Africa	2,305.3	3,143.0	3,179.8
Spain	19.8	91.4	22.3
United Kingdom	23.6	45.2	373.3
USA	41.6	54.8	94.9
Total (incl. others)	2,798.5	4,026.0	4,688.6

NAMIBIA

Statistical Survey

Exports f.o.b.	2006	2007	2008
Angola	192.9	260.9	405.6
Belgium	12.2	12.9	50.8
Canada	127.6	199.3	334.2
Congo, Democratic Republic of	45.4	43.1	51.2
France	53.7	106.4	126.7
Germany	109.0	99.8	48.9
Italy	243.5	570.9	63.9
Netherlands	36.7	74.8	76.0
South Africa	829.2	1,172.3	1,505.0
Spain	202.0	242.8	242.4
United Kingdom	865.2	682.9	709.7
USA	81.7	102.1	260.8
Total (incl. others)	3,375.9	4,040.3	4,729.3

Source: UN, *International Trade Statistics Yearbook*.

Transport

RAILWAYS

	2002/03	2003/04
Freight (million net ton-km)	1,244.6	1,247.4
Passengers carried	125,656	112,033

Source: TransNamib Holdings Ltd, *2004 Annual Report*.

ROAD TRAFFIC
(motor vehicles in use at 31 December)

	1994*	1995*	1996
Passenger cars	61,269	62,500	74,875
Buses and coaches	5,098	5,200	10,175
Lorries and vans	60,041	61,300	59,352
Motorcycles and mopeds	1,450	1,480	1,520

* Estimates.

Total vehicles in use (excl. motorcycles and mopeds): 146,999 in 2000; 152,794 in 2001; 166,998 in 2002.

2002: Passenger cars 82,580; Buses and coaches 4,922; Lorries and vans 79,496; Motorcycles and mopeds 3,416.

2008: Passenger cars 107,825; Buses and coaches 2,396; Lorries and vans 117,410; Motorcycles and mopeds 4,792.

Source: International Road Federation, *World Road Statistics*.

SHIPPING
Merchant Fleet
(at 31 December)

	2007	2008	2009
Number of vessels	173	166	168
Displacement (gross registered tons)	126,062	122,076	121,579

Source: IHS Fairplay, *World Fleet Statistics*.

Sea-borne Freight Traffic
('000 freight tons*, year ending 30 August, unless otherwise indicated)

	2005/06	2006/07	2007/08
Port of Lüderitz:			
Goods loaded	74.5	128.8	56.8
Goods unloaded	171.3	104.3	126.5
Goods transshipped (freight tons)	45	30	29
Containers handled (total TEUs)	10,922	3,241	13,019
Port of Walvis Bay:			
Goods loaded	1,001.0	1,156.9	1,251.3
Goods unloaded	1,878.0	2,299.0	2,702.4
Goods transshipped	329.0	507.3	439.0
Containers handled (total TEUs)	83,263	144,993	170,586

* One freight ton = 40 cu ft (1.133 cu m) of cargo capacity.

Source: Namibian Ports Authority.

CIVIL AVIATION
(traffic on scheduled services)

	2004	2005	2006
Kilometres flown (million)	11	11	11
Passengers carried ('000)	283	399	401
Passenger-km (million)	913	1,569	1,588
Total ton-km (million)	147	157	159

Source: UN, *Statistical Yearbook*.

Tourism

FOREIGN TOURIST ARRIVALS*

Country of origin	2005	2006	2007
Angola	281,365	278,058	336,045
Botswana	22,333	24,720	25,649
Germany	61,222	68,214	80,418
South Africa	230,949	239,886	250,038
United Kingdom	20,978	24,736	28,214
Zimbabwe	22,765	30,623	26,764
Total (incl. others)	777,888	833,344	928,914

* Excluding same-day visitors: 78,000 in 2005; 127,000 in 2006; 119,000 in 2007.

Tourism receipts (US $ million, excl. passenger transport): 349 in 2005; 381 in 2006; 434 in 2007; 382 in 2008.

Source: World Tourism Organization.

Communications Media

	2007	2008	2009
Telephones ('000 main lines in use)	138.1	140.0	142.1
Mobile cellular telephones ('000 subscribers)	800.3	1,052.0	1,217.0
Internet users ('000)	101.0	113.5	127.5
Broadband subscribers ('000)	0.3	0.3	0.4

Personal computers: 500,000 (239.4 per 1,000 persons) in 2007.

Television receivers ('000 in use): 67 in 2000.

Source: International Telecommunication Union.

Daily newspapers (2004): 4 (average circulation 55,800) (Source: UNESCO, *Statistical Yearbook*).

Non-daily newspapers (2004): 3 (average circulation 240,000) (Source: UNESCO, *Statistical Yearbook*).

Education

(2008/09, unless otherwise indicated)

		Students		
	Teachers	Males	Females	Total
Pre-primary	1,314*	16,414†	16,322†	32,736†
Primary	13,516	206,011	200,909	406,920
Secondary	7,031	78,414	90,976	169,390
Tertiary‡	1,204	8,506	11,201	19,707

* Estimate for 1999/2000.
† 2005/06.
‡ 2007/08.

Source: UNESCO, Institute for Statistics.

Pupil-teacher ratio (primary education, UNESCO estimate): 30.1 in 2008/09 (Source: UNESCO Institute for Statistics).

Adult literacy rate (UNESCO estimates): 88.2% (males 88.7%; females 87.7%) in 2008 (Source: UNESCO Institute for Statistics).

Directory

The Government

HEAD OF STATE

President and Commander-in-Chief of the Defence Force: HIFIKEPUNYE POHAMBA (elected by direct suffrage 15–16 November 2004; took office 21 March 2005; re-elected 27–28 November 2009).

THE CABINET
(May 2011)

President: HIFIKEPUNYE POHAMBA.
Prime Minister: NAHAS ANGULA.
Deputy Prime Minister: Dr MARCO HAUSIKU.
Minister of Presidential Affairs and Attorney-General: ALBERT KAWANA.
Minister of Home Affairs and Immigration: ROSALIA NGHIDINWA.
Minister of Safety and Security: NANGOLO MBUMBA.
Minister of Defence: Maj.-Gen. (retd) CHARLES NAMOLOH.
Minister of Foreign Affairs: UTONI NUJOMA.
Minister of Information and Communication Technology: JOEL KAAPANDA.
Minister of Education: Dr ABRAHAM IYAMBO.
Minister of Mines and Energy: ISAK KATALI.
Minister of Justice: PENDUKENI IVULA-ITHANA.
Minister of Trade and Industry: Dr HAGE GEINGOB.
Minister of Agriculture, Water and Forestry: JOHN MUTORWA.
Minister of Finance: SAARA KUUGONGELWA-AMADHILA.
Minister of Health and Social Services: Dr RICHARD KAMWI.
Minister of Labour and Social Welfare: IMMANUEL NGATJIZEKO.
Minister of Regional and Local Government and Housing and Rural Development: JERRY EKANDJO.
Minister of Environment and Tourism: NETUMBO NANDI-NDAITWAH.
Minister of Works, Transport and Communications: ERRKI NGHINTINA.
Minister of Lands, Resettlement and Rehabilitation: ALPHEUS NARUSEB.
Minister of Fisheries and Marine Resources: BEN ESAU.
Minister of Gender Equality and Child Welfare: DOREEN SIOKA.
Minister of Youth, National Service, Sport and Culture: KAZENAMBO KAZENAMBO.
Minister of Veteran Affairs: Dr NICKEY IYAMBO.

Also attending Cabinet

Dir-Gen. of the Namibia Central Intelligence Agency: Lt-Gen. (retd) LUCAS HANGULA.
Dir-Gen. of the National Planning Commission: TOM K. ALWEENDO.

MINISTRIES

Office of the President: State House, Robert Mugabe Ave, PMB 13339, Windhoek; tel. (61) 2707111; fax (61) 221780; e-mail angolo@op.gov.na; internet www.op.gov.na.

Office of the Prime Minister: Robert Mugabe Ave, PMB 13338, Windhoek; tel. (61) 2879111; fax (61) 226189; internet www.opm.gov.na.

Ministry of Agriculture, Water and Forestry: Government Office Park, PMB 13184, Windhoek; tel. (61) 2087111; fax (61) 221733; internet www.mawf.gov.na.

Ministry of Defence: PMB 13307, Windhoek; tel. (61) 2049111; fax (61) 232518; e-mail psecretary@mod.gov.na; internet www.mod.gov.na.

Ministry of Education: Government Office Park, PMB 13186, Windhoek; tel. (61) 2933358; fax (61) 2933368; internet www.mec.gov.na.

Ministry of Environment and Tourism: 2nd Floor, FGI House, Post St Mall, PMB 13346, Windhoek; tel. (61) 2842111; fax (61) 2842216; e-mail kshangula@met.gov.na; internet www.met.gov.na.

Ministry of Finance: Fiscus Bldg, John Meinert St, PMB 13295, Windhoek; tel. (61) 2099111; fax (61) 227702; internet www.mof.gov.na.

Ministry of Fisheries and Marine Resources: Uhland and Goethe Sts, PMB 13355, Windhoek; tel. (61) 2059111; fax (61) 233286; e-mail mfmr@mfmr.gov.na; internet www.mfmr.gov.na.

Ministry of Foreign Affairs: Govt Bldgs, Robert Mugabe Ave, PMB 13347, Windhoek; tel. (61) 2829111; fax (61) 223937; e-mail headquarters@mfa.gov.na; internet www.mfa.gov.na.

Ministry of Gender Equality and Child Welfare: Juvenis Bldg, Independence Ave, PMG 13359, Windhoek; tel. (61) 2833111; fax (61) 238941; e-mail genderequality@mgecw.gov.na; internet www.mgecw.gov.na.

Ministry of Health and Social Services: Old State Hospital, Harvey St, PMB 13198, Windhoek; tel. (61) 2032000; fax (61) 227607; e-mail doccentre@mhss.gov.na; internet www.healthnet.org.na.

Ministry of Home Affairs and Immigration: Cohen Bldg, Kasino St, PMB 13200, Windhoek; tel. (61) 2922111; fax (61) 2922185; internet www.mha.gov.na.

Ministry of Information and Communication Technology: PMB 13344, Windhoek; tel. (61) 2839111; fax (61) 222343; internet www.mict.gov.na.

Ministry of Justice: Justitia Bldg, Independence Ave, PMB 13248, Windhoek; tel. (61) 2805111; fax (61) 221615.

Ministry of Labour and Social Welfare: 32 Mercedes St, Khomasdal, PMB 19005, Windhoek; tel. (61) 2066111; fax (61) 212323; internet www.mol.gov.na.

Ministry of Lands, Resettlement and Rehabilitation: Brendan Simbwaye Bldg, Goethe St, PMB 13343, Windhoek; tel. (61) 2852111; fax (61) 254240.

Ministry of Mines and Energy: 1st Aviation Rd, PMB 13297, Windhoek; tel. (61) 2848111; fax (61) 238643; e-mail info@mme.gov.na; internet www.mme.gov.na.

Ministry of Presidential Affairs: Windhoek.

Ministry of Regional and Local Government and Housing and Rural Development: PMB 13289, Windhoek; tel. (61) 2975111; fax (61) 226049; internet www.mrlgh.gov.na.

Ministry of Safety and Security: Brendan Simbwaye Bldg, Goethe St, PMB 13323, Windhoek; tel. (61) 2846111; fax (61) 233879.

Ministry of Trade and Industry: Block B, Brendan Simbwaye Sq., Goethe St, PMB 13340, Windhoek; tel. (61) 2837111; fax (61) 220227; e-mail tic@mti.gov.na; internet www.mti.gov.na.

Ministry of Veteran Affairs: PMB 13407, Windhoek; tel. (61) 222330; fax (61) 221615.

Ministry of Works, Transport and Communications: 6719 Bell St, Snyman Circle, PMB 13341, Windhoek; tel. (61) 2088111; fax (61) 224381; e-mail jngweda@mwtc.gov.na; internet www.mwtc.gov.na.

Ministry of Youth, National Service, Sport and Culture: NDC Bldg, Goethe St, PMB 13391, Windhoek; tel. (61) 270611; fax (61) 2706303.

President and Legislature

PRESIDENT

Presidential Election, 27–28 November 2009

Candidate	Votes	% of votes
Hifikepunye Pohamba (SWAPO)	611,241	76.42
Hidipo Hamutenya (RDP)	88,640	11.08
Katuutire Kaura (DTA)	24,186	3.02
Kuaima Riruako (NUDO)	23,735	2.97
Justus Garoeb (UDF)	19,258	2.41
Others	32,810	4.10
Total	799,870*	100.00

* Excluding 12,363 invalid votes.

NAMIBIA

NATIONAL ASSEMBLY

Speaker: THEO-BEN GURIRAB.

General Election, 27–28 November 2009

Party	Votes	% of votes	Seats
South West Africa People's Organisation of Namibia (SWAPO)	602,580	75.27	54
Rally for Democracy and Progress (RDP)	90,556	11.31	8
Democratic Turnhalle Alliance of Namibia (DTA)	25,393	3.17	2
National Unity Democratic Organization (NUDO)	24,422	3.05	2
United Democratic Front (UDF)	19,489	2.43	2
All People's Party of Namibia (APP)	10,795	1.35	1
Republican Party (RP)	6,541	0.82	1
Congress of Democrats (CoD)	5,375	0.67	1
South West African National Union (SWANU)	4,989	0.62	1
Others	10,427	1.30	—
Total	800,567*	100.00	72†

* Excluding 10,576 invalid votes.

† In addition to the 72 directly elected members, the President of the Republic is empowered to nominate as many as six non-voting members.

NATIONAL COUNCIL

Chairman: ASSER KUVERI KAPERE.

The second chamber of parliament is the advisory National Council, comprising two representatives from each of the country's 13 Regional Councils, elected for a period of six years.

Election Commission

Electoral Commission of Namibia (ECN): 11 Goethe St, POB 13352, Windhoek; tel. (61) 376200; fax (61) 237618; e-mail mndjarakana@opm.gov.na; internet www.ecn.gov.na; f. 1992; independent; Chair. VICTOR L. TONCHI; Dir of Elections and CEO MOSES K. NDJARAKANA.

Political Organizations

All People's Party of Namibia (APP): f. 2008 in Kavango region; splinter group of the CoD, which split in late 2007; Pres. IGNATIUS SHIXWAMENI.

Communist Party: Windhoek; f. 1989 as Workers' Revolutionary Party; Trotskyist; Leaders WERNER MAMUGWE, ATTIE BEUKES.

Congress of Democrats (CoD): 8 Storch St, POB 40905, Windhoek; tel. (61) 256954; fax (61) 256980; internet www.cod.org.na; f. 1999 after split from SWAPO; Pres. BEN ULENGA; Nat. Chair. ARNOLD LOSPER; Sec.-Gen. TSUDAO GURIRAB.

Democratic Party of Namibia (DPN): Windhoek; f. 2008; Interim Pres. SALOMON DAWID ISAACKS; Sec.-Gen. ADAM ISAAK.

Democratic Turnhalle Alliance of Namibia (DTA): Rand St, Khomasdal, POB 173, Windhoek; tel. (61) 238530; fax (61) 226494; e-mail m.venaani@parliament.gov.na; internet www.dtaofnamibia.org.na; f. 1977 as a coalition of 11 ethnically based political groupings; reorg. in 1991 to allow dual membership of coalition groupings and the main party; Pres. KATUUTIRE KAURA; Chair. JOHAN DE WAAL; Sec.-Gen. MCHENRY VENAANI.

Monitor Action Group (MAG): POB 80808, Olympia, Windhoek; tel. (61) 252008; fax (61) 229242; e-mail mag@iway.na; f. 1991 by mems of the National Party of South West Africa alliance; Leader and Chair. J. W. F. (KOSIE) PRETORIUS.

Namibia Democratic Movement for Change (NDMC): POB 60043, Katutura; tel. and fax (61) 297795; f. 2004; Pres. FRANS GOAGOSEB; Sec.-Gen. JOSEPH KAUANDENGE.

National Democratic Party of Namibia (NDP): Daily Park, POB 2438, Ngweze, Katima Mulilo; f. 2004; Pres. MARTIN LUKATO.

National Unity Democratic Organization (NUDO): Clemence Kapuuo St, Plot 1881, POB 62691, Soweto, Katutura; tel. and fax (61) 211550; e-mail nudoparty@iway.na; internet www.nudoofnamibia.org.na; f. 1964 by the Herero Chiefs' Council; joined the DTA in 1977; broke away from the DTA in 2003; Pres. Chief KUAIMA RIRUAKO; Sec.-Gen. ASSER MBAI.

Rally for Democracy and Progress (RDP): POB 83141, Olympia, Windhoek; tel. (61) 255973; e-mail info@rdp.org.na; internet www.rdp.org.na; f. 2007 by fmr mems of ruling SWAPO party; absorbed the Republican Party in Oct. 2010; Pres. HIDIPO HAMUTENYA; Sec.-Gen. JESAYA NYAMU.

South West African People's Organization of Namibia (SWAPO): Hans-Dietrich Genscher St, Plot 2464, Katutura, POB 1071, Windhoek; tel. (61) 238364; fax (61) 232368; internet www.swapoparty.org; f. 1957 as the Ovamboland People's Congress; renamed South West Africa People's Organisation in 1960; Pres. HIFIKEPUNYE POHAMBA; Vice-Pres. HAGE GEINGOB; Sec.-Gen. PENDUKENI IIVULA-ITHANA.

South West African National Union (SWANU): POB 2976, Windhoek; e-mail swanu@swanu.org.na; internet www.swanu.org.na; f. 1959 by mems of the Herero Chiefs' Council; formed alliance with the Workers' Revolutionary Party in 1999; Pres. USUTUAIJE MAAMBERUA; Vice-Pres. B. B. DE CLERK.

United Democratic Front (UDF): POB 20037, Windhoek; tel. (61) 230683; fax (61) 237175; f. 1989 as a centrist coalition of eight parties; reorg. as a single party in 1999; Nat. Chair. ERIC BIWA; Pres. JUSTUS GAROEB.

The **Caprivi Liberation Army (CLA)**, f. 1998 as the Caprivi Liberation Movement, seeks secession of the Caprivi Strip; conducts military operations from bases in Zambia and Angola; political wing operates from Denmark as the **Caprivi National Union**, led by MISHAKE MUYONGO and BONIFACE MAMILI.

Diplomatic Representation

EMBASSIES AND HIGH COMMISSIONS IN NAMIBIA

Algeria: 24 Robert Mugabe Ave, POB 3079, Windhoek; tel. (61) 221507; fax (61) 236376; e-mail Ambalg.w@mweb.com; Ambassador YOUCEF DELILECHE.

Angola: Angola House, 3 Dr Agostinho Neto St, Ausspannplatz, PMB 12020, Windhoek; tel. (61) 227535; fax (61) 221498; Ambassador MANUEL A. D. RODRIGUEZ.

Botswana: 101 Nelson Mandela Ave, POB 20359, Windhoek; tel. (61) 221941; fax (61) 236034; internet www.botnam.com.na; High Commissioner NORMAN MOLEBOGE.

Brazil: 52 Bismarck St, POB 24166, Windhoek; tel. (61) 237368; fax (61) 233389; e-mail brasemb@mweb.com.na; internet www.brazilianembassy.org.na; Ambassador MARCIO ARAUJO LAGE.

China, People's Republic: 13 Wecke St, POB 22777, Windhoek; tel. (61) 372800; fax (61) 225544; e-mail chinaemb_na@mfa.gov.cn; internet na.chineseembassy.org; Ambassador WEI RUIXING.

Congo, Republic: 9 Korner St, POB 22970, Windhoek; tel. (61) 257517; fax (61) 240796; Ambassador PATRICE NDOUNGA.

Cuba: 37 Quenta St, Ludwigsdorf, POB 23866, Windhoek; tel. (61) 227072; fax (61) 231584; e-mail consular@cubanembassy.net; internet www.cubadiplomatica.cu/namibia; Ambassador CARLOS MANUEL ROJAS LAGO.

Egypt: 10 Berg St, POB 11853, Windhoek; tel. (61) 221501; fax (61) 228856; e-mail embassy.windhoek@mfa.gov.eg; internet www.mfa.gov.eg/windhoek_emb; Ambassador HAZEM RAMADAN.

Finland: 2 Crohn St (cnr Bahnhof St), POB 3649, Windhoek; tel. (61) 221355; fax (61) 221349; e-mail sanomat.win@formin.fi; internet www.finland.org.na; Chargé d'affaires a.i. ASKO LUUKKAINEN.

France: 1 Goethe St, POB 20484, Windhoek; tel. (61) 2276700; fax (61) 231436; e-mail contact@ambafrance-na.org; internet www.ambafrance-na.org; Ambassador JEAN-LOUIS ZOËL.

Germany: Sanlam Centre, 6th Floor, 154 Independence Ave, POB 231, Windhoek; tel. (61) 273100; fax (61) 222981; e-mail germany@iway.na; internet www.windhuk.diplo.de; Ambassador EGON KOCHANKE.

Ghana: 5 Nelson Mandela Ave, POB 24165, Windhoek; tel. (61) 221341; fax (61) 221343; e-mail ghanahc@iwwn.com.na; High Commissioner AFUA DAAKU.

India: 97 Nelson Mandela Ave, POB 1209, Windhoek; tel. (61) 226037; fax (61) 228433; e-mail hicomind@mweb.com.na; internet www.highcommissionofindia.web.na; High Commissioner TSEWANG TOPDEN.

Indonesia: 103 Nelson Mandela Ave, POB 20691, Windhoek; tel. (61) 2851000; fax (61) 2851231; e-mail kbri@iafrica.com; internet www.indonesiawindhoek.org; Ambassador LEONARDUS WIDAYATMO.

Kenya: Kenya House, 5th Floor, 134 Robert Mugabe Ave, POB 2889, Windhoek; tel. (61) 226836; fax (61) 221409; e-mail kenyanet@mweb.com.na; High Commissioner PETER GITAU.

Libya: 69 Burg St, Luxury Hill, POB 124, Windhoek; tel. (61) 234454; fax (61) 234471; Ambassador SALAM MOHAMMED KRAYEM.

NAMIBIA

Malawi: 56 Bismarck St, POB 13254, Windhoek 9000; tel. (61) 221391; High Commissioner F. CHIKUTA.

Malaysia: 12 Babs Street, Ludwigsdorf, POB 312, Windhoek; tel. (61) 259342; fax (61) 259343; e-mail malwdhoek@kln.gov.my; internet www.kln.gov.my/perwakilan/windhoek; High Commissioner MOHD YUSOFF ABU BAKAR.

Nigeria: POB 23547, Windhoek; tel. (61) 232101; fax (61) 221639; e-mail nhcnam@mweb.com.na; internet www.nhcwindhoek.org; High Commissioner ADEGBOYEGA CHRISTOPHER ARIYO.

Russia: 4 Christian St, POB 3826, Windhoek; tel. (61) 228671; fax (61) 229061; e-mail rusemnam@mweb.com.na; Ambassador NIKOLAI M. GRIBKOV.

South Africa: RSA House, cnr Jan Jonker St and Nelson Mandela Ave, POB 23100, Windhoek; tel. (61) 2057111; fax (61) 224140; e-mail dibem@foreign.gov.za; High Commissioner YVETTE MAVIVI MYAKAYAKA-MANZINI.

Spain: 58 Bismarck St, POB 21811, Windhoek-West; tel. (61) 223066; fax (61) 227209; e-mail emb.windhoek@mae.es; internet www.mae.es/embajadas/windhoek/es/home; Ambassador ALFONSO BARNUEVO SEBASTIÁN DE ERICE.

United Kingdom: 116 Robert Mugabe Ave, POB 22202, Windhoek; tel. (61) 274800; fax (61) 228895; e-mail general.windhoek@fco.gov.uk; internet www.ukinnamibia.fco.gov.uk; High Commissioner MARIANNE YOUNG (designate).

USA: 14 Lossen St, PMB 12029, Windhoek; tel. (61) 2958500; fax (61) 2958603; internet windhoek.usembassy.gov; Ambassador WANDA L. NESBITT.

Venezuela: Southern Life Tower, 3rd Floor, 39 Post St Mall, PMB 13353, Windhoek; tel. (61) 227905; fax (61) 227804; Chargé d'affaires a.i. JORGE JIMÉNEZ.

Zambia: 22 Mandume Ndemufayo St, POB 22882, Windhoek; tel. (61) 237610; fax (61) 228162; e-mail zahico@iway.na; internet www.zahico.iway.na; High Commissioner MAVIS MUYUNDA.

Zimbabwe: cnr Independence Ave and Grimm St, POB 23056, Windhoek; tel. (61) 228134; fax (61) 226859; e-mail zimbabwe@mweb.com.na; Ambassador CHIPO ZINDOGA.

Judicial System

Judicial power is exercised by the Supreme Court, the High Court, and a number of Magistrate and Lower Courts. The Constitution provides for the appointment of an Ombudsman.

The Supreme Court: Private Bag 13398, Windhoek; tel. (61) 279900; fax (61) 224979; e-mail cjudge@iway.na; internet www.superiorcourts.org.na/supreme; f. 1990; Chief Justice PETER SHIVUTE; Additional Judge JOHANNES DAWID GERHARDUS MARITZ.

The High Court: Private Bag 13179, Windhoek; tel. (61) 2921111; fax (61) 221686; e-mail chiefregistrar@mtcmobile.com.na; internet www.superiorcourts.org.na/high; Judge Pres. PETRUS DAMASEB.

Additional Judges of the High Court: SYLVESTER MAINGA, ELTON HOFF, KATO NIEKERK, LOUIS MULLER, COLLINS PARKER, NATE NDAUENDAPO.

Religion

It is estimated that about 90% of the population are Christians.

CHRISTIANITY

Council of Churches in Namibia: 8 Mont Blanc St, POB 41, Windhoek; tel. (61) 374054; fax (61) 62786; e-mail ccn.gensec@mweb.com.na; f. 1978; eight mem. churches; Pres. Bishop JOHANNES SINDANO; Gen. Sec. Rev. PHILLIP STRYDOM.

The Anglican Communion

Namibia comprises a single diocese in the Anglican Church of Southern Africa (formerly the Church of the Province of Southern Africa). The Metropolitan of the Province is the Archbishop of Cape Town, South Africa. In 2006 there were an estimated 110,000 Anglicans in the country.

Bishop of Namibia: Rt Rev. NATHANIEL NDAXUMA NAKWATUMBAH, POB 57, Windhoek; tel. (61) 238920; fax (61) 225903; e-mail shirley@mweb.com.na.

Dutch Reformed Church

Dutch Reformed Church in Namibia (Nederduitse Gereformeerde Kerk in Namibië): 46A Schanzen Rd, POB 389, Windhoek; tel. (61) 374350; fax (61) 227287; e-mail clem@ngkn.com.na; internet www.ngkerk.org.za/namibie; f. 1898; Sec. Rev. CLEM MARAIS; 21,281 mems in 44 congregations (2008).

Evangelical Lutheran

Evangelical Lutheran Church in Namibia (ELCIN): POB 2018, Ondangwa; tel. (65) 240241; fax (65) 240472; e-mail gen.sec@elcin.org.na; internet www.elcin.org.na; f. 1870; became autonomous in 1954; Presiding Bishop Dr THOMAS SHIVUTE; Gen. Sec. Rev. ELIKAIM N. K. SHAANIKA; 703,893 mems (2010).

Evangelical Lutheran Church in the Republic of Namibia (ELCRN) (Rhenish Mission Church): POB 5069, 6 Church St, Ausspanplatz, 9000 Windhoek; tel. (61) 224531; fax (61) 226775; e-mail bishop@elcrnam.org; f. 1957; became autonomous in 1972; Pres. Bishop Dr ZEPHANIA KAMEETA; 420,000 mems (2010).

German Evangelical-Lutheran Church in Namibia (ELCIN—GELC): POB 233, 12 Fidel Castro St, Windhoek; tel. (61) 224294; fax (61) 221470; e-mail bishop-office@elcin-gelc.org; internet www.elcin-gelc.org; Pres. Bishop ERICH HERTEL; 5,100 mems (2010).

Methodist

African Methodist Episcopal Church: POB 798, Keetmanshoop; tel. (63) 222347; fax (63) 223026; e-mail erikke5@hotmail.com; bishop resident in Cape Town, South Africa; Rep. Rev. Dr ANDREAS BIWA; c. 8,000 mems in 33 churches.

Methodist Church of Southern Africa: POB 143, Windhoek; tel. (61) 228921; fax (61) 229202; e-mail central@iway.na; internet www.methodist.org.za; Rep. Rev. EDGAR LUKEN.

The Roman Catholic Church

Namibia comprises one archdiocese, one diocese and one apostolic vicariate. Some 18% of the population are Roman Catholics.

Bishops' Conference

Namibian Catholic Bishops' Conference, POB 11525, Windhoek 9000; tel. (61) 224798; fax (61) 228126; e-mail ncbc@windhoek.org.na.

f. 1996; Pres. LIBORIUS NDUMBUKUTI NASHENDA (Archbishop of Windhoek).

Archbishop of Windhoek: LIBORIUS NDUMBUKUTI NASHENDA, POB 272, Windhoek 9000; tel. (61) 227595; fax (61) 229836; e-mail rcarch@iafrica.com.na; internet www.rcchurch.na.

Other Christian Churches

Among other denominations active in Namibia are the Evangelical Reformed Church in Africa, the Presbyterian Church of Southern Africa, Seventh Day Adventists and the United Congregational Church of Southern Africa. At mid-2000 there were an estimated 820,000 Protestants and 192,000 adherents professing other forms of Christianity.

JUDAISM

Windhoek Hebrew Congregation: POB 563, Windhoek; tel. (61) 221990; fax (61) 226444.

BAHÁ'Í FAITH

National Spiritual Assembly: POB 20372, Windhoek; tel. (61) 302663; e-mail bahainamibia@iway.na; Sec. ROSI STEVENSON; mems resident in 215 localities.

The Press

The African Magazine: NCCI, 2 Jenner St, POB 1770, Windhoek; tel. and fax (61) 255018; e-mail info@theafricanmagazin.org; internet www.theafricanmagazin.org.

AgriForum: 114A Robert Mugabe Ave, POB 86641, Eros, Windhoek; tel. (61) 256023; fax (61) 256035; e-mail agriforum@agrinamibia.com.na; internet www.agrinamibia.com.na; f. 1978; monthly; Afrikaans and English; publ. by the Namibia Agricultural Union; Editor MARIETJIE VAN STADEN; circ. 4,000.

Allgemeine Zeitung: 11 Gen. Murtala Muhammed Ave, POB 86695, Eros, Windhoek; tel. (61) 225822; fax (61) 220225; e-mail azinfo@az.com.na; internet www.az.com.na; f. 1916; publ. by Newsprint Namibia; daily; German; Editor-in-Chief STEFAN FISCHER; circ. 5,000.

Insight Namibia: 34 Sam Nujoma Dr., POB 86058, Windhoek; tel. (61) 301438; fax (61) 240385; e-mail editor@insight.com.na; internet www.insight.com.na; f. 2004; monthly; business and current affairs; Editor ROBIN SHERBOURNE.

Namib Times: 8 Sam Nujoma Ave, POB 706, Walvis Bay; tel. (64) 205854; fax (64) 204813; e-mail ntimes@iway.na; internet www.namibtimes.net; f. 1958; 2 a week; Afrikaans, English, German and Portuguese; Editor FLORIS STEENKAMP; circ. 4,300.

NAMIBIA

Namibia Brief: Independence Ave, POB 2123, Windhoek; tel. (61) 251044; fax (61) 237251; e-mail cblatt@iafrica.com.na; 2 a year; English; Editor CATHY BLATT; circ. 7,500.

Namibia Economist: 7 Schuster St, POB 49, Windhoek 9000; tel. (61) 221925; fax (61) 220615; e-mail info@economist.com.na; internet www.economist.com.na; f. 1986; weekly; English; business, finance and economics; Editor DANIEL STEINMANN; circ. 7,000.

Namibia Magazin: POB 6870, Windhoek; tel. and fax (61) 224929; e-mail evonwiet@iafrica.com.na; publ. by Klaus Hess Verlag; German; politics, tourism and culture; Rep. ERIKA VON WIETERSHEIM.

Namibia Review: Directorate Print Media and Regional Offices, Regular Publications, Turnhalle Bldg, Bahnhof St, PMB 13344, Windhoek; tel. (61) 222246; fax (61) 224937; e-mail bupe@webmail.co.za; f. 1992; publ. by the Ministry of Information and Communication Technology; monthly; information on govt policy and developmental issues; Editor ELIZABETH KALAMBO-M'ULE; circ. 5,000.

Namibia Sport: Unit 3, 14 Liliencron St, POB 1246, Windhoek; tel. (61) 224132; fax (61) 224613; e-mail editor@namibiasport.com.na; internet www.namibiasport.com.na; f. 2002; monthly; Editor HELGE SCHUTZ; circ. 2,000.

Namibia Today: 21 Johan Albrecht St, POB 24669, Windhoek; tel. (61) 276730; fax (61) 276381; 2 a week; Afrikaans, English, Otjiherero and Oshiwambo; publ. by SWAPO; Editor ASSER NTINDA; circ. 5,000.

The Namibian: 42 John Meinert St, POB 20783, Windhoek; tel. (61) 279600; fax (61) 279602; e-mail editor@namibian.com.na; internet www.namibian.com.na; daily; English; Editor TANGENI AMUPADHI; circ. 23,000 (Mon.–Thur.), 32,000 (Fri.).

The Namibian Worker: POB 50034, Bachbrecht, Windhoek; tel. (61) 215037; fax (61) 215589; e-mail nunw@mweb.com.na; newsletter publ. by National Union of Namibian Workers; revived in 2003; Afrikaans, English and Oshiwambo; Editor-in-Chief C. RANGA HAIKALI; circ. 1,000.

NCCI Namibia Business Journal: NCCI Head Office, 2 Jenner St, POB 9355, Windhoek; tel. (61) 228809; fax (61) 228009; publ. by the Namibia Chamber of Commerce and Industry; 6 a year; English; CEO TARAH SHAANIKA; Editor CHARITY MWIYA; circ. 4,000.

New Era: Daniel Tjongarero House, cnr Kerby and W. Kulz Sts, PMB 13364, Windhoek; tel. (61) 273300; fax (61) 220584; e-mail editor@newera.com.na; internet www.newera.com.na; f. 1991; daily; publ. by the Ministry of Information and Communication Technology; English; Chair. MATTHEW GOWASEB; CEO SYLVESTER BLACK; Editor RAJAH MUNAMAVA; circ. 10,000.

Plus Weekly: POB 21506, Windhoek; tel. (61) 233635; fax (61) 230478; e-mail info@namibiaplus.com; internet www.namibiaplus.com; publ. by Feddersen Publications; Afrikaans, English and German.

Republikein: 11 Gen. Murtala Muhammed Ave, POB 3436, Eros, Windhoek; tel. (61) 2972000; fax (61) 223721; e-mail republkn@republikein.com.na; internet www.republikein.com.na; f. 1977; daily; Afrikaans and English; publ. by Newsprint Namibia; Exec. Editor CHRIS JACOBIE; circ. 17,500 (Mon.–Wed.), 21,000 (Thur.–Fri.).

Sister Namibia: 163 Nelson Mandela Ave, POB 86753, Windhoek; tel. (61) 230618; fax (61) 236371; e-mail sister@iafrica.com.na; f. 1989; 6 a year; publ. by Sister Namibia human rights org.; women's issues; Editor LIZ FRANK; circ. 9,000.

The Southern Times: cnr Dr W. Külz and Kerby Sts, POB 32235, Windhoek; tel. (61) 301094; fax (61) 301095; internet www.southerntimesafrica.com; f. 2004; weekly (Sun.); owned by New Era and Zimpapers, Zimbabwe; printed in Namibia and Zimbabwe; regional; CEO PETER MIETZNER.

Space Magazine: Sanlam Centre, 3rd Floor, POB 3717, Windhoek; tel. (61) 225155; e-mail space@mweb.com.na; monthly; English; family life; Publr ESTER SMITH; Editor YANNA SMITH.

Windhoek Observer: 6 Schuster St, POB 2255, Windhoek; tel. (61) 221737; fax (61) 226098; e-mail whkob@africaonline.com.na; f. 1978; weekly; English; Editor KUVEE KANGUEEHI; circ. 14,000.

NEWS AGENCY

Namibia Press Agency (Nampa): cnr Keller and Eugene Marais Sts, POB 61354, Windhoek 9000; tel. (61) 374000; fax (61) 221713; e-mail admin@nampa.org; internet www.nampa.org; f. 1991; Chair. MAUREEN HINDA; CEO NGHIDINUA HAMUNIME; Editor TOMMY KATAMILA.

PRESS ASSOCIATION

Press Club Windhoek: POB 2032, Windhoek; tel. (61) 2796000; fax (61) 279602; e-mail carmen@namibian.com.na; Chair. CARMEN HONEY.

Publishers

ELOC Printing Press: PMB 2013, Oniipa, Ondangwa; tel. (65) 240211; fax (65) 240536; e-mail elocbook@iway.na; internet www.elocbook.iway.na; f. 1901; Exec. Dir JOEL AKUDHENGA.

Gamsberg Macmillan Publishers (Pty) Ltd: 19 Faraday St, POB 22830, Windhoek; tel. (61) 232165; fax (61) 233538; e-mail gmp@iafrica.com.na; internet www.macmillan-africa.com; imprints incl. New Namibia Books and Out of Africa; Man. Dir HERMAN VAN WYK.

Longman Namibia: POB 9251, Eros, Windhoek; tel. (61) 231124; fax (61) 224019; Publr LINDA BREDENKAMP.

National Archives of Namibia: 1–9 Eugène Marais St, PMB 13250, Windhoek; tel. (61) 2935211; fax (61) 2935217; e-mail natarch@mec.gov.na; f. 1939; Chief Archivist WERNER HILLEBRECHT.

PUBLISHERS' ASSOCIATION

Association of Namibian Publishers: POB 40219, Windhoek; tel. (61) 228284; fax (61) 231496; f. 1991; Chair. Dr H. MELBER.

Broadcasting and Communications

TELECOMMUNICATIONS

Regulatory Authority

Namibian Communications Comm. (NCC): Communication House, 56 Robert Mugabe Ave, Windhoek; PMB 13309, Windhoek; tel. (61) 222666; fax (61) 222790; e-mail info@ncc.org.na; internet www.ncc.org.na; f. 1992; issues broadcasting licences, supervises broadcasting activities and programme content.

Service Providers

Africa Online Namibia: Ground Floor, NAU Bldg, 114 John Meinert St (cnr of Robert Mugabe Ave), Windhoek; tel. (61) 2058111; fax (61) 2058244; e-mail info@africaonline.com.na; internet www.africaonline.com.na; f. 2000; subsidiary of Africa Online Holdings Ltd (Kenya); Gen. Man. GIDEON NHUNDU.

Mobile Telecommunications Ltd (MTC): cnr Mosé Tjitendero and Hamutenya Wanahepo Ndadi Sts, Olympia, Windhoek; POB 23051, Windhoek; tel. (61) 2802000; fax (61) 2802124; e-mail feedback@mtc.com.na; internet www.mtc.com.na; f. 1995 as jt venture between Namibia Post and Telecommunications Holdings (NPTH), Telia and Swedfund; 34% owned by Portugal Telecom, 64% by NPTH; Chair. DIRK CONRADIE; Man. Dir MIGUEL GERALDES.

Telecom Namibia Ltd (Telecom): POB 297, Windhoek; tel. (61) 2019211; fax (61) 248723; internet www.telecom.na; f. 1992; state-owned; Chair. T. HAIMBILI; Man. Dir FRANS NDOROMA.

BROADCASTING

Radio

In 2007 there were a total of 14 radio stations broadcasting from Windhoek including:

Namibian Broadcasting Corpn (NBC): Pettenkofer St, Windhoek West, POB 321, Windhoek; tel. (61) 2919111; fax (61) 215767; e-mail tnandjaa@nbc.com.na; internet www.nbc.com.na; f. 1990; runs 10 radio stations, broadcasting daily to 90% of the population in English (24 hours), Afrikaans, German and eight indigenous languages (10 hours); Chair. SVEN THIEM; Dir-Gen. ALBERTUS AOCHAMUB.

Channel 7/Kanaal 7: POB 20500, Windhoek; tel. (61) 235815; fax (61) 240190; e-mail channel7@k7.com.na; internet www.k7.com.na; Christian community radio station; English and Afrikaans; Man. NEAL VAN DEN BERGH.

Katutura Community Radio: Clemence Kapuuo St, POB 70448, KHD, Katutura, Windhoek; tel. (61) 263726; fax (61) 236371; f. 1995 by non-governmental orgs; Dir FREDERICK GOWASEB.

Kudu FM: 158 Jan Jonker St, POB 5369, Windhoek; tel. (61) 247262; fax (61) 247259; e-mail radiokudu@radiokudu.com.na; internet www.radiokudu.com.na; f. 1998; commercial station affiliated to Omulunga Radio; English, Afrikaans and German.

Ninety Nine FM (Pty) Ltd (99 FM): POB 11849, Klein-Windhoek, Windhoek; tel. (61) 383450; fax (61) 230964; e-mail 99@99fm.com.na; f. 1994; CEO CHRISNA GREEFF.

Omulunga Radio: POB 40789, Windhoek; tel. (61) 239706; fax (61) 247259; e-mail omulunga@omulunga.com.na; internet www.omulunga.com.na; f. 2002; Ovambo interest station affiliated to Kudu FM; Oshiwambo and English.

Radio Energy (Radio 100): Energy House 17, cnr Bismark and Church Sts, Windhoek West; POB 676, Windhoek; tel. (61) 256380; fax (61) 256379; e-mail energy@iway.na; internet www.energy100fm.com; f. 1996; commercial radio station; Man. Dir JOHN WALENGA.

NAMIBIA

Other radio stations included: Kosmos Radio, Radio France International (via relay), Radio 99, and Radio Wave. There were six community radio stations including: Radio Ecclesia (Catholic), Live FM (in Rehoboth), Ohangwenga Community Radio, and UNAM Radio (University of Namibia). A further four community stations were planned in 2005 at Oshakti, Gobabis, Keetmanshoop and Swakopmund.

Television

Namibian Broadcasting Corpn (NBC): Cullinan St, Northern Industrial, POB 321, Windhoek; tel. (61) 2913111; fax (61) 216209; internet www.nbc.com.na; f. 1990; broadcasts television programmes in English to 45% of the population, 18 hours daily; Chair. SVEN THIEME; Dir-Gen. ALBERTUS AOCHAMUB.

Multi-Choice Namibia: Kenya House, Robert Mugabe Ave, POB 2662, Windhoek; tel. (61) 2705261; fax (61) 2705247; commercial television channels; Gen. Man. KOBUS BEZUIDENHOUT.

One Africa TV: 79 Hosea Kutako Dr., POB 21593, Windhoek; tel. (61) 2891500; fax (61) 259450; internet www.oneafrica.tv.

Trinity Broadcasting Namibia: POB 1587, Swakopmund; tel. (64) 401122; e-mail comments@tbnnamibia.tv; internet www.tbnnamibia.tv; f. 2002; Man. Dir COENIE BOTHA.

Finance

(cap. = capital; res = reserves; dep. = deposits; m. = million; brs = branches; amounts in Namibian dollars)

BANKING

In 2010 there were five commercial banks in Namibia.

Central Bank

Bank of Namibia: 71 Robert Mugabe Ave, POB 2882, Windhoek; tel. (61) 2835111; fax (61) 2835067; e-mail jerome.mutumba@bon.com.na; internet www.bon.com.na; f. 1990; cap. 40.0m., res 1,662.9m., dep. 10,930.5m. (Dec. 2009); Gov. IPUMBU WENDELINUS SHIIMI; Dep. Gov. P. HARTMAN.

Commercial Banks

Bank Windhoek Ltd: Bank Windhoek Bldg, 262 Independence Ave, POB 15, Windhoek; tel. (61) 2991223; fax (61) 223188; e-mail info@bankwindhoek.com.na; internet www.bankwindhoek.com.na; f. 1982; cap. 4.8m., res 1,229.4m., dep. 4,182.2m. (June 2010); Chair. J. C. 'KOOS' BRANDT; Man. Dir JAMES HILL; 32 brs.

FIDES Bank Namibia: Windhoek; internet www.fidesbank.co.na; Chair. MARIA GAOMAS.

First National Bank of Namibia Ltd: 209–211 Independence Ave, POB 195, Windhoek; tel. (61) 2992111; fax (61) 2220979; e-mail info@fnbnamibia.com.na; internet www.fnbnamibia.com.na; f. 1987 as First Nat. Bank of Southern Africa Ltd; present name adopted 1990; res 1,703.6m., dep. 12,179.3m. (June 2010); Chair. H. DIETER VOIGTS; CEO L. J. HAYNES; 28 brs and 12 agencies.

Nedbank Namibia Ltd: 12–20 Dr Frans Indongo St, POB 1, Windhoek; tel. (61) 2959111; fax (61) 2952046; e-mail service@nedbank.com; internet www.nedbank.com.na; f. 1973; fmrly Commercial Bank of Namibia Ltd; subsidiary of Nedbank Ltd, South Africa; cap. 16m., res 110m., dep. 4,436m. (Dec. 2007); Chair. T. J. FRANK; Man. Dir ERASTUS HOVEKA; 16 brs and 3 agencies.

Standard Bank Namibia Ltd: Standard Bank Centre, cnr Werner List St and Post St Mall, POB 3327, Windhoek; tel. (61) 2942126; fax (61) 2942583; e-mail info@standardbank.com.na; internet www.standardbank.com.na; f. 1915; controlled by Standard Bank Africa; cap. 2.0m., res 1,137.7m., dep. 10,969.5m. (Dec. 2009); Chair. LEAKE S. HANGALA; Man. Dir MPUMZI PUPUMA; 23 brs.

Agricultural Bank

Agricultural Bank of Namibia (AgriBank): 10 Post St Mall, POB 13208, Windhoek; tel. (61) 2074111; fax (61) 2074289; e-mail info@agribank.com.na; internet www.agribank.com.na; f. 1922; state-owned; total assets 739.1m. (March 2001); Chair. HANS-GUENTHER STIER; CEO LEONARD N. IIPUMBU.

Development Bank

Development Bank of Namibia (DBN): 12 Daniel Munamava St, POB 235, Windhoek; tel. (61) 2908000; fax (61) 2908049; e-mail info@dbn.com.na; internet www.dbn.com.na; f. 2004; Chair. SVEN THIEME; CEO DAVID NUYOMA.

STOCK EXCHANGE

Namibian Stock Exchange (NSX): Kaiser Krone Centre, Shop 8, Post St Mall, POB 2401, Windhoek; tel. (61) 227647; fax (61) 248531; e-mail info@nsx.com.na; internet www.nsx.com.na; f. 1992; CEO JOHN D. MANDY; Operations Man. MANDA STEYNBERG.

INSURANCE

In 2010 there were 18 long-term and 13 short-term insurance companies operating in Namibia.

Corporate Guarantee and Insurance Co of Namibia Ltd (CGI): Corporate House, Ground Floor, 17 Lüderitz St, POB 416, Windhoek; tel. (61) 259525; fax (61) 255213; e-mail info@corporateguarantee.com; internet www.corporateguarantee.com; f. 1996; wholly owned subsidiary of Nictus Group Ltd since 2001; Chair. F. R. VAN STADEN; Man. Dir and Principal Officer P. J. DE W. TROMP.

Insurance Co of Namibia (INSCON): POB 2877, Windhoek; tel. (61) 275900; fax (61) 233808; f. 1990; short-term insurance; Chair. CHARLES KAURAISA; Man. Dir FERDINAND OTTO.

Legal Shield: 140–142 Robert Mugabe Ave, POB 11363, Windhoek; tel. (61) 2754200; fax (61) 2754090; internet www.legalshield.na; f. 2000; legal, funeral and medical insurance; Man. Dir SANDRA MILLER.

Metropolitan Namibia: Metropolitan Pl., 1st Floor, cnr Bülow and Stubel Sts, POB 3785, Windhoek; tel. (61) 2973000; fax (61) 248191; internet www.metropolitan.com.na; f. 1996; subsidiary of Metropolitan Group, South Africa; acquired Channel Life in 2004; Chair. M. L. SMITH; Man. Dir JASON NANDAGO.

Mutual and Federal Insurance Co Ltd: Mutual and Federal Centre, 5th–7th Floors, 227 Independence Ave, POB 151, Windhoek; tel. (61) 2077111; fax (61) 2077205; f. 1990; subsidiary of Mutual and Federal, South Africa; acquired CGU Holdings Ltd in 2000 and FGI Namibia Ltd in 2001; Man. Dir G. KATJIMUNE; Gen. Man. J. W. B. LE ROUX.

Namibia National Reinsurance Corpn Ltd (NamibRE): Capital Centre, 2nd Floor, Levinson Arcade, POB 716, Windhoek; tel. (61) 256905; fax (61) 256904; e-mail info@namibre.com; internet www.namibre.com; f. 2001; 100% state-owned; Man. Dir ANNA NAKALE-KAWANA.

Old Mutual Life Assurance Co (Namibia) Ltd: Mutual Platz, 5th Floor, Post St Mall, POB 165, Windhoek; tel. (61) 2993999; fax (61) 2993520; e-mail infonamibia@oldmutual.com; internet www.oldmutual.com.na; Chair. G. S. VAN NIEKERK; Chief Exec. BERTIE VAN DER WALT.

Sanlam Namibia: 154 Independence Ave, POB 317, Windhoek; tel. (61) 2947418; fax (61) 2947416; e-mail marketing@sanlam.com.na; internet www.sanlam.com.na; f. 1928; subsidiary of Sanlam Ltd, South Africa; merged with Regent Life Namibia, Capricorn Investments and Nam-Mic Financial Services in Dec. 2004; Chair. KOOS BRANDT; CEO TERTIUS STEARS.

Santam Namibia Ltd: Ausspannplaza Complex, Ausspannplatz, POB 204, Windhoek; tel. (61) 2928000; fax (61) 235225; 60% owned by Santam, South Africa; 33.3% owned by Bank Windhoek Holdings Ltd; acquired Allianz Insurance of Namibia Ltd in 2001; Chief Exec. RIAAN LOUW.

Swabou Insurance Co Ltd: Swabou Bldg, Post St Mall, POB 79, Windhoek; tel. (61) 2997528; fax (61) 2997551; internet www.fnbnamibia.com.na; f. 1990; acquired by FNB Namibia Holdings Ltd in 2004; short-term insurance; Man. Dir RENIER TALJAARD.

Swabou Life Assurance Co Ltd: 209–211 Independence Ave, POB 79, Windhoek; tel. (61) 2997502; fax (61) 2997550; e-mail tgurirab@fnbnamibia.com.na; internet www.fnbnamibia.com.na; f. 1990; acquired by FNB Namibia Holdings Ltd in 2004; life assurance; CEO GERHARD MANS.

Trade and Industry

GOVERNMENT AGENCIES

Karakul Board of Namibia—Swakara Fur Producers and Exporters: PMB 13300, Windhoek; tel. (61) 237750; fax (61) 231990; e-mail swakara@agra.com.na; internet www.swakara.net; f. 1982; promotes development of karakul wool and the pelt industry; Chair. RAIMAR VAN HASE; Man. WESSEL H. VISSER.

Meat Board of Namibia: POB 38, Windhoek; tel. (61) 275830; fax (61) 228310; e-mail info@nammic.com.na; internet www.nammic.com.na; f. 1935; facilitates export of livestock, meat and processed meat products; Chair. POENA POTGIETER; Gen. Man. PAUL STRYDOM.

Meat Corpn of Namibia (Meatco Namibia): POB 3881, Windhoek; tel. (61) 3216400; fax (61) 3217045; e-mail hoffice@meatco.com.na; internet www.meatco.com.na; f. 1986; processors of meat and meat products at four abattoirs and one tannery; CEO KOBUS DU PLESSIS.

Namibian Agronomic Board: 30 David Merero St, POB 5096, Ausspannplatz, Windhoek; tel. (61) 379500; fax (61) 225371; e-mail

NAMIBIA

Directory

nabdesk@nammic.com.na; internet www.nab.com.na; f. 1985; Chair. GERNOT EGGERT; CEO CHRISTOF BROCK.

National Petroleum Corpn of Namibia (NAMCOR): Petroleum House, 1 Aviation Rd, PMB 13196, Windhoek; tel. (61) 2045000; fax (61) 2045061; e-mail info@namcor.com.na; internet www.namcor.com.na; f. 1965 as Southern Oil Exploration Corpn (South-West Africa) (Pty) Ltd—SWAKOR; present name adopted 1990; state petroleum co; responsible for importing 50% of national oil requirements; Chair. F. KISTING; Man. Dir SAMUEL BEUKES.

DEVELOPMENT ORGANIZATIONS

Namibia Investment Centre (NIC): Ministry of Trade and Industry, Brendan Simbwaye Sq., Block B, 6th Floor, Goethe St, PMB 13340, Windhoek; tel. (61) 2837335; fax (61) 220278; e-mail nic@mti.gov.na; f. 1990; promotes foreign and domestic investment; Exec. Dir BERNADETTE ARTIVOR.

Namibia Non-Governmental Organisations' Forum Trust (NANGOF Trust): 9 Strauss St, off Beethoven St, POB 70433, Khomasdal, Windhoek; tel. (61) 212503; fax (61) 211306; e-mail info@nangoftrust.org.na; internet www.nangoftrust.org.na; f. 1991 as NANGOF; renamed NANGOF Trust in July 2007; CEO IVIN LOMBARDT.

National Housing Enterprise: 7 Gen. Murtala Muhammed Ave, Eros, POB 20192, Windhoek; tel. (61) 2927111; fax (61) 222301; internet www.nhe.com.na; f. 1993; replaced Nat. Building and Investment Corpn; provides low-cost housing; manages Housing Trust Fund; 100% state-owned; Chair. V. R. RUKORO; CEO VINCENT HAILULU.

CHAMBERS OF COMMERCE

Chamber of Mines of Namibia (CoM): Channel Life Tower, 4th Floor, Post St Mall, POB 2895, Windhoek; tel. (61) 237925; fax (61) 222638; e-mail dmeyer@chamberofmines.org.na; internet www.chamberofmines.org.na; f. 1979; Pres. MIKE LEECH; Gen. Man. VESTON MALANGO; 60 mems (2009).

Namibia Chamber of Commerce and Industry (NCCI): 2 Jenner St, cnr Simpson and Jenner Sts, POB 9355, Windhoek; tel. (61) 228809; fax (61) 228009; e-mail ncciinfo@ncci.org.na; internet www.ncci.org.na; f. 1990; Chair. JOHN ENDJALA; CEO TARAH SHAANIKA; c. 3,000 mems (2008).

Windhoek Chamber of Commerce and Industries: SWA Building Society Bldg, 3rd Floor, POB 191, Windhoek; tel. (61) 222000; fax (61) 233690; f. 1920; Pres. H. SCHMIDT; Gen. Man. T. D. PARKHOUSE; 230 mems.

EMPLOYERS' ORGANIZATIONS

Construction Industries Federation of Namibia: cnr Stein and Schwabe Sts, POB 1479, Klein Windhoek; tel. (61) 230028; fax (61) 224534; e-mail info@cif.namibia.na; internet www.cifnamibia.com; Pres. KARL HEINZ SCHULZ; Gen. Man. BÄRBEL KIRCHNER; 71 contracting mems, 21 small and medium enterprises members, 17 trade mems, 7 affiliated mems.

Namibia Agricultural Union (NAU): PMB 13255, Windhoek; tel. (61) 237838; fax (61) 220193; e-mail nau@agrinamibia.com.na; internet www.agrinamibia.com.na; f. 1947; represents commercial farmers; Pres. RYNO VAN DER MERWE; Exec. Man. SAKKIE COETZEE.

Namibia National Farmers' Union (NNFU): 4 Axalie Doeseb St, Windhoek West; POB 3117, Windhoek; tel. (61) 271117; fax (61) 271155; e-mail info@nnfu.org.na; internet www.nnfu.org.na; f. 1992; represents communal farmers; Pres. PINTILE DAVIDS.

Namibia Professional Hunting Association (NAPHA): 318 Sam Nujoma Dr., Klein Windhoek; POB 11291, Windhoek; tel. (61) 234455; fax (61) 222567; e-mail napha@mweb.com.na; internet www.napha.com.na; f. 1974; represents hunting guides and professional hunters; Pres. DIETHELM METZGER; c. 400 mems.

UTILITIES

Electricity

Electricity Control Board: 8 Bismarck St, ECB House, POB 2923, Windhoek; tel. (61) 374300; fax (61) 374304; e-mail info@ecb.org.na; internet www.ecb.org.na; f. 2000; CEO SISEHO C. SIMASIKU.

Namibia Power Corpn (Pty) Ltd (NamPower): NamPower Centre, 15 Luther St, POB 2864, Windhoek; tel. (61) 2054111; fax (61) 232805; e-mail paulinus.shilamba@nampower.com.na; internet www.nampower.com.na; f. 1964; state-owned; Chair. ANDRIES LEEVI HUNGAMO; Man. Dir PAULINUS SHILAMBA.

Northern Electricity Distributor (Nored): POB 891, Tsumeb; tel. (67) 222243; fax (67) 222245; private electricity supply co; first regional electricity distributor in Namibia, operating in the north of the country; Chair. SACKEY KAYONE; CEO GOTLIEB AMANYANGA.

Water

Namibia Water Corporation Ltd (NamWater): 176 Iscor St, Northern Industrial Area, POB 13389, Windhoek; tel. (61) 710000; fax (61) 713000; e-mail shigwedhaj@namwater.com.na; internet www.namwater.com.na; f. 1997; state-owned; CEO Dr VAINO SHIVUTE.

TRADE UNIONS

In 2004 there were 27 unions representing more than 100,000 workers.

Trade Union Federations

National Union of Namibian Workers (NUNW): Mungunda St, Katutura; POB 50034, Windhoek; tel. (61) 215037; fax (61) 215589; f. 1972; affiliated to the SWAPO party; Pres. ALPHEUS MUHEUA; Sec.-Gen. EVILASTUS KAARONDA; c. 70,000 mems.

The NUNW has 10 affiliates, which include:

Metal and Allied Namibian Workers' Union (MANWU): Mingunda St, POB 22771, Windhoek 9000; tel. (61) 263100; fax (61) 264300; e-mail manwu@mweb.com.na; f. 1987; Pres. JEFFREY NAOBEB; Gen. Sec. MOSES SHIIKWA; 5,500 mems.

Mineworkers' Union of Namibia (MUN): POB 1566, Windhoek; tel. (61) 261723; fax (61) 217684; f. 1986; Pres. JOHN NDEUTEPO; Sec.-Gen. JONAS LUMBU; 12,500 mems.

Namibia Farm Workers' Union (NAFWU): NUNW Centre, Mungunda Street, Katutura; POB 21007, Windhoek; tel. (61) 218653; e-mail nafwu@iafrica.com.na; internet nafwu.com; f. 1994; Pres. ASSER HENDRICKS; Sec.-Gen. ALFRED ANGULA; 5,700 mems (2009).

Namibia Financial Institutions Union (NAFINU): POB 61791, Windhoek; tel. (61) 239917; fax (61) 215589; f. 2000; Pres. DAVID SHIKULO; Gen. Sec. ASNATH ZAMUEE.

Namibia Food and Allied Workers' Union (NAFAU): Mungunda St, Katutura; POB 1553, Windhoek; tel. (61) 218213; fax (61) 263714; e-mail nafau@mweb.com.na; f. 1986; Pres. ABEL KAZONDUNGE; Gen. Sec. KIROS SACKARIAS; 12,000 mems.

Namibia National Teachers' Union (NANTU): Mungunda St, POB 61009, Katutura, Windhoek; tel. (61) 262247; fax (61) 261926; e-mail nantu@nantu.org.na; internet www.nantu.org.na; f. 1989; Pres. SIMEON KAVILA; Gen. Sec. BASILIUS G. M. HAINGURA.

Namibia Public Workers' Union (NAPWU): POB 50035, Bachbrecht, Windhoek; tel. (61) 261961; fax (61) 263100; e-mail napwu@namibnet.com; f. 1987; Pres. ELIPHAS NDINGARA; Sec.-Gen. PETRUS NEVONGA; 11,000 mems.

Namibia Transport and Allied Workers' Union (NATAU): POB 7516, Katutura, Windhoek; tel. (61) 218514; fax (61) 263767; f. 1988; Pres. DAWID TJOMBE; Gen. Sec. JOHN KWEDHI; 7,500 mems.

Trade Union Congress of Namibia (TUCNA): POB 2111, Windhoek; tel. (61) 246143; fax (61) 212828; f. 2002 following the merger of the Namibia People's Social Movement (f. 1992 as the Namibia Christian Social Trade Unions) and the Namibia Fed. of Trade Unions (f. 1998); Pres. PAULUS HANGO; c. 45,000 mems (2005).

TUCNA has 14 affiliates including:

Local Authorities Union of Namibia (LAUN): Frans Indongo St, Windhoek; POB 22060, Windhoek; tel. (61) 234625; fax (61) 230035; Pres. FRANCOIS ADONIS.

Namibia Building Workers' Union (NABWU): 3930 Verbena St, Khomasdal; POB 22679, Windhoek; tel. (61) 212828.

Namibia Seamen and Allied Workers' Union (NASAWU): Nataniel Maxuilli St, Walvis Bay; POB 1341, Walvis Bay; tel. (64) 204237; fax (64) 205957; Pres. BENNY PETRUS.

Namibia Wholesale and Retail Workers' Union (NWRWU): 19 Verbena St, Khomasdal; POB 22769, Windhoek; tel. (61) 212378; fax (61) 212828; Sec.-Gen. JOSHUA MABUKU.

Public Service Union of Namibia (PSUN): 45–51 Kroon Rd, Khomasdal, Windhoek; POB 21662, Windhoek; tel. (61) 213083; fax (61) 213047; e-mail psun@iway.na; internet www.psun.com.na; f. 1991; successor to the Govt Service Staff Asscn; Pres. JOHANES HOESEB; Sec.-Gen. VICTOR KAZONJATI.

Teachers' Union of Namibia (TUN): PSUN Bldg, Dollar St 4551, Khomasdal, POB 30800, Windhoek; tel. (61) 229115; fax (61) 246360; e-mail tun@mweb.com.na; Pres. MAHONGORA KAVIHUHA.

Transport

RAILWAYS

The main line runs from Nakop, at the border with South Africa, via Keetmanshoop to Windhoek, Kranzberg, Tsumeb, Swakopmund and Walvis Bay. There are three branch lines, from Windhoek to Gobabis,

Otavi to Grootfontein and Keetmanshoop to Lüderitz. The total rail network covers 2,382 route-km. Under phase one of the Northern Railway Line Extension Project, the Kranzberg–Tsumeb line was extended by 248 km to Ondangwa in 2006. Work subsequently commenced on phase two of the project, a further 60-km extension of this line to Oshikango, with the eventual aim of constructing an international link with Oshakati, Angola, under phase three. In 2010 plans were under way for the construction of a trans-Kalahari railway linking Walvis Bay with the Mmamabula coal deposits in Botswana. There were also plans for a railway line connecting the Namibian railway system with Mulobezi, Zambia.

TransNamib Holdings Ltd: TransNamib Bldg, cnr Independence Ave and Bahnhof St, PMB 13204, Windhoek; tel. (61) 2982437; fax (61) 2982386; e-mail pubrelation@transnamib.com.na; internet www.transnamib.com.na; f. 1998; state-owned; Chair. FOIBE JACOBS; CEO TITUS HAIMBILI.

ROADS

Between 2000 and 2002 the total road network decreased from 66,467 km to 42,237 km of roads, of which 12.8% was paved in 2002. A major road link from Walvis Bay to Jwaneng, northern Botswana, the Trans-Kalahari Highway, was completed in 1998, along with the Trans-Caprivi Highway, linking Namibia with northern Botswana, Zambia and Zimbabwe. The Government is also upgrading and expanding the road network in northern Namibia.

SHIPPING

The ports of Walvis Bay and Lüderitz are linked to the main overseas shipping routes and handle almost one-half of Namibia's external trade. Walvis Bay has a container terminal, built in 1999, and eight berths; it is a hub port for the region, serving landlocked countries such as Botswana, Zambia and Zimbabwe. In 2005 NAMPORT added a N $30m. floating dock to the Walvis Bay facilities with a view to servicing vessels used in the region's expanding petroleum industry. Traditionally a fishing port, a new quay was completed at Lüderitz in 2000, with two berths, in response to growing demand from the offshore diamond industry. At the end of 2009 Namibia's merchant fleet comprised 168 vessels, with a combined displacement of 121,579 gross registered tons.

African Portland Industrial Holdings (APIH): Huvest Bldg, 1st Floor, AE/Gams Centre, Sam Nujoma Dr., POB 40047, Windhoek; tel. (61) 248744; fax (61) 239485; e-mail jacques@apiholdings.com; f. 1994; 80% owned by Grindrod (South Africa); bulk port terminal operator; Man. Dir ATHOL EMERTON; Sec. JACQUES CONRADIE.

Namibian Ports Authority (NAMPORT): 17 Rikumbi Kandanga Rd, POB 361, Walvis Bay; tel. (64) 2082207; fax (64) 2082320; e-mail jerome@namport.com.na; internet www.namport.com; f. 1994; Chair. MIKE VAN DER MEER; Man. Dir GERSON ADOLF BISEY UIRAB.

Pan-Ocean Shipping Services Ltd: POB 2613, Walvis Bay; tel. (64) 203959; fax (64) 204199; f. 1995; Man. Dir JÜRGEN HEYNEMANN; Gen. Man. GEORGE KIROV.

CIVIL AVIATION

There are international airports at Windhoek (Hosea Kutako) and Walvis Bay (Rooikop), as well as a number of other airports throughout Namibia and numerous landing strips.

Air Namibia: TransNamib Bldg, cnr Independence Ave and Bahnhof St, POB 731, Windhoek; tel. (61) 2996000; fax (61) 2996101; e-mail aarickerts@airnamibia.com.na; internet www.airnamibia.com.na; f. 1946 as South West Air Transport; present name adopted in 1991; state-owned; part-privatization postponed indefinitely in 2003; services to Angola, Botswana, Ghana, South Africa, Zimbabwe, Germany and the United Kingdom; Chair. HINYANGERWA PIUS ASHEEKE; Man. Dir THEO NAMASES (acting).

Kalahari Express Airlines (KEA): POB 40179, Windhoek; tel. (61) 245665; fax (61) 245612; f. 1995; domestic and regional flights; Exec. Dir PEINGONDJABI SHIPOH.

Namibia Airports Company (NAC) Limited: 5th Floor, Sanlam Centre Independence Ave, POB 23061, Windhoek; tel. (61) 2955000; fax (61) 2955022; e-mail pr@airports.com.na; internet www.airports.com.na; f. 1998; Chair. NDEUHALA KATONYALA; CEO MATTI ASINO (acting).

Tourism

Namibia's principal tourist attractions are its game parks and nature reserves, and the development of 'eco-tourism' is being promoted. Tourist arrivals in Namibia in 2007 totalled 928,914. In 2008 tourism receipts amounted to US $382m.

Namibia Tourism Board: 1st Floor, Channel Life Towers, 39 Post Street Mall, Private Bag 13244, Windhoek; tel. (61) 2906000; fax (61) 254848; e-mail info@namibiatourism.com.na; internet www.namibiatourism.com.na; Chair. ERICKA AKUENJE; CEO DIGU NAOBEB.

Defence

As assessed at November 2010, the Namibian Defence Force numbered an estimated 9,000 men; there was also a 200-strong navy, operating as part of the Ministry of Fisheries and Marine Resources, and a paramilitary force of 6,000.

Defence Expenditure: Budgeted at N $3,100m. for 2010.

Commander-in-Chief of the Defence Force: Pres. HIFIKEPUNYE POHAMBA.

Acting Chief of Staff of the Defence Force: Lt-Gen. EPAPHRAS DENGA NDAITWAH.

Acting Commander of the Army: Brig.-Gen. TOMAS HAMUNYELA.

Commander of the Air Force: Col MARTIN PHINEHAS.

Commander of the Navy: Capt. PETER VILHO.

Education

Education is officially compulsory for 10 years between the ages of six and 16 years, or until primary education has been completed (whichever is the sooner). Primary education consists of seven grades, and secondary education of five. According to UNESCO estimates, in 2008/09 enrolment at primary schools included 89% of children in the relevant age-group (males 87%; females 91%), while the comparable ratio for secondary enrolment in 2006/07 was 54% (males 49%; females 60%). Higher education is provided by the University of Namibia, the Technicon of Namibia, a vocational college and four teacher-training colleges. In 2007/08 19,707 students were enrolled in tertiary education. Various schemes for informal adult education are also in operation in an effort to combat illiteracy. In 2009/10 education received an estimated 18.6% of total government expenditure.

NAURU

Introductory Survey

LOCATION, CLIMATE, LANGUAGE, RELIGION, FLAG, CAPITAL

The Republic of Nauru is a small island in the central Pacific Ocean, lying about 40 km (25 miles) south of the Equator and about 4,000 km (2,500 miles) north-east of Sydney, Australia. Its nearest neighbour is Banaba (formerly Ocean Island), in Kiribati, about 300 km (186 miles) to the east. The climate is tropical, with a westerly monsoon season from November to February. The average annual rainfall is about 2,060 mm (80 ins), but actual rainfall is extremely variable. Day temperatures vary between 24°C and 34°C (75°–93°F). Of the total resident population in 2002, 77% were Nauruans. Their language is Nauruan, but English is also widely understood. The majority of Nauruans are Christians, mostly adherents of the Nauruan Protestant Church. The national flag (proportions 1 by 2) is royal blue, divided by a narrow horizontal yellow stripe, with a 12-pointed white star at the lower hoist. The island state has no official capital, but the seat of the legislature and most government offices are in Yaren district.

CONTEMPORARY POLITICAL HISTORY

Historical Context

Nauru, inhabited by a predominantly Polynesian people, organized in 12 clans, was annexed by Germany in 1888. In 1914, shortly after the outbreak of the First World War, the island was captured by Australian forces. It continued to be administered by Australia under a League of Nations mandate (granted in 1920), which also named the United Kingdom and New Zealand as co-trustees. Between 1942 and 1945 Nauru was occupied by the Japanese, who deported 1,200 islanders to Truk (now Chuuk), Micronesia, where many died in bombing raids or from starvation. In 1947 the island was placed under UN Trusteeship, with Australia as the administering power on behalf of the Governments of Australia, New Zealand and the United Kingdom. The UN Trusteeship Council proposed in 1964 that the indigenous people of Nauru be resettled on Curtis Island, off the Queensland coast. This offer was made in anticipation of the progressive exhaustion of the island's phosphate deposits, and because of the environmental devastation resulting from the mining operations. However, the Nauruans elected to remain on the island. Between 1906 and 1968 41m. metric tons of phosphate were mined. Nauru was accorded a considerable measure of self-government in January 1966, with the establishment of Legislative and Executive Councils, and proceeded to independence on 31 January 1968 (exactly 22 years after the surviving Nauruans returned to the island from exile in Micronesia). In early 1998 Nauru announced its intention to seek UN membership and full Commonwealth membership (Nauru had hitherto been a 'special member' of the Commonwealth, not represented at meetings of Heads of Government). The decision was largely based on the islanders' desire to play a more prominent role in international policies relating to issues that affect them, most notably climate change (see Foreign Affairs). Nauru became a full member of the Commonwealth in May 1999, and a member of the UN in September of that year.

Domestic Political Affairs

The Head Chief of Nauru, Hammer DeRoburt, was elected President in May 1968 and re-elected in 1971 and 1973. Dissatisfaction with his increasingly personal rule led to the election of Bernard Dowiyogo (leader of the recently established, informal Nauru Party) to the presidency in 1976. Dowiyogo was re-elected President after a general election in late 1977. However, DeRoburt's supporters adopted tactics of obstruction in Parliament, and in December 1977 Dowiyogo resigned, in response to Parliament's refusal to approve budgetary legislation; he was re-elected shortly afterwards, but was again forced to resign in April 1978, following the defeat of a legislative proposal concerning phosphate royalties. Lagumot Harris, another member of the Nauru Party, succeeded him, but resigned three weeks later when Parliament rejected a finance measure, and DeRoburt was again elected President. He was re-elected in December of that year, in December 1980 and in May and December 1983.

In September 1986 DeRoburt resigned, following the defeat of a government budget proposal; he was replaced as President by Kennan Adeang, who was elected in Parliament by nine votes to DeRoburt's eight. However, after holding office for only 14 days, Adeang was defeated in a parliamentary vote of no confidence, and DeRoburt subsequently resumed the presidency. Following a general election in December, Adeang was again narrowly elected President, but he was subsequently ousted by another vote of no confidence; DeRoburt was reinstated as President. The atmosphere of political uncertainty generated by the absence of a clear majority in Parliament led DeRoburt to dissolve Parliament in preparation for another general election in January 1987, following which the incumbent was re-elected to the presidency by 11 votes to six. In February Adeang announced the establishment of the Democratic Party of Nauru, essentially a revival of the Nauru Party. Eight members of Parliament subsequently joined the new party, which declared that its aim was to curtail the extension of presidential powers and to promote democracy. In August 1989 a parliamentary motion of no confidence in DeRoburt (proposed by Adeang) was approved by 10 votes to five, and Kenas Aroi, a former Minister of Finance, was subsequently elected President. Aroi resigned in December, owing to ill health, and after a general election in the same month Bernard Dowiyogo was re-elected President, defeating DeRoburt by 10 votes to six. At the next presidential election, held shortly after a general election in November 1992, Dowiyogo defeated Buraro Detudamo.

At a general election held in November 1995, when a total of 67 candidates contested the 18 parliamentary seats, all cabinet members were re-elected. A subsequent presidential election resulted in Lagumot Harris's defeat of the incumbent Dowiyogo by nine parliamentary votes to eight. The resignation of the Chairman of Air Nauru, following allegations of misconduct, prompted Parliament to vote on a motion of no confidence in the Government in November 1996. The motion was narrowly approved and Harris was replaced by Dowiyogo as President. Later that month, however, Dowiyogo's new Government was itself defeated in a parliamentary vote of no confidence, and Kennan Adeang was elected to the presidency. Amid widespread perceptions that the new Government lacked experience, a further motion of no confidence was approved in December, when Adeang was similarly removed from office. At a subsequent presidential contest Reuben Kun, a former Minister of Finance, defeated Adeang by 12 votes to five, on the understanding that his administration would organize a general election. An election duly took place in February 1997, at which four new members were elected to Parliament, following an apparent agreement between the supporters of Harris and those of Dowiyogo to end the political manoeuvring that had resulted in several months of instability in Nauru. At the subsequent election to the presidency Kinza Clodumar (nominated by Dowiyogo) defeated Harris by nine parliamentary votes to eight.

In early 1998 five members of Parliament (including former President Lagumot Harris) were dismissed by Adeang, the Speaker, for refusing to apologize for personal remarks about him that had been published in an opposition newsletter. At the resultant by-elections, held in February 1998, three of the five members were re-elected. A motion expressing no confidence in the President was approved in June, and Dowiyogo was consequently elected to replace Clodumar. In a further vote of no confidence, in April 1999 Dowiyogo was defeated by 10 votes to seven; his replacement was Rene Harris, previously Chairman of the Nauru Phosphate Corporation.

Following the legislative election held on 8 April 2000, Rene Harris was re-elected President, narrowly defeating Dowiyogo by nine parliamentary votes to eight. Ludwig Scotty was elected Speaker of Parliament. However, Scotty and his deputy, Ross Cairn, subsequently resigned, stating only that they were unable to continue under the 'current political circumstances'. Harris therefore tendered his resignation and was replaced by Dowiyogo, whereupon Scotty and Cairn were re-elected to their posts in the legislature.

In early 2001, in another reversal to Dowiyogo's leadership, Anthony Audoa, the Minister of Home Affairs, Culture, Health and Women's Affairs, resigned and requested that Parliament be recalled. He claimed that Dowiyogo had squandered Nauru's wealth during his various tenures as President and that in promoting the island as a tax haven he had allowed Nauru to be used by Russian criminal gangs to launder their illegal funds.

In March 2001 Dowiyogo was ousted from the presidency in a parliamentary vote of no confidence while he was undergoing hospital treatment in Australia. The motion, which was adopted by two votes, led to Rene Harris regaining the presidency. In October, however, Harris was flown to Australia for emergency medical treatment for a diabetes-related illness, during which time Remy Namaduk performed the role of acting President. Allegations that Nauru's 'offshore' financial centre was being used extensively by Russian criminal organizations for laundering the proceeds of their illegal activities had led Dowiyogo to order a full review of the industry in March 1999. In early 2000 President Rene Harris announced that Nauru was to suspend its 'offshore' banking services and improve the accountability of existing banks on the island, as part of the Government's efforts to bring Nauru's financial services regulations into conformity with international standards. Dowiyogo similarly reaffirmed his commitment to reform the 'offshore' sector, following his election in April 2000. However, in February 2001 11 members of Nauru's 18-member legislature signed a petition requesting that Dowiyogo attend a special session of Parliament to answer questions relating to the island's alleged role in laundering significant funds from Russian criminal organizations. The allegations originated in claims by Russia's central bank that some US $70,000m. of illegal funds had been processed in 'offshore' banks in Nauru. It was estimated that 400 such banks existed on the island in early 2001. The Government subsequently drew up an Anti-Money Laundering Act in August 2001, but the Paris-based Financial Action Task Force (FATF, see p. 451) found that the new laws contained several deficiencies and imposed sanctions in December. (The FATF had been established in 1989 on the recommendation of the Group of Seven (G-7) industrialized nations.) The Government announced revised anti-money-laundering legislation in the same month. Meanwhile, following the Islamist attacks on New York and Washington, DC, USA, on 11 September 2001, Nauru's financial system was subject to international scrutiny, amid suspicion that it might have been used as a conduit for the terrorists' funds.

In July 2002 a new political crisis emerged after President Rene Harris decided unilaterally to establish diplomatic relations with the People's Republic of China in place of Taiwan. Several cabinet ministers opposed the President's decision to withdraw recognition from Taiwan, and the controversy increased after Harris accepted aid from China (see Foreign Affairs).

As a result of continued US pressure, Nauru's Parliament approved a new law in February 2004 to address the problem of money-laundering, along with legislation to close down the country's 'offshore' banks. In October 2004 the FATF withdrew counter-measures against the country, and in October 2005, following the implementation of the requisite legislation, Nauru became the last of the Pacific islands to be removed from the FATF list of non-co-operative countries and territories. Nauru's removal from the list coincided with the final preparations for the presentation of the National Sustainable Development Strategy, announced at the international donor meeting held in Nauru at the end of November (see Foreign Affairs). In December 2003, following the island's commitment to improve transparency and to exchange information on tax matters with other countries, Nauru had been removed from a list of unco-operative tax havens, issued in April 2002 by the Organisation for Economic Co-operation and Development (OECD, see p. 376).

In January 2003, meanwhile, President Rene Harris was defeated in a motion of no confidence by eight votes to three and was replaced by Bernard Dowiyogo. The vote followed a political crisis resulting from the defeat of the Government's budget proposals at the end of December 2002, as well as reports of increasing dissatisfaction with Harris's alleged economic mismanagement of the country. Nauru's deteriorating financial situation, in addition to the Government's decision to accept more than 1,000 asylum-seekers in return for aid from Australia (see Processing of Asylum-seekers), were believed to be major factors in the loss of confidence in Harris, which had led to the defection to the opposition of two cabinet ministers, two backbenchers and the Speaker in late 2002. However, Harris applied to the Supreme Court, and on 10 January 2003 an injunction was issued against Dowiyogo accepting the presidency. This decision had been based on the fact that only 11 of the 18 members of Parliament had attended the session when the vote took place, thus rendering it invalid; Harris and his Cabinet had staged a boycott of Parliament when the motion was to be proposed. Despite the injunction, Dowiyogo maintained his position and appointed a new Cabinet. Several days of confusion and political instability ensued. Finally, Harris was reinstated as President, after the intervention of Nauru's Melbourne-based Chief Justice, but he resigned from the presidency on the following day. In the resultant contest Dowiyogo defeated Kinza Clodumar by nine votes to eight to become the new President on 20 January. However, a lack of support for Dowiyogo within Parliament continued to create problems, amid appeals for an early election to resolve the impasse.

Meanwhile, a complete collapse of Nauru's telecommunications system in early January 2003 increased the problems experienced by the island. Nauru thus effectively became cut off from the rest of the world, with external contact possible only when ships equipped with satellite telephones were calling. A speech by Dowiyogo claiming that Nauru was on the verge of bankruptcy, unable to pay its public servants or to send its sick citizens to Australia for treatment, and appealing to donor countries for emergency assistance, could not be transmitted for almost a month. Telecommunications services were restored in March, following a visit from a technician supplied by Australia's government aid agency, AusAID.

In early March 2003 Dowiyogo travelled to Washington, DC, at the request of the US Government, which had threatened to impose harsh economic sanctions on the island and to repossess Air Nauru's only aircraft, if Nauru did not discontinue its 'offshore' banking services. The Administration of George W. Bush was reported to have been angered by the possibility that individuals with links to terrorist organizations might have used the island's financial services to launder their funds; some 400 'offshore' banks were registered on the island in the early 2000s. Consequently, Dowiyogo agreed to sign executive orders not to renew any banking licences or to issue any further so-called 'investor passports'. However, shortly after the meeting, Dowiyogo collapsed and, following emergency heart surgery, died on 9 March. Derog Gioura was appointed acting Head of State and on 20 March was elected President by nine parliamentary votes to seven. Legislation providing for the expiry of most 'offshore' banking licences within 30 days (and for the remainder within six months) was approved by Parliament in late March. At the end of March acting President Derog Gioura himself suffered a heart attack and was flown to Australia for treatment.

A general election took place on 3 May 2003, at which six new members were elected to the legislature. However, the new Speaker resigned one day after his election, and with no further nominations for the position, Parliament was unable to proceed to a presidential election. The impasse was resolved when a Speaker was finally elected in late May and Ludwig Scotty won the subsequent presidential election, defeating Kinza Clodumar by 10 parliamentary votes to seven. Scotty, who named a new six-member Cabinet in June, stated his Government's intention to focus on 'prudent management and financial stability'. However, on 8 August Scotty was ousted from office by a no-confidence motion and replaced by Rene Harris, who became the fourth President of 2003. The reasons for Scotty's removal were not clear, although concerns had been expressed about his plans to close the recently opened embassies in Washington, DC, and the Chinese capital, Beijing, and there had been speculation that he intended to transfer Nauru's diplomatic allegiance from the People's Republic of China back to Taiwan (see Foreign Affairs).

In January 2004 President Rene Harris was flown to Australia, amid rumours that he had suffered a physical collapse and was in a poor state of health. Officials declined to respond to queries surrounding the President, merely stating that Derog Gioura would be acting President in his absence. In the following month the Minister of Justice resigned, precipitating a vote of no confidence in the President. A further political crisis arose when the motion received an equal number of votes in favour and against. Moreover, when Parliament was unable to agree on the election of a new Speaker, following the resignation of the incumbent in early April, the resulting impasse meant that Parliament could not be formally convened. As the country's financial crisis deepened, President Harris travelled to Australia in mid-April to request assistance in averting imminent bankruptcy for the island. On his return to Nauru, Harris confronted angry demonstrations by hundreds of government employees protesting at the hardship imposed on them as a result of their salaries having been unpaid for 12 months. Reports indicated that government employees (who constituted the majority of paid employees on the island) were surviving on subsistence diets of fish and coconuts. In the same month receivers were appointed to manage the assets of the Nauru Phosphate Royalties Trust (including Nauru's extensive property portfolio in Australia), with the company unable to pay off debts of some $A230m. to US interests. Nauruans working in government-owned buildings in Melbourne and Sydney were served with eviction notices. Meanwhile, with neither the Government nor the opposition willing to nominate a Speaker from among its members (thereby giving the other side a majority in Parliament), the legislature was unable to produce a budget. In May, however, during another of Harris's overseas trips, the opposition elected one of its members as Speaker and immediately approved legislation making it illegal for a government to operate without a budget. In the following month, and before the Supreme Court had ruled on the matter, Kinza Clodumar, the Minister of Finance, crossed the floor, thereby allowing the opposition to approve a motion of no confidence in Harris. Ludwig Scotty was subsequently elected to the presidency. In July Australian Treasury official Peter Depta arrived in Nauru to take up the post of Financial Secretary, effectively assuming control of the country's finances.

Nauru's precarious political situation deteriorated during September 2004, and by the end of the month President Ludwig Scotty had dissolved Parliament and declared a state of emergency. His action had been prompted by the Speaker Russell Kun's suspension of the Minister of Health, Kieren Keke, on the grounds that he held dual Nauruan and Australian nationality. Keke's suspension had resulted in the loss of the Government's one-seat majority and a consequent stalemate in Parliament, during which budget legislation had been unable to be approved. Scotty assumed sole responsibility over the government of the country until a general election took place on 23 October. At the election all nine members of Scotty's Government retained their seats in the legislature, while seven of the nine opposition members of parliament were not re-elected. The result thus gave President Scotty an ample majority in Parliament. Within days of its election the new Government approved a budget that included a reduction in public sector salaries and increased import duties. In the following month legislation aimed at discouraging criminals, particularly terrorists, from using the country's financial sector was approved, in addition to the establishment of a procedure for conducting possible future referendums and for reviewing the Constitution. The sudden death of the Speaker, Vassal Gadoengin, from a heart attack in December 2004 led to the election of Valdon Dowiyogo, a new member of Parliament and son of the former President, to the position in the following month.

Meanwhile, in July 2004 President Ludwig Scotty held emergency discussions with the Presidents of Kiribati and Tuvalu regarding at least US $2m. in outstanding salary payments owed to their nationals employed in Nauru by the Nauru Phosphate Corporation. Nauru's financial crisis led it to appeal for assistance from the Pacific region and the international community. In September the Pacific Islands Forum (see p. 413) offered to help pay the salaries of Nauruan government employees, who had been unpaid for many months (see above). The Government of Cuba (with which diplomatic relations had been established in 2001) responded to an appeal for health care workers by sending 11 doctors to Nauru to alleviate an increasingly serious situation, in which only three doctors were available to sick Nauruans.

In January 2005 a committee of members of Parliament began a review of Nauru's Constitution, motivated by a desire to achieve greater political stability in the country and to improve the accountability of public institutions. In 2006 the committee formed the Independent Commission on Constitutional Review, and in mid-2007 a Constitutional Convention, comprising 18 directly elected members and 18 appointees, met to discuss the Commission's conclusions.

In December 2005 Air Nauru, which had consistently operated at a loss and which had suspended all operations in early 2001 following the revelation of various safety concerns, was issued with a court order for the seizure of its only aircraft, on account of the carrier's non-payment of loan instalments to a US bank. In September 2006 Air Nauru was relaunched under the new name of Our Airline, after Taiwan provided sufficient funding for the Government's acquisition of an aircraft with which it could resume services.

At the legislative election held on 25 August 2007 several members and supporters of the Government of Ludwig Scotty were re-elected to Parliament. Later in that month Scotty was re-elected as the island's President, defeating Marcus Stephen by a considerable margin of parliamentary votes. Scotty's new Cabinet retained all the ministers of the previous Government. In December, however, Scotty was removed from office in a vote of no confidence, amid allegations of corruption against the Minister of Foreign Affairs and of Finance, David Adeang, and the withdrawal of support of several members of the Government. Marcus Stephen was subsequently elected to replace Scotty, appointing a Cabinet that included Kieren Keke, who had served as a minister under Scotty.

The new Government's progress was hampered by increasing discord and its lack of a majority in the legislature. In April 2008 Speaker David Adeang, a member of the opposition, announced the suspension of all nine government members of Parliament. Stephen subsequently declared a state of emergency and dissolved Parliament, setting in motion the procedure for the holding of an early election. At the election, conducted on 26 April, the incumbent Government was able to increase its representation in Parliament to 12 of the 18 legislators, at the expense of three members of the opposition who lost their seats. Riddell Akua was elected Speaker. Parliament re-elected Stephen as the country's President and confirmed the membership of the Cabinet, which remained largely unchanged. (Former President Rene Harris lost his seat at the parliamentary election and died in July.) Three of Stephen's supporters subsequently defected to the opposition, amid allegations that Getax, an Australian company that apparently hoped to secure greater control of Nauru's phosphate resources, had attempted to influence the course of the island's politics. Getax had financed a trip to Singapore by 11 of the 18 members of the Nauruan Parliament, including the three who then decided to join the opposition.

Recent developments: the political impasse of 2010

In February 2010 President Stephen survived a parliamentary vote of no confidence relating to alleged irregularities in the use of overseas loans. In a referendum conducted at the end of February, various proposals for constitutional change, which included the direct election of the country's President, were rejected by voters; 78% of the electorate participated in the poll. Parliament was dissolved in March, in preparation for an early election in the following month, when President Stephen hoped to secure wider support.

However, at the election held on 24 April 2010, all 18 incumbent members of Parliament were returned to office, thus resulting in no change to the composition of the legislature and again leaving Parliament evenly divided between the two sides (with nine seats each). As a result, when Parliament convened for its first session, members failed to elect from among themselves a new Speaker to replace Shadlog Bernicke (who had been appointed on an acting basis in March). In mid-May, at its sixth attempt, Parliament chose Godfrey Thoma as Speaker. However, having declared he would resign if a fresh election were not called within four days, Thoma duly announced his resignation when this condition was not met. Meanwhile, President Stephen indicated that he favoured the amendment of the Constitution to permit the selection of the Speaker from outside Parliament, effectively proposing the addition of a 19th member to the legislature, in order to prevent any recurrence of the impasse that had rendered Parliament unable to function. At the beginning of June two opposition legislators were reported to have lent support to the incumbent Government's candidate for the position of Speaker, Dominic Tabuna, whose election was confirmed later that day. However, just three days after taking office, Tabuna resigned, stating that 'recent developments' meant that he no longer had a mandate to remain in office; it was unclear to what Tabuna was referring.

On 11 June 2011, citing the need to approve the national budget, President Stephen declared a state of emergency and called fresh elections for 19 June. However, the poll failed to produce a clear majority for either side: all but one of the 18 incumbent members were returned to office. The sole newcomer, Milton Dube, an independent who won a seat previously held by the opposition, thus held the balance of power. Stephen contended that the results of the second poll indicated a 'rallying' behind his grouping by Nauruans, and urged Dube to lend his support to the interim Government. However, in late June

NAURU

Aloysius Amwano (one of the three opposition members who had withdrawn his support for the Government following the Getax-sponsored trip to Singapore) was elected Speaker; upon taking office, Amwano urged Stephen to resign. The President indicated his willingness to do so, on the condition that a replacement be selected from within his grouping. In early July the interim Government announced that it had secured the support of an opposition member, thereby affording it the majority that it required to form a new government and elect a President. However, Amwano refused to allow the motion to elect a President to be presented to Parliament, prompting Stephen to issue a presidential order demanding the Speaker's removal from office on the grounds that Amwano was in contravention of his constitutional requirements. Amwano declared his intention to challenge the order to vacate the post.

In August 2010 it emerged that the opposition was considering initiating a legal challenge to President Stephen's dismissal of the Speaker and the declaration of a state of emergency in June, claiming that his action had been unconstitutional. The President insisted that the measure was necessary to ensure the continued efficient operation of government and public services during the ongoing parliamentary impasse; in an attempt to answer the claims of autocracy, in mid-September Stephen amended the emergency powers in order to allow challenges to be lodged against the measure with the Supreme Court. The opposition formally lodged its challenge with the Court in early October. In mid-October the Court ruled that the President had acted within his constitutional rights, noting that the Constitution explicitly stated that it was the right of the President, not the Supreme Court, to declare a state of emergency. Stephen welcomed the ruling and announced that he planned to seek a referendum on the proposal to selected a Speaker from outside of the legislature in order to avoid future polls resulting in a hung Parliament. A number of opposition legislators expressed support in principle for the proposal.

In late October 2010 it was revealed that, at the request of President Stephen, Australian federal police had begun investigating allegations of bribery by Getax of members of the Nauruan opposition. Documents allegedly pertaining to unusual financial transactions and the possibility of electoral irregularities were reported to have been given to the Australian High Commissioner in Nauru. Meanwhile, Baron Waqa, leader of the parliamentary opposition, declined to disclose details of the funding that his grouping had received from Getax.

Former President Ludwig Scotty accepted a nomination for the post of Speaker, while reaffirming his position as an opposition legislator, and at the beginning of November 2010 was duly elected. Parliament swiftly re-elected Stephen as President, who removed the state of emergency, thereby appearing finally to have resolved the six-month impasse. Parliament immediately began debating the national budget, which was quickly approved, almost four months after it was scheduled to have been implemented.

In a speech to commemorate the 43rd anniversary of Nauru's independence in January 2011, President Stephen, in a pointed allusion to the protracted impasse, appealed for legislators to eschew 'the politics of divisiveness', arguing that the primary responsibility of elected members was to promote political stability; he urged all legislators to co-operate in order to build consensus on national issues.

Processing of Asylum-seekers

In September 2001 Nauru agreed to accept 310 of 460 predominantly Afghan asylum-seekers who were on board a Norwegian freighter, unable to disembark on Christmas Island, in the Indian Ocean, as Australia refused to grant them entry into its territory (see the chapter on Christmas Island). The Australian Government agreed to fund the processing of the asylum-seekers and to pay an undisclosed sum to Nauru, which was to accommodate the asylum-seekers for three months while their claims for asylum were assessed. Following the interception of several other boats carrying asylum-seekers in Australian waters later the same month, Nauru received a pledge of $A20m. from the Australian Government for agreeing to host 800 asylum-seekers. In December 2001 Nauru signed an agreement with Australia's Minister for Foreign Affairs to accommodate a total of 1,200 at any one time, in return for a further $A10m. of aid, to be allocated to education, health and infrastructure programmes. Local residents and owners of the land upon which the camps were located expressed concern over the delays in processing the asylum-seekers' claims, which were due to be completed by July 2002. However, in December some 700 people remained in the camps, despite the deportation of more than 100 Afghan asylum-seekers. In the same month the President signed a new agreement with Australia's Minister for Foreign Affairs to extend the duration of the camps' operations and to accommodate up to 1,500 asylum-seekers.

In mid-2003 the Australian Government was criticized for its detention of some 100 children in the camps on Nauru and for failing to reunite families held in separate camps for extended periods. Concerns about the conditions at the camps and the welfare of the detainees increased during 2003, and in December some of those held began a hunger strike in order to attract attention to their situation. A reported 40 asylum-seekers participated in the strike. The Nauruan Government's subsequent appeals for medical assistance from Australia to care for the hunger strikers, many of whom required hospital treatment during the following weeks, were refused. The hunger strike ended after about a month, and in mid-January 2004 the Australian Government sent a delegation to inspect medical facilities available to asylum-seekers on the island. However, the resultant report, which found services for those held in detention to be adequate, was widely regarded as flawed, as it had failed to examine any of the detainees and had been compiled solely by Australian government officials. In June the first of 146 Afghan asylum-seekers, approved for entry to Australia, left the detention centre. In November 2005, after four years of detention on the island, a total of 25 asylum-seekers were transferred to Melbourne. It was reported that only two detainees, who had failed to meet security requirements, remained on Nauru; their departure from the centre was finally arranged in late 2006. In early 2007 the claims of 82 Sri Lankan asylum-seekers, who had been intercepted by the Australian navy in February, were being processed on Nauru, along with those of seven detainees from Myanmar. In February 2008 the 21 remaining detainees left Nauru, marking the end of Australia's policy of accommodating asylum-seekers on the island. The Australian Government's decision was not welcomed by all Nauruans, in view of its anticipated impact on the island's economy. In July 2010 President Marcus Stephen expressed Nauru's willingness to reopen the detention centre if approached by Australia. However, the Australian Government of Prime Minister Julia Gillard, which had taken office in the previous month, stated its refusal to consider any such reopening while Nauru remained a non-signatory to the UN's 1951 Convention relating to the Status of Refugees. The Nauruan Government was reported to be considering signing the document in early 2011.

Phosphate-mining Issues

In February 1987 representatives of the British, Australian and New Zealand Governments signed documents effecting the official demise of the British Phosphate Commissioners, who from 1919 until 1970 had overseen the mining of Nauru's phosphate deposits. President DeRoburt subsequently expressed concern about the distribution of the Commissioners' accumulated assets, which were estimated to be worth $A55m. His proposal that part of this sum be spent on the rehabilitation of areas of the island that had been mined before independence was rejected by the three Governments involved. DeRoburt subsequently established a commission of inquiry to investigate proposals for rehabilitation. The commission proposed that the three Governments provide one-third ($A72m.) of the estimated rehabilitation costs. In 1989 Australia's refusal to contribute to the rehabilitation of former phosphate-mining areas prompted Nauru to institute proceedings, claiming compensation from Australia for damage to its environment, at the International Court of Justice. However, in August 1993, following negotiations between President Dowiyogo and the Australian Prime Minister, Paul Keating, a Compact of Settlement was signed, under which the Australian Government was to pay to Nauru a lump sum of $A57m., followed by $A50m. to be paid in instalments over a period of 20 years. New Zealand and the United Kingdom subsequently agreed to contribute $A12m. each towards the settlement. An investigation into methods for the rehabilitation of the damaged areas of the island included plans to use landfill to encourage the restoration of vegetation to the mined areas, and the re-establishment of many of the species of flora and fauna that had previously been abundant on the island. In mid-1995 a report commissioned by the Government published details of a rehabilitation programme extending over the next 20–25 years and costing $A230m. However, the success of the rehabilitation scheme was dependent on the co-operation of landowners, some of whom were expected to continue to allow areas to be mined for residual ore once phosphate reserves had been exhausted. In mid-1997 Parliament approved the Nauru Rehabilitation Corporation (NRC) Act, providing for the establishment of a corporate body to manage the rehabilitation programme. The NRC held its inaugural meeting in May 1999. The rehabilitation programme (which was to be partly financed from the Compact of Settlement with Australia) was expected to transform the mined areas into sites suitable for agriculture, new housing and industrial units, but the project was hampered considerably by delays. In early 2004 the head of the NRC resigned, reportedly in frustration at problems regarding the implementation of a feasibility study into the mining of residual phosphate. Results published in September from a series of test sites on the island indicated that the potential for residual phosphate mining might be greater than had been previously thought. A major refurbishment of the island's mining plant was subsequently undertaken, and exports of phosphates resumed in 2006 (see Economic Affairs). In March 2008 protests reportedly related to the export of phosphates escalated into violence, with a group of approximately 100 demonstrators setting fire to a police station. A team of volunteers was appointed by local Australian police officers to maintain stability on the island. Intense foreign competition for greater control of Nauru's phosphate resources led to the emergence in 2010 of allegations of bribery of local parliamentarians (see Domestic Political Affairs).

Foreign Affairs

In 1989 a UN report on the greenhouse effect (the heating of the earth's atmosphere and a resultant rise in sea-level) listed Nauru as one of the countries that might disappear beneath the sea in the 21st century, unless drastic action were taken. The Government of Nauru strongly criticized Australia's refusal, at the December 1997 Conference of the Parties to the Framework Convention on Climate Change (see UN Environment Programme, see p. 65), in Kyoto, Japan, to reduce its emission of pollutant gases known to contribute to the greenhouse effect. Following a change of government in Australia, the country signed the Kyoto Protocol in December 2007.

Despite such tensions, Nauru maintained generally good relations with Australia, which continued to provide substantial development aid. In August 2009 the two countries signed the Australia-Nauru Partnership for Development. Priority areas included the improvement of the education system and of health facilities in Nauru. In early 2010 the Australian consulate-general in Nauru was upgraded to a full high commission.

In August 2001 Nauru hosted a summit meeting of the Pacific Islands Forum, despite a problematic shortage of accommodation, caused by the presence of large contingents of officials from Australia, refugee agencies, the UN and Eurest (the company subcontracted to operate Nauru's refugee camp). In September 2010 the UN opened a bureau on Nauru combining offices of the UN Development Programme, the UN Population Fund and the UN Children's Fund (UNICEF), which was welcomed by President Marcus Stephen as an opportunity to forge closer co-operation with the organization.

In mid-2002 President Rene Harris announced Nauru's recognition of the People's Republic of China, thus ending 22 years of diplomatic relations with Taiwan. The President swiftly accepted US $60m. in aid and $77m. in debt annulment from the People's Republic of China. Following the switch in allegiance, Taiwan stated its intention to take legal action to recover a loan of $12.5m., which it had arranged to make available to Nauru.

In February 2003 Nauru opened two diplomatic missions, in Washington, DC, and in Beijing. However, suspicions regarding the use of Nauru's facilities by international terrorists were confirmed in the same month when two members of the Islamist al-Qa'ida organization were found to be travelling on Nauruan passports. At the request of the US Government, which had threatened to impose harsh economic sanctions and to repossess Air Nauru's only aircraft if the country did not discontinue its 'offshore' banking services, in March President Dowiyogo flew to the USA for discussions. The Administration of George W. Bush was reported to have been particularly concerned by the possibility that individuals with links to terrorist organizations might have used the island's financial services in order to launder their funds. In July President Scotty announced plans to close the newly opened diplomatic missions, citing economic constraints and his belief that they were not serving their intended purpose. Representatives in China and the USA expressed surprise at the announcement and queried the President's motives, in particular his commitment to ending the lucrative sale of Nauruan passports.

In March 2005 President Ludwig Scotty made an official visit to mainland China, where he took part in discussions on bilateral aid and economic and technical co-operation. However, in May the Chinese Government revealed that Nauru had severed its diplomatic relations with the People's Republic by restoring recognition to Taiwan. In July it was reported that Taiwan was to pay the outstanding salaries of some 1,000 workers from Kiribati and Tuvalu, who had remained stranded on Nauru since the island's financial crisis had resulted in the Government's inability to pay their wages. In March 2006 it was announced that Taiwan was providing US $3m. in overdue salary payments to the former phosphate miners from Kiribati and Tuvalu. In March 2010 Taiwanese President Ma Ying-jeou undertook an official visit to Nauru, where discussions focused on the topics of agricultural co-operation and food safety. In October the Nauruan Minister of Foreign Affairs and Trade, Dr Kieren Keke, visited Taiwan, whereupon he met with President Ma, who stressed the 'very meaningful' effect of the Taiwanese agricultural aid programme in Nauru and thanked the island state for its support of Taiwan's bid to become a member of the International Civil Aviation Organization. During Keke's visit, a bilateral agreement was signed exempting visa requirements for travel between Nauru and Taiwan by diplomatic and government officials. Proposals for an agreement on 'green energy' projects were also discussed.

Nauru was persistently critical of France's use of the South Pacific region for the testing of nuclear weapons, and was one of the most vociferous opponents of the French Government's decision in mid-1995 to resume its testing programme. Diplomatic relations, suspended between the two countries in 1995, were formally resumed in December 1997. In February 2010 Nauru was included on a list of 18 countries and territories deemed unco-operative by the French Government with regard to the issues of transparency in the financial sector and compliance with international tax reporting standards.

Nauru attracted considerable controversy in June 2005 when, at a meeting of the International Whaling Commission (IWC) in the Republic of Korea, it voted with Japan to remove the moratorium on commercial whaling introduced in 1986. Japan was accused by some observers of encouraging small, developing countries to join the IWC and then of attempting to influence their voting with financial incentives. Nauru denied that it had been subjected to any form of manipulation by the Japanese Government, stating that it had voted to remove the ban on whaling in order to preserve its tuna stocks. However, following a covert investigation conducted by a British newspaper, *The Sunday Times*, evidence emerged in June 2010 suggesting that Japan had secured the votes of a number of nations, including the Marshall Islands and Kiribati, through offers of aid donations, cash incentives and funding delegations' visits to whaling meetings. Although Nauru was not mentioned explicitly by the newspaper in connection with the investigation, the exposé did little to quell speculation that its vote had been manipulated by Japan.

Meanwhile, further international controversy ensued in December 2009 when it was revealed that, in exchange for a commitment of Russian aid reportedly totalling US $50m., Nauru had accorded diplomatic recognition to the secessionist republics of Abkhazia and South Ossetia. Nauru's recognition of these separatist regions of Georgia drew much criticism. The Nauruan Minister of Foreign Affairs, Kieren Keke, visited South Ossetia, as well as the Russian capital of Moscow, for discussions. Keke subsequently confirmed the provision of the development aid, but withheld details of the financial arrangements. As part of the agreement, Russia released funding of $9m. in mid-2010, to be disbursed on vital reparation work on Nauru's port and moorings, which commenced in July.

CONSTITUTION AND GOVERNMENT

Under the Constitution of 1968, legislative power is vested in the unicameral Parliament, with 18 members elected by universal adult suffrage for up to three years. Executive authority is vested in a Cabinet, which consists of the President of the Republic, elected by Parliament, and ministers appointed by him. The Cabinet is collectively responsible to Parliament. Responsibilities for administration are divided between the Nauru Local Government Council and the Government. The Council, an elected body of nine members from the country's 14 districts, elects one of its members to be Head Chief.

REGIONAL AND INTERNATIONAL CO-OPERATION

Nauru is a member of the Pacific Community (see p. 410), of the Pacific Islands Forum (see p. 413) and of the Asian Development Bank (ADB, see p. 202), all of which aim to promote regional development. The country is also a member of the UN's Economic and Social Commission for Asia and the Pacific (ESCAP, see p. 37), having joined the UN in 1999.

ECONOMIC AFFAIRS

In 2009, according to the Asian Development Bank (ADB), Nauru's gross domestic product (GDP), measured at current prices, was $A69.5m., equivalent to $A7,117 per head. In 1995–2004, it was estimated, GDP decreased, in real terms, at an average annual rate of 1.5%. The population decreased by an annual average of 1.0% during 2000–08. According to the ADB, real GDP contracted by 27.3% in the fiscal year 2007 (ending in June). Having increased by 1.0% in 2007/08, GDP showed no discernible growth in 2008/09 and 2009/10.

Agricultural activity comprises mainly the small-scale production of tropical fruit, vegetables and livestock, although the production of coffee and copra for export is increasingly significant. According to FAO, agriculture and fishing were expected to engage some 20% of the economically active population in mid-2011. The sector provided an estimated 4.0% of GDP in 2008/09. Following a period of decline, agricultural GDP increased, in real terms, by 25.5% in 2003. Coconuts are the principal crop. Bananas, pineapples and the screw-pine (*Pandanus*) are also cultivated as food crops, while the islanders keep pigs and chickens. Almost all of Nauru's requirements are imported. Increased exploitation of the island's marine resources was envisaged following the approval by Parliament of new fisheries legislation in the late 1990s. However, the sector failed to develop as hoped, and in early 2009 it was reported that a fisheries adviser, funded by Australia, had been engaged. Meanwhile, revenue from fishing licence fees issued to foreign fleets totalled an estimated $A7m. in 2005/06.

Industrial activity (mining, manufacturing, construction and utilities) accounted for 51.2% of GDP in 2008/09. In real terms, industrial GDP declined by 7.5% in 2002 and by 9.8% in 2003.

Mining contributed 14.7% of GDP in 2008/09. Nauru's economy has traditionally been based on the mining of phosphate rock, which constituted four-fifths of the island's surface area. Phosphate extraction was conducted largely by indentured labour, notably by I-Kiribati and Tuvaluan workers. Revenue from phosphate sales was invested in a long-term trust fund, the Nauru Phosphate Royalties Trust (NPRT—see below) and the Nauru Local Government Council. As the depletion of primary (surface) deposits continued, in 2004 an Australian company undertook a successful survey of the island's potential for secondary phosphate mining (see Contemporary Political History). The discovery of substantial new reserves of high-grade phosphate was announced in 2005. In September 2006, following the upgrading of processing facilities, the first major shipment of phosphate for nearly 10 years was exported to India. However, subsequent operations were intermittently disrupted when the island's port facilities were damaged in recurrent storms. In October 2010 Nauru applied to the International Seabed Authority for permission to explore for deep sea minerals in an area of the north-east Pacific Ocean reserved for developing states.

Manufacturing accounted for 24.9% of GDP in 2008/09, while the construction sector contributed 3.3%.

Energy is derived principally from imported petroleum. Output of electrical energy totalled 34.5m. kWh in 2007. Electricity supplies remained intermittent for some years until August 2009, in which month the upgrading of the island's generators was completed.

The services sector, accounting for 44.9% of Nauru's GDP in 2008/09, comprises mainly those employed in public service. The real GDP of services rose by 3.4% in 2002, but decreased by 0.4% in 2003. The sector recorded no growth in 2004, with many salaries remaining in arrears (see Contemporary Political History). There is no tourism sector. Banking services are not widely available.

The country's trade balance deteriorated sharply in 2009, when a deficit of US $44.9m. was recorded (in comparison with a surplus of $31.6m. in the previous year). The deficit on the current account of the balance of payments was estimated at 10.3% of GDP in 2006/07. According to the ADB, in 2006/07 the value of Nauru's exports rose by an estimated 618.6% (owing to the resumption of phosphate sales), a trend that was sustained in the following year. However, the cost of imports also increased substantially, rising by 61.4% in 2008/09 in comparison with the previous year. The principal imports in 2005 were manufactured goods and other manufactured articles (40.4% of total imports), along with machinery and transport equipment, food and live animals. Phosphate has traditionally been the most important export. The main exports in 2005 included manufactured goods and crude materials. The principal export market in 2009 were the Republic of Korea (which purchased 76.7% of the total) and India. The principal sources of Nauru's imports in 2009 were the Republic of Korea (supplying 28.1%) and Australia.

The 2010/11 budget envisaged government expenditure of $A29m., a reduction of 9% in comparison with the previous year. The ADB estimated the budget surplus at the equivalent of 14.2% of GDP in 2009/10, compared with a deficit of 36.3% of GDP in 2005/06. Development assistance from Australia was projected at $A26.6m. for 2010/11. Under the Australia-Nauru Partnership for Development signed in 2009, aid was to be directed to five priority areas, which included Nauru's infrastructure and services, improvements in the public sector and the promotion of the private sector. Nauru's external debt was estimated by the ADB at $A261m. in 2010. In that year the level of international debt was reported to be in excess of the equivalent of eight times the country's GDP, while the Government's domestic debt was estimated at $A265m. Consumer prices increased by 17.9% in 2000, but inflation subsequently moderated. The annual rate of inflation was estimated by the ADB at 2.2% in 2008/09; consumer prices declined by 0.5% in 2009/10. The rate of unemployment in 2002 was estimated at 22.7% of the labour force.

After gaining independence in 1968, Nauru benefited from sole control of earnings from phosphate mining, and as a result its income per head was among the highest in the world. However, the assets of the NPRT were estimated to have decreased from $A1,300m. in 1991 to only $A300m. in 2003, following which the portfolio was placed into receivership. In November 2005 Nauru hosted an international donor meeting, attended by representatives of about 20 donor nations and agencies, at which it requested support for its National Sustainable Development Strategy. The aims of this programme included an increase in revenue from phosphate production, better use of fish resources and the encouragement of agricultural activities, with particular emphasis on local food production. In August 2008 the Pacific Islands Forum agreed to extend its Pacific Regional Assistance to Nauru initiative. Australia's closure in 2008 of an offshore processing centre for asylum-seekers, from which Nauru had derived substantial revenue, had a major impact on the island's economy. Nauru has remained heavily dependent on external support, with budgetary expenditure funded by foreign donors totalling $A11.2m. in 2009/10. The introduction of a mobile phone service in 2009 attracted much interest and greatly stimulated economic activity on the island. The reduction in consumer prices in 2009/10 was partly attributed to the lower costs of telecommunication facilities. However, the increasing costs of imports of fuel and foodstuffs in early 2011 were expected to result in renewed inflationary pressures. The high level of public debt remained a major concern. In addition to the accumulation of a substantial external debt, the Government was reported to owe a further $A265m., largely arising from the insolvency of the Bank of Nauru, while the debts of public enterprises were estimated to total $A368m. in 2010. The economy was further impeded by the suspension of Parliament for much of 2010 (see Contemporary Political History), as a result of which the enactment of the annual budget was delayed by four months. Nevertheless, following two years of stagnation, GDP was forecast by the ADB to increase by 4.0% in 2010/11, mainly owing to improvement in revenue from phosphate exports. The establishment of a new trust fund was under consideration in mid-2011.

PUBLIC HOLIDAYS

2012 (provisional): 2 January (for New Year's Day), 31 January (Independence Day), 6–9 April (Easter), 17 May (Constitution Day), 26 October (Angam Day), 25–26 December (Christmas).

Statistical Survey

Source (unless otherwise indicated): Bureau of Statistics, Ministry of Finance, Government Offices, Yaren District; tel. (674) 444-3142; fax (674) 444-3125; e-mail statistics@naurugov.nr; internet www.spc.int/prism/country/nr/stats.

AREA AND POPULATION

Area: 21.3 sq km (8.2 sq miles).

Population: 8,042 (Nauruan 4,964, Other Pacific Islanders 2,134, Asians 682, Caucasians—mainly Australians and New Zealanders—262) at census of 13 May 1983; 9,919 (males 5,079, females 4,840) at census of 17 April 1992; 10,065 (males 5,136, females 4,929) at census of 23 September 2002. *Mid-2011* (Secretariat of the Pacific Community estimate): 10,186 (Source: Pacific Regional Information System).

Density (at mid-2011): 478.2 per sq km.

Population by Age and Sex (Secretariat of the Pacific Community estimates at mid-2011): *0–14:* 3,607 (males 1,840, females 1,767); *15–64:* 6,445 (males 3,271, females 3,174); *65 and over:* 134 (males 64, females 70); *Total* 10,186 (males 5,175, females 5,011) (Source: Pacific Regional Information System).

Principal Districts (population, 2002 census): Denigomudu 2,381; Meneng 1,323; Aiwo 1,051; Boe 731; Yaren (capital) 632; Buada 673.

Births, Marriages and Deaths (1995): Registered live births 203 (birth rate 18.8 per 1,000); Registered marriages 57 (marriage rate 5.3 per 1,000); Registered deaths 49 (death rate 4.5 per 1,000). *2006* (unless otherwise indicated): Registered live births 120; Registered deaths 75 (2002).

Life Expectancy (years at birth, WHO estimates): 60 (males 57; females 63) in 2008. Source: WHO, *World Health Statistics*.

Economically Active Population (census of 17 April 1992): 2,007 (Elementary occupations 401, Clerks and office workers 355, Craft and related workers 299, Service, shop and market sales workers 250, Professionals 208, Plant, machine operators and assemblers 136, Technicians and associate professionals 115, Legislators, senior officials and managers 18, Agriculture and related workers 2, Not classified 223). *2002* (census of 23 September): Total employed 2,534; Unemployed 746; Total labour force 3,280. *Mid-2011* (estimates): Agriculture, etc. 1,000; Total labour force 5,000 (Source: FAO).

HEALTH AND WELFARE
Key Indicators

Total Fertility Rate (children per woman, 2008): 2.9.

Under-5 Mortality Rate (per 1,000 live births, 2008): 45.

Physicians (per 1,000 head, 2004): 0.8.

Hospital Beds (per 1,000 head, 2004): 5.9.

Health Expenditure (2007): US $ per head (PPP): 812.

Health Expenditure (2007): % of GDP: 15.1.

Health Expenditure (2007): public (% of total): 70.9.

For sources and definitions, see explanatory note on p. vi.

AGRICULTURE, ETC.

Principal Crop and Livestock (2008, FAO estimates): Coconuts 1,800 metric tons; Pigs 3,000 head; Chickens 5,000 head. Note: No data were available for 2009.

Livestock Products (metric tons, 2009, FAO estimates): Pig meat 72; Chicken meat 4; Hen eggs 16.

Fishing (metric tons, live weight of capture, 2008, FAO estimates): Yellowfin tuna 12; Bigeye tuna 3; Skipjack tuna 13; Total catch (incl. other marine fishes) 39.

Source: FAO.

MINING

Phosphate Rock ('000 metric tons, estimates): 84 in 2003; 22 in 2004; 11 in 2005. The phosphoric acid content ('000 metric tons, estimates) was: 26 in 2003; 7 in 2004; 3 in 2005. Source: US Geological Survey.

INDUSTRY

Electric Energy (million kWh): 32.6 in 2005; 33.4 in 2006; 34.5 in 2007. Source: UN Industrial Commodity Statistics Database.

FINANCE

Currency and Exchange Rates: Australian currency: 100 cents = 1 Australian dollar ($A). *Sterling, US Dollar and Euro Equivalents* (31 December 2010): £1 sterling = $A1.5404; US $1 = $A0.9840; €1 = $A1.3148; $A100 = £64.92 = US $101.63 = €76.06. *Average Exchange Rate* (Australian dollars per US $): 1.1922 in 2008; 1.2822 in 2009; 1.0902 in 2010.

Budget ($A '000, year ending 30 June 2007, budget forecasts): *Total Revenue:* 22,288 (Tax revenue 8,646, Non-tax revenue 13,643); *Total Expenditure:* 22,226 (Employee expenses 5,890, Operating expenses 8,543, Property expenses 505, Current transfers 2,150, Gross fixed capital formation 4,682, Other 457).

Gross Domestic Product ($A '000, year ending 30 June at current prices): 27,630 in 2007; 49,520 in 2008; 69,540 in 2009. Source: Asian Development Bank.

Gross Domestic Product by Economic Activity ($A million at current prices, year ending 30 June 2009): Agriculture, hunting and fishing 2.8; Mining 10.2; Manufacturing 17.3; Electricity, gas and water 5.8; Construction 2.3; Trade 6.7; Transport and communications 6.4; Finance 2.9; Public administration 4.9; Other services 10.3; *GDP in market prices* 69.5. Source: Asian Development Bank.

EXTERNAL TRADE

Principal Commodities (US $ '000, year ending 30 June 2005): *Imports:* Food and live animals 4,548; Beverages and tobacco 1,891; Crude materials (except food and fuel) 1,741; Mineral fuels and lubricants 1,528; Animal fats and vegetable oils 1,698; Chemical products 3,300; Manufactured goods 11,898; Machinery and transport equipment 5,375; Miscellaneous manufactured articles 1,705; Total (incl. others) 33,683. *Exports:* Food and live animals 293; Crude materials (except food and fuel) 1,489; Chemical products 408; Manufactured goods 2,039; Machinery and transport equipment 616; Miscellaneous manufactured articles 113; Total (incl. others) 4,959.

Principal Trading Partners (US $ million, year ending 31 December 2009): *Imports:* Australia 18.6; Fiji 0.9; Germany 2.0; Korea, Republic 40.8; USA 3.5; Total (incl. others) 145.1. *Exports:* Canada 0.1; India 17.9; Korea, Republic 76.9; Total (incl. others) 100.2. Source: Asian Development Bank.

Trade Totals (US $ '000, year ending 31 December): *Imports c.i.f.:* 57,514 in 2007; 89,917 in 2008; 145,146 in 2009. *Exports f.o.b.:* 18,135 in 2007; 121,493 in 2008; 100,159 in 2009. Source: Asian Development Bank.

TRANSPORT

Road Traffic (1989): 1,448 registered motor vehicles.

Shipping: *Merchant Fleet* (displacement, '000 grt at 31 December): 15 in 1991 (at 30 June); 5 in 1992; 1 in 1993. Source: Lloyd's Register of Shipping. *International Freight Traffic* (estimates, '000 metric tons, 1990): Goods loaded 1,650; Goods unloaded 59. Source: UN, *Monthly Bulletin of Statistics*.

Civil Aviation (traffic on scheduled services, 2006): Kilometres flown (million) 4; Passengers carried ('000) 219; Passenger-km (million) 376; Total ton-km (million) 37. Source: UN, *Statistical Yearbook*.

COMMUNICATIONS MEDIA

Radio Receivers (1997): 7,000 in use*.

Television Receivers (1997): 500 in use*.

Telephones (main lines, 2009): 1,900 in use†.

Mobile Cellular Telephones (2005): 1,500 subscribers†.

Internet Users: 300 in 2005†.

*Source: UNESCO, *Statistical Yearbook*.
† Source: International Telecommunication Union.

EDUCATION

Pre-primary (2008 unless otherwise indicated): 4 schools (2007); 42 teachers; 663 pupils.

NAURU

Primary (2008 unless otherwise indicated): 2 schools (2007); 56 teachers; 1,254 pupils.
Secondary (2008 unless otherwise indicated): 4 schools (2007); 57 teachers; 816 pupils.
Vocational (2003 unless otherwise indicated): 2 schools (2004); 4 teachers; 38 students.

Pupil-teacher Ratio (primary education, UNESCO estimate): 22.4 in 2007/08 (Source: UNESCO Institute for Statistics).

Note: Nauruans studying at secondary and tertiary levels overseas in 2001 numbered 85.

Source: Department of Education, Yaren, Nauru.

Directory

The Government

HEAD OF STATE

President: MARCUS STEPHEN (elected by Parliament 19 December 2007; re-elected 29 April 2008 and 1 November 2010).

CABINET
(May 2011)

President and Minister of Public Service, Home Affairs, Police, Prisons and Emergency Services, and the Nauru Phosphate Royalties Trust: MARCUS STEPHEN.
Minister of Finance, Foreign Affairs and Trade, responsible for assisting the President: Dr KIEREN KEKE.
Minister of Commerce, Industry and Environment, and Utilities: FREDERICK PITCHER.
Minister of Education, Youth Affairs and Fisheries: ROLAND KUN.
Minister of Health, Sport and Justice: MATTHEW BATSIUA.
Minister of Information and Communications Technology and Transport: SPRENT DABWIDO.

MINISTRIES

Office of the President: Yaren; tel. 444-3772; fax 444-3776; e-mail the.president@naurugov.nr.
Ministry of Commerce, Industry and Resources: Yaren; tel. 444-3133; fax 444-3188; e-mail minister.cir@naurugov.nr.
Ministry of Education: Yaren; tel. 444-3130; fax 444-3718; e-mail minister.education@naurugov.nr.
Ministry of Finance: Government Treasury Bldg, Aiwo; tel. 444-3133; fax 444-3124; e-mail minister.finance@naurugov.nr.
Ministry of Fisheries: e-mail minister.fisheries@naurugov.nr.
Ministry of Foreign Affairs and Trade: Government Offices, Yaren; tel. 444-3133; e-mail minister.foreignaffairs@naurugov.nr.
Ministry of Health: Yaren; tel. 444-3133; fax 444-3188; e-mail minister.health@naurugov.nr.
Ministry of Home Affairs: ; fax 444-3891; e-mail minister.homeaffairs@naurugov.nr.
Ministry of Justice: Yaren; tel. 444-3160; fax 444-3108; e-mail minister.justice@naurugov.nr.
Ministry for the Nauru Phosphate Royalties Trust: e-mail minister.nprt@naurugov.nr.
Ministry of Police: e-mail minister.police@naurugov.nr.
Ministry of Public Service: e-mail minister.publicservice@naurugov.nr.
Ministry of Sport: e-mail minister.sport@naurugov.nr.
Ministry of Telecommunications: e-mail minister.telecommunications@naurugov.nr.
Ministry of Transport: Yaren; tel. 444-3133; fax 444-3136; e-mail minister.transport@naurugov.nr.
Ministry of Utilities: e-mail minister.utilities@naurugov.nr.
Ministry of Youth Affairs: e-mail minister.youthaffairs@naurugov.nr.

Legislature

PARLIAMENT

Parliament comprises 18 members. The general election held on 24 April 2010 failed to produce a conclusive result, with all 18 incumbent legislators being returned to office. A fresh election was therefore conducted on 19 June, when one of the nine opposition members was defeated. However, with Parliament unable to function owing to its failure to select a new Speaker, a state of emergency remained in place until the beginning of November when the impasse was ended.

Speaker: LUDWIG SCOTTY.

Political Organizations

Democratic Party of Nauru: c/o Parliament House, Yaren; f. 1987; revival of Nauru Party (f. 1975); Leader KENNAN ADEANG.
Naoero Amo (Nauru First): c/o Parliament House, Yaren; e-mail visionary@naoeroamo.com; f. 2001; Co-Leaders DAVID ADEANG, KIEREN KEKE.

Diplomatic Representation

EMBASSY AND HIGH COMMISSION IN NAURU

Australia: MQ45 NPC OE, Aiwo; tel. 444-3380; fax 444-3382; e-mail george.fraser@dfat.gov.au; High Commissioner BRUCE COWLED.
Taiwan (Republic of China): Civic Centre, 1st Floor, Aiwo; tel. 444-3239; fax 444-3846; e-mail nru@mofa.gov.tw.

Judicial System

The Chief Justice presides over the Supreme Court, which exercises original, appellate and advisory jurisdiction. The Resident Magistrate presides over the District Court, and he also acts as Coroner under the Inquests Act 1977. The Supreme Court is a court of record. The Family Court consists of three members, one being the Resident Magistrate as Chairman, and two other members drawn from a panel of Nauruans. The Chief Justice is Chairman of the Public Services Appeals Board and of the Police Appeals Board.

Chief Justice of the Supreme Court: GEOFFREY EAMES (non-resident) Yaren; tel. 444-3163; fax 444-3104.
Resident Magistrate of the District Court: G. N. SAKSENA.
Chairman of the Family Court: G. N. SAKSENA.

Religion

Nauruans are predominantly Christians, adhering either to the Nauruan Protestant Church or to the Roman Catholic Church.

Nauruan Protestant Church: Head Office, Nauru; Moderator (vacant).
Roman Catholic Church: POB 16, Nauru; tel. and fax 444-3708; Nauru forms part of the diocese of Tarawa and Nauru, comprising Kiribati and Nauru. The Bishop resides on Tarawa Atoll, Kiribati.

The Press

Central Star News: Nauru; f. 1991; fortnightly.
Nasero Bulletin: Nauru; tel. 444-3847; fax 444-3153; e-mail bulletin@cenpac.net.nr; fortnightly; English; local and overseas news; Editor SEPE BATSIUA; circ. 500.
The Nauru Chronicle: Nauru; Editor RUBY DEDIYA.

NAURU

Broadcasting and Communications

TELECOMMUNICATIONS

A mobile telephone service was introduced in 2009.

Nauru Telecommunications Service: ICT Centre, Civic Centre Complex, Aiwo, Nauru; tel. 444-3324; fax 444-3111; e-mail director.ict@naurugov.nr; Dir (vacant).

BROADCASTING

Radio

Nauru Broadcasting Service: Information and Broadcasting Services, Chief Secretary's Department, POB 77, Nauru; tel. 444-3133; fax 444-3153; f. 1968; state-owned and non-commercial; broadcasts in the mornings in English and Nauruan; operates Radio Nauru; Station Man. RIN TSITSI; Man. Dir GARY TURNER.

Television

Nauru Television (NTV): Nauru; tel. 444-3133; fax 444-3153; began operations in June 1991; govt-owned; broadcasts 24 hrs per day on 3 channels; most of the programmes are supplied by foreign TV companies via satellite or on videotape; a weekly current affairs programme is produced locally; Man. MICHAEL DEKARUBE; Dir of Media GARY TURNER.

Finance

(cap. = capital; res = reserves; dep. = deposits; m. = million; amounts in Australian dollars unless otherwise stated)

BANKING

State Bank

Bank of Nauru: Civic Centre, POB 289, Nauru; tel. 444-3238; fax 444-3203; e-mail bonauru@yahoo.com; f. 1976; state-owned; reported to be insolvent; Chair. NAGENDRA GOSWAMI.

INSURANCE

Nauru Insurance Corporation: POB 82, Nauru; tel. 444-3346; fax 444-3731; f. 1974; sole licensed insurer and reinsurer in Nauru; Chair. NIMES EKWONA.

Trade and Industry

GOVERNMENT AGENCIES

Nauru Agency Corporation: Civic Centre, 1st Floor, POB 300, Aiwo; tel. 444-3782; fax 444-3730; e-mail info@nauruoffshore.com; internet www.nauruoffshore.com; f. 1972; management service to assist entrepreneurs in the incorporation of holding and trading corpns and the procurement of trust and insurance licences; CEO R. MOSES.

Nauru Corporation: Civic Centre, Yaren; f. 1925; operated by the Nauru Council; the major retailer in Nauru; Gen. Man. A. EPHRAIM.

Nauru Fisheries and Marine Resources Authority: POB 449, Aiwo; tel. 444-3733; fax 444-3812; e-mail nfmra@cenpac.net.nr; f. 1997; CEO CHARLESTON DEIYE.

Nauru Phosphate Royalties Trust (NPRT): Nauru; statutory corpn; invests phosphate royalties to provide govt revenue; extensive int. interests, incl. hotels and real estate; assets put into receivership in 2004; Sec. NIRAL FERNANDO.

Nauru Rehabilitation Corporation (NRC): Camp Ibaganiquane, Meneng; tel. and fax 444-3200; e-mail nrcadmin8464@gmail.com; f. 1999; manages and devises programmes for the rehabilitation of those parts of the island damaged by the over-mining of phosphate; CEO VINCI CLODUMAR.

UTILITIES

Eigigu Holding Corporation: Civic Centre, Aiwo; public works, water and waste management; also has interests in supermarket retail and television broadcast distribution; Chair. LESSI OLSSON.

Nauru Central Utilities (Nauru Utilities Authority): Aiwo; tel. 444-3247; fax 444-3521; e-mail wayne.brearley@naurugov.nr; f. 1968; sole electricity provider; CEO APISAKE SOAKAI.

RONPhos Corporation (Republic of Nauru Phosphate Company): Aiwo; tel. 444-3839; fax 444-2752; f. 1967; est. as Nauru Phosphate Corpn; has operated the phosphate industry and several public services of the Republic of Nauru (including provision of electricity) on behalf of the Nauruan people; present name adopted in 2005 following reorganization; Chair. RIDDELL AKUA; Gen. Man. LESI OLSSON.

Transport

RAILWAYS

There are 5.2 km of 0.9-m gauge railway serving the phosphate workings.

ROADS

A sealed road, 16 km long, circles the island, and another serves Buada District.

SHIPPING

In 1998 finance was secured from the Japanese Government for the construction of a harbour in Anibare district, which was opened in 2000.

Nauru Pacific: Government Bldg, Yaren; tel. 444-3133; f. 1969; operates cargo charter services to ports in Australia, New Zealand, Asia, the Pacific and the west coast of the USA; Man. Dir (vacant).

CIVIL AVIATION

Our Airline: Directorate of Civil Aviation, Government Offices, POB 40, Yaren; tel. and fax 444-3746; e-mail info@ourairline.com.au; internet www.ourairline.com.au; f. 1970; fmrly Air Nauru; name changed as above in 2006; operates passenger and cargo services to Kiribati, Fiji, Solomon Islands and Australia; Chair. Capt. KEVIN POWER; CEO KARAM CHAND.

Tourism

There is no tourism industry on the island.

Defence

Nauru has no defence forces. Under an informal agreement, Australia is responsible for the defence of the island.

Education

Education is free and compulsory for children between the ages of six and 16. In 2007 the island had four pre-primary schools, with 663 pupils and 42 teachers in 2008. In 2007 the island had two primary schools and four secondary schools. In 2008 1,254 pupils were enrolled in primary education with 56 teachers, and 816 pupils in secondary education with 57 teachers. In addition, there were two vocational training schools in 2004. An extension centre of the University of the South Pacific, based in Suva, Fiji, was opened in Nauru in the late 1980s.

NEPAL

Introductory Survey

LOCATION, CLIMATE, LANGUAGE, RELIGION, FLAG, CAPITAL

The Federal Democratic Republic of Nepal is a land-locked Asian country in the Himalaya mountain range, with India to the east, south and west, and Tibet (the Xizang Autonomous Region), in the People's Republic of China, to the north. The climate varies sharply with altitude, from arctic on the higher peaks of the Himalaya mountains (where the air temperature is permanently below freezing point) to humid subtropical in the central valley of Kathmandu, which is warm and sunny in summer. Temperatures in Kathmandu, which is 1,337 m (4,386 ft) above sea-level, are generally between 2°C (35°F) and 30°C (86°F), with an annual average of 11°C (52°F). The rainy season is between June and October. Average annual rainfall varies from about 1,000 mm (40 ins) in western Nepal to about 2,500 mm (100 ins) in the east. The official language is Nepali, which was spoken by 48.6% of the population in 2001. Other languages include Maithir (12.3% in 2001) and Bhojpuri (7.5%). Some 80.6% of the population were Hindus in 2001, with 10.7% Buddhists and 4.2% Muslims. The national flag (proportions 4 by 3) is composed of two crimson pennants, each with a blue border. The upper section contains a white crescent moon (horns upwards and surmounted by a disc with eight rays) and the lower section a white sun in splendour. The capital is Kathmandu.

CONTEMPORARY POLITICAL HISTORY

Historical Context

Although Nepal was an hereditary monarchy, for more than 100 years, until 1951, effective control over the country was wielded by the Rana family, who created the post of hereditary Prime Minister. A popular revolution, led by the Nepali Congress Party (NCP), ousted the Ranas and restored King Tribhuvan to power. A limited constitutional monarchy was established in 1951. During most of the 1950s government was controlled by the monarchy, initially under Tribhuvan and then, after his death in 1955, under his son, Mahendra. In February 1959 King Mahendra promulgated Nepal's first Constitution, providing for a bicameral parliament, including a popularly elected lower house. Elections held later that month resulted in victory for the NCP, led by Bisweswor Prasad (B. P.) Koirala, who became Prime Minister. However, the King retained a certain degree of power, and persistent differences between the King and the Prime Minister led to a royal coup in December 1960: Nepal's first brief period of democracy was thus brought to an abrupt end. The King dismissed the Council of Ministers and dissolved Parliament. A royal decree of January 1961 banned political parties. King Mahendra accused the Koirala administration of corruption, and in December 1962 he introduced a new Constitution, reasserting absolute royal power and providing for a 'partyless' system of government, based on the Panchayat (village council), with a Prime Minister appointed by the King. In January 1972 King Mahendra died and was succeeded by his son, Birendra. In December 1975 the Government made major changes to the Constitution, which allowed for a widening of the franchise and more frequent elections to the Rashtriya Panchayat (National Assembly), but in no way were the King's powers eroded.

Domestic Political Affairs

B. P. Koirala, the former Prime Minister and an advocate of parliamentary democracy, was acquitted of treason in February 1978. Returning from abroad a year later, he was placed under house arrest in April 1979, but was subsequently released, partly to appease students who had been demonstrating for reforms. National unrest grew and, after King Birendra announced in May that there would be a national referendum on whether to restore multi-party democracy, Prime Minister Kirti Nidhi Bista resigned and was succeeded by Surya Bahadur Thapa. In the referendum, held in May 1980, 54.8% of the voters supported the Panchayat system with reforms. As a result, the King formed a Constitutional Reforms Commission, and in December he issued a decree under which amendments to the Constitution were made, including the proviso that the appointment of the Prime Minister by the King would henceforth be on the recommendation of the Rashtriya Panchayat. In accordance with the new provisions, direct legislative elections were held in May 1981, the first of their kind since 1959, although still on a non-party basis. Thapa was re-elected by the Rashtriya Panchayat as Prime Minister in June 1981, and the King installed a new Council of Ministers (on the recommendation of the Prime Minister). An extensive ministerial reorganization took place in October 1982, but this failed to stem increasing official corruption and economic mismanagement. In July 1983, for the first time in the 23-year history of the Panchayat system, the incumbent Prime Minister, Thapa, was ousted, and a new Council of Ministers was formed by a former Chairman of the Rashtriya Panchayat, Lokendra Bahadur Chand, who had successfully introduced a motion expressing no confidence in Thapa.

The rise of the Nepali Congress Party and the restoration of multi-party democracy

In March 1985 the NCP held a convention in Kathmandu, and in May it embarked upon a campaign of civil disobedience, aimed at restoring a multi-party political system and parliamentary rule under a constitutional monarchy. In June there was a series of bomb explosions, resulting in loss of life. The explosions were apparently co-ordinated by two newly formed anti-monarchist and anti-Government groups, the Janawadi Morcha (Democratic Front) and the Samyukta Mukti Bahini (United Liberation Torch-bearers). These bombings united an otherwise seriously divided legislature against the terrorists, and forced the predominantly moderate opposition to abandon the campaign of civil disobedience and to disclaim any responsibility for the explosions. In August the Rashtriya Panchayat approved a stringent anti-terrorist law, and more than 1,000 people were arrested in connection with the unrest.

In May 1986 a general election was held. About 64% of the electorate voted, in spite of appeals by the NCP and the pro-China faction of the Communist Party of Nepal (CPN) (neither of which presented candidates) for a boycott of the polls. All the candidates in the election were nominally independents, but it was reported that among the 72 new entrants to the Rashtriya Panchayat (40 members retained their seats) were at least 16 members of the Marxist-Leninist faction of the CPN. In June the King nominated 25 additional members of the new Rashtriya Panchayat, and Marich Man Singh Shrestha (previously Chairman of the Rashtriya Panchayat) was elected unopposed by the Assembly as the new Prime Minister. In late 1986, to counter the growing influence of the communist faction in the Rashtriya Panchayat, several senior figures established a 'Democratic Panchayat Forum', which expressed full support for the non-party system.

In June 1987, in an apparent attempt to improve the image of the Panchayat system, the Government initiated an anti-corruption campaign, during the course of which several senior officials were arrested for drugs-trafficking and other offences. In early 1988 the Government continued its policy of suppressing opposition. In January the President of the NCP was arrested, and in February more than 100 people, who were planning to demonstrate in support of the NCP mayor of Kathmandu (who had been suspended from office for his anti-Panchayat stance), were also detained.

In September 1989 the Government arrested more than 900 NCP supporters, in an apparent effort to prevent them from celebrating the anniversary of the birth of Nepal's first elected Prime Minister, B. P. Koirala (who died in 1982). During these celebrations the NCP demonstrated in protest against the failings of the country's non-party political system. In November the leaders of the NCP held a meeting in Kathmandu with members of several other left-wing and communist political groups, to discuss the proposed formation of a country-wide, peaceful 'movement for the restoration of democracy'; the movement's aims would be the alleviation of Nepal's severe economic problems (including an ongoing trade dispute with India), the restoration of full democracy, the transfer from absolute to constitutional monarchy, the immediate replacement of the Panchayat Government by an interim national government, the removal of the ban on political activities, and the introduction of a multi-party system. In January 1990 a co-ordination committee to conduct the Jana Andolan (People's Movement) was formed by the NCP and the newly formed United Left Front (ULF, which was led by Sahana Pradhan and comprised six factions of the CPN and a labour group), despite the Government's efforts to pre-empt its inauguration by arresting hundreds of activists (including many students) and by banning, or heavily censoring, more newspapers. During the consequent violent confrontations between protesters and police that took place in February, it was officially estimated that 12 people were killed and hundreds more arrested. Violent demonstrations, strikes and mass arrests continued throughout March. At the end of the month the Minister of Foreign Affairs, Shailendra Kumar Upadhayaya, resigned from his post, following differences with the Prime Minister regarding the Government's management of the crisis. A few days later there was an extensive government reorganization, including the dismissal of nine ministers who allegedly opposed the Government's acts of repression against the pro-democracy movement. In an effort to end the political unrest, the King dismissed Shrestha's Government on 6 April and nominated a restricted four-member Council of Ministers, under the leadership of the more moderate Chand. The Government initiated talks with the opposition, and on 8 April the King announced that the 30-year ban on political parties was to be ended, thus enabling the future holding of multi-party elections, and that a commission to study constitutional reform was to be established. At the same time, the Jana Andolan suspended its campaign of demonstrations. However, many political activists continued to agitate, demanding the removal of the formal structure of the Panchayat system. A week later, the King accepted the resignation of Chand from his post as Prime Minister, dismissed the Council of Ministers and announced the dissolution of the Rashtriya Panchayat. King Birendra then invited the opposition alliance of the NCP and the ULF to form an interim government. On 19 April a new coalition Council of Ministers (including two ministers nominated by the King and two independents), under the premiership of the President of the NCP, Krishna Prasad (K. P.) Bhattarai, was sworn in. The new Prime Minister announced that a general election would be held, on a multi-party basis, within a year. The principal task of the interim Government was to prepare a new constitution in accordance with the spirit of multi-party democracy and constitutional monarchy. King Birendra stated that he was committed to transforming his role into that of a constitutional monarch, and, following further violent clashes in Kathmandu between anti-royalists and police, he ordered the army and the police to comply with the orders of the interim Government in order to facilitate a smooth transition to democracy.

In mid-May 1990 King Birendra announced a general amnesty for all religious and political prisoners. On 21 May he delegated the legislative powers of the dissolved Rashtriya Panchayat to the new Council of Ministers, empowering it to enact, amend and repeal legislation in order to bring about the introduction of a multi-party democracy. At the end of the month the King formed a Constitutional Recommendation Commission (based on the suggestions of the Prime Minister), which, after consulting the various parties, was to prepare a draft constitution and present it to the King within three months. In July the death sentence was abolished and the laws restricting freedom of the press and freedom of association were repealed. In addition, the King suspended almost one-half of the articles in the existing Constitution to enable the interim Government to function smoothly. The draft of the new Constitution, which was published at the end of August, recommended the introduction of a constitutional monarchy; a democratic multi-party system and a bicameral legislature, composed of a 205-member House of Representatives (Pratinidhi Sabha) and a 60-member National Assembly (Rashtriya Sabha); the official guarantee of fundamental rights (including freedom of expression); an independent judiciary; and the placing of the army under the control of a three-member National Defence Council, headed by the Prime Minister. Under the draft Constitution, the King would be allowed to declare a state of emergency on the advice of the Council of Ministers, but such declarations would have to be approved by the House of Representatives within three months. A crucial clause under consideration required the King 'to obey and protect' the Constitution: under the old regime, the King was considered to be above the Constitution. The draft Constitution was approved by the Council of Ministers on 15 October and sent to the King for his endorsement. However, King Birendra amended the draft in a final effort to retain sovereign authority and full emergency powers. This retrograde action provoked violent protests. The Council of Ministers rejected most of the proposed amendments in the royal counter-draft, but agreed to the King's proposal to establish a Council of State (Raj Parishad), with a standing committee headed by a royal appointee. The 15-member committee was to be composed of eight royal appointees and seven other members, including the Prime Minister, the Ministers of Defence and Foreign Affairs, the Chief Justice of the Supreme Court, and the Chief of Army Staff. However, Bhattarai stressed that the formation of this committee would not alter the democratic nature of the new Constitution, since it would not function as a parallel body to the Council of Ministers. He also emphasized that the King would only be permitted to act on judicial, executive and legislative matters on the advice of the Council of Ministers. The new Constitution was officially promulgated by the King on 9 November.

The communist movement in Nepal suffered a set-back in December 1990, when four of the seven constituent members of the ULF broke away from the front, citing their lack of representation in the interim coalition Council of Ministers. However, Sahana Pradhan stated that the three remaining factions would continue to operate as the ULF. In January 1991 two major factions of the CPN (the Marxist and Marxist-Leninist factions) merged to form the CPN (Unified Marxist-Leninist—UML).

The general election was held on 12 May 1991. The NCP contested the election alone and not on the basis of an electoral alignment with any of its former Jana Andolan partners. The communists interpreted the NCP's move as the result of an increased understanding between the monarchy and the NCP on the basis that both wanted to forestall the rise of communism in the country. Consequently, relations between the NCP and the UML became strained and competitive. The general election was not only peaceful, but was also characterized by a high turn-out (65.2% of the electorate). The NCP won a comfortable majority, but it was soundly defeated by the UML in the eastern hill districts and in some parts of the Terai. In Kathmandu, supposedly an NCP stronghold, the party lost all of the seats but one. The UML established itself as the second largest party in the House of Representatives, followed by the United People's Front (UPF), an amalgam of radical, Maoist groups. The two promonarchy parties, the Rashtriya Prajatantra Party (Chand) and the Rashtriya Prajatantra Party (Thapa), led by the former Prime Ministers of those names, fared badly in the election, winning only four seats between them. Acting Prime Minister Bhattarai lost his seat in the capital, and was replaced in the premiership by Girija Prasad (G. P.) Koirala, the General Secretary of the NCP and brother of the late B. P. Koirala.

By the end of 1991 unity within the ruling NCP was threatened by growing internal dissent among its leadership, particularly between the senior leader, Ganesh Man Singh, and G. P. Koirala. The Government suffered a further set-back in April 1992 when a *bandh* (general strike), organized by the communist and other opposition parties in Kathmandu in protest against price rises, water shortages and alleged government corruption, resulted in the deaths of at least seven demonstrators following violent clashes with the police. Despite the consequent imposition of curfews in the capital and in the neighbouring town of Lalitpur, the opposition staged a number of anti-Government protest marches and demonstrations during the following week. The success of a second general strike, which was held in May, demonstrated the continuing strength of the radical left. It brought Kathmandu to a standstill and, unlike the earlier general strike, passed off without violent incidents.

Under the leadership of G. P. Koirala, the centrist NCP Government shifted to the right. The public image of the monarchy and leading members of the former Panchayat regime were rehabilitated with government support. No charges were brought against senior officials of the former administration for corruption or human rights violations. Replicating the patronage system of the Panchayat regime, the NCP rapidly began to dominate the public administration structure. The ruling party's persistent failure to democratize its internal bodies and the absence of open election to posts in the party leadership met with criticism both within and outside the NCP. In addition to dissent from within the leadership of his own party, G. P. Koirala was confronted with increasing censure from the opposition parties, which focused on an agreement drawn up by the Prime Minister in December 1991 granting India access to water from the

NEPAL

Tanakpur barrage on the Mahakali River, the terms of which were only subsequently revealed to the Nepalese House of Representatives. Alleging that the agreement constituted a treaty affecting national sovereignty, and therefore requiring a two-thirds' majority in the House of Representatives, the opposition launched a campaign demanding the resignation of Koirala on the grounds of unconstitutional behaviour.

In January–February 1993 the national UML congress abandoned much of the party's Marxist dogma and tacitly acknowledged its commitment to working within a democratic multi-party system. However, the untimely deaths of the party's General Secretary, Madan Bhandari, and Politburo member Jiv Raj Ashrit, following a road accident in mid-May, threw the UML into disarray. The party's rejection of the findings of a government inquiry, which concluded that the deaths had been accidental, provoked nation-wide protests in support of demands for an independent inquiry into the so-called 'Dasdhunga incident'. In late May Madhav Kumar (M. K.) Nepal was appointed as the new General Secretary of the UML.

In the mean time, the rehabilitation of officials of the former Panchayat regime continued. In January 1993 the King appointed senior figures of the old administration, including former Prime Ministers Chand and Shrestha, to the 121-member Council of State. In June the right-wing Rashtriya Prajatantra Party (RPP, formed in February 1992, following a merger of the Chand and Thapa factions) held its first national conference in Kathmandu, an event that would have been inconceivable three years previously, when its leaders were forced into hiding by the democracy movement.

In August 1993 the UML signed an agreement with the NCP, providing for the permanent withdrawal of the UML from anti-Government agitation in return for the ruling party's pledge to establish an independent commission to investigate the Dasdhunga incident. However, the UPF and other left-wing groups continued their campaign of nation-wide general strikes and demonstrations. Further serious rifts became apparent within the NCP when the party's President, K. P. Bhattarai, lost a legislative by-election to the UML candidate in Kathmandu in February 1994; his defeat was widely attributed to G. P. Koirala's public opposition to his candidature. In March the Government survived a vote of no confidence (by 113 votes to 81) presented to the House of Representatives by the UML. The opposition itself suffered from internal dissension in mid-1994 when both the UPF and the CPN (Unity Centre) split into competing factions, while the UML continued to be divided between radical and conservative camps. The crisis within the NCP culminated on 10 July when followers of Ganesh Man Singh withdrew their support for Koirala, who thereby lost his parliamentary majority. Consequently, the Prime Minister offered his resignation, and on the following day the King dissolved the House of Representatives. Koirala was appointed as interim Prime Minister pending the holding of a general election, which was brought forward from mid-1996 to 15 November 1994. At the general election, which attracted a turn-out of 58%, the UML unexpectedly emerged as the single largest party, winning 88 of the 205 seats in the House of Representatives, while the NCP won 85 seats. At the end of the month the UML formed a minority Government under the premiership of its moderate Chairman, Man Mohan Adhikari.

On 11 June 1995 the NCP registered a parliamentary motion of no confidence against the UML Government and, in conjunction with the RPP and the Nepali Sadbhavana Party (NSP), submitted a memorandum to King Birendra, staking their claim to form an alternative government. On the recommendation of the Prime Minister, who wished to avert the approval of the motion, the King dissolved the legislature on 13 June and announced that fresh elections were to be held on 23 November. Adhikari and his Council of Ministers were to function as a caretaker Government, pending the general election. The opposition challenged the dissolution of the House of Representatives in the Supreme Court. In a controversial ruling, declared on 28 August, the Supreme Court decided that the dissolution of the lower house on the advice of a minority administration (when a majority coalition was ready to assume power) had, indeed, been unconstitutional. The House of Representatives was consequently reconvened and the election abandoned. The UML Government was defeated in a vote of no confidence on 10 September, by 107 votes to 88. On 12 September a coalition Government, composed of members of the NCP, the RPP and the NSP, and headed by the NCP's parliamentary leader, Sher Bahadur Deuba, was formed.

Political instability and the onset of the Maoist insurgency

In March 1996 the Government introduced a number of security measures following a series of violent clashes between a group of Maoist activists and the police in western Nepal, which resulted in the deaths of at least 11 people (by the end of the year more than 100 people had been killed as a result of the insurgency). The left-wing extremists (many of whom were members of the underground Communist Party of Nepal (Maoist)—CPN (M)—and the UPF) had launched a 'people's revolutionary war' in the hills of Nepal in February, demanding the abolition of the constitutional monarchy and the establishment of a republic. In May G. P. Koirala was elected to replace Bhattarai as President of the NCP; for the first time since its foundation, the party elected its leader by ballot. The Government suffered a set-back at the end of January 1997 when the UML, already the largest party in the House of Representatives, increased its strength from 87 to 90 deputies, following its success in three by-elections. Deuba's administration collapsed in March when it lost a vote of confidence in the House of Representatives. Chand was appointed as the new Prime Minister (for the fourth time) at the head of a coalition Government composed of members of the RPP, the UML, the NSP and the Nepal Workers' and Peasants' Party. However, the new Government seemed unstable from the outset, since the members of the Thapa faction of the RPP refused to support Prime Minister Chand and the ideological differences between the communists and the former pro-monarchists appeared insuperable. Although Chand held the premiership, the UML, as the largest component of the coalition, was responsible for more ministerial posts than the RPP. In May and June the communists replaced the NCP as the country's dominant force in local government, following resounding successes in local elections. However, these elections were marred by violent clashes between supporters of the main political parties in which about 30 people were killed. In mid-June more than 10,000 NCP supporters demonstrated in Kathmandu in protest against alleged electoral irregularities on the part of the UML during the recent polls. During 1997 the UML suffered from factional infighting, which destabilized the coalition Government further.

In October 1997 the Government lost a parliamentary vote of no confidence tabled by the NCP. King Birendra appointed Thapa, the President of the RPP, to replace Chand as Prime Minister. A new coalition Government, comprising members of the RPP and the NSP, took office on the following day. In December Prime Minister Thapa expanded the Council of Ministers in a reorganization that introduced members of the NCP and a number of independents into the coalition. In January 1998 Nepal was once again confronted with political upheaval when Thapa recommended to the King that he dissolve the House of Representatives and set a date for mid-term elections. The Prime Minister presented the petition for fresh polls following a decision by the UML and dissident members of the RPP (including Chand) to introduce a parliamentary vote of no confidence against the Government. Uncertain as to how to act in this political impasse, the King referred the matter to the Supreme Court (the first time a Nepalese monarch had ever done so). In early February the Court advised King Birendra to convene a special session of the House of Representatives to discuss a no confidence motion against Thapa's Government. Although the Supreme Court's advice was not binding, the King called the parliamentary session. However, the no confidence motion, which was presented on 20 February, was narrowly defeated. Meanwhile, in January Chand and nine other rebel deputies were expelled from the RPP; they immediately re-established a breakaway faction known as the RPP (Chand). In March the UML suffered a serious reverse when about one-half of the party's parliamentary deputies formed a breakaway faction entitled the Communist Party of Nepal (Marxist-Leninist) (ML). Bam Dev Gautam was unanimously elected as the new party's leader. The creation of the new party left the UML with 49 deputies, while the ML claimed the support of 40 deputies.

Under an agreement reached in October 1997 when Thapa assumed power, the Prime Minister was to transfer the leadership of the coalition Government to the NCP within an agreed time frame. In early April 1998, however, Thapa appeared reluctant to relinquish his post, and the NCP threatened to withdraw support for the Government unless the Prime Minister resigned immediately. Thapa consequently tendered his resignation, and the President of the NCP, G. P. Koirala, was appointed Prime Minister in mid-April at the head of an NCP Council of Ministers. In August, in a seeming attempt to strengthen his own precarious administration and to encourage the UML's communist rivals, the Prime Minister invited the ML to join in alliance with the NCP and to form a coalition government. A new coalition administration was subsequently established on 26 August (with the NCP retaining the most important ministries), giving Prime Minister Koirala an adequate parliamentary majority. Meanwhile, the 'people's war' waged by the Maoist activists in the hills of west Nepal gathered momentum. In May the Government launched a large-scale police operation in an effort to curb the guerrilla violence.

In December 1998 the ML withdrew from the coalition Government, alleging that its ruling partner, the NCP, had failed to implement a number of agreements drawn up between the two parties and other political groups in August. Prime Minister G. P. Koirala tendered his resignation, but was asked to head a new coalition Council of Ministers, which was to hold power in an acting capacity pending the holding of a general election. On the recommendation of the Prime Minister, the King appointed a caretaker administration, comprising members of the NCP, the UML and the NSP, and, for the first time in eight years, a nominee of the King, on 25 December. In January 1999 the King dissolved the legislature in preparation for the forthcoming general election.

In May 1999 the NCP won an outright majority in the general election, securing 110 of the 205 seats in the lower house; the UML obtained 68 seats and the RPP (Thapa) took 11 seats, while the ML and the RPP (Chand) both failed to win a single seat. Voting was conducted relatively peacefully, according to government sources, despite threats by the Maoist insurgents to disrupt the electoral process. A new Council of Ministers, headed by the veteran NCP leader, K. P. Bhattarai, and composed solely of NCP members, was appointed at the end of the month.

In November 1999, in an effort to resolve the Maoist insurgency, which, according to government sources, now affected (moderately to severely) 31 of Nepal's 75 districts and had led to the deaths of more than 1,000 people, the Prime Minister offered to grant the guerrillas an amnesty and various rehabilitation measures if they surrendered their arms and entered into negotiations with the Government. In response, the insurgents (who were estimated to number 5,000–6,000 and to have the support of about 8,000 sympathizers) stated that they were not prepared to enter into peace talks until arrest warrants issued against their leaders were withdrawn, official investigations were carried out into alleged extrajudicial killings of suspected militants by the police, and imprisoned activists were released.

Koirala had initially been supportive of Bhattarai's premiership, but had since become a vociferous critic of his rival's administration, particularly with regard to the Government's perceived mismanagement of the Maoist crisis. In February 2000, following a number of internal disagreements within the Government and consequent ministerial resignations, the political unrest culminated in the registration of a vote of no confidence by 58 dissident NCP legislators against Prime Minister Bhattarai; this move led to the immediate resignation of 11 government ministers. The motion was withdrawn, but a second vote of no confidence in Bhattarai was registered by 69 predominantly pro-Koirala legislators in mid-March. Under such pressure, Bhattarai tendered his resignation to the King. It was announced that G. P. Koirala was to be the new Prime Minister (for the fourth time), following his election as parliamentary party leader of the NCP; this election process replaced the party's traditional method of choosing a parliamentary leader through consensus. Koirala and a new Council of Ministers were sworn in by the King on 22 March, and vowed to continue the basic programmes and policies that the previous NCP Government had adopted. In May a Human Rights Commission was formed following accusations by various bodies that both the security forces and the Maoist guerrillas had committed human rights violations, including murder and torture.

In April 2000 Prime Minister Koirala activated the National Defence Council, which, according to the Constitution, comprised the Prime Minister, the Minister of Defence and the Commander-in-Chief of the Royal Nepal Army, to resolve the Maoist crisis. In comparison to the inadequately trained and poorly armed police force, which had suffered numerous casualties, the army was much better equipped to deal with the insurgency, and Koirala expressed his wish to mobilize the armed forces in the ongoing fight against militant activity. At the end of August the Maoist crisis worsened. During two Maoist attacks in Dolpa and Lamjung, 24 police officers were killed and 44 were injured. The Royal Nepal Army was criticized for failing to intervene to protect the police from insurgents, and the Minister of Home Affairs, Govinda Raj Joshi, resigned after admitting his failure to 'maintain law and order in the country'. It was subsequently decided that the Government would employ a dual approach: using the army, as well as encouraging negotiations, in order to resolve the Maoist crisis. At the end of October the first direct, unofficial negotiations began between the Government and the CPN (M); however, they were short-lived, and the violence resumed in early November.

In February 2001 leading opposition parties issued a memorandum to the Prime Minister, demanding his resignation over his alleged involvement in a corrupt aircraft deal and also over the worsening security situation. In March Koirala was confronted by increasing opposition from within and outside his party and a number of ministers resigned. The opposition continued to disrupt parliamentary proceedings, and, as a result, the King prorogued the National Assembly and House of Representatives in early April. At the end of the month the anti-corruption commission cleared the Prime Minister of involvement in the controversial aircraft agreement, but, at the same time, Koirala was accused of accepting bribes in another aircraft deal. The opposition continued to demand his resignation and organized a nation-wide strike in protest against the Government's alleged misuse of power.

The royal family massacre; the Maoist insurgency escalates

On 1 June 2001 King Birendra, Queen Aishwarya and six other members of the royal family were shot dead; the heir to the throne, Crown Prince Dipendra, was gravely wounded. Another family member, Dhirendra Shah, died later in hospital. Initial reports suggested that Prince Dipendra had shot members of his family before shooting himself, following a dispute between himself and his mother regarding his intentions to marry a woman of whom the Queen disapproved. However, Prince Gyanendra, the deceased King Birendra's brother, issued a statement claiming that the deaths were the result of an accidental discharge of an automatic weapon. Immediately after the incident Prince Dipendra was pronounced King, and Prince Gyanendra was appointed regent. On 4 June King Dipendra died and was succeeded by Prince Gyanendra. These events caused considerable unrest in Kathmandu, and a curfew was imposed. Following his accession, King Gyanendra established a commission to investigate the royal deaths. The commission, comprising the Chief Justice and the Speaker of the House of Representatives, duly concluded that Dipendra had been responsible for the shootings and that at the time had been under the influence of drugs and alcohol. King Gyanendra bestowed the title of Queen on his wife, Princess Komal, but did not declare his son, Paras Shah, the Crown Prince until the end of October, owing to the latter's unpopularity among the public, caused by his profligate behaviour.

In June–July 2001 Maoist leaders, taking advantage of the unrest in Nepal, intensified their activities. On 13 July the Deputy Prime Minister, Ram Chandra Poudel, resigned, owing to disagreements with the Prime Minister over government policy towards the insurgency. Several days later a senior Maoist leader declared that he would enter negotiations with the Government on the condition that the Prime Minister resigned. On 19 July Prime Minister Koirala stood down, citing his failure to curb the Maoist insurgency and long-standing corruption allegations; former premier Sher Bahadur Deuba succeeded Koirala as leader of the NCP and Prime Minister.

Immediately after his appointment Prime Minister Deuba persuaded the Maoist leaders to reciprocate his offer of a cease-fire and agree to enter into dialogue. Prior to the negotiations, both sides took part in a series of confidence-building measures, including the reciprocal release of kidnapped police officers and imprisoned Maoist activists. At the same time Parliament adopted legislation to establish a new Armed Police Force and to develop the co-ordination of regional development and security. However, despite the cease-fire, Maoist insurgents continued to carry out violent acts. During the peace talks, which had commenced in August 2001, tens of thousands of people held demonstrations against the fighting. The third round of negotiations, which took place in November, ended in failure, owing to the Maoists' continued demand for the dissolution of the Constitution, the establishment of an interim government, the election of a constituent assembly and, ultimately, a republic.

The Government, in contrast, was prepared to offer a much less radical set of changes. Two days later the leader of the CPN (M), Pushpa Kamal Dahal (better known under his pseudonym, 'Prachanda'—'The Fierce One'), announced the end of the cease-fire. The Maoists established a parallel central government, the 'United People's Revolutionary Government', and resumed their violent campaign in earnest. The Maoists set up parallel governments in 40 of the country's 75 districts, and established direct rule in 22 districts in western Nepal. The violence escalated; on 26 November the King declared a state of emergency and authorized, for the first time, the deployment of the army to curb the insurgency. The King termed the Maoists as 'terrorists' and promulgated the Terrorist and Disruptive Activities Ordinance 2001, which sanctioned a number of counter-terrorist measures, including the suspension of civil liberties and the imposition of media restrictions. In December Prime Minister Deuba declared that he would not resume negotiations with the Maoists until they had surrendered their arms.

In January 2002 the Nepal Rastra Bank froze the bank accounts of individuals and organizations associated with Maoist militants. In mid-February Maoist insurgents launched their heaviest offensive to date against government outposts. More than 150 people, mainly soldiers and police officers, were killed in the fighting. In response to the attacks, the army was instructed to use offensive as well as defensive measures to combat the insurgency. On 21 February the legislature voted to extend the state of emergency for three months. Although the opposition criticized the Government for its handling of the insurgency and for failing to react to warnings that major attacks were imminent, it voted for the extension after the Prime Minister agreed to establish social and economic development programmes in poor rural areas where Maoists were active, and ensured the fair use of the emergency powers.

In the mean time, in February 2002 the UML and its breakaway faction, the ML, merged. The merger of the more moderate communist parties was regarded largely as a move to counter the influence of the Maoist insurgents. In its first annual report, the Human Rights Commission of Nepal accused both the Maoist insurgents as well as the Government of committing serious human rights abuses. The violent insurgency escalated in April, and in early May the army launched an intensive attack against Maoist insurgents in Rolpa district, resulting in the deaths of more than 500 guerrillas, according to government sources. A series of counter-attacks and attacks ensued, leading to further hundreds of fatalities. Deuba tabled a parliamentary motion proposing an extension of the six-month state of emergency (which was due to expire on 25 May), prompting strong opposition from within and outside his party. Growing rifts in the NCP led King Gyanendra to dissolve unexpectedly the House of Representatives on 22 May, on the recommendation of the Prime Minister. A general election was scheduled to take place on 13 November, and the incumbent Government was instructed to rule the country in the interim. Political leaders of all affiliations strongly condemned this decision. On 23 May Deuba was suspended from his party and three days later was expelled from the NCP for three years. In the mean time, three ministers, including the Minister of Finance, resigned in protest against the calling of early elections. In late May King Gyanendra extended the state of emergency by three months.

In June 2002 the NCP officially split during a 'general convention' held by the Deuba faction. Eventually, in September the Election Commission recognized the faction led by G. P. Koirala as the official NCP. Several days later Deuba's minority breakaway faction registered as a new political party, the Nepali Congress Party—Democratic (NCP—D). Meanwhile, in April the NSP split into two factions and in July two communist parties, the National People's Front and the UPF, merged to form the People's Front Nepal (Janamorcha Nepal).

In the mean time, the state of emergency expired in August 2002 and the Maoists consequently intensified their violent campaign. In the following month the Government rejected Prachanda's offer of a cease-fire, on the grounds that it lacked credibility. In early October Deuba requested King Gyanendra to postpone the general election (scheduled for November) by one year, citing the deteriorating law and order situation. However, the King responded by dismissing the Prime Minister and the acting Council of Ministers for reportedly failing to organize the election. He appointed a nine-member interim Government, headed by former premier and monarchist Lokendra Bahadur Chand, and postponed the general election indefinitely. The NCP, UML and legal experts condemned the dismissal of Deuba and his Government and the establishment of a new Council of Ministers as unconstitutional. In December the human rights organization Amnesty International issued a damning report on the human rights situation in Nepal since the collapse of peace talks in November 2001. The army and Armed Police Force were severely criticized for the alleged 'unprecedented levels' of human rights abuses, including torture, arbitrary detention and deaths in custody. In addition, the report accused Maoist insurgents of torturing and killing captives, taking hostages and recruiting children. The report claimed that nearly one-half of the 4,366 people who had died in the conflict since late 2001 were civilians, killed by both security forces and Maoists.

In January 2003 suspected Maoist militants shot dead the chief of the Armed Police Force in Kathmandu. Three days later the CPN (M) and the Government announced an immediate cease-fire and agreed to resume peace negotiations after the Government agreed to declassify Maoist activists as terrorists, to withdraw rewards offered for the arrest of Maoist leaders and to cancel international police warrants issued for the guerrilla leaders. In February a series of informal talks took place; at the end of the month the Maoists presented two conditions for the resumption of formal negotiations: the release of Maoist prisoners and the return of the army to barracks. A 22-point code of conduct was signed by the chief government negotiator and the Maoists' representative in March, according to which the Government would release prisoners gradually and give Maoists equal access to the state-controlled media; however, there was no mention of the army moving back to barracks. Both sides also agreed formally to cease hostilities. The following day a Maoist negotiator declared that, while a communist republic continued to be the CPN (M)'s goal, the militant group would comply with the public's decision on the future of the monarchy.

The interim Government and Maoist representatives commenced formal negotiations at the end of April 2003; it was reported that the CPN (M) demanded the release of Maoist prisoners, participation in an interim government and the creation of a constituent assembly, but did not include the abolition of the monarchy in its agenda. At the second round of peace talks, which took place in May, the Government agreed to release several Maoist detainees and to restrict army troops to within 5 km of their barracks. Both sides also achieved consensus on the composition of a committee to monitor the code of conduct guiding the cease-fire. The third round of negotiations, which took place in mid-August, ended in impasse over the Maoists' demand for an elected assembly to draft a new constitution. In late August Prachanda ended the seven-month cease-fire and withdrew from the peace process, while the Government reclassified the insurgents as 'terrorists'. A few days later thousands of people marched in Kathmandu to demand the resumption of peace talks.

In the mean time, at the end of May 2003 Prime Minister Chand resigned in response to pressure from leaders of the major political parties. On 4 June the King appointed monarchist and former premier Surya Bahadur Thapa as Prime Minister, rejecting the nomination by the five opposition parties of M. K. Nepal, the General Secretary of the UML. One week later the King appointed a new interim Council of Ministers, which was composed entirely of members of the monarchist RPP. Thapa had invited M. K. Nepal and Deuba to join the Government, but they had refused, maintaining that Thapa's appointment had been unconstitutional. Opposition parties held a large demonstration in Kathmandu, demanding Thapa's resignation, the reinstatement of the legislature and the establishment of an all-party government. In August Nepal's major political parties refused Thapa's further appeal for co-operation, instead pledging to launch a new series of nation-wide protests demanding the return of parliamentary democracy. On 1 September, however, the Government banned all demonstrations or public gatherings of five or more people in the Kathmandu valley, citing fears of infiltration by Maoist guerrillas. None the less, about a week later more than 1,000 pro-democracy protesters, including former premier G. P. Koirala, were arrested for defying the ban and taking part in a demonstration.

The CPN (M) fully resumed its violent campaign in September 2003. In the same month it organized a three-day general strike, which severely affected businesses, transport services and schools throughout most of the country. In January 2004 the Maoists announced the formation of autonomous people's governments in 10 districts under their control. At the end of the month the CPN (M) stated that it would give priority to development in these areas, and that representatives of the King and the USA (which had proscribed the Maoist party in October 2003 as a threat to national security and which was providing the Nepalese army with military assistance for its campaign against the insurgents) were banned from operating in districts under Maoist influence. The violence increased, meanwhile, and the Maoists organized a further number of disruptive nation-wide general strikes. The number of people killed in the eight-year 'people's war' had risen sharply to more than 9,130 by mid-March 2004, of whom more than 1,500 had died since the collapse of the cease-fire in August 2003. It was also reported that more than 250 people had 'disappeared' since the end of the cease-fire.

In November 2003 it was reported that the central committee of the RPP had requested Prime Minister Thapa to resign for failing to form an all-party government following his appointment. However, Thapa maintained the support of the King and was thus able to remain in his position. In January 2004 there were almost daily student-led, pro-republic protests held in Kathmandu. At the end of the month the five main opposition parties issued a joint statement offering formal support to the student movement. This action appeared to prove that the NCP, hitherto a committed supporter of the constitutional monarchy, and the UML were reconsidering their views towards the monarchy. The opposition parties criticized the King, claiming that he was not committed to multi-party democracy and the constitutional monarchy, and pledged to intensify their protests against 'regression'. In addition, they maintained that the Thapa Government was illegitimate and should be replaced by an all-party government, which would, in turn, hold elections and enter a peace process with the Maoist militants. In March the five main opposition parties announced that a constitutional monarchy had not been successful and that, henceforth, their movement would be directed at achieving the establishment of a republic. In May the Prime Minister tendered his resignation as a result of the continuing political impasse. The resignation prompted the collapse of the entire Government; King Gyanendra authorized Thapa to remain in office in an acting capacity pending the formation of a new administration.

In June 2004 King Gyanendra appointed Sher Bahadur Deuba as Prime Minister for the third time. Several days later the King appointed two members of the NCP (D) to the new Council of Ministers, in which Deuba held the majority of portfolios. The Council was expanded to 31 members in the following month and incorporated ministers from the four-party coalition (comprising the NCP (D), the UML, the RPP and the NSP) that had been formed following the resignation of Prime Minister Thapa.

In August 2004, for the first time since it had launched its campaign in 1996, the CPN (M) instigated a blockade of Kathmandu, stating that it would be of indefinite duration and would last until the Government released all remaining Maoist prisoners and initiated an investigation into the fates of Maoist activists who had reportedly died while in custody. The blockade was lifted after a week, reportedly in response to pleas from ordinary civilians, who were suffering significant hardship as the prices of food and other essential items had risen steeply. However, the Government's subsequent offer at the end of August 2004 of resuming peace negotiations was rejected by the Maoists. In November Prime Minister Deuba set the rebels a deadline of 13 January 2005 to commence peace talks with the Government. Deuba stated that if the Maoists did not agree to begin discussions, he would ensure that legislative elections were held by April 2005, using the mandate that had been granted to him by King Gyanendra. However, Prachanda rejected the proposed deadline. The rejection reportedly led to disagreement within the Government over the feasibility of holding elections amid the ongoing insurgency. The violence had intensified following the expiry of a short-lived cease-fire in October 2004. The Government was destabilized further in November when the founding President of the RPP, former Prime Minister Thapa, announced that he intended to launch a new political party, effectively creating a split once again within the RPP (the Chand and Thapa factions had reunited in 2000).

King Gyanendra imposes direct rule (2005–06)

In February 2005 the political situation in Nepal seriously deteriorated when King Gyanendra abruptly dismissed Prime Minister Deuba and his Government, declared an indefinite state of emergency in the kingdom and announced that, henceforth, he would rule Nepal directly. All communications links into and out of Nepal were severed temporarily, censorship was imposed on the media and former ministers were placed under house arrest. The King claimed that his actions were a result of the Prime Minister's failure to halt the Maoist insurgency and to hold legislative elections in the country. In an attempt to prevent protests, the King ordered the detention of large numbers of political activists. Maoist rebels subsequently instigated a two-week blockade of national highways in protest against the King's actions. Shortly after he had assumed supreme power, the King appointed a new, 10-member Council of Ministers, under his chairmanship. Former Prime Ministers Dr Tulsi Giri and Kirti Nidhi Bista were appointed to serve as Vice-Chairmen. King Gyanendra's assumption of power met with an unfavourable international response, with Nepal's key allies, India and the United Kingdom, suspending military aid to the country and several nations recalling their ambassadors from Nepal in protest.

In March 2005 Thapa announced the foundation of his new political party, the Rashtriya Janashakti Party (RJP—National People's Power Party). Meanwhile, protests against the King's actions gathered momentum. At the same time, the Maoist insurgency intensified, with several clashes taking place between rebels and government troops. The state of emergency was lifted at the end of April, although public meetings and demonstrations continued to be prohibited, and police powers of arrest and detention were extended. Meanwhile, former Prime Minister Deuba was charged with corruption offences by the newly established Royal Commission for Corruption Control (RCCC); Deuba refused to acknowledge the legitimacy of the body. In June Deuba was cleared by the RCCC of charges relating to the misappropriation of money from the Prime Minister's Relief Fund. However, in the following month the former Prime Minister was convicted of charges of embezzlement relating to the issuing of a water contract and sentenced to a two-year prison term.

Meanwhile, in May 2005 an alliance of seven political parties, including the NCP, announced a joint agenda for the restoration of democracy in Nepal, demanding that King Gyanendra end his period of direct rule and that the House of Representatives, which had been dissolved in 2002, be recalled. In June 2005 Maoist rebels were responsible for the detonation of a land-mine under a bus in the southern district of Chitwan, which resulted in the deaths of 39 civilians. The Maoists subsequently apologized for the attack, claiming that the bomb had been intended to target security forces, and announced that, henceforth, all attacks on unarmed civilians would be suspended.

In August 2005, as opposition to King Gyanendra's ongoing direct rule intensified, it was announced that the seven-party alliance had decided to begin talks with the CPN (M) and to plan joint protests against the King. It cited positive gestures by the Maoist group, such as its suspension of attacks on unarmed civilians, as the reason for co-operation, having consistently maintained that it would be willing to hold discussions with the rebels only if they renounced violence. In September the Maoists announced a three-month, unilateral cease-fire, an offer to which the Government responded cautiously. In October the Government declared that elections would take place to Nepal's municipal councils in February 2006. Shortly afterwards King Gyanendra stated that elections to the House of Representatives would take place in April 2007. In November 2005, following talks with the CPN (M), the opposition alliance announced that it had reached a 12-point agreement with the rebels intended to restore democracy to Nepal. The agreement included a boycott of the February 2006 municipal elections and the election of a constituent assembly, the latter being a long-standing Maoist demand.

In December 2005 an extensive reorganization of the Council of Ministers took place, in which eight ministers were dismissed and several ministers from the RPP and RJP were appointed. In January 2006 the CPN (M) stated that the cease-fire had come to an end, owing to the Government continuing to authorize offensive operations against them. The insurgency subsequently intensified. In the following month the municipal elections were held, taking place in only 36 of the 58 municipal councils owing to an insufficient number of candidates and against the background of a four-day general strike co-ordinated by the Maoists. Turn-out reached an estimated 20% of registered voters, according to official figures, although the major opposition parties, which boycotted the polls, claimed that the figure was significantly lower. Later that month the RCCC was outlawed after the Supreme Court ruled that its orders were not valid. Former Prime Minister Deuba was subsequently freed from prison, having been convicted of corruption offences by the body in the previous year. In March the Maoists instigated an indefinite blockade of Kathmandu in another attempt to force King Gyanendra to end his period of direct rule. Meanwhile, the Government offered an amnesty to any Maoist rebels who surrendered before a mid-June 2006 deadline.

The reinstatement of Parliament

In April 2006 the opposition alliance called a nation-wide general strike. Mass demonstrations followed, in response to which the Government announced the imposition of a 'shoot-on-sight' curfew. As thousands of protesters defied the curfew and violent clashes ensued, King Gyanendra's position appeared increasingly untenable. Following almost three weeks of popular demonstrations, the King offered to permit the opposition alliance to name a new Prime Minister. However, this offer was rejected and the protests continued to escalate. Several days later, in accordance with opposition demands, the King announced that he would reinstate Parliament, thus quelling the unrest. The CPN (M) rejected the royal offer and vowed to continue its insurgency, accusing the political parties of betraying the 12-point agreement. It did, none the less, agree to observe a three-month cease-fire. The opposition alliance subsequently nominated former Prime Minister G. P. Koirala to lead a new Government. The House of Representatives formally convened at the end of April and approved legislation enabling the establishment of a constituent assembly to redraft the country's Constitution. In June Koirala expanded the coalition Council of Ministers to include representatives of a further two members of the seven-party alliance. At this stage all of the seven-party alliance members were represented in the Government, with the exception of the Nepal Workers' and Peasants' Party.

On 3 May 2006 the Council of Ministers had announced a cease-fire with the CPN (M), offering to declassify the group as a terrorist organization and to abandon terrorism charges in exchange for the holding of peace talks. According to government figures, 467 of an estimated 1,000 Maoist prisoners had been freed by 25 May. Despite the Maoists' assertions that they would not enter into negotiations until all their prisoners had been released, and their insistence that the formation of a constituent assembly was subject to the abolition of the existing Constitution, legislature and monarchy, the Government and the CPN (M) engaged in a preliminary round of discussions on 26 May. Meanwhile, on 18 May the House of Representatives approved a resolution divesting the King of his role as Commander-in-Chief of the Army, his authority to make military appointments and nominate an heir, and his legal immunity and exemption from taxes. Nepal was officially transformed from a Hindu state into a secular state in an attempt to extricate the concept of a divinely instituted monarchy from the national ideology. The transfer of power away from the monarchy continued in June: the King was no longer able to veto legislation, he was not required to open and close parliamentary sessions, and he lost the authority to announce government policy.

In June 2006 talks between Koirala and Prachanda in Kathmandu led to the announcement that the CPN (M) would be included in a new interim government, which was to oversee elections for a constituent assembly. At Koirala's request, a UN team arrived in Nepal at the end of July to determine weapons management strategies for the Nepalese army and the People's Liberation Army (PLA) of the Maoists; Koirala reportedly deemed the decommissioning of weapons as a prerequisite of the entry of the CPN (M) into government. Also at the end of July, Prachanda extended the cease-fire by three months. On 9 August Koirala and Prachanda agreed to a system of management for the Nepalese army and the PLA, which stipulated that the former would remain in barracks, while the latter would reside in holding camps. Two days later Lt-Gen. Rukmangad Katuwal assumed the post of Chief of Army Staff, replacing Gen. Pyar Jung Thapa, who had been among those accused of using excessive force to quell the April uprising. In October further talks between the negotiating teams of the Government and the Maoists produced a tentative schedule for elections to the constituent assembly, with a deadline of the end of June 2007 for the assembly's first session. Prachanda reiterated his demand for the declaration of a republic, stating that an agreement to this effect would ensure the disarmament of Maoist forces. He announced a further three-month extension of the cease-fire in October 2006. The Comprehensive Peace Agreement (CPA), which was signed by Koirala and Prachanda on 21 November, provided for the establishment of an interim constitution, assembly and council of ministers by 1 December, and was hailed as the end of a civil war that had claimed the lives of more than 13,000 people. A disarmament agreement soon followed, the terms of which included the complete cessation of hostilities by both sides. The Maoist military forces were to be contained in cantonments and their weapons registered and impounded under UN supervision, while the Nepalese army, which was to remain in barracks, would also have its arms locked away. With the signing of an Interim Constitution in December, constitutional powers of governance were reassigned from the monarchy to the Prime Minister. The National Assembly and House of Representatives were dissolved with the promulgation of the Interim Constitution in mid-January 2007. In their place, an Interim Parliament, or 'Legislature-Parliament', was established; this body included members of the original 1999 Parliament as well as appointees selected by the seven-party alliance and the CPN (M). A few days later the Maoists announced the closure of their 'People's Governments' and 'People's Courts'. The UN Mission in Nepal (UNMIN) was established in January 2007, at the request of the seven-party alliance and the CPN (M). UNMIN's main task was to help in overseeing a fair and free election to the constituent assembly and to monitor the proper enactment of the CPA (including the disarmament and integration of the PLA into the regular army).

However, tensions among the Madhesi people in southern Nepal threatened to hinder the peace process in 2007. Madhesi groups, which were demanding increased independence for their region and greater representation in government, organized demonstrations and called strikes to draw attention to their campaign. The protests were at times violent and clashes with police resulted in several fatalities. At the end of January Koirala, reportedly in response to Madhesi demands, asserted that, under the terms of the forthcoming permanent constitution, Nepal would become a federal state. However, the ethnic unrest continued into the following month amid claims that the Government had not adequately addressed Madhesi needs. A government committee was subsequently established to negotiate with Madhesi groups. Constitutional amendments approved by the Interim Parliament in March provided for proportional representation and a federal style of government, and the revision of constituency boundaries to grant one-half of parliamentary seats to the southern plains, where an estimated 50% of the population resided. Despite these concessions, an element of dissatisfaction remained, with the Madhesi Jana Adhikar Forum Nepal (Madhesi People's Rights Forum Nepal—MPRFN) demanding total autonomy.

Progress in other areas of reform was halting. Conditions in the PLA holding camps were reported to be poor, with hundreds of troops departing, in contravention of the peace agreement. As late as March 2007, Prachanda commented that the arms-decommissioning process had not been completed, and large numbers of Maoist troops had yet to move into the camps. Meanwhile, in February the King's image was removed from bank notes as part of a general move to eradicate symbols of the monarchy from public life; nationalization of the monarchy's assets was also proposed. In the following month Koirala suggested that the voluntary abdication of the King and the Crown Prince would be a positive outcome. According to the Interim Constitution, the future of the monarchy was to be decided at the inaugural session of the constituent assembly.

In April 2007 an Interim Council of Ministers was approved by the Interim Parliament. G. P. Koirala was reappointed interim Prime Minister, heading an administration that included five members of the CPN (M). The UML was assigned responsibility for foreign affairs and the newly created peace and reconstruction portfolio. In May the Government announced the postponement of elections to the constituent assembly until November. In July the CPN (M) registered itself as a political party with the Election Commission of Nepal.

Although it had been agreed that the fate of the monarchy lay with the constituent assembly, demands for the declaration of a republic continued to be made. Seven royal palaces were nationalized by the Government in August 2007. In September the NCP and the NCP (D) announced their merger. In the same month the CPN (M) withdrew from the Government, citing the continuing existence of the monarchy and disagreement over the composition of the constituent assembly as major obstacles to co-operation with its coalition partners. A period of intense negotiations ensued, during which the CPN (M)'s numerous demands were considered by the remaining parties of the governing alliance, amid fears for the future of the peace process. In October the elections were postponed indefinitely. In November the Interim Parliament approved a motion that reiterated the CPN (M)'s key stipulations: the declaration of a republic and the utilization of the proportional representation system for all constituent assembly seats. The Maoists had gained the support of the UML but not the NCP, and the motion, although approved, was consequently unable to garner the two-thirds' majority required for a constitutional amendment. However, in December an amended version of the motion secured the requisite two-thirds of the vote, specifying that, although the monarchy was to be abolished, this change would only come into effect upon the approval of the constituent assembly. More than one-half of the assembly was to be determined by a system of proportional representation, with the bulk of the remainder to be directly elected, in addition to several appointed deputies; elections were scheduled for April 2008. A few days later, the CPN (M) returned to government.

Meanwhile, in the latter half of 2007 tensions remained and the security situation deteriorated in the Terai region, where the MPRFN and numerous other Madhesi groups continued to campaign for autonomy. In December the Minister of Environment, Science and Technology, Mahantha Thakur, resigned, together with several Madhesi members of the Interim Parliament, citing the Government's unwillingness to address the ongoing unrest in the Terai. Shortly after these resignations, the Samyukta Loktantrik Madhesi Morcha (United Democratic Madhesi Front—UDMF), an alliance of three political organizations—the MPRFN, the Sadbhavana Party (a breakaway faction of the NSP) and the Terai Madhes Loktantrik Party—was established. In February 2008 blockades orchestrated by the UDMF caused widespread disruption in the south of the country and led to fuel shortages in Kathmandu and elsewhere. Later in the month the Government and the UDMF signed an agreement ending the blockades and allowing for increased autonomy and representation of Madhesis on party lists and in institutions such as the Nepalese army. However, concerns remained regarding the campaigns of more hard-line Madhesi groups operating outside the negotiations.

The Maoists take power and the monarchy is abolished

At the constituent assembly elections, which were held on 10 April 2008, the CPN (M) won 220 out of a total of 575 elected seats under the mixed electoral system, twice as many as the NCP, which came second with 110 seats. The UML expressed disappointment at its election to only 103 seats, putting it in third place and prompting the resignation of the party's General Secretary, M. K. Nepal, while the MPRFN won 52. Although the period leading up to the polls had been marked by bombings and violent clashes, the day of the election was largely peaceful, with a relatively sizeable proportion of the electorate participating (around 60%). Prachanda declared victory on behalf of the CPN (M) and indicated that he would lead a coalition government. The CPN (M) also urged the King to abdicate voluntarily in advance of the inevitable declaration of a republic. This declaration was duly made following overwhelming approval at the inaugural session of the Constituent Assembly on 28 May, when the monarchy was abolished; King Gyanendra voluntarily vacated the royal palace in Kathmandu in June, opting to move to his summer residence outside the city. Meanwhile, the CPN (M)'s lack of a parliamentary majority proved to be an obstacle in the formation of a new government, with a lack of consensus between the three major parties over the mandate of the new post of president, a position Prachanda was keen to assume. Although by early June the CPN (M) had accepted the notion of a civilian president, the impasse continued, with the CPN (M) ministers of the interim Government tendering their resignations over a dispute with Prime Minister Koirala and the NCP. In June Koirala stated that his resignation would come into effect upon the election of somebody to the presidency, which, it was decided, would be a largely ceremonial role. In a separate development, the seven-party alliance had reportedly been dissolved. A presidential election finally took place in the Constituent Assembly on 19 July, but the leading candidate, Ram Baran Yadav, who was supported by the NCP, was unable to secure a majority. Paramananda Jha, who had been nominated by the MPRFN, was elected Vice-President. At a second round of voting two days later, Yadav defeated the CPN (M) candidate, Ramraja Prasad Singh, securing the support of the UML as well as the MPRFN. Notably, Yadav, Singh and Jha were all Madhesis. Yadav took office on 23 July, and on the following day Subas Chandra Nembang was elected Chairman of the Constituent Assembly. The CPN (M), disgruntled with the alliance between the NCP, the UML and the MPRFN and the resulting failure of its presidential candidate, initially warned that it would decline to form a government. However, with the support of the UML and MPRFN, in mid-August Prachanda defeated NCP candidate and former Prime Minister Sher Bahadur Deuba in a vote held in the Constituent Assembly for the post of prime minister. Prachanda assumed the premiership on 18 August and appointed a new Council of Ministers, comprising members of the CPN (M), the MPRFN, the Sadbhavana Party, the UML, the People's Front Nepal (Janamorcha Nepal) and the Communist Party of Nepal (United) (CPN—U). The NCP remained outside the Government, forming the opposition. On 30 October the country's state title was officially changed from the Kingdom of Nepal to the Federal Democratic Republic of Nepal. In November the Constituent Assembly approved a timetable for the new constitution, with a deadline of May 2010 for its promulgation. The first draft of the constitution was expected to be made public in September 2009. A constitutional committee appointed by the Constituent Assembly began drafting the document in December 2008. However, ongoing disputes between the Government and the opposition, and the unresolved issue of the integration of some 19,000 former Maoist fighters into the army—which strained relations between the Government and the military in early 2009—continued to hamper progress in other areas. In January 2009 the CPN (M) was restyled the Unified Communist Party of Nepal (Maoist)—UCPN (M)—following merger with the CPN (Unity Centre-Masal).

The collapse of the Maoist Government and the ensuing political crisis

On 4 May 2009 Nepal was confronted with a serious political crisis and the peace process appeared increasingly fragile following the resignation of Prime Minister Prachanda and the withdrawal of the UCPN (M) from the ruling coalition. This dramatic development resulted from President Yadav's refusal to accept Prachanda's earlier dismissal of the Chief of Army Staff, Lt-Gen. Rukmangad Katuwal, who was allegedly defying government orders to integrate former rebel fighters into the national army (claiming that they were politically indoctrinated) and was actively recruiting new personnel into the army (in contravention of the peace agreement). A series of protests by Maoist activists demanding the removal of the reinstated army chief subsequently took place in the capital, and a number of clashes occurred between the protesters and riot police. The President set a deadline of 9 May for the formation of a new coalition government, but this date passed without any resolution to the political impasse. The UCPN (M) refused to participate in negotiations unless the President reversed his decision on the reinstatement of Lt-Gen. Katuwal. On 10 May President Yadav directed the Constituent Assembly to elect a new Prime Minister by a majority vote in an attempt to end the political crisis. On 17 May an alliance of 22 political parties, including the NCP and the UML, filed a claim to form a new coalition government and appealed for a parliamentary vote to elect their candidate, the veteran communist leader M. K. Nepal, as the new prime minister. In response, Prachanda stated that the move to form a new administration that excluded that Maoists was a conspiracy to derail the peace process. None the less, M. K. Nepal was elected to the premiership and was sworn in at the end of May at the head of a new, small coalition Government (expanded over the following few weeks).

The Maoists promptly launched a series of anti-Government street protests and strikes in Kathmandu and elsewhere in the country and threatened to renew their revolutionary insurgency. Their demand for the holding of a parliamentary debate on the reinstatement of Lt-Gen. Katuwal (who had since retired) was rejected by Prime Minister Nepal in September 2009. The UCPN (M) responded by continuing to boycott and disrupt the proceedings of the Constituent Assembly; the Maoists succeeded in delaying the approval of the 2009/10 budget for four months, and it was not adopted until November 2009. In December the UCPN (M) led a mass rally in the capital and organized a three-day national strike, which paralyzed the country. The political impasse continued into 2010, and in late April, with only weeks to go before the deadline for the introduction of a new constitution (28 May), the Maoists intensified their protest campaign with the convergence of thousands of their supporters in Kathmandu to attend a mass May Day rally. In an attempt to force the Government to resign, the UCPN (M) announced the enforcement of an indefinite general strike. However, the strike was suspended after less than a week to alleviate the hardships being suffered by the Nepalese people and to recommence negotiations with the Government.

NEPAL

On 28 May 2010, following threats by President Yadav to impose emergency or presidential rule if the political impasse were not resolved, the NCP, the UML and the Maoists agreed to extend the tenure of the Constituent Assembly by one year, on the condition that Prime Minister Nepal resigned to enable the formation of a national consensus government. Accordingly, M. K. Nepal announced his resignation from the premiership on 30 June; however, he and his Government were to remain in their posts in an acting capacity pending the appointment of a consensus administration by 7 July. When the formation of a new government failed to materialize by this deadline, owing to lack of agreement between the three main parties, the President declared that the Constituent Assembly would elect a new prime minister by majority vote. This proved to be an extremely lengthy process. Between July and November the Assembly made 16 unsuccessful attempts to elect a new premier. The main candidates in the first seven rounds of voting were Prachanda of the UCPN (M) and Ram Chandra Poudel of the NCP; the UML's candidate, Jhala Nath Khanal, withdrew from the process following his failure to win a majority of votes in the first two rounds of voting in July. On each of the seven occasions that he participated in the poll, Prachanda received more votes than his rival, but failed to achieve the requisite 301 votes (constituting a majority in the 601-seat Assembly). The deadlock in the voting process was caused by the persistent abstention of the UML and smaller parliamentary parties (notably the various Madhesi organizations), which claimed that neither candidate was acceptable. The prolonged stalemate led to economic instability (with delays in the implementation of the budget and stoppages in work on development projects) and widespread public disillusionment with the political parties and their leaders. The peace process also came to a virtual halt, with thousands of former Maoist militants remaining in UN-monitored holding camps. In late September Sushil Koirala was elected as the new President of the NCP, defeating his closest rival, Sher Bahadur Deuba, by more than 300 votes. At the end of the month, prior to the eighth attempt by the Constituent Assembly to elect a new prime minister, Prachanda withdrew from the contest following a pact with the UML. With the UCPN (M) now abstaining from the voting process, the sole remaining candidate, Poudel, failed to garner the required majority in the nine further polls that were held in 2010 (only 101 legislators participated in the 16th round, which was conducted on 4 November).

Meanwhile, in an effort to resolve numerous outstanding issues over the drafting of the new constitution, a seven-member multi-party task force, headed by Prachanda, was established in October 2010. Following the failure of the Constitutional Council to convene for several months, a number of constitutional bodies, including the Office of the Auditor-General and the Election Commission, lacked permanent office heads and risked becoming dysfunctional. In November the three main parties held a series of crisis talks to discuss the stalled peace process (the stated priority of the NCP and the UML) and power-sharing and government formation (the Maoists' primary concern). In an effort to facilitate the ending of the political vacuum, the Supreme Court ruled in December that no legislators would henceforth be permitted to abstain from voting in the prime ministerial election process. In January 2011, the NCP having withdrawn its candidacy from the scheduled 17th round of prime ministerial elections, President Yadav gave the three main parties a week-long deadline to attempt once again to form a government of national consensus. However, this approach too proved unsuccessful owing to the persistent intransigence of the three parties regarding their respective claims to the leadership of the new government.

On 15 January 2011 UNMIN commenced its withdrawal from Nepal following the decision of the NCP and the UML not to request an extension of the mission's mandate (despite the Maoists' requests to do so). A few days later Prachanda formally handed responsibility for the 19,000 former PLA troops remaining in the holding camps to a special government committee (headed by the Prime Minister), which was to supervise the disarmament, integration and rehabilitation of the ex-militants.

Recent developments: the appointment of Prime Minister Jhala Nath Khanal

The seven-month political stalemate came to an end on 3 February 2011 when the Chairman of the UML, Jhala Nath Khanal, with the support of the UCPN (M) (Prachanda having withdrawn his candidacy at the last minute), was elected as the new Prime Minister by the Constituent Assembly. Khanal won a clear majority, with 368 of the 557 votes cast; Poudel received 122 votes and Bijaya Kumar Gachchhadar of the MPRFN (Democratic) took 67. Khanal was sworn in on 6 February, but appointments to the new Council of Ministers were delayed by several weeks of protracted negotiations with the Maoists over power-sharing arrangements (notably the question of the allocation of the home affairs portfolio). A few days after the inauguration of the new Prime Minister it emerged that, prior to Khanal's election, the UCPN (M) and the UML had signed a secret seven-point agreement regarding their future co-operation in government. Of some controversy were allegations that the agreement had included plans to establish a military body of former Maoist combatants that was to be separate from the country's regular army. The NCP, which had decided to stay in opposition in protest against the secret pact between the UML and the Maoists, claimed that the formation of such a body would prove highly detrimental to the peace process. In early March Khanal expanded his core three-member UML Council of Ministers to include representatives of the UCPN (M); Krishna Bahadur Mahara was assigned one of the deputy premierships, but Khanal himself retained control of the home affairs post. The UML and the Maoists expressed concern at the NCP's refusal to join the Government, claiming that the party's absence from the Council of Ministers would jeopardize the drafting of the constitution (scheduled to be completed by 28 May) and the peace process. In early April the Council of Ministers was further enlarged to incorporate 12 new UML ministers and state ministers. The Maoists persisted in their demand that they be allotted the home affairs portfolio (as agreed in the seven-point accord), but the Prime Minister countered that, prior to the transfer of responsibility for the ministry, greater progress should be made on the rehabilitation and integration of the former PLA soldiers.

In early May, following protracted negotiations with the Maoists, Prime Minister Khanal announced a further expansion of the Council of Ministers, appointing 12 new UCPN (M) ministers and state ministers. In a major concession to the Maoists, Krishna Bahadur Mahara was accorded the disputed home affairs portfolio, in addition to his existing Deputy Prime Minister role. The appointment, which effectively gave the UCPN (M) control over internal security in the country, was strongly criticized by the opposition and by some members of Khanal's UML. The coalition cabinet was further broadened with the addition of three members of the regional MPRFN—party leader Upendra Yadav was appointed Deputy Prime Minister and Minister of Foreign Affairs—and one representative from each of the CPN—U and the ML. The distribution of ministerial posts among the Maoists, especially the allocation of the home affairs portfolio, appeared to further exacerbate internal schisms within the UCPN (M). Barshaman Pun, a leading Maoist candidate for the home affairs position, resigned as Minister of Peace and Reconstruction, a post to which he had been appointed in March; furthermore, by mid-May, as a result of factional disagreements, four Maoist ministerial nominees had refused to take their oaths of office. Owing to the imminent expiry of the latest deadline (28 May) for the drafting of a new constitution, on 12 May the Government tabled a parliamentary bill proposing to extend the tenure of the Constituent Assembly by a further year. The measure required a two-thirds' majority in the House of Representatives.

Regional Affairs

In 1978 the old Trade and Transit Treaty between Nepal and India was replaced by two treaties, one concerning bilateral trade between the two countries, the other allowing Nepal to develop trade with other countries via India. Relations with India deteriorated considerably in March 1989, however, when India decided not to renew the treaties, insisting that a common treaty covering both issues be negotiated. Nepal refused, stressing the importance of keeping the treaties separate, on the grounds that trade issues are negotiable, whereas the right of transit is a recognized basic right of land-locked countries. In response, India closed 13 of the 15 transit points through which most of Nepal's trade was conducted. Severe shortages of food and fuel ensued. It was widely believed that a major issue aggravating the dispute was Nepal's purchase of weapons from the People's Republic of China in 1988, which, according to India, violated the Treaty of Peace and Friendship concluded by India and Nepal in 1950. Diplomatic relations between Nepal and India remained strained throughout 1989, with trade at a virtual standstill. Following several rounds of senior-level talks, a joint communiqué was signed by the two countries in June

1990, restoring trade relations and reopening the transit points, and assuring mutual consultations on matters of security. A few days earlier, as an apparent gesture of goodwill to India, the Nepalese Government had told the Chinese Government to defer indefinitely the delivery of the final consignment of weapons destined for Nepal. The visit to Kathmandu by the Indian Prime Minister in February 1991 (the first official visit to Nepal by an Indian head of government since 1977) helped to reaffirm the traditionally amicable ties between the two countries. Separate trade and transit treaties were signed during a visit by Prime Minister Koirala to India in December 1991; these treaties were both subsequently renewed. A major breakthrough in Indo-Nepalese relations was achieved in February 1996, when the Prime Ministers of the two countries formally signed a treaty in New Delhi, India, regarding the shared utilization of the waters of the Mahakali River basin (for irrigation, general consumption and the production of hydroelectric power). The costs and benefits of the project, which involved the construction of a massive hydroelectric power plant, were to be divided between Nepal and India, although not, some critics claimed, to Nepal's benefit. During a visit to Nepal by the Indian Prime Minister in June 1997, the Mahakali Treaty was formally endorsed, and India granted Nepal access to Bangladeshi ports through a new transit facility across Indian territory via the Karkavita-Phulbari road. Some tension in Indo-Nepalese relations, nevertheless, remained; this centred on border demarcation disputes and, in particular, on the Indian border police's use of territory that Nepal claimed as its own in the far west of the country (namely the strategically situated Kalapani junction between India, Nepal and China, which covers an area of about 35 sq km). In late 2001 India supplied Nepal with two helicopters and arms to assist its neighbour in its campaign against the Maoist insurgency. In early 2002 the Nepalese and Indian Governments held talks on the civil disorder problem in Nepal and India repeated its offer of financial assistance. From early 2003, however, the Indian Government became increasingly concerned about King Gyanendra's perceived disregard for democracy. In February 2005 its concerns were realized when the King dismissed the Government and assumed executive power. India condemned the King's actions and suspended military aid to Nepal. It also intensified security along the shared border, owing to increased fears of infiltration by Maoist insurgents and their possible co-operation with rebels operating in India's fractious north-eastern states. In July India resumed non-lethal military aid to Nepal. During the Maoists' tenure of power in Nepal in 2008–09 there was growing concern expressed among certain sectors of the Indian authorities regarding the Nepalese Maoists' perceived anti-India stance and their links with China and with India's own Maoist insurgencies. In August 2009 the new Prime Minister, M. K. Nepal, made an official visit to India during which the two countries signed a trade treaty and India pledged to assist its neighbour with development projects such as road and rail links (notably the Terai Roads Project, which envisaged the construction of more than 1,450 km of asphalted roads in the Terai region) and the establishment of a police academy. In August 2010, following the resignation of M. K. Nepal's Government, the former Indian foreign secretary and ambassador to Nepal, Shyam Saran, was dispatched by the Indian authorities as a special envoy to Nepal with the aim of persuading the Nepalese parties to reach consensus on the formation of a new administration. The Indian delegation was viewed with suspicion by the Maoists, who believed that India did not wish to see them regain power and was exerting pressure on other parties not to support them. In January 2011 President Yadav undertook a 10-day official visit to India, during which he held discussions with the Indian Government regarding Nepal's ongoing attempts to break the political deadlock.

The People's Republic of China has contributed a considerable amount to the Nepalese economy. The first meeting of a joint committee on economic co-operation took place in 1984. This committee met for a second time (and thenceforth annually) in Kathmandu in 1986, when China agreed to increase its imports from Nepal in order to minimize trade imbalances. Relations between Nepal and China improved further during the late 1980s and 1990s, as indicated by reciprocal visits made by high-ranking Nepalese and Chinese officials (notably, a state visit to Nepal was conducted by the Chinese President, Jiang Zemin, in 1996). In May 2001 the leaders of Nepal and China signed a six-point co-operation agreement to improve cross-border trade, increase road and aviation links, and promote tourism. During the 2000s China continued to expand its investments in Nepal, particularly in the areas of hydroelectricity, telecommunications and road construction.

In 1985 it was agreed that Nepal's border with Tibet (the Xizang Autonomous Region) should be opened. Following the outbreak of ethnic violence in Tibet in 1989, however, the border between Nepal and Tibet was closed indefinitely. The Nepalese authorities have been consistent in their commitment to the 'One China' policy and in their efforts to repatriate refugees fleeing from Tibet. In 1993 G. P. Koirala paid an informal visit to Tibet—the first visit to the region by a Nepalese premier since the 1950s. In 1995, however, the Nepalese authorities banned a proposed peace march by Tibetans through Nepalese territory. During a visit to China by the Nepalese Minister of Foreign Affairs in August 2000 an agreement was reached to allow Nepal increased use of a new road in Tibet. Greater technological and economic co-operation was also achieved, therefore noticeably increasing bilateral trade. Nepal provoked strong criticism from the UN and Western governments in May 2003, after it helped Chinese officials to deport 18 Tibetan refugees from Kathmandu to Tibet (Nepal's usual policy was to transfer Tibetan refugees to officials of the UN High Commissioner for Refugees—UNHCR). It was reported in June that a further 19 Tibetans had been arrested in the western Nepalese district of Accham. In 2008 a series of demonstrations was held by Tibetan refugees in Kathmandu, as the approach of the Beijing Olympic Games in China drew international attention to the Tibet issue. The Nepalese police force was widely criticized for its reportedly violent suppression of the protests and the arrests of hundreds of activists; at the same time, China urged the Nepalese Government to control the demonstrations more stringently.

Ties with Bangladesh are also significant, particularly regarding the utilization of joint water resources. Large-scale migration from Bangladesh has resulted in a notable demographic transformation in Nepal, with the Muslim population increasing from around 4% of the total in the early 1990s to, unofficially, about 10% by the end of the decade. In January 2001 the Nepalese Minister of Foreign Affairs visited Bangladesh, where agreements on greater economic and transport co-operation were reached.

In December 1982 Nepal and Pakistan strengthened their trade links by renewing a 1962 agreement, and in 1983 they established a joint economic commission and a regular air link. In March 2005 the joint economic commission met for the first time in 10 years, when a delegation of Pakistani economic officials visited Nepal. In April 2010 the Pakistani Prime Minister, Yousaf Raza Gilani, met Prime Minister M. K. Nepal during a visit to Kathmandu; the two leaders pledged further to enhance bilateral relations and to work together to ensure peace and security in South Asia.

In late 1991 thousands of Bhutanese of Nepalese origin began to arrive at refugee camps in eastern Nepal, following the outbreak of political and ethnic unrest in Bhutan. By early 1996 nearly 100,000 refugees were living in eight camps in the districts of Jhapa and Morang. In the first half of 1993 talks were held between Bhutanese and Nepalese government officials regarding proposals to resolve the issues at stake. The Nepalese Government steadfastly refused to consider any solution that did not include the resettlement in Bhutan of all ethnic Nepalese refugees living in the camps. This proposal was rejected by the Bhutanese Government, which claimed that the majority of the camp population were not actually Bhutanese. The deadlock was broken, however, when a joint statement was signed by the Ministers of Home Affairs of Bhutan and Nepal in July, which committed each side to establishing a 'high-level joint committee' to work towards a settlement (including the categorization of the refugees). In a notable shift in strategy, in January 1996 the Nepalese Government transferred the responsibility of handling the Bhutanese refugee problem from the Ministry of Home Affairs to the Ministry of Foreign Affairs. In April 1997 more than 10,000 Bhutanese refugees gathered at a mass demonstration in the eastern Nepalese town of Damak to demand UN intervention in the crisis. They also demanded that the Nepal Government either resolve the refugee problem or, failing that, 'internationalize' it. Nepal and Bhutan finally achieved a breakthrough at the 10th round of negotiations in December 2000. Both countries agreed that nationality would be verified on the basis of the head of the refugee family for those under 25 years of age; refugees over 25 years of age would be verified on an individual basis. By the end of January 2001 a Joint Verification Team (JVT) had concluded the inspection of refugee camps, and by late 2001 the verification of individuals in the Khudanabari camp had been completed. However, despite two further rounds of negotiations, the process reached a standstill in early 2002, with Bhutan reluctant to accept the individuals already verified, and both Governments undecided over the most suitable way to continue the verification process. In January 2003 Nepal and Bhutan finally harmonized their positions on the categorization of the refugees into four different groups and arrangements were commenced to conduct the repatriation to Bhutan of about 70 families (comprising around 300 people who were in the category of being Bhutanese nationals who had been forcefully evicted—Category I) by the end of the year. The majority of residents of the Khudanabari camp were categorized as either Bhutanese nationals who had left Bhutan voluntarily (Category II) or as non-Bhutanese (Category III); the remainder were classified as Bhutanese who had committed criminal acts (Category IV). It was agreed that the JVT would review the remaining appeals from people in the Khudunabari camp in November and then begin verification of the Sanischare camp. The two countries also decided that Bhutan would be fully responsible for any Category I persons, while Category II people could apply for either Bhutanese or Nepalese citizenship, in accordance with the respective laws. However, in December the Bhutanese members of the JVT were attacked in the Khudanabari camp by several thousand refugees protesting against the terms and conditions of the agreement. The JVT members were subsequently withdrawn to Thimphu, Bhutan, and talks between Bhutan and Nepal were suspended. In October 2006 the US Government offered to resettle as many as 60,000 of the refugees (who by now totalled around 106,000). This met with a mixed response: some argued that third-country resettlement would amount to an exoneration of Bhutan's actions, while others welcomed the proposal. In the following month Australia, Canada and New Zealand also offered asylum to the refugees, although proposed intake numbers were not supplied. In late 2007 it was reported that the refugees were facing 'severe intimidation' from political leaders who were opposed to the offers of resettlement abroad on the grounds that this would undermine their political struggle to settle all the 'camp people' in Bhutan. Nevertheless, in March 2008 the resettlement of refugees in the USA and New Zealand began. According to UNHCR, by the end of February 2011 more than 43,500 persons claiming Bhutanese refugee status had been resettled in third countries since November 2007: the USA had taken the majority of these (just over 37,000), followed by Canada, Australia, New Zealand, Norway, Denmark, the Netherlands and the United Kingdom. In early 2011 an estimated 69,203 persons remained in seven camps in Nepal, around three-quarters of whom were reported to have expressed an interest in third-country resettlement and were expected to leave by the end of 2014. In February 2011 the Nepalese authorities announced plans to consolidate the seven camps in eastern Nepal into two by the end of 2012. In April 2011 the Bhutanese Prime Minister, Jigmi Yozer Thinley, in his capacity of Chairman of the South Asian Association for Regional Co-operation (SAARC, see p. 417), paid a three-day official visit to Nepal, during which he held talks with his Nepalese counterpart, Jhala Nath Khanal, concerning the resumption of bilateral negotiations on the refugee issue, the proposed establishment of a Nepalese diplomatic mission in the Bhutanese capital, and the formalization of trade and civil aviation agreements. The two leaders agreed to resume talks on the refugee issue (stalled since 2003) at the level of the ministerial joint committee; the date for the resumption of negotiations was to be agreed through diplomatic channels.

CONSTITUTION AND GOVERNMENT

On 15 January 2007 the bicameral legislature instituted by the 1990 Constitution was dissolved upon the promulgation of a new Interim Constitution, and a 330-member Interim Parliament, or 'Legislature-Parliament', was convened by agreement of the seven-party alliance and the Maoists. In accordance with articles stipulated in the Interim Constitution, constitutional powers of governance were reassigned from the monarchy to the acting Prime Minister and the temporary legislature was to facilitate preparations for the democratic election of a constituent assembly by the end of June of that year. The constituent assembly, with a term of two years, would be responsible for drawing up a new permanent constitution. According to the Interim Constitution, the future of the monarchy was to be decided at the first official sitting of the constituent assembly. In December 2007 a parliamentary resolution declaring Nepal a republic received the requisite two-thirds' majority for a constitutional amendment, but this decision did not come into effect until the inaugural session of the Constituent Assembly, held in May 2008. At this stage, the Interim Parliament was dissolved. In mid-2008 the Constituent Assembly elected a new President, Vice-President and Prime Minister; the presidency was a largely ceremonial position. Owing to the ongoing political instability the deadline for the introduction of a new constitution—28 May 2010—was not met, and on that date the Government and the main opposition parties agreed to extend the tenure of the Constituent Assembly by one year. In mid-May 2011 the process of drafting a new constitution remained incomplete and the Government was seeking a further one-year extension of the Constituent Assembly.

For the purposes of local administration, Nepal is divided into 14 zones, 75 districts, 3,913 village development committees and 58 municipalities, which are together grouped into five development regions. Each of the districts is headed by a permanent chief district officer, who is responsible for maintaining law and order and for co-ordinating the work of field agencies of the various government ministries.

REGIONAL AND INTERNATIONAL CO-OPERATION

Nepal is a member of the Asian Development Bank (ADB, see p. 202), the Colombo Plan (see p. 446) and the South Asian Association for Regional Co-operation (SAARC, see p. 417), all of which seek to encourage regional economic development.

Having joined the UN in 1955, Nepal is a member of the Economic and Social Commission for Asia and the Pacific (ESCAP, see p. 37). Nepal became a member of the World Trade Organization (WTO, see p. 430) in 2004.

ECONOMIC AFFAIRS

In 2009, according to estimates by the World Bank, Nepal's gross national income (GNI), measured at average 2007–09 prices, was US $12,985m., equivalent to $440 per head (or $1,180 per head on an international purchasing-power parity basis). During 2000–08, it was estimated, the population increased at an average annual rate of 2.1%, while gross domestic product (GDP) per head increased, in real terms, by an average of 1.7% per year. Overall GDP increased, in real terms, at an average annual rate of 3.7% in 2000–09. According to the Asian Development Bank (ADB), real GDP grew by by 5.8% in 2007/08, by 3.8% in 2008/09 and by 4.0% in 2009/10.

Agriculture (including forestry and fishing) contributed an estimated 32.6% of GDP in the fiscal year ending 15 July 2009. The sector was projected to engage an estimated 92.9% of the economically active population at mid-2011, according to FAO figures. The principal crops are rice, maize, millet, wheat, sugar cane, potatoes and vegetables, and melons. According to the ADB, during 2000–09 agricultural GDP increased by an average of 3.5% per year. The sector grew by 5.8% in 2007/08 and by 3.0% in 2008/09.

Industry (comprising mining, manufacturing, construction and utilities) employed 13.4% of the labour force in 2001, and provided an estimated 15.8% of GDP in 2008/09, according to official figures. About 60% of Nepal's industrial output derives from traditional cottage industries, and the remainder from modern industries. During 2000–09 industrial GDP increased at an average annual rate of 2.5%, according to the ADB. Industrial production rose by 1.7% in 2007/08 but fell by 0.2% in 2008/09.

Mining employed only 0.2% of the labour force in 2001, and contributed an estimated 0.5% of GDP in 2008/09. According to the ADB, during 2000–09 mining GDP increased by an average of 4.4% per year. The sector's GDP rose by 5.5% in 2007/08 but grew by just 0.7% in 2008/09. Mica is mined east of Kathmandu, and there are also small deposits of lignite, copper, talc, limestone, cobalt and iron ore. Geophysical investigations have indicated that the Siwalik range and the Terai belt are potential prospective areas for petroleum.

Manufacturing contributed an estimated 6.8% of GDP in 2008/09, and employed about 8.8% of the labour force in 2001. According to the ADB, manufacturing GDP increased at an average annual rate of 0.6% in 2000–09. Manufacturing production fell by 0.9% in 2007/08 and by 1.0% in 2008/09. The principal branches of the sector include textiles (particularly carpets and rugs), food products, wearing apparel and tobacco products. Traditional cottage industries include basket-making and the production of cotton fabrics and edible oils.

Construction contributed an estimated 6.8% of GDP in 2008/09, and employed about 2.9% of the labour force in 2001. According to the ADB, construction GDP increased at an average annual rate of 3.1% in 2000–09. It rose by 5.1% in 2007/08 and by 0.9% in 2008/09.

Energy is derived principally from traditional sources (particularly fuelwood). However, imports of mineral fuel and lubricants (mainly for the transport sector) comprised an estimated 15.0% of the cost of total imports in 2009/10. In addition, Nepal's rivers are exploited for hydroelectric power (HEP) production, but in mid-2002 it was estimated that only about 1% of the country's huge potential generating capacity (83m. kW) was being utilized. In January 2004 the 144,000-kW Kali Gandaki A HEP plant was officially inaugurated. The project, the country's largest, began generating electricity in 2002. Nepal hoped to export excess electricity to India. Several other HEP projects were under construction in the 2000s. In August 2004 Cairn Energy Co of the United Kingdom signed an agreement with the Nepalese Government to explore for petroleum and gas in a 22,000-sq km area in the Terai plain, near the border with India.

The services sector employed 20.8% of the labour force in 2001. The sector contributed an estimated 51.6% of GDP in 2008/09. The GDP of the services sector increased at an average annual rate of 4.5% in 2000–09, according to the ADB. Sectoral GDP grew by 7.3% in 2007/08 and by 6.3% in 2008/09. By 1996 tourism had emerged as Nepal's major source of foreign exchange; in 1999/2000 revenue from tourism amounted to 12.9% of total foreign-exchange earnings. The Maoist insurgency adversely affected visitor levels in the first half of the 2000s. The cessation of hostilities in 2006 and the subsequent peace agreement between the former insurgents and the political parties' alliance—combined with the introduction of additional airline services between Nepal and other Asian countries—led to a significant recovery in the tourism sector. Between 2006 and 2008 tourist arrivals witnessed massive growth, from 383,926 to a record 500,277. Over the same two-year period, revenue from tourism more than doubled, from US $157.0m. in 2006 to $353.0m. in 2008.

In 2009 Nepal recorded a visible trade deficit of US $3,461.1m., while there was a deficit of $256.1m. on the current account of the balance of payments. In 2007/08 India was the principal source of imports (supplying 65.1% of the total) and the principal market for exports (65.2%). Other major trading partners were the People's Republic of China, the USA, Indonesia and Japan. The principal exports were basic manufactures and manufactured goods (particularly woven articles and garments). The principal imports were basic manufactures, machinery and transport equipment, and mineral fuels and lubricants.

In 2009/10 there was an estimated overall budget deficit of NRs 109,426.2m. Foreign aid plays a vital role in the Nepalese economy. According to the ADB, Nepal's total external debt was US $3,685.2m. at the end of 2008. In that year the cost of debt-servicing was equivalent to 3.6% of receipts from exports of goods and services. The annual rate of inflation averaged 6.4% in 2000–09. Inflation increased by 11.7% in 2007/08, but by October 2008 the rate of inflation had soared to an estimated 14.1%, largely owing to rapidly escalating food and non-food prices. In 2008/09 inflation stood at 11.4%. During the first decade of the 2000s it was estimated that more than 40% of Nepalese workers were underemployed, while urban unemployment, a major problem, particularly among educated youths, stood at around 7%. According to the ADB, the unemployment rate in rural areas in 2004 was 2%.

With an inhospitable terrain comprising isolated valleys and very high mountains and with worrying rates of poverty, Nepal is among the least developed countries in the world. Successive administrations since 1991 have pursued a policy of economic liberalization: many state enterprises have been privatized (although there have been numerous delays in the process), and there have been attempts to reduce the fiscal deficit, to increase revenue mobilization, to restructure and improve the financial sector, and to institute and operate open trade and investment policies. Nepal's accession to the World Trade Organization in 2004 was expected to lead to the further integration of the country into the global economy. However, foreign investment remained negligible, with significant reforms needed if Nepal's attractiveness as an investment destination were to increase. The instability caused by the country's transition from a monarchy to a republic in 2008 and the ensuing political upheaval and general unrest over the following three years did not bode well for the country's short-term economic future. Against a background of Maoist-organized, large-scale demonstrations and strikes, which caused massive disruption to the country's infrastructure, the communist-led coalition Government that assumed power in mid-2009 attempted to impose a degree of economic normalcy: the 2009/10 budget prioritized funding for the rehabilitation of those displaced by the country's civil war and for the rebuilding of vital infrastructure (notably electricity generation to combat serious power shortages). However, the economy was adversely affected by the collapse of the Government in June 2010 and by the seven-month-long political deadlock that followed. The promulgation of the 2010/11 budget was delayed for four months, and numerous development projects were put on hold. In addition, a deceleration in the rate of growth of remittances, together with a widening trade deficit and worsening power outages, all contributed to a projected fall in the GDP growth rate from 4.0% in 2009/10 to 3.8% in 2010/11. On a more positive note, Nepal has enjoyed considerable success in recent years in tackling poverty: the number of those living below the poverty line (about US $160 a year) was estimated to have decreased to 25% of the population in 2010, compared with 31% in 2004. It was also hoped that the tourism sector would help to drive economic recovery in 2011, aided by the resumption of normal governance in February of that year and by the launching of the Nepal Tourism Year 2011 campaign.

PUBLIC HOLIDAYS

The public holidays observed in Nepal vary locally. The dates given below apply to Kathmandu.

2012: 1 January (New Year's Day—Gregorian Calendar), 14 January (Maghi Sankranti), 28 January (Vasant Panchami—Advent of Spring Day), 30 January (Martyrs' Day), 19 February (Rashtriya Prajatantra Divas—National Democracy Day), 20 February (Maha Shivaratri—in honour of Lord Shiva), 22 February (Lhosar, Tibetan New Year), 8 March (Nari Diwas—Women's Day and Phagu Purnima—Holi Festival Day), 22 March (Ghode Jatra—Horse Festival), 1 April (Chaite Dashain/Ram Nawami—Lord Ram's Birthday), 14 April (Navabarsha—New Year's Day), 28 April (Lord Gautam Buddha's Birthday), 1 May (Labour Day), August (Janai Purnima—Sacred Thread Ceremony), August/September (Hartalika Teej—Women's Festival), 10 August (Janmashtami—Lord Krishna's Birthday), September/October (Indra Jatra—Festival of Rain God and, over nine days, Dasain), 16 October (Ghatasthapana), 20–24 October (Durga Puja Festival), 24 October (Vijaya Dashami), 9 November (Constitution Day), 13 November (Laxmi Puja and Diwali—Festival of Lights, over three days), 15 November (Bhai Tika—Brothers' Day).

NEPAL

Statistical Survey

Sources (unless otherwise stated): National Planning Commission Secretariat, Singha Durbar, POB 1284, Kathmandu; tel. (1) 4225879; fax (1) 4226500; e-mail npcs@wlink.com.np; internet www.npc.gov.np; Federation of Nepalese Chambers of Commerce and Industry (FNCCI), Pachali Shahid Shukra FNCCI Milan Marg, Teku, POB 269, Kathmandu; tel. (1) 4262061; fax (1) 4261022; e-mail fncci@mos.com.np; internet www.fncci.org.

Area and Population

AREA, POPULATION AND DENSITY

Area (sq km)	147,181*
Population (census results)	
22 June 1991	18,491,097
22 June 2001†‡	
Males	11,563,921
Females	11,587,502
Total	23,151,423
Population (UN estimates at mid-year)§	
2009	29,331,000
2010	29,853,000
2011	30,376,619
Density (per sq km) at mid-2011	206.4

* 56,827 sq miles.
† Population is *de jure*.
‡ Includes estimates for certain areas in 12 districts where the census could not be conducted, owing to violence and disruption.
§ Source: UN, *World Population Prospects: The 2008 Revision*.

POPULATION BY AGE AND SEX
(UN estimates at mid-2011)

	Males	Females	Total
0–14	5,488,145	5,206,549	10,694,694
15–64	9,026,441	9,394,805	18,421,246
65 and over	566,987	693,692	1,260,679
Total	15,081,573	15,295,046	30,376,619

Source: UN, *World Population Prospects: The 2008 Revision*.

PRINCIPAL TOWNS
(population at 2001 census)

Kathmandu*	671,846	Mahendranagar	80,839
Biratnagar	166,674	Butawal	75,384
Lalitpur	162,991	Janakpur	74,192
Pokhara	156,312	Bhaktapur	72,543
Birgunj	112,484	Hetauda	68,482
Dharan	95,332	Dhangadhi	67,447
Bharatpur	89,323		

* Total for urban agglomeration 1,081,845.

Mid-2010 (incl. suburbs, UN estimate): Kathmandu 1,037,073 (Source: UN, *World Urbanization Prospects: The 2009 Revision*).

BIRTHS AND DEATHS
(annual averages, UN estimates)

	1995–2000	2000–05	2005–10
Birth rate (per 1,000)	34.9	30.1	25.6
Death rate (per 1,000)	9.6	7.7	6.5

Source: UN, *World Population Prospects: The 2008 Revision*.

2001 (estimates): Birth rate 33.1 per 1,000; Death rate 9.6 per 1,000.

Life expectancy (years at birth, WHO estimates): 63 (males 63; females 64) in 2008 (Source: WHO, *World Health Statistics*).

ECONOMICALLY ACTIVE POPULATION
(1999 labour force survey, '000 persons aged 15 years and over)

Agriculture, hunting and forestry	7,190
Fishing	13
Mining and quarrying	8
Manufacturing	553
Electricity, gas and water	26
Construction	344
Wholesale and retail trade	408
Hotels and restaurants	114
Transport, storage and communications	135
Financial intermediation	19
Real estate, renting and business activities	32
Public administration and defence	70
Education	164
Health and social work	34
Other community, social and personal services	57
Private households with employed persons	289
Extra-territorial organizations and bodies	8
Total employed	**9,463**

Source: Central Bureau of Statistics, Kathmandu.

2001 ('000 persons aged 15 years and over): Agriculture, hunting and Forestry 6,496.2; Fishing 8.5; Mining and quarrying 16.0; Manufacturing 872.3; Electricity, gas and water supply 148.2; Construction 286.4; Wholesale and retail trade; repair of motor vehicles, motorcycles and personal and household goods 863.8; Hotels and restaurants 120.9; Transport, storage and communications 161.6; Financial intermediation 46.8; Real estate, renting and business activities 29.9; Public administration and defence and compulsory social security 301.0; Education 228.4; Health and social work 61.8; Other community, social and personal service activities 72.6; Households with employed persons 105.1; Extra-territorial organizations and bodies 58.3; *Sub-total* 9,877.8; Not classifiable by economic activity 22.4; *Total employed* 9,900.2; Unemployed 178.0; *Total labour force* 10,078.2 (Source: ILO).

Mid-2011 (official estimates in '000): Agriculture, etc. 12,367; Total labour force 13,312 (Source: FAO).

Health and Welfare

KEY INDICATORS

Total fertility rate (children per woman, 2008)	2.9
Under-5 mortality rate (per 1,000 live births, 2008)	41
HIV/AIDS (% of persons aged 15–49, 2007)	0.5
Physicians (per 1,000 head, 2004)	0.21
Hospital beds (per 1,000 head, 2001)	0.2
Health expenditure (2007): US $ per head (PPP)	53
Health expenditure (2007): % of GDP	5.1
Health expenditure (2007): public (% of total)	39.7
Access to water (% of persons, 2008)	88
Access to sanitation (% of persons, 2008)	31
Total carbon dioxide emissions ('000 metric tons, 2007)	3,422.2
Carbon dioxide emissions per head (metric tons, 2007)	0.1
Human Development Index (2010): ranking	138
Human Development Index (2010): value	0.428

For sources and definitions, see explanatory note on p. vi.

NEPAL

Agriculture

PRINCIPAL CROPS
('000 metric tons)

	2007	2008	2009
Wheat	1,515	1,572	1,344
Rice, paddy	3,681	4,299	4,524
Barley	28	28	23
Maize	1,820	1,879	1,931
Millet	285	291	293
Potatoes	1,943	2,055	2,424
Sugar cane	2,600	2,485	2,354
Beans, dry*	29	29	n.a.
Pigeon peas	19	19	18
Lentils	165	161	148
Mustard seed	136	134	135
Garlic	30	32	34
Oranges	37	48	49
Apples	35	36	39
Ginger	159	177	n.a.
Jute	17	17	18
Tobacco, unmanufactured	3	3	2

* FAO estimate.

Aggregate production ('000 metric tons, may include official, semi-official or estimated data): Total cereals 7,329 in 2007, 8,069 in 2008, 8,114 in 2009; Total roots and tubers 2,053 in 2007, 2,165 in 2008, 2,534 in 2009; Total vegetables (incl. melons) 2,375 in 2007, 2,602 in 2008, 2,812 in 2009; Total fruits (excl. melons) 1,069 in 2007, 1,128 in 2008, 1,177 in 2009.

Source: FAO.

LIVESTOCK
('000 head, year ending September)

	2007	2008	2009
Cattle	7,044	7,091	7,175
Buffaloes	4,367	4,497	4,680
Pigs	989	1,013	1,044
Sheep	814	809	803
Goats	7,848	8,136	8,473
Chickens	23,925	24,666	24,481

Source: FAO.

LIVESTOCK PRODUCTS
('000 metric tons)

	2007	2008	2009
Cattle meat*	49.3	49.5	24.7
Buffalo meat	147.0	151.7	156.6
Sheep meat	2.7	2.7	2.7
Goat meat	44.9	46.2	48.5
Pig meat	16.0	16.4	17.0
Chicken meat	16.1	16.6	16.7
Cows' milk	392.8	401.0	413.9
Buffaloes' milk	958.6	987.8	1,031.5
Goats' milk*	67.5	67.5	67.5
Hen eggs†	30.0	30.9	30.8

* FAO estimates.
† Unofficial figures.

Source: FAO.

Forestry

ROUNDWOOD REMOVALS
('000 cubic metres, excl. bark, FAO estimates)

	2007	2008	2009
Sawlogs, veneer logs and logs for sleepers	1,260	1,260	1,260
Fuel wood	12,619	12,586	12,555
Total	13,879	13,846	13,815

Source: FAO.

SAWNWOOD PRODUCTION
('000 cubic metres, incl. railway sleepers)

	1999	2000	2001
Coniferous (softwood)*	20	20	20
Broadleaved (hardwood)	610	610	610
Total	630	630	630

* FAO estimates.

2002–09: Production as in 2001 (FAO estimates).

Source: FAO.

Fishing

('000 metric tons, live weight)

	2006	2007	2008
Capture	20.0	20.1	21.5
Aquaculture	25.4	26.7	27.3
Common carp	5.2	5.4	5.5
Bighead carp	3.9	4.1	2.9
Silver carp	7.7	8.1	8.2
Total catch	45.4	46.8	48.8

Source: FAO.

Industry

SELECTED PRODUCTS
('000 metric tons unless otherwise indicated, year ending 15 July)

	2005/06	2006/07	2007/08
Cement	613.6	644.3	670.1*
Raw sugar	98.5	103.4	107.5*
Tea	11.6	12.2	12.7*
Vegetable ghee	179.2	188.2	195.7*
Noodles	32.3	35.6	37.0*
Paper	29.9	31.4	32.7*
Cigarettes ('000 million)	9.5	10.0	10.4*
Soap	44.8	47.1	48.9*
Electric energy (million kWh)	2,514.7	2,723.0	2,768.3

* Annual estimate based on data for first eight months.

Finance

CURRENCY AND EXCHANGE RATES

Monetary Units:
100 paisa (pice) = 1 Nepalese rupee (NR).

Sterling, Dollar and Euro Equivalents (31 December 2010):
£1 sterling = NRs 112.95;
US $1 = NRs 72.15;
€1 = NRs 96.41;
1,000 Nepalese rupees = £8.85 = $13.86 = €10.37.

Average Exchange Rate (rupees per US $):
2008 69.762
2009 77.545
2010 73.155

NEPAL

Statistical Survey

BUDGET
(NRs million, year ending 15 July)*

Revenue†	2004/05	2005/06	2006/07‡
Taxation	54,104.8	57,427.0	69,931.5
Taxes on external trade	15,701.6	15,343.7	18,328.0
Value-added tax	18,885.4	21,613.0	26,423.0
Excise duties	6,445.9	6,508.8	8,587.5
Income and property transfer tax	13,071.9	13,961.5	16,593.0
Other revenue	14,770.3	13,341.5	14,534.3
Interest	1,466.6	1,734.6	925.0
Civil administration	3,943.2	4,705.5	4,719.3
Dividend	4,589.9	3,394.8	3,960.0
Miscellaneous	3,504.0	2,356.0	3,550.0
Total	**68,875.1**	**70,768.5**	**84,465.8**

Expenditure	2004/05	2005/06	2006/07‡
Recurrent expenditure§	61,686.4	67,017.6	83,767.9
General administration	4,359.4	4,891.2	6,260.3
Defence	15,429.4	17,415.7	17,142.9
Social services	23,208.8	25,382.6	33,558.7
Education	15,960.2	17,729.8	20,942.9
Health	4,273.0	4,851.3	7,890.6
Economic services	7,167.8	7,529.8	9,950.9
Agriculture-related	2,117.2	2,437.5	3,045.9
Forestry	1,582.1	1,675.2	1,797.2
Interest payments	6,218.0	6,158.7	7,859.9
Other purposes	5,303.0	5,639.6	8,995.1
Capital expenditure	27,340.7	28,109.4	44,385.5
Administration and defence	3,570.1	3,151.7	1,929.8
Social services	7,940.7	10,151.8	18,314.3
Education	1,260.4	1,609.6	1,825.3
Health	409.3	948.2	1,413.3
Provision of drinking water	1,440.0	1,949.8	5,575.6
Economic services	15,394.9	14,797.1	23,585.3
Irrigation	1,921.5	2,462.7	3,457.1
Transport	4,149.6	4,178.1	7,337.7
Electricity	7,219.1	6,256.4	8,285.7
Total	**89,027.1**	**95,127.0**	**128,153.4**

* Figures refer to the recurrent and capital budgets of the central Government.
† Excluding grants received (NRs million): 14,391.2 in 2004/05; 13,827.5 in 2005/06; 23,728.6 in 2006/07 (budget estimate).
‡ Budget estimates.
§ Excluding net lending (NRs million): −1,247.7 in 2004/05; −16.4 in 2005/06; −319.1 in 2006/07 (budget estimate).

2004/05 (NRs million, revised figures): Total revenue 70,122.8; Total expenditure 90,381.1.

2005/06 (NRs million, revised figures): Total revenue 72,282.1; Total expenditure 110,889.2.

2006/07 (NRs million, revised figures): Total revenue 87,712.1; Total expenditure 133,604.6.

2007/08 (NRs million): Total revenue 107,622.5; Total expenditure 161,349.9.

2008/09 (NRs million, estimates): Total revenue 142,211.3; Total expenditure 213,578.4.

2009/10 (NRs million, budget estimates): Total revenue 176,503.8; Total expenditure 285,930.0.

Source: Nepal Rastra Bank, Kathmandu.

INTERNATIONAL RESERVES
(US $ million at mid-December)

	2003	2004	2005
Gold*	6.5	6.5	5.4
IMF special drawing rights	0.8	9.7	8.8
Reserve position in IMF	8.6	—	—
Foreign exchange	1,213.1	1,452.5	1,490.2
Total	**1,229.0**	**1,468.7**	**1,504.4**

* Valued at US $42.5 per troy ounce in 2003 and 2004, and at $41.9 in 2005.

2007 (US $ million at mid-December): IMF special drawing rights 9.1.

2008 (US $ million at mid-December): IMF special drawing rights 8.3.

2009 (US $ million at mid-December): IMF special drawing rights 99.9.

Source: IMF, *International Financial Statistics*.

MONEY SUPPLY
(NRs million at mid-December)*

	2007	2008	2009
Currency outside depository corporations	85,987	106,106	128,991
Transferable deposits	47,538	53,206	72,063
Other deposits	309,432	455,939	595,233
Broad money	**442,957**	**615,251**	**796,287**

* Excluding Indian currency in circulation.

Source: IMF, *International Financial Statistics*.

COST OF LIVING
(Consumer Price Index; base: 2000 = 100)

	2007	2008	2009
Food (incl. beverages)	139.6	158.8	186.1
Fuel and light	191.4	222.9	218.9
Clothing (excl. footwear)	116.6	121.8	132.1
Rent	137.3	144.2	138.6
All items (incl. others)	140.5	156.9	174.8

Source: ILO.

NATIONAL ACCOUNTS
(NRs million at current prices, year ending 15 July)

Expenditure on the Gross Domestic Product

	2006/07	2007/08*	2008/09†
Final consumption expenditure	656,374	735,470	895,018
Households	576,911	641,085	772,762
Non-profit institutions serving households	12,515	13,721	15,753
General government	66,949	80,663	106,503
Gross capital formation	208,779	247,277	316,097
Gross fixed capital formation	153,337	178,446	211,039
Increase in stocks	55,442	68,831	105,058
Total domestic expenditure	**865,153**	**982,747**	**1,211,115**
Exports of goods and services	93,567	104,207	122,737
Less Imports of goods and services	230,893	271,291	342,536
GDP in purchasers' values	**727,827**	**815,663**	**991,316**
GDP at constant 2000/01 prices	**532,038**	**564,517**	**591,933**

* Revised estimates.
† Preliminary estimates.

Gross Domestic Product by Economic Activity

	2006/07	2007/08*	2008/09†
Agriculture and forestry	223,536	243,323	301,567
Fishing	3,287	3,868	5,147
Mining and quarrying	3,417	4,375	5,084
Manufacturing	52,172	57,185	64,165
Electricity, gas and water	14,841	15,219	15,122
Construction	45,099	54,134	63,683
Wholesale and retail trade	92,648	105,306	125,885
Restaurants and hotels	10,043	11,503	14,031
Transport, storage and communications	69,555	76,818	93,261
Financial intermediation	28,467	33,539	38,545
Real estate, renting and business	70,791	73,636	82,541
Public administration and defence	12,227	14,352	18,532
Education	40,939	48,722	62,875
Health and social work	8,568	10,963	13,959
Other community and social services	21,774	26,505	35,125
Sub-total	**697,364**	**779,448**	**939,522**
Less Imputed bank service charges	21,505	24,186	29,362
Gross value added in basic prices	**675,859**	**755,262**	**910,160**
Indirect taxes, *less* subsidies	51,968	60,401	81,156
GDP in market prices	**727,827**	**815,663**	**991,316**

* Revised estimates.
† Preliminary estimates.

NEPAL

BALANCE OF PAYMENTS
(US $ million)

	2007	2008	2009
Exports of goods f.o.b.	924.9	986.6	840.2
Imports of goods f.o.b.	-2,932.6	-3,519.3	-4,301.3
Trade balance	-2,007.6	-2,532.8	-3,461.1
Exports of services	511.3	723.7	652.4
Imports of services	-722.6	-851.7	-784.7
Balance on goods and services	-2,218.9	-2,660.9	-3,593.4
Other income received	224.3	235.6	210.1
Other income paid	-87.6	-84.6	-52.5
Balance on goods, services and income	-2,082.2	-2,509.8	-3,435.7
Current transfers received	1,993.7	2,945.5	3,289.5
Current transfers paid	-41.5	-51.2	-109.8
Current balance	-130.0	384.5	-256.1
Capital account (net)	75.4	113.6	132.4
Direct investment from abroad	5.7	1.0	38.2
Other investment assets	-161.0	-386.7	-212.5
Investment liabilities	-114.2	299.3	133.7
Net errors and omissions	19.1	-107.5	-187.7
Overall balance	-305.0	304.2	-352.1

Source: IMF, *International Financial Statistics*.

External Trade

PRINCIPAL COMMODITIES
(NRs million, year ending 15 July)

Imports from India

	2006/07	2007/08	2008/09*
Rice	1,614.2	835.5	1,134.2
Textiles	1,753.8	1,663.6	2,441.8
Thread	3,158.8	3,056.3	2,597.1
Medicines	4,442.5	5,434.1	6,558.1
Chemicals	2,590.9	2,719.8	2,764.6
Coal	950.7	910.1	1,517.8
Cement	2,519.9	2,337.0	4,032.1
Petroleum products	33,567.6	40,815.7	41,356.7
Coldrolled sheet (in coil)	2,079.6	4,005.8	6,146.9
Hotrolled sheet (in coil)	2,052.7	3,575.9	3,550.1
Mild steel (MS) billet	4,384.2	8,145.4	5,513.7
Mild steel (MS) wire rod	1,418.7	2,595.3	2,061.0
Transport vehicles and parts	9,798.7	11,874.6	16,157.8
Other machine equipment and parts	3,556.3	4,682.0	7,263.8
Electrical equipment	2,365.2	3,587.3	3,879.8
Agricultural equipment and parts	1,073.1	1,483.8	2,481.5
Total (incl. others)	115,872.3	142,376.5	163,892.4

* Provisional.

IMPORTS FROM OTHER COUNTRIES

	2006/07	2007/08	2008/09*
Crude palm oil	7,121.5	5,746.8	2,949.3
Betel nut	1,418.3	1,857.0	2,922.5
Crude soybean oil	1,924.2	1,600.0	3,658.6
Ready-made garments	1,828.3	1,778.4	1,476.7
Textile dyes	2,344.6	1,376.1	775.5
Textiles	2,455.7	1,966.6	2,253.0
Medicines	1,536.9	1,263.0	3,111.1
Gold	3,519.9	3,750.0	16,574.6
Zinc ingot	2,372.5	458.4	283.8
Copper wire rod, scrapes and sheets	1,878.8	1,941.1	1,813.6
Polyethylene granules	2,959.7	3,718.9	3,616.5
Electrical equipment	2,965.8	3,945.2	7,771.8
Computer parts	2,701.0	2,269.7	3,711.4
Transport equipment and parts	2,705.0	4,391.8	5,459.6
Other machine equipment and parts	2,007.4	3,902.0	5,875.0
Telecommunications equipment and parts	954.1	4,979.4	4,064.4
Aircraft and parts	1,462.8	1,049.9	2,020.4
Total (incl. others)	78,822.3	79,561.2	120,678.6

* Provisional.

EXPORTS TO INDIA

	2006/07	2007/08	2008/09*
Banaspati ghee	4,136.5	2,132.3	9.1
Juice	1,591.3	1,836.4	1,952.2
Cardamom	848.1	1,034.8	1,216.0
Polyester yarn	2,241.0	2,618.0	2,499.2
Thread	4,055.9	4,134.8	2,525.4
Textiles (cotton, synthetic and others)	3,056.9	2,114.8	3,191.5
Jute goods	2,756.8	2,582.5	n.a.
Chemicals	950.2	275.7	166.9
Toothpaste	663.4	475.6	813.2
Galvanized iron sheet	3,579.9	4,416.9	2,821.7
Other wire	1,610.7	1,546.7	895.0
Steel pipes	761.9	979.5	571.2
Total (incl. others)	41,728.8	38,555.7	40,964.1

* Provisional.

EXPORTS TO OTHER COUNTRIES

	2006/07	2007/08	2008/09*
Pulses	488.5	1,458.4	6,247.1
Cardamom	129.6	n.a.	n.a.
Tea	122.5	57.0	61.1
Herbs	43.5	97.9	295.0
Perfume oil	21.4	n.a.	n.a.
Niger seeds	8.8	1.2	1.0
Hide and skins	279.1	248.7	305.4
Ready-made leather goods	111.1	22.9	58.2
Woollen carpet	5,600.2	5,048.2	5,676.3
Ready-made garments	5,212.9	4,755.8	4,813.3
Pashmina goods	931.0	643.4	1,526.9
Nepalese paper and paper products	190.6	347.1	361.2
Handicraft goods (of metal and wood)	250.2	194.0	738.6
Silverware and jewellery	325.4	269.4	262.4
Total (incl. others)	17,654.3	20,710.8	26,283.0

* Provisional.

NEPAL

PRINCIPAL TRADING PARTNERS
(NRs million, year ending 15 July)

Imports	2005/06	2006/07	2007/08
Australia	1,415.3	1,854.7	1,755.8
China, People's Republic	12,083.5	16,678.6	22,255.8
Germany	2,761.8	2,432.7	3,430.3
Hong Kong	930.9	1,029.5	1,177.4
India	107,143.1	115,872.0	144,524.1
Indonesia	5,647.8	11,172.1	9,913.5
Japan	1,935.1	3,229.0	6,148.1
Korea, Republic	1,788.9	2,380.5	2,077.0
Malaysia	2,474.7	2,794.6	3,833.7
New Zealand	1,018.8	841.1	817.9
Saudi Arabia	2,329.7	2,592.7	2,677.7
Singapore	3,375.3	5,496.9	5,268.7
Taiwan	567.9	796.0	1,232.0
Thailand	2,602.1	3,459.5	4,983.5
United Kingdom	961.4	1,727.1	1,643.4
USA	1,677.5	4,260.0	3,718.1
Total (incl. others)	173,780.3	191,708.8	221,937.7

Exports	2005/06	2006/07	2007/08
China, People's Republic	892.6	378.0	736.4
France	1,297.5	904.0	1,001.2
Germany	2,843.8	2,573.7	2,332.1
India	40,714.7	41,874.8	38,626.4
Italy	712.3	684.3	583.8
United Kingdom	1,184.1	998.7	1,066.3
USA	6,993.4	5,571.3	4,598.9
Total (incl. others)	60,234.1	60,795.8	59,266.5

Transport

ROAD TRAFFIC
(vehicles registered)

	2000/01	2001/02	2002/03
Cars, jeeps and vans	5,152	4,374	2,906
Buses and minibuses	1,453	1,343	730
Tractors	3,519	3,189	2,485
Other agro-industrial vehicles	1,271	1,798	1,212
Motorcycles	29,291	38,522	29,404
Total (incl. others)	40,995	49,560	37,610

Source: Department of Transport Management, Kathmandu.

2007 (vehicles in use at 31 December): Passenger cars 86,423; Buses and coaches 18,519; Lorries and vans 43,211; Motorcycles (incl. mopeds) 425,940 (Source: IRF, *World Road Statistics*).

CIVIL AVIATION
(traffic on scheduled services of Royal Nepal Airlines Corporation)

	2004	2005	2006
Kilometres flown (million)	9	10	10
Passengers carried ('000)	445	480	510
Passenger-km (million)	816	873	911
Total ton-km (million)	77	82	86

Source: UN, *Statistical Yearbook*.

Tourism

FOREIGN TOURIST ARRIVALS

Country of residence	2006	2007	2008
Australia	8,231	12,369	13,846
Bangladesh	16,474	24,012	20,067
China, People's Republic	16,800	27,339	35,166
France	14,835	20,250	22,402
Germany	14,361	21,323	18,552
India	93,722	96,010	91,177
Italy	7,736	11,243	7,914
Japan	22,242	27,058	23,383
Korea, Republic	12,917	20,475	18,883
Netherlands	7,207	10,589	10,900
Sri Lanka	27,413	49,947	37,817
Thailand	13,744	20,018	18,689
United Kingdom	22,708	32,367	33,658
USA	19,833	29,783	30,076
Total (incl. others)	383,926	526,633	500,277

Tourism receipts (US $ million, incl. passenger transport): 157.0 in 2006; 234.0 in 2007; 353.0 in 2008.

Source: World Tourism Organization.

Communications Media

	2007	2008	2009
Telephones ('000 main lines in use)	701.1	805.1	812.6
Mobile cellular telephones ('000 subscribers)	3,268.9	4,200.0	5,597.9
Internet users ('000)	398.8	498.4	577.8
Broadband subscribers ('000)	11.0	n.a.	15.6

Radio receivers ('000 in use): 840 in 1997.
Television receivers ('000 in use): 170 in 2000; 193 in 2001.
Daily newspapers (titles): 251 in 2003.
Non-daily newspapers (titles): 3,490 in 2003; 3,465 in 2004.
Personal computers: 132,000 (4.8 per 1,000 persons) in 2005.

Sources: UNESCO, *Statistical Yearbook*; International Telecommunication Union.

Education

(2009/10 unless otherwise indicated)

	Teachers	Students ('000) Males	Females	Total
Pre-primary	19,936*	496.4	450.9	947.3
Primary	153,536	2,446.7	2,453.9	4,900.7
Secondary	83,630	1,228.0*	1,077.2*	2,305.2*
Tertiary†	9,932	174.4	114.8	289.3

* 2007/08.
† 2008/09.

Source: UNESCO Institute for Statistics.

Institutions (2004): Primary 24,746; Lower secondary 7,436; Secondary 4,547. Note: Many schools offer education at more than one level. The total number of primary, lower secondary and secondary institutions was 26,277 (Source: Ministry of Education and Sports, Kathmandu).

Pupil-teacher ratio (primary education, UNESCO estimate): 31.9 in 2009/10 (Source: UNESCO Institute for Statistics).

Adult literacy rate (UNESCO estimates): 57.9% (males 71.1%; females 45.4%) in 2008 (Source: UNESCO Institute for Statistics).

Directory

The Government

HEAD OF STATE

President: Dr RAM BARAN YADAV (assumed office 23 July 2008).
Vice-President: PARAMANANDA JHA.

COUNCIL OF MINISTERS
(May 2011)

A coalition comprising representatives from the Communist Party of Nepal (Unified Marxist-Leninist) (UML), the Unified Communist Party of Nepal (Maoist) (UCPN—M), the Madhesi Jana Adhikar Forum Nepal (Madhesi People's Rights Forum Nepal) (MPRFN), the Communist Party of Nepal (United) (CPN—U) and the Communist Party of Nepal (Marxist-Leninist) (CPN—ML).

Prime Minister: JHALA NATH KHANAL (UML).
Deputy Prime Minister and Minister Responsible for Finance, and Commerce and Supplies: BHARAT MOHAN ADHIKARI (UML).
Deputy Prime Minister and Minister of Home Affairs: KRISHNA BAHADUR MAHARA (UCPN—M).
Deputy Prime Minister and Minister of Foreign Affairs: UPENDRA YADAV (MPRFN).
Minister of Defence: BISHNU PRASAD POUDEL (UML).
Minister of Physical Planning and Works: TOP BAHADUR RAYAMAJHI (UCPN—M).
Minister of Information and Communication: LAXMAN AGNI PRASAD SAPKOTA (UCPN—M).
Minister of Health and Population: SHAKTI BAHADUR BASNET (UCPN—M).
Minister of Peace and Reconstruction: BISWANATH SHAH (UCPN—M).
Minister of Tourism and Civil Aviation: KHADGA BAHADUR BISHWAKARMA (UCPN—M).
Minister of Local Development: URMILA ARYAL (UML).
Minister of Education; Minister Responsible for Science and Technology: GANGA LAL TULADHAR (UML).
Minister of Irrigation: RAGHU BIR MAHASETH (UML).
Minister of Energy: GOKARNA BISTA (UML).
Minister of Forests and Soil Conservation: BHANU BHAKTA JOSHI (UML).
Minister of General Administration: YUBARAJ KARKI (UML).
Minister of Land Reform and Management: RAMCHARAN CHAUDHARI (UCPN—M).
Minister of Law and Justice: PRABHU SHAH (UCPN—M).
Minister of Youth and Sports: HIT BAHADUR TAMANG (UCPN—M).
Minister of Agriculture and Co-operatives: HARI NARAYAN YADAV (MPRF).
Minister of Labour and Transport Management: MOHAMMAD ISTIYAK RAINA (MPRF).
Minister of the Environment: SUNIL KUMAR MANANDHAR (CPN—U).
Minister of Federal Affairs, the Constituent Assembly, Parliamentary Affairs and Culture: KHAGENDRA PRASAD PRASAI (CPN—ML).
Minister without Portfolio: GHANSHYAM BHUSAL (UML).
Minister of State for Local Development: SHATRU GHAN MAHATO (UML).
Minister of State for Irrigation: DAL BAHADUR SUNAR (UML).
Minister of State for Energy: RAMJI SHARMA (UML).
Minister of State for General Administration: DAMBAR SAMBAHAMPHE (UML).
Minister of State for Forests and Soil Conservation: BHAGAWATI CHAUDHARI (UML).
Minister of State for Physical Planning and Works: DEVI KHADKA (UCPN—M).
Minister of State for Health and Population: DHARMASHILA CHAPAGAIN (UCPN—M).
Minister of State for Agriculture and Co-operatives: NANDA KUMAR DATTA (MPRFN).

At mid-May 2011 four ministerial nominees from the UCPN—M had refrained from taking an oath of office in protest against the distribution of portfolios among the Maoists.

MINISTRIES

Prime Minister's Office: Singha Durbar, POB 23312, Kathmandu; tel. (1) 4211000; e-mail info@opmcm.gov.np; internet www.opmcm.gov.np.
Ministry of Agriculture and Co-operatives: Singha Durbar, Kathmandu; tel. (1) 4211706; fax (1) 4211935; e-mail memoac@moac.gov.np; internet www.moac.gov.np.
Ministry of Commerce and Supplies: Singha Durbar, Kathmandu; tel. (1) 4211446; fax (1) 4211167; e-mail info@mocs.gov.np; internet www.mocs.gov.np.
Ministry of Defence: Singha Durbar, Kathmandu; tel. (1) 4211289; fax (1) 4211294; e-mail mod@mos.com.np; internet www.mod.gov.np.
Ministry of Education: Keshar Mahal, Kantipath, Kathmandu; tel. (1) 4412804; fax (1) 4418191; e-mail infomoe@most.gov.np; internet www.moe.gov.np.
Ministry of Energy: Singha Durbar, Kathmandu; tel. (1) 4211516; fax (1) 4211510; e-mail info@moen.gov.np; internet www.mowr.gov.np.
Ministry of the Environment: Singha Durbar, Kathmandu; tel. (1) 4211661; fax (1) 4211754; e-mail info@moenv.gov.np; internet www.moenv.gov.n.
Ministry of Federal Affairs, the Constituent Assembly, Parliamentary Affairs and Culture: Singha Durbar, Kathmandu; tel. (1) 4211628; fax (1) 4211792.
Ministry of Finance: Singha Durbar, Kathmandu; tel. (1) 4211809; fax (1) 4211831; e-mail admindivision@mof.gov.np; internet www.mof.gov.np.
Ministry of Foreign Affairs: Narayanhiti, Kathmandu; tel. (1) 4416011; fax (1) 4416016; e-mail adm@mofa.gov.np; internet www.mofa.gov.np.
Ministry of Forests and Soil Conservation: Singha Durbar, Kathmandu; tel. (1) 4262428; fax (1) 4223868; e-mail mfscmed@ntc.net.np.
Ministry of General Administration: Singha Durbar, Kathmandu; tel. (1) 4245367; fax (1) 4200238; e-mail info@moga.gov.np; internet www.moga.gov.np.
Ministry of Health and Population: Singha Durbar Plaza, Ramshah Path, Kathmandu; tel. (1) 4262862; fax (1) 4262896; e-mail info@moh.gov.np; internet www.moh.gov.np.
Ministry of Home Affairs: Singha Durbar, Kathmandu; tel. (1) 4211204; fax (1) 4211246; e-mail info@moha.gov.np; internet www.moha.gov.np.
Ministry of Industry: Singha Durbar, Kathmandu; tel. (1) 4211579; fax (1) 4211619; e-mail info@moics.gov.np; internet www.moics.gov.np.
Ministry of Information and Communications: Singha Durbar, Kathmandu; tel. (1) 4211556; fax (1) 4211729; e-mail moicppme@ntc.net.np; internet www.moic.gov.np.
Ministry of Irrigation: Singha Durbar, Kathmandu; tel. (1) 4211530; fax (1) 4211510; e-mail info@moir.gov.np; internet www.mowr.gov.np.
Ministry of Labour and Transport Management: Singha Durbar, Kathmandu; tel. (1) 4247842; fax (1) 4256877; e-mail info@moltm.gov.np; internet www.moltm.gov.np.
Ministry of Land Reform and Management: Singha Durbar, Kathmandu; tel. (1) 4211760; fax (1) 4211708; e-mail info@molrm.gov.np; internet www.molrm.gov.np.
Ministry of Law and Justice: Singha Durbar, Kathmandu; tel. (1) 4211987; fax (1) 4211684; e-mail info@moljpa.gov.np; internet www.moljpa.gov.np.
Ministry of Local Development: Shreemahal Pulchwok, Lalitpur; tel. (1) 5523329; fax (1) 5522045; e-mail secretary@mld.gov.np; internet www.mld.gov.np.
Ministry of Peace and Reconstruction: Singha Durbar, Kathmandu; tel. (1) 4211189; fax (1) 4211186; e-mail info@peace.gov.np; internet www.peace.gov.np.
Ministry of Physical Planning and Works: Singha Durbar, Kathmandu; tel. (1) 4211782; fax (1) 4211720; e-mail info@moppw.gov.np; internet www.moppw.gov.np.
Ministry of Science and Technology: Singha Durbar, Kathmandu; tel. (1) 4211637; fax (1) 4211754; e-mail info@most.gov.np; internet www.most.gov.np.
Ministry of Tourism and Civil Aviation: Singha Durbar, Kathmandu; tel. (1) 4232411; fax (1) 4211758; e-mail motca@ntc.net.np; internet www.tourism.gov.np.

NEPAL

Ministry of Women, Children and Social Welfare: Singha Durbar, Kathmandu; tel. (1) 5547013; fax (1) 5521214; e-mail dwd@hons.com.np; internet www.mowcsw.gov.np.

Ministry of Youth and Sports: Kamalpokhari, Kathmandu; tel. (1) 4416507; fax (1) 4416489; e-mail info@moys.gov.np; internet www.moys.gov.np.

Legislature

CONSTITUENT ASSEMBLY

The Constituent Assembly, which is responsible for drafting a new constitution, comprises 601 members, of whom 575 were elected (using the mixed electoral system) and 26 nominated by the incumbent Interim Parliament. The term of office of its members was initially two years, but on 28 May 2010, following the failure of the Assembly to finalize a new constitution, the term of office was extended by one year.

Speaker: SUBAS CHANDRA NEMBANG.
Deputy Speaker: CHITRA LEKHA YADAV.

Election, 10 April 2008

Party	Seats*
Communist Party of Nepal (Maoist—M)†	220
Nepali Congress Party (NCP)	110
Communist Party of Nepal (Unified Marxist-Leninist—UML)	103
Madhesi People's Rights Forum Nepal	52
Terai Madhes Loktantrik Party	20
Sadbhavana Party	9
Communist Party of Nepal (Marxist-Leninist)	8
Rashtriya Prajatantra Party (RPP)‡	8
Janamorcha Nepal	7
Communist Party of Nepal (United)	5
Nepal Workers' and Peasants' Party	4
Rashtriya Prajatantra Party Nepal	4
Rastriya Janamorcha	4
Rashtriya Janashakti Party‡	3
Communist Party of Nepal (Unified)	2
Nepali Janata Dal	2
Nepali Sadbhavana Party (Anandi Devi)	2
Rastriya Janamukti Party	2
Sanghiya Loktantrik Rastriya Manch	2
Churevawar Rastriya Ekata Party Nepal	1
Dalit Janajati Party	1
Nepal Loktantrik Samajbadi Dal	1
Nepal Pariwar Party	1
Nepal Rastriya Party	1
Samajwadi Prajatantrik Janata Party Nepal	2
Independents	2
Nominated	26
Total	**601**

*Includes seats determined by proportional representation and 'first-past-the-post' systems.
† Name changed to Unified Communist Party of Nepal (Maoist) (UCPN—M) following merger in January 2009.
‡ Merged to form Rashtriya Shakti Prajatantra Party in January 2010.

Election Commission

Election Commission of Nepal: Bahadur Bhawan, Kantipath, Kathmandu; tel. (1) 4228663; fax (1) 4229227; e-mail info@election.gov.np; internet www.election.gov.np; independent; appointed by the Prime Minister, on recommendation of a Constitutional Council, for a six-year term; Chief Election Commr NEEL KANTHA UPRETY (acting).

Political Organizations

Communist Party of Nepal (Marxist-Leninist) (CPN—ML): Maitidevi, Kathmandu; tel. (1) 4443589; e-mail cpnml.cc@gmail.com; internet www.cpnml.org.np; re-formed in 2002 following the reunification of the Communist Party of Nepal (Marxist-Leninist) with the Communist Party of Nepal (Unified Marxist-Leninist); C. P. Mainali, co-founder of the original CPN—ML as a break-away faction of the CPN (UML) in 1998, had opposed the merger and formed a separate party under the CPN—ML title; Leader C. P. MAINALI.

Communist Party of Nepal (Unified): Kathmandu; internet cpnunified.org.np; f. 2007; Gen. Sec. RAJ SINGH SHRIS.

Communist Party of Nepal (Unified Marxist-Leninist) (UML): Madan Nagar, Balkhu, POB 5471, Kathmandu; tel. (1) 4278081; fax (1) 4278084; e-mail uml@ntc.net.np; internet www.cpnuml.org; f. 1991 when two major factions of the Communist Party of Nepal (CPN; f. 1949; banned 1960; legalized 1990)—the Marxist and Marxist-Leninist factions—merged; the Communist Party of Nepal (Marxist-Leninist—ML) seceded in 1998 and rejoined the UML in 2002; the Communist Party of Nepal (Verma) merged with the UML in 2001; Chair. JHALA NATH KHANAL; Vice-Chair. BIDYA BHANDARI; Gen. Sec. ISHWAR POKHAREL.

Communist Party of Nepal (United): Kathmandu; f. 2007 following a split in the Communist Party of Nepal (United Marxist); Chair. CHANDRA DEV JOSHI; Gen. Sec. GANESH SHAH.

Madhesi Jana Adhikar Forum Nepal (Madhesi People's Rights Forum Nepal, MPRFN): f. 2006; Chair. UPENDRA YADAV; Gen. Sec. RAM SAHAYA YADAV.

Nepal Workers' and Peasants' Party: Golmadhi Tole-7, Bhaktapur, Kathmandu; tel. (1) 6610974; fax (1) 6613207; e-mail nwpp@ntc.net.np; Chair. NARAYAN MAN BIJUKCHHEN (Comrade Rohit).

Nepali Congress Party (NCP): B. P. Smriti Bhavan, B. P. Nagar, Sanepa, Lalitpur; tel. (1) 5555263; fax (1) 5555188; e-mail ncparty@wlink.com.np; internet www.nepalicongress.org; f. 1947; banned 1960; legalized 1990; Nepali Congress Party—Democratic formed as breakaway faction in 2002, rejoined Sept. 2007; 101,000 active mems, 500,000 ordinary mems; Pres. SUSHIL KOIRALA; Vice-Pres. RAM CHANDRA POUDEL; Gen. Secs K. B. GURUNG, BIMALENDRA NIDHI, Dr RAM BARAN YADAV.

Nepali Janata Dal: Tripureshwor, Kathmandu; tel. (1) 4212389; f. 1990; advocates the consolidation of the multi-party democratic system and supports the campaign against corruption; Chair. HARI CHARAN SHAH.

Nepali Sadbhavana Party (NSP) (Nepal Goodwill Party): Shantinagar, New Baneshwor, Kathmandu; tel. (1) 4488068; fax (1) 4470797; f. 1990; promotes the rights of the Madhesi community, who are of Indian origin and reside in the Terai; demands that the Government recognizes Hindi as an official language, that constituencies in the Terai be allocated on the basis of population, and that the Government grant citizenship to those who settled in Nepal before April 1990; in 2003 the party split into two factions, one led by Badri Prasad Mandal, known as the Mandal Group, and the other led by Anandi Devi Singh, known as the Anandi Devi group.

People's Front Nepal (Janamorcha Nepal): Kathmandu; f. 2002 following merger of Rashtriya Jana Morcha (National People's Front) and United People's Front; split into three factions in Dec. 2006; Chair. LILAMANI POKHAREL (acting).

Rashtriya Prajatantra Party Nepal: Ichchhumati Marga, Baluwatar, Kathmandu; tel. and fax (1) 4430635; internet rppn.org.np; f. 2008 as splinter group of RPP; monarchist; Chair. KAMAL THAPA.

Rastriya Janamorcha: Kathmandu; tel. (1) 4420226; Hindu; pro-royalist; Chair. CHITRA BAHADUR K. C.

Rastriya Janamukti Party: Maha Laxmisthan, Lagan Khel, POB 5569, Kathmandu; tel. (1) 5542212; fax (1) 5525531; e-mail zhedi43@yahoo.com; internet www.janamuktiparty.com; f. 1990; Pres. MALBAR SINGH THAPA; Gen. Sec. SURYA RAJBANSI.

Rastriya Prajatantra Party (RPP): Central Office, Charumati, Chabahil Kathmandu; tel. (1) 4471071; fax (1) 4460324; e-mail rppnepal@enet.com.np; internet rppnepal.org; f. 1990; fmrly divided into two factions led by former Prime Ministers Lokendra Bahadur Chand and Surya Bahadur Thapa, respectively; centre-right, with origins as a monarchist party; Leader LOKENDRA BAHADUR CHAND; Chair. PASHUPATI S.J.B. RANA.

Rastriya Shakti Prajatantra Party (RSPP): Kathmandu; est. February 2010 to facilitate the reunification of Surya Bahadur Thapa's Rastriya Janashakti Party and the Rastriya Prajatantra Party.

Sadbhavana Party: Kathmandu; Chair. RAJENDRA MAHATO.

Samajwadi Prajatantrik Janata Party Nepal: Kathmandu; f. 2008; Chair. PREM BAHADUR SINGH.

Sanghiya Loktantrik Rastriya Manch: Kathmandu; f. 2007; Pres. KAMAL CHARAHANG.

Terai Madhes Loktantrik Party (Terai Madhes Democratic Party): Kathmandu; tel. (1) 4462398; 9 members of the party separated to form a faction called Terai Madhes Loktantrik Party (Nepal) in Dec. 2010; Pres. MAHANTHA THAKUR.

Unified Communist Party of Nepal (Maoist) (UCPN—M): Central Office, Perishdanda, Koteshwor, Kathmandu; tel. (1) 4602290; fax (1) 4602289; e-mail ucpnminfo@gmail.com; internet www.ucpnm.org; f. 1990 as Communist Party of Nepal (Unity Centre), renamed as CPN (Maoist) in 1995; fmr underground political movement, represented in Interim Parliament in 2007; orchestrated 'people's war' in hills of western Nepal (1996–2006); merged with CPN (Unified Marxist-Leninist-Maoist) in Sept. 2007; merged with CPN (Marxist) in Feb. 2008; merged with CPN (Unity Centre-Masal) in Jan. 2009 and name changed as above; 175-mem. cen. cttee; Chair. PUSHPA KAMAL DAHAL ('Prachanda'); Vice-Chair. Dr BABURAM BHATTARAI, MOHAN BAIDYA, NARYANKAJI SHRESTHA; Gen. Sec. RAM BAHADUR THAPA.

Other parties elected to the Constituent Assembly in April 2008 were Churevawar Rastriya Ekata Party Nepal, Dalit Janajati Party, Nepal Loktantrik Samajbadi Dal, Nepal Pariwar Dal and Nepal Rastriya Party.

Diplomatic Representation

EMBASSIES IN NEPAL

Australia: Suraj Niwas, Bansbari, POB 879, Kathmandu; tel. (1) 4371678; fax (1) 4371533; internet www.nepal.embassy.gov.au; Ambassador SUSAN GRACE.

Bangladesh: Shanti Ashram, Ward 4, Kitta 9, Maharajgunj, Chakrapath (Ring Road), Kathmandu 2; tel. (1) 4372843; fax (1) 4373265; e-mail bdootktm@wlink.com.np; Ambassador Dr NEEM CHANDRA BHOWMIK.

China, People's Republic: Baluwatar, POB 4234, Kathmandu; tel. (1) 4411740; fax (1) 4414045; e-mail chinaemb_np@mfa.gov.cn; internet www.fmprc.gov.cn/ce/cenp; Ambassador (vacant).

Denmark: 761 Neel Saraswati Marg, Lazimpat, POB 6332, Kathmandu; tel. (1) 4413010; fax (1) 4411409; e-mail ktmamb@um.dk; internet www.ambkathmandu.um.dk; Ambassador MORTEN JESPERSEN.

Egypt: Naya Bazar Chowk, Saibu Bhaisepati, Lalitpur, POB 792, Kathmandu; tel. (1) 5590544; fax (1) 5592661; e-mail embassy.kathmandu@mfa.gov.eg; Ambassador Dr MOUSTAFA ABDELHAMID MOHAMED GENDY.

Finland: Bishalnagar, POB 2126, Kathmandu; tel. (1) 4416636; fax (1) 4416703; e-mail sanomat.kat@formin.fi; internet www.finland.org.np; Ambassador TERHI HAKALA.

France: Lazimpat, POB 452, Kathmandu; tel. (1) 4412332; fax (1) 4419968; e-mail ambassade@ambafrance-np.org; internet www.ambafrance-np.org; Ambassador JEAN-CHARLES DEMARQUIS.

Germany: 690 Gyaneshwar Marg, POB 226, Kathmandu; tel. (1) 4412786; fax (1) 4416899; e-mail info@kathmandu.diplo.de; internet www.kathmandu.diplo.de; Ambassador VERENA GRÄFIN VON ROEDERN.

India: 336 Kapurdhara Marg, POB 292, Kathmandu; tel. (1) 4410900; fax (1) 4428279; e-mail pic@eoiktm.org; internet www.indianembassy.org.np; Ambassador RAKESH SOOD.

Israel: Bishramalaya House, Lazimpat St, POB 371, Kathmandu; tel. (1) 4411811; fax (1) 4413920; e-mail info@kathmandu.mfa.gov.il; internet kathmandu.mfa.gov.il; Ambassador DAN STAV.

Japan: Panipokhari, POB 264, Kathmandu; tel. (1) 4426680; fax (1) 4414101; e-mail comjpn@mos.com.np; internet www.np.emb-japan.go.jp; Ambassador TATSUO MIZUNO.

Korea, Democratic People's Republic: Jhamsikhel, Lalitpur, Kathmandu; tel. (1) 5521855; fax (1) 5525394; Ambassador KIM YOUNG SU.

Korea, Republic: Ravibhawan, Kathmandu; tel. (1) 4270172; fax (1) 4272041; e-mail konepemb@gmail.com; internet npl.mofat.go.kr; Ambassador HONG SUNG-MOG.

Malaysia: Blk B, 2nd Floor, Karmachari Sanchaya Kosh Bldg, Pulchowk, POB 24372, Lalitpur, Kathmandu; tel. (1) 5010004; fax (1) 5010492; e-mail malkatmandu@kln.gov.my; internet www.kln.gov.my/perwakilan/kathmandu; Ambassador Dato' ILANKOVAN KOLANDAVELU.

Myanmar: Chakupath, Patan Gate, Lalitpur, POB 2437, Kathmandu; tel. (1) 521788; fax (1) 523402; e-mail myanmaremb@wlink.com.np; internet www.mofa.gov.mm/myanmarmissions/nepal; Ambassador THET OO.

Norway: Surya Court, Pulchowk, Lalitpur, POB 20765, Kathmandu; tel. (1) 5545307; fax (1) 5545226; e-mail emb.kathmandu@mfa.no; internet www.norway.org.np; Ambassador THOR GISLESEN.

Pakistan: Pushpanjali, Maharajgunj, Chakrapath, POB 202, Kathmandu; tel. (1) 4374024; fax (1) 4374012; e-mail info@pakemb.org.np; internet mofa.gov.pk/nepal; Ambassador SYED ABRAR HUSSAIN.

Russia: Baluwatar, POB 123, Kathmandu; tel. (1) 4412155; fax (1) 4416571; e-mail ruspos@info.com.np; internet www.nepal.mid.ru; Ambassador Dr SERGEI V. VELICHKIN.

Sri Lanka: 'Shah Villa', Chundevi Rd, Maharajgunj, POB 8802, Kathmandu; tel. (1) 4720623; fax (1) 4720128; e-mail lankaemb@wlink.com.np; Ambassador THOSAPALA HEWAGE.

Switzerland: Jawalakhel, Ekanta Kuna, SDC-Compound, Lalitpur, Kathmandu; tel. (1) 5549225; fax (1) 5549224; e-mail kat.vertretung@eda.admin.ch; internet www.eda.admin.ch/kathmandu; Ambassador THOMAS GASS.

Thailand: 167/4 Ward 3, Maharajgunj-Bansbari Rd, POB 3333, Kathmandu; tel. (1) 4371410; fax (1) 4371409; e-mail thaiemb@wlink.com.np; internet www.thaiembassy.org/kathmandu; Ambassador MARIS SANGIAMPONGSA.

United Kingdom: Lainchaur, POB 106, Kathmandu; tel. (1) 4410583; fax (1) 4411789; e-mail bekathmandu@fco.gov.uk; internet ukinnepal.fco.gov.uk; Ambassador JOHN TUCKNOTT.

USA: Maharajgunj, POB 295, Kathmandu; tel. (1) 4007200; fax (1) 4007272; e-mail usembktm@state.gov; internet nepal.usembassy.gov; Ambassador SCOTT H. DELISI.

Judicial System

According to the Interim Constitution (which was officially endorsed in January 2007), the judicial system has three tiers: the Supreme Court (which is also a Court of Record), the Appellate Courts and the District Courts. The Supreme Court consists of a Chief Justice and a maximum of 14 other judges. The Chief Justice is appointed by the Prime Minister on the recommendation of the Constitutional Council; other Supreme Court, Appellate Court and District Court judges are nominated by the Chief Justice on the recommendation of the Judicial Council. A Constituent Assembly Court was established in February 2008 to deal with election matters.

Supreme Court: Ramashah Path, Kathmandue-mail info@supremecourt.gov.np; internet www.supremecourt.gov.np.

Chief Justice: KHIL RAJ REGMI.

Judges of the Supreme Court: BALA RAM K. C., TAP BAHADUR MAGAR, DAMODAR PRASAD SHARMA, RAM KUMAR PRASAD SHAH, KALYAN SHRESTHA, TAHIR ALI ANSARI, KRISHNA PRASAD UPADHYAYA, PREM SHARMA, RANA BAHADUR BAM, MOHAN PRAKASH SITAULA, ABADESH KUMAR YADAV, GIRISH CHANDRA LAL, SHUSHILA KARKI, PRAKASH CHANDRA SHARMA WASTI, BHARAT RAJ UPRETI.

Registrar: Dr RAM KRISHNA TIMALSENA.

Attorney-General: Prof. Dr YUBARAJ SANGROULA, Ramshah Path, Kathmandu; e-mail info@attorneygeneral.gov.np; internet www.attorneygeneral.gov.np.

Religion

At the 2001 census, an estimated 80.6% of the population professed Hinduism, while 10.7% were Buddhists and 4.2% Muslims. The actual number of Muslims in the country was considered to be much higher, owing to immigration from Bangladesh. There were an estimated 101,976 Christians in Nepal in 2001.

BUDDHISM

All Nepal Bhikkhu Association: Vishwa Shanti Vihara (World Peace Temple), 465 Ekadantamarga, Minbhavan, New Baneshwor, POB 8973 NPC-327, Kathmandu; tel. (1) 4482984; fax (1) 4482250; e-mail vishwa@ntc.net.np; Treas. BHIKSHU BODHIJNANA.

Nepal Buddhist Council: Nahtole, Lalitpur 20; tel. (1) 5534277; e-mail nepalbuddhistcouncil@gmail.com; f. 1977; Chair. MAHISWOR RAJ BAJRACHARYA.

United Trungram Buddhist Foundation: Hattigauda, Bansbari, POB 3157, Kathmandu; tel. (1) 4370089; fax (1) 4370292; internet www.utbf.org; Spiritual Dir GYALTRUL RINPOCHE.

CHRISTIANITY

Protestant Church

Presbyterian Church of the Kingdom of Nepal: POB 3237, Kathmandu; tel. and fax (1) 4524450.

The Roman Catholic Church

The Church is represented in Nepal by a single apostolic prefecture. At 31 December 2007 there were an estimated 6,115 adherents in the country.

Apostolic Vicariate: Church of the Assumption, GPOB 8975, EPC-343, Kathmandu; tel. (1) 5542802; fax (1) 5521710; e-mail anath@wlink.com.np; f. 1983 as Catholic Mission; Vicar Apostolic Bishop ANTHONY FRANCIS SHARMA.

The Press

PRINCIPAL DAILIES

The Commoner: Naradevi, POB 203, Kathmandu; tel. (1) 4228236; f. 1956; English; Publr and Chief Editor GOPAL DASS SHRESTHA; circ. 7,000.

Daily News: Bhimsensthan, POB 171, Kathmandu; tel. (1) 4279147; fax (1) 4279544; e-mail manju_sakya@hotmail.com; f. 1983; Nepali and English; Chief Editor MANJU RATNA SAKYA; Publr SUBHA LAXMI SAKYA; circ. 20,000.

Dainik Nirnaya: Bhairawa; tel. (71) 520117; Nepali; Editor P. K. BHATTACHAN.

Gorkhapatra: Dharma Path, POB 23, Kathmandu; tel. (1) 4244437; fax (1) 4222921; e-mail gopa@gorkhapatra.org.np; internet www.gorkhapatra.org.np; f. 1901; Nepali; govt-owned; Chair. BIJAYA CHALISE; Gen. Man. SHAMBHU SHRESTHA; circ. 75,000.

The Himalayan Times: International Media Network Nepal (Pvt) Ltd, APCA House, Baidya Khana Rd, Anam Nagar, POB 11651, Kathmandu; tel. (1) 4771489; fax (1) 4770701; e-mail editorial@thehimalayantimes.com; internet www.thehimalayantimes.com; f. 2001; English; Editor AJAYA BHADRA KHANAL.

Janadoot: Ga 2-549, Kamal Pokhari (in front of the Police Station), Kathmandu; tel. (1) 4412501; f. 1970; Nepali; Editor GOVINDA BIYOGI; circ. 6,500.

Kantipur: Kantipur Complex, Subhidhanagar, POB 8559, Kathmandu; tel. (1) 4480100; fax (1) 4466320; e-mail corporate@kantipur.com.np; internet www.kantipuronline.com; f. 1993; Nepali; Chair. and Man. Dir KAILASH SIROHIYA; Editor SUDHIR SHARMA; circ. 210,000.

Kathmandu Post: Kantipur Complex, Subhidhanagar, POB 8559, Kathmandu; tel. (1) 4480100; fax (1) 4466320; e-mail au@kantipur.com.np; internet www.kantipuronline.com; f. 1993; English; Editor AKHILESH UPADHYAY; circ. 40,000.

Motherland: POB 1184, Kathmandu; English; Editor MANINDRA RAJ SHRESTHA; circ. 5,000.

Nepal Samacharpatra: Red Cross Marg, Kalimati, POB 2045, Kathmandu; tel. (1) 4287777; fax 4288700; e-mail pushkarlal@newsofnepal.com; internet newsofnepal.com; f. 1945; Nepali; Editor-in-Chief PUSHKAR LAL SHRESTHA; circ. 1,000.

Nepali Hindi Daily: 72 Kalinchok Marg, Maitidevi, POB 49, Kathmandu; tel. (1) 4436374; fax (1) 4435931; e-mail das@ntc.net.np; f. 1954; evening; Hindi; Publr UMA KANT DAS; Chief Editor VIJOY KUMAR DAS; circ. 100,000.

Rajdhani: Kathmandu; internet www.rajdhani.com.np; Editor KAPIL KAFLE; circ. 50,000.

Rising Nepal: Dharma Path, POB 1623, Kathmandu; tel. (1) 4244437; fax (1) 4224381; e-mail trn@gorkhapatra.org.np; internet www.gorkhapatra.org.np; f. 1965; English; Editor-in-Chief AJAY SHUMSHER RANA; circ. 20,000.

Samaj: National Printing Press, Dillibazar, Kathmandu; f. 1954; Nepali; Editor MANI RAJ UPADHYAYA; circ. 5,000.

Samaya: Kamal Press, Ramshah Path, Kathmandu; f. 1954; Nepali; Editor MANIK LALL SHRESTHA; circ. 18,000.

Swatantra Samachar: Kathmandu; tel. (1) 4419285; f. 1957; Editor MADAN DEV SHARMA; circ. 2,000.

SELECTED PERIODICALS

Agricultural Credit: Agricultural Training and Research Institute, Agricultural Development Bank, Head Office, Ramshah Path, Panchayat Plaza, Kathmandu; tel. (1) 4220756; fax (1) 4225329; 2 a year; publ. by the Agricultural Development Bank; Chair. Dr NARAYAN N. KHATRI; Editor RUDRA PD DAHAL.

Arpan: Bhimsensthan, POB 285, Kathmandu; tel. (1) 4244450; fax (1) 4279544; e-mail manju_sakya@hotmail.com; internet www.nepalnews.com.arpan.php; f. 1964; weekly; Nepali; Publr and Chief Editor MANJU RATNA SAKYA; circ. 18,000.

Awake Weekly Chronicle: Kathmandu; English.

Commerce: Bhimsensthan, POB 171, Kathmandu; tel. (1) 4279636; fax (1) 4279544; e-mail manju_sakya@hotmail.com; f. 1971; monthly; English; Publr and Chief Editor MANJU RATNA SAKYA; Editor SUBHA LAXMI SAKYA; circ. 12,000.

Current: Gautam Marg, Kamalpokhari, Kathmandu; tel. (1) 4419484; fax (1) 4445406; f. 1982; weekly; Nepali; publ. by private limited co; Man. Editor KIRAN GAUTAM; Chief Editor DEVENDRA GAUTAM; circ. 10,000.

Cyber Post: Kathmandu; fortnightly; computers, electronics.

Foreign Affairs Journal: 5/287 Lagon, Kathmandu; f. 1976; 3 a year; articles on Nepalese foreign relations and diary of main news events; Publr and Editor BHOLA BIKRUM RANA; circ. 5,000.

Himal Southasian: Patan Dhoka, Lalitpur, POB 24393; tel. (1) 5547279; fax (1) 5552141; e-mail info@himalmag.com; internet www.himalmag.com; f. 1987; monthly; political, business, social and environmental issues throughout South Asia; Editor-in-Chief KANAK MANI DIXIT; Marketing Man. KOMAL MORE.

The Independent: Shankher Deep Bldg, Khichhapokhari, POB 3543, Kathmandu; tel. (1) 4249256; fax (1) 4226293; e-mail independ@mos.com.np; internet www.nepalnews.com/independent.htm; f. 1991; weekly; English; Editor SUBARNA B. CHHETRI.

Janadharana (People's Opinion): Kathmandu; e-mail janadharana@gmail.com; internet www.nepalnews.com.np/janadharana; weekly; independent; Editor NIMKANT PANDEY.

Janmabhumi: Janmabhumi Press, Tahachal, Kathmandu; tel. (1) 4280979; fax (1) 4274795; e-mail sirishnp@hotmail.com; f. 1970; weekly; Nepali; Publr and Editor SHIRISH BALLABH PRADHAN.

Koseli: Kathmandu; weekly; Nepali.

Madhuparka: Dharmapath, POB 23, Kathmandu; tel. (1) 4222278; f. 1986; monthly; Nepali; literary; Editor BIJAYA CHALISE; circ. 20,000.

Matribhoomi (Nepali Weekly): Ga-2-549, Kamal Pokhari (in front of the Police Station), Kathmandu; tel. (1) 4412501; weekly; Nepali; Editor GOVINDA BIYOGI.

Mulyankan: Kathmandu; monthly, left-wing; Editor SHYAM SHRESTHA.

Nepal Chronicle: Maruhiti; weekly; English; Publr and Editor CHANDRA LAL JHA.

Nepal National Weekly: Kantipur Publications Pvt Ltd, Kantipur Complex, Subhidhanagar, POB 8559, Kathmandu; tel. (1) 4480100; fax (1) 4466320; e-mail prashanta@kantipur.com.np; internet www.ekantipur.com/nepal; f. 2000; fortnightly; Nepali; Editor PRASHANT ARYAL; circ. 40,000.

Nepal Overseas Trade Statistics: Trade and Export Promotion Centre, Pulchowk, Lalitpur, POB 825, Kathmandu; tel. (1) 5532642; fax (1) 5525464; e-mail info@tepc.gov.np; internet www.tepc.gov.np; f. 2006; annual; English; Exec. Dir RAMESH KUMAR SHRESTHA.

Nepal Post: 10/31 Gautam Marg, Kamalpokhari, Kathmandu, POB 191; tel. (1) 4419484; fax (1) 4445406; e-mail info@nayanepalpost.com; internet www.nayanepalpost.com; f. 1973; monthly; Chief Editor DEVENDRA GAUTAM.

Nepal Trade and Export Bulletin: Trade and Export Promotion Centre, Pulchowk, Lalitpur, POB 825, Kathmandu; tel. (1) 5532642; fax (1) 5525464; e-mail info@tepc.gov.np; internet www.tepc.gov.np; f. 2006; 3 a year; English; Dir BADRI BAHADUR KARKI (acting).

Nepali Times: Himalmedia Pvt Ltd, POB 7251, Kathmandu; tel. (1) 5250333; fax (1) 5251013; e-mail editors@nepalitimes.com; internet www.nepalitimes.com; f. 2000; weekly; English; publ. by Himalmedia Pvt Ltd; Publr KUNDA DIXIT; Editor RABI THAPA; circ. 15,000.

People's Review: Pipalbot, Dillibazar, POB 3052, Kathmandu; tel. (1) 4417352; fax (1) 4438797; e-mail preview@ntc.net.np; internet www.peoplesreview.com.np; weekly; English; Chief Editor PUSHPA RAJ PRADHAN; circ. 15,000.

Rastrabani: Kathmandu; tel. (1) 4410339; weekly; Nepali; Chief Editor HARI LAMSAL.

Sanghu Weekly: Kathmandu; weekly; Editor GOPAL BUDHATHOKI.

Sanibariya: Kathmandu; weekly.

Saptahik Weekly: Kantipur Complex, Subhidhanagar, POB 8559, Kathmandu; tel. (1) 4480100; fax (1) 4466320; internet www.kantipuronline.com/saptahik; f. 1997; weekly; Nepali; news and entertainment; Editor SUBASH DHAKAL.

Swatantra Manch Weekly: POB 49, Kathmandu; tel. (1) 4436374; fax (1) 4435931; e-mail nepalidaily@rediffmail.com; f. 1985; independent; weekly; Nepali; Publr and Chief Editor VIJOY KUMAR DAS; circ. 40,000.

The Telegraph: Ghattekulo, Laligurans Marg, POB 4063, Kathmandu; tel. (1) 4419370; e-mail tgw@ntc.net.np; internet telegraphnepal.com; weekly; English; Chief Editor NARENDRA P. UPADHYAYA.

Vashudha: Makhan, Kathmandu; monthly; English; social, political and economic affairs; Publr and Editor T. L. SHRESTHA.

NEWS AGENCY

Rastriya Samachar Samiti (RSS): Bhadrakali Plaza, Kathmandu; tel. (1) 4262912; fax (1) 4262744; e-mail info@rss.com.np; f. 1962; state-operated; Chair. BALKRISHNA CHAPAGAIN; Gen. Man. RAM KUMAR KOIRALA (acting).

PRESS ASSOCIATIONS

Federation of Nepalese Journalists (FNJ): Media Village, Sinamangal, Kathmandu; tel. (1) 4490063; fax (1) 4490085; e-mail fnjnepal@mail.com.np; internet www.fnjnepal.org; f. 1956; Pres. DHARMENDRA JHA; Gen. Sec. K. C. POSHAN.

NEPAL   Directory

Nepal Journalists' Association (NJA): Maitighar, POB 285, Kathmandu; tel. (1) 4262426; fax (1) 4279544; e-mail manju_sakya@hotmail.com; internet www.nja.org.np; 5,400 mems; Pres. Manju Ratna Sakya; Gen. Sec. Nirmal Kumar Aryal.

Press Council: Sanchargram, Tilganga, POB 3077, Kathmandu; tel. (1) 4469799; fax (1) 4469894; e-mail prescoun_mdf@wlink.com.np; internet www.presscouncilnepal.org; f. 1970; Chair. Narayan Prasad Sharma; Sec. Shree Dar Gautam.

Publishers

Educational Publishing House: POB 5178, Kathmandu; tel. (1) 4241255; e-mail ishwarbshrestha@yahoo.com; f. 1962; educational and technical; Dir Jyotsna Shrestha.

Himal Books: Himal Association, Patan Dhoka, POB 166, Lalitpur, Kathmandu; tel. (1) 5542544; fax (1) 5541196; e-mail books@himalassociation.org; internet www.himalassociation.org/himalbooks; f. 1992; subsidiary operation of Himal Association; general interest and academic publications in English and Nepali; Exec. Dir Basanta Thapa.

International Standards Books and Periodicals (Pvt) Ltd: Bhotahity Bazaar, Chowk Bhitra, POB 3000, Kathmandu 44601; tel. (1) 4262815; fax (1) 4264179; e-mail u2@ccsl.com.np; f. 1991; Chief Man. Dir Yogyndra Lall Chhipa; Chief Exec. and Man. Dir Ganesh Lall Singh Chhipa.

Lakoul Press: Palpa-Tansen, Kathmandu; educational and physical sciences.

Mahabir Singh Chiniya Main: Makhan Tola, Kathmandu.

Mandass Memorials Publications: Kathmandu; Man. Basant Raj Tuladhar.

Pilgrims Book House: Thamel, POB 3872, Kathmandu; tel. (1) 4700942; fax (1) 4700943; e-mail pilgrims@wlink.com.np; internet www.pilgrimsbooks.com; f. 1986; Asian studies, religion and travel; Propr Pushpa Tiwari.

Pilgrims Publishing Nepal (Pvt) Ltd: Goldhunga 4, POB 21646, Kathmandu; tel. (1) 4356764; fax (1) 4700544; internet www.pilgrimsbooks.com; f. 2000; Exec. Dir John Snyder; Man. Dir Bishow Bhatta.

Ratna Pustak Bhandar: 71 Ga Bank Marg, POB 98, Kathmandu; tel. (1) 4223026; fax (1) 4248421; e-mail rpb@wlink.com.np; f. 1945; textbooks, general, non-fiction and fiction; Propr Govinda Prasad Shrestha.

Royal Nepal Academy: Kamaladi, Kathmandu; tel. (1) 4221241; fax (1) 4221175; f. 1957; languages, literature, social sciences, art and philosophy; Dep. Admin. Chief T. D. Bhandari.

Sajha Prakashan: Pulchowk, Lalitpur, POB 20259, Kathmandu; tel. (1) 5521118; fax (1) 5544236; e-mail sajhap@wlink.com.np; internet www.sajha.org.np; f. 1964; educational, literary and general; Chair. Ram Varos Kapadi Vramar; Gen. Man. Victor Pradhan.

Trans Asian Media Pvt Ltd: Thapathali Crossing, POB 5320, Kathmandu; tel. (1) 4242895; fax (1) 4223889; Man. Editor Shyam Goenka.

GOVERNMENT PUBLISHING HOUSE

Department of Information: Ministry of Information and Communications, Singha Durbar, Kathmandu; tel. (1) 483254; fax (1) 483252; e-mail info@doinepal.gov.np; internet www.doinepal.gov.np.

Broadcasting and Communications

TELECOMMUNICATIONS

Nepal Telecommunications Authority: Bluestar Office Complex, Tripureswor, POB 9754, Kathmandu; tel. (1) 4101030; fax (1)4101034; e-mail info@nta.gov.np; internet www.nta.gov.np; telecommunications regulatory body; f. 1998; Chair. Bhesh Raj Kanel.

Nepal Telecom (Nepal Doorsanchar Co Ltd): Bhadrakali Plaza, POB 11803, Kathmandu; tel. (1) 4210202; fax (1) 4222424; e-mail rkt@ntc.net.np; internet www.ntc.net.np; f. 1975; operates landline and mobile services; 85% state-owned, 10% owned by Nepalese public, 5% owned by Nepal Telecom employees; Chair. Sushil Ghimire; Man. Dir Amarnath Singh.

Spice Nepal (Pvt) Ltd (Ncell): Krishna Tower, Buddhanagar, New Baneshwor, Kathmandu 10; tel. (980) 5554444; fax (980) 5554442; e-mail info@ncell.com.np; internet www.ncell.com.np; f. 2004; subsidiary of Telia Sonera Group (Sweden); launched Nepal's first privately owned GSM mobile network under Mero Mobile brand in 2005; services rebranded as Ncell in 2010; CEO Pasi Koistinen; 4.8m. subscribers (2010).

STM Telecom Sanchar: 768/47 Thirbam Sadak, Baluwatar, Kathmandu; tel. (1) 4445981; fax (1) 44419366; e-mail info@stmtelecom.com; internet www.stmtelecom.com; f. 2003 as jt venture between the USA, Thailand and Nepal; awarded World Bank-funded project to provide rural telecommunication services to eastern region of Nepal; CEO Abhinav Puri.

United Telecom Ltd: Fourth Floor, Triveni Complex, Putali Sadak, Kathmandu; tel. (1) 2222222; fax (1) 2499999; e-mail info@utlnepal.com; internet www.utlnepal.com; f. 2003; jt venture between Indian-owned Mahanagar Telephone Nigam Ltd, Telecommunications Consultants India Ltd, Tata Communications Ltd, and Nepal Ventures Pvt Ltd; CEO S. Kannan.

BROADCASTING

Radio

In August 2009 there were an estimated 186 FM radio stations in operation.

Radio Nepal: Radio Broadcasting Service, Government of Nepal, Singha Durbar, POB 634, Kathmandu; tel. (1) 4211910; fax (1) 4211952; e-mail radio@engg.wlink.com.np; internet www.radionepal.org; f. 1951; broadcasts on short-wave, medium-wave and FM frequencies in 20 regional languages, incl. Nepali and English, for 18 hours daily (incl. two hours of regional broadcasting in the morning and evening); short-wave station at Khumaltar and medium-wave stations at Bhainsepati, Pokhara, Surkhet, Dipayal, Bardibas and Dharan; FM stations at Kathmandu, Kanchanpur, Rupandehi, Chitwan, Makawanpur, Bara, Jumla, Mustang, Ilam, Simikot and Humla; Exec. Dir Tapanath Shukla.

Hits FM: POB 21912, Baneshwor, Kathmandu; tel. (1) 4780534; fax (1) 4780543; e-mail info@hitsfm.com.np; internet www.hitsfm.com.np; f. 1996; broadcasts 24 hrs daily; Exec. Dir Jeevan Shrestha.

Image FM (Kath FM): POB 5566, Kathmandu; tel. (1) 4433141; fax (1) 4427262; e-mail imagefm@wlink.com.np; internet www.imagechannels.com; f. 1999; Station Man. Bharat Shakya.

Janaki FM: Janakpurdham, Nepal; tel. (41) 5527430; fax (41) 5527432; e-mail info@janakifm.org.np; internet www.janakifm.org.np; f. 2007.

Kalika FM: Bharatpur 10, Chitwan; tel. (56) 527158; fax (56) 527161; e-mail kalikafm@techminds.com.np; internet www.kalikafm.com.np; f. 2002.

Kantipur FM: Kantipur Complex, Subhidhanagar, POB 8559, Kathmandu; tel. (1) 4480100; fax (1) 4470178; e-mail kfm@kantimos.com.np; internet www.radiokantipur.com; f. 1998; broadcasts 24 hrs daily; Man. Dir Kailash Sirohiya; Station Man. Prabhat Rimal.

Radio Lumbini: Aanandabane VDC, Ward No. 3, Manigram, Rupandehi, Lumbini; tel. (71) 561003; fax (71) 561545; e-mail lumbinifm@mos.com.np; internet www.radiolumbini.org; f. 2000; CEO Krishna Prasad Nepal.

Radio Sagarmatha: Bakhundol, Lalitpur, GPOB 6958, Kathmandu; tel. (1) 5528091; fax (1) 5530227; e-mail stationmanager@radiosagarmatha.org; internet www.radiosagarmatha.org; f. 1997; independent; Chair. Laxman Upreti; Station Man. Ghama Raj Luitel.

Times FM: GPO 8975, EPC 906, Jawalakhel, Lalitpur, Kathmandu; tel. and fax (1) 4481471; e-mail info@timesfm906.com; internet www.timesfm906.com; Man. Dir R. K. Shrestha.

Television

Nepal Television Corpn: Singha Durbar, POB 3826, Kathmandu; tel. (1) 4220348; fax (1) 4228312; internet neptv.com.np; f. 1985; operates NTV and NTV2; programmes in Nepali (50%), English (25%) and Hindi/Urdu (25%); regional station at Kohalpur; Exec. Chair. Kundan Aryal; Gen. Man. Gambhir Kant Mainali.

Avenues TV: 11 Avenues Plaza, Teku Rd, Ganeshman Marga, Kathmandu; tel. (1) 4227222; fax (1) 4248811; e-mail atv@avenues.tv; internet www.avenues.tv; f. 2003; news service.

Image Channel: POB 5566, Panipokhari, Kathmandu; tel. (1) 4006555; fax (1) 4427262; e-mail ichannel@wlink.com.np; internet www.imagechannels.com; f. 2003; privately owned; Chair. R. K. Manandhar.

Kantipur Television Network (KTV): Kantipur Complex, Subhidhanagar, POB 8559, Kathmandu; tel. (1) 4480100; fax (1) 4470178; e-mail corporate@kantipurtv.com; internet www.kantipurtv.com; f. 2003; Chair. Hem Raj Gyawali; Man. Dir Kailash Sirohiya.

Space-Time Network: Iceberg Bldg, 3rd Floor, Putali Sadak, Kathmandu; tel. (1) 4419133; fax (1) 4419504; f. 1994; satellite transmission services; launched Channel Nepal, the country's first satellite channel, in 2001; Man. Dir (vacant).

NEPAL

Finance

(auth. = authorized; cap. = capital; m. = million; dep. = deposits; res = reserves; brs = branches; amounts in Nepalese rupees)

BANKING

Central Bank

Nepal Rastra Bank: Central Office, Baluwatar, POB 73, Kathmandu; tel. (1) 4410158; fax (1) 4410159; e-mail fxm@nrb.org.np; internet www.nrb.org.np; f. 1956; bank of issue; 100% state-owned; cap. 3,000m., res 43,930m., dep. 75,703m. (July 2009); Gov. and Chair. Dr YUBA RAJ KHATIWADA; 9 brs.

Domestic Commercial Banks

Kumari Bank Ltd: Durbarmarg, POB 21128, Kathmandu; tel. (1) 4221312; fax (1) 4231960; e-mail info@kbl.com.np; internet www.kumaribank.com; f. 2001; auth. cap. 1,070.0m., res 294.9m., dep. 13,274.3m. (July 2008); Chair. MIN BAHADUR GURUNG; CEO RADHESH PANT; 8 brs.

Nepal Bank Ltd: Nepal Bank Bldg, Dharmapath, New Rd, POB 36, Kathmandu; tel. (1) 4222397; fax (1) 4220414; e-mail info@nepalbank.com.np; internet www.nepalbank.com.np; f. 1937; 40% state-owned, 60% owned by Nepalese public; cap. 380.4m., res 5,988.3m., dep. 41,829.4m. (July 2008); Chair. Dr PUSHPA RAJ RAJKARNIKAR; CEO Dr BINOD ATREYA; 105 brs.

Nepal Industrial and Commercial Bank Ltd (NIC Bank): Kamaladi, Ganeshthan, POB 7367, Kathmandu; tel. (1) 4262277; fax (1) 4241865; e-mail kamaladi@nicbank.com.np; internet www.nicbank.com.np; f. 1998; privately owned; cap. 1,140m., res 519m., dep. 16,045m. (July 2009); Chair. JAGDISH PRASAD AGRAWAL; CEO SASHIN JOSHI; 26 brs.

Rastriya Banijya Bank (National Commercial Bank): POB 8368, Singha Durbar Plaza, Kathmandu; tel. (1) 4252595; fax (1) 4252931; e-mail rbb.info@rbb.com.np; internet www.rbb.com.np; f. 1966; 100% state-owned; cap. 1,172m., res and surplus −14,658m., dep. 68,095m. (July 2009); Chair. RAM PRASHAD ADHIKARI; CEO JANARDAN ACHARYA; 128 brs, 5 regional offices.

Joint-venture Banks

Bank of Kathmandu Ltd: Kamal Pokhari, POB 9044, Kathmandu; tel. (1) 4414541; fax (1) 4418990; e-mail info@bok.com.np; internet www.bok.com.np; f. 1993; 58% owned by Nepalese public, 42% by local promoters; cap. 844m., res 862m., dep. 18,335m. (July 2009); Chair. NARENDRA KUMAR BASNYAT; CEO AJAY SHRESTHA; 37 brs.

Everest Bank Ltd (EBL): POB 13384, EBL House, Lazimpath, Kathmandu; tel. (1) 4443377; fax (1) 4443160; e-mail ebl@mos.com.np; internet www.everestbankltd.com; f. 1994; 50% owned by directors, 20% by Punjab National Bank (India) and 30% by the Nepalese public; cap. 838m., res 1,282m., dep. 33,771m. (July 2009); Chair. BISHNU KRISHNA SHRESTHA; CEO P. K. MOHAPATRA; 35 brs.

Global Bank Ltd: Adarshanagar, Birgunj 13, POB 45, Parsa; tel. (1) 530337; fax (1) 530338; e-mail info@globalbank.com.np; internet www.globalbanknepal.com; f. 2006; cap. 1,000m., res 48m., dep. 11,009m. (July 2009); Chair. CHANDRA PRASAD DHAKAL; CEO ANIL GYAWALI.

Himalayan Bank Ltd: Karmachari Sanchaya Kosh Bldg, Tridevi Marg, Thamel, POB 20590, Kathmandu; tel. (1) 4227749; fax (1) 4222800; e-mail hbl@himalayanbank.com; internet www.himalayanbank.com; f. 1993; 20% owned by Habib Bank Ltd (Pakistan); cap. 1,216m., res 1,903m., dep. 35,294m. (July 2009); Chair. MANOJ BAHADUR SHRESTHA; CEO ASOKE S. J. B. RANA; 12 brs.

Laxmi Bank Ltd: Hattisar, POB 19593, Kathmandu; tel. (51) 530394; fax (51) 530393; e-mail info@laxmibank.com; internet www.laxmibank.com; f. 2001; cap. 1,098m., res 245m., dep. 16,417m. (July 2009); Chair. RAJENDRA K. KHETAN; CEO SUMAN JOSHI.

Nabil Bank Ltd (Nabil): Nabil House, Kamaladi, POB 3729, Kathmandu; tel. (1) 4429546; fax (1) 4429548; e-mail nabil@nabilbank.com; internet www.nabilbank.com; f. 1984 as Nepal Arab Bank Ltd; name changed as above Jan. 2000; 50% owned by National Bank of Bangladesh, 30% by the Nepalese public and 20% by Nepalese govt financial institutions; cap. 2,028m., res 1,803m., dep. 47,211m. (July 2010); Chair. SATYENDRA PYARA SHRESTHA; CEO AMRIT CHARAN SHRESTHA; 48 brs.

Nepal Bangladesh Bank Ltd (NB Bank): Bijuli Bazar, New Baneshwor, POB 9062, Kathmandu; tel. (1) 4783976; fax (1) 4780826; e-mail nbblho@nbbl.com.np; internet www.nbbl.com.np; f. 1994; 50% owned by International Finance Investment and Commerce Bank Ltd (Bangladesh), 20% by Nepalese promoters and 30% public issue; CEO GOVIND BABU TIWARI; Chair. TIRTHA MAN SAKYA; 19 brs.

Nepal Credit and Commerce Bank Ltd: NB Bldg, Bagh Bazar, Kathmandu; tel. (1) 4246991; fax (1) 4244610; e-mail corporate@nccbank.com.np; internet www.nccbank.com.np; est. as Nepal Bank of Ceylon; reconstituted as above in Sept. 2002 after Bank of Ceylon (Sri Lanka) sold its shares to NB Group (Nepal); cap. 1,399m., res 239m., dep. 9,143m. (July 2009); Chair. PRITHIVI RAJ LIGAL; CEO RATNA RAJ BAJRACHARYA; 17 brs.

Nepal Investment Bank Ltd (NIBL): Durbar Marg, POB 3412, Kathmandu; tel. (1) 4228229; fax (1) 4226349; e-mail info@nibl.com.np; internet www.nibl.com.np; f. 1986 as Nepal Indosuez Bank Ltd, name changed as above in June 2002; 50% owned by a consortium of Nepalese investors, 20% by general public, 15% by Rastriya Banijya Bank and 15% by Rastriya Beema Sansthan; cap. 2,407m., res 1,383m., dep. 47,830m. (July 2009); Chair. and Chief Exec. PRITHIVI BAHADUR PANDE; 40 brs.

Nepal SBI Bank Ltd: Corporate Office, Hattisar, POB 6049, Kathmandu; tel. (1) 4435516; fax (1) 4435612; e-mail nsblco@nsbl.com.np; internet www.nepalsbi.com.np; f. 1993; 50% owned by State Bank of India, 30% by Nepalese public, 15% by Employees' Provident Fund (Nepal) and 5% by Agricultural Devt Bank (Nepal); Man. Dir N. K. CHARI.

Standard Chartered Bank Nepal Ltd: Grindlays Bhavan, Naya Baneshwor, POB 3990, Kathmandu; tel. (1) 4246753; fax (1) 4226762; e-mail outserve.nepal@standardchartered.com; internet www.standardchartered.com/np; f. 1986 as Nepal Grindlays Bank; name changed in July 2001; 75% owned by Standard Chartered Bank (United Kingdom) and 25% by the Nepalese public; cap. 1,608m., res 1,731m., dep. 35,182m. (July 2010); Chair. NEERAJ SWAROOP; CEO SUJIT MUNDUL; 14 brs.

Banking Organization

Nepal Bankers' Association (NBA): Heritage Plaza, Blk C & D, 2nd Floor, Kamaladi, Kathmandu; tel. (1) 4241278; fax (1) 4243183; e-mail nba@enet.com.np; internet www.nepalbankers.com; Pres. ASHOKE SUMSHER J. B. RANA.

Development Finance Organizations

Agricultural Development Bank Ltd: Ramshah Path, Kathmandu; tel. (1) 4262885; fax (1) 4262616; e-mail info@adbn.gov.np; internet www.adbl.gov.np; f. 1968; 93.6% state-owned, 2.1% owned by the Nepal Rastra Bank, and 4.3% by co-operatives and private individuals; specialized agricultural credit institution providing credit for agricultural development to co-operatives, individuals and asscns; receives deposits from individuals, co-operatives and other asscns to generate savings in the agricultural sector; acts as Government's implementing agency for small farmers' group development project, assisted by the Asian Devt Bank and financed by the UN Devt Programme; operational networks include 14 zonal offices, 37 brs, 92 sub-brs, 52 depots and 160 small farmers' development projects, three Zonal Training Centres, two Appropriate Technology Units; Chair. GOVINDA PRASAD KOIRALA.

Nepal Aawas Finance Ltd: New Baneshwor, POB 5624, Kathmandu; tel. (1) 4780259; fax (1) 4782753; e-mail info@nepalhousing.com; internet www.nepalhousing.com.np; Chair. JITENDRA NATH RIMAL.

STOCK EXCHANGE

Nepal Stock Exchange Ltd (NEPSE): Singha Durbar Plaza, POB 1550, Kathmandu; tel. (1) 4250755; fax (1) 4262538; e-mail info@nepalstock.com; internet www.nepalstock.com.np; f. 1976; reorg. 1984; converted in 1993 from Securities Exchange Centre Ltd to Nepal Stock Exchange Ltd; 147 listed cos, 139 scripts; Chair. TANKA PRASAD PANERU; Gen. Man. SHANKER MAN SINGH.

INSURANCE

Alliance Insurance Co Ltd: POB 10811, Tinkune, Kathmandu; tel. (1) 4499220; fax (1) 4499647; e-mail info@allianceinsurance.com.np; internet www.allianceinsurance.com.np; f. 1996; Chair. GOVINDA DAS SHRESTHA; CEO YUGESH BHAKTA BADE SHRESTHA.

Everest Insurance Co Ltd: Hattisar, POB 10675, Kathmandu; tel. (1) 4425758; fax (1) 4444366; e-mail eveinsco@mos.com.np; internet www.everestinsurance.com; f. 1994; Chair. RAJENDRA K. KHETAN; Gen. Man. KEWAL K. SHRESTHA.

Himalayan General Insurance Co Ltd: Babar Mahal, POB 148, Kathmandu; tel. (1) 4231788; fax (1) 4241517; e-mail ktm@hgi.com.np; internet www.hgi.com.np; f. 1993; Chair. RAJ KRISHNA SHRESTHA; CEO MAHENDRA KRISHNA SHRESTHA.

Neco Insurance Ltd: Star Mall, 7th Floor, Putalisadak, POB 12271, Kathmandu; tel. (1) 4427354; fax (1) 4418761; e-mail info@necoins.com.np; internet www.necoins.com.np; f. 1994; Chair. JANARDAN AACHARYA; Exec. Dir YOGENDRA PRASAD SHRESTHA.

Nepal Insurance Co Ltd: NIC Bldg, Kulratna Marg, Kamaladi, POB 3623, Kathmandu; tel. (1) 4221353; fax (1) 4225446; e-mail nic@wlink.com.np; internet www.nepalinsurance.com.np; f. 1947 as Nepal Malchalani Tatha Beema Co; name changed as above in 1991; Chair. Dr PUSPA RAJ RAJKARNIKAR; Gen. Man. KESHAB DUBADI.

NEPAL

Directory

NLG Insurance Co Ltd: Panipokhari, Lazimpat, POB 20600, Kathmandu; tel. (1) 4442646; fax (1) 4416427; e-mail info@nlgi.com.np; internet www.nlg.com.np; 70% owned by National Life Insurance Co Ltd; Chair. Krishna Prasad Sharma; CEO Vijaya Bahadur Shah.

Premier Insurance Co (Nepal) Ltd: Tripureswor, POB 9183, Kathmandu; tel. (1) 4259567; fax (1) 4249708; e-mail premier@picl.com.np; internet www.premier-insurance.com.np; f. 1994; Chair. Ram Lal Shreshtha; Man. Dir Suresh Lal Shrestha.

Rastriya Beema Sansthan (National Insurance Corpn): POB 527, Kathmandu; tel. (1) 4262520; fax (1) 4262610; e-mail beema@wlink.com.np; internet www.beema.com.np; f. 1967; Gen. Man. Bir Bikram Raxamajhi.

Sagarmatha Insurance Co Ltd: Surakshan Bhavan, Bhagawati Marg, Naxal, POB 12211, Kathmandu; tel. (1) 4412367; fax (1) 4412378; e-mail sagarmatha@insurance.wlink.com.np; internet www.sagarmathainsurance.com.np; f. 1996; Chair. Ram Krishna Manandhar; Exec. Dir Krishna Bahadur Basnyat.

United Insurance Co (Nepal) Ltd: I. J. Plaza, Tindhara Pathshala, 2nd Floor, Durbar Marg, POB 9075, Kathmandu; tel. (1) 4246686; fax (1) 4246687; e-mail uic@mail.com.np; internet www.unitedinsurance.com.np; f. 1993; Chair. Ravi Bhakta Shrestha.

Trade and Industry

GOVERNMENT AGENCY

National Planning Commission (NPC): Singha Durbar, POB 1284, Kathmandu; tel. (1) 4225879; fax (1) 4226500; e-mail npcs@npcnepal.gov.np; internet www.npc.gov.np; Vice-Chair. Jagadish Chandra Pokharel.

DEVELOPMENT ORGANIZATIONS

National Productivity and Economic Development Centre: Balaju Industrial District, POB 1318, Kathmandu; tel. (1) 4350566; fax (1) 4350530; e-mail npedc@wlink.com.np; internet www.npedc-nepal.org; functions as secretariat of National Productivity Council; provides services for industrial promotion and productivity improvement through planning research, consultancy, training, seminars and information services; Gen. Man. Yuddha Bhadur Pant (acting).

National Tea and Coffee Development Board (NTCDB): New Baneshwor, POB 9683, Kathmandu; tel. (1) 4495792; fax (1) 4497941; e-mail ntcdb@hons.com.np; internet teacoffee.gov.np; f. 1992 to promote and expand the Nepalese tea industry; Exec. Dir Binay Kumar Mishra.

National Trading Ltd: Teku, POB 128, Kathmandu; tel. (1) 4225799; fax (1) 4225151; e-mail info@nationaltrading.com.np; internet www.nationaltrading.com.np; f. 1962; govt-owned; imports and distributes construction materials and raw materials for industry; also machinery, vehicles and consumer goods; operates bonded warehouse, duty-free shop and related activities; brs in all major towns; Chair. L. P. Agrawal.

Nepal Foreign Trade Association: Bagmati Chamber, 1st Floor, Milan Marg, Teku, POB 541, Kathmandu; tel. (1) 4223784; fax (1) 4247159; e-mail nfta@mos.com.np; f. 1972; Pres. Ashok Kumar Agrawal; 431 mems.

Nepal Tea Development Corpn Ltd: Triveni Complex, Putali Sadak, Kathmandu; tel. (1) 4224074; fax (1) 4266133; e-mail ntdc@trivenionline.com; internet www.ntdcltd.com; f. 1966; privatized in early 2000s; commercial production of tea; Contact Subhash C. Shanghai.

Trade and Export Promotion Centre (TEPC): Na Tole, Pulchowk, Lalitpur, POB 825, Kathmandu; tel. (1) 5525898; fax (1) 5525464; e-mail info@tepc.gov.np; internet www.tepc.gov.np; f. 1971; govt-owned; Chair. Purshottam Ojha; Exec. Dir Ramesh Kumar Shrestha.

CHAMBERS OF COMMERCE

Federation of Nepalese Chambers of Commerce and Industry (FNCCI): Pachali Shahid Shukra FNCCI Milan Marg, Teku, POB 269, Kathmandu; tel. (1) 4262061; fax (1) 4261022; e-mail fncci@mos.com.np; internet www.fncci.org; f. 1965; comprises 92 District Municipality Chambers (DCCIs), 76 Commodity Associations, 439 leading industrial and commercial undertakings in both the public and private sector, and 10 Bi-national Chambers; publishes annual *Nepal and the World: A Statistical Profile* and directory of members every three years; Chair. Krishna Mohan Shrestha; Gen. Sec. Sanjib Bahadur Koirala.

Birganj Chamber of Commerce and Industries: Hospital Rd, Birganj; tel. (51) 522290; fax (51) 526049; e-mail bicci@wlink.com.np; 605 mems; Pres. Om Prakash Sikariya.

Lalitpur Chamber of Commerce and Industry: Mangal Bazar, Patan Durbar Sq., POB 26, Lalitpur; tel. (1) 5530663; fax (1) 5530661; e-mail lcci@mos.com.np; internet www.lcci.org.np; f. 1967; Pres. Umesh Lal Amatya; Sec.-Gen. Naresh Kumar Shrestha.

Nepal Chamber of Commerce: Chamber Bhavan, Kantipath, POB 198, Kathmandu; tel. (1) 4230947; fax (1) 4229998; e-mail chamber@wlink.com.np; internet www.nepalchamber.org; f. 1952; non-profit org. promoting industrial and commercial development; 8,000 regd cos and 1,600 ordinary mems; Pres. Surendra Bir Malakar; Sec.-Gen. Kishor Kumar Agrawal.

INDUSTRIAL AND TRADE ASSOCIATIONS

Association of Craft Producers: Ravi Bhavan Mode, POB 3701, Kathmandu; tel. (1) 4275108; fax (1) 4272676; e-mail craftacp@mos.com.np; internet acp.org.np; f. 1984; local non-profit org. providing technical, marketing and management services for craft producers; manufacturer, exporter and retailer of handicraft goods; Exec. Dir Meera Bhattarai; Programme Dir Revita Shrestha.

Association of Forest-based Industries and Trade: Thapathali, POB 2798, Kathmandu; tel. (1) 4216020.

Association of Nepalese Rice, Oil and Pulses Industries: POB 20782, Radha Bhavan, Tripureswor, Kathmandu; tel. (1) 4215676; e-mail nfma@mcmail.com.np; Pres. Tola Ram Dugar; Gen. Sec. Chandra Krishna Karmacharya.

Association of Pharmaceutical Producers of Nepal: Babar Mahal, POB 21721, Maitighar, Kathmandu; tel. and fax (1) 4231871; e-mail appon@wlink.com.np; Pres. Pradeep Man Vaidya; Sec.-Gen. Umesh Lal Shrestha.

Cargo Agents' Association of Nepal: Thamel, POB 5355, Kathmandu; tel. (1) 4419019; fax (1) 4419858.

Central Carpet Industries Association of Nepal: Maitighar, Babar Mahal, POB 2419, Kathmandu; tel. (1) 4259400; fax (1) 4262458; e-mail ccia@enet.com.np; internet www.nepalcarpet.org; Pres. Lank Man Roka; Gen. Sec. Chhiring Sherpa.

Computer Association of Nepal: 235/39 Maitidevi Marga, Kathmandu; tel. (1) 4432700; fax (1) 4441998; e-mail info@can.org.np; internet www.can.org.np; f. 1992; asscn of the IT Businessmen's Organization; Pres. Suresh K. Karna.

Confederation of Nepalese Industries: 303 Bagmati Chambers, Teku, Kathmandu; tel. (1) 4243711; fax (1) 4244687; e-mail cni@wlink.com.np; internet www.cnind.org; f. 2000; Pres. Binod Chaudhary.

Federation of Handicraft Associations of Nepal: Upma Marg, Thapathali, POB 784, Kathmandu; tel. (1) 4244231; fax (1) 4222940; e-mail han@wlink.com.np; internet www.nepalhandicraft.org.np; f. 1972; Pres. Bikash Ratna Dhakhwa.

Federation of Nepal Cottage and Small Industries (FNCSI): Chabahil, POB 6530, Kathmandu; tel. (1) 4491528; fax (1) 4468337; e-mail fncsi@ntc.net.np; internet www.fncsi.org.np; business networks in 70 districts; represents interests and promotes development of nation's micro, cottage and small industries; 30,000 general mems (2007); Pres. Lata Pyakurel.

Garment Association of Nepal: Shankhamul Rd, New Baneshwor, POB 21332, Kathmandu; tel. (1) 4780691; fax (1) 4780173; e-mail gan@ntc.net.np; internet www.ganasso.org; Pres. Kiran P. Saakha.

Himalayan Orthodox Tea Producers' Association of Nepal: Bakhundole, Lalitpur; internet www.nepaltea.com.np; f. 1998; non-profit-making org.; represents and promotes the Himalayan tea sector; Chair. Deepak Prakash Baskota.

Leather Footwear and Goods Manufacturers' Association of Nepal: Bag Bazar, POB 19732, Kathmandu; tel. (1) 4219349; e-mail lfgman@ntc.net.np; Pres. Ram Krishna Prasai.

Nepal Forest Industries Association: Naxal, Nag Pokhari, POB 5623, Kathmandu; tel. (1) 4411865; fax (1) 4413838; e-mail padmasri@ccsl.com.np; Pres. Hari Prasad Giri; Sec.-Gen. Rohini Thapaliya.

Nepal Leather Industries Association: POB 9944, Anamnagar, Kathmandu; tel. (1) 4265248; fax (1) 4228978; e-mail giris@atcnet.com.np; Pres. Sanjay Giri; Sec.-Gen. Ramesh Raj Pokharel.

Nepal Plastic Manufacturers' Association: Kandevsthan, Kupandol, POB 2350, Lalitpur; tel. and fax (1) 5528185; Pres. Shailendra Lal Pradhan; Sec.-Gen. Rajeswor Lal Joshi.

Nepal Tea Planters' Association: Bhadrapur-4, Jhapa; tel. (23) 520059; fax (23) 420679; Pres. Chandi Prasad Parajuli; Sec.-Gen. Mal Chand Goyal.

Nepal Textile Industries Association: Krishna Galli, Lalitpur; tel. (1) 5529290; fax (1) 5520291; Pres. Gopal P. Kshatriya; Sec.-Gen. Ram K. Maharjan.

Nepal Trans-Himalayan Trade Association: Jyoti Bhavan, Kantipath, POB 133, Kathmandu; tel. (1) 4225490; fax (1)

4254048; e-mail syamukapu@unilever.wlink.com.np; Pres. Tribhuwan D. Tuladhar; Gen. Sec. Mahesh Tuladhar.

Silk Association of Nepal: Tripureshwor, Kathmandu; tel. (1) 4254093; e-mail san@nepsilk.wlink.com.np; internet www.nepalsilk.org.np; f. 1992; organizes and promotes sericulture and silk devt activities; Pres. Shankar P. Pandeya.

UTILITIES
Electricity

Nepal Electricity Authority: Durbar Marga, POB 10020, Kathmandu; tel. (1) 4153052; fax (1) 4153067; e-mail info@nea.org.np; internet www.nea.org.np; f. 1985 following merger; govt-owned; Chair. Dr Prakash S. Mahat; Man. Dir and CEO Dr Jivendra Jha.

Butwal Power Co Ltd: 313 Ganga Devi Marga, Buddha Nagar, POB 11728, Kathmandu; tel. (1) 4781776; fax (1) 4780994; e-mail info@bpc.com.np; internet www.bpc.com.np; f. 1966; partially privatized in 2003; principal shareholders: 68.95% owned by Shangri-La Energy Ltd, 9.09% by Govt and 6.05% by Interkraft Norway; 5.91% divided between Nepalese energy orgs and employees; public sector retains 10% ownership; owns and operates Jhimruk and Andhi Khola Hydropower Plants; supplies electricity to the national grid; 326 employees; Chair. Padma Jyoti.

Chilime Hydropower Co Ltd: Kalikasthan, POB 25210, Kathmandu; tel. (1) 44439163; fax (1) 4443077; e-mail chpcl@wlink.com.np; internet www.chilime.com.np; 51% owned by Nepal Electricity Authority; Dir Uttar Kumar Shrestha.

Department of Electricity Development: 576 Bhakti Thapa Sadak-4, POB 2507, Anamnagar, Kathmandu; tel. (1) 4496800; fax (1) 4480257; e-mail info@doed.gov.np; internet www.doed.gov.np; f. 1993; fmrly Electricity Development Centre; name changed as above 1999; Dir-Gen. Sunil Bahadur Malla.

Water

Nepal Water Supply Corpn: Tripureshwor Marg, POB 5349, Kathmandu; tel. (1) 4262202; fax (1) 4262229; e-mail info@nwsc.com.np; internet www.nwsc.gov.np; f. 1990; govt-owned; Gen. Man. Gautam Bahadur Amatya.

TRADE UNIONS

Nepal Trade Union Congress—Independent (NTUC—I): POB 5507, Kathmandu; tel. (1) 4107754; fax (1) 4107759; e-mail ntuc@wlink.com.np; internet www.ntuci.org.np; f. 1947 as the Nepal Trade Union Congress; 28 affiliated unions; affiliated to ICFTU; operates in association with Nepali Congress Party; merged with Democratic Confederation of Nepalese Trade Unions in March 2008 and name changed to the above; Pres. Laxman Bahadur Basnet; Gen. Sec. Achayut Raj Pandey; 192,000 mems.

General Federation of Nepalese Trade Unions (GEFONT): Man Mohan Labour Bldg, GEFONT Plaza, Putali Sadak, POB 10652, Kathmandu; tel. (1) 4168000; fax (1) 4168012; e-mail dfa@gefont.org; internet www.gefont.org; f. 1989; 19 affiliated unions; Pres. Bishnu Rimal.

Transport

Department of Transport Management: Ministry of Labour and Transport Management, Singha Durbar, Kathmandu; tel. (1) 4602126; fax (1) 4602440; e-mail info@dotm.gov.np; internet www.dotm.gov.np; Dir-Gen. Krishna Pd. Dawadi (acting).

RAILWAYS

A short narrow-gauge line in Janakpur district is the sole railway in operation. However, a feasibility study into plans for a 1,318-km electric rail network was completed in mid-2010. In addition to a 945-km east–west line, linking the districts of Mechi and Mahakali, the proposed network included a 185-km Kathmandu–Pokhara section and up to six branch lines connecting with the rail network of India.

Nepal Railways Corpn Ltd (NRC): Khajuri, Janakpur; tel. (41) 52082; HQ Jaynagar, India; f. 1937 as Janakpur-Jaynagar Railways; name changed as above June 2004; 53 km open, linking Jaynagar in India with Janakpur and Bijalpura; narrow gauge; 11 steam engines, 25 coaches and vans, and 20 wagons; Gen. Man. Madan Singh Mahat.

ROADS

In mid-March 2008 Nepal had 19,147 km of roads, of which only 30.5% had permanent surfaces, 24.5% were gravel and 45.0% were dirt roads that were regularly washed away by floods. Around Kathmandu, there are short sections of roads suitable for motor vehicles, and there is a 28-km ring road round the valley. A 190-km mountain road, Tribhuwana Rajpath, links the capital with the Indian railhead at Raxaul. The Siddhartha Highway, constructed with Indian assistance, connects the Pokhara valley, in mid-west Nepal, with Sonauli, on the Indian border in Uttar Pradesh. The 114-km Arniko Highway, constructed with Chinese help, connects Kathmandu with Kodari, on the Chinese border. In the early 1990s the final section of the 1,030-km East–West Highway (Mahendra Highway) was constructed. A number of north–south roads were also constructed to connect the district headquarters with the East–West Highway.

A fleet of container trucks operates between Kolkata and Raxaul in India and other points in Nepal for transporting exports to, and imports from, third countries. Trolley buses provide a passenger service over the 13 km between Kathmandu and Bhaktapur.

Roads Board Nepal: POB 11406, Arnico Bldg, Minbhavan, Kathmandu; tel. (1) 4493515; fax (1) 4493542; e-mail roadsboard@wlink.com.np; internet www.roadsboardnepal.org; f. 2002; maintenance and devt of the road network; Exec. Dir Dipak Nath Chalise.

ROPEWAY

A 42-km ropeway links Hetauda and Kathmandu and can carry 22 metric tons of freight per hour throughout the year. Foodgrains, construction goods and heavy goods on this route are transported by the ropeway.

CIVIL AVIATION

Tribhuvan International Airport is situated about 6 km from Kathmandu. In 2007 Nepal had 47 airports, of various standards; in mid-2011, however, only 35 of these airports were in operation. A project to upgrade Janakpur Airport into a regional international airport was scheduled for completion in 2012.

Civil Aviation Authority of Nepal (CAAN): Babar Mahal, Kathmandu; tel. (1) 4262387; fax (1) 4262516; e-mail dgca@caanepal.org.np; internet www.caanepal.org.np; f. 1998; Dir-Gen. Ram Prasad Neupane.

Nepal Airlines Corpn (NAC): NAC Bldg, Kantipath, Kathmandu; tel. (1) 4220757; fax (1) 4225348; e-mail info@nac.com.np; internet nepalairlines.com.np; f. 1958; fmrly Royal Nepal Airlines Corpn (RNAC); 100% state-owned (scheduled for transfer to private ownership); scheduled services to 19 domestic airfields, international scheduled flights to five destinations in the Middle East and the Far East, charter flights; Man. Dir Sr Capt. Kul Bahadur Limbu.

The monopoly of the RNAC in domestic air services came to an end in 1992. By 2007 there were about 16 private airlines in Nepal providing domestic cargo and passenger services.

Agni Air: POB 23650, Prayag Marg, Shantinagar, Kathmandu; tel. (1) 4489386; fax (1) 4107655; e-mail info@agniair.com; internet www.agniair.com; f. 2006; scheduled passenger flights to domestic destinations; 5 aircraft; Chair. Sudhir Basnyat.

Buddha Air: Jawalakhal, Lalitpur, POB 2167, Kathmandu; tel. (1) 5521015; fax (1) 5537726; e-mail buddhaair@buddhaair.com; internet www.buddhaair.com; f. 1997; domestic passenger services; services to Paro, Bhutan, commenced in 2010; Man. Dir Birendra B. Basnet; Chair. Surendra B. Basnet.

Cosmic Air: Kalimatidole, Sinamangal, POB 3488, Kathmandu; tel. (1) 4490146; fax (1) 4497569; e-mail soi@wlink.com.np; internet www.cosmicair.com; f. 1997; operates domestic cargo, passenger and mountain flights; began operating flights to a limited no. of Indian destinations in 2004; Exec. Chair. Sanjaya Pradham; Man. Dir M. B. Mathema; 179 employees.

Gorkha Airlines: Maharajgunj, POB 9451, Kathmandu; tel. (1) 4435122; fax (1) 4444525; e-mail gorkha@mos.com.np; internet www.gorkhaairlines.com; f. 1996; scheduled and charter passenger and cargo flights to domestic destinations; Gen. Man. Rabindra Silwal.

Yeti Airlines: Tilganga, POB 20011, Kathmandu; tel. (1) 4465888; fax (1) 4464977; e-mail yetiair@wlink.com.np; internet www.yetiairlines.com; f. 1998; operates scheduled and chartered domestic flights; Chair. Lhakpa Sonam Sherpa; Man. Dir Ang Tshering Sherpa.

Tourism

Major tourist attractions include Lumbini, the birthplace of Buddha, the lake city of Pokhara and the Himalaya mountain range, including Mt Everest, the world's highest peak. In 1989, in an effort to increase tourism, the Government abolished travel restrictions in 18 areas of north-western Nepal that had previously been inaccessible to foreigners. Following the restoration of parliamentary democracy in 1990, tourist arrivals in Nepal rose considerably. Further travel restrictions in the remote areas of the country were abolished in 1991, and efforts were made to attract foreign investment in the Nepalese tourism industry, but the insurgency in the west hindered development in the early and mid-2000s. Since 2005, in an effort further to promote tourism, access has been granted to an additional 175 mountains, raising the total number of mountains open to climbers to 326. The cessation of Maoist hostilities in 2006 and the subsequent peace agreement between the former insurgents and the political parties' alliance—combined with the introduction of additional airline services between Nepal and other Asian countries—led to a significant recovery in the tourism sector. Tourism arrivals witnessed massive growth, from 383,926 in 2006 to 526,633 in 2007, increasing further, to an estimated 547,040, in 2008. Revenue from tourism increased from US $234.0m. in 2007 to an estimated $353.0m. in 2008.

Nepal Tourism Board: Tourist Service Centre, Bhrikuti Mandap, POB 11018, Kathmandu; tel. (1) 4256909; fax (1) 4256910; e-mail info@ntb.org.np; internet www.welcomenepal.com; f. 1998; Chair. LEELA MANI POUDEL; CEO PRACHANDA MAN SHRESTHA.

Hotel Association Nepal (HAN): Subarna Shamsher Marg, Gairidhara, POB 2151, Kathmandu; tel. (1) 4412705; fax (1) 4424914; e-mail info@hotelassociation.org.np; internet www.hotelassociationnepal.org; f. 1966; Pres. NARENDRA BAJRACHARYA.

Nepal Association of Tour and Travel Agents (NATTA): Gairidhara Rd, Goma Ganesh, Naxal, POB 362, Kathmandu; tel. (1) 4419409; fax (1) 4418684; e-mail info@natta.org.np; internet www.natta.org.np; f. 1966 to promote and regulate development in the tourism industry; non-governmental org.; 360 mems; Pres. RAM KAJI KONEY; Sec.-Gen. D. B. LIMBU.

Tourist Guide Association of Nepal (TURGAN): POB 5344, Kamaladi, Kathmandu; tel. and fax (1) 4225102; e-mail turgan@wlink.com.np; internet www.turgannepal.com; Pres. HARE RAM BARAL.

Trekking Agencies' Association of Nepal (TAAN): Maligaun Ganesthan, POB 3612, Kathmandu; tel. (1) 4427473; fax (1) 4419245; e-mail info@taan.org.np; internet www.taan.org.np; Pres. SITARAM SAPKOTA; Gen. Sec. RAJENDRA BAJAGAIN.

Defence

As assessed at November 2010, Nepal's total armed forces numbered 95,753 men. Paramilitary forces comprised 62,000 men. Military service is voluntary. There was a 15,000-strong Armed Police Force under the Ministry of Home Affairs.

Defence Budget: NRs 18,000m. in 2010.

Chief of Army Staff: Gen. CHHATRAMAN SINGH GURUNG.

Education

Primary education, beginning at six years of age and lasting for five years, is officially compulsory and is provided free of charge in government schools. Secondary education, beginning at the age of 11, lasts for a further five years, comprising a first cycle of three years (lower secondary) and a second of two years (secondary). In 2005/06 the total enrolment at primary and secondary schools was equivalent to an estimated 79% of the school-age population. In 2006/07 enrolment at primary schools included 76.1% of children in the relevant age-group (boys 77.9%; girls 74.2%), while the ratio for secondary enrolment in 2005/06 was equivalent to 43.2% of pupils in the relevant age-group (boys 45.7%; girls 40.5%). Some 8,000 pupils attended the country's 321 primary schools in 1950; in 2004 there were an estimated 24,746 primary schools, with a total of 4,030,045 pupils. The number of secondary schools rose from two in 1950 to 11,983 in 2004. In that year there were an estimated 1,988,761 pupils enrolled at secondary schools.

The oldest of the colleges of higher education in Nepal is Tri Chandra School in Kathmandu, founded in 1918, which provides four-year arts courses. The only other advanced college in existence before the 1951 Revolution was the Sanskrit College in Kathmandu, founded in 1948. A single college of education was established in 1956 for the training of secondary school teachers and other educational personnel. There are also nine primary teacher-training centres. The first 300-bed teaching hospital for 500 pupils, built with Japanese government assistance, was opened in 1984. There are four state universities and one privately funded university. The Tribhuvan University in Kathmandu had 115,608 students in 2001/02. The second state university, the Mahendra Sanskrit Viswavidyalaya in Beljhundi, Dang, was founded in 1986. In 2000/01 the university had an enrolment of 3,252 students. The Purbanchal University, which was opened in 1995, had 2,840 students in 2001/02, and the Pokhara University, which was opened in 1997, had 2,946 students. In addition, there is one private university—the Kathmandu University in Banepa, Kavrepalanchok, which was opened in 1992. In 2001/02 the university had an enrolment of 1,783 students.

Proposed expenditure on education by the central Government in the 2007/08 budget was NRs 28,072m. (16.6% of total spending). According to UNESCO, literacy among the adult population of Nepal was only 56.5% in 2007 (males 70.3%; females 43.6%); it was hoped that an adult literacy rate of 70% would be achieved by the conclusion of the 12th Five-Year Plan in 2017.

THE NETHERLANDS

Introductory Survey

LOCATION, CLIMATE, LANGUAGE, RELIGION, FLAG, CAPITAL

The Kingdom of the Netherlands is situated in Western Europe, bordered to the east by Germany and to the south by Belgium. Its northern and western shores face the North Sea. The Caribbean islands of Bonaire, Saba and Sint (St) Eustatius have the status of *bijzondere gemeente* (special municipalities), while Aruba, Curaçao and Sint (St) Maarten are independent countries within the Kingdom of the Netherlands. The climate is temperate: the average temperature in January is 0°C (32°F), and the summer average is 21°C (70°F). The national language is Dutch. There is a Frisian-speaking minority (numbering about 400,000). About one-third of the inhabitants are Roman Catholics and about one-quarter are Protestants, while most of the remainder do not profess any religion. The national flag (proportions 2 by 3) has three equal horizontal stripes, of red, white and blue. The capital is Amsterdam, but the seat of government is The Hague (Den Haag or 's-Gravenhage).

CONTEMPORARY POLITICAL HISTORY

Historical Context

The Netherlands remained neutral throughout the First World War. During the Second World War the Netherlands was occupied by Germany. Following its liberation in 1945, it became a founder member of the UN. In 1948 the Netherlands formed the Brussels Treaty Organization with Belgium and Luxembourg. The Treaty establishing the Benelux Economic Union (see p. 445) between these three countries was signed in 1958 and came into force in 1960, and a single customs area was established in 1970. The Netherlands was a founder member of the European Community (EC, now European Union—EU, see p. 270). Queen Juliana, who had reigned since 1948, abdicated in favour of her eldest daughter, Beatrix, in April 1980, following the adoption in February of a constitutional amendment that allowed for the accession of the reigning monarch's eldest child, regardless of gender.

Domestic Political Affairs

After the Second World War successive administrations were formed by various coalitions between the several 'confessional' Roman Catholic and Protestant and 'progressive' Socialist and Liberal parties. At a general election held in 1971 left-wing parties made substantial gains. In July 1972 the Government was forced to resign after losing its working majority in the Second Chamber of the States-General. Another general election took place in November, at which the 'confessional' parties suffered a major reverse, and in May 1973 a new Government was formed by a left-of-centre coalition under the leadership of Dr Joop den Uyl of the Partij van de Arbeid (PvdA—Labour Party).

The coalition collapsed in March 1977; a general election followed in May. Attempts to form a left-of-centre coalition between the PvdA, the Christen Democratisch Appèl (CDA—Christian Democratic Appeal)—an alliance of 'confessional' groupings, which united in 1980 to form a single party—and Democraten '66 were unsuccessful, and in December 1977 Andries van Agt, of the CDA, formed a centre-right coalition Government of the CDA and the right-wing Volkspartij voor Vrijheid en Democratie (VVD—People's Party for Freedom and Democracy). Despite retaining only a narrow majority in the Second Chamber and several ministerial disagreements, the Government survived its full term in office. A general election was held in May 1981, and a centre-left coalition Government was formed in September, led by van Agt and comprising the CDA, the PvdA and Democraten '66. The Council of Ministers resigned after only five weeks in office, owing to its failure to agree on economic strategy. In November the coalition partners accepted a compromise economic programme, but deep divisions within the Government continued. The coalition collapsed again in May 1982, when all six PvdA ministers resigned, after which van Agt led a minority interim Government of the CDA and Democraten '66.

Although at a general election held in September 1982 the PvdA became the largest party in the Second Chamber (with 47 of 150 deputies), the election produced a significant swing to the right. In November a centre-right CDA-VVD coalition was established under the leadership of Ruud Lubbers, who had recently succeeded van Agt as Chairman of the CDA. The CDA-VVD coalition was returned to power at a general election in May 1986, having retained its majority in the Second Chamber. A loss of nine seats by the VVD was offset by a corresponding gain by the CDA, which, with 54 seats, became the party with the largest representation in the Second Chamber. The election did, none the less, produce a shift towards the centrist parties, with the PvdA and Democraten '66 (D66, as the party was restyled) both gaining seats at the expense of smaller radical groups. Following the election, Wim Kok replaced den Uyl as parliamentary leader of the PvdA. A new CDA-VVD coalition was formed in July.

In May 1989 the VVD caused the collapse of the Government by refusing to support Lubbers' proposals for the financing of a 20-year National Environment Policy (NEP), which was to involve a reduction in government spending in sectors such as defence and housing, an increase in taxes on motor fuels and the abolition of tax concessions for commuters using private transport. A general election was called for September, at which the CDA again secured 54 seats in the Second Chamber, while the PvdA took 49 seats. The VVD lost five seats. An alliance of left-wing organizations, GroenLinks, won six. In October negotiations between the CDA and the PvdA culminated in the formation of a centre-left coalition, again led by Lubbers. The coalition accord envisaged increased welfare provision, to be funded by a reduction in defence expenditure, as well as a programme of job creation and reductions in certain categories of taxation. Kok was appointed Deputy Prime Minister and Minister of Finance. In August 1990 the Government introduced an amended version of the NEP, designated the National Environment Policy Plus (NEPP), which placed strong emphasis on energy conservation and improvements in waste disposal and recycling.

In November 1992 the Second Chamber ratified the Treaty on European Union, which had been signed by EC Heads of Government at Maastricht in December 1991; the First Chamber (Senate) similarly approved the Treaty in December 1992.

The CDA performed poorly at the May 1994 general election, winning only 34 seats in the Second Chamber. The PvdA became the party with the largest representation in the Chamber, with 37 seats. Both the VVD and D66 improved upon their performances at the previous general election, securing 31 and 24 seats respectively. The remaining 24 seats were distributed among eight smaller parties and special issue groups. Negotiations on a three-party coalition agreement between the PvdA, the VVD and D66 were initially retarded by deeply entrenched disagreement between the VVD and PvdA over the latter's reluctance to sanction severe reductions in social welfare spending. Following several concessions by the PvdA, a tripartite coalition, with Kok as Prime Minister, was eventually agreed in August.

The PvdA won increased representation at the general election to the Second Chamber held on 6 May 1998, taking 45 seats. The VVD secured 38 seats, while the CDA's representation was further reduced, to 29 seats. D66 won only 14 seats, having lost votes to GroenLinks and the Socialistische Partij (SP—Socialist Party). None the less, the PvdA, VVD and D66 agreed to renew their coalition (it was considered that D66 would be useful as an intermediary in conflicts of policy between the two leading partners), and a new Government, led by Kok, was inaugurated in August.

In May 1999 the Senate rejected the Government's proposal to allow the use of referendums on policy issues, a key demand of D66, after the refusal of a prominent member of the VVD to support the measure. D66 subsequently announced that it could no longer work with the VVD, and withdrew from the ruling coalition, prompting the resignation of the Council of Ministers. However, following a series of talks between the three parties, in June the Government formally withdrew its resignation. In January 2001 the three coalition parties reached a new agreement on the introduction of the use of referendums. The new proposals were for a judicially non-binding referendum and would not require a change to the Constitution. The temporary referendum law entered into force on 1 January 2002 and expired three years later. Legislation was subsequently adopted to allow a national referendum to be held exceptionally on the proposed EU constitutional treaty in June 2005 (see below).

In August 2001 Kok announced that he would not seek re-election for a further term in office at the general election, scheduled for May 2002. He also announced that he would step down as Party Leader of the PvdA and subsequently endorsed the appointment of Ad Melkert, the Parliamentary Leader of the party, as his successor. Jaap de Hoop Scheffer, the Parliamentary Leader of the CDA, resigned in September 2001. He was replaced by Jan Peter Balkenende in the following month.

Report on the Srebrenica massacre; the 2002 election

In April 2002 the entire Council of Ministers resigned following the publication of a report by the Netherlands Institute for War Documentation into the massacre of some 7,000 Bosnian Muslims by Bosnian Serb troops in Srebrenica, Bosnia and Herzegovina, in July 1995. The report blamed the Dutch Government, the Dutch military and the UN for their respective roles in failing to prevent the atrocity and claimed that the 100 lightly armed Dutch peace-keeping troops who had been stationed in the town at the time had been ill-trained and had no clear mandate. At the request of Queen Beatrix, the Government agreed to remain in office in a caretaker capacity pending the forthcoming general election, which was scheduled to be held on 15 May 2002.

Further investigations by a parliamentary commission, in November 2002, into the failure of the Dutch authorities to prevent the massacre at Srebrenica in 1995 revealed that the former Government had been aware of the likelihood of atrocities occurring in the UN camp. In January 2003 the commission concluded that the Netherlands bore responsibility for the massacre, that the Government had failed adequately to plan the mission and that the Netherlands army had suppressed details of its failures. In November 2007 a court in The Hague ruled that a case against both the UN and the Netherlands Government brought by a group of relatives of those killed at Srebrenica in 1995 was admissible under Dutch law and in June 2008 civil proceedings began in The Hague. However, in the following month the court ruled that the UN enjoyed immunity from prosecution with regard to its peace-keeping operations. In September the court dismissed a case against the Netherlands Government brought by the relatives of two Bosnian Muslims killed in the 1995 massacre, stating that the Government could not be held liable for the actions of Dutch peace-keepers in Srebrenica, as they had been operating under a UN mandate.

On 6 May 2002 the controversial politician Pim Fortuyn was shot dead in Hilversum, in the central Netherlands, a few days before the general election, in which his newly established party, the populist and anti-immigration Lijst Pim Fortuyn (LPF—Pim Fortuyn List), was expected to secure a substantial proportion of votes. Fortuyn had formed the movement following his dismissal in January as leader of the Leefbaar Nederland (LN—Livable Netherlands) party for his anti-immigration rhetoric. In April 2003 Volkert van der Graaf, an animal-rights activist who claimed that he believed Fortuyn had presented a threat to vulnerable members of society, was convicted of the murder.

At the general election of 15 May 2002 the CDA won 43 of the 150 seats in the Second Chamber, with 27.9% of the valid votes cast. The LPF took 26 seats (with 17.0% of the votes), the VVD 24 (15.4%) and the PvdA 23 (15.1%). In the light of their electoral defeats, both the PvdA and the VVD changed their Parliamentary Leaders, to Jeltje van Nieuwenhoven and Gerrit Zalm, respectively.

Balkenende becomes Prime Minister: 2002–2006

Jan Peter Balkenende was inaugurated as Prime Minister on 21 July 2002, leading a coalition Government comprising the CDA, the LPF and the VVD. However, on the same day, a Suriname-born LPF minister in the Ministry of Emancipation and Family Affairs, Philomena Bijhout, resigned when it was confirmed that she had been linked to a Surinamese militia group involved in political killings in the former Dutch colony in December 1982. The LPF suffered a further reverse when allegations were made by a newspaper that their new leader, Mat Herben, had tried unfairly to influence the selection procedure for the LN's electoral candidates when Fortuyn was still leader and Herben a party member. Herben resigned at the end of July 2002 and was subsequently replaced by Harry Wijnschenk. The new Government detailed policies to reform the health insurance and social security system and reduce the number of illegal immigrants to the Netherlands. In October the Minister of Immigration and Integration opened a new college for the instruction of Muslim religious leaders (*imams*) in Dutch values and social conventions. The course was compulsory for new *imams*, who faced deportation if they practised without passing an examination.

Meanwhile, the LPF was riven by factionalism and personal acrimony. In addition to the expulsion of two party members who objected to Wijnschenk's leadership style, in early October 2002 a feud developed between two ministers. Herman Heinsbroek, the Minister of Economic Affairs, articulated his ambition to assume the deputy premiership, which resulted in a dispute with the incumbent Deputy Prime Minister and Minister of Public Health, Welfare and Sport, Dr Eduard Bomhoff. Despite the subsequent resignations of Heinsbroek and Bomhoff from the Council of Ministers, the LPF's coalition partners refused to co-operate further with the party and the Government resigned on 16 October, after just 87 days in power. Balkenende presided over a minority Government, comprising the CDA and the VVD, pending a general election, which was scheduled for January 2003.

At the general election of 22 January 2003 the CDA won 44 seats in the Second Chamber, while the PvdA increased its number of seats from 23 to 42, under its new leader, Wouter Bos. The LPF, again led by Herben, following the resignation of Wijnschenk in late 2002, secured only eight seats, while D66 obtained six. Although the popularity of the right-wing LPF had declined sharply, the electoral manifestos of the mainstream parties addressed the issues raised by the movement. Of these, immigration became a prominent subject of debate, the VVD echoing Fortuyn's statement that the Netherlands was already 'full'. In late January 2003 negotiations began regarding the formation of a coalition administration under Balkenende. Disagreements between the CDA and the PvdA over Dutch support for an impending US-led military campaign to remove the regime of Saddam Hussain in Iraq hindered progress. In March, in his capacity as Prime Minister of the interim administration, Balkenende announced that, while Dutch troops would not assist in the campaign, some units of the armed forces and weapons would be supplied to help defend Turkey, should the conflict escalate. Negotiations resumed in late March and, as the US-led coalition entered Iraq, both parties expressed their support for the military operation. In early April, however, talks collapsed following the failure of the two sides to agree on reductions in budgetary expenditure necessary to revive a stagnant economy. The following month the CDA negotiated the formation of a centre-right coalition with the VVD and D66, thereby gaining a slender majority of six in the 150-seat Second Chamber. The coalition Government, under the renewed premiership of Balkenende, was formally sworn in on 27 May.

In late May 2003 the Provincial Councils elected a new Senate in which the CDA-VVD-D66 coalition also obtained a majority, securing 41 of the 75 seats. The new Council of Ministers largely resembled the caretaker administration formed in October 2002. The CDA held eight portfolios, the VVD six and D66 two. Two new Deputy Prime Ministers were appointed: Zalm of the VVD, who was also assigned the post of Minister of Finance, and Thom de Graaf of D66, who was also named as Minister of Government Reform and Kingdom Relations.

The Government introduced a number of stringent new policies regarding immigrants and asylum seekers. In late January 2004 the Government announced that, in order to prevent the destabilization of the employment market, a maximum of 22,000 immigrants from the 10 new EU member states (which were scheduled to join the EU on 1 May) would be permitted to settle in the Netherlands. In February parliament approved a bill authorizing the provision of a repatriation payment and a free flight to their country of origin to failed asylum seekers. The law was condemned by human rights groups, but was welcomed by certain sectors of society that felt threatened by the rising level of unemployment. The 'voluntary returns' policy came into effect in June 2004.

In September 2004 the Government announced proposals for an austerity budget for 2005, in an attempt to reduce the budget deficit and prepare for the economic effects of an ageing population. The proposed measures included reforms to unemployment and disability benefits, reductions in health care expenditure and the elimination of tax benefits for those saving for early retirement. The proposals provoked widespread industrial action in September and October, culminating in a demonstration in Amsterdam in early October attended by some 200,000 protesters. However, as a result of negotiations with representatives of the Government, a compromise was reached in November whereby the trade union leaders accepted the proposed disincentive to early retirement and the restriction of eligibility for disability benefits, and agreed to demand only minimal wage increases over the forthcoming year.

The murder in November 2004 of Theo van Gogh, who had made a controversial film about Islamic culture, raised concerns regarding the country's failure to assimilate ethnic minorities. Mohammed Bouyeri, who was convicted of van Gogh's murder and sentenced to life imprisonment in late July 2005, was suspected of membership of a militant Islamist organization, the Hofstad group. Other members of this group were arrested in connection with threats to kill prominent politicians who were openly critical of Islam, including the writer of van Gogh's screenplay, a VVD deputy in the Second Chamber, Ayaan Hirsi Ali. Following van Gogh's murder, a number of arson attacks and acts of vandalism took place, damaging both Islamic and Christian community buildings. The trial of Bouyeri and 13 other alleged members of the Hofstad group on charges of membership of a terrorist organization began in December. In March 2006 nine of the defendants were convicted and sentenced to terms of imprisonment ranging from one to 15 years; Bouyeri was found guilty of leading the organization. In an attempt to improve security, parliament adopted legislation in January 2005 requiring all citizens and foreigners to carry official identification.

In March 2005 de Graaf tendered his resignation as Deputy Prime Minister and Minister of Government Reform, after the rejection by parliament of an electoral reform bill that would have introduced direct election of mayors. The two remaining D66 cabinet members announced that they were also reconsidering their positions, but an agreement was reached that ensured the continuance of the incumbent Government. Pechtold, the Chairman of D66 and the Mayor of Wageningen, was appointed Minister of Government Reform and Kingdom Relations, while the D66 Minister of Economic Affairs, Laurens Jans Brinkhorst, assumed the additional role of Deputy Prime Minister.

In October 2005 the Minister of Immigration and Integration, Rita Verdonk, announced proposals that would prohibit the wearing of traditional Islamic dress, such as the burka and other face veils, in certain public places. Despite criticism by Muslim and human rights organizations, a motion in support of such measures was narrowly approved by the Second Chamber in December. In March 2006, however, following an investigation into the implications of human rights law on such a ban, the Government failed to reach agreement on the issue, and the proposals were to be reconsidered. In the same month further measures to control immigration were introduced, requiring potential immigrants from the majority of non-EU countries to pass an examination in their country of origin on their knowledge of Dutch culture and language.

In May 2006 the Secretary of State for Education, Culture and Science, Mark Rutte, defeated Verdonk in a contest for the VVD leadership, which had emphasized deep divisions within the party, particularly regarding immigration. During the leadership election campaign, Verdonk had publicly questioned the right to Dutch citizenship of her Somali-born parliamentary colleague, Hirsi Ali, and threatened to revoke Hirsi Ali's passport after irregularities were discovered in her original application. Verdonk's intervention was unfavourably received, not only by opposing political parties and the electorate, but within the VVD itself. None the less, later that month Hirsi Ali admitted to falsifying elements of her application for citizenship and announced that she would resign as a member of the Second Chamber. On 27 June, however, Verdonk announced that an inquiry into Hirsi Ali's original application for citizenship had found that her claim was legitimate. Two days later Verdonk survived a motion of censure in the Second Chamber urging her departure from office. The motion had been supported by the D66, the three Government members of which subsequently resigned. On 30 June the remaining members of the Government followed suit. Owing to the timing of the resignations, just prior to the parliamentary summer recess, an early election in September was considered undesirable. Consequently, following discussions between party leaders, a minority interim administration comprising the CDA and the VVD was sworn in on 7 July, with a general election scheduled for November.

The 2006 election and the rising influence of Wilders

A general election was held on 22 November 2006. The three largest parties all suffered a reduction in support among the electorate (80.1% of whom voted). The CDA emerged as the largest party in the Second Chamber, with 26.5% of the valid votes cast (41 seats, a decrease of three on 2003). The PvdA won 21.2% of the valid votes cast (33 seats, from 42 in 2003) and the VVD 14.7%, (22 seats, from 28). The SP achieved the largest electoral gain, winning some 16.6% of the votes (25 seats, from eight) and the 'confessional' ChristenUnie (CU—Christian Union) party also increased its representation, achieving 4.0% of the vote (six seats, from three in the previous parliament). The nationalist Partij voor de Vrijheid (PVV—Freedom Party), which was formed in February 2006 by former VVD parliamentarian Geert Wilders, won 5.9% of the valid votes cast (nine seats).

Following protracted negotiations between the main parties, in late February 2007 a centre-left coalition of the CDA, the PvdA and the CU was formed under the renewed premiership of Balkenende. The PvdA leader, Bos, became Deputy Prime Minister and Minister of Finance, and the CU leader, André Rouvoet, Deputy Prime Minister and Minister of Youth and the Family. In total, the CDA held eight portfolios, the PvdA six and the CU two. The appointment of two foreign-born Muslim Secretaries of State, Ahmed Aboutaleb and Nebahat Albayrak, both of the PvdA, was criticized by Wilders after it was revealed that, in addition to their Dutch citizenship, they retained Moroccan and Turkish nationality, respectively. The PVV and some VVD representatives, including Verdonk, demanded that the two ministers renounce their foreign nationality—despite the fact that this was not legally possible—and proposed legislation to prevent government members from holding dual nationality. The proposal was later withdrawn. The new coalition agreement signalled the Government's intention to reverse some of the policies of the previous administration, including a slowing in the reduction of disability payments and a relaxation of restrictions on immigration. In June the Second Chamber approved a government-proposed amnesty for asylum seekers whose applications had been rejected, reversing legislation approved in February 2004 that allowed for their voluntary repatriation.

The limited progress of the Government in implementing its reform programme allowed nationalist groups to dominate the political agenda in late 2007. In October Verdonk resigned her membership of the VVD, following her expulsion from the party's parliamentary group in September for criticizing the leadership. None the less, Verdonk retained her seat in the Second Chamber and a week later she announced the formation of a new political movement, Trots op Nederland (Proud of the Netherlands), under her leadership; Trots op Nederland was formally inaugurated in April 2008. Meanwhile, in March 2008 Wilders provoked controversy when a film he had produced, entitled *Fitna* (an Arabic word commonly translated as 'strife'), which was critical of the Islamic religion, was broadcast on an internet site. Following the broadcast, the Government accused Wilders of attempting deliberately to cause offence, despite limited criticism from politicians in some Islamic countries, initial reaction to Wilders' film was calm.

None the less, in January 2009 the Amsterdam Court of Appeal ordered that Wilders should be prosecuted for 'initiating hatred and discrimination'. The ruling, which took into account not only Wilders' controversial film, but also a letter that had been published by the Dutch daily *De Volkskrant* in August 2007, in which Wilders described the Koran as 'fascist', reversed an earlier decision by the Dutch prosecution service. In February 2009 Wilders was prevented by the British Government from entering the United Kingdom, on the grounds that he was a potential 'threat to public security'. (Wilders had been invited to attend a screening of *Fitna* in the British Parliament building later that month.) The decision was strongly criticized by Dutch politicians of all parties. Nevertheless, Wilders' PVV enjoyed significant success in elections to the European Parliament in June, securing 17.0% of the votes cast and four seats, second only to the CDA (with 20.1% and five seats). Meanwhile, in October the United Kingdom's Asylum and Immigration Tribunal overturned the British Government's decision to deny Wilders entry after he successfully appealed against the ban. Wilders visited the United Kingdom later in the month, and again in March 2010, provoking demonstrations by both opponents and supporters of his views. Wilders' trial for fomenting hatred and discrimination against the Muslim community began in January 2010 in Amsterdam, and a concurrent demonstration was held outside the court in support of Wilders and freedom of speech; after the completion of the preliminary hearings, the trial was adjourned until later in the year.

Government collapse and the general election of 2010

By late 2008 the Netherlands began to suffer the effects of the global financial crisis. In early October the Government was forced to nationalize the Dutch operations of the Belgian-Dutch financial services group, Fortis. It was also announced later in October that the Dutch Government was to acquire a minority stake in the country's largest bank, ING. By February 2009 the Prime Minister, Jan Peter Balkenende, acknowledged that the Netherlands had entered a deep recession. Following negotiations between the coalition parties, along with business representatives and trade unions, in March the Government announced fiscal stimulus measures valued at some €6,000m., most notably including a reduction in expenditure on health care, increased spending on public infrastructure projects and an extension of the retirement age to 67 years. Nevertheless, the opposition parties criticized the measures, claiming that they were insufficiently radical to address the country's economic decline.

Following long-standing tension within the governing coalition regarding reductions in government spending, particularly on defence, and proposals to raise the retirement age, the PvdA withdrew from the coalition in February 2010 after a disagreement over Dutch involvement in the conflict in Afghanistan, precipitating the collapse of the Government. The PvdA had argued in favour of a withdrawal of Dutch troops from Afghanistan by August, while the CDA was supportive of a NATO request to extend the duration of the Dutch presence, despite a parliamentary vote in October 2009 in favour of an August 2010 withdrawal (which the Government had not endorsed). The CDA and the CU remained in power in a caretaker capacity pending a general election, scheduled for 9 June; all major policy decisions were consequently placed on hold, and the Council of Ministers was reorganized, with the positions vacated by the PvdA being reassigned to CDA and CU members. Notably, Jan Kees de Jager of the CDA, hitherto Secretary of State for Finance, became Minister of Finance, while the Minister of Justice, Ernst Hirsch Ballin, also of the CDA, was additionally allocated the interior portfolio.

The CDA and the PvdA suffered significant losses at the March 2010 local elections; D66 and the VVD were the main beneficiaries. The PVV contested two local authorities, aiming to gain its first representation at local level: it won a majority of seats in Almere and became the second largest party in The Hague. Following the PvdA's poor results, Bos resigned as leader of the party and was replaced by Job Cohen; the SP leader, Agnes Kant, also resigned in March after similarly disappointing results in the local elections, and was replaced by Emile Roemer.

In May 2010 Jack de Vries of the CDA resigned as the State Secretary for Defence, following his admission a few days earlier of an extra-marital affair with an aide. Although de Vries also announced that he would not take up a seat in the Second Chamber after the election in June, commentators believed that the scandal could have an adverse effect on the electoral prospects of the CDA, which espoused Christian family values.

At the general election on 9 June 2010 (in which 74% of the electorate participated) the VVD became the largest party in the Second Chamber, with 31 seats (representing 20.5% of the valid votes cast), compared with 22 seats at the previous general election in 2006. The PvdA won 30 seats (19.6% of the votes), compared with 33 previously. The number of seats held by the PVV increased from nine to 24 (15.5% of the votes), making Wilders' party the third largest in the Second Chamber. The CDA secured only 21 seats (13.6% of the votes), compared with 41 at the previous election. The SP won 15 seats, compared with 25 previously, while D66 and GroenLinks increased their representation to 10 seats each (from three and seven respectively), and the CU won five, a loss of one seat. On the day of his party's severe defeat, Balkenende resigned as Party Leader of the CDA, although he remained as Prime Minister in an interim capacity; the leadership of the CDA was assumed by Maxime Verhagen, the interim Minister of Foreign Affairs and of Development Co-operation (although at mid-May 2011 he had not yet been formally elected to the party position).

Recent developments: the formation of the Government led by Mark Rutte

Negotiations between the various parties on the formation of a new Government began immediately after the June 2010 election and continued for almost four months. Initially, discussions were held between the VVD, the CDA and the PVV, but many members of the CDA (including Ballin, the interim Minister of Justice and of the Interior, and Ab Klink, the interim Minister of Health, Welfare and Sport) were reluctant to share power with the controversial PVV, and there was disagreement concerning both economic policy and the controls on immigration and Islamic practice demanded by the PVV. Discussions between the VVD and three left-wing parties, the PvdA, D66 and GroenLinks, also failed to reach agreement, particularly on the reductions in government spending proposed by the VVD. Eventually, in early October 2010 an agreement was reached whereby the VVD and the CDA would form a minority administration, led by Mark Rutte of the VVD, which would rely on the support of the PVV in the legislature, although no ministerial posts were to be allocated to the PVV. Together the three parties commanded 76 of the 150 seats in the Second Chamber, a majority of only one. The new administration undertook, among other things, to make considerable reductions in public spending by 2015, to increase the police force, impose new limits on immigration, and ban the wearing of the Islamic burka in public. Posts in Rutte's Council of Ministers, announced in mid-October 2010, were shared equally between the VVD and the CDA, each party controlling six ministries and four junior ministries. Notable appointments included Maxime Verhagen, the acting leader of the CDA, as Deputy Prime Minister and Minister of Economic Affairs, Agriculture and Innovation (an amalgamation of two former portfolios), and Uri Rosenthal (VVD) as Minister of Foreign Affairs, while Jan Kees de Jager (CDA) retained the post of Minister of Finance. Two ministries were amalgamated to form a Ministry of Infrastructure and the Environment.

The trial of Geert Wilders on charges of inciting hatred and discrimination, which had been adjourned in January 2010 resumed in October, but at the end of the month a retrial was ordered after Wilders' defence lawyer successfully argued that the judges in the case had given the impression of bias against the defendant. The new trial began in March 2011, and was adjourned until April, when testimony was heard from expert witnesses. At the beginning of May lawyers acting for Wilders urged that the case against him be dropped, on the grounds that a senior court official had exerted undue influence on the decision to prosecute Wilders; the court rejected these claims later in the month. Meanwhile, in November 2010 revelations were published concerning PVV members of the legislature, several of whom, it was reported, had criminal convictions or were under investigation following allegations of misconduct.

Provincial elections took place on 2 March 2011, when the VVD became the largest party in the legislatures of seven provinces (six of which had previously been led by the CDA), the PvdA in three and the CDA in one; in one province, Limburg, the CDA and the PVV led with equal numbers of seats. At the indirect election to the Senate by the Provincial Councils on 23 May, the ruling coalition of the VVD and the CDA, with the support of the PVV, were one seat short of an overall majority, and would therefore need to solicit support from a fundamentalist Christian party, the Staatkundig Gereformeerde Partij, which effectively held the balance of power in the Senate with one seat, in order to pass controversial legislation.

Dutch Dependencies

The Netherlands East Indies (except West New Guinea, now Papua, which remained under Dutch control until 1963) formally seceded from the Union of the Netherlands, to form the United States of Indonesia in December 1949. In 1975 Suriname became independent, leaving the Netherlands Antilles as the only remaining Dutch dependency. Aruba, formerly part of the Netherlands Antilles, was granted separate status within the Kingdom of the Netherlands in 1986. A commission, established jointly by the Governments of the Netherlands and the Netherlands Antilles, recommended in October 2004 that the islands of Curaçao and St Maarten (in the Netherlands Antilles) should be given autonomous status within the Kingdom of the Netherlands (i.e. have *status aparte*, like that of Aruba), while the three other islands of the dependency, Saba, Bonaire and Sint (St) Eustatius, should be placed under direct rule. In a series of non-binding referendums between 2000 and 2005 a majority of voters in Sint (St) Maarten and Curaçao favoured obtaining *status aparte*, while the electorates of both Bonaire and Saba strongly favoured direct rule. St Eustatius was the only island to favour remaining part of the Netherlands Antilles. None the less, in late October 2005 the Dutch Minister of Government Reform and Kingdom Relations, Alexander Pechtold, concluded an outline agreement on constitutional reform with all five islands. Curaçao and St

THE NETHERLANDS

Maarten were to be granted *status aparte*, while Bonaire, Saba and St Eustatius would become *koninkrijkseilanden* (kingdom islands) with direct ties to the Netherlands. The future status of Bonaire, Saba and St Eustatius was subsequently refined to that of *bijzondere gemeente* (special municipalities), similar in most ways to other metropolitan Netherlands municipalities, although with separate social security and currency arrangements, for example. However, the populations of the Antillean municipalities would be able to vote in Dutch and European elections (the province of Noord-Holland offered to include the three territories). Following the negotiation of further details, the Dutch Prime Minister, Jan Peter Balkenende, and the Antillean premier, Emily de Jongh-Elhage, signed an agreement confirming the new status of the five islands at a meeting in Curaçao on 15 December 2008. The agreement entered into effect on 10 October 2010.

Foreign Affairs
Regional relations

The Netherlands was a founder member of the North Atlantic Treaty Organization (NATO, see p. 368) in 1949, abandoning its previous policy of neutrality. The treaty establishing the Benelux Economic Union (see p. 445) between the Netherlands, Belgium and Luxembourg was signed in 1958 and came into force in 1960. At a summit meeting held in The Hague on 17 June 2008 Balkenende, along with the Prime Ministers of Belgium and Luxembourg, signed a new Benelux Treaty on political and economic co-operation. The document expanded the scope of the previous treaty, signed in 1958, to provide for greater co-operation between the three Governments on justice and home affairs, as well as customs and cross-border trade. In recognition of this, the official title of the organization was to change from the Benelux Economic Union to the Benelux Union. The treaty was due to enter into effect two months after ratification by the legislatures of all three member states. The treaty was ratified by the legislatures of the three countries and by the parliaments of the five Belgian federal units by May 2011, and was scheduled to enter into force in July.

The Netherlands was a founder member of the European Community (EC, now European Union—EU, see p. 270). The EU Treaty establishing a Constitution for Europe was signed by the EU heads of state and of government in October 2004. It required ratification by all 25 EU member countries, either through a referendum or by a vote in the national legislature, before it could come into force. In February 2005 the Council of Ministers confirmed that a non-binding referendum on the treaty would take place on 1 June, and undertook to abide by a clear result. At the referendum 61.6% of those who voted (63% of the electorate) were opposed to the treaty's ratification. On the following day the Government formally withdrew the proposed legislation. This decisive rejection of the treaty by Dutch voters, and by French voters a few days earlier, prompted several other member countries to postpone indefinitely their own referendums. In March 2007 Balkenende expressed his new coalition Government's opposition to proposals by Germany and some other EU member countries to introduce a new treaty that would contain some of the main elements of the constitutional treaty, instead favouring a new treaty similar to those signed in Maastricht in 1992 and Amsterdam in 1997. In late June 2007 EU heads of state and of government reached a preliminary agreement for a comprehensive reform treaty. In September Balkenende announced that the new treaty would be submitted to the legislature, thus avoiding the prospect of a further defeat at a national referendum. The Treaty of Lisbon was formally signed by EU leaders on 13 December at a summit meeting in Lisbon, Portugal. The treaty was ratified by parliamentary vote in the Netherlands in July 2008. It came into force on 1 December 2009.

Other external relations

Government plans to commit troops to a NATO peace-keeping mission to southern Afghanistan prompted fierce opposition in late 2005. (Some 350 soldiers from the Netherlands were already stationed in the provinces of Baghlan and Kabul, in the north and east of Afghanistan, while a further 250 were engaged in counter-terrorism operations.) Opponents of further participation in the International Security Assistance Force referred to events in Srebrenica (see above), and claimed that Afghanistan's southern provinces were not sufficiently stable for peace-keeping exercises. However, following a debate in the Second Chamber, in February 2006 the Minister of Defence, Henk Kamp, announced that 1,200 military personnel were to join the mission in the province of Uruzgan, in central Afghanistan, from August. (Dutch troops had been withdrawn from Iraq in March 2005.) In December 2007 the Second Chamber voted to extend the mandate of Dutch troops in Uruzgan province until December 2010. These forces were expected to be withdrawn before the end of the year, despite a NATO request for an extension of the Dutch presence and the collapse of the governing coalition over the issue (see Recent developments). The Netherlands forces were withdrawn from Afghanistan in July. In January 2011, however, the Government agreed to provide personnel, numbering 545, to train police officers in northern Afghanistan, and this was approved by a small majority in the legislature, after assurances that the mission would be civilian in nature: the first 30 members of the mission arrived in February.

CONSTITUTION AND GOVERNMENT

The Netherlands is a constitutional and hereditary monarchy. Legislative power is held by the bicameral States-General (Staten-Generaal). The First Chamber (Eerste Kamer) or Senate (Senaat) has 75 members and is indirectly elected for four years by members of the 12 Provincial Councils. The Second Chamber (Tweede Kamer) comprises 150 members and is directly elected by universal adult suffrage for four years (subject to dissolution), on the basis of proportional representation. The head of state has mainly formal prerogatives, and executive power is exercised by the Council of Ministers, which is led by the Prime Minister and is responsible to the States-General. The monarch appoints the Prime Minister and, on the latter's recommendation, other ministers. Each of the 12 provinces is administered by a directly elected Provincial Council, a Provincial Executive and a Sovereign Commissioner, who is appointed by Royal Decree.

REGIONAL AND INTERNATIONAL CO-OPERATION

The Netherlands was a founder member of the European Community, now the European Union (EU, see p. 270), the Benelux Economic Union (see p. 445), the Organization for Security and Co-operation in Europe (OSCE, see p. 385) and the Council of Europe (see p. 250).

The Netherlands was a founder member of the UN in 1945. As a contracting party to the General Agreement on Tariffs and Trade, it joined the World Trade Organization (WTO, see p. 430) on its establishment in 1995. The Netherlands was also a founder member of the North Atlantic Treaty Organization (NATO, see p. 368) and the Organisation for Economic Co-operation and Development (OECD, see p. 376).

ECONOMIC AFFAIRS

In 2009, according to estimates by the World Bank, the Netherlands' gross national income (GNI), measured at average 2007–09 prices, was US $815,769m., equivalent to $49,350 per head (or $40,510 per head on an international purchasing-power parity basis). During 2000–09, it was estimated, the population grew at an average annual rate of 0.4%, while gross domestic product (GDP) per head increased, in real terms, at an average annual rate of 0.9% over the same period. Overall GDP increased, in real terms, at an average annual rate of 1.3% in 2000–09; real GDP declined by 3.9% in 2009, but increased by 1.8% in 2010.

Agriculture (including hunting, forestry and fishing) contributed an estimated 2.0% of GDP in 2010, although only 2.9% of the employed labour force were engaged in the sector in 2008. The Netherlands is a net exporter of agricultural products: in 2010 exports of food and live animals provided 12.2% of total export earnings. The principal crops are potatoes, sugar beet, wheat and onions. The main agricultural activity is horticulture; market gardening is highly developed, and the production of cut flowers and bulbs has traditionally been a significant industry, although its contribution to export earnings showed some decline in the early years of the 21st century (partly compensated for by re-exports from other growers to European markets). Livestock farming is also an important activity. According to the Central Bureau of Statistics, during 2000–10 agricultural GDP increased, in real terms, at an average annual rate of 1.2%; the sector's GDP rose by 1.4% in 2010.

Industry (including mining, manufacturing, construction and power) contributed an estimated 23.8% of GDP in 2010 and engaged 19.2% of the employed labour force in 2008. The Central Bureau of Statistics put the increase in industrial GDP, in real terms, at an average annual rate of 0.6% in 2000–10; real industrial GDP contracted by 7.1% in 2009, but grew by 3.5% in 2010.

Mining and quarrying provided an estimated 3.1% of GDP in 2010 and engaged 0.1% of the employed labour force in 2008. The principal mineral resource is natural gas. Total production in 2009 was an estimated 62,700m. cu m. Reserves of petroleum and salts are also exploited. The GDP of the mining sector declined, in real terms, at an average annual rate of 0.3% in 2000–10; it declined by 7.1% in 2009, but grew by 11.5% in 2010.

Manufacturing contributed an estimated 13.2% of GDP in 2010, and accounted for 12.2% of the employed labour force in 2008. Several multinational companies are domiciled in the Netherlands, including the electrical firm Philips, the brewer Heineken, and two British-Dutch firms, the food industry company Unilever and the petroleum firm Royal Dutch Shell. According to the Central Bureau of Statistics, manufacturing GDP increased at an average annual rate of 0.9% in 2000–10; it decreased by 8.8% in 2009, but grew by 7.2% in 2010.

The construction sector contributed an estimated 5.3% of GDP in 2010, and engaged 6.4% of the employed labour force in 2008. According to the Central Bureau of Statistics, construction GDP decreased at an average annual rate of 1.0% in 2000–10; it decreased by 4.2% in 2009 and growth further decreased by 10.5% in 2010.

In 2007 natural gas provided 57.2% of total electricity production and coal 27.6%. Imports of mineral fuels and lubricants comprised 10.4% of the value of total imports in 2003; by 2010 this figure had increased to 18.2%. In recent years the gradual depletion of the Groningen natural gas field has prompted the exploration of investment possibilities in smaller fields, while successive Governments have sought to promote the utilization of renewable energy resources.

The services sector contributed an estimated 74.3% of GDP in 2010 and engaged 77.9% of the employed labour force in 2008. Within the sector, financial services, tourism and transport are of considerable importance. The GDP of the services sector increased, in real terms, at an average annual rate of 1.8% in 2000–10; it decreased by 2.6% in 2009, but increased by 1.7% in 2010.

In 2009 the Netherlands recorded a visible trade surplus of €51,066m. and there was a surplus of €36,581m. on the current account of the balance of payments. The principal source of imports in 2010 was Germany (contributing 17.7% of the total); other major suppliers were Belgium, the People's Republic of China, the USA, the United Kingdom and France, according to official estimates. Germany was also the principal market for exports in that year (accounting for 24.2% of the total); other major purchasers in 2010 were Belgium, France, the United Kingdom, and the Italy, according to official estimates. The principal exports in 2010 were machinery and transport equipment (28.9%), chemicals and related products, food and live animals, and petroleum. The principal imports in that year were also machinery and transport equipment (30.1%), followed by mineral fuels, lubricants, chemicals and related products, and basic manufactures.

In 2010, according to official estimates, the Netherlands recorded an overall budgetary deficit of €32,000m., equivalent to 5.4% of GDP. Netherlands's general government gross debt was €353,294m. in 2009, equivalent to 61.8% of GDP. In 2000–09 the annual rate of inflation averaged 2.1%. Consumer prices increased by 1.2% in 2010. The annual average rate of unemployment was 4.8% in 2009.

The Netherlands' small size and dependence on external trade make it particularly vulnerable to external economic conditions. Decreasing industrial production and increasing labour costs in the 2000s, combined with an ageing population and rising levels of unemployment led to increased demands for state-funded pensions, health care and welfare benefits. In an attempt to reduce the budget deficit to comply with the limit of 3% of GDP imposed by the EU's Stability and Growth Pact, the Government introduced measures to encourage participation in the labour market, including a comprehensive reform of the health system, in addition to restricting access to unemployment and disability payments, and the abolition of tax benefits for early retirement. The measures enabled the Government to reduce the budget deficit to the equivalent of 0.2% of GDP in 2005; small surpluses, of 0.8% and 0.6%, were recorded in 2006 and 2007, respectively. However, the global economic crisis in 2008–09 had a significant detrimental effect on the economy. GDP growth remained positive at 2.0% in 2008, although GDP contracted in the third and fourth quarters. Exports and investment declined sharply in the second half of the year, while banks suffered severe losses that required significant state intervention. Following the introduction of necessary fiscal stimulus measures, government finances deteriorated substantially, with a fiscal deficit equivalent to 4.5% of GDP in 2009 and a large increase in the levels of government indebtedness. GDP declined by 3.9% in 2009, although the Netherlands emerged from recession during the third quarter of that year. The swift introduction of the stimulus measures limited the negative impact of the global financial crisis on the country, with real GDP growth of 1.8% in 2010. In that year the budgetary deficit was equivalent to 5.4% of GDP, and government debt was equivalent to 62.7% of GDP, according to government figures. In December 2010 the IMF reported that the Netherlands had been less adversely affected by the economic crisis than many European countries, and that unemployment, then standing at 4.5% of the labour force, was lower than in most other EU member states. The Government that took office in October 2010 introduced reductions in expenditure in order to reduce the budgetary deficit. According to the Government's macroeconomic policy unit, the deficit was expected to decline to the equivalent of 3.6% in 2011, GDP was expected to grow by 1.75% in that year, while unemployment was expected to affect 4.25% of the labour force.

PUBLIC HOLIDAYS

2012: 1 January (New Year's Day), 6 April (Good Friday), 9 April (Easter Monday), 30 April (Queen's Day), 17 May (Ascension Day), 28 May (Whit Monday), 25–26 December (Christmas).

THE NETHERLANDS

Statistical Survey

Source (unless otherwise stated): Netherlands Central Bureau of Statistics, Prinses Beatrixlaan 428, POB 959, 2270 AZ Voorburg; tel. (70) 3373800; fax (70) 3877429; e-mail infoservice@cbs.nl; internet www.cbs.nl.

Area and Population

AREA, POPULATION AND DENSITY

Area (sq km)	
Land	33,873
Inland waters	3,479
Coastal water	4,175
Total	41,528*
Population (census results)†	
1 January 1991‡	15,010,445
1 January 2001‡	
Males	7,909,855
Females	8,077,220
Total	15,987,075
Population (official estimate at 1 January)†	
2009	16,485,787
2010	16,574,989
2011	16,654,455
Density (per sq km of land) at 1 January 2011	491.7§

* 16,034 sq miles.
† Population is *de jure*.
‡ Based on a compilation of continuous accounting and sample surveys.
§ Land area only.

POPULATION BY AGE AND SEX
(official estimates at 1 January 2010)

	Males	Females	Total
0–14	1,490,308	1,422,603	2,912,911
15–64	5,604,519	5,519,231	11,123,750
65 and over	1,108,649	1,429,679	2,538,328
Total	8,203,476	8,371,513	16,574,989

PROVINCES

	Land area (sq km)*	Population (1 January 2009)	Density (per sq km)
Groningen	2,340	574,092	245
Friesland	3,356	644,811	192
Drenthe	2,649	489,918	185
Overijssel	3,337	1,125,435	337
Flevoland	1,421	383,449	270
Gelderland	4,983	1,991,062	400
Utrecht	1,363	1,210,869	888
Noord-Holland	2,657	2,646,445	996
Zuid-Holland	2,867	3,481,558	1,214
Zeeland	1,805	380,984	211
Noord-Brabant	4,929	2,434,560	494
Limburg	2,164	1,122,604	519
Total	33,871	16,485,787	487

* Figures refer to area at 1 January 2000.

PRINCIPAL TOWNS
(population of municipalities at 1 January 2009)*

Amsterdam (capital)†	755,605	Haarlem	148,191
Rotterdam	587,134	Arnhem	145,574
's-Gravenhage/Den Haag (The Hague)†	481,864	Zaanstad	144,055
Utrecht	299,891	Amersfoort	143,212
Eindhoven	212,269	Haarlemmermeer	142,042
Tilburg	203,464	's-Hertogenbosch/Den Bosch	137,775
Almere	185,746	Zoetermeer	120,881
Groningen	184,227	Dordrecht	118,408
Breda	171,916	Maastricht	118,286
Nijmegen	161,817	Leiden	116,787
Enschede	156,071	Zwolle	117,703
Apeldoorn	155,332		

* Provisional figures.
† Amsterdam is the capital, while The Hague is the seat of government.

BIRTHS, MARRIAGES AND DEATHS

	Live births* Number	Rate (per 1,000)	Marriages Number	Rate (per 1,000)	Deaths* Number	Rate (per 1,000)
2002	202,083	12.5	85,808	5.3	142,355	8.8
2003	200,297	12.3	80,427	5.0	141,936	8.7
2004	194,007	11.9	72,231	4.5	136,553	8.4
2005	187,910	11.5	72,263	4.4	136,402	8.4
2006	185,057	11.3	72,369	4.4	135,372	8.3
2007	181,336	11.1	72,485	4.4	133,022	8.1
2008	184,634	11.2	75,438	4.6	135,136	8.2
2009	184,915	11.2	73,477	4.5	134,235	8.1

* Including residents outside the country if listed in a Netherlands population register.

Life expectancy (years at birth, WHO estimates): 80 (males 78; females 82) in 2008 (Source: WHO, *World Health Statistics*).

IMMIGRATION AND EMIGRATION

	2007	2008	2009
Immigrants	116,819	143,516	146,378
Emigrants	122 576	117,779	111,897

ECONOMICALLY ACTIVE POPULATION
('000 persons aged 15 years and over, labour force survey)

	2006	2007	2008
Agriculture, hunting, forestry and fishing	269	252	228
Mining and quarrying	7	11	11
Manufacturing	1,024	1,003	973
Electricity, gas and water supply	43	41	40
Construction	499	500	509
Wholesale and retail trade and repair	1,200	1,211	1,186
Hotels and restaurants	334	352	337
Transport, storage and communications	500	506	512
Financial intermediation	264	258	245
Real estate, renting and business activities	974	1,045	1,099
Public administration, social security and defence	529	541	541
Education	522	534	549
Health and social work	1,249	1,310	1,353
Other community, social and personal service activities	333	381	389

THE NETHERLANDS

—continued	2006	2007	2008
Private households with employed persons	5	5	6
Sub-total	7,749	7,950	7,978
Activities not adequately defined	359	360	479
Total employed	8,108	8,310	8,457
Unemployed	354	300	257
Total labour force	8,462	8,610	8,714
Males	4,649	4,691	4,722
Females	3,813	3,920	3,991

Source: ILO.

Health and Welfare

KEY INDICATORS

Total fertility rate (children per woman, 2008)	1.7
Under-5 mortality rate (per 1,000 live births, 2008)	5
HIV/AIDS (% of persons aged 15–49, 2007)	0.2
Physicians (per 1,000 head, 2005)	3.7
Hospital beds (per 1,000 head, 2003)	5
Health expenditure (2007): US $ per head (PPP)	3,509
Health expenditure (2007): % of GDP	8.9
Health expenditure (2007): public (% of total)	82.0
Total carbon dioxide emissions ('000 metric tons, 2007)	173,102.0
Carbon dioxide emissions per head (metric tons, 2007)	10.6
Human Development Index (2010): ranking	7
Human Development Index (2010): value	0.890

For sources and definitions, see explanatory note on p. vi.

Agriculture

PRINCIPAL CROPS
('000 metric tons)

	2006	2007	2008
Wheat	1,184	990	1,366
Barley	269	260	310
Maize	181	231	252
Rye	11	11	8
Triticale (wheat-rye hybrid)	21	20	19
Potatoes	6,240	6,870	6,923
Sugar beet	5,414	5,512	5,219
Cabbages and other brassicas	210	207*	207†
Lettuce and chicory	72	86	84
Spinach	39	44	43
Tomatoes	680	685	720
Cauliflowers and broccoli	53	62	60
Cucumbers and gherkins	440	430	428
Aubergines (Eggplants)	40	41	40
Chillies and green peppers	318	320	330
Onions and shallots, green†	33	32	32
Onions, dry	942	1,085	1,130
Leeks and other alliaceous vegetables	102†	114	109
Beans, green	70	70	70
Peas, green	34	38	38
Carrots and turnips	541	543	531
Mushrooms and truffles	235	240	240
Apples	365	391	375
Pears	222	260	172
Strawberries	39	43	41

* Unofficial figure.
† FAO estimate(s).

2009: Wheat 1,402; Barley 310; Maize 245; Rye 11; Triticale (wheat-rye hybrid) 17; Potatoes 7,181; Sugar beet 5,735.

Aggregate production ('000 metric tons, may include official, semi-official or estimated data): Total cereals 1,675 in 2006, 1,520 in 2007, 1,963 in 2008, 1,994 in 2009; Total roots and tubers 6,240 in 2006, 6,870 in 2007, 6,923 in 2008, 7,181 in 2009; Total vegetables (incl. melons) 4,104 in 2006, 4,309 in 2007, 4,372 in 2008–09; Total fruits (excl. melons) 640 in 2006, 709 in 2007, 603 in 2008, 603 in 2009.

Source: FAO.

LIVESTOCK
('000 head, year ending September)

	2007	2008	2009
Horses	134	134*	n.a.
Cattle	3,763	3,890	3,996
Chickens	92,763	96,700	97,000*
Sheep	1,369	1,213	1,099
Goats	355	390	416
Pigs	11,663	12,026	12,108

* FAO estimate.

Source: FAO.

LIVESTOCK PRODUCTS
('000 metric tons)

	2007	2008	2009
Cattle meat	386	378	402
Sheep meat	16	14	14
Pig meat	1,290	1,318	1,275
Chicken meat	684	693	764
Turkey meat*	52	52	n.a.
Cows' milk	11,062	11,286	11,469
Hen eggs	621	627	n.a.

* FAO estimates.

Source: FAO.

Forestry

ROUNDWOOD REMOVALS
('000 cubic metres, excl. bark)

	2007	2008	2009
Sawlogs, veneer logs and logs for sleepers	396	416	354
Pulpwood	316	380	324
Other industrial wood	20	31	48
Fuel wood	290	290	290
Total	1,022	1,117	1,016

Source: FAO.

SAWNWOOD PRODUCTION
('000 cubic metres, incl. railway sleepers)

	2007	2008	2009
Coniferous (softwood)	184	159	144
Broadleaved (hardwood)	89	84	66
Total	273	243	210

Source: FAO.

Fishing

('000 metric tons, live weight)

	2006	2007	2008
Capture*	435.3	413.6	416.7
European plaice	23.9	23.1	20.8
Blue whiting	96.6	80.7	78.8
Atlantic herring	95.9	103.1	56.7
Round sardinella	45.4	5.3	67.5
European pilchard	20.3	6.2	9.6
Atlantic horse mackerel	63.6	61.4	63.0
Atlantic mackerel	22.1	24.8	20.4
Aquaculture	45.6	56.8*	46.6*
Blue mussel	31.3	43.7	36.1
Total catch*	480.9	470.4	463.4

* FAO estimate(s).

Note: Figures exclude aquatic mammals, recorded by number rather than by weight. The number of porpoises caught was: 252 in 2006; 173 in 2007; n.a. in 2008.

Source: FAO.

THE NETHERLANDS

Mining
(estimates)

	2006	2007	2008
Crude petroleum ('000 barrels)	11,426	11,250	9,855
Salt ('000 metric tons)	6,056	6,000*	6,000*

* Estimated production.

Source: US Geological Survey.

Natural gas (million cu m, excl. gas flared or recycled): 61,568 in 2006; 60,546 in 2007; 66,628 in 2008; 62,709 in 2009 (Source: BP, *Statistical Review of World Energy*).

Industry

SELECTED PRODUCTS
('000 metric tons unless otherwise indicated)

	2005	2006	2007
Gravel and crushed stone	5,223*	n.a.	n.a.
Margarine	284*	n.a.	n.a.
Cocoa powder (metric tons)	108,050*	n.a.	n.a.
Cocoa butter (metric tons)	182,512*	n.a.	n.a.
Prepared animal feeds	12,479*	n.a.	n.a.
Beer ('000 hectolitres)	23,851*	n.a.	n.a.
Mineral waters ('000 hectolitres)	3,016*	n.a.	n.a.
Soft drinks ('000 hectolitres)	15,713*	n.a.	n.a.
Mechanical wood pulp†	117	109	113
Newsprint†	421	422	421
Printing and writing paper†	931	1,008	924
Wrapping and packaging paper and paperboard†	1,976	1,828	1,764
Packing containers of paper or paperboard	1,736*	1,828	1,764
Synthetic dyestuffs*	10,690	n.a.	n.a.
Synthetic rubber*	273	192	194
Washing powders and detergents	422*	n.a.	n.a.
Jet fuels	6,990	6,914	6,597
Kerosene	469	368	423
Motor spirit (petrol)	14,234	13,794	10,756
Naphthas	13,906	11,643	7,486
Gas-diesel (distillate fuel) oil	21,346	19,685	19,332
White spirit	300	256	192
Residual fuel (Mazout) oils	12,394	12,151	11,974
Lubricating oils	589	581	583
Petroleum bitumen (asphalt)	408	398	521
Liquefied petroleum gas	4,579	4,069	1,518
Coke	2,343	2,265	2,273
Coke-oven gas (terajoules)	19,141	18,515	19,582
Cement‡§	2,400	2,400	2,400
Pig-iron‖	6,031	5,417	6,412
Crude steel‖	6,919	6,372	7,368
Aluminium (unwrought):‡ primary	341	312	301
secondary§	50	25	n.a.
Refined lead: secondary‡§	17	17	16
Zinc (unwrought): primary‡	232	236	232
Passenger vessels launched ('000 grt)	42.7	n.a.	n.a.
Tankers launched ('000 grt)	8.6	n.a.	n.a.
Bicycles ('000)	903*	n.a.	n.a.
Electricity (million kWh)	100,219	96,733	103,241

* Refers to amounts sold by establishments employing 20 persons or more.
† Source: FAO.
‡ Data from US Geological Survey.
§ Estimates.
‖ Source: International Iron and Steel Institute (Brussels).

Source: unless otherwise indicated, UN Industrial Commodity Statistics Database.

2008 ('000 metric tons): Mechanical wood pulp 142; Newsprint 462; Printing and writing paper 708; Wrapping and packaging paper and paperboard 1,690; Crude steel 6,853; Pig-iron 5,998; Cement 2,700 (estimate); Aluminium (unwrought—primary) 301 (estimate); Refined lead (secondary) 16 (estimate); Zinc (unwrought—primary) 240 (Sources: FAO; International Iron and Steel Institute—Brussels; US Geological Survey).

2009 ('000 metric tons): Crude steel 5,194; Mechanical wood pulp 72; Newsprint 273; Printing and writing paper 653; Wrapping and packaging paper and paperboard 1,563 (Source: International Iron and Steel Institute—Brussels; FAO).

Finance

CURRENCY AND EXCHANGE RATES

Monetary Units
100 cent = 1 euro (€).

Sterling and Dollar Equivalents (31 December 2010)
£1 sterling = 1.172 euros;
US $1 = 0.748 euros;
€10 = £8.54 = $13.36.

Average Exchange Rate (euros per US $)
2008 0.6827
2009 0.7198
2010 0.7550

Note: The national currency was formerly the guilder. From the introduction of the euro, with the Netherlands' participation, on 1 January 1999, a fixed exchange rate of €1 = 2.20371 guilders was in operation. Euro notes and coins were introduced on 1 January 2002. The euro and local currency circulated alongside each other until 28 January, after which the euro became the sole legal tender.

GOVERNMENT FINANCE
(general government transactions, non-cash basis, € million)*

Summary of Balances

	2006	2007	2008†
Revenue	248,820	259,805	277,583
Less Expense	244,112	255,951	269,446
Net operating balance	4,708	3,854	8,137
Less Net acquisition of non-financial assets	1,916	2,878	4,107
Net lending/borrowing	2,792	976	4,030

Revenue

	2006	2007	2008†
Tax revenue	132,332	141,050	143,426
Taxes on income, profits and capital gains	57,389	62,463	63,437
Taxes on goods and services	65,427	68,371	70,383
Taxes on property	9,005	9,722	9,093
Social contributions	79,850	81,405	90,647
Social security contribution	75,610	77,000	86,258
Grants	329	267	265
Other revenue	36,309	37,083	43,245
Total	248,820	259,805	277,583

Expense/Outlays

Expense by economic type‡	2006	2007	2008†
Compensation of employees	50,216	52,353	54,490
Use of goods and services	39,024	41,012	44,078
Consumption of fixed capital	13,476	14,283	15,097
Interest	11,893	12,541	12,693
Subsidies	6,149	7,154	7,236
Grants	7,933	7,937	8,497
Social benefits	109,829	114,851	120,273
Other expense	5,592	5,820	7,082
Total	244,112	255,951	269,446

THE NETHERLANDS

Outlays by function of government	2006	2007	2008
General public services	39,231	41,322	43,531
Defence	7,729	7,726	7,919
Public order and safety	9,585	10,269	10,892
Economic affairs	25,324	27,305	29,345
Environment protection	4,473	4,634	5,030
Housing and community amenities	5,396	5,460	6,290
Health	31,542	33,931	35,570
Recreation, culture and religion	7,535	7,605	8,020
Education	27,568	29,658	31,258
Social protection	87,645	90,919	95,698
Total	246,028	258,829	273,553

* Figures represent a consolidation of the operations of the Government, comprising all central and local government accounts.
† Provisional figures.
‡ Including net acquisition of non-financial assets.

2006 (revised figure): Total expense 244,112.
2007 (revised figures): Total revenue 259,772; Total expense 255,961.
2008 (revised figures): Total revenue 277,729; Total expense 270,007.
2009: Total revenue 262,871 (Taxes 137,317; Social contributions 83,372); *Less* Total expense 286,956 (Compensation of employees 57,130; Social benefits 128,994); *Net operating balance* −24,085; *Less* Net acquisition of non-financial assets 6,758; *Net lending/borrowing* −30,843.

Sources: IMF, *Government Finance Statistics Yearbook* and *International Financial Statistics*.

INTERNATIONAL RESERVES
(US $ million at 31 December)

	2007	2008	2009
Gold (Eurosystem valuation)	16,713	17,033	21,739
IMF special drawing rights	981	1,021	7,660
Reserve position in IMF	540	1,087	1,597
Foreign exchange	8,749	9,369	8,613
Total	26,983	28,510	39,609

Source: IMF, *International Financial Statistics*.

MONEY SUPPLY
(incl. shares, depository corporations, national residency criteria, € '000 million at 31 December)

	2007	2008	2009
Currency issued	35.46	39.82	42.91
De Nederlandsche Bank	24.19	24.50	23.04
Demand deposits	184.17	183.63	209.52
Other deposits	511.16	571.56	560.71
Securities other than shares	383.26	385.21	460.76
Shares and other equity	130.94	115.84	126.23
Other items (net)	12.14	11.65	33.12
Total	1,257.14	1,307.71	1,433.26

Source: IMF, *International Financial Statistics*.

COST OF LIVING
(Consumer Price Index; base: 2000 = 100)

	2006	2007	2008
Food	108.3	109.4	115.6
Electricity, gas and other fuels	168.2	170.8	175.3
Clothing (incl. footwear)	97.8	99.0	99.3
Rent	117.7	120.1	122.1
All items (incl. others)	114.4	116.2	119.1

2009: Food 116.8; All items (incl. others) 120.6.
Source: ILO.

NATIONAL ACCOUNTS
(€ million at current prices)
National Income and Product

	2007	2008*	2009*
Compensation of employees	280,309	294,701	298,130
Net operating surplus/mixed income	143,214	148,107	125,799
Domestic primary incomes	423,523	442,808	423,929
Consumption of fixed capital	82,072	85,854	87,857
Gross domestic product (GDP) at factor cost	505,595	528,662	511,786
Taxes on production and imports	74,333	75,630	69,938
Less Subsidies	8,155	8,066	9,745
GDP in market prices	571,773	596,226	571,979
Net primary income from the rest of the world	9,502	−11,327	−15,461
Gross national income (GNI)	581,275	584,899	556,518
Less Consumption of fixed capital	82,072	85,854	87,857
Net national income	499,203	499,045	468,661
Net current transfers from the rest of the world	−8,757	−8,982	−6,713
Net national disposable income	490,446	490,063	461,948

Expenditure on the Gross Domestic Product

	2008	2009	2010†
Government final consumption expenditure	152,325	162,654	167,527
Private final consumption expenditure	270,751	262,585	268,076
Changes in inventories	1,860	−3,530	3,038
Gross fixed capital formation	122,688	108,906	104,721
Total domestic expenditure	547,624	530,615	543,362
Exports of goods and services	456,438	395,949	463,575
Less Imports of goods and services	407,836	354,585	416,616
GDP in purchasers' values	596,226	571,979	590,321
GDP at constant 2000 prices	488,543	469,416	477,622

Gross Domestic Product by Economic Activity

	2008	2009	2010†
Agriculture, hunting, forestry and fishing	9,566	8,798	10,332
Mining and quarrying	21,749	15,211	16,432
Manufacturing	72,605	64,087	69,578
Electricity, gas and water supply	10,373	11,738	11,341
Construction	30,629	30,703	28,138
Wholesale and retail trade; repair of motor vehicles, motorcycles and personal household goods; hotels and restaurants	76,952	71,409	
Transport, storage and communications	35,136	32,067	
Finance, insurance, real estate and other business activities	147,303	143,460	391,939
General government	58,880	61,796	
Care and other service activities	66,126	70,350	
GDP at basic prices	529,319	509,619	527,760
Taxes, less subsidies, on imports	65,785	59,601	61,470
Value-added tax, less imputed bank service charge	1,122	2,759	1,091
GDP in purchasers' values	596,226	571,979	590,321

* Provisional.
† Estimates.

THE NETHERLANDS

BALANCE OF PAYMENTS
(€ million)

	2007	2008	2009
Exports of goods f.o.b.	466,246	536,581	424,804
Imports of goods f.o.b.	−408,828	−474,747	−373,738
Trade balance	57,419	61,833	51,066
Exports of services	96,737	105,568	93,317
Imports of services	−84,527	−92,655	−85,456
Balance on goods and services	69,628	74,746	58,927
Other income received	158,612	133,501	87,214
Other income paid	−159,426	−153,171	−99,215
Balance on goods, services and income	68,815	55,076	46,926
Current transfers received	15,669	17,522	20,612
Current transfers paid	−31,957	−34,650	−30,958
Current balance	52,526	37,949	36,581
Capital account (net)	−2,067	−5,318	−4,194
Direct investment abroad	−53,735	−66,590	−28,094
Direct investment from abroad	124,756	5,691	33,287
Portfolio investment assets	−40,197	7,562	−79,054
Portfolio investment liabilities	−81,746	89,534	44,627
Financial derivatives assets	172,022	238,394	240,260
Financial derivatives liabilities	−168,778	−262,377	−213,587
Other investment assets	−222,248	102,581	124,727
Other investment liabilities	234,340	−125,301	−166,264
Net errors and omissions	−16,282	−21,278	18,670
Overall balance	−1,409	847	6,959

Source: IMF, *International Financial Statistics*.

External Trade

PRINCIPAL COMMODITIES
(distribution by SITC, € million)

Imports c.i.f.	2008	2009	2010*
Food and live animals	27,048	25,721	28,346
Crude materials (inedible) except fuels	13,859	9,831	13,286
Mineral fuels, lubricants, etc.	61,118	42,970	60,464
Petroleum, petroleum products, etc.	49,935	34,534	51,743
Crude petroleum	28,766	18,565	27,380
Chemicals and related products	48,461	43,960	51,148
Organic chemicals	12,258	9,173	11,691
Basic manufactures	38,659	28,288	33,592
Machinery and transport equipment	102,029	82,967	99,827
Office machines and automatic data-processing equipment	25,435	21,660	27,577
Telecommunications and sound equipment	19,746	16,637	20,307
Other electrical machinery, apparatus, etc.	13,485	12,329	15,591
Road vehicles (incl. air-cushion vehicles) and parts (excl. tyres, engines, and electrical parts)	18,081	12,894	15,590
Passenger motor vehicles (excl. buses)	7,838	6,242	7,588
Miscellaneous manufactured articles	37,307	33,829	38,109
Total (incl. others)	335,921	274,020	332,132

Exports f.o.b.	2008	2009	2010*
Food and live animals	42,113	40,157	45,081
Vegetables and fruit	11,714	11,084	12,467
Crude materials (inedible) except fuels	18,142	15,436	19,144
Mineral fuels, lubricants, etc.	56,803	38,309	50,538
Petroleum, petroleum products, etc.	38,176	24,643	35,616
Chemicals and related products	65,968	59,255	70,678
Organic chemicals	16,694	13,266	17,357
Plastics in primary form	11,129	8,839	11,276
Basic manufactures	35,333	26,733	33,179
Machinery and transport equipment	107,390	88,254	106,888
Office machines and automatic data-processing equipment	27,118	24,710	28,460
Automatic data-processing machines	10,332	10,316	13,269
Telecommunications and sound equipment	18,263	15,408	19,051
Other electrical machinery, apparatus, etc.	16,323	14,018	17,718
Thermionic tubes, transistors, etc.	4,328	3,876	5,498
Road vehicles (incl. air-cushion vehicles) and parts (excl. tyres, engines, and electrical parts)	13,533	9,063	11,074
Miscellaneous manufactured articles	32,704	30,512	33,779
Total (incl. others)†	370,480	309,359	370,493

* Estimates.
† Including victuals and stores supplied to foreign ships and aircraft.

PRINCIPAL TRADING PARTNERS
(€ million)

Imports c.i.f.	2008	2009	2010*
Belgium	33,896	27,452	31,825
Brazil	4,854	3,893	4,376
China, People's Republic	25,000	21,948	30,903
Denmark	3,529	2,975	2,745
France	16,884	13,591	15,013
Germany	64,622	52,537	58,911
Hong Kong	1,754	1,800	2,058
Ireland	3,534	3,154	3,835
Italy	7,962	6,322	7,139
Japan	9,492	7,251	9,236
Korea, Republic	2,089	1,740	1,874
Malaysia	4,894	4,309	5,540
Norway	8,531	6,787	8,447
Russia	13,036	9,628	14,028
Saudi Arabia	3,459	1,415	2,294
Singapore	2,567	2,252	2,659
Spain	5,988	4,799	6,934
Sweden	5,737	3,992	5,283
Switzerland	2,058	1,696	2,102
Taiwan	2,116	1,852	2,421
United Kingdom	21,224	17,648	22,313
USA	27,042	22,995	25,076
Total (incl. others)	335,921	274,020	332,132

THE NETHERLANDS

Exports f.o.b.	2008	2009	2010*
Austria	4,871	4,102	4,816
Belgium	42,967	34,619	41,038
Denmark	5,061	4,076	4,764
France	32,375	27,484	32,302
Germany	90,618	75,225	89,664
Italy	19,608	16,007	18,399
Japan	2,945	2,381	3,102
Poland	7,261	5,948	7,429
Spain	12,730	10,512	12,408
Sweden	6,463	5,185	6,613
Switzerland	4,940	4,781	5,408
United Kingdom	33,586	25,879	29,572
USA	16,472	13,928	17,007
Total (incl. others)	370,480	309,359	370,493

* Estimates.

Transport

RAILWAYS
(traffic)

	1996	1997	1998
Passenger-km (million)	14,131	14,485	14,879
Freight ton-km (million)	3,123	3,406	3,778

Passenger-km (million): 15,546 in 2007; 16,180 in 2008; 16,315 in 2009 (Source: Nederlandse Spoorwegen NV, *Annual Report 2009*).

ROAD TRAFFIC
('000 motor vehicles)

	2006	2007	2008
Passenger vehicles	7,092	7,230	7,392
Buses and coaches	11	11	11
Vans and lorries	n.a.	996	1,071
Motorcycles	553	568	1,371

Source: IRF, *World Road Statistics*.

SHIPPING
Inland Waterways
(transport fleet at 1 January)

	1997	1998	1999
Number of vessels	5,067	5,003	4,577
Carrying capacity ('000 metric tons)	5,859	5,589	5,212

Inland Waterways
(freight traffic, million metric tons)

	1996	1997	1998
Internal transport: Commercial	61.2	75.7	79.3
Internal transport: Private	28.2	20.9	19.3
International transport	201.1	224.5	219.7

Merchant Fleet
(at 31 December)

	2007	2008	2009
Number of vessels	1,258	1,296	1332
Displacement ('000 grt)	6,139.4	6,684.2	6,966.2

Source: IHS Fairplay, *World Fleet Statistics*.

Sea-borne Freight Traffic
('000 metric tons)

	1997	1998	1999
Goods loaded	88,667	85,137	92,000
Goods unloaded	312,864	319,684	305,000

CIVIL AVIATION*
(Netherlands scheduled air services)

	2004	2005	2006
Kilometres flown (million)	460	481	503
Passengers carried ('000)	24,627	26,133	27,454
Passenger-km (million)	75,706	82,269	86,833
Total ton-km (million)	12,487	13,235	13,710

* Figures include data for airlines based in the territories and dependencies of the Netherlands.

Source: UN, *Statistical Yearbook*.

2007 ('000): Passengers carried 28,857 (Source: World Bank, World Development Indicators database).

2008 ('000): Passengers carried 29,601 (Source: World Bank, World Development Indicators database).

Tourism

FOREIGN TOURIST ARRIVALS
('000)*

Country of origin	2007	2008	2009
Belgium	1,101	1,109	1,172
France	613	575	574
Germany	2,833	2,669	2,744
Italy	398	370	368
Spain	436	368	351
United Kingdom	1,903	1,639	1,409
Total (incl. others)	11,008	10,104	9,921

* Arrivals at all accommodation establishments.

Tourism receipts (US $ million, incl. passenger transport): 17,529 in 2006; 19,922 in 2007; 20,526 in 2008 (Source: World Tourism Organization).

Communications Media

	2007	2008	2009
Telephones ('000 main lines in use)	7,404.3	7,317.2	7,320.0*
Mobile cellular telephones ('000 subscribers)	19,285	20,627	21,182*
Internet users ('000)†	14,125.8	14,448.5	14,871.6
Broadband subscribers ('000)	5,507‡	5,807	5,902

* At July.
† Estimates.
‡ At September.

Personal computers: 14,900,000 (911.5 per 1,000 persons) in 2006.

Daily newspapers: 37 in 2004 (circulation 5,001,000).

Non-daily newspapers (regional or local): 558 in 2004 (circulation 18,205,000).

Book production (1993): 34,067 titles, excluding pamphlets.

Radio receivers ('000 in use): 15,300 in 1997.

Television receivers ('000 in use): 8,600 in 1997.

Sources: UNESCO, *Statistical Yearbook*; UN, *Statistical Yearbook*; International Telecommunication Union.

Education

(2008/09, provisional)

	Institutions	Students ('000)
Primary	7,223	1,597.4
Secondary	660	935.0
Higher vocational	51	383.7
University	13	220.3

THE NETHERLANDS

Directory

The Government

HEAD OF STATE

Queen of the Netherlands: HM Queen BEATRIX (succeeded to the throne 30 April 1980).

COUNCIL OF MINISTERS
(May 2011)

A coalition of the Volkspartij voor Vrijheid en Democratie (VVD—People's Party for Freedom and Democracy) and the Christen Democratisch Appèl (CDA—Christian Democratic Appeal).

Prime Minister, Minister of General Affairs: MARK RUTTE (VVD).
Deputy Prime Minister, Minister of Economic Affairs, Agriculture and Innovation: MAXIME VERHAGEN (CDA).
Minister of Foreign Affairs: URI ROSENTHAL (VVD).
Minister of the Interior and Kingdom Relations: PIET HEIN DONNER (CDA).
Minister of Immigration and Asylum Policy: GERD LEERS (CDA).
Minister of Security and Justice: IVO OPSTELTEN (VVD).
Minister of Education, Culture and Science: MARJA VAN BIJSTERVELDT-VLIEGENTHART (CDA).
Minister of Finance: JAN KEES DE JAGER (CDA).
Minister of Defence: HANS HILLEN (CDA).
Minister of Infrastructure and the Environment: MELANIE SCHULTZ VAN HAEGEN-MAAS GEESTERANUS (VVD).
Minister of Social Affairs and Employment: HENK KAMP (VVD).
Minister of Health, Welfare and Sport: EDITH SCHIPPERS (VVD).
State Secretary for Education, Culture and Science: HALBE ZIJLSTRA (VVD).
State Secretary for Foreign Affairs: BEN KNAPEN (CDA).
State Secretary for Economic Affairs, Agriculture and Innovation: HENK BLEKER (CDA).
State Secretary for Finance: FRANS WEEKERS (VVD).
State Secretary for Security and Justice: FRED TEEVEN (VVD).
State Secretary for Infrastructure and the Environment: JOOP ATSMA (CDA).
State Secretary for Social Affairs and Employment: PAUL DE KROM (VVD).
State Secretary for Health, Welfare and Sport: MARLIES VELDHUIJZEN VAN ZANTEN-HYLLNER (CDA).

MINISTRIES

Office of the Prime Minister, Ministry of General Affairs: Binnenhof 20, POB 20001, 2500 EA The Hague; tel. (70) 3564100; fax (70) 3564683; internet www.rijksoverheid.nl/ministeries/az.

Ministry of Defence: Plein 4, POB 20701, 2500 ES The Hague; tel. (70) 3188188; fax (70) 3187888; e-mail defensievoorlichting@mindef.nl; internet www.rijksoverheid.nl/ministeries/def.

Ministry of Economic Affairs, Agriculture and Innovation: Bezuidenhoutseweg 30, POB 20101, 2500 EC The Hague; tel. (70) 3798911; internet www.rijksoverheid.nl/ministeries/eleni.

Ministry of Education, Culture and Science: Rijnstraat 50, POB 16375, 2500 BJ The Hague; tel. (70) 4123456; fax (70) 4123450; e-mail ocwinfo@postbus51.nl; internet www.rijksoverheid.nl/ministeries/ocw.

Ministry of Finance: Korte Voorhout 7, POB 20201, 2500 EE The Hague; tel. (70) 3428000; fax (70) 3427900; e-mail webmaster@minfin.nl; internet www.rijksoverheid.nl/ministeries/fin.

Ministry of Foreign Affairs: Bezuidenhoutseweg 67, POB 20061, 2500 EB The Hague; tel. (70) 3486486; fax (70) 3484848; internet www.rijksoverheid.nl/ministeries/bz.

Ministry of Infrastructure and the Environment: Plesmanweg 1–6, POB 20901, 2500 EX The Hague; tel. (70) 4560000; fax (70) 4561111; internet www.rijksoverheid.nl/ministeries/ienm.

Ministry of the Interior and Kingdom Relations: Schedeldoekshaven 200, POB 20011, 2500 EA The Hague; tel. (70) 4266426; fax (70) 3639153; internet www.rijksoverheid.nl/ministeries/bzk.

Ministry of Health, Welfare and Sport: Parnassusplein 5, POB 20350, 2500 EJ The Hague; tel. (70) 3407911; fax (70) 3407834; internet www.rijksoverheid.nl/ministeries/vws.

Ministry of Security and Justice: Schedeldoekshaven 100, POB 20301, 2500 EH The Hague; tel. (70) 3707911; fax (70) 3707900; e-mail voorlichting@minjus.nl; internet www.rijksoverheid.nl/ministeries/venj.

Ministry of Social Affairs and Employment: Anna van Hannoverstraat 4, POB 90801, 2509 LV The Hague; tel. (70) 3334444; fax (70) 3334033; internet www.rijksoverheid.nl/ministeries/szw.

Legislature

STATEN-GENERAAL
(States-General)

Eerste Kamer
(First Chamber)

POB 20017, 2513 AA The Hague; Binnenhof 22, 2513 AA The Hague; tel. (70) 3129200; fax (70) 3129390; e-mail postbus@eerstekamer.nl; internet www.eerstekamer.nl.

President: PIERRE RENÉ HUBERT MARIE VAN DER LINDEN (CDA).

Election, 23 May 2011

Party	Seats
Volkspartij voor Vrijheid en Democratie (VVD)	16
Partij van de Arbeid (PvdA)	14
Christen Democratisch Appèl (CDA)	11
Partij voor de Vrijheid (PVV)	10
Socialistische Partij (SP)	8
Democraten 66 (D66)	5
GroenLinks (GL)	5
ChristenUnie (CU)	2
50Plus	1
Staatkundig Gereformeerde Partij (SGP)	1
Partij voor de Dieren	1
Independent	1
Total	**75**

Tweede Kamer
(Second Chamber)

POB 20018, 2500 EA The Hague; Binnenhof 4, 2513 AA The Hague; tel. (70) 3183040; internet www.tweedekamer.nl.

President: GERDI A. VERBEET (PvdA).

General Election, 9 June 2010

Party	Votes	%	Seats
Volkspartij voor Vrijheid en Democratie (VVD)	1,929,575	20.49	31
Partij van de Arbeid (PvdA)	1,848,805	19.63	30
Partij voor de Vrijheid (PVV)	1,454,493	15.45	24
Christen Democratisch Appèl (CDA)	1,281,886	13.61	21
Socialistische Partij (SP)	924,696	9.82	15
Democraten 66 (D66)	654,167	6.95	10
GroenLinks (GL)	628,096	6.67	10
ChristenUnie (CU)	305,094	3.24	5
Staatkundig Gereformeerde Partij (SGP)	163,581	1.74	2
Partij voor de Dieren	122,317	1.30	2
Others	103,291	1.10	—
Total	**9,416,001**	**100.00**	**150**

Election Commission

Kiesraad (Dutch Electoral Council): Herengracht 21, POB 20011, 2500 EA The Hague; tel. (70) 4266266; fax (70) 4266089; e-mail kiesraad@kiesraad.nl; internet www.kiesraad.nl; f. 1917; independent; Chair. Prof. HENK KUMMELING; Sec.-Dir MELLE BAKKER.

Advisory Councils

Raad van State (Council of State): Paleisstraat 3, POB 20019, 2500 EA The Hague; tel. (70) 4264426; fax (70) 3651380; e-mail voorlichting@raadvanstate.nl; internet www.raadvanstate.nl; comprises a Vice-Pres. and up to 28 mems nominated by the Sovereign, who formally presides over the Council; advises on legislation, constitutional issues, international treaties and all matters of

THE NETHERLANDS

national importance; Vice-Pres. H. D. TJEENK WILLINK; Sec. R. VAN DER BRUG.

Sociaal-Economische Raad (Social and Economic Council): Bezuidenhoutseweg 60, POB 90405, 2509 LK The Hague; tel. (70) 3499499; fax (70) 3832535; e-mail m.vander.burg@ser.nl; internet www.ser.nl; f. 1950; tripartite advisory body; advises Govt on social and economic policy; monitors commodity and industrial boards; 33 mems, of whom 11 belong to trade union federations, 11 belong to the employers' organizations, and 11 are independent experts in social and economic affairs appointed by the Crown; Chair. Dr ALEXANDER RINNOOY KAN; Sec.-Gen. Dr VÉRONIQUE TIMMERHUIS.

Political Organizations

Christen Democratisch Appèl (CDA) (Christian Democratic Appeal): Buitenom 18, POB 30453, 2500 GL The Hague; tel. (70) 3424888; fax (70) 3643417; e-mail cda@cda.nl; internet www.cda.nl; f. 1980 by merger of 3 'confessional' parties; Party Pres. RUTH PEETOOM; Acting Parliamentary Leader MAXIME VERHAGEN; 69,000 mems.

ChristenUnie (CU) (Christian Union): Puntenburgerlaan 91, POB 439, 3800 AK Amersfoort; tel. (33) 4226969; fax (33) 4226968; e-mail bureau@christenunie.nl; internet www.christenunie.nl; f. 2000 by merger of 2 'evangelical' parties, the Gereformeerd Politiek Verbond and the Reformatorische Politieke Federatie; interdenominational, based on biblical precepts; mem. of European Christian Political Movement; Chair. PETER BLOKHUIS; Party Leader ANDRÉ ROUVOET; Parliamentary Leader ARIE SLOB; c. 27,500 mems (2008).

Democraten 66 (D66) (Democrats 66): POB 660, 2501 CR The Hague; Hoge Nieuwstraat 30, 2514 EL The Hague; tel. (70) 3566066; fax (70) 3641917; e-mail info@d66.nl; internet www.d66.nl; f. 1966; Chair. INGRID VAN ENGELSHOVEN; Parliamentary Leader ALEXANDER PECHTOLD; 12,500 mems.

EénNL (One NL): Evenaar 17, 3067 DA Rotterdam; tel. (10) 2518403; fax (10) 2548707; e-mail info@eennl.nl; internet www.eennl.nl; f. 2006 by fmr mems of Leefbaar Rotterdam and List Pim Fortuyn; right-wing, nationalist; agenda broadly similar to that of Pim Fortuyn; Leaders MARCO PASTORS, JOOST EERDMANS.

Fryske Nasjonale Partij (FNP) (Frisian National Party): FNP-hûs, Obrechtstrjitte 32, 8916 EN Ljouwert; tel. (58) 2131422; e-mail fnphus@globalxs.nl; internet www.fnp.nl; f. 1962; promotes federalism and greater regional autonomy; Leader ANNIGJE TOERING-SCHUURMANS; c. 1,300 mems.

De Groenen (The Greens): POB 1251, 3500 BG Utrecht; tel. (30) 2341545; e-mail info@degroenen.nl; internet www.degroenen.nl; f. 1983; founding mem. of the European Green Party; Pres. OTTO TER HAAR (acting); Sec. OTTO TER HAAR.

GroenLinks (GL) (Green Left): Oudegracht 312, POB 8008, 3503 RA Utrecht; tel. (30) 2399900; fax (30) 2300342; e-mail info@groenlinks.nl; internet www.groenlinks.nl; f. 1990 by merger of Communistische Partij van Nederland, Evangelische Volkspartij, Pacifistisch-Socialistische Partij and Politieke Partij Radicalen; Chair. HENK NIJHOF; Parliamentary Leader JOLANDE SAP; c. 20,000 mems.

Nieuwe Communistische Partij Nederland (NCPN) (New Communist Party of the Netherlands): Haarlemmerweg 177, 1051 LB Amsterdam; tel. (20) 6825019; fax (20) 6828276; e-mail manifest@wanadoo.nl; internet www.ncpn.nl; f. 1992; Chair. JOB PRUIJSER.

Nieuwe Midden Partij (NMP) (New Centre Party): POB 2087, 8203 AB Lelijstad; tel. and fax (320) 281412; e-mail info@nmp.nl; internet www.sdnl.nl/nmp.htm; f. 1970; campaigns on economic issues; Leader MARTIN DESSING.

Partij van de Arbeid (PvdA) (Labour Party): Herengracht 54, POB 1310, 1000 BH Amsterdam; tel. (20) 5512155; fax (20) 5512250; e-mail voorzitter@pvda.nl; internet www.pvda.nl; f. 1946 by merger of progressive and liberal organizations; social democratic; Chair. LILIANE PLOUMEN; Party Leader JOB COHEN; Parliamentary Leader MARIËTTE HAMER; c. 55,000 mems.

Partij voor de Dieren (Party for the Animals): POB 17622, 1001 JM Amsterdam; tel. (20) 5203870; e-mail administratie@partijvoordedieren.nl; internet www.partijvoordedieren.nl; f. 2002; promotes animal rights and animal welfare; Chair. MARIANNE THIEME; Sec. PETER BOOGAARD.

Partij voor de Vrijheid (PVV) (Freedom Party): POB 20018, 2500 EA The Hague; internet www.pvv.nl; f. 2004 as Groep Wilders; present name adopted 2006; populist, anti-immigration; Leader GEERT WILDERS.

Socialistische Alternatieve Politiek (SAP) (Socialist Political Alternative): Postbus 2096, 3000 CB Rotterdam; tel. (20) 6259272; e-mail redactie@grenzeloos.nl; internet www.grenzeloos.org; f. 1974; Trotskyist.

Socialistische Partij (SP) (Socialist Party): Vijverhofstraat 65, 3032 SC Rotterdam; tel. (10) 2435555; fax (10) 2435566; e-mail onderzoek@sp.nl; internet www.sp.nl; f. 1972; Chair. JAN MARIJNISSEN; Parliamentary Leader EMILE ROEMER; Gen. Sec. HANS VAN HEIJNINGEN; 46,000 mems.

Staatkundig Gereformeerde Partij (SGP) (Political Reformed Party): Burgemeester van Reenensingel 101, 2803 PA Gouda; tel. (82) 696900; fax (82) 573222; e-mail voorlichting@sgp.nl; internet www.sgp.nl; f. 1918; Calvinist; female membership banned until 2006; Chair. Rev. A. VAN HETEREN; Parliamentary Leader KEES VAN DER STAAIJ; Gen. Sec. V. A. SMIT; 25,900 mems (2005).

Trots op Nederland (TON) (Proud of the Netherlands): POB 60, 2501 CB The Hague; tel. (70) 3155800; e-mail pers@trotsopnederland.com; internet www.trotsopnederland.com; f. 2007; right-wing, nationalist; Leader RITA VERDONK.

Verenigde Senioren Partij (VSP) (United Senior Citizens' Party): Israëlslaan 37, 3431 AS Nieuwegein; tel. (30) 6300208; fax (30) 6300209; e-mail info@verenigdeseniorenpartij.nl; internet www.verenigdeseniorenpartij.nl; Chair. H. J. (HERMAN) TROOST; Sec. JACK KOEHORST.

Volkspartij voor Vrijheid en Democratie (VVD) (People's Party for Freedom and Democracy): Laan Copes van Cattenburch 52, POB 30836, 2500 GV The Hague; tel. (70) 3613061; fax (70) 3608276; e-mail info@vvd.nl; internet www.vvd.nl; f. 1948; advocates free enterprise, individual freedom and responsibility, but its programme also supports social security and recommends the participation of workers in profits and management; Chair. MARK VERHEIJEN (acting); Parliamentary Leader MARK RUTTE; 38,000 mems.

50Plus: J. H. Meijestraat 23, 1214 NG Hilversum; e-mail tonluiting@50pluspartij.nl; internet 50pluspartij.nl; pursuing pensioners interests; f. 2009; Leader JAN NAGEL.

Diplomatic Representation

EMBASSIES IN THE NETHERLANDS

Afghanistan: Laan Van Meerdervoort 2B, 2517 AJ The Hague; tel. (70) 4272540; e-mail afconsulholland@yahoo.com; Ambassador ENAYATULLAH NABIEL.

Albania: Anna Paulownastraat 109B, 2518 BD The Hague; tel. (70) 4272101; fax (70) 4272083; e-mail embalba@xs4all.nl; Ambassador GAZMEND BARBULLUSHI.

Algeria: Van Stolklaan 1–3, 2585 JS The Hague; tel. (70) 3522954; fax (70) 3061961; e-mail ambalg1@wanadoo.nl; internet www.embalgeria.nl; Ambassador NASSIMA BAGHLI.

Argentina: Javastraat 20, 2585 AN The Hague; tel. (70) 3118411; fax (70) 3118410; e-mail argentina@xs4all.nl; internet www.embassyargentina.nl; Ambassador SANTOS GOÑI MARENCO.

Armenia: Laan Van Meerdervoort 90, 2517 AP The Hague; tel. (70) 3311002; e-mail armembnl@mfa.am; Ambassador DZIUNIK AGHAJANIAN.

Australia: Carnegielaan 4, 2517 KH The Hague; tel. (70) 3108200; fax (70) 3107863; e-mail austemb_thehague@dfat.gov.au; internet www.netherlands.embassy.gov.au; Ambassador LYDIA ELIZABETH MORTON.

Austria: Van Alkemadelaan 342, 2597 AS The Hague; tel. (70) 3245470; fax (70) 3282066; e-mail den-haag-ob@bmeia.gv.at; internet www.bmeia.gv.at/denhaag; Ambassador WOLFGANG PAUL.

Azerbaijan: Laan Copes van Cattenburch 127, 2585 EZ The Hague; tel. (70) 3538205; fax (70) 3469604; e-mail info@azembassy.nl; Ambassador FUAD ISKANDAROV.

Bangladesh: Wassenaarseweg 39, 2596 CG The Hague; tel. (70) 3283722; fax (70) 3283524; e-mail amb.thehague@mofa.gov.bd; internet www.bangladeshembassy.nl; Ambassador MUHAMMAD ALI SORCAR.

Belarus: Anna Paulownastraat 34, 2518 BE The Hague; tel. (70) 3631566; fax (70) 3640555; e-mail netherlands@belembassy.org; internet www.netherlands.belembassy.org; Ambassador ELENA GRITSENKO.

Belgium: Alexanderveld 97, 2585 DB The Hague; tel. (70) 3123456; fax (70) 3645579; e-mail thehague@diplobel.fed.be; internet www.diplomatie.be/thehague; Ambassador FRANK GEERKENS.

Bolivia: Nassaulaan 5, 2514 JS The Hague; tel. (70) 3616707; fax (70) 3620039; e-mail embolned@xs4all.nl; Ambassador ROBERTO CALZADILLA SARMIENTO.

Bosnia and Herzegovina: Bezuidenhoutseweg 223, 2495 AL The Hague; tel. (70) 3588505; fax (70) 3584367; e-mail info@bhembassy.nl; Ambassador MIRANDA SIDRAN-KAMIŠALIĆ.

Brazil: Mauritskade 19, 2514 HD The Hague; tel. (70) 3023959; fax (70) 3023950; e-mail brasil@brazilianembassy.nl; internet www.brazilianembassy.nl; Ambassador JOSÉ ARTUR DENOT MEDEIROS.

THE NETHERLANDS

Bulgaria: Duinroosweg 9, 2597 KJ The Hague; tel. (70) 3503051; fax (70) 3584688; e-mail info@embassy-bulgaria.nl; internet www.embassy-bulgaria.nl; Ambassador ZLATIN V. TRAPKOV.

Cameroon: Amaliastraat 14, 2514 JC The Hague; tel. (70) 3469715; fax (70) 3652979; e-mail ambacam-la-haye@planet.nl; internet www.cameroon-embassy.nl; Ambassador ODETTE MELONO.

Canada: Sophialaan 7, POB 30820, 2500 GV The Hague; tel. (70) 3111600; fax (70) 3111620; e-mail info@canada.nl; internet www.canadainternational.gc.ca/netherlands-pays_bas; Ambassador JAMES LAMBERT.

Chile: Mauritskade 51, 2514 HG The Hague; tel. (70) 3123640; fax (70) 3616227; e-mail echilenl@echile.nl; internet www.echile.nl; Ambassador JUAN ANTONIO MARTABIT SCAFF.

China, People's Republic: William Lodewijklaan 10, 2517 JT The Hague; tel. (70) 3065061; fax (70) 3551651; e-mail chinaemb_nl@mfa.gov.cn; internet www.chinaembassy.nl; Ambassador ZHANG JUN.

Colombia: Groot Hertoginnelaan 14, 2517 EG The Hague; tel. (70) 3614545; fax (70) 3614636; e-mail info@colombiaemb.nl; internet www.colombiaemb.nl; Ambassador FRANCISCO JOSÉ LLOREDA MERA.

Congo, Democratic Republic: Violenweg 2, 2597 KL The Hague; tel. (70) 3547904; fax (70) 3541373; Ambassador JACQUES MASANGU-A-MWANZA.

Costa Rica: Laan Copes van Cattenburch 46, 2585 GB The Hague; tel. (70) 3540780; fax (70) 3584754; e-mail embajada@embacrica.demon.nl; Ambassador JORGE ANTONIO URBINA ORTEGA.

Côte d'Ivoire: Laan van Meerdervoort 16, 2517 AK The Hague; tel. (70) 3117878; fax (70) 3924017; e-mail ambacoti.paysbas@yahoo.com; Ambassador KOUADIO ADJOUMANI.

Croatia: Amaliastraat 16, 2514 JC The Hague; tel. (70) 3623638; fax (70) 3623195; e-mail croemb.haag@mvpei.hr; internet nl.mfa.hr; Ambassador VESELA MRÐEN KORAĆ.

Cuba: Scheveningseweg 9, 2517 KS The Hague; tel. (70) 3606061; fax (70) 3647586; e-mail embacuba@embacuba.nl; internet www.embacuba.nl; Ambassador ZELMYS MARIA DOMINGUEZ CORTINA.

Cyprus: Surinamestraat 15, 2585 GG The Hague; tel. (70) 3466499; fax (70) 3924024; e-mail cyprus@xs4all.nl; internet www.mfa.gov.cy/embassythehague; Ambassador JAMES C. DROUSHIOTIS.

Czech Republic: Paleisstraat 4, 2514 JA The Hague; tel. (70) 3130031; fax (70) 3563349; e-mail hague@embassy.mzv.cz; internet www.mfa.cz/hague; Ambassador JAROSLAV HORÁK.

Denmark: Koninginnegracht 30, 2514 AB The Hague; tel. (70) 3025959; fax (70) 3025950; e-mail haaamb@um.dk; internet www.ambhaag.um.dk; Ambassador REIMER REINHOLDT NIELSEN.

Dominican Republic: Raamweg 21–22, 2596 HL The Hague; tel. (70) 3317553; fax (70) 4049890; e-mail embajada@embajadadominicana.nl; Ambassador LUIS ARIAS NÚÑEZ.

Ecuador: Koninginnegracht 84, 2514 AJ The Hague; tel. (70) 3469563; fax (70) 3658910; e-mail info@embassyecuador.eu; internet www.embassyecuador.eu; Chargé d'affaires a.i HELENA YANEZ LOZA.

Egypt: Badhuisweg 92, 2587 CL The Hague; tel. (70) 3542000; fax (70) 3543304; e-mail info@ambeg.nl; Ambassador MAHMOUD AHMED SAMIR SAMY.

El Salvador: Riouwstraat 137, 2585 HP The Hague; tel. (70) 3249855; fax (70) 3247842; Ambassador EDGAR HERNÁN VARELA ALAS.

Eritrea: Nassauplein 13, 2585 EB The Hague; tel. (70) 4276812; fax (70) 4277236; e-mail eritrea@xs4all.nl; Ambassador MOHAMMED SULEIMAN AHMED.

Estonia: Zeestraat 92, 2518 AD The Hague; tel. (70) 3029050; fax (70) 3029051; e-mail embassy.haag@mfa.ee; internet www.estemb.nl; Ambassador GITA KALMET.

Finland: Groot Hertoginnelaan 16, 2517 EG The Hague; tel. (70) 3469754; fax (70) 3107174; e-mail info.haa@formin.fi; internet www.finlande.nl; Ambassador KLAUS KORHONEN.

France: Smidsplein 1, 2514 BT The Hague; tel. (70) 3125800; fax (70) 3125824; e-mail info@ambafrance-nl.org; internet www.ambafrance-nl.org; Ambassador JEAN-FRANÇOIS BLAREL.

Georgia: Groot Hertoginnelaan 28, 2517 EG The Hague; tel. (70) 3029080; fax (70) 3029081; e-mail thehague.emb@mfa.gov.ge; internet www.netherlands.mfa.gov.ge; Ambassador SHOTA GVINERIA.

Germany: Groot Hertoginnelaan 18–20, 2517 EG The Hague; tel. (70) 3420600; fax (70) 3651957; e-mail ambduits@euronet.nl; internet www.den-haag.diplo.de; Ambassador Dr HEINZ-PETER BEHR.

Ghana: Laan Copes van Cattenburch 70, 2585 GD The Hague; tel. (70) 3384384; fax (70) 3062800; e-mail info@ghanaembassy.nl; internet www.ghanaembassy.nl; Ambassador AANAA NAAMUA ENIN.

Greece: Amaliastraat 1, 2514 JC The Hague; tel. (70) 3638700; fax (70) 3563040; e-mail gremb.hag@mfa.gr; internet www.greekembassy.nl; Ambassador JOHN ECONOMIDES.

Guatemala: Javastraat 44, 2585 AP The Hague; tel. (70) 3020253; fax (70) 3602270; e-mail embpaisesbajos@minex.gob.gt; Ambassador ROBERTO PALOMO SILVA.

Holy See: Carnegielaan 5 (Apostolic Nunciature), 2517 KH The Hague; tel. (70) 3503363; fax (70) 3521461; e-mail apost.nuntiatuur@inter.nl.net; Apostolic Nuncio Most Rev. FRANÇOIS BACQUÉ (Titular Archbishop of Gradisca).

Honduras: Burgemeester Patijnlaan 1932, 2585 CB The Hague; tel. (70) 3641684; fax (70) 3649134; e-mail eholan@honduras.demon.nl; Ambassador JULIO ANTONIO RENDÓN BARNICA.

Hungary: Hogeweg 14, 2585 JD The Hague; tel. (70) 3500404; fax (70) 3521749; e-mail mission.hga@kum.hu; internet www.hungarianembassy.nl; Ambassador GYULA SÜMEGHY.

India: Buitenrustweg 2, 2517 KD The Hague; tel. (70) 3469771; fax (70) 3617072; e-mail ambassador@indianembassy.nl; internet www.indianembassy.nl; Ambassador BHASWATI MUKHERJEE.

Indonesia: Tobias Asserlaan 8, 2517 KC The Hague; tel. (70) 3108100; fax (70) 3643331; e-mail bidpen@indonesia.nl; internet www.indonesia.nl; Ambassador JUNUS EFFENDI HABIBIE.

Iran: Duinweg 20–22, 2585 JX The Hague; tel. (70) 3548483; fax (70) 3503224; e-mail info@iranembassy.nl; internet www.iranianembassy.nl; Ambassador KAZEM QARIBABADI.

Iraq: Johan de Wittlaan 16, 2517 JR The Hague; tel. (70) 3101260; fax (70) 3924958; e-mail info@embassyofiraq.nl; internet www.embassyofiraq.nl; Ambassador SAAD ABD AL-MAJEED IBRAHIM IBRAHIM.

Ireland: Scheveningseweg 112, 2584 AE The Hague; tel. (70) 3630993; fax (70) 3617604; e-mail thehagueembassy@dfa.ie; internet www.embassyofireland.nl; Ambassador MARY WHELAN.

Israel: Buitenhof 47, 2513 AH The Hague; tel. (70) 3760500; fax (70) 3760555; e-mail info@hague.mfa.gov.il; internet thehague.mfa.gov.il; Ambassador HARRY KNEY-TAL.

Italy: Alexanderstraat 12, 2514 JL The Hague; tel. (70) 3021030; fax (70) 3614932; e-mail embitaly.denhaag@esteri.it; internet www.amblaja.esteri.it; Ambassador FRANCO GIORDANO.

Japan: Tobias Asserlaan 2, 2517 KC The Hague; tel. (70) 3469544; fax (70) 3106341; e-mail japan.cultural@planet.nl; internet www.nl.emb-japan.go.jp; Ambassador TAKASHI KOEZUKA.

Jordan: Badhuisweg 79, 2587 CD The Hague; tel. (70) 4167200; fax (70) 4167209; e-mail info@jordanembassy.nl; internet www.jordanembassy.nl; Ambassador KHALDOUN TALHOUNI.

Kazakhstan: Nieuwe Parklaan 69, 2597 LB The Hague; tel. (70) 3634757; fax (70) 3657600; e-mail info@kazakhembassy.nl; internet www.kazakhembassy.nl; Ambassador MAINURA S. MURZAMADIYEVA.

Kenya: Nieuwe Parklaan 21, 2597 LA The Hague; tel. (70) 3504215; fax (70) 3553594; e-mail info@kenya-embassy.nl; Ambassador Prof. RUTHIE CHEPKOECH RONO.

Korea, Republic: Verlengde Tolweg 8, 2517 JV The Hague; tel. (70) 3586076; fax (70) 3504712; e-mail koremb@euronet.nl; internet nld.mofat.go.kr; Ambassador Dr KIM YOUNG-WON.

Kosovo: Anna Paulownastraat 56A, 2518 BG The Hague; tel. (70) 3020025; fax (70) 3644473; e-mail embassy.netherlands@ks-gov.net; Ambassador NEXHMI REXHEPI.

Kuwait: Carnegielaan 9, 2517 KH The Hague; tel. (70) 3123400; fax (70) 3924588; e-mail info@kuwaitembassy.nl; Ambassador SALIM AL-AZMI HAFEEZ MUHAMMAD.

Latvia: Balistraat 88, 2585 XX The Hague; tel. (70) 3065000; fax (70) 3065009; e-mail embassy.netherlands@mfa.gov.lv; Ambassador MARIS KLISANS.

Lebanon: Frederikstraat 2, 2514 LK The Hague; tel. (70) 3658906; fax (70) 3620779; e-mail amb.lib@wanadoo.nl; Ambassador ZEIDAN AL-SAGHIR.

Libya: 15 Parkweg, 2585 JH The Hague; tel. (70) 355886; fax (70) 3559075; e-mail embassylibia@ziggo.nl; Chargé d'affaires a.i. AHMED M. TABULI.

Lithuania: Laan van Meerdervoort 20, 2517 AK The Hague; tel. (70) 3855418; fax (70) 3853940; e-mail amb.nl@urm.lt; internet nl.mfa.lt; Ambassador VAIDOTAS VERBA.

Luxembourg: Nassaulaan 8, 2514 JS The Hague; tel. (70) 3647589; fax (70) 3462000; e-mail lahaye.amb@mae.etat.lu; Ambassador JEAN-MARC HOSCHEIT.

Macedonia, former Yugoslav republic: Laan van Meerdervoort 50C, 2517 AM The Hague; tel. (70) 4274464; fax (70) 4274469; e-mail hague@mfa.gov.mk; Ambassador NIKOLA DIMITROV.

Malaysia: Rustenburgweg 2, 2517 KE The Hague; tel. (70) 3506506; fax (70) 3506536; e-mail malaysia@euronet.nl; internet www.kln.gov.my/perwakilan/thehague; Ambassador Dr FAUZIAH MOHD TAIB.

Malta: Carnegielaan 4–14, 2517 KH The Hague; tel. (70) 3561252; fax (70) 3464796; e-mail maltaembassy.thehague@gov.mt; Ambassador Martin Valentino.

Mexico: Nassauplein 28, 2585 EC The Hague; tel. (70) 3602900; fax (70) 3560543; e-mail embamex@embamex-nl.com; internet www.embamex-nl.com; Ambassador Jorge Lomónaco Tonda.

Morocco: Oranjestraat 9, 2514 JB The Hague; tel. (70) 3469617; fax (70) 3562829; e-mail ambamar.lahaye@wanadoo.nl; Ambassador Jawad el-Himdi.

New Zealand: Eisenhowerlaan 77N, 2517 KK The Hague; tel. (70) 3469324; fax (70) 3632983; e-mail nzemb@xs4all.nl; internet www.nzembassy.com/netherlands; Ambassador George Troup.

Nicaragua: Statenlaan 81, 2582 GE, The Hague; tel. (70) 3225063; fax (70) 3508331; e-mail info@embanic.nl; Ambassador Carlos Argüello Gómez.

Nigeria: Wagenaarweg 5, 2597 LL The Hague; tel. (70) 3501703; fax (70) 3551110; e-mail nigembassy@nigerianembassy.nl; internet www.nigerianembassy.nl; Ambassador Dr Nimota Nihinlola Akanbi.

Norway: Lange Vijverberg 11, 2513 AC The Hague; tel. (70) 3117611; fax (70) 3659630; e-mail emb.hague@mfa.no; internet www.noorwegen.nl; Ambassador Eva Bugge.

Oman: Nieuwe Parklaan 9, LA The Hague; tel. (70) 3615800; fax (70) 3605364; e-mail info@embassyofoman.nl; Ambassador Sayyid Muhammad bin Harib bin Abdullah al-Said.

Pakistan: Amaliastraat 8, 2514 JC The Hague; tel. (70) 3648948; fax (70) 3106047; e-mail info@pakembassy.nl; internet www.embassyofpakistan.com; Ambassador Aizaz Ahmad Chaudhry.

Peru: Nassauplein 4, 2585 EA The Hague; tel. (70) 3653500; fax (70) 3651929; e-mail info@embassyofperu.nl; Ambassador Allan Wagner Tizón.

Philippines: Laan Copes van Cattenburch 125, 2585 EZ The Hague; tel. (70) 3604820; fax (70) 3560030; e-mail ph@bart.nl; internet www.philembassy.nl; Ambassador Cardozo M. Luna.

Poland: Alexanderstraat 25, 2514 JM The Hague; tel. (70) 7990100; fax (70) 7990137; e-mail haga.amb.sekretariat@msz.gov.pl; Ambassador Dr Janusz József Stanczyk.

Portugal: Zeestraat 74, 2518 AD The Hague; tel. (70) 3630217; fax (70) 3615589; e-mail info@portembassy.nl; Ambassador Manuel Nuno Tavares de Sousa.

Qatar: Borweg 7, 2597 LR The Hague; tel. (70) 4166666; fax (70) 4166660; e-mail info@embassyofqatar.nl; internet www.embassyofqatar.nl; Ambassador Hamad bin Ali Jabir al-Henzab.

Romania: Catsheuvel 55, 2517 KA The Hague; tel. (70) 3223613; fax (70) 3541587; e-mail roembnl@xs4all.nl; internet haga.mae.ro; Ambassador Călin Fabian.

Russia: Andries Bickerweg 2, 2517 JP The Hague; tel. (70) 3451300; fax (70) 3617960; e-mail ambrusnl@euronet.nl; internet www.netherlands.mid.ru; Ambassador Roman Kolodkin.

Rwanda: Johan van Oldenbarneveltlaan 3, 2582 NE The Hague; tel. 3926571; fax 4275326; e-mail ambalahaye@minaffet.gov.rw; internet www.ambalahaye.nl; Ambassador Immaculee Uwanyiligira.

Saudi Arabia: Alexanderstraat 19, 2514 JM The Hague; tel. (70) 3614391; fax (70) 3561452; e-mail saudiembassy@casema.nl; Ambassador Abdullah A. Z. al-Shaghrood.

Serbia: Groot Hertoginnelaan 30, 2517 EG The Hague; tel. (70) 3636800; fax (70) 3602421; e-mail embassy.hague@mfa.rs; Ambassador Čedomir Rajković.

Slovakia: Parkweg 1, 2585 JG The Hague; tel. (70) 4167777; fax (70) 4167783; e-mail emb.hague@mzv.sk; internet www.haag.mfa.sk; Ambassador Jaroslav Chlebo.

Slovenia: Anna Paulownastraat 11, 2518 BA The Hague; tel. (70) 3108690; fax (70) 3626608; e-mail vhg@gov.si; internet www.haag.veleposlanistvo.si; Ambassador Leon Marc.

South Africa: Wassenaarseweg 40, 2596 CJ The Hague; tel. (70) 3924501; fax (70) 3460669; e-mail info@zuidafrika.nl; internet www.zuidafrika.nl; Ambassador Peter Goosen.

Spain: Lange Voorhout 50, 2514 EG The Hague; tel. (70) 3024999; fax (70) 3617959; e-mail ambassade.spanje@worldonline.nl; internet www.mae.es/embajadas/lahaya; Ambassador Francisco Javier Vallaure de Acha.

Sri Lanka: Jacob de Graeffaan 2, 2517 JM The Hague; tel. (70) 3655910; fax (70) 3465596; e-mail mission@infolanka.nl; Ambassador Grace Ammal Asirwatham.

Sudan: Laan Copes van Cattenburch 81, 2585 EW The Hague; tel. (70) 3620939; fax (70) 3617975; e-mail sudan@tiscali.nl; internet www.sudanembassy-gov-nl.org; Ambassador Sirajuddin Hamid Yousif.

Suriname: Alexander Gogelweg 2, 2517 JH The Hague; tel. (70) 3650844; fax (70) 3617445; e-mail ambassade.suriname@wxs.nl; Ambassador (vacant).

Sweden: Jan Willem Frisolaan 3, 2517, JS The Hague; tel. (70) 4120200; fax (70) 4120211; e-mail ambassaden.haag@foreign.ministry.se; internet www.swedenabroad.com/thehague; Ambassador Håkan Emsgård.

Switzerland: Lange Voorhout 42, 2514 EE The Hague; tel. (70) 3642831; fax (70) 3561238; e-mail hay.vertretung@eda.admin.ch; internet www.eda.admin.ch/denhaag; Ambassador Markus Börlin.

Thailand: Laan Copes van Cattenburch 123, 2585 EZ The Hague; tel. (70) 3450766; fax (70) 3451929; e-mail thaihag@thaihag.demon.nl; internet www.thaiembassy.org/hague; Ambassador Virachai Plasai.

Tunisia: Gentsestraat 98, 2587 HX The Hague; tel. (70) 3512251; fax (70) 3514323; e-mail ambassadetunisie@wanadoo.nl; Ambassador Abbas Mohsen.

Turkey: Jan Evertstraat 15, 2514 BS The Hague; tel. (70) 3604912; fax (70) 3617969; e-mail turkishembassy@euronet.nl; internet www.lahey.be.mfa.gov.tr; Ambassador Uğur Doğan.

Ukraine: Zeestraat 78, 2518 AD The Hague; tel. (70) 3626095; fax (70) 3615565; e-mail embukr@wxs.nl; internet www.oekraine.com; Ambassador Aleksandr Horin.

United Arab Emirates: Eisenhowerlaan 130, 2517 KN The Hague; tel. (70) 3384370; fax (70) 3384373; e-mail info@uae-embassy.nl; internet www.uae-embassy.nl; Ambassador Ali Thani al-Suwaidi.

United Kingdom: Lange Voorhout 10, 2514 ED The Hague; tel. (70) 4270427; fax (70) 4270345; e-mail ukinnl@fco.gov.uk; internet www.britain.nl; Ambassador Paul Arkwright.

USA: Lange Voorhout 102, 2514 EJ The Hague; tel. (70) 3102209; fax (70) 3102307; e-mail ircthehague@state.gov; internet thehague.usembassy.gov; Ambassador Fay Hartog-Levin.

Uruguay: Mauritskade 33, 2514 HD The Hague; tel. (70) 3609815; fax (70) 3562826; e-mail uruholan@wxs.nl; Ambassador Dr Carlos Antonio Mora Medero.

Venezuela: Nassaulaan 2, 2514 JS The Hague; tel. (70) 3651256; fax (70) 3656954; e-mail embvene@xs4all.nl; internet www.embven.nl; Ambassador Haifa Aissami Madah.

Viet Nam: Nassauplein 12, 2585 EB The Hague; tel. (70) 3648917; fax (70) 3648656; e-mail vnembassy.nl@mofa.gov.vn; internet www.vietnamembassy.nl; Ambassador Huynh Minh Chính.

Yemen: Nassaulaan 2A, 2514 JS The Hague; tel. (70) 3653936; fax (70) 3563312; e-mail yemenembassy@planet.nl; internet www.yemen-embassy.nl; Ambassador Dr Nageeb Ahmed Obeid.

Judicial System

Justices and judges must have graduated in law at a Dutch university, and are nominated for life by the Crown. The justices of the Supreme Court are nominated from a list of three compiled by the Second Chamber of the States-General.

SUPREME COURT

De Hoge Raad der Nederlanden

POB 20303, 2500 EH The Hague; Kazernestraat 52, 2514 CV The Hague; tel. (70) 3611311; fax (70) 3658700; internet www.rechtspraak.nl/Gerechten/HogeRaad.

For appeals in cassation against decisions of courts of lower jurisdiction. As a court of first instance, the Supreme Court tries offences committed in their official capacity by members of the States-General and ministers. When dealing with appeals in cassation, the court is composed of five or, in more straightforward cases, of three justices (Raadsheren).

President of the Supreme Court: G. J. M. Corstens.
Procurator-General: J. W. Fokkens.
Secretary of the Court: E. Hartogs.

COURTS OF APPEAL

Gerechtshoven: Five courts: Amsterdam, Arnhem, 's-Hertogenbosch, Leeuwarden, The Hague. A court is composed of three judges (Raadsheren); appeal is from decisions of the District Courts of Justice. Fiscal Divisions (Belastingkamers) of the Courts of Appeal deal with appeals against decisions relating to the enforcement of the fiscal laws (administrative jurisdiction). The court of Arnhem has a Tenancy Division (Pachtkamer), composed of three judges and two assessors (a tenant and a landlord), and a Penitentiary Division (Penitentiaire Kamer), composed of three judges and two experts. The Tenancy Division hears appeals from decisions of all Canton Tenancy Divisions. The Penitentiary Division hears appeals against

THE NETHERLANDS

refusals of release on license, which is usually granted after two-thirds of a prison sentence longer than one year, unless there are special objections from the Minister of Justice. A Companies Division (Ondernemingskamer) is attached to the court at Amsterdam, consisting of three judges and two experts as assessors.

DISTRICT COURTS OF JUSTICE

Arrondissementsrechtbanken: There are 19 courts for important civil and penal cases and for appeals from decisions of the Canton Judges. A court is composed of three judges (Rechter); no jury; summary jurisdiction in civil cases by the President of the Court; simple penal cases, including economic offences, generally by a single judge (Politierechter). Offences committed by juveniles are (with certain exceptions) tried by a specialized judge (Kinderrechter), who is also competent to take certain legal steps when the upbringing of a juvenile is endangered. Economic offences, and in particular environmental offences, are also dealt with by a specialized judge sitting alone.

CANTON COURTS

Kantongerechten: There are 62 courts for civil and penal cases of minor importance. A court consists of a single judge, the Canton Judge (Kantonrechter). Each Canton Court has a Tenancy Division (Pachtkamer), presided over by the Canton Judge who is assisted by two assessors (a landlord and a tenant).

ADMINISTRATIVE COURTS

The administrative courts regulate relations between the authorities and citizens according to the provisions of the General Administrative Law Act. The majority of cases are heard by the Administrative Law Sections of the District Courts, while appeals are heard by the Administrative Law Division of the Council of State (Afdeling Bestuursrechtspraak van de Raad van State), which also acts as the court of sole and last instance in the majority of cases concerning education, the environment and spatial planning. In addition, cases relating to certain areas of administrative law are heard by the following bodies:

Centrale Raad van Beroep (Central Appeals Council): POB 16002, 3500 DA Utrecht; Graadt van Roggenweg 200–250, 3531 AH Utrecht; tel. (30) 8502100; fax (30) 8502198; e-mail crvb@rechtspraak.nl; internet www.rechtspraak.nl/gerechten/crvb; hears appeals against decisions of the District Courts in matters concerning the public service and social security; Pres. T. G. M. SIMONS.

College van Beroep voor het Bedrijfsleven (Trade and Industry Appeals Tribunal): POB 20021, 2500 EA The Hague; Prins Clauslaan 14, POB 20021, 2595 EA The Hague; tel. (70) 3813910; fax (70) 3813999; e-mail cbb@rechtspraak.nl; internet www.rechtspraak.nl/gerechten/cbb; hears in first and last instance appeals against decisions enforcing socio-economic and agricultural legislation made by certain bodies, such as regulatory bodies and Chambers of Commerce, and by certain ministers; Pres. R. R. WINTER.

Administration Law Section, Aliens Division, District Court of The Hague: court of sole and last instance in cases involving immigration; brs in Zwolle, 's-Hertogenbosch, Amsterdam and Haarlem. The introduction of a limited right of further appeal is pending.

Tariefcommissie (Tariff Commission): court of sole and last instance for all customs and excise disputes.

Religion

CHRISTIANITY

Raad van Kerken in Nederland (Council of Churches in the Netherlands): Koningin Wilhelminalaan 5, 3818 HN Amersfoort; tel. (33) 4633844; e-mail rvk@raadvankerken.nl; internet www.raadvankerken.nl; f. 1968; 16 mem. churches; Pres. Drs H. J. VAN HOUT; Gen. Sec. Drs K. VAN DER KAMP.

The Roman Catholic Church

The Netherlands comprises one archdiocese and six dioceses. At 31 December 2006 there were an estimated 4,647,300 adherents in the country (28.6% of the population).

Bishops' Conference

Nederlandse Bisschoppenconferentie, Biltstraat 121, POB 13049, 3507 LA Utrecht; tel. (30) 2334244; fax (30) 2332103; e-mail secrbk@rkk.nl; internet www.katholieknederland.nl/rkkerk.
f. 1986; Pres. Mgr ADRIANUS HERMAN VAN LUYN (Bishop of Rotterdam).

Archbishop of Utrecht: Most Rev. WILLEM JACOBUS (WIM) EIJK, Aartsbisdom, Maliebaan 38–40, 3581 CR Utrecht; tel. (30) 2338033; fax (30) 2311962; e-mail pers@aartsbisdom.nl; internet www.aartsbisdom.nl.

Protestant Churches

Christelijke Gereformeerde Kerken in Nederland (Christian Reformed Churches in the Netherlands): POB 334, 3900 AH Veenendaal; Ghandistr. 2, 3902 KD Veenendaal; tel. (318) 582350; e-mail lkb@cgk.nl; internet www.cgk.nl; f. 1834; Relations Dir Rev. J. G. H. VAN DER VINNE; c. 73,400 mems; 180 churches.

First Church of Christ, Scientist (PEFAAS): Winschoterweg 9, 9723 CG Groningen; e-mail peter.faas@hccnet.nl; churches in Amsterdam, Haarlem and The Hague.

Deutsche Evangelische Gemeinde (German Evangelical Church): Bleijenburg 3B, 2511 VC, The Hague; tel. (70) 3465727; e-mail deg.haag@tiscali.nl; internet www.evangelischekirche-denhaag.nl; Leaders Pastor ECKHARD BENZ-WENZLAFF, Pastor BARBARA WENZLAFF.

Dutch Mennonites: Algemene Doopsgezinde Sociëteit, Singel 454, 1017 AW Amsterdam; tel. (20) 6230914; fax (20) 6278919; e-mail info@doopsgezind.nl; internet www.doopsgezind.nl; f. 1811; Pres. OTTO BLEKER; Sec.-Gen. H. W. STENVERS; 9,000 mems; 118 parishes.

Evangelische Broedergemeente (Hernhutters): Zusterpl. 20, 3703 CB Zeist; tel. (30) 6924833; fax (30) 6922677; e-mail provinciaalbestuur@ebg.nl; internet www.ebg.nl; f. 1746; Pres. RITA HARRY; 10,000 mems in Holland; 7 parishes.

Hersteld Apostolische Zendingkerk (Restored Apostolic Missionary Church): Hogerbeetsstraat 32, 2242 TR Wassenaar; tel. and fax (70) 5113995; e-mail s.de.jong.hazk@hazknederland.org; internet www.hazknederland.org; f. 1863; Pres. Apostle for the Netherlands H. F. RIJNDERS; Sec. J. L. M. STRAETEMANS; 500 mems; 10 parishes.

Protestante Kerk in Nederland (Protestant Church in the Netherlands): POB 8399, 3503 RM Utrecht; tel. (30) 8801435; fax (30) 8801447; e-mail s.freytag@home.nl; internet www.pkn.nl; f. 2004; unification of the Nederlandse Hervormde Kerk with the Gereformeerde Kerken in Nederland and the Evangelisch-Lutherse Kerk; 2m. mems, 3,000 parishes in 77 districts; Pres. Rev. SUSANNE FREYTAG; Sec.-Gen. Rev. Dr B. PLAISIER.

Remonstrantse Broederschap (Remonstrant Church): Nieuwe Gracht 27A, 3512 LC Utrecht; tel. (30) 2316970; fax (30) 2311055; e-mail info@remonstranten.org; internet www.remonstranten.org; f. 1619; Pres. J. W. VAN DER KAMP; Gen. Sec. TOM MIKKERS; 5,800 mems; 44 parishes.

Unie van Baptistengemeenten in Nederland (Union of Baptist Churches in The Netherlands): Raadhuisplein 6–8, NL 3771 ER Barneveld; tel. (342) 712457; e-mail info@baptisten.nl; internet www.baptisten.nl; f. 1881; Pres. JANS HOFMAN; 12,000 mems.

Other Christian Churches

Anglikaans Kerkgenootschap (Anglican Church): Ary van der Spuyweg 1, 2585 HA The Hague; tel. (70) 3555359; e-mail churchoffice@stjohn-stphilip.org; internet www.stjohn-stphilip.org; f. 1698; Chaplain Rev. TONY ROAKE.

Katholiek Apostolische Gemeenten (Catholic Apostolic Church): 1E De Riemerstraat 3, 2513 CT The Hague; tel. (70) 3555018; f. 1867; 7 parishes in the Netherlands and 3 in Belgium.

Oud-Katholieke Kerk van Nederland (Old Catholic Church): Koningin Wilhelminalaan 3, 3818 HN Amersfoort; tel. (33) 4620875; e-mail info@okkn.nl; internet www.okkn.nl; f. 1723 in the Netherlands with Jansenist influence; refuses to accept papal infallibility and other 'new' dogmas of the Roman Catholic Church; in full communion with the Anglican Churches since 1931; Leader and Archbishop of Utrecht Mgr Dr JORIS A. O. L. VERCAMMEN (18 parishes); Bishop of Haarlem Mgr Dr DICK JAN SCHOON (10 parishes); 10,000 mems.

ISLAM

At 1 January 2004 there were around 944,000 Muslims in the Netherlands, representing some 5.8% of the total population.

Contactorgaan Moslims en Overheid (CMO) (Contact Group for Muslims and the Government): Beeklaan 207, 2562 AE The Hague; tel. (70) 3921123; fax (70) 3462409; e-mail info@contactorgaanmoslimsenoverheid.nl; internet www.cmoweb.nl; f. 2004; promotes dialogue between Muslim community and the Government; includes 8 Muslim groups; Pres. Y. ALTUNTAS.

JUDAISM

Nederlands Israëlitisch Kerkgenootschap (Organization of Jewish Communities in the Netherlands): Postbus 7967, 1008 AD Amsterdam; tel. (20) 3018484; fax (20) 3018485; e-mail info@nik.nl; internet www.nik.nl; f. 1814; 36 communities with around 5,000 mems; Rabbi RAPHAEL EVERS.

THE NETHERLANDS

Portugees-Israëlietische Gemeente (Portuguese Synagogue): Mr. Visserplein 3, 1011 RD Amsterdam; tel. (20) 6245351; fax (20) 6254680; e-mail info@portugesesynagoge.com; internet www.portugesesynagoge.com; f. 1675; Gen. Sec. NATHAN MOKED.

BAHÁ'Í FAITH

National Spiritual Assembly (Bahá'í Community of the Netherlands): Riouwstraat 27, 2585 GR The Hague; tel. (70) 3554017; fax (70) 3506161; e-mail secretariaat@bahai.nl; internet www.bahai.nl; f. 1962; mems resident in 180 locations.

The Press

PRINCIPAL DAILIES

Alkmaar

Noordhollands Dagblad: Edisonweg 10, POB 2, 1800 AA Alkmaar; tel. (72) 5196196; fax (72) 5124152; e-mail redactie@nhd.nl; internet www.noordhollandsdagblad.nl; f. 1799; morning; 9 regional editions; Editors GEERT TEN DAM, JAN GEERT MAJOOR; circ. 147,064 (2006).

Amersfoort

AD Amersfoortse Courant: POB 43, 3800 AA Amersfoort; tel. (33) 4647911; fax (33) 4647334; e-mail ac.redactie@ad.nl; internet www.ad.nl/amersfoort; f. 1887; publ. by AD NieuwsMedia; evening; Editor-in-Chief DICK VAN DER MEER (acting).

Amsterdam

Het Financieele Dagblad (Dutch Financial Daily): Prins Bernhardplein 173, POB 216, 1000 AE Amsterdam; tel. (20) 5928888; fax (20) 5928700; e-mail rsc@fd.nl; internet www.fd.nl; f. 1796; morning; Mon.–Sat.; Editor ULKO JONKER; circ. 58,350 (2006).

Metro: Metro Holland BV, Delflandlaan 4, POB 90009, 1006 BA Amsterdam; tel. (20) 5114000; fax (20) 5114090; e-mail info@metronieuws.nl; internet www.metronieuws.nl; f. 2004 in Rotterdam; separate Amsterdam edition since 2005; morning; owned by Metro International SA; Editor ROBERT VAN BRANDWIJK; circ. 560,000 (2008).

Het Parool: Jacob Bontiusplaats 9, POB 433, 1000 AK Amsterdam; tel. (20) 5584444; fax (20) 5584351; e-mail redactie@parool.nl; internet www.parool.nl; f. 1940; evening; Editor BARBARA VAN BEUKERING; circ. 86,656 (2006).

Sp!ts: POB 2620, 1000 CP Amsterdam; tel. (20) 5853045; fax (20) 5853065; e-mail redactie@spitsnieuws.nl; internet www.spitsnieuws.nl; f. 1998; morning; distributed free of charge; publ. by BasisMedia BV; Editor B. BROUWERS; circ. 450,000 (2008).

De Telegraaf: POB 376, 1000 EB Amsterdam; tel. (20) 5859111; fax (20) 5858017; e-mail redactie@telegraaf.nl; internet www.telegraaf.nl; f. 1893; morning; Editor EEF BOS; circ. 714,563 (2006).

Trouw (Loyalty): Jacob Bontiusplaats 9, POB 859, 1000 AW Amsterdam; tel. (20) 5629444; e-mail redactie@trouw.nl; internet www.trouw.nl; f. 1943; morning; Editor WILLEM SCHOONEN; circ. 108,435 (2006).

De Volkskrant (The People's Journal): Jacob Bontiusplaats 9, POB 1002, 1000 BA Amsterdam; tel. (20) 5626222; fax (20) 5626289; e-mail redactie@volkskrant.nl; internet www.volkskrant.nl; f. 1919; morning; Editor PIETER I. BROERTJES; circ. 284,801 (2006).

Apeldoorn

Reformatorisch Dagblad: Laan van Westenenk 12, POB 670, 7300 AR Apeldoorn; tel. (55) 5390222; fax (55) 5412288; e-mail redactie@refdag.nl; internet www.refdag.nl; f. 1971; evening; publ. by Erdee Media Groep; Editor-in-Chief WIM B. KRANENDONK; circ. 58,000 (2008).

De Stentor: Laan van Westenenk 6, POB 99, 7336 AZ Apeldoorn; tel. (55) 5388388; fax (55) 5388200; e-mail redactiesecretariaat@destentor.wegener.nl; internet www.destentor.nl/apeldoorn; f. 2003; evening; publishes 9 regional versions; Editor ALEX ENGBERS; circ. 140,757 (2006).

Barneveld

Nederlands Dagblad: Hermesweg 20, POB 111, 3770 AC Barneveld; tel. (342) 411711; fax (342) 411611; e-mail redactie@nd.nl; internet www.nd.nl; f. 1944; morning; Editor-in-Chief P. A. BERGWERFF; circ. 33,200 (2006).

Breda

BN/De Stem (The Voice): Spinveld 55, POB 3229, 4800 MB Breda; tel. (76) 5312311; fax (76) 5312355; e-mail redactie@bndestem.nl; internet www.bndestem.nl; f. 1998 by merger of Brabants Nieuwsblad and De Stem; owned by Koninklijke Wegener NV; morning; Editor JOHAN VAN UFFELEN; circ. 124,213 (2006).

Dordrecht

AD De Dordtenaar: POB 54, 3300 AB Dordrecht; tel. (78) 6324705; fax (78) 6324729; e-mail dd.redactie@ad.nl; internet www.ad.nl; f. 1946; morning; Editor BART VERKADE.

Eindhoven

Eindhovens Dagblad (ED): Wal 2, POB 534, 5600 AM Eindhoven; tel. (40) 2336336; fax (40) 2436244; e-mail redactie@eindhovensdagblad.nl; internet www.ed.nl; owned by Wegener; Editor HENK VAN WEERT; circ. 116,901 (2006).

Enschede

De Twentsche Courant Tubantia: Getfertsingel 41, POB 28, 7500 AA Enschede; tel. (53) 4842842; fax (53) 4842200; e-mail lezers@tubantia.wegener.nl; internet www.tctubantia.nl; f. 1844; publ. by Koninklijke Wegener NV; Editor ANDRÉ VIS; circ. 124,070 (2006).

's-Gravenhage/Den Haag
(The Hague)

AD Haagsche Courant: POB 16050, 2500 AA The Hague; tel. (70) 3190911; fax (70) 3954783; e-mail hc.lezers@ad.nl; internet www.ad.nl/denhaag; evening; Editor DENNIS MULKENS.

Nederlandse Staatscourant: Prinses Margrietplantsoen 88, POB 20020, 2500 EA The Hague; tel. (70) 3789639; fax (70) 3855505; e-mail staatscourant@sdu.nl; internet www.staatscourant.nl; f. 1814; morning; Editor W. M. C. DE JONG; circ. 5,913 (2006).

Groningen

Dagblad van het Noorden: Lübeckweg 2, POB 60, 9700 MC Groningen; tel. (50) 5844444; fax (50) 5844209; e-mail redactie@dvhn.nl; internet www.dvhn.nl; f. 1888; morning; Editor PIETER SIJPERSMA; circ. 156,247 (2006).

Haarlem

Haarlems Dagblad: Stationsplein 86, POB 507, 2003 PA Haarlem; tel. (88) 8241200; fax (88) 8241212; e-mail stadsredactie@haarlemsdagblad.nl; internet www.haarlemsdagblad.nl; f. 1656; evening; Editors GEERT TEN DAM, JAN GEERT MAJOOR; circ. 44,123 (2006).

IJmuider Courant: Marktplein 1, 1972 GA IJmuiden; tel. (255) 561800; fax (255) 561888; e-mail redactie@ijmuidercourant.nl; internet www.ijmuidercourant.nl; evening; Editors GEERT TEN DAM, JAN GEERT MAJOOR.

's-Hertogenbosch/Den Bosch

Brabants Dagblad: Emmaplein 25, POB 235, 5201 HB 's-Hertogenbosch; tel. (73) 6157157; fax (73) 6157105; e-mail stadsredactie@brabantsdagblad.nl; internet www.brabantsdagblad.nl; f. 1771; morning; publ. by Koninklijke Wegener NV; Editor ANNEMIEKE BESSELING; circ. 136,068 (2006).

Hilversum

De Gooi- en Eemlander: Seinstraat 14, 1223 DA Hilversum; tel. (35) 6477000; fax (35) 6477108; e-mail redactie@gooieneemlander.nl; internet www.gooieneemlander.nl; f. 1871; evening; Editors GEERT TEN DAM, JAN-GEERT MAJOOR; circ. 29,752 (2006).

Leeuwarden

Leeuwarder Courant: Sixmastraat 15, POB 394, 8901 BD Leeuwarden; tel. (58) 2845655; fax (58) 2845419; e-mail redactie@leeuwardercourant.nl; internet www.leeuwardercourant.nl; f. 1752; evening; Editor RIMMER MULDER; circ. 103,489 (2006).

Leiden

Leidsch Dagblad: 3e Binnenvestgracht 23, POB 54, 2300 AB Leiden; tel. (71) 5356356; fax (71) 5356415; e-mail stadsredactie@leidschdagblad.nl; internet www.leidschdagblad.nl; f. 1860; publ. by HDC Media; evening; Editors GEERT TEN DAM, JAN-GEERT MAJOOR; circ. 34,781 (2006).

Nijmegen

De Gelderlander: Voorstadslaan 2, POB 36, 6500 DA Nijmegen; tel. (24) 3650611; fax (24) 3650479; e-mail redactie@gelderlander.nl; internet www.gelderlander.nl; f. 1848; owned by Koninklijke Wegener NV; morning; Editor K. PIJNAPPELS; circ. 163,780 (2006).

THE NETHERLANDS

Rotterdam

AD: Marten Meesweg 35, POB 8983, 3009 TC Rotterdam; tel. (10) 4067211; e-mail ad@ad.nl; internet www.ad.nl; f. 1946; fmrly *Algemeen Dagblad*; morning; Editor JAN BONJER; circ. 524,974 (2006, incl. regional editions).

AD Rotterdams Dagblad: Westblaak 180, POB 2999, 3000 CZ Rotterdam; tel. (10) 4004400; fax (10) 4128509; e-mail rd.redactie@ad.nl; internet www.ad.nl/rotterdam; f. 1991; evening; Editor BART VERKADE.

NRC Handelsblad: Marten Meesweg 35, POB 8987, 3009 TH Rotterdam; tel. (10) 4066111; fax (10) 4066967; e-mail nrc@nrc.nl; internet www.nrc.nl; f. 1970; evening; Editor BIRGIT DONKER; circ. 239,211 (2006).

Sittard

Dagblad De Limburger: POB 1056, 6201 MK Maastricht; tel. (43) 3502000; fax (43) 3501879; e-mail redactievenlo@mgl.nl; internet www.limburger.nl; f. 1845; morning; Editor-in-Chief KITTY BORGHOUTS; circ. 180,000.

Limburgs Dagblad: Mercator 3, 6135 KW Sittard; tel. (46) 4116000; fax (46) 4116471; e-mail marketing@mgl.nl; internet www.limburger.nl; f. 1918; morning; Editor JOS ADRIAENS; circ. 53,904 (2006).

Utrecht

AD Utrechts Nieuwsblad: Essenkade 2, POB 500, 3990 DM Houten; tel. (30) 6399911; fax (30) 6399937; e-mail un.lezers@ad.nl; internet www.ad.nl; f. 1993; evening; Editor-in-Chief DICK VAN DER MEER (acting).

Vlissingen

Provinciale Zeeuwse Courant: POB 31, 4460 AA Goes; tel. (113) 315600; fax (113) 315669; e-mail redactie@pzc.nl; internet www.pzc.nl; f. 1758; morning; Editor PETER JANSEN; circ. 56,868 (2006).

SELECTED WEEKLIES

Adformatie: POB 75462, 1070 AL Amsterdam; tel. (20) 5733644; fax (20) 6793581; e-mail redactie@adformatie.nl; internet www.adformatie.nl; advertising, marketing and media; Editor-in-Chief LÉON BOUWMAN; circ. 40,000.

Avrobode: 's-Gravelandseweg 52, 1217 ET Hilversum; tel. (35) 6717911; fax (35) 717443; e-mail redactie@avrobode.nl; internet www.avrobode.nl; publ. by Algemene Omroepvereniging; radio and TV guide; circ. 791,986.

Boerderij: Hanzestraat 1, POB 4, 7000 BA Doetinchem; tel. (314) 349446; fax (314) 344397; e-mail boerderij@reedbusiness.nl; internet www.boerderij.nl; f. 1915; farming; Editor-in-Chief MARCEL HENST; circ. 65,000.

Donald Duck: Haaksbergsweg 75, 1101 BR Amsterdam; tel. (20) 4300300; fax (20) 4300315; internet www.donaldduck.nl; f. 1952; children's interest; weekly; Publr SUZAN SCHOUTEN HAAGMANS; Editor JESSICA HAAGMANS; circ. 62,784.

Elsevier: POB 152, 1000 AD Amsterdam; tel. (20) 5159944; fax (20) 5159900; e-mail redactie.elsevier@elsevier.nl; internet www.elsevier.nl; f. 1945; current affairs; Chief Editor ARENDO JOUSTRA; circ. 160,000.

Fancy: POB 1610, 2130 JA Hoofddorp; tel. (23) 5565117; fax (23) 5565116; e-mail fancy@sanoma-uitgevers.nl; internet www.fancy.nl; teenage girls' interest; Editor ANNET NITERINK; circ. 120,000.

HP/De Tijd (The Times): POB 95044, 1090 HA Amsterdam; tel. (20) 5979400; fax (20) 5979490; e-mail redactie@hpdetijd.audax.nl; internet www.hpdetijd.nl; f. 1845 as daily; owned by Audax; changed to weekly in 1974; progressive; current affairs; Editor-in-Chief FRANK POORTHUIS; circ. 30,000.

Libelle: POB 1742, 2130 JC Hoofddorp; tel. (23) 5564002; fax (23) 5564003; e-mail libelle@libelle.nl; internet www.libelle.nl; f. 1934; women's interest; Editor-in-Chief FRANSKA STUY; circ. 587,754.

Margriet: POB 1640, 2130 JA Hoofddorp; tel. (23) 5564123; e-mail redactie@margriet.nl; internet www.margriet.nl; f. 1938; women's interest; Editor-in-Chief LEONTINE VAN DEN BOS; circ. 499,868.

Mikro Gids: POB 10050, 1201 DB Hilversum; tel. (35) 6726880; fax (35) 6726878; internet www.mikrogids.nl; f. 1974; radio and TV guide; Editor-in-Chief HANS SANDERS; circ. 468,280.

NCRV-Gids: POB 25900, 1202 HW Hilversum; tel. (35) 6726801; fax (35) 6726863; internet www.ncrvgids.nl; f. 1966; publ. by Nederlandse Christelijke Radio Vereniging; radio and TV guide; Dir C. ABBENHUIS; circ. 419,363.

Nederlands Tijdschrift voor Geneeskunde (Dutch Journal of Medicine): POB 75971, 1070 AZ Amsterdam; tel. (20) 6620150; fax (20) 6735481; e-mail redactie@ntvg.nl; internet www.ntvg.nl; f. 1856; Editors Prof. Dr P. W. DE LEEUW, Prof. Dr F. W. A. VERHEUG, Prof. Dr J. O. M. ZAAT; circ. 30,000.

Nieuwe Revu: Capellalaan 65, POB 41006, 2130 MK Hoofddorp; tel. (88) 7518380; e-mail redactie@revu.nl; internet www.revu.nl; f. 1953; general interest; Editor-in-Chief FRANS LOMANS; circ. 127,802.

Panorama: Ceylonpoort 5–25, 2037 AA Haarlem; tel. (23) 5304304; fax (23) 5361624; e-mail panorama@smm.nl; internet www.panorama.nl; f. 1913; general interest; Editor FRANS LOMANS; circ. 194,466.

Privé: POB 1980, 1000 BZ Amsterdam; tel. (20) 5853375; fax (20) 5854225; e-mail redactie@prive.nl; internet www.prive.nl; f. 1977; women's interest; Editor EVERT SANTEGOEDS; circ. 490,000.

Story: POB 1760, 2130 JD Hoofddorp; tel. (23) 5564894; fax (23) 5564911; internet www.story.nl; f. 1974; women's interest; Editor PETRA BAKKER-SCHUT; circ. 272,700.

TeleVizier: Zeverijnstraat 6, POB 20002, 1202 AB Hilversum; tel. (35) 6726834; fax (35) 6726712; e-mail redactie@televizier.nl; internet www.televizier.nl; publ. by Algemene Omroepvereniging; radio and TV guide; circ. 258,487.

Tina: Ceylonpoort 5–25, 2037 AA Haarlem; tel. (23) 5304304; fax (23) 5352554; f. 1967; teenage interest; circ. 112,191.

TrosKompas: POB 28600, 1202 LR Hilversum; tel. (35) 6728798; fax (35) 6728631; e-mail info@troskompas.nl; internet www.troskompas.nl; f. 1966; owned by Hilversumse Media Compagnie; radio and TV guide; Editor EDGER HAMER.

TV Krant: POB 28600, 1202 LR Hilversum; tel. (35) 6728798; fax (35) 6728631; f. 1990; radio and TV guide; Editor EDGER HAMER.

Vara TV Magazine: POB 175, 1200 AD Hilversum; tel. (35) 6711445; fax (35) 6711429; e-mail tv.magazine@vara.nl; internet vara.nl; radio and TV guide; circ. 500,000.

Veronica: POB 22000, 1202 CA Hilversum; tel. (35) 6463333; fax (35) 6463300; e-mail bladredactie@veronicapublishing.nl; internet www.veronica.nl; f. 1971; radio and TV guide; Editor PETER CONTANT; circ. 1,250,000.

Viva: POB 1630, 2130 JA Hoofddorp; tel. (23) 5565165; fax (23) 5565200; e-mail redactie@viva.nl; internet www.viva.nl; women's interest; Editor KARIN VAN GILST; circ. 149,461.

VNU: Ceylonpoort 5–25, 2037 AA Haarlem; POB 1, 2000 MA Haarlem; tel. (23) 5463463; fax (23) 5463912; e-mail vnupr@hq.vnu.com; circ. 174,250.

VPRO-Gids: POB 11, 1200 JC Hilversum; tel. (35) 6712665; fax (35) 6712285; e-mail gids@vpro.nl; internet www.vpro.nl/gids; radio and TV guide; Dir H. VAN DALFSEN; circ. 254,000.

Vrij Nederland: Raamgracht 4, POB 1254, 1000 BG Amsterdam; tel. (20) 5518711; fax (20) 6247476; e-mail redactie@vn.nl; f. 1940; current affairs; Editor FRITS VAN EXTER; circ. 60,000.

SELECTED PERIODICALS

Art, History and Literature

De Architect: POB 20025, 2501 AG The Hague; tel. (70) 3789911; fax (70) 3854321; e-mail architect@wkths.nl; internet www.dearchitect.nl; Dir HARM TILMAN; circ. 4,859 (2010).

Geschiedenis Magazine: Molukkenstraat 200, 1098 TW Amsterdam; tel. (20) 6652759; fax (20) 6657831; e-mail redactie@geschiedenismagazine.nl; internet www.geschiedenismagazine.nl; f. 1966; monthly; history and archaeology; Editor-in-Chief MARTIJN VAN LIESHOUT; circ. 8,000.

Kunstbeeld: POB 256, 1110 AG Diemen; tel. (20) 5310900; fax (20) 5310971; e-mail redactie@kunstbeeld.nl; internet www.kunstbeeld.nl; monthly; art, sculpture; Editor ROBBERT ROOS; circ. 11,000 (2007).

Tableau Fine Arts Magazine: Delflandlaan 4, 1062 EB Amsterdam; tel. (20) 7581000; e-mail tableau@pelicanmags.nl; internet www.tableaufineartsmagazine.nl; f. 1978; every 2 months; publ. by Pelican Magazines Hearst; Editor (vacant); circ. 14,000.

Economics and Business

Computable: POB 37109, 1030 BA Haarlem; tel. (23) 2042925; e-mail computable@vnumedia.nl; internet www.computable.nl; Editor ALEX BESHUIZEN; circ. 39,914 (2010).

Elektronica + Embedded Systems: POB 58, 7400 AB Deventer; tel. (570) 504381; fax (570) 504399; e-mail h.vries@mybusinessmedia.nl; internet www.engineersonline.nl; f. 1953; 8 a year; electronics design; Editor HENK DE VRIES; circ. 5,000.

Intermediair: POB 1900, 2003 BA Haarlem; tel. (23) 5463455; fax (23) 5465530; e-mail redactie@intermediair.nl; internet www.intermediair.nl; f. 1965; weekly; business recruitment; Editor ALEX BEISHUIZEN; circ. 240,678.

THE NETHERLANDS

Management Team: Paul van Vlissingenstr. 10, 1096 BK Amsterdam; tel. (20) 2620701; e-mail redactie@mt.nl; internet www.mt.nl; f. 1980; monthly; management; Editor EWALD SMITS.

PCM (Personal Computer Magazine): Ceylonpoort 5–25, 2037 AA Haarlem; tel. (23) 5463704; fax (23) 5465524; internet www.pcmweb.nl; f. 1982; monthly; computing; Editor-in-Chief EDWIN AMMERLAAN; circ. 94,997.

Trade Channel: Nieuw Guineastraat 30, 2022 PA Haarlem; tel. (23) 5319022; fax (23) 5317974; e-mail pvroom@tradechannel.com; internet www.tradechannel.com; f. 1945; monthly, 2 edns: Trade Channel Consumer Goods and Trade Channel Industrial & Technical Products; promote imports and exports; Editor HENK VAN CAPELLE; circ. 13,286 (consumer edn), 55,000 (technical edn).

Home, Fashion and General

Ariadne at Home: Capellalaan 65, POB 1919, 2130 YM Hoofddorp; tel. (23) 5566770; fax (23) 5361624; e-mail redactie@ariadneathome.nl; internet www.ariadneathome.nl; f. 1946; monthly; home decoration; Editor BRIGITTE SPEEKMAN; circ. 169,198.

Het Beste uit Reader's Digest: POB 23330, 1100 DV Amsterdam; tel. (20) 56789111; fax (20) 6976422; e-mail hetbeste@readersdigest.nl; internet www.readersdigest.nl; f. 1957; monthly; general interest; Man. Dir OELE STEENKS; circ. 304,453.

Cosmopolitan: Capellalaan 65, POB 1730, 2132 JL Hoofddorp; fax (23) 5565259; e-mail c.straatmans@sanoma-uitgevers.nl; internet www.cosmopolitan.nl; f. 1982; monthly; women's interest; Editor CLAUDIA STRAATMANS; circ. 152,659 (2010).

Delicious: Capellalaan 65, POB 1632, 2130 JA Hoofddorp; tel. (23) 5565466; fax (23) 5565488; e-mail deliciousmagazine@sanoma-uitgevers.nl; internet www.deliciousmagazine.nl; f. 1977; monthly; cookery; Editor-in-Chief MAKKIE MULDER; circ. 62,218 (2010).

Kijk: POB 40091, 2130 KZ Hoofddorp; tel. (20) 4300455; fax (20) 4300450; e-mail info@kijk.nl; internet www.kijk.nl; sports, science, technology and adventure; Editor VIVIANNE BENDERMACHER; circ. 60,023 (2010).

Knipmode: Capellalaan 65, POB 1900, 2130 JL Hoofddorp; tel. and fax (23) 5565006; internet www.knipmode.nl; monthly; DIY fashion; Editor-in-Chief ELLEN DE JONG; Publr WOUTER VERKENNIS; circ. 124,000.

Nouveau: Capellalaan 65, POB 1710, 2132 JC Hoofddorp; tel. (23) 304304; fax (23) 350621; internet www.nouveau.nl; f. 1986; women's interest; Dir K. P. M. VAN DE PAS; circ. 62,708 (2010).

Opzij: Raamgracht 4, POB 2748, 1000 CS Amsterdam; tel. (20) 5518525; fax (20) 6227265; e-mail redactie@opzij.nl; internet www.opzij.nl; f. 1972; monthly; feminist themes; Editor MARGRIET VAN DER LINDEN; circ. 77,540 (2010).

Ouders van Nu: POB 740, 2400 AS Alphen Aan Den Ryn; tel. (23) 5565066; fax (23) 5565095; e-mail ouders@jongezinnen.nl; internet www.oudersvannu.nl; f. 1967; monthly; childcare; Editor K. KROONSTUIVER; circ. 68,029 (2010).

SEN: Mathenesserlaan 179, 3014 HA Rotterdam; fax (102) 092629; e-mail info@senmagazine.com; internet www.senmagazine.com; f. 2004; monthly; women's interest; Publr SENAY OZDEMIR; circ. 20,000.

VT-Wonen: Maassluisstraat 2, POB 1900, 2130 JH Hoofddorp; tel. (30) 822511; fax (30) 898388; e-mail vtwonen@sanoma-utigevers.nl; internet www.vtwonen.nl; f. 1964; monthly; home-owning and decorating; Editors MONIQUE WIEMEYER, FRANCIEN DE VET; circ. 130,640 (2010).

101 Woonideeën: POB 1702, 2130 JC Hoofddorp; tel. (23) 5564590; fax (23) 5564505; e-mail 101woonideeen@sanoma-uitgevers.nl; internet www.101woonideeen.nl; f. 1957; monthly; home ideas; Editor ANNET NITERINK; circ. 72,622 (2010).

Leisure Interests and Sport

Autokampioen: POB 93200, 2509 BA The Hague; tel. (88) 2696688; fax (88) 2696279; e-mail autokampioen@anwb.nl; internet www.anwb.nl/auto; f. 1908; publ. by Royal Dutch Touring Club (ANWB); motoring; fortnightly; Chief Editor JOS VROOMANS; circ. 36,826 (2010).

Grasduinen (Browsing): POB 41000, 2130 2130 MK Hoofddorp; tel. (20) 7518110; fax (20) 7510111; e-mail info@grasduinen.nl; internet www.grasduinen.nl; monthly; leisure, healthy living, art; Editor FANNY GLAZENBURG; circ. 23,661 (2010).

Kampeer en Caravankampioen: POB 93200, 2509 BA The Hague; tel. (88) 2692222; e-mail kck@anwb.nl; internet www.kck-online.nl; f. 1941; monthly; camping and caravanning; publ. by Royal Dutch Touring Club (ANWB); Editor-in-Chief F. VOORBERGEN; circ. 98,892 (2010).

Kampioen: POB 93200, 2509 BA The Hague; tel. (80) 2692222; fax (70) 3146983; e-mail kampioen@anwb.nl; internet www.kampioen.nl; f. 1885; monthly; recreation and tourism; publ. by Royal Dutch Touring Club (ANWB); Editor E. LODEWYKS; circ. 3,608,835 (2010).

Reizen Magazine: POB 93200, 2509 BA The Hague; tel. (88) 2696670; fax (88) 2697610; e-mail reizen@anwb.nl; internet www.reizen.nl; 11 issues a year; tourism, travel; publ. by Royal Dutch Touring Club (ANWB); Editor-in-Chief HARRI THEIRLYNCK; circ. 55,788 (2010).

Voetbal International: WP Sport Media BV, POB 764, 1000 AT Amsterdam; tel. (20) 5518510; e-mail webmaster@vi.nl; internet www.vi.nl; weekly; football; Editor-in-Chief JOHAN DERKSEN; circ. 166,723 (2010).

Waterkampioen: POB 93200, 2509 BA The Hague; tel. (88) 2697049; fax (88) 2697359; e-mail waterkampioen@anwb.nl; internet lwww.anwbwatersport.nl; f. 1927; fortnightly; water sports and yachting; publ. by Royal Dutch Touring Club (ANWB); Editor MARJOLEIN DOOMEN; circ. 38,710 (2010).

Scientific and Medical

Huisarts en Wetenschap: Nederlands Huisartsen Genootschap, POB 3231, 3502 GE Utrecht; tel. (30) 2823500; fax (30) 2823501; e-mail redactie@nhg.org; internet www.henw.org; monthly; medical; Editor Dr JOOST VAAT; circ. 12,463 (2010).

Natuur & Techniek: POB 256, 1110 AG Diemen; tel. (46) 4389444; fax (46) 4370161; e-mail redactie@natutech.nl; internet www.natutech.nl; f. 1932; monthly; Editor R. DOBBELAER; circ. 47,360.

Technische Revue: POB 4, 7000 BA Doetinchem; tel. (314) 349968; fax (314) 361522; internet www.reedbusiness.nl; monthly; review of new products; Chief Editor M. L. MATSER; circ. 28,000.

NEWS AGENCY

Algemeen Nederlands Persbureau (ANP) (Netherlands News Agency): POB 1, 2501 AA The Hague; tel. (70) 4141414; fax (70) 4140560; e-mail redactie@anp.nl; internet www.anp.nl; f. 1934; official agency of the Netherlands Daily Press Asscn; Man. Dir LUC VAN GOMPEL; Editor-in-Chief ERIK VAN GRUIJTHUIJSEN.

PRESS ORGANIZATIONS

Buitenlandse Persvereniging in Nederland (Foreign Press Asscn in the Netherlands): Oudezijds Voorburgwal 129, 1012 EP Amsterdam; tel. (20) 4221209; e-mail ccorder@ap.org; internet www.bpv-fpa.nl; f. 1925; Pres. KERSTIN SCHWEIGHÖFER; 120 mems.

Nederlandse Dagbladpers (NDP) (Dutch Asscn of Daily Newspaper Publrs): Hogehilweg 6, POB 12040, 1100 AA Amsterdam-Zuidoost; tel. (20) 4309171; fax (20) 4309199; e-mail ndp@nuv.nl; internet www.nuv.nl; f. 1908; affiliated to Nederlands Uitgeversverbond; Chair. C. G. G. SPAAN; Gen. Sec. T. NAUTA; 31 mems.

De Nederlandse Nieuwsbladpers (NNP) (Organization of Local News Media in the Netherlands): Hogebrinkerweg 23c, 3871 KM Hoevelaken; tel. (33) 4481650; fax (33) 4481652; e-mail nnpnl@nnp.nl; internet www.nnp.nl; f. 1945; asscn of publrs of non-daily local newspapers and other local news media; Pres. P. V. J. H. (PAUL) JANSSEN; Dir J. P. (PAUL) BOS; 131 mems.

Nederlandse Vereniging van Journalisten (Netherlands Union of Journalists): Johannes Vermeerstraat 22, POB 75997, 1070 AZ Amsterdam; tel. (20) 6766771; fax (20) 6624901; e-mail vereniging@nvj.nl; internet www.villamedia.nl/n/nvj; f. 1884; publ. *De Journalist* (fortnightly); Chair. (vacant); Sec. T. BRUNING; 9,000 mems.

Publishers

Uitgeverij Altamira BV: Zijlweg 308, 2000 AH Haarlem; tel. (23) 5286882; e-mail info@gottmer.nl; internet www.altamira-becht.nl; f. 1985; philosophy, psychology, New Age, health and spirituality.

Uitgeverij Ankh-Hermes BV: Smyrnastraat 5, POB 125, 7400 AC Deventer; tel. (57) 0678900; fax (57) 0624632; e-mail info@ankh-hermes.nl; internet www.ankh-hermes.nl; f. 1972; health, eastern and western religions, astrology, alternative medicine, psychology, esoterics; part of VBK-media since 2011; Dir A. STEENBERGEN; Publrs E. TEN SELDAM, W. DE VEER.

Ambo Anthos: Herengracht 499, 1017 BR Amsterdam; tel. (20) 5245411; fax (20) 4200422; e-mail info@amboanthos.nl; internet www.amboanthos.nl; literature, cultural history, biographies, history, politics; Dir R. AMMERLAAN.

APA (Academic Publishers Associated): POB 806, 1000 AV Amsterdam; tel. (20) 6265544; fax (20) 5285298; e-mail apa@apa-publishers.com; internet www.apa-publishers.com; f. 1966; subsidiaries: Apantiqua, Holland University Press, Fontes Pers, Oriental Press, Philo Press, van Heusden, Hissink & Co; old, new and reprint edns in the arts, humanities and science; Man. Dir G. VAN HEUSDEN.

THE NETHERLANDS

BV Uitgeverij De Arbeiderspers: Herengracht 370–372, POB 2877, 1000 CW Amsterdam; tel. (20) 5247500; fax (20) 6224937; e-mail info@arbeiderspers.nl; internet www.arbeiderspers.nl; participant in Weekbladpers holdings group; general, fiction and non-fiction; Dir LEX JANSEN.

A. Asher & Co BV: Zeeweg 264, POB 258, 1971 AG IJmuiden; tel. (25) 5523839; fax (25) 5510352; e-mail info@asherbooks.com; internet www.asherbooks.com; f. 1830; natural history; Dirs M. J. ROOS, J. W. STEINER.

Bert Bakker BV: Herengracht 540, POB 1662, 1000 BR Amsterdam; tel. (20) 6241934; fax (20) 6225461; e-mail info@pbo.nl; internet www.uitgeverijprometheus.nl/bb; f. 1893; Dutch and international literature, sociology, history, politics, science; Editor JOB LISMAN.

John Benjamins BV: Klaprozenweg 75G, POB 36224, 1020 ME Amsterdam; tel. (20) 6304747; fax (20) 6739773; e-mail customer.services@benjamins.nl; internet www.benjamins.com; f. 1964; linguistics, philology, psychology and art history; antiquarian scholarly periodicals; Man. Dir SELINE BENJAMINS.

Uitgeverij De Bezige Bij BV: Van Miereveldstraat 1, POB 75184, 1070 AD Amsterdam; tel. (20) 3059810; fax (20) 3059824; e-mail info@debezigebij.nl; internet www.debezigebij.nl; f. 1945; Publr MICHIEL GAAF.

Erven J. Bijleveld: Janskerkhof 7, 3512 BK Utrecht, POB 1238, 3500 BE Utrecht; tel. (30) 2317008; fax (30) 2368675; e-mail bijleveld.publishers@wxs.nl; internet www.bijleveldbooks.nl; f. 1865; psychology, sociology, philosophy, religion and history; computer books (as Bijleveld Press); Mans J. B. BOMMELJÉ, L. S. BOMMELJÉ.

Boekencentrum Uitgevers: Goudstraat 50, POB 29, 2700 AA Zoetermeer; tel. (79) 3615481; fax (79) 3615489; e-mail info@boekencentrum.nl; internet www.boekencentrum.nl; bibles, books and magazines; Dir N. A. DE WAAL.

Bohn Stafleu Van Hoghum BV: Het Spoor 2, POB 246, 3990 GA Houten; tel. (30) 6383736; fax (30) 6383999; e-mail klachten@bsl.nl; internet www.bsl.nl; mem. of Wolters Kluwer NV holdings group; social sciences, humanities, medical, dental and nursing; Dir P. J. A. SNAKKERS.

Boom Uitgevers Amsterdam BV: Prinsengracht 747–751, POB 15970, 1001 JX Amsterdam; tel. (20) 6226107; fax (20) 6253227; e-mail info@boomamsterdam.nl; internet www.boomamsterdam.nl; f. 1842; fmrly Boom Pers BV, Meppel; philosophy, educational and social sciences, environment, history; Man. Dir DRIES VAN INGEN.

Brill Academic Publishers: Plantijnstraat 2, POB 9000, 2300 PA Leiden; tel. (71) 5353500; fax (71) 5317532; e-mail marketing@brill.nl; internet www.brill.nl; f. 1683; academic books and periodicals (mainly in English); classics, medieval, renaissance and oriental studies, comparative religion, biology; CEO HERMAN PABBRUWE.

A. W. Bruna Uitgevers BV: Kobaltweg 23–25, POB 40203, 3504 AA Utrecht; tel. (30) 2470411; fax (30) 2410018; e-mail info@awbruna.nl; internet www.awbruna.nl; f. 1868; general fiction and non-fiction; Dir J. A. A. BOEZEMAN.

CRC Press/Balkema–Taylor & Francis Group (CRC Press/Balkema): POB 447, 2300 AK Leiden; Schipholweg 107C, POB 447, 2316 XC Leiden; tel. (71) 5243080; fax (71) 5234571; e-mail pub.nl@tandf.co.uk; internet www.crcpress.com; f. 1901 as Swets & Zeitlinger Publishers; acquired by Taylor & Francis (United Kingdom) in 2003; publr of books in civil engineering, water, geosciences and earth sciences; Sr Publr JANJAAP BLOM.

Uitgeverij Cantecleer BV: Julianalaan 11, POB 309, 3740 AM Baarn; tel. (35) 5486600; fax (35) 5486645; e-mail cantecleer@worldonline.nl; internet www.cantecleer.nl; f. 1948; mem. of Bosch & Keuning Uitgevers group; Man. Dir H. SCHWURMANS.

Uitgeverij De Fontein BV: Herculesplein 20, POB 13288, 3507 LG Utrecht; tel. (35) 5486311; fax (35) 5423855; internet www.defonteinkinderboeken.nl; f. 1981; mem. of NDC/VBK; commercial fiction, non-fiction and children's books; Dir T. AKVELD.

Uitgeverij van Gennep BV: Nieuwezijds Voorburgwal 330, 1012 RW Amsterdam; tel. (20) 6247033; fax (20) 6247035; e-mail info@vangennep-boeken.nl; internet vangennep-boeken.nl; history, social theory, political science, biographies, literature; Dir CHRIS TEN KATE.

Gottmer Uitgevers Groep: Zijlweg 308, POB 317, 2000 CN Haarlem; tel. (23) 5411190; fax (23) 5274404; e-mail info@gottmer.nl; internet www.gottmer.nl; f. 1937; fiction, non-fiction, children's books, religion, spirituality, travel guides; imprints incl. Aramith, Becht, Dominicus and Hollandia; Dir C. G. A. VAN WIJK.

Uitgeverij Holland BV: Spaarne 110, 2011 CM Haarlem; tel. (23) 5323061; fax (23) 5342908; e-mail info@uitgeverijholland.nl; internet www.uitgeverijholland.nl; f. 1922; literature, reference, science, children's books; Publr J. B. VAN ULZEN.

Uitgeefmaatschappij J. H. Kok: IJsseldijk 31, POB 5019, 8260 GA Kampen; tel. (38) 3392555; fax (38) 3327331; e-mail algemeen@kok.nl; internet www.kok.nl; f. 1894; theology, belles-lettres, science, periodicals; mem. of Veen Bosch & Keuning Uitgevers; 9 subsidiaries; Dir B. A. ENDEDIJK.

Ten Have BV: IJsseldijk 31, POB 5018, 8260 GA Kampen; tel. (38) 3328912; fax (38) 3392500; e-mail info@uitgeverijtenhave.nl; internet www.uitgeverijtenhave.nl; f. 1831; imprint of Uitgeefmaatschappij J. H. Kok; religious; Dir B. A. ENDEDIJK; Editor P. DE BOER.

Uitgeverij Voorhoeve: POB 13288, 3507 LG Utrecht; tel. (35) 5418855; fax (35) 5413174; f. 1876; imprint of Uitgeversmaatschappij J. H. Kok; general non-fiction, children's books; Dir B. A. ENDEDIJK.

Kosmos Uitgevers: Herculespl. 20, POB 13288, LG Utrecht; tel. (30) 2528500; fax (30) 2528598; e-mail info@kosmosuitgevers.nl; internet www.kosmosuitgevers.nl; f. 1992; mem. of Veen Bosch & Keuning Uitgevers; Dir GENEVIÈVE WALDMANN.

Lemniscaat BV: Vijverlaan 48, POB 4066, 3006 AB Rotterdam; tel. (10) 2062929; fax (10) 4141560; e-mail info@lemniscaat.nl; internet www.lemniscaat.nl; f. 1963; philosophy, psychology, care of the disabled and mentally handicapped, books for juveniles and young adults, picture books; Dir J. C. BOELE VAN HENSBROEK.

Uitgeverij Leopold BV: Singel 262, POB 3879, 1001 AR Amsterdam; tel. (20) 5511250; fax (20) 4204699; e-mail info@leopold.nl; internet www.leopold.nl; f. 1923; mem. Weekbladpers BV; children's books; Dir ANNETTE PORTEGIES.

Uitgeverij Luitingh-Sijthoff BV: Leidsegracht 105A, POB 289, 1000 AG Amsterdam; tel. (20) 5307340; fax (20) 626251; e-mail info@luitingh-sijthoff.nl; internet www.luitinghsijthoff.nl; f. 1989 following the merger of Sijthoff (f. 1851) and Luitingh (f. 1947); mem. of Veen Bosch en Keuning Uitgevers publishing group; fiction and popular non-fiction; Man. Dir HANCA LEPPINK.

Malmberg BV: Leeghwaterlaan 16, POB 233, 5201 AE Den Bosch; tel. (73) 6288811; fax (73) 6210512; e-mail malmberg@malmberg.nl; internet www.malmberg.nl; f. 1885; part of SanomaWSOY Group (Finland); educational; Dir J. DRIESSEN.

J. M. Meulenhoff BV: Nieuwe Herengracht 507, 1017 BV Amsterdam; tel. (20) 5353135; fax (20) 5353130; e-mail info@meulenhoff.nl; internet www.meulenhoff.nl; f. 1895; literature, historical, political, social/cultural, art, paperbacks and pocket books; Dir ROB HOGENES.

NDC/VBK de Uitgevers B.V.: Sixmastraat 15, POB 394, 8932 PA Leeuwarden; tel. (30) 2845245; e-mail communicatie@ndcvbk.nl; internet www.ndcvbk.nl; f. 2005; merger between NDC Holding BV and Veen Bosch en Keuning Uitgevers NV; Chair. JAN K. W. DE ROOS.

Nienhuis Montessori International BV: Industriepark 14, 7021 AA Zelhem; tel. (314) 627110; fax (314) 627128; e-mail info@nienhuis.nl; internet www.nienhuis.nl; f. 1800; holdings group; publrs and printers specializing in scientific books and periodicals; Dir A. J. NIENHUIS.

Noordhoff Uitgevers: Winschoterdiep 70A, POB 58, 9700 MB Groningen; tel. (50) 5226922; fax (50) 5277599; e-mail info@wolters.nl; internet www.wolters-noordhoff.nl; f. 1836; educational and scientific books, educational software, geographical and historical atlases and maps; Man. Dir Dr A. M. W. HOLL.

Uitgeverij Ploegsma BV: Singel 262, 1016 AC Amsterdam; tel. (20) 5511250; fax (20) 6203509; e-mail info@ploegsma.nl; internet www.ploegsma.nl; subsidiary: Uitgeverij De Brink.

Em. Querido's Uitgeverij BV: Singel 262, POB 3879, 1001 AR Amsterdam; tel. (20) 5511262; fax (20) 6391968; e-mail info@querido.nl; internet www.querido.nl; f. 1915; subsidiary: Uitgeverij Nijgh & van Ditmar; participant in 'Singel 262' holdings group; general fiction, history, children's books, translations from Latin and Greek texts; Dir ARY T. LANGBROEK.

Reed Elsevier NV: Radarweg 29, POB 152, 1043 NX Amsterdam; tel. (20) 5159944; fax (20) 5159900; e-mail redactie.elsevier@elsevier.nl; internet www.elsevier.nl; f. 1979 by merger; subholdings include some 60 subsidiaries in the Netherlands and abroad specializing in reference works, handbooks, weekly magazines, newspapers, trade and technical pubis, (postgraduate) scientific books and journals, audiovisual materials, further education study courses, databases; CEO ERIK ENGSTROM.

Elsevier B.V. Excerpta Medica: Radarweg 29, 1043 NX Amsterdam; tel. (20) 4853975; fax (20) 4853188; e-mail excerptamedica@elsevier.com; internet www.excerptamedica.com; Man. Dir EDWARD ROOS.

Editions Rodopi BV: Tijnmuiden 7, 1046 AK Amsterdam; tel. (20) 6114821; fax (20) 4472979; e-mail info@rodopi.nl; internet www.rodopi.nl; f. 1966; Dir Y. L. SCHIPPERS.

SDU: Prinses Beatrixlaan 116, POB 20025, 2500 EA The Hague; tel. (70) 3789911; fax (70) 3854321; e-mail sdu@sdu.nl; internet www.sdu.nl; Chair. Dr L. JONGSMA.

Springer: Van Godewijckstraat 30, POB 989, 3311 GX Dordrecht; tel. (78) 6576050; fax (78) 6576467; internet www.springeronline.com; merged with Kluwer Academic Publrs in 2004; publrs of books

THE NETHERLANDS

and journals in the fields of science, technology and medicine, incl., *inter alia*, natural sciences, mathematics, engineering, computer science and psychology; CEO DERK HAANK.

Strengholt United Media: Hofstede Oud-Bussem, Flevolaan 41, POB 338, 1400 AH Bussem; tel. (35) 6958430; fax (35) 6958440; e-mail info@utigeverijstrengholt.nl; internet www.uitgeverijstrengholt.nl; f. 1928; health, biography, music, current affairs, psychology, parapsychology, sports, cookery; Dir T. M. JANSEN.

Uitgeverij De Tijdstroom BV: Janskerkhof 26, POB 775, 3500 AT Utrecht; tel. (30) 2364450; fax (30) 23699354; e-mail info@tijdstroom.nl; internet www.tijdstroom.nl; f. 1921; educational and professional publications on health and welfare, periodicals in these fields; Dir N. F. VAN 'T ZET.

Unieboek BV: Papiermolen 14–24, POB 97, 3990 DB Houten; tel. (30) 7998300; fax (30) 7998398; e-mail info@unieboek.nl; internet www.unieboek.nl; f. 1890; holding group incorporating 10 publishing houses; general and juvenile literature, fiction, popular science, history, art, social, economics, religion, textbooks, etc.; Dir W. VAN GILS.

VNU Business Publications BV: Lincolnweg 40, POB 37040, 1030 AA Amsterdam; tel. (20) 2042000; fax (20) 2042001; e-mail info@bp.vnu.com; internet www.vnubp.nl; trade and fashion, careers, IT, personal computer, management, training.

Wolters Kluwer NV: Zuidpoolsingel 2, POB 1030, 2400 BA, Alphen aan den Rijn; tel. (172) 641400; fax (172) 474889; e-mail info@wolterskluwer.com; internet www.wolterskluwer.com; operates in legal, tax, accounting, health, risk & compliance, regulatory and financial services; CEO and Chair., Exec. Bd NANCY MCKINSTRY; CFO BOUDEWIJN BEERKENS.

PUBLISHERS' ASSOCIATIONS

Koninklijke Vereniging van het Boekenvak (KVB) (Royal Ascn for the Book Trade): Herengracht 166, 1016 BP Amsterdam; tel. (20) 6240212; fax (20) 6208871; e-mail info@kvb.nl; internet www.kvb.nl; f. 1815; Chair. L. C. BRINKMAN; Dir ANNA BAKKER; 1,500 mems.

Nederlands Uitgeversverbond (NUV) (Dutch Publrs' Ascn): Hogehilweg 6, POB 12040, 1100 AA Amsterdam Zuidoost; tel. (20) 4309150; fax (20) 4309199; e-mail info@nuv.nl; internet www.nuv.nl; Chair. LOEK HERMANS; Dir J. BOMMER; 250 mems.

Broadcasting and Communications

TELECOMMUNICATIONS

Regulatory Authority

Onafhankelijke Post en Telecommunicatie Autoriteit (OPTA) (The Independent Postal and Telecommunications Authority): POB 90420, 2509 LK The Hague; Muzenstraat 41, 2511 WB The Hague; tel. (70) 3153500; fax (70) 3153501; e-mail info@opta.nl; internet www.opta.nl; f. 1997; supervises compliance with legislation, settles disputes, manages the telephone number database, protects consumers and fights against cyberbrime; Chair. CHRIS A. FONTEIJN.

Service Providers

Koninklijke KPN NV: POB 30000, 2500 The Hague; Maanplein 55, 2516CK The Hague; tel. (70) 3434343; fax (70) 3436568; e-mail webmaster@kpn.com; internet www.kpn.com; privatized 1989; fmrly Koninklijke PTT NV, present name adopted 1998; operates KPN Mobile; acquired Telfort BV in 2005, Enertel NV in 2006 and debitel Nederland BV in 2008; fixed-line operator and internet access provider; Chair. and CEO EELCO BLOK.

  Telfort BV: POB 23079, 1100 DN Amsterdam Zuid-Oost; tel. 0800-1771; internet www.telfort.com; f. 1996; mobile cellular telecommunications and internet access; Man. Dir ROBIN CLEMENTS.

Online: POB 10241, 1001 EE Amsterdam; Muiderstr. 1, 1011 PZ Amsterdam; tel. (20) 5355555; e-mail info@dutchtone.nl; internet www.online.nl; mobile cellular telecommunications and internet access; fmrly called Orange Nederland NV; name changed to present in 2008; owned by Deutsche Telekom; CEO DAVID HOLLIDAY.

T-Mobile: Waldorpstr. 60, 2521 CC The Hague; tel. (61) 4095000; internet www.t-mobile.nl; owned by Deutsche Telekom; mobile telephone operator.

UPC Nederland NV: POB 80900, 1005 DA Amsterdam; Kabelweg 51, 1014 BA Amsterdam; tel. (20) 7755000; fax (20) 7756724; e-mail mediarelations@upc.nl; internet www.upc.nl; subsidiary of UPC Broadband; broadband internet, telephone, digital television and radio service provider; Man. Dir DIEDERIK KARSTEN.

Directory

Vodafone: Ave Ceramique 300, 6221 KX Maastricht; tel. (43) 3555555; e-mail press.nl@vodafone.com; internet www.vodafone.nl; f. 1999; owned by Vodafone Group PLC (United Kingdom); CEO JENS SCHULTE-BOCKUM.

BROADCASTING

Under the Netherlands public broadcasting system the two co-ordinating bodies work with the seven licensed broadcasters to provide a complete range of programmes.

Co-ordinating Bodies

Nederlandse Programma Stichting (NPS) (Dutch National Broadcasting Service): POB 29000, 1202 MA Hilversum; Sumatralaan 49, 1217 GP Hilversum; tel. (35) 6779333; fax (35) 6774959; e-mail publiek@nps.nl; internet www.nps.nl; Chair. GERD LEERS; Dir JOOP DAALMEŸER.

Nederlandse Publieke Omroep (NPO) (Netherlands Public Broadcasting): POB 26444, 1202 JJ Hilversum; Sumatralaan 45, 1217 GP Hilversum; tel. (35) 6779222; fax (35) 6772649; e-mail npo.communicatie@omroep.nl; internet www.omroep.nl; f. 1969; co-ordination of Dutch national public broadcasting and news, sports and teletext programmes on 6 national public radio and 3 television channels; fmrly Nederlandse Omroep Stichting; Chair. HENK N. HAGOORT.

Broadcasting Associations

Algemene Omroepvereniging AVRO: POB 2, 1200 JA Hilversum; 's-Gravelandseweg 80, 1217 EW Hilversum; tel. (35) 6711911; fax (35) 6717439; e-mail info@avro.nl; internet www.avro.nl; f. 1923; independent; general broadcaster; 800,000 mems; Pres. PAUL SMITS.

Evangelische Omroep (EO): POB 21000, 1202 BA Hilversum; Oude Amersfoortseweg 79, 1213 AC Hilversum; tel. (35) 6474747; fax (35) 6474727; e-mail eo@eo.nl; internet www.eo.nl; f. 1967; Protestant; Chair., Supervisory Bd AD DE BOER; Man. Dir ARJAN LOCK.

Katholieke Radio Omroep (KRO): POB 23000, 1202 EA Hilversum; 's-Gravelandseweg 80, 1217 EW Hilversum; tel. (35) 6713911; fax (35) 6713666; e-mail service@kro.nl; internet www.kro.nl; f. 1925; Catholic; 615,000 mems; Pres. Dr KOEN BECKING; Man. Dir Dr YVONNE DE HAAN.

Nederlandse Christelijke Radio Vereniging (NCRV): POB 25000, 1202 HB Hilversum; 's-Gravelandseweg 80, 1217 EW Hilversum; tel. (35) 6719911; fax (35) 6719285; e-mail info@ncrv.nl; internet www.ncrv.nl; f. 1924; Protestant; more than 550,000 mems; Chair. LEO BORN; Dir COEN ABBENHUIS.

Omroepvereniging VARA: POB 175, 1200 AD Hilversum; Sumatralaan 49, 1217 GP Hilversum; tel. (35) 6711911; fax (35) 6711333; e-mail vara@vara.nl; internet vara.nl; f. 1925; social democratic and progressive; 515,000 mems; Pres. MARK MINKMAN.

Omroepvereniging VPRO: POB 11, 1200 JC Hilversum; Villa VPRO, Mediapark, Sumatralaan 49, 1217 GP Hilversum; tel. (35) 6712911; fax (35) 6712100; e-mail info@vpro.nl; internet www.vpro.nl; f. 1926; progressive; 380,000 mems; Pres. PETER VAN LIESHOUT; Dir of Radio GERARD WALHOF; Dirs of Television KAREN DE BOK, FRANK WIERING.

TROS: POB 28450, 1202 LL Hilversum; Lage Naarderweg 45–47, 1217 GN Hilversum; tel. (35) 6715715; fax (35) 6715236; e-mail publiekservice@tros.nl; internet www.tros.nl; f. 1964; independent; general broadcaster; 573,664 mems; Chair. K. VAN DOODEWAERD.

Radio

There are six privately owned national radio stations that are operated on a public service basis, as well as 13 regional stations and about 330 local stations.

Radio 1: internet www.radio1.nl; 24-hour news and sports programming.

Radio 2: Sumatralaan 45, POB 26444, 1202 JJ Hilversum; tel. (35) 6775052; fax (35) 6773311; e-mail info@radio2.nl; internet www.radio2.nl; broadcasts popular music.

3FM: POB 26444, 1202 JJ Hilversume-mail redactie@3fm.nl; internet www.3fm.nl; broadcasts contemporary music.

Radio 4: internet www.radio4.nl; broadcasts popular classical music.

Radio 5: Sumatralaan 45, POB 26444, 1202 JJ Hilversum; tel. (35) 6775052; e-mail info@radio5nostalgia.nl; internet www.radio5.nl; broadcasts popular music, current affairs and cultural programmes; aimed at people aged over 55 years.

Radio 6: e-mail radio6@omroep.nl; internet www.radio6.nl; broadcasts Americana, electronica, folk, jazz and 'world' music.

Television

Television programmes are transmitted on three public channels, each of which is allocated to a different combination of broadcasting

THE NETHERLANDS

associations and other organizations, and on the commercially funded channels operated by RTL Nederland.

RTL Nederland: Postbus 15016, 1200 TV Hilversum; Sumatralaan 47, 1217 GP Hilversum; tel. (35) 6718718; fax (35) 6236892; e-mail info@rtl.nl; internet www.rtl.nl; f. 1996 as Holland Media Groep; present name adopted 2004; operates 5 television channels: RTL 4, RTL 5, RTL 7, RTL 8 and RTL Lounge; subsidiary of RTL Group (Luxembourg); CEO Bert Habets.

SBS 6/NET5: Plantage Rietlandpark 333, POB 18179, 1001 ZB Amsterdam; tel. (20) 8007000; fax (20) 8007001; e-mail sbs6@publieksservice.sbs.nl; internet www.sbs6.nl; private broadcaster; Man. Pascal van Meerten.

United Pan-Europe Communications NV: POB 80900, 1005 DA Amsterdam; Kabelweg 51, 1014 BA Amsterdam; tel. (20) 7755000; fax (20) 7729988; e-mail service@upc.nl; internet www.upc.nl; cable broadcaster; Chair. Michael T. Fries.

Overseas Broadcasting

BVN TV: POB 222, 1200 JG Hilversum; Witte Kruislaan 55, 1217 AM Hilversum; tel. (35) 6724333; fax (35) 6724343; e-mail bvn@rnw.nl; internet www.bvn.tv; f. 1998; by Radio Nederland Wereldomroep, VRT and Nederlandse Publieke Omroep (NPO); daily international transmissions of news and cultural programmes from public service broadcasters in Flanders and the Netherlands; Channel Man. R. van Baaren.

Radio Nederland Wereldomroep (Radio Netherlands International): Witte Kruislaan 55, POB 222, 1200 JG Hilversum; tel. (35) 6724211; fax (35) 6724352; e-mail letters@rnw.nl; internet www.rnw.nl; f. 1947; public service broadcaster; daily transmissions in Arabic, Dutch, English, Indonesian, Papiamento, Portuguese, Sarnami Hindi and Spanish; programme and transcription services for foreign radio and TV stations; Radio Nederland Training Centre (for students from developing countries); Dir-Gen. Jan Hoek.

Finance

(cap. = capital; res = reserves; dep. = deposits; m. = million; br(s). = branch(es); amounts in euros)

BANKING

Central Bank

De Nederlandsche Bank NV: Westeinde 1, POB 98, 1000 AB Amsterdam; tel. (20) 5249111; fax (20) 5242500; e-mail info@dnb.nl; internet www.dnb.nl; f. 1815; nationalized 1948; merged with Pensioen- en Verzekeringskamer (Chamber of Insurance and Pensions) in 2004; cap. 500m., res 17,253m., dep. 26,290m. (Dec. 2007); Pres. A. H. E. M. (Nout) Wellink; Exec. Dirs Henk Brouwer, Prof. Lex H. Hoogduin, Joanne Kellermann.

Principal Commercial Banks

ABN AMRO Bank NV: Gustav Mahlerlaan 10, POB 283, 1082 PP Amsterdam; tel. (20) 6289898; fax (20) 6287740; internet www.abnamro.com; f. 1991 by merger of Algemene Bank Nederland NV and Amsterdam-Rotterdam Bank NV; acquisition by consortium comprising Royal Bank of Scotland PLC (United Kingdom), Grupo Santander (Spain) and Fortis agreed in Oct. 2007; Dutch Govt replaced Fortis as stakeholder in Oct. 2008; cap. 1,852m., res 4,129m., dep. 607,007m. (Dec. 2008); Chair., Management Bd Gerrit Zalm; 915 brs nationally.

Amsterdam Trade Bank NV: Herengracht 469, 1017 BS Amsterdam; tel. (20) 5209429; fax (20) 5209219; e-mail info@atbank.nl; internet www.atbank.nl; f. 1994 as Stolichny Bank International NV; present name adopted 1999; 100% owned by Alfa-Bank (Russia); cap. 117.3m., res 75.4m., dep. 2,550.3m. (Dec. 2008); Chair., Supervisory Bd P. Smida; Man. Dirs Alexei V. Drovossekov, J. P. J. Konijn, Anton H. den Held.

Bank Nederlandse Gemeenten NV (BNG): Koninginnegracht 2, POB 30305, 2500 GH The Hague; tel. (70) 3750750; fax (70) 3454743; e-mail info@bng.nl; internet www.bng.nl; f. 1914 as NV Gemeentelijke Credietbank; present name adopted 1992; 50% Govt-owned, 50% by provincial and municipal authorities; cap. 139m., res 1,832m., dep. 89,517m. (Dec. 2008); Pres. P. O. Vermeulen.

Dexia Bank Nederland NV: Piet Heinkade 55, POB 808, 1000 AV Amsterdam; tel. (20) 3485000; fax (20) 5571414; e-mail klantenservie@dexiabank.nl; internet www.dexiabank.nl; f. 2001 by merger of Bank Labouchere NV (f. 1990) and Kempen and Co NV; owned by Dexia banking group; Chair. B. F. M. Knüppe; 1 br.

Fortis Bank (Nederland) NV: Prins Bernhardplein 200, 1097 JB Amsterdam; tel. (10) 2701010; fax (10) 4148391; e-mail info@fortis.com; internet www.fortis.nl; f. 1999 by merger of VSB Bank and Generale Bank Nederland; nationalized in Oct. 2008; cap. 566m., res 3,333m., dep. 3,314m. (Dec. 2004); Chair. Jan van Rutte.

Friesland Bank NV: Beursplein 1, POB 1, 8900 AA Leeuwarden; tel. (58) 2994499; fax (58) 2994591; e-mail service@frieslandbank.nl; internet www.frieslandbank.nl; f. 1913 as Coöperatieve Zuivel-Bank; present name adopted 1995; dep. 9,323.7m., total assets 10,934.1m. (Dec. 2008); Chair. Dr Robbert Klaasman; Dir A. Vlaskamp; 33 brs.

GE Artesia Bank: Herengracht 539–543, POB 274, 1000 AG Amsterdam; tel. (20) 5204911; fax (20) 6247502; e-mail info@artesia.nl; internet www.geartesiabank.nl; f. 1863 as the Nederlandsche Credit & Depositobank; became Banque Paribas Nederland in 1984; acquired by GE Commercial Finance (USA) in 2006; cap. 73.7m., res 178.5m., dep. 2,933.6m. (Dec. 2008); CEO Steven Prins; Mems, Exec. Bd Johan Benning, John-Harold Every; 9 brs.

ING Bank NV: Amstelveenseweg 500, 1081 KL Amsterdam; tel. (20) 5415411; fax (20) 5415444; e-mail ing@ing.com; internet www.ing.com; f. 1990 by merger of Nationale-Nederlanden and NMB Postbank Groep; Govt acquired an 8.5% stake in Oct. 2008; cap. 525m., res 22,364m., dep. 957,890m. (Dec. 2008); Chair., Supervisory Bd Peter A. F. W. Elverding; more than 400 brs.

KAS BANK NV: Spuistraat 172, POB 24001, 1000 DB Amsterdam; tel. (20) 5575911; fax (20) 5576100; e-mail info@kasbank.com; internet www.kasbank.com; f. 1806 by merger; present name adopted 2002; cap. 15.7m., res 191.7m., dep. 7,136.8m. (Dec. 2008); Chair., Management Bd Albert A. Röell.

F. van Lanschot Bankiers NV: Hooge Steenweg 29, POB 289, 5200 HC 's-Hertogenbosch; tel. (73) 5483548; fax (73) 5483648; e-mail vanlanschot@vanlanschot.nl; internet www.vanlanschot.nl; f. 1737; merger with CenE Bankiers NV completed 2005; cap. 13.3m., res 1,193.7m., dep. 17,821.2m. (Dec. 2008); Chair. F. G. H. Deckers; 32 brs.

Mizuho Corporate Bank Nederland NV: Apollolaan 171, POB 7075, 1007 JB Amsterdam; tel. (20) 5734343; fax (20) 5734372; f. 2000 by merger of Dai Ichi Kangyo Bank Europe NV and Fuji Bank Nederland NV; cap. 141.8m., res 48.3m., dep. 2,057.2m. (Dec. 2008); Man. Dir Tetsuo Hiramatsu.

NIBC Bank NV: Carnegieplein 4, POB 380, 2501 BH The Hague; tel. (70) 3425625; fax (70) 3459129; e-mail info@nibc.com; internet www.nibc.com; f. 1945 as Herstelbank; present name adopted 2005; cap. 80m., res 1,554m., dep. 26,751m. (Dec. 2009); Chair., Management Bd and CEO Jeroen Drost; 1 br.

Postbank NV: Haarlemmerweg 506, POB 21009, 1000 EX Amsterdam; tel. (20) 5846133; fax (20) 5846132; internet www.postbank.nl; f. 1985; retail bank operating through post offices; 100% owned by ING Group NV; Chair. Jan Hommen.

Rabobank Nederland (Coöperatieve Centrale Raiffeisen-Boerenleenbank BA): Croeselaan 18, POB 17100, 3500 HG Utrecht; tel. (30) 2160000; fax (30) 2162672; e-mail rabocomm@rn.rabobank.nl; internet www.rabobank.nl; f. 1972 by merger of Coöperatieve Centrale Raiffeisenbank of Utrecht and Coöperatieve Centrale Boerenleenbank of Eindhoven; dep. 574,555m., total assets 612,120m. (Dec. 2008); Chair. Piet Moerland; 1,727 brs.

SNS Bank NV: Croeselaan 1, 3503 BJ Utrecht; tel. (30) 2915100; fax (30) 2915300; e-mail info@snsbank.nl; internet www.sns.nl; f. 1971 as Bank der Bondsspaarbanken NV; present name adopted 2002; cap. 426m., res 5,182m., dep. 77,297m. (Dec. 2008); Group Chair. and CEO S. van Keulen; 256 brs.

Staalbankiers NV: Lange Houtstraat 8, POB 327, 2501 CH The Hague; tel. (70) 3101510; fax (70) 3396515; e-mail info@staalbankiers.nl; internet www.staalbankiers.nl; f. 1916 as Bankierskantoor Staal & Co NV; present name adopted 2005; mem. of Achmea Groep; dep. 2,692.2m., total assets 3,049.3m. (Dec. 2008); Chair. and CEO P. A. de Ruijter; Man. Dirs P. J. Huurman, D. Beck.

Bankers' Association

Nederlandse Vereniging van Banken (NVB) (Netherlands Bankers' Asscn): Singel 236, POB 3543, 1001 AH Amsterdam; tel. (20) 5502888; fax (20) 6239748; e-mail info@nvb.nl; internet www.nvb.nl; f. 1989; Chair. B. Staal; Dir Hein G. M. Blocks; 93 mems.

STOCK EXCHANGE

A supervisory authority, the Netherlands Securities Board, commenced activities in 1989.

Euronext Amsterdam: Beursplein 5, POB 19163, 1000 GD Amsterdam; tel. (20) 5504444; fax (20) 5504899; e-mail info@euronext.nl; internet www.euronext.com; subsidiary of NYSE Euronext; Euronext NV was formed by merger of Amsterdam, Paris and Brussels stock exchanges and joined in 2002 by the London futures exchange, LIFFE and the Lisbon stock exchange; merged with New York Stock Exchange in 2007 to form NYSE Euronext; unitary stock and options exchange; Chair. Joost van der Does de Willebois.

There are also financial futures, grain, citrus fruits and insurance bourses in the Netherlands; a 'spot' market for petroleum operates from Rotterdam.

THE NETHERLANDS

INSURANCE
Principal Companies

AEGON Nederland: AEGONplein 50, POB 202, 2501 CE The Hague; tel. (70) 3443210; fax (70) 3475238; internet www.aegon.nl; f. 1983 by merger; life, accident, health, general and linked activities; Chair. MARCO B. A. KEIM.

Delta Lloyd Verzekeringen NV: Spaklerweg 4, POB 1000, 1000 BA Amsterdam; tel. (20) 5949111; fax (20) 937968; internet www.deltalloyd.nl; f. 1807; Chair. NIEK HOEK.

De Eerste Nederlandsche/Enfas: POB 325, 1170 AH Badhoevedorp; tel. (562) 445090; fax (562) 445150; e-mail info@eerste.nl; internet www.eerste.nl/over_enfas.htm; Chair. G. VAN PLATERINGEN.

Fiducia Assurantiën: Park Hoornwijck 6B, 2289 CZ Rijswijk; tel. (70) 4150506; fax (70) 4150507; e-mail info@fiducia.nl; internet www.fiducia.nl; f. 1990; home, vehicle, non-life; Dir BJORN DE HAAN.

Fortis ASR Verzekeringsgroep NV: Archimedeslaan 10, POB 2072, 3500 HB Utrecht; tel. (30) 2579111; f. 2000 by merger of ASR Verzekeringsgroep NV (f. 1720) and AMEV Nederland NV (f. 1883); owned by the Fortis group; Group CEO HERMAN VERWILST.

Generali Verzekeringsgroep: Diemerhof 42, 1112 XN Diemen; tel. (20) 6604444; fax (20) 3983000; e-mail info@generali.nl; internet www.generali.nl; f. 1870; life and non-life; Gen. Dir FREEK WANSINK.

ING Groep NV: Amstelveenseweg 500, 1081 KL Amsterdam; tel. (20) 5415411; fax (20) 5415497; e-mail nanne.bos@ing.com; internet www.ing.com; f. 1963; Chair., Management Bd JAN H. M. HOMMEN.

Nationale-Nederlanden NV: Kantoor Delftse Poort, Weena 505, 3013 AL Rotterdam; tel. (10) 5130303; internet www.nn.nl; f. 1863; Chair. LARD FRIESE.

RVS: Loevestein 33, POB 225, 6710 DA Ede; tel. (318) 662054; e-mail rvs@rvs.nl; internet www.rvs.nl; f. 1838; subsidiary of ING Groep NV; mem. of Internationale-Nederlanden group; life and non-life; Chair. MARC VAN DER PLOEG.

Insurance Association

Verbond van Verzekeraars (Asscn of Insurers): Bordewijklaan 2, POB 93450, 2509 AL The Hague; tel. (70) 3338500; fax (70) 3338510; e-mail info@verzekeraars.nl; internet www.verzekeraars.nl; f. 1978; Chair. RONALD R. LATENSTEIN VAN VOORST; Gen. Man. R. WEURDING.

Trade and Industry

GOVERNMENT AGENCY

Netherlands Foreign Investment Agency: Juliana van Stolberglaan 148A, 2595 CL The Hague; tel. (70) 6028818; fax (70) 3796322; e-mail info@nfia.nl; internet www.nfia.nl; f. 1978; govt agency; facilitates foreign direct investment.

CHAMBERS OF COMMERCE

There are 12 autonomous Chambers of Commerce and Industry in the Netherlands. The most important are:

Kamer van Koophandel Amsterdam (Chamber of Commerce and Industry for Amsterdam): De Ruyterkade 5, 1013 AA Amsterdam; POB 2852, 1000 CW Amsterdam; tel. (20) 5314000; fax (20) 5314799; e-mail info@amsterdam.kvk.nl; internet www.amsterdam.kvk.nl; f. 1811; Dir-Gen. H. E. VAN BAARSBANK.

Kamer van Koophandel Rotterdam (Chamber of Commerce for Rotterdam): Blaak 40, POB 450, 3000 AL Rotterdam; tel. (10) 4027777; fax (10) 4145754; e-mail info@rotterdam.kvk.nl; internet www.rotterdam.kvk.nl; f. 1803; Pres. G. J. H. VAN DER VEGT.

EMPLOYERS' ORGANIZATIONS

LTO-Nederland (Netherlands Agricultural Organization): Bezuidenhoutseweg 225, POB 29773, 2502 LT The Hague; tel. (70) 3382700; fax (70) 3382710; e-mail info@lto.nl; internet www.lto.nl; f. 1995; Chair. A. J. MAAT; 50,000 mems.

Nederlands Centrum voor Handelsbevordering (NCH) (Netherlands Council for Trade Promotion): Juliana van Stolberglaan 148, POB 10, 2501 CA The Hague; tel. (70) 3441544; fax (70) 3853531; e-mail info@nchnl.nl; internet www.handelsbevordering.nl; Man. Dir JOCHUM HAAKMA; 800 mem. cos.

Nederlandsche Maatschappij voor Nijverheid en Handel (NMNH) (Netherlands Society for Industry and Trade): Jan van Nassaustraat 75, 2596 BP The Hague; tel. (70) 3141940; fax (70) 3247515; e-mail info@nmnh.nl; internet www.nmnh.nl; f. 1777; Pres. DICK BERLIJN; Dir-Gen. GEERT VAN DER TANG; more than 5,500 mems.

De Nederlandse Tuinbouwraad (NTR) (Netherlands Horticultural Council): Legmeerdijk 313, 1431 GB Aalsmeer; tel. (297) 395005; fax (297) 395012; e-mail informatie@tuinbouwraad.nl;

Directory

internet www.tuinbouwraad.nl; f. 1908; Chair. Dr N. C. A. (NICO) KOOMEN; Sec. GEORGE FRANKE.

NERG (Nederlands Elektronica- en Radiogenootschap): POB 39, 2260 AA Leidschendam; tel. (70) 3325112; fax (70) 3326477; internet www.nerg.nl; f. 1921; Chair. Dr A. VAN OTTERLO; Sec. D. VAN EGMOND; c. 500 mems.

Vereniging VNO-NCW (Confederation of Netherlands Industry and Employers): Bezuidenhoutseweg 12, POB 93002, 2509 AA The Hague; tel. (70) 3490349; fax (70) 3490300; e-mail informatie@vno-ncw.nl; internet www.vno-ncw.nl; f. 1997 as merger of Verbond van Nederlandse Ondernemingen (VNO) and Nederlands Christelijk Werkgeversverbond (NCW); represents almost all sectors of the Dutch economy; Pres. B. E. M. (BERNARD) WIENTJES; mems: 160 asscns representing more than 115,000 enterprises.

UTILITIES
Electricity

ENECO: POB 96, 2900 AB Capelle a/d IJssel; tel. (10) 4576979; fax (10) 4577784; e-mail corporatecommunicatie@eneco.nl; internet www.eneco.nl; Chair. J. F. (JEROEN) DE HAAS; 7,000 employees.

E.ON Benelux: Capelseweg 400, POB 8642, 3009 AP Rotterdam; tel. (10) 2895711; fax (10) 2895088; e-mail info@eon-benelux.com; internet www.eon-benelux.com; f. 2000; replaced Electriciteitsbedrijf Zuid Holland (f. 1941); supplies energy to large-volume customers and distributors; CEO JOOST VAN DIJK.

Essent: Nieuwe Stationsstraat 20, 6811 KS Arnhem; internet www.essent.nl; f. 1999 by merger of Edon Group and Pnem Mega Group; electricity generation and supply, also supplier of gas; CEO PETER TERIUM.

Nuon NV: Spaklerweg 20, POB 41920, 1009 DC Amsterdam; tel. (20) 5972729; fax (20) 5971151; e-mail nuon@nuon.com; internet www.nuon.com; f. 1999; energy and water; Chair., Supervisory Bd ØYSTEIN LØSETH; CEO HUIB MORELISSE (designate).

TenneT BV: Utrechtseweg 310, POB 718, 6800 AS Arnhem; tel. (26) 3731111; fax (26) 3731112; e-mail servicecentre@tennet.org; internet www.tennet.org; f. 1999; independent; Dutch Transmission System operator; manages 220/380-kW national grid and supplies electricity to direct suppliers; Pres. and CEO J. M. (MEL) KROON.

Gas

Full liberalization of the gas market in the Netherlands took effect from the beginning of July 2004. Although retaining ownership of the main transport network, NV Nederlandse Gasunie passed the legal tasks of the national transmission system operator to a new, state-owned organization, Gas Transport Services BV, founded on 2 July 2004.

ENECO: see above**Essent:** see above**Gas Transport Services BV:** Concourslaan 17, POB 181, 9700 AD Groningen; tel. (50) 5212250; fax (50) 3603036; e-mail info@gastransport.nl; internet www.gastransportservices.nl; f. 2004; independent; transmission system operator; CEO GEERT H. GRAAF.

NV Nederlandse Gasunie: Concourslaan 17, POB 19, 9700 MA Groningen; tel. (50) 5219111; fax (50) 5211999; e-mail communicatie@gasunie.nl; internet www.gasunie.nl; f. 2005; Chair. and CEO MARCEL P. KRAMER.

RWE Obragas NV: POB 300, 5700 AH Helmond; tel. (49) 2594888; fax (49) 2594990; internet www.rwe.nl.

Water

Nuon: see above**Vewin:** Sir Winston Churchilllaan 273, POB 1019, 2280 CA Rijswijk; tel. (70) 4144750; fax (70) 4144420; e-mail info@vewin.nl; internet www.vewin.nl; Chair J. A. M. HENDRIKX.

TRADE UNIONS

Central federations and affiliated unions are mainly organized on a religious, political or economic basis. The most important unions are those of the transport, metal, building and textile industries, the civil service and agriculture.

Central Federations

Christelijk Nationaal Vakverbond in Nederland (CNV) (Christian National Federation of Trade Unions): Tiberdreef 4, POB 2475, 3500 GL Utrecht; tel. (30) 7511100; fax (30) 7511109; e-mail cnvinfo@cnv.nl; internet www.cnv.nl; f. 1909; affiliated to ITUC and European Trade Union Confederation; Pres. BERT VAN BOGGELEN; 350,000 mems.

Eleven affiliated unions, of which the principal unions are:

CNV Bedrijvenbond (Industry, Food and Transport): Tiberdreef 4, POB 2525, 3500 GM Utrecht; tel. (30) 7511007; e-mail info@cnv.net; internet www.cnvbedrijvenbond.nl; Chair. JAAP JONGEJAN; 85,000 mems.

CNV Dienstenbond (Service Industries, Media and Printing): Polarisave 175, POB 3135, 2130 KC Hoofddorp; tel. (23) 5651052; fax (23) 5650150; e-mail cnvdienstenbond@cnvdibo.nl; internet www.cnvdienstenbond.nl; f. 1894; Pres. D. SWAGERMAN; Sec. R. J. ROTSHUIZEN; 36,500 mems.

CNV Hout en Bouw (Wood and Building): Oude Haven 1, 3984 KT Odijk; tel. (30) 6597711; fax (30) 6571101; e-mail info@cnvhb.nl; internet www.cnvhb.nl; f. 1900; Chair. A. A. VAN WIJNGAARDEN; Gen. Sec. J. T. SLOK; 48,000 mems.

CNV Onderwijs (Education): Tiberdreef 4, POB 2510, 3500 GM Utrecht; tel. (30) 7511003; fax (30) 7511709; e-mail info@cnvo.nl; internet www.cnvo.nl; f. 2000; Pres. (vacant).

CNV Publieke Zaak (Public Sector Union): Carnegielaan 1, POB 84500, 2508 AM The Hague; tel. (70) 4160600; fax (70) 4160690; e-mail denhaag@cnvpubliekezaak.nl; internet www.cnvpubliekezaak.nl; Pres. ERIC DE MACKER; 79,000 mems.

Federatie Nederlandse Vakbeweging (FNV) (Netherlands Trade Union Confederation): Naritaweg 10, POB 8456, 1005 AL Amsterdam; tel. (20) 5816300; fax (20) 5816319; e-mail persvoorlichting@vc.fnv.nl; internet www.fnv.nl; f. 1975 as confederation of the Netherlands Federation of Trade Unions (f. 1906) and the Netherlands Catholic Trade Union Federation (f. 1909); Pres. AGNES JONGERIUS; Vice-Pres. and Gen. Sec. PETER GORTZAK; 1,234,361 mems.

Seventeen affiliated unions, of which the principal are:

ABVAKABO FNV (Government Personnel, Civil Servants, Private Health Workers, Social Workers, Post and Telecom Workers, Public Utility Workers): Boerhaavelaan 1, POB 3010, 2700 KT Zoetermeer; tel. (79) 3536161; fax (79) 3521226; e-mail post@abvakabo.nl; internet www.abvakabofnv.nl; f. 1982; Pres. EDITH SNOEY; Gen. Sec. XANDER DEN UYL; 365,000 mems.

Algemene Onderwijsbond (AOb) (Education): Jaarbeursplein 22, POB 2875, 3500 GW Utrecht; tel. (30) 2989898; fax (30) 2989862; e-mail info@aob.nl; internet www.aob.nl; f. 1997 as merger between Algemene Bond van Onderwijspersoneel and NGL—Dordrecht; Pres. WALTER DRESSCHER; Gen. Sec. MARTIN KNOOP; 79,000 mems.

FNV Bondgenoten (Transport, Metal and Steel, Information Technology, Electrotechnical, Textiles, Financial Services, Retail, Wholesale, Foods, Agriculture): Varrolaan 100, POB 9208, 3506 GE Utrecht; tel. (30) 2738222; fax (30) 2738225; e-mail info@bg.fnv.nl; internet www.fnvbondgenoten.nl; f. 1998 by merger; Pres. HENK VAN DER KOLK; Sec. ELLEN DEKKERS; 460,000 mems.

FNV Bouw (Building): Houttuinlaan 3, POB 520, 3440 AM Woerden; tel. (88) 5757000; fax (88) 5757003; e-mail info@fnvbouw.nl; internet www.fnvbouw.nl; f. 1917; Pres. DICK VAN HAASTER; 150,000 mems.

FNV KIEM (Printing and Allied Trades): J. Tooropstraat, POB 9354, 1006 AJ Amsterdam; tel. (20) 3553636; fax (20) 3553737; e-mail algemeen@fnv-kiem.nl; internet www.fnv-kiem.nl; Chair. HERMAN LEISINK; Gen. Sec. BEA VAN DEN BOSCH; 40,000 mems.

Nederlandse Politiebond (NPB) (Police): Steinhagenseweg 2D, POB 68, 3440 AB Woerden; tel. (34) 8707444; fax (34) 8707411; e-mail info@politiebond.nl; internet www.politiebond.nl; f. 1946; Pres. HANS VAN DUIJN; Gen. Sec. FRANS VAN DER HEIDEN; 22,500 mems.

Vakcentrale voor Middengroepen en Hoger Personeel (MHP) (Federation for Professional and Managerial Staff): Multatulilaan 12, POB 575, 4100 AN Culemborg; tel. (345) 851900; fax (345) 851915; e-mail info@vc-mhp.nl; internet www.vakcentralemhp.nl; f. 1974; mem. of the European Trade Union Confederation; Pres. RICHARD STEENBORG; 160,000 mems.

Four affiliated unions, of which the following is the largest:

Unie van Onafhankelijke Vakorganisaties (UoV) (United Independent Trade Unions): Multatulilaan 12, POB 400, 4100 AK Culemborg; tel. (345) 851851; fax (345) 851500; e-mail info@unie.nl; internet www.uov.nl; 16 affiliated independent trade unions, including De Unie; 80,000 mems.

Consultative Organization

Stichting van de Arbeid (Labour Foundation): Bezuidenhoutseweg 60, 2509 LK The Hague; tel. (70) 3499499; fax (70) 3832535; internet www.stvda.nl; f. 1945; central organ of co-operation and consultation between employers and employees; 16 bd mems; Jt Pres B. E. M. WIENTJES, Dr A. M. JONGERIUS.

Land Reclamation and Development

Without intensive land-protection schemes, nearly the whole of the north and west of the Netherlands (about one-half of the total area of the country) would be inundated by sea water twice a day. A large part of the country (including a section of the former Zuiderzee, now the IJsselmeer) has already been drained.

The Delta Plan, which was adopted in 1958 and provided for the construction of eight dams, a major canal, several locks and a system of dykes, aimed to shorten the southern coastline by 700 km and to protect the estuaries of Zeeland and Southern Holland. The final cost of the delta works project, which had originally been projected at 2,500m. guilders, totalled around 14,000m. guilders, as the result of a complex adaptation to ensure the preservation of the delta's ecological balance.

Transport

RAILWAYS

About 70% of the Dutch railway network is electrified; the remaining track carries diesel electric and diesel stock. There were approximately 6,500 km of railways in 2007, providing mainly passenger services. The infrastructure of the Dutch railway network remains wholly under public ownership. Until early 2002 the main railway operator, Nederlandse Spoorwegen (NS), was partially privatized, but, following a sharp deterioration in the quality of service, it was taken back under government control. NS retains a majority of the passenger and freight rolling stock, and station premises, while there is a small number of additional, privately owned network service providers.

NS (Nederlandse Spoorwegen NV (Dutch Rail)): Laan van Puntenberg 100, POB 2025, 3500 HA Utrecht; tel. (30) 2359111; fax (30) 2332458; internet www.ns.nl; f. 1937; partially privatized until early 2002, when the Govt reasserted management control; operates passenger services on most railway lines in the Netherlands; Pres. and Man. Dir BERT MEERSTADT.

Arriva Nederland: Trambaan 3, POB 626, 8440 AP Heerenveen; tel. (51) 3655855; fax (51) 3655808; internet www.arriva.nl; f. 1999; operates 50 trains and 920 buses, including cross-border rail services into Germany; Man. Dir ANNE HETTINGA.

ProRail: POB 2038, 3500 GA Utrecht; tel. (30) 2357104; fax (30) 2359056; internet www.prorail.nl; f. 2003; manages and maintains railway infrastructure, and controls passenger and freight traffic; independent; Chair. CLAUDIA ZUIDERWIJK-JACOBS.

Railion Nederland: Moreelspark 1, 3511 Utrecht; tel. (3) 2354127; fax (30) 2359310; e-mail info@railion.nl; internet www.railion.nl; frmly Railon Benelux NV; international goods transport by rail; Man. Dir DETLEF HEYDT.

ROADS

In 2008 there were 2,637 km of motorway, 2,413 km of main roads, 7,848 km of secondary roads and 123,237 km of other roads in the Netherlands.

INLAND WATERWAYS

An extensive network of rivers and canals navigable for ships of 50 metric tons and over, totalling 5,046 km, has led to the outstanding development of Dutch inland shipping. About one-third of goods transported inside the Netherlands are carried on the canals and waterways. Dutch inland shipping has access to Germany and France along the Rhine and its branch rivers, and to France and Belgium along the Meuse and Scheldt (including the Rhine-Scheldt link). Ocean traffic reaches Rotterdam via the New Waterway, and the 21-km long North Sea Canal connects Amsterdam to the North Sea.

SHIPPING

The Netherlands is one of the world's leading shipping countries. At the end of 2009 the merchant fleet comprised 1,332 vessels, with a combined displacement of 7.0m. grt. The Port of Rotterdam complex, incorporating Europoort (for large oil tankers and bulk carriers), is the main European Union port and the busiest in the world.

Principal Companies

Amasus Chartering BV: Zijlvest 26, Farmsum, POB 250, 9930 Delfzijl; tel. (596) 610744; fax (596) 616551; e-mail administration@amasus.nl; internet www.amasus.nl; shipowners, managers and operators.

Hudig Freight Services: Debussystraat 2, POB 1030, 3160 AE Rhoon; tel. (10) 5066550; fax (10) 5012827; e-mail info@hudig.nl; internet www.hudig.com; f. 1795; international freight services; Man. Dir A. D. FONTEIN.

Koninklijke Vopak NV: Westerlaan 10, POB 863, 3000 AW Rotterdam; tel. (10) 4002911; fax (10) 4139829; internet www.vopak.com; f. 1999; Chair. JOHN PAUL BROEDERS.

Koninklijke Wagenborg BV: Marktstraat 10, POB 14, 9930 AA Delfzyl; tel. (596) 636911; fax (596) 636250; e-mail info@wagenborg

.com; internet www.wagenborg.com; shipowners, managers and operators; Man. Dirs Dr E. VUURSTEEN, Dr G. R. WAGENBORG.

Seatrade Groningen BV: Laan Corpus den Hoorn 200, POB 858, 9700 AW Groningen; tel. (50) 5215300; fax (50) 5215399; e-mail info@seatrade.nl; internet www.seatrade.nl; shipowners, managers and operators; Man. Dir Capt. MARK JANSEN.

Spliethoff's Bevrachtingskantoor BV: Radarweg 36, POB 409, 1000 AK Amsterdam; tel. (20) 4488400; fax (20) 4488500; e-mail gogracht@spliethoff.com; internet www.spliethoff.nl; shipowners, managers and operators; Man. ROLF G. W. ERIKSSON.

Stena Line: Stationsweg 10, POB 2, 3150 AA Hoek van Holland; tel. (17) 4389333; fax (17) 4389309; e-mail info.nl@stenaline.nl; internet www.stenaline.nl; operates daily (day and night) ferry services for accompanied private cars, commercial freight vehicles and trailers between Hoek van Holland and Harwich (UK); Man. Dir GUNNAR BLOMDAHL.

Van Uden Maritime BV: POB 1123, 3000 BC, Rotterdam; tel. (10) 2973100; fax (10) 4851044; e-mail group@van-uden.nl; internet www.van-uden.nl; f. 1848; agencies in Rotterdam, Amsterdam; liner operators and representatives; international chartering; Man. D. P. F. DUTILH.

Vroon BV: Haven Westzijde 21, POB 28, 4510 AA Breskens; tel. (117) 384910; fax (117) 384218; e-mail info@vroon.nl; internet www.vroon.nl; shipowners, managers and operators; Man. Dir F. D. VROON.

Wijnne & Barends' Cargadoors- en Agentuurkantonen BV: Handelskade Oost 5, POB 123, 9930 AC Delfzijl; tel. (596) 637777; fax (596) 637790; e-mail info@wijnne-barends.nl; internet www.wijnne-barends.nl; f. 1855; became part of Spliethoff Group in 2003; shipowners, managers and operators; cargo services and agents; Man. Dir D. P. MAKKINJE.

Shipping Associations

Federatie van Werknemers in de Zeevaart (Dutch Seafarers' Federation): Heemraadssingel 323, POB 25131, 3001 HC Rotterdam; tel. (10) 4771188; fax (10) 4773846; e-mail fwz.nl@wxs.nl; internet www.fnv.nl/zeevaart.

Koninklijke Vereniging van Nederlandse Reders (KVNR) (Royal Assen of Netherlands' Shipowners): Wijnhaven 65B, POB 2442, 3000 CK Rotterdam; tel. (10) 4146001; fax (10) 2330081; e-mail kvnr@kvnr.nl; internet www.kvnr.nl; f. 1905; Chair. T. NETELENBOS; Man. Dir G. X. HOLLAAR; 300 mems.

Vereniging Nederlandse Scheepsbouw Industrie (VNSI) (Netherlands Shipbuilding Industry Asscn): Boerhaavelaan 40, POB 138, 2700 AC Zoetermeer; tel. (79) 3531165; fax (79) 3531155; e-mail info@vnsi.nl; internet www.vnsi.nl; promotes Dutch shipbuilding on a national basis; Chair M. J. VAN DER WAL; 95 mems.

CIVIL AVIATION

The main Dutch airport is at Schiphol, near Amsterdam. There are also international airports at Zestienhoven for Rotterdam, Beek for Maastricht, Eelde for Groningen, and at Eindhoven.

KLM (Koninklijke Luchtvaart Maatschappij) NV (Royal Dutch Airlines): Amsterdamseweg 55, 1182 GP Amstelveen; tel. (20) 6499123; fax (20) 6488069; internet www.klm.com; f. 1919; merged with Air France in 2004 to form holding co Air France KLM; regular international air services; subsidiaries: KLM cityhopper, transavia.com; Pres. and CEO PETER F. HARTMAN; Man. Dir JAN ERNST DE GROOT.

Martinair Holland NV: Havenmeesterweg 201, POB 7507, 1118 ZG Schiphol Airport; tel. (20) 6011767; fax (20) 6011303; internet www.martinair.nl; f. 1958; world-wide passenger and cargo services; Pres. and CEO ARIE VERBERK.

transavia.com: Westelijke Randweg 3, POB 7777, 1118 ZM Schiphol Airport; tel. (20) 6046555; fax (20) 6015093; internet transavia.com; f. 1965 as Transavia Limburg N.V.; scheduled and charter services to leisure destinations; subsidiary of KLM; Chair. HANS BAKKER; CEO BRAM GRÄBER.

Tourism

The principal tourist attractions in the Netherlands are the cosmopolitan city of Amsterdam (which receives nearly one-half of all tourist visits), the historic towns, the canals, the cultivated fields of spring flowers, the outlying islands, the art galleries and modern architecture. Some 9.9m. foreign tourists stayed in hotels and boarding houses in the Netherlands in 2009. Receipts from tourism totalled US $20,256m. in 2008.

Royal Dutch Touring Club ANWB: POB 93200, 2596 EC The Hague; tel. (70) 3147147; fax (70) 3146969; e-mail info@anwb.nl; internet www.anwb.nl; f. 1883; CEO GUIDO H. N. L. VAN WOERKOM; 55 brs in Europe; 3.9m. mems.

Toerisme Recreatie Nederlands (Netherlands Board of Tourism): Vlietweg 15, POB 458, 2260 MG Leidschendam; tel. (70) 3705705; fax (70) 3201654; e-mail info@holland.com; internet www.holland.com; f. 1968; Man. Dir HANS VAN DRIEM.

Defence

The Netherlands is a member of the North Atlantic Treaty Organization (NATO). Conscription to the armed forces was ended in August 1996, and a gradual reduction in the number of military personnel is ongoing. The total strength of the armed forces, as assessed at November 2010, was 37,368: army 20,836; navy 8,502; air force 8,030. In addition, the Royal Military Constabulary numbered 5,911. Total reserves stood at 3,189 (army 2,686; air force 821; navy 82; military police 84). In August 1995 a joint Dutch-German army corps, numbering 28,000 troops, was inaugurated, and in January 1996 the operational units of the Royal Netherlands Navy merged with the Belgian navy under the command of the Admiral of the Benelux. In November 2004 the European Union (EU, see p. 270) agreed to create a number of 'battlegroups' (each comprising about 1,500 men), which could be deployed at short notice (within 10 days) to carry out peace-keeping activities at crisis points around the world. The battlegroups, two of which were to be ready for deployment at any one time, following a rotational schedule, reached full operational capacity from 1 January 2007. The Netherlands was committed to contributing troops to two of the battlegroups; one with the participation of Germany and Finland, and one with the United Kingdom.

General Government Defence Expenditure: €7,919m. in 2008, accounting for 2.9% of total expenditure.

Chief of Defence Staff: Gen. PETER J. M. VAN UHM.

Secretary-General of Defence Staff: ANTONIUS HERMANUS CHRISTOFFEL (TON) ANNINK.

Education

There are two types of school in the Netherlands: public schools, which are maintained by municipalities, and attended by about 35% of all school children; and private schools, which are, for the most part, denominational and are attended by almost 70% of the school-going population. Both types of school are fully subsidized by the state. Schools are administered by school boards, responsible to the local authorities or to the private organizations that operate them, thus providing teachers with considerable freedom. The Ministry of Education, Culture and Science, advised by an education council, is responsible for educational legislation and its enforcement.

Full-time education is compulsory in the Netherlands from five to 16 years of age, and part-time education is compulsory for a further two years. Pre-primary education, also known as early childhood education, is offered to educationally disadvantaged children between the ages of two and five years. Almost 99% of children of four years of age attend *Basisschool*, although it is not compulsory until the age of five years. Primary education lasts for eight years and is followed by various types of secondary education. Secondary education lasts to the age of 18 years, and is provided free of charge. In 2007/08 total enrolment in primary education included 99% of children in the relevant age-group, while total enrolment in secondary education included 88% of children in the relevant age-group. Pre-university schools provide various six-year courses that prepare pupils for university education. General secondary education comprises senior and junior secondary schools, providing five- and four-year courses that prepare pupils for higher vocational institutes and senior secondary vocational education, respectively. In all types there is latitude in the choice of subjects taken. Higher education comprises higher professional education *hoger beroepsonderwijs* (HBO) and university education *wetenschappelijk onderwijs* (WO). In 2008/09 some 220,300 students were enrolled at the Netherlands' 13 universities, while some 383,700 students were enrolled at the 51 institutes of higher vocational education. In addition, students can register with the Open Universiteit Nederland (Open University).

General government expenditure on education was €31,258m. in 2008, which represented 11.4% of the total budgetary expenditure.

NETHERLANDS DEPENDENCIES

Ministry of the Interior and Kingdom Relations: Schedeldoekshaven 200, POB 20011, 2500 EA The Hague; tel. (70) 4266426; fax (70) 3639153; internet www.rijksoverheid.nl/ministeries/bzk.
Minister of the Interior and Kingdom Relations: PIET HEIN DONNER.

Netherlands Special Municipalities

Following the dissolution of the Netherlands Antilles on 10 October 2010, Bonaire, Saba and Sint (St) Eustatius adopted the status of *bijzondere gemeente* (special municipalities) within the Kingdom of the Netherlands.

BONAIRE

Introduction

Bonaire lies about 80 km (50 miles) off the coast of Venezuela. The territory consists of Bonaire and, nestled in its western crescent, the uninhabited islet of Klein Bonaire. Together with Aruba and Curaçao, Bonaire forms the Benedenwindse Eilands or Leeward Islands. The climate is tropical, moderated by the sea, with an average annual temperature of 27.5°C (81°F) and little rainfall. The official languages are Dutch and Papiamento (a mixture of Dutch, Spanish, Portuguese, English, Arawak Indian and several West African dialects), which is the dominant language of the Leeward Islands. Almost all of the inhabitants profess Christianity, predominantly Roman Catholicism. The state flag (proportions 2 by 3) has a large blue triangle in the lower right corner and a smaller yellow triangle in the upper left corner. The triangles are separated by a white strip, inside of which is a black compass and a red six-pointed star (each point represents one of the original six villages of Bonaire). The capital is Kralendijk, on the western coast of the island.

The Leeward Islands, already settled by communities of Arawak Indians, were discovered by the Spanish in 1499 and were seized by the Dutch in the 1630s. After frequent changes in possession, the islands (including Aruba) were finally confirmed as Dutch territory in 1816. Together with the Windward Islands (comprising Sint (St) Eustatius, Saba and Sint (St) Maarten), Bonaire was administered as Curaçao and Dependencies between 1845 and 1948. Slavery was abolished in 1863. During the Second World War Queen Wilhelmina of the Netherlands promised independence, and in 1954 a Charter gave the federation of six islands full autonomy in domestic affairs, and declared it to be an integral part of the Kingdom of the Netherlands.

From 1954 until 2010 Bonaire was a constituent part of the Netherlands Antilles (a six-member federation until 1986 when Aruba gained separate status). Political allegiences were generally divided along island, rather than policy, lines. This led to a series of unstable coalitions governing the federation. By the early 1990s it had become clear that although the metropolitan Dutch Government was unwilling to allow the complete disintegration of the federation, it would consider a less centralized system, or the creation of two federations in the separate island groups.

A referendum on status was conducted on Bonaire in October 1994 (simultaneous plebiscites were also held on St Maarten, St Eustatius and Saba). Some 88% of voters favoured continued federation with the Netherlands.

On 8 October 2004 the Jesurun Commission, established by the Dutch and Antillean Governments and headed by Edsel Jesurun (a former Governor of the Netherlands Antilles), recommended the dissolution of the Netherlands Antilles. The Commission proposed that Bonaire, along with Saba and St Eustatius, should be directly administered by the Dutch Government. In September, in an official referendum, a majority of voters (59%) on Bonaire strongly favoured becoming part of the Netherlands. On 3 December 2005 a preliminary agreement with the Dutch Government that the extant federation be dissolved by 1 July 2007 was duly signed in Curaçao. Under the new structure, Bonaire was to become a *koninkrijseilande*, or 'kingdom island', with direct ties to the Netherlands, a status equivalent to that of a Dutch province. The future status of Bonaire was subsequently refined to that of a *bijzondere gemeete*, or 'special municipality', similar in most ways to other metropolitan Dutch municipalities, although with separate social security and currency arrangements.

An agreement confirming Bonaire's impending accession to 'special municipality' status was signed in The Hague, Netherlands, on 12 October 2006, and included provisions for citizens of the island to participate in Dutch national and local elections and in the election of candidates to the European Parliament. A further 'transition accord' was signed by the Netherlands Antilles central Government, the Island Council of Bonaire, and the Netherlands on 12 February 2007, envisaging the Bonaire's complete secession from the federation. Under the terms of this covenant, the Netherlands was to pledge over NA Fl. 1,000m. (in addition to existing financial assistance) to facilitate the process of disintegration, with each participating island receiving individual allocations. The metropolitan administration also agreed to write off almost three-quarters of the Antilles' debt.

Following further negotiations, a meeting was held in Curaçao on 15 December 2008 at which the Dutch Prime Minister, Jan Peter Balkenende, and the Antillean premier, Emily de Jongh-Elhage, signed an agreement confirming the new status of the island. At the end of September 2009, at a meeting of the Dutch State Secretary for the Interior and Kingdom Relations, Ank Bijleveld-Schouten, and representatives of the Netherlands Antilles, it was agreed that the target date for dissolution of the federation would be 10 October 2010.

The Dutch Government postponed the payment of Bonaire's debt in October 2009, after the island's recently formed Executive Council, led by the Partido Demokrátiko Boneriano (PDB), proposed a 'free association' status with the Netherlands, involving greater independence, rather than the planned integration as a municipality. The Dutch Government asserted the island could adopt municipality status, as planned, or assume full self-governance. None the less, the Executive Council proceeded to schedule a referendum on its proposal, initially for 15 January 2010 and subsequently for 26 March. In January the State Secretary for the Interior and Kingdom Relations, Ank Bijleveld-Schouten, requested that Antilles Governor Fritz de los Santos Goedgedrag investigate allegations that a member of Bonaire's Island Council, Anthony Nicolaas, whose withdrawal from the island's former ruling party, the Unión Patriótico Bonairiano (UPB), had forced its administration from office in June 2009, had received financial and political inducements from the PDB in return for his support; Nicolaas and the PDB denied the claims. Acting on the advice of Bonaire's Lieutenant-Governor, in February 2010 Goedgedrag cancelled the referendum due to be conducted in March, on the grounds that it contravened international law, as Dutch nationals who had only resided on Bonaire since January 2007 would have been barred from voting. By the following month, under pressure from the Dutch Government, which was continuing to withhold debt repayments and other funds from Bonaire, the island's Executive Council appeared to have accepted the cancellation of the referendum on the 'free association' status. Nevertheless, the referendum was held in December 2010, although the low turn-out meant the result was declared invalid. The Unión Patriótico Bonariano, which had taken office in September, had urged the electorate to boycott the plebiscite.

On 10 October 2010, following the formal dissolution of the Netherlands Antilles, Bonaire officially became a special municipality of the Netherlands. The US dollar was formally adopted as the island's currency from 1 January 2011, replacing the Netherlands Antilles guilder; the Island Council had opposed the introduction of the euro, the currency of the Netherlands.

At elections to the Island Council on 2 March 2011, the UPB secured four of the nine seats available. The PDB won three seats and the recently formed Movementu Boneiru Liber and Partido Pro Hustisia & Union each won one seat. A coalition government was subsequently formed.

Bonaire's economy is dependent on tourism and petroleum transfers. There was a 9.9% decrease in visitor numbers in 2009, following a fall in tourist arrivals from the lucrative North American market. Although no refining takes place on the island, the Bonaire Petroleum Corporation stores oil for transfer from large tankers to smaller ones and is a significant contributor to the ecomony. Bonaire has reserves of limestone and salt, which are mined; salt production averaged 400,000 metric tons per year. There is also a textile factory. Bonaire is a major exporter of aloes.

PUBLIC HOLIDAYS

In addition to the holidays of the metropolitan Netherlands, Bonaire celebrates the following public holidays.

2012: 1 January (New Year's Day), 20 February (Carnival), 1 May (Labour Day), 17 May (Ascension Day), 6 September (Flag Day), 15 December (Kingdom Day).

For statistical information on Bonaire, see the Statistical Survey in the Curaçao chapter.

Directory

The Government

HEAD OF STATE

Queen of the Netherlands: HM Queen BEATRIX.

Lieutenant-Governor: GLENN A. E. THODE, Bestuurskantoor, Wilhelminaplein 1, Kralendijk; tel. 717-5330; fax 717-2824; e-mail gezag@bonairelive.com; internet www.bonairegov.an.

COUNCIL OF MINISTERS
(May 2011)

The Government is formed by a coalition of the Unión Patriótico Boneriano (UPB), Partido Demokrátiko Boneriano (PDB), Partido Pro Hustisia & Union (PHU) and Movementu Boneiru Liber (MBL).

Island Council: CLARK ABRAHAM (PDB), ROBERT BEUKENBOOM (PDB), NOLLY OLEANA (PDB), MELENA WINKLAAR (UPB), BARNEY EL HAGE (UPB), JEFFERY LEVENSTONE (UPB), MARITZA SILBERIE (UPB), BENITO DIRKSZ (MBL), MICHIEL BIJKERK (PHU).

Island Secretary: NEREIDA GONZALAZ.

Executive Council: PABLO JAMES KROON, ELVIS TJIN ASJOE, ALIANO C. EMERENCIANA, ANTHONY T. C. NICOLAAS.

MINISTRY

Regional Service Centre: Kaya International z/n, POB 357, Kralendijk; tel. 715-8333; fax 715-8330; e-mail info-rsc@rsc-bes.nl.

Political Organizations

Movementu Boneiru Liber (MBL) (Free Bonaire Movement): Kaya Papa Cornes 33, Kralendijk; tel. 717-0390; fax 717-6125; e-mail movementu@gmail.com; internet www.vota-mbl.com; f. 2010; Leader BENITO BENITO; Sec. JOSÉ A. E. CAPELLA.

Partido Demokrátiko Boneriano (PDB) (Bonaire Democratic Party): Kaya America 13A, POB 294, Kralendijk; tel. 717-8903; fax 717-5923; e-mail robbybeuk@gmail.com; internet partido-demokrat.org; f. 1954; also known as Democratische Partij—Bonaire (DPB); liberal, promotes self-governance for Bonaire; known as the Aliansa Demokratika Bonairiana in 2009–10; Leader ROBBY BEUKENBOOM.

Partido Pro Hustisia & Union (PHU): Kralendijk; tel. 796-2650; e-mail m.bijkerk@telbonet.an; f. 2010; Leader MICHIEL BIJKERK; Pres. RAFAEL A. SANTANA.

Unión Patriótico Boneriano (UPB) (Patriotic Union of Bonaire): Kaya Sabana 22, Kralendijk; tel. 717-8906; fax 717-5552; 2,134 mems; Christian democratic; Leader RAMONSITO T. BOOI; Sec.-Gen. C. V. WINKLAAR.

Religion

Almost all of the inhabitants profess Christianity, predominantly Roman Catholicism.

The Press

Arco Bonaire: Kaya Isabel 1, Kralendijk; tel. 717-2427; e-mail info@arcocarib.com; internet www.arcocarib.com; magazine; Editor M. BIJKERK L. M.

Bonaire Reporter: Kaya Gob. Debrot 200-6, POB 407, Kralendijk; tel. and fax 717-8988; e-mail info@bonairenews.com; internet www.bonairereporter.com; English; weekly; Publ. GEORGE DESALVO; Editor-in-Chief LAURA DESALVO.

Broadcasting and Communications

TELECOMMUNICATIONS

Digicel Bonaire: Kaya Grandi 26, Kralendijk; tel. 717-4400; fax 717-4466; e-mail customercare@digicelcuracao.com; internet www.digicelbonaire.com; f. 1999; bought majority shareholding of Antilliano Por NV in April 2006; Digicel acquired mobile business of TELBO (Bonaire) in Dec. 2006; Chair. DENIS O'BRIEN; CEO (Dutch Caribbean, Guyana and Suriname) PHILIP VAN DALSEN.

Telefonia Bonairiano NV (TELBO NV): Kaya Libertador Simon Bolivar 8, POB 94, Kralendijk; tel. 717-7000; fax 717-5007; e-mail telbo@telbo.an; internet www.telbo.net; f. 1983; fixed-line telecommunications and internet service provider; TELBO's mobile operations on Bonaire were purchased by Digicel in Dec. 2006; Gen. Man. GILBERT DE BREE.

BROADCASTING

Radio

Radiodifusión Boneriana NV: Kaya Gobernador Debrot 2, Kralendijk; tel. 717-5947; fax 717-8220; e-mail vozdibonaire@gmail.com; internet www.vozdibonaire.com; f. 1980; Owner FELICIANO DA SILVA PILOTO.

  Alpha FM: broadcasts in Spanish.

  Mega FM: internet www.megahitfm.com; broadcasts in Dutch.

  Voz di Bonaire (PJB2) (Voice of Bonaire): broadcasts in Papiamento.

Trans World Radio (TWR): Kaya Gobernador N. Debrot 64, Kralendijk; tel. 717-8800; fax 717-8808; e-mail 800am@twr.org; internet www.twr.org; f. 1964; religious, educational and cultural station; programmes to South, Central and North America, and Caribbean in five languages; Pres. LAUREN LIBBY; Station Dir JOSEPH BARKER.

Television

Relay stations provide Bonaire with television programmes from Curaçao.

Finance

BANKING

Commercial banks

Maduro & Curiel's Bank (Bonaire), NV: 1 Kaya L. D. Gerharts, Kralendijk; tel. 715-5520; e-mail info@mcbbonaire.com; internet www.mcbbonaire.com; Man. Dir EVERT PIAR.

Banking Associations

Bonaire Bankers' Association: Maduro & Curiel's Bank (Bonaire) NV, Kaya L. D. Gerharts 1, POB 366, Kralendijk; tel. 717-5520; fax 717-5884; Vice-Pres. R. GOMEZ.

Trade and Industry

CHAMBER OF COMMERCE

Bonaire Chamber of Commerce and Industry: Princess Mariestraat, POB 52, Kralendijk; tel. 717-5595; fax 717-8995.

UTILITIES

EcoPower Bonaire BV: Kralendijk; f. 2007; consortium of Econcern (Germany), MAN (Germany) and Enercon (Netherlands); sustainable energy producer; Project Man. HANS VAN HEEL.

Water & Energiebedrijf Bonaire (WEB) NV: Carlos Nicolaas 3, POB 381, Kralendijk; tel. 715-8244; e-mail web@web.an; internet www.web.an.

TRADE UNION

Federashon Bonaireana di Trabou (FEDEBON): Kaya Krabè 6, POB 324, Nikiboko; tel. and fax 717-8845; Pres. GEROLD BERNABELA.

Tourism

Bonaire's attractions include scuba-diving and snorkelling facilities, flamingo and donkey sanctuaries, Bonaire National Marine Park, the historic rock paintings of Caquieto Indians and the white, sandy beaches.

Bonaire Hotel and Tourism Association (BONHATA): Kaya Soeur Bartola 15B, POB 358, Kralendijk; tel. 717-5134; fax 717-8534; e-mail info@bonhata.org; internet www.ilovebonaire.com; f. 1980; Pres. SARA MATERA; Sec. DIRK JAN METHORST.

Tourism Corporation Bonaire (TCB): Kaya Grandi 2, Kralendijk; tel. 717-8322; fax 717-8408; e-mail info@tourismbonaire.com; internet www.tourismbonaire.com; Dir SHARON BOL (acting).

Defence

The Netherlands is responsible for the defence of Bonaire.

Education

The education system is the same as that of the Netherlands. Dutch is the principal language of instruction, although instruction in Papiamento is also used in primary schools. Education was made compulsory on Bonaire in 1992.

SABA

The small, volcanic island of Saba lies in the north-eastern Caribbean Sea, about 27 km north-west of Sint (St) Eustatius. With Sint (St) Maarten, 45 km north of Saba, these three islands comprise the Bovenwindse Eilands, or Windward Islands, although actually in the Leeward group of the Lesser Antilles. The climate is tropical, moderated by the sea, with an average annual temperature of 27.5°C (81°F) and little rainfall. English is the official and principal language, although Dutch is also spoken. Almost all of the inhabitants profess Christianity, predominantly Roman Catholicism. The state flag (proportions 2 by 3) is divided into four triangles, two red at the top, two blue at the bottom. In the centre of the flag is a white diamond, with a yellow five-pointed star in the centre. The capital is The Bottom.

The Dutch captured Saba, once settled by Carib Indians, in 1640. After frequent changes in possession, the islands were finally confirmed as Dutch territory in 1816, administered by the Dutch West Indian Company (WIC). Owing to its difficult terrain, Saba remained sparsely populated. In 1845 Saba was ceded to the Dutch Crown and administered as Curaçao and Dependencies, comprising the Windward Islands and the three territories of the Leeward Islands— Aruba, Bonaire and Curaçao. During the Second World War Queen Wilhelmina of the Netherlands promised independence, and in 1954 a Charter gave the federation of six islands full autonomy in domestic affairs, and declared the Netherlands Antilles to be an integral part of the Kingdom of the Netherlands.

Despite the 1954 Charter, there were demands for further self-government from elements within the federation for most of the latter half of the 20th century. A referendum on the status issue was held on Saba in October 1994; 91% of voters opted for continued membership of the Antillean federation. Nevertheless, similar plebiscites in the other constituent members of the Netherlands Antilles produced differing results and in October 2004 the Jesurun Commission, established by the Dutch and Antillean Governments and headed by Edsel Jesurun (a former Governor of the Netherlands Antilles), recommended the dissolution of the federation. The Commission proposed that Saba (as well as Bonaire and St Eustatius) should be directly administered by the Dutch Government. In November, in another official referendum, a majority of voters (86%) on Saba again voted in favour of becoming part of the Netherlands. On 3 December 2005 a preliminary agreement with the Dutch Government that the extant federation be dissolved by 1 July 2007 was duly signed in Curaçao. Under the new structure, Saba was to become *koninkrijseilande*, or 'kingdom island', with direct ties to the Netherlands, a status equivalent to that of a Dutch province. The future status of Saba was subsequently refined to that of a *bijzondere gemeete*, or 'special municipality', similar in most ways to other metropolitan Dutch municipalities, although with separate social security and currency arrangements.

An agreement confirming Saba's impending accession to 'special municipality' status was signed in The Hague, Netherlands, on 12 October 2006, and included provisions for citizens of the island to participate in Dutch national and local elections and in the election of candidates to the European Parliament. A further 'transition accord' was signed by the Netherlands Antilles central Government, the Island Council, and the Netherlands on 12 February 2007, envisaging the island's complete secession from the federation. Under the terms of this covenant, the Netherlands was to pledge over NA Fl. 1,000m. (in addition to existing financial assistance) to facilitate the process of disintegration, with Saba, Bonaire and St Eustatius receiving individual allocations. The metropolitan administration also agreed to write off almost three-quarters of the Antilles' debt. Following further negotiations, a meeting was held in Curaçao on 15 December 2008 at which the Dutch Prime Minister, Jan Peter Balkenende, and the Antillean premier, Emily de Jongh-Elhage, signed an agreement confirming the new status of the island.

The Antilles Government's announcement in August 2009 that a general election would be held in January 2010, despite plans for the dissolution of the Netherlands Antilles to take place later that year, prompted the Executive Council of Saba to declare its intention to become independent from the Netherlands Antilles. The Island Council argued that the central Government lacked the political will to complete the transition process. However, it was generally agreed that Saba's secession from the federation at this stage would not be legally feasible. At the end of September 2009, at a meeting of the Dutch State Secretary for the Interior and Kingdom Relations, Ank Bijleveld-Schouten, and representatives of the Netherlands Antilles, it was agreed that the target date for dissolution of the Netherlands Antilles would be 10 October 2010, at which date Saba would become a special municipality of the Netherlands. The US dollar was formally adopted as the island's currency from 1 January 2011, replacing the Netherlands Antilles guilder; the Island Council had opposed the introduction of the euro, the currency of the Netherlands.

Elections to Saba's Island Council were held on 2 March 2011. The Windward Islands People's Movement won four of the five available seats, while the Saba Labour Party secured the remaining seat. The new Council was sworn into office on 11 March.

Lieutenant-Governor: JONATHAN JOHNSON, 1 Power St, The Bottom; tel. 416-3215; fax 416-3274; e-mail lt.gov@sabagov.com; internet www.sabagovernment.com.

Island Council: ROLANDO WILSON, CARL BUNCAMPER, ISHMAEL LEVENSTONE, EVITON HEYLIGER, SHAMARA NICHOLSON.

Island Secretary: MENNO VAN DER VELDE.

Executive Council: BRUCA ZAGERS, CHRIS JOHNSON.

Regional Service Centre: The Bottom; tel. 416-3934; e-mail info-rsc@rsc-bes.nl.

SINT EUSTATIUS

Sint (St) Eustatius (also known as Statia—from the original Spanish name St Anastasia) is a volcanic island in the north-eastern Caribbean Sea, about 20 km north-east of Saint Christopher (St Kitts) and Nevis. Together with Saba and St Maarten, St Eustatius comprises the Bovenwindse Eilands or Windward Islands (although actually in the Leeward group of the Lesser Antilles). The climate is tropical, moderated by the sea, with an average annual temperature of 27.5°C (81°F) and little rainfall. English is the official and principal language, although Dutch is also spoken. Almost all of the inhabitants profess Christianity, predominantly Protestantism. The state flag (proportions 2 by 3) is divided into four five-sided blue squares with red borders. In the centre of the flag is a white diamond, in which an outline of the island appears. At the top of the diamond is a five-pointed gold star. The capital is Oranjestad.

The Dutch settled the Windward Islands, once settled by Carib Indians, in the mid-17th century. St Eustatius came under Dutch control in 1635. After frequent changes in possession, the islands were finally confirmed as Dutch territory in 1816. Together with the Leeward Islands (comprising Aruba, Bonaire and Curaçao), the Windward islands were administered as Curaçao and Dependencies between 1845 and 1948. In the early 18th century St Eustatius prospered as a trading centre and transshipment centre for African slaves. During the Second World War Queen Wilhelmina of the Netherlands promised independence, and in 1954 a Charter gave the federation of six islands full autonomy in domestic affairs, and declared it to be an integral part of the Kingdom of the Netherlands.

Political allegience within the federation was traditionally along island, rather than party lines. These divisions increased following Aruba's secession from the federation in 1986. Calls for further autonomy increased in Curaçao and St Maarten, although the population of St Eustatius remained broadly in favour of maintaining the status quo. In a referendum on status held in October 1994 some

86% of voters opted for continued membership of the Antillean federation. Nevertheless, plebiscites in the other constituent parts of the federation produced differing results, and in the 1990s and early 2000s movements to obtain autonomy in Curaçao and St Maarten increased. In October 2004 the Jesurun Commission, established by the Dutch and Antillean Governments and headed by Edsel Jesurun (a former Governor of the Netherlands Antilles), recommended the dissolution of the federation; support for the continued union had, it was argued, virtually disintegrated on most of the islands. The Commission proposed that Curaçao and St Maarten should become autonomous states within the Netherlands (i.e. have *status aparte*), while Saba, Bonaire and St Eustatius should be directly administered by the Dutch Government. A further referendum on the constitutional futures of St Eustatius took place on 8 April 2005: from a voter turn-out of 55%, 76% of the electorate favoured remaining part of the Netherlands Antilles, while 20% voted for closer ties with the Netherlands and 1% preferred to seek complete independence for the tiny island. On 3 December 2005 a preliminary agreement with the Dutch Government that the extant federation be dissolved by 1 July 2007 was duly signed in Curaçao. Under the new structure, St Eustatius was to become a *koninkrijseilande*, or 'kingdom island', with direct ties to the Netherlands, a status equivalent to that of a Dutch province. The future status of St Eustatius was subsequently refined to that of a *bijzondere gemeete*, or 'special municipality', similar in most ways to other metropolitan Dutch municipalities, although with separate social security and currency arrangements.

An agreement confirming St Eustatius's impending accession to 'special municipality' status was signed in The Hague, Netherlands, on 12 October 2006, and included provisions for citizens of the island to participate in Dutch national and local elections and in the election of candidates to the European Parliament. A further 'transition accord' was signed by the Netherlands Antilles central Government, the Island Council of St Eustatius, and the Netherlands on 12 February 2007, envisaging the island's complete secession from the federation. Under the terms of this covenant, the Netherlands was to pledge over NA Fl. 1,000m. (in addition to existing financial assistance) to facilitate the process of disintegration, with St Eustatius, Saba and Bonaire receiving individual allocations. The metropolitan administration also agreed to write off almost three-quarters of the Antilles' debt.

Following further negotiations, a meeting was held in Curaçao on 15 December 2008 at which the Dutch Prime Minister, Jan Peter Balkenende, and the Antillean premier, Emily de Jongh-Elhage, signed an agreement confirming the new status of the island. At the end of September 2009, at a meeting of the Dutch State Secretary for the Interior and Kingdom Relations, Ank Bijleveld-Schouten, and representatives of the Netherlands Antilles, it was agreed that the target date for dissolution of the federation would be 10 October 2010, at which date St Eustatius would become a special municipality of the Netherlands. The US dollar was formally adopted as the island's currency from 1 January 2011, replacing the Netherlands Antilles guilder; the Island Council had opposed the introduction of the euro, the currency of the Netherlands.

In elections to the new five-member Island Council held on 2 March 2011, the Democratic Party of St Eustatius won two seats, while the Progressive Labour Party, the United People's Coalition and the St Eustatius Empowerment Party each won one seat. The new members of the Council were sworn into office on 11 March.

Lieutenant-Governor: GERARD BERKEL, Govt Bldg, Oranjestad; tel. 318-2552; fax 318-2324; e-mail lt.governor@statiagovernment.com; internet www.statiagovernment.com.

Island Council: KOOS SNEEK, REUBEN MERKMAN, FRANKLIN BROWN, REGINALD C. ZAANDAM, MILLICENT LIJFROCK-MARSDEN.

Island Secretary: EDRIS BENNETT-MERKMAN (acting).

Executive Council: Commr GLENNVILLE SCHMIDT, Commr CLYDE I. VAN PUTTEN.

Regional Service Centre: Mazinga Complex A and B, Fort Oranjestraat, Oranjestad; tel. 318-3370; e-mail info-rsc@rsc-bes.nl.

NETHERLANDS DEPENDENCIES

Netherlands Autonomous Countries

Under the 1983 Constitution, the Kingdom of the Netherlands comprises territories in Europe (the Netherlands) and in the Caribbean (Aruba, Curaçao and Sint (St) Maarten). The Charter for the Kingdom of the Netherlands, signed by Queen Juliana in 1954, designates these territories as a single realm, ruled by the House of Orange-Nassau. Aruba gained *status aparte* (separate status) within the Kingdom on 1 January 1986. Following further constitutional amendments, on 10 October 2010 Curaçao and St Maarten, formerly part of the Netherlands Antilles, also became independent countries within the Kingdom of the Netherlands.

ARUBA

Introductory Survey

LOCATION, CLIMATE, LANGUAGE, RELIGION, FLAG, CAPITAL

Aruba is one of the Benedenwindse Eilands or Leeward Islands, which it forms with Bonaire and Curaçao, and lies in the southern Caribbean Sea, 25 km north of Venezuela and 68 km west of Curaçao. The climate is tropical, with an average annual temperature of 28°C (82°F), but is tempered by north-easterly winds. Rainfall is very low, averaging only about 426 mm (16.8 ins) annually. The official language is Dutch, but the dominant language is Papiamento (a mixture of Dutch, Spanish, English, Arawak Indian and several West African dialects). Spanish and English are also spoken. Most of the inhabitants profess Christianity and belong to the Roman Catholic Church, although a wide variety of other denominations are represented. The national flag (proportions 2 by 3) is blue, with two narrow yellow horizontal stripes in the lower section and a white-bordered four-pointed red star in the upper hoist. The capital is Oranjestad.

CONTEMPORARY POLITICAL HISTORY

Historical Context

The Caribbean island of Aruba was claimed for Spain in 1499, but was first colonized by the Dutch in 1636 and subsequently formed part of the Dutch possessions in the West Indies. Administered from Curaçao after 1845, in 1954 Aruba became a member of the autonomous federation of the Netherlands Antilles. The establishment in 1929 of a large petroleum refinery on the island, at Sint (St) Nicolaas, led to the rapid expansion of the economy and a high standard of living for the islanders. However, many Arubans resented the administrative dominance of Curaçao, and what they regarded as the excessive demands made upon Aruban wealth and resources by the other five islands within the Netherlands Antilles. The island's principal political party, the Movimentu Electoral di Pueblo (MEP), campaigned, from its foundation in 1971 onwards, for Aruban independence and separation from the other islands. In a referendum held in Aruba in March 1977 82% of voters supported independence and withdrawal from the Antillean federation. The MEP used its position in the coalition Government of the Netherlands Antilles, formed in 1979, to press for concessions from the other islands towards early independence for Aruba. In 1981 (after the MEP had withdrawn from the Government of the Netherlands Antilles) a provisional agreement regarding Aruba's future was reached between the Dutch and Antillean Governments. Following further discussions, it was agreed in March 1983 that Aruba should receive *status aparte* (separate status), within the Kingdom of the Netherlands, from 1 January 1986, achieving full independence in 1996. The Dutch Government would remain responsible for defence and external relations until independence, while Aruba was to form a co-operative union with the Netherlands Antilles (the Antilles of the Five) in economic and monetary affairs.

Domestic Political Affairs

At local elections in April 1983 the MEP increased its representation to 13 of the 21 seats in the Staten (parliament), and the leader of the MEP, Gilberto F. (Betico) Croes, remained as leader of the island Government. Austerity measures introduced in late 1984 provoked a series of strikes and demonstrations by civil servants in protest at wage reductions and price rises. The MEP consequently lost popular support and, following elections to the Staten in November 1985, was succeeded in government by a coalition of four opposition parties led by the Arubaanse Volkspartij (AVP). Aruba achieved *status aparte*, as planned, on 1 January 1986, and Jan Hendrik Albert (Henny) Eman, leader of the AVP, became its first Prime Minister. Croes died in November 1986; he was succeeded as leader of the MEP by Nelson O. Oduber.

From 1988 Aruba began to enjoy an economic recovery, based on tourism. However, the MEP claimed that the benefits to the whole community were limited, and also criticized Eman's stated reservations about independence in 1996 and his refusal to negotiate with the Netherlands about transitional arrangements. At a general election in January 1989 the MEP came within 28 votes of securing an absolute majority in the Staten. The number of seats held by the MEP increased from eight to 10, and in February Oduber formed a Government in coalition with the Partido Patriótico Arubano (PPA) and the Acción Democrático Nacional (ADN). (Both these parties had been in the previous Government, and retained one seat each at the election.)

The MEP and the AVP each secured nine seats in the Staten at the January 1993 general election, while the three remaining seats were won by the ADN, the PPA and the Organisacion Liberal Arubano (OLA). Despite gaining fewer votes than the AVP, the MEP administration remained in office, renewing the coalition with the ADN and the PPA. In April 1994, however, Oduber announced the Government's resignation, following the withdrawal of the ADN and the PPA from the coalition. A fresh general election was held on 29 July: the AVP secured 10 seats, while the MEP won nine seats and the OLA the remaining two. In August Eman formed a Government in coalition with the OLA.

In March 1994 the Governments of Aruba, the Netherlands and the Netherlands Antilles convened in The Hague, Netherlands, and decided to cancel plans for Aruba's transition to full independence, due to take place in 1996. The possibility of a transition to full independence at a later date was not excluded, but was not considered a priority, and would, moreover, require the approval of the Aruban people, by referendum, as well as the support of a two-thirds' majority in the Staten.

In September 1997 the Staten was dissolved after the OLA withdrew from the coalition. A general election was thus held on 12 December; this resulted in a political composition identical to that of the 1993 polls. Following protracted negotiations, the AVP and the OLA renewed their coalition in mid-1998, and a new Council of Ministers, headed by Eman, was appointed.

In June 2001 the governing coalition collapsed, following the withdrawal of the OLA's support for the AVP's plan to privatize the Aruba Tourism Authority. As a result, a general election was held on 28 September. The MEP comfortably defeated the incumbent AVP, securing 52% of the votes cast and 12 seats in the Staten. The AVP legislative representation was reduced to six seats. The three remaining seats were shared between the PPA (two) and the OLA (one). Oduber was once again appointed Prime Minister and a new single-party Government, with an unprecedented opportunity to pass legislation through the Staten, took office in November.

In early 2004, after several months of discussion, the Aruban and Dutch Governments agreed to appoint Fredis Refunjol, hitherto Minister of Education, as Governor. The Dutch Government objected to the fact that there was only one candidate for the position and argued that the appointment was overtly political. Nevertheless, since Refunjol's candidature had strong cross-party support in the Staten, he was duly sworn in on 7 May. The erstwhile President of the Staten, Francisco Walfrido Croes, assumed the vacant education portfolio. Meanwhile, in January the Staten voted against becoming an Ultra Periphery Area of the European Union (EU, see p. 270). The island thus remained an Overseas Territory of the EU.

At a general election on 23 September 2005 the MEP again won a majority of seats (11, in 43% of the popular vote) in the 21-seat Staten. The victory came in spite of broad public criticism of the Government's unwillingness to defend wage levels from the downward pressure caused by large-scale immigration from South America. Notably, the minimum wage had not been adjusted for five years. The AVP won eight seats, an improvement on its result in the 2001 election, and the Movimento Patriotico Arubano and RED Democratico each won one legislative seat. The electoral turn-out among those eligible to vote was 85%. Oduber, who continued as Prime Minister, defended his economic policies.

NETHERLANDS DEPENDENCIES

Aruba

Recent developments: the AVP in power

The AVP defeated the governing MEP in a general election held on 25 September 2009, winning 12 of the Staten's 21 seats, with 48% of the votes cast. The MEP obtained eight seats and Democracia Real secured the remaining seat. A voter participation rate of 86% was recorded. The AVP, led since 2003 by Michiel Eman (the brother of former Prime Minister Henny Eman), had focused on Aruba's economic difficulties during the electoral campaign, pledging to revive the tourism sector, which was suffering as a result of the global economic downturn, and to eliminate an unpopular 3% business turnover tax. Oduber attributed his party's loss to Dutch interference in Aruba's affairs (see Foreign Affairs) and to the recent closure of the petroleum refinery at St Nicolaas (see Economic Affairs). Eman took office as Prime Minister on 30 October.

The Eman Government's early policies focused on the economy, including reviving the important tourism industry and reopening the Valero refinery. In January 2010 the administration succeeded in resolving a long-running dispute over tax with the refinery owners; the refinery finally resumed operations until January 2011.

Foreign Affairs

Aruba's relations with the Antilles of the Five improved after 1986. In 1987 Aruba agreed to undertake economic co-operation, and in 1988 the three Dutch Leeward Islands initiated a joint project for the development of tourism. Aruba's relations with the 'metropolitan' Netherlands were dominated at this time by the latter's pressure for more control to be exercised over the large amount of aid that it gave to Aruba, and by the issue of independence, in particular the future arrangements for the island's security: Aruba's strategic position, close to the South American mainland, and the possibility of it being used as a base for drugs-trafficking, were matters of particular concern. In 1990 Aruba adopted the 1988 UN Convention on measures to combat trade in illegal drugs; a joint Dutch and Aruban team was formed to conduct investigations. In December 1996, however, the USA included Aruba on its list of major drugs-producing or transit countries. New legislation to facilitate the extradition of suspected drugs-traffickers and money-launderers took effect in the following year and in 1999 US naval and air force patrols began operating from a base in Aruba in an effort to counter the transport of illicit drugs. In 2001 the Caribbean Financial Action Task Force commended the Government on its efforts in combating money-laundering. In the same year the territory was removed from the list of so-called 'unco-operative tax havens' drawn up by the Organisation for Economic Co-operation and Development (OECD, based in Paris, France), after the Government pledged to reform the territory's financial sector in order to conform to OECD's guidelines by 2005. In November 2003 Aruba signed an agreement with the USA to exchange tax information in order to combat illegal financial activities, such as money-laundering, that are associated with international terrorism and drugs-trafficking. However, in April 2009 Aruba was included in OECD's so-called 'grey list' of territories that had committed to improving financial transparency, but had yet substantially to implement reform. Following efforts to conclude further bilateral agreements on the exchange of tax information in the second half of the year, Aruba was removed from the list. Relations between Aruba and the Netherlands deteriorated in 2005 when the Dutch Government forced Aruba to introduce a more stringent policy on visa conditions. Tensions arose again in 2008–09 as a result of persistent allegations made by Dutch politicians of corruption on Aruba. In mid-2009 Prime Minister Oduber criticized plans by the Kingdom Government to conduct an investigation into the corruption claims, accusing the Dutch authorities of interfering in Aruban internal affairs. The new AVP Government that took office in Aruba in October that year pledged to improve relations with the Netherlands.

After acquiring *status aparte*, Aruba fostered relations with some of its Caribbean neighbours and with countries in Latin America. This included the development of ties with Venezuela, which had traditionally laid claim to the Dutch Leeward Islands, including Aruba, and the signing of a memorandum of understanding with Brazil in September 2006, which sought to promote more extensive air transport links. In late 2009 the Dutch Minister of Foreign Affairs refuted allegations by the Venezuelan Government that the US military was being permitted to use airbases on Aruba and Curaçao to launch reconnaissance flights over Venezuelan territory.

CONSTITUTION AND GOVERNMENT

Aruba has separate status (*status aparte*) within the Kingdom of the Netherlands. Legislative power is held by the unicameral Staten (parliament) of 21 members, elected by universal adult suffrage for four years (subject to dissolution). Executive power in all domestic affairs is vested in the Council of Ministers (led by the Prime Minister), responsible to the Staten. The Governor, appointed by the Dutch Crown for a term of six years, represents the monarch of the Netherlands on Aruba and holds responsibility for external affairs and defence. The Governor is assisted by an advisory council. The Government of Aruba appoints a minister plenipotentiary to represent it in the Government of the Kingdom.

REGIONAL AND INTERNATIONAL CO-OPERATION

Aruba forms a co-operative union with Curaçao and Sint (St) Maarten in monetary and economic affairs, and has observer status with the Caribbean Community and Common Market (CARICOM, see p. 219). As part of the Kingdom of the Netherlands, Aruba is classed as an Overseas Territory in association with the European Union (EU, see p. 270).

ECONOMIC AFFAIRS

In 2008, according to the UN, Aruba's gross national income (GNI) was US $2,562m. During 2000–10 the population increased at an average annual rate of 1.9%. According to the central bank, gross domestic product (GDP) per head decreased, in real terms, by an average of 1.0% per year in 2000–10. Overall GDP decreased, in real terms, at an average annual rate of 0.8% in 2000–10. Real GDP decreased by 10.5% in 2009 and by 3.7% in 2010.

The agricultural sector engaged 0.7% of the employed labour force in 2007, according to the International Labour Organization, and contributed 0.4% of total GDP in 2009, according to UN estimates. Owing to the poor quality of the soil and the prohibitive cost of desalinated water, the only significant agricultural activity is the cultivation of aloes (used in the manufacture of cosmetics and pharmaceuticals); aloe-based products are exported. Some livestock is raised, and there is a small fishing industry.

The industrial sector contributed an estimated 20.2% of GDP in 2009, and engaged 20.3% of the employed labour force in 2007. The industrial sector, and the island's economy, was based on the refining and transshipment of imported petroleum and petroleum products. The petroleum refinery at St Nicolaas, purchased by the US-based Valero Energy Corporation in 2004, produced an average of 280,000 barrels per day (b/d). In August 2009, however, Valero announced the closure of the refinery, which it hoped to sell. The refinery reopened in January 2011. In 2008 Aruba refined 58.3m. barrels of crude petroleum; production fell to 35.8m. in 2009 and was non-existent in 2010. Imports of crude petroleum were valued at A Fl. 8,513m. in 2008, before falling to A Fl. 2,504m. in the following year. Exports of refined petroleum were valued at A Fl. 9,216m. in 2008 and A Fl. 3,194m. in 2009.(total exports excluding mineral fuels and free trade zone transactions amounted to just A Fl. 41.6m. in 2009). There is a large petroleum transshipment terminal on Aruba, and a small petrochemicals industry. An advanced-technology coker plant supplies liquefied petroleum gas, largely for export to the USA. There are believed to be exploitable reserves of hydrocarbons within Aruban territory, and Aruba also has reserves of salt.

Manufacturing contributed an estimated 3.9% of GDP in 2009 and, along with electricity, gas and water, engaged 7.6% of the employed labour force in 2007. Light industry is engaged in the production of beverages, building materials, paints and solvents, paper and plastic products, candles, detergents, disinfectants, soaps and aloe-based cosmetics. There is a 'free zone', and the ports of Oranjestad and Barcadera provide bunkering and repair facilities for ships.

The construction sector, which grew steadily in the 1980s, declined in importance following a moratorium on the construction of new hotels in 1992. In 2005–07, however, some US $150m. was allocated to the renovation and expansion of existing hotels and resorts in an attempt to reinvigorate the sector.

Services are Aruba's principal economic activity, employing 78.9% of the active labour force in 2007, and contributing an estimated 79.3% of the island's GDP in 2009. Aruba's principal source of income is tourism; the hotels and restaurants sector alone was estimated to provide 10.5% of Aruba's GDP in 2002. The number of visitor arrivals fluctuates from year to year. The number of stop-over arrivals decreased by 1.7% in 2009, to 812,623, but increased by 1.6% in 2010, to 825,451. Conversely, the number of cruise ship passengers increased in 2009 (to 606,768 from 556,090 in the previous year), but then fell in 2010 (to 569,424). Receipts from tourism decreased to A Fl. 2,314.1m. in 2009, and further, to A Fl. 2,212,0m. in the following year. Financial services are well established in Aruba, particularly the data-processing sector, an important service to US companies in particular.

Aruba is obliged to import most of its requirements, particularly machinery and electrical equipment (which accounted for 23.0% of the total value of imports in 2009), foodstuffs and chemical products; in 2009 the island recorded a trade deficit of US $473.8m. There was a surplus on the current account of the balance of payments of US $157.1m. in the same year. In 2009 the principal source of imports, excluding the petroleum sector and the free zone, was the USA (54.1% of the total value); other major sources were the Netherlands, the Netherlands Antilles and Panama. The principal export commodity was refined petroleum (see above). Excluding the petroleum sector and the free zone, the principal market for exports in 2009 was also the Netherlands Antilles (accounting for 27.0% of the total

NETHERLANDS DEPENDENCIES

Aruba

value of exports), followed by the USA, the Netherlands and Venezuela.

In 2009 Aruba recorded a budget deficit of A Fl. 120.3m., equivalent to 2.7% of GDP in that year. At the end of 2009 total government debt was A Fl. 2,179.6m. (equivalent to 46.4% of GDP), much of which was owed to the Government of the Netherlands. The average annual rate of inflation was 3.2% in 2000–10; consumer prices increased by 6.8% in 2009, but fell by 0.7% in 2009. Some 10.3% of the labour force were unemployed in 2009.

Aruba was considered one of the most prosperous islands in the Caribbean, and generally maintained reasonably low levels of inflation and of unemployment. Concern, however, was expressed that Aruba's high public sector wage bill and the generous nature of the island's social welfare system, combined with its ageing population, would threaten the future stability of public finances, already hindered by a narrow taxation base and poor revenue collection. In an attempt to expand the vital tourism industry, investments of over US $350m. were implemented during 2007 (including the renovation and upgrade of the island's cruise ship terminals, facility improvements at Queen Beatrix International Airport, the inauguration of a new private jet terminal, and extensive hotel and resort renovation and expansion), and the number of tourist arrivals increased significantly overall in 2008. However, the onset of the global financial crisis in that year meant that numbers began to decline from September. Although cruise ship tourism proved to be resilient in 2009, the number of stop-over arrivals decreased, as did receipts. The closure of the petroleum refinery from July 2009 to January 2011 represented a serious reverse for the economy, given its importance in terms of employment, export earnings and fiscal revenues. This, combined with the international economic downturn, resulted in real GDP decreasing sharply in 2009, by 10.5%, one of the most severe contractions in the Caribbean. The Government that took office in October 2009 introduced reforms to the health care and pensions sector, but the IMF recommended further structural adjustments, including the introduction of value added tax. The Fund also urged a reduction in the public deficit to less than 1% of GDP by 2014 in an attempt to bolster the economy against further external factors.

PUBLIC HOLIDAYS

2012: 1 January (New Year's Day), 25 January (Gilberto F. Croes's Birthday), 20 February (Lenten Carnival), 18 March (National Anthem and Flag Day), 6–9 April (Easter), 30 April (Queen's Day), 1 May (Labour Day), 17 May (Ascension Day), 25–26 December (Christmas).

Statistical Survey

Sources (unless otherwise stated): Central Bureau of Statistics, Ministry of Finance and Economic Affairs, Sun Plaza Bldg, 3rd Floor, L. G. Smith Blvd 160, Oranjestad; tel. 5837433; fax 5838057; internet www.cbs.aw; Centrale Bank van Aruba, J. E. Irausquin Blvd 8, POB 18, Oranjestad; tel. 5252100; fax 5252101; e-mail cbaua@setarnet.aw; internet www.cbaruba.org.

AREA AND POPULATION

Area: 180 sq km (69.5 sq miles).

Population: 90,506 (males 43,434, females 47,072) at census of 14 October 2000; 107,138 (males 51,343, females 55,795) at 31 December 2009 (official estimate). *Mid-2011* (UN estimate): 108,011 (Source: UN, *World Population Prospects: The 2008 Revision*.

Density (at mid-2011): 600.1 per sq km.

Population by Age and Sex (UN estimates at mid-2011): *0–14:* 20,056 (males 10,142, females 9,914); *15–64:* 77,169 (males 36,968, females 40,201); *65 and over:* 10,786 (males 4,665, females 6,121); *Total* 108,011 (males 51,775, females 56,236). Source: UN, *World Population Prospects: The 2008 Revision*.

Principal Town (UN estimate, mid-2009): Oranjestad (capital) 33,112. Source: UN, *World Urbanization Prospects: The 2009 Revision*.

Births, Marriages and Deaths (2009 unless otherwise indicated): Live births 1,213 (birth rate 11.3 per 1,000); Marriages 832 (marriage rate 7.8 per 1,000) in 2008; Deaths 623 (death rate 5.8 per 1,000).

Life Expectancy (years at birth, 2010): 75.5 (males 72.5; females 78.6). Source: Pan American Health Organization.

Immigration and Emigration (2009): Immigration 2,833; Emigration 2,333.

Economically Active Population (persons aged 15 years and over, October 2007): Agriculture, hunting and forestry 352; Mining and quarrying 17; Manufacturing, electricity, gas and water 3,945; Construction 6,500; Wholesale and retail trade, repairs 7,283; Hotels and restaurants 8,712; Transport, storage and communications 2,832; Financial intermediation 1,905; Real estate, renting and business activities 6,811; Public administration, defence and social security 3,983; Education 1,589; Health and social work 3,177; Other community, social and personal services 3,218; Private households with employed persons 1,163; Extra-territorial organizations and bodies 33; *Sub-total* 51,520; Activities not adequately defined 87; *Total employed* 51,607; Unemployed 3,124; *Total labour force* 54,731 (males 28,629, females 26,102). Source: ILO.

HEALTH AND WELFARE

Total Fertility Rate (children per woman, 2010): 1.9.

Under-5 Mortality Rate (per 1,000 live births, 2010): 16.8.

Physicians (per 1,000 head, 2008): 1.51.

Hospital Beds (per 1,000 head, 2003): 3.2.

Health Expenditure (% of GDP, 2010): 10.0.

Total Carbon Dioxide Emissions ('000 metric tons, 2007): 2,396.3.

Carbon Dioxide Emissions Per Head (metric tons, 2007): 23.0.

Source: partly Pan American Health Organization.

For definitions, see explanatory note on p. vi.

FISHING

Total catch (metric tons, live weight, 2008): 151 (Groupers 16, Snappers and jobfishes 40, Wahoo 50, Other marine fishes 45). Source: FAO.

INDUSTRY

Electric Energy (million kWh, 2009): 924.3.

FINANCE

Currency and Exchange Rates: 100 cents = 1 Aruban gulden (guilder) or florin (A Fl.). *Sterling, Dollar and Euro Equivalents* (31 December 2010): £1 sterling = A Fl. 2.802; US $1 = A Fl. 1.790; €1 = A Fl. 2.392; A Fl. 100 = £35.69= $55.87 = €41.81. Note: the Aruban florin was introduced in January 1986, replacing (at par) the Netherlands Antilles guilder or florin (NA Fl.). Since its introduction, the currency has had a fixed exchange rate of US $1 = A Fl. 1.79.

Budget (A Fl. million, 2009, provisional): *Revenue:* Tax revenue 928.9; Non-tax revenue 180.0 (incl. grants 52.4); Total 1,108.9. *Expenditure:* Wages 315.0; Wage subsidies 153.8; Goods and services 205.2; Interest payments 116.4; Investments 41.2; Transfer to the General Health Insurance (AZV) 127.6; Total (incl. others) 1,229.2.

International Reserves (US $ million at 31 December 2009): Gold 122.9; Foreign exchange 578.2; *Total* 701.1. Source: IMF, *International Financial Statistics*.

Money Supply (A Fl. million at 31 December 2009): Currency outside banks 174.6; Demand deposits at commercial banks 1,366.1; Total money (incl. others) 1,540.7. Source: IMF, *International Financial Statistics*.

Cost of Living (Consumer Price Index; base: 2006 = 100): All items 107.9 in 2008; 115.2 in 2009; 114.4 in 2010.

Gross Domestic Product (A Fl. million at constant 2000 prices): 2,014.8 in 2007; 2,029.1 in 2008; 1,875.0 in 2009.

Expenditure on the Gross Domestic Product (A Fl. million at current prices, 2009, estimates): Final consumption expenditure 3,616; Gross capital formation 1,361; *Total domestic expenditure* 4,976; Exports of goods and services 3,051; *Less* Imports of goods and services 3,332; *GDP in purchasers' values* 4,695.

Gross Domestic Product by Economic Activity (A Fl. million at current prices, 2009): Agriculture, hunting, forestry and fishing 18; Mining and utilities 417; Manufacturing 175; Construction 324; Wholesale, retail trade, restaurants and hotels 929; Transport, storage and communications 380; Other activities 2,282; *Total gross value added* 4,526; Net taxes on products 169 (figure obtained as a residual); *GDP in purchasers' values* 4,695. Source: UN National Accounts Main Aggregates Database.

Balance of Payments (US $ million, 2009): Exports of goods f.o.b. 1,445.3; Imports of goods f.o.b. –1,919.1; *Trade balance* –473.8; Exports of services 1,600.7; Imports of services –826.1; *Balance on goods and services* 300.8; Other income received 50.0; Other income paid –118.1; *Balance on goods, services and income* 232.8; Current transfers received 69.6; Current transfers paid –145.3; *Current balance* 157.1; Capital account (net) 34.1; Direct investment abroad

−0.6; Direct investment from abroad 79.9; Portfolio investment assets −6.6; Portfolio investment liabilities 12.1; Financial derivatives assets 0.6; Financial derivatives liabilities −1.6; Other investment assets −161.5; Other investment liabilities −68.2; Net errors and omissions −11.1; *Overall balance* 34.2. Source: IMF, *International Financial Statistics*.

EXTERNAL TRADE

Principal Commodities (A Fl. million, 2009): *Imports c.i.f.:* Live animals and animal products 121.1; Food products 213.5; Chemical products 200.5; Base metals and articles thereof 103.2; Machinery and electrical equipment 409.7; Transport equipment 103.3; Total (incl. others) 1,783.1. *Exports f.o.b.:* Live animals and animal products 0.8; Machinery and electrical equipment 9.0; Transport equipment 7.5; Art objects and collectors' items 10.1; Total (incl. others) 55.1. Note: Figures exclude transactions involving mineral fuels and those of the Free Trade Zone of Aruba.

Principal Trading Partners (A Fl. million, 2009): *Imports c.i.f.:* Brazil 28.8; Colombia 33.7; Japan 31.3; Netherlands 306.6; Netherlands Antilles 43.7; Panama 58.9; USA 964.8; Venezuela 27.5; Total (incl. others) 1,783.1. *Exports f.o.b.:* Colombia 0.9; Netherlands 11.0; Netherlands Antilles 14.9; USA 14.5; Venezuela 2.1; Total (incl. others) 55.1. Note: Figures exclude transactions of the petroleum sector and those of the Free Trade Zone of Aruba.

TRANSPORT

Road Traffic (motor vehicles registered, December 2009): Passenger cars 49,255; Lorries 910; Buses 285; Taxis 365; Rental cars 3,545; Government cars 457; Motorcycles 1,638; Total (incl. others) 56,602.

Shipping: *Arrivals* (2008): 1,433 vessels. *Merchant Fleet* (vessels registered at 31 December 2009): Number of vessels 1; Total displacement 221 grt (Source: IHS Fairplay, *World Fleet Statistics*).

Civil Aviation: *Aircraft Landings:* 16,842 in 2006; 17,177 in 2007; 18,563 in 2008. *Passenger Arrivals:* 810,322 in 2006; 896,605 in 2007; 967,710 in 2008.

TOURISM

Tourist Arrivals: 1,253,848 (772,073 stop-over visitors, 481,775 cruise ship passengers) in 2007; 1,382,864 (826,774 stop-over visitors, 556,090 cruise ship passengers) in 2008; 1,419,391 (812,623 stop-over visitors, 606,768 cruise ship passengers) in 2009.

Tourism Receipts (A Fl. million): 2,242.3 in 2007; 2,522.4 in 2008; 2,314.1 in 2009.

COMMUNICATIONS MEDIA

Radio Receivers (1997): 50,000 in use.

Television Receivers (1997): 20,000 in use.

Telephones (2009): 38,300 main lines in use.

Mobile Cellular Telephones (2009): 128,000 subscribers.

Internet Users (2009): 24,000.

Broadband Subscribers (2009): 22,000.

Personal Computers: 10,000 (97.4 per 1,000 persons) in 2006.

Daily Newspapers (1996): 13 titles (estimated circulation 73,000 copies per issue).

Sources: mainly UNESCO, *Statistical Yearbook*; International Telecommunication Union; UN, *Statistical Yearbook*.

EDUCATION

Pre-primary (September 2008 unless otherwise indicated): 28 schools; 2,686 pupils (2008/09); 140 teachers.

Primary (September 2008 unless otherwise indicated): 39 schools; 9,336 pupils (2008/09); 500 teachers.

General Secondary (September 2008 unless otherwise indicated): 15 schools; 7,635 pupils (2008/09); 558 teachers.

Technical-Vocational (September 2008 unless otherwise indicated): 2 schools (2008/09); 2,013 pupils; 194 teachers.

Community College (1999/2000): 1 school; 1,187 pupils; 106 teachers.

University (September 2008): 1 university; 136 students; 18 tutors.

Teacher Training (September 2008): 1 institution; 183 students; 59 teachers.

Special Education (September 2008): 5 schools; 524 pupils; 75 teachers.

Private, Non-aided (September 2008): 7 schools; 530 pupils; 47 teachers.

International School (2000/01): 1 school; 154 pupils; 25 teachers.

Pupil-teacher Ratio (primary education, UNESCO estimate): 17.1 in 2008/09 (Source: UNESCO Institute for Statistics).

Adult Literacy Rate (UNESCO estimates, 2008): 98.1% (males 98.2%; females 98.0%) (Source: UNESCO Institute for Statistics).

Directory

The Government

HEAD OF STATE

Queen of the Netherlands: HM Queen BEATRIX.
Governor: FREDIS J. REFUNJOL (took office 7 May 2004).

COUNCIL OF MINISTERS
(May 2011)

The Government is formed by the Arubaanse Volkspartij.

Prime Minister and Minister of General Affairs: MICHIEL GODFRIED EMAN.
Minister of Integration, Infrastructure and the Environment: OSLIN BENITO SEVINGER.
Minister of Finance, Communications, Utilities and Energy: MIKE ERIC DE MEZA.
Minister of Tourism, Transport and Labour: OTMAR ENRIQUE ODUBER.
Minister of Justice and Education: ARTHUR LAWRENCE DOWERS.
Minister of the Economy, Social Affairs and Culture: MICHELLE JANICE HOOYBOER-WINKLAAR.
Minister of Public Health and Sports: RICHARD WAYNE MILTON VISSER.
Minister Plenipotentiary and Member of the Council of Ministers of the Realm for Aruba in the Netherlands: EDWIN BIBIANO ABATH.
Minister Plenipotentiary of the Realm for Aruba in Washington, DC (USA): JOCELYNE CROES.

MINISTRIES

Office of the Governor: Plaza Henny Eman 3, POB 53, Oranjestad; tel. 5834445; fax 5820730; e-mail info@kabga.aw; internet www.kabga.aw.

Office of the Prime Minister: Government Offices, L. G. Smith Blvd 76, Oranjestad; tel. 5880300; fax 5880024.

Ministry of the Economy, Social Affairs and Culture: L. G. Smith Blvd 76, Oranjestad; tel. 5885455; fax 5827526.

Ministry of Finance, Communications, Utilities and Energy: L. G. Smith Blvd 76, Oranjestad; tel. 5835455; fax 5827538.

Ministry of General Affairs: L. G. Smith Blvd 76, Oranjestad; tel. 5830001; fax 5827513; e-mail rekenkamer@aruba.gov.aw.

Ministry of Integration, Infrastructure and the Environment: L. G. Smith Blvd 76, Oranjestad; tel. 5828368; fax 5827564.

Ministry of Justice and Education: L. G. Smith Blvd 76, Oranjestad; tel. 5830004; fax 5827518.

Ministry of Public Health and Sports: L. G. Smith Blvd 76, Oranjestad; tel. 5825751; fax 5827569.

Ministry of Tourism, Transport and Labour: L. G. Smith Blvd 76, Oranjestad; tel. 5827718; fax 5827556.

Office of the Minister Plenipotentiary for Aruba in the Netherlands: R. J. Schimmelpennincklaan 1, 2517 JN The Hague, Netherlands; tel. (70) 3566200; fax (70) 3451446; e-mail info@arubahuis.nl; internet www.arubahuis.nl.

Office of the Minister Plenipotentiary for Aruba in Washington, DC: 4200 Linnean Ave, NW, Washington, DC 20008, USA; tel. (202) 274-2601; fax (202) 237-8303; e-mail was-plvcdp@minbuza.nl.

Legislature

STATEN

President: RENDOLF A. LEE.

NETHERLANDS DEPENDENCIES

General Election, 25 September 2009

Party	Seats
Arubaanse Volkspartij	12
Movimentu Electoral di Pueblo	8
Democracia Real	1
Total	**21**

Political Organizations

Arubaanse Volkspartij (AVP) (Aruba People's Party): Avda Alo Tromp 56, Oranjestad; tel. 5830911; fax 5837963; e-mail info@avparuba.net; internet www.avparuba.net; f. 1942; advocates Aruba's separate status; Leader MICHIEL GODFRIED EMAN.

Democracia Real (Real Democracy): Oranjestad; f. 2004; Leader AINDIN BIKKER.

Movimentu Electoral di Pueblo (MEP) (People's Electoral Movement): Santa Cruz 74D, Oranjestad; tel. 5854495; fax 5850768; e-mail mep@setarnet.aw; internet www.mep.aw; f. 1971; socialist; 1,200 mems; Pres. and Leader NELSON ORLANDO ODUBER.

Movimento Patriotico Arubano (MPA) (Aruban Patriotic Movement): Oranjestad; Leader MONICA KOCK ARENDS.

Organisacion Liberal Arubano (OLA) (Aruban Liberal Organization): Oranjestad; f. 1991; Leader GLENBERT FRANCOIS CROES.

Partido Patriotico di Arubà (PPA) (Patriotic Party of Aruba): Clavelstraat 5, Sint Nicolaas; tel. 5844609; e-mail nisbet@ppa-aruba.org; internet www.ppa-aruba.org; f. 1949; social democratic; opposed to complete independence for Aruba; Leader BENEDICT (BENNY) JOCELYN MONTGOMERY NISBET.

RED Democratico (RED Democratic Network): Belgiestraat 14, Oranjestad; tel. 5820213; e-mail info@red.aw; internet www.red.aw; f. 2003; Leader ARMANDO LAMPE.

Judicial System

Legal authority is exercised by the Court of First Instance. Appeals are heard by the Joint High Court of Justice of Aruba, Curaçao and St Maarten.

Attorney-General of Aruba: ROBERT PIETERSZ.

Solicitor-General of Aruba: TACO STEIN.

Courts of Justice: J. G. Emanstraat 51, Oranjestad; tel. 5822294; fax 5821241; e-mail griffiekopie@setarnet.aw.

Religion

CHRISTIANITY

The Roman Catholic Church

Roman Catholics form the largest religious community, numbering more than 80% of the population. Aruba forms part of the diocese of Willemstad, comprising Aruba and the former constituent parts of the Netherlands Antilles. The Bishop resides in Willemstad (Curaçao).

Roman Catholic Church: J. Yrausquin Plein 3, POB 445, Oranjestad; tel. 5821434; fax 5821276; e-mail parokiasanfrancisco@yahoo.com.

The Anglican Communion

Within the Church in the Province of the West Indies, Aruba forms part of the diocese of the North Eastern Caribbean and Aruba. The Bishop is resident in The Valley, Anguilla.

Anglican Church: Holy Cross, Weg Seroe Pretoe 31, Sint Nicolaas; tel. 5845142; fax 5843394; e-mail holycross@setarnet.aw.

Protestant Churches

Baptist Church: Aruba Baptist Mission, SBC, Paradera 98-C; tel. 5883893.

Church of Christ: Pastoor Hendrikstraat 107, POB 2206, Sint Nicolaas; tel. 5848172; e-mail lwaymire@setarnet.aw; Minister LARRY WAYMIRE.

Church of Jesus Christ of Latter Day Saints: Dadelstraat 16, Oranjestad; tel. 5823507.

Dutch Protestant Church: Wilhelminastraat 1, Oranjestad; tel. 5821435.

Evangelical Church of San Nicolas: Jasmijnstraat 7, Sint Nicolaas; tel. 5848973; e-mail ecsnaua@gmail.com; f. 1970.

Faith Revival Center: Rooi Afo 10, Paradera; tel. 5831010; fax 5833070; e-mail frc_aruba@yahoo.com; internet faithrevival.googlepages.com.

Iglesia Evangelica Pentecostal: Asamblea di Dios, Reamurstraat 2, Oranjestad; tel. 5831940.

Jehovah's Witnesses: Guyabastraat 3, Oranjestad; tel. 5828963.

Methodist Church: Bernhardstraat 245, Sint Nicolaas; tel. 5845243; fax 5934810; e-mail relismartinriley@yahoo.com; Supt Rev. RELIS F. MARTIN-RILEY.

New Apostolic Church: Goletstraat 5A, Oranjestad; tel. 5833762.

Pentacostal Apostolic Assembly: Bernhardstraat 185; tel. 5848710; fax 5845699.

Seventh-day Adventist: Weststraat, Oranjestad; tel. 5845896; Pastor K. LUIS.

JUDAISM

Beth Israel Synagogue: Adriaan Laclé Blvd 2, Oranjestad; tel. 5823272; fax 5823534; e-mail jcommaruba@gmail.com; internet bethisrael-aruba.blogspot.com; Rabbi MARIO GUREVICH.

BAHÁ'Í FAITH

Spiritual Assembly: Bucutiweg 19, Oranjestad; tel. 5823104; Contact M. CHRISTIAN.

The Press

DAILIES

Amigoe di Aruba: Bilderdijkstraat 16-2, POB 323, Oranjestad; tel. 5824333; fax 5822368; e-mail amigoearuba@setarnet.aw; internet www.amigoe.com; f. 1884; Dutch; Dir WILLEM DA COSTA GOMEZ; Editor JEAN MENTENS; circ. 12,000.

Aruba Today: Weststraat 22, Oranjestad; tel. 5827800; fax 5827093; e-mail info@arubatoday.com; internet www.arubatoday.com; English; Editor-in-Chief JULIA C. RENFRO.

Bon Dia Aruba: Weststraat 22, Oranjestad; tel. 5827800; fax 5827044; e-mail infor@bondia.com; internet www.bondia.com; Papiamento; Dirs JOHN CHEMALY, JOHN CHEMALY, Jr.

Diario: Engelandstraat 29, POB 577, Oranjestad; tel. 5826747; fax 5828551; e-mail noticia@diarioaruba.com; internet www.diarioaruba.com; f. 1980; Papiamento; morning; Editor and Man. JOSSY M. MANSUR; circ. 15,000.

The News: Italiestraat 5, POB 300, Oranjestad; tel. 5824725; fax 5889430; e-mail thenewsaruba@setarnet.aw; f. 1951; English; Dir SONIA WEVER-SCHOUTEN; Editor-in-Chief MARGARET BONARRIVA-WEVER; circ. 6,900.

La Prensa: Bachstraat 6, POB 566, Oranjestad; tel. 5821199; fax 5828634; e-mail laprensa@laprensacur.com; internet www.laprensacur.com; f. 1929; Papiamento; Editor THOMAS C. PIETERSZ.

NEWS AGENCIES

Algemeen Nederlands Persbureau (ANP) (The Netherlands): Caya G. F. (Betico) Croes 110, POB 323, Oranjestad; tel. 5824333; fax 5822368; internet www.anp.nl.

Aruba News Agencies: Bachstraat 6, Oranjestad; tel. 5821243.

Publishers

Aruba Experience Publications NV: Verbindingsweg 2, POB 634, Oranjestad; tel. 5834467; fax 5384520; e-mail info@arubaexperience.com; internet www.arubaexperience.com; f. 1985; Gen. Man. FRANCO SNEEK.

Caribbean Publishing Co Ltd (CPC): L. G. Smith Blvd 116, Oranjestad; tel. 5820485; fax 5820484.

De Wit Stores NV: L. G. Smith Blvd 110, POB 386, Oranjestad; tel. 5823500; fax 5821575; e-mail info@dewitvandorp.com; f. 1948; Gen. Man. LYANNE BEAUJON.

Editorial Charuba: Lagoenweg 31, Oranjestad; tel. 7301512; fax 5884574; e-mail alivaro@hotmail.com; f. 1982; Pres. ALICE VAN ROMONDT.

Gold Book Publishing: L. G. Smith Blvd 116, Oranjestad; tel. 5820485; fax 5820484; internet www.caribbeanhotelassociation.com; a division of the Caribbean Hotel and Tourism Asscn, based in Miami, FL, USA; Chair. WARREN BINDER.

Oranjestad Printing NV: Italiestraat 5, POB 300, Oranjestad; Man. Dir GERARDUS J. SCHOUTEN.

ProGraphics Inc: Italiestraat 5, POB 201, Oranjestad; tel. 5824550; fax 5833072; e-mail prographics@setarnet.aw; f. 2001; fmrly VAD Printers Inc; Publr H. VAN DER PUTTEN.

Aruba

Van Dorp Aruba NV: Caya G. F. (Betico) Croes 77, POB 596, Oranjestad; tel. 5823076; fax 5823573.

Broadcasting and Communications

TELECOMMUNICATIONS

Digicel Aruba: Marisol Bldg, L. G. Smith Blvd 60, POB 662, Oranjestad; tel. 5222222; fax 5222223; e-mail customercarearuba@digicelgroup.com; internet www.digicelaruba.com; f. 2003; owned by an Irish consortium; established a mobile cellular telephone network connecting Aruba with Bonaire and Curaçao in July 2006; Chair. DENIS O'BRIEN; CEO (Dutch Caribbean) HANS LUTE; Gen. Man. (Aruba) BERT SCHREUDERS.

Servicio di Telecomunicacion di Aruba NV (SETAR): Seroe Blanco z/n, POB 13, Oranjestad; tel. 5251000; fax 5251515; e-mail sysop@setarnet.aw; internet www.setar.aw; f. 1986; Man. Dir ROLAND CROES.

BROADCASTING

Radio

Canal 90 FM Stereo: Van Leeuwenhoekstraat 26, Oranjestad; tel. 5828952; fax 837340; e-mail info@canal90fm.aw; internet www.canal90fm.aw/index2.htm; Producer M. GRAVENHORST.

Cristal Sound 101.7 FM: J. G. Emanstraat 124A, Oranjestad; tel. 5820017; fax 5820144.

Hit 94 FM: Caya Ernesto Petronia 68, Oranjestad; tel. 5820694; fax 5820494; e-mail hit94@setarnet.aw; internet www.hit94fm.com; f. 1993; Dir JOHNNY HABIBE.

Magic 96.5 FM: Caya G.F. Betico Croes 164, Oranjestad; tel. 5865353; fax 5835354; internet www.magic965.com; Owner and Dir ERIN J. CROES; Producer RUBEN GARCIA.

Radio 1270 AM: Bernardstraat 138, POB 28, Sint Nicolaas; tel. 5845602; fax 5827753; commercial station; programmes in Dutch, English, Spanish and Papiamento; Dir F. A. LEAUER; Station Man. J. A. C. ALDERS.

Radio Carina FM: Datustraat 10A, Oranjestad; tel. 5821450; fax 5831955; commercial station; programmes in Dutch, English, Spanish and Papiamento; Dir-Gen. ALBERT R. DIEFFENTHALER.

Radio Caruso Booy FM: G. M. de Bruynewijk 49, Savaneta; tel. 5847752; fax 5843351; e-mail sira@setarnet.aw; commercial station; broadcasts for 24 hrs a day; programmes in Dutch, English, Spanish and Papiamento; Pres. HUBERT ERQUILLES ANTONIO BOOY; Gen. Man. SIRA BOOY.

Radio Kelkboom: Bloemond 14, POB 146, Oranjestad; tel. 5821899; fax 5834825; e-mail radiokelkboom@setarnet.aw; internet www.watapana-aruba.com; f. 1954; commercial radio station; affiliated with Radio Nederland Wereldomroep (Netherlands) and Voice of America (USA); programmes in Papiamento, Dutch, English and Spanish; Man. Dir EMILE A. M. KELKBOOM.

Radio Victoria: Washington 23A, POB 5291, Oranjestad; tel. and fax 5873444; e-mail radiovictoria@setarnet.aw; internet www.radiovictoriaaruba.org; f. 1958; religious and cultural FM radio station owned by the Radio Victoria Foundation; programmes in Dutch, English, Spanish, Papiamento, Dutch, Tagalog, Creole and Mandarin; Pres. N. J. F. ARTS.

Voz di Aruba (Voice of Aruba): Van Leeuwenhoekstraat 26, POB 219, Oranjestad; tel. 5823355; fax 5837340; commercial radio station; programmes in Dutch, English, Spanish and Papiamento; also operates Canal 90 on FM; Dir A. M. ARENDS, Jr.

Television

ABC Aruba Broadcasting Co NV (ATV): Royal Plaza Suite 223, POB 5040, Oranjestad; tel. 5838150; fax 5838110; e-mail 15atv@setarnet.aw.

Telearuba NV: Pos Chiquito 1A, POB 392, Oranjestad; tel. 5851000; fax 5851111; e-mail info@telearuba.aw; internet www.telearuba.aw; f. 1963; fmrly operated by Netherlands Antilles Television Co; commercial; acquired by SETAR in March 2005; Gen. Man. M. MARCHENA.

Finance

(cap. = capital; res = reserves; dep. = deposits; m. = million; brs = branches; amounts in Aruban florin, unless otherwise stated)

BANKING

Central Bank

Centrale Bank van Aruba: J. E. Irausquin Blvd 8, POB 18, Oranjestad; tel. 5252100; fax 5252101; e-mail cbaua@setarnet.aw; internet www.cbaruba.org; f. 1986; cap. 10.0m., res 224.9m., dep. 814.2m. (Dec. 2008); Chair. C. G. MADURO; Pres. JANE R. FIGAROA-SEMELEER.

Commercial Banks

Aruba Bank NV: Camacuri 12, POB 192, Oranjestad; tel. 5277777; fax 5277715; e-mail info@arubabank.com; internet www.arubabank.com; f. 1925; acquired Interbank Aruba NV in Dec. 2003; total assets US $260m. (Dec. 2004); Chair. B. W. H. GUIS; Man. Dir and CEO EDWIN TROMP; 5 brs.

Banco di Caribe NV: Vondellaan 31, POB 493, Oranjestad; tel. 5232000; fax 5832422; e-mail bdcaua@setarnet.aw; internet www.bancodicaribe.com; f. 1987; Gen. Man. and CEO IDEFONS D. SIMON; Man. (Aruba) EDUARDO DE KORT; 1 br.

Caribbean Mercantile Bank Aruba: Caya G. F. (Betico) Croes 53, POB 28, Oranjestad; tel. 5823118; fax 5830919; e-mail executive_office@cmbnv.com; internet www.cmbnv.com; f. 1963; cap. 4.0m., res 109.6m., dep. 1,110.8m. (Dec. 2008); Chair. LIONEL CAPRILES, II; Gen. Man. Dir J. E. WOLTER; 6 brs.

RBTT Bank Aruba NV: Italiestraat 36, Sasakiweg, Oranjestad; tel. 5233100; fax 58821576; e-mail info@tt.rbtt.com; internet www.rbtt.com; f. 2001; fmrly First National Bank of Aruba NV (f. 1985 and acquired by Royal Bank of Trinidad and Tobago Ltd in 1998); total assets US $111.5m. (Dec. 2003); Chair. PETER J. JULY; 6 brs.

Investment Bank

AIB Bank NV: Wilhelminastraat 34–36, POB 1011, Oranjestad; tel. 5827327; fax 5827461; e-mail info@aib-bank.com; internet www.aib-bank.com; f. 1987 as Aruban Investment Bank; name changed as above in April 2004; total assets 149.0m. (Dec. 2005); Man. Dir FRENDSEL W. GIEL; Asst Man. Dir HERRY M. KOOLMAN.

Mortgage Bank

Fundacion Cas pa Comunidad Arubano (FCCA): Sabana Blanco 66, Oranjestad; tel. 5238800; fax 5836272; e-mail info@fcca.com; internet www.fcca.com; f. 1979; Man. Dir PETER VAN POPPEL.

INSURANCE

There were eight life insurance companies and 13 non-life insurance companies active in Aruba in December 2007.

Association

Insurance Association of Aruba (IAA): Sun Plaza 202, Oranjestad; tel. 5825500; fax 5822126; e-mail prakash.gupta@aig.com; Pres. PRAKASH GUPTA; 17 mems.

Trade and Industry

DEVELOPMENT ORGANIZATIONS

Department of Agriculture, Husbandry and Fisheries: Piedra Plat 114A, Oranjestad; tel. 5858102; fax 5855639; e-mail dlvv@aruba.gov.aw; internet www.overheid.aw; f. 1976; Dir T. G. DAMIAN.

Department of Economic Affairs, Commerce and Industry (Directie Economische Zaken, Handel en Industrie): Sun Plaza Bldg, L. G. Smith Blvd 160, Oranjestad; tel. 5821181; fax 5834494; e-mail deaci@setarnet.aw; internet www.arubaeconomicaffairs.aw; f. 1986; Dir MARIA DIJKHOFF-PITA.

CHAMBER OF COMMERCE AND INDUSTRY

Chamber of Commerce and Industry Aruba: J. E. Irausquin Blvd 10, POB 140, Oranjestad; tel. 5821120; fax 5883200; e-mail secretariat@arubachamber.com; internet www.arubachamber.com; f. 1930; Pres. EDWIN A. ROOS; Exec. Dir LORRAINE C. DE SOUZA.

TRADE ASSOCIATION

Aruba Trade and Industry Association (ATIA): ATIA Bldg, Pedro Gallegostraat 6, Dakota, POB 562, Oranjestad; tel. 5827593; fax 5833068; e-mail atiaruba@setarnet.aw; internet www.atiaruba.org; f. 1945; Pres. STEPHEN DAAL; Chair. and Sec. FRANK SNIJDERS; 250 mems.

UTILITIES

Electricity and Water

Utilities Aruba NV: Arulex Center, Punta Brabo z/n; tel. 5828277; fax 5828682; e-mail utilities.aruba.hhenriquez@gmail.com; govt-owned holding co; Man. Dir HAROLD HENRIQUEZ.

Electriciteit-Maatschappij Aruba (ELMAR) NV: Wilhelminastraat 110, POB 202, Oranjestad; tel. 5237100; fax 5828991; e-mail info@elmar.aw; internet www.elmar.aw; independently managed co, residing under Utilities Aruba NV; electricity distribution; Man. Dir A. O. RAFINÉ; 160 employees.

Water en Energiebedrijf Aruba (WEB) NV: Balashi 76, POB 575, Oranjestad; tel. 5254600; fax 5857681; e-mail info@webaruba.com; internet www.webaruba.com; f. 1991; independently managed co, residing under Utilities Aruba NV; production and distribution of industrial and potable water, and electricity generation; Man. Dir JOSSY M. LACLÉ.

Gas

Aruba Gas Supply Company Ltd (ARUGAS): Barcadera z/n, POB 190, Oranjestad; tel. 5851198; fax 5852187; e-mail webmaster@arugas.com; internet www.arugas.com; f. 1940.

BOC Gases Aruba NV: Balashi z/n, POB 387, Oranjestad; tel. 5852624; fax 5852823; e-mail bocaruba@setarnet.aw; internet www.boc-gases.com; acquired by the Linde Group global industrial gases and engineering org. in 2006; Man. Dir J. KENT MASTERS (responsible for Americas, South Pacific and Africa).

TRADE UNIONS

Federacion di Trahadornan di Aruba (FTA) (Aruban Workers' Federation): Bernhardstraat 23, Sint Nicolaas; tel. 5845448; fax 5845504; e-mail fetraua@setarnet.aw; f. 1964; independent; affiliated with the International Trade Union Confederation; Pres. JOSÉ RUDOLF (RUDY) GEERMAN; Vice-Pres. JANE ANASTACIA BRAAFHART.

There are also several unions for government and semi-government workers and employees.

Transport

There are no railways, but Aruba has a network of all-weather roads.

Arubus NV: Sabana Blanco 67, Oranjestad; tel. 5882300; fax 5828633; e-mail info@arubus.com; internet www.arubus.com; f. 1979; state-owned company providing public transport services; runs a fleet of 48 buses; Dir FRANKLIN KUIPERI.

SHIPPING

The island's principal seaport is Oranjestad, whose harbour can accommodate ocean-going vessels. There are also ports at Barcadera and Sint Nicolaas.

Aruba Ports Authority NV: Port Administration Bldg, L. G. Smith Blvd 23, Oranjestad; tel. 5826633; fax 5832896; e-mail info@arubaports.com; internet www.arubaports.com; f. 1981; responsible for the administration of the ports of Oranjestad and Barcadera; Man. Dir JUAN ALFONSO BOEKHOUDT.

Valero Aruba Refining Co NV: Lagoweg 5, POB 2150, Sint Nicolaas; tel. 5894904; fax 5849087; internet www.valero.com; f. 1989; acquired by Valero in 2004; petroleum refinery, responsible for the administration of the port of Sint Nicolaas; closed in Sept. 2009; negotiations to sell refinery ongoing in mid-2010; Gen. Man. RAYMOND A. BUCKLEY.

Principal Shipping Companies

Aruba Stevedoring Co (ASTEC), NV: Port Administration Bldg, L. G. Smith Blvd 23, Oranjestad; tel. 5822558; fax 5834570; e-mail astec_admin@setarnet.aw.

SEL Maduro & Sons (Aruba) Inc: Rockefellerstraat 1, Oranjestad; tel. 5282343; fax 5826003; internet www.selmaduro.com; ship husbandry and port agent; also provides container services, cargo services, moving services, real estate and travel services; Man. Dir HANS VAN ESVELD; Man. GRACEO DUNLOCK (Shipping and Container Services).

Valero Aruba Marine Services: Lagoweg, POB 2150, Sint Nicolaas; tel. 5894742; fax 5894554.

VR Shipping NV: Executive Bldg, Frankrijkstraat 1, POB 633, Oranjestad; tel. 5821953; fax 5825988; e-mail info@vrshipping.com; internet www.vrshipping.com; f. 1975 as Anthony Veder & Co; name changed as above 2000.

CIVIL AVIATION

The Queen Beatrix International Airport (Aeropuerto Internacional Reina Beatrix), about 2.5 km from Oranjestad, is served by numerous airlines (including Dutch Antilles Express, based in Curaçao), linking the island with destinations in the Caribbean, Europe, the USA, and Central and South America. The airport handles an estimated 2.2m. passengers per year. In 2000 the national carrier, Air Aruba, was declared bankrupt.

Aruba Airport Authority NV: Queen Beatrix International Airport, Wayaca z/n, Oranjestad; tel. 5242424; fax 5834229; e-mail p.steinmetz@airportaruba.com; internet www.airportaruba.com; Man. Dir PETER STEINMETZ.

Tiara Air: Sabana Blanco 70E, Suite 11, Oranjestad; tel. 5884272; fax 5885002; e-mail sales@tiara-air.com; internet www.tiara-air.com; Pres. ALEJANDRO MUYALE.

Tourism

Aruba's white sandy beaches, particularly along the southern coast, are an attraction for foreign visitors, and tourism is a major industry. The number of hotel rooms totalled 7,441 in 2009. In 2010 some 1,394,875 tourists visited Aruba, of which 825,451 were stop-over visitors and 569,424 were cruise ship passengers. Most stop-over visitors came from the USA (65% in 2010), Venezuela (11%) and the Netherlands (5.0%). Receipts from tourism totalled A Fl. 2,212.0m. in 2010.

Aruba Cruise Tourism: Suite 230, Royal Plaza Mall, L. G. Smith Blvd 94, POB 5254, Oranjestad; tel. 5833648; fax 5835088; e-mail info@arubabycruise.com; internet www.arubabycruise.com; f. 1995 as the Cruise Tourism Authority—Aruba; name changed as above in 2005; non-profit government organization; Exec. Dir KATHLEEN ROJER.

Aruba Hotel and Tourism Association (AHATA): L. G. Smith Blvd 174, POB 542, Oranjestad; tel. 5822607; fax 5824202; e-mail info@ahata.com; internet www.ahata.com; f. 1965; 101 mems; Pres. and CEO JAMES HEPPLE; Chair. EWALD BIEMANS.

Aruba Tourism Authority (ATA): L. G. Smith Blvd 172, Eagle, Oranjestad; tel. 5823777; fax 5834702; e-mail ata.aruba@aruba.com; internet www.aruba.com; f. 1953; Man. Dir MYRNA JANSEN-FELICIANO.

Defence

The Netherlands is responsible for Aruba's defence, and military service is compulsory. The Dutch-appointed Governor is Commander-in-Chief of the armed forces on the island. A Dutch naval contingent is stationed in Curaçao and Aruba. In May 1999 the USA began air force and navy patrols from a base on Aruba as part of efforts to prevent the transport of illegal drugs.

Education

A Compulsory Education Act was introduced in 1999 for those aged between four and 16. Kindergarten begins at four years of age. Primary education begins at six years of age and lasts for six years. Secondary education, beginning at the age of 12, lasts for up to six years. In 2007/08 enrolment at primary schools included 99% of pupils in the relevant age-group, while the comparable ratio at secondary schools was 75%. The main language of instruction is Dutch, but Papiamento (using a different spelling system from that of Bonaire and Curaçao) is used in kindergarten and primary education and in the lower levels of technical and vocational education. Papiamento is also being introduced into the curriculum in all schools. Aruba has two institutes of higher education: the University of Aruba, comprising the School of Law and the School of Business Administration, and the Teachers' College. There is also a community college. However, the majority of students continue their studies abroad, generally in the Netherlands. General government expenditure on education in 2008 amounted to A Fl. 308.3m., equivalent to 17.5% of total expenditure.

CURAÇAO

Introductory Survey

LOCATION, CLIMATE, LANGUAGE, RELIGION, FLAG, CAPITAL

Curaçao, a dependency of the Netherlands, lies about 55 km (34 miles) off the coast of Venezuela in the Caribbean Sea. Together with Aruba and Bonaire, the island forms the Benedenwindse Eilands or Leeward Islands. The climate is tropical, moderated by the sea, with an average annual temperature of 27.5°C (81°F) and little rainfall. The official languages are Dutch and Papiamento (a mixture of Dutch, Spanish, Portuguese, English, Arawak Indian and several West African dialects). Almost all of the inhabitants profess Christianity, predominantly Roman Catholicism. The state flag (proportions 2 by 3) is blue, with a yellow horizontal stripe just below the midline and two white, five-pointed stars in the canton. The capital is Willemstad.

Until October 2010 Curaçao formed part of the Netherlands Antilles, with Bonaire, Sint (St) Maarten, Saba and Sint (St) Eustatius. On 10 October 2010 the Netherlands Antilles was formally dissolved as a federation and Curaçao assumed the new status of an autonomous country within the Kingdom of the Netherlands.

CONTEMPORARY POLITICAL HISTORY

Historical Context

The Leeward Islands, already settled by communities of Arawak Indians, were discovered by the Spanish in 1499 and were seized by the Dutch in the 1630s. Curaçao became prosperous in the late 17th and 18th centuries as an entrepôt for trade in the Caribbean. After frequent changes in possession, the Leeward Islands were finally confirmed as a Dutch territory in 1816. The islands (including Aruba and the Windward Islands—comprising St Eustatius, Saba and St Maarten) were administered as Curaçao and Dependencies between 1845 and 1948. Slavery was abolished in 1863, and the islands suffered from an economic decline until the establishment of a petroleum refinery on Curaçao in 1918. During the Second World War Queen Wilhelmina of the Netherlands promised independence, and in 1954 a Charter gave the federation of six islands full autonomy in domestic affairs, and declared it to be an integral part of the Kingdom of the Netherlands.

Domestic Political Affairs

Divisions of political allegience within the Netherlands Antilles were along island, rather than policy, lines, and Curaçao traditionally dominated administrative affairs. Following Aruba's secession from the federation to assume *status aparte* (separate status) within the Kingdom in 1986, the Antilles of the Five was ruled by a series of unstable coalition Governments. By the early 1990s the 'metropolitan' Government in the Netherlands indicated it was willing to consider the creation of two federations in separate island groups. A referendum was held on Curaçao in November 1993 regarding its constitutional status; 74% of the electorate voted for a continuance of the island's status as a member of the Antillean federation. The option of *status aparte*, favoured by the Government, received only 18% of the votes cast. As a result of this defeat, the Government collapsed. A general election took place in February 1994, at which a new, Curaçao-based party, the Partido Antía Restrukturá (PAR), led by Miguel A. Pourier, became the largest single party in the Staten. Pourier assumed the leadership of a broadly based coalition Government, which was inaugurated in March.

The PAR lost four of its eight seats in the Staten at a general election in January 1998 and Pourier lacked the support needed to form a new administration. Dissatisfaction with the new Government's attempts to reduce the fiscal deficit in October 1999 led to its collapse and that of the island Government of Curaçao. In the following month former Prime Minister Pourier formed a new broad-based coalition Government, which had the support of 18 of the 22 members of the Staten. The general election of 18 January 2002 was won by the Curaçao-based Frente Obrero i Liberashon 30 di mei (FOL), led by Anthony Godett, which had campaigned against the stringent measures imposed by the IMF. However, the FOL was unable to form a government because of allegations of corruption and mismanagement of funds by party leaders. Eventually, in June, a coalition Government under the leadership of the new PAR leader, Etienne Ys, replaced Pourier's caretaker administration.

The Ys Government ruled until April 2003, when the cabinet resigned to allow a fresh governing coalition. Ys was eventually replaced by Mirna Luisa Godett, the sister of Anthony, in August, who formed a FOL-dominated coalition. The dominance of the FOL heralded a deterioration of the island's political relationship with the Netherlands, which had improved under the PAR leadership. The new Prime Minister immediately announced that a delegation of Dutch MPs would not be officially received when they visited the territory. Godett's administration further alienated the Dutch Government by its support of a proposal to remove a body scanner at Curaçao's international airport, which had been installed in an attempt to combat the increasing drugs trade between the Netherlands and the Caribbean. Relations continued to worsen, and in January 2004 Godett accused Dutch officials of spying on her Government after it emerged that local justice officials had met two visiting Dutch ministers without her knowledge. Prime Minister Godett was forced to resign in April 2004 amid allegations of corruption among FOL members. The next federal Government was formed by a seven-party coalition, once again led by Ys.

In October 2004 the Jesurun Commission, established by the Dutch and Antillean Governments and headed by Edsel Jesurun (a former Governor of the territory), recommended the dissolution of the Netherlands Antilles; support for the federation had, it was argued, virtually disintegrated on most of the islands. The Commission proposed that Curaçao and St Maarten should become autonomous states within the Netherlands (i.e. have *status aparte*). A further referendums on the constitutional future of Curaçao took place on 8 April 2005: 68% of participants in Curaçao favoured *status aparte*, in line with the recommendations of the Commission, 23% voted for closer ties with the Netherlands and 5% voted for complete independence—there was a 54% voter turn-out. On 3 December 2005 a preliminary agreement with the Dutch Government that the extant federation be dissolved by 1 July 2007 was duly signed in Curaçao. Under the new structure, Curaçao was, as expected, to become an autonomous member of the Kingdom of the Netherlands.

On 2 November 2006 the Dutch Government granted Curaçao independent governance within the Kingdom of the Netherlands; endorsement of this latter agreement was contingent upon the island ceding authority for the administration of defence, foreign policy and law enforcement matters to the Dutch Government. However, on 28 November, Curaçao's Island Council voted by a decisive 13–6 majority against the accord, averring that further negotiations were required in order to safeguard the interests of the island's citizens, specifically over the administration of justice (over which they regarded the Dutch Government as having too great an influence). Particular concern had been expressed by the detractors with regard to stipulations for the management of the islands' respective budgets—entailing submission to a joint central bank—and the supervision of their judicial and police departments by the Dutch Government; furthermore, potential deficiencies had been identified within the Dutch system regarding the regulation of political practices, freedom of expression, the synthesis of European Union (EU, see p. 270) directives with national democratic tenets, and the integration of foreign nationals into Dutch society. Representatives of the PAR and conservative Partido Nashonal di Pueblo (PNP), who had voted in favour of the final agreement, left the Island Council in protest at the decision. Their departure left Curaçao without a legitimate government. Furthermore, in January 2007 the Netherlands Government rejected the island's request for a renegotiation of the 2 November accord. Curaçao's abstention was regarded as having jeopardized certain provisions of the agreement that were dependent upon all five islands becoming signatories and provoked polarized responses from the island's people. The urgency of addressing Curaçao's already burdensome public debt, estimated as constituting approximately one-half of the entire federation's total obligation, was rendered more acute in light of the fact that the island would no longer benefit from the debt relief awarded by the Netherlands to signatories of the 2 November agreement.

Curaçao was also conspicuously absent from the provisions of a further 'transition accord' signed by the Netherlands Antilles central Government and the other four Island Councils on 12 February 2007, envisaging the islands' complete secession from the federation. Under the terms of this covenant, the Netherlands was to pledge over NA Fl. 1,000m. (in addition to existing financial assistance) to facilitate the process of disintegration; of this sum, NA Fl. 224m. was designated specifically for debt relief, while the remaining funds were to be disseminated through social and economic development programmes and budgetary aid, with each of the four participating islands receiving individual allocations. Curaçao's exclusion from the restructured Netherlands Antilles precipitated serious concerns for the island's pursuit of autonomy and its future status and relations with the Dutch Government, and, consequently, on 9 July the Curaçao Island Council signed the November accord's 'closing statement', although its late accession to the arrangement precluded the island from the Netherlands Government's debt-restructuring provisions. Opposition-led protests took place in late 2007 in Curaçao in response to the continuing constitutional negotiations with the Dutch Government. The demonstrators objected to the Dutch Government having the power to intervene in the island's future financial and legal affairs. One week later the Island Council formally ratified the results of the 2005 referendum: at a second peaceful demonstration held in December and attended by several thousand people, opposition parties demanded an end to the negotiations and for the Government to seek to achieve the autonomous status of Curaçao, in accordance with the results of the ballot.

A round table conference was held in Curaçao's capital, Willemstad, on 14–16 December 2008, at which it was established that Curaçao (and St Maarten) would gain autonomy, while the other three islands would become Dutch municipalities. Agreement was reached on the extent of the administrative powers of the Netherlands Government within the two seceding territories. In return for retaining some legal and financial controls over Curaçao and St Maarten, the Netherlands agreed to write off almost three-quarters of the Antilles' debt, beginning in 2009. The agreement was narrowly endorsed, by 52% of participants, in a referendum in Curaçao on 15 May 2009.

Recent developments: towards autonomy

At the end of September 2009, at a meeting of the Dutch State Secretary for the Interior and Kingdom Relations, Ank Bijleveld-Schouten, and representatives of the Netherlands Antilles, Curaçao and St Maarten, it was agreed that the target date for dissolution of the Netherlands Antilles would be 10 October 2010. Prior to securing autonomy, Curaçao (and St Maarten) would be required to introduce an appropriate legislative framework and to prepare their public authorities for the additional tasks entailed in administering an independent state. If the two islands failed to meet the criteria for becoming independent countries within the Kingdom, a strategic plan to implement necessary changes would be devised, with developments to be monitored by a progress committee.

An election to Curaçao's new designated legislature, the Estates of Curaçao, was held on 27 August 2010. The PAR won eight of the 21 seats, followed by the newly formed Movementu Futuro Korsou (MFK), led by Gerrit Schotte, which gained five seats, and the Pueblo Soberano with four seats. The Movimentu Antiyas Nobo (MAN) garnered two seats while the FOL and the PNP each secured one seat each. The MFK subsequently formed a coalition with the Pueblo Soberano and the MAN and on 10 October Schotte was sworn in as Curaçao's first Prime Minister. On the same day Fritz Goedgedrag took office as the autonomous territory's Governor.

CONSTITUTION AND GOVERNMENT

The Constitution of Curaçao was approved by the Island Council in September 2010 and came into effect on 10 October 2010. The Governor of Curaçao, appointed by the Dutch Government for a term of six years, represents the monarch of the Netherlands in the territory. The Governor is assisted by an advisory council. Executive power in internal affairs is invested in the Council of Ministers. The Council of Ministers is responsible to the Estates of Curaçao, the 21-seat parliament, elected by universal adult suffrage.

ECONOMIC AFFAIRS

In 2009 the gross national income (GNI) of the Netherlands Antilles, measured at current prices, was an estimated US $4,032m., equivalent to some $20,341 per head. Gross domestic product (GDP) was some $4,022m. in 2009 (equivalent to $20,295 per head), according to UN estimates. In 2000–09 the population increased at an average annual rate of 1.0%, while GDP per head increased, in real terms, by an average of 2.8% per year. According to UN estimates, the GDP of the Netherlands Antilles increased, in real terms, at an average annual rate of 1.6% in 2000–09; real GDP increased by 2.1% in 2008, but fell by 0.2% in 2009.

Agriculture, together with forestry, fishing and mining, contributed only 0.7% of GDP in the Netherlands Antilles in 2009, according to UN estimates. The sector employed an average of 1.2% of the working population on Curaçao in 2007–09. Some 8% of the total land area is cultivated. The chief products are sorghum, divi-divi, groundnuts, beans, fresh vegetables and tropical fruit. A bitter variety of orange is used in the production of Curaçao liqueur. There is also some fishing.

Industry (comprising manufacturing, construction, utilities and mining) contributed 16.2% of GDP in the Netherlands Antilles in 2009, according to UN estimates, and employed an average of 18.3% of the working population on Curaçao in 2007–09.

The mining and quarrying sector employed only 0.3% of the working population on Curaçao in 2000. Curaçao has few significant mineral reserves.

Manufacturing contributed 6.4% of GDP in the Netherlands Antilles in 2009, according to UN estimates, and employed an average of 6.9% of the working population on Curaçao in 2007–09; activities include food-processing, production of Curaçao liqueur, and the manufacture of paint, paper, soap and cigarettes. Curaçao's free trade zone is of considerable importance in the economy, but there are very few manufacturing activities. Petroleum-refining (using petroleum imported from Venezuela) is the principal industrial activity, with the Curaçao refinery leased to the Venezuelan state petroleum company. Production capacity at the refinery was 116.8m. barrels per year in 2001, according to the US Geological Survey. In March 2010 the Venezuelan Government threatened to halt operations at the refinery in connection with its earlier allegations (denied by the Dutch Government) that the US military was being permitted to use airbases on Curaçao (and Aruba) to launch reconnaissance flights over Venezuelan territory. Petroleum trans-shipment is also important, and ship repairs at the Curaçao dry dock make a significant contribution to the economy. In 2002 petroleum imports comprised 68.4% of total merchandise imports in the Netherlands Antilles.

Construction contributed 5.7% of GDP in the Netherlands Antilles in 2009, according to UN estimates, and employed an average of 8.7% of the working population on Curaçao in 2007–09.

The services sector contributed 83.1% of GDP in 2009, according to UN estimates, and engaged an average of 81.7% of the employed labour force on Curaçao in 2007–09. The Netherlands Antilles was a major 'offshore' financial centre. In 2002, after improving the accountability and transparency of its financial services, the Netherlands Antilles was removed from the Organisation for Economic Co-operation and Development's (OECD, based in Paris, France) list of those countries deemed to be 'unco-operative tax havens'. Nevertheless, in April 2009 the Netherlands Antilles was included on OECD's so-called 'grey list' of territories that had committed to improving financial transparency, but had yet substantially to implement reform. In response, the Government increased efforts to conclude bilateral agreements on the exchange of tax information, signing 14 such accords in the second half of the year and thus securing the territory's removal from the 'grey list'. The financial and business services sector contributed 31.6% of GDP in the Netherlands Antilles in 2004, and employed an average of 17.9% of the Curaçao working population in 2006–08. Operational income from the 'offshore' sector increased significantly from the 1990s. A major industry is tourism, which is the largest employer after the public sector. The number of stop-over tourists generally increased steadily between 2003 and 2008 (with the exception of a modest decline in 2005), while the number of cruise ship passengers rose in every year from 2001–08. In addition to tourism, Curaçao has sought to establish itself as a centre for regional trade, exploiting its excellent harbours. In 1998 a free trade zone was established at the island's airport, which further enhanced Curaçao's entrepôt status.

In 2009 the Netherlands Antilles recorded a visible trade deficit of US $1,796.9m., and there was a deficit of $827.4m. on the current account of the balance of payments. The petroleum industry dominated the trade figures of the Netherlands Antilles, particularly of the Leeward Islands. In 2008 the principal source of imports (39.4%) was the USA and the principal market for exports (34.2%) was the Netherlands. Panama, Venezuela, Japan and other Caribbean countries were also important trading partners. Petroleum is the principal commodity for both import and export and, according to unofficial figures compiled from partner countries, accounted for 45.9% of imports and 66.0% of exports in 2009.

In 2009 the central Government of the Netherlands Antilles recorded a budgetary surplus of NA Fl. 364.5m., which was equivalent to 5.1% of GDP. At the end of 2008 total domestic debt amounted to NA Fl. 4,998.1m. (70.6% of GDP), while total foreign debt stood at NA Fl. 805.2m. (11.4% of GDP). The average annual rate of inflation was 2.5% in 2000–09; consumer prices increased by an average of 1.7% in 2009. According to a sample survey of the labour force, 9.7% of the Curaçao work-force were unemployed in 2007–09.

The relative isolation of the individual islands of the Netherlands Antilles led to the development of semi-independent economies, and economic conditions vary considerably between them. However, recent years have witnessed a progressive weakening of the economy, leading to a prolonged recession, high unemployment and increasing rates of emigration. Following stringent measures announced by the Government in 2001, the Dutch Government released NA Fl. 153m. to encourage sustained economic development; the release of a further €125m. was approved in 2003. Growth in activity in Curaçao's free trade zone and a consequent increase in arrivals from Venezuela and the Dominican Republic also provided an important boost for the tourism and retail sectors. In 2008 stop-over visitors to Curaçao from Venezuela increased by 137%. However, because of the favourable fixed exchange rate and a limit to how much US currency Venezuelans can buy, many Venezuelan visitors travel to Curaçao in order to purchase dollars, which they then sell on the 'black market' at an inflated exchange rate. The lowering of Venezuelans' travel allowances was expected negatively to affect the Netherlands Antilles tourism sector, as was the recession in the USA. Under the agreement to dissolve the Netherlands Antilles (see Domestic Political Affairs), in 2009 the Dutch Government began to restructure some 70% of the islands' public debt, a large proportion of which was owed to the Netherlands. Real GDP growth slowed in 2009, to an estimated 0.7% in each of the first three quarters of the year, as the global economic downturn took effect.

NETHERLANDS DEPENDENCIES   *Curaçao*

PUBLIC HOLIDAYS

2012: 1 January (New Year's Day), 20 February (Lenten Carnival), 6–9 April (Easter), 30 April (Queen's Day), 1 May (Labour Day), 17 May (Ascension Day), 2 July (Curaçao Day), 25–26 December (Christmas).

Statistical Survey

Note: The Netherlands Antilles was officially dissolved on 10 October 2010. The figures in this Statistical Survey refer to the pre-dissolution five-member Netherlands Antilles unless otherwise indicated.

Sources (unless otherwise stated): Centraal Bureau voor de Statistiek, Fort Amsterdam, Willemstad, Curaçao; tel. (9) 461-1031; fax (9) 461-1696; internet www.central-bureau-of-statistics.an; Bank van de Nederlandse Antillen, Simon Bolivar Plein 1, Willemstad, Curaçao; tel. (9) 434-5500; fax (9) 461-5004; e-mail info@centralbank.an; internet www.centralbank.an.

AREA AND POPULATION

Area (sq km): Curaçao 444; Bonaire 288; St Maarten (Dutch sector) 34; St Eustatius 21; Saba 13; Total 800 (309 sq miles).

Population: 189,474 at census of 27 January 1992 (excluding adjustment for underenumeration, estimated at 3.2%); 175,653 (males 82,521, females 93,132) at census of 29 January 2001; 197,621 at 1 January 2010 (official estimate). *By Island* (official estimates at 1 January 2010): Curaçao 142,180; Bonaire 13,389; St Maarten (Dutch sector) 37,429; St Eustatius 2,886; Saba 1,737.

Density (per sq km at 1 January 2010): 247.0. *By Island:* Curaçao 320.2; Bonaire 46.5; St Maarten (Dutch sector) 1,100.9; St Eustatius 137.4; Saba 133.6.

Population by Age and Sex (official estimates at 1 January 2009): *0–14:* 43,578 (males 22,105, females 21,472); *15–64:* 136,582 (males 63,116, females 73,467); *65 and over:* 19,766 (males 8,118, females 11,648); *Total* 199,926 (males 93,339, females 106,587).

Principal Town: Willemstad (capital), population (incl. suburbs, UN estimate) 123,355 at mid-2009. Source: UN, *World Urbanization Prospects: The 2009 Revision*.

Births, Marriages and Deaths (2009 unless otherwise indicated): Registered live births 2,661 (birth rate 13.5 per 1,000); Registered marriages 1,104 (marriage rate 5.8 per 1,000) in 2006; Registered deaths 1,342 (death rate 6.7 per 1,000).

Life Expectancy (years at birth): 76.9 (males 74.5; females 79.3) in 2010. Source: Pan American Health Organization.

Economically Active Population (sample survey, Curaçao only, persons aged 15 years and over, average 2007–09): Agriculture, forestry, fishing and mining 705; Manufacturing 3,914; Electricity, gas and water 806; Construction 4,911; Wholesale and retail trade, repairs 9,993; Hotels and restaurants 4,247; Transport, storage and communications 3,894; Financial intermediation 4,132; Real estate, renting and business activities 6,118; Public administration, defence and social security 4,307; Education 2,739; Health and social work 5,071; Other community, social and personal services 3,383; Private households with employed persons 2,176; Extra-territorial organizations and bodies 186; *Total employed* 56,582; Unemployed 6,045; *Total labour force* 62,627.

HEALTH AND WELFARE

Total Fertility Rate (children per woman, 2010): 2.0.

Under-5 Mortality Rate (per 1,000 live births, 2010): 13.5.

Physicians (per 1,000 head, 1999): 1.4.

Hospital Beds (per 1,000 head, 2002): 7.24.

Health Expenditure (% of GDP, 2005): 4.8.

Total Carbon Dioxide Emissions ('000 metric tons, 2007): 6,232.5.

Total Carbon Dioxide Emissions Per Head (metric tons, 2007): 32.4.

Source: mostly Pan American Health Organization.

For other sources and definitions, see explanatory note on p. vi.

AGRICULTURE, ETC.

Livestock ('000 head, year ending September 2008, FAO estimates): Cattle 0.7; Pigs 2.6; Goats 13.6; Sheep 9.1; Chickens 140. Note: No data were available for 2009.

Livestock Products (metric tons, 2009 unless otherwise indicated, FAO estimates): Pig meat 189; Chicken meat 300; Cows' milk 450 (2008); Hen eggs 530 (2008).

Fishing (metric tons, live weight, 2008): Skipjack tuna 6,436; Yellowfin tuna 7,351; Bigeye tuna 1,721; *Total catch* (incl. others) 16,698 (FAO estimate).

Source: FAO.

MINING

Production ('000 metric tons, estimate): Salt 500 in 2003–08. Source: US Geological Survey.

INDUSTRY

Production ('000 metric tons, 2007, unless otherwise indicated): Jet fuel 783; Kerosene 46 (2004); Residual fuel oils 4,056; Lubricating oils 327; Petroleum bitumen (asphalt) 1,128; Liquefied petroleum gas, refined 83; Motor spirit (petrol) 1,987; Aviation gasoline 18; Distillate fuel oils (gas-diesel oil) 2,350; Sulphur (recovered) 23 (2008); Electric energy (million kWh) 1,294.

Sources: mainly UN Industrial Commodity Statistics Database and Yearbook, and US Geological Survey.

FINANCE

Currency and Exchange Rates: 100 cents = 1 Netherlands Antilles gulden (guilder) or florin (NA Fl.). *Sterling, Dollar and Euro Equivalents* (31 December 2010): £1 sterling = NA Fl. 2.802; US $1 = NA Fl. 1.790; €1 = NA Fl. 2.392; NA Fl. 100 = £35.69 = $55.87 = €41.81. *Exchange Rate:* In December 1971 the central bank's midpoint rate was fixed at US $1 = NA Fl. 1.80. In 1989 this was adjusted to $1 = NA Fl. 1.79. The US dollar also circulates on St Maarten. In December 2009 it was announced that the US dollar would replace the Netherlands Antilles guilder and florin in Bonaire, St Eustatius and Saba from 1 January 2011, following the dissolution of the previous federation of the Netherlands Antilles in October 2010. In Curaçao and St Maarten, the Netherlands Antilles guilder was to be replaced with a newly created Caribbean guilder from 1 January 2012.

Central Government Budget (NA Fl. million, 2009): *Revenue:* Tax revenue 788.8 (Taxes on property 40.4, Taxes on goods and services 559.2, Taxes on international trade and transactions 179.9, Other taxes 9.3); Non-tax revenue 105.6 (Entrepreneurial and property income 90.1, Administrative fees and charges, non-industrial and incidental sales 10.3, Other 5.2); Grants (from other levels of government, excluding overseas development aid) 571.5; Total 1,465.9. *Expenditure:* Wages and salaries 342.4; Other goods and services 123.5; Interest payments 170.9; Subsidies 0.0; Current transfers 427.4; Capital expenditure (incl. transfers and net lending) 37.2; Total 1,101.4.

International Reserves (US $ million at 31 December 2009): Gold (national valuation) 356; Foreign exchange 867; Total 1,223. Source: IMF, *International Financial Statistics*.

Money Supply (NA Fl. million at 31 December 2009): Currency outside banks 334.1; Demand deposits at commercial banks 2,106.0; Total (incl. others) 2,758.2. Source: IMF, *International Financial Statistics*.

Cost of Living (Consumer Price Index; base: 2005 = 100): All items 106.3 in 2007; 113.6 in 2008; 115.6 in 2009. Source: IMF, *International Financial Statistics*.

Gross Domestic Product (US $ million at constant 2005 prices): 3,473 in 2007; 3,546 in 2008; 3,539 in 2009. Source: UN Statistics Division, National Accounts Main Aggregates Database.

Expenditure on the Gross Domestic Product (million NA Fl. at current prices, 2009): Final consumption expenditure 5,618 (Government 1,356, Households and non-profit institutions serving households 4,263); Gross fixed capital formation 2,089; *Total domestic expenditure* 7,707; Exports of goods and services 5,548; *Less* Imports of goods and services 6,056; *GDP in market prices* 7,200. Source: UN Statistics Division, National Accounts Main Aggregates Database.

Gross Domestic Product (million NA Fl. at current prices, 2009): Agriculture, hunting, forestry and fishing 44.0; Mining, electricity, gas and water 262.5; Manufacturing 416.1; Construction 370.6; Trade, restaurants and hotels 1,223.2; Transport, storage and communications 651.2; Other activities 3,515.2; *Sub-total* 6,482.6; Net of indirect taxes 717.4 (obtained as a residual); *GDP in purchasers' values* 7,200.0. Source: UN National Accounts Main Aggregates Database.

Balance of Payments (US $ million, 2009): Exports of goods f.o.b. 810.1; Imports of goods f.o.b. –2,606.92; *Trade balance* –1,796.9; Exports of services 2,035.4; Imports of services –929.7; *Balance on goods and services* –691.1; Other income received 109.6; Other

NETHERLANDS DEPENDENCIES

income paid –206.1; *Balance on goods, services and income* –787.7; Current transfers received 375.0; Current transfers paid –414.8; *Current balance* –827.4; Capital account (net) 112.1; Direct investment abroad –7.3; Direct investment from abroad 116.9; Portfolio investment assets –39.4; Portfolio investment liabilities –66.2; Financial derivatives assets 0.2; Other investment assets 504.7; Other investment liabilities –44.2; Net errors and omissions 74.7; *Overall balance* –176.0. Source: IMF, *International Financial Statistics*.

EXTERNAL TRADE

(Note: Although the import and export of petroleum and petroleum products, largely for refinery, transshipment and storage purposes, made a significant contribution to the economy of the Netherlands Antilles, such transactions are not included in official trade statistics.)

Principal Commodities (US $ million, distribution by HS, 2008, excl. petroleum): *Imports c.i.f.:* Meat and edible meat offal 43.3; Beverages, spirits and vinegar 43.6; Pharmaceutical products 56.2; Products of iron or steel 57.7; Nuclear reactors, boilers, machinery, etc. 171.2; Electrical and electronic equipment 136.3; Vehicles other than railway, tramway 128.8; Total (incl. others) 1,437.0. *Exports f.o.b.:* Cocoa and cocoa preparations 16.0; Miscellaneous edible preparations 10.4; Salt, sulphur, earth, stone, etc. 6.5; Soaps, lubricants, waxes, candles and modelling pastes 4.8; Pearls, precious stones, metals, coins, etc. 15.3; Nuclear reactors, boilers, machinery, etc. 16.1; Electrical and electronic equipment 5.2; Vehicles other than railway, tramway 6.7; Aircraft, spacecraft, and parts thereof 18.8; Optical, photo, technical and medical apparatus 4.7; Total (incl. others) 146.2. Source: Trade Map-Trade Competitiveness Map, International Trade Centre, www.intracen.org/marketanalysis.

Principal Trading Partners (US $ million, 2008, excl. petroleum): *Imports c.i.f.:* Aruba 24.1; Brazil 30.0; China, People's Republic 30.5; Colombia 37.3; Germany 17.0; Hong Kong 14.4; Japan 39.0; Korea, Republic 20.7; Netherlands 332.3; Panama 51.8; USA 566.1; Venezuela 51.6; Total (incl. others) 1,437.0. *Exports f.o.b.:* Antigua and Barbuda 2.1; Aruba 14.9; Belgium 1.5; Canada 1.7; France 1.7; Germany 4.0; Namibia 2.2; Netherlands 50.0; USA 33.6; Venezuela 3.7; Total (incl. others) 146.2. Source: Trade Map-Trade Competitiveness Map, International Trade Centre, www.intracen.org/marketanalysis.

TRANSPORT

Road Traffic (Curaçao and Bonaire, motor vehicles registered, excl. government-owned vehicles, 2008): Passenger cars 82,281; Lorries 18,458; Buses 460; Taxis 220; Other cars 296; Motorcycles 2,457.

Shipping: *International Sea-borne Freight Traffic* (Curaçao, TEUs moved, 2008): 102,082. *Merchant Fleet* (registered at 31 December 2009): Number of vessels 171; Total displacement 1,406,987 grt (Source: IHS Fairplay, *World Fleet Statistics*).

Civil Aviation (aircraft landings, 2008): *Bonaire* 16,908 (Commercial 14,843). *Curaçao* 22,373 (Commercial 18,461).

TOURISM

Tourist Arrivals: *Stop-overs:* 782,249 in 2006; 862,102 in 2007; 970,680 in 2008. *Cruise ship passengers* (Bonaire, Curaçao and St Maarten only): 1,805,040 in 2006; 1,860,448 in 2007; 1,873,411 in 2008.

Tourism Receipts (NA Fl. million, incl. passenger transport): 1,683.5 in 2002; 1,761.0 in 2003; 1,906.5 in 2004.

COMMUNICATIONS MEDIA

Radio Receivers (1997): 217,000 in use.
Television Receivers (1999): 71,000 in use.
Telephones (2009): 89,000 main lines in use.
Mobile Cellular Telephones (2008): 200,000 subscribers.
Internet Users (1999, UN estimate): 2,000.
Daily Newspapers: 6 titles (estimated circulation 70,000 copies per issue) in 1996; 5 in 2004.

Sources: UNESCO, *Statistical Yearbook*; UNESCO Institute for Statistics; UN, *Statistical Yearbook*; International Telecommunication Union.

EDUCATION

Pre-primary (2002/03): 5,972 pupils; 309 teachers.
Primary (2002/03): 22,667 pupils; 1,145 teachers.
General Secondary (2002/03): 9,180 pupils; 639 teachers.
Vocational (2002/03): 6,088 pupils; 542 teachers.

Curaçao

Tertiary (2001/02): 2,285 students; 340 teachers.
English Language Secondary (2000/01): 377 pupils.
Special Education (2000/01): 2,337 pupils; 178 teachers.
Teacher Training (2000/01): 133 students; 22 teachers.
Pupil-teacher Ratio (primary education, UNESCO estimate): 19.8 in 2002/03.
Adult Literacy Rate (2008, UNESCO estimates): 96.3% (males 96.3%; females 96.3%).

Source: partly UNESCO Institute for Statistics.

Directory

The Government

HEAD OF STATE

Queen of the Netherlands: HM Queen BEATRIX.
Governor: Dr FRITZ M. DE LOS SANTOS GOEDGEDRAG.
Lieutenant-Governor: LIZANNE M. RICHARDS-DINDIAL.

COUNCIL OF MINISTERS
(May 2011)

The Government is formed by a coalition of the Movementu Futuro Korsou, the the Pueblo Soberano and the Movimentu Antia Nobo.

Prime Minister and Minister of General Affairs: GERRIT F. SCHOTTE.
Deputy Prime Minister and Minister of Traffic, Transport and Urban Planning: CHARLES F. COOPER.
Minister of Social Affairs, Labour and Welfare: HENSLEY F. KOEIMAN.
Minister of Public Health, the Environment and Nature: JACINTHA V. A. CONSTANCIA.
Minister of Justice: ELMER R. WILSOE.
Minister of Finance: GEORGE R. M. JAMALOODIN.
Minister of Economic Development: ABDUL NASSER EL HAKIM.
State Secretary of Education, Science, Culture and Sports: RENE V. ROSALIA.
State Secretary of Governmental Affairs, Planning and Public Service: (vacant).
Minister Plenipotentiary of Curaçao in the Netherlands: SHELDRY P. OSEPA.

MINISTRIES

Office of the Governor: Fort Amsterdam 2, Willemstad; tel. (9) 461-1289; fax (9) 461-1412; e-mail rojer@kgna.an; internet www.gouverneur.an.
Office of the Lieutenant-Governor: Breedestraat 39C, Willemstad; tel. (9) 433-3131; fax (9) 433-3130; e-mail info@curacao-gov.an; internet www.curacao-gov.an.
Office of the Prime Minister: Fort Amsterdam 17, Willemstad; tel. (9) 463-0495; fax (9) 461-7199.
Ministry of Traffic, Transport and Urban Planning: Concordiastraat 24, Willemstad; tel. (9) 463-3215; fax (9) 461-1213.
Ministry of Social Affairs, Labour and Welfare: Concordiastraat 24, Willemstad; tel. (9) 463-3224; fax (9) 465-8738.
Ministry of Public Health, the Environment and Nature: LVV, Klein Kwartier 33, Willemstad; tel. (9) 738-1466; fax (9) 461-0106.
Ministry of Justice: Wilhelminaplein z/n, Willemstad; tel. (9) 463-0628; fax (9) 461-0598.
Ministry of Finance: Pietermaai 17, Willemstad; tel. (9) 463-0470; fax (9) 463-0477.
Ministry of Economic Development: Dienst Economische Zaken, Pietermaai 25B, Willemstad; tel. (9) 463-0461; fax (9) 461-5420.
Ministry of Education, Science, Culture and Sports: APNA gebouw D, 1e verdieping Schouwburgweg, Willemstad; tel. (9) 434-3772; fax (9) 465-0271.
Ministry of Governmental Affairs, Planning and Public Service: Fort Amsterdam 17, Willemstad; tel. (9) 463-0569; fax 461-5845.
Office of the Minister Plenipotentiary for Curaçao in the Netherlands: Kabinet van de Gevolmachtigde Minister van de Nederlanse Antillen, Badhuisweg 173-175, POB 90706, 2509 LS The Hague, Netherlands; tel. (70) 3066111; fax (70) 3066110; internet www.vertegenwoordigingcuracao.nl.

NETHERLANDS DEPENDENCIES   *Curaçao*

Legislature

ESTATES OF CURAÇAO

Election, 27 August 2010

Party	Votes	% of votes	Seats
Partido Antía Restrukturá (PAR)	22,474	30.23	8
Movementu Futuro Korsou	15,953	21.46	5
Pueblo Soberano	13,886	18.68	4
Movmentu Antia Nobo (MAN)	6,531	8.79	2
Frente Obrero i Liberashon 30 di mei	4,813	6.47	1
Partido Nashonal di Pueblo (PNP)	4,588	6.17	1
Others	6,095	8.20	—
Total	**74,340**	**100.00**	**21**

*In addition, there were 1,231 invalid votes, including 241 blank votes.

Political Organizations

Democratische Partij—Curaçao (DP—C) (Democratic Party—Curaçao): Neptunusweg 28, Willemstad; f. 1944; Leader NORBERTO VIERA RIBEIRO.

Frente Obrero i Liberashon 30 di mei (FOL) (Workers' Liberation Front of 30 May): Mayaguanaweg 16, Willemstad; tel. (9) 461-8105; f. 1969; socialist; Leader ANTHONY GODETT.

Lista di Kambio (LdK) (List of Change): Willemstad; electoral alliance; Leader CHARLES COOPER.

Forsa Kòrsou: F. D. Rooseveltweg 347, Willemstad; tel. (9) 888-3041; fax (9) 888-3504; e-mail forsakorsou@onenet.an; internet www.forsakorsou.com; Pres. NELSON NAVARRO; Leader GREGORY DAMOEN.

Movementu Antia Nobo (MAN) (Movement for a New Antilles): Landhuis Morgenster, Willemstad; tel. (9) 468-4781; internet www.new.partidoman.org; f. 1971; socialist; Pres. EUGENE CLEOPA; Leader EUNICE EISDEN.

Niun Paso Atras: Willemstad; Leader CARLOS MONK.

Movementu Futuro Korsou (Movement for the Future of Curaçao): Willemstad; f. 2010; Leader GERRIT SCHOTTE.

Partido Adelanto i Inovashon Soshal (PAIS): Willemstad; f. 2010; Leader ALEX ROSARIA.

Partido Antía Restrukturá (PAR) (Restructured Antilles Party): Fokkerweg 26, Unit 3, Willemstad; tel. (9) 465-2566; fax (9) 465-2622; e-mail omi7@ibm.net; internet www.cura.net/archives/par/frame.html; f. 1993; social-Christian ideology; Leader MIGUEL ARCHANGEL POURIER; Pres. GLENN SULVARAN.

Partido Laboral Krusado Popular (PLKP): Winston Churchillweg 57, Willemstad; tel. (9) 868-1924; internet www.plkp.an; f. 1997; progressive; Leader ERROL GOELOE.

Partido Nashonal di Pueblo (PNP) (National People's Party): Winston Churchillweg 133, Willemstad; tel. (9) 869-6777; fax (9) 869-6688; f. 1958; also known as Nationale Volkspartij; social-Christian party; Pres. FAROE METRY; Leader HUMPHREY DAVELAAR.

Pueblo Soberano: Willemstad; Leader HELMIN WIELS.

Judicial System

Legal authority is exercised by the Court of First Instance and in appeal by the Joint High Court of Justice of Curaçao, St Maarten and Aruba. The members of the Joint High Court of Justice sit singly as judges in the Courts of First Instance. The Chief Justice of the Joint High Court of Justice, its members and the Attorney-General of Curaçao is appointed for life by the Dutch monarch, after consultation with the Government of Curaçao. The Supreme Court of the Netherlands (based in The Hague) is the court of Final Instance for any appeal. Reforms to the judicial system were implemented from 2007 prior to the dissolution of the Netherlands Antilles.

Joint High Court of Justice

Wilhelminaplein 4, Willemstad; tel. (9) 463-4111; fax (9) 461-8341; e-mail hofcur@cura.net.

Chief Justice of the Joint High Court: LISBETH HOEFDRAAD.

Secretary-Executive of the Joint High Court: M. E. N. ROJER-DE FREITAS (acting).

Religion

CHRISTIANITY

Most of the population are Christian, the predominant denomination being Roman Catholicism. There are also small communities of Jews, Muslims and Bahá'ís.

Curaçaose Raad van Kerken (Curaçao Council of Churches): Periclesstraat 6, Willemstad; tel. (9) 465-3207; fax (9) 461-0733; e-mail ddtic@yahoo.com; f. 1958; six mem. churches; Chair. IDA VISSER; Exec. Sec. PAUL VAN DER WAAL.

The Roman Catholic Church

Roman Catholics form the largest single group on Curaçao. Curaçao and the other former constituent territories of the Netherlands Antilles, as well as Aruba, together form the diocese of Willemstad, suffragan to the archdiocese of Port of Spain (Trinidad and Tobago). The Bishop participates in the Antilles Episcopal Conference, currently based in Trinidad and Tobago.

Bishop of Willemstad: Rt Rev. LUIGI ANTONIO SECCO, Bisdom, Breedestraat 31, Otrobanda, Willemstad; tel. (9) 462-5857; fax (9) 462-7437; e-mail bisdomwstad@curinfo.an.

Other Churches

The largest of the other churches in the Netherlands Antilles, according to the 2001 census, were the Pentecostal (5% of the population), Protestant (3%), Seventh-day Adventist (3%) and Methodist (3%). According to the 2001 census, around 1% of the population of the Netherlands Antilles were Anglicans. Other denominations included the Moravian, Apostolic Faith, Wesleyan Holiness and Norwegian Seamen's Churches, the Baptists, Calvinists, Jehovah's Witnesses, Evangelists, the Church of Christ, and the New Testament Church of God.

Iglesia Protestant Uni (United Protestant Church): Fortkerk, Fort Amsterdam, Willemstad; tel. (9) 461-1139; fax (9) 465-7481; e-mail vpg-cur@curlink.com; internet www.vpg-curacao.com; f. 1825 by union of Dutch Reformed and Evangelical Lutheran Churches; associated with the World Council of Churches; Pres. MARITZA BEAUJON-BAKHUIS; 3 congregations; 11,280 adherents; 3,200 mems.

JUDAISM

According to the 2001 census, around 1% of the population of the Netherlands Antilles were Jews.

Congregation 'Shaarei Tsedek' Ashkenazi Orthodox Jewish Community: 37 Magdalenaweg, Willemstad; tel. and fax (9) 738-5949; e-mail rel_yes@yahoo.com; 140 mems; Rabbi ARIEL YESHURUN.

Reconstructionist Shephardi Congregation Mikvé Israel-Emanuel: Hanchi di Snoa 29, POB 322, Willemstad; tel. (9) 461-1067; fax (9) 465-4141; e-mail information@snoa.com; internet www.snoa.com; f. 1732 on present site; Pres. RENÉ LEVY MADURO; about 150 mems.

The Press

Algemeen Dagblad: ABCourant NV, Prof. Kernkampweg z/n, POB 725, Willemstad; tel. (9) 747-2200; fax (9) 747-2257; e-mail algemeen@antilliaansdagblad.com; internet www.antilliaansdagblad.com; daily; Dutch; Editor NOUD KÖPER.

Amigoe: Kaya Fraternan di Skèrpenè z/n, POB 577; tel. (9) 767-2000; fax (9) 767-4084; e-mail management@amigoe.com; internet www.amigoe.com; f. 1884; Christian; daily; evening; Dutch; Dir ERNEST VOGES; Editor-in-Chief WILLEM DA COSTA GOMEZ; circ. 12,000.

Bala: Noord Zapateer nst 13, Willemstad; tel. (9) 467-1646; fax (9) 467-1041; e-mail bala@cura.net; daily; Papiamento.

Beurs en Nieuwsberichten: A. M. Chumaceiro Blvd 5, POB 741, Willemstad; tel. (9) 465-4544; fax (9) 465-3411; f. 1935; daily; evening; Dutch; Editor L. SCHENK; circ. 8,000.

Bonaire Holiday: POB 569, Willemstad; tel. (9) 767-1403; fax (9) 767-2003; f. 1971; tourist guide; English; 3 a year; circ. 95,000.

The Business Journal: Indjuweg 30A, Willemstad; tel. (9) 461-1367; fax (9) 461-1955; monthly; English.

Curaçao Holiday: POB 569; tel. (9) 767-1403; fax (9) 767-2003; f. 1960; tourist guide; English; 3 a year; circ. 300,000.

De Curaçaosche Courant: Frederikstraat 123, POB 15, Willemstad; tel. (9) 461-2766; fax (9) 462-6535; f. 1812; weekly; Dutch; Editor J. KORIDON.

Extra: W. I. Compagniestraat 41, Willemstad; tel. (9) 462-4595; fax (9) 462-7575; e-mail redactie@extra.an; daily; morning; Papiamento; Man. R. YRAUSQUIN; Editor MIKE OEHLERS; circ. 20,000.

Newsletter of Curaçao Trade and Industry Association: Kaya Junior Salas 1, POB 49, Willemstad; tel. (9) 461-1210; fax (9) 461-

NETHERLANDS DEPENDENCIES

5422; f. 1972; monthly; English and Dutch; economic and industrial paper.

Nobo: Scherpenheuvel w/n, POB 323, Willemstad; tel. (9) 467-3500; fax (9) 467-2783; daily; evening; Papiamento; Editor CARLOS DAANTJE; circ. 15,000.

Nos Isla: Refineria Isla (Curazao) SA, Emmastad; 2 a month; Papiamento; circ. 1,200.

La Prensa: W. I. Compagniestraat 41, Willemstad; tel. (9) 462-3850; fax (9) 462-5983; e-mail webmaster@laprensacur.com; internet news.laprensacur.com; f. 1929; daily; evening; Papiamento; Man. R. YRAUSQUIN; Editor SIGFRIED RIGAUD; circ. 10,750.

Ultimo Noticia: Frederikstraat 123, Willemstad; tel. (9) 462-3444; fax (9) 462-6535; daily; morning; Papiamento; Editor A. A. JONCKHEER.

La Unión: Rotaprint NV, Willemstad; weekly; Papiamento.

NEWS AGENCY

Algemeen Nederlands Persbureau (ANP) (Netherlands): Panoramaweg 5, POB 439, Willemstad; tel. (9) 461-2233; fax (9) 461-7431; Representative RONNIE RENS.

Publishers

Drukkerij Scherpenheuvel NV: Lindberghweg 28 A; tel. (9) 465-6801.

Drukkerij de Stad NV: W. I. Compagniestraat 41, POB 3011, Willemstad; tel. (9) 462-3566; fax (9) 462-2175; e-mail management@destad.an; internet www.destad.an; f. 1929; Dir KENRICK A. YRAUSQUIN.

Ediciones Populares: W. I. Compagniestraat 41, Willemstad; f. 1929; Dir RONALD YRAUSQUIN.

Broadcasting and Communications

TELECOMMUNICATIONS

Digicel Curaçao: Biesheuvel 24–25; tel. (9) 736-1056; fax (9) 736-1057; e-mail customercare@digicelcuracao.com; internet www.digicelcuracao.com; f. 1999 as Curaçao Telecom; bought by Digicel (Ireland) in 2005, present name adopted 2006; telephone and internet services; Chair. DENIS O'BRIEN; CEO (Dutch Caribbean, Guyana and Suriname) PHILIP VAN DALSEN.

Scarlet: Fokkerweg 26, Suite 106, Willemstad; tel. (9) 766-0000; fax (9) 461-8301; internet www.scarlet.an; telecommunications provider in Curaçao and St Maarten; CEO ERIC E. STAKLAND.

United Telecom Services (UTS): UTS Headquarters, Rigelweg 2, Willemstad; tel. (9) 777-0101; fax (9) 777-1284; e-mail info@uts.an; internet www.uts.an; f. 1999 following merger of Antelecom NV (f. 1908) and SETEL (f. 1979); Antelecom and SETEL still operate under own names; Chair. DAVID DICK; CEO PAUL DE GEUS.

  Servicio de Telekomunikashon (UTS Wireless Curaçao) (SETEL): UTS Headquarters, Rigelweg 2, Willemstad; tel. (9) 777-0101; fax (9) 777-1284; e-mail info@uts.an; internet www.uts.an; f. 1979; telecommunications equipment and network provider; forms part of UTS; state-owned, but privatization pending; Pres. ANGEL R. KOOK; Man. Dir JULIO CONSTANCIA; 400 employees.

BROADCASTING

Radio

Curom Broadcasting Inc: Roodeweg 64, POB 2169, Willemstad; tel. (9) 462-2020; fax (9) 462-5796; e-mail z86@curom.com; internet www.curom.com; f. 1933; broadcasts in English, Papiamento, Dutch and Spanish; Dir ORLANDO CUALES.

  Mi 95: f. 1988; FM; music station, aimed at adults.

  Z-86: news station.

  88 Ròckòrsou: rock music station, aimed at young people.

Easy 97.9 FM: Arikokweg 19A, Willemstad; tel. (9) 462-3162; fax (9) 462-8712; e-mail radio@easyfm.com; internet www.easyfm.com; f. 1995; Dir KEVIN CARTHY.

Gold 91.5 FM Curaçao: De Rouvilleweg 7, Ingang Klipstraat, POB 6103, Willemstad; tel. (9) 426-1803; fax (9) 461-9103; e-mail info@gold915.com; internet gold915.an; music station.

Paradise FM: De Rouvilleweg 7, Ingang Klipstraat, POB 6103, Willemstad; tel. (9) 426-1803; fax (9) 461-9103; e-mail studio@paradisefm.an; internet paradisefm.an; news station.

Radio Caribe: Ledaweg 35, Brievengat, Willemstad; tel. (9) 736-9564; fax (9) 736-9569; f. 1955; commercial station; programmes in Dutch, English, Spanish and Papiamento; Dir-Gen. C. R. HEILLEGGER.

Curaçao

Radio Exito: Julianaplein 39, Willemstad; tel. (9) 462-5577; fax (9) 462-5580.

Radio Hoyer NV: Plasa Horacio Hoyer 21, Willemstad; tel. (9) 461-1678; fax (9) 461-6528; e-mail hoyer1@radiohoyer.com; internet www.radiohoyer.com; f. 1954; commercial; two stations: Radio Hoyer I (mainly Papiamento, also Spanish) and II (mainly Dutch, also English) in Curaçao; Man. Dir HELEN HOYER.

Radio Korsou FM: Bataljonweg 7, POB 3250, Willemstad; tel. (9) 737-3012; fax (9) 737-2888; e-mail studio@korsou.com; internet www.korsou.com; f. 1976; 24 hrs a day; programmes in Papiamento and Dutch; Gen. Man. ALAN H. EVERTSZ.

Radio Tropical: Kaya W. F. G. Mensing, Willemstad; tel. (9) 465-0190; fax (9) 465-2470; e-mail tropi@cura.net; Dir DWIGHT RUDOLPHINA.

Television

Antilliaanse Televisie Maatschappij NV (TeleCuraçao): Berg Ararat z/n, POB 415, Willemstad; tel. (9) 461-1288; fax (9) 461-4138; e-mail web@telecuracao.com; internet www.telecuracao.com; f. 1960; fmrly operated Tele-Aruba; commercial; owned by United Telecommunication Services; also operates cable service, offering programmes from US satellite television and two Venezuelan channels; Dir PAUL DE GEUS; Gen. Man. HUGO LEW JEN TAI.

Five television channels can be received on Curaçao in total. Curaçao has a publicly owned cable television service, TDS.

Finance

(cap. = capital; res = reserves; dep. = deposits; m. = million; br.(s) = branch(es); amounts in Netherlands Antilles guilders unless otherwise stated)

BANKING

Central Bank

Bank van Curaçao en Sint Maarten (Bank of Curaçao and Sint Maarten): Simon Bolivar Plein 1, Willemstad; tel. (9) 434-5500; fax (9) 461-5004; e-mail info@centralbank.an; internet centralbank.an; f. 1828 as Curaçaosche Bank, renamed Bank van de Nederlandse Antillen in 1962, present name adopted in 2010; cap. 30.0m., res 519.9m., dep. 2,447.4m. (Dec. 2008); Pres. Dr EMSLEY D. TROMP; br. on St Maarten.

Commercial Banks

Banco di Caribe NV: Schottegatweg Oost 205, POB 3785, Willemstad; tel. (9) 432-3000; fax (9) 461-5220; e-mail info@bancodicaribe.com; internet www.bancodicaribe.com; f. 1973; cap. 4.7m., res 120.1m., dep. 1,028.2m. (Dec. 2008); Chair. HUSHANG ANSARY; CEO and Gen. Man. Dir IDEFONS D. SIMON; Man. Dirs EDUARDO A. DE KORT, PERCIVAL VIRGINIA; 5 brs.

Banco Industrial de Venezuela, SA: Handelskade N-12, Punda; tel. (9) 461-6534; subsidiary of state-owned Banco Industrial de Venezuela, SA.

CITCO Banking Corporation NV: De Ruyterkade 62, POB 707, Willemstad; tel. (9) 732-2322; fax (9) 732-2330; e-mail curacao-bank@citco.com; internet www.citco.com; f. 1980 as Curaçao Banking Corpn NV; Man. Dir and Gen. Man. SCOTT CASE; Man. Dirs GLENDA E. C. LALLJEE-TRAPENBERG, RUPERT E. WALLÉ.

FirstCaribbean International Bank (Curaçao) NV: De Ruyterkade 61, POB 3144, Willemstad; tel. (9) 433-8338; fax (9) 433-8198; e-mail bank.curacao@firstcaribbeanbank.com; internet www.firstcaribbeanbank.com/curacao; f. 1964 as ABN AMRO Bank NV; part of FirstCaribbean Group, based in Barbados; 91.5% owned by CIBC, Canada; Exec. Chair. MICHAEL MANSOOR; Man. Dir (Dutch Caribbean) W. M. (PIM) VAN DER BERG; 6 brs.

Girobank NV: Scharlooweg 35, Willemstad; tel. (9) 433-9999; fax (9) 461-7861; e-mail info@gironet.com; internet www.girobank.net; Man. Dirs ERIC GARCIA, MANUEL SUENO.

Maduro & Curiel's Bank NV: Plaza Jojo Correa 2–4, POB 305, Willemstad; tel. (9) 466-1100; fax (9) 466-1122; e-mail info@mcb-bank.com; internet www.mcb-bank.com; f. 1916 as NV Maduro's Bank; merged with Curiel's Bank in 1931; affiliated with Bank of Nova Scotia NV, Toronto, Canada; br. in Bonaire; cap. 50.7m., res 168.6m., dep. 4,762.2m. (Dec. 2008); Pres. and CEO LIONEL CAPRILES; Man. Dir RONALD GOMES CASSERES; 31 brs.

Meespierson (Curaçao) NV: Berg Ararat 1, POB 3889, Willemstad; tel. (9) 463-9200; fax (9) 461-3769; e-mail privatebanking_curacao@meespierson.com; internet www.meespierson.an; f. 1952 as Pierson, Heldring and Pierson (Curaçao) NV; became Meespierson (Curaçao) NV in 1993; name changed to Fortis Bank (Curaçao) NV in 2000, and reverted to Meespierson (Curaçao) NV in 2009; international banking/trust co; Man. Dir WILLIE BEUMER; Gen. Man. FRANK LAMMERS.

NETHERLANDS DEPENDENCIES

Curaçao

Orco Bank NV: Dr Henry Fergusonweg 10, POB 4928, Willemstad; tel. (9) 737-2000; fax (9) 737-6741; e-mail info@orcobank.com; internet www.orcobank.com; f. 1986; cap. 7.8m., res 11.1m., dep. 393.6m. (Dec. 2008); Man. Dirs M. N. S. SPROCK, K. R. CANWORD; 1 br.

Rabobank Curaçao NV: Zeelandia Office Park, Kaya W. F. G. (Jombi), Mensing 14, POB 3876, Willemstad; tel. (9) 465-2011; fax (9) 465-2066; e-mail l.an.curacao.ops@rabobank.com; internet www.rabobank.com; f. 1978; cap. US $53.0m., res $17.8m., dep. $4,535.2m. (Dec. 2003); Chair. BERT HEEMSKERK; Gen. Man. J. S. KLEP.

RBTT Bank NV: Kaya Flamboyan 1, Rooi Catootje, Willemstad; tel. (9) 763-8438; fax (9) 737-0620; e-mail info@tt.rbtt.com; internet www.rbtt.com; f. 1997 as Antilles Banking Corpn; name changed to RBTT Bank Antilles in 2001; name changed as above in 2002; cap. 114.5m., res 132.6m., dep. 3,393.2m. (Dec. 2008); Pres. and Country Head (Curaçao) DAISY A. TYROL-CAROLUS; Man. Dir RICHARD RAJACK; 4 brs.

'Offshore' Banks

Abu Dhabi International Bank NV: Kaya W. F. G. (Jombi), Mensing 36, POB 3141, Willemstad; tel. (9) 461-1299; fax (9) 461-5392; internet www.nbad.com; f. 1981; cap. US $20.0m., res $30.0m., dep. $112.2m. (Dec. 2006); Pres. QAMBAR AL MULLA; Man. Dir NAGY S. KOLTA.

FirstCaribbean International Wealth Management (Curaçao) NV: De Ruyterkade 61; tel. (9) 433-8000; fax (9) 433-8198; f. 1976 as ABN AMRO Bank Asset Management (Curaçao) NV; acquired by FirstCaribbean Bank in Dec. 2005; Man. Dir E. J. W. HERMENS.

F. Van Lanschot Bankiers (Curaçao) NV: Schottegatweg Oost 32, POB 4799, Willemstad; tel. (9) 737-1011; fax (9) 737-1086; e-mail info@vanlanschot.an; internet www.vanlanschot.nl; f. 1962; wholly owned by F. Van Lanschot Bankiers NV (Netherlands); Man. A. VAN GEEST.

Development Banks

Ontwikkelingsbank van de Nederlandse Antillen NV: Schottegatweg Oost 3C, POB 267, Willemstad; tel. (9) 747-3000; fax (9) 747-3320; e-mail obna@obna-bank.com; f. 1981; Man. Dir DENNIS CIJNTJE.

Stichting Korporashon pa Desaroyo di Korsou (Curaçao Development Corporation—KORPODEKO): Schottegatweg Oost 36, Willemstad; tel. (9) 738-1799; fax (9) 738-1766; e-mail info@korpodeko.an; internet www.korpodeko.an.

Savings Banks

Postspaarbank van de Nederlandse Antillen: Waaigatplein 1, Willemstad; tel. (9) 433-1100; fax (9) 461-7561; e-mail info@postpaarbank.com; internet www.postspaarbank.com/English; f. 1905; post office savings bank; Chair. H. J. J. VICTORIA; cap. 21m.; 20 brs.

Spaar- en Beleenbank van Curaçao NV: MCB Salinja Bldg, Schottegatweg Oost 130, Willemstad; tel. (9) 466-1585; fax (9) 466-1590; e-mail chbsbb@mcb-bank.com.

There are also several mortgage banks and credit unions.

Banking Associations

Association of International Bankers in the Netherlands Antilles (IBNA): A. M. Chumaceiro Blvd 3, POB 3369, Willemstad; tel. (9) 461-5367; fax (9) 461-5369; e-mail info@ibna.an; internet www.ibna.an; f. 1980; 32 mems; Pres. ARTHUR ADAMS; Sec. ANTONIO TORRES.

Curaçao Bankers' Association (CBA): Girobank NV, Scharlooweg 35, Willemstad; tel. (9) 433-9999; fax (9) 461-7861; e-mail florisela.bentoera@an.rbtt.com; f. 1972; Pres. E. GARCIA; Sec. FLORISELA BENTOERA.

Federashon di Kooperativanan di Spar i Kredito Antiyano (Fekoskan): Curaçaostraat 50, Willemstad; tel. (9) 462-3676; fax (9) 462-4995; e-mail fekoskan@attglobal.net; Pres. W. DE LIMA.

International Bankers' Association in the Netherlands Antilles: A. M. Chumaceiro Blvd 3, Willemstad; tel. (9) 461-5367; fax (9) 461-5369; Pres. F. GIRIGORI.

INSURANCE

Amersfoortse Antillen NV: Kaya W. F. G. Mensing 19, Willemstad; tel. (9) 461-6399; fax (9) 461-6709.

Aseguro di Kooperativa Antiyano (ASKA) NV: Scharlooweg 15, Willemstad; tel. (9) 461-7765; fax (9) 461-5991; accident and health, motor vehicle, property.

Ennia Caribe Schaden NV: J. B. Gorsiraweg 6, POB 581, Willemstad; tel. (9) 434-3800; fax (9) 434-3873; e-mail mail@ennia.com; f. 1948; general; life insurance as Ennia Caribe Leven NV; Pres. DONALD BAKHUIS; Man. Dir ALBARTUS WILLEMSEN.

ING Fatum: Cas Coraweg 2, Willemstad; tel. (9) 777-7777; fax (9) 461-2023; f. 1904; property insurance.

MCB Group Insurance NV: MCB Bldg Scharloo, Scharloo, Willemstad; tel. (9) 466-1370; fax (9) 466-1327.

Netherlands Antilles and Aruba Assurance Company (NA&A) NV: Pietermaai 135, Willemstad; tel. (9) 465-7146; fax (9) 461-6269; accident and health, motor vehicle, property.

Seguros Antilliano NV: S. b. N. Doormanweg/Reigerweg 5, Willemstad; tel. (9) 736-6877; fax (9) 736-5794; general.

A number of foreign companies also have offices in Curaçao, mainly British, Canadian, Dutch and US firms.

Insurance Association

Insurance Association of the Netherlands Antilles (NAVV): c/o ING Fatum, Cas Coraweg 2, POB 3002, Willemstad; tel. (9) 777-7777; fax (9) 736-9658; Pres. R. C. MARTINA-JOE.

Trade and Industry

DEVELOPMENT ORGANIZATIONS

Curaçao Industrial and International Trade Development Company NV (CURINDE): Emancipatie Blvd 7, Landhuis Koningsplein; tel. (9) 737-6000; fax (9) 737-1336; e-mail info@curinde.com; internet www.curinde.com; f. 1980; state-owned; manages the harbour free zone, the airport free zone and the industrial zone; Man. Dir ERIC R. SMEULDERS.

Foreign Investment Agency Curaçao (FIAC): Luchthavenweg 55, 5657 EA Eindhoven, Netherlands; tel. (40) 2518674; fax (40) 2572098.

World Trade Center Curaçao: POB 6005, Piscadera Bay; tel. (9) 463-6132; fax (9) 463-6573; e-mail info@wtccuracao.com; internet www.worldtradecentercuracao.com; Man. Dir LUIS E. BELTRAN M.

CHAMBER OF COMMERCE

Curaçao Chamber of Commerce and Industry: Kaya Junior Salas 1, Pietermaai, World Trade Centre Bldg, POB 10, Piscadera Bay; tel. (9) 461-1451; fax (9) 461-5652; e-mail management@curacao-chamber.an; internet www.curacao-chamber.an/info; f. 1884; Chair. RUUD THUIS; Exec. Dir JOHN H. JACOBS.

INDUSTRIAL AND TRADE ASSOCIATIONS

Curaçao Exporters' Association (CEA): c/o Seawings NV, Maduro Plaza z/n CEA, POB 6049, Willemstad; tel. (9) 733-1591; fax (9) 733-1599; e-mail albert.elens@seawings-curacao.com; f. 1993; Dir ALBERT ELENS.

Curaçao International Financial Services Association (CIFA): Chumaceiro Blvd 3, POB 220, Willemstad; tel. (9) 461-5371; fax (9) 461-5378; e-mail info@cifa-curacao.com; internet www.cifa-curacao.com; Chair. ETIENNE YS.

Curaçao Trade and Industry Association (Vereniging Bedrijfsleven Curaçao—VBC): Kaya Junior Salas 1, POB 49, Willemstad; tel. (9) 461-1210; fax (9) 461-5422; e-mail info@vbc.an; internet www.vbc.an; f. 1944; Pres. BASTIAN KOOYMAN; Exec. Dir JOHAN LIEUW.

UTILITY

Electricity and Water

Aqualectra Production NV (KAE): Rector Zwijsenstraat 1, POB 2097; tel. (9) 463-2200; fax (9) 463-2228; e-mail info@aqualectra.com; internet www.aqualectra.com; present name adopted in 2001 following the restructuring of Curaçao's energy sector; CEO ANTHON CASPERSON.

TRADE UNIONS

Algemene Bond van Overheidspersoneel (ABVO) (General Union of Civil Servants): POB 3604, Willemstad; tel. (9) 737-6097; fax (9) 737-3145; e-mail abvo_na@cura.net; internet www.abvo-informa.org; f. 1936; Pres. ROLAND H. IGNACIO; Sec. R. C. SAEZ; 4,000 mems.

Central General di Trahado di Corsow (CGTC) (General Headquarters for Workers of Curaçao): POB 2078, Willemstad; tel. (9) 737-6097; fax (9) 737-3145; e-mail abvo_na@cura.net; f. 1949; Sec.-Gen. ROLAND H. IGNACIO.

Curaçaosche Federatie van Werknemers (Curaçao Federation of Workers): Schouwburgweg 44, Willemstad; tel. (9) 737-6300; fax (9) 737-1426; f. 1964; Pres. WILFRED SPENCER; Sec.-Gen. GILBERT POULINA; 204 affiliated unions; about 2,000 mems.

Petroleum Workers' Federation of Curaçao: Willemstad; tel. (9) 737-0255; fax (9) 737-5250; affiliated to Int. Petroleum and Chemical Workers' Federation; f. 1955; Pres. R. G. GIJSBERTHA; approx. 1,500 mems.

NETHERLANDS DEPENDENCIES

Sentral di Sindikatonan di Korsou (SSK) (Central Trade Unions of Curaçao): Schouwburgweg 44, POB 3036, Willemstad; tel. (9) 737-0255; fax (9) 737-5250; Pres. Pablo Cova; 6,000 mems.

Sindikato di Trahado den Edukashon na Korsou (SITEK) (Curaçao Schoolteachers' Trade Union): Landhuis Stenen Koraal, POB 3545, Willemstad; tel. (9) 468-2902; fax (9) 469-0552; 1,234 mems.

Transport

RAILWAYS

There are no railways.

ROADS

Curaçao has a good system of all-weather roads. There were 845 km of roads in the Netherlands Antilles as a whole in 2004, of which 31% were paved.

SHIPPING

Curaçao is an important centre for the refining and transshipment of Venezuelan and Middle Eastern petroleum. Willemstad is served by the Schottegat harbour, set in a wide bay with a long channel and deep water. A Mega Cruise Facility, with capacity for the largest cruise ships, has been constructed on the Otrobanda side of St Anna Bay. Ports at Bullen Bay and Caracas Bay also serve Curaçao.

Curaçao Ports Authority: Werf de Wilde z/n, POB 689, Willemstad; tel. (9) 434-5999; fax (9) 461-3907; e-mail info@curports.com; internet curports.com; Man. Dir Agustín Díaz.

Curaçao Shipping Association (SVC): c/o Dammers & van der Heide (Antilles) Inc, Kaya Flamboyan 11, Willemstad; tel. (9) 737-0600; fax (9) 737-3875; Pres. K. Ponsen.

Principal Shipping Companies

Anthony Veder & Co NV: Zeelandia z/n, POB 3677; tel. (9) 461-4700; fax (9) 461-2576; e-mail anveder@vrshipping.com; Man. Dir Joop van Vliet.

Caribbean Moving Services NV: Caracasbaaiweg 328, POB 442, Willemstad; tel. (9) 767-2588; fax 747-1155; internet www.ccs.an; fmrly Caribbean Cargo Services NV; Man. Dir Loes van der Woude.

Curaçao Dry-dock Co Inc: POB 3012; tel. (9) 733-0000; fax (9) 736-5580; e-mail info@cdmnv.com; f. 1958; Man. Dir Mario Raymond Evertsz.

Curaçao Ports Services Inc NV (CPS): Curaçao Container Terminal, POB 170; tel. (9) 461-5177; fax (9) 461-6536; e-mail cps@cps.an; Man. Dir Karel Jan O. Aster.

Dammers Ship Agencies Inc: Dammers Bldg, Kaya Flamboyan 11, POB 3018, Willemstad; tel. (9) 737-0600; fax (9) 737-3875; e-mail directorate@dammers-curacao.com; internet www.dammers-curacao.com; f. 1964; fmrly Dammers & van der Heide, Shipping and Trading (Antilles) Inc; Man. Dir (Finance) Peter Govers; Man. Dir (Marketing and Sales) Robert van Heulen.

Gomez Transport NV: Zeelandia z/n, Willemstad; tel. (9) 461-5900; fax (9) 461-3358; e-mail info@gomezshipping.an; Man. Fernando da Costa Gómez.

Hal Antillen NV: De Ruyterkade 63, POB 812.

Intermodal Container Services NV: Salinja Galleries, 1st Floor Unit 201, POB 3747; tel. (9) 461-3330; fax (9) 461-3432; Mans A. R. Beaujon, N. N. Harms.

Lagendijk Maritime Services: POB 3481; tel. (9) 465-5766; fax (9) 465-5998; e-mail ims@ibm.net.

S. E. L. Maduro Shipping: Dokweg 19, Maduro Plaza; tel. (9) 733-1510; fax (9) 733-1538; e-mail maduroship@madurosons.com; internet www.madurosons.com; f. 1837; Vice-Pres. Ronald Corsen.

CIVIL AVIATION

Curaçao International Airport is located at Hato, 12 km from Willemstad. In 1998 a free trade zone was inaugurated at the airport and in 2006 a new passenger terminal building was opened.

Dutch Antilles Express: Pietermaai 33–35, POB 4101, Willemstad; tel. 461-2502; fax 461-2508; e-mail curacao@flydae.com; internet www.flydae.com; f. 2005; scheduled passenger flights within the Netherlands Dependencies and to other Caribbean and South American destinations.

InselAir: Curaçao International Airport, Hato; tel. (9) 737-0444; e-mail customerrelations@fly-inselair.com; internet www.fly-inselair.com; f. 2006; flights within Caribbean and to USA (Charlotte, NC); CEO Albert J. Kluijver.

Tourism

Tourism is a major industry on Curaçao. The principal attractions for tourists are the white, sandy beaches, marine wildlife and diving facilities. Visitor arrivals to Curaçao totalled 366,837 in 2009, a decrease of 11.5% on the previous year's total. The majority of visitors were from the Netherlands (34%) and Venezuela (29%).

Curaçao Tourist Board: Pietermaai 19, POB 3266, Willemstad; tel. (9) 434-8200; fax (9) 461-5017; e-mail info@curacao.com; internet www.curacao.com; f. 1989; supervised by the Curaçao Tourism Development Bureau; CEO Ghatim Kabbara.

Curaçao Hospitality and Tourism Association (CHATA): Kaya Junior Salas 01, Willemstad; tel. (9) 465-1005; fax (9) 465-1052; e-mail info@chata.org; internet www.chata.org; f. 1967 as Curaçao Hotel Asscn; Pres. Jeanette Bonet.

Defence

Although defence is the responsibility of the Netherlands, compulsory military service is laid down in an Antilles Ordinance. The Governor is the Commander-in-Chief of the armed forces, and a Dutch contingent is stationed in Willemstad. In 1999 the US air force and navy began patrols from a base on Curaçao to combat the transport of illegal drugs.

Commander of the Navy: Commodore Peter W. Lenselink.

Education

Education was made compulsory in 1992. The island's educational facilities are generally of a high standard. The education system is the same as that of the Netherlands. Dutch is the principal language of instruction, although lessons in Papiamento have been introduced in primary schools. Primary education begins at six years of age and lasts for six years. Secondary education lasts for a further five years. The University of the Netherlands Antilles had 2,104 students in 2008/09.

SINT MAARTEN

Introduction

Sint (St) Maarten lies in the north-eastern Caribbean Sea, 20 km to the north of Saint-Barthélemy, a French Overseas Collectivity. St Maarten shares a land border with Saint-Martin, the northern half of the island and another Overseas Collectivity of France. St Maarten, as well as Saba (45 km to the south) and Sint (St) Eustatius (56 km south) are known as the Bovenwindse Eilands or Windward Islands (although actually in the Leeward group of the Lesser Antilles). The climate is tropical, moderated by the sea, with an average annual temperature of 27.5°C (81°F) and little rainfall. The official language is English, although Dutch is also spoken. Almost all of the inhabitants profess Christianity, predominantly Protestantism. The state flag (proportions 2 by 3) comprises two equal horizontal stripes, red over blue, with a white triangle at the hoist. In the centre of the triangle is the territory's coat of arms. The capital is Philipsburg.

The Dutch settled the Windward Islands, once inhabited by Carib Indians, in the mid-17th century. The island of St Maarten was divided between the Dutch and the French in 1648, but conflicts over ownership continued for many decades before finally, in 1817, the current partition line between the Dutch and French territories was established. The Dutch part of the island then prospered as a slave-based plantation economy and a major exporter of salt. Together with the Leeward Islands (comprising Aruba, Bonaire and Curaçao), the Windward islands were administered as Curaçao and Dependencies between 1845 and 1948. The territory attracted immigration from Europe, particularly Dutch Protestants but also some French. During the Second World War Queen Wilhelmina of the Netherlands promised independence, and following the end of the war calls for independence became more persistent in St Maarten (as well as Curaçao—see separate chapter). In 1954 the Dutch Government gave the federation of six islands full autonomy in domestic affairs,

NETHERLANDS DEPENDENCIES

Sint Maarten

and declared it to be an integral part of the Kingdom of the Netherlands.

Political allegience within the federation was traditionally along island, rather than party lines. These divisions increased following Aruba's secession from the federation in 1986. Calls for further autonomy increased in Curaçao and St Maarten, By the early 1990s it appeared that, while the 'metropolitan' Government was unwilling to allow the complete disintegration of the federation, it was prepared to consider a less centralized system or the creation of two federations in the separate island groups. Nevertheless, in a referendum on the status issue held in St Maarten in October 1994, 60% of the electorate voted to remain within the Antillean federation, while the option of *status aparte* (separate status) received 32% of the vote.

A further referendum on the constitutional future of St Maarten took place on 23 June 2000. Only 4% of participants favoured maintaining the status quo. Some 69% favoured obtaining *status aparte* within the Kingdom of the Netherlands, 14% favoured complete independence and 12% preferred a restructuring of the Antilles of the Five. However, the Dutch Government indicated that it would not support a request by St Maarten to receive *status aparte*. In February 2003 the Dutch Minister of Interior and Kingdom Relations confirmed that the Netherlands would not permit St Maarten to leave the federation. Despite this set-back, St Maarten had signed an agreement with the central Antilles Government in August 2002, which would permit the island's Executive Council to take out loans on its own initiative, without seeking permission from the central bank. Furthermore, in late 2002 the Executive Council proposed to the central bank that discussions should begin on a separate monetary system for St Maarten.

The Jesurun Commission, established by the Dutch and Antillean Governments and headed by Edsel Jesurun (a former Governor of the territory), on 8 October 2004 recommended the dissolution of the Netherlands Antilles; support for the federation had, it was argued, virtually disintegrated on most of the islands. The Commission proposed that St Maarten (and Curaçao) should become an autonomous state within the Netherlands (i.e. have *status aparte*), while Saba, Bonaire and St Eustatius should be directly administered by the Dutch Government. A preliminary agreement with the Dutch Government was signed in Curaçao on 3 December 2005; the accord set out that the extant federation be dissolved by 1 July 2007 and that St Maarten would become an autonomous member of the Kingdom of the Netherlands.

On 2 November 2006 the Dutch Government granted St Maarten (and Curaçao) independent governance within the Kingdom of the Netherlands, with the exception of matters of defence, foreign policy and law enforcement matters to the Dutch Government. The Common Court of Justice of the Netherlands Antilles and Aruba was to be retained as the islands' principal judicial authority. The metropolitan administration would assume responsibility for the Netherlands Antilles' substantial collective debt, estimated at NA Fl. 5,000m. St Maarten's Island Council aceeded to the proposed agreement on 28 November; however, progress towards dissolving the federation was delayed by the Curaçao Island Council's voting against ratification of the accord, citing concern over provisions relating to judicial matters, policing and debt relief (for further details see the Curaçao chapter). The Dutch Government refused to countenance renegotiation of the terms of the agreement. Nevertheless, on 12 February 2007, at a meeting in Philipsburg, a further 'transition accord' was signed by the Island Councils of Saba, Bonaire, St Eustatius and St Maarten, and the Netherlands, establishing a target date of 15 December 2008 for the dissolution of the federation.

In January 2007 draft legislation was submitted to the Island Council of St Maarten for the proposed repatriation of persons who had assumed illegal residence on the island since 2005. It was estimated that over 25,000 people were living in the territory at that time, although the proportion of this number to which compulsory expulsion would apply was unclear. The measure appeared to coincide with requirements for immigration and security reforms ahead of the proposed redesignation of the territory within the Kingdom of the Netherlands. In late 2009 a six-week programme was implemented to grant residency and working rights to illegal immigrants who could prove that they had been living in the territory since the end of 2006, or who possessed a valid contract from an employer. It was estimated that up to 70,000 immigrants were residing illegally on the islands.

During 2008 it became increasingly clear that the December deadline for constitutional change would not be met. Negotiations continued throughout that year and at a round-table conference in Willemstad, Curaçao, on 14–16 December 2008, representatives of all five islands of the federation and the Dutch Prime Minister, Jan Pieter Balkenende, agreed on the new political structure of the Netherlands Antilles. St Maarten would become self-governing except in matters of defence, foreign policy, justice and finance. In return for retaining some legal and financial controls over St Maarten, the Dutch Government agreed to write off almost three-quarters of the Antilles' debt, beginning in 2009. Negotiations stalled, however, other matters, particularly policing and sound financial management (the latter despite the establishment of a financial supervision body, the College financieel toezicht. In September 2009 it was agreed that a second proposed dissolution date of January 2010 was unattainable, and that constitutional change would be set for 10 October of that year. Prior to securing autonomy, St Maarten would be required to introduce an appropriate legislative framework and to prepare its public authorities for the additional tasks entailed in administering an independent state. If the criteria was not met, a strategic plan to implement necessary changes would be devised, with developments to be monitored by a progress committee.

An election was held on 17 September 2010 to St Maarten's new 15-seat legislature. The National Alliance, comprising the Sint Maarten Patriotic Alliance and the National Progressive Party, gained seven seats, while the United People's Party (UP) won six seats and the Democratic Party (DP) the remaining two seats. Following the ballot, the UP and the DP agreed to form a coalition government following the introduction of the new Constitution. The DP's leader, Sarah Wescott-Williams took office as the autonomous territory's first Prime Minister on 10 October 2010, on the same day that the first meeting of parliament was convened. Eugene Holiday assumed the office of Governor.

The major economic activity in St Maarten is tourism. The addition of a new US $87m. terminal at the Princess Juliana International Airport in 2006 expanded the airport's passenger-handling capabilities by 2.5m. Aggregate is also quarried and consumed primarily by the local construction industry. Figures from the 2001 census showed that the rate of unemployment in St Maarten stood at 12.2%, with the rate of youth unemployment at 24.1%.

PUBLIC HOLIDAYS

2012: 1 January (New Year's Day), 6–9 April (Easter), 30 April (Queen's Day), 1 May (Labour Day), 17 May (Ascension Day), 28 May (Whit Monday), 11 November (St Maarten Day), 15 December (Kingdom Day), 25–26 December (Christmas).

For statistical information on St Maarten, see the Statistical Survey in the Curaçao chapter.

Directory

The Government

HEAD OF STATE

Queen of the Netherlands: HM Queen BEATRIX.
Governor: EUGENE HOLIDAY.

COUNCIL OF MINISTERS
(May 2011)

Prime Minister and Minister of General Affairs: SARAH WESCOT-WILLIAMS.

Minister of Housing and Spatial Planning, Environment and Infrastructure: THEODORE HEYLIGER.

Minister of Finance: HIROSHI SHIGEMOTO.

Minister of Justice: ROLAND DUNCAN.

Minister of Education, Culture, Youth and Sports Affairs: RHODA ARRINDELL.

Minister of Health Care, Social Development and Labour: CORNELIUS DE WEEVER.

Minister of Tourism, Economic Affairs, Transport and Telecommunication: FRANKLIN MEYERS.

Minister Plenipotentiary of Sint Maarten in the Netherlands: MATHIAS VOGES.

MINISTRIES

Office of the Governor: Government Administration Bldg, Clem Labega Sq., POB 943, Philipsburg; tel. 542-6085; fax 542-4172; e-mail dircab@governorsxm.com; internet www.governorsxm.com.

All government offices are located in Philipsburg.

NETHERLANDS DEPENDENCIES

Legislature

ESTATES OF SINT MAARTEN

General Election, 17 September 2010

Party	Votes	% of votes	Seats
National Alliance (NA)	6,298	45.94	7
United People's Party (UP)	4,943	36.06	6
Democratische Partij (DP)	2,339	17.06	2
Others	128	0.94	—
Total	13,708	100.00	15

Political Organizations

Democratische Partij—Sint Maarten (DP—StM): Tamarind Tree Dr. 4, Union Rd, Cole Bay; tel. 543-1166; fax 542-4296; Leader SARAH WESCOTT-WILLIAMS.

National Alliance (NA): Philipsburg; internet www.sxmnationalalliance.com; comprises the Sint Maarten Patriotic Alliance and the National Progressive Party; Leader WILLIAM MARLIN.

United People's Party (UP): Philipsburg; internet www.upparty.com; Leader THEO HEYLIGER.

Religion

Almost all of Sint (St) Maarten's population profess Christianity. Roman Catholicism forms the largest single group on St Maarten. St Maarten and the other former constituent territories of the Netherlands Antilles, as well as Aruba, together form the diocese of Willemstad, suffragan to the archdiocese of Port of Spain (Trinidad and Tobago). The Bishop participates in the Antilles Episcopal Conference, currently based in Trinidad and Tobago. Within the Anglican Communion, St Maarten forms part of the diocese of the North Eastern Caribbean and Aruba, within the Church in the Province of the West Indies. The Bishop is resident in The Valley, Anguilla.

The Press

Daily Herald: Bush Rd 22, POB 828, Philipsburg; tel. 542-5253; fax 542-5913; e-mail editorial@thedailyherald.com; internet www.thedailyherald.com; daily; English.

St Maarten Guardian: Vlaun Bldg, Pondfill, POB 1046, Philipsburg; tel. 542-6022; fax 542-6043; e-mail guardian@sintmaarten.net; f. 1989; daily; English; Man. Dir RICHARD F. GIBSON; Man. Editor JOSEPH DOMINIQUE; circ. 4,000.

Teen Times: c/o The Daily Herald, Bush Rd 22, POB 828, Philipsburg; tel. 542-5597; e-mail info@teentimes.com; for teenagers by teenagers; sponsored by *The Daily Herald*; English; Editor-in-Chief MICHAEL GRANGER.

Broadcasting and Communications

TELECOMMUNICATIONS

East Caribbean Cellular NV (ECC): 13 Richardson St, Philipsburg; tel. 542-4100; fax 542-5678; e-mail info@eastcaribbeancellular.com; internet www.eastcaribbeancellular.com; f. 1989.

Scarlet: see Curaçao—Telecommunications.

St Maarten Telecommunications Group: Soualiga Blvd 5, Philipsburg; tel. 542-0200; fax 543-0101; e-mail info@telemgroup.an; internet www.telemgroup.an; f. 1975; comprises TelEm (providing local services), TelCell NV (digital mobile services), TelNet Communications NV (internet services) and SMITCOMS NV (international services); 15,000 subscribers (TelEm); Chair. RAFAEL BOASMAN; CEO PIETER DRENTH.

BROADCASTING

Radio

Laser 101 (101.1 FM): Suite 2, 106 A. T. Illidge Rd, Philipsburg; tel. 543-2200; fax 543-2229; e-mail master@laser101.com; internet www.laser101.fm; 24 hours a day; music; English and Papiamento.

Voice of St Maarten (PJD2 Radio): Plaza 21, Backstreet, POB 366, Philipsburg; tel. 542-2580; fax 542-4905; also operates PJD3 on FM (24 hrs); commercial; programmes in English; Gen. Man. DON R. HUGHES.

Sint Maarten

Television

Leeward Broadcasting Corporation—Television: POB 375, Philipsburg; tel. (5) 23491; transmissions for approx. 10 hours daily. Relay stations provide St Maarten with programmes from Puerto Rico.

Finance

BANKING

Central Bank

Bank van Curaçao en Sint Maarten: see Curaçao—Banking.

Commercial Bank

Windward Islands Bank Ltd: Clem Labega Sq. 7, POB 220, Philipsburg; tel. 542-2313; fax 542-4761; e-mail info@wib-bank.net; internet www.wib-bank.net; affiliated to Maduro & Curiel's Bank NV; f. 1960; cap. and res 53.2m., dep. 662.2m. (Dec. 2006); Man. Dir JAN J. BEAUJON.

Banking Association

St Maarten Bankers' Association: Clem Labega Sq. 7, Philipsburg; tel. 542-2313; fax 542-6355; Pres. J. BEAUJON.

Trade and Industry

CHAMBER OF COMMERCE

St Maarten Chamber of Commerce and Industry: Cannegieterstraat 11, POB 454, Philipsburg; tel. 542-3590; fax 542-3512; e-mail info@sxmcoci.org; internet www.sxmcoci.org; f. 1979; Pres. GLEN CARTY; Exec. Dir LUDWIG OUENNICHE (acting).

INDUSTRIAL AND TRADE ASSOCIATION

St Maarten Hospitality and Trade Association: W. J. A. Nisbeth Rd 33A, POB 486, Philipsburg; tel. 542-0108; fax 542-0107; e-mail info@shta.com; internet www.shta.com; Pres. EMIL LEE; Exec. Project Man. ROBERT DUBOURCQ.

ULTILITY

GEBE NV: W. J. A. Nisbeth Rd 35, Pond Fill, POB 123, Philipsburg; tel. 542-2213; fax 542-4810; e-mail gebesxm@nvgebe.com; internet www.nvgebe.com; f. 1961; generates and distributes electricity via island network; operates island water supply system; Man. Dir WILLIAM GODFREY BROOKS.

TRADE UNION

Windward Islands' Federation of Labour (WIFOL): Long Wall Rd, POB 1097, Pond Fill, Philipsburg; tel. 542-2797; fax 542-6631; e-mail wifol@sintmaarten.net; Pres. THEOPHILUS THOMPSON.

Transport

SHIPPING

St Maarten is one of the Caribbean's leading ports for visits by cruise ships, and in 2001 new pier facilities were opened that could accommodate up to four cruise ships and add more cargo space.

St Maarten Ports Authority: J. Yrausquin Blvd, POB 146, Philipsburg; tel. 542-2307; fax 542-5048; e-mail Executive_Desk@portofstmaarten.com; internet www.portofstmaarten.com; f. 1989; Man. Dir MARK MINGO.

CIVIL AVIATION

Princess Juliana International Airport is located 16 km from Philipsburg. The second phase of a US $118m. project to expand the airport was completed in 2006. The development comprised a new terminal, enhancing the airport's passenger-handling capacity by 2.5m.

Windward Express Airways: Princess Juliana International Airport; tel. 545-2001; fax 545-2224; e-mail windwardexpressreservations@hotmail.com; internet www.windwardexpress.com; domestic and limited Caribbean island charter flights, incl. destinations with restricted access; passenger and cargo flights; Man. Dir CURLETTA HALLEY.

Windward Islands Airways International (WIA—Winair) NV: POB 2088, Princess Juliana International Airport; tel. 545-4237; fax 545-2002; e-mail info@fly-winair.com; internet www.fly-winair.com; f. 1961; govt-owned since 1974; scheduled and charter flights throughout north-eastern Caribbean; Man. Dir EDWIN HODGE.

Tourism

St Maarten Tourist Bureau: Vineyard Office Park, W. G. Buncamper Rd 33, Philipsburg; tel. 542-2337; fax 542-2734; e-mail info@e-stmaarten.com; internet www.vacationstmaarten.com; Dir REGINA LA BEGA.

Defence

The Netherlands is responsible for the defence of St Maarten. Military service is compulsory. The Governor is Commander-in-Chief of the armed forces in the territory. A Coast Guard Force operates from St Maarten.

Education

Education was made compulsory in 1992. The education system is the same as that of the Netherlands, and is generally of a high standard. English is the official language of instruction. Primary education begins at six years of age and lasts for six years. Secondary education lasts for a further five years.

NEW ZEALAND

Introductory Survey

LOCATION, CLIMATE, LANGUAGE, RELIGION, FLAG, CAPITAL

The Dominion of New Zealand lies in the South Pacific Ocean, about 1,750 km (1,100 miles) south-east of Australia. It consists of North Island and South Island, separated by the narrow Cook Strait, and several smaller islands, including Stewart Island (or Rakiura) in the south. The climate is temperate and moist, with an average temperature of 12°C (52°F), except in the far north, where higher temperatures are reached. The official languages are English and Maori. At the 2001 census, 15.7% of respondents professed adherence to the Anglican Church, 13.0% being Roman Catholics and 11.5% Presbyterians. At the 2006 census, 55.6% of respondents professed adherence to the Christian religion. The national flag (proportions 1 by 2) is dark blue, with a representation of the United Kingdom flag as a canton in the upper hoist. In the fly are four five-pointed red stars, edged in white, in the form of the Southern Cross constellation. The capital is Wellington, on North Island.

CONTEMPORARY POLITICAL HISTORY

Historical Context

New Zealand is a former British colony. It became a dominion, under the British Crown, in 1907 and achieved full independence by the Statute of Westminster, adopted by the British Parliament in 1931 and accepted by New Zealand in 1947. With Australia and the USA, New Zealand signed the ANZUS Security Treaty (see p. 459) in 1951. In 1962 Western Samoa (now Samoa, q.v.), formerly administered by New Zealand, achieved independence, and in 1965 the Cook Islands attained full internal self-government, but retained many links, including common citizenship, with New Zealand. In October 1974 Niue, one of New Zealand's island territories, obtained similar status 'in free association with New Zealand'. New Zealand retains two Dependent Territories, Ross Dependency and Tokelau (see the chapter on New Zealand's Dependent Territories).

Domestic Political Affairs

In December 1972 the first Labour Government for more than 12 years came to power, under the leadership of Norman Kirk, after a succession of New Zealand National Party administrations, most recently led by John Marshall, who had replaced Sir Keith Holyoake upon Marshall's retirement in February of that year. The New Zealand Labour Party took office at a time when the economy was thriving, mainly as a result of a sharp increase in international prices for agricultural commodities. However, this prosperity was accompanied by inflation, and the international energy crisis of 1973–74 led to a rapid deterioration in the country's economy.

Norman Kirk died in August 1974, and Wallace Rowling, hitherto Minister of Finance, became Prime Minister in September. The economic recession worsened, and in November 1975 a general election resulted in victory for the National Party, which won 55 of the 87 seats in the House of Representatives, while the Labour Party took the remaining 32 seats. The new Government, under Robert (later Sir Robert) Muldoon, who had led the National Party since July 1974, introduced austere economic policies, and in 1976 reduced the annual intake of migrants from 30,000 to 5,000, while conducting a campaign against illegal immigrants.

Popular dissatisfaction with Muldoon's sometimes controversial leadership was reflected at the general election in November 1978. The National Party retained power, with 50 of the 92 seats in the enlarged House of Representatives, but its share of the total vote decreased markedly. Labour won 41 seats. The Social Credit Party substantially increased its share of the votes cast but obtained only one seat. In the November 1981 election Muldoon's majority was further reduced. The National Party won 47 of the 92 seats in the House, while Labour, which again received more votes, won 43 seats and Social Credit (despite obtaining 20.6% of votes cast) only two.

In February 1984 Muldoon's Government antagonized New Zealand's trade unions by effecting legislation to ban 'closed shop' agreements with employers, thus giving employees the right to choose whether or not to join a trade union. Further legislation was used in June to compel striking construction workers to return to work. In the same month, owing to dissent within his own party, Muldoon called an early general election for July. The Labour Party secured 56 of the 95 seats in an enlarged House of Representatives, while the National Party took 37 seats. It was thought that the National Party had lost considerable support to the newly formed New Zealand Party; this right-wing party won more than 12% of the votes cast but no seats, after campaigning for a minimum of government intervention in the economy. David Lange (the leader of the Labour Party since February 1983) became Prime Minister. James McLay, who had been deputy leader of the National Party since March 1984, defeated Muldoon in an election for the leadership of the party in November 1984, but he was replaced as party leader by his deputy, James (Jim) Bolger, in March 1986.

The Labour Government introduced controversial deregulatory measures to improve the country's economic situation. The initial success of these measures, together with widespread popular support for the Government's anti-nuclear policy (see below), contributed to a second victory for the Labour Party in a general election in August 1987. Of the 97 seats in the expanded House of Representatives, the Labour Party secured 58, and the National Party 39. (The Democratic Party lost both the seats that its predecessor, the Social Credit Party, had won at the 1984 election.)

In 1987 Lange's Government initiated a controversial policy of privatization of state-owned enterprises. In November 1988 policy disagreements prompted Lange to dismiss the minister responsible for the privatization programme, Richard Prebble. Lange was accused by cabinet colleagues of acting without consultation, and in December Roger (later Sir Roger) Douglas, the Minister of Finance, declared that he would not serve another term under Lange. Douglas was promptly dismissed from office, and later that month unsuccessfully challenged Lange for the leadership of the Labour Party. In May 1989 the formation of the NewLabour Party (led by a former president of the Labour Party, Jim Anderton) was announced: the party aimed to appeal to disillusioned Labour supporters. In early August Douglas was elected by Labour MPs to a vacant cabinet post, thus prompting Lange to resign. Shortly afterwards, Geoffrey Palmer, hitherto the deputy leader of the Labour Party, was elected the Labour Party's parliamentary leader and Prime Minister.

In January 1990 Palmer effected an extensive government reorganization. The return of Richard Prebble to the Cabinet, in his former post as Minister for State-Owned Enterprises, provoked considerable anger within the Labour Party. The Government aroused further hostility by its introduction of a substantial fee for tertiary-level students. The continued sale of state assets, especially that of the telecommunications company, Telecom, was also unpopular. In September 1990, less than eight weeks before the next general election, Palmer resigned as Prime Minister. Public opinion polls had indicated that Labour, under his leadership, had lost support to the National Party, and members of the Cabinet had consequently urged him to resign. Michael Moore, the Minister of External Relations and Trade (who had also contested the August 1989 leadership election), replaced Palmer as Prime Minister and Labour Party leader. Moore promised to act promptly to avert the enormous budget deficit forecast for 1991/92; two weeks later he secured an agreement with the country's trade union leaders regarding restricted pay settlements. At the general election of October 1990, none the less, the National Party took 67 of the 97 seats in the House of Representatives. The Labour Party won 29 seats, while the NewLabour Party retained its sole seat. Jim Bolger, as leader of the National Party, thus became Prime Minister at the head of a Government that promised to continue Labour's strict budgetary and monetary controls. The sale of state assets would also continue.

In November 1990 the new Government's first economic proposals were outlined. They included the repeal of legislation on equal pay for women, and envisaged reductions in public spending, particularly in the field of social welfare. In December the Government announced measures that entailed proposed reductions in unemployment benefit, family benefits, and in medical and sickness payments, in preparation for the introduction of a system whereby users of medical and educational services (hitherto provided free of charge) would be required to pay, according to a means test. These measures were received with anger by social and church groups. Protest marches took place in April 1991, and plans for a 'freeze' in the levels of old-age pensions prompted groups representing the elderly unsuccessfully to petition the British monarch (through the Governor-General) to dismiss the Government. Two National Party members of the House of Representatives resigned from the party in August, in protest against the proposals, and the Minister of Maori Affairs, Winston Peters (who had openly criticized the Government's economic strategy), was dismissed in October. In November Sir Robert Muldoon announced that he would resign from the legislature in early 1992, in protest against the Government's economic policies. Earlier in the month criticism had prompted the Government to withdraw its stringent means-testing measures for the allocation of state pensions, but the overall level of payments remained lower than previously.

In December 1991 a coalition was formed by minor parties as a challenge to the two main parties. The grouping, known as the Alliance, consisted of the NewLabour Party, the New Zealand Democratic Party, the Green Party of Aotearoa—New Zealand and Mana Motuhake. In September 1992 a preliminary referendum on proposed electoral reform was held. The electorate voted overwhelmingly in favour of the abolition of the 'first-past-the-post' system and for its replacement by a form of proportional representation; of the four alternatives offered, the mixed member proportional (MMP) system (similar to that used in Germany) received the greatest support. The new rules were to be implemented at the 1996 election, following a second, binding referendum.

In March 1993 the outspoken Winston Peters resigned from his parliamentary seat in order to stand for re-election as an independent candidate. The by-election in April resulted in an overwhelming victory for Peters, the major political parties having declined to present candidates. In July Peters established New Zealand First, and announced that the party would contest all 99 seats at the forthcoming general election.

At the election, held in November 1993, the National Party, which had campaigned mainly on the Government's record of economic recovery, was narrowly returned to office, securing 50 seats in the House of Representatives. The Labour Party won 45 seats, the Alliance two and New Zealand First two. At a concurrent, second referendum on electoral reform, 54% of voters favoured the adoption of the MMP system. A new Government was appointed in late November.

In October 1994 Peter Dunne, a former cabinet minister, resigned from the Labour Party, following differences over the party's policy on taxation, and declared his intention to remain in the House of Representatives as an independent member. He subsequently established a new party, Future New Zealand. The traditional two-party system was further challenged in early 1995, when support for ACT New Zealand, co-founded by Sir Roger Douglas (reformist Minister of Finance in 1984–88), who had recently announced his return to politics, began to increase rapidly. In June 1995, however, the position of the ruling party was strengthened by the formation of United Future New Zealand (UFNZ) by seven members of the House of Representatives (four National, two Labour and the leader of Future New Zealand, Peter Dunne). The new grouping pledged its support for the Government on issues of confidence. In February 1996, for the first time since the early 1930s, a formal coalition Government was established when the National Party formed an official alliance with United New Zealand. In the ensuing government reorganization, Peter Dunne joined the Cabinet as Minister of Revenue and Internal Affairs. As a result of a number of parliamentary defections and realignments, by April 1996 the number of parliamentary seats held by the National Party had been reduced to 41. In March, meanwhile, Sir Michael Hardie Boys replaced Dame Catherine Tizard as Governor-General.

The first general election under the MMP system was held in October 1996. No party achieved an outright majority. The National Party received 34.1% of the votes cast and took 44 of the 120 seats in the expanded House of Representatives, the Labour Party (28.3%) secured 37 seats and New Zealand First (13.1%) garnered 17 seats, while the Alliance won 13 seats, ACT New Zealand eight and United New Zealand one. A notable development was the increase in the number of Maori MPs from six to 15, a figure almost equivalent to the proportion of Maori (the country's aboriginal inhabitants) in the population as a whole. Although the election result initially appeared to favour the formation of a centre-left coalition under the leadership of Helen Clark, complex negotiations finally led to the establishment in December of an alliance between the National Party and New Zealand First, led by Winston Peters.

Jim Bolger thus continued as Prime Minister, while Winston Peters was appointed Deputy Prime Minister and Treasurer, the latter newly created post carrying responsibility for the drafting of the country's budget. Although Peters had previously discounted the possibility of a reconciliation and of entering into a coalition with the National Party, he had unexpectedly altered his stance in exchange for concessions on economic policy. The incoming Cabinet incorporated a total of five members of New Zealand First. Don McKinnon of the National Party retained the foreign affairs portfolio, and Bill Birch continued to hold nominal responsibility for finance.

In September 1997 proposals for the introduction of a compulsory retirement savings scheme were overwhelmingly rejected by the electorate in a referendum. The holding of the referendum had been a condition of New Zealand First's participation in the ruling coalition, but the Prime Minister had also actively supported the proposed pension reforms. In the following month thousands of protesters took to the streets to demand the resignation of the Government, its policies on health and education having drawn particular criticism.

In November 1997, following a leadership challenge from Jenny Shipley, a cabinet minister whose portfolios now included transport and women's affairs, the Prime Minister announced his intention to resign. Shipley was thus sworn in as New Zealand's first woman Prime Minister in December, reiterating the National Party's commitment to a continuation of the partnership with New Zealand First. In the ensuing government reorganization, most supporters of Jim Bolger retained their portfolios but were downgraded. Winston Peters continued as Deputy Prime Minister, while other members of New Zealand First also remained in the Cabinet.

In November 1997, meanwhile, following the Alliance's rejection of a Greens' proposal to establish a coalition arrangement, the Green Party of Aotearoa decided that at the next general election it would stand as a separate political party but would remain a member of the Alliance until that time. In January 1998 the Liberal Party announced that it was to be dissolved and would merge with the Alliance.

In May 1998 the outcome of a parliamentary by-election to fill the seat vacated by Jim Bolger confirmed the electorate's growing disillusionment with the coalition Government. Although the seat was retained by the National Party, its majority was greatly reduced. In August, following an acrimonious dispute regarding the sale of the Government's stake in Wellington airport, Winston Peters was dismissed from the post of Deputy Prime Minister and Treasurer; the dissolution of the coalition Government was announced. Rejecting demands for an early general election, Jenny Shipley reallocated many cabinet portfolios. Although Tau Henare (who in late 1998 founded a new party, Mauri Pacific, having been removed as deputy leader of New Zealand First in July), the Minister of Maori Affairs, was the only former New Zealand First minister to retain his post within the Cabinet, three other erstwhile members of the National Party's former coalition partner remained as ministers outside the Cabinet. Despite the defection of Winston Peters to the opposition, the Prime Minister was able to secure the support of eight of the 16 New Zealand First representatives in the legislature, and in September she survived a vote of confidence in the House. In the same month, in an attempt to raise public concern over the social effects of government policy, in particular the plight of low-income families, the Anglican Church initiated an ecumenical 'Hikoi of Hope', in which protesters from both ends of the country marched to Wellington and converged upon the House of Representatives.

In December 1998 the minority Government's position was further weakened by the unexpected resignation of a supporting independent (and former New Zealand First) MP, following the administration's decision to proceed with its acquisition of 28 F-16 fighter aircraft from the USA. The Prime Minister was placed under further pressure in early 1999, when it was alleged that the Minister of Tourism, Murray McCully, had acted inappropriately with regard to the handling of a major contract for the advertising business of the New Zealand Tourism Board. In February, as the Prime Minister became personally implicated in the affair and as opposition MPs accused her of deliberately misleading the legislature over her association with the head of the advertising agency in question, the Government won a motion of no confidence by 61 votes to 59. Claiming that the ruling party had intended to exploit its links with the agency during the next general election campaign, the Labour Party demanded an inquiry into the Government's alleged payments to departing members of the New Zealand Tourism Board and into the Board's expenditure on overseas promotions. In March the $NZ53m. marketing contract with the agency was terminated. McCully relinquished the tourism portfolio in April.

The Labour Party's return to power

At the general election, conducted in late November 1999, the opposition Labour Party won the largest share of votes cast. A recount of votes in one constituency, where the Green Party candidate then unexpectedly took the seat from the incumbent National MP, combined with the incorporation of 'special votes' (which included those cast by New Zealanders overseas), led to a substantial modification of the initial results. Having secured 38.7% of the votes cast, the Labour Party was finally allocated 49 of the 120 seats in the House of Representatives, while the National Party, which had won 30.5% of the votes, received 39 seats. The Alliance was allocated 10 seats and ACT New Zealand nine seats. Under the recently introduced system of proportional representation, the Green Party's victory in the one constituency automatically entitled the movement to a further six seats in the legislature. New Zealand First's representation declined to five seats; the party's leader, Winston Peters, only narrowly retained his seat. United New Zealand took the one remaining seat. Having previously discounted any co-operation with the Green Party, the Labour Party was thus obliged to seek the support not only of the Alliance but also of the seven Green MPs.

The leader of the Labour Party, Helen Clark (who had served as Deputy Prime Minister in 1989–90), thus became Prime Minister. The minority Government, which incorporated several members of the Alliance, took office in December 1999. Jim Anderton, the leader of the Alliance, was appointed Deputy Prime Minister, Minister for Economic Development and Minister for Industry and Regional Development. The treasury and finance portfolios were assigned to Dr Michael Cullen, while Phil Goff became Minister of Foreign Affairs and Trade and also assumed responsibility for the justice portfolio.

In a non-binding, citizen-initiated referendum held on the same day as the general election, a majority of voters favoured a reduction in the number of members of the House of Representatives from 120 to 99; voters also favoured a reform of the criminal justice system.

One of the new Government's stated priorities was the 'Closing the Gaps' initiative, which aimed to address the socio-economic disparities between the Maori and non-Maori communities, particularly in health, housing, education, income and the incidence of crime. Among its first actions were the repeal of the Employment Contracts Act, the restoration of the state monopoly in the provision of accident compensation and the cancellation of the contract to lease 28 F-16 fighter aircraft from the USA. The new Government was strongly criticized by opposition politicians and accused of racism, following its decision in mid-2000 to sell a 25% share of a lucrative radiowaves company to a Maori trust under its 'Closing the Gaps' policy.

In June 2000 the Prime Minister was obliged to dismiss the Minister of Maori Affairs, Dover Samuels, following allegations of sexual misconduct. On 4 April 2001 Dame Silvia Cartwright (New Zealand's first female High Court Judge) took office as Governor-General. Her appointment represented a significant achievement for women in New Zealand public life, and created an unprecedented situation in which the five most important public roles in the country (those of Prime Minister, Leader of the Opposition, Attorney-General and Chief Justice, along with that of Governor-General) were all occupied by women.

In October 2001 Jenny Shipley resigned as leader of the National Party and was replaced by Bill English, a former Minister of Health. The incoming leader renamed the party the New National Party. In December Jim Anderton was placed under considerable pressure from left-wing members of the Alliance to withdraw his support for the Government's involvement in the US-led military campaign in Afghanistan (see the chapter on Afghanistan). In early April 2002, after months of discord, the Alliance split. Anderton and six other members of the party agreed to form a breakaway party, later named the Progressive Coalition, but continued to support the ruling coalition. The seven members of the legislature were expelled from the Alliance in late April. At the same time Laila Harré, Minister of Women's Affairs, Youth Affairs and Statistics, succeeded Anderton as leader of the Alliance and confirmed her support for the Government until the next legislative election. In June the Prime Minister announced that the next election was to be held earlier than planned, in late July, largely owing to the disintegration of the Alliance, and a dispute between the Labour Party and the Greens over the Government's decision not to renew a moratorium banning the commercial release of genetically modified organisms (which expired in October 2003).

In April 2002, following extensive consultations, the Government announced the proposed replacement of the monarch's Privy Council (based in London, United Kingdom) as New Zealand's court of final appeal by an independent Supreme Court, consisting of five judges headed by the Chief Justice. The requisite legislation was approved in October 2003; the new court began functioning in July 2004.

Some 77% of registered voters participated in the general election, which took place on 27 July 2002. The Labour Party won 41% of the party votes cast, thereby gaining a second term in office. However, the party failed to secure an overall majority in the House of Representatives, winning 52 of the 120 seats. The National Party performed badly, winning only 21% of the party votes; its representation declined by 12 seats to 27. New Zealand First secured 13 seats, ACT New Zealand nine, the Greens nine and UFNZ eight. The Progressive Coalition took two seats, while the Alliance failed to secure any parliamentary representation. Unable to reach an agreement with the Greens on the issue of genetically modified organisms, Clark formed a minority coalition Government with the Progressive Coalition. The Labour Party leader secured the support of UFNZ. In May 2003 the Prime Minister carried out a government reorganization.

In June 2003 Clark announced that the Government intended to draw up new legislation to ensure that the country's coastline and seabed were owned by the Crown, following a ruling by the Court of Appeal that Maori tribes could pursue their own claims to ownership of the Marlborough Sands foreshore and seabed in South Island. Maori condemned the Government's 'draconian' and 'colonialist' actions. In October the legislature voted overwhelmingly in favour of the Anti-Terrorism Act, which widened the powers of the police force. The act, an extension of the 2002 Terrorism Suppression Act, created various new offences. The Green Party opposed the legislation, claiming that the law would infringe upon civil liberties.

In February 2004 the Minister of Commerce and of Immigration, Lianne Dalziel, was forced to resign after it transpired that she had lied over the disclosure to the media of a document relating to the deportation of a Sri Lankan youth. The Prime Minister ordered an inquiry into the acquisition by Dalziel of a confidential legal document and into officials' involvement in its subsequent circulation. A cabinet reorganization was subsequently effected. Meanwhile, in the same month the new leader of the opposition National Party, Don Brash, a former governor of the central bank, announced that if he won power he would discontinue all forms of positive discrimination for Maori, considering 'special privileges' to be unnecessary and divisive. Brash also pledged to abolish the parliamentary seats reserved for Maori and to repeal 'divisive, race-based' legislation. Clark accused Brash of creating disharmony by breaking the national consensus on dealing with Maori affairs; nevertheless, two days later she promised a review of state assistance for Maori, agreeing that policies should be based on need and not on any perceived privilege. In the February government reorganization, Clark also created the post of Co-ordinating Minister for Race Relations after opinion polls showed a decline in support for her administration over its policies towards the Maori. The portfolio was assigned to the Minister of Education, of State Services, and for Sport and Recreation, Trevor Mallard; he was given the immediate responsibility of conducting a full review of government policy.

In April 2004 the Progressive Coalition was renamed the Progressive Party. In the same month Clark dismissed the Associate Minister of Maori Affairs, Tariana Turia, after Turia stated that she intended to vote against the Government's Foreshore and Seabed Bill, which ensured that coastal areas were owned by the Crown, on the grounds that the new legislation was in contravention of the rights of indigenous Maori. Following her dismissal, in the following month Turia resigned from the Labour Party and the House of Representatives. In May the Prime Minister secured a narrow victory in a vote of no confidence precipitated by Turia's resignation. Meanwhile, a two-week hikoi (protest march) against the planned legislation, which had commenced in mid-April, arrived outside the Parliament building in Wellington.

In July 2004 Tariana Turia secured victory in a by-election to the seat of Te Tai Hauauru on North Island, necessitated by her resignation from the House of Representatives in the previous month. Turia was the candidate of the newly formed Maori Party. In November the controversial Foreshore and Seabed Bill was narrowly approved by the House of Representatives, after the Government secured the support of New Zealand First. (However, the legislation was repealed in June 2010—see Maori Land Rights and the Waitangi Tribunal Process.) Also in November 2004 the Minister of Youth Affairs, for Land Information and of Statistics, John Tamihere, resigned following the revelation that a report on his activities had been sent to the Serious Fraud Office for investigation. In December a major government reorganization was announced, in which Tamihere's portfolios were reassigned. The appointments took effect in February 2005, when Attorney-General Margaret Wilson left the Cabinet in order to succeed Jonathan Hunt as Speaker of the House of Representatives. Deputy Prime Minister Michael Cullen became the new Attorney-General, while retaining his existing portfolios. In March the Serious Fraud Office announced that, following its investigation, it did not intend to charge Tamihere with any offence.

In May 2005 Minister of Fisheries David Benson-Pope resigned from his cabinet post, following the commencement of a police inquiry into allegations that he had abused children during his former career as a teacher. However, he was reinstated to the Cabinet in the following month. In July Prime Minister Helen Clark announced that a general election would take place in September. At the election, which was held on 17 September, Clark's Labour Party secured victory by a narrow margin, winning 41.1% of the votes cast and 50 seats. The National Party won 39.1% of the votes and 48 seats, a significant improvement in comparison with its performance at the 2002 election. The newly formed Maori Party secured 2.1% of the vote, winning four of the seven seats reserved for Maoris. As the Labour Party had failed to gain an overall majority, it subsequently entered into a coalition with the Progressive Party, which had won only one seat. With the support of New Zealand First and UFNZ, secured on a more informal basis, this brought the total number of seats controlled by the Government in the new legislature to 61.

In October 2005 the new Government was sworn in. Controversial New Zealand First leader Winston Peters was appointed Minister of Foreign Affairs. Peter Dunne of UFNZ was allocated the revenue portfolio, but with the unusual provision that both would remain outside the Cabinet. The appointment of Peters drew widespread criticism, owing to his anti-immigration views. In March 2006 David Parker, who had been appointed as Attorney-General in the new Government, resigned from the position, having admitted that he had made an error while filing an annual return for a company with which he was involved. However, he retained the cabinet portfolios of energy and transport. Deputy Prime Minister Michael Cullen subsequently became Attorney-General for the second time, holding the post concurrently with the finance and tertiary education portfolios. In the same month Maj.-Gen. Jerry Mateparae, hitherto Chief of the Army, became the first Maori to be appointed Chief of the New Zealand Defence Force; he took up the position in May. In August 2006 Te Arikinui (Dame Te Atairangikaahu, the Maori Queen) died, bringing to an end her 40-year reign. Te Arikinui's son, Tuheitia Paki, took the throne, shortly before a traditional Maori funeral ceremony for Dame Te Ata, which was attended by thousands of mourners, including Prime Minister Clark. Also in August Anand (later Sir Anand) Satyanand, a retired judge of Indo-Fijian descent, replaced Dame Silvia Cartwright as Governor-General upon the expiry of her term of office.

In October 2006 the Auditor-General, Kevin Brady, published a report on an investigation into campaign funding during the 2005 legislative election. Brady found that the Labour Party had improperly spent $NZ768,000 of taxpayers' money on its election campaign; several other parties, including New Zealand First and the Green Party, were similarly implicated in breaches of regulations, albeit for smaller sums. Labour promptly announced that it was to reimburse the funds. Legislation retrospectively validating the relevant election campaign expenditure was swiftly enacted by the House of Representatives, but controversy continued. In November 2006 Don Brash resigned as leader of the National Party, citing concerns that increased speculation about his position was having a negative effect on the party. Brash had applied for an injunction against the publication of his e-mails in a book that attempted to prove a link between himself and the Exclusive Brethren, a business-orientated Christian group that had allegedly been involved in improperly influencing the outcome of the 2005 election; he denied allegations of irregular campaign practices and maintained that his resignation was not related to the impending publication of the book. John Key, hitherto the National Party's finance spokesman and a former investment banker, was subsequently elected unopposed to the National Party leadership.

In July 2007 David Benson-Pope, the Minister for Social Development and Employment and for the Environment, resigned in connection with the allegedly unfair dismissal of an employee of the Ministry for the Environment. Amid opinion poll results suggesting an increase in support for the National Party, Prime Minister Clark announced a ministerial reorganization in October 2007. Steve Chadwick was appointed Minister of Conservation and of Women's Affairs, Maryan Street Minister for the Accident Compensation Corporation and of Housing, and Shane Jones Minister for Building and Construction. Another notable change was the allocation of the justice portfolio to Annette King, in addition to her existing responsibilities for transport and police.

In October 2007 a nation-wide police operation, carried out in various cities as well as in a remote part of North Island, resulted in the arrest of 17 people under the Terrorism Suppression Act. Some of the detainees were reported to be activists for causes including Maori independence and the environment, and were alleged to have been involved in illegal training camps where firearms and other weapons were found. Tame Iti, a well-known Maori campaigner, was among those arrested. Hundreds of people took part in demonstrations to protest against the police action. However, in November the Solicitor-General concluded that the detainees could not be charged under the Terrorism Suppression Act.

In August 2008 the Minister of Foreign Affairs and for Racing, Winston Peters, relinquished his portfolios, following the commencement of an investigation by the Serious Fraud Office into allegations of irregularities with regard to donations intended for his New Zealand First party. Prime Minister Helen Clark assumed responsibility for the portfolios, pending the outcome of the inquiry. In October the investigation concluded that Peters had not committed any fraud. However, he did not resume his ministerial role, owing to the imminence of the general election, which was scheduled for November.

The National Party's formation of a coalition Government

At the election held on 8 November 2008, the National Party won 58 of the 122 seats in the House of Representatives, having received 44.9% of the party votes cast. The Labour Party took 43 seats, with 34.0% of the votes. Nine seats were won by the Green Party. The rate of participation in the polls was almost 79.5% of the registered electorate. In the absence of an overall majority of parliamentary seats for the National Party, John Key announced his intention to establish an informal coalition administration, and he proceeded to secure the support of members of ACT New Zealand (which had won five seats), the Maori Party (also five seats) and UFNZ (one seat). Following the defeat of the Labour Party, Helen Clark resigned as leader; she was replaced by Phil Goff, whose portfolios in the outgoing Government had included that of defence.

On 19 November 2008 John Key was sworn in as Prime Minister, at the head of a coalition Government. Key also assumed the tourism portfolio. Bill English was appointed as Deputy Prime Minister and Minister of Finance. Other notable appointments to the new Cabinet included Murray McCully as Minister of Foreign Affairs, who in addition was allocated responsibility for sport and recreation. The new Government also included New Zealand's first minister of Asian origin, Pansy Wong, who was appointed as Minister for Ethnic and Women's Affairs. Five 'support party ministers' included Dr Pita Sharples as Minister of Maori Affairs; Tariana Turia, also a member of the Maori Party, as Minister for the Community and Voluntary Sector; and Peter Dunne of UFNZ as Minister of Revenue. As global financial conditions rapidly deteriorated and as New Zealand entered recession, the incoming Government underlined that its immediate priority was to address the country's economic difficulties.

In June 2009 the Prime Minister accepted the resignation of John Worth, Minister for Land Information, Archives New Zealand and the National Library, and Associate Minister for Justice, following a series of allegations of inappropriate behaviour and a police investigation into accusations of harassment. Taito Phillip Field, a former Labour cabinet member, was sentenced to a six-year prison term in October after being found guilty in August of corruption, bribery and perverting the course of justice; he thus became the first senior New Zealand politician to be convicted of such charges. Field had given favourable treatment to eight Thai immigrants in exchange for free labour on his properties in Auckland and Samoa; he lodged an appeal against his conviction at the end of October. The case also raised cultural issues, Field having been New Zealand's first MP of Pacific island descent. In February 2010 the Minister of Fisheries and of Housing, Phil Heatley, submitted his resignation in response to allegations of irregularities relating to claims for parliamentary expenses. However, he was subsequently exonerated, following an investigation by the Auditor-General, and reinstated in his cabinet position.

In November 2009 parliamentary approval was narrowly secured for the Government's contentious emissions trading scheme (ETS), intended to encourage the reduction of greenhouse gas emissions. The opposition Labour Party regarded the ETS as a weaker version of a similar initiative that it had proposed in 2008 and argued that insufficient incentives were available to polluters to curtail their carbon emissions. Labour and the Greens also expressed concern at the cost of the ETS and at the hurried nature of the review process prior to the bill's approval. Nevertheless, the first phase of the trading scheme entered into effect in July 2010, and the second, and final, phase was implemented in September.

Following the Government's announcement in March 2010 of proposals to replace the divisive Foreshore and Seabed Act (see Maori Land Rights and the Waitangi Tribunal Process), in April the Government unexpectedly declared its support for the controversial UN Declaration on the Rights of Indigenous Peoples, thereby officially acknowledging the Maori right to self-determination (within the boundaries of New Zealand law). Labour had refused to support the non-binding Declaration in 2007, owing to fears that it would conflict with the Waitangi Tribunal process and the Constitution by potentially prompting further Maori land claims, while bestowing additional rights upon the Maori but excluding the remainder of the country's population.

In April 2010 the Government launched a new welfare initiative, Whanau Ora (family wellness). By providing social services through a single consolidated agency, the programme was primarily intended to redress the consistently low social indicators of Maori, although it was emphasized that the scheme was open to all. The new agency was to address families' health and welfare needs through a holistic approach. Tariana Turia, the co-leader of the Maori Party, was appointed to head the programme, the portfolio being added to the Minister's existing responsibilities. Although the Whanau Ora initiative was criticized by the opposition parties for its lack of clarity, the initial phase of the scheme was scheduled to commence in July. (See also Maori Land Rights and the Waitangi Tribunal Process.)

Demonstrators converged in Auckland in May 2010 to protest against controversial government plans to initiate mining operations in protected conservation zones. Police estimates placed the total number of protesters at around 20,000, a much higher number than had been anticipated, in what was reportedly the largest demonstration in the country for some 20 years.

Recent developments: preparations for the 2011 election

Legislation to reform the electoral finance system prior to the holding of the next general election, due in late 2011, was introduced into Parliament in April 2010. The legislation, which, *inter alia*, clarified regulations governing matters such as donations to political parties, secured parliamentary approval in mid-December, by 116 votes to five, replacing the complex, and unpopular, 2007 Electoral Finance Act, which had been repealed in late 2009. Meanwhile, in September 2010 the Government announced that voters who had participated in previous elections would for the first time be able to complete the re-enrolment process for the 2011 poll online; after the 2011 election, the system was to be expanded to include enrolment for first-time voters. It was hoped that simplifying the enrolment procedure would result in a greater rate of electoral participation, particularly among young members of the electorate. At the beginning of October 2010 the functions of the Electoral Commission and of the Chief Electoral Officer were transferred to a new Electoral Commission. Legislation was introduced in mid-November providing for the transfer to the new Electoral Commission of the functions of the Chief Registrar of Electors, thereby completing the consolidation of all electoral administrative responsibilities within the new Commission.

In February 2011 Prime Minister John Key announced that the general election was to be held on 26 November. A referendum on the issue of the MMP system was to be held concurrently with the election, at which voters were to be asked two questions: first, if they favoured the retention of the current system; and, second, which alternative system they preferred from a range of options. At the same time Key ruled out the possibility of working with New Zealand First should Winston Peters' party hold the balance of power at the election between the National Party and Labour. Key dismissed Peters' parliamentary outlook as 'rearward-looking', and declared that if New Zealand First did hold the balance of power there would be a Labour government.

Meanwhile, in mid-November 2010 Pansy Wong tendered her resignation as Minister for Ethnic Affairs and of Women's Affairs, following allegations of misuse of a parliamentary travel allowance, a claim that related to an internal flight in China taken by her husband in 2008. Wong acknowledged that, in contravention of the rules governing ministerial travel entitlements (which stipulated that entitlements could be used for personal travel exclusively), her husband had conducted some private business during the trip. Prime Minister Key accepted Wong's resignation, expressing his belief that, as the minister had been unable to assure him that the transgression was an isolated breach of ministerial rules, her decision to resign had been 'appropriate'. Wong was exonerated of serious misuse of her travel allowance on 3 December 2010, following the publication of a report detailing the findings of a parliamentary investigation into her use of ministerial travel entitlements, which found that the trip has been 'unplanned and inadvertent'. The report, which revealed that Wong and her husband had claimed $NZ54,149 for 13 overseas trips, and $NZ93,935 for domestic trips, since 2000, elicited strong criticism from a number of opposition legislators, including Phil Goff, who urged that the issue be referred to the Auditor-General for further review. Hekia Parata, of the National Party, was appointed as the new Minister for Ethnic Affairs and of Women's Affairs on 6 December 2010. On the following day Prime Minister Key announced that the Government was to introduce legislation that would provide for ministerial allowances to be controlled by the independent Remuneration Authority; hitherto, all ministerial entitlements were determined by the Prime Minister and Speaker, with the Remuneration Authority responsible only for setting ministers' base salaries. On 14 December Pansy Wong resigned from the House of Representatives, stating that the ongoing debate over her misuse of travel entitlements was causing 'unnecessary distractions' to the Government. A by-election for the parliamentary seat vacated by Wong in the electoral district of Botany was held on 5 March 2011, and was won by Jami-Lee Ross, who retained the seat for the National Party, but with its majority reduced, according to preliminary results.

At the end of January 2011 Prime Minister Key announced the creation of a new Ministry of Science and Innovation, following the merger of the Ministry of Research, Science and Technology and the Foundation for Research, Science and Technology. The new ministry was to be headed by Dr Wayne Mapp, hitherto Minister of Research, Science and Technology. Following an earthquake 10 km south-east of Christchurch in mid-February, which claimed the lives of at least 65 people and caused widespread damage to buildings and infrastructure, Key effected a minor reallocation of ministerial portfolios, in order to allow the Minister for Economic Development and of Energy and Resources, Gerry Brownlee, who had also been appointed Minister for Earthquake Recovery following an earlier earthquake that had struck about 40 km west of Christchurch in September 2010, to focus exclusively on recovery efforts in the aftermath of the second, more serious disaster: the economic development portfolio was transferred, on an interim basis, to David Carter, while Hekia Parata became acting Minister of Energy and Resources and Simon Power was appointed acting Leader of the House of Representatives.

Maori Land Rights and the Waitangi Tribunal Process

During 1987 there were protests by the Maori concerning their cultural and economic rights and, in particular, their claims to land in accordance with the Treaty of Waitangi, concluded in 1840 by the British Government and Maori leaders, whereby sovereignty had been ceded to the United Kingdom in return for the Maori people's retention of hunting and fishing grounds. In November 1987 a ruling by the Waitangi Tribunal, reconvened in 1975 to consider retrospectively the claims of Maori land rights activists, recommended the restoration of an Auckland harbour headland to the Maori people. By 1994 about 75% of the country was subject to land claims by Maori groups. In December of that year the Government offered the sum of $NZ1,000m., payable over a 10-year period, in full and final settlement of outstanding claims for compensation. However, the condition that all future land claims be renounced was rejected by most Maori groups. In the same month an historic agreement between the Government and the Tainui people of Waikato provided for the return of land confiscated in 1863 and for the deposit over a period of five years of $NZ65m. in a land acquisition trust.

In May 1995 the Prime Minister and the Queen of the Tainui people signed an agreement relating to a full and final settlement, valued at $NZ170m., of land grievances dating back to 1863. However, increasing ethnic tension was demonstrated by the destruction in September 1995 of an old school building by Maori protesters involved in a land dispute and by the burning down in October of an historic church, the 'Maori Cathedral', at Otaki, in an apparent retaliatory arson attack by white extremists. In November, in a highly significant ceremony in Wellington, Queen Elizabeth II gave her personal assent to the legislation ending the Tainui grievances when she signed the Waikato Raupatu Claims Settlement Act: this implemented the $NZ170m. agreement, including the return of 15,780 ha of land, and incorporated an apology from the Crown for the loss of lives and for the confiscation of property. A final settlement payment of $NZ13m. was made to the Tainui tribe in late 2000. In October 1996, as more modest agreements continued to be reached, the Government announced a $NZ170m. provisional settlement with the South Island's Ngai Tahu (one of New Zealand's smallest Maori tribes) regarding the group's long-standing claim for compensation. In early 1997 Maori leaders, pursuing a claim first lodged by tribal advocates in 1991, embarked upon a lawsuit aimed at the official alteration of New Zealand's name to Aotearoa ('Land of the Long White Cloud').

In July 1997 a Maori tribe that had been driven off its land in the 1840s lodged a claim to the site of the Parliament building in Wellington. The Ngati Tama also presented claims to other areas of the capital, while declaring their willingness to negotiate. At a ceremony in Wellington in September 1997, following six years of negotiations, the Government and the Ngai Tahu reached a formal agreement, subject to approval by the tribe's members, regarding the compensation of $NZ170m. The Government's offer also included the right to name mountains and rivers, often in combination with the English equivalents, and incorporated a full apology from the Crown. In November, the tribal beneficiaries having voted overwhelmingly in favour of the arrangements, the historic deed of full and final settlement was signed by the Prime Minister and representatives of the Ngai Tahu. In March 1998 the Ngai Tahu Claims Settlement Bill was duly submitted to the House of Representatives, where it received approval six months later. In July, exercising for the first time its power of compulsory recommendation, the Waitangi Tribunal ordered the Government to return to the Ngati Turangitukua land (now valued at $NZ6.1m.) that had been confiscated from its Maori owners more than 30 years previously to permit the construction of housing for workers engaged on an electric power project in the central North Island.

In early 2000 a joint land claim was lodged by five Maori tribes of the central North Island. With the forestry claim alone worth an estimated $NZ588m., the application was potentially the largest ever submitted to the Waitangi Tribunal. In March 2001 the Ngati Ruanui became the first Taranaki tribe to conclude a deed of settlement with the Government, amounting to $NZ41m. In early 2003 the Ngati Awa voted in favour of a treaty settlement with the Government, which included an apology from the Crown, the return of 64 ha of land and $NZ42m. In August 2005 Prime Minister Helen Clark announced that all Maori land claims under the Treaty of Waitangi would have to be filed by 1 September 2008, in order that they could be settled by 2020. According to reports, by 2007 the Waitangi Tribunal had been able to settle only about 20 claims. On the closing date for registration the Waitangi Tribunal received more than 1,000 new historical grievance claims from Maori communities. In October 2007 the Government instigated a campaign to persuade Maoris living in Australia to return to New Zealand.

In June 2008, in a settlement valued at $NZ418m., the New Zealand Government signed an agreement with seven Maori tribes to transfer ownership of 176,000 ha of Crown forestry land in the central North Island, originally ceded under the Treaty of Waitangi. The Maori tribes, which represented approximately 100,000 people, also stood to receive backdated forest rental payments of $NZ223m., in addition to future annual rental income and carbon credits.

In February 2009 the Government awarded $NZ300m. in compensation to eight Maori tribes, comprising more than 12,000 members, in recognition of historic injustices arising from violations of the Treaty of Waitangi and illegal seizures of land. Furthermore, in the first such decision relating to an issue of intellectual property, the Government recognized that the Ka Mate haka, the 'war dance' traditionally performed by the New Zealand rugby team at international games but increasingly being used for commercial exploitation, had been written in the 1820s by Maori chief Te Rauparaha, an ancestor of the Ngati Toa tribe. A $NZ25m. settlement encompassing the greater Wellington region was agreed in July 2009; significantly, the *iwi* (tribe) involved in the agreement issued an unprecedented formal statement of forgiveness to the Crown.

The Ngati Kuia concluded a deed of settlement with the Crown in October 2010, the first such agreement in South Island since 1997; the settlement included an apology from the Crown, the return of culturally sensitive land and $NZ24m. in compensation. The Ngati Porou, New Zealand's second largest *iwi*, comprising about 72,000 members, signed a deed of settlement with the Crown in December 2010, which included the return of approximately 5,900 ha of land and $NZ110m. in compensation.

Maori fishing rights

In response to Maori grievances over fishing rights, in 1988 the Government introduced a Maori Fisheries Bill, under the provisions of which 2.5% of current fishing quotas were to be restored to the Maori people annually for the following 19 years. However, Maori activists alleged that the proposed legislation was racially discriminatory, since it stipulated that no other Maori fishing claim would be considered by the Waitangi Tribunal until the 19 years had elapsed. The bill was also condemned by some white New Zealanders, as, if implemented as proposed, it would guarantee the Maori people about 50% of the country's entire fishing rights by 2008. In November 1992, in the hope of reaching a permanent settlement, the Government advanced the sum of $NZ150m. to a Maori consortium to enable the latter's purchase of a 50% stake in the country's biggest inshore fishing company.

In early 1996 the Treaty of Waitangi Fisheries Commission, established to resolve the issue of the allocation among Maori of resources valued at $NZ200m., had yet to deliver its recommendations. In April the Court of Appeal declared that, despite having no coastline, urban Maori constituted an *iwi* and were therefore directly entitled to a share of these fishery assets. The case was subsequently referred to the Privy Council in London. Its decision, announced in January 1997, overruled the Court of Appeal's definition of an *iwi*.

In April 1997 urban Maori were outraged at a proposal by the Treaty of Waitangi Fisheries Commission to allocate up to $NZ300m. of fishery assets on a tribal basis, rather than according to *iwi* size as the populous northern tribes demanded. The Ngai Tahu and other *iwi*, meanwhile, argued that the length of coastline and traditional fishing grounds should determine the allocation of assets. In early 1998 it was announced that new regulations were to govern the management of 'customary' fishing by *tangata whenua* (people of the land), whereby Maori were permitted to take an unlimited amount of seafood provided that it was not for pecuniary gain.

In mid-1998 the Waitangi Tribunal ruled that urban Maori without blood ties should be accorded similar negotiating rights to those of traditional *iwi*. The historic decision thus acknowledged urban Maori trusts as modern tribes. In August, however, a High Court judge ruled in favour of traditional Maori tribes, effectively declaring that urban Maori groups had no claim to fishery assets. In October 1999, furthermore, the urban Maori claim was rejected by the Court of Appeal. In June 2004 it was reported that Maori tribes had been offered 20% of all new aquaculture or marine farming areas and 20% of aquaculture areas that had been allocated since 1992 in an attempt to resolve the 1992 fisheries settlement. The offer was believed to be, in part, an inducement to Maori to accept the controversial Foreshore and Seabed Bill.

In March 2010 the Government announced proposals to replace the Foreshore and Seabed Act with new legislation, following a ministerial review in 2009, which had concluded that the legislation failed to balance the interests of all New Zealanders in the foreshore and seabed, and was discriminatory against Maori, and advised repealing the legislation. In June 2010 Prime Minister John Key announced that the Government, the Maori Party and *iwi* leaders had reached an agreement providing for the repeal of the Act and its replacement with new legislation that would abrogate Crown ownership of the coastal areas in question and place them in the public domain, thereby also preventing Maori ownership claims, while allowing Maori groups to seek recognition of their customary rights from the Government or by application to the High Court—a right that had been denied to them under the Foreshore and Seabed Act. The Marine and Coastal Area (Takutai Moana) Bill was introduced to Parliament in August, whereupon it encountered significant opposition from some quarters, including Maori Party legislator Hone Harawira, who argued that the draft legislation was 'a fraud' since Maori seeking to claim customary rights over foreshore and seabed areas would be required to prove unbroken tenure of the areas in question since 1840, which, he contended, 98% of Maori would be unable to do. Conversely, the Coastal Coalition, an umbrella organization comprising those who believed the foreshore and seabed to be 'the birthright and common heritage of all New Zealanders equally' and should remain under the ownership of the Crown, opposed the bill as a 'massive coastal land grab for the Maori'. At early 2011 the Marine and Coastal Area (Takutai Moana) Bill remained under parliamentary consideration. An opinion poll conducted in late February indicated that just 11% of Maori approved of the Government's proposed legislation.

Foreign Affairs

The Labour Government that took office at the end of 1972 adopted a more independent policy than that of its predecessors. It phased out New Zealand's military commitments under the South-East Asia Treaty Organization and established diplomatic relations with the People's Republic of China. New Zealand became committed to the objective of the global elimination of all nuclear weapons, and in November 1996 was a co-sponsor of a UN resolution, overwhelmingly adopted by the General Assembly, to promote the establishment of a nuclear-weapons-free southern hemisphere. In October 2000 New Zealand ratified the Waigani Convention, which banned the export of hazardous and radioactive waste to the Pacific islands.

Regional relations

New Zealand has played an active role in Pacific island affairs. In 1997, in the quest for peace in Papua New Guinea, it participated in a peace-keeping force on the secessionist island of Bougainville. New Zealand hosted discussions between the Papua New Guinea Government and representatives of the secessionist movement, and in January 1998 a permanent ceasefire agreement was signed in Christchurch. The agreement was successfully implemented in April. New Zealand strongly condemned the coup in Fiji in May 2000, which led to the overthrow of the Indian-led, elected Government of the country and prompted outbreaks of racially motivated violence throughout the islands. New Zealand's Minister of Foreign Affairs and Trade, Phil Goff, led a Commonwealth delegation, together with his Australian counterpart, to negotiate with the ethnic militias involved in a coup in Solomon Islands in June 2000. A New Zealand naval frigate, *Te Kaha*, was dispatched to the islands to serve as a venue for peace talks, and the country pledged to contribute to a group of international peace-keepers following the signing of a ceasefire agreement in October. In mid-2003 New Zealand troops joined forces from Australia and several Pacific islands to provide a peace-keeping force in Solomon Islands. New Zealand, together with Australia, deployed security forces to Tonga in November 2006 to restore stability following violent demonstrations.

In December 2006 Prime Minister Clark condemned the military coup in Fiji as an 'outrage'; the Government subsequently imposed defence, travel and development sanctions. Further sanctions were announced in June 2007 after New Zealand's high commissioner to Fiji was expelled because of his alleged interference in the country's internal affairs. In December 2008, as the restoration of democracy in Fiji appeared increasingly unlikely, the acting high commissioner of New Zealand in Fiji was expelled, in response to which her Fijian counterpart was asked to leave New Zealand. Nevertheless, New Zealand was one of several nations swiftly to offer, via non-governmental agencies, aid to the emergency flood relief effort in Fiji in January 2009. In April New Zealand was particularly critical of the abrogation of the Fijian Constitution and subsequent developments in the country (see the chapter on Fiji). The country's high commissioner to Fiji was expelled again in November in response to the New Zealand Government's continuing firm stance towards the Fijian regime. A reciprocal expulsion by New Zealand followed soon afterwards. Although senior diplomats returned to the respective missions in early 2010, the exchange was not at ambassadorial level. None the less, New Zealand continued to supply relief aid to Fiji, most recently following a cyclone in the islands in March 2010.

Meanwhile, in June 2008 the New Zealand Government released details of its Pacific Development Strategy Plan, which envisaged expenditure of $NZ2,000m. in official development assistance to the Pacific region over an eight-year period. This new initiative aimed to improve health services and education facilities, to strengthen governance, to reduce poverty and to promote economic growth in the Pacific islands.

Although New Zealand's trade with the People's Republic of China assumed increasing significance from the 1990s, relations were strained by the issue of China's nuclear-testing programme. Relations were further strained in September 1996 when the Dalai Lama, the exiled spiritual leader of Tibet, paid a four-day visit to New Zealand, where he was welcomed by the Prime Minister. In September 1997, however, the New Zealand Deputy Prime Minister expressed support for China's application to join the World Trade Organization (WTO, see p. 430). In November 1998 New Zealand's decision to accord Taiwanese government officials similar privileges to those granted to representatives of the People's Republic provoked serious concern in China. During a visit to China in July 1999, however, the Prime Minister of New Zealand reaffirmed her country's support for the 'one China' policy. An official visit to China by the Prime Minister in April 2001 was intended to improve New Zealand's trading position with the country, prior to its accession to the WTO. The Chinese Premier, Wen Jiabao, paid an official visit to New Zealand in April 2006. In March 2008 it was reported that China had agreed to grant 'most favoured nation' status to New Zealand as part of a free trade agreement between the two countries, which was signed in the following month. During his first official visit to China in April 2009 Prime Minister John Key expressed his firm commitment to the consolidation of the bilateral trading relationship and also urged an expansion in cultural exchanges with China, which had become the largest source of New Zealand's students from overseas. In February 2011 the New Zealand Government announced that total bilateral trade between China and New Zealand had increased by more than one-third since the implementation of the free trade agreement. In late 2010 Key and Wen Jiabao pledged their commitment to effecting a doubling of bilateral trade by 2015. Meanwhile, in March 2010 a Closer Economic Partnership Agreement was signed with Hong Kong, New Zealand's ninth largest export market in 2009; the agreement entered into force in January 2011.

In January 1997 New Zealand lodged a strong protest with the Japanese Government regarding the proposed route of a ship transporting nuclear waste to Japan from France. In March 1998 the New Zealand Prime Minister travelled to Japan, the first official visit by the country's head of government for 22 years. Relations with Japan, however, continued to be strained by a fishing dispute relating to Japan's perceived failure to conserve stocks of southern bluefin tuna, as agreed in a treaty of 1993, of which Australia was also a signatory. In July 1998, following a protest to Japan's ambassador in Wellington, New Zealand closed its ports to all Japanese tuna-fishing vessels. In August 1999 an international tribunal ruled in favour of New Zealand and Australia. In early 2000, the Labour Party's commitment to the protection of the environment having been reaffirmed, the new Government of New Zealand became embroiled in a further dispute with Japan, this time relating to the latter's controversial whaling programme. The Prime Minister, Helen Clark, announced her intention to raise the issue with Japan on an official visit to that country in April 2001, and she expressed her Government's desire to pursue proposals for a southern seas whale sanctuary through the International Whaling Commission (see p. 439). In December 2000 New Zealand reiterated its opposition to nuclear waste shipments in response to the news that a shipment of high-level waste had left the United Kingdom for Japan, warning that the vessel must not enter New Zealand's exclusive economic zone.

Relations with the countries of South-East Asia continued to assume greater significance. In June 2001 President Abdurrahman Wahid undertook an official visit to New Zealand, the first by an Indonesian head of state for 26 years. In July 2005 New Zealand signed the Treaty of Amity and Co-operation of the Association of Southeast Asian Nations (ASEAN, see p. 206). In December New Zealand was represented at the inaugural East Asia Summit meeting, convened in Malaysia and attended by leaders of ASEAN members and various other countries of the Asia-Pacific region. In February 2009 (along with Australia) New Zealand signed a free trade agreement with ASEAN, which entered into force in January 2010. A separate free trade agreement with Malaysia, a significant export market for New Zealand, was signed in October 2009 and entered into force in July 2010; the agreement provided for the elimination of trade tariffs on 99.5% of New Zealand's exports to Malaysia within seven years. Minister of Foreign Affairs Murray McCully visited Indonesia and Malaysia in October 2010; during his visit to the former, the Indonesia-New Zealand Friendship Council was established, with the aim of fostering closer co-operation.

New Zealand's foreign policy has continued to be influenced by the country's need to diversify its export markets, particularly within Asia; the Republic of Korea (South Korea), for example, has become a significant trading partner, and at early 2011 negotiations over a New Zealand-South Korean free trade agreement were ongoing. Closer relations with Singapore, Thailand and Viet Nam have also been developed.

About 3,500 New Zealand soldiers served in Viet Nam between 1964 and 1971. However, New Zealand's decision to contribute troops in support of the US war effort was not popular, and it was only in May 2008 that the New Zealand Prime Minister issued a public apology to the veterans for their lack of recognition. A series of bilateral events and exchanges were organized in 2010 to commemorate the 35th anniversary of the establishment of diplomatic relations between New Zealand and Viet Nam.

Within the ANZUS pact, from 1984 New Zealand's relations with both Australia and the USA were severely tested by the issue of the nuclear ban (see The ANZUS Treaty and other relations with the USA). In 1982 New Zealand signed an agreement for a 'closer economic relationship' (CER) with Australia; trade barriers between the two countries were eliminated in July 1990. In September 2001 relations with Australia were strained by the failure of Ansett, the Melbourne-based airline. Ansett's owner, Air New Zealand, had been unable to find a purchaser for the loss-making company, which was therefore placed in receivership. In Melbourne irate Ansett staff blockaded an aircraft upon which the New Zealand Prime Minister was due to travel, and the Australian media demanded a boycott of New Zealand products. Nevertheless, in the same month the New Zealand Government helped Australia to resolve an international crisis, when it agreed to accept up to 150 of the refugees stranded aboard a Norwegian vessel (see the chapter on Christmas Island). During her first state visit to New Zealand since acceding to the Australian premiership in June 2010, Prime Minister Julia Gillard met with her New Zealand counterpart, John Key, in Wellington, whereupon the two leaders pledged to hold bilateral prime ministerial discussions on an annual basis henceforth.

The ANZUS Treaty and other relations with the USA

In 1984 the Lange Government's pledge to ban from New Zealand's ports all vessels believed to be carrying nuclear weapons, or powered by nuclear energy, caused considerable strain in the country's relations with Australia and the USA, its partners in ANZUS. The ban was duly imposed in February 1985. In July 1986 the US Government announced its intention to devise new, bilateral defence arrangements with Australia, and in August the USA's military obligations to New Zealand under the ANZUS Treaty were formally suspended. In February 1987 the US Government announced its decision not to renew a 1982 memorandum of understanding, whereby New Zealand was able to purchase military equipment from the USA at favourable prices. The Lange Government subsequently defined a new defence strategy, based on increased self-reliance for the country's military forces. In June 1987 legislation banning nuclear-armed ships was formally enacted by the House of Representatives, despite strong opposition from the National Party. In September 1989 New Zealand agreed the terms for a joint venture with Australia to build as many as 12 naval frigates to patrol the South Pacific. The decision proved to be very contentious because of the high costs and because of allegations that the Government was succumbing to political pressure from Australia to return to the ANZUS alliance and abandon its independent anti-nuclear stance. In March 1990 the opposition National Party announced its support for the anti-nuclear policy, a position that it retained after its election to office in October.

Following the US Government's decision, in September 1991, to remove nuclear weapons from surface naval vessels, Bolger announced that his administration would reconsider the law banning visits from nuclear-armed and nuclear-propelled warships. In July 1992 the USA announced that its warships no longer carried tactical nuclear weapons. In December the report commissioned by the Prime Minister was released. The committee of scientists concluded that the dangers of permitting nuclear-powered vessels to enter New Zealand waters were minimal. Despite these findings, no immediate change to the anti-nuclear legislation was envisaged. In February 1994 the Prime Minister welcomed the US decision to resume senior-level contacts with New Zealand, suspended since 1985. In August 1998, during a visit by Madeleine Albright, the US Secretary of State, the Prime Minister of New Zealand strongly reiterated her country's long-standing ban on visits by nuclear-armed or nuclear-powered vessels. In July 2005 a private member's bill proposing the removal of the ban was rejected by a large majority by the House of Representatives.

After attending the summit meeting of the Asia-Pacific Economic Co-operation (APEC, see p. 197) forum held in Auckland in September 1999, US President Bill Clinton announced the end of the 14-year ban on New Zealand's participation in military exercises with the USA, in preparation for the dispatch of a multinational peace-keeping force to East Timor (now Timor-Leste, q.v.), of which New Zealand troops were to form part. Meanwhile, New Zealand's trading relations with the USA were strained during 1999 by the latter's imposition of tariffs on imports of New Zealand lamb. However, in December 2000 the WTO ruled in favour of New Zealand's case against the tariffs, and upheld the decision when the USA appealed against the ruling.

The Government quickly expressed support for the USA following the suicide attacks of 11 September 2001 and offered to share intelligence in the effort to combat terrorism. In October New Zealand provided troops from the Special Air Service (SAS) for the US-led military campaign against the al-Qa'ida organization, held principally responsible for the attacks, and its Taliban hosts in Afghanistan. However, US policy in the 'war on terror' was a source of concern in New Zealand. In 2003, during preparations for the US-led military campaign to remove the regime of Saddam Hussain in Iraq, the Government stated that it would favour action in Iraq only through the UN, a stance that was popularly supported in New Zealand. In May Prime Minister Clark warned the USA and the United Kingdom that they had set a dangerous precedent by invading Iraq without the endorsement of a UN resolution. None the less, New Zealand decided to provide humanitarian support for Iraq and assistance in the rehabilitation of the country once the UN had authorized reconstruction efforts following the ousting of Saddam Hussain. The Government had already sent forces to Afghanistan to assist in the reconstruction there, and in March 2004 it agreed to send SAS troops back to the South Asian country to take part in the search for senior al-Qa'ida leaders. In February 2005 the Prime Minister announced an extension to the New Zealand Defence Force's deployment in Afghanistan; the deployment was subsequently further extended on several occasions—most latterly in May 2010, until September 2011. A further SAS deployment in Afghanistan was effected in September 2009, following a US request for additional military assistance; in February 2011 it was announced that the deployment was to be extended for 12 months, effective from April, but with a reduction in the number of personnel, from 70 to 35 troops. In August 2010 New Zealand suffered its first military fatality in Afghanistan, when one solder was killed and two others were seriously injured in an ambush in the Afghan province of Bamian (Bamyan). Meanwhile, in August 2007 it emerged that earlier in the year Air New Zealand, the national carrier, had flown Australian soldiers to Kuwait and the United Arab Emirates, en route to military service in Iraq; the revelation was reported to have appalled Prime Minister Clark.

A subsequent improvement in relations with the USA was exemplified in July 2008 by the visit to New Zealand of Condoleezza Rice, the US Secretary of State and thus the most senior representative of the US Government to visit the country since the late 1990s. Rice's discussions with Prime Minister Clark and with the Minister of Foreign Affairs focused on trade issues, renewing hopes that a free trade agreement between the two countries might be negotiated. Further discussions on a free trade agreement were held between Prime Minister Key and US Vice-President Joseph Biden in April 2010, although no substantive progress was reported. US Secretary of State Hillary Clinton visited Wellington in November, whereupon she and the New Zealand Minister of Foreign Affairs, Murray McCully, signed a strategic co-operation agreement, which effectively formalized the amelioration in bilateral relations and greater engagement between the two countries in recent years. The so-called Wellington Declaration focused on enhancing dialogue and practical co-operation between New Zealand and the USA across a wide range of bilateral, Pacific and international issues, including combating the effects of climate change, the pursuit of renewable energy initiatives, and the co-ordination of disaster recovery initiatives. The Wellington Declaration also committed the two countries to regular diplomatic, trade and defence discussions.

Other external relations

In July 1985 the *Rainbow Warrior*, the flagship of the anti-nuclear environmentalist group Greenpeace (which was to have led a flotilla to Mururoa Atoll, in French Polynesia, to protest against France's testing of nuclear weapons in the South Pacific), was blown up and sunk in Auckland Harbour. One member of the crew was killed as a result of the explosion. Two agents of the French secret service were tried for manslaughter in November and sentenced to 10 years' imprisonment, initially in Auckland. The French Government made repeated requests for the release or repatriation of the agents, and in July 1986 the two Governments eventually reached an agreement, whereby the agents were to be transferred to detention on Hao Atoll, in French Polynesia, for three years. The French Government made a formal apology for its part in the sabotage operation, and paid the New Zealand Government $NZ7m. in compensation. By May 1988, however, both the agents had been taken back to France, ostensibly for medical reasons. When neither agent was returned to the atoll, Lange referred the matter to the UN: in May 1990 an arbitration panel ruled that France's repatriation of the agents constituted a substantial violation of the 1986 agreement, but it announced that the agents would not be required to return to Hao Atoll. France agreed to pay an initial US $2m. into a joint fund intended to foster close and friendly relations between the two countries. In April 1991 the French Prime Minister, Michel Rocard, visited New Zealand and again apologized for the sinking of the *Rainbow Warrior*, while reiterating that French testing of nuclear weapons in the Pacific was to continue. Relations between the two countries deteriorated in July, following the French Government's announcement that it had conferred an honour for distinguished service on one of the two agents responsible for the sabotage of the *Rainbow Warrior*. In July 2005 an article in a French newspaper confirmed that the sinking of the *Rainbow Warrior* had been authorized by the then French President, François Mitterrand. Meanwhile, France announced the suspension of its nuclear testing in the South Pacific in April 1992.

In June 1995 President Jacques Chirac's announcement that France was to resume its nuclear-testing programme in the South Pacific aroused international condemnation. New Zealand suspended military relations with France, and the New Zealand ambassador to Paris was recalled. The first in the new series of tests was carried out in September. Later in the month the International Court of Justice ruled that it could not reopen New Zealand's case against France, brought in 1973. France's continuation of its testing programme, in defiance of world opinion, was a major issue at the Commonwealth heads of government meeting held in Auckland in November 1995. New Zealand's relations with the United Kingdom were strained by the British Prime Minister's apparent support for France's position; upon his arrival in Auckland, thousands of anti-nuclear demonstrators took to the streets to express their outrage. In March 1996 (the French tests having been concluded) France, the United Kingdom and the USA finally acceded to the South Pacific Nuclear-Free Zone Treaty (Treaty of Rarotonga—Pacific Islands Forum, see p. 413), thus opening the way to improved relations with New Zealand and other Pacific nations. In October 1997, following a two-day official visit to Paris by the New Zealand Prime Minister, the resumption of normal relations with France was declared.

In December 1996 the New Zealand Government announced that it was to finance a lawsuit against the United Kingdom that was being prepared by former servicemen (and veterans' widows) who had long campaigned for compensation for their exposure to the effects of British hydrogen bomb tests conducted in the South Pacific region in the late 1950s. As part of her golden jubilee tour of the Commonwealth, Queen Elizabeth II visited New Zealand in February 2002. Having previously stated that New Zealand's eventual transition to a republic was inevitable, the Prime Minister attracted some criticism for her absence from the country on the day of the Queen's arrival.

In July 2004 New Zealand's relations with Israel were strained when two alleged agents from the Israeli secret service, Mossad, were fined and sentenced to six-month prison terms by the Auckland High Court, having been convicted of fraudulently attempting to obtain New Zealand passports. Prime Minister Helen Clark stated that the available evidence strongly suggested that the men were acting as Israeli agents, but that no explanation had been forthcoming from the Israeli Government. New Zealand subsequently suspended senior-level diplomatic contact with Israel, demanding an apology for the incident. In September, having been released from prison early, the Israelis were deported from the country. However, in June 2005 the Israeli Government issued a formal apology for the incident, following which cordial diplomatic relations were restored.

Negotiations between New Zealand and India on a bilateral free trade agreement commenced in Wellington in April 2010. Subsequent rounds of negotiations were held in August (in Delhi) and October (in Wellington); a fourth round was due in mid-2011. Meanwhile, in November 2010 the Indian Minister of State for Commerce and Industry, Jyotiraditya Scindia, stated that the Indian Government expected an agreement to be concluded by the end of 2011. The pact was expected to be wide-ranging, with agricultural produce, biotechnology, education, health care, technology and tourism considered likely to be among the areas covered. Trade between the two countries amounted to $NZ985m. in 2009, representing an increase of 180% on that recorded in 2001.

CONSTITUTION AND GOVERNMENT

New Zealand has no written Constitution. Executive power is vested in the British monarch, as Head of State, and is exercisable by an appointed representative, the Governor-General, who must be guided by the advice of the Executive Council (Cabinet), led by the Prime Minister. Legislative power is vested in the unicameral House of Representatives, elected for three years by universal adult suffrage. A system of mixed member proportional representation was introduced in 1996. At the 2008 election the legislature was expanded to 122 seats: 70 electorate members, including seven seats reserved for Maori, and 52 being chosen from party lists. The Governor-General appoints the Prime Minister and, on the latter's recommendation, other Ministers. The Cabinet is responsible to the House.

REGIONAL AND INTERNATIONAL CO-OPERATION

New Zealand is a member of Asia-Pacific Economic Co-operation (APEC, see p. 197), the Pacific Community (see p. 410), the Pacific Islands Forum (see p. 413) and the Cairns Group (see p. 502). The country is also a member of the Colombo Plan (see p. 446) and of the UN's Economic and Social Commission for Asia and the Pacific (ESCAP, see p. 37).

New Zealand joined the UN in 1945. As a contracting party to the General Agreement on Tariffs and Trade (GATT), the country joined the World Trade Organization (WTO, see p. 430) upon its establishment in 1995. New Zealand is also a member of the Organisation for Economic Co-operation and Development (see p. 376).

ECONOMIC AFFAIRS

In 2008, according to estimates by the World Bank, New Zealand's gross national income (GNI), measured at average 2006–08 prices, was US $114,518m., equivalent to US $26,830 per head (or US $26,430 per head on an international purchasing-power parity basis). During 2000–09, it was estimated, the population increased at an average annual rate of 1.3%, while gross domestic product (GDP) per head increased, in real terms, by an average of 1.4% per year. Overall GDP increased, in real terms, at an average annual rate of 2.7% in 2000–09. GDP grew by 3.0% in 2007 but declined by 0.5% in 2008 and by the same percentage in 2009.

Agriculture (including fishing, forestry and logging) contributed 5.4% of GDP in the year ending March 2007. About 7.0% of the employed labour force were engaged in the sector in 2008. The principal crops are barley, maize and wheat. Fruit (particularly kiwi fruit, apples and pears) and vegetables are also cultivated. New Zealand is a major producer of wool, although its significance as a source of export earnings has declined in recent years. Meat and dairy products are important, contributing 11.7% and 23.9% of export earnings, respectively, in 2010. The forestry industry showed strong expansion in the early 1990s. In 2010 exports of logs, wood and wood articles totalled a provisional $NZ2,950m. (equivalent to 6.8% of total export earnings). The fisheries sector is of increasing significance, with exports worth a provisional $NZ1,308m. (equivalent to 3.0% of total export earnings) in 2010. According to World Bank estimates, agricultural GDP (including fishing and forestry) increased at an average annual rate of 1.7% in 2000–07. Compared with the previous year, the GDP of the sector grew by 0.6% in 2006 but declined by 1.9% in 2007.

Industry (including mining, manufacturing, construction and utilities) engaged 21.7% of the employed labour force in 2008. The industrial sector provided 23.8% of GDP in the year ending March 2007. In 2000–07 industrial GDP increased at an average annual rate of 2.6%. Compared with the previous year, industrial GDP decreased by 1.5% in 2006 but grew by 3.1% in 2007.

Mining contributed only 1.3% of GDP in the year ending March 2007; the sector engaged just 0.2% of the employed labour force in 2008. New Zealand has substantial coal reserves; petroleum, natural gas, iron, gold and silica are also exploited. A considerable amount of natural gas is used to produce synthetic petrol.

Manufacturing contributed an estimated 14.3% of GDP in the year ending March 2007. The sector engaged 12.8% of the employed labour force in 2008. The principal branches of manufacturing are food products, printing and publishing, wood and paper products, chemicals, metals and metal products, machinery and transport equipment. In 2000–05 manufacturing GDP increased by an average of 2.2% per year. Manufacturing GDP contracted by 1.6% in 2005. After seven consecutive quarters of contraction, manufacturing activity was reported to have expanded in the final quarter of 2009.

Construction contributed 5.4% of GDP in the year ending March 2007. The sector engaged 8.2% of the employed labour force in 2008.

Energy is derived mainly from domestic supplies of natural gas, coal and petroleum. Hydroelectric power supplied about 53.6% of total electricity output in 2007, gas 27.3% and coal 7.1%. Imports of petroleum and its products comprised 15.3% of the total value of merchandise imports in 2010.

The services sector provided 70.8% of GDP in 2006/07. This sector engaged 71.3% of the employed labour force in 2008. Tourism became the single largest source of foreign exchange in the late 1980s. Visitor arrivals decreased marginally, to 2.4m., in 2009, but recovered to exceed 2.5m. in 2010, in which year tourist receipts rose to $NZ6,278m.

New Zealand trade balance moved into surplus in 2009. In that year a surplus of US $1,316m. was recorded, although there was a deficit of US $3,624m. on the current account of the balance of payments. In 2010 the principal sources of imports were Australia (18.2%), the People's Republic of China the USA and Japan. China was the principal market for exports in that year (purchasing 11.1%), followed by the USA and Japan. The principal exports in 2010 were dairy products, meat, logs, wood and wood articles, machinery and equipment, and fruit. The principal imports were petroleum and petroleum products, boilers and mechanical appliances, vehicles, parts and accessories, and electrical machinery and equipment.

In the year ending June 2011 a budgetary deficit of $NZ9,636m. was forecast. In December 2010 total overseas debt was estimated by the central bank at $NZ248,488m. (comprising $NZ215,922m. owed by the corporate sector and $NZ32,566m. of official government debt), equivalent to 127.7% of GDP. New Zealand's general government gross debt was $NZ48,583m. in 2009, equivalent to 26.2% of GDP. According to the IMF, the average rate of unemployment was 6.4% of the labour force in 2009. Annual inflation averaged 2.7% in 2000–09. Consumer prices increased by 4.0% in 2008 and by 2.1% in 2009.

The Government of John Key took office in November 2008, having pledged to reduce taxes, to increase expenditure on the country's infrastructure and to implement a programme of regulatory reform. However, the immediate challenge for the incoming Prime Minister was to address the deterioration in the economy: in mid-2008, for the first time in nine years, New Zealand entered recession, as business confidence weakened, investment decreased and the availability of credit declined sharply. In order to address the repercussions of the global economic crisis, in December 2008 the new Government announced a financial stimulus programme. In late 2010 the value of the New Zealand dollar stood at a relatively high level, leading to some concern that, if sustained, the strength of the currency would lead to increasing difficulties for the country's exporters. Following a succession of decreases, at the end of April 2009 the interest rate set by the Reserve Bank of New Zealand stood at a record low level of 2.5%, a percentage at which it remained until April 2010 when it was raised to 3.0%. In March 2011, however, with the objective of mitigating the economic impact of the Christchurch earthquake in the previous month, the rate was again reduced to 2.5%. In the longer term, New Zealand's trade prospects were greatly enhanced in April 2008 by the signing of a free trade agreement with the People's Republic of China, a major trading partner. Although GDP contracted by 0.2% in the third quarter of 2010, it expanded by 0.2% in the final quarter. Narrowly avoiding a third consecutive year of recession, therefore, in 2010 as a whole the economy grew by an estimated 0.5%. Inflationary pressures increased substantially in the latter part of 2010, and by March 2011 the annual rate of inflation had reached 4.5%. The 2011/12 budget provided funding of $NZ1,600m. (over a four-year period) for the purposes of infrastructural improvements. By reducing expenditure in other areas, the Government envisaged that the budget would return to surplus by 2014/15. The Government planned to reduce its stake in Air New Zealand and to dispose of other state assets.

PUBLIC HOLIDAYS

2012 (provisional): 2–3 January (for New Year), 6 February (for Waitangi Day, anniversary of 1840 treaty), 6–9 April (Easter), 25 April (for ANZAC Day, anniversary of 1915 landing at Gallipoli), 4 June (Queen's Official Birthday), 22 October (Labour Day), 25–26 December (Christmas).

In addition to these national holidays, each region celebrates an anniversary day.

NEW ZEALAND

Statistical Survey

Source (unless otherwise stated): Statistics New Zealand, Aorangi House, 85 Molesworth St, POB 2922, Wellington 1; tel. (4) 931-4600; fax (4) 931-9135; e-mail info@stats.govt.nz; internet www.stats.govt.nz.

Area and Population

AREA, POPULATION AND DENSITY

Area (sq km)	270,534*
Population (census results)†	
6 March 2001	3,737,277
7 March 2006	
Males	1,965,618
Females	2,062,329
Total	4,027,947
Population (official estimates at mid-year)	
2008	4,268,900
2009	4,315,800
2010	4,367,800
Density (per sq km) at mid-2010	16.1

* 104,454 sq miles.
† Figures refer to the population usually resident. The total population (including foreign visitors) was: 3,820,749 in 2001; 4,143,282 in 2006.

POPULATION BY AGE AND SEX
(official provisional estimates at mid-2010)

	Males	Females	Total
0–14	458,500	435,960	894,450
15–64	1,427,030	1,477,140	2,904,170
65 and over	259,070	310,080	569,150
Total	2,144,600	2,223,200	4,367,800

Note: Totals may not be equal to the sum of components, owing to rounding.

ADMINISTRATIVE REGIONS
(census of March 2006)

	Area (sq km)	Population	Density (per sq km)
North Island			
Northland	13,296	148,470	11.2
Auckland	5,048	1,303,068	258.1
Waikato	26,170	382,713	14.6
Bay of Plenty	11,428	257,379	22.5
Gisborne	8,355	44,499	5.3
Hawke's Bay Region	13,764	147,783	10.7
Taranaki	7,227	104,124	14.4
Manawatu-Wanganui	22,687	222,423	9.8
Wellington	8,056	448,959	55.7
Total North Island	116,031	3,059,418	26.4
South Island			
Tasman	14,538	44,625	3.1
Nelson	444	42,891	96.6
Marlborough	12,493	42,558	3.4
West Coast	23,351	31,326	1.3
Canterbury	45,845	521,832	11.4
Otago	31,476	193,800	6.2
Southland	25,392	90,876	3.6
Total South Island	153,540	967,908	38.1
Area outside regions	963	618	0.6
Total	270,534	4,027,947	14.9

Note: Totals may not be equal to the sum of components, owing to rounding.

PRINCIPAL CENTRES OF POPULATION
(census of March 2006, enumerated totals, incl. visitors)

Auckland city	404,658	Palmerston North	75,543
Christchurch	348,435	Hastings district	70,842
Wellington (capital)	179,466	Rotorua district	65,901
Hamilton	129,249	Napier	55,359
Dunedin	118,683	Nelson	42,888
Tauranga	103,635		

BIRTHS, MARRIAGES AND DEATHS

	Live births*		Marriages†		Deaths*	
	Number	Rate (per '000)	Number	Rate (per '000)	Number	Rate (per '000)
2003	56,134	13.9	21,419	5.3	28,010	7.0
2004	58,073	14.2	21,006	5.1	28,419	7.0
2005	57,745	14.0	20,470	5.0	27,034	6.5
2006	59,193	14.1	21,423	5.1	28,245	6.8
2007	64,044	15.1	21,494	5.1	28,522	6.7
2008	64,343	15.1	21,948	5.1	29,188	6.8
2009	62,543	14.5‡	21,628	5.0	28,964	6.7‡
2010	63,897	14.6‡	n.a.	n.a.	28,438	6.5‡

* Data for births and deaths are tabulated by year of registration rather than by year of occurrence.
† Based on the resident population concept, replacing the previous de facto concept.
‡ Provisional.

Life expectancy (years at birth, WHO estimates): 81 (males 78; females 83) in 2008 (Source: WHO, *World Health Statistics*).

IMMIGRATION AND EMIGRATION

	2008	2009	2010
Long-term immigrants*	87,463	86,410	82,469
Long-term emigrants†	83,649	65,157	72,018

* Figures refer to persons intending to remain in New Zealand for 12 months or more, and New Zealand citizens returning after an absence of 12 months or more.
† Figures refer to New Zealand citizens intending to remain abroad for 12 months or more, and overseas migrants departing after a stay of 12 months or more.

ECONOMICALLY ACTIVE POPULATION
('000 persons aged 15 years and over, excl. armed forces)

	2006	2007	2008
Agriculture, hunting and forestry	150.6	153.5	149.4
Fishing	1.8	2.4	2.6
Mining and quarrying	4.8	5.2	4.0
Manufacturing	280.6	279.2	278.0
Electricity, gas and water	8.3	8.8	12.0
Construction	185.1	185.3	179.2
Wholesale and retail trade; repair of motor vehicles, motorcycles and personal and household goods	368.4	377.7	387.1
Restaurants and hotels	97.1	108.2	101.0
Transport, storage and communications	118.7	118.1	123.1
Financial intermediation	70.2	70.8	68.1
Real estate, renting and business activities	246.3	248.7	254.0
Public administration and defence; compulsory social security	136.6	138.1	132.7
Education	166.0	169.6	175.4
Health and social work	196.2	203.5	207.8
Other community, social and personal service activities	92.4	91.1	99.9
Private households with employed persons	3.3	3.7	2.2
Sub-total	2,126.5	2,163.8	2,176.4
Activities not adequately defined	8.2	10.7	11.8
Total employed	2,134.7	2,174.5	2,188.2
Unemployed	85.4	82.8	95.0
Total labour force	2,220.1	2,257.3	2,283.2
Males	1,188.6	1,206.0	1,214.7
Females	1,031.5	1,051.2	1,068.4

Source: ILO.

NEW ZEALAND

Health and Welfare

KEY INDICATORS

Total fertility rate (children per woman, 2008)	2.0
Under-5 mortality rate (per 1,000 live births, 2008)	6
HIV/AIDS (% of persons aged 15–49, 2007)	0.1
Physicians (per 1,000 head, 2002)	2.1
Hospital beds (per 1,000 head, 2002)	6.0
Health expenditure (2007): US $ per head (PPP)	2,497
Health expenditure (2007): % of GDP	9.0
Health expenditure (2007): public (% of total)	78.9
Total carbon dioxide emissions ('000 metric tons, 2007)	32,635.2
Carbon dioxide emissions per head (metric tons, 2007)	7.7
Human Development Index (2010): ranking	3
Human Development Index (2010): value	0.907

For sources and definitions, see explanatory note on p. vi.

Agriculture

PRINCIPAL CROPS
('000 metric tons)

	2007	2008	2009
Wheat	344	343	403
Barley	356	409	435
Maize	186	206	238
Oats	28	25	34
Potatoes*	432	473	490
Peas, dry	22	20	21
Cabbages and other brassicas*	44	44	44
Lettuce and chicory*	34	33	32
Tomatoes*	110	90	92
Cauliflowers and broccoli*	45	45	42
Pumpkins, squash and gourds*	185	175	160
Onions and shallots, green*	210	200	203
Peas, green*	50	47	43
Carrots and turnips*	65	65	65
Maize, green*	90	90	92
Grapes	190*	190*	n.a.
Apples	355*	355*	n.a.
Pears	35*	35*	n.a.
Kiwi fruit	365*	365*	n.a.

* FAO estimate(s).

Aggregate production ('000 metric tons, may include official, semi-official or estimated data): Total cereals 927 in 2007, 999 in 2008, 1,126 in 2009; Total roots and tubers 447 in 2007, 486 in 2008, 502 in 2009; Total vegetables (incl. melons) 1,012 in 2007, 967 in 2008, 951 in 2009; Total fruits (excl. melons) 1,060 in 2007–09.

Source: FAO.

LIVESTOCK
('000 head at 30 June)

	2007	2008	2009
Cattle	9,654	9,715	9,961
Sheep	38,460	34,088	32,384
Goats	112	96	82
Pigs	367	325	323
Horses	80*	63	65
Chickens	19,829	19,733	13,147
Ducks*	170	170	n.a.
Geese and guinea fowls*	80	80	n.a.
Turkeys*	76	76	n.a.

* FAO estimate(s).
Source: FAO.

Statistical Survey

LIVESTOCK PRODUCTS
('000 metric tons)

	2007	2008	2009
Cattle meat	632.4	634.6	637.0
Sheep meat	573.2	598.1	478.4
Pig meat	50.6	51.4	46.7
Chicken meat	147.3	145.4	135.0
Game meat	32.9	32.3	27.2
Cows' milk	15,618	15,217	n.a.
Hen eggs	69.3	69.3*	n.a.
Other poultry eggs*	2.5	2.5	n.a.
Honey	9.7	12.4	n.a.
Wool, greasy	217.9	217.9*	n.a.

* FAO estimate(s).
Source: FAO.

Forestry

ROUNDWOOD REMOVALS
('000 cubic metres)

	2007	2008	2009
Sawlogs, veneer logs and logs for sleepers	8,966	8,966	8,966
Pulpwood	3,284	3,492	3,119
Other industrial roundwood	7,664	7,852	8,125
Total	19,914	20,310	20,210

Source: FAO.

SAWNWOOD PRODUCTION
('000 cubic metres, year ending 31 March)

Species	2007/08	2008/09	2009/10
Radiata pine	4,122	3,435	3,551
Other introduced pines	4	2	0
Douglas fir	175	138	115
Rimu and miro	3	3	2
Total (incl. others)	4,341	3,610	3,695

Source: Forestry Statistics Section, Ministry of Agriculture and Forestry, Wellington.

Fishing

('000 metric tons, live weight)

	2006	2007	2008
Capture*	476.6	494.5	451.1
Southern blue whiting	23.4	23.9	29.3
Blue grenadier (Hoki)	105.0	101.9	96.0
Oreo dories	16.9	17.8	15.6
Jack and horse mackerels	36.3	46.4	47.3
Snoek (Barracouta)	25.9	28.6	27.4
Skipjack tuna	21.7	33.7	25.2
Wellington flying squid	69.2	70.8†	55.6
Aquaculture	107.5	111.9†	112.4†
New Zealand mussel	97.0	99.5	100.1
Total catch	584.1	606.4†	563.4†

* Excluding catches made by chartered vessels and landed outside New Zealand.
† FAO estimate.

Note: Figures exclude aquatic plants (metric tons, all capture); 225 in 2006; 192 in 2007; 196 in 2008. Also excluded are aquatic mammals (recorded by number rather than by weight). The number of whales and dolphins caught was: 11 in 2006; 28 in 2007; 5 in 2008.

Source: FAO.

NEW ZEALAND

Mining

('000 metric tons, unless otherwise indicated)

	2007	2008	2009
Coal (incl. lignite)	4,835	4,909	4,563
Gold (kg)	10,628	13,403	13,442
Crude petroleum ('000 barrels)	15,011	21,436	19,617
Gross natural gas (million cu m)	4,712	4,484	4,644
Liquid petroleum gas ('000 barrels)	1,263	979	900*
Ironsands	1,723	2,020	585
Silica sand	86.5	48.6	43.5
Limestone	5,092	4,810	4,481

* Estimate.

Source: US Geological Survey.

Industry

SELECTED PRODUCTS
(metric tons, unless otherwise indicated)

	2002	2003	2004
Wine (million litres)	89.0	55.0	119.2
Beer (sales, '000 hectolitres)	3,093	3,127	2,902
Chemical wood pulp*	711,361	623,437	743,671
Mechanical wood pulp*	838,963	795,394	852,787
Newsprint*	351,585	362,130	379,913
Other paper and paperboard*	518,155	447,512	537,350
Fibre board (cu m)*	880,301	868,539	873,408
Particle board (cu m)*	204,650	221,855	243,798
Veneer (cu m)*	552,738	637,556	680,687
Plywood (cu m)*	299,056	343,715	402,147
Jet fuels ('000 metric tons)	869	832	930
Motor spirit—petrol ('000 metric tons)	1,530	1,520	1,627
Gas-diesel (Distillate fuel) oils ('000 metric tons)	2,049	2,018	1,763
Residual fuel oils ('000 metric tons)	427	359	350
Cement ('000 metric tons)	1,090	1,100	1,110
Aluminium—unwrought ('000 metric tons):			
primary	335.0	342.0	351.4
secondary†	21.5	21.5	21.5
Electric energy (million kWh)	40,346	40,441	41,813

* Source: Ministry of Agriculture and Forestry, Wellington.
† Estimates.

Sources (unless otherwise stated): UN, *Industrial Commodity Statistics Yearbook* and *Monthly Bulletin of Statistics*; US Geological Survey; New Zealand Wine Online.

2005: Wine (million litres) 102.0; Chemical wood pulp (metric tons, provisional) 747,768; Mechanical wood pulp (metric tons, provisional) 852,961; Newsprint (metric tons) 379,628; Other paper and paperboard (metric tons) 541,711; Fibre board (cu m) 845,663; Particle board (cu m) 229,971; Veneer (cu m) 694,301; Plywood (cu m) 408,635 (Sources: New Zealand Wine Online; Ministry of Agriculture and Forestry, Wellington).

2006: Wine (million litres) 133.2; Chemical wood pulp (metric tons, provisional) 751,349; Mechanical wood pulp (metric tons, provisional) 749,679; Newsprint (metric tons) 367,064; Other paper and paperboard (metric tons) 573,396; Fibre board (cu m) 906,938; Particle board (cu m) 238,205; Veneer (cu m) 665,206; Plywood (cu m) 403,808 (Sources: New Zealand Wine Online; Ministry of Agriculture and Forestry, Wellington).

2007: Wine (million litres) 147.6; Newsprint (metric tons) 292,015; Other paper and paperboard (metric tons) 579,931; Fibre board (cu m) 836,755; Particle board (cu m) 256,239; Veneer (cu m) 688,312; Plywood (cu m) 421,794 (Sources: New Zealand Wine Online; Ministry of Agriculture and Forestry, Wellington).

2008: Wine (million litres) 205.2; Newsprint (metric tons) 285,654; Other paper and paperboard (metric tons) 585,429; Fibre board (cu m) 765,044; Particle board (cu m) 245,309; Veneer (cu m) 512,575; Plywood (cu m) 416,383 (Sources: New Zealand Wine Online; Ministry of Agriculture and Forestry, Wellington).

2009: Wine (million litres) 205.2; Newsprint (metric tons) 291,297; Other paper and paperboard (metric tons) 578,746 (Sources: New Zealand Wine Online; Ministry of Agriculture and Forestry, Wellington).

Finance

CURRENCY AND EXCHANGE RATES

Monetary Units
100 cents = 1 New Zealand dollar ($NZ).

Sterling, US Dollar and Euro Equivalents (31 December 2010)
£1 sterling = $NZ2.116;
US $1 = $NZ1.351;
€1 = $NZ1.806;
$NZ100 = £47.27 = US $74.00 = €55.38.

Average Exchange Rate (New Zealand dollars per US $)
2008 1.4227
2009 1.6002
2010 1.3874

BUDGET
($NZ million, year ending 30 June)

Revenue	2006/07	2007/08*	2008/09*
Taxation	53,064	56,186	55,911
Compulsory fees, fines, penalties and levies	3,496	3,851	4,037
Sales of goods and services	12,613	13,682	14,222
Interest revenue and dividends	2,995	3,203	3,358
Other	2,421	2,891	2,591
Total	**74,589**	**79,813**	**80,119**

Expenditure	2006/07	2007/08*	2008/09*
Social security and welfare	19,829	22,274	22,843
GSF pension expenses	645	714	652
Health	10,661	10,765	12,024
Education	9,853	10,803	11,017
Core government services	4,628	3,163	3,412
Law and order	2,822	3,192	3,341
Defence	1,478	1,524	1,697
Transport and communications	6,990	7,185	8,027
Economic and industrial services	4,723	7,433	7,918
Primary services	1,233	1,404	1,364
Heritage, culture and recreation	2,043	2,366	3,130
Housing and community development	865	965	1,036
Other	74	84	83
Finance costs	2,885	2,954	2,503
Future spending forecast	—	—	249
Adjustment	—	−240	−495
Total (incl. others)	**68,729**	**74,586**	**78,801**

* Forecasts.

2009/10 (estimates): *Revenue:* Tax revenue 55,875; Non-tax revenue 7,328; Capital receipts 1,635; Total 64,838. *Expenditure:* Education 11,740; Health 12,624; Social development 20,394; Total (incl. others) 76,168.

2010/11 (forecasts): *Revenue:* Tax revenue 60,469; Non-tax revenue 7,314; Capital receipts 1,865; Total 69,647. *Expenditure:* Education 11,969; Health 13,574; Social development 21,429; Total (incl. others) 79,283.

Source: New Zealand Treasury, Wellington.

INTERNATIONAL RESERVES
(excl. gold, US $ million at 31 December)

	2008	2009	2010
IMF special drawing rights	22	1,340	1,317
Reserve position in IMF	175	273	273
Foreign exchange	10,855	13,982	15,133
Total	**11,052**	**15,594**	**16,723**

Source: IMF, *International Financial Statistics*.

NEW ZEALAND

MONEY SUPPLY
($NZ million at 31 December)

	2008	2009	2010
Currency outside banks	3,526	3,580	3,799
Demand deposits at banking institutions	31,361	31,316	31,468
Total money	34,888	34,896	35,267

Source: IMF, *International Financial Statistics*.

COST OF LIVING
(Consumer Price Index; base: 2000 = 100)

	2007	2008	2009
Food (incl. beverages)	120.6	130.2	137.7
Fuel and light	149.5	160.2	167.4
Clothing (incl. footwear)	101.6	101.5	103.5
Rent	105.2	108.5	110.1
All items (incl. others)	119.6	124.4	127.0

Source: ILO.

NATIONAL ACCOUNTS
($NZ million at current prices, year ending 31 March)

Expenditure on the Gross Domestic Product

	2007/08	2008/09	2009/10
Government final consumption expenditure	34,202	37,265	38,213
Private final consumption expenditure	105,770	108,602	110,834
Change in inventories	1,585	1,197	−1,324
Gross fixed capital formation	41,902	40,315	36,845
Total domestic expenditure	183,459	187,379	184,568
Exports of goods and services	51,607	57,196	52,424
Less Imports of goods and services	53,146	59,597	49,690
GDP in market prices	181,920	184,979	187,302

Gross Domestic Product by Economic Activity

	2004/05	2005/06	2006/07
Agriculture	7,666	6,795	7,450
Fishing	257	235	247
Forestry and logging	998	1,005	1,067
Mining and quarrying	1,553	1,830	2,047
Manufacturing	21,759	22,779	23,229
Electricity, gas and water	3,886	4,284	4,502
Construction	7,777	8,473	8,825
Wholesale and retail trade	19,196	20,007	20,282
Hotels and restaurants	2,836	2,939	3,108
Transport, storage and communications	10,592	11,019	11,312
Financial intermediation (incl. insurance)	9,173	10,010	10,780
Property and business activities	22275	24459	25,922
Ownership of dwellings	11,604	12,247	12,671
Public administration and defence	6,363	7,083	7,928
Education	6,167	6,473	6,963
Health and community services	8,124	8,971	9,551
Cultural and recreational services	3,528	3,640	3,720
Personal and other services	2,280	2,391	2,474
Sub-total	146,034	154,640	162,075
Less Financial intermediation services indirectly measured	5,139	5,907	6,552
Gross value added at basic prices	140,896	148,735	155,523
Goods and services tax on production	10,273	10,842	11,472
Import duties	870	997	1,668
GDP in market prices	152,038	160,573	168,663

BALANCE OF PAYMENTS
(US $ million)

	2007	2008	2009
Exports of goods f.o.b.	27,288	31,192	25,336
Imports of goods f.o.b.	−29,078	−32,897	−24,020
Trade balance	−1,790	−1,705	1,316
Exports of services	9,406	9,264	7,873
Imports of services	−9,187	−9,692	−7,932
Balance on goods and services	−1,571	−2,133	1,257
Other income received	4,751	3,787	2,729
Other income paid	−14,290	−13,789	−7,877
Balance on goods, services and income	−11,110	−12,136	−3,892
Current transfers received	1,425	1,695	1,189
Current transfers paid	−1,022	−984	−921
Current balance	−10,706	−11,424	−3,624
Capital account (net)	−553	−446	271
Direct investment abroad	−3,642	−973	613
Direct investment from abroad	3,079	5,121	−1,259
Portfolio investment assets	−1,350	−702	−3,426
Portfolio investment liabilities	12,019	−5,696	6,128
Other investment assets	−1,634	1,621	−1,650
Other investment liabilities	4,574	459	3,160
Net errors and omissions	1,300	7,043	3,442
Overall balance	3,088	−4,997	3,653

Source: IMF, *International Financial Statistics*.

External Trade

PRINCIPAL COMMODITIES
($NZ million)

Imports c.i.f.	2008	2009	2010
Vehicles, parts and accessories	5,061	3,226	4,267
Boilers, machinery and mechanical appliances	6,218	5,024	5,197
Petroleum, petroleum products, etc.	8,577	5,855	6,490
Electrical machinery and equipment	4,000	3,968	3,630
Paper and paperboard	1,045	955	995
Plastic and plastic articles	1,723	1,488	1,612
Iron and steel and articles	1,762	1,124	1,187
Optical, medical and measuring equipment	1,297	1,371	1,328
Total (incl. others)	48,514	40,222	42,375

Exports f.o.b.	2008	2009	2010
Dairy produce; birds' eggs; natural honey; edible products of animal origin, not elsewhere specified or included	9,285	8,116	10,414
Meat and edible offal	5,145	5,142	5,089
Logs, wood and wood articles	2,184	2,319	2,950
Boilers, machinery and mechanical appliances; parts thereof	1,881	1,658	1,722
Fruit and nuts; peel of citrus fruit or melons	1,445	1,601	1,471
Fish, crustaceans and molluscs	1,217	1,262	1,308
Aluminium and aluminium articles	1,428	883	1,213
Electrical machinery and equipment	1,075	982	1,029
Total (incl. others)*	42,915	39,672	43,500

* Including re-exports.

NEW ZEALAND

PRINCIPAL TRADING PARTNERS
($NZ million)

Imports (c.i.f.)*	2008	2009	2010
Australia	8,738	7,397	7,704
Belgium	340	262	290
Canada	727	538	521
China, People's Republic	6,444	6,066	6,763
France	804	1,331	596
Germany	2,076	1,684	1,741
Indonesia	1,155	720	647
Italy	978	728	701
Japan	3,956	2,981	3,107
Korea, Republic	1,318	1,357	1,387
Malaysia	1,986	1,085	1,524
Netherlands	388	337	309
Qatar	1,523	945	825
Saudi Arabia	550	272	310
Singapore	2,252	1,625	1,622
Sweden	378	227	279
Taiwan	973	607	731
Thailand	1,318	1,062	1,372
United Arab Emirates	784	466	885
United Kingdom	1,084	937	955
USA	4,600	4,328	4,393
Total (incl. others)	48,514	40,222	42,375

* Excluding specie and gold.

Exports*	2008	2009	2010
Australia	9,995	9,132	1,003
Belgium	507	490	360
Canada	511	501	497
China, People's Republic	2,534	3,628	4,825
Fiji	363	306	313
France	502	508	457
Germany	895	765	658
Hong Kong	700	794	866
Indonesia	1,006	963	930
Italy	471	404	437
Japan	3,613	2,821	3,376
Korea, Republic	1,358	1,240	1,414
Malaysia	949	705	776
Mexico	432	375	363
Netherlands	509	480	494
Philippines	734	570	729
Saudi Arabia	729	475	615
Singapore	863	1,100	826
Taiwan	752	756	843
Thailand	826	453	679
United Kingdom	1,672	1,696	1,528
USA	4,382	3,953	3,759
Venezuela	654	362	463
Total (incl. others)	42,900	39,672	43,500

* Including re-exports, but excluding specie and gold.

Transport

RAILWAYS
(traffic, year ending 30 June)

	2000/01	2001/02	2002/03
Freight ('000 metric tons)	14,461	14,330	14,822
Passengers ('000)	12,714	12,521	12,300*

* Excludes passengers on the Tranz Scenic network.
Source: Tranz Rail Ltd, Wellington.

ROAD TRAFFIC
(vehicles licensed at June)

	2008	2009	2010
Passenger cars	2,311,006	2,330,312	2,337,934
Taxis	7,823	7,855	7,575
Buses and service coaches	18,419	19,067	19,388
Trailers and caravans	446,745	453,488	459,912
Motorcycles and mopeds	75,140	78,217	76,548
Tractors	28,212	28,703	29,030
Trucks	425,894	427,525	426,491

Source: New Zealand Transport Agency.

SHIPPING

Merchant Fleet
(registered at 31 December)

	2007	2008	2009
Number of vessels	174	172	176
Displacement (grt)	210,208	214,142	213,084

Source: IHS Fairplay, *World Fleet Statistics*.

Vessels Handled
(international, '000 grt)

	1993	1994	1995
Entered	37,603	39,700	48,827
Cleared	35,128	37,421	42,985

Source: UN, *Statistical Yearbook*.

International Sea-borne Freight Traffic
('000 metric tons, year ending 30 June)

	2004/05	2005/06	2006/07*
Goods loaded	21,894	21,840	22,986
Goods unloaded	19,164	18,119	18,499

* Provisional.

CIVIL AVIATION
(domestic and international traffic on scheduled services)

	2004	2005	2006
Kilometres flown (million)	176	185	195
Passengers carried ('000)	11,305	11,952	12,382
Passenger-km (million)	24,710	26,093	27,032
Total metric ton-km (million)	3,307	3,486	3,621

Source: UN, *Statistical Yearbook*.

Tourism

VISITOR ARRIVALS

Country of residence	2008	2009	2010*
Australia	976,200	1,082,680	1,154,830
China, People's Republic	112,398	102,259	105,500
Germany	62,300	64,564	66,270
Japan	102,482	78,426	88,190
Korea, Republic	79,061	52,921	66,580
United Kingdom	285,094	258,438	245,430
USA	212,410	197,792	198,120
Total (incl. others)	2,447,208	2,447,346	2,537,680

* Estimates.

Tourism receipts ($NZ million): 5,947 in 2008; 6,187 in 2009; 6,278 in 2010 (estimate).

Source: Tourism Research Council, Wellington.

NEW ZEALAND

Communications Media

	2007	2008	2009
Telephones ('000 main lines in use)	1,747	1,750	1,870
Mobile cellular telephones ('000 subscribers)	4,251	4,620*	4,700
Internet users ('000)	2,925	3,047	3,400
Broadband subscribers ('000)	853	915	981

* At September.

Personal computers: 2,200,000 (525.7 per 1,000 persons) in 2006.

Television receivers ('000 in use): 2,130 in 2001.

Radio receivers ('000 in use): 3,750 in 1997.

Daily newspapers: 23 (circulation 739,000 copies) in 2004.

Non-daily newspapers: 129 titles in 2004; 311,380 copies in 2002.

Book production (1999): 4,800 titles.

Sources: partly International Telecommunication Union; UNESCO, *Statistical Yearbook*; UN, *Statistical Yearbook*.

Education

(July 2010 unless otherwise indicated)

	Institutions	Teachers (full-time equivalent)	Students
Early childhood services	5,152	13,294	188,924[1]
Primary schools[2]	2,018	25,141[3]	435,051
Composite schools[4]	155	2,603[3]	50,524
Secondary schools[5]	340	18,930[3]	275,945
Special schools	46	1,019[3]	2,878
Polytechnics	20[6]	4,194	180,709[7]
Colleges of education	4[6]	301[8]	66,897[7]
Universities	8[6]	7,869[7]	154,866[7]
Wananga[9]	3[6]	572[7]	42,566[7]
Private training establishments receiving government grants	522[6]	4,177[6]	59,158[10]

[1] Includes children on the regular roll of kindergartens, playcentres, the Correspondence School, Te Kohanga Reo, Early Childhood Development Unit funded playgroups, Early Childhood Development Unit funded Pacific Islands language groups, education and care centres (including home-based child care).
[2] Primary schools include Full Primary Years 1–8, Contributing Years 1–6, Intermediate Years 7–8.
[3] Teachers employed in state schools at 1 April 2010.
[4] Composite schools provide both primary and secondary education (includes area schools and the Correspondence School).
[5] Secondary schools include Years 7–15, Years 9–15.
[6] 2003 figure.
[7] 2009 figure.
[8] 2006 figure.
[9] Tertiary institutions providing polytechnic and university level programmes specifically for Maori students, with an emphasis on Maori language and culture.
[10] 2004 figure.

Source: Ministry of Education, Wellington.

Pupil-teacher ratio (primary education, UNESCO estimate): 15.3 in 2007/08 (Source: UNESCO Institute for Statistics).

Directory

The Government

Head of State: HM Queen ELIZABETH II (acceded to the throne 6 February 1952).

Governor-General and Commander-in-Chief: Sir ANAND SATYANAND (assumed office 23 August 2006).

CABINET
(May 2011)

The Government is formed by the National Party, in coalition with ACT New Zealand, the Maori Party and United Future New Zealand.

Prime Minister and Minister of Tourism: JOHN KEY.
Deputy Prime Minister, Minister of Finance and for Infrastructure: BILL ENGLISH.
Minister for Canterbury Earthquake Recovery, for Economic Development and of Energy and Resources: GERRY BROWNLEE.
Minister of Justice, of Commerce and of Consumer Affairs: SIMON POWER.
Minister of Health, for State-Owned Enterprises and of State Services: TONY RYALL.
Minister for the Environment, for Climate Change Issues and for the Accident Compensation Corporation: Dr NICK SMITH.
Minister of Police, of Corrections and of Veterans' Affairs: JUDITH COLLINS.
Minister of Education: ANNE TOLLEY.
Attorney-General and Minister for Treaty of Waitangi Negotiations and for Arts, Culture and Heritage: CHRISTOPHER FINLAYSON.
Minister of Agriculture, for Biosecurity and of Forestry: DAVID CARTER.
Minister of Foreign Affairs and for Sport and Recreation and for the Rugby World Cup: MURRAY MCCULLY.
Minister of Trade: TIM GROSER.
Minister of Defence and of Science and Innovation: Dr WAYNE MAPP.
Minister of Transport, for Communications and Information Technology and for Tertiary Education: STEVEN JOYCE.
Minister for Courts, of Pacific Island Affairs and for Disarmament and Arms Control: GEORGINA TE HEUHEU.
Minister for Social Development and Employment and of Youth Affairs: PAULA BENNETT.
Minister of Fisheries and Aquaculture and of Housing: PHIL HEATLEY.
Minister of Immigration and of Broadcasting: Dr JONATHAN COLEMAN.
Minister of Conservation, of Labour and for Food Safety: KATE WILKINSON.
Minister for Ethnic Affairs and of Women's Affairs: HEKIA PARATA.

MINISTERS OUTSIDE CABINET

Minister for Building and Construction, of Customs, for Land Information, of Statistics and for Small Business: MAURICE WILLIAMSON.
Minister of Civil Defence, for Senior Citizens and for Racing: JOHN CARTER.
Minister of Internal Affairs: NATHAN GUY.

SUPPORT PARTY MINISTERS

Minister of Local Government and for Regulatory Reform: RODNEY HIDE.
Minister of Maori Affairs: Dr PITA SHARPLES.

NEW ZEALAND

Minister for the Community and Voluntary Sector and for Disability Issues: Tariana Turia.
Minister of Revenue: Peter Dunne.

MINISTRIES AND GOVERNMENT DEPARTMENTS

Department of the Prime Minister and Cabinet: Executive Wing, Parliament Bldgs, Wellington 6011; tel. (4) 817-9682; fax (4) 472-3181; e-mail finance@dpmc.govt.nz; internet www.dpmc.govt.nz.

Ministry of Agriculture and Forestry: 25 The Terrace, POB 2526, Wellington 6140; tel. (4) 894-0100; fax (4) 894-0720; e-mail info@maf.govt.nz; internet www.maf.govt.nz.

Department of Building and Housing: Level 6, 86 Customhouse Quay, POB 10-729, Wellington; tel. (4) 494-0260; fax (4) 494-0290; e-mail info@dbh.govt.nz; internet www.dbh.govt.nz.

Ministry of Civil Defence and Emergency Management: Level 9, 22 The Terrace, POB 5010, Wellington; tel. (4) 473-7363; fax (4) 473-7369; e-mail emergency.management@dia.govt.nz; internet www.civildefence.govt.nz.

Department of Conservation: POB 10-420, Wellington 6143; tel. (4) 471-0726; fax (4) 381-3057; e-mail enquiries@doc.govt.nz; internet www.doc.govt.nz.

Ministry of Consumer Affairs: Level 7, 33 Bowen St, POB 1473, Wellington 6140; tel. (4) 474-2750; fax (4) 473-9400; e-mail mcainfo@mca.govt.nz; internet www.consumeraffairs.govt.nz.

Department of Corrections: POB 1206, Wellington 6140; tel. (4) 460-3000; fax (4) 460-3208; e-mail info@corrections.govt.nz; internet www.corrections.govt.nz.

Ministry for Culture and Heritage: POB 5364, Wellington; tel. (4) 499-4229; fax (4) 499-4490; e-mail info@mch.govt.nz; internet www.mch.govt.nz.

Ministry of Defence: Molesworth St, POB 12-703, Wellington 6144; tel. (4) 496-0999; fax (4) 496-0859; e-mail info@defence.govt.nz; internet www.defence.govt.nz.

Ministry of Economic Development: 33 Bowen St, POB 1473, Wellington; tel. (4) 472-0030; fax (4) 473-4638; e-mail info@med.govt.nz; internet www.med.govt.nz.

Ministry of Education: 45–47 Pipitea St, POB 1666, Thorndon, Wellington 6140; tel. (4) 463-8000; fax (4) 463-8001; e-mail enquiries.national@minedu.govt.nz; internet www.minedu.govt.nz.

Ministry for the Environment: POB 10-362, Wellington 6143; tel. (4) 439-7400; fax (4) 439-7700; e-mail info@mfe.govt.nz; internet www.mfe.govt.nz.

Ministry of Fisheries: ASB Bank House, 101–103 The Terrace, POB 1020, Wellington; tel. (4) 819-4600; fax (4) 819-4601; e-mail info@fish.govt.nz; internet www.fish.govt.nz.

Ministry of Foreign Affairs and Trade: Private Bag 18901, Wellington 5045; tel. (4) 439-8000; fax (4) 439-8505; e-mail enquiries@mfat.govt.nz; internet www.mfat.govt.nz.

Ministry of Health: POB 5013, Wellington; tel. (4) 496-2000; fax (4) 496-2340; e-mail emailmoh@moh.govt.nz; internet www.moh.govt.nz.

Department of Inland Revenue: POB 39010, Wellington Mail Centre, Lower Hutt 5045; tel. (4) 978-0779; e-mail nonres@ird.govt.nz; internet www.ird.govt.nz.

Department of Internal Affairs: POB 805, Wellington 6140; tel. (4) 495-7200; e-mail info@dia.govt.nz; internet www.dia.govt.nz.

Ministry of Justice: Vogel Centre, 19 Aitken St, POB 180, Wellington; tel. (4) 918-8800; fax (4) 918-8820; e-mail reception@justice.govt.nz; internet www.justice.govt.nz.

Department of Labour: POB 3705, Wellington; tel. (4) 915-4400; fax (4) 915-4015; e-mail info@dol.govt.nz; internet www.dol.govt.nz.

Ministry of Maori Development (Te Puni Kokiri): POB 3943, Wellington 6140; tel. (4) 819-6000; fax (4) 819-6299; e-mail info@tpk.govt.nz; internet www.tpk.govt.nz.

Ministry of Pacific Island Affairs: POB 833, Wellington 6140; tel. (4) 473-4493; fax (4) 473-4301; e-mail contact@mpia.govt.nz; internet www.mpia.govt.nz.

Ministry of Science and Innovation: POB 5336, Wellington 6145; tel. (4) 917-2900; fax (4) 471-1284; e-mail info@msi.govt.nz; internet www.msi.govt.nz.

Ministry of Social Development: POB 1556, Wellington 6140; tel. (4) 916-3300; fax (4) 918-0099; e-mail information@msd.govt.nz; internet www.msd.govt.nz.

State Services Commission: POB 329, Wellington 6140; tel. (4) 495-6600; fax (4) 495-6686; e-mail commission@ssc.govt.nz; internet www.ssc.govt.nz.

Statistics New Zealand (Tatauranga Aotearoa): POB 2922, Wellington 6140; tel. (4) 931-4600; fax (4) 931-4030; e-mail info@stats.govt.nz; internet www.stats.govt.nz.

Ministry of Tourism: 33 Bowen St, POB 5640, Wellington; tel. (4) 498-7440; fax (4) 498-7445; e-mail info@tourism.govt.nz; internet www.tourism.govt.nz.

Ministry of Transport: POB 3175, Wellington 6140; tel. (4) 439-9000; fax (4) 439-9005; e-mail informationmanagement@transport.govt.nz; internet www.transport.govt.nz.

Treasury: POB 3724, Wellington 6140; tel. (4) 472-2733; fax (4) 473-0982; e-mail info@treasury.govt.nz; internet www.treasury.govt.nz.

Ministry of Women's Affairs: POB 10-049, Wellington; tel. (4) 915-7112; fax (4) 916-1604; e-mail mwa@mwa.govt.nz; internet www.mwa.govt.nz.

Ministry of Youth Development: POB 1556, Wellington 6140; tel. (4) 916-3300; fax (4) 918-0091; e-mail mydinfo@myd.govt.nz; internet www.myd.govt.nz.

Legislature

HOUSE OF REPRESENTATIVES

Speaker: Lockwood Smith.
General Election, 8 November 2008

Party	Number of party votes	% of votes	Party seats	List seats	Total seats
NZ National Party	1,053,398	44.93	41	17	58
NZ Labour Party	796,880	33.99	21	22	43
Green Party	157,613	6.72	—	9	9
ACT New Zealand	85,496	3.65	1	4	5
Maori Party	55,980	2.39	5	—	5
Progressive Party	21,241	0.91	1	—	1
United Future NZ	20,497	0.87	1	—	1
New Zealand First	95,356	4.07	—	—	—
Total (incl. others)	2,356,536	100.00	70	52	122

Election Commission

Electoral Commission of New Zealand: POB 3050, Wellington 6140; tel. (4) 474-0670; fax (4) 474-0674; e-mail info@elections.govt.nz; internet www.elections.org.nz; f. 2010; independent Crown entity; assumed responsibilities of Chief Electoral Office and previous Electoral Commission in Oct. 2010; Chair. Sir Hugh Williams; Chief Electoral Officer Robert Peden.

Political Organizations

In March 2010 19 political parties were registered.

ACT New Zealand: 309 Broadway, POB 99-651, Newmarket, Auckland; tel. (9) 523-0470; fax (9) 523-0472; e-mail info@act.org.nz; internet www.act.org.nz; f. 1994; supports free enterprise, tax reform and choice in education and health; Pres. Chris Simmonds; Leader Rodney Hide.

Green Party of Aotearoa—New Zealand: POB 11652, Wellington; tel. (4) 801-5102; fax (4) 801-5104; e-mail greenparty@greens.org.nz; internet www.greens.org.nz; f. 1989; fmrly Values Party, f. 1972; Co-Leaders Russel Norman, Metiria Turei.

Maori Party: POB 50-271, Porirua; tel. (4) 471-9900; fax (4) 499-7269; e-mail hekeretari2@maoriparty.com; internet www.maoriparty.org; f. 2004; Co-Leaders Dr Pita Sharples, Tariana Turia; Pres. Dr Whatarangi Winiata.

NZ Democrats for Social Credit: POB 18-907, New Brighton, Christchurch 8641; tel. and fax (3) 382-9544; e-mail democrats@democrats.org.nz; internet www.democrats.org.nz; f. 1953; est. as Social Credit Political League; subsequently known as New Zealand Democratic Party Inc; liberal; Pres. Neville Aitchison; Leader Stephnie de Ruyter.

New Zealand First: Albany, North Shore City, POB 301158, Auckland 0752; tel. (7) 827-4932; fax (7) 827-4931; e-mail info@nzfirst.org.nz; internet www.nzfirst.org.nz; f. 1993; est. by fmr Nat. Party mems; Leader Winston Peters; Pres. George Groombridge.

New Zealand Labour Party: Fraser House, POB 784, Wellington; tel. (4) 384-7649; fax (4) 384-8060; e-mail office@labourparty.org.nz; internet www.labour.org.nz, www.labourparty.org.nz; f. 1916; advocates an organized economy guaranteeing an adequate standard of living to every person able and willing to work; Pres. ANDREW LITTLE; Parl. Leader PHIL GOFF; Gen. Sec. CHRIS FLATT.

New Zealand National Party: Willbank House, Level 14, 57 Willis St, POB 1155, Wellington 6001; tel. (4) 472-5211; fax (4) 478-1622; e-mail hq@national.org.nz; internet www.national.org.nz; f. 1936; centre-right; supports private enterprise and competitive business, together with maximum personal freedom; Pres. PETER GOODFELLOW; Parl. Leader JOHN KEY.

Progressive Party: POB 33-243, Christchurch 8030; tel. (3) 377-7679; fax (3) 377-7673; e-mail contact@progressive.org.nz; internet www.progressive.org.nz; f. 2002; est. as Progressive Coalition to contest 2002 general election; name changed as above April 2004; Leader JIM ANDERTON; Gen. Sec. PHIL CLEARWATER.

United Future New Zealand (UFNZ): Bowen House, Parliament Bldgs, Wellington; tel. (4) 471-9410; e-mail frankowen@xtra.co.nz; internet www.unitedfuture.org.nz; f. 1995; est. by 4 mems of Nat. Party, 2 mems of Labour Party and leader of Future New Zealand; Leader PETER DUNNE; Pres. JUDY TURNER.

Other parties that contested the 2008 election included the Alliance, the Aotearoa Legalise Cannabis Party, the Family Party, Libertarianz, the Kiwi Party, the New Zealand Pacific Party, the Republic of New Zealand Party and the Workers' Party.

Diplomatic Representation

EMBASSIES AND HIGH COMMISSIONS IN NEW ZEALAND

Argentina: Level 14, 142 Lambton Quay, POB 5430, Wellington; tel. (4) 472-8330; fax (4) 472-8331; e-mail enzel@arg.org.nz; internet www.arg.org.nz; Ambassador PEDRO R. HERRERA.

Australia: 72–76 Hobson St, Thorndon, POB 4036, Wellington; tel. (4) 473-6411; fax (4) 498-7135; e-mail nzinbox@dfat.gov.au; internet www.australia.org.nz; High Commissioner PAUL O'SULLIVAN.

Brazil: Deloitte House, Level 9, 10 Brandon St, POB 5432, Wellington 6011; tel. (4) 473-3516; fax (4) 473-3517; e-mail brasemb@brazil.org.nz; internet www.brazil.org.nz; Ambassador RENATE STILLE.

Canada: 125 The Terrace, Level 11, POB 8047, Wellington; tel. (4) 473-9577; fax (4) 471-2082; e-mail wlgtn@international.gc.ca; internet www.canadainternational.gc.ca/new_zealand-nouvelle_zelande; High Commissioner CAROLINE CHRÉTIEN.

Chile: 19 Bolton St, POB 3861, Wellington; tel. (4) 471-6270; fax (4) 472-5324; e-mail echile@embchile.co.nz; internet www.embchile.co.nz; Ambassador LUIS LILLO.

China, People's Republic: 2–6 Glenmore St, Kelburn, Wellington; tel. (4) 472-1382; fax (4) 499-0419; e-mail administration@chinaembassy.org.nz; internet www.chinaembassy.org.nz; Ambassador XU JIANGUO.

Cuba: 35 Hobson St, Thorndon, POB 3294, Wellington; tel. (4) 472-3748; fax (4) 473-2958; e-mail embajada@xtra.co.nz; Ambassador JOSÉ LUIS ROBAINA GARCÍA.

Fiji: 31 Pipitea St, Thorndon, POB 3940, Wellington; tel. (4) 473-5401; fax (4) 499-1011; e-mail viti@paradise.net.nz; internet www.fiji.org.nz; Head of Mission MERE TORA (acting).

France: Sovereign House, Level 13, 34–42 Manners St, POB 11-343, Wellington 6142; tel. (4) 384-2555; fax (4) 384-2577; e-mail amba.france@actrix.co.nz; internet www.ambafrance-nz.org; Ambassador FRANCIS ETIENNE.

Germany: 90–92 Hobson St, POB 1687, Wellington; tel. (4) 473-6063; fax (4) 473-6069; e-mail info@wellington.diplo.de; internet www.wellington.diplo.de; Ambassador THOMAS H. MEISTER.

Greece: Petherick Tower, Level 11, 38–42 Waring Taylor St, POB 24-066, Wellington; tel. (4) 473-7775; fax (4) 473-7441; e-mail gremb.wel@mfa.gr; internet www.mfa.gr/wellington; Ambassador DIMITRIOS ANNINOS.

Holy See: Apostolic Nunciature, 112 Queens Dr., Lyall Bay, POB 14-044, Wellington 6241; tel. (4) 387-3470; fax (4) 387-8170; e-mail nuntius@ihug.co.nz; Apostolic Nuncio Most Rev. CHARLES D. BALVO (Titular Archbishop of Castello).

India: 180 Molesworth St, POB 4045, Wellington 6015; tel. (4) 473-6390; fax (4) 499-0665; e-mail hicomind@hicomind.org.nz; internet www.hicomind.org.nz; High Commissioner Adm. SUREESH MEHTA.

Indonesia: 70 Glen Rd, Kelburn, POB 3543, Wellington; tel. (4) 475-8698; fax (4) 475-9374; e-mail info@indonesianembassy.org.nz; internet www.indonesianembassy.org.nz; Ambassador ANTONIUS AGUS SRIYONO.

Iran: POB 14733, Kilbirnie, Wellington; tel. (4) 386-2983; fax (4) 939-8108; e-mail info@iranembassy.org.nz; internet www.iranembassy.org.nz; Ambassador MORTEZA RAHMANI-MOVAHED.

Israel: Greenock House, 39 The Terrace, Wellington 6011; tel. (4) 471-0079; fax (4) 498-2959; e-mail info@wellington.mfa.gov.il; internet users.iconz.co.nz/israel; Ambassador SHEMI TZUR.

Italy: 34–38 Grant Rd, Thorndon, POB 463, Wellington; tel. (4) 473-5339; fax (4) 472-7255; e-mail ambasciata.wellington@esteri.it; internet www.ambwellington.esteri.it/ambasciata_wellington; Ambassador Dr GIOACCHINO TRIZZINO.

Japan: POB 6340, Marion Sq., Wellington 6141; tel. (4) 473-1540; fax (4) 471-2951; e-mail japan.emb@eoj.org.nz; internet www.nz.emb-japan.go.jp; Ambassador HIDETO MITAMURA.

Korea, Republic: ASB Bank Tower, Level 11, 2 Hunter St, POB 11-143, Wellington; tel. (4) 473-9073; fax (4) 472-3865; e-mail info@koreanembassy.org.nz; internet www.koreanembassy.org.nz; Ambassador NOH KWANG-IL.

Malaysia: 10 Washington Ave, Brooklyn, POB 9422, Wellington; tel. (4) 385-2439; fax (4) 385-6973; e-mail mwwelton@xtra.co.nz; internet www.kln.gov.my/web/nzl_wellington; High Commissioner Dato' HASNUDIN HAMZAH.

Mexico: AMP Chambers, Level 2, 185–187 Featherston St, POB 11-510, Wellington; tel. (4) 472-0555; fax (4) 496-3559; e-mail mexico@xtra.co.nz; internet www.sre.gob.mx/nuevazelandia; Chargé d'affaires a.i. LUIS ENRIQUE FRANCO.

Netherlands: POB 840, Wellington 6140; tel. (4) 471-6390; fax (4) 471-2923; e-mail wel@minbuza.nl; internet www.netherlandsembassy.co.nz; Ambassador ARIE VAN DER WIEL.

Pakistan: 182 Onslow Rd, Khandallah, Wellington 6035; tel. (4) 479-0026; fax (4) 479-4315; e-mail pakhcwellington@xtra.co.nz; internet www.mofa.gov.pk/newzealand; High Commissioner SYED IBNE ABBAS.

Papua New Guinea: 279 Willis St, POB 197, Wellington; tel. (4) 385-2474; fax (4) 385-2477; e-mail pngnz@globe.net.nz; internet www.pngnz.org/highcom; High Commissioner WILLIAM DIHM.

Peru: Cigna House, Level 8, 40 Mercer St, POB 2566, Wellington; tel. (4) 499-8087; fax (4) 499-8057; e-mail embassy.peru@xtra.co.nz; internet www.embassyofperu.org.nz; Ambassador CARLOS ZAPATA.

Philippines: 50 Hobson St, Thorndon, Wellington 6011; tel. (4) 472-9848; fax (4) 472-5170; e-mail embassy@wellington-pe.co.nz; internet www.philembassy.org.nz; Ambassador Dr BIENVENIDO V. TEJANO.

Poland: City Chambers, Level 9, 142–144 Featherston St, POB 10211, Wellington; tel. (4) 475-9453; fax (4) 475-9458; e-mail polishembassy@xtra.co.nz; internet www.wellington.polemb.net; Ambassador BEATA STOCZYŃSKA.

Russia: 57 Messines Rd, Karori, Wellington; tel. (4) 476-6113; fax (4) 476-3843; e-mail info@rus.co.nz; internet www.russianembassy.co.nz; Ambassador ANDREI A. TATARINOV.

Samoa: 1A Wesley Rd, Kelburn, POB 1430, Wellington; tel. (4) 472-0953; fax (4) 471-2479; e-mail shc@paradise.net.nz; High Commissioner ASI TUIATAGA J. F. BLAKELOCK.

Singapore: 17 Kabul St, Khandallah, POB 13140, Wellington; tel. (4) 470-0850; fax (4) 479-4066; e-mail singhc_wlg@sgmfa.gov.sg; internet www.mfa.gov.sg/wellington; High Commissioner M. P. H. RUBIN.

South Africa: State Insurance Bldg, Level 7, 1 Willis St, POB 25406, Wellington; tel. (4) 815-8484; fax (4) 472-5010; e-mail wellington@foreign.gov.za; High Commissioner ANTHONY LE CLERK KGWADU MONGALO.

Spain: BNZ Trust House Bldg, Level 11, 50 Manners St, POB 24-150, Wellington 6142; tel. (4) 802-5665; fax (4) 801-7701; e-mail emb.wellington@maec.es; internet www.maec.es/subwebs/embajadas/wellington; Ambassador MARCOS GÓMEZ MARTÍNEZ.

Switzerland: POB 25004, Wellington 6146; tel. (4) 472-1593; fax (4) 499-6302; e-mail wel.vertretung@eda.admin.ch; internet www.eda.admin.ch/wellington; Ambassador Dr MARION WEICHELT KRUPSKI.

Thailand: 2 Cook St, Karori, POB 17-226, Wellington; tel. (4) 476-8619; fax (4) 476-8610; e-mail thaiembassynz@xtra.co.nz; internet www.thaiembassynz.org.nz; Ambassador NOPPADON THEPPITAK.

Tonga: 41 Bay St, Petone, Lower Hutt, Wellington 5012; tel. (4) 566-3884; fax (4) 566-3887; e-mail thc.wellington@gmail.com; High Commissioner SIAOSI TAIMANI 'AHO.

Turkey: 15–17 Murphy St, Level 8, POB 12-248, Thorndon, Wellington; tel. (4) 472-1292; fax (4) 472-1277; e-mail turkem@xtra.co.nz; Ambassador MEHMET TASER.

United Kingdom: 44 Hill St, POB 1812, Wellington; tel. (4) 924-2888; fax (4) 473-4982; e-mail ppa.mailbox@fco.gov.uk; internet ukinnewzealand.fco.gov.uk; High Commissioner VICTORIA TREADELL.

NEW ZEALAND

USA: 29 Fitzherbert Terrace, POB 1190, Wellington; tel. (4) 462-6000; fax (4) 499-0490; internet newzealand.usembassy.gov; Ambassador Dr DAVID HUEBNER.

Viet Nam: Grand Plimmer Tower, Level 21, 2–6 Gilmer Terrace, POB 8042, Wellington; tel. (4) 473-5912; fax (4) 473-5913; e-mail embassyvn@clear.net.nz; internet www.vietnamembassy-newzealand.org; Ambassador VUONG HAI NAM.

Judicial System

The Judicial System of New Zealand comprises a Supreme Court, a Court of Appeal, a High Court and District Courts, all of which have civil and criminal jurisdiction, and the specialist courts, the Employment Court, the Family Court, the Youth Court and the Maori Land Court. On 1 January 2004 the newly established Supreme Court replaced the Judicial Committee of the Privy Council in the United Kingdom as the final appellate court. The right to appeal to the Supreme Court was granted only if the Court was satisfied that the case involved a matter of general or public importance or commercial significance, or in order to correct or prevent a substantial miscarriage of justice.

The Court of Appeal hears appeals from the High Court and from District Court Jury Trials, although it does have some original jurisdiction. Its decisions are final, except in cases that may be appealed to the Supreme Court. Appeals regarding convictions and sentences handed down by the High Court or District Trial Courts are by leave only.

The High Court has jurisdiction to hear cases involving crimes, admiralty law and civil matters. It hears appeals from lower courts and tribunals, and reviews administrative actions.

District Courts have an extensive criminal and civil law jurisdiction. They hear civil cases, while Justices of the Peace can hear minor criminal and traffic matters. The Family Court, which is a division of the District Courts, has the jurisdiction to deal with dissolution of marriages, adoption, guardianship applications, domestic actions, matrimonial property, child support, care and protection applications regarding children and young persons, and similar matters.

The tribunals are as follows: the Employment Tribunal (administered by the Department of Labour), Disputes Tribunal, Complaints Review Tribunal, Residential Tenancies Tribunal, Waitangi Tribunal, Environment Court, Deportation Review Tribunal and Motor Vehicles Disputes Tribunal.

In criminal cases involving indictable offences (major crimes), the defendant has the right to a jury. In criminal cases involving summary offences (minor crimes), the defendant may elect to have a jury if the sentence corresponding to the charge is three months or greater.

Attorney-General: CHRISTOPHER FINLAYSON.

Chief Justice: Dame SIAN ELIAS.

THE SUPREME COURT

Judges: Dame SIAN ELIAS, Sir PETER BLANCHARD, Sir ANDREW TIPPING, Sir JOHN MCGRATH, Sir WILLIAM YOUNG, 85 Lambton Quay, Wellington; tel. (4) 918-8222; internet www.courtsofnz.govt.nz/about/supreme.

THE COURT OF APPEAL

President: MARK O'REGAN, cnr Molesworth and Aitken Sts, Wellington; tel. (4) 914-3540; fax (4) 914-3570.

Judges: SUSAN GLAZEBROOK, GRANT HAMMOND, ROBERT CHAMBERS, TERENCE ARNOLD, ELLEN FRANCE, ANTHONY RANDERSON, RHYS HARRISON, LYNTON LAURENCE STEVENS, JOHN RICHARD WILD.

THE HIGH COURT

Permanent Judges: HELEN WINKELMANN (Chief High Court Judge), LOWELL GODDARD, GRAHAM PANCKHURST, LESTER CHISHOLM, WARWICK GENDALL, JUDITH POTTER, JOHN WILD, RODNEY HANSEN, JOHN PRIESTLEY, RONALD YOUNG, PAUL HEATH, GEOFFREY VENNING, PATRICK KEANE, JOHN FOGARTY, ALAN MACKENZIE, FORREST MILLER, MARK COOPER, CHRISTOPHER ALLAN, PATRICIA COURTNEY, SIMON FRANCE, RAYNOR ASHER, GRAHAM LANG, DENIS CLIFFORD, PAMELA ANDREWS, JILLIAN MALLON, PETER WOODHOUSE, AILSA DUFFY, ROBERT ANDREW DOBSON, CHRISTINE FRENCH, EDWIN WYLIE, JOSEPH WILLIAMS, DOUGLAS WHITE, REBECCA ELLIS, TIMOTHY CHARLES BREWER, MARY PETERS, MARK WOOLFORD, CHRISTIAN NATHANIAL WHATA, CHRISTOPHER HOLDEN TOOGOOD, JOHN STEPHEN KÓS.

Religion

CHRISTIANITY

Te Runanga Whakawhanaunga i Nga Hahi o Aotearoa (Maori Council of Churches in New Zealand): Private Bag 11903, Ellerslie, Auckland; tel. (9) 525-4179; fax (9) 525-4346; f. 1982; 4 mem. churches; Administrator TE RUA GRETHA.

The Anglican Communion

The Anglican Church in Aotearoa, New Zealand and Polynesia comprises Te Pihopatanga o Aotearoa and eight dioceses (one of which is Polynesia). In 1996 the Church had an estimated 631,764 members in New Zealand.

Primate of the Anglican Church in Aotearoa, New Zealand and Polynesia, and Bishop of Aotearoa: Rt Rev. WILLIAM BROWN TUREI, POB 568, Gisborne 4040; tel. (6) 867-88561; fax (9) 377-6962; e-mail browntmihi@xtra.co.nz.

General Secretary and Treasurer of the Anglican Church in Aotearoa, New Zealand and Polynesia: JACKIE PEARSE, POB 87-188, Meadowbank, Auckland 1742; tel. (9) 521-4439; fax (9) 521-4490; e-mail gensec@ang.org.nz; internet www.anglican.org.nz.

The Roman Catholic Church

For ecclesiastical purposes, New Zealand comprises one archdiocese and five dioceses. At 31 December 2007 there were an estimated 524,645 adherents.

Bishops' Conference

New Zealand Catholic Bishops' Conference, Catholic Centre, 22–30 Hill St, POB 1937, Wellington 6140; tel. (4) 496-1747; fax (4) 496-17461; e-mail adickinson@nzcbc.org.nz; internet www.catholic.org.nz.

f. 1974; Pres. Most Rev. DENIS BROWNE (Bishop of Hamilton); Sec. Archbishop JOHN A. DEW (Archbishop of Wellington); Exec. Officer ANNE DICKINSON.

Archbishop of Wellington: Most Rev. JOHN A. DEW, Catholic Centre, 22–30 Hill St, POB 1937, Wellington 6140; tel. (4) 496-1766; fax (4) 496-1330; e-mail g.burns@wn.catholic.org.nz; internet www.wn.catholic.org.nz.

Other Christian Churches

Baptist Churches of New Zealand: 473 Great South Rd, POB 12149, Penrose, Auckland; tel. (9) 526-0333; fax (9) 526-0334; e-mail info@baptist.org.nz; internet www.baptist.org.nz; f. 1882; 22,928 mems; Pres. LYN CAMPBELL; Nat. Leader Rev. RODNEY MACANN.

Congregational Union of New Zealand: 8C Kirrie Dr., Te Atatu South, Auckland; tel. (9) 837-2220; fax (9) 620-8291; e-mail cunz@xtra.co.nz; internet www.congregational.org.nz; f. 1884; 600 mems, 14 churches; Sec. ROGER FROST; Chair. PETER ECCLES.

Methodist Church of New Zealand: Connexional Office, POB 931, Christchurch 8140; tel. (3) 366-6049; fax (3) 364-9439; e-mail info@methodist.org.nz; internet www.methodist.org.nz; 18,548 mems; Gen. Sec. Rev. JILL VAN DE GEER.

Presbyterian Church of Aotearoa New Zealand: Level 1, Terralink House, 275–283 Cuba St, POB 9049, Wellington; tel. (4) 801-6000; fax (4) 801-6001; e-mail info@presbyterian.org.nz; internet www.presbyterian.org.nz; f. 1840; 30,000 mems; Moderator Rev. Dr GRAHAM REDDING; Assembly Convenor Rev. EMMA KEOWN.

There are several Maori Churches in New Zealand, with a total membership of over 30,000. These include the Ratana Church of New Zealand, Ringatu Church, Church of Te Kooti Rikirangi, Absolute Maori Established Church, Destiny Church and United Maori Mission. The Antiochian Orthodox Church, the Assemblies of God, the Greek Orthodox Church of New Zealand, the Liberal Catholic Church and the Society of Friends (Quakers) are also active.

BAHÁ'Í FAITH

National Spiritual Assembly of the Bahá'ís of New Zealand: POB 21-551, Henderson, Auckland 1231; tel. (9) 837-4866; fax (9) 837-4898; e-mail admin@bahai.org.nz; internet www.bahai.org.nz; f. 1957; CEO MURRAY R. SMITH.

The Press

NEWSPAPERS AND PERIODICALS

Principal Dailies

In 2006 there were 28 daily newspapers in New Zealand.

NEW ZEALAND

Ashburton Guardian: 161 Burnett St, POB 77, Ashburton; tel. (3) 307-7900; fax (3) 307-7980; e-mail enquiries@theguardian.co.nz; internet www.ashburtonguardian.co.nz; f. 1879; morning; Mon.–Sat.; Editor Peter O'Neill; Man. Dir Bruce Bell; circ. 5,243 (2010).

Bay of Plenty Times: 108 Durham St, Private Bag 12002, Tauranga; tel. (7) 577-7770; fax (7) 578-0047; e-mail editor@bopp.co.nz; internet www.bayofplentytimes.co.nz; f. 1872; evening; Mon.–Sat.; Gen. Man. David Mackenzie; Editor Scott Inglis; circ. 20,352 (2010).

The Daily Post: 1143 Hinemoa St, POB 1442, Rotorua; tel. (7) 348-6199; fax (7) 348-0220; e-mail editor@dailypost.co.nz; internet www.dailypost.co.nz; f. 1885; evening; Gen. Man. Greg Alexander; Editor Kim Gillespie; circ. 10,294 (2010).

Dominion Post: Dominion Post House, 40 Boulcott St, POB 3740, Wellington; tel. (4) 474-0000; fax (4) 474-0584; e-mail editor@dompost.co.nz; internet www.dompost.co.nz; f. 2002; est. by merger of *The Evening Post* and *The Dominion*; morning; Mon.–Sat.; Gen. Man. Paul Elenio; Editor Bernadette Courtney; circ. 84,047 (2010).

Gisborne Herald: 64 Gladstone Rd, POB 1143, Gisborne; tel. (6) 869-0600; fax (6) 869-0643; e-mail info@gisborneherald.co.nz; internet www.gisborneherald.co.nz; f. 1874; evening; Man. Dir Michael Muir; Editor Jeremy Muir; circ. 7,705 (2010).

Greymouth Star: Werita St, POB 3, Greymouth; tel. (3) 768-7121; fax (3) 768-6205; internet www.greystar.co.nz; f. 1866; Mon.–Sat. (evening); Gen. Man. John Goulding; Editor Paul Madgwick; circ. 4,284 (2010).

Hawke's Bay Today: 113 Karamu Rd, POB 180, Hastings; tel. (6) 873-0800; fax (6) 873-0812; e-mail editor@hbtoday.co.nz; internet www.hbtoday.co.nz; f. 1999; evening; conservative; Gen. Man. Russell Broughton; Editor Antony Phillips; circ. 24,682 (2010).

Manuwatu Standard: 57–64 The Square, POB 3, Palmerston North; tel. (6) 356-9009; fax (6) 350-9545; e-mail editor@msl.co.nz; internet www.manawatustandard.co.nz; f. 1880; evening; Gen. Man. Craig Nash; Editor Michael Cummings; circ. 17,000 (2010).

Marlborough Express: 62–66 Arthur St, POB 242, Blenheim 7274; tel. (3) 520-8900; fax (3) 520-8911; e-mail smason@marlexpress.co.nz; internet www.marlboroughexpress.co.nz; f. 1866; Gen. Man. Roger G. Rose; Editor Steve Mason; circ. 8,986 (2010).

The Nelson Mail: 15 Bridge St, POB 244, Nelson; tel. (3) 548-7079; fax (3) 546-2802; e-mail mailbox@nelsonmail.co.nz; internet www.stuff.co.nz/nelsonmail; f. 1866; evening; Gen. Man. Craig Dennis; Editor Paul McIntyre; circ. 15,609 (2010).

New Zealand Herald: POB 32, Auckland; tel. (9) 379-5050; fax (9) 373-6421; internet www.nzherald.co.nz; f. 1863; morning; CEO Martin Simons; Editor-in-Chief Tim Murphy; circ. 170,677 (2010).

The Northern Advocate: 88 Robert St, POB 210, Whangarei; tel. (9) 470-2899; fax (9) 470-2869; e-mail daily@northernadvocate.co.nz; internet www.northernadvocate.co.nz; f. 1875; evening; 6 a week; Gen. Man. Alex Lawson; Editor Craig Cooper; circ. 13,292 (2010).

The Oamaru Mail: 80 Thames St, POB 343, Oamaru; tel. (3) 434-9970; fax (3) 433-0549; e-mail news@oamarumail.co.nz; internet www.oamarumail.co.nz; f. 1876; Mon.–Fri.; morning; Gen. Man. Tony Nielsen; Editor Sally Brooker; circ. 2,869 (2010).

Otago Daily Times: 52 Stuart St, POB 517, Dunedin; tel. (3) 477-4760; fax (3) 474-7422; e-mail odt.editorial@alliedpress.co.nz; internet www.odt.co.nz; f. 1861; morning; 6 a week; Man. Dir Julian C. S. Smith; Editor Robin Charteris; circ. 39,097 (2010).

The Press: 22 Cathedral Sq., Private Bag 4722, Christchurch 8140; tel. (3) 379-0940; fax (3) 364-8492; e-mail letters@press.co.nz; internet www.press.co.nz; f. 1861; morning; Gen. Man. Andrew Boyle; Editor Andrew Holden; circ. 81,017 (2010).

Southland Times: 67 Esk St, POB 805, Invercargill; tel. (3) 211-1130; fax (3) 214-9905; e-mail letters@stl.co.nz; internet www.southlandtimes.co.nz; f. 1862; morning; Mon.–Sat.; Gen. Man. Gareth Codd; Editor Fred Tulett; circ. 28,066 (2010).

Taranaki Daily News: 49–65 Currie St, POB 444, New Plymouth; tel. (6) 757-6862; fax (6) 758-4653; e-mail editor@dailynews.co.nz; internet www.stuff.co.nz/dailynews; f. 1857; morning; Gen. Man. Mike Brewer; Editor Roy Pilott; circ. 23,005 (2010).

Timaru Herald: POB 46, Timaru; tel. (3) 684-4129; fax (3) 688-1042; e-mail editor@timaruherald.co.nz; internet www.timaruherald.co.nz; f. 1864; morning; Gen. Man. Chris McAuslin; Editor David King; circ. 14,010 (2010).

Waikato Times: Private Bag 3086, Hamilton; tel. (7) 849-6180; fax (7) 849-9554; e-mail editor@waikatotimes.co.nz; internet www.stuff.co.nz/waikatotimes; f. 1872; evening; independent; Gen. Man. Gerard Watt; Editor Jonathan Mackenzie; circ. 40,096 (2010).

Wairarapa Times-Age: Cnr Perry St and Chapel St, POB 445, Masterton; tel. (6) 378-9999; fax (6) 378-2371; internet www.times-age.co.nz; f. 1938; evening; 6 a week; Gen. Man. Peter Wilson; Editor Dave Saunders; circ. 6,566 (2010).

Wanganui Chronicle: 59 Taupo Quay, POB 433, Wanganui; tel. (6) 349-0710; fax (6) 349-0721; e-mail news@wanganuichronicle.co.nz; internet www.wanganuichronicle.co.nz; f. 1856; morning; Gen. Man. Andy Jarden; Editor Ross Pringle; circ. 11,217 (2010).

Weeklies and Other Newspapers

Best Bets: 155 New North Rd, Eden Terrace, POB 1327, Auckland; tel. (9) 302-1300; fax (9) 366-4565; e-mail alan.caddy@best-bets.co.nz; Sun. and Thur.; horse-racing, trotting and greyhounds; Editor Alan Caddy; circ. 10,000.

Herald on Sunday: 58 Albert St, POB 32, Auckland; tel. (9) 373-9323; fax (9) 373-9372; internet www.heraldonsunday.co.nz; f. 2004; Editor Bryce Johns; circ. 96,069 (2010).

MG Business: POB 20-034 Bishopdale, Christchurch 8543; tel. (3) 358-3219; fax (3) 358-4490; internet www.mgpublications.co.nz; f. 1876; fmrly Mercantile Gazette; fortnightly; economics, finance, management, stock market, politics; Editor Bill Horsley; circ. 16,300.

The National Business Review: POB 1734, Auckland 1140; tel. (9) 307-1629; fax (9) 373-3997; e-mail editor@nbr.co.nz; internet www.nbr.co.nz; f. 1970; weekly; Editor-in-Chief Nevil Gibson; circ. 9,093 (2010).

New Zealand Gazette: POB 805, Wellington 6140; tel. (4) 495-7200; fax (4) 470-2932; e-mail info@dia.govt.nz; internet www.gazette.govt.nz; official govt publ; f. 1840; weekly; Chief Exec Brendan Boyle; circ. 1,000.

New Zealand Truth Weekly: Truth Publications Ltd, POB 9613, Newmarket, Auckland 1149; tel. (9) 909-3660; fax (9) 373-5410; e-mail editor@truth.co.nz; internet www.truth.co.nz; f. 1905; Friday; local news and features, TV and entertainment, sports; owned by Truth Publs Ltd; Editor Wayne Butler; circ. 24,000.

North Shore Times: POB 33-235, Takapuna, Auckland; tel. (9) 489-4189; fax (9) 486-6700; e-mail janet.ainsworth@snl.co.nz; 3 a week; Man. Janet Ainsworth; Editor Peter Eley; circ. 69,834 (2010).

The Star: POB 1467, Christchurch; tel. (3) 379-7100; fax (3) 366-0180; e-mail star.reporters@starcanterbury.co.nz; internet www.starcanterbury.co.nz; f. 1868; fmrly Christchurch Star; 2 a week; Editor Barry Clarke; circ. 118,170.

Sunday News: POB 1327, Auckland; tel. (9) 302-1300; fax (9) 358-3003; e-mail editor@sunday-news.co.nz; internet www.sundaynews.co.nz; Man. Editor Mitchell Murphy; circ. 51,740 (2010).

Sunday Star-Times: POB 1327, Auckland 1140; tel. (9) 302-1300; fax (9) 309-0258; e-mail letters@star-times.co.nz; internet www.stuff.co.nz/sunday-star-times; f. 1994 by merger; Editor David Kemeys; circ. 160,592 (2010).

Taieri Herald: 92 Gordon Rd, POB 105, Mosgiel; tel. (3) 489-7123; fax (3) 489-7668; e-mail sue.gregory@stl.co.nz; f. 1962; weekly; morning; Editor Daryl Holden; circ. 13,049 (2010).

Wairarapa News: Media House, 89 Chapel St, POB 902, Masterton; tel. (6) 370-5690; fax (6) 370-5699; e-mail editor@wainews.co.nz; f. 1869; weekly; Editor Walt Dickson; circ. 21,019 (2010).

Other Periodicals

AA Directions: POB 5, Auckland 1010; tel. (9) 966-8800; fax (9) 966-8975; e-mail editor@aa.co.nz; internet www.aa.co.nz/Online; f. 1991; quarterly; official magazine of The New Zealand Automobile Asscn; Editor Kathryn Webster; circ. 542,242 (2010).

Architecture New Zealand: AGM Publishing Ltd, Private Bag 99-915, Newmarket, Auckland; tel. (9) 846-4068; fax (9) 846-8742; e-mail john.walsh@agm.co.nz; internet www.agm.co.nz; f. 1987; every 2 months; Man. Dir Ian Close; Editor John Walsh; circ. 5,609 (2010).

Australian Women's Weekly (NZ edition): Private Bag 92-512, Wellesley St, Auckland; tel. (9) 308-2945; fax (9) 302-0667; e-mail aww@acpmagazines.co.nz; f. 1987; monthly; Editor Leonie Barlow; circ. 80,032 (2010).

Dairying Today: POB 3855, Shortland St, Auckland 1140; tel. (9) 307-0399; fax (9) 307-0122; e-mail sudeshk@ruralnews.co.nz; internet www.ruralnews.co.nz; fortnightly; Editor Sudesh Kissun; circ. 26,792 (2007).

Fashion Quarterly: ACP Media Centre, Private Bag 92-512, Auckland; tel. (9) 308-2409; fax (9) 302-0667; e-mail fq@acpmagazines.co.nz; f. 1982; 5 a year; Editor Fiona Hawtin; circ. 25,778 (2010).

Grapevine: Private Bag 92-124, Auckland; tel. (9) 813-4956; fax (9) 813-4957; e-mail info@grapevine.org.nz; internet www.grapevine.org.nz; f. 1981; 4 issues a year; family magazine; Editor John Cooney; circ. 160,000.

Home New Zealand: ACP Media Centre, cnr Fanshawe and Beaumont Sts, Private Bag 92-512, Auckland; tel. (9) 308-2739; e-mail homenewzealand@acpmagazines.co.nz; f. 1936; fmrly *NZ Home and Entertaining*; bi-monthly; design, architecture, lifestyle; Editor Jeremy Hansen; circ. 13,472 (2010).

NEW ZEALAND

Info-Link: AGM Publishing Ltd, 409 New North Rd, Kingsland, Auckland; tel. (9) 846-4068; fax (9) 846-8742; e-mail infolink@agm.co.nz; internet www.info-link.co.nz; quarterly; Publr PARUL SHEOPURI; Editor MARK LONGLEY; circ. 19,303 (2008).

Inwood Magazine: POB 17124, Greenlane, Auckland 1546; tel. (9) 921-257; fax (9) 535-7295; e-mail info@inwoodmag.com; internet www.inwoodmag.com; f. 1993; monthly; forestry; Man. Dir TONY NEILSON; circ. 8,000.

Landfall: Otago University Press, POB 56, Dunedin; tel. (3) 479-4194; fax (3) 479-8385; e-mail wendy.harrex@otago.ac.nz; internet www.otago.ac.nz/press/landfall; f. 1947; 2 a year; new fiction, poetry, biographical and critical essays, cultural commentary; Publr WENDY HARREX; Editor DAVID EGGLETON; circ. 1,200.

Mana Magazine: POB 1101, Rotorua; tel. (7) 349-0260; fax (7) 349-0258; e-mail editor@manaonline.co.nz; internet www.manaonline.co.nz; Maori news magazine; Editor DEREK FOX.

New Idea New Zealand: 48 Greys Ave, 4th Floor, Auckland; tel. (9) 979-2726; fax (9) 979-2721; f. 1992; weekly; women's interest; Editor HAYLEY MCLARIN; circ. 50,563 (2010).

New Zealand Dairy Exporter: 8 Weld St, POB 529, Feilding; tel. (6) 323-7104; fax (6) 323-7101; e-mail amelia.grant@nzx.com; internet www.dairymag.co.nz; f. 1925; monthly; Editor GLENYS CHRISTIAN; circ. 7,201 (2010).

New Zealand Gardener: POB 6341, Wellesley St, Auckland 1141; tel. (4) 909-6800; fax (9) 909-6802; e-mail mailbox@nzgardener.co.nz; internet www.nzgardener.co.nz; f. 1944; monthly; Editor LYNDA HALLIMAN; circ. 48,699 (2010).

New Zealand Horse and Pony: POB 12965, Penrose, Auckland; tel. (9) 634-1800; fax (9) 634-2948; e-mail rowan.dixon@horse-pony.co.nz; internet www.horse-pony.co.nz; f. 1959; monthly; Editor ROWAN DIXON; circ. 10,901 (2010).

New Zealand Management: Mediaweb, Wellesley St, POB 5544, Auckland 1141; tel. (9) 968-8400; fax (9) 968-0126; e-mail editor@management.co.nz; internet www.management.co.nz; f. 1955; monthly; business; Editor ELLEN READ; circ. 7,782 (2010).

New Zealand Medical Journal: Dept of Surgery, Christchurch Hospital, POB 4345, Christchurch; tel. (3) 364-1277; fax (3) 364-1683; e-mail nzmj@cdhb.govt.nz; internet www.nzma.org.nz/journal; f. 1887; publ. by New Zealand Medical Asscn; online publ.; articles free to non-subscribers 6 months after publ; 20 a year; Editor Prof. FRANK A. FRIZELLE; circ. 5,000.

New Zealand Science Review: POB 1874, Wellington; tel. (021) 487-284; e-mail editor@scientists.org.nz; internet www.scientists.org.nz; f. 1942; 4 a year; reviews, policy and philosophy of science; Editor ALLEN PETREY.

New Zealand Woman's Day: Wellesley St, Private Bag 92-512, Auckland; tel. (9) 308-2718; fax (9) 357-0978; e-mail wdaynz@acpmagazines.co.nz; weekly; Editor SIDO KITCHIN; circ. 105,127 (2010).

New Zealand Woman's Weekly: POB 90-119, Victoria St West, Auckland 1142; tel. (9) 373-9400; fax (9) 373-9405; e-mail editor@nzww.co.nz; internet www.nzwomansweekly.co.nz; f. 1932; Mon.; women's issues and general interest; Editor SARAH STUART; circ. 80,439 (2010).

Next: Level 4, cnr Fanshawe and Beaumont Sts, Westhaven, Private Bag 92-512, Auckland 1036; tel. (9) 308-2775; fax (9) 377-6725; e-mail next@acpmagazines.co.nz; internet www.acpmedia.co.nz; f. 1991; monthly; home and lifestyle; owned by ACP Media; Editor CHRISTINA SAYERS WICKSTEAD; circ. 46,489 (2010).

North & South: Wellesley St, Private Bag 92-512, Auckland; tel. (9) 366-5337; fax (9) 308-9498; e-mail northsouth@acpmedia.co.nz; f. 2011; f. 1986; monthly; current affairs and lifestyle; Editor VIRGINIA LARSON; circ. 26,819 (2010).

NZ Catholic: POB 147-000, Ponsonby, Auckland 1034; tel. (9) 360-3067; fax (9) 360-3065; e-mail contact@nzcatholic.org.nz; internet www.nzcatholic.org.nz; f. 1996; fortnightly; Roman Catholic; Man. Editor PETER GRACE; circ. 6,700.

NZ House and Garden: 317 New North Rd, Eden Terrace, Auckland; tel. (9) 909-6913; fax (9) 909-6802; e-mail sally.duggan@nzhouseandgarden.co.nz; internet www.nzhouseandgarden.co.nz; f. 1994; monthly; Editor KATE COUGHLAN; circ. 48,752 (2010).

NZ Listener: POB 90-783, Victoria St West, Auckland 1142; tel. (9) 373-9400; fax (9) 373-9406; e-mail submissions@listener.co.nz; internet www.listener.co.nz; f. 1939; weekly; current affairs and entertainment; Editor PAMELA STIRLING; Publr and Chief Exec. SARAH SANDLEY; circ. 73,404.

Otago Southland Farmer: POB 105, Mosgiel; tel. (3) 489-7123; fax (3) 489-7668; e-mail newspapersales@stl.co.nz; f. 1982; fortnightly; Editor TAM MATANGI; circ. 22,180 (2008).

Pacific Wings: POB 57163, Mana, Porirua 5247; tel. (4) 233-8368; e-mail editor@pacificwingsmagazine.com; internet www.pacificwingsmagazine.com; f. 1932; monthly; aviation; Editor and Publr ROB NEIL; circ. 20,000.

PC World: POB 6813, Wellesley St, Auckland; tel. (9) 926-9108; fax (9) 909-6989; e-mail ted.gibbons@ffxbusinessgroup.co.nz; internet pcworld.co.nz; f. 1988; monthly; Editor ZARA BAXTER; circ. 12,120 (2010).

Prodesign: AGM Publishing Ltd, Private Bag 99-915, Newmarket, Auckland; tel. (9) 846-2722; fax (9) 846-8742; e-mail michael.barrett@agm.co.nz; f. 1992; every 2 months; publ. of the Designers' Institute of New Zealand; Editor MICHAEL BARRETT; circ. 5,717 (2010).

PSA Journal: PSA House, 11 Aurora Terrace, POB 3817, Wellington 6140; tel. (4) 495-7633; fax (4) 917-2051; e-mail enquiries@psa.org.nz; internet www.psa.org.nz; f. 1913; 4 a year; journal of the NZ Public Service Asscn; Pres. PAULA SCHOLES; circ. 52,000.

Reader's Digest: POB 90-487, Mail Service Centre, Auckland; e-mail editor@readersdigest.co.nz; internet www.readersdigest.co.nz; f. 1950; monthly; Editor TONY SPENCER-SMITH; circ. 91,145 (2008).

RSA Review: RNZRSA National Headquarters, POB 27248, Wellington 6030; tel. (6) 384-7994; fax (6) 385-3325; e-mail subscribe@rnzrsa.org.nz; internet www.rsa.org.nz; quarterly; official magazine of the Royal New Zealand Returned and Services' Asscn; Editor BARRY ALLISON; circ. 95,000.

Rural News: POB 3855, Auckland; tel. (9) 307-0399; fax (9) 307-0122; e-mail editor@ruralnews.co.nz; fortnightly; Editor HAMISH CARNACHAN; circ. 81,811 (2007).

Spanz: POB 9049, Wellington; tel. (4) 801-6000; fax (4) 801-6001; e-mail amanda@presbyterian.org.nz; internet www.presbyterian.org.nz; f. 1987; bi-monthly; magazine of Presbyterian Church; circ. 21,500.

Straight Furrow: c/o Rural Press, POB 4233, Auckland; tel. (9) 524-1177; fax (9) 524-1170; e-mail straightfurrow@ruralpress.com; internet www.straightfurrow.co.nz; f. 1933; weekly; Group Editor JEFF SMITH; circ. 85,000.

Time New Zealand: POB 198, Auckland 1015; fax (9) 366-4706; internet www.time.com; weekly; circ. 23,970 (2008).

TV Guide (NZ): 317–319 New North Rd, Eden Terrace, POB 6341, Auckland; tel. (9) 909-6902; fax (9) 909-6912; e-mail julie.eley@tv-guide.co.nz; internet www.stuff.co.nz/entertainment/tv; f. 1986; weekly; Editor JULIE ELEY; circ. 155,591 (2011).

United Nations Association New Zealand: UNANZ, POB 24494, Wellington 6142; tel. (4) 496-9638; e-mail office@unanz.org.nz; internet www.unanz.org.nz; f. 1946; every 2 months; Pres. ANTONY VALLYON.

NEWS AGENCIES

New Zealand Press Association: 93 Boulcott St, POB 1599, Wellington 6040; tel. (4) 472-7910; fax (4) 473-7480; e-mail editor@nzpa.co.nz; internet www.nzpa.co.nz; f. 1879; non-political; Editor KEVIN NORQUAY.

South Pacific News Service Ltd (Sopacnews): Lambton Quay, POB 5026, Wellington; tel. and fax (3) 472-8329; e-mail farthing@deepsouth.co.nz; f. 1948; Man. Editor NEALE MCMILLAN.

PRESS COUNCIL

New Zealand Press Council: The Terrace, 79 Boulcott St, POB 10879, Wellington; tel. (4) 473-5220; fax (4) 471-1785; e-mail info@presscouncil.org.nz; internet www.presscouncil.org.nz; f. 1972; Chair. BARRY PATERSON; Exec. Dir M. E. MAJOR.

PRESS ASSOCIATIONS

Commonwealth Press Union (New Zealand Section): POB 1066, Wellington; tel. (4) 472-6223; fax (4) 471-0987; Sec. LINCOLN GOULD.

Newspaper Publishers' Association of New Zealand (Inc): Newspaper House, 93 Boulcott St, POB 1066, Wellington 6015; tel. (4) 472-6223; fax (4) 471-0987; e-mail npa@npa.co.nz; internet www.npa.co.nz; f. 1898; 31 mems; Pres. MICHAEL MUIR; CEO TIM PANKHURST.

Publishers

Auckland University Press: Private Bag 92019, University of Auckland, Auckland; tel. (9) 373-7528; fax (9) 373-7465; e-mail aup@auckland.ac.nz; internet www.auckland.ac.nz/aup; f. 1966; scholarly press; Dir SAM ELWORTHY.

The Caxton Press Ltd: 113 Victoria St, POB 25-088, Christchurch 8013; tel. (3) 366-8516; fax (3) 365-7840; e-mail peter@caxton.co.nz;

NEW ZEALAND

internet www.caxton.co.nz; f. 1935; human and general interest, local and NZ history, tourist pubs; Man. Dir Bruce Bascand.

Dunmore Publishing Ltd: POB 250-80, Wellington 6146; tel. (4) 472-2705; fax (4) 471-0604; e-mail books@dunmore.co.nz; internet www.dunmore.co.nz; f. 1975; non-fiction, educational; Publrs Murray Gatenby, Sharmian Firth.

Hachette New Zealand Ltd: POB 100-749, North Shore Mail Centre, Auckland 0745; tel. (9) 477-5550; fax (9) 477-5560; e-mail admin@hachette.co.nz; f. 1971; fmrly Hachette Livre NZ Ltd; Man. Dir Kevin Chapman.

HarperCollins Publishers (New Zealand) Ltd: POB 1, Shortland St, Auckland 1140; tel. (9) 443-9400; fax (9) 443-9403; e-mail editors@harpercollins.co.nz; internet www.harpercollins.co.nz; f. 1888; general and educational; CEO Jim Demetriou (acting); Man. Dir Tony Fisk.

Learning Media Ltd: POB 3293, Wellington; tel. (4) 472-5522; fax (4) 472-6444; e-mail info@learningmedia.co.nz; internet www.learningmedia.co.nz; f. 1947; est. as School Publs; state-owned enterprise; contract publishing, professional devt services, and educational products in a range of media and languages; Chief Exec. David Glover.

Legislation Direct: POB 12357, Wellington 6144; tel. (4) 568-0005; fax (4) 568-0003; e-mail Ldorders@legislationdirect.co.nz; internet www.legislationdirect.co.nz; general publishers and leading distributor of government publs; fmrly Govt Printing Office/GP Publications; Publications Man. Wendy Caylor.

LexisNexis NZ Ltd: Level 1, 181 Wakefield St, POB 472, Wellington 6140; tel. (4) 385-1479; fax (4) 385-1598; internet www.lexisnexis.co.nz; legal; Gen. Man. Darryn Keiller.

McGraw-Hill Book Co, New Zealand Ltd: Private Bag 11904, Ellerslie, Auckland 1005; tel. (9) 526-6200; fax (9) 526-6216; e-mail cservice_auckland@mcgraw-hill.com; internet www.mcgraw-hill.com.au/; f. 1974; educational; Man. Dir Murray St Leger.

New Zealand Council for Educational Research: POB 3237, Wellington 6140; tel. (4) 384-7939; fax (4) 384-7933; e-mail sales@nzcer.org.nz; internet www.nzcer.org.nz; f. 1934; scholarly, research monographs, educational, academic, periodicals; Chair. Peter Allen; Dir Robyn Baker.

Otago University Press: POB 56, Dunedin; tel. (3) 479-8807; fax (3) 479-8385; e-mail university.press@otago.ac.nz; internet www.otago.ac.nz/press; f. 1958; publishes titles on New Zealand, the Pacific and Asia, with special emphasis on history, literature, the arts and natural and social sciences; also educational titles and journals; Publr Wendy Harrex.

Pearson Education New Zealand Ltd: Private Bag 102-902, North Shore City, Auckland 0745; tel. (9) 414-9980; fax (9) 414-9981; e-mail customer.service@pearsonnz.co.nz; internet www.pearsoned.co.nz; f. 1968; fmrly Addison Wesley Longman; educational; Dirs Rosemary Stagg, P. Field.

Penguin Group (NZ) Ltd: Private Bag 102-902, North Shore Mail Centre, Auckland 0745; tel. (9) 442-7400; fax (9) 442-7401; e-mail publishing@penguin.co.nz; internet www.penguin.co.nz; f. 1973; Publ. Dir Geoff Walker; Man. Dir Tony Harkins.

Wendy Pye Ltd: Private Bag 17-905, Greenlane, Auckland; tel. (9) 525-3575; fax (9) 525-4205; e-mail admin@sunshine.co.nz; internet www.sunshinebooks.com.au/; children's fiction and educational; Man. Dir Wendy Pye.

Random House New Zealand Ltd: Private Bag 102-950, North Shore Mail Centre, Auckland; tel. (9) 444-7197; fax (9) 444-7524; e-mail admin@randomhouse.co.nz; internet www.randomhouse.co.nz; f. 1977; general; Chair. Michael Moynahan; Man. Dir Karen Ferns.

Victoria University Press: POB 600, Wellington; tel. (4) 463-3680; fax (4) 463-6581; e-mail victoria-press@vuw.ac.nz; internet www.victoria.ac.nz/vup; f. 1970; Publr Fergus Barrowman.

PUBLISHERS' ASSOCIATION

Publishers' Association of New Zealand Inc: Private Bag 102006, North Shore City, Auckland 0745; tel. (9) 477-5589; fax (9) 477-5570; e-mail admin@publishers.org.nz; internet www.publishers.org.nz; f. 1977; Dir Anne de Lautour.

Broadcasting and Communications

TELECOMMUNICATIONS

CallPlus: Level 4, 110 Symonds St, POB 108-109, Auckland; tel. (9) 915-7575; e-mail info@callplus.co.nz; internet www.callplus.co.nz; f. 1996; 100% New Zealand owned; full-service telecommunications co; Gen. Man. Kelvin Hussey.

Compass Communications Ltd: Level 2, Compass House, 162 Grafton Rd, Grafton, POB 2533, Auckland; tel. (9) 965-2200; fax (9) 965-2270; internet www.compass.net.nz; f. 1995; CEO Karim Hussona.

Kordia: Level 4, Fidelity House, 81 Carlton Gore Rd, Auckland 1023; tel. (9) 916-6400; fax (9) 916-6402; internet www.kordiasolutions.com; fmrly known as THL Group; name changed as above 2006; telecommunications, broadcasting and converged solutions; operates in New Zealand and Australia; Chair. David Clarke; CEO Geoff Hunt.

Orcon Internet Ltd: POB 302362, North Harbour, Auckland 0751; tel. (9) 444-4414; e-mail support@orcon.net.nz; internet www.orcon.net.nz; state-owned; provides mobile and internet services; CEO Scott Bartlett.

Telecom Corpn of New Zealand Ltd: Telecom House, 8 Hereford St, Auckland 1011; tel. (4) 801-9000; fax (4) 385-3469; internet www.telecom.co.nz; Chair. Wayne Boyd; Chief Exec. Paul Reynolds.

Telecommunications Users Association of New Zealand (TUANZ): POB 33-1014, Takapuna North Shore Mail Centre 0740; tel. (9) 488-1888; fax (9) 489-9515; e-mail bernice@tuanz.org.nz; internet www.tuanz.org.nz; f. 1986; non-profit asscn representing corporate telecommunications users; Chair. Pat O'Connell; CEO (vacant); 500 corporate mems.

TelstraClear: Private Bag 92-143, Auckland 1142; tel. (9) 913-9150; fax (9) 982-6232; internet www.telstraclear.co.nz; f. 1990; est. as Clear Communications Ltd; merged with TelstraSaturn Ltd 2001; owned by Australian telecommunications co Telstra; business solutions, local and toll services, enhanced internet, etc.; Chair. David Thodey; CEO Dr Allan Freeth.

Two Degrees Mobile Ltd: Symonds St, POB 8355, Auckland 1150; tel. 222002000; e-mail info@2degreesmobile.co.nz; internet www.2degreesmobile.co.nz; CEO Eric Hertz.

Vodafone New Zealand Ltd: POB 7281, Wellesley St, Auckland 1141; tel. (9) 355-2007; fax (9) 962-9300; internet www.vodafone.co.nz; fmrly Bell South; cellular network; CEO Russell Stanners.

Woosh Wireless Ltd: 11–15 Railway St, POB 9635, Newmarket, Auckland; tel. (9) 940-0111; fax (9) 520-3447; internet www.woosh.com; f. 1999 as Walker Wireless Ltd; name changed as above 2003; provides internet and telephony services; Chair. Rod Inglis; CEO Kevin Wiley.

WorldxChange Communications Ltd: Level 9, Tower Two, 55–65 Shortland St, POB 3296, Auckland; tel. (9) 950-1300; e-mail service@wxc.co.nz; internet www.wxc.co.nz; CEO Cecil Alexander.

Regulatory Authority

Telecommunications Policy Section, Ministry of Economic Development: 33 Bowen St, POB 1473, Wellington; tel. (4) 472-0030; fax (4) 473-4638; e-mail info@med.govt.nz; internet www.med.govt.nz.

BROADCASTING

Radio

Radio Broadcasters' Association (NZ) Inc: POB 3762, Auckland; tel. (9) 378-0788; fax (9) 378-8180; e-mail janine@rba.co.nz; internet www.rba.co.nz; represents commercial radio industry; Exec. Council Chair. John McElhinney; Exec. Dir David Innes; 13 mems.

Radio New Zealand Ltd: RNZ House, 155 The Terrace, POB 123, Wellington; tel. (4) 474-1999; fax (4) 474-1459; e-mail rnz@radionz.co.nz; internet www.radionz.co.nz; f. 1936; Crown-owned entity, operating non-commercial national networks: Radio New Zealand National and Radio New Zealand Concert; parliamentary broadcasts on AM Network; Radio New Zealand News and Current Affairs; short-wave service, Radio New Zealand International; Chair. Richard Griffin; CEO Peter Cavanagh.

The Radio Network of New Zealand Ltd: 54 Cook St, Private Bag 92-198, Auckland; tel. (9) 373-0000; e-mail enquiry@radionetwork.co.nz; internet www.radionetwork.co.nz; operates 129 commercial stations, reaching 1.4m. people; Chief Exec. John McElhinney.

Television

Television New Zealand (TVNZ) Ltd: Television Centre, 100 Victoria St West, POB 3819, Auckland; tel. (9) 916-7000; e-mail news@tvnz.co.uk; fax (9) 916-7934; internet www.tvnz.co.nz; f. 1960; the television service is responsible for the production of programmes for five TV networks: TV One, TV2, TVNZ Sport Extra, TVNZ 6 and TVNZ 7; networks are commercial all week and transmit in colour; channels broadcast 24 hours a day, seven days a week, and reach 99.9% of the population; Chair. Sir John Anderson; CEO Rick Ellis.

Maori Television: 9–15 Davis Cres., POB 113-017, Newmarket, Auckland; tel. (9) 539-7000; fax (9) 539-7199; e-mail info@maoritelevision.com; internet www.maoritelevision.com; f. 2003; owned by the Crown and Te Putahi Paoho; operates two stations; Te

NEW ZEALAND

Reo station, launched in early 2008, broadcasts Maori-language programmes daily; Maori Television channel broadcasts Maori- and English-language programmes; Chair. GARRY MURIWAI; CEO JIM MATHER.

Private Television

Auckland Independent Television Services Ltd: POB 1629, Auckland.

Sky Network Television Limited: 10 Panorama Rd, POB 9059, Newmarket, Auckland; tel. (9) 579-9999; fax (9) 579-0910; internet www.skytv.co.nz; f. 1990; UHF service on seven channels, satellite service; 720,919 subscribers (Dec. 2007); Chair. PETER MACOURT; CEO JOHN FELLET.

TV3 Network Services Ltd: Symonds St, Private Bag 92-624, Auckland; tel. (9) 377-9730; fax (9) 366-5949; internet www.tv3.co.nz; f. 1989; operated by MediaWorks NZ; Man. Dir RICK FRIESEN.

Finance

(cap. = capital; res = reserves; dep. = deposits; m. = million; br(s). = branch(es); amounts in New Zealand dollars)

BANKING

Central Bank

Reserve Bank of New Zealand (RBNZ): 2 The Terrace, POB 2498, Wellington; tel. (4) 472-2029; fax (4) 473-8554; e-mail rbnz-info@rbnz.govt.nz; internet www.rbnz.govt.nz; f. 1933; cap. 1,600m., res 1,085m., dep. 19,464m. (June 2010); Gov. ALAN BOLLARD; Chair. Dr ARTHUR GRIMES.

Regulatory Authority

Financial Markets Authority: Level 8, Unisys House, 56 The Terrace, POB 1179, Wellington 6140; tel. (4) 472-9830; fax (4) 472-8076; internet www.fma.govt.nz; f. 2011; regulatory body for securities exchanges, financial advisers and brokers, trustees and issuers, and auditors; Chair. SIMON ALLEN; CEO SEAN HUGHES.

Registered Banks

As a result of legislation that took effect in 1987, several foreign banks were incorporated into the domestic banking system. In March 2011 there were 20 registered banks in New Zealand.

ANZ National Bank Ltd: Level 14, ANZ Tower, 215–229 Lambton Quay, Wellington; tel. (4) 470-3142; fax (4) 494-4000; internet www.anz.com/nz; f. 1979; subsidiary of Australia and New Zealand Banking Group Ltd of Melbourne, Australia; fmrly ANZ Banking Group (New Zealand) Ltd; name changed as above 2004 following merger with Nat. Bank of New Zealand Ltd; cap. 9,817m., res 889m., dep. 277,039m. (Sept. 2007); Chair. Sir DRYDEN SPRING; CEO DAVID HISCO; 143 brs and sub-brs.

ASB Bank Ltd: Level 28, ASB Bank Centre, 135 Albert Sts, POB 35, Auckland 1010; tel. (9) 306-3000; fax (9) 358-3511; e-mail helpdesk@asbbank.co.nz; internet www.asbbank.co.nz; f. 1847; est. as Auckland Savings Bank, name changed 1988; cap. 2,798m., res –121m., dep. 58,662m. (June 2010); Chair. G. J. JUDD; Man. Dir BARBARA CHAPMAN; 138 brs.

Bank of India (New Zealand) Ltd: Level 18, PWC Towers, Quay St, Auckland; e-mail boi.nz@bankofindia.co.in; internet www.bankofindia.co.nz.

Bank of New Zealand (BNZ): BNZ Tower, 125 Queen St, Auckland; tel. (9) 302-4955; fax (9) 375-9537; internet www.bnz.co.nz; f. 1861; owned by Nat. Australia Bank; cap. 2,161m., res –3m., dep. 63,366m. (Sept. 2009); Chair. JOHN WALLER; Man. Dir and CEO ANDREW THORBURN; 179 domestic brs and 1 overseas br.

Citibank NA (USA): Level 11, Citibank Centre, 23 Customs St East, POB 3429, Auckland 1140; tel. (9) 307-1902; fax (9) 308-9928; e-mail citinewzealand@citi.com; internet www.citi.co.nz; Chief Country Officer STEPHEN ROBERTS; 2 brs.

Deutsche Bank New Zealand: Level 11, ASB Bank Centre, Wellesley St, POB 6900, Auckland; tel. (9) 351-1000; fax (9) 351-1001; e-mail deutsche-ausnz.press@db.com; internet www.deutsche-bank.co.nz; f. 1986; fmrly Bankers Trust New Zealand; Chair. JOSEPH ACKERNMAN.

Hongkong and Shanghai Banking Corporation Ltd (Hong Kong): 1 Queen St, Level 9, POB 5947, Auckland 1010; tel. (9) 918-8688; fax (9) 918-8797; e-mail premier@hsbc.co.nz; internet www.hsbc.co.nz; CEO DAVID JAMES GRIFFITHS; 6 brs.

Kiwibank Ltd: Private Bag 39888, Wellington Mail Centre, Lower Hutt 5045; tel. (4) 473-1133; fax (4) 462-7922; internet www.kiwibank.co.nz; f. 2002; 100% New Zealand-owned; savings bank for small depositors; cap. 295m., res 60.1m., dep. 10,436.9m. (June 2009); Chair. IAN FITZGERALD; Chief Exec. PAUL BROCK.

Directory

Rabobank (New Zealand): POB 38-396, Wellington Mail Centre, Wellington; tel. (4) 819-2700; fax (4) 819-2706; e-mail wellington.enquiry@rabobank.com; internet www.rabobank.co.nz; f. 1996; full subsidiary of Rabobank Nederland; Chair. PIET MOERLAND; CEO BRUCE DICK; 30 brs.

TSB Bank Ltd: POB 240, New Plymouth; tel. (6) 872-2265; fax (6) 968-3815; internet www.tsbbank.co.nz; f. 1850; cap. 10m., res 4.2m., dep. 4,025.1m. (March 2010); Chair. ELAINE GILL; Man. Dir KEVIN MURPHY; 24 brs.

Westpac New Zealand: 188 Quay St, Auckland; tel. (9) 912-8000; fax (4) 498-1350; e-mail customer_support@westpac.co.nz; internet www.westpac.co.nz; acquired Trust Bank New Zealand; New Zealand division of Westpac Banking Corpn (Australia); Chair. PETER WILSON; CEO GEORGE FRAZIS; 200 brs.

Association

New Zealand Bankers' Association: Level 14, Kordia House, 109–125 Willis St, POB 3043, Wellington 6140; tel. (4) 802-3358; fax (4) 473-1698; e-mail nzba@nzba.org.nz; internet www.nzba.org.nz; f. 1891; Chief Exec. SARAH MEHRTENS.

STOCK EXCHANGES

Dunedin Stock Exchange: POB 298, Dunedin; tel. (3) 477-5900; Chair. E. S. EDGAR; Sec. R. P. LEWIS.

New Zealand Exchange Ltd (NZX): Level 2, NZX Centre, 11 Cable St, POB 2959, Wellington 6140; tel. (4) 472-7599; fax (4) 496-2893; e-mail info@nzx.com; internet www.nzx.com; Chair. ANDREW HARMOS; CEO MARK WELDON.

Supervisory Body

New Zealand Securities Commission: POB 1179, Wellington 6011; tel. (4) 472-9830; fax (4) 472-8076; e-mail seccom@seccom.govt.nz; internet www.seccom.govt.nz; f. 1978; Chair. JANE DIPLOCK.

INSURANCE

ACE Insurance NZ Ltd: POB 734, Auckland 1010; tel. (9) 377-1459; fax (9) 303-1909; e-mail michael.poole@ace-ina.com; internet www.aceinsurance.co.nz; CEO GILES WARD.

AMI Insurance Ltd: 29–35 Latimer Sq., POB 2116, Christchurch 8001; tel. (3) 371-9000; fax (3) 371-8340; internet www.ami.co.nz; f. 1926; Chair. KERRY G. L. NOLAN; CEO JOHN B. BALMFORTH.

Atradius: POB 2404, Auckland 1140; tel. (9) 302-4560; fax (9) 353-1244; e-mail info.nz@atradius.com; internet www.atradius.co.nz; f. 1925; fmrly known as Gerling NCM; name changed as above following acquisition by Deutsche Bank and Swiss Re; trade credit insurance services.

AXA New Zealand Ltd: POB 1692, Wellington 6140; tel. (4) 474-4500; fax (4) 161-699; e-mail askus@axa.co.nz; internet www.axa.co.nz; Gen. Man. SID MILLER.

BNZ Life Insurance Ltd: POB 1299, Wellington; tel. (4) 382-2577; fax (4) 474-6883; internet www.bnz.co.nz; Chair. JOHN WALLER; Man. Dir and CEO ANDREW THORBURN.

Farmers' Mutual Group: POB 1943, Palmerston North Central, Palmerston North 4440; tel. (6) 356-9456; fax (6) 356-4603; e-mail contact@fmg.co.nz; internet fmg.co.nz; f. 1905; comprises Farmers' Mutual Finance Ltd and other cos; insurance investment and financial services for the New Zealand rural sector; Chair. GREG GENT.

ING Life (NZ) Ltd: Private Bag 92131, Victoria St West, Auckland 1142; tel. (9) 442-4800; fax (9) 442-4801; e-mail clientserviceslife@onepath.co.nz; internet www.inglife.co.nz; operates ANZ- and The Nat. Bank-branded insurance policies; CEO HELEN TROUP; Man. Dir, Insurance NAOMI BALLANTYNE.

New Zealand Insurance: NZI, Private Bag 92130, Auckland 1030; tel. (9) 969-6000; fax (9) 309-7097; internet www.nzi.co.nz; owned by Insurance Australia Group New Zealand Ltd; Exec. Gen. Man. KARL ARMSTRONG.

New Zealand Local Government Insurance Corporation Ltd (Civic Assurance): POB 5521, Wellington 6145; tel. (4) 978-1250; fax (4) 978-1260; e-mail info@civicassurance.co.nz; internet www.civicassurance.co.nz; f. 1960; local govt insurance provider; fire, motor, all risks, accident; Chief Exec. TIM SOLE.

QBE Insurance (International) Ltd: Level 6, AMP Centre, 29 Customs St West, Auckland; tel. (9) 366-9920; fax (9) 308-8526; internet www.qbe.co.nz/insurance.html; f. 1890; Gen. Man. ROSS CHAPMAN.

Sovereign Ltd: Private Bag Sovereign, Auckland Mail Centre 1142; tel. (9) 487-9000; fax (9) 487-8003; e-mail enquire@sovereign.co.nz; internet www.sovereign.co.nz; f. 1989; life insurance and investment; Chief Exec. CHARLES ANDERSON.

NEW ZEALAND

State Insurance Ltd: POB 3233, Wellington 6140; tel. (9) 969-1150; fax (4) 476-9664; internet www.state.co.nz; f. 1905; mem. NRMA Insurance Group; Man. Dir T. C. Sole.

Tower Insurance Ltd: Level 11, Tower Centre, 22 Fanshawe St, POB 90347, Auckland; tel. (9) 369-2000; fax (9) 369-2040; e-mail contactus@tower.co.nz; internet www.tower.co.nz; f. 1869; fmrly Nat. Insurance Co of New Zealand; Chair. Tony Gibbs; Group Man. Dir Rob Flannagan.

Associations

Insurance Council of New Zealand: iSoft House, Level 7, 111–115 Customhouse Quay, POB 474, Wellington; tel. (4) 472-5230; fax (4) 473-3011; e-mail icnz@icnz.org.nz; internet www.icnz.org.nz; f. 1895; Chief Exec. Christopher Ryan.

Investment Savings and Insurance Association of New Zealand Inc: City Chambers, Cnr Johnston and Featherston Sts, POB 1514, Wellington, 6140; tel. (4) 473-8730; fax (4) 471-1881; e-mail isi@isi.org.nz; internet www.isi.org.nz; f. 1996 from Life Office Asscn and Investment Funds Asscn; represents cos that act as manager, trustee, issuer, insurer, etc. of managed funds, life insurance and superannuation; Chair. Sean Carroll; Chief Exec. Peter Neilson.

Trade and Industry

GOVERNMENT AGENCY

New Zealand Trade and Enterprise (NZTE): POB 2878, Wellington 6140; tel. (4) 816-8100; fax (4) 816-8101; e-mail info@nzte.govt.nz; internet www.nzte.govt.nz; f. 2003; national govt devt agency, with global network of offices; provides businesses, organizations and investors with access to goods and services; facilitates partnerships with New Zealand businesses and investment opportunities; Chair. Jon Mayson; CEO Peter Chrisp.

CHAMBERS OF COMMERCE

Auckland Regional Chamber of Commerce and Industry: POB 47, Auckland 1140; tel. (9) 309-6100; fax (9) 309-0081; e-mail auckland@chamber.co.nz; internet www.chamber.co.nz; CEO Michael Barnett; Chair. John Lindsay.

Canterbury Employers' Chamber of Commerce: 57 Kilmore St, POB 359, Christchurch 8140; tel. (3) 366-5096; fax (3) 379-5454; e-mail info@cecc.org.nz; internet www.cecc.org.nz; f. 1859; formed through merger of Employers' Fed. and Chamber of Commerce; employment and business support services including legal consultancy and international trade advice, business performance and training, networking and advocacy; Chief Exec. Peter Townsend; Pres. Allan Pollard.

Employers' Chamber of Commerce Central: POB 1087, Wellington 6140; tel. (4) 473-7224; fax (4) 473-4501; e-mail ema@emacentral.org.nz; internet www.eccc.org.nz; f. 1997 as Employers' and Manufacturers' Association (Central Inc); renamed as above following merger with Wellington Regional Chamber of Commerce; CEO Paul Winter; 2,200 mems.

Otago Chamber of Commerce Inc: Ground Floor, Burns House, 10 George St, POB 5173, Dunedin 9058; tel. (3) 479-0181; fax (3) 477-0341; e-mail office@otagochamber.co.nz; internet www.otagochamber.co.nz; f. 1861; CEO J. A. Christie; Pres. M. Willis.

Wellington Employers' Chamber of Commerce: POB 1590, Wellington 6140; tel. (4) 473-7224; fax (4) 473-4501; e-mail info@wecc.org.nz; internet www.wecc.org.nz; f. 1856; fmrly Wellington Regional Chamber of Commerce; Chief Exec. Ken Harris; Pres. Richard Stone; 1,000 mems.

INDUSTRIAL AND TRADE ASSOCIATIONS

Employers' and Manufacturers' Association (Northern Inc): 159 Khyber Pass Rd, Grafton, Private Bag 92066, Auckland; tel. (9) 367-0900; fax (9) 367-0902; e-mail ema@ema.co.nz; internet www.ema.co.nz; f. 1886; fmrly Auckland Manufacturers' Asscn; Chief Exec. Alasdair Thompson; Pres. Graham Mountfort; 5,000 mems.

ENZA: 405 Williams St, POB 279, Hastings; tel. (9) 878-1898; fax (9) 878-1850; e-mail info@enza.co.nz; internet www.enza.co.nz; f. 1956; owned by Turners and Growers Ltd; fmrly New Zealand Apple and Pear Marketing Bd; export apples, pears and kiwifruit; creates new apple varieties; Man. Dir Jeff Wesley; Gen. Man. Snow Hardy.

Federated Farmers of New Zealand (Inc): POB 715, Wellington; tel. (4) 473-7269; fax (4) 473-1081; e-mail receptionwgton@fedfarm.org.nz; internet www.fedfarm.org.nz; f. 1945; Pres. Don Nicolson; CEO Conor English; 16,000 mems.

Horticulture New Zealand: POB 10232, The Terrace, Wellington 6143; tel. (4) 472-3795; fax (4) 471-2861; e-mail info@hortnz.co.nz; internet www.hortnz.co.nz; est. by merger of New Zealand Fruitgrowers' Fed., New Zealand Berryfruit Fed. and New Zealand Vegetable and Potato Growers' Fed; 7,000 mems; Pres. and Chair. Andrew Fenton; CEO Peter Silcock.

Kiwifruit New Zealand (KNZ): POB 4683, Mt Maunganui South 3149; tel. (7) 572-3685; fax (7) 572-5934; e-mail richard.procter@knz.co.nz; f. 2000; Chair. Sir Brian Elwood.

Meat and Wool New Zealand: POB 121, Wellington 6140; tel. (4) 473-9150; fax (4) 474-0800; e-mail enquiries@beeflambnz.com; internet www.meatandwoolnz.com; Chair. Mike Petersen; CEO Dr Scott Champion.

Meat Industry Association of New Zealand (Inc) (MIA): Level 5, Wellington Chambers, 154 Featherston St, Wellington 6011; tel. (4) 473-6465; fax (4) 473-1731; e-mail info@mia.co.nz; internet www.mia.co.nz; Chair. W. J. (Bill) Falconer; CEO Tim Ritche.

National Beekeepers' Association of New Zealand (Inc): Level 6, Adecco House, 330 Lambton Quay, POB 10792, Wellington; tel. (6) 471-6254; fax (6) 499-0876; e-mail secretary@nba.org.nz; internet www.nba.org.nz; f. 1913; 400 mems; Pres. Seth Belson; Secretaries Jessica Williams, Pauline Downie.

New Zealand Animal By-Products Exporters' Association: 11 Longhurst Terrace, POB 12-222, Christchurch; tel. (3) 332-2895; fax (3) 332-2825; 25 mems; Sec. J. L. Naysmith.

New Zealand Council of Wool Exporters Inc: POB 2857, Christchurch; tel. (3) 353-1049; fax (3) 374-6925; e-mail cwe@woolexport.net; internet www.woolexport.net; f. 1893; Exec. Man. R. H. F. Nicholson; Pres. John Dawson.

The New Zealand Forest Owners' Association: POB 1208, Wellington 6140; tel. (4) 473-4769; fax (4) 499-8893; e-mail nzfoa@nzfoa.org.nz; internet www.nzfoa.org.nz; f. 1926; Pres. Peter Berg; Chief Exec. David Rhodes.

New Zealand Fruit Wine and Cider Makers Inc: POB 912, New Plymouth; tel. and fax (6) 769-9009; e-mail admin@fruitwines.co.nz; internet www.fruitwines.co.nz; f. 1985; 40 mems; represents all non-grape wine, cider, perry and mead makers in New Zealand; Chair. Justin Hall; Exec. Officer Christine Garnham.

New Zealand Manufacturers' and Exporters' Association (MEA): POB 13152, Armagh, Christchurch 8141; tel. (3) 353-2540; fax (3) 353-2549; e-mail cma@cma.org.nz; internet www.mea.org.nz; f. 2007; est. by merger of Canterbury Manufacturers' Asscn and New Zealand Engineers' Fed; CEO John L Walley; Pres. Allen Voss.

New Zealand Meat Board: POB 121, Wellington 6140; tel. (4) 473-9150; fax (4) 474-0801; e-mail info@nzmeatboard.org; internet www.nzmeatboard.org; f. 1922; Chair. Mike Petersen; 10 mems.

New Zealand Pork Industry Board (New Zealand Pork): Level 4, 94 Dixon St, POB 4048, Wellington; tel. (4) 917-4750; fax (4) 385-8522; e-mail info@pork.co.nz; internet www.pork.co.nz; f. 1937; Chair. C. Trengrove; CEO S. McIvor.

New Zealand Retailers' Association Inc: POB 12086, Wellington 6144; tel. (4) 805-0830; fax (4) 805-0831; e-mail helpline@retail.org.nz; internet www.retail.org.nz; 6,000 direct mems; Pres. Ray Clarke; CEO John Albertson.

New Zealand Seafood Industry Council: Private Bag 24901, Manners St, Wellington 6142; tel. (4) 385-4005; fax (4) 385-2727; e-mail info@seafood.co.nz; internet www.seafood.co.nz; CEO Peter Bodeker; Chair. David Sharp.

New Zealand Timber Industry Federation: POB 308, Wellington; tel. (4) 473-5200; fax (4) 473-6536; e-mail inquiries@nztif.co.nz; internet www.nztif.co.nz; f. 1983; 350 mems; Exec. Dir Wayne S. Coffey.

Registered Master Builders' Federation (Inc): Level 6, 234 Wakefield St, POB 1796, Wellington; tel. (4) 385-8999; fax (4) 385-8995; e-mail mbfinfo@masterbuilder.org.nz; internet www.masterbuilder.org.nz; Chief Exec. Warwick Quinn.

EMPLOYERS' ORGANIZATION

Business New Zealand: Level 6, Lumley House, 3–11 Hunter St, POB 1925, Wellington; tel. (4) 496-6555; fax (4) 496-6550; e-mail admin@businessnz.org.nz; internet www.businessnz.org.nz; f. 2001; Chief Exec. Phil O'Reilly.

UTILITIES

Energy Efficiency and Conservation Authority (EECA): POB 388, Wellington 6140; tel. (4) 470-2200; fax (4) 499-5330; e-mail info@eeca.govt.nz; internet www.eeca.govt.nz; f. 2000; Chair. Roger Sutton; Chief Exec. Mike Underhill.

Electricity

Following parliamentary approval of the Electricity Industry Bill in September 2010, the new Electricity Authority was established on 1 November in place of the Electricity Commission.

Electricity Authority: Level 7, ASB Bank Tower, 2 Hunter St, POB 10041, Wellington 6143; tel. (4) 460-8860; fax (4) 460-8879; e-mail

NEW ZEALAND

info@ea.govt.nz; internet www.ea.govt.nz; f. 2010; to replace the Electricity Commission; independent; regulatory body supervising electricity sector; Chair. Dr BRENT LAYTON; Chief Exec. CARL HANSEN.

Bay of Plenty Energy (BOPE): 52 Commerce St, POB 404, Whakatane; tel. (7) 922-2700; fax (7) 307-0922; e-mail enquiries@bopelec.co.nz; internet www.bope.co.nz; f. 1995; generation, purchase and supply of electricity and natural gas; Commercial Man. CHRIS POWER; CEO DAVID BULLEY.

Contact Energy Ltd: Level 1, Harbour City Tower, 29 Brandon St, POB 10742, Wellington; tel. (4) 449-4001; fax (4) 499-4003; e-mail help@contact-energy.co.nz; internet www.contactenergy.co.nz; f. 1996; generation of electricity, wholesale and retail of energy; Chair. GRANT KING; CEO DENNIS BARNES.

Genesis Energy Ltd: POB 17-188, Greenlane, Auckland 1546; tel. (9) 838-7863; fax (9) 580-4891; internet www.genesisenergy.co.nz; f. 1999; state-owned; generation and retail of electricity and gas; Chair. Dame JENNY SHIPLEY; Chief Exec. ALBERT BRANTLEY.

The Marketplace Co Ltd (M-CO): Level 2, NZX Ltd, NZX Center, 11 Cable St, POB 2959, Wellington 6140; tel. (4) 473-5240; fax (4) 473-5247; e-mail info@m-co.com; internet www.nz.m-co.com; f. 1993; administers wholesale electricity market; acquired by NZX Ltd in 2009; Chief Exec. CARL HANSEN.

Meridian Energy Ltd: POB 2128, Christchurch; tel. (3) 353-9500; fax (3) 353-9501; e-mail contactus@meridianenergy.co.nz; internet www.meridianenergy.co.nz; state-owned; generation and retail of electricity; Chair. CHRIS MOLLER; Chief Exec. TIM LUSK.

Mighty River Power Ltd: Level 14, 23–29 Albert St, POB 90-399, Auckland; tel. (9) 308-8200; fax (9) 308-8209; e-mail enquiries@mightyriver.co.nz; internet www.mightyriverpower.co.nz; f. 1998; electricity generation and retail; cos include Vector Electricity; Chair. JOAN WITHERS; Chief Exec. DOUG HEFFERMAN.

Nova Energy Ltd: POB 10-141, Wellington 6143; tel. (4) 668-236; fax (4) 472-6264; e-mail info@novaenergy.co.nz; internet www.novaenergy.co.nz; fmrly Nova Gas Ltd; supplier of electricity, gas, LPG and solar energy; Group Gas Man. HAMISH TWEEDIE.

Orion New Zealand Ltd: POB 13896, Christchurch 8141; tel. (3) 363-9898; fax (3) 363-9899; e-mail info@oriongroup.co.nz; internet www.oriongroup.co.nz; f. 1998; electricity distribution network; Chair. CRAIG BOYCE; CEO ROGER SUTTON.

Todd Energy Ltd: 95 Customhouse Quay, POB 3141, Wellington; tel. (4) 471-6555; fax (4) 472-2474; e-mail energy@toddenergy.co.nz; internet www.toddenergy.co.nz; Man. Dir and CEO RICHARD TWEEDIE.

Transpower New Zealand Ltd: Level 7, Transpower House, 96 The Terrace, POB 1021, Wellington; tel. (4) 495-7000; fax (4) 495-7100; internet www.transpower.co.nz; f. 1994; manages national grid; Chair. MARK VERBIEST; Chief Exec. PATRICK STRANGE.

TrustPower Ltd: Private Bag 12-023, Tauranga Mail Centre, Tauranga 3143, Auckland; tel. (7) 574-4754; fax (7) 574-4803; e-mail enquiries@trustpower.co.nz; internet www.trustpower.co.nz; f. 1920 as Tauranga Electric Power Board; independent generator; Chair. Dr BRUCE HARKER; CEO VINCE HAWKSWORTH.

Vector Electricity Ltd: Vector, POB 99-882, Newmarket, Auckland 1149; tel. (9) 303-0626; fax (9) 978-7799; e-mail info@vector.co.nz; internet www.vector.co.nz; owned by Vector Ltd; fmrly Mercury Energy Ltd; operates power networks in Auckland, Manukau and Papakura; distributes natural gas in Auckland; Group CEO SIMON MACKENZIE.

Gas

Bay of Plenty Electricity Ltd: see Electricity, above.

E-gas Ltd: Level 13, Forsyth Barr House, cnr Lambton Quay and Johnston St, POB 2577, Wellington; tel. (4) 499-4964; fax (4) 499-4965; e-mail info@e-gas.co.nz; internet www.e-gas.co.nz; supplier of natural gas.

Genesis Energy Ltd: see Electricity, above.

NGC Holdings Ltd: Level 8, NGC Bldg, 44 The Terrace, Private Bag 39-980, Wellington Mail Centre, Wellington; tel. (4) 462-8700; fax (4) 462-8600; internet www.ngc.co.nz; f. 1992; fmrly Natural Gas Corpn Holdings Ltd; name changed as above 2002; purchase, processing and transport of natural gas; wholesale and retail sales; Chair. MICHAEL STIASSNY; Chief Exec. BRYAN CRAWFORD.

Nova Energy Ltd: see Electricity, above.

Vector Gas Ltd: see Electricity, above.

Wanganui Gas Ltd: 179 Hill St, POB 32, Wanganui; tel. (6) 349-0909; fax (6) 345-4931; e-mail enquiries@wanganuigas.co.nz; internet www.wanganuigas.co.nz; f. 1879; supplier of gas on North Island; Chair. MATTHEW J DOYLE; Chief Exec. TREVOR GOODWIN.

Water

Waste Management NZ Ltd: 86 Lunn Ave, Mt Wellington, Private Bag 14-919, Panmure, Auckland 1741; tel. (9) 527-1300; fax (9) 570-1417; internet www.wastemanagement.co.nz; f. 1985; waste collection, recovery and disposal; liquid waste collection and processing; recycling; Man. Dir GREGG CAMPBELL; Regional Man. KEVIN BONNIFACE.

Watercare Services Ltd: Private Bag 92521, Wellesley St, Auckland 1141; tel. (9) 442-2222; fax (9) 970-1461; e-mail info@water.co.nz; internet www.watercare.co.nz; f. 1993; provides water and waste water services in the Auckland area; Chair. ROSS KEENAN; Chief Exec. MARK FORD.

TRADE UNIONS

In December 2000 a total of 134 unions were in operation; 318,519 workers belonged to a union.

New Zealand Council of Trade Unions: Education House, West Block, 178 Willis St, POB 6645, Wellington 6141; tel. (4) 385-1334; fax (4) 385-6051; e-mail helenk@nzctu.org.nz; internet www.union.org.nz; f. 1937; present name since 1987; affiliated to ITUC; 40 affiliated unions with more than 350,000 mems; Pres. HELEN KELLY; Sec. PETER CONWAY.

Principal Affiliated Unions

Association of Staff in Tertiary Education (ASTE)/Te Hau Takitini o Aotearoa: POB 27141, Wellington; tel. (4) 801-5098; fax (4) 385-8826; e-mail enquiry@aste.ac.nz; internet www.aste.ac.nz; f. 1988; 3,500 mems; Nat. Sec. SHARN RIGGS.

Central Amalgamated Workers Union (CAWU): 307 Willis St, POB 27-291, Wellington; tel. (4) 384-4049; fax (4) 801-7306; e-mail info@cawu.org.nz; internet www.cawu.org.nz; Sec. HAROLD LEWIS.

FinSec Finance and Information Workers Union: POB 27-355, Wellington; tel. (4) 385-7723; fax (4) 385-2214; e-mail union@finsec.org.nz; internet www.finsec.org.nz; Pres. KELVIN PYCROFT; Sec. ANDREW CASIDY.

Maritime Union of New Zealand: POB 2773, Wellington; tel. (4) 385-9288; fax (4) 384-8766; e-mail john.whiting@muno.org.nz; internet www.munz.org.nz; 2,800 mems; Gen. Sec. JOHN WHITING.

New Zealand Dairy Workers Union, Inc: TUC Bldg, 34 Harwood St, POB 9046, Hamilton; tel. (7) 839-0239; fax (7) 838-0398; e-mail nzdwu@nzdwu.org.nz; internet www.nzdwu.org.nz; f. 1992; 7,000 mems; Sec. JAMES RITCHIE; Pres. SINCLAIR WATSON.

New Zealand Educational Institute (NZEI) (Te Riu Roa): 178–182 Willis St, POB 466, Wellington 6140; tel. (4) 384-9689; fax (4) 385-1772; e-mail nzei@nzei.org.nz; internet www.nzei.org.nz; f. 1883; Pres. IAN LECKIE; Sec. PAUL GOULTER.

New Zealand Engineering, Printing & Manufacturing Union (EPMU): POB 14-277, Kilbirnie 7, McGregor St, Rongotai, Wellington; tel. (4) 387-4681; fax (4) 387-4673; e-mail andrew.little@epmu.org.nz; internet www.epmu.org.nz; Sec. ANDREW LITTLE.

New Zealand Meat Workers and Related Trades Union: POB 13-048, Christchurch; tel. (3) 366-5105; fax (3) 379-7763; e-mail nzmeatworkersunion@clear.net.nz; internet www.nzmeatworkersunion.co.nz; 13,788 mems; Pres. MIKE NAHU; Gen. Sec. DAVID EASTLAKE.

New Zealand Nurses' Organisation: POB 2128, Wellington 6140; tel. (4) 931-6730; fax (4) 384-4951; e-mail nurses@nzno.org.nz; internet www.nzno.org.nz; 38,000 mems; CEO GEOFF ANNALS.

New Zealand Post Primary Teachers' Association: POB 2119, Wellington; tel. (4) 384-9964; fax (4) 382-8763; e-mail enquiries@ppta.org.nz; internet www.ppta.org.nz; f. 1952; Pres. ROBIN DUFF; Gen. Sec. KEVIN BUNKER.

New Zealand Public Service Association (PSA): PSA House, 11 Aurora Terrace, POB 3817, Wellington 6140; tel. (4) 495-7633; fax (4) 917-2051; e-mail enquiries@psa.org.nz; internet www.psa.org.nz; 56,000 mems; Pres. PAULA SCHOLES.

Rail & Maritime Transport Union Inc: POB 1103, Wellington; tel. (4) 499-2066; fax (4) 471-0896; e-mail tvalster@rmtunion.org.nz; internet www.rmtunion.org.nz; 4,100 mems; Pres. J. KELLY; Gen. Sec. W. BUTSON.

Service and Food Workers' Union: Private Bag 68-914, Newton, Auckland 1145; tel. (9) 375-2680; fax (9) 375-2681; e-mail info@sfwu.org.nz; internet www.sfwu.org.nz; 23,000 mems; Pres. BARBARA WYETH; Sec. JOHN RYALL.

Tertiary Education Union (TEU): POB 11-767, Wellington 6142; tel. (4) 801-5098; fax (4) 385-8826; e-mail scr.im/nzteu; internet www.teu.ac.nz; fmrly Asscn of University Staff; 6,000 mems; Nat. Pres. TOM RYAN.

Other Unions

Manufacturing & Construction Workers Union: 126 Vivian St, Te Aro, Wellington 6011; tel. (4) 385-8264; fax (4) 384-8007; e-mail m.c.union@tradeshall.org.nz; Gen. Sec. GRAEME CLARKE.

National Distribution Union (NDU): 120 Church St, Private Bag 92-904, Onehunga, Auckland; tel. (9) 622-8355; fax (9) 622-8353; e-mail info@ndu.org.nz; internet www.ndu.org.nz; f. 1986; 18,500 mems; Pres. DENNIS DAWSON; Gen. Sec. ROBERT REID.

New Zealand Building Trades Union: POB 13-594, Christchurch; tel. (4) 366-4033; fax (4) 366-4032; e-mail national@nzbtu.org.nz; internet www.nzbtu.org.nz; f. 1860; Pres. P. REIDY; Sec. DAVID O'CONNELL.

New Zealand Seafarers' Union: Marion Sq., POB 9288, Wellington; tel. (4) 385-9288; fax (4) 384-9288; e-mail admin@seafarers.org.nz; f. 1993; Pres. DAVE MORGAN.

Transport

RAILWAYS

There were 3,898 km of railways in New Zealand in 2003, of which more than 500 km were electrified.

New Zealand Railways Corporation (NZRC—KiwiRail): POB 593, Wellington 6140; tel. 800-801-070; fax (4) 473-1589; e-mail kiwirail@kiwirail.co.nz; internet www.kiwirail.co.nz; f. 2008; state-owned enterprise, est. following Govt's purchase of rail and inter-island ferry operations of Toll NZ Ltd; Chair. JOHN SPENCER; Chief Exec. JIM QUINN.

ROADS

In 2009 there were a total of 93,910 km of maintained roads in New Zealand, including 10,909 km of state highways and motorways, 17,510 km of urban local roads and 65,492 km of rural and special purpose roads.

New Zealand Transport Agency: Victoria Arcade, 44 Victoria St, Private Bag 6995, Wellington 6141; tel. (4) 894-5400; fax (4) 894-6100; e-mail info@nzta.govt.nz; internet www.nzta.govt.nz; f. 2008; formed by merger of Land Transport NZ and Transit NZ; Crown entity charged with contributing to an integrated, safe, responsive and sustainable land transport system; Chair. CHRIS MOLLER; Chief Exec. GEOFF DANGERFIELD.

SHIPPING

There are 13 main seaports, of which the most important are Auckland, Tauranga, Wellington, Lyttleton (the port of Christchurch) and Port Chalmers (Dunedin). In December 2009 the New Zealand merchant fleet comprised 176 vessels, with a total displacement of 213,084 grt.

Principal Companies

Maersk New Zealand: The CPO, Level 3, 12 Queen St, Auckland; tel. (9) 359-3499; fax (9) 359-3488; e-mail nezcsedir@maersk.com; internet www.maerskline.com; f. 1928; CEO EIVIND KOLDING.

Reef Shipping Ltd: 68 Anzac Ave, Auckland; tel. (9) 302-2204; fax (9) 302-0096; e-mail shipping@reefship.co.nz; internet www.reefship.co.nz; f. 1975; operates services between New Zealand and the Pacific Islands; Gen. Man. JASON WARD.

Sofrana Unilines NZ Ltd: 38 Ponsonby Rd, POB 3614, Auckland; tel. (9) 356-1400; fax (9) 356-1429; e-mail info@sofrana.co.nz; internet www.sofrana.co.nz; Chair. DIDIER LEROUX; Man. Dir BENOIT MARCENAC.

Other major shipping companies operating services to New Zealand include Blue Star Line (NZ) Ltd and Columbus Line, which link New Zealand with Australia, the Pacific Islands, South-East Asia and the USA.

CIVIL AVIATION

There are international airports at Auckland, Christchurch and Wellington.

Civil Aviation Authority of New Zealand: Asteron Centre, 55 Featherston St, POB 3555, Wellington; tel. (4) 560-9400; fax (4) 569-2024; e-mail info@caa.govt.nz; internet www.caa.govt.nz; Dir of Civil Aviation STEVE DOUGLAS.

Principal Airlines

Air Nelson: Private Bag 32, Nelson 7042; tel. (3) 547-8700; fax (3) 547-8788; e-mail airnelsonadmin@airnz.co.nz; internet www.airnelson.co.nz; f. 1979; owned by Air New Zealand; present name adopted 1986; operates services throughout New Zealand; Gen. Man. GRANT KERR.

Air New Zealand: Private Bag 92007, Auckland 1142; tel. (9) 336-2287; fax (9) 366-2664; e-mail investor@airnz.co.nz; internet www.airnewzealand.co.nz; f. 1942; privatized in 1989, recapitalized by the Govt 2001; 76% govt-owned; services to and from Australia, the Pacific Islands, Asia, Europe and North America, as well as regular daily services to regional New Zealand; Chair. JOHN PALMER; CEO ROB FYFE.

Pacific Blue Airlines (NZ) Ltd: e-mail sales.corporate@virginblue.com.au; internet www.flypacificblue.com; f. 2003; wholly owned subsidiary of Australian Virgin Blue; domestic services and services to Australia and the Pacific Islands; announced plans to terminate domestic services in late 2010; CEO MARK PITT.

Tourism

New Zealand's principal tourist attractions are its mountains, lakes, forests, volcanoes, hot springs and beaches. The sector makes a substantial contribution to the country's economy, and receipts from tourism totalled an estimated $NZ6,278m. in 2010. In the same year New Zealand received more than 2.5m. international visitors. The majority of visitors are from Australia, the United Kingdom and the USA.

Tourism New Zealand: POB 95, Wellington; tel. (4) 462-8000; fax (4) 915-3817; e-mail reception@tnz.govt.nz; internet www.newzealand.com; f. 1901; responsible for marketing of New Zealand as a tourism destination; offices in Auckland, Wellington and Christchurch; 13 offices overseas; Chair. GREG MUIR; Chief Exec. GEORGE HICKTON.

Defence

As assessed at November 2010, the total strength of the regular forces was 9,673: army 4,905, navy 2,161 and air force 2,607. In addition, there were approximately 2,314 regular reserves (army 1,789, navy 339, air force 186) and 1,789 territorial reserves. Military service is voluntary. New Zealand is a participant in the Five-Power Defence Arrangements with Australia, Malaysia, Singapore and the United Kingdom. In early 2011 New Zealand's overseas deployments included 231 personnel in Afghanistan, 80 in Timor-Leste and 45 in Solomon Islands.

Defence Expenditure: Budgeted at $NZ2,210m. for 2010.
Chief of Defence Force: Lt-Gen. RICHARD RHYS JONES.
Chief of Army: Maj.-Gen. TIM KEATING.
Chief of Navy: Rear-Adm. ANTONY J. PARR.
Chief of Air Force: Air Vice-Marshal PETER JAMES STOCKWELL.
Commander Joint Forces New Zealand: Maj.-Gen. ARTHUR DAVID GAWN.

Education

Education in New Zealand is free and secular in state schools. It is compulsory for all children aged six to 16 years, although in practice almost 100% start at the age of five years. Budgetary expenditure on education by the central Government in 2010/11 was forecast at $NZ11,969m., representing 15.1% of total spending.

In July 2010 there were 188,924 children enrolled in early childhood education services, while 435,051 pupils were enrolled in primary classes at 2,018 schools. A total of 275,945 pupils attended 340 secondary schools. Composite schools, which were attended by 50,524 pupils, provide education at both primary and secondary levels. A total of 154,866 students were enrolled at the various universities in 2009.

NEW ZEALAND'S DEPENDENT TERRITORIES

New Zealand's two Dependent Territories are the Ross Dependency, which is situated in Antarctica, and Tokelau, located in the Pacific Ocean.

ROSS DEPENDENCY

The Ross Dependency comprises the sector of Antarctica between 160°E and 150°W (moving eastward) and the islands lying between those degrees of longitude and south of latitude 60°S. It has been administered by New Zealand since 1923 and has a total area of 750,310 sq km (289,700 sq miles), comprising a land area of 413,540 sq km and an ice shelf of 336,770 sq km. The Territory rises to a height of 3,794 m above sea-level at the peak of the volcano, Mount Erebus.

Scott Base was established in 1957 on Ross Island, and in the following year the Ross Dependency Research Committee was formed to supervise New Zealand activity on the Territory. In 1968 a new scientific station was set up at Lake Vanda, about 130 km (80 miles) west of Scott Base. In 1986 traces of petroleum were discovered in the Territory, more than 600 m below the sea-bed. The Ross Dependency Research Committee was disbanded in 1995.

Legislation approved in the mid-1990s consolidated measures aimed at conserving the region's flora and fauna (which includes 18 species of penguin, six species of seal and several rare species of whale) included in the Antarctic Treaty (see p. 612), and reinforced the Convention for the Conservation of Antarctic Marine Living Resources. Since 1997 New Zealand has conducted exploratory fishing for toothfish in the Ross Sea. In April 2006 it was announced that an Estonian summer-only research station was to be built at Edmonson Point South, 350 km north-west of Scott Base, to provide facilities for six personnel. Following a visit by the New Zealand Minister of Research, Science and Technology in November 2006, new proposals, including emphasis on the provision of renewable energy resources and the encouragement of greater investment in scientific projects in the territory, were announced.

TOKELAU

Introductory Survey

LOCATION, CLIMATE, LANGUAGE, RELIGION, FLAG, CAPITAL

Tokelau consists of three atolls (Atafu, Nukunonu and Fakaofo), which lie about 480 km (300 miles) north of Samoa, in the Pacific Ocean. The annual average temperature is 28°C (82°F), July being the coolest month and May the warmest; rainfall is heavy but inconsistent. The principal language is Tokelauan (a Polynesian language), although English is also widely spoken. The population is almost entirely Christian, with 67% adhering to the Congregational Christian Church (a Protestant denomination) and 30% to the Roman Catholic Church. The national flag (proportions 1 by 2) is dark blue, with four five-pointed white stars in the form of the Southern Cross constellation in the upper hoist and a yellow canoe in full sail facing towards the hoist across the bottom. Tokelau has no capital, each atoll having its own administrative centre. However, the seat of government, the Office of the Council for the Ongoing Government of Tokelau (formerly the Council of Faipule), is recognized as 'the capital' and is rotated on a yearly basis among the three atolls.

CONTEMPORARY POLITICAL HISTORY

Historical Context

The Tokelau (formerly Union) Islands became a British protectorate in 1877. At the request of the inhabitants, the United Kingdom annexed the islands in 1916 and included them within the Gilbert and Ellice Islands Colony (now Kiribati and Tuvalu). The British Government transferred administrative control of the islands to New Zealand by legislation enacted in 1925, effective from February 1926. The group was officially designated the Tokelau Islands in 1946, and sovereignty was transferred to New Zealand by legislation of 1948, effective from January 1949. From 1962 until the end of 1971 the High Commissioner for New Zealand in Western Samoa (now Samoa) was also the Administrator of the Tokelau Islands. In November 1974 the administration of the Tokelau Islands was transferred to the Ministry of Foreign Affairs in New Zealand. In 1976 the Tokelau Islands were officially redesignated Tokelau.

New Zealand has undertaken to assist Tokelau towards increased self-government and economic self-sufficiency. The Territory was visited by the UN Special Committee on Decolonization in 1976 and 1981, but on both occasions the mission reported that the people of Tokelau did not wish to change the nature of the existing relationship between Tokelau and New Zealand. This opinion was reiterated by an emissary of the General Fono, the Territory's highest advisory body, in 1987, and by the Official Secretary in 1992. In June 1987, however, in a statement to the UN Special Committee, Tokelau had expressed a desire to achieve a greater degree of political autonomy, while maintaining its relationship with New Zealand. A report by the UN Special Committee in 2002 listed Tokelau as one of 16 dependent territories it was seeking to encourage towards independence. However, a UN decolonization mission, which visited the islands in September of that year, was informed that the majority of Tokelauans wanted to remain part of New Zealand and that the Territory was far too dependent on that country to change its status.

In 1989 a UN report on the greenhouse effect (the heating of the earth's atmosphere as a result of pollution) listed Tokelau as one of the island groups that would completely disappear beneath the sea in the 21st century, unless drastic action were taken.

Domestic Political Affairs

A programme of constitutional change, agreed in 1992 and formalized in January 1994, provided for a more defined role for Tokelau's political institutions, as well as for their expansion. A process of relocating the Tokelau Public Service (hitherto based in Apia, Western Samoa—now Samoa) to the Territory began in 1994, and by 1995 all government departments, except Transport and Communications and part of the Administration and Finance Department, had been transferred to Tokelauan soil. However, the Tokelau Apia Liaison Office (formerly the Office for Tokelau Affairs) was to remain in Western Samoa, owing to that country's more developed communications facilities.

The development of Tokelau's institutions at a national level prompted renewed interest in the islands' prospects for greater internal autonomy. In June 1994 the General Fono adopted a National Strategic Plan, which gave details of Tokelau's progression (over the next five to 10 years) towards increased self-determination and, possibly, free association with New Zealand. The executive and administrative powers of the Administrator were formally transferred, in that year, to the General Fono and, when the Fono was not in session, to the Council of Faipule (cabinet). A draft constitution was subsequently drawn up. In May 1996 the New Zealand House of Representatives approved the Tokelau Amendment Bill, granting the General Fono the power to enact legislation, to impose taxes and to declare public holidays, effective from 1 August 1996 (although New Zealand was to retain the right to legislate for Tokelau).

Following electoral reforms introduced in the latter half of the 1990s, delegates were, for the first time, elected to the General Fono for a three-year term in January 1999; they had previously been nominated by each Taupulega (Island Council or Council of Elders). As part of the same reform process, the number of delegates to the

General Fono was reduced from 27 to 18. At the elections two of the Territory's Faipule (political leaders) were re-elected, while the third Faipule and all three Pulenuku (village mayor) posts were secured by new candidates. At elections in January 2002 all three incumbent Faipule and one Pulenuku were re-elected to office; two new Pulenuku were elected. In January 2005 the three Faipule were again re-elected, along with one of the Pulenuku; two new Pulenuku were chosen.

Meanwhile, mounting fears among islanders that, despite their wishes, New Zealand was seeking to loosen its ties with Tokelau, led the New Zealand Minister of Foreign Affairs and Trade to state in April 2000 that his country would not impose independence on the Territory and that any change in its political status would only occur with the consent of Tokelauans. In early 2001 the head of the Tokelau Public Service Commission, Aleki Silau, reiterated the islanders' reluctance to renounce New Zealand citizenship, and emphasized that both sides had until 2010 to reach a decision. A mission from the UN Special Committee on Decolonization visited the islands in September 2002 (see Historical Context). Under legislation approved in 1999, management of the islands' public service was formally transferred to Tokelau in July 2001. In July 2003 responsibility for the islands' budget was transferred to the General Fono. In October of that year a number of constitutional changes were instituted. The Council of Faipule was renamed the Council for the Ongoing Government of Tokelau, henceforth to comprise the three Faipule and the three Pulenuku. In the following month New Zealand's Governor-General, Dame Sylvia Cartwright, made an official visit to Tokelau to sign the Principles of Partnership agreement. The document was described by New Zealand's Minister of Foreign Affairs, Phil Goff, as a step closer to decolonization for the islands. Goff reiterated that the final decision on Tokelau's future would be made by its inhabitants, although he also confirmed that he expected the islands to adopt a system of self-government in free association with New Zealand, similar to that existing in Niue and the Cook Islands. In March 2004 it was announced that new powers were to be granted to the three atolls' Taupulega, giving them greater control over local affairs. In May a senior government member reiterated the view that, despite the ambition of New Zealand and the UN for Tokelau to achieve self-determination, the islanders themselves were extremely reluctant to change their status. In June the Administrator's powers were formally transferred from the General Fono to the three Taupulega, as part of the Modern House of Tokelau Project.

In August 2004 New Zealand's Prime Minister, Helen Clark, made an official visit to Tokelau (the first such visit in more than 20 years). During the visit Clark announced the provision of a grant worth some US $0.3m. towards improvements for boat access to the islands and a review of the islands' communications infrastructure. The Prime Minister also expressed her confidence that the islanders would vote in favour of free association with New Zealand when the issue was finally put to a referendum. In November leaders from Tokelau travelled to New Zealand for a series of meetings with the latter's Minister of Foreign Affairs, Phil Goff, following which certain elements to be included in a treaty of free association with New Zealand were agreed upon. However, contrary to the New Zealand Government's expectations, at a referendum on the issue of the future status of Tokelau held between 11 and 15 February 2006 the requisite two-thirds' majority in favour of the proposed change to free association with New Zealand was not received: 349 votes were cast in favour of greater self-government, while 232 voters wanted Tokelau to remain a Dependent Territory. The referendum was observed by several international organizations, including representatives of the UN. The result was regarded as a major set-back for the New Zealand Government. However, in June 2006 it was announced that the General Fono had agreed to the holding of another referendum on the issue of Tokelau's status.

In October 2006 David Payton replaced Neil Walter as Tokelau's Administrator. The decision to appoint a New Zealand diplomat to the position gave rise to some controversy, and it was suggested that the appointment indicated a lack of confidence in the people of Tokelau and their ability to manage their own affairs. In November regional inter-governmental groups, led by the Secretariat of the Pacific Community (see p. 410), began a fact-finding operation in Tokelau, the aim of which was to identify the islands' particular needs and priorities and to formulate a three-year strategy.

At the second referendum on Tokelau's status, conducted in October 2007, the level of participation was reported to be almost 100%; UN officials were again present as observers. However, support for self-government was not sufficient to produce the requisite two-thirds' majority, with 246 out of 692 voters rejecting the proposal. There was speculation about the influence of Tokelauans living in New Zealand, although expatriates were not permitted to cast a vote. Prime Minister Clark pledged her Government's 'ongoing friendship and support'. Elections to the General Fono were held on 18–19 January 2008, when 20 delegates were elected. In the same month one new Faipule was elected to office and two incumbent Faipule were re-elected, while three new Pulenuku were also chosen.

In February 2005, meanwhile, all three atolls were struck by Cyclone Percy, which caused widespread damage to infrastructure, homes and crops. Nukunonu was subjected to severe flooding as a result of the storm. The New Zealand Government approved some $NZ0.5m. in emergency aid in the form of food supplies and temporary shelters (to be shipped from Samoa) and the restoration of essential services.

Tokelau was badly affected by an outbreak of influenza in March 2009. About 150 people, mostly children, were reported to have been taken ill, with several requiring hospital treatment. Owing to the islands' isolation, the level of immunity to the virus was low. As the authorities attempted to limit the spread of the illness, sick islanders were urged to stay at home. Schools were closed and public gatherings were cancelled. New Zealand and the World Health Organization (WHO) supplied vaccines and offered medical advice.

Recent developments

On 7 September 2009, in a development regarded as important in advancing the islands' identity, the New Zealand Governor-General, Sir Anand Satyanand, formally presented Tokelau with an official flag, in place of the New Zealand flag used hitherto.

The islands' isolation has remained a significant issue for Tokelau, access to which has been possible only by a boat journey of at least 24 hours from Samoa. Long-standing demands for a new ferry for the islands gained fresh impetus in mid-2009 following the sinking of a ferry in Tonga with the loss of 74 lives. Without an airstrip, the only means of transport to and from Tokelau was a single vessel donated to the islands by New Zealand in the 1970s, which had become unseaworthy, according to the Tokelauan authorities. New Zealand Prime Minister John Key undertook to review the issue, but expressed concern at the high cost of a replacement ferry (estimated at some $NZ140m. over a 25-year period). In August 2010 it was announced that the New Zealand Government was considering the construction of an airstrip in Tokelau, with a replacement ferry to be made available in the interim. Foua Taloa, Faipule for Fakaofo and Tokelau's Minister of Transport, responded to the announcement by stating that the General Fono had made it clear to the New Zealand Government that an airstrip was neither a priority nor feasible at that time, insisting that a permanent replacement ferry would more effectively serve the islands' needs. However, Pio Tuia, Faipule of Nukunonu, expressed support for the proposal, suggesting that it would help islanders in need of evacuation from Tokelau to the Samoan capital, Apia. In October Polynesia Airlines of Samoa expressed interest in a potential arrangement with any company planning to launch air services to Tokelau.

In April 2010 Tokelau announced that it intended to ban whaling in its territorial waters. The New Zealand Ministry of Foreign Affairs was not consulted prior to this declaration, despite the fact that the implementation of such a whale sanctuary would require New Zealand's assistance. However, the New Zealand Government indicated that it would support Tokelau's bid to implement the ban on whaling.

Elections to the General Fono were held in January 2011. In the same month two new Faipule and two new Pulenuku were elected to office. Also in early 2011 Jonathan Kings replaced John Allen as the islands' Administrator. Allen had replaced David Payton in an acting capacity in 2009.

Foreign Affairs

New Zealand is responsible for the external relations of Tokelau. Strong links are maintained with Samoa, to the people of which the Tokelauans are closely related. There is considerable co-operation in health and education matters.

In December 1980 New Zealand and the USA signed a treaty whereby a US claim to Tokelau, dating from 1856, was relinquished. At the same time New Zealand abandoned a claim, on behalf of Tokelau, to Swains Island, which had been administered by the USA since 1925 as part of American Samoa. The treaty was ratified in August 1983, although there was some dissent in Tokelau. In March 2007 the Faipule of Fakaofo, Kolouei O'Brien, declared that if the islands achieved greater autonomy then Tokelau would wish to enter immediate negotiations with the USA regarding the return of Swains Island.

In 1989 Tokelau supported efforts by the South Pacific Forum to impose a regional ban on drift-net fishing (which was believed to have resulted in a serious depletion in tuna stocks). In November New Zealand prohibited drift-net fishing within Tokelau's exclusive economic zone (which extends to 200 nautical miles (370 km) from the islands' coastline). At the annual meeting of the Pacific Islands Forum (formerly the South Pacific Forum) in August 2002 New Zealand endorsed Tokelau's membership of the Forum Fisheries Agency.

A visit to the islands by the Prime Minister of Tuvalu in mid-1996, for the signing of a mutual co-operation agreement (covering shipping, trade and fisheries), was widely interpreted as an indication of Tokelau's increased autonomy. A further co-operation agreement was established in March 2003, following a five-day visit to the islands by the Prime Minister of Samoa. Tokelau's traditional leaders agreed a framework for annual meetings with the Samoan Government to discuss issues of concern and mutual benefit in what was regarded as a sign of the growing relationship between the two parties.

CONSTITUTION AND GOVERNMENT

Tokelau is administered under the authority of the Tokelau Islands Act 1948, incorporating subsequent amendments and regulations. The administration of Tokelau is the responsibility of the Minister of Foreign Affairs and Trade of New Zealand, who is empowered to appoint an Administrator to the Territory. In practice, most of the Administrator's powers are delegated to the Official Secretary, who heads the Tokelau Apia Liaison Office, as well as to the General Fono and the Council for the Ongoing Government of Tokelau (formerly the Council of Faipule). Each atoll has its own Taupulega (Island Council or Council of Elders), which comprises the heads of family groups together with two elected members, the Faipule and the Pulenuku. The Faipule represents the atoll in its dealings with the administering power and the public service, and presides over the Council and the court. The Pulenuku is responsible for the administration of village affairs. The Faipule and the Pulenuku are democratically elected by universal adult suffrage every three years. The three Faipule, who hold ministerial portfolios and along with the three Pulenuku form the six-member Council for the Ongoing Government of Tokelau, choose one of their number to hold the title Ulu-O-Tokelau (Head of Tokelau) for a term of one year. The Ulu-O-Tokelau chairs sessions of the territorial assembly, the General Fono. The General Fono is a meeting of 20 delegates, who are elected by universal adult suffrage for a three-year term (including the three Faipule and the three Pulenuku) and who represent the entire Territory. There are two or three meetings of the General Fono each year, which may take place on any of the atolls.

REGIONAL AND INTERNATIONAL CO-OPERATION

Tokelau is a member of the Pacific Community (see p. 410), and, as a Dependent Territory of New Zealand, has been represented by that country in the Pacific Islands Forum (see p. 413) and other international organizations. In October 2005 Tokelau was granted observer status at the Pacific Islands Forum.

ECONOMIC AFFAIRS

According to estimates by the UN Development Programme (UNDP), in 1982 Tokelau's gross national product (GNP) was US $1.2m., equivalent to US $760 per head. Gross domestic product (GDP) was estimated at US $1.5m. in 1993. During 1996–2004 the population increased at an average rate of 0.8% per year.

Agriculture (including fishing) is, excluding copra production, of a basic subsistence nature. Coconuts (the source of copra) are the only cash crop, for which there is an increasingly limited market. Pulaka, breadfruit, papayas, the screw-pine (*Pandanus*) and bananas are cultivated as food crops. Livestock comprises pigs, ducks and other poultry. Ocean and lagoon fish and shellfish are staple constituents of the islanders' diet. In early 2004 the Secretariat of the Pacific Community produced a fisheries management plan for Tokelau. The plan, which was to be implemented in mid-2004, focused on community-based activities and included the increased exploitation of the islands' giant-clam resources. A five-year development plan for the fisheries sector was drafted for 2006–10. Meanwhile, the sale to foreign fleets of fishing licences permitting them to operate in Tokelau's exclusive economic zone (EEZ) provides an important, albeit fluctuating, source of income (see below).

The industrial sector has been constrained by a lack of resources. Manufacturing comprises mainly the production of handicrafts, notably woven items such as mats. However, the opening on Atafu, in 1990, of a factory processing highly priced yellowfin tuna provided another important source of income. The principal markets for the product were New Zealand and Japan.

Energy is provided by diesel-powered generators, the fuel for which is imported via Samoa. With funding from New Zealand, a major power project to supply all three atolls with a more reliable source of electricity was initiated in 2002. In the longer term, greater emphasis was to be given to renewable forms of energy, particularly solar power. In conjunction with the Governments of New Zealand and France, UNDP and UNESCO, in 2003 Tokelau embarked on a programme aimed at utilizing the territory's solar energy potential for grid-connected power generation.

The services sector is dominated by village services and public administration. The tourism sector is limited, having remained undeveloped owing to the lack of air services and the difficulty of access. There is just one recognized hotel, on the central atoll of Nukunonu. Fewer than 30 tourists visited the islands in 2001. Since 1982 the General Fono has levied a tax on the salaries of public servants who are unavailable for the community service labour levy. Public salaries and employment account for the single largest item of government expenditure (about one-third in the early 1990s). Following the purchase by a Dutch entrepreneur of the islands' internet domain address '.tk' in 2001, more than 1.6m. names had been registered to the facility by 2007. Although the Government's precise earnings from Dot TK were not disclosed, the services of this joint venture with Teletok, the islands' communications company, were reported to be proving highly lucrative. The establishment of Dot TK was believed to have increased annual government revenue by about 10%. Furthermore, the attendant upgrading of Tokelau's communications infrastructure, including a broadband connection via satellite, greatly enhanced the islanders' own information technology facilities. In March 2007, however, a leading information technology publication reported that '.tk' was the most insecure web domain in the world. A content-filtering system was subsequently installed, in an attempt to reduce the risks. Furthermore, in March 2008 an international software security company reported that, along with Niue, in per caput terms Tokelau was one of the world's worst offenders with regard to the relaying of unsolicited e-mails.

Imports to the value of $NZ1.7m. were purchased in 2002. The principal imports in that year were food and live animals (which cost 55.2% of total imports), mineral fuels (11.6%) and miscellaneous manufactured goods (11.0%).

In 1999/2000 there was a budgetary deficit of $NZ0.9m. Tokelau's budget for 2001/02 was to include at least $NZ4.2m. from New Zealand and an estimated $NZ1.7m. to be obtained from local revenues such as fisheries licensing, duty, taxes, philatelic sales, freight charges and interest earned. Tokelau assumed responsibility for the management of its own budgetary affairs in 2003. Since then most of New Zealand's bilateral assistance has been transferred directly to the Territory's budget, thereby enabling Tokelau to finance its recurrent expenditure on services such as transport, education and health. Local revenue was estimated to have reached about $NZ2m. in 2005. Receipts from EEZ fees rose from $NZ286,000 in 2004 to an estimated $NZ569,000 in 2005. Fees from shipping, radio excises and customs duties have provided another source of revenue; local receipts from such duties increased from $NZ372,000 in 2004 to an estimated $NZ388,000 in 2005. The sale of postage stamps and souvenir coins (which are legal tender, although New Zealand currency is in general use) also makes a significant contribution to the Territory's income. Receipts from this source increased from $NZ54,000 in 2004 to an estimated $NZ70,000 in 2005. Some revenue is provided by remittances from Tokelauans working abroad, mainly in New Zealand. Official development assistance from New Zealand reached almost $NZ17.3m. in 2010/11. In addition to its links to New Zealand, Tokelau maintains a bilateral development assistance plan with Australia, focused upon human resource development.

Tokelau's agricultural development has been constrained by the lack of suitable cultivable soil and by the adverse effects of inclement weather. In February 2005 Cyclone Percy caused serious destruction on the islands, coinciding with 'king tides' that flooded the Territory resulting in widespread damage. Moreover, the Territory's small size, remote location, lack of land-based resources and the population's continuing migration to New Zealand have severely hindered economic development. In September 2002 renewed proposals were announced for the construction of wharves and improved access for shipping to facilitate the export of fish. The construction of an airport, to encourage tourism, has been intermittently considered. It was hoped that Tokelau would derive greater benefits from its fisheries resources as a result of a plan initiated by the Secretariat of the Pacific Community in 2004. In that year the Tokelau International Trust Fund (TITF) was established, with assistance from New Zealand and with the objective of enhancing the Territory's prospects for long-term self-reliance. Australia and the United Kingdom also contributed to the TITF, along with Tokelau itself. Following New Zealand's contribution of $NZ15m. in November 2008, the assets of the TITF totalled $NZ52m., and by 2010 this had risen to $NZ56m. A three-year Economic Support Arrangement was implemented under the direction of the New Zealand Government during 2007–10, with a projected total budget of $NZ43m. Areas targeted for development included transport, communications, information technology, education and health. The maintenance of adequate shipping services remained a major focus in 2010. Under the Administrative Assistance scheme (part of the Principles of Partnership agreement—see Contemporary Political History), the limited capacity of the Tokelau Public Service is supplemented by the resources of various New Zealand government departments.

PUBLIC HOLIDAYS

2012 (provisional): 2 January (for New Year's Day), 6 February (Waitangi Day, anniversary of 1840 treaty), 4–9 April (Easter), 25 April (ANZAC Day, anniversary of 1915 landing at Gallipoli), 4 June (Queen's Official Birthday), 29 October (Labour Day), 25–26 December (Christmas).

Statistical Survey

Source (unless otherwise indicated): Tokelau Apia Liaison Office, POB 805, Apia, Samoa; tel. 20822; fax 21761; e-mail f.aukuso@clear.net.nz; internet www.spc.int/prism/country/tk/stats/.

AREA AND POPULATION

Area: Atafu 3.5 sq km; Nukunonu 4.7 sq km; Fakaofo 4.0 sq km; Total 12.2 sq km (4.7 sq miles).

Population: 1,537 (males 761, females 776) at census of 11 October 2001; 1,074 (males 543, females 531) at census of 19 October 2006 (excluding 392 persons usually resident but absent on census night). *By Atoll* (2006 census): Atafu 417; Nukunonu 287; Fakaofo 370; Total 1,074. Note: Data for census of 19 October 2006 refer to the population usually resident on census night; actual population count was 1,151. *Mid-2011* (Secretariat of the Pacific Community estimate): 1,162 (Source: Pacific Regional Information System).

Density (mid-2011): 95.2 per sq km.

Population by Age and Sex (Secretariat of the Pacific Community estimates at mid-2011): *0–14:* 378 (males 191, females 187); *15–64:* 686 (males 353, females 333); *65 and over:* 98 (males 45, females 53); *Total* 1,162 (males 589, females 573) (Source: Pacific Regional Information System).

Births and Deaths (1996): Birth rate 33.1 per 1,000; Death rate 8.2 per 1,000. *2010* (Secretariat of the Pacific Community estimates): Live births 26 (birth rate 22.1 per 1,000); Registered deaths 9 (death rate 7.6 per 1,000) (Source: Pacific Regional Information System).

Life Expectancy (years at birth, 1996, official estimates): Males 68; Females 70. Source: Ministry of Foreign Affairs and Trade, Wellington.

Economically Active Population (2001 census, persons aged 15 years and over): Construction 78; Retail trade 12; Hotels and restaurants 4; Transport 7; Communications 20; Village services 182; Public administration 59; Education 53; Medical 23; Total 438. *2006 Census:* Total in paid employment 375.

HEALTH AND WELFARE
Key Indicators

Access to Water (% of households, 2004): 88.

Access to Sanitation (% of households, 2004): 78.

For sources and definitions, see explanatory note on p. vi.

AGRICULTURE, ETC.

Crop Production (metric tons, 2008 unless otherwise indicated, FAO estimates): Coconuts 3,000; Roots and tubers 300 (2009); Bananas 15.

Livestock (year ending September 2008, FAO estimates): Pigs 1,000; Chickens 5,000. Note: Data for 2009 were not available.

Livestock Products (metric tons, 2008 unless otherwise indicated, FAO estimates): Pig meat 19; Chicken meat 4 (2009); Hen eggs 8.

Fishing (metric tons, live weight, 2008, FAO estimate): Total catch 200.

Source: FAO.

INDUSTRY

Production (1990, estimate): Electric energy 300,000 kWh.

FINANCE

Currency and Exchange Rates: New Zealand currency is legal tender. Tokelau souvenir coins have also been issued. New Zealand currency: 100 cents = 1 New Zealand dollar ($NZ); *Sterling, US Dollar and Euro Equivalents* (31 December 2010): £1 sterling = $NZ2.1155; US $1 = $NZ1.3514; €1 = $NZ1.8057; $NZ100 = £47.27 = US $74.00 = €55.38. *Average Exchange Rate* ($NZ per US $): 1.4227 in 2008; 1.6002 in 2009; 1.3874 in 2010.

Budget ($NZ, year ending 30 June 1998): *Revenue:* Local 734,950; New Zealand subsidy 4,600,000; Total 5,334,950. *Expenditure:* Total 5,208,449.

Overseas Aid (projection, $NZ '000, 2002/03): Official development assistance from New Zealand 8,100 (of which Budget support 4,750, Projects and training 2,650). *2010/11:* Total development assistance from New Zealand $NZ17.25m.

EXTERNAL TRADE

Principal Commodities ($NZ, 2002): *Imports:* Food and live animals 923,766; Mineral fuels, lubricants, etc. 194,779; Animal and vegetable oils, fats and waxes 50,012; Chemicals and related products 45,429; Manufactured goods 183,488; Total (incl. others) 1,673,389.

COMMUNICATIONS MEDIA

Radio Receivers (1997, estimate): 1,000 in use.

EDUCATION

Schools (1999): 3 (one school for all levels on each atoll).

Teachers (2003): Primary 23; Secondary 17.

Pupils (2003): Primary 182; General secondary 176.

Students Overseas (1999): Secondary 22; Tertiary 20.

Pupil-teacher Ratio (primary education, UNESCO estimate): 5.8 in 2003/04 (Source: UNESCO Institute for Statistics).

Directory

The Government
(May 2011)

Administrator: JONATHAN KINGS (took office in 2011).

FAIPULE

The title of Ulu-O-Tokelau (Head of Tokelau) is held on a one-year rotational basis by each Faipule in turn. At elections held on Atafu on 19 January and on Nukunonu on 20 January 2011 new Faipule were chosen on both atolls.

Faipule of Fakaofo: FOUA TOLOA.
Faipule of Nukunonu: SALESIO LUI.
Faipule of Atafu: KELISIANO KALOLO.

PULENUKU

At elections in January 2011 a new Pulenuku (Village Mayor) was chosen on Atafu, while the incumbent Pulenuku of Nukunonu was re-elected.

Pulenuku of Fakaofo: OTINIELU TUUMULI.
Pulenuku of Nukunonu: PANAPA SAKARIA.
Pulenuku of Atafu: SAASETAI TAUMANU.

GOVERNMENT OFFICES

Council for the Ongoing Government of Tokelau: POB 3298, Apia, Samoa; tel. 32325; fax 32338; e-mail jsuveinakama@yahoo.com; internet www.tokelau.org.nz; Gen. Man. JOVILISI SUVEINAKAMA.

Tokelau Apia Liaison Office/Ofiha o Fehokotakiga Tokelau Ma Apia: POB 865, Savalalo, Apia, Samoa; tel. 20822; fax 21761; e-mail maka@lesamoa.net; internet www.tokelau-govt.info; responsible for transport, accounting and consular functions; Gen. Man. FALANI AUKUSO.

The Tokelau Public Service has seven departments, divided among the three atolls, with a supervising administrative official located in each village. Two departments are established on each atoll, while the seventh department, the Council for the Ongoing Government of Tokelau (formerly the Council of Faipule), rotates on a yearly basis in conjunction with the position of Ulu-O-Tokelau. Management of the Tokelau Public Service was formally transferred to Tokelau in July 2001.

Legislature
GENERAL FONO

The General Fono, or territorial assembly, is a meeting of delegates representing the Territory, and includes the Faipule and Pulenuku; it is the highest advisory body and must be consulted by the administration about all policy affecting the Territory. The General Fono has responsibility for the territorial budget and has the power to enact legislation, impose taxes and declare public holidays. The assembly is elected by universal suffrage and, since the legislative elections of 2002, the number of representatives from each atoll has been determined by its proportion of the total population. Members of the General Fono elect a Chairman, and hold between three and four sessions a year on the Ulu-O-Tokelau's atoll.

Chairman: MOSE PELASIO.

NEW ZEALAND'S DEPENDENT TERRITORIES

Judicial System

Tokelau's legislative and judicial systems are based on the Tokelau Islands Act 1948 and subsequent amendments and regulations. The Act provided for a variety of British regulations to continue in force and, where no other legislation applies, the law of England and Wales in 1840 (the year in which British sovereignty over New Zealand was established) was to be applicable. New Zealand statute law applies in Tokelau only if specifically extended there. In 1986 legislation formalized the transfer of High Court civil and criminal jurisdiction from Niue to New Zealand. Most cases are judged by the Commissioner established on each atoll, who has limited jurisdiction in civil and criminal matters. Commissioners are appointed by the New Zealand Governor-General, after consultation with the elders of the atoll.

Commissioner of Fakaofo: PENEHE TULAFONO.
Commissioner of Nukunonu: IOANE TUMUA.
Commissioner of Atafu: SALASOPA SEMU IUPATI.

Religion

On Atafu almost all inhabitants are members of the Congregational Christian Church, on Nukunonu all are Roman Catholic, while both denominations are represented on Fakaofo. In the late 1990s some 70% of the total population adhered to the Congregational Christian Church, and 30% to the Roman Catholic Church.

CHRISTIANITY

Roman Catholic Church

The Church is represented in Tokelau by a Mission, established in 1992. There were an estimated 500 adherents at 31 December 2007.

Superior: Mgr PATRICK EDWARD O'CONNOR, Catholic Mission, Nukunonu, Tokelau (via Apia, Samoa); tel. 4160; fax 3146; e-mail dr.tovite@clear.net.n3.

Broadcasting and Communications

Each atoll has a radio station to broadcast shipping and weather reports. Radio-telephone provided the main communications link with other areas until the late 1990s. A new telecommunications system established at a cost of US $2.76m. (US $1m. of which was provided by New Zealand) and operating through an earth station, linked to a communications satellite, on each atoll, became operational in 1997. A new weekly radio programme, called Vakai, broadcast by Samoa Broadcasting Service to Tokelau's three atolls, began in October 2004.

TELECOMMUNICATIONS

Telecommunications Tokelau Corporation (TeleTok): Fenuafala, Fakaofo; tel. 3100; fax 3108; e-mail apvitale@clear.net.nz; f. 1996; govt-owned; Gen. Man. AUKUSITINO VITALE.

Finance

There are no banks in operation in Tokelau; however, the Office of Tokelau Affairs provides a facility for deposits and withdrawals, and pays interest on accounts. Commercial and other banking facilities are available in Apia, Samoa.

Trade and Industry

A village co-operative store was established on each atoll in 1977. These stores are operated by village management committees, which work with the public service administration to reduce the costs of imported goods. Most imports are purchased from Samoa, with an increasing amount coming from New Zealand and Fiji. Local industries include copra production, woodwork and plaited craft goods, and the processing of tuna. Electricity is provided by diesel generators based in the village on each atoll.

Transport

There are no roads or motor vehicles. Unscheduled inter-atoll voyages, by sea, are forbidden because the risk of missing landfall is too great. Passengers and cargo are transported by vessels that anchor off shore, as there are no harbour facilities. A scheme to provide wharves (primarily to facilitate the export of fish) was proposed in September 2002. Most shipping links are with Samoa, but a monthly service from Fiji was introduced in 1986. The vessel *Forum Tokelau*, operated by Pacific Forum Line, began a monthly service between Tokelau and Apia, Samoa, in mid-1997. A New Zealand-funded interatoll vessel commenced service in 1991, providing the first regular link between the atolls for 40 years. Plans to construct an airstrip on each atoll were postponed in 1987 in favour of the development of shipping links. Proposals for the introduction of air links have encountered resistance from the island communities.

Education

Education is provided free of charge, and attendance is virtually 100%. Kindergarten facilities are available for children from the age of three years, while primary education takes place between the ages of five and 14. The provision of an additional year of schooling, for those aged 15, is rotated among the Territory's three schools every five years. In 2003 there were 23 primary school teachers and 17 secondary school teachers. Pupil enrolment in that year at primary level totalled 182 and at secondary level totalled 176. The New Zealand Department of Education provides advisory services and some educational equipment. The Education Department of Samoa organizes daily radio broadcasts. Scholarships are awarded for secondary and tertiary education, and for vocational training, in New Zealand, Australia and other Pacific countries. Link arrangements exist between Tokelau and the Fiji-based University of the South Pacific, which has an outpost on each atoll that is electronically connected. In 2004 a total of 53 Tokelauans over the age of 15 years were studying overseas under the Tokelau Sponsorship Scheme (34 in Samoa, 12 in New Zealand and seven in Fiji). In 2001 there were some 169 Tokelauan pupils enrolled at the Samoa Secondary School. Australia also provides scholarships.

NEW ZEALAND'S ASSOCIATED STATES

New Zealand's two Associated States are the self-governing Cook Islands and Niue, both of which are situated in the Pacific Ocean.

THE COOK ISLANDS

Introductory Survey

LOCATION, CLIMATE, LANGUAGE, RELIGION, FLAG, CAPITAL

The 13 inhabited and two uninhabited islands of the Cook Islands are located in the southern Pacific Ocean and lie between American Samoa, to the west, and French Polynesia, to the east. The islands extend over about 2m. sq km (more than 750,000 sq miles) of ocean, and form two groups: the Northern Cooks, which are all atolls and include Pukapuka, Rakahanga and Manihiki, and the Southern Cooks, including Aitutaki, Mangaia and Rarotonga, which are all volcanic islands. From December to March the climate is warm and humid, with the possibility of severe storms; from April to November the climate is mild and equable. The average annual rainfall on Rarotonga is 2,012 mm (79 ins). The official languages are English and Cook Islands Maori. The principal religion is Christianity, with the majority of the population adhering to the Cook Islands Congregational Christian Church. The islands' flag (proportions 1 by 2) displays 15 five-pointed white stars (representing the islands of the group) on a royal blue field, with the United Kingdom's Union Flag as a canton in the upper hoist. The capital is Avarua, on Rarotonga.

CONTEMPORARY POLITICAL HISTORY

Historical Context

The first Europeans to visit the islands were members of a British expedition, led by Capt. James Cook (after whom the islands are named), in 1773. The Cook Islands were proclaimed a British protectorate in 1888, and a part of New Zealand in 1901.

On 4 August 1965 the Cook Islands became a self-governing Territory in free association with New Zealand. The people are New Zealand citizens. Sir Albert Henry, leader of the Cook Islands Party (CIP), was elected Premier in 1965 and re-elected in 1971, 1974 and March 1978. However, in July 1978, following an inquiry into alleged electoral malpractice, the Chief Justice disallowed votes cast in the elections to the Legislative Assembly (later renamed Parliament) by Cook Islands expatriates who had been flown from New Zealand, with their fares paid from public funds. The amended ballot gave a majority to the Democratic Party (DP), and its leader, Dr (later Sir) Thomas Davis, was sworn in as Premier by the Chief Justice. In August 1979 Sir Albert Henry was convicted of conspiracy to defraud, and was formally stripped of his knighthood.

Domestic Political Affairs

In May 1981 the Cook Islands' Constitution was amended to increase the membership of Parliament from 22 to 24, and to extend the parliamentary term from four to five years. In March 1983 Sir Thomas Davis lost power to the CIP, under Geoffrey (later Sir Geoffrey) Henry, cousin of the former Premier. However, with one seat already subject to re-election, Henry's majority of three was reduced by the death of one CIP member of Parliament and the transfer of allegiance to the DP by another. Henry resigned in August, and a general election in November returned the DP to power under Davis. In August 1984 Davis announced wide-ranging government changes, with three of the seven posts going to members of the CIP, to form a coalition Government, with Henry as Deputy Prime Minister. In mid-1985, however, Davis dismissed Henry, who had endorsed an unsuccessful motion expressing no confidence in the Government, and Henry's supporters withdrew from the coalition. Henry's successor as Deputy Prime Minister was Dr (later Sir) Terepai Maoate, one of four CIP members who continued to support the Davis Government, in defiance of the CIP central committee.

Davis was forced to resign as Prime Minister in July 1987, after the approval of a parliamentary motion expressing no confidence in his administration. He was succeeded by Dr Pupuke Robati, a member of the Cabinet and a leading figure in the DP. Geoffrey Henry again became Prime Minister following a general election victory for the CIP in January 1989. The defection in mid-1990 of a member of Parliament from the DP to the CIP provided the latter with 15 seats in Parliament and thus the minimum two-thirds' majority support necessary to amend the Constitution. In August 1991 a constitutional amendment was approved to increase the number of members of Parliament to 25, and at an election to the newly created seat a CIP candidate was successful. The amendment also provided for an increase in the number of cabinet members from seven to nine (including the Prime Minister).

At a general election in March 1994 the CIP increased its majority, winning 20 seats in Parliament; the DP secured three seats and the Alliance Party (established in 1992 by Norman George, the former DP parliamentary whip, who had been expelled from the party following a dispute over spending) two. Davis, who failed to win a seat, subsequently resigned as leader of the DP. A referendum held simultaneously revealed that a majority of the electorate favoured retaining the current name (69.8% of voters) and national anthem (80.2%), while 48.5% favoured the retention of the flag of the Cook Islands. (At subsequent by-elections the CIP lost two seats and the DP and Alliance Party each gained one seat.)

A financial scandal was narrowly averted following reports that during 1994 the Government had issued loan guarantees for foreign companies worth more than $NZ1,200m. (the island's total revenue for 1994/95 was estimated at $NZ50m.). An investigation into the affair by the central bank found that the Government had not been guilty of fraud, but rather had been coerced into the activity by unscrupulous foreign business interests. However, the affair led many investors to remove their funds from the islands, provoking a financial crisis that resulted in Henry's decision in mid-1995 to withdraw the Cook Islands dollar from circulation, and to implement a programme of retrenchment measures. The crisis deepened during 1995 as new allegations emerged, and Henry's Government was severely criticized by New Zealand for failing to co-operate with an official inquiry into accusations of fraud and tax evasion involving several New Zealand companies. Henry maintained that the islands' bank secrecy laws prevented the disclosure of information relating to financial transactions. The situation deteriorated further when it was revealed that the Government had defaulted on a debt of some US $100m. to an Italian bank. In response to pressure from New Zealand, and in an attempt to restore a degree of financial stability to the islands, Henry (whose management of the crisis had been questioned both by his own party and by the opposition) announced a severe restructuring programme in April 1996. The measures included a 50% reduction in the pay of public sector workers, the closure of almost all diplomatic missions overseas, a 60% reduction in the number of government departments and ministries, and the privatization of the majority of government-owned authorities. A marked increase in 1995/96 in the emigration rate and a decline in the number of Cook Islanders returning to the islands following a period of residency overseas was attributed to the austere economic conditions created by the financial crisis.

In August 1997 Parliament approved the Outer Islands Local Government Act, providing for a new budgetary system to allocate funds for projects in the outer islands and for increased powers for local authorities, with the aim of reducing significantly central government administration of the outer islands. As part of the plan, three new government bodies were elected in April 1998.

Henry's administration continued to attract controversy, with the announcement in December 1997 of the closure of the Ministry of Public Works, Survey, Housing, Water Supply and Environment Services for exceeding its budget. The minister responsible, Tihina Tom Marsters, resigned in protest against the closure, which resulted in the loss of more than 100 public servants' jobs, problems with the supply of utilities (particularly water) and the suspension of several development projects.

At the legislative election of June 1999 the CIP won 11 of the 25 seats in Parliament, the Democratic Alliance Party (DAP, a grouping that included the DP) 10 seats and the New Alliance Party (NAP, formerly the Alliance Party) four seats. Sir Geoffrey Henry of the CIP was reappointed Prime Minister and formed a new Cabinet, following the establishment of a political coalition with the NAP; the leader of the NAP, Norman George, became Deputy Prime Minister. However, three members of the CIP subsequently left the party to form a coalition with the DAP, in protest against the alliance with the NAP, and at the end of July Henry resigned and was replaced by a 'rebel' CIP member, Dr Joe Williams. Williams was confirmed as the new Prime Minister by 13 votes to 12 in a vote of confidence by the Parliament. Williams' appointment provoked a public protest in Rarotonga, exacerbated by general discontent at the nomination of a Prime Minister whose parliamentary constituency was outside the

Cook Islands (having been elected to the seat reserved for non-resident voters). The result of the contest for the Pukapuka seat, which had been won by former Prime Minister Inatio Akaruru by just one vote, was challenged by the DAP. The matter was taken to the Court of Appeal, which subsequently declared the result invalid, stripping the Government of its one-seat majority. A by-election was held in late September 1999 to decide the Pukapuka seat; however, the result was again said to be invalid and a further by-election was scheduled. The Government became a minority administration in mid-October when the Prime Minister dismissed his deputy, Norman George, along with the Minister of Education, following their defection to the opposition. Despite the appointment of three new ministers, Williams failed to regain a majority in Parliament. In November Williams resigned, shortly before a vote of no confidence was to be tabled against him by Dr Terepai Maoate, now the leader of the opposition DAP. Maoate won the vote by 14 votes to 11 and was appointed Prime Minister, forming a new coalition Government with the NAP. He subsequently reappointed Norman George to the post of Deputy Prime Minister.

In early 2000 the islands of Penrhyn, Pukapuka, Rakahanga and Manihiki expressed their desire to become fully devolved and to take sole control over areas such as administration, public expenditure and justice. In response, the Government pledged gradually to phase out the Ministry of Outer Islands Development, as well as the post of Government Representative in the outer islands. In December of that year an additional US $2m. in funding under the Cotonou Agreement with the European Union (see p. 270) was designated for projects on the outer islands.

As the rate of emigration from the islands continued to increase, in late 2000 it was announced that some 1,400 residents had left the islands during that year (compared with 641 in the previous year). This resulted in a reduction in the population of the islands to its lowest level in more than 50 years, the majority of the loss being from the outer islands, and prompted the Government to campaign in Australia and New Zealand to encourage former citizens to return to the Cook Islands. Private sector businesses, many of which had experienced difficulties in recruiting workers in sufficient numbers, were also involved in the campaign. At the census of 2001 the resident population was recorded at only 14,990. In August 2002 the Government announced that it would allocate US $23,350 for the campaign.

Meanwhile, Maoate dismissed Norman George in July 2001 on the grounds that he was attempting to undermine him; this was the second time that George had lost the position of Deputy Prime Minister. He was replaced by Dr Robert Woonton. However, Woonton strongly criticized Maoate's leadership in the same month. In late 2001 the rift between the Prime Minister and his Cabinet widened. Woonton announced his resignation, which Maoate refused to accept. This led to a motion of no confidence in the Prime Minister, which he only narrowly survived. In February 2002 Maoate's leadership was again challenged: 15 of the 25 members of Parliament voted against him in a second motion of no confidence. He was therefore replaced by Robert Woonton. In an extensive ministerial reorganization Sir Geoffrey Henry returned to the Cabinet as Deputy Prime Minister.

In November 2002 Parliament approved a constitutional amendment abolishing the requirement for electoral candidates to reside in the islands for a qualifying period of three months. This action was widely interpreted as a way of retaining the overseas voters' parliamentary seat for the CIP leader, Dr Joe Williams, who lived permanently in New Zealand. In the same month the CIP and the DP formed a coalition Government (the fifth such coalition since the previous election), which left Norman George, who had been recently dismissed from his position in the Cabinet, as the sole opposition member of Parliament. The Government's action prompted a demonstration outside the parliament building by some 150 people, organized by a recently formed organization, the Group for Political Change. The protesters claimed that the virtual absence of an opposition constituted an erosion of democracy and appealed to the Prime Minister to commit to an early general election. However, in January 2003 the CIP was ousted from the coalition. The continued political manoeuvring was widely denounced, particularly among the business community, for creating a climate of instability in the islands. Public dissatisfaction with the situation resulted in the presentation of a petition to the Government in March signed by a significant percentage of the population. The petition demanded a number of political reforms including a reduction in the number of members of Parliament, the introduction of a shorter parliamentary term and the abolition of the overseas seat. Moreover, businessman Teariki Heather announced the formation of a new political party, the Cook Islands National, in the same month. In September legislation was approved providing for the abolition of the overseas seat and for a referendum (to be held concurrently with the next general election) on a proposal to shorten the parliamentary term from five years to four. (An earlier referendum on this issue in 1999 had narrowly failed to receive the support of the two-thirds' majority required to amend the Constitution.)

In November 2003 Dr Terepai Maoate, who had been appointed Deputy Prime Minister earlier in the year, and the Minister of Justice, Tangata Vavia, resigned following an unsuccessful attempt by Maoate to propose a motion of no confidence in the Government. The Government was the focus of further criticism in December when about 200 people marched through Avarua to protest against the granting of a residency permit to New Zealander Mark Lyon. The protesters claimed that Lyon, a wealthy businessman with recent convictions for weapons possession and a reputation for behaviour deemed disrespectful to island traditions, was not a suitable candidate for residency in the islands, and demanded the resignation of the Prime Minister and his chief adviser, Norman George, over the matter.

The elections of 2004 and 2006; other events

At a general election in September 2004 the DP won 14 of the 24 seats, the CIP secured nine and an independent candidate won the remaining seat. Prime Minister Robert Woonton regained his seat by only four votes, amid accusations that he had secured the support of some voters through bribery. In the concurrent referendum 82.3% of participating voters indicated their support for the shortening of the parliamentary term from five years to four. The period immediately after the election was characterized by political manoeuvring and the initiation of several legal cases challenging the outcome in a number of constituencies. In November Woonton announced that his party was to form a coalition government with the CIP. This decision was widely opposed within the DP, the leadership questioned the legality, and prompted the resignation of the Deputy Prime Minister, Aunty Mau Munokoa. Further controversy was caused by the appointment of Norman George to the position of Speaker. In December, with the DP effectively divided over Woonton's actions, Jim Marurai, of the minority Democratic Tumu Party, was elected Prime Minister and a governing coalition was formed between his party and the CIP. It was understood that Marurai would serve as Prime Minister for the first two years of the parliamentary term and would then be replaced by Sir Geoffrey Henry of the CIP. However, in August 2005 Henry was dismissed and replaced by DP leader Dr Terepai Maoate. In September two further CIP cabinet ministers were dismissed and replaced by DP members. Marurai declared that the coalition had been dissolved, claiming that the action followed threats to his leadership.

The islands suffered considerable damage in February and March 2005 when five cyclones struck in just over four weeks. The resultant damage to housing, infrastructure and crops was estimated at $NZ25m. A rehabilitation programme was implemented, and in October 2005 discussions took place between Jim Marurai and the Prime Minister of New Zealand, Helen Clark, regarding the progress made. The islands' economic situation was also discussed.

In October 2005 Peri Vaevae Pare, the Minister of Health and Internal Affairs, whose other portfolios included social services, was suspended from office pending police investigations into allegations of fraud. In November he was convicted on three charges of intent to defraud and gain pecuniary advantage, each conviction carrying a maximum sentence of five years' imprisonment. In early 2006 the Prime Minister requested the formal resignation of the suspended Minister, who was subsequently replaced. Dr Terepai Maoate continued as Deputy Prime Minister, retaining responsibility for the finance portfolio, while Wilkie Rasmussen remained responsible for foreign affairs. In March Robert Woonton, who had previously been appointed as the islands' High Commissioner to New Zealand, was dismissed from that post, following allegations that he had been involved in an attempt to oust the islands' Government.

In July 2006 a by-election victory for the opposition CIP gave it a parliamentary majority, prompting the Queen's Representative, Sir Frederick Goodwin, to dissolve the legislature and to call an early election. Votes on a motion of no confidence in Prime Minister Marurai and a motion in favour of his replacement by Sir Geoffrey Henry, submitted at a parliamentary session following the decision, were invalidated by the dissolution of Parliament. Marurai retained the role of Prime Minister in an interim capacity pending the election, which was scheduled for September. Henry announced his retirement as leader of the CIP in August.

Provisional results of the election, held on 26 September 2006, indicated that the DP had secured 15 of the 24 parliamentary seats and the CIP seven, with one seat being taken by an independent candidate. Henry Puna, who had succeeded Sir Geoffrey Henry as leader of the CIP, failed to retain his seat. A by-election to resolve the tied result in the remaining constituency resulted in victory for the CIP candidate in November. In the following month it was announced that a by-election would also be held in Titikaveka after the eligibility of the winning candidate, Robert Wigmore of the DP, was called into question. Wigmore won the Titikaveka by-election in February 2007, thus taking the final result of the 2006 election to 15 seats for the DP and eight for the CIP, along with one independent. Jim Marurai, who had returned to the DP, thus retained the position of Prime Minister, although Maoate continued as leader of the DP. In August 2007 Wilkie Rasmussen, the cabinet member responsible for foreign affairs among other portfolios, was elected deputy leader of the DP, having left the CIP prior to the 2006 election. Meanwhile, in July 2007 a report by the Fiji-based Pacific Institute of Advanced Studies in Development and Governance on seven Pacific island nations gave the Cook Islands the highest rating in the area of good governance.

Preparations for the 2009 South Pacific Mini Games, which were to be hosted by the islands in September of that year, attracted considerable media attention in 2007–08, with the Ministry of Finance and Economic Management warning against the acceptance of a grant from the People's Republic of China to finance the construction of a sports complex, maintaining that it would neither be cost-effective nor serve the long-term economic interests of the islands (see Foreign Affairs). Preparations were marred by allegations of financial mismanagement, and in March 2009 the Government announced an audit into the finances of Pacific Mini Games Company, the enterprise responsible for organizing the event. The rising cost of the Mini Games forced the Government to allocate additional funding in a supplementary budget in April, and in June the President of the Pacific Games Council expressed doubt in the islands' ability to host the event. Nevertheless, the Mini Games were staged successfully in September and provided a short-term increase in economic activity.

Meanwhile, Brian Donnelly was appointed to replace John Bryan as New Zealand's High Commissioner to the Cook Islands, taking office in February 2008. In August, however, Donnelly was himself compelled to resign owing to poor health, and was replaced in December by Tia Barrett. Following the death of Barrett in November 2009, he was replaced, in an acting capacity, by Nicola Ngawati. Ngawati was replaced as acting High Commissioner in March 2010 by Linda Te Puni, who was confirmed in the role in June. In February 2011 it was announced that John Carter was to replace Te Puni from August.

Recent developments: the election of 2010

Following the dismissal from the Cabinet of Wilkie Rasmussen in July 2009, on the grounds that he had allegedly colluded with members of the opposition in order to establish a new government (claims that were denied by Rasmussen), the foreign affairs portfolio was reassigned to the Deputy Prime Minister, Sir Terepai Maoate. However, in December Prime Minister Jim Marurai dismissed Maoate owing to his role in an abortive deal to purchase a fuel depot, which had lost the Government some $NZ2m. Three DP ministers resigned in protest against his dismissal. In the subsequent cabinet reorganization in January 2010, Robert Wigmore became Deputy Prime Minister and was also allocated responsibility for foreign affairs. Rasmussen was reappointed to the Cabinet, securing the finance portfolio, among other responsibilities, despite having denounced Marurai as 'totally incompetent' at the time of his dismissal in July 2009.

In February 2010 the island of Aitutaki was devastated by Cyclone Pat, which reportedly damaged up to 90% of the island's housing and disabled communications and electricity lines. Following the declaration of a state of disaster, the New Zealand Government pledged $NZ5.5m. in reconstruction aid in March. Despite demands from the DP and the CIP for Marurai to recall Parliament so that official approval could be given to the New Zealand aid programme, the Prime Minister controversially revealed that he would not reconvene the legislature until September, apparently owing to a threat of a motion of no confidence being tabled by the opposition. The Government was also censured for the slow pace of the recovery effort on Aitutaki.

Following a lengthy trial, Norman George was found not guilty of corruption in May 2010. George alleged that the charges against him, dating from 1999 to 2002, had been politically motivated and accused Maoate of having used his former position as Attorney-General to influence the police investigation.

In an escalating dispute within the DP regarding the dismissal of Sir Terepai, all six members of the Cabinet, including Marurai, were expelled from the party in March 2010, prompting rumours of the creation of a new party prior to the legislative election scheduled for later in the year. However, at a conference held in June the six were readmitted to the party; Wigmore was elected party Leader in place of Maoate, with Rasmussen returned as his deputy; Sean Willis was elected as the new party President replacing Makiuti Tonga. Maoate was reported to have responded angrily to the developments and pledged to take further action, which was interpreted by some as a threat of legal action over his removal as party Leader, although nothing to this end immediately materialized. In September 2010 Maoate's ambitions were further thwarted when he was defeated in his bid to secure election as the DP candidate for the Rarotonga seat of Ngatangiia; the former premier subsequently announced that he would be contesting the election as an independent candidate and expressed his belief that the DP would soon cease to exist as an integral entity.

Meanwhile, in mid-August 2010 Marurai announced that the next legislative election was to be held in mid-November, and that a popular referendum on parliamentary reform, comprising a proposal to reduce the number of parliamentary seats, was to take place concurrently. Parliament was formally dissolved in mid-September, although it had been reconvened only briefly by Marurai in July and again in August in order to secure approval of the national budget. Some 70 candidates registered to contest the elections, including 24 candidates presented by the CIP and 23 by the DP. The participation of some 16 independents (12 more than in the 2006 election), together with the emergence of, and the fielding of six candidates by, Te Kura O Te Au represented a significant challenge to the traditional two-party contest. A political movement established earlier in the year, Te Kura O Te Au pledged to pursue political reform that remained 'in tune with spiritual and cultural values'.

However, in the event, the election held on 17 November 2010 was, as in previous polls, entirely dominated by the two main parties. According to final results announced on 29 November, the CIP secured a commanding victory, winning 16 of the 24 seats, and thus a two-thirds' majority, with the DP managing to secure just eight seats. Turn-out, at about 78%, was considerably lower than in previous polls. Shortly prior to the election, outgoing Prime Minister Marurai had acknowledged that the DP was highly unlikely to secure re-election after its fractious past 12 months. According to the results of the referendum on parliamentary reform, 59.2% of voters cast their ballot in support of the proposal to reduce the number of seats, thus short of the two-thirds' majority required to force Parliament to take action. CIP Leader Henry Puna, who won back the seat that he had lost in 2006, criticized the handling of the referendum, contending that many people, particularly those on the outer islands, had not been sufficiently apprised of the issues, with some remaining unaware even that a referendum was being held.

Henry Puna was inaugurated as Prime Minister on 1 December 2010. On the following day he announced the composition of his Cabinet, which included Tom Marsters as Deputy Prime Minister. Norman George, who had publicly questioned the competence of Puna shortly after the election, was not included. Ministerial portfolios were assigned to the cabinet ministers a few days later, with Puna taking, *inter alia*, the portfolios of justice and of energy and renewable energy, Marsters being accorded additional responsibility for foreign affairs, immigration, transport, and mineral and natural resources. Other appointments included that of Mark Brown as, *inter alia*, Minister of Finance and Economic Management and of Internal Affairs, and that of Teariki Heather as Minister of Infrastructure and Planning, Cultural Development and House of Ariki. Puna identified the national economy as the main priority of the new Government. Sir Geoffrey Henry was appointed parliamentary Speaker in February 2011.

Meanwhile, in mid-December 2010 the DP lodged a formal petition against the results in three constituencies, alleging electoral irregularities. A further challenge was subsequently lodged against a fourth election result. A hearing into the petitions commenced at the beginning of February 2011. All but one of the petitions were rejected later that month by the Chief Justice. However, a by-election was ordered in Pukapuka, the DP's petition about the improper conduct of voting in that constituency having been upheld. Also in February the Secretary of Justice, Mark Short, was suspended indefinitely pending an investigation into the apparent mismanagement of funds during the election; in his role as Chief Registrar of Elections, Short was alleged to have been responsible for significant over-spending.

The 'Offshore' Financial Sector

A reported increase in the number of Russian nationals opening accounts in the Cook Islands led to allegations in early 1999 that the islands' 'offshore' financial centre was being used extensively by criminal organizations for 'laundering' the proceeds of their activities. The claims were vigorously denied by officials in the sector. However, in June 2000 the naming of the islands by the Paris-based Financial Action Task Force (FATF, see p. 451) as one of a number of countries and territories that had failed to co-operate in regional efforts to combat money-laundering, along with the islands' identification by the Organisation for Economic Co-operation and Development (OECD, see p. 376) as a tax 'haven' that lacked financial transparency, led to increased international pressure on the Government to implement stricter controls over its 'offshore' financial centre. Consequently, legislation was approved in August of that year providing for the creation of the Money Laundering Authority and the introduction of new regulations aimed at reducing criminal activity in the sector. In February 2005 the Cook Islands were finally removed from the FATF list of non-co-operative countries and territories.

In February 2009 the Government introduced legislation into Parliament to abolish 'offshore' banks in the Cook Islands, arguing that the cost of regulating such organizations outweighed any financial benefits that they brought to the country. However, in April OECD included the Cook Islands on its so-called 'grey list' of countries that, while committed to the internationally agreed tax standard, had yet to implement substantial measures to combat tax evasion. In response, the Government made significant progress in negotiating agreements on tax information exchange with other nations, and by mid-2010 the Cook Islands had signed 11 such agreements, one short of the 12 required to be removed from the 'grey list'. Nevertheless, in February 2010 the French Government included the Cook Islands on a 'black list' of nations accused of a lack of transparency in tax reporting. Consequently, the French Government announced that it would impose a 50% tax upon transactions between France and the black-listed nations. The Banking Amendment Bill was approved by islands' Parliament in August. The closure of 'offshore' banks operating without the requisite domestic licence was envisaged by mid-2011.

Meanwhile, the operating licence of the Wall Street Banking Corporation Bank (WSBC Bank) was revoked in April 2009. The WSBC Bank had links to a New Zealand financial services company, WSD Global Markets, which was being investigated by the New Zealand Serious Fraud Office in connection with suspected money-laundering activities. Further controversy ensued in the second half of 2010 when concerns were raised over the legitimacy of the transfer to WSD of assets worth an estimated $NZ20m. from former clients of WSBC Bank.

Foreign Affairs

Since 1965 the Cooks Islands has developed a distinct identity in its external relations. Although not a sovereign state, by mid-2011 it had established diplomatic relations with more than 20 countries and international organizations, most latterly with Switzerland (in March 2011).

In August 1985 eight members of the South Pacific Forum (subsequently restyled the Pacific Islands Forum, see p. 413), including the Cook Islands, signed a treaty on Rarotonga, designating a 'nuclear-free' zone in the South Pacific. The treaty imposed a ban on the manufacture, testing, storage and use of nuclear weapons, and the dumping of nuclear waste, in the region.

In January 1986, following the rift between New Zealand and the USA in respect of the ANZUS (see p. 459) security arrangements, Sir Thomas Davis declared the Cook Islands a neutral country, because he considered that New Zealand (which has control over the islands' defence and foreign policy) was no longer in a position to defend the islands. The proclamation of neutrality meant that the Cook Islands would not enter into a military relationship with any foreign power, and, in particular, would prohibit visits by US warships. Visits by US naval vessels were allowed to resume by the Government of Geoffrey (later Sir Geoffrey) Henry. In November 2007 the Cook Islands and the USA signed agreements on maritime surveillance and anti-trafficking measures.

In October 1991 the Cook Islands signed a treaty of friendship and co-operation with France, covering economic development, trade and surveillance of the islands' exclusive economic zone (EEZ). The establishment of closer relations with France was widely regarded as an expression of the Cook Islands Government's dissatisfaction with existing arrangements with New Zealand. However, relations deteriorated considerably when the French Government resumed its programme of nuclear-weapons testing at Mururoa Atoll in September 1995. Henry was fiercely critical of the decision and dispatched a *vaka* (traditional voyaging canoe) with a crew of Cook Islands' traditional warriors to protest near the test site. The tests were concluded in January 1996. Full diplomatic relations with France were established in early 2000.

Meanwhile, the islands established diplomatic relations at ambassadorial level with the People's Republic of China in July 1997. In November 1998 Henry made an official visit to China, during which the two countries signed a bilateral trade agreement and each conferred the status of 'most favoured nation' on the other. Henry stated that the move constituted a further attempt by his Government to reduce the islands' dependence on New Zealand. In February 2008 the Government accepted a loan of US $10.2m. from China, the bulk of which was to fund preparations for the 2009 South Pacific Mini Games, which were to be hosted by the Cook Islands in September of that year; the decision resulted in threats of legal action from the local Chamber of Commerce. In March 2009 China agreed to provide a further loan of nearly $28m., of which $11m. was to be allocated to the construction of a sports stadium and the remainder was to finance infrastructure projects. The announcement prompted further demands for a public inquiry from the opposition, which claimed that the Cook Islands could not afford to repay such a large loan. The Deputy Prime Minister, Sir Terepai Maoate, who was also responsible for the finance portfolio, was alleged to have stated that repayments would be made with New Zealand aid; however, a New Zealand government official was reported as stating that such requests for aid were likely to be rejected. In March 2010 Minister of Finance Wilkie Rasmussen stated that the Government was extremely reluctant to accept a $NZ37.5m. Chinese loan for projects to upgrade the road and water systems in Rarotonga owing to the islands' already high external debt levels. In January 2011 it was announced that China had signed an agreement providing for a $NZ1.9m. grant to the islands, to be spent according to the Cook Islands Government's wishes.

During her visit to the islands in June 2001, Helen Clark, the New Zealand Prime Minister, stated that if the Cook Islands desired complete independence, and membership of international organizations, the process would not be obstructed by New Zealand. However, Cook Islanders would then be obliged to renounce their New Zealand citizenship. In mid-December 2010 the New Zealand Minister of Foreign Affairs, Murray McCully, made an official four-day visit to the Cook Islands, where he met with incoming Prime Minister Henry Puna and his newly announced Cabinet. During his stay, McCully visited Aitutaki to see the reconstruction efforts following Cyclone Pat in February (see Domestic Political Affairs). He was reported to have discussed a wide range of issues with the Puna Government, including New Zealand's programme of development assistance to the islands, with education, health care and tourism identified as the main priorities for assistance. Further bilateral talks were held in the Cook Islands in early 2011, during which New Zealand budgetary support for the islands and infrastructure co-operation were among the issues discussed.

In September 2008 the Cook Islands became a member of the International Maritime Organization (IMO) after securing the approval of two-thirds of the organization's members, rendering it eligible for IMO funding and assistance. Meanwhile, in April 2009 the Cook Islands Government submitted a claim to the UN to extend its seabed boundaries by over 400,000 sq km. The application, the first such claim to be lodged by a Pacific island nation, was motivated by the Government's desire to gain access to potential reserves of petroleum, gas and manganese.

CONSTITUTION AND GOVERNMENT

Under the Constitution of 1965, the Cook Islands is an internally self-governing state in free association with New Zealand, which is responsible for the Cook Islands' external affairs and defence (although the Territory has progressively assumed control over much of its foreign policy). Executive authority is vested in the British monarch, who is Head of State, and is exercised through her official representative; a representative of the New Zealand Government (redesignated High Commissioner in 1994) resides on Rarotonga. Executive government is carried out by the Cabinet, consisting of the Prime Minister and between five and seven other ministers. The Cabinet is collectively responsible to the Parliament, which is formed of 24 members (decreased from 25 in 2004, following the abolition of the seat for a member chosen by non-resident voters) who are elected by universal adult suffrage every four years (reduced from five years by a referendum in 2004). The House of Ariki, which comprises up to 15 members who are hereditary chiefs, can advise the Government, but has no legislative powers. The Koutu Nui is a similar body, comprising sub-chiefs. Each of the main islands, except Rarotonga, has an elected island council, and a government representative who is appointed by the Prime Minister.

REGIONAL AND INTERNATIONAL CO-OPERATION

The Cook Islands has membership of the Pacific Community (see p. 410) and the Pacific Islands Forum (see p. 413) and is an associate member of the UN Economic and Social Commission for Asia and the Pacific (ESCAP, see p. 37). In 1999 the Cook Islands were granted observer status at the Lomé Conventions with the European Union (subsequently superseded by the Cotonou Agreement, see p. 327).

ECONOMIC AFFAIRS

In 2009, according to official sources, the Cook Islands' gross domestic product (GDP), measured at current prices, totalled an estimated $NZ330.5m. GDP, measured at average 2006 prices, increased, in real terms, at an estimated average annual rate of 1.1% in 2000–09. In 2009 GDP per head was estimated at $NZ14,623. During 2000–09, it was estimated, the population increased at an average annual rate of about 2.6%. Overall GDP increased by 5.0%, in real terms, in 2006, but declined each year between 2007 and 2009 (when real GDP decreased by 3.6%).

Agriculture (including fishing) contributed 4.8% of GDP in 2009. The sector is estimated to have engaged 25.0% of the total economically active population in mid-2011, according to FAO figures. The real GDP of the agricultural sector (including pearl farming) decreased by an average of 5.2% per year in 2000–09. The sector's GDP declined, in real terms, by 5.7% in 2009. Cash crops include coconuts and tropical fruits such as mangoes, pineapples, bananas and papayas. Cassava, sweet potatoes and vegetables are cultivated as food crops. Pigs and poultry are the main livestock kept. The sale of fishing licences to foreign fleets provides an important source of income. Revenue from the export of fresh and chilled fish reached an estimated $NZ2.0m. in 2009, providing 44.4% of export earnings. Pearl oyster farming is also an important industry. Receipts from pearl exports totalled an estimated $NZ1.2m. (equivalent to 27.2% of total export earnings) in 2009.

NEW ZEALAND'S ASSOCIATED STATES

The Cook Islands

Industry (comprising mining and quarrying, manufacturing, construction and utilities) provided 10.0% of GDP in 2009. The sector engaged 13.3% of employees in 2001. Industrial GDP increased, in real terms, at an average rate of 2.9% per year during 2000–09, but the sector's real GDP declined by 5.0% in 2009.

The manufacturing sector engaged 6.0% of employees in 2001. The manufacturing and mining sectors together accounted for 3.6% of GDP in 2009. The real GDP of manufacturing and mining increased at an average rate of 1.8% per year during 2000–09. The two subsectors' combined GDP increased, in real terms, by 5.0% in 2008, but declined by 0.4% in 2009.

Construction contributed 4.2% of GDP in 2009; the sector engaged 5.9% of the employed labour force in 2001. GDP of construction increased at an average rate of 4.4% per year during 2000–09; the sector's GDP increased by 1.7% in 2008 but declined by an estimated 10.6% in 2009.

The islands depend on imports for their energy requirements. According to official estimates, mineral fuels and lubricants accounted for 31.4% of total imports in 2009. Tax rebates on the purchase of solar panels and water tanks by home-owners were under consideration in 2008. It was also reported in 2008 that the Government intended to increase fuel storage capacity on the islands.

Service industries contributed 85.2% of GDP in 2009. The sector engaged 79.5% of the employed labour force in 2001. The GDP of the services sector increased, in real terms, at an average annual rate of 1.9% in 2000–09; services GDP decreased by 1.6%, in real terms, in 2009. Tourism expanded considerably from the late 1980s, and generated revenue of an estimated US $105m. in 2008. Visitor arrivals were reported to have risen from 101,060 in 2009 to an estimated 102,156 in 2010. The restaurants and hotels sector contributed an estimated 15.1% of GDP in 2009. 'Offshore' banking, introduced to the islands in 1982, expanded rapidly, with more than 2,000 international companies registered by 1987. In August 2010, however, legislation to abolish 'offshore' banks operating without a domestic licence was approved by Parliament. The banks concerned were to be given 12 months in which to cease their operations. The financial and business services sector provided an estimated 12.0% of GDP in 2009 and engaged 5.4% of the employed labour force (including persons occupied in the real estate sector) in 2001. Significant revenue is provided by remittances from emigrants (who outnumber the residents of the islands).

In 2009 the cost of imports rose to $NZ290.2m. (according to official estimates), while export revenue totalled less than $NZ4.4m., thus resulting in a trade deficit of nearly $NZ285.8m. According to the Asian Development Bank (ADB), the deficit on the current account of the balance of payments totalled US $11m. in 2010, when it stood at the equivalent of 4.9% of GDP. The principal exports in 2009 were fresh and chilled fish and pearls. The principal imports, according to official estimates, in that year were mineral fuels and lubricants, machinery and transport equipment, food and live animals, and basic manufactures. The principal source of imports in 2009 was New Zealand (62.8% of the total). In the same year, Japan (49.2%) and New Zealand were the principal markets for exports.

In the financial year ending June 2009 the overall budgetary deficit (including grants) was estimated at $NZ7.7m. Development assistance is provided mainly by New Zealand and Australia. In 2004 New Zealand and Australia agreed to combine their programmes of aid to the Cook Islands in order to improve their effectiveness. Between 2009/10 and 2011/12 aid to the Cook Islands from New Zealand and Australia was expected to total $NZ51m. The islands were also to receive €3.3m. per year between 2008 and 2013 (to be spent on improvements to the environment, water supply and sanitation, including waste disposal) under the Cotonou Agreement with the European Union. It was estimated by the ADB that in December 2009 the islands' external debt stood at US $41m. and that the cost of debt-servicing in that year was equivalent to 69.1% of the value of exports of goods and services (in comparison with 41.5% in the previous year). The annual rate of inflation in Rarotonga averaged 4.2% in 2000–09. Consumer prices rose by an average of 6.6% in 2009, but declined by 0.3% in 2010. The ADB estimated the unemployment rate to be 8.9% of the labour force in 2006.

The National Sustainable Development Plan and the Infrastructure Master Plan, the latter to encompass a 20-year period, were announced in 2007. These long-term programmes envisaged substantial capital expenditure. In October 2009, following the deterioration in global conditions, an economic recovery programme was implemented, the provisions of which included support for vulnerable families and funding for various infrastructural projects. The economy has become heavily dependent on tourism, despite concerns that the Cook Islands might be unable to sustain such rapid development in the longer term. In August 2009 a leading international ratings agency reassessed the Cook Islands' prospects as negative; this downgrading was due largely to concerns regarding the maintenance of tourist numbers and the high level of government debt that continued to prevail. Nevertheless, in 2010 the Government of the Cook Islands continued to subsidize Air New Zealand flights on the Los Angeles–Rarotonga route, in order to ensure the continuation of the carrier's vital service to the islands. The inauguration of direct flights from the Australian city of Sydney in 2010 also enhanced the capacity of the tourism sector. Visitor arrivals rose by an estimated 7% in 2009 but by only 1% in 2010, partly as a result of the cyclone damaged suffered by the popular island of Aitutaki in February. The fisheries sector displayed strong growth in 2010, with the value of its exports estimated to have increased by 16%. However, the islands' total exports declined in value by more than 20% (mainly owing to a substantial decline in exports of pearls), while the cost of imports increased by more than 40%, thereby resulting in a sharp increase in the trade deficit in 2010. The need to import materials for infrastructural projects was expected to lead to a further deterioration in the trade balance in 2011. Moreover, inflationary pressures were reported to be re-emerging in early 2011, mainly owing to the higher costs of food, energy and transport. Upon taking office in late 2010, incoming Prime Minister Henry Puna declared the islands' economy to be his administration's main priority. Following expansion of 0.5% in the previous year, the ADB projected GDP growth of 2.0% in 2010/11.

PUBLIC HOLIDAYS

2012 (provisional): 2 January (for New Year's Day), 3 January (for Second day of New Year), 6–9 April (Easter), 25 April (for ANZAC Day, anniversary of 1915 landing at Gallipoli), 4 June (Queen's Official Birthday), 6 August (for Constitution Day), 26 October (Cook Islands Gospel Day), 25–26 December (Christmas).

Statistical Survey

Sources (unless otherwise stated): Cook Islands Statistics Office, Ministry of Finance and Economic Management, POB 41, Rarotonga; tel. 29511; fax 21511; e-mail info@stats.gov.ck; internet www.stats.gov.ck; Prime Minister's Department, Government of the Cook Islands, Avarua, Rarotonga; tel. 29300; fax 22856.

AREA AND POPULATION

Area: 236.7 sq km (91.4 sq miles).

Population: 18,027 (males 9,303, females 8,724) at census of 1 December 2001 (resident population 14,990); 19,342 (males 9,816, females 9,526) at census of 1 December 2006. *Cook Island Maoris Resident in New Zealand* (New Zealand census of 6 March 2001): 52,569. *By Island* (resident population at 2006 census): Rarotonga (including the capital, Avarua) 10,226; Aitutaki 1,975; Atiu 558; Mangaia 631; Manihiki 344; Mauke 372; Mitiaro 193; Nassau 75; Palmerston (Avarua) 62; Penrhyn (Tongareva) 254; Pukapuka 507; Rakahanga 127; Total 15,324. *Mid-2009* (official estimate): 22,600.

Density (mid-2009): 95.5 per sq km.

Population by Age and Sex (resident population at 2006 census): *0–14:* 5,049 (males 2,619, females 2,430); *15–64:* 12,821 (males 6,430, females 6,391); *65 and over:* 1,472 (males 767, females 705); *Total* 19,342 (males 9,816, females 9,526).

Principal Town (UN population estimate at mid-2003, incl. suburbs): Avarua (capital) 12,507. Source: UN, *World Urbanization Prospects: The 2003 Revision*.

Births, Marriages and Deaths (2009, provisional): Registered live births 255 (birth rate 11.1 per 1,000); Registered marriages 754 (marriage rate 32.9 per 1,000); Registered deaths 74 (death rate 3.2 per 1,000).

Life Expectancy (years at birth, WHO estimates): 74 (males 72; females 76) in 2008. Source: WHO, *World Health Statistics*.

Economically Active Population (resident population aged 15 years and over, 2001 census): Agriculture, hunting, forestry and fishing 427; Mining and quarrying 3; Manufacturing 357; Electricity, gas and water 79; Construction 347; Trade, restaurants and hotels 1,938; Transport, storage and communications 587; Financing, insurance, real estate and business services 323; Community, social and personal services 1,867; Total employed 5,928 (males 3,386, females 2,542); Unemployed 892 (males 449, females 443); *Total labour force* 6,820 (males 3,835, females 2,985). *Mid-2011* (estimates): Agriculture, etc. 2,000; Total labour force 8,000 (Source: FAO).

HEALTH AND WELFARE

Key Indicators

Total Fertility Rate (children per woman, 2008): 2.6.

Under-5 Mortality Rate (per 1,000 live births, 2008): 15.

Physicians (per 1,000 head, 2004): 1.2.

NEW ZEALAND'S ASSOCIATED STATES

The Cook Islands

Hospital Beds (per 1,000 head, 2005): 6.3.
Health Expenditure (2007): US $ per head (PPP): 381.
Health Expenditure (2007): % of GDP: 4.4.
Health Expenditure (2007): public (% of total): 91.7.
Access to Water (% of persons, 2006): 95.

For sources and definitions, see explanatory note on p. vi.

AGRICULTURE, ETC.

Principal Crops (metric tons, 2008, FAO estimates): Cassava 1,500; Sweet potatoes 700; Coconuts 2,000; Tomatoes 700; Watermelons 75; Guavas, mangosteens and mangoes 300; Papayas 800; Bananas 60; Oranges 100. Note: Data were not available for individual crops in 2009. *Aggregate Production* (metric tons, may include official, semi-official or estimated data, 2009): Roots and tubers 4,700; Vegetables (incl. melons) 2,277; Fruits (excl. melons) 1,725.
Livestock (head, year ending September 2008, FAO estimates): Cattle 125; Pigs 32,200; Goats 1,010; Poultry 20,000; Horses 305. Note: data were not available for 2009.
Livestock Products (metric tons, 2009 unless otherwise indicated, FAO estimates): Hen eggs 35 (2008); Pig meat 555; Chicken meat 20.
Forestry ('000 cu m, 2009, FAO estimate): Roundwood removals (excl. bark) 5.
Fishing (metric tons, live weight, 2008): Albacore 1,905; Yellowfin tuna 228; Bigeye tuna 244; Total catch (incl. others) 3,000 (FAO estimate).

Source: FAO.

INDUSTRY

Electric Energy (production, million kWh): 34 in 2007; 34 in 2008; 33 in 2009.

FINANCE

Currency and Exchange Rates: New Zealand currency is legal tender. In mid-1995 it was announced that the Cook Islands dollar (formerly the local currency, at par with the New Zealand dollar) was to be withdrawn from circulation. New Zealand currency: 100 cents = 1 New Zealand dollar ($NZ); for details of exchange rates, see Tokelau.
Budget ($NZ '000, year ending 30 June 2009, provisional): *Revenue:* Total revenue 95,491 (Tax 80,963, Other current 7,857, Capital 6,671). (Note: Revenue excludes grants of 21,174). *Expenditure:* Total expenditure 124,355 (Current 109,330, Capital 15,025).
Overseas Aid ($NZ '000): Official development assistance from New Zealand (incl. $A1.5m. annual contributions from Australia, but administered by New Zealand) 51,000 for 2009/10–2011/12. Source: Ministry of Foreign Affairs and Trade, Wellington.
Cost of Living (Consumer Price Index for Rarotonga, average of quarterly figures; base: December 2006 = 100): All items 110.4 in 2008; 117.7 in 2009; 117.4 in 2010.
Gross Domestic Product ($NZ '000 at constant 2006 prices): 289,097 in 2007; 278,937 in 2008; 268,977 in 2009.
Gross Domestic Product by Economic Activity ($NZ '000 in current prices, 2009): Agriculture and fishing 16,857; Mining, quarrying and manufacturing 12,556; Electricity, gas and water 7,425; Construction 14,667; Wholesale and retail trade 66,204; Restaurants and hotels 52,602; Transport and communications 59,034; Finance and business services 41,586; Education and health services 18,268; Public administration 28,841; Other community, social and personal services 9,767; Ownership of dwellings 20,128; *Sub-total* 347,935; *Less* Imputed bank service charge 17,451; GDP in purchasers' values 330,486.

EXTERNAL TRADE

Principal Commodities ($NZ '000, 2009, estimates): *Imports c.i.f.:* Food and live animals 35,477; Mineral fuels, lubricants, etc. 91,001; Chemicals 10,077; Basic manufactures 34,854; Machinery and transport equipment 55,208; Miscellaneous manufactured articles 39,227; Total (incl. others) 290,228. *Exports f.o.b.:* Fish, fresh or chilled 1,950; Pearls 1,197; Total (incl. others) 4,396.
Principal Trading Partners ($NZ '000, 2009, estimates): *Imports:* Australia 19,675; Fiji 51,240; Japan 6,660; New Zealand 182,243; USA 7,662; Total (incl. others) 290,228. *Exports:* Australia 130; Japan 2,164; New Zealand 290; USA 89; Total (incl. others) 4,396.

TRANSPORT

Road Traffic (registered vehicles, April 1983): 6,555. *New Motor Vehicles Registered* (Rarotonga, 2009): Motorcycles 442; Cars and jeeps 163; Vans and pick-ups 73; Trucks and buses 25; Others 19; *Total* 722.
Shipping: *Merchant Fleet* (registered at 31 December 2009): 107 vessels, displacement 150,020 grt (Source: IHS Fairplay, *World Fleet Statistics*); *International Sea-borne Freight Traffic* ('000 metric tons, estimates): Goods unloaded 32.6 (2001); Goods loaded 9; Goods unloaded 32 (1990) (Source: UN, *Monthly Bulletin of Statistics*).
Civil Aviation (2009): *Aircraft Movements:* 732 departures. *Freight Traffic* (metric tons): Goods loaded 75; Goods unloaded 1,056.

TOURISM

Foreign Tourist Arrivals: 97,316 in 2007; 94,776 in 2008; 101,060 in 2009 (provisional).
Tourist Arrivals by Place of Residence (2009, provisional): Australia 14,765; Canada 2,086; Europe 12,452; New Zealand 63,429; USA 3,981; Total (incl. others) 101,060.
Tourism Revenue (US $ million, incl. passenger transport): 90 in 2006; 107 in 2007; 105 in 2008. Source: World Tourism Organization.

COMMUNICATIONS MEDIA

Radio Receivers (1997): 14,000 in use*.
Television Receivers (1997): 4,000 in use*.
Telephones (main lines, 2009): 6,900 in use†.
Mobile Cellular Telephones (2009): 7,000 subscribers†.
Internet Users (2009): 6,000†.
Broadband Subscribers (2009): 1,500†.
Daily Newspaper (2004, unless otherwise indicated): 1; circulation 2,000 (1996)*.
Non-daily Newspaper (1996): 1; circulation 1,000*.
*Source: UNESCO, *Statistical Yearbook*.
†Source: International Telecommunication Union.

EDUCATION

Pre-primary (2007, unless otherwise indicated): 26 schools (1998); 31 teachers (2000); 479 pupils.
Primary (2007, unless otherwise indicated): 28 schools (1998); 144 teachers (2000); 2,031 pupils.
Secondary* (1998, unless otherwise indicated): 23 schools; 129 teachers; 1,951 pupils (2007).
Higher (1980): 41 teachers; 360 pupils†.
*Includes high school education.
†Source: UNESCO, *Statistical Yearbook*.
Pupil-teacher Ratio (primary education, UNESCO estimate): 15.0 in 2009/10 (Source: UNESCO Institute for Statistics).

Directory

The Government

Queen's Representative: Sir FREDERICK GOODWIN.
New Zealand High Commissioner: LINDA TE PUNI.

CABINET
(May 2011)

The Government is formed by the Cook Islands Party.

Prime Minister and Minister for the Public Service Commission, Office of the Head of State, Attorney-General, Parliamentary Services, Police, Minister of Justice, Ombudsman, National Environment Service, Energy and Renewable Energy, and Emergency Management: HENRY PUNA.
Deputy Prime Minister and Minister of Foreign Affairs, Immigration, Transport, and Mineral and Natural Resources: TOM MARSTERS.
Minister of Finance and Economic Management, Business Trade and Investment Board, Cook Islands Investment Corporation, Internal Affairs, Commerce Commission, Financial Intelligence Unit, Telecommunication, Financial Services Development Authority, Financial Supervisory Commission, National Superannuation, and Public Expenditure and Review Committee Audit (PERCA): MARK BROWN.
Minister of Infrastructure and Planning, Cultural Development and House of Ariki: TEARIKI HEATHER.

NEW ZEALAND'S ASSOCIATED STATES

Minister of Health and Agriculture: NANDI GLASSIE.
Minister of Education, Marine Resources, Tourism, and National Human Resource Development: TEINA BISHOP.

GOVERNMENT OFFICES

Office of the Queen's Representative: POB 134, Titikaveka, Rarotonga; tel. and fax 29311; e-mail queenrep@oyster.net.ck.
Office of the Prime Minister: Government of the Cook Islands, Private Bag, Avarua, Rarotonga; tel. 25494; fax 20856; e-mail coso@pmoffice.gov.ck; internet www.pmoffice.gov.ck.
Office of the Public Service Commissioner: POB 24, Rarotonga; tel. 29421; fax 21321; e-mail epati@psc.gov.ck; internet www.psc.gov.ck.
New Zealand High Commission: 1st Floor, Philatelic Bureau Bldg, Takuvaine Rd, Avarua, POB 21, Rarotonga; tel. 22201; fax 21241; e-mail nzhcraro@oyster.net.ck.

Ministries

Ministry of Agriculture: POB 96, Rarotonga; tel. 28711; fax 21881; e-mail cimoa@oyster.net.ck; internet www.agriculture.gov.ck.
Ministry of Cultural Development: POB 8, Rarotonga; tel. 20725; fax 23725; e-mail sonny@oyster.net.ck; internet www.mocd.gov.ck.
Ministry of Education: POB 97, Rarotonga; tel. 29357; fax 28357; e-mail cieducat@oyster.net.ck; internet www.education.gov.ck.
Ministry of Energy: POB 72, Rarotonga; tel. 24484; fax 24483; e-mail punanga@energy.gov.ck.
Ministry of Finance and Economic Management: POB 120, Rarotonga; tel. 22878; fax 23877; e-mail etuatina@mfem.gov.ck; internet www.mfem.gov.ck.
Ministry of Foreign Affairs and Immigration: POB 105, Rarotonga; tel. 29347; fax 21247; e-mail secfa@mfai.gov.ck.
Ministry of Health: POB 109, Rarotonga; tel. 29664; fax 23109; e-mail aremaki@health.gov.ck; internet www.health.gov.ck.
Ministry of Infrastructure and Planning: POB 102, Rarotonga; tel. 20034; fax 21134; e-mail t.taoro@moip.gov.ck; internet www.moip.gov.ck.
Ministry of Internal Affairs: POB 98, Rarotonga; tel. 29370; fax 23608; e-mail secintaff@intaff.gov.ck.
Ministry of Justice: POB 111, Rarotonga; tel. 29410; fax 29610; e-mail offices@justice.gov.ck.
Ministry of Marine Resources: POB 85, Rarotonga; tel. 28721; fax 29721; e-mail I.Bertram@mmr.gov.ck.
Ministry of Transport: POB 61, Rarotonga; tel. 28810; fax 28816; e-mail transport@oyster.net.ck.
National Environment Service: POB 371, Rarotonga; tel. 21256; fax 22256; e-mail resources@environment.org.ck; internet www.environment.org.ck.

Advisory Chambers

House of Ariki: POB 13, Rarotonga; tel. 26500; fax 21260; Pres. TRAVEL TOU ARIKI.
Koutu Nui: POB 13, Rarotonga; tel. 29317; fax 21260; e-mail nvaloa@parliament.gov.ck; Pres. TETIKA MATAIAPO DORICE REID.

Legislature

PARLIAMENT

Parliamentary Service
POB 13, Rarotonga; tel. 26500; fax 21260; e-mail nvaloa@parliament.gov.ck.
Speaker: Sir GEOFFREY HENRY.
General Election, 17 November 2010

Party	Seats
Cook Islands Party (CIP)	16
Democratic Party (DP)	8
Total	**24**

Political Organizations

Cook Islands Labour Party: Rarotonga; f. 1988; anti-nuclear; Leader RENA ARIKI JONASSEN.
Cook Islands Party (CIP): Rarotonga; f. 1965; Leader HENRY PUNA; Deputy Leader MARK BROWN.

Democratic Party (DP): POB 73, Rarotonga; tel. 21224; e-mail demo1@oyster.net.ck; internet www.democookislands.com; f. 1972; Pres. SEAN WILLIS; Leader ROBERT WIGMORE.
Party Tumu: c/o Parliament, POB 13, Rarotonga; f. 2010; est. as Cook Islands Party Tumu; obliged to change name as above following court ruling; Leader ALBERT NICHOLAS.
Te Kura O Te Au: Rarotonga; f. 2010; based upon People's Movement; advocates reform in accordance with spiritual and cultural values; opposed to Sunday flights to Aitutaki; Leader TARAOTA TOM.

Judicial System

The judiciary comprises the Privy Council, the Court of Appeal and the High Court. The High Court exercises jurisdiction in respect of civil, criminal and land titles cases on all the islands, except for Mangaia, Pukapuka and Mitiaro, where disputes over land titles are settled according to custom. The Court of Appeal hears appeals against decisions of the High Court. The Privy Council, sitting in the United Kingdom, is the final appellate tribunal for the country in civil, criminal and land matters.

Attorney-General: HENRY PUNA.
Solicitor-General: TINGIKA ELIKANA.
President of the Court of Appeal: Sir IAN BARKER.
Chief Justice of the High Court: TOM WESTON, Avarua, Rarotonga; e-mail offices@justice.gov.ck.
Judges of the High Court: GLENDYN CARTER, COLIN NICHOLSON, HETA HINGSTON, CHRISTINE GRICE.

Religion

CHRISTIANITY

The principal denomination is the Cook Islands (Congregational) Christian Church, to which the majority of islanders belong.
Religious Advisory Council of the Cook Islands: POB 763, Rarotonga; tel. 23778; fax 21767; e-mail tpere@oyster.net.ck; f. 1972; six mem. churches; Pres. Pastor TUTAI PERE.

The Roman Catholic Church

The Cook Islands form the diocese of Rarotonga, suffragan to the archdiocese of Suva (Fiji). At 31 December 2007 the diocese contained an estimated 2,471 adherents. The Bishop participates in the Catholic Bishops' Conference of the Pacific, based in Suva.
Bishop of Rarotonga: Rt Rev. STUART FRANCE O'CONNELL, Catholic Diocese, POB 147, Avarua, Rarotonga; tel. 20817; fax 29817; e-mail sbish@oyster.net.ck.

The Anglican Communion

The Cook Islands are within the diocese of Polynesia, part of the Church of the Province of New Zealand. The Bishop of Polynesia is resident in Fiji.

Protestant Churches

Cook Islands Christian Church: Takamoa, POB 93, Rarotonga; tel. 26452; 11,193 mems (1986); Pres. Rev. TANGIMETUA TANGATATUTA; Gen. Sec. WILLIE JOHN.
Seventh-day Adventists: POB 31, Rarotonga; tel. 22851; fax 22852; e-mail umakatu@oyster.net.ck; 732 mems (1998); Pres. UMA KATU.

Other churches active in the islands include the Assembly of God, the Church of Latter-day Saints (Mormons), the Apostolic Church, the Jehovah's Witnesses and the Baptist Church.

BAHÁ'Í FAITH

Administrative Committee of the Bahá'ís of Cook Islands: POB 1, Rarotonga; tel. 20658; e-mail nsacooks@bahai.org.ck; mems resident in six localities; Sec. JANE LAMB.

The Press

Cook Islands Herald: POB 126, Tutakimoa, Rarotonga; e-mail bestread@ciherald.co.ck; internet www.ciherald.co.ck; weekly; Publr GEORGE PITT; Editor CHARLES PITT.
Cook Islands News: POB 15, Rarotonga; tel. 22999; fax 25303; e-mail editor@cookislandsnews.com; internet www.cinews.co.ck; f. 1954; est. by Govt; transferred to private ownership in 1989; 6 a week; mainly English; Editor JOHN WOODS; circ. 2,100.
Cook Islands Star: POB 798, Rarotonga; tel. 29965; e-mail jason@oyster.net.ck; fortnightly; Chief Reporter JASON BROWN.

NEW ZEALAND'S ASSOCIATED STATES

Broadcasting and Communications

TELECOMMUNICATIONS

Telecom Cook Islands Ltd: POB 106, Avarua, Rarotonga; tel. 29680; fax 26174; e-mail sales@telecom.co.ck; internet www.telecom.co.ck; CEO JULES MAHER.

BROADCASTING

Radio

Cook Islands Broadcasting Corpn (CIBC): POB 126, Avarua, Rarotonga; tel. 29460; fax 21907; f. 1989; est. to operate new TV service, and radio service of former Broadcasting and Newspaper Corpn; state-owned; Gen. Man. EMILE KAIRUA.

Radio Cook Islands: tel. 20100; e-mail tunein@radio.co.ck; internet www.radio.co.ck; broadcasts in English and Maori 18 hours daily.

KC Radio: POB 521, Avarua, Rarotonga; tel. 23203; f. 1979; est. as Radio Ikurangi; commercial; operates station ZK1ZD; broadcasts 18 hours daily on FM; Man. Dir and Gen. Man. DAVID SCHMIDT.

Television

Cook Islands Broadcasting Corpn (CIBC): see Radio.

Cook Islands TV (CITV): POB 126, Rarotonga; tel. 29460; fax 21907; f. 1989; operated by Elijah Communications; broadcasts nightly, in English and Maori; 10 hours of local programmes per week; remainder provided by Television New Zealand.

Finance

(cap. = capital; dep. = deposits; m. = million; brs = branches)

Financial Supervisory Commission: POB 594, Avarua, Rarotonga; tel. 20798; fax 21798; e-mail Inquire@fsc.gov.ck; internet www.fsc.gov.ck; f. 1981; est. as Cook Islands Monetary Bd; present name adopted 2003; supervises banks and insurance cos; licenses trustee cos; registers international cos, limited liability cos, trusts, financial institutions, etc.; Commr JOHN HOBBS; Chair. RAYMOND NEWNHAM.

Trustee Companies Association (TCA): Rarotonga; controlling body for the 'offshore' financial sector; Sec. LOU COLVEY.

BANKING

Legislation was adopted in 1981 to facilitate the establishment of 'offshore' banking operations.

Development Bank

Bank of the Cook Islands (BCI): POB 113, Avarua, Rarotonga; tel. 29341; fax 29343; e-mail cash@bci.co.ck; internet www.bci.co.ck; f. 2003; est. by merger of Cook Islands Devt Bank and Cook Islands Savings Bank; 100% state-owned; finances devt projects in all areas of the economy and helps islanders to establish small businesses and industries by providing loans and management advisory assistance; Man. Dir VAINE ARIOKA; 10 brs throughout the Cook Islands.

Commercial Banks

ANZ Cook Islands: ANZ House, Maire Nui Dr., POB 907, Avarua, Rarotonga; tel. 21750; fax 21760; e-mail murphyp@anz.co.uk; internet www.anz.com/cookislands; Gen. Man. PHIL HAYNES.

Capital Security Bank Ltd: POB 906, ANZ House, Rarotonga; tel. 22505; fax 22506; e-mail info@csb.co.ck; internet www.capitalsecuritybank.com; cap. US $1.2m., res US $.4m., dep. US $166.5m. (Dec. 2009); Chair. BRIAN MASON.

Westpac Banking Corpn (Australia): Main Rd, POB 42, Avarua, Rarotonga; tel. 22014; fax 20802; e-mail westpaccookislands@westpac.com.au; internet www.westpac.co.ck/pacific; Man. TERRY SMITH.

INSURANCE

Cook Islands Insurance: POB 44, Rarotonga.

International General Insurance (Cook Islands) Ltd: POB 11, Avarua, Rarotonga; tel. 20514; fax 20667; e-mail info@internationalgeneral.com; internet www.internationalgeneral.com; f. 1982.

Trade and Industry

GOVERNMENT AGENCIES

Business Trade Investment Board: Private Bag, Avarua, Rarotonga; tel. 24296; fax 24298; e-mail info@btib.gov.ck; internet www.btib.gov.ck; f. 1996; est. as replacement for Devt Investment Council; present name adopted 2009, following a merger between the Development Investment Board (DIB) and Small Business Enterprise Centre (SBEC); promotes, monitors and regulates foreign investment, promotes international trade, advises the private sector and Govt, and provides training in business skills; Chair. JAMES BEER; CEO TERRY RANGI.

Cook Islands Investment Corporation: Rarotonga; tel. 29391; fax 29381; e-mail ciic@oyster.net.ck; f. 1998; manages govt assets and shareholding interests; Chair. JULIAN DASHWOOD; CEO JOHN TINI.

Cook Islands Public Service Commission: POB 24, Rarotonga; tel. 29421; fax 21321; e-mail epati@psc.gov.ck; internet www.psc.gov.ck; Commr NAVY EPATI; CEO PRISCILLA MARUARIKI.

Cook Islands Trading Corporation (CITC): Private Bag 1, Avarua, Rarotonga; tel. 22000; fax 20857; e-mail directors@citc.co.ck; internet kiaorana.net/citc; f. 1891; principal importer, distributor, wholesaler and retailer of products in the Cook Islands; Exec. Chair. TREVOR CLARKE; Gen. Man. GAYE WHITTA.

CHAMBER OF COMMERCE

Chamber of Commerce: POB 242, Rarotonga; tel. 20925; fax 20969; e-mail chamber@commerce.co.ck; internet www.cookislandschamber.org; f. 1956; represents the private sector in the Cook Islands; Pres. STEVE ANDERSON.

INDUSTRIAL AND TRADE ASSOCIATION

Pearl Guild of the Cook Islands: POB 257, Rarotonga; tel. 21902; fax 21903; e-mail trevon@oyster.net.ck; f. 1994; monitors standards of quality within the pearl industry and develops marketing strategies; Pres. TREVON BERGMAN.

UTILITIES

Electricity

Te Aponga Uira O Tumutevarovaro (TAUOT) (Rarotonga Electricity Authority): POB 112, Rarotonga; tel. 20054; fax 21944; Chair. TAMARII TUTANGATA.

Water

Water Supply Department: POB 102, Arorangi, Rarotonga; tel. 20034; fax 21134.

TRADE UNIONS

Airport Workers' Association: Rarotonga Int. Airport, POB 90, Rarotonga; tel. 25890; fax 21890; e-mail jessie@airport.gov.ck; f. 1985; Pres. (vacant).

Cook Islands Industrial Union of Waterside Workers: Avarua, Rarotonga.

Cook Islands Workers' Association (CIWA): POB 403, Avarua, Rarotonga; tel. 24422; fax 24423; e-mail ciwa@oyster.net.ck; largest union in the Cook Islands; Pres. ANTHONY TURUA; Gen. Sec. TUAINE MAUNGA; 700 mems (2006).

Transport

ROADS

On Rarotonga a 33-km sealed road encircles the island's coastline. A partly sealed inland road, parallel to the coastal road and known as the Ara Metua, is also suitable for vehicles. In February 2006 it was announced that construction of a cyclone-proof road, which would encompass the flood-prone area west of Rarotonga airport, was to be initiated with aid from the People's Republic of China. Roads on the other islands are mainly unsealed.

SHIPPING

The main ports are on Rarotonga (Avatiu), Penrhyn, Mangaia and Aitutaki. The Cook Islands National Line operates a three-weekly cargo service between the Cook Islands, Tonga, Samoa and American Samoa. In August 2002 the Government approved proposals to enlarge Avatiu Harbour. The project received additional funding from the Ports Authority and from New Zealand. In October 2008 plans further to upgrade Avatiu Wharf, to enable large ships to berth in the harbour, were endorsed by the Government. The Asian Development Bank agreed to lend US $15.5m. for the three-year project.

Apex Maritime: POB 378, Rarotonga; tel. 27651; fax 21138.

Cook Islands National Line: POB 264, Rarotonga; tel. 20374; fax 20855; 30% govt-owned; operates three fleet cargo services between the Cook Islands, Niue, Samoa, Norfolk Island, Tonga and New Zealand; Dirs CHRIS VAILE, GEORGE ELLIS.

Cook Islands Shipping Ltd: POB 2001, Arorangi, Rarotonga; tel. 24905; fax 24906.

NEW ZEALAND'S ASSOCIATED STATES

Ports Authority: POB 84, Rarotonga and Aitutaki; tel. 21921; fax 21191; e-mail info@ports.co.ck; internet www.ports.co.ck; Gen. Man. ANDREW MCBIRNEY.

Reef Shipping Ltd: operates services between New Zealand and the Pacific Islands.

Taio Shipping Ltd: Teremoana Taio, POB 2001, Rarotonga; tel. 24905; fax 24906.

Triad Maritime (1988) Ltd: Rarotonga; fax 20855.

CIVIL AVIATION

An international airport was opened on Rarotonga in 1974. An airport rebuilding project was completed in 2010. Air New Zealand is among the airlines operating services between Rarotonga and other airports in the region. Air Pacific (Fiji) began a twice-weekly service between Nadi and Rarotonga in June 2000, and in August of that year Air New Zealand began a direct service from Rarotonga to Los Angeles, USA.

Airport Authority, Cook Islands: POB 90, Rarotonga; tel. 25890; fax 21890; e-mail aaci@airport.gov.ck; f. 1986; CEO JOE NGAMATA.

Air Rarotonga: POB 79, Rarotonga; tel. 22888; fax 23288; e-mail admin@airraro.co.ck; internet www.airraro.com; f. 1978; privately owned; operates internal passenger and cargo services and charter services to Niue and French Polynesia; Man. Dir EWAN F. SMITH.

Tourism

Tourism is the most important industry in the Cook Islands. According to provisional estimates, in 2009 the number of foreign tourist arrivals reached 101,060, the majority of whom came from New Zealand. Australia and Europe are also important sources of tourists. Visitor arrivals were estimated to have increased to 102,156 in 2010. There were 1,874 beds available at hotels and similar establishments in the islands in 1999. Most of the tourist facilities are to be found on Rarotonga and Aitutaki, but the outer islands also offer attractive scenery. Revenue from tourism was estimated at some US $105m. in 2008.

Cook Islands Tourism Corporation: POB 14, Rarotonga; tel. 29435; fax 21435; e-mail tourism@cookislands.gov.ck; internet www.cookislands.travel; Chair. EWAN F. SMITH; CEO CARMEL BEATTIE.

Education

Free secular education is compulsory for all children between six and 15 years of age. In 1998 there were 26 pre-primary schools, 28 primary schools and 23 secondary schools. In 2007 there were 479 pupils enrolled in pre-primary education, 2,031 in primary education and 1,951 in secondary education. Under the New Zealand Training Scheme, the New Zealand Government offers overseas scholarships in New Zealand, Fiji, Papua New Guinea, Australia and Samoa for secondary and tertiary education, career-training and short-term in-service training. There is an extension centre of the University of the South Pacific (based in Fiji) in the Cook Islands. Budgetary expenditure on education was estimated at $NZ14.7m. in 2007/08, equivalent to 15.4% of total expenditure.

NIUE

Introductory Survey

LOCATION, CLIMATE, LANGUAGE, RELIGION, FLAG, CAPITAL

Niue is a coral island, located in the Pacific Ocean, about 480 km (300 miles) east of Tonga and 930 km (580 miles) west of the southern Cook Islands. Rainfall occurs predominantly during the hottest months, from December to March, when the average temperature is 27°C (81°F). Average annual rainfall is 7,715 mm (298 ins). Niuean, a Polynesian language, and English are spoken. The population is predominantly Christian, with 66% belonging to the Ekalesia Niue, a Protestant church, in 1991. Niue's flag (proportions 1 by 2) is yellow, bearing, in the upper hoist corner, the United Kingdom's Union Flag with a yellow five-pointed star on each arm of the cross of St George and a slightly larger yellow five-pointed star on a blue disc in the centre of the cross. Some 30% of the population resides in Alofi, which is the capital and administrative centre of Niue. Plans to relocate the capital to Fonuakula on the upper plateau of the island were announced following the widespread devastation caused by Cyclone Heta in January 2004.

CONTEMPORARY POLITICAL HISTORY

Historical Context

The first Europeans to discover Niue were members of a British expedition, led by Capt. James Cook, in 1774. Missionaries visited the island throughout the 19th century, and in 1900 Niue was declared a British protectorate. In 1901 Niue was formally annexed to New Zealand as part of the Cook Islands, but in 1904 it was granted a separate administration.

In October 1974 Niue attained 'self-government in free association with New Zealand'. Niueans retain New Zealand citizenship, and a sizeable resident Niuean community exists in New Zealand. The 1991 population census revealed an 11.5% decrease since 1986, and many more Niueans live in New Zealand than on Niue. Robert (from 1982, Sir Robert) Rex, who had been the island's political leader since the early 1950s, was Niue's Premier when it became self-governing, and retained the post at three-yearly general elections in 1975–90.

Domestic Political Affairs

The migration of Niueans to New Zealand has been a cause of concern, and in October 1985 the Government of New Zealand announced its intention to review its constitutional relationship with Niue, with the express aim of preventing further depopulation of the island. In 1987 a six-member committee, comprising four New Zealanders and two Niueans, was formed to examine Niue's economic and social conditions, and to consider the possibility of the island's reversion to the status of a New Zealand-administered territory.

At the 1987 general election all except three of the 20 members of the Niue Assembly were re-elected. The newly founded Niue People's Action Party (NPAP) secured one seat. The NPAP, Niue's only political party, criticized the Government's economic policy, and in particular its apparent inability to account for a substantial amount of the budgetary aid received from New Zealand. A declared aim of the party was to persuade Niueans residing in New Zealand to invest in projects on Niue.

In April 1989 the New Zealand Auditor-General issued a report that was highly critical of the Niuean Government's use of aid money from New Zealand, in particular Rex's preferential treatment of public servants in the allocation of grants. In June Young Vivian, leader of the unofficial NPAP opposition in the Niue Assembly, proposed a motion expressing no confidence in the Government, which was defeated by 13 votes to seven. In November proposed legislation that envisaged the replacement of New Zealand's Governor-General by a Niuean citizen was rejected by the Niue Assembly, owing to the implications for relations with New Zealand.

At the 1990 general election candidates of the NPAP and its sympathizers won 12 of the 20 seats. Earlier disagreements in the NPAP leadership, however, allowed Rex to secure the support of four members previously opposed to his Government. Rex therefore remained Premier.

The announcement in mid-1991 by the New Zealand Government that it was to reduce its aid payments to Niue by about $NZ1m. (a decrease of some 10% on the average annual allocation) caused considerable concern on the island. More than one-quarter of the paid labour force on Niue were employed by the Niue Government, and, following the reduction in aid in July, about 150 (some 25%) lost their jobs. Members of the Government subsequently travelled to New Zealand to appeal against the decision and to request the provision of redundancy payments for the dismissed employees. However, their attempts failed, with the New Zealand Government reiterating its claim that aid had been inefficiently used in the past.

In December 1992 Sir Robert Rex died, and Young Vivian (who had been serving as acting Premier at the time of Rex's death) was unanimously elected Premier by the Government. Legislative elections took place in February 1993, and in the following month the Niue Assembly elected Frank Lui, a former cabinet minister, as Premier. Lui, who defeated Young Vivian by 11 votes to nine, announced a new Cabinet following the election; among the new Premier's stated objectives were the development of tourism and further plans to encourage Niueans resident in New Zealand to return to the island.

In March 1994 Vivian proposed an unsuccessful motion of no confidence in the Government, and a further attempt by the opposition to introduce a similar motion was invalidated in the High Court in October on a procedural matter. However, during the ensuing debate, the Minister of National Planning and Economic Development, Sani Lakatani, resigned in order to join the opposition as its deputy leader, thus leaving the Government with only 10 official supporters in the Niue Assembly. Subsequent opposition demands for the intervention of the Governor-General of New Zealand in dissolving the legislature, in preparation for a fresh general election, were rejected, and, despite Lui's assurance that an early election would take place in order to end the atmosphere of increasing political uncertainty, polls were not held until February 1996. The Premier and his three cabinet ministers were re-elected to their seats, although support among the electorate for candidates of the Niue People's Party (NPP, as the NPAP had been renamed in 1995) and independents appeared fairly equally divided; in one village the result was decided by the toss of a coin when both candidates received an equal number of votes. Frank Lui was re-elected by the Niue Assembly as Premier, defeating Robert Rex, Jr (son of Niue's first Premier) by 11 votes to nine.

The issue of Niue's declining population continued to cause concern, particularly when provisional census figures, published in late 1997, revealed that the island's population was at its lowest recorded level. The Government expressed disappointment that its policy of encouraging Niueans resident in New Zealand to return to the island had failed and announced its intention to consider introducing more lenient immigration laws in an attempt to increase the population.

At a general election on 19 March 1999 Lui lost his seat and subsequently announced his retirement from politics. The Minister of Finance, Aukuso Pavihi, also failed to be re-elected. On 29 March Sani Lakatani, leader of the NPP, was elected Premier by the new Assembly, defeating O'Love Jacobsen by 14 votes to six. Lakatani's stated priority as Premier was to increase Niue's population to at least 3,000; he claimed that the sharp decline in the number of residents constituted a threat to the island's self-governing status.

At the general election, held on 20 April 2002, all 20 incumbent members were returned to the Niue Assembly. Independent candidate Toke Talagi polled the highest number of votes (445), but overall the NPP was victorious. However, despite having polled the second-highest number of votes (428), Sani Lakatani did not command the general support of his party, and a leadership challenge was mounted by his deputy, Young Vivian. Following several days of lobbying within the NPP, Vivian was chosen as Premier. Vivian announced that the party had the support of 10 elected members, having formed a coalition with several independents associated with Toke Talagi. Lakatani was appointed Deputy Premier, however, later that year.

In July 2003 Niue's only formal political party, the Niue People's Party, was dissolved as a result of ongoing disagreement among its membership and the failure of several projects. Opposition member Terry Coe expressed satisfaction with the news, stating that he hoped that party politics would cease henceforth in Niue. Observers also commented that Robert Rex (Niue's widely respected first Premier) had strongly opposed party politics, believing it to cause rifts in families and communities.

In September 2003 the opposition expressed concern that too many government members were travelling overseas on business, and that a significant amount of public money was being used to fund these trips. At the time of the statement seven of the Niue Assembly's 20 members (including two cabinet ministers) were absent on engagements overseas. In the same month it was announced that Niue was to receive US $90,000 from the People's Republic of China in order to build new accommodation for the 300 delegates and visitors who were expected to visit the island for the Pacific Islands Forum (see p. 413) summit meeting in 2004. However, the meeting was relocated, following the widespread devastation of the island by Cyclone Heta in January 2004.

Cyclone Heta, which was described as the worst in the island's recent history, caused the deaths of two people and the destruction of many buildings, along with the loss of most food crops. In addition, there was extensive damage to Niue's infrastructure, communications and coral reef. Relief supplies were sent from New Zealand as part of an initial aid programme worth some US $3.5m. It was estimated that US $23m. would be needed for a rebuilding programme to be carried out over a five-year period. The destruction of Alofi was so severe that the Government announced plans to relocate the island's capital to Fonuakula on the upper plateau.

The Government conducted a survey in September 2004 to assess the current population of the island. However, its apparent reluctance to release the information prompted speculation that more people had left Niue than official reports had previously indicated. When its findings were made public in October some observers disputed the figure of 1,550 (which many believed was higher than the reality, in order to attract more favourable levels of economic assistance). A local newspaper conducted a similar survey and estimated a resident population of some 1,300. In July 2005 the Premier announced that ongoing efforts to attract Niueans back to the island, notably by promoting the farming and fisheries sectors, were to be increased. The people of Niue were also to be granted better access to health care following an agreement concluded in November 2005 between the Niue Ministry for Health and the Counties Manukau District Health Board of New Zealand. The agreement was expected to facilitate the referral of Niuean patients to New Zealand.

In November 2004 Niue's High Commissioner to New Zealand, Hima Takelesi Douglas (hereafter referred to as Hima Takelesi), announced his intention to return to the island to stand for parliament in the forthcoming elections. His stated motivation was a desire to form a stronger partnership with the 20,000 Niueans resident in New Zealand, in an attempt to ensure that Niue retained its current status and did not become incorporated into New Zealand. At the election, held on 30 April 2005, Hima Takelesi succeeded in securing a seat in the Niue Assembly. Young Vivian was re-elected Premier several days later, defeating O'Love Jacobsen (who had founded the Alliance of Independents in December 1991) by 17 votes to three. Vivian's stated priorities for the new Assembly included ongoing efforts to increase Niue's population (see above), the clearing of some 350 derelict homes and continued efforts to increase economic prospects for the island. Moreover, in June Vivian announced his intention to propose political reforms to the legislature, including an increase in the parliamentary term from three years to five years and an increase in the number of cabinet ministers from four to six members.

In February 2007, in an attempt to ease its financial difficulties, the Government announced a 10% decrease in public servants' salaries, along with a reduction in working hours for certain employees and decreases in local grants. In the following month a parliamentary motion of no confidence submitted by the opposition against Premier Vivian, in protest against the Government's alleged financial mismanagement, was defeated. Niue's financial problems were again highlighted in late 2007, when a member of the opposition reported that the island's financial secretary had admitted the Government's bankruptcy.

Recent developments: the 2008 and 2011 elections

On 7 June 2008 a general election was held, with 11 of the 20 parliamentary seats being contested. Three new members were elected to the Niue Assembly, including Togia Sioneholo, hitherto the Secretary of Justice, who defeated Hima Takelesi, the former High Commissioner to New Zealand. On 26 June Toke Talagi, a former Minister of Finance, was elected Premier by 14 parliamentary votes to five, thereby succeeding the incumbent Young Vivian. Talagi assumed responsibility for numerous ministerial portfolios, including planning, economic development, finance, external affairs and environment. O'Love Jacobsen was allocated the portfolios of health and women's affairs, among others. Togia Sioneholo received the justice portfolio, along with other responsibilities. Pokotoa Sipeli was appointed Minister of Agriculture, Forestry and Fisheries, Posts and Telecommunications, and Administrative Services. The new Premier declared that his immediate priority was to address the island's economic situation.

In February 2009, after a delay of almost two years, modified legislation providing for the introduction of a new consumption tax, which would be applicable to visitors to the island, was finally approved by the Niue Assembly. Owing to its likely impact on low-income families, the controversial tax had encountered widespread opposition within the Assembly, and led to the filing of a motion of no confidence in Toke Talagi in early February. However, the Premier easily defeated the motion, by 11 votes to six.

In December 2010 the Cabinet approved, in principle, a proposal mooted by Toke Talagi to construct a casino on Niue in a bid to expand the island's tourism industry. The proposal, if pursued, was expected to require the introduction of legislation to ensure the proper management and operation of the casino.

A general election was held on 7 May 2011, following which Toke Talagi was re-elected as Premier, having secured the support of 12 of the 20 incoming assembly members. Prior to the poll the parliamentary Speaker, Siakimotu Atapana, had announced his retirement after nine years in office. Ahohiva Levi was chosen as his replacement. A new cabinet was appointed.

The 'Offshore' Financial Sector

In late 1999 allegations made by a foreign news agency that Niue was being used by criminal organizations for 'laundering' the proceeds of their illegal activities were strongly denied by Sani Lakatani, the island's Premier. However, the naming of the island in a report by the Financial Action Task Force (FATF, see p. 451) in June 2000 as one of a number of countries and territories that had failed to co-operate in regional efforts to combat money-laundering led the Government to suspend the issue of any further 'offshore' banking licences until stricter regulations governing the financial sector had been introduced. In early 2001 the USA imposed sanctions on Niue (including a ban on transactions with US banks), claiming that the island had not implemented all the recommendations of the report. Lakatani appealed directly to US President George W. Bush to end the embargo, which he described as having had a devastating effect on Niue's economy. The Government stressed its commitment to meeting international requirements in its financial sector but claimed that it was having difficulty in doing so, given its limited legal resources. Moreover, the Premier expressed strong disapproval that a nation as powerful as the USA should inflict such hardship on a small, economically vulnerable island, and he urged other Pacific islands targeted by the report to unite in protest against such impositions. In June 2001 the Government engaged a US law firm in an effort to persuade two banks, Chase Manhattan and Bank of New York, to remove their bans on the transfer of some $NZ1m. to Niue via the business registry in Panama that the Government used for its 'offshore' tax activity.

Having failed to meet an FATF deadline in August 2001, in February 2002 Niue pledged to repeal its 'offshore' banking legislation. Premier Sani Lakatani was also considering closing down international business registrations based in Niue. The FATF announced in April that, in view of the island's commitment to improving the transparency of its tax and regulatory systems, the organization was to remove Niue from its list of non-co-operative territories; the decision was duly implemented in October. The bank-licensing legislation was repealed in June.

Although by 2002 most 'offshore' financial activity had ostensibly ended, the sector once again became the focus of scrutiny in February 2010 after the French Government included Niue on a 'black list' of nations accused of a lack of transparency in tax reporting. Consequently, the French Government announced that it would impose a 50% tax upon transactions between France and the black-listed nations. Furthermore, in April 2009 Niue was placed on a 'grey list' of nations compiled by the Organisation for Economic Co-operation and Development (OECD, see p. 376) owing to the island's failure to have established the requisite number of tax information exchange agreements. Niue remained on the 'grey list' in mid-2011.

Relations with New Zealand

In March 2000 a Niue-New Zealand joint consultative committee met, for the first time, in Alofi to consider the two sides' future constitutional relationship. Later that year the committee proposed to conduct a survey of islanders' views and to consider all options, from reintegration with New Zealand to full independence. A meeting of the joint committee took place in March 2001 in Wellington at which the issues of New Zealand aid and reciprocal immigration laws were discussed, as well as options for Niue's future constitutional status. In early 2001 Hima Takelesi was appointed Niue's first High Commissioner to New Zealand. New Zealand remained committed to annual assistance of $NZ6.3m. in the years 2001–03. At New Zealand's 2001 census, a total of 20,148 Niueans were recorded as resident in New Zealand. Discussions took place in Wellington in March 2003 between the New Zealand Prime Minister, Helen Clark, and Niue's Premier, Young Vivian. Topics debated included budgetary assistance, a review of the island's development plan and the continued migration of islanders from the territory to New Zealand.

In October 2004 Helen Clark made an official visit to Niue to celebrate the 30-year anniversary of the island's attainment of self-governing status. She urged expatriate Niueans to return to the island and support efforts to regenerate its infrastructure and economy. She also announced a programme to introduce the Niuean language into the education curriculum from pre-school level onwards by 2006, as part of Taoga Niue, an initiative aimed at preserving traditional customs and cultural practices on the island. The Halavaka ke he Monuina Arrangement (HkhMA), a bilateral agreement signed in October 2004, aimed to facilitate closer co-operation between the various government agencies of Niue and New Zealand. The arrangement represented a major shift in New Zealand's approach to the management of its relationship with Niue. In addition, Clark confirmed that $NZ6m. was to be made available to rebuild the hospital destroyed by Cyclone Heta. The new hospital, located at Kaimiti, opened in March 2006. In April of that year New Zealand and France agreed jointly to finance the construction of a government administration building on Niue. Meanwhile, in February Anton Ojala replaced Kurt Meyer as New Zealand High Commissioner to Niue; Ojala was in turn replaced by Brian Smythe in January 2008. Smythe departed from the post in January 2010, to take up a diplomatic appointment in Malaysia, and was replaced on an interim basis by John Bryan. In September Mark Blumsky was appointed as his permanent replacement.

The New Zealand Minister of Foreign Affairs, Murray McCully, visited Niue in January 2009 and again in October. The Government of Niue hoped that New Zealand might provide financial assistance for the reopening of a fish-processing plant, a joint venture between the Niuean Government and the Auckland-based Reef Group, which had closed in 2007 and resulted in many job losses (see Economic Affairs). However, McCully was reluctant to support the reopening of the plant, since a similar operation in neighbouring American Samoa had closed in September 2009. In August 2010 Reef announced that it was seeking bids for a stake in, or sole ownership of, the plant.

Premier Talagi criticized the New Zealand Government in June 2009 for withholding investment funds pledged as part of the HkhMA, particularly a $NZ2m. tranche that had been allocated for the island's tourism industry. In the following month, during New Zealand Prime Minister John Key's first visit to Niue and amid rising tensions, Key emphasized that the tourism aid would not be dispensed without a more detailed plan of how it was to be spent. In late 2009 the New Zealand Government expressed a willingness to finance an expansion of the island's sole hotel resort, alongside concurrent reforms to the taxation and property ownership laws in Niue; however, no funds had been released by mid-2011. In May 2010 Minister of Foreign Affairs McCully stated that international hotel groups had expressed an interest in involvement in the expansion of the resort.

A report published by a New Zealand parliamentary committee in December 2010 included a critical assessment of Niue, contending that 40 years of New Zealand aid to the island had yielded 'almost no return'. The report urged Niue to reduce the size of its parliament, arguing that a 20-member legislature for an electorate comprising just 600 voters was 'an abuse of trust and responsibility', and noted that the island was caught in a 'vicious cycle' in which its economic difficulties were both exacerbated by, and reflected in, its ongoing population decline. The committee concluded that Niue could never be a sustainable economic entity, and proposed that the island be redesignated as a retirement village in which inhabitants would be granted access to the same services as other New Zealand citizens. The proposals received a mixed response, with some, including the Niuean Minister of Health, Public Works, Women's Affairs and the Niue Power Corporation, O'Love Jacobsen, arguing that the proposal raised serious questions about the long-term constitutionality of Niue; others contended that a harmonization of services between New Zealand and Niue would attract expatriate Niueans back to the island, which would provide a stimulus to its economy. In late December Premier Toke Talagi contested that the island economy was viable and that the most significant impediment to economic growth and development was the New Zealand Government, which, he argued, was frustrating efforts to expand the Niuean tourism sector owing to a reluctance to release funds. In March 2011 opposition legislator Terry Coe suggested that Niue forgo development aid pledged by New Zealand for the next few years and that the funds be redirected to help rebuild Christchurch following two earthquakes that caused significant damage to the New Zealand city in September 2010 and February 2011.

Foreign Affairs

Following almost 10 years of technical and political consultations, Niue and the USA signed a maritime boundary treaty in May 1997, delineating the precise boundary between the territorial waters of Niue and American Samoa. In October 2003 Niue's Premier issued a statement inviting the residents of Tuvalu (whose continued existence on those islands was increasingly threatened by rising sea levels) to migrate to Niue. The Government of Tuvalu subsequently requested that Niue produce a memorandum of understanding giving formal details of this invitation and of the rights that Tuvaluans would enjoy on Niue. Further discussions between officials from the two Governments took place in June 2005. In October 2006 Niue agreed to join the Regional Assistance Mission to Solomon Islands (RAMSI), with the deployment of two Niuean police officers to Solomon Islands. In August 2008 Niue hosted the annual summit meeting of the Pacific Islands Forum, at which the Niue Declaration on Climate Change was endorsed. In May 2009 an FAO conference on Pacific food security, and a meeting of the Pacific Islands Forum Fisheries Agency, were convened in Niue. The island hosted a meeting of the Pacific Island Forum ministers responsible for economic affairs in October 2010 and the Pacific Climate Change Roundtable in March 2011.

In August 2010 China expressed interest in financing an expansion of Niue's hotel resort and sent a delegation to the island to discuss the proposal with the Niuean Government. A deal was subsequently agreed providing for Chinese funding of a new US $1.5m. hotel on Niue, which was expected to open in 2012. In February 2011 China was reported to have provided funding for an extension of Niue's airport terminal and the erection of security fencing at the airport. Following a meeting with the Chinese ambassador in that month, Premier Toke Talagi hailed the burgeoning bilateral relationship and expressed his belief that closer co-operation would be forged between the two countries, particularly in the tourism and fisheries sectors.

CONSTITUTION AND GOVERNMENT

Under the Niue Constitution Act 1974, the island enjoys self-government in free association with New Zealand. The New Zealand Government remains responsible for the island's defence and external affairs, although in practice Niue may conduct its own external relations. Executive government is carried out by the Premier and three other ministers. Legislation is the responsibility of the Niue Assembly, which has 20 members (14 village representatives and six elected on a common roll), but New Zealand, if called upon to do so by the Assembly, will also legislate for the island. There is a New

Zealand representative in Niue, whose status was upgraded to that of High Commissioner in 1993.

REGIONAL AND INTERNATIONAL CO-OPERATION

Niue is a member of the Pacific Community (see p. 410) and of the Pacific Islands Forum (see p. 413). It is an associate member of the UN's Economic and Social Commission for Asia and the Pacific (ESCAP, see p. 37). In 2000 Niue became a signatory of the Cotonou Agreement (see p. 327) with the European Union (EU).

ECONOMIC AFFAIRS

Niue's gross domestic product (GDP) was estimated at $NZ17.3m. in 2003, when GDP per head was estimated at $NZ10,048. The population decreased at an average annual rate of 2.3% in 1991–2001.

Agriculture, forestry and fishing contributed 25.6% of GDP in 2006. According to the census of 2006, the sector engaged 15.9% of the employed labour force. Two-thirds of the land surface is uncultivable, but many households practise subsistence gardening. The principal crops are coconuts, taro, yams, cassava and sweet potatoes. A taro export scheme was successfully introduced in the early 1990s, and production of the crop increased by more than 500% in 1993. Exports of taro, principally to New Zealand, contributed nearly 93% of total export earnings in 2003, being facilitated by a new regular shipping service. Plans to increase the production of vanilla as an export crop were discussed in 2003, but the promising crop was destroyed by the cyclone of early 2004. The reintroduction of vanilla cultivation, as well as that of organic nonu (or noni, a fruit renowned for its medicinal properties), for export was initiated during 2004 as part of the Government's post-cyclone recovery programme. Honey is also produced for export. Pigs, poultry, goats and beef cattle are raised, mainly for local consumption. An island development plan for 2003 included proposals to develop Niue's fishing industry by employing a fleet of used Korean fishing vessels. The construction of a fish-processing factory at Amanau was completed in 2004. It was estimated that the new plant might raise $NZ9m. annually in revenue. Fishing licences to five New Zealand vessels and four Samoan vessels were issued. However, a series of problems resulted in operational difficulties. Operations were suspended in 2007. Niue remained hopeful that the plant, an important source of employment for islanders, might resume activities. A buyer for the plant was being sought in early 2011.

Industry (including mining, manufacturing, construction and utilities) contributed only 5.3% of GDP in 2006. In the same year industry engaged 17.1% of the labour force. The manufacturing sector has been very limited, accounting for only 1.5% of GDP in 2006. A noni juice factory also opened in October 2004. Exploration for deposits of uranium continued on the island in 2005, but in November it was announced that no commercially viable resources had been identified. The extensive damage caused by Cyclone Heta led to much activity in the construction sector from early 2004, as rebuilding programmes commenced.

The island remains dependent upon imported diesel fuel for its energy requirements. In collaboration with the international environmentalist group Greenpeace, in December 2005 Niue confirmed its commitment to the development of wind power, hoping to become one of the first locations in the world to be completely reliant on renewable energy sources. In April 2009 Niue signed a memorandum of understanding on the Pacific Petroleum Project, a regional initiative that aimed to reduce the energy costs of the Pacific islands through collective negotiations for the bulk procurement of petroleum supplies.

The services sector contributed 69.1% of GDP in 2006. In that year the sector engaged 66.9% of the labour force. The Government is the most important employer, engaging 512 members of the paid labour force in December 2004, when an estimated 269 people were employed in the private sector. Tourism has begun to make a significant contribution to the economy, and arrivals by air reached 4,662 in 2009. In comparison with the previous year, visitor arrivals were reported to have increased by 33.3% in 2010, with arrivals from Germany and the United Kingdom estimated to have doubled. Receipts from tourism amounted to US $2.0m. in 2008. From the 1990s various attempts to secure new sources of revenue in Niue included the leasing of the island's telecommunications facilities to foreign companies for use in specialist telephone services. However, this enterprise (which earned the island an estimated $NZ1.5m. per year) caused considerable controversy when it was revealed that Niue's telephone code had been made available to companies offering personal services considered indecent by the majority of islanders. The sale of the internet domain name '.nu' yielded significant revenue but proved similarly controversial (see below).

Niue records an annual trade deficit, with imports generally far exceeding exports. The value of Niue's exports totalled only $NZ27,000 in 2008, while the cost of the island's imports reached almost $NZ11.0m. New Zealand is the island's main trading partner, supplying more than 95% of its imports in 2008. The principal exports in 2008 were taro, coconut and vanilla The principal imports were mineral products (which constituted 38.3% of the total cost of imports), base metals, machinery and prepared foodstuffs.

The budget for 2008/09 projected expenditure of $NZ20.3m. and revenue of $NZ20.4m. In 2009/10 development assistance from New Zealand totalled $NZ9.2m., of which $NZ7.6m. was for the purposes of budgetary support. Development assistance from New Zealand totalled $NZ 19.0m. in 2010/11. Meanwhile, the Halavaka Arrangement announced in late 2004 (see Contemporary Political History) provided funding of $NZ20m., to be disbursed over five years. Other donors include Australia, the People's Republic of China and France. With the objective of providing Niue with an independent source of future revenue, in 2006 the Niue International Trust Fund was established, with a total contribution of $NZ10m. from New Zealand and Australia. By 2010 the trust fund's assets stood at $NZ36m. Revenue from the fund was not expected to be drawn before 2014. The annual rate of inflation averaged 4.2% in 2000–08. Compared with the previous year, consumer prices increased by 9.1% in 2008 and by 11.6% in 2009. The unemployment rate was estimated at 13.8% of the labour force in 2001.

Niue's entire economy was severely affected by Cyclone Heta, which struck the island in January 2004 causing extensive damage to housing, infrastructure and crops. The subsequent recovery programme, known as New Niue or Niue Foou, emphasized rebuilding works and industrial projects. New Zealand assisted Niue's post-cyclone recovery programme. In addition to the revenue derived from the leasing of telecommunications facilities to overseas companies (see above), Niue's earnings from the sale of its internet domain name '.nu' led to further controversy when a report published in July 2004 claimed that the island was hosting some 3m. pages of pornographic material via its nu domain. In March 2008, furthermore, an international software security company reported that, along with Tokelau, in per caput terms Niue had become one of the world's worst offenders with regard to the relaying of unsolicited e-mails. Upon taking office in June 2008, Premier Toke Talagi stated that his immediate intention was to focus on the economy of Niue. The priorities of his administration were to be the control of government expenditure and the creation of new sources of revenue. In April 2009 a controversial new consumption tax entered into effect (see Contemporary Political History). Levied at a rate of 12.5%, the tax on goods and services was expected to make a substantial contribution to government revenue. Revised tax legislation was also implemented. The banking sector has remained undeveloped, but in early 2011 it was reported that the island's first automated teller machines were to be installed. The Government of Toke Talagi identified the tourism sector as a potential source of higher income. However, constraints on development included the lack of business expertise and dearth of professional skills among the islanders. A major project to extend the Matavai Resort, Niue's main hotel, was under way in 2011. The refurbishment was to be funded by New Zealand aid of almost US $5m., and a trust company was established to oversee the project. Meanwhile, the establishment of a casino was under consideration, and capacity on Air New Zealand's weekly flight to Niue was increased. Furthermore, a Chinese-financed hotel was scheduled to open in 2012. Fisheries and mining have been identified as additional sources of potential revenue.

PUBLIC HOLIDAYS

2012 (provisional): 2 January (for New Year's Day), 3 January (for Commission Day), 6 February (Waitangi Day, anniversary of 1840 treaty), 6–9 April (Easter), 25 April (ANZAC Day, anniversary of 1915 landing at Gallipoli), 4 June (Queen's Official Birthday), 16 October (Constitution Day celebrations), 22 October (Peniamina's Day), 25–26 December (Christmas).

Statistical Survey

Source (unless otherwise indicated): Statistics Unit, Economics, Planning, Development Office, Government of Niue, POB 95, Alofi; tel. 4219; fax 4148; e-mail statsniue@mail.gov.nu; internet www.spc.int/prism/country/nu/stats.

AREA AND POPULATION

Area: 261.5 sq km (100.9 sq miles).

Population: 1,788 at census of 7 September 2001; 1,625 (males 802, females 823) at census of September 2006. An estimated 22,473 Niueans lived in New Zealand at the time of the 2006 census. Mid-2010 (official estimate, on-island residents): 1,494.

Density (at mid-2010): 5.7 per sq km.

Population by Age and Sex (official estimates at mid-2011, on-island residents): 0–14: 383 (males 187, females 196); 15–64: 929

NEW ZEALAND'S ASSOCIATED STATES

Niue

(males 482, females 447); *65 and over:* 182 (males 85, females 97); *Total* 1,494 (males 754, females 740).

Ethnic Groups (2001 census, declared ethnicity): Niuean 1,399; Caucasian 81; Pacific Islander 182; Niuean/Caucasian 28; Niuean/Pacific Islander 42; Asian 4.

Principal Villages (population at mid-2010, official estimates): Alofi (capital) 540; Hakupu 138; Avatele 137; Tamakautoga 115; Tuapa 105.

Births, Marriages and Deaths: *2009* (including Niueans temporarily resident in New Zealand): Live births 31; Marriages 12; Deaths 12. *2010* (Secretariat of the Pacific Community estimate): Birth rate 14.8 per 1,000; Death rate 9.7 per 1,000 (Source: Pacific Regional Information System).

Life Expectancy (years at birth, WHO estimates): 71 (males 64; females 79) in 2008. Source: WHO, *World Health Statistics*.

Immigration and Emigration (2009): Arrivals 6,380; Departures 6,426.

Economically Active Population (2006 census, persons aged 15 years and over): Agriculture, forestry and fishing 119; Mining, electricity, gas, water and construction 61; Manufacturing 67; Trade, restaurants and hotels 84; Transport, storage and communications 43; Finance, real estate, business activities 33; Public administration 180; Education and health 117; Community, social and personal services 43; *Total employed* 747. Note: figures exclude subsistence workers. *Paid Employment* (December 2004): Government sector 512 (males 294, females 218); Private sector (estimates) 269 (males 143, females 126).

HEALTH AND WELFARE

Key Indicators

Total Fertility Rate (children per woman, 2006): 2.6.

Under-5 Mortality Rate (per 1,000 live births, 2008): 28.

Physicians (per 1,000 head, 2004): 2.0.

Hospital Beds (per 1,000 head, 2006): 4.9.

Health Expenditure (2007): US $ per head (PPP): 1,123.

Health Expenditure (2007): % of GDP: 18.6.

Health Expenditure (2007): public (% of total): 98.9.

For sources and definitions, see explanatory note on p. vi.

AGRICULTURE, ETC.

Principal Crops (metric tons, 2008, FAO estimates): Taro 3,300; Sweet potatoes 260; Yams 130; Coconuts 2,600; Bananas 80; Lemons and limes 130. Note: No data were available for individual crops in 2009. *Aggregate Production* ('000 metric tons, 2009, may include official, semi-official or estimated data): Vegetables (incl. melons) 130; Fruits (excl. melons) 610.

Livestock (year ending September 2008, FAO estimates): Cattle 115; Pigs 2,100; Chickens 15,000. Note: No data were available for 2009.

Livestock Products (metric tons, 2008 unless otherwise stated, FAO estimates): Pig meat 65; Chicken meat 18; Cows' milk 55; Hen eggs 12 (2009); Honey 7.

Forestry (cu m, 1985): Roundwood removals 613; Sawnwood production 201.

Fishing (metric tons, live weight, 2008, FAO estimate): Total catch 200.

Source: FAO.

INDUSTRY

Production (2007, estimate): Electric energy 3 million kWh. Source: UN Industrial Commodity Statistics Database.

FINANCE

Currency and Exchange Rates: 100 cents = 1 New Zealand dollar ($NZ). For details, see Tokelau.

Budget ($NZ '000, year ending 30 June 2006, provisional): Internal revenue 14,206; New Zealand budgetary support 6,953; *Total revenue* 21,159; Recurrent expenditure 21,417; Capital 90; *Total expenditure* 21,507. *2006/07* ($NZ '000, forecasts): Internal revenue 16,499; New Zealand budgetary support 6,915; Total revenue 23,414; Recurrent expenditure 23,364; Capital projects 50; Total expenditure 23,414. *2008/09* ($NZ '000, forecasts): Total revenue 20,441; Total expenditure 20,259.

Overseas Aid ($NZ '000, 2010/11, provisional): Official development assistance from New Zealand 19,000. Source: Ministry of Foreign Affairs and Trade, Wellington.

Cost of Living (Consumer Price Index, average of quarterly figures; base: July–Sept. 2003 = 100): All items 113.6 in 2007; 123.9 in 2008; 138.3 in 2009.

Gross Domestic Product ($NZ '000 in current prices): 17,771 in 2004; 19,441 in 2005; 20,541 in 2006.

Gross Domestic Product by Economic Activity ($NZ '000 in current prices, 2006): Agriculture, forestry and fishing 4,913; Mining and quarrying 47; Manufacturing 282; Electricity, gas and water 494; Construction 196; Trade 2,344; Restaurants and hotels 819; Transport, storage and communications 1,057; Financial and business services, real estate, etc. 1,596; Public administration 6,941; Other community, social and personal services 534; *Sub-total* 19,223; *Less* Imputed bank service charge 334; *GDP at factor cost* 18,889; Indirect taxes *Less* Subsidies 1,664; *GDP in purchasers' values* 20,541.

EXTERNAL TRADE

Principal Commodities ($NZ '000, 2008): *Imports c.i.f.*: Animals and animal products 679; Prepared foodstuffs 1,250; Mineral products 4,206; Chemical products 321; Plastics and rubber 195; Wood and wood products 403; Base metals and articles thereof 1,176; Machinery, mechanical appliances and electrical equipment 915; Miscellaneous manufactured articles 461; Total (incl. others) 10,968. *Exports f.o.b.*: Taro 24; Coconut 2; Vanilla 1; Total (incl. others) 27.

Principal Trading Partners ($NZ '000, 2008): *Imports c.i.f.*: China, People's Republic 113; Japan 296; New Zealand 10,478; Total (incl. others) 10,968. *Exports f.o.b.*: Total 27.

TRANSPORT

Road Traffic (2001 census): Passenger cars 323; Motorcycles 134; Vans 170; Trucks 74; Pick-ups 76; Buses 11.

International Shipping: *Ship Arrivals* (1989): Yachts 20; Merchant vessels 22; Total 42. *Freight Traffic* (metric tons, 1989, official estimates): Unloaded 3,410; Loaded 10.

Civil Aviation: *Passengers* (1992): Arrivals 3,500; Departures 3,345. *Freight Traffic* (metric tons, 1992): Unloaded 41.6; Loaded 15.7.

TOURISM

Foreign Tourist Arrivals (by air): 3,463 in 2007; 4,748 in 2008; 4,662 in 2009.

Tourist Arrivals by Country of Residence (2009): Australia 461; New Zealand 2,690; United Kingdom 47; USA 157; Total (incl. others) 4,662.

Tourism Receipts (US $ million, incl. passenger transport): 1.1 in 2006; 1.6 in 2007; 2.0 in 2008. Source: World Tourism Organization.

COMMUNICATIONS MEDIA

Telephones (2009): 1,100 main lines in use*.

Mobile Cellular Telephones (2009): 1,100 units in use*.

Radio Receivers (2006 census): 373 per 1,000 persons.

Television Receivers (2006 census): 519 per 1,000 persons.

Personal Computers (2001 census): 77 in use.

Internet Users (2009): 1,100*.

Daily Newspaper (2004): 1.

Non-daily Newspaper (2004): 1†.

*Source: International Telecommunication Union.
†Source: UNESCO.

EDUCATION

Pre-primary and Primary (2006): 1 school; 212 pupils (males 104, females 108); 20 teachers (males 3, females 17).

Secondary (2006): 1 school; 191 pupils (males 102, females 89); 31 teachers (males 9, females 22).

Source: Department of Education, Niue.

Pupil-teacher Ratio (primary education, UNESCO estimate): 11.9 in 2004/05. Source: UNESCO Institute for Statistics.

Directory

The Government

New Zealand High Commissioner: Mark Blumsky.
Secretary to Government: Richard Hipa.

CABINET
(May 2011)

Premier, Chairman of the Cabinet and Minister responsible for Finance, Customs and Revenue and Government Assets, Premier's Department (Civil Aviation, Crown Law, External Affairs, Planning, Economic Development and Statistics), Infrastructure, Transport, Public Service Commission, Police and National Security, Tourism, Meteorological Services and Climate Change, Environment, Youth and Sports, Religion and Taoga Niue: Toke Tufukia Talagi.
Minister of Education, Agriculture, Forestry and Fisheries, Administrative Services and Niue Broadcasting Corpn: Pokotoa Sipeli.
Minister of Public Works, Niue Power Corpn, Posts and Telecommunications and Bulk Fuel: Kupa Magatogia.
Minister of Health, Community Affairs, and Justice, Lands and Survey: Joan Viliamu.

GOVERNMENT OFFICES

All ministries are in Alofi.
Office of the New Zealand High Commissioner: POB 78, Tapeu, Alofi; tel. 4022; fax 4173; e-mail sog.hipa@mail.gov.nu; internet www.nu.
Office of the Secretary to Government: POB 40, Alofi; tel. 4220; fax 4232; e-mail ctatui.sog@mail.gov.nu.

Legislature

ASSEMBLY

The Niue Assembly or Fono Ekepule has 20 members (14 village representatives and six members elected on a common roll). The most recent general election was held on 7 May 2011.
Speaker: Ahohiva Levi.

Political Organizations

There have been no active political parties on Niue since the disbanding, in 2003, of the Niue People's Pary (f. 1987—Niue's sole political party to date). All politicians on the island are de facto independents.

Judicial System

The Chief Justice of the High Court, which exercises civil and criminal jurisdiction, and the Judge of the Land Court, which is concerned with litigation over land and titles, visit Niue quarterly. In addition, locally appointed lay justices exercise limited criminal and civil jurisdiction. Appeals against High Court judgments are heard in the Court of Appeal of Niue, while appeals against Land Court judgments are heard in the Land Appellate Court. Established in 1992, sessions of the Court of Appeal of Niue are usually held in the New Zealand capital of Wellington. In April 2009, however, for the first time the four New Zealand judges heard various cases, including several land disputes, on Niue itself.
Chief Justice of the High Court: Patrick Savage.
Registrar of the High Court: Justin Kamupala.

Religion

About 63% of the population belong to the Ekalesia Niue, a Protestant organization, which had 1,093 adherents at the time of the 2001 census. Within the Roman Catholic Church, which had 128 adherents (equivalent to 7.4% of the population) in 2001, Niue forms part of the diocese of Tonga. The Church of Jesus Christ of Latter-day Saints (Mormon—which had 158 adherents in 2001), the Seventh-day Adventists, the Jehovah's Witnesses and the Church of God of Jerusalem are also represented.
Ekalesia Niue: Head Office, POB 25, Alofi; tel. 4195; fax 4352; e-mail ekalesia.niue@niue.nu; f. 1846; est. by London Missionary Society, became Ekalesia Niue in 1966; Pres. Rev. Matagi Vilitama; Gen. Sec. Rev. Arthur Pihigia.

The Press

Niue Business News: 20 Lautamina Rd, Mutalau 110175; tel. 3317; fax 4010; e-mail sioneholof@gmail.com; f. 2000; owned by Tropical Suppliers; electronic; previously publ. in print as *Niue Economic Review*; CEO Frank Sioneholo.
Niue Star: weekly; Niuean and English; publ. in Alofi until destruction of office by Cyclone Heta in 2004; operations transferred to Auckland, New Zealand; Publr Mike Jackson; circ. 800.

Broadcasting and Communications

TELECOMMUNICATIONS

In 2003 Niue became the first location in the world to have a national wireless internet system allowing access from anywhere on the island by means of solar-powered aerials attached to coconut palms. A four-fold expansion of the island's internet capacity was announced in March 2010.
Director of Posts and Telecommunications: POB 37, Alofi; tel. 4000; fax 4010.
Telecom Niue: POB 37, Alofi; tel. 4002; Dir Tuli Heka (acting).

BROADCASTING

Radio

Broadcasting Corporation of Niue: POB 68, Alofi; tel. 4026; fax 4217; operates radio and TV services; govt-owned; Chair. Neal Morrissey; CEO Trevor Tiakia; Gen. Man. Patrick Lino.
Radio Sunshine: broadcasts in English and Niuean between 6 a.m. and 10 p.m. Mon.–Sat.

Television

Broadcasting Corporation of Niue: see Radio.
Television Niue broadcasts in English and Niuean six days a week from 5 p.m. to 11 p.m.

Finance

DEVELOPMENT BANK

Niue Development Bank: POB 34, Alofi; tel. 4335; fax 4290; e-mail devbank@niue.nu; f. 1993; govt-owned; began operations July 1994; Chair. Misiata Tasmania; Gen. Man. Vaine Pasisi.

COMMERCIAL BANK

Bank South Pacific Ltd: POB 76, Main St, Alofi; tel. 4220; fax 4043; e-mail bsp@niue.nu; internet www.bsp.com.pg/niue/niue.htm; acquired from Westpac Banking Corpn in Sept. 2004; Man. Ann Pesamino.

Trade and Industry

GOVERNMENT AGENCIES

Business Advisory Service: Alofi; tel. 4228.
Office of Economic Affairs, Planning and Development, Statistics and Trade and Investment: POB 42, Alofi; tel. 4148; e-mail business.epdsu@mail.gov.nu; responsible for planning and financing activities in the agricultural, tourism, industrial sectors, business advisory and trade and investment.

CHAMBER OF COMMERCE

Niue Chamber of Commerce: POB 160, Alofi; tel. 4399; fax 4010; e-mail chamber@niue.nu; internet live.niuechamber.com; Pres. Avi Rubin.

UTILITIES

Niue Power Corporation: POB 198, Alofi; tel. 4119; fax 4385; e-mail gm.npc@mail.gov.nu; Gen. Man. Speedo Hetutu.

TRADE UNION

Public Service Association: Alofi.

Transport

ROADS

There are 123 km of all-weather roads and 106 km of access and plantation roads. A total of 788 motor vehicles were registered in 2001. The road network was extensively damaged by Cyclone Heta in January 2004. In mid-2004 it was estimated that some 48 km of sealed roads were clear and in good condition.

SHIPPING

The best anchorage is an open roadstead at Alofi, the largest of Niue's 14 villages. Work to extend a small wharf at Alofi began in mid-1998 with US assistance. The New Zealand Shipping Corporation operates a monthly service between New Zealand, Nauru and Niue. Fuel supplies are delivered by a tanker (the *Pacific Explorer*) from Fiji. In December 2002 the Government signed an agreement with Reef Shipping Ltd to provide a service to New Zealand every three to four weeks.

CIVIL AVIATION

Hanan International Airport has a total sealed runway of 2,350 m, following the completion of a 700 m extension in 1995, with New Zealand assistance. In 2005 Air New Zealand began a weekly service between Auckland and Niue. In early 2011 the provision of funding by the People's Republic of China, to finance improvements that included the extension of the airport terminal, was confirmed.

Tourism

Niue has a small but significant tourism industry (specializing in holidays based on activities such as diving, rock-climbing, caving and game fishing), which has benefited from an increase in the frequency of flights between the island and New Zealand. The Matavai Resort provides the main tourist facilities; the resort was in the process of being extended in 2011. A second hotel, financed by Chinese interests, was expected to open in 2012. Tourist receipts (including passenger transport) totalled US $2.0m. in 2008. A total of 4,662 people arrived by air to visit Niue in 2009. Most visitors are from New Zealand. In comparison with the previous year, visitor arrivals were reported to have increased by 33.3% in 2010, with arrivals from Germany and the United Kingdom estimated to have doubled.

Niue Tourism Office: POB 42, Alofi; tel. 4224; fax 4225; e-mail niuetourism@mail.gov.nu; internet www.niueisland.com; Dir of Tourism TANYA LIAMOTU (acting).

Education

Education is free and compulsory between six and 16 years of age (the school-leaving age having been raised from 14 in 1998). In 1987 the island's seven village primary schools were closed and a single national primary school was opened at Halamahaga. In 2006 this bilingual (Niuean/English) primary school had 20 teachers and an enrolment of 212 pupils. There was one secondary school at Paliati, with a teaching staff of 31 and a total enrolment of 191 pupils in 2006. Higher education takes place at the Niue Extension Centre of the University of the South Pacific (based in Fiji), on government training schemes or by correspondence. Some study overseas, in the Pacific region and New Zealand. A private medical school opened in Niue in 2000 but closed in the following year. A private university offering online business and information technology courses opened in late 2003.

NICARAGUA

Introductory Survey

LOCATION, CLIMATE, LANGUAGE, RELIGION, FLAG, CAPITAL

The Republic of Nicaragua lies in the Central American isthmus, bounded by the Pacific Ocean to the west and by the Caribbean Sea to the east. Its neighbours are Honduras, to the north, and Costa Rica, to the south. The climate is tropical, with an annual average temperature of 25.5°C (78°F). The rainy season extends from May to October. The national language is Spanish, although English is also spoken on the Caribbean coast. Almost all of the inhabitants profess Christianity, and a majority are Roman Catholics. The national flag (proportions 3 by 5) has three equal horizontal stripes, of blue, white and blue, with the state emblem (a triangle enclosing a dark blue sea from which rise five volcanoes, in green, surmounted by a Phrygian cap from which extend white rays and, at the top, a rainbow, all encircled by the words, in gold capitals, 'República de Nicaragua' and 'América Central') in the centre of the white stripe; the same flag without the state emblem is an alternative version of the civil flag. The capital is Managua.

CONTEMPORARY POLITICAL HISTORY

Historical Context

Nicaragua was under Spanish rule from the 16th century until 1821. It then became part of the Central American Federation until 1838. From 1927 US troops were based in Nicaragua at the request of the Government, which was opposed by a guerrilla group, led by Augusto César Sandino. In 1933, following the establishment of the National Guard (commanded by Gen. Anastasio Somoza García), the US troops left Nicaragua. Sandino was assassinated in 1934, but some of his followers ('Sandinistas') continued actively to oppose the new regime. Somoza seized power in a coup in 1935 and took office as President in 1936. Apart from a brief interlude in the late 1940s, Somoza remained as President until September 1956, when he was assassinated. However, the Somoza family continued to dominate Nicaraguan politics until 1979.

Domestic Political Affairs

In 1962 the left-wing Frente Sandinista de Liberación Nacional (FSLN—Sandinista National Liberation Front) was formed with the object of overthrowing the Somozas by revolution. Gen. Anastasio Somoza Debayle, son of the former dictator, became President in May 1967, holding office until April 1972. The Congreso Nacional (National Congress) was dissolved, and a triumvirate ruled until Gen. Somoza was re-elected President in September 1974. In January 1978 the murder of Pedro Joaquín Chamorro Cardenal, the leader of the opposition coalition and the editor of *La Prensa* (the country's only independent newspaper), provoked violent demonstrations against the Government.

In June 1979 the FSLN announced the formation of a provisional Junta of National Reconstruction. With the FSLN in command of many towns and preparing for the final onslaught on Managua, President Somoza resigned and left the country in July. (He was assassinated in Paraguay in September 1980.) After the Sandinistas had gained control of the capital, the Junta and its Provisional Governing Council took power on 20 July as the Government of National Reconstruction. The 1974 Constitution was abrogated, and the bicameral Congreso Nacional dissolved. The National Guard was disbanded and replaced by the Ejército Popular Sandinista (EPS—Sandinista People's Army), officially established in August. In that month the Junta issued a 'Statute on Rights and Guarantees for the Citizens of Nicaragua', providing for basic personal freedoms and restoring freedom of the press and broadcasting. Civil rights were restored in January 1980.

On taking office, the Junta had issued a Basic Statute, providing for the creation of an appointed Council of State to act as an interim legislature. In March 1981 Commdr Daniel Ortega Saavedra was appointed Co-ordinator of the Junta and of its new consultative body, the Council of Government.

By 1981 discontent at the postponement of elections and the increasing hegemony of the Sandinistas had led to the creation of counter-revolutionary forces ('Contras'), who were mostly members of the former National Guard and operated from camps in Honduras. Meanwhile, relations between the US and Nicaraguan Governments had seriously deteriorated, culminating in the suspension of US economic aid in April. In the same year the US Government donated US $10m. in support of the Contras, while covert operations by the US Central Intelligence Agency (CIA) attempted to destabilize the Sandinista regime. In March 1982 the Sandinista Government declared a state of emergency. However, the intensity of attacks by the Fuerzas Democráticas Nicaragüenses (FDN), anti-Sandinista guerrillas based in Honduras, increased. A Contra group, the Alianza Revolucionaria Democrática (ARDE), was also established in Costa Rica, led by Edén Pastora Gómez, a prominent figure in the revolution who had become disillusioned with the Sandinistas. In December the Sandinistas reaffirmed their support for the initiatives of the 'Contadora group' (Colombia, Mexico, Panama and Venezuela), which was attempting to find peaceful solutions to the disputes involving Central America, and adopted a more conciliatory approach towards the opposition.

In June 1984 talks commenced between the Nicaraguan and US Governments in order to foster the peace negotiations proposed by the Contadora group. However, although the Sandinistas agreed in September to sign a peace agreement, the USA rejected the agreement on the grounds that the forthcoming Nicaraguan elections would not be fairly conducted. In June 1985 the US Congress voted to allocate US $27m. in non-military aid to the Contras. None the less, the Nicaraguan Government reaffirmed its desire to resume negotiations with the USA. Concurrently, however, the civil conflict escalated, and clashes along Nicaragua's borders with Costa Rica and Honduras became increasingly frequent. In July thousands of Miskito Indians, who had allied themselves with the Contras in the early 1980s, began to return to their ancestral homelands in northern Nicaragua, following talks with the Government concerning autonomy for the region.

A presidential election and elections to a constituent assembly were held on 4 November 1984. The assembly was to draw up a constitution within two years of taking office. In August the Government had restored the majority of the civil rights that had been suspended in September 1982, in order to permit parties to campaign without restrictions. Ortega, the FSLN candidate won the presidential ballot, and his party won a majority of seats in the National Constituent Assembly, which replaced the Council of State. Ortega's new Government and the National Constituent Assembly were inaugurated in January 1985.

In August 1986 the US Congress approved assistance for the Contras worth US $100m. In November the US Government disclosed that funds accruing from its clandestine sales of military equipment to Iran had been used to support the Contras.

In January 1987 a new Constitution was promulgated; on the same day, however, civil liberties, guaranteed in the Constitution, were again suspended by the renewal of the five-year-old state of emergency. In February the Governments of Costa Rica, El Salvador, Guatemala and Honduras approved a peace plan for Nicaragua, largely based on earlier Contadora proposals, but placing greater emphasis on democratization, including the ending of the state of emergency. Following some modification, in August the peace plan was signed by the Presidents of the five nations, in Guatemala. In accordance with the plan's requirements, a four-member National Commission for Reconciliation was created, chaired by Cardinal Miguel Obando y Bravo, the Archbishop of Managua, a leading critic of the Government. In January 1988 the Government ended the state of emergency, and consented to participate directly in negotiations with the Contras. In March negotiations between representatives of the Government and the Contras resulted in agreement on a 60-day cease-fire, as a prelude to detailed peace negotiations (this was later unilaterally extended by the Government until November 1989). The Government agreed to the gradual release of political prisoners and to the participation of the Contras in domestic political dialogue and, eventually, in elections. In August 1988 the US Senate approved the provision of US $27m. in humanitarian aid for the Contras. As the hope of further military aid diminished, the Contras retreated into Honduras.

In February 1989 the five Central American Presidents met in El Salvador to discuss the reactivation of the regional peace plan. At the meeting it was agreed that, in return for the dismantling of Contra bases in Honduras, there would be moves towards greater democracy in Nicaragua. These included a pledge to hold a general election, open to opposition parties, by February 1990. A number of electoral reforms were introduced: Contra rebels were to be permitted to return to vote, on condition that they relinquished their armed struggle under a proposed demobilization plan.

In August 1989 the five Central American Presidents met in Tela, Honduras, where they signed an agreement providing for the voluntary demobilization, repatriation or relocation of the Contra forces within a 90-day period. To facilitate this process, an International Commission of Support and Verification (CIAV) was established by the UN and the Organization of American States (OAS, see p. 391). Following mediation (conducted by former US President Jimmy Carter), the Government concluded an agreement with the leaders of the Miskito Indians of the Caribbean coast. The rebels agreed to renounce their armed struggle and to join the political process. Meanwhile, the recently formed Unión Nacional Opositora (UNO), comprising 14 opposition parties of varying political views, designated Violeta Barrios de Chamorro (the owner and director of *La Prensa* since the assassination of her husband, Pedro Chamorro, in 1978) as its presidential candidate in the forthcoming election. Daniel Ortega was nominated as the candidate of the FSLN.

In November 1989 President Ortega declared the ending of the cease-fire with the Contras, on the grounds that the rebels had made insufficient progress in implementing the Tela agreement and disbanding their forces stationed in Honduras. In response, the UN Security Council established the UN Observer Group in Central America (ONUCA) to monitor compliance with the Tela agreement, to prevent cross-border incursions by rebels and to assist in supervising the forthcoming Nicaraguan elections.

Chamorro in power

The elections of February 1990 resulted in an unexpected victory for Chamorro. Foreign observers confirmed the conduct of the polls to have been free and fair. After the elections, the Sandinista Government decreed an immediate cease-fire. The President-elect pledged to 'depoliticize' the military and security forces, and urged the Contra rebels to disband and return to civilian life. However, the UNO had not secured a sufficient majority of seats in the Asamblea Nacional to make amendments to the Constitution. Before the transfer of power on 25 April, Ortega introduced a number of reforms. A General Amnesty and National Reconciliation Law was adopted: this was designed to pre-empt retaliatory measures against outgoing officials and to quash legal proceedings against those who had committed politically motivated crimes against the State since 1979.

On 19 April 1990 a cease-fire was agreed by the Contras and the Sandinista armed forces. The Contras agreed to surrender their weapons by 10 June, and to assemble in 'security zones' supervised by UN troops. A transitional agreement between the outgoing Sandinista Government and the newly elected UNO administration provided for a reduction in the strength of the security forces and their subordination to civilian authority. In return for a commitment from the Contras to sign the demobilization accords, the Government agreed to the establishment of a special police force, composed of former Contra rebels, in order to guarantee security within the demobilization zones. Demobilization of the Contra rebels was officially concluded on 27 June, signifying the end of 11 years of civil war in Nicaragua.

On assuming office, the UNO Government immediately attempted to reverse much Sandinista policy. The suspension of the civil service law in May 1990 provoked a public sector strike. Chamorro was forced to concede wage increases of 100% and the establishment of a joint commission of trade union and government representatives to revise the civil service law. In July another general strike, involving 100,000 workers, was held in support of demands for wage increases and also in protest at the implementation of legislation allowing the restoration to private ownership of land that had been nationalized and redistributed under the Sandinista regime. Once again the Government made concessions, a move condemned by the Vice-President, Virgilio Godoy Reyes. In October the Government announced the formation of a National Agrarian Commission to study problems of land distribution and illegal land seizures. In mid-1991, however, the emergence of groups of rearmed Contra rebels (known as Re-contras) became apparent with the reported occupation of several cities in the northern province of Jinotega. The Re-contras' stated aim was to publicize the grievances of thousands of demobilized Contras in the north of the country who had not received land and aid promised to them under the terms of the Government's resettlement plan.

In August 1991 a National Security Commission was established to disarm civilians. The phased disarmament of the Re-contras and the Re-compas (groups of rearmed Sandinistas) began in January 1992. However, in April groups of the former combatants began joining forces to form the Revueltos, demanding land and credit promised to them prior to demobilization. In May the Government allocated 800 plots of land outside the capital to the Revueltos, as a gesture of its intention to address the groups' grievances. However, rebel activity continued, despite successive government ultimatums requiring the rebels to disarm or face military intervention. In February 1994 a peace agreement was signed that provided for the demobilization of a prominent Re-contra group, the Frente Norte 3-80, by April, in return for which the rebels were granted an amnesty and the right to be incorporated into the national police force. Nevertheless, violent incidents involving further groups of Re-contras continued. The Government deployed security forces to combat the rebels' activities, which, it asserted, were criminal and not related to legitimate demands for land.

In June 1991 the FSLN withdrew its 39 deputies from the Asamblea Nacional in protest against the proposal to revoke two laws concerning redistribution of property. The so-called *piñata* laws had been introduced by the FSLN in March 1990, immediately prior to the transfer of power to the Chamorro administration. They guaranteed the property rights of the thousands of people who had benefited from the land expropriation that had been conducted by the Sandinistas. In August 1991 the legislature approved the abrogation of the *piñata* laws, but in the following month President Chamorro vetoed parts of the bill that she deemed to be unconstitutional. Disagreement over the property issue had by now led to the alienation by Chamorro of the majority of UNO deputies, and the legislature only narrowly failed to overturn the veto in December.

In May 1992 the US Congress suspended aid to Nicaragua, on the grounds that the Nicaraguan Government had failed to compensate US citizens for land expropriated under the Sandinista regime. In September Chamorro signed decrees establishing a property ombudsman's office and other provisions to expedite the processing of property claims. In addition, the President signed an agreement specifying that all unjustly confiscated property would be returned (or the rightful owners compensated).

A serious legislative crisis arose in September 1992, when the President of the Asamblea Nacional, Alfredo César, convened the legislature in the absence of the deputies of the FSLN and the Grupo de Centro (GC—dissident UNO deputies who had maintained their allegiance to the Government, thus depriving the UNO of its parliamentary majority), recruiting substitute deputies in order to elect new legislative authorities. Chamorro announced that no laws approved by the legislature would be promulgated until the Asamblea recognized a Supreme Court decision ruling César's actions to be unconstitutional and declaring all subsequent rulings by the legislature null and void. In December Chamorro ordered the army to occupy the assembly building and appointed a provisional administration to manage parliamentary affairs pending the election of new legislative authorities.

In October 1993 the Alianza Política Opositora (APO—as the UNO had become) and the FSLN signed an agreement providing for the implementation of partial constitutional reforms. The APO stipulated that it would support the reforms only on condition that its parliamentary majority be restored (through the dismissal of the GC deputies and their replacement by APO members) and that it gain control of the legislative authorities. The Asamblea Nacional reconvened in January 1994, and a new working alliance elected new legislative authorities. In November the Asamblea Nacional approved amendments to some 67 of the Constitution's 202 articles, which adjusted the balance of authority in favour of the legislature. In particular, the Government would be required to seek legislative approval for external loans, debt negotiations and international trade agreements. A further amendment, prohibiting close relatives of a serving # NICARAGUA

President from contesting the presidential election, was widely considered to be intended specifically to prevent Antonio Lacayo, Chamorro's son-in-law and Minister of the Presidency, from securing presidential office at the next election. Other reforms included a reduction in the presidential and legislative terms and the withdrawal of the absolute ban on presidential re-election, although consecutive terms remained prohibited. The amendments were deemed illegal by the FSLN leadership but won the support of FSLN deputies, reflecting the divisions within the party.

In February 1995 the constitutional amendments were signed. However, following Chamorro's refusal to promulgate the reforms, the Asamblea Nacional released the amendments for publication, thereby enacting them. In June a resolution to the dispute was achieved by the signing of a political accord between the Government and the legislature. Under the terms of the agreement, many of the amendments intended to reduce presidential authority were to be moderated. Legislation defining the interpretation and implementation of the amendments was approved by the Asamblea Nacional in July, and was subsequently promulgated by Chamorro.

Alemán in power

Presidential and legislative elections were held in October 1996. Arnoldo Alemán Lacayo of the Partido Liberal Constitucionalista (PLC), the candidate of the Alianza Liberal (an electoral alliance comprising mainly liberal parties), secured the presidency. The Alianza Liberal also won the largest number of seats in the Asamblea Nacional, although it failed to gain a majority. The FSLN boycotted the newly inaugurated Asamblea Nacional in January 1997 in protest at the decision of the Consejo Supremo Electoral (CSE—Supreme Electoral Council) to conduct an open ballot (rather than a secret vote) to elect the legislative authorities.

In November 1999 the Comptroller-General, Agustín Jarquín, was arrested on charges of committing fraud against the State. Jarquín, a vigorous critic of corruption in the Government, had launched numerous investigations into corrupt practices by members of the Alemán administration, the most notable of which had resulted in the publication of a report revealing that Alemán had increased his personal wealth by 900% during his terms of office as Mayor of Managua and as President, and that he had failed to declare these assets to the Office of the Comptroller-General, as required by law. Jarquín's supporters alleged that the accusations made against him were politically motivated. In December Jarquín was acquitted of the charges against him, and formally renewed the corruption charges against Alemán.

Meanwhile, in June 1999 the Government and the FSLN reached an agreement to begin negotiations on constitutional and electoral reform. In January 2000 a series of constitutional reforms came into force. The principal amendments included a reduction in the proportion of votes necessary for a President to be elected outright from 45% to 35%, thus increasing the likelihood of an FSLN victory. In return, Alemán was guaranteed a seat in the Asamblea Nacional after leaving office, thus making him virtually immune from prosecution. Other reforms included the restructuring of the judiciary, electoral authorities and the Office of the Comptroller-General—which was to be headed by a five-member board, thereby effectively removing the threat to the Alemán administration of Jarquín.

The Bolaños Government

Presidential and legislative elections took place on 4 November 2001, amid tight security. The final results of the presidential poll gave former Vice-President and PLC candidate Enrique Bolaños Geyer 56% of votes cast, while Ortega, standing again for the FSLN, secured 42%. The PLC also won a majority of seats in the Asamblea Nacional. The FSLN made allegations of electoral irregularities, but the complaints were rejected by the Supreme Constitutional Court.

Bolaños took office on 10 January 2002. Almost immediately he encountered opposition from within his own party, when members of the PLC rejected his preferred candidate for President of the Asamblea Nacional, Jaime Cuadra, and voted with the majority in favour of former President Alemán. In March the Attorney-General announced that former President Alemán was to face charges of fraud and embezzlement. In the months that followed President Bolaños made several attempts to remove Alemán's congressional immunity; however, internal divisions within the PLC (which had divided into pro-Alemán and pro-Bolaños factions) meant that the President lacked the votes necessary to have the motion approved. In August thousands of protesters marched through Managua to demand an end to the former head of state's immunity.

In September 2002 several of Alemán's relatives and former members of his Government were convicted of laundering some US $100m. from state communications, infrastructure, insurance and petroleum enterprises. One week later Alemán, who faced the same charges, suspended a parliamentary session at which the removal of his congressional immunity was to be discussed. The following day FSLN members joined the Bolaños faction of the PLC to vote in favour of Alemán's dismissal. Cuadra was installed as President of the Asamblea and a new legislative commission formed to determine whether Alemán's immunity should be revoked. The former President's financial assets in Panama and those of his family in the USA were frozen while investigations into the charges were made. The USA also suspended Alemán's right to enter its territory. In December the Asamblea Nacional approved a motion revoking Alemán's congressional immunity; the former President was immediately put under house arrest.

In October 2002 Bolaños himself became the subject of allegations of fraud. In response to charges filed with the Supreme Court, that he and his Vice-President, José Rizo Castellón, had used an illegal fund controlled by Alemán to finance his 2001 electoral campaign, Bolaños promised to renounce his presidential immunity at a date named by his prosecutors. In November Bolaños and Rizo were formally charged with embezzling US $4.1m. from public funds.

Alemán's arrest further deepened divisions within the PLC. In January 2003 Bolaños's veto of parts of the budget, in order to comply with conditions stipulated by the IMF for Nicaragua to qualify for debt relief, was opposed by both the pro-Alemán faction of the PLC and the FSLN. In March the pro-Alemán faction of the PLC officially announced that it was in opposition to the Government, in protest at the Government's alliance with the FSLN. The departure of the deputies left Bolaños with the unconditional support of only nine PLC members in the Asamblea (although six members of the Alemán faction later declared their allegiance to the President).

In December 2003 Alemán was found guilty of money-laundering, fraud and theft of state funds and was sentenced to 20 years' imprisonment. He was also fined US $17m. Owing to ill health, however, he was to serve his prison term under house arrest. In the same month the alliance between the FSLN and the pro-Bolaños PLC members collapsed, following the latter's insistence that the release of Alemán was essential if the pact were to continue. In January 2004 the two factions of the PLC attempted a fragile truce in order to select a new directorate of the Asamblea. The new legislative President, Carlos Noguera Pastora, was an Alemán supporter, while the six remaining seats were divided evenly between the two factions of the party.

In March 2004 the Asamblea began to debate a series of measures proposed by President Bolaños. The proposed reforms included the introduction of an independently appointed judiciary, adoption of a five-year national budget and reform of the electoral system. The proposed judicial reform prompted protests in the Asamblea from judges. Throughout most of 2004 the PLC- and FSLN-dominated Asamblea blocked the reform proposals, although in October the creation of an independent judicial council to appoint judges did receive legislative approval.

Also in March 2004 President Bolaños, Vice-President Rizo and 31 other senior members of the PLC were accused of illegal campaign-financing during the previous presidential election. Seven PLC members were arrested, including party president Jorge Castillo Quant. In October the Comptroller-General, Juan Gutiérrez, requested that President Bolaños be removed from power and fined two months' salary for withholding information regarding the financing of his 2001 election campaign. Supporters of the President claimed the request was politically motivated, as the office of the Comptroller-General was controlled by the FSLN and the anti-Bolaños faction of the PLC. At the invitation of Bolaños, a delegation arrived from the OAS to investigate the Comptroller-General's findings. Following a meeting with the OAS representatives, Ortega agreed to withdraw FSLN support for the initiation of impeachment proceedings against the President until after the November municipal elections.

The FSLN won a decisive victory in the local elections of November 2004. The following day a two-thirds' majority in the Asamblea Nacional voted in support of constitutional reform legislation limiting presidential powers. The reforms would require the President to seek legislative ratification for key appointments such as ministers, ambassadors, the chief prosecutor and banking superintendent, and would enable the Asamblea to remove officials deemed to be incompetent. A further reform provided for the transfer of control of the state energy, water and telecommunications services from the President to one regulatory body, the Surperintendencia de Servicios Públicos (Sisep). In December President Bolaños appealed to the Supreme Court, contending that the reforms, supported by the FSLN and the PLC, were unconstitutional. In January 2005 the Central American Court of Justice (CCJ) ruled that ratification of the controversial constitutional amendments should be suspended. None the less, one week later the Asamblea approved the legislation. In mid-January, two days before the legislation was due to come into effect, the Presidents of El Salvador, Guatemala and Honduras issued a joint statement of support for President Bolaños. Following further negotiations between factions supporting Bolaños, Ortega and Alemán, the President agreed to promulgate the controversial reforms in return for a pledge from the opposition that it would work towards a consensus with the executive on such matters as the budget and social security reform.

In July 2005 Alemán was released on probation for the remainder of his sentence, allegedly for health reasons. The Court of Appeal overruled the decision three days later, ordering that he return to house arrest. However, Alemán's probation was upheld in August by the Supreme Court, thereby permitting the former President to travel within the province of Managua and to participate in political activities.

Meanwhile, accusations against Bolaños and his associates of illegal campaign-financing during the 2001 elections persisted. In early September 2005 seven Central American heads of state gathered in Managua to demonstrate their support for Bolaños. None the less, later that month the Asamblea Nacional removed the immunity from prosecution of three ministers and three deputy ministers.

Dissent over the proposed constitutional reforms impeded the Government's legislative agenda in 2005, including efforts to gain approval for the proposed Dominican Republic-Central American Free Trade Agreement (DR-CAFTA, comprising Nicaragua, Costa Rica, the Dominican Republic, El Salvador, Guatemala, Honduras and the USA). Following the intervention of the US Assistant Secretary of State, who publicly criticized the PLC-FSLN legislative pact and proposed the implementation of DR-CAFTA without Nicaragua, in October the FSLN withdrew its opposition to the trade agreement, which was swiftly approved by the Asamblea Nacional.

The return of Ortega

Presidential and legislative elections took place on 5 November 2006. Ortega, who had sought to distance himself from the more extreme Sandinista policies of the 1980s, was elected to the presidency with 38.0% of the votes cast. Eduardo Montealegre Rivas of the Alianza Liberal Nicaragüense (ALN), a recently founded party composed primarily of dissident former PLC members opposed to Alemán, secured 28.3%, while former Vice-President Rizo, a close ally of Alemán, took 27.1% on behalf of the PLC. The poor performance of the Movimiento Renovador Sandinista (MRS) candidate, Edmundo Jarquín, who, with 6.3%, obtained a substantially lower share of the vote than most polls had predicted, suggested that Ortega's moderate tone prior to the elections had succeeded in persuading dissident Sandinistas to return to the FSLN. The FSLN also became the largest party in the Asamblea Nacional, winning 38 seats; the PLC took 25 seats (compared with 47 in the 2001 elections), the ALN 22 and the MRS the remaining five elective seats. Montealegre and Bolaños were both awarded supplementary legislative seats, in accordance with electoral rules. An estimated 16,000 domestic and international observers monitored the elections, with the OAS mission concluding that the process had generally been conducted peacefully and transparently. An estimated 69% of the electorate participated in the poll.

Ortega took office on 10 January 2007. His new Cabinet included Samuel Santos López, mayor of Managua during Ortega's previous period in office, as Minister of Foreign Affairs, Ana Isabel Morales Mazún as Minister of the Interior and Alberto Guevara Obregón as Minister of Finance and Public Credit. Ortega's wife, Rosario Murillo Zambrana, was appointed to the newly created cabinet position of Co-ordinator of the Communication and Citizenship Council, in which role she was to be responsible for all government publicity. Later that month the President issued a decree more than halving his own salary and substantially lowering those of government ministers and other senior officials. In late January the Asamblea Nacional adopted amendments to legislation on the organization and duties of the executive. Proposed by Ortega, and supported by the PLC, these 'urgent' reforms gave the President greater control over the police force and the military and allowed the President to create 'Citizen Power Councils' by decree. Amid concerns regarding the potential power of these Councils, which were intended to encourage direct democracy by co-ordinating the work of non-governmental organizations and public institutions on a regional and local level, opposition parties insisted that they should be purely consultative and not assume any of the functions of government ministries.

Also in late January 2007 the legislature approved the further postponement, for one year, of the constitutional amendments limiting presidential powers that had been due to take effect that month. A special commission, comprising seven deputies, was charged in February with drafting new constitutional reform legislation. In January 2008 the Supreme Court annulled the law postponing the implementation of the constitutional reforms, although it also declared invalid the majority of the reforms themselves, including the transfer of control of utilities to Sisep. However, it did not annul the law requiring the President to seek legislative approval of key appointments, with the result that this reform duly entered into force.

The Commission for Verification, Reconciliation, Peace and Justice was formally constituted in May 2007 under the chairmanship of Cardinal Obando y Bravo. Its stated remit was to continue the work of the commission established following the peace accords of 1987, ensuring that former combatants and victims of the war had received land and compensation as stipulated in the accords.

The national prison service granted Alemán complete freedom of movement within Nicaragua in March 2007. Montealegre claimed that the decision to ease the restrictions on the former President had been made on the orders of Ortega, in a joint attempt by the FSLN and the PLC to ensure that the country's liberal factions remained divided. Alemán's status continued to be exploited by the Government throughout 2007 to ensure PLC support for its programme. In January 2009 Alemán was definitively absolved from his conviction by the Supreme Court.

The 2008 municipal elections

Events surrounding the municipal elections of November 2008 caused substantial tension between the FSLN and its opponents. In April the Government announced its decision to postpone the elections in the Región Autónoma Atlántico Norte (RAAN) until 2009, owing to the damage caused by Hurricane Felix in September 2007. Anti-Government protesters claimed that the FSLN was acting to avoid an electoral defeat in the autonomous region, and riots led to two deaths in Bilwi. In June 2008 the CSE revoked the legal status of two political parties for administrative reasons, provoking criticism that the PLC-FSLN legislative pact remained in place and continued to pose a threat to multiparty democracy. The CSE, composed of seven magistrates, all of whom were aligned with either the FSLN or the PLC, voted to ban the MRS on the grounds that it had failed to present the necessary documentation, and the Partido Conservador (PC) for failing to nominate candidates in 80% of municipalities. In the elections, which were held on 9 November, the FSLN secured 105 of the 146 contested mayoralties, including that of Managua, while the PLC took 37. However, allegations of widespread fraud, supported by the discovery of burned and discarded ballots, undermined the results. A recount in Managua was negotiated, but demands that it be monitored by independent observers were rejected, and the recount confirmed the victory of the FSLN candidate, Alexis Argüello. Standing in opposition to Argüello was former presidential candidate Eduardo Montealegre, whose movement, Vamos con Eduardo (VCE), had formed a political alliance with the PLC in March 2008. The PLC-VCE alliance, supported by the monitoring authority Etica y Transparencia (which the Government had refused to accredit), maintained that Montealegre was the rightful mayor of Managua. Despite riots and demonstrations across Nicaragua, a bill proposed by the PLC to annul the November elections failed to generate sufficient support in the Asamblea Nacional. The Asamblea was suspended at the end of November owing to the prevailing election crisis, but reconvened in January 2009. The FSLN made significant gains in the delayed municipal elections held in the RAAN in January. A report published in March by the non-governmental anti-corruption organization Transparency International alleged that fraud had occurred in at least 40 of the

146 municipalities contested in November 2008. At elections to the Atlantic Coast Regional Councils in March 2010, which were marked by a high rate of abstention, the FSLN remained the largest party in the RAAN, as did the PLC in the Región Autónoma Atlántico Sur, although neither secured a majority of seats.

Recent developments: judicial controversy

The Government continued to attract controversy during 2009, managing in October to secure the removal of the one-term limit on presidential tenure by means of a ruling by the constitutional panel of the highly politicized Supreme Court. The ruling, which was deemed illegal on the basis that only the Asamblea Nacional can effect constitutional change, was condemned by opposition parties and by the US authorities. Further tension was provoked in January 2010, when the President issued a decree extending the terms of incumbent electoral and judicial officials, defying a constitutional provision according the Asamblea Nacional responsibility for such appointments. An opposition boycott of the legislature ensued in protest against the decree. Following the refusal of two FSLN-aligned Supreme Court judges to leave their posts on the expiry of their terms in April, opposition deputies attempted to convene with the aim of overturning Ortega's controversial decree, but were forcibly prevented from doing so by government supporters. The dismissal of several mayors (belonging to both the FSLN and opposition parties) during May and June was attributed by analysts to their hostility to Ortega's bid for re-election. In July, at a party congress, the PLC endorsed Alemán as its presidential candidate in the election due in late 2011. The crisis within the Supreme Court escalated in August 2010, with the replacement of seven PLC-affiliated judges who had refused to participate in court sessions in protest against the continuance in office of the two FSLN judges whose terms had expired; five of the substitute judges were aligned with the ruling party and two with the opposition.

In two contentious judgments in September 2010, the Supreme Court upheld both the decree issued by Ortega in January extending the mandates of electoral and judicial officials and the ruling by its constitutional panel in October 2009 that revoked the constitutional provision prohibiting consecutive presidential re-election. In October 2010, moreover, the Asamblea Nacional approved the publication in the previous month of a new version of the Constitution, incorporating Ortega's January decree. In February 2011 the FSLN officially designated Ortega as its candidate for the forthcoming presidential election, which was scheduled to take place on 6 November, concurrently with legislative polls. In addition to Alemán, Ortega's main rival for the presidency was expected to be former PLC member Fabio Gadea Mantilla, representing the Unidad Nicaragüense por la Esperanza, an alliance of various opposition parties and movements, including the VCE and the MRS.

Foreign Affairs

Relations with the USA

Full military relations between Nicaragua and the USA, suspended since 1980, were re-established in 2001. In 2004 the Government agreed to destroy one-half of its stockpile of surface-to-air missiles. However, dissatisfaction with a lack of progress on the issue prompted the US Administration to suspend military aid to Nicaragua in April–October 2005. In July 2007 President Daniel Ortega proposed the destruction of 651 missiles, leaving 400 for the purposes of national defence, in exchange for military helicopters and medical equipment from the USA. Talks between the two countries concerning the destruction of the missiles took place during 2008, although no agreement had been reached by early 2011.

The dispute regarding the results of the municipal elections of November 2008 put a strain on international relations: in that month the European Union and the USA both suspended budgetary aid to Nicaragua due to the country's failure to resolve the dispute. In June 2009 the US Government's Millennium Challenge Corporation announced the 'definitive' cancellation of US $62m. (of a total $175m.) of funds to Nicaragua. Ortega criticized the decision and declared that the shortfall would in part be compensated by assistance from the Venezuelan Bolivarian Alliance for the Peoples of our America (Alianza Bolivariana para los Pueblos de Nuestra América—ALBA). In September 2010 the USA included Nicaragua for the first time on its list of major illicit drugs-transit or drugs-producing countries.

Other regional relations

In June 1995, prompted by frequent disputes concerning fishing rights in the Gulf of Fonseca, Nicaragua signed an accord with Honduras providing for the visible demarcation of each country's territorial waters. A demarcation process began in May 1998. In December 1999, following further confrontations, Nicaragua initiated proceedings at the International Court of Justice (ICJ, see p. 23) in The Hague, Netherlands, to determine the maritime delimitation in the Gulf of Fonseca. In that month a dispute arose prompting Nicaragua to sever commercial ties with, and impose import taxes on, Honduras, in direct contravention of Central American free trade undertakings. Following mediation by the OAS, in January 2000 Nicaragua ended its trade sanctions against Honduras, and in March both countries signed an accord committing them to observe a maritime exclusion zone in the Caribbean and to reduce troop numbers on their common border. However, following further illegal incursions by both sides, in early 2001 Nicaragua submitted documentation to the ICJ contesting the treaty. Nicaragua also refused to participate in the joint patrol of the Gulf of Fonseca. In March delegates from both Governments attended OAS-sponsored discussions in Washington, DC, USA. In June Nicaragua and Honduras concluded a confidence-building agreement, which provided for OAS observers to monitor the actions of army and navy forces on both sides of the common border. None the less, in July 2002 the situation deteriorated when the Nicaraguan Government announced plans to sell oil-drilling rights in the disputed area. The ICJ ruled on a revised maritime border approximately midway between the two countries in October 2007. Both the Nicaraguan and Honduran Governments declared themselves satisfied with the ruling.

In 1997 relations with Costa Rica became strained when the latter began deporting Nicaraguans who were residing illegally in the country. Remittances from Nicaraguans in Costa Rica represented a significant contribution to the Nicaraguan economy, averaging US $240m.–$300m. per year. Further antagonism had developed between the two countries in 1998 when Nicaragua prohibited Costa Rican civil guards from carrying arms while navigating the San Juan river, which forms the border between the two countries. According to a long-standing treaty, the river, which is Nicaraguan territory, was only to be used by Costa Rica for commercial purposes. Following protests by Costa Rica, agreement was reached allowing for that country's civil guard to carry arms on the river while under escort by the Nicaraguan authorities. In August, however, following concerted pressure by opposition parties, the media and the Roman Catholic Church in Nicaragua, which accused the Government of surrendering part of the nation's sovereignty, Nicaragua annulled the accord. In June 2000 both Governments agreed a procedure that would allow armed Costa Rican police officers to patrol the river. However, following continued tensions over Costa Rica's use of the river, in September 2002 the two countries agreed to attempt to resolve the dispute within three years. Failure to agree on Costa Rica's navigational rights within the stipulated period prompted the country to refer the matter to the ICJ in September 2005. In response, President Bolaños recalled the Nicaraguan ambassador to Costa Rica, ordered the troops patrolling the border area to prohibit the passage of armed Costa Rican police officers, and imposed a 35% tariff on Costa Rican imports. In July 2009 the ICJ upheld Nicaragua's right to regulate traffic on the river and ruled that, although Costa Rica had the right to navigate freely on the river for commercial purposes, Costa Rican vessels undertaking police functions were not permitted to use the river. Bilateral tensions were renewed in October 2010, however, when the Costa Rican Government deployed armed police officers to the joint border, alleging that Nicaraguan troops had violated Costa Rican territory while dredging the river. In November, in response to a request from Costa Rica, the OAS sought to mediate, notably urging both countries to withdraw their armed personnel from the disputed area. Following Ortega's rejection of OAS involvement and refusal to withdraw Nicaraguan troops, Costa Rica referred the matter to the ICJ, additionally accusing Nicaragua of constructing a canal across Costa Rican territory. Pending a definitive ruling, in March 2011 the Court ordered both sides to withdraw police, security and civilian personnel from the disputed area (with the exception of Costa Rican officials charged with protecting the environment), but did not accede to a Costa Rican demand that Nicaraguan dredging operations be suspended.

NICARAGUA

Introductory Survey

In November 2001 a dispute with Colombia arose after a Nicaraguan fishing vessel was captured allegedly in Colombian waters. It was the third time in that year that a Nicaraguan vessel had been apprehended in the area. In the following month Nicaragua presented a request to the ICJ that its claim over territorial waters in the Caribbean Sea and around the islands of San Andrés and Providencia be recognized. The ICJ dismissed Nicaragua's claim to the San Andrés archipelago in December 2007, although it had yet to rule on jurisdiction of the other disputed waters. In 2011 Costa Rica and Honduras, despite citing interests in the disputed territory, were denied permission from the ICJ to participate in the ongoing case.

Developing strong regional relations appeared to be a priority for Ortega following his election as President in November 2006: he toured four other Central American countries in that month, before visiting the leaders of Cuba and Venezuela, with whom he already had close links. At the same time, Ortega adopted a conciliatory approach towards the USA, stating that he would seek to foster a 'respectful' bilateral relationship. None the less, on taking office in January 2007 Ortega sought to strengthen relations with other left-wing administrations in Latin America. He immediately confirmed Nicaragua's participation in ALBA, which had been devised by Venezuela as an alternative model to the US-promoted Free Trade Area of the Americas. Furthermore, Ortega signed a number of economic agreements with the Venezuelan President, Hugo Chávez, who pledged substantial financial assistance to Nicaragua, including the construction of a petroleum refinery, capable of processing 100,000–150,000 barrels of oil per day, and the provision of low-interest loans for impoverished Nicaraguans living in rural areas. In March a joint Nicaraguan-Venezuelan committee was formed to advance plans for bilateral co-operation, particularly in the energy sector. Venezuela was to supply Nicaragua with 10,000 barrels of petroleum per day at preferential rates and 32 electricity generators to alleviate severe energy shortages. Speaking at the launch of the joint committee in Managua, Ortega compared ALBA favourably with DR-CAFTA, praising the former's focus on the principles of social justice. Following a visit to Managua by Chávez, in May 2010 Ortega announced that ALBA funds would be used to finance the provision of monthly bonuses of US $25 for some 120,000 (later increased to 147,500) public sector workers.

CONSTITUTION AND GOVERNMENT

A new Constitution was approved by the National Constituent Assembly on 19 November 1986 and promulgated on 9 January 1987. Amendments to the Constitution were approved by the Asamblea Nacional (National Assembly) in July 1995 and January 2000.

Executive power is vested in the President, who is elected by popular vote for a five-year term. The President is assisted by a Vice-President and an appointed Cabinet. Legislative power is held by the Asamblea Nacional, elected by universal adult suffrage, under a system of proportional representation, for a five-year term.

REGIONAL AND INTERNATIONAL CO-OPERATION

Nicaragua is a member of the Central American Common Market (CACM, see p. 224), which aims eventually to liberalize intra-regional trade, and of the Inter-American Development Bank (IDB, see p. 333). Negotiations towards a free trade agreement, to be known as the Central American Free Trade Agreement, were concluded between El Salvador, Guatemala, Honduras, Nicaragua and the USA in December 2003. The agreement entailed the gradual elimination of tariffs on most industrial and agricultural products over the following 10 and 20 years, respectively. Implementation of the Dominican Republic-Central American Free Trade Agreement (DR-CAFTA) with the USA took place in April 2006. Nicaragua is a founder member of the UN. As a contracting party to the General Agreement on Tariffs and Trade, Nicaragua joined the World Trade Organization (see p. 430) on its establishment in 1995. Nicaragua is a member of the Group of 77 (see p. 447).

ECONOMIC AFFAIRS

In 2009, according to estimates by the World Bank, Nicaragua's gross national income (GNI), measured at average 2007–09 prices, was US $5,765m., equivalent to $1,000 per head (or $2,450 per head on an international purchasing-power parity basis). During 2000–09 the population increased at an average annual rate of 1.3%, while gross domestic product (GDP) per head grew, in real terms, by an average of 1.4% per year.

Nicaragua's GDP increased, in real terms, by an average of 2.8% per year in 2000–09; GDP expanded by 2.8% in 2008, but decreased by an estimated 1.5% in the following year.

Agriculture (including forestry and fishing) contributed an estimated 17.8% of GDP in 2009 and, according to the FAO, the sector was estimated to engage some 14.2% of the employed work-force in mid-2011. The principal cash crops are coffee (which accounted for 17.0% of export earnings in 2009), groundnuts, sugar cane and beans. Maize, rice and beans are the principal food crops. Meat and meat products accounted for 16.6% of export earnings in 2009. According to official estimates, agricultural GDP increased at an average annual rate of 2.3% during 2001–09; agricultural GDP grew by 6.7% in 2008, but the sector remained stagnant in 2009.

Industry (including mining, manufacturing, construction and power) engaged 18.6% of the employed labour force and provided an estimated 27.7% of GDP in 2009. According to official estimates, industrial GDP increased by an average of 2.7% per year during 2001–09; however, growth remained almost stagnant in 2008 and in 2009.

Mining contributed an estimated 1.2% of GDP and engaged 0.3% of the employed labour force in in 2009. Nicaragua has workable deposits of gold, silver, copper, lead, antimony, zinc and iron; its non-metallic minerals include limestone, gypsum, bentonite and marble. In 2009 gold accounted for 5.8% of export earnings. According to official estimates, the GDP of the mining sector decreased at an average annual rate of 2.4% in 2001–09; the sector's GDP declined by an estimated 10.5% in 2009.

Manufacturing contributed some 18.7% of GDP and engaged 13.1% of the employed labour force in 2009. The principal branches of manufacturing were food products, beverages and tobacco. The *maquila*, or assembly, sector expanded rapidly in the 1990s, although growth slowed in the 2000s. The principal products were clothing, footwear, aluminium frames and jewellery. Manufacturing GDP increased, according to official figures, by an average of 3.8% per year in 2001–09; the sector's GDP grew by 1.1% in 2008, but fell by 2.7% in 2009.

Construction contributed some 5.0% of GDP and engaged 4.7% of the employed labour force in 2009. Construction GDP fell, according to official figures, by an average of 1.5% per year in 2001–09; the sector's GDP decreased by 4.1% in 2009.

Energy is derived principally from imported petroleum (about 71.1% in 2007), although two hydroelectric plants in the department of Jinotega account for some 10% of the electrical energy generated in the country. Imports of crude petroleum comprised 10.0% of the total value of imports in 2009. In 2008 Nicaragua produced an estimated 3,327.4 GWh of electrical energy.

The services sector contributed an estimated 54.5% of GDP and engaged 52.7% of the employed labour force in 2009. The tourism sector has become increasingly significant in recent years; in 2008 annual income totalled US $276m., with arrivals put at 857,901, an increase of 7.2% on the previous year's figures. According to official figures, the GDP of the services sector increased by an average of 3.5% per year in 2001–09; the sector remained stagnant in 2008 and in 2009.

In 2009 Nicaragua recorded a visible trade deficit of US $1,540.4m., and there was a deficit of $841.1m. on the current account of the balance of payments. In 2009 the principal source of imports (supplying 19.9% of total imports) was the USA; other major suppliers were Nicaragua's partners in the Central American Common Market (CACM—Costa Rica, El Salvador, Guatemala and Honduras, see p. 224), as well as Venezuela and Mexico. The USA was also the principal market for exports (accounting for 29.5% of total exports) in 2009; other notable purchasers were the countries of the CACM, Mexico and Canada. The principal exports in 2009 were coffee, meat and groundnuts. The principal imports were non-durable consumer goods, primary materials and intermediate goods for industry and crude petroleum.

In 2009 Nicaragua recorded a budgetary deficit of an estimated 2,853.9m. gold córdobas, according to central bank figures, equivalent to 2.3% of GDP. Nicaragua's general government gross debt was 101,658m. gold córdobas in 2009, equivalent to 81.3% of GDP. At the end of 2008 Nicaragua's total external debt was US $3,558m., of which $2,259m. was public and publicly guaranteed debt. The cost of servicing external debt in that year was equivalent to 7.3% of the value of goods and services. In 2001–09 the average annual rate of increase in consumer prices was 8.3%. Consumer prices rose by an annual average of 19.8% in 2008 but the rate of growth was estimated to have decelerated to

NICARAGUA

3.7% in 2009. An estimated 8.2% of the labour force was unemployed in 2009.

In 2011 Nicaragua remained the second poorest country in Latin America (after Haiti), heavily dependent on international aid. In 2003 Nicaragua qualified for debt alleviation under the World Bank's heavily indebted poor countries (HIPC) initiative, making it eligible for some US $4,500m. in loans in 2004; in December of the following year the IMF approved 100% debt relief on Nicaragua's multilateral debt incurred prior to 2005, totalling some $201m. ($132m., excluding the remaining HIPC funding). The administration of Daniel Ortega, which took office in January 2007, pledged to promote fiscal prudence. His Government's focus on social policies resulted in a reduction in maternal mortality and poverty rates, increased school enrolment and literacy, and improved access to safe water. In addition, programmes were initiated to stimulate agricultural productivity, with microcredits offered to small-scale farmers. Meanwhile, following disputed municipal elections in November 2008 (see Contemporary Political History), the USA withheld disbursement of some $62m. in development aid; total foreign aid declined by 12% in 2009, although contributions from Venezuela, which have been substantial during Ortega's presidency, remained largely stable. The economy remained vulnerable to external shocks, including natural disasters and fluctuations in the international price of commodities (notably petroleum imports).

The economy was adversely affected by the global financial crisis, not least because of the decline in income from exports (particularly textiles sales to the USA) and remittances from workers abroad (predominantly in the USA and Costa Rica). Real GDP contracted by 1.5% in 2009. Amid improving external conditions, Nicaragua's economy returned to growth in 2010, with GDP increasing by an estimated 4.5%. Export earnings and remittances rose, the latter by 7.1%, to reach $822.8m., equivalent to 12.6% of GDP. However, a resurgence in the rate of inflation, which averaged 9.2% in 2010, was of concern, and GDP growth was forecast to decelerate slightly in 2011. In November 2010 the IMF agreed to a one-year extension of a three-year Extended Credit Facility for Nicaragua first approved in October 2007.

PUBLIC HOLIDAYS

2012: 1 January (New Year's Day), 5 April (Maundy Thursday), 6 April (Good Friday), 1 May (Labour Day), 30 May (Mothers' Day, afternoon only), 19 July (Liberation Day), 1 and 10 August (Managua local holidays), 14 September (Battle of San Jacinto), 15 September (Independence Day), 2 November (All Souls' Day, afternoon only), 8 December (Immaculate Conception), 25 December (Christmas Day).

Various local holidays are also observed.

Statistical Survey

Sources (unless otherwise stated): Banco Central de Nicaragua, Carretera Sur, Km 7, Apdos 2252/3, Zona 5, Managua; tel. 265-0500; fax 265-2272; e-mail bcn@cabcn.gob.ni; internet www.bcn.gob.ni; Instituto Nacional de Información de Desarrollo, Los Arcos, Frente Hospital Fonseca, Managua; tel. 266-6178; e-mail webmaster@inide.gob.ni; internet www.inide.gob.ni.

Area and Population

AREA, POPULATION AND DENSITY

Area (sq km)	
Land	120,340
Inland water	10,034
Total	130,373*
Population (census results)	
25 April 1995	4,357,099
28 May–11 June 2005	
Males	2,534,491
Females	2,607,607
Total	5,142,098
Population (official estimates at mid-year)	
2009	5,742,309
2010	5,815,524
2011	5,888,945
Density (per sq km) at mid-2011	48.9†

* 50,337 sq miles.
† Land area only.

POPULATION BY AGE AND SEX
(official estimates at mid-2010)

	Males	Females	Total
0–14	1,024,450	984,664	2,009,114
15–64	1,733,454	1,813,383	3,546,837
65 and over	120,619	138,954	259,573
Total	2,878,523	2,937,001	5,815,524

ADMINISTRATIVE DIVISIONS
(land area only, population estimates at mid-2010)

	Area (sq km)	Population	Density (per sq km)	Capital
Departments:				
Chinandega	4,822.4	412,731	85.6	Chinandega
León	5,138.0	394,512	76.8	León
Managua	3,465.1	1,401,272	404.4	Managua
Masaya	610.8	336,877	551.5	Masaya
Carazo	1,081.4	179,108	165.6	Jinotepe
Granada	1,039.7	193,065	185.7	Granada
Rivas	2,161.8	168,594	78.0	Rivas
Estelí	2,229.7	218,660	98.1	Estelí
Madriz	1,708.2	149,983	87.8	Somoto
Nueva Segovia	3,491.3	235,381	67.4	Ocotal
Jinotega	9,222.4	393,356	42.7	Jinotega
Matagalpa	6,803.9	518,699	76.2	Matagalpa
Boaco	4,176.7	167,270	40.0	Boaco
Chontales	6,481.3	177,279	27.4	Juigalpa
Río San Juan	7,540.9	109,353	14.5	San Carlos
Autonomous Regions:				
Atlántico Norte (RAAN)	32,819.7	407,397	12.4	Bilwi
Atlántico Sur (RAAS)	27,546.3	351,987	12.8	Bluefields
Total	120,339.5	5,815,524	48.3	—

PRINCIPAL TOWNS
(population at 2005 census)

Managua (capital)	937,489	Chinandega	121,793
León	174,051	Estelí	112,084
Masaya	139,582	Granada	105,171
Matagalpa	133,416	Tipitapa	101,685

NICARAGUA

BIRTHS, MARRIAGES AND DEATHS
(annual averages, UN estimates)

	1995–2000	2000–05	2005–10
Birth rate (per 1,000)	30.1	26.3	24.8
Death rate (per 1,000)	5.6	5.0	4.7

Source: UN, *World Population Prospects: The 2008 Revision.*

2005: Registered live births 121,380; Registered marriages 23,069; Registered deaths 16,770. Note: Registration believed to be incomplete.

2006: Registered live births 123,886; Registered marriages 23,320; Registered deaths 16,595. Note: Registration believed to be incomplete.

2007: Registered live births 128,171; Registered marriages 20,918; Registered deaths 17,288. Note: Registration believed to be incomplete.

Life expectancy (years at birth, WHO estimates): 74 (males 71; females 77) in 2008 (Source: WHO, *World Health Statistics*).

EMPLOYMENT
(population aged 10 years and over, 2005 census)

	Male	Female	Total
Agriculture, forestry and fishing	537,209	33,611	570,820
Mining and quarrying	5,005	503	5,508
Manufacturing	118,919	89,074	207,993
Electricity, gas and water	3,830	954	4,784
Construction	86,574	2,182	88,756
Trade, restaurants and hotels	166,863	150,580	317,443
Transport and communications	60,346	5,338	65,684
Financial services	7,104	7,320	14,424
Government services	150,992	232,220	383,212
Other activities	9,817	7,109	16,926
Total employed	**1,146,659**	**528,891**	**1,675,550**

2009 (population 10 years and over, '000): Agriculture, forestry and fishing 600.8; Mining and quarrying 5.7; Manufacturing 274.6; Construction 99.4; Electricity, gas and water supply 10.9; Trade 485.9; Public administration 90.2; Transport and communication 86.6; Financial services 82.7; Social and personal services 359.6; *Total employed* 2,096.5; Unemployed 186.2; *Total labour force* 2,282.7.

Mid-2011 (estimates in '000): Agriculture, etc. 349; Total labour force 2,462 (Source: FAO).

Health and Welfare

KEY INDICATORS

Total fertility rate (children per woman, 2008)	2.7
Under-5 mortality rate (per 1,000 live births, 2008)	27
HIV/AIDS (% of persons aged 15–49, 2007)	0.2
Physicians (per 1,000 head, 2003)	0.4
Hospital beds (per 1,000 head, 2005)	0.9
Health expenditure (2007): US $ per head (PPP)	232
Health expenditure (2007): % of GDP	8.3
Health expenditure (2007): public (% of total)	54.9
Access to water (% of persons, 2008)	85
Access to sanitation (% of persons, 2008)	52
Total carbon emissions ('000 metric tons, 2007)	4,587.3
Carbon dioxide emissions per head (metric tons, 2007)	0.8
Human Development Index (2010): ranking	115
Human Development Index (2010): value	0.565

For sources and definitions, see explanatory note on p. vi.

Agriculture

PRINCIPAL CROPS
('000 metric tons)

	2006	2007	2008
Rice, paddy	319.6	269.9	321.9
Maize	501.9	486.7	423.9
Sorghum	73.2	107.6	74.6
Cassava (Manioc)*	105.0	115.0	115.0
Sugar cane	4,505.0	4,480.9	4,304.9
Beans, dry	179.7	170.4	176.7
Groundnuts, in shell	145.7†	156.8†	139.3
Oil palm fruit*	58.7	60.0	60.0
Bananas	42.6	44.4	36.3
Plantains*	55.0	55.0	55.0
Oranges*	72.0	85.0	85.0
Pineapples*	50.0	51.0	51.0
Coffee, green	70.5	100.0	72.7

* FAO estimates.
† Unofficial figure.

Note: No data were available for individual crops in 2009.

Aggregate production ('000 metric tons, may include official, semi-official or estimated data): Total cereals 894 in 2006, 864 in 2007, 820 in 2008–09; Total roots and tubers 149 in 2006, 163 in 2007–09; Total vegetables (incl. melons) 36 in 2006–09; Total fruits (excl. melons) 232 in 2006, 248 in 2007, 240 in 2008–09.

Source: FAO.

LIVESTOCK
('000 head, year ending September, FAO estimates)

	2005	2006	2007
Cattle	3,500	3,600	3,600
Pigs	463	472	473
Goats	7	7	7
Horses	268	268	268
Asses	9	9	9
Mules	48	48	48
Poultry	18,000	18,000	18,000

2008: Figures assumed to be unchanged from 2007 (FAO estimates).
Source: FAO.

LIVESTOCK PRODUCTS
('000 metric tons)

	2006	2007	2008
Cattle meat	84.3	92.8	96.1
Pig meat	6.8	6.9	7.1
Horse meat*	2.1	2.1	2.1
Chicken meat	83.6	89.8	91.0
Cows' milk	664.5	691.1	718.9
Hen eggs	21.1	21.5	21.6

* FAO estimates.

2009: Pig meat 7.5 (FAO estimate).
Source: FAO.

Forestry

ROUNDWOOD REMOVALS
('000 cubic metres, excl. bark, FAO estimates)

	2007	2008	2009
Sawlogs, veneer logs and logs for sleepers	93	93	54
Fuel wood	6,003	6,033	6,064
Total	**6,096**	**6,126**	**6,118**

Source: FAO.

NICARAGUA

SAWNWOOD PRODUCTION
('000 cubic metres, incl. railway sleepers, FAO estimates)

	2007	2008	2009
Coniferous	19.5	19.5	12.0
Broadleaved	34.6	34.6	40.0
Total	54.1	54.1	52.0

Source: FAO.

Fishing

('000 metric tons, live weight)

	2006	2007	2008
Capture	29.6	27.1	29.8
Snooks	1.1	1.1	1.1
Snappers	0.7	2.6	1.6
Yellowfin tuna	7.6	5.9	5.5
Skipjack tuna	5.3	2.4	6.0
Common dolphinfish	0.2	0.2	0.4
Caribbean spiny lobsters	3.6	3.7	4.2
Penaeus shrimp	2.3	2.5	1.8
Aquaculture	11.2	11.5	16.1
Whiteleg shrimp	10.9	11.1	14.7
Total catch	40.8	38.6	45.9

Source: FAO.

Mining

	2005	2006	2007
Gold (kg)	3,674	3,395	1,650
Silver (kg)	2,999	2,929	n.a.
Gypsum and anhydrite (metric tons)	36,456	42,191	n.a.

Gold (kg): 1,226 in 2008; 1,337 in 2009.

Source: US Geological Survey.

Industry

SELECTED PRODUCTS
('000 barrels, unless otherwise indicated)

	2006	2007	2008*
Liquid gas	178	185	110
Motor spirit	774	721	714
Kerosene	211	239	201
Diesel	1,486	1,515	1,398
Fuel oil	2,691	2,633	2,305
Bitumen (asphalt)	73	92	74
Electric energy (million kWh)	3,137.2	3,208.8	3,327.4

* Preliminary figures.

Cement ('000 metric tons, estimates): 530 in 2006–09 (Source: US Geological Survey).

Finance

CURRENCY AND EXCHANGE RATES

Monetary Units
100 centavos = 1 córdoba oro (gold córdoba).

Sterling, Dollar and Euro Equivalents (31 December 2010)
£1 sterling = 34.257 gold córdobas;
US $1 = 21.883 gold córdobas;
€1 = 29.239 gold córdobas;
1,000 gold córdobas = £29.19 = $45.70 = €34.20.

Average Exchange Rate (gold córdobas per US dollar)
2008   19.3719
2009   20.3395
2010   21.3564

Note: In February 1988 a new córdoba, equivalent to 1,000 of the former units, was introduced, and a uniform exchange rate of US $1 = 10 new córdobas was established. Subsequently, the exchange rate was frequently adjusted. A new currency, the córdoba oro (gold córdoba), was introduced as a unit of account in May 1990 and began to be circulated in August. The value of the gold córdoba was initially fixed at par with the US dollar, but in March 1991 the exchange rate was revised to $1 = 25,000,000 new córdobas (or 5 gold córdobas). On 30 April 1991 the gold córdoba became the sole legal tender.

BUDGET
(million gold córdobas)

Revenue*	2007	2008	2009†
Taxation	18,984.2	21,730.3	22,175.2
Income tax	5,746.0	7,001.9	7,817.7
Value-added tax	8,025.3	9,005.6	8,924.3
Taxes on petroleum products	2,107.6	2,162.2	2,276.6
Taxes on imports	1,093.3	1,183.2	970.2
Other revenue	1,594.6	1,737.8	1,684.1
Total	20,578.8	23,468.0	23,859.3

Expenditure‡	2007	2008	2009†
Compensation of employees	7,247.3	9,050.6	10,177.9
Goods and services	2,526.5	3,947.6	3,313.1
Interest payments	1,579.8	1,447.4	1,711.3
Current transfers	3,863.8	4,498.8	5,084.2
Capital transfers	3,211.3	3,528.7	3,013.7
Social security contributions	528.7	903.8	1,324.0
Other expenditure	1,166.5	1,654.9	1,534.0
Total	20,124.0	25,031.8	26,158.3

* Excluding grants received (million gold córdobas): 3,912.1 in 2007; 3,573.9 in 2008; 3,079.5 in 2009.
† Preliminary figures.
‡ Excluding net acquisition of non-financial assets (million gold córdobas): 3,926.2 in 2007; 3,448.1 in 2008; 3,634.4 in 2009.

INTERNATIONAL RESERVES
(excluding gold, US $ million at 31 December)

	2008	2009	2010
IMF special drawing rights	0.14	164.48	161.48
Foreign exchange	1,140.70	1,408.60	1,637.50
Total	1,140.84	1,573.08	1,798.98

Source: IMF, *International Financial Statistics*.

MONEY SUPPLY
(million gold córdobas at 31 December)

	2008	2009	2010
Currency outside depository corporations	5,498.8	6,157.7	8,224.8
Transferable deposits	10,711.1	13,967.4	18,674.5
Other deposits	29,784.0	32,463.8	37,087.5
Broad money	45,993.9	52,589.0	63,986.8

Source: IMF, *International Financial Statistics*.

NICARAGUA

COST OF LIVING
(Consumer Price Index; base: 1999 = 100)

	2007	2008	2009
Food	188.9	242.8	252.4
Clothing	129.5	140.0	149.5
Rent, fuel and light	189.7	219.3	213.8
All items (incl. others)	178.8	214.2	222.2

Source: ILO.

NATIONAL ACCOUNTS
(million gold córdobas at current prices)

Expenditure on the Gross Domestic Product

	2007*	2008*	2009†
Final consumption expenditure	104,844.3	127,226.9	128,324.4
Gross capital formation	34,245.6	40,687.5	29,324.3
Total domestic expenditure	139,090.0	167,914.4	157,648.6
Exports of goods and services	35,517.2	42,719.9	43,867.0
Less Imports of goods and services	71,318.2	89,608.0	76,447.1
GDP in purchasers' values	103,289.0	121,026.3	125,068.6
GDP at constant 1994 prices	33,951.7	34,888.7	34,382.0

* Preliminary figures.
† Estimates.

Gross Domestic Product by Economic Activity

	2007*	2008*	2009†
Agriculture, hunting, forestry and fishing	16,669.0	20,700.4	21,003.5
Mining and quarrying	1,211.4	1,479.4	1,433.9
Manufacturing	17,584.0	21,112.2	22,085.9
Electricity, gas and water	2,730.7	3,356.4	3,257.5
Construction	5,169.0	5,848.7	5,893.6
Wholesale and retail trade	14,594.5	17,087.3	17,713.3
Transport and communications	5,914.9	6,589.0	6,835.2
Finance, insurance and business services	5,469.4	6,420.7	6,372.0
General government services	11,882.2	14,580.9	15,750.5
Other services	14,560.4	16,337.8	17,604.4
Sub-total	95,785.4	113,512.9	117,949.7
Net taxes on products	13,285.9	14,788.5	14,368.0
Less Imputed bank service charge	5,782.3	7,275.1	7,249.2
GDP in purchasers' values	103,289.0	121,026.3	125,068.6

* Preliminary figures.
† Estimates.

BALANCE OF PAYMENTS
(US $ million)

	2007	2008	2009
Exports of goods f.o.b.	2,335.7	2,537.6	2,386.8
Imports of goods f.o.b.	−4,094.3	−4,748.9	−3,927.2
Trade balance	−1,758.6	−2,211.3	−1,540.4
Exports of services	373.1	399.1	470.1
Imports of services	−555.1	−608.2	−554.7
Balance on goods and services	−1,940.6	−2,420.4	−1,625.0
Other income received	48.2	22.9	5.7
Other income paid	−182.8	−183.5	−240.2
Balance on goods, services and income	−2,075.2	−2,581.0	−1,859.5
Current transfers (net)	1,074.6	1,068.1	1,018.4
Current balance	−1,000.6	−1,512.9	−841.1
Capital (net)	416.2	523.9	511.0
Direct investment from abroad	381.7	626.1	434.2
Portfolio investment	−12.2	—	—
Other investment assets	−186.3	−276.6	−218.7
Other investment liabilities	284.1	137.9	36.0
Net errors and omissions	20.4	330.0	32.4
Overall balance	−96.7	−171.6	−46.3

Source: IMF, *International Financial Statistics*.

External Trade

PRINCIPAL COMMODITIES
(US $ million)

Imports c.i.f.	2007	2008	2009
Consumer goods	1,072.5	1,255.9	1,125.8
Non-durable consumer goods	843.5	1,009.1	940.6
Durable consumer goods	229.0	246.8	185.2
Petroleum, mineral fuels and lubricants	813.4	1,000.2	684.1
Crude petroleum	403.5	503.1	346.8
Mineral fuels and lubricants	409.9	497.1	337.2
Intermediate goods	1,009.5	1,226.3	824.6
Primary materials and intermediate goods for agriculture and fishing	113.9	172.2	138.4
Primary materials and intermediate goods for industry	678.5	808.5	686.2
Construction materials	217.2	245.7	161.6
Capital goods	695.2	846.0	670.6
For agriculture and fishing	35.6	44.0	28.2
For industry	405.5	536.7	436.1
For transport	254.0	265.3	206.2
Miscellaneous	7.2	9.4	10.8
Total	3,597.8	4,337.8	3,477.4

Exports f.o.b.	2007	2008	2009
Coffee	188.1	278.3	236.7
Groundnuts	56.0	90.2	65.9
Cattle on hoof	42.2	26.8	17.7
Beans	39.9	79.8	61.3
Bananas	9.9	9.6	11.7
Lobster	46.8	39.5	31.2
Fresh fish	14.1	14.0	13.4
Shrimp	46.1	48.3	38.3
Tobacco (leaf)	4.8	5.4	5.1
Gold	61.4	78.2	81.2
Meat and meat products	179.5	210.7	230.6
Refined sugars, etc.	74.3	50.4	50.0
Cheese	49.7	66.2	76.9
Wood products	6.3	4.9	4.7
Chemical products	49.6	63.8	66.9
Refined petroleum	10.1	15.7	11.3
Porcelain products	12.1	10.0	4.5
Total (incl. others)	1,224.8	1,488.7	1,390.9

PRINCIPAL TRADING PARTNERS
(US $ million)

Imports c.i.f.	2007	2008	2009
Canada	27.5	37.9	24.2
Costa Rica	303.9	341.1	319.5
Ecuador	136.0	107.0	41.4
El Salvador	172.4	229.3	170.0
Germany	42.6	50.8	42.4
Guatemala	222.8	264.6	217.4
Honduras	108.4	135.3	125.4
Japan	121.5	124.3	80.2
Mexico	492.8	361.7	243.6
Panama	16.0	19.7	12.1
Spain	36.9	46.9	51.7
Sweden	21.0	19.3	12.9
Taiwan	15.4	21.0	13.6
USA	781.3	899.9	692.9
Venezuela	255.8	625.2	586.6
Total (incl. others)	3,597.8	4,337.8	3,477.4

NICARAGUA

Exports f.o.b.	2007	2008	2009
Belgium	25.2	28.6	15.7
Canada	69.4	75.0	42.3
Costa Rica	87.6	102.97	86.0
El Salvador	168.1	217.2	199.4
France	10.3	12.6	19.0
Germany	24.0	26.8	14.8
Guatemala	65.6	74.9	61.7
Honduras	111.1	101.4	100.6
Italy	11.3	14.6	7.4
Mexico	57.9	78.9	56.8
Spain	43.3	43.3	36.2
USA	353.6	439.0	410.4
Total (incl. others)	1,224.8	1,488.7	1,390.9

Transport

RAILWAYS
(traffic)

	1990	1991	1992
Passenger-km (million)	3	3	6

Freight ton-km (million): 4 in 1985.

Source: UN, *Statistical Yearbook*.

ROAD TRAFFIC
(motor vehicles in use)

	2002	2003	2004
Passenger cars	83,168	86,020	94,998
Buses and coaches	6,947	13,782	16,139
Lorries and vans	111,797	120,408	136,674
Motorcycles and mopeds	28,973	42,153	47,547

Source: IRF, *World Road Statistics*.

2007 (motor vehicles in use): Passenger cars 115,432; Buses and coaches 18,668; Lorries and vans 156,295; Motorcycles and mopeds 56,525.

SHIPPING
Merchant fleet
(registered at 31 December)

	2007	2008	2009
Number of vessels	28	29	31
Total displacement ('000 grt)	5.7	6.5	7.9

Source: IHS Fairplay, *World Fleet Statistics*.

International Sea-Borne Freight Traffic
('000 metric tons)

	1997	1998	1999
Imports	1,272.7	1,964.7	1,180.7
Exports	329.3	204.5	183.6

Total international cargo movements ('000 metric tons): 2,831.5 in 2009.

CIVIL AVIATION
(traffic on scheduled services)

	1998	1999	2000
Kilometres flown (million)	1.2	0.8	0.8
Passengers carried ('000)	52	59	61
Passenger-km (million)	93	67	72
Freight ton-km (million)	n.a.	0.5	0.5

Source: UN Economic Commission for Latin America and the Caribbean.
2006: 1,047,000 passengers carried; 19,240 metric tons of cargo carried.

Tourism

TOURIST ARRIVALS BY COUNTRY OF ORIGIN

	2006	2007	2008
Canada	19,319	16,800	20,233
Costa Rica	80,009	71,370	70,733
El Salvador	103,537	118,252	123,501
Guatemala	56,662	69,629	68,819
Honduras	153,168	173,816	182,511
Panama	15,412	15,479	14,924
USA	164,273	170,662	196,602
Total (incl. others)	749,184	799,996	857,901

Tourism receipts (US $ million, excl. passenger transport): 231 in 2006; 255 in 2007; 276 in 2008.

Source: World Tourism Organization.

Communications Media

	2007	2008	2009
Telephones ('000 main lines in use)	249.0	252.0	255.0
Mobile cellular telephones ('000 subscribers)	2,502.3	3,108.0	3,204.4
Internet users ('000)	170.1	184.8	199.8
Broadband subscribers ('000)	27.6	36.1	47.0

Personal computers: 220,000 (40.3 per 1,000 persons) in 2005.
Radio receivers ('000 in use): 1,240 in 1997.
Television receivers ('000 in use): 350 in 2000.
Daily newspapers: 6 in 2004 (average circulation 135,000 copies in 1996).

Sources: UNESCO, *Statistical Yearbook*; International Telecommunication Union.

Education

(2007/08, unless otherwise indicated)

	Institutions*	Teachers	Students Males	Females	Total
Pre-primary	5,980	11,032	111,938	108,591	220,529
Primary	8,251	32,349	486,898	457,443	944,341
Secondary: general	1,249	16,164	212,449	234,419	446,868
Tertiary: university level	35	3,630†	47,683‡	51,222‡	98,905‡
Tertiary: other higher	73	210†	1,902‡	2,770‡	4,672‡

* 2002/03 figures.
† 2001/02 figure.
‡ 2003/04 figure.

Sources: UNESCO, *Statistical Yearbook*; Ministry of Education.
Pupil-teacher ratio (primary education, UNESCO estimate): 29.2 in 2007/08 (Source: UNESCO Institute for Statistics).
Adult literacy rate (UNESCO estimates): 80.5% (males 79.7%; females 81.4%) in 2007 (Source: UNESCO Institute for Statistics).

Directory

The Government

HEAD OF STATE

President: José Daniel Ortega Saavedra (elected 5 November 2006; took office 10 January 2007).
Vice-President: Jaime René Morales Carazo.

CABINET
(May 2011)

The Government is formed by the Frente Sandinista de Liberación Nacional.

Minister of Foreign Affairs: Samuel Santos López.
Minister of the Interior: Ana Isabel Morales Mazún.
Secretary-General of Defence with Ministerial Rank: Ruth Esperanza Tapia Roa.
Minister of Finance and Public Credit: Alberto José Guevara Obregón.
Minister of Development, Industry and Trade: Dr Orlando Solórzano Delgadillo.
Minister of Labour: Jeannette Chávez Gómez.
Minister of the Environment and Natural Resources: Juana Argeñal Sandoval.
Minister of Transport and Infrastructure: Pablo Fernando Martínez Espinoza.
Minister of Agriculture and Forestry: Ariel Bucardo Rocha.
Minister of Health: Dr Sonia Castro González.
Minister of Education: Miriam Ráudez.
Minister of the Family, Adolescence and Childhood: Marcia Ramírez Mercado.
Minister of Energy and Mines: Emilio Rappaccioli Baltodano.
Secretary to the Presidency: Salvador Vanegas Guido.
Co-ordinator of the Communication and Citizenship Council: Rosario Murillo Zambrana.

MINISTRIES

Office of the President: Casa Presidencial, Managua; e-mail daniel@presidencia.gob.ni; internet www.presidencia.gob.ni.
Ministry of Agriculture and Forestry: Km 8½, Carretera a Masaya, Managua; tel. 2276-0200; fax 2276-0204; e-mail ministro@magfor.gob.ni; internet www.magfor.gob.ni.
Ministry of Defence: De los semáforos el Redentor, 4 c. arriba, donde fue la casa 'Ricardo Morales Aviles', Managua; tel. 2222-2201; fax 2222-5439; e-mail prensa.midef@midef.gob.ni; internet www.midef.gob.ni.
Ministry of Development, Industry and Trade: Edif. Central, Km 6, Carretera a Masaya, Apdo 8, Managua; tel. 2278-8702; fax 2270-095; internet www.mific.gob.ni.
Ministry of Education: Complejo Cívico Camilo Ortega Saavedra, Managua; tel. 2265-1451; fax 2265-1595; e-mail webmaster@mined.gob.ni; internet www.mined.gob.ni.
Ministry of Energy and Mines: Hospital Bautista, 1 c. al oeste, 1 c. al norte, Managua; tel. 2280-9500; fax 2280-9516; e-mail informacion@mem.gob.ni; internet www.mem.gob.ni.
Ministry of the Environment and Natural Resources: Km 12½, Carretera Norte, Apdo 5123, Managua; tel. 2233-1111; fax 2263-1274; e-mail jargenal@marena.gob.ni; internet www.marena.gob.ni.
Ministry of the Family, Adolescence and Childhood: De donde fue ENEL Central, 100 m al sur, Managua; tel. 2278-1620; e-mail webmaster@mifamilia.gob.ni; internet www.mifamilia.gob.ni.
Ministry of Finance and Public Credit: Frente a la Asamblea Nacional, Apdo 2170, Managua; tel. 2222-6530; fax 2222-6430; e-mail webmaster@mhcp.gob.ni; internet www.hacienda.gob.ni.
Ministry of Foreign Affairs: Del Antiguo Cine González 1 c. al sur, sobre Avda Bolívar, Managua; tel. 2244-8000; fax 2228-5102; e-mail despacho.ministro@cancilleria.gob.ni; internet www.cancilleria.gob.ni.
Ministry of Health: Complejo Nacional de Salud 'Dra Concepción Palacios', costado oeste Colonia Primero de Mayo, Apdo 107, Managua; tel. 2289-7164; e-mail webmaster@minsa.gob.ni; internet www.minsa.gob.ni.
Ministry of the Interior: Apdo 68, Managua; tel. 2228-2284; fax 2222-2789; e-mail webmaster@migob.gob.ni; internet www.migob.gob.ni.
Ministry of Labour: Estadio Nacional, 400 m al norte, Apdo 487, Managua; tel. 2222-2115; fax 2228-2103; e-mail info@mitrab.gob.ni; internet www.mitrab.gob.ni.
Ministry of Transport and Infrastructure: Frente al Estadio Nacional, Apdo 26, Managua; tel. 2228-2061; fax 2222-5111; e-mail webmaster@mti.gob.ni; internet www.mti.gob.ni.

President and Legislature

PRESIDENT

Election, 5 November 2006

Candidate	Votes	% of total
José Daniel Ortega Saavedra (FSLN)	930,862	37.99
Eduardo Montealegre Rivas (ALN)	693,391	28.30
José Rizo Castellón (PLC)	664,225	27.11
Edmundo Jarquín Calderón (MRS)	154,224	6.29
Edén Pastora Gómez (AC)	7,200	0.29
Total	**2,449,902**	**100.00**

ASAMBLEA NACIONAL

National Assembly: Avda Bolívar, Contiguo a la Presidencia de la República, Managua; e-mail webmaster@correo.asamblea.gob.ni; internet www.asamblea.gob.ni.
President: René Núñez Téllez.
First Vice-President: Oscar Moncada Reyes.
Second Vice-President: Carlos García.
Third Vice-President: Juan Ramón Jiménez.

Election, 5 November 2006

Party	Votes	% of total	Seats
Frente Sandinista de Liberación Nacional (FSLN)	1,837,901	37.47	38
Partido Liberal Constitucionalista (PLC)	1,355,594	27.63	25
Alianza Liberal Nicaragüense (ALN)	1,279,859	26.09	22
Movimiento Renovador Sandinista (MRS)	405,149	8.26	5
Alternativa por el Cambio (AC)	27,135	0.55	—
Total	**4,905,638***	**100.00**	**90†**

* Each elector had two votes: one for representatives at regional level (for which there were 70 seats) and one for representatives at national level (20 seats). The total number of votes cast at regional level was 2,487,448, while at national level 2,418,190 votes were cast.
† In addition to the 90 elected members, supplementary seats in the Asamblea Nacional are awarded to the unsuccessful candidates at the presidential election who were not nominated for the legislature but who received, in the presidential poll, a number of votes at least equal to the average required for one of the 70 legislative seats decided at a regional level. On this basis, the ALN obtained one additional seat in the Asamblea Nacional. A legislative seat is also awarded to the outgoing President, bringing the total number of seats in the Asamblea Nacional to 92.

Election Commission

Consejo Supremo Electoral (CSE): Iglesia Las Palmas, 1 c. al sur, Apdo 2241, Managua; tel. 2268-7948; e-mail info@cse.gob.ni; internet www.cse.gob.ni; Pres. Roberto José Rivas Reyes.

Political Organizations

Alianza Liberal Nicaragüense (ALN): Managua; fmrly Movimiento de Salvación Liberal; adopted current name in 2006; formed alliance with Partido Conservador (q.v.) ahead of 2006 elections; Pres. Alejandro Mejía Ferreti; Sec.-Gen. Carlos García.

Alianza por la República (APRE): Casa 211, Col. Los Robles, Funeraria Monte de los Olivos 1.5 c. al norte, Managua; f. 2004 by

NICARAGUA

supporters of President Enrique Bolaños Geyer; Pres. MIGUEL LÓPEZ BALDIZÓN.

Movimiento Democrático Nicaragüense (MDN): Casa L-39, Ciudad Jardín Bnd, 50 m al sur, Managua; tel. 2243-898; f. 1978; Leader ROBERTO SEQUEIRA GÓMEZ.

Partido Social Cristiano (PSC): Ciudad Jardín, Pizza María, 1 c. al lago, Managua; tel. 2222-026; f. 1957; 42,000 mems; Pres. ABEL REYES TELLEZ.

Alternativa por el Cambio (AC): Managua; f. as Alternativa Cristiana; fmr faction of Frente Sandinista de Liberación Nacional (q.v.); name changed as above in 2006; Pres. Dr ORLANDO J. TARDENCILLA ESPINOZA.

Camino Cristiano Nicaragüense (CCN): Managua; Pres. GUILLERMO ANTONIO OSORNO MOLINA.

Frente Sandinista de Liberación Nacional (FSLN) (Sandinista National Liberation Front): Costado oeste Parque El Carmen, Managua; tel. and fax 2266-8173; internet www.fsln.org.ni; f. 1960; led by a 15-mem. directorate; embraces Izquierda Democrática Sandinista 'orthodox revolutionary' faction, led by Daniel Ortega Saavedra; leads Nicaragua Triunfa electoral alliance; 120,000 mems; Gen. Sec. JOSÉ DANIEL ORTEGA SAAVEDRA.

Movimiento de Unidad Cristiana (MUC): Managua; mem. of Convergencia Nacional alliance; Pres. Pastor DANIEL ORTEGA REYES.

Partido Conservador (PC): Colegio Centroamérica, 500 m al sur, Managua; tel. 2267-0484; e-mail contactenos@partidoconservador.org.ni; f. 1992 following merger between Partido Conservador Demócrata and Partido Socialconservadurismo; formed alliance with Alianza Liberal Nicaragüense (q.v.) ahead of 2006 elections; legal status annulled by the Consejo Supremo Electoral in June 2008; Pres. AZALIA AVILÉS.

Partido Indígena Multiétnico (PIM): Residencial Los Robles, de Farmacentro 1 c. al este, 80 varas al sur, Managua; Pres. CARLA WHITE HODGSON.

Partido Liberal Constitucionalista (PLC): Semáforos Country Club 100 m al este, Apdo 4569, Managua; tel. 2278-8705; fax 2278-1800; f. 1967; Pres. JORGE CASTILLO QUANT; Nat. Sec. Dr NOEL RAMÍREZ SÁNCHEZ.

Partido Liberal Nacionalista (PLN): Managua; f. 1913; Pres. CONSTANTINO VELÁSQUEZ ZEPEDA.

Partido Movimiento de Unidad Costeña (PAMUC): Bilwi Puerto Cabeza; Pres. KENNETH SERAPIO HUNTER.

Partido Neo-Liberal (Pali): Cine Dorado, 2 c. al sur, 50 m arriba, Managua; tel. 2266-5166; f. 1986; Pres. ADOLFO GARCÍA ESQUIVEL.

Partido Resistencia Nicaragüense (PRN): Edif. VINSA, frente a Autonica, Carretera Sur, Managua; tel. and fax 2270-6508; e-mail salvata@ibw.com.ni; f. 1993; nationalist party; Pres. JULIO CÉSAR BLANDÓN SÁNCHEZ (KALIMÁN).

Partido Socialista (PS): Hospital Militar, 100 m al norte, 100 m al oeste, 100 m al sur, Managua; tel. 2266-2321; fax 2266-2936; f. 1944; social democratic party; Sec.-Gen. Dr GUSTAVO TABLADA ZELAYA.

Partido Unionista Centroamericano (PUCA): Cine Cabrera, 1 c. al este, 20 m al norte, Managua; tel. 2227-472; f. 1904; Pres. BLANCA ROJAS ECHAVERRY.

Unidad Nicaragüense por la Esperanza (UNE): Managua; f. 2010 to support the presidential candidacy of Fabio Gadea Mantilla in 2011 elections; electoral coalition; Leader FABIO GADEA MANTILLA; mems include:

Movimiento Renovador Sandinista (MRS): De los semáforos del Ministerio de Gobernación, 1/2 cuadra al norte, Managua; tel. 2250-9461; fax 2278-0268; e-mail info@partidomrs.com; internet www.partidomrs.com; f. 1995; fmr faction of Frente Sandinista de Liberación Nacional (q.v.); formed the Alianza Patriótica in advance of the 2011 elections; Pres. ENRIQUE SÁENZ; Sec. ANA MARGARITA VIJIL.

Vamos con Eduardo (VCE): Managua; internet www.vamosconeduardo.org; f. 2005; merged with the Partido Liberal Independiente in 2009; Pres EDUARDO MONTEALEGRE.

Unión Demócrata Cristiana (UDC): De Iglesia Santa Ana, 2 c. abajo, Barrio Santa Ana, Apdo 3089, Managua; tel. 2266-2576; f. 1976 as Partido Popular Social Cristiano; name officially changed as above in Dec. 1993; mem. of Convergencia Nacional alliance; Pres. AGUSTÍN JARQUÍN ANAYA.

Yatama (Yapti Tasba Masraka Nanih Aslatakanka): Of. de Odacan, Busto José Martí, 1 c. al este y 1/2 c. al norte, Managua; tel. 2228-1494; Atlantic coast Miskito org.; mem. of FSLN-led electoral alliance, Nicaragua Triunfa; Leader BROOKLYN RIVERA BRYAN.

Diplomatic Representation

EMBASSIES IN NICARAGUA

Argentina: Reparto Las Colinas, Calle Prado Ecuestre 235B (interseción con Calle los Mangos), Apdo 703, Managua; tel. 2283-7066; fax 2270-2343; e-mail embargentina@amnet.com.ni; Ambassador JORGE TELESFORO PEREIRA.

Brazil: Km $7^{3}/_{4}$, Carretera Sur, Quinta los Pinos, Apdo 264, Managua; tel. 2265-0035; fax 2265-2206; e-mail ebrasil@ibw.com.ni; Ambassador FLAVIO HELMOLD MACIEIRA.

Chile: Entrada principal los Robles, Semáforos Hotel Milton Princess, 1 c. abajo, 1 c. al sur, Apdo 1289, Managua; tel. 2278-0619; fax 2270-4073; e-mail echileni@cablenet.com.ni; Ambassador NATACHA MOLINA GARCÍA.

Colombia: 2da Entrada a Las Colinas, 1 c. arriba, 1/2 c. al lago, Casa 97, Apdo 1062, Managua; tel. 2276-2149; fax 2276-0644; e-mail emanagua@cancilleria.gov.co; Ambassador ANTONIO GONZÁLEZ CASTAÑO.

Costa Rica: Reparto Las Colinas, Calle Prado Ecuestre 304, 1°, Managua; tel. 2276-1352; fax 2276-0115; e-mail infembcr@cablenet.com.ni; Ambassador (vacant).

Cuba: 3a Entrada a Las Colinas, 400 varas arriba, 75 al sur, Managua; tel. 2276-0742; fax 2276-0166; e-mail embacuba@embacuba.net.ni; internet embacu.cubaminrex.cu/nicaragua; Ambassador EDUARDO MARTÍNEZ BORBONET.

Denmark: De la Plaza España, 1 c. abajo, 2 c. al lago, 1/2 c. abajo, Apdo 4942, Managua; tel. 2268-0250; fax 2266-8095; e-mail mgaambu@um.dk; internet www.ambmanagua.um.dk; Ambassador SØREN VØHTZ.

Dominican Republic: Reparto Las Colinas, Prado Ecuestre 100, con Curva de los Gallos, Apdo 614, Managua; tel. 2276-2029; fax 2276-0654; e-mail embdom@cablenet.com.ni; Ambassador PEDRO DESIDERIO BLANDINO CANTO.

Ecuador: Barrio Bolonia, Sede Central Los Pipitos, 1 1/2 c. oeste, Managua; tel. 2268-1098; fax 2266-8081; e-mail ecuador@ibw.com.ni; Ambassador ANTONIO EUTIMIO PRECIADO BEDOYA.

El Salvador: Reparto Las Colinas, Avda del Campo y Pasaje, Los Cerros 142, Apdo 149, Managua; tel. 2276-0712; fax 2276-0711; e-mail embelsa@cablenet.com.ni; internet www.embelsanica.org.ni; Ambassador ALFREDO FRANCISCO UNGO RIVAS LAGUARDIA.

Finland: Sucursal Jorge Navarro, Apdo 2219, Managua; tel. 2278-1216; fax 2278-2840; e-mail sanomat.mgu@formin.fi; internet www.finlandia.org.ni; Ambassador EIJA ROTINEN.

France: Iglesia el Carmen 1 1/2 c. abajo, Apdo 1227, Managua; tel. 2222-6210; fax 2268-5630; e-mail info@ambafrance-ni.org; internet www.ambafrance-ni.org; Ambassador THIERRY PIERRE FRAYSSÉ.

Germany: Bolonia, de la Rotonda El Güegüense, 1 1/2 c. al lago, contiguo a Optica Nicaragüense, Apdo 29, Managua; tel. 2266-3917; fax 2266-7667; e-mail alemania@cablenet.com.ni; internet www.managua.diplo.de; Ambassador ANNA BETINA KERN.

Guatemala: Km 11 1/2, Carretera a Masaya, Apdo E-1, Managua; tel. 2279-9609; fax 2279-9610; e-mail embnic@minex.gob.gt; Ambassador EDGAR RUANO NAJARRO.

Holy See: Apostolic Nunciature, Km 10.8, Carretera Sur, Apdo 506, Managua; tel. 2265-8657; fax 2265-7416; e-mail nuntius@cablenet.com.ni; Apostolic Nuncio Most Rev. HENRYK JÓZEF NOWACKI (Titular Archbishop of Blera).

Honduras: Reparto Las Colinas, Prado Ecuestre 298, frente a Residencia de la Embajada de China (Taiwán), Apdo 321, Managua; tel. 2276-2406; fax 2276-1998; e-mail embhonduras@cablenet.com.ni; Chargé d'affaires a.i. VICTORIA MARGARITA RODAS AMAYA.

Iran: Del Club Terraza, 300 m al este, de la principal entrada de las Cumbres, 3 c. al sur, No E4, Managua; tel. 2270-0954; fax 2255-0565; e-mail embirannic@cablenet.com.ni; Ambassador AKBAR ESMAEIL POUR.

Italy: Residencial Bolonia, Rotonda El Güegüense, 1 c. al norte, 1/2 c. al oeste, Apdo 2092, Managua 4; tel. 2266-2961; fax 2266-3987; e-mail ambasciata.managua@esteri.it; internet www.ambmanagua.esteri.it; Ambassador OMBRETTA PACILIO.

Japan: Plaza España, 1 c. abajo y 1 c. al lago, Bolonia, Apdo 1789, Managua; tel. 2266-8668; fax 2266-8566; e-mail embjpnic@ibw.com.ni; internet www.ni.emb-japan.go.jp; Ambassador JIRO SHIBASAKI.

Korea, Republic: De la Rotonda El Güegüense 3. al Oeste, 1/2 c. al sur, casa A-45, Apdo LV101, Managua; tel. 2254-8107; fax 2254-8131; e-mail nicaragua@mofat.go.kr; Ambassador LEE SANG-PAL.

Libya: Del portón principal del Hopsital Militar 1 c. al lago, 1 c. abajo y 1/2 al lago, Reparto Bolonia, Managua; tel. 2266-8540; fax 2266-8542; e-mail ofilibia@ibw.com.ni; Sec. of the People's Bureau ABDULLAH MUHAMMAD MATOUG.

Luxembourg: Residencial Bolonia del Hospital Militar, 1c. al lago y 1 1/2 abajo, Contiguo al Hotel Maracas Inn, Apdo 969, Managua; tel.

NICARAGUA

2268-1881; fax 2266-7965; e-mail secretariat.managua@mae.etat.lu; Chargé d'affaires a.i. RENÉ LAUER.

Mexico: Contiguo a Optica Matamoros, Km 4½, Carretera a Masaya, 25 varas Arriba, Altamira, Apdo 834, Managua; tel. 2278-4919; fax 2278-2886; e-mail embamex@turbonett.com.ni; Ambassador RAÚL LÓPEZ-LIRA NAVA.

Netherlands: Calle Erasmus de Rotterdam, Carretera a Masaya Km 5, del Colegio Teresiano 1 c. al sur, 1 c. abajo, Apdo 3688, Managua; tel. 2276-8630; fax 2276-0399; e-mail mng@minbuza.nl; internet www.embajadaholanda-nic.com; Ambassador LAMBERTUS CHRISTIAAN GRIJNS.

Norway: Rotonda El Güegüense, 100 m el Oeste, Apdo 2090, Correo Central, Managua; tel. 2266-4199; fax 2266-3303; e-mail emb.managua@mfa.no; internet www.noruega.org.ni; Ambassador TOM TYRIHJELL.

Panama: Casa 93, Reparto Mántica, del Cuartel General de Bomberos 1 c. abajo, Apdo 1, Managua; tel. 2266-8633; fax 2266-2224; e-mail embdpma@enitel.com.ni; Ambassador OLIMPO ANIBAL SÁENZ MARCUCI.

Peru: Del Hospital Militar, 1 c. al norte, 2 c. hacia oeste, casa 325, Apdo 211, Managua; tel. 2266-8678; fax 2266-8679; e-mail embajada@peruennicaragua.com.ni; internet www.peruennicaragua.com.ni; Ambassador CARLOS BÉRNINZON DEVÉSCOVI.

Russia: Reparto Las Colinas, Calle Vista Alegre 214, Apdo 249, Managua; tel. 2276-0374; fax 2276-0179; e-mail rossia@cablenet.com.ni; internet www.nicaragua.mid.ru; Ambassador IGOR S. KONDRASHEV.

Spain: Avda Central 13, Las Colinas, Apdo 284, Managua; tel. 2276-0966; fax 2276-0937; e-mail emb.managua@mae.es; internet www.mae.es/embajadas/managua; Ambassador ANTONIO PÉREZ-HERNÁNDEZ TORRA.

Taiwan (Republic of China): Optica Matamoros, 2 c. abajo, ½ c. al lago, Carretera a Masaya, Planes de Altamira, Apdo 4653, Managua; tel. 2277-1333; fax 2267-4025; e-mail nic@mofa.gov.tw; internet www.roc-taiwan.org.ni; Ambassador WU CHIN-MU.

USA: Km 5½, Carretera Sur, Apdo 327, Managua; tel. 2252-7100; fax 2252-7304; e-mail consularmanagua@state.gov; internet nicaragua.usembassy.gov; Ambassador ROBERT J. CALLAHAN.

Venezuela: Costado norte de la Iglesia Santo Domingo, Las Sierritas, Casa 27, Apdo 406, Managua; tel. 2272-0267; fax 2272-2265; e-mail embaveznica@cablenet.com.ni; Chargé d'affaires a.i. PEDRO LUIS PENSO SÁNCHEZ.

Judicial System

The Supreme Court

Km 7½, Carretera Norte, Managua; tel. 2233-0083; fax 2233-0581; e-mail webmaster@csj.gob.ni; internet www.poderjudicial.gob.ni.

Deals with both civil and criminal cases, acts as a Court of Cassation, appoints Judges of First Instance, and generally supervises the legal administration of the country.

President: Dr ALBA LUZ RAMOS VANEGAS.
Vice-President: MARVIN AGUILAR GARCÍA.
Attorney-General: Dr HERNÁN ESTRADA.

Religion

All religions are tolerated. Almost all of Nicaragua's inhabitants profess Christianity, and the majority belong to the Roman Catholic Church. The Moravian Church predominates on the Caribbean coast.

CHRISTIANITY

The Roman Catholic Church

Nicaragua comprises one archdiocese, six dioceses and the Apostolic Vicariate of Bluefields. According to the latest available census figures (2005), some 58% of the population aged five years and above are Roman Catholics.

Bishops' Conference

Conferencia Episcopal de Nicaragua, Ferretería Lang 1 c. al norte, 1 c. al este, Zona 3, Las Piedrecitas, Apdo 2407, Managua; tel. 2266-6292; fax 2266-8069; e-mail cen@tmx.com.ni.

f. 1975; statute approved 1987; Pres. LEOPOLDO JOSÉ BRENES SOLÓRZANO (Archbishop of Managua).

Archbishop of Managua: LEOPOLDO JOSÉ BRENES SOLÓRZANO, Arzobispado, Apdo 2008, Managua; tel. 2276-0129; fax 2276-0130; e-mail mob@unica.edu.ni.

The Anglican Communion

Nicaragua comprises one of the five dioceses of the Iglesia Anglicana de la Región Central de América.

Bishop of Nicaragua: Rt Rev. STURDIE W. DOWNS, Apdo 1207, Managua; tel. 2222-5174; fax 2222-6701; e-mail episcnic@tmx.com.ni.

Protestant Churches

Some 22% of the population aged five years and above are members of evangelical churches, according to the last census (2005).

Baptist Convention of Nicaragua: Apdo 2593, Managua; tel. 2225-785; fax 2224-131; f. 1917; 135 churches, 20,000 mems (2006); Pres. ABEL MENDOZA; Sec. DALIA NAVARRETE.

The Moravian Church in Nicaragua: Iglesia Morava, Bilwi; tel. and fax 2282-2222; 199 churches, 83,000 mems; Leader Rt Rev. JOHN WILSON.

The Nicaraguan Lutheran Church of Faith and Hope: Apdo 151, Managua; tel. 2266-4467; fax 2266-4609; e-mail luterana@turbonett.com.ni; f. 1994; 7,000 mems (2007); Pres. Rev. VICTORIA CORTEZ RODRÍGUEZ.

The Press

NEWSPAPERS AND PERIODICALS

Bolsa de Noticias: Col. Centroamérica, Grupo L 852, Apdo VF-90, Managua; tel. 2270-0546; fax 2277-4931; e-mail prensa@bolsadenoticias.com.ni; internet www.bolsadenoticias.com.ni; f. 1974; daily; Dir MARÍA ELSA SUÁREZ GARCÍA; Editor-in-Chief MARÍA ELENA PALACIOS.

Confidencial: De Pharoahs Casino, 2 c. abajo, 2 c. al sur, Managua; tel. 2277-5134; fax 2270-7017; e-mail info@confidencial.com.ni; internet www.confidencial.com.ni; weekly; political analysis; Dir CARLOS F. CHAMORRO; Editors IVÁN OLIVARES, CARLOS SALINAS.

La Gaceta, Diario Oficial: De la Rotonda de Plaza Inter, 1 c. arriba, 2 c. al lago, Managua; tel. 2228-3791; fax 2228-4001; e-mail lagaceta@presidencia.gob.ni; internet www.lagaceta.gob.ni; f. 1912; morning; daily; official; Dir Dr LEOPOLDO CASTRILLO.

Novedades: Pista P. Joaquín Chamorro, Km 4, Carretera Norte, Apdo 576, Managua; evening; daily.

Nuevo Diario: Pista P. Joaquín Chamorro, Km 4, Carretera Norte, Apdo 4591, Managua; tel. 2249-0499; fax 2249-0700; e-mail info@elnuevodiario.com.ni; internet www.elnuevodiario.com.ni; f. 1980; morning; daily; independent; Dir FRANCISCO CHAMORRO; Editor-in-Chief ROBERTO COLLADO; circ. 45,000.

El Observador Económico: De Pricesmart, 2 c. al lago, Apdo 2074, Managua; tel. 2266-8708; fax 2266-8711; e-mail info@elobservadoreconomico.com; internet www.elobservadoreconomico.com; Dir-Gen. ALEJANDRO MARTÍNEZ CUENCA.

La Prensa: Km 4½, Carretera Norte, Apdo 192, Managua; tel. 2249-8405; fax 2249-6926; e-mail info@laprensa.com.ni; internet www.laprensa.com.ni; f. 1926; morning; daily; independent; Pres. JAIME CHAMORRO CARDENAL; Editor F. POTOY; circ. 30,000.

Prensa Proletaria: Managua; tel. 2222-594; fortnightly; official publ. of the Movimiento de Acción Popular Marxista-Leninista.

Revista 7 Días: Altamira de lo Vicky, 5½ al lago, Managua; tel. 2270-6509; e-mail 7dias@ibw.com.ni; internet www.7dias.com.ni.

Revista Encuentro: Universidad Centroamericana, Apdo 69, Managua; tel. 2278-3923; fax 2267-0106; e-mail ucapubli@ns.uca.edu.ni; internet www.uca.edu.ni:8080/encuentro; f. 1968; termly; academic publ. of the Universidad Centroamericana; Dir JORGE ALBERTO PÉREZ HUETE.

Revista Envío: Edif. Nitlapán, 2°, Campus Universidad Centroamericana, Apdo A-194, Managua; tel. 2278-2557; fax 2278-1402; e-mail envio@ns.uca.edu.ni; internet www.envio.org.ni; f. 1981; 11 a year; political economic and social analysis; edns in Spanish, English and Italian; Dir JUAN RAMIRO MARTÍNEZ; Chief Editor MARÍA LÓPEZ VIGIL.

Tiempos del Mundo: Apdo 3525, Managua; tel. 2270-3418; fax 2270-3419; e-mail tiempos@tdm.com.ni; f. 1996; weekly; Gen. Man. TAKUYA ISHII; circ. 5,000.

La Tribuna: Detrás del Banco Mercantil, Plaza España, Apdo 1469, Managua; tel. 2266-9282; fax 2266-5167; e-mail tribuna@latribuna.com.ni; f. 1993; morning; daily; Dir HAROLDO J. MONTEALEGRE; Gen. Man. MARIO GONZÁLEZ.

NICARAGUA

Trinchera de la Noticia: Managua; tel. 2240-0114; e-mail info@trinchera.com.ni; internet www.trinchera.com.ni; daily; Dir XAVIER REYES ALBA; Man. EMILIO NÚÑEZ TENORIO.

Visión Sandinista: Costado este, Parque El Carmen, Managua; tel. and fax 2268-1565; internet www.visionsandinista.com; f. 1980; weekly; official publ. of the Frente Sandinista de Liberación Nacional; Dir MAYRA REYES SANDOVAL.

Association

Unión de Periodistas de Nicaragua (UPN): Apdo 4006, Managua; tel. 2271-2436; e-mail uperiodistasnic@yahoo.com; internet www.aquinicaragua.com/periodistas2.html; Pres. RÓGER SUÁREZ.

Publishers

Academia Nicaragüense de la Lengua: Avda del Campo, 42 Las Colinas, Apdo 2711, Managua; fax 2249-5389; e-mail pavsa@mundinet.com.ni; f. 1928; languages; Dir JORGE EDUARDO ARELLANO SANDINO.

Ediciones Océano, SA: Km. 7 1/2, Carretera a Masaya, Contiguo a Nitalsa, Managua; tel. 2276-1372; fax 2276-1443; e-mail edocanic@ibw.com.ni; internet www.oceano.com; Spanish culture and language; Dir-Gen. ELVIN CANO.

Editora de Arte SA: Etapa 53, Col. Los Robles III, Managua; tel. 2278-5854; e-mail editarte@editarte.com.ni; internet www.editarte.com.ni.

Editorial Nueva Nicaragua: Paseo Salvador Allende, Km 3½, Carretera Sur, Apdo 073, Managua; fax 266-6520; f. 1981; Pres. Dr SERGIO RAMÍREZ MERCADO; Dir-Gen. ROBERTO DÍAZ CASTILLO.

Editorial Unión: Altagracia Rest Los Ranchos, 4 1/2 c. al Sur, Managua; tel. 2266-0019; travel.

Librería Hispanoamericana (HISPAMER): Costado este de la UCA, Apdo A-221, Managua; tel. 2278-1210; fax 2278-0825; e-mail hispamer@hispamer.com.ni; internet hispamer.com.ni; f. 1991; Man. JESÚS DE SANTIAGO.

UCA Publicaciónes: Avda Universitaria, Rotonda Rubén Darío 150 m. al oeste, Apdo 69, Managua; tel. 2278-5951; fax 2278-5951; e-mail comsj@ns.uca.edu.ni; internet www.uca.edu.ni; academic publishing dept of the Universidad Centroamericana; Publ. Dir GUNTER GADEA BARBERENA.

Universidad Nacional Agraria: Km 12½ Carretera Norte, Apdo 453, Managua; tel. 233-1950; e-mail info@una.edu.ni; internet www.una.edu.ni; sciences.

Broadcasting and Communications

TELECOMMUNICATIONS

Regulatory Body

Instituto Nicaragüense de Telecomunicaciones y Correos (Telcor): Edif. Telcor, Avda Bolívar diagonal a Cancillería, Apdo 2264, Managua; tel. 2222-7350; fax 2222-7554; e-mail mgutierrez@telcor.gob.ni; internet www.telcor.gob.ni; Exec. Pres. ORLANDO CASTILLO.

Major Service Providers

Telefonía Celular de Nicaragua, SA (Movistar Nicaragua—TCN): Edif. Movistar, Km. 6 1/2, Carretera a Masaya, Managua; tel. 2277-0731; fax 2268-0389; e-mail gerardo.mena@telefonica.com.ni; internet www.movistar.com.ni; Man. MATÍAS SEÑORÁN.

Claro: Villafontana, 2°, Apdo 232, Managua; tel. 2277-3057; fax 2270-2128; e-mail cliente@claro.com.ni; internet www.claro.com.ni; f. 2006 by merger of ALÓ PCS (f. 2002) and Empresa Nicaragüense de Telecomunicaciones (Enitel, f. 1925); subsidiary of América Móvil, SA de CV (Mexico); Chair. PATRICIO SLIM DOMIT; CEO DANIEL HAJJ ABOUMRAD.

Telefónica SA Nicaragua: Km 6½, Carretera a Masaya, Managua; tel. 2277-0731; internet www.movistar.com.ni; fmrly BellSouth; owned by Grupo Telefónica Móviles (Spain); mobile cellular telephone provider; Vice-Pres. HUMBERTO PATO-VINUESA; Gen. Man. MARÍA JOSEFINA PERALTA.

BROADCASTING

Radio

La Nueva Radio Ya: Pista de la Resistencia, Frente a la Universidad Centroamericana, Managua; tel. 2278-8335; fax 2278-8334; e-mail info@nuevaya.com.ni; internet www.nuevaya.com.ni; f. 1990 as Radio Ya; restyled as above in 1999; operated by Entretenimiento Digital, SA; Dir-Gen. DENNIS SCHWARTZ.

Radio Católica: Altamira D'Este 621, 3°, Apdo 2183, Managua; tel. 2278-0836; fax 2278-2544; e-mail oramos@radiocatolica.org; internet www.radiocatolica.org; f. 1961; controlled by Conferencia Episcopal de Nicaragua; Dir Fr ROLANDO ÁLVAREZ; Gen. Man. ALBERTO CARBALLO MADRIGAL.

Radio Corporación, Gadea y Cía: Avda Ponciano Lombillo, Ciudad Jardín Q-20, Apdo 24242, Managua; tel. 2249-1619; fax 2244-3824; e-mail rc540@radio-corporacion.com; internet www.radio-corporacion.com; f. 1995; Gen. Man. FABIO GADEA MANTILLA; Asst Man. CARLOS GADEA MANTILLA.

Radio Estrella: Sierritas de Santo Domingo, Frente al Cementerio, Apdo UNICA 104, Managua; tel. 2276-0241; fax 2276-0062; e-mail radiosm@radioestrelladelmar.com; internet www.radioestrelladelmar.com; f. 1997; Catholic.

Radio Mundial: 36 Avda Oeste, Reparto Loma Verde, Apdo 3170, Managua; tel. 2266-6767; fax 2266-4630; f. 1948; commercial; Dir-Gen. ALMA ROSA ARANA HARTIG.

Radio Nicaragua: Villa Fontana, Contiguo a Enitel, Apdo 4665, Managua; tel. 2227-2330; fax 2267-1448; e-mail director@radionicaragua.com.ni; internet www.radionicaragua.com.ni; f. 1960; govt station; Dir-Gen. ALBERTO CARBALLO MADRIGAL.

Radio Ondas de Luz: Costado Sur del Hospital Bautista, Apdo 607, Managua; tel. and fax 2249-7058; f. 1959; religious and cultural station; Pres. GUILLERMO OSORNO MOLINA.

Radio Sandino: Paseo Tiscapa Este, Contiguo al Restaurante Mirador, Apdo 4776, Managua; tel. 2228-1330; fax 2262-4052; internet www.lasandino.com.ni; f. 1977; station controlled by the Frente Sandinista de Liberación Nacional; Pres. RAFAEL ORTEGA MURILLO.

Radio Segovia: Ocotal, Nueva Segovia; tel. 2732-2870; fax 2732-2271; e-mail info@radiosegovia.net; internet www.radiosegovia.net; f. 1980; commercial.

Radio Tiempo: Altamira D'este, Casa No 776, de donde fue Lozelsa, 1 c. al lago, 1 c. al abajo, Managua; tel. 2278-2540; fax 2277-1964; f. 1976; Dir DANILO LACAYO LANZAS.

Radio Universidad: Avda Card, 3 c. abajo, Apdo 2883, Managua; tel. 2278-4743; fax 2277-5057; internet www.ladelcolor.com; f. 1984; Dir LUIS LÓPEZ RUIZ.

There are some 50 other radio stations.

Television

Canal 4: Montoya, 1 c. al sur, 2 c. arriba, Managua; tel. 2228-1310; fax 2222-4067; internet www.multinoticias.tv; owned by Radio y Televisión de Nicaragua, SA (RATENSA).

Nicavisión, Canal 12: Bolonia Dual Card, 1 c. abajo, ½ c. al sur, Apdo 2766, Managua; tel. 2266-0691; fax 2266-1424; f. 1993; Dir MARIANO VALLE PETERS.

Televicentro de Nicaragua, SA, Canal 2: Casa del Obrero, 6½ c. al sur, Apdo 688, Managua; tel. 2268-2222; fax 2266-3688; e-mail tvnoticias@canal2.com.ni; internet www.canal2.com.ni; f. 1965; Pres. OCTAVIO SACASA RASKOSKY; Gen. Man. ALEJANDRO SACASA PASOS.

Televisión Internacional, Canal 23: Casa L-852, Col. Centroamérica, Managua; tel. 2268-7466; fax 2266-0625; e-mail canal23@ibw.com.ni; f. 1993; Pres. CÉSAR RIGUERO.

Televisora Nicaragüense, SA (Telenica 8): De la Mansión Teodolinda, 1 c. al sur, ½ c. abajo, Bolonia, Apdo 3611, Managua; tel. 2266-5021; fax 2266-5024; internet www.telenica.com.ni; f. 1989; sold to private buyer in 2010; Pres. (vacant).

Ultravisión de Nicaragua, SA: Casa 567, Rotonda los Cocos, Altamira, Managua; tel. 2277-3524; Pres. CRISEYDA OLIVAS VEGA.

Finance

(cap. = capital; res = reserves; dep. = deposits; m. = million; amounts in gold córdobas)

BANKING

All Nicaraguan banks were nationalized in July 1979. Foreign banks operating in the country are no longer permitted to secure local deposits. All foreign exchange transactions must be made through the Banco Central or its agencies. Under a decree issued in May 1985, the establishment of private exchange houses was permitted. In 1990 legislation allowing for the establishment of private banks was enacted.

Supervisory Authority

Superintendencia de Bancos y de Otras Instituciones Financieras: Edif. SIBOIF, Km 7, Carretera Sur, Apdo 788, Managua; tel. 2265-1555; fax 2265-0965; e-mail correo@sibiof.gob.ni; internet www

NICARAGUA

.superintendencia.gob.ni; f. 1991; Supt Dr VICTOR M. URCUYO VIDAURRE.

Central Bank

Banco Central de Nicaragua: Carretera Sur, Km 7, Apdos 2252/3, Zona 5, Managua; tel. 2255-7171; fax 2265-0561; e-mail oaip@bcn.gob.ni; internet www.bcn.gob.ni; f. 1961; bank of issue and govt fiscal agent; cap. and res –1,142.0m., dep. 42,382.0m. (Dec. 2008); Pres. Dr ANTENOR ROSALES BOLAÑOS; Gen. Man. JOSÉ DE JESÚS ROJAS RODRÍGUEZ.

Private Banks

Banco de América Central (BAC): Km 4½, Carretera a Masaya, Managua; tel. 2274-4444; fax 2274-4620; e-mail serviciocliente@bac.com.ni; internet www.bancodeamericacentral.com; f. 1991; total assets 10,516m. (1999); Pres. CARLOS PELLAS CHAMORRO; Gen. Man. CARLOS MATUS TAPIA.

Banco de Crédito Centroamericano (BANCENTRO): Edif. BANCENTRO, Km 4½ Carretera a Masaya, Managua; tel. 2278-2777; fax 2278-6001; e-mail info@bancentro.com.ni; internet www.bancentro.com.ni; f. 1991; total assets 282m. (2005); Pres. ROBERTO J. ZAMORA LLANES; Gen. Man. CARLOS A. BRICEÑO RÍOS.

Banco Uno, SA: Plaza España, Rotonda el Güegüense 20 m al oeste, Managua; tel. 2278-7171; fax 2277-3154; e-mail info@bancouno.com.ni; internet www.bancouno.com.ni; dep. 2,372m. (Dec. 2002); fmrly Banco de la Exportación (BANEXPO), present name adopted in Nov. 2002; acquired by Citibank in 2007; Dir ADOLFO ARGÜELLO LACAYO.

STOCK EXCHANGE

Bolsa de Valores de Nicaragua: Edif. Oscar Pérez Cassar, Centro BANIC, Km 5½, Carretera Masaya, Apdo 121, Managua; tel. 2278-3830; fax 2278-3836; e-mail info@bolsanic.com; internet bolsanic.com; f. 1993; Pres. Dr RAÚL LACAYO SOLÓRZANO; Gen. Man. GERARDO ARGÜELLO LEIVA.

INSURANCE

State Company

Instituto Nicaragüense de Seguros y Reaseguros (INISER): Centro Comercial Camino de Oriente, Km 6, Carretera a Masaya, Apdo 1147, Managua; tel. 2255-7575; e-mail iniser@iniser.com.ni; internet www.iniser.com.ni; f. 1979 to assume the activities of all the pre-revolution national private insurance cos; Exec. Pres. EDUARDO HALLESLEVENS; Vice-Pres GUILLERMO JIMÉNEZ, JUAN JOSÉ UBEDA.

Private Companies

Aseguradora Mundial Nicaragua: Edif. Invercasa, 1°, Managua; tel. 2276-8890; fax 2278-6358; e-mail lucia.ramirez@amundial.com.ni; internet www.amundial.com; Pres. ORLANDO EDMUNDO SÁNCHEZ AVILÉS; Gen. Man. LUCÍA RAMÍREZ.

Metropolitana Compañía de Seguros, SA: Reparto Serrano Plaza El Sol, 400 m al norte, Managua; tel. 2276-9000; fax 2276-9002; e-mail metroseg@metroseg.com; internet www.metroseg.com; Pres. Dr LEONEL ARGÜELLO RAMÍREZ; Sec. HORACIO ARGÜELLO CARAZO.

Seguros América, SA: Centro BAC, Km 5½ Carretera a Masaya, Apdo 6114, Managua; tel. 2274-4200; fax 2274-4202; e-mail sergioulvert@segamerica.com.ni; internet www.segurosamerica.com.ni; f. 1996; Pres. CARLOS F. PELLAS CHAMORRO; Man. SERGIO ULVERT SÁNCHEZ.

Seguros Lafise, SA: Centro Financiero Lafise, Km 5½ Carretera a Masaya, Managua; tel. 2270-3505; fax 2270-3558; e-mail seguros@seguroslafise.com.ni; internet www.seguroslafise.com.ni; fmrly Seguros Centroamericanos (Segurossa); Pres. ROBERTO ZAMORA LLANES; Gen. Man. CLAUDIO TABOADA RODRÍGUEZ.

Trade and Industry

GOVERNMENT AGENCIES

Empresa Nicaragüense de Alimentos Básicos (ENABAS): Salida a Carretera Norte, Apdo 1041, Managua; tel. 2248-1640; e-mail direccion.administrativa@enabas.gob.ni; internet www.enabas.gob.ni; f. 1979; controls trading in basic foodstuffs; Exec. Dir HERMINIO ESCOTO GARCÍA.

Instituto de Desarrollo Rural (IDR) (Institute of Rural Development): B3, Camino de Oriente, Apdo 3593, Managua; tel. 2255-8777; e-mail divulgacion@idr.gob.ni; internet www.idr.gob.ni; f. 1995; Exec. Dir PEDRO HASLAM MENDOZA.

Instituto Nicaragüense de Apoyo a la Pequeña y Mediana Empresa (INPYME): De la Shell Plaza el Sol, 1 c. al sur, 300 m abajo, Apdo 449, Managua; tel. 2278-7836; e-mail bcantillo@inpyme.gob.ni; internet www.inpyme.gob.ni; supports small and medium-sized enterprises; Exec. Dir MARÍA LIDIA ESPINALES.

Instituto Nicaragüense de Tecnología Agropecuaria (INTA): Col. Centroamérica, contiguo al Distrito 5, Apdo 1247, Managua; tel. 2227-2290; fax 2278-0373; e-mail bayserfe@inta.gob.ni; internet www.inta.gob.ni; f. 1993; Dir-Gen. EVA ACEVEDO GUTIÉRREZ.

Instituto de la Vivienda Urbana y Rural (INVUR): Km 4.5, Carretera Sur, contiguo a INISER, Managua; tel. 2226-6112; e-mail gmartinez@invur.gob.ni; internet www.invur.gob.ni; housing devt; Pres. JUDITH SILVA.

DEVELOPMENT ORGANIZATIONS

Asociación de Productores y Exportadores de Nicaragua (APEN): Del Hotel Intercontinental, 2 c. al sur y 2 c. abajo, Bolonia, Managua; tel. 2268-6053; fax 2266-5160; internet www.apen.org.ni; Pres. ENRIQUE ZAMORA LLANES; Gen. Man. AZUCENA CASTILLO.

Cámara de Industrias de Nicaragua: Rotonda el Güegüense, Plaza España 300 m al sur, Apdo 1436, Managua; tel. 2266-8847; fax 2266-1891; e-mail cadin@cadin.org.ni; internet www.cadin.org.ni; f. 1964; Pres. ALFREDO MARÍN XIMÉNEZ; Vice-Pres. LUZ ARGENTINA CANO ZAMBRANA.

Cámara Nacional de la Mediana y Pequeña Industria (CONAPI): Plaza 19 de Julio, Frente a la UCA, Apdo 153, Managua; tel. 2278-4892; fax 2267-0192; e-mail conapi@nicarao.org.ni; Pres. FLORA VARGAS LOAISIGA; Gen. Man. URIEL ARGEÑAL C.

Cámara Nicaragüense de la Construcción (CNC): Bolonia de Aval Card, 2 c. abajo, 50 varas al sur, Managua; tel. 2226-3363; fax 2266-3327; e-mail info@construccion.org.ni; internet www.construccion.org.ni; f. 1961; construction industry; Pres. MARIO ZELAYA BLANDÓN; Gen. Man. BRUNO VIDAURRE.

Instituto Nicaragüense de Fomento Municipal (INIFOM): Edif. Central, Carretera a la Refinería, entrada principal residencial Los Arcos, Apdo 3097, Managua; tel. and fax 2266-6050; e-mail eduardo.centeno@inifom.gob.ni; internet www.inifom.gob.ni; Pres. EDUARDO CENTENO GADEA.

CHAMBERS OF COMMERCE

Cámara de Comercio Americana de Nicaragua: Plaza España, Rotonda el Güegüense 400 m al este, 75 m al este, detrás de American Airlines, Managua; tel. and fax 2266-2758; e-mail amcham@ns.tmx.com.ni; internet www.amcham.org.ni; f. 1974; Pres. ROGER ARTEAGA CANO.

Cámara de Comercio de Nicaragua (CACONIC): Rotonda el Güegüense 400 m al sur, 20 m al oeste, Managua; tel. 2268-3505; fax 2268-3600; e-mail comercio@caconic.org.ni; internet www.caconic.org.ni; f. 1892; 904 mems; Pres. MARIO GONZÁLES LACAYO; Exec. Dir EDUARDO FONSECA.

Cámara Oficial Española de Comercio de Nicaragua: Restaurante la Marseilleisa, ½ c. arriba, Los Robles, Apdo 4103, Managua; tel. 2278-9047; fax 2278-9088; e-mail camacoesnic@cablenet.com.ni; internet www.camacoesnic.com.ni; Pres. JOSÉ DE LA JARA AHLERS; Sec.-Gen. MARÍA AUXILIADORA MIRANDA DE GUERRERO.

EMPLOYERS' ORGANIZATIONS

Asociación de Café Especiales de Nicaragua (ACEN): Oficentro Norte, Km 5, Carretera Panamericana Norte, Managua; tel. 2249-0180; fax 2249-0182; internet www.acen.org.ni; coffee producers and exporters; Pres. JULIO PERALTA; Sec. LEANA FERREY.

Consejo Superior de la Empresa Privada (COSEP): De Telcor Zacarías Guerra, 1 c. abajo, Apdo 5430, Managua; tel. 2276-3333; fax 2276-1666; e-mail cosep@cablenet.com.ni; internet www.cosep.org.ni; f. 1972; private businesses; consists of Cámara de Industrias de Nicaragua (CADIN), Unión de Productores Agropecuarios de Nicaragua (UPANIC), Cámara de Comercio, Cámara de la Construcción, Confederación Nacional de Profesionales (CONAPRO), Instituto Nicaragüense de Desarrollo (INDE); mem. of Coordinadora Democrática Nicaragüense; Pres. Dr JOSÉ ADÁN AGUERRI; Exec. Dir MARÍA GERMANIA CARRIÓN SOTO.

Instituto Nicaragüense de Desarrollo (INDE): Col. Los Robles, del Hotel Colón 1 c. al sur, 1 c. abajo, mano izquierda, frente a Funeraria Reñazco, Managua; tel. 2252-5800; fax 2270-9866; e-mail inde@inde.org.ni; internet www.inde.org.ni; f. 1963; private business org.; 650 mems; Pres. MARCO ZAVALA; Sec. LIGIA ROBLETO.

Unión Nacional de Agricultores y Ganaderos (UNAG): Managua; tel. 2268-7429; fax 2266-1675; e-mail unag@unag.org.ni; internet www.unag.org.ni; f. 1981; Pres. ALVARO FIALLOS OYANGUREN; Sec. DOUGLAS ALEMÁN.

Unión de Productores Agropecuarios de Nicaragua (UPANIC): Edif. Jorge Salazar, Reparto Serrano, DGI Central, 1 c. al norte ½ c. al este, Apdo 2351, Managua; tel. 2251-0340; fax 2251-0307; e-mail upanic@ibw.com.ni; internet www.upanic.org.ni; pri-

NICARAGUA

vate agriculturalists' asscn; Pres. MANUEL ALVAREZ SOLÓRZANO; Sec. FERNANDO MANSELL VILLANUEVA.

UTILITIES

Regulatory Bodies

Comisión Nacional de Energía y Minas (CNEM): Hospital Bautista, 1 c. al oeste, 1 c. al norte, Managua; Pres. EMILIO RAPPACCIOLI BALTODANO (Minister of Energy and Mines).

Instituto Nicaragüense de Acueductos y Alcantarillados (INAA): De la Mansión Teodolinda, 3 c. al sur, Bolonia, Apdo 1084, Managua; tel. 2266-7882; fax 2266-7917; e-mail inaa@inaa.gob.ni; internet www.inaa.gob.ni; f. 1979; water regulator; Exec. Pres. CARLOS SCHUTZE SUGRAÑES.

Instituto Nicaragüense de Energía (INE): Edif. Petronic, 4°, Managua; tel. 2277-5317; fax 2228-3104; e-mail dac@ine.gob.ni; internet www.ine.gob.ni; Pres. JOSÉ DAVID CASTILLO SÁNCHEZ; Exec. Sec. MARIELA DEL CARMEN CERRATO VÁSQUEZ.

Electricity

Empresa Nicaragüense de Electricidad (ENEL): Ofs Centrales, Pista Juan Pablo II y Avda Bolívar, Managua; tel. 2277-4160; fax 2267-2683; e-mail relapub@ibw.com.ni; internet www.enel.gob.ni; responsible for planning, organization, management, administration, research and development of energy resources; split into a transmission co, 2 distribution businesses and 4 generation cos in 1999; Pres. EMILIO RAPPACCIOLI BALTODANO (Minister of Energy and Mines); Sec. RAÚL CASTRO CASCO.

Empresa Nacional de Transmisión Eléctrica, SA (ENATREL): Intersección Avda Bolívar y Pista Juan Pablo II, Apdo 283, Managua; tel. 2277-4159; fax 2267-4379; internet www.enatrel.gob.ni; operates the electricity transmission network; Exec. Pres. SALVADOR MANSELL CASTRILLO.

Generadora Eléctrica Central, SA (GECSA): electricity generation co; 79 MW capacity thermal plant; almost obsolete and therefore difficult to privatize, GECSA was likely to be retained for emergency purposes.

Generadora Eléctrica Occidental, SA (GEOSA): electricity generation co; 112 MW capacity thermal plant; sold to Coastal Power International (USA) in Jan. 2002.

HIDROGESA: electricity generation co; 94 MW capacity hydroelectric plant; privatized in 2002; Gen. Man. JUSTO SANDINO.

ORMAT Momotombo Power Co: Momotombo; internet www.ormat.com; f. 1999 on acquisition of 15-year concession to rehabilitate and operate Momotombo power plant; 30 MW capacity geothermal plant; subsidiary of ORMAT International, Inc; CEO YEHUDIT (DITA) BRONICKI; Gen. Man. RÓGER ARCIA LACAYO.

Unión Fenosa DISSUR y DISNORTE: Managua; tel. 2274-4700; e-mail comunicacion@ni.unionfenosa.com; internet www.disnorte-dissur.com.ni; electricity distribution co; privatized in 2000; distributes some 1460 GWh (DISSUR 658 GWh, DISNORTE 802 GWh); Country Man. CARLOS HERNÁNDEZ.

Water

Empresa Nicaragüense de Acueductos y Alcantarillados Sanitarios (ENACAL): Km 5, Carretera Sur 505, Asososca; tel. 2266-7875; e-mail ccomunicacion@enacal.com.ni; internet www.enacal.com.ni; Exec. Pres. (vacant).

TRADE UNIONS

Asociación Nacional de Educadores de Nicaragua (ANDEN): Managua; tel. 517-0018; e-mail anden@guegue.com.ni; Sec.-Gen. JOSÉ ANTONIO ZEPEDA; 19 affiliates, 15,000 mems.

Asociación de Trabajadores del Campo (ATC) (Association of Rural Workers): Rotonda Metrocentro, 120 m al oeste, Complejo el CIPRES, Apdo A-244, Managua; tel. 2278-4576; fax 2278-4575; e-mail atcnic@ibw.com.ni; internet www.movimientos.org/cloc/atc-ni; f. 1977; Gen. Sec. EDGARDO GARCÍA; 52,000 mems.

Central Sandinista de Trabajadores (CST): Iglesia del Carmen, 1 c. al oeste, ½ c. al sur, Managua; tel. 2265-1096; fax 2240-1285; Sec.-Gen. ROBERTO GONZÁLEZ GAITÁN; 40,000 mems.

Central de Trabajadores de Nicaragua (CTN) (Nicaraguan Workers' Congress): De la Iglesia del Carmen, 1 c. al sur, ½ c. arriba y 75 varas al sur, Managua; tel. 2268-3061; fax 2265-2056; f. 1962; mem. of Coordinadora Democrática Nicaragüense; Pres. ANTONIO JARQUÍN.

Confederación de Acción y Unidad Sindical (CAUS) (Confederation for Trade Union Action and Unity): Semáforos de Rubenia, 2 c. abajo y 2 c. al lago, Barrio Venezuela, Managua; tel. and fax 244-2587; f. 1973; trade union wing of Partido Comunista de Nicaragua; Sec.-Gen. EMILIO MÁRQUEZ.

Confederación General de Trabajadores Independientes (CGT-i) (Independent General Confederation of Labour): Centro Comercial Nejapa, 1 c. arriba y 3 c. al lago, Managua; tel. 2222-5195; fax 2228-7505; f. 1953; Sec.-Gen. NILO M. SALAZAR AGUILAR; 4,843 mems (est.) from 6 federations with 40 local unions, and 6 non-federated local unions.

Confederación de Unificación Sindical (CUS) (Confederation of United Trade Unions): Casa Q3, del Colegio la Tenderi 2½ c. arriba, Ciudad Jardín, Managua; tel. 2248-3681; fax 2240-1330; f. 1972; affiliated to the Inter-American Regional Organization of Workers; mem. of Coordinadora Democrática Nicaragüense; Sec.-Gen. JOSÉ ESPINOZA NAVAS.

Enrique Schmidt Cuadra Federation (FESC): Managua; e-mail fschmidt@tmx.com.ni; communications and postal workers' union.

Federación de Trabajadores Nicaragüenses (FTN): workers' federation; Leader DOMINGO PÉREZ.

Federación de Trabajadores de la Salud (FETSALUD) (Federation of Health Workers): Optica Nicaragüense, 2 c. arriba ½ c. al sur, Apdo 1402, Managua; tel. and fax 2266-3065; e-mail fntsid@ibw.com.ni; Sec.-Gen. GUSTAVO PORRAS; 25,000 mems.

Federación de Transportistas de Carga de Nicaragua (FETRACANIC) (Cargo Transport Workers' Federation of Nicaragua): Avda del Ejército del Arbolito, 2½ c. al sur, Casa 410, Managua; tel. 2266-5255; fax 2254-7381; e-mail fetracanic@hotmail.com; internet www.fetracanic.com; f. 1986; part of Consejo Centroamericano del Transporte (CONCETRANS); Pres. JOSÉ FRANCISCO GUERRA CABRERA.

Frente Nacional de los Trabajadores (FNT) (National Workers' Front): Residencial Bolonia, de la Optica Nicaragüense, 2 c. arriba, 30 varas al sur, Managua; tel. 2266-3065; fax 2266-7457; e-mail prensa@fnt.org.ni; internet www.fnt.org.ni; f. 1979; affiliated to Frente Sandinista de Liberación Nacional; Leader Dr GUSTAVO PORRAS CORTÉS.

Unión Nacional de Caficultores de Nicaragua (UNCAFENIC) (National Union of Coffee Growers of Nicaragua): Reparto San Juan, Casa 300, Apdo 3447, Managua; tel. 2782-2225; fax 2772-3330; Pres. FREDDY TORRES.

Unión Nacional de Empleados (UNE): Managua; e-mail cocentrafemenino@xerox.com.ni; f. 1978; public sector workers' union; Sec.-Gen. DOMINGO PÉREZ; 18,000 mems.

Transport

RAILWAYS

There are no functioning railways. The state-owned rail operator, Ferrocarril de Nicaragua, which formerly operated a network of 287 km, ceased operations in 1994, and the only remaining private line closed in 2001.

ROADS

In 2007 there were an estimated 20,333 km of roads, of which 1,081 km were highways and 999 km were secondary roads. In 2010 the Inter-American Development Bank approved a $20m. loan for road improvements, including reduction of vulnerability due to climate change impacts. Some 8,000 km of roads were damaged by Hurricane Mitch, which struck in late 1998. The Pan-American Highway runs for 384 km in Nicaragua and links Managua with the Honduran and Costa Rican frontiers and the Atlantic and Pacific Highways, connecting Managua with the coastal regions.

SHIPPING

Corinto, Puerto Sandino, San Juan del Sur and Potosí, on the Pacific, and Puerto Cabezas, El Bluff (Bluefields) and El Rama, on the Caribbean, are the principal ports. Corinto deals with about 60% of trade. In addition to sea ports, there are small ports on two inland lakes.

Empresa Portuaria Nacional (EPN): Residencial Bolonia, de la Optica Nicaragüense 1 c. abajo, Managua; tel. 2266-3039; fax 2266-3488; e-mail epn_puertos@epn.com.ni; internet www.epn.com.ni; Pres. VIRGILIO SILVA MUNGUÍA.

CIVIL AVIATION

The principal airport is the Augusto Sandino International Airport, in Managua. There are some 185 additional airports in Nicaragua.

Empresa Administradora de Aeropuertos Internacionales (EAAI): POB 5179, 11 Km Carretera Norte, Managua; tel. 2233-1624; fax 2263-1072; e-mail czamora@eaai.com.ni; internet www.eaai.com.ni; autonomous govt entity; operates Managua International Airport and 3 national airports: Bluefields, Puerto Cabezas and Corn Island; Pres. DANILO LACAYO RAPPACIOLI; Gen. Man. ORLANDO CASTILLO GUERRERO.

La Costeña: Managua International Airport, Km 10.5 North Hwy, Managua; tel. 2263-2142; fax 2263-1281; e-mail info@lacostena.com.ni; internet www.lacostena.com.ni; Gen. Man. ALFREDO CABALLERO.

Tourism

In 2008 tourist arrivals totalled 857,901 and receipts from tourism totalled US $276m.

Asociación Nicaragüense de Agencias de Viajes y Turismo (ANAVYT): Edif. Policlínica Nicaragüense, Reparto Bolonia, Apdo 1045, Managua; tel. 2266-9742; fax 2266-4474; e-mail aeromund@cablenet.com.ni; f. 1966; Pres. ANA MARÍA ROCHA C.

Cámara Nacional de Turismo (CANATUR): Contiguo al Ministerio de Turismo, Apdo 2105, Managua; tel. 2278-9971; e-mail direccion@canaturnicaragua.org; internet www.canaturnicaragua.org; f. 1976; Exec. Dir GRETHEL COLLINS.

Instituto Nicaragüense de Turismo (INTUR): Del Hotel Crowne Plaza, 1 c. al sur, 1 c. al oeste, Apdo 5088, Managua; tel. 2254-5191; fax 2222-6610; e-mail promocion@intur.gob.ni; internet www.intur.gob.ni; f. 1998; Pres. MARÍA NELLY RIVAS BLANCO; Sec.-Gen. IAN CORONEL.

Defence

As assessed at November 2010, Nicaragua's professional armed forces numbered an estimated 12,000: army 10,000, navy 800 and air force 1,200. There is a voluntary military service which lasts 18–36 months.

Defence Budget: 809m. gold córdobas (US $38m.) in 2010.
Commander-in-Chief: Gen. JULIO CÉSAR AVILÉS CASTILLO.

Education

Primary and secondary education in Nicaragua is provided free of charge. Primary education, which is officially compulsory, begins at seven years of age and lasts for six years. Secondary education, beginning at the age of 13, lasts for up to five years, comprising a first cycle of three years and a second of two years. In 2007/08 enrolment at primary schools included 92% of children in the relevant age-group. Secondary enrolment in that year included 45% of children in the relevant age-group, according to UNESCO estimates. There are many commercial schools and eight universities. In 2003/04 some 103,577 students attended universities and other higher education institutes. In the same year expenditure on education accounted for 15.0% of total government expenditure.

NIGER

Introductory Survey

LOCATION, CLIMATE, LANGUAGE, RELIGION, FLAG, CAPITAL

The Republic of Niger is a land-locked country in western Africa, with Algeria and Libya to the north, Nigeria and Benin to the south, Mali and Burkina Faso to the west, and Chad to the east. The climate is hot and dry, with an average temperature of 29°C (84°F). The official language is French, but numerous indigenous languages, including Hausa (spoken by about one-half of the population), Tuareg, Djerma and Fulani, are also used (the 1991 sovereign National Conference identified 10 'national' languages). Some 95% of the population are Muslims, the most influential Islamic groups being the Tijaniyya, the Senoussi and the Hamallists. Most of the remainder of the population follow traditional beliefs, and there is a small Christian minority. The national flag (proportions 6 by 7) has three equal horizontal stripes, of orange, white and green, with an orange disc in the centre of the white stripe. The capital is Niamey.

CONTEMPORARY POLITICAL HISTORY

Historical Context

Formerly a part of French West Africa, Niger became a self-governing member of the French Community in December 1958 and was granted independence on 3 August 1960. Hamani Diori, leader of the Parti progressiste nigérien (the local section of the Ivorian-dominated Rassemblement démocratique africain) and Prime Minister since December 1958, became Head of State. Diori was elected President in November 1960, and re-elected in 1965 and 1970. Close links were maintained with France.

The Sahelian drought of 1968–74 was particularly damaging to the Nigerien economy and was a major factor in precipitating a military coup in April 1974 following which Lt-Col (later Maj.-Gen.) Seyni Kountché, the armed forces Chief of Staff, became President. The new administration, headed by a Conseil militaire suprême (CMS), suspended the Constitution; the legislature was replaced by a consultative Conseil national de développement (CND), and political activity was banned. Kountché obtained the withdrawal of French troops and reduced French influence over the exploitation of Niger's deposits of uranium (which France had initiated in 1968).

From 1977 the proportion of army officers in the Government was progressively reduced and in January 1983 a civilian, Oumarou Mamane, was appointed to the newly created post of Prime Minister. In November Mamane, who in August had been appointed President of the CND, was replaced as premier by Hamid Algabid.

Domestic Political Affairs

A draft 'national charter' was approved by a reported 99.6% of voters in a referendum in June 1987. In November Kountché died while undergoing medical treatment in France, and Col (later Brig.) Ali Saïbou, the army Chief of Staff, was inaugurated as Chairman of the CMS and Head of State. In July 1988 Mamane (who had been replaced as President of the CND in September 1987) was reinstated as Prime Minister, and the CND was given the task of drafting a new constitution. In August 1988 Brig. Saïbou formed a new ruling party, the Mouvement national pour la société de développement (MNSD).

In May 1989 an MNSD congress elected a Conseil supérieur d'orientation nationale (CSON) to succeed the CMS. The draft Constitution was endorsed by a reported 99.3% of voters in a referendum in September. At elections in December Saïbou (as President of the CSON and the sole candidate) was confirmed as President of the Republic, for a seven-year term, by 99.6% of those who voted, while 99.5% of voters endorsed a single list of CSON-approved deputies to a new, 93-member Assemblée nationale. In March 1990 a prominent industrialist, Aliou Mahamidou, was appointed Prime Minister in an extensive government reorganization. In November Saïbou announced that a multi-party political system would be established. A national conference on political reform was to be convened in mid-1991, and multi-party national elections would take place in 1992.

In March 1991 the armed forces Chief of Staff announced that the armed forces were to distance themselves from the MNSD—Nassara (as the MNSD had been restyled) with immediate effect. In July Saïbou resigned as Chairman of the MNSD—Nassara, in preparation for the National Conference, which was convened in Niamey later that month and attended by about 1,200 delegates, including representatives of the organs of state, 24 political organizations, the military and civil society. It declared itself sovereign, voting to suspend the Constitution and dissolve the legislature. Saïbou would remain in office as Head of State on an interim basis, but the Conference would supervise the exercise of his (now largely ceremonial) powers. The Government was dissolved in September, and in October the Conference appointed Cheiffou Amadou to head a transitional Council of Ministers, which was intended to hold office until the inauguration of democratically elected institutions, now scheduled for early 1993. Prior to the conclusion of the Conference, in November 1991, its President, André Salifou, was designated Chairman of a 15-member interim legislative body, the Haut conseil de la République (HCR), which was, *inter alia*, to supervise the drafting of a new constitution.

The new Constitution was approved by 89.8% of those who voted in a referendum held on 26 December 1992. The MNSD—Nassara won the greatest number of seats (29) at elections to the 83-member Assemblée nationale, held on 14 February 1993 and contested by 12 political parties, but was prevented from resuming power by the rapid formation, following the elections, of the Alliance des forces de changement (AFC) by six parties with a total of 50 seats in the legislature. Principal members of the AFC were the Convention démocratique et sociale—Rahama (CDS), the Parti nigérien pour la démocratie et le socialisme—Tarayya (PNDS), and the Alliance nigérienne pour la démocratie et le progrès social—Zaman Lahiya (ANDP). At the first round of the presidential election, held on 27 February and contested by eight candidates, Col (retd) Mamadou Tandja, Saïbou's successor as leader of the MNSD—Nassara, won the greatest proportion of votes cast (34.2%). He and his nearest rival, Mahamane Ousmane (the leader of the CDS, with 26.6%), proceeded to a second round on 27 March, at which Ousmane was elected President by 55.4% of voters; his inauguration took place on 16 April. Ousmane appointed Mahamadou Issoufou of the PNDS as Prime Minister. Despite an attempt by the MNSD—Nassara to block the appointment, in May Moumouni Adamou Djermakoye of the ANDP became President of the Assemblée nationale.

The new regime's efforts to curb public expenditure, combined with the effects of the 50% devaluation of the CFA franc in January 1994, provoked considerable disquiet among workers and students. In September the PNDS withdrew from the AFC, and Issoufou resigned the premiership, in protest at the perceived transfer of certain prime ministerial powers to the President. A new minority Government, led by Souley Abdoulaye of the CDS, failed to withstand a parliamentary motion of 'no confidence' proposed by the MNSD—Nassara and the PNDS in October. Ousmane therefore dissolved the Assemblée nationale.

At legislative elections held in mid-January 1995 the MNSD—Nassara won 29 seats and subsequently led a 43-strong majority group in the Assemblée nationale. Although the CDS increased its representation to 24 seats, the AFC secured only 40 seats. Ousmane declined to accept the new majority's nominee to the premiership, Hama Amadou (the Secretary-General of the MNSD—Nassara), instead appointing another member of that party, Amadou Aboubacar Cissé, a former official of the World Bank. The MNSD—Nassara and its allies announced that they would not co-operate with his administration, and Cissé was expelled from the party. Meanwhile, Issoufou was elected President of the Assemblée nationale. In February the legislature approved a motion of censure against Cissé, and Ousmane accepted the nomination of Amadou as Prime Minister. This political 'cohabitation' encountered serious difficulties, as the President and Prime Minister disputed their respective competencies, in particular with regard to a proposed programme for the reorganization and privatization of state enterprises, which Ousmane opposed. Following several months of industrial unrest, Ousmane's rejection of the Government's draft budget, in January 1996, resulted in a new impasse in relations.

Ousmane overthrown

On 27 January 1996 the elected organs of state were overthrown by the military. The coup leaders, who formed a Conseil de salut national (CSN), chaired by Col (later Brig.-Gen.) Ibrahim Baré Maïnassara, armed forces Chief of Staff since March 1995 and a former aide-de-camp to Kountché, asserted that their seizure of power had been necessitated by Niger's descent into political chaos. The CSN annulled the Constitution and dissolved the Assemblée nationale, while political parties were suspended. A national forum was to be convened to consider the revision of the Constitution and the electoral code, and to determine a timetable for a return to civilian rule. The CSN appointed Boukary Adji, the Deputy Governor of the Banque centrale des états de l'Afrique de l'ouest as Prime Minister. Adji's transitional Government, named in February 1996, was composed entirely of civilians.

Two consultative bodies were established to prepare for the restoration of civilian government, the advisory Conseil des sages and the co-ordinating committee of the national forum. The National Forum for Democratic Renewal, which was convened in April 1996, adopted revisions to the Constitution that aimed to guarantee greater institutional stability, essentially by conferring executive power solely on the President. In April Ousmane, Amadou and Issoufou accompanied Maïnassara to northern Niger to celebrate National Concord Day, on the first anniversary of the signing of the peace agreement with the Tuareg movement (see below).

The revised Constitution was approved by some 92.3% of the votes cast at a referendum on 12 May 1996 (about 35% of the electorate participated). The ban on political activity was lifted shortly afterwards. Voting in the presidential election commenced, as scheduled, on 7 July 1996, but was quickly halted in several areas where preparations were incomplete: polling took place in these areas on 8 July. According to the Supreme Court, Maïnassara won the election, with some 52.2% of the votes cast; Ousmane secured 19.8% and Tandja 15.7%. Maïnassara was installed as President on 7 August. A new Government, with Adji as Prime Minister, also included Abdoulaye and Cissé. Members of the CDS, the MNSD—Nassara and the PNDS who had accepted government posts were subsequently expelled from these parties.

Legislative elections proceeded on 23 November 1996, contested by 11 parties and movements. According to official results, the pro-Maïnassara Union nationale des indépendants pour le renouveau démocratique (UNIRD) won 52 of the Assemblée nationale's 83 seats. International observers pronounced themselves satisfied with the organization and conduct of the election. (The Supreme Court later annulled the results in three constituencies won by the UNIRD, on the grounds of fraud.) A new Government was formed, with Cissé as Prime Minister. In November 1997 Maïnassara dismissed the entire Government and subsequently appointed Ibrahim Hassane Maiyaki, hitherto Minister of Foreign Affairs and Co-operation, as Prime Minister.

The death of Maïnassara

On 9 April 1999 Maiyaki made a broadcast to the nation, announcing the death of Maïnassara in an 'unfortunate accident' at a military airbase in Niamey. The Prime Minister stated that the defence and security forces would continue to be the guarantors of republican order and national unity, and announced the dissolution of the Assemblée nationale, as well as the temporary suspension of all party political activity. Despite the official explanation for his death, it was generally perceived that members of the presidential guard had assassinated Maïnassara in a coup d'état. Although members of the Assemblée nationale initially rejected its dissolution, on 11 April the Constitution was suspended and its institutions dissolved. A military Conseil de réconciliation nationale (CRN), under the chairmanship of Maj. Daouda Mallam Wanké (hitherto head of the presidential guard), was to exercise executive and legislative authority during a nine-month transitional period, prior to the restoration of elected civilian institutions. Wanké immediately signed an ordinance on interim political authority, which was to function as a constitutional document during the transitional period. Maiyaki was reappointed as Prime Minister of the transitional Government on 12 April; a new Council of Ministers was named shortly afterwards. Moussa Moumouni Djermakoye, who had been succeeded as armed forces Chief of Staff by Lt-Col Soumara Zanguina, became Minister of National Defence. In July, in a minor reshuffle, the Minister of the Interior and Territorial Administration, Lt-Col Moumouni Boureima, was appointed armed forces Chief of Staff, while Zanguina became an adviser to the Head of State.

The new draft Constitution was submitted to referendum on 18 July 1999, when it was approved by 89.6% of those who voted (about one-third of the registered electorate). The Constitution envisaged a balance of powers between the President, the Government and the legislature, but, none the less, vested strong powers in the Head of State, who was to be politically liable only in the case of high treason. The Government, under a Prime Minister appointed by the President, was to be responsible to the Assemblée nationale, which would be competent to remove the Prime Minister by vote of censure. A clause in the Constitution guaranteeing all those involved in the military take-overs of 1996 and 1999 immunity from prosecution provoked controversy and was condemned by Amnesty International, in a report in September, as undermining the rule of law. The report was regarded as particularly significant in that it published the testimony of a witness who alleged that Maïnassara had been killed by the presidential guard under Wanké's command. The Wanké regime continued to assert that Maïnassara's death had been accidental, and that a commission of inquiry into the death had been ordered in response to a complaint lodged by the late President's family.

Voting at the presidential election, which was contested by seven candidates, took place on 17 October 1999, and was considered both by the CENI and by independent observers to have been largely transparent and peaceful. Tandja, representing the MNSD—Nassara, won 32.3% of the votes cast, followed by Issoufou, of the PNDS, with 22.8%, and Ousmane, of the CDS, with 22.5%. The rate of participation by voters was 43.7%. Tandja and Issoufou proceeded to a second round on 24 November. Having secured the support of Ousmane, Tandja was elected President, with 59.9% of the votes cast. About 39% of the registered electorate voted. The MNSD—Nassara was similarly successful in the concurrent elections to the Assemblée nationale, winning 38 of the 83 seats; the CDS took 17, the PNDS 16, the pro-Maïnassara Rassemblement pour la démocratie et le progrès—Djamaa (RDP) eight and the ANDP four. Tandja, who had served in the CMS under Kountché and was Minister of the Interior in the early 1990s, was inaugurated as President on 22 December. Hama Amadou was subsequently appointed Prime Minister, and a new Council of Ministers was named in January 2000.

In January 2000 the Assemblée nationale adopted draft amnesty legislation, as provided for in the Constitution. The amnesty was opposed by the RDP, and many party activists joined a demonstration in February to denounce the legislation and to demand an international inquiry into the death of Maïnassara. In March 12 opposition parties, led by the PNDS, formed a coalition, the Coordination des forces démocratiques (CFD). Similarly, 17 parties loyal to the President, most notably the MNSD—Nassara and the CDS, formed the Alliance des forces démocratiques (AFD). In May Col Bourahima Moumouni was appointed armed forces Chief of Staff. None the less, rumours persisted of dissent within the army. In July the ANDP withdrew from the opposition CFD alliance and joined the AFD, thereby increasing the Government's parliamentary majority by four seats. Explaining his party's shift in allegiances, the leader of the ANDP, Moumouni Adamou Djermakoye, accused the CFD of intolerance and of failing to ease social tensions.

Tandja implemented a major government reorganization in November 2002, as a result of which the position of allies of Prime Minister Amadou was reportedly strengthened. At the end of December the Assemblée nationale approved legislation providing for the creation of a special military tribunal to try those accused of involvement in the rebellion earlier in the year (a total of 268 arrests were reported); elements within the opposition alleged that the legislation violated several articles of the Constitution. However, many soldiers were reportedly released during 2003, owing to a lack of evidence, and the three highest-ranking officers arrested were provisionally freed in February 2004. (Six of the mutineers were awarded custodial sentences at a military tribunal in early 2006.)

In mid-October 2003 the Council of Ministers announced proposals to increase the number of deputies in the Assemblée nationale from 83 to 113, in order to reflect the growth in the population recorded between the national censuses of 1988 and 2001. A minor government reshuffle was effected later in October

2003. Also in that month the Council of Ministers approved the abolition of the State Security Court.

The 2004 presidential election

In the first round of the presidential election, held on 16 November 2004, Tandja won 40.7% of votes cast, followed by Issoufou, who received 24.6% and both, therefore, proceeded to a second round of voting, while the four eliminated candidates all urged their supporters to transfer their allegiance to Tandja. In the second round of voting, held on 4 December, Tandja was victorious, receiving 65.5% of votes cast. (Turn-out in the first round was reported to be 48.5% of registered voters, declining slightly, to 45.0%, in the second round.) At elections to the newly enlarged 113-seat Assemblée nationale, held concurrently with the second round of voting in the presidential election, the MNSD—Nassara won the largest number of seats, obtaining 47, while allied pro-presidential parties secured a further 41 seats. An opposition coalition formed around the PNDS, which also comprised the Parti nigérien pour l'autogestion (PNA), the Parti progressiste nigérien—Rassemblement démocratique africain (PPN—RDA), the Union pour la démocratie et la République (UDR) and the Union des Nigeriens indépendants (UNI), won a total of 25 seats. Ousmane was subsequently re-elected as President of the Assemblée nationale, 13 seats in which, in accordance with legislation adopted in 2001, were reserved for women. Later in December President Tandja announced the formation of a new Government, in which Amadou remained as Prime Minister.

In mid-March 2005 up to 20,000 people were reported to have participated in demonstrations in Niamey against the recent introduction of a 19% value-added tax on basic commodities. The demonstration was organized by an alliance of some 30 groups, including trade unions, human rights organizations and consumer movements known as the Coalition contre la vie chère (CCVC). In the following week, after the Government refused to authorize a second protest march, the CCVC staged a one-day strike, which halted most activity in the capital. The authorities subsequently agreed to hold talks with the CCVC, although they emphasized that the tax would not be withdrawn. However, before the proposed meeting, five leaders of the Coalition were arrested and accused of establishing an unauthorized association and plotting against state security. The radio station Alternative FM, which had broadcast interviews with prominent supporters of the CCVC, was also closed by police, prompting protests from international press freedom groups. (The director of the station, Moussa Tchangari, was among those arrested.) During a further one-day strike, held a few days later, protesters erected barricades and burned tyres in Maradi and Tahoua, leading to more arrests. A third strike was suspended by the Coalition in early April in the hope that a compromise could be reached with the Government. The five leaders of the CCVC were subsequently released and, following negotiations between the Government and the leadership of the CCVC, agreement was reached on numerous concessions.

None the less, public discontent with the Government arose again in mid-2005 over severe food shortages, which had largely resulted from a poor harvest in 2004, when low rainfall had been combined with an invasion of locusts. According to the Ministry of Agricultural Development, there was a shortfall of more than 223,000 metric tons of grain, representing the country's largest deficit for more than 20 years. In early June up to 2,000 people marched through Niamey in protest at the Government's failure to respond adequately to the crisis and in support of opposition-backed demands for the distribution of free food. The Government, which had been supplying cereals at subsidized prices in the most stricken areas, appealed for international assistance, but insisted that it did not have the resources to distribute free food and instead announced plans to 'loan' grain to farmers most at risk until they could reimburse the Government after the harvest later in the year.

President Tandja effected a major government reorganization in March 2007, in which the number of ministers was increased from 26 to 31. Although the key portfolios remained largely unchanged, both the Minister for Agricultural Development, Labo Moussa, and the Minister for Secondary and Higher Education, Research and Technology, Ousmane Galadima, were removed from office. Two new ministerial posts were created, to assume responsibility for education and anti-desertification, and for relations with institutions of the Republic. In May the Government was dissolved following a vote of 'no confidence' in the Assemblée nationale, supported by 62 of the 113 deputies. The following month President Tandja named Seyni Oumarou as Prime Minister, an appointment which drew considerable criticism from opposition members. Oumarou was nevertheless sworn in and he later announced a new Council of Ministers in which many key portfolios remained unchanged.

Increased measures by the authorities against the independent media was reported, including the closure of the private radio station Sahara FM by the media regulatory authority in April 2008, after it had broadcast testimonies from victims of attacks by the Nigerien military. Despite being considered a potential candidate to succeed Tandja as President, former Prime Minister Hama Amadou was arrested and charged with corruption in June. Around 100 people protested outside the High Court of Justice in response to his arrest and were dispersed by police; in October several thousand demonstrators took to the streets of Niamey to call for his release. Amadou denied the charges against him, claiming that they were part of a campaign to prevent him contesting the presidential elections, scheduled for December 2009.

Political crisis and Constitution of the Sixth Republic

The campaign to prolong Tandja's presidency gained momentum in December 2008, when a further demonstration was staged in the capital in support of the extension of his term in office, and a change to the Constitution to allow the President to serve beyond the two-term limit stipulated therein. There were reports of similar rallies taking place elsewhere in the country, while counter-demonstrations by opponents of a third mandate for Tandja also followed. In March 2009 Tandja announced that, although he would be willing to remain in power after the end of his second term, he would not amend the Constitution in order to do so. An extraordinary congress of the MNSD—Nassara, held in Zinder in February, designated Oumarou as President of the party, replacing Amadou, whose supporters declared the change of leadership to be illegal, on the grounds that it contravened party regulations. Amadou was released from prison in April, owing to ill health, and subsequently fled abroad.

In early May 2009 Tandja declared his intention to conduct a constitutional referendum on the extension of his mandate. His announcement was widely criticized by opposition parties, non-governmental organizations and trade unions; the PNDS subsequently organized a large opposition protest in Niamey. As part of a government reorganization in mid-May, ministers from the ANDP who opposed a referendum were replaced. On 26 May, after the Constitutional Court ruled in response to an appeal by opposition parliamentary deputies that a referendum on his retention of power would be illegal, the President dissolved the Assemblée nationale. In early June Tandja created a committee to draft a new constitution (of what was to be designated the Sixth Republic) that would enable him to remain in office for a transitional period of three years if endorsed at a national referendum (subsequently scheduled for 4 August). However, on 12 June the Constitutional Court annulled the decree on the organization of the referendum. Following denouncement of Tandja's plan, a large protest was staged by opposition supporters in Niamey. The CENI subsequently declared that legislative elections would take place on 20 August, while the CDS withdrew its eight ministers from the Government, in recognition of the ruling by the Constitutional Court.

Following the Constitutional Court's refusal to review its decision regarding the referendum, on 26 June 2009 Tandja assumed emergency powers to rule by decree, subsequently dissolving the Court and suspending the Constitution. Opposition leaders accused Tandja of staging a coup and trade unions organized a one-day general strike in protest, which was only partially observed. Amid mounting international concern, in early July the European Commission threatened to suspend aid to the country; the Economic Community of West African States (ECOWAS) had also earlier threatened economic and diplomatic sanctions, while other international donors, including the UN, France and the USA, urged the Nigerien Government to respect the constitutional order. Nevertheless, Tandja appointed members to a new Constitutional Court, prompting condemnation from the opposition, and again decreed that a constitutional referendum would be held on 4 August. Later in July a joint delegation of the UN, the African Union (AU, see p. 183) and ECOWAS visited Niamey in an effort to resolve the political crisis; however, the referendum proceeded, as scheduled, on 4 August. According to results released by the CENI, 92.5% of those that participated in the vote (68.3% of the electorate) were in favour of the new Constitution, which, in addition to prolonging Tandja's mandate by three years, provided for the removal of the limit on presidential terms, the significant expansion of the powers of the President and the creation of a Senate. An opposition coalition of political parties, trade unions and human rights groups, known as Coordination des Forces pour la Démocratie et la République (CFDR), which had urged voters to boycott the referendum, disputed the results, and claimed that the overall turn-out was less than 5% of the electorate. Nevertheless, on 14 August the Constitutional Court endorsed the validity of the result. On 18 August the Constitution of the Sixth Republic entered into force by presidential decree. Oumarou's Government was reappointed by Tandja on 19 August. On the same day a presidential decree declared that early legislative elections would be held on 20 October. The CFDR condemned the arrest in early September of 30 former deputies on charges of embezzlement of public funds, maintaining that Tandja had ordered measures against opposition members. On 24 September it was announced that Oumarou and two ministers had resigned from their posts in order to contest the legislative elections. On 2 October Tandja appointed Ali Badjo Gamatié, hitherto Vice-Governor of the Central Bank of West African States, as the new Prime Minister.

Despite international pressure for a postponement of the poll and a further opposition boycott, the elections to the Assemblée nationale proceeded on 20 October 2009. ECOWAS announced the suspension of Niger's membership of the organization until the restoration of constitutional order, and announced that it would not recognize the outcome of the elections, while the European Union (EU, see p. 270) also warned of punitive measures. According to official results, which were released by the CENI, on 24 October, the MNSD—Nassara secured 76 seats (compared with 47 in 2004), while the remaining seats were won by parties or candidates allied to the MNSD—Nassara, with the Rassemblement social-démocratique—Gaskiya (RSD) receiving 15 seats and the RDP seven seats. In early November the Constitutional Court endorsed the validity of the election results. The EU suspended development aid to Niger and issued an ultimatum that discussions begin on a return to constitutional order. In December the CFDR organized a mass demonstration in Niamey demanding that Tandja relinquish power by 22 December, the date marking the expiry of his presidential mandate under the previous Constitution. Later that month negotiations began between government and opposition representatives, mediated by former Nigerian President Abdulsalami Abubakar on behalf of ECOWAS, in an effort to resolve the impasse. On 23 December the US State Department announced that the country had suspended non-humanitarian assistance to the Government and had imposed travel restrictions on members and supporters of Tandja's regime. In January 2010 Abubakar presented negotiating representatives with a plan to resolve the crisis, which would allow Tandja to retain power for a transitional period under a 'government of national reconciliation'. However, in early February the discussions, which had repeatedly been adjourned, were abandoned after government and opposition representatives failed to reach agreement on Abubakar's draft plan, prompting a large anti-Government demonstration outside the parliamentary building.

Military coup

On 18 February 2010 members of the armed forces stormed the presidential office during a cabinet meeting and captured Tandja, together with all the government members; it was reported that some 10 people had been killed. The coup leaders, the self-styled Conseil suprême pour la restauration de la démocratie (CSRD), announced the suspension of the Constitution and dissolution of all state organs; following meetings with UN, AU and ECOWAS delegations, they pledged to restore democratic rule and oversee the drafting of a new constitution. The President of the Conseil, a senior army officer, Squadron Commdr Salou Djibo, was named as acting Head of State and Head of Government. On the following day the AU suspended Niger's membership of the organization and demanded the restoration of constitutional rule; the UN and ECOWAS also condemned the military coup. Meanwhile, the CFDR organized a large rally in Niamey in support of the ousting of Tandja and intervention of the military junta. On 23 February Djibo appointed Mahamadou Danda, who was not a member of a political party and had served in the transitional administration after the April 1999 coup, as acting Prime Minister. On 2 March Djibo announced the appointment of a 20-member transitional Government, comprising 15, largely technocratic civilians and five military officers; Gen. Mamadou Ousseini, the former army chief of staff, became Minister of National Defence, while a further two senior army officers who had served under Tandja were allocated portfolios. Djibo declared that no member of the CSRD or of the transitional Government would be permitted to contest a pledged presidential election. Later in March Djibo replaced eight regional governors with army officers. Also in March Djibo appointed military officers to replace civilian regional governors who had been dismissed following the coup, and installed a 131-member advisory council for the transitional period, the Conseil consultatif national, chaired by civil society activist Marou Amadou. In late March Oumarou and 13 other former ministers and officials loyal to Tandja (who remained in detention in the presidential buildings in Niamey) were arrested and accused of involvement in 'subversive activities' aimed at undermining the transitional process; they were released several days later.

In April 2010 Djibo appointed a 16-member committee to draft a new constitution, electoral law and charter governing political parties. In early May, in an announcement that was welcomed by ECOWAS, the CSRD declared that the transition to civilian rule would be completed by 18 February 2011, following a constitutional referendum and local, legislative and presidential elections. Later in May 2010 Djibo promulgated a new electoral code, based on the recommendations of the Conseil consultatif national, which notably reduced the presidential term from five years to four (renewable only once) and required presidential candidates to be aged between 40 and 70 years and to possess a university degree. A new CENI was inaugurated in mid-June, under the chairmanship of a judge, Abdourahmane Ghousmane. On 3 July Ghousmane announced that a constitutional referendum would take place on 31 October, followed by legislative elections and the first round of a presidential election on 3 January 2011. Also on 3 July 2010 ECOWAS announced that Niger was to be reinstated as an observer member. In mid-July the leaders of 17 member parties of the CFDR, including the CDS, the PNDS and the Mouvement démocratique nigérien (Moden—established by supporters of former Prime Minister Hama Amadou), signed an accord in which they pledged to support whoever of their candidates succeeded in reaching the second round of the presidential election. In September the CENI announced a postponement of the elections owing to organizational difficulties; according to the revised timetable, local elections were to be conducted on 8 January 2011, followed by legislative elections and the first round of the presidential election on 31 January (with a second round scheduled for 12 March). A proposal by the European Commission for a gradual resumption of EU development aid to Niger, conditional on continued progress towards the restoration of constitutional order in the country, was approved by EU member governments on 27 September 2010. In October four army officers, including Abdoulaye Badie, the second most senior member of the CSRD, and Abdou Sidikou, a commander in the national guard, were arrested on suspicion of conspiring to overthrow Djibo, after the transitional Government announced that a coup attempt had been thwarted.

Recent developments: presidential and legislative elections

At the national referendum, which took place, as scheduled, on 31 October 2010, the Constitution of the Seventh Republic was endorsed by 90.2% of votes cast, with a recorded participation rate of about 52.0%. The new Constitution included provisions restricting the President to two five-year terms in office, prohibited members of the armed forces from seeking the presidency, and also granted an amnesty to the protagonists of the military coup in February. The Constitution was promulgated by Djibo on 26 November, after the Constitutional Court confirmed the results. At a CDS congress in November, Ousmane was re-elected unopposed as the party's President.

In January 2011, as campaigning for the forthcoming elections began, it was reported that Tandja had been transferred from house arrest to prison, after being formally charged with misappropriation of public funds. Local and regional elections were conducted on 11 January (after a delay of three days). The first round of the presidential election, which was contested by 10 candidates took place, concurrently with the legislative elections, on 31 January as scheduled. In the legislative elections, the PNDS secured 39 of the 113 seats, while the MNSD—Nassara took 26 and Moden 24 seats, according to provisional results. In the presidential poll, PNDS leader Issoufou secured the highest number of votes, with 36.2%, followed by former premiers Oumarou (23.2%) and Amadou (19.8%), and former President Ousmane (8.3%). The second round of the presidential election between Issoufou and Oumarou took place on 12 March: the CENI announced that Issoufou had been elected to the presidency, with about 58% of votes cast, according to provisional results. ECOWAS and AU observers commended the successful organization of the presidential election. Issoufou's inauguration as President on 7 April officially marked the end of military rule. He immediately appointed a member of the Tuareg community and former minister, Brigi Rafini, as Prime Minister. Later that month a new, 24-member Government, which included six women, was announced.

Tuareg issues

Ethnic unrest followed the return to northern Niger, during the late 1980s, of large numbers of Tuareg nomads who had migrated to Libya and Algeria in the early 1980s to escape the Sahelian drought. It was widely believed that the perceived failure of the Saïbou administration to assist in the rehabilitation of returnees was a significant factor contributing to the subsequent Tuareg uprising. In January 1992 the transitional authorities intensified security measures in the north and, for the first time, formally acknowledged that there was a rebellion in the country. Rhissa Ag Boula, the leader of the rebel Front de libération de l'Aïr et l'Azaouad (FLAA), subsequently stated that the Tuareg rebels were seeking to achieve the establishment of a federal system of governance. Although the Government and the FLAA concluded a truce agreement in May, violence swiftly resumed. In August the security forces launched a major offensive against rebel Tuareg groups. Military authority was reinforced in October by the appointment of senior members of the security forces to northern administrative posts. In November, none the less, a commission that had been appointed by the transitional Government recommended a far-reaching programme of decentralization, according legal status and financial authority to local communities.

In January 1993 a Minister of State for National Reconciliation, whose main responsibility would be to seek a solution to the Tuareg issue, was appointed to the Government. In March, following Algerian mediation, Ag Boula (who was based in Algeria) agreed that the FLAA would observe a truce for the duration of the campaign for the second round of the presidential election. Shortly afterwards Tuareg representatives in Niamey signed a similar (French-brokered) agreement.

In mid-1993 a three-month truce agreement between representatives of the Government and the Tuaregs, which provided for the demilitarization of the north, and envisaged negotiations on the Tuaregs' political demands, was signed in Paris, France. However, a new group, the Armée révolutionnaire de libération du nord-Niger (ARLN), emerged to denounce the truce, and supporters of the truce (led by Mano Dayak, the Tuareg signatory to the agreement) broke away from the FLAA to form the Front de libération de Tamoust (FLT): Ag Boula and the remainder of the FLAA stated that they could not support any agreement that contained no specific commitment to discussion of federalism. In September the FLT and the Government agreed to extend the truce for a further three months. Although the FLAA and the ARLN refused to sign the accord, in October they joined with the FLT in a Coordination de la résistance armée (CRA), with the aim of presenting a cohesive programme in future negotiations.

Tentative agreement was reached in June 1994 on the creation of ethnically based autonomous regions, each of which was to have its own elected assembly and governor to function in parallel with the organs of central government. Despite renewed unrest, in September the CRA presented Nigerien government negotiators with a plan for the restoration of peace. Formal negotiations resumed, with mediation by the Burkinabè President, Blaise Compaoré, as well as representatives of France and Algeria, in Ouagadougou (Burkina Faso) in October. A new peace accord resulted, emphasizing that Niger was 'unitary and indivisible', while proposing the establishment of elected assemblies or councils for territorial communities, which would be responsible for the implementation of economic, social and cultural policies. A renewable three-month truce was to take immediate effect, to be monitored by French and Burkinabè military units. By the time of the conclusion of the Ouagadougou agreement the number of deaths since the escalation of the Tuareg rebellion in late 1991 was officially estimated at 150. A commission was established in January 1995 to consider the administrative reorganization of the country.

Ag Boula, who had withdrawn from the CRA, and refused to participate in the decentralization committee, in protest at alleged delays in the implementation of the provisions of the October 1994 agreement, emerged as the leader of the Tuareg delegation (now renamed the Organisation de la résistance armée—ORA) at negotiations in Ouagadougou in March 1995.

In April it was announced that a lasting peace agreement had been reached. Demobilized rebels were to be integrated into the Nigerien military and public sector; particular emphasis was to be placed on the economic, social and cultural development of the north, and the Government undertook to support the decentralization process. There was to be a general amnesty for all parties involved in the Tuareg rebellion and its suppression, and a day of national reconciliation was to be instituted in memory of the victims of the conflict. The peace agreement was formally signed by Ag Boula and a representative of the Nigerien Government on 24 April 1995, one day before the cease-fire took effect.

Meanwhile, there was increasing ethnic unrest in the Lake Chad region of south-east Niger, where several thousand (mainly Toubou) Chadian refugees had settled since the overthrow of President Hissène Habré in late 1990. The Front démocratique du renouveau (FDR) emerged in October 1994 to demand increased autonomy for the Toubou population of the south-east. In November, in compliance with a request by the UN, Niger established a committee to disarm militias and to combat arms-trafficking, which was reportedly prevalent in the Agadez and Lake Chad regions. A Comité spécial de la paix (CSP) was inaugurated in May 1995, and a military observer group, comprising representatives of Burkina and France, was deployed in the north in July. The Prime Minister approved an amnesty in that month, and all Tuareg prisoners were reported to have been released shortly afterwards. The peace process was undermined, however, by evidence that Dayak and other Tuareg groups in a revived CRA were making common cause with the FDR in demanding autonomy for their respective regions. In December Dayak was one of three leading CRA members to be killed in an air crash. In January 1996 the new leader of the FLT (and acting leader of the CRA), Mohamed Akotai, indicated that his movement favoured inter-Tuareg reconciliation and a dialogue with the Government.

Following the *coup d'état* of January 1996, the CSN expressed its commitment to the peace process. Nevertheless, insecurity persisted, particularly in the east and violent clashes were reported in March 1997, involving several hundred soldiers and Toubou rebels. In July the FDR announced its withdrawal from the peace process, stating that Nigerien and Chadian military units had attacked one of its bases; the FDR reported that 17 members of the armed forces had been killed in clashes with its fighters. The Nigerien authorities denied that any engagement had taken place. In November a peace accord, known as the Algiers addendum protocol, providing for an immediate cease-fire, was signed in Algeria between the Nigerien Government and several opposition movements. In March 1998 the ORA and CRA surrendered their weapons stocks at Agadez. Meanwhile, Ag Boula was appointed as Minister-delegate responsible for Tourism in December 1997.

Following the death of President Maïnassara, in April 1999, the military CRN gave assurances that the peace process would be continued. Ag Boula was promoted to the rank of minister in the transitional Government and retained his ministerial post in the new Government of Hama Amadou, formed in January 2000. Concerns remained, however, that progress still had to be made in the implementation of moves towards greater administrative decentralization, as well as regarding the delayed fulfilment of quotas for Tuaregs in military formations. In late September more than 1,200 guns, surrendered by the disarmed factions, were ceremoniously burned in Agadez, in the presence of President Mamadou Tandja, leaders of other West African nations and UN representatives. Furthermore, the dissolution of several of the rebel groups and militias was announced.

In February 2004 Ag Boula was dismissed from his ministerial post and detained on a charge of complicity in the murder of an MNSD—Nassara activist (in order to maintain Tuareg representation in the Government, Mohamed Anako was appointed as a Minister-delegate at the Ministry of the Economy and Finance). The Government subsequently denied rumours that elements of FLAA had resumed insurgent activities in the north; however, following a clash with government forces in October, in which five people were reported to have died, Ag Boula's brother, Mohamed Ag Boula, claimed responsibility for the attack, citing the failure of the Government to implement the 1995 peace agreements, and the continuing detention of certain former insurgents, as motivation for the attack. Also in late 2004 four government soldiers were taken hostage in northern Niger; once more, Mohamed Ag Boula declared responsibility for the action, as the leader of a revived FLAA. Following mediation by the Libyan authorities, the hostages were released, after some five months in captivity, in February 2005; Rhissa Ag Boula was released from prison (where he had been awaiting trial) one month later. The authorities reportedly denied Ag Boula's release was linked to that of the hostages, although Mohamed Ag Boula had previously refused to free the kidnapped soldiers while his brother remained in detention. In July 2008 Rhissa Ag Boula (who had fled to France following his release) was convicted for the murder of the MNSD—Nassara activist and sentenced to death *in absentia*.

In February 2007 a lesser known Tuareg rebel group, the MNJ, claimed responsibility for an attack on a military base north of Niamey, prompting concerns that ethnic unrest was once again increasing. Further attacks were reported in mid-2007. Despite repeated demands from the rebel group for fairer distribution of revenue generated by mining the uranium resources of the northern region, the Government refused to enter into negotiations, insisting that the attacks were not considered to be a rebellion. However, by August the situation had worsened, with the number of Tuareg attacks increasing, and in that month President Tandja declared a three-month state of emergency in the region and granted additional powers of arrest to the security forces. Meanwhile, residents fled the towns of northern Niger as the rebel group used landmines to block roads and prevent the delivery of food supplies.

The MNJ claimed that it was responsible for an attack on the town of Tanhout in January 2008, in which seven soldiers were reported to have been killed and several more captured; the civilian administrator of the town was also taken prisoner. There was further violence in March when Tuareg gunmen attacked a vehicle that was transporting uranium to a port in Benin, killing one civilian, and in the same month the Nigerien armed forces launched an offensive against the MNJ in the north. The MNJ denied army claims that 10 rebels had been killed. In May the army announced that it had killed a further 11 Tuareg rebels in a new operation against rebel bases in the north (the MNJ again denied this claim), while President Tandja issued a decree extending the state of emergency declared in August 2007. In June 2008 four French executives working for the nuclear power company, Areva, were kidnapped by Tuareg rebels; they were held for four days before being handed over to the International Committee of the Red Cross. In the following month further clashes between government forces and the MNJ resulted in the death of a senior member of that organization, Mohamed Acherif.

In August 2008 a government spokesman falsely claimed that the Tuareg rebels had agreed to cease hostilities after holding peace talks with Libyan Revolutionary Leader Col Muammar al-Qaddafi. Nevertheless, a senior MNJ member stated that the rebels were willing to engage in peace talks with the Government, on the condition that they were conducted outside Niger. Despite this development there were reports in October that MNJ forces had attacked an army convoy near the town of Arlit, and in December another Tuareg rebel organization, the Front des forces de redressement (FFR), claimed responsibility for the kidnapping of a Canadian diplomat, Robert Fowler; the FFR, however, later retracted its claim. An Algerian-based rebel group styled al-Qa'ida Organization in the Islamic Maghreb (AQIM—previously known as the Groupe salafiste pour la prédication et le combat) subsequently claimed that it had Fowler in captivity, and in March 2009 demanded the return of 20 of its members detained in Mali and elsewhere, as a condition for his release and that of several other Western hostages. Meanwhile, in the same month, numerous members of the MNJ split from the group to form the Front patriotique du Niger (FPN), which sought to enter into negotiations with the Government to restore peace. Days later al-Qaddafi appealed to all Tuareg rebels in Niger and Mali to engage in a peace process, and in April the Government dispatched a senior security official to Libya for mediation with the rebels.

After two days of Libyan-sponsored talks held in early April 2009, delegates from the Nigerien Government, the MNJ, the FPN and the FFR reportedly committed themselves to restoring peace in the north. President Tandja held talks with representatives of the three Tuareg groups for the first time in early May in Agadez, offering an amnesty if the rebels disarmed; shortly beforehand, the MNJ announced the release of the last remaining hostage. In mid-May the MNJ and the FPN were reported to have agreed to a cease-fire during discussions with Prime Minister Oumarou, which were, however, boycotted by the FFR. In early October the MNJ symbolically surrendered its weapons at a ceremony in southern Libya, attended by al-Qaddafi; this was followed by an official disarmament ceremony near Arlit in January 2010. It was reported that the FPN and the FFR had also agreed to disarm. The leaders of the main Tuareg movements returned to Niamey after Tandja was overthrown in February to seek involvement in the transitional process and to apply pressure on the new military authorities to accelerate the reintegration of former rebels. However, Ag Boula was arrested in the capital in March in connection with his 2008 conviction.

In September 2010 five French nationals, together with one from Togo and one from Madagascar, were seized by an armed group in northern Niger; AQIM claimed responsibility for the kidnapping. The French Government subsequently announced that it had deployed 80 military personnel to Niamey to assist Niger's military forces in locating the hostages. In January 2011 a further two French nationals, who had been taken hostage by suspected AQIM militants in Niamey, were killed during a failed rescue operation by Nigerien troops and French special forces. In February three of the hostages who had been seized in the previous September (one French, one Togolese and one Malagasy) were released.

Foreign Affairs
Regional relations

Countries of the region with which Maïnassara had forged close relations condemned the military take-over of April 1999: Libya notably denounced the new regime, although relations between the CRN and the Libyan Government had normalized by the end of the year. In December the two countries signed an agreement envisaging the establishment of a joint company to distribute oil and liquefied natural gas; it was also agreed to expedite the establishment of a joint company for petroleum exploration and production. On a visit to Agadez in early July, Libyan leader Col Muammar al-Qaddafi pledged support for the Tuareg peace process. In November Libya pledged to grant financial support for several construction and development projects in Niger. Meanwhile, some 1,000 Nigerien citizens were repatriated from Libya in October, following instances of inter-ethnic violence between Libyan Arabs and black Africans in that country. On 24 April 2006, the 11th anniversary of the signing of the peace agreement, President Tandja announced that a rehabilitation programme was to be launched to assist more than 3,000 former Tuareg rebels. On surrendering their weapons in 1995 the rebels were forced onto barren land in the north of the country, but, with funds from the project amounting to 850m. francs CFA, it was hoped that the Tuaregs would develop prosperous farming and agricultural communities. Following a meeting in April 2009 between the Libyan Secretary for Public Security, Gen. Abd al-Fattah Yunis al-Abaidi, and Nigerien Minister of the Interior, Albadé Abouba, the two countries agreed to establish a joint organization to combat organized crime, narcotics trafficking and illegal migration through their common borders.

In May 2000 a long-term dispute between Niger and Benin regarding the ownership of a number of small islands along their common border at the Niger river escalated, reportedly following the sabotage of a Beninois administrative building on the island of Lété, apparently by Nigerien soldiers. A meeting between representatives of the two Governments failed to resolve the dispute, which was subsequently referred to the Organization of African Unity (OAU, now the African Union, see p. 183) for arbitration. Further clashes between rival groups of farmers were reported on Lété in late August. In April 2002 the two Governments officially ratified an agreement (signed in 2001) to refer the issue of ownership of the islands to the International Court of Justice, ICJ (see p. 23) in The Hague, Netherlands, for arbitration. In November 2003 a five-member chamber formed to consider the case held its first public sitting. Both countries subsequently submitted counter-arguments, and a third written pleading was submitted by both parties in December of that year. Meanwhile, in late 2004 Nigerien traders and haulage contractors boycotted Cotonou port in Benin in reaction to the shooting of two Nigerien citizens by Beninois gendarmes in the city in September. The boycott was ended in January 2005 following a visit to Niamey by the Beninois Minister of Foreign Affairs and African Integration, Rogatien Biaou, during which he announced that the Beninois Government would compensate the victims' families. In July the ICJ issued a final ruling to the effect that 16 of the 25 disputed islands, including Lété, belonged to Niger; the Governments of both countries announced their acceptance of the ruling.

In June 2001 Niger and Nigeria announced that joint border patrols of their common frontier would be instigated, in order to combat increasing cross-border crime and smuggling in the region. It was reported that the introduction of *Shari'a* law in several northern Nigerian states, from 2000, had been instrumental in encouraging Nigerian criminal gangs to operate from within Niger. Further concerns regarding regional security were raised in early 2004, when Islamic militants reportedly attacked a group of tourists in northern Niger. Following clashes between the militants and Chadian and Nigerien troops in March, it was announced that the Governments of Algeria, Chad, Mali and Niger were to reinforce security co-operation in the regions of their common borders. In January 2005 President Tandja was elected Chairman of the Economic Community of West African States (see p. 257).

In October 2006 the Government announced that it was to forcibly remove some 150,000 Mahamid Arabs from eastern Niger and return them to their native Chad. Several thousand Chadians had crossed the border into Niger during the 1970s to escape widespread drought, which had caused outbreaks of violence in their homeland. During the 1980s thousands more fled to Niger when conflict escalated into civil war in Chad. Mahamid communities continued to establish themselves in the Diffa region, but there followed complaints of deteriorating relations between the Mahamids and the local population, and it was feared that the Chadians' presence posed a serious threat to national security. The office of the UN High Commissioner for Refugees responded with claims that the Mahamid communities did not hold refugee status and stipulated that it be ensured that those forced to leave would not become victims of discrimination on their return to Chad. The Niger authorities then reversed the earlier decision, stating instead that the Mahamids would be asked to move to land better suited to their agricultural needs. In late October several thousand Nigeriens protested against that ruling, threatening that they would be forced to take action to protect their land and property if the Mahamids were not returned to Chad. The Nigerien Government subsequently announced that only those who did not have the required documents would be sent back; according to the census of 2001, the majority of the Arab community held identity cards issued by the local authorities.

Other external relations

There was a notable deterioration in relations with the USA in the immediate aftermath of the 1996 presidential election in Niger. The assumption of power by the CRN in April 1999, following the death of Maïnassara, was condemned by the USA, France and Niger's other Western creditors. Relations with the USA improved following the re-installation of an elected Government; in February 2000 Niger's Minister of Foreign Affairs, Co-operation and African Integration visited Washington, DC, and in March the USA announced an end to the sanctions imposed after Maïnassara's death. In August President Tandja met President Bill Clinton and other US representatives in Abuja, Nigeria, where the USA announced increased support for Niger in areas including food security, the promotion of democracy, education and health care. The actions of Tandja attracted strong condemnation from the USA and other international creditors, in response to the constitutional crisis from May 2009 (see Domestic Political Affairs); in December the USA suspended all non-humanitarian assistance to Niger.

The EU suspended all assistance to Niger in the aftermath of the military take-over in April 1999 and made its resumption dependent on a full investigation into Maïnassara's death; the CRN subsequently stated that its report had been lodged with organizations including the EU, and EU aid recommenced in June 2000. France also suspended military and civilian co-operation with Niger in April 1999. Following a visit to France by Mamadou Tandja in January 2000, when the newly installed Nigerien President met President Jacques Chirac and Prime Minister Lionel Jospin, the resumption of French co-operation was formalized, with the announcement of exceptional assistance principally to allow payment of outstanding salaries in the public sector. Chirac visited Niger in October 2003, when he praised 'the return of democratic life' to the country. In early November 2009 the EU suspended development aid to Niger, accusing President Tandja of violating the Constitution; the gradual resumption of EU development aid to Niger, concurrent with the transitional process, was approved by EU member governments in September 2010.

CONSTITUTION AND GOVERNMENT

On 31 October 2010 90.2% of those who voted in a national referendum approved the text of the Constitution of the Seventh Republic. On 26 November the new Constitution was promulgated by the President of the Conseil suprême pour la restauration de la démocratie, Salou Djibo.

For the purposes of local administration, Niger comprises seven regions and the municipality of Niamey. A reorganization of Niger's administrative structures, with the aim of devolving increased autonomy to local and regional authorities, was undertaken in the second half of the 1990s.

REGIONAL AND INTERNATIONAL CO-OPERATION

Niger is a member of numerous regional organizations, including the Economic Community of West African States (ECOWAS, see p. 257), the West African organs of the Franc Zone (see p. 332), the Conseil de l'Entente (see p. 446), the Lake Chad Basin Commission (see p. 448), the Liptako–Gourma Integrated Development Authority (see p. 448), the Niger Basin Authority (see p. 448) and the Permanent Inter-State Committee on Drought Control in the Sahel (see p. 449). On 20 October 2009 Niger's membership of ECOWAS was suspended (see Domestic Political Affairs); in July 2010 the country was reinstated as an observer member. On 19 February the African Union (see p. 183) also suspended Niger's membership, in response to a military coup.

Niger became a member of the UN in 1960 and was admitted to the World Trade Organization (WTO, see p. 430) in 1996. Niger participates in the Group of 77 (G77, see p. 447) developing countries.

ECONOMIC AFFAIRS

In 2009, according to estimates by the World Bank, Niger's gross national income (GNI), measured at average 2007–09 prices, was US $5,197m., equivalent to $340 per head (or $660 on an international purchasing-power parity basis). During 2000–09, it was estimated, the population increased at an average annual rate of 3.7%, while gross domestic product (GDP) per head increased, in real terms, by an average of 0.8% per year. Overall GDP increased, in real terms, at an average annual rate of 4.5% in 2000–09; growth was 1.0% in 2009.

Agriculture (including hunting, forestry and fishing) contributed 44.0% of GDP in 2009, according to estimates provided by the African Development Bank (AfDB) and in 2007, according to official figures, 2.0% of the labour force were employed in the sector. The principal cash crops are cow-peas, onions, groundnuts and cotton. The principal subsistence crops are millet and sorghum. Niger is able to achieve self-sufficiency in basic foodstuffs in non-drought years. Agricultural production in northern Niger in 2004/05 was severely affected by drought and by the swarms of locusts that invaded the Sahel region from mid-2004, resulting in a grain deficit of 223,487 tons for that agricultural year. However, by 2006 a surplus had been re-established. The effects of drought and locust invasion were also thought to have caused significant damage to pasture land: livestock-rearing in Niger is especially important among the nomadic population, and live animals intended chiefly for food accounted for 17.1% of total export earnings in 2008, constituting the second most important source of export revenue, after uranium. Major anti-desertification and re-afforestation programmes are in progress. According to the World Bank, agricultural GDP increased by an average of 7.0% per year in 2000–03. Agricultural GDP increased by 16.2% in 2008, but decreased by 6.9% in 2009, according to the AfDB.

Industry (including mining, manufacturing, construction and power) contributed 16.1% of GDP in 2009, according to AfDB estimates. Some 40.6% of the labour force were employed in industrial activities in 2007, according to official figures. According to the World Bank, industrial GDP increased by an average of 3.1% per year in 2000–03; growth was 4.0% in 2003.

Mining contributed 6.5% of GDP in 2009, according to AfDB data, but employed only 0.8% of the labour force in 2007, according to official figures. Niger is among the world's foremost producers of uranium (the fifth largest, after Kazakhstan, Canada, Australia, and Namibia, in 2010), although the contribution of uranium-mining to the domestic economy has declined, as production costs have exceeded world prices for the mineral. In 2008 exports of uranium accounted for 57.5% of total export earnings. In addition, gypsum, coal, salt and cassiterite are also extracted, and commercial exploitation of gold (previously mined on a small scale) at the Samira Hill mine began in 2004, with production of 79,300 oz of gold in 2007. In that year the Government awarded the US firm Caracal Gold Burkina two permits for gold exploration in western Niger. According to the IMF, the GDP of the mining sector increased at an average annual rate of

2.3% in 1998–2005; mining GDP decreased by an estimated 2.1% in 2008, but increased by 6.0% in 2009, according to the AfDB.

According to AfDB estimates, manufacturing contributed 5.5% of GDP in 2009 and employed 25.7% of the labour force in 2007. The processing of agricultural products (groundnuts, cereals, cotton and rice) constitutes the principal activity. Some light industries, including a textiles plant, a brewery and a cement works, supply the internal market. According to the World Bank, manufacturing GDP increased by an average of 3.9% per year in 2000–03. Manufacturing GDP increased by 3.2% in 2009, according to the AfDB.

The construction sector contributed 2.8% of GDP in 2009 and employed 11.9% of the labour force in 2007. The sector recorded growth of 6.3% in 2009, according to the AfDB.

The domestic generation of electricity (almost entirely thermal) provides a little less than one-half of Niger's electrical energy requirements, much of the remainder being imported from Nigeria. Construction of a hydroelectric installation at Kandadji, on the Niger, is planned. Imports of mineral fuels accounted for 16.6% of the value of merchandise imports in 2008.

The services sector contributed 39.9% of GDP in 2009, according to AfDB estimates, and employed 57.3% of the labour force in 2007. The GDP of the sector increased by an average of 3.6% per year in 2000–03, according to the World Bank; growth was 3.1% in 2003.

In 2008 Niger recorded a visible trade deficit of an estimated 174,200m. francs CFA, while there was a deficit of 301,100m. francs CFA on the current account of the balance of payments. France was Niger's principal source of imports in 2008, supplying 13.2%; other major suppliers were the People's Republic of China, Netherlands, the USA, and Côte d'Ivoire. The principal markets for exports in that year were France (33.3%), the USA, Nigeria and Japan. The principal exports in 2008 were uranium and food and live animals. The principal imports in that year were machinery and transport equipment, food and live animals, mineral fuels, lubricants, and chemicals and related products.

Niger's overall budget deficit for 2010 was projected at 112,700m. francs CFA. Niger's general government gross debt was 391,814m. francs in 2009, equivalent to 15.8% of GDP. Niger's total external debt was US $966m. at the end of 2008, of which $883m. was public and publicly guaranteed debt. Consumer prices increased by an annual average of 3.1% during 2000–09. Consumer prices increased by 4.3% in 2009. Some 64,987 people were registered as unemployed in 2001.

Niger is one of the world's poorest countries, and has consistently been among the lowest ranking countries in the United Nations Development Programme's Human Development Report. Niger's narrow export base, which is dominated by uranium, and political instability have adversely affected economic performance. In July 2005 Niger was among 18 countries to be granted 100% debt relief on multilateral debt by the Group of Eight leading industrialized nations (G8), while a new three-year Poverty Reduction and Growth Facility (PRGF) of US $35.3m. became effective in June 2008. In September 2009 an IMF assessment mission considered that Niger's economy had been largely unaffected by the international financial crisis. However, a protracted political crisis from May (see Domestic Political Affairs) resulted in the virtual suspension of Niger's relations with international donor nations and organizations; the Economic Community of West African States (ECOWAS, see p. 257) suspended the country's membership in October, while the EU withheld non-humanitarian assistance in November and the USA in December. In February 2010 the IMF issued its third review of Niger's economic performance under a programme supported by an Extended Credit Facility (which had succeeded the PRGF) and approved a disbursement of $5m. Following a military coup on 18 February, the African Union (see p. 183) also suspended Niger's membership; the international community demanded the restoration of democratic rule prior to the normalization of relations with Niger. In March the transitional Government announced that $123m. of international assistance was necessary to overcome impending food shortages (resulting from poor regional rainfall). NGOs and UN agencies subsequently praised the military Government, headed by Salou Djibo, for helping to facilitate a prompt response to the food crisis. An improved harvest in 2010 and the gradual resumption of external donor financing in the second half of that year markedly improved the economic outlook, while a number of significant mining and oil projects were expected potentially to generate further growth. By mid-2011 the transition to democratic rule had reached a successful conclusion, following legislative and presidential elections.

PUBLIC HOLIDAYS

2012: 1 January (New Year's Day), 4 February* (Mouloud, Birth of the Prophet), 9 April (Easter Monday), 24 April (National Concord Day), 1 May (Labour Day), 3 August (Independence Day), 18 August* (Id al-Fitr, end of Ramadan), 26 October* (Tabaski, Feast of the Sacrifice), 15 November* (Islamic New Year), 18 December (Republic Day).

*These holidays are dependent on the Islamic lunar calendar and may vary by one or two days from the dates given.

Statistical Survey

Source (unless otherwise stated): Institut national de la Statistique, Immeuble sis à la Rue Sirba, derrière la Présidence de la république, BP 720, Niamey; tel. 20-72-35-60; fax 20-72-21-74; e-mail insniger@ins.ne; internet www.stat-niger.org.

Area and Population

AREA, POPULATION AND DENSITY

Area (sq km)	1,267,000*
Population (census results)	
20 May 1988	7,248,100
20 May 2001	
Males	5,516,588
Females	5,543,703
Total	11,060,291
Population (UN estimates at mid-year)†	
2009	15,290,102
2010	15,891,482
2011	16,507,290
Density (per sq km) at mid-2011	13.0

*489,191 sq miles.
†Source: UN, *World Population Prospects: The 2008 Revision*.

POPULATION BY AGE AND SEX
(UN estimates at mid-2011)

	Males	Females	Total
0–14	4,238,283	4,057,725	8,296,008
15–64	3,882,962	3,998,712	7,881,674
65 and over	150,116	179,492	329,608
Total	8,271,361	8,235,929	16,507,290

Source: UN, *World Population Prospects: The 2008 Revision*.

NIGER

ETHNIC GROUPS
(2001 census, Nigerien citizens only)

	Population	%
Hausa	6,069,731	55.36
Djerma-Sonraï	2,300,874	20.99
Tuareg	1,016,883	9.27
Peulh	935,517	8.53
Kanouri-Manga	513,116	4.68
Toubou	42,172	0.38
Arab	40,085	0.37
Gourmantché	39,797	0.36
Others	5,951	0.05
Total	**10,964,126**	**100.00**

ADMINISTRATIVE DIVISIONS
(2010)

Agadez	487,313	Niamey (city)	1,222,066
Diffa	473,563	Tahoua	2,658,099
Dosso	2,016,690	Tillabéri	2,500,454
Maradi	3,021,169	Zinder	1,394,184

PRINCIPAL TOWNS
(population at 2001 census)

Niamey (capital)	707,951	Agadez	78,289
Zinder	170,575	Tahoua	73,002
Maradi	148,017	Arlit	69,435

Mid-2010 (incl. suburbs, UN estimate): Niamey 1,048,000 (Source: UN, *World Urbanization Prospects: The 2009 Revision*).

BIRTHS AND DEATHS
(annual averages, UN estimates)

	1995–2000	2000–05	2005–10
Birth rate (per 1,000)	54.0	52.2	54.1
Death rate (per 1,000)	20.5	17.4	15.2

Source: UN, *World Population Prospects: The 2008 Revision*.

2006: Birth rate 53.5 per 1,000; Death rate 15.8 per 1,000 (Source: African Development Bank).
2007: Birth rate 53.6 per 1,000; Death rate 15.3 per 1,000 (Source: African Development Bank).
2008: Birth rate 53.5 per 1,000; Death rate 14.9 per 1,000 (Source: African Development Bank).
2009: Birth rate 53.2 per 1,000; Death rate 14.5 per 1,000 (Source: African Development Bank).

Life expectancy (years at birth, WHO estimates): 52 (males 51; females 53) in 2008 (Source: WHO, *World Health Statistics*).

EMPLOYMENT
('000 persons at 31 December)

	2005	2006	2007*
Agriculture, hunting, forestry and fishing	59	60	72
Mining and quarrying	21	24	29
Manufacturing	845	846	907
Electricity, gas and water	71	71	79
Construction	380	411	421
Trade, restaurants and hotels	592	678	704
Transport, storage and communications	312	319	342
Financing, insurance, real estate and business services	195	196	205
Community, social and personal services	650	666	776
Total	**3,125**	**3,271**	**3,535**

* Provisional figures.

2001 census (persons aged 10 years and over): Total employed 4,015,951 (males 2,706,910, females 1,309,041), Unemployed 64,987 (males 49,437, females 15,550), Total labour force 4,080,938 (males 2,756,347, females 1,324,591).

Statistical Survey

Health and Welfare

KEY INDICATORS

Total fertility rate (children per woman, 2008)	7.1
Under-5 mortality rate (per 1,000 live births, 2008)	167
HIV/AIDS (% of persons aged 15–49, 2007)	0.8
Physicians (per 1,000 head, 2004)	0.03
Hospital beds (per 1,000 head, 1998)	0.12
Health expenditure (2007): US $ per head (PPP)	35
Health expenditure (2007): % of GDP	5.3
Health expenditure (2007): public (% of total)	52.8
Access to water (% of persons, 2008)	48
Access to sanitation (% of persons, 2008)	9
Total carbon dioxide emissions ('000 metric tons, 2007)	908.7
Carbon dioxide emissions per head (metric tons per, 2007)	0.1
Human Development Index (2010): ranking	167
Human Development Index (2010): value	0.261

For sources and definitions, see explanatory note on p. vi.

Agriculture

PRINCIPAL CROPS
('000 metric tons)

	2006	2007	2008
Wheat	7.8	9.0	8.5
Rice, paddy	78.4	70.0	28.5*
Millet	3,009	2,782	3,889
Sorghum	929	975	1,331
Potatoes	32.3	32.3	22.6
Sweet potatoes	92	123	58
Cassava (Manioc)	138	146	110
Sugar cane	240†	240†	188
Cow peas, dry	703.3	1,013.3	1,569.3
Groundnuts, with shell	152.6*	147.7	307.8*
Sesame seed	44	22	51*
Cottonseed	5*	7†	7†
Cabbages and other brassicas	130†	150†	171
Lettuce and chicory	50†	60†	77
Tomatoes†	130	130	130
Chillies and peppers, green	20†	22†	26
Onions, dry	330†	350†	374
Garlic	8†	8†	8
Beans, green†	25	25	25
Carrots and turnips†	20	20	20
Dates	10†	13†	17
Tobacco, unmanufactured†	1.0	1.0	1.0

* Unofficial figure.
† FAO estimate(s).

Aggregate production ('000 metric tons, may include official, semi-official or estimated data): Total cereals 4,030 in 2006, 3,859 in 2007, 4,851 in 2008–09; Total roots and tubers 262 in 2006, 301 in 2007, 191 in 2008–09; Total vegetables (incl. melons) 801 in 2006, 859 in 2007, 929 in 2008–09; Total pulses 727 in 2006, 1,037 in 2007, 1,593 in 2008–09.

2009 (FAO estimate): Cotton seed 6.

Source: FAO.

LIVESTOCK
('000 head, year ending September)

	2006	2007	2008
Cattle	7,776	8,243	8,737
Sheep	9,514	9,847	10,191
Goats	11,688	12,155	12,641
Pigs*	40	40	40
Horses	233	235	237
Asses	1,507	1,537	1,567
Camels	1,586	1,606	1,627
Chickens	10,977	11,120	11,000*

* FAO estimate(s).

2009 (FAO estimate): Sheep 10,200.

Source: FAO.

NIGER

LIVESTOCK PRODUCTS
('000 metric tons, FAO estimates)

	2007	2008	2009
Game meat	23	23	n.a.
Horse meat	1	1	1
Goat meat	50.4	52.8	n.a.
Sheep meat	39.2	35.2	41.6
Chicken meat	10.7	10.6	10.6
Hen eggs	7.6	7.6	8.0

Source: FAO.

Forestry

ROUNDWOOD REMOVALS
('000 cubic metres, excl. bark, FAO estimates)

	1999	2000	2001
Industrial wood	411	411	411
Fuel wood	7,611	7,805	2,857
Total	8,022	8,216	3,268

2002–09: Production assumed to be unchanged from 2001 (FAO estimates).
Source: FAO.

SAWNWOOD PRODUCTION
('000 cubic metres, incl. railway sleepers, FAO estimates)

	1991	1992	1993
Total (all broadleaved)	0	1	4

1994–2009: Figures assumed to be unchanged from 1993 (FAO estimates).
Source: FAO.

Fishing
(metric tons, live weight)

	2006	2007	2008
Capture (freshwater fishes)	29,835	29,728	29,960
Aquaculture	40	40	40
Total catch	29,875	29,768	30,000

Source: FAO.

Mining
('000 metric tons, unless otherwise indicated)

	2005	2006	2007
Hard coal	182.1	176.3	171.3
Tin (metric tons)*†	14.0	13.0	n.a.
Uranium (metric tons)*	3,093	3,431	3,153
Gold (kg)	4,962	2,615	2,649
Gypsum	17.4	13.0	n.a.

* Data refer to the metal content of ore.
† Artisanal production only.

2008: Hard coal 182.9; Uranium (metal content of ore) 2,993.
2009: Hard coal 225.2; Uranium (metal content of ore) 3,241.

Industry

SELECTED PRODUCTS
('000 metric tons, unless otherwise indicated)

	2005	2006	2007
Raw sugar*	10	10	10
Cement	83.4	62.0	42.0
Soap	9.4	9.4	9.4
Textile fabrics (million metres)	2.0	1.9	2.6
Beer ('000 bottles)	94.9	97.5	99.9
Electric energy (million kWh)*	195	179	197

* Source: UN Industrial Commodity Statistics Database.

Source: partly IMF, *Niger: Selected Issues and Statistical Appendix* (February 2009).

Finance

CURRENCY AND EXCHANGE RATES

Monetary Units
100 centimes = 1 franc de la Communauté financière africaine (CFA).

Sterling, Dollar and Euro Equivalents (31 December 2010)
£1 sterling = 768.523 francs CFA;
US $1 = 490.912 francs CFA;
€1 = 655.957 francs CFA;
10,000 francs CFA = £13.01 = $20.37 = €15.24.

Average Exchange Rate (francs CFA per US $)
2008   447.805
2009   472.186
2010   495.277

Note: An exchange rate of 1 French franc = 50 francs CFA, established in 1948, remained in force until January 1994, when the CFA franc was devalued by 50%, with the exchange rate adjusted to 1 French franc = 100 francs CFA. This relationship to French currency remained in effect with the introduction of the euro on 1 January 1999. From that date, accordingly, a fixed exchange rate of €1 = 655.957 francs CFA has been in operation.

BUDGET
('000 million francs CFA)

Revenue*	2008†	2009‡	2010‡
Tax revenue	281.1	329.4	356.1
International trade	110.7	116.1	121.1
Non-tax revenue	158.8	15.3	20.0
Annexed budgets and special accounts	2.1	2.9	2.5
Total	442.0	347.6	378.6

Expenditure	2008†	2009‡	2010‡
Current expenditure	300.8	310.5	308.3
Wages and salaries	83.8	93.3	107.0
Materials and supplies	63.4	65.3	77.5
Subsidies and transfers	102.1	114.5	91.9
Interest	5.5	5.6	7.5
Capital expenditure	247.1	288.7	294.1
Total	547.9	599.2	602.4

* Excluding grants received ('000 million francs CFA): 141.9 in 2008 (estimate); 117.0 in 2009 (budget projection); 111.1 in 2010 (budget projection).
† Estimates.
‡ Budget projections.

Source: IMF, *Niger: Third Review Under the Three-Year Arrangement Under the Extended Credit Facility—Staff Report; Supplement; Press Release on the Executive Board Discussion; and Statement by the Executive Director for Niger* (May 2010).

NIGER

INTERNATIONAL RESERVES
(US $ million at 31 December, excl. gold)

	2007	2008	2009
IMF special drawing rights	0.1	1.5	85.1
Reserve position in IMF	13.6	13.3	13.5
Foreign exchange	579.3	690.5	556.9
Total	593.0	705.2	655.5

2010: IMF special drawing rights 83.6; Reserve position in IMF 13.3.

Source: IMF, *International Financial Statistics*.

MONEY SUPPLY
('000 million francs CFA at 31 December)

	2007	2008	2009
Currency outside banks	133.3	147.7	187.9
Demand deposits at deposit money banks*	134.5	141.8	166.6
Checking deposits at post office	1.4	1.5	1.7
Total money (incl. others)*	269.3	291.2	356.4

* Excluding the deposits of public enterprises of an administrative or social nature.

Source: IMF, *International Financial Statistics*.

COST OF LIVING
(Consumer Price Index for Niamey, annual averages; base: 2000 = 100)

	2007	2008	2009
Food	117.6	141.8	n.a.
Clothing	99.8	103.8	101.0
Rent	108.1	113.4	115.7
All items (incl. others)	113.6	126.5	131.9

Source: ILO.

NATIONAL ACCOUNTS
('000 million francs CFA at current prices)

Expenditure on the Gross Domestic Product

	2007	2008	2009
Government final consumption expenditure	321.9	363.1	425.5
Private final consumption expenditure	1,517.1	1,714.6	1,840.6
Gross fixed capital formation	468.0	672.6	721.1
Changes in inventories	6.7	30.0	—
Total domestic expenditure	2,313.7	2,780.3	2,987.2
Exports of goods and services	358.5	454.9	490.5
Less Imports of goods and services	615.4	830.9	1,001.7
GDP at purchasers' values	2,056.7	2,404.2	2,476.0

Gross Domestic Product by Economic Activity

	2007	2008	2009
Agriculture, hunting, forestry and fishing	842.0	1,044.8	1,019.0
Mining and quarrying	90.8	139.2	149.8
Manufacturing	106.6	117.7	127.8
Electricity, gas and water supply	26.0	29.7	32.0
Construction	51.6	57.5	64.5
Wholesale and retail trade; restaurants and hotels	290.8	325.6	342.8
Finance, insurance and real estate	134.9	145.7	158.6
Transport and communications	116.0	122.6	127.8
Public administration and defence	184.5	191.8	213.6
Other services	68.8	73.0	81.3
Sub-total	1,912.0	2,247.7	2,317.2
Indirect taxes (net)	144.7	156.5	158.8
GDP at purchasers' values	2,056.7	2,404.2	2,476.0

Source: African Development Bank.

BALANCE OF PAYMENTS
('000 million francs CFA)

	2007	2008*	2009†
Exports of goods f.o.b.	318.3	397.9	390.1
Imports of goods f.o.b.	−429.4	−572.1	−748.8
Trade balance	−111.1	−174.2	−358.7
Services (net)	−136.5	−190.8	−269.2
Balance on goods and services	−247.8	−365.0	−627.9
Income (net)	−0.2	−7.4	−42.9
Balance on goods, services and income	−247.8	−372.4	−670.8
Private unrequited transfers (net)	44.0	47.0	55.4
Public unrequited transfers (net)	20.5	24.3	73.0
Current balance	−183.4	−301.1	−542.6
Capital account (net)	153.4	113.4	128.4
Direct investment (net)	58.0	225.0	348.9
Portfolio investment (net)	−3.0	−3.2	2.0
Other investment (net)	47.4	21.4	54.1
Net errors and omissions	−3.6	—	—
Overall balance	68.9	55.5	−9.2

* Estimates.
† Projections.

Source: IMF, *Niger: Second Review Under the Three-Year Arrangement Under the Poverty Reduction and Growth Facility and Request for Modification of Performance Criteria—Staff Report; Press Release on the Executive Board Discussion* (May 2009).

External Trade

PRINCIPAL COMMODITIES
(distribution by SITC, US $ million)

Imports c.i.f.	2006	2007	2008
Food and live animals	183.9	172.8	247.8
Dairy products and birds' eggs	25.1	15.7	32.4
Milk and cream	24.8	15.4	31.9
Milk and cream, preserved, concentrated or sweetened	24.3	15.0	31.2
Cereals and cereal preparations	100.5	94.6	141.7
Rice, semi-milled or wholly milled	64.0	50.9	106.1
Rice, semi-milled or milled (unbroken)	63.5	50.9	89.5
Sugar, sugar preparations and honey	21.2	22.2	28.2
Beverages and tobacco	22.0	27.6	29.1
Cigarettes	19.0	24.5	25.5
Crude materials (inedible) except fuel	50.4	61.2	87.0
Textile fibres (not wool tops) and their wastes (not in yarn)	34.7	40.6	56.1
Bulk textile waste, old clothing, traded in bulk or in bales	34.5	40.4	55.4
Mineral fuels, lubricants, etc. (incl. electric current)	124.3	162.4	207.2
Petroleum, petroleum products, etc.	108.6	145.7	189.2
Petroleum products, refined	106.9	144.5	185.9
Animal and vegetable oils, fats and waxes	30.0	22.9	32.4
Fixed vegetable oils and fats	27.9	20.4	27.4
Palm oil	23.4	15.9	19.2
Chemicals and related products	82.5	120.1	175.1
Medicinal and pharmaceutical products	36.3	75.4	118.7

NIGER

Statistical Survey

Imports c.i.f.—continued	2006	2007	2008
Basic manufactures	122.4	124.4	161.1
Textile yarn, fabrics, made-up articles, etc.	22.3	20.6	26.3
Cotton fabrics, woven (not incl. narrow or special fabrics)	13.3	13.6	18.0
Machinery and transport equipment	193.2	213.7	251.6
Telecommunications, sound recording and reproducing equipment	30.6	25.7	24.9
Road vehicles	59.5	85.1	76.4
Passenger motor vehicles (excl. buses)	21.7	28.3	29.7
Miscellaneous manufactured articles	51.5	46.8	56.2
Total (incl. others)	860.2	955.7	1,247.5

Exports f.o.b.	2006	2007	2008
Food and live animals	78.8	86.7	85.9
Live animals chiefly for food	38.7	35.0	46.3
Animals of the bovine species (incl. buffaloes), live	20.1	18.2	21.0
Sheep and goats, live	13.7	12.7	18.4
Fish, crustaceans and molluscs, and preparations thereof	0.5	0.3	0.4
Vegetables and fruit	26.1	31.8	17.8
Vegetables, fresh or simply preserved; roots and tubers	25.3	31.1	17.1
Other fresh or chilled vegetables	23.8	27.6	12.2
Beverages and tobacco	8.2	6.9	8.1
Cigarettes	7.9	6.6	7.8
Crude materials (inedible) except fuels	175.1	325.1	321.9
Textile fibres (not wool tops) and their wastes (not in yarn)	20.5	24.5	30.8
Ores and concentrates of uranium and thorium	152.0	298.8	289.4
Mineral fuels, lubricants, etc., (incl. electric current)	9.3	14.5	16.4
Petroleum, petroleum products, etc.	9.3	14.5	16.3
Basic manufactures	19.0	18.0	22.8
Fabrics, woven, 85% plus of cotton, bleached, dyed, etc., or otherwise finished	18.6	17.7	22.7
Total (incl. others)	393.8	550.1	503.1

Source: UN, *International Trade Statistics Yearbook*.

PRINCIPAL TRADING PARTNERS
(US $ million)

Imports c.i.f.	2006	2007	2008
Argentina	12.7	6.5	13.0
Belgium	22.4	25.2	31.1
Benin	42.5	23.0	12.0
Brazil	19.0	26.1	25.4
Burkina Faso	9.4	9.5	10.7
Cameroon	4.8	9.1	13.2
China, People's Republic	107.3	66.3	156.8
Côte d'Ivoire	55.4	75.5	62.5
France (incl. Monaco)	132.3	179.5	164.1
Germany	12.2	28.8	26.8
Ghana	14.7	13.6	17.7
India	40.0	30.5	29.0
Italy	8.4	12.2	14.2
Japan	32.6	46.0	44.5
Malaysia	12.9	14.2	26.0

Imports c.i.f.—continued	2006	2007	2008
Netherlands	16.0	23.0	89.4
Nigeria	52.3	45.4	58.1
Pakistan	16.4	18.6	42.3
South Africa	12.9	13.5	11.2
Thailand	6.8	7.5	43.7
Togo	20.2	36.7	49.4
United Kingdom	10.1	36.2	40.3
USA	86.5	86.5	95.4
Viet Nam	8.9	3.3	18.4
Total (incl. others)	860.2	955.7	1,247.5

Exports f.o.b.	2006	2007	2008
Belgium	7.6	3.5	3.8
Benin	9.3	3.0	0.9
Brazil	3.9	6.8	7.6
Burkina Faso	3.7	4.8	3.8
Cameroon	0.5	—	2.9
China, People's Republic	7.4	7.6	5.5
Côte d'Ivoire	10.3	21.4	17.9
France (incl. Monaco)	120.3	216.2	167.3
Germany	5.7	1.1	2.3
Ghana	14.4	17.5	7.1
Italy	0.6	2.0	3.7
Japan	53.2	68.7	49.8
Korea, Democratic People's Republic	—	2.8	6.4
Mali	0.7	0.2	0.1
Netherlands	1.7	3.2	8.7
Nigeria	51.3	41.3	59.2
South Africa	2.8	5.5	—
Spain	8.2	15.0	8.5
Sri Lanka	2.1	3.9	—
Switzerland-Liechtenstein	32.4	59.1	21.8
Thailand	2.1	3.9	10.0
Togo	9.7	0.8	0.3
United Kingdom	1.6	0.5	0.5
USA	21.9	32.1	88.7
Total (incl. others)	393.8	550.1	503.1

Source: UN, *International Trade Statistics Yearbook*.

Transport

ROAD TRAFFIC
(motor vehicles in use at 31 December, estimates)

	2003	2004	2005
Passenger cars	47,676	52,992	57,732
Buses and coaches	2,264	2,430	2,613
Lorries and vans	13,153	14,562	15,716

Source: IRF, *World Road Statistics*.

CIVIL AVIATION
(traffic on scheduled services)*

	1999	2000	2001
Kilometres flown (million)	3	3	1
Passengers carried ('000)	84	77	46
Passenger-km (million)	235	216	130
Total ton-km (million)	36	32	19

* Including an apportionment of the traffic of Air Afrique.

Source: UN, *Statistical Yearbook*.

NIGER

Tourism

FOREIGN TOURIST ARRIVALS BY NATIONALITY*

	2006	2007	2008
Africa	36,199	23,770	39,680
America	4,223	3,898	3,720
East Asia and the Pacific	3,017	1,778	2,656
Europe	16,893	17,589	15,500
France	13,448	12,084	10,649
Total (incl. others)	60,332	47,539	73,154

* Figures refer to arrivals at national borders.

Receipts from tourism (US $ million, excl. passenger transport): 36.0 in 2006, 41.0 in 2007, 45.0 in 2008.

Source: World Tourism Organization.

Communications Media

	2007	2008	2009
Telephones ('000 main lines in use)	41.7	64.7	65.0
Mobile cellular telephones ('000 subscribers)	900.0*	1,897.6	2,599.0
Internet users ('000)	55.2	102.9	115.9
Broadband subscribers	500	600	1,000

* Estimated figure.

Personal computers: 10,000 (0.8 per 1,000 persons) in 2005.

Television receivers ('000 in use): 395 in 2000.

Radio receivers ('000 in use): 680 in 1997.

Daily newspapers: 1 (average circulation 2,000 copies) in 1997; 1 (average circulation 2,000 copies) in 1998; 1 (average circulation 2,500 copies) in 2004.

Non-daily newspapers: 5 (average circulation 14,000 copies) in 1996; 28 (average circulation 34,000 copies) in 2004.

Books published (first editions): titles 5; copies 11,000 in 1991.

Sources: UNESCO, *Statistical Yearbook*; UNESCO Institute for Statistics; UN, *Statistical Yearbook*; International Telecommunication Union.

Education

(2008/09 unless otherwise indicated)

	Institutions	Teachers	Students
Pre-primary	621	1,568	48,119
Primary	11,609	40,021	1,554,102
Secondary	751	8,689	250,143
Tertiary*	7	278	4,953
University	2	297	9,882

* 2004/05 figures.

Pupil-teacher ratio (primary education, UNESCO estimate): 38.8 in 2008/09 (Source: UNESCO Institute for Statistics).

Adult literacy rate (UNESCO estimates): 30.4% (males 44.3%; females 16.4%) in 2007 (Source: UNESCO Institute for Statistics).

Directory

The Government

HEAD OF STATE

President: MAHAMADOU ISSOUFOU (inaugurated 7 April 2011).

COUNCIL OF MINISTERS
(May 2011)

Prime Minister: BRIGI RAFINI.
Minister of State, Minister of Foreign Affairs, African Integration and Nigeriens Abroad: BAZOUM MOHAMED.
Minister of State, Minister of Planning, Land Settlement and Community Development: AMADOU BOUBACAR CISSÉ.
Minister of State, Minister of the Interior, Public Security, Decentralization and Religious Affairs: ABDOU LABO.
Minister of Public Health: SOUMANA SANDA.
Minister of Mines and Energy: FOUMAKOYE GADO.
Minister of Justice, Keeper of the Seals and Government Spokesperson: MAROU AMADOU.
Minister of Equipment: KALLA HANKORAOU.
Minister of Town Planning, Housing and Sanitation: MOUSSA BAKO ABDOULKARIM.
Minister of Trade and the Promotion of the Private Sector: SALEY SAIDOU.
Minister of Communication and New Information Technology, in charge of Relations with the Institutions: SALIFOU LABO BOUCHÉ.
Minister of Population, the Promotion of Women and the Protection of Children: MAIKIBI KADIDIATOU DAN DOBI.
Minister of National Defence: KARIDJO MAHAMADOU.
Minister of Finance: OUHOUMOUDOU MAHAMADOU.
Minister of Professional Training and Employment: NGADÉ NANA HADIZA NOMA KAKA.
Minister of Higher Education and Scientific Research: MAMADOU YOUBA DIALLO.
Minister of National Education, Literacy and the Promotion of National Languages: ALI MARIAMA ELHADJ IBRAHIM.
Minister of Agriculture: OUHA SAIDOU.
Minister of Hydraulics and the Environment: ISSOUFOU ISSAKA.
Minister of Stockbreeding: MAHAMANE ELHADJ OUSMANE.
Minister of Transport: SALAMI MAIMOUNA ALMOU.
Minister of Youth, Sports and Culture: HASSANE KOUNOU.
Minister of Industrial Development, Handicrafts and Tourism: YAHAYA BAARÉ HAOUA ABDOU.
Minister of the Civil Service and Labour: SABO FATOUMA ZARA BOUBACAR.

MINISTRIES

Office of the President: BP 550, Niamey; tel. 20-72-23-80; fax 20-72-33-96; internet www.presidence.ne.
Office of the Prime Minister: BP 893, Niamey; tel. 20-72-26-99; fax 20-73-58-59.
Ministry of Agricultural Development: BP 12091, Niamey; tel. 20-73-35-41; fax 20-73-20-08.
Ministry of Animal Resources: BP 12091, Niamey; tel. 20-73-79-59; fax 20-73-31-86.

NIGER

Ministry of Basic Education and Literacy: BP 557, Niamey; tel. 20-72-28-33; fax 20-72-21-05; e-mail scdameb@intnet.ne.

Ministry of Capital Works: BP 403, Niamey; tel. 20-73-53-57; fax 20-72-21-71.

Ministry of the Civil Service and Labour: BP 11107, Niamey; tel. 20-73-22-31; fax 20-73-61-69; e-mail sani.yakouba@caramail.com.

Ministry of Culture, the Arts and Communication: BP 452, Niamey; tel. 20-72-28-74; fax 20-73-36-85.

Ministry of the Economy and Finance: BP 389, Niamey; tel. 20-72-23-74; fax 20-73-59-34.

Ministry of Equipment: Niamey.

Ministry of Foreign Affairs and Co-operation: BP 396, Niamey; tel. 20-72-29-07; fax 20-73-52-31.

Ministry of the Interior, Public Security and Decentralization: BP 622, Niamey; tel. 20-72-32-62; fax 20-72-21-76.

Ministry of Justice: BP 466, Niamey; tel. 20-72-31-31; fax 20-72-37-77.

Ministry of Land Settlement and Community Development: BP 403, Niamey; tel. 20-73-53-57; fax 20-72-21-71.

Ministry of Mines and Energy: BP 11700, Niamey; tel. 20-73-45-82; fax 20-73-27-59.

Ministry of National Defence: BP 626, Niamey; tel. 20-72-20-76; fax 20-72-40-78.

Ministry of Population and Social Reform: BP 11286, Niamey; tel. 20-72-23-30; fax 20-73-61-65.

Ministry of Privatization and the Restructuring of Enterprises: Immeuble CCCP, BP 862, Niamey; tel. 20-73-27-50; fax 20-73-59-91; e-mail ccpp@intnet.ne.

Ministry of Professional and Technical Training: BP 628, Niamey; tel. 20-72-26-20; fax 20-72-40-40.

Ministry for the Promotion of Women and the Protection of Children: BP 11286, Niamey; tel. 20-72-23-30; fax 20-72-61-65.

Ministry of Public Health and the Fight against Epidemics: BP 623, Niamey; tel. 20-72-28-08; fax 20-73-35-70.

Ministry of Secondary and Higher Education, Research and Technology: BP 628, Niamey; tel. 20-72-26-20; fax 20-72-40-40; e-mail mesnt@intnet.ne.

Ministry of Tourism and Crafts: BP 480, Niamey; tel. 20-73-65-22; fax 20-72-23-87; internet www.niger-tourisme.com.

Ministry of Town Planning and Living Conditions: BP 403, Niamey; tel. 20-73-53-57; fax 20-72-21-71.

Ministry of Trade, Industry and the Promotion of the Private Sector: BP 480, Niamey; tel. 20-73-29-74; fax 20-73-21-50; e-mail nicom@intnet.ne.

Ministry of Transport: BP 12130, Niamey; tel. 20-72-28-21; fax 20-73-36-85.

Ministry of Water Resources, the Environment and Anti-desertification: BP 257, Niamey; tel. 20-73-47-22; fax 20-72-40-15.

Ministry of Youth, Sports and the Games of La Francophonie: BP 215, Niamey; tel. 20-72-32-35; fax 20-72-23-36.

President and Legislature

PRESIDENT

Presidential Election, First Round, 31 January 2011

Candidate	Votes	% of votes
Mahamadou Issoufou (PNDS—Tarayya)	1,192,945	36.16
Seyni Oumarou (MNSD—Nassara)	766,215	23.23
Hama Amadou (Moden)	653,737	19.82
Mahamane Ousmane (CDS)	274,676	8.33
Cheiffou Amadou (RSD—Gaskiya)	134,732	4.08
Moumouni Adamou Djermakoye (ANDP—Zaman Lahiya)	129,954	3.94
Ousmane Isoufou Oubandawaki (ARD)	63,378	1.92
Amadou Boubacar Cissé (UDR—Tabbat)	52,779	1.60
Abdoulaye Amadou Traoré (Ind.)	17,630	0.53
Mme Bayard Mariama Gamatié (RaCINN)	12,595	0.38
Total	**3,298,641**	**100.00**

Second Round, 12 March 2011, provisional results

Candidate	Votes	% of votes
Mahamadou Issoufou (PNDS—Tarayya)	1,820,639	57.95
Seyni Oumarou (MNSD—Nassara)	1,321,248	42.05
Total	**3,141,887**	**100.00**

LEGISLATURE

Assemblée nationale

pl. de la Concertation, BP 12234, Niamey; tel. 20-72-27-38; fax 20-72-43-08; e-mail an@assemblee.ne; internet www.assemblee.ne.

President: HAMA AMADOU.

General Election, 31 January 2011, provisional results

Party	Votes	% of votes	Seats
PNDS—Tarayya	1,143,263	33.02	39
MNSD—Nassara	707,191	20.43	26
Moden	684,583	19.77	24
ANDP—Zaman Lahiya	252,857	7.30	8
RDP—Djamaa	232,105	6.70	7
UDR—Tabbat	185,473	5.36	6
CDS—Rahama	109,536	3.16	2
RSD—Gaskiya	60,048	1.73	—
UNI	32,277	0.93	1
Others	54,552	1.58	—
Total	**3,461,885**	**100.00**	**113***

*Including eight special seats, five of which were allocated to the PNDS—Tarayya, two to Moden and one to the MNSD—Nassara.

Election Commission

Commission électorale nationale indépendante (CENI): Niamey; internet www.ceni-niger.net; Pres. ABDOURAHMANE GHOUSMANE.

Political Organizations

A total of 23 political parties contested the legislative elections of January 2011.

Alliance nigérienne pour la démocratie et le progrès social—Zaman Lahiya (ANDP): Quartier Abidjan, Niamey; tel. 20-74-07-50; Pres. MOUSSA MOUMOUNI DJERMAKOYE.

Alliance pour la démocratie et le progrès—Zumunci (ADP): Niamey; tel. 20-73-67-57; e-mail adp@zumunci.com; internet www.adpzumunci.com; f. 1992; Chair. ISSOUFOU BACHAR.

Convention démocratique et sociale—Rahama (CDS): BP 11973, Niamey; tel. 20-74-19-85; f. 1991; mem. of Alliance des forces démocratiques (AFD); Pres. MAHAMANE OUSMANE.

Mouvement démocratique nigérien (Moden): Niamey; e-mail mdnloumana@gmail.com; internet mdn-lumana.populus.org; f. 2009 by supporters of former Prime Minister Hama Amadou; Pres. HAMA AMADOU; Sec.-Gen. OMAR HAMIDOU TCHIANA.

Mouvement national pour la société de développement—Nassara (MNSD—Nassara): rue Issa Beri 30, cnr blvd de Zarmaganda, porte 72, BP 881, Niamey; tel. 20-73-39-07; fax 20-72-41-74; e-mail presi@mnsd-nassara.org; internet www.mnsd.ne; f. 1988; sole party 1988–90; restyled as MNSD—Nassara in 1991; Chair. Col (retd) MAMADOU TANDJA; Pres. SEYNI OUMAROU.

Mouvement des Nigériens pour la justice (MNJ): ; e-mail mnj.contact@gmail.com; internet m-n-j.blogspot.com; f. 2007; Pres. AGHALI ALAMBO.

Parti des masses pour le travail—al Barka (PMT—al Barka): Niamey; tel. 20-74-02-15; MAMALO ABDOULKARIM.

Parti nigérien pour l'autogestion—al Umat (PNA): Quartier Zabarkian, Niamey; tel. 20-72-33-05; f. 1997; Leader SANOUSSI JACKOU.

Parti nigérien pour la démocratie et le socialisme—Tarayya (PNDS): pl. Toumo, Niamey; tel. 20-74-48-78; internet pnds-tarayya.net; f. 1990; Pres. MAHAMADOU ISSOUFOU; Sec.-Gen. FOUMAKOYE GADO.

Parti progressiste nigérien—Rassemblement démocratique africain (PPN—RDA): Quartier Sonni, Niamey; tel. 20-74-16-70; associated with the late Pres. Diori; Chair. ABDOULAYE DIORI.

Parti social-démocrate nigérien—Alheri (PSDN): tel. 20-72-28-52; Pres. Labo Issaka.

Rassemblement pour la démocratie et le progrès—Djamaa (RDP): pl. Toumo, Niamey; tel. 20-74-23-82; party of late Pres. Maïnassara; Chair. Hamid Algabid; Sec.-Gen. Mahamane Souley Labi.

Rassemblement des patriotes Nigériens—al Kalami (RPN—al Kalami): Niamey; f. 2009; Pres. Ousmane Issoufou Oubandawaki.

Rassemblement social-démocratique—Gaskiya (RSD): Quartier Poudrière, Niamey; tel. 20-74-00-90; f. 2004 following split in the CDS; Pres. Cheiffou Amadou.

Rassemblement pour un Sahel vert—Ni'ima (RSV): BP 12515, Niamey; tel. and fax 20-74-11-25; e-mail agarba_99@yahoo.com; f. 1991; Pres. Adamou Garba.

Union pour la démocratie et le progrès social—Amana (UDPS): internet www.udps-amana.com; represents interests of Tuaregs; Chair. Rhissa Ag Boula.

Union pour la démocratie et la République—Tabbat (UDR): Quartier Plateau, Niamey; f. 2002; Pres. Amadou Bouabacar Cissé.

Union des forces populaires pour la démocratie et le progrès—Sawaba (UFPDP): Niamey; tel. 20-73-51-38; Leader Ibrahim Baoua Souley.

Union des Nigeriens indépendants (UNI): Quartier Zabarkan, Niamey; tel. 20-74-23-81; Leader Amadou Djibo.

Union des patriotes démocratiques et progressistes—Shamuwa (UPDP): Niamey; tel. 20-74-12-59; Chair. Prof. André Salifou.

Union des socialistes nigériens—Talaka (USN): f. 2001 by mems of the UFPDP; Leader Issoufou Assoumane.

Diplomatic Representation

EMBASSIES IN NIGER

Algeria: route des Ambassades-Goudel, BP 142, Niamey; tel. 20-72-35-83; fax 20-72-35-93; Ambassador Hamid Boukrif.

Benin: BP 11544, Niamey; tel. 20-72-28-60; Ambassador Awahou Labouda.

Chad: POB 12820, Niamey; tel. 20-75-34-64; fax 20-72-43-61; Ambassador Mahamat Nour Mallaye.

China, People's Republic: BP 873, Niamey; tel. 20-72-32-83; fax 20-72-32-85; e-mail embchina@intnet.ne; Ambassador Xia Huang.

Cuba: rue Tillaberi, angle rue de la Cure Salée, face lycée Franco-Arabe, Plateau, BP 13886, Niamey; tel. 20-72-46-00; fax 20-72-39-32; e-mail embacuba@niger.cubaminrex.cu; internet emba.cubaminrex.cu/nigerfr; Ambassador Roberto Rodríguez Pena.

Egypt: Terminus Rond-Point Grand Hôtel, BP 254, Niamey; tel. 20-73-33-55; fax 20-73-38-91; Chargé d'affaires Kareem Hussein.

France: route de Tondibia, Quartier Yantala, BP 10660, Niamey; tel. 20-72-24-32; fax 20-72-25-18; e-mail webmestre@mail.com; internet www.ambafrance-ne.org; Ambassador Alain Holleville.

Germany: 71 ave du Général de Gaulle, BP 629, Niamey; tel. 20-72-35-10; fax 20-72-39-85; e-mail amb-all-ny@web.de; Ambassador Rüdiger John.

Iran: 11 rue de la Présidence, BP 10543, Niamey; tel. 20-72-21-98; fax 20-72-28-10; e-mail aliakbar_100@yahoo.com; Ambassador Mohamad Nikkhah.

Korea, Democratic People's Republic: Niamey; Ambassador Pak Song Il.

Libya: route de Goudel, BP 683, Niamey; tel. 20-72-40-19; fax 20-72-40-97; e-mail boukhari@intnet.ne; Ambassador Boukhari Salem Hoda.

Morocco: ave du Président Lubke, face Clinique Kaba, BP 12403, Niamey; tel. 20-73-40-84; fax 20-73-80-27; e-mail ambmang@intnet.ne; Ambassador Tayeb Raouf.

Nigeria: rue Goudel, BP 11130, Niamey; tel. 20-73-24-10; fax 20-73-35-00; e-mail embnig@intnet.ne; Ambassador Batouré Lawal.

Pakistan: 90 rue YN 001, ave des Zarmakoye, Yantala Plateau, BP 10426, Niamey; tel. 20-75-32-57; fax 20-75-32-55; e-mail parepniamey@yahoo.com; internet www.brain.net.pk/~farata; Ambassador (vacant).

Saudi Arabia: route de Tillabery, BP 339, Niamey; tel. 20-75-32-15; fax 20-75-24-42; e-mail neemb@mofa.gov.sa; Ambassador Abdul Kareem Mohammad Al-Maliki.

Spain: 151 rue de la Radio, BP 11888, Niamey; tel. 20-75-59-61; e-mail emb.niamey@maec.es; Ambassador María Soledad Fuentes Gómez.

USA: rue des Ambassades, BP 11201, Niamey; tel. 20-73-31-69; fax 20-73-55-60; e-mail NiameyPASN@state.gov; internet niamey.usembassy.gov; Ambassador Bisa Williams.

Judicial System

Following the suspension of the Constitution promulgated on 18 August 2009, the Supreme Court and the Constitutional Court were replaced by the Court of State and a Constitutional Committee, respectively.

Religion

It is estimated that some 95% of the population are Muslims, 0.5% are Christians and the remainder follow traditional beliefs.

ISLAM

The most influential Islamic groups in Niger are the Tijaniyya, the Senoussi and the Hamallists.

Association Islamique du Niger: BP 2220, Niamey; tel. 20-74-08-90; Dir Cheikh Oumarou Ismael.

CHRISTIANITY

The Roman Catholic Church

Niger comprises two dioceses, directly responsible to the Holy See. The Bishops participate in the Bishops' Conference of Burkina Faso and Niger (based in Ouagadougou, Burkina Faso).

Bishop of Maradi: Rt Rev. Ambroise Ouédraogo, Evêché, BP 447, Maradi; tel. and fax 20-41-03-30; fax 20-41-13-86; e-mail evechemi@intnet.ne.

Bishop of Niamey: Rt Rev. Michel Christian Cartatéguy, Evêché, BP 10270, Niamey; tel. 20-73-32-59; fax 20-73-80-01; e-mail cartateguymi@voila.fr; internet www.multimania.com/cathoniger.

The Press

The published press expanded considerably in Niger after 1993, when the requirement to obtain prior authorization for each edition was lifted, although legislation continued to require that a copy of each publication be deposited at the office of the Procurator of the Republic. For the most part, however, economic difficulties have ensured that few publications have maintained a regular, sustained appearance. The following were among those newspapers and periodicals believed to be appearing regularly in the late 2000s:

L'Action: Quartier Yantala, Niamey; tel. 96-96-92-22; e-mail action_ne@yahoo.fr; internet www.tamtaminfo.com/action.pdf; f. 2003; fortnightly; popular newspaper intended for youth audience; Dir of Publication Boussada Ben Ali; circ. 2,000 (2003).

Anfani: Immeuble DMK, rue du Damagaram, BP 2096, Niamey; tel. 20-74-08-80; fax 20-74-00-52; e-mail anfani@intnet.ne; f. 1992; 2 a month; Editor-in-Chief Ibbo Daddy Abdoulaye; circ. 3,000.

Al-Salam: BP 451, Niamey; tel. 20-74-29-12; e-mail assa_lam@yahoo.fr; monthly; Dir Ibbo Daddy Abdoulaye.

L'Alternative: BP 10948, Niamey; tel. 20-74-24-39; fax 20-74-24-82; e-mail alter@intnet.ne; internet www.alternative.ne; f. 1994; weekly; in French and Hausa; Dir Moussa Tchangari; Editor-in-Chief Abdramane Ousmane.

Le Canard Déchainé: BP 383, Niamey; tel. 93-92-66-64; satirical; weekly; Dir of Publication Abdoulaye Tiémogo; Editor-in-Chief Ibrahim Manzo.

Le Canard Libéré: BP 11631, Niamey; tel. 20-75-43-52; fax 20-75-39-89; e-mail canardlibere@caramail.com; satirical; weekly; Dir of Publication Traoré Daouda Amadou; Editorial Dir Oumarou Nalan Moussa.

Le Démocrate: 21 rue 067, NB Terminus, BP 11064, Niamey; tel. 20-73-24-25; e-mail le_democrate@caramail.com; internet www.tamtaminfo.com/democrate.pdf; weekly; independent; f. 1992; Dir of Publication Albert Chaïbou; Editor-in-Chief Ousseini Issa.

Les Echos du Sahel: Villa 4012, 105 Logements, BP 12750, Niamey; tel. and fax 20-74-32-17; e-mail ecosahel@intnet.ne; f. 1999; rural issues and devt; quarterly; Dir Ibbo Daddy Abdoulaye.

L'Enquêteur: BP 172, Niamey; tel. 93-90-18-74; e-mail lenqueteur@yahoo.fr; fortnightly; Publr Tahirou Gouro; Editor Ibrahim Souley.

Haské: BP 297, Niamey; tel. 20-74-18-44; fax 20-73-20-06; e-mail webmaster@planetafrique.com; internet www.haske.uni.cc; f. 1990; weekly; also Haské Magazine, quarterly; Dir Cheikh Ibrahim Diop.

NIGER
Directory

Journal Officiel de la République du Niger: BP 116, Niamey; tel. 20-72-39-30; fax 20-72-39-43; f. 1960; fortnightly; govt bulletin; Man. Editor BONKOULA AMINATOU MAYAKI; circ. 800.

Libération: BP 10483, Niamey; tel. 96-97-96-22; f. 1995; weekly; Dir BOUBACAR DIALLO; circ. 1,000 (2003).

Matinfo: BP 11631, Niamey; tel. 20-75-43-52; fax 20-75-39-89; e-mail matinfo@caramail.com; daily; independent; Dir DAOUDA AMADOU TRAORÉ.

Nigerama: BP 11158, Niamey; tel. 20-74-08-09; e-mail anpniger@intnet.ne; quarterly; publ. by the Agence Nigérienne de Presse.

Le Républicain: Nouvelle Imprimerie du Niger, pl. du Petit Marché, BP 12015, Niamey; tel. 20-73-47-98; fax 20-73-41-42; e-mail webmasters@republicain-niger.com; internet www.republicain-niger.com; f. 1991; weekly; independent; Dir of Publication MAMANE ABOU; circ. 2,500.

La Roue de l'Histoire: Zabarkan, rue du SNEN, BP 5005, Niamey; tel. 20-74-05-69; internet www.tamtaminfo.com/roue.pdf; weekly; Propr SANOUSSI JACKOU; Dir ABARAD MOUDOUR ZAKARA.

Le Sahel Quotidien: BP 13182, ONEP, Niamey; tel. 20-73-34-87; fax 20-73-30-90; e-mail onep@intnet.ne; internet www.lesahel.org; f. 1960; publ. by Office National d'Edition et de Presse; daily; Dir IBRAHIM MAMANE TANTAN; Editor-in-Chief ALASSANE ASOKOFARE; circ. 3,000; also Sahel-Dimanche, Sundays; circ. 5,000.

Sauyi: BP 10948, Niamey; tel. 20-74-24-39; fax 20-74-24-82; e-mail sarji@alternative.ne; fortnightly; Hausa; publ. by Groupe Alternative; Hausa; rural interest; Dir SAÏDOU ARJI.

La Source: Academie des Arts, BP 5320, Niamey; tel. 96-53-95-77; e-mail amanimb9@yahoo.fr; weekly; Dir of Publication AMANI MOUNKAÏLA; circ. 1,000.

Stadium: BP 10948, Niamey; tel. 20-74-08-80; e-mail kiabba@yahoo.fr; sports; 2 a month; Dir ABDOU TIKIRÉ.

Le Témoin: BP 10483, Niamey; tel. 96-96-58-51; e-mail istemoin@yahoo.fr; internet www.tamtaminfo.com/temoin.pdf; 2 a month; Dir of Publication IBRAHIM SOUMANA GAOH; Editors AMADOU TIÉMOGO, MOUSSA DAN TCHOUKOU, I. S. GAOH; circ. 1,000 (2005).

Ténéré Express: BP 13600, Niamey; tel. 20-73-35-76; fax 20-73-77-75; e-mail tenerefm@intnet.ne; daily; independent; current affairs; Dir ABDOULAYE MOUSSA MASSALATCHI.

La Tribune du Peuple: Niamey; tel. 20-73-34-28; e-mail tribune@intnet.ne; f. 1993; weekly; Man. Editor IBRAHIM HAMIDOU.

Le Trophée: BP 2000, Niamey; tel. 20-74-12-79; e-mail strophee@caramail.com; sports; 2 a month; Dir ISSA HAMIDOU MAYAKI.

Le Visionnaire: quartier Plateau, Niamey; tel. 98-15-62-40; weekly; Dir of Publication SALIFOU SOUMAÏLA ABDOULKARIM; circ. 1,000.

NEWS AGENCIES

Agence Nigérienne de Presse (ANP): BP 11158, Niamey; tel. 20-74-08-09; e-mail anpniger@intnet.ne; f. 1987; state-owned; Dir YAYE HASSANE.

Sahel—Office National d'Edition et de Presse (ONEP): BP 13182, Niamey; tel. 20-73-34-86; f. 1989; Dir ALI OUSSEÏNI.

Publishers

La Nouvelle Imprimerie du Niger (NIN): pl. du Petit Marché, BP 61, Niamey; tel. 20-73-47-98; fax 20-73-41-42; e-mail imprim@intnet.ne; f. 1962 as Imprimerie Nationale du Niger; govt publishing house; brs in Agadez and Maradi; Dir MAMAN ABOU.

Réseau Sahélien de Recherche et de Publication: Niamey; tel. 20-73-36-90; fax 20-73-39-43; e-mail resadep@ilimi.uam.ne; press of the Université Abdou Moumouni; Co-ordinator BOUREIMA DIADIE.

Broadcasting and Communications

REGULATORY AUTHORITY

Following the assumption of power by the Conseil suprême pour la restauration de la démocratie, the Conseil supérieur de la communication was replaced by the Observatoire national de la communication.

TELECOMMUNICATIONS

Airtel Niger: route de l'Aéroport, BP 11922, Niamey; tel. 20-73-23-46; fax 20-73-23-85; e-mail info.ne@zain.com; internet africa.airtel.com/niger; f. 2001 to operate mobile cellular telecommunications network in Niamey and Maradi; fmrly Zain Niger, present name adopted in 2010; Dir-Gen. ALAIN KAHASHA.

Orange Niger: internet www.orange.ne; provides mobile, fixed-line and internet services; Dir-Gen. JEAN LOUIS BRANCO.

Société Nigérienne des Télécommunications (SONITEL): ave du Général de Gaulle, BP 208, Niamey; tel. 20-72-29-98; fax 20-72-24-78; e-mail info@sonitel.ne; internet www.sonitel.ne; f. 1998; 51% jtly owned by ZTE Corpn (People's Republic of China) and Laaico (Libya), 46% state-owned; Dir-Gen. MOUSSA BOUBACAR.

Sahel Com: BP 208, Niamey; internet www.sahelcom.ne; f. 2002; mobile cellular telecommunications in Niamey.

Telecel Niger: Niamey; tel. 20-74-44-44; e-mail telecel@telecelniger.com; internet www.telecelniger.com; f. 2001 to operate mobile cellular telecommunications network, initially in Niamey and western regions, expanding to cover Maradi and Zinder by 2003, and Tahoua and Agadez by 2004; 68% owned by Orascom Telecom (Egypt); Dir HIMA SOULEY.

BROADCASTING
Radio

Independent radio stations have been permitted to operate since 1994, although the majority are concentrated in the capital, Niamey. In 2000 the first of a network of rural stations, RURANET, which were to broadcast mainly programmes concerned with development issues, mostly in national languages, was established.

Anfani FM: blvd Nali-Béro, BP 2096, Wadata, Niamey; tel. 20-74-08-80; fax 20-74-00-52; e-mail anfani@intnet.ne; private radio station, broadcasting to Niamey, Zinder, Maradi and Diffa; Dir ISMAËL MOUTARI.

Office de Radiodiffusion-Télévision du Niger (ORTN): BP 309, Niamey; tel. 20-72-31-63; fax 20-72-35-48; internet www.ortn.ne; f. 1967; state broadcasting authority; Dir-Gen. YAYÉ HAROUNA.

Ténéré FM: BP 13600, Niamey; tel. 20-73-65-76; fax 20-73-46-94; e-mail tenerefm@intnet.ne; f. 1998; Dir ABIBOU GARBA; Editor-in-Chief SOULEYMANE ISSA MAÏGA.

La Voix du Sahel: BP 361, Niamey; tel. 20-72-22-02; fax 20-72-35-48; e-mail ortny@intnet.ne; internet www.ortn.ne; f. 1958; govt-controlled radio service; programmes in French, Hausa, Djerma, Kanuri, Fulfuldé, Tamajak, Toubou, Gourmantché, Boudouma and Arabic; Dir IBRO NA-ALLAH AMADOU.

RURANET: Niamey; internet membres.lycos.fr/nigeradio; f. 2000; network of rural radio stations, broadcasting 80% in national languages, with 80% of programmes concerned with devt issues; 31 stations operative in April 2002.

La Voix de l'Hémicycle: BP 12234, Niamey; f. 2002 as the radio station of the Assemblée nationale; broadcasts parliamentary debates and analysis for 15 hours daily in French and national languages to Niamey and environs.

Sudan FM: Dosso; auth. 2000; private radio station; Dir HIMA ADAMOU.

Television

Office de Radiodiffusion-Télévision du Niger (ORTN): see Radio.

Tal TV: BP 309, Niamey; f. 2001; broadcasts 72 hours of programmes each week.

Télé-Sahel: BP 309, Niamey; tel. 20-72-31-55; fax 20-72-35-48; govt-controlled television service; broadcasts daily from 13 transmission posts and six retransmission posts, covering most of Niger; Dir-Gen. ABDOU SOULEY.

Télévision Ténéré (TTV): BP 13600, Niamey; tel. 20-73-65-76; fax 20-73-77-75; e-mail tenerefm@intnet.ne; f. 2000; independent broadcaster in Niamey; Dir ABIBOU GARBA.

The independent operator, Télé Star, broadcasts several international or foreign channels in Niamey and environs, including TV5 Monde, Canal Horizon, CFI, RTL9, CNN and Euro News.

Finance

(cap. = capital; res = reserves; dep. = deposits; m. = million; brs = branches; amounts in francs CFA)

BANKING

In 2009 there were 10 commercial banks and one financial institution in Niger.

Central Bank

Banque centrale des états de l'Afrique de l'ouest (BCEAO): rue de l'Uranium, BP 487, Niamey; tel. 20-72-24-91; fax 20-73-47-43; HQ in Dakar, Senegal; f. 1962; bank of issue for the mem. states of the Union économique et monétaire ouest-africaine (UEMOA, comprising Benin, Burkina Faso, Côte d'Ivoire, Guinea-Bissau, Mali, Niger,

NIGER

Senegal and Togo); cap. 134,120m., res 1,474,195m., dep. 2,124,051m. (Dec. 2009); Interim Gov. JEAN-BAPTISTE MARIE PASCAL COMPAORÉ; Dir in Niger ABDOULAYE SOUMANA; brs at Maradi and Zinder.

Commercial Banks

Bank of Africa—Niger (BOA—Niger): Immeuble BOA, rue du Gawèye, BP 10973, Niamey; tel. 20-73-36-20; fax 20-73-38-18; e-mail information@boaniger.com; internet www.boaniger.com; f. 1994 to acquire assets of Nigeria International Bank Niamey; 42.6% owned by African Financial Holding; cap. 3,500m., res 4,072m., dep. 92,026m. (Dec. 2009); Pres. PAUL DERREUMAUX; Dir-Gen. MAMADOU SÉNÉ; 8 brs.

Banque Atlantique Niger: BP 375, Rond Point Liberté, Niamey; tel. 20-73-98-88; fax 20-73-98-91; e-mail ban@banqueatlantique.net; internet www.banqueatlantique.net; f. 2005; 73% owned by Atlantic Financial Group, Lomé; total assets US $19.5m. (Dec. 2006); Chair. KONE DOSSONGUI; Man. Dir AMADOU MOUSTAPHA DIOUF.

Banque Commerciale du Niger (BCN): rue du Combattant, BP 11363, Niamey; tel. 20-73-39-15; fax 20-73-21-63; e-mail info@bcn .ne; internet www.bcn-niger.com; f. 1978; 83.15% owned by Libyan Arab Foreign Bank, 16.85% state-owned; cap. and res 1,477m., total assets 14,618m. (Dec. 2003); Administrator BASHIR M. SAMALOUS.

Banque Internationale pour l'Afrique au Niger (BIA—Niger): ave de la Mairie, BP 10350, Niamey; tel. 20-73-31-01; fax 20-73-35-95; e-mail bia@intnet.ne; internet www.bianiger.com; f. 1980; 35% owned by Groupe Belgolaise (Belgium); cap. 2,800m., res −25m., dep. 78,367m. (Dec. 2008); Pres. AMADOU HIMA SOULEY; Dir-Gen. DANIEL HASSER; 11 brs.

Banque Islamique du Niger pour le Commerce et l'Investissement (BINCI): Immeuble El Nasr, BP 12754, Niamey; tel. 20-73-27-30; fax 20-73-47-35; e-mail binci@intnet.ne; f. 1983; fmrly Banque Masraf Faisal Islami; 33% owned by Dar al-Maal al-Islami (Switzerland), 33% by Islamic Development Bank (Saudi Arabia); cap. 1,810m., total assets 7,453m. (Dec. 2003); Pres. ABDERRAOUF BENESSAÏAH; Dir-Gen. AISSANI OMAR.

Ecobank Niger: blvd de la Liberté, angle rue des Bâtisseurs, BP 13804, Niamey; tel. 20-73-71-81; fax 20-73-72-04; e-mail ecobankni@ ecobank.com; internet www.ecobank.com; f. 1999; 99.85% owned by Ecobank Transnational Inc, Lomé; total assets 100,385m. (Dec. 2009); Chair. IBRAHIM IDDI ANGO; Dir-Gen. MOUKARAMOU CHANOU.

Société Nigérienne de Banque (SONIBANK): ave de la Mairie, BP 891, Niamey; tel. 20-73-47-40; fax 20-73-46-93; e-mail sonibank@ intnet.ne; internet www.sonibank.net; f. 1990; 25% owned by Société Tunisienne de Banque; cap. 2,000m., res 7,587m., dep. 90,264m. (Dec. 2009); Pres. ILLA KANÉ; Dir-Gen. MOUSSA HAITOU; 6 brs.

Development Banks

Caisse de Prêts aux Collectivités Territoriales (CPCT): route Torodi, BP 730, Niamey; tel. 20-72-34-12; fax 20-72-30-80; f. 1970; 100% state-owned (94% by organs of local govt); cap. and res 744m., total assets 2,541m. (Dec. 2003); Administrator ABDOU DJIBO (acting).

Crédit du Niger (CDN): 11 blvd de la République, BP 213, Niger; tel. 20-72-27-01; fax 20-72-23-90; e-mail cdb-nig@intnet.ne; f. 1958; 54% state-owned, 20% owned by Caisse Nationale de Sécurité Sociale; transfer to full private ownership pending; cap. and res 1,058m., total assets 3,602m. (Dec. 2003); Administrator ABDOU DJIBO (acting).

Fonds d'Intervention en Faveur des Petites et Moyennes Entreprises Nigériennes (FIPMEN): Immeuble Sonara II, BP 252, Niamey; tel. 20-73-20-98; f. 1990; state-owned; cap. and res 124m. (Dec. 1991); Chair. AMADOU SALLA HASSANE; Man. Dir IBRAHIM BEIDARI.

Savings Bank

FINAPOSTE: BP 11778, Niamey; tel. 20-73-24-98; fax 20-73-35-69; fmrly Caisse Nationale d'Epargne; Chair. Mme PALFI; Man. Dir HASSOUME MATA.

STOCK EXCHANGE

Bourse Régionale des Valeurs Mobilières (BRVM): c/o Chambre de Commerce et d'Industrie du Niger, pl. de la Concertation, BP 13299, Niamey; tel. 20-73-66-92; fax 20-73-69-47; e-mail imagagi@ brvm.org; internet www.brvm.org; f. 1998; national branch of BRVM (regional stock exchange based in Abidjan, Côte d'Ivoire, serving the member states of UEMOA); Man. IDRISSA S. MAGAGI.

INSURANCE

Agence d'Assurance du Sahel: BP 10661, Niamey; tel. 20-74-05-47.

Agence Nigérienne d'Assurances (ANA): pl. de la Mairie, BP 423, Niamey; tel. 20-72-20-71; f. 1959; cap. 1.5m.; owned by L'Union des Assurances de Paris; Dir JEAN LASCAUD.

Caren Assurance: BP 733, Niamey; tel. 20-73-34-70; fax 20-73-24-93; e-mail carenas@intnet.ne; insurance and reinsurance; Dir-Gen. IBRAHIM IDI ANGO.

Leyma—Société Nigérienne d'Assurances et de Réassurances (SNAR—Leyma): BP 426, Niamey; tel. 20-73-57-72; fax 20-73-40-44; f. 1973; restructured 2001; Pres. AMADOU HIMA SOULEY; Dir-Gen. GARBA ABDOURAHAMANE.

La Nigérienne d'Assurance et de Réassurance: BP 13300, Niamey; tel. 20-73-63-36; fax 20-73-73-37; Dir-Gen. OUMAROU ALMA.

Union Générale des Assurances du Niger (UGAN): rue de Kalley, BP 11935, Niamey; tel. 20-73-54-06; fax 20-73-41-85; f. 1985; cap. 500m.; Pres. PATHÉ DIONE; Dir-Gen. MAMADOU TALATA; 7 brs.

Trade and Industry

GOVERNMENT AGENCIES

Cellule de Coordination de la Programme de Privatisation: Immeuble Sonibanque, BP 862, Niamey; tel. 20-73-29-10; fax 20-73-29-58; responsible for co-ordination of privatization programme; Co-ordinator IDÉ ISSOUFOU.

Centre National de'Energie Solaire (ONERSOL): BP 621, Niamey; tel. 20-72-39-23; e-mail cnes@intnet.ne; frmly Office National de l'Energie Solaire (ONERSOL), present name adopted 1998; govt agency for research and devt, commercial production and exploitation of solar devices; Dir ABDOUSSALAM BA.

Office des Eaux du Sous-Sol (OFEDES): BP 734, Niamey; tel. 20-74-01-19; fax 20-74-16-68; govt agency for the maintenance and devt of wells and boreholes; Pres. DJIBO HAMANI.

Office du Lait du Niger (OLANI): BP 404, Niamey; tel. 20-73-23-69; fax 20-73-36-74; f. 1971; devt and marketing of milk products; transferred to majority private ownership in 1998; Dir-Gen. M. DIENG.

Office National des Ressources Minières du Niger (ONAREM): Rond-Point Kennedy, BP 12716, Niamey; tel. 20-73-59-28; fax 20-73-28-12; f. 1976; govt agency for exploration, exploitation and marketing of all minerals; Pres. MOUDY MOHAMED; Dir-Gen. A. A. ASKIA.

Office des Produits Vivriers du Niger (OPVN): pl. du petit Marché, BP 474, Niamey; tel. 20-73-44-43; fax 20-73-24-68; e-mail opvn@opvn.net; internet www.opvn.net; govt agency for developing agricultural and food production; Dir-Gen. SEYDOU SADOU.

Riz du Niger (RINI): BP 476, Niamey; tel. 20-71-13-29; fax 20-73-42-04; f. 1967; cap. 825m. francs CFA; 30% state-owned; transfer to 100% private ownership proposed; production and marketing of rice; Pres. YOUSSOUF MOHAMED ELMOCTAR; Dir-Gen. M. HAROUNA.

DEVELOPMENT ORGANIZATIONS

Agence Française de Développement (AFD): 203 ave du Gountou-Yéna, BP 212, Niamey; tel. 20-72-33-93; fax 20-72-26-05; e-mail afdniamey@groupe-afd.org; internet www.afd.fr; Country Dir EMMANUEL DEBROISE.

Mission Française de Coopération et d'Action Culturelle: BP 494, Niamey; tel. 20-72-20-66; administers bilateral aid from France; Dir JEAN BOULOGNE.

Stichting Nederlandse Vrijwilligers Niger (SNV): ave des Zarmakoye, BP 10110, Niamey; tel. 20-75-36-33; fax 20-75-35-06; e-mail snvniger@snv.ne; internet www.snvniger.org; present in Niger since 1978; projects concerning food security, agriculture, the environment, savings and credit, marketing, water and communications; operations in Tillabéri, Zinder and Tahoua provinces; Dir-Gen. NIKO PATER.

CHAMBER OF COMMERCE

Chambre de Commerce d'Agriculture, d'Industrie et d'Artisanat du Niger: BP 209, Niamey; tel. 20-73-22-10; fax 20-73-46-68; e-mail cham209n@intnet.ne; internet www.ccaian.org; BP 201, Agadez; tel. 20-44-01-61; BP 91, Diffa; tel. 20-54-03-92; BP 79, Maradi; tel. 20-41-03-76; BP 172, Tahoua; tel. 20-61-03-84; BP 83, Zinder; tel. 20-51-00-78; f. 1954; comprises 80 full mems and 40 dep. mems; Pres. IBRAHIM IDI ANGO; Sec.-Gen. SADOU AISSATA.

INDUSTRIAL AND TRADE ORGANIZATIONS

Centre Nigérien du Commerce Extérieur (CNCE): pl. de la Concertation, BP 12480, Niamey; tel. 20-73-22-88; fax 20-73-46-68; f. 1984; promotes and co-ordinates all aspects of foreign trade; Dir AÏSSA DIALLO.

NIGER

Directory

Société Nationale de Commerce et de Production du Niger (COPRO-Niger): Niamey; tel. 20-73-28-41; fax 20-73-57-71; f. 1962; monopoly importer of foodstuffs; cap. 1,000m. francs CFA; 47% state-owned; Man. Dir DJIBRILLA HIMA.

EMPLOYERS' ORGANIZATIONS

Syndicat des Commerçants Importateurs et Exportateurs du Niger (SCIMPEXNI): Chambre de Commerce, d'Agriculture, d'Industrie et d'Artisanat du Niger, Niamey; tel. 20-73-33-17; Pres. M. SILVA; Sec.-Gen. INOUSSA MAÏGA.

Syndicat National des Petites et Moyennes Entreprises et Industries Nigériennes (SYNAPEMEIN): Chambre de Commerce, d'Agriculture, d'Industrie et d'Artisanat du Niger, Niamey; tel. 20-73-50-97; Pres. ALZOUMA SALEY; Sec.-Gen. HASSANE LAWAL KADER.

Syndicat Patronal des Entreprises et Industries du Niger (SPEIN): BP 415, Niamey; tel. 20-73-24-01; fax 20-73-47-07; f. 1994; Pres. AMADOU OUSMANE; Sec.-Gen. NOUHOU TARI.

UTILITIES

Electricity

Société Nigérienne d'Electricité (NIGELEC): 46 ave du Gen. de Gaulle, BP 11202, Niamey; tel. 20-72-26-92; fax 20-72-32-88; e-mail nigelec@intnet.ne; f. 1968; 95% state-owned; 51% transfer to private ownership proposed; production and distribution of electricity; Dir-Gen. ABDOULKARIM NOMA KAKA.

Water

Société d'Exploitation des Eaux du Niger (SEEN): blvd Zarmaganda, BP 12209, Niamey; tel. 20-72-25-00; fax 20-73-46-40; fmrly Société Nationale des Eaux; 51% owned by Veolia Environnement (France); production and distribution of drinking water; Pres. ABARY DAN BOUZOUA SOULEYMENE; Dir-Gen. SEYNI SALOU.

TRADE UNION FEDERATIONS

Confédération Démocratique des Travailleurs du Niger (CDTN): 1046 ave de l'Islam, BP 10766, Niamey; tel. 20-74-38-34; fax 20-74-28-55; e-mail c_cdtn@yahoo.fr; f. 2000; Sec.-Gen. ISSOUFOU SIDIBE.

Confédération des Travailleurs du Niger (CTN): Niamey; Sec.-Gen. MAMADOU SAKO.

Entente des Travailleurs du Niger (ETN): Bourse du Travail, BP 388, Niamey; tel. and fax 20-73-52-56; f. 2005 by merger of Confédération Nigérienne du Travail, Union Generale des Travailleurs du Niger and Union des Syndicats des Travailleurs du Niger.

Transport

ROADS

Niger is crossed by highways running from east to west and from north to south, giving access to neighbouring countries. A road is under construction to Lomé, Togo, via Burkina Faso, and the 428-km Zinder–Agadez road, scheduled to form part of the Trans-Sahara Highway, has been upgraded. In 2006 there were 18,550 km of classified roads, of which 3,803 km were paved.

Société Nationale des Transports Nigériens (SNTN): BP 135, Niamey; tel. 20-72-24-55; fax 20-74-47-07; e-mail stratech@intnet.ne; f. 1963; operates passenger and freight road-transport services; 49% state-owned; Chair. MOHAMED ABDOULAHI; Man. Dir BARKE M. MOUSTAPHA.

RAILWAYS

There are as yet no railways in Niger.

Organisation Commune Bénin-Niger des Chemins de Fer et des Transports (OCBN): BP 38, Niamey; tel. 20-73-27-90; f. 1959; 50% owned by Govt of Niger, 50% by Govt of Benin; manages the Benin-Niger railway project (begun in 1978); also operates more than 500 km within Benin (q.v.); extension to Niger proposed; transfer to private ownership proposed; Dir-Gen. RIGOBERT AZON.

INLAND WATERWAYS

The River Niger is navigable for 300 km within the country. Access to the sea is available by a river route from Gaya, in south-western Niger, to the coast at Port Harcourt, Nigeria, between September and March. Port facilities at Lomé, Togo, are used as a commercial outlet for land-locked Niger.

Société Nigérienne de Transit (NITRA): Zone Industrielle, BP 560, Niamey; tel. 20-73-22-53; fax 20-73-26-38; f. 1974; 48% owned by SNTN; customs agent, freight-handling, warehousing, etc.; manages Nigerien port facilities at Lomé, Togo; Pres. MOUNKAILA SEYDOU; Man. Dir SADE FATIMATA.

Société Nigérienne des Transports Fluviaux et Maritimes (SNTFM): Niamey; tel. 20-73-39-69; river and sea transport; cap. 64.6m. francs CFA; 99% state-owned; Man. Dir BERTRAND DEJEAN.

CIVIL AVIATION

There are international airports at Niamey (Hamani Diori), Agadez (Mano Dayak) and Zinder, and major domestic airports at Diffa, Maradi and Tahoua.

Air Continental: Niamey; f. 2003 to replace Air Niger International (f. 2002); 60% owned by private Nigerian interests, 20% by private Nigerien interests, 5% by Govt of Niger; regional and international services.

Air Inter Afrique: Niamey; tel. 20-73-85-85; fax 20-73-69-73; f. 2001; operates services within West Africa; CEO CHEIKH OUSMANE DIALLO.

Air Inter Niger: Agadez; f. 1997 to operate services to Tamanrasset (Algeria).

Niger Air Continental: Niamey; e-mail info@nigeraircontinental.com; f. 2003.

Nigeravia: BP 10454, Niamey; tel. 20-73-30-64; fax 20-74-18-42; e-mail nigavia@intnet.ne; internet www.nigeravia.com; f. 1991; operates domestic, regional and international services; Pres. and Dir-Gen. JEAN SYLVESTRE.

Sahel Airlines: rue de Rivoli, BP 10154, Niamey; tel. 20-73-65-71; fax 20-73-65-33; e-mail sahelair@intnet.ne; Dir-Gen. ABDOUL AZIZ LARABOU.

Société Nigérienne des Transports Aériens (SONITA): Niamey; f. 1991; owned by private Nigerien (81%) and Cypriot (19%) interests; operates domestic and regional services; Man. Dir ABDOULAYE MAIGA GOUDOUBABA.

Tourism

The Aïr and Ténéré Nature Reserve, covering an area of 77,000 sq km, was established in 1988. In 2008 some 73,154 tourists entered Niger, while receipts from tourism totalled $45m.

Centre Nigerien de Promotion Touristique (CNPT): ave de Président H. Luebke, BP 612, Niamey; tel. 20-73-24-47; fax 20-73-28-07; e-mail CNPT2@yahoo.fr; internet www.maisontourism-niger.com; Dirs BOULOU AKANO, IBRAHIM HALIDOU, KIEPIW TOYÉ FANTA.

Defence

As assessed at November 2010, Niger's armed forces totalled 5,300 men (army 5,200; air force 100). Paramilitary forces numbered 5,400 men, comprising the gendarmerie (1,400 men), the republican guard (2,500) and the national police force (1,500). Conscription is selective and lasts for two years.

Defence Expenditure: Estimated at 24,000m. francs CFA in 2009.

Chief of General Staff of the Armed Forces: Brig.-Gen. SOULEYMANE SALOU.

Chief of General Staff of the Land Army: Col SALIFOU MODY.

Chief of General Staff of the Air Force: Col HASSANE MOSSI.

Education

Education is available free of charge, and is officially compulsory for eight years between the ages of seven and 15 years. Primary education begins at the age of seven and lasts for six years. Secondary education begins at the age of 13 years, and comprises a four-year cycle followed by a three-year cycle. According to UNESCO estimates, primary enrolment in 2008/09 included 54% of children in the appropriate age-group (boys 60%; girls 48%). Secondary enrolment in 2006/07 included only 9% of the relevant age-group (boys 11%; girls 7%). The Abdou Moumouni University (formerly the University of Niamey) was inaugurated in 1973, and the Islamic University of Niger, at Say (to the south of the capital), was opened in 1987. Some 9,882 students were enrolled at those institutions in 2008/09. In December 2001 the Assemblée nationale approved legislation providing for the introduction of teaching in all local languages, with the aim of improving the literacy rate—one of the lowest in the world. Expenditure on education in 2008 represented 15.5% of total spending.

NIGERIA

Introductory Survey

LOCATION, CLIMATE, LANGUAGE, RELIGION, FLAG, CAPITAL

The Federal Republic of Nigeria is a West African coastal state on the shores of the Gulf of Guinea, with Benin to the west, Niger to the north, Chad to the north-east, and Cameroon to the east and south-east. The climate is tropical in the southern coastal areas, with an average annual temperature of 32°C (90°F) and high humidity. It is drier and semi-tropical in the north. Average annual rainfall is more than 2,500 mm (98 ins) in parts of the south-east, but in certain areas of the north is as low as 600 mm (24 ins). English is the country's official language. In 1963 the principal religious groups were Muslims (47.2%) and Christians (34.5%), while 18% of the total population followed animist beliefs. The national flag (proportions 1 by 2) has three equal vertical stripes, of green, white and green. The capital is Abuja, to which the Federal Government was formally transferred in December 1991; however, many non-government institutions remained in the former capital, Lagos.

CONTEMPORARY POLITICAL HISTORY

Historical Context

The territory of present-day Nigeria, except for the section of former German-controlled Cameroon (see below), was conquered by the United Kingdom, in several stages, during the second half of the 19th century and the first decade of the 20th century. The British dependencies of Northern and Southern Nigeria were merged into a single territory in 1914, administered largely by traditional native rulers, under the supervision of the colonial authorities. In 1947 the United Kingdom introduced a new Nigerian Constitution, establishing a federal system of government, based on three regions: Northern, Western and Eastern. The federal arrangement was an attempt to reconcile religious and regional tensions, and to accommodate Nigeria's diverse ethnic groups, notably the Ibo (in the east), the Yoruba (in the west) and the Hausa and Fulani (in the north). The Northern Region, which was predominantly Muslim, contained about one-half of Nigeria's total population.

In 1954 the federation became self-governing, and the first federal Prime Minister, Alhaji Abubakar Tafawa Balewa (a Muslim northerner), was appointed in August 1957. A constitutional conference, convened in 1958, agreed that Nigeria should become independent in 1960, and elections to an enlarged federal legislature took place in December 1959. The Northern People's Congress (NPC), which was politically dominant in the north, became the single largest party in the new legislature, although lacking an overall majority. Tafawa Balewa (a prominent member of the NPC) continued to head a coalition government of the NPC and the National Council for Nigeria and the Cameroons (NCNC), which attracted most support in the Eastern Region.

On 1 October 1960, as scheduled, the Federation of Nigeria achieved independence, initially as a constitutional monarchy. In June 1961 the northern part of the UN Trust Territory of British Cameroons was incorporated into Nigeria's Northern Region as the province of Sardauna, and in August 1963 a fourth region, the Mid-Western Region, was created by dividing the existing Western Region. On 1 October a revised Constitution was adopted, and the country was renamed the Federal Republic of Nigeria, although it remained a member of the Commonwealth. Dr Nnamdi Azikiwe of the NCNC took office as Nigeria's first President (then a non-executive post).

Domestic Political Affairs

In January 1966 Balewa's civilian Government was overthrown by junior army officers (mainly Ibos from the Eastern Region). The Commander-in-Chief of the Armed Forces, Maj.-Gen. Johnson Aguiyi-Aronsi (an Ibo), formed a Supreme Military Council, suspended the Constitution and imposed emergency rule. In July Aguiyi-Aronsi was killed in a further coup, staged by northern troops, and power was transferred to the Chief of Army Staff, Lt-Col (later Gen.) Yakubu Gowon, a Christian northerner. Gowon subsequently reintroduced the federal system, which had been suppressed after the January coup, and in April 1968 the four existing regions were replaced by 12 states.

Increasing opposition to Gowon's regime culminated in his overthrow in July 1975. Gowon was replaced as Head of State by Brig. (later Gen.) Murtala Ramat Muhammed, hitherto Federal Commissioner for Communications, who, in October, announced a detailed timetable for a transition to civilian rule. In February 1976, however, Muhammed was assassinated during an unsuccessful coup attempt. Power was immediately assumed by Lt-Gen. (later Gen.) Olusegun Obasanjo, the Chief of Army Staff, who promised to fulfil his predecessor's programme for the restoration of civilian rule.

In March 1976 the number of states was increased from 12 to 19, and it was announced that a new federal capital was to be constructed near Abuja, in central Nigeria. In September 1978 a new Constitution was promulgated, and the state of emergency, in force since 1966, was ended. At the same time the 12-year ban on political activity was revoked. Elections took place in July 1979 to a new bicameral National Assembly (comprising a Senate and a House of Representatives), and for State Assemblies and State Governors. The National Party of Nigeria (NPN), which included many prominent members of the former NPC, received the most widespread support in all the elections. The NPN's presidential candidate, Alhaji Shehu Shagari (who had served as an NPC federal minister prior to 1966 and as a federal commissioner in 1970–75), was elected to the new post of executive President in August 1979. He took office on 1 October, whereupon the military regime transferred power to the newly elected civilian authorities and the new Constitution came into effect.

In December 1983 the civilian Government was deposed in a bloodless military coup, led by Maj.-Gen. Muhammadu Buhari, who had been Federal Commissioner for Petroleum in 1976–78. The Government was replaced by a Supreme Military Council (SMC), headed by Buhari; the National Assembly was dissolved, and all political parties were banned. However, in August 1985 Buhari's administration was deposed in a bloodless coup, led by Maj.-Gen. (later Gen.) Ibrahim Babangida, the Chief of Army Staff and a member of the SMC. A new military administration, the Armed Forces Ruling Council (AFRC), was established, with Babangida as President.

Babangida's announcement in February 1986 that Nigeria had been accepted as a full member of the Organization of the Islamic Conference (OIC, see p. 400) prompted concern in the non-Muslim sector of the population at increasing 'Islamization' in Nigeria. In July 1987 Babangida announced details of a programme to transfer power to a civilian government on 1 October 1992. The ban on party politics was to be revoked in 1989, and a maximum of two associations were to be approved to contest elections. In August 1987 the Government established a National Electoral Commission (NEC); in September the number of states was increased to 21. In May 1988 a Constituent Assembly, comprising 450 members elected by local government and 117 members nominated by the AFRC, commenced preparation of a draft constitution. The progress of the Constituent Assembly was impeded, however, by controversy over the proposed inclusion of Islamic (*Shari'a*) courts in the new document.

In May 1989 Babangida announced the end of the prohibition on political parties, and the new Constitution (which was scheduled to take effect on 1 October 1992) was promulgated. Only 13 of the existing parties managed to fulfil the requirements for registration by the stipulated date in July 1989. In September the NEC submitted six political associations to the AFRC for consideration; in October, however, it was decided to dissolve all the newly formed political parties, on the grounds that they were too closely associated with discredited former parties. In their place, the AFRC created two new organizations, the Social Democratic Party (SDP) and the National Republican Convention (NRC), provoking widespread criticism.

Following the completion of registration for membership of the SDP and the NRC, party executives were elected for each state in July 1990, taking the place of government-appointed administrators. In August Babangida replaced nine government ministers, and the position of Chief of General Staff, held by Vice-Adm.

(later Adm.) Augustus Aikhomu, was replaced by the office of Vice-President (to which Aikhomu was immediately appointed). Babangida subsequently announced plans to reduce substantially the size of the armed forces.

In October 1990 the Movement for the Survival of the Ogoni People (MOSOP) was formed to co-ordinate opposition to the exploitation of petroleum reserves in territory of the Ogoni ethnic group (Ogoniland), in the south-central Rivers State, by the Shell Petroleum Development Co of Nigeria. Following a demonstration, organized by MOSOP in protest at environmental damage resulting from petroleum production, it was reported that security forces had killed some 80 Ogonis.

In September 1991, in an apparent attempt to relieve ethnic tensions, nine new states were created, increasing the size of the federation to 30 states. On 12 December the Federal Government was formally transferred from Lagos to Abuja, the new federal capital. In January 1992 Babangida formed a new Council of Ministers, in which several portfolios were restructured. In the same month the Government announced that elections to a bicameral National Assembly, comprising a 593-member House of Representatives and a 91-member Senate, would take place on 7 November, and would be followed by a presidential election on 5 December. The formal installation of a civilian government (and the implementation of the new Constitution) was consequently scheduled for 2 January 1993, rather than, as previously planned, on 1 October 1992.

The 1992 elections

Elections to the National Assembly were brought forward to 4 July 1992. The SDP secured a majority in both chambers, with 52 seats in the Senate and 314 seats in the House of Representatives, while the NRC won 37 seats in the Senate and 275 seats in the House of Representatives. The formal inauguration of the National Assembly, due to take place on 27 July, was, however, postponed until 5 December, the stipulated date for the presidential election, prompting concern at the AFRC's apparent reluctance to relinquish legislative power.

Voting in primary elections for presidential candidates took place in September 1992. In October, however, shortly before a final round of voting was due to take place, Babangida suspended the primary elections, pending the outcome of an investigation by the NEC into alleged incidents of electoral malpractice. In November Babangida postponed the presidential election until 12 June 1993.

On 5 December 1992 Babangida inaugurated the National Assembly. On 2 January 1993 the AFRC and the Council of Ministers were dissolved, and a civilian Transitional Council and the National Defence and Security Council (NDSC—which comprised the President, Vice-President, the heads of the armed forces and senior members of the Transitional Council) were formally installed. The Chairman of the Transitional Council, Chief Ernest Adegunle Shonekan, was officially designated Head of Government (although supreme power was vested in the NDSC and the President), while Aikhomu retained the post of Vice-President. In accordance with the new programme for the transition to civilian rule, party congresses to select presidential candidates were conducted in February–March; the NRC elected Alhaji Bashir Othman Tofa and the SDP Chief Moshood Kastumawo Olawale Abiola to contest the presidential election.

Following a series of court rulings provoking widespread confusion, the results of the presidential election, which took place on 12 June 1993, were declared invalid by the Abuja High Court. It had been reported that Abiola had secured the majority of votes in 19 states, and Tofa in 11. On 23 June, in what it claimed was an effort to uphold the judicial system, the NDSC annulled the results of the presidential election, suspended the NEC and halted all proceedings pertaining to the election. Babangida subsequently announced that the poll had been marred by widespread irregularities (despite reports by international observers that voting had been conducted fairly), but insisted that he remained committed to the transition to civilian rule on 27 August. The SDP and the NRC were to select two new presidential candidates, under the supervision of a reconstituted NEC. The annulment of the election attracted international criticism, particularly from the USA and the United Kingdom, which announced the imposition of military sanctions against Nigeria. In July the NDSC announced that a new presidential election was to take place on 14 August. Legal proceedings initiated by Abiola in the Lagos Supreme Court, in an attempt to uphold his claim to the presidency, were abandoned after Babangida introduced legislation that prohibited any legal challenges to the annulment of the election.

At the end of July 1993 Babangida announced that an Interim National Government (ING) was to be established, on the grounds that there was insufficient time to permit the scheduled transition to civilian rule on 27 August. On 26 August Babangida resigned; on the following day a 32-member interim Federal Executive Council (FEC), headed by Shonekan as the new President, was installed, while the transitional period for the return to civilian rule was extended to 31 March 1994. Supporters of democracy criticized the inclusion in the ING of several members of the now-dissolved NDSC, including Gen. Sani Abacha, who was appointed to the new post of Vice-President. Shonekan pledged his commitment to the democratic process and, in an effort to restore order, initiated negotiations with the Nigerian Labour Congress (NLC), which had announced industrial action in protest at the continuation of military rule, and effected the release of several journalists and opposition figures.

In September 1993 a series of military appointments, which included the nomination of Lt-Gen. Oladipo Diya to the office of Chief of Defence Staff, effectively removed supporters of Babangida from significant posts within the armed forces, thereby strengthening Abacha's position. Later in September the NRC and SDP agreed to a new timetable whereby local government elections and a presidential election would take place concurrently in February 1994.

On 17 November 1993, following a meeting with senior military officials, Shonekan resigned as Head of State and immediately transferred power to Abacha (confirming widespread speculation that the latter had effectively assumed control of the Government following Babangida's resignation). On the following day Abacha dissolved all state institutions that had been established under the transitional process, replaced the State Governors with military administrators, prohibited political activity (thereby proscribing the NRC and the SDP), and announced the formation of a Provisional Ruling Council (PRC), which was to comprise senior military officials and principal members of a new FEC. He insisted, however, that he intended to relinquish power to a civilian government, and pledged to convene a conference with a mandate to determine the constitutional future of the country. Restrictions on the media were revoked. On 21 November Abacha introduced legislation that formally restored the 1979 Constitution and provided for the establishment of the new government organs. In an apparent attempt to counter domestic and international criticism, several prominent supporters of Abiola, including Baba Gana Kingibe, and four former members of the ING were appointed to the PRC and FEC, which were installed on 24 November. Abacha subsequently removed 17 senior military officers who were believed to be loyal to Babangida. Also in November the NLC agreed to abandon strike action after the Government acted to limit the increase in the price of petroleum products.

In December 1993 the United Kingdom announced that member nations of the European Union (EU, see p. 270) were to impose further sanctions against Nigeria, including restrictions on the export of armaments. In April 1994 the Government announced a programme for the establishment of a National Constitutional Conference (NCC), which was to submit recommendations, including proposals for a new draft constitution, to the PRC in October. The ban on political activity was to end in January 1995. In May 1994 a new pro-democracy organization, comprising former politicians, retired military officers and human rights activists, the National Democratic Coalition (NADECO), demanded that Abacha relinquish power by the end of that month and urged a boycott of the NCC. In the same month the leader of MOSOP, Ken Saro-Wiwa, was arrested in connection with the deaths, during political violence, of four Ogoni traditional leaders. Saro-Wiwa was alleged to have incited his supporters to commit the murders.

Following a public gathering, at which he declared himself Head of State and President of a parallel government, Abiola was arrested by security forces. He was arraigned before a special High Court in Abuja in July 1994 and charged with treason, although his trial was repeatedly adjourned as a consequence of legal action challenging the jurisdiction of the special High Court in Abuja with regard to an offence that had been allegedly committed in Lagos.

In January 1995 the NCC, which had been scheduled to complete the preparations for a draft constitution in October 1994, adjourned until March 1995, prompting increasing concern that its protracted deliberations served to prolong the tenure of the military administration. The trial of Saro-Wiwa and a further 14 Ogoni campaigners, on charges of complicity in the murder of the four Ogoni traditional leaders, commenced in mid-January; the defendants were to challenge the legitimacy of the government-appointed Special Military Tribunal, at Port Harcourt. In February the Federal Court of Appeal dismissed Abiola's legal action challenging the jurisdiction of the High Court in Abuja.

In February 1995 Abacha dissolved the FEC, after a number of ministers announced their intention of engaging in political activity in the forthcoming transitional period. In March some 150 military officials were arrested, and the authorities subsequently confirmed reports of a conspiracy to overthrow the Government. The arrest of the former Head of State, Olusegun Obasanjo, and his former deputy, Maj.-Gen. (retd) Shehu Musa Yar'Adua, together with other prominent critics of the Government, prompted international protests. In mid-March Abacha appointed a new, 36-member FEC. In May more than 40 people, including Obasanjo and Yar'Adua, were arraigned before a Special Military Tribunal in Lagos, in connection with the alleged coup attempt in March.

Transition to civilian rule

In June 1995 the NCC submitted a draft Constitution to Abacha, who rescinded the ban on political activity; a programme for transition to civilian rule was to be announced on 1 October. (A number of political organizations subsequently emerged, in response to the removal of the ban.) At the end of June it was reported that Yar'Adua and a further 13 military officers had been sentenced to death for conspiring to overthrow the Government, while several other defendants, including Obasanjo, received custodial terms. The Government subsequently confirmed that a total of 43 had been convicted in connection with the coup attempt, prompting protests and appeals for clemency from the international community. On 1 October, however, Abacha officially commuted the death sentences to terms of imprisonment and reduced the custodial sentences (although he did not withdraw the capital charges against Abiola). At the same time he announced the approval of the new Constitution (which was due to be formally endorsed in 1998) and the adoption of a three-year programme for transition to civilian rule, whereby a new President was to be inaugurated on 1 October 1998, following elections at local, state and national level. (The duration of the transitional period was received with disapproval by the international community.)

At the end of October 1995 Saro-Wiwa and a further eight Ogoni activists were sentenced to death by the Special Military Tribunal in Port Harcourt, having been convicted of involvement in the murder of the four Ogoni leaders in May 1994; six defendants were acquitted. Although the defendants were not implicated directly in the incident, the nine convictions were based on the premise that the MOSOP activists had effectively incited the killings. An international campaign against the convictions and numerous appeals for clemency ensued. However, on 10 November the nine convicted Ogonis were executed, prompting immediate condemnation by the international community. Nigeria was suspended from the Commonwealth, and threatened with expulsion if the Government failed to restore democracy within a period of two years. Later that month the EU reaffirmed its commitment to existing sanctions that had been imposed in 1993 (notably an embargo on the export of armaments and military equipment to Nigeria), and extended visa restrictions to civilian members of the administration. The Governments of the USA, South Africa and the EU member nations recalled their diplomatic representatives from Nigeria in protest at the executions. The Nigerian Government condemned the imposition of sanctions and, in turn, withdrew its diplomatic representatives from the USA, South Africa and the EU member countries.

In June 1996 Nigerian officials met the Commonwealth Ministerial Action Group (CMAG) in an attempt to avert the threatened imposition of sanctions against Nigeria; the Nigerian delegation demanded that Nigeria be readmitted to the Commonwealth in exchange for the Government's adoption of the programme for transition to civilian rule by October 1998. The Commonwealth dismissed the programme as unsatisfactory, but remained divided regarding the adoption of consequent measures. It was finally agreed that the Commonwealth would suspend the adoption of sanctions, but that the situation would subsequently be reviewed. Canada, however, announced its opposition to this decision and unilaterally imposed a number of sanctions (similar to those already adopted by the EU). In September 1996 CMAG agreed that the Commonwealth delegation would visit Nigeria, despite conditions imposed by the military authorities, which insisted that it would not be permitted access to opposition activists or political prisoners.

In June 1996 legislation governing the formation of political parties was promulgated. Five of 15 political organizations that applied for registration were granted legal status in September. NADECO condemned the disqualification of the remaining 10 parties, which were subsequently dissolved by decree; it was widely believed that the associations that had been granted registration were largely sympathetic towards the military administration. In October Abacha announced the creation of a further six states, increasing the total size of the federation to 36 states.

In early 1997 escalating tension between the Ijaw and Itsekiri ethnic groups in the town of Warri, in south-western Nigeria, severely disrupted operations in the region of the Niger Delta by the Shell Petroleum Development Company of Nigeria. In March Ijaw protesters seized Shell installations and took about 100 employees hostage, in an attempt to force the Government to accede to their demands. The disruption in petroleum production resulted in a national fuel shortage, effectively suspending the transportation system in much of the country. Further attacks on Shell installations were reported in May. Later that month the authorities established a commission of inquiry to investigate the cause of the unrest and submit recommendations for restoring order in the region. Persistent attacks by Ijaw activists against petroleum installations resulted in the imposition of a state of emergency at the end of December 1998.

Meanwhile, at a summit meeting of the Commonwealth Heads of Government, which took place in Edinburgh, United Kingdom, in October 1997, Nigeria's suspension from the organization was extended for an additional year; it was further indicated that the country would be expelled from the Commonwealth if Abacha reneged on his pledge to restore democratic rule by 1 October 1998. The Government had announced a new electoral timetable and it was maintained that the new elected organs of government would be installed by 1 October 1998. Elections to the state legislatures, which were contested by the five registered parties, took place on 6 December 1997; the United Nigeria Congress Party (UNCP) won 637 of the 970 contested seats, securing a majority in 29 of the 36 State Assemblies. The other four parties (the Congress for National Consensus, the Democratic Party of Nigeria, the Grassroots Democratic Movement and the National Centre Party of Nigeria) subsequently attributed the electoral success of the UNCP to malpractice on the part of the authorities, and threatened to withdraw from the remainder of the electoral process. In mid-December Abacha nominated a new FEC, in which most of the ministers who had served in the previous administration were replaced.

On 8 June 1998 Abacha died unexpectedly from heart failure. The PRC designated the Chief of Defence Staff, Maj.-Gen. Abdulsalami Abubakar, as Abacha's successor, and on 9 June he was inaugurated as Head of State (having been promoted to the rank of General). Abubakar pledged to continue the Abacha Government's scheduled transition to civilian rule. In mid-June Abubakar ordered the release of about 26 political prisoners, including Obasanjo (ostensibly on grounds of ill health). In July, following discussions with UN officials, the authorities agreed to release Abiola from detention. Shortly after his release, however, Abiola collapsed and subsequently died. Violent rioting ensued, amid widespread speculation that the authorities were responsible for Abiola's death. Although an autopsy confirmed that he had died of heart failure, it was indicated that his period in detention had contributed to his poor health. Later in July Abubakar announced that the transition to civilian rule would be completed on 29 May 1999 (rather than 1 October 1998). The Government annulled the results of the elections that had previously been conducted, and dissolved the five authorized political parties. In August a new, 31-member FEC, which included a number of civilians, was appointed to remain in office pending the formal transition to civilian rule; an Independent National Electoral Commission (INEC) was also established. Later that month the INEC announced that local government elections would take place on 5 December 1998 and state legislative elections on 9 January 1999, followed by elections to a bicameral national legislature on 20 February and a presidential election on 27 February. On 7 September 1998 the Government published the draft Constitution that had been submitted by the NCC in June 1995.

Some 25 new political organizations submitted applications for registration to the INEC. The commission provisionally approved nine political associations, notably the People's

Democratic Party (PDP), which principally comprised former opponents of the Abacha administration. In October 1998 CMAG recommended that Commonwealth member states end sanctions against Nigeria, in preparation for the country's readmission to the Commonwealth. At the end of that month, in response to the democratization measures undertaken by the Government, the EU ended a number of sanctions against Nigeria (while maintaining the embargo on the export of armaments).

In January 1999 several prominent members of former administrations announced that they intended to seek nomination to contest the forthcoming presidential election. In early February the All Nigeria People's Party (ANPP) and the Alliance for Democracy (AD), which, despite the stated opposition of the INEC, had established an electoral alliance, nominated a joint candidate, Samuel Oluyemisi Falae (a former Minister of Finance in the Babangida administration). Later that month Obasanjo (who had joined the PDP in October 1998) was elected as the presidential candidate of that party. At the elections to the bicameral legislature, which took place on 20 February, the PDP secured 215 seats in the 360-member House of Representatives and 66 seats in the 109-member Senate. (Voting in the Niger Delta region was postponed, owing to continued unrest, and a further by-election for the vacant seat to the National Assembly took place in March.)

Obasanjo becomes President

On 27 February 1999 Obasanjo was elected to the presidency with 62.8% of votes cast. The Constitution was promulgated on 5 May and Obasanjo was formally inaugurated as President on 29 May; on the same day Nigeria was readmitted as a full member of the Commonwealth. On 3 June the inaugural session of the National Assembly took place. Obasanjo nominated a new Cabinet, principally comprising members of the PDP, which was approved by the Senate later that month. He also undertook a reorganization of the armed forces, removing more than 150 military officers who had served under the Abacha Government.

The Christian Association of Nigeria threatened to initiate a legal challenge to the introduction of Islamic *Shari'a* law, announced in Kano and Zamfara States in December 1999 and January 2000, respectively, on the grounds that it contravened the principle of secularity enshrined in the Constitution. In February a demonstration by Christians in the northern town of Kaduna in protest at the proposed imposition of *Shari'a* in Kaduna State precipitated violent hostilities between Muslims and Christians, in which more than 300 people were killed; government troops eventually suppressed the unrest and a curfew was imposed in the town. However, more than 50 people were killed in further clashes between Christians and Muslims in the south-eastern towns of Aba and Umuahia, which ensued in reprisal for the violence in the north. By the end of the month thousands of Christians had fled the north of the country, fearing possible retaliatory massacres. At an emergency meeting at the end of February, chaired by Obasanjo, the Governors of the 18 northern states agreed, in the interests of peace, to withdraw the new legislation introducing *Shari'a* law, and to revert to the provisions for *Shari'a* in the existing penal code, in accordance with the federal Constitution. However, the Governors of a number of the states subsequently announced that they would not comply with the federal government order, but would proceed with the implementation of *Shari'a* law. In March religious rioting in Niger State (where the adoption of the *Shari'a* law had been declared) was reported. In May some 150 people were killed in further clashes between Christians and Muslims in Kaduna; government troops were again deployed in the town to restore order.

In August 2000, following persistent dissension between the executive and the legislature over the issue of government corruption, the President of the Senate was removed from office and charged with misusing public funds. In the same month *Shari'a* law was formally adopted in the northern states of Katsina, Jigawa and Yobe (to enter into effect later that year). In September the Governor of Borno State also announced the adoption of *Shari'a*. Although the Governors of most of these states had declared that Christians would be exempt from the provisions of *Shari'a,* social segregation of men and women and the application of punishments stipulated under Islamic law had been widely implemented in Zamfara and Kano States. In view of the violence in Kaduna State, the Governor announced that the form of *Shari'a* to be introduced in the state was to be modified to allow Islamic courts to exist in conjunction with special courts upholding secular laws.

In June 2001 religious and ethnic unrest in northern and central Nigeria intensified; some 1,000 people were killed in fighting between Christians and Muslims in Bauchi (which had become the 10th northern state to adopt *Shari'a* law). In early 2002 the death sentence imposed on a woman in northern Sokoto State, who had been convicted in October 2001 under *Shari'a* law on charges of adultery, attracted increasing international attention. Following pressure from the international community, in March the Minister of Justice urged the 12 State Governors who had adopted *Shari'a* law to discontinue its strict enforcement, on the grounds that it contravened the Constitution for reasons of discrimination (applying only to Muslims). A Court of Appeal subsequently overturned the sentence against the convicted woman, ruling that there was insufficient evidence to justify the death penalty. However, the Governors of several northern states insisted that they would continue to implement *Shari'a*.

In June 2002 the INEC announced that, of 24 political parties that had applied for official registration, only three had been recognized (increasing the total number of legal associations to six). Also in June, after a long-standing dispute between Obasanjo and the Senate over control of public finances, the President survived an impeachment attempt by the upper chamber. In August the House of Representatives adopted by an overwhelming majority a resolution demanding that Obasanjo resign from office or face impeachment, on charges of mismanagement and abuse of power. Obasanjo refused to comply with the resolution, and at the end of that month the PDP voted in favour of drafting a list of charges against the President.

In December 2002 the INEC granted registration to a further 24 political associations, after the Supreme Court upheld an appeal by five opposition parties against their exclusion, and ordered less restrictive regulations for legalization. Later that month the Commission announced that legislative elections were to be conducted on 12 April 2003, followed by a presidential election on 19 April and elections to regional Houses of Assembly on 3 May. In January Obasanjo was formally elected as the presidential candidate of the PDP. A further 18 political leaders subsequently announced their intention to contest the presidential election.

Obasanjo's second term

Incidences of violence and malpractice were reported during the federal legislative elections on 12 April 2003. The PDP secured an overwhelming majority in both legislative chambers (213 seats in the House of Representatives and 73 in the Senate), while the ANPP was the only other party to win significant representation (95 seats in the House of Representatives and 28 in the Senate). At the presidential election on 19 April (the first to be organized by civilian authorities for 19 years), Obasanjo was elected for a second term by 61.9% of the valid votes cast, while Maj.-Gen. Muhammadu Buhari received 32.2% of votes. Opposition leaders, notably Buhari, contested the results, claiming that widespread electoral malpractice had been perpetrated, and indicated that violent protests might ensue. International monitors, although generally satisfied with the organization of the elections, declared that irregularities had taken place, particularly in the region of the Niger Delta. At gubernatorial elections, which also took place on 19 April, the PDP gained eight state governorships from the ANPP and AD, losing only one (that of Kano). Later that month Obasanjo criticized a statement by EU monitors, who claimed that they had obtained evidence of electoral malpractice perpetrated in 13 states. Meanwhile, at the end of April four offshore petroleum rigs, operated by a US enterprise, Transocean, in the Niger Delta were seized by protesting Nigerian employees, who took hostage 97 foreign national workers. Military naval forces were dispatched to the region and all hostages were airlifted from the rigs.

Obasanjo officially dissolved the Federal Government on 21 May 2003. He was sworn in on 29 May (after a legal challenge against his inauguration by Buhari was rejected by the federal Court of Appeal), and in early June began to nominate ministers to his new administration. In mid-July Obasanjo finally inaugurated the new, 40-member Federal Government, which included the hitherto Vice-President of the World Bank, Dr Ngozi Okonja-Iweala, as the Minister of Finance and the Economy (an appointment that reflected the authorities' stated intention to eliminate corruption and implement economic reforms).

In early April 2004 the Government announced that some 20 army officials had been arrested, following the discovery of a conspiracy to seize power, believed to have been instigated by a former head of security in the Abacha administration, Maj. Hama al-Mustapha. (In October three senior military officers, including al-Mustapha, were charged with planning to overthrow the Government with an attack on the presidential helicopter.) Later in April reports emerged of severe clashes between Christian and Muslim tribes in farming villages on the border of Plateau State, reportedly as a result of land ownership disputes; by early May some 650 people, mainly Muslims, had been killed in the fighting. Muslims subsequently rioted in Kano in reprisal for the deaths; it was announced that 600 Christians had been killed and that a further 30,000 had fled from the region. Later in May Obasanjo dispatched security forces to restore order and imposed a state of emergency in Plateau State (which was ended in November).

In September 2004 renewed hostilities between the Ijaw and Itsekiri in the Niger Delta prompted further concern on the part of the authorities, particularly after an Ijaw militia, the Niger Delta People's Volunteer Force (NDPVF), threatened a campaign to disrupt petroleum supplies by attacking installations. Consequently, the Government announced a further substantial increase in the price of fuel in that month, prompting the NLC to organize a general strike in October. Further planned strike action by the NLC and allied organizations was suspended in November, after the Government agreed to a reduction in the price. Following a peace accord between the Government and the activists, reached in October, fighting in the Niger Delta region declined significantly. However, Ijaw militia had failed to disarm by the scheduled date at the end of December, and a campaign of peaceful protests was threatened, on the grounds that the Government had not complied with the terms of the agreement.

In September 2005 tension increased in the Niger Delta region, following the arrest of the leader of the NDPVF; Mujahid Dokubo-Asari had threatened to continue hostilities unless his demands that the Ijaw people of the region be granted self-determination were met. Petroleum installations, which had temporarily closed, resumed operations after Dokubo-Asari urged his supporters to maintain civil order. In October he was officially charged with treason before the Abuja Federal High Court. Later that month the leader of the Movement for the Actualization of the Sovereign State of Biafra (MASSOB), Chief Ralph Uwazurike, was arrested and subsequently charged with treason (on the grounds that he had attempted to overthrow the Federal Government). Protests by members of MASSOB against the arrest of their leader culminated in clashes, in which some 20 people were killed.

In January 2006 four foreign nationals employed by companies subcontracted by the Shell Petroleum Development Co were seized by militants in Bayelsa State; a hitherto unknown organization, the Movement for the Emancipation of the Niger Delta (MEND), claimed responsibility for the kidnappings. At the end of January MEND announced the release of the hostages on humanitarian grounds, but maintained that it would continue attacks in the Niger Delta region and seized a further nine foreign nationals employed by a subcontracted US enterprise, Willbros. Six of the hostages were released one week later, while the remaining three (two US and one British national) were released in late March. Also in February a High Court in Port Harcourt ruled that the Shell Petroleum Development Co pay $1,500m. in compensation to the Ijaw population in the Niger Delta for environmental damage, in compliance with a decision by the National Assembly in 2000.

The situation worsened during mid-2006 and in June five Nigerian soldiers were killed in a raid by MEND on a petroleum installation. In August Obasanjo ordered the establishment of a joint operation between the armed forces and the police to patrol the Niger Delta region. Shortly after the operation commenced, it was reported that the security forces had opened fire in the region, forcing civilians to flee from the area. Concerns were raised that the order from the President would aggravate an already volatile situation; in October the number of kidnappings multiplied and the disturbances led to the reduction of petroleum production by some 25%.

In early 2006 the Nigerian Constitutional Committee conducted a series of public debates on proposed amendments to the Constitution, which would allow Obasanjo to seek a third term in office. In April relations between Obasanjo and the Vice-President, Alhaji Atiku Abubakar (who had protested at the proposals to end the constitutional restriction on two presidential terms), significantly deteriorated. In May the National Assembly rejected the proposals, thus preventing Obasanjo from contesting the 2007 presidential election.

The 2007 elections

In the months leading up to the presidential and legislative elections, scheduled to be held on 14 and 21 April 2007, several government reorganizations were effected. In June 2006 Obasanjo reassigned Okonja-Iweala to the foreign affairs portfolio amid concerns over the durability of the Government's financial management and economic reforms. However, Okonja-Iweala resigned from the new position in August, having been dismissed from her role as head of the economic reform team; Prof. Joy Ogwu replaced her at the Ministry of Foreign Affairs. Further changes to the Government were carried out in mid-January 2007 when almost one-third of the ministries were dissolved or merged to simplify the administration's structure and improve its efficiency ahead of the forthcoming elections.

With Obasanjo prohibited from contesting the presidential election, Abubakar emerged as the primary presidential candidate. However, his relationship with the President had become increasingly strained and Obasanjo strongly opposed Abubakar's candidacy. In September 2006 Obasanjo submitted a report to the Senate containing allegations of fraudulent activity involving Abubakar, who was subsequently indicted by the Economic and Financial Crimes Commission (EFCC), which had been established by Obasanjo in 2004. As Vice-President, Abubakar held immunity against prosecution unless impeached. Later in September 2006 he was suspended from the PDP for three months; although he retained his position as Vice-President, the suspension prevented him from seeking nomination from the PDP to stand as its presidential candidate. Abubakar continually denied the allegations against him, and it subsequently emerged that he would represent the Action Congress of Nigeria (ACN), a new party formed in September by the merger of several minor political parties, in the presidential election. Abubakar was disqualified from contesting the election by the INEC in mid-March 2007, owing to his indictment for corruption, but following a number of legal challenges, his candidature was confirmed by a Supreme Court ruling on 16 April.

Gubernatorial and state assembly elections took place on 14 April 2007: the PDP secured control of 28 states and the ANPP of five. Ensuing outbreaks of violence marred the conduct of the presidential election, which was held concurrently with the elections to the National Assembly, as scheduled, on 21 April. According to official results, the PDP candidate, Alhaji Umaru Musa Yar'Adua (the younger brother of the late Maj.-Gen. (retd) Shehu Musa Yar'Adua, former Vice-President in Obasanjo's military Government during the 1960s), secured a decisive victory, receiving about 70.0% of the votes cast. Buhari, who contested the election as the candidate of the ANPP, was second placed with 18.7% of the ballots, while Abubakar secured 7.3%. In the legislative elections, the PDP increased its majority in both the House of Representatives and the Senate, winning 263 seats and 87 seats, respectively, while the ANPP secured 63 seats in the lower house and 14 seats in the upper chamber. Despite claims by the INEC that the elections had been successfully held, international observers cast doubt on the credibility of the polls as reports emerged that no voting took place in some states due to delays in the distribution of ballot papers. Opposition parties rejected the outcome of the presidential election, and Buhari and Abubakar instigated legal proceedings to have the results of the ballot annulled. Yar'Adua was sworn in as President on 29 May. In June the House of Representatives for the first time elected a woman, Patricia Etteh, as Speaker. (However, following allegations regarding the misappropriation of funds, Etteh resigned in November, and was replaced by Dimeji Bankole.)

President Yar'Adua named a new Cabinet in August 2007, which included Mahmud Yayale Ahmed as Minister of Defence, Ojo Maduekwe as Minister of Foreign Affairs and Shamsudeen Usman as Minister of Finance; in October four more ministers were sworn in, having received approval from the Senate. Yar'Adua assumed responsibility for the petroleum resources portfolio, as Obasanjo had before him, and pledged to continue with reforms to the energy sector that had been commenced under the previous administration. Furthermore the new President ordered investigations, which were launched in August, into the award of numerous petroleum and gas contracts.

At a final hearing in Abuja in February 2008 five judges dismissed the case brought by Buhari and Abubakar, citing insufficient grounds for overruling the result of the presidential election. The two defeated candidates announced their intention to appeal against the decision in the Supreme Court. By this time the election of eight State Governors had been nullified by the

Court of Appeal, following challenges by opposition candidates, and in April the election of a further two Governors was also ruled invalid; polls were subsequently repeated in those states.

The Yar'Adua presidency

In mid-August 2008 Yar'Adua announced an overhaul of the command structure of the armed forces, replacing the Chief of Defence Staff, Gen. Andrew Owoye Azazi, with Air Marshall Paul Dike; the chiefs of staff of the army, navy and air force were also removed, although intense media speculation that the changes were effected as a result of a perceived threat to the Government were denied by the presidency. In September Yar'Adua approved the restructuring of several government departments, including the creation of a new Ministry of Niger Delta Affairs and the division of the Ministry of Energy into two separate ministries, namely the Ministry of Power and the Ministry of Petroleum Resources. He also dismissed the Secretary to the Government of the Federation, Baba Gana Kingibe, following suggestions in the media that he planned to challenge for the presidency. A total of eight ministers and 12 ministers of state were removed from the Cabinet in November in preparation for a major reorganization of the structure of the federal ministries. In the following month Yar'Adua named his new Government, in which only three members of the outgoing administration retained their positions. The new Cabinet featured 19 new appointees: most notably, Dr Rilwanu Lukman (the Secretary-General of the Organization of the Petroleum Exporting Countries, see p. 405 in 1995–2000), was appointed Minister of Petroleum Resources and Dr Shettima Mustapha was named as the new Minister of Defence, while Chief Ufot Ekaette, a former Secretary to the Government of the Federation, was awarded responsibility for the Niger Delta affairs portfolio.

Meanwhile, in late November 2008 there was significant unrest in the Plateau State town of Jos; violent clashes between Christian and Muslim groups resulted in the deaths of some 400 people, while thousands more were displaced. The rioting followed a dispute over local elections in mid-November (the first for some 10 years) at which the PDP defeated the largely Muslim-supported ANPP, and swiftly escalated into sectarian violence. A report published by Human Rights Watch in early 2009 claimed that police had carried out summary executions of some 90 youths while suppressing the disturbances.

Unrest continued in the Niger Delta region throughout 2007 with numerous kidnappings and abductions reported, and in the months preceding the elections there had also been an escalation of attacks on oil installations and several car bombings in Port Harcourt; by mid-February some 52 hostages had been taken, the majority of whom had links to the petroleum sector. As part of President Yar'Adua's pledge that his administration would give special priority to the problems of the Niger Delta, militia leader Dokubo-Asari, who had been in detention since October 2005, was released on bail in June 2007. However, in August a cease-fire negotiated by the Nigerian Government and MEND in May broke down and further abductions and disruptions to petroleum production were reported during late 2007. In February 2008 MEND leader Henry Okah and another senior member of the movement, Edward Atatah, were extradited from Angola, where they had been arrested in September 2007 on weapons charges; in March 2008 treason charges were filed against both men. MEND claimed responsibility for a number of attacks on oil installations and pipelines owned by Royal Dutch Shell in April and May. The company was reportedly forced to halt production equivalent to some 169,000 barrels per day as a result, and in June shut down production at its facility in the offshore Bonga oil field, after it was attacked. In September the Nigerian military carried out a large-scale bombardment of a MEND position in Rivers State, prompting the declaration of an 'oil war' by the rebels: after a week of intensified attacks on oil installations, MEND declared a cease-fire. However, there was a resumption of hostilities in early 2009, after rebels affiliated to MEND launched an assault on an oil platform and kidnapped six crew members. On 31 January MEND officially ended its cease-fire in response to a military offensive against one of its bases; attacks on oil and gas installations continued, and there was an increase in the number of foreign nationals and oil workers being kidnapped in the region, leading to a two-day strike by workers at the French company Total, who were concerned about the continuing unrest and insecurity. In May MEND warned oil companies to evacuate their employees, after the Government launched a further large-scale military operation against insurgent positions. In early June settlement was reached on a protracted legal case brought against Royal Dutch Shell in the USA by relatives of Ken Saro-Wiwa and other Ogoni leaders executed in 1995, who accused the corporation of complicity in human rights atrocities committed against the Ogoni people of the Niger Delta in the 1990s, including the executions; Royal Dutch Shell admitted no accountability but agreed to pay US $15.5m. to establish a trust fund for the Ogoni people shortly before the trial was due to start. Later in June 2009 Yar'Adua proposed a 60-day period of amnesty for all members of MEND, including its leaders, to allow a process of disarmament, which would begin in early August. In July Okah was released from prison, after accepting the presidential offer of amnesty.

In late July 2009 police in Bauchi State arrested several suspected leaders of a militant Islamist group opposed to Western education and culture, known as Boko Haram prompting retaliatory attacks against police stations by its followers in Bauchi and other northern states. Government forces were deployed in the capital of Borno State, Maidaguri, believed to be the base of Boko Haram, and launched an offensive against the compound of the movement's leader, Ustaz Mohammed Yusuf, and a nearby mosque. It was reported that Yusuf and some 300 militants had escaped; however, at the end of July he was captured by security forces and killed in custody, according to the police statement while trying to escape. The authorities estimated that a total of 700 people had been killed during the clashes. Human rights organizations subsequently accused the police of the unlawful killing of Yusuf and demanded an inquiry into events. In early August Yar'Adua announced that he had ordered an official investigation into the security operation launched against Boko Haram.

After the period of amnesty for insurgents entered into effect in early August 2009, it was reported that other prominent leaders of MEND had accepted a government pardon by early October and that large numbers of rebels had surrendered their armaments. Later that month Yar'Adua approved a plan (which was subject to confirmation by the legislature) to allocate 10% of revenue from Nigeria's oil and gas ventures to the population of the Niger Delta, in an effort to satisfy the longstanding demands of the insurgents. It was reported that MEND had responded favourably to the proposal, announcing an indefinite cease-fire. However, at the end of January 2010 MEND announced an end to its cease-fire, on the grounds that the Government had failed to fulfil pledges made in exchange for disarmament.

Goodluck Jonathan becomes President

The emergency hospitalization of President Yar'Adua in Saudi Arabia in late November 2009 prompted increasing demands for his resignation. In early December 56 politicians, including prominent PDP members, issued a statement urging Yar'Adua to transfer power to Vice-President Dr Goodluck Ebele Jonathan. However, the Government agreed unanimously that there were no grounds upon which to seek the resignation of Yar'Adua, who resisted pressure to cede power. In January 2010 the Federal High Court, rejecting an appeal by the Nigerian Bar Association, ruled that Yar'Adua was not obliged under the Constitution to transfer power or to inform the legislature of his absence; the Government issued a statement that he remained capable of governing. However, Yar'Adua's continued medical treatment for a heart condition in Saudi Arabia created an impasse regarding the adoption of the 2010 budget and attracted widespread criticism, including from within factions of the PDP, with opposition rallies and demands for the President's impeachment. In early February Yar'Adua announced his decision to transfer power to Jonathan. On 10 February Jonathan became Acting President and Commander-in-Chief of the Armed Forces, after both legislative chambers adopted motions allowing him to assume interim executive powers while Yar'Adua was unfit for office. Jonathan immediately reorganized the Government; changes included the replacement as Minister of Justice of Michael Kaase Aondoakaa, who had opposed the transfer of presidential power. Jonathan pledged to address severe energy shortages and continue the amnesty process for insurgents in the Niger Delta. Yar'Adua unexpectedly returned to Nigeria in late February, but failed to appear in public.

Meanwhile, in January 2010 it was reported that some 400 people had been killed in further clashes between Muslim and Christian groups in Jos; in early March it was reported that about 500 members of the Christian Berom community had been killed by Muslim Hausa-Fulani herders near Jos, apparently in reprisal for the violence in January. The recurrent hostilities were widely attributed to longstanding divisions between mainly Christian indigenous ethnic groups and predominantly Muslim ethnic groups, who were classified as settlers, over land and resources in the region. In mid-March MEND claimed responsibility for two bomb explosions, in which four people were killed, at a government building on the occasion of an amnesty conference at Warri; the movement claimed that these had been intended as an attack against the Governor of Delta State in retaliation for his declaration in the press that the movement was a 'media creation'.

In early March 2010 Jonathan removed the National Security Adviser, a close associate of Yar'Adua, replacing him with Aliyu Gusau. On 17 March Jonathan dissolved the Cabinet; his decision was widely believed to be an effort to remove associates of Yar'Adua and consolidate power. He subsequently submitted a number of ministerial nominees for approval by the Senate. On 6 April a new Government (which included 13 members of the previous administration) was installed. Olusegun Olutoyin Aganga, hitherto a senior executive at an investment bank in the United Kingdom, became the new Minister of Finance and was also appointed Chairman of a new National Economic Team, which was entasked with effecting economic recovery.

On 5 May 2010 the death of Yar'Adua was announced; on the following day Jonathan was sworn in as Head of State. A period of national mourning lasting seven days was also declared. Later that month Jonathan nominated the Governor of Kaduna State, Namadi Sambo, to be his Vice-President. Sambo's appointment to the vice-presidency was confirmed by the House of Representatives and the Senate on 18 May. In September internationally renowned Nigerian writer 'Wole' Soyinka officially established a new party, the Democratic Front for a People's Federation, which was to contest the 2011 elections.

On 1 October 2010 12 people were killed and 17 others injured, when two car bombs exploded in Abuja during a celebration marking the 50th anniversary of Nigeria's independence; MEND declared responsibility for the bomb attacks and claimed that it had given advance notice to the security services. Okah was again detained in Johannesburg, South Africa, and charged with engaging in terrorist activity; several other suspects, including Okah's son and brother, were also arrested and charged in connection with the attacks. Later in October the Government deployed some 400 armed police officers and troops in the north-eastern town of Maiduguri, following a series of violent incidents that were attributed to Boko Haram, including the killings of five police officers and six civilians. Further sectarian attacks were also reported near Jos. In early November seven foreign nationals (including two US citizens) were seized by MEND militia from the Okoro oilfield, in the Niger Delta. After the Nigerian military launched a major offensive against MEND bases in the region, the seven foreign nationals, together with 12 Nigerian hostages, were released by the rebels later that month; however, MEND issued a statement declaring its intention to continue its insurgent campaign. In May 2011 Royal Dutch Shell lost a legal appeal against a court ruling that the corporation pay rent to the local community of the Niger Delta for the use of land where its major oil terminal was located.

Recent developments: the 2011 presidential and legislative elections

In November 2010 the INEC announced that the presidential election, which had been scheduled for January 2011, had been postponed until 9 April to allow more time for preparation; it was confirmed that the legislative elections would be conducted on 2 April, and the gubernatorial and state legislative elections on 16 April. Reports of violent incidents increased during December 2010; these included attacks against churches by members of Boko Haram, and further clashes at the end of the month between Muslims and Christians in Jos, in which some 80 people were killed. On 14 January 2011 Jonathan was elected as the PDP candidate for the forthcoming presidential election, securing 2,736 votes, while his closest contender, Abubakar, received 805 votes. The nomination of Jonathan (a southern Christian) prompted a number of protests against senior PDP officials in northern cities (the PDP having previously agreed to adopt election candidates alternately from the north and the south of the country). In the same month Buhari was selected as the presidential candidate of the Congress for Progressive Change (CPC), which had been established by former members of the ANPP in 2009 and which he had joined in March 2010. In early February 2011 public demonstrations in Plateau State were banned, after some 20 people were killed in further sectarian clashes in Jos. In the same month 11 people were killed in a stampede at an election campaign rally for Jonathan at a sports stadium in Port Harcourt, when a police officer fired a gun to disperse supporters. On 22 February the House of Representatives approved legislation increasing the powers of the authorities with regard to counter-terrorism; notably, judges were henceforth permitted to order the detention of suspects for up to 30 days without charge. In March three people were killed in a bomb attack staged against a PDP election rally in Abuja, while numerous other incidents included an explosion at INEC offices in the town of Suleja, near the capital, in which eight people were killed.

In early April 2011 the INEC rescheduled all the forthcoming elections for several days later, owing to organizational difficulties, including the delivery of ballot papers. The legislative elections were finally conducted on 9 April: partial results indicated a significant loss in the parliamentary strength of the PDP, which obtained 123 of the 234 seats declared in the House of Representatives, while the ACN took 47 seats, the CPC 30 seats and the ANPP 25 seats; the PDP received 45 and the ACN 13 of the 74 seats declared in the elections to the Senate. (The INEC had announced that polls in 15 senatorial districts and 48 federal constituencies were to be postponed further, until 26 April.) The presidential election, which was contested by 19 candidates, took place on 16 April: according to provisional results, Jonathan secured a decisive majority of 58.9% of votes cast, while Buhari of the CPC was second placed, with about 32% of the votes (mainly receiving support in northern regions). Voter turnout of 58.7% was recorded. International election observers, including an EU mission, generally declared that the conduct of the polls demonstrated a significant improvement compared with those of 2007. On 18 April 2011 the INEC announced that Jonathan had won the presidential election; the outcome prompted rioting in the northern regions, particularly in the towns of Kano and Kaduna, where protesters attacked the residences of Jonathan's supporters. Buhari, claiming that widespread electoral irregularities, particularly in the south of the country, had been observed, declared that the CPC would submit a legal challenge to the results and appealed for an end to the disturbances. However, increasing violence directed against Christians in the north, which had prompted reprisal attacks against Muslims, had by late April resulted in the deaths of more than 500 people and the displacement of some 48,000. On 25 April three people were killed in four bomb attacks in Maiduguri, which were attributed to Boko Haram. Together with the remaining federal legislative polls, the gubernatorial and state assembly elections proceeded in 24 of the 26 contested states on 26 April (owing to previously repeated polls in 10 states, after challenges to the April 2007 election results, the mandate of 10 Governors had not expired); despite the explosion of further bombs in Maiduguri, the elections were considered to have taken place relatively peacefully. On 28 April 2011 the final gubernatorial and state assembly elections took place in Kano and Bauchi States, where voting had been delayed for two days as a result of the unrest. According to preliminary results, PDP candidates were elected Governors in 18 states, the ACN in three and the ANPP in three; consequently the PDP controlled 23 of the 36 states overall, compared with 27 previously. On 8 May the CPC submitted a legal appeal against the election of Jonathan, on the grounds of alleged electoral malpractice in a number of regions.

Foreign Affairs

Nigeria has taken a leading role in African affairs and is a prominent member of the Economic Community of West African States (ECOWAS, see p. 257) and other regional organizations. The Nigerian Government has contributed a significant number of troops to the ECOWAS Monitoring Group (ECOMOG, see p. 261), which was deployed in Liberia from August 1990 in response to the conflict between government forces and rebels in that country. In 1993 Nigerian troops were dispatched to Sierra Leone, in response to a formal request by the Sierra Leonean Government for military assistance to repulse attacks by rebels in Liberia. Following the completion of the transition to civilian rule in Nigeria in May 1999, a phased withdrawal of Nigerian troops from Sierra Leone commenced. By the end of April 2000 all Nigerian troops belonging to ECOMOG had left Sierra Leone; however, Nigeria continued to contribute troops to the UN Mission in Sierra Leone (UNAMSIL). In September an official visit to Nigeria by the US President, Bill Clinton, the first by a US Head of State since 1978, provided for a number of new trade and development initiatives. After further full-scale conflict in Liberia in mid-2003 (see the chapter on Liberia), the Liberian President, Charles Taylor, finally accepted an offer of asylum from Obasanjo, following pressure from the international community, and took up residence in Calabar, in south-eastern

Nigeria, in early August. Some 1,500 Nigerian troops, which were deployed in the country, under an ECOWAS mandate, at the end of August, were instrumental in restoring peace and were incorporated into the replacement contingent, the UN Mission in Liberia (UNMIL, see p. 91), on 1 October. In October the Nigerian Government strongly protested at the US authorities' approval of the offer of a reward of some US $2m. for the arrest of Taylor (who had been indicted by the Special Court established in Sierra Leone to try war crime suspects). In March 2006 Nigeria announced that it had received a formal request from the new Liberian Government to extradite Taylor to the Special Court. Obasanjo agreed to return him to the Liberian authorities, but failed to comply with demands by the Chief Prosecutor of the Special Court and the USA to take him into custody. Taylor fled from his residence in Calabar, but was apprehended two days later in Borno State, near the border with Cameroon, and dispatched to Liberia, from where he was immediately extradited by UNMIL peace-keepers to the Special Court.

In 1991 the Nigerian Government claimed that Cameroonian security forces had annexed several Nigerian fishing settlements in Cross River State (in south-eastern Nigeria), following a long-standing border dispute, based on a 1913 agreement between Germany and the United Kingdom that ceded the Bakassi peninsula in the Gulf of Guinea (a region with significant petroleum reserves) to Cameroon. Subsequent negotiations between Nigerian and Cameroonian officials in an effort to resolve the dispute achieved little progress, and in February 1994 the Cameroonian Government announced that it was to submit the dispute for adjudication by the UN, the Organization of African Unity (OAU, now the African Union, see p. 183) and the International Court of Justice (ICJ). Subsequent reports of clashes between Cameroonian and Nigerian forces in the region prompted fears of a full-scale conflict between the two nations.

In March 1996 the ICJ ruled that Cameroon had failed to provide sufficient evidence to support its contention that Nigeria had instigated the border dispute, and ordered both nations to cease military operations in this respect, to withdraw troops to former positions, and to co-operate with a UN investigative mission that was to be dispatched to the region. In April, however, clashes continued, with each Government accusing the other of initiating the attacks. Although tension in the region remained high, diplomatic efforts to avoid further conflict were intensified in May; in that month a Cameroonian delegation visited Nigeria, while Abacha accepted an invitation to attend an OAU summit meeting, which was to be convened in Yaoundé in July. The UN investigative mission visited the Bakassi region in September. In May 1997 the Cameroonian Government denied further allegations by Nigeria that it had initiated hostilities; the UN requested that the Togolese President continue mediation efforts. Further clashes between Nigerian and Cameroonian forces were reported in December 1997 and February 1998. In March the Nigerian Government contested the jurisdiction of the ICJ to rule on the Bakassi issue, on the grounds that the two countries had agreed to settle the dispute through bilateral negotiations. In June, however, the Court pronounced that it held the necessary jurisdiction.

In October 2002 the ICJ finally ruled that the disputed Bakassi region was part of Cameroon, under the terms of the 1913 agreement. Obasanjo criticized the decision, in support of strong opposition expressed by the Nigerian majority inhabitants of the peninsula, although he subsequently pledged to abide by the ruling. In August 2003, following UN mediation, Nigeria and Cameroon finally adopted a framework agreement for the implementation of the ICJ's judgment; all military and administrative personnel were to be withdrawn from the Bakassi region, and a commission, comprising Nigerian, Cameroonian and UN officials, was to resolve outstanding issues for the redemarcation of boundaries between the two countries, in a process that was expected to continue for up to three years. In December the Nigerian Government ceded control of some 33 villages on its north-eastern border to Cameroon, but sovereignty over the disputed territory with petroleum resources remained under discussion by the commission. However, the Nigerian Government announced that the transfer of authority in the peninsula, scheduled for September 2004, had been postponed, citing technical difficulties in the final redemarcation of the joint border. Following a meeting in May 2005 between Obasanjo and the Head of State of Cameroon, conducted in Geneva, Switzerland, under the aegis of the UN Secretary-General, it was announced that the two sides had agreed to draft a new programme for Nigeria's withdrawal from the Bakassi peninsula. On 12 June 2006 an accord was signed, according to which Nigeria agreed to withdraw troops from the region within 60 days, and on 14 August Nigerian troops left the peninsula. Although the territory would remain under Nigerian control during the interim period, a full transfer of the Bakassi peninsula was to be completed by June 2008. The situation remained calm during October 2006 as steady progress was made in the demarcation of the border between the countries and agreement was reached on the relocation of 13 villages. However, in November 2007 21 Cameroonian soldiers were reported to have been killed by Nigerian troops, raising concerns that the security of the region was under threat. The Nigerian authorities denied involvement in the attack and local sources blamed a faction of MEND; however, a group styling itself the Liberators of the Southern Cameroons later claimed responsibility, alleging that the soldiers who had been killed had been implicated in illegal arms trading with Nigerian forces. Meanwhile, that same month the Nigerian Senate approved a motion to declare the handover of the Bakassi peninsula to be illegal and that no Nigerian territory could be ceded without amendments to the Constitution.

An agreement was reached in March 2008 which finalized the position of the two countries' long-disputed maritime boundary in the Gulf of Guinea, and the transfer of the Bakassi peninsula to Cameroon was scheduled for August that year. There was further violence in the peninsula in June, when five Cameroonian troops and a local government official, Felix Morfan, were abducted and later killed; soldiers from both Nigeria and Cameroon stationed in the region were placed on high alert, although it was not clear who was responsible for the murders. In the following month Nigerian gunmen opened fire on a Cameroonian security patrol in Bakassi: the attack was launched by the Niger Delta Defence and Security Council (NDDSC), a rebel group seeking to prevent the agreed transfer of the Bakassi peninsula from proceeding as planned. The NDDSC claimed responsibility for a further attack on a Cameroon military post in the same month, in which the Cameroonian military claimed to have killed 10 of the rebels. There were also reports in July that another militant group, the Bakassi Freedom Fighters, had merged its forces with the NDDSC in a final attempt to disrupt the handover scheduled for the following month. None the less, on 14 August the transfer was finally completed with an official flag-exchange ceremony which, for security reasons, took place in the city of Calabar, more than 100 miles from the peninsula. Formal delineation of the boundary began in December 2009.

CONSTITUTION AND GOVERNMENT

Under the terms of the Constitution of the Federal Republic of Nigeria, which entered into effect on 31 May 1999, executive power is vested in the President, who is the Head of State. The President, who is elected for a term of four years (and is restricted to two mandates), nominates a Vice-President and a Cabinet, subject to confirmation by the Senate. Legislative power is vested in the bicameral National Assembly, which comprises a 360-member House of Representatives and a 109-member Senate, and is elected by universal suffrage for a four-year term. Nigeria is a federation of 36 states, composed of 774 local government areas. The executive power of a state is vested in the Governor of that state, who is elected for a four-year term, and the legislative power in the House of Assembly of that state.

REGIONAL AND INTERNATIONAL CO-OPERATION

Nigeria is a member of the African Union (see p. 183) and of the Economic Community of West African States (see p. 257), which aims to promote trade and co-operation in West Africa.

Nigeria became a member of the UN in 1960 and was admitted to the World Trade Organization (WTO, see p. 430) in 1995. Nigeria participates in the Group of 15 (G15, see p. 447) and the Group of 77 (G77, see p. 447) developing countries, and is a member of the Organization of the Petroleum Exporting Countries (OPEC, see p. 405). In October 2009 Nigeria was elected as a non-permanent member of the UN Security Council for 2010 and 2011.

ECONOMIC AFFAIRS

In 2009, according to estimates by the World Bank, Nigeria's gross national income (GNI), measured at average 2007–09 prices, was US $175,774m., equivalent to $1,140 per head (or $1,980 per head on an international purchasing-power parity basis). During 2000–09, it was estimated, the population increased, in real terms, at an average annual rate of 2.4%, while gross domestic product (GDP) per head rose by 3.3%. Overall GDP increased, in real terms, at an average annual rate of 5.8% in 2000–09; growth was 2.9% in 2009.

Agriculture (including hunting, forestry and fishing) contributed an estimated 37.2% of GDP in 2009. An estimated 57.9% of the employed labour force were engaged in the sector in 2007. According to FAO estimates, agriculture engaged 24.1% of the total labour force in mid-2011. The principal cash crops are cocoa (which accounted for only 0.3% of total merchandise exports in 2006), rubber and oil palm. Staple food crops include cassava, yams, maize, millet, taro, rice and sorghum. Timber production, the raising of livestock (principally goats, sheep, cattle and poultry), and artisanal fisheries are also important. According to the African Development Bank (AfDB), agricultural GDP increased at an average annual rate of 4.8% in 2000–07. Growth in agricultural GDP was 6.2% in 2009.

Industry (including mining, manufacturing, construction and power) engaged an estimated 3.4% of the employed labour force in 2006, and contributed an estimated 33.9% of GDP in 2009. According to the AfDB, industrial GDP increased at an average annual rate of 3.7% in 2000–07. Sectoral growth declined by 0.4% in 2006, but increased by 3.2% in 2007.

Mining contributed an estimated 29.8% of GDP in 2009, although the sector engaged just 0.1% of the employed labour force in 2007. The principal mineral is petroleum, of which Nigeria is Africa's leading producer (providing an estimated 92.0% of total export earnings in 2008 and 34.5% of GDP in 2009). As a member of OPEC, Nigeria is subject to production quotas agreed by the Organization's Conference. Nigeria also possesses substantial deposits of natural gas and coal. In late 1999 the Nigerian Government commenced exports of liquefied natural gas, and by 2004 natural gas accounted for 8.8% of earnings. A 678-km pipeline, which would transport natural gas from the Escravos field, in Delta State, to Benin, Togo and Ghana, commenced operations in April 2007. In June 2009 it was announced that Russian state-controlled natural gas company Gazprom had signed an agreement investing some US $2,500m. in a joint venture with the Nigerian National Petroleum Corporation to explore and develop the country's gas reserves. Tin and iron ore are also mined, while there are plans to exploit deposits of uranium. The GDP of the mining sector was estimated by the IMF to have declined by an average of 0.1% per year in 1997–2001; mining GDP increased by 0.6% in 2001. According to AfDB, mining GDP declined by 1.0% in 2009.

Manufacturing contributed an estimated 2.5% of GDP in 2009, and engaged about 1.5% of the employed labour force in 2007. The principal sectors are food-processing, brewing, petroleum-refining, iron and steel, motor vehicles (using imported components), textiles, cigarettes, footwear, pharmaceuticals, pulp and paper, and cement. According to the AfDB, manufacturing GDP increased at an average annual rate of 7.3% in 2000–07. Manufacturing GDP increased by 8.5% in 2009.

The construction sector contributed an estimated 1.4% of GDP in 2009, and engaged 0.6% of the employed labour force in 2007. According to the AfDB, construction GDP increased by 12.9% in 2009.

Energy is derived principally from natural gas, which provided some 67.2% of electricity in 2007, and hydroelectric power (27.9%); petroleum provided 4.9%. Mineral fuels comprised 1.6% of the value of merchandise imports in 2008.

The services sector contributed an estimated 28.9% of GDP in 2009, and engaged 39.1% of the employed labour force in 2007. According to the AfDB, the GDP of the services sector increased at an average annual rate of 9.6% in 2000–07. The GDP of the services sector increased by 2.0% in 2007.

In 2009 Nigeria recorded a trade surplus of US $29,042m., and there was a surplus of $21,659m. on the current account of the balance of payments. In 2008 the principal source of imports (8.1%) was the USA; the other major supplier was Germany. The USA was also the principal market for exports (42.3%) in that year; the other significant purchaser was Brazil. The principal export in 2008 was petroleum. The principal imports in 2008 were machinery and transport equipment, basic manufacturers, chemicals and related products, and food and live animals.

Nigeria's overall budget surplus for 2009 was an estimated ₦1,338,000m., equivalent to around 5.2% of GDP. Nigeria's general government gross debt was ₦ 3,887,840m. in 2009, equivalent to 15.5% of GDP. The country's external debt totalled US $11,221m. at the end of 2008, of which $3,590m. was public and publicly guaranteed debt. In 2007 the cost of debt-servicing was equivalent to 1.4% of the value of exports of goods, services and income. The annual rate of inflation averaged 12.4% in 2003–10; consumer prices increased by 13.2% in 2009 and by 12.9% in 2010. An estimated 4.5% of the labour force were unemployed at the end of 1997.

Nigeria is one of Africa's most powerful economies, but, despite considerable agricultural and mineral resources, political instability has severely impeded economic reform, and it is classified as a low-income country by the World Bank. High levels of external debt continued to cause concern in the early 2000s; however, Nigeria settled its entire debt to the 'Paris Club' in early 2006, under a debt-reduction agreement that was part of an IMF-approved government reform programme. From 2006 an escalation of unrest in the Niger Delta region, with a series of attacks against petroleum pipelines and seizures of foreign nationals as hostages, threatened national stability. Militant groups in the region continued to demand the withdrawal of all foreign enterprises exploiting the country's resources, and the violence resulted in frequent disruptions and partial suspensions in oil production. Meanwhile, the West African Gas Pipeline became operational in April 2007. In late 2009 the IMF concluded that the adverse affects of the international financial crisis on Nigeria's economy had been mitigated by previous reforms, particularly a fiscal regulation (introduced in 2004), whereby excess oil revenue generated at times of high prices was transferred to a savings fund. However, continuing insurgent activity in the Niger Delta, together with production quotas imposed by the Organization of the Petroleum Exporting Countries (see p. 405), restricted the level of oil production in 2009. Despite earlier reforms in the banking sector, deteriorating asset quality had increased pressure on the system, necessitating the Central Bank's intervention to prevent bank failures. Goodluck Ebele Jonathan, who became Head of State following the death of President Umaru Yar'Adua in May 2010, undertook further stabilization measures, including the establishment of a new National Economic Team entasked with economic recovery. In the same month it was announced that the Government had secured a concessionary loan of US $915m. from the World Bank, which was to finance infrastructural development over a five-year period. Despite the efforts of the authorities to negotiate with the main insurgent group, the Movement for the Emancipation of the Niger Delta, the militia ended a cease-fire in January 2010, and attacks on oil installations and kidnappings continued in the region later that year, prompting concerns that foreign investors would withdraw from the country. In August the Government announced a programme of privatization of the successor companies of the Power Holding Company of Nigeria, as part of extensive reforms to address long-standing energy shortages. In February 2011 the IMF issued a generally favourable assessment of Nigeria's economy, which, however, stated that the authorities' monetary policy had resulted in high inflation and a depletion of international reserves; the Governor of the Central Bank contested the Fund's conclusions, and attributed the reduction in reserves to investment in new power projects and oil installations. Revenue from oil exports had risen by 46% in 2010, owing to an increase in international oil prices and higher output, and the oil sector contributed significantly to overall GDP growth of more than 8% in that year (according to the IMF).

PUBLIC HOLIDAYS

2012: 1 January (New Year's Day), 4 February* (Mouloud, Birth of the Prophet), 6–9 April (Easter), 18 August* (Id al-Fitr, end of Ramadan), 1 October (National Day), 26 October* (Id al-Kabir, Feast of the Sacrifice), 25–26 December (Christmas).

* These holidays are dependent on the Islamic lunar calendar, and may vary by one or two days from the dates given.

NIGERIA

Statistical Survey

Sources (unless otherwise stated): National Bureau of Statistics, Plot 762, Independence Avenue, Central Business District, PMB 127, Garki, Abuja; tel. (9) 2731085; fax (9) 2731084; internet www.nigerianstat.gov.ng; Central Bank of Nigeria, Central Business District, PMB 187, Garki, Abuja; tel. (9) 61639701; fax (9) 61636012; e-mail info@cenbank.org; internet www.cenbank.org.

Area and Population

AREA, POPULATION AND DENSITY

Area (sq km)	909,890*
Population (census results)	
28–30 November 1991†	88,992,220
21–27 March 2006	
Males	71,345,488
Females	69,086,302
Total	140,431,790
Population (UN estimates at mid-year)‡	
2009	154,728,895
2010	158,258,917
2011	161,796,038
Density (per sq km) at mid-2011	177.8

* 351,310 sq miles.
† Revised 15 September 2001.
‡ Source: UN, *World Population Prospects: The 2008 Revision*.

POPULATION BY AGE AND SEX
(UN estimates at mid-2011)

	Males	Females	Total
0–14	34,583,851	33,627,624	68,211,475
15–64	44,210,742	44,276,277	88,487,019
65 and over	2,348,053	2,749,491	5,097,544
Total	81,142,646	80,653,392	161,796,038

Source: UN, *World Population Prospects: The 2008 Revision*.

STATES
(population at 2006 census)

	Area (sq km)	Population	Density (per sq km)	Capital
Abia	4,900	2,845,380	581	Umuahia
Adamawa	38,700	3,178,950	82	Yola
Akwa Ibom	6,900	3,902,051	556	Uyo
Anambra	4,865	4,177,828	859	Awka
Bauchi	49,119	4,653,066	95	Bauchi
Bayelsa	9,059	1,704,515	188	Yenogoa
Benue	30,800	4,253,641	138	Makurdi
Borno	72,609	4,171,104	57	Maiduguri
Cross River	21,787	2,892,988	133	Calabar
Delta	17,108	4,112,445	240	Asaba
Ebonyi	6,400	2,176,947	340	Abakaliki
Edo	19,187	3,233,366	169	Benin City
Ekiti	5,435	2,398,957	441	Ado-Ekiti
Enugu	7,534	3,267,837	434	Enugu
Gombe	17,100	2,365,040	138	Gombe
Imo	5,288	3,927,563	743	Owerri
Jigawa	23,287	4,361,002	187	Dutse
Kaduna	42,481	6,113,503	144	Kaduna
Kano	20,280	9,401,288	464	Kano
Katsina	23,561	5,801,584	246	Katsina
Kebbi	36,985	3,256,541	88	Birnin Kebbi
Kogi	27,747	3,314,043	119	Lokoja
Kwara	35,705	2,365,353	66	Ilorin
Lagos	3,671	9,113,605	2,483	Ikeja
Nassarawa	28,735	1,869,377	65	Lafia
Niger	68,925	3,954,772	57	Minna
Ogun	16,400	3,751,140	229	Abeokuta
Ondo	15,820	3,460,877	219	Akure
Osun	9,026	3,416,959	379	Oshogbo
Oyo	26,500	5,580,894	211	Ibadan
Plateau	27,147	3,206,531	118	Jos
Rivers	10,575	5,198,716	492	Port Harcourt
Sokoto	27,825	3,702,676	133	Sokoto
Taraba	56,282	2,294,800	41	Jalingo
Yobe	46,609	2,321,339	50	Damaturu
Zamfara	37,931	3,278,873	86	Gusau
Federal Capital Territory (Abuja)	7,607	1,406,239	185	Abuja
Total	909,890	140,431,790	154	—

PRINCIPAL TOWNS
(unrevised census of November 1991)

Lagos (federal capital)*	5,195,247	Enugu	407,756
Kano	2,166,554	Oyo	369,894
Ibadan	1,835,300	Warri	363,382
Kaduna	933,642	Abeokuta	352,735
Benin City	762,719	Onitsha	350,280
Port Harcourt	703,421	Sokoto	329,639
Maiduguri	618,278	Okene	312,775
Zaria	612,257	Calabar	310,839
Ilorin	532,089	Katsina	259,315
Jos	510,300	Oshogbo	250,951
Aba	500,183	Akure	239,124
Ogbomosho	433,030	Bauchi	206,537

* Federal capital moved to Abuja (population 107,069) in December 1991.

Mid-2010 ('000 incl. suburbs, UN estimates): Lagos 10,578; Kano 3,395; Ibadan 2,837; Kaduna 1,561; Benin City 1,302; Port Harcourt 1,104; Ogbomosho 1,032; Maiduguri 970; Zaria 963 (Source: UN, *World Urbanization Prospects: The 2009 Revision*).

BIRTHS AND DEATHS
(annual averages, UN estimates)

	1995–2000	2000–05	2005–10
Birth rate (per 1,000)	43.5	41.8	40.1
Death rate (per 1,000)	18.8	17.4	16.5

Source: UN, *World Population Prospects: The 2008 Revision*.

Life expectancy (years at birth, WHO estimates): 49 (males 49; females 49) in 2008 (Source: WHO, *World Health Statistics*).

NIGERIA

EMPLOYMENT
('000 persons aged 14 years and over)

	2005	2006	2007
Agriculture, hunting, forestry and fishing	29,017	30,682	31,278
Mining and quarrying	69	73	81
Manufacturing	908	960	821
Electricity, gas and water	427	451	n.a.
Construction	273	289	n.a.
Wholesale and retail trade; repairs of motor vehicles and motorcycles and personal and household articles	104	110	140
Hotels and restaurants	96	102	130
Transport, storage and communications	416	440	1,108
Financial intermediation	281	297	303
Real estate, renting and business activities	60	64	81
Public administration, defence and compulsory social security	5,067	5,358	5,338
Education	9,473	10,017	10,444
Health and social welfare	296	313	308
Other community, social and personal service activities	2,999	3,171	3,280
Total employed	49,486	52,327	54,030

Mid-2011 (estimates in '000): Agriculture, etc. 12,203; Total labour force 50,556 (Source: FAO).

Health and Welfare

KEY INDICATORS

Total fertility rate (children per woman, 2008)	5.3
Under-5 mortality rate (per 1,000 live births, 2008)	186
HIV/AIDS (% of persons aged 15–49, 2007)	3.1
Physicians (per 1,000 head, 2003)	0.28
Hospital beds (per 1,000 head, 2004)	0.5
Health expenditure (2007): US $ per head (PPP)	131
Health expenditure (2007): % of GDP	6.6
Health expenditure (2007): public (% of total)	25.3
Access to water (% of persons, 2008)	58
Access to sanitation (% of persons, 2008)	32
Total carbon dioxide emissions ('000 metric tons, 2007)	95,194.4
Carbon dioxide emissions per head (metric tons, 2007)	0.6
Human Development Index (2010): ranking	142
Human Development Index (2010): value	0.423

For sources and definitions, see explanatory note on p. vi.

Agriculture

PRINCIPAL CROPS
('000 metric tons)

	2006	2007	2008
Wheat	71	44	53
Rice, paddy	4,042	3,186	4,179
Maize	7,100	6,724	7,525
Millet	7,705	8,090	9,064
Sorghum	9,866	9,058	9,318
Potatoes	838	662	1,105
Sweet potatoes	3,462	2,432	3,318
Cassava	45,721	43,410	44,582
Taro (Coco yam)	5,473	4,996	5,387
Yams	36,720	31,136	35,017
Sugar cane	987	1,506	1,500*
Cow peas, dry	3,040	2,800*	2,916
Cashew nuts	636	660*	660*
Kolanuts*	86	88	88
Soybeans (Soya beans)	605	580†	591
Groundnuts, with shell	3,825	3,836*	3,900*
Coconuts	225	226	234
Oil palm fruit*	8,300	8,500	8,500
Sesame seed†	100	105	110
Melonseed	483	490	493

—continued	2006	2007	2008
Tomatoes	896*	1,079	1,701
Chillies and peppers, green*	722	723	725
Onions and shallots, green*	221	225	226
Onions, dry*	616	618	621
Carrots and turnips*	240	243	243
Okra	1,000*	1,280	1,039
Maize, green*	577	579	579
Plantains	2,785	2,991*	2,727
Citrus fruits*	3,300	3,325	3,400
Guavas, mangoes and mangosteens*	732	734	734
Pineapples*	895	900	900
Papayas*	759	765	765
Cocoa beans	485	500†	500*
Ginger	134	138*	140*
Tobacco, unmanufactured	14	9	12
Natural rubber*	143	143	143

* FAO estimate(s).
† Unofficial figure(s).

2009: Soybeans (Soya beans) 610 (unofficial figure).

Aggregate production ('000 metric tons, may include official, semi-official or estimated data): Total cereals 28,864 in 2006, 27,171 in 2007, 30,209 in 2008–09; Total roots and tubers 92,214 in 2006, 82,636 in 2007, 89,409 in 2008–09; Total vegetables (incl. melons) 9,923 in 2006, 9,609 in 2007, 10,839 in 2008–09; Total fruits (excl. melons) 9,671 in 2006, 9,799 in 2007, 9,502 in 2008–09.

Source: FAO.

LIVESTOCK
('000 head, year ending September)

	2006	2007	2008
Horses*	207	208	208
Asses*	1,050	1,050	1,050
Cattle	16,066*	16,153	16,293
Camels*	19	19	19
Pigs	6,390*	6,642	6,908
Sheep	32,314*	33,080	33,874
Goats	51,224*	52,488	53,800
Chickens	158,400*	166,127	175,000*

* FAO estimate(s).

2009: Cattle 16,400 (FAO estimate).

Source: FAO.

LIVESTOCK PRODUCTS
('000 metric tons, FAO estimates)

	2006	2007	2008
Cattle meat	284.1	287.5	293.8
Sheep meat	141.4	144.7	145.3
Goat meat	264.3	270.7	270.7
Pig meat	201.3	209.3	217.6
Chicken meat	232.1	243.3	243.3
Game meat	120	121	121
Cows' milk	463	468	469
Hen eggs	526	553	553

2009: Cattle meat 298.4; Pig meat 217.6.

Source: FAO.

Forestry

ROUNDWOOD REMOVALS
('000 cubic metres, excluding bark, FAO estimates)

	2007	2008	2009
Sawlogs, veneer logs and logs for sleepers	7,100	7,100	7,100
Pulpwood	39	39	39
Other industrial wood	2,279	2,279	2,279
Fuel wood	62,000	62,389	62,793
Total	71,418	71,807	72,211

Source: FAO.

SAWNWOOD PRODUCTION
('000 cubic metres, including railway sleepers)

	1995	1996	1997
Broadleaved (hardwood)	2,356	2,178	2,000

1998–2009: Broadleaved (hardwood) production as in 1997.
Source: FAO.

Fishing

('000 metric tons, live weight)

	2006	2007	2008
Capture	552.3	530.4	541.4
Tilapias	30.5	38.9	47.6
Elephant snout fishes	18.7	26.1	22.4
Torpedo-shaped catfishes	14.9	14.3	32.8
Sea catfishes	23.5	18.2	20.8
West African croakers	12.5	10.0	11.3
Sardinellas	72.7	65.9	3.5
Bonga shad	22.6	21.7	22.1
Southern pink shrimp	11.9	10.9	11.4
Other shrimps and prawns	16.1	11.4	1.9
Aquaculture	84.6	85.1	143.2
Total catch	636.9	615.5	684.6

Source: FAO.

Mining

(metric tons, unless otherwise indicated)

	2007	2008	2009
Coal, bituminous	5,30,000	5,00,000	4,50,000
Kaolin	100,000	100,000	1,00,000
Gypsum	579,000	300,000	3,00,000
Crude petroleum ('000 barrels)	803,000	768,800	780,348
Tin concentrates*	180	185	180

* Metal content.
Source: US Geological Survey.

Natural gas (million cu m, excl. gas flared or recycled): 35,014 in 2007; 35,027 in 2008; 24,899 in 2009 (Source: BP, *Statistical Review of World Energy*).

Industry

SELECTED PRODUCTS
('000 metric tons, unless otherwise indicated)

	2005	2006	2007
Palm oil*	1,170	1,287	1,300†
Wheat flour‡	1,564	1,730	1,598
Beer of barley*†	1,180	1,253	1,350
Plywood ('000 cubic metres)‡	55	55	55
Wood pulp*†	23	23	23
Paper and paperboard*†	19	19	19
Raw sugar‡	n.a.	30	55
Liquefied petroleum gas ('000 barrels)	700†	n.a.	16
Motor spirit—petrol ('000 barrels)	14,800†	8,500†	2,450
Kerosene ('000 barrels)	10,100†	6,100†	2,550
Gas-diesel (distillate fuel) oil ('000 barrels)	15,800†	9,400†	4,645
Residual fuel oils ('000 barrels)	19,200†	14,400†	6,670
Cement†	2,700	3,300	4,700
Electric energy (million kWh)‡	20,468	23,110	22,978

* Source: FAO.
† Estimate(s).
‡ Source: UN Industrial Commodity Statistics Database.
Source (unless otherwise indicated): US Geological Survey.

2008 ('000 metric tons, unless otherwise indicated): Palm oil 1,330 (FAO estimate); Beer of barley 1,540 (unofficial figure); Liquefied petroleum gas ('000 barrels) 300; Motor spirit—petrol ('000 barrels) 5,958; Kerosene ('000 barrels) 5,179; Gas-diesel (distillate fuel) oil ('000 barrels) 8,698; Residual fuel oils ('000 barrels) 9,629; Cement 5,000 (Sources: FAO and US Geological Survey).

2009 ('000 metric tons, unless otherwise indicated): Palm oil 1,380 (FAO estimate); Beer of barley 1,600 (unofficial figure); Liquefied petroleum gas ('000 barrels) 294; Motor spirit—petrol ('000 barrels) 3,102; Kerosene ('000 barrels) 2,530; Gas-diesel (distillate fuel) oil ('000 barrels) 4,168; Residual fuel oils ('000 barrels) 4,060; Cement 5,000 (Sources: FAO and US Geological Survey).

Finance

CURRENCY AND EXCHANGE RATES

Monetary Units
100 kobo = 1 naira (₦).

Sterling, Dollar and Euro Equivalents (31 August 2010)
£1 sterling = 229.196 naira;
US $1 = 148.790 naira;
€1 = 188.666 naira;
1,000 naira = £4.36 = $6.72 = €5.30.

Average Exchange Rate (naira per US $)
2007 125.808
2008 118.546
2009 148.902

FEDERAL BUDGET
(₦ '000 million)

Revenue	2006	2007*	2008†
Petroleum revenue	2,166	1,734	2,411
Crude receipts, cash calls (net) and derivation	926	683	1,105
Profit tax and royalty	989	851	1,153
Non-petroleum revenue	258	476	484
Import and excise duties	80	111	131
Companies' income tax	114	156	182
Value-added tax	31	42	51
Total	2,424	2,211	2,895

NIGERIA

Statistical Survey

Expenditure	2006	2007*	2008†
Recurrent expenditure	1,169	1,471	1,600
Goods and services	888	1,139	1,210
Personnel and pension	665	864	943
Overhead cost	223	275	267
Interest payments	187	208	203
Transfers	94	141	188
Capital expenditure	495	705	850
Total	**1,664**	**2,176**	**2,451**

* Estimates.
† Projected.

Source: IMF, *Nigeria: 2007 Article IV Consultation—Staff Report; Staff Supplement and Statement; Public Information Notice on the Executive Board Discussion; and Statement by the Executive Director for Nigeria* (February 2008).

2007 (₦ '000 million, revised figures): *Revenue:* Total revenue 2,311 (Petroleum revenue 1,767, Non-petroleum revenue 544). *Expenditure:* Total expenditure 2,425 (Recurrent expenditure 1,593, Capital expenditure 833) (Source: IMF, *Nigeria: 2010 - Article IV Consultation—Staff Report; Debt Sustainability Analysis; Informational Annex; Public Information Notice on the Executive Board Discussion; and Statement by the Executive Director for Nigeria*—February 2011).

2008 (₦ '000 million, revised figures): *Revenue:* Total revenue 3,029 (Petroleum revenue 2,539, Non-petroleum revenue 490). *Expenditure:* Total expenditure 2,784 (Recurrent expenditure 2,075, Capital expenditure 710) (Source: IMF, *Nigeria: 2010 - Article IV Consultation—Staff Report; Debt Sustainability Analysis; Informational Annex; Public Information Notice on the Executive Board Discussion; and Statement by the Executive Director for Nigeria*—February 2011).

2009 (₦ '000 million, revised figures): *Revenue:* Total revenue 1,614 (Petroleum revenue 1,079, Non-petroleum revenue 535). *Expenditure:* Total expenditure 2,952 (Recurrent expenditure 2,294, Capital expenditure 658) (Source: IMF, *Nigeria: 2010 - Article IV Consultation—Staff Report; Debt Sustainability Analysis; Informational Annex; Public Information Notice on the Executive Board Discussion; and Statement by the Executive Director for Nigeria*—February 2011).

2010 (₦ '000 million, budget projections): *Revenue:* Total revenue 2,852 (Petroleum revenue 2,193, Non-petroleum revenue 659). *Expenditure:* Total expenditure 4,602 (Recurrent expenditure 3,444, Capital expenditure 1,158) (Source: IMF, *Nigeria: 2010 - Article IV Consultation—Staff Report; Debt Sustainability Analysis; Informational Annex; Public Information Notice on the Executive Board Discussion; and Statement by the Executive Director for Nigeria*—February 2011).

INTERNATIONAL RESERVES
(US $ million at 31 December)

	2008	2009	2010
Gold (national valuation)	0	0	0
IMF special drawing rights	1	2,380	2,580
Foreign exchange	53,000	42,382	32,339
Total	**53,002**	**44,763**	**34,919**

Source: IMF, *International Financial Statistics*.

MONEY SUPPLY
(₦ '000 million at 31 December)

	2007	2008	2009
Currency outside depository corporations	732.9	892.9	927.2
Transferable deposits	2,431.5	3,785.3	3,575.5
Other deposits	2,686.8	4,247.8	5,708.0
Broad money	**5,851.3**	**8,926.0**	**10,210.7**

Source: IMF, *International Financial Statistics*.

COST OF LIVING
(Consumer Price Index at May; base: May 2003 = 100)

	2008	2009	2010
Food (excl. beverages)	174.2	201.6	227.9
Alcoholic beverages, tobacco and kola	166.1	165.7	172.8
Clothing (incl. footwear)	149.8	159.6	174.8
Rent, fuel and light	207.4	228.7	247.5
Household goods and maintenance	158.1	167.6	193.7
Medical care and health	153.0	167.5	177.0
Transport	168.6	184.0	203.8
Education	181.6	223.8	263.4
All items (incl. others)	**177.6**	**201.0**	**227.0**

NATIONAL ACCOUNTS
(₦ '000 million at current basic prices)

Expenditure on the Gross Domestic Product

	2007	2008	2009
Government final consumption expenditure	1,642.0	1,400.2	1,434.8
Private final consumption expenditure	16,135.9	17,166.5	17,930.8
Increase in stocks	1.8	2.0	1.9
Gross fixed capital formation	1,915.3	2,030.5	2,442.7
Total domestic expenditure	**19,695.1**	**20,599.2**	**21,810.2**
Exports of goods and non-factor services	7,091.3	9,799.7	10,063.3
Less Imports of goods and non-petroleum services	5,912.2	4,973.9	6,383.5
GDP in basic prices	**20,874.2**	**25,424.9**	**25,490.0**
GDP in constant basic 1990 prices	648.4	735.8	n.a.

Gross Domestic Product by Economic Activity

	2007	2008	2009
Agriculture, hunting, forestry and fishing	6,757.9	7,981.4	9,193.9
Mining and quarrying	7,564.5	9,133.9	7,359.9
Crude petroleum	7,533.0	9,097.8	7,319.3
Manufacturing	520.9	585.6	612.6
Electricity, gas and water	45.8	52.7	62.2
Construction	266.5	306.6	347.7
Wholesale and retail trade	3,044.8	3,503.2	4,091.8
Hotels and restaurants	72.8	86.1	99.0
Transport, storage and communications	719.7	731.8	765.6
Finance, insurance	340.9	392.0	444.2
Real estate and business services	925.6	1,064.4	1,213.0
Government services	193.4	223.4	255.4
Other community, social and personal services	204.6	235.3	267.4
GDP at factor cost	**20,657.3**	**24,296.3**	**24,712.7**
Indirect taxes	247.8	1,164.2	806.0
Less Subsidies	31.0	35.6	33.3
Statistical discrepancy	—	—	4.6
Total GDP in basic prices	**20,874.2**	**25,424.9**	**25,490.0**

BALANCE OF PAYMENTS
(US $ million)

	2007	2008	2009
Exports of goods f.o.b.	66,040	83,587	59,318
Imports of goods f.o.b.	−28,291	−39,844	−30,276
Trade balance	**37,748**	**43,743**	**29,042**
Exports of services	1,443	2,264	2,228
Imports of services	−17,663	−23,755	−17,567
Balance on goods and services	**21,528**	**25,252**	**13,702**
Other income received	2,564	2,352	1,036
Other income paid	−14,311	−14,702	−11,055
Balance on goods, services and income	**9,780**	**9,902**	**3,683**

NIGERIA

Statistical Survey

—continued	2007	2008	2009
Current transfers received	18,013	19,275	18,440
Current transfers paid	–150	–531	–464
Current balance	27,643	28,646	21,659
Direct investment abroad	–471	–356	–140
Direct investment from abroad	6,035	5,487	5,787
Portfolio investment assets	–1,843	–4,729	–912
Portfolio investment liabilities	2,643	1,326	724
Other investment assets	–5,783	–7,320	–1,828
Other investment liabilities	818	554	2,937
Net errors and omissions	–20,083	–21,952	–38,743
Overall balance	8,959	1,657	–10,515

Source: IMF, *International Financial Statistics*.

External Trade

PRINCIPAL COMMODITIES
(₦ '000 million)

Imports c.i.f.	2006	2007	2008
Food and live animals	498.7	777.1	288.9
Beverages and tobacco	14.4	31.0	18.7
Crude materials, inedible (excluding fuels)	29.0	49.1	49.9
Mineral fuels	84.3	73.5	52.4
Chemicals and related products	473.1	684.7	400.9
Basic manufactures	497.9	942.0	791.5
Machinery and transport equipment	1,208.1	1,427.1	1,525.5
Miscellaneous manufactured articles	105.7	123.7	156.6
Total (incl. others)	2,922.2	4,127.7	3,299.1

Exports f.o.b.	2006	2007	2008
Mineral products (mainly petroleum)	7,422.3	6,531.9	8,804.5
Total (incl. others)	6,621.3	7,555.1	9,568.9

PRINCIPAL TRADING PARTNERS
(₦ '000 million)*

Imports c.i.f.	2006	2007	2008
Brazil	58.6	142.3	57.7
France (incl. Monaco)	128.7	158.6	155.7
Germany	163.2	201.2	223.0
Italy	99.7	105.1	85.4
Japan	96.6	95.4	88.8
Netherlands	90.1	129.5	52.2
South Africa	51.5	81.7	59.9
Spain	24.3	28.7	9.7
Togo	8.4	49.6	97.4
United Kingdom	344.6	218.8	143.6
USA	455.2	623.6	267.7
Total (incl. others)	2,922.1	4,127.7	3,299.1

Exports f.o.b.	2006	2007	2008
Brazil	319.5	441.2	620.8
Cameroon	136.4	66.3	—
Canada	291.7	141.0	175.9
Côte d'Ivoire	273.3	151.2	135.5
France (incl. Monaco)	427.5	251.4	394.2
Gabon	—	—	214.3
Germany	0.5	159.9	148.0
Guinea-Bissau	—	—	109.3
Italy	187.4	74.5	314.3
Japan	142.0	45.8	34.5
Netherlands	195.0	22.3	385.4
Senegal	—	9.4	306.1
South Africa	135.9	176.3	1.4
Spain	603.0	91.6	327.3
United Kingdom	4.1	36.1	156.9
USA	3,400.6	3,207.7	4,051.3
Total (incl. others)	7,555.1	6,881.5	9,568.9

* Imports by country of consignment; exports by country of destination.

Transport

RAILWAYS
(traffic)

	2006	2007	2008
Passenger journeys ('000)	708.8	1,478.7	1,996.3
Passenger-km (million)	256.6	535.3	722.7
Freight ('000 metric tons)	41,219	31,405	47,409
Net freight ton-km (million)	34.3	26.0	41.1

ROAD TRAFFIC
(motor vehicles in use, estimates)

	1995	1996
Passenger cars	820,069	885,080
Buses and coaches	1,284,251	903,449
Lorries and vans	673,425	912,579
Motorcycles and mopeds	481,345	441,651

2007 ('000 motor vehicles in use): Passenger cars 4,560; Motorcycles and mopeds 3,040.

Source: IRF, *World Road Statistics*.

SHIPPING

Merchant Fleet
(registered at 31 December)

	2007	2008	2009
Number of vessels	379	470	516
Displacement ('000 grt)	407.7	611.6	679.2

Source: IHS Fairplay, *World Fleet Statistics*.

International Sea-borne Freight Traffic
(estimates, '000 metric tons)

	1991	1992	1993
Goods loaded	82,768	84,797	86,993
Goods unloaded	10,960	11,143	11,346

Source: UN Economic Commission for Africa, *African Statistical Yearbook*.

NIGERIA

CIVIL AVIATION
(traffic on scheduled services)

	2004	2005	2006
Kilometres flown (million)	12	14	21
Passengers carried ('000)	540	748	1,308
Passenger-km (million)	683	935	1,767
Total ton-km (million)	64	89	161

Source: UN, *Statistical Yearbook*.

2007: Passengers carried ('000) 1,363.4 (Source: World Bank, World Development Indicators database).

2008: Passengers carried ('000) 1,460.9 (Source: World Bank, World Development Indicators database).

Tourism

ARRIVALS BY NATIONALITY*

Country	2006	2007	2008
Benin	432,537	740,367	822,695
Cameroon	117,818	201,586	223,984
Chad	93,584	160,290	178,100
France	68,058	116,704	129,668
Germany	66,383	113,842	126,488
Ghana	22,755	39,078	43,420
Italy	72,152	123,697	137,473
Liberia	118,141	202,638	225,153
Niger	642,724	1,101,959	1,224,399
Sudan	69,350	118,916	132,130
Total (incl. others)	3,055,800	5,238,545	5,820,497

* Figures refer to arrival at frontiers of visitors from abroad, including same-day visitors (excursionists).

Tourism receipts (US $ million, incl. passenger transport): 90 in 2006; 337 in 2007; 586 in 2008.

Source: World Tourism Organization.

Communications Media

	2007	2008	2009
Telephones ('000 main lines in use)	1,579.7	1,307.6	1,482.0
Mobile cellular telephones ('000 in use)	40,395.6	62,988.5	74,518.3
Internet users ('000)	10,000.8	23,982.3	43,989.4
Broadband subscribers ('000)	53.6	67.8	82.0

Radio receivers ('000 in use): 23,500 in 1997.
Television receivers ('000 in use): 12,000 in 2001.
Book production (titles, including pamphlets): 1,314 in 1995.
Daily newspapers: 25 (estimated average circulation 2,760,000 copies) in 1998.
Personal computers: 1,200,000 (8.5 per 1,000 persons) in 2005.

Sources: International Telecommunication Union; UNESCO Institute for Statistics.

Education

(2008, unless otherwise specified)

	Institutions	Teachers	Males	Females	Total
Primary*	54,434	586,930	11,483,943	9,810,575	21,294,518
Secondary*	18,238	270,650	3,682,141	2,943,802	6,625,943
Poly/Monotechnic†	178	16,499	n.a.	n.a.	237,708
University	95	23,535†	n.a.	n.a.	724,856†

* Provisional.
† 2005 figure.

Pupil-teacher ratio (primary education, UNESCO estimate): 46.3 in 2006/07 (Source: UNESCO Institute for Statistics).

Adult literacy rate (UNESCO estimates): 60.1% (males 71.5%; females 48.8%) in 2008 (Source: UNESCO Institute for Statistics).

Directory

Federal Government

HEAD OF STATE

President and Commander-in-Chief of the Armed Forces, Minister responsible for Power: Dr GOODLUCK EBELE JONATHAN (sworn in 6 May 2010; re-elected 16 April 2011).

Vice-President: NAMADI SAMBO.

CABINET
(May 2011)

Attorney-General and Minister of Justice: MOHAMMED BELLO ADOKE.
Minister of Agriculture: Prof. SHEIKH AHMED ABDULLAH.
Minister of Aviation: FIDELIA NJEZE.
Minister of Commerce and Industry: JIBRIL MARTINS KUYE.
Minister of Culture and Tourism: ABUBAKAR SADIQ A. MOHAMMED.
Minister of Defence: Chief ADETOKUNBO KAYODE.
Minister of Education: Prof. RUQAYYATU RUFA'I.
Minister of the Environment: JOHN OGAR ODEY.
Minister of the Federal Capital Territory: BALA MUHAMMED.
Minister of Finance: OLUSEGUN OLUTOYIN AGANGA.
Minister of Foreign Affairs: HENRY ODEIN AJUMOGOBIA.
Minister of Health: Prof. CHRISTIAN OTU ONYEBUCHI.
Minister of Information and Communication: LABARAN MAKU.
Minister of Labour and Productivity and Acting Minister of the Interior: CHUKWUEMEKA NGOZI WOGU.
Minister of Lands, Housing and Urban Development: NDUESE ESSIEN.
Minister of Mines and Steel Development: MUSA MOHAMMED SADA.
Minister of Niger Delta Affairs: PETER GODSDAY ORUBEBE.
Minister of Petroleum Resources: DEZIANI ALISON-MADUEKE.
Minister of Police Affairs: HUMPHREY ABBAH.
Minister of Science and Technology: Prof. MUHAMMED K. ABUBAKAR.
Minister of Special Duties and Acting Minister of Sports: Prof. TAOHEED ADEDOJA.
Minister of Transport: YUSUF SULAIMAN.
Minister of Water Resources: OBADIAH ANDO.
Minister of Women's Affairs: IYOM JOSEPHINE ANENIH.
Minister of Works: SANUSI M. DAGASH.
Minister of Youth Development: AKINLABI OLASUNKANMI.
Minister, Chairman of the National Planning Commission: Dr SHAMSUDEEN USMAN.

There were, in addition, 10 Ministers of State.

MINISTRIES

Office of the Head of State: New Federal Secretariat Complex, Shehu Shagari Way, Central Area District, Abuja; tel. (9) 5233536.
Ministry of Agriculture: Area 11, Secretariat Complex, Garki, PMB 135, Abuja; tel. (9) 3141931; e-mail aruma@nigeria.gov.ng.
Ministry of Aviation: New Federal Secretariat Complex, Shehu Shagari Way, Central Area District, PMB 146, Abuja; tel. (9) 5237487.

NIGERIA

Directory

Ministry of Commerce and Industry: Area 1, Secretariat Complex, Garki, PMB 88, Abuja; e-mail fmi@fmind.gov.ng; tel. (9) 2341662.

Ministry of Culture and Tourism: Phase II Federal Secretariat, Block A, 1st Floor, Shehu Shagari Way, Abuja; tel. (9) 2348311; fax (9) 23408297; e-mail akayode@nigeria.gov.ng; internet www.visit-nigeria.gov.ng.

Ministry of Defence: Ship House, Central Area, Abuja; tel. (9) 2340534; fax (9) 2340714; e-mail mamed@nigeria.gov.ng.

Ministry of Education: New Federal Secretariat Complex, Shehu Shagari Way, Central Area District, PMB 146, Abuja; tel. (9) 5237838; e-mail enquires@fme.gov.ng; internet www.fme.gov.ng.

Ministry of Energy: Annex 3, Federal Secretariat Complex, Shehu Shagari Way, Central Area, PMB 278, Garki, Abuja; tel. (9) 5239462; fax (9) 5236652; e-mail info@mpr.gov.ng.

Ministry of the Environment: Federal Secretariat Towers, Shehu Shagari Way, Central Area, PMB 468, Garki, Abuja; tel. (9) 5234014; fax (9) 5211847; e-mail haloa@nigeria.gov.ng; internet www.environmentnigeria.org.

Ministry of the Federal Capital Territory: Kapital St, off Obafemi Awolowo St, Garki Area 11, PMB 25, Garki, Abuja; tel. (9) 2341525; fax (9) 3143859; e-mail presunit@fct.gov.ng; internet www.fct.gov.ng.

Ministry of Finance: Ahmadu Bello Way, Central Area, PMB 14, Garki, Abuja; tel. (9) 2346290; e-mail susman@nigeria.gov.ng; internet www.fmf.gov.ng.

Ministry of Foreign Affairs: Sir Tafawa Balewa House, Federal Secretariat, PMB 130, Abuja; tel. (9) 5230570; e-mail omaduekwe@nigeria.gov.ng; internet www.mfa.gov.ng.

Ministry of Health: New Federal Secretariat Complex, Ahmadu Bello Way, Central Business District, PMB 083, Garki, Abuja; tel. (9) 5238362; e-mail agrange@nigeria.gov.ng.

Ministry of Housing: Mabushi District, Garki, Abuja; tel. (9) 2346550; fax (9) 2340174.

Ministry of Information and Communication: New Federal Secretariat Complex, Shehu Shagari Way, Central Area District, PMB 1278, Abuja; tel. (9) 5237183; e-mail jodey@nigeria.gov.ng.

Ministry of the Interior: Area 1, Secretariat Complex, Garki, PMB 16, Abuja; tel. (9) 2341934; fax (9) 2342426; e-mail gabbe@nigeria.gov.ng; internet www.fmia.gov.ng.

Ministry of Justice: New Federal Secretariat Complex, Shehu Shagari Way, Central Area, PMB 192, Garki, Abuja; tel. (9) 5235208; fax (9) 5235194.

Ministry of Labour and Productivity: New Federal Secretariat Complex, Shehu Shagari Way, Central Area, PMB 04, Garki, Abuja; tel. (9) 5235980; e-mail hlawal@nigeria.gov.ng.

Ministry of Mines and Steel Development: New Federal Secretariat Complex, Shehu Shagari Way, Central Area, PMB 107, Garki, Abuja; tel. (9) 5235830; fax (9) 5235831.

Ministry of Niger Delta Affairs: Abuja.

Ministry of Petroleum Resources: 1st and 2nd Floors, New Federal Secretariat Complex, Shehu Shagari Way, Garki, Abuja; tel. (9) 5230763.

Ministry of Police Affairs: 8th Floor, New Federal Secretariat Complex, Shehu Shagari Way, Garki, Abuja; tel. (9) 2340422; internet www.policeaffairs.gov.ng.

Ministry of Power: Abuja.

Ministry of Science and Technology: New Federal Secretariat Complex, Shehu Shagari Way, Central Area, PMB 331, Garki, Abuja; tel. (9) 5233397; fax (9) 5235204.

Ministry of Special Duties: Block 3, 3rd Floor, Phase II New Federal Secretariat Complex, Shehu Shagari Way, Garki, Abuja.

Ministry of Transport: Dipcharima House, Central Business District, off 3rd Ave, PMB 0336, Garki, Abuja; tel. (9) 2347451; fax (9) 2347453; e-mail info@fmt.gov.ng; internet www.fmt.gov.ng.

Ministry of Water Resources: Area 11, Secretariat Complex, Garki, PMB 135, Abuja; tel. (9) 3141931; e-mail aruma@nigeria.gov.ng.

Ministry of Women's Affairs: New Federal Secretariat Complex, Shehu Shagari Way, Central Area, PMB 229, Garki, Abuja; tel. (9) 5237112; fax (9) 5233644; e-mail sbungudu@nigeria.gov.ng; internet www.fmwa.gov.ng.

Ministry of Works: Mabushi District, Garki, Abuja; tel. (9) 2346550; fax (9) 2340174.

Ministry of Youth Development: Federal Secretariat, Phase II, Shehu Shagari Way, PMB 229, Abuja; tel. (9) 5237112; fax (9) 5233644; e-mail aolasunkanmi@nigeria.gov.ng.

National Planning Commission: Old Central Bank Bldg, 4th Floor, Garki, PMB 234, Abuja; e-mail info@nigerianeconomy.com; internet www.npc.gov.ng.

National Sports Commission: New Federal Secretariat Complex, Shehu Shagari Way, Maitama, Abuja; tel. (9) 5235905; fax (9) 5235901; e-mail agimba@nigeria.gov.ng.

President and Legislature

PRESIDENT

Presidential Election, 16 April 2011, provisional results

Candidate	Votes	% of votes
Goodluck Ebele Jonathan (People's Democratic Party)	22,495,187	58.87
Muhammadu Buhari (Congress for Progressive Change)	12,214,853	31.97
Malam Nuhu Ahmed Ribadu (Action Congress of Nigeria)	2,079,151	5.44
Ibrahim Shekarau (All Nigeria People's Party)	917,012	2.40
Mahmud Mudi Waziri (People For Democratic Change)	82,243	0.22
Others*	421,532	1.10
Total	**38,209,978**	**100.00**

* There were 15 other candidates.

NATIONAL ASSEMBLY

House of Representatives

Speaker of the House of Representatives: DIMEJI BANKOLE.

Election, 9 April 2011, provisional results

Party	Seats
People's Democratic Party	123
Action Congress of Nigeria	47
Congress for Progressive Change	30
All Nigeria People's Party	25
Others	9
Total	**234***

* There are 360 seats; however results in 126 constituencies were not immediately made available.

Senate

Speaker of the Senate: DAVID MARK.

Election, 9 April 2011, provisional results

Party	Seats
People's Democratic Party	45
Action Congress of Nigeria	13
All Nigeria People's Party	7
Congress for Progressive Change	5
Others	4
Total	**74**

* There are 109 seats; however, full results of the senatorial elections were not immediately made available.

Election Commission

Independent National Electoral Commission (INEC): Plot 436 Zambezi Cres., Maitama District, PMB 0184, Garki, Abuja; tel. (9) 2224632; e-mail contact@inecnigeria.org; internet www.inecnigeria.org; f. 1998; Chair. Prof. ATTAHIRU JEGA.

Political Organizations

Following the death of the military Head of State in June 1998, the existing authorized political parties were dissolved. The Government established a new Independent National Electoral Commission (INEC), which officially approved three political parties to contest elections in February 1999. Prior to legislative and presidential elections in April 2003, three political associations were granted registration in June 2002, as were a further 24 in December. According to the INEC, by 2011 63 parties had been officially registered.

Action Congress of Nigeria (ACN): PMB 141, Garki, Abuja; tel. (9) 2730102; internet www.acnigeria.com; f. 2006 by a merger of the

NIGERIA

Alliance for Democracy, the Justice Party, the Advanced Congress of Democrats and several minor parties; Chair. Dr USMAN BUGAJE; Nat. Sec. Chief BISI AKANDE.

Alliance for Democracy (AD): Plot 2096, Bumbona Close, Zone 1, Wuse, Abuja; tel. (9) 5239357; e-mail info@alliancefordemocracy.org; f. 1998; Chair. MOJISOLUWA AKINFEWA.

Justice Party (JP): 2nd Ave, Gwarimpa, Abuja; tel. 8057764363 (mobile); Chair. RALPH OBIOHA; Nat. Sec. SHADE MABUNORI.

Advanced Congress of Democrats (ACD): Suite 35/36, Mazafala Complex, Kuru, Abuja; tel. 8044107989 (mobile); Chair. YUSUF BABA; Nat. Sec. Dr KENNETH KALU.

All Nigeria People's Party (ANPP): Bassan Plaza, Plot 759, Central Business Area, Abuja; tel. (9) 2347556; f. 1998; Chair. Chief OKEY NWOSU; Nat. Sec. SAIDU KUMOR.

All Progressives Grand Alliance (APGA): House 4, Rd 116, Gwarimpa Housing Estate, Abuja; e-mail feedback@apganigeria.com; internet apganigeria.com; regd June 2002; Chair. VICTOR C. UMEH; Nat. Sec. Alhaji SHIKAFI.

Congress for Progressive Change (CPC): Suite 212, Banex Plaza, Plot 750, Aminu Kano Cres., Zone A7, Wuse II, Abuja; Nat. Chair. RUFAI HANGA; Nat. Sec. BADMUS MUTALLIB.

Democratic People's Party (DPP): 20 Oro Ago St, opp. Holy Trinity Hospital, off Muhammadu Buhari Way, old CBN, Garki II, Abuja; Chair. BIODUN OGUNBIYI; Nat. Sec. Dr ADEMOLA ADEBO.

Fresh Democratic Party: 4 Park Close, Aguyi Ironsi St, Maitma, Abuja; Chair. Rev. CHRIS OKOTIE; Nat. Sec. SOLA SALAKO.

Movement for the Actualization of the Sovereign State of Biafra (MASSOB): Okwe, Imo; tel. 7039015000 (mobile); e-mail massob_1999@yahoo.com; f. 1999; Leader Chief RALPH UWAZURIKE.

Movement for the Emancipation of the Niger Delta (MEND): f. 2005; main Ijaw militant group operating in the Niger Delta; Leader Maj.-Gen. GODSWILL TAMUNO.

Movement for the Survival of the Ogoni People (MOSOP): 17 Kenule St, Bori, Khana Local Govt Area, Ogoni; tel. (84) 233907; e-mail info@mosop.org; internet www.mosop.org; f. 1990 to organize opposition to petroleum production in Ogoni territory; Pres. LEDUM MITEE; Sec.-Gen. MOSES DAMGBOR.

National Conscience Party (NCP): 18 Phase 1 Low Cost Housing Estate, Lake City Ave, Gwagwalada, Abuja; tel. (9) 4937279; internet www.nigeriancp.net; Leader GANI FAWEHINMI; Chair. OSAGIE OBAYUWANA.

National Democratic Party (NDP): Plot 39, Durban St, off Ademola Adetokunbo Cres., Wuse II, Abuja; tel. (9) 6704070; regd June 2002; Chair. Alhaji ALIYU HABU FARI; Nat. Sec. ADEMOLA AYOADE.

Niger Delta People's Volunteer Force (NDPVF): prominent Ijaw militant group operating in the Niger Delta; Leader Alhaji MUJAHID DOKUBO-ASARI.

People For Democratic Change (PDC): Kalabari St, Karu Site, Karu, Abuja; Nat. Chair. MAHMUD MUDI WAZIRI; Nat. Sec. BENJAMIN EMEKA IGWE.

People's Democratic Party (PDP): Wadata Plaza, Michael Okpara Way, Zone 5, Wuse, Abuja; tel. (9) 5232589; e-mail info@peopledemocraticparty.org; internet www.peopledemocraticparty.org; f. 1998 by fmr opponents of the Govt of Gen. Sani Abacha; supports greater federalism; ruling party; Chair. Alhaji HALIRU MOHAMMED BELLO (acting); Nat. Sec, Alhaji ABUBAKAR BARAJE.

People's Redemption Party (PRP): City Plaza, Area 11, Garki, Abuja; tel. 8033495403 (mobile); regd Dec. 2002; Chair. Alhaji ABDULKADIR B. MUSA; Nat. Sec. Dr E. NGOZI OKAFOR.

People's Salvation Party (PSP): 451 Oron St, Wuse Zone 1, Abuja; tel. (9) 5235359; regd Dec. 2002; Chair. Dr JUNAIDU MOHAMMED; Nat. Sec. Dr V. A. AMOSU.

Progressive People's Alliance (PPA): 36 Moses A. Majekodunmi Cres., Utako District, Abuja; tel. 7038263544 (mobile); internet ppanigeria.com; Chair. SAM NKIRE; Nat. Sec. DAHIRU MUSA MOHAMMED.

United Nigeria People's Party (UNPP): Plot 1467, Safana Close, Garki 11, Abuja; tel. (9) 2340091; regd June 2002; Chair. MALLAM SALEH JAMBO; Nat. Sec. Dr UKEJE NWOKEFORO.

Diplomatic Representation

EMBASSIES AND HIGH COMMISSIONS IN NIGERIA

Algeria: Plot 203, Etim Inyang Cres., POB 55238, Falomo, Lagos; tel. (1) 612092; fax (1) 2624017; Ambassador HAFRAD ALI.

Angola: 5 Kasumu Ekomode St, Victoria Island, POB 50437, Falomo Ikoyi, Lagos; tel. (1) 611702; fax (1) 618675; Ambassador EVARISTO DOMINGOS KIMBA.

Argentina: 1611 Yusuf Maitama Sule St, Asokoro District, Abuja; tel. (9) 7800651; fax (9) 3148683; e-mail enige@mrecic.gov.ar; internet www.nigeria.embajada-argentina.gov.ar; Ambassador MARIA SUSANA PATARO.

Australia: 5th Floor, Oakland Centre, 48 Aguiyi Ironsi St, Maitama, Abuja; PMB 5152, Abuja; tel. (9) 4612780; fax (9) 4612782; e-mail ahc.abuja@dfat.gov.au; internet www.nigeria.embassy.gov.au; High Commissioner IAN MCCONVILLE.

Austria: Plot 9, Usuma St, Maitama, Abuja; tel. 7064183226 (mobile); fax (9) 4612715; e-mail abuja-ob@bmeia.gv.at; Ambassador Dr STEFAN SCHOLZ.

Belgium: 9 Usuma St, Maitama, Abuja; tel. (9) 4131859; fax (9) 4132015; e-mail abuja@diplobel.fed.be; internet www.diplomatie.be/abuja; Ambassador DIRK VERHEYEN.

Benin: 4 Abudu Smith St, Victoria Island, POB 5705, Lagos; tel. (1) 2614411; fax (1) 2612385; Ambassador PATRICE HOUNGAVOU.

Brazil: Plot 173, Mississippi St, Maitama, Abuja; tel. (9) 4134067; fax (9) 4134066; Ambassador ANA CANDIDA PEREZ.

Bulgaria: 10 Euphrates St, off Aminu Kano Cres., Maitama, Abuja; tel. (9) 4130034; fax (9) 4132741; e-mail bulembassy@yahoo.com; internet www.mfa.bg/abuja; Ambassador MIROSLAV NIKOLAEV KOMAROV.

Burkina Faso: No. 4, Freetown St, off Ademola Adetokunbo Cres., Wuse II, Abuja; tel. (9) 4130491; fax (9) 4130492; e-mail ebfn@nova.net.ng; Ambassador DRAMANE YAMÉOGO.

Cameroon: 469, Lobito Cres., Wuse II, Abuja; tel. (1) 4611355; e-mail haucocamabuja@yahoo.fr; High Commissioner ABBAS IBRAHIMA SALAHEDDINE.

Canada: 15 Bobo St, Maitama, POB 5144, Abuja; tel. (9) 4612900; fax (9) 4612901; e-mail abuja@international.gc.ca; internet www.canadainternational.gc.ca/nigeria; High Commissioner CHRISTOPHER COOTER.

Chad: 10 Mississippi St, PMB 488, Abuja; tel. (9) 4130751; fax (9) 4130752; Ambassador MAHAMAT HABIB DOUTOUM.

China, People's Republic: Plot 302–303, Central Area, Abuja; tel. (9) 4618661; fax (9) 4618660; e-mail chinaemb_ng@mfa.gov.cn; internet ng.china-embassy.org; Ambassador DENG BOQING.

Congo, Republic: 447 Lobito Cres., Abuja; tel. (9) 4137407; fax (9) 4130157; Ambassador PETER NGUI.

Côte d'Ivoire: 2630 Gourara St, Abuja; tel. (9) 4133087; fax (9) 4133137; e-mail cotedivoire@micro.com.ng; Ambassador AMIDOU DIARA.

Cuba: Plot 339, Diplomatic Zone, Area 10, Garki, Abuja; tel. (9) 4614821; fax (9) 4614820; e-mail embajada@ng.embacuba.cu; internet emba.cubaminrex.cu/nigeriaing; Ambassador ELIO SAVÓN OLIVA.

Czech Republic: Plot 1223, 5 Gnassingbé Eyadéma St, Asokoro District, POB 4628, Abuja; tel. (9) 3141245; fax (9) 3141248; e-mail abuja@embassy.mzv.cz; internet www.mzv.cz/abuja; Ambassador JAROSLAV SIRO.

Egypt: 8 Buzi Close, off Amazon St, Maitama, Abuja; PMB 5069, Wuse, Abuja; tel. (9) 4136091; fax (9) 4132602; Ambassador YOUSSEF HASSAN SHAWKI.

Equatorial Guinea: 20 Dakala St, off Parakou Cres., off Aminu Kano Cres., Wuse II, Abuja; tel. and fax (9) 7816867; e-mail egembassyabj@hotmail.com; Ambassador JOB OBIANG ESONO MBENGONO.

Eritrea: Plot 1510, Yedseram St, off IBB Way, Maitama, Abuja; tel. 8139856889 (mobile); fax (9) 4136085; e-mail eriemba_nigeria@yahoo.com; Ambassador MOHAMMED ALI OMARO.

Ethiopia: 19 Ona Cres., Maitama, POB 2488, Abuja; tel. (1) 4131691; fax (1) 4131692; e-mail etabuja@primair.net; Ambassador YOHANESS GENDA.

Finland: 9 Iro Dan Musa St, Asokoro, Abuja; tel. (9) 3147256; fax (9) 3147252; e-mail sanomat.aba@formin.fi; internet www.finlandnigeria.org; Ambassador ANNELI VUORINEN.

France: 37 Udi Hills St, off Aso Dr., Abuja; tel. (9) 5235510; fax (9) 5235482; e-mail sec-amb.abuja-amba@diplomatie.gouv.fr; internet www.ambafrance-ng.org; Ambassador JEAN-MICHEL DUMOND.

Gabon: 8 Norman Williams St, SW Ikoyi, POB 5989, Lagos; tel. (1) 684566; fax (1) 2690692; Ambassador CORENTIN HERVO-AKENDENGUE.

The Gambia: 7 Misratah St, off Parakou Cres., Wuse II, PMB 5058, Abuja; tel. (9) 5241224; fax (9) 5241228; e-mail ghcabuja@yahoo.com; High Commissioner ANGELA COLLEY.

Germany: 9 Lake Maracaibo Close, off Amazon St, Maitama, Abuja; tel. (9) 4130962; fax (9) 4130949; e-mail info@abuja.diplo.de; internet www.abuja.diplo.de; Ambassador JOACHIM CHRISTOPH SCHMILLEN.

Ghana: 21–25 King George V Rd, POB 889, Lagos; tel. (1) 2630015; fax (1) 2630338; High Commissioner ALHAJI BABA KAMARA.

NIGERIA

Greece: 6 Seguela St, Wuse II, POB 11525, Abuja; tel. (9) 4612775; fax (9) 4612778; e-mail gremb.abj@mfa.gr; internet www.mfa.gr/abuja; Ambassador HARALAMBOS DAFARANOS.

Guinea: No. 349, Central Business District, opp. United Nations Premises, POB 591, Abuja; tel. (9) 4618612; fax (9) 4618611; e-mail ambaguinig@yahoo.com; Ambassador Dr CHEICK ABDOUL CAMARA.

Holy See: Pope John Paul II Cres., Maitama, PMB 541, Garki, Abuja; tel. (9) 4138381; fax (9) 4136653; e-mail nuntiusabj@hotmail.com; Apostolic Nuncio AUGUSTINE KASUJJA (Titular Archbishop of Caesarea in Numidia).

Hungary: 61 Jose Marti Cres., Asokoro, POB 5299, Abuja; tel. 7064786188 (mobile); e-mail mission.abv@kum.hu; internet www.mfa.gov.hu/emb/abuja; Chargé d'affaires a.i. JÁNOS KOVÁCS.

India: 15 Rio Negro Close, off Yedseram St, Maitama, Abuja; tel. (9) 4602800; fax (9) 4602805; e-mail hoc.abuja@mea.gov.in; internet www.indianhcabuja.com; High Commissioner MAHESH SACHDEV.

Indonesia: 5B Anifowoshe St, Victoria Island, POB 3473, Marina, Lagos; tel. (1) 2614601; fax (1) 2613301; e-mail unitkomigs@hyperia.com; Ambassador SUDIRMAN HASENG.

Iran: 1 Udi Hills St, off Aso Dr., Maitama, Abuja; tel. (1) 5238048; fax (1) 5237785; e-mail iranabuja@gmail.com; Ambassador JAWAD TORKABADI.

Ireland: 11 Negro Cres., Maitama District, Abuja; tel. (9) 4620611; fax (9) 4620613; e-mail abujaembassy@dfa.ie; internet www.embassyofireland.org.ng; Ambassador KYLE O'SULLIVAN.

Israel: Plot 12, Mary Slessor St, Asokoro, POB 10924, Abuja; tel. (9) 4605500; e-mail info@abuja.mfa.gov.il; internet abuja.mfa.gov.il; Ambassador MOSHE RAM.

Italy: 21st Cres., off Constitution Ave, Central Business District, Abuja; tel. (9) 4614722; fax (9) 4614709; e-mail ambasciata.abuja@esteri.it; internet www.ambabuja.esteri.it; Ambassador ROBERTO COLAMINÈ.

Jamaica: Plot 247, Muhammadu Buhari Way, Central Area District, Abuja; tel. and fax (9) 2345107; e-mail jamaicanembassy@yahoo.com; High Commissioner ROBERT MILLER.

Japan: 9 Bobo St, off Gana St, Maitama, PMB 5070, Abuja; tel. (9) 4138898; fax (870) 600-315-545 (satellite); Ambassador TOSHITSUGU UESAWA.

Kenya: 18 Yedseram St, Maitama, PMB 5160, Abuja; tel. (9) 4139155; fax (9) 4139157; e-mail abuja@mfa.go.ke; High Commissioner DANIEL MEPUKORI KOIKAI.

Korea, Democratic People's Republic: Plot 350, Central Area, Cadastral Zone, AO, POB 407, Garki, Abuja; tel. (9) 2347200; fax (9) 2347199; Ambassador JONG HAK SE.

Korea, Republic: 9 Ovia Cres., off Pope John Paul St, Maitama, POB 6870, Abuja; tel. (9) 4612701; fax (9) 4612702; e-mail emb-ng@mofat.go.kr; internet nga-abuja.mofat.go.kr; Ambassador PARK YOUNG-KUK.

Liberia: 3 Idejo St, Plot 162, off Adeola Odeku St, Victoria Island, POB 70841, Lagos; tel. (1) 2618899; Ambassador Prof. AL-HASSAN CONTEH.

Libya: Plot 1591, Mike Okoye Cl., off George Sowemimo St, Asokoro Ext., POB 435, Garki, Abuja; tel. (9) 3148356; fax (9) 3148354; Ambassador Eng. MANSOUR O. OSMAN.

Malaysia: 2 Pechora Close, off Panama St, Maitama PMB 5217, Abuja; tel. (9) 7822091; e-mail malabuja@kln.gov.my; High Commissioner NIK MUSTAFA KAMAL NIK.

Morocco: 5 Mary Slessor St, off Udo Udoma Cres., Asokoro, Abuja; tel. (9) 8746697; fax (9) 3141959; e-mail mcherkaoui45@yahoo.fr; Ambassador MUSTAPHA CHERQAOUI.

Namibia: Plot 1738 T. Y., Danyuma St, Cadasdral Zone, A4 Asokoro, Abuja; tel. (9) 3142740; fax (9) 3142743; e-mail namibiahighcomabuja@yahoo.com; High Commissioner DANIEL SMITH.

Netherlands: 21st Cres., off Constitution Ave, Central Business District, Abuja; tel. (9) 4611200; fax (9) 4611240; e-mail abj@minbuza.nl; internet nigeria.nlembassy.org; Ambassador BERT RONHAAR.

Niger: 15 Adeola Odeku St, Victoria Island, PMB 2736, Lagos; tel. (9) 4136206; fax (9) 4136205; Ambassador MOUSSA ELHADJI IBRAHIM.

Norway: 54 T.Y. Danjuma St, Asokoro, Abuja; tel. (9) 8746989; fax (9) 3149309; e-mail emb.abuja@mfa.no; internet www.emb-norway.com.ng; Ambassador KJELL LILLERUD.

Pakistan: 4 Samora Machel Street, Asokoro, Abuja; tel. (9) 3141650; fax (9) 3141652; e-mail pahicabuja@yahoo.com; High Commissioner ASIF DURAIZ AKHTAR.

Philippines: 2 Kainji St, cnr Lake Chad Cres., Maitama, Abuja; tel. (9) 4137981; fax (9) 4137650; e-mail pe.abuja@dfa.gov.ph; Ambassador NESTOR NABAYRA PADALHIN.

Poland: 10 Ona Cres., off Lake Chad Cres., Maitama, 900271, Abuja; tel. 8052000204 (mobile); e-mail contact@abuja-polemb.net; internet www.abuja.polemb.net; Ambassador PRZEMYSŁAW NIESIOŁOWSKI.

Portugal: 27B Gana St, Maitama, Abuja; tel. (9) 4137211; fax (9) 4137214; e-mail portemb@rosecom.net; Ambassador MARIA DE FÁTIMA DE PINA PERESTRELLO.

Romania: Nelson Mandela St, No. 76, Plot 498, Asokoro; tel. (9) 3142304; fax (9) 3142306; e-mail romembabujaconsularsection@gmail.com; internet www.romnig.com; Chargé d'affaires a.i. MIRCEA LEUCEA.

Russia: 5 Walter Carrington Cres., Victoria Island, POB 2723, Lagos; tel. (1) 2613359; fax (1) 4619994; Ambassador ALEXANDER DIMITRIEVICH POLYAKOV.

Saudi Arabia: Plot 347H, off Adetokunbo Ademola Cres., Wuse II, Abuja; tel. (9) 4131880; fax (9) 4134906; Ambassador ANWAR A. ABD-RABBUH.

Senegal: 14 Kofo Abayomi Rd, Victoria Island, PMB 2197, Lagos; tel. (1) 2611722; Ambassador AMADOU THIALAW DIOP.

Serbia: 11, Rio Negro Close, off Yedseram St, Cadastral Zone A6, Maitama District, Abuja; tel. 8059738141 (mobile); fax (9) 4130078; e-mail mail@ambnig.com; Ambassador RIFAT RONDIC.

Sierra Leone: Plot 308 Mission Rd, opp Ministry of Defence (Ship House), Diplomatic Zone, Central Business District, Abuja; tel. (9) 2349332; fax (9) 2349890; e-mail slhcnig@yahoo.com; High Commissioner HENRY O. MACAULEY.

Slovakia: POB 1290, Lagos; tel. (1) 2621585; fax (1) 2612103; e-mail obeo.sk@micro.com.ng; Ambassador MIROSLAV HACEK.

Somalia: Plot 1270, off Adeola Odeka St, POB 6355, Lagos; tel. (1) 2611283; Ambassador M. S. HASSAN.

South Africa: 71 Usuma St, off Gana St, Maitama, Abuja; tel. (9) 4133776; fax (9) 4133829; e-mail sahcabuja@yahoo.co.uk; High Commissioner J. N. K. MAMABOLO.

Spain: 8 Bobo Close, Maitama, PMB 5120, Wuse, Abuja; tel. (9) 4613258; fax (9) 4613259; e-mail emb.abuja@maec.es; internet www.maec.es/embajadas/abuja; Ambassador ÁNGEL LOSADA FERNÁNDEZ.

Sudan: Plot 337, Misson Rd Zone, Central Area District, Abuja; tel. (9) 6700668; fax (9) 2346265; e-mail sudaniabj@hotmail.com; Ambassador AHMED ALTIGANI SALEH.

Sweden: PMB 569, Garki, Abuja; tel. (9) 8746913; fax (870) 782-248-789 (satellite); e-mail ambassaden.abuja@foreign.ministry.se; internet www.swedenabroad.com/abuja; Ambassador PER LINDGÄRDE.

Switzerland: 157 Adetokumbo Ademola Cres., Wuse II, Abuja; tel. (9) 4610540; fax (9) 4610548; e-mail abu.vertretung@eda.admin.ch; internet www.eda.admin.ch/abuja; Ambassador Dr ANDREAS BAUM.

Syria: 25 Kofo Abayomi St, Victoria Island, Lagos; tel. (1) 2615860; Chargé d'affaires a.i. MUSTAFA HAJ-ALI.

Tanzania: 8 Agoro Odiyan St, Victoria Island, POB 6417, Lagos; tel. (1) 613604; fax (1) 610016; e-mail tanabuja@lytos.com; High Commissioner ABDUL CISCO MTIRO.

Thailand: 24 Tennesse Cres., off Panama St, Maitama, Abuja; tel. (9) 8723746; fax (9) 4135193; e-mail thaiabj@mfa.go.th; Ambassador N. SATHAPORN.

Togo: Plot 976, Oju Olobun Close, Victoria Island, POB 1435, Lagos; tel. (1) 2617449; fax (1) 617478; Ambassador FOLI-AGBENOZAN TETTEKPOE.

Trinidad and Tobago: 7 Casablanca St, off Nairobi St, off Amino Kano Cres., Wuse II, Abuja; tel. (9) 6411118; fax (9) 4611117; e-mail trinitobagoabj@yahoo.co.uk; internet www.ttmissionsnigeria.com; High Commissioner NYAHUMA MENTHUHOTEP OBIKA.

Turkey: 5 Amazon St, Minister's Hill, Maitama, Abuja; tel. (9) 4139787; fax (9) 4139457; e-mail turkishembassyabuja@gmail.com; internet www.abuja.emb.mfa.gov.tr; Ambassador ALI RIFAT KÖKSAL.

Ukraine: Plot 15, Moundou St, Wuse II, Abuja; tel. (9) 5239577; fax (9) 5239578; e-mail emb_ng@mfa.gov.ua; internet www.mfa.gov.ua/nigeria; Ambassador VALERII VASYLIEV.

United Kingdom: Dangote House, Aguiyi Ironsi St, Wuse, Abuja; tel. (9) 4132010; fax (9) 4623223; e-mail information.abuja@fco.gov.uk; internet www.ukinnigeria.fco.gov.uk; High Commissioner ANDREW LLOYD.

USA: Plot 1075, Diplomatic Dr., Central District Area, Abuja; tel. (9) 4614000; fax (9) 4614171; e-mail consularabuja@state.gov; internet abuja.usembassy.gov; Ambassador TERENCE PATRICK MCCULLEY.

Venezuela: Plot 1361 Hon, Justice Sowemino St, Asokoro District, Abuja; tel. (9) 3140900; fax (9) 3140903; e-mail evenigeria@yahoo.com; Ambassador BORIS ENRÍQUEZ MARTÍNEZ.

Zambia: 351 Mission Rd, Central Area District, Garki, Abuja; tel. (9) 4618605; fax (9) 4618602; e-mail zambiahc@yahoo.com; High Commissioner ALEXIS LUHILA.

NIGERIA

Zimbabwe: 19 Tiamiyu Savage St, POB 50247, Victoria Island, Lagos; tel. (1) 2619328; e-mail zimabuja@yahoo.co.uk; High Commissioner Dr JOHN SHUMBA MVUNDURA.

Judicial System

Supreme Court
Three Arms Complex, Central District, PMB 308, Abuja; tel. (9) 2346594.
Consists of a Chief Justice and up to 15 Justices, appointed by the President, on the recommendation of the National Judicial Council (subject to the approval of the Senate); has original jurisdiction in any dispute between the Federation and a state, or between states, and hears appeals from the Federal Court of Appeal.
Chief Justice: IYORGHER IGNATIUS KATSINA-ALU.
Court of Appeal: consists of a President and at least 35 Justices, of whom three must be experts in Islamic (*Shari'a*) law and three experts in Customary law; has 12 divisions in various states.
Federal High Court: Abuja; internet www.fhc-ng.com; Chief Judge ABDULLAHI MUSTAPHA.
Each state has a **High Court**, consisting of a Chief Judge and a number of judges, appointed by the Governor of the state on the recommendation of the National Judicial Council (subject to the approval of the House of Assembly of the state). If required, a state may have a **Shari'a Court of Appeal** (dealing with Islamic civil law) and a **Customary Court of Appeal**. **Special Military Tribunals** have been established to try offenders accused of crimes such as corruption, drugs-trafficking and armed robbery; appeals against rulings of the Special Military Tribunals are referred to a **Special Appeals Tribunal**, which comprises retired judges.

Religion

ISLAM
According to the 2003 Nigeria Demographic and Health Survey, Muslims comprised 50.5% of the total population.
Spiritual Head: Col MUHAMMADU SA'AD ABUBAKAR (the Sultan of Sokoto).

CHRISTIANITY
According to the 2003 Nigeria Demographic and Health Survey, 48.2% of the population were Christians.
Christian Council of Nigeria: 139 Ogunlana Dr., Surulere, POB 2838, Lagos; tel. (1) 7923495; f. 1929; 15 full mems and six assoc. mems; Pres. Rt Rev. ROGERS O. UWADI; Gen. Sec. Rev. IKECNUKWU OKORIE.

The Anglican Communion
Anglicans are adherents of the Church of the Province of Nigeria, comprising 139 dioceses. Nigeria, formerly part of the Province of West Africa, became a separate Province in 1979; in 1997 it was divided into three separate provinces and a 10-Province structure for the Church of Nigeria (Anglican Communion) was proclaimed in January 2003.
Primate, Archbishop of the Province of Bendel and Bishop of Esan: Rt Rev. Dr F. J. IMAEKHAI, Bishopscourt, Cable Point, POB 216, Asaba; tel. (56) 280682; e-mail primate@anglican-nig.org; internet www.anglican-nig.org.
Archbishop of the Province of Abuja: Most Rev. NICHOLAS DIKERIEHI OKOH, 24 Douala St, Wuse Zone 5, POB 212, Abuja; tel. (9) 5236950; fax (9) 5230986.
Archbishop of the Province of Ibadan and Bishop of Ibadan: Most Rev. JOSEPH AKINFENWA, POB 3075, Mapo; tel. (2) 8101400; fax (2) 8101413; e-mail ibadan@anglican.skannet.com.ng.
Archbishop of the Province of Jos and Bishop of Maiduguri: Most Rev. EMMANUEL KANA MANI, Bishopscourt, off Lagos St, GRA POB 1693, Maiduguri; tel. (76) 234010; e-mail maiduguri@anglican-nig.org.
Archbishop of the Province of Kaduna and Bishop of Kaduna: Most Rev. JOSIAH IDOWU-FEARON, POB 72, Kaduna; tel. (62) 240085; fax (62) 244408; e-mail manasoko@infoweb.abs.net.
Archbishop of the Province of Lagos and Bishop of Lagos: Most Rev. EPHRAIM ADEBOLA ADEMOWO, 29 Marina, POB 13, Lagos; tel. (1) 2636026; fax (1) 2636536; e-mail lagos@anglican.skannet.com.ng.
Archbishop of the Province of the Niger and Bishop of Awka: Most Rev. MAXWELL SAMUEL CHIKE ANIKWENWA, Bishopscourt, Ifite Rd, POB 130, Awka; tel. (48) 550058; fax (48) 550052; e-mail angawka@infoweb.abs.net.
Archbishop of the Niger Delta and Bishop of Aba: Most Rev. UGOCHUCKWU UWAOMA EZUOKE, Bishopscourt, 70/72 St Michael's Rd, POB 212, Aba; tel. (82) 227666; e-mail aba@anglican-nig.org.
Archbishop of the Province of Ondo and Bishop of Ekiti: Most Rev. SAMUEL ADEDAYE ABE, Bishopscourt, POB 12, Okesa St, Ado-Ekiti, Ekiti; tel. (30) 250305; e-mail ekiti@anglican.skannet.com.ng.
Archbishop of the Province of Owerri and Bishop of Orlu: Most Rev. BENNETT C. I. OKORO, Bishopscourt, POB 260, Nkwerre; tel. (82) 440538.
General Secretary: Ven. EMMANUEL ADEKUNLE, 24 Douala St, Wuse Zone 5, POB 212, Abuja; tel. (9) 5236950; fax (9) 5230987; e-mail general_secretary@anglican-nig.org.

The Roman Catholic Church
Nigeria comprises nine archdioceses, 41 dioceses and two Apostolic Vicariates. An estimated 15% of the population were Roman Catholics.
Catholic Bishops' Conference of Nigeria
6 Force Rd, POB 951, Lagos; tel. (1) 2635849; fax (1) 2636670; e-mail cathsec1@infoweb.abs.net.
f. 1976; Pres. Most Rev. FELIX ALABA ADEOSIN JOB (Archbishop of Ibadan); Sec.-Gen. of Secretariat Rev. Fr MATTHEW HASSAN KUKAH.
Archbishop of Abuja: Most Rev. JOHN O. ONAIYEKAN, Archdiocesan Secretariat, POB 286, Garki, Abuja; tel. (9) 2340661; fax (9) 2340662; e-mail onaiyekan7@hotmail.com.
Archbishop of Benin City: AUGUSTINE OBIORA AKUBEZE, Archdiocesan Secretariat, POB 35, Benin City, Edo; tel. (52) 253787; fax (52) 255763; e-mail cadobc@infoweb.abs.net.
Archbishop of Calabar: Most Rev. JOSEPH EDRA UKPO, Catholic Secretariat, PMB 1044, 1 Bishop Moynagh Ave, Calabar, Cross River; tel. (87) 231666; fax (87) 239177; e-mail archdical@yahoo.com.
Archbishop of Ibadan: Most Rev. FELIX ALABA JOB, Archbishop's House, PMB 5057, 8 Bale Latosa Rd, Onireke, Ibadan, Oyo; tel. (22) 2413544; fax (22) 2414855; e-mail archdiocese.ibadan@skannet.com.
Archbishop of Jos: Most Rev. IGNATIUS AYAU KAIGAMA, Archdiocesan Secretariat, 20 Joseph Gomwalk Rd, POB 494, Jos, Plateau; tel. (73) 452878; fax (73) 451547; e-mail josarch@hisen.org.
Archbishop of Kaduna: Most Rev. MATTHEW MAN-OSO NDAGOSO, Archbishop's House, 71 Tafawa Balewa Way, POB 248, Kaduna; tel. (62) 246076; fax (62) 240026; e-mail catholickaduna@yahoo.com.
Archbishop of Lagos: Cardinal ANTHONY OLUBUNMI OKOGIE, Archdiocesan Secretariat, 19 Catholic Mission St, POB 8, Lagos; tel. (1) 2635729; fax (1) 2633841; e-mail arclagos@yahoo.com.
Archbishop of Onitsha: Most Rev. VALERIAN OKEKE, Archdiocesan Secretariat, POB 411, Onitsha, Anambra; tel. (46) 413298; fax (46) 413913; e-mail secretariat@onitsha-archdiocese.org.
Archbishop of Owerri: Most Rev. ANTHONY JOHN VALENTINE OBINNA, Villa Assumpta, POB 85, Owerri, Imo; tel. (83) 250115; fax (83) 230760; e-mail owcatsec@owerriarchdiocese.org.

Other Christian Churches
Brethren Church of Nigeria: c/o Kulp Bible School, POB 1, Mubi, Adamawa; f. 1923; Gen. Sec. Rev. JINATU WAMDEO; 100,000 mems.
Church of the Lord (Aladura): Anthony Village, Ikorodu Rd, POB 308, Ikeja, Lagos; tel. (1) 4964749; f. 1930; Primate Dr E. O. A. ADEJOBI; 1.1m. mems.
Lutheran Church of Christ in Nigeria: POB 21, Hospital Rd, Numan, Adamawa; tel. (75) 772330; fax (75) 625093; e-mail nemuelbabba@hotmail.com; Pres. Archbishop NEMUEL A. BABBA; 1.9m. mems (2010).
Lutheran Church of Nigeria: POB 49, Obot Idim Ibesikpo, Uyo, Akwa Ibom; tel. (85) 200505; fax (85) 200451; e-mail chrisekonglcn@yahoo.com; internet www.lutheranchurchnigeria.org; f. 1936; Pres. Most Rev. CHRISTIAN EKONG; 142,000 mems (2010).
Methodist Church Nigeria: Wesley House, 21–22 Marina, POB 2011, Lagos; tel. (1) 2702563; fax (1) 2702710; 483,500 mems; Patriarch Rev. Dr SUNDAY OLA KAKINDE.
Nigerian Baptist Convention: Baptist Bldg, PMB 5113, Ibadan; tel. (2) 2412667; fax (2) 2413561; e-mail baptconv@nigerianbaptist.org; internet nigerianbaptist.org; Pres. Rev. Dr REUBEN I. CHUGA; Gen. Sec. Dr S. ADEMOLA ISHOLA; 3.5m. mems.
The Presbyterian Church of Nigeria: 26–29 Ehere Rd, Ogbor Hill, POB 2635, Aba, Imo; tel. (82) 222551; f. 1846; Moderator Rt Rev. Dr UBON B. USUNG; Synod Clerk Rev. Dr BENEBO F. FUBARA-MANUEL; 1m. mems.

The Redeemed Church of Christ, the Church of the Foursquare Gospel, the Qua Iboe Church and the Salvation Army are prominent among numerous other Christian churches active in Nigeria.

NIGERIA   *Directory*

AFRICAN RELIGIONS

The beliefs, rites and practices of the people of Nigeria are very diverse, varying between ethnic groups and between families in the same group.

The Press

DAILIES

Al-Mizan: internet almizan.faithweb.com; Hausa.

Aminiya: 20 POW Mafemi Cres., off Solomon Lar Way, Utako, Abuja; tel. (9) 6726241; internet aminiya.dailytrust.com; Hausa; Editor-in-Chief MANNIR DAN ALI.

BusinessDay: 72 Festac Link Rd, Amuwo Odofin, Lagos; tel. 8034694482 (mobile); internet www.businessdayonline.com; Editor PHILLIP ISAKPA.

Daily Champion: Isolo Industrial Estate, Oshodi-Apapa, Lagos; fax (1) 4526011; e-mail letters@champion-newspapers.com; internet www.champion-newspapers.com; Man. Editor UGO ONUOHA.

Daily Independent: Independent Newspapers Ltd, Block 5, Plot 7D, Wempco Rd, Ogba, PMB 21777, Ikeja, Lagos; tel. (1) 4962136; e-mail newseditor@independentngonline.com; internet www.independentngonline.com; f. 2001; Editor IKECHUKWU AMAECHI.

Daily Triumph: Triumph Publishing Co Ltd, Gidan Sa'adu Zungur, PMB 3155, Kano; tel. (64) 633875; fax (64) 630273; internet www.triumphnewspapers.com; Editor MUSA AHMAD TIJJANI.

Daily Trust: 20 POW Mafemi Cres., off Solomon Lar Way, Utako, Abuja; tel. (9) 6726241; internet www.dailytrust.com; f. 2001; Editor MAHMUD JEGA.

The Guardian: Guardian Newspapers Ltd, Rutam House, Isolo Expressway, Isolo, PMB 1217, Oshodi, Lagos; tel. (1) 4524111; fax (1) 4524080; e-mail editday@ngrguardiannews.com; internet www.ngrguardiannews.com; f. 1983; independent; Editor-in-Chief EMEKA IZEZE; Editor DEBO ADESINA; circ. 80,000.

Leadership: 8A Umuozu Close, off Samuel Ladoke Akintola Blvd, POB 9514, Garki, Abuja; tel. (9) 2345055; fax (9) 2345360; e-mail leadershipnigeria@yahoo.com; internet leadershipnigeria.com.

The Nation: Vintage Press Ltd, 27B Fatai Atere Way, Matori, Mushin, Lagos; tel. (1) 8168361; e-mail info@thenationonlineng.com; internet www.thenationonlineng.net; f. 2006; Editor GBENGA OMOTOSO.

National Daily: e-mail editor@nationaldailyngr.com; internet www.nationaldailyngr.com; f. 2006; Exec. Editor SYLVESTER EBHODAGHE; circ. 50,000.

New Age: Lagos; e-mail ebiz@newage-online.com; internet www.newage-online.com; Editor STEVE OSUJI.

New Nigerian: New Nigerian Newspapers Ltd, 4/5 Ahmadu Bello Way, POB 254, Kaduna; tel. (62) 245220; fax (62) 245221; internet www.newnigeriannews.com; f. 1965; govt-owned; Editor-in-Chief NDANUSA ALAO; circ. 80,000.

Next: Timbuktu Media, 235 Igbosere Rd, Lapal Plaza, 2nd Floor, Lagos; tel. (1) 8977685; e-mail MediaRelations@TimbuktuMedia.com; internet 234next.com; Editor MUFU OGUNBUNMI.

Nigerian Compass: 10 Western Industrial Ave, Compass Media Village, Isheri, Ogun; tel. (1) 7400001; internet www.compassnews.net; Editor GABRIEL AKINADEWO.

Nigerian Observer: Bendel Newspaper Co Ltd, 24 Airport Rd, PMB 1334, Benin City; tel. (52) 240050; e-mail info@nigerianobservernews.com; internet nigerianobservernews.com; f. 1968; Editor TONY IKEAKANAM; circ. 150,000.

Nigerian Tribune: African Newspapers of Nigeria Ltd, Imalefalafi St, Oke-Ado, POB 78, Ibadan; tel. (2) 2312844; e-mail editornigeriantribune@yahoo.com; internet www.tribune.com.ng; f. 1949; Editor EDWARD DICKSON; circ. 109,000.

Peoples Daily: 35 Ajose Adeogun St, Peace Park Plaza, 1st Floor, Utako, Abuja; tel. (9) 9702136; e-mail editor@peoplesdaily-online.com; internet www.peoplesdaily-online.com; Editor AHMED SHEKARAU.

The Port Harcourt Telegraph: NUJ Bldg, Ernest Ikoli Press Centre, Moscow Rd, Port Harcourt; tel. 8036002239 (mobile); e-mail phtelegraph@yahoo.com; internet www.thephctelegraph.com; Editor-in-Chief OGBONNA NWUKE.

The Punch: 1 Olu Aboderin St, Onipetesi, PMB 21204, Ikeja, Lagos; tel. (1) 7748081; e-mail editor@punchontheweb.com; internet www.punchng.com; f. 1976; Editor-in-Chief ADEMOLA OSINUBI; circ. 150,000.

The Sun: The Sun Publishing Ltd, 2 Coscharis St, Kirikiri Industrial Layout, Apapa, PMB 21776 Ikeja, Lagos; tel. (1) 5875560; fax (1) 5875561; e-mail thesun@sunnewsonline.com; internet www.sunnewsonline.com; f. 2003; Editor STEVE NWOSU.

This Day: 35 Creek Rd, Apapa, Lagos; tel. 8022924721; fax (1) 4600276; e-mail info@thisdayonline.com; internet www.thisdayonline.com; f. 1995; Editor SIMON KOLAWOLE.

The Tide: Rivers State Newspaper Corpn, 4 Ikwerre Rd, POB 5072, Port Harcourt; internet www.thetidenewsonline.com; f. 1971; Editor SOYE WILSON JAMABO; circ. 30,000.

Vanguard: Kirikiri Canal, PMB 1007, Apapa; e-mail vanguard@linkserve.com.ng; internet www.vanguardngr.com; f. 1984; Editor MIDENO BAYAGBON.

SUNDAY NEWSPAPERS

New Nigerian on Sunday: 4/5 Ahmadu Bello Way, POB 254, Kaduna; tel. (62) 245220; fax (62) 245221; e-mail auduson@newnigerian.com; internet www.newnigeriannews.com/sunday; f. 1981; weekly; Editor MALAM TUKUR ABDULRAHMAN; circ. 120,000.

Next on Sunday: Timbuktu Media, 235 Igbosere Rd, Lapal Plaza, 2nd Floor, Lagos; tel. (1) 8977685; e-mail MediaRelations@TimbuktuMedia.com; internet 234next.com; Editor MUFU OGUNBUNMI.

Sunday Compass: 10 Western Industrial Ave, Compass Media Village, Isheri, Ogun; tel. (1) 7400001; internet www.compassnews.net; Editor DOTUN OLADIPO.

Sunday Observer: Bendel Newspapers Co Ltd, 24 Airport Rd, PMB 1334, Benin City; e-mail info@nigerianobservernews.com; internet www.nigerianobservernews.com; f. 1968; Editor T. O. BORHA; circ. 60,000.

Sunday Sun: The Sun Publishing Ltd, 2 Coscharis St, Kirikiri Industrial Layout, Apapa, PMB 21776 Ikeja, Lagos; tel. 5875560; fax (1) 5875561; e-mail thesun@sunnewsonline.com; internet www.sunnewsonline.com; Editor FUNKE EGBEMODE.

Sunday Tide: Rivers State Newspaper Corpn, 4 Ikwerre Rd, POB 5072, Port Harcourt; f. 1971; Editor AUGUSTINE NJOAGWUANI.

Sunday Tribune: Imalefalafi St, POB 78, Oke-Ado, Ibadan; tel. (2) 2310886; e-mail editornigeriantribune@yahoo.com; internet www.tribune.com.ng; Editor DEBO ABDULLAHI.

Sunday Triumph: Triumph Publishing Co Ltd, Gidan Sa'adu Zungur, PMB 3155, Kano; tel. (64) 633875; fax (64) 630273; internet www.triumphnewspapers.com; Editor MUSA AHMAD TIJJANI.

WEEKLIES

Business Hallmark: 109B Adeniyi Jones Ave, Ikeja, Lagos; tel. (1) 7397013; fax (1) 7397008; e-mail info@bizhallmark.com; internet bizhallmark.com; Editor-in-Chief PRINCE EMEKA OBASI.

Business World: 7B Regina Omolara St, off Opebi Rd, Opebi, Lagos; tel. (1) 8742199; e-mail info@businessworldng.com; internet businessworldng.com/web; Editor NIK OGBULI.

The News: 27 Acme Rd, Agidingbi, PMB 21531, Ikeja, Lagos; tel. (1) 7939286; e-mail info@thenewsng.com; internet thenewsng.com; independent; Editor-in-Chief JENKINS ALUMONA.

Newswatch: 3 Billingsway Rd, Oregun, Ikeja, Lagos; tel. (1) 7619660; e-mail newswatch@newswatchngr.com; internet www.newswatchngr.com; f. 1985; English; CEO RAY EKPU; Editor-in-Chief DAN AGBESE.

Technology Times: Suite B316, 81 Ikeja Plaza, Mobolaji Bank Anthony Way, Ikeja, Lagos; tel. (1) 8968161; e-mail info@technologytimesng.com; internet www.technologytimesng.com; Man. Editor TOYIN OGUNSEINDE.

Tell Magazine: PMB 21749, Ikeja, Lagos; tel. (1) 7747910; internet www.tellng.com; Editor AYO AKINKUOTU.

Truth (The Muslim Weekly): 45 Idumagbo Ave, POB 418, Lagos; tel. (1) 2668455; f. 1951; Editor S. O. LAWAL.

Weekly Insight: 33 Oron Road, Uyo; contemporary issues; Editor AUGUSTINE DAVID; circ. 5,000.

Weekly Trust: 20 POW Mafemi Cres., off Solomon Lar Way, Utako, Abuja; tel. (9) 6726241; internet www.weekly.dailytrust.com; Editor ABDULKAREEM BABA AMINU (acting).

ENGLISH-LANGUAGE PERIODICALS

Benin Review: Ethiope Publishing Corpn, PMB 1332, Benin City; f. 1974; African art and culture; 2 a year; circ. 50,000.

The Catholic Ambassador: PMB 2011, Iperu-Remo, Ogun; tel. 8023503748; e-mail ambassadorpublications@yahoo.com; internet www.mspfathers.org; f. 1980; quarterly; Roman Catholic; Editor-in-Chief Rev. Fr PATRICK EBITO AKEKPE; circ. 20,000.

Economic Confidential: Abuja; e-mail info@economicconfidential.com; internet www.economicconfidential.com; f. 2007; monthly; Editor DONATUS ETUKUDO.

Financial Standard: 2 IPM Ave, CBD, Alausa-Ikeja, Lagos; tel. (1) 4934894; fax (1) 4934891; e-mail info@financialstandardnews.com;

NIGERIA

internet www.financialstandardnews.com; f. 1999; Mon.–Fri.; Editor-in-Chief SUNDAY SAMUEL ADEBOLA ONANUGA; circ. 60,000.

Headlines: Daily Times of Nigeria Ltd, New Isheri Rd, Agindingbi, PMB 21340, Ikeja, Lagos; f. 1973; monthly; Editor ADAMS ALIU; circ. 500,000.

Home Studies: Daily Times Publications, 3–7 Kakawa St, Lagos; f. 1964; 2 a month; Editor Dr ELIZABETH E. IKEM; circ. 40,000.

Lagos Education Review: Faculty of Education, University of Lagos Akoka, Lagos; tel. (1) 5820396; fax (1) 4932669; e-mail dajeyalemi@unilag.edu.ng; f. 1978; 2 a year; African education; Editor Prof. DURO AJEYALEMI.

The Leader: 19A Assumpta Press Ave, Industrial Layout, PMB 1017, Owerri, Imo; tel. 8088227344 (mobile); e-mail leaderpress@yahoo.com; internet www.leadernewspaperowerri.com; f. 1956; weekly; Roman Catholic; Editor-in-Chief Rev. CHIMARAOKE SAMUEL OFFURUM.

Management in Nigeria: Plot 22, Idowu Taylor St, Victoria Island, POB 2557, Lagos; tel. (1) 2615105; fax (1) 614116; e-mail nim@rcl.nig.com; quarterly; journal of Nigerian Inst. of Management; Editor Rev. DEJI OLOKESUSI; circ. 25,000.

Nigerian Journal of Economic and Social Studies: Nigerian Economic Society, c/o Dept of Economics, University of Ibadan, PMB 22004, Ibadan, Oyo; tel. (2) 8700395; e-mail journaleditor@nigerianeconomicsociety.org; internet www.nigerianeconomicsociety.org; f. 1957; 3 a year; Editor Prof. ABDUL GANIYU GARBA.

Nigerian Journal of Science: Science Asscn of Nigeria, c/o Dept of Computer Science, University of Ibadan, POB 4039, Ibadan, Oyo; tel. 8023382550 (mobile); e-mail iyifawole@yahoo.com; internet www.sciencenigeria.org; publ. of the Science Asscn of Nigeria; f. 1966; 2 a year; Editor Prof. I. FAWOLE; circ. 1,000.

Nigerian Medical Journal: Office of the Nigerian Medical Journal, Department of Surgery, Nnamdi Azikiwe Univ. Teaching Hospital, PMB 5025, Nnewi; e-mail nmj@nigeriannma.org; internet www.nigeriannma.org; quarterly; Editor Prof. STANLEY N. C. ANYANWU.

Savanna: Ahmadu Bello University Press Ltd, PMB 1094, Zaria; tel. (69) 550054; e-mail abupl@wwlkad.com; f. 1972; 2 a year; Editor Prof. J. A. ARIYO; circ. 1,000.

VERNACULAR PERIODICAL

Gaskiya ta fi Kwabo: New Nigerian Newspapers Ltd, 4/5 Ahmadu Bello Way, POB 254, Kaduna; tel. (62) 245220; fax (62) 245221; internet www.newnigeriannews.com; f. 1939; 3 a week; Hausa; Editor ALHAJI NASIRU GARBA TOFA (acting).

NEWS AGENCIES

Independent Media Centre (IMC): POB 894, Benin City; e-mail nigeriaimc@yahoo.com; internet www.nigeria.indymedia.org.

News Agency of Nigeria (NAN): Independence Avenue, Central Business District, PMB 7006, Garki, Abuja; tel. (9) 6732189; e-mail nanhq@nanngr.com; internet www.nannewsngr.com; f. 1976; state-owned; Man. Dir OLUREMI OYO; Editor-in-Chief DIPO OGBEDE.

Publishers

Africana First Publishers Ltd: Book House Trust, 1 Africana-First Dr., PMB 1639, Onitsha; tel. (46) 485031; f. 1973; study guides, general science, textbooks; Chair. RALPH O. EKPEH; Man. Dir J. C. ODIKE.

Ahmadu Bello University Press: PMB 1094, Zaria; tel. (69) 550054; f. 1972; history, Africana, social sciences, education, literature and arts; Man. Dir SA'IDU HASSAN ADAMU.

Albah International Publishers: 100 Kurawa, Bompai-Kano, POB 6177, Kano City; f. 1978; Africana, Islamic, educational and general, in Hausa; Chair. BASHARI F. ROUKBAH.

Aromolaran Publishing Co Ltd: POB 1800, Ibadan; tel. (2) 715980; f. 1968; educational and general; Man. Dir Dr ADEKUNLE AROMOLARAN.

Cross Continent Press Ltd: 25 Egbeyemi Rd, Ilupeju, POB 282, Yaba, Lagos; tel. and fax (1) 7746348; e-mail crosscontinent@yahoo.com; f. 1974; general, educational and academic; Man. Dir Dr T. C. NWOSU.

Daar Communications PLC: Daar Communications Centre, Kpaduma Hills, off Gen. T. Y. Danjuma St, Asokoro, Abuja; tel. (9) 3144802; fax (9) 3300512; broadcasting and information services; Man. Dir LADI LAWAL.

Daystar Press: Daystar House, POB 1261, Ibadan; tel. (2) 8102670; f. 1962; religious and educational; Man. PHILLIP ADELAKUN LADOKUN.

ECWA Productions Ltd: PMB 2010, Jos; tel. (73) 52230; f. 1973; religious and educational; Gen. Man. Rev. J. K. BOLARIN.

Ethiope Publishing Corpn: Ring Rd, PMB 1332, Benin City; tel. (52) 243036; f. 1970; general fiction and non-fiction, textbooks, reference, science, arts and history; Man. Dir SUNDAY N. OLAYE.

Evans Brothers (Nigeria Publishers) Ltd: Jericho Rd, PMB 5164, Ibadan; tel. (2) 2414394; fax (2) 2410757; f. 1966; general and educational; Chair. Dr ADEKUNLE OJORA; Man. Dir GBENRO ADEGBOLE.

Fourth Dimension Publishing Co Ltd: 16 Fifth Ave, City Layout, PMB 01164, Enugu; tel. (42) 459969; fax (42) 456904; e-mail nwankwov@infoweb.abs.net; internet www.fdpbooks.com; f. 1977; periodicals, fiction, verse, educational and children's; Chair. ARTHUR NWANKWO; Man. Dir V. U. NWANKWO.

Gbabeks Publishers Ltd: POB 37252, Ibadan; tel. (62) 2315705; e-mail gbabeks@hotmail.com; f. 1982; educational and technical; Man. Dir TAYO OGUNBEKUN.

HEBN Publishers PLC: 1 Ighodaro Rd, Jericho, PMB 5205, Ibadan; tel. (2) 2412268; fax (2) 2411089; e-mail info@hebnpublishers.com; internet www.hebnpublishers.com; f. 1962; educational, law, medical and general; Chair. AIGBOJE HIGO; Man. Dir AYO OJENIYI.

Heritage Books: The Poet's Cottage, Artistes Village, Ilogbo-Eremi, Badagry Expressway, POB 610, Apapa, Lagos; tel. (1) 5871333; f. 1971; general; Chair. NAIWU OSAHON.

Ibadan University Press: Publishing House, University of Ibadan, PMB 16, IU Post Office, Ibadan; tel. (2) 400550; e-mail iup-unibadan@yahoo.com; f. 1951; scholarly, science, law, general and educational; Dir F. A. ADESANOYE.

Ilesanmi Press Ltd: Akure Rd, POB 204, Ilesha; tel. 2062; f. 1955; general and educational; Man. Dir G. E. ILESANMI.

John West Publications Ltd: Plot 2, Block A, Acme Rd, Ogba Industrial Estate, PMB 21001, Ikeja, Lagos; tel. (1) 4925459; f. 1964; general; Man. Dir Alhaji L. K. JAKAUDE.

Literamed Publications Ltd (Lantern Books): Plot 45, Alausa Bus-stop, Oregun Industrial Estate, Ikeja, PMB 21068, Lagos; tel. (1) 7901129; fax (1) 7936521; e-mail information@lantern-books.com; internet www.lantern-books.com; f. 1969; children's, medical and scientific; Chair. O. M. LAWAL-SOLARIN.

Longman Nigeria Ltd: 52 Oba Akran Ave, PMB 21036, Ikeja, Lagos; tel. (1) 4978925; fax (1) 4964370; e-mail longman@linkserve.com; f. 1961; general and educational; Man. Dir J. A. OLOWONIYI.

Macmillan Nigeria Publishers Ltd: Ilupeju Industrial Estate, 4 Industrial Ave, POB 264, Yaba, Lagos; tel. (1) 4962185; e-mail macmillan@hotmail.com; internet www.macmillan.nigeria.com; f. 1965; educational and general; Exec. Chair. J. O. EMANUEL; Man. Dir Dr A. I. ADELEKAN.

Minaj Systems Ltd: Ivie House, 4–6 Ajose Adeogun St, POB 70811, Victoria Island, Lagos; tel. (1) 2621168; fax (1) 2621167; e-mail minaj@minaj.com; broadcasting, printing and publishing; Chair. Chief MIKE NNANYE I. AJEGBO.

Northern Nigerian Publishing Co Ltd: Gaskiya Bldg, POB 412, Zaria; tel. (69) 332087; fax (69) 331348; internet www.nnpchausa.com; f. 1966; general, educational and vernacular texts; Gen. Man. MAHMUD BARAU BAMBALE.

NPS Educational Publishers Ltd: Trusthouse, Ring Rd, off Akinyemi Way, POB 62, Ibadan; tel. (2) 316006; f. 1969; academic, scholarly and educational; CEO T. D. OTESANYA.

Nwamife Publishers: 10 Ibiam St, Uwani, POB 430, Enugu; tel. (42) 338254; f. 1971; general and educational; Chair. FELIX C. ADI.

Obafemi Awolowo University Press Ltd: Obafemi Awolowo University, Ile-Ife; tel. (36) 230284; f. 1968; educational, scholarly and periodicals; Man. Dir AKIN FATOKUN.

Obobo Books: The Poet's Cottage, Artistes Village, Ilogbo-Eremi, Badagry Expressway, POB 610, Apapa, Lagos; tel. and fax (1) 5871333; e-mail theendofknowledge@yahoo.com; internet www.theendofknowledge.com; f. 1981; children's books; Editorial Dir BAKIN KUNAMA.

Ogunsanya Press Publishers and Bookstores Ltd: SW9/1133 Orita Challenge, Idiroko, POB 95, Ibadan; tel. (2) 310924; f. 1970; educational; Man. Dir Chief LUCAS JUSTUS POPO-OLA OGUNSANYA.

Onibonoje Press and Book Industries (Nigeria) Ltd: Felele Layout, Challenge, POB 3109, Ibadan; tel. (2) 313956; f. 1958; educational and general; Chair. G. ONIBONOJE; Man. Dir J. O. ONIBONOJE.

Spectrum Books Ltd: Spectrum House, Ring Rd, PMB 5612, Ibadan; tel. (2) 2310058; fax (2) 2318502; e-mail admin1@spectrumbooksonline.com; internet www.spectrumbooksonline.com; f. 1978; educational and fiction; Chair. JOOP BERKHOUT; Man. Dir SINA OKEOWO.

University of Lagos Press: University of Lagos, POB 132, Akoka, Yaba, Lagos; tel. (1) 825048; e-mail library@rcl.nig.com; university textbooks, monographs, lectures and journals; Man. Dir S. BODUNDE BANKOLE.

NIGERIA
Directory

University Press Ltd: Three Crowns Bldg, Eleyele Rd, Jericho, PMB 5095, Ibadan; tel. (2) 2411356; fax (2) 2412056; e-mail unipress@skannet.com.ng; f. 1978; associated with Oxford University Press; educational; Man. Dir WAHEED O. OLAJIDE.

University Publishing Co: 11 Central School Rd, POB 386, Onitsha; tel. (46) 210013; f. 1959; primary, secondary and university textbooks; Chair. E. O. UGWUEGBULEM.

Vanguard Media Ltd: Vanguard Ave, off Mile 2/Apapa Expressway, Kirikiri Canal; tel. (1) 5871200; fax (1) 5872662; e-mail vanguard@linkserve.com.ng; Publr SAM AMUKA.

Vista Books Ltd: 59 Awolowo Rd, S. W. Ikoyi, POB 282, Yaba, Lagos; tel. (1) 7746348; e-mail vista-books@yahoo.com; f. 1991; general fiction and non-fiction, arts, children's and educational; Man. Dir Dr T. C. NWOSU.

West African Book Publishers Ltd: Ilupeju Industrial Estate, 28–32 Industrial Ave, POB 3445, Lagos; tel. (1) 7754518; fax (1) 2799127; e-mail w_bookafricapubl@hotmail.com; internet www.wabp.com; f. 1963; textbooks, children's, periodicals and general; Chair. B. A. IDRIS-ANIMASHAUN; Man. Dir FOLASHADE B. OMO-EBOH.

PUBLISHERS' ASSOCIATION

Nigerian Publishers' Association: Book House, NPA Permanent Secretariat, Jericho G.R.A., POB 2541, Ibadan; tel. (2) 2413396; f. 1965; Pres. S. B. BANKOLE.

Broadcasting and Communications

TELECOMMUNICATIONS

Nigerian Communications Commission (NCC): Plot 423, Aguiyi Ironsi St, Maitama, Abuja; tel. (9) 4617000; fax (9) 4617514; e-mail ncc@ncc.gov.ng; internet www.ncc.gov.ng; f. 1932 as an independent regulatory body for the supply of telecommunications services and facilities; Chair. Alhaji AHMED JODA; CEO ERNEST C. A. NDUKWE.

Airtel Nigeria: Plot L2, Banana Island, Foreshore Estate, Ikoyi, Lagos; tel. 8021900000; fax (1) 3200477; e-mail customercare.ng@airtel.com; internet www.ng.airtel.com; f. 2000; fmrly Celtel Nigeria, subsequently Zain Nigeria, present name adopted in 2010; CEO ALAIN SAINTE-MARIE.

Globacom Nigeria Ltd: Mike Adenuga Towers, 1 Mike Adenuga Cl., off Adeola Odeku, Victoria Island, Lagos; e-mail customercare@gloworld.com; internet www.gloworld.com; f. 2003; Chair. Dr MIKE ADENUGA, Jr; 9m. subscribers (2007).

Intercellular Nigeria Ltd: UBA House, 57, Marina, PMB 80078, Victoria Island, Lagos; tel. (1) 4703010; fax (1) 2643014; internet www.intercellular-ng.com; f. 1993; internet and international telephone services; 70% owned by Sudatel (Sudan); CEO ARVID KNUTSEN.

Motophone Ltd: C. & C. Towers, Plot 1684, Sanusi Fafumwa St, Victoria Island, Lagos; tel. (1) 2624168; fax (1) 2620079; e-mail motophone@hyperia.com; internet www.motophone.com; f. 1990; Man. Dir ERIC CHAMCHOUM.

MTN Nigeria Communications Ltd: Golden Plaza Bldg, Awolowo Rd, Falomo, Ikoyi, PMB 80147, Lagos; tel. 8032005638; fax 8039029636; e-mail info@mtnnigeria.net; internet www.mtnonline.com; f. 2001; CEO AHMAD FARROUKH.

Multi-Links Telecommunication Ltd: 231 Adeola Odeku St, Victoria Island, POB 3453, Marina, Lagos; tel. (1) 7740000; fax (1) 7912345; internet www.multilinks.com; f. 1994; Chair. R. J. SEPTEMBER; Man. Dir T. G. MSIMANGO.

Nigerian Mobile Telecommunications Ltd (M-TEL): 2 Bissau St, off Herbert Macaulay Way, Wuse Zone 6, Abuja; tel. (9) 5233031; internet www.mtelnigeria.com; f. 1996; Chair. OLULADE ADEGBOYEGA.

Nigerian Telecommunications Ltd (NITEL): 2 Bissau St, off Herbert Macaulay Way, Wuse Zone 6, Abuja; tel. (9) 5233021; f. 1984; 51% owned by Transnational Corporation of Nigeria PLC, 49% govt-owned; undergoing privatization in 2009; Chair. Dr MARTINS IGBOKWE.

Starcomms: Starcomms House, Plot 1261 Bishop Kale Close, off Saka Tinubu St, Victoria Island, Lagos; tel. (1) 8041234; fax (1) 8110301; e-mail customerservice@starcomms.com; internet www.starcomms.com; f. 1999; Chair. Chief MANN LABABIDI; CEO MAHER QUBAIN.

Telnet (Nigeria) Ltd: Plot 242, Kofo Abayomi St, Victoria Island, POB 53656, Falomi Ikoyi, Lagos; tel. (1) 2611729; fax (1) 2619945; e-mail contact@iteco.com; internet www.telnetng.com; f. 1985; telecommunications engineering and consultancy services; Man. Dir GBENGA ODUJINRIN.

BROADCASTING

Regulatory Authority

National Broadcasting Commission: Plot 20, Ibrahim Taiwo St, Asokoro District, POB 5747, Garki, Abuja; tel. (9) 3147527; fax (9) 3147522; e-mail infonbc@nbc.gov.ng; internet www.nbc.gov.ng; Dir-Gen. Eng. YOMI BOLARINWA.

Radio

Federal Radio Corpn of Nigeria (FRCN): Radio House, PMB 452, Garki, Abuja; tel. (9) 2345230; fax (9) 2346486; e-mail info@radionigeria.net; internet www.radionigeria.net; f. 1976; controlled by the Fed. Govt and divided into five zones: Lagos (English); Enugu (English, Igbo, Izon, Efik and Tiv); Ibadan (English, Yoruba, Edo, Urhobo and Igala); Kaduna (English, Hausa, Kanuri, Fulfulde and Nupe); Abuja (English, Hausa, Igbo and Yoruba); Dir-Gen. YUSUF NUHU.

Imo Broadcasting Corpn: Egbu Rd, PMB 1129, Owerri, Imo; tel. (42) 250327; operates one radio station in Imo State; CEO SAMFO NWANKWO.

Voice of Nigeria (VON): 6th and 7th Floor, Radio House, Herbert Macaulay Way, Area 10, Garki, Abuja; tel. (9) 2344017; fax (9) 2346970; e-mail info@voiceofnigeria.org; internet www.voiceofnigeria.org; f. 1990; controlled by the Fed. Govt; external services in English, French, Arabic, Ki-Swahili, Hausa and Fulfulde; Dir-Gen. Alhaji ABUBAKAR BOBBOYI JIJIWA.

Menage Holding's Broadcasting System Ltd: Umuahia, Imo; commenced broadcasting Jan. 1996; commercial.

Ray Power Radio 100.5 FM: Abeokuta Express Way, Ilapo, Alagbado, Lagos; tel. (1) 2644814; fax (1) 2644817; 100% owned by DAAR Communications Ltd; commenced broadcasting Sept. 1994; commercial; Chair. Chief ALEOGHO RAYMOND DOKPESI.

Television

Nigerian Television Authority (NTA): Television House, Area 11, Garki, PMB 13, Abuja; tel. (9) 2345907; fax (9) 2345914; internet www.nta.com.ng; f. 1976; controlled by the Fed. Govt; operates a network of 31 terrestrial broadcasters, which share national programming but also broadcast local programmes; also operates c. 70 regional channels; Chair. YAKUBULL HUSSAINI; Dir-Gen. Dr MAGAWATA MOHAMMED USMAN.

Africa Independent Television (AIT): Kpaduma Hill, off T. Y. Danjuma, Asokoro Extension, Abuja; e-mail info@daargroup.com; internet www.daargroup.com; f. 1994; 100% owned by DAAR Communications Ltd; Exec. Chair. Dr ALEOGHO RAYMOND DOKPESI.

Minaj Broadcast International (MBI): Minaj Media Group, 130/132, Ladipo St, Materi, Mushin, POB 70811, Victoria Island, Lagos; tel. (1) 4529203; fax (1) 4528500; e-mail info@minajmedia.com; internet www.minajmedia.com; provides free-to-air services; Chair. Chief MIKE AJEGBO.

Murhi International Television (MITV): MITV Plaza, Ikeja Central Business District, Obafemi Awolowo Way, Alausa, Lagos; tel. (1) 4931271; fax (1) 4931272; e-mail mitv@murhi-international.com; Chair. MURI GBADEYANKA BUSARI.

Finance

(cap. = capital; res = reserves; dep. = deposits; m. = million; brs = branches; amounts in naira)

BANKING

In early 2011 there were 24 commercial banks and five development finance institutions in Nigeria.

Central Bank

Central Bank of Nigeria: Plot 33, Abubakar Tafawa Balewa Way, Central Business District, Cadestral Zone, PMB 0187, Garki, Abuja; tel. (9) 46239701; fax (9) 46236012; e-mail info@cenbank.org; internet www.cenbank.org; f. 1958; bank of issue; cap. 5,000m., res 320,165m., dep. 4,971,643m. (Dec. 2006); Gov. SANUSI LAMIDO AMINU SANUSI; 28 brs.

Commercial Banks

Access Bank: Plot 1665, Oyin Jolayemi St, Victoria Island, Lagos; tel. (1) 2805628; e-mail contactcenter@accessbankplc.com; internet www.accessbankplc.com; Chair. GBENGA OYEBODE; CEO AIGBOJE AIG-IMOUKHUEDE.

Bank PHB: 1 Bank PHB Cres., Victoria Island, Lagos; tel. (1) 4485742; e-mail phblink@bankphb.com; internet www.bankphb.com; Chair. KOLA ABIOLA.

NIGERIA

Afribank Nigeria Ltd: 51–55 Broad St, PMB 12021, Lagos; tel. (1) 2641566; fax (1) 2669763; e-mail info@afribank.com; internet www.afribank.com; f. 1969 as International Bank for West Africa Ltd; cap. 3,065.0m., res 31,822.0m., dep. 280,290.1m. (March 2008); Chair. Osa Osunde; Man. Dir and CEO Nebolisa O. Arah; 137 brs.

Citibank Nigeria Ltd: 27 Kofo Abayomi St, Victoria Island, POB 6391, Lagos; tel. (1) 2798400; fax (1) 2618916; internet www.citibanknigeria.com; f. 1984; cap. 2,793.7m., res 34,900.5m., dep. 97,969.5m. (Dec. 2008); Chair. Olayemi Cardoso; Country Officer Emeka Emuwa; 4 brs.

Diamond Bank PLC: Plot 1261, Adeola Hopewell St, Victoria Island, POB 70381, Lagos; tel. (1) 2701500; fax (1) 2619728; e-mail info@diamondbank.com; internet www.diamondbank.com; f. 2005 by merger with Lion Bank of Nigeria PLC; cap. 6,579.6m., res. 100,941.0m., dep. 410,094.0m. (April 2008); Chair. Igwe Nnaemeka Alfred Achebe; Man. Dir and CEO Alex Otti.

Ecobank Nigeria Ltd: Plot 21, Ahmadu Bello Way, Victoria Island, POB 72688, Lagos; tel. (1) 2706985; fax (1) 2706986; e-mail ecobankng@ecobank.com; internet www.ecobank.com; f. 1989; cap. 3,609.0m., res 26,419.7m., dep. 380,287.5m. (Dec. 2008); Chair. Olor'ogun Sonny Folorunsho Kuku; Man. Dir Jibril J. Aku; 23 brs.

First Bank of Nigeria PLC: Samuel Asabia House, 35 Marina, POB 5216, Lagos; tel. (1) 2665900; fax (1) 2669073; e-mail firstcontact@firstbanknigeria.com; internet www.firstbanknigeria.com; f. 1894 as Bank of British West Africa; cap. 12,432m., res. 338,622m., dep. 1,150,816m. (March 2009); Chair. Dr Oba Otudeko; CEO and Man. Dir Stephen Olabisi Onasanya; 302 brs.

Guaranty Trust Bank PLC: The Plural House, Plot 1669, Oyin Jolayemi St, PMB 75455, Victoria Island, Lagos; tel. (1) 4480740; fax (1) 2715227; e-mail corpaff@gtbank.com; internet www.gtbank.com; f. 1990; cap. 9,326.9m., res 160,507.5m., dep. 728,859.7m. (Dec. 2009); Chair. Oluwole S. Oduyemi; Man. Dir and CEO Tayo Aderinokun; 161 brs.

Intercontinental Bank PLC: Danmole St, Plot 999c, Adela Odeku, PMB 80150, Victoria Island, Lagos; tel. (1) 2773300; fax (1) 2622981; e-mail customercaredepartment@intercontinentalbankplc.com; internet www.intercontinentalbankplc.com; cap. 9,733.0m., res 168,519.0m., dep. 1,058,920.0m. (Feb. 2008); Chair. Raymond Obieri; Chief Exec. Mahmoud Alabi; 42 brs.

Oceanic Bank International PLC: Plot 270, Ozumba Mbadiwe Ave, Waterfront Plaza, Victoria Island, Lagos; tel. (1) 2705010; fax (1) 2705066; e-mail info@oceanicbanknigeria.com; internet www.oceanicbanknigeria.com; f. 1990; name changed as above June 2005; cap. 11,110m., res. 193,775m., dep. 911,471m. (Dec. 2008); Chair. Apostle Hayford Alile; Man. Dir and CEO John Aboh.

Skye Bank PLC: 3 Akin Adesola St, Victoria Island, Lagos; tel. (1) 2701600; e-mail info@skyebankng.com; internet www.skyebankng.com; Chair. Moronkeji Onasanya; Group Man. Dir Kehinde Durosinmi-Etti.

Spring Bank PLC: 143 Ahmadu Bello Way, Victoria Island, Lagos; tel. (1) 2623780; internet www.springbankplc.com; f. 2004 by merger of ACB International Bank PLC, Citizens International Bank PLC, Fountain Trust Bank PLC, Guardian Express Bank PLC, Omegabank (Nigeria) PLC and Trans International Bank PLC; acquired by Platinum Habib Bank Group in 2008; Man. Dir Benardina Olusola Ayodele.

Stanbic IBTC Bank PLC: I.B.T.C. Place, Walter Carrington Cres., POB 71707, Victoria Island, Lagos; tel. (1) 2712400; fax (1) 2806998; e-mail customercarenigeria@stanbic.com; internet www.ibtc.com/portal/site/nigeria; f. 1989 as Investment Banking & Trust Co Ltd; name changed as above 2008 following merger with Stanbic Bank (Nigeria) Ltd; cap. 9,375.0m., res 67,241.7m., dep. 181,093.1m. (Dec. 2008); Chair. Atedo N. A. Peterside; CEO Sola David-Borha; 57 brs.

Sterling Bank: Sterling Towers, 20 Marina, POB 12735, Lagos; tel. (1) 2600420; fax (1) 2633294; e-mail tradeservices@sterlingbankng.com; internet www.sterlingbankng.com; f. 2005 following merger of Indo-Nigerian Bank Ltd, Magnum Trust Bank, NAL Bank PLC, NBM Bank and Trust Bank of Africa Ltd; cap. 6,281.5m., res. 23,957.3m., dep. 184,730.2m. (Sept. 2008); Chair. Alhaji Suleiman Adebola Adegunwa; Man. Dir Razack Adeyemi Adeola.

Union Bank of Nigeria Ltd: 36 Marina, PMB 2027, Lagos; tel. (1) 2630361; fax (1) 2669873; e-mail info@unionbankng.com; internet www.unionbankng.com; f. 1969 as Barclays Bank of Nigeria Ltd; cap. 101,049m., res 1,493m., dep. 482,382m. (March 2007); Chair. Prof. Musa G. Yakubu; Man. Dir and CEO Olunfunke Iyabo Osibodu; 235 brs.

United Bank for Africa (Nigeria) Ltd: UBA House, 57 Marina, POB 2406, Lagos; tel. (1) 2808822; fax (1) 2808448; e-mail cic@ubagroup.com; internet www.ubagroup.com; f. 1961; cap. 8,622m., res 179,533m., dep. 1,258,035m. (Sept. 2008); Chair. Ferdinand Ngogo Alabraba; Man. Dir Tony O. Elumelu; 428 brs.

Unity Bank PLC: Plot 785, Herbert Macaulay Way, Central Business District, POB 52463, Abuja; tel. (9) 4616700; fax (9) 4616730; e-mail we_care@unitybankng.com; internet www.unitybankng.com; f. 2005; cap. 21,752.9m., res. 9,015.0m., dep. 79,683.5m. (June 2006); Chair. Prof. Akin L. Mabogunje; Man. Dir and CEO Alhaji Falalu Bello.

Wema Bank Ltd: Wema Towers, PMB 12862, 54 Marina, Lagos; tel. (1) 2668043; fax (1) 2669236; e-mail info@wemabank.com; internet www.wemabank.com; f. 1945; cap. 5,035.0m., res 19,781.7m., dep. 125,476.0m. (March 2007); Chair. Chief Samuel Bolarinde; Man. Dir Segun Oloketuyi; 146 brs.

Zenith Bank PLC: Plot 84, Ajose Adeogun St, Victoria Island, POB 75315, Lagos; tel. (1) 2788000; fax (1) 2618212; e-mail enquiry@zenithbank.com; internet www.zenithbank.com; f. 1990; name changed as above in 2004; cap. 8,372.4m., res. 330,111.7m., dep. 1,167,335.2m. (Sept. 2008); Man. Dir Jim Ovia.

Merchant Banks

FBN Capital Ltd: 16 Keffi St, off Awolowo Rd, Ikoyi, Lagos; tel. (1) 2707180; fax (1) 2633600; e-mail info@fbncapital.com; internet www.fbncapital.com; Chair. Oyekanmi Hassan-Odukale; Man. Dir and CEO Osaze Osifo.

Fidelity Bank PLC: 2 Kofo Abayomi St, Victoria Island, Lagos; tel. (1) 2713487; fax (1) 2610414; e-mail info@fidelitybankplc.com; internet www.fidelitybankplc.com; f. 1988; cap. 14,481.3m., res 114,892.5m., dep. 356,137.3m. (June 2009); Chair. Chief Christopher Ezeh; CEO Reginald Ihejiahi; 20 brs.

First City Monument Bank Ltd: Primrose Tower, 17A Tinubu St, POB 9117, Lagos; tel. (1) 2665944; fax (1) 2665126; e-mail fcmb@fcmb-ltd.com; internet www.firstcitygroup.com; f. 1983; cap. 8,136.0m., res 119,322.0m., dep. 349,441.8m. (April 2009); Chair. Dr Jonathan A. D. Long; Man. Dir and CEO Ladi Balogun; 12 brs.

Development Finance Institutions

Bank of Industry (BOI) Ltd: 23 Marina, POB 2357, Lagos; tel. (1) 2665528; fax (1) 2665286; e-mail info@boi-ng.com; internet www.boinigeria.com; f. 1964 as the Nigerian Industrial Development Bank Ltd to provide medium and long-term finance to industry, manufacturing, non-petroleum mining and tourism; name changed as above Oct. 2001; cap. 6,585.1m., dep. 3,500m. (Dec. 2005); Chair. Alhaji Abdulsamad Rabiu; Man. Dir Dr Eveln N. Oputu; 8 brs.

The Federal Mortgage Bank of Nigeria (FMBN): Mortgage House, Plot 266, Cadastral AO, Central Business District, PMB 2273, Garki, Abuja; tel. (9) 4602102; e-mail info@fmbnigeria.org; internet www.fmbnigeria.org; f. 1956 as Nigerian Building Society (NBS); Chair. Alhaji Adedamola Atta; Man. Dir Gimba Ya'u Kumo.

Nigerian Agricultural, Co-operative and Rural Development Bank Ltd (NACRDB): Yakubu Gowoh, PMB 2155, Kaduna; tel. (62) 244417; fax (62) 244612; e-mail nacb@infoweb.abs.net; internet www.nacrdb.com; f. 1973 for funds to farmers and co-operatives to improve production techniques; name changed as above Oct. 2000, following merger with People's Bank of Nigeria; cap. 1,000m. (2002); Chair. Chief Gordon Bozimo; Man. Dir Dr Mohammed Santuraki; 200 brs.

The Nigerian Export-Import Bank (NEXIM): NEXIM House, Plot 975, Cadastral Zone AO, Central Business District, PMB 276, Garki, Abuja; tel. (9) 6281630; fax (9) 6281640; e-mail neximabj@neximbank.com.ng; internet www.neximbank.com.ng; f. 1991; CEO Roberts U. Orya.

The Urban Development Bank of Nigeria PLC (UDBN): Plot 977, Central Business Area, PMB 272, Garki, Abuja; tel. (9) 6710863; e-mail enquiries@udbng.com; internet www.udbng.com; f. 1992; Chair. Hakeem O. Sanusi.

Bankers' Association

Chartered Institute of Bankers of Nigeria: PC 19 Adeola Hopewell St, POB 72273, Victoria Island, Lagos; tel. (1) 2703494; fax (1) 4618930; e-mail cibn@cibng.org; internet www.cibng.org; Chair. Joseph Laoye Jaiyeola; CEO Dr Uju M. Ogubunka.

STOCK EXCHANGE

Securities and Exchange Commission (SEC): SEC Towers, Plot 272, Samuel Adesujo Ademulegun St, Central Business District, PMB 315, Garki, Abuja; tel. (9) 6330000; fax (9) 2346276; internet www.sec.gov.ng; f. 1979 as govt agency to regulate and develop capital market and to supervise stock exchange operations; Chair. Udoma Udo Udoma; Dir-Gen. Arunma Oteh.

Nigerian Stock Exchange: Stock Exchange House, 2–4 Customs St, POB 2457, Lagos; tel. (1) 2660287; fax (1) 2668724; e-mail info@nigerianstockexchange.biz; internet www.nigerianstockexchange.com; f. 1960; Pres. Dr Oba Otudeko; CEO Oscar Onyema; 6 brs.

NIGERIA

Directory

INSURANCE

In early 2011 the insurance sector comprised 51 registered companies, seven life insurance companies, 23 non-life insurance companies, 19 composite companies and two reinsurance companies. Since 1978 they have been required to reinsure 20% of the sum insured with the Nigeria Reinsurance Corpn.

Regulatory Authority

National Insurance Commission (NAICOM): Shippers Plaza, Micheal Okpara St, Wuse Zone 5, PMB 457, Graki Abuja; tel. (9) 6733520; fax (9) 6735649; e-mail info@naicom.gov.org; internet www.naicom.gov.ng; f. 1992 as National Insurance Supervisory Board; present name adopted 1997; Chair. Hajia INNA MARYAM CIROMA; Commr for Insurance FOLA DANIEL.

Insurance Companies

African Alliance Insurance Co Ltd: 112 Broad St, POB 2276, Lagos; tel. (1) 7227666; fax (1) 2660943; e-mail info@africanallianceinsurance.com; internet www.africanallianceinsurance.com; f. 1960; life assurance and pensions; Man. Dir ALPHONSUS OKPOR; 30 brs.

Aiico International Insurance (AIICO): AIICO Plaza, Plot PC 12, Afribank St, Victoria Island, POB 2577, Lagos; tel. (1) 2610651; fax (1) 2799800; e-mail info@aiicoplc.com; internet www.aiicoplc.com; CEO S. D. A SOBANJO.

Ark Insurance Group: Glass House, 11A Karimu Kotun St, Victoria Island, POB 3771, Marina, Lagos; tel. (1) 2615826; fax (1) 2615850; e-mail info@arkinsurancegroup.com; internet www.arkinsurancegroup.com; Chair. FRANCIS OLUWOLE AWOGBORO.

Continental Reinsurance Co Ltd: St. Nicholas House, 8th Floor, 6 Catholic Mission St, POB 2401, Lagos; tel. (1) 2665350; fax (1) 2665370; e-mail info@continental-re.com; internet www.continental-re.com; Chair. S. A. LAGUDA; CEO Dr FEMI OYETUNJI.

Cornerstone Insurance Co PLC: POB 75370, Victoria Island, Lagos; tel. (1) 2631832; fax (1) 2633079; e-mail marketing@cornerstone.com.ng; internet www.cornerstone.com.ng; f. 1991; Chair. ADEDOTUN SULAIMAN; Man. Dir and CEO LIVINGSTONE MAGORIMBO.

CrystaLife: 12th and 13th Floor, Eleganza House, 15B Joseph St, POB 1514, Lagos; tel. (1) 2636800; fax (1) 2637095; e-mail equilifekn@equity-lifeinsurance.com; internet www.crystalifeassurance.com; Chair. AKINSOLA AKINFEMIWA; Man. Dir and CEO OLUSEYI IFATUROTI.

Equity Assurance PLC: 19 Circular Road, Presidential Estate, POB 2709, Port Harcourt; tel. (84) 236114; fax (84) 236115; e-mail portharcourt@equityassuranceplc.com; f. 1991; Chair. OLUFEMI SOMOLU; COO OLUMIDE FALOHUN.

Great Nigeria Insurance Co Ltd: 8 Omo-Osaghie St, off Obafemi Awolono Rd, Ikoyi S/W, Ikoyi, POB 2314, Lagos; tel. (1) 2695805; fax (1) 2693483; e-mail info@gniplc.com; internet www.gniplc.com; f. 1960; all classes; Chair. SEGUN OLOKETUYI; Man. Dir CECILIA O. SIPITAN.

Guinea Insurance PLC: Reinsurance Bldg, 10th Floor, 46 Marine, POB 1136, Lagos; tel. (1) 2665201; e-mail info@guineainsurance.com; internet www.guineainsurance.com; f. 1958; all classes; Man. Dir and CEO SOJI EMIOLA.

Industrial and General Insurance Co Ltd: Plot 741, Adeola Hopewell St, PMB 80181, Victoria Island, Lagos; tel. (1) 6215010; fax (1) 2621146; e-mail info@iginigeria.com; internet www.iginigeria.com; Chair. YAKUBU GOWON.

Law Union and Rock Insurance PLC: 14 Hughes Ave, Alagomeji, Yaba, POB 944, Lagos; e-mail enquiry@lur-ng.com; tel. (1) 8995010; fax (1) 3425077; internet www.lawunioninsurance.com; fire, accident and marine; Chair. AKINSOLA AKINFEMIWA; Man. Dir and CEO YINKA BOLARINWA; 6 brs.

Leadway Assurance Co Ltd: NN 28–29 Constitution Rd, POB 458, Kaduna; tel. (62) 246776; fax (62) 246838; e-mail insure@leadway.com; internet www.leadway.com; f. 1970; all classes; Man. Dir OYEKANMI ABIODUN HASSAN-ODUKALE.

Lion of Africa Insurance Co Ltd: St Peter's House, 3 Ajele St, POB 2055, Lagos; tel. (1) 2600950; fax (1) 2636111; internet thelionofafrica.org; f. 1952; all classes; Man. Dir and CEO PETER MONYE.

National Insurance Corpn of Nigeria (NICON): 5 Customs St, POB 1100, Lagos; tel. (1) 2640230; fax (1) 2666556; f. 1969; all classes; cap. 200m.; Chair. JIMOH IBRAHIM; 28 brs.

N.E.M. Insurance Co (Nigeria) Ltd: 138/146 Broad St, POB 654, Lagos; tel. (1) 5861920; internet www.nem-insurance.com; all classes; Chair. Chief ADEWALE TELUWO; Man. Dir TOPE SMART.

Niger Insurance PLC: 48/50 Odunlami St, POB 2718, Marina, Lagos; tel. (1) 2631329; fax (1) 2662196; e-mail info@nigerinsurance.com; internet www.nigerinsurance.com; f. 1962; all classes; Chair. BALA ZAKARIYA'U; Man. Dir Dr JUSTUS URANTA; 6 brs.

Nigeria Reinsurance Corpn: 46 Marina, PMB 12766, Lagos; tel. (1) 2667049; fax (1) 2668041; e-mail info@nigeriare.com; internet www.nigeriareinsurance.com; all classes of reinsurance; Man. Dir T. T. MIRILLA.

Nigerian General Insurance Co Ltd: 1 Nnamdi Azikiwe St, Tirubu Square, POB 2210, Lagos; tel. (1) 2662552; e-mail odua@odua.com; f. 1951; all classes; Chair. O. O. OKEYODE; Man. Dir J. A. OLANIHUN; 15 brs.

Royal Exchange Assurance (Nigeria) Group: New Africa House, 31 Marina, POB 112, Lagos; tel. (1) 2663120; fax (1) 2664431; e-mail info@royalexchangeplc.com; internet portal.royalexchangeplc.com; all classes; Chair. Alhaji MUHTAR BELLO YOLA; Man. Dir ALLAN WALMSLEY; 6 brs.

Sun Insurance Office (Nigeria) Ltd: Unity House, 37 Marina, POB 2694, Lagos; tel. (1) 2661318; all classes except life; Man. Dir A. T. ADENIJI; 6 brs.

United Nigeria Insurance Co Ltd (UNIC): 53 Marina, POB 588, Lagos; tel. (1) 2663201; fax (1) 2664282; f. 1965; all classes except life; CEO E. O. A. ADETUNJI; 17 brs.

UnityKapital Assurance PLC: 497 Abogo Largema St, off Constitution Ave, Central Business District, POB 2044, Abuja; tel. (9) 4619900; fax (9) 4619901; e-mail info@unitykapital.com; internet www.unitykapital.com; f. 1973; Chair. Alhaji FALALU BELLO; CEO MOHAMMED KARI.

Unity Life and Fire Insurance Co Ltd: 25 Nnamdi Azikiwe St, POB 3681, Lagos; tel. (1) 2662517; fax (1) 2662599; all classes; Man. Dir R. A. ODINIGWE.

West African Provincial Insurance Co: WAPIC House, 119 Awolowo Rd, POB 55508, Falomo-Ikoyi, Lagos; tel. (1) 2672770; fax (1) 2693838; e-mail wapic@alpha.linkserve.com; Man. Dir D. O. AMUSAN.

Insurance Association

Nigerian Insurers' Association (NIA): 42 Saka Tinubu St, Victoria Island, POB 9551, Lagos; tel. (1) 2629616; fax (1) 2621298; e-mail info@nigeriainsurers.com; internet www.nigeriainsurers.com; f. 1971; Chair. OLUSOLA LADIPO AJAYI; Dir-Gen. SUNDAY THOMAS.

Trade and Industry

GOVERNMENT AGENCIES

Bureau of Public Enterprises: Secretariat of the National Council on Privatization, 1 Osun Cres., off IBB Way, Maitama District, PMB 442, Garki, Abuja; tel. (9) 4134636; fax (9) 4134657; e-mail bpe@bpeng.org; internet www.bpeng.org; Dir-Gen. BOLANLE ONAGORUWA.

Corporate Affairs Commission: Plot 420, Tigris Cres., off Aguiyi Ironsi St, Maitama, PMB 198, Garki, Abuja; tel. (9) 4618800; fax (9) 2342669; e-mail info@cac.gov.ng; internet www.cac.gov.ng; Chair. Chief Dr JIMOH IBRAHIM; Registrar-Gen./CEO BELLO MAHMUD.

National Council on Privatisation: Bureau of Public Enterprises, NDIC Bldg, Constitution Ave, Central Business District, PMB 442, Garki, Abuja; tel. (9) 5237405; fax (9) 5237396; e-mail bpegen@micro.com.ng; internet www.bpe.gov.ng; Chair. NAMADI SAMBO.

Nigeria Export Processing Zones Authority (NEPZA): 2 Zambezi Cres., Cadastral Zone A6, off Aguiyi Ironsi St, Maitama, PMB 037, Garki, Abuja; tel. (9) 2343059; fax (9) 2343061; e-mail info@nepza.gov.ng; Man. Dir SINA A. AGBOLUAJE.

DEVELOPMENT ORGANIZATIONS

Benin–Owena River Basin Development Authority: 24 Benin-Sapele Rd, PMB 1381, Obayantor, Benin City; tel. (52) 254415; f. 1976 to conduct irrigation; Gen. Man. Dr G. E. OTEZE.

Chad Basin Development Authority (CBDA): Dikwa Rd, PMB 1130, Maiduguri; tel. (76) 232015; f. 1973; irrigation and agriculture-allied industries; Man. Dir Dr ABUBAKAR GARBA ILLIYA; Gen. Man. Alhaji BUNU S. MUSA.

Cross River Basin Development Authority (CRBDA): 32 Target Rd, PMB 1249, Calabar; tel. (87) 223163; f. 1976; Gen. Man. SIXTUS ABETIANBE.

Federal Institute of Industrial Research, Oshodi (FIIRO): Blind Center St, by Cappa Bus Stop, off Agege Motor Rd, Oshodi, Ikeja, PMB 21023, Lagos; tel. (1) 4701846; fax (1) 4525880; e-mail info@fiiro-ng.org; internet www.fiiro-ng.org; f. 1956; plans and directs scientific research for industrial and technological development; provides tech. assistance and information to industry;

NIGERIA

specializes in foods, minerals, textiles, natural products and industrial intermediates; Dir-Gen. Dr OLUWOLE OLATUNJI.

Industrial Training Fund: 1, Kufang Village, Miango Rd, PMB 2199, Jos, Plateau; tel. and fax (73) 462395; e-mail dp@itf-nigeria.com; internet www.itf-nigeria.com; f. 1971 to promote and encourage skilled workers in trade and industry; Dir-Gen. Prof. OLU E. AKEREJOLA.

Kaduna Industrial and Finance Co Ltd: Investment House, 27 Ali Akilu Rd, PMB 2230, Kaduna; tel. 8037035577 (mobile); fax (62) 290781; e-mail info@kadunainvest.com; internet www.kadunainvest.com; f. 1989; provides devt finance; Man. Dir and CEO ALHAJI SHEHU MUHAMMAD SHITU.

Kwara State Investment Corpn: Charlets, 109–112 Fate Rd, PMB 1344, Ilorin, Kwara; tel. (31) 220510.

Lagos State Development and Property Corpn: 2/4 Town Planning Way, Ilupeju Industrial Estate, PMB 21050, Lagos; tel. (1) 7621424; e-mail info@lsdpc.gov.ng; internet www.lsdpc.gov.ng; f. 1972; planning and devt of Lagos; Man. Dir BIODUN OKI.

New Nigerian Development Co Ltd: 18/19 Ahmadu Bello Way, Ahmed Talib House, PMB 2120, Kaduna; tel. (62) 249355; fax (62) 245482; e-mail nndc@skannet.com.ng; f. 1949; owned by the govts of 19 northern states; investment finance; 8 subsidiaries, 83 assoc. cos; Chair. Prof. HALIDU IBRAHIM ABUBAKAR.

Niger Delta Development Commission (NDDC): 6 Olumeni St, Port Harcourt; internet nddc.gov.org; f. 2000; Chair. Air Vice-Marshall (retd) LARRY KOINYAN; Man. Dir CHIBUZOR UGWOHA.

Nigerian Enterprises Promotion Board: 15–19 Keffi St, Ikoyi, Lagos; tel. (1) 2680929; f. 1972 to promote indigenization; Chair. MINSO GADZAMA.

Northern Nigeria Investments Ltd: 4 Waff Rd, POB 138, Kaduna; tel. (62) 239654; fax (62) 230770; f. 1959 to identify and invest in industrial and agricultural projects in 16 northern states; cap. p.u. 20m.; Chair. Alhaji ABUBAKAR G. ADAMU; Man. Dir GIMBA H. IBRAHIM.

Odu'a Investment Co Ltd: Cocoa House Complex, Oba Adebimpe Rd, PMB 5435, Ibadan; tel. (2) 2001037; fax (2) 413000; e-mail odua@oduainvestmentcompany.com; internet www.oduainvestmentcompany.com; f. 1976; jtly owned by Ogun, Ondo and Oyo States; Man. Dir A. K. JIMOH.

Plateau State Water Resources Development Board: Jos; incorporates the fmr Plateau River Basin Devt Authority and Plateau State Water Resources Devt Board.

Projects Development Institute (PRODA): Emene Industrial Layout, Proda Rd, POB 01609, Enugu; tel. (42) 451593; fax (42) 457691; f. 1977; promotes the establishment of new industries and develops industrial projects utilizing local raw materials; Dir BASIL K. C. UGWA.

Raw Materials Research and Development Council (RMRDC): Plot 427, Aguiyi, Ironsi St, Maitama District, PMB 232, Garki Abuja; tel. (9) 4134716; fax (9) 4136034; e-mail icsd_liaison@rmrdc.gov.ng; internet www.rmrdc.gov.ng; f. 1988; Dir.-Gen. Prof. A. P. ONWUALU.

Rubber Research Institute of Nigeria (RRIB): PMB 1049, Benin City; tel. 8033197241; e-mail rubberresearchnig@yahoo.com; f. 1961; conducts research into the production of rubber and other latex products; Exec. Dir M.U.B. MOKWUNYE; Chair Air Cdre DAN SULEIMAN.

Trans Investments Co Ltd: Bale Oyewole Rd, PMB 5085, Ibadan; tel. (2) 416000; f. 1986; initiates and finances industrial and agricultural schemes; Gen. Man. M. A. ADESIYUN.

CHAMBERS OF COMMERCE

Nigerian Association of Chambers of Commerce, Industry, Mines and Agriculture: 8A Oba Akinjobi Way, PMB 12816, Lagos; tel. (1) 4964727; fax (1) 4964737; e-mail contact@naccima.com; internet www.naccima.com; f. 1960; Pres. Dr HERBERT ADEMOLA AJAYI; Dir-Gen. JOHN ISEMEDE.

Aba Chamber of Commerce and Industry: UBA Bldg, Ikot Expene Rd/Georges St, POB 1596, Aba; tel. (82) 352084; fax (82) 352067; f. 1971; Pres. Chief KALU OMOJI KALU.

Abeokuta Chamber of Commerce and Industry: Commerce House, Nr Govt House, Oke Igbehin, Ibaha, POB 937, Abeokuta; tel. (39) 241230; Pres. Chief S. O. AKINREMI.

Abuja Chamber of Commerce, Industry, Mines & Agriculture: International Trade Fair Complex, KM8, Airport Rd, PMB 86, Garki, Abuja; tel. 8033139347 (mobile); e-mail abuccima@hotmail.com; f. 1986; Pres. DELE KELVIN OYE.

Adamawa Chamber of Commerce and Industry: c/o Palace Hotel, POB 8, Jimeta, Yola; tel. (75) 255136; Pres. Alhaji ISA HAMMANYERO.

Akure Chamber of Commerce and Industry: 57 Oyemekun Rd, POB 866, Akure; tel. (34) 242540; f. 1984; Pres. OMOLADE OWOSENI.

Awka Chamber of Commerce and Industry: 220 Zik Ave, POB 780, Awka; tel. (45) 550105; Pres. Lt-Col (retd) D. ORUGBU.

Bauchi Chamber of Commerce and Industry: 96 Maiduguri Rd, POB 911, Bauchi; tel. (77) 43727; f. 1976; Pres. Alhaji MAGAJI MU'AZU.

Benin Chamber of Commerce, Industry, Mines and Agriculture: 10 Murtala Muhammed Way, POB 2087, Benin City; tel. (52) 255761; Pres. Chief SIMON UDUIGHO EKWENUKE.

Benue Chamber of Commerce, Industry, Mines and Agriculture: Suite 7, IBB Sq, High Level, PMB 102344, Makurdi; tel. (44) 32573; Chair. Col (retd) R. V. I. ASAM.

Borno Chamber of Commerce and Industry: Grand Stand, Ramat Sq., off Central Bank, PMB 1636, Maiduguri; tel. (76) 232832; e-mail bsumar@hotmail.com; f. 1973; Pres. Alhaji MOHAMMED RIJYA; Sec.-Gen. BABA SHEHU BUKAR.

Calabar Chamber of Commerce and Industry: Desan House Bldg, 38 Ndidem Iso Rd, POB 76, Calabar, Cross River; tel. (87) 221558; 92 mems; Pres. Chief TAM OFORIOKUMA.

Enugu Chamber of Commerce, Industry, Mines and Agriculture (ECCIMA): International Trade Fair Complex, Abakaliki Rd, POB 734, Enugu; tel. (42) 290481; fax (42) 252186; e-mail enuguchamber@yahoo.com; internet www.enuguchamber.net; f. 1963; Pres. OKECHUKWU NWADINOBI; Dir-Gen. EMEKA OKEREKE.

Franco-Nigerian Chamber of Commerce: 5th Floor, Big Leaf House, 7 Oyin Jolayemi St, POB 70001, Victoria Island, Lagos; tel. (1) 4611201; fax (1) 4613501; e-mail fncci@ccife.org; internet franco-nigerian.com; f. 1985; Pres. MARCEL HOCHET; Gen. Man. AKIN AKINBOLA.

Gongola Chamber of Commerce and Industry: Palace Hotel, POB 8, Jimeta-Yola; tel. (75) 255136; Pres. Alhaji ALIYU IBRAHIM.

Ibadan Chamber of Commerce and Industry: Commerce House, Ring Rd, Challenge, PMB 5168, Ibadan; tel. (2) 317223; Pres. JIDE ABIMBOLA.

Ijebu Chamber of Commerce and Industry: 51 Ibadan Rd, POB 604, Ijebu Ode; tel. (37) 432880; Pres. DOYIN DEGUN.

Ikot Ekpene Chamber of Commerce and Industry: 47 Aba Rd, POB 50, Ikot Ekpene; tel. (85) 400153; Pres. G. U. EKANEM.

Kaduna Chamber of Commerce, Industry, Mines and Agriculture: POB 728, Kaduna; tel. 7023228854 (mobile); fax 7023228908 (mobile); e-mail kadunachamberofcommerce@yahoo.com; internet kadccima.net; Pres. Alhaji MOHAMMED SANI AMINU.

Kano Chamber of Commerce, Industry, Mines and Agriculture: Trade Fair Complex, Zoo Rd, POB 10, Kano City, Kano; tel. (64) 666936; fax (64) 667138; Pres. Alhaji AHMAD RABIU.

Katsina Chamber of Commerce and Industry: IBB Way, POB 789, Katsina; tel. (65) 31974; Pres. ABBA ALI.

Kwara Chamber of Commerce, Industry, Mines and Agriculture: 9A Kwara Hotel Premises, Ahmadu Bello Ave, POB 1634, Ilorin; tel. (31) 223069; fax (31) 224131; e-mail kwaccima@yahoo.com; internet www.kwaccima.com; f. 1965; Pres. Dr HEZEKIAH ADEDIJI.

Lagos Chamber of Commerce and Industry: Commerce House, 1 Idowu Taylor St, Victoria Island, POB 109, Lagos; tel. (1) 7746617; fax (1) 2701009; e-mail inform@micro.com.ng; internet www.lagoschamber.com; f. 1888; 1,500 mems; Pres. Chief OLUSOLA FALEYE.

Niger Chamber of Commerce and Industry: Trade Fair Site, Paiko Rd, POB 370, Minna; tel. (66) 223153; Pres. Alhaji U. S. NDANUSA.

Nnewi Chamber of Commerce, Industry, Mines and Agriculture: 31A Nnobi Rd, POB 1471, Nnewi, Anambra State; tel. (70) 35187662; f. 1987; Pres. PRINCE EMEKA A. AYABAZU.

Osogbo Chamber of Commerce and Industry: Obafemi Awolowo Way, Ajegunle, POB 870, Osogbo, Osun; tel. (35) 231098; Pres. Prince VICTOR ADEMLE.

Owerri Chamber of Commerce and Industry: OCCIMA Secretariat, 123 Okigwe Rd, POB 1439, Owerri; tel. (83) 234849.

Oyo Chamber of Commerce and Industry: Ogbomosho Rd, opp. Apaara Methodist Church, POB 588, Oyo; tel. (38) 240691; Pres. B. A. LASEBIKAN.

Plateau State Chambers of Commerce, Industry, Mines and Agriculture: POB 74, 21A Nassarawa Rd, Jos; tel. (73) 453918; f. 1976; Pres. SILAS JANGA.

Port Harcourt Chamber of Commerce, Industry, Mines and Agriculture: Alesa Eleme, POB 585, Port Harcourt; tel. (84) 239536; f. 1952; Pres. VINCENT FURO.

Remo Chamber of Commerce and Industry: 7 Sho Manager Way, POB 1172, Shagamu; tel. (37) 640962; Pres. Chief ADENIYI OGUNSANYA.

NIGERIA

Sapele Chamber of Commerce and Industry: 144 New Ogorode Rd, POB 154, Sapele; tel. and fax (54) 42323; Pres. Chief DAVID IWETA.

Sokoto Chamber of Commerce and Industry: 12 Racecourse Rd, POB 2234, Sokoto; tel. (60) 231805; Pres. Alhaji ALIYU WAZIRI BODINGA.

Umahia Chamber of Commerce: 44 Azikiwe Rd, Umahia; tel. (88) 223373; fax (88) 222299; Pres. GEORGE AKOMAS.

Uyo Chamber of Commerce and Industry: 141 Abak Rd, POB 2960, Uyo, Akwa Ibom; Pres. Chief DANIEL ITA-EKPOTT.

Warri Chamber of Commerce, Industry, Mines and Agriculture: Block 1, Edewor Shopping Centre, PMB 302, Warri; tel. (53) 253709; internet www.waccima.com; f. 1963; Pres. AUSTIN E. EGBEGBADIA.

INDUSTRIAL AND TRADE ASSOCIATIONS

Nigerian Export Promotion Council (NEPC): Plot 40, Blantyre St, Wuse 2, Abuja; tel. (9) 5230932; fax (9) 5230931; e-mail info@nepc.gov.ng; internet www.nepc.gov.ng; f. 1977; Chair. Alhaji ISIAKA ADELEKE; CEO DAVID ADULUGBA.

Nigerian Investment Promotion Commission (NIPC): Plot 1181, Aguiyi Ironsi St, Maitama District, PMB 381, Garki Abuja; tel. (9) 4134380; e-mail infodesk@nipc.gov.ng; internet www.nipc.gov.ng; Chair. FELIX OMOIKHOJE AIZOBEOJE OHIWEREI; Exec. Sec. Alhaji MUSTAFA BELLO.

EMPLOYERS' ORGANIZATIONS

Association of Advertising Agencies of Nigeria (AAAN): Plot 8, Otunba Jobi Fele-Way, Central Business District, Alausa, Ikeja, Lagos; tel. and fax (1) 4970842; e-mail lekan@aaanigeria.com; internet www.aaanigeria.com; Pres. FUNMI ONABOLU; CEO LEKAN FADOLAPO.

Chartered Institute of Bankers of Nigeria: PC 19 Adeola Hopewell St, POB 72273, Victoria Island, Lagos; tel. (1) 2703494; fax (1) 4618930; e-mail cibn@cibng.org; internet www.cibng.org; Chair. JOSEPH LAOYE JAIYEOLA; CEO Dr UJU M. OGUBUNKA.

Institute of Chartered Accountants of Nigeria: Plot 16, Professional Layout Centre, Idowu Taylor St, Victoria Island, POB 1580, Lagos; tel. (1) 2622394; fax (1) 4627048; e-mail info.ican@ican.org.ng; internet www.ican-ngr.org; f. 1965; CEO and Registrar OLUTOYIN ADEPATE; Pres. SEBASTIAN ACHULIKE OWUAMA.

Nigeria Employers' Consultative Association: NECA House, Plot A2, Hakeem Balogun St, Central Business District, Alausa, Ikeja, POB 2231, Marina, Lagos; tel. (1) 7746352; fax (1) 7912941; e-mail neca@necang.org; internet www.necang.org; f. 1957; Pres. R. U. UCHE; Dir-Gen. O. A. OSHINOWO.

Nigerian Institute of Architects (NIA): 2 Kukawa Close, off Gimbiya St, Area 11, Garki, Abuja; tel. (9) 4802518; e-mail info@niarchitects.org; internet niarchitects.org; f. 1960; Pres. OLATUNJI OLUMIDE BOLU.

Nigerian Institute of Building (NIOB): House No 24, Road 37, Gwarinpa Housing Estate, Abuja; tel. and fax (9) 7831243; e-mail niob@niobuilding.org; internet www.niobuilding.org; f. 1967; Pres. DACHOLLOM DALYOP JAMBOL.

Nigerian Institution of Estate Surveyors and Valuers: Plot 759, BASSAN Plaza, Wing C, Last Floor, Central Business District, Independence Ave, PMB 5147 Abuja; tel. (9) 4604710; e-mail admin@niesv.org.ng; internet www.niesv.org.ng; f. 1969; Pres. BODE ADEDIJI; Nat. Sec. ROWLAND E. ABONTA.

Nigerian Society of Engineers (NSE): National Engineering Centre, off National Mosque-Labour House Rd, Central Business Area, Abuja; tel. (9) 6735096; e-mail info@nseng.org; internet www.nse.org.ng; f. 1958; Pres. OLUMUYIWA AJIBOLA.

UTILITIES

Electricity

Nigerian Electricity Regulatory Commission (NERC): Adamawa Plaza, Plot 1099, First Ave, off Shehu Shagari Way, Central Business District, PMB 136, Garki, Abuja; tel. (9) 6700991; e-mail info@nercng.org; internet www.nercng.org; f. 2005; Chair. Dr SAM AMADI; CEO Mallam IMAMUDDEEN TALBA.

Power Holding Company of Nigeria (PHCN): Plot 1071, Area 3, Garki, Abuja; tel. (9) 5236899; internet www.phcnonline.com; f. 1972 as National Electric Power Authority, by merger of the Electricity Corpn of Nigeria and the Niger Dams Authority; renamed as above April 2005; assets were to be diverted to six generating companies and 11 distribution companies, prior to privatization; CEO HUSEIN LABO.

Gas

Nigeria Liquefied Natural Gas Co Ltd (NLNG): C. & C. Towers, Plot 1684, Sanusi Fafunwa St, Victoria Island, PMB 12774, Marina, Lagos; tel. (1) 2624190; fax (1) 2616976; internet www.nigerialng.com; f. 1989; Man. Dir CHIMA IBENECHE.

TRADE UNIONS

Federation

Nigerian Labour Congress (NLC): Labour House, Plot 820/821, Central Business District, Abuja; tel. (9) 6276042; fax (9) 6274342; e-mail gsec@nlcng.org; internet www.nlcng.org; f. 1978; comprised 36 affiliated industrial unions in 2009; Pres. ABDULWAHED IBRAHIM OMAR.

Trade Union Congress of Nigeria (TUC): Express House, 338 ikorodu Rd, Maryland, Lagos; tel. (1) 4701699; e-mail info@tucnigeria.org; internet www.tucnigeria.org; Pres.-Gen. PETER ESELE; Gen. Sec. JOHN KOLAWOLE; 24 mem. orgs.

Principal Unions

Amalgamated Union of Public Corpns, Civil Service, and Technical and Recreational Services Employees (AUPCTRE): 9 Aje St, PMB 1064, Yaba, Lagos; tel. (1) 5863722; Gen. Sec. SYLVESTER EJIOFOR.

National Union of Journalists: Lagos; Pres. LANRE OGUNDIPE; Sec. MOHAMMED KHALID.

National Union of Petroleum Workers and Natural Gas (NUPENG): 9 Jibowu St, off Ikorodu Rd, Yaba, Lagos; tel. (1) 8770277; fax (1) 3425310; e-mail headoffice@nupeng.org; internet nupeng.org; f. 1977; Gen. Sec. ELIJAH OKOUGBO.

Nigerian Union of Civil Engineering, Construction, Furniture and Woodworkers: 51 Kano St, Ebute Metta, PMB 1064, Lagos; tel. (1) 5800263.

Nigerian Union of Mine Workers: 95 Enugu St, POB 763, Jos; tel. (73) 52401.

Petroleum and Natural Gas Senior Staff Association of Nigeria (PENGASSAN): U. M. Okoro House, 288 Ikorodu Rd, Anthony, Lagos; tel. (1) 2790715; fax (1) 2790717; e-mail headoffice@pengassan.org; internet www.pengassan.org; f. 1978; Gen. Sec. M. A. OLOWOSHILE.

Transport

RAILWAYS

In 2005 there were about 3,528 km of mainly narrow-gauge railways. The two principal lines connect Lagos with Nguru and Port Harcourt with Maiduguri. In 2010 there were plans for the construction of a 21-km monorail in Enugu. There were also plans for a light rail project in Lagos.

Nigerian Railway Corpn: PMB 1037, Ebute-Metta, Lagos; tel. (1) 7747320; fax (1) 5831367; e-mail info.nrc@nrc-ng.org; internet www.nrc-ng.org; f. 1955; restructured in 1993 into three separate units: Nigerian Railway Track Authority; Nigerian Railways; and Nigerian Railway Engineering Ltd; Chair. Dr BELLO HALIRU MOHAMMED; Man. Dir ADESEYI SIJUWADE.

ROADS

In 2004 the Nigerian road network totalled 193,200 km, including 15,688 km of highways and 18,719 km of secondary roads; some 9,660 km were paved.

Nigerian Road Federation: Ministry of Transport, National Maritime Agency Bldg, Central Area, Abuja; tel. (9) 5237053.

INLAND WATERWAYS

National Inland Waterways Authority (NIWA): PMB 1004, Adankolo, Lokoja, Kogi State; tel. (58) 2220965; f. 1997; responsible for all navigable waterways; Man. Dir AHMED AMINU.

SHIPPING

The principal ports are the Delta Port complex (including Warri, Koko, Burutu and Sapele ports), Port Harcourt and Calabar; other significant ports are situated at Apapa and Tin Can Island, near Lagos. The main petroleum ports are Bonny and Burutu.

Nigerian Maritime Administration and Safety Agency (NIMASA): f. 2007 following merger of National Maritime Authority and Joint Maritime Labour Industrial Council; Dir-Gen. RAYMOND TEMSARE OMATSEYE.

Nigerian Ports Authority: 26/28 Marina, PMB 12588, Lagos; tel. (1) 2600620; fax (1) 2636719; e-mail telnpo@infoweb.abs.net; internet www.nigerianports.org; f. 1955; Man. Dir MALLAM ABDUL SALAM MUHAMMED.

Nigerian Green Lines Ltd: Yinka Folawiyo Plaza, 38 Yinka Folawiyo Ave (fmrly Warehouse Rd), Apapa; tel. (1) 5450436; fax

NIGERIA

(1) 5450204; f. 1972; Yinka Folawiyo Group; 2 vessels totalling 30,751 grt; Chair. Alhaji W. I. FOLAWIYO.

Association

Nigerian Shippers' Council: Shippers' Tower, 4 Park Lane, Apapa, Lagos; tel. (1) 5452307; fax (1) 5452906; e-mail info@shipperscouncil.com; internet www.shipperscouncil.com; Chair. Chief Dr MARIAN ALI; CEO Capt. ADAMU A. BIU.

CIVIL AVIATION

The principal international airports are at Lagos (Murtala Mohammed Airport), Kano, Port Harcourt and Abuja. There are also 14 airports servicing domestic flights.

Federal Airports Authority of Nigeria (FAAN): Murtala Mohammed Airport, PMB 21607, Ikeja, Lagos; tel. (1) 4970335; fax (1) 4970342; e-mail contact@faannigeria.org; internet www.faannigeria.org; Chair. Capt. E. UKEJE; CEO RICHARD AISUEBEOGUN.

Principal Airlines

Air Nigeria: 3rd Floor, Ark Towers, Plot 17, Ligali Ayorinde St, Victoria Island Extension, Ikeja, Lagos; tel. (1) 4600505; internet www.flyairnigeria.com; f. Sept. 2004, name changed as above in 2010; private flag carrier; owned by Air Nigeria Development Ltd; scheduled domestic regional and international services; Chair. JIMOH IBRAHIM; CEO KINFE KAHASSAYE.

Arik Air: Murtala Mohammed Airport, POB 10468, Ikeja, Lagos; tel. (1) 2799900; fax (1) 4975940; e-mail info@arikair.com; internet www.arikair.com; f. 2002; Chair. JOSEPH ARUMEMI-IKHIDE; Group CEO Dr MICHAEL ARUMEMI-IKHIDE.

Tourism

Potential attractions for tourists include fine coastal scenery, dense forests and the rich diversity of Nigeria's arts. A total of 5,820,497 tourists visited Nigeria in 2008. Receipts from tourism in that year amounted to US $586m.

Nigerian Tourism Development Corpn: Old Federal Secretariat, Area 1, Garki, PMB 167, Abuja; tel. (9) 2342764; fax (9) 2342775; e-mail ntdc@metrong.com; internet www.nigeria.tourism.com; Chair. Prince ADESUYI HAASTRUP; CEO OMOTAYO OMOTOSHO.

Defence

As assessed at November 2010, the total strength of the armed forces was 80,000: the army totalled 62,000 men, the navy 8,000 and the air force 10,000. There was also a paramilitary force of 82,000. Military service is voluntary.

Defence Expenditure: Budgeted at ₦232,000m. in 2010.
Commander-in-Chief of the Armed Forces: Dr GOODLUCK EBELE JONATHAN.
Chief of Defence Staff: Air Marshall OLUSEYI PETINRIN.
Chief of Army Staff: Maj.-Gen. O. A. IHEJIRIKA.
Chief of Naval Staff: Rear-Adm. O. S. IBRAHIM.
Chief of Air Staff: Air Vice-Marshal M. D. UMAR.

Education

Education is partly the responsibility of the state governments, although the Federal Government has played an increasingly important role since 1970. Primary education begins at six years of age and lasts for six years. Secondary education begins at 12 years of age and lasts for a further six years, comprising two three-year cycles. Education to junior secondary level (from six to 15 years of age) is free and compulsory. According to UNESCO estimates, in 2006/07 61% of children in the relevant age-group (males 64%; females 58%) were enrolled in primary education, while the comparable ratio for secondary enrolment in that year was 26% (males 29%; females 22%). In 2005 724,856 students were enrolled at Nigerian universities. Expenditure on education by the Federal Government in 2005 was ₦82,797m., equivalent to 5.0% of total spending in the federal budget.

NORWAY

Introductory Survey

LOCATION, CLIMATE, LANGUAGE, RELIGION, FLAG, CAPITAL

The Kingdom of Norway forms the western part of Scandinavia, in northern Europe. It is bordered to the east by Sweden and, within the Arctic Circle, by Finland and Russia. A long, indented coast faces the Atlantic Ocean. Norway exercises sovereignty over the Svalbard archipelago, Jan Mayen island and the uninhabited dependencies of Bouvetøya and Peter I Øy. Dronning Maud Land, in Antarctica, is also a Norwegian dependency. Norway's climate is temperate on the west coast, but colder inland. Average temperatures range from −2°C (28°F) to 8°C (46°F). There are two forms of the Norwegian language, which are officially recognized as equal. About 80% of children in schools use the older form, *Bokmål*, as their principal language, whereas only 20% use the newer form, *Nynorsk* (Neo-Norwegian). Lappish is also spoken by the Sámi population, in northern Norway. Almost all of the inhabitants profess Christianity: the Evangelical Lutheran Church is the established religion, with about 82% of the population professing adherence in 2010. The civil flag (proportions 8 by 11) has a dark blue cross, bordered with white, on a red background, the upright of the cross being to the left of centre; the state flag (16 by 27) displays the same cross, but forms a triple swallow-tail at the fly. The capital is Oslo.

CONTEMPORARY POLITICAL HISTORY

Historical Context

Norway, formerly linked to the Swedish crown, declared its independence in 1905. The union with Sweden was peacefully dissolved and the Norwegians elected their own monarch, Prince Karl of Denmark, who took the title of King Håkon VII. He reigned until his death in 1957, and was succeeded by his son, Olav V. Olav's son, Crown Prince Harald (who had acted as regent since May 1990, when his father suffered a stroke), became King Harald V upon Olav's death in January 1991.

During the Second World War Norway was occupied by German forces between 1940 and 1945. Norway abandoned its traditional policy of neutrality after the war, joining the North Atlantic Treaty Organization (NATO, see p. 368) in 1949. Norway was also a founder member of the Nordic Council (see p. 461) in 1952 and of the European Free Trade Association (EFTA, see p. 447) in 1960.

Domestic Political Affairs

Det norske Arbeiderparti (DnA—Norwegian Labour Party) governed from 1935 to 1965, except for the period of German occupation, when a pro-Nazi 'puppet' regime was administered by Vidkun Quisling, and an interlude of one month in 1963. Norway applied for membership of the European Community (EC, now European Union—EU, see p. 270) in 1962, and again in 1967. A general election to the Storting (parliament) in September 1965 resulted in a defeat for the DnA Government of Einar Gerhardsen, who had been Prime Minister almost continuously since 1955. His administration was replaced in October 1965 by a non-socialist coalition under Per Borten, leader of the Senterpartiet (Sp—Centre Party). However, in March 1971 Borten resigned, following revelations that he had deliberately disclosed confidential details of Norway's negotiations with the EC. He was succeeded by a minority DnA Government, led by Trygve Bratteli. The terms of Norway's entry into the EC were agreed in December 1971, and a preliminary Treaty of Accession was signed in January 1972. In September, however, a consultative referendum on the agreed terms produced a 53.3% majority against entering the EC. The application was withdrawn, and Bratteli resigned in October. A coalition of Venstre (Liberals), the Sp and the Kristelig Folkeparti (KrF—Christian Democratic Party) formed a new minority Government, with Lars Korvald of the KrF as Prime Minister.

Following the general election of September 1973, Bratteli formed another minority DnA Government, dependent on the support of a socialist alliance known from 1975 as the Socialistisk Venstreparti (SV—Socialist Left Party). In January 1976 Odvar Nordli replaced Bratteli as Prime Minister. Nordli resigned in February 1981, citing reasons of ill health, and was succeeded by Gro Harlem Brundtland. At the general election in September DnA lost support to centre-right groups. In October a minority administration, led by Kåre Willoch, became Norway's first Høyre (Conservative) Government since 1928. In June 1983 a coalition of Høyre with the Sp and the KrF was formed, with 79 of the 165 parliamentary seats. Willoch's Government was returned to power, although lacking an overall majority in the Storting, following the general election in September 1985. In May 1986 Willoch resigned when the Storting narrowly rejected a proposal to increase taxation on petrol. The Norwegian Constitution did not permit a general election before the expiry of the Storting's term (due in 1989). Brundtland accepted an invitation by the King to form a minority DnA administration. The new Government devalued the krone by 12%, and a revised budget was approved by the Storting in June 1986.

At the general election in September 1989 both DnA and Høyre lost support to more radical parties. The SV gained nine seats, to achieve a total of 17 seats. The Fremskrittspartiet (FrP—Progress Party) increased its representation from two to 22 seats, despite attracting allegations of racism during the election campaign. Brundtland's Government resigned in October, following an agreement made by Høyre, the Sp and the KrF to form a coalition. The new Government, led by Jan Syse of Høyre, controlled only 62 seats in the Storting and was dependent upon the support of the FrP. Also in September 1989 the Sámi (Lapps) of northern Norway elected 39 representatives for a new Sameting (Consultative Assembly), to be based in Karasjok. This followed an amendment to the Constitution the previous year, which recognized the Sámi as an indigenous people and an ethnic minority. There was considerable support among the Sámi for a degree of autonomy, in order to protect their traditional way of life. The Sámi had officially ceased to exist by 1900, with their culture and language being declared illegal, but by 2000 they had formed a joint council comprising Sámi populations in Norway, Sweden, Finland and Russia, and received a parliament building, opened in November by King Harald V. The issue of land rights, however, remained unresolved. This was aggravated by the discovery, in 2001, of substantial platinum deposits in Finnmark, an area to which the Sámi laid claim.

While Høyre had supported EC membership since 1988, the Sp remained strongly opposed to it. In October 1990 the Government announced that the Norwegian krone was to be linked to the European Currency Unit (ECU). Later in that month the coalition collapsed, following disagreement between Høyre and the Sp regarding Norwegian demands in the negotiations between EFTA and the EC on the creation of a joint European Economic Area (EEA). In November DnA formed another minority Government, led by Brundtland.

In October 1991 agreement was finally reached on the terms of the EEA treaty, including arrangements whereby EC countries were to be allowed to take extra quotas of fish from Norwegian waters, while Norwegian fish products were to have increased access to EC markets. Many Norwegians remained opposed to membership of the EC, fearing, in particular, that government subsidies to remote rural and coastal communities would no longer be permitted. The EEA treaty was ratified by the Storting in October 1992. (The treaty entered into effect on 1 January 1994.) A proposal by Brundtland to apply for EC membership was endorsed by the Storting in November 1992, and an application was duly submitted.

At the September 1993 general election DnA increased its representation in the Storting, from 63 to 67 seats. The Sp increased its total from 11 to 32 seats, thereby becoming the second largest party in the Storting, while Høyre won only 28 seats, compared with 37 at the previous election.

Negotiations on Norway's entry to the EU, as the EC had been restyled, were concluded in March 1994. However, at a national referendum held on 27–28 November (shortly after Sweden and Finland had voted to join the Union), 52.4% of voters rejected EU membership. The success of the campaign opposing Norway's entry to the EU was attributed to several factors: in particular, farmers feared the impact of an influx of cheaper agricultural goods from the EU, and fisheries workers feared that fish stocks would be severely depleted if EU boats were granted increased access to Norwegian waters. There was also widespread concern that national sovereignty would be compromised by the transfer to the EU of certain executive responsibilities.

The general elections of 1997 and 2001

In October 1996 Brundtland resigned as Prime Minister and was succeeded by Thorbjørn Jagland, who had replaced Brundtland as DnA leader in November 1992. Jagland pledged to continue the previous Government's cautious fiscal policy. By the end of the year, however, the Government's credibility had been seriously undermined, after Terje Röd-Larsen, the newly appointed Minister of National Planning, and Grete Faremo, the Minister of Petroleum and Energy, were forced to resign, following, respectively, allegations of financial irregularities and abuse of power.

At the general election in September 1997 DnA attracted the largest level of support, winning 65 seats, ahead of the FrP and the KrF with 25 seats each and Høyre with 23 seats. In October Jagland resigned, honouring a pre-election pledge to stand down should DnA fail to attain the level of popular support that it attracted at the 1993 poll. Kjell Magne Bondevik, the parliamentary leader of the KrF, had organized an alliance of the KrF, the Sp and Venstre (with representation totalling 42 seats), and was invited to form a coalition government on that basis. The new Council of State was dominated by the KrF. There was some uncertainty regarding the durability of the Government after the Prime Minister took more than three weeks' leave from his post from the end of August 1998, owing to depression. Bondevik was reported to have been under intense pressure as a result of recent economic instability, largely attributable to the sharp decline in international prices for petroleum, necessitating the postponement of a child-care scheme promoted by Bondevik. In November, furthermore, the Government was obliged to abandon proposed tax increases in order to secure the support of the FrP (and thus parliamentary approval) for the 1999 budget.

In March 2000 Bondevik resigned following his defeat in a confidence motion in the Storting. The vote was called to resolve a dispute over government plans to postpone the construction of gas-fired power plants. Jens Stoltenberg, who had replaced Jagland as leader of DnA in February, subsequently formed a single-party minority government. The new Council of State included Jagland as Minister of Foreign Affairs. The new Government pledged to reform the public sector, resume the country's privatization programme, forge stronger links with Europe and continue Norway's role as a mediator in international peace negotiations.

At a general election conducted on 10 September 2001, DnA received only 24.3% of the valid votes cast (its poorest electoral performance since 1909), attaining 43 seats. Høyre secured 38 seats, the FrP 26, the SV 23 and the KrF 22. DnA formed a minority Government, but was unable to attract enough political support to hold a majority in the Storting. Stoltenberg consequently resigned on 17 October, and DnA was replaced in government by a minority centre-right coalition comprising Høyre, the KrF and Venstre, with Bondevik as Prime Minister. The coalition gained a majority in the Storting with the informal support of the FrP.

In February 2003 the Government announced its decision to expel Mullah Krekar, the Iraqi-born leader of the Kurdish guerrilla organization Ansar al-Islam, who was suspected by both the USA and the UN of having links to terrorism, and possibly to the Islamist al-Qa'ida organization. However, Krekar, who had stated that he would not leave Norway voluntarily, was not taken into custody or otherwise compelled to leave the country. The following month the Government announced that the case merited further investigation, and that the launch of the US-led military action in Iraq that month posed difficulties for his repatriation. A request from Jordan for him to be extradited for drugs offences was also to be investigated. Krekar was eventually detained following an appearance on Dutch television during which he stated that Ansar al-Islam had suicide bombers ready to attack US citizens, but did not remain in custody for long. Krekar was arrested again in December and charged with plotting the murder of his political rivals in Iraq in 2000–01, and was imprisoned in January 2004 while prosecutors investigated the charges against him. Despite the prosecutors' efforts to keep Krekar in custody, he was freed by the Lagmannsrett (Court of Appeal) in February. The charges against Krekar were withdrawn in June owing to insufficient evidence. In 2005 Krekar's expulsion was further delayed pending a guarantee from the Iraqi authorities that he would not face the death penalty. (Norwegian law forbids extradition to countries with the death penalty.) In November 2007 the Høyesterett (Supreme Court) upheld the decision to expel Krekar. However, in April 2008 it was reported that the Government had failed to reach an agreement with the Iraqi authorities over his extradition and that Krekar was to be allowed to remain in Norway indefinitely. In January 2010 Krekar survived a suspected assassination attempt at his home in Oslo.

In 2004 Norway introduced transitional rules aimed at limiting (for an initial period of two years) the entry of migrant workers from the eight Central and Eastern European countries that joined the EU on 1 May. While Norway was not itself a member of the EU, it nevertheless had commitments arising from its membership of the EEA and the EU's Schengen agreement.

Stoltenberg regains the premiership

At the general election of 12 September 2005, DnA received 32.7% of the votes cast and won 61 of the 169 seats in the enlarged Storting, thus retaining its position as the largest parliamentary party. DnA contested the election at the head of a centre-left alliance also comprising the SV (which secured 15 seats, with 8.8% of the votes cast) and the Sp (11 seats, with 6.5%). The FrP won 22.1% of the votes cast (38 seats), while Høyre secured 14.1% (23 seats), the KrF 6.8% (11 seats) and Venstre 5.9% (10 seats). DnA, the SV and the Sp subsequently formed the first majority Government since 1985, led by Jens Stoltenberg. The new coalition Government's programme included proposals to increase welfare spending, raise taxes and eradicate social inequality.

In late September 2006 Dag Terje Andersen, of DnA, succeeded party colleague Odd Eriksen as Minister of Trade and Industry. At a DnA party conference held in April 2007, Stoltenberg announced that the Government intended to reduce Norway's emissions of carbon dioxide by 30% (from 1990 levels) by 2020 and to achieve a reduction in emissions world-wide equivalent to 100% of Norwegian emissions by 2050, subsequently brought forward to 2030, mainly through a system of trading in emissions with other countries.

In September 2007 Odd Roger Enoksen resigned as Minister of Petroleum and Energy. The appointment of his successor, the leader of the Sp, Aslaug Haga, created Norway's first government composed of a majority of women, who occupied 10 of the 19 ministerial positions. A minor government reorganization took place in October and included new appointments by the SV, following significant losses for the party in nation-wide local elections in September, which were widely attributed to popular disenchantment with the SV members of the Cabinet. Helen Bjørnøy and Øystein Djupedal, responsible for the environment and education portfolios, respectively, were removed from the Cabinet, while DnA's Manuela Ramin-Osmundsen was appointed Minister of Children and Equality. In February 2008, however, Ramin-Osmundsen left the Cabinet, following media allegations of favouritism over her decision to appoint a government lawyer, Ida Hjort Kraby, as children's ombudsman. Stoltenberg, who initially offered his support to Ramin-Osmundsen, announced her dismissal from the Cabinet after it emerged that she had withheld information from the Prime Minister. Ramin-Osmundsen had acknowledged that she knew Hjort Kraby, but denied that they were close friends. However, the media subsequently documented professional and social links between the two women dating back 20 years. She was succeeded later that month by Anniken Huitfeldt. Hjort Kraby subsequently resigned from the post of children's ombudsman.

In June 2008 Haga resigned both as Minister of Petroleum and Energy and as leader of the Sp, citing ill health, following media accusations of tax irregularities in connection with the letting of a holiday home. Stoltenberg subsequently effected a reorganization of the Council of State. The Sp's Terje Riis-Johansen, hitherto Minister of Agriculture and Food, was appointed as Minister of Petroleum and Energy, while Lars Peder Brekk, who had been appointed as interim leader of the Sp, assumed the portfolio formerly held by Riis-Johansen. In September the Minister of Transport and Communications, Liv Signe Navarsete, was elected as leader of the Sp.

On 19 June 2009 the Lagting and the Odelsting, the upper and lower houses of the Storting, met for the final time as separate bodies in their 195-year history, in accordance with a bill approved in February 2007 providing for their abolition. Previously members of the Storting had elected one-quarter of their own body to constitute the Lagting, while the other three-quarters had constituted the Odelsting. In practice, debates in the Lagting had become an unnecessary formality, since the composition of parties in both chambers was so similar that decisions made in the upper house were virtually identical to those in the lower house.

Recent developments: the 2009 general election

At the general election of 14 September 2009 DnA, led by Jens Stoltenberg, remained the largest party in the Storting after securing 35.4% of the votes cast, increasing its parliamentary representation by three seats, to 64. The other two members of the DnA-led, centre-left coalition—the SV and the Sp—obtained 11 seats each in the 169-seat legislature, with both parties attracting 6.2% of the votes cast, thereby giving the three incumbent parties a total of 86 seats and a very slim majority (of two seats). The two main right-wing parties, the FrP and Høyre, increased their standing in the Storting, winning 41 seats (22.9% of the vote) and 30 seats (17.2%), respectively, while the KrF secured 10 seats (5.5%) and Venstre two (3.9%). The rate of participation by the electorate was 76.4%. Environmental issues, immigration and asylum, and education were subsequently announced as the main priorities of the new administration.

Stoltenberg reorganized the Council of State in October 2009, assigning one-half of the cabinet positions to women. Notably, the finance portfolio was allocated to Sigbjørn Johnsen, Minister of Finance during 1990–96, while his predecessor, SV leader Kristin Halvorsen, became Minister of Education, with a former Minister of Defence, Anne-Grete Strøm-Erichsen, being reassigned to the health ministry after being replaced by Grete Faremo. Meanwhile, in November the Government was accused of reneging on earlier promises to tackle climate change, when a tax on biodiesel, previously exempt, received legislative approval, attracting widespread criticism and causing division within the ruling coalition.

Terje Riis-Johansen resigned as Minister of Petroleum and Energy in March 2011, having sustained repeated criticism regarding his ministerial competence: in particular, he had been blamed by many commentators for allowing a pioneering plan to install a carbon capture and storage facility at the Mongstad gas-fired power station to fall well behind schedule. (In May 2010 Riis-Johansen had announced that the Government would delay making the decision to finance the project until 2014, beyond the end of the current legislative term, and further delays were announced in February 2011.) He was also responsible for a highly controversial decision to erect overhead power lines through the scenic Hardanger district in western Norway, which had been finalized earlier in March. Ole Borten Moe, also of the Sp, was appointed to replace him.

The *Lebensborn* project

In March 1999 the Storting approved compensation valued at US $57.5m. for the country's Holocaust victims and their descendants. The programme was to include compensation for plundered property, as well as funding for contemporary Jewish community projects. In October 2001 a lawsuit was brought against the Norwegian Government by surviving victims of the Nazi *Lebensborn* (Source of Life) project. The survivors, children of German soldiers and Norwegian women, were conceived during the Nazi occupation of Norway in the Second World War as part of a scheme to create a 'master race'. They alleged that, following the liberation of Norway, they and their mothers were subjected to systematic abuse and discrimination, and that the Government not only allowed this abuse to occur, but also attempted to conceal it. The lawsuit was rejected on the grounds that the alleged offences occurred too long ago to be brought to court. However, in late 2002 the Storting's Justice Committee recommended that the Government 'make amends'. In March 2007 the European Court of Human Rights rejected as inadmissible a lawsuit against the Norwegian Government brought by a group of 159 *Lebensborn* survivors.

Foreign Affairs

Regional relations

Norway was also a founder member of the Nordic Council (see p. 461) in 1952 and of the European Free Trade Association (EFTA, see p. 447) in 1960. Norway declared an exclusive economic zone extending to 200 nautical miles (370 km) from its coastline in 1977, and also unilaterally established a fisheries protection zone around its territory of Svalbard. The declaration of an economic zone around Jan Mayen island in 1980 led to agreements with Iceland, in 1980 and 1981, over conflicting claims to fishing and mineral rights. A similar dispute with Denmark, acting for Greenland, was not resolved, and in 1988 Denmark requested arbitration by the International Court of Justice, in The Hague, Netherlands, which gave its judgment on the delimitation of the disputed zones in June 1993 (see under Jan Mayen). During 1994 incidents were reported between vessels of the Norwegian coastguard and Icelandic fishing boats, within the economic zone surrounding the Norwegian island of Spitsbergen (see under Svalbard). In October 2005 Norway detained two Russian vessels that were illegally transferring fish within the same zone.

In April 2009 the UN Commission on the Limits of the Continental Shelf finalized its recommendations on the extension of the Norwegian continental shelf, assigning responsibility for an additional 235,000 sq km of seabed in the Arctic Ocean to Norway, including the right to exploit any mineral resources present. However, the delimitation of Norwegian and Russian waters in the Barents Sea, a point of contention since 1974, remained in dispute until April 2010, when agreement was reached on the maritime border; the accord, which was signed in September, opened the possibility for the two countries to begin exploration for petroleum and natural gas in the Barents Sea.

Other external relations

Norway was a founder member of the North Atlantic Treaty Organization (NATO, see p. 368) in 1949. From 1999 Norway contributed 520 troops to the NATO-led Kosovo Force (KFOR) peace-keeping mission in Kosovo, consisting of a mechanized infantry battalion and a smaller rapid reaction force that was specially trained in riot control. In 2004 Norway increased its contribution to KFOR, sending four helicopters and support personnel. By November 2010 Norway's contribution had been reduced to just five troops.

During 1993 the Norwegian Government was instrumental in conducting secret negotiations between the Israeli Government and the Palestine Liberation Organization (PLO), which led to agreement on Palestinian self-rule in certain areas occupied by Israel. Norway won international acclaim for its role in furthering peace in the Middle East through these negotiations, and continued to be involved in the advancement of the peace process in the late 1990s and first half of the 2000s.

In February 2000 Norway extended its role as an international mediator, agreeing to broker negotiations between the Sri Lankan Government and Tamil separatists in an attempt to end the 17-year conflict. A cease-fire agreement was signed by the two parties in February 2002, supervised by the Norwegian-led Sri Lanka Monitoring Mission (SLMM). However, the SLMM's activities were terminated in January 2008, following an escalation of violence in the country and the Government's withdrawal from the cease-fire agreement.

In April 2001 Norway agreed to host peace negotiations between the Philippine Government and the Philippine dissident communist alliance, the National Democratic Front. These formal negotiations stalled in 2004 and in 2005, although Norway continued to act as a mediator between the two parties. Representatives of both parties held informal discussions in Oslo in November 2008. However, the talks collapsed without agreement owing to the Philippine Government's insistence upon a cease-fire as a precondition for the resumption of formal negotiations. Formal talks resumed in Oslo in February 2011, at the end of which the two parties agreed to work towards ending the conflict by June 2012.

Following a moratorium on commercial whaling, adopted by the International Whaling Commission (IWC, see p. 439) in 1982 with effect from 1986, Norway continued to hunt small numbers of whales ostensibly for the purpose of scientific research. Norway registered an objection to the moratorium on hunting minke whales, claiming that (according to the findings of the IWC's scientific commission) this species was plentiful enough to allow whaling on a sustainable basis and that many Norwegian coastal communities depended on whaling for their existence. In 1992 the Norwegian Government declared that it would allow the resumption of commercial hunting of minke whales in 1993, as it was not bound by the moratorium, having reserved its position when the ban was introduced. In December 2005 the Norwegian Government announced an increase in its quota for minke whales from 797 in 2005 to 1,052 in 2006, the highest quota since 1993. The narrow approval, at an IWC meeting in June 2006, of a Norwegian-backed resolution for an eventual resumption of commercial whaling provoked strong protests from countries opposed to whaling. Although the vote was not binding, it was considered to represent a further step towards a return for

NORWAY

the IWC to a role of setting limits for the capture of whales, rather than one of protection.

In January 2002, following the US-led military campaign against the Taliban and al-Qa'ida militants in Afghanistan in 2001, Norway contributed 180 troops to the International Security Assistance Force (ISAF), deployed in the Afghan capital, Kabul, and at Bagram airbase to help maintain security in the area. In January 2004, at the request of the Loya Jirga (the Afghan Grand Assembly), the Norwegian troops extended their mission in Afghanistan until August of that year. Norway also contributed special forces troops from its Naval Ranger Command and the Norwegian Army's Ranger Command to the US-led operation 'Enduring Freedom', the main aim of which was to combat al-Qa'ida's terrorist network in Afghanistan. In August 2004 the mandate of Norway's ISAF troops in northern Afghanistan was extended indefinitely. In January 2006 Norway withdrew almost all its remaining troops from 'Enduring Freedom' and instead increased its commitment to ISAF. In December 2009 approximately 500 Norwegian troops were stationed in Afghanistan. The Government confirmed that there were no plans to increase this number, following the US announcement, earlier in the year, of the deployment of an additional 17,000 US troops and pleas for NATO allies to expand their commitment to Afghanistan.

In July 2003 Norway sent 150 soldiers from the Telemark Engineer Squadron to Iraq to help British troops south of Basra repair roads and bridges and to clear land mines, following the success of the US-led military action in removing the regime of Saddam Hussain earlier in the year. Norway had not supported the war, and insisted that its troops were in Iraq as part of a humanitarian 'stabilizing force' mandated by UN Security Council Resolution 1483, and that they would remain separate from peace-keeping forces dispatched by the USA, the United Kingdom, Denmark and Poland. Norway withdrew its troops from Iraq in mid-2004. However, a small number of staff officers, who were attached to a Polish brigade, remained until late December 2005.

Relations with Iran were strained in December 2009, when Norway (and Sweden) condemned the confiscation of human rights campaigner Shirin Ebadi's Nobel Peace Prize medal, an act that was denied by the Iranian authorities. Further tension arose in early 2010 following the resignation of an Iranian diplomat in Norway, Mohammed Reza Heydari, in protest against the suppression of anti-Government demonstrations in Iran; Heydari was subsequently granted asylum in Norway, despite Iran expressing discontent at the decision.

The award by the Norwegian Nobel Committee of the 2010 Nobel Peace Prize to the Chinese political rights activist Liu Xiaobo badly damaged relations between Norway and the People's Republic of China, which responded to the announcement of the award in October of that year by refusing to attend negotiations on a proposed free trade agreement. In November it was reported that China had suspended the trade negotiations indefinitely. China withheld its ambassador from Liu's award ceremony in Oslo in December (which Liu himself was prevented from attending by the Chinese authorities) and urged other nations to do likewise.

CONSTITUTION AND GOVERNMENT

Norway is a constitutional monarchy. Legislative power is held by the Storting (parliament), with 169 members elected for four years by universal adult suffrage, on the basis of proportional representation. Under a constitutional amendment that took effect from October 2009, the internal division of the Storting into two chambers, the Lagting (upper house) and the Odelsting (lower house), was abolished. Executive power is nominally held by the monarch, but is, in effect, exercised by the Statsråd (Council of State), led by the Prime Minister. The Council is appointed by the monarch in accordance with the will of the Storting, to which the Council is responsible. Norway comprises 19 counties (*fylker*) and 430 municipalities (*kommuner*).

REGIONAL AND INTERNATIONAL CO-OPERATION

Norway is a founding member of the Nordic Council (see p. 461) and the Nordic Council of Ministers (see p. 461). In addition to its membership of EFTA, Norway is a member of the European Economic Area (EEA), which incorporates Norway (together with Iceland and Liechtenstein) into the internal market of the European Union (EU, see p. 270). Although Norway is not a member of the EU, it joined the EU's Schengen agreement on the abolition of border controls in May 1999 (Denmark, Finland and Sweden—all EU members—had already joined in 1996) by virtue of its membership in the Nordic passport union. Norway is a member of the Arctic Council (see p. 445), which is based in Norway, and was a founder member of both the Council of Europe (see p. 250) and the Council of the Baltic Sea States (see p. 248). It participates in the Organization for Security and Co-operation in Europe (OSCE, see p. 385)

Norway was a founder member of the UN in 1945. As a contracting party to the General Agreement on Tariffs and Trade, Norway joined the World Trade Organization (WTO, see p. 430) on its establishment in 1995. It is a founder member of the North Atlantic Treaty Organization (NATO, see p. 368), and participates in the Organisation for Economic Co-operation and Development (OECD, see p. 376).

ECONOMIC AFFAIRS

In 2009, according to estimates by the World Bank, Norway's gross national income (GNI), measured at average 2007–09 prices, was US $417,260m., equivalent to $86,440 per head (or $56,050 per head on an international purchasing-power parity basis). During 2000–09, it was estimated, the population increased by an average of 0.8% per year, while gross domestic product (GDP) per head increased, in real terms, by an average of 1.0% per year. Norway's overall GDP increased, in real terms, at an average annual rate of 1.8% in 2000–09; real GDP increased by 1.8% in 2008, but declined by 1.6% in 2009.

The contribution of agriculture (including hunting, forestry and fishing) to GDP in 2010 was estimated at 1.6%. In the same year, the agricultural sector engaged 2.5% of the employed labour force. Around 3.4% of the land surface is cultivated, and the most important branch of the sector is livestock-rearing. Fish farming has been intensively developed by the Government since the early 1970s. The fishing industry provided an estimated 5.8% of total export revenue in 2009. In 2006 Norway produced some 626,400 metric tons of farmed salmon. According to official figures, agricultural GDP increased at an average annual rate of 3.4% during 2000–08. Agricultural GDP decreased by 2.7% in 2009, but grew by 10.1% in 2010.

Industry (including mining, manufacturing, construction, power and public utilities) contributed an estimated 40.8% of GDP in 2010, and engaged 19.6% of the employed labour force in that year. During 2000–08 industrial GDP increased, in real terms, at an average annual rate of 0.2%, according to official figures. Industrial GDP (including service activities incidental to the oil and gas sector) increased by 1.4% in 2008.

Mining (including gas and petroleum extraction) provided an estimated 23.5% of GDP in 2010, and engaged 1.8% of the employed labour force in the same year. Extraction of petroleum and natural gas dominates the sector, accounting for 29.0% of GDP in 2008 and 0.8% of employment in 2010. Norway possesses substantial reserves of petroleum and natural gas (exports of petroleum and petroleum products accounted for 37.4% of total export earnings in 2009). Most of the reserves are located off shore. During 1995–2005 the production of crude petroleum from fields on the Norwegian continental shelf decreased at an average annual rate of 0.6%, while output of natural gas grew at an average rate of 11.8% per year, according to the Norwegian Petroleum Directorate. Norway's other mineral reserves include iron ore, iron pyrites, copper, lead and zinc. A large terminal to pump natural gas via a 1,200-km pipeline to the United Kingdom was completed in Aukra, on the island of Gossa, in 2007.

Manufacturing contributed 9.2% of GDP in 2010, and employed 9.4% of the working population in the same year. In 2006 the most important branches of manufacturing were food products, transport equipment (including ships and oil platforms), metals and metal products, electrical and optical equipment, chemicals and chemical products, and pulp and paper products. During 2000–07, according to the World Bank, manufacturing GDP increased, in real terms, by an average of 3.3% per year. Manufacturing GDP increased by 3.0% in 2008.

In 2009 hydroelectric power accounted for 95.7% of Norway's electricity production, thermal power for 3.5% and wind power for 0.8%. Domestic energy demands are easily supplied, and Norway has exported hydroelectricity since 1993. Norway's extensive reserves of petroleum and natural gas are mainly exploited for sale to foreign markets, since the domestic market is limited.

Construction contributed 5.3% of GDP in 2010, while the sector engaged some 7.1% of the employed labour force in that year.

NORWAY

The services sector contributed 57.6% of GDP in 2010, and engaged 77.9% of the employed labour force in the same year. The GDP of the services sector increased, in real terms, by an average of 2.9% per year during 2000–08, according to the World Bank. Services GDP grew by 3.3% in 2008.

Although shipbuilding has declined since the early 1970s, Norway remains a leading shipping nation. The establishment of the Norwegian International Ship Register in 1987 allowed an expansion of the merchant fleet by more than 300%, in terms of gross tonnage. At 31 December 2009 the combined displacement of the merchant fleet totalled 16.6m. grt, of which the Norwegian International Ship Register accounted for 13.9m. grt.

In 2009, according to IMF figures, Norway recorded a visible trade surplus of US $54,405m., and there was a surplus of $50,122m. on the current account of the balance of payments. In 2010 the EU (excluding the Nordic countries) provided 63.4% of imports and took 80.7% of exports; fellow members of the European Free Trade Association (EFTA, see p. 447) accounted for 1.3% of Norway's imports and 0.9% of exports in the same year. The principal source of imports in 2010 was Sweden (providing 14.1% of the total), followed by Germany, the People's Republic of China and Denmark; the principal market for exports was the United Kingdom (taking 26.7%), followed by the Netherlands, Germany and Sweden. In 2010 the principal exports were petroleum and petroleum products (accounting for 40.4% of total exports), natural gas, basic manufactures (most notably aluminium) and machinery and transport equipment; the principal imports were machinery and transport equipment (38.3%), miscellaneous manufactured articles, basic manufactures and chemicals and related products.

In 2010 Norway recorded an overall surplus of 265,547m. kroner in the general budget (equivalent to some 10.6% of GDP in purchasers' values). Norway's general government gross debt was 1,291.776m. kroner in 2009, equivalent to 54.3% of GDP. During 2000–10 the average annual rate of inflation was 2.0%; consumer prices increased by 2.5% in 2010. The average annual rate of unemployment was 3.6% in 2010, according to official figures.

The Norwegian economy is highly dependent on its hydrocarbons sector. It has traditionally maintained a stable exchange rate and a prudent fiscal position, reinvesting a substantial proportion of petroleum revenues abroad through the Government Pension Fund—Global (formerly the Government Petroleum Fund), partly in preparation for future increased demands on pensions and also to offer a degree of protection to the economy against fluctuations in the petroleum sector. Budgetary guidelines introduced in 2001 state that government spending of hydrocarbons revenues should equate to the expected annual return on the Pension Fund (assumed to be 4%) in the long term, while allowing for a more expansionary fiscal policy during an economic downturn. In the first years of the 21st century a strong policy framework underpinned enviable prosperity and a high degree of social equity in Norway. Norway's traditionally high social cohesiveness and solidarity ensured that the use of the petroleum wealth benefited people at all levels of society, and would continue to benefit future generations well after the petroleum itself was depleted. Strong economic expansion was achieved during 2004–07, not least because of high international prices for petroleum and gas; however, the economy slowed in 2008, before contracting by an estimated 1.6% in 2009, as it suffered the adverse effects of the global financial crisis. In January 2009 the Government announced fiscal measures designed to stimulate economic growth, which included a significant increase in public spending, principally on infrastructure projects, as well as reductions in the level of taxation for businesses. Such measures were considered effective at lessening the effects of the global downturn, and the fiscal stimulus was expected to be gradually withdrawn from 2011 as the economy recovered. Low production levels in the petroleum sector contributed to an overall GDP growth rate of just 0.4% in 2010, although 'mainland' GDP (which excludes the off-shore industries) grew by 2.2%, an expansion that was driven mainly by an increase in household consumption fuelled by increased export revenue from the petroleum sector owing to higher commodity prices. According to official forecasts, overall GDP was projected to increase by 2.1% in 2011.

PUBLIC HOLIDAYS

2012: 1 January (New Year's Day), 5 April (Maundy Thursday), 6 April (Good Friday), 9 April (Easter Monday), 1 May (Labour Day), 17 May (Constitution Day and Ascension Day), 28 May (Whit Monday), 25–26 December (Christmas).

Statistical Survey

Sources (unless otherwise stated): Statistics Norway, Kongensgt. 6, Oslo; tel. 21-09-00-00; fax 21-09-49-73; e-mail biblioteket@ssb.no; internet www.ssb.no
Nordic Statistical Secretariat (Copenhagen), *Yearbook of Nordic Statistics*.

Area and Population

AREA, POPULATION AND DENSITY

Area (sq km)	
Land	304,248
Inland water	19,539
Total	323,787*
Population (census results)	
3 November 1990	4,247,546
3 November 2001	
Males	2,240,281
Females	2,280,666
Total	4,520,947
Population (official estimates at 1 January)	
2009	4,799,252
2010	4,858,199
2011	4,920,305
Density (per sq km) at 1 January 2011†	16.2

* 125,015 sq miles.
† Excluding inland water.

POPULATION BY AGE AND SEX
(official estimates at 1 January 2011)

	Males	Females	Total
0–14	472,060	449,649	921,709
15–64	1,662,852	1,593,501	3,256,353
65 and over	325,937	416,306	742,243
Total	2,460,849	2,459,456	4,920,305

COUNTIES
(official population estimates at 1 January 2011)

	Land area (sq km)*	Population	Density (per sq km)
Østfold	3,888	274,827	70.7
Akershus	4,579	545,653	119.2
Oslo	426	599,230	1,406.6
Hedmark	26,084	191,622	7.3
Oppland	23,784	186,087	7.8
Buskerud	13,796	261,110	18.9
Vestfold	2,147	233,705	108.9
Telemark	13,854	169,185	12.2
Aust-Agder	8,314	110,048	13.2
Vest-Agder	6,677	172,408	25.8

NORWAY

—continued

	Land area (sq km)*	Population	Density (per sq km)
Rogaland	8,589	436,087	50.8
Hordaland	14,525	484,240	33.3
Sogn og Fjordane	17,676	107,742	6.1
Møre og Romsdal	14,583	253,904	17.4
Sør-Trøndelag	17,840	294,066	16.5
Nord-Trøndelag	20,778	132,140	6.4
Nordland	36,079	237,280	6.6
Troms	24,866	157,554	6.3
Finnmark	45,762	73,417	1.6
Total	304,248	4,920,305	16.2

* Excluding inland waters, totalling 19,539 sq km.

PRINCIPAL TOWNS
(estimated population of urban settlements at 1 January 2009)

Oslo (capital)	876,391	Tønsberg	47,465
Bergen	227,752	Ålesund	46,471
Stavanger/Sandnes	189,828	Haugesund	42,850
Trondheim	160,072	Moss	41,725
Fredrikstad/Sarpsborg	101,698	Sandefjord	40,877
Drammen	96,563	Bodø	36,482
Porsgrunn/Skien	86,923	Arendal	32,439
Kristiansand	67,547	Hamar	30,015
Tromsø	55,057	Larvik	23,899

BIRTHS, MARRIAGES AND DEATHS

	Registered live births		Registered marriages*		Registered deaths†	
	Number	Rate (per 1,000)	Number	Rate (per 1,000)	Number	Rate (per 1,000)
2002	55,434	12.3	24,069	5.3	44,465	9.8
2003	56,458	12.4	22,361	4.9	42,478	9.3
2004	56,951	12.4	22,354	4.9	41,200	9.0
2005	56,756	12.3	22,392	4.9	41,232	8.9
2006	58,545	12.6	21,721	4.7	41,253	8.9
2007	58,459	12.5	23,471	5.0	41,954	9.0
2008	60,497	12.8	25,125	5.3	41,712	8.8
2009	61,807	12.7	24,582‡	5.1‡	41,449	8.5

* Where bridegroom or older spouse (for same-sex marriages) is resident in Norway.
† Including deaths of residents temporarily abroad.
‡ Including same-sex marriages.

2010 (incl. same-sex): Marriages 23,577.

Life expectancy (years at birth, WHO estimates): 81 (males 78; females 83) in 2008 (Source: WHO, *World Health Statistics*).

IMMIGRATION AND EMIGRATION

	2007	2008	2009
Immigrants	61,774	66,961	65,186
Emigrants	22,122	23,615	26,549

ECONOMICALLY ACTIVE POPULATION
('000 persons aged 16 to 74 years)*

	2008	2009	2010
Agriculture, fishing and forestry	67	67	63
Mining and quarrying (incl. petroleum and gas)	42	45	46
Manufacturing	262	247	236
Electricity, gas and water	29	31	31
Construction	187	180	179
Trade, restaurants and hotels	426	413	414
Transport and communications	233	227	230
Financing, insurance, real estate and business services	315	317	311
Public administration and defence	149	157	157
Education	220	206	208
Health and social work	500	518	529
Other services	88	98	102
Sub-total	2,518	2,506	2,506
Activities not adequately described	6	2	2
Total employed	2,524	2,508	2,508
Unemployed	67	82	94
Total labour force	2,591	2,590	2,602
Males	1,370	1,366	1,378
Females	1,222	1,224	1,224

* Figures are annual averages, based on quarterly sample surveys.

Health and Welfare

KEY INDICATORS

Total fertility rate (children per woman, 2008)	1.9
Under-5 mortality rate (per 1,000 live births, 2008)	3
HIV/AIDS (% of persons aged 15–49, 2007)	0.1
Physicians (per 1,000 head, 2006)	3.8
Hospital beds (per 1,000 head, 2006)	4.1
Health expenditure (2007): US $ per head (PPP)	4,763
Health expenditure (2007): % of GDP	8.9
Health expenditure (2007): public (% of total)	84.1
Total carbon dioxide emissions ('000 metric tons, 2007)	42,722.2
Carbon dioxide emissions per head (metric tons, 2007)	9.1
Human Development Index (2010): ranking	1
Human Development Index (2010): value	0.938

For sources and definitions, see explanatory note on p. vi.

Agriculture

PRINCIPAL CROPS
('000 metric tons)*

	2007	2008	2009
Wheat	401.1	453.3	240.0
Barley	485.3	558.2	435.0
Rye	40.0	47.6	26.5
Oats	276.0	327.8	245.0
Potatoes	329.8	398.4	332.7
Rapeseed	9.7	9.5	10.0†
Cabbages and other brassicas	29.3	31.6	34.7
Tomatoes	15.5	12.0	10.9
Cucumbers and gherkins	20.4	17.0	18.3
Onions and shallots, green	19.2	22.3	20.6
Carrots and turnips	43.1	44.5	48.3
Apples	10.9	17.0	13.8

* Figures refer to holdings with at least 0.5 ha of agricultural area in use.
† Unofficial figure.

Aggregate production ('000 metric tons, may include official, semi-official or estimated data): Total cereals 1,202 in 2007, 1,387 in 2008, 947 in 2009; Total roots and tubers 330 in 2007, 398 in 2008, 333 in 2009; Total vegetables (incl. melons) 174 in 2007, 182 in 2008, 189 in 2009; Total fruits (excl. melons) 26 in 2007, 34 in 2008, 32 in 2009.

Source: FAO.

NORWAY

LIVESTOCK
('000 head)*

	2007	2008	2009
Horses	32.9	34.3	35.5
Cattle	905.5	891.2	877.7
Sheep	2,267.1	2,250.5	2,296.1
Goats	72.0	69.9	67.8
Pigs	837.9	828.2	839.3
Chickens	3,542	3,668	3,834

* Figures refer to holdings with at least 0.5 ha of agricultural area in use.

Source: FAO.

LIVESTOCK PRODUCTS
('000 metric tons)

	2007	2008	2009*
Cattle meat	84.7	86.4	86.0
Sheep meat	23.5	24.2	24.5
Pig meat	117.7	122.7	115.0
Chicken meat	62.6	74.8	69.0
Cows' milk	1,595.5	1,580.0	1,520.0
Goats' milk	20.9	20.7	18.0
Hen eggs	53.2	55.9	58.0
Honey	1.4	1.5	1.4
Wool, greasy	4.5	4.5	4.5

* FAO estimates.

Source: FAO.

Forestry

ROUNDWOOD REMOVALS
('000 cubic metres, excl. bark)

	2007	2008	2009
Sawlogs, veneer logs and logs for sleepers	4,353	3,969	3,060
Pulpwood	3,830	4,067	3,549
Other industrial wood	29	34	22
Fuel wood	2,253	2,253	2,253
Total	10,465	10,324	8,884

Source: FAO.

SAWNWOOD PRODUCTION
('000 cubic metres, incl. railway sleepers)

	2007	2008	2009
Coniferous (softwood)	2,374	2,200	1,850
Broadleaved (hardwood)	28	28	0
Total	2,402	2,228	1,850

Source: FAO.

Fishing
('000 metric tons, live weight)

	2006	2007	2008
Capture	2,256.4	2,378.8	2,430.8
Atlantic cod	221.3	217.5	216.3
Saithe (Pollock)	256.9	224.5	227.6
Blue whiting (Poutassou)	642.5	539.6	418.3
Sandeels (Sandlances)	5.8	51.1	81.6
Capelin	2.0	41.1	40.9
Atlantic herring	710.6	884.7	1,025.5
Atlantic mackerel	122.0	131.7	121.5
Aquaculture	712.4	841.6	843.7
Atlantic salmon	629.9	744.2	743.0
Total catch	2,968.8	3,220.4	3,274.6

Note: Figures exclude aquatic plants ('000 metric tons, wet weight, capture): 145.4 in 2006; 134.7 in 2007; n.a. in 2008. Also excluded are aquatic mammals, recorded by number rather than by weight. The number of minke whales caught was: 545 in 2006; 597 in 2007; 536 in 2008. The number of harp seals caught was: 13,390 in 2006; 13,981 in 2007; 891 in 2008. The number of hooded seals caught was: 3,647 in 2006; 62 in 2007; nil in 2008.

Source: FAO.

Mining
('000 metric tons unless otherwise indicated)

	2006	2007	2008
Coal (all grades)	236	322	343
Crude petroleum	128,712	118,561	114,054
Natural gas (million cu m)	87,613	89,662	99,245
Iron ore*	620	1,437	2,046

* Metal content of ore.

2009: Crude petroleum 108,323,000 metric tons; Natural gas 103,470m. cu m.

Source: US Geological Survey; BP, *Statistical Review of World Energy*.

Industry

SELECTED PRODUCTS
('000 metric tons unless otherwise indicated)

	2006	2007	2008
Margarine	42.5	n.a.	n.a.
Mechanical wood pulp (dry weight)*	1,536	1,473	1,354
Chemical wood pulp (dry weight)*	744	730	739
Particle board ('000 cu m)*	382	383	309
Paper and paperboard*	2,109	2,010	1,900
Kerosene ('000 barrels)	5,800	5,800†	n.a.
Naphthas ('000 barrels)	10,000	10,000†	n.a.
Gas-diesel (distillate fuel) oil ('000 barrels)	50,000	50,000†	n.a.
Residual fuel oil ('000 barrels)	12,000	12,000†	n.a.
Cement	1,850	1,800	1,800
Ferro-silicon (75% basis)	93	90	90
Other ferro-alloys	60	60	60
Crude steel	679	740	560
Nickel (refined): primary	82.0	87.6	88.7
Copper (refined): primary and secondary	40	34	32†
Aluminium (refined): primary	1,422.0	1,304.4	1,360.0†
Aluminium (refined): secondary	349.2	350.0	350.0†
Zinc (refined): primary	160.7	157.0	145.5
Electric energy (million kWh)	121,580	137,471	n.a.

* Source: FAO.
† Estimated or unofficial figure.

Sources (unless otherwise indicated): UN Industrial Commodity Statistics Database; US Geological Survey.

NORWAY

Finance

CURRENCY AND EXCHANGE RATES

Monetary Units
100 øre = 1 Norwegian krone (plural: kroner).

Sterling, Dollar and Euro Equivalents (31 December 2010)
£1 sterling = 9.217 kroner;
US $1 = 5.888 kroner;
€1 = 7.867 kroner;
100 Norwegian kroner = £10.85 = $16.98 = €12.71.

Average Exchange Rate (kroner per US $)
2008   5.6400
2009   6.2883
2010   6.0432

GENERAL BUDGET
(accrued values, million kroner)

Revenue	2008	2009	2010
Taxation	1,078,686	1,000,408	1,066,854
Taxes on income, profits and wealth	564,820	478,701	516,910
Taxes on goods and services	285,013	284,535	304,349
Capital taxes	1,973	2,431	2,377
Social security contributions	226,880	234,741	243,218
Property income	350,188	274,872	265,815
Interest	114,580	91,434	86,792
Dividends	73,982	74,790	70,221
Withdrawals from income of quasi-corporations	156,182	101,314	102,158
Land rent, road rent, etc.	5,444	7,334	6,644
Administrative fees and charges	60,111	62,826	65,832
Current transfers	9,338	9,915	10,953
Total	**1,498,323**	**1,348,021**	**1,409,453**

Expenditure	2008	2009	2010
General public services	109,724	114,286	115,921
Defence	40,169	41,183	38,233
Public order and safety	22,523	24,445	25,468
Economic affairs	94,319	104,703	111,341
Environmental protection	14,673	15,620	17,105
Housing and community amenities	15,546	16,548	17,918
Health	170,294	179,836	188,875
Recreation, culture and religion	28,636	32,739	33,122
Education	131,756	142,191	148,323
Social protection	390,295	426,871	449,777
Statistical discrepancy	—	−3	−2,177
Total	**1,017,935**	**1,098,419**	**1,143,906**

INTERNATIONAL RESERVES
(excluding gold, US $ million at 31 December)

	2008	2009	2010
IMF special drawing rights	436.6	2,508.7	2,455.5
Reserve position in IMF	299.1	632.1	602.2
Foreign exchange	50,214.1	45,718.6	49,801.8
Total	**50,949.8**	**48,859.3**	**52,859.5**

Source: IMF, *International Financial Statistics*.

MONEY SUPPLY
('000 million kroner at 31 December)

	2004	2005	2006
Currency outside banks	43.34	46.57	48.25
Demand deposits at commercial and savings banks	700.07	791.12	923.21
Total money (incl. others)	**743.44**	**839.01**	**971.48**

Source: IMF, *International Financial Statistics*.

COST OF LIVING
(Consumer Price Index; base: 1998 = 100)

	2008	2009	2010
Food and non-alcoholic beverages	117.3	122.2	122.4
Alcoholic beverages and tobacco	136.0	142.8	147.8
Housing and utilities	148.4	151.0	159.0
Clothing and footwear	62.1	60.0	57.6
All items (incl. others)	**123.1**	**125.7**	**128.8**

NATIONAL ACCOUNTS
(million kroner at current prices)

Expenditure on the Gross Domestic Product

	2008	2009	2010
Government final consumption expenditure	491,861	533,106	555,094
Private final consumption expenditure	988,809	1,015,261	1,072,575
Increase in stocks*	9,238	−39,549	39,401
Gross fixed capital formation	545,827	519,563	496,022
Total domestic expenditure	**2,035,735**	**2,028,381**	**2,163,092**
Exports of goods and services	1,223,846	1,008,761	1,050,512
Less Imports of goods and services	742,780	656,294	708,526
GDP in purchasers' values	**2,516,800**	**2,380,851**	**2,505,076**
GDP at constant 2007 prices	2,288,673	2,255,991	2,266,079

*Including statistical discrepancy.

Gross Domestic Product by Economic Activity

	2008	2009	2010
Agriculture, hunting and forestry	16,362	13,966	16,538
Fishing and fish farming	11,026	12,049	18,572
Petroleum and gas extraction	650,314	486,353	519,495
Other mining and quarrying	4,973	4,243	3,931
Manufacturing	206,472	204,843	206,133
Electricity, gas and water	59,410	52,229	62,027
Construction	109,910	111,934	119,160
Wholesale and retail trade; repair of motor vehicles	181,244	175,836	180,939
Hotels and restaurants	32,465	32,714	34,430
Transport, storage and communications*	146,383	137,843	127,983
Financing, insurance, real estate and business services	313,631	325,918	344,144
Private services in households	87,034	89,679	93,814
Public administration and defence	99,461	106,068	110,500
Education	91,568	97,890	102,559
Health and social work	195,308	210,353	221,576
Other social and personal services	60,363	64,972	70,160
Sub-total	**2,265,924**	**2,126,890**	**2,231,961**
Value-added tax and investment levy	184,842	186,211	199,120
Other taxes on products (net)	70,678	69,399	74,502
Statistical discrepancy	−4,644	−1,647	−507
GDP in purchasers' values	**2,516,800**	**2,380,851**	**2,505,076**

*Including transportation of petroleum and gas by pipeline.

BALANCE OF PAYMENTS
(US $ million)

	2007	2008	2009
Exports of goods f.o.b.	137,297	173,599	121,929
Imports of goods f.o.b.	−77,026	−87,127	−67,525
Trade balance	**60,271**	**86,472**	**54,405**
Exports of services	40,592	45,388	38,758
Imports of services	−39,758	−45,154	−36,972
Balance on goods and services	**61,105**	**86,706**	**56,191**
Other income received	39,273	43,884	27,089
Other income paid	−37,272	−47,031	−28,750
Balance on goods, services and income	**63,106**	**83,559**	**54,531**

NORWAY

—continued

	2007	2008	2009
Current transfers received	3,554	3,560	3,229
Current transfers paid	−6,201	−7,031	−7,637
Current balance	60,459	80,088	50,122
Capital account (net)	−163	−210	−173
Direct investment abroad	−12,500	−23,708	−27,218
Direct investment from abroad	3,788	7,252	11,270
Portfolio investment assets	−68,808	−133,044	−3,013
Portfolio investment liabilities	44,283	20,545	4,316
Other investment assets	−47,671	36,560	27,199
Other investment liabilities	50,238	17,376	−84,565
Net errors and omissions	−28,581	−246	4,993
Overall balance	1,045	4,612	−17,068

Source: IMF, *International Financial Statistics*.

OFFICIAL ASSISTANCE TO DEVELOPING COUNTRIES
(million kroner)

	2001	2002	2003
Bilateral assistance	7,901	8,493	9,646
Technical assistance	1,140	1,551	1,878
Investments	532	412	378
Sector-related project and programme aid	3,510	3,496	3,310
Non-sector related project and programme aid	2,357	3,132	3,983
Associated financing	9	69	—
Loan assistance	—	—	—
Norfund	61	57	96
Multilateral assistance	3,374	4,400	4,107
Contributions to multilateral organizations	273	—	—
Humanitarian relief work	273	—	—
Administration	595	652	704
Total official development assistance	11,870	13,545	14,457

2004 (million kroner): Bilateral assistance 6,932; Multilateral-bilateral assistance 2,629; Multilateral assistance 4,463; Administration 793; Total official development assistance 14,817.

2005 (million kroner): Bilateral assistance 7,850; Multilateral-bilateral assistance 4,053; Multilateral assistance 5,157; Administration 885; Total official development assistance 17,946.

2006 (million kroner): Bilateral assistance 8,487; Multilateral-bilateral assistance 4,127; Multilateral assistance 5,283; Administration 1,053; Total official development assistance 18,950.

2007 (million kroner): Bilateral assistance 10,331; Multilateral-bilateral assistance 5,459; Multilateral assistance 4,952; Administration 1,098; Total official development assistance 21,840.

2008 (million kroner, provisional figures): Bilateral assistance 10,037; Multilateral-bilateral assistance 5,992; Multilateral assistance 5,391; Administration 1,200; Total official development assistance 22,621.

External Trade

(Note: Figures include all ships bought and sold but exclude trade in military supplies under defence agreements.)

PRINCIPAL COMMODITIES
(distribution by SITC, million kroner)

Imports c.i.f.*	2008	2009	2010
Food and live animals	26,469	26,889	27,560
Crude materials (inedible) except fuels	38,178	24,889	32,741
Metalliferous ores and metal scrap	26,710	15,371	22,247
Mineral fuels, lubricants, etc. (incl. electric current)	24,995	22,140	31,977
Petroleum, petroleum products, etc.	21,084	18,736	22,851
Chemicals and related products	45,198	43,327	47,659
Basic manufactures	80,926	64,633	68,500
Metal manufactures	23,112	18,617	18,256
Machinery and transport equipment	208,700	174,990	177,807
Machinery specialized for particular industries	21,300	16,457	15,828
General industrial machinery, equipment and parts	30,394	26,010	21,901
Office machines and automatic data-processing equipment	16,060	14,571	15,152
Telecommunications and sound equipment	18,652	18,115	18,607
Other electrical machinery, apparatus, etc.	24,686	22,333	22,795
Road vehicles and parts†	44,477	34,988	43,811
Other transport equipment†	39,603	31,261	30,863
Miscellaneous manufactured articles	71,082	66,972	69,388
Clothing and accessories (excl. footwear)	14,292	14,274	15,146
Total (incl. others)	504,481	432,378	464,653

* Equipment imported directly to the Norwegian sector of the continental shelf is excluded.
† Excluding tyres, engines and electrical parts.

Exports f.o.b.	2008	2009	2010
Food and live animals	40,041	46,293	55,495
Fish and fish preparations*	37,369	43,481	52,424
Mineral fuels, lubricants, etc. (incl. electric current)	663,644	492,962	510,421
Petroleum, petroleum products, etc.	412,974	279,709	320,643
Gas (natural and manufactured)	241,105	207,190	185,805
Chemicals and related products	44,046	37,153	44,954
Basic manufactures	88,253	63,539	74,745
Non-ferrous metals	48,275	33,732	44,084
Machinery and transport equipment	87,324	85,079	73,634
Miscellaneous manufactured articles	22,350	20,612	20,511
Total (incl. others)	959,002	756,811	794,425

* Including crustaceans and molluscs.

NORWAY

PRINCIPAL TRADING PARTNERS
(million kroner)

Imports c.i.f.	2008	2009	2010
Belgium	9,885.6	8,345.6	8,600.0
Canada	14,036.5	9,499.9	15,004.4
China, People's Repub.	32,097.5	33,384.8	39,617.1
Denmark	34,152.2	29,008.0	29,053.0
Finland	16,782.8	12,526.2	11,923.8
France	18,075.6	15,583.1	16,580.7
Germany	66,620.1	54,962.9	57,510.4
Ireland	5,144.0	5,522.7	4,811.8
Italy	16,480.3	13,370.8	12,646.7
Japan	10,980.7	10,656.8	10,236.7
Korea, Republic	6,627.3	8,160.7	14,158.3
Netherlands	20,270.1	16,711.4	17,415.6
Poland	12,204.3	11,743.2	11,730.6
Russia	11,083.4	7,062.1	11,926.9
Spain	10,119.7	9,574.7	6,129.8
Sweden	70,861.1	59,295.3	65,480.3
Switzerland	5,421.2	4,766.0	4,800.7
Taiwan	3,870.2	3,373.2	3,981.8
United Kingdom	29,513.7	25,723.2	27,330.5
USA	26,874.4	26,424.9	24,933.4
Total (incl. others)	504,481.2	432,377.7	464,653.4

Exports f.o.b.	2008	2009	2010
Belgium	24,337.6	20,119.6	21,280.8
Canada	22,464.8	16,245.4	13,077.0
China, People's Repub.	10,673.0	15,210.2	14,187.0
Denmark	34,404.2	29,895.4	25,184.3
Finland	13,473.2	8,878.3	9,842.6
France	89,753.1	61,387.0	51,069.4
Germany	119,709.7	99,012.7	90,501.2
Ireland	9,856.2	7,309.0	8,475.6
Italy	30,009.0	23,818.5	19,824.7
Japan	8,126.0	7,846.6	9,509.4
Korea, Republic	9,062.1	14,575.5	12,143.6
Netherlands	100,146.7	86,227.6	95,884.8
Spain	18,273.0	17,426.5	14,909.8
Sweden	59,908.6	43,110.2	55,733.5
United Kingdom	260,329.4	175,893.0	212,212.9
USA	41,167.6	36,065.3	39,520.7
Total (incl. others)	959,001.9	756,810.6	794,425.4

Transport

STATE RAILWAYS
(traffic)

	2006	2007	2008
Passengers carried (million)	54.7	56.8	59.1
Goods carried ('000 metric tons)	24,802	25,131	24,888
Passenger-km (million)	2,832	2,957	3,122
Freight ton-km (million)	3,351	3,502	3,550

ROAD TRAFFIC
(motor vehicles registered at 31 December)

	2007	2008	2009
Passenger cars (incl. station wagons and ambulances)	2,154,837	2,197,193	2,244,039
Buses	25,204	23,324	21,474
Vans	361,911	379,343	387,546
Combined vehicles	67,020	59,657	53,911
Goods vehicles, etc.	84,742	84,350	82,694
Tractors and special purpose vehicles	245,692	248,463	250,995
Motorcycles	126,207	134,721	141,235
Snow scooters	61,145	63,631	66,426
Mopeds	156,287	161,662	165,557

SHIPPING
Merchant Fleet
(registered at 31 December)

	2007	2008	2009
Number of vessels	2,088	2,055	2,023
Total displacement ('000 grt)	18,156.0	18,311.3	16,614.3

Note: Figures include vessels on the Norwegian International Ship Register.

Source: IHS Fairplay, *World Fleet Statistics*.

International Sea-borne Freight Traffic*
('000 metric tons)

	2007	2008	2009
Goods loaded	136,104	132,840	122,904
Goods unloaded	26,136	24,888	20,700

* Figures exclude transit traffic (other than Swedish iron ore), packing and re-export.

Source: UN, *Monthly Bulletin of Statistics*.

CIVIL AVIATION
(traffic on scheduled services)*

	2004	2005	2006
Kilometres flown (million)	128	110	107
Passengers carried ('000)	12,277	10,398	10,344
Passenger-km (million)	10,321	9,408	9,779
Total ton-km (million)	1,199	1,125	1,183

* Including an apportionment (2/7) of the international services of Scandinavian Airlines System (SAS), operated jointly with Denmark and Sweden.

Source: UN, *Statistical Yearbook*.

Tourism

VISITOR ARRIVALS BY COUNTRY OF ORIGIN*

	2006	2007	2008
Denmark	587,565	565,643	540,630
Finland	67,295	73,120	67,649
France	205,741	202,870	201,231
Germany	746,031	720,138	729,381
Italy	163,982	164,578	139,001
Japan	122,132	110,908	103,796
Netherlands	285,178	320,576	309,379
Spain	243,163	268,108	213,336
Sweden	526,764	560,289	579,329
United Kingdom	651,545	645,809	562,212
USA	316,954	312,855	289,944
Total (incl. others)	4,914,019	5,067,552	4,893,806

* Non-residents staying in all types of accommodation establishments.

Tourism receipts (US $ million, incl. passenger transport): 4,251 in 2006; 5,037 in 2007; 5,559 in 2008.

Source: World Tourism Organization.

NORWAY

Communications Media

	2007	2008	2009
Telephones ('000 main lines in use)	1,988	1,896	1,783
Mobile cellular telephones ('000 subscribers)	5,037.6	5,211.2	5,359.6
Internet users ('000)*	4,103	4,317	4,431
Broadband subscribers ('000)	1,436.0	1,586.0	1,637.5

* Estimated figures.

Personal computers: 2,931,000 (628.9 per 1,000 persons) in 2006.

Source: International Telecommunication Union.

Television receivers (2000): 3,000,000 in use.

Radio receivers (1997): 4,030,000 in use*.

Books published (1999): 4,985 titles†.

Daily newspapers (2004): 74; total average circulation ('000 copies) 2,378‡.

Non-daily newspapers (2004): 151; total average circulation ('000 copies) 641‡.

* Source: UNESCO, *Statistical Yearbook*.
† Source: UN, *Statistical Yearbook*.
‡ Source: UNESCO Institute for Statistics.

Education

(2009, unless otherwise indicated)

	Institutions	Teachers	Students
Pre-primary	6,675	68,096	270,174
Primary and lower secondary	2,997	65,376*	613,928
Upper secondary	439	21,067†	257,755
Folk high schools	n.a.	n.a.	6,850
Other upper secondary programmes	n.a.	n.a.	11,441‡

* 2003.
† Full-time equivalent 'man years'.
‡ Private educational programmes between lower secondary and higher education, but not consistent with upper secondary education (e.g. bible schools).

Higher and further education (2009 unless otherwise indicated): *Institutions* (2003): 59 colleges of higher education and 11 universities (or equivalent). *Teachers* (full-time equivalent 'man years'): 18,239. *Students:* Higher vocational 11,721; other higher education (incl. university) 235,300. Note: In addition 469,669 students were engaged in adult education, and 18,376 students were enrolled in distance learning programmes, in 2009.

Pupil-teacher ratio (primary education, UNESCO estimate): 10.5 in 2003/04 (Source: UNESCO Institute for Statistics).

Directory

The Government

HEAD OF STATE

Sovereign: HM King HARALD V (succeeded to the throne 17 January 1991; sworn in 21 January 1991).

COUNCIL OF STATE
(Statsråd)
(May 2011)

A coalition of Det norske Arbeiderparti (DnA), the Sosialistisk Venstreparti (SV) and the Senterpartiet (Sp).

Prime Minister: JENS STOLTENBERG (DnA).
Minister of Education: KRISTIN HALVORSEN (SV).
Minister of Local Government and Regional Development: LIV SIGNE NAVARSETE (Sp).
Minister of Foreign Affairs: JONAS GAHR STØRE (DnA).
Minister of Defence: GRETE FAREMO (DnA).
Minister of Finance: SIGBJØRN JOHNSEN (DnA).
Minister of Trade and Industry: TROND GISKE (DnA).
Minister of Transport and Communications: MAGNHILD MELTVEIT KLEPPA (Sp).
Minister of Health and Care Services: ANNE-GRETE STRØM-ERICHSEN (DnA).
Minister of the Environment and International Development: ERIK SOLHEIM (SV).
Minister of Justice and the Police: KNUT STORBERGET (DnA).
Minister of Petroleum and Energy: OLA BORTEN MOE (Sp).
Minister in the Office of the Prime Minister: KARL EIRIK SCHJØTT-PEDERSEN (DnA).
Minister of Research and Higher Education: TORA AASLAND (SV).
Minister of Culture: ANNIKEN HUITFELDT (DnA).
Minister of Agriculture and Food: LARS PEDER BREKK (Sp).
Minister of Government Administration, Reform and Church Affairs: RIGMOR AASRUD (DnA).
Minister of Labour: HANNE INGER BJURSTRØM (DnA).
Minister of Fisheries and Coastal Affairs: LISBETH BERG-HANSEN (DnA).
Minister of Children, Equality and Social Inclusion: AUDUN LYSBAKKEN (SV).

MINISTRIES

Office of the Prime Minister: Akersgt. 42, POB 8001 Dep., 0030 Oslo; tel. 22-24-90-90; fax 22-24-95-00; e-mail postmottak@smk.dep.no; internet www.regjeringen.no/smk.

Ministry of Agriculture and Food: Akersgt. 59 (R5), POB 8007 Dep., 0030 Oslo; tel. 22-24-90-90; fax 22-24-95-55; e-mail postmottak@lmd.dep.no; internet www.regjeringen.no/lmd.

Ministry of Children, Equality and Social Inclusion: Akersgt. 59, POB 8036 Dep., 0030 Oslo; tel. 22-24-90-90; fax 22-24-95-15; e-mail postmottak@bld.dep.no; internet www.regjeringen.no/bld.

Ministry of Culture: Akersgt. 59, POB 8030 Dep., 0030 Oslo; tel. 22-24-78-39; fax 22-24-95-50; e-mail postmottak@kud.dep.no; internet www.regjeringen.no/kud.

Ministry of Defence: Glacisgt. 1, POB 8126 Dep., 0032 Oslo; tel. 23-09-80-00; fax 23-09-60-75; e-mail postmottak@fd.dep.no; internet www.regjeringen.no/fd.

Ministry of Education and Research: Akersgt. 44, POB 8119 Dep., 0032 Oslo; tel. 22-24-90-90; fax 22-24-95-40; e-mail postmottak@kd.dep.no; internet www.regjeringen.no/kd.

Ministry of the Environment: Myntgt. 2, POB 8013 Dep., 0030 Oslo; tel. 22-24-90-90; fax 22-24-95-60; e-mail postmottak@md.dep.no; internet www.regjeringen.no/md.

Ministry of Finance: Akersgt. 40, POB 8008 Dep., 0030 Oslo; tel. 22-24-90-90; fax 22-24-95-10; e-mail postmottak@fin.dep.no; internet www.regjeringen.no/fin.

Ministry of Fisheries and Coastal Affairs: Grubbegt. 1, POB 8118 Dep., 0032 Oslo; tel. 22-24-90-90; fax 22-24-95-85; e-mail postmottak@fkd.dep.no; internet www.regjeringen.no/fkd.

Ministry of Foreign Affairs: 7 juni pl., POB 8114 Dep., 0032 Oslo; tel. 22-24-36-00; fax 22-24-95-80; e-mail post@mfa.no; internet www.regjeringen.no/ud; also incl. Ministry of International Development.

Ministry of Government Administration, Reform and Church Affairs: Akersgt. 59, POB 8004 Dep., 0030 Oslo; tel. 22-24-90-90; fax 22-24-95-16; e-mail postmottak@fad.dep.no; internet www.regjeringen.no/fad.

Ministry of Health and Care Services: Einar Gerhardsens pl. 3, POB 8011 Dep., 0030 Oslo; tel. 22-24-90-90; e-mail postmottak@hod.dep.no; internet www.regjeringen.no/hod.

Ministry of Justice and the Police: Akersgt. 42, POB 8005 Dep., 0030 Oslo; tel. 22-24-90-90; e-mail postmottak@jd.dep.no; internet www.regjeringen.no/jd.

Ministry of Labour: Einar Gerhardsens pl. 3, POB 8019 Dep., 0030 Oslo; tel. 22-24-90-90; fax 22-24-87-11; e-mail postmottak@ad.dep.no; internet www.regjeringen.no/ad.

Ministry of Local Government and Regional Development: Akersgt. 59, POB 8112 Dep., 0032 Oslo; tel. 22-24-90-90; e-mail postmottak@krd.dep.no; internet www.regjeringen.no/krd.

Ministry of Petroleum and Energy: Einar Gerhardsens pl. 1, POB 8148 Dep., 0033 Oslo; tel. 22-24-90-90; fax 22-24-95-96; e-mail postmottak@oed.dep.no; internet www.regjeringen.no/oed.

NORWAY

Ministry of Trade and Industry: Einar Gerhardsens pl. 1, POB 8014 Dep., 0030 Oslo; tel. 22-24-90-90; fax 22-24-01-30; e-mail postmottak@nhd.dep.no; internet www.regjeringen.no/nhd.

Ministry of Transport and Communications: Akersgt. 59 (R5), POB 8010 Dep., 0030 Oslo; tel. 22-24-90-90; fax 22-24-95-71; e-mail postmottak@sd.dep.no; internet www.regjeringen.no/sd.

Legislature

Storting

Karl Johansgt. 22, 0026 Oslo; tel. 23-31-30-50; fax 23-31-38-17; e-mail info@stortinget.no; internet www.stortinget.no.

President: DAG TERJE ANDERSEN (DnA).
First Vice-President: ØYVIND KORSBERG (FrP).

General Election, 14 September 2009

Party	Votes	% of votes	Seats
Det norske Arbeiderparti (DnA)	949,060	35.37	64
Fremskrittspartiet (FrP)	614,724	22.91	41
Høyre (H)	462,465	17.24	30
Sosialistisk Venstreparti (SV)	166,366	6.20	11
Senterpartiet (Sp)	165,014	6.15	11
Kristelig Folkeparti (KrF)	148,750	5.54	10
Venstre (V)	104,148	3.88	2
Rødt (R)	36,220	1.35	—
Others	36,201	1.35	—
Total	2,682,948	100.00	169

Political Organizations

Fremskrittspartiet (FrP) (Progress Party): Karl Johans gt. 25, 0159 Oslo; tel. 23-13-54-00; fax 23-13-54-01; e-mail frp@frp.no; internet www.frp.no; f. 1973 as Anders Langes Parti; present name adopted 1977; anti-tax; favours privatization, the diminution of the welfare state and less immigration; Chair. SIV JENSEN; Sec.-Gen. GEIR A. MO.

Høyre (H) (Conservative): Stortingsgt. 20, POB 1536 Vika, 0117 Oslo; tel. 22-82-90-00; fax 22-82-90-80; e-mail politikk@hoyre.no; internet www.hoyre.no; f. 1884; aims to promote economic growth and sound state finances, to achieve a property-owning democracy, and to uphold democratic govt, social security, private property, private initiative and personal liberty; 67,000 mems; Leader ERNA SOLBERG; Sec.-Gen. LARS ARNE RYSSDAL.

Kristelig Folkeparti (KrF) (Christian Democratic Party): Øvre Slottsgt. 18–20, POB 478 Sentrum, 0105 Oslo; tel. 23-10-28-00; fax 23-10-28-10; e-mail krf@krf.no; internet www.krf.no; f. 1933; aims to promote a democratic policy based on Christian values; Chair. DAGFINN HØYBRÅTEN; Sec.-Gen. KNUT H. JAHR.

Kystpartiet (Coastal Party): Grennsen 8B, 0159 Oslo; tel. 22-33-68-10; e-mail post@kystpartiet.no; internet www.kystpartiet.no; nationalist; Leader ERLING SKÅTØY; Sec. PER-JØRGEN HANSSEN.

Miljøpartiet De Grønne (Green Party of Norway): Karl Johans gt. 6B, 0159 Oslo; tel. 23-69-94-11; e-mail mdg@mdg.no; internet www.mdg.no; f. 1988; Principal Speakers HARALD NISSEN, HANNA ELISE MARCUSSEN.

Norges Kommunistiske Parti (NKP) (Communist Party of Norway): Helgesensgt. 21, POB 9288 Grønland, 0134 Oslo; tel. 22-71-60-44; fax 22-71-79-07; e-mail nkp@nkp.no; internet www.nkp.no; f. 1923; Chair. ZAFER GÖZET.

Det norske Arbeiderparti (DnA) (Norwegian Labour Party): Youngstorget 2A, 5th floor, POB 8743, 0028 Oslo; tel. 24-14-40-00; fax 24-14-40-01; e-mail post@arbeiderpartiet.no; internet www.arbeiderpartiet.no; f. 1887; social democratic; 50,269 mems (Dec. 2009); Leader JENS STOLTENBERG; Gen. Sec. RAYMOND JOHANSEN.

Pensjonistpartiet (Pensioners' Party): Møllergt. 6, 0179 Oslo; tel. 45-28-90-10; fax 22-42-77-00; e-mail post@pensjonistpartiet.no; internet www.pensjonistpartiet.no; Leader TERJE WOLD.

Rødt (R): Osterhausgt. 27, 0183 Oslo; tel. 22-98-90-50; fax 22-98-90-55; e-mail raudt@raudt.no; internet rodet.no; f. 2007 by merger of Rød Valgallianse (Red Electoral Alliance) and Arbeidernes Kommunistparti (Workers' Communist Party); left-wing group; Leader TURID THOMASSEN; Sec. BETH HARTMANN.

Senterpartiet (Sp) (Centre Party): Akersgt. 35, 3rd Floor, POB 1191 Sentrum, 0107 Oslo; tel. 23-69-01-00; fax 23-69-01-01; e-mail epost@senterpartiet.no; internet www.senterpartiet.no; f. 1920 as the Bondepartiet (Farmers' Party), name changed 1959; advocates a decentralized society that will secure employment and diversified settlements in all parts of the country; opposes Norwegian membership of the EU; encourages the devt of an ecologically balanced society; Leader LIV SIGNE NAVARSETE; Sec.-Gen. KNUT M. OLSEN.

Sosialistisk Venstreparti (SV) (Socialist Left Party): Akersgt. 35, 0158 Oslo; tel. 21-93-33-00; fax 21-93-33-01; e-mail post@sv.no; internet www.sv.no; f. 1975 by merger of the Socialist People's Party, the Democratic Socialists and other socialist forces united previously in the Socialist Electoral League; advocates non-alignment and socialism independent of international centres, based on workers' control, decentralized powers, gender equality and ecological principles; Chair. KRISTIN HALVORSEN; Sec. SILJE SCHEI TVEITDAL.

Venstre (V) (Liberal): Møllergt. 16, 0179 Oslo; tel. 22-40-43-50; fax 22-40-43-51; e-mail venstre@venstre.no; internet www.venstre.no; f. 1884; in 1988 reunited with Det Liberale Folkepartiet (Liberal Democratic Party, f. 1972); advocates the promotion of national and democratic progress on the basis of the present system by gradual economic, social and cultural reforms; Leader TRINE SKEI GRANDE; Sec.-Gen. TERJE BREIVIK.

Diplomatic Representation

EMBASSIES IN NORWAY

Afghanistan: Kronprinsensgt. 17, 0251 Oslo; tel. 23-23-92-20; fax 22-83-84-11; e-mail info@afghanemb.com; internet www.afghanistanembassy.no; Ambassador MANIZHA BAKHTARI.

Algeria: Inkognitogt. 35, 0265 Oslo; tel. 22-55-75-31; fax 25-55-75-30; e-mail ambalgoslo@live.fr; Ambassador BOUBAKEUR OGAB.

Argentina: Drammensvn 39, 0244 Oslo; tel. 22-55-24-49; fax 22-44-16-41; e-mail enoru@online.no; Ambassador JUAN MANUEL ORTIZ DE ROSAS.

Austria: Thomas Heftyesgt. 19–21, 0244 Oslo; tel. 22-54-02-00; fax 22-55-43-61; e-mail oslo-ob@bmeia.gv.at; Ambassador Dr LORENZ GRAF.

Belgium: Drammensvn 103D, 0244 Oslo; tel. 23-13-32-20; fax 23-13-32-32; e-mail oslo@diplobel.fed.be; internet www.diplomatie.be/oslo; Ambassador CHRISTIAN MONNOYER.

Bosnia and Herzegovina: Bygdøy allé 10, POB 2407 Solli, 0201 Oslo; tel. 22-54-09-63; fax 22-55-27-50; e-mail gkbih@gkbih.com; Ambassador ELMA KOVAČEVIĆ.

Brazil: Sigurd Syrsgt. 4, 0244 Oslo; tel. 22-54-07-30; fax 22-44-39-64; e-mail brasil@brasil.no; internet www.brasil.no; Ambassador CARLOS HENRIQUE CARDIM.

Bulgaria: Tidemandsgt. 11, 0244 Oslo; tel. 22-55-40-40; fax 22-55-40-24; e-mail bulgemb@online.no; internet www.mfa.bg/oslo; Ambassador NIKOLAS IVANOV KARADIMOV.

Canada: Wergelandsvn 7, 4th Floor, 0244 Oslo; tel. 22-99-53-00; fax 22-99-53-01; e-mail oslo@international.gc.ca; internet www.canadainternational.gc.ca/norway-norvege; Ambassador JOHN HANNAFORD.

Chile: Meltzersgt. 5, 0244 Oslo; tel. 22-44-89-55; fax 22-44-24-21; e-mail secretary@chile.no; internet www.chile.no; Ambassador JUAN ANÍBAL BARRÍA GARCÍA.

China, People's Republic: Tuengen allé 2B, Vinderen, 0244 Oslo; tel. 22-49-20-52; fax 22-92-19-78; e-mail webmaster@chinese-embassy.no; internet www.chinese-embassy.no; Ambassador TANG GUOQIANG.

Colombia: Oscarsgt. 34, 0258 Oslo; tel. 23-12-01-50; fax 23-12-01-51; e-mail eoslo@cancilleria.gov.co; Chargé d'affaires a.i. SANTIAGO SALCEDO BUITRAGO.

Costa Rica: Skippergt. 33, 8th Floor, 0154 Oslo; tel. 22-42-58-23; fax 22-33-04-08; e-mail embassy@costarica.no; Chargé d'affaires a.i. LILLIAM RODRÍGUEZ.

Croatia: Drammensvn 82, 0244 Oslo; tel. 23-01-40-50; fax 23-01-40-60; e-mail croemb.oslo@mvpei.hr; Ambassador MARIO HORVATIĆ.

Cuba: Oscarsgt. 78B, 0244 Oslo; tel. 23-08-32-60; fax 23-08-32-61; e-mail enoruega@online.no; internet www.embacuba.no; Ambassador ROGERIO SANTANA.

Czech Republic: Fritznersgt. 14, 0244 Oslo; tel. 22-12-10-31; fax 22-55-33-95; e-mail oslo@embassy.mzv.cz; internet www.mzv.cz/oslo; Ambassador LUBOŠ NOVÝ.

Denmark: Olav Kyrresgt. 7, 0244 Oslo; tel. 22-54-08-00; fax 22-55-46-34; e-mail oslamb@um.dk; internet www.amboslo.um.dk; Ambassador HUGO ØSTERGAARD-ANDERSEN.

Egypt: Drammensvn 90A, 0244 Oslo; tel. 23-08-42-00; fax 22-56-22-68; e-mail information@egypt-embassy.no; internet www.egypt-embassy.no; Ambassador TAMER ABD AL-AZIZ A. KHALIL.

NORWAY

Estonia: Parkvn 51A, 0244 Oslo; tel. 22-54-00-70; fax 22-54-00-71; e-mail embassy.oslo@mfa.ee; internet www.estemb.no; Ambassador ARTI HILPUS.

Finland: Thomas Heftyesgt. 1, 0244 Oslo; tel. 22-12-49-00; fax 22-12-49-49; e-mail sanomat.osl@formin.fi; internet www.finland.no; Ambassador MAIMO SUSANNE HENRIKSSON.

France: Drammensvn 69, 0244 Oslo; tel. 23-28-46-00; fax 23-28-46-70; e-mail ambafrance.oslo@diplomatie.gouv.fr; internet www.ambafrance-no.org; Ambassador BRIGITTE COLLET.

Germany: Oscarsgt. 45, 0244 Oslo; tel. 23-27-54-00; fax 22-44-76-72; e-mail info@oslo.diplo.de; internet www.oslo.diplo.de; Ambassador DETLEV RÜNGER.

Greece: Nobelsgt. 45, 0244 Oslo; tel. 22-44-27-28; fax 22-56-00-72; e-mail gremb.osl@mfa.gr; Ambassador ANTONIOS VLAVIANOS.

Guatemala: Drammensvn 126B, 0277 Oslo; tel. 22-55-60-04; fax 22-55-60-47; e-mail guatemala@embajada.no; Ambassador JUAN LEÓN ALVARADO.

Hungary: Sophus Liesgt. 3, 0244 Oslo; tel. 22-55-24-18; fax 22-44-76-93; e-mail mission.osl@kum.hu; internet www.mfa.gov.hu/kulkepviselet/no; Ambassador LAJOS BOZI.

Iceland: Stortingsgt. 30, 0244 Oslo; tel. 23-23-75-30; fax 22-83-07-04; e-mail emb.oslo@mfa.is; internet www.island.no; Chargé d'affaires a.i. TÓMAS ORRI RAGNARSSON.

India: Niels Juelsgt. 30, 0244 Oslo; tel. 24-11-59-10; fax 24-11-59-12; e-mail amb.oslo@mea.gov.in; internet www.indemb.no; Chargé d'affaires a.i. BALACHANDRAN PULIYAMPOTTA.

Indonesia: Fritznersgt. 12, 0244 Oslo; tel. 22-12-51-30; fax 22-12-51-31; e-mail kbrioslo@online.no; internet www.indonesia-oslo.no; Ambassador ESTI ANDAYANI.

Iran: Drammensvn 88E, 0244 Oslo; tel. 23-27-29-60; fax 22-55-49-19; e-mail iremb@iran-embassy-oslo.no; internet www.iran-embassy-oslo.no; Ambassador SAYED HUSSAIN REZVANI.

Iraq: Torgbygget rom 301, Nydalsvn 33, 0484 Oslo; tel. 21-52-02-17; fax 21-52-01-71; e-mail oslemb@iraqmfamail.com; Ambassador SUNDUS OMAR ALBAYRAQDAR.

Ireland: Haakon VIIs gt. 1, 0244 Oslo; tel. 22-01-72-00; fax 22-01-72-01; e-mail osloembassy@dfa.ie; internet www.embassyofireland.no; Ambassador GERALD F. ANSBRO.

Israel: Parkvn 35, POB 534 Skøyen, 0214 Oslo; tel. 21-01-95-00; fax 21-01-95-30; e-mail israel@oslo.mfa.gov.il; internet oslo.mfa.gov.il; Ambassador MICHAEL ELIGAL.

Italy: Inkognitogt. 7, 0244 Oslo; tel. 23-08-49-00; fax 22-44-34-36; e-mail ambasciata.oslo@esteri.it; internet www.amboslo.esteri.it; Ambassador ANTONIO BANDINI.

Japan: Wergelandsveien 15, 0244 Oslo; tel. 22-99-16-00; fax 22-44-25-05; e-mail info@japan-embassy.no; internet www.no.emb-japan.go.jp; Ambassador AKIO SHIROTA.

Kazakhstan: Nedre Vollgt. 3, 2nd Floor, 0158 Oslo; tel. 22-42-06-40; fax 22-42-06-42; e-mail mail@kazembassy.no; internet www.kazembassy.no; Chargé d'affaires a.i. NURLAN MUSSIN.

Korea, Republic: Inkognitogt. 3, 0244, Oslo; tel. 22-54-70-90; fax 22-56-14-11; e-mail kornor@mofat.go.kr; internet nor.mofat.go.kr; Ambassador LEE BYONG-HYUN.

Latvia: Bygdøy allé 76, POB 3163 Elisenberg, 0208 Oslo; tel. 22-54-22-80; fax 22-54-64-26; e-mail embassy.norway@mfa.gov.lv; Ambassador ANDRIS SEKACIS.

Lithuania: Dronningensgt. 3, 0244 Oslo; tel. 22-12-92-00; fax 22-12-92-01; e-mail amb.no@urm.lt; internet no.mfa.lt; Ambassador ANDRIUS NAMAVIČIUS.

Macedonia, former Yugoslav republic: Skjalgssonsgt. 19B, 0267 Oslo; tel. 22-55-15-44; fax 22-55-06-22; e-mail goran.cekov@mfa.gov.mk; Chargé d'affaires a.i. GORAN CEKOV.

Morocco: Holtegt. 28, 0355 Oslo; tel. 23-19-71-50; fax 23-19-71-51; e-mail oslosifam@yahoo.com; Ambassador YAHDIH BOUCHAÂB.

Netherlands: Oscarsgt. 29, 0244 Oslo; tel. 23-33-36-00; fax 23-33-36-01; e-mail osl@minbuza.nl; internet www.netherlands-embassy.no; Ambassador RICHARD VAN RIJSSEN.

Pakistan: Eckersbergsgt. 20, 0244 Oslo; tel. 23-13-60-80; fax 22-55-50-97; e-mail info@pakistanembassy.no; internet www.pakistanembassy.no; Chargé d'affaires a.i. NAEEM SABIR KHAN.

Philippines: Nedre Vollgt. 4, 0158 Oslo; tel. 22-40-09-00; fax 22-41-74-01; e-mail ambassador@philembassy.no; internet www.philembassy.no; Ambassador (vacant).

Poland: Olav Kyrres pl. 1, 0244 Oslo; tel. 24-11-08-50; fax 22-44-48-39; e-mail ambassador@oslo.polemb.net; internet www.oslo.polemb.net; Ambassador WOJCIECH LUDWIK KOLAŃCZYK.

Portugal: Josefinesgt. 37, 0244 Oslo; tel. 23-33-28-53; fax 22-56-43-55; e-mail portuguese.embassy@scosl.dgaccp.pt; Ambassador JOÃO DE LIMA PIMENTEL.

Romania: Oscarsgt. 51, 0244 Oslo; tel. 22-44-15-12; fax 22-43-16-74; e-mail oslo@mae.ro; internet oslo.mae.ro; Ambassador Dr CRISTIAN ISTRATE.

Russia: Drammensvn 74, 0244 Oslo; tel. 22-55-32-78; fax 22-55-00-70; e-mail rembassy@online.no; internet www.norway.mid.ru; Ambassador VYACHESLAV PAVLOVSKY.

Serbia: Drammensvn 105, 0244 Oslo; tel. 23-08-68-58; fax 22-55-29-92; e-mail ambasada@serbianembassy.no; internet www.serbianembassy.no; Ambassador MILAN SIMURDIĆ.

Slovakia: Thomas Heftyesgt. 24, 0244 Oslo; tel. 22-04-94-70; fax 22-04-94-74; e-mail emb.oslo@mzv.sk; internet www.oslo.mfa.sk; Ambassador DUŠAN ROZBORA.

South Africa: Drammensvn 88C, POB 2822 Solli, 0204 Oslo; tel. 23-27-32-20; fax 22-44-39-75; e-mail oslo.reception@foreign.gov.za; internet www.saemboslo.no; Ambassador BERYL ROSE SISULU.

Spain: Oscarsgt. 35, 0244 Oslo; tel. 22-92-66-90; fax 22-55-98-22; e-mail embespno@mail.mae.es; internet www.maec.es/embajadas/oslo; Ambassador SANTIAGO SALAS COLLANTES.

Sri Lanka: Sjølyst pl. 4, 0158 Oslo; tel. 23-13-69-50; fax 23-31-70-90; e-mail embassy@srilanka.no; internet www.srilanka.no; Ambassador E. RODNEY M. PERERA.

Sudan: Holtegt. 28, 0355 Oslo; tel. 22-60-33-55; fax 22-69-83-44; e-mail sudanembassy@sudanoslo.com; Chargé d'affaires a.i. SWAR EL-DAHAB.

Sweden: Nobelsgt. 16, 0244 Oslo; tel. 24-11-42-00; fax 22-55-15-96; e-mail ambassaden.oslo@foreign.ministry.se; internet www.swedenabroad.com/oslo; Ambassador INGRID HJELT AF TROLLE.

Switzerland: Bygdøy allé 78, 0244 Oslo; tel. 22-43-05-90; fax 22-44-63-50; e-mail osl.vertretung@eda.admin.ch; internet www.eda.admin.ch/oslo; Ambassador DENIS FELDMEYER.

Thailand: Eilert Sundtsgt. 4, 0244 Oslo; tel. 22-12-86-75; fax 22-04-99-69; e-mail thaioslo@online.no; internet www.thaiembassy.no; Ambassador JULLAPONG NONSRICHAI.

Tunisia: Fridtjof Nansenspl. 9, 0160 Oslo; tel. 22-41-72-01; fax 22-41-72-04; e-mail at.oslo@online.no; Chargé d'affaires a.i. SIHEM SELTENE.

Turkey: Halvdan Svartesgt. 5, 0244 Oslo; tel. 22-12-87-50; fax 22-55-62-63; e-mail postmaster@oslo-turkish-embassy.com; Ambassador HAYATI GÜVEN.

Ukraine: Arbinsgt. 4, 0253 Oslo; tel. 22-83-55-60; fax 22-83-55-57; e-mail embassy@ukremb.no; internet www.mfa.gov.ua/norway; Ambassador OLEKSANDR H. TSVYETKOV.

United Kingdom: Thomas Heftyesgt. 8, 0264 Oslo; tel. 23-13-27-00; fax 23-13-27-41; e-mail britemb@online.no; internet www.britain.no; Ambassador JANE OWEN.

USA: Henrik Ibsensgt. 48, 0244 Oslo; tel. 21-30-85-40; e-mail osloirc@state.gov; internet norway.usembassy.gov; Ambassador BARRY B. WHITE.

Venezuela: Drammensvn 82, POB 2820 Solli, 0204 Oslo; tel. 22-43-06-60; fax 22-43-14-70; e-mail consulado@venezuela.no; Ambassador JOSÉ DE JESÚS SOJO REYES.

Viet Nam: St Olavsgt. 21B, 0165 Oslo; tel. 99-34-38-77; e-mail vietnamnorway@gmail.com; Ambassador TA VAN THONG.

Judicial System

The judicial system in Norway is organized on three levels. The courts of first instance are the District (Herredsrett) and City (Byrett) Courts. The country is divided into 93 judicial areas, most of which are served by one professional judge and one or two deputies (in the major cities the number of judges ranges from three to 52). The Court of Appeal (Lagmannsrett) consists of six jurisdictions, each with between 10 and 52 judges, and two divisions (Appeals and Criminal Divisions). The Supreme Court (Høyesterett) sits in Oslo and decides cases in the last instance. The Court, which is served by 19 judges appointed by the Crown and presided over by a Chief Justice, is competent to try all factual and legal aspects of cases in civil and criminal cause. In criminal cases, however, the competence of the Court is limited to questions concerning the application of the law, the nature of the penalty, and procedural errors of the lower courts. Appeals to the Supreme Court may not be based on errors in the assessment of evidence in connection with the question of guilt.

SUPREME COURT

Høyesterett

Høyesteretts pl., POB 8016 Dep., 0030 Oslo; tel. 22-03-59-00; fax 22-33-23-55; e-mail post@hoyesterett.no; internet www.domstol.no/hoyesterett.

f. 1815; pronounces judgment in the final instance; hears both civil and criminal cases, and has jurisdiction in all areas of law; composed

NORWAY

of 18 ordinary justices of the Supreme Court and one Chief Justice; individual cases are heard by five justices—in some instances cases are heard by all of the justices sitting in plenary session; works in two parallel and equal divisions; Supreme Court justices also sit on the Appeals Selection Committee of the Supreme Court, which is classed as a separate court; cases brought before the Appeals Selection Committee are heard by three justices; any matter brought before the Supreme Court must initially be considered by the Appeals Selection Committee; justices sit in both divisions of the Supreme Court and on the Appeals Selection Committee in accordance with a rota system.

Chief Justice of the Supreme Court: TORE SCHEI.

Justices of the Supreme Court: LIV GJØLSTAD, WILHELM MATHESON, KARENANNE GUSSGARD, AAGE THOR FALKANGER, KIRSTI COWARD, HANS FLOCK, MAGNUS MATNINGSDAL, KARIN MARIA BRUZELIUS, JENS EDVIN A. SKOGHØY, KARL ARNE UTGÅRD, INGER-ELSE STABEL, OLE BJØRN STØLE, TORIL MARIE ØIE, BÅRD TØNDER, CLEMENT ENDRESEN, HILDE INDREBERG, ARFINN BÅRDSEN, ERIK MØSE, BERGLJOT WEBSTER.

COURTS OF APPEAL

Agder Lagmannsrett (Court of Appeal in Skien): Gjerpensgt. 16, POB 2644, 3702 Skien; tel. 35-54-05-00; fax 35-52-10-09; e-mail agder.lagmannsrett@domstol.no; internet www.domstol.no/agder; Presiding Judge DAG BUGGE NORDÉN.

Borgarting Lagmannsrett (Court of Appeal in Oslo): Keysersgt. 13, POB 8017 Dep., 0030 Oslo; tel. 21-55-80-00; fax 21-55-80-38; e-mail borgadm@domstol.no; internet www.domstol.no/borgarting; Presiding Judge NILS ERIK LIE.

Eidsivating Lagmannsrett (Court of Appeal in Hamar): Hamar tinghus, Østregt. 41, POB 4450, 2326 Hamar; tel. 62-55-06-00; fax 62-55-06-20; e-mail elag@domstol.no; internet www.domstol.no/elag; Presiding Judge ODD JARL PEDERSEN.

Frostating Lagmannsrett (Court of Appeal in Trondheim): Trondheim tinghus, Munkegt. 20, POB 2315, 7004 Trondheim; tel. 73-54-24-60; fax 73-54-24-84; e-mail frostating.lagmannsrett@domstol.no; internet www.frostating.no; Presiding Judge AAGE RUNDBERGET.

Gulating Lagmannsrett (Court of Appeal in Bergen): Bergen tinghus, Tårnpl. 2, POB 7414, 5020 Bergen; tel. 55-69-95-00; fax 55-23-07-24; e-mail gulating@domstol.no; internet www.domstol.no/gulating; Presiding Judge BJØRN SOLBAKKEN.

Hålogaland Lagmannsrett (Court of Appeal in Tromsø): Fridtjof Nansens pl. 17, POB 2511, 9271 Tromsø; tel. 77-66-00-35; fax 77-66-00-60; e-mail halogaland.lagmannsrett@domstol.no; internet www.domstol.no/halogaland; Presiding Judge ARILD O. EIDESEN.

CIVIL COURTS

In each municipality there is a Conciliation Board (Forliksråd) consisting of three lay members elected by the municipal council for four years. With a few exceptions, no case may be taken to a court of justice without a prior attempt at mediation by a Conciliation Board. In addition to mediation, the Conciliation Board has a judicial capacity and is intended to settle minor cases in a simple manner without great expense to the parties involved.

The ordinary lower courts are the District and City Courts, which decide all cases not adjudicated upon by the Conciliation Board, and they also act as courts of appeal from judgments given in the Conciliation Board. During the main hearing, the court is generally convened with only one professional judge, but each of the parties may request that the court be convened with two lay judges, in addition to the professional judge. When the court finds it advisable, it may also summon lay judges on its own initiative.

Judgments delivered in the District and City Courts may be taken, on appeal, to the Court of Appeal or to the Supreme Court. In the Court of Appeal cases are judged by three professional judges, but, if requested by one of the parties, lay judges may be summoned.

CRIMINAL COURTS

The criminal courts are: the Court of Examination and Summary Jurisdiction (Forhørsretten), the District and City Courts, the Court of Appeal and the Supreme Court. In the Court of Examination and Summary Jurisdiction the professional judge presides alone, but in the District and City Courts two lay judges also sit. Following the implementation of a major reform in 1995, all criminal cases now begin in a District or City Court. The gravest offences were previously tried directly before a jury in the Court of Appeal and the possibilities for appeal were thus limited. Now, however, the issue of guilt can be appealed to the Court of Appeal in all cases. (Such cases are tried either by three professional judges, and four lay judges with equal votes, or by three professional judges and a jury of 10 members. For a guilty verdict to be upheld in the latter case, at least seven members of the jury must support the original decision of the lower court. In other cases appeal is directly to the Supreme Court.) The maximum penalty permissible under Norwegian law is 21 years of imprisonment.

OMBUDSMAN

The office of Parliamentary Ombudsman was established in 1962. An Ombudsman is elected by the Storting after every general election for a four-year term (with the possibility of re-election). The Ombudsman is accessible to all citizens, and attempts to ensure against the public administration committing any injustice to the individual citizen. The Ombudsman does not cover private legal affairs, and does not have the right to reverse an official decision, but his pronouncements are normally complied with.

Sivilombudsmannen—Stortingets ombudsmann for forvaltningen (Parliamentary Ombudsman for Public Administration): Akersgt. 8, 6th Floor, POB 3 Sentrum, 0101 Oslo; tel. 22-82-85-00; fax 22-82-85-11; e-mail postmottak@sivilombudsmannen.no; internet www.sivilombudsmannen.no; Ombudsman ARNE FLIFLET.

Religion

CHRISTIANITY

Citizens are considered to be members of the National Church unless they explicitly associate themselves with another denomination; around 80.7% of the population nominally belonged to the Church at January 2009, although actual church attendance is low. Other Protestant Christian denominations accounted for some 4.5% of the population. There are a very small number of Orthodox Christians in Norway.

The National Church

Church of Norway

The Church Synod, Rådhusgt. 1-3, POB 799 Sentrum, 0106 Oslo; tel. 23-08-12-00; fax 23-08-12-01; e-mail berit.hagen.agoy@kirken.no; internet www.kirken.no.

The Evangelical Lutheran Church is the established religion; there are 11 dioceses, 103 archdeaconries, 620 clerical districts and 1,285 parishes. The highest representative body of the Church is the Synod, summoned for the first time in 1984. In 2010 3,992,295 persons belonged to the Church of Norway.

Bishop of Oslo: OLE CHRISTIAN MÆLEN KVARME.

Bishop of Borg: HELGA HAUGLAND BYFUGLIEN.

Bishop of Hamar: SOLVEIG FISKE.

Bishop of Tunsberg: LAILA RIKSAASEN DAHL.

Bishop of Agder and Telemark: OLAV SKJEVESLAND.

Bishop of Stavanger: ERLING J. PETTERSEN.

Bishop of Bjørgvin: HALVOR NORDHAUG.

Bishop of Møre: INGEBORG SYNØVE MIDTTØMME.

Bishop of Nidaros: TOR SINGSAAS.

Bishop of Sør-Hålogaland: TOR BERGER JØRGENSEN.

Bishop of Nord-Hålogaland: PER OSKAR KJØLAAS.

The Roman Catholic Church

For ecclesiastical purposes, Norway comprises the diocese of Oslo and the territorial prelatures of Tromsø and Trondheim. The diocese and the prelatures are directly responsible to the Holy See. At 31 December 2006 there were an estimated 62,934 adherents in Norway, equivalent to about 1.3% of the population. The Bishop of Oslo participates in the Scandinavian Episcopal Conference (based in Västra Frölunda, Sweden).

Bishop of Oslo: Rt Rev. BERNT IVAR (MARKUS) EIDSVIG, Oslo Katolske Bispedømme, Akersvn 5, POB 8270, 0177 Oslo; tel. 23-21-95-00; fax 23-21-95-01; e-mail okb@katolsk.no; internet www.katolsk.no.

Other Churches

Church of England (Anglican Chaplaincy in Norway): St Edmund's Anglican Church, Møllergt. 30, Oslo; tel. 22-69-22-14; e-mail j-heil@online.no; internet www.osloanglicans.net; 1,800 mems (2010); also in Stavanger, Bergen and Trondheim; part of the Diocese of Gibraltar in Europe; Chaplain Rev. Canon JANET HEIL.

Evangelical Lutheran Free Church of Norway: Kongsvn. 82, POB 23, Bekkelagshøgda, 1109 Oslo; tel. 22-74-86-00; fax 22-74-86-01; e-mail post@frikirken.no; internet www.frikirken.no; f. 1877; c. 21,848 mems (2010); Chair. of Synod ARNFINN LØYNING.

Norwegian Baptist Union: Micheletsvei 62C, 1368 Stabekk; tel. 67-10-35-60; fax 67-10-35-69; e-mail post@baptist.no; internet www.baptist.no; f. 1860; 10,200 mems (2011); Gen. Sec. TERJE AADNE.

Pinse Bevegelsen i Norge (Pentecostal Movement): POB 2, 0617 Oslo; tel. 40-41-30-43; fax 94-87-45-72; e-mail post@pinsebevegelsen.no; internet www.pinsebevegelsen.no; 39,590 mems (2009).

NORWAY

United Methodist Church: POB 2744 St Hanshaugen, 0131 Oslo; tel. 23-33-27-00; fax 23-33-27-01; e-mail post@metodistkirken.no; internet www.metodistkirken.no; f. 1856; 12,000 mems (2009); Council Dir GUNNAR BRADLEY.

In 2009 there were 14,976 Jehovah's Witnesses in Norway and 5,086 Seventh-day Adventists.

OTHER RELIGIONS

In 2009 there were 92,744 Muslims, 12,252 Buddhists, 5,238 Hindus, 2,713 Sikhs and 803 Jews in Norway.

The Press

The principle of press freedom is safeguarded in the Norwegian Constitution. There is no law specifically dealing with the press. Editors bear wide responsibility in law for the content of their papers, especially regarding such matters as libel. Although a journalist is legally entitled to conceal his source he may be required to disclose this information under penalty of imprisonment, but such instances are rare. A three-member Council of Conduct gives judgments in cases of complaint against a paper or of disputes between papers. It has no powers of enforcement but its judgments are highly respected. The Press Association has a code of ethics aimed at maintaining the standards and reputation of the profession.

The eastern region dominates press activity. Oslo dailies are especially influential throughout this area, and four of these—*Aftenposten*, *Dagsavisen*, *Dagbladet* and *Verdens Gang*—have a national readership. Nevertheless, in Norway's other major cities the large local dailies easily lead in their own districts. In 2007 the most popular newspapers were *Verdens Gang* (Oslo), *Aftenposten* (Oslo), *Dagbladet* (Oslo), *Bergens Tidende* (Bergen) and *Adresseavisen* (Trondheim), with a combined average circulation of almost 900,000.

PRINCIPAL NEWSPAPERS

(circulation figures refer to the year 2007, unless otherwise indicated)

Ålesund

Sunnmørsposten: POB 123, 6001 Ålesund; tel. 70-12-00-00; fax 70-12-46-42; e-mail redaksjon@smp.no; internet www.smp.no; f. 1882; Liberal; Editor HARALD KJØLÅS; circ. 33,712.

Arendal

Agderposten: POB 8, 4801 Arendal; tel. 37-00-37-00; fax 37-00-38-38; e-mail agderposten@agderposten.no; internet www.agderposten.no; f. 1874; independent; Editor STEIN GAUSLAA; circ. 23,746.

Bergen

Bergens Tidende: Krinkelkroken 1, POB 7240, 5020 Bergen; tel. 55-21-45-02; fax 55-21-48-48; e-mail webmaster@bt.no; internet www.bergens-tidende.no; f. 1868; Editor HANS ERIK MATRE; circ. 87,668.

Bergensavisen: Chr. Michelsensgt. 4, POB 824 Sentrum, 5807 Bergen; tel. 55-23-50-00; fax 55-31-00-30; e-mail nyhet@ba.no; internet www.ba.no; f. 1927; independent, social democratic; Editor-in-Chief OLAV BERGO; circ. 29,311.

Dagen: POB 76/77, 5002 Bergen; tel. 55-31-17-55; fax 55-31-71-06; f. 1919; religious daily; Editor FINN JARLE SÆLE; circ. 9.033.

Billingstad

Budstikka: POB 133, 1376 Billingstad; tel. 66-77-00-00; fax 66-77-00-60; e-mail redaksjonen@budstikka.no; internet www.budstikka.no; f. 1898; 6 a week; fmrly *Asker og Baerums Budstikke*; Conservative; Editor ANDREAS GJØLME; circ. 28,264.

Bodø

Avisa Nordland: Storgt. 38, 8002 Bodø; tel. 75-50-50-00; fax 75-50-50-60; e-mail kundeservice@an.no; internet www.an.no; f. 1910; Labour; Editor JAN-ELRIK HANSSEN; circ. 23,959.

Drammen

Drammens Tidende: POB 7033, 3007 Drammen; tel. 32-20-40-00; fax 32-20-40-61; e-mail redaksjonen@dt.no; internet www.dt.no; f. 1832 and 1883; Conservative daily; Dir FINN GRUNDT; Editor HANS ARNE ODDE; circ. 40,954.

Fredrikstad

Fredrikstad Blad: POB 143, 1606 Fredrikstad; tel. 46-80-77-77; e-mail tips@f-b.no; internet www.f-b.no; f. 1889; Conservative; Editor ERLING OMVIK; circ. 23,442.

Gjøvik

Oppland Arbeiderblad: POB 24, 2801 Gjøvik; tel. 61-18-93-00; fax 61-17-98-56; e-mail redaksjonen@oa.no; internet www.oa.no; f. 1924; daily; Labour; Editor-in-Chief JENS OLAI JENSSEN; circ. 27,173.

Hamar

Hamar Arbeiderblad: Torggt. 51, POB 333, 2301 Hamar; tel. 62-51-96-99; fax 62-51-96-18; e-mail post@ha-nett.no; internet www.ha-nett.no; f. 1925; daily; Labour; Editor ROLV AMDAL; circ. 27,363.

Harstad

Harstad Tidende: Storgt. 11, POB 85, 9481 Harstad; tel. 77-01-80-00; fax 77-01-80-05; e-mail redaksjonen@ht.no; internet www.ht.no; f. 1887; Conservative; Editor BÅRD MICHALSEN; circ. 13,503.

Haugesund

Haugesunds Avis: POB 2024, 5504 Haugesund; tel. 52-72-00-00; fax 52-72-04-44; e-mail redaksjonen@haugesunds-avis.no; internet www.h-avis.no; f. 1895; independent; Editor-in-Chief TONNY NUNDAL; circ. 33,013.

Hønefoss

Ringerikes Blad: POB 68, 3502 Hønefoss; tel. 32-17-95-00; fax 32-17-95-01; e-mail redaksjonen@ringblad.no; internet www.ringblad.no; f. 1845; independent; Editor TORE ROLAND; circ. 12,694.

Kongsvinger

Glåmdalen: POB 757, 2204 Kongsvinger; tel. 62-88-25-00; fax 62-88-25-01; e-mail redaksjon@glomdalen.no; internet www.glomdalen.no; f. 1926; daily; Labour; Editor ROLF NORDBERG; circ. 19,848.

Kristiansand

Fædrelandsvennen: POB 369, 4664 Kristiansand; tel. 38-11-30-00; fax 38-11-30-01; e-mail 03811@fvn.no; internet www.fvn.no; f. 1875; daily; Liberal independent; Editor EIVIND LJØSTAD; circ. 37,934.

Lillehammer

Gudbrandsdølen Dagningen: POB 954, 2604 Lillehammer; tel. 61-22-10-00; fax 61-26-09-60; e-mail redaksjonen@gd.no; internet www.gd.no; f. 1841 and 1894; independent; Editor-in-Chief KRISTIAN SKULLERUD; circ. 26,723.

Lillestrøm

Romerikes Blad: POB 235, 2001 Lillestrøm; tel. 63-80-50-50; fax 63-80-50-60; e-mail redaksjonen@rb.no; internet www.rb.no; f. 1913; Labour; Editor-in-Chief THOR WOJE; circ. 43,238.

Molde

Romsdals Budstikke: POB 2100, 6402 Molde; tel. 71-25-00-00; fax 71-25-00-11; e-mail redaksjon@r-b.no; internet www.rbnett.no; f. 1843; Conservative independent; Editor NILS-KRISTIAN MYHRE; circ. 18,205.

Moss

Moss Avis: POB 248/250, 1530 Moss; tel. 69-20-50-00; fax 69-20-50-02; e-mail jan.tollefsen@moss-avis.no; internet www.moss-avis.no; f. 1876; Liberal/Conservative independent; Editor JAN TOLLEFSEN; circ. 15,304.

Oslo

Aftenposten: POB 1 Sentrum, 0051 Oslo; tel. 22-86-30-00; fax 22-42-63-25; e-mail aftenposten@aftenposten.no; internet www.aftenposten.no; f. 1860; Conservative independent; Editor-in-Chief HANS ERIK MATRE; circ. morning 250,179, evening 131,089.

Akers Avis/Groruddalen Budstikke: POB 100 Grorud, 0905 Oslo; tel. 22-91-88-20; e-mail redaksjonen@groruddalen.no; internet www.groruddalen.no; fax 22-16-01-05; f. 1928; 2 a week; non-political; Editor HJALMAR KIELLAND; circ. 15,171.

Dagbladet: POB 1184 Sentrum, 0107 Oslo; tel. 22-31-06-00; fax 22-31-05-10; e-mail annb@dagbladet.no; internet www.dagbladet.no; f. 1869; daily; Editor-in-Chief ANNE AASHEIM; circ. 135,611.

Dagens Næringsliv: POB 1182 Sentrum, 0107 Oslo; tel. 22-00-11-90; fax 22-00-10-70; e-mail redaksjonen@dn.no; internet www.dn.no; Editor SVEIN-THORE GRAN; circ. 81,391.

Dagsavisen: POB 1183 Sentrum, 0107 Oslo; tel. 22-72-60-00; fax 22-64-92-82; e-mail abonnement@dagsavisen.no; internet www.dagsavisen.no; f. 1884; Labour; Editor-in-Chief ARVID JACOBSEN; circ. 31,403.

NORWAY

Nationen: POB 9390 Grønland, 0135 Oslo; tel. 21-31-00-00; fax 21-31-00-90; e-mail hans.eldegard@nationen.no; internet www.nationen.no; f. 1918; daily; Centre; Editor-in-Chief TOVE LIE; circ. 15,871.

Vårt Land: POB 1180 Sentrum, 0107 Oslo; tel. 22-31-03-10; fax 22-31-03-05; e-mail sentral@vl.no; internet www.vl.no; f. 1945; independent, religious daily; Editor HELGE SIMONNES; circ. 27,146.

Verdens Gang (VG): Akersgt. 55, POB 1185 Sentrum, 0107 Oslo; tel. 22-00-00-00; fax 22-42-68-70; e-mail redaksjonen@vg.no; internet www.vg.no; f. 1945; independent; Editor-in-Chief TORRY PEDERSEN; circ. 309,610.

Sandefjord

Sandefjords Blad: POB 143, 3201 Sandefjord; tel. 33-42-00-00; fax 33-46-29-91; e-mail redaksjonen@sb.no; internet www.sb.no; f. 1861; Conservative; Editor LEIF MAGNE FLEMMEN; circ. 14,260.

Sarpsborg

Sarpsborg Arbeiderblad: POB 83, 1701 Sarpsborg; tel. 69-11-11-11; fax 69-11-11-00; e-mail redaksjonen@sa.no; internet www.sa.no; f. 1929; independent; Editor EIRIK MOE; circ. 15,016.

Skien

Telemarksavisa AS: POB 2833, Kjørbekk, 3702 Skien; tel. 35-58-55-00; fax 35-52-82-09; e-mail redaksjonen@ta.no; internet www.ta.no; f. 1921; independent; Editor OVE MELLINGEN; circ. 22,346.

Varden: POB 2873 Kjørbekk, 3702 Skien; tel. 35-54-30-00; fax 35-52-83-23; e-mail info@varden.no; internet www.varden.no; f. 1874; Conservative; Editor MAJ-LIS STORDAL; circ. 27,341.

Stavanger

Stavanger Aftenblad: POB 229, 4001 Stavanger; tel. 05150; fax 51-89-30-05; e-mail redaksjonen@aftenbladet.no; internet www.aftenbladet.no; independent; f. 1893; Editor-in-Chief TOM HETLAND; circ. 68,010.

Steinkjer

Trønder-Avisa: Hamnegt., 7738 Steinkjer; tel. 74-12-12-00; fax 74-12-13-13; e-mail redaksjonen@t-a.no; internet www.t-a.no; Centre/Liberal; Editor ARVE LØBERG; circ. 23,268.

Tønsberg

Tønsbergs Blad: POB 2003, Postterminalen, 3103 Tønsberg; tel. 33-37-00-00; fax 33-37-30-10; e-mail redaksjonen@tb.no; internet www.tb.no; f. 1870; Conservative; Editor-in-Chief HÅKON BORUD; circ. 30,354.

Tromsø

Nordlys: Rådhusgt. 3, POB 2515, 9272 Tromsø; tel. 77-62-35-00; fax 77-62-35-01; e-mail firmapost@nordlys.no; internet www.nordlys.no; f. 1902; Labour; Editor HANS KRISTIAN AMUNDSEN; circ. 27,647.

Trondheim

Adresseavisen: 7003 Trondheim; tel. 07200; fax 72-50-15-16; e-mail redaksjon@adresseavisen.no; internet www.adressa.no; f. 1767; Editor ROLF DYRNES SVENDSEN; circ. 79,789.

POPULAR PERIODICALS

Allers: Stenersgt. 2, POB 1169, 0107 Oslo; tel. 21-30-10-00; fax 21-30-12-04; e-mail elisabeth@allers.no; internet www.allers.no; family weekly; Editor-in-Chief ELISABETH LUND-ANDERSEN; circ. 123,578.

Bedre Helse: Gullhaugvn 1, 0441 Oslo; tel. 22-58-50-00; fax 22-58-58-79; e-mail bedre-helse@hm-media.no; internet www.bedrehelse.com; health; Editor INGVILD HAGEN; circ. 35,000 (2007).

Bonytt: Gullhaugvn 1, 0441 Oslo; tel. 22-58-50-00; fax 22-58-05-85; e-mail bonytt@hm-media.no; internet www.klikk.no/bonytt; home and furnishing; 14 a year; Editor JAN THORESEN; circ. 68,000 (2003).

Byavisa: Munkegt. 66E, 7011 Trondheim; tel. 73-95-49-00; fax 73-99-05-60; e-mail redaksjon@byavisa.no; internet www.byavisa.no; f. 1996; weekly; Editor-in-Chief PAUL JOSTEIN AUNE; circ. 82,000.

Familien: Gullhaugvn 1, 0441 Oslo; tel. 22-58-57-00; fax 22-58-07-64; e-mail abo-familien@hm-media.no; internet www.familien.no; family fortnightly; Editor-in-Chief IVAR MOE; circ. 111,448 (2009).

Foreldre & Barn: 0441 Oslo; tel. 22-58-50-00; fax 22-58-05-80; e-mail foreldreogbarn@hm-media.no; internet www.foreldreogbarn.no; 11 a year; for parents of young children; Editor TJODUNN ELTVIK DYRNES; circ. 59,210.

Foreldremagasinet: Gullhaugvn 1, 0483 Oslo; tel. 22-58-55-39; e-mail vibeke.ostelie@hm-media.no; monthly; for parents; circ. 20,470.

Henne: Stenersgt 2–8, POB 1169 Sentrum, 0107 Oslo; tel. 21-30-10-00; e-mail redaksjonen@henne.no; internet www.henne.no; women's interest; Editor-in-Chief ELLEN ARNSTAD; circ. 45,586.

Hjemmepc: Gullhaugvn 1, 0441 Oslo; tel. 22-58-50-00; e-mail hjemmepc@hm-media.no; internet www.hjemmepc.no; home computers; Editor-in-Chief HALLVARD LUNDE; circ. 28,963 (2003).

Hjemmet: Gullhaugvn 1, 0441 Oslo; tel. 22-58-50-00; fax 22-58-05-70; e-mail hjemmet@hm-media.no; internet www.hm-media.no; family weekly; Editor-in-Chief LISE HANSEN; circ. 228,313 (2004).

Hytteliv: Gullhaugvn 1, 0441 Oslo; tel. 22-58-50-00; fax 22-58-58-59; e-mail hytteliv@hm-media.no; internet www.klikk.no/produkthjemmesider/hytteliv; f. 1972; 9 a year; for second-home owners; Editor TURID RØSTE; circ. 55,000.

I form: Trim.no AS, 6789 Loen; tel. 22-37-30-50; fax 91-38-59-26; e-mail redaksjonen@trim.no; internet www.iform.no; monthly; health and fitness; Editor-in-Chief GEIR TVERDAL; circ. 46,551.

Jærbladet: POB 23, 4349 Bryne; tel. 51-77-99-00; fax 51-48-37-40; internet redaksjon@jbl.no; internet www.jbl.no; 3 days a week; independent; Editor IVAR RUSDAL; circ. 12,477.

KK (Kvinner og Klær): Stenersgt. 2–8, POB 1169 Sentrum, 0107 Oslo; tel. 21-30-10-00; fax 22-63-61-02; e-mail leserservice@kk.no; internet www.kk.no; women's weekly; Editor-in-Chief PETTER DANBOLT; circ. 88,158.

Mann: Gullhaugvn 1, 0441 Oslo; tel. 22-58-50-00; fax 22-58-05-69; e-mail post@mann.no; internet www.mann.no; men's magazine; Editor-in-Chief KNUT CHRISTIAN MOENG; circ. 20,000.

Mat & Drikke: POB 40, 0411 Oslo; tel. 90-04-64-40; e-mail olav@matogdrikke.no; internet www.matogdrikke.no; 7 a year; food and wine; Editor-in-Chief LINDAN SANNUM; circ. 23,032.

Norsk Ukeblad: Gullhaugvn 1, 0441 Oslo; tel. 22-58-58-00; fax 22-58-05-69; e-mail nu-tips@hm-media.no; internet www.norskukeblad.no; family weekly; Editor-in-Chief KJERSTI MOEN; circ. 102,347 (2009).

Det Nye: Gullhaugvn 1, 0441 Oslo; tel. 22-58-50-00; fax 22-58-58-09; e-mail detnye@hm-media.no; internet www.detnye.com; for young women; 14 a year; Editor-in-Chief KJERSTI MO (acting); circ. 72,000.

Programbladet: POB 1151 Sentrum, 0107 Oslo; tel. 22-31-03-10; fax 22-31-04-55; e-mail elins@programbladet.no; internet www.programbladet.no; f. 1946; radio and television weekly; Editor TRUDE HUSJORD; circ. 65,000.

Se og Hør: POB 1169 Sentrum, 0107 Oslo; tel. 22-41-51-80; fax 22-41-51-70; f. 1978; news weekly (radio and TV); Editors-in-Chief KNUT HÅVIK, ODD J. NELVIK; circ. 174,552 (2009).

TOPP: POB 169 Sentrum, 0107 Oslo; tel. 21-30-12-28; e-mail vilvite@topp.no; internet www.topp.no; monthly; for young people aged between 10 and 17 years; Editor PETTER DANBOLT; circ. 48,011.

Vi Menn: Gullhaugvn 1, 0441 Oslo; tel. 22-58-50-00; fax 22-58-05-71; e-mail vimenn@hm-media.no; internet www.vimenn.no; f. 1951; men's weekly; publ. by Hjemmet Mortensen; Editor-in-Chief ALEXANDER OEYSTAA; circ. 81,500.

SPECIALIST PERIODICALS

Alt om Fiske: Gullhaugvn 1, 0441 Oslo; tel. 22-58-50-00; fax 22-58-59-59; e-mail fiske@hm-media.no; internet www.klikk.no/altomfiske; angling; circ. 22,906 (2005); Chief Editor JON LENÆS.

Barnemagasinet BAM: Gullhaugvn 1, 0484 Oslo; tel. 23-00-81-80; fax 23-00-81-89; e-mail postmaster@bam.no; internet www.bam.no; for expectant and new parents; 3 additional titles, *BAM Gravid*, *BAM Nyfødt* and *BAM Spedbarn*; circ. 80,000 (2000).

Batmagasinet: Stenersgt. 2A, POB 1169 Sentrum, 0107 Oslo; tel. 21-30-10-00; fax 21-30-12-59; e-mail hans.due@aller.no; internet www.batmagasinet.no; f. 1985; owned by Aller Media AS; 12 a year; boating, powerboats; Editor-in-Chief HANS DUE; circ. 22,500.

Bilforlaget AS: Hovfaret 17B, POB 63 Vaterland, 0134 Oslo; tel. 23-03-66-00; fax 23-03-66-40; e-mail info@bilforlaget.no; internet www.bilnorge.no; f. 1975; 10 a year; motoring; Editor TRYGVE BÆRA; circ. 51,388.

Bondebladet: POB 9303 Grønland, 0135 Oslo; tel. 21-31-44-00; fax 21-31-44-01; e-mail redaksjon@bondebladet.no; internet www.bondebladet.no; f. 1974; weekly; farming; Editor LARS OLAV HAUG; circ. 85,593.

Fjell og Vidde: Den Norske Turistforening, Youngstorget 1, 0181 Oslo; tel. 40-00-18-68; fax 22-42-64-27; e-mail redaksjonen@turistforeningen.no; internet www.turistforeningen.no; f. 1967; 6 a year; organ of The Norwegian Mountain Touring Asscn; Editor HELLE ANDRESEN; circ. 131,000.

Hagen for alle: POB 433, Sentrum, 0103 Oslo; tel. 22-40-12-00; e-mail post@hagenforalle.no; internet www.hagenforalle.no; monthly; gardening; Editor ARILD SANDGREN; circ. 30,000.

NORWAY

Directory

Hundesport: POB 163 Bryn, 0611 Oslo; tel. 21-60-09-00; fax 21-60-09-01; e-mail hundesport@nkk.no; internet www.nkk.no; monthly; for dog-owners; circ. 60,000.

IngeniørNytt AS: POB 164, 1332 Østerås; Nils Lassons vei 5, 1359 Eiksmarka; tel. 67-16-34-99; fax 67-16-34-55; e-mail post@ingeniornytt.no; internet www.ingeniornytt.no; every 2 weeks; engineering, architecture; Editor EIRIK IVELAND (acting); circ. 65,000.

Jakt & Fiske: POB 94, 1378 Nesbru; tel. 66-79-22-00; fax 66-90-15-87; e-mail jaktogfiske@njff.no; internet www.jaktogfiske.info; monthly; hunting and angling; Editor VIGGO KRISTIANSEN; circ. 76,710.

Kampanje: Prinsengracht 22, 0157 Oslo; tel. 22-33-50-00; fax 22-15-40-86; e-mail kampanje@kampanje.com; internet www.kampanje.com; marketing and media; Editor-in-Chief KNUT KRISTIAN HAUGER; circ. 11,340 (2000).

Kapital: POB 724 Skøyen, 0214 Oslo; tel. 23-29-63-00; fax 23-29-63-01; e-mail wenchew@kapital.no; internet www.hegnar.no; fortnightly; business, management; Editor-in-Chief FINN ØYSTEIN BERGH; circ. 40,000.

Kommuniké: POB 9202, 0134 Oslo; tel. 21-03-36-00; fax 21-03-36-50; e-mail post@delta.no; internet www.kommunike.no; f. 1936; 9 a year; organ of Norwegian Confederation of Municipal Employees; Editor AUDUN HOPLAND; circ. 54,000.

Motor: POB 494 Sentrum, 0105 Oslo; tel. 22-58-50-00; fax 22-58-59-59; e-mail svein.ola@motor.no; internet www.naf.no; 8 a year; motoring, travel and leisure; publ. by Norwegian Automobile Federation (NAF); Editor SVEIN OLA HOPE; circ. 400,000.

Norsk Hagetidend: POB 53 Manglerud, 0612 Oslo; tel. 23-03-16-00; fax 23-03-16-01; e-mail postkasse@hageselskapet.no; internet www.hageselskapet.no; f. 1885; monthly; gardening; Editor BERGLJOT GUNDERSEN; circ. 41,878.

Norsk Landbruk: POB 9309 Grønland, 0135 Oslo; tel. 21-31-44-09; fax 21-31-44-92; e-mail norsk.landbruk@tunmedia.no; internet www.norsklandbruk.no; f. 1882; 22 a year; agriculture, horticulture and forestry; Editor-in-Chief MARIANNE RØHME; circ. 16,172.

Okonomisk Rapport: POB 1180 Skøyen, 0213 Oslo; tel. 22-31-02-10; fax 22-40-41-01; e-mail rapport@orapp.no; internet www.orapp.no; business; Editor TERJE AURDAL; circ. 24,946 (2000).

PCPro: Gullhaugvn 1, 0441 Oslo; POB 5001 Majorstuen, 0301 Oslo; tel. 22-58-50-00; e-mail pcpro@hm-media.no; internet www.pcpro.no; f. 2000; 8 a year; computing; circ. 25,000; Editor-in-Chief KJETIL ENSTAD.

Seilmagasinet: Gartnerveien 1, 1394 Nesbru; tel. 21-37-77-90; fax 66-77-40-61; e-mail morten.jensen@seilmagasinet.no; internet www.seilmagasinet.no; f. 1975; publ. by MediaNavigering A/S; 10 a year; sailing; Editor MORTEN JENSEN; circ. 14,000.

SKOGeieren: POB 1438 Vika, 0115 Oslo; tel. 22-01-05-50; fax 22-42-16-90; e-mail anders.hals@skog.no; f. 1914; 12 a year; forestry; Editor ANDERS HALS; circ. 46,100.

Snø og Ski: Kongevn 5, 0787 Oslo; tel. 22-92-32-00; fax 22-92-32-50; quarterly; winter and summer sports; Editor KRISTIN MOE KROHN; circ. 42,000.

Teknisk Ukeblad (Technology Review Weekly): POB 5844 Majorstuen, 0308 Oslo; tel. 23-19-93-00; fax 23-19-93-01; e-mail redaksjonen@tu.no; internet www.tu.no; f. 1854; technology, industry, management, marketing and economics journal; Editor-in-Chief TORMOD HAUGSTAD; circ. 93,542.

Tidsskriftet Sykepleien: POB 456 Sentrum, 0104 Oslo; tel. 22-04-32-00; fax 22-04-33-756; internet www.sykepleien.no; f. 1912; 21 a year; health personnel, nursing; Editor-in-Chief BARTH THOLENS; circ. 69,000.

Utdanning: POB 9191 Grønland, 0134 Oslo; tel. 24-14-20-00; fax 24-14-21-55; e-mail redaksjonen@utdanning.ws; internet www.utdanning.ws; f. 1934; fmrly *Norsk Skoleblad*; weekly; teaching; Editor KNUT HOVLAND; circ. 129,423.

Utsyn: Sinsenvn 25, 0572 Oslo; tel. 22-00-72-00; fax 22-00-72-02; e-mail utsyn@nlm.no; internet www.utsyn.no; 25 a year; organ of Norsk Luthersk Misjonssamband (Norwegian Lutheran Mission); circ. 17,000.

Vi Menn Båt: Gullhaugvn 1, 0441 Oslo; tel. 22-58-50-00; fax 22-58-05-66; e-mail inger.storodegord@hm-media.no; internet www.vimenn.no; f. 1992; 7 a year; boats; Editor ALEXANDER ØYSTÅ; circ. 77,000 (2004).

Vi Menn Bil: Oslo; Gullhaugvn 1, 0441 Oslo; tel. 22-58-50-00; fax 22-58-05-66; e-mail wiggo.frantzen@hm-media.no; internet www.vimenn.no; f. 1996; 10 a year; cars; Editor ALEXANDER ØYSTÅ.

Vi Menn Fotball: Gullhaugvn 1, 0441 Oslo; tel. 22-58-50-00; e-mail erika-o.asker@hm-media.no; internet www.vimenn.no; football; circ. 30,000 (2000).

Villmarksliv: Gullhaugvn 1, 0441 Oslo; tel. 22-58-50-00; fax 22-58-59-59; e-mail knut.brevik@hm-media.no; internet www.villmarksliv.no; f. 1972; monthly; angling, hunting, photography; Editor-in-Chief KNUT BREVIK; circ. 45,600 (2006).

NEWS AGENCIES

Bulls Pressetjeneste A/S: Ebbellsgt. 3, 0179 Oslo; tel. 22-98-26-60; fax 22-20-49-78; e-mail info@bulls.no; internet www.bulls.no; Man. PAUL E. VATNE.

A/S Norsk Telegrambyrå (NTB) (Norwegian News Agency): Akersgt. 55, POB 6817 St Olavs pl., 0130 Oslo; tel. 22-03-44-00; fax 22-20-12-29; e-mail ntb@ntb.no; internet www.ntb.no; f. 1867; Editor-in-Chief PÅL BJERKETVEDT.

PRESS ASSOCIATIONS

Mediebedriftenes Landsforening (Norwegian Media Businesses' Asscn): Tollbugt. 27, 0157 Oslo; tel. 22-86-12-00; fax 22-42-26-11; e-mail info@mediebedriftene.no; internet www.mediebedriftene.no; Man. Dir ARVID SAND.

Den Norske Fagpresses Forening (Specialized Press Asscn): Akersgt. 41, 0158 Oslo; tel. 24-14-61-00; fax 24-14-61-10.

Norsk Journalistlag (Norwegian Union of Journalists): Torggt. 5, 5th Floor, POB 8793 Youngstorget, 0028 Oslo; tel. 22-05-39-50; fax 22-41-33-70; e-mail nj@nj.no; internet www.nj.no; f. 1946; Sec.-Gen. JAHN-ARNE OLSEN; 8,770 mems (2004).

Norsk Presseforbund (Norwegian Press Asscn): Rådhusgt. 17, POB 46 Sentrum, 0101 Oslo; tel. 22-40-50-40; fax 22-40-50-55; e-mail np@presse.no; internet www.presse.no; f. 1910; asscn of newspapermen, editors and journalists; Pres. KJETIL HAANES; Sec.-Gen. PER EDGAR KOKKVOLD.

Publishers

Antropos Forlag: Josefinesgt. 12, 0351 Oslo; tel. 22-46-03-74; fax 22-69-64-50; e-mail bokhandel@antropos.no; internet www.antropos.no.

H. Aschehoug & Co (W. Nygaard): Sehestedsgt. 3, POB 363 Sentrum, 0102 Oslo; tel. 22-40-04-00; fax 22-20-63-95; e-mail epost@aschehoug.no; internet www.aschehoug.no; f. 1872; general non-fiction, fiction, reference, children's, educational, textbooks; Man. Dir WILLIAM NYGÅRD.

Boksenteret Erik Pettersen & Co A/S: Krusesgt. 11, POB 3125 Elisenberg, 0207 Oslo; tel. 22-54-07-00; fax 22-54-07-07; e-mail bs@boksenteret.no; internet www.boksenteret.no; f. 1999; illustrated, non-fiction, craft, DIY; Man. Dir ERIK PETTERSEN.

Bokvennen Forlag: POB 6794, 0133 Oslo; tel. 22-19-14-25; fax 22-19-14-26; e-mail post@bokvennen.no; internet www.vidarforlaget.no; f. 1989; fiction, essays, biographies; Mans MORTEN CLAUSSEN, JAN M. CLAUSSEN.

Cappelen Akademisk Forlag: POB 350 Sentrum, 0055 Oslo; tel. 21-61-65-00; fax 21-61-65-01; e-mail cafinfo@cappelen.no; internet www.cappelendamm.no; f. 1946; textbooks for universities and colleges, social sciences, law, economics, medicine, health and nursing, educational science, psychology; Publr ESTER MOEN.

Cappelen Damm AS: Akersgt. 47, 0180 Oslo; tel. 21-61-65-00; fax 21-61-65-01; e-mail web@cappelen.no; internet www.cappelendamm.no; f. 1829; general, educational, popular science, fiction, maps, children's, encyclopaedias; Man. Dir PIP HALLÉN.

Dreyers Forlag: POB 2336 Solli, 0201 Oslo; tel. 23-13-69-38; fax 23-13-69-39; e-mail post@dreyersforlag.no; internet www.dreyersforlag.no; fmrly Andresen & Butenschøn A/S.

Egmont Hjemmet Mortensen A/S: Gullhaugvn 1, Nydalen, 0441 Oslo; tel. 22-58-50-00; fax 22-58-50-68; e-mail firmapost@hm-media.no; internet www.hm-media.no; f. 1941; fiction, non-fiction, children's; Man. Dir ANNE BRITT BERENSTEN.

Eide Forlag A/S: POB 6050 Postterminalen, 5892 Bergen; tel. 55-38-88-00; fax 55-38-88-01; e-mail post@eideforlag.no; internet www.eideforlag.no; f. 1880; general, children's, textbooks, fiction, non-fiction; Publrs ARNO VIGMOSTAD, ARNSTEIN BJORKE.

Fagbokforlaget: POB 6050, Postterminalen, 5892 Bergen; tel. 55-38-88-00; fax 55-38-88-01; e-mail fagbokforlaget@fagbokforlaget.no; internet www.fagbokforlaget.no; f. 1992; general and scientific; also owns Forlaget Fag og Kultur A/S; Publrs ARNO VIGMOSTAD, ARNSTEIN BJØRKE.

Falken Forlag: Helgesens gt. 21, 0553 Oslo; tel. 22-35-54-00; e-mail falkenforlag@falkenforlag.no; internet www.falkenforlag.no; f. 1946; fiction, non-fiction; Publr KIRSTI KRISTIANSEN.

Fonna Forlag: Underhaugsveien 9A, 0354 Oslo; tel. 22-69-10-10; fax 22-20-12-01; e-mail fonna@fonna.no; internet www.fonna.no; f. 1934; limited co; general, fiction; Man. Dir ARNT ÅRNES.

NORWAY

Frifant Forlag A/S: Leinvn 10, 1453 Bjørnemyr; tel. 66-91-29-40; fax 66-91-29-41; e-mail frifor@online.no; internet www.frifant.no; f. 1997.

Genesis Forlag: Fetveien 1D, POB 83, 2027 Kjeller; tel. 63-80-30-99; fax 63-81-69-22; e-mail genesis@genesis.no; internet www.genesis.no; f. 1996; Dir SVEIN ANDERSEN.

John Grieg Forlag A/S: Spelhaugen 20, 5147 Bergen; tel. 55-16-13-44; fax 66-16-13-44; e-mail post@grieg1721.no; internet www.grieg1721.no; f. 1721; children's, art, education, aquaculture; Publr SVEIN SKOTHEIM.

Gyldendal Akademisk: Sehestedsgt. 4, POB 6860, St Olavs pl., 0130 Oslo; tel. 22-03-41-00; fax 22-03-43-05; e-mail akademisk@gyldendal.no; internet www.gyldendal.no/akademisk; f. 1992; university textbooks; Man. Dir FREDRIK NISSEN.

Gyldendal Norsk Forlag A/S: Sehestedsgt. 4, POB 6860 St Olavs pl., 0130 Oslo; tel. 22-03-41-00; fax 22-03-41-05; internet www.gyldendal.no; f. 1925; general, non-fiction, fiction, biography, religion, cookery, school and university textbooks, children's, manuals; Man. Dir BJØRGUN HYSING.

Imprintforlaget A/S: Huitfeldtsgt. 15, POB 2336 Solli, 0201 Oslo; tel. 23-13-69-30; fax 23-13-69-39; e-mail imprint@imprint.no; internet www.imprint.no; imprints: Omnipax, Pegasus, Unipax; Publr BJØRN SMITH-SIMONSEN.

Kolibri Forlag A/S: POB 44 Øvre Ullern, 0311 Oslo; tel. 92-45-25-29; e-mail post@kolibriforlag.no; internet www.kolibriforlag.no; f. 1982; fantasy, non-fiction, cookery, children's, humour, leisure; Publr ELSE LILL BJØNNES.

Kolon Forlag: Sehestedsgt. 4, POB 6860 St Olavs pl., 0130 Oslo; tel. 22-03-42-02; fax 22-03-41-05; e-mail kolon@gyldendal.no; internet www.kolonforlag.no; f. 1995; modern Norwegian poetry and fiction; Publr BJØRN AAGENÆS.

Kunnskapsforlaget: Gullhaug Torg 1, POB 4432 Nydalen, 0403 Oslo; tel. 22-02-22-00; fax 22-02-22-99; e-mail resepsjonen@kunnskapsforlaget.no; internet www.kunnskapsforlaget.no; f. 1975; reference books, encyclopaedias, dictionaries, atlases, electronic reference titles; Man. Dir MARIANNE BRATTLAND.

Libretto Forlag: Øvre Vollgt. 15, 0158 Oslo; tel. 22-41-03-85; fax 22-20-42-81; e-mail post@librettoforlaget.no; internet www.librettoforlag.no; f. 1990; children's, gift books and handbooks; Publr TOM THORSTEINSEN.

Lunde Forlag A/S: Sinsenvn 25, 0572 Oslo; tel. 22-00-73-50; fax 22-00-73-73; e-mail post@lundeforlag.no; internet www.lundeforlag.no; f. 1905; religious, general, fiction, children's; Dir TORLEIF BELT.

Luther Forlag: Grensen 3, 0159 Oslo; tel. 22-00-87-80; fax 22-00-87-81; e-mail postkasse@lutherforlag.no; internet www.lutherforlag.no; religious, fiction, general; Dir ASLE DINGSTAD.

Lydbokforlaget A/S: Søreggen 2, POB 64, 7224 Melhus; tel. 72-85-60-70; fax 72-85-60-90; e-mail info@lydbokforlaget.no; internet www.lydbokforlaget.no; f. 1987; owned by H. Aschehoug & Co (33%), Gyldendal Norsk Forlag (33%) and Stiftergruppen (34%); Publr HERBORG HONGSET.

Messel Forlag: Øvre Vollgt. 15, 0158 Oslo; tel. 22-42-14-20; e-mail info@messelforlag.no; internet www.messelforlag.no; f. 1992; Pub. Dir ANNE-GRETHE MESSEL.

NKI Forlaget: Hans Burumsvn 30, POB 111, 1319 Bekkestua; tel. 67-58-89-00; fax 67-58-19-02; e-mail faordre@nki.no; internet www.nkiforlaget.no; f. 1972; textbooks for secondary and technical schools and colleges; Publr MARIANNE LØVDAHL.

Norsk Bokreidingslag: POB 6045, 5892 Bergen; tel. 55-30-18-99; fax 55-32-03-56; e-mail post@bodonihus.no; internet www.bokreidingslaget.no; f. 1939; fiction, folklore, linguistics, cultural history; Man. FROYDIS LEHMANN.

Det Norske Samlaget: Jens Bjelkesgt. 12, POB 4672 Sofienberg, 0506 Oslo; tel. 22-70-78-00; fax 22-68-75-02; e-mail kontakt@samlaget.no; internet www.samlaget.no; f. 1868; fiction, non-fiction, poetry, children's, textbooks; Man. Dir TOVE LIE.

Forlaget Oktober A/S: Kr. Augustsgt. 11, POB 6848 St Olavs pl., 0130 Oslo; tel. 23-35-46-20; fax 23-35-46-21; e-mail oktober@oktober.no; internet www.oktober.no; f. 1970; fiction, politics, social and cultural books; Publr GEIR BERDAHL.

Pantagruel Forlag A/S: Inkognitogt. 33, POB 2370 Solli, 0201 Oslo; tel. 23-27-28-10; fax 23-27-28-15; e-mail alle@pantagruel.no; internet www.pantagruel.no; Pub. Dir ALEXANDER ELGURÉN.

Pax Forlag A/S: Huitfeldtgt. 15, POB 2336 Solli, 0201 Oslo; tel. 23-13-69-00; fax 23-13-69-19; e-mail pax@pax.no; internet www.pax.no; f. 1964; fiction, non-fiction, feminism, social sciences; Man. Dir BJØRN SMITH-SIMONSEN.

Schibsted Forlagene AS: Apotekergt. 12, POB 6974 St Olavs pl., 0130 Oslo; tel. 24-14-68-00; fax 24-14-68-01; e-mail post@schibstedforlag.no; internet www.schibstedforlag.no; f. 2004 by merger of Chr. Schibsteds Forlagene A/S (f. 1839) and other units within Schibsted Group; reference, biographies, handbooks, children's, food and drink, sports, foreign language, guides, fiction, comics; Group Dir ROLV ERIK RYSSDAL.

Snøfugl Forlag: POB 95, 7221 Melhus; tel. 72-87-24-11; fax 72-87-10-13; e-mail snoefugl@online.no; internet www.snoefugl.no; f. 1972; fiction, general; Man. ASMUND SNØFUGL.

Solum Forlag A/S: Hoffsvn 18, POB 140 Skøyen, 0212 Oslo; tel. 22-50-04-00; fax 22-50-14-53; e-mail info@solumforlag.no; internet www.solumforlag.no; f. 1974; fiction, human sciences, general; Man. Dir KNUT ENDRE SOLUM.

Spartacus Forlag A/S: POB 2587 Solli, 0203 Oslo; tel. 22-44-56-70; fax 22-44-46-50; e-mail post@spartacus.no; internet www.spartacus.no; f. 1989; Publr PER NORDANGER.

Spektrum Forlag AS: Rosencrantzgt. 22, 0160 Oslo; tel. 22-00-82-60; fax 85-03-64-78; e-mail post@spektrum-forlag.no; internet www.spektrum-forlag.no; f. 1992; Pub. Dir CYRUS BRANTENBERG.

Stabenfeldt A/S: Sothammargeilen 3, 4029 Stavanger; tel. 51-84-54-00; fax 51-84-54-90; f. 1913; general fiction, adventure, reference; Man. Dir JENS OTTO HANSEN.

Tell Forlag A/S: Slemmestadveien 416, 1390 Vollen; tel. 66-78-09-18; fax 66-90-05-72; e-mail post@tell.no; internet www.tell.no; f. 1987; textbooks and educational books; Man. TELL-CHR. WAGLE.

Tiden Norsk Forlag: Sehestedsgt. 4, POB 6704 St Olavs pl., 0130 Oslo; tel. 23-32-76-60; fax 23-32-76-97; e-mail tiden@tiden.no; internet www.tiden.no; f. 1933; literary fiction, crime, thrillers, fantasy, non-fiction; Pub. Dir RICHARD AARØ.

Tun Forlag A/S: Schweigaardsgt. 34A POB 9303 Grønland, 0135 Oslo; tel. 21-31-44-00; e-mail post@tunforlag.no; internet www.boktunet.no; f. 2005; agriculture, hunting, fishing, outdoor, handicrafts, culture, horses, dogs; Man. HEIDI JANNICKE ANDERSEN.

Universitetsforlaget AS: Sehestedsgt. 3, POB 508 Sentrum, 0105 Oslo; tel. 24-14-75-00; fax 24-14-75-01; e-mail post@universitetsforlaget.no; internet www.universitetsforlaget.no; f. 1950; publishers to the Universities of Oslo, Bergen, Trondheim and Tromsø and various learned societies; school books, university textbooks, specialized journals; Man. Dir SVEIN SKARHEIM.

Verbum Forlag: Bernhard Getzgt. 3, POB 6624 St Olavs pl., 0129 Oslo; tel. 22-93-27-00; fax 22-93-27-27; e-mail verbumforlag@verbumforlag.no; internet www.verbumforlag.no; f. 1820; Christian literature; Man. TURID BARTH PETTERSEN.

Forlaget Vett & Viten AS: Ramstadsletta 15, 1363 Høvik; tel. 66-84-90-40; fax 66-53-11-52; e-mail vv@vettviten.no; internet www.vettviten.no; f. 1987; medical, technical and engineering textbooks; Man. Dir MORTEN LIEN.

Wigestrand Forlag A/S: POB 621, 4003 Stavanger; tel. 51-51-76-10; fax 51-51-76-40; e-mail forlag@wigestrand.no; internet www.wigestrand.no; f. 1998; Publr ØYVIND WIGESTRAND.

PUBLISHERS' ASSOCIATION

Den norske Forleggerforening (Norwegian Publishers' Asscn): Øvre Vollgt. 15, 0158 Oslo; tel. 22-00-75-80; fax 22-33-38-30; e-mail dnf@forleggerforeningen.no; internet www.forleggerforeningen.no; f. 1895; Chair. GEIR BERDAHL; Sec. PER CHRISTIAN OPSAHL; 52 mem. firms.

Broadcasting and Communications

REGULATORY AUTHORITY

Post- og Teletilsynet (NPT) (Norwegian Post and Telecommunications Authority): Nygård 1, POB 93, 4791 Lillesand; tel. 22-82-46-00; fax 22-82-46-40; e-mail firmapost@npt.no; internet www.npt.no; f. 1987; issues and supervises regulations, concessions and licences; expanded to incorporate postal matters in 1997; Dir-Gen. WILLY JENSEN.

TELECOMMUNICATIONS

NetCom AS: Sandakervn 140, 0484 Oslo; tel. 92-40-50-50; internet www.netcom.no; f. 1990; mobile cellular telecommunications; owned by TeliaSonera AB (Sweden); Man. Dir AUGUST BAUMANN.

Network Norway AS: Innspurten 15, 0663 Oslo; tel. 51-84-64-00; fax 51-84-64-01; e-mail 09060@networknorway.no; internet www.networknorway.no; f. 2005; mobile cellular telecommunications and broadband internet services; Man. Dir ARILD E. HUSTAD.

Norkring AS: Telenor Broadcast, 1331 Fornebu; tel. 67-89-20-00; fax 67-89-36-11; e-mail norkring@telenor.com; internet www.norkring.no; f. 1996; provides fixed and mobile telephone services; owned by Telenor Broadcast Holding A/S; CEO TORBJOERN TEIGEN.

Telenor ASA: Snarøyvn 30, 1331 Fornebu; tel. 67-89-00-00; e-mail infomaster@telenor.no; internet www.telenor.no; offers fixed-line telecommunications, broadband internet and digital television services; f. 1855; 53.97% stake owned by Ministry of Trade and Industry; Man. Dir RAGNAR KÅRHUS.

djuice: Snarøyvn 30, 1331 Fornebu; tel. 81-07-70-00; fax 67-89-00-00; e-mail infomaster@telenor.com; internet www.djuice.no; mobile cellular telecommunications; subsidiary of Telenor ASA.

Tele2 Norge AS: Brynsengfaret 6B, 0667 Oslo; tel. 21-31-90-00; fax 21-31-91-00; internet www.tele2.no; f. 1995; fixed-line and mobile cellular telecommunications services, also broadband internet access; subsidiary of Tele2 AB (Sweden); Man. Dir HAAKON DYRNES.

BROADCASTING

Radio

Norsk Rikskringkasting (NRK) (Norwegian Broadcasting Corpn): Bj. Bjørnsons pl. 1, 0340 Oslo; tel. 23-04-70-00; fax 75-12-27-77; e-mail info@nrk.no; internet www.nrk.no; autonomous public corpn; operates 3 national services (including a youth programme), 18 regional services (including 1 in the language of the Sámi—Lappish) and an international service, Radio Norway International; Chair. WILLIAM NYGAARD; CEO (Broadcasting) HANS-TORE BJERKAAS.

P4—Radio Hele Norge ASA: Serviceboks, 2626 Lillehammer; tel. 61-24-84-44; fax 61-24-84-47; e-mail p4@p4.no; internet www.p4.no; f. 1993; private commercial station; Man. Dir KALLE LISBERG.

Radio Norge: Kråkerøyvn 2 POB 144, 1601 Fredrikstad; tel. 69-70-76-00; fax 69-70-76-01; e-mail redaksjon@radionorge.com; internet www.radionorge.com; f. 2004 as Kanal24; present name adopted 2008; 77% stake owned by SBS Radio Norge AS; Man. Dir BENTE KLEMETSDAL.

Television

Digital terrestrial broadcasting began in 2007. Analogue signals were discontinued in December 2009.

Canal Digital Norge AS: POB 1036, 3905 Porsgrunn; fax 81-53-20-30; internet www.canaldigital.no; digital satellite and cable television services; also broadband internet access; owned by Telenor ASA; Man. Dir SVEIN ERIK DAVIDSEN.

Norsk Rikskringkasting (NRK) (Norwegian Broadcasting Corpn): Dir of Television HANS-TORE BJERKAAS.

RiksTV AS: Økernvn 145, POB 393, Økern, 0513 Oslo; tel. 22-88-37-90; fax 22-88-37-91; e-mail post@rikstv.no; internet www.rikstv.no; f. 2005; a digital terrestrial, cable and satellite television service, offering up to 26 channels; co-owned by NRK, Telenor Broadcast Holding and TV 2 Gruppen; Man. Dir CHRISTIAN BIRKELAND (acting).

TV-2: Nøstegaten 72, POB 7222, 5020 Bergen; tel. 02255; fax 21-00-60-03; e-mail 02255@tv2.no; internet www.tv2.no; f. 1992; private commercial station; Man. Dir ALF HILDRUM; Dir of Programmes NILS KETIL ANDRESEN.

TV Norge AS: Nydalen Allé 37, POB 4800, 0484 Oslo; tel. 21-02-20-00; fax 22-05-10-00; e-mail tvnorge@tvnorge.no; internet www.tvnorge.no; private commercial television channel; owned by ProSiebenSat1 (Germany); Man. Dir HARALD STRØMME; Dir of Programmes EIVIND LANDSVERK.

Finance

At May 2011 there were 19 commercial banks (comprising the major banks, some large regional banks and a number of smaller regional and local banks) and 113 savings banks.

Finanstilsynet (Financial Supervisory Authority of Norway): Revierstredet 3, POB 1187, Sentrum, 0107 Oslo; tel. 22-93-98-00; fax 22-63-02-26; e-mail post@finanstilsynet.no; internet www.finanstilsynet.no; f. 1986; finance inspectorate; Dir-Gen. BJØRN SKOGSTAD AAMO.

BANKING

(cap. = capital; res = reserves; dep. = deposits; m. = million; brs = branches; amounts in kroner, unless otherwise specified)

Central Bank

Norges Bank: Bankplassen 2, POB 1179 Sentrum, 0107 Oslo; tel. 22-31-60-00; fax 22-41-31-05; e-mail central.bank@norges-bank.no; internet www.norges-bank.no; f. 1816; holds the exclusive right of note issue; cap. and res 59,887m., dep. 2,690,419m. (Dec. 2008); Chair., Supervisory Bd REIDAR SANDAL; Gov. SVEIN GJEDREM; 12 brs.

Principal Commercial Banks

Bank 1 Oslo AS: Hammersborggt. 2, POB 778 Sentrum, 0106 Oslo; tel. 07040; fax 21-02-50-51; e-mail bank1@sparebank1.no; internet www.oslo.sparebank1.no; f. 1898; present name adopted 2000; cap. 291m., res 844m., dep. 15,069m. (Dec. 2007); CEO TORBJØRN VIK; Chair. ELDAR MATHISEN; 10 brs.

DnB NOR Bank ASA: Aker Brygge, Stranden 21, 0021 Oslo; tel. 91-50-30-00; fax 24-02-53-00; e-mail 04800@dnbnor.no; internet www.dnbnor.no; f. 2004 by merger of Den norske Bank ASA and Union Bank of Norway; cap. 17,514m., res 54,948m., dep. 1,337,672m. (Dec. 2009); Chair. ANNE CARINE TANUM; Pres. and CEO RUNE BJERKE; 187 brs.

Fokus Bank ASA: Søndregt. 13-15, 7466 Trondheim; tel. 85-40-90-00; fax 81-00-09-01; e-mail fokus@fokus.no; internet www.fokus.no; f. 1987 by merger of Bøndernes Bank A/S, Buskerudbanken A/S, Forretningsbanken A/S and Vestlandsbanken; present name adopted 1996; owned by Danske Bank A/S (Denmark); Chair. SØREN MØLLER NIELSEN; Man. Dir TROND F. MELLINGSÆTER; 55 brs.

Nordea Bank Norge ASA: Middelthunsgt. 17, POB 1166 Sentrum, 0107 Oslo; tel. 22-48-50-00; fax 22-48-47-49; internet www.nordea.no; fmrly Christiania Bank og Kreditkasse ASA; present name adopted 2001; part of Nordea Bank Group (Sweden); cap. €5,102m., res €–518m., dep. €444,034m. (Dec. 2009); Group Pres. and CEO CHRISTIAN CLAUSEN; Senior Exec., Norway GUNN WÆRSTED; 130 brs.

Nordlandsbanken ASA: Molov. 16, 8002 Bodø; tel. 91-50-89-00; fax 75-55-87-89; e-mail post@nordlandsbanken.no; internet www.nordlandsbanken.no; f. 1893; owned by DnB NOR Bank ASA; cap. 625m., res 1,107m., dep. 32,112m. (Dec. 2009); Chair. PÅL SKOE; CEO MORTEN STØVER; 16 brs.

Principal Savings Banks

Sparebank 1 Nord-Norge: Storgt. 65, POB 6800, 9298 Tromsø; tel. 91-50-22-44; fax 77-62-22-91; e-mail 02244@snn.no; internet www.snn.no; f. 1989 as Sparebanken Nord-Norge, following merger of Sparebanken Nord and Tromsø Sparebank; present name adopted 2008; cap. 1,019m., res 3,433m., dep. 58,393m. (Dec. 2008); Chair. KJELL OLAV PETTERSEN; CEO HANS OLAV KARDE; 81 brs.

Sparebank 1 SMN: Sondregt. 4, 7467 Trondheim; tel. 73-58-51-11; fax 73-58-64-50; e-mail smn@smn.no; internet www.smn.no; f. 1823 as Trondhjems Sparebank; fmrly Sparebanken Midt-Norge; present name adopted 2008; cap. 1,447m., res 3,254m., dep. 73,166m. (Dec. 2008); Chair. PER AXEL KOCHE; Man. Dir FINN HAUGAN; 56 brs.

SpareBank 1 SR-Bank: Bjergsted Terrasse 1, POB 250, 4066 Stavanger; tel. 91-50-20-02; fax 51-53-54-67; e-mail kundesenter@sr-bank.no; internet www.sr-bank.no; f. 1839 as Egersund Sparebank; merged with 22 savings banks in 1976; present name adopted 2007; cap. 1,865m., res 3,262m., dep. 113,747m. (Dec. 2008); CEO TERJE VAREBERG; 52 brs.

Sparebanken Hedmark: Strandgt. 15, POB 203, 2302 Hamar; tel. 62-51-20-00; fax 62-53-29-75; e-mail kundesenter@sparebanken-hedmark.no; internet www.sparebanken-hedmark.no; f. 1845; cap. 3,840m., dep. 30,267m. (Dec. 2007); Chair. RICHARD H. HEIBERG; Man. Dir HARRY KONTERUD; 29 brs.

Sparebanken Møre: Keiser Wilhelmsgt. 29–33, POB 121, 6002 Ålesund; tel. 70-11-30-00; fax 70-12-26-70; e-mail kundeservice@sbm.no; internet www.sbm.no; f. 1985; cap. 710m., res 1,868m., dep. 24,175m. (Dec. 2008); CEO OLAV-ARNE FISKERSTRAND; 31 brs.

Sparebanken Pluss: Rådhusgt. 7–9, POB 200, 4662 Kristiansand; tel. 38-17-35-00; fax 38-17-35-04; e-mail firmapost@sparebankenpluss.no; internet www.sparebankenpluss.no; f. 1824; merged with 4 savings banks in 1987; dep. 22,738m., total assets 25,676m. (Dec. 2007); Chair. ARVID GRUNDEKJØN; Man. Dir STEIN HANNEVIK.

Sparebanken Sør: Vestervn. 1, POB 782, 4800 Arendal; tel. 37-02-50-00; fax 37-02-19-36; e-mail international@sor.no; internet www.sor.no; f. 1825; cap. 2,423m., res 51m., dep. 31,966m. (Dec. 2009); Chair. ALICE JERVELL; Man. Dir MORTEN KRAFT; 27 brs.

Sparebanken Vest: Kaigt. 4, POB 7999, 5016 Bergen; tel. 91-50-55-55; fax 55-21-73-50; e-mail sparebanken.vest@spv.no; internet www.spv.no; f. 1823 as Bergens Sparebank; merger 1982 of 25 savings banks; cap. 267m., res 4,068m., dep. 87,086m. (Dec. 2008); Man. Dir STEIN KLAKEGG; 59 brs.

Bankers' Associations

Finansnæringens Fellesorganisasjon (FNO) (Finance Norway): Hansteensgt. 2, POB 2473 Solli, 0202 Oslo; tel. 23-28-42-00; fax 23-28-42-01; e-mail fno@fno.no; internet www.fno.no; f. 2010; trade organization for banks, insurance companies and other financial institutions; 180 mems; Chair. RUNE BJERKE; Man. Dir ARNE HYTTNES.

Sparebankforeningen i Norge (Savings Banks Asscn): Universitetsgt. 8, St Olavs pl., POB 6772, 0130 Oslo; tel. 22-11-00-75; fax 22-36-25-33; e-mail firmapost@sparebankforeningen.no; internet www.sparebankforeningen.no; f. 1914; Pres. TERJE VAREBERG (Sparebank 1 SR-Bank); Man. Dir ARNE HYTTNES; 121 mems.

NORWAY

STOCK EXCHANGE

Oslo Børs (Oslo Stock Exchange): Tollbugt. 2, POB 460 Sentrum, 0105 Oslo; tel. 22-34-17-00; e-mail communications@oslobors.no; internet www.oslobors.no; f. 1819; owned by Oslo Børs VPS Holding ASA; Pres. and CEO BENTE A. LANDSNES.

INSURANCE

Assuranceforeningen Skuld: Ruseløkkvn. 26, POB 1376 Vika, 0114 Oslo; tel. 22-00-22-00; fax 22-42-42-22; e-mail osl@skuld.com; internet www.skuld.com; f. 1897; mutual, shipowners' protection and indemnity; Chair. ERIK GLØERSEN; Pres. and CEO DOUGLAS JACOBSOHN.

Gjensidige Forsikring ASA: Drammensvn 228, POB 276, 1326 Lysaker; tel. 91-50-31-00; fax 22-96-92-00; e-mail epost@gjensidigenor.no; internet www.gjensidige.com; f. 1847; merged with Forenede Norge Forsikring and Forenede Skadeforsikring in 1993; Chair. INGE K. HANSEN; Group CEO HELGE LEIRO BAASTAD.

Nordea Liv AS: POB 7078, 5020 Bergen; tel. 22-48-50-00; fax 55-17-33-80; internet www.nordealink.no; f. by merger of Norske Liv AS and Vesta Liv AS; life insurance; Dir JØRUND VANDVIK.

TrygVesta: Folke Bernadottesvei 50, 5020 Bergen; tel. 89-56-35-21; e-mail kundeservice@trygvesta.no; internet www.trygvesta.com; f. 1884 as Vesta; bought by Tryg-Baltica in 1999; current name adopted 2002; includes Skadeforsikringsselskapet Vesta A/S (general insurance), Vesta Liv A/S (life insurance), Vesta Finans A/S (financial services); Chair. MIKAEL OLUFSEN; CEO STINE BOSS.

Uni Storebrand: Prof. Kohtsvei 9, POB 500, 1327 Lysaker; tel. 22-31-50-50; e-mail international@storebrand.no; internet www.storebrand.no; f. 1991 by merger of Storebrand (f. 1947) and Uni Forsikring (f. 1984); group includes life, non-life and international reinsurance operations; taken over by govt administrators in 1992 and new holding co (Uni Storebrand New) formed, following suspension of payments to creditors; CEO IDAR KREUTZER.

Vital Insurance: Folke Bernadottesvei 40, POB 7500, 5020 Bergen; tel. 55-17-70-00; fax 55-17-86-99; e-mail kundesenter@vital.no; internet www.vital.no; f. 1990 by a merger between NKP Forsikring and Hygea; life and pension insurance; Dir-Gen. TOM RATHKE.

Insurance Association

Finansnaeringens Hovedorganisasjon (FNH) (Norwegian Financial Services Asscn): (see Bankers' Associations, above).

Trade and Industry

GOVERNMENT AGENCIES

Enova SF: Prof. Brochsgt. 2, POB 5700 Sluppen, 7437 Trondheim; tel. 73-19-04-30; e-mail post@enova.no; internet www.enova.no; f. 2001; owned by the Ministry of Petroleum and Energy; advises the Ministry on matters related to energy efficiency and new renewable energy; Man. Dir NILS KRISTIAN NAKSTAD.

Innovasjon Norge (Innovation Norway): Akersgt. 13, POB 448 Sentrum, 0104 Oslo; tel. 22-00-25-00; fax 22-00-25-01; e-mail post@invanor.no; internet www.invanor.no; f. 2004 to replace Norges Turistråd (Norwegian Tourist Board), Norges Eksportråd (Norwegian Trade Council), Statens nærings- og distriktsutviklingsfond (SND-Industrial and Regional Development Fund) and Statens Veiledningskontor for Oppfinnere (SVO-Government Consultative Office for Inventors); state-owned; operates in all Norwegian counties and more than 30 countries world-wide; Pres. KJELL A. STOREIDE; Man. Dir GUNN OVESEN.

CHAMBERS OF COMMERCE

Bergen Næringsråd (Bergen Chamber of Commerce and Industry): POB 843, Sentrum, 5807 Bergen; tel. 55-55-39-00; fax 55-55-39-01; e-mail firmapost@bergen-chamber.no; internet www.bergen-chamber.no; f. 1915; Pres. ERIK BØCKMANN; Man. Dir MARIT WARNCKE.

Oslo Handelskammer (Oslo Chamber of Commerce): Drammensvn 30, POB 2874 Solli, 0230 Oslo; tel. 22-12-94-00; fax 22-12-94-01; e-mail mail@chamber.no; internet www.chamber.no; Man. Dir LARS-KÅRE LEGERNES.

INDUSTRIAL AND TRADE ASSOCIATION

Norges Skogeierforbund (Norwegian Forest Owners' Fed.): Roald Amundsensgt. 6, POB 1438 Vika, 0115 Oslo; tel. 23-00-07-50; fax 22-42-16-90; e-mail nsf@skog.no; internet www.skog.no; f. 1913; aims to promote the economic and technical interests of forest owners, a general forest policy in the interests of private ownership and co-operation between the affiliated asscns; Man. Dir GUDBRAND KVAAL; 38,000 mems.

EMPLOYERS' ASSOCIATIONS

Næringslivets Hovedorganisasjon (NHO) (Confederation of Norwegian Business and Industry): Middelthunsgt. 27, POB 5250 Majorstua, 0303 Oslo; tel. 23-08-80-00; fax 23-08-80-01; e-mail firmapost@nho.no; internet www.nho.no; f. 1989; rep. org. for industry, crafts and service industries; Pres. KRISTIN SKOGEN LUND; Dir-Gen. JOHN G. BERNANDER; c. 18,500 mems who must also belong to one of the 20 affiliated national asscns, chief among which are the following:

Bensinforhandlernes Bransjeforening (BBF) (Petrol Retailers' Organization): POB 5488, Majorstua, 0305 Oslo; tel. 23-08-87-50; fax 23-08-87-51; e-mail bbf@nho.no; internet www.bensinforhandlerne.no; Man. Dir JAN CARHO; 700 mems.

Energi Norge (Energy Norway): Middelthunsgt. 27, POB 7184 Majorstua, 0307 Oslo; tel. 23-08-89-00; fax 23-08-89-01; e-mail post@energinorge.no; internet www.energinorge.no; fmrly Energibedriftenes Landsforening; present name adopted in 2009; Chair. OLA MØRKVED RINNAN.

Fiskeri- og Havbruksnæringens Landsforening (FHL) (Fish and Aquaculture Industries): Middelthunsgt. 27, POB 5471 Majorstua, 0305 Oslo; tel. 23-08-87-30; fax 23-08-87-31; e-mail firmapost@fhl.no; internet www.fhl.no; Dir-Gen. GEIR ANDREASSEN.

NHO Grafisk (Fed. of Graphic Arts Enterprises): Middelthunsgt. 27, 0369, POB 5495, Majorstua, 0305 Oslo; tel. 23-08-78-70; fax 23-08-78-71; e-mail post@nhografisk.no; internet www.nhografisk.no; f. 1906; fmrly Visuell Kommunikasjon Norge; Dir-Gen. ROBERT WRIGHT; 240 mems.

NHO Håndverk (Norwegian Fed. of Craft Industries): Middelthunsgt. 27, POB 5250, Majorstua, 0303 Oslo; tel. 23-08-80-00; fax 23-08-87-61; e-mail handverk@nho.no; internet www.nhohandverk.no; f. 1993; Chair. VIBEKE GISKE RØISLAND; 2,200 mems.

NHO Luftfart (Fed. of Norwegian Aviation Industries): POB 5474 Majorstua, 0305 Oslo; tel. 23-08-85-70; fax 23-08-85-71; e-mail nholuftfart@nho.no; internet www.nholuftfart.no; Dir TORBJØRN LOTHE.

NHO Mat og Drikke (Fed. of Norwegian Food and Drink Industry): Middelthunsgt. 27, POB 5472 Majorstua, 0305 Oslo; tel. 23-08-87-00; fax 23-08-87-20; e-mail firmapost@nhomd.no; internet www.nhomatogdrikke.no; Admin. Dir KNUT MARONI.

NHO Reiseliv (Norwegian Hospitality Asscn): Middelthunsgt. 27, POB 5465 Majorstua 0305 Oslo; tel. 23-08-86-20; fax 23-08-86-21; e-mail firmapost@nhoreiseliv.no; internet www.nhoreiseliv.no; f. 1997 as Reiselivsbedriftenes Landsforening; present name adopted 2006; Pres. RAGNAR HEGGDAL; 2,300 mems.

NHO Service (Nat. Fed. of Service Industries): Middelthunsgt. 27, POB 5473, Majorstua, 0305 Oslo; tel. 23-08-86-50; fax 23-08-86-59; e-mail firmapost@sbl.no; internet www.nhoservice.no; Admin. Dir PETTER FURULUND; 1,187 mems.

NHO Transport (TL) (Fed. of Norwegian Transport Cos): Middelthunsgt. 27, POB 5477 Majorstuen, 0305 Oslo; tel. 23-08-86-00; fax 23-08-86-01; e-mail post@transport.no; internet www.transport.no; Dir-Gen. JON H. STORDRANGE.

Norges Bilbransjeforbund (NBF) (Asscn of Norwegian Motor Car Dealers and Services): Drammensvn 97, POB 2804 Solli, 0204 Oslo; tel. 22-54-21-00; fax 22-44-10-56; e-mail firmapost@nbf.no; internet www.nbf.no; f. 1928; Admin. Dir SYVER LEIVESTAD; 1,200 mems.

Norsk Industri (Fed. of Norwegian Industries): Middelthunsgt. 27, POB 7072 Majorstuen, 0306 Oslo; tel. 23-08-88-00; fax 22-59-00-01; e-mail post@norskindustri.no; internet www.norskindustri.no; f. 2005 by merger of Teknologibedriftenes Landsforening (Fed. of Norwegian Manufacturing Industries) and Prosessindustriens Landsforening (Fed. of Norwegian Process Industries); Chair. PER A. SØRLIE; Man. Dir STEIN LIER-HANSEN; c. 2,200 mems.

Skogbrukets Landsforening (SL) (Forestry Asscn): Essendropsgt. 6, POB 5496, Majorstuen 0305 Oslo; tel. 23-08-86-80; fax 23-08-86-75; e-mail firmapost@skogbruk.no; internet www.skogbruk.no; f. 1928; Man. Dir HAAVARD ELSTRAND.

Treforedlingsindustriens Bransjeforening (TFB) (Norwegian Pulp and Paper Association): Middelthunsgt. 27, POB 7072, Majorstuen, 0306 Oslo; tel. 23-08-88-08; fax 23-08-78-99; e-mail mhf@norskindustri.no; internet www.norskindustri.no/treforedling; f. 1891; Man. Dir MARIT HOLTERMANN FOSS; 18 mems.

Bryggeri- og Drikkevareforeningen (Norwegian Breweries and Soft Drink Producers): POB 7087 Majorstua, 0306 Oslo; tel. 23-08-86-96; fax 22-60-30-04; e-mail info@bryggeriforeningen.no; internet www.bryggeri-ogdrikkevareforeningen.no; f. 1901; Man. Dir HALFDAN KVERNELAND OLAFSSON; 11 mems.

Entreprenørforeningen—Bygg og Anlegg (General Contractors): Middelthunsgt. 27, POB 5485 Majorstua, 0305 Oslo; tel. 23-08-

NORWAY

75-00; fax 23-08-75-30; e-mail firmapost@ebanett.no; internet www.ebanett.no; Chair. Dag Andresen; 220 mems.

Handels- og Servicenæringens Hovedorganisasjon (HSH) (Federation of Commercial and Service Enterprises): Henrik Ibsensgt. 90, POB 2900 Solli, 0230 Oslo; tel. 22-54-17-00; fax 22-06-09-30; e-mail info@hsh-org.no; internet www.hsh-org.no; f. 1990 by merger; 14,000 mem. cos; Pres. Carl Otto Løvenskiold.

Oljeindustriens Landsforening (OLF) (Oil Industry): Vassbotnen 1, POB 8065, 4068 Stavanger; tel. 51-84-65-00; fax 51-84-65-01; e-mail firmapost@olf.no; internet www.olf.no; Admin. Dir Gro Brækken.

TBL Møbel- og Innredning (Asscn of Norwegian Furnishing Industries): POB 7072 Majorstuen, 0306 Oslo; tel. 22-59-00-00; fax 22-59-00-01; e-mail tbl@tbl.no; Exec. Man. Egil Sundet.

UTILITIES

Electricity

Bergenshalvøens Kommunale Kraftselskap AS (BKK): Kokstadvegen 37, POB 7050, 5020 Bergen; tel. 55-12-70-00; fax 55-12-70-01; e-mail firmapost@bkk.no; internet www.bkk.no; f. 1920; production, distribution and supply of electricity; supplies customers throughout western Norway; 49.9% stake owned by Statkraft AS, 37.75% owned by Bergen city council, 12.35% owned by 16 other municipalities; Chair. Martin Smith-Sivertsen; CEO Atle Neteland.

Fjordkraft AS: Folke Bernadottes Vei 38, POB 3507, Fyllingsdalen, 5845 Bergen; tel. 06-11-0; fax 33-46-63-73; e-mail kundeservice@fjordkraft.no; internet www.fjordkraft.no; electricity supplier; owned by BKK, Skagerak Energi and Statkraft; Man. Dir Sverre Gjessing; c. 325,000 customers.

Hafslund ASA: Drammensvn 144, 0247 Oslo; tel. 22-43-50-00; internet www.hafslund.no; f. 1898; electrical generation (9 hydroelectric plants), sales, distribution, safety, installation, security and network infrastructure; Pres. and CEO Christian Berg; Chair. Christian Brinch.

Lyse Energi AS: Breiflåtvn 18, POB 8124, 4017 Stavanger; tel. 51-90-80-00; internet www.lyse.no; production, distribution and supply of electricity; also supplier of natural gas and telecommunications services; owned by 16 municipalities in south Rogaland (incl. Stavanger city council); Chair. Ivar Rusdal; Man. Dir Eimund Nygaard.

Nordkraft AS: Teknologivn 2, POB 55, 8517 Narvik; tel. 76-96-10-00; fax 76-94-10-67; e-mail post@nordkraft.no; internet www.nordkraft.no; f. 2006 by merger of Nordkraft AS and Narvik Energi AS; production of electricity (hydroelectric power plants and wind power farms); 50.01% stake owned by Narvik municipal council, 33.33% owned by DONG Energy A/S (Denmark), 16.66% owned by Hålogaland Kraft AS; Chair. Sigve Nils Stokland; Man. Dir Olaf Andreas Larsen.

Salten Kraftsamband AS (SKS): Eliasbakken 7, 8205 Fauske; tel. 75-40-22-00; e-mail firmapost@sks.no; internet www.sks.no; production, distribution and supply of electricity nation-wide; 40% stake owned by Bodø municipal council, 23.7% by DONG Energy A/S (Denmark); Man. Dir Leif Finsveen.

Statnett SF: Husebybakken 28B, POB 5192 Majorstua, 0302 Oslo; tel. 22-52-70-00; fax 22-52-70-01; e-mail firmapost@statnett.no; internet www.statnett.no; f. 1992; national power grid co; supervises and co-ordinates the operation of the entire Norwegian power system, also operates own transmission lines and submarine cables, as well as sub-stations and switching stations; state-owned co under the jurisdiction of the Ministry of Petroleum and Energy; Pres. and CEO Auke Lont.

Trondheim Energi AS: 7005 Trondheim; tel. 73-96-10-11; fax 73-96-11-90; e-mail informasjon@trondheimenergi.no; internet www.trondheimenergi.no; f. 1901 as Trondheim Energiverk; present name adopted 2007; production and supply of electricity in Sør-Trøndelag; owned by Statkraft AS; Chair. Jon Brandsar.

Ustekveikja Energi AS: Geilovegen 68, 3580 Geilo; tel. 32-08-70-00; fax 32-08-70-10; e-mail post@ustekveikja.no; internet www.ustekveikja.no; f. 1992; producer and retailer of electricity; supplies customers throughout Norway; Man. Dir Bjørn Skaret.

Other major production and distribution companies include Agder Energi AS, Akershus Energi AS, Bodø Energi AS, Fredrikstad Energi AS, Haugeland Kraft AS, HelgelundsKraft AS, Istad AS, Oppland Energi AS, Østfold Energi AS, Skagerrak Energi AS, Sira-Kvina Kraftselskap, Troms Kraft AS, TrønderEnergi AS and Vest-Agder Energiverk.

Water

Responsibility for water supply in Norway lies with the municipalities.

TRADE UNIONS

National Confederations

Landsorganisasjonen i Norge (LO) (Norwegian Confederation of Trade Unions): Folkets Hus, Youngstorget 11, 0181 Oslo; tel. 23-06-10-50; fax 23-06-17-43; e-mail inter@lo.no; internet www.lo.no; f. 1899; Pres. Roar Flåthen; 860,000 mems in 21 affiliated unions (2009).

Unio (Confed. of Unions for Professionals): Stortingsgt 2, 0158 Oslo; tel. 22-70-88-50; fax 22-70-88-50; e-mail post@unio.no; internet www.unio.no; f. 2001; Pres. Anders Folkestad; 280,979 mems in 10 affiliated unions (Jan. 2009).

Yrkesorganisasjonenes Sentralforbund (YS) (Confed. of Vocational Unions): Brugt. 19, 0134 Grønland, Oslo; tel. 21-01-36-00; fax 21-01-37-20; e-mail post@ys.no; internet www.ys.no; f. 1977; Pres. Tore Eugen Kvalheim; 213,288 mems in 22 affiliated unions (July 2008).

Principal Affiliated Unions

Delta (Public and Private Sector Services Union): Brugt. 19, POB 9202, 0134 Oslo; tel. 21-01-36-00; fax 21-01-36-50; e-mail post@delta.no; internet www.delta.no; affiliated to YS; Pres. Gunn Olander; 61,590 mems (July 2008).

EL & IT Forbundet (Electricians and Information Technology Workers): Youngstorget 11, 0181 Oslo; tel. 23-06-34-00; fax 23-06-34-01; e-mail firmapost@elogit.no; internet www.elogit.no; f. 1999 by merger of Tele- og Dataforbundet (TD) and Norsk Elektriker- og Kraftstasjonsforbundet (NEKF); affiliated to LO; Pres. Hans Olav Felix; 37,000 mems.

Fagforbundet (Norwegian Union of Municipal and General Employees): POB 7003, Keysersgt 15, 0165 Oslo; tel. 23-06-40-00; fax 23-06-40-01; e-mail servicetorget@fagforbundet.no; internet www.fagforbundet.no; f. 2003; affiliated to LO; Pres. Jan Davidsen; 305,000 mems.

Fellesforbundet (The Norwegian United Federation of Trade Unions): Lilletorget 1, 0184 Oslo; tel. 23-06-31-00; fax 23-06-31-01; e-mail fellesforbundet@fellesforbundet.no; internet www.fellesforbundet.no; f. 1988; affiliated to LO; Pres. Arve Bakke; 156,000 mems.

Fellesorganisasjonen (FO) (Social Educators and Social Workers): Mariboesgt. 13, POB 4693 Sofienberg, 0506 Oslo; tel. 23-06-11-70; fax 23-06-11-14; e-mail kontor@fo.no; internet www.fo.no; f. 1992; affiliated to LO; Pres. Randi Reese; 24,000 mems.

Finansforbundet (Financial Services Union): Schweigaards gt. 14, 5th Floor, 0185 Oslo; tel. 22-05-63-00; fax 22-17-06-90; e-mail post@finansforbundet.no; internet www.finansforbundet.no; f. 2000 by merger of 3 separate unions; affiliated to YS; Pres. Jorun Berland; 37,388 mems (July 2008).

Handel og Kontor i Norge (Commercial and Office Employees): Youngstorget 11, 0181 Oslo; tel. 22-03-11-80; fax 22-03-12-06; internet www.handelogkontor.no; f. 1908; affiliated to LO; Pres. Sture Arntzen; 62,000 mems.

Industri Energi (IE): Youngstorget 11, 0181 Oslo; tel. 23-06-22-30; fax 22-03-22-60; e-mail post@industrienergi.no; internet www.industrienergi.no; f. 2006 by merger of Norsk Olje- og Petrokjemisk Fagforbund (Norwegian Oil and Petrochemical Industry Union) and Norsk Kjemisk Industriarbeiderforbund (Norwegian Chemical Industry Union); affiliated to LO; Pres. Leif Sande; 55,000 mems.

LO Stat (Government Employees): Møllergt. 10, 0179 Oslo; tel. 23-06-10-53; fax 22-42-00-75; e-mail lostat@lostat.no; internet www.lostat.no; f. 1939 as Statstjenestemannskartellet; present name adopted 1996; affiliated to LO; Pres. Morten Øye; 105,867 mems.

Norsk Arbeidsmandsforbund (Norwegian General Workers): Møllergt. 3, POB 8704, Youngstorget, 0028 Oslo; tel. 23-06-10-50; fax 23-06-10-92; e-mail norsk@arb-mand.no; internet www.arbeidsmandsforbundet.no; f. 1895; affiliated to LO; Pres. Erna Hagensen; 34,000 mems.

Norsk Næring- og Nytelsesmiddelforbund (NNN) (Norwegian Food and Allied Workers): Arbeidersamfunnets pl. 1, 0181 Oslo; POB 8719 Youngstorget, 0028 Oslo; tel. 23-10-29-60; fax 23-10-29-61; e-mail firmapost@nnn.no; internet www.nnn.no; f. 1923; affiliated to LO; Pres. Jan-Egil Pedersen; 30,556 mems (Dec. 2008).

Norsk Post- og Kommunikasjonsforbund (Postkom) (Norwegian Union of Postal and Communications Workers): Møllergt. 10, 0179 Oslo; tel. 23-06-22-50; e-mail postkom@postkom.no; internet www.postkom.no; f. 2000; affiliated to LO; Pres. Odd-Christian Øverland; 22,000 mems.

Norsk Sjømannsforbund (Norwegian Seamen): Maritimt Hus, Rosenkrantz gt. 15-17, 0125 Oslo; POB 2000, Vika, 0125 Oslo; tel. 22-82-58-00; fax 22-33-66-18; e-mail firmapost@sjomannsunion.no; internet www.sjomannsforbundet.no; f. 1910; affiliated to LO; Pres. Jacqueline Smith; 11,500 mems.

NORWAY

Directory

Norsk Sykepleierforbund (Norwegian Nurses' Union): Tollbugt 22, POB 456, Sentrum, 0104 Oslo; tel. 22-04-33-04; fax 22-04-32-99; e-mail post@sykepleierforbundet.no; internet www.sykepleierforbundet.no; f. 1912; affiliated to Unio; Pres. LISBETH NORMANN; 87,083 mems (Jan. 2009).

Norsk Tjenestemannslag (Norwegian Civil Service Union): Møllergt. 10, 0179 Oslo; tel. 23-06-15-99; fax 23-06-15-55; e-mail post@ntl.no; internet www.ntl.no; f. 1947; affiliated to LO; Pres. TURID LILLEHEIE; 47,000 mems.

Norsk Transportarbeiderforbund (Norwegian Transport Workers): Hammersborg Torg 3, 0179 Oslo; tel. 40-64-64-64; fax 22-20-50-89; e-mail ntf@transportabeider.no; internet www.transportarbeider.no; f. 1896; affiliated to LO; Pres. ROGER HANSEN; 20,000 mems.

Utdanningsforbundet (Union of Education): Hausmannsgt 17, 0182 Oslo; tel. 24-14-20-00; fax 24-14-21-00; e-mail post@utdanningsforbundet.no; internet www.utdanningsforbundet.no; f. 2002 by merger of the Norwegian Union of Teachers (Norsk Lærerlag) and the Teachers' Union of Norway (Lærerforbundet); affiliated to Unio; Pres. HELGA HJETLAND; 146,543 mems (Jan. 2009).

Transport

RAILWAYS

In 2008 there were 4,087 km of state railways (standard gauge), of which 2,599 km were electrified.

Jernbaneverket (JBV) (Norwegian National Rail Administration): POB 4350, 2308 Hamar; tel. 22-45-50-00; fax 22-45-54-99; e-mail dsft@jbv.no; internet www.jernbaneverket.no; f. 1996; manages railway infrastructure; Dir-Gen. ELISABETH ENGER.

Norges Statsbaner AS (NSB) (Norwegian State Railways): Prinsensgt. 7–9, 0048 Oslo; tel. 23-15-00-00; fax 23-15-33-00; internet www.nsb.no; f. 1854 as private line; govt-owned; Chair. INGEBORG MOEN BORGERUD; CEO EINAR ENGER.

ROADS

In 2008 there were 93,247 km of public roads in Norway, of which 253 km were motorways and 27,216 km were national main roads.

Statens vegvesen Vegdirektoratet: Brynsengfaret 6A, POB 8142 Dep., 0033 Oslo; tel. 22-07-35-00; fax 22-07-37-68; e-mail firmapost@vegvesen.no; internet www.vegvesen.no; f. 1864; Dir TERJE MOE GUSTAVSEN.

SHIPPING

At 31 December 2009 the Norwegian merchant fleet numbered 2,033 vessels, with a combined displacement of 16.6m. grt. The total includes vessels on the Norwegian International Ship Register (established in 1987), which numbered 560 vessels at 31 December 2009, with a combined displacement of 13.9m. grt.

Port Authorities

Ålesund Port Authority: Ålesund Havn KF, Skansekaia, 6002 Ålesund; tel. 70-16-34-00; fax 70-16-34-01; e-mail post@alesund.havn.no; internet www.alesund.havn.no.

Bergen Port Authority: Bergen & Omland Havnevesen, Slottsgt. 1, 5003 Bergen; tel. 55-56-89-50; fax 55-56-89-86; e-mail bergen.havn@bergen-kommune.telemax.no; internet www.bergenhavn.no; Harbour Master GUNVALD ISAKSEN.

Bodø Port Authority: Bodø Havnevesen, POB 138, 8001 Bodø; tel. 75-58-15-80; fax 75-58-39-90; e-mail firmapost@bodo-havnevesen.no; Harbour Master TERJE DOKSRØD.

Borg Harbour Port Authority: Borg Havnevesen, Oravn 27, POB 1205 Gamle, 1631 Fredrikstad; tel. 69-35-89-00; fax 69-35-89-20; e-mail borghavnevesen@borghavn.of.no; Port Capt. SVEN-JAN JOHANSEN.

Flekkefjord Port Authority: Flekkefjord Havnevesen, Kirkegt.50, 4400 Flekkefjord; tel. 38-32-80-00; fax 38-32-80-09; e-mail petter.tagholdt@flekkefjord.kommune.no; internet flekkefjord.kommune.no; Harbour Master PETTER TAGHOLDT.

Flora Hamn og Næring KF Port Authority: POB 17, 6901 Florø; tel. 57-75-67-40; fax 57-74-09-16; e-mail hamn@flora.kommune.no; internet www.flora.kommune.no; Harbour Master NILS ARILD HOVLAND.

Grenland Port Authority: Grenland Havnevesen, POB 20, 3951 Brevik; tel. 35-93-10-00; fax 35-93-10-11; e-mail ghv@grenland-havn.no; internet www.port.of.grenland.com; Port Capt. TORJUS JOHNSEN.

Halden Port Authority: Halden Havnevesen, Wiels Pass 4, 1771 Halden; tel. 69-17-48-30; fax 69-17-46-83; e-mail post@haldenhavn.no; internet www.haldenhavn.no; Harbour Master ØYVIND JOHANNESSEN.

Hammerfest Port Authority: Hammerfest Havnevesen KF, POB 123, 9615 Hammerfest; tel. 78-40-74-00; fax 78-40-74-01; e-mail post@hammerfest.havn.no; internet www.hammerfesthavn.no; f. 1828; Harbour Master ROLL STIANSEN.

Haugesund Port Authority: Karmsund Interkommunale Havnevesen, Garpaskjaerskaien, POB 186, 55001 Haugesund; tel. 52-70-37-50; fax 52-70-37-69; e-mail postmottak@karmsund-havn.no; internet www.karmsund-havn.no.

Horten Port Authority: Borre Havnevesen, POB 167, 3192 Horten; tel. 33-03-17-17; fax 33-04-47-27; tel. horten.havnevesen@horten.kommune.no; internet www.hortenhavn.no; Harbour Master HANS CHRISTIAN GUNNENG.

Kirkenes Port Authority: Municipality of Sør-Varanger, Rådhusplassen, POB 406, 9915 Kirkenes; tel. 78-97-74-99; fax 78-97-75-89; e-mail post@kirkenes-havn.no; internet www.kirkenes-havn.no.

Kopervik Port Authority: Karmsund Havnevesen, POB 134, 4291 Kopervik; tel. 52-84-43-00; fax 52-84-43-10; e-mail postmattak@karmsund-havn.no; internet www.karmsund-havn.no; Harbour Master O. E. MAELAND.

Kragerø Port Authority: Board of Harbour Commissioners, POB 158, 3791 Kragerø; tel. 35-98-17-50; fax 35-99-13-34; e-mail post@kragero-havnevesen.no; Harbour Master Capt. BORGAR F. THORSEN.

Kristiansand Port Authority: Kristiansand Havn KF, Gravane 4, 4661 Kristiansand; tel. 38-00-60-00; fax 38-02-70-99; e-mail post@kristiansand-havn.no; internet www.kristiansand-havn.no; Port Dir STEIN E. HAARTVEIT.

Kristiansund Port Authority: Kristiansund og Nordmøre Havn IKS, Kaibakken 1, 6509 Kristiansund; tel. 40-00-65-04; fax 71-67-14-83; e-mail info@knhavn.no; internet www.knhavn.no; Harbour Master JAN OLAV BJERKESTRAND.

Larvik Port Authority: Larvik Havn KF, POB 246 Sentrum, Havnegt. 5, 3251 Larvik; tel. 33-16-57-50; fax 33-16-57-59; e-mail post@larvik.havn.no; internet www.larvik.havn.no; Port Dir JAN FREDRIK JONAS.

Malm Port Authority: Fosdalens Bergverks Aktie, 7720 Malm; tel. 74-15-71-00; fax 74-15-78-76; Agent OLAV VAARDAL.

Mandal Port of Agder Port Authority: Mandal Havnevesen KF, POB 905, 4509 Mandal; tel. 40-00-51-52; fax 38-26-34-76; e-mail mandalhavn@mandal.kommune.no; internet www.mandal-kommune.no/mandalhavn; Harbour Master JONNY O. HANSEN.

Mongstad Port Authority: Statoil Mongstad, 5954 Mongstad; tel. 56-34-40-00; fax 56-34-47-29; e-mail jja@statoilhydro.com; internet www.statoilhydro.com/mongstad; Port Capt. JON M. JAKOBSEN.

Mosjøen Port Authority: Mosjøen Havnevesen, Mosjøen 8663; tel. 75-10-18-70; fax 75-10-18-71; e-mail torbjorn.jorgensen@vefsn.kommune.no; Port Man. GUNNAR JOHANSEN.

Moss Port Authority: Moss Havnevesen, Moss Maritime Centre, POB 118, 1501 Moss; tel. 69-20-87-00; fax 69-20-87-01; e-mail firmapost@moss-havn.no; internet www.moss-havn.no; Harbour Master REIDAR MAGNUS HANSEN.

Narvik Port Authority: Narvik Havn KF, POB 627, 8508 Narvik; tel. 76-95-03-70; fax 76-95-03-84; e-mail post@narvikhavn.no; internet www.portofnarvik.com; Port Man. RUNE J. ARNØY.

Odda Port Authority: Odda Havnevesen, Opheimsgt 31, 5750 Odda; tel. 53-64-84-00; fax 53-64-12-92; e-mail svenn.berglie@odda.kommune.no; Harbour Master OLAV BJØERKE.

Orkanger Port Authority: Orkanger Havnevesen, 7300 Orkanger; tel. 72-48-00-09; fax 72-48-10-03; e-mail tom.hamborg@orkdal.kommune.no; Port Man. TOM HAMBORG.

Oslo Port Authority: Oslo Havnevesen, POB 230 Sentrum, 0103 Oslo 1; tel. 81-50-06-06; fax 23-49-26-01; e-mail postmottak@havnevesenet.oslo.kommune.no; internet www.ohv.oslo.no; Port Dir ANNE SIGRID HAMRAN.

Risør Port Authority: Risør Havnekontor, 4950 Risør; tel. 37-15-05-00; fax 37-15-00-58; Agent KJELL SKARHEIM.

Sandefjord Port Authority: Sandefjord Havnevesen, Tollbugt. 5, 3200 Sandefjord; tel. 33-45-60-38; fax 33-46-26-13; e-mail info@visitsandefjord.com; internet www.cruisesandefjord.com; Harbour Master LEIF ALLUM.

Sauda Port Authority: Sauda Havnekontor, 4200 Sauda; tel. 52-78-62-21; fax 52-78-69-68; Harbour Master HARALD HALVORSEN LOELAND.

Stavanger Port Authority: Stavanger Interkommunale Havn IKS, Nedre Strandgt. 51, 4005 Stavanger; tel. 51-50-12-00; fax 51-50-12-22; e-mail info@stavanger.havn.no; internet www.stavanger.havn.no; Port Dir BJØRN HELGOY.

Tønsberg Port Authority: Tønsberg Havnevesen, Nedre Langgate 36, 3126 Tønsberg; tel. 33-35-45-00; fax 33-33-26-75; e-mail tonsberg.havn@tonsberg.havn.no; internet www.tonsberghavn.no; Harbour Master PER SVENNAR.

Tromsø Port Authority: Tromsø Havnevesen, POB 392, 9254 Tromsø; tel. 77-66-18-50; fax 77-66-18-51; e-mail adm@tromso.havn.no; internet www.tromso.havn.no; f. 1827; Port Capt. HALVAR PETTERSEN.

Trondheim Port Authority: Trondheim Havn, Pirsenteret, 7462 Trondheim; tel. 73-99-17-00; fax 73-99-17-17; fax firmapost@trondheim.havn.no; internet www.trondheim.havn.no; Port Capt. SIGURD KLEIVEN.

Vardø Port Authority: Vardø Havn KF, POB 50, 9951 Vardø; tel. 78-98-72-76; fax 78-98-78-28; tel. vardhavn@online.no; internet www.vardoport.no; Harbour Master INGOLF ERIKSEN.

Shipping Organizations

Nordisk Skibsrederforening (Nordisk Defence Club): Kristinelundvn 22, POB 3033 Elisenberg, 0207 Oslo; tel. 22-13-56-00; fax 22-43-00-35; e-mail post@nordisk.no; internet www.nordisk.no; f. 1889; Pres. MORTEN WERRING; Man. Dir GEORG SCHEEL.

Norges Rederiforbund (Norwegian Shipowners' Asscn): POB 1452 Vika, 0116 Oslo; tel. 22-40-15-00; fax 22-40-15-15; e-mail post@rederi.no; internet www.rederi.no; f. 1909; Dir-Gen. STURLA HENRIKSEN.

Norsk Skipsmeglerforbund (Norwegian Shipbrokers' Asscn): Rådhusgt. 25, 0158 Oslo; tel. 22-33-02-00; fax 22-42-74-13; e-mail mail@shipbroker.no; internet www.shipbroker.no; f. 1919; Pres. LARS PETTER STORFJORD; Gen. Man. KNUT FRODE ERIKSEN; 138 mems.

Det Norske Veritas (DNV): Veritasvn 1, POB 300, 1322 Høvik; tel. 67-57-99-00; f. 1864; global provider of services for managing risk; acts on behalf of 130 national maritime authorities; CEO HENRIK O. MADSEN.

Rederienes Landsforening (Federation of Norwegian Coastal Shipping): Essendropsgt. 6, POB 5201 Majorstua, 0302 Oslo; tel. 23-08-85-60; fax 23-08-85-61; e-mail rlf@rlf.no; internet www.rlf.no; Man. Dir HARALD THOMASSEN.

Principal Companies

Actinor Shipping ASA: Rådhusgt. 27, 0158 Oslo; tel. 22-42-78-30; fax 22-42-72-04; Pres. ALF OLSEN.

Bergshav Management AS: POB 8, 4891 Grimstad; tel. 37-25-63-00; fax 37-25-63-01; e-mail mgmt@bergshav.com; internet www.bergshav.com; Chair. ATLE BERGSHAVEN.

Bona Shipping AS: Rådhusgt. 27, POB 470 Sentrum, 0105 Oslo; tel. 22-31-00-00; fax 22-31-00-01; internet www.bona.no; Pres. RAGNAR BELCK-OLSEN.

BW Gas ASA: Drammensvn 106, POB 2800 Solli, 0204 Oslo; tel. 22-12-05-05; fax 22-12-05-00; e-mail bwgas@bwgas.com; internet www.bwgas.com; f. 1935; fmrly Bergesen d.y. ASA; Chair. MORTEN SIG. BERGESEN; Man. Dir SVEIN ERIK AMUNDSEN.

Grieg Shipping AS: POB 781, 5804 Bergen; tel. 55-57-66-00; fax 55-57-68-55; internet www.grieg.no; Chair. ELISABETH GRIEG.

Leif Høegh & Co ASA: Wergelandsvn 7, POB 2596 Solli, 0203 Oslo; tel. 22-86-97-00; fax 22-20-14-08; e-mail ihc@hoegh.no; internet www.hoegh.no; f. 1927; vessels for the transport of liquefied gas, ores and other bulk materials, car and ro-ro ships and reefers; world-wide services; Chief Exec. THOR J. GUTTORMSEN; Chair. WESTYE HØEGH.

Jahre-Wallem AS: Strandpromenaden 9, POB 271, 3201 Sandefjord; tel. 33-48-44-44; fax 33-48-44-43; e-mail jawa@jawa.no; Dir HENRIK LIAN.

Jebsens Management AS: POB 4145 Dreggen, 5015 Bergen; tel. 55-31-03-20; fax 55-31-72-70; f. 1929; services in Scandinavia, and to Europe, Far East, Australia and the Americas; Owner ATLE JEBSEN.

Torvald Klaveness & Co AS: Harbitzalleen 2A, POB 182 Skøyen, 0212 Oslo; tel. 22-52-60-00; fax 22-50-67-31; e-mail management@klaveness.com; internet www.klaveness.com; Chair. TOM ERIK KLAVENESS; Man. Dir TROND HARALD KLAVENESS.

Knutsen OAS Shipping AS: Smedasundet 40, POB 2017, 5504 Haugesund; tel. 52-70-40-00; fax 52-70-40-40; e-mail firmapost@knutsenoas.com; internet www.knutsenoas.com; Man. JENS ULLTVEIT MOE.

AS J. Ludwig Mowinckels Rederi: Bradbenken 1, POB 4070 Dreggen, 5835 Bergen; tel. 55-21-63-00; fax 55-21-63-05; e-mail mailbox@jlmr.no; internet www.jlmr.no; f. 1898; tankers and cargo services; Man. Dir BØRGE ROSENBERG.

Norbroker Shipping & Trading AS: POB 34, 4401 Flekkefjord; Strandgt. 36, 4400 Flekkefjord; tel. 38-32-61-00; fax 38-32-61-01; e-mail drycargo@norbroker.no; internet www.norbroker.no; Man. Dir ARNT IVAR BJOERNELI.

Odfjell ASA: Conrad Mohrsveg 29, 5892 Bergen; POB 6101 Postterminalen, 5892 Bergen; tel. 55-27-00-00; fax 55-28-47-41; e-mail bgo.mail@odfjell.com; internet www.odfjell.no; f. 1916; transportation and storage of liquid chemicals; Chair. BERNT DANIEL ODFJELL.

Fred.Olsen Marine Services AS: Prinsensgt. 2B, POB 374 Sentrum, 0101 Oslo; tel. 22-34-11-00; fax 22-42-13-14; e-mail foms@foms.no; internet www.fredolsen-marine.com; Man. Dir LEIF LAURITZEN.

OSM Ship Management AS: POB 69, 4661 Kristiansand; tel. 38-04-12-00; fax 38-04-12-01; e-mail osm.krs@osm.no; internet www.osm.no; part of OSM Group; frmly Rasmussen Maritime Services AS; Man. Dir OIVIND STAERK.

Det Stavangerske Dampskibsselskab: POB 848, 4004 Stavanger; tel. 51-84-56-00; fax 51-84-56-01; e-mail mail@dsd-shipping.no; tel. www.dsd-shipping.no; Chair. HENRIK AGER-HANSSEN.

Uglands Rederi AS: POB 128, 4891 Grimstad; tel. 37-29-26-00; fax 37-04-47-22; e-mail jjuc@jjuc.no; internet www.jjuc.no; f. 1930; part of J. J. Ugland Cos.

A. Wilhelmsen Gruppen AS: Beddingen 8, Aker Brygge, POB 1583 Vika, 0118 Oslo; tel. 22-01-42-00; fax 22-01-43-72; e-mail thagen@awilco.no; Chair. ARNE WILHELMSEN; Man. Dir KNUT INGER NOSSEN.

Wilh. Wilhelmsen ASA: Strandvn 20, POB 33, 1324 Lysaker; tel. 67-58-40-00; fax 67-58-40-80; e-mail ww@wilhelmsen.com; internet www.wilhelmsen.com; f. 1861; regular fast freight services worldwide; Chair. WILHELM WILHELMSEN; Man. Dir INGAR SKAUG.

CIVIL AVIATION

In 2008 there were 46 airports in Norway, the principal international airport being Gardermoen Airport, 47 km north of Oslo.

Avinor AS: POB 150, 2061 Gardermoen; Oslo Atrium, Christian Fredriksplass 6, 0154 Oslo; tel. 81-53-05-50; fax 67-03-00-01; e-mail post@avinor.no; internet www.avinor.no; f. 2003; state-owned; owns and operates 46 airports in Norway and responsible for air traffic control services; Chair. INGE K. HANSEN; CEO SVERRE QUALE.

Luftfartstilsynet (Civil Aviation Authority): POB 243, 8001 Bodø; tel. 75-58-50-00; fax 75-58-50-05; e-mail postmottak@caa.no; internet www.caa.no; f. 2000; independent administrative body under the Ministry of Transport and Communications; Dir-Gen. HEINE RICHARDSEN.

Principal Airlines

SAS Norge ASA: 0800 Oslo; tel. 64-81-77-00; fax 67-58-78-77; internet www.sas.no; f. 2004 as SAS Braathens; present name adopted 2007; wholly owned subsidiary of the Scandinavian Airlines System (SAS) Group; Gen. Man. OLA H. STRAND.

Scandinavian Airlines System (SAS): Head Office: Snarøyvn 57, 0080 Oslo; tel. 64-81-60-50; e-mail cr@sas.no; internet www.sas.no; f. 1946; the national carrier of Denmark, Norway and Sweden; consortium owned two-sevenths by SAS Danmark A/S, two-sevenths by SAS Norge ASA and three-sevenths by SAS Sverige AB; parent org. 50% owned by the Govt and 50% by private shareholders; SAS group includes the consortium and the subsidiaries in which the consortium has a majority or otherwise controlling interest; the Board consists of 2 members from each of the parent cos and the chairmanship rotates among the 3 national chairmen on an annual basis; strategic alliance with Lufthansa (Germany) formed in 1995; Chair. FRITZ H. SCHUR; Pres. and CEO RICKARD GUSTAFSON.

Norwegian Air Shuttle ASA: Oksenøyvn 10A, POB 115, 1330 Fornebu; tel. 67-59-30-00; fax 67-59-30-01; e-mail post@norwegian.no; internet www.norwegian.no; f. 1966; present name since 1993; low-cost carrier, offering flights to domestic and European destinations; CEO BJØRN KJOS.

Widerøes Flyveselskap AS: Langstranda 6, POB 257, 8001 Bodø; tel. 75-51-35-00; fax 75-51-35-81; e-mail kundservice@wideroe.no; internet www.wideroe.no; f. 1934; subsidiary of Scandinavian Airlines System (SAS) Group; scheduled domestic service and flights to destinations in Denmark, Russia, Sweden and the United Kingdom; Pres. and CEO LARS KOBBERSTAD.

Tourism

Norway is a popular resort for tourists who prefer holidays in rugged, peaceful surroundings. It is also a centre for winter sports. In 2008 visitor arrivals totalled 4.9m., while receipts from tourism amounted to US $5,559m.

Innovasjon Norge (Innovation Norway): Akersgt 13, POB 448 Sentrum, 0104 Oslo; tel. 22-00-25-00; fax 22-00-25-01; e-mail post@invanor.no; internet www.visitnorway.com; f. 2004 to replace Norges Turistråd (Norwegian Tourist Board), Norges Eksportråd (Norwegian Trade Council), Statens nærings- og distriktsutviklingsfond (SND-Industrial and Regional Development Fund) and Statens Veiledningskontor for Oppfinnere (SVO-Government Consultative Office for Inventors); state-owned; operates in all Norwegian counties and more than 30 countries world-wide; Pres. KJELL A. STOREIDE; Man. Dir GUNN OVESEN.

NORWAY

Defence

Norway is a member of the North Atlantic Treaty Organization (NATO), and became an associate member of Western European Union (WEU) in 1992. Every male is liable for 12 months' national service at the age of 19. Periodical refresher programmes are also compulsory until the age of 44. The total strength of the armed forces, as assessed at November 2010, was 24,450 (including 7,700 conscripts): army 8,900 (4,400 conscripts); navy 3,750 (1,450 conscripts); air force 3,550 (including 850 conscripts); home guard 500; and central support, administration and command 7,750 (conscripts 1,000). There is also a mobilization reserve of 45,190 (army 270, navy 320, home guard 44,250 and central support 350). In November 2004 the European Union (EU) ministers responsible for defence agreed to create 13 'battlegroups' (each numbering about 1,500 men), which could be deployed at short notice to crisis areas around the world. The EU battlegroups, two of which were to be ready for deployment at any one time, following a rotational schedule, reached full operational capacity from 1 January 2007. In December 2004 the Storting gave qualified approval for Norway's participation, with Finland and Sweden, in a joint Nordic Battlegroup, which was subsequently joined by Estonia and Ireland. Norway provides 150 of the group's 2,850 soldiers (most of whom are provided by Sweden).

Defence Expenditure: Budget estimated at 39,200m. kroner for 2011.

Chief of Defence: Gen. HARALD SUNDE.

Chief of Defence Staff: Vice-Adm. JAN EIRIK FINSETH.

Chief of the Army Staff: Maj.-Gen. PER SVERRET OPEDAL.

Chief of the Naval Staff: Rear Adm. HAAKON BRUUN-HANSSEN.

Chief of the Air Force Staff: Maj.-Gen. FINN KRISTIAN HANNESTAD.

Chief of the Home Guard Staff: Maj.-Gen. KRISTIN LUND.

Education

The Ministry of Education and Research has overall responsibility for education and manages tertiary education directly. Compulsory education is supervised by the municipal authorities, while upper secondary education is managed by the county authorities. Non-compulsory pre-primary education is offered to children less than six years of age. Compulsory education begins at six years of age and lasts for 10 years. Elementary education is divided into two phases. The primary phase (*Barnetrinnet*) is meant for children between the ages of six and 12 years, and the lower secondary phase (*Ungdomstrinnet*) for children between 13 and 16 years of age. Completion of lower secondary entitles pupils to transfer to an upper secondary school (*Videregående skole*) for a course lasting three years. Primary enrolment in 2007/08 included 99% of children in the relevant age-group, while the comparable rate for secondary enrolment was 96%. Adults who did not complete compulsory education, or who wish to refresh their competence, have a statutory right to lower secondary education. This also applies to special education. Upon completion of a three-year course at an upper secondary school, pupils may seek admission to one of Norway's seven universities or other colleges. In 2008/09 there were 77 institutes of higher education (including universities) in Norway. From the age of 25 years adults have the right to be assessed for admittance to higher education based on non-formal learning. A broader system of higher professional education has been organized on a regional basis, including colleges of education and technology. At 1 October 2009 91,783 students were enrolled at universities and their equivalent. Expenditure on education by all levels of government in 2010 was estimated at 148,323m. kroner (equivalent to 12.9% of total government expenditure).

NORWEGIAN EXTERNAL TERRITORIES
SVALBARD

Introductory Survey

LOCATION AND CLIMATE

The Svalbard archipelago is the northernmost part of the Kingdom of Norway. It lies in the Arctic Sea, 657 km north of mainland Norway, between latitudes 74°N and 81°N and longitudes 10°E and 35°E, comprising a total area of 61,022 sq km (23,561 sq miles). The group consists of nine principal islands—Spitsbergen (formerly Vestspitsbergen), the main island, Kvitøya, Edgeøya, Barentsøya, Nordaustlandet, Prins Karls Forland, Kong Karls Land, Hopen and Bjørnøya (Bear Island), some 204 km to the south of the main island—together with numerous small islands. Mild Atlantic winds lessen the severity of the Arctic climate, but almost 60% of the land area is covered with glaciers. Average temperatures range from −16°C (3°F) to 6°C (43°F), and precipitation in the lowlands averages some 200 mm per year.

CONTEMPORARY POLITICAL HISTORY

The existence of Svalbard has probably been known since Viking exploration in the 12th century. There were conflicting claims to sovereignty by Britain, the Netherlands and Denmark-Norway in the 17th century, when the area was an important centre for whale hunting, but interest subsequently lapsed until the early years of the 20th century, when coal deposits were discovered. On 9 February 1920 14 nations signed a treaty recognizing Norwegian sovereignty over Svalbard. International rights of access and economic exploitation were agreed, but the use of the islands for bellicose purposes and the construction of fortifications were expressly forbidden. Svalbard has been part of the Kingdom of Norway since it was formally incorporated in 1925. Owing to its international rights of access, Svalbard, unlike mainland Norway, is not covered by the terms of the Schengen agreement of the European Union (EU), which abolishes border controls between signatories. In order to aid compliance with the Schengen agreement, in February 2011 the Norwegian authorities introduced identity controls for all arrivals in Svalbard, including Norwegian nationals.

In 1941 the population was evacuated by Allied forces for the duration of the war, and three years later the USSR, to which Svalbard was of considerable strategic interest, unsuccessfully sought Norway's agreement to a revision of the 1920 treaty whereby part of the archipelago would become a Soviet-Norwegian condominium. Russia currently maintains a helicopter station and a mobile radar station adjoining its coal-mining settlement at Barentsburg on Spitsbergen. Russia (and, before it, the USSR) refused to recognize Norway's unilateral declaration of a fisheries protection zone around Svalbard from 1977.

Particularly since a Royal Decree of 1971, the Norwegian administration has endeavoured to protect the flora, fauna and environment of Svalbard. The protected areas, which total 39,815 sq km of land, or 64% of the land area, and 76,293 km of sea, include seven national parks, the most recently created (September 2005) being at Indre Wijdefjorden in northern Spitsbergen. From April 2007 visitors to Svalbard were required to pay an 'environment fee', the income from which was to be added to the territory's environmental protection fund.

Apart from a small permanent research station established by Poland, only Norway and Russia maintain permanent settlements on Svalbard. In order to continue Norwegian occupation of Svalbard, thus ensuring its future as a Norwegian territory and protecting it from potential, rival claims for sovereignty, notably from Russia, in 2000 the Svalbard administration proposed the opening of a new coal mine on Spitsbergen to exploit newly discovered reserves. Svalbard has also been promoted as a centre for scientific research; at the end of 2000 there were more than 20 scientific stations from foreign countries on the islands. In January 2004 representatives of the Norwegian Ministry of Foreign Affairs met with Russia's Deputy Minister of Foreign Affairs to discuss possible bilateral co-operation in Svalbard, in the areas of energy, fisheries and environmental protection. In February 2008 the Svalbard Global Seed Vault was inaugurated by the Norwegian Prime Minister, Jens Stoltenberg. Established at a depth of 130 m in the permafrost of a mountain at Longyearbyen, the vault was designed to store up to 4.5m. seed samples from around the world, in order to preserve biological diversity for future generations.

In November 2001 Norwegians resident on Spitsbergen conducted, for the first time, an election for a local council. The new Longyearbyen Council (Longyearbyen Lokalstyre) replaced the incumbent Svalbard Council, which had been partly appointed by the state-owned mining company, Store Norske Spitsbergen Kulkompani. The new 15-seat Council was to exercise only limited power in issues relating to health, education and the Church, which would all continue to be controlled by the state. The rate of participation in the local election was only 51.5% of the electorate; a multi-party grouping won eight seats on the Council, while Det norske Arbeiderparti (DnA—Norwegian Labour Party) secured six seats; Høyre (Conservative) took the remaining seat. At the elections held in October 2003, DnA won six seats on the Council, while the multi-party grouping won five seats; the Fremskrittspartiet (FrP—Progress Party) and Høyre each won two seats. The Council's mandate was increased from two to four years. DnA again emerged as the largest party following the elections of October 2007, winning seven seats on the Council; the multi-party grouping won four seats, while Høyre received three seats and the FrP lost its representation. The rate of voter participation was recorded at just 40.3% of the electorate.

CONSTITUTION AND GOVERNMENT

Svalbard has been part of the Kingdom of Norway since it was formally incorporated in 1925. The territory is administered by a Sysselmann (Governor), resident at Longyearbyen, on Spitsbergen, which is the administrative centre of the archipelago. The Sysselmann is responsible to the Polar Department of the Ministry of Justice and the Police. The Norwegian Polar Institute acts in an advisory capacity to the administration. Svalbard lies within the same judicial jurisdiction as the city of Tromsø.

In accordance with the Svalbard Treaty of 1920, the Norwegian Government prescribed a mining code in 1925, regulating all mineral prospecting and exploitation in the islands and their territorial waters extending to 4 nautical miles (7.4 km). The Mining Code is administered by the Directorate for Mineral Management of Mines at Svalbard (Direktoratet for mineralforvaltning med Bergmesteren for Svalbard).

ECONOMIC AFFAIRS

The total population of Svalbard at 1 July 2010 was 2,529, of whom 2,071 were resident in Norwegian settlements (including 324 foreign nationals), 449 were in Russian settlements and 9 in the Polish settlement. There are limited recreational, transport, financial and educational facilities on Svalbard. There are hospitals in the capital, Longyearbyen (which had a population of 2,075 in March 2007), and in Barentsburg.

Mining and quarrying is the dominant industry, with coal the islands' main product. In 2006 2,419,745 metric tons were shipped from mines on Svalbard (2,331,605 tons from Norwegian mines). The Norwegian state-owned company Store Norske Spitsbergen Grubekompani (SNSG) directly employs some 370 people. SNSG produced some 2.6m. tons of coal in 2009, a decline of 23.0% compared to the previous year. SNSG's most productive mine, at Svea Nord, about 60 km from Longyearbyen, was opened in 2001 to exploit significant newly discovered reserves of coal. The coal was of high calorific value and therefore burnt more cleanly than normal coal. In April 2011 SNSG received permission from the Svalbard Sysselmann (Governor) to open a new mine at Lunkefjell, some 2 km from Svea Nord. Subject to approval by the Norwegian Ministry of the Environment, the Lunkefjell mine was scheduled to begin production in 2014, in which year stocks at Svea Nord were expected to be exhausted. Svea is extremely well-placed for exporting coal to Europe, as it is located only 10 km from the port; the mine is linked to the port by road, and in 2004 a conveyor belt was constructed to transport the coal directly to the ships. A second Norwegian coal-mining camp, Gruve 7, some 15 km from Longyearbyen, is used largely to supply a coal-burning power station, which provides electricity for Longyearbyen.

Russia had only one camp on Svalbard in early 2010, at Barentsburg; in 2006 88,140 tons of coal were produced at Barentsburg and shipped to Russia. Barentsburg, located about 40 km south-west of Longyearbyen, with a population of 470 in January 2009, has its own coal-fired power station.

Deep drillings for petroleum have been carried out by Norwegian and other companies, but no commercial results have been reported. In 2003 Store Norske Gull, a subsidiary of the Store Norske group, was founded in order to explore the potential for gold mining in Svalbard. In January 2011 the company reported that gold deposits had been discovered, although it was not yet clear if they were significant enough to be commercially exploited. Svalbard's other mineral resources include reserves of phosphate, asbestos, iron ore, anhydrite, limestone and various sulphides.

Total turnover in Svalbard in 2009 was 3,968m. kroner. The construction sector comprised 15 companies in 2009, which had a turnover of 377.8m. kroner in that year, accounting for 9.5% of the total.

NORWEGIAN EXTERNAL TERRITORIES — *Svalbard*

Tourism has been encouraged on Svalbard; cruise ships make stops at the islands and there is also a small industry in skiing and trekking across the wilderness. In 2010 visitors spent a total of 76,713 nights in Svalbard, of which 43,570 were spent by those visiting for recreational purposes. The services sector has grown substantially in recent years, particularly in the areas of education and research. Many jobs are connected to Norwegian government organizations, such as Statsbygg, the state-owned building agency, and Longyearbyen Elementary and High School.

For 2005 the Svalbard budget was 195.2m. kroner, of which 135.9m. kroner was a direct subsidy from the Norwegian state budget. Svalbard raises some revenue from the sale of hunting and fishing licences.

Statistical Survey

Source: Statistics Norway, Kongensgt. 6, Oslo; tel. 21-09-00-00; fax 21-09-49-73; e-mail biblioteket@ssb.no; internet www.ssb.no.

AREA AND POPULATION

Area: 61,020 sq km (23,561 sq miles).

Population (official estimate at mid-2010): 2,529 (Norwegian settlements 2,071—including 324 foreign nationals, Russian settlements 449, Polish settlement 9).

Density (at mid-2010): 0.04 per sq km.

Population by Age and Sex (official estimates at mid-2010, Norwegian settlements only): *0–14:* 351 (males 183, females 168); *15–64:* 1,680 (males 965, females 715); *65 and over:* 40 (males 28, females 12); *Total* 2,071 (males 1,176, females 895).

Economically Active Population (2003): Mining and quarrying 233; Manufacturing 8; Construction 194; Wholesale and retail trade 107; Hotels and restaurants 100; Transport and storage 177; Supporting and auxiliary transport activities 120; Public administration 147; Education, health and social work 133; Other community, social and personal service activities 15; *Total* 1,234.

MINING

Coal Shipments ('000 metric tons): 2,991.2 (Norwegian mines 2,859.1) in 2004; 1,863 (Norwegian mines 1,768.3) in 2005; 2,419.7 (Norwegian mines 2,331.6) in 2006.

FINANCE

(Norwegian currency is used)

Budget (million kroner, 2005): Estimated revenue 195.2 (incl. direct grant of 135.9 from central Govt); Budgeted expenditure 195.2.

TRANSPORT

Road Traffic (vehicles registered at 31 December 2004): Passenger cars 930; Buses 41; Goods vehicles 394; Mopeds and motorcycles 130; Snow scooters 1,468.

Civil Aviation (2004, metric tons unless otherwise specified): Passengers (number) 92,958; Goods received 541; Goods sent 42; Mail received 341; Mail sent 42.

TOURISM

Overnight Stays (Longyearbyen): 77,926 in 2004; 76,570 in 2005; 83,049 in 2006.

EDUCATION

(2006, unless otherwise indicated)

Pre-primary: Schools 2; Teachers 29; Pupils 106.

Primary and Lower Secondary: Schools 1; Pupils 198.

Upper Secondary (2004): Schools 1; Pupils 55.

Directory

The Government

(May 2011)

ADMINISTRATION

Governor (Sysselmann): ODD OLSEN INGERØ.

OFFICES

Office of the Governor: Kontoret til Sysselmannen på Svalbard, POB 633, 9171 Longyearbyen, Svalbard; tel. 79-02-43-00; fax 79-02-11-66; e-mail firmapost@sysselmannen.no; internet www.sysselmannen.no.

Ministry of Justice and the Police (Polar Affairs Department): Akersgt. 42, POB 8005 Dep., 0030 Oslo; tel. 22-24-56-01; fax 22-24-95-30; e-mail postmottak@jd.dep.no; responsible for the administration of Svalbard and Jan Mayen, and for the Norwegian Antarctic dependencies.

Norsk Polarinstitutt på Svalbard (Norwegian Polar Institute in Svalbard): Forskningsparken, POB 505, 9171 Longyearbyen, Svalbard; tel. 79-02-26-00; fax 79-02-26-04; e-mail post@npolar.no; internet npweb.npolar.no; f. 1928 as Norges Svalbard- og Ishavsundersøkelser; adopted present name and expanded functions in 1948; branch of Norwegian Polar Institute, Tromsø; mapping and research institute; responsible for advising Govt on matters concerning Svalbard, Jan Mayen and the Antarctic dependencies; monitors and investigates environment of the territories; organizes regular Antarctic research expeditions; establishes and maintains aids to navigation in Svalbard waters; Dir JAN-GUNNAR WINTHER.

Norsk Polarinstitutts Forskningsstasjon (Norwegian Polar Institute Research Station): Sverdrupstasjonen, 9173 Ny-Alesund, Svalbard; tel. 79-02-74-00; fax 79-02-70-02; permanent research base in Svalbard.

LONGYEARBYEN COUNCIL

Longyearbyen Lokalstyre: POB 350, 9171 Longyearbyen, Svalbard; tel. 79-02-21-50; fax 79-02-21-51; e-mail postmottak@lokalstyre.no; internet www.lokalstyre.no; f. 2002; first locally elected body in Svalbard; replaced Svalbard Council; 15 mems; Leader KJELL MORK.

Svalbard, as an integral part of the Kingdom of Norway, has provision for its Norwegian inhabitants to participate in the national elections. For judicial matters Svalbard lies in the jurisdiction of the Nord-Troms District Court (based in Tromsø). The state Evangelical Lutheran Church provides religious services.

Press

There is only one newspaper published in the Svalbard archipelago.

Svalbardposten: POB 503, 9171 Longyearbyen, Svalbard; tel. 79-02-47-00; fax 79-02-47-01; e-mail post@svalbardposten.no; internet www.svalbardposten.no; f. 1948; weekly; Editor-in-Chief BIRGER AMUNDSEN; circ. 3,380 (2004).

Finance

Norwegian currency is used. Most banking facilities are available.

Sparebank 1 Nord-Norge: POB 518, 9171 Longyearbyen, Svalbard; tel. 79-02-29-10; fax 79-02-29-11; e-mail kundesenter@snn.no; internet www.snn.no; Man. Dir HANS OLAV KARDE; savings bank.

Trade and Industry

Bydrift Longyearbyen A/S: POB 350, 9171 Longyearbyen, Svalbard; tel. 79-02-21-50; fax 79-02-23-01; e-mail bydrift@lokalstyre.no; internet www.lokalstyre.no; state-owned; operates most local services, incl. utilities, and undertakes infrastructure devt; Admin. Dir IVAR UNDHEIM.

Direktoratet for mineralforvaltning med Bergmesteren for Svalbard (Directorate for Mineral Management of Mines at Svalbard): POB 520,9171 Longyearbyen; tel. 79-02-12-92; fax 79-02-14-24; e-mail per.brekke@dirmin.no; from 2003 the Commissioner of Mines at Svalbard was merged into the Norwegian Directorate of Mining; name changed from the Directorate of Mines at Svalbard in Jan. 2010; Dir PER ZAKKEN BREKKE.

Store Norske Spitsbergen Kulkompani A/S (SNSK): POB 613, 9171 Longyearbyen, Svalbard; tel. 79-02-52-00; fax 79-02-18-41; e-mail firmapost@snsk.no; internet www.snsk.no; state-owned; develops the Store Norske group's proprietary and coal mining rights on Svalbard, with the exception of the Svea area; Chair. BÅRD MIKKELSEN; CEO BJØRN ARNESTAD.

Store Norske Spitsbergen Grubekompani A/S (SNSG): f. 2002; manages all assets, rights, contractual obligations and liabilities in connection with the Svea Nord mine, responsible for coal production and sales in Longyearbyen and Svea, and for exploration at both its own and SNSK's claims; 350 employees.

Store Norske Boliger A/S: f. 2002; manages the group's accommodation in Longyearbyen and some of the accommodation in Svea.

Transport

The airport near Longyearbyen was opened in 1975. SAS operates services to Oslo, via Tromsø, up to six times per week. There are air strips at Ny-Ålesund and Svea, and a Russian helicopter facility at Barentsburg. Apart from helicopters, and a fixed-wing service between Longyearbyen and Ny-Ålesund, internal traffic is little developed.

AIRPORT

Svalbard Airport: POB 550, 9170 Longyearbyen, Svalbard; tel. 67-03-54-00; fax 67-03-54-01; e-mail ole.m.rambech@avinor.no; internet www.avinor.no/lufthavn/svalbard; f. 1975; owned by Avinor; Man. OLE M. RAMBECH.

Tourism

Svalbard Reiseliv AS: POB 232, 9171 Longyearbyen, Svalbard; tel. 79-02-55-50; fax 79-02-55-51; e-mail info@svalbard.net; internet www.svalbard.net; f. 2001; represents and promotes tourism-related enterprises in Svalbard; produces brochures for tourists and collates statistics.

JAN MAYEN

The lofty volcanic island of Jan Mayen is located in the Arctic Ocean, some 910 km west-north-west of Bodø on the Norwegian mainland, 610 km north-north-east of Iceland and 480 km east of Greenland (Denmark). The island is 53 km in length and has a total area of 377 sq km (145 sq miles). The highest point is the summit of Mt Beerenberg, which is an active volcano (2,277 m above sea level). The climate is severe, cold and usually misty.

The sea north and west of Jan Mayen (which was frequented by various whalers and hunters for a brief period in the 17th century) has been an important area for sealing by Norwegians since the mid-19th century. Partly to assist their navigation, the Norwegian Meteorological Institute instigated activities on the island in the early 20th century. In 1922 Jan Mayen was declared annexed by the Institute, and on 8 May 1929 Norwegian sovereignty was proclaimed by Royal Decree. The island was made an integral part of the Kingdom of Norway by the Jan Mayen Act of 1930. Jan Mayen is not included in the Svalbard Treaty.

The island has no known exploitable mineral resources and is largely barren. However, geologists believe that the Jan Mayen Ridge, which lies beneath the surrounding waters, may contain reserves of petroleum. Fishing in the surrounding waters is intermittently productive. In 1970 there was a violent volcanic eruption on the island, the first since the early 19th century. In the course of the first few days of the eruption a huge glacier melted and millions of cubic metres of ice disappeared as steam. Lava poured into the sea and formed about 3.5 sq km of new land. The last volcanic eruption on the island occurred in 1985. The island's main use remains as a meteorological, navigational and radio station.

During the Second World War Jan Mayen remained the only part of Norway under Norwegian rule, following the German invasion of the mainland. Despite some conflict, the Norwegian Government and its allies maintained the strategic meteorological station and established a radio-locating station on the island during the war.

In 1946 a new base was established at Nordlaguna, both as a meteorological and a coastal radio station. As a result of a North Atlantic defence co-operation exercise in 1959–60, a long-range navigation (LORAN) network was established, with one base on Jan Mayen. At the same time, it was decided to build an airstrip near the new LORAN C base, and in 1962 the personnel of the weather and coastal radio services also moved to the same area.

Following negotiations with Iceland in 1980, the Norwegian Government declared an economic zone extending for 200 nautical miles (370 km) around the coast of Jan Mayen. In 1981 a further agreement was made with Iceland, regarding mineral and fishing rights. A dispute with Denmark, acting on behalf of Greenland, concerning the delimitation of maritime economic zones between Greenland and Jan Mayen was referred by Denmark to the International Court of Justice (based in The Hague, Netherlands) in 1988. The Court delivered its judgment in June 1993, deciding that 57% of the disputed area belonged to Norway. A subsequent accord on maritime delimitation, agreed between the Governments of Norway, Greenland and Iceland in November 1997, established the boundaries of a 1,934-sq km area of Arctic sea that had been excluded from the terms of the 1993 settlement.

In September 2009, following a visit to the island by the Minister of Petroleum and Energy, Terje Riis-Johansen, the Norwegian Government initiated the process of opening the territorial waters surrounding Jan Mayen to possible future petroleum exploration. Earlier in 2009 the Icelandic Government had offered petroleum exploration licences for the portion of the undersea Jan Mayen Ridge that lay within Iceland's territorial waters. In October 2010 the Norwegian Government allocated 10m. kroner towards an environmental impact assessment in connection with the proposed opening of the Jan Mayen waters to petroleum exploration; as part of these investigations, the Norwegian Petroleum Directorate (Oljedirektoratet) intended to carry out seismic surveys in mid-2011.

The commanding officer in charge of the LORAN C base is the chief administrative official of the island. The officer is responsible for the 15–25 inhabitants (who usually remain on the island for only one year at a time), and is accountable to the Chief of Police for Salten district (headquartered in Bodø), and the Ministry of Justice and the Police (as in Svalbard). The commander may grant permission for visits of not more than 24 hours. For longer visits, the Chief of Police or the Ministry must approve the application. Visits are normally allowed only for scientific purposes and only if private provision has been made for transport. There is no public transport or accommodation on Jan Mayen.

Station Commander: OLE ØISETH, LORAN C Base, 8099 Jan Mayen; tel. 32-17-79-00; fax 32-17-79-01; e-mail post@www.jan-mayen.no; internet www.jan-mayen.no.

Chief of Police (Salten district): TONE VANGEN, Kongensgt. 81, POB 1023, 8001 Bodø; tel. 75-54-58-00; e-mail post.salten@politiet.no; internet www.politi.no/salten.

For the Ministry of Justice and the Police and the Norsk Polarinstitutt (Norwegian Polar Institute), see under Svalbard.

NORWEGIAN DEPENDENCIES

Norway's so-called 'Antarctic' dependencies are all uninhabited and were acquired as a result of Norwegian whaling interests in the region since the 1890s. The three territories are dependencies of the Kingdom of Norway, and are administered by the Polar Affairs Department of the Ministry of Justice and the Police, with the advice of the Norsk Polarinstitutt (Norwegian Polar Institute: for details, see under Svalbard) and the assistance of the Ministry of the Environment.

Bouvetøya

Bouvetøya (Bouvet Island) is a volcanic island in the South Atlantic Ocean, some 2,400 km south-west of the Cape of Good Hope (South Africa) and 1,600 km north of Antarctica. The island lies north of the Antarctic Circle (it is not, therefore, encompassed by the terms of the Antarctic Treaty). Bouvetøya has an area of 49 sq km, but about 93% of the surface is covered by ice. The climate is maritime antarctic, with a mean annual temperature of −1°C and a persistent heavy fog.

Regular landings on the island occurred only as part of Norwegian Antarctic expeditions in the 1920s and 1930s. Bouvetøya was claimed for Norway in 1927, placed under its sovereignty in 1928, and declared a Norwegian dependency in 1930. A Royal Decree of 1971 declared the entire island to be a nature reserve. An automatic weather station was established in 1977, and the island is regularly visited by Norwegian scientific expeditions.

Dronning Maud Land

Dronning Maud Land (Queen Maud Land) is that sector of the Antarctic continent lying between the longitudes of 20°W (adjoining the British Antarctic Territory to the west) and 45°E (neighbouring the Australian Antarctic Territory). The territory is, in area, several times the size of Norway, and 98% of its surface is covered by ice. The climate is severe, the usual temperature always being below 0°C and, in the winter months of mid-year, falling to −60°C on the coast and −88°C inland. The territory's coast is divided into five named sectors (the exact delimitations of which, and of the territory as a whole, have varied at different periods): Kronprinsesse Märtha Kyst (Crown Princess Märtha Coast), Prinsesse Astrid Kyst, Prinsesse Ragnhild Kyst, Prins Harald Kyst and Kronprins Olav Kyst.

The first Norwegian territorial claims in Antarctica were made in 1929, following many years of Norwegian involvement in the exploration and survey of the continent. Further claims were made in 1931 and 1936–37. These claims were formalized by the Norwegian authorities, and the land placed under their sovereignty, only in 1939. The extent of Dronning Maud Land then received its current limits, between the British and Australian claims. Norway now follows a policy which upholds its claim to sovereignty but supports the pattern of international co-operation, particularly that established under the terms of the Antarctic Treaty (signed in 1959, see p. 612), to which the Kingdom of Norway is an original signatory. In 2005 the Troll research station, previously suitable only for summer use, reopened as an all-year station; an airstrip to serve the facility was also opened. A further, summer-only research station is also in operation.

Peter I Øy

Peter I Øy (Peter I Island) is located in the Bellingshausen Sea, some 450 km north of Antarctica and more than 1,800 km south-west of Chile, the nearest inhabited territory. It covers an area of some 156 sq km, 95% of which is covered by ice. The island lies within the Antarctic Circle and the area covered by the terms of the Antarctic Treaty. The first recorded landing on the island was not made until 1929, by a Norwegian expedition, which then claimed the island. A Royal Proclamation placed Peter I Øy under Norwegian sovereignty in 1931, and the island was declared a dependency in 1933. Few landings have been made since, but in 1987 the Norsk Polarinstitutt (Norwegian Polar Institute) conducted a relatively long survey and established an automatic weather station on the island.

OMAN

Introductory Survey

LOCATION, CLIMATE, LANGUAGE, RELIGION, FLAG, CAPITAL

The Sultanate of Oman occupies the extreme east and south-east of the Arabian peninsula. It is bordered to the west by the United Arab Emirates (UAE), Saudi Arabia and Yemen. A detached portion of Oman, separated from the rest of the country by UAE territory, lies at the tip of the Musandam peninsula, on the southern shore of the Strait of Hormuz. Oman has a coastline of more than 1,600 km (1,000 miles) on the Indian Ocean, and is separated from Iran by the Gulf of Oman. In Muscat average annual rainfall is 100 mm and the average temperature varies between 21°C (70°F) and 35°C (95°F). Rainfall is heavier on the hills of the interior, and the south-western province of Dhofar is the only part of Arabia to benefit from the summer monsoon. The official language is Arabic. Islam is the official religion. The majority of the population are Ibadi Muslims; there are also Sunni Muslim, Hindu and Christian minorities. The national flag (proportions 1 by 2) has three equal horizontal stripes, of white, red and green, with a vertical red stripe at the hoist. In the upper hoist is a representation, in white, of the state emblem, two crossed swords and a dagger (*khanjar*), surmounted by a belt. The capital is Muscat.

CONTEMPORARY POLITICAL HISTORY

Historical Context

Officially known as Muscat and Oman until 1970, the Sultanate has had a special relationship with the United Kingdom since the 19th century. Full independence was confirmed by a treaty of friendship with the United Kingdom on 20 December 1951, although the armed forces and police retain some British officers on loan service. Sultan Said bin Taimur succeeded his father in 1932 and maintained a strictly conservative and isolationist rule until July 1970, when he was overthrown by his son in a bloodless palace coup. The new Sultan, Qaboos bin Said al-Said, then began a liberalization of the regime, and spending on development was increased.

Domestic Political Affairs

A Consultative Assembly (comprising representatives of the Government, the private sector and the regions, appointed by the Sultan) was created in 1981, in order to advise Sultan Qaboos on economic and social development. In November 1990 it was announced that the Assembly was to be replaced by a Consultative Council (Majlis al-Shoura), comprising regional representatives, which was intended to extend participation by Omani citizens in national affairs. A selection process was duly announced whereby representatives of each of the country's 59 districts (*wilayat*—increased to 61 in 2006) would nominate three candidates; the nominations would then be submitted to the Deputy Prime Minister for Legal Affairs, who, with the Sultan's approval, would choose one representative for each district to join the new Majlis. No government official or civil servant would be eligible for election to the new body. The President of the Majlis al-Shoura would be appointed by royal decree; other executive officers and committee members would be designated by, and from among, the local delegates. Although the role of the Majlis was strictly advisory, government ministers were to be obliged to submit reports to the assembly and to answer any questions addressed to them. The Majlis was formally established by royal decree in November 1991 and was convened in January 1992, when its members were sworn in for a three-year term. In 1994 membership of the Majlis was increased from 59 to 80, to include an additional member for any district with 30,000 or more inhabitants. For the first time, women were nominated as candidates in six regions in and around the capital; two women were subsequently appointed to the enlarged Majlis.

In mid-1994 the Government was reported to be employing stringent measures to curb an apparent rise in Islamist militancy in Oman. In August the security forces arrested more than 200 members of an allegedly foreign-sponsored Islamist organization, including two junior ministers, university lecturers, students and soldiers. Most were later released, but in November several of those against whom charges had been brought were sentenced to death, having been found guilty of conspiracy to foment sedition; the Sultan subsequently commuted the death sentences to terms of imprisonment. In November 1995 139 prisoners were released, under a general amnesty granted by Sultan Qaboos.

The Basic Statute of the State and the formation of the Majlis Oman

In November 1996 Sultan Qaboos issued a decree promulgating a Basic Statute of the State, a constitutional document defining for the first time the organs and guiding principles of the state. The Statute provided for a Council of Oman (Majlis Oman), to be composed of the Majlis al-Shoura and a new State Council (Majlis al-Dawlah). The latter was to be appointed from among prominent Omanis, and would liaise between the Government and the people of Oman. In December a Defence Council was established by royal decree, comprising the Minister of the Royal Court, the heads of the armed and police forces, and the chief of internal security. The Basic Statute defined a process of succession to the Sultan, requiring that the ruling family determine a successor within three days of the throne's falling vacant, failing which the Defence Council would confirm the appointment of a successor predetermined by the Sultan.

Voting was organized in October 1997 to select candidates for appointment to the Majlis al-Shoura. Women from all regions were permitted to seek nomination. Of a total of 736 candidates, 164 were chosen, from whom the Sultan selected the 82 members of the newly expanded Majlis in November. The two female members of the outgoing Majlis were returned to office. In December Sultan Qaboos issued a decree appointing the 41 members of the Majlis al-Dawlah, which was reportedly dominated by former politicians, business leaders and academics. A further decree established the Majlis Oman, which was formally inaugurated by the Sultan on 27 December.

The elections to the Majlis al-Shoura held on 14 September 2000 were the first in which members were directly elected rather than appointed by the Sultan. However, voting rights were restricted to prominent business leaders, intellectuals, professionals and tribal chiefs. Of a total of 541 candidates, 21 of whom were women, 83 (including two women) were elected to the (further expanded) Majlis. The number of eligible voters had tripled, to some 150,000, since the previous election; according to official figures, an estimated 90% of the electorate participated in the poll. A new Majlis al-Dawlah was appointed in October, and the Majlis Oman convened for its second term on 4 November.

In March 2003 Sultan Qaboos issued a decree establishing a Public Authority for Craft Industries. The President of the Authority, Sheikha Aisha bint Khalfan bin Jumiel al-Siyabiah, was given the rank of Minister, and thus became the first female to be appointed to that level of government. Elections to the Majlis al-Shoura were held on 4 October, for which voting rights were granted to all Omani citizens over 21 years of age—some 820,000 people. A total of 506 candidates, 15 of them women, stood for election to the 83-seat assembly. Critics of the polls claimed that tribal loyalties had guided the decision-making of most voters, resulting in a predictable set of results—a situation that was exacerbated by the lack of legislative power wielded by council members. Moreover, turn-out was recorded at just 32%. A royal decree issued later in October extended the term of office for members of both the Majlis al-Shoura and the Majlis al-Dawlah from three to four years. In November a new Majlis al-Dawlah was appointed, with an expanded membership of 57 (including eight women); membership of the Majlis was subsequently increased to 59 (nine of whom were women) and then again, to 70 (see below).

A royal decree signed in March 2004 appointed Dr Rawya bint Saud bin Ahmad al-Busaidiyah as Minister of Higher Education (the first female member of the Council of Ministers) and Sheikh Yahya bin Mahfoudh al-Mantheri as President of the Majlis al-Dawlah. In June the Sultan created a Ministry of Tourism; another woman, Rajha bint Abd al-Amir bin Ali, was appointed as the new minister. When, in October, Dr Sharifah bint Khalfan bin Nasser al-Yahiyaia was given the role of Minister of Social Development, she became the third woman to be appointed to the Council of Ministers.

Following the approval of a press and broadcasting law in 2004, which allowed the establishment of private television and radio stations, the country's first private radio stations received licences in 2005 and began broadcasting in 2007. Although Omanis can, against the wishes of the state, receive private broadcasts from foreign broadcasters, this represented a significant concession to reformist elements in society. Nevertheless, despite such reforms, the views of two popular writers, Abdullah al-Riyami and Muhammad al-Harthy, were reportedly suppressed in the media after they had criticized the Government in 2004; in 2005 al-Riyami was arrested and detained for a week without charges being brought.

In September 2007 Sultan Qaboos carried out a reorganization of the Council of Ministers, which included the creation of new Ministries of Fisheries and of Environment and Climate Affairs. A Public Authority for Electricity and Water was also established to plan and supervise the development of Oman's utilities. Sheikh Ahmad bin Muhammad al-Issai was appointed as President of the Majlis al-Shoura, elections to which were held on 27 October. Membership of the Majlis was increased from 83 to 84. The polls were contested by 632 candidates, 21 of them women; however, none of the contested seats were secured by women. The majority of elected members of the new Majlis al-Shoura were reported to be tribal leaders or businessmen. Turn-out of some 62.7% was recorded. A new Majlis al-Dawlah, comprising 70 members (including 14 women), was appointed on 5 November.

A report issued by the US Department of State in June 2008, which classified Oman as one of the countries failing to tackle the problem of human-trafficking, led to forceful protests from the Omani authorities. Sultan Qaboos issued a new law in November that specifically addressed human-trafficking, and specified prison sentences of up to 15 years and fines of up to RO 100,000 for those convicted of the crime. Also in November a new National Commission for Human Rights was established; the body, which was described as 'autonomous', was to be attached to the Majlis al-Dawlah, the members of which are directly appointed by the Sultan. In October 2009 11 people were sentenced to seven years' imprisonment following their conviction for involvement in a human-trafficking operation, involving the illegal transit of a group of women to the Sultanate from Bahrain. By February 2010, according to the Inspector-General of Police and Customs, 33 people, including 14 non-Omani nationals, had been indicted under the human-trafficking law promulgated in 2008.

The Government had, in 1998, introduced measures aimed at reducing the number of expatriates in the labour force and replacing them with trained Omani personnel, a process termed 'Omanization'. By 2000 the proportion of Omanis employed in the state services sector exceeded the set target of 72%. Several amendments to Oman's Labour Law were introduced in November 2009, imposing stringent regulations on the utilization of foreign labour, including the provision of prison sentences and fines for employers or sponsors of illegal workers, and stipulating increased financial penalties for employers failing to meet Omanization targets. According to unofficial estimates, there were up to 125,000 unregistered or illegal expatriate workers in Oman in 2009. In January 2010 the Government announced a two-month amnesty programme to enable foreign nationals employed illegally in the country to either acquire correct documentation or leave the Sultanate without prosecution. The amnesty was subsequently extended until 31 May and then again, to 31 July. However, it was reported in August that only 20,000 people had responded to the initiative.

In March 2010 Ahmad bin Muhammad bin Obaid al-Saeedi was appointed Minister of Health, replacing Dr Ali bin Muhammad bin Mousa. In late July Sultan Qaboos celebrated the 40th anniversary of his accession to power. Rajha bint Abd al-Amir bin Ali, the Minister of Tourism since 2004, died in early February 2011. Eng. Mohsin bin Muhammad bin Ali al-Sheikh was named as her successor as part of a reorganization of the Council of Ministers later that month; however, al-Sheikh was himself among the ministers replaced in an extensive reorganization of the Government in early March (see below).

Recent developments: the protests of early 2011

Amid a series of popular uprisings taking place in the Middle East and North Africa during the early part of 2011, on 17 January a demonstration was held in Muscat by protesters who demanded lower food prices and the removal of government ministers perceived to be involved in corruption. A second rally was held in the capital on 18 February, at which the demands further included political reform and job creation. On 25 February the protests intensified, and two days later violence erupted in the northern industrial port of Sohar, with many official buildings reportedly being vandalized and shops set on fire. As protesters in Sohar began a sit-in, blocking access roads to the port, and some reportedly tried to break into a police station, the police used tear-gas and rubber bullets in an attempt to control the situation. Two protesters were said to have died in clashes with security forces. The unrest spread to other cities, including Muscat and Salalah, despite a pledge by Sultan Qaboos to create 50,000 public sector jobs and to introduce unemployment benefits. Nevertheless, unlike the instigators of pro-democracy protests in other parts of the Gulf and wider region, Omanis did not directly challenge the rule of their leader. On 26 February Sultan Qaboos replaced six cabinet ministers and promised improved benefits to students. On 6 March the Sultan effected a further limited reshuffle of the Council of Ministers, which included the replacement of the Minister of the Royal Palace Office, Gen. Ali bin Majid al-Ma'amari. Then, on 7 March Qaboos announced a more substantial reorganization of the 29-member Government: 12 ministers were removed from office and several other portfolios changed hands. It was announced that the Ministry of National Economy—the minister of which, Ahmad bin Abd al-Nabi Macki, had been a target of the protesters' anger—was to be dissolved, while the former Minister of Commerce and Industry, Maqbool bin Ali Sultan (who had on 26 February been awarded the transport and communications portfolio), was also removed from his post. Saad bin Muhammad bin Said al-Mardhouf al-Saadi became the new Minister of Commerce and Industry. Darwish bin Ismail bin Ali al-Balushi, previously Secretary-General for Financial Affairs at the Ministry of National Economy, was named as the new Minister Responsible for Financial Affairs. The Minister of the Interior, Saud bin Ibrahim al-Busaidi, also lost his post, as did the Minister of the Diwan of the Royal Court, Sayed Ali bin Hamoud al-Busaidi; the former was replaced by Hamoud bin Faisal bin Said al-Busaidi and the latter by Khalid bin Hilal bin Saud al-Busaidi. Six of the newly appointed ministers were reported to be elected members of the Majlis al-Shoura.

On 13 March 2011 Sultan Qaboos issued a decree in which he pledged to grant legislative and audit powers to both chambers of the Majlis Oman. The decree provided for the establishment of a technical committee of experts, which would formulate a draft amendment to the Basic Statute of the State and submit a report to the Sultan within 30 days. On the same day Qaboos appointed Lt-Gen. Hassan bin Mohsen bin Salim Al Shraiqi to succeed Lt-Gen. Malik bin Suleiman al-Ma'amari as Inspector-General of Police and Customs, with the rank of Minister. However, despite the Sultan's actions, the protests continued during March, and a reported 7,000 Omanis signed a petition urging the Government to bring corruption charges against three of the ministers recently removed from office, Macki, Sultan and Gen. Ali al-Ma'amari. (There were subsequent demands by the protesters for other serving cabinet ministers to leave office in order to face allegations of corruption.) However, the Public Prosecutor ruled at the end of the month that it would not investigate the claims against the three former ministers owing to a lack of evidence, prompting demands for the Attorney-General to stand down. Meanwhile, the security forces attempted to bring an end to the sit-in that protesters had staged in Sohar for the past month, and made around 50 arrests. The authorities described those detained as 'law-breaking vandals', who were charged with a range of violations including damage to property, obstructing free movement and damaging the country's reputation.

Foreign Affairs
Regional relations

An agreement on the demarcation of Oman's border with Yemen, which had been the subject of a lengthy dispute with the former People's Democratic Republic of Yemen, was signed in October 1992 and ratified in December; demarcation was completed in June 1995. In July 1996 Oman withdrew an estimated 15,000 troops from the last of the disputed territories on the Yemeni border, in accordance with the 1992 agreement, and in May 1997 the border demarcation maps were signed in Muscat. Several bilateral economic co-operation accords were announced in September 1998, and a free trade zone was subsequently established near the border at Al-Mazyona. In late March 2011 the Omani authorities were reported to be increasing security along the country's border with Yemen, where a series of demonstrations by protesters demanding the resignation of President Ali Abdullah Saleh were in some cases being violently suppressed by security forces. The Omani Government feared that, unless border security was improved, a possible influx of Yemeni refugees fleeing the escalating violence might use the free trade zone at Al-Mazyona to enter Oman illegally.

Having signed a preliminary border accord in June 2002, Oman and the UAE reached agreement on the final delineation of their mutual land borders in July 2008. Although the two countries have traditionally enjoyed good relations, at the end of January 2011 the Omani authorities revealed that they were investigating the existence of an espionage network originating in the UAE, which was allegedly engaged in spying on the Omani Government and security forces. Although the UAE Government denied any knowledge of such a network, it pledged to co-operate fully with the Omani investigation into the matter.

The 29th Annual Summit of the Supreme Council of the Co-operation Council for the Arab States of the Gulf (Gulf Co-operation Council—GCC) was held in Muscat on 29–30 December 2008. The foremost topics on the agenda were the Gulf's impending monetary union and the regional impact of the global financial crisis. The Council approved a monetary union agreement covering the legislative and institutional framework of the union, and reaffirmed its commitment to ratify the agreement and introduce a single currency by 1 January 2010. However, since 2006 Oman had made clear its intention to abstain from a single currency, preferring to maintain the rial's pegging to the US dollar. The Government did not rule out joining such a currency at a later date, but was adamant that joining by 2010 would jeopardize the Sultanate's ongoing development plans. Although four GCC member states, excluding Oman and the UAE, had ratified the monetary union agreement by the beginning of 2010, the introduction of a single currency was postponed until at least 2015.

Despite Oman's strong relations with the USA and other Western powers, the Sultanate also maintains close ties with Iran, supporting the right of the Iranian regime to pursue the peaceful development of nuclear energy and opposing any use of military force against Iran. Since June 2007 Oman and Iran have been engaged in negotiations concerning a joint venture to develop Iran's Kish gasfield, at an estimated cost of more than US $9,000m. The proposed deal would involve Oman providing finance for the project in exchange for a guaranteed gas supply of at least 1,000m. cu ft per day. Sayyid Fahd bin Mahmoud al-Said, Oman's Deputy Prime Minister, led a high-level delegation to the Iranian capital, Tehran, in April 2008 for talks on bilateral relations, including the Kish development project. In April 2009 Minister Responsible for Foreign Affairs Yousuf bin al-Alawi bin Abdullah conducted an official visit to Iran, during which he held discussions on bilateral relations and regional affairs with the Iranian President, Mahmoud Ahmadinejad, and the Iranian Minister of Foreign Affairs, Manouchehr Mottaki. Relations were strengthened further in August when Sultan Qaboos, accompanied by a senior-level ministerial delegation, completed his first visit to Iran since the Islamic Revolution in 1979. The three-day visit was the first by a foreign head of state since the disputed Iranian presidential election in June 2009 (see the chapter on Iran). During the visit several co-operation agreements were signed in the fields of security and education, and the establishment of a US $800m. petrochemicals joint venture was announced. However, no agreement was reached concerning the ongoing gas supply negotiations. High-level Omani-Iranian consultations continued in subsequent months, and in January 2010 the establishment of an Iranian trade centre in Oman was announced, the first such initiative in a GCC member state. In early August the two countries' respective ministers of defence signed a military co-operation accord in Muscat.

In April 1994 the Israeli Deputy Minister of Foreign Affairs, Yossi Beilin, participated in talks in Oman. This constituted the first official visit by an Israeli government member to an Arab Gulf state since Israel's declaration of independence in 1948. In September 1994, moreover, Oman and the other GCC member states announced the partial ending of their economic boycott of Israel. In December the Israeli Prime Minister, Itzhak Rabin, made an official visit to Oman to discuss the Middle East peace process, and in February 1995 it was announced that low-level diplomatic relations were to be established between Oman and Israel. An Omani trade office was opened in Tel-Aviv, Israel, in August 1996, despite concerns that bilateral relations would be undermined by the uncompromising stance adopted by the new Israeli Government of Binyamin Netanyahu. In March 1997 ministers responsible for foreign affairs of the countries of the League of Arab States (Arab League, see p. 361) recommended, in condemnation of Israeli settlement policy, the suspension of involvement in multilateral negotiations with Israel, a reassertion of the primary economic boycott and the ending, by means of closing representative offices in Tel-Aviv, of efforts to normalize bilateral relations. In April Oman prohibited Israeli participation at a Muscat trade fair. In October 2000, in view of the deepening crisis in Israeli–Palestinian relations, Oman closed both its trade office in Tel-Aviv and the Israeli trade office in Muscat. Oman hosted the annual summit meeting of GCC heads of state in December 2001, at the close of which a statement was issued blaming Israel for the collapse of the peace process and expressing support for the Palestinian leadership. Demonstrations subsequently took place in Muscat to demand an end to Israeli military incursions into Palestinian territory. Nevertheless, according to reports in the Israeli daily newspaper *Ha'aretz*, senior officials from Israel's Ministry of Foreign Affairs visited Muscat in November 2009, ostensibly to attend a conference on water desalination, and held discussions on the Middle East peace process with their Omani counterparts.

Other external relations

Negotiations between Oman and the USA concerning a bilateral free trade agreement took place in March–October 2005, and the deal was signed following their conclusion. The accord was ratified by both countries' institutions in 2006 and came into force on 1 January 2009. The US-Omani agreement followed similar accords between the USA and Bahrain, Israel, Jordan and Morocco, with a view to establishing a wider free trade area across the Middle East. The development of US-Omani relations was expected to displease the Saudi Government, which had previously argued that the GCC should negotiate a trade deal as a single body and in 2004 claimed that the US accord with Bahrain contravened the GCC's external tariff agreement.

Dr Manmohan Singh, the Prime Minister of India, visited Oman in November 2008 for a two-day state visit—the first by an Indian premier for more than a decade. Since the establishment of an India-Oman Joint Commission in 1995 bilateral relations progressed considerably, with the signing of several agreements on trade and defence co-operation. During Prime Minister Singh's visit two significant memorandums of understanding were signed: one concerning labour co-operation and another on the establishment of an India-Oman Joint Investment Fund, with initial capital of US $100m. and the potential to expand eventually to $1,500m.

CONSTITUTION AND GOVERNMENT

The Basic Statute of the State, which was promulgated by Royal Decree on 6 November 1996, defines Oman's organs of government. The Sultan, who is Head of State, is empowered to promulgate and ratify legislation. He is assisted in formulating and implementing the general policy of the state by a Council of Ministers. Members of the Council of Ministers are appointed by the Sultan, who presides, or may appoint a Prime Minister to preside, over the Council. There is no legislature. However, a Majlis al-Shoura (Consultative Council) is now elected for four years at national polls. With effect from elections held in October 2003, voting rights have been granted to all Omani citizens over 21 years of age. The Majlis is composed of one representative from each *wilaya* (district) with fewer than 30,000 inhabitants, and two from each *wilaya* with 30,000 or more inhabitants. The Majlis al-Shoura elected in October 2007 comprised 84 members. A Majlis al-Dawlah (State Council) is appointed by the Sultan from among prominent Omanis; currently, it comprises 70 members, who also serve a four-year term of office. The two Councils together comprise the Majlis Oman (Council of Oman). Sultan Qaboos issued a decree on 13 March 2011, stating his intention to grant legislative and audit powers to both chambers of the Majlis Oman. Under the terms of the decree, a technical committee of experts was to formulate a draft amendment to the Basic Statute of the State and to submit a report to the Sultan within 30 days.

Oman comprises four governorates and five regions, which are subdivided into 60 *wilayat*; each *wilaya* has its own governor (*wali*).

REGIONAL AND INTERNATIONAL CO-OPERATION

Oman was a founder member of the Co-operation Council for the Arab States of the Gulf (the Gulf Co-operation Council—GCC, see p. 243). The GCC's six members established a unified regional customs tariff in 2003. The economic convergence criteria for a common market and monetary union were agreed at a GCC summit in Abu Dhabi, the UAE, in 2005. However, it was announced in February 2007 that the Omani authorities had decided to withdraw their participation from the proposed monetary union, owing to concerns regarding the convergence criteria. The common market was officially launched in January 2008. Oman is also a member of the League of Arab States (Arab League, see p. 361).

Oman became a member of the UN in October 1971 and was admitted to the World Trade Organization (WTO, see p. 430) in November 2000. The country also participates in the Organization of the Islamic Conference (OIC, see p. 400) and the Group of 77 developing countries (G77, see p. 447).

ECONOMIC AFFAIRS

In 2008, according to estimates by the World Bank, Oman's gross national income (GNI), measured at average 2006–08 prices, was US $49,834m., equivalent to $17,890 per head (or $24,370 per head on an international purchasing-power parity basis). During 2000–09, it was estimated, the population increased at an average annual rate of 1.9%, while real gross domestic product (GDP) per head increased, in real terms, by an average of 3.4% per year during 2000–08. Overall GDP increased, in real terms, at an average annual rate of 4.6% in 2000–09; growth was 12.8% in 2008, but declined to just 1.1% in 2009, according to provisional official figures.

Agriculture (including fishing) contributed 1.4% of GDP in 2009, according to provisional figures, while 27.8% of the labour force was estimated to be engaged in the sector in mid-2011, according to FAO data. The major crops are dates, tomatoes, watermelons, bananas and other fruits. The production of frankincense, formerly an important export commodity, has been revived. Livestock and fishing are also important. The real GDP of the agricultural sector increased by an average of 1.6% annually in 2000–09. Real agricultural GDP expanded by 3.6% in 2009, according to provisional official figures.

Industry (including mining and quarrying, manufacturing, construction, and power) provided 57.8% of GDP in 2009, according to provisional figures, and employed 27.9% of the working population in 2003. According to provisional official figures, real industrial GDP increased by an average of 2.8% annually in 2000–09. The sector's real GDP increased by 6.1% in 2009.

The mining sector contributed more than one-third of the country's GDP in 2009, at 40.2%, according to provisional figures, and engaged 2.8% of the employed labour force in 2003. The principal mineral reserves are petroleum and natural gas, which together provided around 39.7% of GDP in 2009. There were proven petroleum reserves of 5,572m. barrels at the end of 2009, sufficient to maintain output at that year's levels—which averaged an estimated 810,000 barrels per day (b/d)—for almost 19 years. Exports of Omani crude petroleum provided 50.4% of total export earnings in 2009. Natural gas is also an important mineral resource; there were proven reserves of some 980,000m. cu m at the end of 2009, sustainable for just under 40 years at that year's production levels (output in 2009 totalled 24,800m. cu m). Budgetary revenue from petroleum and natural gas contributed some 77.4% of the total in 2009. Chromite, gold, silver, salt, marble, gypsum and limestone are also mined, and the exploitation of coal deposits is planned. The GDP of the mining sector (including petroleum activities) declined at an average annual rate of 1.3% in 2000–09; however, according to provisional official figures, mining GDP (including petroleum activities) recorded an increase of 6.5% in 2009.

Manufacturing contributed 10.1% of GDP in 2009, according to provisional figures, and engaged 8.2% of the employed labour force in 2003. The most important branches of the sector are petroleum-refining, construction materials, cement production and copper-smelting. Assembly industries, light engineering and food-processing are being encouraged at Oman's seven industrial estates, which include estates at Nizwa, Sohar, Al-Buraymi and Sur. The Government is also promoting light industry in free trade zones at Sohar and Salalah Ports. The GDP of the manufacturing sector increased, in real terms, at an average rate of 10.3% annually in 2000–09. The sector's real GDP grew by 10.0% in 2008, but declined by 3.9% in 2009, according to provisional official figures.

Construction contributed 6.4% of GDP in 2009, according to provisional figures, and engaged 16.1% of the labour force in 2003. The real GDP of the construction sector increased at an average annual rate of 23.7% in 2000–09. Real construction GDP expanded by some 30.1% in 2008 and by 16.8% in 2009, according to provisional official figures.

Energy is derived almost exclusively from domestic supplies of natural gas (which accounted for 82.0% of electricity produced in 2007) and petroleum. Imports of fuel products comprised just 5.5% of total imports in 2009. A regional electricity grid, linking countries of the Co-operation Council for the Arab States of the Gulf (Gulf Co-operation Council), was completed in 2006 and aimed eventually to achieve regional self-sufficiency up to 2058. After the grids of Bahrain, Kuwait, Qatar and Saudi Arabia were linked in late 2009, those of Oman and the United Arab Emirates (UAE) were expected to be connected during 2011–12.

Services provided 40.8% of GDP in 2009, according to provisional figures, and engaged 64.0% of the employed population in 2003. With the Government seeking to diversify Oman's petroleum-dependent economy, the construction of several large-scale tourism projects have been initiated in recent years. Pre-eminent among these was Al-Madina al-Zarqa (Blue City) resort, the plans for which were announced in June 2005, and which was expected to take some 15 years to complete. However, in April 2011 the Government assumed control of the US $20,000m. project, after it had been beset by a series of problems, including a legal dispute over ownership, funding difficulties and a disappointing level of interest in the properties for sale. The Government intended to increase the number of tourist arrivals from an estimated 1.7m. in 2010 to 12m. by 2020. The GDP of the services sector increased, in real terms, at an average rate of 7.2% per year during 2000–09. Real services GDP expanded by an estimated 14.2% in 2008, but declined slightly by 1.6% in 2009, according to provisional official figures.

In 2009 Oman recorded a visible trade surplus of US $11,600m., while there was a deficit of $287m. on the current account of the balance of payments. In that year the principal source of imports was the UAE (which supplied 23.8% of total imports). Japan, the USA, and India were also important suppliers. The most important market for non-petroleum exports in 2009 was the UAE (taking 35.6%). Iran, India, Saudi Arabia and China were also important markets for non-petroleum exports. Petroleum and natural gas is, by far, the principal export category, comprising 65.3% of the total in 2009. Mineral products made the most notable contribution to export revenue of all non-oil exports of Omani origin in the same year. The principal imports in that year were machinery and transport equipment, basic manufactures, food and live animals, and chemicals and related products.

Oman recorded an estimated overall budgetary deficit of RO 680m. in 2009 (equivalent to some 3.8% of GDP in that year). However, the preliminary figures of 2010 indicated a surplus of RO 635m. Oman's general government gross debt was RO 1,162m. in 2008, equivalent to 5.0% of GDP. At the end of 2006 Oman's total external debt was US $4,819m., of which $819m. was long-term public debt. The cost of debt-servicing in that year was equivalent to 1.3% of the total value of exports of goods and services. Annual inflation increased by an average of 2.9% in 2000–10, and consumer prices grew by an average of 3.2% in 2010, compared with some 12.4% in 2008. Although Oman has traditionally relied on a high level of immigrant labour (non-Omanis accounted for 57.6% of the employed labour force in 2003), employment opportunities for young Omanis declined in the early 1990s and, according to census results, unemployment among Omanis stood at 11.9% in 1993; the figure was estimated at 12%–15% in 2006, although unemployment in rural areas was assumed to be far greater.

Oman's limited petroleum reserves and fluctuations in the price of petroleum have necessitated a series of five-year development plans to diversify the country's economic base, in particular through the expansion of the private sector (a programme initiated in 1994). Petroleum production declined steadily during 2001–07. However, following sustained government investment in enhanced recovery techniques, this trend has subsequently been reversed; in 2010 production increased by 6.4%, to some 864,600 b/d (compared with 812,500 b/d in 2009), according to official figures. By mid-2009 around 20 foreign oil companies were engaged in exploration and production projects in Oman, and a number of potentially significant oil and gas discoveries were announced by the state-owned Petroleum Development Oman in February 2010. Under the eighth

Development Plan (2011–15), emphasis was to be placed on improvements to the health, education and transport systems. However, despite ongoing efforts to develop the non-petroleum sector (with gas-based industry and tourism being notable targets), an estimated RO 6,000m. of the allocated RO 30,000m. was to be spent on the oil industry. Under the Plan, the Government aimed to achieve annual GDP growth of at least 3% and to maintain an average annual inflation rate of 4%. The Plan also envisaged the further development of the so-called 'Omanization' policy, which sought to create more jobs for Omani nationals and to limit the employment of expatriate workers. The Government was committed to developing the tourism sector's infrastructure, including the construction of six airports and the expansion, by 2014, of Muscat International and Salalah airports. Having benefited from foreign investment, tourism's contribution to GDP reportedly increased from an estimated 0.9% in 2008 to almost 3% in 2010. Meanwhile, the implementation of a bilateral free trade agreement with the USA in January 2009 increased trading opportunities for Omani businesses. In an analysis of Oman's economic performance during 2009–10, published in April 2011, the IMF observed that the financial sector had proved notably resilient during the global financial crisis, owing to 'prudent macroeconomic management of oil wealth', a strong regulatory environment and structural reforms aimed at stimulating non-hydrocarbons growth. Although GDP growth slowed to 1.1% in 2009, the IMF projected an increase, to 4.1%, in 2010. In its 2010 Human Development Report, the UN Development Programme placed Oman first in terms of improvements to human development achieved since 1970. The draft budget for 2011 included a 13% increase in government spending, with the focus on economic and social infrastructure investment; revenues were also set to increase by around 14%, and the proposed fiscal deficit was expected to be covered by higher than anticipated oil prices. In February 2011, amid unprecedented popular protests (see Contemporary Political History), the Government increased the minimum monthly wage for Omani private sector workers from RO 140 to RO 200.

PUBLIC HOLIDAYS

2012: 4 February* (Mouloud, Birth of the Prophet), 16 June* (Leilat al-Meiraj, Ascension of the Prophet), 19 July* (Ramadan begins), 23 July (Renaissance Day), 18 August* (Id al-Fitr, end of Ramadan), 25 October* (Id al-Adha, Feast of the Sacrifice), 14 November* (Muharram, Islamic New Year), 18 November (National Day), 19 November (Birthday of Sultan Qaboos).

* These holidays are dependent on the Islamic lunar calendar and may vary by one or two days from the dates given.

Statistical Survey

Sources (unless otherwise stated): Information and Publication Centre, Ministry of National Economy, POB 506, Muscat 113; tel. 24604285; fax 24698467; e-mail mone@omantel.net.om; internet www.mone.gov.om; Central Bank of Oman, POB 1161, 44 Mutrah Commercial Centre, Ruwi 112; tel. 24777777; fax 24788995; e-mail cboccr@omantel.net.om; internet www.cbo-oman.org.

Area and Population

AREA, POPULATION AND DENSITY

Area (sq km)	309,500*
Population (census results)	
1 December 2003	
Males	1,313,239
Females	1,027,576
Total	2,340,815†
12 December 2010 (preliminary)	2,694,094‡
Population (official estimates at mid-year)	
2007	2,743,499
2008	2,867,428
2009	3,173,917§
Density (per sq km) at mid-2009	10.3

* 119,500 sq miles.
† Comprising 1,781,558 Omani nationals and 559,257 non-Omanis.
‡ Comprising approximately 1,951,000 Omani nationals and 743,000 non-Omanis. Note: The number of non-Omanis was believed to have been significantly reduced by the proximity of the census to the Christmas holiday season.
§ Comprising 2,017,559 Omani nationals and 1,156,358 non-Omanis.

POPULATION BY AGE AND SEX
(official estimates at mid-2009)

	Males	Females	Total
0–14	394,354	377,426	771,780
15–64	1,551,055	802,097	2,353,152
65 and over	25,706	23,279	48,985
Total	1,971,115	1,202,802	3,173,917

ADMINISTRATIVE DIVISIONS
(population at mid-2009, official estimates)

	Area (sq km)*	Population	Density (per sq km)
Muscat Governorate	3,900	949,694	243.5
Al-Batinah Region	12,500	818,650	65.5
Musandam Governorate	1,800	40,460	22.5
Al-Dhahira Region	44,000	169,350	6.6
Al-Dakhliya Region	31,900	332,772	10.4
Al-Sharqiya Region	36,400	402,425	11.1
Al-Wosta Region	79,700	32,757	0.4
Dhofar Governorate	99,300	307,834	3.1
Al-Buraymi Governorate	n.a.	119,975	n.a.
Total	309,500	3,173,917	10.3

* Area data predate the creation, from al-Dhahira Region, of al-Buraymi Governorate in October 2006.

Note: Figures for area are rounded, and totals may not be equal to the sum of components as a result.

PRINCIPAL TOWNS
(population at 2003 census)

Salalah	156,530	Nizwa	68,785
		Al-Buraymi	
Sohar	104,312	(Buraimi)	67,963
Ibri	97,429	Sur	66,785
Al-Rustaq	74,224	Muscat (capital)	24,893

Source: Thomas Brinkhoff, *City Population* (internet www.citypopulation.de).

Mid-2009 (incl. suburbs, UN estimate): Muscat 634,074 (Source: UN, *World Urbanization Prospects: The 2009 Revision*).

OMAN

BIRTHS AND DEATHS
(Omani nationals only, official estimates)

	2007	2008	2009
Live births	47,928	53,754	59,461
Birth rate (per 1,000)	25.0	27.3	29.5
Deaths	5,917	6,398	6,092
Death rate (per 1,000)	3.1	3.3	3.0

Registered marriages: 25,423 (marriage rate 12.6 per 1,000) in 2009.

Life expectancy (years at birth, official figures): 72.7 (males 70.0; females 75.7) in 2009.

EMPLOYMENT
(persons aged 15 years and over, 2003 census)

	Omanis	Non-Omanis	Total
Agriculture and fishing	14,210	43,904	58,114
Mining and quarrying	11,998	8,117	20,115
Manufacturing	13,831	45,661	59,492
Electricity, gas and water	1,826	2,219	4,045
Construction	10,128	108,129	118,257
Trade, hotels and restaurants	24,999	84,158	109,157
Transport, storage and communications	17,202	10,472	27,674
Finance, insurance and real estate	12,657	12,543	25,200
Public administration and defence	144,699	18,043	162,742
Other community, social and personal services	54,923	83,299	138,222
Sub-total	306,473	416,545	723,018
Activities not adequately defined	5,973	7,633	13,606
Total employed	312,446	424,178	736,624
Males	258,655	364,337	622,992
Females	53,791	59,841	113,632

Mid-2011 (estimates in '000): Agriculture, etc. 321; Total labour force 1,153 (Source: FAO).

Health and Welfare

KEY INDICATORS

Total fertility rate (children per woman, 2008)	3.0
Under-5 mortality rate (per 1,000 live births, 2008)	12
HIV/AIDS (% of persons aged 15–49, 2003)	0.1
Physicians (per 1,000 head, 2005)	1.7
Hospital beds (per 1,000 head, 2006)	2.1
Health expenditure (2007): US $ per head (PPP)	688
Health expenditure (2007): % of GDP	2.4
Health expenditure (2007): public (% of total)	78.7
Access to water (% of persons, 2008)	88
Access to sanitation (% of persons, 2002)	89
Total carbon dioxide emissions ('000 metric tons, 2007)	37,288.5
Carbon dioxide emissions per head (metric tons, 2007)	13.7
Human Development Index (2007): ranking	56
Human Development Index (2007): value	0.846

For sources and definitions, see explanatory note on p. vi.

Agriculture

PRINCIPAL CROPS
('000 metric tons)

	2005	2006	2007
Sorghum	9.5	8.8	10.4
Potatoes	5.9	5.4	9.1
Tomatoes	39.4	40.4	41.4
Onions, dry	5.4	4.2	9.1
Watermelons	27.0	11.1	17.2
Bananas	26.7	26.0	28.9
Lemons and limes	6.2	5.9	6.0
Mangoes, mangosteens and guavas	7.7	6.9	6.4
Dates	247.3	258.7	255.9
Papayas	1.4	1.4	1.9

2008: Production assumed to be unchanged from 2007 (FAO estimates). Note: No data were available for individual crops in 2009.

Aggregate production ('000 metric tons, may include official, semi-official or estimated data): Total cereals 15.1 in 2005, 14.2 in 2006, 16.2 in 2007, 16.4 in 2008, 16.6 in 2009; Total roots and tubers 5.9 in 2005, 5.4 in 2006, 9.1 in 2007–09; Total vegetables (incl. melons) 206.1 in 2005, 189.1 in 2006, 207.7 in 2007–09; Total fruits (excl. melons) 289.3 in 2005, 298.9 in 2006, 299.0 in 2007–09.

Source: FAO.

LIVESTOCK
('000 head, year ending September)

	2006	2007	2008
Asses*	28.5	28.5	28.5
Cattle	308	314	314
Camels	120	122	125
Sheep	358	366	374
Goats	1,598	1,620	1,620
Chickens*	4,200	4,200	4,200

* FAO estimates.

2009: Camels 124.

Source: FAO.

LIVESTOCK PRODUCTS
('000 metric tons)

	2007	2008	2009
Cattle meat*	4.2	4.2	4.2
Camel meat*	6.8	6.7	6.7
Sheep meat	12.6	10.8*	10.8*
Goat meat*	23.5	23.5	24.0
Chicken meat*	5.9	5.8	5.8
Cows' milk	47.6	35.7*	35.7*
Sheep's milk*	4.0	4.0	4.0
Goats' milk*	85.0	84.7	84.7
Hen eggs*	9.0	9.0	n.a.

* FAO estimate(s).

Source: FAO.

OMAN
Statistical Survey

Fishing

('000 metric tons, live weight)

	2006	2007	2008
Capture	147.7	151.7	145.6
Groupers	4.6	4.7	4.5
Emperors (Scavengers)	8.1	8.6	8.2
Porgies and seabreams	6.2	6.5	6.2
Hairtails and scabbardfishes	5.6	5.5	5.3
Demersal percomorphs	5.6	4.9	4.7
Indian oil sardine	36.2	34.3	32.9
Longtail tuna	7.9	7.8	7.4
Yellowfin tuna	17.5	19.8	19.1
Indian mackerel	4.4	7.0	6.7
Sharks, rays, skates, etc.	6.0	5.3	5.1
Cuttlefish and bobtail squids	9.2	10.8	10.4
Aquaculture	0.1	0.2*	0.1
Total catch	**147.8**	**151.9***	**145.8**

* FAO estimate.
Source: FAO.

Mining

('000 metric tons unless otherwise indicated)

	2007	2008	2009
Crude petroleum	34,506	35,947	38,507
Natural gas (million cu m)	24,040	24,056	24,760
Chromium	407.8	859.7	636.5
Gold (kg)	125	49	28
Marble	311.9	501.4	587.9
Salt	10.5	11.4	30.6
Gypsum	183.2	348.8	333.4

Sources: BP, *Statistical Review of World Energy*; US Geological Survey.

Industry

SELECTED PRODUCTS
('000 barrels, unless otherwise indicated, estimates)

	2007	2008	2009
Jet fuel and kerosene	2,160	3,037	3,225
Motor spirit (petrol)	3,908	6,514	6,604
Gas-diesel (distillate fuel) oils	2,849	8,132	6,662
Residual fuel oils	13,177	18,561	19,697
Electric energy (million kWh)	14,443	16,048	18,445

Source: mainly US Geological Survey.

Electric energy (million kWh): 19,844 in 2010.

Finance

CURRENCY AND EXCHANGE RATES

Monetary Units
1,000 baiza = 1 rial Omani (RO).

Sterling, Dollar and Euro Equivalents (31 December 2010)
£1 sterling = 601.9 baiza;
US $1 = 384.5 baiza;
€1 = 513.8 baiza;
10 rials Omani = £16.61 = $26.01 = €19.46.

Exchange Rate: Since January 1986 the official exchange rate has been fixed at US $1 = 384.5 baiza (1 rial Omani = $2.6008).

BUDGET
(RO million)

Revenue	2007	2008	2009
Petroleum revenue (net)	3,678.2	5,093.1	4,490.5
Gas revenues	810.9	909.9	731.3
Other current revenue	1,344.9	1,553.8	1,492.6
Taxes and fees	468.1	630.0	701.4
Income tax on enterprises	187.1	237.4	370.1
Customs duties	159.6	226.6	158.1
Non-tax revenue	876.8	923.8	791.2
Surplus from public authorities	5.9	6.7	24.8
Income from government investments	393.3	600.1	378.9
Capital revenue	66.2	68.3	24.0
Capital repayments	20.4	13.6	10.0
Total	**5,920.6**	**7,638.7**	**6,748.4**

Expenditure	2007	2008	2009
Current expenditure	3,857.5	4,420.4	4,218.5
Defence and national security	1,663.4	1,775.1	1,726.4
Civil ministries	1,898.7	2,348.4	2,216.7
Investment expenditure	1,697.3	2,280.9	2,690.9
Share of PDO expenditure*	476.9	649.1	696.1
Participation and subsidies	325.6	859.0	519.3
Total	**5,880.4**	**7,560.3**	**7,428.7**

* Referring to the Government's share of current and capital expenditure by Petroleum Development Oman.

2010 (RO million, provisional): Total revenue 7,023.0 (Net petroleum revenue 4,890.8, Gas revenues 824.8, Other current revenue 1,280.8, Capital revenue 26.6); Total expenditure 6,388.4 (Defence and national security 1,552.5; Civil ministries 1,979.6).

INTERNATIONAL RESERVES
(US $ million at 31 December)

	2008	2009	2010
Gold (national valuation)	0.5	0.7	0.9
IMF special drawing rights	19.8	290.8	285.8
Reserve position in IMF	21.0	55.9	67.2
Foreign exchange	11,541.1	11,856.3	12,671.3
Total	**11,582.4**	**12,203.7**	**13,025.2**

Source: IMF, *International Financial Statistics*.

MONEY SUPPLY
(RO million at 31 December)

	2008	2009	2010
Currency outside depository corporations	628.6	624.2	702.0
Transferable deposits	1,660.8	2,073.1	2,596.1
Other deposits	5,243.9	5,192.6	5,369.5
Securities other than shares	—	—	117.2
Broad money	**7,533.2**	**7,889.9**	**8,784.8**

Source: IMF, *International Financial Statistics*.

OMAN

COST OF LIVING
(Consumer Price Index; base: 2000 = 100)

	2008	2009	2010
Food, beverages and tobacco	150.6	151.3	154.4
Textiles, clothing and footwear	102.2	104.5	104.5
Rent, electricity, water and fuel	118.9	129.3	134.3
All items (incl. others)	125.2	129.5	133.7

NATIONAL ACCOUNTS
(RO million in current prices)

Expenditure on the Gross Domestic Product

	2007	2008	2009*
Final consumption expenditure	8,329.3	10,507.8	10,899.1
General government	3,043.9	3,316.4	3,591.7
Households	5,272.3	7,179.2	7,286.9
Non-profit institutions serving households	13.1	12.2	20.5
Gross capital formation	5,113.6	7,796.4	5,11.0
Gross fixed capital formation	4,927.5	6,873.9	6,055.2
Changes in inventories	186.1	922.5	−945.0
Total domestic expenditure	13,442.9	18,304.2	16,009.3
Balance on goods and services	2,668.0	4,984.0	2,010.0
GDP in purchasers' values	16,110.9	23,287.8	18,019.7
GDP at constant 2000 prices	9,794.2	11,051.9	11,176.1

* Provisional figures.

Gross Domestic Product by Economic Activity

	2007	2008	2009*
Agriculture and fishing	210.1	244.0	258.6
Mining and quarrying	7,181.9	11,845.0	7,399.5
Crude petroleum	6,538.6	10,915.0	6,610.2
Natural gas	600.4	859.8	707.0
Non-petroleum	42.9	70.2	82.3
Manufacturing	1,748.6	2,463.4	1,853.3
Electricity and water	176.2	188.9	210.3
Construction	791.8	1,116.5	1,179.3
Wholesale and retail trade	1,489.4	2,060.5	1,730.9
Hotels and restaurants	143.4	175.9	175.1
Transport, storage and communications	909.0	1,176.9	1,082.3
Financial intermediation	698.0	846.3	856.0
Real estate	692.4	817.8	934.0
Public administration and defence	1,192.2	1,282.1	1,333.9
Other community, social and personal services	1,123.4	1,291.4	1,406.8
Sub-total	16,356.4	23,508.5	18,420.1
Less Financial intermediation services indirectly measured	293.5	359.5	420.3
Gross value added in basic prices	16,062.9	23,149.0	17,999.8
Taxes on imports	48.0	138.8	19.9
GDP in purchasers' values	16,110.9	23,287.8	18,019.7

* Provisional figures.

Note: Totals may not be equal to the sum of components, owing to rounding.

BALANCE OF PAYMENTS
(US $ million)

	2007	2008	2009
Exports of goods f.o.b.	24,692	37,719	27,651
Imports of goods f.o.b.	−14,343	−20,707	−16,052
Trade balance	10,349	17,012	11,600
Exports of services	1,685	1,831	1,792
Imports of services	−5,096	−5,881	−5,555
Balance on goods and services	6,937	12,962	7,836
Other income received	2,162	1,097	819
Other income paid	−2,966	−3,858	−3,629
Balance on goods, services and income	6,133	10,201	5,026

—continued	2007	2008	2009
Current transfers paid	−3,670	−5,181	−5,313
Current account	2,463	5,020	−287
Capital account (net)	827	−52	55
Direct investment abroad	37	−584	−405
Direct investment from abroad	3,332	2,359	2,210
Portfolio investment assets	−123	−151	512
Portfolio investment liabilities	1,605	−1,525	240
Other investment assets	−4,932	−7,033	−762
Other investment liabilities	2,862	3,133	354
Net errors and omissions	179	660	−840
Overall balance	6,250	1,827	1,076

Source: IMF, *International Financial Statistics*.

External Trade

PRINCIPAL COMMODITIES
(RO million)

Imports c.i.f. (distribution by SITC)*	2007	2008	2009
Food and live animals	509.2	824.2	639.5
Beverages and tobacco	42.5	48.6	60.9
Crude materials (inedible) except fuels	114.5	153.0	166.9
Minerals, fuels, lubricants, etc.	214.3	235.5	387.4
Chemicals and related products	395.6	548.0	578.5
Basic manufactures	1,283.6	1,873.9	1,202.7
Machinery and transport equipment	3,165.1	4,403.3	3,368.2
Miscellaneous manufactured articles	340.7	599.3	385.4
Commodities not elsewhere classified	32.6	46.3	24.9
Total (incl. others)	6,144.1	8,814.2	6,863.8

Exports f.o.b.	2007	2008	2009
Petroleum and natural gas	7,199.9	11,024.2	6,947.9
Crude petroleum	5,553.5	8,415.9	5,359.5
Refined petroleum	466.0	1,007.0	618.9
Natural gas	1,180.4	1,601.3	969.5
Non-oil and -gas exports	1,290.7	1,962.9	1,849.5
Live animals and animal products	98.5	192.0	131.0
Mineral products	451.9	640.0	645.0
Chemicals and related products	185.0	315.5	320.3
Total†	9,493.9	14,502.9	10,632.0

* Excluding unrecorded imports (RO million): 17.3 in 2007; 81.8 in 2008; 31.8 in 2009.

† Including re-exports (RO million): 1,003.3 in 2007; 1,515.8 in 2008; 1,834.6 in 2009.

PRINCIPAL TRADING PARTNERS
(RO million)

Imports c.i.f.	2007	2008	2009
Australia	121.8	153.0	138.7
Bahrain	56.3	82.7	42.4
Belgium	57.2	155.5	77.0
China, People's Republic	183.4	403.0	329.4
France	149.2	118.0	103.1
Germany	325.8	371.8	296.1
India	400.1	400.7	404.7
Italy	144.9	176.0	158.6
Japan	969.1	1,372.1	1,031.0
Korea, Republic	212.6	372.7	242.2
Kuwait	11.8	38.4	83.2

OMAN

Imports c.i.f.—continued

	2007	2008	2009
Malaysia	60.5	89.6	177.1
Netherlands	131.2	132.4	113.3
Pakistan	40.3	159.8	72.1
Saudi Arabia	149.7	225.3	242.0
Singapore	42.2	154.2	68.9
Thailand	122.6	174.5	163.1
United Arab Emirates	1,625.2	2,397.5	1,632.1
United Kingdom	181.7	197.3	157.3
USA	354.8	504.2	442.7
Total (incl. others)	6,144.2	8,814.5	6,864.2

Exports f.o.b.*	2007	2008	2009
China, People's Republic	54.0	134.7	184.4
Egypt	12.8	16.7	52.4
Hong Kong	36.2	33.2	51.3
India	185.7	257.7	241.3
Indonesia	1.1	8.4	37.3
Iran	129.1	177.9	246.4
Iraq	22.2	88.3	69.1
Jordan	6.1	12.8	14.2
Korea, Republic	27.2	34.2	73.1
Kuwait	18.1	35.7	19.1
Libya	7.5	22.3	32.7
Netherlands	32.6	44.5	37.5
Pakistan	39.0	43.3	84.1
Qatar	61.3	101.5	129.5
Saudi Arabia	96.8	188.4	216.3
Singapore	32.5	69.9	171.6
Somalia	16.2	23.4	40.9
United Arab Emirates	1,081.0	1,581.4	1,309.8
United Kingdom	44.3	46.2	42.4
USA	25.6	72.0	75.6
Yemen	39.7	43.5	55.6
Total (incl. others)	2,294.1	3,478.7	3,684.1

* Excluding petroleum exports.

Transport

ROAD TRAFFIC
(registered vehicles at 31 December)

	2001	2002	2003
Private cars	309,217	335,771	284,902
Taxis	20,901	23,639	23,761
Commercial	132,920	140,270	109,118
Government	27,788	29,175	14,861
Motorcycles	5,195	5,436	3,977
Diplomatic	1,274	1,386	561
Other	23,631	24,625	7,320
Total	520,926	560,302	444,500

2007 (registered vehicles at 31 December): Passenger cars 453,362; Buses 26,387; Vans and Lorries 113,341; Motorcycles and mopeds 6,297 (Source: IRF, *World Road Statistics*).

SHIPPING
Merchant Fleet
(registered at 31 December)

	2007	2008	2009
Number of vessels	36	38	40
Total displacement ('000 grt)	24.1	26.1	27.3

Source: IHS Fairplay, *World Fleet Statistics*.

International Sea-borne Freight Traffic
('000 metric tons unless otherwise specified)

	2008	2009	2010
Port Sultan Qaboos:			
Vessels entered (number)	2,125	1,737	1,826
Goods loaded	1,069	838	860
Goods unloaded	5,211	4,366	4,082
Salalah Port:			
Vessels entered (number)	964	1,591	1,639
Goods loaded	2,759	2,970	5,345
Goods unloaded	710	752	935
Mina al-Fahal Coastal Area			
Vessels entered (number)	407	447	n.a.
Petroleum loaded	29,496	33,328	n.a.
Petroleum products unloaded	1,215	1,677	n.a.

CIVIL AVIATION
(aircraft movements, passengers and cargo handled at Muscat International Airport)

	2008	2009	2010*
International flights:			
flights (number)	52,537	49,012	60,467
passengers ('000)	3,545	4,063	5,195
goods handled (metric tons)	56,772	62,485	n.a.
Domestic flights:			
flights (number)	5,809	6,066	6,269
passengers ('000)	457	491	555
goods handled (metric tons)	1,112	1,273	n.a.

* Preliminary figures.

Tourism

FOREIGN TOURIST ARRIVALS*

Country of nationality	2006	2007	2008
Bahrain	38,038	25,428	12,258
Egypt	15,594	15,662	20,718
France	36,785	36,198	35,771
Germany	129,848	95,607	93,106
India	116,166	145,749	141,451
Kuwait	14,883	12,545	14,630
Netherlands	14,004	13,528	18,905
Pakistan	16,324	24,954	19,454
Saudi Arabia	25,961	20,167	22,102
Switzerland	38,340	19,768	22,425
Tanzania	441	463	n.a.
United Arab Emirates	97,674	79,206	102,293
United Kingdom	221,242	99,218	112,228
USA	34,616	28,729	35,539
Total (incl. others)	1,336,441	1,124,068	1,273,441

* Figures refer to international arrivals at hotels and similar establishments.

Tourism receipts (US $ million, incl. passenger transport): 749 in 2006; 908 in 2007; 1,111 in 2008.

Source: World Tourism Organization.

OMAN

Communications Media

	2007	2008	2009
Telephones ('000 main lines in use)	294.9	304.7	299.8
Mobile cellular telephones ('000 subscribers)	2,500.0	3,219.3	3,970.6
Internet users ('000)	454.7	557.1	1,465.4*
Broadband subscribers ('000)	20.2	32.0	41.1

*Estimate.

Personal computers: 460,264 (168.8 per 1,000 persons) in 2007.
Daily newspapers (number): 6 in 2004.
Non-daily newspapers and other periodicals (number): 23 in 2004.
Television receivers (number in use): 1,430,000 in 2000.
Radio receivers (number in use): 1,400,000 in 1997.
Book production (number of titles): 7 in 1996; 136 in 1998; 12 in 1999.
Sources: mainly UNESCO, *Statistical Yearbook*, and International Telecommunication Union.

Education

(state schools; 2009/10 unless otherwise indicated)

			Pupils/Students		
	Institutions	Teachers	Males	Females	Total
Pre-primary*	5	529	4,973	4,456	9,429
Basic†	802	30,856	167,630	163,632	331,262
General†:					
Grades 1–6	238	1,153	14,372	14,256	28,628
Grades 7–9		3,102	24,675	23,707	48,382
Grades 10–12		9,186	63,467	59,654	123,121
Higher‡§	34	1,608	12,282	11,004	23,286
University	1	1,074	7,942	7,415	15,357

* 2005/06.
† The Basic education system began to replace the General education system from 1998/99.
‡ Comprising six teacher-training colleges, the College of *Shari'a* and Law, five technical colleges, the Academy of Tourism and Catering, the College of Banking and Financial Studies, 16 institutes of health, and four vocational-training centres.
§ 2004/05.

Pupil-teacher ratio (primary education, UNESCO estimate): 11.8 in 2008/09 (Source: UNESCO Institute for Statistics).

Adult literacy rate (UNESCO estimates): 86.7% (males 90.0%; females 80.9%) in 2008 (Source: UNESCO Institute for Statistics).

Directory

The Government

HEAD OF STATE

Sultan: QABOOS BIN SAID AL-SAID (assumed power on 23 July 1970, after deposing his father).

COUNCIL OF MINISTERS
(May 2011)

Prime Minister and Minister of Foreign Affairs, Defence and Finance: Sultan QABOOS BIN SAID AL-SAID.
Deputy Prime Minister for the Council of Ministers: Sayyid FAHD BIN MAHMOUD AL-SAID.
Minister Responsible for Defence Affairs: Sayyid BADR BIN SAUD BIN HAREB AL-BUSAIDI.
Minister of Legal Affairs: Dr ABDULLAH BIN MUHAMMAD BIN SAID AL-SAEEDI.
Minister of Oil and Gas: Dr MUHAMMAD BIN HAMAD BIN SAIF AL-RUMHI.
Minister of Justice: Sheikh MUHAMMAD BIN ABDULLAH BIN ZAHIR AL-HINAI.
Minister Responsible for Financial Affairs: DARWISH BIN ISMAIL BIN ALI AL-BALUSHI.
Minister of Awqaf (Religious Endowments) and Religious Affairs: Sheikh ABDULLAH BIN MUHAMMAD BIN ABDULLAH AL-SALIMI.
Minister Responsible for Foreign Affairs: YOUSUF BIN AL-ALAWI BIN ABDULLAH.
Minister of Information: HAMAD BIN MUHAMMAD BIN MUHSIN AL-RASHDI.
Minister of Housing: Sheikh SAIF BIN MUHAMMAD AL-SHABAIBI.
Minister of Education: MADEEHA BINT AHMAD BIN NASIR AL-SHIBANIYAH.
Minister of Higher Education: Dr RAWYA BINT SAUD BIN AHMAD AL-BUSAIDIYAH.
Minister of Heritage and Culture: Sayyid HAITHAM BIN TARIQ AL-SAID.
Minister of Tourism: Sheikh ABD AL-MALIK BIN ABDULLAH BIN ALI AL-KHALILI.
Minister of Social Development: Sheikh MUHAMMAD BIN SAID BIN SAIF AL-KALBANI.
Minister of Manpower: ABDULLAH BIN NASSER AL-BAKRI.
Minister of Sports Affairs: Eng. ALI BIN MASSOUD BIN ALI AL-SINAIDI.
Minister of Transport and Communications: AHMAD BIN MUHAMMAD BIN SALIM AL-FUTAISI.
Minister of the Interior: Sayyid HAMOUD BIN FAISAL BIN SAID AL-BUSAIDI.
Minister of Commerce and Industry: SAAD BIN MUHAMMAD BIN SAID AL-MARDHOUF AL-SAADI.
Minister of Agriculture and Fisheries: Dr FUAD BIN JAAFAR BIN MUHAMMAD AL-SAJWANI.
Minister of Environment and Climate Affairs: MUHAMMAD BIN SALIM BIN SAID AL-TOOBI.
Minister of Health: Dr AHMAD BIN MUHAMMAD BIN OBAID AL-SAEEDI.
Minister of Regional Municipalities and Water Resources: AHMAD BIN ABDULLAH BIN MUHAMMAD AL-SHUHI.
Minister of the Civil Service: Sheikh KHALID BIN OMAR BIN SAID AL-MARHOON.
Minister of State and Governor of Muscat: Sayyid SAUD BIN HILAL BIN HAMAD AL-BUSAIDI.
Minister of State and Governor of Dhofar: Sheikh MUHAMMAD BIN MARHOUD AL-MA'AMARI.
Minister of the Diwan of the Royal Court: Sayyid KHALID BIN HILAL BIN SAUD AL-BUSAIDI.
Minister of the Royal Office: Lt-Gen. SULTAN BIN MUHAMMAD AL-NUMANI.

MINISTRIES

Diwan of the Royal Court: POB 632, Muscat 113; tel. 24738711; fax 24739427.
Ministry of Agriculture and Fisheries: POB 3738, Ruwi 112; tel. 24700896; fax 24707939; e-mail info@maf.gov.om; internet www.maf.gov.om.
Ministry of Awqaf (Religious Endowments) and Religious Affairs: POB 3232, Ruwi 112; tel. 24696870; e-mail info@mara.gov.om; internet www.maraoman.net.
Ministry of the Civil Service: POB 3994, Ruwi 112; tel. 24696000; fax 24601365; internet www.mocs.gov.om.
Ministry of Commerce and Industry: POB 550, Muscat 113; tel. 24813500; fax 24817238; e-mail info@mocioman.gov.om; internet www.mocioman.gov.om.
Ministry of Defence: POB 113, Muscat 113; tel. 24312605; fax 24702521.

OMAN

Ministry of Education: POB 3, Muscat 113; tel. 24773181; fax 24704465; e-mail moe@moe.gov.om; internet www.moe.gov.om.

Ministry of Environment and Climate Affairs: POB 323, Muscat 100; tel. 24404805; fax 24603993.

Ministry of Finance: POB 506, Muscat 100; tel. 24738201; fax 24737028; e-mail info@mof.gov.om; internet www.mof.gov.om.

Ministry of Foreign Affairs: POB 252, Muscat 112; tel. 24699453; fax 24696141; e-mail info@mofa.gov.om; internet www.mofa.gov.om.

Ministry of Health: POB 393, Muscat 113; tel. 24600527; fax 24602647; e-mail moh@moh.gov.om; internet www.moh.gov.om.

Ministry of Heritage and Culture: POB 668, Muscat 113; tel. 24641300; fax 24641331; e-mail info@mhc.gov.om; internet www.mhc.gov.om.

Ministry of Higher Education: POB 82, Ruwi 112; tel. 24693148; e-mail press@mohe.gov.om; internet www.mohe.gov.om.

Ministry of Housing: POB 1491, Ruwi 112; tel. 24603906; fax 24699180.

Ministry of Information: POB 600, Muscat 113; tel. 24603222; fax 24693770; e-mail omanet@omantel.net.om; internet www.omanet.om.

Ministry of the Interior: POB 127, Ruwi 112; tel. 24602244; fax 24696660; internet www.moi.gov.om.

Ministry of Justice: POB 354, Ruwi 112; tel. 24697699; e-mail webmaster@moj.gov.om; internet www.moj.gov.om.

Ministry of Legal Affairs: POB 578, Ruwi 112; tel. 24605802; fax 24482309; e-mail inquiry@mola.gov.om; internet www.mola.gov.om.

Ministry of Manpower: POB 413, Muscat 113; tel. 24816739; fax 24816234; internet www.manpower.gov.om.

Ministry of Oil and Gas: POB 551, Muscat 113; tel. 24603333; fax 24696972.

Ministry of Regional Municipalities and Water Resources: POB 461, Muscat 112; tel. 24692550; fax 24694015; e-mail admin@mrmwr.gov.om; internet www.mrmwr.gov.om.

Ministry of the Royal Office: POB 2227, Ruwi 112; tel. 24600841.

Ministry of Sports Affairs: POB 211, Muscat 113; tel. 24755240; fax 24704558; e-mail feedback@sportsoman.com; internet www.sportsoman.com.

Ministry of Tourism: Madinat al-Sultan Qaboos, POB 200, Muscat 115; tel. 24588700; fax 24588880; e-mail info@omantourism.gov.om; internet www.mot.gov.om.

Ministry of Transport and Communications: POB 338, Ruwi 112; tel. 24697888; fax 24696817; e-mail dgroads@omantel.net.om; internet www.motc.gov.om.

MAJLIS OMAN
(Council of Oman)

In a decree issued on 13 March 2011, Sultan Qaboos bin Said al-Said stated his intention to grant legislative and audit powers to both chambers of the Majlis Oman. A technical committee of experts was to be constituted and entrusted with the task of formulating a draft amendment to the Basic Statute of the State. Under the terms of the decree, the committee was bound to submit a report to Sultan Qaboos within 30 days of its issue.

Majlis al-Shoura
(Consultative Council)

POB 981, Muscat; tel. 24510444; fax 24510560; e-mail info@shura.om; internet www.shura.om.

President: Sheikh AHMAD BIN MUHAMMAD AL-ISSAI.

The Majlis al-Shoura was established by royal decree in November 1991. Initially, members of the Majlis were appointed by the Sultan from among nominees selected at national polls, but from the September 2000 elections members were directly elected. Two representatives are appointed from four candidates in each *wilaya* (district) of more than 30,000 inhabitants, and one from two candidates in each *wilaya* of fewer than 30,000 inhabitants. Members of the Majlis are appointed for a single four-year term of office. The Majlis elected in October 2007 comprised 84 members. The Majlis is an advisory body, the duties of which include the review of all social and economic draft laws prior to their enactment; public service ministries are required to submit reports and answer questions regarding their performance, plans and achievements. The President of the Majlis al-Shoura is appointed by royal decree.

Majlis al-Dawlah
(State Council)

POB 59, Muscat; tel. 24699677; fax 24698719; e-mail statecouncil@statecouncil.om.

President: Sheikh YAHYA BIN MAHFOUDH AL-MANTHERI.

The Majlis al-Dawlah was established in December 1997, in accordance with the terms of the Basic Statute of the State. Like the Majlis al-Shoura, it is an advisory body, the function of which is to serve as a liaison between the Government and the people of Oman. Its members are appointed by the Sultan for a four-year term. A new Majlis, comprising 70 members, was appointed in November 2007.

Political Organizations

There are no political organizations in Oman.

Diplomatic Representation

EMBASSIES IN OMAN

Algeria: POB 216, Muscat 115; tel. 24694945; fax 24694419; e-mail afcongem@omantel.net.om; Ambassador MUHAMMAD YOUSFI.

Austria: al-Kharijia St, Villa No. 898, Way No. 3013, POB 2070, Ruwi 112; tel. 24694127; fax 24699265; e-mail maskat-ob@bmeia.gv.at; Ambassador Dr ANDREAS KARABACZEK.

Bahrain: al-Khuwair, POB 66, Madinat Qaboos; tel. 24605133; fax 24605072; e-mail muscat.mission@mofa.gov.bh; Ambassador FOUAD SALMAN AL-MUAWDA.

Bangladesh: St 664, Bldg 5903, POB 3959, Ruwi 112; tel. 24567379; fax 24567502; e-mail bania@omantel.net.om; Ambassador NURUL ALAM CHOWDHURY.

Brazil: al-Khuwair, Villa 1424, Way 1521, POB 1149, Muscat; Ambassador MITZI GURGEL VALENTE DA COSTA.

Brunei: Shatti al-Qurum, St 3050, Villa 4062, POB 91, Ruwi 112; tel. 24603533; fax 24605910; e-mail kbopuni@omantel.net.om; Ambassador Dato' Seri Setia Dr Haji BESAR BIN Haji BAKAR.

China, People's Republic: House No. 1368, Shatti al-Qurum, POB 315, Muscat 112; tel. 24696698; fax 24602322; e-mail chinaemb_om@mfa.gov.cn; Ambassador WU JIUHONG.

Egypt: Jamiat al-Dowal al-Arabiya St, Diplomatic City, al-Khuwair, POB 2252, Ruwi 112; tel. 24600411; fax 24603626; e-mail eg.emb_muscat@mfa.gov.eg; Ambassador MUHAMMAD EL-MOKALI.

France: Diplomatic City, al-Khuwair, POB 208, Madinat Qaboos 115; tel. 24681800; fax 24681843; e-mail diplofr1@omantel.net.om; internet www.ambafrance-om.org; Ambassador MALIKA BERAK.

Germany: POB 128, Ruwi 112; tel. 24832482; fax 24835690; e-mail info@maskat.diplo.de; internet www.maskat.diplo.de; Ambassador ANGELIKA RENATE STORZ-CHAKARJI.

India: New Chancery Complex, Jamiat al-Dowal al-Arabiya St, al-Khuwair, POB 1727, Ruwi 112; tel. 24684500; fax 24698291; e-mail indiamct@omantel.net.om; internet www.indemb-oman.org; Ambassador ANIL WADHWA.

Iran: Diplomatic Area, Jamiat al-Dowal al-Arabiya St, POB 3155, Ruwi 112; tel. 24696944; fax 24696888; e-mail iranembassy@hotmail.com; internet www.iranembassy.gov.om; Ambassador HUSSEIN NOSH ABADI.

Iraq: Shatti al-Qurum, Way 3015, House No. 1073, POB 262, Muscat 115; tel. 24603642; fax 24602026; e-mail musemb@iraqmofamail.net; internet www.iraqem.com; Ambassador MUIZ KADIM SALMAN AL-NOAH.

Italy: Shatti al-Qurum, Way No. 3034, House No. 2697, POB 3727, Ruwi 112; tel. 24693727; fax 24695161; e-mail ambasciata.mascate@esteri.it; internet www.ambmascate.esteri.it; Ambassador PAOLO DIONISI.

Japan: Shatti al-Qurum, Villa No. 760, Way No. 3011, Jamiat al-Dowal al-Arabiya St, POB 3511, Ruwi 112; tel. 24601028; fax 24698720; e-mail embjapan@omantel.net.om; internet www.oman.emb-japan.go.jp; Ambassador SEIJI MORIMOTO.

Jordan: Diplomatic City, Arab League St, POB 70, al-Adhaiba 130; tel. 24692760; fax 24692762; e-mail embhkjom@omantel.net.om; Ambassador MAZIN MIDHAT JUMAH.

Korea, Republic: POB 377, Madinat Qaboos 115; tel. 24691490; fax 24691495; e-mail emboman@mofat.go.kr; internet omn.mofat.go.kr; Ambassador CHOE JONG-HYUN.

Kuwait: Diplomatic Area, al-Khuwair, Arab League St, Blk 13, Bldg 58, POB 1798, Ruwi 112; tel. 24699626; fax 24604732; e-mail muscat@mofa.gov.kw; Ambassador SALIM GHASAB AL-ZIMNAN.

Lebanon: Shatti al-Qurum, Way 3019, Villa 1613, al-Harthy Complex, POB 67, Muscat 118; tel. 24695844; fax 24695633; e-mail lebanon1@omantel.net.om; Ambassador AFIF AYYUB.

Malaysia: Shatti al-Qurum, Villa No. 1611, Way No. 3019, POB 3939, Ruwi 112; tel. 24698329; fax 24605031; e-mail mwmuscat@omantel.net.om; internet www.kln.gov.my/perwakilan/muscat; Chargé d'affaires a.i. MUHAMMAD NORHISYAM MUHAMMAD YOUSUF.

OMAN

Morocco: Shatti al-Qurum, Villa No. 2443, Way No. 3030, POB 3125, Ruwi 112; tel. 24696152; fax 24601114; e-mail sifamamu@omantel.net.om; Ambassador Dr NOUREDDINE BENOMAR.

Netherlands: Shatti al-Qurum, Way No. 3017, Villa No. 1366, POB 3302, Ruwi 112; tel. 24603706; fax 24603778; e-mail mus@minbuza.nl; internet www.mfa.nl/mus; Ambassador STEFAN VAN WERSCH.

Pakistan: Way No. 2133, POB 1302, Madinat Qaboos, Ruwi 112; tel. 24603439; fax 24697462; e-mail parepmuscat@hotmail.com; internet www.mofa.gov.pk/oman; Ambassador SOHAIL AMIN.

Philippines: POB 420, Madinat Qaboos 115; tel. 24605140; fax 24605176; e-mail muscatpe@omantel.net.om; Ambassador ACMAD D. OMAR.

Qatar: Diplomatic City, Jamiat al-Dowal al-Arabiya St, al-Khuwair, POB 802, Muscat 113; tel. 24691152; fax 24691156; e-mail sad707@omantel.net.om; Ambassador ABDULLAH BIN MUHAMMAD BIN KHALID AL-KHATIR.

Russia: Shatti al-Qurum, Way No. 3032, Surfait Compound, POB 80, Ruwi 112; tel. 24602894; fax 24604189; e-mail rusoman@omantel.net.om; Ambassador Dr SERGEI E. EVANOV.

Saudi Arabia: Diplomatic City, Jamiat al-Dowal al-Arabiya St, POB 1411, Ruwi 112; tel. 24601744; fax 24603540; e-mail omemb@mofa.gov.sa; Ambassador ABD AL-AZIZ BIN SULAIMAN AL-TURKI.

Senegal: Muscat; Ambassador CHEIKH TIDIANE SY.

Somalia: Mumtaz St, Villa Hassan Jumaa Baker, POB 1767, Ruwi 112; tel. and fax 24697977; e-mail danjsiad@omantel.net.om; Ambassador HASSAN MOHAMED SYAAD BERI.

South Africa: al-Harthy Complex, POB 231, Muscat 118; tel. 24694791; fax 24694792; e-mail solomona@foreign.gov.za; internet www.saembassymuscat.gov.om; Ambassador YOUSEF SALOJI.

Spain: Shatti al-Qurum, Way No. 2834, House No. 2573, POB 3492, Ruwi 112; tel. 24691101; fax 24698969; e-mail emb.mascate@mae.es; Ambassador TOMÁS RODRÍGUEZ-PANTOJA MÁRQUEZ.

Sri Lanka: POB 95, Madinat Qaboos 115; tel. 24697841; fax 24697336; e-mail lankaemb@omantel.net.om; Ambassador MUDIYANSELAGE MAHINDA RANARJA.

Sudan: Diplomatic City, al-Khuwair, POB 3971, Ruwi 112; tel. 24697875; fax 24699065; e-mail suanimt@gto.net.om; Ambassador JAMAL AL-SHEIKH AHMAD OTHMAN.

Syria: al-Ensharah St, Villa 201, POB 85, Madinat Qaboos, Muscat 115; tel. 24697904; fax 24603895; e-mail syria@omantel.net.om; internet www.syrianembassy.gov.om; Ambassador FAROUK MAHMOUD QADDOUR.

Thailand: Shatti al-Qurum, Villa No. 1339, Way No. 3017, POB 60, Ruwi 115; tel. 24602684; fax 24605714; e-mail thaimct@omantel.net.om; Ambassador VORAVEE WIRASAMBAN.

Tunisia: al-Ensharah St, Way 1507, POB 220, Muscat 115; tel. 24603486; fax 24697778; Ambassador MAHMOUD KHEMRI.

Turkey: Shatti al-Qurum, Bldg No. 3270, St No. 3042, POB 47, Mutrah 115; tel. 24697050; fax 24697053; e-mail turemmus@omantel.net.om; Ambassador MEHMET KHAIRI AYROL.

United Arab Emirates: Diplomatic City, al-Khuwair, POB 551, Muscat 111; tel. 24600302; fax 24604182; e-mail uaeoman@omantel.net.om; Ambassador MUHAMMAD ALI ABD AL-RAHMAN AL-OSAIMI.

United Kingdom: POB 185, Mina al-Fahal 116; tel. 24609000; fax 24609010; e-mail enquiries.muscat@fco.gov.uk; internet ukinoman.fco.gov.uk; Ambassador Dr NOEL GUCKIAN.

USA: Jamiat al-Dowal al-Arabiya St, POB 202, Madinat Qaboos, Muscat 115; tel. 24643400; fax 24699771; e-mail answersom@state.gov; internet oman.usembassy.gov; Ambassador RICHARD J. SCHMIERER.

Yemen: Shatti al-Qurum, Area 258, Way No. 2840, Bldg No. 2981, POB 105, Madinat Qaboos 115; tel. 24600815; fax 24605008; Ambassador ABD AL-RAHMAN KHAMIS UBAID.

Judicial System

Oman's Basic Statute guarantees the independence of the judiciary. The foundation for the legal system is *Shari'a* (Islamic law), which is the basis for family law, dealing with matters such as inheritance and divorce. Separate courts have been established to deal with commercial disputes and other matters to which *Shari'a* does not apply.

Courts of the First Instance are competent to try cases of criminal misdemeanour; serious crimes are tried by the Criminal Courts; the Court of Appeal is in Muscat. There are district courts throughout the country. Special courts deal with military crimes committed by members of the armed and security forces.

The Basic Statute provides for a Supreme Council to supervise the proper functioning of the courts.

An Administrative Court, to review the decisions of government bodies, was instituted in April 2001.

The office of Public Prosecutor was established in 1999, and the first such appointment was made in June 2001.

Religion

ISLAM

The majority of the population (estimated at 89.2% in 2001) are Muslims, of whom approximately three-quarters are of the Ibadi sect and about one-quarter are Sunni Muslims.

Grand Mufti of Oman: Sheikh AHMAD BIN HAMAD AL-KHALILI.

HINDUISM

According to 2001 estimates, 6.0% of the population are Hindus.

CHRISTIANITY

According to 2001 estimates, 2.9% of the population are Christians.

Protestantism

The Protestant Church in Oman: POB 1982, Ruwi 112; tel. 24702372; fax 24789943; e-mail pcomct@omantel.net.om; internet 76.12.38.165/occ2003/skur/history.htm; joint chaplaincy of the Anglican Church and the Reformed Church of America; four interdenominational churches in Oman, at Ruwi and Ghala in Muscat, at Sohar, and at Salalah; Senior Pastor Rev. MICHAEL PEPPIN.

The Roman Catholic Church

A small number of adherents, mainly expatriates, form part of the Apostolic Vicariate of Southern Arabia. The Vicar Apostolic is resident in the United Arab Emirates.

The Press

Article 31 of Oman's Basic Statute guarantees the freedom of the press, printing and publishing, according to the terms and conditions specified by the law. Published matter 'leading to discord, harming the State's security or abusing human dignity or rights' is prohibited.

NEWSPAPERS

Oman: POB 3002, Ruwi 112; tel. 24699689; fax 24697443; e-mail editor@omandaily.com; internet www.omandaily.com; daily; Arabic; publ. by Oman Establishment for Press, News, Publication and Advertising; Editor-in-Chief ABDULLAH BIN NASSER AL-RAHBI; circ. 26,000.

Al-Shabiba (Youth): POB 2998, Ruwi 112; tel. 24814373; fax 24811722; e-mail editor@shabiba.com; internet www.shabiba.com; f. 1993; daily; Arabic; culture, leisure and sports; publ. by Muscat Press and Publishing House SAOC; Editor-in-Chief AHMAD BIN ESSA AL-ZEDJALI; circ. 15,000.

Al-Watan (The Nation): POB 463, Muscat 113; tel. 24491919; fax 24491280; e-mail alwatan@omantel.net.om; internet www.alwatan.com; f. 1971; daily; Arabic; Editor-in-Chief MUHAMMAD BIN SULAYMAN AL-TAI; circ. 40,000.

English Language

Oman Daily Observer: POB 3002, Ruwi 112; tel. 24699647; fax 24600362; e-mail editor@omanobserver.com; internet www.omanobserver.com; f. 1981; daily; publ. by Oman Establishment for Press, News, Publication and Advertising; Chair. ABDULLAH BIN NASSER AL-RAHBI; Editor IBRAHIM BIN SAIF AL-HAMDANI; circ. 22,000.

Oman Tribune: POB 463, Muscat 113; tel. 24491919; fax 24498444; e-mail eomantribune@omantribune.com; internet www.omantribune.com; f. 2004; Chair. MUHAMMAD BIN SULAYMAN AL-TAI; Editor-in-Chief ABD AL-HAMID BIN SULAYMAN AL-TAI.

Times of Oman: POB 770, Ruwi 112; tel. 24811953; fax 24813153; e-mail online@timesofoman.com; internet www.timesofoman.com; f. 1975; daily; publ. by Muscat Press and Publishing House SAOC; Founder, Chair. and Editor-in-Chief ESSA BIN MUHAMMAD AL-ZEDJALI; Man. Dir ANIS BIN ESSA AL-ZEDJALI; circ. 34,000.

TheWeek: POB 2616, Ruwi 112, Muscat; tel. 24799388; fax 24793316; e-mail theweek@apexstuff.com; internet www.theweek.co.om; f. 2003; weekly; free; publ. by Apex Press and Publishing; CEO and Man. Editor MOHANA PRABHAKAR; circ. 50,743 (copies per week).

PERIODICALS

Al-Ain al-Sahira (The Vigilant Eye): Royal Oman Police, POB 302, Mina' al-Fahl 116; tel. 24569270; fax 24567161; internet www.rop.gov.om; quarterly magazine of Royal Oman Police; Editor-in-Chief Col ABDULLAH BIN ALI AL-HARTHI.

OMAN

Alam Aliktisaad Wala'mal (World of Economy and Business): POB 3305, Ruwi 112; tel. 24700896; fax 24707939; f. 2007; monthly; Arabic; business magazine; publ. by United Press and Publishing LLC.

Al-'Aqida (The Faith): POB 1001, Ruwi 112; tel. 24701000; fax 24709917; weekly illustrated magazine; Arabic; political; Editor SAID AL-SAMHAN AL-KATHIRI; circ. 10,000.

Business Today: POB 2616, Ruwi 112; tel. 24799388; fax 24793316; e-mail editorial@apexstuff.com; internet www.businesstoday.co.om; monthly; publ. by Apex Press and Publishing; Man. Editor MOHANA PRABHAKAR.

The Commercial: POB 2002, Ruwi 112; tel. 24704022; fax 24795885; e-mail omanad@omantel.net.om; f. 1978; monthly; Arabic and English; business news; Man. MUHAMMAD AYOOB; Chief Editor ALI BIN ABDULLAH AL-KASBI; circ. 10,000.

Al-Ghorfa (The Chamber): POB 1400, Ruwi 112; tel. 24703082; fax 24708497; e-mail alghorfa@chamberoman.com; internet www.chamberoman.com; f. 1978; bi-monthly; English and Arabic; business; publ. by Oman Chamber of Commerce and Industry; Editor HAMOOD HAMAD AL-MAHROUQ; circ. 10,500.

Al-Jarida al-Rasmiya (Official Gazette): POB 578, Ruwi 112; tel. 24605802; fax 24605697; f. 1972; fortnightly; publ. by Ministry of Legal Affairs.

Jund Oman (Soldiers of Oman): Ministry of Defence, POB 113, Muscat 113; tel. 24613615; fax 24613369; f. 1974; monthly; Arabic; illustrated magazine of the Ministry of Defence; Supervisor Chief of Staff of the Sultan's Armed Forces.

Al-Mar'a (Woman): United Media Services, POB 3305, Ruwi 112; tel. 24700896; fax 24707939; e-mail almara@umsoman.com; internet www.almaraonline.com; monthly; Arabic and English; women's interest; publ. by United Press and Publishing LLC.

Al-Markazi (The Central): POB 1161, Ruwi 112; tel. 24702222; fax 24707913; e-mail cboccr@omantel.net.om; internet www.cbo-oman.org; f. 1975; bi-monthly economic magazine; Arabic and English; publ. by Cen. Bank of Oman; Editor-in-Chief HAIDER BIN ABD AL-REDHA AL-LAWATI.

Al-Nahda (The Renaissance): POB 979, Muscat 113; tel. 24563104; fax 24563106; weekly illustrated magazine; Arabic; political and social; Editor TALEB SAID AL-MEAWALY; circ. 10,000.

Nizwa: POB 855, 117 Wadi Kabir; tel. 24601608; fax 24694254; e-mail nizwa99@nizwa.com; internet www.nizwa.com; f. 1994; quarterly; Arabic; literary and cultural; publ. by Oman Establishment for Press, News, Publication and Advertising; Editor-in-Chief SAIF AL-RAHBI.

Oman Economic Review: POB 3305, Ruwi 112; tel. 24700896; fax 24707939; e-mail editor@oeronline.com; internet www.oeronline.com; f. 1998; monthly; English; business news; publ. by United Press and Publishing LLC; Editor-in-Chief Sayyid TARIK BIN SHABIB; circ. 25,000.

Oman Today: POB 2616, Ruwi 112; tel. 24799388; fax 24793316; e-mail editorial@apexstuff.com; internet www.omantoday.co.om; f. 1981; monthly; English; leisure and sports; publ. by Apex Press and Publishing; Man. Editor MOHANA PRABHAKAR; circ. 20,000.

Al-Omaniya (Omani Woman): POB 3303, Ruwi 112; tel. 24792700; fax 24707765; f. 1982; monthly; Arabic; Editor AIDA BINT SALIM AL-HUJRI; circ. 10,500.

Risalat al-Masjid (The Mosque Message): POB 6066, Muscat; tel. 24561178; fax 24560607; issued by Diwan of the Royal Court Protocol Dept (Schools and Mosques Section); Editor JOUMA BIN MUHAMMAD BIN SALEM AL-WAHAIBI.

Al-Usra (The Family): POB 440, Mutrah 114; tel. 24794922; fax 24795348; e-mail admeds@omantel.net.om; f. 1974; fortnightly; Arabic; socio-economic illustrated magazine; Chief Editor SADEK ABDOWANI; circ. 15,000.

NEWS AGENCY

Oman News Agency: Ministry of Information, POB 3659, Ruwi 112; tel. 24698891; fax 24699657; e-mail onaoman@omantel.net.om; internet www.omannews.gov.om; f. 1986; Dir-Gen. and Editor-in-Chief MAJID BIN MUHAMMAD BIN FARAJ AL-ROWAS.

Publishers

Apex Press and Publishing: POB 2616, Ruwi 112, Muscat; tel. 24799388; fax 24793316; e-mail editorial@apexstuff.com; internet www.apexstuff.com; f. 1980; art, history, trade directories, maps, leisure and business magazines, and guidebooks; publs incl. *TheWeek* (English weekly), *Business Today* (business monthly), *Oman Today* (leisure monthly); Pres. SALEH M. TALIB AL-ZAKWANI; Man. Editor MOHANA PRABHAKAR.

Dar al-Usra: POB 440, Mutrah 114; tel. 24794922; fax 24795348; e-mail alusra@omantel.net.om.

Muscat Press and Publishing House SAOC: POB 770, Ruwi 112; tel. 24811953; fax 24813153; publs incl. *Times of Oman* (English daily) and *Al-Shabiba* (Arabic daily); Chair. ESSA MUHAMMAD AL-ZEDJALI; CEO AHMAD BIN ESSA AL-ZEDJALI.

National Publishing and Advertising LLC: POB 3112, Ruwi 112; tel. 24793098; fax 24708445; e-mail advertising@npaoman.com; internet www.npaoman.com; f. 1987; Man. ASHOK SUVARNA.

Oman Establishment for Press, News, Publication and Advertising (OEPNPA): POB 974, al-Qurum, Muscat 113; tel. 24699170; f. 1996 as Oman Newspaper House; publs include *Oman* (Arabic daily), *Oman Daily Observer* (English language) and *Nizwa* (magazine); three regional offices in Dhofar, Nizwa and Sohar; Chair. ABDULLAH BIN NASSER AL-RAHBI.

United Press and Publishing LLC (UPP): POB 3305, Ruwi 112; tel. 24700896; fax 24707939; e-mail info@renaissanceoman.com; internet www.renaissanceoman.com; f. 1995; part of Renaissance Services SAOG; publishes *Alam Aliktisaad Wala'mal* (Arabic monthly) and *Oman Economic Review* (English monthly); Gen. Man. SANDEEP SEHGAL.

Broadcasting and Communications

TELECOMMUNICATIONS

Regulatory Authority

Telecommunications Regulatory Authority: POB 579, Ruwi 112; tel. 24574300; fax 24565464; e-mail traoman@tra.gov.om; internet www.tra.gov.om; f. 2002 to oversee the privatization of Omantel (see below) and to set tariffs and regulate the sale of operating licences; Chair. MUHAMMAD BIN NASSER AL-KHUSAIBI.

Service Providers

Oman Telecommunications Company SAOC (Omantel): POB 789, Ruwi 112; tel. 24631417; fax 24697066; e-mail info@omantel.net.om; internet www.omantel.net.om; f. 1999 as successor to Gen. Telecommunications Org.; provider of fixed-line, mobile and internet services; held a monopoly on fixed-line services until 2008; state-owned, but undergoing privatization; Chair. Eng. SULTAN BIN HAMDOUN AL-HARTHY; Exec. Pres. Dr AMER BIN AWADH AL-RAWAS.

Oman Mobile Telecommunications Company LLC (Oman Mobile): POB 694, al-Azaiba 130; tel. 24474000; e-mail enquiry@omanmobile.om; internet www.omanmobile.om; f. 2004; Chair. Eng. SULTAN BIN HAMDOUN AL-HARTHI.

Omani Qatari Telecommunications Co SAOC (Nawras): POB 874, Muscat 111; tel. 95011500; fax 95011555; e-mail customerservice@nawras.om; internet www.nawras.om; f. 2004; awarded Oman's second mobile cellular telecommunications licence 2004; awarded Oman's second fixed-line licence 2008; jt venture between Qatar Telecommunications Corpn (Q-Tel), TDC A/S (Denmark) and several Omani investors; Chair. Sheikh SALIM BIN MUSTAHIL AL-MA'ASHANI; CEO ROSS CORMACK.

BROADCASTING

The Law on Private Radio and Television Stations, enacted in 2004, provided for the establishment of private broadcasters for the first time.

Radio

Sultanate of Oman Radio: Ministry of Information, POB 600, Muscat 113; tel. 24602058; fax 24601393; e-mail omanet@omantel.net.om; internet www.oman-radio.gov.om; f. 1970; operates four services: General Arabic Channel, Al-Shabab Channel (youth service), English-language FM service, Holy Koran Channel; Dir-Gen. NASSER SULAYMAN AL-SAIBANI.

The first private radio licences were issued in 2005, and broadcasts began in 2007 with the launch of Hala FM (Arabic, entertainment and music) and Hi FM (English, entertainment and music). A third private station, Al-Wisal FM, began broadcasting in Arabic in 2008.

Television

Sultanate of Oman Television: Ministry of Information, POB 600, Muscat 113; tel. 24603222; fax 24605032; e-mail feedback_tv@oman-tv.gov.om; internet www.oman-tv.gov.om; began broadcasting in 1974; programmes broadcast via Arabsat and Nilesat satellite networks.

OMAN

Finance

(cap. = capital; res = reserves; dep. = deposits; m. = million; brs = branches; amounts in rials Omani)

BANKING

At the end of March 2010 there were 17 commercial banks (seven local and 10 foreign) and two specialized banks, with a total network of 451 domestic branch offices operating throughout Oman.

Central Bank

Central Bank of Oman: POB 1161, 44 Mutrah Commercial Centre, Ruwi 112; tel. 24777777; fax 24788995; e-mail cboccr@omantel.net.om; internet www.cbo-oman.org; f. 1974; cap. 400m., res 774m., dep. 2,851m. (Dec. 2009); 100% state-owned; Dep. Chair. Dr ALI BIN MUHAMMAD BIN MOUSA; 2 brs.

Commercial Banks

Ahli Bank SAOG: POB 545, Mina al-Fahal 116; tel. 24577000; fax 24568001; e-mail info@ahlibank-oman.com; internet www.ahlibank-oman.com; f. 1997 as Alliance Housing Bank; renamed as above 2008; privately owned; cap. 67.8m., res 12.6m., dep. 501.8m. (Dec. 2009); Chair. HAMDAN ALI NASSER AL-HINAI; CEO ABD AL-AZIZ AL-BALUSHI; 12 brs.

Bank Dhofar SAOG: POB 1507, Ruwi 112; tel. 24790466; fax 24797246; e-mail info@bankdhofar.com; internet www.bankdhofar.com; f. 1990 as Bank Dhofar al-Omani al-Fransi SAOG; renamed as above in 2004 after merger with Majan Int. Bank SAOC; cap. 73.9m., res 95.0m., dep. 1,201.3m. (Dec. 2009); Chair. Eng. ABD AL-HAFIDH SALIM RAJAB AL-AUJAILI; CEO KRIS BABICCI; 54 brs.

BankMuscat SAOG: POB 134, Ruwi 112; tel. 24768888; fax 24785572; e-mail banking@bkmuscat.com; internet www.bankmuscat.com; f. 1993 by merger as Bank Muscat Al-Ahli Al-Omani; renamed Bank Muscat Int. in 1998, and as above in 1999; merged with Commercial Bank of Oman Ltd SAOG in 2000 and with Industrial Bank of Oman in 2002; 88.8% owned by Omani shareholders; cap. 107.7m., res 482.3m., dep. 4,673.5m. (Dec. 2009); Chair. Sheikh ABD AL-MALEK BIN ABDULLAH AL-KHALILI; Chief Exec. ABD AL-RAZAK ALI ISSA; 129 brs in Oman, 2 brs abroad.

Bank Sohar SAOG: POB 44, Hay al-Mina, Muttrah 114; tel. 24730000; fax 24793972; e-mail info@banksohar.net; internet www.banksohar.net; f. 2007; 32.5% owned by Oman Govt, 12% by Al Ghadir Al Arabia LLC, 55.5% by various Omani shareholders; cap. 100.0m., res 2.9m., dep. 892.8m. (Dec. 2009); Chair. Sheikh Dr SALIM SAID AL-FANNAH AL-ARAIMI; CEO Dr MUHAMMAD ABD AL-AZIZ KALMOOR; 11 brs.

National Bank of Oman SAOG (NBO): POB 751, Ruwi 112; tel. 24778000; fax 24778585; e-mail ask@nbo.co.om; internet www.nbo.co.om; f. 1973; 100% Omani-owned; cap. 108.1m., res 92.5m., dep. 1,480.4m. (Dec. 2009); Chair. OMAR HUSSAIN AL-FARDAN; CEO SALAAM BIN SAEED AL-SHAKSY; 64 brs in Oman, 6 brs abroad.

Oman Arab Bank SAOC: POB 2010, Ruwi 112; tel. 24706265; fax 24797736; e-mail mktoab@omantel.net.om; internet www.omanab.com; f. 1984; purchased Omani European Bank SAOG in 1994; 51% Omani-owned, 49% by Arab Bank PLC (Jordan); cap. 75m., res 47m., dep. 698m. (Dec. 2009); Chair. RASHAD MUHAMMAD AL-ZUBAIR; CEO ABD AL-QADER ASKALAN; 46 brs.

Oman International Bank SAOG: POB 1727, Muscat 111; tel. 24682500; fax 24682800; e-mail oibgm@omantel.net.om; internet www.oiboman.com; f. 1984; 100% Omani-owned; cap. 91.3m., res 57.7m., dep. 813.2m. (Dec. 2009); Chair. REEM BINT OMAR AL-ZAWAWI; Gen. Man. DOUGLAS EMMETT; 83 brs in Oman, 4 brs abroad.

Development Banks

Oman Development Bank SAOC: POB 3077, Ruwi 112; tel. 24812507; fax 24813100; e-mail customer.care@odboman.net; internet www.odboman.net; f. 1977; absorbed Oman Bank for Agriculture and Fisheries in 1997; provides finance for devt projects in industry, agriculture and fishing; state-owned; cap. 58m., res 7m., dep. 3m. (Dec. 2009); Chair. Sheikh YAQOOB BIN HAMAD AL-HARTHY; Gen. Man. SAMIR BIN BECHIR AL-SAID; 9 brs.

Oman Housing Bank SAOC: POB 2555, Ruwi 112; tel. 24704444; fax 24704071; e-mail ohb@ohb.co.om; internet www.ohb.co.om; f. 1977; long-term finance for housing devt; 100% state-owned; cap. 30.0m., res 44.5m., total assets 176.5m. (Dec. 2007); Gen. Man. ADNAN HAIDAR DARWISH AL-ZA'ABI; 9 brs.

STOCK EXCHANGE

Muscat Securities Market (MSM): POB 3265, Muscat 112; tel. 24823600; fax 24815776; e-mail info@msm.gov.om; internet www.msm.gov.om; 221 cos listed (Jan. 2009); f. 1989; Chair. HASSAN BIN ALI JAWAD AL-LAWATI; Dir-Gen. AHMAD SALEH AL-MARHOON.

Supervisory Body

Capital Market Authority (CMA): POB 3359, Ruwi 112; tel. 24823224; fax 24817471; e-mail info@cma.gov.om; internet www.cma.gov.om; f. 1998 to regulate capital market and insurance sector; Chair. SAAD BIN MUHAMMAD BIN SAID AL-MARDHOUF AL-SAADI (Minister of Commerce and Industry); Exec. Pres. YAHYA BIN SAID ABDULLAH AL-JABRI.

INSURANCE

In 2008 there were 23 licensed insurance companies operating in Oman. Of these, 11 were local firms and the remainder were branches of non-resident companies.

Al-Ahlia Insurance Co SAOG: POB 1463, Ruwi 112; tel. 24766800; fax 24797151; e-mail aaic@alahliaoman.com; internet www.alahliaoman.com; f. 1985; cap. 6.0m., total assets 63.1m. (June 2008); Chair. KHALID HILAL AL-MAAWALI; Gen. Man. A. R. SRINIVASAN.

Dhofar Insurance Co SAOG: POB 1002, Ruwi 112; tel. 24705305; fax 24793641; e-mail dhofar@dhofarinsurance.com; internet www.dhofarinsurance.com; f. 1989; cap. 20.0m. (Dec. 2007); Chair. Sheikh SALIM BIN MUBARAK AL-SHANFARI; Man. Dir and CEO TAHER T. AL-HERAKI.

Falcon Insurance Co SAOC: POB 2279, Ruwi 112; tel. 24660900; fax 24566476; e-mail info@falconinsuranceaoc.com; internet www.falconinsuranceaoc.com; f. 1977 as Al-Ittihad al-Watani; assoc. co of Al Anwar Holdings SAOG; cap. 5.4m.; Gen. Man. MICHAEL JAN WRIGHT.

Al Madina Gulf Insurance Co SAOC: POB 1805, Athaiba 130; tel. 24771888; fax 24771899; e-mail contact@amgioman.com; internet www.amgioman.com; f. 2006; cap. 10m. (Dec. 2006); CEO GAUTAM DATTA.

Muscat Insurance Co SAOC: POB 72, Ruwi 112; tel. 24478897; fax 24481847; e-mail info@muscatlife.com; internet www.omzest.com/mic.htm; f. 1995 as Muscat Insurance Co SAOG; restructured in 1999 as Muscat Nat. Holding Co SAOG (parent co), Muscat Insurance Co SAOC and Muscat Life Assurance Co SAOC; subsidiary of Omar Zawawi Establishment (OMZEST); Gen. Man. ANDREW M. WOODWARD.

National Life and General Insurance Co SAOC: POB 798, Wadi Kabir 117; tel. 24730999; fax 24795222; e-mail natlife@nlicgulf.com; internet www.nlicgulf.com; f. 1983; subsidiary of Oman Nat. Investment Corpn Holding SAOG; Gen. Man. S. VENKATACHALAM.

Oman Qatar Insurance Co SAOC: POB 3660, Ruwi 112; tel. 24700798; fax 24700815; e-mail contact@oqic.com; internet www.qatarinsurance.com/net_oman.htm; subsidiary of Qatar Insurance Co; CEO GEOFFREY BLOFELD.

Oman United Insurance Co SAOG: POB 1522, Ruwi 112; tel. 24477300; fax 24477334; e-mail info@omanutd.com; internet www.ouic-oman.com; f. 1985; cap. 10.0m., total assets 65.4m. (Dec. 2007); Chair. and CEO SAID SALIM BIN NASSIR AL-BUSAIDI.

Royal and Sun Alliance Oman (RSA Oman): POB 889, Muscat 100; tel. 24478318; fax 24482296; e-mail rsaoman@om.rsagroup.com; internet www.rsa.com.om; f. 2004; 67% owned by Royal and Sun Alliance Group (United Kingdom); CEO SANJEEV JHA.

Trade and Industry

GOVERNMENT AGENCY

Omani Centre for Investment Promotion and Export Development (OCIPED): POB 25, al-Wadi Kabir 117, Muscat; tel. 24826699; fax 24810890; e-mail info@ociped.com; internet www.ociped.com; f. 1996; promotes investment to Oman and the devt of non-oil Omani exports; Chair. SAAD BIN MUHAMMAD BIN SAID AL-MARDHOUF AL-SAADI (Minister of Commerce and Industry); CEO SALEM BIN NASSER AL-ISMAILY.

CHAMBER OF COMMERCE

Oman Chamber of Commerce and Industry: POB 1400, Ruwi 112; tel. 24707674; fax 24708497; e-mail occi@chamberoman.com; internet www.chamberoman.com; f. 1973; Chair. KHALIL BIN ABDULLAH BIN MUHAMMAD AL-KHONJI; 142,881 mems (Sept. 2008).

STATE HYDROCARBONS COMPANIES

National Gas Co SAOG: POB 95, Rusayl 124; tel. 24446073; fax 24446307; e-mail info@nationalgasco.net; internet www.nationalgasco.net; f. 1979; bottling of LPG; Chair. Sheikh KHALID AHMAD SULTAN AL-HOSNI; Gen. Man. PRADYOT KUMAR BAGCHI; 158 employees.

Oman Gas Co SOAC (OGC): POB 799, al-Khuwair 133; tel. 24681600; fax 24681678; e-mail info@oman-gas.com.om; internet www.oman-gas.com.om; f. 2000; govt-owned (80% Ministry of Oil

OMAN

Directory

and Gas; 20% Oman Oil Co SAOC); operates gas network and builds pipelines to supply power plants and other industries in Oman; Chair. Dr MUHAMMAD BIN HAMAD BIN SAIF AL-RUMHI (Minister of Oil and Gas); CEO YOUSUF BIN MUHAMMAD AL-OJAILI.

Oman LNG LLC: POB 560, Mina al-Fahal 116; tel. 24609999; fax 24609900; e-mail info@omanlng.co.om; internet www.omanlng.com; f. 1994; 51% state-owned; Royal Dutch Shell 30%; manages 6.6m.-metric-tons-per-year LNG plant at Qalhat; manufacturing, shipping and marketing; Chair. NASSER BIN KHAMIS AL-JASHMI; CEO and Gen. Man. Dr BRIAN BUCKLEY; 225 employees.

Oman Oil Co SAOC (OOC): POB 261, Ruwi 118; tel. 24573100; fax 24573101; e-mail info@oman-oil.com; internet www.oman-oil.com; f. late 1980s to invest in foreign commercial enterprises and oil-trading operations; incorporated 1996; 100% state-owned; Chair. NASSIR BIN KHAMIS AL-JASHMI; CEO AHMAD AL-WAHAIBI.

Oman Refineries and Petrochemicals Co LLC (ORPC): POB 3568, Ruwi 112; tel. 24561200; fax 24561384; internet www.orpc.co .om; f. 2007 after merger of Oman Refinery Co (f. 1982) and Sohar Refinery Co LLC; production of light petroleum products; production capacity 222,000 b/d (2008); 75% owned by Oman Govt, 25% by Oman Oil Co SAOC; Chair. Dr MUHAMMAD BIN HAMAD BIN SAIF AL-RUMHI (Minister of Oil and Gas); CEO Dr ADIL BIN ABD AL-AZIZ AL-KINDY; 355 employees.

Petroleum Development Oman LLC (PDO): POB 81, Muscat 113; tel. 24678111; fax 24677106; e-mail external-affairs@pdo.co.om; internet www.pdo.co.om; incorporated in Sultanate of Oman by royal decree as an LLC since 1980; 60% owned by Oman Govt, 34% by Royal Dutch Shell; exploration and production of crude petroleum and gas; crude petroleum production (2007) averaged 561,000 b/d from over 100 fields, linked by a pipeline system to terminal at Mina al-Fahal, near Muscat; gas production (2007) totalled 63.3m. cu m/d; Chair. Dr MUHAMMAD BIN HAMAD BIN SAIF AL-RUMHI (Minister of Oil and Gas); Man. Dir JOHN MALCOLM; 5,000 employees.

Qalhat LNG SAOC: POB 514, al-Khuwair 133; tel. 24574004; fax 24574090; e-mail info@qalhatlng.co.om; internet www.qalhatlng .com; f. 2003; production of LNG; 46.84% owned by Oman Govt, 36.80% by Oman LNG LLC, 16.36% by foreign investors; Chair. Sheikh AL-FADHIL BIN MUHAMMAD AL-HARTHY; CEO HARIB AL-KITANI.

UTILITIES

As part of its privatization programme, the Omani Government is divesting the utilities on a project-by-project basis. Private investors have already been found for several municipal wastewater projects, desalination plants and regional electricity providers.

Supervisory Body

Public Authority for Electricity and Water (PAEW): POB 1889, al-Azaiba 130; tel. 24611100; fax 24611133; e-mail dg-project@paew .gov.om; internet www.paew.gov.om; f. 2007 following restructuring of fmr Ministry of Housing, Electricity and Water; Chair. MUHAMMAD BIN ABDULLAH BIN MUHAMMAD AL-MAHROUQI.

Electricity

Authority for Electricity Regulation (AER): POB 954, al-Khuwair 133; tel. 24609700; fax 24609701; e-mail enquiries@aer-oman .org; internet www.aer-oman.org; f. 2004 to regulate and facilitate the privatization of the electricity and related water sector; Chair. Dr SALEH MUHAMMAD AL-ALAWI; Exec. Dir JOHN CUNEEN.

Electricity Holding Co SAOC (EHC): POB 850, Mina al-Fahal 116; tel. 24559200; fax 24559288; e-mail ehcoman@omantel.net.om; internet www.ehcoman.com; f. 2005; state-owned; established to hold Govt's ownership in nine utility cos and to facilitate the commercial restructuring of the sector; Al-Rusail Power Co was privatized in 2007; of the remaining eight successor cos, six are currently scheduled for privatization; Chair. MUHAMMAD BIN ABDULLAH BIN MUHAMMAD AL-MAHROUQI; CEO KARL MATACZ.

Principal subsidiaries of the EHC include:

Muscat Electricity Distribution Co SAOC (MEDC): POB 3732, al-Ghubrah 112; tel. 24588600; fax 24588666; e-mail medc@medcoman.com; internet www.medcoman.com; f. 2005; responsible for all distribution in the Governorate of Muscat; Chair. Eng. SALEH AL-FARSI; Gen. Man. Eng. ZAHIR AL-ABRI.

Oman Electricity Transmission Co SAOC (OETC): POB 1224, al-Hamriya 131; tel. 24573221; fax 24573222; e-mail info@ omangrid.com; internet www.omangrid.com; f. 2003; owns and operates the Main Interconnected System, which covers the north of Oman and accounts for 90% of the Sultanate's electricity transmission; scheduled for privatization; Chair. Eng. SAIF ABDULLAH RASHID AL-SUMRY; Gen. Man. ALI AL-HADABI.

Oman Power and Water Procurement Co SAOC: POB 1388, Ruwi 112; e-mail vacancies@omanpwp.com; internet www .omanpwp.co.om; f. 2003; responsible for forecasting and managing the supply and demand of electricity and water; Chair. SAUD NASSIR AL-SHUKAILY; CEO BOB WHITELAW.

Other subsidiaries of the EHC are: Al-Ghubrah Power and Desalination Co, Majan Electricity Co, Mazoon Electricity Co, Rural Areas Electricity Co and Wadi Jizzi Power Co.

Water

Ministry of Regional Municipalities and Water Resources: (see The Government); assesses, manages, develops and conserves water resources.

Oman Power and Water Procurement Co SAOC: see Electricity.

Oman Wastewater Services Co SAOC (Haya Water): POB 1047, al-Khuwair 133; tel. 24590544; fax 24693418; e-mail customerservice@omanwsc.com; internet www.owsc.com.om; f. 2002; devt and operation of a wastewater system in the Governorate of Muscat; govt-owned; CEO OMAR KHALFAN AL-WAHAIBI.

Transport

RAILWAYS

There are no railways in Oman, although plans for a regional rail network, connecting Oman with member countries of the Co-operation Council for the Arab States of the Gulf (or Gulf Co-operation Council—GCC), were finalized in late 2009. A feasibility study into the proposed first phase of the Omani section of the GCC network, a 230-km line linking Sohar and Muscat, was carried out by a French contractor in 2009. Tenders for contracts to design and manage the Omani rail project were issued in April 2010.

ROADS

A network of adequate graded roads links all the main centres of population, and only a few mountain villages are inaccessible by off-road vehicles. In 2009 there were 56,361 km of roads, of which 1,625 km were dual carriageways and a further 25,926 km were asphalted roads. The eighth Development Plan (2011–15) provided for several large-scale road-building projects, including the third phase of a new 240-km Batinah coastal road linking Barka and Sohar with Khatmat Malaha on the border with the United Arab Emirates. A new 81-km dual carriageway linking Sohar with Buraimi, in north-eastern Oman, was inaugurated in January 2010.

Directorate-General of Roads: Ministry of Transport and Communications, POB 338, Ruwi 112; tel. 24697870; fax 24696817; e-mail dgroads@omantel.net.om; internet www.motc.gov.om/en/ edgr/edgr.html; Dir-Gen. of Roads Sheikh MUHAMMAD BIN HILAL AL-KHALILI.

Oman National Transport Co SAOG (ONTC): POB 620, Muscat 113; tel. 24490046; fax 24490152; e-mail info@ontcoman.com; internet www.ontcoman.com; f. 1972; re-established in 1984; operates local, regional and long-distance bus services from Muscat; Chair. MAJID SAID SALIM AL-RUWAHI; Gen. Man. MAJID AL-MANDHRY.

SHIPPING

Port Sultan Qaboos (Mina Sultan Qaboos), at the entrance to the Persian (Arabian) Gulf, was built in 1974 to provide nine deep-water berths varying in length from 250 ft to 750 ft (76 m to 228 m), with draughts of up to 43 ft (13 m), and three berths for shallow-draught vessels drawing 12 ft to 16 ft (3.7 m to 4.9 m) of water. A total of 12 new berths have been opened, and two of the existing berths have been upgraded to a container terminal capable of handling 60 containers per hour. The port also has a 3,000-metric-ton-capacity cold store, which belongs to the Oman Fisheries Co. In the 1990s Port Sultan Qaboos underwent a further upgrade and expansion. A new terminal for passenger cruise ships was inaugurated in February 2010.

The oil terminal at Mina al-Fahal can also accommodate the largest super-tankers on offshore loading buoys. Similar facilities for the import of refined petroleum products exist at Mina al-Fahal. Salalah Port, formerly known as Mina Raysut, is Oman's largest transshipment terminal and serves as a major transshipment centre for the region. Salalah has been developed into an all-weather port, and, in addition to container facilities, has six deep-water berths with an annual capacity of 4.5m. 20-ft equivalent units; plans for the construction of three additional deep-water berths were announced in 2008. A major redevelopment of the port at Duqm, on the Gulf of Masirah, was announced in 2007. In 2008 the authorities announced that the project would be significantly expanded to provide: deep-water berths of 18 m; a deepened approach channel; breakwaters expanded to 7.7 km; a new dry dock for ships of up to 400,000 tons; and a new ship repair yard. The project was allocated an initial RO 700m. in government investment and was expected to be completed by 2012.

OMAN

Port Authorities and Regulatory Body

Directorate-General of Ports and Maritime Affairs: POB 684, Ruwi 113; tel. 24685994; fax 24685992; e-mail dgpma@omantel.net.om; Dir-Gen. Eng. QASSIM AHMAD ABD AL-MOHSEN AL-SHIZAWI.

Port Services Corpn SAOG (PSC): POB 133, Muscat 113; tel. 24714000; fax 24714007; e-mail mktg@pscoman.com; internet www.pscoman.com; f. 1976; jointly owned by the Govt of Oman and private shareholders; responsible for management of Port Sultan Qaboos; cap. RO 7.9m. (2007); Exec. Pres. SAUD BIN AHMAD AL-NAHARI.

Salalah Port Services Co SAOG (SPS): POB 105, Muscat 118; tel. 24601003; fax 24600736; e-mail info@salalahport.com; internet www.salalahport.com; f. 1997; holds a 30-year concession to manage and develop Salalah Port; CEO PETER FORD.

Principal Shipping Companies

National Ferries Co SAOC: Jibroo, Blk 1, Muscat; tel. 24715252; fax 24711333; e-mail reservation@nfcoman.com; internet www.nfcoman.com; govt-owned; operates a high-speed, passenger and vehicle ferry service between Muscat and Khasab, on the Strait of Hormuz; Chair. MEHDI AL-ABDUWANI.

Oman Shipping Co SAOC (OSC): al-Harthy Complex, POB 104, Muscat 118; tel. 24400900; fax 24400922; e-mail info@omanship.co.om; internet www.omanship.co.om; f. 2003; govt-owned (Ministry of Finance 80%, Oman Oil Co SAOC 20%); owns and operates a fleet of over 30 vessels; transportation of LNG, crude petroleum and petrochemical products; subsidiaries include: Oman Charter Co, Duqm Maritime Transportation Co, Liwa Maritime Transportation Co, Energy Spring LNG Carrier SA, Oasis LNG Carrier SA; Dep. Chair. AHMAD BIN MUHAMMAD BIN SALIM AL-FUTAISI (Minister of Transport and Communications).

CIVIL AVIATION

Domestic and international flights operate from Muscat International Airport (known as Seeb International Airport prior to February 2008). In 2009 4.6m. passengers passed through the airport; a project designed to increase annual passenger capacity to 12m. was expected to be completed by 2014. Oman's second international airport, at Salalah, was completed in 1978; in 2009 426,000 passengers passed through the airport. Both Seeb and Salalah were effectively privatized in October 2001. Responsibility for the management and refurbishment of the airports passed to Oman Airports Management Co (OAMC), 75% of which was owned by foreign investors and 25% by the Omani Government; however, following the failure of the Government successfully to agree financial terms for the privatization and ongoing development of the airports with OAMC, the 25-year contract was cancelled in October 2004 and Seeb and Salalah airports were returned to state control. OAMC continues to manage and operate Oman's airports, but it is now a wholly government-owned entity. Plans for substantial development and expansion of both international airports to provide additional terminals and increase passenger-handling capacity were announced as part of the Government's seventh Development Plan in 2006. There are also airports at Sur, Masirah, Khasab and Diba, with six further airports planned for Sohar, Duqm, Ras Al Hadd, Adam, Haima and Shaleem. Three new private airfields, owned and operated by Petroleum Development Oman, were opened in 2008 at Marmul, Qarn Alam and Fahud.

Directorate-General of Civil Aviation and Meteorology: POB 1, CPO Muscat International Airport, Muscat 111; tel. 24519356; fax 24519880; internet www.met.gov.om; Dir-Gen. Eng. AHMAD BIN SAID BIN SALIM AL-RAWAHY.

Oman Air SAOC: POB 58, Muscat International Airport 111; tel. 24531111; fax 24765121; e-mail wycallcenter@omanair.aero; internet www.omanair.aero/wy; f. 1993 as a subsidiary of Oman Aviation Services Co (f. 1981), whole corpn renamed Oman Air 2008; state-owned; cap. US $1,300m.; air-charter, maintenance, handling and catering; operators of Oman's domestic and international commercial airline; operates a fleet of 21 aircraft; carried over 2.3m. passengers in 2009; Chair. DARWISH BIN ISMAIL BIN ALI AL-BALUSHI (Minister Responsible for Financial Affairs); CEO PETER HILL.

Oman Airports Management Co SOAC: POB 1707, Muscat 111; tel. 24518030; fax 24518088; e-mail oamcinfo@omanairports.com; f. 2002; originally 75% owned by private investors; 100% owned by Oman Govt since 2004; operates Muscat International and Salalah airports; Chair. AHMAD BIN MUHAMMAD BIN SALIM AL-FUTAISI (Minister of Transport and Communications); CEO GEORGE BELLEW.

Tourism

Tourism, introduced in 1985, is strictly controlled. Oman's attractions, apart from the capital itself, include Nizwa, ancient capital of the interior, Dhofar, and the forts of Nakhl, Rustaq and al-Hazm. The country also possesses an attractive and clean environment, including around 1,700 km of sandy beaches. The tourism sector has been undergoing a period of intensive investment and development in recent years, overseen by the Oman Tourism Development Co (Omran). The emphasis has been on the development of extensive luxury resorts in areas of outstanding natural beauty. By the end of 2009 there were 10,420 hotel rooms, with plans to increase this to 18,000 by 2015. In 2008 there were 1,273,441 visitor arrivals in Oman, and tourism receipts totalled US $1,111m.

Directorate-General of Tourism: Madinat al-Sultan Qaboos, POB 200, Muscat 115; tel. 24588700; fax 24588880; e-mail info@omantourism.gov.om; internet www.omantourism.gov.om; Dir-Gen. MUHAMMAD ALI SAID.

Oman Tourism Development Co (Omran): POB 479, Muttrah 114; tel. 24773700; fax 24793929; e-mail enquiries@omran.om; internet www.omran.om; f. 2005; CEO WAEL BIN AHMAD AL-LAWATI.

Defence

Chief of Staff of the Sultan's Armed Forces: Lt-Gen. AHMED BIN HARITH AL-NABHANI.

Commander of the Royal Army of Oman: Maj.-Gen. SAID BIN NASSIR AL-SALMI.

Commander of the Royal Air Force of Oman: Air Vice-Marshal YAHIA BIN RASHID AL-JUMAA.

Defence and National Security Expenditure (2010 budget): RO 1,553m.

Military service: voluntary.

Total armed forces (as assessed at November 2010): 42,600: army 25,000; navy 4,200; air force 5,000; plus 2,000 expatriate personnel. There is a 6,400-strong Royal Guard.

Paramilitary forces: 4,400: tribal Home Guard (*Firqat*) 4,000; police coastguard 400.

Education

Great advances have been made in education since 1970, when Sultan Qaboos came to power. Although education is still not compulsory, it is provided free to Omani citizens from primary to tertiary level, and attendance has increased greatly. Primary education begins at six years of age and lasts for six years. The next level of education, divided into two equal stages (preparatory and secondary), lasts for a further six years. In 1998/99 a new system, comprising 10 years of basic education and two years of secondary education, was introduced in 17 schools; it was to be implemented gradually throughout the country. In 2009/10 there were 1,043 schools in the state sector, as well as 343 private kindergartens and schools regulated by the Ministry of Education. In total, 531,283 students were in state education and 56,204 in private education in 2009/10. As a proportion of the school-age population, the total enrolment at primary, preparatory and secondary schools increased from 25% (boys 36%; girls 14%) in 1975 to 76% (boys 78%; girls 74%) in 1997/98. Primary enrolment in 2008/09 included 77% of children in the relevant age-group, while secondary enrolment included 82% of children in the relevant age-group. In 2005/06 there were six teacher-training colleges, four vocational institutes, six technical colleges and 16 institutes of health, together with the College of Shari'a and Law, the Academy of Tourism and Catering, and the College of Banking and Financial Studies. There are five private universities and several private technical colleges. Oman's first national university, named after Sultan Qaboos, was opened in late 1986, and had 15,357 students in 2009/10. In the 2010 budget RO 874m. was allocated to education (equivalent to 12% of total budgetary expenditure).

PAKISTAN

Introductory Survey

LOCATION, CLIMATE, LANGUAGE, RELIGION, FLAG, CAPITAL

The Islamic Republic of Pakistan lies in southern Asia, bordered by India to the east and by Afghanistan and Iran to the west. It has a short frontier with the People's Republic of China in the far north-east. The climate is dry and generally hot, with an annual average temperature of 27°C (80°F), except in the mountains, which have very cold winters. Temperatures in Karachi are generally between 13°C (55°F) and 34°C (93°F), with negligible rainfall. The principal languages are Punjabi (the language usually spoken in 44.2% of households in 1998), Pushto (Pashtu) (15.4%), Sindhi (14.1%) and Saraiki (10.5%). Urdu (7.6%) is the national language, and English is extensively used. The state religion is Islam, embracing more than 96% of the population in 1998, the remainder being mainly Hindus or Christians. The national flag (proportions 2 by 3) has a vertical white stripe at the hoist, while the remainder is dark green, with a white crescent moon and a five-pointed star in the centre. The capital is Islamabad.

CONTEMPORARY POLITICAL HISTORY

Historical Context

Pakistan was created in August 1947 by the partition of the United Kingdom's former Indian Empire into the independent states of India and Pakistan, in response to demands by elements of the Muslim population in the subcontinent for the establishment of a specifically Islamic state. Pakistan originally comprised two distinct regions: East Pakistan and West Pakistan, separated by some 1,600 km (1,000 miles) of Indian territory, and united only by a common religion. Although the majority of the population lived in the smaller East Pakistan, political and military power was concentrated in the west, where the Muslim League was the dominant political movement. The leader of the Muslim League, Muhammad Ali Jinnah, popularly known as Quaid-i-Azam ('Great Leader'), became the first Governor-General of Pakistan but died in 1948. The country, formerly a dominion with the British monarch as Head of State, became a republic on 23 March 1956, when Pakistan's first Constitution was promulgated. At the same time Maj.-Gen. Iskander Mirza was appointed as Pakistan's first President.

Pakistan came under military rule in early October 1958, when President Mirza abrogated the Constitution, declared martial law, dismissed the national and provincial governments and dissolved all political parties. In late October, however, Gen. (later Field Marshal) Muhammad Ayub Khan, the Martial Law Administrator appointed by Mirza, removed Mirza from office and became President himself. Ayub Khan's autocratic but modernizing regime lasted until March 1969, when he was forced to resign following widespread unrest. Gen. Agha Muhammad Yahya Khan, the Commander-in-Chief of the Army, replaced him, and martial law was reimposed.

In December 1970 the country's first general election was held for a national assembly. Sheikh Mujibur Rahman's Awami League, which advocated autonomy for East Pakistan, won almost all the seats in the east (thus gaining an absolute majority in the National Assembly), while the Pakistan People's Party (PPP), led by Zulfikar Ali Bhutto, won a majority of seats in the west. Following the failure of negotiations to achieve a coalition government of the two parties, on 23 March 1971 East Pakistan declared its independence as the People's Republic of Bangladesh. Civil war immediately broke out, as Pakistani troops clashed with Bengali irregular forces. In December the Indian army intervened in the conflict to support the Bengalis, and the Pakistani army was forced to withdraw, thus permitting Bangladesh to establish firmly its independence. In the truncated Pakistan that remained in the west Yahya Khan resigned, military rule was ended, and Bhutto became the new President.

Domestic Political Affairs

Premiership of Zulfikar Ali Bhutto (1973–77)

A new Constitution, which came into effect in August 1973, provided for a parliamentary system of government. Bhutto was appointed executive Prime Minister, while Fazal Elahi Chaudry, hitherto Speaker of the National Assembly, became constitutional President. The PPP won an overwhelming majority of seats in elections to the National Assembly in March 1977. However, the opposition Pakistan National Alliance (PNA) accused the PPP of widespread electoral malpractice and launched a nation-wide campaign of civil disobedience. An estimated 1,000 people died in subsequent clashes between troops and demonstrators, and some 40,000 people were arrested. In July the armed forces intervened in the crisis: Bhutto was deposed in a bloodless military coup and a martial law regime was instituted, with Gen. Mohammad Zia ul-Haq, the Army Chief of Staff, as Chief Martial Law Administrator. President Chaudry remained in office as Head of State. Bhutto was subsequently charged with instigating the murder of a PPP dissident and a member of the dissident's family in 1974. He was sentenced to death in March 1978 and executed in April 1979.

Pakistan under Gen. Mohammad Zia ul-Haq (1977–88)

In September 1978 President Chaudry resigned and Gen. Zia became President. General elections were postponed several times by the military administration, and in October 1979 Gen. Zia announced an indefinite postponement of the polls. Opposition to the military regime was severely suppressed. In March 1981 nine political parties formed an opposition alliance, the Movement for the Restoration of Democracy (MRD), which advocated an end to military rule. Several opposition politicians were subsequently interned or placed under house arrest. In August 1983 the MRD, led by the PPP, launched a civil disobedience campaign to press for the restoration of parliamentary democracy on the basis of the 1973 Constitution. The campaign enjoyed considerable support in Sindh province, where anti-Government protests resulted in numerous deaths. However, there was limited popular support elsewhere in the country, and the campaign ended in December 1983. Many political leaders and activists, including Benazir Bhutto (daughter of the former President and herself a leading PPP activist), were subsequently imprisoned or went into exile.

Gen. Zia's regime zealously pursued a policy of 'Islamization' of the country's institutions, including the enforcement of Islamic penal codes, and the introduction of Islamic economic principles, such as interest-free banking. In December 1984 a referendum was held, which sought affirmation of the Islamization process and, indirectly, endorsement of a further five-year term for Gen. Zia. The referendum was boycotted by the MRD, but, according to official figures, 98% of those participating supported the proposal. However, there were widespread allegations of electoral malpractice.

In February 1985 a general election was held for a national assembly, followed shortly afterwards by elections to four provincial assemblies. The elections were held on a non-party basis, but widespread dissatisfaction with the regime was indicated by the defeat of several of Zia's cabinet ministers and close supporters. The largest two groupings in the new National Assembly were formed by a faction of the Pakistan Muslim League (PML, the successor to the Muslim League), known as the Pagara Group, and former members of the PPP. In late March Gen. Zia appointed Muhammad Khan Junejo, a member of the PML (Pagara Group), as Prime Minister, and an almost entirely civilian Cabinet was formed.

In October 1985 the National Assembly approved changes to the Constitution (the 'Eighth Amendment'), proposed by Gen. Zia, which introduced a powerful executive presidency and indemnified all actions of the military regime during the previous eight years. On 30 December Gen. Zia announced the repeal of martial law and the restoration of the Constitution (as amended in October). The military courts were dissolved, and military personnel were removed from civilian posts, with the exception of Gen. Zia, who remained as President and head of the armed forces. Junejo retained the post of Prime Minister in a new Cabinet. However, the MRD continued to demand the restoration of the unamended 1973 Constitution. In April 1986 the opposition's cause was strengthened by the return from exile of

Benazir Bhutto, who travelled throughout the country holding political rallies which attracted thousands of supporters. She demanded the resignation of President Zia and the holding of a free general election, open to all political parties. In May Benazir Bhutto and her mother, Nusrat Bhutto, were elected as Co-Chairwomen of the PPP. In August the Government adopted a less tolerant approach towards the MRD by banning all rallies scheduled for Independence Day and by detaining hundreds of opposition members, including Benazir Bhutto. The arrests provoked violent anti-Government demonstrations in a number of cities.

In late 1986 violent clashes occurred in Karachi, Quetta and Hyderabad as a result of disputes between rival ethnic groups—primarily between the Pathans, originally from the North-West Frontier Province (NWFP, renamed Khyber Pakhtoonkhwa in 2010) and Afghanistan, and the Urdu-speaking Mohajirs, who migrated from India when the subcontinent was partitioned in 1947. The violence was most severe in Karachi, where some 170 people were killed in December. The rise of ethnic communalism in Pakistan was reflected in the results of local elections held throughout the country in November 1987. The party of the Mohajirs, the Mohajir Qaumi Movement (MQM), won the majority of seats in Karachi and was also successful in other urban areas of Sindh province.

In May 1988, in accordance with the authority vested in him through the Eighth Amendment, President Zia dismissed the Prime Minister and his Cabinet, and dissolved the National Assembly and the four provincial assemblies. Zia became head of an interim administration, which was to govern until a general election was held. In July Zia announced that the elections would be held in November. However, on 17 August 1988 President Zia was killed in an air crash in eastern Pakistan. Subsequent speculation that the cause of the crash was sabotage was not officially confirmed. The Chairman of the Senate, Ghulam Ishaq Khan, was appointed acting President, and an emergency National Council (composed of senior military officers, the four provincial governors and four federal ministers) was appointed to take charge of government.

Benazir Bhutto and the Pakistan People's Party assume power (1988–90)

Despite the imposition of a state of emergency after the death of Zia, the general election took place, as scheduled, in November 1988. The PPP won 93 of the 207 directly elected seats in the National Assembly, and was the only party to secure seats in each of Pakistan's four provinces. The Islamic Democratic Alliance (IDA), a grouping of nine Islamic and right-wing parties (including the PML), gained 54 seats. However, the PPP did not achieve such a high level of support in the elections to the provincial assemblies, held three days later. The PPP was able to form coalition governments in Sindh and the NWFP, but the IDA took power in Punjab, the most populous province. At the federal level, a coalition Government was formed by the PPP and the MQM, which together had a working majority in the National Assembly (the MQM held 14 seats). Benazir Bhutto, the leader of the PPP, was appointed Prime Minister on 1 December, thus becoming the first female leader of a Muslim country. The state of emergency was repealed on the same day. A new Cabinet was formed, and later in December an electoral college (comprising the Senate, the National Assembly and the four provincial assemblies) elected Ghulam Ishaq Khan as President.

Benazir Bhutto's attempts, in early 1989, to repeal the Eighth Amendment to the Constitution, which severely constrained her powers as Prime Minister, were unsuccessful. Moreover, the fragile coalitions that the PPP had formed in the provincial assemblies soon came under pressure. In April the coalition Government formed by the PPP and the Awami National Party (ANP) in the NWFP collapsed. In May the coalition with the MQM in Sindh province also failed, following renewed ethnic conflict in the region. In the same month the opposition was strengthened by the formation of an informal parliamentary grouping, the Combined Opposition Party (COP), comprising the IDA, the ANP, Jamiat-e-Ulema-e-Islam (JUI) and the Pakistan Awami Ittehad. In October the Government suffered a serious reversal when the MQM withdrew its parliamentary support for the PPP and transferred it to the opposition, claiming that the PPP had failed to honour any of the promises made in the original co-operation agreement between the two parties. In November a parliamentary motion of no confidence, proposed by the COP against the Government, was narrowly defeated. In January 1990 the COP organized a campaign to undermine the Government, accusing it of corruption, political bribery and mismanagement. Rallies and demonstrations in Sindh province culminated in violence between supporters of the PPP and the MQM; in May about 100 people were killed during violent clashes between police and demonstrators in the region. Calm was temporarily restored by the deployment of army units.

By mid-1990 the initial popularity of the PPP Government appeared to have declined considerably: the maintenance of law and order had worsened; no significant new legislation had been introduced; the economic situation was deteriorating; and there were widespread allegations of corruption against high-ranking officials. On 6 August the President, in accordance with his constitutional powers, dissolved the National Assembly, dismissed the Prime Minister and her Cabinet and declared a state of emergency. He also announced that a general election would take place in late October. The President alleged that the ousted Government had violated the Constitution, accusing it of corruption, nepotism and incompetence. Ghulam Mustafa Jatoi, the leader of the COP in the National Assembly, was appointed acting Prime Minister in an interim Government. The four provincial assemblies were also dissolved, and 'caretaker' Chief Ministers appointed. Benazir Bhutto claimed that the dissolution of her administration was illegal and strongly denied the various charges made against her Government. At the end of August several of Benazir Bhutto's former ministers were arrested, and in the following month she herself was indicted on more than 10 charges of corruption and abuse of power. In early October Benazir Bhutto's husband, Asif Ali Zardari, was arrested on charges of extortion, kidnapping and financial irregularities (he was later acquitted on all counts).

Mohammad Nawaz Sharif and the Islamic Democratic Alliance head the Government (1990–93)

At the general election, which took place, as scheduled, on 24 October 1990, the IDA doubled its representation in the National Assembly, leaving it only four seats short of an absolute majority, while the People's Democratic Alliance (PDA, an electoral alliance comprising the PPP and three smaller parties) suffered a heavy defeat. Support for the PPP also declined in the provincial elections, where it unexpectedly lost control of its traditional stronghold in Sindh and fared badly elsewhere. Regional and ethnic parties continued to expand their influence, notably the MQM in urban areas of Sindh, and the ANP in the NWFP. On 6 November Mohammad Nawaz Sharif, the leader of the IDA and the former Chief Minister of Punjab, was elected as the new Prime Minister. He officially ended the three-month-long state of emergency, and appointed a new Cabinet, which included several ministers who had served under President Zia. Nawaz Sharif promised that one of the Government's major priorities was to establish lasting peace in Sindh, where ethnic conflict and general lawlessness continued to prevail. However, it was alleged that the Government's subsequent campaign of suppression in the province, in response to numerous local murders and kidnappings, was aimed primarily at supporters of the PPP, hundreds of whom were arrested.

In May 1991 the National Assembly adopted legislation imposing the incorporation of *Shari'a*, the Islamic legal code, in Pakistan's legal system. The Assembly also adopted legislation providing for the Islamization of the educational, economic and judicial systems. Benazir Bhutto criticized the legislation as being extreme and fundamentalist, while the right-wing JUI claimed that the new law's provisions were not stringent enough. The fundamentalist Jamaat-e-Islami Pakistan left the IDA in May 1992, in protest at the Government's decision to support the new moderate *mujahidin* Government in Kabul, Afghanistan and at its failure to effect the full Islamization of Pakistan.

In response to continuing violence in Sindh, the Government launched 'Operation Clean-up' in May 1992, whereby the army was to apprehend criminals and terrorists, and seize unauthorized weapons. A violent clash between two factions of the MQM (the majority Altaf faction and the small breakaway Haqiqi faction) in Karachi in June provided the armed forces with the opportunity to suppress the extremist elements within the MQM. More than 500 people were arrested; caches of arms were located and seized; and 'torture cells', allegedly operated by the MQM, were discovered. The leader of the MQM (A), Altaf Hussain, accused the Government of attempting to crush the MQM through the military operation. In protest, 12 of the 15 MQM members in the National Assembly and 24 of the 27 members in the Sindh assembly resigned their seats. However, the Government repeatedly gave assurances that the operations were against criminals, and not specifically against the MQM.

In November 1992 the PDA intensified its campaign of political agitation and was now supported by the majority of the components of the newly formed opposition National Democratic Alliance (NDA), including the National People's Party (NPP—which had been expelled from the IDA in March). The large-scale demonstrations and marches organized by Benazir Bhutto were ruthlessly suppressed by the Government. However, by mid-December tensions between the Government and opposition had eased considerably, and in January 1993, in an apparently conciliatory move on the part of Nawaz Sharif's administration, Benazir Bhutto was elected Chairperson of the National Assembly's Standing Committee on Foreign Affairs. Shortly after Benazir Bhutto had accepted the nomination, her husband was released on bail.

In March 1993 a growing rift between the Prime Minister and the President became evident when the Government initiated discussions regarding proposed modifications to the provisions of the Eighth Constitutional Amendment, which afforded the President the power to dismiss the Government and dissolve assemblies, and to appoint judicial and military chiefs. In late March three cabinet ministers resigned in protest at Nawaz Sharif's nomination as President of the PML (Junejo Group), to succeed Muhammad Khan Junejo (who had died earlier that month), and voiced their support for Ghulam Ishaq Khan in his political struggle with the Prime Minister. In a seemingly final attempt at reconciliation, the Cabinet unanimously decided, in early April, to nominate Ghulam Ishaq Khan as the PML's candidate for the forthcoming presidential election. By mid-April, however, a total of eight ministers had resigned from the Cabinet in protest at Nawaz Sharif's continued tenure of the premiership. On 18 April the President dissolved the National Assembly and dismissed the Prime Minister and his Cabinet, accusing Nawaz Sharif of 'maladministration, nepotism and corruption'. However, the provincial assemblies and governments remained in power, despite demands by the PDA and the NDA for their dissolution. A member of the dissolved National Assembly, Mir Balakh Sher Mazari, was sworn in as acting Prime Minister. It was announced that elections to the National Assembly would be held on 14 July. In late April a broadly based interim Cabinet, including Benazir Bhutto's husband, was sworn in. In early May the PML (Junejo Group) split into two factions: one led by Nawaz Sharif, the other by Hamid Nasir Chattha (with the support of the President).

On 26 May 1993, in an historic and unexpected judgment, the Supreme Court ordered that the National Assembly, the Prime Minister and the Cabinet (dismissed in April) should be restored to power immediately, stating that President Khan's order had been unconstitutional. The President agreed to honour the Court's ruling, and the National Assembly and Nawaz Sharif's Government were reinstated with immediate effect. On the following day Nawaz Sharif's return to power was consolidated when he won a vote of confidence in the National Assembly. A few days later, however, there was renewed political turmoil following the dissolution, through the machinations of supporters of the President, of the provincial assemblies in Punjab and the NWFP. Lacking effective authority in each of the four provinces, Nawaz Sharif resorted to the imposition of federal government's rule on Punjab through a resolution passed by the National Assembly in late June. However, the Punjab provincial government refused to obey the federal Government's orders, claiming that they subverted provincial autonomy, prompting the Government to threaten the imposition of a military administration. Meanwhile, an All Parties Conference (APC), including, among others, Benazir Bhutto and the Chief Ministers of Punjab and the NWFP, convened in Lahore to pass a resolution, urging the President to dissolve the legislature, dismiss Nawaz Sharif's Government and hold fresh elections. In early July the Chief of Army Staff, following an emergency meeting of senior army officers, acted as an intermediary in talks between the President and Prime Minister in an attempt to resolve the political crisis. On 18 July, in accordance with an agreement reached under the auspices of the army, both Khan and Nawaz Sharif resigned from their posts, the federal legislature and the provincial assemblies were dissolved, the holding of a general election in October was announced, and neutral administrations were established at both federal and provincial level. As specified in the Constitution, Khan was succeeded by the Chairman of the Senate, Wasim Sajjad Jan, who was to hold the presidency for the remaining tenure of the deposed President. A small, apolitical Cabinet was sworn in, headed by Moeenuddin Ahmad Qureshi, a former Executive Vice-President of the World Bank, as interim Prime Minister.

Benazir Bhutto's second term as Prime Minister (1993–96)

The general election, held in early October 1993 under military supervision, was widely considered to have been fair, although the turn-out, which some officials estimated to be less than 50%, was disappointing. The polling was closely contested between the PML faction led by Nawaz Sharif—PML (Nawaz—N)—and the PPP (the MQM boycotted the elections to the National Assembly, claiming systematic intimidation by the army, but took part in the provincial assembly elections a few days later). Neither of the two leading parties won an outright majority in the federal elections, and in the provincial elections an outright majority was only achieved by the PPP in Sindh. Following intensive negotiations with smaller parties and independents in the National Assembly, on 19 October Benazir Bhutto was elected to head a coalition Government. On the following day a PPP-led coalition assumed control of the provincial administration in Punjab (traditionally a PML stronghold). However, the provincial governments in the NWFP and in Balochistan were headed by alliances led by the PML (N).

In November 1993 the PPP's candidate, Sardar Farooq Ahmad Khan Leghari, was elected President, comfortably defeating the incumbent acting President, Wasim Sajjad Jan, who stood as the candidate of the PML (N). On assuming office, Leghari stated that he intended to end his political ties with the PPP and that he hoped for the early repeal or modification of the controversial Eighth Constitutional Amendment.

In February 1994 the President imposed governor's rule in the NWFP, following the thwarted introduction of a vote of no confidence against the PML (N)-led coalition by the PPP. In April a PPP member was elected as Chief Minister of the newly revived provincial government in the NWFP; the opposition alliance boycotted the proceedings.

September 1994 witnessed an upsurge in political unrest when Nawaz Sharif organized a nation-wide general strike; in response, the Government arrested hundreds of PML supporters. In November the Government was confronted with a series of uprisings staged by heavily armed tribesmen in the mountainous regions of Malakand and Swat demanding the enforcement of *Shari'a*. The fundamentalist revolt was suppressed by paramilitary forces (but only after the deaths of several hundred people), and *Shari'a* measures were implemented in the tribal areas. By the end of the year, however, the police and paramilitary forces appeared to be losing control of Karachi, which was riven by rapidly escalating ethnic and criminal violence; nearly 170 people were killed in the city in December alone, following the lengthy 'Operation Clean-up' and the withdrawal of the army in the previous month. Much of the violence stemmed from the bloody rivalry between the opposing factions of the MQM, while other killings were linked to drugs mafias and to sectarian disputes between Sunni and Shi'a Muslims.

In early 1995, despite the arrest of large numbers of suspected Islamist militants, there was an upsurge in religious violence between Sunni and Shi'a Muslims in Karachi. In March the murder of two US consular officials by unidentified gunmen in the troubled Sindh capital provoked international condemnation. There was no respite from the violence in the following months, and by June the security forces had lost control of large areas of Karachi to MQM activists. It was estimated that during 1995 almost 2,000 people (including about 250 members of the security forces) were killed as a result of the political and ethnic violence in Karachi. In November 18 people were killed when a car bomb exploded at the Egyptian embassy in Islamabad; within hours of the attack three militant Islamist groups in Egypt had claimed responsibility for the bombing. During the previous year the Pakistani Government had been co-operating with Egypt in attempts to apprehend and extradite members of illegal Islamist militant organizations operating in the NWFP or across the border in Afghanistan. (In 1993–95 the Pakistani authorities, concerned at the country's growing reputation as a refuge for Islamist extremists, expelled more than 2,000 Arabs, the majority of whom were reported to have been involved in the civil war in Afghanistan.) Acts of violence and terrorism in Pakistan continued throughout late 1995 and early 1996.

A new political force emerged in Pakistan in early 1996 when the popular former international cricketer Imran Khan (of late a prominent benefactor of charitable causes) established a political

PAKISTAN

reform movement, known as the Tehreekk-e-Insaf (Movement for Justice), to oppose Benazir Bhutto's administration.

In March 1996 the Supreme Court in Karachi ruled that the Government no longer had the exclusive mandate to appoint judges to the higher courts; these appointments would, in future, be required to have the consent of the Chief Justices of the High Courts and the Chief Justice of Pakistan. This ruling provoked considerable controversy since it deprived the executive of substantial authority within the national judicial system.

The Government's popularity was undermined by the necessary introduction of an austere budget in June 1996, in an attempt to reduce the budget deficit. The volatile political situation was intensified by a bomb explosion at Lahore airport in late July, a series of debilitating public-sector strikes and by a resurgence of violence in Karachi. In addition, the appointment of the Prime Minister's unpopular husband, Asif Ali Zardari, as Minister of Investment, in July, aroused much controversy and criticism. At the end of that month the Government's position appeared even less secure when about 16 opposition parties, including the PML (N), the MQM and the JIP, established an informal alliance with a one-point agenda: to oust Prime Minister Bhutto and her Government. Pakistan was thrown into further political turmoil in September following the fatal shooting of Benazir Bhutto's estranged brother, Mir Murtaza Bhutto, in a gun battle with police in Karachi. A number of opposition politicians accused the Prime Minister and her husband of complicity in the killing, while Benazir Bhutto implied in a number of public statements that she believed that the President and the army were to blame. In 1995 Mir Murtaza Bhutto had established a rival faction of the PPP, known as the PPP (Shaheed Bhutto Group), charging his sister's Government with corruption and misrule; however, the breakaway faction attracted no substantial support and posed little threat to the Prime Minister. Meanwhile, growing discord between Benazir Bhutto and President Leghari was becoming more apparent.

Amid mounting public discontent, President Leghari dismissed Prime Minister Benazir Bhutto and her Government and dissolved the National Assembly on 5 November 1996 (the state assemblies were dissolved over the following week), citing as justification the deteriorating law and order situation, severe economic problems, widespread corruption, disregard for judicial authority and the violation of various constitutional provisions. A former Speaker of the National Assembly, Malik Meraj Khaled, who claimed no affiliation to any political party, was named as acting Prime Minister and an interim Cabinet was appointed. Following the dismissal of her Government, it was reported that several leading members of Benazir Bhutto's PPP, including her husband, had been arrested. In mid-November the President promulgated a decree providing for a five-year disqualification from public office of politicians (with the exception of the President and members of the judiciary and armed forces) involved in corruption and abuses of power. Sectarian violence between Sunni and Shi'a Muslims escalated in January 1997, culminating in a bomb blast outside a district court in Lahore, which killed 25 people, including the leader of the Sunni extremist group Sipah-e-Sahaba Pakistan. Meanwhile, in early January the President instituted an official advisory role for the military, with the formation of a 10-member Council of Defence and National Security (CDNS), which was to advise the Government on a broad range of issues from national security to the economy. The President chaired the new body, which comprised the Prime Minister, four senior cabinet ministers, the Chairman of the Joint Chiefs of Staff and the three armed services chiefs, and could refer any matter to it without previously consulting the Prime Minister. In response to this unexpected development, many political parties, including the PPP, but with the notable exception of the PML (N), accused the President of an unconstitutional usurpation of authority. However, the Government insisted that the role of the CDNS would be purely advisory.

Mohammad Nawaz Sharif's second term as Prime Minister (1997–99)

The general election, which was held on 3 February 1997, was marred by an extremely low turn-out (an estimated 30%–40%). The PML (N) won a decisive victory, obtaining 134 seats in the National Assembly, while the PPP was routed, winning only 18 seats. The MQM emerged as the country's third political force (obtaining 12 seats), while Imran Khan's Tehreekk-e-Insaf failed to win a single seat. Nawaz Sharif was sworn in as Prime Minister on 17 February and a small Cabinet was appointed the following week.

Nawaz Sharif's political authority was strengthened considerably in April 1997, when both the National Assembly and the Senate voted unanimously to repeal the major components of the 1985 Eighth Constitutional Amendment, thereby divesting the President of the power to appoint and dismiss the Prime Minister and Cabinet, to dissolve the legislature, to order a national referendum on any national issue, and to appoint provincial Governors, the Chairman of the Joint Chiefs of Staff and the three armed forces chiefs (these functions and appointments were, in future, to be carried out subject to mandatory advice from the Prime Minister). The President thus became a largely ceremonial figure whose main executive role was the appointment of judges. President Leghari was reported to have 'willingly agreed' to the constitutional changes.

In July 1997 Asif Ali Zardari was formally charged with ordering the killing of Mir Murtaza Bhutto. In September the Swiss police ordered four banks in Geneva to freeze the accounts of Benazir Bhutto and her family after Pakistan's Accountability Commission alleged that up to US $80m. had been illegally transferred to them. In March 1998 the Sindh High Court issued an arrest warrant for the leader of the PPP on a charge of misuse of power during her final term in office as Prime Minister. In April the High Court in Lahore ordered that all assets belonging to Benazir Bhutto, her husband and her mother be frozen as the government investigation into allegations of corruption continued.

Meanwhile, in the latter half of 1997 a serious rift developed between Nawaz Sharif and the Chief Justice of the Supreme Court, Sajjad Ali Shah, over the appointment of new judges to the Court. In early November, however, a compromise was reached between the Supreme Court and the Government, allowing the former to appoint five new judges while confirming the right of the legislature to determine the total number of judges. Yet, despite this outcome, later that month the Supreme Court charged Nawaz Sharif with contempt for slandering the Court and defying its orders in October. The Prime Minister, who, if found guilty, was liable to be disqualified from office, denied the charges. However, the Chief Justice was forced to adjourn Nawaz Sharif's trial in late November, when thousands of the Prime Minister's supporters stormed the Supreme Court in Islamabad. The constitutional crisis came to a dramatic end on 2 December when the Chief Justice was suspended from office by rebel members of the Supreme Court; on the same day President Leghari also stood down from office. The Chairman of the Senate, Wasim Sajjad Jan, assumed the position of acting President. It was widely speculated that the army, in tacitly supporting the Prime Minister, had exerted considerable influence in resolving the constitutional impasse. Nawaz Sharif strengthened his hold on power on 31 December when his nominee and fellow Punjabi, Mohammad Rafiq Tarar, won the presidential election by a record margin.

In January 1998 sectarian violence erupted again in Lahore when at least 24 Shi'a Muslims were massacred by a clandestine Sunni group. In response, the Government approved measures to control illicit weapons in an attempt to curb terrorism. (A controversial anti-terrorist law had been passed in August 1997, giving the security forces extensive powers of arrest and enabling the Government to ban any group or association without parliamentary approval.) However, in February 1998 two Iranian engineers were murdered by unidentified terrorists in Karachi, and in the following month more than 20 people were killed in two bomb explosions on passenger trains in Lahore.

Despite the temporary public euphoria and heightened popularity of the Prime Minister arising from the conduct of controversial nuclear tests in May 1998 (see Foreign Affairs), the repercussions (particularly the international sanctions) left Pakistan in dire financial straits. In August the Prime Minister introduced the Fifteenth Constitutional Amendment Bill to the National Assembly, seeking to replace Pakistan's legal code with *Shari'a*. Nawaz Sharif attempted to allay fears of a move towards Islamist extremism by promising to uphold women's rights and to safeguard minorities. The Bill was passed in the National Assembly in October (it remained to be ratified by the Senate); it was denounced by human rights activists as 'regressive'.

The Government suffered a severe reverse in October 1998 when the Muttahida Qaumi Movement—MQM (A)—(formerly known as the Mohajir Qaumi Movement) withdrew its support for the PML (N)-led provincial administration in Sindh. On 30 October the provincial legislature was suspended and the province was placed under governor's rule in an effort to curb the violence. In November the Prime Minister announced the establishment of anti-terrorist military courts in Karachi, and the suspension of civil rights in Sindh.

In April 1999 the Lahore High Court found Benazir Bhutto (now in self-imposed exile abroad) and her husband guilty of corruption; they were each sentenced to five years' imprisonment, their property was confiscated and they were jointly fined US $8.6m. The verdict automatically removed the former Prime Minister and Asif Ali Zardari (who was already in prison serving a separate sentence) from their seats in the National Assembly and Senate, respectively.

Meanwhile, in early January 1999 the Prime Minister escaped an apparent assassination attempt when a bomb exploded near his country residence in Punjab, killing four people. The following day there was an upsurge in sectarian violence in the province when unidentified gunmen murdered 17 worshippers in a Shi'a mosque near Multan. Sindh became the focus of political attention later in the month when the Supreme Court declared unlawful the central Government's decision (made in November 1998) to remove the powers of the Speaker and Deputy Speaker of the suspended Sindh assembly. In February 1999 the Supreme Court ruled that military trials could not be used for cases against civilians, thus sparing 14 people from death sentences imposed in the military tribunals in Sindh and effectively barring the establishment of military courts throughout the country (as the Government had proposed). The Supreme Court ordered the transfer of the cases to civilian anti-terrorist courts.

A dangerous escalation in the Kashmir crisis between Pakistan and India in mid-1999 (see Foreign Affairs) elicited considerable international condemnation and appeared to represent a major turning-point in the fortunes of the PML Government. Many of Nawaz Sharif's opponents in Pakistan declared that the Prime Minister's seeming haste to concede defeat and to agree to a Pakistani withdrawal in the face of US pressure constituted a national 'betrayal'. In September Nawaz Sharif's position looked increasingly precarious following the formation of a Grand Democratic Alliance by 19 conservative and centrist opposition parties, including the PPP, the MQM (A) and the ANP, which demanded the Prime Minister's immediate resignation. The various Islamist parties, including the JIP, also stepped up their anti-Government protests and rallies throughout the country. However, the opposition was weakened to some extent by the fact that Benazir Bhutto was unwilling to return to Pakistan for fear of being arrested.

Pakistan under Gen. Pervez Musharraf (1999–2008)

Events took a dramatic turn on 12 October 1999, when, shortly after Nawaz Sharif's announcement of a decision to dismiss the Chief of Army Staff and Chairman of the Joint Chiefs of Staff Committee, Gen. Pervez Musharraf, the army chief flew back from an official tour in Sri Lanka and promptly mounted a bloodless military coup in Islamabad. Nawaz Sharif and his Government were overthrown, and the deposed Prime Minister was placed under house arrest. On 15 October Gen. Musharraf assumed the position of Chief Executive, declared a nation-wide state of emergency and suspended the Constitution, the National Assembly, the Senate, the four provincial legislatures and all political officials, with the exception of the President and judiciary. He also ensured, by means of a Provisional Constitution Order (PCO), that his actions could not be challenged by any court of law, thus imposing virtual martial law. On 18 October the Commonwealth Ministerial Action Group (CMAG) condemned the coup and demanded a time-frame for the restoration of democracy; Pakistan was suspended from participation in meetings of the Commonwealth with immediate effect (it was not readmitted to full membership until May 2004). On 22 October 1999 Musharraf appointed four new provincial governors, and on 26 October he installed a three-member Cabinet (which was later expanded) and named the members of a National Security Council (NSC), which was expected to be the supreme executive body of the country.

Following his seizure of power, Musharraf attempted to win over international opinion by portraying himself as a moderate, liberal leader. He was aided in this respect by the fact that the majority of the Pakistani people appeared to support the army's coup (it was a widely held opinion that the military had no provincial bias and represented all levels of society—rather than purely the landed élite). Although expressing regret at Pakistan's effective suspension from the Commonwealth, the military regime was more concerned with the reaction of the USA and international financial organizations to the coup. The US Government's initial relations with the new administration in Pakistan appeared cautious but conciliatory. Musharraf promised an eventual return to civilian rule and announced wide-ranging measures to tackle corruption, regional instability and religious extremism. The new regime's stated major priority was the revival of the almost bankrupt economy.

In November 1999 Nawaz Sharif and six other senior officials (including Muhammad Shahbaz Sharif, the brother of the ousted Prime Minister and the former Chief Minister of Punjab) were arrested on charges of criminal conspiracy, hijacking, kidnapping and attempted murder in relation to the alleged refusal of landing rights to the aircraft carrying Musharraf from Sri Lanka to Karachi on 12 October. The military authorities also charged Nawaz Sharif and his brother in November with corruption and non-repayment of bank loans. Later that month a new law was enacted barring politicians from holding public office for 21 years if found guilty of corruption or of defaulting on loans. The bill also allowed for the establishment of special courts to conduct trials within 30 days and gave the newly formed National Accountability Bureau far-reaching powers of investigation.

In April 2000 Nawaz Sharif was sentenced to life imprisonment on charges of terrorism (a charge subsequently lifted following appeal) and hijacking; in addition, all of the former Prime Minister's property in Pakistan was to be confiscated by the State. The six other defendants were acquitted. In July Nawaz Sharif was convicted of corruption and sentenced to 14 years' imprisonment, and barred from holding public office for 21 years. In August the Chief Executive issued a decree disqualifying all those convicted of criminal offences and of terrorist acts from holding public office. The decision was viewed by many as a ban on convicted political leaders, notably former Prime Ministers Benazir Bhutto and Nawaz Sharif.

Meanwhile, in January 2000 Musharraf was accused of undemocratic conduct and of attempting to erode the independence of the judiciary when he dismissed the country's Chief Justice, Saeeduzzaman Siddiqui, together with five other judges of the Supreme Court, following their refusal to swear allegiance to the military regime under a new oath. In May Musharraf's regime was strengthened by a unanimous decision by the now pro-military Supreme Court to validate the October 1999 coup as having been necessary to spare the country from chaos and bankruptcy. At the same time, the Court announced that the Chief Executive should name a date not later than 90 days before the expiry of the three-year period from 12 October 1999 for the holding of elections to the National Assembly, the provincial assemblies and the Senate. Musharraf stated that he would comply with the Supreme Court ruling regarding the restoration of democracy.

In July 2000 Musharraf issued a decree to revive the Islamic provisions of the suspended Constitution and to incorporate them in the PCO, thereby supporting a ban on the passing of any law that conflicted with Islamic principles. In August the NSC was reconstituted and redefined as the supreme executive body, comprising the three chiefs of staff and the Ministers of Foreign Affairs, of Interior, of Finance and of Commerce.

In late 2000 Nawaz Sharif and Benazir Bhutto, together with the heads of 16 other smaller political parties, formed the Alliance for the Restoration of Democracy (ARD), with the aim of ending military rule and accelerating a return to democracy. The new alliance superseded the PPP-led Grand Democratic Alliance. On 10 December Nawaz Sharif was unexpectedly released from prison and sent into exile in Saudi Arabia, with his wife and other members of his family. The Government announced that the deposed Prime Minister had been granted a 'presidential pardon' and had been permitted to leave the country to seek medical treatment. In return, Nawaz Sharif relinquished his personal and business assets, promised not to return to Pakistan for 10 years, and agreed not to take part in Pakistani politics for 21 years. In May 2001 a warrant was issued for Benazir Bhutto's arrest on her return to Pakistan. However, owing to her continued exile in Dubai (United Arab Emirates), in June she was sentenced, *in absentia,* to three years' imprisonment for failing to appear in court to answer these latest corruption allegations; this criminal conviction effectively disqualified Bhutto from holding further public office in Pakistan.

Meanwhile, in December 2000 the first phase of local elections was held. According to the Government, the turn-out reached 43.5%. However, the opposition PPP claimed that less than 20% of the electorate had participated, attributing the low turn-out to the ban on political parties. The next three phases of local elections took place in March, May and July 2001. Elections to the legislative assembly in Azad Kashmir also took place in July. Meanwhile, Musharraf insisted that a ban on party political activity in public would be maintained until after the forthcoming parliamentary elections, and opposition attempts at organizing pro-democracy rallies in March and May were suppressed by the authorities, who detained thousands of ARD supporters prior to the planned demonstrations.

On 20 June 2001 Musharraf unexpectedly assumed the presidency, having dismissed Mohammad Rafiq Tarar. Musharraf immediately issued a formal dissolution of both houses of the federal legislature (which had been suspended since October 1999) in preparation for the elections. In August Musharraf confirmed that elections to the four provincial legislatures and to the bicameral federal parliament would be conducted between 1 and 11 October 2002, thereby providing for the full restoration of democratic institutions by 12 October (the deadline established by the Supreme Court).

In response to a continuing escalation in sectarian and ethnically motivated violence, in June 2001 the Government approved new legislation to tackle terrorist activity. Earlier in the month Musharraf had complained that Pakistan's growing reputation as a centre for militant religious intolerance and fundamentalism was having a detrimental effect on the country's international standing and on its economic prospects. In August Musharraf announced an immediate ban on the activities of two militant Islamist groups: the Sunni Lashkar-e-Jhangvi and the Shi'a Sipah-e-Mohammad.

As one of only three states to have recognized the legitimacy of the Taliban administration in Afghanistan, and as the most significant trading partner and political associate of the regime, Pakistan's support was crucial to the efforts of the US-led anti-terrorism coalition in the aftermath of the 11 September 2001 terrorist attacks on the US mainland, and Musharraf was left in little doubt that his refusal to co-operate with the campaign to apprehend those members of the al-Qa'ida organization held responsible for the attacks would result in Pakistan's increased economic and political isolation. Therefore, Musharraf's political opponents in the PML and PPP appeared to accept his declaration of co-operation with US requests for shared intelligence and use of air space with resignation. However, large-scale popular opposition to the President's decision was inevitable, particularly in the NWFP bordering Afghanistan, which was home to large numbers of Pakhtoon (Pashtun) Pakistanis who were fiercely opposed to any assault on the Pashtun-dominated Taliban. Despite Musharraf's insistence that the US-led activities in the region did not represent an attack on Islam, protests against the action spread throughout the country. There was further opposition to Pakistan's support for the intervention in Afghanistan from within the armed forces and the Inter-Services Intelligence (ISI) agency, both having nurtured particularly close links with the Taliban. In October, having extended indefinitely his term of office as Chief of Army Staff, Musharraf implemented a radical reorganization of the military high command and the intelligence service, replacing a number of senior personnel with known sympathies for the country's militant Islamist cause, including Lt-Gen. Mahmood Ahmed, head of the ISI. However, popular protests against co-operation with the US-led coalition continued. None the less, Musharraf's resolve remained firm (strengthened, in part, by the promise of financial recognition of his political support from the USA and the European Union—EU), and despite the uncompromising response of the security forces to sporadic rioting there were surprisingly few casualties. In early November the leaders of the JUI and the JIP were detained following allegations that they were continuing to promote anti-Government activities and demonstrations. In the border regions of the NWFP and Balochistan reports began to emerge of large numbers of armed local tribesmen crossing the border as willing recruits for the Taliban and it was alleged that supply lines for the Taliban were being maintained into north-western Pakistan. However, by mid-November the anti-Taliban forces of the United National Islamic Front for the Salvation of Afghanistan (commonly known as the United Front or Northern Alliance), with the support of the US-led coalition had taken Kabul (the Afghan capital). As the rout of Taliban forces in Afghanistan continued in December and the USA intensified its bombardment of suspected al-Qa'ida positions in southern Afghanistan, Pakistan substantially reinforced security personnel along its north-western border in order to intercept fleeing combatants.

Meanwhile, relations with India had become openly hostile as a result of the deteriorating security situation in Kashmir and the increasingly violent activities of Pakistan's militant Islamist groups in India. Following intense international pressure (particularly from the USA) to address the continuing security risk presented by these groups, in December 2001 the security forces began to detain some of their most prominent members, financial assets were frozen and offices closed down. Moreover, in January 2002 Musharraf announced an indefinite ban on the activities of five predominantly separatist groups (Tehrik-e-Nifaz-e-Shariat-e-Mohammadi, Sipah-e-Sahaba Pakistan, Jaish-e-Mohammed, Tehrik-e-Jafria and Lashkar-e-Taiba) and plans to reform and regulate the country's system of *madrassa* religious schools, many of which were accused of promoting extremism and theocracy.

In early April 2002 the Government approved a plan to hold a national referendum seeking endorsement for Musharraf's term of office as President to be extended by five years and approval of the Government's political and economic programme. Opposition parties and the independent Human Rights Commission of Pakistan condemned the decision as unconstitutional and resolved to boycott the vote; however, on 27 April the Supreme Court ruled that the referendum was legitimate, allowing the poll to take place three days later. According to official figures, 98% of those participating supported the proposal. However, there were widespread allegations of gross irregularities and fraud. The Government claimed that the turn-out was 70%, but opposition parties and independent monitors estimated that it was only about 5%. In late June Musharraf dismissed the head of the political wing of the ISI and chief organizer of the presidential referendum, Maj.-Gen. Ehtesam Zamir, after being forced to admit that his referendum victory had been fraudulent. In an alleged attempt to reduce the political influence wielded by feudal landowning families, on 24 June the President issued a Chief Executive's Order stipulating that all candidates for future elections to federal and provincial legislatures should hold a university degree (this measure, which was widely held to have been designed by Musharraf to sideline many of his political opponents, was repealed by the Supreme Court in 2008). Several days later Musharraf announced a set of radical proposals for constitutional reform. The suggested reforms were strongly criticized by political parties, constitutional experts and human rights groups for attempting to remodel Pakistan's prime ministerial system into a presidential one and to undermine the authority of any elected government. Among the changes put forward by Musharraf were proposals to reduce the parliamentary term from five years to four, to lower the voting age from 21 years to 18 years, to restrict the number of terms premiers or provincial chief ministers could hold in office to two, and to disqualify those members of the legislature who had criminal convictions, had defaulted on loans or had absconded. The last two amendments were widely considered to be aimed at preventing former Prime Ministers Benazir Bhutto and Nawaz Sharif from returning to office. Furthermore, in July 2002 Musharraf issued a decree barring former premiers and chief ministers from seeking a third term in office. Several days later Musharraf announced that elections to the federal and provincial legislatures would be held on 10 October.

Instead of presenting the proposed constitutional amendments before the next legislature, on 21 August 2002 President Musharraf unilaterally enacted the Legal Framework Order (LFO), which introduced 29 amendments to the Constitution (including those listed above) and validated all the military decrees approved since the coup in 1999. The amendments were to take effect from 12 October 2002. As a result, the President's powers were enlarged and the military was ensured influence in decision-making beyond the parliamentary elections in October. One of the most significant amendments, the permanent establishment of an NSC, which would include Musharraf in his capacity as President and Chief of Army Staff, as well as the three other armed forces chiefs, the Prime Minister, the provincial chief ministers, the leader of the parliamentary opposition and Speakers of both houses of the federal legislature, was also authorized. The NSC would provide consultation to the elected government on strategic issues. The President was also restored the right to dissolve the National Assembly, and to dismiss the Prime Minister and Cabinet; furthermore, he was given the authority to override parliamentary majorities and provincial assemblies in order to appoint a Prime Minister and provincial governors himself if necessary. The amendments allowed the President to appoint Supreme Court judges and to extend his term in office. The changes were heavily criticized by the PML (N) and PPP. However, Musharraf insisted that a formal role for the military in governing the country was necessary to ensure a stable transition to democracy and to forestall a potential military coup. According to the LFO, the size of the National Assembly would be increased to 342 members, with 60 seats reserved for women and 10 seats reserved for non-Muslims. The Senate would consist of 100 members.

Meanwhile, in July 2002 Benazir Bhutto was re-elected as leader of the PPP. However, the decree barring parties from contesting an election if any of its office-holders had a criminal conviction prompted the PPP in early August to create the Pakistan People's Party Parliamentarians (PPPP) under new leadership to contest the forthcoming general election. At the same time Shahbaz Sharif was elected leader of the PML (N). Bhutto's plans to return to the political arena were thwarted in late August when election officials in Sindh province rejected her candidacy in the National Assembly elections, owing to her criminal conviction. In response, Nawaz Sharif withdrew his nomination papers (although they had been accepted by the Election Commission), reportedly in solidarity with Bhutto. In September Shahbaz Sharif was disqualified from entering the general election for defaulting on a bank loan. Meanwhile, a pro-Musharraf faction of the PML, the Quaid-e-Azam group, was reportedly receiving covert support from the Government.

On 9 October 2002 Musharraf declared that he was relinquishing the title of Chief Executive. The following day elections for the National Assembly and provincial assemblies took place. In elections to the National Assembly the PML (Quaid-e-Azam—Q) won 77 of the 272 directly elective seats (25.7% of the vote). The PPPP won 25.8% of the vote, but only 63 seats. A surprising outcome was the success of the Muttahida Majlis-e-Amal (MMA), an alliance of six Islamist parties, in securing 45 seats (11.3% of the vote). The PML (N) won only 14 seats (9.4% of the vote). According to the Election Commission, the turn-out at the election was 41.8%. Opposition parties, independent analysts and the Human Rights Commission of Pakistan claimed that the army had provided financial and other support to the PML (Q), while hampering other parties' campaign efforts. Benazir Bhutto claimed that the election had been rigged and EU election monitors reported that the poll was 'seriously flawed'. The emergence of the MMA as a third political force suggested that a significant proportion of the population objected to Musharraf's support for the US-led military action against the Taliban and al-Qa'ida in Afghanistan, and the ongoing campaign against al-Qa'ida in Pakistan. In late October the three leading parties entered intensive and protracted negotiations on forming a governing coalition: the PML (Q) and PPPP each attempted to gain the support of the MMA. By mid-November the parties had yet to reach a compromise; nevertheless, the National Assembly convened and elected a Speaker and Deputy Speaker. Shortly beforehand, the President revived the 1973 Constitution, which had been in abeyance since he assumed power in 1999—it was believed that the Constitution incorporated the controversial LFO—and took an oath to begin his new five-year term as President. On 21 November the PML (Q) candidate, Zafarullah Khan Jamali, was elected Prime Minister by the National Assembly. Jamali's victory ensured a PML (Q)-led, pro-army Government with a slim majority, which was sworn in two days later. Meanwhile, Musharraf agreed to transfer power to the elected Government, but emphasized that he would continue to carry out his 'important role'.

In the provincial elections held in October 2002 the MMA won a majority in the NWFP and formed a coalition government in Balochistan with the PML (Q). The PML (Q) assumed power in Punjab, and a coalition government comprising the PML (Q), the MMA and several smaller parties was appointed in Sindh in December (following the failure of the PPPP—which had won the largest number of seats—to form a provincial administration). The delay in forming the new federal and provincial governments meant that the Senate elections were not held until 25–27 February 2003. Some 88 of the 100 seats in the Senate were elected by the four provincial assemblies. The remaining 12 seats were chosen by the National Assembly from a list of candidates provided by the Federally Administered Tribal Areas (FATA) and the federal capital. The PML (Q) secured 34 seats, making it the largest single party in the Senate. The Senate convened on 12 March. The PML (Q) candidate, Mohammad Mian Soomro, was elected unopposed as Chairman of the Senate after the eight opposition parties boycotted the vote in protest at the President's LFO and the alleged military interference in the Senate elections.

At the end of April 2003 the National Assembly suspended its session, following a month of disruption caused by opposition parties. The MMA, PPPP and other opposition parties had refused to allow Musharraf to address the legislature (a constitutional requirement before it could begin to legislate) and repeatedly demanded that the President submit the LFO to approval by the National Assembly. The President refused to accede to this demand and the opposition's campaign of boycott and agitation of parliamentary proceedings continued.

In June 2003 the MMA-led legislative assembly in the NWFP unanimously voted in favour of legislation to implement *Shari'a* throughout the province (giving Islamic law precedence over secular provincial law). During a visit to the NWFP later that month Musharraf warned against the adoption of Taliban-style Islam, promoting instead the practice of 'tolerant, progressive and civilized' Islam.

In September 2003 the Cabinet unanimously endorsed a modified version of the LFO. Although the PML (N) and PPPP appeared to be willing to compromise regarding their opposition to the measures, the MMA remained dissatisfied and negotiations between the Government and opposition continued. Finally, in December Musharraf announced seven further concessionary amendments to the LFO, including his commitment to resign as Chief of Army Staff by December 2004. On 29 December 2003 the National Assembly passed the Constitution (Seventeenth Amendment) Bill, which comprised the seven modifications. The opposition ARD boycotted the parliamentary proceedings, dismissing the concessions as 'cosmetic'. According to the Bill, which became law on 31 December following the Senate's approval, the existing NSC, which had been inactive since its creation one year previously, disbanded. A new NSC was to be established by an act of parliament, rather than be incorporated into the Constitution by the LFO. Furthermore, while the President would have the right to dismiss the National Assembly, he would be obliged to refer the matter to the Supreme Court within 15 days. Despite the concessions, Musharraf retained most of the special powers that he had awarded himself in 2002. In early January 2004 the federal and provincial legislatures passed votes of confidence in Musharraf, allowing him to complete his five-year term as President (which was due to expire in 2007). In April 2004 the National Assembly passed an item of legislation on the establishment of the NSC amid strong protest by opposition members. The Council was to comprise the President, the Prime Minister, the Chairman of the Senate, the Speaker of the National Assembly, the leader of the parliamentary opposition, the provincial chief ministers and the three other chiefs of armed forces. The new Chief of Army Staff (who was to be appointed in late 2004 following Musharraf's resignation from the position) would also be a member. The NSC law, approved by the Senate several days later, gave the armed forces a formal, albeit supervisory, role in civilian politics for the first time in Pakistan's history.

In August 2003 Asif Ali Zardari was acquitted of all charges relating to the 1998 murder of Sajjad Hussain, the former Chairman of Pakistan Steel Mills. In November 2003 opposition parties held widespread protests on the seventh anniversary of Zardari's arrest to demand his release from prison. Zardari, now largely considered a political prisoner, was implicated in 14 pending criminal cases, but had been convicted on only one corruption charge. In November 2004 the Supreme Court ordered that Zardari be released on bail. Meanwhile, his wife, Benazir Bhutto, faced further corruption cases in Pakistan, Switzerland, the United Kingdom and the USA. In November 2005 Bhutto claimed that President Musharraf had offered to abandon all remaining charges against her, on the condition that she declined to contest elections scheduled for 2007; she asserted that she was unable to accept the condition.

In 2003 sectarian violence between Sunni and Shi'a Muslims escalated, and in October the legislator and leader of Millat-e-Islamia Pakistan, Maulana Azam Tariq, was assassinated in Islamabad. In addition, attacks by militant Islamists on Western targets, continued to take place. Although Musharraf decided not to support the USA in its attempt to gain UN endorsement of the planned military campaign to remove the regime of Saddam Hussain in Iraq in March, the President was condemned by some sectors of the Pakistani community for not opposing the war in stronger terms. In November Musharraf proscribed six militant Islamist groups under the 1997 Anti-Terrorist Act. Three of the organizations—Islami Tehrik-e-Pakistan (formerly Tehrik-e-Jafria-e-Pakistan), Millat-e-Islamia Pakistan (formerly Sipah-e-Sahaba) and Khudam ul-Islam (formerly Jaish-e-Mohammed)—had disregarded an earlier ban by changing their names. Some commentators doubted the effectiveness of Musharraf's approach to militant Islamism, claiming that the groups would continue to receive covert support from the army and judiciary. Indeed, in December 2003 the President narrowly escaped two assassination attempts by suspected Islamist militants near his residence in Rawalpindi. No one was hurt in the first suicide bomb attack, but the second killed at least 17 people. It was suggested that al-Qa'ida, which in September had issued a death threat to Musharraf, blaming him for the arrest of hundreds of its members, was responsible for organizing the attacks. There was also speculation that the extremists had infiltrated Musharraf's security apparatus in order to gain secret information on his travel plans. Notably, among those sentenced to death in 2005 for their part in the assassination attempts were five junior members of the Pakistani armed forces.

In December 2003 the Government admitted that it was investigating allegations that Pakistan had transferred nuclear technology to other countries, and that Dr Abdul Qadeer Khan, the founder of Pakistan's nuclear weapons programme, was being questioned. However, the authorities were quick to deny any official involvement, suggesting that 'rogue' individuals motivated by personal greed were to blame. Khan was reportedly placed under house arrest and in January 2004 was removed from his post as scientific adviser to the Prime Minister. The following month Khan confessed on television that during the past 15 years he had provided Iran, the Democratic People's Republic of Korea (North Korea) and Libya with designs and technology to develop nuclear weapons. Taking full responsibility for his actions, he denied any government involvement and absolved the military and his fellow scientists. Dr Khan's plea for clemency was promptly granted by Musharraf, who stated, nevertheless, that the scientist would remain under strict surveillance. It was widely acknowledged that prosecuting Dr Khan would have led to unrest throughout the country (he had been long revered as the 'father' of Pakistan's nuclear bomb and had the status of a national hero) and to political problems (there were fears that if put on trial the scientist would provide evidence that incriminated Pakistani leaders and generals). Military analysts doubted that Khan was solely responsible, declaring that it was unlikely that the transfer of nuclear materials could have been conducted without the knowledge and involvement of at least parts of the military.

In June 2004 Prime Minister Jamali tendered his resignation, having been placed under considerable pressure to do so by Musharraf. The President was reportedly frustrated at the weakness of Jamali's Government and, in particular, its apparent inability to curb sectarian violence in Pakistan. Later in the same month Musharraf's nominee, Chaudhry Shujaat Hussain, President of the newly formed PML (which had been created following the merger of several factions of the PML and the Sindh Democratic Alliance), was elected to serve as interim Prime Minister. It was reported that Minister of Finance Shaukat Aziz was Musharraf's choice to serve in the post permanently, but, as Aziz was a Senator, he would first need to be elected to the House of Representatives. In August, following victories in two constituency by-elections, Aziz was elected as Prime Minister and leader of the house by the National Assembly. In the following month a new Cabinet was appointed, which included the 20 members of Chaudhry Shujaat Hussain's interim Government and incorporated an additional 13 members.

In October 2004 the National Assembly approved legislation enabling Musharraf to retain his dual role as President and Chief of Army Staff, contrary to his December 2003 pledge that he would resign from his military position by the end of 2004. To counter opposition protests that the bill was unconstitutional, the Government claimed that the ongoing terrorist threat necessitated Musharraf's retention of both roles. In November, having been approved by the Senate, the bill was signed into law. In the following month Musharraf formally confirmed that he intended to retain his military position until the end of his presidential term, in 2007. In April 2005 the Supreme Court dismissed all petitions challenging Musharraf's dual role as unconstitutional.

The issue of religious extremism continued to resonate in Pakistani society, with rising levels of sectarian violence continuing to disrupt and unsettle the country's major cities. In July 2005, following the discovery that at least two of the four British Muslim suicide bombers who had attacked the transport network in London, United Kingdom, in that month had previously visited Pakistan and had allegedly received instruction at one of the country's many *madrassas*, President Musharraf announced the implementation of a more stringent policy to prevent the spread of Islamist extremism. Hundreds of suspected Islamist militants were arrested and several *madrassas* suspected of being involved in extremism were raided. In August the National Assembly gave its assent to legislation requiring all *madrassas* to register with the Government and to submit annual reports. The schools were also barred from encouraging militancy and propagating religious hatred. Furthermore, all foreign students studying at *madrassas* in Pakistan were to be expelled.

In October 2005 a huge earthquake devastated Azad Kashmir and much of the NWFP, resulting in the deaths of more than 81,000 people and leaving many thousands homeless. The response of the Government and armed forces to the disaster attracted criticism for its tardiness and lack of co-ordination, although the logistical challenge of delivering relief to many of the remote areas affected was considerable. At a meeting of donors held in November in Islamabad, a total of US $5,800m. was pledged by the international community for the relief and reconstruction effort.

In November 2006 the federal legislature passed the Women's Protection Bill, giving civil courts jurisdiction in rape cases and revoking the death penalty for extra-marital sexual intercourse. Religious groups voiced their opposition to the bill, arguing that it was 'un-Islamic', while others complained that it did not go far enough. In March 2007 Musharraf suspended the Chief Justice of the Supreme Court, Iftikhar Mohammad Chaudhry—who was widely recognized for his independent stance on controversial issues and for his investigations into human rights violations—on charges of abuse of office. This controversial action provoked the holding of large-scale, violent demonstrations by the legal community and the resignation of several senior judicial officials. The authorities' decision to dispatch riot police to contain the protests precipitated further unrest. In May Chaudhry arrived in Karachi to address a political rally organized by his supporters, but was unable to leave the airport because the roads into the city were blocked. Demonstrations in Karachi subsequently escalated into violent clashes between supporters of the Government and the opposition, resulting in some 41 fatalities. The campaign to reinstate Chaudhry appeared to have succeeded when the Supreme Court voted to restore him to the position of Chief Justice in July.

Sectarian violence and terrorist attacks continued to pose a threat to internal security and stability throughout the country in 2006 and 2007. The growing prominence of religious leaders of the Lal Masjid (Red Mosque) in central Islamabad posed a further threat to the Government's attempts to stabilize the situation. Members of the Lal Masjid and its two *madrassas* had been involved in increasingly overt challenges to authority, issuing a *fatwa* (Islamic edict) against a government minister and even abducting security officers and alleged prostitutes. Matters came to a head in July 2007 with violent clashes between paramilitary forces and occupants of the Lal Masjid compound. Following the collapse of negotiations between the two sides, the security forces invaded the compound. It was later estimated that some 100 people, many of them Lal Masjid followers, had been killed, but some estimates put the death toll much higher. The siege aggravated anti-Government sentiment in certain quarters, and resulted in a spate of retaliatory attacks.

Meanwhile, conjecture about the possible return to Pakistan of Benazir Bhutto and Nawaz Sharif intensified. In August 2007 the Supreme Court decided that, regardless of the terms of his exile agreement, Nawaz Sharif was entitled to return to the country; however, upon his arrival in Islamabad in the following month, Nawaz Sharif was sent back to Saudi Arabia, prompting a legal challenge to the deportation. In early October Musharraf passed a National Reconciliation Ordinance, giving Bhutto and other politicians immunity from prosecution under charges brought during 1986–99. Despite the absence of a conclusive agreement, Bhutto entered Pakistan later that month. She was greeted by hundreds of thousands of supporters in Karachi, but fears for her safety were confirmed when a bomb attack on her procession resulted in approximately 139 fatalities. Bhutto herself was unharmed.

On 6 October 2007 Musharraf was re-elected as President by the incumbent national and provincial legislatures, securing 671 votes against the eight received by former Supreme Court judge Wajihuddin Ahmed. Members of the MMA, the PML (N) and other opposition parties had resigned from the National Assembly in protest prior to the ballot, while the PPP abstained from the vote. Just before the vote, the Supreme Court had ruled that the victor could not be declared until the legality of the election had been confirmed pending legal challenges from the opposition. The Supreme Court was also expected to rule on the legality of the National Reconciliation Ordinance. On 3 November Musharraf declared a state of emergency and suspended the Constitution, citing, among other contributing factors, the deteriorating law and order situation and the judiciary's interference in government affairs. Immediate measures included the dismissal of Chief Justice Chaudhry and the swearing in of Abdul Hameed Dogar as his replacement. Members of the judiciary were reportedly among those detained, together with lawyers, opposition figures and human rights activists who had taken part in demonstrations to protest against the imposition of emergency measures. Meanwhile, the police force was accorded special powers, and the broadcasting of private and international television channels was suspended. The National Assembly was dissolved on 15 November, and the Chairman of the Senate, Mohammad Mian Soomro, was sworn in to lead an interim government the following day. The Punjab, Balochistan and Sindh provincial legislatures were subsequently dissolved, the provincial assembly of NWFP having been dissolved in October. On 20 November the Chief Election Commissioner confirmed that parliamentary and provincial assembly elections would be held on 8 January 2008. Musharraf resigned as Chief of Army Staff on 28 November 2007, following the Supreme Court's dismissal, on 22 November, of the final legal challenge to Musharraf's re-election as President, thus facilitating Musharraf's inauguration as civilian head of state (which duly took place on 29 November). Meanwhile, also on 22 November, the Commonwealth Ministerial Action Group on the Harare Declaration suspended Pakistan from the Councils of the Commonwealth. Musharraf revoked the state of emergency on 15 December.

Meanwhile, the possibility of a power-sharing agreement between Musharraf and Bhutto appeared increasingly unlikely as PPP supporters joined the ranks of opposition members detained under the emergency measures, and Bhutto herself was placed under temporary house arrest to prevent her participation in political rallies. In mid-November 2007 Bhutto announced an end to negotiations, demanded Musharraf's resignation from the post of President as well as the head of the military, and indicated a willingness to consider the formation of a coalition government with other opposition parties. Nawaz Sharif was permitted to return to Pakistan at the end of November, following the reported intervention of the King of Saudi Arabia. However, in late December, as the country prepared for elections, there was a dramatic turn of events when Benazir Bhutto was killed in a suicide bomb attack on a PPP rally in Rawalpindi. The Government was criticized for not arranging adequate security measures, and some voiced suspicion about the perpetrators' possible links to sections of the Government or the intelligence establishment, a claim that Musharraf vehemently denied. According to officials, Baitullah Mehsud, an extremist from the FATA, and al-Qa'ida were involved in the attack. News of the assassination provoked rioting in several cities, resulting in more than 45 deaths. On 30 December 19-year-old Bilawal Bhutto Zardari was named to succeed his mother as leader of the PPP upon the completion of his university studies, with Asif Ali Zardari assuming the role in an interim capacity.

At the legislative elections, which were held later than scheduled, on 18 February 2008, the PPPP secured a total of 121 seats in the National Assembly (including seats reserved for women and non-muslims). The PML (N) won 91 seats, while the PML, which supported Musharraf, took just 54 seats. Turn-out was estimated at some 45% of the electorate. The PML was also defeated in all of the provincial assemblies except Balochistan. A coalition Government, mainly composed of PPP and PML (N) members, was sworn in at the end of March, under the premiership of Yousaf Raza Gilani of the PPP. Shortly after assuming office, Gilani ordered the release of several judges arrested in November 2007. Following the reinstallation of a democratically elected government, the Commonwealth readmitted Pakistan as a full member in May 2008.

Musharraf steps down and Asif Ali Zardari assumes the presidency

The fragility of the new coalition Government was demonstrated almost immediately, when a disagreement over the reinstatement of the judges who had been dismissed in November 2007 necessitated prolonged negotiations between the PPP and the PML (N) in April–May 2008. The PML (N) wanted to return Chaudhry and the other judges to their positions, while the PPP was hesitant, perhaps fearing the consequences of their reinstatement (i.e. the rescinding of the National Reconciliation Ordinance). In the absence of a resolution, in mid-May the PML (N) announced the withdrawal of its ministers from the Cabinet, although Nawaz Sharif gave an assurance of his party's continuing support for the coalition in the legislature. In the following month a campaign instigated by lawyers to reinstate the judges gained momentum and increasingly targeted the President, with thousands of people participating in a march from Lahore to Islamabad. In August Musharraf announced his resignation as President, prompted by the prospect of impending impeachment proceedings (on charges of violating the Constitution and gross misconduct) initiated by the PPP and the PML (N). The Chairman of the Senate, Mohammad Mian Soomro, was appointed President in an acting capacity, pending the parliamentary election of a successor.

At the presidential election held on 6 September 2008, Zardari defeated the PML (N) candidate, former Chief Justice of the Supreme Court Saeeduzzaman Siddiqui, by 481 votes to 153; a third candidate, Mushahid Hussain Syed, supported by the PML (Q), received only 44 votes. The rift between the PPP and the PML (N) appeared to widen in February 2009, when the Supreme Court upheld a verdict barring Nawaz Sharif and his brother, Shahbaz Sharif, from elected office on account of their previous criminal convictions. The latter was dismissed from his position as Chief Minister of Punjab, and governor's rule was imposed in the province. Nawaz Sharif protested against the ruling, claiming that Zardari was behind the decision and reiterating his demand for the reinstatement of the judges. In mid-March, in an apparent attempt to defuse the political crisis and to end the agitation by the lawyers and PML (N) activists that threatened to destabilize the country, the Government agreed to reinstate Chaudhry as Chief Justice. In response, Nawaz Sharif called off a 'long march' protest that was heading for Islamabad. At the end of the month, in a further conciliatory move, President Zardari lifted central rule in Punjab and the Supreme Court restored Shahbaz Sharif as Chief Minister of the province.

On 31 July 2009 the Supreme Court proclaimed that the state of emergency declared by Gen. Musharraf in November 2007 had been unconstitutional and that decrees based on it (including the dismissal of Chaudhry and other judges) were consequently illegal. In December 2009 the Supreme Court ruled that the National Reconciliation Ordinance of October 2007 (which had allowed for the return of Benazir Bhutto and her husband, Zardari, to take an active role in Pakistani politics, as well as acting as a political amnesty for thousands of other politicians and officials) was unconstitutional and ordered that it be abolished with immediate effect. Although Zardari was immune from criminal prosecution while he held the presidency, Nawaz Sharif demanded his resignation on moral grounds. As well as the President's political future looking increasingly unstable, a number of his government colleagues, including the Minister of the Interior, Rehman Malik, were also confronted by the prospect of renewed charges of corruption. In March 2010 the Supreme Court threatened to apprehend the Chairman of the National Accountability Bureau, Naveed Ahsan, on the grounds of contempt of court, unless he reopened hundreds of corruption cases. A few days later Ahsan announced that the Swiss authorities had been requested to reopen a money-laundering case against President Zardari. However, the Swiss authorities claimed that they were unable to reopen the case since Zardari had legal immunity as head of state.

These political developments took place against a background of increasing instability and violence in Pakistan. As fighting and bombings continued in the NWFP and FATA, there were concerns about the expanding power base of the militants. Numerous terrorist attacks (many of which were perpetrated by suspected Islamist extremists) took place in major cities throughout Pakistan in 2008 and 2009. The emergence of the Tehrik-e-Taliban Pakistan, or the so-called Pakistani Taliban, a coalition of more than 10 militant factions operating in northwest Pakistan and reportedly led by Baitullah Mehsud, was a disturbing development for the Government. In his capacity as new Prime Minister, Gilani vowed to tackle terrorism, but he also declared a willingness to negotiate with militants on the condition of their cessation of violence. Receiving particular media attention was the situation in the Swat Valley, where the provincial government was reported to have signed a peace agreement with pro-Taliban radicals in May 2008. However, sporadic fighting continued, as did attacks on girls' schools. In February 2009 a further cease-fire agreement was announced, under the terms of which large parts of the NWFP's Malakand

Division (which includes the Swat Valley, Lower Dir and Buner) would be brought under *Shari'a* law. However, in April, following a clear warning from the USA about a possible Taliban takeover of Pakistan, government forces launched a fresh offensive against the Taliban militants who—in violation of the peace agreement—were attempting to expand their power base southwards into Buner (only around 100 km from Islamabad). In early May it was reported that thousands of civilians were fleeing their homes in the Swat Valley as the peace agreement between the Taliban militants and the government troops appeared to have collapsed, with increasingly frequent violent clashes (centred around the town of Mingora) and rising casualties on both sides. There was huge public and media support for the army's intervention and in mid-May most political parties signed a joint declaration of support for the armed forces. By the end of May, as fighting intensified and the army entered Mingora, an estimated 2.4m. people had fled Swat and neighbouring regions. With the threat of a serious humanitarian catastrophe, the UN appealed for international assistance of US $600m., but by June only $140m. had been pledged. The USA had committed $750m. in aid to tribal regions, but much of this had been wasted by inefficient and corrupt local administrations. In July the Pakistani Government, having taken control of Mingora, declared that its offensive in the Swat Valley had been a success; however, despite the return of tens of thousands of refugees the cycle of violence continued. In August the army's struggle against the militants was given a major boost when Baitullah Mehsud was reported to have been killed by a US missile strike; he was replaced as leader of the Tehrik-e-Taliban Pakistan by Hakimullah Mehsud. Baitullah Mehsud had been blamed for recent bomb blasts in various Pakistani cities as well as for the assassination of Benazir Bhutto in December 2007.

In September 2009 there was a notable upsurge in militant attacks (particularly suicide bombings) against civilian and army targets in the NWFP. The army itself was also accused of carrying out human rights violations (including extrajudicial killings) against the Taliban fighters. In mid-October the army launched a fresh offensive against the Taliban militants in South Waziristan, one of the agencies of the FATA. The fierce fighting that ensued led to another exodus of refugees from the area of conflict and also prompted an escalation in retaliatory suicide bombings and armed attacks against government, military and civilian targets throughout Pakistan. One of the worst such incidents took place in Peshawar in late October when a car bomb killed at least 118 people in a crowded market. In December the army claimed to have achieved a victory against the militants in South Waziristan, but subsequent reports of terrorist activity appeared to verify that the Taliban remained active in the region. Unverified claims that the Pakistani Taliban leader, Hakimullah Mehsud, had been mortally wounded in January 2010 were strongly denied by the militants, whose assertions appeared to be supported by video footage of Mehsud allegedly recorded in April.

Recent developments: the abolition of the Seventeenth Amendment; increasing unrest and instability

In April 2010 a number of far-reaching constitutional reforms (the Eighteenth Amendment Bill), ceding key presidential powers to the Prime Minister and legislature, were signed into law, following unanimous approval by the National Assembly and Senate earlier that month. The main components of the amendments, which effectively terminated the Seventeenth Amendment enacted by President Musharraf in December 2003 (including the LFO) and transformed the president into a largely titular head of state, were: the divestment of the presidential mandate to dismiss elected governments and to appoint military chiefs and the transferral of these powers to the prime minister; the appointment of judges was transferred from the president to a judicial commission headed by the Chief Justice (with nominations to be approved by a parliamentary committee); the chief election commissioner was no longer to be appointed by the president; the election of the prime minister and of provincial chief ministers was no longer to be conducted by secret ballot; the president no longer had the power unilaterally to impose emergency rule in a province; the two-term limit on the holding of the premiership was lifted (thus allowing for Nawaz Sharif potentially to stand for another term as prime minister); and the NWFP was renamed Khyber Pakhtoonkhwa (a long-standing demand of the ethnic Pashtuns who dominate that region).

Political events in Pakistan were overshadowed by devastating floods that began in late July 2010 following unusually heavy monsoon rains. The floods, which were described as the country's worst in more than 80 years, affected around 100,000 sq km of land throughout the Indus river basin, killing at least 1,600 people, damaging or destroying around 1.6m. homes, destroying vast areas of agricultural land and adversely affecting 20m. people. With up to 8m. people in urgent need of emergency relief, in early August the UN appealed for US $460m. in international aid. Severe damage to roads, bridges and other infrastructure greatly impeded efforts by the Government and aid agencies to provide relief to victims in remote districts. Widespread public anger at the perceived ineffectiveness of the authorities' relief operation was reported in numerous areas, and consequently the profile of various Islamic charities that provided relief to flood victims was raised considerably, prompting concerns that a number of these charities had links to militant groups. In addition, the Government's civilian authority was undermined by the dominant role played by the army in the relief effort. President Zardari came under particular criticism for completing a European tour during the height of the flooding. By January 2011 the International Federation of Red Cross and Red Crescent Societies estimated that some four million people were still homeless as a result of the disaster.

Meanwhile, Karachi, the country's largest city and its main commercial centre, which had enjoyed a period of relative stability over the previous decade, suffered an intensification of political and sectarian violence in 2010. In August, following the assassination of a leading local MQM politician, Raza Haider, at least 100 people were reported to have been killed in the ensuing clashes. Further unrest erupted in September following the murder in London, United Kingdom, of a founding member of the MQM, Dr Imran Farooq. More than 50 people were killed during several days of intense violence following a by-election for Haider's former parliamentary seat in October, fuelling a growing sense of crisis in the city. According to the Government, more than 500 people were killed in violent incidents in Karachi during 2010; human rights organizations estimated the death toll to be considerably higher. The climate of violence and unrest persisted in early 2011.

During 2010 minority religious groups (including Shi'a Muslims, Christians and members of the Sufi branch of Islam) were increasingly targeted by extremists. In April Taliban militants were suspected of having carried out attacks on two mosques (belonging to the minority Ahmadi sect) in Lahore which left around 90 people dead. The issue of the persecution of religious minorities in Pakistan came to the fore in November when a court near Lahore sentenced to death a Christian woman, Asia Bibi, for blasphemy (the first woman in Pakistan to face the death charge). The conviction prompted a public debate about reforming the controversial blasphemy laws, which sanctioned the death penalty as a punishment for insulting Islam. However, opponents of reform mounted large demonstrations throughout the country from late December, demanding the retention of the existing legislation, and public support for reform was gradually stifled by increasingly menacing threats of violent retaliation issued by extremist groups against would-be supporters of liberalization. Events took a grave turn on 4 January 2011 when the PPP Governor of Punjab, Salman Taseer, who had demanded the reform of the blasphemy laws and had described Bibi's sentence as 'disgraceful', was murdered by one of his own bodyguards in Islamabad. The liberal sectors of Pakistan's population expressed their disapproval when the assassination was welcomed by Islamist extremists throughout Pakistan and the murderer was hailed as a hero of Islam. However, the Government itself failed directly to condemn Taseer's murder (despite the Governor having been a close associate of President Zardari), and the Minister of the Interior, Rehman Malik, pledged to prevent any attempt to amend the blasphemy laws. Pakistan's faltering image as a moderate Islamic state was further undermined on 2 March when Minister of Minorities Shahbaz Bhatti, the only Christian member of the Cabinet, was killed by suspected Islamist activists in Islamabad. Bhatti was apparently targeted because of his support for the rights of religious minorities and his opposition to the blasphemy legislation. Responsibility for the attack was reportedly claimed by Tehrik-e-Taliban Pakistan.

In the mean time, as agreed in the Eighteenth Amendment Bill, in early December 2010 the Cabinet approved the devolution of five federal ministries to the provinces (another five ministries were to be devolved by the end of June 2011). In mid-December the Government suffered a setback when the JUI (Fazl—F) left the coalition following the dismissal of one its members from the Cabinet and the subsequent resignation of two other JUI (F) ministers. On 2 January 2011 the Government appeared even more fragile when the MQM withdrew from the coalition in protest against the introduction of economic reforms, including the introduction of a sales tax and the imposition of a fuel price increase (instigated under pressure from the IMF). To prevent the collapse of the Government, Prime Minister Gilani cancelled the controversial reforms; on 7 January the MQM pledged to transfer its support back to the coalition (but not to rejoin the Cabinet). The following month, as part of the Government's plans to reduce public expenditure in response to the deteriorating economic situation, the number of cabinet ministers was reduced from 42 to 22.

In mid-February 2011 an anti-terrorism court in Rawalpindi issued a warrant for the arrest of Pervez Musharraf with regard to the 2007 assassination of Benazir Bhutto, claiming that the former President had failed to provide adequate security protection for the PPP leader. Musharraf, from his self-imposed exile in London, the United Kingdom, refuted all the allegations.

At the end of April 2011, in an effort to address the Government's narrowing parliamentary majority, a new coalition agreement between the PPP and the PML—still widely known in Pakistan as the PML (Q)—was concluded. On 2 May Prime Minister Gilani incorporated 14 new PML ministers and ministers of state into the Cabinet. Chaudhry Pervaiz Elahi, a senior PML official and leader of the party's Punjab wing, was appointed Senior Minister, a post that was regarded as the de facto deputy premiership, and allocated additional responsibility for Defence Production and for Industries. The Government was further strengthened by the decision of the MQM to rejoin the Cabinet; three MQM members were inducted into the Cabinet on 11 May. However, the new coalition arrangement appeared to intensify internal divisions within the PML; in mid-May the newly appointed PML Minister for Production, Amir Muqam, resigned in protest against the terms of the coalition deal, and several members of the PML announced their intention to support the opposition in the National Assembly. In mid-May the Lahore High Court ruled that President Zardari's dual role as head of state and Co-Chairman of the ruling PPP was unconstitutional, as the President was required to function with impartiality. The ruling prompted opposition demands for Zardari's resignation from the presidency.

The Government came under intense domestic and international pressure following the killing of Osama bin Laden, the founder of al-Qa'ida, by US special forces during a raid on a fortified compound in Abbottabad, Khyber Pakhtoonkhwa, on 2 May 2011. Four other inhabitants of the compound, including one of bin Laden's sons, were reportedly killed during the operation, which was apparently carried out without consultation with the Pakistani authorities. The discovery of the al-Qa'ida leader in a town containing a prominent Pakistani military academy and located less than 120 km from Islamabad prompted widespread assertions that senior Pakistani officials, most likely from the ISI or the army, must have sanctioned bin Laden's presence in the country. While the Pakistani Government welcomed bin Laden's demise, Prime Minister Gilani described the operation as a violation of national sovereignty, and rejected all allegations of official involvement in harbouring the militant leader. However, the Government's professed ignorance of the presence of the notorious fugitive and their inability to prevent the USA from conducting a unilateral military operation within Pakistani territory exposed them to persistent accusations of weakness and incompetence. The incident also reinforced existing doubts about the Government's ability to exert control over the security apparatus in Pakistan. Gilani initiated an internal investigation into the circumstances of bin Laden's presence in Pakistan; however, whichever version of events turned out to be accurate, the Government's authority appeared to have been considerably undermined by the incident. On 13 May at least 80 people were killed and more than 100 injured in a double suicide bomb attack on a training base of the paramilitary Frontier Constabulary in Charsadda District, Khyber Pakhtoonkhwa. Tehrik-e-Taliban Pakistan issued a statement claiming that they had carried out the attack in reprisal for the killing of bin Laden and vowed to launch further violent retaliatory attacks.

Foreign Affairs
Relations with India

Relations with India have dominated Pakistan's foreign policy since the creation of the two states in 1947. Relations deteriorated during the late 1970s and early 1980s, owing to Pakistan's programme to develop nuclear weapons, and as a result of major US weapons deliveries to Pakistan. The other major contentious issue between the two states was the disputed region of Kashmir, where, since 1949, a cease-fire line, known as the Line of Control (LoC), has separated Indian-controlled Kashmir (the state of Jammu and Kashmir) and Pakistani Kashmir, which comprises Azad (Free) Kashmir and the Northern Areas. While Pakistan demanded that the sovereignty of the region be decided in accordance with earlier UN resolutions (which advocated a plebiscite in both parts of the region), India argued that a solution should be reached through bilateral negotiations.

Relations between Pakistan and India reached a crisis in late 1989, when the outlawed Jammu and Kashmir Liberation Front (JKLF) and several other Muslim groups in Indian-controlled Kashmir intensified their campaigns of terrorism, strikes and civil unrest, in support of demands for an independent Kashmir or unification with Pakistan. In response, the Indian Government dispatched troops to Jammu and Kashmir. By February 1990 it was officially estimated that about 80 people (mostly civilians) had been killed in resulting clashes between troops and protesters. The opposition parties in Pakistan organized nation-wide strikes, to express their sympathy for the Muslims in Jammu and Kashmir, and urged the Government to adopt more active measures regarding the crisis.

In December 1990 discussions were held between the Ministers of External Affairs of Pakistan and India, at which an agreement not to attack each other's nuclear facilities was finalized, but no solution was found to the Kashmiri problem. Further high-level talks held between the two countries during the first half of the 1990s made no progress in resolving the crisis, and skirmishes between Pakistani and Indian troops along the border in Kashmir continued. In February 1995 (and again in February 1996) Benazir Bhutto's Government organized a nation-wide general strike to express solidarity with the independence movement in Jammu and Kashmir and to protest against alleged atrocities carried out by the Indian forces. In January 1996 relations between the two countries deteriorated when the Pakistani Government accused the Indian forces of having launched a rocket attack on a mosque in Azad Kashmir, which killed 20 people. The Indian authorities claimed that the deaths had been caused by misfired Pakistani rockets. Tensions between Pakistan and India were also exacerbated in early 1996 by allegations that each side was on the verge of conducting nuclear tests. Later that year, India's holding of state assembly elections in Jammu and Kashmir (described as 'farcical' by Benazir Bhutto) and its refusal to sign the Comprehensive Test Ban Treaty (CTBT) did nothing to encourage an improvement in relations between Islamabad and New Delhi. Despite the resumption in March 1997 of bilateral talks (which had been suspended since 1994), both at official and at ministerial level, little progress was made during the course of the year to ease tension between the two countries.

In April 1998 Pakistan provoked stern condemnation from the recently elected right-wing Government in India following its successful test-firing of a new intermediate-range missile (capable of reaching deep into Indian territory). The arms race escalated dramatically and to potentially dangerous proportions in the following month when India conducted five underground nuclear test explosions. The test programme was condemned world-wide, and the USA imposed economic sanctions against India. The US President, Bill Clinton, and the UN Security Council urged Pakistan to show restraint in not carrying out its own retaliatory test explosions. However, at the end of May Pakistan carried out six underground atomic test explosions. In early June the Pakistani Government ordered a 50% reduction in public expenditure in an attempt to mitigate the effects of the resultant economic sanctions imposed by various foreign countries, including the USA. Immediately after the nuclear tests, India and Pakistan announced self-imposed moratoriums on further testing and engaged in intense diplomatic activity. In September, however, the Pakistani Minister of Foreign Affairs categorically stated that Pakistan would not sign the CTBT until all of the sanctions were lifted and other legitimate concerns addressed.

Indo-Pakistani talks at foreign secretary level regarding Kashmir and other issues were resumed in Islamabad in October

1998. In February 1999 relations appeared to improve considerably when the Indian Prime Minister, Atal Bihari Vajpayee, made an historic journey (inaugurating the first passenger bus service between India and Pakistan) over the border to Lahore. Following his welcome by the Pakistani Prime Minister, the two leaders held a summit meeting (the first to be conducted in Pakistan for 10 years), at the end of which they signed the Lahore Declaration, which, with its pledges regarding peace and nuclear security, seemed designed to allay world-wide fears of a nuclear 'flashpoint' in South Asia. However, the contentious subject of Jammu and Kashmir was largely avoided. Concern over the escalating arms race in South Asia again heightened in April, following a series of ballistic missile tests carried out first by India and subsequently by Pakistan (however, both countries appeared to have adhered to the procedures incorporated in the Lahore Declaration, by informing each other of their test plans well in advance).

In May 1999 the Kashmir conflict intensified to reach what was termed a 'near-war situation' following the reported infiltration of 600–900 well-armed Islamist militants, reinforced by regular Pakistani troops, across the LoC into the area around Kargil in the Indian-held sector of Kashmir. It was widely believed that the incursion of the guerrillas had been planned months in advance by the Pakistani army and intelligence agents; however, the Pakistani Government claimed that it had no direct involvement whatsoever with the Islamist insurgents. In response, the Indian troops launched a series of airstrikes against the militants at the end of the month, a move that represented a serious provocation to Pakistan since it constituted the first peacetime use of air power in Kashmir. Within days tensions were heightened when a militant Kashmiri group claimed responsibility for shooting down an Indian helicopter gunship and Pakistani troops destroyed two Indian fighter aircraft, which had reportedly strayed into Pakistani airspace. Artillery exchanges increased along the LoC (with both sides suffering heavy casualties) and reports of the massing of troops and evacuation of villages along the international border aroused considerable concern. In early July, however, Indian military dominance combined with US diplomatic pressure prompted Nawaz Sharif's precipitate visit to Washington, DC, in the USA for talks with President Clinton. The resultant Washington Declaration effectively ended the Kargil crisis through the Pakistan leader's agreement to the withdrawal of all 'intruders' from Indian-controlled Kashmir. In August there was renewed tension between Pakistan and India when India shot down a Pakistani naval reconnaissance aircraft near Pakistan's border with Gujarat, killing all 16 personnel on board; Pakistan retaliated the following day by opening fire on Indian military aircraft in the same area.

In October–November 1999 there was a notable increase in terrorist incidents in Kashmir, and Indian and Pakistani forces were reported to have resumed skirmishes across the LoC. Relations between the two countries worsened in early November after the success of Vajpayee in promoting an official condemnation of the new Pakistani military regime by the Commonwealth heads of government, following the military coup in Pakistan in October. In December the Indian Government stated that it would not resume dialogue with Pakistan until the latter halted 'cross-border terrorism'. In late December the Kashmir conflict came to international attention when five Islamist fundamentalists hijacked an Indian Airlines aircraft and held its passengers captive at Qandahar airport in southern Afghanistan for one week. Among the hijackers' demands was the release from Indian prisons of 36 Muslim militants who supported the Kashmiri separatist movement. Under increasing domestic pressure to prioritize the safety of the hostages, the Indian Government agreed to release three of the prisoners in exchange for the safe return of the captive passengers and crew. Despite Indian accusations of complicity, the Pakistani Government denied any links with the hijackers.

In November 2000 the Indian Government declared the suspension of combat operations against Kashmiri militants during the Muslim holy month of Ramadan. The unilateral cease-fire began at the end of November (and was subsequently extended, at intervals, until the end of May); however, Indian security forces were authorized to retaliate if fired upon. The Pakistani authorities described the cease-fire as 'meaningless' without simultaneous constructive dialogue. The moderate All-Party Hurriyat Conference in Indian-administered Kashmir welcomed the development and offered to enter negotiations with Pakistani authorities in order to prepare for tripartite discussions. However, the Hizbul Mujahideen and other militant groups in Pakistan-administered Kashmir rejected the offer of talks and continued their campaign of violence, extending their activities as far as the Red Fort in Old Delhi, where three people were shot dead in December. In January 2001 the Indian High Commissioner to Pakistan held talks with Gen. Musharraf. This meeting signified the first high-level contact since the military coup in Pakistan in 1999. The two officials urged an early resumption of negotiations on the Kashmir question.

Relations with India appeared to improve following the earthquake in Gujarat in January 2001, when Pakistan offered humanitarian relief to India and the leaders of the two countries thus established contact. In July Prime Minister Vajpayee and Gen. Musharraf held bilateral negotiations in Agra. However, there was no breakthrough on the issue of Kashmir, with the divergent views of the two sides on the priority issue in the dispute (cross-border terrorism according to India, and Kashmiri self-determination in the opinion of Pakistan) appearing to be more firmly entrenched than ever. Tension with India was heightened considerably following a guerrilla-style attack on the state assembly building in Srinagar on 1 October. An estimated 38 people (including two of the four assailants) were killed in the attack and in the subsequent confrontation with security forces. The Indian Government attributed responsibility for the attack to the Pakistan-based Jaish-e-Mohammed and Lashkar-e-Taiba groups. Tensions were exacerbated later in the month when Gen. Musharraf rejected official Indian requests to ban the activities of the organizations in Pakistan, although he did publicly condemn the attack.

On 13 December 2001 five armed assailants attempted to launch an apparent suicide attack on the Indian union parliament building in New Delhi. Although no parliamentary deputies were hurt in the attack, nine people were killed in the botched assault (as were the five assailants). The Indian authorities again attributed responsibility for the attack to the Jaish-e-Mohammed and Lashkar-e-Taiba groups, and suggested that the assailants appeared to be of Pakistani origin. Pakistan, which had been among the numerous countries to express immediate condemnation of the attack, demanded concrete proof to support the allegations made by the Indian Government, while the US Administration urged the Indian authorities to exercise restraint in their response. Tensions between India and Pakistan continued to mount when Mohammed Afzal, a member of Jaish-e-Mohammed arrested in Kashmir on suspicion of complicity in the incident, admitted his involvement and alleged publicly that Pakistani security and intelligence agencies had provided support to those directly responsible for the attack. India recalled its High Commissioner from Islamabad and announced that overground transport services between the two countries would be suspended from 1 January 2002. As positions were reinforced with troops and weapons on both sides of the LoC, there was considerable international concern that such brinkmanship might propel the two countries into renewed armed conflict. Mindful of the potential detriment to security at Pakistan's border with Afghanistan that could result from escalated conflict in Kashmir, the USA applied increased pressure on the beleaguered Pakistani Government (already facing vociferous domestic opposition to its accommodation of US activities in Afghanistan) to adopt a more conciliatory attitude towards India's security concerns, and in late December the Pakistani authorities followed the US Government's lead in freezing the assets of the two groups held responsible for the attack by India. Although the leaders of the two groups were later detained by the Pakistani authorities, the Indian Government dismissed much of the Pakistani response as superficial and demanded that the two leaders be extradited to stand trial in India.

In January 2002 Musharraf yielded to relentless international pressure by publicly condemning the activities of militant extremists based in Pakistan and announcing the introduction of a broad range of measures to combat terrorist activity and religious zealotry, including the proscription of five extremist organizations (among them Jaish-e-Mohammed and Lashkar-e-Taiba). However, in mid-May suspected Islamist militants attacked an Indian army camp in Jammu and Kashmir, killing more than 30 people. In response, India expelled Pakistan's High Commissioner from New Delhi. Indo-Pakistani relations deteriorated further following the assassination of Abdul Ghani Lone, the leader of the moderate All-Party Hurriyat Conference on 21 May, by suspected Islamist militants. India accused the Pakistani Government of supporting the extremists. Despite US attempts to calm tensions, artillery fire was exchanged along the

LoC. More than 1m. soldiers were mobilized on both sides of the border as the two countries appeared once more to be on the brink of war. In June, following intense diplomatic efforts by British and US officials, the threat of conflict appeared to diminish. However, the killing of 27 Hindu civilians by suspected Islamist militants in Jammu in July disrupted attempts to improve diplomatic relations between India and Pakistan, and the Indian Government decided to delay the appointment of a new High Commissioner to Pakistan. Both countries conducted 'routine' ballistic-missile tests in October. President Musharraf dismissed elections in Jammu and Kashmir in September–October as a 'sham'.

Relations with India deteriorated in early 2003. Tensions were exacerbated by India conducting its latest set of 'routine' ballistic-missile tests without advance warning (Pakistan responded in kind), the continuing violence in Kashmir and India's new military agreement with Russia. Diplomatic relations between Pakistan and India were severed in February amid allegations of espionage and the funding of terrorism. Nevertheless, in May the two neighbours agreed to restore diplomatic relations and civil aviation links. Two months later the bus service between Lahore and New Delhi was renewed. However, India continued to insist on a complete cessation of cross-border infiltration by militant Islamists as a precondition for direct peace talks. In October a series of confidence-building measures (including more transport links) announced by the Indian Government was met with a cautious welcome on the part of Pakistan, and in November Pakistani Prime Minister Zafarullah Khan Jamali announced a unilateral cease-fire along the LoC. India reciprocated the gesture, but reserved the right to fire at so-called 'infiltrators'. In December Indian and Pakistani officials signed a three-year agreement on the restoration from mid-January 2004 of a passenger and freight train service between New Delhi and Lahore. Direct aviation links were resumed on 1 January 2004. Meanwhile, in November 2003 President Musharraf banned six Islamist militant groups (three of which had been banned in 2002 but had re-emerged under different names), closed down their offices and froze their bank accounts.

At a ground-breaking summit meeting of the South Asian Association for Regional Co-operation (SAARC, see p. 417) in Islamabad in January 2004, Musharraf assured Vajpayee that he would not permit any territory under Pakistan's control to be used to support terrorism; in return Vajpayee agreed to begin negotiations on all bilateral issues, including Kashmir. Indian and Pakistani senior officials opened discussions in Islamabad in February and a timetable for future dialogue was established. In June several rounds of discussions took place between Indian and Pakistani officials in New Delhi. In a joint statement issued at the end of the month, both sides stressed their renewed commitment to reaching a negotiated final settlement on the Kashmir issue and agreed to restore their diplomatic missions to full strength and, in principle, to reopen their respective consulates in Mumbai and Karachi. In September Pakistan and India held their first, official, ministerial-level talks in more than three years in New Delhi. As a result, the two sides again agreed to implement a series of confidence-building measures, including the restoration of bilateral transport links.

In November 2004 Pakistan welcomed a move by India to reduce the number of troops deployed in Jammu and Kashmir. Despite the holding of a number of high-level talks in late 2004, tensions between the two countries resurfaced in early 2005 when each side accused the other of violating the cease-fire along the LoC. However, in February, following talks at foreign minister level, the two countries agreed to open a bus service across the LoC, linking Srinagar with Muzaffarabad. Despite militant threats of disruption, and several attacks on the proposed route, the service opened in early April. Plans were also announced to reopen the consulates in Mumbai and Karachi. However, in March India made clear its disapproval of the US decision to supply Pakistan with F-16 fighter aircraft, stating its concerns that the deal would exacerbate security tensions in the region. In mid-April Musharraf travelled to India for the first time since 2001 and met with Prime Minister Manmohan Singh in Delhi for further peace talks; the two leaders subsequently issued a statement referring to the peace process as 'irreversible' and agreeing to improve trade and transport links over the LoC.

In October 2005 the devastating consequences of the massive earthquake centred in Azad Kashmir had significant implications for the ongoing peace process. In the aftermath of the disaster, Pakistan accepted an Indian offer of aid. Following a series of negotiations, the two countries subsequently agreed to open a number of crossing points on the LoC, in order to permit the reunification of divided families. However, fears on the part of both countries that the other would take advantage of the situation to conduct military surveillance hampered prospects for more extensive co-operation. Despite speculation that many militants operating in the area had been killed by the earthquake, sporadic separatist violence continued. In February 2006 a second rail link was opened between the two countries, linking the town of Khokrapar in Sindh with the Indian town of Munabao in Rajasthan.

In March 2006 the peace process advanced further when the two countries agreed that trade links would be further developed, as part of efforts to restore normal relations through the improvement of economic and commercial ties. Relations became temporarily strained in the aftermath of the Mumbai train bombings in July (see chapter on India), when, despite Musharraf's condemnation of the atrocities, Singh suggested the perpetrators had links to Pakistan. In November, during foreign secretary-level talks, the two countries agreed to form an intelligence-sharing panel to combat terrorism; the panel's first meeting took place in Islamabad in March 2007.

The Indian Minister of External Affairs, Pranab Mukherjee, travelled to Pakistan in January 2007 amid relative optimism about the resolution of outstanding issues such as Kashmir; further rounds of talks on the issue were scheduled to be held later that year. The explosions on the Delhi–Lahore Samjhauta Express train in February, which claimed 68 lives, were widely believed to have been a deliberate attempt to sabotage negotiations between Pakistan and India. Fighting across the LoC in July 2008 threatened to destabilize relations between the two countries, with India accusing Pakistan of the most 'serious violation' of the cease-fire yet. In the same month a suicide bombing at the Indian embassy in Kabul, Afghanistan, resulted in more than 40 fatalities; the Indian Government intimated that the plot had originated in Pakistan. In the aftermath of the November Mumbai attacks, when more than 170 people were killed in co-ordinated offensives against public targets, including two hotels, a hospital, a railway station and a Jewish centre, the Indian Government suggested that the perpetrators were all from Pakistan. The Pakistani authorities initially issued a denial, but subsequently conceded that the sole gunman captured alive, Mohammed Ajmal Amir Qasab, was indeed a Pakistani citizen. Moreover, in February 2009, in an unexpected turnaround, a senior official of the Pakistani Government publicly admitted that the Mumbai attacks had been partly planned in Pakistan and stated that six suspects belonging to Lashkar-e-Taiba had been arrested. The Indian Government described this groundbreaking admission as a 'positive development' and demanded that the suspects be extradited to India; however, Pakistan insisted that any prosecutions be carried out internally (Qasab was sentenced to death by a court in Mumbai in early May 2010). In February 2010 India and Pakistan held their first high-level direct talks since the 2008 Mumbai attacks in the hope of easing tension between the two countries. However, the talks, which were held in New Delhi, proved fruitless, with both sides accusing each other of supporting terrorism and of tolerating human rights abuses. In May 2010 tension was further exacerbated by the Pakistan Supreme Court's decision to release from custody the founder of Lashkar-e-Taiba, Hafiz Mohammad Saeed, who the Indian authorities believed to have been one of the masterminds behind the Mumbai attacks. In July the Indian Minister of External Affairs met his Pakistani counterpart in Islamabad in an attempt to relaunch formal peace negotiations. However, the Pakistani minister accused the Indian delegation of being ill-prepared for the talks and refusing to discuss the Kashmir issue; the summit culminated in mutual recriminations. A controversial accusation made just prior to the negotiations, by Indian Home Secretary G. K. Pillai, in which he claimed that the ISI had co-ordinated the 2008 Mumbai attacks, the first time that an Indian official had accused the Pakistani authorities of a direct role in the attacks, had done little to alleviate mutual tensions.

Following a high-level diplomatic meeting between the two sides, held in Bhutan in early February 2011, it was announced that Pakistan and India had agreed to a formal resumption of comprehensive bilateral discussions at foreign minister level, to be held in July in New Delhi. In late March relations appeared to thaw somewhat further when Pakistani Prime Minister Yousaf Raza Gilani made his first official visit to India, having accepted an invitation from Indian Prime Minister Singh to attend an international cricket match in Punjab. During his visit the premiers held a range of discussions reportedly covering 'all outstanding issues' concerning bilateral relations. Both leaders stressed the positive outcome of their talks and affirmed their commitment to resolve all bilateral problems through dialogue and to promote peace and prosperity in the region. Meanwhile, following a meeting between the Indian and Pakistani Home Secretaries, held in New Delhi in advance of the prime-ministerial summit, agreement was reportedly reached on a number of measures to improve co-operation in counter-terrorism efforts; in addition, security officials from Pakistan and India were to be permitted access to each other's countries to facilitate investigations into the 2008 Mumbai attacks.

Other regional relations

Relations with Afghanistan were strained during the 1980s and early 1990s, as rebel Afghan tribesmen (*mujahidin*) used areas inside Pakistan (notably the city of Peshawar) as bases for their activities. In early 1988 there were an estimated 3.2m. Afghan refugees in Pakistan, most of them in the NWFP. The presence of the refugees prompted cross-border attacks against *mujahidin* bases by Soviet and Afghan government troops. In 1988 Pakistan signed the Geneva Accords on the withdrawal of Soviet troops from Afghanistan, which included agreements on the voluntary repatriation of Afghan refugees from Pakistan. Following the withdrawal of Soviet troops from Afghanistan in 1989, Pakistan maintained its support for the guerrillas' cause, while denying accusations by the Afghan Government that it was taking an active military part in the conflict, or that it was acting as a conduit for arms supplies to the *mujahidin*. The Pakistani Government welcomed the overthrow of the Afghan regime by the guerrillas in April 1992 and supported the interim coalition Government that was formed to administer Afghanistan pending the holding of free elections. However, relations between Pakistan and Afghanistan deteriorated in 1994. The turbulence and increasing anti-Pakistan feeling in Afghanistan not only threatened to result in an extension of the violence into the Pakhtoon (Pashtun) areas of the NWFP, but also obstructed the trade route from the Central Asian republics of the former USSR to the Arabian Sea at Karachi. The situation worsened in September 1995 when the Pakistani embassy in Kabul was ransacked and burned down by a mob of about 5,000 Afghans protesting at Pakistan's alleged active support for the Islamist Taliban militia who opposed the more moderate *mujahidin* Government. In the following month the Afghan ambassador to Pakistan was expelled from the country. Following the capture of Kabul by Taliban troops in September 1996 and their assumption of power, the Pakistani Government issued a statement recognizing the Taliban militia as the new Afghan Government.

In December 1999 there were signs of distinct changes in Pakistan's policy towards Afghanistan. Following the imposition of UN-mandated sanctions on Afghanistan the previous month for refusing to hand over the Saudi-born terrorist suspect Osama bin Laden, Pakistan appeared to be exerting pressure on the Taliban to accede to Western demands by closing down a number of Afghan banking operations in Pakistan. The Pakistani Government continued to offer financial and diplomatic support to the Taliban, although Gen. Musharraf repeatedly and strongly denied giving military assistance. However, allegations regarding the involvement of Pakistan's special forces in the Taliban campaign against the forces of the opposition *mujahidin* grew following the Taliban's successful offensive in August–September 2000. The Pakistani Government agreed to implement the UN sanctions imposed on Afghanistan in January 2001, but announced that it would attempt to mitigate the effect of the restrictions, warning of a steep increase in refugee numbers and a worsening of the civil war. The failure of (somewhat unconvincing) attempts by senior Pakistani military officers to persuade the Taliban administration to comply with US demands that bin Laden and members of his al-Qa'ida terrorist organization thought to be resident in Afghanistan should be handed over to the US authorities to answer charges of responsibility for the September 2001 terrorist attacks on the US mainland, ultimately resulted in a US-led military campaign to remove the Taliban from power. Despite considerable opposition from ethnic Pashtuns in north-western Pakistan and from elements of the armed forces who had spent years consolidating relations with the Taliban regime (the majority of which was composed of Pashtuns), Musharraf was forced to co-operate with the US-led coalition to avoid potentially devastating economic and political isolation. Long-standing enmity between the Pakistani Government and the Afghan forces of the United Front, arising from Pakistani sponsorship of the Taliban regime, was exacerbated by the participation of Pakistani nationals in the armed resistance to the United Front's renewed military campaign (supported by the international coalition) to recapture Afghanistan. As the United Front continued to make impressive territorial gains in Afghanistan, culminating in the capture of the capital, Kabul, and the collapse of the Taliban regime in mid-November, the Pakistani Government announced the closure of all Taliban consular offices in Pakistan, including the embassy in Islamabad. It was hoped that the broad-based ethnicity of the Afghan Interim Administration (which included Pashtun representatives) installed in December would help to foster improved relations between the Pakistani authorities and the United Front.

Publicly, Musharraf supported Hamid Karzai, President of the new Afghan Transitional Administration. However, Afghan officials were convinced that the Pakistani ISI was giving sanctuary to senior Taliban members and other Afghan military commanders, such as Gulbuddin Hekmatyar, who were opposed to the new Government in Kabul. In February 2003 the Pakistani and Afghan military intelligence services held talks in Rome, Italy, in an attempt to resolve deep-rooted differences. Some two months later, during an official visit to Pakistan, President Karzai urged the Pakistani Government to assist in curbing cross-border attacks by militant Islamists. Relations were strained when Pakistan delivered a formal protest to Afghanistan in June over the dumping of the bodies of some 21 Taliban fighters on its territory; the Afghan authorities were forced to recover the bodies after Pakistani border guards discovered that the dead were, in fact, not Pakistani, but Afghan citizens. One month later the Pakistani embassy in Afghanistan was stormed and raided by hundreds of Afghans in protest against alleged incursions by Pakistani border troops into Afghan territory. In January 2004 the Pakistani Prime Minister paid his first ever official visit to Afghanistan; the two countries agreed to work together to combat cross-border infiltration. In 2005–06, however, despite a number of meetings between Afghan and Pakistani officials, relations were strained, with President Karzai and his Pakistani counterpart engaging in public recriminations over cross-border activities and the fight against the Taliban.

In late 2006 the announcement of Pakistan's plans to lay landmines and construct a series of fences along sections of the Afghan–Pakistani border to prevent insurgents based in Pakistan from launching cross-border raids, while also reducing drugs-smuggling from Afghanistan, elicited a negative response from Karzai, who complained that the strategy was divisive. Preparatory work on the fence carried out by Pakistani officials in March 2007 raised further protests from the Afghan Government, which argued that the demarcation of the border was in dispute, but construction continued. Relations between the two countries appeared to improve with the holding of a joint 'peace *jirga* (council)' in Kabul in August. The four-day meeting, which was attended by some 650 tribal leaders from both countries, along with Karzai, President Musharraf and other senior government officials, was convened with the aim of addressing shared issues such as security and terrorism. In February 2008 the Pakistani ambassador to Afghanistan was abducted by suspected Taliban militants in the Khyber Agency in Pakistan; he was released unharmed in May. In February 2009 the new US Secretary of State, Hillary Rodham Clinton, hosted a meeting with the foreign ministers of Pakistan and Afghanistan in Washington, DC, and announced that these trilateral negotiations would be held on a regular basis to discuss mutually strategic issues. In August President Karzai and the Pakistani Prime Minister, Yousaf Raza Gilani, agreed to co-operate in combating terrorism and militancy. In early 2010 the Pakistani authorities appeared to be adhering to their pledge to co-operate in the fight against the insurgents when a number of high-ranking Afghan Taliban figures were arrested in Pakistan.

Relations between Pakistan and Afghanistan were given a major boost in October 2010 when the two sides signed a US-sponsored Afghan-Pakistan Transit Trade Agreement (APTTA), which was to replace a 1965 bilateral trade agreement and would facilitate the transport of Afghan exports through Pakistan to markets in India, as well as providing access to Central Asian markets for Pakistani exports. However, the official implementation of the APTTA, which was scheduled to take place in February 2011, was postponed until June owing to a number of unresolved technical issues. The positive trend in relations continued in December 2010 following Prime Minister Gilani's first official visit to Afghanistan during which he held wide-ranging discussions with President Karzai. In early January

2011 members of the Afghan High Peace Council, which had been established by Karzai in September 2010 and which was led by former Afghan President Prof. Burhanuddin Rabbani, held talks with the Pakistani President and Prime Minister in Islamabad regarding Pakistan's future role in peace negotiations with the Afghan Taliban. In mid-April 2011 Gilani returned to Afghanistan to finalize plans for the establishment of a senior-level joint commission on peace and reconciliation; the planned participation in the commission of senior Afghan and Pakistani military and intelligence officials, in addition to the ministers responsible for foreign affairs, was interpreted as a significant breakthrough in security co-operation.

According to the UN High Commissioner for Refugees (UNHCR), by April 2002 (following the decisive defeat of Taliban forces in most of Afghanistan) repatriation offices in Pakistan were processing the return of as many as 50,000 Afghan refugees each week. At the end of 2002 UNHCR announced that more than 1.5m. Afghan refugees in Pakistan had returned to their homeland, surpassing all expectations; a further 400,000 returned in 2003 and approximately 384,000 in 2004. In early 2005 the Pakistani Government and UNHCR launched a census intended to determine how many Afghan refugees remained in Pakistan, in order to aid the development of policies to assist them. According to reports, between early 2002 and April 2007 more than 3m. refugees returned to Afghanistan from Pakistan. In March 2010 the UNHCR welcomed the decision of the Pakistani authorities to permit almost 1.7m. Afghan refugees (the majority of whom were living in designated villages or among host communities) to remain in the country for three more years.

Relations between Pakistan and Bangladesh improved in 1976: ambassadors were exchanged, and trade, postal and telecommunication links were resumed. In September 1991 Pakistan finally agreed to initiate a process of phased repatriation and rehabilitation of some 250,000 Urdu-speaking Bihari Muslims (who openly supported Pakistan in Bangladesh's war of liberation in 1971) still remaining in refugee camps in Bangladesh. The first group of Bihari refugees returned to Pakistan from Bangladesh in January 1993, but the implementation of the repatriation process has proved very slow. (In May 2008 the Dhaka High Court concluded that approximately 150,000 Biharis—those who had been minors in 1971 or who had been born in the intervening years—could become citizens of Bangladesh.) A diplomatic row arose in September 2000 over who was responsible for the events during Bangladesh's war of liberation, culminating in the withdrawal of the Pakistani Deputy High Commissioner to Bangladesh. In July 2002 Pakistani President Pervez Musharraf paid a visit to Bangladesh, during which he expressed regret for the atrocities committed by Pakistani troops during the 1971 war. In February 2006 Bangladeshi Prime Minister Khaleda Zia visited Islamabad to hold talks with her Pakistani counterpart, Shaukat Aziz; the latter hailed the visit, during which the two sides signed four memorandums of understanding on trade, agriculture, tourism, and standardization and quality control, as a turning point in bilateral relations. A fifth round of Pakistan-Bangladesh bilateral consultations (primarily covering trade and investment) was held, after a three-year hiatus, in Islamabad in November 2010, during which the Bangladeshi delegation requested a formal apology from Pakistan for the war of liberation; other issues discussed reportedly included the proposed repatriation of more Bihari refugees and the division of state assets pertaining to the period before Bangladesh's independence. In addition, the Bangladeshi delegation formally raised the issue of war reparations for the first time.

Other external relations

In foreign relations Pakistan has traditionally pursued a policy of maintaining close links with Islamic states in the Middle East and Africa and with the People's Republic of China, while continuing to seek aid and assistance from the USA. Pakistan's controversial nuclear programme prompted the USA to terminate development aid in April 1979, but, as a result of the Soviet invasion of Afghanistan in December of that year, military and economic assistance was renewed in 1981. However, increased concern about Pakistan's ability to develop nuclear weapons and its refusal to sign the Nuclear Non-Proliferation Treaty (NPT) led to the suspension of military and economic aid by the US Government again in 1990 (under the Pressler Amendment). In February 1992 the Pakistani Government admitted for the first time that Pakistan had nuclear-weapons capability, but added that it had frozen its nuclear programme at the level of October 1989, when its capabilities were insufficient to produce a nuclear device. In September 1995 the US Senate voted in favour of the Brown Amendment, which allowed a limited resumption of defence supplies to Pakistan. The Brown Amendment (which was ratified by the US President, Bill Clinton, in January 1996) also deleted the Pressler Amendment requirements for economic sanctions, thus paving the way for the resumption of US economic aid to Pakistan. In August 1996 the first consignment of military equipment released by the US Government after a six-year delay arrived in Pakistan. In December 1998 Prime Minister Nawaz Sharif held talks with President Clinton in the US capital in an attempt to gain support for Pakistan's ailing economy and to persuade the US leader further to ease sanctions imposed on Pakistan following nuclear tests carried out by the latter in May. During 1998–99 the USA lifted some of the sanctions imposed on Pakistan and India, while reiterating requests that the two countries sign the CTBT and exercise restraint in their respective missile development programmes. During 2000 US foreign policy appeared to favour closer co-operation with India at the expense of improved relations with Pakistan. However, Pakistan's strategic importance to US efforts to dismantle the Taliban regime in Afghanistan and thus apprehend members of the al-Qa'ida terrorist organization held responsible for the devastating attacks on New York and Washington, DC, USA, in September 2001 resulted in attempts by the USA to promote Pakistan's political rehabilitation in the Western international community. Although in September the US Government withdrew sanctions imposed on Pakistan in May 1998, and Gen. Musharraf was warmly received on official visits to the USA in November 2001 and February 2002, a 1990 suspension order on the delivery to Pakistan of 28 US F-16 fighter aircraft was not lifted, to the evident disappointment of the Pakistani President.

Despite the international acclaim that greeted Musharraf's public declaration of his commitment to the eradication of militant religious extremism in January 2002, US concerns persisted about the proliferation of armed fundamentalist groups in Pakistan's border regions, and the possibility of their assisting scattered al-Qa'ida units to regroup in these areas. A US journalist, Daniel Pearl, was abducted in Karachi in January by a previously unknown group called the National Movement for the Restoration of Pakistani Sovereignty; the group made a number of demands in exchange for his safe return, including the release of all Pakistani nationals captured by US forces in Afghanistan and transported (together with other suspected al-Qa'ida members) to a detention centre at the US military base in Guantánamo Bay, Cuba. Despite the prompt arrest by the Pakistani authorities of a British-born militant Islamist, Ahmed Omar Saeed Sheikh, who was believed to have organized the kidnapping, it soon emerged that Pearl had been murdered by his abductors. Confounding speculation that suspects in the case would be extradited for trial in the USA, in March Saeed Sheikh and three alleged accomplices appeared in a specially instituted anti-terrorism court in Karachi on charges of kidnapping, murder and terrorism. The men were convicted of the charges in July; Saeed Sheikh was sentenced to death and his co-defendants were each sentenced to life imprisonment. Following an anti-US grenade attack on the Protestant International Church in Islamabad in March, in which five people (including the wife and daughter of a US diplomat) were killed, Musharraf dismissed five senior police officers for what he considered a serious lapse in security. It was widely believed that intelligence proceeding from Pakistani investigations to discover the identities of the assailants was a crucial factor in the arrest of Abu Zubaydah, one of al-Qa'ida's most senior commanders, by officers of the US Federal Bureau of Investigation (FBI) in Faisalabad at the end of March. However, another attack occurred in June outside the US consulate in Karachi, killing 12 people. One month later two Pakistani members of the al-Alami faction of the banned Harakat ul-Mujahideen claimed responsibility for the attack on the US consulate as well as other attacks on Western targets. In September Pakistani security forces arrested 12 alleged members of al-Qa'ida in Karachi, including the Yemeni-born Ramzi Binalshibh, a principal suspect in the attacks on the USA on 11 September 2001. The USA took custody of Binalshibh and four other al-Qa'ida suspects.

In an apparent breakthrough in the campaign against religious extremism, the alleged operations chief of the al-Qa'ida network, Khalid Sheikh Mohammed, who was suspected of having planned the attacks on the USA in September 2001, was arrested in Rawalpindi in March 2003. It was hoped that the suspect, who was promptly taken into US custody, would provide information on the identity and whereabouts of al-Qa'ida cells in Pakistan and elsewhere in the world. Two other suspected Islamist militants were also arrested. The ISI's involvement in the arrest of the alleged militants suggested that the intelligence agency was genuinely attempting to curb militant activity. Furthermore, in early March the ISI declared that since 11 September 2001 Pakistan had arrested 442 suspected foreign militants, of whom 346 had been handed over to US custody. However, the discovery of Mohammed in a house owned by an army officer's brother raised questions about links between al-Qa'ida and the Pakistani military. Furthermore, the proprietor's prominent role in the Jamaat-e-Islami Pakistan generated speculation about that political party's connections with al-Qa'ida. Later in March 2003 Pakistan, influenced by widespread large-scale protest marches against US-led military action to remove the regime of Saddam Hussain in Iraq, stated that it would not support the USA in this action. In the same month the USA removed all remaining sanctions imposed on Pakistan after the 1999 military coup and in early April 2003 agreed to waive a total of US $1,000m. in debt, in recognition of Pakistan's efforts in the 'war on terror'. During Musharraf's visit to the USA in June, the Pakistani President expressed his hopes of securing further pledges of co-operation, economic aid and possibly military sales in return for his support. Indeed, the US President, George W. Bush, offered an aid package of $3,000m. in financial and military assistance over the next five years. However, the Bush Administration declined to cancel a further $1,800m. debt, owing to reservations over whether the Pakistani authorities were acting sufficiently to curb militant activity and to prevent the infiltration of separatist militants into Indian-controlled Kashmir.

In October 2003, following reports of increased militant activity in South Waziristan, particularly in conservative Pashtun areas where Taliban members were known to enjoy support, Pakistani forces mounted several operations targeting militants and tribal elders who were suspected of providing them with shelter. However, despite the apparent attempts to combat Taliban activity in the tribal areas, there were claims that Pakistani troops continued to allow Taliban movement across the Afghan–Pakistani border and that senior Taliban members were openly living in Quetta in Balochistan. In the first half of 2004 the search for suspected militants remained focused on South Waziristan, where the USA believed Osama bin Laden and other al-Qa'ida leaders were receiving shelter. Several thousand Pakistani troops were deployed to force al-Qa'ida fugitives across the border into Afghanistan, where US soldiers were active (US troops were not permitted to operate from Pakistani soil). Fighting between Pakistani troops and militants in March resulted in the deaths of more than 100 people, although many militants were believed to have evaded capture and escaped.

Meanwhile, during a visit to Pakistan in March 2004, the US Secretary of State announced that, in recognition of the close military relations between the two countries, the USA had decided to designate Pakistan a 'major non-North Atlantic Treaty Organization (NATO) ally'. Shortly afterwards President Bush announced that all remaining US sanctions against Pakistan would be lifted. However, concerns continued to be expressed by the USA that more progress was not being made in the campaign against al-Qa'ida. In July it was announced that several suspected al-Qa'ida members, including the Tanzanian Ahmed Khalfan Ghailani, who was wanted in connection with the 1998 bombing of US embassies in Kenya and Tanzania, had been arrested in the town of Gujrat in Punjab. Ghailani was later placed in the custody of the USA.

In February 2005, in a move indicative of the improved relations between the two countries, the USA revived the deal that it had suspended in 1990 to supply Pakistan with F-16 fighter aircraft. The agreement constituted part of a US $3,000m., five-year assistance programme. Following the devastating earthquake of October 2005, however, the purchase of the aircraft was postponed, in order that the funds could be allocated instead to the reconstruction effort. Meanwhile, in May it was announced that Abu Faraj al-Libbi, reported to be the operational head of al-Qa'ida in Pakistan, had been captured in the city of Mardan in the NWFP. Al-Libbi was subsequently transferred into US custody for interrogation.

In September 2006 the signing of a peace accord by the Government and tribal leaders in North Waziristan prompted criticism from international observers for what was seen as a strategy of appeasement: under the terms of the agreement the Government was to downgrade its military presence in the area in exchange for a cessation of rebel offensives against the army and across the border with Afghanistan. In March 2007 the Government signed a peace agreement with tribal elders in the Bajaur region of the FATA under which the latter confirmed that they would not provide refuge to foreign militants, while the Government, on its part, was obliged to consult tribal elders before launching operations in the region. Despite these attempts at reconciliation, however, the violence between the army and the militants did not cease and the death toll on both sides continued to rise. In July Baitullah Mehsud (a militant later accused of involvement in Benazir Bhutto's assassination in December), along with a group of tribal leaders, declared an end to the cease-fire in North Waziristan. Clashes between militants and security forces resulted in many deaths in North and South Waziristan in 2007 and 2008. Accounts of attacks by unmanned US aircraft ('drones') in the FATA and cross-border incursions served to strain relations between Pakistan and the USA, with the former demanding the latter respect its sovereignty. The reportedly high civilian death toll was also perceived to have an extremely counter-productive effect on public sentiment. The new US President, Barack Obama, who took office in January 2009, emphasized his 'commitment to a strong partnership' with Pakistan in February, including an increase in the provision of non-military aid. However, there was a marked increase in the frequency of the controversial US drone attacks in north-west Pakistan (particularly in North Waziristan) in 2009–10, as the USA intensified its struggle against the Islamist militants who were based in that area.

In October 2009 the US Administration pledged US $7,500m. in non-military aid to Pakistan over a five-year period, on the condition that the country remained committed to fighting terrorism; that it did not permit its territory to be used as a base for attacks against other countries; that it committed itself to nuclear non-proliferation; and that the army did not interfere in Pakistan's political or judicial processes. The conditions attached to the so-called Kerry-Lugar-Berman Bill, which were to be strictly monitored and certified by US officials within Pakistan itself, prompted serious criticism within certain quarters in Pakistan (notably the armed forces) on the grounds that they undermined the country's sovereignty by allowing the USA to exert excessive influence over Pakistani policies. In February 2010 US-Pakistani co-operation in the fight against Islamist terrorism appeared to be working effectively when US officials reported the capture of the high-ranking Afghan Taliban military commander, Mullah Abdul Ghani Baradar, who was widely believed to be second-in-command to Mullah Mohammad Omar, in Karachi. There appeared to be an improvement in mutual understanding and trust between Pakistan and the USA in late March when the Pakistani Minister of Foreign Affairs and the Pakistani Chief of Army Staff met their US counterparts on an official visit to Washington. In May the US authorities arrested a Pakistani-born US citizen and two Pakistani nationals for their alleged involvement in a failed bomb attack in the centre of New York, USA, that was foiled earlier that month. In October a plot by another Pakistani-born US national to carry out a bomb attack on the Metrorail system in Washington, DC, was uncovered by the US authorities; the suspect, Farooque Ahmed, was sentenced to 23 years in prison in April 2011. Meanwhile, in June 2010 it was reported that a founding member of al-Qa'ida, Mustafa Abu al-Yazid, who was alleged to have aided the financing of the September 2001 attacks in the USA, had been killed in a US drone attack in north-west Pakistan.

During the latter half of 2010 the USA exerted increasing pressure on Pakistan to launch a major offensive against the militants in North Waziristan. Pakistan's military leadership resisted the US demands, claiming that their troops were already overstretched. In November it was reported that the USA was seeking to expand the areas inside Pakistan where unmanned aircraft (used for surveillance and to launch missile strikes) could operate. Pakistan responded by stating categorically that it would never allow such an expansion of US drone operations. Furthermore, in the following month Pakistan warned the USA that their counter-terrorism partnership would be terminated if there was any encroachment by US ground forces across the Afghan border into Pakistani territory (as the US military was reported to have recently requested).

In late January 2011 Pakistani-US relations were severely strained following the fatal shooting in Lahore of two Pakistani civilians by a US national, Raymond Davis, who, it later transpired, was employed by the US Central Intelligence Agency (CIA). Davis, who claimed to have been acting in self-defence, was charged with murder but was acquitted by a Pakistani court in March when relatives of the victims accepted so-called 'blood money' in exchange for his release. However, the incident provoked a marked increase in anti-US sentiment throughout Pakistan. In April it was reported that Pakistan had requested that the USA reduce the number of CIA agents in the country, provide detailed information regarding the assignments of the agency's remaining personnel, and limit the number of drone attacks in the north-west tribal areas (such attacks, the number of which had doubled in 2010, compared with the previous year, were estimated to have killed hundreds of civilians in addition to the numerous targeted Taliban and al-Qa'ida militants).

Bilateral relations were brought to a crisis point following the covert US raid in Abbottabad at the beginning of May 2011 during which Osama bin Laden, the founder of al-Qa'ida and the USA's 'most-wanted' terrorist target, was killed (see Domestic Political Affairs). The US decision apparently to conduct the operation without consulting the Pakistani authorities illustrated the low level of trust that existed between the two countries, especially with regard to counter-terrorism and security issues. The Pakistani Government angrily rejected suggestions emanating from the USA that the al-Qa'ida leader could not have taken refuge in Abbottabad without the co-operation of senior Pakistani officials. The incident provoked intense political debate in both the USA and Pakistan concerning the viability of the strategic alliance between the two countries. Members of the US Senate urged the Obama Administration to halt military aid to Pakistan until the Pakistani authorities demonstrated greater commitment to supporting US counter-terrorism objectives in the region; Pakistan had received some US $20,000m. in military and non-military aid since 2001. In mid-May 2011 John Kerry, Chairman of the US Senate Foreign Affairs Committee, travelled to Islamabad for talks with Pakistan's civilian and military leaders concerning the bin Laden incident and the crisis facing bilateral relations. Kerry stated that the US Administration had 'grave concerns' regarding bin Laden's refuge in Pakistan but insisted that the USA was committed to rebuilding trust between the allies. None the less, in an official visit to China during the same week, organized to mark the 60th anniversary of the establishment of bilateral relations, Prime Minister Gilani thanked China for its unwavering support and solidarity and described the host nation as Pakistan's 'best and most trusted friend'. The Chinese Premier, Wen Jiabao, stated that China had recently issued the USA with a formal request to respect Pakistani sovereignty. During the summit China finalized arrangements for the supply of 50 JF-17 fighter aircraft to Pakistan; details of a joint venture agreement to produce additional fighter aircraft in Pakistan were also announced.

Pakistan withdrew from the Commonwealth in January 1972, in protest at the United Kingdom's role in the East Pakistan crisis. Pakistan recognized Bangladesh in February 1974, but attempts to rejoin the Commonwealth in the late 1970s and early 1980s were thwarted by India. However, in January 1989 India announced that it would no longer oppose Pakistan's application to rejoin the organization, and in July, during an official visit to the United Kingdom by Benazir Bhutto, Pakistan was formally invited to rejoin the Commonwealth, which it did on 1 October 1989. However, in October 1999, following the military coup, Pakistan was suspended from participation in meetings of the Commonwealth. In September 2003 the CMAG agreed to maintain Pakistan's suspension from participation in meetings, as it was not convinced that democracy had been completely restored in the country. However, in May 2004 the CMAG agreed to restore fully Pakistan's Commonwealth membership, stating that it had decided that the country had consolidated the progress made towards democracy following the October 2002 general election, owing to President Musharraf's statement that he would step down as Chief of Army Staff by the end of 2004 and the subsequent legislative vote of confidence in his leadership. In February 2005 the CMAG criticized Musharraf for reneging on his pledge to become a civilian president and insisted that he must relinquish his military role by 2007. Following Musharraf's imposition of a state of emergency and suspension of the Constitution in November 2007, the CMAG once again suspended Pakistan from participation in meetings. However, full membership was restored in May 2008 as a result of the restoration of democratic government in February.

In 1995 Pakistan, the People's Republic of China, Kazakhstan and Kyrgyzstan signed a transit trade agreement, restoring Pakistan's overland trade route with Central Asia, through China. During a commemorative visit to Pakistan by the Chinese Premier, organized in May 2001 to celebrate 50 years of bilateral relations, the two countries concluded a number of agreements on technical and economic co-operation. In January 2002 it was reported that China had supplied several dozen fighter aircraft and air defence missiles to Pakistan. In May 2004 the two countries signed an agreement to construct a second nuclear power plant at Chashma in Punjab province, with substantial assistance from the Chinese National Nuclear Corporation (a first plant having opened in 2001); the second Chashma facility was inaugurated in May 2011. Relations between Pakistan and China were further strengthened by the signing of a Treaty of Friendship, Co-operation and Good-Neighbourly Relations in April 2005 and of a landmark free-trade agreement in November 2006. It was hoped that the latter accord would lead to the tripling of bilateral trade within five years. In April 2008 the Pakistani navy took delivery of the first of four advanced Chinese-constructed frigates that had been ordered in 2005. The new Pakistani President, Asif Ali Zardari, made China the destination of his first official state visit in October 2008, during which it was reported that the two countries agreed to expand their nuclear co-operation. In April 2009 Pakistan and China signed an agreement to construct a further two nuclear power plants at Chashma. In mid-2010 the USA and India expressed their concern at the proposed expansion of Pakistan's nuclear sector, but China insisted that its civilian nuclear co-operation with Pakistan was for purely peaceful purposes. According to the guidelines of the Nuclear Suppliers' Group (NSG, which China had joined in 2004), member states should not export civil nuclear technology to countries that had not signed the NPT (Pakistan being one of these). China argued, however, that its nuclear co-operation programme with Pakistan predated its joining the NSG. China's role as a counterweight to US influence in Pakistan was underlined in May 2011 when Chinese Premier Wen Jiabao, in the midst of a US-Pakistani diplomatic crisis following the killing of Osama bin Laden (see above), extended to Prime Minister Gilani China's unqualified support, and substantial military aid, during a bilateral summit in Beijing.

In February 2003 President Musharraf visited Moscow, the first official visit by a Pakistani head of state to the Russian capital in 33 years. In April 2007, during the holding of official talks in Islamabad, the Prime Ministers of Pakistan and Russia pledged further to strengthen bilateral ties, particularly in the fields of trade and the economy. In March 2009 the two countries agreed to establish a Pakistan-Russia Business Forum.

In early 1992 the Economic Co-operation Organization (ECO, see p. 264), comprising Pakistan, Iran and Turkey, was reactivated, and by the end of the year had been expanded to include Afghanistan, Azerbaijan and the five Central Asian, mainly Muslim, republics of the former USSR; the 'Turkish Republic of Northern Cyprus' joined ECO in 1993. Trade delegations from Turkey and the new republics visited Pakistan, and an agreement for the restoration and construction of highways in Afghanistan, to link Pakistan with these republics, was signed. In October 2010 the Pakistani Government formally approved the framework agreement for the construction of the 1,680-km Turkmenistan-Afghanistan-Pakistan-India (TAPI) gas pipeline. The pipeline, which was to be funded by the Asian Development Bank (ADB, see p. 202) at an estimated cost of US $7,600m. and was projected to be operational by 2014, was to extend from the Dauletabad gas field in Turkmenistan to the town of Fazilka in the Indian state of Punjab (via Afghanistan and Pakistan).

CONSTITUTION AND GOVERNMENT

The Constitution was promulgated on 10 April 1973, and amended on a number of subsequent occasions. Several provisions were suspended following the imposition of martial law in 1977. The (amended) Constitution was restored on 30 December 1985. The Constitution was placed in abeyance on 15 October 1999 following the overthrow of the Government in a military coup. The Constitution, incorporating a Legal Framework Order (LFO), which greatly increased the powers held by the President, was revived on 15 November 2002. The LFO, however, was effectively repealed by the Eighteenth Amendment Bill, which was passed in April 2010 and which transformed the President into a largely titular Head of State.

The President is a constitutional Head of State, who is normally elected for five years by an electoral college, comprising the Federal Legislature and the four provincial assemblies. The former consists of a lower and upper house—the National

Assembly and Senate. There are 342 seats in the National Assembly, with 272 members directly elected (on the basis of adult suffrage), 60 seats reserved for women and 10 for non-Muslims. The term of the National Assembly is five years. The Senate comprises 104 seats; the provincial assemblies directly elect 92 members—of whom four have to be non-Muslims, 16 have to be women and a further 16 technocrats (including *ulema*, Muslim legal scholars)—and of the remaining 12 members, the Federally Administered Tribal Areas return eight members and the remaining four are elected from the Federal Capital Territory by members of the Provincial Assemblies. The term of the Senate is six years, with one-half of the membership being renewed every three years. The Prime Minister is elected by the National Assembly and he/she and the other ministers in the Cabinet are responsible to it.

Pakistan comprises four provinces (each with an appointed Governor and provincial government), the federal capital of Islamabad and the Federally Administered Tribal Areas (FATA).

REGIONAL AND INTERNATIONAL CO-OPERATION

Pakistan is a member of the South Asian Association for Regional Co-operation (SAARC, see p. 417), of the Asian Development Bank (ADB, see p. 202), and of the Colombo Plan (see p. 446). Pakistan is also a founder member of the Islamic Financial Services Board.

Having joined the UN in 1947, Pakistan is a member of the Economic and Social Commission for Asia and the Pacific (ESCAP, see p. 37). As a contracting party to the General Agreement on Tariffs and Trade (GATT), Pakistan joined the World Trade Organization (WTO, see p. 430) on its establishment in 1995.

ECONOMIC AFFAIRS

In 2009, according to estimates by the World Bank, Pakistan's gross national income (GNI), measured at average 2007–09 prices, was US $172,855m., equivalent to $1,020 per head (or $2,710 per head on an international purchasing-power parity basis). During 2000–09, it was estimated, the population grew at an average annual rate of 2.3%, while gross domestic product (GDP) per head increased, in real terms, by an average of 2.4% per year. Overall GDP rose, in real terms, at an average annual rate of 4.7% in 2000–09. According to official provisional figures, growth reached 3.6% in 2008/09, and 4.4% in 2009/10.

Agriculture (including forestry and fishing) contributed an estimated 21.8% of GDP in 2009/10. Some 44.7% of the employed labour force was engaged in the sector at 30 June 2008. The principal cash crops are cotton (which accounted for around 16.8% of export earnings in 2009/10) and rice; sugar cane, wheat and maize are also major crops. Fishing and leather production provide significant export revenues. According to the Asian Development Bank (ADB, see p. 202), during 2000–09 agricultural GDP increased at an average annual rate of 2.9%; it rose by 1.0% in 2007/08, and 4.0% in 2008/09.

Industry (including mining, manufacturing, power and construction) engaged an estimated 20.1% of the employed labour force at 30 June 2008, and provided an estimated 23.6% of GDP in 2009/10. During 2000–09, according to the ADB, industrial GDP increased by an average of 5.6% per year; industrial GDP grew by 1.4% in 2007/08, but fell by 1.9% in 2008/09.

Mining and quarrying contributed an estimated 2.5% of GDP in 2009/10, and, according to the International Labour Organization (ILO), engaged only 0.1% of the employed labour force at 30 June 2008. Petroleum and petroleum products are the major mineral exports. Limestone, rock salt, gypsum, silica sand, natural gas and coal are also mined. In addition, Pakistan has reserves of graphite, copper and manganese. The GDP of the mining sector increased at an average annual rate of 6.1% during 2000–09; according to the ADB, mining GDP grew by 4.4% in 2007/08, but fell by 0.2% in 2008/09.

Manufacturing contributed an estimated 17.1% of GDP in 2009/10, and engaged about 13.0% of the employed labour force at 30 June 2008. The most important sectors include the manufacture of textiles, food products, automobiles and electrical goods and also petroleum refineries. During 2000–09 manufacturing GDP increased at an average annual rate of 7.4%; according to the ADB, manufacturing GDP rose by 4.8% in 2007/08, but fell by 3.7% in 2008/09.

Construction contributed an estimated 2.2% of GDP in 2009/10, while the sector engaged some 6.3% of the employed labour force at 30 June 2008. According to the ADB, construction GDP increased at an average annual rate of 2.9% during 2000–09; sectoral GDP fell by 5.5% in 2007/08, and declined substantially, by a further 11.2%, in 2008/09.

Energy is derived principally from natural gas (providing 34.4% of the total electrical energy supply in 2007), hydroelectric power (30.0%) and petroleum (32.2%). Imports of mineral fuels, lubricants, etc. comprised about 30.4% of the cost of total imports in 2009/10.

Services engaged 35.2% of the employed labour force at 30 June 2008, and provided an estimated 54.6% of GDP in 2009/10. The combined GDP of the service sectors increased at an average rate of 5.4% per year in 2000–09; according to the ADB, the GDP of services expanded by 6.0% in 2007/08, and by 1.6% in 2008/09.

According to the IMF, Pakistan recorded a visible trade deficit of US $10,270m. in 2009 and there was a deficit of $3,993m. on the current account of the balance of payments. The flow of remittances from Pakistanis working abroad showed strong and steady growth during the 2000s, increasing from $4,600m. in 2005/06, to $5,490m. in 2006/07 and to a record $6,451m. in 2007/08. The principal source of imports in 2008/09 was Saudi Arabia (which provided 12.3% of the total); other major suppliers were the People's Republic of China, Kuwait and the USA. The principal market for exports was the USA (which accounted for 18.9% of the total); other major purchasers were the United Arab Emirates and Afghanistan. The principal exports in 2009/10 were garments and hosiery, cotton fabrics, yarn and thread, and rice. The principal imports were mineral fuels and lubricants, machinery and transport equipment, and chemicals and related products.

For the financial year ending 30 June 2010, there was an estimated budgetary deficit of Rs 525,074m. (equivalent to approximately 3.6% of GDP). Pakistan's general government gross debt was Rs 7,298,140m. in 2009, equivalent to 57.3% of GDP. According to the ADB, Pakistan's total external debt was US $50,759m. at the end of 2009. The cost of debt-servicing in that year was equivalent to 18.7% of earnings from exports of goods and services. During 2000–09, according to the ILO, the average annual rate of inflation was 8.3%. Consumer prices rose by 20.8% in 2008/09 and by 11.7% in 2009/10. About 5.2% of the labour force was estimated to be unemployed at 30 June 2008.

Following a period of steady growth in the first half of the 2000s, in 2007/08 the Pakistan economy reached crisis point, with massive increases in levels of external debt, the trade deficit and the current-account deficit. Increases in food prices, worsening political strife, energy shortages and poor export figures combined to have a negative impact on GDP growth. The threat to Pakistan's economic stability was somewhat alleviated by the implementation of an IMF-supported stabilization programme (worth US $7,600m.) in November 2008. In April 2009 a meeting of Pakistan's donors, hosted by Japan and the IMF in Tokyo, pledged a total of $5,280m. in aid to Pakistan over a two-year period in an attempt to bolster its faltering economy and boost infrastructural investment. In July 2010 the World Bank approved a four-year lending programme for Pakistan worth a total of $6,200m.; the goals of the programme included the development of conflict-affected areas and improvements to energy supplies and the collection of tax revenues. However, economic progress suffered a substantial setback when devastating floods from late July led to a reduction in agricultural output and severely damaged the country's transport and communications networks. Flood damage was estimated to total approximately $9,500m. Partly owing to an improvement in the current account balance, the rate of growth of GDP was an estimated 4.1% in 2009/10, compared with 1.2% the previous year, but, owing to the floods, was projected to fall back to 2.5% in 2010/11. Likewise, the rate of inflation, which had decreased from 20.8% in 2008/09 to 11.7% in 2009/10, was expected to rise again in 2010/11. During 2010 and the early part of 2011 levels of foreign direct investment continued to fall in response to widespread concerns over security and inadequate infrastructure. Large-scale losses incurred by state-owned enterprises and increases in the wages of government employees helped to raise the budget deficit from 5.3% of GDP in 2008/09 to 6.3% of GDP in 2009/10. In November 2010 the Government requested the international donor community to write off Pakistan's foreign debt of $55,000m., claiming that the country had already sustained losses equivalent to $140,000m. in its counter-terrorist campaign. In January 2011 the Pakistani Government was criticized by the IMF for succumbing to political pressure and cancelling the planned introduction of power tariffs and a new general sales tax. Talks held between the Government and the

PAKISTAN

IMF in March 2011 were described as 'constructive', but the IMF continued to refuse to revive its suspended standby arrangement programme (with remaining disbursements of up to $3,700m. withheld since May 2010) until Pakistan made further progress with economic reform.

PUBLIC HOLIDAYS

2012: 4 February* (Eid-i-Milad-un-Nabi, Birth of the Prophet), 23 March (Pakistan Day, proclamation of republic in 1956), 1 May (Labour Day), 19 July* (Ramadan begins), 14 August (Independence Day), 18 August* (Id al-Fitr, end of Ramadan), 6 September (Defence of Pakistan Day), 11 September (Anniversary of Death of Quaid-i-Azam), 25 October* (Id al-Adha, Feast of the Sacrifice), 9 November (Allama Iqbal Day), 14 November* (Muharram, Islamic New Year), 23 November* (Ashoura), 25 December (Birthday of Quaid-i-Azam).

* These holidays are dependent on the Islamic lunar calendar and may vary by one or two days from the dates given.

Statistical Survey

Sources (unless otherwise stated): Federal Bureau of Statistics, 5-SLIC Building, F-6/4, Blue Area, Islamabad; fax (51) 99203233; e-mail statpak@isb.paknet.com.pk; internet www.statpak.gov.pk/depts/index.html; State Bank of Pakistan, Karachi; internet www.sbp.org.pk.

Area and Population

AREA, POPULATION AND DENSITY*

Area (sq km)	796,095†
Population (census results)	
1 March 1981	84,253,644
2 March 1998	
Males	68,873,686
Females	63,478,593
Total	132,352,279
Population (official estimates at mid-year)‡	
2008	166,410,000
2009	169,940,000
2010	173,510,000
Density (per sq km) at mid-2010	218.0

* Excluding data for the disputed territory of Jammu and Kashmir. The Pakistani-held parts of this region are known as Azad ('Free') Kashmir, with an area of 11,639 sq km (4,494 sq miles) and a population of 1,980,000 in 1981, and Gilgit-Baltistan (the former Northern Areas), with an area of 72,971 sq km (28,174 sq miles) and a population of 870,347 in 1998. Also excluded are Junagardh and Manavadar. The population figures exclude refugees from Afghanistan (estimated to number 765,000 in late 2008).
† 307,374 sq miles.
‡ Source: Sub Group II on Population Projections for the 10th Five Year People's Plan 2010–2015, Ministry of Finance, *Economic Survey, 2009/10*.

POPULATION BY AGE AND SEX
(population at 1998 census)

	Males	Females	Total
0–14	29,241,025	26,823,722	56,064,747
15–64	35,504,033	33,082,093	68,586,126
65 and over	2,476,581	2,048,494	4,525,075
Total	67,221,639	61,954,309	129,175,948

Note: Figures exclude population of Federally Administered Tribal Areas (FATA), numbering 3,176,331.

ADMINISTRATIVE DIVISIONS
(population at 1998 census)

	Area (sq km)	Population	Density (per sq km)
Provinces:			
Balochistan	347,190	6,565,885	18.9
North-West Frontier Province*	74,521	17,743,645	238.1
Punjab	205,344	73,621,290	358.5
Sindh	140,914	30,439,893	216.0
Federally Administered Tribal Areas	27,220	3,176,331	116.7
Federal Capital Territory:			
Islamabad	906	805,235	888.8
Total	796,095	132,352,279	166.3

* Renamed Khyber Pakhtoonkhwa in April 2010.

PRINCIPAL TOWNS
(population at 1998 census)

Karachi	9,269,265		Bahawalpur	408,395
Lahore	5,143,495		Sukkur	335,551
Faisalabad (Lyallpur)	2,008,861		Jhang Maghiana (Jhang Sadar)	293,366
Rawalpindi	1,409,768		Shekhupura	280,263
Multan	1,197,384		Larkana	270,283
Hyderabad	1,166,894		Gujrat	251,792
Gujranwala	1,042,509		Mardan	244,511
Peshawar	988,005		Kasur	241,649
Quetta	565,137		Rahimyar Khan	233,537
Islamabad (capital)	529,180		Sahiwal	207,388
Sargodha	455,360		Okara	201,815
Sialkot	421,502			

2010 (official estimates): Karachi 13,386,730; Lahore 7,214,954; Faisalabad (Lyallpur) 2,912,269; Rawalpindi 2,013,876; Gujranwala 1,676,357; Multan 1,610,180; Hyderabad 1,521,231; Peshawar 1,386,529; Islamabad 972,669; Quetta 871,643.

BIRTHS AND DEATHS
(annual averages, UN estimates)

	1995–2000	2000–05	2005–10
Birth rate (per 1,000)	34.0	31.7	30.2
Death rate (per 1,000)	8.5	7.6	7.0

Source: UN, *World Population Prospects: The 2008 Revision*.

2010: Crude birth rate 28.0 per 1,000; Crude death rate 7.4 per 1,000 (Source: Ministry of Finance, *Economic Survey, 2009/10*).

Life expectancy (years at birth, WHO estimates): 63 (males 63; females 64) in 2008 (Source: WHO, *World Health Statistics*).

PAKISTAN

ECONOMICALLY ACTIVE POPULATION
('000 persons aged 10 years and over, excl. armed forces, at 30 June)

	2006	2007	2008
Agriculture, hunting, forestry and fishing	20,364	20,780	21,919
Mining and quarrying	43	52	57
Manufacturing	6,499	6,454	6,377
Electricity, gas and water	308	360	343
Construction	2,880	3,127	3,088
Wholesale and retail trade, and restaurants and hotels	6,886	6,872	7,178
Transport, storage and communication	2,697	2,569	2,681
Financing, insurance, real estate and business services	518	544	692
Community, social and personal services	6,739	6,868	6,706
Sub-total	46,934	47,626	49,041
Activities not adequately defined	18	25	49
Total employed	46,952	47,651	49,090
Unemployed	3,103	2,680	2,694
Total labour force	50,055	50,331	51,784
Males	39,974	39,925	40,825
Females	10,081	10,406	10,959

Source: ILO.

2009 ('000 persons aged 10 years and over, excl. armed forces, at 30 June): Total employed 50,790; Unemployed 2,930; Total labour force 53,720 (Source: Ministry of Finance, *Economic Survey, 2009/10*).

Health and Welfare

KEY INDICATORS

Total fertility rate (children per woman, 2008)	4.0
Under-5 mortality rate (per 1,000 live births, 2008)	89
HIV/AIDS (% of persons aged 15–49, 2007)	0.1
Physicians (per 1,000 head, 2005)	0.8
Hospital beds (per 1,000 head, 2005)	1.2
Health expenditure (2007): US $ per head (PPP)	64
Health expenditure (2007): % of GDP	2.7
Health expenditure (2007): public (% of total)	30.0
Access to water (% of persons, 2008)	90
Access to sanitation (% of persons, 2008)	45
Total carbon dioxide emissions ('000 metric tons, 2007)	156,265.9
Carbon dioxide emissions per head (metric tons, 2007)	1.0
Human Development Index (2010): ranking	125
Human Development Index (2010): value	0.490

For sources and definitions, see explanatory note on p. vi.

Agriculture

PRINCIPAL CROPS
('000 metric tons)

	2006	2007	2008
Wheat	21,277	23,295	20,959
Rice, paddy	8,158	8,345	10,428
Barley	88	93	87
Maize	3,088	3,605	4,036
Millet	238	305	296
Sorghum	180	170	165
Potatoes	1,568	2,582	2,539
Sugar cane	44,666	54,742	63,920
Sugar beet	93	84	64
Beans, dry	154	195	171
Chick peas	480	838	475
Groundnuts, with shell	74	83	86
Sunflower seed	348	407	604
Rapeseed	350	368	390
Tomatoes	468	502	536
Cauliflower and broccoli	209	212	216
Pumpkins, squash and gourds	256	252	260
Onions, dry	2,056	1,816	2,015
Carrots and turnips	244	237	237

—*continued*	2006	2007	2008
Okra	112	104	115
Watermelons	383	362	412
Cantaloupes and other melons	256	241	275
Bananas	150	158	159
Oranges	1,721	1,721*	1,721*
Tangerines, mandarins, clementines and satsumas	639	640*	640*
Lemons and limes	98	99*	99*
Apples	348	442	583
Apricots	177	240	326
Peaches and nectarines	71	82	94
Plums and sloes	60	73	73*
Guavas, mangoes and mangosteens	1,754	1,719	1,754
Dates	426	557	680
Pimento and allspice	62	130†	130*
Tobacco, unmanufactured	113	103	108

* FAO estimate.
† Unofficial figure.

2009: Wheat 24,033; Rice 10,325; Barley 82; Maize 3,487; Millet 293; Sorghum 154; Potatoes 2,941; Sugar cane 50,045; Beans, dry 130; Chick peas 741; Sunflower seed 598; Rapeseed 276.

Aggregate production ('000 metric tons, may include official, semi-official or estimated data): Total cereals 33,028 in 2006, 35,813 in 2007, 35,528 in 2008, 38,374 in 2009; Total roots and tubers 2,048 in 2006, 3,060 in 2007, 3,018 in 2008, 3,420 in 2009; Total vegetables (incl. melons) 5,434 in 2006, 5,165 in 2007, 5,481 in 2008–09; Total fruits (excl. melons) 6,341 in 2006; 6,649 in 2007, 7,095 in 2008–09.

Source: FAO.

LIVESTOCK
('000 head, year ending September)

	2007	2008	2009
Cattle	30,673	31,830	33,000
Buffaloes	28,165	29,000	29,900
Sheep	26,794	27,111	27,400
Goats	55,244	56,742	58,300
Horses	346	348	400
Asses	4,347	4,427	4,500
Mules	158	162	200
Camels	933	945	1,000
Chickens*	251,000	273,000	296,000
Ducks*	3,500	3,500	3,500

* FAO estimates.

Source: FAO.

LIVESTOCK PRODUCTS
('000 metric tons)

	2007	2008	2009
Cattle meat	656	680	703
Buffalo meat	688	708	738
Sheep meat	151	154	158
Goat meat	256	261	267
Chicken meat	554	601	652
Cows' milk	11,130	11,550	11,985
Buffaloes' milk	20,372	20,985	21,622
Sheep's milk	35	35	36
Goats' milk	682	700	719
Hen eggs*	479.3	503.4	529.1
Other poultry eggs†	7.2	7.2	n.a.
Wool, greasy	40.6	41.0	n.a.

* Unofficial figures.
† FAO estimates.

Source: FAO.

PAKISTAN

Forestry

ROUNDWOOD REMOVALS
('000 cubic metres, excl. bark)

	2007	2008	2009*
Sawlogs, veneer logs and logs for sleepers	2,008	2,023	2,023
Pulpwood	56	59	59
Other industrial wood	897	908	908
Fuel wood	29,520	29,660	29,493
Total	32,481	32,650	32,483

* FAO estimates.
Source: FAO.

SAWNWOOD PRODUCTION
('000 cubic metres, incl. railway sleepers)

	2006	2007	2008
Coniferous (softwood)	432	453	462
Broadleaved (hardwood)	881	910	919
Total	1,313	1,363	1,381

2009: Production assumed to be unchanged from 2008 (FAO estimates).
Source: FAO.

Fishing

('000 metric tons, live weight)

	2006	2007	2008
Capture	489.4	440.2	451.4
Freshwater fishes	140.0	100.0	108.0
Sea catfishes	28.7	28.2	28.2
Croakers and drums	14.7	14.6	14.7
Largehead hairtail	23.5	22.6	22.7
Indian oil sardine	31.0	31.3	31.5
Other clupeoids	16.9	16.2	16.3
Jacks and crevalles	4.9	5.0	5.0
Requiem sharks	10.7	8.5	8.5
Skates, rays and mantas	8.9	7.3	7.3
Aquaculture	121.8	130.0	135.1
Total catch	611.2	570.3	586.5

Source: FAO.

Mining

('000 metric tons unless otherwise indicated)

	2007/08	2008/09	2009/10
Barite	50	63	47
Chromite	115	90	256
Limestone	31,789	33,186	37,129
Gypsum	660	800	854
Rock salt	1,849	1,917	1,944
Coal	4,066	3,679	3,499
Crude petroleum (million barrels)	26	24	24
Natural gas ('000 million cu feet)	1,454	1,461	1,483

Natural gas (million cu m, excluding flared or recycled gas): 37,900 in 2009 (Source: BP, *Statistical Review of World Energy*).

Industry

SELECTED PRODUCTS
('000 metric tons, unless otherwise indicated, year ending 30 June)

	2006/07	2007/08	2008/09
Cotton cloth (million sq m)	1,013	1,016	1,019
Cotton yarn	2,728	2,809	2,274
Refined sugar	3,527	4,733	3,190
Vegetable ghee	1,180	1,137	1,059
Cement	22,739	26,751	28,380
Urea	4,733	4,925	4,918
Superphosphate	149	162	187
Sulphuric acid	96	103	98
Soda ash	331	365	365
Caustic soda	242	248	244
Chlorine gas	17	18	17
Cigarettes ('000 million)	66	67	76
Ammonium nitrate	331	344	344
Nitrophosphate	326	330	306
Pig-iron	1,009	993	791
Paper and paperboard	627	640	703
Tractors (number)	54,610	53,256	59,968
Bicycles ('000)	486	536	428
Motor tyres and tubes ('000)	17,304	16,617	21,616
Bicycle tyres and tubes ('000)	15,602	13,467	10,081
Electric energy (million kWh)	98,384	95,860	91,843

Finance

CURRENCY AND EXCHANGE RATES

Monetary Units
100 paisa = 1 Pakistani rupee.

Sterling, Dollar and Euro Equivalents (31 December 2010)
£1 sterling = 134.18 rupees;
US $1 = 85.71 rupees;
€1 = 114.53 rupees;
1,000 Pakistani rupees = £7.45 = $11.67 = €8.73.

Average Exchange Rate (Pakistani rupees per US $)
2008 70.408
2009 81.713
2010 85.194

CENTRAL GOVERNMENT BUDGET
(million rupees, year ending 30 June)

Revenue	2008/09	2009/10	2010/11*
Tax revenue	1,251,462	1,483,046	1,778,715
Income and corporate taxes†	477,000	520,400	633,000
Other direct taxes	19,000	20,000	24,700
Excise duty	112,000	134,400	153,600
Sales tax†	472,000	540,300	674,900
Taxes on international trade	170,000	164,900	180,800
Other taxes revenue	1,462	103,046	111,715
Non-tax revenue (incl. surcharges)	427,800	568,899	632,279
Total	1,679,262	2,051,945	2,410,994

Expenditure	2008/09	2009/10	2010/11*
Current expenditure	1,649,224	2,017,254	1,997,893
General public service	1,132,595	1,471,743	1,387,664
Defence†	311,303	378,135	442,173
Economic affairs	136,678	80,608	66,897
Development expenditure	237,857	316,446	311,885
Capital expenditure	214,394	243,319	187,695
Total	2,101,475	2,577,019	2,497,473

* Budget estimates.
† Exclusively federal.

PAKISTAN

INTERNATIONAL RESERVES
(US $ million, last Thursday of the year)

	2008	2009	2010
Gold*	1,709	2,452	2,864
IMF special drawing rights	183	1,381	1,230
Foreign exchange	7,011	9,938	13,115
Total	8,903	13,771	17,209

*Revalued annually, in June, on the basis of London market prices.

Source: IMF, *International Financial Statistics*.

MONEY SUPPLY
(million rupees, last Thursday of the year)

	2008	2009	2010
Currency outside depository corporations	1,127,591	1,292,190	1,508,986
Transferable deposits	2,191,921	2,566,930	3,040,414
Other deposits	1,310,964	1,456,625	1,566,688
Securities other than shares	1,816	233	111
Broad money	4,632,293	5,315,979	6,116,199

Source: IMF, *International Financial Statistics*.

COST OF LIVING
(Consumer Price Index; base: 2000/01 = 100; year ending 30 June)

	2007/08	2008/09	2009/10
Food, beverages and tobacco	174.4	215.7	242.6
Clothing and footwear	133.8	152.8	162.5
Rent	154.5	180.9	205.9
Energy	165.2	198.9	226.9
All items (incl. others)	158.9	191.9	214.4

NATIONAL ACCOUNTS
(million rupees at current prices, year ending 30 June)

Expenditure on the Gross Domestic Product

	2007/08	2008/09	2009/10*
Government final consumption expenditure	1,278,431	1,029,156	1,312,520
Private final consumption expenditure	7,835,310	10,254,625	11,815,289
Gross fixed capital formation	2,094,743	2,210,920	2,196,969
Increase in stocks	163,885	203,829	234,695
Total domestic expenditure	11,372,369	13,698,530	15,559,473
Exports of goods and services	1,316,439	1,636,196	1,892,553
Less Imports of goods and services	2,446,008	2,595,390	2,783,598
Gross domestic product (GDP) in market prices	10,242,800	12,739,336	14,668,428
GDP at constant 1999/2000 prices	5,565,375	5,767,538	6,018,865

*Provisional figures.

Gross Domestic Product by Economic Activity

	2007/08	2008/09	2009/10*
Agriculture, forestry and fishing	2,017,181	2,603,826	3,016,565
Mining and quarrying	301,469	346,810	346,256
Manufacturing	1,950,522	2,067,494	2,369,029
Electricity and gas distribution	145,874	222,249	246,086
Construction	260,340	294,990	308,425
Wholesale and retail trade	1,829,944	2,100,661	2,391,058
Transport, storage and communications	1,155,873	1,630,278	1,894,188
Finance and insurance	556,679	625,471	667,550
Ownership of dwellings	239,010	298,789	345,759
Public administration and defence	530,074	662,723	794,439
Community, social and personal services	934,618	1,228,665	1,464,134
GDP at factor cost	9,921,584	12,081,956	13,843,489
Indirect taxes	667,604	763,501	896,702
Less Subsidies	346,389	106,121	71,763
GDP in market prices	10,242,799	12,739,336	14,668,428

*Provisional figures.

Source: Ministry of Finance, *Economic Survey, 2009/10*.

BALANCE OF PAYMENTS
(US $ million)

	2007	2008	2009
Exports of goods f.o.b.	18,188	21,214	18,347
Imports of goods f.o.b.	−28,775	−38,216	−28,617
Trade balance	−10,587	−17,003	−10,270
Exports of services	3,767	4,263	3,983
Imports of services	−8,811	−9,717	−6,551
Balance on goods and services	−15,631	−22,457	−12,838
Other income received	1,357	1,285	607
Other income paid	−5,097	−5,619	−4,221
Balance on goods, services and income	−19,371	−26,791	−16,452
Current transfers received	11,216	11,252	12,552
Current transfers paid	−131	−116	−93
Current balance	−8,286	−15,655	−3,993
Capital account (net)	176	146	484
Direct investment abroad	−98	−49	−71
Direct investment from abroad	5,590	5,438	2,338
Portfolio investment assets	5	−26	−26
Portfolio investment liabilities	2,081	−243	−582
Other investment assets	284	−494	−3
Other investment liabilities	2,794	2,045	3,325
Net errors and omissions	−29	−167	191
Overall balance	2,517	−9,005	1,662

Source: IMF, *International Financial Statistics*.

External Trade

Note: Data exclude trade in military goods.

PRINCIPAL COMMODITIES
(million rupees, year ending 30 June)

Imports c.i.f. (excl. re-imports)	2007/08	2008/09	2009/10
Food and live animals	121,756.6	183,414.8	141,005.7
Mineral fuels, lubricants, etc.	773,199.2	797,188.9	883,653.4
Animal and vegetable oils, fats and waxes	115,459.7	124,316.2	120,975.4
Chemicals and related products	364,136.3	409,810.3	492,227.1
Basic manufactures	238,769.1	271,679.1	294,972.2
Machinery and transport equipment	602,387.0	626,010.2	616,893.3
Total (incl. others)	2,512,071.7	2,723,569.9	2,910,975.3

PAKISTAN

Exports f.o.b. (excl. re-exports)	2007/08	2008/09	2009/10
Rice	117,088.1	154,762.9	183,370.3
Fish and fish preparations	13,327.5	18,464.9	19,049.8
Raw cotton	4,426.1	6,826.5	16,365.5
Leather, leather manufactures and dressed furskins	26,026.3	23,393.0	28,698.3
Carpets and rugs	13,295.4	11,158.8	11,119.1
Cotton fabrics, cotton yarn and thread	207,918.5	240,850.6	271,703.4
Garments and hosiery	227,351.4	272,100.6	294,059.9
Sports goods	19,012.9	21,391.3	25,020.8
Total (incl. others)	1,196,637.6	1,383,717.5	1,617,457.6

PRINCIPAL TRADING PARTNERS
(million rupees, year ending 30 June)

Imports c.i.f. (excl. re-imports)	2006/07	2007/08	2008/09
Australia	17,984	32,589	39,039
Belgium	13,617	14,946	20,828
Canada	29,982	31,927	37,419
China, People's Republic	214,275	294,684	319,640
France	25,399	30,776	30,422
Germany	73,073	79,950	102,534
Hong Kong	11,714	11,797	9,469
India	74,938	106,872	93,471
Indonesia	51,333	73,998	65,742
Iran	24,596	34,654	72,111
Italy	32,977	34,639	66,338
Japan	105,484	114,510	98,549
Korea, Republic	40,699	42,567	50,449
Kuwait	104,850	188,502	180,947
Malaysia	57,319	96,935	125,582
Netherlands	14,894	22,282	27,682
Saudi Arabia	211,751	336,590	334,132
Singapore	29,225	48,764	43,140
Switzerland	19,488	23,475	24,894
Thailand	36,201	37,259	46,102
Turkey	9,283	9,742	10,093
United Arab Emirates	167,907	214,561	n.a.
United Kingdom	42,383	48,373	71,652
USA	139,453	153,278	146,205
Total (incl. others)	1,851,806	2,512,072	2,723,570

Exports f.o.b. (excl. re-exports)	2006/07	2007/08	2008/09
Afghanistan	45,686	71,974	109,330
Australia	7,462	8,689	7,494
Bangladesh	15,884	21,501	30,073
Belgium	21,833	25,743	30,803
Canada	12,222	12,347	13,595
China, People's Republic	34,927	43,164	54,888
France	20,988	22,905	24,601
Germany	42,527	51,255	57,731
Hong Kong	39,645	32,595	29,602
Italy	38,794	45,391	45,321
Japan	7,524	8,585	8,668
Korea, Republic	10,556	12,523	11,625
Netherlands	26,799	32,303	36,343
Saudi Arabia	17,530	23,981	35,699
Spain	28,231	33,992	31,674
Turkey	23,645	27,244	31,547
United Arab Emirates	83,990	130,549	114,752
United Kingdom	57,610	64,597	68,470
USA	253,584	232,758	261,362
Total (incl. others)	1,020,312	1,196,638	1,383,718

Transport

RAILWAYS
(year ending 30 June)

	2006/07	2007/08	2008/09
Passenger journeys ('000)	83,890	79,990	82,540
Passenger-km (million)	26,446	24,731	25,702
Freight ('000 metric tons)	6,420	7,230	6,940
Net freight ton-km (million)	5,453	6,178	5,896

Source: Ministry of Finance, *Economic Survey, 2009/10*.

ROAD TRAFFIC
('000 vehicles in use, year ending 30 June)

	2006/07	2007/08	2008/09
Motorcycles and scooters	4,463.8	5,037.0	5,368.0
Passenger cars	1,682.2	1,853.5	2,029.1
Jeeps	85.4	82.9	79.0
Station wagons	169.1	163.2	155.6
Road tractors	877.8	900.5	911.7
Buses	108.4	109.9	111.1
Taxicabs	119.1	129.8	138.6
Rickshaws	79.0	89.3	88.4
Delivery vans and pick-ups	253.5	278.8	292.7
Trucks and tankers	182.1	187.6	192.7

Source: Ministry of Finance, *Economic Survey, 2009/10*.

SHIPPING

Merchant Fleet
(displacement at 31 December)

	2007	2008	2009
Number of vessels	53	55	54
Total displacement ('000 grt)	349.0	409.0	295.5

Source: IHS Fairplay, *World Fleet Statistics*.

International Sea-borne Shipping
(port of Karachi, year ending 30 June)

	2006/07	2007/08	2008/09
Goods ('000 long tons):			
loaded	7,517	11,676	13,365
unloaded	23,329	25,517	25,367

Source: Ministry of Finance, *Economic Survey, 2009/10*.

CIVIL AVIATION
(PIA only, domestic and international flights, '000, year ending 30 June)

	2006/07	2007/08	2008/09
Kilometres flown	80,302	80,759	79,580
Passengers carried	5,732	5,415	5,617
Passenger-km ('000)	15,124	13,680	13,925

Source: Ministry of Finance, *Economic Survey, 2009/10*.

PAKISTAN

Tourism

FOREIGN TOURIST ARRIVALS
('000)

Country of nationality	2007	2008	2009
Afghanistan	80.5	66.4	96.6
Canada	36.5	39.9	43.0
China, People's Republic	30.4	30.1	30.1
Germany	23.9	22.4	21.4
India	48.2	54.1	42.7
Japan	11.0	8.3	6.7
United Kingdom	275.5	285.7	275.4
USA	121.9	114.1	117.5
Total (incl. others)	839.5	822.8	854.9

Receipts from tourism (US $ million, incl. passenger transport): 919 in 2006; 912 in 2007; 915 in 2008.

Source: partly World Tourism Organization.

Communications Media

	2007	2008	2009
Television receivers (number in use)*	9,003,882	9,940,078	n.a.
Telephones ('000 main lines in use)	4,806.2	4,416.4	3,523.2
Mobile cellular telephones ('000 subscribers)	62,856.7	88,019.7	94,342.0
Internet users ('000)	17,500	18,500	20,431.3
Broadband subscribers ('000)	45.2	148.5	302.8
Daily newspapers:			
number	437	324	252
average circulation	9,934,951	6,067,998	n.a.
Other newspapers and periodicals:			
number	1,383	875	454
average circulation	3,797,835	1,137,287	n.a.

Radio receivers ('000 in use): 13,500 in 1997.

Personal computers: 680,000 (4.7 per 1,000 persons) in 2002.

*Estimates as at 30 June; includes Azad Kashmir and Gilgit-Baltistan (former Northern Areas).

Sources: partly UNESCO, *Statistical Yearbook*; International Telecommunication Union.

Education

(2009/10, estimates)

	Institutions	Teachers	Students
Primary*	156,364	469,151	18,714,582
Middle	41,456	323,824	5,445,247
Secondary	24,822	447,117	2,699,589
Higher:			
arts and science colleges	3,399	78,656	1,147,807
professional	1,275	21,385	458,835
universities/degree-awarding institutes	132	56,839	948,364

*Including mosque schools.

Source: Ministry of Finance, *Economic Survey, 2009/10*.

Pupil-teacher ratio (primary education, UNESCO estimate): 39.7 in 2008/09 (Source: UNESCO Institute for Statistics).

Adult literacy rate (UNESCO estimates): 53.7% (males 66.8%; females 40.0%) in 2008 (Source: UNESCO Institute for Statistics).

Directory

The Government

HEAD OF STATE

President: Asif Ali Zardari (sworn in 9 September 2008).

CABINET
(May 2011)

A coalition Government comprising members of the Pakistan People's Party (PPP), the Awami National Party (ANP), the Balochistan National Party—Awami (BNP—A), the Muttahida Qaumi Movement (MQM), the Pakistan Muslim League (PML), the Pakistan Muslim League—Functional (PML—F), and independents (Ind.).

Prime Minister and Minister-in-charge of Information Technology, of Petroleum and Natural Resources, of Ports and Shipping, and of Telecommunications: Yousaf Raza Gilani (PPP).

Senior Minister and Minister Responsible for Defence Production, and for Industries: Chaudhry Pervaiz Elahi (PML).

Minister of Commerce: Makhdoom Amin Fahim (PPP).

Minister of Communications: Dr Arbab Alamgir Khan (PPP).

Minister of Defence: Chaudhry Ahmed Mukhtar (PPP).

Minister of the Environment; Minister responsible for Women's Development: Samina Khalid Ghurki (PPP).

Minister of Finance, Planning and Development, Economic Affairs, Revenue and Statistics: Dr Abdul Hafeez Shaikh (Ind.).

Minister of Food and Agriculture: Mir Israr Ullah Zehri (BNP—A).

Minister of Health: Riaz Hussain Pirzada (PML).

Minister of Housing and Works: Makhdoom Syed Faisal Saleh Hayat (PML).

Minister of Information and Broadcasting: Firdous Ashiq Awan (PPP).

Minister of the Interior: Rehman Malik (PPP).

Minister of Kashmir Affairs and Gilgit-Baltistan: Mian Manzoor Ahmad Wattoo (PPP).

Minister of Law, Justice and Parliamentary Affairs: Maula Bakhsh Chandio (PPP).

Minister of Narcotics Control: Haji Khuda Bux Rajar (PML—F).

Minister for Overseas Pakistanis: Chaudhry Wajahat Hussain (PML).

Minister of Postal Services: Sardar Al-Haj Mohammad Umar Gorgage (PPP).

Minister of Privatisation: Ghous Bakhsh Khan Mahar (PML).

Minister of Production: ANWAR ALI CHEEMA (PML).

Minister of Railways: Haji GHULAM AHMAD BILOUR (ANP).

Minister of Religious Affairs; Minister responsible for Labour and Manpower: SYED KHURSHEED AHMED SHAH (PPP).

Minister of Science and Technology: Mir CHANGEZ KHAN JAMALI (PPP).

Minister of States and Frontier Regions; Minister responsible for Sports: SHAUKAT ULLAH (Ind.).

Minister of the Textile Industry: MAKHDOOM SHAHABUDDIN (PPP).

Minister of Water and Power: SYED NAVEED QAMAR (PPP).

In addition, there were nine Ministers of State, five Advisers to the Prime Minister (with the status of Federal Minister), and three Special Assistants to the Prime Minister (with the status of Minister of State).

MINISTRIES

Office of the President: Aiwan-e-Sadr, Islamabad; tel. (51) 9206060; fax (51) 9208046; internet www.presidentofpakistan.gov.pk.

Office of the Prime Minister's Secretariat: Cabinet Secretariat, Cabinet Div., Islamabad; tel. (51) 925190512; e-mail contact@cabinet.gov.pk; internet www.cabinet.gov.pk.

Ministry of Commerce: Blk A, Pakistan Secretariat, Islamabad; tel. (51) 9205708; fax (51) 9205241; e-mail mincom@commerce.gov.pk; internet www.commerce.gov.pk.

Ministry of Communications: Islamabad; tel. (51) 9203738; fax (51) 9220899; internet 202.83.164.26/wps/portal/Mocomm.

Ministry of Culture: NFCH, 12th Floor, Green Tower, Blue Area, F-6/3, Islamabad; tel. (51) 9201304; fax (51) 9201970; internet www.culture.gov.pk.

Ministry of Defence: Pakistan Secretariat, No. II, Rawalpindi 46000; tel. (51) 9271107; fax (51) 9271113; e-mail tahir@mod.gov.pk; internet www.mod.gov.pk.

Ministry of Defence Production: Islamabad; internet www.modp.gov.pk.

Ministry of Economic Affairs and Statistics: Islamabad; tel. (51) 9213204; e-mail minister@finance.gov.pk.

Ministry of Education: Blk D, Pakistan Secretariat, Islamabad; tel. (51) 9201392; fax (51) 9202851; e-mail minister@moe.gov.pk; internet www.moe.gov.pk.

Ministry of Environment: G-5/2, Islamabad; tel. and fax (51) 9218293; e-mail contact@moenv.gov.pk; internet 202.83.164.26/wps/portal/Moe.

Ministry of Finance, Revenue and Planning and Development: Blk Q, Pakistan Secretariat, Islamabad; tel. (51) 9202576; fax (51) 9206354; e-mail webmaster@finance.gov.pk; internet www.finance.gov.pk.

Ministry of Food and Agriculture: Blk B, Pakistan Secretariat, Islamabad; tel. (51) 9210088; fax (51) 9205912; e-mail minister@minfal.gov.pk; internet www.minfal.gov.pk.

Ministry of Foreign Affairs: Constitution Ave, Islamabad; tel. (51) 9210335; fax (51) 9207600; internet www.mofa.gov.pk.

Ministry of Health: Blk C, Pakistan Secretariat, Islamabad; tel. (51) 9203944; fax (51) 9208139; e-mail minister@health.gov.pk; internet www.health.gov.pk.

Ministry of Housing and Works: Blk B, Pakistan Secretariat, Islamabad; tel. (51) 9214121; fax (51) 9209125; e-mail minister@housing.gov.pk; internet www.pha.gov.pk.

Ministry of Human Rights: 3rd Floor, Old USAID Bldg, Attaturk Ave, G-5/1, Islamabad; tel. (51) 9206022; fax (51) 9201631; internet www.mohr.gov.pk.

Ministry of Industries and Production: Blk A, Pakistan Secretariat, Islamabad; tel. (51) 9212164; fax (51) 9205130; e-mail moip@moip.gov.pk; internet www.moip.gov.pk.

Ministry of Information and Broadcasting: Cyber Wing, 4th Floor, Cabinet Blk, Pakistan Secretariat, Islamabad; tel. (51) 9206176; fax (51) 9207629; e-mail webmaster@infopak.gov.pk; internet www.infopak.gov.pk.

Ministry of Information Technology: 4th Floor, Evacuee Trust Bldg, Aga Khan Rd, F-5/1, Islamabad; tel. (51) 9201990; fax (51) 9205233; e-mail minister@moitt.gov.pk; internet www.moitt.gov.pk.

Ministry of the Interior: Blk R, Room 404, Pakistan Secretariat, Islamabad; tel. (51) 9212026; fax (51) 9202624; e-mail ministry.interior@gmail.com; internet www.interior.gov.pk.

Ministry of Inter Provincial Co-ordination: Cabinet Secretariat, Cabinet Div., Islamabad; tel. (51) 9203248; fax (51) 9207760; internet www.ipc.gov.pk.

Ministry of Kashmir Affairs and Gilgit-Baltistan: Blk R, Pakistan Secretariat, Islamabad; tel. (51) 9208442; fax (51) 9207084; e-mail minister@moka.gov.pk; internet www.kana.gov.pk.

Ministry of Labour and Manpower: Blk B, Pakistan Secretariat, Islamabad; tel. (51) 9213686; fax (51) 9203462; e-mail mol_gov@yahoo.com; internet 202.83.164.26/wps/portal/Molmop.

Ministry of Law, Justice and Parliamentary Affairs: Blk R, Pakistan Secretariat, Islamabad; tel. (51) 9211278; fax (51) 9201722; e-mail contact@molaw.gov.pk; internet 202.83.164.26/wps/portal/Moljhr.

Ministry of Minorities Affairs: Islamabad; tel. (51) 9203904; fax (51) 9203905; e-mail minister@minorities.gov.pk; internet www.minorities.gov.pk.

Ministry of Narcotics Control: 30 St 48, F-8/4, Islamabad; tel. (51) 9260535; fax (51) 9260208; e-mail mnc@anf.gov.pk; internet 202.83.164.26/wps/portal/Monc.

Ministry of Overseas Pakistanis: Shahrah-e-Jamhuriat, Sector G-5/2, POB 1470, Islamabad; tel. (51) 9203267; fax (51) 9224335; internet www.opf.org.pk.

Ministry of Petroleum and Natural Resources: 3rd Floor, Blk A, Pakistan Secretariat, Islamabad; tel. (51) 9210220; fax (51) 9213180; e-mail minister@mpnr.gov.pk; internet www.mpnr.gov.pk.

Ministry of Ports and Shipping: 3rd Floor, Block D, Pakistan Secretariat, Islamabad; tel. (51) 9210322; fax (51) 9215740; e-mail minister@mops.gov.pk; internet www.mops.gov.pk.

Ministry of Postal Services: Islamabad; tel. (51) 9260179; fax (51) 9261570; internet www.pakpost.gov.pk.

Ministry of Privatisation: 5-A, EAC Bldg, Constitution Ave, Islamabad 44000; tel. (51) 9205146; fax (51) 9203076; e-mail info@privatisation.gov.pk; internet www.privatisation.gov.pk.

Ministry of Railways: Blk D, Pakistan Secretariat, Islamabad; tel. (51) 9218515; fax (51) 9210247; e-mail minister@railways.gov.pk; internet www.railways.gov.pk.

Ministry of Religious Affairs: 20 Civic Centre, G-6 Markaz, Islamabad; tel. (51) 9214856; fax (51) 9205833; e-mail minister@mora.gov.pk; internet www.mora.gov.pk.

Ministry of Science and Technology: 4th Floor, Evacuee Trust Complex, Aga Khan Rd, F-5/1, Islamabad; tel. (51) 9208026; fax (51) 9204541; e-mail minister@most.gov.pk; internet www.most.gov.pk.

Ministry of Social Welfare and Special Education: opp. Noori Hospital, G-8/4, Islamabad; tel. (51) 9107550; fax (51) 9107552; internet www.moswse.gov.pk.

Ministry of Sports: Pakistan Sports Complex, nr Aabpara, Islamabad; tel. (51) 9202812; fax (51) 9205529; e-mail minister@mosp.gov.pk; internet 202.83.164.26/wps/portal/Mos.

Ministry of States and Frontier Regions (SAFRON): Islamabad; tel. 9211405; fax 9218772; e-mail minister@safron.gov.pk.

Ministry of the Textile Industry: 2nd Floor, FBC Bldg, Attaturk Ave, G-5/2, Islamabad; tel. (51) 9212799; fax (51) 9214015; e-mail minister@textile.gov.pk; internet www.textile.gov.pk.

Ministry of Tourism: Green Trust Towers, 7th Floor, Jinnah Ave, Blue Area, Islamabad 44000; tel. (51) 9203772; fax (51) 9207427; e-mail secretary@tourism.gov.pk; internet www.tourism.gov.pk.

Ministry of Water and Power: Blk A, 15th Floor, Shaheed-e-Millat, Pakistan Secretariat, Islamabad; tel. (51) 9212442; fax (51) 9224825; e-mail fminister@mowp.gov.pk; internet www.mowp.gov.pk.

Ministry of Women Development.: Islamabad; tel. (51) 9217129; e-mail raizhussain2009@hotmail.com; internet www.mowd.gov.pk.

Federal Legislature

SENATE

The Eighteenth Amendment Bill, promulgated in April 2010, increased the number of seats in the Senate from 100 to 104. The provincial assemblies were directly to elect 92 members—of whom four were to be non-Muslims, 16 were to be women and a further 16 technocrats (including *ulema*, Muslim legal scholars)—and of the remaining 12 members the Federally Administered Tribal Areas were to return eight members and four were to be elected from the Federal Capital Territory by members of the Provincial Assemblies. The term of office of the Senate is six years, but one-half of its membership is renewed after three years. The most recent election was held on 6 March 2006.

Chairman: FAROOQ HAMEED NAIK.

Deputy Chairman: JAN MOHAMMAD KHAN JAMALI.

PAKISTAN

Distribution of Seats, March 2006

	Seats
Pakistan Muslim League (Quaid-e-Azam Group)	38
Muttahida Majlis-e-Amal*	17
Pakistan People's Party Parliamentarians	9
Muttahida Qaumi Movement	6
Pakistan Muslim League (Nawaz Group)	4
Pakistan People's Party (Sherpao Group)	3
Pakhtoonkhwa Milli Awami Party	3
Awami National Party	2
Balochistan National Party (Awami)	1
Balochistan National Party (Maingal)	1
Jamoori Watan Party	1
Jamiat-e-Ulema-e-Islam (F)	1
National Alliance†	1
Pakistan Muslim League (Functional)	1
Independents	12
Total	**100**

* Coalition comprising Jamaat-e-Islami Pakistan, Jamiat-e-Ulema-e-Pakistan, Jamiat-e-Ulema-e-Islam (S), Jamiat-e-Ulema-e-Islam (F), Islami Tehreek Pakistan and Jamiat Ahl-e-Hadith.
† Coalition comprising the National People's Party, the Millat Party, the Sindh National Front, the Sindh Democratic Alliance and the Awami National Party.

NATIONAL ASSEMBLY

Speaker: Dr FEHMIDA MIRZA.
Deputy Speaker: FAISAL KARIM KUNDI.

General Election, 18 February 2008

	Seats
Pakistan People's Party Parliamentarians	89
Pakistan Muslim League (Nawaz Group)	68
Pakistan Muslim League	42
Muttahida Qaumi Movement	19
Awami National Party	10
Muttahida Majlis-e-Amal	6
Pakistan Muslim League (Functional Group)	4
Balochistan National Party (Awami)	1
National People's Party	1
Pakistan People's Party (Sherpao Group)	1
Independents and others	29
Reserved	70
Vacant	2
Total	**342**

Provincial Governments

(May 2011)

Pakistan comprises the four provinces of Sindh, Balochistan, Punjab and Khyber Pakhtoonkhwa (the former North-West Frontier Province), plus the federal capital and Federally Administered Tribal Areas.

BALOCHISTAN
(Capital—Quetta)

Governor: Nawab ZULFIQAR ALI MAGSI.
Chief Minister: Nawab MOHAMMAD ASLAM RAISANI.
Legislative Assembly: 65 seats (Pakistan People's Party Parliamentarians 14, Like Minded Group 13, Jamiat-e-Ulema-e-Islam 10, Balochistan National Party—Awami 7, Pakistan Muslim League—Quaid-e-Azam Group 6 Awami National Party 3, Jamiat-e-Ulema-e-Islam—Ideological 1, National Party 1, Pakistan Muslim League—Nawaz 1, independents 8, vacant 1.

KHYBER PAKHTOONKHWA
(Capital—Peshawar)

Governor: SYED MASOOD KAUSAR.
Chief Minister: AMIR HAIDER KHAN HOTI.
Legislative Assembly: 124 seats (Awami National Party 48, Pakistan People's Party Parliamentarians 30, Muttahida Majlis-e-Amal 15, Pakistan Muslim League—Nawaz 9, Pakistan People's Party—Sherpao 6, Pakistan Muslim League—Quaid-e-Azam Group 6, independents 10).

PUNJAB
(Capital—Lahore)

Governor: SARDAR MUHAMMAD LATIF KHAN KHOSA.
Chief Minister: MUHAMMAD SHAHBAZ SHARIF.
Legislative Assembly: 371 seats (Pakistan Muslim League—Nawaz 171, Pakistan People's Party Parliamentarians 106, Pakistan Muslim League—Quaid-e-Azam Group 81, Pakistan Muslim League—Functional 3, Muttahida Majlis-e-Amal 2, Pakistan Muslim League—Zia 1, independents 6, vacant or withheld 1).

SINDH
(Capital—Karachi)

Governor: Dr ISHRATUL EBAD KHAN.
Chief Minister: SYED QAIM ALI SHAH.
Legislative Assembly: 168 seats (Pakistan People's Party Parliamentarians 93, Muttahida Qaumi Movement 51, Pakistan Muslim League—Quaid-e-Azam Group 11, Pakistan Muslim League—Functional 8, National People's Party 3, Awami National Party 2).

Election Commission

Election Commission of Pakistan: Secretariat, Election House, Constitution Ave, G-5/2, Islamabad; e-mail info@ecp.gov.pk; internet www.ecp.gov.pk; independent; Chief Election Commr Justice HAMID ALI MIRZA.

Political Organizations

All Jammu and Kashmir Muslim Conference: f. 1948; advocates the holding of a free plebiscite in the whole of Kashmir; Leader Sardar ATTIQ AHMED KHAN.

Awami Muslim League (AML): Lal Haveli, Rawalpindi; tel. (51) 5554242; fax (51) 5772708; e-mail info@aml.org.pk; internet www.aml.org.pk; f. 2008; Pres. SHEIKH RASHID AHMED.

Awami National Party (ANP) (People's National Party): Bacha Khan Markaz, Pajagai Rd, POB 306, Peshawar; tel. (91) 2246851-3; fax (91) 2252406; e-mail info@anp.org.pk; internet www.anp.org.pk; f. 1986 by the merger of the National Democratic Party, the Awami Tehrik (People's Movement) and the Mazdoor Kissan (Labourers' and Peasants' Party); federalist and nationalist; the Pakhtoonkhawa Qaumi Party merged with the ANP in February 2006, followed by the National Awami Party Pakistan in June of the same year; Pres. ASFANDYAR WALI KHAN.

Awami Qiyadat Party (People's Leadership Party): 1 Nat. Park Rd, Rawalpindi Cantt; f. 1995; Chair. Gen. (retd) MIRZA ASLAM BEG.

Balochistan National Party—Awami (BNP—A): Istaqlal Bldg, Quarry Rd, Quetta; Leader SYED EHSAN SHAH; Pres. Sardar AKHTER JAN MANGAL.

Balochistan National Party—Maingal (BNP—M): Quetta; e-mail bnpwebadmin@balochistan.net; Leader Sardar MOHAMMAD AKHTAR MAINGAL.

Jamaat-e-Islami Pakistan (JIP): Mansoorah, Multan Rd, Lahore 54570; tel. (42) 37844605; fax (42) 37832194; e-mail info@jamaat.org; internet www.jamaat.org; f. 1941; seeks the establishment of Islamic order through adherence to teaching of Maulana MAUDUDI, founder of the party; revivalist; right-wing; Chair. Amir S. MUNAWAR HASSAN; c. 5m. mems (2005).

Jamhoori Watan Party (Bugti) Balochistan: Bugti House, Dera Bugti, Quetta; tel. (81) 32827743; fax (81) 32845559; Pres. Nawab TALAL AKBAR KHAN BUGTI.

Jamiat-e-Ulema-e-Islam (JUI): Jamia al-Maarf, al-Sharia, Dera Ismail Khan; f. 1950; mem. Muttahida Majlis-e-Amal alliance; advocates adoption of a constitution in accordance with (Sunni) Islamic teachings; split into factions led by Maulana Fazlur Rehman (JUI—F; Sec.-Gen. Maulana Abdul Ghafoor Haideri) and Sami ul-Haq (JUI—S).

Jamiat-e-Ulema-e-Pakistan (JUP): Burns Rd, Karachi; f. 1948; mem. Muttahida Majlis-e-Amal alliance; advocates progressive (Sunni) Islamic principles and enforcement of Islamic laws in Pakistan; Pres. Dr ABUL KHAIR MOHAMMAD ZUBAIR (acting); Gen. Sec. QARI ZAWWAR BAHADUR.

Millat Party: 20 Bridge Colony, Lahore; tel. (42) 35757805; fax (42) 35756718; e-mail millat@lhr.comsats.net.pk; advocates 'true federalism'; Chair. FAROOQ AHMAD KHAN LEGHARI.

Muttahida Qaumi Movement (MQM): 494/8 Azizabad, Federal Area B, Karachi; tel. (21) 36313690; fax (21) 36329955; e-mail mqm@mqm.org; internet www.mqm.org; f. 1984 as Mohajir Qaumi Movement; name changed to Muttahida Qaumi Movement in 1997;

associated with the All Pakistan Muttahida Students' Organization (f. 1978 as the All Pakistan Mohajir Students' Organization; name changed July 2006); represents the interests of Muslim, Urdu-speaking immigrants (from India) in Pakistan; seeks the designation of Mohajir as fifth nationality (after Sindhi, Punjabi, Pathan and Balochi); aims to abolish the prevailing feudal political system and to establish democracy; Founder and Leader ALTAF HUSSAIN; Pres. AFTAB SHEIKH.

National Party: Firdosi Bldg, 4th Floor, Rustam G Line, Jinnah Rd, Quetta; f. 2003 following merger of Balochistan National Movement and Balochistan National Democratic Party; Chair. Dr ABDUL HAYEE BALOCH.

National People's Party (NPP): 18 Khayaban-e-Shamsheer, Defence Housing Authority, Phase V, Karachi; tel. (21) 35854522; fax (21) 35853500; f. 1986; centre left-wing party advocating a just, democratic welfare state for Pakistan; breakaway faction from PPP; Chair. GHULAM MUSTAFA JATOI; Parl. Leader ARIF MUSTAFA JATOI.

Pakhtoonkhwa Milli Awami Party: Central Secretariat, Jinnah Rd, Quetta; Leader MEHMOOD KHAN ACHAKZAI.

Pakistan Awami Tehreek (PAT): 365M Model Town, Lahore; fax (42) 35169114; e-mail info@pat.com.pk; internet www.pat.com.pk; Pres. MUHAMMAD TAHIR UL-QADRI; Sec.-Gen. Dr ANWAAR AKHTAR.

Pakistan Democratic Party (PDP): 8 Davis Rd, Lahore; tel. (42) 34220430; f. 1969; advocates democratic and Islamic values; Pres. NAWABZADA MANSOOR AHMED KHAN.

Pakistan Muslim League (PML): PML House, F-7/3, Islamabad; tel. (51) 9217364; e-mail mushahid.hussain@gmail.com; internet www.pml.org.pk; f. 2004 following merger of PML Quaid-e-Azam Group, PML (Junejo), PML (Functional), PML (Zia-ul-Haq Shaheed), PML (Jinnah) and the Sindh Democratic Alliance; PML (Functional) subsequently split from party; commonly known as PML (Q) within Pakistan; Pres. CHAUDHRY SHUJAAT HUSSAIN; Sec.-Gen. Sen. MUSHAHID HUSSAIN SYED.

Pakistan Muslim League—Functional (PML—F): Islamabad; merged with PML Quaid-e-Azam Group, PML (Junejo), PML (Zia-ul-Haq Shaheed), PML (Jinnah) and the Sindh Democratic Alliance in 2004 but subsequently split from party; Leader PIR PAGARA.

Pakistan Muslim League—Nawaz (PML—N): 20-H, St 10, F-8/3, Islamabad; tel. and fax (51) 2852662; e-mail pmlisb@hotmail.com; internet www.pmln.org.pk; f. 1993 as faction of Pakistan Muslim League (Junejo); Leader NAWAZ SHARIF; Pres. SHAHBAZ SHARIF; Chair. RAJA ZAFARUL HAQ.

Pakistan People's Party (PPP): 8, St 19, F-8/2, Islamabad; tel. (51) 2255264; fax (51) 2282741; e-mail ppp@comsats.net.pk; internet www.ppp.org.pk; formed Pakistan People's Party Parliamentarians (PPPP) 2002 in order to meet electoral requirements; advocates Islamic socialism, democracy and a non-aligned foreign policy; Leaders BILAWAL BHUTTO ZARDARI, ASIF ALI ZARDARI.

Pakistan People's Party (Shaheed Bhutto Group): 70 Clifton, Karachi; tel. (21) 35865370; fax (21) 35861224; f. 1995 as a breakaway faction of the PPP; Chair. GHINWA BHUTTO; Sec.-Gen. Dr MUBASHIR HASAN.

Punjabi Pakhtoon Ittehad (PPI): f. 1987 to represent the interests of Punjabis and Pakhtoons in Karachi; Pres. MALIK MIR HAZAR KHAN.

Sindh National Front (SNF): Pres. MUMTAZ BHUTTO.

Sindh Taraqi Passand Party (STPP): Leader Dr QADIR MAGSI.

Tehreek-e-Insaf (Movement for Justice): 2, St 84, Sector G-6/4, Islamabad; tel. (51) 2270744; fax (51) 2873893; e-mail info@insaf.org.pk; internet www.insaf.org.pk; f. 1996; Leader IMRAN KHAN; Sec.-Gen. ARIF ALVI.

Diplomatic Representation

EMBASSIES AND HIGH COMMISSIONS IN PAKISTAN

Afghanistan: 8, St 90, G-6/3, Islamabad 44000; tel. (51) 32824505; fax (51) 32824504; e-mail contact@islamabad.mfa.gov.af; internet islamabad.mfa.gov.af; Ambassador MUHAMMAD DAUDZAI.

Algeria: 107, St 9, E-7, POB 1038, Islamabad; tel. (51) 2653773; fax (51) 2653795; Ambassador AHMED BENFLIS.

Argentina: 60, St 1, F-6/3, POB 1015, Islamabad; tel. (51) 8438120; fax (51) 2825564; e-mail epaki@mrecic.gov.ar; internet www.pakistan.embajada-argentina.gov.ar; Ambassador RODOLFO MARTIN-SARAVIA.

Australia: Diplomatic Enclave 1, Constitution Ave and Isphani Rd, G-5/4, POB 1046, Islamabad; tel. (51) 8355500; fax (51) 2820112; e-mail consular.islm@dfat.gov.au; internet www.pakistan.embassy.gov.au; High Commissioner TIMOTHY GEORGE.

Austria: 13, St 1, F-6/3, POB 1018, Islamabad 44000; tel. (51) 2209710; fax (51) 2828366; e-mail islamabad-ob@bmeia.gv.at; Ambassador Dr MICHAEL STIGELBAUER.

Azerbaijan: House 14, St 87, G-6/3, Atatürk Ave, Islamabad; tel. (51) 2829345; fax (51) 2820898; e-mail azeremb@isb.paknet.com.pk; internet www.azembassy.com.pk; Ambassador DASHGIN SHIKAROV.

Bahrain: House 5, St 83, G-6/4, Islamabad; tel. (51) 2831060; fax (51) 2206732; Ambassador MUHAMMAD EBRAHIM MUHAMMAD ABD AL-QADIR.

Bangladesh: 1, St 5, F-6/3, Islamabad; tel. (51) 2279267; fax (51) 2279266; e-mail bdhcisb@yahoo.com; internet www.bdhcpk.org; High Commissioner YASMEEN MURSHED.

Belgium: 24, St 4, F-6/3, Islamabad; tel. (51) 2822293; fax (51) 2820972; e-mail islamabad@diplobel.fed.be; internet www.diplomatie.be/islamabad; Ambassador KINT CHRISTIAN-HAUS.

Bosnia and Herzegovina: 195, St 10, E-7, Islamabad; tel. (51) 32654018; fax (51) 32654017; e-mail ambassador@bosnianembassypakistan.org; internet www.bosnianembassypakistan.org; Chargé d'affaires VEJSIL GODINJAK.

Brazil: 23, St 19, F-6/2, Islamabad; tel. (51) 32279690; fax (51) 32823034; e-mail brasembp@isb.compol.com; Ambassador ALFREDO CESAR MARTINHO LEONI.

Brunei: House 5, St 6, F-6/3, Islamabad; tel. (51) 32879636; fax (51) 32823688; e-mail islamabad.pakistan@mfa.gov.bn; High Commissioner Pehin Dato' Haji Panglima Col (retd) Haji ABDUL JALIL BIN Haji AHMAD.

Bulgaria: Plot 6–11, Diplomatic Enclave, Ramna 5, POB 1483, Islamabad; tel. (51) 32279196; fax (51) 32279159; e-mail bul@isd.wol.net.pk; internet www.mfa.bg/en/56/; Ambassador ROUMEN PIRONCTHEV.

Canada: Diplomatic Enclave, Sector G-5, POB 1042, Islamabad; tel. (51) 327291007; fax (51) 32279110; e-mail isbad@international.gc.ca; internet www.international.gc.ca/missions/pakistan; High Commissioner ROSS HYNES.

China, People's Republic: Diplomatic Enclave, Ramna 4, Islamabad; tel. (51) 2877279; fax (51) 2279600; e-mail chinaemb_pk@mfa.gov.cn; internet pk.china-embassy.org; Ambassador LIU JIAN.

Cuba: 37 School Rd, F-6/2, Islamabad; tel. (51) 2824077; fax (51) 2824076; e-mail eocuba2@nayatel.pk; Ambassador GUSTAVO MACHÍN GÓMEZ.

Czech Republic: 49, St 27, Shalimar F-6/2, POB 1335, Islamabad; tel. (51) 2274304; fax (51) 2825327; e-mail islamabad@embassy.mzv.cz; internet www.mzv.cz/islamabad; Ambassador PAVOL SEPELAK.

Denmark: 16, St 21, F-6/2, POB 1118, Islamabad; tel. (51) 2824722; fax (51) 2823483; e-mail isbamb@um.dk; internet www.ambislamabad.um.dk; Ambassador ANDERS C. HOUGAARD.

Egypt: 38–51, UN Blvd, Diplomatic Enclave, Ramna 5/4, POB 2088, Islamabad; tel. (51) 2209072; fax (51) 2279552; Ambassador MAGDY MAHMOUD HELMY AMER.

Eritrea: 28, St 33, F-8/1, Islamabad; tel. (51) 2816131; fax (51) 2816133; Ambassador ABDUL MOHAMED HEGGI.

Finland: 11, St 90, G-6/3, Islamabad; tel. (51) 2828426; fax (51) 2828427; e-mail finnemb@isd.wol.net.pk; Ambassador OSMO LIPONNEN.

France: Diplomatic Enclave 1, Ramna 5, Islamabad; tel. (51) 2011414; fax (51) 2011400; e-mail ambafra@isb.comsats.net.pk; internet www.ambafra-pk.org; Ambassador DANIEL JOUANNEAU.

Germany: Diplomatic Enclave, Ramna 5, POB 1027, Islamabad 44000; tel. (51) 2279430; fax (51) 2279436; e-mail info@isla.diplo.de; internet www.islamabad.diplo.de; Ambassador Dr MICHAEL KOCH.

Greece: 33A, School Rd, F-6/2, Islamabad; tel. (51) 2822558; fax (51) 8358985; e-mail gremb.isl@mfa.gr; Ambassador PETROS MAVROIDIS.

Holy See: Apostolic Nunciature, St 5, G-5, Diplomatic Enclave 1, POB 1106, Islamabad 44000; tel. (51) 2278218; fax (51) 2820847; e-mail vatipak@dsl.net.pk; Apostolic Nuncio Most Rev. EDGAR PEÑA PARRA.

Hungary: 12, Margalla Rd, F-6/3, POB 1103, Islamabad; tel. (51) 2823352; fax (51) 2825256; e-mail mission.isl@kum.hu; internet www.mfa.gov.hu/emb/islamabad; Ambassador ISTVAN DARVASI.

India: G-5, St 5, Diplomatic Enclave, Islamabad; tel. (51) 2206950; fax (51) 2823102; e-mail hoc.islamabad@mea.gov.in; internet www.india.org.pk; High Commissioner SHARAT SABHARWAL.

Indonesia: St 5, G-5/4, Diplomatic Enclave 1, Ramna 5/4, POB 1019, Islamabad; tel. (51) 2826390; fax (51) 2832013; e-mail unitkom@kbri-islamabad.go.id; internet www.kbri-islamabad.go.id; Ambassador ISHAK LATUCONSINA.

Iran: Plot No. 222–238, St 2, F-5/1, Islamabad; tel. (51) 2833070; fax (51) 2833075; e-mail info@iranembassy.pk; internet www.iranembassy.pk; Ambassador MASHALLAH SHAKERI.

PAKISTAN

Iraq: 57, St 48, F-8/4, Islamabad; tel. (51) 2253734; fax (51) 2253688; e-mail iraqiya@sat.net.pk; Ambassador Dr RUSHDI MAHMOOD RASHEED.

Italy: 54 Margalla Rd, F-6/3, POB 1008, Islamabad; tel. (51) 2828982; fax (51) 2829026; e-mail segreteria.ambislamabad@esteri.it; internet www.ambislamabad.esteri.it; Ambassador VINCENZO PRATI.

Japan: Plot No. 53-70, Diplomatic Enclave 1, Ramna 5/4, Islamabad 44000; tel. (51) 2279320; fax (51) 2279340; e-mail japanemb@comsats.net.pk; internet www.pk.emb-japan.go.jp; Ambassador HIROSHI OE.

Jordan: 99, Main Double Rd, F-10/1, Islamabad; tel. (51) 2297383; fax (51) 2211630; e-mail islamabad@fm.gov.jo; Ambassador Dr SALEH AL-JAWARNEH.

Kazakhstan: 11, St 45, F-8/1, Islamabad; tel. (51) 2262926; fax (51) 2262806; e-mail embkaz@isb.comsats.net.pk; Ambassador BAKHITBEK SHABARKAYE.

Kenya: 8A, Embassy Rd, F-6/4, POB 2097, Islamabad; tel. (51) 2876024; fax (51) 2876027; e-mail kenreppk@apollo.et.pk; High Commissioner MISHI MASIKA MWATSAHU.

Korea, Democratic People's Republic: 9, St 18, F-8/2, Islamabad; tel. and fax (51) 2252756; fax (51) 2252754; Ambassador RO KYONG CHOL.

Korea, Republic: Block 13, St 29, G-5/4, Diplomatic Enclave 2, POB 1087, Islamabad; tel. (51) 2279380; fax (51) 2279391; e-mail pakistan@mofat.go.kr; internet pak-islamabad.mofat.go.kr/eng/index.jsp; Ambassador CHOI CHOONG-JOO.

Kuwait: Plot Nos 1, 2 and 24, University Rd, G-5, Diplomatic Enclave, POB 1030, Islamabad; tel. (51) 2297411; fax (51) 2829487; Ambassador NAWAF AL-ENEZI.

Kyrgyzstan: 163, St 36, F-10/1, Islamabad; tel. (51) 2212196; fax (51) 2212169; e-mail kyrgyzembassy@dsl.net.pk; Ambassador BEKTUR ASANOV.

Lebanon: 6, St 27, F-6/2, Islamabad; tel. (51) 2278338; fax (51) 2826410; e-mail lebemb@comsats.net.pk; Ambassador WAFIC MUHAMMAD REHAIME.

Libya: 736, Margalla Rd, F-10/2, Islamabad; tel. (51) 2214348; fax (51) 2290093; Ambassador IBRAHIM AL-ABID MUKHTAR.

Malaysia: 34, St 56, F-7/4, Islamabad; tel. (51) 2656092; fax (51) 2656012; e-mail malislamb@kln.gov.my; internet www.kln.gov.my/perwakilan/islamabad; High Commissioner Dato' AHMAD ANWAR BIN ADNAN.

Maldives: Islamabad; High Commissioner Dr AISHATH SHEHENAZ ADAM.

Mauritius: 13, St 26, F-6/2, POB 1084, Islamabad; tel. (51) 2824658; fax (51) 2824656; e-mail mauripak@dsl.net.pk; High Commissioner DEEPAK PRABHAKAR GOKULSING (acting).

Morocco: 6, Gomal Rd, E-7, POB 1179, Islamabad; tel. (51) 2654744; fax (51) 2654741; e-mail sifamapak@morocco-embassy.com.pk; internet www.morocco-embassy.com.pk; Ambassador MUHAMMAD RIDA EL-FASSI.

Myanmar: 240, St 51, F-10/4, Islamabad; tel. (51) 2114148; fax (51) 2114149; e-mail embassy_myanmar@yahoo.com; Ambassador SAN MYINT OO.

Nepal: 11A, St 13, F-7/2, Islamabad; tel. (51) 2655182; fax (51) 2655184; e-mail nepem@isb.comsats.net.pk; Ambassador BAL BAHADUR KUNWAR.

Netherlands: Plot No. 167, St 15, G-5, Diplomatic Enclave, Islamabad; tel. (51) 2004444; fax (51) 2004333; e-mail isl@minbuza.nl; internet www.mfa.nl/isl-en; Ambassador JOOST REINTJES.

Nigeria: 132–135, Isphani Rd, G-5/4, Diplomatic Enclave 1, POB 1075, Islamabad; tel. (51) 2823542; fax (51) 2824104; e-mail nigeria@isb.comsats.net.pk; High Commissioner ADAMU SAIDU DAURA.

Norway: 25, St 19, F-6/2, Islamabad; tel. (51) 2279720; fax (51) 2279726; e-mail emb.islamabad@mfa.no; internet www.norway.org.pk; Ambassador ROBERT KVILE.

Oman: 53, St 48, F-8/4, POB 1194, Islamabad; tel. (51) 2254955; fax (51) 2255074; Ambassador MUHAMMAD BIN SAID BIN MUHAMMAD AL-LAWATI.

Philippines: 12, St 12, F-7/2, Islamabad; tel. (51) 2653661; fax (51) 2653665; e-mail isdpe@isb.comsats.net.pk; Ambassador JAIME J. YAMBAO.

Poland: St 24, G-5/4, Diplomatic Enclave 2, POB 1032, Islamabad; tel. (51) 2600844; fax (51) 2600852; e-mail polemb@dsl.net.pk; internet www.islamabad.polemb.net; Ambassador Dr ANDRZEJ ANANICZ.

Portugal: 466, Main Margalla Rd, F-7/2, Islamabad; tel. (51) 2652491; fax (51) 2652492; e-mail portugal@dsl.net.pk; Ambassador Dr ANTONIO JOSÉ M. SANTOS BRAGA.

Qatar: 20, Khayaban-e-Iqbal, F-6/3, Islamabad; tel. (51) 2270833; fax (51) 2270207; e-mail islamabad@mofa.gov.qa; Ambassador HAMAD ALI AL-HENZAB.

Romania: 13, St 88, G-6/3, Islamabad; tel. (51) 2826514; fax (51) 2826515; e-mail amb.rom.isb@gmail.com; Ambassador EMILIAN ION.

Russia: Khayaban-e-Suhrawardy, Diplomatic Enclave, Ramna 4, Islamabad; tel. (51) 2278670; fax (51) 2826552; e-mail russia2@isb.comsats.net.pk; internet www.pakistan.mid.ru; Ambassador BUDNIK ANDREY.

Saudi Arabia: 14, Hill Rd, F-6/3, Islamabad; tel. (51) 2600900; fax (51) 2278816; Ambassador IBRAHIM BIN SALIH AL-GHADEER.

Somalia: 17, St 60, F-8/4, Islamabad; tel. and fax (51) 32854733; Ambassador ABDISALAM Haji AHMED LIBAN.

South Africa: 48, Main Margalla Rd, Khayaban-e-Iqbal, F-8/2, Islamabad; tel. (51) 2262354; fax (51) 2250114; e-mail xhosa@isb.comsats.net.pk; High Commissioner DANIEL JABULANI MAVIMBELA.

Spain: St 6, G-5, Diplomatic Enclave 1, POB 1144, Islamabad; tel. (51) 2088777; fax (51) 2088774; e-mail embspain@dsl.net.pk; Ambassador GONZALO MARIA QUINTERO SARAVIA.

Sri Lanka: 2C, St 55, F-6/4, POB 1497, Islamabad; tel. (51) 2828723; fax (51) 2828751; e-mail srilanka@isb.net.pk; High Commissioner Air Chief Marshal (retd) JAYALATH WEERAKKODY.

Sudan: 1A, St 32, F-8/1, Islamabad; tel. (51) 2263926; fax (51) 2264404; e-mail sudanipk@isb.compol.com; Ambassador MOHAMMED OMER MUSA.

Sweden: 4, St 5, F-6/3, Islamabad; tel. (51) 2828712; fax (51) 2825284; e-mail ambassaden.islamabad@foreign.ministry.se; internet www.swedenabroad.com/Start___28997.aspx; Ambassador ULRIKA SUNDBERG.

Switzerland: St 6, G-5/4, Diplomatic Enclave, POB 1073, Islamabad; tel. (51) 2279291; fax (51) 2279286; e-mail isl.vertretung@eda.admin.ch; internet www.eda.admin.ch/islamabad; Ambassador MARKUS PETER.

Syria: 30 Hill Rd, F-6/3, Islamabad; tel. (51) 2279470; fax (51) 2279472; Ambassador ALI AL-MOHRA.

Tajikistan: 90, Main Double Rd, F-10/1, Islamabad; tel. (51) 2101254; fax (51) 2299710; e-mail tajemb_islamabad@inbox.ru; Ambassador ZUBAYDULLO ZUUBAYDOV.

Thailand: 10, St 33, F-8/1, Islamabad; tel. (51) 2280909; fax (51) 5837422; e-mail thaiemb@dslplus.net.pk; internet www.mfa.go.th/web/1330.php?depid=231; Ambassador MARUT JITPATIMA.

Tunisia: 221, St 21, E-7, Islamabad; tel. (51) 2827869; fax (51) 2653564; Ambassador MOURAD BOUREHLA.

Turkey: St 1, Diplomatic Enclave, Islamabad; tel. (51) 8319800; fax (51) 2278752; e-mail turkemb@dsl.net.pk; internet www.turkishembassy.org.pk; Ambassador MUSTAFA BABUR HEZLAN.

Turkmenistan: 22A, Nazim-Ud-Din Rd, F-7/1, Islamabad; tel. (51) 2274913; fax (51) 2278790; e-mail turkmen@comsats.net.pk; Ambassador SAPOR BERDINIYAZOV.

Ukraine: 20, St 18, F-6/2, Islamabad; tel. (51) 2274732; fax (51) 2274643; e-mail emb_pk@mfa.gov.ua; Ambassador Dr IHOR PASKO.

United Arab Emirates: Plot No. 1-22, Quaid-e-Azam University Rd, Diplomatic Enclave, POB 1111, Islamabad; tel. (51) 2279052; fax (51) 2279063; e-mail uaeempk@isb.paknet.pk; Ambassador ALI SAIF SULTAN AL-AWANI.

United Kingdom: Diplomatic Enclave, Ramna 5, POB 1122, Islamabad; tel. (51) 2012000; fax (51) 2012043; e-mail bhcmedia@isb.comsats.net.pk; internet ukinpakistan.fco.gov.uk; High Commissioner ADAM THOMSON.

USA: Diplomatic Enclave, Ramna 5, POB 1048, Islamabad; tel. (51) 2080000; fax (51) 2276427; e-mail webmasterisb@state.gov; internet islamabad.usembassy.gov; Ambassador CAMERON MUNTER.

Uzbekistan: 2, St 21, E-7, Kaghan Rd, Islamabad; tel. (51) 2821146; fax (51) 2261739; e-mail uzbekemb@isb.comsats.net.pk; internet www.pakistan.mfa.uz; Ambassador OYBEK A. USMANOV.

Viet Nam: 117, St 11, E-7, Islamabad; tel. (51) 2850581; fax (51) 2850582; e-mail dsqvn.pakistan@yahoo.com; Ambassador NGUYEN VIET HUNG.

Yemen: 90, Main Double Rd, F-10/2, Islamabad; tel. (51) 2102448; fax (51) 2102417; e-mail yemen22@isb.apollo.net.pk; Ambassador ABDO ALI ABDUL RAHMAN.

Judicial System

A constitutional amendment bill was passed in the National Assembly in October 1998 replacing the country's existing legal code with full Islamic *Shari'a*. However, the bill remained to be approved by the Senate.

PAKISTAN   *Directory*

SUPREME COURT
Chief Justice: IFTIKHAR CHAUDHRY.
Attorney-General: Maulvi ANWAR UL-HAQ.

FEDERAL SHARIAT COURT
Chief Justice: AGHA RAFIQ AHMED KHAN.

Religion

ISLAM
Islam is the state religion. The majority of the population are Sunni Muslims, while estimates of the Shi'a sect vary between 5% and 20% of the population. Only about 0.001% are of the Ahmadi sect.

CHRISTIANITY
About 3% of the population are Christians.
National Council of Churches in Pakistan: 32-B, Shahrah-e-Fatima Jinnah, POB 357, Lahore 54000; tel. (42) 37592167; fax (42) 37569782; e-mail nccp@lhr.comsats.net.pk; internet nccpakistan.org.pk; f. 1949; four mem. bodies, 14 assoc. mems; Gen. Sec. VICTOR AZARIAH.

The Roman Catholic Church
For ecclesiastical purposes, Pakistan comprises two archdioceses, four dioceses and one apostolic prefecture. At 31 December 2007 there were an estimated 1,139,333 adherents in the country.
Bishops' Conference: Pakistan Catholic Bishops' Conference, St 55, F-8/4, Kaghan Rd, Islamabad 44000; e-mail cbcp2000@isb.comsats.net.pk; internet www.pcbcsite.org; f. 1976; Pres. Most Rev. LAWRENCE J. SALDANHA (Archbishop of Lahore); Sec.-Gen. Rt Rev. ANTHONY LOBO (Bishop of Islamabad-Rawalpindi).
Archbishop of Karachi: Most Rev. EVARIST PINTO, St Patrick's Cathedral, Shahrah-e-Iraq, Karachi 74400; tel. (21) 37781533; fax (21) 37781532.
Archbishop of Lahore: (vacant), Sacred Heart Cathedral, 1 Mian Mohammad Shafi Rd, POB 909, Lahore 54000; tel. (42) 6366137; fax (42) 6368336; e-mail info@archdioceselahore.org; internet www.archdioceselahore.org.

Protestant Churches
Church of Pakistan: Moderator Rt Rev. Dr ALEXANDER JOHN MALIK (Bishop of Lahore), Bishopsbourne, Cathedral Close, The Mall, Lahore 54000; tel. (42) 7233560; fax (42) 7221270; e-mail bishop_lahore@hotmail.com; f. 1970 by union of the fmr Anglican Church in Pakistan, the United Methodist Church in Pakistan, the United Church in Pakistan (Scots Presbyterians) and the Pakistani Lutheran Church; eight dioceses; c. 700,000 mems (1993); Gen. Sec. HUMPHREY PETERS.
Presbyterian Church of Pakistan: Gujranwala Theological Seminary, Civil Lines, POB 13, Gujranwala; tel. (431) 259512; fax (431) 258314; e-mail kamil65@gjr.paknet.com.pk; f. 1961; c. 340,000 mems (1989); Moderator Rev. Dr ARTHUR JAMES; Sec. Rev. Dr MAGSOOD KAMIL.

Other denominations active in the country include the Associated Reformed Presbyterian Church and the Pakistan Salvation Army.

HINDUISM
Hindus comprise about 1.8% of the population.

BAHÁ'Í FAITH
National Spiritual Assembly: 56, H-8/4, Islamabad; tel. (51) 4444699; fax (51) 4444691; e-mail nsapakistan@cyber.net.pk; internet www.bahai.org; f. 1956; Gen. Sec. Prof. MEHRDAD YOSUF.

The Press

The Urdu press comprises almost 800 newspapers, with the *Daily Jang*, *Daily Khabrain*, *Nawa-i-Waqt*, *Daily Express* and *Jasarat* among the most influential. The daily newspaper with the largest circulation is the *Daily Jang*. Although the English-language press reaches only a small percentage of the population, it is influential in political, academic and professional circles. The four main press groups in Pakistan are Jang Publications (the *Daily Jang*, *The News*, the *Daily News* and the weekly *Akhbar-e-Jehan*), the Dawn or Herald Group (the *Dawn*, and the monthly *Herald* and *Spider*), the Khabrain Group (the *Daily Khabrain*) and the Nawa-i-Waqt Group (the *Nawa-i-Waqt*, *The Nation*, the *Daily Express* and the weekly *Family*).

PRINCIPAL DAILIES

Islamabad
Al-Akhbar: 44, St 2, I-10/3, Islamabad; tel. (51) 4438862; fax (51) 4438860; e-mail alakabar@dsl.net.pk; Urdu; also publ. in Muzaffarabad; Editor GHULAM AKBAR.
Daily Khabrain: 12 Lawrence Rd, Lahore; tel. (42) 36309155; fax (42) 36314658; e-mail khabrain@khabrain.com; internet www.khabrain.com; Urdu; Editor and Proprietor ZIA SHAHID.
The Nation: Nawa-i-Waqt House, Zero Point, Islamabad; tel. (51) 2202641; fax (51) 2202645; e-mail editor@nation.com.pk; internet www.nation.com.pk; English; Man. Dir and Editor-in-Chief MAJID NIZAMI; circ. 15,000.
Pakistan Observer: Al-Akbar House, Markaz G-8, Islamabad 44870; tel. (51) 2852027; fax (51) 2262258; e-mail observer@pakobserver.net; internet www.pakobserver.net; f. 1988; English; independent; Editor-in-Chief ZAHID MALIK.

Karachi
Aghaz: 11 Japan Mansion, Preedy St, Sadar, Karachi 74400; tel. (21) 32720228; fax (21) 32722125; e-mail ex101@hotmail.com; f. 1962; evening; Urdu; Chief Editor MOHAMMAD ANWAR FAROOQI.
Amn: Deen Muhammad Wafai Rd, opposite NED City Campus, Karachi; tel. (21) 32634451; fax (21) 32634454; e-mail amn@cyber.net.pk; Urdu; Editor AJMAL DEHLVI.
Anjam Daily: 2nd Floor, New Block No. 12, Hockey Stadium, Liaquat Barrack, nr Jinnah Hospital, Karachi; tel. (21) 35672940; e-mail dailyanjam@yahoo.com; Editor ABDUL JABBAR KHATTAK.
Awami Awaz: 2nd Floor, New Central Block No. 2, Hockey Stadium, Liaquat Barracks, off Shahrah-e-Faisal, Karachi; tel. (21) 35672949; fax (21) 35672946; e-mail awamiawaz@hotmail.com; Man. Editor Dr KHAIR MUHAMMAD JUNO.
Barsat: 246/D-6, PECHS, Karachi; tel. (21) 34535228; fax (21) 34535227; Editor MUHAMMAD SALEEM DAUDPOTA.
Beopar: 205 Alfalah Court, I. I. Chundrigar Rd, Karachi; tel. (21) 32636442; fax (21) 32630784; e-mail beopar@yahoo.com.
Business Daily: Suite 209, 2nd Floor, Prime Office Lobby, Pak Towers, Clifton, Karachi; tel. (21) 35820100; fax (21) 35821655; Editor QAISAR MAHMOOD.
Business Recorder: Recorder House, 53 Business Recorder Rd, Karachi 74550; tel. (21) 32250071; fax (21) 32228644; e-mail ed.khi@br-mail.com; internet www.brecorder.com; f. 1965; English; Editor-in-Chief WAMIQ A. ZUBERI.
Daily Awam: Printing House, I. I. Chundrigar Rd, POB 52, Karachi; tel. (21) 32637111; fax (21) 32636066; e-mail awam@awam.com.pk; f. 1994; evening; Urdu; Editor-in-Chief Mir SHAKIL-UR-RAHMAN.
Daily Express: 5 Expressway, off Korangi Rd, Karachi; tel. (21) 35800051-6; fax (21) 358000510; Urdu; Editor TAHIR NAJMI.
Daily Islam: Nazimabad 4, Karachi; tel. (21) 36682380; fax (21) 36622240; e-mail editor@dailyislam.pk; internet www.dailyislam.pk; Editor MUFTI ABDUL RASHEED.
Daily Jang: HQ Printing House, I. I. Chundrigar Rd, POB 52, Karachi; tel. (21) 32637111; fax (21) 32636066; e-mail jangkarachi@janggroup.com.pk; internet www.jang.com.pk; f. 1940; morning; Urdu; also publ. in Quetta, Rawalpindi, Lahore and London; Editor-in-Chief Mir SHAKIL-UR-RAHMAN; combined circ. 750,000.
Daily Khabar: A-8 Sheraton Centre, F. B. Area, Karachi; tel. (21) 3210059; Urdu; Exec. Editor FAROOQ PARACHA; Editor and Publr SAEED ALI HAMEED.
Daily Naya Akhbar: Zia Shahid Printer and Publisher, Muzammil Press, 1301, Mehmoodabad No. 6, Masjid-e-Awais Qarni, Block 7, Karachi; tel. (21) 111-55-88-55; fax (21) 5382271; CEO ZIA SHAHID; Editor AMTNAN SHAHID.
Daily News: Al-Rahman Bldg, I. I. Chundrigar Rd, Karachi; tel. (21) 32637111; fax (21) 32634395; e-mail dailynews@janggroup.com.pk; f. 1962; evening; English; Editor S. M. FAZAL; circ. 25,000.
Daily Public: Falak Printing Press, 191 Altaf Hussain Rd, New Challi, Karachi; tel. (21) 35687522; Man. Editor INQUILAB MATRI; Editor ANWAR SANROY.
Daily Sindh Sujag: Suite 414, 6th Floor, Amber Medical Centre, M. A. Jinnah Rd, Karachi; tel. (21) 32700252; fax (21) 32700249; e-mail sindhsujag786@yahoo.com; Sindhi; political; Editor NASIR DAD BALOCH.
Daily Times: Plot No. SR 5/12/1, 2nd Floor, Nelson Chamber, I. I. Chundrigar Rd, Karachi; tel. (21) 32213822; fax (21) 32213874; e-mail yousaf@dailytimes.com.pk; internet www.dailytimes.com.pk; Resident Editor YOUSAF RAFIQ.
Daily Ummat: Room No 1, Block IV, Hockey Club of Pakistan Stadium, Liaquat Barracks, Karachi; tel. (21) 35655270; fax (21) 35655275; e-mail info@ummatpublication.com; Editor NASEER HASHMI.

PAKISTAN

Dawn: Haroon House, Dr Ziauddin Ahmed Rd, POB 3740, Karachi 74200; tel. (21) 111-444-777; fax (21) 35683801; e-mail editor@dawn.com; internet www.dawn.com; f. 1947; English; also publ. from Islamabad, Rawalpindi and Lahore; Chief Exec. HAMEED HAROON; Editor ABBAS NASIR; circ. 110,000 (weekdays), 125,000 (Sundays).

Deyanet: 4th Floor, Al Warid Centre, off I. I. Chundrigar Rd, Karachi; tel. (21) 32263556; fax (21) 32631888; Urdu; also publ. in Sukkur and Islamabad; Editor NAJMUDDIN SHAIKH.

The Finance: 903–905 Uni Towers, I. I. Chundrigar Rd, Karachi; tel. (21) 32411665; fax (21) 32422560; e-mail tfinance@super.net.pk; English; Chief Editor S. H. SHAH.

Financial Daily: 11-C, Jami Commercial St No. 11, Phase VII, DHA, Karachi; tel. (21) 35311893; e-mail info@thefinancialdaily.com; internet thefinancialdaily.com; publ. by Data Research & Communications.

Financial Post: Bldg No. 106/C, 11 Commercial St, Phase II, Extension, Defence Housing Authority, Karachi; tel. (21) 35381626; fax (21) 35802760; e-mail fpost@gerrys.net; internet www.dailyfpost.com; f. 1994; English; Chief Editor and CEO QUDSIA K. KHAN; Publr WAJID JAWAD.

Hilal-e-Pakistan: Court View Bldg, 2nd Floor, M. A. Jinnah Rd, POB 3737, Karachi 74200; tel. (21) 32624997; fax (21) 32624996; Sindhi; Editor MOHAMMAD IQBAL DAL.

Jago: Karachi; tel. (21) 32635544; fax (21) 32628137; f. 1990; Sindhi; political; Editor AGHA SALEEM.

Janbaz: 9th Floor, Uni Tower, I. I. Chundrigar Rd, Karachi; tel. (21) 32411665; fax (21) 32422560; Editor ALI AKHBAR RIZVI.

Jasarat: 3rd Floor, Syed House, I. I. Chundrigar Rd, Karachi 74200; tel. (21) 32630391; fax (21) 32629344; e-mail jasarat@cyber.net.pk; f. 1970; Urdu; Editor ATHAR HASHMI; circ. 50,000.

Jurat: Jurat House, off I. I. Chundrigar Rd, Karachi; tel. (21) 32637641; fax (21) 32637640; Editor MUKHTAR AAQIL.

The Leader: Block 5, 609, Clifton Centre, Clifton, Karachi 75600; tel. (21) 35820801; fax (21) 35872206; e-mail info@theleader.com.pk; f. 1958; English; independent; Man. Editor MUNIR M. LADHA; circ. 7,000.

Mazdur: Spencer Bldg, I. I. Chundrigar Rd, Karachi 2; f. 1984; Urdu; Editor MOHAMMAD ANWAR BIN ABBAS.

Millat: 310 B, Pak Arab Society, Ferozepore Rd, Lahore; tel. (30) 08452590; fax (42) 45924421; e-mail editor@millat.com; internet www.millat.com; f. 1998; Urdu and English; independent; Editor ASADULLAH GHALIB; circ. 22,550.

Mohasib: Karachi; fax (21) 32632763; Urdu; also publ. from Abbotabad; Chief Editor ZAFAR MAJAZI; Editor NAEEM AHMAD.

The Nation: Block-I, Hockey Stadium, off Khayaban-e-Shamsher, Phase V, Defence Housing Authority, Karachi; tel. (21) 35846622; fax (21) 35848892; e-mail editor@nation.com.pk; internet www.nation.com.pk; English; Editor MAJEED NIZAMI.

The News International: Al-Rahman Bldg, I. I. Chundrigar Rd, POB 52, Karachi; tel. (21) 32630611; fax (21) 32418343; e-mail thenewskarachi@thenews.com.pk; f. 1990; English; also publ. from Lahore and Rawalpindi/Islamabad; Editor-in-Chief Mir SHAKIL-UR-RAHMAN; Editor TALAT ASLAM.

Qaumi Akhbar: 14 Ramzan Mansion, Dr Bilmoria St, off I. I. Chundrigar Rd, Karachi; tel. (21) 32633381; fax (21) 32635774; f. 1988; Urdu; offices in Islamabad; Editor ILYAS SHAKIR.

Savera: 108 Adam Arcade, Shaheed-e-Millat Rd, Karachi; tel. (21) 419616; Urdu; Editor RUKHSANA SAHAM MIRZA.

Sindh Tribune: No. 246-D/6, PECHS, Karachi; tel. (21) 34535227; fax (21) 4332680; English; political; Editor YOUSUF SHAHEEN.

Lahore

Daily Pakistan: 41 Jail Rd, Lahore; tel. (42) 37576301; fax (42) 37586251; f. 1990; Urdu; Chief Editor MUJIBUR RAHMAN SHAMI.

Daily Times: Media Times (Pvt) Ltd, 41-N, Industrial Area, Gulberg II, Lahore; tel. (42) 35878614; fax (42) 35878620; e-mail editor@dailytimes.com.pk; internet www.dailytimes.com.pk; Editor NAJAM SETHI.

Daily Wifaq: 6A Warris Rd, Lahore; tel. (42) 36367467; e-mail wifaqtimes@yahoo.com; Urdu; also publ. in Rawalpindi, Sargodha and Rahimyar Khan; Editor MUTAHHIR WAQAR; circ. 50,000.

Mahgribi Pakistan: Lahore; tel. (42) 353490; Urdu; also publ. in Bahawalpur and Sukkur; Editor M. SHAFAAT.

The Nation: NIPCO House, 4 Sharah-e-Fatima Jinnah, POB 1815, Lahore 54000; tel. (42) 36367580; fax (42) 36367005; e-mail editor@nation.com; internet www.nation.com.pk; f. 1986; English; Chair. MAJEED NIZAMI; Editor ARIF NIZAMI; circ. 52,000.

Nawa-i-Waqt (Voice of the Time): 4 Sharah-e-Fatima Jinnah, Lahore 54000; tel. (42) 36367580; fax (42) 36367005; internet www.nawaiwaqt.com.pk; f. 1940; English, Urdu; also publ. edns in Karachi, Islamabad and Multan; Editor MAJID NIZAMI; combined circ. 560,000.

The Sun International: 15-L, Gulberg III, Ferozepur Rd, Lahore; tel. (42) 35883540; fax (42) 35839951; Editor MAHMOOD SADIQ.

Tijarat: 14 Abbot Rd, opp. Nishat Cinema, Lahore; tel. (42) 36312462; fax (42) 36362767; Urdu; Editor JAMIL ATHAR.

Rawalpindi

Daily Asas: Asas Plaza, B-27, Murree Road, Rawalpindi; tel. (51) 111272711; fax (51) 4428315; e-mail info@dailyasas.com.pk; internet www.dailyasas.com.pk; f. 1993; also printed from Islamabad, Lahore, Karachi and Faisalabad; Editor DANISH IFTIKHAR.

Daily Jang: Murree Rd, Rawalpindi; tel. (51) 5962444; fax (51) 5962277; internet www.jang.com.pk; f. 1940; also publ. in Quetta, Karachi, Lahore and London; Urdu; independent; Editor Mir JAVED REHMAN; circ. (Rawalpindi) 65,000.

Daily Wifaq: Mohallah Waris Khan 604, Murree Rd, Rawalpindi; tel. (51) 553979; e-mail dailywifaq@hotmail.com; f. 1959; also publ. in Lahore, Sargodha and Rahimyar Khan; daily publ. in Urdu, monthly magazine in English *The Times*; Editor MUSTAFA SADIQ.

The News: Al-Rehman Bldg, Murree Rd, Rawalpindi; tel. (51) 5962444; fax (51) 5962277; e-mail thenews@isb.comsats.net.pk; internet www.jang-group.com; f. 1991; also publ. in Lahore and Karachi; English; independent; Chief Editor Mir SHAKIL-UR-RAHMAN.

Other Towns

Aftab: Opposite WASA Office, Bagh Langay Khan Rd, Multan; tel. (61) 4546080; fax (61) 4786083; e-mail aftabmultan@aftabdaily.com; Sindhi; Editor ASAD MUMTAZ SEYAL.

Al Falah: Al Falah House, Al Falah Bazar, nr State Life Bldg, Mall Rd, Peshawar; tel. (91) 5853694; f. 1939; Urdu and Pashtu; Editor SYED BADRUDDIN SHAH.

Al-Jamiat-e-Sarhad: Kocha Gilania Chakagali, Karimpura Bazar, Peshawar; tel. (91) 2567757; e-mail sagha@brain.net.pk; f. 1941; Urdu and Pashtu; Propr and Chief Editor S. M. HASSAN GILANI.

Balochistan Times: Jinnah Rd, Quetta; Editor SYED FASIH IQBAL.

Basharat: Peshawar; Urdu; general; also publ. in Islamabad; Chief Editor ANWAR-UL-HAQ; Editor KHALID ATHER.

Daily Awaz: Peshawar; political; Man. Editor ALI RAZA MALIK.

Daily Business Report: Railway Rd, Faisalabad; tel. (41) 2642131; fax (41) 2621207; f. 1948; Editor ABDUL RASHID GHAZI; circ. 26,000.

Daily Ibrat Hyderabad: Ibrat Building, Gadi Khata, Hyderabad; tel. (22) 2728571; fax (22) 2784300; e-mail ibrat@hyd.paknet.com.pk; internet www.dailyibrat.com; Sindhi; Man. Editor Qazi ASAD ABID.

Daily Khadim-e-Waten: B-2, Civil Lines, Hyderabad; Editor MUSHTAQ AHMAD.

Daily Rehber: 17-B East Trust Colony, Bahawalpur; tel. (621) 884664; fax (621) 874032; e-mail rehberbwp@yahoo.co.uk; f. 1951; Urdu; Chief Editor AKHTER HUSSAIN ANJUM; circ. 250,000.

Daily Sarwan: 11-EGOR Colony, Hyderabad; tel. (221) 781382; Sindhi; Chief Editor GHULAM HUSSAIN.

Daily Shabaz: Peshawar; tel. (521) 220188; fax (521) 216483; Urdu; organ of the Awami National Party; Chief Editor Begum NASEEM WALI KHAN.

Frontier Post: 32 Stadium Rd, Peshawar; tel. (521) 79174; fax (521) 76575; e-mail editor@frontierpost.com.pk; f. 1985; English; left-wing; also publ. in Lahore; closed down temporarily in January 2001, reopened in June; Editor-in-Chief REHMAT SHAH AFRIDI; Editor MUZAFFAR SHAH AFRIDI.

Jihad: 15A Islamia Club Bldg, Khyber Bazar, Peshawar; tel. (521) 210522; e-mail jehad@pes.comsats.net.pk; also publ. in Karachi, Rawalpindi, Islamabad and Lahore; Editor SHARIF FAROOQ.

Kaleem: Shahi Bazar, Thalla, POB 88, Sukkur; tel. (71) 5627833; fax (71) 5622087; e-mail kaleemsukkur@yahoo.com; Urdu; Editor SHAHID MEHR SHAMSI.

Kavish: Sindh Printing and Publishing House, Civil Lines, POB 43, Hyderabad; Chief Editor MUHAMMAD AYUB QAZI; Publr/Editor ASLAM A. QAZI.

Nawai Asma'n: Mubarak Ali Shah Rd, Hyderabad; tel. and fax (221) 21925; Urdu, Sindhi and Pashtu; Chief Editor DOST MUHAMMAD.

The News: Qaumi Printing Press, Peshawar; English; Editor KHURSHID AHMAD.

Punjab News: Iftikhar Heights, Aminpur Bazar, POB 419, Faisalabad; tel. (41) 633102; fax (41) 615731; e-mail imranlateef1@hotmail.com; f. 1968; Chief Editor and Publr Sheikh Sultan MAHMOOD; circ. 10,000.

Sindh Guardian: Tulsi Das Rd, POB 300, Hyderabad; tel. and fax (221) 21926; English; Chief Editor DOST MUHAMMAD.

PAKISTAN

Sindh News: Gadi Khata, Hyderabad; tel. (221) 20793; fax (221) 781867; Editor Kazi SAEED AKBER.

Sindh Observer: POB 43, Garikhata, Hyderabad; tel. (221) 27302; English; Editor ASLAM AKBER KAZI.

Sindhu: Popular Printers, Ibrat Bldg, Gadi Khata, Hyderabad; tel. (221) 783571; fax (221) 783570; Sindhi; political.

Watan: 10 Nazar Bagh Flat, Peshawar.

Zamana: Jinnah Rd, Quetta; tel. (81) 71217; Urdu; Editor SYED FASIH IQBAL; circ. 5,000.

SELECTED WEEKLIES

Akhbar-e-Jehan: Printing House, off I. I. Chundrigar Rd, Karachi; tel. (21) 32634368; fax (21) 32635693; e-mail editor-in-chief@akhbar-e-jehan.com; internet www.akhbar-e-jehan.com; f. 1967; Urdu; independent; illustrated family magazine; Editor-in-Chief Mir JAVED RAHMAN; circ. 285,000.

Amal: Shah Qabool Colony, POB 185, Peshawar; tel. (91) 5704673; e-mail maab_kaifi@hotmail.com; f. 1958; Urdu, Pashtu and English; Chief Editor F. M. ZAFAR KAIFI; Publr MUNAZIMA MAAB KAIFI.

Chatan: Chatan Bldg, 88 McLeod Rd, Lahore; tel. (42) 36311336; fax (42) 36374690; f. 1948; Urdu; Editor MASUD SHORISH.

Family Magazine: 4 Shara-i-Fatima Jinnah, Lahore 54000; tel. (42) 36367551; fax (42) 36367583; circ. 100,000.

The Friday Times: 72-F. C. C. Gulberg IV, Lahore; tel. (42) 35673510; fax (42) 35751025; e-mail tft@lhr.comsats.net.pk; internet www.thefridaytimes.com; independent; Editor/Owner NAJAM SETHI.

Hilal: Hilal Rd, Rawalpindi 46000; tel. (51) 56134605; fax (51) 565017; f. 1951; Friday; Urdu; illustrated armed forces; Editor MUMTAZ IQBAL MALIK; circ. 90,000.

Insaf: P/929, Banni, Rawalpindi 46000; tel. and fax (51) 5550903; e-mail insafrwp@isb.paknet.com.pk; f. 1955; Editor Mir WAQAR AZIZ.

Lahore: Galaxy Law Chambers, 1st Floor, Room 1, Turner Rd, Lahore 5; f. 1952; Editor SAQIB ZEERVI; circ. 8,500.

Memaar-i-Nao: 39 KMC Bldg, Leamarket, Karachi; Urdu; labour magazine; Editor M. M. MUBASIR.

The Muslim World: 49-B, Block 8, Gulshan-e-Iqbal, Karachi 75300; POB 5030, Karachi 74000; English; current affairs.

Nairang Khayal: 8 Mohammadi Market, Rawalpindi; f. 1924; Urdu; Chief Editor Sultan RASHK.

Nida-i-Millat: 4 Sharah-e-Fatima Jinnah, Lahore 54000.

Noor Jehan Weekly: 32A National Auto Plaza, POB 8833, Karachi 74400; tel. and fax (21) 37723946; f. 1948; Urdu; film journal; Editor KHALID CHAWLA.

Pak Kashmir: Pak Kashmir Office, Soikarno Chowk, Liaquat Rd, Rawalpindi; tel. (51) 74845; f. 1951; Urdu; Editor M. MUSADDIQ ABBASI.

Pakistan and Gulf Economist: 1st Floor, 20-C, Sunset Lane 9, Phase 2 Extension, D. H. A., Karachi 75500; tel. (21) 35883967; fax (21) 35883295; e-mail information@pakistaneconomist.com; internet www.pakistaneconomist.com; f. 1960; English; Editor ALI HAIDER GOKAL; circ. 30,000.

Parsi Sansar and Loke Sevak: 8 Mehrabad, 5 McNeil Rd, Karachi 75530; tel. and fax (21) 35656217; e-mail organ@cyber.net.pk; f. 1909; English and Gujarati; Editor NUSSERWANJI OGRA.

Parwaz: Madina Office, Bahawalpur; Urdu; Editor MUSTAQ AHMED.

Qalandar: Peshawar; f. 1950; Urdu; Editor M. A. K. SHERWANI.

Shahab-e-Saqib: Shahab Saqib Rd, Maulana St, Peshawar; f. 1950; Urdu; Editor S. M. RIZVI.

Takbeer: A-1, 3rd Floor, 'Namco Centre', Campbell St, Karachi 74200; tel. (21) 32626613; fax (21) 32627742; e-mail irfanfaruqi@usa.com; f. 1984; Urdu; Sr Exec. IRFAN KALIM FAROOQ; circ. 70,000.

Tarjaman-i-Sarhad: Peshawar; Urdu and Pashtu; Editor MOHAMMAD SHAFI SABIR.

Times of Kashmir: P/929, Banni, Rawalpindi 46000; tel. (51) 5550903; fax (51) 4411348; e-mail insafrwp@isb.paknet.com.pk; f. 1982; English; Editor Mir IQBAL AZIZ.

Ufaq: 44H, Block No. 2, PECHS, Karachi; tel. (21) 437992; f. 1978; Editor WAHAJUDDIN CHISHTI; circ. 2,000.

SELECTED PERIODICALS

Aadab Arz: 190 N. Ghazali Rd, Saman Abad, Lahore 54500; tel. (42) 37582449; monthly; Editor KHALID BIN HAMID.

Aalami Digest: B-1, Momin Sq., Rashid Minhas Rd, Gulshan-e-Iqbal, Karachi; monthly; Urdu; Editor ZAHEDA HINA.

Akhbar-e-Watan: 68-C, 13th Commercial St, Phase-II, Extension Defence, Karachi; tel. (21) 5886071; fax (21) 5890179; e-mail akhbarewatan@hotmail.com; f. 1977; monthly; Urdu; cricket; Man. Editor MUNIR HUSSAIN; circ. 63,000.

Albalagh Darul Uloom: Korangi Rd, Karachi; monthly; Editor MOHAMMED TAQI USMANI.

Al-Ma'arif: Institute of Islamic Culture, Club Rd, Lahore 54000; tel. (42) 6363127; f. 1950; quarterly; Urdu; Dir and Editor-in-Chief Dr RASHID AHMAD JALLONDHRI.

Anchal: 24 Saeed Mansion, I. I. Chundrigar Rd, Karachi; monthly.

Archi Times: B-34, Block 15, Gulshan-e-Iqbal, Karachi; tel. (21) 34977652; fax (21) 34967656; e-mail architimes@cyber.net.pk; internet www.archpresspk.com; f. 1986; monthly; English; architecture; Editor MURTAZA SHIKOH.

Architecture and Interiors: B-34, Blk 15, Gulshan-e-Iqbal, Karachi 75300; tel. (21) 34977652; fax (21) 34967656; e-mail aplusi@cyber.net.pk; internet www.archpresspk.com; f. 2001; quarterly; English; Editor MUTJUBA HUSSAIN; Man. Editor MURTUZA SHIKOH.

Asia Travel News: 101 Muhammadi House, I. I. Chundrigar Rd, Karachi 74000; tel. (21) 32424837; fax (21) 32420797; fortnightly; travel trade, tourism and hospitality industry; Editor JAVED MUSHTAQ.

Auto Times: 5 S. J. Kayani Shaheed Rd, off Garden Rd, Karachi; tel. (21) 713595; fortnightly; English; Editor MUHAMMAD SHAHZAD.

Bachoon Ka Risala: 108–110 Adam Arcade, Shaheed-e-Millat Rd, Karachi; tel. (21) 3419616; monthly; Urdu; children's; Editor RUKHSANA SEHAM MIRZA.

Bagh: 777/18 Federal B Area, POB 485, Karachi; tel. (21) 449662; monthly; Urdu; Editor RAHIL IQBAL.

Bayyenat: Jamia Uloom-e-Islamia, Binnori Town, Karachi 74800; tel. (21) 34927233; f. 1962; monthly; Urdu; religious and social issues.

Beauty: Plot No. 4-C, 14th Commercial St, Defence Housing Authority, Phase II Extension, Karachi; tel. (21) 35805391; fax (21) 35896269; e-mail riazmansuri@hotmail.com; f. 2000; bi-monthly; English; Chief Editor RIAZ AHMED MANSURI.

Beemakar (Insurer): 58 Press Chambers, I. I. Chundrigar Rd, Karachi; e-mail tahakn@cyber.net.pk; f. 1990; monthly; Urdu; Man. Editor SHAMSHAD AHMAD; Editor AYAZ KHAN.

Chand: 190 N. Ghazali Rd, Saman Abad, Lahore 54500; tel. (42) 7582449; monthly; Editor MASOOD HAMID.

The Cricketer: Plot No. 4-C, 14th Commercial St, Defence Housing Authority, Phase II Extension, Karachi; tel. (21) 35805391; fax (21) 35896269; e-mail riazmansuri@hotmail.com; f. 1972; monthly; English/Urdu; Chief Editor RIAZ AHMED MANSURI.

Dastarkhuan: Plot No. 4-C, 14th Commercial St, Defence Housing Authority, Phase II Extension, Karachi; tel. (21) 35805391; fax (21) 35896269; e-mail riazmansuri@hotmail.com; f. 1998; monthly; Urdu; Chief Editor RIAZ AHMED MANSURI.

Defence Journal: SMS Block, Defence Hockey Stadium, Phase-V, Karachi; tel. (21) 35843502; fax (21) 35843416; e-mail defjrnl@pathfinder9.com; internet www.defencejournal.com; f. 1975; monthly; English; Editor-in-Chief IKRAM SEHGAL.

Dentist: 70/7, Nazimabad No. 3, Karachi 18; f. 1984; monthly; English and Urdu; Editor NAEEMULLAH HUSAIN.

Dosheeza: 108–110 Adam Arcade, Shaheed-e-Millat Rd, Karachi; tel. (21) 34930470; fax (21) 34934369; monthly; Urdu; Editor RUKHSANA SEHAM MIRZA.

Duniya-e-Tibb: Eveready Chambers, 2nd Floor, Mohd Bin Qasim Rd, off I. I. Chundrigar Rd, POB 1385, Karachi 1; tel. (21) 32630985; fax (21) 32637624; e-mail mcm@digicom.net.pk; f. 1986; monthly; Urdu; modern and Asian medicine; Editor QUTUBUDDIN; circ. 12,000.

Economic Review: Al-Masiha, 3rd Floor, 47 Abdullah Haroon Rd, POB 7843, Karachi 74400; tel. (21) 37728963; fax (21) 37728957; f. 1969; monthly; economic, industrial and investment research; Editor AHMAD MUHAMMAD KHAN.

Engineering Horizons: 13-J, Markaz F-7, Islamabad 44000; tel. (51) 2650174; fax (51) 2650943; e-mail islamabad@engghorizons.com; internet www.engghorizons.com; f. 1988; English; Chief Editor IMTIAZ SHEIKH.

Engineering Review: 305 Spotlit Chambers, Dr Billimoria St, off I. I. Chundrigar Rd, POB 807, Karachi 74200; tel. (21) 32632567; fax (21) 32639378; e-mail engineeringreview@yahoo.com; internet www.engineeringreview.com.pk; f. 1975; fortnightly; English; circ. 5,000.

Film Asia: 68-C, 13th Commercial St, Phase-II, Extension Defence, Karachi; tel. (21) 35886071; fax (21) 35890179; e-mail akhbarewatan@hotmail.com; f. 1973; monthly; film, television, fashion, art and culture; Man. Editor MUNIR HUSSAIN; circ. 38,000.

Good Food: Plot No. 4-C, 14th Commercial St, Defence Housing Authority, Phase II Extension, Karachi; tel. (21) 35805391; fax (21) 35896269; e-mail riazmansuri@hotmail.com; f. 1997; bi-monthly; English; Chief Editor RIAZ AHMED MANSURI.

Hamdard-i-Sehat: Hamdard Foundation Pakistan, Nazimabad 3, Karachi 74600; tel. (21) 36620945; fax (21) 36611755; e-mail hfp@hamdardfoundation.org; internet hamdardfoundation.org; f. 1933; monthly; Urdu; Editor-in-Chief SADIA RASHID; circ. 13,000.

PAKISTAN

Hamdard Islamicus: Hamdard Foundation Pakistan, Hamdard Centre, Nazimabad 3, Karachi 74600; tel. (21) 36620949; fax (21) 36611755; e-mail hfp@hamdardfoundation.org; internet hamdardfoundation.org; f. 1978; quarterly; English; Editor-in-Chief SADIA RASHID; circ. 750.

Hamdard Medicus: Hamdard Foundation Pakistan, Nazimabad 3, Karachi 74600; tel. (21) 36620949; fax (21) 36611755; e-mail hfp@hamdardfoundation.org; internet hamdardfoundation.org; f. 1957; quarterly; English; Editor-in-Chief SADIA RASHID; circ. 1,000.

Hamdard Naunehal: Hamdard Foundation Pakistan, Nazimabad 3, Karachi 74600; tel. (21) 36620949; fax (21) 36611755; e-mail hfp@hamdardfoundation.org; internet hamdardfoundation.org; f. 1952; monthly; Urdu; Editor MASOOD AHMAD BARAKATI; circ. 34,000.

The Herald: Haroon House, Dr Ziauddin Ahmed Rd, Karachi 74200; tel. (21) 35670001; fax (21) 35683188; e-mail letters.herald@dawn.com; internet www.dawn.com/herald; f. 1970; monthly; English; Editor ARIFA NOOR; circ. 38,000.

Hikayat: 26 Patiala Ground, Link McLeod Rd, Lahore; monthly; Editor SHAHID JAMIL; circ. 25,000.

Islamic Studies: Islamic Research Institute, Faisal Masjid Campus, POB 1035, Islamabad 44000; tel. (51) 2281289; fax (51) 2254879; e-mail islamicstudies.iri@gmail.com; internet iri.iiu.edu.pk; f. 1962; quarterly; English, Urdu (Fikro-Nazar) and Arabic (Al Dirasat al-Islamiyyah) edns; Islamic literature, religion, history, geography, language and the arts; Editor Dr ZAFAR ISHAQ ANSARI (acting); circ. 3,000.

Jamal: Institute of Islamic Culture, 2 Club Rd, Lahore 54000; tel. (42) 36363127; f. 1950; annual; English; Dir and Editor-in-Chief Dr JULUNDHRI RASHEED.

Journal of the Pakistan Historical Society: Hamdard Foundation Pakistan, Nazimabad 3, Karachi 74600; tel. (21) 36620945; fax (21) 36611755; e-mail hfp@hamdardfoundation.org; internet hamdardfoundation.org; f. 1953; quarterly; English; Editor Dr ANSAR ZAHID KHAN; circ. 700.

Khel-Ke-Duniya: 6/13 Alyusaf Chamber, POB 340, Karachi; tel. (21) 3216888.

Khwateen Digest: Urdu Bazar, M. A. Jinnah Rd, Karachi; monthly; Urdu; Editor MAHMUD RIAZ.

Kiran: 37 Urdu Bazar, M. A. Jinnah Rd, Karachi; Editor MAHMUD BABAR FAISAL.

The Leather News: Iftikhar Chambers, opp. UNI Plaza, Altaf Hussain Rd, POB 4323, Karachi 74000; tel. (21) 32630861; fax (21) 32631545; e-mail arsintl@yahoo.com; f. 1989; Editor ABDUL RAFAY SIDDIQI.

Ma'arif Feature: D-35, Block 5, Federal 'B' Area, Karachi 75950; tel. (21) 36349840; fax (21) 36361040; e-mail info@irak.pk; internet www.irak.pk; f. 1999; journal of the Islamic Research Acad; fortnightly; Urdu; Editor SYED SHAHID HASHMI.

Medical Variety: 108–110 Adam Arcade, Shaheed-e-Millat Rd, Karachi; tel. (21) 3419616; monthly; English; Editor RUKHSANA SEHAM MIRZA.

Muslim World Business: 20 Sasi Arcade, 4th Floor, Main Clifton Rd, POB 10417, Karachi 6; f. 1989; monthly; English; political and business; Editor-in-Chief MUZAFFAR HASSAN.

Naey-Ufaq: 24 Saeed Mansion, I. I. Chundrigar Rd, Karachi; fortnightly.

NGM Communication: POB 3540, Post Mall, Gulberg, Lahore 54660; tel. (42) 35879524; e-mail anjeeam@yahoo.com; f. 1980; owned by Nizam Nizami; English; lists newly released Pakistani publications on the internet; updated weekly; Editor GHUFRAN NIZAMI.

Pakistan Journal of Applied Economics: Applied Economics Research Centre, University of Karachi, POB 8403, Karachi 75270; tel. (21) 99261541; fax (21) 99261545; e-mail pjae@aerc.edu.pk; internet www.aerc.edu.pk; twice a year; Editor MUHAMMAD SABIHUDDIN BUTT.

Pakistan Journal of Scientific and Industrial Research: Pakistan Council of Scientific and Industrial Research, Scientific Information Centre, PCSIR Laboratories Campus, off University Rd, Karachi 75280; tel. (21) 34651740; fax (21) 34651738; e-mail pcsir@cyber.net.pk; f. 1958; bi-monthly; English; Exec. Editor Dr KANIZ FIZZA AZHAR; circ. 1,000.

Pakistan Management Review: Pakistan Institute of Management, Management House, Shahrah Iran, Clifton, Karachi 75600; tel. (21) 99251711; e-mail pimkhi@pim.com.pk; internet www.pim.com.pk; f. 1960; quarterly; English; Editor IQBAL A. QAZI.

Pakistan Textile Journal: Suite No. 213, Anum Blessings, Block Nos 7 & 8, KMCHS, Shahrah-e-Faisal, Karachi; tel. (21) 34431674; fax (21) 35206188; Editor NADEEM MAZHAR.

Pasban: Faiz Modh Rd, Quetta; fortnightly; Urdu; Editor MOLVI MOHD ABDULLAH.

Phool: 23 Queen's Rd, Lahore 54000; tel. (42) 36314099; fax (42) 36309661; e-mail editor@phool.com.pk; internet www.phool.com.pk; f. 1989; monthly; children's; Chief Editor MAJID NIZAMI; Editor MUHAMMAD SHOAIB MIRZA; circ. 50,000.

Progress: 4th Floor, PIDC House, Dr Ziauddin Ahmed Rd, Karachi 75530; tel. (21) 111-568-568; fax (21) 35680005; e-mail h_saquib@ppl.com.pk; f. 1956; monthly; publ. by Pakistan Petroleum Ltd; Editor and Publr NUSRAT NASARULLAH; Chief Exec./Man. Dir S. MUNSIF RAZA.

Qaumi Digest: 50 Lower Mall, Lahore; tel. (42) 37225143; fax (42) 37233261; monthly; Editor MUJIBUR REHMAN SHAMI.

Sabrang Digest: 47–48 Press Chambers, I. I. Chundrigar Rd, Karachi 1; f. 1970; monthly; Urdu; Editor SHAKEEL ADIL ZADAH; circ. 150,000.

Sach-Chee Kahaniyan: 108–110 Adam Arcade, Shaheed-e-Millat Rd, Karachi; tel. (21) 34930470; fax (21) 34934369; monthly; Urdu; Editor RUKHSANA SEHAM MIRZA.

Sayyarah: Aiwan-e-Adab, Urdu Bazar, Lahore 54000; tel. (42) 37321842; f. 1962; monthly; Urdu; literary; Man. Editor HAFEEZ-UR-RAHMAN AHSAN.

Sayyarah Digest: 244, Main Market Riwaz Garden, Lahore 54000; tel. (42) 37245412; fax (42) 37325080; e-mail sayyaradigest@brain.com.pk; f. 1963; monthly; Urdu; Chief Editor AMJAD RAUF KHAN; Editor KAMRAN AMJAD KHAN; circ. 40,000.

Science Magazine: Science Book Foundation, Haji Bldg, Hassan Ali Efendi Rd, Karachi; tel. (21) 32625647; monthly; Urdu; Editor QASIM MAHMOOD.

Seep: Alam Market, Block No. 16, Federal B Area, Karachi; quarterly; Editor NASIM DURRANI.

Show Business: 108–110 Adam Arcade, Shaheed-e-Millat Rd, POB 12540, Karachi; monthly; Urdu; Editor RUKHSANA SEHAM MIRZA.

Sindh Quarterly: 36D Karachi Administrative Co-operative Housing Society, off Shaheed-e-Millat Rd, Karachi 75350; tel. (21) 34531988; f. 1973; Editor SAYID GHULAM MUSTAFA SHAH.

Smash: Plot No. 4-C, 14th Commercial St, Defence Housing Authority, Phase II Extension, Karachi; tel. (21) 35805391; fax (21) 35896269; e-mail riazmansuri@hotmail.com; f. 2000; monthly; English; Chief Editor RIAZ AHMED MANSURI.

Spider: Haroon House, Dr Ziauddin Ahmed Rd, Karachi 74200; tel. (21) 111-444-777; fax (21) 35681544; e-mail reba@spider.tm; internet www.spider.tm; f. 1998; internet monthly; Editor REBA SHAHID; CEO HAMEED HAROON.

Sports International: Arshi Market, Firdaus Colony, Nazimabad, Karachi 74600; tel. (21) 36602171; fax (21) 36683768; e-mail ibp-khi@cyber.net.pk; f. 1972; fortnightly; Urdu and English; Chief Editor KANWAR ABDUL MAJEED; Editor RAHEEL MAJEED.

Taj: Jamia Tajia, St 13, Sector 14/B, Buffer Zone, Karachi 75850; monthly; Editor BABA M. ATIF SHAH ANWARI ZAHEENI TAJI.

Talimo Tarbiat: Ferozsons (Pvt) Ltd, 60 Shahrah-e-Quaid-e-Azam, Lahore 54000; tel. (42) 36301196; fax (42) 36369204; e-mail support@ferozsons.com.pk; f. 1941; children's monthly; Urdu; Publr and Editor ZAHEER SALAM; circ. 50,000.

Textile Times: Arshi Market, Firdaus Colony, Nazimabad, Karachi 74600; tel. (21) 36683768; e-mail ibp-khi@cyber.net.pk; f. 1993; monthly; English; Chief Editor KANWAR ABDUL MAJEED; Exec. Editor RAHEEL MAJEED KHAN.

Trade Chronicle: Iftikhar Chambers, Altaf Hussain Rd, POB 5257, Karachi 74000; tel. (21) 32631587; fax (21) 32635007; e-mail arsidiqi@ptcl.net; f. 1953; monthly; English; trade, politics, finance and economics; Editor ABDUL RAB SIDDIQI; circ. 6,000.

Trade Link International: Zahoor Mansion, Tariq Rd, Karachi; monthly; English; Man. Editor M. IMRAN BAIG; Editor IKRAMULLAH QUREISHI.

TV Times: Plot No. 4-C, 14th Commercial St, Defence Housing Authority, Phase II Extension, Karachi; tel. (21) 35805391; fax (21) 35896269; e-mail rmansuri@fascom.com; f. 1987; monthly; English; Chief Editor RIAZ AHMED MANSURI.

UNESCO Payami: 30 UNESCO House, Sector H-8/1, Islamabad; tel. (51) 434196; fax (51) 431815; monthly; Urdu; publ. by Pakistan National Commission for UNESCO; Editor Dr MUNIR A. ABRO.

Urdu Digest: 21-Acre Scheme, Samanabad, Lahore 54500; tel. (42) 37589957; fax (42) 37563646; e-mail urdudigest42@hotmail.com; monthly; Urdu; Editor ALTAF HASAN QURESHEE.

Voice of Islam: Jamiatul Falah Bldg, Akbar Rd, Saddar, POB 7141, Karachi 74400; tel. (21) 37721394; f. 1952; monthly; Islamic Cultural Centre magazine; English; Editor Prof. ABDUL QADEER SALEEM; Man. Editor Prof. WAQAR ZUBAIRI.

Wings: 101 Muhammadi House, I. I. Chundrigar Rd, Karachi 74000; tel. (21) 32412591; fax (21) 32420797; monthly; aviation and defence; English; Editor and Publr JAVED MUSHTAQ.

PAKISTAN

Women's Own: Plot No. 4-C, 14th Commercial St, Defence Housing Authority, Phase II Extension, Karachi; tel. (21) 35805391; fax (21) 35896269; e-mail riazmansuri@hotmail.com; f. 1987; monthly; English; Chief Editor RIAZ AHMED MANSURI.

Yaqeen International: Darut Tasnif (Pvt) Ltd, Main Hub River Rd, Mujahidabad, Karachi 75760; tel. (21) 32814432; fax (21) 32811304; e-mail daruttasnif@yaqeendtl.com; f. 1952; English and Arabic; Islamic organ; Editor Dr HAFIZ MUHAMMAD ADIL.

Yaran-e-Watan: Overseas Pakistanis Foundation, Shahrah-e-Jamhuriate, G-5/2, POB 1470, Islamabad 44000; tel. (51) 9224518; fax (51) 9211613; e-mail yw@opf.org.pk; f. 1982; monthly; Urdu; publ. by the Overseas Pakistanis Foundation; Editor TANVIR HUSSAIN.

Youth World International: 104/C Central C/A, Tariq Rd, Karachi; f. 1987; monthly; English; Editor SYED ADIL EBRAHIM.

NEWS AGENCIES

Agence France Press: House 90, Atatürk Ave, G-6/3, Islamabad; tel. (51) 2822738; fax (51) 2822203; Bureau Chief JEAN-HERVÉ DEILLER.

Associated Press of Pakistan (APP): 18 Mauve Area, Zero Point, G-7/1, POB 1258, Islamabad; tel. (51) 2203073; fax (51) 2203074; e-mail news@app.com.pk; internet app.com.pk; f. 1948; Dir-Gen. MANSOOR SOHAIL.

International News Network (INN): Suite 803, 8th Floor, Regal Trade Sq., Saddar, Karachi; tel. (21) 37767810; fax (21) 32767810; Chief Editor MUHAMMAD AKRAM.

Kyodo News Agency (Japan): House 31, St 28, F-10/1, Islamabad; tel. (51) 2291577; fax (51) 2297031; Bureau Chief KIMURA KAZUHIRO.

National News Agency (NNA): 491-C, Margalla Town, Islamabad 45510; tel. (51) 2840896; fax (51) 2841746; e-mail nnaisb@yahoo.com; f. 1990; Chief Editor SUHAIL ILYAS.

News Network International: 2nd Floor, Redco Plaza, Islamabad 44000; tel. (51) 2874344; fax (51) 2826289; e-mail nni2005@isb.paknet.com.pk; internet www.nni-news.com; f. 1992; independent international news agency; news in Arabic, Urdu and English; provides services to 435 newspapers and radio and television channels in South Asia, Europe, the Middle East, the Far East and the USA; Editor-in-Chief QAISAR JAVED; Editor MUHAMMAD TAHIR KHAN.

Pakistan—International Press Agency (PPA): 6, St 39, G-6/2, Islamabad 44000; tel. (51) 2279830; fax (51) 2272405; e-mail khalidathar@gmail.com; f. 1991; Urdu and English; Chief Editor KHALID ATHAR.

Pakistan Press International (PPI): Press Centre, Shahrah Kamal Atatürk, POB 541, Karachi; tel. (21) 32633215; fax (21) 32217069; e-mail ppi@ppinewsagency.com; f. 1956; pvt ltd co; Chair. OWAIS ASLAM ALI.

Sharp Eye: 111 Lytton Rd, Qurtaba Chowk (Mozang Chungi), Lahore; tel. (42) 37313401; fax (42) 37313404; e-mail editor@sharpeye.com.pk; internet www.sharpeye.pk; f. 2000; Chief Editor MIAN MUHAMMAD AZHAR AMIN.

United Press of Pakistan (Pvt) Ltd (UPP): 1 Victoria Chambers, Haji Abdullah Haroon Rd, Karachi 74400; tel. (21) 35683235; fax (21) 35682694; e-mail pnrupp2000@yahoo.com; f. 1949; Chair. MAHMUD UL-AZIZ; 5 brs.

Voice of America (VOA): House 1, St 89, G-6/3, Islamabad; tel. (51) 2278784; fax (51) 2277349.

PRESS ASSOCIATIONS

All Pakistan Newspaper Employees Confederation: Karachi Press Club, M. R. Kayani Rd, Karachi; f. 1976; confed. of all press industry trade unions; Pres. MAZHAR ABBAS; Sec.-Gen. PERVAIZ SHAUKAT.

All Pakistan Newspapers Society: 32 Farid Chambers, Abdullah Haroon Rd, POB 74400, Karachi 3; tel. (21) 35671256; fax (21) 35671310; e-mail apns@apns.com.pk; internet www.apns.com.pk; f. 1949; Pres. HAMEED HAROON; Sec.-Gen. SARMAD ALI.

Council of Pakistan Newspaper Editors: c/o United Press of Pakistan, 1 Victoria Chambers, Haji Abdullah Haroon Rd, Karachi 74400; tel. and fax (21) 35682694; f. 1957; Pres. JAMAL AKHTAR KAZI; Sec.-Gen. ILYAS SHAKIR.

Pakistan Federal Union of Journalists (PFUJ): 12 Nazimuddin Rd, F-6/1, Islamabad; tel. (51) 2870220; fax (51) 2870223; Pres. PERWAIZ SHAUKAT; Sec.-Gen. SHAMSUL ISLAM NAZ.

Pakistan Press Foundation: Press Centre, Shahrah Kamal Ataturk, Karachi 74200; tel. (21) 32633215; fax (21) 32631275; e-mail aboutus@pakistanpressfoundation.org; internet www.pakistanpressfoundation.org; f. 1967; independent media research and training centre for promotion of press freedom; Sec.-Gen. OWAIS ASLAM ALI.

Publishers

Alhamra Publishing: Al-Babar Centre, Office 6, 1st Floor, F-8 Markaz, Islamabad 44000; tel. (51) 2818033; fax (51) 2855150; e-mail contact@alhamra.com; internet www.alhamra.com; f. 2000; publs broad range of subjects incl. fiction, literary criticism, languages, history, education and religion in Urdu and English translations; Man. Dir SHAFIQ NAZ.

Al-Noor Publishers: 15x DHA, Ghazi Rd, Lahore; tel. (42) 35733700; e-mail alnoorcentraloffice@yahoo.com; CEO NIGHAT YASMIN HASHMI.

Anjuman Taraqqi-e-Urdu Pakistan: D-159, Block 7, Gulshan-e-Iqbal, Karachi 75300; tel. (21) 34811406; fax (21) 34973296; e-mail quami.zaban@yahoo.com; f. 1903; literature, religion, textbooks, Urdu dictionaries, literary and critical texts; Pres. AFTAB AHMED KHAN; Hon. Sec. JAMIL UDDIN AALI.

Book Group: 187/2–C, Block No. 2, PECHS, Karachi; tel. (21) 34310641; fax (21) 34395264; e-mail info@bookgroup.org.pk; internet www.bookgroup.org.pk; Chair. SYED SAMI MUSTAFA.

Camran Publishers: Jalaluddin Hospital Bldg, Circular Rd, Lahore; f. 1964; general, technical, textbooks; Propr ABDUL HAMID.

Chronicle Publications: Iftikhar Chambers, Altaf Hussain Rd, POB 5257, Karachi 74000; tel. (21) 32631587; fax (21) 32635007; e-mail arsidiqi@ptcl.net; f. 1953; reference, directories, religious books; Dir ABDUL RAUF SIDDIQI.

Darussalam Publishers and Distributors: D.C.H.S., Tariq Rd, Karachi; tel. (21) 34393937; e-mail mayubsipra@hotmail.com; internet www.darussalampk.com; Man. Dir MUHAMMAD AYUB SIPRA.

Dasnavi Book House: Book St, G-6, Mazang Rd, Lahore; tel. (42) 32231518; e-mail bookhome@hotmail.com.

Dawah Academy International Islamic University: Faisal Masjid, Islamabad; tel. (51) 2262031; fax (51) 9263442; e-mail hairankhatak@yahoo.com; internet www.dawahacademy.com; Dir Dr SAJID UR-RAHMAN.

Economic and Industrial Publications: Al-Masiha, 3rd Floor, 47 Abdullah Haroon Rd, POB 7843, Karachi 74400; tel. (21) 37728963; fax (21) 37728434; f. 1965; industrial, economic and investment research.

Educational Resource Development Centre: A 735, Blk H, North Nazimabad, Karachi; tel. (21) 36723454; fax (21) 36678748; e-mail info@erdconline.org; internet www.erdconline.org; Dir SALMAN ASIF SIDDIQUI.

Elite Publishers Ltd: D-118, SITE, Karachi 75700; tel. (21) 32573435; fax (21) 32564720; e-mail elite@elite.com.pk; internet www.elite.com.pk; f. 1951; general commercial printing and packaging; Chair. AHMED MIRZA JAMIL; Chief Exec. KHALID JAMIL.

Fazlee's Book Super Market: 507/3, Temple Rd, Urdu Bazar, Nr Radio Pakistan, Karachi; tel. (21) 32629724; fax (21) 32633887; e-mail fazleebook@hotmail.com; internet www.fazleebooks.com; Propr SAJID REHMAN.

Ferozsons (Pvt) Ltd: 60 Shahrah-e-Quaid-e-Azam, Lahore; tel. (42) 111-626-262; fax (42) 36369204; e-mail support@ferozsons.com.pk; internet www.ferozsons.com.pk; f. 1894; general books, school books, periodicals, maps, atlases, stationery products; Man. Dir ZAHEER SALAM; Dir (Business Development) MUQEET SALAM.

Fiction House: 18, Mozang House, Lahore; publs quarterly social science journal Tareekh.

Frontline Publishing Co: 22, Urdu Bazar, Lahore; tel. (42) 37247310; fax (42) 37247323; e-mail azam.fpc@gmail.com; f. 1951; academic and general; Dirs AZAM MUHAMMAD, AMIR MUHAMMAD.

Gaba Educational Books: Urdu Bazar, 1/2 Urdu Manzil, Karachi; tel. (21) 32628266; fax (21) 32630606; e-mail gebpak@cyber.net.pk; internet www.gabaedu.com; Man. Dir MUHAMMAD HAROON GABA.

Sh. Ghulam Ali and Sons (Pvt) Ltd: 14 Lawrence Rd, Lahore 54000; tel. (42) 37352908; fax (42) 36315478; e-mail info@ghulamali.com.pk; internet www.ghulamali.com.pk; f. 1887; general, religion, technical, textbooks; Dirs NIAZ AHMAD, ASAD NIAZ.

Gohar Publishers: 1 and 2 Quran Mahal, Urdu Bazar, M. A. Jinnah Rd, Karachi; tel. (21) 32639320; fax (21) 32623884; e-mail gohar.publishers@live.com; internet goharpublishers.com; academic; Dir ABU ZAR GHAFFARI.

Harf Academy: G/307, Amena Plaza, Peshawar Rd, Rawalpindi.

Idara Taraqqi-i-Urdu: S-1/363 Saudabad, Karachi 27; f. 1949; general literature, technical and professional books and magazines; Propr IKRAM AHMED.

Ilmi Kitab Khana: Kabeer St, Urdu Bazar, Lahore; tel. (42) 37248129; f. 1948; technical, professional, historical and law; Propr Haji SARDAR MOHAMMAD.

INAYAT Sons: YMCA Bldg, 16 The Mall, Lahore 54000; tel. (42) 38401335; fax (42) 37231896; e-mail general@inayatsons.com; internet www.inayatsons.com; f. 1971; Propr S. PERVEZ.

PAKISTAN

Indus Publications: 25 Fared Chambers, Abdullah Haroon Rd, Karachi; tel. (21) 35660242; e-mail muzaffar_indus@hotmail.com; f. 1959; printers, publishers and importers of books; Dir AATIF SAFDAR.

Iqbal Sons Educational Publishers: Urdu Bazar, M. A. Jinnah Rd, Karachi; tel. (21) 32218838; fax (21) 34387943; e-mail aliqbalsons@yahoo.com; internet www.al-iqbaledu.com; Propr MUHAMMAD SOHAIL IQBAL GABA.

Islamic Book Centre: 25B Masson Rd, POB 1625, Lahore 54000; tel. (42) 36361803; fax (42) 36360955; e-mail lsaeed@paknetl.ptc.pk; religion in Arabic, Urdu and English; Islamic history, textbooks, dictionaries and reprints; Propr and Man. Dir SUMBLEYNA SAJID SAEED.

Islamic Publications (Pvt) Ltd: 3 Court St, Lower Mall, Lahore 54000; tel. (42) 37248676; fax (42) 37214974; e-mail islamicpak@hotmail.com; internet www.islamicpak.com.pk; f. 1959; Islamic literature in Urdu and English; Man. Dir Prof. MUHAMMAD AMIN JAVED; Gen. Man. AMANAT ALI.

Jamiatul Falah Publications: Jamiatul Falah Bldg, Akbar Rd, Saddar, POB 7141, Karachi 74400; tel. (21) 37721394; f. 1952; Islamic history and culture; Pres. MUZAFFAR AHMED HASHMI; Sec. Prof. SHAHZADUL HASAN CHISHTI.

Kazi Publications: 121 Zulqarnain Chambers, Ganpat Rd, POB 1845, Lahore; tel. (42) 37311359; fax (42) 37350805; e-mail kazipublications@hotmail.com; internet www.brain.net.pk/~kazip; f. 1978; Islamic literature, religion, law, biographies; Propr/Man. MUHAMMAD IKRAM SIDDIQI; Chief Editor MUHAMMAD ASIM BILAL.

Lark Publishers: Urdu Bazar, Karachi 1; f. 1955; general literature, magazines; Propr MAHMOOD RIAZ.

Liberty Books (Pvt) Ltd: 3 Rafiq Plaza, M. R. Kayani Rd, Saddar, Karachi; tel. (21) 35656567; fax (21) 35684319; e-mail info@libertybooks.com; internet www.libertybooks.com; f. 1980.

Lion Art Press (Pvt) Ltd: 112 The Mall, Lahore 54000; tel. (42) 36304444; fax (42) 36367728; e-mail lionart786@hotmail.com; f. 1919; general pubs in English and Urdu; Chief Exec. KHALID A. SHEIKH; Dir ASMA KHALID.

Maktaba Darut Tasnif: Main Hub River Rd, Mujahidabad, Karachi 75760; tel. (21) 32814432; fax (21) 32811307; e-mail daruttasnif@yaqeendtl.com; f. 1951; Koran Majeed and Islamic literature; Dir ABDUL BAQI FAROOQI.

Malik Sirajuddin & Sons: 48-C, Lower Mall, Lahore 54000; tel. (42) 37225809; fax (42) 37224586; e-mail sirajco@brain.net.pk; f. 1905; general, religion, law, textbooks; Man. MALIK ABDUL ROUF.

Malik Sons: Karkhana Bazar, Faisalabad.

Medina Publishing Co: M. A. Jinnah Rd, Karachi 1; f. 1960; general literature, textbooks; Propr HAKIM MOHAMMAD TAQI.

Mehtab Co: Ghazni St, Urdu Bazar, Lahore; tel. (42) 37120071; fax (42) 37353489; e-mail shashraf@brain.net.pk; f. 1978; Islamic literature; Propr SHAHZAD RIAZ SHEIKH.

Mohammad Hussain and Sons: 17 Urdu Bazar, Lahore 2; tel. (42) 37244114; f. 1941; religion, textbooks; Partners MOHAMMAD HUSSAIN, AZHAR ALI SHEIKH, PERVEZ ALI SHEIKH.

Sh. Muhammad Ashraf: 7 Aibak Rd, New Anarkali, Lahore 7; tel. (42) 37353171; fax (42) 37353489; e-mail shashraf@brain.net.pk; f. 1923; books in English on all aspects of Islam; Man. Dir SHAHZAD RIAZ SHEIKH.

Nafees Academy: Qasr-e-Maryam, Govali Lane No. 3, Ratan Talab, Urdu Bazar, Karachi; tel. (21) 32722080; fax (21) 32751247; e-mail nafeesacademy@cyber.net.pk; Dir KHAWAR IFTIKHAR.

National Book Foundation: G 8/4, 6 Mauve Area, Islamabad; tel. (51) 9261036; fax (51) 9261534; e-mail books@nbf.org.pk; internet www.nbf.org.pk; Man. Dir MAZHAR-UL-ISLAM.

National Book Service: 22 Urdu Bazar, Lahore; tel. (42) 37247310; fax (42) 37247323; e-mail fpc_pak@hotmail.com; internet www.fpcpk.com; f. 1950; academic and primary, secondary and ELT school books; Execs MUHAMMAD ARIF, MUHAMMAD AMIR, MUHAMMAD ASIM.

Oxford University Press: Plot No. 38, Sector 15, Korangi Industrial Area, Karachi; tel. (21) 34265945; fax (21) 35071586; e-mail oup.pk@oup.com; internet www.oup.com.pk; academic, educational and general; Man. Dir AMEENA SAIYID.

Pak Book Corpn: Star Centre, Main Tariq Rd, PECHS, Karachi; tel. (21) 34536375; fax (21) 34386971; e-mail info@pakbook.com; internet www.pakbook.com; Man. Dir MUHAMMAD IQBAL CHEEMA.

Pakistan Law House: Pakistan Chowk, POB 90, Karachi 1; tel. (21) 32212455; fax (21) 32627549; e-mail plh_law_house@hotmail.com; internet www.pakistanlawhouse.com; f. 1950; importers and exporters of legal books and reference books; Man. K. NOORANI.

Pakistan Publishing House: Victoria Chambers 2, A. Haroon Rd, Karachi 75400; tel. (21) 35681457; fax (21) 32627549; e-mail danyalbooks@hotmail.com; f. 1959; Propr HOORI NOORANI; Gen. Man. AAMIR HUSSEIN.

Paramount Books: 152/0, Blk 2, PECHS, Karachi 75400; tel. (21) 34310030; fax (21) 34553772; e-mail paramount@cyber.net.pk; internet www.paramountbooks.com.pk.

Pioneer Book House: M. A. Jinnah Rd, Karachi; tel. (21) 32628739; internet www.pioneerbookhouse.com; agent for state and federal govt publications; periodicals, gazettes, maps and reference works in English, Urdu and other regional languages.

Premier Bookhouse: Shahin Market, Room 2, Anarkali, POB 1888, Lahore; tel. (42) 37321174; Islamic and law.

Publishers United (Pvt) Ltd: c/o Gulam Ali Medicine Market, Chowk Lohari Gate, POB 1689, Lahore 54000; tel. (42) 36361306; fax (42) 36316015; e-mail smalipub2@hotmail.com; f. 1950; Islamic studies, history, art, archaeology, literature, Oriental studies, genealogy, scientific, medical, humanities and social sciences; Man. Dir ASAD NIAZ.

Punjab Religious Books Society: Anarkali, Lahore 2; educational, religious, law and general; Gen. Man. A. R. IRSHAD; Sec. NAEEM SHAKIR.

Reprints Ltd: 16 Bahadur Shah Market, M. A. Jinnah Rd, Karachi; f. 1983; Pakistani edns of foreign works; Chair. A. D. KHALID; Man. Dir AZIZ KHALID.

Royal Book Co: BG-5, Rex Centre, Basement, Fatima Jinnah Rd, Karachi 75530; tel. (21) 35653418; e-mail royalbook@hotmail.com.

Sang-e-Meel Publications: 25 Lower Mall, Lahore 54000; tel. (42) 37220100; fax (42) 37245101; e-mail smp@sang-e-meel.com; internet www.sang-e-meel.com; f. 1962; Marketing and Sales Exec. ALI KAMRAN.

Say Publishing (Pvt) Ltd: SA 1-3, Shahnawaz Arcade, Shahid-e-Millat Rd, Karachi; tel. (21) 34945541; fax (21) 35834777; e-mail saybooks@gerrys.net; f. 1982; Man. Dir AHSON JAFFRI.

Sindh Education Foundation: Plot No. 9, Blk 7, Clifton 5, Karachi 75600; tel. (21) 111-424-111; fax (21) 99251652; e-mail info@sef.org.pk; internet www.sef.org.pk; Man. Dir ANITA GHULAM ALI.

Sindhi Adabi Board (Sindhi Literary and Publishing Organization): Hyderabad; tel. (221) 771276; e-mail bookinfo@sindhiadabiboard.org; internet www.sindhiadabiboard.org; f. 1951; history, literature, culture of Sindh; in Sindhi, Urdu, English, Persian and Arabic; translations into Sindhi, especially of literature and history; chaired by Minister of Education and Literacy, Sindh; Sec. INAM SHEIKH.

Taj Co Ltd: Qissa Khani Bazar, Peshawar; tel. (91) 2580245; fax (91) 2580247; internet www.tajcom.com; f. 1929; religious books; Man. Dir A. H. KHOKHAR.

The Times Press (Pvt) Ltd: C-18, Al-Hilal Society, off University Rd, Karachi 74800; tel. (21) 34932931; fax (21) 34935602; e-mail timekhi@cyber.net.pk; internet www.timespress.8m.com; f. 1948; printers, publishers and stationery manufacturers, incl. security printing (postal stationery and stamps); registered publishers of Koran, school textbooks, etc.; Dir S. M. MINHAJUDDIN.

Tooba Publishers: 85 Sikandar Block, Allama Iqbal Town, Lahore; tel. (42) 35410185; e-mail haroonkallem@hotmail.com; f. 1983; poetry; Man. HAROON KALEEM USMANI.

Urdu Academy Sind: Main Urdu Bazar, M. A. Jinnah Rd, Karachi; tel. (21) 32628655; fax (21) 32625992; e-mail urduacademy@cyber.net.pk; f. 1947; brs in Hyderabad and Lahore; academic, reference, general and textbooks; Man. Dir AZIZ KHALID.

Vanguard Books (Pvt) Ltd: 72-FCC, Gulberg IV, Lahore; tel. (42) 35763510; fax (42) 35751025; e-mail vbl@brain.net.pk; Chief Exec. NAJAM SETHI.

West-Pak Publishing Co (Pvt) Ltd: 17 Urdu Bazar, Lahore; tel. (42) 37230555; fax (42) 37120077; e-mail pakcompany@hotmail.com; f. 1932; textbooks and religious books; Chief Exec. SYED AHSAN MAHMUD.

GOVERNMENT PUBLISHING HOUSE

Government Publications: Office of the Deputy Controller, Stationery and Forms, nr Old Sabzi Mandi, University Rd, Karachi 74800; tel. (21) 99231989; publ. Gazette of Pakistan; Dep. Controller MUHAMMAD AMIN BUTT.

PUBLISHERS' ASSOCIATION

Pakistan Publishers' and Booksellers' Association: 6 Gunpat Rd, Lahore; tel. (42) 37722043; Chair. NAJAM SETHI; Sec. ZUBAIR SAEED.

Broadcasting and Communications

TELECOMMUNICATIONS

Pakistan Telecommunication Authority (PTA): F-5/1, Islamabad 44000; tel. (51) 2878143; fax (51) 2878155; e-mail administration@pta.gov.pk; internet www.pta.gov.pk; f. 1997; regulatory authority; Chair. Dr MOHAMMAD YASEEN; Dir-Gen. CH. MOHAMMAD DIN.

Burraq Telecom (Pvt) Ltd: Plot 94A, St 7, Sector I-10/3, Islamabad; tel. (51) 111-287-727; fax (51) 2112380; e-mail info@burraqtel.com.pk; internet www.burraqtel.com.pk; f. 2004; CEO SADIQ YOUSAF YALMAZ.

Callmate Telips Telecom Ltd: 99-CF, 1/5 Clifton, Karachi; tel. (21) 35867696; fax (21) 35833006; e-mail info@cttelecom.net; internet www.cttelecom.net; f. 2003; telecommunications services.

Carrier Telephone Industries (Pvt) Ltd: 1-9/2 Industrial Area, POB 1098, Islamabad 44000; tel. (51) 4434981; fax (51) 4449581; e-mail niamatullah.khan.ext@siemens.com; internet www.ctipak.com.pk; f. 1969; Man. Dir MALIK MOHAMMAD AMIN.

China Mobile Pakistan Ltd: 68E Jinnah Ave, Blue Area, Islamabad; tel. (51) 111222111; fax (51) 111031031; internet www.zong.com.pk; f. 2008; Chair. WANG JIANZHOU.

Instaphone: 75 East, Fazal-ul-Haq Rd, Blue Area, POB 1681, Islamabad; tel. (51) 2277400; fax (51) 111-501501; internet www.instaphone.com; private mobile telephone co; CEO SHAHID FEROZ.

Megatech Communications (Pvt) Ltd: 47 Banglore Town, off Tipu Sultan Rd, Karachi 75350; tel. (21) 34528954; fax (21) 34533768; e-mail info@megatech.com.pk; internet www.megatech.com.pk; f. 1992; supplier of new digital telephone systems integrated with ISDN/BRI; Sales Dir FARHAT ABBAS.

Mobilink: 42 Kulsum Plaza, 1st Floor, Blue Area, Islamabad; tel. (21) 32273984; fax (21) 32826999; e-mail customercare@mobilink.net; internet www.mobilinkgsm.com; subsidiary of Orascom Telecom; Pres. and CEO ZOUHAIR ABDUL KHALIQ.

National Telecommunication Corporation: NTC Building, F-5/1, Islamabad; tel. (51) 9206450; e-mail infolhr@ntc.net.pk; internet www.ntc.net.pk; f. 1996 by government; Chair. NOOR-UD-DIN BAQAI.

Pakistan Telecommunications (Pvt) Ltd (PTCL): Block E, G-8/4, Islamabad 44000; tel. (51) 4844463; fax (51) 4843991; e-mail info@ptcl.net.pk; internet www.ptcl.com.pk; f. 1990; 74% state-owned; 26% owned by Etisalat (United Arab Emirates); Chair. HIFZ-UR-REHMAN; Pres. and CEO WALID IRSHAID.

TeleCard Ltd: 7th Floor, World Trade Centre, 10 Khayaban-e-Roomi, Block 5, Clifton, Karachi 75600; tel. (21) 111-222-124; e-mail customerservices@telecard.com.pk; internet www.telecard.com.pk; Chief Exec. SHAHID FIROZ.

Telenor: 13-K, Moaiz Centre, F-7 Markaz, Islamabad; tel. (51) 111-345-700; fax (51) 2651923; internet www.telenor.com.pk; f. 2004; private mobile telephone co; CEO CHRISTIAN ALBECH.

Telephone Industries of Pakistan (TIP): Khanpur Rd, Haripur 22630, NWFP; tel. (995) 611469; fax (995) 610490; e-mail mdtip@tip.org.pk; internet www.tip.org.pk; f. 1952; Man. Dir NADEEM KHAN; mfrs of telecommunications equipment.

Ufone: 13-B, F-7 Markaz, Jinnah Super Market, Islamabad; fax (51) 111-333-100; e-mail customercare@ufonegsm.net; internet www.ufone.com; f. 2001; subsidiary of Pakistan Telecommunications (Pvt) Ltd; private mobile telephone co; Pres. and Chief Exec. ABDUL AZIZ.

Warid Telecom (Pvt) Ltd: 9th Floor, EFU Bldg, Jail Rd, Lahore; e-mail customerservice@waridtel.com; internet www.waridtel.com; owned by Abu Dhabi Group; CEO MUNEER FAROOQUI.

Wateen Telecom (Pvt) Ltd: POB 3527, Lahore; fax (21) 34324096; e-mail info@wateen.com; internet www.wateen.com; subsidiary of the Abu Dhabi Group, UAE; mobile and fixed line telephone services; internet, television and multimedia provider; CEO TARIQ MALIK.

BROADCASTING

Regulatory Authority

Pakistan Electronic Media Regulatory Authority (PEMRA): 6th Floor, Green Trust Tower, Blue Area, Islamabad; tel. (51) 9107105; fax (51) 9107107; e-mail exec_member@pemra.gov.pk; internet www.pemra.gov.pk; regulates the establishment and operation of broadcast media and distribution services; Chair. MUSHTAQ MALIK.

Radio

Pakistan Broadcasting Corporation: National Broadcasting House, Constitution Ave, Islamabad 4400; tel. (51) 9208306; fax (51) 9223827; e-mail info@radio.gov.pk; internet www.radio.gov.pk; f. 1947 as Radio Pakistan; national broadcasting network of 33 stations; home service 24 hrs daily in 17 languages and dialects; external services 11 hrs daily in 15 languages; world service 11 hrs daily in two languages; 80 news bulletins daily; Dir-Gen. ASHFAQ GONDAL; Programme Dir NAYYAR MEHMOOD.

Pakistan Broadcasting Foundation: Planning and Development, Headquarters, Constitution Ave, Islamabad; tel. (51) 9216942; fax (51) 9204363.

Azad Kashmir Radio: Muzaffarabad; state-owned; Station Dir MASUD KASHFI; Dep. Controller (Eng.) SYED AHMED.

Capital FM: Islamabad; f. 1995; privately owned; broadcasts music and audience participation shows 24 hrs daily.

CityFM89: Penthouse, Anum Empire, Block 7 & 8, KCHS, Karachi; tel. (21) 34390155; fax (21) 34390160; e-mail info@cityFM89.com; internet cityfm89.com; f. 2004; owned by Kohinoor Airwaves (Pvt) Ltd; broadcasts in Karachi, Lahore, Islamabad and Faisalabad; Chief Operating Officer NERMEEN CHINOY.

FM-100: Karachi; tel. (21) 32630611; fax (21) 32629311; music station; broadcasts in Karachi, Lahore and Islamabad.

Television

Aaj TV: 531 Recorder House, Business Recorder Rd, Karachi 74550; fax (21) 32237067; e-mail aajcomments@aaj.tv; internet www.aaj.tv; privately owned by Business Recorder Group; digital satellite channel broadcasting news, current affairs and entertainment programmes; also operates from Islamabad and Lahore; Dir MASOOM USMANI.

ARY One World: 6th Floor, Madina City Mall, Abdullah Haroon Rd, Saddar, Karachi; tel. (21) 35212815; fax (21) 35655700; internet www.thearynews.com.

ATV Shalimar Television Network Channel (Shalimar Recording and Broadcasting Co Ltd): 36, H-9, POB 1246, Islamabad; tel. (51) 9257396; fax (51) 4434830; e-mail contact@srbc.com.pk; internet www.srbc.com.pk; f. 1976 as Shalimar Recording Co; 92.81% state-owned, 7.19% privately owned; 20 terrestrial stations throughout Pakistan; Man. Dir and CEO MUHAMMAD AZAM.

CNBC Pakistan: Techno City Corporate Tower, 17/F Altaf Hussain Rd, Karachi; tel. (21) 32270850; fax (21) 32270852; internet www.cnbcpakistan.com.

Geo TV: I. I. Chundrigar Rd, Jang Building, Karachi; tel. (21) 32628614; fax (21) 32636937; e-mail distribution@geo.tv; internet www.geo.tv; f. 2003; Pakistan's first private broadcasting network; broadcasts in Urdu; operates four channels; Pres. IMRAN ASLAM.

HUM TV: Plot 10/11, Hassan Ali St, Karachi; tel. (21) 35374258; fax (21) 32628840.

Indus TV Network: 2nd Floor, Shafi Court, Civil Lines, Mereweather Rd, Karachi; tel. (21) 35693801; fax (21) 35693813; internet www.indus.tv; f. 2000; Pakistan's first independent satellite channel; CEO GHAZANFAR ALI.

Pakistan Television Corpn Ltd: Federal TV Complex, Constitution Ave, POB 1221, Islamabad; tel. (51) 9208651; fax (51) 9211184; e-mail md@ptv.com.pk; internet ptv.com.pk; f. 1964; transmits 24 hrs daily; four channels; Chair. SYED ANWAR MEHMOOD; Man. Dir ARSHAD KHAN.

SAMAA TV: Techno City Corporate Tower, Karachi; tel. (21) 111222275; fax (21) 32270848; internet www.samaa.tv.

WAQT Television: NIPCO House, 4 Sharah Fatimah Jinnah, Lahore; tel. (42) 36367551; fax (42) 36367616.

Finance

(cap. = capital; auth. = authorized; p.u. = paid up; res = reserves; dep. = deposits; m. = million; brs = branches; amounts in rupees unless otherwise stated)

BANKING

Central Bank

State Bank of Pakistan: Central Directorate, I. I. Chundrigar Rd, POB 4456, Karachi 2; tel. (21) 99212400; fax (21) 99217234; e-mail info@sbp.org.pk; internet www.sbp.org.pk; f. 1948; bank of issue; controls and regulates currency and foreign exchange; cap. 1.0m., res 349.7m., dep. 512.7m. (June 2009); Gov. SHAHID H. KARDAR; 16 brs.

Commercial Banks

Allied Bank Ltd: Central Office, Main Clifton Rd, Bath Island, Karachi; tel. (21) 35370499; fax (21) 35370500; e-mail info@abl.com.pk; internet www.abl.com.pk; f. 1942 as Australasia Bank Ltd; name changed as above 2005; cap. 6,463.6m., res 7,355.3m., dep. 300,427.8m. (Dec. 2008); 49% state-owned; Pres. and Chief Exec.

PAKISTAN

Mohammad Aftab Manzoor; Chair. Mohammad Naeem Mukhtar; 741 brs in Pakistan.

Askari Bank Ltd: AWT Plaza, The Mall, POB 1084, Rawalpindi; tel. (51) 99063000; fax (51) 99272455; e-mail president@askaribank.com.pk; internet www.askaribank.com.pk; f. 1992; cap. 4,058.8m., res 8,603.6m., dep. 170,261.4m. (Dec. 2008); Chair. Lt-Gen. Zaved Zia; Pres. and Chief Exec. Muhammad Rafiquddin Mehkari; 121 brs.

Bank Al Habib Ltd: Mackinnons Bldg, I. I. Chundrigar Rd, Karachi; tel. (21) 32412421; fax (21) 32419752; e-mail info@bankalhabib.com; internet www.bankalhabib.com; f. 1991; cap. 4,785.4m, res 4,728.6m., dep. 144,389.6m. (Dec. 2008); Chief Exec. and Man. Dir Abbas D. Habib; 263 brs in Pakistan and abroad.

Bank Alfalah Ltd: BA Bldg, I. I. Chundrigar Rd, POB 6773, Karachi; tel. (21) 32416811; fax (21) 32424901; e-mail figroup@bankalfalah.com; internet www.bankalfalah.com; f. 1992 as Habib Credit and Exchange Ltd; name changed as above 1998; cap. 7,995.0m., res 5,602.3m., dep. 304,184.9m. (Dec. 2008); 60.65% owned by Abu Dhabi Consortium, 15.61% non-residents, 23.24% general public, employees and cos, 0.50% others; Chair. Sheikh Hamdan Bin Mubarak Al Nahayan; 231 brs.

The Bank of Khyber: 24 The Mall, Peshawar; tel. (521) 111-959-595; fax (915) 278146; e-mail bokforex@psh.paknet.com.pk; internet www.bok.com.pk; f. 1991; cap. 5,004.0m., res 1,133.0m., dep. 26,739.8m. (Dec. 2009); 51% state-owned; 49% public shareholders; the main branch in Peshawar began Islamic banking operations in June 2003; Man. Dir Bilal Mustafa; Chair. Ghulam Dastgir Akhtar; 34 brs.

The Bank of Punjab: BOP Tower, 10-B, Blk-E-II, Main Blvd, Gulberg-III, POB 2254, Lahore; tel. (42) 35783700; e-mail sajjad.hussain@bop.com.pk; internet www.bop.com.pk; f. 1989; cap. 5,287.9m., res 6,113.8m., dep. 165,292.3m. (Dec. 2008); 51% owned by provincial govt; Chair. Javed Mehmood; Pres. and CEO Naeemuddin Khan; 271 brs.

Faysal Bank Ltd: ST-02, Faysal House, 4th Floor, FIG, Main Shahrah-e-Faisal, Karachi; tel. (21) 32795306; fax (21) 32793131; e-mail fbl@faysalbank.com; internet www.faysalbank.com; f. 1995; merged with Al-Faysal Investment Bank Ltd 2002; took over Royal Bank of Scotland (RBS) Pakistan in Jan. 2011; cap. 5,296.4m., res 4,426.1m., dep. 104,313.3m. (Dec. 2008); Pres. and CEO Naved A. Khan; 107 brs.

Habib Bank Ltd: 22 Habib Bank Plaza, I. I. Chundrigar Rd, Karachi 75650; tel. (21) 32411530; fax (21) 32411556; e-mail zmahmood@hblpk.com; internet www.habibbankltd.com; f. 1941; cap. 7,590.0m., res 25,895.3m., dep. 606,918.6m. (Dec. 2009); transferred to private sector Feb. 2004; 51% owned by Agha Khan Fund for Economic Development (United Kingdom), 41% by State Bank of Pakistan and 8% by Government and National Bank of Pakistan; Pres. and CEO Zakir Mahmood; 1,437 brs in Pakistan; 39 foreign brs.

Habib Metropolitan Bank Ltd: Mezzanine Floor, Spencer's Bldg, I. I. Chundrigar Rd, POB 1289, Karachi; tel. (21) 32638080; fax (21) 32630404; e-mail info@hmb.com.pk; internet www.hmb.com.pk; f. 1992; fmrly Metropolitan Bank; merged with Habib Bank AG Zurich in 2006; cap. 7,527.5m., res 7,439.2m., dep. 145,568.8m. (Dec. 2009); Chair. Kassim Parekh; Pres. and CEO Anjum Zahoor Iqbal; 110 brs (incl. four Islamic banking brs).

JS Bank Ltd: 1st Floor, Shaheen Commercial Complex, Dr Ziauddin Ahmed Rd, Karachi 74200; tel. (21) 111-572-265; fax (21) 32631803; e-mail info@jsbl.com; internet www.jsbl.com; f. 2006; cap. 5,106.3m., res 59.5m., dep. 14,407.0m. (Dec. 2007); Pres. and CEO Naveed Qazi; Chair. Jahangir Siddiqui; 39 brs.

KASB Bank Ltd: Business and Finance Centre, I. I. Chundrigar Rd, Karachi 74000; tel. (21) 32446005; fax (21) 32446781; e-mail international@kasb.com; internet www.kasbbank.com; f. 1995 as Platinum Commercial Bank Ltd; name changed as above 2003; cap. 4,014.9m., res 6,159.4m., dep. 35,305.0m. (Dec. 2008); Pres. and CEO Muneer Kamal; 73 brs.

Khushhali Bank: 94 West, 4th Floor, Jinnah Ave, Blue Area, POB 3111, Islamabad; tel. (51) 111-092-092; fax (51) 9206080; internet www.khushhalibank.com.pk; cap. 1,705.0m., res 15,023.4m. (Dec. 2004); Pres. Ghalib Nishtar.

MCB Bank Ltd: MCB Tower, I. I. Chundrigar Rd, POB 4976, Karachi 74000; tel. (21) 32270075; fax (21) 32270076; e-mail atif.bajwa@mcb.com.pk; internet www.mcb.com.pk; f. 1947; cap. 6,282.8m., res 42,960.0m., dep. 340,825.6m. (Dec. 2008); Chair. Mian Muhammad Mansha; Pres. and CEO Atif Aslam Bajwa; 1,057 brs in Pakistan, 4 brs abroad.

Mybank Ltd: 10th Floor, Business & Finance Centre, I. I. Chundrigar Rd, Karachi; tel. (21) 111-692-265; fax (21) 2471951; e-mail president@mybankltd.com; internet mybankltd.com; f. 1991; fmrly Bolan Bank Ltd; cap. 5,303.6m., res 1,193.6m., dep. 27,179.6m. (Dec. 2009); Chair. Iqbal Alimohamed; Pres. and CEO Muhammad Bilal Sheikh; 60 brs.

National Bank of Pakistan (NBP): NBP Bldg, I. I. Chundrigar Rd, POB 4937, Karachi 2; tel. (21) 99212100; fax (21) 99212774; e-mail nbp@nbp.com.pk; internet www.nbp.com.pk; f. 1949; cap. 10,763.7m., res 47,446.2m., dep. 737,085.9m. (Dec. 2009); 100% state-owned; Pres. Qamar Hussain; 1,491 brs in Pakistan and 22 brs abroad.

NIB Bank Ltd: Muhammadi House, I. I. Chundrigar Rd, Karachi; tel. (21) 32420333; fax (21) 32472258; e-mail info@nibpk.com; internet www.nibpk.com; f. 2003; PICIC Commercial Bank Ltd and Prime Commercial Bank Ltd merged into NIB in December 2007; cap. 28,437.3m., res 19,018.5m., dep. 106,018.3m. (Dec. 2008); Pres. and CEO Khawaja Iqbal Hassan; 240 brs (2008).

Samba Bank Ltd: 5th & 6th Floor, Sidco Avenue Centre, Maulana Deen Mohammad Wafai Rd, Karachi 74000; tel. (21) 111-999-333; internet www.cresbank.com; f. 2002 as Crescent Commercial Bank Ltd; cap. 8,769.5m., res 2,235.5m., dep. 12,598.8m. (Dec. 2009); Pres. and CEO Tawfiq A. Husain; Chair. Syed Sajjad Razvi; 18 brs.

Silkbank: Saudi Pak Bldg, I. I. Chundrigar Rd, Karachi; tel. (21) 32460466; fax (21) 32460464; fmrly Saudi Pak Commercial Bank Ltd, rebranded as above in 2009; cap. 9,003.2m., res 1,790.8m., dep. 49,610.0m. (Dec. 2009); Chair. Munnawar Hamid; Pres. and CEO Azmat Tarin; 38 brs.

Soneri Bank Ltd: 87 Shahrah-e-Quaid-e-Azam, POB 49, Lahore; tel. (42) 36368142; fax (42) 36368138; e-mail main.lahore@soneribank.com; internet www.soneribank.com; f. 1991; cap. 5,019.3m., res 2,625.6m., dep. 82,933.7m. (Dec. 2009); Chair. Alauddin Feerasta; Pres. and CEO Safar Ali K. Lakhani; 117 brs.

Standard Chartered Bank (Pakistan) Ltd: 3rd Floor, Main Br., POB 5556, I. I. Chundrigar Rd, Karachi; tel. (21) 32450288; fax (21) 32414914; e-mail badar.kazmi@pk.standardchartered.com; internet www.standardchartered.com/pk; f. 2006; cap. 38,715.9m., res 559.5m., dep. 178,848.2m. (Dec. 2008); Pres. and CEO Badar Kazmi; 144 brs.

Summit Bank Ltd: 6B, F-6, Supermarket, Islamabad; tel. (21) 111-124-725; fax (21) 2463566; e-mail syedadnanali@arifhabibbank.com; internet www.summitbank.com.pk; f. 2006 as Arif Habib Bank Ltd; name changed as above in August 2010; cap. 5,000.0m., res 1,314.8m., dep. 16,616.5m. (Dec. 2008); Pres. and Chief Exec. Husain Lawai; Chair. Nasser Abdullah Hussain Lootah; 80 brs and sub brs.

United Bank Ltd: State Life Bldg, No. 1, I. I. Chundrigar Rd, POB 4306, Karachi 74000; tel. (21) 32417021; fax (21) 32413492; e-mail president@ubl.com.pk; internet www.ubl.com.pk; f. 1959; cap. 11,128.9m., res 27,620.0m., dep. 497,183.4m. (Dec. 2009); privatized in 2002; Pres. and CEO Atif Bokhari; 1,172 brs in Pakistan and 16 brs abroad.

Leasing Banks (*Modarabas*)

The number of leasing banks (*modarabas*), which conform to the strictures placed upon the banking system by *Shari'a* (the Islamic legal code), rose from four in 1988 to about 45 in 2002. The following are among the most important *modarabas* in Pakistan.

Asian Leasing Corporation Ltd: 85-B Jail Rd, Gulberg, POB 3176, Lahore; tel. (42) 484417; fax (42) 484418.

Atlas Lease Ltd: Ground Floor, Federation House, Shahrah-e-Firdousi, Main Clifton, Karachi 75600; tel. (21) 35866817; fax (21) 35870543; e-mail all@atlasgrouppk.com; Chair. Yusuf H. Shirazi.

B. R. R. International Modaraba: 1500A Saima Trade Towers, I. I Chundrigar Rd, Karachi 74000; tel. (21) 32271874; fax (21) 32271912; e-mail brr@firstdawood.com; internet www.firstdawood.com/brr.

Dadabhoy Leasing Co Ltd: 5th Floor, Maqbool Commercial Complex, JCHS Block, Main Shahrah-e-Faisal, Karachi; tel. (21) 34548171; fax (21) 34547301; Man. (Finance) Mohammad Ayub.

English Leasing Ltd: D-16, Block 3, Clifton, Scheme 5, Karachi; tel. (21) 35810453; fax (21) 35375770; e-mail info@engl.com.pk; Chair. Asim Mahboob Sheikh.

First Habib Bank Modaraba: 18 Habib Bank Plaza, I. I. Chundrigar Rd, Karachi 75650; tel. (21) 32635949; fax (21) 32627373; e-mail fhm@habibmodaraba.com; internet www.habibmodaraba.com; f. 1991; wholly owned subsidiary of Habib Bank Ltd; Chair. Wazir Mumtaz Ahmed; CEO Muhammad Shoaib.

Orix Leasing Pakistan Ltd: Overseas Investors Chamber of Commerce Bldg, Talpur Rd, Karachi 74000; tel. (21) 32425896; fax (21) 32425897; e-mail olp@orixpakistan.com; internet www.orixpakistan.com; f. 1986; cap. US $10m. (June 2004); Chief Exec. Taiza Kiset.

Pakistan Industrial and Commercial Leasing Ltd: 504 Park Ave, 24-A, Blk 6, PECHS, Shahrah-e-Faisal, Karachi 75210; tel. (21) 324551045; fax (21) 32452065; e-mail picl@super.net.pk; internet www.piclltd.com; f. 1987; Exec. Chair. Zaheerul Haque.

Standard Chartered Modaraba: Standard Services of Pakistan (Pvt) Ltd, Standard Bank Bldg, I. I. Chundrigar Rd, POB 5556,

Karachi 74000; tel. (21) 32450378; fax (21) 38140801; e-mail contact@scmodaraba.com; internet www.scmodaraba.com; fmrly First Grindlays Modaraba; Man. Dir SYED ZAHIR MEHDI.

Islamic Banks

BankIslami Pakistan Ltd: 11th Floor, Executive Tower One, Dolmen City, Marine Dr., Blk 4, Clifton, Karachi; tel. (21) 35839906; fax (21) 35378373; e-mail info@bankislami.com.pk; internet www.bankislami.com.pk; CEO MAHBOOB AHMED.

Dawood Islamic Bank Ltd: Trade Centre, I. I. Chundrigar Rd, Karachi 74000; tel. (21) 32637174; fax (21) 32272466; e-mail info@dawoodislamic.com; internet www.dawoodislamic.com; cap. 5,010.5m., res 16.7m., dep. 7,937.4m. (Dec. 2009); Pres. and CEO PERVEZ SAID.

Dubai Islamic Bank Pakistan Ltd: Hassan Chambers, Plot DC-7, Blk 7, Clifton, Karachi; tel. (21) 35368556; fax (21) 35821071; e-mail saad.zaman@dib.ae; internet www.dibpak.com; CEO M. A. MANNAN.

Emirates Global Islamic Bank Ltd: Shopping Arcade, Karachi Sheraton Hotel and Towers, Club Rd, Karachi; tel. (21) 35633418; fax (21) 35633427; e-mail feedback@egibl.com; internet www.egibl.com; sponsored by Emirates Investment Group LLC, UAE, and Saudi Arabian investors; Pres. and CEO SYED TARIQ HUSSAIN.

Meezan Bank Ltd: 2nd & 3rd Floor, PNSC Bldg, Moulvi Tamizuddin Khan Rd, Karachi 74000; tel. (21) 35610582; fax (21) 35610375; e-mail info@meezanbank.com; internet www.meezanbank.com; f. 1997 as Al-Meezan Investment Bank; became commercial bank 2002 and name changed as above; cap. 4,926.0m., res 478.9m., dep. 75,299.4m. (Dec. 2008); Pres. and CEO IRFAN SIDDIQUI; Gen. Man. ARIFUL ISLAM; 37 brs.

Co-operative Banks

In 1976 all existing co-operative banks were dissolved and given the option of becoming a branch of the appropriate Provincial Co-operative Bank, or of reverting to the status of a credit society.

Federal Bank for Co-operatives: State Bank Bldg, G-5/2, POB 1218, Islamabad; tel. (51) 9204518; fax (51) 9204534; f. 1976; owned jtly by the fed. Govt, the prov. govts and the State Bank of Pakistan; provides credit facilities to each of six prov. co-operative banks and regulates their operations; they in turn provide credit facilities through co-operative socs; supervises policy of prov. co-operative banks and of multi-unit co-operative socs; assists fed. and prov. govts in formulating schemes for development and revitalization of co-operative movement; carries out research on rural credit, etc.; Man. Dir M. AFZAL HUSSAIN; four regional offices.

Investment Banks

Asset Investment Bank Ltd: Rm 1-B, 1st Floor, Ali Plaza, Khayaban-e-Quaid-e-Azam, Blue Area, Islamabad; tel. (51) 2270625; fax (51) 2272506; Chief Exec. SYED NAVEED ZAIDI.

Atlas Investment Bank Ltd: 3rd Floor, Federation House, Abdullah shah Ghazi Rd, Main Clifton, Karachi; tel. (21) 111-333-225; fax (21) 35870543; e-mail info@atlasbank.com.pk; internet www.atlasbank.com.pk; 15% owned by Bank of Tokyo-Mitsubishi UFJ Ltd; Chair. YUSUF H. SHIRAZI; CEO AZIZ RAJKOTWALA.

Escorts Investment Bank Ltd: Escorts House, 26 Davis Rd, Lahore; tel. (42) 36371931; fax (42) 36375950; e-mail mailmanager@escortsbank.net; internet escortsbank.net; Pres. and CEO RASHID MANSUR.

IGI Investment Bank Ltd: 7th Floor, The Forum, Suite 701–703, 4-20, Blk 9, Khayaban-e-Jami, Clifton, Karachi; tel. (21) 111-234-234; fax (21) 111-567-567; e-mail contact.center@igi.com.pk; internet www.igiinvestmentbank.com.pk; Man. Dir and CEO SYED BABAR ALI.

Orix Investment Bank Pakistan Ltd: 2nd Floor, Islamic Chamber of Commerce Bldg, St 2/A, Block 9, Clifton, Karachi 75600; tel. (21) 35861266; fax (21) 35868862; e-mail oibpl@orixbank.com; internet www.orixbank.com; f. 1995; Man. Dir and CEO NAIM FAROOQUI.

Development Finance Organizations

Bankers' Skill Development Centre: Hamilton Court, 1st Floor, Suite 206/A, G-1, Main Clifton Rd, Block 7, Karachi 75600; tel. (21) 35306244; fax (21) 35306245; Pres. and CEO Dr AHSAN H. KHAN.

First MicroFinanceBank Ltd: President's Secretariat, 62-C, 25th Commercial St, Tauheed Commercial Area, DHA Phase V, Karachi; tel. (21) 35822432; fax (21) 35822434; e-mail information@mfb.com.pk; internet www.mfb.com.pk; Pres. and CEO HUSSAIN TEJANY.

First Women Bank Ltd: S.T.S.M. Foundation Bldg, CL-10/20/2 Beaumont Rd, Civil Lines, Karachi 75530; tel. (21) 111-676-767; fax (21) 35657756; e-mail info@fwbl.com.pk; internet www.fwbl.com.pk; f. 1989; cap. and res 590m., dep. 8,690m. (Dec. 2004); Pres. SHAFQAT SULTANA; 38 brs.

House Building Finance Corpn: Finance and Trade Centre, 3rd Floor, Shahrah-e-Faisal, Karachi 74400; tel. (21) 99202301; fax (21) 99202360; e-mail info@hbfc.com.pk; internet www.hbfc.com.pk; provides loans for the construction and purchase of housing units; Man. Dir and CEO AZHAR A. JAFFRI.

Industrial Development Bank of Pakistan: State Life Bldg No. 2, Wallace Rd, off I. I. Chundrigar Rd, POB 5082, Karachi 74000; tel. (21) 99213601; fax (21) 99213644; e-mail idbp@idbp.com.pk; internet www.idbp.com.pk; f. 1961; provides credit facilities for small and medium-sized industrial enterprises in the private sector; 100% state-owned; Chair. and Man. Dir JAMAL NASIM; 19 brs.

Investment Corpn of Pakistan: NBP Bldg, 5th Floor, I. I. Chundrigar Rd, POB 5410, Karachi 74400; tel. (21) 99212360; fax (21) 99212388; e-mail icp@paknet3.ptc.pk; f. 1966 by the Govt to encourage and broaden the base of investments and to develop the capital market; Man. Dir ISTIQBAL MEHDI; 10 brs.

Khushhali Bank: 94W, 4th Floor, Jinnah Ave, Blue Area, Islamabad 44000; tel. (51) 111-092-092; fax (51) 9245120; internet www.khushhalibank.com.pk; f. 2000 by the Govt under the Asian Development Bank's micro-finance sector development programme; provides micro-loans to the poor and finances reforms in the micro-finance sector; cap. 1,705m. (Aug. 2000); Pres. GHALIB NISHTAR.

National Investment Trust Ltd: NBP Bldg, 6th Floor, I. I. Chundrigar Rd, POB 5671, Karachi; tel. (21) 32419061; fax (21) 32430623; e-mail info@nit.com.pk; internet www.nit.com.pk; f. 1962; an open-ended mutual fund, mobilizes domestic savings to meet the requirements of growing economic development and enables investors to share in the industrial and economic prosperity of the country; 67,000 unit holders (1999/2000); Man. Dir TARIQ IQBAL KHAN.

Network Microfinance Bank Ltd: 202 Azayam Plaza, opp. FTC Bldg, SMCHS, Shahrah-e-Faisal, Karachi; fax (21) 34311722; e-mail info@networkmicrobank.com; internet www.networkmicrobank.com; Pres. and CEO M. MOAZZAM KHAN.

Pak Oman Microfinance Bank Ltd: 2nd Floor, Tower C, Finance and Trade Centre, Shahrah-e-Faisal, Karachi; tel. (21) 35630941; fax (21) 35630999; e-mail info@pomicro.com; internet www.pomicro.com; f. 2005; Pres. and CEO MUNAWAR SULEMAN.

Pakistan Industrial Credit and Investment Corpn Ltd (PICIC): State Life Bldg No. 1, I. I. Chundrigar Rd, POB 5080, Karachi 74000; tel. (21) 32414220; fax (21) 32419100; f. 1957 as an industrial development bank to provide financial assistance in both local and foreign currencies, for the establishment of new industries in the private sector and balancing modernization, replacement and expansion of existing industries; merchant banking and foreign exchange activities; total assets 33,949m., cap. 2,736m., res 4,188m. (June 2005); held 97.9% and 2.1% by local and foreign investors respectively; Man. Dir MOHAMMAD ALI KHOJA; Chair. ALTAF M. SALEEM; 19 brs.

Pakistan Kuwait Investment Co (Pvt) Ltd: Tower 'C', 4th Floor, Finance and Trade Centre, Shahrah-e-Faisal, POB 901, Karachi 74400; tel. (21) 35630901; fax (21) 35630939; e-mail info@pkic.com; internet www.pkic.com; jt venture between the Govt and Kuwait to promote investment in industrial and agro-based enterprises; Man. Dir SHAMSUL HASAN.

Pak-Libya Holding Co (Pvt) Ltd: Finance and Trade Centre, 5th Floor, Tower 'C', Shahrah-e-Faisal, POB 10425, Karachi 74400; tel. (21) 111-111-115; fax (21) 35630665; e-mail info@paklibya.com.pk; internet www.paklibya.com.pk; jt venture between the Govts of Pakistan and Libya to promote industrial investment in Pakistan; Chair. RAMADAN A. HAGGIAGI; Man. Dir KAMAL UDDIN KHAN.

Saudi Pak Industrial and Agricultural Investment Co (Pvt) Ltd: Saudi Pak Tower, 61-A Jinnah Ave, Islamabad; tel. (51) 111-222-003; fax (51) 111-222-004; e-mail saudipak@saudipak.com; internet www.saudipak.com; f. 1981 jtly by Saudi Arabia and Pakistan to finance industrial and agro-based projects and undertake investment-related activities in Pakistan; cap. 2,000m., res 732m., dep. 5,900m. (March 2001); CEO MUHAMMAD RASHID ZAHIR; Chair. ABDULLAH T. AL-THENAYAN; 1 br.

SME Bank Ltd: Jang Plaza, 2nd Floor, 40 Fazal-ul-Haq Rd, Blue Area, POB 1587, Islamabad; tel. (51) 9217000; fax (51) 9217001; e-mail info@smebank.org; internet www.smebank.org; formed through merger of Regional Development Finance Corpn (RDFC) and Small Business Finance Corpn (SBFC); provides loans for small businesses; Pres. and CEO R. A. CHUGHTAI.

Zarai Taraqiati Bank Ltd (ZTBL): 1 Faisal Ave, POB 1400, Islamabad; tel. (51) 9252805; fax (51) 9252737; e-mail contactus@ztbl.com.pk; internet www.ztbl.com.pk; f. 1961; provides credit facilities to agriculturists (particularly small-scale farmers) and cottage industrialists in the rural areas and for allied projects; 100% state-owned; Pres. MUHAMMAD ZAKA ASHRAF; 24 zonal offices and 342 brs.

PAKISTAN

Banking Associations

Investment Banks Association of Pakistan: 7th Floor, Shaheen Commercial Complex, Dr Ziauddin Ahmed Rd, POB 1345, Karachi; tel. (21) 32631396; fax (21) 32630678; internet www.ibap.biz; Chair. RASHID MANSUR.

Modaraba Association of Pakistan: 6th Floor, Progressive Centre, 30A, Blk 6, PECHS, Shahrah-e-Faisal, Karachi; tel. (21) 34322439; fax (21) 34322440; internet www.modarabas.com.pk; Chair. MUHAMMAD SHOAIB.

Pakistan Banks' Association: D-126, Blk 4, Clifton, Karachi 2; tel. (21) 35822986; fax (21) 35823418; e-mail pba@pakistanbanks.org; internet www.pakistanbanks.org; Chair. M. YOUNAS KHAN; Sec. A. GHAFFAR K. HAFIZ.

Banking Organizations

Banking Mohtasib Pakistan: Secretariat, 5th Floor, Shaheen Complex, POB 604, M. R. Kiyani Rd, Karachi; tel. (21) 99217334; fax (21) 99217375; e-mail info@bankingmohtasib.gov.pk; internet www.bankingmohtasib.gov.pk; resolves public grievances against banks and disputes between banking institutions; offices in Quetta, Lahore, Rawalpindi and Peshawar; Banking Ombudsman AZHAR HAMID.

Pakistan Banking Council: Habib Bank Plaza, I. I. Chundrigar Rd, Karachi; f. 1973; acts as a co-ordinating body between the nationalized banks and the Ministry of Finance; Chair. MUHAMMAD ZAKI; Sec. Mir WASIF ALI.

Pakistan Development Banking Institute: 4th Floor, Sidco Ave Centre, Stratchen Rd, Karachi; tel. (21) 35688049; fax (21) 35688460.

STOCK EXCHANGES

Securities and Exchange Commission of Pakistan: NIC Bldg, 63 Jinnah Ave, Blue Area, Islamabad 44000; tel. (51) 9218585; fax (51) 9204915; e-mail enquiries@secp.gov.pk; internet www.secp.gov.pk; oversees and co-ordinates operations of exchanges and registration of companies; registration offices in Faisalabad (356-A, 1st Floor, Al-Jamil Plaza, People's Colony, Small D Ground, Faisalabad; tel. (41) 713841), Karachi (No. 2, 4th Floor, State Life Building, North Wing, Karachi; tel. (21) 2415855), Lahore (3rd and 4th Floors, Associated House, 7 Egerton Rd, Lahore; tel. (42) 9202044), Multan (61 Abdali Rd, Multan; tel. (61) 542609), Peshawar (Hussain Commercial Bldg, 3 Arbab Rd, Peshawar), Quetta (382/3, IDBP House, Shahrah-e-Hall, Quetta; tel. (81) 844138) and Sukkur (B-30, Sindhi Muslim Housing Society, Airport Rd, Sukkur; tel. (71) 30517); Chair. RAZI-UR-RAHMAN KHAN.

Islamabad Stock Exchange (Guarantee) Ltd: 4th Floor, Stock Exchange Bldg, 101E Faz-ul-haq Rd, Blue Area, Islamabad; tel. (51) 2275045; fax (51) 2275044; e-mail ise@ise.com.pk; internet www.ise.com.pk; f. 1991; 103 mems; Chair. SHAHARYAR AHMAD; Sec. YOUSUF H. MAKHDOOMI.

Karachi Stock Exchange (Guarantee) Ltd: Stock Exchange Bldg, Stock Exchange Rd, Karachi 74000; tel. (21) 111-001-122; fax (21) 32410825; e-mail info@kse.com.pk; internet www.kse.com.pk; f. 1947; 200 mems, 654 listed cos (Jan. 2007); Chair. ZUBYR SOOMRO; Man. Dir ADNAN AFRIDI.

Lahore Stock Exchange (Guarantee) Ltd: Lahore Stock Exchange Bldg, 19 Khayaban-e-Aiwan-e-Iqbal, POB 1315, Lahore 54000; tel. (42) 36368000; fax (42) 36368484; e-mail secretary@lahorestock.com; internet www.lahorestock.com; f. 1970; 511 listed cos, 151 mems; Chair. ARIF SAEED; Man. Dir/CEO MIAN SHAKEEL ASLAM.

National Commodity Exchange Ltd: 9th Floor, PIC Towers, 32-A Lalazar Drive, M. T. Khan Rd, Karachi; tel. (21) 111-623-623; fax (21) 35611263; e-mail info@ncel.com.pk; internet www.ncel.com.pk; f. 2002; online commodity futures exchange; regulated by Securities and Exchange Commission of Pakistan; Chair. KAMRAN Y. MIRZA; Man. Dir ASSIM JANG.

Central Depository Co: CDC House, 99-B, Block B, S. M. C. H. Society, Main Shahrah-e-Faisal, Karachi 74400; tel. (21) 32416774; fax (21) 34326016; e-mail info@cdcpak.com; internet www.cdcpakistan.com; f. 1993 to manage and operate Central Depository System of the financial services industry; regulated by the Securities and Exchange Commission of Pakistan; CEO HANIF JAKHURA.

INSURANCE

Insurance Division: Securities and Exchange Commission, 4th Floor, NIC Bldg, Jinnah Ave, Islamabad; tel. (51) 9207091; fax (51) 9204915; e-mail enquiries@secp.gov.pk; internet www.secp.gov.pk; under the Ministry of Finance; Commissioner of Insurance TARIQ A. HUSSAIN; Exec. Dir S. GULREZ YAZDANI.

Life Insurance

American Life Insurance Co (Pakistan) Ltd: Dolmen City Mall, 13th Floor (Level 16), Blk 4, Scheme 5, Clifton, Karachi 75600; tel. (21) 111-111-711; fax (21) 35290042; e-mail alico@cyber.net.pk; internet www.alico.com.pk; Chair. and Chief Exec. ARIF SULTAN MUFTI.

Asia Care Health and Life Insurance Co Ltd: 15C and 17C, 2nd Floor, Zamzama 5th Commercial Lane, Karachi; tel. (21) 35302072; fax (21) 35302076; e-mail info@asiacare.net; Man. Dir MEHDI KAZMI.

EFU Life Assurance Ltd: 37-K, Blk 6, PECHS, Karachi; tel. (21) 111-338-111; fax (21) 34535079; e-mail info@efulife.com; internet www.efulife.com; f. 1932; Chair. SAIFUDDIN N. ZOOMKAWALA; Man. Dir and CEO TAHER G. SACHAK.

Postal Life Insurance Organization: 2nd and 3rd Floors, Karachi GPO Bldg, I. I. Chundrigar Rd, Karachi; tel. (21) 99211102; e-mail dg@pakpost.gov.pk; f. 1884; life and group insurance; Dir-Gen. ABDUL HAMEED.

State Life Insurance Corpn of Pakistan: State Life Bldg No. 9, Dr Ziauddin Ahmed Rd, POB 5725, Karachi 75530; tel. (21) 111-111-888; fax (21) 99202868; e-mail dhasp@statelife.com.pk; internet www.statelife.com.pk; f. 1972; life and group insurance and pension schemes; Chair. SHAHID AZIZ SIDDIQI.

General Insurance

ACE Insurance Ltd: 6th Floor, NIC Bldg, Abbasi Shaheed Rd, off Shahrah-e-Faisal, Karachi; tel. (21) 35681320; fax (21) 35683935; e-mail zehra.naqvi@acegroup.com; internet www.ace-ina.com; f. 1948; Chief Exec. ZEHRA NAQVI.

Adamjee Insurance Co Ltd: Adamjee House, 6th Floor, I. I. Chundrigar Rd, POB 4850, Karachi 74000; tel. (21) 32410145; fax (21) 32419162; e-mail info@adamjeeinsurance.com; internet www.adamjeeinsurance.com; f. 1960; Man. Dir MUHAMMAD ALI ZEB.

Agro General Insurance Co Ltd: 612 Qamar House, M. A. Jinnah Rd, Karachi 74000; tel. (21) 2313181; fax (21) 2313182; e-mail agiho@cyber.net.pk; f. 1987; Man. Dir and CEO M. JALILULLAH.

AIG Pakistan New Hampshire Insurance Co: 7th Floor, Dawood Centre, M. T. Khan Rd, Karachi 75530; tel. (21) 111-111-244; fax (21) 35634022; e-mail info-pakistan@aig.com; internet www.aigpakistan.com; f. 1869; Country Man. GOKTUG GUR.

Alfalah Insurance Co Ltd: 5 Saint Mary Park, Gulberg, Lahore; tel. (42) 111-786-234; fax (42) 35774329; e-mail afi@alfalahinsurance.com; internet www.alfalahinsurance.com; Chair. and Chief Exec. Sheikh HAMDAN BIN MUBARAK AL-NAHAYAN.

Alpha Insurance Co Ltd: State Life Bldg No. 1B–1C, 2nd Floor, off I. I. Chundrigar Rd, POB 4359, Karachi 74000; tel. (21) 32416041; fax (21) 32419968; internet www.alphainsurance.com.pk; f. 1952; Man. Dir NASIR JAVED KHAN; 9 brs.

Amicus Insurance Co Ltd: F-50, Blk 7, Feroze Nana Rd, Bath Island, POB 3971, Karachi; tel. (21) 35831082; fax (21) 35870220; f. 1991; Chair. M. IRSHAD UDDIN.

Asia Insurance Co Ltd: 18E III, Model Town, Lahore; tel. (42) 35858532; fax (42) 35865579; e-mail asiains@nexlinx.net.pk; f. 1979; Chief Exec. IHTESHAM-UL-HAQ QURESHI.

Askari General Insurance Co Ltd: 4th Floor, AWT Plaza, The Mall, POB 843, Rawalpindi; tel. (51) 9272425; fax (51) 927242; e-mail agicoho@agico.com.pk; internet www.agico.com.pk; f. 1995; Chair. NADEEM TAJ.

Atlas Insurance Ltd: 3 Bank Sq., Shahrah-e-Quaid-e-Azam, Lahore; tel. (42) 37320542; fax (42) 37234742; e-mail info@atlasinsurance.com; internet www.atlasinsurance.com.pk; f. 1935; Chair. YUSUF H. SHIRAZI; Chief Exec. ARSHAD P. RANA.

Beema Pakistan Co Ltd: 412–427 Muhammadi House, I. I. Chundrigar Rd, POB 5626, Karachi 74000; tel. (21) 32429530; fax (21) 32429534; e-mail info@beemapakistan.com; internet www.beemapakistan.com; f. 1960 as Khyber Insurance Ltd; renamed as above in 2000; Chair. MUHAMMAD SHAHNAWAZ AGHA.

Business and Industrial Insurance Co Ltd: 65 East Pak Pavilions, 1st Floor, Fazal-e-Haq Rd, Blue Area, Islamabad; tel. (51) 2278757; fax (51) 2271914; e-mail biic.ltd@yahoo.com; f. 1995; Chair. and Chief Exec. Mian MUMTAZ ABDULLAH.

Capital Insurance Co Ltd: Muradia Rd, Nr Lone House Model Town, Sialkot; tel. (52) 3563771; fax (52) 3552958; e-mail info@capital-insurance.net; internet www.capital-insurance.net; f. 1998; Chief Exec. NAVID IQBAL SHEIKH.

Central Insurance Co Ltd: Dawood Centre, 5th Floor, M. T. Khan Rd, POB 3988, Karachi 75530; tel. (21) 35686001; fax (21) 35680218; e-mail info.cic@dawoodgroup.com; internet www.ceninsure.com; f. 1960; owned by the Dawood Group; Chair. ISAR AHMAD; Chief Exec. A. SAMAD DAWOOD.

Century Insurance Co Ltd: 11th Floor, Lakson Square Bldg No. 3, Sarwar Sheheed Rd, POB 4895, Karachi 74200; tel. (21) 35698000;

fax (21) 35671665; e-mail info@cicl.com.pk; internet www.cicl.com.pk; f. 1988; Chair. and Chief Exec. IQBALALI LAKHANI; Man. Dir and CEO TINKU IRFAN JOHNSON.

CGU Inter Insurance PLC: 74/1-A, Lalazar, M. T. Khan Rd, POB 4895, Karachi 74000; tel. (21) 35611802; fax (21) 35611456; f. 1861; general and life insurance; Country Chief MOIN M. FUDDA; 3 brs.

Commerce Insurance Co Ltd: 11 Shahrah-e-Quaid-e-Azam, POB 1132, Lahore 54000; tel. (42) 37325330; fax (42) 37230828; f. 1992; Chief Exec. SYED MOIN-UD-DIN.

Co-operative Insurance Society of Pakistan Ltd: Co-operative Insurance Bldg, Shahrah-e-Quaid-e-Azam, POB 147, Lahore; tel. (42) 37352306; fax (42) 37352794; f. 1949; Chief Exec. and Gen. Man. MUZAFFAR SHAH.

Credit Insurance Co Ltd: Asmat Chambers, 68 Mazang Rd, Lahore; tel. (42) 36316774; fax (42) 36368868; f. 1995; Chief Exec. MUHAMMAD IKHLAQ BUTT.

Crescent Star Insurance Co Ltd: Nadir House, I. I. Chundrigar Rd, POB 4616, Karachi 74000; tel. (21) 32415471; fax (21) 32415474; internet www.cstar.com.pk; f. 1957; Man. Dir MUNIR I. MILLWALA.

Dadabhoy Insurance Co Ltd: Maqbool Commercial Complex, JCHS Block, Main Shahrah-e-Faisal, Karachi; tel. (21) 34545704; fax (21) 34548625; f. 1983; Chief Exec. USMAN DADABHOY.

Delta Insurance Co Ltd: 101 Baghpatee Bldg, Altaf Hussain Rd, New Challi, Karachi; tel. (21) 32632297; fax (21) 32422942; f. 1991; Man. Dir SYED ASIF ALI.

East West Insurance Co Ltd: 410, EFU House, M. A. Jinnah Rd, POB 6693, Karachi 74000; tel. (21) 32313304; fax (21) 32310851; e-mail info@eastwestlifeco.com; internet www.eastwestlifeco.com; f. 1983; Chair. MIAN MAHBOOB AHMAD.

EFU General Insurance Co Ltd: EFU House, M. A. Jinnah Rd, Karachi 74000; tel. (21) 32313471; fax (21) 32310450; e-mail info@efuinsurance.com; internet www.efuinsurance.com; f. 1932; Man. Dir and Chief Exec. SAIFUDDIN N. ZOOMKAWALA.

Excel Insurance Co Ltd: 38/C-1, Blk 6, PECH Society, Shahrah-e-Faisal, Karachi 75400; tel. (21) 111-777-666; fax (21) 34548076; e-mail eicl@cyber.net.pk; f. 1991; Man. Dir GHULAM H. ALI MOHAMMAD.

Gulf Insurance Co Ltd: Gulf House, 1-A Link McLeod Rd, Patiala Grounds, Lahore; tel. (42) 37312028; fax (42) 37234987; f. 1988; Chief Exec. S. ARIF SALAM.

Habib Insurance Co Ltd: Insurance House, 6 Habib Sq., M. A. Jinnah Rd, POB 5217, Karachi 74000; tel. (21) 32424038; fax (21) 32421600; e-mail info@habibinsurance.net; internet www.habibinsurance.net; f. 1942; Chair. RAFIQ A. HABIB; Man. Dir and Chief Exec. ALI RAZA D. HABIB.

IGI Insurance Ltd: 7th Floor, The Forum, Suite 701–713m G-20, Blk 9, Khayaban-e-Jami, Clifton, Karachi 75600; tel. (21) 35301726; fax (21) 35301729; e-mail skhalid@igi.com.pk; internet www.igiinsurance.com.pk; Chair. SYED BABAR ALI.

Ittefaq General Insurance Co Ltd: H-16 Murree Rd, Rawalpindi; tel. (51) 5771333; f. 1982; Chief Exec. and Man. Dir Dr SYED ISHTIAQ HUSSAIN SHAH.

National General Insurance Co Ltd: 401-B, Satellite Town, nr Commercial Market, Rawalpindi; tel. (51) 4411792; fax (51) 4427361; f. 1969; Gen. Man. F. A. JAFFERY.

National Insurance Corpn: NIC Bldg, Abbasi Shaheed Rd, Karachi 74400; tel. (21) 99202741; fax (21) 99202779; e-mail info@nicl.com.pk; internet www.nicl.com.pk; govt-owned; sole govt insurance co; Chair. and CEO MUHAMMAD AYYAZ NIAZI.

New Jubilee Insurance Co Ltd: 2nd Floor, Jubilee Insurance House, I. I. Chundrigar Rd, POB 4795, Karachi 74000; tel. (21) 32416022; fax (21) 32416728; e-mail nji@cyber.net.pk; internet www.nji.com.pk; f. 1953; Chair. TOWFIQ H. CHINOY.

North Star Insurance Co Ltd: 37–38 Basement, Sadiq Plaza, 69 The Mall, Lahore 54000; tel. (42) 36314308; fax (42) 36375366; e-mail northstarins@hotmail.com; f. 1995; Chief Exec./Man. Dir M. RAFIQ CHAUDHRY.

Orient Insurance Co Ltd: 2nd Floor, Dean Arcade, Blk No. 8, Kahkeshan, Clifton, Karachi; tel. (21) 35865327; fax (21) 35865724; f. 1987; Man. Dir FAZAL REHMAN.

Pak Equity Insurance Co Ltd: M. K. Arcade, 32 Davis Rd, Lahore; tel. (42) 36316536; fax (42) 36365959; f. 1984; Chief Exec. CH. ATHAR ZAHOOR.

Pakistan General Insurance Co Ltd: 3 Bank Sq., Shahrah-e-Quaid-e-Azam, POB 1364, Lahore; tel. (42) 37323569; fax (42) 37230634; f. 1948; Chair. CH. MANZOOR AHMAD; Pres. and CEO CH. ZAHOOR AHMAD.

Pakistan Guarantee Insurance Co Ltd: Al-Falah Court, 3rd and 5th Floors, I. I. Chundrigar Rd, POB 5436, Karachi 74000; tel. (21) 32636111; fax (21) 32638740; f. 1965; Chief Exec. SHAKIL RAZA SYED.

Pakistan Reinsurance Co Ltd: PRC Towers, 32 A Lalazar Dr., M. T. Khan Rd, POB 4777, Karachi 74000; tel. (21) 99202908; fax (21) 99202921; e-mail prcl@pakre.org.pk; internet www.pakre.org.pk; Chair. RUKHSANA SALEEM.

PICIC Insurance Ltd: 8th Floor, Shaheen Complex, M. R. Kiyani Rd, Karachi; tel. (21) 32219550; fax (21) 32219561; e-mail info@picicinsurance.com; internet www.picicinsurance.com; Man. Dir and CEO AHMED SALAHUDDIN.

Premier Insurance Ltd: 2-A State Life Bldg, 5th Floor, Wallace Rd, off I. I. Chundrigar Rd, POB 4140, Karachi 74000; tel. (21) 32416331; fax (21) 32416572; e-mail prinscop@super.net.pk; internet www.pil.com.pk; f. 1952; Chair. ZAHID BASHIR; CEO FAKHIR A. RAHMAN.

Prime Insurance Co Ltd: 505–507, Japan Plaza, M. A. Jinnah Rd, POB 1390, Karachi; tel. (21) 37770801; fax (21) 37725427; f. 1989; Chief Exec. ABDUL MAJEED.

Progressive Insurance Co Ltd: 2nd Floor, Sasi Arcade, Blk 7, Main Clifton Rd, Clifton, Karachi; tel. (21) 35823560; fax (21) 35823561; f. 1989; Man. Dir and CEO ABDUL MAJEED.

Raja Insurance Co Ltd: Panorama Centre, 5th Floor, 256 Fatimah Jinnah Rd, POB 10422, Karachi 4; tel. (21) 35670619; fax (21) 35681501; f. 1981; Chair. RAJA ABDUL RAHMAN; Man. Dir Sheikh HUMAYUN SAYEED.

Reliance Insurance Co Ltd: Reliance Insurance House, 181-A, Sindhi Muslim Co-operative Housing Society, POB 13356, Karachi 74400; tel. (21) 34539415; fax (21) 34539412; e-mail reli-ins@cyber.net.pk; internet www.relianceins.com; Chair. ISMAIL H. ZAKARIA.

Royal Exchange Assurance: P&O Plaza, I. I. Chundrigar Rd, POB 315, Karachi 74000; tel. (21) 32635141; fax (21) 32631369; Man. (Pakistan) Dr MUMTAZ A. HASHMI.

Saudi Pak Insurance Co Ltd: 2nd Floor, State Life Bldg, No. 2A, Wallace Rd, Karachi; tel. (21) 32418430; fax (21) 32417885; e-mail info@saudipakinsurance.com.pk; internet www.saudipakinsurance.com.pk; Man. Dir and CEO Capt. AZHAR EHTESHAM AHMED.

Seafield Insurance Co Ltd: 86-Q, Blk 2, Allama Iqbal Rd, PECHS, Karachi; tel. (21) 34527592; fax (21) 34527593; e-mail sifcpk89@hotmail.com; f. 1989; Man. Dir ADNAN HAFEEZ.

Security General Insurance Co Ltd: 18-C/E-1, SGI House, Gulberg III, Lahore; tel. (42) 35775024; fax (42) 35775030; e-mail sgi@sgicl.com; f. 1996; CEO NABIHA SAMAD.

Shaheen Insurance Co Ltd: 10th Floor, Shaheen Complex, M. R. Kayani Rd, Karachi 74200; tel. (21) 2630370; fax (21) 2626674; e-mail sihfc@cyber.net.pk; internet www.shaheeninsurance.com; f. 1996; Chief Exec. ASIF SULEMAN.

Silver Star Insurance Co Ltd: Silver Star House, 2nd Floor, 5 Bank Sq., POB 2533, Lahore 54000; tel. (42) 37324488; fax (42) 37229966; e-mail info@silverstarinsurance.com; internet www.silverstarinsurance.com; f. 1984; Man. Dir and Chief Exec. ZAHIR MUHAMMAD SADIQ; Chair. CHAUDHRY MUHAMMAD SADIQ.

TPL Direct Insurance Ltd: 172-B, 2nd Floor, Najeeb Centre, Blk 2, PECHS., Karachi; tel. (21) 34322555; fax (21) 34322515; e-mail insurance@trakkerdirect.com; internet tplinsurance.com; CEO SAAD NISSAR.

UBL Insurers Ltd: 8th Floor, State Life Bldg, No. 2, Wallace Rd, off I. I. Chundrigar Rd, Karachi; tel. (21) 111–845–111; fax (21) 2463117; e-mail khalid.hamid@ublinsurers.com; internet www.ublinsurers.com; CEO and Man. Dir KHALID HAMID.

Union Insurance Co of Pakistan Ltd: Adamjee House, 9th Floor, I. I. Chundrigar Rd, Karachi; tel. (21) 32416171; fax (21) 32420174; e-mail unionins@cyber.net.pk; Pres. NISHAT RAFFIQ.

United Insurance Co of Pakistan Ltd: Nizam Chambers, 5th Floor, Shahrah-e-Fatima Jinnah, POB 532, Lahore; tel. (42) 36361471; fax (42) 36375036; e-mail uicp@xcess.net.pk; internet www.theunitedinsurance.com; f. 1959; Chair. and CEO M. A. SHAHID.

Universal Insurance Co Ltd: Universal Insurance House, 63 Shahrah-e-Quaid-e-Azam, POB 539, Lahore; tel. (42) 37353458; fax (42) 37230326; e-mail tuic@nexlinx.net.pk; internet www.uic.com.pk; f. 1958; Chief Exec. Begum ZEB GAUHAR AYUB KHAN; Man. Dir SARDAR KHAN.

Insurance Associations

Insurance Association of Pakistan: 1713–1715, 17th Floor, Saima Trade Tower A, I. I. Chundrigar Rd, POB 4932, Karachi 74000; tel. (21) 32277165; fax (21) 32277170; e-mail iapho@cyber.net.pk; internet www.iap.net.pk; f. 1948; mems comprise 39 non-life insurance cos and 4 life insurance cos; establishes rules for insurance in the country; regional office in Lahore; Chair. HASANALI ABDULLAH; Sec. N. A. USMANI.

Pakistan Insurance Institute: 3030– B, Lalazar Drive, M. T. Khan Rd, Karachi; tel. 35611063; f. 1951 to encourage insurance education; Chair. FARZANA SIDDIQUE.

Trade and Industry

GOVERNMENT AGENCIES

Alternative Energy Development Board (AEDB): Ministry of Water and Power, 1, Nazmuddin Rd, F-10/4, Islamabad; tel. (51) 2215308; fax (51) 2215356; e-mail support@aedb.org; internet www.aedb.org; f. 2003; mandate incl. development of national plans and policies, undertaking promotion and dissemination of activities in field of renewable energy technologies, facilitation of power generation projects using alternative or renewable energy resources; CEO ARIF ALAUDDIN.

Board of Investment (BOI): Government of Pakistan, Ataturk Ave, Sector G-5/1, Islamabad; tel. (51) 9204339; fax (51) 9215554; e-mail secretary@pakboi.gov.pk; internet www.pakboi.gov.pk; operates under the presidency of the Prime Minister of Pakistan and chairmanship of the Minister of Privatisation; Chair. SALEEM H. MANDVI WALLA; Sec. TARIQ IQBAL PURI.

Central Board of Revenue: Constitution Ave, G-5, Islamabad; tel. (51) 9207545; fax (51) 9207540; e-mail helpline@cbr.gov.pk; internet www.cbr.gov.pk; tax authority; Chair. SOHAIL AHMED.

Competition Commission of Pakistan: 4-C, Diplomatic Enclave, G-5, Islamabad; tel. (51) 9247545; fax (51) 9247559; e-mail kmirza@cc.gov.pk; internet www.cc.gov.pk; Chair. KHALID A. MIRZA.

Corporate and Industrial Restructuring Corpn: 13-C-II, M. M. Alam Rd, Gulberg III, Lahore; tel. (42) 5871532; fax (42) 5761650; e-mail info@circ-gov.com.

Earthquake Reconstruction and Rehabilitation Authority (ERRA): Prime Minister's Secretariat (Public), Constitution Ave, Islamabad; tel. (51) 9201254; fax (51) 9209525; e-mail chairman@erra.gov.pk; internet www.erra.gov.pk; f. 2005; Chair. HAMID YAR HIRAJ.

Electronic Government Directorate: 10-D, 3rd Floor, Taimur Chambers, Blue Area West, Islamabad; tel. (51) 9205992; fax (51) 9205981; e-mail contact@e-government.gov.pk; internet www.pakistan.gov.pk/e-government-directorate; f. 2002; fmrly the Information Technology Commission; subsidiary department of the Ministry of Information Technology; Dir-Gen. of Projects SYED RAZA ABBAS SHAH.

Engineering Development Board: 5-A, Constitution Ave, SEDC Bldg (STP), Sector F-5/1, Islamabad 44000; tel. (51) 9205595; fax (51) 9203584; e-mail ceo@edb.gov.pk; internet www.engineeringpakistan.com; CEO ASAD ELAHI.

Environmental Protection Agency: 311 Margalla Rd, F-11/3, Islamabad 44000; tel. (51) 9267621; fax (51) 9267625; e-mail greenlib@isb.paknet.com.pk; internet www.environment.gov.pk; Dir-Gen. ASIF S. KHAN.

Export Processing Zones Authority (EPZA): Landhi Industrial Area Extension, Mehran Highway, Landhi, Karachi 75150; tel. (21) 111-777-222; fax (21) 35082009; e-mail info@epza.gov.pk; internet www.epza.gov.pk; Chair. AFTAB AHMED MEMON.

Family Planning Association of Pakistan (Rahnuma—FPAP): 3-A Temple Rd, Lahore 54000; tel. (42) 111-223-366; fax (42) 36368692; e-mail info@fpapak.org; internet www.fpapak.org; f. 1953; executes diversified community uplift programmes and activities; Pres. Begum SURAYYA JABEEN; CEO SYED KAMAL SHAH.

Geological Survey of Pakistan: Sariab Rd, POB 15, Quetta; tel. (81) 9211032; fax (81) 9211018; e-mail qta@gsp.gov.pk; internet www.gsp.gov.pk; Dir-Gen. MIRZA TALIB HASAN; Asst Dir MOHSIN ANWAR KAZIM.

Higher Education Commission: H-9, Islamabad; tel. (51) 9040305; fax (51) 9290120; e-mail info@hec.gov.pk; internet www.hec.gov.pk; Chair. JAVED LAGHARI.

Intellectual Property Organization of Pakistan (IPO-PAKISTAN): House 23, St 87, Ataturk Ave (West), G-6/3, Islamabad; tel. (51) 9208587; fax (51) 9208157; e-mail info@ipo.gov.pk; internet www.ipo.gov.pk; f. 2005; Chair. PERVAIZ KAUSAR.

National Accountability Bureau: Atatürk Ave, G-5/2, Islamabad; tel. (51) 111-622-622; fax (51) 9214502; e-mail infonab@nab.gov.pk; internet www.nab.gov.pk; Chair. DEEDAR HUSSAIN SHAH.

National Aliens Registration Authority (NARA): C-82, Block 2, Clifton, Karachi; tel. (21) 39251083; f. 2001; registers all foreign nationals who wish to work in Pakistan.

National Commission for Human Development: 14th Floor, Shaheed-e-Millat Secretariat, Jinnah Ave, Islamabad; tel. (51) 9216200; fax (51) 9216164; e-mail info@nchd.org.pk; internet www.nchd.org.pk; f. 2002.

National Database and Registration Authority (NADRA): State Bank of Pakistan Bldg, Shahrah-e-Jamhuriat, G-5/2, Islamabad; tel. (51) 9201120; e-mail info@nadra.gov.pk; internet www.nadra.gov.pk.

National Disaster Management Authority (NDMA): Prime Minister's Secretariat, Rm No 233–B, Islamabad; tel. (51) 9204429; fax (51) 9213082; e-mail an@ndma.gov.pk; internet www.ndma.gov.pk; Chair. (vacant).

National Economic Council: supreme economic body; the governors and chief ministers of the four provinces and fed. ministers in charge of economic ministries are its mems; sr fed. and provincial officials in the economic field are also associated; Chair. Prime Minister.

National Electric Power Regulatory Authority (NEPRA): (see Utilities).

National Energy Conservation Centre (ENERCON): ENERCON Bldg, G-5/2, Islamabad; tel. (51) 9206005; fax (51) 9206004; e-mail ferts@enercon.gov.pk; internet www.enercon.gov.pk; Man. Dir FARIDULLAH KHAN.

National Highway Authority (NHA): (see Transport: Roads).

National Housing Authority: Prime Minister's Office, Islamabad; tel. (51) 9202279; fax (51) 9217813; e-mail info@nhagov.pk; internet www.nhagov.pk; Dir-Gen. TALIT MIYAN.

National Tariff Commission: State Life Bldg, No. 5, Blue Area, Jinnah Ave, POB 1689, Islamabad 44000; tel. (51) 9202839; fax (51) 9221205; e-mail ntc@ntc.gov.pk; internet www.ntc.gov.pk; f. 1990; Chair. M. IKRAM ARIF.

National Testing Service (NTS): 402, St 34, I-8/2, Islamabad; tel. (51) 9258478; fax (51) 9258480; e-mail support@nts.org.pk; internet www.nts.org.pk; conducts assessment programs for students at all educational levels; facilitates employment and career development through subject testing.

Oil and Gas Regulatory Authority: Tariq Chambers, Civic Centre, G-6, Islamabad; tel. (51) 9204524; fax (51) 9204762; e-mail secretary@ogra.org.pk; internet www.ogra.org.pk; regulates oil and gas sector.

Pakistan Electronic Media Regulatory Authority: Islamabad; tel. (51) 9202174; fax (51) 9219634; e-mail info@pemra.gov.pk; internet www.pemra.gov.pk; f. 2002; Chair. IFTIKHAR RASHID; Dir-Gen. RANA ALTAF MAJID.

Pakistan National Accreditation Council (PNAC): Ministry of Science and Technology, 4th Floor, Evacuee Trust Complex, Aga Khan Rd, F-5/1, Islamabad; tel. (51) 9222310; fax (51) 9222312; e-mail info@pnac.org.pk; internet www.pnac.org.pk; f. 1998; Dir-Gen. ABDUL RASHID KHAN.

Pakistan Software Export Board (Guarantee) Ltd: 2nd Floor, Evacuee Trust Complex, F-5/1, Aga Khan Rd, Islamabad; tel. (51) 9204074; fax (51) 9204075; e-mail info@pseb.org.pk; internet www.pseb.org.pk; Man. Dir ZIA IMRAN.

Pakistan Standards and Quality Control Authority (PSQCA): Pakistan Secretariat, Block 77, Karachi 74400; tel. and fax (21) 99206290; fax (21) 99206263; e-mail psqcadg@super.net.pk; internet www.psqca.com.pk; f. 1996; regulates standards in industry; Dir-Gen. ABDUL GHAFFAR SOOMRO.

Pakistan Stone Development Co: I. C. C. I. Bldg, 2nd Floor, Mauve Area, G-8/A, Islamabad; tel. (51) 9263465; fax (51) 9263464; internet www.pasdec.org; f. 2006; promotes devt of marble and granite sector; Chair. IHSANULLAH KHAN.

Pakistan Telecommunication Authority: (see Telecommunications).

Pakistan Tobacco Board: 46-B Office Enclave, Phase-V, Hayatabad, POB 188, Peshawar; tel. (91) 9217156; fax (91) 9217149; e-mail mail@ptb.gov.pk; internet www.ptb.gov.pk; f. 1968; regulates, controls and promotes the export of tobacco and related products, and fixes grading standards; Chair. Maj. SAHIBZADA MUHAMMAD KHALID; Research and Devt Dir MOHAMMAD TARIQ.

Privatisation Commission: Experts Advisory Cell Bldg, 5A Constitution Ave, Islamabad 44000; tel. (51) 9205146; fax (51) 9203076; e-mail info@privatisation.gov.pk; internet www.privatisation.gov.pk; supervised by Ministry of Privatisation.

Sindh Board of Investment: 108F, Blk 2, PECHS, Karachi; tel. (21) 34300971; fax (21) 34300974.

Sindh Privatisation Commission: Sindh Secretariat, 4-A, Block 15, Court Rd, Karachi; tel. (21) 99202077; fax (21) 99202071; e-mail spcsecretary@yahoo.com; Sec. SYED ZULFIQAR ALI SHAH.

Sustainable Development Policy Institute (SDPI): 20 Hill Rd, F-6/3, Islamabad; tel. (51) 2278134; fax (51) 2278135; e-mail main@sdpi.org; internet www.sdpi.org; f. 1992; Chair. H. U. BEG.

Trade Development Authority of Pakistan (TDAP): Finance and Trade Centre, Block A, 5th Floor, POB 1293, Shahrah-e-Faisal, Karachi 75200; tel. (21) 1114441; fax (21) 99206487; e-mail tdap@tdap.gov.pk; internet www.tdap.gov.pk; f. 1963 as Export Promotion Bureau (EPB) affiliated to the Ministry of Commerce; Trade Development Authority was established in Nov. 2006 by an Ordinance of President Musharraf to assume all functions fmrly dispatched by the EPB; Chair. TARIQ IKRAM; Sec. ZAFAR MAHMOOD.

PAKISTAN

Trading Corporation of Pakistan: 4th and 5th Floors, Finance and Trade Centre, Main Shahrah-e-Faisal, Karachi 75530; tel. (21) 99202947; fax (21) 99202722; e-mail tcp@tcp.gov.pk; internet www.tcp.gov.pk; f. 1967; Chair. SAEED AHMED.

Utility Stores Corporation of Pakistan: Plot No. 2039, G-7/F-7, POB 1339, Jinnah Ave, Blue Area, Islamabad; tel. (51) 9245030; fax (51) 9210982; e-mail usc_ho@yahoo.com; internet www.usc.com.pk; f. 1971; Man. Dir MUHAMMAD ARIF KHAN.

DEVELOPMENT ORGANIZATIONS

Balochistan Development Authority: Civil Secretariat, Block 7, Quetta; tel. (81) 9202491; created for economic devt of Balochistan; exploration and exploitation of mineral resources; development of infrastructure, water resources, etc.

Capital Development Authority: G-7/4, Islamabad; tel. (51) 9252638; fax (51) 9252612; e-mail info@cda.gov.pk; internet www.cda.gov.pk; Chair. IMTIAZ ENAYAT ELAHI.

Center for International Private Enterprise (Pakistan) (CIPE): Glass Tower, Suite 214–15, 2 Ft 3, adjacent to PSO House, Main Clifton Rd, Karachi 75530; tel. (21) 35656993; e-mail pakistan@cipe.org; internet www.cipe.org; international org.; affiliate of US Chamber of Commerce and key member of National Endowment for Democracy; US Agency for International Development supports programs of CIPE; Country Dir M. MOIN FUDDA.

Council for Works and Housing Research (CWHR): F-40, SITE Area Hub River Rd, Karachi 75730; tel. (23) 32577236; fax (23) 32577235; e-mail cwhr@khi.comsats.net.pk; internet www.cwhr.gov.pk; f. 1964; Chair. NAJMUL HASAN TAQVI.

Faisalabad Industrial Estate Development & Management Co (FIEDMC): Faisalabad; tel. (41) 8523106; fax (41) 8522884; e-mail fiedmc@fiedmc.com.pk; internet www.fiedmc.com.pk; established by the Punjab state government under the Public Private Partnership system to promote devt of industrial estates; Chair. Mian MUHAMMAD LATIF; CEO KHURRAM IFTIKHAR.

Gwadar Development Authority: Governor House Rd, Gwadar; tel. and fax (86) 4211775; fax (86) 4211779; e-mail info@gda.gov.pk; internet www.gda.gov.pk; f. 2003; Dir-Gen. GHULAM MUHIUDDIN MARRI.

Infrastructure Project Development Facility (IPDF): House No. 2, St 59, F-7/4, Islamabad; tel. (51) 2656252; fax (51) 2656251; e-mail adil.anwar@ipdf.gov.pk; internet ipdf.gov.pk; devt of public infrastructure projects.

Lahore Development Authority (LDA): LDA Plaza, 9th Floor, Egerton Rd, Lahore; tel. (42) 99201510; internet www.lda.gop.pk; f. 1975; Dir of Admin. ABDUL HAMEED CHAUDHRY.

Lasbella Industrial Estate Development Authority (LIEDA): Hub Industrial Trading Estate, Lasbella, Balochistan; tel. (853) 303361; fax (853) 302470; e-mail lieda@lieda.gov.pk; est. under section 3 of Government of Balochistan Ordinance IX (1989); promotes devt of industrial concerns over 1,000 acre Coastal Highway region; Man. Dir MUHAMMAD ASLAM SHAKIR.

Malir Development Authority: Main Northern By-Pass, Scheme No. 45, Taisar Town, Karachi; Dir-Gen. AMEERZADA KOHATI; Chair. SYED MUSTAFA KAMAL.

National Commission for Human Development: Shaheed-e-Millat Secretariat, 14th Floor, Jinnah Ave, Islamabad; tel. (51) 9216200; fax (51) 9216164; e-mail info@nchd.org.pk; internet www.nchd.org.pk; f. 2001 by presidential decree; facilitates programmes towards achievement of the UNDP Millennium Development Goals; Chair. FARROKH K. CAPTAIN.

Pakistan Agricultural Resources Council: 20, Ataturk Ave, G-5/1, Islamabad; tel. (51) 8442280; fax (51) 9202968; agricultural research.

Pakistan Engineering Council: Ataturk Ave (East), G-5/2, Islamabad; tel. (51) 2829348; fax (51) 2276224; e-mail info@pec.org.pk; internet www.pec.org.pk; f. 1976; Chair. RUKHSANA ZUBERI.

Pakistan Gems & Jewellery Development Co (PGJDC): Regent Plaza Hotel and Convention Centre, M-3 Mezzanine Floor, Shahra-e-Faisal, Karachi; tel. (21) 35631394; fax (21) 35631398; e-mail info@pgjdc.org; internet www.pgjdc.org; f. 2006; supervised by the Ministry of Industries and Production; subsidiary of Pakistan Industrial Devt Corpn; promotes devt of Pakistan's gem and jewellery industry; CEO BASHIR AHMED ABBASI.

Pakistan Industrial Technical Assistance Centre (PITAC): 234 Maulana Jalaluddin Roomi Rd (old Ferozepur Rd), Lahore 54600; tel. (42) 99230699; fax (42) 99230589; e-mail info@pitac.gov.pk; internet www.pitac.gov.pk; f. 1962 by the Govt to provide prototype tooling facilities and spare parts to manufacturing industries and advanced training to industrial personnel in the fields of metal trades and tool engineering design and related fields; under Ministry of Industries and Production; provides human resource devt programmes; Chair. MANZAR SHAMIM; Gen. Man. Lt-Col (retd) KHAN M. NAZIR.

Pakistan Poverty Alleviation Fund: House No. 1, St 20, F-7/2, Islamabad; tel. (51) 111-000-102; fax (51) 2652246; e-mail info@ppaf.org.pk; internet www.ppaf.org.pk; f. 1997 by the Government; funded by the World Bank; works with non-governmental organizations and private-sector institutions to alleviate poverty; 68 partner orgs nationwide; Chief Exec. and Man. Dir KAMAL HAYAT.

Provincial Disaster Management Authority (Sindh): C-52, Blk 2, Clifton, Karachi; tel. (21) 99925158; fax (21) 35830087; e-mail info@pdma.gos.pk; crisis management, resource mobilization, planning; headed by the Chief Minister of Sindh.

Quetta Development Authority: Sarai Rd, Quetta; tel. (81) 9211069.

Sarhad Development Authority (SDA): PIA Bldg, Arbab Rd, POB 172, Peshawar; tel. (91) 9211608; fax (91) 9211605; e-mail sda.psh@ntc.net.pk; internet www.sda.org.pk; f. 1972; promotes industrial and commercial devt in the North-West Frontier Province; Chair. GHULAM DASTGIR AKHTAR.

Sindh Katchi Abadis Authority (SKAA): Maulana Din Muhammad Wafai Rd, Karachi 74200; tel. (21) 99211278; fax (21) 99211272; e-mail skaa@khi.compol.com; f. 1987; govt agency established to regulate and improve slums in Pakistan's southern province; Dir-Gen. MIR NASIR ABBAS.

Small and Medium Enterprises Development Authority (SMEDA): 6th Floor, LDA Plaza, Egerton Rd, Lahore; tel. (42) 111-111-456; fax (42) 36304926; e-mail helpdesk@smeda.org.pk; internet www.smeda.org.pk; f. 1998; four brs; 18 regional business centres; CEO SHAHAB KHAWAJA.

CHAMBERS OF COMMERCE

The Federation of Pakistan Chambers of Commerce and Industry: Federation House, Main Clifton, Sharea Firdousi, Karachi 75600; tel. (21) 35873691; fax (21) 35874332; e-mail info@fpcci.com.pk; internet www.fpcci.com.pk; f. 1950; 132 mem. bodies; Pres. HAJI GHULAM ALI; Sec.-Gen. SYED MASOOD ALAM RIZVI.

Islamic Chamber of Commerce and Industry: St 2/A, Block 9, KDA Scheme 5, Clifton, Karachi 75600; tel. (21) 35874756; fax (21) 35870765; e-mail icci@icci-oic.org; internet www.iccionline.net; f. 1979; Pres. Sheikh SALEH BIN ABDULLAH KAMEL; Sec.-Gen. Dr ALVI SHIHAB.

Overseas Investors' Chamber of Commerce and Industry: Chamber of Commerce Bldg, Talpur Rd, POB 4833, Karachi 74000; tel. (21) 32426076; fax (21) 32427315; e-mail info@oicci.org; internet www.oicci.org; f. 1860 as the Karachi Chamber of Commerce, name changed to above in 1968; 175 mem. bodies; Pres. FARRUKH H. KHAN; Sec.-Gen. UNJELA SIDDIQI.

Principal Affiliated Chambers

Attock Chamber of Commerce and Industry: Rehman Villas, Attock; tel. (57) 2611776; fax (57) 2610888; Pres. MIRZA ABDUL REHMAN.

Bahawalpur Chamber of Commerce and Industry: 43-A/1, Tipu Shaheed Rd, Model Town A, Bahawalpur; tel. and fax (62) 2883192; fax (62) 2889283; e-mail info@bahawalpurchamber.com; internet www.bahawalpurchamber.com; Pres. CHAUDHRY MAHMOOD MAJEED.

Chaman Chamber of Commerce and Industry: Commerce House, Trunch Rd, Chaman; tel. (826) 613308; fax (826) 615376; e-mail Cccichaman@Yahoo.Com; Pres. Haji HAMEEDULLAH KHAN.

Dadu Chamber of Commerce and Industry: C-15, Larkana Rd, Dadu; tel. (25) 4610093; fax (25) 4610092; e-mail daduchamber@hotmail.com; Pres. OSMAN DADABHOY.

Dera Ghazi Khan Chamber of Commerce and Industry: Block 34, Khakwani House, Dera Ghazi Khan, Punjab; tel. (64) 9260503; fax (64) 9260507; Pres. Dr MUHAMMAD HARIS.

Faisalabad Chamber of Commerce and Industry: East Canal Rd, Canal Park, Faisalabad; tel. (41) 9230265; fax (41) 9230270; e-mail info@fcci.com.pk; internet www.fcci.com.pk; Pres. Mian HAMID JAVED; Vice-Pres. MIAN ZAFAR IQBAL.

Gujranwala Chamber of Commerce and Industry: Aiwan-e-Tijarat Rd, Gujranwala; tel. (55) 3256701; fax (55) 3254440; e-mail info@gcci.org.pk; internet www.gcci.org.pk; f. 1978; Pres. CHADDA KHALID MEHMOOD; Sec. SYED ALI ASIM.

Gujrat Chamber of Commerce and Industry: G. T. Rd, Gujrat; tel. (53) 3523012; fax (53) 3523011; e-mail gujrat.chamber@yahoo.com; f. 1994; Pres. CH. ARFAN YOUSAF.

Haripur Chamber of Commerce and Industry: Chamber House, GPO Rd, Haripur; tel. (995) 613364; fax (995) 614664; e-mail haripur-chamber@yahoo.com; Pres. Haji FAKHAR-E-ALAM; Sec.-Gen. FAQIR MUHAMMAD KHAN.

PAKISTAN

Hyderabad Chamber of Commerce and Industry: Aiwan-e-Tijarat Rd, Saddar, POB 99, Hyderabad 71000; tel. (22) 2784972; fax (22) 2784977; e-mail hcci@muchomail.com; internet www.hcci.com.pk; f. 1961; Pres. GOHARULLAH; Sec.-Gen. Dr MOHAMAD ALI MIAN.

Islamabad Chamber of Commerce and Industry: Aiwan-e-Sana't-o-Tijarat Rd, Mauve Area, Sector G-8/1, Islamabad; tel. (51) 2250526; fax (51) 2252950; e-mail icci@brain.net.pk; internet www.icci.com.pk; f. 1984; Pres. MIAN SHAUKAT MASUD; Sec.-Gen. MAJID SHABBIR.

Jhang Chamber of Commerce and Industry: Aamir Colony, Yousaf Shah Rd, Jhang; tel. (47) 7611780; fax (47) 7612371; e-mail jcci@paknet4.ptc.pk; Pres. Haji ABAD HUSSAIN KHOKHAR.

Jhelum Chamber of Commerce and Industry: G. T. Rd, Jhelum; tel. (544) 646532; fax (544) 646229; e-mail jhelumcci@gmail.com; internet www.jlmcci.com; f. 1993; Pres. MALIK KHAWAR SHAHZAD; Sec.-Gen. NAZAR MUHAMMAD.

Karachi Chamber of Commerce and Industry: Aiwan-e-Tijarat Rd, off Shahrah-e-Liaquat, POB 4158, Karachi 74000; tel. (21) 99218001; fax (21) 99218010; e-mail info@karachichamber.com; internet www.karachichamber.com; f. 1959; 11,705 mems; Pres. ABDUL MAJID Haji MUHAMMAD; Sec. MAZAHIR RIZVI.

Khanewal Chamber of Commerce and Industry: Sadar Bazar, Jahanian, Khanewal; tel. (65) 563223; Pres. WAHEED SINDU.

Lahore Chamber of Commerce and Industry: 11 Shahrah-e-Aiwan-e-Tijarat, POB 597, Lahore; tel. (42) 36305538; fax (42) 36368854; e-mail sect@lcci.org.pk; internet www.lcci.org.pk; f. 1923; 8,000 mems; Pres. SHAHZAD ALI MALIK; Sec.-Gen. MUHAMMAD YASEEN.

Larkana Chamber of Commerce and Industry: 21–23 Kenedy Market, POB 78, Larkana, Sindh; tel. (741) 457136; fax (741) 440709; e-mail president@larkanachamber.com; Pres. MASOOD AHMED SHAIKH.

Lasbela Chamber of Commerce and Industry: LIEDA Office Bldg, Ground Floor, Hub District, Lasbela, Balochistan; tel. (853) 303410; fax (853) 302431; e-mail info@lasbelachamber.com; internet www.lasbelachamber.com; f. 1995; Pres. MUHAMMAD ASLAM.

Mardan Chamber of Commerce and Industry: Saleem Manzil, Muqam Mandi, Malakand Rd, Mardan; tel. (37) 9230215; fax (37) 9230214; e-mail mrd_chamber@yahoo.com; Pres. NASEEM UR REHMAN.

Multan Chamber of Commerce and Industry: Shahrah-e-Aiwan-e-Tijarat-o-Sanat, Multan; tel. (61) 4517087; fax (61) 4570463; e-mail mccimultan@hotmail.com; internet www.mcci.org.pk; Pres. SHAHID NASEEM KHOKHAR; Sec. KHURRAM JAVED.

Okara Chamber of Commerce and Industry: 9 M. A. Jinnah Rd, Okara; tel. (44) 2551901; fax (44) 2552005; internet www.occi.org.pk; Pres. CH. SHAFQAT RASOOL.

Quetta Chamber of Commerce and Industry: Zarghoon Rd, POB 117, Quetta 87300; tel. (81) 2821943; fax (81) 2821948; e-mail qcci@hotmail.com; Pres. GHULAM FAROOQ; Sec. MUHAMMAD AHMED.

Rawalpindi Chamber of Commerce and Industry: 39 Mayo Rd, Civil Lines, Rawalpindi; tel. (51) 5110514; fax (51) 5111055; e-mail rcci@isd.wol.net.pk; internet www.rcci.org.pk; f. 1952; Pres. KASHIF SHABBIR; Sec. MUHAMMAD IFTIKHAR-UD-DIN.

SAARC Chamber of Commerce and Industry: House No. 397, St No. 64, I-8/3, Islamabad; tel. (51) 4860611; fax (51) 8316024; e-mail info@saarcchamber.com; internet www.saarcchamber.com; f. 1993; Pres. ANNISUL HUQ.

Sahiwal Chamber of Commerce and Industry: Liaqat Rd, Sahiwal; tel. (40) 4221429; fax (4) 4221039; e-mail scciswl@brain.net.pk; Pres. CHAUDHRY SULTAN MAHMOOD.

Sargodha Chamber of Commerce and Industry: 80/2-A, Satellite Town, Sargodha 40100; tel. (48) 9230883; fax (48) 9230835; e-mail info@scci.pk; internet www.scci.pk; f. 1986; Pres. TARIQ YAQOOB MIAN; Sec.-Gen. KHALIQUE AHMAD KHAN.

Sarhad Chamber of Commerce and Industry: Sarhad Chamber House, Family Park, G. T. Rd, Peshawar; tel. (91) 9213314; fax (91) 9213316; e-mail sccip@brain.net.pk; internet www.scci.org.pk; f. 1958; 3,159 mems; Pres. SHARAFAT ALI MUBARAK; Sec. FAQIR MUHAMMAD.

Sheikhupura Chamber of Commerce and Industry: Chamber House, km 23 Lahore–Sheikhupura Rd, Qila Sattar Shah, Sheikhupura; tel. (42) 37971367; fax (42) 37970667; e-mail info@scci.net.pk; internet www.scci.net.pk; Pres. TARIQ IQBAL MUGHAL.

Sialkot Chamber of Commerce and Industry: Shahrah-e-Aiwan-e-Sanat-o-Tijarat, POB 1870, Sialkot 51310; tel. (52) 4261881; fax (52) 4268835; e-mail directorrnd@scci.com.pk; internet www.scci.com.pk; f. 1982; 7,500 mems; Pres. HASSAN ALI BHATTI; Sec. NAWAZ AHMED TOOR.

South Punjab Women's Chamber of Commerce and Industry: 116, Metro Plaza, Qasim Rd, Multan; tel. (61) 4002389; fax (61) 4027621; e-mail spwcci@hotmail.com; Pres. ANEELA IFTIKHAR.

Sukkur Chamber of Commerce and Industry: Sukkur Chamber House, 1st Floor, opp. Mehran View Plaza, Bunder Rd, Sukkur; tel. (71) 5623938; fax (71) 5623059; e-mail info@sukkurcci.org.pk; internet www.sukkurcci.org.pk; Pres. SHAKEEL AHMED MUKHTAR; Sec. MIRZA IQBAL BEG.

INDUSTRIAL AND TRADE ASSOCIATIONS

Air Cargo Agents' Association of Pakistan: Suite 305, 3rd Floor, Fortune Centre, 45-A, Block 6, PECHS, Shahrah-e-Faisal, Karachi 75400; tel. (21) 34383501; fax (21) 34383502; e-mail acaap@pk.netsolir.com; Chair. JAMSHED QURESHI.

All Pakistan Cement Manufacturers' Association: House 27-28/3A FCC, Gulberg-IV, Lahore; tel. (42) 5871632; fax (42) 5874442; e-mail apcma@apcma.com; internet apcma.com; Chair. Maj.-Gen. (retd.) REHMAT KHAN.

All Pakistan Cloth Merchants' Association: 4th Floor, Hasan Ali Centre, Hussaini Cloth Market, nr Mereweather Tower, M. A. Jinnah Rd, Karachi; tel. (21) 32444274; fax (21) 32401423; e-mail pcma@cyber.net.pk; f. 1947; Chair. AHMED CHINOY; Sec.-Gen. RAFIQ KHAN.

All Pakistan Cotton Powerlooms' Association: P-79/3, Montgomery Bazaar, Faisalabad; tel. (41) 2612929; fax (41) 2613636; Chair. KHALID MAHMOOD CHEEMA.

All Pakistan Furniture Exporters' Association: Karachi; tel. (21) 35861963; Chair. TURHAN BAIG MOHAMMAD.

All Pakistan Textile Mills' Association (APTMA): APTMA House, 44A Lalazar, off Moulvi Tamizuddin Khan Rd, POB 5446, Karachi 74000; tel. (21) 111-700-000; fax (21) 35611305; e-mail aptma@cyber.net.pk; internet www.aptma.org.pk; f. 1959; Chair. TARIQ MEHMOOD.

Association of Builders and Developers of Pakistan: ABAD House, St 1/D, Blk 16, Gulistan-e-Jauhar, Karachi 75290; tel. (21) 34613645; fax (21) 34613648; e-mail info@abad.com.pk; internet www.abad.com.pk; f. 1972; Chair. FAROOQ-UZ-ZAMAN KHAN.

Cigarette Manufacturers' Association of Pakistan: Caesars Towers (opp. Aisha Bawany Academy), Rm 102, 1st Floor, Main Shahrah-e-Faisal, Karachi 75400; tel. and fax (21) 32789555; e-mail cmaofpak@cyber.net.pk; Sec. TARIQ FAROOQ.

Cotton Board: Dr Abbasi Clinic Bldg, 76 Strachan Rd, Karachi 74200; fax (21) 35680422; f. 1950; Dep. Sec. Dr MUHAMMAD USMAN.

Federal 'B' Area Association of Trade and Industry: ST-7, Block 22, Federal 'B' Area, Karachi 75950; tel. (21) 36340362; fax (21) 36360203; e-mail info@fbati.com; internet www.fbati.com; Chair. M. IDREES GIGI.

Karachi Cotton Association: The Cotton Exchange, I. I. Chundrigar Rd, Karachi; e-mail kcapak@cyber.net.pk; internet www.kcapk.org; Chair. MOHAMMAD ATIF DADA; Sec. S. A. JAWED.

Korangi Association of Trade and Industry: ST-4/2, 1st Floor, Aiwan-e-Sanat, Sector 23, Korangi Industrial Area, Karachi 74900; tel. (21) 35061211; fax (21) 35061215; e-mail kati@kati.pk; internet www.kati.com.pk; Chair. SYED JOHAR QANDHARI; Sec.-Gen. NIHAL AKHTAR.

Management Association of Pakistan: 36-A/4, Lalazar, opp. Beach Luxury Hotel, Karachi 74000; tel. (21) 35610903; fax (21) 35611683; e-mail info@mappk.org; internet www.mappk.org; f. 1964; Pres. WAQAR A. MALIK.

Pakistan Advertising Association: Rm 318, 3rd Floor, Hotel Metropole, Club Rd, Karachi; tel. (21) 35671567; fax (21) 35671571; e-mail info@paa.com.pk; internet www.paa.com.pk; Chair. MANSOOR ALI ZAIDI; Sec. S. NAJMUL HASSAN.

Pakistan Agricultural Machinery and Implements Manufacturers' Association: Samundra Rd, Faisalabad; tel. (41) 714517; fax (41) 722721; e-mail iqra@fsd.comsats.net.pk.

Pakistan Arms and Ammunition Merchants' and Manufacturers' Association: Metropole Cinema Bldg, Rm 7, Abbot Rd, Lahore; tel. (42) 37239973; fax (42) 37230170; e-mail ssalimali@hotmail.com.

Pakistan Art Silk Fabrics and Garments Exporters' Association: 60, The Mall, Lahore; tel. (42) 36360919; fax (42) 36361291; e-mail pasfgea@hotmail.com; internet www.pasfgea.org; Chair. JAMIL MEHBOOB MAGOON; Sec.-Gen. IFTIKHAR AHMED KHAN.

Pakistan Association of Automotive Parts and Accessories Manufacturers: 501, 5th Floor, Mehdi Towers, SMCHS, Main Shahrah-e-Faisal, Karachi; tel. (21) 35412514; fax (42) 37237613; e-mail chairman@paapam.com; internet www.paapam.com; Chair. JAWAID SHAIKH.

Pakistan Association of Printing and Graphic Arts: 214, Mashriq Centre, 2nd Floor, Stadium Rd, Karachi; tel. (21) 34920175; fax (21) 34926625; e-mail info@papgai.com.pk; internet www.papgai.com.pk; f. 1959; affiliated with the federation of Pakistan Chambers of Commerce and Industry; promotion and

PAKISTAN

devt of the printing and graphic arts industry; Chair. MUHAMMAD SAEED PRESSWALA.

Pakistan Automotive Manufacturers' Association: 1st Floor, Block-C, Finance & Trade Centre, Shahrah-e-Faisal, Karachi; tel. (21) 35630992; fax (21) 35630995; e-mail pamaftc@cyber.net.pk; internet www.pama.org.pk; Chair. ALI S. HABIB.

Pakistan Bedwear Exporters' Association: 245-1-V, Block 6, PECHS, Karachi; tel. (21) 34541149; fax (21) 34541192; e-mail bedwear@fascom.com; Chair. SHABIR AHMED; Sec. S. IFTIKHAR HUSSAIN.

Pakistan Beverage Manufacturers' Association: C, 1st Floor, Kiran Centre, M-28, Model Town Extension, Lahore; tel. (42) 35167306; fax (42) 35167316.

Pakistan Broadcasters Association (PBA): 177/2, 1st Floor, I.E.P Bldg, Liaquat Barracks, Shahrah-e-Faisal, Karachi; tel. (21) 32793075; fax (21) 32793045; e-mail info@pba.org.pk; internet www.pba.org.pk; Exec. Dir MUHAMMAD ALI BUTT.

Pakistan Canvas and Tents Manufacturers' and Exporters' Association: 15/63, Shadman Commercial Market, Afridi Mansion, Lahore 3; tel. (42) 37577522; fax (42) 37578836; e-mail pctmea@wol.net.pk; internet www.pctmea.org; f. 1984; Chair. MUHAMMAD MAQSOOD SABIR ANSARI; Sec.-Gen. IJAZ HUSSAIN.

Pakistan Carpet Manufacturers' and Exporters' Association: 23–D, Block 6, PECHS, Shahrah-e-Faisal, Karachi; tel. (21) 34382728; fax (21) 34382739; e-mail pcmeaho@gerrys.net; Chair. ABDUL GHAFOOR SAJID.

Pakistan Chemicals and Dyes Merchants' Association: Chemicals and Dyes House, Rambharti St, Jodia Bazar, Karachi; tel. (21) 32432752; fax (21) 32430117; e-mail pcdma@super.net.pk; Chair. SHAUKAT RIAZ.

Pakistan Commercial Exporters of Towels Association: PCETA House, 7-H, Block 6, PECHS, Karachi; tel. (21) 34535757; fax (21) 34522372; e-mail pceta@cyber.net.pk; Chair. ALI ASHRAF KHAN.

Pakistan Cotton Fashion Apparel Manufacturers' and Exporters' Association: 5 & 6, Amber Court, 2nd Floor, Shahrah-e-Faisal, Shaheed-e-Millat Rd, Karachi 75350; tel. (21) 34522936; fax (21) 34546711; e-mail pcfa@cyber.net.pk; internet www.pcfa.pk; f. 1982; 650 mems; Chair. KHAWAJA M. USMAN.

Pakistan Cotton Ginners' Association: PCGA House, M.D.A. Rd, Multan; tel. (61) 4549815; fax (61) 4549817; e-mail pcga@pgca.org; internet www.pcga.org; Chair. MUHAMMAD AKRAM; Sec. AIJAZUDDIN GHAURI.

Pakistan Dairy Association: 11/19-B, Link Shami Rd, Lahore; tel. (42) 36680041; fax (42) 36682042; e-mail pakdairy@yahoo.com.

Pakistan Electronics Manufacturers' Association: 3rd Floor, Lakson Square Bldg 1, Sarwar Shaheed Rd, Karachi; tel. (21) 35658872; fax (21) 35620877; Chair. SARFRAZUDDIN.

Pakistan Engineering Council: Atatürk Ave (East), Sector G-5/2, Islamabad; tel. (51) 9206974; fax (51) 2276224; e-mail info@pec.org.pk; internet www.pec.org.pk; f. 1976; Chair. RUKSHANA ZUBERI.

Pakistan Film Producers' Association: Regal Cinema Bldg, Shahrah-e-Quaid-e-Azam, Lahore; tel. (42) 37322904; fax (42) 37241264; Chair. Mian AMJAD FARZEND; Sec. SAMI DEHLVI.

Pakistan Flour Mills' Association: 676, Shadman Colony-1, Lahore; tel. (42) 37596330; fax (42) 37573967; e-mail info@thepfma.com; internet www.thepfma.com; f. 1961; Chair. ASIM RAZA AHMAD.

Pakistan Footwear Manufacturers' Association: 6-F, Rehman Business Centre, 32-B-III, Gulberg III, Lahore 54660; tel. (42) 35750051; fax (42) 35780276; e-mail pfma@pakfootwear.org; internet www.pakfootwear.org; f. 1984; Chair. MUHAMMAD ALI; Sec.-Gen. Col (retd) ARSHAD AYYAZ.

Pakistan Glass Manufacturers' Association: 33A, St 13, F-7/2, Islamabad; tel. (51) 2825045; fax (51) 5857692.

Pakistan Gloves Manufacturers' and Exporters' Association: PGMEA Bldg, Kashmir Rd, POB 1330, Sialkot; tel. (52) 4272959; fax (52) 4274860; e-mail pgmea@brain.net.pk; internet www.brain.net.pk/~pgmea; f. 1978; Chair. MALIK NASEER AHMED.

Pakistan Hardware Merchants' Association: 47 Nishtar Rd, Lahore 54000; tel. (42) 37631182; e-mail phmasbcircle@hotmail.com; internet www.phma.info; f. 1961; more than 1,500 mems; Chair. BASIT ALAVI; Sec. SYED ZAFRUN NABI.

Pakistan Hosiery Manufacturers' Association: PHMA House, 37-H, Block 6, PECHS, Karachi; tel. (21) 34544765; fax (21) 34543774; e-mail info@phmaonline.com; internet www.phmaonline.com; f. 1960; Chair. SALEEM PAREKH.

Pakistan Iron and Steel Merchants' Association: Mustafa Cloth Market, M. A. Jinnah Rd, Karachi; tel. (21) 32464567; fax (21) 32464568; Chair. AKBAR ABDULLAH.

Pakistan Jute Mills' Association: PJMA House, 18 D-E, 2 Gulberg III, Lahore 546600; tel. (42) 35774400; fax (42) 35774402; e-mail secretary@pjma.com.pk; internet www.pjma.com.pk; Chair. MALIK MUHAMMAD ASIF.

Pakistan Knitwear and Sweaters Exporters' Association: Rms Nos 1014–1016, 10th Floor, Park Ave, Block 6, PECHS, Shahrah-e-Faisal, Karachi 95350; tel. (21) 34544035; fax (21) 34544039; Chair. RAFIQ H. GABOL.

Pakistan Leather Garments Manufacturers' and Exporters' Association: 60-C, Mezzanine Floor, 11th Commercial St, DHA Phase II (Extension), Karachi; tel. (21) 35387365; fax (21) 35388799; e-mail plgmea@cyber.net.pk; internet www.plgmea.com; f. 2001; Chair. FAWAD IJAZ KHAN.

Pakistan Paint Manufacturers' Association: St 6/A, Block 14, Federal 'B' Area, Karachi 38; tel. (21) 36321103; fax (21) 32560468; f. 1953; Chair. WASSIM A. KHAN; Sec. SYED AZHAR ALI.

Pakistan Petroleum Exploration and Production Companies' Association: 1 St 49, Sector F-6/4, Islamabad; tel. (51) 2823928; fax (51) 2276084; e-mail mail@ppepca.com; internet www.ppepca.com; f. 1995; Chair. JANOS FEHRER; Sec.-Gen. MAZHAR FAROOQ.

Pakistan Pharmaceutical Manufacturers' Association: 430–431, Hotel Metropole, Karachi; tel. (21) 35211773; fax (21) 35675608; e-mail ppma@cyber.net.pk; internet www.ppma.org.pk; Chair. RANA MOHAMMAD MUSHTAQ KHAN.

Pakistan Plastic Manufacturers' Association: 4th Floor, 410, St 6/A, Blk 14, Gulshan-e-Iqbal, Karachi; tel. (21) 34942336; fax (21) 34944222; e-mail pakppma@pk.netsolir.com; Chair. SHAKEEL AHMED.

Pakistan Polypropylene Woven Sacks Manufacturers' Association: Karachi; Chair. SHOUKAT AHMED.

Pakistan Poultry Association: 219 Mashriq Centre, Block 14, Sir Shah Muhammad Suleman Rd, Gulshan-e-Iqbal, Karachi; tel. (21) 34940362; fax (21) 34940364; e-mail ppasee@cyber.net.pk.

Pakistan Pulp, Paper and Board Mills' Association: 402 Burhani Chambers, Abdullah Haroon Rd, Karachi 74400; tel. (21) 37726150; Chair. KAMRAN KHAN.

Pakistan Readymade Garments Manufacturers' and Exporters' Association (PRGMEA): Shaheen View Bldg, Mezzanine Floor, Plot No. 18A, Block 6, PECH Society, Shahrah-e-Faisal, Karachi 75400; tel. (21) 34547912; fax (21) 34539669; e-mail info@prgmea.org; internet www.prgmea.org; f. 1981; Chair. IJAZ A. KHOKHAR.

Pakistan Seafood Industries' Association: A-2, Fish Harbour, West Wharf, Karachi; tel. (21) 32311117; fax (21) 32310939; e-mail psiapk@hotmail.com.

Pakistan Ship Breakers' Association: 608, S. S. Chamber, Siemens Chowrangi, S.I.T.E., Karachi; tel. (21) 3293958; fax (21) 3256533.

Pakistan Silk and Rayon Mills' Association: Rms Nos 44, 48 & 49, Textile Plaza, 5th Floor, M. A. Jinnah Rd, Karachi 2; tel. (21) 32410288; fax (21) 32415261; e-mail ctech@edu.pk; f. 1974; Chair. KHALID AMIN.

Pakistan Small Units Powerlooms' Association: 2nd Floor, Waqas Plaza, Aminpura Bazar, POB 8647, Faisalabad; tel. (411) 627992; fax (411) 633567.

Pakistan Soap Manufacturers' Association: 148 Sunny Plaza, Hasrat Mohani Rd, Karachi 74200; tel. (21) 32218937; fax (21) 32634648; e-mail pakistansma@yahoo.com; Chair. MUHAMMAD KALI ZIA.

Pakistan Software Houses Association (PASHA): 172/P Najeeb Corner, 4th Floor, Block 2, PECHS, Karachi; tel. (21) 35418121; fax (21) 34547759; e-mail karachi@pasha.org.pk; internet www.pasha.org.pk; f. 1992; Pres. JEHAN ARA.

Pakistan Sports Goods Manufacturers' and Exporters' Association: 298–99 Shah Faisal Rd, Model Town, Sialkot 51310; tel. (52) 3256930; fax (52) 3256920; e-mail psga@brain.net.pk; Chair. MOHAMMAD YOUNUS SONY.

Pakistan Steel Melters' Association: 30-S, Gulberg Centre, 84-D/1, Main Boulevard, Gulberg-III, Lahore; tel. (42) 35759284; fax (42) 35712028; e-mail steelmelters@angelfire.com; Chair. ILYAS AZIZ MALIK.

Pakistan Steel Re-rolling Mills' Association: Rashid Chambers, 6-Link McLeod Rd, Lahore 54000; tel. (42) 37227136; fax (42) 37231154; e-mail steel_re_rollers@hotmail.com; Chair. Mian TARIQ WAHEED.

Pakistan Sugar Mills' Association: 24D Rashid Plaza Mezzanine Floor, Jinnah Ave, Islamabad; tel. (51) 2270525; fax (51) 2274153; e-mail center@psmaonline.com; internet www.psmaonline.com; Chair. ISKANDAR M. KHAN; Sec.-Gen. K. ALI QAZILBASH.

PAKISTAN

Pakistan Tanners' Association: Plot No. 46-C, 21st Commercial St, Phase II Extension, Defence Housing Authority, Karachi 75500; tel. (21) 35880180; fax (21) 35880093; e-mail info@pakistantanners.org; internet www.pakistantanners.org; Chair. KHURSHID ALAM.

Pakistan Tea Association: Suite 307, Business Plaza, Mumtaz Hassan Rd, off I. I. Chundrigar Rd, Karachi; tel. (21) 32422161; fax (21) 32422209; e-mail pta@cyber.net.pk; Chair. HAMID SAEED KHAWAJA.

Pakistan Textile Exporters Association: 30/7, Civil Lines, Faisalabad; tel. (41) 644750; fax (41) 617985; e-mail info@ptea.org; internet www.ptea.org; Chair. KHURRAM MUKHTAR SADAQAT.

Pakistan Vanaspati Manufacturers' Association: 7, I-8/2, Main Service Rd, Islamabad; tel. (51) 2502004; fax (51) 4430125; Chair. ABDUL MAJID HAJI MOHAMMAD.

Pakistan Wool and Hair Merchants' Association: 27 Idris Chambers, Talpur Rd, Karachi; Pres. Mian MOHAMMAD SIDDIQ KHAN; Sec. KHALID LATEEF.

Pakistan Woollen Mills' Association: 25A, Davis Rd, Lahore 54000; tel. (42) 36307691; fax (42) 36306881; e-mail pwma@brain.net.pk; Chair. Mian MUZAFFAR ALI; Sec. MUHAMMAD RAHEEL CHOHAN.

Pakistan Yarn Merchants' Association: Rms Nos 802–803, Business Centre, 8th Floor, Dunolly Rd, Karachi 74000; tel. (21) 32410320; fax (21) 32424896; e-mail pakyarn@cyber.net.pk; internet www.pyma.com.pk; Chair. SAQIB NAEEM.

Rice Exports Association of Pakistan: 4th Floor, Sadiq Plaza, The Mall, Lahore; tel. and fax (42) 36280146; e-mail reap@cyber.net.pk; internet www.reap.com.pk; Chair. SHAHAD ALI MALIK.

Towel Manufacturers' Association of Pakistan: 77-A, Block A, Sindhi Muslim Co-operative Housing Society, Karachi 74400; tel. (21) 111-360-360; fax (21) 34551628; e-mail tma@towelassociation.com; internet www.towelassociation.com; Chair. WAQAR ALAM.

EMPLOYERS' ORGANIZATION

Employers' Federation of Pakistan: 2nd Floor, State Life Bldg No. 2, Wallace Rd, off I. I. Chundrigar Rd, POB 4338, Karachi 74000; tel. (21) 32411049; fax (21) 32439347; e-mail efpak@cyber.net.pk; internet www.efp.org.pk; f. 1950; Pres. ASHRAF WALI MOHAMMAD TABANI; Sec.-Gen. Prof. M. MATIN KHAN.

UTILITIES

Water and Power Development Authority (WAPDA): WAPDA House, Shahrah-e-Quaid-e-Azam, Lahore; tel. (42) 99202222; fax (42) 99202505; e-mail chairman@wapda.gov.pk; internet www.wapda.gov.pk; f. 1958 for devt of irrigation, water supply and drainage, building of replacement works under the World Bank-sponsored Indo-Pakistan Indus Basin Treaty; flood-control and watershed management; reclamation of waterlogged and saline lands; inland navigation; generation, transmission and distribution of hydroelectric and thermal power; partial transfer to private ownership carried out in 1996; Chair. SHAKIL DURRANI.

Electricity

National Electric Power Regulatory Authority (NEPRA): OPF Bldg, 2nd Floor, Shahrah-e-Jamhuriat, G-5/2, Islamabad 44000; tel. (51) 9207200; fax (51) 9210215; e-mail info@nepra.org.pk; internet www.nepra.org.pk; f. 1997; fixes the power tariff; Chair. Lt-Gen. (retd) SAEED UZ ZAFAR.

Hub Power Co Ltd (Hubco): Islamic Chamber Bldg, 3rd Floor, St 2/A, Block No. 9, Clifton, POB 13841, Karachi 75600; tel. (21) 35874677; fax (21) 35870397; e-mail info@hubpower.com; internet www.hubpower.com; f. 1991; supplies electricity; Chair. MOHAMMAD AHMED ZAINAL ALIREZA; Chief Exec. VINCE R. HARRIS.

Karachi Electric Supply Corpn Ltd (KESC): Aimai House, Abdullah Haroon Rd, POB 7197, Karachi; tel. (21) 35685492; fax (21) 35682408; internet www.kesc.com.pk; f. 1913; Chair. ABDUL AZIZ HAMEED AL-JOMAIH; CEO TABISH GAUHAR.

Kohinoor Energy Ltd: Near Tablighi Ijtima, PO Kohinoor Energy, Raiwind Bypass, Lahore; tel. (42) 35392317; fax (42) 35393415; e-mail info@kel.com.pk; internet www.kel.com.pk; f. 1994; jt venture of Saigols Group of Cos and Toyota Tsusho Corpn; Chair. M. NASEEM SAIGOL; CEO MUNEKI UDAKA.

Kot Addu Power Co (KAPCO): 404 Siddiq Trade Centre, 72-Main Blvd, Gulberg, Lahore; tel. (42) 35781631; fax (42) 35781636; e-mail info@kapco.com.pk; internet www.kapco.com.pk; f. 1996; 46% owned by Pakistan Water and Power Development Authority; Chair. SHAKIL DURRANI.

National Power Construction Corpn (Pvt) Ltd: 9 Shadman II, Lahore 54000; tel. (42) 37566019; fax (42) 37566022; e-mail npcc@wol.net.pk; internet www.npcc.com.pk; f. 1974; execution of power projects on turnkey basis, e.g. extra high voltage transmission lines, distribution networks, substations, power generation plants, industrial electrification, external lighting of housing complexes, etc.; Chair. MUHAMMAD ISMAIL QURESHI; Man. Dir MUHAMMAD AJAZ MALIK; project office in Jeddah (Saudi Arabia).

Pakistan Atomic Energy Commission (PAEC): POB 1114, Islamabad; tel. (51) 9206384; fax (51) 9204908; e-mail feedback@paec.gov.pk; internet www.paec.gov.pk; operates Karachi Nuclear Power Plant—KANUPP (POB 3183, nr Paradise Point, Hawksbay Rd, Karachi 75400; tel. (21) 9202222; fax (21) 7737488; e-mail knpc@khi.comsats.net.pk) and Chashma Nuclear Power Plant (CHASNUPP) at Chashma District, Mianwali (tel. (459) 9224430; fax (0459) 241505; email chasnupp1@ntc.net.pk); a second nuclear power station at Chashma opened in 2011; responsible for harnessing nuclear energy for devt of nuclear technology as part of the nuclear power programme; establishing research centres, incl. Pakistan Institute of Nuclear Science and Technology (PINSTECH); promoting peaceful use of atomic energy in agriculture, medicine, industry and hydrology; searching for indigenous nuclear mineral deposits; Chair. ANSAR PARVEZ; Dir-Gen. (KANUPP) JAWED IQBAL; Dir-Gen. (CHASNUPP) SAFDER HABIB.

Pakistan Electric Power Co: WAPDA House, Lahore; tel. (42) 99203846; fax (42) 99202402; e-mail info@pepco.gov.pk; internet www.pepco.gov.pk; f. 1998; Man. Dir FAZL AHMED KHAN.

Pakistan Nuclear Regulatory Authority (PNRA): POB 1912, Islamabad 44000; tel. (51) 9263017; fax (51) 9263007; e-mail officialmail@pnra.org; internet www.pnra.org; f. 2001 by presidential ordinance; Chair. JAMSHED AZIM HASHMI.

Private Power and Infrastructure Board (PPIB): 50 Nazimuddin Rd, F-7/4, Islamabad; tel. (51) 9205421; fax (51) 9217735; e-mail ppib@ppib.gov.pk; internet www.ppib.gov.pk; f. 1994; facilitates participation of private sector in national power generation; Man. Dir MOHAMMAD YOUSUF MEMON.

Quetta Electric Supply Co Ltd (QESCO): Zarghoon Rd, Quetta Cantt, Balochistan; tel. (81) 9202211; fax (81) 836554; e-mail qesco@qta.infolink.net.pk; internet www.qesco.com.pk; f. 1998; CEO MUHAMMAD KHATTAK.

Gas

Hydrocarbon Development Institute of Pakistan: Plot 18, Street 6, H-9/1, POB 1308, Islamabad; tel. (51) 9258301; fax (51) 9258310; e-mail info@hdip.com.pk; internet www.hdip.com.pk; f. 1975; re-established Jan. 2006 under Ministry of Petroleum and Natural Resources; national petroleum research and devt org.; provides consultancy and laboratory services to petroleum industry; Chair. ASIM HUSSAIN; Dir-Gen. and Chief Exec. HILAL A. RAZA.

Mari Gas Co Ltd (MGCL): 21 Mauve Area, 3rd Rd, Sector G-10/4, POB 1614, Islamabad; tel. (51) 111-410-410; fax (51) 2297686; e-mail info@marigas.com.pk; internet www.marigas.com.pk; 20% govt-owned; Chair. Lt-Gen. (retd) SYED ARIF HASSAN; Resident Gen. Man. Col (retd) AMJAD JAVED.

Oil and Gas Development Co Ltd (OGDCL): OGDC House, Blue Area, Islamabad; tel. (51) 9209882; fax (51) 9209859; f. 1961; became a publicly limited co in 1997; 85% govt-owned; plans, promotes, organizes and implements programmes for the exploration and devt of petroleum and gas resources, and the production, refining and sale of petroleum and gas; transfer to private ownership pending; Man. Dir and CEO MUHAMMAD NAEEM MALIK; 11,624 employees (Aug. 2005).

Oil and Gas Regulatory Authority: Tariq Chambers, Main Civic Centre, Islamabad; tel. (51) 9204524; fax (51) 9204762; e-mail registrar@ogra.org.pk; internet www.ogra.org.pk; f. 2002; Chair. TAUQIR SADIQ; Vice-Chair. RASHID FAROOQ.

Pakistan Petroleum Ltd (PPL): PIDC House, 4th Floor, Dr Ziauddin Ahmed Rd, POB 3942, Karachi 75530, Sindh; tel. (21) 111-568-568; fax (21) 35680005; e-mail info@ppl.com.pk; internet www.ppl.com.pk; 78.4% govt-owned, 15.5% owned by private Pakistani shareholders and 6.1% owned by International Finance Corpn; Pakistan's largest producer of natural gas; cap. and res Rs 18,393m., sales Rs 10,732m. (July–Dec. 2004); Chief Exec./Man. Dir KHALID RAHMAN; 2,520 employees (2006).

Petroleum Institute of Pakistan (PIP): Federation House, 1st Floor, St 28, Block V, Kehkashan, Clifton, Karachi 75600; tel. (21) 35378701; fax (21) 35378704; e-mail info@pip.org.pk; internet www.pip.org.pk; f. 1963; represents all sectors of the petroleum industry (incl. exploration, production, refining, marketing and natural gas); promotes and co-ordinates industry activities; mem. of the International Gas Union and World Petroleum Council; 25 Industrial Collective mems, over 860 individual industry mems; Chair. TARIQ KHAMISANI.

Sui Northern Gas Pipelines Ltd: Gas House, 21 Kashmir Rd, Lahore; tel. (42) 99201451; fax (42) 99201302; e-mail info@sngpl.com.pk; internet www.sngpl.com.pk; f. 1964; 36% state-owned; transmission and distribution of natural gas in northern Pakistan; sales

PAKISTAN

Rs 107,897.3m. (2005/06); Chair. MIAN MISBAH UR-RAHMAN; Man. Dir ABDUL RASHID LONE.

Sui Southern Gas Co Ltd: 4B Sir Shah Suleman Rd, Block 14, Gulshan-e-Iqbal, Karachi 75000; tel. (21) 99231602; fax (21) 99231604; e-mail info@ssgc.com.pk; internet www.ssgc.com.pk; f. 1988; 70% state-owned; Chair. SALIM ABBAS JILANI; Man. Dir Dr FAIZULLAH ABBASI.

Water

Faisalabad Development Authority (Water and Sanitation Agency) (FDA): Jail Rd, POB 229, Faisalabad; tel. (41) 9210053; fax (41) 9210054; e-mail wasa_fsd@yahoo.com; internet www.wasa.fda.gov.pk; f. 1978; Man. Dir Dr IJAZ AHMAD RANDHAWA.

Karachi Water and Sewerage Board: 9th Mile, Karsaz, Shahrah-e-Faisal, Karachi; tel. (21) 99231882; fax (21) 99231814; e-mail mdkwsb@yahoo.co.uk; internet www.kwsb.gos.pk; f. 1983; Man. Dir FAZAL-UR-REHMAN.

Lahore Development Authority (Water and Sanitation Agency): 4-A Gulberg V, Jail Rd, Lahore; tel. (42) 35752483; fax (42) 35752960; internet www.lda.gop.pk; f. 1967; Dir-Gen. RAJA MUHAMMAD ABBAS.

TRADE UNIONS

National Trade Union Federation Pakistan: Bharocha Bldg, 2-B/6, Commercial Area, Nazimabad No. 2, Karachi 74600; tel. (21) 3628339; fax (21) 36622529; e-mail ntuf@super.net.pk; f. 1999; 50 affiliated unions; covers following fields: steel, agriculture, textiles, garments, leather, automobiles, pharmaceuticals, chemicals, transport, printing, food, shipbuilding, engineering and power; Pres. MUHAMMAD RAFIQUE; Gen. Sec. SALEEM RAZA.

Pakistan Workers Federation (PWF): Bakhtiar Labour Hall, 28 Nisbet Rd, Lahore; tel. (42) 37229192; fax (42) 37239529; e-mail cpr@pwf.org.pk; internet www.pwf.org.pk; f. 2005 following the merger of the All Pakistan Federation of Trade Unions, Pakistan National Federation of Trade Unions and All Pakistan Federation of Labour; affiliated with the International Confederation of Free Trade Unions; 10 regional offices; Pres. CH. TALIB NAWAZ; Chair. MUHAMMAD AHMED; Gen. Sec. KHURSHID AHMED.

The principal affiliated federations are:

Muttahida Labour Federation: 24, Circular Bldg, Risala Rd, Hyderabad; c. 120,000 mems; Pres. KHAMASH GUL KHATTAK; Sec.-Gen. NABI AHMED.

National Labour Federation (NLF): 28, Circular Rd, Hyderabad; Pres. RANA MAHMOOD ALI KHAN.

Pakistan Central Federation of Trade Unions: 220 Al-Noor Chambers, M. A. Jinnah Rd, Karachi; tel. (21) 728891.

Pakistan Railway Employees' Union (PREM): City Railway Station, Karachi; tel. (21) 32415721; Divisional Sec. BASHIRUDDIN SIDDIQUI.

Pakistan Trade Union Federation: Khamosh Colony, Karachi; Pres. KANIZ FATIMA; Gen. Sec. SALEEM RAZA.

Pakistan Transport Workers' Federation: 110 McLeod Rd, Lahore; 17 unions; 92,512 mems; Pres. MEHBOOB-UL-HAQ; Gen. Sec. CH. UMAR DIN.

Other affiliated federations include: Pakistan Bank Employees' Federation, Pakistan Insurance Employees' Federation, Automobile, Engineering and Metal Workers' Federation, Pakistan Teachers Organizations' Council, Sarhad WAPDA Employees' Federation, and Balochistan Ittehad Trade Union Federation.

Transport

RAILWAYS

Pakistan Railways: Empress Rd, Lahore; tel. (42) 99201700; fax (42) 99201669; e-mail gmopr@pr.gov.pk; internet www.pakrail.com; state-owned; 11,515 km of track and 7,791 route km; seven divisions (Karachi, Lahore, Multan, Quetta, Rawalpindi, Peshawar and Sukkur); Chair. MOHAMMAD KASHIF MURTAZA; Man. Dir JAVEED IQBAL.

ROADS

The total length of roads in June 2006 was 260,420 km, 65.36% of which were paved, including 11,488 km of highways and motorways.

National Highways Authority: 27 Mauve Area, G-9/1, Islamabad; tel. (51)111-000–642; e-mail info@nha.gov.pk; internet www.nha.gov.pk; f. 1991; responsible for planning, maintenance and devt of nat. highways and strategic roads; Chair. ALTAF AHMED CHOWDHRY; Dir-Gen. ATHAR HUSSAIN KHAN.

SHIPPING

The chief port is Karachi. A second port, Port Qasim, started partial operation in 1980 and another port, Port Pasni, which is situated on the Balochistan coast, was completed in 1988. A fourth port, Port Gwadar, has been developed as a deep-water seaport; the port opened in 2007.

Mercantile Marine Dept: 70/4, Timber Pond, N. M. Reclamation, Keamari, Karachi 74000; tel. (21) 99263014; fax (21) 99263018; e-mail info@mercantilemarine.gov.pk; internet www.mercantilemarine.gov.pk; f. 1930; ensures safety of life and property at sea and prevention of marine pollution through implementation of nat. legislation and international conventions; Prin. Officer TARIQ SARDAR.

Ports and Shipping Division: Ministry of Ports and Shipping; see Ministries; Sec. MUHAMMAD SALEEM KHAN.

Al-Hamd International Container Terminal (Pvt) Ltd: Plot No. 28, O & L Trans Lyari Quarters, Hawkesbay Rd, New Truck Stand, Karachi; tel. (21) 32352660; fax (21) 32351556; e-mail sshipping@cyber.net.pk; internet www.aictpakistan.com; CEO HUSSAIN ISLAM; Gen. Man. Col (retd) SHAHZADA FARRUKH ZAMAN.

Engro Vopak Terminal Ltd: 1st Floor, Bahrai Complex 1, 24 M. T. Khan Rd, POB 5736, Karachi 74000; tel. (21) 37301213; e-mail saqadri@engro.com; internet www.vopak.com; Man. SYED ATIQUDDIN QADRI.

Gwadar Port Authority: GPA Complex, Fish Harbour Rd, Gwadar 92100; tel. (864) 210073; fax (864) 210075; e-mail gwadarport@hotmail.com.

Karachi International Container Terminal (KICT): Administration Bldg, Berths 28–30, Dockyard Rd, West Wharf, Karachi 74000; tel. (21) 35273599; fax (21) 32313816; e-mail info@kictl.com; internet www.kictl.com; f. 1996; Chief Exec. ANJUM SAJID.

Karachi Port Trust (KPT): Eduljee Dinshaw Rd, Karachi 74000; tel. (21) 99214312; fax (21) 99214329; e-mail chairman@kpt.org.pk; internet www.kpt.gov.pk; Chair. NASREEN HAQUE; Gen. Operations Man. Rear-Adm. AGHA DANISH; Sec. KHALID MOBIN ARSHAD.

Karachi Shipyard and Engineering Works Ltd: POB 4419, West Wharf, Dockyard Rd, Karachi 74000; tel. (21) 99214045; fax (21) 99214020; e-mail contact@karachishipyard.com.pk; internet www.karachishipyard.com.pk; f. 1953; building and repairing ships; general engineering; Man. Dir Vice-Adm. IFTIKHAR AHMED RAO.

Korangi Fisheries Harbour Authority: Ghashma Goth, Landhi, POB 15804, Karachi 75160; tel. (21) 35013315; fax (21) 35015096; e-mail kfha@sat.net.pk.

Pakistan International Container Terminal Ltd: 2nd Floor, Business Plaza, Mumtaz Hussain Rd, Karachi 74000; tel. (21) 32855701; fax (21) 32855715; e-mail info@pict.com.pk; internet www.pictcntrtrack.com; Chair. Capt. HALEEM A. SIDDIQI; CEO Capt. ZAFAR IQBAL AWAN.

Pakistan National Shipping Corpn: PNSC Bldg, M. T. Khan Rd, POB 5350, Karachi 74000; tel. (21) 99203980; fax (21) 99203974; e-mail communication@pnsc.com.pk; internet www.pnsc.com.pk; f. 1979 by merger; state-owned; national flag carrier; undertakes global shipping operations; Chair. Vice Adm. AHMED SALEEM MENAI; Sec. ZAINAB SULEMAN.

Port Qasim Authority (PQA): Bin Qasim, Karachi 75020; tel. (21) 99272111; fax (21) 34730108; e-mail webmaster@portqasim.org.pk; internet www.portqasim.org.pk; f. 1973; Chair. Vice-Adm. MUHAMMAD SHAFI; Sec. ANWAR MEHTAB ZAIDI.

Qasim International Container Terminal: Berths 5–7, Marginal Wharfs, POB 6425, Port Mohammad Bin Qasim, Karachi 75020; tel. (21) 34739100; fax (21) 34730021; e-mail info@qict.net; internet www.dpworldkarachi.com; f. 1994; CEO CHANGEZ NIAZI.

Associations

All Pakistan Shipping Association: 01-E, 1st Floor, Sattar Chambers, West Wharf Rd, Karachi; tel. (21) 32200742; fax (21) 32200743; e-mail apsa-pak@cyber.net.pk; Chair. MUHAMMAD F. QAISER.

Pakistan Ship's Agents Association (PSAA): GSA House, Suite 1, 1st Floor, 19 Timber Pound, Keamari, Karachi 75620; tel. (21) 32850837; fax (21) 32850836; e-mail psaa@cyber.net.pk; internet www.psaa.org.pk; f. 1976; Chair. MOHAMMED A. RAJPAR.

Terminal Association of Pakistan: 8th Floor, Adamjee House, I. I. Chundrigar Rd, Karachi 74000; tel. (21) 32417131; fax (21) 32416477; e-mail terasspak@cyber.net.pk; Chair. MOHAMMED KASIM HASHIM; Sec. AKHTAR SULTAN.

CIVIL AVIATION

Islamabad, Karachi, Lahore, Rawalpindi, Peshawar and Quetta have international airports. In 2007 the first phase of construction for the development of a new international airport at Islamabad commenced following a series of postponements; the project was to

PAKISTAN

cost an estimated Rs 35,000m. and would handle 6.5m. passengers annually upon completion, which was scheduled for late 2011.

Civil Aviation Authority: Terminal 1 Bldg, Karachi Airport, Karachi; tel. (21) 99242070; fax (21) 99242071; e-mail chief.hr@caapakistan.com.pk; internet www.caapakistan.com.pk; controls all the civil airports; Chair. Lt. Gen. (retd) SYED ATHAR ALI; Sec. ASHRAF M. HAYAT.

Air Blue Ltd: 55B, Jinnah Ave, Islamabad; tel. (51) 111-247-258; e-mail writetous@airblue.com; internet www.airblue.com; f. 2004; Man. Dir SYED NASIR ALI.

Pakistan International Airlines Corpn (PIA): Jinnah International Airport, Karachi 75200; tel. (21) 111-786-786; fax (21) 34570419; e-mail info@piac.com.pk; internet www.piac.com.pk; f. 1955; merged with Orient Airways in 1955; 57.7% govt-owned; operates domestic services to 35 destinations and international services to 40 destinations in 31 countries; reduced number of weekly flights to Europe and the USA from 42 to 24 in March 2007 in response to proscriptive new European Union safety regulations; Chair. CHAUDHRY AHMED MUKHTAR; Man. Dir NADEEM KHAN YOUSUFZAI.

Shaheen Air International: Jinnah International Airport, Karachi 75200; tel. (21) 99242951; fax (21) 99242965; e-mail info@shaheenair.com; internet www.shaheenair.com; f. 1993; operates scheduled domestic services and international services to the Gulf region; Chair. and CEO KHALID M. SEHBAI.

Tourism

The Himalayan hill stations of Pakistan provide magnificent scenery, a fine climate and excellent opportunities for field sports, mountaineering, trekking and winter sports. The archaeological remains and historical buildings are also impressive.

In 2009 Pakistan received some 854,900 foreign visitors and receipts from tourism (excluding passenger transport) amounted to an estimated US $208m.

Pakistan Tourism Development Corpn (PTDC): Flashman's Hotel, The Mall, Rawalpindi; tel. (51) 9271592; fax (51) 9271591; e-mail info@tourism.gov.pk; internet www.tourism.gov.pk; f. 1970; chaired by the Minister for Tourism; Man. Dir SAREER MOHAMMAD KHAN.

Travel Agents' Association of Pakistan (TAAP): 115, Central Hotel Bldg, 1st Floor, Mereweather Rd, Karachi 75530; tel. (21) 35656022; fax (21) 35684469; e-mail taap.khi@gmail.com; internet www.taap.org.pk; f. 1974; Chair. YAYHA POLANI; Sec.-Gen. MOHAMMAD SALEEM.

Defence

As assessed at November 2010, the total strength of the armed forces was 617,000: army 550,000, navy 22,000, air force 45,000. There was also a paramilitary force of as many as 304,000 (including a National Guard of 185,000). Military service is voluntary.

Defence Expenditure: The projected defence budget for 2010/11 was Rs 442,200m. at the federal level.

Chairman of Joint Chiefs of Staff Cttee: Gen. KHALID SHAMIM WYNE.

Chief of Army Staff: Gen. ASHFAQ PERVEZ KAYANI.

Chief of Air Staff: Air Marshal RAO QAMAR SULEMAN.

Chief of Naval Staff: Adm. NOMAN BASHIR.

Education

Universal and free primary education is a constitutional right, but education is not compulsory. Primary education begins at five years of age and lasts for five years. Secondary education, beginning at the age of 10, is divided into two stages, of three and four years respectively. In 2009/10 there were an estimated 156,364 primary schools (including mosque schools), and total enrolment at those institutions amounted to 18,714,582. With the assistance of the World Bank, a Primary Education Project has been launched to increase educational facilities and improve the quality of instruction.

There were an estimated 41,456 middle schools and 24,822 secondary schools in 2009/10. Enrolment in that year was estimated at about 5.4m. in middle schools and 2.7m. in secondary schools. The secondary education sector includes secondary vocational institutes (an estimated 3,121 schools and 263,000 enrolled pupils in 2007/08).

In 2007/08 66% of children in the relevant age-group (72% of males; 60% of females) were enrolled at primary schools, while enrolment at secondary level in the same year included an estimated 33% of pupils of the relevant age (37% of males; 28% of females).

In 2009/10, according to estimates, there were 3,399 arts and science colleges and 1,275 professional colleges (including educational colleges); enrolment totalled 1,147,80 and 458,835, respectively. There were 132 universities (including degree-awarding institutes) and 948,364 enrolments in 2009/10. The Open University has been established with the technical support of the British Open University.

With the assistance of the Asian Development Bank, 11 polytechnic institutes and a national teacher-training college have been established by the federal Government. Training is provided for teachers at polytechnic, commercial and vocational institutes.

In 2008, according to UNESCO, the adult literacy rate in Pakistan was an estimated 53.7% (males 66.8%; females 40.0%).

RELATED TERRITORIES

The status of Jammu and Kashmir has remained unresolved since the 1949 cease-fire agreement, whereby the area was divided into sectors administered by India and Pakistan separately. Pakistan administers Azad (Free) Kashmir and Gilgit-Baltistan (the former Northern Areas) as *de facto* dependencies, being responsible for foreign affairs, defence, coinage, currency and the implementation of UN resolutions concerning Kashmir.

AZAD KASHMIR

Area: 11,639 sq km (4,494 sq miles).
Population: 1,980,000 (1981 census).
Administration: Government is based on the Azad Jammu and Kashmir Interim Constitution Act of 1974. There are seven administrative districts: Bagh, Bhimber, Kotli, Mirpur, Muzaffarabad, Poonch and Sudhnuti.
Legislative Assembly: consists of 48 members: 40 directly elected and eight indirectly elected, including five women.

Azad Jammu and Kashmir Council: consists of the President of Pakistan as Chairman, the President of Azad Kashmir as Vice-Chairman, five members nominated by the President of Pakistan, six members by the Legislative Assembly, and, *ex officio*, the Pakistan Minister of Kashmir Affairs and Gilgit-Baltistan.
President of Azad Kashmir: RAJA ZULQARNAIN KHAN.
Chief Minister of Azad Kashmir: SARDAR ATTIQUE AHMED KHAN.

GILGIT-BALTISTAN

Area: 72,971 sq km (28,174 sq miles).
Population: 870,347 (1998 census).
Administration: There are two divisions, Gilgit and Baltistan, which are, in turn, divided into seven districts: the Baltistan districts of Skardu and Ghanche, and the Gilgit districts of Gilgit, Ghizer, Diamer, Astore and Hunza-Nagar.
Legislative Assembly: consists of 33 members: 24 directly elected and nine indirectly elected (six women and three technocrats), headed by a Chief Minister.

Gilgit-Baltistan Council: consists of the Prime Minister of Pakistan as Chairman and the Governor of Gilgit-Baltistan as Vice-Chairman.
Governor of Gilgit-Baltistan: PIR KARAM ALI SHAH.
Chief Minister of Gilgit-Baltistan: SYED MEHDI SHAH.

PALAU

Introductory Survey

LOCATION, CLIMATE, LANGUAGE, RELIGION, FLAG, CAPITAL

The Republic of Palau (also known as Belau) consists of more than 200 islands, in a chain about 650 km (400 miles) long, lying about 7,150 km (4,450 miles) south-west of Hawaii and about 1,160 km (720 miles) south of Guam. With the Federated States of Micronesia (q.v.), Palau forms the archipelago of the Caroline Islands. Palau is subject to heavy rainfall, and seasonal variations in precipitation and temperature are generally small. Palauan and English are the official languages. The principal religion is Christianity, much of the population being Roman Catholic. The flag (proportions 3 by 5) features a large golden disc (representing the moon), placed off-centre, towards the hoist, on a light blue background. The capital is Ngerulmud, in the state of Melekeok, which is located on the island of Babeldaob.

CONTEMPORARY POLITICAL HISTORY

Historical Context

The Republic of Palau's independence, under the Compact of Free Association, in October 1994 marked the end of the Trust Territory of the Pacific Islands, of which Palau was the final component (for history up to 1965, see the chapter on the Marshall Islands). From 1965 there were increasing demands for local autonomy within the Trust Territory. In that year the Congress of Micronesia was formed, and in 1967 a commission was established to examine the future political status of the islands. In 1970 the commission declared Micronesians' rights to sovereignty over their own lands, self-determination, the right to their own constitution and to revoke any form of free association with the USA. In May 1977, after eight years of negotiations, US President Jimmy Carter announced that his Administration intended to adopt measures to terminate the trusteeship agreement by 1981. In the Palau District a referendum in July 1979 approved a proposed local Constitution, which came into effect on 1 January 1981, when the district became the Republic of Palau.

The USA signed the Compact of Free Association with the Republic of Palau in August 1982, and reached agreement with the Marshall Islands and the Federated States of Micronesia in October. The trusteeship of the islands was due to end after the principle and terms of the Compacts had been approved by the respective peoples and legislatures of the new countries, by the US Congress and by the UN Security Council. Under the Compacts, the four countries (including the Northern Mariana Islands) would be independent of each other and would manage both their internal and foreign affairs separately, while the USA would be responsible for defence and security. In addition, the USA was to allocate some US $3,000m. in aid to the islands.

Domestic Political Affairs

More than 60% of Palauans voted in February 1983 to support their Compact, but fewer than the required 75% approved changing the Constitution to allow the transit and storage of nuclear materials. A revised Compact, which contained no reference to nuclear issues, was approved by 66% of votes cast in a referendum in September 1984. However, the US Government had hoped for a favourable majority of 75% of the votes cast, which would have allowed the terms of the Compact to override the provisions of the Palau Constitution in the event of a conflict between the two.

In June 1985 President Haruo Remeliik of Palau was assassinated. Relatives of a rival candidate in the 1984 presidential election, Roman Tmetuchl, were convicted of the murder, but remained at liberty pending an appeal; this was upheld, on the grounds of unreliable evidence, by Palau's Supreme Court in August 1987. Lazarus Salii was elected President in September 1985.

In January 1986 representatives of the Palau and US administrations reached a preliminary agreement on a new Compact, whereby the USA consented to provide US $421m. in economic assistance to the islands. However, the proportion of votes in favour of the new Compact at a referendum in the following month was still less than that required for the constitutional ban on nuclear material to be waived. Both Salii and US President Ronald Reagan supported the terms of the Compact, arguing that a simple majority would suffice for its approval, as the USA had guaranteed that it would observe the constitutional ban on nuclear material.

In May 1986 the UN Trusteeship Council endorsed the US Administration's request for the termination of the existing trusteeship agreement with the islands. However, a writ was subsequently submitted to the Palau High Court, in which it was claimed that approval of the Compact with the USA was unconstitutional because it had failed to obtain the requisite 75% of votes. The High Court ruled in favour of the writ, but the Palau Government appealed against the ruling and in October the Compact was approved by the US Congress. At a new plebiscite in December, however, only 66% of Palauans voted in favour of the Compact; ratification of the Compact thus remained impossible. A fifth plebiscite on the proposed Compact, in June 1987, again failed to secure the 75% endorsement required by the Constitution. Under alleged physical intimidation by pro-nuclear supporters of the Compact, the House of Delegates (the lower house of the Palau National Congress) agreed to a further referendum in August. In this referendum an amendment to the Constitution was approved, ensuring that a simple majority would henceforth be sufficient to approve the Compact. This was duly achieved in a further referendum in the same month. When a writ was entered with the Supreme Court challenging the legality of the decision to allow approval of the Compact by a simple majority, a campaign of arson and bombing followed, and one person was murdered.

In February 1988 a team from the US General Accounting Office travelled to Palau to investigate allegations of corruption and intimidation on the part of the Palau Government. Approval of the Compact by the US Congress was to be delayed until the investigators had published their findings. However, in April a ruling by Palau's Supreme Court invalidated the procedure by which the Compact had finally been approved by a simple majority in the previous August. Three government employees, including Salii's personal assistant, were imprisoned in April, after being found guilty of firing on the home of Santos Olikong, Speaker of Palau's House of Delegates. The attack was widely considered to have been prompted by Olikong's public opposition to the Compact.

In August 1988 Salii, the principal subject of the bribery allegations, apparently committed suicide. At an election in November Ngiratkel Etpison was elected President, with just over 26% of the total votes. Although Etpison advocated the proposed Compact and was supported by the pro-Compact Ta Belau Party, his closest challenger, Tmetuchl, opposed it and was supported by the anti-nuclear Coalition for Open, Honest and Just Government, which had demanded that a special prosecutor from the USA be dispatched to Palau to investigate alleged corruption and violent attacks against opponents of the Compact. Only 60% of voters approved the proposed Compact at a seventh referendum in February 1990. In July the US Department of the Interior declared its intention to impose stricter controls on the administration of Palau, particularly in financial matters.

During 1991 the US authorities reopened investigations into the assassination of Remeliik in 1985. In March 1992 Palau's Minister of State, John Ngiraked, his wife, Emerita Kerradel, and Sulial Heinrick (already serving a prison sentence for another killing) were charged with Remeliik's murder. In March 1993 Ngiraked and Kerradel were found guilty of aiding and abetting the assassination of the President, while Heinrick was acquitted.

Legislative and presidential elections were held in November 1992. (The electoral system had been modified earlier in the year to include primary elections for the selection of two presidential candidates.) At the presidential election the incumbent Vice-President, Kuniwo Nakamura, narrowly defeated Johnson Toribiong to become President. A concurrent referendum endorsed a proposal that, in future polls, a simple majority be sufficient to approve the adoption of the Compact of Free Association. Some

62% of voters were in favour of the proposal, which was approved in 14 of Palau's 16 states. A further referendum on the proposed Compact took place in November 1993. Some 68.3% of participating voters approved the proposed Compact, giving the Government a mandate to proceed with its adoption. Despite continued opposition to the changes, two legal challenges to the amendments, which claimed that the Compact's approval had been procured by coercion, were dismissed, and on 1 October Palau achieved independence under the Compact of Free Association. At independence celebrations, Nakamura appealed to opponents of the Compact to support Palau's new status, and announced that his Government's principal concern was the regeneration of the country's economy, which he aimed to initiate with an economic programme financed by funds from the Compact. Palau was admitted to the UN in December 1994, and became a member of the IMF in December 1997.

A preliminary round of voting in the presidential election took place in September 1996; Kuniwo Nakamura secured 52.4% of total votes, Johnson Toribiong received 33.5%, and Yutaka Gibbons 14.2%. Nakamura and Toribiong were, therefore, expected to proceed to a second election due to take place in November. However, in late September a serious crisis struck Palau when the bridge linking the islands of Koror and Babeldaob collapsed, killing two people and injuring several others. The collapse of the bridge left the capital isolated from the international airport on Babeldaob, with disastrous economic repercussions for Palau, which was reliant on the route for all domestic and international communications. It was subsequently revealed that major repairs had recently been carried out on the bridge, at a cost of US $3.2m., and several reports implied that inappropriate changes made to its structure during the work were responsible for the disaster. Toribiong was harshly critical of Nakamura, who had commissioned the repair work, and demanded his resignation along with those of the public works officials involved. However, following the revelation that Toribiong's running-mate in the election for the vice-presidency was one of the officials involved in the work, Toribiong withdrew his candidacy from the second round of the presidential election. Yutaka Gibbons thus re-entered the contest by default; none the less, at the second round of the presidential poll, held concurrently with legislative elections on 5 November, Nakamura was re-elected with 62.0% of total votes.

In October 1998 the Senate approved legislation providing for the establishment of an 'offshore' financial centre in Palau. The measure was strongly opposed by President Nakamura, who believed that it might attract criminal organizations seeking to launder the proceeds of their illegal activities. In December 1999, following discussions with US government officials, Nakamura signed an executive order establishing a National Banking Review Commission, with the aim of maintaining a legally responsible banking environment in Palau: both the Bank of New York (of the USA) and Deutsche Bank (of Germany) had alleged that Palau's 'offshore' banks were facilitating money-laundering. The new body was given wide-ranging powers to examine banking operations in the country and to evaluate current banking regulations.

At the presidential election conducted on 7 November 2000, Thomas E. Remengesau, Jr, hitherto the Vice-President of Palau, received 52% of the votes cast, thus defeating Senator Peter Sugiyama. Sandra Pierantozzi was elected as Vice-President. Remengesau was officially inaugurated on 19 January 2001. In July Remengesau introduced a formal resolution proposing the reduction of the legislature to a single chamber, to replace the existing House of Delegates and the Senate, claiming that a unicameral legislature would reduce bureaucracy. However, owing to a lack of legislative progress on the necessary constitutional changes, in early 2004 Remengesau endorsed a congressional resolution to conduct a popular referendum. The poll, which would first require the signatures of 25% of the electorate, was scheduled to take place in November. The proposals included the creation of a unicameral legislature and restrictions on legislators' terms of office; furthermore, it was proposed that Palauans resident in the USA be offered the opportunity of dual citizenship.

Despite President Remengesau's inauguration pledges to improve transparency in public office, there were several instances of fraudulent use of official funds in the early 2000s. In December 2002 the Speaker of the House of Delegates, Mario Gulibert, was arrested on charges relating to the alleged misuse of travel expenses (he was dismissed on unrelated charges in March 2004). In February 2003 the former Governor of Ngardmau state, Albert Ngirmekur, was fined and sentenced to six months' imprisonment following his impeachment for theft. In late 2003 President Remengesau was obliged to veto an attempt by legislators to eliminate the Office of the Special Prosecutor, which had conducted a number of investigations into alleged misuse of public funds. In February 2004, however, members of the National Congress under investigation for alleged misuse of expenses agreed to pay some US $250,000 on condition that the cases against them be withdrawn. In November the Senate overturned President Remengesau's veto of a bill to ease bank-licensing restrictions, although this decision was reversed in December, following the threat of international financial sanctions.

At the presidential election of 2 November 2004, President Remengesau was re-elected with 6,494 of the votes cast; his opponent, Polycarp Basilius, received 3,268 votes. Elias Camsek Chin was elected Vice-President. Following his re-election, Remengesau announced that the priorities of his new administration would include increasing government revenues, promoting economic diversification and tourism, and maintaining programmes of infrastructural development. Concurrent to the presidential election, voters also approved various amendments to the Constitution: to restrict members of the National Congress to three terms of four years, to permit dual US-Palauan citizenship, to provide for the joint election of the country's President and Vice-President as a team, and to adjust congressional members' salaries. The proposal to create a unicameral legislature, however, was rejected. A plan to hold a constitutional convention was approved by 5,085 votes (some 53% of the votes cast), with 3,742 votes (some 39%) against the motion. In April 2005 16 state delegates and nine delegates-at-large were elected to the Constitutional Convention, which in June ended its deliberations, following consultations with the general public and special-interest groups. The Convention concluded with 251 proposals, of which 22 were to be submitted for the electorate's consideration at a referendum to be held concurrently with the elections scheduled for 2008.

Financial issues and the elections of 2008

The issue of misuse of public funds was highlighted by several political developments in 2006–08. In March 2006 the legislature of Peleliu state approved a resolution to impeach Governor Jackson Ngiraingas on charges of treason, unlawful spending of state finances and the lodging of accusations, against President Remengesau and others, purporting to be on the state's behalf. In April Ngiraingas failed to gain the support of a majority in the state legislature to revoke the impeachment and was removed from office; he subsequently filed a civil suit, claiming that the allegations against him were false and not necessarily grounds for impeachment, and that his removal from office was unconstitutional. The Supreme Court invalidated the legislature's resolution in the following month, deciding that Ngiraingas had been denied due process. Meanwhile, in March the Ngardmau state legislature adopted a resolution to impeach Governor J. Schwartz Tudong. Tudong was accused of illegally spending state funds and making payments to himself without legal authority; a trial court later decided that it did not have the jurisdiction to rule on his appeal against the impeachment, and in May Akiko C. Sugiyama was elected to succeed him. In August Augustine Mesebeluu, the Speaker of the House of Delegates, was charged on numerous counts related to personal use of public finances. (Mesebeluu later entered into settlement agreements to repay costs that he had incurred during trips off the island.)

The closure of the Pacific Savings Bank, which went into receivership in late 2006, was followed by charges against the bank's President, Timothy Taunton, and other employees in 2007. However, Taunton fled from Palau shortly after the failure of the bank and at early 2011 nothing was known of his whereabouts. Meanwhile, in October 2008 the charges against the defunct bank's former employees were dismissed by the Independent Counsel, Lewis Harley, with the exception of the charges against Taunton, which remained pending. In December 2010 the Palauan Government announced that it was to reimburse some depositors of the bank, following the provision of a US $900,000 grant from Taiwan, which was to be released in instalments; as a result, only those depositors with an unpaid claim not in excess of $4,000 would initially be eligible for a refund.

Meanwhile, in October 2006 the relocation of Palau's seat of government from Koror to the new capital, Melekeok, on the island of Babeldaob, was marked with official ceremonies and celebrations. In March 2007 the President of the Senate, Johnny

Reklai, was killed in a fishing accident. Joshua Koshiba was subsequently elected as his successor, but, following a successful legal appeal by some members of the Senate, Surangel Whipps replaced Koshiba. A special election to fill the Senate vacancy took place in May. By February 2008 three candidates, Whipps, Koshiba and Johnson Toribiong, had announced plans to contest the forthcoming presidential election, scheduled for November.

In June 2008 the US General Accountability Office (GAO) published an audit report examining Palau's financial accountability and the provisions of the Compact with the USA, which was due to expire in 2009. The report judged that Palau had made progress in providing financial accountability and that the country had complied with most of the Compact's conditions. However, problems of internal control persisted. Meanwhile, preparations for a review of the Compact were under way with the establishment earlier in 2008 of the Palau Compact Review Commission.

Elections took place on 4 November 2008 for the 16 seats in the House of Delegates and the 13 seats in the newly expanded Senate, concurrently with polling for the country's presidency. In the presidential contest (for which primary elections to determine the candidates had been held in September) Johnson Toribiong defeated Vice-President Elias Camsek Chin by a narrow margin, having obtained 5,040 of the votes cast, compared with the 4,828 received by Chin. The level of voter participation was 74%. Kerai Mariur was elected as the country's new Vice-President. President Toribiong took office in January 2009; Vice-President Mariur also assumed the role of Minister of Administration and of Finance. In the legislative elections several incumbents were re-elected to the House of Delegates and to the Senate. Despite a legal challenge, other members of the National Congress, including a number of long-serving Senators, were unable to stand for re-election owing to the implementation of a limit of a maximum of three terms of office. Outgoing President Thomas Remengesau was elected to a seat in the Senate, as were two women, who thus became the country's first female Senators. A total of 22 proposed constitutional amendments were submitted to the electorate in a concurrent referendum held on 4 November 2008; voters endorsed a proposal henceforth to elect the President and Vice-President separately.

In January 2009 the Speaker of the Koror state legislature, Timothy Uehara, was convicted of perjury and of misconduct in public office. Uehara was found to have subleased government properties and embezzled tenants' rental payments from the Koror State Public Lands Authority. In March he received a six-year prison sentence and a fine of US $10,000; however, he was to serve only one year of the prison sentence, with the remainder being suspended. In April the Governor of Melekeok State, Lazarus Kodep, was formally charged with misconduct. It was alleged that between 2003 and 2007 Kodep had used public funds to repay a personal bank loan. Kodep subsequently pleaded guilty to misconduct and misuse of public funds, and resigned as Governor in March 2010; in April he was sentenced to five years' imprisonment, four-and-a-half of which were suspended, and was fined $10,000. Meanwhile, in December 2009 Senator Remengesau was fined $156,000, following his conviction in the previous month on 12 counts of failure to disclose assets during his term as President.

Recent developments: renewal of the Compact of Free Association

In March 2009 the Compact with the USA was extended for one year from the end of September, following a meeting in Washington, DC, between President Toribiong and US Secretary of State Hillary Clinton. Negotiations to reach a new long-term agreement were held during the latter half of the year. In October an offer extended by the USA of direct economic assistance to the sum of US $156m. for the period 2010–24 was summarily rejected by Palau, which dismissed the stipulated amount as 'inadequate' and stated that it expected the level of assistance to remain at current levels. However, agreement was finally reached at the start of 2010, when Palau accepted a $250m. aid programme for the next 15 years; representatives of the two sides convened in Hawaii to finalize the terms of the arrangement at the end of January.

However, the signing of the agreement was delayed for a number of months, owing to several unresolved points of contention, including a US demand that the US $250m. aid programme incorporate a $21m. subsidy pledged for postal services. Of this subsidy, $16.8m. was intended for US postal services to the Marshall Islands and the Federated States of Micronesia and was therefore of no benefit to Palau—a provision that was strongly contested by the Palauan Government. In early September 2010 a Palauan delegation headed by President Toribiong travelled to Hawaii to meet with US officials to discuss the outstanding issues. In the following week Palau and the USA finally signed the agreement, formally renewing the Compact for a further 15 years. The contentious inclusion of the $21m. postal subsidy remained within the final agreed terms, but the US delegation made concessions on certain other demands, including the stipulation that charitable donations no longer be tax deductible, a measure that the Palauan Government had denounced as 'highly intrusive'. The terms of the agreement provided for the creation of a economic and financial reforms body, the composition of which was to be approved by the US Government. The final agreement on the Compact was referred to a US Congress foreign affairs sub-committee, which conducted an initial hearing, attended by a Palauan delegation, on the aid programme in late September. In mid-February 2011 the Compact was introduced into the US Senate, from where it was referred to the Senate's Committee on Energy and Natural Resources; a committee hearing on the terms of the agreement was expected to be convened in April. President Toribiong urged the US Senate to approve the Compact, warning that failure to do so threatened to erode the confidence of Palauans in their relations with the USA.

Meanwhile, in November 2010 Toribiong introduced to the Senate draft legislation proposing to increase incrementally the minimum hourly wage from US $2.50 (at which level it had remained since its implementation in 1998) to $3.50 from October 2011.

Regional Affairs

In mid-1999 a delegation from Solomon Islands visited Palau to discuss the possibility of allowing Solomon Islanders to work in Palau, in an attempt to resolve the latter's severe labour shortage. In August 2001, however, the Government imposed a ban on the hiring of Indian and Sri Lankan workers, citing rising tensions and disputes with local employers which the Government claimed were largely due to religious differences. The ban was to remain in place until legislation to create official recruitment agencies in Palau had been approved. In July 2002 the Senate approved a bill that would amend the islands' immigration law in order to give greater authority over immigration affairs to the President of Palau. (Non-Palauan nationals were estimated to represent about 73% of the islands' population in 2003.) In March 2003 the Government introduced a measure to extend employment permits for foreign workers, which allowed a new maximum extension of two years. In April some 200 Chinese migrant employees of a failed clothing business were stranded in Palau and placed under house arrest. However, the migrants were subsequently repatriated, following diplomatic intervention from the People's Republic of China. In January 2006 legislation banning the employment of Bangladeshi nationals in Palau for a period of one year was implemented, making an exception for those Bangladeshis already contracted to work in the country, who would be allowed to complete their terms; in December the House of Delegates voted to extend the ban indefinitely, subject to ongoing review. The ban was subsequently extended on several occasions, latterly in October 2009. In the same month President Johnson Toribiong banned the employment of Myanma nationals, citing a lack of diplomatic relations and cultural differences, and issued an executive order introducing a quota for the number of foreign workers in Palau. At that time there were reported to be some 5,432 foreign nationals employed in the country; as a result of the executive order, this number would not be permitted to increase beyond 6,000. In July 2010 President Toribiong was forced to defend a newly introduced law requiring foreign nationals to register with, and pay an administrative fee to, the Government. Critics of the legislation argued that it constituted a tax on foreigners, but the President insisted that the new measure was intended merely to give a clear indication of the number of foreigners resident on the island. The Supreme Court repealed the legislation in February 2011.

Diplomatic relations were established, at ambassadorial level, with Taiwan in late 1999. The first Taiwanese ambassador to Palau was formally appointed in April 2000. Reports in December of that year that the Palau Government was considering establishing diplomatic relations with the People's Republic of China were denied, and President-elect Remengesau reaffirmed Palau's diplomatic relations with Taiwan. In early 2000, meanwhile, Palau and Taiwan signed an agreement undertaking to develop bilateral projects in a number of areas, including agriculture, fisheries and tourism. In late January 2005 President Chen Shui-bian of Taiwan visited Palau to discuss economic co-operation and to strengthen bilateral political relations. President Remengesau travelled to Taiwan in May 2008 to attend the inauguration of President Ma Ying-jeou. In March 2010 President Ma paid a reciprocal visit to Palau, on the last stage of a tour of Taiwan's six Pacific allies; during his stay he met with President Toribiong and various members of the Cabinet. Cultural exchanges constituted the theme of the Taiwanese President's visit to Palau. A bilateral memorandum of understanding, which was intended to foster greater co-operation in the fields of aquaculture, food-processing and tourism, was signed in October 2010. Palau and Taiwan also agreed to convene regularly to facilitate the exchange of information that would help to strengthen the economic development of the Pacific nation.

Palau maintains strong diplomatic links with Japan, which has been a leading source of tourist revenue since the 1980s. The Japanese Government provided US $25m. for the reconstruction of the Koror bridge (see above) and contributed to the construction of a new terminal building at Palau International Airport, which opened in May 2003. In June 2002 President Remengesau undertook his first state visit to the Republic of Korea. His itinerary incorporated visits to a number of infrastructural development projects. Palauan support for Japan's position on international whaling (see the chapter on Japan) was withdrawn in June 2010; announcing the change in strategy, President Toribiong stated that Palau would henceforth be advocating a quota system by which it was envisaged that the hunting of whales would be reduced by one-half.

In October 2001 the Government sought to establish diplomatic relations with Malaysia and Indonesia in an attempt to facilitate the resolution of disputes about overlapping territorial boundaries, amid concern over increasing instances of illegal fishing in Palauan waters. (Palau introduced more stringent regulations to counter illegal fishing in 2002 and 2003.) Diplomatic relations with Indonesia were established in July 2007. In July 2009 former Malaysian Prime Minister Abdullah Badawi headed a delegation to Palau, dispatched to discuss the possibility of establishing diplomatic and trade links. Meanwhile, in March 2009 Palau and the Philippines held discussions regarding the delineation of their maritime border. In March 2010 President Toribiong created a task force to negotiate Palau's maritime boundaries with the Philippines and Indonesia; the Extended Continental Shelf Task Force was to submit to the President a report of its findings and recommendations at the end of 2011.

Palau established diplomatic relations with Solomon Islands in September 2009 and with the United Arab Emirates in October. Palau's consulates on Saipan (the Northern Mariana Islands) and Guam were closed owing to a lack of funding in December 2009 and March 2010, respectively. However, the 2010/11 budget allocated funding to enable the reopening of the Guam consulate, prompting an angry response from Palauans resident on Saipan, who appealed to the Government similarly to reopen the Saipan consulate. Although the Palau Minister of Natural Resources announced in July 2010 that a new consulate was to be opened at a new location on Saipan later in the year, at mid-2011 this had yet to transpire. Meanwhile, in August 2010 Palau and Australia signed a development agreement, which was welcomed by both sides as the beginning of a 'new era' of bilateral co-operation which, it was hoped, would lead to improved living standards and national development in Palau.

CONSTITUTION AND GOVERNMENT

In October 1994 Palau, the last remaining component of the Trust Territory of the Pacific Islands (a United Nations Trusteeship administered by the USA), achieved independence under the Compact of Free Association. Administrative authority was transferred to the Government of Palau (with the USA retaining responsibility for the islands' defence).

A locally drafted Constitution of the Republic of Palau entered into effect on 1 January 1981. Under the Constitution, executive authority is vested in the President, elected by direct suffrage for a four-year term. Legislative power is exercised by the Olbiil era Kelulau ('House of Whispered Decisions', or Palau National Congress), composed of the directly elected House of Delegates (comprising one Delegate from each of the 16 states of Palau) and the Senate (comprising 13 Senators after the elections of 2008). Members of the National Congress are elected for a four-year term.

Local governmental units are the municipalities and villages. Elected Magistrates and Councils govern the municipalities. Village government is largely traditional.

REGIONAL AND INTERNATIONAL CO-OPERATION

Palau is a member of the Pacific Community (see p. 410), the Pacific Islands Forum (see p. 413) and the Asian Development Bank (ADB, see p. 202); it is also an associate member of the UN's Economic and Social Commission for Asia and the Pacific (ESCAP, see p. 37), having been admitted to the UN in 1994.

ECONOMIC AFFAIRS

In 2009, according to estimates by the World Bank, Palau's gross national income (GNI), measured at average 2007–09 prices, totalled US $182m., equivalent to $8,940 per head. During 2000–09, it was estimated, the population increased at an average annual rate of 0.7%, while gross domestic product (GDP) per head increased, in real terms, by an average of 0.2% per year. In 2000–09 overall GDP expanded, in real terms, at an average annual rate of 1.0%. The Asian Development Bank (ADB) estimated that real GDP contracted by 2.1% in 2009 but expanded by 2.0% in 2010.

Agriculture (including forestry and fishing) is mainly on a subsistence level, the principal crops being coconuts, root crops and bananas. Pigs and chickens are kept for domestic consumption. Eggs are produced commercially, and the introduction of cattle-ranching on Babeldaob was under consideration in the early 2000s. The agricultural sector engaged 7.8% of the employed labour force in 2005 and, according to provisional figures, provided 3.5% of GDP in 2007. Fishing licences have been sold to foreign fleets, including those of Taiwan, the USA, Japan and the Philippines. Fish has traditionally been a leading export, accounting for almost US $8.9m. of exports in 2004. According to the ADB, the agricultural sector's GDP contracted, in real terms, by 7.1% in 2008 but expanded by 6.0% in 2009.

The industrial sector (including mining and quarrying, manufacturing, construction and utilities) engaged 18.7% of the employed labour force in 2005. The sector provided an estimated 20.7% of GDP in 2007, according to provisional figures. The only manufacturing activity of any significance is the production of garments; the sector has employed mainly foreign workers. Manufacturing accounted for 2.3% of employment in 2005, but only 0.5% of GDP in 2007. Construction is the most important industrial activity, contributing 15.7% of GDP in 2007 and engaging 14.0% of the employed labour force in 2005. Electrical energy, output of which totalled an estimated 154m. kWh in 2007, is produced by two power plants at Aimeliik and Malakal. In July 2008 it was announced that the World Bank was to provide financial and technical assistance in the exploration for reserves of petroleum and gas in an area north-east of Babeldaob. According to the ADB, the industrial sector's GDP contracted by 30.7% in 2008 and by 11.6% in 2009.

Service industries dominate Palau's economy, providing some 75.8% of GDP in 2007, according to provisional results, and engaging 73.5% of the employed labour force in 2005. The Government is a significant employer within the sector, public administration engaging 17.7% of the total employed labour force in 2005. The tourism sector has expanded rapidly since the 1980s, to become an important source of foreign exchange. Receipts from tourism (including passenger transport) totalled US $90m. in 2006. The trade, hotels and restaurants sector engaged 17.1% of the employed labour force and provided 30.8% of GDP in 2005. Visitor arrivals (mostly from Japan, Taiwan and the Republic of Korea) were reported to have increased substantially in 2010 to reach 85,593. The Micronesian Games were held in Palau in August 2010. The real GDP of the services sector decreased by 1.9% in 2008 and by 1.8% in 2009, according to the ADB.

In the year ending September 2009 the visible trade deficit was provisionally estimated at US $91.7m. The deficit on the current account of the balance of payments, including grants, was estimated at $29.1m. in the same year. Import costs were a provisional $91.3m. in the year ending September 2007, while revenue from exports totalled a provisional $10.1m. The principal sources of imports were the USA (including Guam, which supplied 45.0% of the total in 2004) and Singapore (27.9%). Other significant suppliers were Japan, the Republic of Korea and Taiwan. The principal imports in that year were machinery and transport

PALAU

equipment, mineral fuels and lubricants, and food and live animals.

The islands record a persistent budget deficit, which reached US $21.3m. in the year ending 30 September 2009 (including net lending). Financial assistance from the USA contributes a large part of the islands' external revenue. Upon implementation of the Compact of Free Association with the USA in 1994, Palau became eligible for an initial grant of $142m. and for annual aid of $23m. over the period until 2009, following which the Compact was renegotiated; the USA was to provide $250m. over a 15-year period (see Contemporary Political History). Palau's external debt was estimated by the ADB to have risen from $18m. in 2006 to $23m. in 2007. The cost of debt-servicing decreased to the equivalent of 1.0% of the value of exports of goods and services in 2007. The annual rate of inflation averaged 2.0% between 2000 and 2007. The inflation rate rose significantly in 2008, to reach 11.3%, before declining to 5.2% in 2009 and to 3.8% in 2010, according to the ADB. At the 2005 census 4.2% of the total labour force were unemployed.

The economy of Palau has benefited greatly from the substantial aid payments from the US Government that followed the implementation in 1994 of the Compact of Free Association, which was renegotiated in early 2010 (see above). Grants accounted for more than 50% of government revenue in 2008/09. The decline in real GDP that prevailed for several years until 2009 was attributed mainly to the contraction in tourist arrivals, which decreased by 10% in 2008 and by a similar percentage in 2009. Compounding the impact of unfavourable global economic conditions, flight schedules from Taiwan were disrupted by airline difficulties in 2008. However, the tourism sector registered a substantial improvement in 2010, in tandem with economic recovery in Asia, while overseas marketing campaigns were intensified. In January 2011 it was announced that (as in the previous year) the Government of Taiwan was to provide stimulus funding of US $10m. for the purposes of economic development: the 22 projects thus financed by Taiwan again included agricultural schemes, such as livestock development, and infrastructural improvements, notably the rehabilitation of the road network. Inflationary pressures, emanating largely from the higher costs of foodstuffs and fuel, re-emerged in the latter part of 2010 and were expected to depress consumer spending. Palau's trust fund remained vulnerable to the volatility of global stock markets, as demonstrated in 2008 when the value of the fund's assets decreased by an estimated 28%. The US General Accountability Office (GAO) estimated that by the fiscal year ending in September 2009 US aid to Palau since 1995 would total more than $852m., with direct assistance under the Compact accounting for 48% of this. The GAO also drew attention to the need for fiscal reform and for an improvement in investment conditions, in order to encourage the growth of the private sector. The shortage of investment for the purposes of public infrastructure programmes remained an issue of some concern. None the less, the ADB forecast that the economic recovery of 2010 would be sustained and that GDP would expand by about 2.0% in the following year.

PUBLIC HOLIDAYS

2012 (provisional): 2 January (for New Year's Day), 15 March (Youth Day), 4 May (for Senior Citizens' Day), 1 June (Presidents' Day), 9 July (Constitution Day), 3 September (Labor Day), 1 October (Independence Day), 24 October (United Nations Day), 22 November (Thanksgiving), 25 December (Christmas Day).

Statistical Survey

Source (unless otherwise indicated): Office of Planning and Statistics, Ministry of Finance, POB 6011, Koror; tel. 767-1269; fax 767-5642; e-mail ops@palaugov.net; internet www.palaugov.net/stats/index.htm.

AREA AND POPULATION

Area: 508 sq km (196 sq miles); Babeldaob (Babeldaop, Babelthuap) island 409 sq km (158 sq miles).

Population: 19,129 at census of 15 April 2000; 19,907 (males 10,699, females 9,208) at census of 1 April 2005. *Mid-2011* (Secretariat of the Pacific Community estimate): 20,643 (Source: Pacific Regional Information System).

Density (at mid-2011): 40.6 per sq km.

Population by Age and Sex (Secretariat of the Pacific Community estimates at mid-2011): *0–14:* 4,136 (males 2,123, females 2,013); *15–64:* 15,288 (males 8,395, females 6,893); *65 and over:* 1,219 (males 536, females 683); *Total* 20,643 (males 11,054, females 9,589) (Source: Pacific Regional Information System).

Principal Towns (population at 2005 census): Koror (capital) 10,743; Meyuns 1,153. Source: Thomas Brinkhoff, *City Population* (internet www.citypopulation.de).

Births and Deaths (2006): Registered live births 259 (birth rate 12.9 per 1,000); Registered deaths 144 (death rate 7.2 per 1,000).

Life Expectancy (years at birth, WHO estimates): 72 (males 68; females 77) in 2008. Source: WHO, *World Health Statistics*.

Economically Active Population (persons aged 16 years and over, 2005 census): Agriculture 451; Forestry and fishing 310; Mining 34; Manufacturing 225; Utilities and sanitary services 208; Construction 1,365; Transport and communications 561; Trade, restaurants, etc. 1,670; Finance, insurance and real estate 132; Public administration 1,734; Professional and related services 1,466; Private households 915; Other personal services 387; Other services 319; *Total employed* 9,777 (males 5,982, females 3,795); Unemployed 426 (males 232, females 194); *Total labour force* 10,203 (males 6,214, females 3,989).

HEALTH AND WELFARE
Key Indicators

Total Fertility Rate (children per woman, 2008): 1.9.

Under-5 Mortality Rate (per 1,000 live births, 2008): 15.

Physicians (per 1,000 head, 2000): 1.6.

Hospital Beds (per 1,000 head, 2006): 5.9.

Health Expenditure (2007): US $ per head (PPP): 812.

Health Expenditure (2007): % of GDP: 10.8.

Health Expenditure (2007): public (% of total): 78.4.

Total Carbon Dioxide Emissions ('000 metric tons, 2007): 212.5.

Carbon Dioxide Emissions Per Head (metric tons, 2007): 10.5.

For sources and definitions, see explanatory note on p. vi.

AGRICULTURE, ETC.

Fishing (metric tons, live weight, 2008): Marine fishes 1,002; Total catch (incl. others) 1,027 (FAO estimate). Source: FAO.

INDUSTRY

Production (2007): Electric energy 154 million kWh (estimate). Source: UN Industrial Commodity Statistics Database.

FINANCE

Currency and Exchange Rates: United States currency is used: 100 cents = 1 United States dollar (US $). *Sterling and Euro Equivalents* (31 December 2010): £1 sterling = US $1.5655; €1 = US $1.3362; US $100 = £63.88 = €74.84.

Budget (US $ million, year ending 30 September 2009, provisional): *Revenue:* Current revenue 37.8 (Taxes 29.7, Non-tax revenue 8.2); Grants 43.4; Total 81.3. *Expenditure:* Current expenditure 73.7; Capital expenditure 21.3; Net lending 7.6; Total 102.6. Source: Asian Development Bank.

Cost of Living (Consumer Price Index, base: June 2008 = 100): All items 90.1 in 2007; 100.9 in 2008; 102.3 in 2009.

Gross Domestic Product (US $ '000 at current prices, provisional): 164,289 in 2007; 180,716 in 2008; 179,631 in 2009. Source: Asian Development Bank.

Gross Domestic Product by Economic Activity (US $ '000 at current prices, 2007, provisional): Agriculture and fishing 5,597; Mining 180; Manufacturing 822; Electricity, gas and water 7,027; Construction 25,099; Trade 34,369; Transport and communications 12,655; Finance 6,188; Public administration 32,340; Other services

35,730; *Sub-total* 160,007; Import duties 7,367; *Less* Imputed bank service charges 3,087; *GDP in purchasers' values* 164,289. Source: Asian Development Bank.

Balance of Payments (US $ million, year ending September 2009, provisional): Exports of goods f.o.b. 11.8; Imports of goods f.o.b. −103.5; *Trade balance* −91.7; Services and income (net) 51.7; *Balance on goods, services and income* −40.0; Current transfers (net) 10.9; *Current balance* −29.1; Capital and financial account (net) 34.3; Net errors and omissions 5.2; *Overall balance* 10.4. Source: Asian Development Bank.

EXTERNAL TRADE

Principal Commodities (US $ '000): *Imports f.o.b.* (2004): Food and live animals 10,862; Beverages and tobacco 4,947; Mineral fuels, lubricants, etc. 30,061; Chemicals 5,772; Basic manufactures 8,597; Machinery and transport equipment 47,405; Miscellaneous manufactured articles 7,129; Total (incl. others) 116,499. *Exports* (2004/05): 13,414 (including trochus shells, tuna, copra and handicrafts). *2009* (year ending 30 September, provisional): Total imports 103,500; Total exports 11,800. Source: Asian Development Bank.

Principal Trading Partners (US $ '000, year ending September 2004): *Imports:* Japan 8,531; Korea, Republic 5,411; Philippines 6,934; Singapore 29,885; Taiwan 5,343; USA (incl. Guam) 48,225; Total (incl. others) 107,280. *Exports:* Total 5,882.

TRANSPORT

International Shipping (freight traffic, metric tons, 2006): Goods loaded 8,767; Goods unloaded 94,693.

Civil Aviation (2006): Aircraft movements 1,054; Passengers enplaned 98,808; Cargo loaded 2,170,648 lbs.

TOURISM

Tourist Arrivals: 84,566 in 2007; 75,829 in 2008; 68,329 in 2009.

Tourist Arrivals by Country of Residence (2009): Guam 2,779; Japan 26,340; Korea, Republic 12,901; Philippines 626; Taiwan 16,105; USA (mainland) 4,236; Total (incl. others) 68,329.

Tourism Receipts (US $ million, incl. passenger transport): 97 in 2004; 97 in 2005; 90 in 2006.

Source: World Tourism Organization.

COMMUNICATIONS MEDIA

Radio Receivers (1997): 12,000 in use.
Television Receivers (1997): 11,000 in use.
Telephones (2009): 7,100 main lines in use.
Mobile Cellular Telephones (2009): 13,200 subscribers.
Internet Users (2008): 5,400.
Broadband Subscribers (2009): 200.

Source: partly International Telecommunication Union.

EDUCATION

Pre-primary (public institutions only, 2006/07): 13 schools; 30 teachers; 509 pupils.

Enrolment (2006/07): *Elementary:* Total 2,683 (Public 2,135, Private 548). *Secondary:* Total 1,309 (Public 810, Private 499).

Teachers (1999/2000, estimates): *Elementary:* 124. *Secondary:* 126.

Institutions (2006/07): *Elementary:* Total 21 (Public 19, Private 2). *Secondary:* Total 6 (Public 1, Private 5).

Tertiary (Palau Community College): 54 teachers (full-time and part-time, 2005/06); 545 students (at 2005 census).

Pupil-teacher Ratio (primary education, UNESCO estimate): 12.5 in 2004/05 (Source: UNESCO Institute for Statistics).

Directory

The Government

HEAD OF STATE

President: JOHNSON TORIBIONG (took office 15 January 2009).
Vice-President and Minister of Administration and of Finance: KERAI MARIUR.

CABINET
(May 2011)

Minister of Health: Dr STEVENSON KUARTEI.
Minister of Public Infrastructure, Industries and Commerce: JACKSON NGIRAINGAS.
Minister of Natural Resources, Environment and Tourism: HARRY FRITZ.
Minister of Education: MASA-AKI EMESIOCHEL.
Minister of Justice: JOHNNY GIBBONS.
Minister of Community and Cultural Affairs: FAUSTINA K. REHUHER-MARUGG.
Minister of State: VICTOR YANO.

COUNCIL CHIEFS

The Constitution provides for an advisory body for the President, comprising the 16 highest traditional chiefs from the 16 states. The chiefs advise on all traditional laws and customs, and on any other public matter in which their participation is required.

Chairman: Ibedul YUTAKA GIBBONS (Koror).

GOVERNMENT OFFICES AND MINISTRIES

Office of the President: POB 6051, Koror, PW 96940; tel. 488-2403; fax 488-1662; e-mail pres@palaunet.com.

Department of the Interior, Office of Insular Affairs (OIA): OIA Field Office, POB 6031, Koror, PW 96946; tel. 488-2601; fax 488-2649; internet www.doi.gov/oia/Islandpages/palaupage.htm; Field Rep. (vacant); Co-ordinator HAURO WILLTER.

Ministry of Community and Cultural Affairs: POB 100, Koror, PW 96940; tel. 767-1126; fax 767-3354; e-mail mcca@palaunet.com.

Ministry of Education: POB 819, Koror, PW 96940; tel. 767-1464; fax 767-1465; e-mail moe@palaumoe.net; internet www.palaumoe.net.

Ministry of Finance: POB 6011, Koror, PW 96940; tel. 767-2501; fax 767-2168; e-mail bpss@palaugov.net.

Ministry of Health: POB 6027, Koror, PW 96940; tel. 767-5552488; fax 767-0722; e-mail moh@palau-health.net; internet www.palau-health.net.

Ministry of Justice: POB 3022, Koror, PW 96940; tel. 488-3198; fax 488-4567; e-mail justice@palaunet.com.

Ministry of Natural Resources, Environment and Tourism: Exec. Bldg, 1st Floor, Ngerulmud, PW 96939; tel. 767-5435; fax 767-3380; e-mail mnret@palaugov.net.

Ministry of Public Infrastructure, Industries and Commerce: POB 1471, Ngerulmud, PW 96940; tel. 767-2111; fax 767-3207; e-mail mincat@palaunet.com.

Ministry of State: Ngerulmud, Melekeok; tel. 767-2509; fax 767-2443; e-mail state@palaugov.net.

All national government offices were transferred from Koror to the new capital Ngerulmud, in the state of Melekeok, in October 2006. Each state has its own administrative headquarters.

President and Legislature

PRESIDENT

At the presidential election held on 4 November 2008, Johnson Toribiong defeated his opponent, Elias Camsek Chin, by a narrow margin. Toribiong secured 5,040 votes, and Chin received 4,828.

OLBIIL ERA KELULAU
(Palau National Congress)

The Palau National Congress comprises two chambers, the Senate and the House of Delegates. The Senate has 13 elected members, and the House of Delegates consists of 16 elected members. The most recent election was held on 4 November 2008.

President of the Senate: MLIB TMETUCHL.
Vice-President of the Senate: KATHY KESOLEI.
Speaker of the House of Delegates: NOAH IDECHONG.

PALAU

Vice-Speaker of the House of Delegates: ALEXANDER MEREP.
National Congress: National Capitol Bldg, Ngerulmud, Melekeok State; tel. 767-2455; fax 767-2633; e-mail senate@palaunet.com; internet www.palauoek.net.

Election Commission

Palau Election Commission: POB 826, Koror, PW 96940; tel. 488-1554; fax 488-3327; Chair. SANTOS BORJA.

Political Organizations

(There are currently no active political parties in Palau)

Palau Nationalist Party: c/o Olbiil era Kelulau, Koror, PW 96940; inactive; Leader JOHNSON TORIBIONG.
Ta Belau Party: c/o Olbiil era Kelulau, Koror, PW 96940; inactive; Leader KUNIWO NAKAMURA.

Diplomatic Representation

EMBASSIES IN PALAU

Japan: POB 6050, Palau Pacific Resort, Arakebesang, Koror, PW 96940; tel. 488-6455; fax 488-6458; Ambassador YOSHIYUKI SADAOKA.
Philippines: Minami Bldg, 2nd Floor, Iyebukel Hamlet, POB 1447, Koror, PW 96940; tel. 488-5077; fax 488-6310; e-mail philkor@palaunet.com; Ambassador RAMONCITO MARIÑO.
Taiwan (Republic of China): WCTC Bldg, Of. 3F, POB 9087, Koror, PW 96940; tel. 488-8150; fax 488-8151; e-mail roc@palautelecoms.com; Ambassador MAGGIE TIEN.
USA: POB 6028, Koror, PW 96940; tel. 587-2920; fax 587-2911; e-mail usembassykoror@palaunet.com; internet palau.usembassy.gov; Ambassador HELEN REED-ROWE.

Judicial System

The judicial system of the Republic of Palau consists of the Supreme Court (including Trial and Appellate Divisions), presided over by the Chief Justice, the National Court (inactive), the Court of Common Pleas and the Land Court.

Supreme Court of the Republic of Palau: POB 248, Koror, PW 96940; tel. 488-4979; fax 488-1597; e-mail cjngiraklsong@palaunet.com; Chief Justice ARTHUR NGIRAKLSONG.
Office of the Attorney-General: 1365 Koror, PW 96940; tel. 488-2481; fax 488-3329; e-mail agoffice@palaunet.com; Attorney-Gen. ERNESTINE RENGIIL.

Religion

The population is predominantly Christian, mainly Roman Catholic. The Assembly of God, Baptists, Seventh-day Adventists, the Church of Jesus Christ of Latter-day Saints (Mormons), and the Bahá'í and Modignai (or Modeknai) faiths are also represented.

CHRISTIANITY

The Roman Catholic Church

Palau forms part of the diocese of the Caroline Islands, suffragan to the archdiocese of Agaña (Guam). The Bishop, who is resident in Chuuk, Eastern Caroline Islands (see the Federated States of Micronesia), participates in the Catholic Bishops' Conference of the Pacific, based in Suva, Fiji.

MODIGNAI FAITH

Modignai Church: Koror, PW 96940; an indigenous, non-Christian religion; also operates a high school.

The Press

Moonshadow Publications: POB 9006, Koror, PW 96940; tel. 488-8655; fax 779-3440; e-mail jerome@palaunet.com; internet jerometemengil.synthasite.com; Publr JEROME TEMENGIL.
Palau Gazette: POB 100, Koror, PW 96940; tel. 488-3257; fax 488-1662; e-mail roppresoffice@palaunet.com; newsletter publ. by Govt; monthly; Publr ROMAN YANO.

Roureur Belau: POB 477, Koror, PW 96940; tel. 488-6365; fax 488-4810; e-mail myu@palaunet.com; weekly; Publr CLIFFORD 'SPADE' EBAS.
Tia Belau (This is Palau): POB 477, Koror, PW 96940; tel. 488-6365; fax 488-4810; e-mail tiabelau@palaunet.com; f. 1992; weekly; English and Palauan; Editor RAOUL G. BRIONES; Publr MOSES ULUDONG; circ. 1,500.

Broadcasting and Communications

TELECOMMUNICATIONS

Palau National Communications Corpn (PNCC): POB 99, Koror, PW 96940; tel. 587-9000; fax 587-1888; e-mail pncc@palaunet.com; internet www.palaunet.com; f. 1982; mem. of the Pacific Islands Broadcasting Asscn; tel., internet and digital TV operator; 24 hrs daily; Chair. LEILANI REKLAI; Gen. Man. RICHARD L. MISECH.
Palau Mobile Corpn (PMC): POB 8084, Koror, PW 96940; tel. 488-4088; fax 488-2111; e-mail marklin@palaumobile.com; internet www.palaumobile.com; mobile tel. operator.

BROADCASTING

Radio

High Adventure Ministries: POB 66, Koror, PW 96940; tel. 488-2162; fax 488-2163; e-mail hamadmin@palaunet.com; f. 1992; broadcasts religious material; Engineering Man. BENTLEY CHAN.
KRFM: Sure Save Store, Koror, PW 96940; tel. 488-1359; e-mail rudimch@palaunet.com.
T8AA (Eco Paradise): POB 279, Koror, PW 96940; tel. 488-2417; fax 488-1932; broadcasts news, entertainment and music; govt-owned.
WSZB Broadcasting Station: POB 279, Koror, PW 96940; tel. 488-2417; fax 488-1932; Station Man. ALBERT SALUSTIANO.
WWFM: POB 1327, Koror, PW 96940; tel. 488-4848; fax 488-4420; e-mail wwfm@palaunet.com; internet www.brouhaha.net/palau/wwfm.html; Man. ALFONSO DIAZ.

Television

PNCC Digital Television: POB 39, Koror, PW 96940; tel. 587-3515; fax 587-1888; e-mail pncc@palaunet.com; internet www.palaunet.com; owned by the Palau Nat. Communications Corpn; fmrly Island Cable Television.
STV-TV Koror: POB 2000, Koror, PW 96940; tel. 488-1357; fax 488-1207; broadcasts 12 hrs daily; Man. DAVID NOLAN; Technical Man. RAY OMELEN.

Finance

(cap. = capital; res = reserves; amounts in US dollars)

BANKING

Bank of Guam: POB 338, Koror, PW 96940; tel. 488-2696; fax 488-1384; internet www.bankofguam.com; Man. KATHERINE LUJAN.
Bank of Hawaii (USA): POB 340, Koror, PW 96940; tel. 488-2602; fax 488-2427; internet www.boh.com.
Bank Pacific: Lebuu St, Tngerongel Hamlet, Koror; tel. 488-5635; fax 488-4752; internet www.bankpacific.com; Sr Country Officer JOSEPH KOSHIBA.
National Development Bank of Palau: POB 816, Koror, PW 96940; tel. 587-2578; fax 587-2579; e-mail ndbp@palaunet.com; internet www.ndbp.com; f. 1982; cap. and res 11.5m. (Sept. 2002); 100% govt-owned; Pres. KALEB ADUI, Jr; Chair. RINGSANG RECHIREI.

INSURANCE

Century Insurance Co: POB 318, Koror, PW 96940; tel. 488-8580; fax 488-8632; e-mail knakamura@palaunet.com.
Moylan's Insurance Underwriters Palau: POB 156, Koror, PW 96940; tel. 488-2765; fax 488-2744; e-mail palau@moylans.net; internet www.moylansinsurance.com; Branch Man. KENJI DENGOKL.
NECO Insurance Underwriters Ltd: POB 129, Koror, PW 96940; tel. 488-2325; fax 488-2880; e-mail necogroup@palaunet.com.
Poltalia National Insurance: POB 12, Koror, PW 96940; tel. 488-2254; fax 488-2834; e-mail psata@palaunet.com; f. 1974; Pres. and CEO EPHRAM POLYCARP.

Trade and Industry

CHAMBER OF COMMERCE

Palau Chamber of Commerce: POB 6021, Koror, PW 96940; tel. 488-4581; fax 488-2732; e-mail reklai@reklai.com; f. 1984; Pres. SURANGEL WHIPPS, Jr.

CO-OPERATIVES

These include the Palau Fishermen's Co-operative, the Palau Boatbuilders' Asscn and the Palau Handicraft and Woodworkers' Guild. In 1990, of the 13 registered co-operatives, eight were fishermen's co-operatives, three consumers' co-operatives (only two in normal operation) and two farmers' co-operatives (one in normal operation).

DEVELOPMENT ORGANIZATION

Palau Conservation Society: POB 1811, Koror, PW 96940; tel. 488-3993; fax 488-3990; e-mail pcs@palaunet.com; internet www.palauconservation.org; f. 1994; sustainable devt, environmental protection; Chair. MAURA GORDON; Exec. Dir ELBUCHEL SADANG.

Transport

ROADS

Tarmac and concrete roads are found in the more important islands. Other islands have stone- and coral-surfaced roads and tracks. The Government is responsible for 36 km (22 miles) of paved roads and 25 km (15 miles) of coral- and gravel-surfaced roads. Most paved roads are located on Koror. A major project to construct a new 85-km (53-mile) road around Babeldaob was completed in 2007, funded with US $150m. from the Compact of Free Association.

SHIPPING

Most shipping in Palau is government-organized. However, the Micronesia Transport Line operates a service from Sydney (Australia) to Palau. A twice-weekly inter-island service operates between Koror and Peleliu. There is one commercial port at Malakal Harbor, which is operated by the privately owned Belau Transfer and Terminal Company.

CIVIL AVIATION

There is an international airport on Babeldaob. Domestic airfields (former Japanese military airstrips) are located on Angaur and Peleliu. Continental Micronesia (Northern Mariana Islands and Guam) provides daily flights to Koror from Guam, and twice-weekly flights from Manila (Philippines). Cebu Pacific operates direct flights from Davao (Philippines) to Koror. In May 2008 China Airlines began operating charter flights between Taiwan and Palau. Palau Trans Pacific also operates from Taiwan. In July 2008 two South Korean carriers, Korean Air and Asiana Airlines, reached an agreement with the Palau Government, allowing for up to seven passenger flights and four cargo flights per week. Following the suspension by Japan Airlines of its charter flights from Tokyo, US carrier Delta Airlines inaugurated a regular service between the Japanese capital and Palau in December 2010.

Pacific Flier: POB 37, Koror, PW 96940; tel. 488-2604; e-mail palautravel@palaunet.com; internet www.pacificflier.com.

Rock Island Airlines: managed by Aloha Airlines (Hawaii).

Tourism

Tourism is becoming increasingly important in Palau. The islands are particularly rich in their marine environment, and the Government has implemented measures to conserve and protect these natural resources. The myriad Rock Islands, now known as the Floating Garden Islands, are a noted reserve in the lagoon to the west of the main group of islands. There were 959 hotel rooms in 2004. In 2010 Palau reportedly received 85,593 visitors, most of whom were from Taiwan, Japan and the Republic of Korea. Tourist revenue reached US $90m. in 2006. The Seventh Micronesian Games were held in Palau in August 2010.

Belau Tourism Association: POB 9032, Koror, PW 96940; tel. 488-4377; fax 488-1725; e-mail bta@palaunet.com; Pres. MARY FRANCES VOGT.

Palau Visitors' Authority: POB 256, Koror, PW 96940; tel. 488-2793; fax 488-1453; e-mail pva@visit-palau.com; internet www.visit-palau.com; f. 1982; Man. Dir DARIN DE LEON.

Defence

The USA is responsible for the defence of Palau, according to the Compact of Free Association implemented in October 1994, and has exclusive military access to Palau's waters, as well as the right to operate two military bases on the islands. The US Pacific Command is based in Hawaii.

Education

The educational system is similar to that of the USA. The Government of Palau is now responsible for the state school system, which most children attend. Education is free and compulsory between the ages of six and 14, and secondary education may be obtained at the public High School or one of the five private ones.

In 2006/07 there were 509 pupils enrolled in pre-primary public schools, 2,683 in primary schools, and 1,309 in secondary schools. According to the results of the 2005 census, there were 545 students in tertiary education in that year. In 2006/07 government schools totalled 20, one of which was a secondary school. The Micronesian Occupational College, based in Koror, provides two-year training programmes. Government expenditure on education totalled US $9.1m. in 1999/2000, equivalent to 10.7% of total budgetary expenditure.

PALESTINIAN AUTONOMOUS AREAS

Introductory Survey

LOCATION, CLIMATE, LANGUAGE, RELIGION, FLAG, CAPITAL

The Palestinian Autonomous Areas are located in the West Bank and the Gaza Strip. (For a more detailed description of the location of the Palestinian territories, see Constitution and Government.) The West Bank lies in western Asia, to the west of the Jordan river and the Dead Sea, with the State of Israel to the north, west and south. The Gaza Strip lies on the easternmost coast of the Mediterranean, with Israel to the north and east, and Egypt to the south. The Interim Agreement of September 1995 (see Contemporary Political History) provides for the creation of a corridor, or safe passage, linking the Gaza Strip with the West Bank. A 'southern' safe passage between Hebron and Gaza was opened in October 1999 (although it has been closed since October 2000). Including East Jerusalem, the West Bank covers an area of 5,655 sq km. Precipitation ranges between 600 mm and 800 mm on the Mount Hebron massif and 200 mm in the Jordan valley. Apart from the urban centres of Beit Lahm (Bethlehem) and Al-Khalil (Hebron) to the south, the majority of the Palestinian population is concentrated in the northern localities around Ram Allah (Ramallah), Nabulus (Nablus), Janin (Jenin) and Tulkarm. The Gaza Strip covers an area of 365 sq km. Annual average rainfall is 300 mm. The language of Palestinians in the West Bank and Gaza is Arabic. The majority of the Palestinian population are Muslims, with a Christian minority representing about 2% of the Palestinian population of the territories. This minority, in turn, represents about 45% of all Palestinian Christians. The national flag (proportion 1 by 2) comprises three equal horizontal stripes of black, white and green, with a red triangle with its base corresponding to the hoist. Gaza City is the main population centre and the centre of administration for the Palestinian (National) Authority (PA), appointed in May 1994. Ramallah is the PA's administrative centre in the West Bank. In November 1988 the Palestine National Council (PNC) proclaimed Jerusalem as the capital of the newly declared independent State of Palestine. Israel (q.v.) declares Jerusalem as its capital. In 1967 East Jerusalem was formally annexed by the Israeli authorities, although the annexation has never been recognized by the UN. The permanent status of Jerusalem remains subject to negotiation on so-called 'final status' issues under the Oslo accords (see Contemporary Political History).

CONTEMPORARY POLITICAL HISTORY

Historical Context

Until the end of the 1948 Arab–Israeli War, the West Bank formed part of the British Mandate of Palestine, before becoming part of the Hashemite Kingdom of Jordan under the Armistice Agreement of 1949. It remained under Jordanian sovereignty, despite Israeli occupation in 1967, until King Hussein of Jordan formally relinquished legal and administrative control on 31 July 1988. Under Israeli military occupation, the West Bank was administered by a military government, which divided the territory into seven sub-districts. The Civil Administration, as it was later termed, did not extend its jurisdiction to the many Israeli settlements that were established under the Israeli occupation; settlements remained subject to the Israeli legal and administrative system. By October 2000 approximately 17.2% of the West Bank was under exclusive Palestinian jurisdiction and security control, although Israel retained authority over access to and from the zone; about 23.8% was under Israeli military control, with responsibility for civil administration and public order transferred to the Palestinian (National) Authority (PA); the remaining 59% was under Israeli occupation.

An administrative province under the British Mandate of Palestine, Gaza was transferred to Egypt after the 1949 armistice and remained under Egyptian administration until June 1967, when it was invaded by Israel. Following Israeli occupation, the Gaza Strip, like the West Bank, became an 'administered territory'. Until the provisions of the Declaration of Principles on Palestinian Self-Rule (see The Palestinian–Israeli Conflict) began to take effect, the management of day-to-day affairs was the responsibility of the area's Israeli military commander. Neither Israeli laws nor governmental and public bodies—including the Supreme Court—could review or alter the orders of the military command to any great extent. In 2001 an estimated 42% of the Gaza Strip was under Israeli control, including Jewish settlements, military bases, bypass roads and a 'buffer zone' along the border with Israel. However, Israel withdrew its settlers and military personnel from Gaza in August–September 2005 (see The Palestinian–Israeli Conflict).

The Palestinian–Israeli Conflict

The Oslo accords

In accordance with the Declaration of Principles on Palestinian Self-Rule of 13 September 1993, and the Cairo Agreement on the Gaza Strip and Jericho of 4 May 1994, the Palestine Liberation Organization (PLO) assumed control of the Jericho area of the West Bank, and of the Gaza Strip, on 17 May 1994. In November and December 1995, under the terms of the Israeli-Palestinian Interim Agreement on the West Bank and the Gaza Strip concluded on 28 September 1995, Israeli armed forces withdrew from the West Bank towns of Nablus, Ramallah, Jenin, Tulkarm, Qalqilya and Bethlehem. (These three agreements and associated accords are referred to collectively as the 'Oslo accords', owing to the role played by Norwegian diplomacy in their negotiation.) In late December the PLO assumed responsibility in some 17 areas of civil administration in the town of Hebron, with a view to eventually assuming full responsibility for civil affairs in the 400 surrounding villages. However, despite a partial withdrawal from Hebron in January 1997, Israeli armed forces were to retain freedom of movement to act against potential hostilities there and also to provide security for some 400 Jewish settlers. Responsibility for security in the rest of Hebron (excluding access roads) passed to the Palestinian police force. Following the first phase of the redeployment and the holding, on its completion, of elections to a Palestinian Legislative Council and for a Palestinian Executive President, Israel was to have completed a second redeployment from rural areas by July 1997. The Israeli occupation was to be maintained in military installations, Jewish settlements, East Jerusalem and the settlements around Jerusalem until the conclusion of 'final status' negotiations between Israel and the Palestinians, scheduled for May 1999.

Diplomatic developments within the context of the Oslo peace process led to a new timetable for Israeli redeployment, which envisaged two phases, subsequent to the Hebron withdrawal, to be completed by October 1997 and August 1998. Discussions on 'final status' issues—borders, Jerusalem, Jewish settlements and Palestinian refugees—were to commence within two months of the signing of the agreement on Hebron. As guarantor of the Oslo accords, the USA undertook to obtain the release from Israeli custody of Palestinian prisoners, and to ensure that Israel continued to engage in negotiations for the establishment of a Palestinian airport in the Gaza Strip and for safe passage for Palestinians between the West Bank and Gaza. The USA also endeavoured to ensure that the Palestinians would continue to combat terrorism, complete the revision of the Palestinian National Charter (or PLO Covenant), adopted in 1964 and amended in 1968, and consider Israeli requests to extradite Palestinians suspected of involvement in attacks in Israel.

In February 1997 the Israeli Government of Binyamin Netanyahu announced the construction of a new Jewish settlement at Jabal Abu Ghunaim (Har Homa in Hebrew), near Beit Sahur, which would prejudice 'final status' negotiations concerning Jerusalem because it would effectively separate East Jerusalem from the West Bank. In response, the PA withdrew from 'final status' talks scheduled to commence in March. The start of construction work at Jabal Abu Ghunaim provoked rioting among Palestinians and a resumption of attacks by the military wing of the Islamic Resistance Movement (Hamas) on Israeli civilian targets. Israel responded by ordering a general closure of the West Bank and Gaza. Both the Jabal Abu Ghunaim construction and Israel's unilateral decision to redeploy its armed forces from only 9% of West Bank territory (announced in March)

PALESTINIAN AUTONOMOUS AREAS

Introductory Survey

were regarded by many observers as a vitiation of both the Oslo and the subsequent post-Hebron agreements. Moreover, the Israeli newspaper *Ha'aretz* later reported that Israeli plans, evolved within the framework of the Oslo accords, to relinquish 90% of the West Bank had been revised to a 40% redeployment.

In June 1997 the US House of Representatives voted in favour of recognizing Jerusalem as the undivided capital of Israel and of transferring the US embassy to the city from Tel-Aviv. The vote (which was opposed by US President Bill Clinton) coincided with violent clashes between Palestinian civilians and Israeli troops in Gaza and Hebron. In July, on the eve of a scheduled visit by Dennis Ross, the US Special Co-ordinator to the Middle East, to reactivate negotiations between Israel and the PA, Hamas carried out a suicide bomb attack at a Jewish market in Jerusalem, in which 14 civilians were killed. Ross cancelled his visit, and the Israeli Government immediately halted payment of tax revenues to the PA and closed the Gaza Strip and the West Bank. In the aftermath of the bombing the PA undertook a campaign to detain members of Hamas and another militant organization, Islamic Jihad. As a result of US diplomacy, Israeli and Palestinian officials agreed to resume negotiations focusing on the outstanding issues of the Oslo accords in October.

It was reported in December 1997 that, under further US pressure, the Israeli Cabinet had agreed in principle to withdraw troops from an unspecified area of the West Bank. However, the Israeli Government subsequently reiterated that it would not conduct such a redeployment until the Palestinian leadership had adopted effective measures to counter terrorism, reduced the strength of its security forces from 40,000 to 24,000, and revised the Palestinian National Charter to recognize explicitly Israel's right to exist. Moreover, prior to a summit meeting in January 1998 between Clinton and Netanyahu in Washington, DC, USA, the Israeli Cabinet issued a communiqué detailing 'vital and national interests' in the West Bank (amounting to some 60% of the entire territory) that it was not prepared to relinquish, including the territory surrounding Jerusalem. In late January direct contacts between Palestinian representatives and the Israeli Prime Minister collapsed.

In March 1998 it emerged that the USA planned to present new proposals regarding the withdrawal of Israeli armed forces from the West Bank at separate meetings in Europe between US Secretary of State Madeleine Albright and the PA President, Yasser Arafat, and Israeli Prime Minister Netanyahu. However, it was evident that, even if agreement could be reached on the extent of territory involved, the issue of whether a subsequent withdrawal should take place prior to the commencement of 'final status' talks remained far more contentious. The Israeli Cabinet rejected the new US initiative. During a visit to Gaza City on behalf of the European Union (EU), in May the British Prime Minister, Tony Blair, hosted a summit meeting attended by Netanyahu, Arafat and Albright. At its conclusion, the US Secretary of State invited Netanyahu and Arafat to attend a further meeting with Bill Clinton in Washington, DC, to discuss the apparent US proposal that Israeli and Palestinian officials could proceed to 'final status' negotiations as soon as the scope of the next Israeli withdrawal from the West Bank had been agreed. In June details of the latest US initiative were unofficially disclosed in the Israeli press: Israel would be required to agree to 'no significant expansion' of Jewish settlements and to relinquish slightly more than 13% of West Bank territory over a period of 12 weeks, in exchange for increased Palestinian co-operation on security issues. The adoption by the Israeli Cabinet later that month of a plan to extend the boundaries of Jerusalem and construct homes there for a further 1m. people prompted accusations by the PA that it amounted to a de facto annexation of territories that were officially subject to 'final status' discussions.

On 7 July 1998 the UN General Assembly overwhelmingly approved a resolution to upgrade the status of the PLO at the UN. The new provision, which the USA and Israel had opposed, allowed the PLO to participate in debates, co-sponsor resolutions and raise points of order during discussions of Middle East affairs.

The Wye River Memorandum and subsequent US-sponsored peace negotiations

On 19–22 July 1998 Israeli and Palestinian delegations held direct negotiations in order to discuss the US peace initiative disclosed in the previous month. In September Netanyahu and Arafat met in Washington, DC, and agreed to participate in a peace conference in the USA. This summit meeting, also attended by President Clinton, commenced at the Wye Plantation, Maryland, USA, on 15 October 1998, and culminated in the signing, on 23 October, of the Wye River Memorandum, which was intended to facilitate the implementation of the Oslo accords. Under the terms of the Wye Memorandum, to be implemented within three months of its signing, Israel was to transfer a further 13.1% of West Bank territory from exclusive Israeli control to joint Israeli-Palestinian control. An additional 14% of the West Bank was to be transferred from joint Israeli-Palestinian control to exclusive Palestinian control. The Wye Memorandum also stipulated that: negotiations with regard to a third Israeli redeployment (under the terms of the Oslo accords) should proceed concurrently with 'final status' discussions; the PA should reinforce anti-terrorism measures and arrest 30 suspected terrorists; the strength of the Palestinian police force should be reduced by 25%; Israel should carry out the phased release of 750 Palestinian prisoners (including political detainees); the Palestine National Council (PNC) should annul those clauses of the PLO Covenant deemed to be anti-Israeli; Gaza International Airport was to become operational with an Israeli security presence; and an access corridor between the West Bank and the Gaza Strip should be opened. The Memorandum was endorsed by both the Israeli Cabinet and the Knesset (parliament) by mid-November. On 20 November Israel redeployed its armed forces from about 500 sq km of the West Bank (with the PA assuming responsibilty for all civil affairs and for security affairs in some 400 sq km); released some 250 (mainly non-political) Palestinian prisoners; and signed a protocol for the opening of Gaza International Airport. Israel retained the right to decide which airlines could use the airport, which was officially inaugurated by Arafat on 24 November.

However, implementation of the Wye Memorandum did not proceed smoothly. In December 1998, prior to a planned visit by Bill Clinton to Israel and the Gaza Strip, violent clashes erupted in the West Bank between Palestinians and Israeli security forces. One cause of the unrest was a decision by the Israeli Cabinet to suspend further releases of Palestinian prisoners under the terms of the Memorandum, and its insistence that no Palestinians convicted of killing Israelis, nor members of Hamas or Islamic Jihad, would be released. On 14 December, meanwhile, in the presence of President Clinton, the PNC voted to annul articles of the Palestinian National Charter that were deemed to be anti-Israeli. However, at a summit meeting the following day between Clinton, Netanyahu and Arafat at the Erez checkpoint between Israel and the Gaza Strip, the Israeli Prime Minister further demanded that the Palestinians should cease incitement to violence and formally relinquish plans for a unilateral declaration of Palestinian statehood on 4 May 1999 (the original deadline as established by the Oslo accords). Netanyahu announced that Israel would not proceed with the second scheduled redeployment of its armed forces on 18 December 1998, and on 20 December the Israeli Cabinet voted to suspend implementation of the Wye Memorandum.

Palestinians reacted to the death of King Hussein of Jordan in February 1999 with public grief—about 65% of the kingdom's inhabitants are believed to be of Palestinian origin—especially in the West Bank, which King Hussein ruled for 15 years until June 1967. For Arafat, the death of Hussein was a major political reverse since the King had frequently supported him when the peace process with Israel appeared to be on the verge of collapse. Arafat subsequently surprised many Jordanians by proposing the establishment of a Palestinian-Jordanian confederation. The proposal (which had been put forward as part of a peace initiative in 1985, but was rejected by King Hussein) was not welcomed in Jordan, where it was considered to be premature while the West Bank was still largely under Israeli occupation.

President Arafat came under intense international pressure to postpone a unilateral declaration of Palestinian statehood, at least until after the Israeli elections scheduled for May 1999. In late April PLO chief negotiators Mahmud Abbas and Saeb Erakat (the Minister of Local Government) visited Washington, DC, in order to secure certain assurances from the USA in return for an extension of the 4 May deadline. Following a meeting of the Palestinian Central Council (PCC), together with Hamas representatives, in Gaza, it was announced that a declaration on Palestinian statehood would be postponed until after the Israeli elections. The decision was applauded internationally, but provoked violent demonstrations among many Palestinians.

Meeting at Sharm el-Sheikh, Egypt, on 4 September 1999, during a visit to the region by US Secretary of State Albright, Arafat and the new Israeli Prime Minister, Ehud Barak, signed the Sharm el-Sheikh Memorandum (or Wye Two accords), outlining a revised timetable for implementation of the outstanding provisions of the original Wye agreement. Under the terms of the Memorandum, on 9 September Israel released some 200 Palestinian 'security' prisoners, and the following day Israel transferred a further 7% of the West Bank to PA control. A ceremonial opening of 'final status' negotiations between Israel and the PA was held at the Erez checkpoint on 13 September; shortly afterwards details emerged of a secret meeting between Barak and Arafat to discuss an agenda for such talks. However, in early October the Palestinians' chief negotiator and Minister of Culture and Information, Yasser Abd al-Rabbuh, warned that the PA would boycott 'final status' talks unless Israel ended its settlement expansion programme. In mid-October Barak, also under pressure from left-wing groups in Israel, responded by dismantling 12 'settlement outposts' in the West Bank which he deemed to be illegal. Meanwhile, Israel released a further 151 Palestinian prisoners under the terms of Wye Two. The first 'safe passage' between the West Bank and Gaza was inaugurated on 25 October. Israel asserted that it would maintain almost complete control over the so-called 'southern route', which linked Hebron to the Erez checkpoint.

'Final status' negotiations between Israel and the PA commenced in Ramallah on 8 November 1999, following a summit meeting held earlier in the month in Oslo, Norway, between Arafat, Barak and Clinton. A further redeployment of Israeli armed forces from 5% of the West Bank, scheduled for 15 November, was postponed owing to disagreement over the areas to be transferred. In early December Palestinian negotiators walked out of the talks, following reports that settlement activity had intensified under Barak. Apparently in response to US pressure, the Israeli Prime Minister subsequently announced a halt to settlement construction until the close of negotiations regarding a framework agreement on 'final status'. In late December Arafat conducted talks in Ramallah with Barak, who became the first Israeli premier to hold peace discussions on Palestinian territory. At the end of the month Israel released some 26 Palestinian 'security' prisoners as a gesture of 'goodwill'. Israeli armed forces withdrew from a further 5% of the West Bank on 6–7 January 2000. However, Israel announced in mid-January that a third redeployment from 6.1% of the territory (scheduled to take place on 20 January) would be postponed until Barak had returned from the USA, where revived talks on the Israeli-Syrian track of the peace process ended in failure. During a subsequent meeting with Arafat, Barak was reported to have proposed that the deadline for reaching a framework agreement be postponed for two months. The approval by the Israeli Cabinet of a withdrawal of its troops from a sparsely populated area of the West Bank led the PA to break off negotiations in early February. On 19–20 March Israel released 15 Palestinian 'security' prisoners, and the resumption of 'final status' talks was announced on 21 March. On the same day Israeli armed forces withdrew from a further 6.1% of the West Bank.

In mid-April 2000, following talks between Barak and Clinton in Washington, DC, Israel was said to have agreed to Palestinian demands for greater US involvement in future discussions. Moreover, the Israeli premier reportedly indicated that a Palestinian entity could be established in what was now PA-controlled territory—covering 60%–70% of the West Bank—although he refused to speak of a Palestinian 'state'. The third round of 'final status' talks between Israel and the PA opened at the Israeli port of Eilat on 30 April, at which Palestinian negotiators denounced a recent decision by the Israeli Government to construct 174 new Jewish homes in the West Bank. At crisis talks between Arafat and Barak in Ramallah in early May, mediated by Dennis Ross, Barak reportedly proposed the transfer to full PA control of three Palestinian villages close to Jerusalem, on condition that the third West Bank redeployment (scheduled to be implemented in June) be postponed. After PA negotiators admitted that the 13 May deadline for reaching a framework agreement would not be met, 'final status' talks were suspended. Moreover, on 21 May Israel suspended 'secret' talks being conducted between Israeli and Palestinian representatives in Stockholm, Sweden, after an Israeli child was seriously wounded in continuing violence in the West Bank. (The latest unrest came after Palestinians declared 15 May—the anniversary of the declaration of the State of Israel in 1948—to be a 'day of rage' and amid growing anger over the apparent unaccountability of the PA leadership.) The Israeli Government also reversed its decision to transfer the three Arab villages to PA control, demanding that Arafat take action to curb Palestinian unrest.

On 21 June 2000, two days prior to the scheduled date, the PA reportedly agreed to a postponement of the third redeployment of Israeli forces from the West Bank. The PCC convened on 2 July, and after two days of discussions stated that the PLO would declare a State of Palestine on or before 13 September. On 11 July 2000 Bill Clinton inaugurated a peace summit between Arafat and Barak at the US presidential retreat at Camp David, Maryland, with the aim of achieving a framework agreement on 'final status'. However, the talks ended without agreement on 25 July. Despite reported progress regarding the borders of a future Palestinian entity and the question of Palestinian refugees, disagreements over the future status of Jerusalem had been the principal obstacle to an accord. Israel was said to have offered the Palestinians municipal authority over certain parts of East Jerusalem, as well as access to the Islamic holy sites. PA officials, however, demanded full sovereignty over the holy sites (in particular the al-Aqsa Mosque and the Dome of the Rock), with East Jerusalem as the capital of a Palestinian state. Nevertheless, Israel and the PA pledged to continue peace negotiations and to avoid 'unilateral actions'—interpreted as Arafat's threat unilaterally to declare an independent Palestinian state on 13 September. After Arafat came under intense international pressure not to take such action, the PCC convened in Gaza on 9–10 September and agreed to postpone the declaration of statehood for an indefinite period (although 15 November was reportedly designated as the new target date). Later in September negotiations between Israeli and PA officials resumed in the USA, and on 20 September an agreement was signed allowing for construction of the Gaza seaport to begin (although the work failed to progress owing to the worsening security situation).

The al-Aqsa intifada

From late September 2000 the West Bank and Gaza Strip became engulfed in what became known as the al-Aqsa *intifada* (uprising—the first *intifada* lasted from 1987 to 1993), as Palestinians demonstrated their frustration at the lack of progress in the Oslo peace process and at their failure to achieve statehood. The outbreak of violence was triggered by the visit of Ariel Sharon, leader of Israel's right-wing Likud party, to Temple Mount/Haram al-Sharif in Jerusalem—the site of the al-Aqsa Mosque and the Dome of the Rock—on 28 September. Sharon's visit to the Islamic holy sites provoked violent protests and stone-throwing by Palestinians, to which Israeli security forces responded forcefully. The clashes spread rapidly to other Palestinian towns: by the end of October at least 140 people had died—all but eight of them Palestinians—and thousands had been wounded. In early October Arafat and Barak travelled to Paris, France, for negotiations led by the US Secretary of State, Madeleine Albright, but no agreement was reached on the composition of an international commission of inquiry into the causes of the violence. The Israeli authorities subsequently sealed off the borders of the West Bank and Gaza, and on 7 October the UN Security Council issued a resolution condemning the 'provocation carried out' at Temple Mount/Haram al-Sharif and the 'excessive use of force' employed by the Israeli security forces against Palestinians. Meanwhile, Israel accused Arafat of failing to intervene to halt the violence, as members of Arafat's own Fatah movement joined Hamas and other militant groups in the quickly escalating *intifada*. In an attempt to prevent the crisis from developing into a major regional conflict, a US-sponsored summit meeting between Barak and Arafat was convened on 16–17 October at Sharm el-Sheikh. At the close of the meeting US President Clinton announced that the Israeli and Palestinian leaders had agreed the terms of a 'truce' to halt the spiralling violence. The two sides had also reportedly agreed on the formation of a US-appointed committee to investigate the clashes. Barak, however, demanded that Arafat rearrest some 60 militant Islamists whom the PA had freed in early October.

At the end of October 2000 Islamic Jihad claimed responsibility for a suicide bombing on an Israeli army post in Gaza, signalling a new campaign against Israeli forces by militant Palestinian organizations opposed to the Oslo process. Israel responded by launching air-strikes on Fatah military bases, and declared a new strategy of targeting leading officials of militant Islamist groups suspected of terrorist activities. On 1 November Arafat held a crisis meeting in Gaza with the Israeli Minister for Regional Co-operation, Shimon Peres; the two sides were reported to have agreed a 'cease-fire', based on the truce brokered in Egypt in October. The following day, however, a car bomb exploded in Jerusalem, for which Islamic Jihad claimed responsibility. In early November President Clinton appointed the five-member international commission of inquiry, to be chaired by former US Senator George Mitchell; their investigations into the violence began in mid-December. Meeting with Clinton in the USA in early November 2000, meanwhile, Arafat demanded that the USA support Palestinian requests for the establishment of a UN peace-keeping force in the self-rule areas, despite Barak's opposition to such a force. Israel imposed an economic blockade on the West Bank and Gaza in mid-November, and launched airstrikes against PA offices in Gaza later that month, in reprisal for the deaths of two people in the bombing of a school bus for Jewish settlers. At the end of November the Palestinians rejected a partial peace plan, announced by Barak, whereby Israel would withdraw its armed forces from additional West Bank territory provided that the PA agreed to postpone any discussion of the remaining 'final status' issues.

A further round of peace talks opened in mid-December 2000, at which Clinton was reported to have proposed a peace deal that included plans for a future Palestinian state covering the Gaza Strip and some 95% of the West Bank, as well as granting the Palestinians sovereignty over the Islamic holy sites in the Old City of Jerusalem. However, the US plan also required that Palestinians renounce the right of return for 3.7m. refugees, which the PA deemed unacceptable. The negotiations broke down in late December after two Israelis died in bombings by Palestinian militants in Tel-Aviv and the Gaza Strip. In January 2001 Israel confirmed its policy of assassinating local Palestinian officials who were regarded as endangering Israeli society, which it referred to as 'targeted killings'.

The election of Ariel Sharon to the Israeli premiership in early February 2001 provoked violent demonstrations by Palestinians, who held Sharon responsible—as Israel's Minister of Defence at that time—for the Phalangist massacre of Palestinian refugees in Lebanese camps in 1982 (see the chapters on Israel and Lebanon). Immediately after Sharon's election Palestinian militants carried out a car bombing in Jerusalem, and in midFebruary a Palestinian bus driver launched an attack on Israeli soldiers and civilians in Tel-Aviv, killing nine people. Israel again responded by sealing off the Palestinian territories.

At the beginning of June 2001 21 Israelis were killed in a suicide bomb attack, apparently perpetrated by Hamas, at a TelAviv nightclub. The PA agreed the following day to implement the recommendations listed in the final report of the international commission of inquiry under George Mitchell (the Sharm el-Sheikh Fact-Finding Committee, or 'Mitchell Committee'), published in late May. The Mitchell Report recommended a freeze on Israeli settlement expansion; a clear statement by the PA demanding an end to Palestinian violence; an 'immediate and unconditional' end to the conflict and the disengagement of forces by both sides; and the resumption of security co-operation. Moreover, in mid-June the PA also agreed to an extended cease-fire brokered by the US Central Intelligence Agency (CIA) Director, George Tenet, although in early July both Hamas and Islamic Jihad formally announced that the cease-fire was ended.

Following a Hamas suicide bombing in early August 2001 that killed at least 15 Israelis at a restaurant in central Jerusalem, Israel ordered its armed forces to occupy several PA offices including Orient House, the PA's de facto headquarters in East Jerusalem. Israeli troops entered the West Bank town of Jenin in mid-August—the first Israeli reoccupation of territory transferred to full PA control under the terms of the Oslo accords. Palestinian officials called the action a 'declaration of war'. Later in the month Abu Ali Moustafa, the leader of the Popular Front for the Liberation of Palestine (PFLP), was assassinated by Israeli forces in the West Bank.

The unprecedented scale of the suicide attacks launched against New York and Washington, DC, on 11 September 2001—for which the USA held the al-Qa'ida network led by the Saudi-born militant Islamist Osama bin Laden principally responsible—precipitated efforts by the US Administration to encourage Israel and the PA to end the violence in the Palestinian territories, as President George W. Bush (who had been elected to the presidency in November 2000) sought to garner support for an international 'war on terror'. In mid-September 2001 Yasser Arafat, who had condemned the attacks in the strongest terms, declared that he had ordered militant Palestinian groups to halt their actions against Israelis, while Israel agreed to withdraw from PA-controlled areas of the West Bank. However, Sharon stated that his Government required 48 hours without violence prior to any resumption of peace talks. Arafat and Peres finally met in the Gaza Strip in late September, in an attempt to consolidate the cease-fire arrangements outlined in the Mitchell Report. However, on the first anniversary of the al-Aqsa *intifada* five Palestinians were shot dead by Israeli forces in Gaza, and retaliatory attacks between the two sides resumed.

President Bush disclosed for the first time in early October 2001 that the USA would accept the creation of a Palestinian state, on condition that Israel's existence was not threatened. The assassination in Jerusalem of Israel's ultra-nationalist Minister of Tourism, Rechavam Ze'evi, by three members of the PFLP—apparently in revenge for the murder of the PFLP leader in August—led Israel, in late October, to order its armed forces into six major West Bank towns. Shortly after Ze'evi's death Arafat banned all military factions of Palestinian political groups, and his security forces arrested several PFLP militants; however, the PA refused Israeli demands for their extradition. At least five Palestinians reportedly died in Beit Rima, near Ramallah, in a raid by Israeli forces searching for Ze'evi's assassins. Towards the end of October Israel stated that it would carry out a phased withdrawal from the six West Bank towns; however, its 'anti-terrorist' operation continued in Jenin and Tulkarm, and Israeli tanks continued to surround Ramallah.

The Israeli blockade of Arafat's West Bank headquarters

Hamas claimed responsibility for a series of attacks in Jerusalem and Haifa over a 24-hour period in early December 2001, in which at least 25 Israelis were killed. Palestinian security forces subsequently claimed to have arrested more than 150 militants, mostly in Jenin, and also reportedly placed the spiritual leader of Hamas, Sheikh Ahmad Yassin, under house arrest. Meanwhile, an Israeli missile strike on Arafat's official residence in Gaza destroyed two of his helicopters, while in Ramallah Israeli tanks advanced to the edge of the presidential compound, where Arafat was then residing. The Israeli Prime Minister increasingly began to draw parallels between Israel's efforts to suppress the *intifada* and the USA's 'war on terror', describing the PA as a 'terror-supporting entity'. In mid-December Israel responded to an assault on a settlers' bus in the West Bank (in which some 10 Israelis died) by declaring the PA leader to be 'irrelevant', owing to his failure to prevent such attacks, and announced that it was severing all contacts with Arafat. The Israeli military launched air-raids across the West Bank and Gaza, reoccupied large areas of Ramallah, and reinforced its military blockade of Arafat's headquarters; several Palestinian police officers and civilians were killed during the Israeli operations. Meanwhile, the USA again vetoed a proposed UN resolution calling for international observers to be deployed in the Palestinian areas. In a televised speech Arafat issued a strong condemnation of groups that carried out gun attacks and suicide bombings against Israelis, although Sharon insisted that Arafat would not be permitted to leave Ramallah until the PA arrested the perpetrators of Ze'evi's murder.

In January 2002 Arafat ordered an investigation into Israeli and US claims that the PA was complicit in a massive shipment of largely Iranian-produced weaponry—including *Katyusha* rockets, mortar shells and anti-tank missiles—which Israeli forces had intercepted in the Red Sea; the freighter, the *Karine A*, was apparently en route for the Gaza Strip to be used in attacks against Israeli targets. In February the Palestinian President accepted responsibility on behalf of his administration for the shipment. Following a gun attack by members of another militant group, the Al-Aqsa Martyrs Brigades, that killed six guests at a bar mitzvah ceremony in Hadera, northern Israel, Sharon ordered tanks and armoured vehicles to tighten their blockade of Arafat's Ramallah headquarters, and also reoccupied Tulkarm in order to arrest known Palestinian militants. Although the troops withdrew a day later, it was reported to be the largest military incursion since the start of the al-Aqsa *intifada*. Meanwhile, EU officials increasingly distanced themselves from the US position towards the conflict, reaffirming their support for Arafat as a crucial partner in the peace process. The EU also issued a formal complaint to Israel, listing EU-funded projects in the West Bank and Gaza that had undergone physical damage during recent military operations.

In early February 2002 Israel carried out the 'targeted killing' of at least four members of the radical Democratic Front for the Liberation of Palestine (DFLP) in the Gaza Strip. The violence came at a time of renewed efforts to restart peace negotiations. Ariel Sharon met leading PA representatives, while Shimon Peres held a series of discussions with the Palestinian Legislative Council (PLC) Speaker, Ahmad Quray. However, Israeli

PALESTINIAN AUTONOMOUS AREAS

officials were angered when a large number of Palestinian militants were freed during Israeli air-strikes on the PA's security headquarters in Nablus. Requests for calm by the UN and attempts by the EU to launch a new peace initiative in the second week of February—reportedly based on the convening of new elections to the PLC—failed to prevent an escalation of violence in the territories, particularly in Gaza. As Hamas appeared to be intensifying its attacks on Israelis by firing a new type of missile, the *Qassam-2*, against Jewish settlers, four Palestinian security officers died during incursions by the Israeli army into three Gazan towns. Israel also accelerated its military offensive in Hebron and Ramallah. In late February up to 30 Palestinians were reportedly killed in Israeli military operations across the West Bank and Gaza in retaliation for the shooting of six Israelis at an army checkpoint near Ramallah. The Israeli Cabinet subsequently agreed to withdraw its tanks from Arafat's compound in Ramallah, but refused to allow the Palestinian leader freedom of movement beyond the town: Sharon stated that the travel ban would remain in place despite the arrest by Palestinian security forces of three militants believed to have been responsible for Ze'evi's murder. The Israeli position led PA security officials to suspend the recently resumed bilateral talks.

Gun battles took place across the West Bank, despite efforts by Crown Prince Abdullah of Saudi Arabia to promote his proposals for peace in the Middle East prior to a summit meeting of the League of Arab States (the Arab League, see p. 361) Council, due to be held in Beirut, Lebanon, in March 2002. Abdullah's proposals centred on Arab recognition of the State of Israel and the normalization of diplomatic relations, in exchange for agreement by Israel to withdraw from all Arab land occupied since 1967 and on the establishment of a Palestinian state with East Jerusalem as its capital. Arafat announced that he would not attend the Beirut conference owing to threats by Sharon to prevent his return to the West Bank and Gaza. Meanwhile, in response to a suicide bombing by a Palestinian woman at an Israeli army checkpoint, Israel for the first time sent ground troops into two refugee camps in the West Bank which it claimed were centres of Islamist militancy: the Balata camp near Nablus and the camp at Jenin. Fierce fighting ensued, and the PA announced subsequently that it was suspending all contacts with the Israeli Government. The USA, meanwhile, urged Israel to show restraint, while UN and EU officials demanded an immediate Israeli withdrawal from the camps.

PA officials categorically rejected an offer made by Ariel Sharon in early March 2002 that Yasser Arafat should agree to go into voluntary exile. At the same time Israel refused to allow senior UN and EU diplomats to visit Arafat. A number of Palestinians were killed as Israeli forces entered Ramallah, Bethlehem and Tulkarm in an attempt to find those responsible for two attacks apparently perpetrated by the Al-Aqsa Martyrs Brigades, in which 20 Israelis had died. The US Secretary of State, Gen. Colin Powell, publicly criticized Sharon's declared aim of forcing the PA to return to peace talks by defeating them militarily. On 8 March five Jewish settler students were killed by Hamas gunmen in Gaza; an estimated 40 Palestinians died during the fierce fighting that ensued. Meanwhile, Sharon declared that Arafat had met the conditions required for his release after a fifth suspect in Ze'evi's murder was arrested by Palestinian security forces in the first week of March. However, after a suicide bombing in Jerusalem, killing 11 Israelis, and a shooting in Netanya in which two died, Israel's 'inner' Security Cabinet voted to intensify its military offensive. Tanks entered Qalqilya and the Jabalia refugee camp in Gaza (where 18 Palestinians, including four Hamas members, were reported to have been killed), while Arafat's headquarters in Gaza were destroyed by Israeli helicopters and gunboats.

On 11 March 2002 Israel announced that it was lifting its travel ban on Arafat, although the Palestinian leader would still not be permitted to travel abroad. The following day some 20,000 Israeli troops began a massive ground offensive in the Palestinian territories as part of a campaign to dismantle the 'infrastructure of terror'; hundreds of Palestinian men were detained for questioning, and several civilians died during the incursions. This was reported to be the largest Israeli operation against Palestinian militants since the 1982 invasion of Lebanon. Israeli forces again took control of most of Ramallah, with tanks coming to within a short distance of Arafat's presidential compound. On 12 March 2002 the UN Security Council adopted Resolution 1397, affirming its 'vision' of both Israeli and Palestinian states 'within secure and recognized borders'; the US-drafted resolution also demanded an immediate end to 'all acts of violence' by both sides, and called upon Israel and the Palestinians to co-operate in implementation of the Mitchell Report and George Tenet's recommendations. US special envoy to the Middle East Anthony Zinni returned to the region on the following day. Under pressure to withdraw as a 'goodwill' gesture to Zinni, the Israeli army later withdrew from Ramallah, Tulkarm and Qalqilya, although it continued to surround the towns. Following discussions between Zinni and Arafat, and US-brokered talks between Israeli and PA security officials in Jerusalem, Israel also agreed to redeploy its troops from Bethlehem and Beit Jala. After the security talks ended without agreement on 21 March, the Israeli Government again ordered troops into much of the West Bank and detained several alleged militants. A further suicide attack by the Al-Aqsa Martyrs Brigades, which killed three Israelis in central Jerusalem, prompted the USA to add the group to its list of proscribed terrorist organizations.

The Arab League summit proceeded in Beirut on 27–28 March 2002, in the notable absence of both President Hosni Mubarak of Egypt and King Abdullah of Jordan; the two leaders had apparently boycotted the meeting as a gesture of support for the PA President. Palestinian officials were angered when the Lebanese hosts refused to permit Arafat to address the session via a live satellite link from Ramallah: the Lebanese authorities had stated that they feared an Israeli disruption of such a broadcast. At the close of the conference, the participating Arab states unanimously endorsed the Saudi peace initiative, which also included a clause calling for a 'just solution' to the question of Palestinian refugees. Israel rejected the plan, however, stating that its terms would lead to the destruction of the Jewish state.

The Netanya bombing and 'Operation Defensive Shield'

The Israeli–Palestinian crisis deepened at the end of March 2002, following an attack by a Hamas suicide bomber at a hotel in the Israeli town of Netanya, where Jews were celebrating the festival of Passover; 30 people died as a result of the attack. Although Arafat personally condemned the bombing, and reportedly ordered the immediate arrest of four prominent West Bank militants, Sharon blamed the PA for its failure to prevent such attacks. In response to what was swiftly called the 'Passover massacre', Israel mobilized about 20,000 army reservists and convened an emergency cabinet meeting, at which 'extensive operational activity against Palestinian terrorism' was agreed. With Arafat effectively isolated at his compound in Ramallah, on 29 March Israeli armed forces began a huge campaign of incursions into West Bank towns—code-named 'Operation Defensive Shield'—with the declared aim of dismantling the Palestinian 'terrorist infrastructure' in order to prevent future suicide bombings against Israeli citizens. During the offensive Israeli forces entered and conducted house-to-house searches for militants in Ramallah, Bethlehem, Beit Jala, Qalqilya, Tulkarm, Jenin and Nablus. On 30 March the UN Security Council met in emergency session and demanded, in Resolution 1402, an immediate Israeli withdrawal from all towns that had been transferred to the PA under the Oslo accords. At the end of the month a Hamas suicide bomber from Jenin killed 15 Israelis at a café in Haifa. Sharon declared that Israel was 'at war', and his 'inner' Security Cabinet gave the army permission to broaden its offensive in the West Bank. Israeli armed forces reoccupied Ramallah and declared it to be a 'closed military area'.

In early April 2002 Yasser Arafat again dismissed a suggestion by Sharon that the Palestinian leader should go into exile. On 2 April fighting between Israelis and Palestinians in Bethlehem escalated into a siege at the Church of the Nativity—believed by Christians to be the birthplace of Jesus Christ. As many as 200 people—Palestinian civilians and priests, as well as some 30 armed militants wanted by Israel—sought shelter from Israeli troops inside the church. On 3 April Israeli tanks entered Jenin and its refugee camp. By the following day Israel had effectively reoccupied all but two major towns (Jericho and Hebron) in the West Bank and detained more than 1,000 Palestinians; Bethlehem, like Ramallah, was declared a 'closed military area'. On 4 April Israeli troops reportedly withdrew from Nablus but entered Hebron. Israel also intensified its offensive in the Jenin refugee camp, the alleged base of several of the suicide bombers. According to PA reports, more than 80 Palestinians died during the first week of Israeli military operations in Jenin. The UN Security Council unanimously adopted a resolution (No. 1403) that demanded the implementation of Resolution 1402 (i.e. an Israeli withdrawal from Palestinian territories) 'without delay'. On 9 April 13 Israeli army reservists were killed in ambushes in the Jenin camp, and the following day, in response to the deaths of at least eight people in the Hamas suicide bombing of a bus near Haifa, Israel ruled out the prospect of further withdrawals from the West Bank.

During mid-April 2002 Palestinians made increasingly vocal allegations of an Israeli 'massacre' at the Jenin refugee camp, claiming that Israeli armed forces were guilty of war crimes. Palestinian sources suggested that at least 100 Palestinians had died during the Israeli invasion; 23 Israelis were believed to have died. (In May the US-based Human Rights Watch issued a report stating that Israeli forces had been guilty of 'excessive force' and of war crimes in Jenin, but that there had been no massacre, findings echoed by a UN report released in August.) Also in mid-April Marwan Barghouthi, the Fatah leader in the West Bank (who Israel also claimed was the commander of the Al-Aqsa Martyrs Brigades), was arrested by Israeli forces in Ramallah; his trial, on charges of leading Palestinian 'terrorist' groups in the West Bank and of orchestrating a number of suicide bombings against Israeli citizens, began in August. (Barghouthi claimed that the Israeli judiciary had no jurisdiction over him, as an elected member of the PLC.) Meanwhile, Sharon announced on 21 April 2002 that the first stage of Operation Defensive Shield had been completed; however, Israeli forces were to remain in Ramallah and Bethlehem. Some reports stated that more than 4,000 Palestinians were detained during the offensive, although many were subsequently released. According to the Palestine Red Crescent Society (PRCS), by the end of April at least 1,500 Palestinians had been killed, and more than 19,000 injured, since the start of the al-Aqsa *intifada* in September 2000. According to Israeli sources, more than 470 Israelis had been killed, and many more wounded, as a result of the violence.

Yasser Arafat was freed by the Israeli authorities on 1 May 2002. His release came after the USA secured an arrangement whereby Israel agreed to end its siege of Ramallah, including Arafat's headquarters, on condition that the PA leader handed over six prisoners sheltering in the presidential compound who were wanted by Israel in connection with 'terrorist' activities. In late April four of the prisoners were convicted of direct involvement in the assassination of Rechavam Ze'evi by an ad hoc Palestinian court inside the compound, and were sentenced to between one and 18 years' imprisonment. The other two detainees were the PFLP leader, Ahmad Saadat, and a militant implicated in the *Karine A* affair. In early May the six prisoners were moved from Ramallah to a gaol in Jericho, where they were to remain in 'international custody' under US and British guard. Despite Arafat's release, US President Bush declared that he was not yet willing to meet the Palestinian leader. Following protracted negotiations, the siege at the Church of the Nativity in Bethlehem finally came to an end, after more than five weeks, on 10 May, when 13 remaining militants were transferred under international guard to Cyprus pending their dispersal to permanent exile elsewhere in Europe. The agreement ending the siege envisaged that 26 other militants who were removed to the Gaza Strip should be tried by a Palestinian court there. It was reported in mid-June that Israel had begun construction of an electrified (later, partially concrete) 'security fence', which would eventually extend along the length of its border with the West Bank, in an attempt to prevent further suicide bombings. In response to a series of fatal suicide attacks against Israeli citizens by Palestinian militants in late June, Israel again ordered its armed forces into several towns in the West Bank and Gaza.

The Israeli Cabinet responded to the latest suicide bombing in Tel-Aviv in September 2002 by announcing that it would seek to 'isolate' Yasser Arafat. Sharon declared that Arafat had failed to arrest militant Islamists known to advocate violence against Israeli citizens, and Israeli forces began the systematic destruction of Arafat's compound in Ramallah while the Palestinian leader reportedly remained inside one of the office buildings. At the same time Israeli armed forces launched a series of incursions into the Gaza Strip, which increasingly became the focus of Israeli military operations. At the end of September the Israeli siege of Arafat's headquarters was brought to an end, after the UN Security Council had issued a resolution (No. 1435), demanding the immediate cessation of Israeli military actions in and around Ramallah.

The 'roadmap' peace plan and the construction of Israel's 'security fence'

The stalled peace process was temporarily revived by the publication of the 'roadmap' peace plan (sponsored by the Quartet group, comprising the USA, Russia, the UN and the EU) on 30 April 2003. The release of the roadmap, which had originally been agreed in December 2002, was conditional on the announcement of a new Palestinian Cabinet under Prime Minister Mahmud Abbas (see Domestic Political Affairs). However, it also affirmed George W. Bush's pledge to focus attention on Israeli-Palestinian affairs following the successful US-led coalition's campaign during March–April 2003 to overthrow the regime of Saddam Hussain in Iraq. The roadmap envisaged an end to Israeli–Palestinian conflict and the establishment of a sovereign Palestinian state by 2005–06 (for further details, see the chapter on Israel). Broadly speaking, Palestinian responsibilities under the terms of the roadmap were restricted to a commitment to ending militant actions against Israeli targets and the establishment of a civilian and government infrastructure; otherwise, crucial issues concerning the Palestinian population, such as the borders of a future state, the status of refugees and Jerusalem, were to be decided during Israel's negotiations with Lebanon, Syria and other Arab states. Initially, Sharon objected to the issue of the right to return of Palestinian refugees and refused to consider the dismantling of Jewish settlements, but on 25 May 2003 the Israeli Cabinet accepted the terms of the roadmap. At the end of the month Sharon made the unprecedented acknowledgement that Israel was indeed in occupation of the Palestinian areas. In early June Sharon, Abbas and President Bush met in Aqaba, Jordan, to discuss the implementation of the roadmap, particularly the contentious issue of Jewish settlements.

Israeli troops had begun dismantling settlements in the West Bank in early June 2003, but this positive development in the peace process was overshadowed by a resumption of violence: on 10 June Israel attempted to kill the prominent Hamas leader, Abd al-Aziz al-Rantisi, leading to a retaliatory suicide attack against a bus in Jerusalem, in which 16 people died. Subsequently, Israeli helicopter gunships attacked targets in Gaza. Twenty-six people were killed in the renewed fighting, and the USA condemned the attempted Israeli assassination of al-Rantisi. Nevertheless, Israel continued to dismantle some Jewish settlements, to withdraw troops from certain areas of the West Bank and Gaza, and to release Palestinian prisoners. This latter development was not a condition of the roadmap, but was viewed as a 'goodwill' gesture to Mahmud Abbas, who was now apparently engaged in a power struggle with Yasser Arafat. Some 400 prisoners were released in August, but excluded those members of Hamas and Islamic Jihad who had been involved in planning or executing attacks against Israeli targets. Along with Fatah, these two militant groups had declared a three-month cease-fire at the end of June. Following the cease-fire declaration, Israeli troops withdrew from key parts of northern and central Gaza and removed roadblocks from the arterial north–south highway. In July Bethlehem was handed over to Palestinian control.

The successful implementation of the roadmap was threatened, however, by Israel's ongoing construction of a 'security fence' in the West Bank, which had begun in mid-2002. Ostensibly intended to act as a barrier against Palestinian militants who infiltrated Israel to carry out attacks, by mid-2003 Israel was being accused of seeking to annex Palestinian territory. However, construction of the barrier continued despite international criticism, and Israel also maintained its policy of targeting and killing Palestinian militant leaders. A senior commander of Islamic Jihad in Hebron was killed by Israeli forces on 14 August; on 19 August a suicide bomber killed 20 Israelis on a bus in Jerusalem, an attack for which both Hamas and Islamic Jihad claimed responsibility; and Israel raided militant targets in both the West Bank and Gaza Strip. The resumption of hostilities between Israel and the Palestinian militant groups effectively marked the end of the cease-fire declared in June. A prominent member of Hamas, Ismael Abu Shanab, was killed in an Israeli missile attack on 21 August; the following day Israel reimposed roadblocks on the main north–south Gaza highway.

In September 2003 it was reported that the Israeli Cabinet had agreed in principle to the removal of Yasser Arafat as 'a total obstacle to peace'. It was not made clear whether Israel sought to eliminate Arafat or to send him into exile, and, although the US Administration declared that it was opposed to either outcome, the USA vetoed a UN Security Council resolution on 16 September condemning Israel's new policy, on the grounds that the resolution did not condemn the actions of Palestinian militant groups. At the end of October Sharon denied that Israel had any

PALESTINIAN AUTONOMOUS AREAS

intention of 'removing' Yasser Arafat from power. Earlier in the month the Israeli Cabinet had approved the next phase of the 'security fence', and, although the new sections were not contiguous to those already built, they would completely enclose Jewish settlements in the West Bank.

Senior Palestinian and Israeli political figures launched a new peace plan in Geneva, Switzerland, in early December 2003. Yasser Abd al-Rabbuh, the former Palestinian Minister of Information, and Yossi Beilin, Israel's former Minister of Justice, were the most prominent supporters of the so-called 'Geneva Accords', which did not have the official approval of either the Israeli or Palestinian administrations. The Geneva Accords outlined a two-state solution to the Israeli–Palestinian issue, including proposals that: Palestinians would receive compensation for giving up the right of return; most settlements in the West Bank and Gaza (except those neighbouring Jerusalem) would be dismantled; and Jerusalem (to become the capital of two states) would be divided administratively rather than physically.

On 19 December 2003 Israel declared that, unless the PA started disarming and disbanding Palestinian militant groups, it was prepared to initiate a 'disengagement plan', consisting of the accelerated construction of the 'security fence' in the West Bank and the physical separation of Israel from the Palestinian territories. In February 2004 Ariel Sharon announced in an interview published in *Ha'aretz* that a plan had been drawn up for the evacuation of all Jewish settlements in the Gaza Strip: this would reportedly affect 7,500 settlers in 17 settlements (although details of the plan were subsequently amended—see below). This news was welcomed by the recently appointed Palestinian Prime Minister, Ahmad Quray. On 14 March 10 Israelis were killed in a double suicide bombing at the southern Israeli port of Ashdod, an attack for which both Hamas and the Al-Aqsa Martyrs Brigades claimed responsibility. In retaliation for the attack Ariel Sharon and his 'inner' Security Cabinet ordered Israel's most high profile 'targeted killing'. On 22 March Israeli helicopter gunships in the Gaza Strip attacked the founder and spiritual leader of Hamas, Sheikh Ahmad Yassin, and his entourage as they left a mosque, killing the cleric and several others. Yassin's assassination prompted international condemnation, especially from Iran and from Arab countries, where mass protests took place. However, a UN Security Council resolution condemning the killing was vetoed by the USA, which criticized the absence of any reference to Hamas as a 'terrorist organization'. Immediately after Yassin's assassination, Abd al-Aziz al-Rantisi was appointed to the leadership of Hamas in Gaza; however, al-Rantisi himself was killed in a targeted airstrike by Israeli forces in Gaza City on 17 April. EU leaders condemned both of the 'targeted killings' as illegal and unjustified. Hamas did not disclose the identity of al-Rantisi's successor and reportedly adopted a policy of 'collective leadership' in order to prevent future leaders of the organization from being victims of Israel's strategy. Khalid Meshaal apparently remained the head of the group's political bureau, based in Damascus, Syria. Meanwhile, details of Sharon's 'disengagement plan' were published in Israeli newspapers: it combined a complete Israeli withdrawal from the Gaza Strip, and evacuation of all Jewish settlements there, with the consolidation of six settlement blocs in the West Bank. In October the Israeli Knesset voted in favour of Sharon's proposal to dismantle all 21 settlements in Gaza, and four in the northern West Bank, entailing the eviction of about 9,000 Jewish settlers. The removal of settlements in Gaza was scheduled to commence in July 2005, but was later postponed until August (see below).

In May 2004 imprisoned Fatah leader Marwan Barghouthi was convicted by a Tel-Aviv court on five counts of murder and of leading a 'terrorist organization' which had launched Palestinian militant assaults on Israeli forces and settlers, although lack of evidence forced the court to acquit Barghouthi on 33 counts of resistance attacks. The court's verdict provoked strong criticism from the PA, which called the conviction 'illegal, immoral and unjust'. In early June Barghouthi was sentenced to five terms of life imprisonment and two additional 20-year terms.

Following a ruling by the Israeli Supreme Court, in June 2004 Israel altered the route of part of the 'security fence', including a 30-km section in a Palestinian village, Beit Sourik. In early July the International Court of Justice (ICJ) in The Hague, Netherlands, issued a non-binding ruling that the barrier breached international law and effectively constituted the annexation of Palestinian land. The ICJ urged Israel to remove sections of the fence and to pay compensation to affected Palestinians. Sharon rejected the court's recommendations, while the Palestinian leadership hoped that the decision would mobilize public opinion. In late July the UN General Assembly voted to demand that Israel comply with the ICJ ruling and take down the barrier (the USA voted against the resolution). Meanwhile, in August Sharon approved the construction of 1,000 new Jewish settlements in the West Bank.

In September 2004, following a double suicide bombing by Hamas in Beersheba, Israel, that killed 16 people, Israeli tanks and aircraft attacked a Hamas training camp in the centre of the Gaza Strip. In October the UN reported that 135 Palestinians had been killed and an estimated 95 homes destroyed following a 16-day Israeli military assault in northern and southern Gaza, prompted by a Hamas rocket that killed two children in Sderot, close to the border with Gaza. Following the death of Yasser Arafat in November (see Domestic Political Affairs), Sharon expressed hope that the new Palestinian leadership would understand the need to end 'terrorist' attacks before relations between the two sides could be improved and outstanding issues resolved.

Israel and Egypt agreed in early December 2004 that 750 Egyptian troops would be deployed along the country's border with Gaza in advance of Israel's planned withdrawal; however, Jewish settlers in Gaza vowed to resist eviction. In mid-December Mahmud Abbas issued a call (rejected by Hamas) for an end to the continuing use of violence in resistance to Israeli occupation. Despite referring to Israel as 'the Zionist enemy' when Israeli armed forces responded to Palestinian mortar attacks by firing two shells into a field in Beit Lahiya in early January 2005, killing seven Palestinians, Abbas continued to express hopes of implementing the roadmap and of achieving peace with Israel in the event of his election to the Palestinian presidency. Israel announced that it would withdraw troops from Palestinian areas prior to the election, and that its military would remain outside towns in the West Bank and Gaza Strip for 72 hours. Towards the end of December 2004 Israel released 159 Palestinian prisoners as a gesture of 'goodwill' prior to the Palestinian election.

In mid-January 2005 the deaths of six Israelis in a Palestinian militant attack at the Karni crossing prompted Sharon to sever ties with the Palestinian leadership and to order the Israeli army to raid several areas of Gaza. Following a demand by the PLO leadership that Palestinians should cease all military action against Israel, Sharon called off the offensive and announced that Israel would co-operate on security issues, although he instructed his troops to prepare for a full-scale assault on an area in the northern Gaza Strip from where rockets were being fired on Israeli targets, and in late January Palestinian security forces were deployed in the area to prevent such attacks. Despite talks being held between Hamas, Islamic Jihad and other militant groups chaired by newly elected PA President Abbas, Hamas continued to insist on its right to retaliate against Israeli attacks and demanded that Israel release more than 7,000 Palestinian prisoners and end its policy of targeting militants before it would enter into negotiations.

Negotiations with Israel following the election of President Mahmud Abbas

Security talks between Palestinian and Israeli officials began in late January 2005, and, despite attacks on Palestinian police vehicles by Jewish settlers, an agreement was reached on the deployment of Palestinian security forces in the southern Gaza Strip within 24 hours to reduce attacks on Israeli targets. (By this time 2,500 Palestinian security forces were patrolling northern Gaza, on the orders of the new Palestinian President.) Later in the month the former Palestinian Minister of Security, Muhammad Dahlan, and the Israeli Minister of Defence, Lt-Gen. Shaul Mofaz, agreed to the withdrawal of Israeli troops and the deployment of PA security forces in the five West Bank towns of Ramallah, Qalqilya, Tulkarm, Jericho and Bethlehem.

Abbas and Sharon finally met in early February 2005 at a summit meeting held in Sharm el-Sheikh, with Egypt's President Mubarak and King Abdullah of Jordan also in attendance. At the summit, Abbas announced a Palestinian cease-fire and Sharon declared that Israeli military operations would end if Palestinian militant attacks stopped, emphasizing that Israel would not compromise in its fight against 'terrorism'; Sharon also agreed to release 500 Palestinian prisoners as a 'goodwill' gesture. However, although some Palestinian militant groups signed up to the cease-fire, Hamas asserted that it would not be bound by it, criticizing the fact that it had been negotiated unilaterally, and demanded that Israel cease all acts of aggression against Palestinians and release all Palestinian prisoners before agreeing to a formal cease-fire, although they apparently agreed to an informal 'truce'. Soon after the Sharm el-Sheikh meeting, Israel permitted 56 deported Palestinians to return to the West Bank, and also transferred the bodies of 15 Palestinian bombers to the PA. The relative lull in violence was interrupted in late February by a suicide bomb attack by Islamic Jihad outside a nightclub in Tel-Aviv that killed four Israelis, halting Israeli plans to withdraw from the five West Bank towns.

In mid-March 2005 Israel officially surrendered Jericho to Palestinian security control, and also announced plans to remove all 24 outposts constructed since Sharon was elected to the premiership in February 2001, after a ministerial report condemned the illegal use of budget funds to develop the outposts. Although this development fulfilled a condition of the roadmap, it was criticized for the fact that not all of the 105 outposts, which were deemed by many to be illegal, would be dismantled. In late March 2005 Israeli forces withdrew from the West Bank town of Tulkarm.

Meanwhile, in February 2005 Israel announced plans to alter the route of the 'security fence' so that it would cut out 7% of the territory of the West Bank instead of the 16% outlined in the original route. In March the Israeli Government announced that the barrier (to be completed by the end of 2005) would divide the town of Bethlehem and also separate East Jerusalem and the settlement of Ma'aleh Edomin from the rest of the West Bank; the decision provoked protests by Palestinians, who demanded that the ICJ's recommendations be implemented and expressed concern at the unilateralism of the move and the negative impact that this could have on future peace talks with Israel.

Abbas travelled to Washington, DC, in May 2005 for his first meeting with President Bush since becoming President of the PA. Bush reportedly offered US $50m. in direct aid to the PA to develop the Gaza Strip after the Israeli withdrawal. The US President also urged Israel to dismantle illegal settlement outposts in the West Bank, to end the expansion of settlements and to ensure that the 'security fence' did not become a 'political border'. Abbas later advocated the start of 'final status' negotiations with Israel after its disengagement from the Gaza Strip. Meanwhile, in accordance with the agreement reached by Abbas and Sharon in February at Sharm el-Sheikh, the Israeli Government approved the release of 400 Palestinian prisoners. (A total of 398 prisoners were released in early June—two had chosen to remain in gaol.) Israel had released 500 prisoners shortly after the February summit meeting, but had delayed further releases, urging the PA to curb terrorism more effectively.

Following a series of Palestinian militant attacks on Israeli and Jewish targets (which the militants justified as retaliation for Israeli violations of the cease-fire), in late June 2005 Israel carried out raids across the West Bank and detained around 50 members of Islamic Jihad. Israeli forces also launched a missile strike on Gaza in a failed attempt to kill an Islamic Jihad activist. Palestinian Minister of the Interior and National Security Maj.-Gen. Nasser Yousuf declared a state of emergency in the Gaza Strip, and gave his forces permission to prevent militants from launching rocket and mortar attacks on targets in Israel. As clashes broke out between members of the Palestinian security services and Hamas militants, Israel carried out further air attacks on Hamas targets, killing seven fighters. Islamic Jihad claimed responsibility for a suicide bomb attack near a shopping mall in Netanya in mid-July that killed four Israelis. Israeli troops re-entered Tulkarm after it was reported that the suicide bomber had come from a nearby village. Meanwhile, Hamas launched a series of rocket attacks from Gaza, killing an Israeli woman and prompting Israel to carry out air-strikes on targets in Gaza used by the militant group. Abbas and Sharon held their second summit meeting since Abbas's election to the presidency in Jerusalem in late July, when Sharon again urged Abbas to rein in militants and suppress terrorism.

Israel completed its withdrawal from the Gaza Strip (according to the terms of its unilateral Disengagement Plan) ahead of schedule on 12 September 2005, when the last Israeli forces left Gaza. Although in July Israeli and Palestinian officials had reportedly agreed in principle to establish a 'safe passage' between the West Bank and Gaza Strip following the withdrawal, the status of Gaza's southern crossing into Egypt at Rafah was still disputed. Soon after it had completed the disengagement, Israel declared that the crossing would be closed for six months. In November, following intervention by US Secretary of State Condoleezza Rice, Israel reached an agreement with Palestinian officials to reopen the Rafah crossing later that month. The PA was to manage the crossing, with additional Israeli and EU observers monitoring the site remotely from a control centre via live television cameras.

In September 2005 21 people were killed when a Palestinian truck carrying rockets exploded during a Hamas parade in the Jabalia refugee camp in the Gaza Strip. Hamas accused Israel of having fired a missile at the truck from a remote-controlled drone aircraft; both Israel and the PA denied the accusation. However, Hamas responded by launching mortars into Sderot. The Israeli Government decided at an emergency meeting to permit the army to use any means necessary to suppress militants. Accordingly, the Israeli army stationed tanks and artillery batteries on Gaza's eastern and northern borders, began seizing Hamas and Islamic Jihad activists in the West Bank, and used air-strikes to kill militants in Gaza and to destroy a weapons store and weapons-production facilities, despite a pledge from Hamas to end attacks and return to the cease-fire. In October Israeli security forces also killed two senior Islamic Jihad militants in Tulkarm and arrested five other members of the Tulkarm cell, which it believed to be responsible for the suicide attacks in Tel-Aviv in February and in Netanya in July. Islamic Jihad avenged the 'targeted killings' by launching a suicide bomb attack on a market in Hadera, resulting in the deaths of five Israelis. Israeli Prime Minister Ariel Sharon declared a 'broad and continuous' offensive against militant Islamist groups, and hours later the Israeli army launched an air-strike on a car carrying two senior Islamic Jihad militants in Gaza: eight Palestinians, mostly civilians, died. In December Islamic Jihad launched a further suicide attack on the shopping mall in Netanya that it had targeted in July, killing another five Israelis.

Developments following Hamas's 2006 electoral victory

Israel reacted to Hamas's victory in the legislative elections held in January 2006 (see Domestic Political Affairs) by declaring that it would not negotiate with a Palestinian authority that included 'an armed terrorist organization' that advocated Israel's destruction. US President Bush announced that his country would also refuse to deal with Hamas until it renounced its call to destroy Israel, and stated that the USA would consider halting aid to the Palestinians. At the end of the month the Quartet group announced that financial assistance to a future Palestinian administration would depend on the extent to which Hamas fulfilled the following conditions: that it renounce violence, respect agreements approved under the Fatah regime and recognize Israel's right to exist. Egypt and Jordan also demanded that the militant organization reject violence and accept Israel's existence. The head of Hamas's political bureau, Khalid Meshaal, announced that his organization could enter into a long-term truce with Israel under certain conditions, including the return of Israel to its pre-1967 borders. However, Meshaal asserted that violent resistance to the occupation was legal.

Israel announced in February 2006 that, in order to punish the new Palestinian regime until it renounced violence and recognized Israel's right to exist, it would stop collecting customs and tax revenues on Palestinians' behalf, and would ask foreign donors to cease all payments to the PA; however, it would permit the transfer of humanitarian aid to Palestinians. President Abbas announced that the PA faced a financial crisis, while Hamas asserted that Arab and Islamic countries would compensate for a reduction in aid from Israel and the West. Later in the month the EU, which—like Israel and the USA—considered Hamas to be a terrorist organization, announced that it was to give the PA US $140m. worth of aid to save the interim administration from financial collapse. However, following the installation of the new Hamas-led Cabinet on 28 March, both the USA and the EU announced that they were withdrawing direct aid to the PA until Hamas fulfilled the three conditions placed on it by the Quartet group.

Meanwhile, as Israel continued to kill militants in the Palestinian territories following further missile strikes, it declared that, should Hamas resume attacks on Israel, all members of the organization would be deemed to be legitimate targets for assassinations, including Prime Minister-designate Ismail Haniya and future ministers. In March 2006 Israeli forces stormed the gaol in Jericho in which the Secretary-General of the PFLP, Ahmad Saadat, was being held prisoner, detaining him and other inmates suspected of involvement in attacks against Israel. US and British monitors had left the gaol immediately prior to the raid, ostensibly to protest against poor security arrangements there. A Palestinian high court had announced in 2002 that there

PALESTINIAN AUTONOMOUS AREAS

was no evidence that Saadat had been involved in Rechavam Ze'evi's murder, and both President Abbas and Hamas had recently announced plans to release him, as he had been elected to the PLC at the elections in January 2006. Israel, however, still wished to interrogate Saadat in connection with the murder, and therefore resolved to detain him before the Palestinian authorities released him. The raid, in which two Palestinians were killed, provoked unrest throughout the territories. Palestinians set fire to the British Council building in Jericho in protest at perceived British collusion with the Israeli authorities, and gunmen briefly kidnapped 11 foreign workers. The PFLP vowed to avenge Saadat's capture, which President Abbas condemned as a crime and a humiliation for Palestinians. In April the Israeli Ministry of Justice announced that a pre-trial inquiry had not produced enough evidence to try Saadat for Ze'evi's murder, but that he would be tried for other security offences. However, four other militant PFLP members detained with him were charged with the murder, among them the man accused of firing the fatal shot.

Israel's new Government under Prime Minister Ehud Olmert, which was appointed in May 2006, was at this time pursuing plans to establish Israel's permanent borders, if necessary unilaterally, by 2010. Olmert's so-called Convergence Plan entailed the annexation of West Bank settlement blocs to Israel and the transfer of other, majority-Palestinian, sections of the West Bank to full PA control. (Israel would retain the whole of Jerusalem under the plans.) The Israeli premier affirmed that Israel was, however, seeking to secure an internationally supported peace plan with Hamas, but that such a solution required the group to reject violence and adhere to peace agreements signed by Israel and the previous Fatah administration. Khalid Meshaal dismissed the Convergence Plan as allowing Israel to: illegally retain its possession of the largest section of the West Bank and its 'security fence'; reject concessions on the status of Jerusalem; and thwart the 'right of return' of Palestinian refugees.

In June 2006 Palestinians claimed that the shelling of a beach in the northern Gaza Strip, in which seven members of one family were killed, had been carried out by Israeli forces firing from gunboats. (The Israeli Prime Minister later declared that a technical failure had been to blame for the deaths, and issued an apology to the Palestinian authorities.) On 25 June Hamas militants from Gaza launched a cross-border raid, which resulted in the kidnapping of an Israeli soldier, Corporal Gilad Shalit; two other Israeli soldiers were killed during the raid, as were two of the militants. The following day Palestinian militant groups issued a statement demanding that Israel release all female Palestinian prisoners and detainees under 18 years of age in exchange for Shalit. Israel responded by launching air-strikes on Gaza and entering the southern part of the Strip. Israel's military actions (code-named 'Operation Summer Rains') to seek to secure the release of Corporal Shalit in the Gaza Strip continued despite the conflict that began between Israel and Hezbollah in July (see the chapters on Israel and Lebanon). Several bridges and official buildings were bombed by the Israeli military, while the territory's only power plant was also destroyed, leaving thousands of Gazans without electricity or water.

On 29 June 2006 Israeli security forces arrested 64 senior Palestinian officials, including eight Hamas ministers from the Cabinet and 20 other parliamentarians, for questioning in relation to their alleged involvement in attacks against Israeli targets. On the following day an Israeli missile destroyed the offices of the Ministry of the Interior and Civil Affairs in Gaza City. On 2 July an Israeli air-strike destroyed the office of the Palestinian Prime Minister, Ismail Haniya. The crisis continued to escalate during July, and many Palestinians died in the ensuing violence: it was estimated that Israeli troops killed more than 160 Palestinians in the period between late June and 23 July. Israel arrested the Speaker of the PLC, Dr Aziz Duweik, on 6 August, while some of the cabinet ministers arrested in June were released during subsequent weeks.

In November 2006 Israeli armed forces began a new military offensive in the town of Beit Hanoun, in northern Gaza. 'Operation Autumn Clouds' was aimed at destroying the infrastructure and weapons supplies used by Palestinian militants across the border in order to prevent the firing of rockets into Israel by the armed groups. It was reported that more than 50 Palestinians, including many civilians, were killed in the operation. However, a cease-fire between the sides was secured by President Abbas towards the end of the month, and Israel withdrew its troops from Gaza. Nevertheless, relations between

Introductory Survey

Israel and the PA deteriorated once again in early 2007, after the truce was broken by militant Palestinian groups, who continued to launch large numbers of rockets against Israeli targets such as the town of Sderot. Two human rights organizations claimed that the number of Palestinians killed by Israeli security forces in the West Bank and Gaza had tripled in 2006. A report issued by Israel's B'Tselem in December put the death toll at 657 people (including 140 minors); of this total, 322 Palestinians were assessed as being unarmed civilians. In May 2007 Amnesty International also reported that at least 650 Palestinians (including 120 minors) had been killed by Israeli troops in 2006, of whom more than 50% were civilians. Most of these fatalities had occurred in the Gaza Strip, following the intensification of Israeli bombardments of the territory from mid-2006. In mid-April 2007 Abbas and Olmert held discussions concerning a future Palestinian state and a possible prisoner exchange, in what was intended to be the first of a series of regular fortnightly meetings between the two leaders. However, in late April Hamas militants, announcing that they were ending the truce brokered in November 2006, resumed the firing of rockets into Israel from Gaza. Israel responded in May 2007 by conducting a series of air-strikes against alleged militant targets in Gaza; a number of Hamas legislators, ministers and local government officials were also detained by Israeli security forces.

Following the takeover of the Gaza Strip by militants of Hamas on 14 June 2007 and the subsequent naming of an Emergency Cabinet—consisting principally of independents and technocrats—by President Abbas in the West Bank on 17 June (see Domestic Political Affairs), on 24 June the Israeli Government agreed to transfer tax revenues to the PA that it had withdrawn following Hamas's election victory of January 2006. On 25 June 2007 a summit meeting was held in Sharm el-Sheikh between Egypt's President Mubarak, King Abdullah of Jordan, Israeli Prime Minister Ehud Olmert and President Abbas, aimed at expressing solidarity with Abbas's newly appointed Emergency Cabinet in the West Bank. Olmert declared that Israel was to free 250 Palestinian security prisoners as a gesture of 'goodwill' to the Palestinian President; a final total of 255 (mainly Fatah-affiliated) prisoners were duly released on 20 July. In that month Israel also granted an amnesty for some 180 Fatah militants who were sought by the Israeli security forces in the West Bank, provided that the men renounced violence against Israel and handed themselves over to the PA.

Abbas held discussions with Olmert in Jericho on 6 August 2007—the first meeting between Israeli and Palestinian leaders on Palestinian territory since May 2000—in preparation for the US-sponsored Middle East peace meeting scheduled for November. The two leaders held further talks on 'fundamental issues' in late August and early September 2007. On 5 September Israel's Supreme Court issued a ruling that the route of a further section of the 'security fence' along Israel's boundary with the West Bank should be altered in order to improve the living conditions of Palestinians residing at the affected village of Bil'in whose homes had been separated from the land they were cultivating. During 26–27 September the Israeli military took firm action against the continued launching by Palestinian militants of *Qassam* rockets against northern Israel by carrying out air raids and sending tanks into the north of the Gaza Strip; at least 12 Palestinians were reported to have died during the military campaign. Nevertheless, Israel released another 57 (mainly Fatah) Palestinian prisoners to the West Bank and 29 to the Gaza Strip on 1 and 2 October, respectively. In mid-October President Abbas for the first time outlined his specific demands with regard to the territory on which a future Palestinian state should be established: Abbas demanded that the state should cover 6,205 sq km (2,400 sq miles) of the West Bank and Gaza Strip—the exact amount of territory occupied by Israel in 1967. Towards the end of October 2007 the Israeli Government responded to the launching of missiles into northern Israel by Gazan militants by confirming a policy of reducing fuel and electricity supplies to Gaza, which it now classified as a 'hostile entity'. (An intervention by the Supreme Court prevented the authorities from phasing out electricity supplies until they could prove that this would not impede vital services such as hospitals and sanitation provision, although the fuel sanctions were permitted.)

The Annapolis conference on peace in the Middle East

An international peace meeting intended officially to relaunch the Middle East peace process was held in Annapolis, Maryland, USA, on 27 November 2007, with members of the Quartet group and the Arab League in attendance. Prior to the meeting the US

PALESTINIAN AUTONOMOUS AREAS

Introductory Survey

Secretary of State, Condoleezza Rice, had stated that it must advance the prospect of Palestinians achieving statehood, and had affirmed that reaching a two-state solution between Israelis and Palestinians was one of the priorities of the Bush Administration. At the close of the Annapolis summit, US President George W. Bush read a statement of 'joint understanding' between Ehud Olmert and Mahmud Abbas, who expressed their commitment to achieving a final settlement of the outstanding issues of contention between Israelis and Palestinians by the end of 2008. It was announced that: an Israeli-Palestinian steering committee would oversee 'vigorous, ongoing and continuous' negotiations between the two sides; the Israeli and Palestinian leaders would continue to meet on a fortnightly basis; and both Israel and the PA would comply with their obligations as agreed under the terms of the roadmap signed in 2003. However, on 4 December 2007 Palestinians complained that Israel had again contravened its obligations by issuing tenders for 307 new homes to be built at the Jabal Abu Ghunaim settlement in East Jerusalem. Moreover, Olmert appeared to indicate that Israel would not be required to conclude a peace treaty with the PA by the end of 2008 if it considered that the Palestinians had not met their security obligations; the Israeli leader was reported to have told his Cabinet that there was 'no commitment to a specific timetable' made at Annapolis. A Hamas spokesman reportedly responded to the Annapolis meeting by pledging that Palestinian 'resistance' to Israeli occupation would continue. Nevertheless, the Israeli authorities released a further 429 Palestinian prisoners (408 to the West Bank and 21 to Gaza—none of whom had been involved in attacks against Israelis) on 3 December 2007 as a further 'goodwill' gesture to President Abbas; most of those freed were Fatah members from the West Bank, with no Hamas or Islamic Jihad detainees on the list.

Meanwhile, on 2 December 2007 Hamdi Koran, one of the PFLP militants who had been seized when Israeli forces stormed the gaol in Jericho in March 2006, was sentenced in a court in Jerusalem to a term of life imprisonment (and an additional 100 years in prison), after he had been convicted of having assassinated the Israeli Minister of Tourism, Rechavam Ze'evi, in October 2001 (see above), as well as involvement in other attacks against Israeli citizens.

The first session of the Israeli-Palestinian steering committee established at the Annapolis peace meeting was held on 12 December 2007. However, against the backdrop of increased violence between Israeli forces and Palestinian militants in the Gaza Strip, and following the announcement of Israel's proposed settlement expansion, the talks failed to achieve significant progress. An international donors' conference was held in Paris on 17 December, with 68 states and international institutions in attendance. At the meeting, donors pledged funds worth US $7,400m. to ease the PA's budgetary crisis and to assist with proposed Palestinian development projects. Meanwhile, Israeli air-strikes against alleged militant targets in the Gaza Strip continued during December, with several members of Islamic Jihad believed to have fired rockets into Sderot being targeted. According to B'Tselem at the end of December, 344 Palestinians had been killed as a result of inter-factional violence in 2007—the highest number since the start of the second *intifada* in 2000.

The Palestinian death toll increased rapidly in early January 2008, as Israel intensified its military campaign in Gaza following a Palestinian rocket assault on the Israeli town of Ashkelon; Israeli officials explained the high number of casualties by claiming that militants were deliberately firing on Israeli security forces from civilian areas. By mid-January it was estimated that at least 100 Palestinians (mostly militants) had been killed by Israeli forces in Gaza since the Annapolis peace conference in November 2007. Nevertheless, B'Tselem reported at the end of 2007 that there had been a decline in the number of fatalities in the Israeli–Palestinian conflict in that year, compared with 2006: some 373 Palestinians were killed by Israeli troops during 2007, of whom 131 were estimated to be civilians and 53 minors; 290 of the deaths occurred in the Gaza Strip. During a visit to Israel and the West Bank in the second week of January 2008, US President Bush asserted that a future Palestinian state should be contiguous territory and not a 'Swiss cheese' of separate cantons; he also urged Israel to withdraw from Arab territory that its forces had occupied in 1967. Bush reiterated his demand that the PA dismantle the territories' militias.

On 17 January 2008 Israel imposed virtually a complete blockade on the Gaza Strip, which prompted vehement international criticism: the Israeli response to Palestinian violence targeted at its citizens was widely viewed as 'collective punishment' of the people of Gaza for the actions of a minority of militants. The blockade resulted in severe disruption to Gaza's electricity supplies, although Olmert did subsequently agree to allow some essential supplies into the Strip. None the less, on 23 January hundreds of thousands of Palestinians entered Egypt from Gaza in search of food, fuel and medical supplies, after Hamas militants had breached the Rafah crossing separating the two territories. (The crossing had been almost permanently closed since Hamas's takeover of the Strip in June 2007 because the Egyptian Government, as did Israel, refused to recognize Hamas as the legitimate administration there.) Egyptian officials responded by offering their backing to a plan proposed by President Abbas that would allow for the PA, rather than Hamas, to assume control of the Egypt–Gaza border. Although the breaches in the border were repaired by 3 February 2008, there were reports of exchanges of gunfire between Egyptian security forces and Palestinian gunmen as tensions continued. The UN estimated that 700,000 Gazans (about 50% of the territory's population) had crossed the border into Egypt. On 4 February the Al-Aqsa Martyrs Brigades reportedly claimed responsibility for the first suicide bombing in Israel for more than a year, in the southern town of Dimona (in which an Israeli woman died), although a Hamas representative apparently alleged that militants from its Hebron branch had in fact carried out the attack. The Israeli Government implied that the perpetrator of the bombing, whom it believed to be Gazan, must have entered Israel via Egypt as a direct result of the border having been breached. As Israeli officials threatened a full-scale invasion of the Gaza Strip and also pledged to restart the policy of 'targeted killings' of Hamas and other militants, Olmert declared that he considered the status of Jerusalem to be the final 'core issue' to be negotiated by the two parties—a proposal that was rejected strongly by many Palestinians.

In March 2008 a militant Palestinian, believed to be a resident of East Jerusalem, entered a Jewish religious college in West Jerusalem and shot dead eight students. As with the Dimona bombing, the issue of whether ultimate responsibility for the shooting could be attributed to Hamas remained unclear. Although the Israeli Government affirmed that it would not break off peace negotiations with the PA, the likelihood of a swift breakthrough in the peace process was again impeded when, shortly after the Jerusalem shooting, Olmert approved a plan to construct a further 330 homes for Jewish settlers in the West Bank. At the end of April 12 Palestinian militant factions (excluding Fatah and Hamas), meeting in Cairo under the auspices of the Egyptian Government, reportedly agreed to new proposals for a cease-fire to be reached with Israel: a cessation of violence was to be implemented gradually, beginning in the Gaza Strip and then being undertaken in the West Bank, provided that Israel also ended its economic blockade of Gaza. Talks between Abbas and Olmert, under the terms agreed at Annapolis, had resumed earlier that month. However, with regard to a proposed cease-fire deal between Israel and Hamas, Olmert emphasized during discussions in Jerusalem with the Egyptian intelligence chief, Lt-Gen. Omar Suleiman, that Israel demanded an end to the weapons-smuggling by Palestinian militants into Gaza and the release of its abducted soldier Corporal Gilad Shalit in order for any sustainable truce to be realized. A Hamas spokesman subsequently rejected any linkage between Shalit's release and a period of calm, asserting that the organization required the release of 450 Palestinian prisoners in exchange for Shalit.

Following several violent incidents in previous weeks, in mid-June 2008 a formal cease-fire was finally agreed between Israel and Hamas representatives in the Gaza Strip, after lengthy negotiations led by Egyptian mediators. Israel was to end its economic blockade of the Strip and cease military action in the territory, on condition that Hamas militants and those of other Palestinian groups refrained from conducting any cross-border attacks on Israeli targets. The truce was to remain in place for at least six months, but to take effect in stages. Yet towards the end of June Israeli officials complained of a 'grave violation' of the cease-fire by Palestinian militants who had launched a rocket attack against the town of Sderot, and responded by closing Israel's border crossings into Gaza. The rocket attack was alleged to have been carried out by Islamic Jihad in retaliation for an Israeli military raid in the West Bank, which caused two Palestinian deaths. Hamas asserted in July that, since Israel was not abiding by the terms of the recent truce, it had suspended bilateral negotiations concerning a proposed prisoner exchange

PALESTINIAN AUTONOMOUS AREAS

involving the release of Corporal Shalit. Meanwhile, three Israelis were killed by a Palestinian militant in Jerusalem. In August the Israeli Government released 198 Palestinian prisoners as a gesture of 'goodwill' to President Abbas. The list included two of the longest-serving Palestinian detainees, who—contrary to Israel's usual policy of not freeing those with 'blood on their hands'—had been responsible for the deaths of two Israeli citizens in the 1970s.

In November 2008 the first direct clashes between Israeli armed forces and Hamas militants since the cease-fire agreement of June took place in the Gaza Strip. Israel launched a renewed military campaign in the territory and reimposed its blockade, while Hamas and Islamic Jihad fighters responded by firing rockets into northern Israel. Officials from the US Administration conceded that it was no longer possible to achieve an Israeli-Palestinian peace agreement by the end of the year, as envisaged by the November 2007 Annapolis meeting. Nevertheless, at the first meeting held between Abbas and Olmert for two months, Olmert promised to free a further 250 Palestinian prisoners as a 'confidence-building measure' towards the Palestinian President. After a government committee agreed to the release of only 230 Palestinians, on 15 December 2008 a total of 227 prisoners (none of whom were from Hamas or Islamic Jihad) were freed. On 16 December the UN Security Council approved Resolution 1850, which reiterated its endorsement of a two-state solution to the Israeli–Palestinian conflict and affirmed that the peace process was 'irreversible'. The resolution urged all parties involved in the negotiations to intensify their efforts to achieve a comprehensive and lasting peace in the Middle East.

'Operation Cast Lead'

However, on 19 December 2008, following discussions with other Palestinian factions in the Gaza Strip, Hamas formally declared an end to its six-month truce with Israel, asserting that Israel had not adhered to its requirements under the terms of the agreement. Rocket and mortar attacks by Palestinian militants against towns in northern Israel followed, and Israel launched air-strikes against Gaza. On 27 December Olmert ordered a campaign of intensive air-strikes against targets in the Strip, as the first phase of its offensive code-named 'Operation Cast Lead', undertaken in response to the increased cross-border attacks. The principal targets initially appeared to be security headquarters and police stations, as well as the tunnels used by militants to smuggle weapons used to launch attacks against Israelis. At least 225 Palestinians were reported to have been killed on the first day of the Israeli military operation. On 27 December the Commissioner-General of the UN Relief and Works Agency for Palestine Refugees in the Near East (UNRWA) expressed horror at the extensive destruction and loss of life caused by the Israeli action and, while recognizing Israel's legitimate security concerns, urged the Israeli military to cease the bombardment and to respect all international conventions regarding the protection of non-combatants in times of conflict to which Israel is a signatory. Meeting on the following day, the UN Security Council expressed 'serious concern at the escalation of the situation in Gaza' and urged an immediate halt to all violence.

Having declared an 'all-out war against Hamas' on 29 December 2008, the Israeli Government sanctioned a wider campaign of air-strikes, which now targeted government offices, presidential buildings and the Islamic University in Gaza. On 31 December UNRWA stated that the ongoing Israeli bombardment had inflicted considerable damage on the Gaza Strip's already fragile public infrastructure, and that it had erased the territory's public service capacity. On 3 January 2009 Israel launched a major ground assault into the Strip. The declared aim of the operation, which effectively divided the enclave into two, was to guarantee the long-term security of Israel's citizens by preventing the continued firing of rockets and mortars by Hamas militants against towns in southern Israel; the Israeli military sought to destroy Hamas's infrastructure, weapons factories and supplies. Heavy fighting ensued in densely populated districts of Gaza City and other urban centres. There was condemnation from the international community on 6 January, when an Israeli mortar attack close to an UNRWA-administered school in the Jabalia refugee camp resulted in the deaths of 43 Palestinians; at that time around 25 UNRWA-run schools were serving as temporary shelters to Palestinians who had been displaced by the ongoing violence, and a further two of these had also come under attack. Soon afterwards UNRWA temporarily suspended its movements through Gaza (including food distribution activities) owing to Israeli air-strikes on humanitarian convoys that had caused several fatalities. On 8 January the UN Security

Introductory Survey

Council adopted Resolution 1860, which demanded: an immediate and durable cease-fire in Gaza, culminating in the full withdrawal of Israeli forces; the unimpeded provision throughout Gaza of food, fuel and medical treatment; improved international arrangements to prevent arms- and ammunition-smuggling; intra-Palestinian reconciliation; and renewed efforts to achieve a comprehensive long-term peace between Israel and the Palestinians. The USA abstained from the vote. Hostilities continued, however, and on 15 January UNRWA's Gaza field headquarters was struck and set alight by Israeli shells that reportedly contained incendiary white phosphorus; the UN Secretary-General, Ban Ki-Moon, protested strongly against the attack. On the same day Said Siyam, the Minister of the Interior and Civil Affairs in the Hamas administration, was killed, along with two members of his family, in an Israeli aerial attack on the Jabalia camp.

On 17 January 2009 the Israeli Government declared a unilateral cease-fire in its conflict with Hamas, with Prime Minister Olmert asserting that the objectives of Operation Cast Lead had been achieved. Hours after the cease-fire entered into effect, on 18 January, Hamas also announced a week-long cessation of hostilities against Israeli targets, in order to permit Israel to withdraw its armed forces from the Gaza Strip; the Israeli withdrawal was completed on 21 January. UNRWA reported that by the time of the cease-fire 1,340 Palestinians had been killed (including 460 children and 106 women), and some 5,320 wounded (including 1,855 children and 795 women), during the 22-day Israeli offensive. In addition, thousands of Palestinian homes, as well as commercial and industrial buildings, had been destroyed by Israeli forces. Some 13 Israelis (including 10 soldiers) were reported to have died, and at least 680 to have been injured. A report published by B'Tselem on 9 September claimed that 1,387 Palestinians had been killed during Operation Cast Lead, of whom 773 were civilians (including 320 children and 109 women), 330 were combatants and 248 were Hamas police officers who died in an Israeli bombing raid at the start of the offensive; the status of the remaining 36 was unknown. These figures differed markedly from those of the Israeli Defence Forces (IDF), which reportedly assessed that 1,166 Palestinians had been killed during the campaign, of whom 295 were civilians and 709 were Hamas fighters; the IDF claimed that 162 of the fatalities had an unclear status.

According to the PRCS, by the end of December 2008 (therefore excluding most of the duration of Operation Cast Lead) some 5,365 Palestinians had been killed, and 33,639 injured, since the start of the al-Aqsa *intifada* in September 2000. By the end of December 2009 the number of Palestinian deaths was estimated by the Palestinian Central Bureau of Statistics to have increased to 7,235.

In early 2009 international diplomatic efforts were conducted in the region with the aim of securing a more formal, permanent truce between Israel and Hamas, thereby ensuring that international arrangements would be put in place to prevent the smuggling of weapons into Gaza, and to allow for the unimpeded provision of humanitarian aid within Gaza and the subsequent reconstruction of the territory's infrastructure. On 18 January an international summit was held in Sharm el-Sheikh, hosted by Egypt's President Mubarak and attended principally by leaders of European nations and the Arab League (including President Abbas). Delegates at the Sharm el-Sheikh summit agreed to intensify efforts to provide much-needed humanitarian aid to Gaza's population, to support Egypt in its ongoing mediation between Hamas and Israel, and to maintain a dialogue with the Israeli Government. On 19–20 January, at an Arab Economic, Social and Development Summit taking place in Kuwait City, King Abdullah of Saudi Arabia warned Israel that the Arab League peace initiative originally proposed in 2002 would not remain on offer indefinitely; the King also denounced Israel's 'excessive use of force' in Gaza. In February 2009 the Israeli Government stated that, until the release of Corporal Gilad Shalit, who was still being held captive by Hamas, border crossings into Gaza would not be reopened and an official long-term cease-fire would not be concluded. International donors, convened in Sharm el-Sheikh in March, pledged some US $5,200m. in funds that were to provide humanitarian aid and rebuilding assistance for Gaza, as well as budgetary support to the PA.

PALESTINIAN AUTONOMOUS AREAS

A new Israeli Government led by Binyamin Netanyahu and the continued suspension of the peace process

The inauguration of Barack Obama as US President on 20 January 2009 resulted in renewed efforts by the USA to engage constructively in efforts to resolve the Israeli–Palestinian situation, and, indeed, wider Middle East conflict. In early March the new US Secretary of State, Hillary Clinton, declared her support for the creation of a Palestinian state in the West Bank and Gaza. However, at the end of March a new Israeli Government took office under the premiership of Binyamin Netanyahu, who, shortly after his appointment, stated that he would not endorse a two-state solution to the Israeli–Palestinian crisis. Moreover, the new Israeli Minister of Foreign Affairs, Avigdor Lieberman, declared that decisions reached at the November 2007 Annapolis meeting had 'no validity'. In early April 2009 President Obama restated the US Administration's strong support for the commitments made at Annapolis. Furthermore, in mid-May, during a meeting with Netanyahu in Washington, DC, the US President declared his commitment to a two-state solution to the Israeli–Palestinian conflict, and identified the expansion of Israeli settlements as the chief obstacle to the resumption of peace negotiations. Meanwhile, in April the UN Human Rights Council (UNHRC) appointed a fact-finding team, headed by South African judge Richard Goldstone, to investigate violations of human rights and humanitarian law committed in the context of the December 2008–January 2009 conflict in Gaza.

In mid-June 2009 Prime Minister Netanyahu indicated, for the first time during his premiership, his acceptance of the idea of a sovereign Palestinian state. However, he insisted that the formation of such a state would be conditional on the complete demilitarization of the Palestinian territories and Arab recognition of Israel as a Jewish state, with an undivided Jerusalem as its capital. Netanyahu also rejected the 'right of return' of Palestinian refugees. The proposal was rejected by the Palestinian leadership, on the grounds that it placed unacceptable limitations on the sovereignty of a future Palestinian state. An invitation to resume direct negotiations, issued to President Abbas in mid-July, was rejected, with the Palestinians refusing to resume peace talks, frozen since the launch of the Israeli offensive in the Gaza Strip in December 2008, until a complete cessation of Israeli settlement activity had been implemented.

Between June and August 2009 George Mitchell, the US Special Envoy to the Middle East, and other senior-level US diplomats were engaged in intensive efforts aimed at reviving the peace process. However, the prospects for a revival of peace talks were undermined in early September when the Israeli Ministry of Defence granted approval for the construction of 455 new housing units in Jewish settlements in the West Bank. Later in the month further efforts on the part of Mitchell to foster an agreement on settlements were unsuccessful. It was reported that Netanyahu was proposing a temporary moratorium on new housing units in the West Bank, but this was deemed inadequate by the Palestinian negotiators, who continued to demand a complete cessation of all settlement construction in the West Bank and East Jerusalem. No significant breakthrough was achieved when President Obama hosted a meeting between Netanyahu and Abbas during a session of the UN General Assembly in New York on 22 September. Abbas met with US Secretary of State Hillary Clinton in Abu Dhabi, United Arab Emirates (UAE), on 31 October, where he again rejected a resumption of talks based on a partial suspension of settlement activity. During a visit to Jerusalem later that day Clinton praised Netanyahu's proposals on restraining settlement activity, describing his proposed concessions as 'unprecedented'. This apparent softening of the US position on Israeli settlements provoked strong criticism from the Palestinian leadership.

Meanwhile, the UN Fact Finding Mission on the Gaza Conflict, headed by Richard Goldstone, issued its final report on 15 September 2009. The report concluded that both the Israeli armed forces and Hamas militants had committed war crimes during the conflict, and outlined evidence of possible crimes against humanity committed by both sides. The most serious allegations were levelled against Israel's armed forces, who were accused of: launching a disproportionate operation, which aimed to 'punish, humiliate and terrorize' the civilian population of Gaza; targeting civilian and commercial infrastructure; and using inappropriate armaments, including white phosphorous. On the Palestinian side, the report highlighted: indiscriminate rocket attacks against Israel; the possible use of 'human shields' by militants in Gaza; and arbitrary arrests and extra-judicial executions carried out by the authorities in both Gaza and the West Bank. Hamas denied the report's claims regarding its own conduct, but supported its referral to the UN Security Council. In a surprising development on 2 October, shortly before a scheduled vote at the UNHRC concerning referral of the report to the Security Council, PA representatives requested that the vote be deferred for six months. The decision was reportedly made under intense pressure from US diplomats, who warned that the report could endanger efforts to revive the peace process; other sources suggested that Israel had threatened to tighten economic restrictions on the West Bank if the report was forwarded to the UN Security Council. The decision proved hugely unpopular with many Palestinians and drew strong criticism from the leaders of several Arab states; a planned visit by Abbas to Damascus was cancelled by the Syrian authorities. Following public protests against Abbas in the Gaza Strip and the West Bank, the President, in a televised address on 11 October, explained that the deferral had been implemented in order to secure greater support for a future resolution on the report. None the less, Abbas reversed his earlier decision and announced that the PA would resubmit the report to the UNHRC. The council endorsed the Gaza report on 16 October, and in early November the UN General Assembly endorsed a resolution demanding that Israel conduct an investigation into allegations that its forces had committed war crimes. In late January 2010 the de facto Hamas administration in Gaza submitted to the UNHRC the findings of an internal investigation into the findings of the Goldstone report. According to the report, Hamas militants had been instructed to attack military targets only, and any civilian casualties resulting from Hamas operations were, therefore, accidental. The report apparently contained an unprecedented apology for Israeli civilian casualties caused by Hamas rockets. However, following condemnation from several Palestinian factions, the apology was subsequently retracted and denounced by Hamas officials. Human Rights Watch rejected the findings of the Hamas report and insisted that militants had deliberately targeted Israeli civilians during the Gaza conflict.

In early October 2009 the Israeli authorities freed 20 female Palestinian prisoners in exchange for a video recording that appeared to show that Corporal Gilad Shalit, who had been kidnapped by Hamas militants in June 2006, was alive and in good health. Israel denied that the release, in late May 2010, of Muhammad Abu Tir—a senior Hamas member of the PLC who had been among scores of Palestinian officials to be arrested after Shalit's abduction—was connected to a prisoner exchange deal involving Shalit's release. (Abu Tir became the 10th Hamas parliamentarian to be freed by the Israeli authorities in recent months, although he was rearrested in early July and threatened with deportation, together with three other Hamas-backed politicians.) By mid-December 2010 such a deal had yet to be concluded, with the Israeli authorities reportedly refusing to meet Hamas's demand that hundreds of Palestinian detainees (including several high-ranking militants) be included in the transaction. It was reported at this time that President Abbas had urged Hamas to release Shalit, apparently without preconditions, comparing his situation to that of Palestinians held in Israeli detention; however, the President acknowledged that he had limited authority over the Islamist organization in de facto control of the Gaza Strip.

Although there had been a notable decrease in the number of rockets being launched across the border into Israel by Palestinian militants since the conflict in Gaza, Israelis were alarmed by reports in early November 2009 that Hamas had test-fired a longer-range missile that could, in theory, reach as far as Tel-Aviv. Indeed, the violence across Israel's border with Gaza continued into 2010: at the end of March, following further Palestinian rocket attacks, an incursion by Israeli forces into Gaza resulted in two Israeli soldiers and two Palestinian militants being killed.

Following pressure from the US Administration, on 25 November 2009 Netanyahu formally announced the imposition of a 10-month moratorium on the construction of new housing units in Jewish settlements in the West Bank, excluding some 3,000 units that were already under construction or for which permission had already been granted. Crucially, the moratorium did not apply to settlements within East Jerusalem, which Netanyahu described as part of Israel's 'sovereign capital'. The issue of settlements remained an insurmountable obstacle to peace negotiations during 2010. In mid-February it was revealed by the Israeli Ministry of Defence that construction work had continued in some 29 settlements in the West Bank, despite the moratorium on settlement-building activity. In March the start of the so-called 'proximity talks' (see below) was delayed after the Israeli authorities approved plans for a further 1,600 new homes to be built in the settlement of Ramat Shlomo, in East Jerusalem.

Meanwhile, following the assassination of Mahmoud al-Mabhouh, a senior member of Hamas, in Dubai, UAE, on 19 January 2010, Hamas accused the Israeli external intelligence service, Mossad, of involvement in the killing. The Israeli Government insisted that there was no evidence to support such a claim. In mid-February the authorities in Dubai issued details of 11 individuals suspected of involvement in the assassination, all of whom had travelled to the emirate using false or stolen British, Australian, Irish, French and German passports, and announced that they were '99% certain' of Mossad's involvement in the operation. It was subsequently reported that police in Dubai were investigating the possibility that al-Mabhouh had been betrayed by a Hamas associate. Meanwhile, reports emanating from Gaza emphasized the alleged involvement of two former members of Fatah's security service, who had been arrested in Jordan in connection with the investigation into al-Mabhouh's death.

A short-lived resumption of peace negotiations and partial easing of the Gaza blockade

It was reported in late January 2010 that a US proposal to revive the peace process through indirect negotiations, to be mediated by George Mitchell and other US diplomats, was under consideration by Palestinian and Israeli officials. Abbas resolved to consult with other Arab leaders before accepting the proposal. At the beginning of March the Arab League granted approval to the plan, although with the provision of a four-month time limit; the PLO voted in favour of indirect talks a few days later. Netanyahu's acceptance of the proposal represented a potential departure in Israel's policy on peace talks: the Jewish state had traditionally rejected the concept of proximity talks, preferring to limit the involvement of international diplomats in such negotiations. In early May, reportedly after Netanyahu had assured President Obama that Israel would temporarily delay the expansion of Ramat Shlomo and would not approve the construction of any large new settlements in Jerusalem while the talks were under way, the indirect negotiations began when George Mitchell visited Ramallah for talks with Abbas; Mitchell returned to the region later that month to continue the dialogue. However, although direct Palestinian-Israeli negotiations were intended to begin within four months of the start of the proximity talks, no tangible progress had apparently been made after the first two rounds of discussions. Moreover, both the Israeli and Palestinian electorates were highly sceptical about the prospects for a successful outcome, while Hamas declared its opposition to the decision of the PA in the West Bank to enter into indirect negotiations with Israel.

Plans announced by the Israeli Government in late February 2010 to incorporate into a Jewish heritage project two holy sites in the West Bank, Rachel's Tomb in Bethlehem and the Tomb of the Patriarchs in Hebron (both of which are venerated by Jews, Muslims and Christians), provoked violent protests by Palestinians in Hebron. The reopening of the Hurva synagogue in East Jerusalem in mid-March was also deemed a provocative measure by many Palestinians, who believed it reflected a programme to promote the Jewish character of the Old City. Hamas called for a 'day of rage' in response. Widespread rioting occurred in the city on 16 March. Israeli riot police were deployed in Jerusalem at the end of March when Palestinian protesters attacked visitors to the al-Aqsa mosque, in the belief that they were Jewish extremists intending to pray at the site. In late June Israeli municipal authorities in East Jerusalem endorsed a plan to demolish 22 Palestinian homes in the Silwan district of the city as part of a significant redevelopment involving the construction of an archaeological park. The UN Secretary-General, US Department of State officials and even senior Israeli cabinet ministers such as the Deputy Prime Minister and Minister of Defence, Ehud Barak, criticized the decision as being detrimental to attempts to further the Palestinian-Israeli peace negotiations.

On 31 May 2010 nine pro-Palestinian Turkish activists were killed, and many more injured, during a raid by Israeli naval forces on a ship which was part of a flotilla attempting to breach the Israeli blockade of Gaza in order to deliver humanitarian aid and materials to the population there. Although the Israeli military, seven of whose naval commandos were also wounded, insisted that its forces had acted in self-defence, their actions were widely condemned by foreign governments and international organizations. On 1 June Egypt opened the Rafah crossing on its border with Gaza for an indefinite period to permit the free movement of both people and humanitarian supplies. On 5 June the Israeli Government rejected a recommendation by the UN Secretary-General that a multinational inquiry be launched into what exactly occurred on the Turkish ship. Instead, the Israeli leadership declared on 8 June that two internal committees—one military and one government—would be formed to investigate the incident; the latter would include two foreign observers. Following a meeting with President Obama in Washington, DC, on 9 June, President Abbas received an assurance from the US President that his Administration would provide a further US $400m. to the Palestinian territories and that it was seeking to persuade Israel to reconsider its blockade of the Gaza Strip. On 14 June the International Committee of the Red Cross described the Israeli blockade as 'a collective punishment' of the people of Gaza, which was 'in clear violation of Israel's obligations under international humanitarian law'. The Israeli Government did announce an easing of the blockade on 17 June, following discussions between Netanyahu and the former British Prime Minister, Tony Blair, in his capacity as the international Quartet group's special envoy to the Middle East. Henceforth, only weapons and other items that could be used by Hamas militants to target Israelis were to be banned from entry into Gaza, thus allowing into the territory humanitarian aid, food and so-called 'dual-use' materials intended to be used in internationally supervised civilian reconstruction projects; Israel also pledged to improve the efficiency of its procedures for checking both goods and people at the border crossings. Nevertheless, a report issued by 21 international charities and human rights organizations at the end of November demanded that Israel bring an immediate end to the blockade, assessing that, five months after the partial easing, there was little evidence that it had improved the lives of the Gazan population since many vital supplies were still being prevented from reaching their intended destination. On 22 September the UNHRC published its report into the events of 31 May, which described the violent actions of the Israeli naval commandos who boarded the Turkish aid vessel as 'totally unnecessary'.

Direct negotiations between Prime Minister Netanyahu and President Abbas commenced in Washington, DC, on 2 September 2010, chaired by US Secretary of State Hillary Clinton and attended by George Mitchell. These negotiations—the first direct Israeli-Palestinian talks since December 2008—followed meetings held on the previous day between President Obama and both leaders, as well as with King Abdullah of Jordan and President Mubarak of Egypt. However, the talks were preceded by further violence in the West Bank, where four Jewish settlers were killed by Hamas militants. During September Obama urged the Israeli premier to extend the 10-month moratorium on settlement-building in the West Bank, which came to an end on 26 September; however, Netanyahu was unwilling to implement a complete freeze on construction. A second round of direct negotiations took place in Sharm el-Sheikh on 14 September and in Jerusalem on the following day. However, while it appeared that some progress was being made in the talks (for example, the Israeli and Palestinian leaders reportedly agreed to hold further fortnightly meetings), the end of Israel's temporary settlement ban—a prerequisite for the PA and the Arab League as far as continuing the discussions was concerned—together with the fact that Hamas did not recognize the legitimacy of the talks, meant that the peace process effectively remained deadlocked once again at mid-December. In early November 2010 Clinton had announced that the US Administration was offering the PA another US $150m. to ameliorate its financial situation and to assist with the further development of Palestinian institutions and security forces. In early December US diplomats acknowledged that their attempts to persuade the Israeli Government to impose a new partial suspension of settlement-building in the West Bank had failed, although they insisted that the Obama Administration remained committed to pursuing a comprehensive peace in the Middle East. Netanyahu had reportedly been unable to persuade the right-wing parties in his governing coalition to agree to another cessation of Jewish settlement expansion. By early 2011, however, the prospect of a resumption of peace talks had been further diminished by a number of violent incidents. In early March five members of a Jewish family, including three children, were killed in their home at the Itamar settlement in the West Bank; the following month, following an extensive Israeli investigation, two Palestinian men were arrested on suspicion of carrying out the killings, which were condemned by Abbas as 'immoral and inhuman'. In mid-March one person was killed and up to 50 injured in a bomb explosion near the Central Bus Station in Jerusalem; Palestinian militants were widely suspected of carrying out the attack, although no group officially acknowledged responsibility. Later that month militants in the Gaza Strip launched a series of rocket attacks against towns in southern Israel, prompting Israeli air-strikes against Hamas and Islamic Jihad targets, in which at least eight people were reported to have been killed. In early May the Israeli Government criticized the conclusion of a so-called unity agreement between Hamas and Fatah (see Domestic Political Affairs), and announced that it was to suspend the transfer of tax revenues to the PA, citing concerns that the funds could be used to finance operations against Israeli interests by Hamas militants.

Domestic Political Affairs

Legislative elections took place on 20 January 1996, with the participation of some 79% of the estimated 1m. eligible Palestinian voters, selecting 88 deputies to the 89-seat PLC. (One seat was reserved for the President of the Council's executive body—the Palestinian President.) At the concurrent election for a Palestinian Executive President, Yasser Arafat defeated his only rival, Samiha Khalil, winning 88.1% of the votes cast, and took office as President on 12 February. Deputies returned to the PLC automatically became members of the PNC, the existing 483 members of which were subsequently permitted to return from exile by the Israeli authorities. The PLC held its first session in Gaza City on 7 March, electing Ahmad Quray as its Speaker. At the 21st session of the PNC, held in Gaza City on 22–24 April, the PNC voted to amend the Palestinian National Charter (or PLO Covenant) by annulling those clauses that sought the destruction of the State of Israel and those that were inconsistent with the agreement of mutual recognition concluded by Israel and the PLO in September 1993. At the close of its session, the PNC elected a new PLO Executive Committee, and in May 1996 President Arafat appointed a Palestinian Cabinet. The appointments were approved by the PLC in July.

In April 1997 Arafat's audit office disclosed evidence of the misappropriation by PA ministers of some US $326m. of public funds. In August the findings of a parliamentary committee appointed by Arafat to investigate the affair led to the resignation of the Cabinet. New appointments were made in early 1998, but the Cabinet resigned again in June, apparently in order to obstruct a second vote of no confidence in Arafat's leadership, in protest partly at alleged corruption within the PA. A new Cabinet was appointed by Arafat in August, but soon attracted criticism from officials of the principal international organizations granting funds to the PA. In November donors pledged aid worth more than $3,000m., to be disbursed over the next five years. In October 1998 the PA was again accused of financial mismanagement, after customs revenues amounting to some $70m. allegedly failed to be deposited at the PA treasury.

US officials reportedly confirmed in March 1998 that the CIA was assisting the Palestinian security forces in the spheres of espionage, information-gathering and interrogation, in an attempt to reassure the Israeli Government of the PA's ability to take effective action against groups involved in attacks on Israeli targets. (Under the terms of the Wye Memorandum—see The Palestinian–Israeli Conflict—the CIA was to monitor the PA's compliance with the security provisions of the accord.) In October the PA detained 11 journalists who had attempted to obtain an interview with the spiritual leader of Hamas, Sheikh Ahmad Yassin (who was subsequently placed under house arrest). In subsequent weeks several radio and television stations, as well as press offices, were closed down by the PA, and numerous journalists were imprisoned. There was also a marked increase in self-censorship in the state-controlled and pro-administration media.

In January 1999 the PLC approved a motion urging an end to political detentions and the release of all those imprisoned on exclusively political charges; the motion further demanded the formation of a special committee to assess the case of every political prisoner in the Palestinian territories and to recommend prisoner releases. The committee was duly appointed in February, under the chairmanship of the Minister of Justice. However, despite the release of 37 political prisoners by the PA, in late January Hamas and Islamic Jihad activists began a hunger strike in Jericho and Nablus, in protest against their continued detention without trial. In February some 3,000 protesters marched to the headquarters of the PA, which they accused of 'subservience to Israel and the CIA'. In March a security agent and former member of Hamas's military wing was sentenced to death for the killing of a Palestinian intelligence officer in Rafah. The verdict provoked serious clashes between Palestinian police and protesters in the Gaza Strip, and Arafat was forced to curtail an official visit to Jordan to address the domestic security crisis. In November 20 leading Palestinian intellectuals (including members of the PLC) issued a joint statement in which they criticized alleged corruption, mismanagement and abuse of power within the PA, and accused Palestinian officials of ineffectiveness in the peace talks with Israel. An official crackdown on Arafat's critics was subsequently instigated, during which several of the document's signatories were detained or placed under house arrest (they were later released on bail). The establishment, announced in January 2000, of a Higher Council for Development under Arafat's chairmanship was welcomed by foreign donors as a major step towards ending corruption and mismanagement within the Palestinian administration.

In August 1999 a Palestinian national dialogue conference was held in Cairo, Egypt, between representatives of Fatah and the PFLP. Later in August Arafat and the Secretary-General of the DFLP, Nayef Hawatmeh, met, also in Cairo, for the first time since 1993. At the end of the month representatives of nine Palestinian political factions, meeting in Ramallah, agreed on an agenda for a comprehensive national dialogue; Hamas and Islamic Jihad, however, refused to participate. In September 1999 the PFLP's deputy leader, Abu Ali Moustafa, was permitted by the Israeli Government to return to the West Bank from exile in Jordan, in order to participate in reconciliation talks with Arafat. George Habash stepped down as leader of the PFLP in April 2000, and Abu Ali Moustafa was elected to lead the organization in July. (Following Moustafa's assassination in August 2001, Ahmad Saadat assumed the party leadership.)

The start of the al-Aqsa *intifada* by Palestinians in September 2000 (see The Palestinian–Israeli Conflict) moved some analysts to suggest that Arafat's influence over Palestinians might be waning, as other Fatah leaders began to pursue their own agendas and to speak out against the President: Marwan Barghouthi, in particular, was said to be attracting considerable support among Palestinians in the West Bank, where he was the regional leader of Fatah. In August 2001 a group of Palestinians were sentenced to death, and at least 100 others arrested, on charges of having collaborated with Israeli security services in recent attacks against Hamas officials. In October three Palestinians were killed by security forces in Gaza during violent protests in support of Osama bin Laden. Although the al-Qa'ida leader claimed to have launched the previous month's suicide attacks against the USA partly in protest against Israel's occupation of Palestinian territory, the PA sought to distance itself from the atrocities.

A report published by Human Rights Watch in November 2001 accused the PA of systematic abuses of human rights since the start of the al-Aqsa *intifada*, citing incidences of arbitrary arrests, detention without trial and torture of prisoners. When Sheikh Ahmad Yassin was placed under house arrest in December, hundreds of Hamas supporters demanded his release, resulting in clashes between Hamas gunmen and security forces. Fierce protests by militants also ensued in January 2002 when Palestinian security services in Ramallah arrested the PFLP leader, Ahmad Saadat. There was also an increasing number of 'vigilante killings': in February a crowd led by members of the security services entered a military court in Jenin and killed three defendants, two of whom had just been sentenced to death for the murder of a security official; and during one day in April 11 suspected collaborators were reportedly murdered by Palestinians in Tulkarm, Qalqilya and Bethlehem.

In June 2002, following Arafat's release from Israeli house arrest in the previous month, the President implemented major government changes: membership of the Cabinet was reduced from 31 ministers to 21, with several ministries being either merged or abolished. Maj.-Gen. Abd al-Razzaq al-Yahya was appointed Minister of the Interior—a position previously held by Arafat. Dr Salam Fayyad was named as the new Minister of Finance. The new Cabinet was described as an interim administration, its main task to be the preparation and supervision of far-reaching reforms, including the organization of municipal elections towards the end of 2002 and of presidential and legislative elections by early 2003. The planned reforms would also include the streamlining of the Palestinian security services. Perhaps most importantly, draft legislation was prepared in order to create a new post of Prime Minister, to be responsible for the day-to-day administration of the PA. In September 2002 the entire Palestinian Cabinet resigned in order to prevent a vote of no confidence being brought in the legislature; a new administration was announced in the following month. Meanwhile, the PA President set 20 January 2003 as the day on which legislative and presidential elections were to be held. However, in December 2002 Arafat announced a postponement of the polls, claiming that it would be untenable to hold elections while Israel continued to occupy PA-controlled population centres in the West Bank and Gaza.

In March 2003 the PLC endorsed a bill defining the role to be played by a future Palestinian Prime Minister, after having rejected amendments to the legislation proposed by Arafat according to which the President would retain authority over the appointment of cabinet ministers. In the proposed power-sharing arrangement, the President was reportedly to control security and foreign affairs and would also have the authority to appoint and dismiss a premier, while the Prime Minister would nominate ministers and retain responsibility for domestic affairs. Mahmud Abbas, the Secretary-General of the PLO Executive Committee, formally accepted the post of Prime Minister on 19 March; on 29 April the Palestinian legislature endorsed his appointment. A newly expanded Palestinian Cabinet was announced on that day, comprising 25 ministers under the premiership of Mahmud Abbas (who also became Minister of the Interior). Muhammad Dahlan was confirmed as the Minister of State for Security Affairs, while Dr Nabil Shaath was named as the Minister of External Affairs and Saeb Erakat as the Minister of Negotiation Affairs. The announcement of the new PA Cabinet prompted the publication of the Quartet-sponsored 'roadmap' peace plan (see The Palestinian–Israeli Conflict).

Ongoing tensions between Arafat and Abbas appeared to be the principal reason for the resignation of Erakat in May 2003. Regarded as an Arafat ally, Erakat had traditionally been at the forefront of Palestinian negotiations with Israel; however, his resignation was interpreted as a protest against his omission from the Palestinian delegation, which included Abbas, Muhammad Dahlan and the Speaker of the PLC, Ahmad Quray, scheduled to hold talks with Ariel Sharon and leading Israeli officials. Immediately following the summit with Sharon, Abbas had engaged in a round of discussions with Hamas and Islamic Jihad, which in June resulted in the implementation of a cease-fire in attacks by those groups against Israeli targets, with the support of Fatah. However, in September Abbas resigned as Prime Minister, seemingly representing the culmination of his power struggle with Arafat over control of the Palestinian security apparatus. Arafat nominated Quray to replace him. Meanwhile, Erakat was reinstated as the Minister of Negotiation Affairs, and it appeared that Arafat had effectively regained control of the PA. In October the Palestinian President declared a state of emergency in the West Bank and Gaza, following Israel's continuing construction of the 'security fence' (see The Palestinian–Israeli Conflict) and the arrest of a key member of Islamic Jihad; he also announced the establishment of an eight-member Emergency Cabinet. In early November the PLC approved Ahmad Quray's first full Cabinet. Ministers who retained their portfolios from the previous administration under Mahmud Abbas included Shaath as Minister of Foreign Affairs and Fayyad as Minister of Finance; notable new appointments included Hakam Balawi as Minister of the Interior and Nahid al-Rayyis as Minister of Justice. Rafiq al-Natsheh was elected Speaker of the PLC (but was replaced by Rawhi Fattouh in March 2004).

An audit of the PA's finances carried out by the IMF in 2003 estimated that during 1995–2000 nearly US $900m. had been diverted into accounts controlled by Yasser Arafat. Moreover, documents seized by Israeli forces during the reoccupation of Palestinian areas in 2001 reportedly revealed that some EU funds intended for the PA had in fact been used by the Al-Aqsa Martyrs Brigades. In February 2004 Israeli soldiers raided banks in Ramallah in an operation to seize funds reputedly belonging to Palestinian militant groups. The Arab Bank and the Cairo-Amman Bank were among those raided, and it was later reported that nearly $9m. had been confiscated.

Arafat's authority was further threatened in July 2004 by mass disorder in the Gaza Strip, in protest against PA corruption and incompetence, as well as a threat by Prime Minister Quray to bring about the collapse of the administration if his powers were not increased. In mid-July Arafat took measures against the growing anarchy in Gaza, discharging two senior security commanders, declaring a state of emergency and sending loyal troops to protect official buildings in Gaza. He also replaced the national police chief and the commander of general security forces in Gaza (the latter with his cousin, Musa Arafat), and amalgamated eight rival security forces into three. However, Fatah members demanding reforms rejected those introduced by the President as 'superficial and unconvincing', and pressure on Arafat (especially from the Al-Aqsa Martyrs Brigades) apparently forced him to reverse his decision to appoint his cousin as head of security. In late July Quray reportedly announced his resignation (which was rejected by Arafat) after chaos erupted in Gaza following the kidnapping of the Palestinian police commander, a colonel in the PA security forces and four French aid workers. However, Quray later announced his intention to stay in office as caretaker Prime Minister, having, according to one of his ministers, urged Arafat to forgo some of his powers to prevent the PA from collapsing further. Yet Quray did little to combat the widespread poverty in the Palestinian territories—a principal cause of popular anger—nor to address the power struggle within the Fatah movement, and in August al-Rayyis resigned as Minister of Justice, citing the ongoing disorder in Gaza.

Developments following the death of Yasser Arafat

It was announced on 11 November 2004 that Yasser Arafat, who had been undergoing treatment at a military hospital in France, had died. In accordance with Palestinian law, the Speaker of the PLC, Rawhi Fattouh, was sworn in as acting President, pending an election due to take place in the territories within 60 days. Mahmud Abbas assumed the chairmanship of the PLO, and Quray was chosen to head the Palestinian National Security Council (PNSC) in addition to taking charge of the administration of the PA. Farouk Kaddoumi was appointed leader of Fatah. In late November Abbas was nominated as Fatah's only candidate in the forthcoming election, which in early December both Hamas and Islamic Jihad announced they would boycott. Palestinian election officials declared that a total of 10 candidates had qualified for registration, including a human rights activist, Mustafa Barghouthi, who was to stand as an independent. Having initially registered his candidacy, Marwan Barghouthi later withdrew from the campaign, following pressure on him to give Abbas the best chance of securing the presidency; it had been feared that, had Marwan Barghouthi won the ballot, Israel would have refused to negotiate with him due to his imprisonment.

The first municipal elections to be held in the West Bank since 1976 began on 23 December 2004, at which Hamas, participating in an election in the Palestinian territories for the first time, won 16 councils and Fatah secured nine, with the two movements to share control of one municipality. At the local elections held in the Gaza Strip in late January 2005, Hamas secured control of seven of the 10 councils. The lack of support for Fatah was attributed to its association with corruption, while voters were encouraged by Hamas's provision of welfare and educational services and by its opposition to Israel.

The election to appoint a successor to Yasser Arafat was held in the West Bank, Gaza Strip and East Jerusalem on 9 January 2005. The Palestinian Central Elections Commission (CEC) asserted that the presence of Israeli forces in Jerusalem interfered with the voting process, forcing international observers to intervene. Nevertheless, these observers considered the overall conduct of the election to have been free and fair. Final results showed that, from the seven candidates, Abbas had received 62.5% of votes cast and Mustafa Barghouthi 19.5%. The other candidates had all secured less than 4% of the votes. Abbas was sworn in as Executive President of the PA on 15 January.

In February 2005 the PLC voted to approve a new Cabinet under Prime Minister Ahmad Quray. Dr Nabil Shaath was appointed Deputy Prime Minister and Minister of Information; Shaath's previous role as Minister of Foreign Affairs was assumed by Dr Nasser al-Kidwa, hitherto the Palestinian representative to the UN. Maj.-Gen. Nasr Yousuf became Minister of the Interior and National Security. Quray pledged the new administration's determination to heighten security and combat poverty. In March, after militants from the Fatah-affiliated Al-Aqsa Martyrs Brigades reportedly shot at the presidential compound in Ramallah, President Abbas removed the military chief in the West Bank and the Ramallah district commander, explaining that the security apparatus had failed and needed to be reorganized. In an effort to consolidate various (often rival) factions into a unified command, in the following month Abbas nominated four new heads of security forces in the West Bank and Gaza Strip, and ordered 10 senior officers to resign.

A reported 82% of eligible voters took part in a second round of municipal elections in the West Bank and Gaza Strip on 5 May

2005. According to official results, 45 of the 84 municipal districts contested were to be governed by councils with a majority of Fatah representatives (which took 56% of votes). Hamas, which had not participated in the presidential election, took 23 councils (33% of votes), and left-wing and independent lists secured 16 councils. Later in the month the CEC declared that elections to the PLC, scheduled for July, would be delayed while the PLC ratified a new elections law, intended to replace the system of simple majority by which the 1996 general election had been held, with a 'mixed' electoral system. The PLC ratified the new law in June 2005. In August Abbas issued a decree setting 25 January 2006 as the date for the legislative elections. A third round of municipal elections was held in 82 towns and villages in the West Bank on 29 September 2005. Fatah won a reported 54% of the votes, and Hamas took 26%. At local elections in some of the largest cities in the West Bank conducted on 15 December, Fatah secured 35% of the 414 contested seats, while Hamas won 26%. However, although Fatah retained control of Ramallah, Hamas notably gained control of Nablus and Jenin.

Factional conflict following Hamas's victory in the 2006 legislative elections

Israel announced in late December 2005 that it would not allow Arabs in East Jerusalem to vote if Hamas participated in the forthcoming legislative elections. After PA officials threatened to postpone the elections, and amid international pressure, in mid-January 2006 Israel declared that it would allow a small number of Arabs in East Jerusalem to vote on 25 January, and that candidates from groups other than Hamas could campaign there. In the event, Hamas, competing as the Change and Reform list in order to avoid a ban on its direct participation, secured 74 of the 132 seats, and Fatah only 45. A large part of Change and Reform's election campaign had focused on the movement's social welfare programme and its strong stance against official corruption. Other groups, including the PFLP (contesting the poll as Martyr Abu Ali Moustafa) and independents, also achieved representation. Quray announced the resignation of his administration on 26 January.

The new PLC was inaugurated on 18 February 2006. Dr Aziz Duweik was appointed to replace Rawhi Fattouh as Speaker, and President Abbas called on Hamas to establish a new administration. Hamas subsequently held discussions with Abbas and other factions, including Fatah, concerning the possibility of forming a coalition administration of national unity, and nominated Ismail Haniya as Prime Minister. Haniya, who had led the organization's national list for the elections, had held senior positions within Hamas; imprisoned in Israeli gaols in 1987–89 for his participation in the first *intifada* and leading one of Hamas's security apparatuses, Haniya had survived an Israeli assassination attempt in 2003, five years after assuming control of Sheikh Ahmad Yassin's office. Hamas began to assert its authority at a PLC session in early March 2006 when it reversed legislation that the Fatah-led parliament had approved immediately prior to its dissolution. Fatah deputies walked out of the session, asserting that Hamas had no right to reverse their decisions. The new laws had given President Abbas further powers, apparently in an attempt to increase his authority and curb that of parliament, in anticipation of Hamas's domination of the legislature. One of the rulings had provided for the establishment of a constitutional court and granted Abbas the right to elect its members.

Hamas leaders continued their attempts to persuade Fatah to enter into an administration of national unity. However, in late March 2006, after weeks of discussions between the two factions, Fatah rejected Hamas's offer, and the Islamist organization decided to form a cabinet alone. One of the most important matters of dispute had been Hamas's rejection of bilateral Israeli-Palestinian agreements approved by the former legislature: Hamas considered that by recognizing these accords it would be accepting Israeli occupation of Palestinian territory. The PLC approved Hamas's proposed Cabinet on 28 March, and President Abbas inaugurated the new administration on the following day. Notable appointees included Nasser al-Shaer as Deputy Prime Minister and Minister of Education and Higher Education, Mahmud al-Zahhar as Minister of Foreign Affairs, and Said Siyam as Minister of the Interior and Civil Affairs.

In the weeks following the elections to the PLC, there were sporadic violent clashes between rival militias and security forces of Hamas and Fatah. The increased tensions in the Palestinian territories were aggravated by the decision of the USA and the EU to withdraw all direct aid to the PA until Hamas fulfilled the three conditions that the Quartet group had placed on it (see The Palestinian–Israeli Conflict). Nevertheless, in June 2006 Hamas and Fatah reportedly agreed to a joint political platform which contained implicit recognition of Israel's existence. The representatives approved a document drawn up in May by a group of Palestinian political prisoners in Israeli gaols, led by Marwan Barghouthi and Sheikh Abd al-Khaliq al-Natsheh of Hamas, which detailed 18 points for a return to negotiations with Israel. The so-called 'prisoners' document' called for the formation of an administration of national unity in which all political parties that accepted the terms of the document would be represented, as well as the establishment of a 'unified resistance front' against Israeli occupation. Shortly afterwards Hamas endorsed the prisoners' document and agreed in principle to share power with Fatah in an administration committed to a two-state settlement and negotiations with Israel on the basis of an independent Palestinian state on territories occupied in 1967. (The group had been under intense pressure from President Abbas to accept the proposals or face a referendum.) However, the agreement was rejected by Hamas's military wing and the organization's political leaders-in-exile. Moreover, it failed to achieve the immediate resumption of foreign aid to the PA, which was urgently required in order to allow the authorities to begin paying workers' salaries.

In September 2006 a general strike was organized by public sector workers in protest against unpaid wages. In early November Arab ministers responsible for foreign relations, meeting in Cairo, pledged to increase levels of financial assistance given to the PA; Iran also gave funds to the Hamas-led administration in the following month. In mid-November it was announced that Fatah and Hamas had agreed to nominate Muhammad Shbeir, a former head of the Islamic University in Gaza, as Prime Minister in a coalition administration. However, despite lengthy discussions, it proved impossible for Shbeir to form a cabinet. On 8 February 2007 Fatah and Hamas—represented by President Abbas and Khalid Meshaal, respectively—signed an agreement to form a national unity administration; the accord followed two days of discussions in Mecca, Saudi Arabia, held at the invitation of King Abdullah. Although Hamas continued to reject an acceptance of Israel's right to exist, it was reported that the organization had agreed, for the first time, to 'respect and work to implement' the 'land-for-peace' proposal adopted at the Beirut summit in 2002 (see The Palestinian–Israeli Conflict).

Finally, on 17 March 2007 the PLC approved the composition of a new Cabinet, which replaced the former Hamas-dominated administration with a coalition of ministers from Hamas and Fatah, together with independents and representatives from the DFLP and the Palestinian People's Party. Hamas's Ismail Haniya retained the post of Prime Minister, while Azzam al-Ahmad, of Fatah, became Deputy Prime Minister. Three prominent ministries were allocated to independents: Hani Talab al-Qawasmeh was appointed Minister of the Interior, Dr Ziad Abu Amr Minister of Foreign Affairs and Dr Salam Fayyad was again named as Minister of Finance. At the end of March EU ministers responsible for foreign affairs, meeting in Germany, declared their support for the peace initiative revived in Saudi Arabia a few days previously, and announced that they would be willing to have contacts with non-Hamas members of the new Palestinian Cabinet. Israel declared that it would continue its boycott of the PA, however, until the new administration met the conditions demanded by the Quartet group. The resignation from the Cabinet of al-Qawasmeh in May appeared to demonstrate the divisions within the administration with regard to the difficult security issues facing the West Bank and Gaza; Prime Minister Haniya assumed the interior portfolio in an acting capacity.

Abbas announced in March 2007 that he had appointed Muhammad Dahlan as Secretary of the newly re-established PNSC, which in theory meant that he became general commander of the Palestinian security forces; Dahlan, however, was profoundly disliked by Hamas. Following several unsuccessful attempts to achieve a lasting cease-fire between the rival militias in the Palestinian territories, a new security plan to restore order in Gaza was announced by the Cabinet in May. Yet the factional fighting between gunmen from Hamas and Fatah continued, leading Abbas, speaking in June on the 40th anniversary of Israeli occupation, to warn of the threat of a Palestinian civil war. In mid-2007 scores of Palestinians were killed in the violence, some of which even occurred within hospital buildings. On 12 June gun battles between Hamas and Fatah fighters intensified across the Gaza Strip. As Hamas began to demonstrate its military superiority, it seized control of the headquarters of security forces in the north and south of the Strip, before taking over Gaza City itself. At the same time Fatah militias in the West Bank stormed Hamas-controlled institutions, seeking revenge for the Islamist movement's takeover of the Strip. On 14 June Abbas dissolved the national unity Cabinet under Haniya's premiership, declared a state of emergency and appointed Salam Fayyad as Prime Minister. As a respected economist and former employee of the World Bank and the IMF, Fayyad had wide support in Israel, the USA and the EU. Meanwhile, Haniya sought to consolidate his power over Gaza by naming a new chief of security in the territory, Maj.-Gen. Said Fanouna.

An Emergency Cabinet, consisting principally of independents and technocrats, as well as one Fatah representative, was sworn in by President Abbas in Ramallah on 17 June 2007. Besides assuming the premiership, Fayyad also held charge of the finance portfolio and, briefly, that of foreign affairs. (Riyad al-Maliki assumed responsibility for the latter from September.) Fatah's Abd al-Razzaq al-Yahya became Minister of the Interior and of Civil Affairs. The hope was that this administration would restore law and order throughout the Palestinian territories, but it became apparent that divisions between the Fatah-controlled West Bank and Hamas-administered Gaza Strip were widening. Abbas refused to enter into a dialogue with Hamas until it withdrew its militias from former Fatah positions in Gaza. Moreover, the President granted himself the power to take decisions without the endorsement of the PLC, where Hamas held a majority of the seats. Abbas also declared that he was outlawing Hamas's paramilitary wing and other militias associated with the Islamist group. On 18 June the USA and the EU, in a demonstration of support for President Abbas and his formation of an administration that excluded Hamas ministers, lifted their 15-month economic and political boycott of the PA. The Bush Administration additionally pledged assistance valued at some US $190m. to the Ramallah-based Cabinet.

Upon the expiry of the 30-day state of emergency, on 13 July 2007 President Abbas accepted the resignation of the Emergency Cabinet and appointed three new ministers to a reorganized Cabinet, which was to function as a caretaker administration until either the PLC convened or new legislative elections were called. (Hamas was unwilling for a vote to be held in the PLC as, with so many of its legislators in Israeli detention, it would lose its parliamentary majority.) Hamas leaders again refused to recognize the legitimacy of this interim administration. On 4 July, three days after Israel began transferring US $117m. of withheld Palestinian taxes to the Fayyad administration, thousands of Palestinian civil servants began receiving their first full salaries since March 2006. However, the West Bank administration continued to withhold the salaries of thousands of civil servants in the Gaza Strip. On 19 July 2007, at the first meeting of the international Quartet group since the appointment of former British Prime Minister Tony Blair as its special envoy to the Middle East, members of the Quartet affirmed their joint refusal to deal with Hamas. Muhammad Dahlan resigned as National Security Adviser on 26 July, citing ill health; however, some reports alleged that Dahlan had been asked to resign after his security forces in Gaza had allowed Hamas militants to oust Fatah from power in Gaza (when Dahlan was undergoing medical treatment abroad). Nevertheless, the resignation was essentially a formality since President Abbas had dissolved the PNSC following Hamas's takeover of Gaza. In August Fayyad issued a statement outlining the conditions required for inter-Palestinian dialogue to begin: Hamas should renounce any claims to be the legal authority governing Gaza (although Fayyad did not insist on an annulment of the 2006 election results) and disband all armed militias. This demand apparently included the Hamas Executive Force, which was responsible for maintaining law and order in Gaza.

In October 2007 Haniya appeared to demonstrate a move towards reconciliation with Fatah, when he described Hamas's administration of the Gaza Strip as 'temporary'. In early November President Abbas hosted Hamas representatives for discussions at his Ramallah headquarters; it was hoped that there would soon be a resumption of complete negotiations with Abbas's faction, with a view to restoring Palestinian unity. However, the third anniversary of the death of Yasser Arafat in November provoked a further outbreak of factional violence; eight Palestinians were reported to have died in clashes between rival Fatah and Hamas supporters in Gaza City.

International aid organizations stated in early March 2008 that the humanitarian crisis afflicting the Gazan population was the worst in the territory since 1967; in that month both the USA and the EU released to the PA the first instalments of funds pledged at the December 2007 donors' conference. In late March 2008 Hamas and Fatah signed a reconciliation agreement brokered by the Yemeni President, Ali Abdullah Saleh, and thus termed the San'a Declaration, which included a pledge to resume direct discussions between the feuding parties and affirmed the 'unity of the Palestinian people, territory and authority'. However, doubts were immediately expressed as to exactly what preconditions had been agreed, and productive dialogue was not pursued. In July a bomb exploded near the beach at Gaza City, killing six people, including five who were reported to be Hamas members and a child. The Hamas-controlled security forces subsequently arrested up to 160 people associated with Fatah, which Hamas publicly blamed for the crime. Fatah, meanwhile, denied involvement and claimed that the atrocity had resulted from infighting within Hamas; an increase in numbers of Hamas members detained by Fatah-controlled PA security forces in the West Bank ensued. In August the two factions agreed to participate in a national committee aimed at calming the spate of politically motivated arrests and facilitating the release of detainees.

In September 2008 Abbas declared that he would remain President beyond the formal expiry, on 8 January 2009, of his term of office, pending the organization of national elections. In early October 2008 it was reported that the Fatah and Hamas leaderships, as well as representatives of other Palestinian factions, had agreed to meet to discuss national reconciliation under mediation by Egyptian government officials. Later in October the Egyptian Government, following a series of consultations with relevant parties, released a draft proposal for achieving Palestinian national unity, urging the immediate formation of a united government that would have responsibility for rebuilding the Palestinian security forces and for organizing legislative and presidential elections, for which a date was to be scheduled without delay. Under the Egyptian proposal, the currently Fatah- and Hamas-controlled security forces were to be managed at the national level and thereby removed from involvement in factional politics. In addition, any future peace deal reached by President Abbas with the Israeli Government was to be submitted to a national referendum or else presented to a restructured PLO that was to encompass Hamas and other factions opposed to the peace process. On 8 November, however, Hamas, alleging that politically motivated arrests of its members were continuing to be ordered by the PA in the West Bank, announced its withdrawal from a conference that had been planned for the following day to discuss the Egyptian proposal.

Hamas-Fatah reconciliation negotiations

The reconciliation process received new impetus in early 2009 in the aftermath of Israel's devastating Operation Cast Lead, targeted at Hamas's administration in the Gaza Strip (see The Palestinian–Israeli Conflict). As reports emerged that intra-Palestinian tensions were causing delays in transfers of aid to Gaza, and that many international donors considered it preferable to pledge assistance to a united government, it appeared that continuing political divisions might undermine urgently required reconstruction activities in the Strip. In late February representatives of Fatah, Hamas and 11 other Palestinian factions met in Cairo to begin a newly arranged series of Egyptian-mediated negotiations, with the principal aims of pursuing reconciliation, and reaching agreement on the staging of elections and the formation of a national unity coalition. Five negotiating committees were established to discuss: reconciliation; elections; the proposed interim government; security; and PLO-Hamas integration. The participants also decided to draft a new agreement to govern use of the Rafah crossing between Gaza and Egypt. In mid-March the parties to the negotiations jointly determined that concurrent presidential and legislative elections should be held by 25 January 2010. Progress on the formation of the planned national unity administration, however, remained deadlocked over several contentious issues, including conflicting perspectives on Israel's right to exist, on the use of state violence and on the legitimacy of existing Israeli-Palestinian agreements.

In an effort to facilitate the reconciliation negotiations, Prime Minister Fayyad submitted his resignation, and that of his Cabinet, on 7 March 2009. At the beginning of April Fayyad announced that, at the request of President Abbas, he would remain in office until the conclusion of the ongoing Egyptian-mediated negotiations. At the end of April a new round of the talks ended without agreement, and with Hamas having rejected a compromise proposal, suggested by the Egyptian mediators, under which Abbas would appoint, pending the January 2010 elections, a transitional government without Hamas representation. Shortly before the new round of talks, scheduled for 16 May 2009, Abbas announced his readiness to swear in the newly proposed transitional government; however, the President was persuaded to postpone the inauguration until the completion of the new round of negotiations. The fifth round of reconciliation talks ended without agreement in Cairo on 18 May, and on 19 May Abbas appointed a new transitional government led by Prime Minister Fayyad, which excluded representatives of Hamas. The new, enlarged Cabinet consisted principally of Fatah members, independents and representatives of smaller Palestinian factions including the DFLP, the Palestinian Popular Struggle Front (PPSF) and the Palestinian Democratic Union—FIDA. Several ministers, including Minister of Foreign Affairs Riyad al-Maliki, retained positions they had held in the previous administration; newly appointed cabinet members included Saeed Abu Ali, a Fatah official, who was appointed Minister of the Interior. President Abbas stated that he did not intend to abandon the reconciliation negotiations with Hamas, and promised that the transitional government would be disbanded upon the conclusion of any Fatah-Hamas reconciliation agreement. However, Hamas refused to recognize the legitimacy of the administration and warned that its appointment would deepen intra-Palestinian divisions and imperil the prospects for the reconciliation negotiations. At the end of June the PA's Minister of Jerusalem Affairs, Hatem Abd al-Qader, became the first cabinet member to offer his resignation: al-Qader was reported to be angered by the inadequate level of funding allocated to his department and the insufficient support offered by the PA to those Palestinian residents of East Jerusalem who were subject to house demolitions by Israeli forces. In mid-July it was reported that Fayyad would assume responsibility for the relevant ministry, and al-Qader subsequently became an adviser to the President on Jerusalem affairs.

Factional tensions increased at the end of May 2009, when an attempt by PA security forces to arrest a senior Hamas militant in the West Bank town of Qalqilya escalated into a gun battle; three police officers, two Hamas militants and a civilian were killed in the fighting. The PA security forces mounted a series of raids on suspected militants around Qalqilya in the following days; another police officer and two Hamas fighters were killed in an operation on 4 June. In reprisal, Hamas security forces reportedly arrested numerous Fatah supporters in the Gaza Strip. Nevertheless, representatives of the two factions reconvened in Cairo on 28 June for a new round of negotiations, subject to a deadline of 7 July for conclusion of an agreement. However, despite reports that progress had been made concerning electoral reform and a joint security force, on 1 July the negotiations were suspended, with new talks scheduled for 25 July and the deadline for reaching an agreement extended until 28 July. Preliminary discussions in mid-July were hampered by discord over security operations and political prisoners, and the new round of negotiations was postponed until 25 August. Meanwhile, representatives of smaller Palestinian factions, including the PFLP, the DFLP, the PPSF and FIDA, continued to protest against their exclusion from the Egyptian-brokered reconciliation talks.

The long-awaited sixth Fatah convention opened in Bethlehem, in the West Bank, on 4 August 2009 (the last party conference having been held in Tunisia in 1989). The weeklong convention, which was attended by more than 2,000 delegates, many of whom were making a rare return from exile in Syria, Lebanon and Jordan, marked the emergence of a new generation to the party leadership. Fourteen new members secured representation in the first elections in more than 20 years to the 23-member Fatah Central Committee. Newly elected representatives to the faction's ruling body included Marwan Barghouthi, who was serving five sentences of life imprisonment in Israel, and Muhammad Dahlan, Fatah's leading official in the Gaza Strip and the erstwhile PA security chief. Prominent members of the old guard who lost their seats on the Committee included former Prime Minister Ahmad Quray and Farouk Kaddoumi, hitherto Secretary-General of the Central Committee. Abbas, who was reappointed Chairman of the Central Committee, reaffirmed Fatah's commitment to the pursuit of a negotiated peace settlement with Israel, but also reiterated the organization's entitlement to engage in 'resistance' against Israel if necessary. More than 400 Gaza-based delegates were reportedly prevented from attending the convention after Hamas barred them from travelling to the West Bank; Hamas had demanded the release of hundreds of its prisoners in the West Bank in exchange for granting exit permits to Fatah members. On 26–27 August a special session of the PNC was convened in Ramallah to replace members of the 18-member PLO Executive Committee who had died since the last such meeting in 1996 (including former President Yasser Arafat). Among the six new members were Quray, Saeb Erakat, and parliamentary deputy and former cabinet minister Hanan Ashrawi, who became the first woman to join the Executive Committee. Also in August 2009 Prime Minister Fayyad launched a plan intended to achieve unilateral Palestinian statehood by 2011; Palestinian officials began actively to secure international backing for the proposal.

In early October 2009 it was announced that a new Egyptian-brokered reconciliation agreement was expected to be signed by the end of that month. Representatives of Fatah reportedly signed the agreement, which included the proposal to hold presidential and legislative elections on 28 June 2010; however, Hamas demanded further amendments, including an increase in the proposed 25% of parliamentary seats to be elected by district, rather than proportional, representation to at least 40%. Hamas subsequently withdrew from the negotiations, partly in protest against Abbas's decision to delay Palestinian endorsement of the report of the UN Fact Finding Mission on the Gaza conflict, headed by South African judge Richard Goldstone (see The Palestinian–Israeli Conflict). Furthermore, on 16 October Fayyad accepted the resignation of the PA Minister of National Economy, Bassem Khoury, who disagreed with the administration's decision not to discuss the Goldstone report; he was succeeded on 25 October by Dr Hasan Abu-Libdeh, founder of the Palestinian Central Bureau of Statistics and a former Chairman of the Palestine Securities Exchange. Other members of the PA Cabinet, of Fatah and of the PLO were also strongly critical of the President's stance with regard to the UN report, and the PLO announced the holding of a domestic inquiry into the PA's decision-making processes. Meanwhile, following the suspension of the reconciliation talks, on 23 October Abbas declared that legislative and presidential elections would be held on 24 January 2010, on the expiry of the PLC's term. Hamas leaders rejected the declaration and announced that they would prevent the holding of elections in the Gaza Strip; furthermore, the Islamist faction warned that such elections would serve to exacerbate the internal Palestinian divisions. Earlier in October 2009 the head of Hamas's political bureau, Khalid Meshaal, had described Abbas as 'an illegal president' whose term of office had ended on 9 January, exactly four years after his election victory. In early November Abbas announced that he would not stand for re-election in the forthcoming presidential election, citing his frustration at the failure of PA efforts to restart peace talks with Israel and, in particular, at the policy of the new US Administration under President Obama with regard to Israeli settlement expansion in the West Bank. However, on 19 November, in response to recommendations from the CEC, the President announced the postponement of the planned elections. In mid-December the Central Council of the PLO approved a decision to extend indefinitely the terms of President Abbas and the PLC, pending a resolution of the Hamas–Fatah schism, and the holding of fresh elections.

Hamas-Fatah negotiations resumed in early 2010; however, progress was hampered by a dispute concerning the status of both the interim Cabinet in the West Bank and the de facto Hamas administration in Gaza, following the expiry of the PLC's scheduled term on 24 January. A further dispute arose in early February when the interim Cabinet in Ramallah scheduled municipal elections in the West Bank and Gaza for 17 July. Following Hamas's decision to boycott the forthcoming municipal elections, in late April 2010 it was announced that, while voting would be postponed in the Gaza Strip, it would proceed as scheduled in the West Bank. In mid-February, meanwhile, President Abbas suspended from office his chief of staff, Rafiq al-Husseini, following allegations of impropriety regarding the allocation of jobs to female applicants, details of which were broadcast on an Israeli television channel, along with further allegations of widespread financial corruption among PA officials. Although cleared of corruption charges by an internal PA inquiry, al-Husseini was dismissed from his post in mid-April for 'tarnishing the office of the President'. In early June the Cabinet announced that it had decided to postpone the municipal elections due to be held in the West Bank on 17 July for an indefinite period. Officials from the Ministry of Local Government explained that the elections were being delayed in the interests of maintaining unity between the West Bank and Gaza. However, the two Palestinian territories remained divided between the two rival administrations led by Fatah and Hamas, respectively, at the end of 2010.

Seemingly inspired by the anti-government uprisings across the Middle East and north Africa, a series of rallies by protesters demanding an end to the ongoing tensions between the main political factions took place in towns across the West Bank and Gaza in mid-March 2011, including Ramallah and Gaza City. In mid-February Prime Minister Fayyad had tendered the resignation of his administration to President Abbas, in order to facilitate a long-awaited cabinet reorganization; Fayyad was immediately requested by Abbas to lead the new administration. The CEC had earlier that month announced that municipal elections would be held on 9 July, and PA officials indicated that presidential and legislative elections would finally take place in September, despite warnings from Hamas that it would prevent the polls from being extended to Gaza. In an unexpected development, it was reported in late April that the newly installed Egyptian Government had initiated talks between Hamas and Fatah aimed at ending the dispute between the two factions, and, at a meeting in Cairo on 3 May, representatives of 13 Palestinian groups, including Hamas and Fatah, signed a so-called 'unity' agreement, which was expected to lead to the formation of a joint administration for both the West Bank and Gaza. The following day Abbas and Meshaal travelled to the Egyptian capital for a formal ceremony to mark the agreement. It was expected that a new government comprised principally of figures independent of both main factions would take office later that month; however, Palestinian media reported that Fayyad would be replaced as Prime Minister.

CONSTITUTION AND GOVERNMENT

In accordance with the Declaration of Principles on Palestinian Self-Rule and the Cairo Agreement on the Gaza Strip and Jericho (see Contemporary Political History), the PLO assumed control of the Jericho area of the West Bank and of the Gaza Strip on 17 May 1994. In November and December 1995, under the terms of the Israeli-Palestinian Interim Agreement on the West Bank and the Gaza Strip concluded in September 1995, Israeli armed forces withdrew from the West Bank towns of Nablus, Ramallah, Jenin, Tulkarm, Qalqilya and Bethlehem. In late December the PLO assumed responsibility in some 17 areas of civil administration in the town of Hebron. The Interim Agreement divided the West Bank into three zones: Areas A, B and C. As of July 1998, the PA had sole jurisdiction and security control in Area A (2% of the West Bank), but Israel retained authority over movement into and out of the area. In Area B (26% of the West Bank) the PA had some limited authority while Israel remained in control of security. Area C, the remaining 72% of the West Bank, was under Israeli military occupation. In accordance with the Wye Memorandum of October 1998 (see Contemporary Political History), Israel effected a further redeployment of its armed forces from approximately 500 sq km of West Bank territory in November. Of this, about 400 sq km became Area A territory and the remainder Area B territory. The Sharm el-Sheikh Memorandum of September 1999 was intended to facilitate completion of outstanding commitments under agreements previously signed, as well as to enable the resumption of 'final status' negotiations with Israel. By October 2000 approximately 17.2% of the West Bank (Area A) was under sole Palestinian jurisdiction and security control, although Israel retained authority over access to and from the zone; about 23.8% (Area B) was under Israeli military control, with the PA responsible for civil administration and public order; the remaining 59% (Area C) remained under Israeli military occupation. Israel implemented its unilateral Disengagement Plan, according to which it dismantled Israeli military installations and settlements in the Gaza Strip, and withdrew from four settlements in the West Bank, in August–September 2005 (see Contemporary Political History). The total area of the territory over which the PA will eventually assume control, and the extent of its jurisdiction there, remain subject to 'final status' talks.

REGIONAL AND INTERNATIONAL CO-OPERATION

The Palestinian (National) Authority acts as an observer at the UN General Assembly. It is also represented at the League of Arab States (Arab League, see p. 361) and the Organization of the Islamic Conference (see p. 400).

ECONOMIC AFFAIRS

In 2005, according to estimates by the World Bank, the gross national income (GNI) of the West Bank and the Gaza Strip, measured at average 2003–05 prices, was US $4,452m., equivalent to $1,230 per head. During 2000–09, it was estimated, the population increased at an average annual rate of 3.4%, while in 2000–07 gross domestic product (GDP) per head decreased, in real terms, by an average of 5.1% per year. According to official estimates, overall GDP increased, in real terms, at an average annual rate of 2.0% in 2000–08; growth in real GDP of 5.9% was recorded in 2008.

Agriculture and fishing contributed 6.5% of the GDP of the West Bank and Gaza Strip in 2008, according to official figures. In the same year agriculture (including hunting, forestry and fishing) engaged 15.6% of the classified employed Palestinian labour force. Citrus fruits are the principal export crop, and horticulture also makes a significant contribution to trade. Other important crops are tomatoes, cucumbers, olives and grapes. The livestock sector is also significant. Agricultural GDP decreased at an average annual rate of 4.4% during 2000–08. The GDP of the sector grew by 13.4% in 2008.

Industry (including mining, manufacturing, electricity and water supply, and construction) contributed 19.9% of GDP in the West Bank and Gaza Strip in 2008. The industrial sector engaged 13.5% of the classified employed labour force of the West Bank and Gaza in that year. During 2000–08 industrial GDP increased at an average rate of 1.6% annually. The sector's GDP increased by 3.7% in 2008.

Mining and quarrying contributed 0.7% of GDP in the West Bank and Gaza Strip in 2008, and engaged 0.3% of the classified employed labour force in that year. Two significant gasfields were discovered off the Gazan coast in 1999; however, the exploration and supply of this offshore gas is dependent upon agreement being reached with Israel, which was expected to be the principal purchaser before its own discovery of significant offshore gas reserves in 2009.

Manufacturing contributed 12.1% of the GDP of the West Bank and Gaza Strip in 2008. In 2007 12.3% of the classified employed labour force were engaged in the sector. Palestinian manufacturing is characterized by small-scale enterprises, which typically engage in food-processing and the production of textiles and footwear. The frequent closure of the West Bank and Gaza by the Israeli authorities has prompted the development of free trade industrial zones on the Palestinian side of the boundaries separating Israel from the territories: Israeli and Palestinian enterprises can continue to take advantage of low-cost Palestinian labour at times of closure, and the zones also benefit from tax exemptions and export incentives. Manufacturing GDP contracted at an average annual rate of 1.7% during 2000–08. The GDP of the sector increased by 2.2% in 2008.

Construction accounted for 4.4% of GDP in 2008, while it employed 12.7% of the classified employed labour force in that year. During 2000–08 construction GDP contracted at an average annual rate of 1.9%. The sector's GDP decreased by 4.2% in 2007, but increased by 5.1% in 2008.

The energy sector (comprising electricity and water supply) accounted for an estimated 2.7% of GDP in the West Bank and Gaza Strip in 2008. Electricity, gas and water utilities together employed 0.5% of the employed labour force of the West Bank and Gaza in that year. In the West Bank, the Jerusalem District Electric Company supplies electric power to Jerusalem, Bethlehem, Jericho, Ramallah and Al-Birah, while the National Electric Company operates in the northern West Bank. The Israel Electric Corporation (IEC) was the only source of electricity to municipalities in the Gaza Strip prior to the establishment of the Palestine Electric Company in 1999, and Palestinian utility firms remain principally reliant on the purchase of electricity from the IEC.

In 2008 the services sector contributed 73.6% of GDP in the West Bank and Gaza Strip. Services engaged 71.0% of the classified employed labour force in the same year. Although in recent years the Palestinian tourism industry was all but halted by the ongoing violence in the territories, tourism officials reported a record number of almost 5m. visitors in 2010, when the sector's contribution to GDP was close to 15%. The GDP of the services sector increased at an average rate of 2.1% per year during 2000–08. Real GDP of the services sector grew by 7.4% in 2008.

In 2008, according to preliminary estimates, the West Bank and Gaza Strip recorded a visible trade deficit of US $3,453.8m. while there was a surplus of $535.1m. on the current account of the balance of payments. In the absence of seaport facilities and of an airport (Gaza International Airport was opened in 1998 but closed by the Israeli authorities in 2001), foreign trade (in terms of value) has been conducted almost exclusively with Israel since occupation. In 2008 Israel was the source of 77.6% of all imports and took 89.4% of all exports; Jordan was the second most significant trading partner, taking 6.1% of all exports in that year. Most Palestinian exports are of agricultural or horticultural products. One notable feature of this trade is that Palestinian goods have often been exported to Israel, and subsequently re-exported as originating in Israel.

In 2010, according to the Ministry of Finance figures, the PA recorded an overall budget deficit of US $1,143.0m. The annual rate of inflation in the West Bank and Gaza averaged 4.1% in 2000–09; consumer prices increased by an average of 2.8% in 2009. According to official estimates, some 26.0% of the labour force in the Palestinian territories (19.0% in the West Bank; 40.6% in Gaza) were unemployed in 2008.

The prospects for an improvement in economic conditions in the Palestinian Autonomous Areas, which remain highly dependent on Israel, are inextricably linked to the full implementation of the Oslo accords (see Contemporary Political History) and the outcome of (currently stalled) 'final status' negotiations between the PA and Israel. Agriculture remains focused mainly on meeting local demand, although the sector supplies the bulk of Palestinian exports and there is proven demand for Palestinian products beyond the Israeli market. The expansion of Palestinian agriculture is also limited by problems with irrigation since access to water supplies is subject to 'final status' discussions. Economic conditions in the West Bank and Gaza have deteriorated markedly since 1993, largely as a result of frequent border closures enforced by the Israeli authorities in reprisal for terrorist attacks by militant Islamist groups. Such closures lead to an immediate rise in the rate of unemployment among Palestinians, raise transportation costs for Palestinian goods and, at times, halt trade entirely. The Oslo accords provide for the development of seaport facilities and for the opening of Gaza International Airport and of a safe passage linking the Gaza Strip with the West Bank.

The victory of the Islamic Resistance Movement (Hamas) in the legislative elections of 2006 provoked a financial crisis in the Palestinian Autonomous Areas, as the European Union (see p. 270) and the USA withdrew direct aid to the Palestinian (National) Authority (PA), which had consisted of annual payments of some US $600m. and $400m., respectively; transfers of direct humanitarian aid were to continue. Furthermore, Israel halted payments of tax and customs duties to the PA. The takeover of the Gaza Strip by Hamas militants in June 2007 resulted in a de facto separation between an emergency administration in the West Bank and a Hamas-led cabinet in Gaza. The establishment by President Abbas of a Cabinet that excluded ministers from Hamas did, however, result in the international embargo imposed on the West Bank being lifted. In late 2007 the PA's Prime Minister in the West Bank, Dr Salam Fayyad, launched a Palestinian Reform and Development Plan for 2008–10, which was intended to stimulate the economy and to encourage private sector development. At an international donors' conference held in Paris in December 2007, around $7,400m. was pledged in support to the PA, both to alleviate the budgetary crisis and to fund proposed development projects. The cost of rebuilding infrastructure destroyed during Operation Cast Lead, the Israeli offensive that targeted Hamas-administered Gaza in late 2008–early 2009, was estimated at $1,100m. Another donors' conference, convened in Sharm el-Sheikh, Egypt, in March 2009, raised pledges totalling $5,200m. to finance humanitarian aid and rebuilding assistance for Gaza, as well as further budgetary support to the PA. According to IMF estimates, real GDP growth of 6.8% was achieved in 2009, owing to the generous flow of foreign aid, the PA-administered West Bank's ongoing programme of institutional and economic reforms, and the Israeli Government's lifting of some restrictions on access and movement in the West Bank. However, there is a growing disparity between the economic performance of the West Bank and that of the Gaza Strip: in 2009 GDP growth reached 8.5% in the West Bank, but only 1% in the Gaza Strip, where economic activity remained severely constrained by the economic blockade imposed by the Israeli authorities. The acute problem of unemployment in Gaza was reported to have worsened following Operation Cast Lead: at April 2010 the Palestinian Central Bureau of Statistics estimated the unemployment rate to have risen to 44.3%, compared with 21.1% in the West Bank. The Israeli human rights organization B'Tselem reported in that month that 95% of Gaza's factories and workshops had been forced to close as a result of the blockade. By early 2011 the Palestinian economy remained largely unaffected by the global financial crisis from late 2008, principally owing to its isolation from foreign markets, although there were concerns that the economic downturn in many donor countries had affected the disbursement of aid during 2010. In June, following widespread criticism of Israel's continued blockade of Gaza after the interception of a Turkish-led convoy attempting to deliver essential aid and supplies to the territory, the Israeli Government announced that it would ease restrictions on the transfer of goods into Gaza, instituting a list of prohibited items deemed to have a potential military use. Nevertheless, a report issued by international aid agencies and human rights organizations in November noted that this partial easing had offered little relief to the Gazan population since Israel was still preventing the transfer of many vital materials. Following the conclusion of a unity agreement between Hamas and Fatah in early 2011, the Israeli Government suspended transfers of tax and customs duties to the PA.

PUBLIC HOLIDAYS

2012: 4 February* (Mouloud/Yum al-Nabi, Birth of Muhammad), 16 June* (Leilat al-Meiraj, Ascension of Muhammad), 18 August* (Id al-Fitr, end of Ramadan), 25 October* (Id al-Adha, Feast of the Sacrifice), 15 November (Independence Day).

* These holidays are dependent on the Islamic lunar calendar and may vary by one or two days from the dates given.

Christian holidays are observed by the Christian Arab community.

PALESTINIAN AUTONOMOUS AREAS

Statistical Survey

Source (unless otherwise indicated): Palestinian Central Bureau of Statistics (PCBS), POB 1647, Ramallah; tel. (2) 2406340; fax (2) 2406343; e-mail diwan@pcbs.gov.ps; internet www.pcbs.gov.ps.

Note: Unless otherwise indicated, data include East Jerusalem, annexed by Israel in 1967.

Area and Population

AREA, POPULATION AND DENSITY

Area (sq km)	6,020*
Population (census of 9 December 1997)†	2,895,683
Population (census of December 2007)‡	
Males	1,877,028
Females	1,821,229
Total	3,698,257
Population (official projected estimates at mid-year)	
2008	3,825,512
2009	3,935,249
2010	4,048,403
Density (per sq km) at mid-2010	672.5

* 2,324 sq miles. The total comprises: West Bank 5,655 sq km (2,183 sq miles); Gaza Strip 365 sq km (141 sq miles).
† Figures include an estimate of 210,209 for East Jerusalem and an adjustment of 83,805 for estimated underenumeration. The total comprises 1,873,476 (males 951,693, females 921,783) in the West Bank (including East Jerusalem) and 1,022,207 (males 518,813, females 503,394) in the Gaza Strip. The data exclude Jewish settlers. According to official Israeli estimates, the population of Israelis residing in Jewish localities in the West Bank (excluding East Jerusalem) and Gaza Strip was 243,900 at 31 December 2004 (West Bank 235,700, Gaza Strip 8,200). The withdrawal of Israeli settlers residing in Jewish localities in the Gaza Strip was completed in September 2005.
‡ Includes population counted between 25 December 2007 and 8 January 2008, and estimates for underenumeration.

Note: Official projected estimates of a total world-wide Palestinian population of 10,094,565 at 31 December 2006 included 1,134,293 Palestinians resident in Israel and 2,799,440 resident in Jordan.

POPULATION BY AGE AND SEX
(UN estimates at mid-2011)

	Males	Females	Total
0–14	1,022,120	978,939	2,001,059
15–64	1,234,427	1,175,420	2,409,847
65 and over	55,734	76,184	131,918
Total	2,312,281	2,230,543	4,542,824

Source: UN, *World Population Prospects: The 2008 Revision*.

GOVERNORATES
(census of December 2007)

	Area (sq km)	Population*	Density (per sq km)
West Bank			
Janin (Jenin)	583	251,807	431.9
Tubas	402	48,164	119.8
Tulkarm	246	156,792	637.4
Qalqilya	166	88,574	533.6
Salfeet	204	58,800	288.2
Nabulus (Nablus)	605	315,956	522.2
Ram Allah (Ramallah) and Al-Birah	855	262,941	307.5
Al-Quds (Jerusalem)†	345	350,051	1,014.6
Ariha (Jericho) and Al-Aghwar	593	40,403	68.1
Beit Lahm (Bethlehem)	659	169,966	257.9
Al-Khalil (Hebron)	997	538,260	539.9
Gaza Strip			
North Gaza	61	270,246	4,430.3
Gaza	74	496,411	6,708.3
Deir al-Balah	58	205,535	3,543.7
Khan Yunus (Khan Yunis)	108	270,979	2,509.1
Rafah	64	173,372	2,708.9
Total	6,020	3,698,257	614.3

* Figures exclude Jewish settlers.
† Figures refer only to the eastern sector of the city.

PRINCIPAL LOCALITIES
(estimated population at mid-2002, excluding Jewish settlers)

West Bank

Al-Quds (Jerusalem)	242,081*	Al-Dhahiriya	25,348
Al-Khalil (Hebron)	147,291	Al-Ram and Dahiyat al-Bareed	23,038
Nabulus (Nablus)	121,344	Ram Allah (Ramallah)	22,493
Tulkarm	41,109	Halhul	19,345
Qalqilya	39,580	Dura	19,124
Yattah (Yatta)	38,023	Ariha (Jericho)	18,239
Al-Birah	34,920	Qabatiya	17,788
Janin (Jenin)	32,300		
Beit Lahm (Bethlehem)	26,847		

Gaza Strip

Ghazzah (Gaza)	361,651	Beit Lahya	50,576
Khan Yunus (Khan Yunis)	110,677	Deir al-Balah	43,593
		Bani Suhaylah	28,761
Jabalyah (Jabalia)	104,620	Beit Hanoun	27,341
Rafah	62,452	Tel al-Sultan Camp	21,477
Al-Nuseirat	56,449	Al-Maghazi Camp	21,278

* The figure refers only to the eastern sector of the city.

Mid-2009 (incl. suburbs, UN estimate): Ramallah 69,000 (Source: UN, *World Urbanization Prospects: The 2009 Revision*).

BIRTHS AND DEATHS
(official estimates)*

	2006	2007	2008
Live births:			
West Bank	61,366	59,235	62,600
Gaza Strip	49,352	49,439	n.a.
Deaths:			
West Bank	4,712	5,481	5,809
Gaza Strip	4,490	4,406	n.a.

* Excluding Jewish settlers.

Birth rate (official estimates per 1,000): 32.5 in 2007; 32.7 in 2008; 32.7 in 2009.

Death rate (official estimates per 1,000): 4.4 in 2007; 4.4 in 2008; 4.3 in 2009.

MARRIAGES
(number registered)

	2007	2008	2009
West Bank	18,576	19,006	19,821
Gaza Strip	14,109	14,768	n.a.

Marriage rate (rates per 1,000, official estimates): West Bank: 8.0 in 2007; 8.0 in 2008; 8.1 in 2009. Gaza Strip: 10.1 in 2007; 10.3 in 2008; n.a. in 2009.

ECONOMICALLY ACTIVE POPULATION
(persons aged 15 years and over)

	2006	2007	2008
Agriculture, hunting, forestry and fishing	107,024	103,721	86,447
Mining and quarrying	2,237	1,542	1,462
Manufacturing	80,543	81,964	n.a.
Electricity and gas	2,500	2,230	2,780
Construction	73,905	72,722	70,688
Wholesale and retail trade	114,662	116,408	111,537
Hotels and restaurants	13,492	13,407	19,599
Transport, storage and communications	38,242	37,404	32,046
Financial intermediation	4,503	4,214	4,916
Real estate, renting and business activities	11,217	11,380	n.a.
Public administration and defence	98,922	99,584	101,723
Education	67,704	68,034	71,114

PALESTINIAN AUTONOMOUS AREAS

—continued	2006	2007	2008
Health and social work	24,400	24,525	27,265
Services	19,426	20,594	19,189
Extra-territorial organizations and bodies	7,221	7,411	6,449
Households with employed persons	348	182	483
Sub-total	666,345	665,322	555,698
Unclassified	30	298	91,324
Total employed	666,375	665,620	647,022
Unemployed	206,150	183,689	227,990
Total labour force	872,525	849,309	875,012
Males	721,153	691,695	715,822
Females	151,372	157,615	159,192

Source: ILO.

Health and Welfare

KEY INDICATORS

Total fertility rate (children per woman, 2007)	4.6
Under-5 mortality rate (per 1,000 live births, 2005–06)	28.2
Physicians (per 1,000 head, 2008, official estimate)	1.9
Hospital beds (per 1,000 head, 2008, official estimate)	1.3
Access to water (% of persons, 2008)	91
Access to sanitation (% of persons, 2008)	89
Total carbon dioxide emissions ('000 metric tons, 2007)	2,323.0
Carbon dioxide emissions per head (metric tons, 2007)	0.6
Human Development Index (2007): ranking	110
Human Development Index (2007): value	0.737

For other sources and definitions, see explanatory note on p. vi.

Agriculture

PRINCIPAL CROPS
('000 metric tons)

	2006	2007	2008
Wheat	42.4	39.8	39.8
Barley	21.9	15.0	9.7
Potatoes	65.5	62.8	69.2
Sweet potatoes	8.8	5.6	4.9
Olives	50.6	85.7	85.8
Cabbages and other brassicas	25.3	25.2	22.8
Tomatoes	207.2	204.0	207.6
Cauliflowers and broccoli	27.4	26.2	24.8
Cucumbers and gherkins	150.0	160.0	208.2
Aubergines (Eggplants)	56.3	54.2	59.7
Onions, dry	40.8	38.4	40.1
Watermelons	15.6	19.4	17.3
Grapes	52.5	64.8	55.2
Plums and sloes	8.4	8.8	8.7
Oranges	36.3	35.4	38.4
Tangerines, mandarins, clementines and satsumas	8.2	5.6	7.3
Lemons and limes	18.1	13.6	15.4
Grapefruit and pomelos	1.8	1.8	1.8
Bananas	8.0	6.2	5.1
Strawberries	5.3	4.0*	3.2

* FAO estimate.

2009: Wheat 45.0 (FAO estimate).

Aggregate production ('000 metric tons, may include official, semi-official or estimated data): Total cereals 66.0 in 2006, 55.1 in 2007, 49.8 in 2008, 55.0 in 2009; Total roots and tubers 77.7 in 2006, 70.8 in 2007, 76.3 in 2008–09; Total vegetables (incl. melons) 668.2 in 2006, 668.1 in 2007, 710.7 in 2008–09; Total fruits (excl. melons) 166.4 in 2006, 166.7 in 2007, 169.1 in 2008–09.

Source: FAO.

LIVESTOCK
('000 head)

	2006	2007	2008
Cattle	36.3	34.2	33.0
Sheep	793.9	744.8	688.9
Goats	387.1	343.6	322.1
Chickens*	8,520	7,200	7,500

* FAO estimates.

Note: No data were available for 2009.

Source: FAO.

LIVESTOCK PRODUCTS
('000 metric tons)

	2006	2007	2008
Cattle meat	5.4	4.9	5.1
Chicken meat	53.6	45.2	47.1
Goat meat*	4.7	4.9	4.9
Sheep meat*	13.1	12.4	11.8
Cows' milk	102.6	93.7	95.4
Hen eggs†	37.9	41.0	39.4

* FAO estimates.
† Unofficial figures.

2009: Goat meat 4.9 (FAO estimate).

Source: FAO.

Fishing

GAZA STRIP
(metric tons, live weight)

	2006	2007	2008
Bogue	21	26	27
Jack and horse mackerels	44	28	44
Sardinellas	1,516	1,953	1,983
Chub mackerel	94	77	109
Cuttlefish and bobtail squids	38	23	18
Total catch (incl. others)	2,323	2,702	2,843

Source: FAO.

Finance

CURRENCY AND EXCHANGE RATES

Monetary Units:
At present, there is no domestic Palestinian currency in use. The Israeli shekel, the Jordanian dinar and the US dollar all circulate within the West Bank and the Gaza Strip.

BUDGET OF THE PALESTINIAN AUTHORITY
(US $ million, estimates)

Revenue	2002	2003*	2004†
Domestic revenue	185	259	298
Revenue clearances‡	150	442	508
Total	335	701	806

PALESTINIAN AUTONOMOUS AREAS

Expenditure	2002	2003*	2004†
Central administration	141.8	128.0	109.2
Public security and order	310.4	392.1	433.9
Financial affairs	292.5	352.2	410.7
Foreign affairs	13.8	17.2	25.6
Economic development	35.8	39.8	43.1
Social services	340.5	432.9	526.6
Cultural and information services	25.4	29.2	32.8
Transport and communication services	10.4	12.1	14.2
Total	1,170.6	1,403.5	1,596.1

* Revised estimates.
† Provisional figures.
‡ Figures refer to an apportionment of an agreed pool of selected tax revenues arising as a result of the de facto customs union between Israel and the Palestinian territories. Israel is the collecting agent for these receipts and periodically makes transfers to the Palestinian Authority.

Source: Ministry of Finance, Ramallah.

2008 (US $ million): *Revenue:* Local taxes 419; Clearing 1,067; Total 1,486; *Expenditure and net lending:* Wages and salaries 1,481; Other current expenditure 964; Net lending 400; Total 2,845.

2009 (US $ million): *Revenue:* Local taxes 625; Clearing 1,005; Total 1,630; *Expenditure and net lending:* Wages and salaries 1,410; Other current expenditure 989; Net lending 380; Total 2,779.

2010 (US $ million): *Revenue:* Local taxes 707; Clearing 1,320; Total 2,027; *Expenditure and net lending:* Wages and salaries 1,550; Other current expenditure 1,370; Net lending 250; Total 3,170.

Source: Ministry of Finance, Palestinian National Authority.

COST OF LIVING
(Consumer Price Index; base: 2000 = 100)

	2006	2007	2008
Food	118.8	124.3	147.4
Electricity, gas and other fuels	135.8	140.3	160.8
Clothing	103.5	102.7	102.4
Rent	109.0	100.8	119.5
All items (incl. others)	123.5	126.9	139.2

2009: Food 152.7; All items (incl. others) 143.1.

Source: ILO.

NATIONAL ACCOUNTS*
(US $ million at current prices)

Expenditure on the Gross Domestic Product

	2006	2007	2008
Final consumption expenditure	5,722.1	6,604.4	7,799.0
Households	4,662.6	5,331.1	6,228.2
Non-profit institutions serving households	189.8	247.2	328.1
General government	869.7	1,026.1	1,242.7
Gross capital formation	1,420.2	1,586.1	1,643.7
Gross fixed capital formation	1,393.6	1,542.2	1,609.5
Changes in inventories	26.6	43.9	34.2
Total domestic expenditure	7,142.3	8,190.5	9,442.7
Exports of goods and services	678.3	911.3	880.0
Less Imports of goods and services	3,201.5	3,919.4	4,214.5
GDP in purchasers' values	4,619.1	5,182.4	6,108.2

Gross Domestic Product by Economic Activity

	2006	2007	2008
Agriculture and fishing	267.5	292.8	355.7
Mining and quarrying	22.7	14.3	39.8
Manufacturing	563.9	675.5	657.9
Electricity and water supply	130.5	132.1	145.4
Construction	352.9	266.3	240.8
Wholesale and retail trade	489.4	671.9	879.1
Transport, storage and communications	275.7	372.5	576.2
Financial intermediation	183.9	328.0	342.2
Real estate, renting and business services	464.4	371.0	397.8
Community, social and personal services	48.4	72.8	125.7
Hotels and restaurants	41.6	70.0	65.0

—*continued*	2006	2007	2008
Education	339.5	388.4	493.2
Health and social work	106.3	158.2	214.6
Public administration and defence	616.8	628.7	734.7
Households with employed persons	2.9	3.6	3.3
Other services	199.4	179.2	177.8
Sub-total	4,105.8	4,625.3	5,449.2
Less Financial intermediation services indirectly measured	128.6	198.4	275.4
Gross value added	3,977.2	4,426.9	5,173.8
Taxes on imports	641.9	755.5	934.4
GDP in purchasers' values	4,619.1	5,182.4	6,108.2

* Referring to the West Bank and Gaza Strip, but excluding that part of Jerusalem annexed in 1967.

BALANCE OF PAYMENTS
(US $ million, preliminary estimates)

	2006	2007	2008
Exports of goods f.o.b.	450.4	646.5	669.6
Imports of goods f.o.b.	−3,245.4	−3,824.7	−4,123.4
Trade balance	−2,795.0	−3,178.2	−3,453.8
Exports of services	259.9	369.5	498.2
Imports of services	−560.3	−742.6	−838.5
Balance on goods and services	−3,095.4	−3,551.3	−3,794.1
Other income received (net)	691.9	765.7	910.9
Balance on goods, services and income	−2,403.5	−2,785.6	−2,883.2
Current transfers (net)	1,490.6	2,368.3	3,418.3
Current balance	−912.9	−417.3	535.1
Capital account (net)	274.8	401.5	398.8
Direct investment abroad (net)	−106.5	36.3	59.8
Portfolio investment (net)	−8.4	−130.7	−24.7
Other investment (net)	816.7	86.8	−399.6
Net errors and omissions	−41.5	114.7	−35.6
Overall balance	22.3	91.3	533.8

External Trade

PRINCIPAL COMMODITIES
(US $ million)

Imports c.i.f.	2006	2007	2008
Food and live animals	452.2	493.3	513.5
Beverages and tobacco	102.4	134.5	124.7
Crude materials (inedible) except fuels	62.0	27.1	29.9
Mineral fuels, lubricants, etc.	718.3	1,291.7	1,460.2
Animal and vegetable oils and fats	20.3	15.9	19.6
Chemicals and related products	223.0	223.1	244.4
Basic manufactures	490.5	448.3	493.0
Machinery and transport equipment	433.9	466.3	408.1
Miscellaneous manufactured articles	147.5	183.8	172.3
Commodities not classified elsewhere	17.4	—	50.2
Total	2,667.6	3,284.0	3,466.2

PALESTINIAN AUTONOMOUS AREAS

Exports f.o.b.	2006	2007	2008
Food and live animals	38.8	68.5	63.1
Beverages and tobacco	10.0	15.6	19.4
Crude materials (inedible) except fuels	18.5	13.2	9.5
Mineral fuels, lubricants, etc.	3.3	8.2	3.2
Animal and vegetable oils and fats	13.7	17.8	21.1
Chemicals and related products	35.2	66.7	72.7
Basic manufactures	155.4	222.0	240.2
Machinery and transport equipment	22.1	28.3	32.3
Miscellaneous manufactured articles	69.6	71.7	97.0
Other commodities and transactions	—	0.9	—
Total	366.7	513.0	558.4

PRINCIPAL TRADING PARTNERS
(US $ million)

Imports c.i.f.	2006	2007	2008
China, People's Republic	114.3	143.8	126.0
Egypt	31.4	27.5	23.5
France (incl. Monaco)	24.2	23.5	27.6
Germany	38.7	57.3	82.9
Israel	2,002.2	2,307.9	2,767.7
Italy	31.8	30.9	69.9
Japan	87.1	103.1	17.0
Jordan	33.0	44.8	52.2
Korea, Republic	2.5	12.9	27.7
Spain	24.9	27.5	23.4
Sweden	42.9	21.2	13.9
Switzerland	16.0	35.3	52.8
Thailand	9.4	25.5	8.3
Turkey	92.5	82.0	68.5
United Kingdom	16.0	20.7	16.7
USA	21.6	24.3	37.7
Total (incl. others)	2,758.7	3,141.3	3,568.7

Exports f.o.b.	2006	2007	2008
Algeria	3.5	1.0	0.8
Israel	326.6	455.2	499.4
Jordan	23.0	27.8	34.1
Netherlands	—	8.8	0.3
Saudi Arabia	2.1	1.8	3.6
United Arab Emirates	2.4	2.4	3.7
USA	2.4	3.4	3.6
Total (incl. others)	366.7	513.0	558.4

Source: UN, *International Trade Statistics Yearbook*.

Transport

ROAD TRAFFIC
(registered motor vehicles holding Palestinian licence, 2009, unless otherwise indicated)

	West Bank	Gaza Strip*
Private cars	91,132	42,372
Taxis	8,947	3,392
Buses	1,579	203
Trucks and commercial cars	20,266	10,788
Motorcycles and mopeds	156	219
Tractors	825	1,416

* 2006 figures.

Tourism

ARRIVALS OF VISITORS AT HOTELS*

	2007	2008	2009
Total	315,866	446,133	452,625

* Including Palestinians.

2006: Total guest nights in hotels 383,603 (Palestinians 52,309; European Union members 142,980; Israelis 44,602; Asians 47,421).

2007: Total guest nights in hotels 673,458 (Palestinians 51,698; European Union members 115,279; Israelis 47,846; Asians 16,882).

2008: Total guest nights in hotels 1,127,286 (Palestinians 114,416; European Union members 514,097; Israelis 47,581; Asians 103,066).

2009: Total guest nights in hotels 1,042,290.

Communications Media

	2007	2008	2009
Telephones ('000 main lines in use)	348	348	348
Mobile cellular telephones ('000 subscribers)	1,026	1,153	1,224
Internet users ('000)	851*	1,010	1,379
Broadband subscribers ('000)	56	100	233

* Estimated figure.

Personal Computers: 195,000 (54.6 per 1,000 persons) in 2005.

Source: International Telecommunication Union.

Book production (1996): 114 titles; 571,000 copies (Source: UNESCO, *Statistical Yearbook*).

Daily newspapers (titles): 3 (total average circulation 35,000) in 2004 (Source: UNESCO Institute for Statistics).

Non-daily newspapers (titles): 10 (total average circulation 21,554) in 2004 (Source: UNESCO Institute for Statistics).

Education

(2010/11, preliminary, unless otherwise indicated)

	Institutions	Teachers	Students
Pre-primary*	972	3,285	84,289
Primary	1,742	43,560*	975,460
Secondary	905		152,891
Higher: universities, etc.	11†	5,939‡	182,453‡
other	23†		

* 2007/08.
† 2006/07.
‡ 2009/10.

Pupil-teacher ratio (primary education, UNESCO estimate): 28.0 in 2008/09 (Source: UNESCO Institute for Statistics).

Adult literacy rate (persons aged 15 and over, official estimates): 94.1% (males 97.1%; females 90.9%) in 2008.

PALESTINIAN AUTONOMOUS AREAS

Directory

Administration

PALESTINIAN NATIONAL AUTHORITY

Appointed in May 1994, the Palestinian National Authority, generally known internationally as the Palestinian Authority (PA), has assumed some of the civil responsibilities formerly exercised by the Israeli Civil Administration in the Gaza Strip and parts of the West Bank.

Executive President: Mahmud Abbas (assumed office 15 January 2005).

CABINET
(May 2011)

On 14 February 2011 Prime Minister Dr Salam Khaled Abdullah Fayyad tendered the resignation of his administration to the Executive President of the Palestinian (National) Authority, Mahmud Abbas. Later that day Abbas reappointed Fayyad as premier and instructed him to form a new Cabinet. However, following the signature on 3 May of a so-called unity agreement by 13 Palestinian factions at a ceremony in Cairo, Egypt, it was expected that a joint, non-aligned administration for both the West Bank and the Gaza Strip (which had, de facto, been governed by the Islamic Resistance Movement—Hamas—since June 2007) would be formed.

Prime Minister, Minister of Finance and Acting Minister of Information: Dr Salam Khaled Abdullah Fayyad (Ind.).
Minister of the Interior: Saeed Abu Ali (Fatah).
Minister of Foreign Affairs: Dr Riyad Najib al-Maliki (Ind.).
Minister of Local Government: Khaled al-Qawasmi (Fatah).
Minister of Tourism and Antiquities: Khouloud Ihadeb Daibes (Ind.).
Minister of National Economy: Hasan Abu-Libdeh (Fatah).
Minister of Education and Higher Education: Lamis al-Alami (Ind.).
Minister of Planning and Administrative Development: Dr Ali al-Jarbawi (Ind.).
Minister of Health: Dr Fathi Abdullah Abu Mughli (Ind.).
Minister of Awqaf (Religious Endowments): Mahmud Sidqi al-Habbash (Ind.).
Minister of Transport: Dr Saadi al-Qarmuz (Fatah).
Minister of Telecommunications and Information Technology: Dr Mashhour Muhammad Abu Daqqa (Ind.).
Minister of Detainees' Affairs: Issa Qaraqe' (Fatah).
Minister of Women's Affairs: Rabiha Thiab (Fatah).
Minister of Social Affairs: Majida al-Masri (Democratic Front for the Liberation of Palestine).
Minister of Justice: Dr Ali Ahmad Salim Khashan (Ind.).
Minister of Labour: Dr Ahmad al-Majdalani (Palestinian Popular Struggle Front).
Minister of Agriculture: Ismail D'eiq (Ind.).
Minister of Culture: Siham al-Barghouthi (Palestinian Democratic Union—FIDA).
Minister of Public Works: (vacant).
Secretary-General of the Cabinet: Dr Naim Abu Hommos (Fatah).
Head of the Department of Jerusalem Affairs in the Office of the President: Ahmad al-Ruweidi (Fatah).
Minister of State: Maher Ghanim (Fatah).

MINISTRIES

Office of the President: Ramallah.
Department of Jerusalem Affairs in the Office of the President: POB 20479, Jerusalem; tel. (2) 6273330; fax (2) 6286820.
Ministry of Agriculture: POB 197, Ramallah; tel. (2) 2961080; fax (2) 2961212; e-mail moa@planet.edu.
Ministry of Awqaf (Religious Endowments): POB 17412, Jerusalem; tel. (2) 6282085; fax (2) 2986401.
Ministry of Civil Affairs: Ramallah; tel. (2) 2987336; fax (2) 2987335.
Ministry of Culture: POB 147, Ramallah; tel. (2) 2986205; fax (2) 2986204; e-mail moc@moc.pna.ps.
Ministry of Detainees' Affairs: Ramallah; tel. (2) 2961713; internet www.mod.gov.ps.
Ministry of Education and Higher Education: POB 576, al-Masioun, Ramallah; POB 5285, al-Wihda St, Gaza; tel. (2) 2983200; fax (2) 2983222; e-mail irp@mohe.gov.ps; tel. (8) 2866809; fax (8) 2865909; e-mail hope@hally.net; internet www.moehe.gov.ps.
Ministry of Finance: POB 795, Sateh Marhaba, al-Birah/Ramallah; POB 4007, Gaza; tel. (2) 2400650; fax (2) 2400595; tel. (8) 2826188; fax (8) 2820696; e-mail cbomof@palnet.com; internet www.mof.gov.ps.
Ministry of Foreign Affairs: POB 1336, Ramallah; POB 4017, Gaza; tel. (2) 2405040; fax (2) 2403772; tel. (8) 2829260; fax (8) 2868971; e-mail mofapal@gmail.com; internet www.mofa.gov.ps.
Ministry of Health: POB 14, al-Mukhtar St, Nablus; POB 1035, Abu Khadra Center, Gaza; tel. (9) 2384772; fax (9) 2384777; e-mail moh@gov.ps; tel. (8) 2829173; fax (8) 2826295; internet www.moh.gov.ps.
Ministry of Information: al-Masyoun Area, Ramallah; tel. (2) 2954042; fax (2) 2954043; e-mail minfo@minfo.gov.ps; internet www.minfo.gov.ps.
Ministry of the Interior: Ramallah; tel. (2) 2429873; fax (2) 2429872.
Ministry of Justice: POB 267, Ramallah; POB 1012, Gaza; tel. (2) 2987661; fax (2) 2974491; e-mail info@moj.gov.ps; internet www.moj.gov.ps.
Ministry of Labour: POB 350, al-Irsal St, Ramallah; tel. (2) 2900375; fax (2) 2900607; e-mail info@mol.pna.org; internet www.mol.gov.ps.
Ministry of Local Government: POB 731, Albaloo, al-Birah/Ramallah; Gaza; tel. (2) 2401092; fax (2) 2401091; tel. (8) 2820272; fax (8) 2828474; e-mail info@molg.gov.ps; internet www.molg.pna.ps.
Ministry of National Economy: Umm al-Sharayet, Ramallah; Maqqusi Bldg, al-Nasser St, Gaza; tel. (2) 2981218; fax (2) 2981207; tel. (8) 2874146; fax (8) 2874145; e-mail info@met.gov.ps; internet www.met.gov.ps.
Ministry of Planning and Administrative Development: POB 4557, al-Birah/Ramallah; POB 4017, Gaza; tel. (2) 2973010; fax (2) 2973012; tel. (8) 2828825; fax (8) 2830509; e-mail mop@gov.ps; internet www.mop-gov.ps.
Ministry of Public Works: Gaza; tel. (8) 2829232; fax (8) 2823653; e-mail mopgaza@palnet.com.
Ministry of Social Affairs: POB 3525, Ramallah; tel. (2) 2986181; fax (2) 2985239; e-mail msa@hally.net; internet www.mosa.gov.ps.
Ministry of Telecommunications and Information Technology: Ramallah; Gaza; tel. (2) 2409354; fax (2) 2409352; tel. (8) 2829171; fax (8) 2824555; e-mail mdiwan@mtit.gov.ps; internet www.mtit.gov.ps.
Ministry of Tourism and Antiquities: POB 534, Manger St, Bethlehem; Gaza; tel. (2) 2741581; fax (2) 2743753; tel. (7) 2824866; fax (7) 2824856; e-mail mota@visit-palestine.com; internet www.visit-palestine.com.
Ministry of Transport: POB 399, Ramallah; tel. (2) 2986945; fax (2) 2986943.
Ministry of Women's Affairs: al-Birah/Ramallah; tel. (2) 2403315; e-mail contactus@mowa.ps; internet www.mowa.gov.ps.

President and Legislature

Presidential and legislative elections had been due to take place by 25 January 2010; however, the polls were postponed indefinitely owing to the ongoing dispute between the Palestinian (National) Authority Cabinet and the de facto Hamas administration in the Gaza Strip. Following the signature of a unity agreement by the main Palestinian factions in early May 2011, elections were expected to take place later that year.

PALESTINIAN AUTONOMOUS AREAS

PRESIDENT
Election, 9 January 2005

Candidates	Votes	%
Mahmud Abbas (Fatah)	501,448	62.52
Mustafa Barghouthi (Ind.)	156,227	19.48
Tayseer Khalid (DFLP)	26,848	3.35
Abd al-Halim al-Ashqar (Ind.)	22,171	2.76
Bassam el-Salhi (PPP)	21,429	2.67
Al-Said Baraka (Ind.)	10,406	1.30
Abd al-Karim Shbeir (Ind.)	5,717	0.71
Invalid votes	57,831	7.21
Total	802,077	100.00

Palestinian Legislative Council
e-mail info@plc.gov.ps; internet www.plc.gov.ps.
Speaker: Dr AZIZ DUWEIK.

General Election, 25 January 2006

Parties, Lists and Coalitions	Majority system	Proportional system	Total
Change and Reform*	29	45	74
Fatah	28	17	45
Martyr Abu Ali Moustafa†	3	0	3
The Third Way	2	0	2
The Alternative‡	2	0	2
Independent Palestine§	2	0	2
Independents	0	4	4
Total	66	66	132

* The Islamic Resistance Movement (Hamas) contested the elections as Change and Reform.
† The Popular Front for the Liberation of Palestine contested the elections as Martyr Abu Ali Moustafa.
‡ Electoral list comprising the Palestinian Democratic Union, the Coalition of the Democratic Front (representing the Democratic Front for the Liberation of Palestine) and the Palestinian People's Party.
§ Coalition comprising independents and representatives of the Palestinian National Initiative.

Election Commission

Central Elections Commission (CEC): POB 2319, Qasr al-Murjan Bldg, Al-Balou, nr Jawwal Circle, Ramallah; tel. (2) 2969700; fax (2) 2969712; e-mail info@elections.ps; internet www.elections.ps; f. 2002; independent; comprises nine mems, appointed by the Exec. Pres. of the PA; Chair. Dr HANNA NASIR; Sec.-Gen. Dr RAMI HAMDALLAH.

Political Organizations

Alliance of Palestinian Forces: f. 1994; comprises representatives of the PLF, the PPSF, the PRCP and the PFLP—GC; opposes the Declaration of Principles on Palestinian Self-Rule signed by Israel and the PLO in September 1993, and subsequent agreements concluded within its framework (the 'Oslo accords'). The PFLP and DFLP left the Alliance in 1996. The **Fatah Revolutionary Council**, headed by Sabri Khalil al-Banna, alias 'Abu Nidal', split from Fatah in 1973. Its headquarters were formerly in Baghdad, Iraq, but the office was closed down and its staff expelled from the country by the Iraqi authorities in November 1983; a new base was established in Damascus, Syria, in December. Al-Banna was readmitted to Iraq in 1984, having fled Syria. With 'Abu Musa' (whose rebel Fatah group is called **Al-Intifada** or 'Uprising'), Abu Nidal formed a joint rebel Fatah command in February 1985, and both had offices in Damascus until June 1987, when those of Abu Nidal were closed by the Syrian Government. Forces loyal to Abu Nidal surrendered to Fatah forces at the Rashidiyeh Palestinian refugee camp near Tyre, northern Lebanon, in 1990. Abu Nidal was reportedly found dead in Baghdad in August 2002.

Arab Liberation Front (ALF): Ramallah; f. 1969; fmrly supported by Iraq's Arab Baath Socialist Party under the leadership of former President Saddam Hussein; member of the PLO; opposes Oslo accords; Sec.-Gen. RAKAD SALIM (imprisoned in 2002).

Democratic Front for the Liberation of Palestine (DFLP) (Al-Jabha al-Dimuqratiyya li-Tahrir Filastin): Damascus, Syria; tel. (11) 4448993; fax (11) 4442380; Ramallah; tel. (2) 2954438; fax (2) 2980401; e-mail dflp-palestine@dflp-palestine.org; internet www.dflp-palestine.org; f. 1969 following split with PFLP; Marxist-Leninist; contested Jan. 2006 legislative elections on The Alternative electoral list as the Coalition of the Democratic Front; Sec.-Gen. NAIF HAWATMEH (Damascus).

Fatah (Harakat al-Tahrir al-Watani al-Filastin—Palestine National Liberation Movement): POB 1965, Ramallah; tel. (2) 2986892; fax (2) 2987947; e-mail fact@palnet.com; internet www.fateh.ps; f. 1957; militant group that became the single largest Palestinian org. and strongest faction in both the administration and Palestinian Legislative Council until the legislative elections of Jan. 2006; leadership is nominally shared by the members of the Cen. Cttee, who were elected at Fatah's Sixth Gen. Conference on 10 Aug. 2009; Chair. of Cen. Cttee MAHMUD ABBAS.

Islamic Jihad (Al-Jihad al-Islami): Damascus, Syria; f. 1979–80 by Palestinian students in Egypt; militant Islamist; opposed to the Oslo accords; Sec.-Gen. RAMADAN ABDULLAH SHALLAH.

Islamic Resistance Movement (Hamas—Harakat al-Muqawama al-Islamiyya): Gaza; Damascus, Syria; f. 1987; originally welfare organization Mujama (f. 1973) led by the late Sheikh AHMAD YASSIN (killed by Israeli forces in March 2004); militant Islamist; opposes the Oslo accords; following the killing by Israeli forces of Hamas's leader in the Gaza Strip, Abd al-Aziz al-Rantisi, in April 2004, the group announced that it was adopting a policy of 'collective leadership'; contested Jan. 2006 legislative elections as Change and Reform; Head of Political Bureau KHALID MESHAAL (Damascus); Gen. Commdr of military wing, Izz al-Din al-Qassam Brigades, MUHAMMAD DEIF (in hiding from the Israeli authorities since 1992, though presumed to be in Gaza).

Palestine Liberation Front (PLF): f. 1977 following split with PFLP—GC; the PLF split into three factions in the early 1980s, all of which retained the name PLF; one faction (Leader MUHAMMAD 'ABU' ABBAS) was based in Tunis, Tunisia, and Baghdad, Iraq, and remained nominally loyal to Yasser Arafat; the second faction (Leader TALAAT YAQOUB) belonged to the anti-Arafat National Salvation Front and opened offices in Damascus, Syria, and Libya; a third group derived from the PLF was reportedly formed by its Central Cttee Secretary, ABD AL-FATTAH GHANIM, in June 1986; the factions of Yaqoub and Ghanim were reconciled in early 1985; at the 18th session of the PNC a programme for the unification of the PLF was announced, with Yaqoub (died November 1988) named as Secretary-General and Abu Abbas appointed to the PLO Executive Committee, while unification talks were held. The merging of the two factions was announced in June 1987, with Abu Abbas becoming Deputy Secretary-General. Abu Abbas was apprehended by US-led coalition forces in Iraq in April 2003, and reportedly died of natural causes in March 2004 while still in US custody; Sec.-Gen. ABU NIDAL AL-ASHQAR.

Palestine Liberation Organization (PLO) (Munazzimat al-Tahrir al-Filastiniyya): Negotiations Affairs Dept, POB 4120, Ramallah; tel. (2) 2963741; fax (2) 2963740; internet www.nad-plo.org; f. 1964; the supreme organ of the PLO is the Palestine Nat. Council (PNC; Pres. SALIM AL-ZA'NUN), while the PLO Exec. Cttee (Chair. MAHMUD ABBAS; Sec.-Gen. FAROUK KADDOUMI) deals with day-to-day business. Fatah (the Palestine Nat. Liberation Movement) joined the PNC in 1968, and all the guerrilla orgs joined the Council in 1969. In 1973 the Palestinian Cen. Council (PCC; Chair. SALIM AL-ZA'NUN) was established to act as an intermediary between the PNC and the Exec. Cttee. The Council meets when the PNC is not in session and approves major policy decisions on its behalf; Chair. MAHMUD ABBAS.

Palestine Revolutionary Communist Party (PRCP) (Al-Hizb al-Shuyu'i al-Thawri al-Filastini): principally based in Lebanon; promotes armed struggle in order to achieve its aims; Sec.-Gen. ARABI AWAD.

Palestinian Democratic Union (FIDA): POB 247, Ramallah; tel. 2954072; fax (2) 2954071; e-mail info@fida.ps; internet www.fida.ps; f. 1990 following split from the DFLP; contested Jan. 2006 legislative elections on The Alternative electoral list; Leader YASSER ABD AL-RABBUH; Sec.-Gen. SALEH RA'FAT.

Palestinian National Initiative (Al-Mubadara): Ramallah; tel. (5) 9293006; e-mail almubadara@almubadara.org; internet www.almubadara.org; f. 2002; seeks peaceful resolution of conflict with Israel through establishment of an independent, unified, viable and democratic Palestinian state, with East Jerusalem as its capital; advocates reform of internal political structures, and aims to fight corruption and injustice, and to uphold citizens' rights; contested Jan. 2006 legislative elections as part of the Independent Palestine coalition; Sec.-Gen. Dr MUSTAFA BARGHOUTHI.

Palestinian People's Party (PPP) (Hezb al-Sha'ab): Ramallah; tel. (2) 2963593; fax (2) 2963592; e-mail shaab@palpeople.org; internet www.palpeople.org; f. 1921 as Palestine Communist Party;

PALESTINIAN AUTONOMOUS AREAS

adopted current name in 1991; admitted to the PNC at its 18th session in 1987; contested Jan. 2006 legislative elections on The Alternative electoral list; Sec.-Gen. BASSAM EL-SALHI.

Palestinian Popular Struggle Front (PPSF) (Jabhat al-Nidal al-Sha'biyya al-Filastiniyya): f. 1967; has reportedly split into two factions which either support or oppose the PA; the pro-PA faction (Leader AHMAD AL-MAJDALANI) is based in the West Bank; the anti-PA faction (Leader KHALID ABD AL-MAJID) is based in Damascus, Syria.

Popular Front for the Liberation of Palestine (PFLP) (Al-Jabha al-Sha'biyya li-Tahrir Filastin): Damascus, Syria; internet www.pflp.ps; f. 1967; Marxist-Leninist; publr of *Democratic Palestine* (English; monthly); contested Jan. 2006 legislative elections as Martyr Abu Ali Moustafa; Sec.-Gen. AHMAD SAADAT (imprisoned in 2002).

Popular Front for the Liberation of Palestine—General Command (PFLP—GC): Damascus, Syria; f. 1968 following split from the PFLP; pro-Syrian; Leader AHMAD JIBRIL.

Popular Front for the Liberation of Palestine—National General Command: Amman, Jordan; split from the PFLP—GC in 1999; aims to co-operate with the PA; Leader ATIF YUNUS.

Al-Saiqa (Thunderbolt, or Vanguard of the Popular Liberation War): f. 1968; Syrian-backed; pan-Arab; opposed to the Oslo accords; Sec.-Gen. ISSAM AL-QADI.

The formation of the **Right Movement for Championing the Palestinian People's Sons** by former members of Hamas was announced in April 1995. The movement, based in Gaza City, was reported to support the PA. The **Al-Aqsa Martyrs Brigades**, consisting of a number of Fatah-affiliated activists, emerged soon after the start of the al-Aqsa *intifada* in September 2000, and have carried out attacks against Israeli targets in Israel, the West Bank and Gaza Strip.

Diplomatic Representation

Countries with which the PLO maintains diplomatic relations include:

Afghanistan, Albania, Algeria, Angola, Argentina, Austria, Bahrain, Bangladesh, Benin, Bhutan, Bolivia, Botswana, Brazil, Brunei, Bulgaria, Burkina Faso, Burundi, Cambodia, Cameroon, Cape Verde, Central African Republic, Chad, Chile, China (People's Rep.), Comoros, Congo (Dem. Rep.), Congo (Rep.), Costa Rica, Côte d'Ivoire, Cuba, Cyprus, Czech Republic, Djibouti, Dominican Republic, Ecuador, Egypt, Equatorial Guinea, Ethiopia, Gabon, Gambia, Ghana, Guinea, Guinea-Bissau, Guyana, the Holy See, Hungary, India, Indonesia, Iran, Iraq, Jordan, Korea (Dem. People's Rep.), Kuwait, Laos, Lebanon, Libya, Madagascar, Malaysia, Maldives, Mali, Malta, Mauritania, Mauritius, Mongolia, Morocco, Mozambique, Nepal, Nicaragua, Niger, Nigeria, Norway, Oman, Pakistan, Peru, Philippines, Poland, Qatar, Romania, Russia, Rwanda, São Tomé and Príncipe, Saudi Arabia, Senegal, Serbia, Seychelles, Sierra Leone, Somalia, Sri Lanka, Sudan, Suriname, Swaziland, Sweden, Tanzania, Togo, Tunisia, Turkey, Uganda, Uruguay, the United Arab Emirates (UAE), Uzbekistan, Vanuatu, Venezuela, Viet Nam, Yemen, Zambia and Zimbabwe.

The following states, while they do not recognize the State of Palestine, allow the PLO to maintain a regional office: Belgium, France, Germany, Greece, Italy, Japan, the Netherlands, Portugal, Spain, Switzerland and the United Kingdom.

Judicial System

In the Gaza Strip, the West Bank towns of Jericho, Nablus, Ramallah, Jenin, Tulkarm, Qalqilya, Bethlehem and Hebron, and in other, smaller population centres in the West Bank, the PA has assumed limited jurisdiction with regard to civil affairs. However, the situation is confused owing to the various and sometimes conflicting legal systems which have operated in the territories occupied by Israel in 1967: Israeli military and civilian law; Jordanian law; and acts, orders-in-council and ordinances that remain from the period of the British Mandate in Palestine. Religious and military courts have been established under the auspices of the PA. In February 1995 the PA established a Higher State Security Court in Gaza to decide on security crimes both inside and outside the PA's area of jurisdiction; and to implement all valid Palestinian laws, regulations, rules and orders in accordance with Article 69 of the Constitutional Law of the Gaza Strip of 5 March 1962.

General Prosecutor of the PA: AHMAD AL-MOGHANI.

Religion

The vast majority of Palestinians in the West Bank and Gaza are Muslims, while a small (and declining) minority are Christians of the Greek Orthodox and Roman Catholic rites.

ISLAM

The PA-appointed Grand Mufti of Jerusalem and the Palestinian Lands is the most senior Muslim cleric in the Palestinian territories.

Mufti of Jerusalem: Sheikh MUHAMMAD AHMAD HUSSEIN.

CHRISTIANITY

The Roman Catholic Church

Latin Rite

The Patriarchate of Jerusalem covers Israel and the Occupied Territories, the Palestinian Autonomous Areas, Jordan, and Cyprus. At 31 December 2006 there were an estimated 78,215 adherents.

Patriarchate of Jerusalem: Patriarcat Latin, POB 14152, Jerusalem 91141; tel. (2) 6282323; fax (2) 6271652; e-mail latinvic@latinpat.org; internet www.lpj.org; Patriarch His Beatitude Archbishop FOUAD TWAL; Vicar-General Emeritus for Jerusalem KAMAL HANNA BATHISH (Titular Bishop of Jericho); Vicar-General for Israel GIACINTO-BOULOS MARCUZZO (Titular Bishop of Emmaus Nicopolis).

Melkite Rite

The Greek-Melkite Patriarch of Antioch and all the East, of Alexandria, and of Jerusalem (GRÉGOIRE III LAHAM) is resident in Damascus, Syria.

Patriarchal Vicariate of Jerusalem: Patriarcat Grec-Melkite Catholique, POB 14130, Porte de Jaffa, Jerusalem 91141; tel. (2) 6282023; fax (2) 6289606; e-mail gcpjer@p-ol.com; about 3,300 adherents (31 December 2007); Protosyncellus Archim. Archbishop JOSEPH JULES ZEREY (Titular Archbishop of Damietta).

The Greek Orthodox Church

The Patriarchate of Jerusalem contains an estimated 260,000 adherents in Israel and the Occupied Territories, the Palestinian Autonomous Areas, Jordan, Kuwait, the UAE, and Saudi Arabia.

Patriarchate of Jerusalem: POB 14518, Jerusalem 91145; tel. (2) 6274941; fax (2) 6282048; e-mail secretariat@jerusalem-patriarchate.info; internet www.jerusalem-patriarchate.info; Patriarch THEOPHILOS III.

The Press

NEWSPAPERS

Al-Ayyam: POB 1987, al-Ayyam St, Commercial Area, Ramallah; tel. (2) 2987341; fax (2) 2987342; e-mail info@al-ayyam.com; internet www.al-ayyam.ps; f. 1995; weekly; Arabic; publ. by Al-Ayyam Press, Printing, Publishing and Distribution Co; Editor-in-Chief AKRAM HANIYA.

Al-Ayyam al-Arabi: POB 1987, al-Ayyam St, Commercial Area, Ramallah; tel. 2-2987341; fax 2-2987342; e-mail info@al-ayyam.com; internet www.al-ayyam.com; f. 1995; daily; Arabic; publ. by Al-Ayyam Press, Printing, Publishing and Distribution Co; Editor-in-Chief AKRAM HANIYA.

Filastin al-Thawra (Palestine of the Revolution): fmrly publ. in Beirut, Lebanon, but resumed publication from Cyprus in November 1982; weekly newspaper of the PLO; Arabic.

Al-Hadaf (The Target): e-mail alhadaf@alhadafmagazine.com; internet www.alhadafmagazine.com; f. 1969 in Beirut, Lebanon; weekly; Arabic; organ of the Popular Front for the Liberation of Palestine.

Al-Hayat al-Jadidah: POB 1822, Ramallah; tel. (2) 2407251; fax (2) 2407250; e-mail info1@alhayat-j.com; internet www.alhayat-j.com; f. 1994; weekly; Arabic; Editor NADIL AMR.

Al-Hourriah (Liberation): POB 11488, Damascus, Syria; tel. (1) 6319455; fax (1) 6319125; e-mail hourriah@hotmail.com; internet www.alhourriah.org; Arabic; organ of the Democratic Front for the Liberation of Palestine; publ. in Beirut (Lebanon) and Damascus; Editor-in-Chief HAMADEH MUTASIM.

Al-Istiqlal (Independence): al-Thawra St, Gaza City; e-mail alesteqlal@p-i-s.com; weekly; Arabic; organ of Islamic Jihad; Sec. TAWFIQ AL-SAYYID SALIM.

Palestine Times: POB 10355, London, NW2 3WH, United Kingdom; e-mail palestimes@ptimes.org; internet www.ptimes.org; f. 2006; monthly; English; privately owned; independent; Editor-in-Chief AHMAD KARMAWI; circ. 5,000.

PALESTINIAN AUTONOMOUS AREAS

Al-Quds (Jerusalem): POB 19788, Jerusalem; tel. (2) 5833501; fax (2) 5856937; e-mail info@alquds.com; internet www.alquds.com; Arabic; independent; pro-PA; supports peace negotiations; reportedly has largest circulation of all Palestinian newspapers; daily; Editor MAHER AL-ALAMI.

Al-Risala (Letter): Gaza City; weekly; Arabic; affiliated with the Islamic Resistance Movement (Hamas); Editor-in-Chief GHAZI HAMAD.

Al-Watan: Gaza City; weekly; Arabic; supports Hamas.

PERIODICALS

Filastin (Palestine): Gaza City; e-mail adel@falasteen.com; internet www.falasteen.com; f. 1994; weekly; Arabic; pro-Hamas, banned from publication and distribution in the West Bank; Editor-in-Chief MUSTAFA AL-SAWWAF.

The Jerusalem Times: POB 20185, 19 Nablus Rd, Jerusalem; tel. (2) 6264883; fax (2) 6287893; e-mail webmaster@jerusalem-times.net; internet www.jerusalem-times.net; f. 1994; weekly; English; independent; Publr HANNA SINIORA; Man. Editor SAMI KAMAL.

Al-Karmel Magazine: POB 1887, Ramallah; tel. (2) 2965934; fax (2) 2987374; e-mail editor@alkarmel.org; internet www.alkarmel.org; f. 1981 in Beirut, Lebanon; literature; Editor-in-Chief MAHMOUD DARWISH.

Madar: Madar—al-Markaz al-Filastini lil-Dirasat al-Israiliyah, Ramallah; publ. by Madar—The Palestinian Centre for Israeli Studies; political; Editor SALMAN NATOUR.

Palestine Report: Jerusalem Media and Communications Centre, POB 25047, 7 Nablus Rd, Jerusalem 97300; tel. (2) 5838266; fax (2) 5836837; e-mail jmcc@jmcc.org; internet www.jmcc.org; f. 1990; weekly; English; current affairs; publ. by the Jerusalem Media and Communications Centre; Editor-in-Chief JOHARAH BAKER; Man. Dir OMAR KARMI.

The Youth Times: Orabi Bldg, 2 Ramallah St, Jerusalem; tel. (2) 2426280; fax (2) 2426281; e-mail pyalara@pyalara.org; internet www.pyalara.org; f. 1998; monthly; Arabic and English; publ. by the Palestinian Youth Association for Leadership and Rights Activation; Editor-in-Chief HANIA BITAR.

NEWS AGENCY

Wikalat Anbaa' Filastiniya (WAFA, Palestine News Agency): POB 5300, Gaza City; tel. (8) 2824036; fax (8) 2824046; e-mail edit@wafa.ps; internet www.wafa.ps; official PLO news agency; Editor ZIAD ABD AL-FATTAH.

Publishers

Al-Ayyam Press, Printing, Publishing and Distribution Co: POB 1987, Ramallah; tel. (2) 2987341; fax (2) 2987342; e-mail info@al-ayyam.com; internet www.al-ayyam.com; f. 1995; publishes *Al-Ayyam al-Arabi* daily newspaper, *Al-Ayyam* weekly newspaper, books and magazines.

Beit Al-Maqdes for Publishing and Distribution: Ramallah; history, politics, fiction, children's.

Centre for Palestine Research and Studies (CPRS): POB 132, Nablus; tel. (9) 2380383; fax (9) 2380384; f. 1993; history, politics, strategic studies and economics; Dir SAID KANAAN.

Ogarit Centre for Publishing and Distribution: Ramallah; nonfiction, children's.

Broadcasting and Communications

TELECOMMUNICATIONS

A monopoly on fixed-line services is held by the Palestine Telecommunications Co PLC (PalTel). However, a second mobile telephone licence was awarded to Wataniya Mobile in 2006.

Palestine Telecommunications Co PLC (PalTel): POB 1570, Nablus; tel. (9) 2390108; fax (9) 2350140; e-mail paltel@palnet.net; internet www.paltel.ps; f. 1995; following acquisition of 56% stake by Zain Kuwait in May 2009, PalTel was merged with Zain Jordan; provider of fixed-line, mobile (cellular) and internet services; CEO, Levant Region Dr ABD AL-MALEK JABER; Gen. Man. MUHAMMAD HEAJAWI.

Palestine Cellular Co (Jawwal): POB 3999, al-Birah/Ramallah; tel. (2) 2402440; fax (2) 2968636; e-mail atyourservice@jawwal.ps; internet www.jawwal.ps/index.php; f. 1999; wholly owned subsidiary of PalTel; 700,000 subscribers (May 2006), representing some 55% of the Palestinian mobile (cellular) telecommunications market; CEO AMMAR AKER.

Wataniya Mobile: POB 4236, al-Birah/Ramallah; tel. (2) 2415000; fax (2) 2423044; e-mail mohammad.nassar@wataniya.ps; internet www.wataniya-palestine.com; awarded the second mobile telephone licence 2006; commenced services in the West Bank Nov. 2009; 57% owned by Wataniya Telecom (Kuwait), 43% owned by Palestine Investment Fund; Chair. MUHAMMAD MUSTAFA; CEO ALAN RICHARDSON.

BROADCASTING

Palestinian Broadcasting Co (PBC): POB 984, al-Birah/Ramallah; tel. (2) 2959894; fax (2) 2959893; e-mail pbcinfo@pbc.gov.ps; internet www.pbc.gov.ps/English/about_us.htm; f. 1994; state-controlled; Chair. BASEM ABU SUMAYA.

Sawt Filastin (Voice of Palestine): c/o Police HQ, Jericho; tel. (2) 921220; f. 1994; official radio station of the PA; broadcasts in Arabic from Jericho and Ramallah; Dir RADWAN ABU AYYASH.

Palestine Television: f. 1994; broadcasts from Ramallah and Gaza City; broadcasts online on JumpTV; Dir RADWAN ABU AYYASH.

Finance

(cap. = capital; p.u. = paid up; res = reserves; dep. = deposits; brs = branches; m. = million)

BANKING

The Palestine Monetary Authority (PMA) is the financial regulatory body in the Palestinian Autonomous Areas, and is expected to evolve into the Central Bank of Palestine. Three currencies circulate in the Palestinian economy—the Jordanian dinar, the Israeli shekel and the US dollar—and the PMA currently has no right of issue. According to the PMA, there were 19 banks with a network of more than 200 branches operating in the West Bank and Gaza in mid-2010.

Palestine Monetary Authority (PMA): POB 452, Nablus Rd, Ramallah; POB 4026, Nasrah St, Gaza; tel. (2) 2415250; fax (2) 2409922; tel. (8) 2407779; fax (8) 2409646; e-mail info@pma.ps; internet www.pma.ps; f. 1994; began licensing, inspection and supervision of the Palestinian and foreign commercial banks operating in the Gaza Strip and the Jericho enclave in the West Bank in July 1995; assumed responsibility for 13 banks in the Palestinian territories over which the Central Bank of Israel had hitherto exercised control in Dec. 1995; Gov. Dr JIHAD AL-WAZIR.

National Banks

Bank of Palestine PLC (BOP): POB 471, Court St, Ain Misbah, Ramallah; tel. (2) 2965010; fax (2) 2964703; e-mail info@bankofpalestine.com; internet www.bankofpalestine.com; f. 1960; cap. US $100m., res $26m., dep. $1,086m. (Dec. 2009) Gen. Man. Dr HANI HASHEM SHAWA; 31 brs and sub-brs in West Bank and Gaza.

Palestine Commercial Bank: POB 1799, Michael Tanous Bldg, Alawda St, Ramallah; tel. (2) 2979999; fax (2) 2979977; internet www.pcb.ps; f. 1992; as Commercial Bank of Palestine; name changed as above 2009; cap. US $35m. (May 2008); Pres. MAHMOUD ZUHDI MALHAS; 5 brs.

Palestine International Bank: al-Birah/Ramallah; tel. (2) 2983300; fax (2) 2983344; e-mail issam@ias.intranets.com; internet www.pibank.net; f. 1997; cap. US $20m.; Chair. OSAMA MUHAMMAD KHADIR; 4 brs.

Investment Banks

Arab Palestinian Investment Bank: POB 1260, al-Harji Bldg, Ramallah; tel. (2) 2987126; fax (2) 2987125; e-mail apibank@palnet.com; internet www.apibank.ps; f. 1996; Arab Bank of Jordan has a 51% share; cap. US $15m.; Dir ABD AL-MAJID SHOMAN; Gen. Man. BESHARA DABBAH.

Palestine Investment Bank PLC: POB 3675, al-Helal St, al-Birah/Ramallah; tel. (2) 2407880; fax (2) 2407887; e-mail info@pinvbank.com; internet www.pinvbank.com; f. 1995 by the PA; some shareholders based in Jordan and the Gulf states; cap. US $60m.; provides full commercial and investment banking services throughout the West Bank and Gaza; Chair. ABD AL-AZIZ ABU DAYYEH; 7 brs.

Al-Quds Bank for Development and Investment (Quds Bank): POB 2471, Ramallah; tel. (2) 2961750; fax (2) 2961754; e-mail quds@qudsbank.ps; internet www.alqudsbank.ps; f. 1995; merchant bank; cap. p.u. US $50m.; Gen. Man. AZZAM A. SHAWWA; 8 brs and 12 offices.

Islamic Banks

Arab Islamic Bank: POB 631, Nablus St, al-Birah/Ramallah; tel. (2) 2407060; fax (2) 2407065; e-mail aib@arabislamicbank.com; internet www.arabislamicbank.com; f. 1995; cap. US $40m., res $9m., dep. $238m. (Dec. 2009); Chair. WALID T. FAKHOURI; Gen. Man. ATIYEH A. SHANANIER; 8 brs.

PALESTINIAN AUTONOMOUS AREAS

Palestine Islamic Bank: POB 1244, Omar al-Mukhtar St, Gaza City; tel. (8) 2827360; fax (8) 2825269; e-mail info@islamicbank.ps; internet www.islamicbank.ps; f. 1996; Chair. MUHAMMED FAYEZ JABER ZAKARNEH.

STOCK EXCHANGE

Palestine Exchange (PEX): POB 128, 4th Floor, Amman St, Nablus; tel. (9) 2390999; fax (9) 2390998; e-mail pex@pex.ps; internet www.pex.ps; f. 1995; CEO AHMAD AWEIDAH.

INSURANCE

A very small insurance industry exists in the West Bank and Gaza.

Ahleia Insurance Group Ltd (AIG): POB 1214, al-Jalaa Tower, Remal, Gaza; tel. (8) 2824035; fax (8) 2824015; e-mail info@aig.ps; internet www.aig.ps; f. 1994; Chair. and CEO Dr MUHAMMAD AL-SABAWI; 11 brs.

Arab Insurance Establishment Co Ltd (AIE): POB 166, al-Qasr St, Nablus; tel. (9) 2341040; fax (9) 2341033; e-mail info@aie.com.ps; f. 1975; Chair. WALID ALOUL.

National Insurance Co: POB 1819, 34 Municipality St, al-Birah/Ramallah; tel. (2) 2983800; fax (2) 2407460; e-mail nic@nic-pal.com; internet www.nic-pal.com; f. 1992; Chair. MUHAMMAD MAHMOUD MASROUJI; Gen. Man. AZIZ MAHMOUD ABD AL-JAWAD; 8 brs.

DEVELOPMENT FINANCE ORGANIZATIONS

Arab Palestinian Investment Co Ltd: POB 2396, Kharaz Center, Yafa St, Industrial Zone, Ramallah; tel. (2) 2981060; fax (2) 2981065; e-mail apic@apic.com.jo; internet www.apic.ps; f. 1995; headquarters in Amman, Jordan; Chair. and CEO TAREK OMAR AGGAD.

Jerusalem Real Estate Investment Co: POB 1876, Ramallah; tel. (2) 2965215; fax (2) 2965217; e-mail jrei@palnet.com; f. 1996; Chair. AWNI ALSAKET.

Palestine Development & Investment Co (PADICO): POB 316, Nablus; tel. (9) 2384480; fax (9) 2384355; e-mail padico@padico.com; internet www.padico.com; f. 1993; 12 subsidiary and affiliate cos; Chair. MUNIB R. AL-MASRI; CEO Dr SAMIR HULILEH.

Palestine Real Estate Investment Co (Aqaria): POB 4049, Gaza; tel. (8) 2824815; fax (8) 2824845; e-mail aqaria@rannet.com; internet www.aqaria.com; f. 1994; Chair. NABIL SARAF; Vice-Chair. OMAR AL-ALAMI.

Palestinian Economic Council for Development and Reconstruction (PECDAR): POB 54910, Dahiyat al-Barid, Jerusalem; tel. (2) 2974300; fax (2) 2974331; e-mail info@pecdar.pna.net; internet www.pecdar.org; privately owned; Pres. Dr MUHAMMAD SHTAYYEH.

Trade and Industry

CHAMBERS OF COMMERCE

Federation of Chambers of Commerce, Industry and Agriculture: tel. (2) 2344923; fax (2) 2344924; e-mail fpccia@palnet.com; internet www.pal-chambers.org; f. 1989; 14 chambers, 32,000 mems.

Bethlehem Chamber of Commerce and Industry: POB 59, Bethlehem; tel. (2) 2742742; fax (2) 2764402; e-mail bcham@palnet.com; internet www.bethlehem-chamber.org; f. 1952; 2,800 mems; Chair. of Bd SAMIR HAZBOUN.

Gaza Chamber of Commerce, Industry and Agriculture: POB 33, Sabra Quarter, Gaza; tel. and fax (8) 2864588; e-mail gazacham@palnet.com; internet www.gazacham.ps; f. 1954; Chair. MUHAMMAD QUDWAH; Man. Dir BASSAM MORTAJA; 14,000 mems.

Hebron Chamber of Commerce and Industry: POB 272, Hebron; tel. (2) 2228218; fax (2) 2227490; e-mail info@hebroncci.org; internet www.hebroncci.org; f. 1954; Chair. HASHEM NATSHEH; 7,350 mems.

Jenin Chamber of Commerce, Industry and Agriculture: Jenin; tel. (4) 2501107; fax (4) 2503388; e-mail jencham@hally.net; internet www.pal-chambers.org/chambers/jenin.html; f. 1953; 3,800 mems.

Jericho Chamber of Commerce, Industry and Agriculture: POB 91, Jericho 00970; tel. (2) 2323313; fax (2) 2322394; e-mail jericho@pal-chambers.org; internet www.pal-chambers.org/chambers/jericho.html; f. 1953; 400 mems; Chair. HAJ MANSOUR SALAYMEH; Sec.-Gen. SELMI HAMAD.

Jerusalem Arab Chamber of Commerce and Industry: POB 19151, Jerusalem 91191; tel. (2) 2344923; fax (2) 2344914; e-mail chamber@jerusalemchamber.org; internet www.jerusalemchamber.org; f. 1936; 2,050 mems; Chair. AHMAD HASHEM ZUGHAYAR; Dir AZZAM ABU SAUD.

Nablus Chamber of Commerce and Industry: POB 35, Nablus; tel. (9) 2380335; fax (9) 2377605; e-mail nabluschamber@gmail.com; internet www.pal-chambers.org/chambers/nablus.html; f. 1943; Pres. MA'AZ NABULSI; Dir TAJ EL-DIN BITAR; 7,000 mems.

Palestinian-European Chamber of Commerce: Jerusalem; tel. (2) 894883; Chair. HANNA SINIORA.

Qalqilya Chamber of Commerce, Industry and Agriculture: POB 13, Qalqilya; tel. (9) 2941473; fax (9) 2940164; e-mail chamberq@hally.net; internet www.pal-chambers.org/chambers/qalqilya.html; f. 1972; 1,068 mems.

Ramallah Chamber of Commerce and Industry: POB 256, al-Birah/Ramallah; tel. (2) 2955052; fax (2) 2984691; e-mail info@ramallahcci.org; internet www.ramallahcci.org; f. 1950; Chair. MUHAMMAD AHMAD AMIN; Vice-Chair. YOUSUF AL-SHARIF; 4,100 mems.

Salfeet Chamber of Commerce, Industry and Agriculture: Salfeet; tel. and fax (9) 2515970; e-mail salfeetchamber@hotmail.com; internet www.pal-chambers.org/chambers/salfeet1.html; f. 1997; Chair. FOUAD AWAD.

Tulkarm Chamber of Commerce, Industry and Agriculture: POB 51, Tulkarm; tel. (9) 2671010; fax (9) 2675623; e-mail tulkarm@palnet.com; internet www.tulkarmchamber.org; f. 1945; 2,000 mems; Chair. SHUKRI AHMAD JALLAD.

TRADE AND INDUSTRIAL ORGANIZATIONS

Palestinian General Federation of Trade Unions (PGFTU): POB 1216, Nablus; tel. (9) 2385136; fax (9) 2384374; e-mail pgftu@pgftu.org; internet www.pgftu.org; f. 1965; Sec.-Gen. SHAHER SAED.

Union of Industrialists: POB 1296, Gaza; tel. (8) 2866222; fax (8) 2862013; Chair. MUHAMMAD YAZIJI.

UTILITIES

Electricity

Palestinian Energy Authority (PEA): POB 3591, Nablus St, al-Birah/Ramallah; POB 3041, Gaza; tel. (2) 2986190; fax (2) 2986191; tel. (8) 2821702; fax (8) 2824849; e-mail pea@palnet.com; internet pea-pal.tripod.com; f. 1994; Chair. Dr ABD AL-RAHMAN T. HAMAD.

Jerusalem District Electricity Co (JDECO): POB 19118, 15 Salah el-Din St, Jerusalem; (2) 6269333; fax (2) 6282441; e-mail info@jdeco.net; internet www.jdeco.net; Gen. Man. HISHAM OMARI.

National Electric Co (NEC): West Bank; f. 2000.

Palestine Electric Co (PEC): POB 1336, Gaza; tel. (8) 2823800; fax (8) 2823297; e-mail info@pec-gpgc.com; internet www.pec-gpgc.com; f. 1999; 33% state-owned; Chair. SAID KHOURY; CEO WALID SALMAN.

Water

Palestinian Water Authority (PWA): POB 2174, Baghdad St, Ramallah; tel. (2) 2429022; fax (2) 2429341; e-mail pwa@pwa.ps; internet www.pwa.ps; f. 1995; Dir Dr SHADDAD AL-ATTILI.

Transport

ROADS

In 2006, according to estimates by the International Road Federation, the Palestinian territories had 5,147 km of paved roads, of which 535 km were highways or main roads, 438 km were secondary roads and 4,175 km were other roads.

CIVIL AVIATION

Palestinian Civil Aviation Authority (PCAA): Yasser Arafat International Airport, POB 4043, Rafah, Gaza; tel. and fax (8) 2827844; e-mail abuhalib@gaza-airport.org; internet www.gaza-airport.org; f. 1994; Gaza International Airport (renamed as above after Arafat's death in Nov. 2004) was formally inaugurated in November 1998 to operate services by Palestinian Airlines (its subsidiary), EgyptAir and Royal Jordanian Airline; Royal Air Maroc began to operate services to Amman (Jordan), Abu Dhabi and Dubai (both UAE), Cairo (Egypt), Doha (Qatar), Jeddah (Saudi Arabia), Istanbul (Turkey) and Larnaca (Cyprus), and intends to expand its network to Europe; the airport was closed by the Israeli authorities in February 2001 and the runway seriously damaged by Israeli airstrikes in late 2001 and early 2002; Dir-Gen. SALMAN ABU HALIB; Admin. Man. JAMAL AL-MASHHARAWI.

Palestinian Airlines: POB 4043, Gaza; tel. and fax (8) 2827844; e-mail commercial@palairlines.com; internet www.palairlines.com; f. 1994; state-owned; operates flights from el-Arish, Egypt, and Amman, Jordan; Dir-Gen. Capt. ZEYAD ALBADDA; Commercial. Dir YASSER IRQAYEQ.

Tourism

Although the tourism industry in the West Bank was virtually destroyed as a result of the 1967 Arab–Israeli War, by the late 1990s the sector was expanding significantly, with a number of hotels being opened or under construction. Much of the tourism in the West Bank centres around the historical and biblical sites of Jerusalem and Bethlehem. However, the renewed outbreak of Israeli–Palestinian conflict in the West Bank and Gaza Strip from late 2000, as well as the recent increase in inter-Palestinian violence, has generally prevented the recovery of the tourism industry.

Ministry of Tourism and Antiquities: See Administration.

NET—Near East Tourist Agency: POB 19015, 30 Mount of Olives Rd, Jerusalem 91190; tel. (2) 5328720; fax (2) 5328701; internet new.netours.com; f. 1964; CEO SAMI ABU DAYYEH; Man. STEVE USTIN.

Defence

Commander of the Palestinian National Security Forces: Maj.-Gen. DIAB AL-ALI.

Commander of the Interior Forces and the Civil Police: Brig.-Gen. ALAA HUSNI RABAIA.

Commander of General Intelligence: Maj.-Gen. TARIQ ABU RAJAB.

Estimated Public Security and Order Budget (2004): US $433.9m.

Paramilitary Forces (as assessed at November 2010): Paramilitary forces in the Gaza Strip and in the areas of the West Bank where the PA has assumed responsibility for security totalled an estimated 56,000; however, figures for personnel strength in the various forces were impossible to confirm, owing to the uncertain situation in the Palestinian territories at that time. There is, *inter alia*, a Presidential Security Force, a Preventative Security Force, a Civil Defence Force and a Police Force. Units of the Palestine National Liberation Army (PNLA) have been garrisoned in various countries in the Middle East and North Africa; however, much of the PNLA's personnel strength has now been incorporated into the PA's various security forces.

Education

According to the World Bank, Palestinians are among the most highly educated of any Arab group. However, basic and secondary education facilities in the West Bank and Gaza Strip are described as poor. In the West Bank, the Jordanian education system is in operation. Services are provided by the Israeli Civil Administration, the UN Relief and Works Agency for Palestine Refugees in the Near East (UNRWA) and private, mainly charitable, organizations. Vocational education is offered by the Civil Administration and UNRWA. All university and most community college education is provided by private, voluntary organizations. There are 20 community and teacher training colleges in the West Bank, and six universities (including an open university). The Egyptian system of education operates in the Gaza Strip, where there are three universities and one teacher training college. Palestinian education has been severely disrupted since the first *intifada* (uprising) of 1987, and more recently as a result of the al-Aqsa *intifada*, which began in late 2000. Universities have played a major role in the political activities of the West Bank and Gaza, and were closed by the Israeli Civil Administration during 1987–1992.

Since May 1994 the PA has assumed responsibility for education in Gaza and parts of the West Bank. In 2007/08, according to the Palestinian Central Bureau of Statistics (PCBS), 84,289 pupils attended 972 pre-primary institutions. In 2010/11 975,460 pupils attended 1,742 primary institutions and in the same year 152,891 students were enrolled at 905 secondary institutions. The number of teachers at pre-primary institutions in 2007/08 was 3,267, and in 2008/09 there were 43,560 teachers at primary and secondary schools. In 2009/10 182,453 students attended universities or equivalent third-level institutions, while teachers numbered 5,939. In 2010/11 UNRWA operated 97 schools in the West Bank and 228 in the Gaza Strip, providing education to 55,679 pupils in the West Bank and to 206,114 pupils in Gaza. Education personnel in that year numbered 3,098 in the West Bank and 8,512 in Gaza. In addition, UNRWA operated five vocational training centres. In 2009/10 UNRWA budgeted some US $187.1m. for expenditure on education in the Palestinian territories.

PANAMA

Introductory Survey

LOCATION, CLIMATE, LANGUAGE, RELIGION, FLAG, CAPITAL

The Republic of Panama is a narrow country situated at the southern end of the isthmus separating North and South America. It is bounded to the west by Costa Rica and to the east by Colombia in South America. The Caribbean Sea is to the north, and the Pacific Ocean to the south. Panama has a tropical maritime climate (warm, humid days and cool nights). There is little seasonal variation in temperatures, which average 23°C–27°C (73°F–81°F) in coastal areas. The rainy season is from April until December. Spanish is the official language. Almost all of the inhabitants profess Christianity, and some 83% are Roman Catholics. The national flag (proportions 2 by 3) is composed of four equal rectangles: on the top row the quarter at the hoist is white, with a five-pointed blue star in the centre, while the quarter in the fly is red; on the bottom row the quarter at the hoist is blue, and the quarter in the fly is white, with a five-pointed red star in the centre. The capital is Panamá (Panama City).

CONTEMPORARY POLITICAL HISTORY

Historical Context

Panama was subject to Spanish rule from the 16th century until 1821, when it became independent as part of Gran Colombia. Panama remained part of Colombia until 1903, when it declared its separate independence with the support of the USA. In that year the USA purchased the concession for construction of the Panama Canal, which was opened in 1914. The 82-km Canal links the Atlantic and Pacific Oceans, and is a major international sea route. Under the terms of the 1903 treaty between Panama and the USA concerning the construction and administration of the Canal, the USA was granted ('in perpetuity') control of a strip of Panamanian territory, called the Canal Zone, extending for 8 km on either side of the Canal route. The treaty also established Panama as a protectorate of the USA. In exchange for transferring the Canal Zone, Panama was to receive an annuity from the USA.

In 1939 a revised treaty with the USA ended Panama's protectorate status. A new Constitution for Panama was adopted in 1946. Following a period of rapidly changing governments, the 1952 presidential election was won by Col José Antonio Remón, formerly Chief of Police. During his term of office, President Remón negotiated a more favourable treaty with the USA, whereby the annuity payable to Panama was increased. In January 1955, however, before the treaty came into force, Remón was assassinated. He was succeeded by José Ramón Guizado, hitherto the First Vice-President, but, less than two weeks after assuming power, the new President was implicated in the plot to assassinate Remón. Guizado was removed from office and later imprisoned. Remón's Second Vice-President, Ricardo Arias Espinosa, completed the presidential term, which expired in 1956, when Ernesto de la Guardia was elected President. The next presidential election was won by Roberto Chiari, who held office in 1960–64, and his successor was Marco Aurelio Robles (1964–68). During this period there were frequent public demands for the transfer to Panama of sovereignty over the Canal Zone.

The presidential election of May 1968 was won by Dr Arnulfo Arias Madrid, the candidate supported by the coalition Unión Nacional (which included his own Partido Panameñista). Dr Arias had been President in 1940–41 and 1949–51, but both terms had ended in his forcible removal from power. He took office for a third term in October 1968 but, after only 11 days, he was deposed by the National Guard (Panama's only military body), led by Col (later Brig.-Gen.) Omar Torrijos Herrera, who accused him of planning to establish a dictatorship. The Asamblea Nacional (National Assembly) was dissolved, and political activity suspended. Political parties were banned in February 1969.

Domestic Political Affairs

In August 1972 elections were held to a new legislative body, the 505-member Asamblea Nacional de Corregidores (National Assembly of Community Representatives). In October the Asamblea conferred extraordinary powers on Gen. Torrijos as Chief of Government for six years.

In February 1974 representatives of Panama and the USA concluded an agreement on principles for a new treaty whereby the USA would surrender its jurisdiction over the Canal Zone. Intensified talks in 1977 resulted in two new Canal treaties, which were approved by referendum in October and became effective from October 1979. Panama assumed control of the former Canal Zone, which was abolished. Administration of the Canal was placed under the control of a joint Panama Canal Commission until the end of 1999. US military forces in Panama were to remain until 2000, and the USA was to be entitled to defend the Canal's neutrality thereafter.

In August 1978 elections were held to the Asamblea Nacional de Corregidores; in October the new representatives elected Dr Arístides Royo Sánchez to be President for a six-year term. Gen. Torrijos resigned as Chief of Government, but continued in the post of Commander of the National Guard, and effectively retained power until his death in an air crash in July 1981. President Royo failed to gain the support of the National Guard, and in July 1982 he was forced to resign by Col Rubén Darío Paredes, who had ousted Col Florencio Flores as Commander-in-Chief in March. The Vice-President, Ricardo de la Espriella, was installed as President, and, under the direction of Col Paredes, promoted business interests and pursued a foreign policy more favourable to the USA.

In April 1983 a series of amendments to the Constitution were approved by referendum. However, in spite of new constitutional measures to limit the power of the National Guard, de facto power remained with the armed forces, whose position was strengthened by a decision in September to unite all security forces within one organization (subsequently known as the National Defence Forces). In June Paredes was succeeded as Commander-in-Chief by Brig. (later Gen.) Manuel Antonio Noriega Morena. In February 1984 Dr Jorge Illueca, hitherto the Vice-President, became Head of State after the sudden resignation of President de la Espriella, who was believed to have been ousted from power by the National Defence Forces.

Elections to the presidency and the legislature (the new 67-member Asamblea Legislativa—Legislative Assembly) took place in May 1984. Despite allegations of electoral fraud, Dr Nicolás Ardito Barletta, the candidate of the Partido Revolucionario Democrático (PRD), who received the electoral support of the armed forces, was eventually declared President-elect, narrowly defeating Arias Madrid, representing the Partido Panameñista Auténtico (PPA). However, Ardito was unable to secure a political base to support his administration, and in September 1985 he resigned. There was considerable speculation that Ardito had been forced to resign by Gen. Noriega, to prevent a public scandal over the alleged involvement of the National Defence Forces in the murder of Dr Hugo Spadafora, a leading critic of Noriega. Ardito was succeeded as President in September by Eric Arturo Delvalle, formerly First Vice-President.

In June 1986 US sources alleged that Noriega was involved in the trafficking of illegal drugs and weapons and in the transfer of proceeds from these activities through Panamanian banks. In addition, Noriega was implicated in the sale of US national security information and restricted technology to Cuba. There were also renewed allegations of his involvement in the murder of Dr Spadafora and in electoral fraud during the 1984 presidential election. Strikes and demonstrations in support of demands for Noriega's dismissal resulted in violent clashes with the National Defence Forces. Following this outbreak of violence, the US Senate approved a resolution urging the establishment of democracy in Panama, the suspension of Noriega and the holding of an independent investigation into the allegations against him. The Panamanian Government responded by accusing the USA of interfering in Panamanian affairs, and a wave of anti-US sentiment was unleashed, including an attack on the US embassy building by protesters in July 1987. The USA subsequently suspended economic and military aid to Panama and downgraded its official links with the country. Protests against

Noriega continued, in an atmosphere of mounting political and economic insecurity.

In February 1988 Noriega was indicted in the USA on charges of drugs-smuggling and racketeering. President Delvalle subsequently dismissed Noriega from his post, following his refusal to resign. However, leading members of the ruling coalition and the National Defence Forces united in support of their Commander-in-Chief, and on the following day the Asamblea Legislativa voted to remove President Delvalle from office. The Minister of Education, Manuel Solís Palma, was appointed acting President. Delvalle refused to accept his dismissal, and the US Administration declined to recognize the new leadership. At the end of the month, following Delvalle's demand that the US Government impose an economic boycott on Panama, US courts authorized a 'freeze' on Panamanian assets held in US banks. This move, coupled with a general strike organized by the Cruzada Civilista Nacional (an opposition grouping led by the business sector), brought economic chaos to Panama, prompting the closure of all banks for more than two months.

In March 1988 a coup attempt by the chief of police, Col Leónidas Macías, was thwarted by members of the National Defence Forces loyal to Noriega. The attempted coup represented the first indication of opposition to Noriega from within the security forces. The Government announced a state of emergency (revoked in April) and the suspension of civil rights. Negotiations between Noriega and a representative of the US Administration, during which the USA was reported to have proposed the withdrawal of charges against Noriega in exchange for his departure into exile before the elections scheduled for 1989, ended acrimoniously in late March. The US Administration subsequently reinforced economic sanctions against Panamanian interests.

Presidential and legislative elections were held on 7 May 1989. The presidential candidate of the pro-Government electoral alliance, the Coalición de Liberación Nacional (COLINA), was Carlos Duque Jaén, the leader of the PRD and a close associate of Noriega. Guillermo Endara Galimany of the PPA was the presidential candidate of the opposition Alianza Democrática de Oposición Civilista (ADOC). The election campaign was dominated by accusations of electoral malpractice, and, following the voting, both ADOC and COLINA claimed victory, despite indications from exit polls and unofficial sources that ADOC had received between 50% and 75% of votes cast. A group of international observers declared that the election had been conducted fraudulently. Endara declared himself President-elect; in subsequent demonstrations crowds clashed with the National Defence Forces, and many members of the opposition, including Endara and other leaders, were severely beaten. On 10 May the election results were annulled by the Electoral Tribunal, which cited US interference.

On 31 August 1989, following intervention by the Organization of American States (OAS, see p. 391), Panama's General State Council announced the appointment of a provisional Government and a 41-member Legislative Commission to preserve 'institutional order'. The holding of elections was to be considered within six months, but this was to be largely dependent upon the cessation of US 'hostilities' and the withdrawal of US economic sanctions. On 1 September Francisco Rodríguez, a known associate of Noriega, was inaugurated as President. The USA immediately severed diplomatic relations with Panama. In October an attempted coup was suppressed by forces loyal to Noriega.

US invasion and removal of Noriega

In November 1989 the Asamblea Nacional de Corregidores was provisionally restored. This body, now numbering 510 members, was intended to fulfil a consultative and (limited) legislative function. Noriega was elected as its 'national co-ordinator'. In December the Asamblea adopted a resolution declaring Noriega to be Head of Government and 'leader of the struggle for national liberation', and announced that a state of war existed with the USA. On 20 December a US military offensive ('Operation Just Cause'), involving some 24,000 troops, was launched against Noriega and the headquarters of the National Defence Forces from US bases within Panama. The objects of the assault were swiftly brought under US control, although sporadic attacks on US bases by loyalist forces continued for several days, and Noriega eluded capture long enough to take refuge in the residence of the Papal Nuncio in Panama. On 21 December Endara was officially inaugurated as President. President Endara declared that the Panamanian judicial system was inadequate to try Noriega. Following his surrender to US forces in January 1990, Noriega was immediately transported to the USA and arraigned on several charges of involvement in drugs-trafficking and money-laundering operations. In April 1992 Noriega was found guilty on eight charges of conspiracy to manufacture and distribute cocaine and received a prison sentence of 40 years (reduced to 30 years in 1999).

International criticism of the USA's military operation was widespread, although the Administration cited the right to self-defence, under Article 51 of the UN Charter, as a legal justification for armed intervention, and US President George Bush asserted that military action was necessary for the protection of US citizens and the Panama Canal, support for Panama's 'democratically elected' officials and the pursuit of an indicted criminal. According to the US Government, 'Operation Just Cause' resulted in about 500 Panamanian casualties, but a total of at least 1,000 Panamanian deaths was estimated by the Roman Catholic Church and other unofficial sources; 23 US troops were killed, and more than 300 wounded, during the invasion.

Following the appointment of a new Cabinet in December 1989, the Endara administration declared itself to be a 'democratic Government of reconstruction and national reconciliation'. Shortly afterwards the Electoral Tribunal revoked its annulment of the May elections and announced that ADOC had obtained 62% of the votes cast in the presidential election, according to copies of incomplete results that had been held in safe keeping by the Bishops' Conference of the Roman Catholic Church. In February 1990 the composition of the Asamblea Legislativa was announced, based on the same documentation. The National Defence Forces were officially disbanded, and a new, 'non-political' Public Force was created.

Although the overthrow of Noriega immediately released US $375m. in assets that had previously been withheld by the US Government, the new administration inherited serious economic difficulties. The cost of 'Operation Just Cause', in terms of damage and lost revenues alone, was estimated to be at least $2,000m. In April 1990 the USA revoked the economic restrictions that had been imposed two years previously, and in May Congress approved financial assistance to Panama totalling $420m. Disbursement of a substantial tranche was to be dependent upon the successful negotiation of a Mutual Legal Assistance Treaty between the two countries, whereby the US authorities sought to gain greater access to information amassed by Panama City's 'offshore' international finance centre, in order to combat the illegal laundering of money.

Claims that the security forces had not been adequately purged following the ousting of Noriega were seemingly justified by a succession of coup attempts during the early 1990s. Meanwhile, public concern at the Government's failure to restore civil and economic order was reflected in the results of elections held in January 1991 for nine unallocated seats in the Asamblea Legislativa. Member parties of COLINA secured five seats, while parties represented in the governing alliance won only four. Serious concern had been expressed at the increasing level of influence exerted by the US Government over the President, particularly when it became known that in July 1990 the Government had accepted US funds to establish, by decree, a 100-strong Council for Public Security, which would maintain close links with the US Central Intelligence Agency.

Long-standing political differences within the Government reached a crisis in March 1991 when one of the parties in the ruling coalition, the Partido Demócrata Cristiano (PDC), initiated proceedings to impeach Endara for involving the US armed forces in suppressing an uprising in December 1990 (a technical violation of the 1977 Panama Canal Treaty). Although the proposal was rejected by the Asamblea Legislativa, Endara dismissed the five PDC members of his Cabinet. In October 1991 and February 1992 two further alleged coup attempts were suppressed, and resulted in the creation, in March 1992, of a presidential police force. In November the President suffered a serious reverse, when proposals for more than 50 reforms (including the constitutional abolition of the armed forces) were rejected by 64% of voters in a referendum.

The acquittal, in September 1993, of seven former soldiers tried for involvement in the 1985 assassination of Dr Spadafora provoked widespread public outrage. Noriega was tried in connection with the affair *in absentia* and, in October 1993, was found guilty and sentenced to 20 years' imprisonment for ordering his murder. Further convictions followed in 1994 and 2001. Noriega completed his prison sentence in the USA in September 2007, having served 17 years, but remained in detention pending the outcome of an extradition request from France. In April 2009 the US federal Court of Appeal ruled that Noriega could be extradited to France, where he had been convicted *in absentia* on money-laundering charges in 1999. In February 2010 the US Supreme Court refused to hear an appeal by Noriega against his extradition, which was effected in April. Following a retrial, in July a French court sentenced Noriega to seven years' imprisonment and ordered the seizure of €2.3m. of his assets.

Presidents Pérez Balladares and Moscoso, 1994–2004

At a presidential election held in May 1994, Ernesto Pérez Balladares, the candidate of the Pueblo Unido alliance (that included the PRD), won a narrow victory over Mireya Moscoso de Gruber (the widow of former President Arias Madrid). Moscoso was the nominee of the Alianza Democrática, comprising the Partido Arnulfista (PA, formerly a faction of the PPA), the Partido Liberal (PL), the Partido Liberal Auténtico (PLA), the Unión Democrática Independiente and the Partido Nacionalista Popular (PNP). Post-electoral political manoeuvring resulted in the creation of the Alianza Pueblo Unido y Solidaridad, Pérez Balladares' electoral alliance having secured the additional support of the Partido Solidaridad in the Asamblea. Pérez Balladares assumed the presidency on 1 September 1994. A new Cabinet, installed on the same day, included former members of the PA and the PDC who had resigned their party membership in order to take up their posts. In June 1996 the position of President Pérez Balladares was undermined by reports that an alleged drugs-trafficker had contributed some US $51,000 to his 1994 presidential campaign. Pérez Balladares was forced to admit that his campaign fund had 'unwittingly' received the payment.

At a presidential election conducted in May 1999, Mireya Moscoso de Gruber, the candidate of the Unión por Panamá alliance (comprising the PA, Movimiento Liberal Republicano Nacionalista—MOLIRENA, Movimiento de Renovación Nacional and Cambio Democrático), was elected, ahead of Martín Torrijos Espino, son of former dictator Omar Torrijos, the candidate of the Nueva Nación alliance (comprising the PRD, the Partido Solidaridad, the Partido Liberal Nacional—PLN—and the Movimiento Papa Egoró—MPE). However, the Unión por Panamá failed to secure a majority in the concurrent legislative election. Moscoso assumed the presidency on 1 September. A new Cabinet, installed on the same day, included members of the Partido Solidaridad, the PLN, the PDC and the Partido Renovación Civilista (PRC), each of which had abandoned their respective electoral alliances in order to form a 'Government of national unity', thereby giving Moscoso a narrow majority in the legislature. However, in August of the following year the governing coalition lost its majority after the PRD and the PDC formed an alliance.

On 31 December 1999 the USA officially relinquished ownership of the Canal to Panama.

Following the discovery of human remains in a former military barracks in Tocumen, in December 2000 President Moscoso announced the establishment of a Truth Commission to investigate 'disappearances' during the military dictatorships of 1968–89. Following excavations in 12 separate areas, the Commission reported in October 2001 that 72 of the 189 people believed to have 'disappeared' had been killed or tortured by state forces. In March 2004 the Asamblea approved the establishment of a Special Prosecutor's Office to investigate crimes committed during the military dictatorships.

President Moscoso's administration encountered problems in the wake of an agreement signed in February 2002, which provided for US authorities to join the Panamanian National Maritime Service in patrolling its territorial waters, in an attempt to control the illegal trade in narcotics. The agreement was strongly criticized by opposition members. However, in September a number of defections from the opposition to the governing coalition restored Moscoso's majority in the Asamblea. An additional accord, which provided the USA with increased powers to inspect Panama's financial and tax records as part of its campaign against money-laundering, provoked protests from opposition parties. In April of that year Panama was removed from the Organisation for Economic Co-operation and Development's (OECD) list of 'un-co-operative tax havens' after the Government committed to making its financial sector more transparent.

In September 2003 President Moscoso dismissed Juan Jované as Director of the social security fund, the Caja de Seguro Social (CSS), which had been running at a loss for years, after he refused to agree on a balanced budget with the other members of the CSS board. However, Jované subsequently alleged that he had been removed to allow for the privatization of the CSS. Following protests, Moscoso signed a declaration pledging not to sell off the CSS.

Presidential and legislative elections took place in May 2004. Martín Torrijos Espino, the candidate of the PRD (which contested the elections as part of the Patria Nueva electoral alliance with the Partido Popular), won the presidential ballot, with 47% of the votes cast. Former President Endara, representing the Partido Solidaridad, came second with 31% of the ballot. The Patria Nueva also performed well in the concurrently held elections to the enlarged, 78-seat Asamblea Legislativa, securing a total of 43 seats, 42 of which were won by the PRD. Torrijos assumed office on 1 September.

The presidency of Martín Torrijos, 2004–09

Even before he assumed the presidency, Torrijos was successful in bringing about several constitutional amendments. In July 2004 his proposed reform of the Asamblea Legislativa received legislative approval. The number of seats in the legislature—which was renamed the Asamblea Nacional (National Assembly)—was to be reduced to 71 (from 78) from 2009. Furthermore, parliamentary immunity from prosecution was abolished and the authority to ratify constitutional amendments transferred from the legislature to a constituent assembly. Torrijos also pledged to address the problem of official corruption. One week after Torrijos' Government took office, Panama's ambassador to Cuba was arrested as part of an investigation into the alleged sale of Panamanian visas to Cuban citizens. Then, in November the Government announced that corruption charges had been filed against former Minister of Finance and the Treasury Norberto Delgado.

In October 2004 some 5,000 people participated in a protest march organized by the Frente Nacional por la Defensa de la Seguridad Social (FRENADESSO), the social organization established to resist privatization of the CSS. The new Government denied intentions fully to privatize the CSS, but emphasized the need for reform in light of the institution's estimated deficit of between US $2,500m. and $3,000m. Proposed social security reforms included an increase in the retirement age, a reduction in retirement benefits and the transfer of some pensions into private funds. Despite further protests, the pension reforms were approved by the Asamblea Nacional in June 2005. However, they included a number of concessions, including a reduction in the proposed pensionable retirement age for women from 62 years of age to 60 (hitherto 57). None the less, industrial unrest continued, and one week later medical workers joined the ongoing strike. In late June the Government partially suspended implementation of the new law, and a revised series of measures (which maintained the retirement age for women at 57 years of age and increased the minimum qualifying number of monthly pension contributions from 180 to just 240—rather than 300 as initially suggested) was voted into law in December.

In April 2006 the Autoridad del Canal de Panamá (ACP) announced plans to expand the Canal's capacity to allow the passage of larger commercial container vessels, by constructing a third set of locks at either end of the waterway. The projected cost of US $5,250m. to build the wider locks was to be funded by toll revenues and loans totalling an estimated $2,270m. President Torrijos pledged to hold a national debate and an eventual referendum on the ACP's proposals. While widely considered to be vital to the future of the Canal, concerns were raised relating to the environmental consequences of the expansion and the possible relocation of farmers in communities bordering the Canal. At the end of the month Héctor Alemán and Ricaurte Vázquez Morales, previously Ministers of the Interior and Justice and of the Economy and Finance, respectively, were appointed co-ordinators of the national debate. In July the Asamblea Nacional overwhelmingly approved the ACP's plan to expand the Canal. At the referendum duly conducted on 22 October, the project was approved by 78% of those voting, although voter participation was much lower than expected, at just 43% of the electorate. A ceremony to launch the project took place in September 2007. In July 2009 the contract for the construction of the new locks was awarded to a consortium led by a Spanish construction company. It was anticipated that work on enlarging the Canal, which would not disrupt normal operations, would be completed in 2014.

The Asamblea Nacional approved legislation aimed at improving internal security in May 2008. The Government claimed the new law introduced a more uncompromising stance against crime, increasing maximum prison sentences, and recognizing 37 new offences. In the following month the legislature granted Torrijos temporary powers to introduce security reforms by decree. The reforms included the creation of a single national intelligence and security service (SENIS—Servicio Nacional de Intelligencia y Seguridad), a proposal that met with widespread opposition owing to fears that the agency would wield excessive power. The Constitution was also amended to validate the recent nomination of former soldier Jaime Ruiz as chief of police, following criticism that the appointment of a military official was a constitutional violation. FRENADESO (Frente Nacional por la Defensa de los Derechos Económicos y Sociales, as FRENADESSO had been restyled) mobilized over 15,000 people in marches in the capital and other cities on 14 August to protest against both the SENIS decree and rising living costs. A national strike took place on 5 September; as well as protesting against the security laws, strikers also demanded a 20% salary increase and a halt to price increases.

Cabinet changes continued throughout Torrijos' final year in power. The most significant dismissal was that of the Minister of the Interior and Justice, Daniel Delgado Diamante, in October 2008 following allegations by a newspaper that, as a lieutenant in the national guard in 1970, he had murdered a corporal. Delgado admitted the killing, but claimed that the case was a police matter and had already been investigated; however, he volunteered to step down from his position temporarily in order to clear his name. Meanwhile, in September Herrera secured the PRD's presidential candidacy. Her campaign was damaged in March 2009 by allegations that Colombian financier David Murcia Guzmán, who was in gaol for fraud, had contributed US $3m. to her presidential campaign.

Recent developments: Martinelli in power

The presidential election, which was held on 3 May 2009, was won decisively by Ricardo Martinelli Berrocal, the owner of a large chain of supermarkets, on behalf of the Alianza por el Cambio, comprising his own Cambio Democrático party, the Partido Panameñista (PP, as the PA had been renamed in 2005), MOLIRENA and the Unión Patriótica (UP), which had been formed in 2007 by the merger of the PLN and the Partido Solidaridad. Martinelli, whose campaign had concentrated on crime and poverty reduction, secured 60.0% of the valid votes cast, while Herrera, representing the PRD-led Un País para Todos alliance, obtained 37.7%; former President Endara, of the Vanguardia Moral de la Patria, took just 2.3%. A turn-out of 74.0% was recorded. In the concurrent legislative elections, the Alianza por el Cambio won an overall majority in the Asamblea Nacional, securing a total of 42 of the 71 seats, while Un País para Todos won 27 seats, with the PRD's representation reduced to 26 seats. One week after his victory, Martinelli announced the composition of his Cabinet, appointing his Vice-President-elect, Juan Carlos Varela Rodríguez, the leader of the PP, as Minister of Foreign Affairs and Alberto Vallarino Clement, also of the PP, as Minister of the Economy and Finance. The President of the UP, José Raúl Mulino, was allocated the interior and justice portfolio. The leadership of the PRD resigned in October as part of efforts to renew the party following its electoral defeat; Francisco Sánchez Cárdenas and Mitchell Doens were elected to succeed Herrera and Torrijos as PRD President and Secretary-General, respectively.

Martinelli took office on 1 July 2009. The new President acted swiftly to initiate the implementation of several of the pledges he made during his electoral campaign: a salary increase of US $100 per month for police officers; monthly payments, also of $100, for those aged over 70 without pensions; and the creation of a government agency to supervise the construction of a metro system in Panama City. Martinelli's administration also sought to demonstrate its commitment to addressing government corruption. A judicial investigation into allegations that the Moscoso Government had bribed PRD deputies in December 2001 was reopened in July 2009, and two former PRD Ministers of Education in the Torrijos Government, Belgis Castro and Salvador Rodríguez, were arrested on charges of embezzlement in September and December. In January 2010, moreover, former President Pérez Balladares was placed under house arrest after being charged with money-laundering. (He was acquitted of this charge in April 2011.) However, Martinelli's appointment of two close allies to fill vacant positions in the Supreme Court of Justice in December 2009 provoked criticism, particularly from civil society groups, as did his suspected involvement in the following month in the Court's decision to suspend the PRD-appointed Ana Matilde Gómez from the post of Procurator-General pending an investigation into her alleged abuse of office (on the grounds that she had failed to seek the Court's approval before authorizing the interception of conversations involving a prosecutor being investigated for corruption). Gómez was dismissed in August, after being convicted of abuse of office by the Supreme Court, but claimed that the verdict was politically motivated, an allegation that received significant support from the media and civil society groups. Her replacement, Guiseppe Bonissi, resigned in December, amid allegations that his office had been infiltrated by organized criminals, following the release from custody in November of four suspected drugs-traffickers.

In March 2010, meanwhile, some 10,000 people participated in protests organized by FRENADESO against recently approved tax reforms, most notably an increase in the rate of value-added tax from 5% to 7%. Government changes were announced in April and took effect in June: José Raúl Mulino, hitherto Minister of the Interior and Justice, was appointed to head a newly created Ministry of Public Security, while Roxana Méndez, the Deputy Mayor of Panama City, joined the Government as Minister of the Interior.

Considerable controversy was provoked in June 2010 by the approval of legislation that reformed regulations affecting a wide range of areas, including civil aviation, the environment, the police and the labour code. Most contentious were the amendments to the labour code—which notably permitted the suspension of the contracts of striking workers—and the abolishment of the requirement for environmental impact studies to be conducted into projects declared to be 'in the social interest'. The labour reforms were suspended for 90 days in July, pending discussions with trade unions, following violent clashes between protesters and the police in the province of Bocas del Toro in which three people were killed and more than 100 injured. Following these discussions, President Martinelli agreed to repeal the law entirely in October, although the Government intended to propose separate bills addressing each of the various areas individually. The new legislation covering labour rights and environmental protection, which was adopted by the Asamblea Nacional later that month, omitted the controversial elements of the previous law. However, the reforms relating to the police, which were enacted at the beginning of November, retained a provision (that had also been criticized) preventing police officers accused of committing crimes on duty from being suspended or held in custody until they had been convicted; trade union officials claimed that the legislation contradicted agreements reached during the negotiations with the Government. In March 2011 President Martinelli was forced to revoke another controversial law, adopted the previous month, which would have allowed investment by foreign governments in the mining sector, following widespread protests by environmentalists and civil society groups, as well as by indigenous communities fearing the development of mineral reserves within their territories.

In January 2011 the constitutional committee of the Asamblea Nacional rejected a bill proposed by a deputy from Cambio Democrático to amend the Constitution to permit the President to seek a second consecutive term in office. However, President Martinelli announced his intention to seek the approval of other constitutional reforms, including a reduction in the number of years that a former President was required to wait before contesting the presidency again from 10 to five. The UP merged into Cambio Democrático in March, while FRENADESO applied for registration as a political party, the Frente Amplio por la Democracia.

Foreign Affairs

In July 1997, in the light of the increasing number of incursions by Colombian guerrillas and paramilitary groups into Panamanian territory, the Government deployed more than 1,200 members of the security forces to Darién Province to secure the border with Colombia. In previous months Colombian paramilitary members were reported to have forcibly occupied several settlements in the area while in pursuit of guerrillas who had taken refuge over the border. Following discussions between Pérez Balladares and his Colombian counterpart, Andrés Pastrana Arango, an agreement on improved co-operation concerning border security was reached. In June 1999, following further incursions by Colombian guerrillas into Darién Province, Panama and Colombia reached agreement on the strengthening of military patrols on both sides of the countries' joint border. In January 2010 the Panamanian Government announced plans to strengthen security co-operation with Colombia. Negotiations towards a bilateral free trade agreement commenced in March. However, bilateral relations were strained in November, after the Panamanian Government granted asylum to a former director of the Colombian intelligence service, who had been implicated in an intelligence-gathering scandal in Colombia.

PANAMA

In 1993 President Endara signed a protocol to establish Panama's membership of the Central American Parliament (Parlacen), a regional political forum with its headquarters in Guatemala. Endara, together with the five Presidents of the member nations of the Central American Common Market (CACM, see p. 224), also signed a protocol to the 1960 General Treaty on Central American Integration, committing Panama to fuller economic integration in the region. However, at a meeting of Central American Presidents in 1994, Pérez Balladares (attending as an observer) stated that his administration considered further regional economic integration to be disadvantageous to Panama, owing to the differences between Panama's services-based economy and the reliance on the agricultural sector of the other Central American states. A free trade agreement with El Salvador entered into force in April 2003, and similar accords with Costa Rica, Honduras, Guatemala and Nicaragua took effect between November 2008 and November 2009. In late 2009 Panama unilaterally withdrew from Parlacen, fulfilling a pre-election pledge made by President Martinelli, who claimed that membership of the body had been of no benefit to Panama. However, in March 2010 the President of Parlacen announced that he had protested against the Panamanian Government's decision to the Central American Court of Justice, maintaining that Panama required the consent of the Presidents of the other member states to withdraw from Parlacen and owed the organization some US $1.1m. in outstanding dues. In a ruling in October, the Court confirmed that Panama's departure from Parlacen required the approval of the remaining Parlacen members, but the Government rejected the Court's verdict, announcing Panama's formal withdrawal from the Parliament in the following month.

Although Panama was excluded from the negotiations towards a Dominican Republic-Central American Free Trade Agreement with the USA, a bilateral free trade agreement with the USA was finally signed in June 2007. However, the accord was subject to ratification by the US legislature. In June 2009 the outgoing Torrijos Government announced the adoption of US-advocated amendments to labour legislation, which, inter alia, facilitated the formation of trade unions, but opponents of the trade agreement within the US Congress asserted that ratification of the trade agreement should be made conditional on efforts by Panama to reduce international tax evasion. In April Panama had been included on OECD's so-called 'grey list' of territories that had committed to improving financial transparency, but had yet substantially to implement reform. After taking office in July, President Martinelli declared that securing US congressional approval of the free trade accord was a priority for his administration and sought to conclude bilateral agreements on double taxation; although nine such accords had been signed by October 2010, it was uncertain whether the provisions of these treaties conformed fully with OECD standards. In November, however, Panama and the USA signed a tax information exchange agreement that complied with OECD requirements; it was hoped that this would facilitate the approval of the bilateral trade agreement by the US Congress. Panama's ambassador to the USA, Jaime Alemán, resigned in the following month, after the publication of a US diplomatic cable by WikiLeaks, an organization publishing leaked private and classified content, that questioned the propriety of the awarding in July 2009 of the contract for the construction of new locks for the Panama Canal to a Spanish-led consortium, to which Alemán had apparently provided legal representation. Meanwhile, in May 2010 negotiations were concluded on an association agreement between Central American countries, including Panama, and the European Union (see p. 270), while the Panamanian Government also signed a free trade agreement with Canada; the accord with Canada was ratified by Panama's legislature in October.

CONSTITUTION AND GOVERNMENT

Legislative power is vested in the unicameral Asamblea Nacional (National Assembly), with a total of 71 members elected for five years by universal adult suffrage. Executive power is held by the President, also directly elected for a term of five years, assisted by two elected Vice-Presidents and an appointed Cabinet. Panama is divided into nine provinces and three autonomous Indian Reservations. Each province has a governor, appointed by the President.

REGIONAL AND INTERNATIONAL CO-OPERATION

Panama is a member of the Central American Integration System (see p. 224), the Inter-American Development Bank (see p. 333) and the Organization of American States (see p. 391), and has observer status within the Andean Community of Nations (see p. 189). Panama was a founder member of the UN in 1945 and was admitted to the World Trade Organization (see p. 430) in 1997. Free trade agreements with El Salvador, Taiwan and Chile entered into force in April 2003, January 2004 and March 2008, while similar accords with Costa Rica, Honduras, Guatemala and Nicaragua took effect successively between November 2008 and November 2009. In December 2006 negotiations towards a free trade agreement with the USA were finally concluded. The accord was to remove 90% of tariffs on Panamanian-US trade, with the remaining 10% to be eliminated over the next 10 years; however, by May 2011 the agreement had still to be ratified by the US Congress. In May 2010 Panama signed a free trade agreement with Canada, and was party to a Central American association agreement concluded with the European Union (see p. 270).

ECONOMIC AFFAIRS

In 2009, according to estimates by the World Bank, Panama's gross national income (GNI), measured at average 2007–09 prices, was US $23,174m., equivalent to $6,710 per head (or $12,530 on an international purchasing-power parity basis). During 2000–09, it was estimated, the population increased at an average annual rate of 1.8%, while gross domestic product (GDP) per head increased, in real terms, by an average of 4.3% per year. Overall GDP increased, in real terms, at an average annual rate of 6.1% in 2000–09; according to official estimates, growth was 3.2% in 2009.

According to the World Bank, agriculture (including hunting, forestry and fishing) contributed an estimated 6.0% of GDP in 2009. The sector engaged some 13.9% of the employed labour force in 2008. Rice, maize and beans are cultivated as subsistence crops, while the principal cash crops are melons (which accounted for an estimated 10.0% of total export earnings in 2009), bananas, sugar cane and coffee. Cattle-raising, tropical timber and fisheries (particularly shrimps and yellowfin tuna for export) are also important. In an attempt to diversify the agricultural sector, new crops such as oil palm, cocoa, coconuts, various winter vegetables and tropical fruits were introduced in the 1990s. Fish exports were increasingly important. In 2009 exports of yellowfin tuna and fish fillet accounted for an estimated 29.9% of export revenue. According to World Bank figures, agricultural GDP increased by an average of 3.5% annually during 2000–09. According to official figures, the sector decreased by an estimated 7.2% in 2009.

According to the World Bank, industry (including mining, manufacturing, construction and power) contributed an estimated 17.4% of GDP in 2009. The sector engaged 19.6% of the employed labour force in 2008. According to World Bank figures, industrial GDP increased at an average annual rate of 4.7% during 2000–09; the sector's GDP increased by an estimated 3.1% in 2009.

Mining contributed an estimated 1.2% of GDP and engaged 0.2% of the employed labour force in 2008. Panama has significant deposits of copper and coal. The GDP of the mining sector increased by an estimated average of 18.7% per year in 2005–09; the sector expanded by an estimated 4.4% in 2009.

According to the World Bank, manufacturing contributed an estimated 6.6% of GDP in 2009. The sector engaged an estimated 8.6% of the employed labour force in 2008. The most important sectors were refined petroleum products, food-processing, beverages, and cement, lime and plaster. Manufacturing GDP increased by an average of 0.9% annually during 2000–09; the sector declined by an estimated 0.4% in 2009.

The construction sector contributed an estimated 6.2% of GDP and engaged some 10.2% of the employed labour force in 2008. The sector increased by an estimated 4.5% in 2009.

The country's topography and climate make it ideal for hydroelectric power, and in 2007 approximately 56.6% of Panama's total output of electricity was water-generated. Construction of a hydroelectric project on the Bonyic river, costing US $49m. began in October 2007. Petroleum accounted for most of the remainder (43.1%) of the country's generating capacity. In 2009 imports of mineral products accounted for 18.1% of the value of merchandise imports.

Panama's economy is dependent upon the services sector, which, according to the World Bank, contributed an estimated

76.5% of GDP in 2009. The sector engaged 66.5% of the employed labour force in 2008. The Panama Canal contributed an estimated 6.3% of the country's GDP in 2007. Panama is an important 'offshore' financial centre, and in 2006 financial, property and business services contributed an estimated 26.4% of GDP. Important contributions to the economy are also made by trade in the Colón Free Zone (CFZ—in which some 2,500 companies were situated in 2010), and by the registration of merchant ships under a 'flag of convenience' in Panama. The tourism sector also increased steadily from the 1990s. In 2008 tourism receipts totalled US $2,223m., compared with $1,806m. in the previous year. According to the World Bank, the GDP of the services sector increased by an average of 6.8% per year in 2000–09; the sector grew by an estimated 4.2% in 2009.

In 2009 Panama recorded a visible trade deficit of US $2,026.3m., and there was a deficit of $3.5m. on the current account of the balance of payments. According to preliminary figures, in 2009 the principal source of imports (29.1%) was the USA, which was also the principal market for exports (42.6%). Other major trading partners are Costa Rica, the Netherlands, Mexico, Spain and the People's Republic of China. The principal exports in 2009 were fresh and frozen fish and fillets, melons and bananas. The principal imports in that year were machinery and apparatus, mineral products, and food and live animals.

In 2009 there was an estimated overall budgetary surplus of 1,008.8m. balboas, equivalent to 4.2% of GDP. Panama's general government gross debt was 9,911m. m. balboas in 2009, equivalent to 39.9% of GDP. Panama's external debt at the end of 2008 was US $10,722m., of which $9,661m. was public and publicly guaranteed debt. In that year the cost of debt-servicing was equivalent to 9.2% of the value of exports of goods, services and income. Annual inflation averaged 3.5% in 2003–09; consumer prices increased by 2.4% in 2009. Some 6.3% of the labour force were unemployed in August 2009.

Following the cession to Panamanian control of the Panama Canal at the end of 1999, the waterway was operated as a profit-making venture, providing the Government with a considerable source of funds. In 2006 plans to expand the Canal (at a cost of US $5,250m.) were approved. On completion (scheduled for 2014), the expanded Canal was expected to increase GDP growth by 1%–2% per year until 2025. The Asamblea Nacional approved the Fiscal Responsibility Law in May 2008 in order to limit the deficit to 1% of GDP for the non-financial public sector, excluding the Panama Canal Authority, and achieve a debt target of 40% of GDP by 2015. Strong growth in 2006–08 was driven primarily by foreign investment, the expansion of the construction and financial sectors and increasing Canal traffic. Growth slowed substantially in 2009, to 3.2%, as a result of the impact of the global economic downturn, and export earnings declined sharply. None the less, Panama's economic performance remained relatively strong compared with that of other countries within the region. The construction sector continued to expand, and was expected to be further boosted by the enlargement of the Canal and a project to construct a metro system in Panama City. In March 2010 President Ricardo Martinelli Berrocal enacted taxation reforms intended to increase annual revenue by $200m.: notably, value-added tax was raised from 5% to 7%, although income tax rates were reduced. The economy strengthened in 2010, reflecting improved international conditions, with real GDP increasing by an estimated 7.5%, the fastest growing sector being transport and communications, which expanded by 15.5%; the growth rate accelerated throughout the year, to reach 8.7% in the final quarter. Growth was driven by a large rise in investment, linked to the expansion of the Canal and other infrastructure projects, as well as by renewed domestic demand. The budget for 2011 envisaged GDP growth of 6.5% in that year.

PUBLIC HOLIDAYS

2012: 1 January (New Year's Day), 9 January (National Martyrs' Day), 20–21 February (Carnival), 22 February (Ash Wednesday), 5 April (Maundy Thursday), 6 April (Good Friday), 1 May (Labour Day), 15 August (Foundation of Panama City, Panama City only)*, 11 October (Revolution Day), 1 November (National Anthem Day)*, 2 November (Day of the Dead), 3 November (Independence from Colombia), 4 November (Flag Day)*, 5 November (Independence Day, Colón only), 10 November (First Call for Independence), 26 November (for Independence from Spain), 8 December (Immaculate Conception, Mothers' Day), 25 December (Christmas).

* Official holiday: banks and government offices closed.

Statistical Survey

Sources (unless otherwise stated): Instituto Nacional de Estadística y Censo, Contraloría General de la República, Avda Balboa y Federico Boyd, Apdo 5213, Panamá 5; tel. 210-4800; fax 210-4801; e-mail cgrdec@contraloria.gob.pa; internet www.contraloria.gob.pa/inec/; Ministry of the Economy and Finance, Edif. Ogawa, Vía España, Apdo 5245, Panamá 5; e-mail webmaster@mef.gob.pa; internet www.mef.gob.pa.

Note: The former Canal Zone was incorporated into Panama on 1 October 1979.

Area and Population

AREA, POPULATION AND DENSITY

Area (sq km)	75,517*
Population (census results)	
14 May 2000	2,839,177
16 May 2010	
Males	1,712,584
Females	1,693,229
Total	3,405,813
Density (per sq km) at 2010 census	45.1

* 29,157 sq miles.

POPULATION BY AGE AND SEX
(population at 2010 census)

	Males	Females	Total
0–14	507,674	486,405	994,079
15–64	1,083,592	1,076,601	2,160,193
65 and over	121,318	130,223	251,541
Total	1,712,584	1,693,229	3,405,813

ADMINISTRATIVE DIVISIONS
(population at 2010 census)

Province	Population	Capital (and population)*
Bocas del Toro	125,461	Bocas del Toro (16,135)
Chiriquí	416,873	David (144,858)
Coclé	233,708	Penonomé (85,737)
Colón	241,928	Colón (206,553)
Comarca Emberá	10,001	—
Comarca Kuna Yala	33,109	—
Comarca Ngöbe-Buglé	156,747	—
Darién	48,378	Chepigana (30,110)
Herrera	109,955	Chitré (50,684)
Los Santos	89,592	Las Tablas (27,146)
Panamá	1,713,070	Panamá (880,691)
Veraguas	226,991	Santiago (88,997)
Total	3,405,813	—

* Population of district in which capital is located.

Note: Population figures include the former Canal Zone.

PANAMA

PRINCIPAL TOWNS
(population at 2010 census)

Panamá (Panama City, capital)	430,299	Puerto Armuelles	55,775
San Miguelito	315,019	Pacora	52,494
Santiago	88,997	Pedregal	51,641
David	82,907	Nuevo Arraiján	41,041
Tocumen	74,952	Colón	34,655
La Chorrera	62,803	Changuinola	31,223

Mid-2010 (incl. suburbs, UN estimate): Panama City 1,378,470 (Source: UN, *World Urbanization Prospects: The 2009 Revision*).

BIRTHS, MARRIAGES AND DEATHS

	Registered live births Number	Rate (per 1,000)†	Registered marriages* Number	Rate (per 1,000)†	Registered deaths Number	Rate (per 1,000)†
2002	61,671	20.2	9,558	3.1	12,428	4.1
2003	61,753	19.8	10,310	3.3	13,248	4.3
2004	62,743	19.8	10,290	3.2	13,475	4.2
2005	63,645	19.7	10,512	3.3	14,180	4.4
2006	65,764	20.0	10,747	3.3	14,358	4.4
2007	67,364	20.2	11,516	3.4	14,775	4.4
2008	68,759	20.3	11,508	3.4	15,115	4.5
2009	68,364	19.8	12,273	3.6	15,498	4.5

* Excludes tribal Indian population.
† Based on official mid-year population estimates.

Life expectancy (years at birth, WHO estimates): 76 (males 74; females 79) in 2008 (Source: WHO, *World Health Statistics*).

ECONOMICALLY ACTIVE POPULATION
('000 persons aged 15 years and over, August of each year)

	2006	2007	2008
Agriculture, hunting and forestry	183.1	176.5	176.5
Fishing	9.9	9.8	9.1
Mining and quarrying	2.3	3.6	3.3
Manufacturing	105.2	109.6	114.1
Electricity, gas and water supply	8.4	8.1	6.9
Construction	102.8	122.4	136.7
Wholesale and retail trade; repair of motor vehicles, motorcycles and personal and household goods	229.6	240.7	258.6
Hotels and restaurants	64.5	69.5	70.8
Transport, storage and communications	90.8	91.9	100.9
Financial intermediation	26.4	28.8	28.4
Real estate, renting and business activities	62.6	67.0	71.7
Public administration and defence; compulsory social service	70.3	79.6	78.7
Education	62.7	65.3	74.6
Health and social work	48.3	50.6	55.1
Other community, social and personal service activities	68.0	63.8	70.0
Private households with employed persons	74.9	76.1	77.4
Extra-territorial organizations and bodies	0.8	0.7	0.9
Total employed	1,210.7	1,264.0	1,333.8
Unemployed	121.4	92.0	82.9
Total labour force	1,332.1	1,355.9	1,416.7

Source: ILO.

Health and Welfare

KEY INDICATORS

Total fertility rate (children per woman, 2008)	2.5
Under-5 mortality rate (per 1,000 live births, 2008)	23
HIV/AIDS (% of persons aged 15–49, 2007)	1.0
Physicians (per 1,000 head, 2000)	1.5
Hospital beds (per 1,000 head, 2005)	1.8
Health expenditure (2007): US $ per head (PPP)	773
Health expenditure (2007): % of GDP	6.7
Health expenditure (2007): public (% of total)	64.6
Access to water (% of persons, 2008)	93
Access to sanitation (% of persons, 2008)	69
Total carbon dioxide emissions ('000 metric tons, 2007)	7,243.7
Carbon dioxide emissions per head (metric tons, 2007)	2.2
Human Development Index (2010): ranking	54
Human Development Index (2010): value	0.755

For sources and definitions, see explanatory note on p. vi.

Agriculture

PRINCIPAL CROPS
('000 metric tons)

	2006	2007	2008
Rice, paddy	232.4	237.0	231.3
Maize	84.4	86.1	83.9
Sugar cane	1,771.5	1,797.5	1,822.7
Watermelons	92.3	120.7	100.0
Cantaloupes and other melons	100.3	116.6	101.5
Bananas	538.9	544.6	357.9
Plantains	110.0	108.1	105.0
Oranges	44.7	46.1	46.3
Coffee, green	12.8	13.8	13.0
Tobacco, unmanufactured*	2.6	2.8	2.8

* FAO estimates.

Note: No data were available for individual crops in 2009.

Aggregate production ('000 metric tons, may include official, semi-official or estimated data): Total cereals 324.7 in 2006, 332.0 in 2007, 394.6 in 2008–09; Total roots and tubers 83.4 in 2006, 78.2 in 2007, 72.9 in 2008–09; Total vegetables (incl. melons) 294.5 in 2006, 361.3 in 2007, 379.1 in 2008–09; Total fruits (excl. melons) 782.2 in 2006, 816.0 in 2007, 629.0 in 2008–09.

Source: FAO.

LIVESTOCK
('000 head, year ending September)

	2006	2007	2008
Horses*	185	190	190
Mules*	4	4	4
Cattle	1,562	1,526	1,603
Pigs	278	325	318
Goats*	6	6	6
Chickens	14,535	15,141	17,484
Ducks*	230	235	235
Turkeys*	35	40	40

* FAO estimates.

2009: Cattle 1,614; Pigs 273; Chickens 16,483.

Source: FAO.

LIVESTOCK PRODUCTS
('000 metric tons)

	2006	2007	2008
Cattle meat	67.1	65.4	68.0
Pig meat	25.0	30.5	34.7
Chicken meat	95.9	113.2	114.9
Cows' milk	178.6	181.5	188.6
Hen eggs	25.7	28.2	28.2

Source: FAO.

PANAMA

Forestry

ROUNDWOOD REMOVALS
('000 cubic metres, excluding bark)

	2007	2008	2009
Sawlogs, veneer logs and logs for sleepers	70	74	79
Other industrial wood	1	1	1
Fuel wood*	1,173	1,158	1,143
Pulp wood*	90	90	90
Total*	1,334	1,323	1,313

* FAO estimates.
Source: FAO.

SAWNWOOD PRODUCTION
('000 cubic metres, incl. railway sleepers)

	2007	2008	2009
Total (all broadleaved)	30	9	9

Source: FAO.

Fishing

('000 metric tons, live weight)

	2006	2007	2008
Capture	227.0	208.5	222.5*
Snappers and jobfishes	8.8	6.7	6.5
Pacific thread herring	30.3	17.7	36.8
Pacific anchoveta	53.4	62.2	47.4
Skipjack tuna	56.7	39.8	50.8
Yellowfin tuna	38.0	39.7	33.9
Bigeye tuna	12.0	10.8	11.0
Marine fishes	8.7	7.7	10.3
Aquaculture	8.7	8.8	8.2
Whiteleg shrimp	8.1	8.2	7.8
Total catch	235.7	217.3	230.7*

* FAO estimate.
Note: Figures exclude crocodiles. The number of spectacled caimans caught was: 2,210 in 2006; 2,752 in 2007; 1,155 in 2008.
Source: FAO.

Industry

SELECTED PRODUCTS
('000 metric tons, unless otherwise indicated)

	2007	2008	2009*
Salt	20	21	20
Sugar	164	151	141
Beer (million litres)	195	214	230
Wines and spirits (million litres)	13	14	13
Evaporated, condensed and powdered milk	19	23	23
Fish oil	7	6	10
Footwear ('000 pairs)	14	26	9
Electricity (million kWh, net)	6,156	6,171	6,638

* Preliminary.

Finance

CURRENCY AND EXCHANGE RATES

Monetary Units
100 centésimos = 1 balboa (B).

Sterling, Dollar and Euro Equivalents (31 December 2010)
£1 sterling = 1.565 balboas;
US $1 = 1.000 balboas;
€1 = 1.336 balboas;
100 balboas = £63.88 = $100.00 = €74.84.

Exchange Rate: The balboa's value is fixed at par with that of the US dollar.

BUDGET
(consolidated general government budget, '000 balboas)

Revenue	2007	2008	2009*
Central government revenue	4,433,157	5,204,123	6,474,147
Current revenue	3,682,164	4,389,933	4,333,890
Tax revenue	2,132,803	2,484,570	2,739,413
Direct taxes	1,134,342	1,302,843	1,511,981
Income tax	985,184	1,137,593	1,310,105
Taxes on property and inheritance	109,316	120,002	150,914
Educational insurance	39,842	45,248	50,962
Indirect taxes	998,461	1,181,727	1,227,432
Non-tax revenue	1,460,182	1,818,725	1,477,376
Panama Canal	463,414	n.a.	n.a.
Transfers from balance of public sector	2,754	4,487	5,084
Other current revenue	89,179	86,638	117,101
Surplus on cash account	357	21,110	12,167
Capital revenue	750,636	793,080	2,128,090
Decentralized institutional revenue	2,369,000	2,786,700	3,577,000
State enterprises	2,150,300	2,451,000	2,341,000
Non-financial	792,000	934,800	778,500
Financial	1,358,300	1,516,200	1,562,500
Municipalities	129,800	140,100	140,200
Total revenue	9,082,257	10,581,923	12,532,347

Expenditure	2007	2008	2009*
Central government expenditure	4,432,114	5,171,665	6,468,305
Current expenditure	3,462,913	3,810,639	4,928,625
National Assembly	56,305	72,739	69,561
State treasury	40,688	43,323	47,620
Ministry of the Presidency	60,607	65,149	63,563
Ministry of the Interior and Justice	247,908	295,707	329,565
Ministry of Foreign Affairs	39,326	40,967	44,877
Ministry of Social Development	15,384	18,643	56,521
Ministry of the Economy and Finance	112,053	207,730	160,233
Ministry of Education	639,408	715,349	760,699
Ministry of Commerce and Industry	29,660	51,040	28,431
Ministry of Public Works	26,439	27,305	27,751
Ministry of Agricultural Development	42,792	51,252	48,744
Ministry of Public Health	598,101	671,832	725,451
Ministry of Labour and Social Welfare	8,649	18,868	15,918
Ministry of Housing	13,627	14,123	15,520
Judiciary	43,068	50,958	55,388
Ombudsman	49,486	47,250	—

PANAMA

Expenditure—continued	2007	2008	2009*
Electoral tribunal	29,031	51,345	51,311
Other institutions	—	1,918	49,696
Other expenditures of administration	11,478	11,697	12,059
Debt-servicing	1,362,504	1,290,635	2,288,623
Education fund	36,399	62,809	77,094
Ministerial development expenditure	969,201	1,361,026	1,539,680
Decentralized institutional expenditure	1,996,800	2,453,300	2,722,400
State enterprises	1,896,300	2,298,900	2,204,400
Municipalities	119,800	134,100	128,400
Total	**8,445,000**	**10,058,000**	**11,523,500**

* Preliminary figures.

Note: Totals may not be equal to the sum of components, as some figures have been rounded.

INTERNATIONAL RESERVES
(US $ million at 31 December*)

	2008	2009	2010
IMF special drawing rights	0.8	268.2	263.3
Reserve position in IMF	18.3	18.6	18.3
Foreign exchange	2,404.7	2,741.5	2,432.9
Total	**2,423.8**	**3,028.3**	**2,714.5**

* Excludes gold, valued at US $476,000 in 1991–93.

Note: US treasury notes and coins form the bulk of the currency in circulation in Panama.

Source: IMF, *International Financial Statistics*.

MONEY SUPPLY
(million balboas at 31 December)

	2008	2009	2010
Transferable deposits	3,763.6	4,403.5	5,230.4
Other deposits	15,837.2	17,378.7	18,963.7
Securities other than shares	179.4	29.9	40.1
Broad money	**19,780.2**	**21,812.1**	**24,234.2**

Source: IMF, *International Financial Statistics*.

COST OF LIVING
(Consumer Price Index, base: 2000 = 100)

	2005	2006	2007
Food (incl. beverages)	105.6	107.0	114.2
Rent, fuel and light	104.0	109.3	114.3
Clothing (incl. footwear)	97.1	96.3	94.9
All items (incl. others)	**103.3**	**105.9**	**110.3**

2008: Food (incl. beverages) 131.3; All items (incl. others) 119.9.
2009: Food (incl. beverages) 138.8; All items (incl. others) 122.8.

Source: ILO.

NATIONAL ACCOUNTS
National Income and Product
(million balboas at current prices)

	2007	2008	2009*
Compensation of employees	6,405.5	6,886.9	7,183.7
Operating surplus	7,788.7	9,793.0	10,525.2
Net mixed income	2,602.8	3,094.3	3,101.6
Domestic factor incomes	**16,797.0**	**19,774.2**	**20,810.5**
Consumption of fixed capital	1,369.7	1,362.8	1,260.3
Gross domestic product (GDP) at factor cost	**18,166.7**	**21,137.0**	**22,070.8**
Indirect taxes	1,801.0	2,084.7	2,186.1
Less Subsidies	174.1	220.0	176.7
GDP in purchasers' values	**19,793.7**	**23,001.6**	**24,080.1**
Less Net factor income paid to the rest of the world	1,741.2	2,035.6	1,835.7
Gross national product	**18,052.5**	**20,966.0**	**22,244.4**
Less Consumption of fixed capital	1,369.7	1,362.8	1,260.3
National income in market prices	**16,682.8**	**19,603.2**	**20,984.1**
Other current transfers from abroad (net)	150.3	122.8	82.2
National disposable income	**16,833.0**	**19,726.0**	**21,066.3**

* Preliminary figures.

Expenditure on the Gross Domestic Product
(million balboas at current prices)

	2007	2008	2009*
Government final consumption expenditure	2,236.3	2,389.0	2,591.8
Private final consumption expenditure	11,345.4	12,142.8	11,068.5
Increase in stocks	221.0	254.7	241.7
Gross fixed capital formation	4,554.7	6,100.5	5,932.0
Total domestic expenditure	**18,357.4**	**20,887.0**	**19,834.0**
Exports of goods and services	16,071.9	19,595.5	19,624.8
Less Imports of goods and services	14,635.6	17,480.9	15,378.7
GDP in purchasers' values	**19,793.7**	**23,001.6**	**24,080.1**
GDP at constant 1996 prices	**17,084.4**	**18,812.9**	**19,414.1**

* Preliminary figures.

Gross Domestic Product by Economic Activity
(million balboas at constant 1996 prices)

	2007	2008	2009*
Agriculture, hunting, forestry and fishing	1,045.0	1,131.6	1,050.3
Mining and quarrying	197.8	259.0	270.4
Manufacturing	1,126.7	1,170.9	1,165.7
Electricity, gas and water	484.3	502.9	540.8
Construction	857.2	1,120.3	1,170.4
Wholesale and retail trade, repair of vehicles, motorcycles and other household goods	2,517.7	2,695.2	2,737.4
Hotels and restaurants	494.9	535.9	549.7
Transport, storage and communications	3,417.5	3,945.8	4,206.3
Financial intermediation	1,414.7	1,614.6	1,640.1
Renting, real estate and business services	2,607.8	2,795.6	2,919.9
General government services	1,272.7	1,321.0	1,353.3
Social services and private education and health	269.0	285.7	303.5
Other community, social and personal services	513.1	548.3	572.1
Private households with employed persons	112.6	114.7	113.6
Sub-total	**16,331.0**	**18,041.5**	**18,593.5**
Less Financial intermediation services indirectly measured	379.8	403.9	430.4
Gross value added in basic prices	**15,951.2**	**17,637.6**	**18,163.1**
Import duties and other taxes, less subsidies	1,133.2	1,175.3	1,251.0
GDP in market prices	**17,084.4**	**18,812.9**	**19,414.1**

* Preliminary figures.

PANAMA

Statistical Survey

BALANCE OF PAYMENTS
(US $ million)*

	2007	2008	2009
Exports of goods f.o.b.	9,333.7	10,323.2	10,904.3
Imports of goods f.o.b.	-12,523.8	-14,869.1	-12,930.6
Trade balance	**-3,190.1**	**-4,545.9**	**-2,026.3**
Exports of services	4,958.1	5,825.9	5,438.2
Imports of services	-2,121.8	-2,621.2	-2,165.9
Balance on goods and services	**-353.8**	**-1,341.2**	**1,246.0**
Other income received	1,864.2	1,891.9	1,504.6
Other income paid	-3,170.6	-3,465.7	-2,964.5
Balance on goods, services and income	**-1,660.2**	**-2,915.0**	**-213.9**
Current transfers received	416.4	449.5	463.1
Current transfers paid	-163.2	-211.6	-252.7
Current balance	**-1,407.0**	**-2,677.1**	**-3.5**
Capital account (net)	43.7	56.9	23.1
Direct investment from abroad	1,776.5	2,401.7	1,772.8
Portfolio investment assets	-1,081.6	-464.3	-864.1
Portfolio investment liabilities	450.0	-62.3	1,323.0
Other investment assets	-5,118.5	-3,000.6	-1,106.7
Other investment liabilities	6,432.8	4,034.7	116.5
Net errors and omissions	-476.0	296.3	-652.3
Overall balance	**619.9**	**585.3**	**608.8**

* Including the transactions of enterprises operating in the Colón Free Zone.

Source: IMF, *International Financial Statistics*.

External Trade

PRINCIPAL COMMODITIES
('000 balboas)

Imports c.i.f.	2007	2008	2009*
Food and live animals	737,830	990,839	925,954
Mineral products	1,331,529	2,003,609	1,412,569
Chemicals and chemical products	643,643	780,094	798,431
Plastics, rubber and articles thereof	282,982	343,952	319,501
Textiles and articles thereof	223,895	276,245	345,210
Metals and manufactures of metal	530,211	826,700	600,656
Machinery and apparatus	1,415,090	1,768,606	1,537,350
Transport materials	813,776	932,841	794,387
Total (incl. others)	**6,869,921**	**9,009,934**	**7,800,571**

Exports f.o.b.†	2007	2008	2009*
Sugar	17,637	15,149	13,149
Bananas	111,615	98,748	61,181
Melons	202,523	214,084	81,856
Pineapples	42,855	36,503	33,063
Coffee	16,303	16,049	9,630
Shellfish	56,367	40,683	43,925
Fresh and frozen fish and fillets (incl. yellowfin tuna)	293,154	275,133	245,517
Meat from cattle	13,906	14,502	14,047
Standing cattle	16,429	478	198
Total (incl. others)	**1,126,799**	**1,144,046**	**820,999**

* Preliminary.
† Including re-exports.

PRINCIPAL TRADING PARTNERS*
('000 balboas)

Imports c.i.f.†	2007	2008	2009
Brazil	140,703	140,285	144,397
China, People's Republic	358,725	454,407	327,345
Colombia	192,109	240,779	258,376
Costa Rica	326,226	456,011	408,555
El Salvador	72,337	93,309	83,784
Germany	87,350	125,560	103,350
Guatemala	107,372	145,125	162,098
Japan	328,945	385,137	284,277
Korea, Republic	267,671	263,550	206,527
Mexico	212,027	312,615	355,054
Netherlands Antilles‡	489,156	50,881	5,242
Peru	69,029	107,026	45,644
Spain	106,958	142,131	113,853
USA	2,079,584	2,683,527	2,266,973
Venezuela	55,401	44,957	28,974
Total (incl. others)	**6,869,921**	**9,009,934**	**7,800,571**

Exports f.o.b.	2007	2008	2009§
Belgium-Luxembourg	42,347	11,628	6,343
China, People's Republic	68,032	46,374	20,298
Colombia	19,138	11,793	15,716
Costa Rica	57,101	65,976	60,737
Dominican Republic	13,440	16,815	19,297
El Salvador	8,022	7,521	5,375
Guatemala	16,712	8,147	5,582
Honduras	20,923	17,156	11,521
Hong Kong	5,337	2,587	3,953
India	7,791	6,611	4,532
Italy	18,309	29,744	17,011
Mexico	9,252	8,871	7,913
Netherlands	114,640	122,789	53,938
Nicaragua	12,879	13,508	10,613
Portugal	13,076	3,848	4,752
Puerto Rico	9,045	12,894	7,772
Spain	55,792	56,870	50,808
Sweden	62,150	62,295	48,763
Taiwan	38,920	49,407	24,006
United Kingdom	61,239	61,762	12,057
USA	391,402	434,890	349,745
Total (incl. others)	**1,126,799**	**1,144,046**	**820,999**

* Including trade with the Colón Free Zone (CFZ) ('000 balboas): *Imports*: 714,614 in 2007; 823,952 in 2008; 919,572 in 2009 (preliminary). *Exports*: 20,229 in 2007; 19,676 in 2008; 18,007 in 2009 (preliminary).
† Including imports to the Petroleum Free Zone ('000 balboas): 360,009 in 2007; 1,381,650 in 2008, 1,091,316 in 2009 (preliminary).
‡ Curaçao only.
§ Preliminary.

Transport

RAILWAYS
(traffic)

	2002*	2003	2004
Passenger-km (million)	35,693	52,324	53,377
Freight ton-km (million)	20,665	41,863	52,946

* Panama Railway only.

Source: UN, *Statistical Yearbook*.

ROAD TRAFFIC
(motor vehicles in use)

	2000	2001	2002
Cars	223,433	219,372	224,504
Buses and coaches	16,865	15,558	16,371
Lorries and vans	75,454	73,139	74,247

2007: Cars 436,205; Buses and coaches 20,133; Lorries and vans 174,482; Motorcycles and mopeds 20,133.

Source: IRF, *World Road Statistics*.

PANAMA

SHIPPING

Merchant Fleet
(registered at 31 December)

	2007	2008	2009
Number of vessels	7,605	8,065	8,100
Total displacement ('000 grt)	168,165.5	183,503.5	190,663.1

Source: IHS Fairplay, *World Fleet Statistics*.

International Sea-borne Freight Traffic
('000 metric tons)

	2001	2002	2003
Goods loaded	108,456	110,556	99,516
Goods unloaded	84,864	99,288	76,152

Panama Canal Traffic

	2007/08	2008/09	2009/10
Transits	14,702	14,342	14,230
Cargo ('000 long tons)	209,763.1	198,014.3	204,816.3

Source: Panama Canal Authority.

CIVIL AVIATION
(traffic on scheduled services)

	2006	2007	2008
Kilometres flown (million)	67	81	95
Passenger-km (million)	6,078	7,940	9,316
Total ton-km (million)	40	33	42

Source: UN Economic Commission for Latin America and the Caribbean, *Statistical Yearbook*.

Tourism

VISITOR ARRIVALS BY COUNTRY OF ORIGIN
(arrivals at Tocumen International Airport)

	2006	2007	2008
Argentina	14,230	19,093	22,911
Canada	29,392	39,097	47,166
Chile	9,985	13,478	16,127
Colombia	129,418	174,476	209,182
Costa Rica	31,248	42,158	50,460
Dominican Republic	9,049	11,917	14,322
Ecuador	35,024	47,387	56,521
El Salvador	11,545	15,567	18,612
France	9,396	11,752	14,079
Germany	6,275	8,517	10,231
Guatemala	17,361	23,494	27,955
Honduras	8,143	10,950	13,096
Italy	10,584	14,952	17,930
Jamaica	6,890	9,636	11,449
Mexico	34,507	46,787	55,913
Nicaragua	7,332	9,903	11,850
Peru	15,416	20,761	24,831
Puerto Rico	10,585	14,920	17,744
Spain	12,267	16,555	19,929
USA	191,094	258,249	308,991
Venezuela	23,113	31,157	37,345
Total (incl. others)	703,745	948,946	1,136,079

Tourism receipts (US$ million, incl. passenger transport): 1,425 in 2006; 1,806 in 2007; 2,223 in 2008.

Source: World Tourism Organization.

Communications Media

	2007	2008	2009
Telephones ('000 main lines in use)	495.2	524.0	537.1
Mobile cellular telephones ('000 subscribers)	3,010.6	3,915.2	5,677.1
Internet users ('000)	745.3	936.5	959.8
Broadband subscribers ('000)	150.3	196.2	201.1

Personal computers: 96,823 (28.5 per 1,000 persons) in 2008.
Radio receivers ('000 in use): 815 in 1997.
Television receivers ('000 in use): 550 in 2000.
Daily newspapers: 8 in 2004.

Sources: UNESCO, *Statistical Yearbook*; UN, *Statistical Yearbook*; International Telecommunication Union.

Education

(2007/08 unless otherwise indicated, provisional)

	Institutions*	Teachers	Males	Females	Total
Pre-primary	1,662	5,315	48,356	46,572	94,928
Primary	3,116	18,364	230,645	214,462	445,107
Secondary	442	17,337	130,846	135,914	266,760
General	n.a.	13,814	108,793	115,124	223,917
Vocational	n.a.	3,523	22,053	20,790	42,843
Tertiary†	24	12,209	52,287	80,373	132,660

* 2001/02 figures.
† 2006/07.

Sources: Ministry of Education; UNESCO, *Statistical Yearbook*; UNESCO Institute for Statistics.

Pupil-teacher ratio (primary education, UNESCO estimate): 24.2 in 2007/08 (Source: UNESCO Institute for Statistics).
Adult literacy rate (UNESCO estimates): 93.5% (males 94.1%; females 92.8%) in 2008 (Source: UNESCO Institute for Statistics).

Directory

The Government

HEAD OF STATE

President: RICARDO A. MARTINELLI BERROCAL (took office 1 July 2009).
Vice-President: JUAN CARLOS VARELA RODRÍGUEZ.

THE CABINET
(May 2011)

The Government is formed by a coalition, comprising representatives of Cambio Democrático (CD), the Partido Panameñista (PP) and the Unión Patriótica (UP), several Independents (Ind.) and a dissident member of the Partido Revolucionario Democrático (PRD).

Minister of Foreign Affairs: JUAN CARLOS VARELA RODRÍGUEZ (PP).
Minister of Public Security: JOSÉ RAÚL MULINO (UP).
Minister of the Interior: ROXANA MÉNDEZ (CD).
Minister of Public Works: FEDERICO JOSÉ SUÁREZ (Ind.).
Minister of the Economy and Finance: ALBERTO VALLARINO CLÉMENT (PP).
Minister of Agricultural Development: EMILIO KIESWETTER (CD).
Minister of Commerce and Industry: ROBERTO HENRÍQUEZ (CD).
Minister of Health: FRANKLIN VERGARA J. (Ind.).
Minister of Labour and Social Welfare: ALMA LORENA CORTÉS AGUILAR (CD).
Minister of Education: LUCINDA MOLINAR (Ind.).
Minister of Housing: CARLOS ALBERTO DUBOY SIERRA (PP).
Minister of the Presidency: DEMETRIO PAPADIMITRIU (CD).
Minister of Social Development: GUILLERMO ANTONIO FERRUFINO BENÍTEZ (CD).
Minister of Canal Affairs: RÓMULO ROUX (Ind.).
Minister of Tourism: SALOMÓN SHAMAH ZUCHIN (Ind.).
Minister of Micro-, Small and Medium-sized Enterprises: GISELLE BURILLO SÁIZ (PRD dissident).

MINISTRIES

Office of the President: Palacio de Las Garzas, Corregimiento de San Felipe, Panamá 1; tel. 527-9600; fax 527-7693; e-mail web@presidencia.gob.pa; internet www.presidencia.gob.pa.

Ministry of Agricultural Development: Edif. 576, Calle Manuel E. Melo, Altos de Curundú, Apdo 5390, Panamá 5; tel. 507-0600; e-mail infomida@mida.gob.pa; internet www.mida.gob.pa.

Ministry of Commerce and Industry: Plaza Edison, Sector El Paical, 2° y 3°, Apdo 0815-0111, Panamá 4; tel. 560-0600; fax 560-0663; e-mail contactenos@mici.gob.pa; internet www.mici.gob.pa.

Ministry of the Economy and Finance: (Economy) Edif. Ogawa, Vía España, Calle del Santuario Nacional, Apdo 5245, Panamá 5; (Finance) Antiguo Edif. de Hacienda y Tesoro, Calle 34 y 35, Avda Perú, Calidonia, Panamá; tel. (Economy) 507-7000; tel. (Finance) 507-7600; e-mail prensa@mef.gob.pa; internet www.mef.gob.pa.

Ministry of Education: Villa Cárdenas, Ancón, Apdo 0816-04049, Panamá 3; tel. 511-4400; fax 511-4440; e-mail meduca@meduca.gob.pa; internet www.meduca.gob.pa.

Ministry of Foreign Affairs: Edif. 26, Palacio Bolívar, Calle 3, San Felipe, Panamá 4; tel. 511-4100; fax 511-4022; e-mail prensa@mire.gob.pa; internet www.mire.gob.pa.

Ministry of Health: Apdo 2048, Panamá 1; tel. and fax 512-9202; e-mail saludaldia@minsa.gob.pa; internet www.minsa.gob.pa.

Ministry of Housing: Edif. Plaza Edison, 4°, Avda Ricardo J. Alfaro, Apdo 5228, Panamá 5; tel. 579-9200; fax 579-9651; e-mail info@mivi.gob.pa; internet www.mivi.gob.pa.

Ministry of the Interior: Avda 7 y Calle 3, Central San Felipe, Apdo 1628, Panamá 1; tel. 512-7600; fax 512-2126; e-mail despachosuperior@mingob.gob.pa; internet www.mingob.gob.pa.

Ministry of Labour and Social Welfare: Plaza Edison, 5°, Avda Ricardo J. Alfaro (Tumba Muerto) Betania, Apdo 2441, Panamá 3; tel. 560-1100; fax 560-1117; e-mail mitradel@mitradel.gob.pa; internet www.mitradel.gob.pa.

Ministry of the Presidency: Palacio de Las Garzas, Corregimiento de San Felipe, Apdo 2189, Panamá 1; tel. 527-9600; e-mail ofasin@presidencia.gob.pa; internet www.presidencia.gob.pa.

Ministry of Public Security: Avda 7 y Calle 3, Central San Felipe, Apdo 1628, Panamá 1; tel. 512-7600; internet www.minseg.gob.pa.

Ministry of Public Works: Edif. Principal 1019, Curundú, Zona 1, Apdo 1632, Panamá 1; tel. 507-9400; fax 507-9419; e-mail info@mop.gob.pa; internet www.mop.gob.pa.

Ministry of Social Development: Plaza Edison, 4°, Avda Ricardo J. Alfaro, Apdo 680-50, El Dorado, Panamá; tel. 500-6001; fax 500-6020; e-mail mides@mides.gob.pa; internet www.mides.gob.pa.

President and Legislature

PRESIDENT

Election, 3 May 2009

Candidate	Votes	% of valid votes
Ricardo A. Martinelli Berrocal (Alianza por el Cambio*)	952,333	60.03
Balbina del Carmen Herrera Araúz (Un País para Todos†)	597,227	37.65
Guillermo Endara Galimany (Vanguardia Moral de la Patria)	36,867	2.32
Total valid votes‡	**1,586,427**	**100.00**

* Electoral alliance comprising Cambio Democrático, the Partido Panameñista, the Movimiento Liberal Republicano Nacionalista and the Unión Patriótica.
† Electoral alliance comprising the Partido Revolucionario Democrático, the Partido Popular and the Partido Liberal.
‡ In addition, there were 19,105 blank and 30,976 invalid ballots.

ASAMBLEA NACIONAL
(National Assembly)

President: JOSÉ LUIS VARELA RODRÍGUEZ.

General Election, 3 May 2009

Affiliation/Party	% of votes	Seats
Alianza por el Cambio	56.0	42
Partido Panameñista	22.2	22
Cambio Democrático	23.4	14
Unión Patriótica	5.7	4
Movimiento Liberal Republicano Nacionalista	4.7	2
Un País para Todos	40.6	27
Partido Revolucionario Democrático	35.7	26
Partido Popular	3.7	1
Partido Liberal	1.2	—
Vanguardia Moral de la Patria	1.0	—
Independents	2.4	2
Total	**100.0**	**71**

Election Commission

Tribunal Electoral: Edif. del Tribunal Electoral-Dirección Superior, Avda Ecuador y Calle 33, Apdo 5281, Panamá 5; tel. 507-8000; e-mail secretaria-general@tribunal-electoral.gob.pa; internet www.tribunal-electoral.gob.pa; f. 1956; independent; Pres. GERARDO FELIPE SOLÍS DÍAZ.

Political Organizations

Cambio Democrático (CD): Parque Lefevre, Plaza Carolina, arriba de la Juguetería del Super 99, Panamá; tel. 217-2643; fax 217-2645; e-mail cambio.democratico@hotmail.com; internet www.cambiodemocratico.org.pa; formally registered 1998; contested the 2009 elections as part of the Alianza por el Cambio; merged with the Unión Patriótica in March 2011; Pres. RICARDO A. MARTINELLI BERROCAL; Sec.-Gen. GIACOMO TAMBURELLI.

Frente Amplio por la Democracia (FAD): Panamá; tel. 396-6679; e-mail frenadeso@frenadesonoticias.com; internet www.frenadesonoticias.org; f. 2011 by Frente Nacional por la Defensa de los Derechos Económicos y Sociales (FRENADESO); Pres. FERNANDO CEBAMANOS.

Movimiento Liberal Republicano Nacionalista (MOLIRENA): Calle 66 (Calle Belén), Casa Duplex 46-A, Corregimiento de

PANAMA

San Francisco, Panamá; tel. 399-5280; fax 399-5288; formally registered 1982; conservative; contested the 2009 elections as part of the Alianza por el Cambio; Pres. SERGIO GONZÁLEZ RUIZ; Sec.-Gen. CLAUDIO LACAYO ALVAREZ.

Partido Liberal: Edif. Torre Universal, 11°, Avda Federico Boyd, Panamá; tel. 209-2574; fax 209-2575; e-mail partidoliberal@elveloz.com; f. 2005; contested the 2009 elections as part of the Un Pais para Todos alliance; Pres. JOAQUÍN F. FRANCO VÁSQUEZ; Sec.-Gen. AUGUSTO C. AROSEMENA.

Partido Panameñista (PP): Avda Perú y Calle 37, No 37–41, al lado de Casa la Esperanza, Apdo 9610, Panamá 4; tel. 227-0028; fax 227-0951; e-mail partidopanamenista@hotmail.com; f. 1990 by Arnulfista faction of the Partido Panameñista Auténtico as Partido Arnulfista (PA); name changed as above in Jan. 2005; contested the 2009 elections as part of the Alianza por el Cambio; Pres. JUAN CARLOS VARELA RODRÍGUEZ; Sec.-Gen. FRANCISCO ALEMÁN MENDOZA.

Partido Popular: Avda Perú, frente al Parque Porras, Apdo 6322, Panamá 5; tel. 225-2381; fax 227-3944; e-mail pdc@cwpanama.net; f. 1960 as Partido Demócrata Cristiano; name changed as above in 2001; contested the 2009 elections as part of the Un País para Todos alliance; Pres. MILTON COHEN-HENRÍQUEZ; Sec.-Gen. ROBERTO MÉNDEZ MOREIRA.

Partido Revolucionario Democrático (PRD): Avda México, entre Calle 27 y 28, Apdo 3-85, Panamá 3; tel. 225-8460; fax 225-8476; e-mail prdpanama@yahoo.com; f. 1979; supports policies of late Gen. Omar Torrijos Herrera; combination of Marxists, Christian Democrats and some business interests; contested the 2009 elections as part of the Un País para Todos alliance; Pres. FRANCISCO SÁNCHEZ CÁRDENAS; Sec.-Gen. MITCHELL CONSTANTINO DOENS.

Vanguardia Moral de la Patria (VMP): Edif. Río Plaza, No 10, planta baja, Calle Décima, esq. con Calle La Pulida, Corregimiento de Río Abajo, Panamá; tel. 221-9337; f. 2004; Pres. (vacant); Gen. Sec. ANA MAE DÍAZ DE ENDARA.

Diplomatic Representation

EMBASSIES IN PANAMA

Argentina: PH Torre Global, 24°, Calle 50, Apdo 832-0458, Panamá 1; tel. 302-0005; fax 302-0004; e-mail embajada@embargen.org; internet www.embargen.org; Ambassador JORGE ALBERTO ARGUINDEGUI.

Belize: Villa de la Fuente 1, F-32, Calle 22, POB 0819-12255, Panamá; tel. 236-3762; fax 236-4132; e-mail nmusag@cwpanama.net; Ambassador ALFREDO MARTÍNEZ.

Bolivia: Calle G, Casa 3, El Cangrejo, Apdo 0823-05603, Panamá; tel. 269-0274; fax 264-3868; e-mail emb_bol_pan@cwpanama.net; internet embolivia-panama.com.pa; Ambassador EDGAR SOLIZ MORALES.

Brazil: Edif. El Dorado 24, 1°, Calle Elvira Méndez y Avda Ricardo Arango, Urb. Campo Alegre, Apdo 4287, Panamá 5; tel. 263-5322; fax 269-6316; e-mail embrasil@embrasil.org.pa; internet www.embrasil.org.pa; Ambassador EDUARDO PRISCO PARAÍSO RAMOS.

Canada: Edif. World Trade Center, Torres de las Américas, Torre A, 11°, Punta Pacífica, Apdo 0832-2446, Panamá; tel. 294-2500; fax 294-2514; e-mail panam@international.gc.ca; internet www.canadainternational.gc.ca/panama; Ambassador PATRICIA LANGAN-TORELL.

Chile: Torres de las Américas, 7°, Punta Pacífica, Apdo 7341, Panamá 5; tel. 294-8901; fax 294-8904; e-mail echilepa@tdla.com.pa; internet chileabroad.gov.cl/panama; Ambassador ALBERTO LABBÉ GALILEA.

Colombia: Edif. World Trade Center, Of. 1801, 18°, Calle 53, Urb. Marbella, Panamá; tel. 264-9513; fax 223-1134; e-mail epanama@cancilleria.gov.co; internet www.embajadaenpanama.gov.co; Ambassador GINA BENEDETTI DE VÉLEZ.

Costa Rica: Edif. Plaza Omega, 3°, Calle Samuel Lewis, Apdo 0816-02038, Panamá; tel. 264-2980; fax 264-4057; e-mail embajadacr@cwpanama.net; Ambassador MELVIN SÁENZ BIOLLEY.

Cuba: Avda Cuba y Ecuador 33, Apdo 6-2291, Bellavista, Panamá; tel. 227-5277; fax 225-6681; e-mail respanama@sinfo.net; Ambassador REINALDO CARLOS CALVIAC LAFERTÉ.

Dominican Republic: Torre Delta, 16°, Calle Elvira Méndez, Área Bancaria, Apdo 6250, Panamá 5; tel. 263-6324; fax 263-7725; e-mail embajadadompa.zlg@cableonda.net; Ambassador GRECIA FIORDALICIA PICHARDO POLANCO.

Ecuador: Edif. Torre 2000, 6°, Calle 50, Marbella, Bellavista, Panamá; tel. 264-2654; fax 223-0159; e-mail ecuador@cwpanama.net; Ambassador ELSA BEATRIZ VILLACÍS ROCA.

Egypt: Calle 55, No 15, El Cangrejo, Apdo 7080, Panamá 5; tel. 263-5020; fax 264-8406; e-mail egempma@hotmail.com; Ambassador REDA HALIM FAHMY IBRAHIM.

El Salvador: Edif. ADR, 8°, Avda Samuel Lewis y Calle 58, Apdo 0823-05432, Panamá; tel. 223-3020; fax 264-6148; e-mail embasalva@cwpanama.net; Ambassador EFRÉN ARNOLDO BERNAL CHÉVEZ.

France: Plaza de Francia 1, Las Bovedas, San Felipe, Apdo 0816-07945, Panamá 1; tel. 211-6200; fax 211-6201; e-mail cad.panama-amba@diplomatie.gouv.fr; internet www.ambafrance-pa.org; Ambassador HUGUES GOISBAULT.

Germany: Edif. World Trade Center, 20°, Calle 53E, Marbella, Apdo 0832-0536, Panamá 5; tel. 263-7733; fax 223-6664; e-mail germpanama@cwp.net.pa; internet www.panama.diplo.de; Ambassador MICHAEL GRAU.

Guatemala: Edif. World Trade Center, 2°, Of. 203, Calle 53, Urb. Marbella, Panamá 9; tel. 269-3475; fax 223-1922; e-mail embpanama@minex.gob.gt; Ambassador STELLA RIEGER DE GARCÍA-GRANADOS.

Haiti: Edif. Dora Luz, 2°, Calle 1, El Cangrejo, Apdo 442, Panamá 9; tel. 269-3443; fax 223-1767; e-mail embhaitipan@cableonda.net; Chargé d'affaires a.i. BOCCHIT EDMOND.

Holy See: Punta Paitilla, Avda Balboa y Vía Italia, Apdo 0816-00457, Panamá 5 (Apostolic Nunciature); tel. 269-2102; fax 264-2116; e-mail nuncio@cableonda.net; Apostolic Nuncio Most Rev. ANDRÉS CARRASCOSA COSO (Titular Archbishop of Elo).

Honduras: Edif. Bay Mall, 1°, Avda Balboa 112, Apdo 0816-03427, Panamá 5; tel. 264-5513; fax 264-4628; e-mail info@embajadadehonduras.com.pa; internet www.embajadadehonduras.com.pa; Ambassador NERY M. FÚNES PADILLA.

India: Avda Federico Boyd y Calle 51, Bella Vista, Apdo 0823-05815, Panamá 7; tel. 264-3043; fax 209-6779; e-mail ambassador@indempan.org; internet www.indempan.org; Ambassador VISHNU NAMDEO HADE.

Israel: Edif. Torre Banco General, 17°, Calle Aquilino De La Guardia, Urb. Marbella, Panamá; tel. 208-4700; fax 208-4755; e-mail info@panama.mfa.gov.il; internet panama.mfa.gov.il; Ambassador YOED MAGEN.

Italy: Torre Banco Exterior, 25°, Avda Balboa, Apdo 0816-04453, Panamá 9; tel. 225-8950; fax 227-4906; e-mail ambpana.mail@esteri.it; internet www.ambpanama.esteri.it; Ambassador PLACIDO VIGO.

Japan: Calle 50 y 60E, Urb. Obarrio, Apdo 0816-06807, Panamá 1; tel. 263-6155; fax 263-6019; e-mail taiship2@cwpanama.net; internet www.panama.emb-japan.go.jp; Ambassador IKUO MIZUKI.

Korea, Republic: Edif. Victoria Plaza, 4°, Calle 53, Urb. Obarrio, Apdo 8096, Panamá 7; tel. 264-8203; fax 264-8825; e-mail panama@mofat.go.kr; internet pan.mofat.go.kr; Ambassador DOO JUNG-SOO.

Libya: Avda Balboa y Calle 32 (frente al Edif. Atalaya), Apdo 6-894, El Dorado, Panamá; tel. 227-3342; fax 227-3886; Chargé d'affaires a.i. NAGI A. S. KSUDA.

Mexico: Edif. Torre ADR, 10°, Avda Samuel Lewis y Calle 58, Urb. Obarrio, Corregimiento de Bella Vista, Apdo 0823-05788, Panamá; tel. 263-4900; fax 263-5446; e-mail embamexpan@cwpanama.net; internet www.sre.gob.mx/panama; Ambassador YANERIT CRISTINA MORGAN SOTOMAYOR.

Nicaragua: Edif. De Lessep's, 3°, Calle Manuel Maria Icaza, Urb. Obarrio, Panamá; tel. 264-3080; fax 264-5425; e-mail embapana@sinfo.net; Ambassador ANTENOR ALBERTO FERREY PERNUDI.

Paraguay: Edif. Galerías Balboa, 3°, Of. 45, Avda Balboa y Aquilino de la Guardia, Bella Vista, Panamá; tel. 263-4782; fax 269-4247; e-mail embapar_pa@cwpanama.net; Ambassador JUAN CARLOS RAMIREZ MONTALBETTI.

Peru: Edif. World Trade Center, 12°, Calle 53, Urb. Marbella, Apdo 4516, Panamá 5; tel. 223-1112; fax 269-6809; e-mail embaperu@cableonda.net; Ambassador GABRIEL GARCÍA PIKE.

Russia: Torre IBC, 10°, Avda Manuel Espinosa Batista, Apdo 6-4697, El Dorado, Panamá; tel. 264-1408; fax 264-1588; e-mail emruspan@sinfo.net; internet www.panama.mid.ru; Ambassador ALEXEI A. ERMAKOV.

Spain: Plaza de Belisario Porras, entre Avda Perú y Calle 33A, Apdo 0816-06600, Panamá 1; tel. 227-5122; fax 227-6284; e-mail emb.panama@mae.es; Ambassador JESÚS SILVA FERNÁNDEZ.

Taiwan (Republic of China): Edif. Torre Hong Kong Bank, 10°, Avda Samuel Lewis, Apdo 7492, Panamá 5; tel. 269-1347; fax 264-9118; e-mail panama@mail.gio.gov.tw; internet www.taiwanembassy.org/pa; Ambassador SHEN-YEAW KO.

United Kingdom: MMG Tower, 4°, Calle 53, Urb. Marbella, Apdo 0816-07946, Panamá 1; tel. 269-0866; fax 263-5138; e-mail britemb@cwpanama.net; internet ukinpanama.fco.gov.uk; Ambassador MICHAEL JOHN HOLLOWAY.

PANAMA

USA: Edif. 783, Avda Demetrio Basilio Lakas, Apdo 0816-02561, Clayton, Panamá 5; tel. 207-7000; fax 317-5568; e-mail panamaweb@state.gov; internet panama.usembassy.gov; Ambassador PHYLLIS MARIE POWERS.
Uruguay: Edif. Los Delfines, Of. 8, Avda Balboa, Calle 50E Este, Apdo 0816-03616, Panamá 5; tel. 264-2838; fax 264-8908; e-mail urupanam@cwpanama.net; internet www.urupana.org; Ambassador FRANCISCO HEBER PURIFICATTI GAMARRA.
Venezuela: Torre HSBC, 5°, Avda Samuel Lewis, Apdo 661, Panamá 1; tel. 269-1244; fax 269-1916; e-mail info@venezuela.org.pa; internet www.venezuela.org.pa; Ambassador JORGE LUIS DURÁN CENTENO.
Viet Nam: 52 José Gabriel Duque, La Cresta, Apdo 12434-6A, El Dorado, Panamá; tel. 264-2551; fax 265-6056; e-mail convietnam@cwpanama.net; Ambassador HOANG CONG THUY.

Judicial System

The judiciary in Panama comprises the following courts and judges: Corte Suprema de Justicia (Supreme Court of Justice), with nine judges appointed for a 10-year term; 10 Tribunales Superiores de Distrito Judicial (High Courts) with 36 magistrates; 54 Jueces de Circuito (Circuit Judges), and 89 Jueces Municipales (Municipal Judges).

Panama is divided into four judicial districts and has seven High Courts of Appeal. The first judicial district covers the provinces of Panamá, Colón, Darién and the region of Kuna Yala and contains two High Courts of Appeal, one dealing with criminal cases, the other dealing with civil cases. The second judicial district covers the provinces of Coclé and Veraguas and contains the third High Court of Appeal, located in Penonomé. The third judicial district covers the provinces of Chiriquí and Bocas del Toro and contains the fourth High Court of Appeal, located in David. The fourth judicial district covers the provinces of Herrera and Los Santos and contains the fifth High Court of Appeal, located in Las Tablas. Each of these courts deals with civil and criminal cases in their respective provinces. There are two additional special High Courts of Appeal. The first hears maritime, labour, family and infancy cases; the second deals with anti-trust cases and consumer affairs.

Corte Suprema de Justicia
Edif. 236, Calle Culebra, Ancón, Apdo 1770, Panamá 1; tel. 262-9833; e-mail prensa@organojudicial.gob.pa; internet www.organojudicial.gob.pa.
President of the Supreme Court of Justice: ANÍBAL SALAS CÉSPEDES.
Procurator-General: JOSÉ EDUARDO AYÚ PRADO CANALS.

Religion

The Constitution recognizes freedom of worship and the Roman Catholic Church as the religion of the majority of the population.

CHRISTIANITY

The Roman Catholic Church
For ecclesiastical purposes, Panama comprises one archdiocese, five dioceses, the territorial prelature of Bocas del Toro and the Apostolic Vicariate of Darién. Some 83% of the population are Roman Catholics.

Bishops' Conference
Conferencia Episcopal de Panamá, Secretariado General, Apdo 870933, Panamá 7; tel. 223-0075; fax 223-0042; internet www.iglesia.org.pa.
f. 1958; statutes approved 1986; Pres. Rt Rev. JOSÉ LUIS LACUNZA MAESTROJUAN (Bishop of David).
Archbishop of Panamá: Most Rev. JOSÉ DIMAS CEDEÑO DELGADO, Arzobispado Metropolitano, Calle 1a Sur Carrasquilla, Apdo 6386, Panamá 5; tel. 261-0002; fax 261-0820; e-mail asccn4@keops.utp.ac.pa.

The Baptist Church
The Baptist Convention of Panama (Convención Bautista de Panamá): Apdo 0816-01761, Panamá 5; tel. and fax 259-5485; e-mail convencionbautistadepanama@hotmail.com; f. 1959; Pres. FRANCISCO MEDINA; Sec. ESMERALDA DE TUY; 7,573 mems.

The Anglican Communion
Panama comprises one of the five dioceses of the Iglesia Anglicana de la Región Central de América.

Bishop of Panama: Rt Rev. JULIO MURRAY, Edif. 331A, Calle Culebra, Apdo R, Balboa; tel. 212-0062; fax 262-2097.

BAHÁ'Í FAITH
National Spiritual Assembly of the Bahá'ís: Apdo 850-625, Las Cumbres, Panamá 15; tel. 231-1191; fax 231-6909; e-mail panbahai@cwpanama.net; internet panamabahai.net; mems resident in 529 localities; Nat. Sec. YOLANDA RODRÍGUEZ VILLAREAL.

The Press

DAILIES

Crítica Libre: Vía Fernández de Córdoba, Apdo B-4, Panamá 9A; tel. 261-0575; fax 230-0132; e-mail esotop@epasa.com; internet www.critica.com.pa; f. 1925; morning; Pres. ROSARIO ARIAS DE GALINDO; Dir JUAN PRITSIOLAS; circ. 40,000.
DIA a DIA: Vía Ricardo J. Alfaro, al lado de la USMA, Apdo B-4, Panamá 9A; tel. 230-7777; fax 230-2279; e-mail editor.diaadia@epasa.com; internet www.diaadia.com.pa; Pres. FRANCISCO ARIAS V.; Gen. Man. RAMÓN R. VALLARINO A.
La Estrella de Panamá: Calle Alejandro Duque, Vía Transístmica y Frangipani, Panamá; tel. 227-0555; fax 227-1026; e-mail laestre@estrelladepanama.com; internet www.estrelladepanama.com; f. 1853; morning; Pres. EBRAHIM ASVAT; Editor GERARDO BERROA; circ. 10,000.
El Panamá América: Vía Ricardo J. Alfaro, al lado de la USMA, Apdo 0834-02787, Panamá 9A; tel. 230-7777; fax 230-7773; e-mail director@epasa.com; internet pa-digital.com.pa; f. 1925; morning; independent; affiliated to Interamerican Press Asscn; Pres. FRANCISCO ARIAS V.; Dir GUIDO RODRÍGUEZ LUGARI; circ. 25,000.
La Prensa: Avda 12 de Octubre y Calle C, Hato Pintado, Pueblo Nuevo, Apdo 0819-05620, Panamá; tel. 222-1222; fax 221-7328; e-mail editor@prensa.com; internet www.prensa.com; f. 1980; morning; independent; Pres. RICARDO ALBERTO ARIAS; Editor FERNANDO BERGUIDO; circ. 38,000.
El Siglo: Calle 58 Obarrio, Panamá; tel. 264-3921; fax 269-6954; e-mail redaccion@elsiglo.com; internet www.elsiglo.com; f. 1985; morning; acquired by Geo-Media, SA, in 2001; Pres. Dr NIVIA ROSSANA CASTRELLÓN; Editor OCTAVIO COGLEY; circ. 30,000.

PERIODICALS

FOB Colón Free Zone: Apdo 0819-06908, El Dorado, Panamá; tel. 225-6638; fax 225-0466; e-mail focusint@sinfo.net; internet www.colonfreezone.com; annual; bilingual trade directory; publ. by Focus Publications (Int.), SA; Editor ISRAEL ARGUEDAS; circ. 60,000.
Focus Panama: 742 Calle 2A, Perejil, Panamá; tel. 225-6638; fax 225-0466; e-mail focusint@sinfo.net; internet www.focuspublicationsint.com; f. 1970; 2 a year; publ. by Focus Publications; visitors' guide; separate English and Spanish edns; Dir KENNETH J. JONES; circ. 100,000.
Informativo Industrial: Apdo 6-4798, El Dorado, Panamá 1; tel. 230-0482; fax 230-0805; monthly; organ of the Sindicato de Industriales de Panamá; Pres. GASPAR GARCÍA DE PAREDES.
Instituto Nacional de Estadística y Censo: Avda Balboa y Federico Boyd, Apdo 0816-01521, Panamá 5; tel. 510-4800; fax 510-4801; e-mail cie_dec@contraloria.gob.pa; internet www.contraloria.gob.pa/inec; f. 1941; publ. by la Contraloría General de la República; statistical survey in series according to subjects; Controller-Gen. GIOCONDA TORRES DE BIANCHINI; Dir of Statistics and Census DANIS P. CEDEÑO H.
Mi Diario, La Voz de Panamá: Avda 12 de Octubre y Calle C, Hato Pintado, Pueblo Nuevo, Apdo 0819-05620, Panamá; tel. 222-9000; fax 222-9090; e-mail midiario@midiario.com; internet www.midiario.com; f. 2003 by La Prensa (q.v.); Dir LORENZO ABREGO.
Revista SIETE: Vía Ricardo J. Alfaro, al lado de la USMA, Apdo B-4, Panamá 9A; tel. 230-7777; fax 230-1033; e-mail revista.siete@epasa.com; internet www.epasa.com/siete; weekly; Editor NAYLA G. MONTENEGRO.

PRESS ASSOCIATION
Sindicato de Periodistas de Panamá: Avda Gorgas 287, Panamá; tel. 214-0163; fax 214-0164; e-mail sindiperpana@yahoo.com; f. 1949; Sec.-Gen. FILEMÓN MEDINA RAMOS.

Publishers

Editora Géminis, SA: Edif. Don Tomás, Planta Baja, Calle 7, Vista Hermosa, Apdo 0819-04188, El Dorado, Panamá; tel. 229-2972; fax 229-1010; e-mail info@editorageminis.com; internet www

PANAMA

.editorageminis.com; f. 1985; dictionaries, general fiction, school texts; Dir-Gen. RAÚL ESQUIVEL.

Editora Panamá América, SA (EPASA): Avda Ricardo J. Alfaro, al lado de la USMA, Apdo 0834-02787, Panamá R; tel. 230-7777; fax 230-7773; e-mail gerente.general@epasa.com; internet www.epasa .com; Pres. RICARDO CHANIS CORREA; Gen. Man. LUIS STANZIOLA S.

Editora Sibauste, SA: Panamá; tel. 229-4577; fax 229-4582; e-mail esibauste@cwpanama.net; Editor DENIS DE SIBAUSTE.

Exedra Books: esq. de Vía España y Vía Brasil, diagonal a Galerias Obarrio, Apdo 0831-00125, Paitilla, Panamá; tel. 264-4252; fax 264-4266; e-mail info@exedrabooks.com; internet www.exedrabooks.com; general fiction and non-fiction; Dir-Gen. SHEILA DE TERÁN.

Focus Publications: Calle 2a 742, Perejil, Apdo 0819-06908, El Dorado, Panamá; tel. 225-6638; fax 225-0466; e-mail focusint@sinfo .net; internet www.focuspublicationsint.com; f. 1970; guides, trade directories, yearbooks and maps; Pres. KENNETH J. JONES.

Piggy Press, SA: Apdo 0413-00110, Boquete, Chiriquí; tel. 720-1072; e-mail info@piggypress.com; internet www.piggypress.com; f. 2001; multilingual children's literarture; Pres. PAT ALVARADO.

Ruth Casa Editorial: Edif. Los Cristales, Of. 6, Calle 38 y Avda Cuba, Apdo 2235, Zona 9A, Panamá; e-mail ruthcasaeditorial@yahoo .com; internet www.ruthcasaeditorial.org; Pres. FRANÇOIS HOUTART.

Serapis Bey Editores, SA: Parque Lefevre, Calle W-2, Casa 46-B-21, Apdo 0834-01726, Panamá; tel. 302-0213; fax 302-0214; e-mail jorgecarrizo@serapisbey.com; internet www.serapisbey.com; f. 1989; spiritual literature; Gen. Man. JORGE A. CARRIZO.

SIJUSA (Sistemas Juridicos, SA): Edif. Bank Boston, 2°, Vía España y Calle Elvira Méndez, Panamá; tel. 223-2764; fax 223-2766; e-mail servicioalcliente@sijusa.com; internet www.sijusa.com; f. 1989; law and politics; Dir-Gen. JOSÉ ALEJANDRO ESPINO.

Susaeta Ediciones Panamá, SA: Apdo. 0819-08750, Panamá; tel. 220-0833; fax 220-4561; e-mail susaeta@susaetapanama.com; internet www.susaetapanama.net; f. 1982; children's literature; includes the imprints Ediesco, Nacho and Susaeta; Dir-Gen. MIRNA DE DÍAZ.

GOVERNMENT PUBLISHING HOUSE

Editorial Mariano Arosemena: Instituto Nacional de Cultura, Apdo 662, Panamá 1; tel. 501-4000; fax 211-4016; e-mail secretariageneral@inac.gob.pa; internet www.inac.gob.pa; f. 1974; division of National Institute of Culture; literature, history, social sciences, archaeology; Dir-Gen. MARIA EUGENIA HERRERA DE VICTORIA.

ASSOCIATION

Cámara Panameña del Libro: Edif. Tula, Of. 6C, Vía España, entrada de Vía Argentina, arriba del Blockbuster, Apdo 0823-04289, Panamá; tel. 390-4738; fax 390-4739; e-mail info@capali.com.pa; internet www.capali.com.pa; f. 1997; organizes international book fairs; 28 active mems, 3 honorary mems, 2 associate mems; Pres. RENÉE AVILA; Sec. MIRNA DE DÍAZ.

Broadcasting and Communications

REGULATORY AUTHORITY

Autoridad Nacional de los Servicios Públicos: Vía España, Edif. Office Park, Apdo 0816-01235, Panamá 5; tel. 508-4500; fax 508-4600; e-mail adminweb@asep.gob.pa; internet www.asep.gob.pa; f. 1996 as Ente Regulador de los Servicios Públicos; name changed as above in 2006; state regulator with responsibility for television, radio, telecommunications, water and electricity; Administrator-Gen. ZELMAR RODRÍGUEZ CRESPO.

TELECOMMUNICATIONS

Dirección Nacional de Medios de Comunicación Social: Avda Cuba y Calle 29, Apdo 1628, Panamá 1; tel. 512-2000; fax 262-9495.

Major Service Providers

Digicel: Edif. Digicel, Vía Transístimica, Panamá; tel. 306-0600; fax 300-0469; e-mail servicioalcliente.pa@digicelgroup.com; internet www.digicelpanama.com; f. 2001; Exec. Pres. and CEO EDUARDO RYAN; 11m. subscribers.

Cable & Wireless Panama: Box 0834-00659, Panamá; e-mail cwp@cwpanama.com; internet www.cwpanama.com.pa; 49% govt-owned, 49% owned by Cable & Wireless; major telecommunications provider; Pres. JORGE NICOLAU.

Movistar: Edif. Magna, Area Bancaria, Calle 51 Este y Manuel M. Icaza, Panamá; tel. 265-0955; internet www.movistar.com.pa; f. 1996 as BellSouth Panamá, SA; acquired by Telefónica Móviles, SA (Spain) in Oct. 2004; name changed as above in April 2005; mobile telephone services; Gen. Man. ISAAC SUÁREZ.

Optynex Telecom, SA: Edif. Plaza 2000, 9°, Calle 50 y 53, Urb. Marbella, Apdo 0832-2650, Panamá; tel. 380-0000; fax 380-0099; e-mail info@optynex.com; internet www.optynex.com; f. 2002; Gen. Man. ERIC MEYER.

BROADCASTING

Radio

In 2004 there were 109 AM (Medium Wave) and 181 FM stations registered in Panama. Most stations are commercial.

La Mega 98.3 FM: Casa 35, Calle 50 y 77 San Francisco, Panamá; tel. 270-3242; fax 226-1021; e-mail ventas@lamegapanama.com; internet www.lamegapanama.com; f. 2000.

Omega Stereo: Calle G, El Cangrejo 3, Panamá; e-mail omegaste@omegastereo.com; internet www.omegastereo.com; f. 1981; Pres. GUILLERMO ANTONIO ADAMES.

RPC Radio: Avda 12 de Octubre, Panamá; tel. 390-6700; e-mail mtalessandria@medcom.com.pa; internet www.rpcradio.com; f. 1949; broadcasts news, sports and commentary; Man. MARÍA TERESA ALESSANDRÍA.

SuperQ: Edif. Dominó, 1°, Of. 9, Via España, Apdo 0816-03034, Panamá; tel. 263-5298; fax 263-0362; e-mail info@superqpanama .com; internet www.superqpanama.net; f. 1984; Pres. G. ARIS DE ICAZA.

WAO 97.5: Edif. Plaza 50, 2°, Calle 50 y Vía Brasil, Panamá; tel. 223-8348; fax 223-8351; e-mail info@wao975.fm; internet www.wao975 .fm; Gen. Man. ROGELIO CAMPOS.

Television

In 2005 there were 133 authorized television channels broadcasting in Panama.

Fundación para la Educación en la Televisión—FETV (Canal 5): Vía Ricardo J. Alfaro, Apdo 6-7295, El Dorado, Panamá; tel. 230-8000; fax 230-1955; e-mail comentarios@fetv.org; internet www.fetv .org; f. 1992; Pres. JOSÉ DIMAS CEDEÑO DELGADO; Dir MANUEL SANTIAGO BLANQUER I PLANELLS; Gen. Man. TERESA WONG DE FONG.

Medcom: Avda 12 de Octubre, Hato Pintado, Apdo 0827-00116, Panamá 8; tel. 390-6700; fax 390-6895; e-mail murrutia@medcom .com.pa; internet www.rpctv.com; f. 1998 by merger of RPC Televisión (Canal 4) and Telemetro (Canal 13); commercial; also owns Cable Onda 90 and RPC Radio; Pres. FERNANDO ELETA; CEO NICOLÁS GONZÁLEZ-REVILLA.

Sistema Estatal de Radio y Televisión (Canal 11): Curundu, diagonal al Ministerio de Obras Públicas, Apdo 0843-0256, Panamá; tel. 507-1500; e-mail aportal@sertv.gob.pa; internet www.sertv.gob .pa; f. 1978 as Radio y Televisión Educativa; was restructured and assumed present name in 2005; educational and cultural; Dir-Gen. MARISÍN LUZCANDO.

Televisora Nacional—TVN (Canal 2): Edif. TVN-TV–MAX, Avda Ricardo J. Alfaro, Apdo 0819-07129, Panamá; tel. 294-6400; fax 236-2987; e-mail tvn@tvn-2.com; internet www.tvn-2.com; f. 1962; Dir JAIME ALBERTO ARIAS.

Broadcasting Association

Asociación Panameña de Radiodifusión: Apdo 7387, Estafeta de Paitilla, Panamá; tel. 263-5252; fax 226-4396; Pres. FERNANDO CORREA.

Finance

(cap. = capital; res = reserves; dep. = deposits; m. = million; br.(s) = branch(es); amounts in balboas, unless otherwise stated)

BANKING

Superintendencia de Bancos (Banking Superintendency): Torre HSBC, 18°, Avda Samuel Lewis, Apdo 0832-2397, Panamá 1; tel. 506-7800; fax 506-7706; e-mail superbancos@superbancos.gob.pa; internet www.superbancos.gob.pa; f. 1970 as Comisión Bancaria Nacional (National Banking Commission); licenses and controls banking activities within and from Panamanian territory; Comisión Bancaria Nacional superseded by Superintendencia de Bancos in June 1998 with enhanced powers to supervise banking activity; Supt ALBERTO DIAMOND.

National Bank

Banco Nacional de Panamá: Casa Matriz, Vía España, Apdo 5220, Panamá 5; tel. 505-2000; fax 269-0091; e-mail sugerencia@banconal .com.pa; internet www.banconal.com.pa; f. 1904; govt-owned; cap. 500.0m., res −2.9m., dep. 4,911.0m. (Dec. 2008); Pres. CARLOS R.

HENRÍQUEZ LÓPEZ; Gen. Man. DARIO ERNESTO BERBEY DE LA ROSA; 53 brs.

Savings Bank

Caja de Ahorros: Vía España y Calle Thays de Pons, Apdo 1740, Panamá 1; tel. 205-1000; fax 269-3674; e-mail atencionalcliente@cajadeahorros.com.pa; internet www.cajadeahorros.com.pa; f. 1934; govt-owned; cap. 150.7m., res 47.9m., dep. 170.9m. (Dec. 2006); Pres. RICCARDO FRANCOLINI AROSEMENA; Gen. Man. JAYSON E. PASTOR; 37 brs.

Domestic Private Banks

Banco Continental de Panamá, SA: Calle 50 y Avda Aquilino de la Guardia, Apdo 135, Panamá 9A; tel. 215-7000; fax 215-7134; e-mail bcp@bcocontinental.com; internet www.bbvabancocontinental.com; f. 1972; merged with Banco Internacional de Panamá in 2002; took over Banco Atlántico (Panamá), SA in 2006; cap. 126.7m., res 29.0m., dep. 3,079.8m. (Dec. 2006); Chair. PEDRO BRESCIA CAFFERATA; Gen. Man. EDUARDO TORRES-LLOSA VILLACORTA; 36 brs.

Banco Cuscatlán de Panamá: Edif. Panabank, Casa Matriz, Calle 50, Apdo 1828, Panamá 1; tel. 208-8300; fax 269-1537; e-mail gerencia@panabank.com; internet www.bancocuscatlan.com/panama; f. 1983; acquired Banco Panamericano (Panabank) in 2004; acquired by Citi in 2007; Chair. MAURICIO SAMAYOA; Gen. Man. GUIDO J. MARTINELLI, Jr.

Banco General, SA: Calle Aquilino de la Guardia, Apdo 0816-00843, Panamá 5; tel. 227-3200; fax 265-0210; e-mail info@bgeneral.com; internet www.bgeneral.com; f. 1955; purchased Banco Comercial de Panamá (BANCOMER) in 2000; cap. 500.0m., res 62.7m., dep. 5,719.9m. (Dec. 2008); Chair. and CEO FEDERICO HUMBERT; Exec. Vice-Pres. and Gen. Man. RAÚL ALEMÁN Z.; 36 brs.

Banco Panameño de la Vivienda (BANVIVIENDA): Edif. Grupo Mundial, Avda Balboa, Calle 41 E, Bella Vista, Apdo 0816-03366, Panamá 5; tel. 300-4700; fax 300-1133; e-mail bpvger@pty.com; internet www.banvivienda.com; f. 1981; cap. 12.4m., dep. 128.0m., total assets 150.3m. (2004); Pres. FERNANDO LEWIS NAVARRO; Gen. Man. JUAN RICARDO DE DIANOUS; 3 brs.

Banco Pichincha Panamá: Edif. PH Parque Urraca, entre Avda Federico Boyd y Avda Balboa, Panamá; tel. 297-4500; fax 264-6129; e-mail banco@pichinchapanama.com; internet wwwp2.pichinchapanama.com; f. 2006; Gen. Man. FRANCISCO JAVIER LEJARRAGA LÓPEZ DE ARROYABE.

Banco Trasatlántico, SA: Calle 50 y 55 Este, Apdo 0823-00207, Panamá; tel. 366-7600; fax 269-44748; internet www.bancotrasatlantico.com; f. 1979 as Banco Comercial Trasatlántico, current name adopted 1981; Pres. RAÚL DE MENA; Gen. Man. ROBERTO DÍAZ FÁBREGA; 2 brs.

Banco Universal: Edif. Miguel A. Brenes, Calle B Norte y Avda 1ra, Apdo 0426-00564, David, Chiriquí; tel. 775-4394; fax 775-2308; e-mail cosorio@bancouniversal.com; internet www.bancouniversal.com; f. 1970 as Asociación Chiricana de Ahorros y Préstamos para la Vivienda; present name adopted 1994; Pres. JOSÉ ISAAC VIRZI LÓPEZ; Gen. Man. CARLOS RAÚL BARRIOS ICAZA.

Global Bank Corporation: Torre Global Bank, Calle 50, Apdo 0831-01843, Paitilla, Panamá; tel. 206-2000; fax 263-3518; e-mail global@pan.gbm.net; internet www.globalbank.com.pa; f. 1994; Pres. LAWRENCE MADURO; Gen. Man. JORGE VALLARINO S.

Multibank: Edif. Prosperidad, planta baja, Vía España 127, Apdo 8210, Panamá 7; tel. 294-3500; fax 264-4014; e-mail banco@grupomulticredit.com; internet www.multibank.com.pa; f. 1990 as Multi Credit Bank; current name adopted 2008; total assets 536.1m. (Dec. 2005); Pres. ALBERTO S. BTESH; Gen. Man. RAFAEL SÁNCHEZ GARRÓS.

Towerbank International Inc: Edif. Tower Plaza, Calle 50 y Beatriz M. de Cabal, Apdo 0819-04318, Panamá; tel. 269-6900; fax 269-6800; e-mail towerbank@towerbank.com; internet www.towerbank.com; f. 1971; cap. 68.0m., res –3.1m., dep. 498.2m. (Dec. 2008); Pres. FRED KARDONSKI; Gen. Man. JOSÉ CAMPA.

Foreign Banks

Principal Foreign Banks with General Licence

BAC International Bank (Panamá), Inc (USA): Edif. BAC Credomatic, Calle Aquilino de la Guardia, Apdo 6-3654, Panamá; tel. 213-0822; fax 269-3879; e-mail infobac@pa.bac.net; internet www.bac.net/panama; f. 1995; Chair. CARLOS PELLAS; Gen. Man. RODOLFO TABASH.

Balboa Bank & Trust Corpn: Torre Generali, 19°, Avda Samuel Lewis y Calle 54, Urb. Obarrio, Panamá; tel. 208-7300; fax 263-4165; e-mail customerservice@balboabanktrust.com; internet www.balboabanktrust.com; f. 2003 as Stanford Bank (Panamá), SA; taken over by the Superintendencia de Bancos de Panamá in 2009; renamed in April 2010; Pres. GEORGE FRANCIS NOVEY DE LA GUARDIA.

BANCAFE (Panamá), SA (Colombia): Avda Manuel María Icaza y Calle 52E, No 18, Apdo 0834-00384, Panamá 9A; tel. 264-6066; fax 263-6115; e-mail bancafe@bancafe-pa.com; internet www.bancafe-pa.com; f. 1966 as Banco Cafetero; current name adopted in 1995; Pres. JORGE CASTELLANOS RUEDA; Gen. Man. JAIME DE GAMBOA GAMBOA; 2 brs.

Banco Aliado, SA: Calle 50 y 56, Urb. Obarrio, 0831-02109 Paitilla, Panamá; tel. 302-1555; fax 302-1556; e-mail bkaliado@bancoaliado.com; internet www.bancoaliado.com; f. 1992; Pres. MOISÉS CHREIM; Gen. Man. ALEXIS A. ARJONA.

Banco Bilbao Vizcaya Argentaria (Panama), SA (Spain): Torre BBVA, Avda Balboa, Calles 42 y 43, Apdo 8673, Panamá 5; tel. 227-0973; fax 227-3663; e-mail fperezp@bbvapanama.com; internet www.bbvapanama.com; f. 1982; cap. 28.7m., res 56.7m., dep. 1,383.0m. (Dec. 2008); Chair. MANUEL ZUBIRÍA PASTOR; Gen. Man. FÉLIX PÉREZ PARRA; 15 brs.

Banco Delta, SA (BMF): Edif. Torre Delta, planta baja, Vía España 122 y Calle Elvira Méndez, Apdo 0816-07831, Panamá; tel. 340-0000; fax 340-0019; e-mail mguerra@bandelta.com; internet www.bandelta.com; f. 2006; Pres. ARTURO MÜLLER; Gen. Man. ARIEL ANTONIO SANMARTÍN MÉNDEZ.

Banco Internacional de Costa Rica, SA: Casa Matriz, Calle Manuel M. Icaza 25, Apdo 0816-07810, Panamá 1; tel. 208-9500; fax 208-9581; e-mail informacion@bicaspan.net; internet www.bicsa.com; f. 1976; Gen. Man. FEDERICO CARRILLO ZURCHER.

Banco Latinoamericano de Comercio Exterior SA (BLADEX) (Multinational): Casa Matriz, Calles 50 y Aquilino de la Guardia, Apdo 0819-08730, El Dorado, Panamá; tel. 210-8500; fax 269-6333; e-mail infobla@blx.com; internet www.blx.com; f. 1979 as Banco Latinoamericano de Exportaciones; name changed as above in 2009; groups together 254 Latin American commercial and central banks, 22 international banks and some 3,000 New York Stock Exchange shareholders; cap. US $415.6m., res $–109.7m., dep. $2,396.1m. (Dec. 2008); CEO JAIME RIVERA; Chair. GONZALO MENÉNDEZ DUQUE.

Citibank Panamá (USA): Edif. Banco Cuscatlán, Calle Aquilino de la Guardia, Apdo 555, Panamá 9A; tel. 210-5900; fax 210-5901; internet www.citibank.com.pa; f. 1904; Gen. Man. FRANCISCO CONTO; 4 brs.

Credicorp Bank, SA: Edif. Plaza Credicorp Bank, Nicanor de Obarrio, Calle 50, Apdo 833-0125, Panamá; tel. 210-1111; fax 210-0100; internet www.credicorpbank.com; f. 1992; cap. 34.1m., res –0.2m., dep. 659.5m. (Dec. 2008); Pres. RAYMOND HARARI; Gen. Man. MAX J. HARARI.

Helm Bank (Panama), SA: Edif. World Trade Center, 19°, Calle 53, Urb. Marbella, Apdo 0819-07070, Panamá; tel. 265-2820; fax 214-9715; e-mail servicioalcliente@helmpanama.com; internet www.helmpanama.com; f. as Banco de Crédito (Panama) SA, renamed in 2002 as Banco de Crédito Helm Financial Sevices (Panama), and as above in 2009; owned by Helm Bank SA (Colombia); cap. 25.0m., res 1.5m., dep. 386.8m. (Dec. 2009); Gen. Man. CARLOS HUMBERTO ROJAS M.

HSBC Bank (Panama), SA: Plaza HSBC, Calle Aquilino de La Guardia, Urb. Marbella, Panamá; tel. 263-5855; fax 263-6009; e-mail panama_investrel@hsbc.com.pa; internet www.hsbc.com.pa; cap. US $1,293.7m., dep. $11,137.7m. (Dec. 2009); acquired the Panama operations of Chase Manhattan Bank in 2000 and Primer Banco del Istmo (Banistmo) in 2006; CEO ERNESTO FERNANDES; 62 brs.

Principal Foreign Banks with International Licence

Austrobank Overseas (Panamá), SA: Torre Morgan y Morgan, planta baja, Calle 53, Este Marbella, Apdo 0819-07030, El Dorado, Panamá 6; tel. 223-5105; fax 264-6918; e-mail gerencia@austrobank.com; internet www.austrobank.com; f. 1995; Gen. Man. GUILLERMO WILLIS.

Banco Agrícola (Panamá), SA: Edif. Global Bank, 17°, Local E y F, Calle 50, Apdo 6-2637, Panamá; tel. 263-5762; fax 263-5626; e-mail info@bancoagricola.com; internet www.bancoagricolapanama.com; f. 2002; Exec. Pres. JOSÉ ROBERTO ORELLANA MILLA.

Banco de la Nación Argentina: Edif. World Trade Center 501, Calle 53, Urb. Marbella, Panamá; tel. 269-4666; fax 269-6719; e-mail bnapanama@bna.com.pa; internet www.bna.com.ar; f. 1977; Pres. JUAN CARLOS FABREGA; Gen. Man. RUBÉN DARÍO NOCERA.

Banco de Occidente (Panama), SA: Edif. American International, Calle 50 y Aquilino de la Guardia, Apdo 6-7430, Panamá; tel. 263-8144; fax 269-3261; internet www.bancoccidente.com.pa; f. 1982; cap. US $8.0m., res $5.9m., dep. $345.8m. (Dec. 2007); Pres. EFRAÍN OTERO ALVAREZ; Gen. Man. OSCAR LUNA GORDILLO.

Banco del Pacífico (Panama), SA: Calle Aquilino de la Guardia y Calle 52, esq. Edif. Banco del Pacifico, Apdo 0819-07070, El Dorado, Panamá; tel. 263-5833; fax 263-7481; e-mail bpacificopanama@pacifico.fin.ec; internet www.bancodelpacifico.com.pa; f. 1980; Pres. and Gen. Man. ANA ESCOBAR.

PANAMA

Bancolombia (Panama), SA: Edif. Bancolombia, Plaza Marbella, Calle Aquilino de la Guardia y Calle 47, Apdo 0816-03320, Panamá; tel. 263-6955; fax 269-1138; e-mail bancolombiapanama@allus.com.co; internet www.bancolombiapanama.com; f. 1973; current name adopted in 1999; cap. US $14.0m., res $4.3m., dep. $5,622.5m. (Dec. 2007); Gen. Man. María Isabel Uribe Ramírez.

FPB International Bank Inc: Ofs A y C, 16°, Calle 50 y Aquilino de la Guardia, Panamá; tel. 210-6600; fax 263-0919; f. 2005; Gen. Man. José Aparecido Paulucci.

GNB Sudameris Bank, SA: Area Bancaria, Calle Manuel María Icaza 19, Panamá; tel. 206-6900; fax 206-6901; internet www.gnbsudameris.com; f. 1970; Gen. Man. Angelmiro Castillo H.

Popular Bank Ltd Inc: Edif. Torre Banco General, Calle 47E y Avda Aquilini de la Guardia, Marbella, Apdo 0816-00265, Panamá; tel. 269-4166; fax 269-1309; e-mail contactenos@popularbank.com.pa; internet www.popularbank.com.pa; f. 1983 as Banco Popular Dominicano (Panama), SA; current name adopted in 2003; cap. 50.4m., res 0.1m., dep. 487.9m. (Dec. 2008); Pres. Rafael A. Rodríguez; Gen. Man. Gianni Versari.

Banking Association

Asociación Bancaria de Panamá (ABP): Torre Hong Kong Bank, 15°, Avda Samuel Lewis, Apdo 4554, Panamá 5; tel. 263-7044; fax 223-5480; e-mail abp@orbi.net; internet www.asociacionbancaria.com; f. 1962; 79 mems; Pres. Moisés D. Cohen M.; Exec. Vice-Pres. and Gen. Man. Alberto Conde.

STOCK EXCHANGE

Bolsa de Valores de Panamá: Edif. Vallarino, planta baja, Calles Elvira Méndez y 52, Apdo 87-0878, Panamá; tel. 269-1966; fax 269-2457; e-mail bvp@pty.com; internet www.panabolsa.com; f. 1960; Pres. Ricardo Arango; Gen. Man. Roberto Brenes Pérez.

INSURANCE

Arca Internacional de Reaseguros, SA: Edif. Bolsa de Valores, 1°, Avda Federico Boyd, Frente al Restaurante Rinos, Panamá; tel. 300-2858; fax 300-2859; f. 1996; Gen. Man. Carlos G. De La Lastra.

Aseguradora Ancón, SA: Avda Samuel Lewis y Calle 54, Urb. Obarrio, Panamá; tel. 210-8700; fax 210-8790; e-mail info@aseguranacon.com; internet www.aseguranacon.com; f. 1992; Pres. Tobias Carrero Nacar; Gen. Man. Carlos G. Chamorro.

Aseguradora Mundial, SA: Edif. Aseguradora Mundial, Avda Balboa y Calle 41, Apdo 8911, Panamá 5; tel. 207-6600; fax 207-8787; e-mail info@mundial.com; internet www.amundial.com; f. 1937; general; Pres. Orlando Edmundo Sánchez Áviles.

ASSA Cía de Seguros, SA: Edif. ASSA, Avda Nicanor de Obarrio (Calle 50), Apdo 0816-01622, Panamá 5; tel. 300-2772; fax 300-2729; e-mail assamercadeo@assanet.com; internet www.assanet.com; f. 1973; Pres. Stanley Motta.

Assicurazioni Generali, Spa: Torre Generali, Avda Samuel Lewis y Calle 54, Urb. Obarrio, Apdo 0816-02206, 507 Panamá; tel. 206-9100; fax 206-9101; e-mail mercadeo@generali.com.pa; internet www.generali.com.pa; f. 1977; Gen. Man. Gabriel R. de Obarrio, III.

Cía Interoceánica de Seguros, SA: Plaza Margella, Frente Banco HSBC, Calle Alquilino de la Guardia, Panamá; tel. 205-0700; fax 264-7668; e-mail info@interoceanica.com; internet www.interoceanica.com; f. 1978; Gen. Man. Salvador Morales Baca.

Empresa General de Seguros, SA: Edif. Bancomer, Enre Piso, Calles 50 y 53, Panamá; tel. 269-1896; fax 264-1107; internet www.asecomer.com; f. 1987; Gen. Man. Luis E. Bandera.

HSBC Seguros (Panamá), SA (CONASE): Edif. HSBC, No 62, Calle 50, Apdo 5303, Panamá 5; tel. 205-0300; fax 223-1146; e-mail ines.m.arosemena@hsbc.com.pa; f. 1957 as Cía Nacional de Seguros, SA; current name adopted July 2007; Pres. Joseph Salterio.

Internacional de Seguros, SA: Avda Cuba y Calles 35 y 36, Apdo 1036, Panamá 1; tel. 227-4000; e-mail conase@conase.net; internet www.iseguros.com; f. 1910; Pres. Richard A. Ford.

Mitsui Sumitomo Insurance Co Ltd: Of. 701, 7°, Plaza Credicorp Bank Panamá, Panamá; tel. 210-0133; fax 210-0122; internet www.msilm.com; f. 1979; Gen. Man. Ta Kashi Morimoto.

Provincial Re Panamá, SA: Edif. Alexandra, Of. 3A, Avda Octavio de Icaza, Panamá; tel. 260-5078; fax 260-5055; f. 1984; Gen. Man. Frank Castagnet.

QBE del Istmo Cía de Reaseguros, Inc: Costa del Este, Avda Paseo del Mar y Calle Vista del Pacífico, Apdo 51, Panamá; tel. 301-0610; fax 223-0479; internet www.istmore.com; f. 1979; Pres. and CEO Ramón E. Fernández.

La Seguridad de Panamá, Cía de Seguros, SA: Edif. American International, Calle 50, esq. Aquilino de la Guardia, Apdo 5306, Panamá 5; tel. 263-6700; f. 1986; Gen. Man. Mariela Osorio.

Trade and Industry

Colón Free Zone (CFZ): Avda Roosevelt, Apdo 1118, Colón; tel. 445-1033; fax 445-2165; e-mail zonalibre@zolicol.org; internet www.zonalibredecolon.com.pa; f. 1948 to manufacture, import, handle and re-export all types of merchandise; some 1,800 companies were established in 2005; well-known international banks operate in the CFZ, where there are also customs, postal and telegraph services; the main exporters to the CFZ are Japan, the USA, Hong Kong, Taiwan, the Republic of Korea, Colombia, France, Italy and the United Kingdom; the main importers from the CFZ are Brazil, Venezuela, Mexico, Ecuador, the Netherlands Dependencies, Bolivia, the USA, Chile, Argentina and Colombia; the total area of the CFZ was 450 ha in 2011; Gen. Man. Leopoldo Benedetti.

GOVERNMENT AGENCIES

Autoridad de la Micro, Pequeña y Mediana Empresa: Calle Maritza Alabarca, Edif. 1005 y 1010, Clayton, Panamá; tel. 500-5602; e-mail atencionalcliente@ampyme.gob.pa; internet www.ampyme.gob.pa; f. 2000; promotes the devt of micro-, small and medium enterprises; Dir-Gen. Giselle Burillo Sáiz.

CHAMBERS OF COMMERCE

American Chamber of Commerce and Industry of Panama: POB 0843-00152, Panamá; tel. 301-3881; fax 301-3882; e-mail amcham@panamcham.com; internet www.panamcham.com; Pres. Donald N. Elder; Exec. Dir David Hunt.

Cámara de Comercio, Industrias y Agricultura de Panamá: Avda Cuba y Ecuador 33A, Apdo 74, Panamá 1; tel. 207-3440; fax 207-3422; e-mail infocciap@cciap.com; internet www.panacamara.com; f. 1915; Pres. Fernando Arango; Exec. Dir Rafael Zuñiga Brid; 1,300 mems.

Cámara Oficial Española de Comercio: Avda Balboa, Edif. Banco BBVA, Torre Menor, 7°, Apdo 1857, Panamá 1; tel. 225-1487; fax 225-6608; e-mail caespan@cwpanama.net; internet www.caespan.com.pa; Pres. Noel Riande; Exec. Dir María Jesús Alonso Ros.

INDUSTRIAL AND TRADE ASSOCIATIONS

Asociación Panameña de Exportadores (APEX): Edif. Ricardo Galindo Quelquejeu, Avda Ricardo J. Alfaro, Urb. Sara Sotillo, Panamá; tel. 230-0169; e-mail apex@cableonda.net; internet www.apexpanama.org; f. 1971; export asscn; Pres. Manuel Fernández; Sec. Jaime Ortiz.

Cámara Panameña de la Construcción: Calle Aquilino de la Guardia y Calle 52, Área Bancaria, diagonal al Hotel Ejecutivo, Apdo 0816-02350, Panamá 5; tel. 265-2500; fax 265-2571; e-mail informacion@capac.org; internet www.capac.org; represents interests of construction sector; Pres. Jaime A. Jované C.; Dir-Gen. Eduardo Rodríguez.

Corporación Azucarera La Victoria: Vía Transístmica, San Miguelito; tel. 229-4794; state sugar corpn; scheduled for transfer to private ownership; Dir Prof. Alejandro Vernaza.

Corporación para el Desarrollo Integral del Bayano: Avda Balboa, al lado de la estación del tren, Estafeta El Dorado, Panamá 2; tel. 232-6160; f. 1978; state agriculture, forestry and cattle-breeding corpn.

Dirección General de Industrias: Edif. Plaza Edison, 3°, Apdo 9658, Panamá 4; tel. 360-0720; govt body that undertakes feasibility studies, analyses and promotion; Dir-Gen. Lucía Fuentes de Ferguson; Nat. Dir of Business Devt Francisco de la Barrera.

Sindicato de Industriales de Panamá: Vía Ricardo J. Alfaro, Entrada Urb. Sara Sotillo, Apdo 6-4798, Estafeta El Dorado, Panamá; tel. 230-0169; fax 230-0805; e-mail sip@cableonda.net; internet www.industriales.org; f. 1945; represents and promotes activities of industrial sector; Pres. Juan F. Kiener; Sec.-Gen. Máximo Gallardo.

EMPLOYERS' ORGANIZATIONS

Asociación Panameña de Ejecutivos de Empresas (APEDE): Avda Justo Arosemena, Calle 31, frente a la Piscina Adán Gordón, Apdo 0816-06785, Panamá; tel. 204-1500; fax 204-1510; e-mail apede@apede.org; internet www.apede.org; Pres. Rubén M. Castillo Gill; Exec. Dir Jackeline Aizpurúa.

Consejo Nacional de la Empresa Privada (CONEP): Avda Morgan, Balboa, Ancón, Casa 302A-B, Zona 1, Apdo 0816-07197, Panamá 1; tel. 211-2672; fax 211-2694; e-mail conep1@cwpanama.net; internet www.conep.org.pa; Pres. Antonio Fletcher; Exec. Dir Alfredo Burgos.

PANAMA

UTILITIES

Regulatory Authority

Autoridad Nacional de los Servicios Públicos: see Broadcasting and Communications—Regulatory Authority.

Electricity

The partial divestment of generation and distribution services was completed in December 1998. The restructuring of the state-owned Instituto de Recursos Hidráulicos y Electrificación (IRHE) resulted in the sale of four generation and three distribution companies. However, transmission operations remained under state control.

AES Panama: Torre Banco Continental, 25°, Calle 50 y Aquilino de la Guardia, CP 0816-01990, Panamá; tel. 206-2600; fax 206-2645; e-mail aespanama@aes.com; internet www.aespanama.com; f. 1998 upon acquisition by AES Corpn of 49% interest in Empresa de Generación Electrica Bayano and Empresa de Generación Electrica Chiriquí; operates three hydroelectric facilities in Bayano (248 MW), Estí (120 MW) and Chiriquí (90 MW) and one 43-MW thermal facility; Pres. JAIME TUPPER; Gen. Man. JAVIER GIORGIO.

Elektra Noreste, SA (ENSA): Costa del Este, Business Park-Torre Oeste, 3°, Panamá; tel. 340-4600; internet www.ensa.com.pa; electricity distribution; Gen. Man. JAVIER PARIENTE.

Empresa de Transmisión Eléctrica, SA (ETESA): Plaza Sun Tower, 3°, Avda Ricardo J. Alfaro, El Dorado, Panamá; tel. 501-3800; fax 501-3506; e-mail gerinfo@etesa.com.pa; internet www.etesa.com.pa; f. 1998; state-owned transmission co; Pres. FRANK DE LIMA; Gen. Man. RENÉ E. RIVERA.

Unión FENOSA—EDEMET EDECHI: Albrook, Panamá; internet www.ufpanama.com; f. 1998 by acquisition from IRHE of Empresa de Distribución Eléctrica Metro Oeste (EDEMET) and Empresa de Distribución Eléctrica Chiriquí (EDECHI) by Unión FENOSA, Spain; Exec. Pres. RICARDO BARRANCO.

Water

Instituto de Acueductos y Alcantarillados Nacionales (IDAAN) (National Waterworks and Sewage Systems Institute): Apdo 5234, Panamá; tel. 523-8567; e-mail relaciones.publicas@idaan.gob.pa; internet www.idaan.gob.pa; Pres. JOSÉ ANTONIO DÍAZ; Exec. Dir MANUEL GONZÁLEZ RUÍZ.

TRADE UNIONS

Central General Autónoma de Trabajadores de Panamá (CGTP): Edif. CGTP, Calle 3a Perejil, detrás del Colegio Javier, Panamá; tel. 269-9741; fax 223-5287; e-mail cgtpan@cwpanama.net; internet www.cgtp.org.pa; fmrly Central Istmeña de Trabajadores; Sec.-Gen. MARIANO E. MENA.

Confederación Nacional de Unidad Sindical Independiente (CONUSI): 0421B Calle Venado, Ancón, Apdo 830344, Zona 3, Panamá; tel. 212-3865; fax 212-2565; e-mail conusipanama@hotmail.com; Sec.-Gen. GENARO LÓPEZ.

Confederación de Trabajadores de la República de Panamá (CTRP) (Confederation of Workers of the Republic of Panama): Calle 31, entre Avdas México y Justo Arosemena 3-50, Apdo 0816-03647, Panamá 5; tel. 225-0293; fax 225-0259; e-mail ctrp@cableonda.net; f. 1956; admitted to ITUC/ORIT; Sec.-Gen. GUILLERMO PUGA; 62,000 mems from 13 affiliated groups.

Consejo Nacional de Trabajadores Organizados (CONATO) (National Council of Organized Labour): Edif. 777, 2°, Balboa-Ancón, Panamá; tel. and fax 228-0224; e-mail conato@cwpanama.net; Co-ordinator MIGUEL EDWARDS; 150,000 mems.

Convergencia Sindical: Casa 2490, Balboa-Ancón, Calle Bomparte Wise, Apdo 0815-00863, Panamá 4; tel. and fax 314-1615; e-mail conversind@cwpanama.net; f. 1995; Sec.-Gen. VÍCTOR MANUEL TORRES.

Federación Nacional de Servidores Públicos (FENASEP) (National Federation of Public Employees): Galerías Alvear, 2°, Of. 301, Vía Argentina, Apdo 66-48, Zona 5, Panamá; tel. and fax 269-1316; e-mail fenasep@sinfo.net; f. 1984; Sec.-Gen. ALFREDO BERROCAL.

A number of unions exist without affiliation to a national centre.

Transport

RAILWAYS

In 1998 there was an estimated 485 km of track in Panama. In 2000 a US $75m. project to modernize the line between the ports at either end of the Panama Canal began. In July 2001 the 83-km Trans-Isthmian railway, originally founded in 1855, reopened. The construction of an underground railway (metro) system in Panama City was planned by the Government of Ricardo Martinelli that took office in 2009. In 2011 construction began in the Consorcio Línea 1, the first phase of the subway project funded by the Corporación Andina de Fomento (CAF) with $400m. Operations were expected to begin in 2014 and the Government was expected to launch a tender for the second subway line in the same year. Four such lines were planned, one of which was to run above the canal.

Ferrocarril Nacional de Chiriquí: Apdo 12B, David City, Chiriquí; tel. 775-4241; fax 775-4105; 126 km linking Puerto Armuelles and David.

Panama Canal Railway Company: Edif. T-376, Corozal Oeste, Apdo 2669, Balboa Ancón, Panamá; tel. 317-6070; fax 317-6061; e-mail info@panarail.com; internet www.panarail.com; private investment under 50-year govt concession; 83 km linking Panama City and Colón, running parallel to Panama Canal; operation on concession by Kansas City Southern (KS, USA) and Mi-Jack Products (IL, USA); modernization programme completed in 2001; operates daily passenger and cargo service; Marketing Dir THOMAS KENNA.

ROADS

In 2008, according to preliminary figures, there were 13,727 km of roads, of which some 38% were paved. The two most important highways are the Pan-American Highway and the Boyd-Roosevelt, or Trans-Isthmian, linking Panama City and Colón. The Pan-American Highway to Mexico City runs for 545 km in Panama and is expected to be extended towards Colombia. There is also a highway to San José, Costa Rica. The Coastal Beltway or Cinta Costera road development project aimed to reduce congestion in the road network of Panama City by providing a bypass route past the city. The first phase of the project was completed in 2009 at a cost of US $189.1m. In the same year, the Government approved $52m. for the second phase of the project. In 2010 the third and final phase of the Cinto Costera project, expected to cost $776.9m., was approved. There were at least 16 bridge projects and three highway programmes in progress in early 2011.

SHIPPING

The Panama Canal opened in 1914. Some 5% of all the world's sea-borne trade passes through the waterway. It is 82 km long, and ships take an average of nine hours to complete a transit. In 2009/10 some 14,230 transits were recorded. The Canal can accommodate ships with a maximum draught of 12 m (39 ft), beams of up to approximately 32.3 m (106 ft) and lengths of up to about 290 m (950 ft), roughly equivalent to ships with a maximum capacity of 65,000–70,000 dwt. A five-year modernization project was completed in 2005. The project included: a general improvement of facilities; the implementation of a satellite traffic-management system; the construction of a bridge; and the widening of the narrowest section of the Canal, the Culebra Cut. Plans were also announced to construct a 203-ha international cargo-handling platform at the Atlantic end of the Canal, including terminals, a railway and an international airport. Terminal ports are Balboa, on the Pacific Ocean, and Cristóbal, on the Caribbean Sea. Further expansion of the Canal's capacity to allow the passage of larger commercial container vessels, by constructing a third set of locks at either end of the waterway, was expected to be completed in 2014.

Autoridad del Canal de Panamá (ACP): Administration Bldg, Balboa, Ancón, Panamá; tel. 272-7602; fax 272-7693; e-mail info@pancanal.com; internet www.pancanal.com; f. 1997; manages, operates and maintains the Panama Canal; succeeded the Panama Canal Commission, a US govt agency, on 31 December 1999, when the waterway was ceded to the Govt of Panama; the ACP is the autonomous agency of the Govt of Panama; there is a Board of 11 mems; Chair. RÓMULO ROUX; Administrator ALBERTO ALEMÁN ZUBIETA; Dep. Administrator JOSÉ BARRIOS NG.

Autoridad Marítima de Panamá: Edif. PanCanal Albrook, Diablo Heights, Balboa, Ancón, Apdo 0843-0533, Panamá 7; tel. 501-5196; fax 501-5406; e-mail ampadmin@amp.gob.pa; internet www.amp.gob.pa; f. 1998 to unite and optimize the function of all state institutions with involvement in the maritime sector; Administrator ROBERTO LINARES TRIBALDOS.

Panama City Port Authority and Foreign Trade Zone 65: Apdo 15095, Panamá; FL 32406, USA; tel. 767-3220; e-mail wstubbs@portpanamacityusa.com; internet www.portpanamacityusa.com; Chair. GEORGE NORRIS; Exec. Dir WAYNE STUBBS.

There are deep-water ports at Balboa and Cristóbal (including general cargo ships, containers, shipyards, industrial facilities); Coco Solo (general cargo and containers); Bahía Las Minas (general bulk and containers); Vacamonte (main port for fishing industry); Puerto Armuelles and Almirante (bananas); Aguadulce and Pedregal (export of crude sugar and molasses, transport of fertilizers and chemical products); and Charco Azul and Chiriquí Grande (crude petroleum).

PANAMA

The Panamanian merchant fleet was the largest in the world in December 2009, numbering 8,100 vessels with total displacement of 190.7m. gross registered tons.

CIVIL AVIATION

Tocumen (formerly Omar Torrijos) International Airport, situated 19 km (12 miles) outside Panamá (Panama City), is the country's principal airport and is served by many international airlines. A project to expand the airport's facilities, at a cost of US $20m., was completed in 2006. The France Airport in Colón and the Rio Hato Airport in Coclé province have both been declared international airports. There are also 11 smaller airports in the country.

Aerolíneas Pacífico Atlántico, SA (Aeroperlas): Apdo 6-3596, El Dorado, Panamá; tel. 315-7500; fax 315-0331; e-mail info@aeroperlas.com; internet www.aeroperlas.com; f. 1970; fmrly state-owned, transferred to private ownership in 1987; operates scheduled regional and domestic flights to 16 destinations; initiated international flights in 2000; Dir JAN ROHDE.

Air Panama: Marcos A. Gelabert Airport, Albrook, Panamá; tel. 316-9000; e-mail info@flyairpanama.com; internet www.flyairpanama.com; operates flights throughout Panama and to Costa Rica; Gen. Man. EDUARDO STAGG.

Compañía Panameña de Aviación, SA (COPA): Avda Justo Arosemena 230 y Calle 39, Apdo 1572, Panamá 1; tel. 227-2522; fax 227-1952; e-mail proquebert@mail.copa.com.pa; internet www.copaair.com; f. 1947; scheduled passenger and cargo services from Panamá (Panama City) to Central America, South America, the Caribbean and the USA; Chair. ALBERTO MOTTA; CEO PEDRO O. HEILBRON.

Tourism

Panama's attractions include Panamá (Panama City), the ruins of Portobelo and 800 sandy tropical islands, including the resort of Contadora, one of the Pearl Islands in the Gulf of Panama, and the San Blas Islands, lying off the Atlantic coast. In 2008 the number of visitor arrivals at Tocumen International Airport stood at 1,136,079. Income from tourism was some US $2,223m. in that year.

Asociación Panameña de Agencias de Viajes y Turismo (APAVIT): Edif. Balmoral, Vía Argentina, diagonal a la Universidad de Panamá, Panamá; tel. 264-9171; fax 264-5355; e-mail apavit@cableonda.net; f. 1957; Pres. ERNESTO REINA.

Autoridad de Turismo Panamá (IPAT): Centro de Convenciones ATLAPA, Vía Israel, Apdo 4421, Panamá 5; tel. 526-7000; fax 526-7100; e-mail gerencia@atp.gob.pa; internet www.atp.gob.pa; f. 1960; Dir-Gen. SALOMÓN SHAMAH ZUCHIN.

Defence

In 1990, following the overthrow of Gen. Manuel Antonio Noriega Morena, the National Defence Forces were disbanded and a new Public Force was created. The new force was representative of the size of the population and affiliated to no political party. As assessed at November 2010, the Public Force numbered an estimated 12,000, comprising the National Police (11,000) the National Air Service (400) and the National Maritime Service (an estimated 600).

Security Expenditure: budgeted at an estimated US $230m. in 2010.

Director of National Civil Protection System: ARTURO ALVARADO DE ICAZA.

Director of National Police: GUSTAVO PÉREZ.

Director of National Aero-Naval Service: JACINTO TOM.

Education

The education system in Panama is divided into elementary, secondary and university schooling, each of six years' duration. Education is free up to university level and is officially compulsory between six and 15 years of age. Primary education begins at the age of six and secondary education, which comprises two three-year cycles, at the age of 12. In 2007/08 enrolment at primary schools included 98% of children in the relevant age-group, while secondary enrolment included 66% of children in the relevant age-group. There are four public universities and 11 private ones, including one that specializes in distance learning. In 2011 a plan to improve educational standards in indigenous schools was announced. The project was to be financed by a US $30m. loan from the Inter-American Development Bank. Budgetary expenditure on education by the central Government in 2007 amounted to a preliminary 639.4m. balboas (equivalent to 18.5% of total current expenditure).

PAPUA NEW GUINEA

Introductory Survey

LOCATION, CLIMATE, LANGUAGE, RELIGION, FLAG, CAPITAL

The Independent State of Papua New Guinea lies east of Indonesia and north of the north-eastern extremity of Australia. It comprises the eastern section of the island of New Guinea (the western section being Papua (West Papua), formerly Irian Jaya, which forms part of Indonesia) and about 600 smaller islands, including the Bismarck Archipelago (mainly New Britain, New Ireland and Manus) and the northern part of the Solomon Islands (mainly Bougainville and Buka). The climate is hot and humid throughout the year, with an average maximum temperature of 33°C (91°F) and an average minimum of 22°C (72°F). Rainfall is high on the coast but lower inland: the annual average varies from about 1,000 mm (40 ins) to 6,350 mm (250 ins). There are more than 850 native languages, but Pidgin and, to a lesser extent, standard English are also spoken, and, together with Motu, are the official languages in Parliament. More than 90% of the population profess Christianity. The national flag (proportions 3 by 4) is divided diagonally from the upper hoist to the lower fly: the upper portion displays a golden bird of paradise in silhouette on a red ground, while the lower portion has five white five-pointed stars, in the form of the Southern Cross constellation, on a black ground. The capital is Port Moresby.

CONTEMPORARY POLITICAL HISTORY

Historical Context

Papua New Guinea was formed by the merger of the Territory of Papua, under Australian rule from 1906, with the Trust Territory of New Guinea, a former German possession which Australia administered from 1914, first under a military Government, then under a League of Nations mandate, established in 1921, and later under a trusteeship agreement with the UN. During the Second World War, parts of both territories were occupied by Japanese forces from 1942 to 1945.

A joint administration for the two territories was established by Australia in July 1949. The union was named the Territory of Papua and New Guinea. A Legislative Council was established in November 1951 and was replaced by a House of Assembly, with an elected indigenous majority, in June 1964. The territory was renamed Papua New Guinea in July 1971. It achieved internal self-government in December 1973 and full independence on 16 September 1975, when the House of Assembly became the National Parliament.

Domestic Political Affairs

Michael Somare, who from 1972 served as Chief Minister in an interim coalition Government, became Prime Minister on independence. He remained in office until 1980, despite widespread allegations of inefficiency in government ministries and of discrimination against the Highland provinces. The first elections since independence were held in mid-1977, following which Somare's Pangu (Papua New Guinea Unity) Pati formed a governing coalition, first with the People's Progress Party (PPP) and later with the United Party (UP).

In March 1980 the Government lost a vote of confidence, the fourth in 15 months, and Sir Julius Chan, the leader of the PPP and a former Deputy Prime Minister, succeeded to the premiership. Somare became Prime Minister again following a general election in June 1982. In 1983 the Somare Government effected a constitutional change to provide the central authorities with greater control of the provincial governments as a means of preventing abuse of their powers. As a result, between 1983 and 1991 a total of nine provincial governments were suspended by the central Government for alleged maladministration.

In March 1985 a motion expressing no confidence in Somare's Government was introduced in Parliament by Chan, who nominated Paias Wingti (hitherto Deputy Prime Minister and a member of the Pangu Pati) as alternative Prime Minister. Somare quickly formed a coalition, comprising the ruling Pangu Pati, the National Party (NP) and the Melanesian Alliance (MA), and the no confidence motion was defeated. Fourteen Members of Parliament (MPs) who had supported the motion were expelled from the Pangu Pati, and subsequently formed a new political party, the People's Democratic Movement (PDM), under the leadership of Wingti.

In August 1985 the NP withdrew from Somare's coalition Government, and in November Chan presented another motion of no confidence, criticizing Somare's handling of the economy. Somare was defeated and Wingti took office as Prime Minister, heading a new five-party coalition Government (comprising the PDM, the PPP, the NP, the UP and the MA), with Chan as Deputy Prime Minister.

At the mid-1987 election to the National Parliament Somare's Pangu Pati won 26 of the 109 elective seats, while Wingti's PDM obtained 18. However, by forming a coalition with minor parties, Wingti succeeded in securing a parliamentary majority and was re-elected Prime Minister. In July 1988 Wingti was defeated in a no confidence motion, proposed by Rabbie Namaliu, who had replaced Somare as leader of the Pangu Pati. As a result, Namaliu took office as Prime Minister and announced a new coalition Government, comprising members of the Pangu Pati and five minor parties: the People's Action Party (PAP), the MA, the NP, the League for National Advancement (LNA) and the Papua Party. In August Ted Diro, the leader of the PAP, was acquitted on a charge of perjury by the Supreme Court (having been accused of illegally appropriating funds for his party). An amendment to the Constitution, whereby a motion expressing no confidence in the Prime Minister could not be proposed until the premier had completed 18 months in office, was approved by Parliament in August 1990 and incorporated into the Constitution in July 1991.

In September 1991 a leadership tribunal found Ted Diro, the leader of the PAP, guilty of 81 charges of misconduct in government office. However, the Governor-General, Sir Serei Eri, refused to ratify the tribunal's decision and reinstated Diro as Deputy Prime Minister, despite recommendations that he be dismissed. A constitutional crisis subsequently arose, during which a government envoy was sent to the United Kingdom to request that the Queen dismiss Eri, but in early October the resignation of the Governor-General was announced; this was followed shortly afterwards by that of Diro. A new Governor-General, Wiwa Korowi, was elected by the National Parliament in November.

In 1992 the Government continued to be troubled by allegations of corruption and misconduct (notably bribery and misuse of public funds). Campaigning for the 1992 general election began amid serious fighting among the various political factions, which led to rioting, in April, by some 10,000 supporters of rival candidates. At the election in June a total of 59 members of the legislature (including 15 ministers) lost their seats. The final result gave the Pangu Pati 22 of the 109 elective seats, while the PDM secured 15. Independent candidates won a total of 31 seats. Paias Wingti of the PDM was subsequently elected Prime Minister by the National Parliament, defeating Rabbie Namaliu of the Pangu Pati by a single vote. Wingti formed a coalition Government, comprising PDM, PPP and LNA members, as well as several independents. As part of the new administration's anti-corruption policy, Wingti suspended six provincial governments for financial mismanagement in October, and threatened to abolish the entire local government system.

In early 1993 a resurgence of tribal violence, mainly in the Enga Province, resulted in the deaths of more than 100 people. This development, together with a continued increase in violent crime throughout the country (despite the implementation in 1991 of severe measures to combat crime, including the introduction of the death penalty) prompted the National Parliament to approve a new internal security act in May 1993. The measures, which included an amendment of the legal system that required defendants accused of serious crimes to prove their innocence, rather than be proven guilty, were criticized by the opposition as oppressive. In May 1994 the Supreme Court nullified six of the 26 sections of the act (most of which concerned the extension of police powers), denouncing them as unconstitutional.

In September 1993 Prime Minister Wingti announced his resignation to Parliament. The Speaker immediately requested nominations for the premiership, and Wingti was re-elected unopposed with 59 of the 109 votes. According to the Constitution (as amended in 1991), a motion of no confidence in the Prime Minister could not be presented for at least 18 months, and Wingti claimed that his action had been necessary in order to secure a period of political stability for the country. However, opposition members described the events as an abuse of the democratic process, and several thousand demonstrators gathered in the capital to demand Wingti's resignation. In December 1993 the National Court rejected a constitutional challenge from the opposition to Wingti's re-election, but in August 1994 the Supreme Court declared Wingti's re-election in September 1993 invalid. Wingti did not contest the ensuing parliamentary vote for a new Prime Minister, in which Sir Julius Chan of the PPP defeated the Speaker, Bill Skate, by 66 votes to 32; Chris Haiveta, the leader of the Pangu Pati, was appointed Deputy Prime Minister.

The abolition of the directly elected provincial government system, as proposed by Wingti, was rejected by Chan's Government, although there was still considerable support among members of the opposition for the planned changes and, as a result, it was decided that Parliament would vote on a series of motions to amend the Constitution accordingly; the first of these was approved in March 1995. However, in June the Pangu Pati withdrew its support for the reforms, and considerable opposition to the proposals was expressed by the provincial governments. Nevertheless, the controversial legislation was approved later that month on condition that Chan lent his support to several opposition amendments to be considered later in the year. Chan subsequently dismissed six ministers for failing to vote for the legislation and effected a major reorganization of portfolios. The new regional authorities, comprising national politicians and selected local councillors and led by appointed governors, were appointed in that month. Wingti resigned as parliamentary leader of the opposition in order to assume the post of Governor in the Western Highlands Province, and was replaced by another PDM member, Roy Yaki.

The involvement of mercenaries to counter the secessionist movement on the island of Bougainville in early 1997 led to a period of extreme instability throughout the country, culminating in Chan's temporary resignation and the appointment of John Giheno as acting Prime Minister for about two months. The atmosphere of political uncertainty was exacerbated by serious outbreaks of violence in the weeks preceding the legislative election (which had been set for mid-June). The Government imposed a dusk-to-dawn curfew and a nation-wide ban on the sale of alcohol. Many senior politicians, including Giheno and Wingti, failed to secure re-election at the polls. Outbreaks of violence were reported in several Highlands constituencies as the results were declared. A period of intense political manoeuvring followed the election, as various members sought to form coalitions and groupings in an attempt to achieve a majority in Parliament. In July Bill Skate of the People's National Congress (PNC), who was the former Speaker and Governor of the National Capital District (NCD), was elected Prime Minister, defeating Sir Michael Somare (who had established a new party—the National Alliance—in 1996) by 71 votes to 35. Skate was supported by a coalition of the PNC, PDM, PPP, Pangu Pati and independent members. A new Government was appointed in late July 1997, and extensive changes in the functional responsibilities of ministries were announced.

In September 1997 the Government declared a national disaster following a prolonged period of drought. By December more than 1,000 people had died. Several countries and organizations that had provided relief funds during the disaster were highly critical of the Government's management of the aid it received. The Minister for Finance, Roy Yaki, was dismissed, in part for his role in the affair, and responsibility for the administration of relief funds was subsequently transferred from the Department of Finance to the Department of Provincial Affairs. In March 1998 (when the drought was deemed to have ended following heavy rainfall) it was revealed that less than one-half of the relief aid received had been deployed to help the victims of the disaster.

In mid-November 1997 Silas (later Sir Silas) Atopare was appointed Governor-General, defeating Sir Getake Gam, head of the Evangelical Lutheran Church, by 54 votes to 44 in the legislature. A serious political scandal erupted in late November, following allegations of corruption against the Prime Minister. The accusations centred on a videotape broadcast on Australian television, which appeared to show Skate arranging bribes and boasting of his strong connections with criminal elements in Port Moresby. The Prime Minister dismissed his recorded comments (and the resultant allegations) stating that he had been drunk at the time of filming. Several senior politicians, including Somare, demanded his resignation over the affair. Meanwhile, Skate dismissed the leaders of the Pangu Pati and the PPP (Chris Haiveta and Andrew Baing, respectively), his coalition partners, accusing them of conspiring against him. The situation intensified with the resignation of seven Pangu Pati members from the Government in early December, and the announcement that the Pangu Pati and the PPP would join the opposition. However, the PPP rejoined the Government shortly afterwards, having voted to replace Baing as leader of the party with Michael Nali. Similarly, four Pangu Pati ministers rejoined the Government, thereby restoring Skate's majority in the National Parliament. A major ministerial reorganization was subsequently announced, in which Nali was appointed Deputy Prime Minister.

In April 1998 the Prime Minister announced the formation of a new political grouping, the Papua New Guinea First Party (which absorbed the PNC, the Christian Country Party and several other minor parties); Skate also effected a ministerial reorganization. However, the Government's majority was subsequently undermined, following a series of decisions by the Court of Disputed Returns during mid-1998, which declared the election in 1997 of seven government MPs to be null and void. Furthermore, in June 1998 the Pangu Pati officially joined the opposition, thereby reducing the Government's representation to 61 members in the National Parliament. Rumours of a forthcoming motion of no confidence in the Prime Minister prompted the establishment of a new pro-Skate coalition in the National Parliament in late July 1998. In the same month Skate announced a number of major reforms in the structure of the Government and an extensive ministerial reorganization. In October the PPP left the governing coalition and, in a subsequent ministerial reorganization, the party's leader, Nali, was replaced as Deputy Prime Minister by Iairo Lasaro.

In late 1998 there was a series of scandals relating to the various serious misdemeanours of a number of provincial governors. Moreover, outbreaks of tribal fighting continued to cause problems (particularly in the Highlands) in 1998–99. A serious conflict in the Eastern Highlands in early 1999, which involved villagers using rocket launchers and grenades, resulted in numerous deaths. In mid-1999 a state of emergency was declared in the Southern Highlands, following serious disturbances provoked by the death of a former provincial Governor, Dick Mune, in a road accident.

The establishment of a new political party, the PNG Liberal Party, in May 1999 by the Speaker, John Pundari (relaunched in June as the Advance PNG Party—APP), encouraged rumours of a forthcoming vote of no confidence against the Prime Minister. In early June, as part of a government reorganization, Skate dismissed the PDM leader, Sir Mekere Morauta (a former Governor of the central bank), and three other PDM ministers, replacing them with four Pangu Pati members, including Haiveta. Later that month both the PDM and the United Resource Party (URP) announced their decision to withdraw completely from the coalition Government, following the resignation of nine government ministers. Both parties were expected to support the APP, in an attempt to subject the Prime Minister to a vote of no confidence. In early July, however, Skate unexpectedly resigned, but declared that he would remain in power in an acting capacity, pending the appointment of a new prime minister. The opposition alliance announced Morauta as their candidate for the premiership. Skate claimed that the APP had pledged support for the Government, thereby ensuring that it would have a sufficient majority to defeat any motion of no confidence. At the opening session of the National Parliament in mid-July, Lasaro, the incumbent Prime Minister's nominee, defeated the opposition candidate, Bernard Narokobi of the PDM, by 57 votes to 45, to become Speaker. However, on the next day Morauta was elected Prime Minister by an overwhelming majority, following his nomination by Pundari, who had transferred his allegiance from Skate, having refused to accept the latter's nomination of himself as candidate for the premiership. Lasaro immediately resigned as Speaker, and Narokobi was elected unopposed to the position. Morauta subsequently appointed a new coalition Government, with Pundari as Deputy Prime Minister.

The Morauta administration

In early August 1999 Sir Mekere Morauta presented a 'mini-budget', in an attempt to combat various economic problems

PAPUA NEW GUINEA

which, he claimed, were a consequence of the previous Government's mismanagement. In October legislation was drafted to prevent ministers transferring political allegiances. In early December the Prime Minister expelled the APP from the coalition Government and dismissed Pundari from his post as Deputy Prime Minister, claiming that this constituted a further move towards the restoration of political stability. (Pundari was rumoured to have conspired with the opposition leader, Skate, to oust the Prime Minister.) Pundari was replaced by the former Minister of Works and deputy leader of the PDM, Mao Zeming. Following Pundari's sudden dismissal, four small political parties within the governing coalition—the National Alliance, the People's National Party, the Melanesian Alliance and the Movement for Greater Autonomy—joined together to form the People's National Alliance (subsequently known as the National Alliance). Also in that month, Skate (who had been charged with attempted fraud during his term in office as Governor of the National Capital District Commission), announced that his party, the PNC, which had 10 MPs, was to join the coalition Government; in May he assumed leadership of the party. Later in December, the resignation of the Minister of Agriculture and Livestock, Ted Diro, prompted Morauta to carry out a government reorganization.

Morauta dismissed three ministers in March 2000, on the grounds that they had allegedly conspired to introduce a parliamentary motion of no confidence in the Prime Minister. The parliamentary strength of the ruling coalition was increased to 76 MPs in April, following the readmission of the APP to government, including the appointment of Pundari to the post of Minister of Lands and Physical Planning. In an attempt to increase government stability, Morauta proposed legislation in August that would restrict the ability of MPs to change their party allegiance within a parliamentary session. Moreover, Morauta also announced the adjournment of Parliament between January and July 2001, the only period during which votes of no confidence could be tabled. (The Constitution forbade such votes in the 18 months following the election of a Prime Minister, and in the 12 months prior to a general election.) In November 2000, however, a revolt by 25 MPs (including six government ministers) prevented a vote on the so-called Political Parties Integrity Bill. The rebellion prompted a major government reorganization, in which all of the ministers involved in the revolt, including the Deputy Prime Minister, Mao Zeming, were dismissed. Further changes to the composition of the Government were made in December, notably the dismissal of Michael Somare, the Minister for Foreign Affairs and Trade, following which Morauta secured the parliamentary approval of the bill. The Prime Minister claimed that the introduction of the new legislation represented the most important constitutional change in Papua New Guinea since independence and would greatly enhance the political stability of the country, as it required MPs who wished to change party allegiance to stand down and contest a by-election.

Allegations of corruption and mismanagement resulted in the suspension of four provincial governments (Western Province, Southern Highlands, Enga and the NCD) in late 2000 and early 2001. The central Government claimed that a failure to deliver services had resulted from the misuse of public funds. Moreover, in January 2001 the Minister for Provincial and Local Government, Iairo Lasaro, was arrested for the alleged misappropriation of public funds, and in mid-March Bill Skate was charged with the same crime, having been acquitted earlier in the month of conspiring to defraud an insurance company (the trial was abandoned in December owing to lack of evidence).

A Commonwealth report into the Papua New Guinea Defence Force, published in January 2001, recommended reducing the number of army personnel by one-third. Subsequent plans by the Government to make more than 2,000 soldiers redundant (equivalent to some 50% of the entire Defence Force) resulted in a revolt at the Port Moresby barracks in March. It was believed that senior officers had helped to distribute weapons to the rebels, who demanded the resignation of the Prime Minister and the transfer of power to an interim administration. The rebellion ended two weeks later with an amnesty for the soldiers involved, during which hundreds of looted weapons were surrendered. In March 2002 another rebellion by soldiers protesting against the proposed reductions in defence personnel took place at the Moem barracks on the northern coast. The leader of the rebellion, Nebare Dege, was sentenced to 15 years' imprisonment in December.

Introductory Survey

In April 2001 the Advance PNG Party, led by John Pundari, was dissolved and merged with the PDM, led by the Prime Minister. In May, following a minor ministerial reorganization in March, Morauta expelled the National Alliance from the ruling coalition and dismissed the party's ministers (including Bart Philemon, Minister for Foreign Affairs) from the National Executive Council, accusing Somare, the party's leader, of attempting to destabilize the Government. In late June, following several days of protests against the Government's economic reforms, police used tear gas to disperse hundreds of demonstrators outside the Prime Minister's office in Port Moresby. In a separate incident, four students were killed and several injured when riot police allegedly entered the premises of the University of Papua New Guinea and opened fire. A temporary curfew was imposed, and a commission of inquiry was established; in December relatives of one of the dead students began legal action against the police force.

In October 2001 the Prime Minister effected another reallocation of ministerial portfolios. At the end of the month, furthermore, the Minister for Foreign Affairs, John Pundari, was dismissed. His removal from office followed his criticism of the Government's participation in Australia's 'Pacific Solution', whereby 216 refugees, who had attempted to enter Australia by boat, were being housed in a former military prison on Manus Island. In December negotiations with Australia were under way to accommodate a further 1,000 asylum-seekers, and Australia had requested the Government to hold the refugees for an additional six months, although no formal agreement was made. In January 2002 the Government decided to accept 784 additional asylum-seekers. It was understood that they were to remain only until their asylum claims were processed. The agreement with Australia to accommodate the asylum-seekers on Manus Island was extended for a further 12 months in October 2002 and was to provide for the reception of an additional 1,000 people. In August 2003 the Australian Government announced that it intended to close the facility.

A legislative election was held in mid-2002. Voting commenced on 15 June and was to extend over a two-week period. However, many polling stations failed to open as scheduled, amid reports of the theft of ballot papers and subsequent strike action by electoral staff. Some 25 people were killed and dozens injured in election-related violence, much of which occurred in the Highlands provinces as a result of disputes between clan-based candidates. A Commonwealth inquiry was subsequently planned to investigate the events surrounding the election, which was described as the worst in the country's history. In the final results, announced in August, six seats in the Highlands provinces remained vacant where voting had been unable to proceed (elections for these seats were held in April and May 2003). Of the 103 seats determined, Somare's National Alliance won 19 and Morauta's PDM secured 12. Independent candidates won 17 seats, with the remainder divided among a large number of minor parties, many of which had been formed specifically to contest the election.

Somare's third term as Prime Minister

On 5 August 2002 Sir Michael Somare was elected unopposed as Prime Minister, receiving 88 parliamentary votes. Bill Skate, who had played an important part in Somare's campaign, was elected Speaker. After appointing a 28-member National Executive Council (which included 19 newly elected MPs), Somare began his third term as Prime Minister, pledging to restore stability, halt the privatization programme initiated by his predecessor and reduce state expenditure. Instability within the parliamentary opposition in late 2002 resulted in the dismissal of Morauta as leader of the opposition in December.

In June 2003 the Government submitted proposals for a number of changes to the political system, including a mandatory general election following the approval of a no confidence motion and stricter rules governing the switching of party allegiances among members of the National Parliament. In late 2003 the Government proposed legislation that would extend the period during which a new government should be exempt from votes of no confidence, from 18 months to three years. Both attempts to introduce these constitutional changes were unsuccessful, despite government inducements of some US $25,000 for MPs to support the proposals.

In mid-September 2003 Sir Albert Kipalan defeated Sir Paulias Matane by a single vote in the final poll to elect a new Governor-General. Kipalan was expected to assume the position in mid-November, when the term of the incumbent, Sir Silas Atopare, expired. However, questions concerning possible irregularities in the polling procedure arose in the following week, casting doubt on the validity of the election, and the Supreme Court subsequently declared it to be defective and invalid. The parliamentary Speaker, Bill Skate, was appointed acting Governor-General pending a fresh election. At the poll, which was duly held in early December, Sir Pato Kakaraya was the successful candidate. However, Kipalan, who had also contested the election, challenged the result and was granted a legal injunction against Kakaraya's inauguration, which had been due to take place in late January 2004. In March the Supreme Court declared the election of Sir Pato Kakaraya to be null and void. Somare consequently ordered the recall of the National Parliament in order that another election for the post could be organized. Following four rounds of voting Sir Paulias Matane, a former Minister for Foreign Affairs, was narrowly elected Governor-General in late May and, after the Supreme Court had refused to grant an injunction against his appointment as requested by Kakaraya, he was duly sworn in the following month.

In May 2004 Somare dismissed the Deputy Prime Minister, Moses Maladina, together with all the PNC members of the National Executive Council who had refused to support proposed government legislation and who were believed to be planning a vote of no confidence in the Government. In early August the National Parliament was adjourned for a period of three months after both the Government and the opposition expressed concern over the number of legislators who were reported to be bringing firearms into the parliament building. In January 2005 Somare announced a reorganization of ministerial portfolios, which included the appointment of his son, Arthur, to the role of Minister for National Planning and Monitoring. In February 2006, however, Arthur Somare resigned from his government position following allegations of misappropriation of public funds; he was referred to the Public Prosecutor for failing to submit annual statements on time and to account for the application of local grants. The Minister for Forestry, Patrick Pruaitch, was appointed to the vacant post in an acting capacity. In a reallocation of portfolios in early April, Pruaitch also assumed responsibility for the finance portfolio, which was removed from Bart Philemon, who nevertheless remained as Minister for Treasury. Mark Maipakai, hitherto Minister of Justice, was appointed Minister for Housing and Urban Resettlement, being replaced in the former position by Bire Kimisopa. Kimisopa had previously served as Minister for Internal Security, a post to which Alphonse Willie was appointed. A major reorganization of the National Executive Council was carried out in July; five ministers, including the Minister for Treasury, Bart Philemon, and the Minister for Defence, Mathew Gubag, were dismissed. Sir Michael Somare himself took the foreign affairs portfolio from Rabbie Namaliu, who became Minister for Treasury, while Arthur Somare, whose case with the Public Prosecutor was still pending, was reappointed to the Government as Minister for State Enterprise, Communication and Information. In November the Prime Minister assigned the foreign affairs portfolio to Paul Tiensten.

In early 2007 the Prime Minister announced further government changes, including the appointment of Michael Nali as Minister for Commerce and Industry and Nick Kuman as Minister for Culture and Tourism. In late February Martin Aini, the Minister for Defence, was dismissed by Somare, reportedly for reasons related to the Julian Moti affair (see Regional Affairs).

Meanwhile, in April 2006 it was reported that the Public Prosecutor had found enough evidence to justify the establishment of a leadership tribunal to investigate alleged misconduct on the part of Puka Temu, the Minister for Lands and Physical Planning, and Andrew Baing, the Deputy Leader of the Opposition. In February 2007 a tribunal was formed to examine allegations of misconduct against Melchior Pep, who had previously served as Minister for Correctional and Administrative Services. In May a leadership tribunal recommended the dismissal of Sir Moi Avei, the former Deputy Prime Minister who had subsequently held the government portfolio of petroleum and energy, over charges of financial misconduct; however, a final decision was postponed pending his appeal.

Recent developments: the election of 2007 and subsequent events

In June 2007 the Minister for Commerce and Industry, Michael Nali, and the Minister for Culture and Tourism, Nick Kuman, resigned in order to contest the forthcoming legislative election as PNC candidates. Polling took place, under a new 'limited preferential voting' system, in relatively peaceful circumstances between 30 June and 15 July, although there were some fatalities. The National Alliance won 27 of the 109 parliamentary seats, with its nearest rival, the PNG Party, taking only eight. The PAP won six seats, while the Pangu Pati, the PDM and the URP each took five seats. Following coalition negotiations with several smaller parties, including the PAP, the Pangu Pati and the URP, along with additional support from independents, Sir Michael Somare was re-elected as Prime Minister in mid-August; Sir Mekere Morauta became leader of the opposition soon after. In late August the composition of the new National Executive Council was announced. The National Alliance, which provided a total of 13 ministers, was allocated a number of important portfolios: Puka Temu was appointed Deputy Prime Minister and Minister for Lands, Physical Planning and Mining, while Patrick Pruaitch assumed responsibility for the finance and treasury portfolio, and a new government appointee, Samuel Abal, became Minister for Foreign Affairs and Trade. Bob Dadae of the UP was appointed Minister for Defence, and Allan Marat of the Melanesian Labour Party (MLP) received the justice portfolio. Other parties represented included the PAP and the PNC. The Minister for Education, Michael Laimo, was forced to relinquish his portfolio when a court invalidated the election result in his parliamentary constituency in February 2008; Somare then assumed responsibility for education in an acting capacity.

In July 2009 the National Parliament approved the formation of two new provinces, to take effect in 2012: Hela (hitherto part of Southern Highlands Province) and Jiwaka (hitherto part of Western Highlands). This would bring the total number of provinces to 22. Later in July 2009 the National Parliament was adjourned until November: the opposition claimed that this action had been taken by the Government in order to avoid a motion of no confidence. At the end of July a total of 14 members of the governing coalition parties joined the opposition, claiming that the Government was corrupt and that they had been warned that if they did not support the administration funds would not be allocated to their local districts. In August the Minister for Works, Transport and Civil Aviation, Don Polye, was obliged to resign after the National Court ruled that his election to the legislature in 2007 had been invalid; he was reinstated in January 2010, following a by-election. Later in January, following several recent prison escapes involving more than 100 prisoners, Somare dismissed the Minister for Correctional Services and assumed responsibility for the portfolio himself. In February the Chief Justice announced the appointment of a leadership tribunal to investigate allegations of financial misconduct on the part of the Minister for Finance and Treasury, Patrick Pruaitch (in June the Supreme Court ordered the suspension of Pruaitch from his post, pending an appeal against his referral to the tribunal). Later in February the National Alliance announced that, in anticipation of Somare's retirement, it would elect a new parliamentary party leader in August, to take over the leadership in August 2011, although Somare was expected to remain as Prime Minister until 2012. Disagreements were reportedly caused within the party by Somare's ambition to have his son, Arthur, elected to the leadership.

In March 2010 the Governor of the NCD, Powes Parkop, founded a new political party, with the aim of combating corruption and ensuring the fair distribution of resources, in particular those derived from the imminent exploitation of the country's reserves of natural gas. (Initially known as the United Democratic Front, the party subsequently assumed the name of Social Democratic Party.) Also in March, a commission of inquiry, established three years previously, reported that the Department of Finance had paid large sums, amounting to hundreds of millions of kina, in response to fraudulent claims against the state. In the same month the Ombudsman Commission, which had been examining the conduct of the Government in the Moti affair (see Regional Affairs), concluded that both Somare and Polye had acted wrongly, and recommended a criminal investigation; however, the National Parliament voted to reject the Commission's report. The legislature approved a constitutional amendment in March allowing the maximum number of ministers in the National Executive Council to be increased from 28 to 31, despite objections by the opposition that the expansion would result in unnecessary expense. In early May the Minister for Justice and Attorney-General, Dr Allan Marat, resigned from his posts (under pressure from the Prime Minister to do so), following his public criticism of the Government's reduction of the powers of the Ombudsman Commission and his expression of concern regarding certain factors of the Government's mining policies; Marat was replaced in both positions by Ano Pala of the National Alliance. Following his resignation, Marat announced that the party that he headed, the Melanesian Liberal Party, would rescind its links with the Government, denouncing the ruling coalition for not permitting internal dissent. In mid-May Parliament proposed legislation to create 22 reserved seats in the national legislature for women before the next general election in 2012; this proposal had first been mooted by the country's sole female MP, Dame Carol Kidu, on her election in 2007. Later in May 2010 Parliament approved amendments to the Defence Force Act to allow the legal participation of troops from Papua New Guinea in international combat or civil operations. As part of the same bill, Parliament agreed to establish an International Relations Committee, which was to advise the National Executive Council on international issues.

The six-year term of the Governor-General was due to expire at the end of June 2010. In preparation for the election to choose a replacement for Sir Paulias Matane, in mid-May the parliamentary Speaker, Jeffery Nape, invited nominations for the post. Four candidates, including the incumbent Matane, presented themselves for election. However, the election process descended into uproar on 25 June when, under extremely controversial and confusing circumstances, the National Parliament appeared unwittingly to approve a second term uncontested for Matane. The Speaker had initially requested the MPs to conduct an open ballot on the eligibility of Matane seeking a second term in office and, this vote having been carried by an absolute majority, the Prime Minister subsequently presented a motion for Parliament to resolve that Matane be supported in his second term as Governor-General. Amid expressions of outrage by the opposition, the Government claimed that the MPs' earlier approval of Matane's eligibility circumvented any need for the holding of a secret multi-candidate ballot, since the MPs had, in effect, already voted in favour of returning the Governor-General to office. The leader of the opposition, Sir Mekere Morauta, claimed that this action by the Government constituted an abuse of parliamentary democracy and pledged to challenge the decision in court.

In early July 2010 the Supreme Court ruled that a law governing the conduct of MPs and political parties was unconstitutional: since the Organic Law on the Integrity of Political Parties and Candidates (OLIPAC, which had been introduced in 2001) prohibited MPs from voting against a party resolution or switching allegiance, it was deemed to contravene their rights and freedom of choice. The annulment of the OLIPAC meant that Parliament was now constitutionally free to introduce a vote of no confidence against the Prime Minister. As the opposition made plans and garnered support for such a vote, three government ministers (Deputy Prime Minister Puka Temu, Minister for Forestry Belden Namah and Minister for Culture and Tourism Charles Abel) and Attorney-General Ano Pala announced their defection to the opposition. Following an unsuccessful attempt to present a parliamentary motion of no confidence against the Prime Minister in late July (the Government avoided the vote by adjourning Parliament until November), the opposition stated its intention to force an early recall of Parliament through the judiciary (claiming that the legislature had not convened for the minimum number of 63 days, as specified in the Constitution). Prime Minister Somare subsequently effected a government reorganization, appointing eight new ministers and promoting Don Polye to the post of Deputy Prime Minister. In addition, three new portfolios—climate change, trade and immigration—were created. In early August Somare attracted further criticism when he abrogated the constitution of the National Alliance and cancelled a party conference in an apparent attempt to allow his son, Arthur, to assume the party leadership unchallenged. In October Morauta announced his resignation as leader of the Papua New Guinea Party (being replaced by Belden Namah), while remaining as parliamentary leader of the opposition.

Prime Minister Somare's political future appeared increasingly unstable in early December 2010 when the acting Public Prosecutor announced plans to refer the premier to a leadership tribunal to answer charges of alleged misconduct in office (with some of the charges dating back nearly 20 years). Somare's referral to the tribunal was expected to force him to resign from the premiership and be replaced by the Deputy Prime Minister. In a seeming attempt to bolster his support within government prior to his departure, Somare unexpectedly carried out a ministerial reorganization, which included the replacement of Deputy Prime Minister Polye with Samuel Abal. In addition, former Chief Justice Sir Arnold Amet was appointed as the new Attorney-General. The Government came under greater pressure on 10 December when the Supreme Court ruled that the parliamentary Speaker, Jeffery Nape, had acted unconstitutionally by reappointing Matane to a second term as Governor-General in June. Matane's reappointment was consequently ruled invalid and Nape became acting Governor-General pending the election of a permanent replacement. Nape was replaced as Speaker by Francis Marus, who assumed the role in an interim capacity.

In an unexpected development, Prime Minister Somare announced in mid-December 2010 that he was temporarily relinquishing the premiership pending the investigation by the leadership tribunal into the allegations of financial misconduct that had been made against him; he was replaced, in an acting capacity, by the newly appointed Deputy Prime Minister Abal. In response, the opposition claimed that Abal's appointment as Deputy Prime Minister (together with the other ministerial reallocations effected by Somare earlier that month) had been unconstitutional and that, therefore, Polye was still the official Deputy Prime Minister. In the mean time, Polye refused to take up his new cabinet portfolio of foreign affairs and immigration. In early January 2011 the political situation became more confused when acting Prime Minister Abal announced that, rather than Somare having 'stepped aside' from the premiership in the previous month, he had simply gone on holiday and intended to resume his duties as Prime Minister whenever he deemed it appropriate. The opposition initiated an unsuccessful attempt to introduce a parliamentary vote of no confidence in Somare. On 14 January Michael Ogio, the incumbent Minister for Higher Education, Research, Science and Technology and the candidate favoured by the National Alliance, was elected as the new Governor-General, defeating Sir Pato Kakaraya by 65 votes to 23. Immediately after the election Parliament adjourned until May. (In late February, however, Parliament was recalled for a special sitting officially to swear in Ogio.)

In mid-January 2011 it was reported that Somare had resumed the premiership, and Abal was thus reappointed as Deputy Prime Minister. Following the establishment in late February of the leadership tribunal (comprising three judges from the United Kingdom, Australia and New Zealand) that was to hear the charges of misconduct against Somare, the Prime Minister stated that he intended to remain in office and allow the tribunal to decide whether he should be suspended from the premiership or not. In the same month the Government provoked further disapproval from the opposition following the dismissal of the acting Public Prosecutor, Jim Tamata (who had referred Somare to the leadership tribunal in late 2010), for alleged non-performance in his role. In mid-March the leadership tribunal ruled that Somare could continue as Prime Minister during the misconduct hearing. On 24 March the tribunal found Somare guilty on 13 counts of official misconduct for failing properly to lodge financial returns. Although the Public Prosecution Office demanded that the tribunal impose the maximum penalty of dismissal from office, Somare was merely suspended from the premiership, without pay, for two weeks, commencing on 4 April. The opposition reacted by claiming that this relatively lenient sentence made a mockery of the rule of law in Papua New Guinea.

Bougainville and the Issue of Secession

From the late 1980s the status of Bougainville (the island which, with the smaller neighbouring islands, forms the easternmost part of Papua New Guinea, and is geographically and ethnically distinct from the rest of the country) became a matter of dispute that developed into civil unrest and a long-term national crisis. In April 1988 landowners on the island of Bougainville submitted claims for financial compensation for land that had been mined by the Australian-owned Bougainville Copper Ltd since 1972. When no payment was forthcoming, acts of sabotage were perpetrated in late 1988 by the Bougainville Revolutionary Army (BRA), led by Francis Ona, a former mine surveyor and landowner, and the copper mine was obliged to suspend operations. Members of the national security forces were deployed in the area and production at the mine recommenced in December, but a curfew was imposed after further violence in January 1989.

The BRA increasingly favoured secession from Papua New Guinea for Bougainville (and for North Solomons Province as a whole), together with the closure of the mine until their demands for compensation and secession had been met. In May 1989, as the violent campaign on the island intensified, the mine was forced once more to suspend production, and in June the Papua

New Guinea Government declared a state of emergency on Bougainville, sending 2,000 security personnel to the island. In September a minister in the Bougainville provincial government, who had been negotiating an agreement with Bougainville landowners to increase their share of mining royalties from 5% to 20%, was shot dead. The signing of the accord, due to take place the following day, was postponed indefinitely. In early 1990 the owners of Bougainville Copper Ltd completed a full withdrawal and Australian nationals were evacuated by their Government.

In March 1990 the Government negotiated a cease-fire with the BRA and withdrew its security forces; later in that month it imposed an economic blockade on Bougainville, now under the control of the BRA. The blockade was intensified in May, when banking, telecommunications and public services on the island were suspended. Also in May, Ona proclaimed Bougainville's independence and declared himself interim President. The unilateral declaration of independence was immediately dismissed by the central Government as unconstitutional and invalid. Negotiations between the BRA and the Government in July resulted in the BRA representatives agreeing to defer implementation of the May declaration of independence and to hold further discussions on the political status of the island. The Government agreed to end the blockade, and to restore essential services to the island. However, there was a resurgence in violence between the BRA and armed forces in September, leading to many reported deaths, after the Government sent troops to take control of the island of Buka, claiming that Buka islanders had petitioned for help.

In January 1991 further negotiations between representatives of the Papua New Guinea Government and of Bougainville in Honiara, the capital of Solomon Islands, resulted in the 'Honiara Accord'. The Papua New Guinea Government agreed not to station its security forces on Bougainville if the BRA disbanded and surrendered all prisoners and weapons to a multinational peace-keeping force. The Bougainville secessionists were guaranteed immunity from prosecution. However, the agreement made no provision for any change in the political status of Bougainville, and by early March it appeared to have failed. Government troops launched a further attack on Bougainville in April. In June Col Leo Nuia was dismissed from his post as Commander of the Papua New Guinea Defence Force, after admitting that his troops had committed atrocities during fighting on Bougainville in early 1990. Further allegations of human rights abuses and summary executions of BRA members and sympathizers by government troops prompted the Prime Minister, Rabbie Namaliu, to announce plans for an independent inquiry into the claims. (The report, published in late 1996, identified numerous problems contributing to a lack of discipline among the troops, and recommended a thorough reorganization of the country's armed forces.)

Fighting continued throughout 1991, and in early 1992, in an attempt to force the Government to end its economic blockade of the island, the BRA intercepted and set fire to a supply ship, and held its crew hostage. As a result, all shipping and air services to Bougainville were suspended, and in October government troops began a major offensive against rebel-held areas of Bougainville. Violence on the island intensified in early 1993, and allegations of atrocities and violations of human rights by both sides were widely reported.

Talks between government representatives and Bougainville secessionists in Honiara during 1994 led to the signing of a cease-fire agreement in September. Under the terms of the agreement, a regional peace-keeping force, composed of troops from Fiji, Vanuatu and Tonga, was deployed in October (with the Governments of Australia and New Zealand in a supervisory role) and the economic blockade of Bougainville was ended. In the following month Prime Minister Chan and a group of non-BRA Bougainville leaders signed the Charter of Mirigini, which provided for the establishment of a transitional Bougainville government. The BRA declared its opposition to the proposed authority, reiterating its goal of outright secession.

In April 1995, following the suspension of the Bougainville provincial government, Theodore Miriong, a former legal adviser to Ona, was sworn in as Premier of a 32-member transitional administration. Three seats reserved for the BRA leaders, Ona, Gen. Sam Kauona and Joseph Kabui (a former Premier of North Solomons Province), remained vacant, as the rebels urged their supporters to reject the new administration. The murder of several more members of the security forces in March 1996 led the Government to abandon all talks with the secessionists and to reimpose a military blockade on Bougainville. An escalation of violence in mid-1996 culminated in a major military offensive against rebel-held areas in June. By August it was estimated that some 67,000 Bougainvilleans were taking refuge in 59 government 'care centres'. In the same month defence forces arrested Miriong, accusing him of incitement regarding the killing of 13 government soldiers at an army camp. In October Miriong was assassinated by unidentified gunmen, later found by an official inquiry to be a group of government soldiers, assisted by pro-Government civilians (known as 'resistance fighters'). Meanwhile, Gerard Sinato was elected as the new Premier of the Bougainville Transitional Government.

In February 1997, in response to unofficial reports, Prime Minister Chan confirmed that a company based in the United Kingdom, Sandline International (a subsidiary of Executive Outcomes, a supplier of private armed forces in Africa), had been commissioned to provide military advice and training for soldiers on Bougainville. Subsequent reports of mercenary activity on the island and of the large-scale purchase of military equipment and of weapons provoked condemnation from numerous international sources. The situation developed into a major crisis in mid-March when the Commander of the Defence Force, Brig.-Gen. (later Maj.-Gen.) Jerry Singirok, announced that the mercenaries (most of whom were from South Africa) had been captured by the armed forces and were being detained while arrangements were made for their deportation. Singirok demanded the immediate resignation of Chan, but denied that his actions constituted a coup attempt. On the following day the Prime Minister dismissed Singirok, replacing him with Col Alfred Aikung. However, the armed forces rejected the new leadership, remaining loyal to Singirok. Popular support for the army's stance became increasingly vocal, as several thousand demonstrators rampaged through the streets of the capital, looting and clashing with security forces. The contract with Sandline International was suspended and the remaining mercenaries left the country. Aikung was replaced as Commander of the Defence Force by Col Jack Tuat. However, demands for the Prime Minister's resignation intensified. Following large-scale demonstrations, an (unsuccessful) parliamentary motion of no confidence and the appeals of military, political and religious leaders, as well as the Governor-General, Chan resigned from office, along with the Deputy Prime Minister and the Minister for Defence. John Giheno, the erstwhile Minister for Mining and Petroleum, was subsequently elected acting Prime Minister.

In June 1997 an inquiry into the mercenary affair concluded that Chan had not been guilty of misconduct and, as a result (despite Giheno's stated intention to continue as acting Prime Minister until a general election had taken place), Chan announced his immediate resumption of his former position. Shortly after resuming office, Chan again provoked controversy by re-appointing Col Leo Nuia to the position of Commander of the Defence Force.

A second inquiry into the mercenary affair, begun following the election of a new Government and based on broader criteria, concluded in September 1998 that former Deputy Prime Minister Chris Haiveta had been the beneficiary of corrupt payments from Sandline, but upheld the first inquiry's finding that Chan had not been guilty of any wrongdoing. Meanwhile, in March government soldiers reacted angrily to the prosecution of military leaders involved in the operation to oust Sandline mercenaries from Bougainville. Nuia was imprisoned in his barracks by members of the Defence Force, while Maj. Walter Enuma, who was being held while awaiting trial on charges of 'raising an illegal force', was freed by rebel soldiers.

Throughout 1997 talks were held at the Burnham army base in New Zealand between secessionists and representatives of the Bougainville Transitional Government, which concluded in October with the signing of the 'Burnham Truce'. Both sides agreed to a series of interim measures, which included refraining from acts of armed confrontation pending a formal meeting of government and secessionist leaders in early 1998. The Prime Ministers of both Papua New Guinea and Solomon Islands made an extended visit to Bougainville in December 1997 to demonstrate their united support for the truce; however, Ona, who appeared to be becoming increasingly marginalized within the BRA, refused to give his support. Further talks held at Lincoln University in Christchurch, New Zealand, in January 1998 resulted in the 'Lincoln Agreement', providing for an extension to the truce, the initiation of a disarmament process and the phased withdrawal of government troops from the island. The Prime Minister also issued a public apology for the mistakes of

PAPUA NEW GUINEA

successive administrations during the conflict, which was estimated to have resulted in the deaths of some 20,000 people.

A permanent cease-fire agreement was signed in Arawa, the main town on Bougainville, on 30 April 1998. Ona declined to take part in the ceremony, reiterating his opposition to the peace agreement. In June government troops were withdrawn from Arawa, and reconstruction projects on Bougainville were initiated.

Bougainville's progression to autonomy

In August 1998 more than 2,000 representatives from different groups in Bougainville met in Buin (in the south of the island) to discuss their response to the 'Burnham Truce'. In the resultant 'Buin Declaration' the islanders stated their united aspiration for independence through peaceful negotiation. In October the National Parliament voted to amend the Constitution to allow the Bougainville Reconciliation Government to replace the Bougainville Transitional Government. The new authority came into existence on 1 January 1999, following the renewed suspension of the Bougainville provincial government, and at its first sitting elected Sinato and Kabui as its co-leaders. In April an agreement signed by Bougainville and Papua New Guinea government representatives (although not acknowledged by the BRA), known as the Matakana and Okataina Understanding, reaffirmed both sides' commitment to the cease-fire, while undertaking to discuss options for the political future of the island.

Elections to the Bougainville People's Congress (BPC, formerly the Bougainville Reconciliation Government) were held in early May 1999, and were reported to have proceeded smoothly. At the first session of the BPC, Kabui was elected President by an overwhelming majority, securing 77 of the 87 votes, thus defeating his former co-leader, Sinato, who received only 10 votes. Kabui subsequently appointed 29 members to the Congressional Executive Council. Ona refused Kabui's invitation to join the BPC. At a subsequent session of the Council, Kabui announced his intention to campaign for independence for Bougainville. In response, Prime Minister Bill Skate stated that, although there was no possibility of independence (as this was not provided for in the Constitution), Parliament would consider terms for greater autonomy for the island. In August the suspension of the Bougainville provincial government was extended for a further six months in an attempt to find a peaceful resolution to the autonomy issue. The Minister for Bougainville Affairs and for Foreign Affairs, Sir Michael Somare (as he had become), stated that the Government was willing to allow Bougainville to be self-governing in all matters except foreign affairs, defence and policing, all of which would remain the responsibility of the central Government. The proposal was welcomed by members of the BPC, although they also announced their intention not to surrender their weapons until the Government had agreed to hold a referendum on independence.

In October 1999 a Supreme Court ruling declared the suspension of the Bougainville provincial government illegal on technical grounds. On 9 December the provincial government was formally recognized, in theory: in effect, however, the provincial government comprised only four members—the Bougainville Regional Member of Parliament, John Momis, who thus became Governor-elect (although he agreed not to exercise his powers for the time being) and the three other Bougainville parliamentarians. Further talks regarding the future status of Bougainville between Somare and members of the BPC, the BRA and elders of the island took place in December 1999 and March 2000, and an agreement was subsequently signed. Known as the Loloata Understanding, this allowed for the eventual holding of a referendum on independence, once full autonomy had been implemented, and the formal establishment of the Bougainville Interim Provincial Government (BIPG), composed of an Executive Council and a 25-member Provincial Assembly (including the four original members).

At the end of March 2000 the Provincial Assembly and the Executive Council were sworn in by the Governor-General. Six seats were left vacant in the Provincial Assembly for other Bougainville officials such as Kabui and Ona; however, Kabui stated that, rather than joining the BIPG, he would await the establishment of a fully autonomous government (which he hoped would be in place by early 2001). In May 2000 the Office of Bougainville Affairs was renamed the Office of Peace and Reconstruction. Uncertainties regarding the proposed date of a referendum, as well as concerns about renewed Australian funding of the Papua New Guinea Defence Force troops stationed on Bougainville and the BRA's failure to begin disarmament, continued to delay the progress of negotiations. Following

Introductory Survey

a further round of peace talks in November, Kabui confirmed that he had secured an agreement from Somare that a future referendum would include a legally binding option of independence, although disagreement over how soon the vote should be held persisted.

In February 2001 agreement on the terms of the referendum was finally reached, following the intervention of the Australian Minister for Foreign Affairs. The agreement stated that the referendum would be held in 10–15 years' time and would contain the option of independence. In the interim the provincial government was to be granted increased autonomy and the BRA would be expected to disarm. In early May commanders of the BRA and the Bougainville Resistance Force (BRF, a militia that was allied to the Government during the civil conflict on Bougainville) signed an agreement to surrender their weapons. In late June an agreement was reached on autonomy for the island, with the Government ceding to demands that Bougainville be accorded its own system of criminal law and an autonomous police force. It was also agreed that the Papua New Guinea Defence Force's jurisdiction on the island would be strictly limited. On 30 August the Government and island leaders signed the Bougainville Peace Agreement in Arawa. Although he signed the accord, which was still to be approved by the National Parliament, Ishmael Toroama, the BRA's Chief of Defence, stated that the BRA would campaign for the referendum to be held in three–five years' time and would continue to seek full independence. (Francis Ona did not attend the signing ceremony; he died in July 2005.)

Weapons disposal by the BRA and BRF began in early December 2001, and the UN Observer Mission on Bougainville (UNOMB) formally acknowledged the Bougainville Peace Agreement later in that month. In January 2002 the National Parliament unanimously endorsed the Organic Law enacting the Bougainville Peace Agreement, along with a bill containing the requisite constitutional amendment. A second vote, held in late March, ratified the legislation, and the Papua New Guinea Defence Force began its withdrawal from Bougainville. The withdrawal of troops was completed in late December.

In August 2003 the Government of Papua New Guinea formally announced its plan for autonomy in Bougainville, allowing provincial authorities to proceed with the establishment of a constitution and the eventual organization of elections for an autonomous government leader and local assembly. In March 2004 the BIPG approved legislation providing for its merger with the BPC to establish the Bougainville Constituent Assembly (BCA), which was finally convened later that month to consider the third and final draft of the proposed constitution. In mid-December the Government of Papua New Guinea finally approved Bougainville's Constitution, and the UN agreed to extend its Observer Mission by a further six months to cover the period of the forthcoming election. Elections for the President of the new Autonomous Bougainville Government (ABG) and for 39 members of the first local assembly began on 20 May 2005 and continued for two weeks to allow islanders, some of whom had to travel for several days on foot or by canoe, sufficient time to reach the polling stations. Despite attempts by armed rebels to disrupt the election process, it was deemed to have been largely successful. Joseph Kabui was declared to be Bougainville's first President, with 37,928 votes, defeating several other candidates (the closest of whom, former Governor John Momis, received 23,861 votes). The inauguration of the autonomous assembly, the Bougainville House of Representatives, took place on 14 June, with the President occupying the 40th seat. Kabui appointed a 10-member Bougainville Executive Council several days later.

The leader of the Observer Mission left Papua New Guinea at the beginning of August 2005. Also in August the Government announced its commitment to ensuring that a referendum on the independence of Bougainville be carried out by 2020. Some areas of rebel resistance remained in 'no go zones', such as Me'ekamui in the south-west of Bougainville, where the self-styled 'king', Noah Musingku, an alleged fraudster, was reportedly assisted by Fijian mercenaries.

In September 2000 a group of landowners from Bougainville had initiated legal action in a US court against Rio Tinto, the operator of the Panguna copper mine between 1972 and 1988. The group was reported to be suing the company for the environmental and social damage caused by its activities, including health problems experienced by workers and islanders living near the mine. Moreover, their case alleged that the company had effectively transformed the Papua New Guinea Defence

PAPUA NEW GUINEA

Force into its own private army and was therefore responsible for the deaths of some 15,000 civilians in military action and a further 10,000 as a result of the economic blockade on the island. In 2007 the US Ninth Court of Appeals upheld the Bougainville residents' right to sue. A committee was established by the provincial Government in late 2005 to work on reopening the mine following an overwhelming vote in favour of the proposal.

In early June 2008 Joseph Kabui, the President of Bougainville, died of a heart attack. John Tabinaman was appointed as his temporary replacement, pending the scheduling of an election. Although it was initially proposed that a new president be chosen by the Bougainville House of Representatives, at a by-election in December, James Tanis, a former BRA commander and an unsuccessful opponent of Kabui in the first presidential election in 2005, secured victory, taking office in January 2009. Tanis undertook to remove roadblocks in the remaining 'no go zones', and in March it was reported that the ABG had concluded an agreement with the principal rebel group in the Me'ekamui area. In March 2010 it was announced that legislative and presidential elections would be held in May. Tanis was to be a candidate for the presidency again, while John Momis was to contest the presidential election as leader of the New Bougainville Party, along with five other candidates. The possible reopening of the Panguna copper mine was a major topic of debate during the election campaign. (In February 2011 the Chairman of Bougainville Copper Ltd, Peter Taylor, stated that the reopening of the mine was feasible and that he would welcome all parties who wished to discuss such a possibility.)

Polling commenced on 7 May 2010 and lasted for a fortnight; the election process was monitored by a team from the Pacific Islands Forum. In an indication of the efficacy of the peace process, for the first time since the signing of the 2001 peace agreement polling was to be permitted by rebel leaders in the areas surrounding the Panguna mine. Having secured 43,047 votes (more than 52% of the total cast), John Momis was subsequently declared the new President. James Tanis, his nearest rival, received 17,205 votes (21%). More than three-quarters of incumbent legislators lost their seats in the House of Representatives in a vote that was widely held to reflect the public's disenchantment with the ABG's perceived lack of progress in recent years. Independent candidates were reported to have won 23 seats and the New Bougainville Party 14 seats. On assuming the presidency on 15 June, Momis pledged to work towards fully implementing autonomy in preparation for the holding of the referendum on independence between 2015 and 2020, to complete the weapons-disposal programme, to combat corruption, to improve the general welfare of the population through economic development and to investigate means of generating revenue for the completion of much-needed infrastructure projects. During an official visit to the People's Republic of China by President Momis in November 2010 a number of agreements were signed regarding future joint business ventures, including the proposed establishment of an airline company in Bougainville.

Exploitation of Natural Resources and Tribal Conflict

Papua New Guinea's wealth of mineral deposits and forestry resources are important for the country's economy and have attracted considerable foreign investment. However, the operations of foreign business interests have sometimes caused serious environmental damage, with the interests of local inhabitants frequently being ignored, and legislative controls proving difficult to enforce.

In 1989 the Government gave Ok Tedi Mining Ltd (OTML), the owners of a gold and copper mine in Western Province, permission to discharge 150,000 metric tons of toxic waste per day into the Fly River. In 1994 6,000 people living in the region began a compensation claim against the Australian company operating the mine for damage caused by the resultant pollution. A settlement worth some $A110m. was reached in an Australian court in 1995 (and a further settlement worth $A400m. for the establishment of a containment system was concluded in mid-1996), despite opposition from the Papua New Guinea Government, which feared that such action might adversely affect the country's prospects of attracting foreign investment in the future. Similar claims were initiated by people living near the Australian-controlled Porgera gold-mine in Enga Province in early 1996 for pollution of the Strickland River system, as well as by landowners near the Kutubu oilfield, while the Panguna copper mine on Bougainville was also alleged to have caused severe environmental problems. The results of an independent review, carried out by the World Bank and published in March 2000, recommended the closure of the Ok Tedi mine on environmental grounds, but also emphasized the potentially damaging impact of the mine's early closure on both the local economy and world copper markets. In October 2001 BHP Billiton, the Australian operator, announced its withdrawal from the OTML venture and in early 2002 it transferred its 52% stake in the company to a development fund called the PNG Sustainable Development Programme Ltd. In early 2006 the managing director of OTML acknowledged that mining operations had caused major damage to the Ok Tedi and Fly River systems, resulting in flooding and forest dieback. Furthermore, the toxic effects of this waste were now believed to be threatening supplies of ground and drinking water. In 2009 OTML achieved record sales, amounting to US $1,500m., and was reportedly the single largest business contributor to the Papua New Guinea economy. In December it was announced that the Ok Tedi mine would cease commercial operations in 2013.

Activity in the forestry sector increased dramatically in the early 1990s, and an official report published in 1994 indicated that the current rate of logging was three times the sustainable yield of the country's forests. However, attempts to introduce new regulations to govern the industry were strongly opposed by several Malaysian logging companies with operations in the country. In early 2000, however, environmentalists welcomed a commitment by the Papua New Guinea Government to impose a moratorium on all new forestry licences and to review all existing licences. Concern continued among conservation organizations as the Government failed to enforce laws promoting sustainable forestry activity, which, if upheld, were deemed sufficient to ensure the long-term survival of the forestry sector. Conservationists hoped that pressure from consumers in the destination countries might lead to a reduction in illegal logging. In March 2011 the UN expressed its concern to the Government of Papua New Guinea that it was involved in the allocation of large areas of forestry land for 'logging by stealth' through Special Agricultural Business Leases.

Controversy surrounding the role of foreign interests in the exploitation of the country's natural resources re-emerged in early 2005 when a group representing tribal landowners near the Porgera gold mine protested at the mysterious deaths of villagers while panning for alluvial gold near the mine. The group claimed that a number of local people (totalling 29 by early May) had been shot dead by Porgera security personnel and that others had been seriously assaulted. Mine officials denied the allegations, stating that most of the deaths had been accidental, and that any shootings by their security guards had been carried out in self-defence. Violent incidents between miners and villagers living near the Porgera mine continued sporadically. In May 2009 villagers reportedly claimed that their homes had been destroyed by security personnel who had been sent to the mine in the previous month, to quell alleged tribal warfare and halt illegal mining activities. Also in May, violence between local workers and foreign employees over the issue of labour conditions broke out at the Chinese-owned Ramu nickel/cobalt mine, in Madang Province, forcing it to close temporarily; a further closure was effected by local landowners in January 2010, protesting at delays in the previously agreed relocation of residents.

Tribal conflicts, principally between the Ujimap and Wagia tribes, broke out near Mendi, the capital of Southern Highlands Province, in December 2001. It was alleged that national and local politicians, along with tribal leaders, had made little effort to end the fighting, which had originated in a dispute over the governorship of the province in 1997; furthermore, many were dissatisfied at the election of Tom Tomiape as Governor, in late November 2001, and at the widespread political corruption and deteriorating public services in the province. Tomiape's election was ruled invalid by the Supreme Court in December, and Wambi Nondi was appointed acting Governor. A brief cease-fire was brokered in early January 2002 and an independent peace commission was established in February, headed by Francis Awesa, a local businessman. By early 2002 more than 120 people had been killed since the onset of the fighting.

Ethnic and tribal violence continued in several regions of the country during 2003. Eight people were killed in fighting near Port Moresby in May, and 17 died during inter-clan violence involving more than 1,000 people in Enga Province in July. By mid-2004 further ethnic violence in Enga, Morobe, Chimbu and East Highlands Provinces had resulted in many more deaths, including those of several children. Concerns regarding the conduct of the national police force in tackling such conflicts intensified following an incident in August when a confrontation between security personnel and a group of youths in Enga

Province resulted in police setting fire to an entire village, shooting dead a villager and injuring several others, and killing domestic animals. Earlier in the year the former Commander-in-Chief of the Defence Force, Jerry Singirok, stated his belief that the marked increase in ownership of illegal firearms, particularly in the Highlands region, was the single most significant problem in Papua New Guinea. Ethnic violence continued in 2005. Some 5,000 villagers were left homeless following fighting in Chimbu Province in April. Further violence during the year, particularly in the Highlands provinces, resulted in many more deaths. In one outbreak of fighting in July, resulting from a land dispute, an estimated 7,000 guns were believed to have been used and police officers declined to intervene as they were considerably less well-armed. In another incident fuel shortages prevented police from attending a serious tribal conflict in which many people were killed. A report published in July claimed that the majority of illegal firearms in circulation in the country originated from the Papua New Guinea Defence Force or from police stocks. Another report released in early 2006 confirmed that many of the weapons used in these inter-tribal conflicts had been bought or stolen from the security forces, who appeared to be unable or unwilling to intervene in such incidents, while home-made shotguns were increasingly being replaced by more sophisticated weaponry. (See also Relations with Australia.)

In early August 2006 a state of emergency was declared in Southern Highlands Province in response to widespread lawlessness and allegations of financial mismanagement and corruption within the regional administration; the provincial Government was later suspended. In February 2007 the central Government extended the state of emergency for a further nine months, but in the following month the Supreme Court annulled the Government's decision, maintaining that, despite a breakdown in law and order, conditions in Southern Highlands Province did not warrant such extreme measures.

A reported increase in murders involving allegations of sorcery was a source of concern for officials in 2008. In January 2009 the police estimated that as many as one-half of all the murders in the country in the previous year were linked to accusations of 'black magic', which, according to human rights organizations, frequently led to the persecution of innocent individuals. In June senior police officers in Port Moresby reported that they lacked the personnel and vehicles necessary to enforce the law effectively. In November tribal fighting was reported to have led to several deaths and serious damage in Chimbu Province, and in December expatriate medical staff left a hospital in Southern Highlands Province after numerous attacks on staff and patients.

During 2009 it became evident that plans for the exploitation of natural gas deposits in Southern Highlands and Gulf Provinces, although expected to result in an enormous increase in the national income, were also a cause of conflict among rival groups claiming to be the traditional landowners at the construction sites. The signing of a benefit-sharing agreement by the Government and representatives of some 60,000 landowners was postponed from March until May, in order to identify legitimate claimants, and demands for recognition were still being made by other groups in early 2010. In January the Minister for Internal Security, Mark Maipaki, appealed to aggrieved landowners to cease threatening government officials and developers over delays in the payment of business development grants and funds. In February construction work on an airport forming part of the project in Southern Highlands Province was halted owing to insecurity in the area.

In May 2010, according to official reports, more than 10,000 mainly Sepik settlers had been displaced and two killed as a result of the violent unrest between the settlers and the local Watut and Patep people in the Bulolo mining township in Morobe Province.

Other Environmental Concerns and Health Issues

Fears that rising sea levels caused by global warming might have very serious consequences for Pacific islanders intensified in May 2003 when an emergency operation was undertaken to save the inhabitants of Carteret and Mortlock Islands, near Bougainville. Food supplies were sent to the islands, the 2,000 inhabitants of which were reported to be suffering from starvation and health problems related to poor diet, since the failure of their crops, which had been flooded by sea water. Some islanders were reluctant to accept a government proposal to relocate them to the main island of Bougainville, fearing the loss of their distinct Polynesian culture and way of life. None the less, in 2009 the relocation of the world's first so-called climate change refugees, from the Carteret Islands, commenced, although the process of their transfer from the islands was reported to be delayed by lack of funds and by negotiations over the allocation of land to the resettled families.

A series of severe floods in late 2003 and early 2004 affected 5,000 people in Morobe Province and more than 10,000 in West Highlands Province. In November 2007 Cyclone Guba struck Papua New Guinea, causing major floods that resulted in the deaths of at least 163 people and the displacement of thousands more. A state of emergency was declared in Oro Province, the worst-affected region. In December of the following year the northern coast was hit by tsunamis, which affected an estimated 75,000 people.

Between September and December 2009 outbreaks of cholera and dysentery were reported in several provinces, and the representative of the World Health Organization (WHO) in Papua New Guinea warned that outbreaks would continue if the country's sanitation and water supply systems were not improved. By May 2010 the cholera outbreak was reported to have reached Port Moresby. In April, meanwhile, WHO described the occurrence of HIV and AIDS in Papua New Guinea as an epidemic, while communicable diseases, such as malaria and tuberculosis, were still the principal cause of death. In November an outbreak of dysentery and suspected cholera at Baisu prison in Mount Hagen in the Western Highlands Province led to an attempted mass escape during which seven prisoners were shot dead by warders. A group of inmates had earlier requested a transfer from the prison following the reported deaths of four prisoners from dysentery, but had been told that nothing could be done to ameliorate the situation owing to a lack of funds.

Regional Affairs

Papua New Guinea's most influential relationships have been with its immediate neighbours, Australia (the former ruling power), Indonesia and Solomon Islands. The country's large mineral resources have also attracted considerable investment from China and Japan. Papua New Guinea is a member of the Commonwealth and of numerous other international and regional organizations (see Regional and International Co-operation).

Relations with Australia and the Pacific Islands

Relations with Australia, the former administrative power and a major source of investment and aid, have remained close, although affected by various developments. In December 2003, following the apparent success of the intervention in Solomon Islands earlier in the year, Australia announced the deployment of some 250 of its security personnel to different regions of Papua New Guinea, as part of plans for a five-year operation costing US $325m., aimed at restoring order to troubled areas of the country. Moreover, the Australian Government was to send up to 70 officials to Papua New Guinea to assume senior public roles in the spheres of finance, justice, public sector management, immigration, border security and transport safety. The agreement, known as the Enhanced Co-operation Program (ECP), was officially concluded in June 2004 and incorporated a substantial aid programme. Prime Minister Somare had initially been reluctant to accept Australia's expanded role in the country, fearing that it would erode national sovereignty, but had been obliged to reconsider when the Australian Prime Minister, John Howard, implied that aid payments to Papua New Guinea were dependent on the country's co-operation. A report by the Australian Strategic Policy Institute, published in December 2004, claimed that Papua New Guinea risked economic and social collapse. It urged the Australian Government to intervene further in the country by radically increasing the amount of aid it provided and by taking control of some aspects of government, particularly immigration. Research by the organization indicated that government and state institutions had become too weak to prevent drugs and weapons smuggling, human trafficking and money-laundering activities, operated by international criminal groups, which had relocated to Papua New Guinea from South-East Asia in recent years. Furthermore, an investigation carried out by Australian journalists, the results of which were published in early 2005, alleged that Chinese mafia groups had infiltrated the highest levels of Papua New Guinea's police force. According to the report, the corruption of the country's authorities was facilitating serious criminal activities that posed a threat to the national security of Australia. It was also believed that the criminals had been recruiting Port Moresby's notorious 'raskol' gangs (groups of heavily armed, disaffected young men responsible for much of the violent crime in the capital) to commit armed robberies, assaults and other crimes in support of their activities.

The ECP suffered a serious reversal in May 2005 when Papua New Guinea's Supreme Court ruled that the deployment of Australian security personnel in the country was unconstitutional (principally because they had been given immunity from prosecution). Personnel began to return to Australia shortly after the ruling. Relations between the two countries had deteriorated in March when the Prime Minister of Papua New Guinea, Sir Michael Somare, had been subjected to a security search at the Australian airport of Brisbane. In October, following revisions to the ECP, it was announced that Australia was to commit up to 40 police officers to assist the local forces in a renewed attempt to curb the increasing levels of violence and crime in Papua New Guinea. In February 2006 an internal police investigation that had begun in 2003 revealed that as many as 66 Papua New Guinea police officers had been implicated in corrupt activities, such as receiving funds from Asian crime syndicates.

Relations with Australia became increasingly strained towards the end of 2006 over the extradition of the newly appointed Solomon Islands Attorney-General, Julian Moti, who was wanted by the authorities in Australia on a child molestation charge (see the chapter on Australia). Moti had been arrested in Port Moresby in September, but escaped to Solomon Islands at the beginning of October, reportedly on an aircraft of the Papua New Guinea Defence Force. Prime Minister Somare denied any knowledge of the operation. Australia subsequently imposed a ban on ministerial exchanges with Papua New Guinea and ministerial-level travel to Australia. In November it was reported that the Papua New Guinea Chief Secretary, the Commander of the Defence Force and the acting Police Commissioner had been suspended, ostensibly owing to the Moti affair. The progress of a Papua New Guinea Defence Force inquiry was closely scrutinized by both countries in early 2007. In February, following a testimony that Somare had given instructions to fly Moti out to Solomon Islands, the inquiry issued a summons to the Prime Minister, prompting him to criticize it for exceeding its jurisdiction. Somare's dismissal of the Minister for Defence, Martin Aini, who had established the board of inquiry and admitted that the Prime Minister had exerted pressure on him to disband it, prompted further speculation over Somare's involvement. In September 2007 the National Court overruled Somare's attempt to dismiss the inquiry's conclusions. According to media sources, the report alleged that Somare had given the order to fly Moti out of the country and was therefore liable to prosecution. In October the new Minister for Defence, Bob Dadae, rejected the findings of the report on the basis that the 'composition of the board was not legally constituted'. The Australian Government removed its ban on contact between ministers of the two countries in September. The new Australian Prime Minister, Kevin Rudd, paid a three-day visit to Papua New Guinea in March 2008, and announced an increase in aid to Papua New Guinea, specifically for improvements in infrastructure, employment opportunities, primary education, health services and governance. In April 2009, during a return visit to Australia by Somare, Rudd criticized the distribution of Australia's aid in Papua New Guinea, stating that too much aid was being spent on the engagement of consultants. Somare disputed Rudd's claim, maintaining that resources were being devoted to areas where funding was most needed.

In December 2009 an Australian court ordered that the charges against Moti be abandoned. In March 2010 Papua New Guinea's Ombudsman Commission, which had been conducting its own investigation into the Moti affair, concluded that Somare had been responsible for the order to transport Moti to Solomon Islands, and recommended a criminal investigation; however, the Commission's findings were rejected by the legislature (see Recent Developments).

In March 2011 the Australian authorities stated that they would adopt a 'zero tolerance' approach towards fraud in their annual aid programme to Papua New Guinea; it had recently been reported that out of Australia's total international aid programme a disproportionately large percentage of fraudulent dealings occurred in Papua New Guinea. In May the Australian Government announced that it intended to review the effectiveness of its aid programmes, following complaints by Papua New Guinea that large sums of money were being squandered on the salaries of consultants and advisers rather than being directly invested in needy sectors such as health and education.

From 1990 relations with Solomon Islands were overshadowed by the conflict on Bougainville. Solomon Islands (the inhabitants of which are culturally and ethnically very similar to Bougainville islanders) protested against repeated incursions by Papua New Guinea defence forces into Solomon Islands' territorial waters, while the Papua New Guinea Government consistently accused Solomon Islands of harbouring members of the BRA and providing them with supplies. Despite several attempts during the 1990s to improve the situation between the two countries (including an agreement by Solomon Islands in 1993 to close the BRA office in the capital, Honiara), relations remained tense. In April 1997 the Solomon Islands Government announced that it was considering the initiation of proceedings against the Papua New Guinea Government concerning the latter's attempted use of mercenaries on Bougainville. In June of that year Papua New Guinea and Solomon Islands concluded a maritime border agreement, following several years of negotiations. The purpose of the agreement (which took effect in January 1998) was not only to delineate the sea boundary between the two countries but also to provide a framework for co-operation in matters of security, natural disaster, customs, quarantine, immigration and conservation. In March 2004 the two countries signed a number of treaties and agreements relating to the management of their common border area.

Concerns were expressed in mid-2003 that the rebel Solomon Islands leader Harold Keke (alleged to be responsible for a campaign of terror in Solomon Islands) was recruiting new members for his Guadalcanal Liberation Force in Bougainville and strengthening his links with the BRA. These fears were exacerbated by sightings of Keke in Buka and Bougainville and attacks against journalists who had reported on the activities of Keke's supporters (including the stockpiling of weapons) along the border between Papua New Guinea and Solomon Islands. However, in August the Governor of Bougainville, John Momis, officially stated that he did not believe that any link existed between Keke and the BRA. In that month Keke surrendered and was arrested by the regional peace-keeping force in Solomon Islands.

In May 2010 the importance attached to relations between Papua New Guinea and Solomon Islands was underlined by the official opening of a new chancery building in Port Moresby; this building constituted the first permanent location for the High Commission of Solomon Islands in any country with which it maintained diplomatic relations.

In March 1988, meanwhile, Papua New Guinea signed an agreement with Vanuatu and Solomon Islands to form the Melanesian Spearhead Group, which was subsequently joined by Fiji. The grouping was dedicated to the preservation of Melanesian cultural traditions and to achieving independence for the French Overseas Territory of New Caledonia. In March 2007 the members of the Melanesian Spearhead Group signed a constitution.

Relations with Asia

In 1989 Papua New Guinea increased its links with South-East Asia, signing a Treaty of Amity and Co-operation with the Association of Southeast Asian Nations (ASEAN, see p. 206). During an official visit to the Philippines in April 2009, and a visit by the Indonesian President to Papua New Guinea in March 2010, Somare appealed for the support of both countries for Papua New Guinea's ambition to attain full membership of ASEAN.

In 1984 more than 9,000 refugees crossed into Papua New Guinea from the western section of the island of New Guinea, the Indonesian province of Irian Jaya (officially known as Papua from January 2002), as a consequence of operations by the Indonesian army against Melanesian rebels of the pro-independence Organisasi Papua Merdeka (Free Papua Movement—OPM). For many years relations between Papua New Guinea and Indonesia had been strained by the conflict in Irian Jaya, not least because the independence movement drew sympathy from many among the largely Melanesian population of Papua New Guinea. A new border treaty was signed in October 1984, and attempts were made to repatriate the refugees, based on assurances by the Indonesian Government that there would be no reprisals against those who returned. In October 1985 representatives of the Papua New Guinea and Indonesian Governments signed a treaty providing for the settlement of disputes by consultation, arbitration and 'other peaceful means'. However, the treaty provoked strong criticism among opposition politicians in Papua New Guinea, who claimed that it effectively precluded the censure of any violation of human rights in Irian Jaya. In 1988 the Government condemned incursions by Indonesian soldiers into Papua New Guinea, in search of OPM members, and the resultant violence and killings, as a breach of bilateral accords, and affirmed that Papua New Guinea would not support Indonesia in its attempt to suppress the OPM. In late 1995 violent confrontations resulted in the killing of several rebels and security personnel and the kidnapping by OPM activists of some 200 villagers. Australia urged the Papua New Guinea Government to accept several thousand refugees living in camps along the border, and in May 1996 the Government announced that 3,500 Irian Jayans would be allowed to remain in Papua New Guinea on condition that they were not involved in OPM activities. In mid-1998 the Governments of Papua New Guinea and Indonesia concluded an agreement on bilateral relations, which was expected to provide the basis for closer co-operation in political, economic and defence matters. Under the terms of the agreement, troop numbers along the border were increased in March 1999. During 2000 hundreds of refugees were voluntarily repatriated to Indonesia (including more than 600 in a major operation in early September), although approximately 7,000 were believed to remain in Papua New Guinea in September. In late 2000 it was reported that Indonesian security forces had made some 400 incursions into Papua New Guinea in the previous two months while pursuing separatists. In December the border with Irian Jaya was officially closed.

In January 2003 the Papua New Guinea Government denied a number of security breaches, which were reported to have occurred along its border with Indonesia. The number of Indonesian troops along the border increased from about 150 in late 2002 to a reported 1,500 in early 2003. In late January the Government of Papua New Guinea ordered its security forces to arrest OPM rebels believed to be staying in refugee camps along the border, following complaints from the Indonesian authorities that rebels based there were carrying out operations in the province of Papua. The Government also confirmed in April that it had been unable to persuade more than 400 West Papuans living in a camp near the border town of Vanimo to return to Indonesia, despite assurances that their safety would not be at risk. In July 2004 it was announced that Vanuatu would host a series of negotiations between the Indonesian authorities and Papuan separatists. In January 2009 it was reported that 700 West Papuans would voluntarily return to Indonesia, although observers were sceptical about their reasons for departing. In March 2010 the President of Indonesia, Susilo Bambang Yudhoyono, paid an official visit to Papua New Guinea; agreements on co-operation in defence, agricultural development and commerce were concluded during the visit, and Yudhoyono expressed satisfaction that Somare had reaffirmed his Government's acknowledgement of Papua as part of Indonesia.

In January 2011 the Government of Papua New Guinea launched a joint forces security operation, reportedly at the request of the people of West Sepik Province, in an alleged attempt to curb illegal weapons- and drugs-trafficking, poaching activities and people smuggling. By early February more than 170 people (many of whom were reported to be suspected OPM activists) had been arrested and detained for their purported illegal movement across the border from Indonesia. Many of the detainees were subsequently sent to a UN refugee camp in Western Province.

Diplomatic relations with the People's Republic of China were established in 1976. In February 2004 Prime Minister Sir Michael Somare led a delegation of 80 officials (the largest such group Papua New Guinea had ever sent on a state visit) to China. Almost one-half of the delegates were representatives from the mining sector, who were hoping to secure agreements with Chinese interests relating to petroleum, gas and other mineral developments in Papua New Guinea. Major Chinese investments in Papua New Guinea include the Ramu mine in Madang Province, extracting nickel and cobalt, and China was expected to be one of the principal customers for Papua New Guinea's liquefied natural gas (LNG) after the planned commencement of exports in 2014/15. In May 2009 disturbances in Port Moresby and Lae were reported to reflect resentment against expatriate Chinese entrepreneurs who owned many urban businesses. In March 2010 it was announced that China was to finance and develop a US $53m. integrated electronic information system for the Papua New Guinea Government. Bilateral relations were further strengthened in August when two Chinese warships docked at Port Moresby during a three-day intensive exchange programme between technical naval staff of the two countries.

Relations with Taiwan came under international scrutiny in May 2008, when two senior members of the Taiwanese Government were forced to resign over a major funding controversy involving the use of intermediaries to secure diplomatic recognition for Taiwan by Papua New Guinea. The affair, which highlighted the practice of so-called 'chequebook diplomacy', prompted Somare to issue a denial of any involvement. In March 2010 a contract was signed for the supply of Papua New Guinea's LNG to Taiwan over a period of 20 years from the expected commencement of production in 2014.

In December 2009 it was announced that two Japanese companies had won the contract for providing the production and processing facilities for Papua New Guinea's LNG project. During an official visit to Japan in March 2010 Somare announced that Japan was to buy more than 50% of Papua New Guinea's LNG output.

During her two-week tour of the Asia-Pacific region in October–November 2010, US Secretary of State Hillary Clinton made a brief visit to Port Moresby, during which she had discussions with the Government on a wide-ranging variety of issues, including the development of Papua New Guinea's petroleum and gas reserves, climate change, military co-operation in the Pacific and elsewhere, and the global empowerment of women.

CONSTITUTION AND GOVERNMENT

Executive power is vested in the British monarch (the Head of State), represented locally by the Governor-General, who is appointed on the proposal of the National Executive Council (the Cabinet) in accordance with the decision of the National Parliament by simple majority vote. The Governor-General acts on the advice of the National Executive Council, which is led by the Prime Minister. The Prime Minister is appointed and dismissed by the Head of State on the proposal of the National Parliament. Legislative power is vested in the unicameral National Parliament, with 109 members elected by universal adult suffrage for a term of five years. The National Executive Council is responsible to the National Parliament. The local government system underwent extensive reform in 1995, when the directly elected provincial governments were replaced by new regional authorities, composed of members of the National Parliament and local councillors, and led by an appointed Governor. The National Capital District (NCD) has its own governing body. Papua New Guinea comprises 20 provinces (to be increased to 22 in 2012).

In January 2005 the National Government approved the final draft of the proposed Constitution for the province of Bougainville, and elections for the President of the new autonomous Government and for the 39 members of the House of Representatives commenced in May (see Contemporary Political History). In mid-June the new President was duly sworn in and the House of Representatives was inaugurated. The second Bougainville elections took place in mid-2010.

REGIONAL AND INTERNATIONAL CO-OPERATION

Papua New Guinea is a member of Asia-Pacific Economic Co-operation (APEC, see p. 197), the Asian Development Bank (ADB, see p. 202), the Colombo Plan (see p. 446), the Pacific Community (see p. 410), the Pacific Islands Forum (see p. 413) and the UN's Economic and Social Commission for Asia and the Pacific (ESCAP, see p. 37). Papua New Guinea is also a member of the Melanesian Spearhead Group, which, besides other benefits, provides for free trade among member countries (the others being Fiji, Solomon Islands and Vanuatu).

The country was admitted to the World Trade Organization (WTO, see p. 430) in 1996. Papua New Guinea is also a member of the International Cocoa Organization (see p. 443) and of the International Coffee Organization (see p. 443).

ECONOMIC AFFAIRS

In 2009, according to estimates by the World Bank, Papua New Guinea's gross national income (GNI), measured at average 2007–09 prices, was US $7,911m., equivalent to $1,180 per head (or $2,270 per head on an international purchasing-power parity basis). During 2000–09, it was estimated, the population increased at an average annual rate of 2.5%, while gross domestic product (GDP) per head increased at an average annual rate of 0.7% in real terms. Overall GDP grew, in real terms, at an average annual rate of 3.2% in 2000–09. According to the Asian Development Bank (ADB), real GDP increased by 5.5% in 2009 and by 7.1% in 2010.

Agriculture (including hunting, forestry and fishing) contributed 34.5% of GDP in 2009. In mid-2011, according to FAO, the sector engaged an estimated 68.8% of the labour force. The principal cash crops are oil palm and coffee. Other significant crops are cocoa and coconuts (for the production of copra and coconut oil), rubber, tea and vanilla. Roots and tubers, vegetables, bananas and melons are grown as food crops. Forestry is an important activity, and Papua New Guinea is one of the world's largest exporters of unprocessed tropical timber. However, serious concerns have been raised with regard to the environmental damage caused by extensive logging activity in the country (see Contemporary Political History). Exports of forest products accounted for 3.9% of total export earnings in 2009, when revenue reached K476.8m. The sale of fishing licences to foreign fleets has provided a substantial source of revenue. During 2000–09, according to figures from the World Bank, agricultural GDP increased at an average annual rate of 1.7%. According to the ADB, the GDP of the agricultural sector increased by 0.7% in 2009 and by 3.5% in 2010.

Industry (including mining, manufacturing, construction and power) contributed an estimated 42.1% of GDP in 2009. During 2000–09 industrial GDP increased by an average of 3.9% per year, according to figures from the World Bank. The ADB estimated that industrial GDP increased by 6.9% in 2009 and by 9.3% in 2010.

Mining and quarrying provided an estimated 20.9% of GDP in 2009. Gold, which accounted for an estimated 44.9% of the country's total export revenue in 2009, copper (16.8%) and crude petroleum (13.6%) are the sector's major exports. Other mineral deposits include cobalt, nickel, silver, chromite and quartz. The country's largest petroleum refinery, at Napa Napa, began production in 2004. Papua New Guinea also has substantial reserves of natural gas. Construction of a 700-km pipeline from Southern Highlands Province to the capital of Port Moresby commenced in 2010, part of a liquefied natural gas project (LNG), which was scheduled for completion in 2013/14 (see below). The GDP of the mining sector was estimated to have declined at an average annual rate of 2.5% during 2000–09; sectoral GDP decreased by 1.8% in 2009, according to ADB data.

Manufacturing contributed an estimated 6.5% of GDP in 2009. The sector is limited, employing only 1.1% of the working population in 2000. The principal branches of manufacturing are food products, beverages, tobacco, wood products, metal products, machinery and transport equipment. Several fish canneries have been established since the 1990s. In addition to a large tuna-loining plant in Wewak, it was announced in May 2009 that a major tuna cannery was to be built with Chinese assistance in Morobe Province; the project was expected to create 3,000 jobs. According to the World Bank, during 2000–09 manufacturing GDP increased by an average of 3.1% per year. Compared with the previous year, the sector's GDP expanded by 4.5% in 2009, according to provisional figures from the ADB.

Construction contributed an estimated 12.5% of GDP in 2009. According to ADB data, during 2000–09 the GDP of the construction sector increased by an estimated annual average of 13.7%; the sector's GDP expanded by 15.0% in 2008 and by 9.5% in 2009.

Energy is derived principally from hydroelectric power, which in 2000 accounted for more than 50% of electricity supplies. Output of electric energy reached 3,049m. kWh in 2007. However, more than 90% of the population are estimated to have no access to electricity, and in early 2009, with assistance from the ADB, the Government was in the process of formulating a new development plan for the country's power sector. In 2004 fuel imports accounted for 16.9% of the value of total merchandise imports.

The services sector contributed an estimated 23.4% of GDP in 2009. Tourism is an expanding industry, although political instability and reports of widespread violent crime have had a detrimental effect on the sector. Total foreign visitor arrivals were reported to have increased from 125,891 in 2009 to 146,928 in 2010. Tourism receipts were worth an estimated US $3.7m. in 2005. The GDP of the services sector increased at an average annual rate of 4.2% in 2000–09, according to figures from the World Bank. The sector's GDP expanded by 9.4% in 2009 and by 8.5% in 2010, according to the ADB.

In 2009 Papua New Guinea recorded a visible trade surplus of K4,192m., while there was a deficit of K1,611m. on the current account of the balance of payments. In 2009 the principal source of imports (43.3%) was Australia; other major suppliers were the People's Republic of China, Singapore and the USA. In that year Australia was also the principal market for exports (29.9%), followed by Japan and China. The principal exports were gold, copper and crude petroleum.

The budget for 2010 (excluding grants from abroad and net lending) projected a deficit of K1,357.7m. Of the total expenditure of K7,493.5m., K3,393.8m. was allocated to the development budget. Papua New Guinea receives grants for budgetary aid from Australia. In 2010/11 official development assistance from Australia was projected at $A457.2m. New Zealand's allocation of aid totalled $NZ29.0m. in 2010/11. According to the ADB, Papua New Guinea's external debt totalled US $891m. at the end of 2010. In that year the cost of debt-servicing was equivalent to 1.2% of the value of exports of goods and services. A large informal sector supports the majority of the population. At the census of 2000, 2.8% of the registered labour force were reported to be unemployed. In urban areas, however, the unemployment rate was estimated at some 70%. In the rural areas underemployment remained a serious problem. The annual rate of inflation averaged 6.6% in 2000–09. Consumer prices increased by 6.0% in 2010.

The Government's Medium-Term Development Plan for 2011–15 focused on the effective utilization of the substantial revenue inflows expected from the US $16,000m. LNG project (see above); among the proposed measures was the establishment of a sovereign wealth fund. The Government planned to open up a number of state-owned enterprises, such as electricity provision and ports, to private sector competition. It was also proposed to improve general living standards by rehabilitating infrastructure and upgrading basic services. Despite the continuing economic growth of the resource-rich country, the incidence of poverty was still believed to be about 50% of the population. Papua New Guinea remained vulnerable to extreme climatic conditions and to variations in world commodity prices. Following a large decrease in the value of merchandise exports in 2009, they made an impressive recovery in 2010, growing by around 27%, as a result of a resurgence in international commodity prices (notably for gold, copper, petroleum, palm oil, copra and timber). Meanwhile, plans to revitalize the coffee industry, encompassing the period 2008–18, were to be implemented, in an attempt to counter the variations in global coffee prices and the changes in the country's climatic conditions of recent years. In the Highlands region crops of both coffee and tea were adversely affected by the prolonged drought conditions experienced in 2010. Although inflationary pressures eased in 2009–10, the level of inflation remained relatively high; renewed pressure on prices was reported in early 2011, partly owing to the devaluation of the kina in the previous year and to the rising costs of imported food items. Economic growth accelerated in 2010 as construction work began on the LNG project, which was being developed in collaboration with an international consortium. With the scheme providing many local employment opportunities, production of LNG for export was expected to commence in 2014 or 2015; at full operating capacity, the project was forecast to have an annual output of 6.6m. metric tons of LNG. In 2011 plans were under way for the establishment of a second LNG project, in Gulf Province. Having expanded for the ninth consecutive year in 2010, GDP was forecast by the ADB to increase by 8.5% in 2011.

PUBLIC HOLIDAYS

2012: 2 January (for New Year's Day), 6–9 April (Easter), 11 June (Queen's Official Birthday), 23 July (Remembrance Day), 17 September (for Independence Day and Constitution Day), 25–26 December (Christmas).

PAPUA NEW GUINEA

Statistical Survey

Source (unless otherwise stated): Papua New Guinea National Statistical Office, POB 337, Waigani, NCD; tel. 3011200; fax 3251869; e-mail pmaime@nso.gov.pg; internet www.nso.gov.pg.

Area and Population

AREA, POPULATION AND DENSITY

Area (sq km)	462,840*
Population (census results)	
11 July 1990†	3,607,954
9 July 2000	
Males	2,691,744
Females	2,499,042
Total	5,190,786
Population (UN estimates at mid-year)‡	
2009	6,732,157
2010	6,888,387
2011	7,045,417
Density (per sq km) at mid-2011	15.2

* 178,704 sq miles.
† Excluding North Solomons Province (estimated population 154,000).
‡ Source: UN, *World Population Prospects: The 2008 Revision*.

POPULATION BY AGE AND SEX
(UN estimates at mid-2011)

	Males	Females	Total
0–14	1,424,609	1,328,947	2,753,556
15–64	2,070,415	2,042,527	4,112,942
65 and over	84,434	94,485	178,919
Total	3,579,458	3,465,959	7,045,417

Source: UN, *World Population Prospects: The 2008 Revision*.

PRINCIPAL TOWNS
(census of 9 July 2000, provisional)

Port Moresby (capital)	254,158	Mount Hagen	27,782
Lae	78,038	Madang	27,394
Arawa	36,443	Kokopo/Vunamami	20,262

Source: Thomas Brinkhoff, *City Population* (internet www.citypopulation.de).

Mid-2009 (incl. suburbs, UN estimate): Port Moresby 313,593 (Source: UN, *World Urbanization Prospects: The 2009 Revision*).

BIRTHS AND DEATHS
(annual averages, UN estimates)

	1995–2000	2000–05	2005–10
Birth rate (per 1,000)	36.9	34.1	31.7
Death rate (per 1,000)	10.0	8.7	8.0

Source: UN, *World Population Prospects: The 2008 Revision*.

2003 (incomplete registration): Registered live births 192,817; Registered deaths 7,054 (Source: UN, *Population and Vital Statistics Report*).

Life expectancy (years at birth, WHO estimates): 62 (males 61; females 64) in 2008 (Source: WHO, *World Health Statistics*).

ECONOMICALLY ACTIVE POPULATION
(census of 9 July 2000, persons aged 10 years and over)

Agriculture, hunting and forestry	1,666,247
Fishing	30,024
Mining and quarrying	9,282
Manufacturing	25,557
Electricity, gas and water	2,208
Construction	48,312
Wholesale and retail trade; repair of motor vehicles, motorcycles and personal and household goods	353,186
Hotels and restaurants	4,395
Transport, storage and communications	24,513
Financial intermediation	3,670
Real estate, renting and business activities	27,459
Public administration and defence; compulsory social security	32,043
Education	27,118
Health and social work	12,341
Other community, social and personal service activities	31,409
Private households with employed persons	15,523
Extra-territorial organizations and bodies	163
Activities not adequately defined	31,284
Total employed	**2,344,734**
Unemployed	68,623
Total labour force	**2,413,357**
Males	1,256,887
Females	1,156,470

Source: ILO.

Mid-2011 (estimates in '000): Agriculture, etc. 2,166; Total labour force 3,149 (Source: FAO).

Health and Welfare

KEY INDICATORS

Total fertility rate (children per woman, 2008)	4.1
Under-5 mortality rate (per 1,000 live births, 2008)	69
HIV/AIDS (% of persons aged 15–49, 2007)	1.5
Physicians (per 1,000 head, 2000)	0.05
Hospital beds (per 1,000 head, 1990)	4.0
Health expenditure (2007): US $ per head (PPP)	65
Health expenditure (2007): % of GDP	3.2
Health expenditure (2007): public (% of total)	81.3
Access to water (% of persons, 2008)	40
Access to sanitation (% of persons, 2008)	45
Total carbon dioxide emissions ('000 metric tons, 2007)	3,363.6
Carbon dioxide emissions per head (metric tons, 2007)	0.5
Human Development Index (2010): ranking	137
Human Development Index (2010): value	0.431

For sources and definitions, see explanatory note on p. vi.

Agriculture

PRINCIPAL CROPS
('000 metric tons, FAO estimates)

	2006	2007	2008
Cassava (Manioc)	135	145	145
Sweet potatoes	560	580	580
Yams	290	310	310
Taro (Cocoyam)	260	285	285
Sugar cane	320	320	320
Coconuts	660	677	677
Oil palm fruit	1,350	1,400	1,400
Pineapples	20	20	20
Bananas	920	940	940
Coffee, green	67.5	75.4	75.4
Cocoa beans	51.1	47.3	48.8
Tea	9	9	9
Natural rubber	4.5	4.7	4.7

Note: No data were available for individual crops in 2009.

Aggregate production ('000 metric tons, may include official, semi-official or estimated data): Total cereals 11.3 in 2006; 12.3 in 2007–09; Total oil crops 495 in 2006, 516 in 2007, 519 in 2008–09; Total vegetables (incl. melons) 501 in 2006–09; Total fruits (excl. melons) 1,942 in 2006, 2,007 in 2007–09.

Source: FAO.

PAPUA NEW GUINEA

LIVESTOCK
('000 head, year ending September, FAO estimates)

	2005	2006	2007
Horses	2	2	2
Cattle	92	93	94
Pigs	1,800	1,800	1,800
Sheep	7	7	7
Goats	3	3	3
Chickens	4,000	4,000	4,000

2008: Figures assumed to be unchanged from 2007 (FAO estimates). Note: No data were available for 2009.

Source: FAO.

LIVESTOCK PRODUCTS
('000 metric tons, FAO estimates)

	2005	2006	2007
Cattle meat	3.1	3.2	3.2
Pig meat	68	68	68
Chicken meat	5.7	5.9	5.9
Game meat	330	355	365
Hen eggs	5.0	5.0	5.0

2008–09: Production assumed to be unchanged from 2007 (FAO estimates).

Source: FAO.

Forestry

ROUNDWOOD REMOVALS
('000 cubic metres, excluding bark)

	2005	2006	2007
Sawlogs, veneer logs and logs for sleepers	2,536*	2,908*	2,958†
Pulpwood	78	82	82†
Fuel wood†	5,533	5,533	5,533
Total†	8,147	8,523	8,573

* Unofficial figure.
† FAO estimate(s).

2008–09: Production assumed to be unchanged from 2007 (FAO estimates).

Source: FAO.

SAWNWOOD PRODUCTION
('000 cubic metres, including railway sleepers)

	2003	2004*	2005*
Coniferous (softwood)	10*	10	10
Broadleaved (hardwood)	50†	50	51
Total	60†	61	61

* Unofficial figure(s).
† FAO estimate.

2006–09: Production assumed to be unchanged from 2005 (unofficial figures).

Source: FAO.

Fishing

('000 metric tons, live weight)

	2006	2007	2008
Capture	298.3	268.9	223.6
Mozambique tilapia*	2.3	2.3	2.3
Other freshwater fishes*	6.7	6.7	6.7
Sea catfishes*	1.9	1.9	1.9
Skipjack tuna	184.1	181.5	147.0
Yellowfin tuna	41.4	42.6	53.3
Aquaculture	0.1	0.1	0.1
Total catch*	298.3	268.9	223.7

* FAO estimates.

Note: Figures exclude crocodiles, recorded by number rather than weight. The number of estuarine crocodiles caught was: 10,208 in 2006; 12,675 in 2007; 4,937 in 2008. The number of New Guinea crocodiles caught was: 22,070 in 2006; 15,904 in 2007; 5,599 in 2008. Figures also exclude shells ('000 metric tons): 0.4 in 2006; 0.4 in 2007; 0.2 in 2008.

Source: FAO.

Mining

	2007	2008	2009*
Petroleum, crude ('000 barrels)	15,418	13,993	12,806
Copper ('000 metric tons)†	169.2	159.7	166.7
Silver (metric tons)†	48.7	51.3	50.0
Gold (metric tons)†	57.5	67.5	63.6

* Preliminary figures.
† Figures refer to metal content of ore.

Source: US Geological Survey.

Industry

SELECTED PRODUCTS
('000 metric tons unless otherwise indicated)

	2005	2006	2007
Beer of barley*	36	39	60
Palm oil*	310	365	395
Raw sugar	44	35	35
Electric energy (million kWh)	3,002	3,012	3,049†

* Unofficial figures.
† Estimate.

2008 ('000 metric tons): Beer of barley 65 (unofficial figure); Palm oil 382 (FAO estimate).

2009 ('000 metric tons): Beer of barley 60 (unofficial figure).

Wood products ('000 cu m, excl. furniture): 1,611 in 2003.

Sources: FAO; UN Industrial Commodity Statistics Database; Asian Development Bank.

Finance

CURRENCY AND EXCHANGE RATES

Monetary Units
100 toea = 1 kina (K).

Sterling, Dollar and Euro Equivalents (30 November 2010)
£1 sterling = 4.092 kina;
US $1 = 2.635 kina;
€1 = 3.425 kina;
100 kina = £24.44 = $37.95 = €29.20.

Average Exchange Rate (kina per US $)
2007   2.9654
2008   2.7001
2009   2.7551

Note: The foregoing information refers to the mid-point exchange rate of the central bank. In October 1994 it was announced that the kina would be allowed to 'float' on foreign exchange markets.

PAPUA NEW GUINEA

BUDGET
(million kina)

Revenue*	2008	2009	2010†
Taxation	5,756.1	4,974.5	5,735.3
Personal tax	1,108.8	1,241.8	1,420.2
Company tax	2,849.9	1,121.4	2,196.5
Other direct tax	393.9	1,156.5	413.0
Import duties	158.0	143.7	168.1
Excise duties	491.5	493.9	573.4
Export tax	126.8	108.7	122.3
Goods and services tax	610.9	703.0	835.7
Other indirect tax	16.2	5.5	6.1
Non-tax revenue	282.6	765.8	400.5
Dividends	188.0	138.0	285.2
Interest revenue/fees	1.2	6.9	9.0
Other internal revenue	93.4	99.9	106.3
Injection from Trust Accounts	—	521.0	—
Total	**6,038.6**	**5,740.3**	**6,135.8**

Expenditure‡	2008	2009	2010†
Recurrent expenditure	3,768.9	4,169.7	4,099.7
National departmental	2,276.1	2,403.4	2,380.2
Provincial governments	802.8	1,046.6	983.0
Interest payments	381.1	449.2	467.1
Foreign	292.1	59.2	67.0
Domestic	89.0	390.0	400.1
Other grants and expenditure	308.9	270.5	269.4
Development expenditure	1,630.1	2,348.7	3,393.8
National projects	1,304.1	1,879.0	2,715.0
Provincial projects	326.0	469.7	678.8
Additional priority expenditure	1,376.0	—	—
Reappropriation to trust account	779.0	172.5	—
Total	**7,554.0**	**6,690.0**	**7,493.5**

* Excluding grants received from abroad, tax credits and trust accounts (million kina): 1,034.6 in 2008; 911.0 in 2009; 1,353.9 in 2010 (budget figure).
† Budget figures.
‡ Excluding net lending (million kina): −2.2 in 2008; −3.3 in 2009; −4.0 in 2010 (budget figure).

Source: Bank of Papua New Guinea, Port Moresby.

INTERNATIONAL RESERVES
(US $ million at 31 December)

	2007	2008	2009
Gold (national valuation)	32.84	33.73	46.40
IMF special drawing rights	0.09	0.11	182.19
Reserve position in IMF	0.69	0.67	0.69
Foreign exchange	2,052.92	1,952.62	2,377.73
Total	**2,086.54**	**1,987.13**	**2,607.01**

2010: IMF special drawing rights 15.50; Reserve position in IMF 0.67.

Source: IMF, *International Financial Statistics*.

MONEY SUPPLY
(million kina at 31 December)

	2008	2009	2010
Currency outside depository corporations	675.93	788.95	954.42
Transferable deposits	4,843.68	5,443.73	6,748.75
Other deposits	4,170.12	5,537.23	5,238.79
Securities other than shares	—	52.66	61.87
Broad money	**9,689.73**	**11,822.57**	**13,003.83**

Source: IMF, *International Financial Statistics*.

COST OF LIVING
(Consumer Price Index; base: 1977 = 100)

	2007	2008	2009
Food	831.3	969.6	1,039.1
Clothing and footwear	514.1	525.6	531.2
Rent, fuel and power	374.2	429.2	384.8
All items (incl. others)	**822.2**	**910.7**	**973.6**

NATIONAL ACCOUNTS
(million kina at current prices)

National Income and Product

	2004	2005	2006
Compensation of employees	2,450.5	2,491.1	2,550.9
Operating surplus	9,163.8	10,505.1	11,994.5
Domestic factor incomes	**11,614.3**	**12,996.2**	**14,545.4**
Consumption of fixed capital	828.9	876.7	985.0
Gross domestic product (GDP) at factor cost	**12,443.2**	**13,872.9**	**15,530.4**
Indirect taxes / *Less* Subsidies	1,016.3	1,221.8	1,366.2
GDP in purchasers' values	**13,459.3**	**15,094.7**	**16,896.5**
Net factor income from abroad	−1,408.8	−1,670.0	−2,462.0
Gross national product	**12,050.7**	**13,424.7**	**14,434.6**
Less Consumption of fixed capital	828.9	876.7	985.0
National income in market prices	**11,221.8**	**12,548.0**	**13,449.6**

Source: Bank of Papua New Guinea, Port Moresby.

Expenditure on the Gross Domestic Product

	2004	2005	2006
Government final consumption expenditure	2,237.6	2,437.6	2,837.6
Private final consumption expenditure	7,047.5	7,239.2	7,959.0
Increase in stocks	580.2	150.0	350.0
Gross fixed capital formation	2,294.3	2,489.3	2,302.6
Total domestic expenditure	**12,159.6**	**12,316.1**	**13,449.2**
Exports of goods and services	9,143.4	11,245.7	13,986.2
Less Imports of goods and services	7,843.7	8,467.1	10,538.9
GDP in purchasers' values	**13,459.3**	**15,094.7**	**16,896.5**
GDP at constant 1998 prices	**8,299.1**	**8,625.2**	**8,823.1**

Source: Bank of Papua New Guinea, Port Moresby.

Gross Domestic Product by Economic Activity
(million kina, provisional)

	2007	2008	2009
Agriculture, hunting, forestry and fishing	5,901.7	6,909.2	7,328.8
Mining and quarrying	5,440.9	5,926.8	4,438.2
Manufacturing	1,064.2	1,247.6	1,385.9
Electricity, gas and water	361.8	404.1	451.0
Construction	1,750.5	2,226.2	2,661.9
Wholesale and retail trade	1,177.3	1,393.3	1,550.7
Transport, storage and communications	364.2	440.3	585.7
Finance, insurance, real estate and business services*	638.6	760.0	852.3
Community, social and personal services (incl. defence)	1,635.0	1,818.8	1,990.6
Sub-total	**18,334.0**	**21,126.3**	**21,245.1**
Import duties, *less* subsidies	464.4	499.5	536.6
GDP in purchasers' values	**18,798.4**	**21,625.8**	**21,781.7**

* Including services of owner occupied dwellings.

Source: Asian Development Bank.

PAPUA NEW GUINEA

BALANCE OF PAYMENTS
(million kina)

	2007	2008	2009
Exports of goods f.o.b.	14,079	15,675	12,101
Imports of goods f.o.b.	−7,797	−8,479	−7,909
Trade balance	6,282	7,196	4,192
Exports of services	1,069	980	511
Imports of services	−5,409	−4,727	−5,070
Balance on goods and services	1,942	3,449	−367
Other income received	310	230	128
Other income paid	−2,444	−1,970	−1,849
Balance on goods, services and income	−192	1,709	−2,088
Current transfers received	1,219	1,060	1,046
Current transfers paid	−477	−624	−569
Current balance	550	2,145	−1,611
Capital account (net)	113	67	74
Direct investment abroad	−23	—	−12
Direct investment from abroad	284	−82	1,166
Portfolio investment assets	1,210	941	414
Portfolio investment liabilities	—	—	−1
Financial derivatives assets	−274	−356	58
Other investment assets	26	−2,579	1,232
Other investment liabilities	−335	−787	363
Net errors and omissions	41	53	42
Overall balance	1,592	−598	1,725

Source: Bank of Papua New Guinea, Port Moresby.

External Trade

PRINCIPAL COMMODITIES
(US $ million)

Imports f.o.b.*	2002	2003	2004
Food and live animals	176.8	192.4	237.3
Meat and meat preparations	32.9	34.8	40.8
Cereals and cereal preparations	81.4	94.6	122.7
Rice	53.2	61.5	90.8
Milled or semi-milled rice	23.5	20.5	88.6
Mineral fuels, lubricants and related materials	153.9	173.2	264.5
Petroleum and petroleum products	150.0	169.9	262.1
Chemicals and related products	90.6	109.6	128.9
Basic manufactures	239.2	233.6	247.5
Iron and steel	35.5	39.2	41.2
Manufactures of other metals	100.1	82.0	80.2
Machinery and transport equipment	399.9	454.3	541.6
Power-generating machinery and equipment	36.1	51.2	57.1
Machinery specialized for particular industries	89.5	90.6	123.6
General industrial machinery and equipment	84.3	92.4	102.4
Electrical machinery, apparatus and appliances, etc.	40.3	46.7	48.1
Road vehicles and parts†	63.2	68.1	101.0
Motor vehicles for goods transport	24.0	24.2	43.1
Other transport equipment and parts†	27.9	46.4	52.8
Miscellaneous manufactured articles	90.3	100.7	102.6
Total (incl. others)	1,186.0	1,302.4	1,567.2

Exports f.o.b.	2002	2003	2004
Food and live animals	206.3	285.0	280.4
Coffee, tea, cocoa and spices, etc.	127.9	193.2	192.0
Crude materials, inedible, except fuels	588.8	1,107.2	753.3
Cork and wood	96.4	54.3	167.6
Metalliferous ores and metal scrap	478.9	1,043.4	572.8
Ores and concentrates of precious metals	263.2	645.0	91.3
Mineral fuels, lubricants and related materials	367.8	459.3	543.1
Crude petroleum and oils obtained from bituminous materials	367.7	458.1	513.3
Animal and vegetable oils, fats and waxes	107.0	146.5	140.2
Palm oil	86.0	122.8	113.2
Gold, non-monetary, unwrought or semi-manufactured	278.7	143.9	880.7
Total (incl. others)	1,625.1	2,260.2	2,722.2

*Figures include migrants' and travellers' dutiable effects, but exclude military equipment and some parcel post.
†Data on parts exclude tyres, engines and electrical parts.

Source: UN, *International Trade Statistics Yearbook*.

2005 (million kina): *Imports c.i.f.*: Total 4,732. *Exports f.o.b.*: Gold 2,834; Crude petroleum 2,283; Copper 2,498; Forestry products 476; Coffee beans 471; Palm oil 391; Cocoa 199; Total (incl. others) 10,168 (Source: Asian Development Bank).

2006 (million kina): *Imports c.i.f.*: Total 6,084. *Exports f.o.b.*: Gold 3,091; Crude petroleum 2,989; Copper 4,330; Forestry products 527; Coffee beans 337; Palm oil 430; Cocoa 204; Total (incl. others) 12,752 (Source: Asian Development Bank).

2007 (million kina): *Imports c.i.f.*: Total 7,603. *Exports f.o.b.*: Gold 3,672; Crude petroleum 2,984; Copper 4,173; Forestry products 631; Coffee beans 408; Palm oil 672; Cocoa 261; Total (incl. others) 13,866 (Source: Asian Development Bank).

2008 (million kina): *Imports c.i.f.*: Total 8,413.3. *Exports f.o.b.*: Gold 4,669.3; Crude petroleum 3,506.1; Copper 3,616.7; Forestry products 537.9; Total (incl. others) 15,423.4 (Source: Bank of Papua New Guinea, Port Moresby).

2009 (million kina): *Imports c.i.f.*: Total 7,886.5. *Exports f.o.b.*: Gold 5,419.2; Crude petroleum 1,645.3; Copper 2,025.9; Forestry products 476.8; Total (incl. others) 12,079.8 (Source: Bank of Papua New Guinea, Port Moresby).

PRINCIPAL TRADING PARTNERS
(US $ million)

Imports c.i.f.	2007	2008	2009
Australia	1,523.0	1,469.0	1,620.6
China, People's Republic	234.2	378.1	499.7
Indonesia	76.9	89.1	58.0
Japan	167.7	198.8	173.1
Korea, Republic	20.2	34.5	30.5
Malaysia	106.5	149.0	130.3
New Zealand	97.0	107.8	105.7
Singapore	344.8	538.8	359.3
Thailand	66.3	98.8	96.5
USA	72.3	76.9	239.6
Total (incl. others)	2,964.4	3,487.0	3,744.5

PAPUA NEW GUINEA

Exports f.o.b.	2007	2008	2009
Australia	2,022.2	2,469.5	2,314.9
China, People's Republic	425.8	464.7	236.6
Germany	244.4	311.8	198.9
India	196.0	198.3	175.1
Japan	703.9	814.3	576.1
Korea, Republic	124.8	207.9	183.7
Philippines	105.8	132.3	113.8
Spain	63.7	143.4	109.8
United Kingdom	70.6	106.8	76.8
USA	104.4	101.7	97.5
Total (incl. others)	7,516.7	9,049.4	7,740.0

Note: Data reflect the IMF's direction of trade methodology and, as a result, the totals may not be equal to those presented for trade in commodities.

Source: Asian Development Bank.

Transport

ROAD TRAFFIC
('000 vehicles in use)

	1999	2000	2001
Passenger cars	18.8	24.9	24.9
Commercial vehicles	87.0	87.8	87.8

Source: UN, *Statistical Yearbook*.

2007 ('000 vehicles in use at 31 December): Passenger cars 38,173; Coaches and buses 6,561; Vans and lorries 11,333; Motorcycles and mopeds 1,193 (Source: IRF, *World Road Statistics*).

SHIPPING
Merchant Fleet
(registered at 31 December)

	2007	2008	2009
Number of vessels	125	124	135
Total displacement ('000 grt)	85.2	90.3	97.8

Source: IHS Fairplay, *World Fleet Statistics*.

International Sea-borne Freight Traffic

	1997	1998	1999
Cargo unloaded ('000 metric tons)	2,208.6	2,209.0	2,062.8
Cargo loaded ('000 metric tons)	735.9	823.3	788.1

Source: Papua New Guinea Harbours Board, *Monthly Shipping Register Form*.

CIVIL AVIATION
(traffic on scheduled services)

	2004	2005	2006
Kilometres flown (million)	12	12	14
Passengers carried ('000)	763	819	919
Passenger-km (million)	667	695	771
Total ton-km (million)	84	92	100

Source: UN, *Statistical Yearbook*.

2007: Passenger carried ('000) 918.7 (Source: World Bank, World Development Indicators database).

2008: Passenger carried ('000) 904.9 (Source: World Bank, World Development Indicators database).

Tourism

FOREIGN TOURIST ARRIVALS

Country of origin	2006	2007	2008
Australia	40,642	54,098	58,724
Canada	981	1,385	1,745
Germany	818	1,492	1,408
Japan	3,966	3,347	3,865
Malaysia	3,155	4,490	4,772
New Zealand	2,867	4,643	5,399
Philippines	3,784	6,478	7,661
United Kingdom	1,783	3,515	3,800
USA	6,228	6,159	6,109
Total (incl. others)	77,730	104,122	114,182

Receipts from tourism (US $ million, incl. passenger transport): 5.9 in 2004; 3.7 in 2005.

Source: World Tourism Organization.

Communications Media

	2007	2008	2009
Telephones ('000 main lines in use)	60	60	60
Mobile cellular telephones ('000 subscribers)	300	600	900
Internet users ('000)	115	120	125

Personal computers: 391,000 (63.9 per 1,000 persons) in 2005.

Daily newspapers (2004): 2 (combined circulation 51,000 copies).

Radio receivers (1997): 410,000 in use.

Television receivers (2001): 110,000 in use.

Sources: UNESCO, *Statistical Yearbook*; International Telecommunication Union.

Education

(2005/06, unless otherwise indicated)

	Institutions*	Teachers	Students
Pre-primary	29	2,697†	95,121†
Primary	2,790	14,860	532,250
Secondary	n.a.	8,420‡	173,214‡
Tertiary§	n.a.	815	13,761

* 1994/95 figures.
† 2001/02 figure.
‡ 2002/03 figure.
§ 1998/99 figures.

Sources: National Department of Education, *The State of Education in PNG* (March 2001); UN, *Statistical Yearbook for Asia and the Pacific*; UNESCO Institute for Statistics.

Pupil-teacher ratio (primary education, UNESCO estimate): 35.8 in 2005/06 (Source: UNESCO Institute for Statistics).

Adult literacy rate (UNESCO estimates): 59.6% (males 63.6%; females 55.6%) in 2008 (Source: UNESCO Institute for Statistics).

PAPUA NEW GUINEA

Directory

The Government

HEAD OF STATE

Queen: HM Queen ELIZABETH II.
Governor-General: MICHAEL OGIO (sworn in 25 February 2011).

NATIONAL EXECUTIVE COUNCIL
(May 2011)

The cabinet comprises members of the National Alliance (NA), the People's Action Party (PAP), the United Resources Party (URP), the Pangu Pati (PANGU), the People's National Congress (PNC), the People's Democratic Movement (PDC), the Rural Development Party (RDP), the United Party (UP), the People's Party (PP) and the Melanesian Alliance (MA).

Prime Minister and Minister for Autonomy and Autonomous Regions: Sir MICHAEL SOMARE (NA).
Deputy Prime Minister and Minister for Works: SAMUEL TEI ABAL (NA).
Minister for Foreign Affairs and Immigration: DON POLYE (NA).
Minister for Finance and Treasury: PETER O'NEILL (PNC).
Minister for Commerce and Industry: GABRIEL KAPRIS (PAP).
Minister for Defence: BOB DADAE (UP).
Minister for Internal Security: MARK MAIPAKAI (NA).
Minister for Justice and Attorney-General: Sir ARNOLD AMET (NA).
Minister for Agriculture and Livestock: ANO PALA (NA).
Minister for Communications and Information: PATRICK TAMMUR (NA).
Minister for Culture and Tourism: GUMA WAU (URP).
Minister for Environment and Conservation: BENNY ALLEN (URP).
Minister for Mining: JOHN PUNDARI (PP).
Minister for Fisheries: BEN SEMRI (PAP).
Minister for Forestry: TIMOTHY BONGA (NA).
Minister for Public Service: MOSES MALADINA (RDP).
Minister for Administrative Services and Transport and Minister assisting the Prime Minister on Constitutional Matters: FRANCIS POTAPE (PRP).
Minister for Health and HIV/AIDS: SASA ZIBE (NA).
Minister for Education: JAMES MARAPE (NA).
Minister for Higher Education, Research, Science and Technology: PARU AIHI (NA).
Minister for Housing and Urban Development: ANDREW KUMBAKOR (PANGU).
Minister for Inter-Government Relations and Provincial and Local Government Affairs: JOB POMAT (PNC).
Minister for Labour and Industrial Relations: SANI RAMBI (NA).
Minister for National Planning and Rural Development: PAUL TIENSTEN (NA).
Minister for Petroleum and Energy: WILLIAM DUMA (URP).
Minister for Public Enterprise: ARTHUR SOMARE (NA).
Minister for Lands: LUCAS DEKENA (NA).
Minister for Civil Aviation: BENJAMIN POPONAWA (NA).
Minister for Trade and Bougainville Affairs: FIDELIS SEMOSO (NA).
Minister for Community Development, Women and Religion: Dame CAROL KIDU (MA).
Minister for Sports: PHILEMON EMBEL (PANGU).
Minister for Corrective Services: TONY AIMO (PAP).

GOVERNMENT DEPARTMENTS AND OFFICES

Office of the Prime Minister: POB 639, Waigani, NCD; tel. 3277316; fax 3277328; e-mail chiefsectogov@pmnec.gov.pg; internet www.pm.gov.pg.
Department of Agriculture and Livestock: POB 417, Konedobu 125; tel. 3231848; fax 3230563; e-mail dalit@daltron.com.pg; internet www.agriculture.gov.pg.
Department of the Attorney-General: POB 591, Waigani, NCD; tel. 3230138; fax 3230241.
Department of Communications and Information: POB 1122, Waigani, NCD; tel. 3250148; fax 3250412; e-mail hiduhu@gopng.gov.pg.
Department of Community Development: POB 7354, Boroko, NCD; tel. 3244526; fax 3250133; internet www.pngfamilies.gov.pg.
Department of Defence: Murray Barracks, Free Mail Bag, Boroko 111, NCD; tel. 3242494; fax 3277480; internet www.defence.gov.pg.
Department of Education: Fincorp Haus, POB 446, Waigani, NCD; tel. 3013555; fax 3254648; internet www.education.gov.pg.
Department of Environment and Conservation: POB 6601, Boroko 111, NCD; tel. 3250182; fax 3250180; e-mail wamini@dec.gov.pg; internet www.dec.gov.pg.
Department of Family and Church Affairs: Ori Lavi Haus, Nita St, POB 7354, Boroko, NCD; tel. 3254566; fax 3251230.
Department of Finance: POB 710, Waigani, Vulupindi Haus, NCD; tel. 3288455; fax 3232239; e-mail inquires@finance.gov.pg; internet www.finance.gov.pg.
Department of Fisheries and Marine Resources: POB 2016, Port Moresby; tel. 3271799; fax 3202074.
Department of Foreign Affairs and Trade: POB 422, Waigani 131, NCD; tel. 3156047; fax 3254263.
Department of Health: POB 807, Waigani, NCD; tel. 3013827; fax 3013742; internet www.health.gov.pg.
Department of Housing and Urban Resettlement: POB 1550, Boroko, NCD; tel. 3247200; fax 3259918.
Department of Justice: POB 591, Waigani, NCD.
Department of Labour and Industrial Relations: POB 5644, Boroko, NCD; tel. 3235758; fax 3256655; e-mail enquiries@workpermits.gov.pg; internet www.workpermits.gov.pg.
Department of Lands and Physical Planning: Aopi Centre, Tower 2, Levels 2, 3 and 4, Waigani Drive, Boroko, NCD; tel. 3013206; fax 3013205; e-mail onnoj@lands.gov.pg; internet www.lands.gov.pg.
Department of Mining: PMB, Port Moresby Post Office, Port Moresby 121; tel. 3214011; fax 3217958; internet www.mineral.gov.pg.
Department of National Planning and Monitoring: POB 631, Waigani, NCD; tel. 3288302; fax 3288444; e-mail dnpm_enquiries@planning.gov.pg; internet www.planning.gov.pg.
Department of Personnel Management: POB 519, Wards Strip, Waigani, NCD; tel. 3276422; fax 3250520; e-mail perrtsiamalili@dpm.gov.pg.
Department of Petroleum and Energy: POB 1993, Port Moresby, NCD; tel. 3224200; fax 3224222; e-mail enquiry@petroleum.gov.pg; internet www.petroleum.gov.pg.
Department of Police: Police Headquarters, POB 85, Konedobu, NCD; tel. 3226100; fax 3226113.
Department of Provincial and Local Government Affairs: POB 1287, Boroko, NCD; tel. 3011002; fax 3250553; e-mail paffairs@dalton.com.pg; internet www.dplga.gov.pg.
Department of Social Welfare and Development, Youth and Women: POB 7354, Boroko, NCD; tel. 3254967; fax 3213821.
Department of State: Haus To Makala, 5th Floor, Post Office, Wards Strip, Waigani, NCD; tel. 3276758; fax 3214861.
Department of Transport and Civil Aviation: POB 1489, Port Moresby; tel. 3222580; fax 3200236.
Department of Treasury: POB 542, Waigani 131, NCD; tel. 3128817; fax 3128844; e-mail enquiries@treasury.gov.pg; internet www.treasury.gov.pg.
Department of Works and Implementation: POB 1108, Boroko 111, NCD; tel. 3222500; fax 3200236; e-mail webmaster@works.gov.pg; internet www.works.gov.pg.
Correctional Service: POB 6889, Boroko, NCD III; tel. 3231437; fax 3230407; e-mail rsikani@hq.cs.gov.pg.
Papua New Guinea Forest Authority: POB 5055, Boroko, NCD; tel. 3277841; fax 3254433; e-mail info_general@pngfa.gov.pg; internet www.forestry.gov.pg.

Legislature

NATIONAL PARLIAMENT

The unicameral legislature has 109 elective seats: 89 representing open constituencies and 20 representing provincial constituencies. There is constitutional provision for up to three nominated members.
Speaker: FRANCIS MARUS (acting).

PAPUA NEW GUINEA

General Election, 30 June–15 July 2007 (provisional results)

Party	Seats
National Alliance	27
Papua New Guinea Party	8
People's Action Party	6
Pangu Pati	5
People's Democratic Movement	5
United Resource Party	5
New Generation Party	4
People's National Congress	4
People's Progress Party	4
Rural Development Party	4
People's Party	3
Melanesian Liberal Party	2
People's Labour Party	2
PNG Country Party	2
United Party	2
Melanesian Alliance Party	1
National Advance Party	1
Pipol First Party	1
PNG Conservative Party	1
PNG Labour Party	1
PNG National Party	1
Independents and others	20
Total	**109**

Note: in many cases party affiliations were subject to review in the immediate aftermath of the election. The National Alliance was subsequently reported to have secured the support of 30 members of the legislature.

Autonomous Region

BOUGAINVILLE ASSEMBLY

Elections for 39 of the 40 seats in Bougainville's second autonomous assembly and for the President of the Autonomous Bougainville Government took place over a period of two weeks commencing on 7 May 2010. John Momis of the New Bougainville Party was elected President of the ABG, winning 52.3% of the total votes cast, thus defeating the incumbent James Tanis (20.9%) and five other candidates. More than three-quarters of incumbent legislators lost their seats in the House of Representatives. Independent candidates were reported to have won 23 seats and the New Bougainville Party 14 seats. Three of the 39 seats are reserved for women and three for former combatants. The President occupies the 40th seat in the assembly. The incoming President and the House of Representatives were inaugurated on 15 June 2010.

President: John Momis.

Vice-President: Patrick Nisira.

Speaker: Andrew Miriki.

Election Commission

Election Commission of Papua New Guinea: POB 5348, Boroko, NCD; tel. 3258187; fax 3258650; e-mail info@pngec.gov.pg; internet www.pngec.gov.pg; Electoral Commr Andrew Trawen.

Political Organizations

Bougainville Revolutionary Army (BRA): f. 1988; demands full independence for island of Bougainville; Leader Ishmael Toroama.

Christian Democratic Party: Leader Dr Banare Bun.

Customary Land Rights-holders Party: f. 2011; promotes wealth creation, co-operation and equal development among all customary land rights-holders and citizens; Pres. Peter Donigi.

Melanesian Alliance (MA): Port Moresby; tel. 3277635; f. 1978; socialist; Chair. Sir Moi Avei; Gen. Sec. Fabian Wau Kawa.

Melanesian Labour Party: Port Moresby; Leader Paul Mondia.

Movement for Greater Autonomy: Manus Province; Leader Stephen Pokawin.

National Alliance: c/o National Parliament, Port Moresby; f. 1996; est. to combat corruption in public life; Pres. Simon Kaiwi; Parliamentary Leader Sir Michael Somare.

National Party (NP): Private Bag, Boroko, NCD; f. 1979; fmrly People's United Front; Leader Michael Mel.

New Bougainville Party (NBP): Bougainville; f. 2005; aims to combat corruption, review peace process and issue of disposal of guns, and to involve youths, women, church groups and businesses in devt of Bougainville; Leader John Momis; Pres. Linus Sahoto.

New Generation Party: c/o National Parliament, Port Moresby; Leader Bart Philemon.

Pangu Pati (PANGU) (Papua New Guinea Unity): POB 289, Waigani, NCD; tel. 3277628; fax 3277611; f. 1968; urban- and rural-based; Leader Andrew Kumbakor; Deputy Leader Philemon Embel.

Papua New Guinea Greens Party: f. 2001; Pres. Dorothy Tekwie.

Papua New Guinea Party: f. 2007; Leader Belden Namah.

People's Action Party (PAP): Boroko, NCD; tel. 3251343; f. 1985.

People's Democratic Movement (PDM): POB 972, Boroko, NCD; f. 1985; merged with Advance PNG Party in 2001; Leader Paias Wingti.

People's National Congress (PNC): c/o National Parliament, Port Moresby; Leader Peter O'Neill.

People's National Party: Port Moresby.

People's Party: Leader Peter Ipatas.

People's Progress Party (PPP): POB 6030, Boroko, NCD; f. 1970; Parliamentary Leader Julius Chan; Nat. Pres. Alex Anisi; Gen. Sec. Emos Daniels.

Rural Development Party: Leader Moses Maladina.

Social Democratic Party: f. 2010; est. as United Democratic Front; aims to eliminate corruption and 'power politics, power-play and politics of convenience'; Leader Powes Parkop; Pres. Wesley Sanarup.

United Party: c/o National Parliament, Port Moresby; Leader Bob Dadae.

United Resources Party (URP): Port Moresby; f. 1997; aims to secure greater representation in govt for resource owners; Leader Tim Neville.

Other parties that contested the 2007 election included the Melanesian Liberal Party, the National Advance Party, the People's Labour Party, the Pipol First Party, the PNG Conservative Party, the PNG Country Party (Leader Jamie Maxtone-Graham), the PNG Labour Party and the PNG National Party.

Diplomatic Representation

EMBASSIES AND HIGH COMMISSIONS IN PAPUA NEW GUINEA

Australia: Godwit Rd, Waigani, NCD; tel. 3259333; fax 3256647; internet www.png.embassy.gov.au; High Commissioner Ian Kemish.

China, People's Republic: POB 1351, Boroko, NCD; tel. 3259836; fax 3258247; e-mail chinaemb_pg@mfa.gov.cn; internet www.chinaembassy.org.pg; Ambassador Qiu Bohua.

Fiji: Defens Haus, 4th Floor, Champion Parade, Port Moresby; tel. 3211914; fax 3217220; High Commissioner Dr Niumaia Tabunakawai.

France: Defens Haus, 6th Floor, Champion Parade, POB 1155, Port Moresby; tel. 3215550; fax 3215549; e-mail ambfrpom@global.net.pg; internet www.ambafrance-pg.org; Ambassador Alain Waquet.

Holy See: POB 98, Port Moresby; tel. 3256021; fax 3252844; e-mail nunciaturepng@datec.net.pg; Apostolic Nuncio Most Rev. Francisco Montecillo Padilla (Titular Archbishop of Nebbio).

India: Lot 20, Section 8, Unit 2, Tanatana St, Boroko, NCD; tel. 3254757; fax 3253138; e-mail hcipom@datec.net.pg; High Commissioner S. P. Mann.

Indonesia: POB 7165, Boroko, NCD; tel. 3253116; fax 3250535; e-mail kbripom@daltron.com.pg; internet www.deplu.go.id/portmoresby; Ambassador Andreas Sitepu.

Japan: POB 1040, Port Moresby; tel. 3211800; fax 3214868; e-mail sceoj@online.net.pg; Ambassador Hiroharu Iwasaki.

Korea, Republic: POB 381, Port Moresby; tel. 3215822; fax 3215828; e-mail embpng@mofat.go.kr; internet png.mofat.go.kr; Ambassador Han Won-Jung.

Malaysia: POB 1400, Port Moresby; tel. 3252076; fax 3252784; e-mail malpmresby@kln.gov.my; internet www.kln.gov.my/web/png_port-moresby; Ambassador Datin Blanche Olbery.

New Zealand: POB 1051, Waigani, NCD; tel. 3259444; fax 3250565; e-mail nzhcpom@dg.com.pg; High Commissioner Marion Crawshaw.

Philippines: POB 5916, Boroko, NCD; tel. 3256414; fax 3231803; e-mail pompe@datec.net.pg; Ambassador Shirley Ho-Vicario.

PAPUA NEW GUINEA

Solomon Islands: Waigani, Port Moresby; e-mail sihicomm@daltron.com.pg; High Commissioner BERNARD BATA'ANISIA.

United Kingdom: Locked Bag 212, Waigani 131, NCD; tel. 3251677; fax 3253547; e-mail ukinpng@datec.net.pg; internet www.ukinpng.fco.gov.uk; High Commissioner JACQUELINE BARSON.

USA: POB 1492, Port Moresby; tel. 3211455; fax 3211593; e-mail png@state.gov; internet portmoresby.usembassy.gov; Ambassador TEDDY TAYLOR.

Judicial System

The Supreme Court is the highest judicial authority in the country, and deals with all matters involving the interpretation of the Constitution, and with appeals from the National Court. The National Court has unlimited jurisdiction in both civil and criminal matters. All National Court Judges (except acting Judges) are Judges of the Supreme Court. District Courts are responsible for civil cases involving compensation, for some indictable offences and for the more serious summary offences, while Local Courts deal with minor offences and with such matters as custody of children under the provision of Custom. There are also Children's Courts, which judge cases involving minors. Appeal from the District, Local and Children's Courts lies to the National Court. District and Local Land Courts deal with disputes relating to Customary land, and Warden's Courts with civil cases relating to mining. In addition, there are other courts with responsibility for determining ownership of government land and for assessing the right of Customary landowners to compensation. Village Courts, which are presided over by Magistrates with no formal legal qualification, are responsible for all Customary matters not dealt with by other courts.

Chief Justice of the Supreme Court of Papua New Guinea: Sir SALAMO INJIA, POB 7018, Boroko, NCD; tel. 3245700; fax 3234492; internet www.pngjudiciary.gov.pg.

Attorney-General: Sir ARNOLD AMET.

Religion

The belief in magic or sorcery is widespread, even among the significant proportion of the population that has adopted Christianity (nominally 97% in 1990). Pantheism also survives. There are many missionary societies.

CHRISTIANITY

Papua New Guinea Council of Churches: POB 1015, Boroko, NCD; tel. 3259961; fax 3251206; f. 1965; seven mem. churches; Chair. EDEA KIDU; Gen. Sec. SOPHIA W. R. GEGEYO.

The Anglican Communion

Formerly part of the Province of Queensland within the Church of England in Australia (now the Anglican Church of Australia), Papua New Guinea became an independent Province in 1977. The Anglican Church of Papua New Guinea comprises five dioceses and had 246,000 members in 2000.

Archbishop of Papua New Guinea and Bishop of Aipo Rongo: Most Rev. JAMES AYONG, POB 893, Mount Hagen, Western Highlands Province; tel. 5421131; fax 5421181; e-mail acpnghgn@global.net.pg.

General Secretary: MARTIN GARDHAM, POB 673, Lae, Morobe Province; tel. 4724111; fax 4721852; e-mail acpng@global.net.pg.

The Roman Catholic Church

For ecclesiastical purposes, Papua New Guinea comprises four archdioceses and 15 dioceses. At 31 December 2007 there were 1,826,012 adherents.

Catholic Bishops' Conference of Papua New Guinea and Solomon Islands

POB 398, Waigani, NCD; tel. 3259577; fax 3232551; e-mail cbc@dg.com.pg; internet www.catholicpng.org.pg; f. 1959; Pres. Most Rev. FRANCESCO SAREGO (Bishop of Goroka); Gen. Sec. LAWRENCE STEPHENS.

Archbishop of Madang: Most Rev. STEPHEN JOSEPH REICHERT, Archbishop's Residence, POB 750, Madang 511; tel. 8522599; fax 8522596; e-mail Kurtz_caom@global.net.pg.

Archbishop of Mount Hagen: Most Rev. DOUGLAS YOUNG, Archbishop's Office, POB 54, Mount Hagen, Western Highlands Province 281; tel. 5421285; fax 5422128; e-mail dwyoung@global.net.pg.

Archbishop of Port Moresby: Most Rev. JOHN RIBAT, Archbishop's House, POB 1032, Boroko, NCD 111; tel. 3251192; fax 3256731; e-mail archpom@daltron.com.pg.

Archbishop of Rabaul: Most Rev. KARL HESSE, Archbishop's House, POB 357, Kokopo 613, East New Britain Province; tel. 9829384; fax 9828404; e-mail abkhesse@online.net.pg.

Other Christian Churches

Baptist Union of Papua New Guinea Inc: POB 705, Mount Hagen, Western Highlands Province; tel. 5522364; fax 5522402; e-mail bupng@global.net.pg; f. 1976; Gen. Sec. JOHN KAENKI; 48,000 mems.

Evangelical Lutheran Church of Papua New Guinea: Bishop Rt Rev. WESLEY KIGASUNG, POB 80, Lae, Morobe Province; tel. 4723711; fax 4721056; e-mail bishop.admin@global.net.pg; f. 1956; Sec. ISAAC TEO; 900,000 mems.

Gutnius Lutheran Church of Papua New Guinea: Bishop Rev. DAVID P. PISO, POB 111, 291 Wabag, Enga Province; tel. 5471280; fax 5471235; e-mail dpisoglc@online.net.pg; f. 1948; Gen. Sec. RICHARD R. MOSES; 138,000 mems.

Papua New Guinea Union Mission of the Seventh-day Adventist Church: POB 86, Lae, Morobe Province 411; tel. 4721488; fax 4721873; Pres. Pastor WILSON STEPHEN; Sec. Pastor BRADLEY RICHARD KEMP; 200,000 adherents.

The United Church in Papua New Guinea: POB 1401, Port Moresby; tel. 3211744; fax 3214930; e-mail assmbly.office@ucpng.com; internet www.ucpng.com; f. 1968; formed by union of the Methodist Church in Melanesia, the Papua Ekalesia and United Church, Port Moresby; Moderator Sir SAMSON LOWA; 700,000 mems; Gen. Sec. Rev. SIULANGI KAVORA.

BAHÁ'Í FAITH

National Spiritual Assembly: PMB, Boroko, NCD; tel. 3250286; fax 3236474.

ISLAM

In 2000 the Muslim community in Papua New Guinea numbered about 1,500, of whom approximately two-thirds were believed to be expatriates. The religion was introduced to the island in the 1970s. The country's first mosque was opened in 2000 at Poreporena Highway, Hohola, Port Moresby; Imam MIKHAIL KORAH (acting).

The Press

There are numerous newspapers and magazines published by government departments, statutory organizations, missions, sporting organizations, local government councils and regional authorities. They are variously in English, Tok Pisin (Pidgin), Motu and vernacular languages.

Ailans Nius: POB 1239, Rabaul, East New Britain Province; weekly.

Foreign Affairs Review: Dept of Foreign Affairs, Central Government Offices, Kumul Ave, Post Office, Wards Strip, Waigani, NCD; tel. 3271401; fax 3254886.

Hailans Nius: Mount Hagen, Western Highlands Province; weekly.

Lae Nius: POB 759, Lae, Morobe Province; 2 a week.

The National: POB 6817, Boroko, NCD; tel. 3246888; fax 3246868; e-mail national@thenational.com.pg; internet www.thenational.com.pg; f. 1993; daily; Editor DANIEL KORIMBAU; circ. 30,000.

Papua and New Guinea Education Gazette: Dept of Education, Fincorp Haus, POB 446, Waigani, NCD; tel. 3272413; fax 3254648; monthly; Editor J. OBERLENTER; circ. 8,000.

Papua New Guinea Post-Courier: POB 85, Port Moresby; tel. 3091000; fax 3212721; e-mail postcourier@ssp.com.pg; internet www.postcourier.com.pg; f. 1969; daily; English; published by News Corpn; Gen. Man. TONY YIANNI; Editor OSEAH PHILEMON; circ. 25,044.

Sunkamap Times: POB 322, Buka, Bougainville, North Solomons Province; e-mail stephen@viscom.co.nz; internet www.viscom.co.nz/SunkamapTimes; monthly; f. 2004; community newsletter.

Wantok (Friend) Niuspepa: POB 1982, Boroko, NCD; tel. 3252500; fax 3252579; e-mail word@global.net.pg; f. 1970; weekly in New Guinea Pidgin; mainly rural readership; Publr ANNA SOLOMON; Editor NEVILLE CHOI; circ. 10,000.

Publishers

Gordon and Gotch (PNG) Pty Ltd: POB 107, Boroko, NCD; tel. 3254855; fax 3250950; e-mail ggpng@online.net.pg; f. 1970; books, magazines and stationery; Gen. Man. PETER G. PORTER.

Scripture Union of Papua New Guinea: POB 280, University, Boroko, NCD; tel. and fax 3253987; f. 1966; religious; Chair. RAVA TAVIRI.

PAPUA NEW GUINEA

Word Publishing Co Pty Ltd: POB 1982, Boroko, NCD; tel. 3252500; fax 3252579; e-mail word@global.net.pg; f. 1982; 60% owned by the Roman Catholic Church, 20% by Evangelical Lutheran, 10% by Anglican and 10% by United Churches; Gen. Man. JEREMY BURGESS.

Broadcasting and Communications

TELECOMMUNICATIONS

Department of Information and Communication: POB 1122, Waigani; tel. 3250148; fax 3250412; e-mail hiduhu@gopng.gov.pg; internet www.communication.gov.pg; Sec. HENAO IDUHU.

Digicel (PNG) Ltd: POB 1618, Port Moresby, NCD; e-mail customercarepng@digicelgroup.com; internet www.digicelpng.com; GSM services; CEO JOHN MANGOS.

Pacific Mobile Communications Company Ltd: POB 6973, Boroko, NCD; tel. 3232555; fax 3232554; e-mail pmc@tiare.net.pg; internet www.pacificmobile.com.pg; Chair. Dr FLORIAN GUBON.

Papua New Guinea Radiocommunications and Telecommunications Technical Authority (Pangtel): POB 8444, Boroko, NCD; tel. 3258633; fax 3256868; e-mail licensing@pangtel.gov.pg; internet www.pangtel.gov.pg; f. 1997; CEO CHARLES PUNAHA.

Telikom PNG Pty Ltd: POB 291, Waigan, Port Moresby, NCD; tel. 3004010; fax 3250665; e-mail webadmin@telikompng.com.pg; internet www.telikompng.com.pg; Chair. GEREA AOPI; CEO PETER LOKO.

In 2006 Green Communications (GreenCom), an Indonesian company, acquired a licence to expand into Papua New Guinea.

BROADCASTING

Radio

National Broadcasting Corporation of Papua New Guinea: POB 1359, Boroko, NCD; tel. 3255233; fax 3256296; e-mail info@nbc.com.pg; internet www.nbc.com.pg; f. 1973; commercial and free govt radio programmes services; broadcasting in English, Melanesian, Pidgin, Motu and 30 vernacular languages; Chair. CHRIS RANGATIN; Man. Dir Dr MEMAFU KAPERA (acting).

Kalang Service (FM): POB 1359, Boroko, NCD; tel. 3255233; commercial radio co established by National Broadcasting Commission; Chair. CAROLUS KETSIMUR.

Nau FM/Yumi FM: POB 774, Port Moresby; tel. 3201996; fax 3201995; f. 1994; Gen. Mans MARK ROGERS, JUSTIN KILI.

Television

EM TV: POB 443, Boroko, NCD; tel. 3257322; fax 3254450; e-mail emtv@emtv.com.pg; internet www.emtv.com.pg; f. 1988; operated by Media Niugini Pty Ltd; Gen. Man. GLENN ARMSTRONG.

Media Niugini Pty Ltd: POB 443, Boroko, NCD; tel. 3257322; fax 3254450; e-mail emtv@emtv.com.pg; internet www.emtv.com.pg; f. 1987; owned by Fijity Ltd; Gen. Man. GLENN ARMSTRONG.

Finance

(cap. = capital; res = reserves; dep. = deposits; m. = million; brs = branches; amounts in kina unless otherwise stated)

BANKING

Central Bank

Bank of Papua New Guinea: POB 121, Port Moresby 121; tel. 3227200; fax 3211617; e-mail info@bankpng.gov.pg; internet www.bankpng.gov.pg; f. 1973; bank of issue since 1975; sold to Bank of South Pacific in 2002; cap. 145.5m., res 246.8m., dep. 4,926.6m. (Dec. 2008); Gov. LOI MARTIN BAKANI; Deputy Gov. BENNY POPOITAI.

Commercial Banks

Australia and New Zealand Banking Group (PNG) Ltd: POB 1152, Port Moresby 121; tel. 3211079; fax 3223302; e-mail cshdpg@anz.com; internet www.anz.com/Png/; f. 1976; cap. 5.0m., res 2.2m., dep. 3,055.3m. (Sept. 2008); Chair. JOHN MORSCHEL; Man. Dir GARRY TUNSTALL; 12 brs.

Bank of South Pacific Ltd: POB 78, Cnr Douglas and Musgrave Sts, Port Moresby; tel. 3211999; fax 3211954; e-mail servicebsp@bsp.com.pg; internet www.bsp.com.pg; f. 1974; acquired from National Australia Bank Ltd by Papua New Guinea consortium (National Investment Holdings, now BSP Holdings Ltd) in 1993; merged with Papua New Guinea Banking Corpn in 2002; 10% stake acquired by International Finance Corporation in mid-2010; cap. 318.0m., res 66.4m., dep. 6,771.8m. (Dec. 2009); Chair. NOREO BEANGKE; CEO IAN B. CLYNE; 35 brs.

Finance Corpn Ltd (FinCorp): Aopi Centre, Ground Floor, Waigani Dr., Port Moresby; tel. 3232399; fax 3230167; e-mail sales@fincorp.com.pg; internet www.fincorp.com.pg; Chair. KERENGA KUA; Man. Dir and CEO TONY WITHAM; 5 brs.

Maybank (PNG) Ltd: Cnr Waigani Rd and Islander Dr., POB 882, Waigani, NCD; tel. 3258028; fax 3256128; e-mail maybankpom@datec.net.pg; internet maybank.com.my/maybank-worldwide/papua-new-guinea; f. 1995; Chair. ALISTER MAITLAND.

Westpac Bank—PNG—Ltd: POB 706, Port Moresby; tel. 3220511; fax 3220636; e-mail westpacpng@westpac.com.au; internet www.westpac.com.pg; f. 1910; est. as Bank of New South Wales, present name adopted 1982; 93.5% owned by Westpac Banking Corpn (Australia); cap. 5.8m., res 78.5m., dep. 2,206m. (Sept. 2010); Man. Dir GAIL KELLY; 16 brs.

Development Bank

National Development Bank (NDB): POB 686, Waigani, NCD; tel. 3247500; fax 3259817; e-mail rbank@devbank.com.pg; internet www.ndb.com.pg; f. 1967; est. as Agriculture Bank of Papua New Guinea; later known as Rural Development Bank of Papua New Guinea; name changed as above in 2007; statutory govt agency; Chair. WILLIAM LAMUR; Man. Dir RICHARD MARU; 18 brs.

Savings and Loan Societies

Registry of Savings and Loan Societies: Bank of Papua New Guinea, Banking Supervision Dept, POB 121, Port Moresby; tel. 3227200; fax 3214548; e-mail gawap@bankpng.gov.pg; internet www.bankpng.gov.pg; 21 savings and loan societies; 243,003 mems (2010); total funds 756.8m., loans outstanding 219.4m., investments 341.1m. (Dec. 2010); Man. GEORGE AWAP.

STOCK EXCHANGE

Port Moresby Stock Exchange (POMSoX) Ltd: POB 1531, Port Moresby; tel. 3201980; fax 3201981; e-mail pomsox@pomsox.com.pg; internet www.pomsox.com.pg; f. 1999; Chair. GEREA AOPI; Gen. Man. VINCENT IVOSA.

INSURANCE

Capital Life Insurance Co: 2nd Floor, Tisa Haus, Wardship, Waigani, Port Moresby; tel. 3234036; fax 3232533; e-mail marketing@tsl.org.pg; f. 1993; fmrly Pan Asia Pacific Assurance (PNG); 100% owned by Teachers' Savings & Loan Society Ltd (TISA).

Kwila Insurance Corpn: POB 1457, Boroko, NCD; tel. 3258811; fax 3112867; e-mail jmcllvena@kwilainsurance.com.pg; internet www.kwilainsurance.com.pg; f. 1977; Gen. Man. JASON R. MCILVENA.

Pacific MMI Insurance Ltd: POB 331, Port Moresby; tel. 3214077; fax 3218437; e-mail enquiries@pacificmmi.com; internet www.pacificmmi.com; f. 1998; fmrly Niugini Insurance Corpn Ltd; jt venture; general and life insurance; financial services; Chair. Dr JOHN MUA; Man. Dir WAYNE DORGAN.

There are branches of several Australian and United Kingdom insurance companies in Port Moresby, Rabaul, Lae and Kieta.

Trade and Industry

GOVERNMENT AGENCIES

Independent Public Business Corpn (IPBC): POB 320, Port Moresby, NCD; tel. 3212977; fax 3212916; e-mail ipbc@ipbc.com.pg; internet www.ipbc.com.pg; f. 2002; assets manager of all govt enterprises of Papua New Guinea; Chair. GEREA AOPI; Man. Dir GLENN BLAKE.

Investment Promotion Authority (IPA): POB 5053, Boroko, NCD 111; tel. 3213900; fax 3213049; e-mail ipa@ipa.gov.pg; internet www.ipa.gov.pg; f. 1992; est. following reorganization of National Investment and Development Authority; statutory body responsible for the promotion of foreign investment; recommends priority areas for investment to the Govt; also co-ordinates investment proposals; Man. Dir IVAN POMALEU.

Mineral Resources Authority (MRA): POB 1906, Port Moresby; tel. 3213511; fax 3215711; e-mail info@mra.gov.pg; internet www.mra.gov.pg; f. 2006; Man. Dir KEPAS WALI.

DEVELOPMENT ORGANIZATION

Industrial Centres Development Corporation (ICDC): POB 1571, Boroko, NCD; tel. 3112211; fax 3112212; e-mail henlytaka@hotmail.com; internet www.icdc.gov.pg; f. 1990; promotes foreign investment in non-mining sectors through establishment of industrial estates; Sr Marketing Officer HENLY TAKA.

PAPUA NEW GUINEA

CHAMBERS OF COMMERCE

Lae Chamber of Commerce Inc: POB 265, Lae, Morobe Province; tel. 4722340; fax 4726038; e-mail lcci@global.net.pg; internet www.lcci.org.pg; Pres. ALAN MCLAY.

Papua New Guinea Chamber of Commerce and Industry: POB 1621, Port Moresby; tel. 3213057; fax 3210566; e-mail pngcci@global.net.pg; internet www.pngcci.org.pg; Pres. JOHN LEAHY; Vice-Pres. MICHAEL MAYBERRY.

Port Moresby Chamber of Commerce and Industry: POB 75, Port Moresby; tel. 3213077; fax 3214203; e-mail bizcentre@pomcci.org.pg; internet www.pomcci.com; Pres. RON SEDDON; Chief Exec. DAVID CONN.

INDUSTRIAL AND TRADE ASSOCIATIONS

Cocoa Board of Papua New Guinea: POB 532, Rabaul, East New Britain Province; tel. 9829083; fax 9828712; e-mail l.tautea@global.net.pg; f. 1974; Chair. JIMMY SIMITAB; CEO LAVATAU TAUTEA.

Coffee Industry Corpn Ltd: POB 137, Goroka, Eastern Highlands Province; tel. 7321266; fax 7321214; e-mail cicgka@daltron.com.pg; internet www.coffeecorp.org.pg; CEO RICKY MITIO.

Fishing Industry Association (PNG) Inc: POB 5860, Boroko, NCD; tel. 3258222; fax 3258994; e-mail netshop1@daltron.com.pg; Chair. MAURICE BROWNJOHN.

Forest Industries Association: POB 229, Waigani, NCD; internet www.fiapng.com; Pres. ANTHONY HONEY; CEO ROBERT TATE.

Kokonas Indastri Korporesen (KIK): POB 81, Port Moresby; tel. 3211133; fax 3214257; e-mail infor@kik.com.pg; regulates and markets all copra and coconut products in Papua New Guinea; represents producers; fmrly Copra Marketing Board of Papua New Guinea (f. 1950s); name changed as above 2002; govt-owned; Chair. JOE ARARUA; Man. Dir TORE OVASURU.

Manufacturers' Council of Papua New Guinea: POB 598, Port Moresby; tel. 3259512; fax 3230199; e-mail pngmade@global.com.pg; Chair. WAYNE GOLDING; CEO BRUCE REVILLE.

Mineral Resources Development Corporation: POB 1076, Port Moresby, NCD 121; tel. 3255822; fax 3252633; e-mail enquiry@mrdc.com.pg; internet www.mrdc.com.pg; f. 1975; manages landowner and provincial govt interests in major mineral resources projects; subsidiaries incl. Mineral Resources Star Mountains Ltd, Mineral Resources Ok Tedi No 2 Ltd, Mineral Resources Enga Ltd, Petroleum Resources Kutubu Ltd, Petroleum Resources Gobe Ltd and Petroleum Resources Moran Ltd; Chair. SIMON TOSALI; Man. Dir AUGUSTINE SANGA MANO.

National Fisheries Authority: POB 2016, Port Moresby; tel. 3212643; fax 3202061; e-mail nfa@fisheries.gov.pg; internet www.fisheries.gov.pg; Man. Dir SYLVESTER POKAJAM.

National Housing Corpn (NHC): POB 1550, Boroko, NCD; tel. 3252124; fax 3259918; e-mail managingdirector@nhc.gov.pg; f. 1990; man. and promotion of nat. housing projects; Man. Dir TARCISSIUS MUGANAUA (acting).

Palm Oil Producers Association: Port Moresby; Chair. BROWN BAI.

Papua New Guinea Chamber of Mines and Petroleum: POB 1032, Port Moresby; tel. 3212988; fax 3217107; e-mail conf@pngchamberminpet.com.pg; internet www.pngchamberminpet.com.pg; Exec. Dir GREG ANDERSON; Pres. Dr ILA TEMU.

Papua New Guinea Forest Authority: POB 5055, Boroko, NCD; tel. 3277800; fax 3254433; e-mail info_general@pngfa.gov.pg; internet www.forestry.gov.pg; Man. Dir KANAWI POURU; Chair. JOSEPH LELANG.

Papua New Guinea Growers Association: POB 14, Kokopo, East New Britain Province 613; tel. 9829123; fax 9829264; e-mail growers@global.net.pg; Pres. PAUL ARNOLD; Exec. Dir DAVID LOH.

Rural Industries Council: POB 1530, Port Moresby; tel. 3215773; fax 3217223; e-mail ric@daltron.com.pg; Chair. BROWN BAI.

UTILITIES

Electricity

PNG Power Ltd (PPL): POB 1105, Boroko, NCD; tel. 3243200; fax 3250072; e-mail marketing@pngpower.com.pg; internet www.pngpower.com.pg; prev. PNG Electricity Commission (Elcom); Commission privatized and name changed to above in 2002; undertakes regulatory role on behalf of Consumer and Competition Commission; Chair. WILLIAM KENJIBI; Chief Exec. TONY KOIRI.

Water

Eda Ranu (Our Water): PMB, Waigani, NCD; tel. 3122100; fax 3122194; e-mail info@edaranu.com.pg; internet www.edaranu.com.pg; fmrly Port Moresby Water Supply Company; Gen. Man. BILLY IMAR.

PNG Waterboard: POB 2779, Boroko, NCD; tel. 3235700; fax 3256298; e-mail pamini@pngwater.com.pg; f. 1986; govt-owned; operates 17 water supply systems throughout the country; Man. Dir PATRICK AMINI.

TRADE UNIONS

Papua New Guinea Trade Unions Congress (PNGTUC): POB 4279, Boroko, NCD; tel. 3257642; fax 3257890; e-mail tucl@daltron.com.pg; Pres. MICHAEL MALABAG; Gen. Sec. JOHN PASKA; 52 affiliates, 76,000 mems.

The following are among the major trade unions:

Bougainville Mining Workers' Union: POB 777, Panguna, North Solomons Province; tel. 9958272; Pres. MATHEW TUKAN; Gen. Sec. ALFRED ELISHA TAGORNOM.

Central Province Building and Construction Industry Workers' Union: POB 265, Port Moresby.

Central Province Transport Drivers' and Workers' Union: POB 265, Port Moresby.

Employers' Federation of Papua New Guinea: POB 6057, Boroko, NCD; tel. 3258266; fax 3258272; e-mail information@efpng.org.pg; internet www.efpng.org.pg; f. 1963; Pres. ROBERT DEBROUWERE; Exec. Dir FLORENCE WILLIE.

National Federation of Timber Workers: Madang; f. 1993; Gen. Sec. MATHIAS KENUANGI (acting).

Papua New Guinea Communication Workers' Union: Pres. BOB MAGARU; Gen. Sec. EMMANUEL KAIRU.

Papua New Guinea National Doctors' Association: Pres. Dr BOB DANAYA; 225 mems.

Papua New Guinea Teachers' Association: POB 1027, Waigani, NCD; tel. 3409291; fax 3261514; e-mail pngta@gmail.com; f. 1971; Pres. TOMMY HECKO; Gen. Sec. UGWALUBU MOWANA; 20,049 mems.

Papua New Guinea Waterside Workers' and Seamen's Union: POB 76, Kimbe 621; tel. 9835603; f. 1979; an amalgamation of four unions; Sec. DOUGLAS GADEBO.

Police Association of Papua New Guinea: tel. 3214172; f. 1964; Pres. ROBERT ALI; 4,596 mems.

Port Moresby Council of Trade Unions: POB 265, Boroko, NCD; Gen. Sec. JOHN KOSI.

Port Moresby Miscellaneous Workers' Union: POB 265, Boroko, NCD.

Printing and Kindred Industries Union: Port Moresby.

Public Employees' Association: POB 965, Boroko, NCD; tel. 3252955; fax 3252186; f. 1974; Pres. NAPOLEON LIOSI; Gen. Sec. JACK N. KUTAL; 28,000 mems.

Transport

There are no railways in Papua New Guinea. The capital city, Port Moresby, is not connected by road to other major population centres. Therefore, air and sea travel are of particular importance.

ROADS

In 2000 there were an estimated 19,600 km of roads in Papua New Guinea, of which 3.5% were paved.

National Roads Authority: Lae, Morobe Province; f. 2004; statutory authority; maintains the road network, particularly the Highlands Highway; Chair. ALLAN MCLAY.

SHIPPING

Papua New Guinea has 16 major ports and a coastal fleet of about 300 vessels.

PNG Ports Corporation Ltd: POB 671, Port Moresby, NCD; tel. 3084200; fax 3211546; e-mail corporatecommunications@pngports.com.pg; internet www.pngports.com.pg; CEO BRIAN RICHES.

Port Authority of Kieta: POB 149, Kieta, North Solomons Province; tel. 9956066; fax 9956255; Port Man. CHARLES TARURAVA.

Port Authority of Lae: POB 563, Lae, Morobe Province; tel. 4723464; fax 4723543; Port Man. SAKEUS GEM.

Port Authority of Port Moresby: POB 671, Port Moresby; tel. 211400; fax 3211546; Gen. Man. BEN PUKAI.

Port Authority of Rabaul: POB 592, Rabaul, East New Britain Province; tel. 9821533; fax 9821535; Port Man. JOHN TUNGAPIK.

Shipping Companies

Coastal Shipping Co Ltd: Sulphur Creek Rd, POB 423, Rabaul, East New Britain Province; tel. 9821746; fax 9821734; e-mail coastco@global.net.pg; f. 1967; Man. Dir HENRY CHOW.

Lutheran Shipping: POB 789, Madang; tel. 8522577; fax 8522180; e-mail finance.luship@global.net.pg.

Morehead Shipping Pty Ltd: POB 1908, Lae, Morobe Province; tel. 4423602.

New Guinea Australia Line Pty Ltd: POB 145, Stanley Esplanade, Port Moresby, NCD 121; tel. 3212377; fax 3201825; f. 1952; est. by The China Navigation Co, a fully owned shipping wing of John Swire & Sons (PNG) Ltd; operates regular container services between Australia, Papua New Guinea, Singapore, Indonesia, Vanuatu, Tuvalu and Solomon Islands; Chair. JAMES HUGHES-HALLETT.

P & O Maritime Services (PNG) Ltd: MMI House, 3rd Floor, Champion Parade, POB 1403, Port Moresby; tel. 3229200; fax 3229251; e-mail jhulse@pom.popng.com.pg; owned by P & O (Australia); Country Man. JOHN HULSE.

Papua New Guinea Shipping Corporation Pty Ltd: POB 634, Port Moresby; tel. 3220290; fax 3212815; e-mail shipping@steamships.com.pg; f. 1977; owned by Steamships Trading Co Ltd; provides a container/break-bulk service to Australia and the Pacific islands; Chair. CHRISTOPHER PRATT; Man. Dir JOHN DUNLOP.

South Sea Lines Proprietary Ltd: POB 5, Lae, Morobe Province; tel. 4423455; fax 4424884; Man. Dir R. CUNNINGHAM.

Steamships Trading Co Ltd: Champion Parade, POB 1, Port Moresby; tel. 3220222; fax 3213595; internet www.steamships.com.pg; f. 1924; Chair. W. L. ROTHERY; Man. Dir D. H. COX.

Western Tug & Barge Co P/L: POB 1403, Port Moresby; tel. 3229290; fax 3229251; division of P & O PNG; operates 24 vessels.

CIVIL AVIATION

There is an international airport, Jackson's Airport, at Port Moresby, and there are more than 400 other airports and airstrips throughout the country. International services from Lae and Mount Hagen airports began in 1999.

Air Niugini: POB 7186, Boroko, NCD; tel. 3259000; fax 3273482; e-mail airniugini@airniugini.com.pg; internet www.airniugini.com.pg; f. 1973; govt-owned national airline; operates scheduled domestic cargo and passenger services within Papua New Guinea and international services to Australia, Fiji, Solomon Islands, Philippines, Hong Kong, Singapore and Japan; fleet comprises 20 aircraft (2010); Chair. JIM TJOENG; CEO WASANTHA KUMARASIRI.

Airlines PNG: POB 170, Boroko, NCD; tel. 3252011; fax 3252219; e-mail apng@apng.com; internet www.apng.com; f. 1984; est. as Milne Bay Air (MBA); operates domestic scheduled and charter services; Chair. SIMON WILD; CEO GARRY TOOMEY.

National Aviation Services: Boroko, NCD; f. 2005; provides services between all small airstrips in Central, Oro, Gulf and Western Provinces, primarily for the transport of agricultural products to markets; Operations Man. GILBERT YENBARI; Propr and CEO TED DIRO.

Tourism

Papua New Guinea's attractions include the tribal customs, spectacular scenery and abundant wildlife. Foreign visitor arrivals reportedly rose from 125,891 in 2009 to 146,928 in 2010. The industry earned an estimated US $3.7m. in 2005.

PNG Tourism Promotion Authority: POB 1291, Port Moresby; tel. 3200211; fax 3200223; e-mail info@pngtourism.org.pg; internet www.pngtourism.org.pg; CEO PETER VINCENT.

Tour Operators Association of Papua New Guinea (TOAPNG): tel. 3200211; fax 3200223; e-mail toapng@pngtourism.org.pg; internet www.toa.org.pg; f. 2005; Pres. MICHAEL BULEAU; Treas. AARON HAYES.

Defence

As assessed at November 2010, the Papua New Guinea Defence Force had a total strength of some 3,100 (army 2,500, navy 400 and air force 200). Military service is voluntary. Australian training forces stationed in the country totalled 38. Government expenditure on defence in 2010 was budgeted at K116m.

Commander-in-Chief of Papua New Guinea Defence Force: Brig.-Gen. FRANCIS WANGI AGWI.

Education

Education facilities remain inadequate and unevenly distributed. In 2005/06 there were 2,790 primary schools, with 532,250 pupils and 14,860 teachers. In 1986 there were 116 secondary schools and 103 technical and vocational schools. Secondary-school pupils totalled 173,214 and the teachers numbered 8,420 in 2002/03. There are two universities.

Children attend school from seven years of age. At the age of 13 they move from community schools to provincial high schools for a further three years and are then eligible to spend another two years at the national high schools, where they are prepared for entrance to tertiary education. Fees and charges for equipment have been introduced.

In 2005/06 the total enrolment at primary schools was equivalent to 55% of that school-age population (males 59%; females 50%). In 1995 secondary enrolment was equivalent to only 14% of children in the relevant age-group (boys 17%; girls 11%). In some areas, such as East New Britain and Port Moresby, almost all eligible children attend primary schools, whereas in others, such as the Highlands provinces, attendance is as low as 34%. Access to secondary education ranges from 7% in the Eastern Highlands to almost 50% in East New Britain. In 2007, according to UNESCO estimates, adult literacy averaged 57.8% (males 62.1%; females 53.4%).

Budgetary expenditure on education by the central Government in 2006 totalled an estimated K43m.

PARAGUAY

Introductory Survey

LOCATION, CLIMATE, LANGUAGE, RELIGION, FLAG, CAPITAL

The Republic of Paraguay is a land-locked country in central South America. It is bordered by Bolivia to the north, by Brazil to the east, and by Argentina to the south and west. The climate is sub-tropical. Temperatures range from an average maximum of 34.3°C (93.7°F) in January to an average minimum of 14°C (51°F) in June. The official languages are Spanish and Guaraní, the latter, an indigenous Indian language, being spoken by the majority of the population. Almost all of the inhabitants profess Christianity, and some 92% adhere to the Roman Catholic Church, the country's established religion. There is a small Protestant minority. The national flag (proportions 3 by 5) has three equal horizontal stripes, of red, white and blue. It is the only national flag with a different design on each side, having a varying emblem in the centre of the white stripe: the obverse side bears the state emblem (a white disc with a red ring bearing the words 'República del Paraguay', in yellow capitals, framing a blue disc with the five-pointed 'May Star', in yellow, surrounded by a wreath, in green), while the reverse side carries the seal of the Treasury (a white disc with a red ribbon bearing the words 'Paz y Justicia' in yellow capitals above a lion supporting a staff, surmounted by the red 'Cap of Liberty'). The capital is Asunción.

CONTEMPORARY POLITICAL HISTORY

Historical Context

Paraguay, ruled by Spain from the 16th century, achieved independence in 1811. In 1865 Paraguay was involved in a disastrous war against Brazil, Argentina and Uruguay (the Triple Alliance), resulting in the loss of more than one-half of its population. Paraguay also suffered heavy losses in the Chaco Wars of 1928–30 and 1932–35 against Bolivia, but won a large part of the disputed territory when the boundary was fixed in 1938. Gen. Higinio Morínigo established an authoritarian regime in 1940, but the return of a number of political exiles in 1947 precipitated a civil war in which supporters of the right-wing Asociación Nacional Republicana—Partido Colorado (ANR—PC, commonly known as the Partido Colorado) defeated the Liberals and the Partido Revolucionario Febrerista, leading to the overthrow of Gen. Morínigo in June 1948. A period of great instability ensued. In May 1954 Gen. Alfredo Stroessner Mattiauda, the Army Commander-in-Chief, assumed power in a military coup. He nominated himself for the presidency, as the Colorado candidate, and was elected unopposed in July to complete the term of office of his predecessor, Federico Chávez. In 1955 Stroessner assumed extensive powers, and established a state of siege. Regular purges of the Partido Colorado membership, together with the mutual co-operation of the ruling party, the armed forces and the business community, enabled Stroessner to become the longest-serving dictator in South America: he was re-elected President, by large majorities, at five-yearly elections in 1958–88.

Domestic Political Affairs

In February 1978 President Stroessner revoked the state of siege in all areas except Asunción. The assassination of the former Nicaraguan dictator, Gen. Anastasio Somoza Debayle, in Asunción in September 1980, however, prompted Stroessner to reimpose the state of siege throughout the country; harassment of leaders of the political opposition and of peasant and labour groups continued. The leader of the Partido Demócrata Cristiano, Luis Alfonso Resck, was expelled from the country in June 1981, and Domingo Laíno, leader of the Partido Liberal Radical Auténtico (PLRA), was deported in December 1982. After Ronald Reagan took office as President of the USA in 1981, Paraguay encountered less pressure from the US Administration to curb abuses of human rights, and the use of torture against detainees reportedly became widespread once more. It was estimated at this time that more than 60% of all Paraguayans resided outside the country.

The majority of opposition parties boycotted the presidential and legislative elections of February 1983, enabling Stroessner to obtain more than 90% of the votes cast in the presidential poll, and in August he formally took office for a further five-year term. In May 1983 the Government instigated a campaign of repression against students and trade unionists. In February 1984 opposition parties organized demonstrations in Asunción for the first time in 30 years.

Divisions over Stroessner's continuance in office led to factionalism within the Partido Colorado in the mid-1980s. In April 1987 Stroessner announced that the state of siege was to be ended. (Later in the month Laíno was finally allowed to return to Paraguay.) However, the suppression of civil liberties and of political activity continued under the new penal code that replaced the state of siege. Stroessner received 89% of the votes cast in the 1988 presidential election. However, opposition leaders (who had urged voters to boycott the elections) complained of electoral malpractice, and denounced Stroessner's re-election as fraudulent.

On 3 February 1989 Gen. Stroessner was overthrown in a coup led by Gen. Andrés Rodríguez, the second-in-command of the armed forces. Stroessner was allowed to leave for exile in Brazil, as Gen. Rodríguez assumed the presidency and appointed a new Council of Ministers. The interim President pledged to respect human rights and to strengthen links with neighbouring countries. At the presidential election in May Rodríguez, the candidate of the Partido Colorado, was confirmed as President. The Partido Colorado also won the largest number of seats in both the Cámara de Diputados (Chamber of Deputies) and the Senado (Senate). Despite widespread allegations of electoral fraud, all parties agreed to respect the results.

In July 1989 the Cámara ratified the San José Pact on Human Rights, adopted by the Organization of American States (OAS, see p. 391) in 1978. In August 1989 the Congreso Nacional (National Congress—comprising the Cámara de Diputados and the Senado) initiated judicial proceedings against former government officials for violations of human rights. Following the repeal, in August, of laws that had provided a basis for political repression under the Stroessner regime, the Partido Comunista Paraguayo (PCP) was formally legalized. In November 1990, however, Rodríguez vetoed congressional proposals for the establishment of a legislative commission to investigate alleged violations of human rights.

In August 1991 the Congreso Nacional approved proposals for a complete revision of the 1967 Constitution. In anticipation of the elections to a National Constituent Assembly, President Rodríguez and military leaders made concerted efforts to forge unity within the Partido Colorado, with the result that the party's three main factions, the 'Renovadores', the 'Democráticos' and the 'Autónomos', were persuaded to present a single list of candidates, under the title 'Tradicionalistas'. In the December elections the Partido Colorado secured an overwhelming majority of the Assembly's 198 seats. The new body was convened in January 1992.

In November 1991 new legislation, drafted by President Rodríguez in co-operation with military leaders, was approved by the Congreso Nacional. The law appeared to guarantee the autonomy of the armed forces, and the definition of the role of the military was expanded to include responsibility, at the request of the Head of State, for civil defence and internal order. Apparently in contradiction of the 1990 electoral code, no restrictions were placed on political activities by serving members of the armed forces. Provision was made for the President to delegate the functions of Commander-in-Chief of the Armed Forces to a senior military officer (with the Head of State retaining only ceremonial powers as the military commander). Opposition parties protested that, should the new legislation be entrenched in the new Constitution, the armed forces would remain a 'parallel' political force, following the transition to civilian rule.

On 20 June 1992 the new Constitution was promulgated before the Constituent Assembly. Under the new Constitution, the President and Vice-President (a new post) were to be elected by a simple majority of votes. The Constituent Assembly had ostensibly disregarded the November 1991 military legislation by confirming the President as Commander-in-Chief of the

Armed Forces and excluding officers on active duty from participating directly in politics.

In August 1992, following the party's first direct internal elections, Blas Riquelme was appointed President of the Partido Colorado. However, serious divisions within the party persisted. An internal election, conducted in December, to select the party's presidential candidate was declared to have been won by Luis María Argaña (who had resigned the position in 1992), the candidate of the far right. However, the candidate believed to be favoured by Rodríguez, Juan Carlos Wasmosy, refused to recognize the result, claiming that the vote had been fraudulent. An electoral tribunal failed to resolve the issue, and, following intense pressure and alleged death threats by both factions, several members of the tribunal resigned. Wasmosy was eventually confirmed as the presidential candidate of the Partido Colorado.

Wasmosy's presidency, 1993–98

At the general election of May 1993 Wasmosy was elected President with 40% of the votes cast. However, the Partido Colorado failed to gain a majority in either the Cámara or the Senado. Moreover, the faction of the Partido Colorado led by Argaña, the Movimiento de Reconciliación Colorada, negotiated with the PLRA and the Partido Encuentro Nacional (PEN) to exclude supporters of the President-elect from appointment to important posts in the Congreso Nacional. Wasmosy was inaugurated as President on 15 August. The opposition expressed some concern over the composition of his first Council of Ministers, many of whom had served in the administrations of Rodríguez and Stroessner. Despite Wasmosy's apparent desire to restrict the influence of the military, the designation of Gen. Lino César Oviedo Silva as Commander of the Army provoked further criticism, since, prior to the elections, Oviedo had publicly stated that the army would not accept an opposition victory.

A preliminary agreement on a 'governability pact' between the Government and the opposition, initiated in an attempt to facilitate the implementation of a coherent economic and legislative programme, was signed in October 1993, and this, in turn, facilitated an agreement between the Government and the legislature towards resolving the controversial question of judicial reform. Under the latter agreement, the two were to appoint members of the Supreme Court and the Supreme Electoral Tribunal by consensus. In January 1994 Riquelme resigned as President of the Partido Colorado, following disagreements with Wasmosy.

In May 1995 an investigation into corruption at the Central Bank revealed the existence of an illegal 'parallel' financial system involving a network of institutions, including the Central Bank. The investigation precipitated the collapse of the system and a severe liquidity crisis. In December the Government issued an emergency decree extending the powers of intervention of the Central Bank, with the aim of resolving the financial crisis and restoring confidence in the banking sector. By late December the Central Bank had disbursed almost US $400m. of reserves in order to contain the liquidity crisis, which had resulted in the closure of several financial institutions.

In April 1996 a serious confrontation arose between President Wasmosy and Gen. Oviedo, with the result that a military coup was only narrowly averted. Following an attempt by Oviedo to postpone the internal elections of the Partido Colorado, Wasmosy accused Oviedo of contravening the ban on political activity by serving members of the military, and, on 22 April, demanded his resignation as Commander of the Army. When Oviedo refused to resign, Wasmosy dismissed him. Oviedo rejected the decision, and installed himself at the army headquarters in Asunción, from where he issued demands for Wasmosy's resignation and threatened, with the support of the army, violently to overthrow the Government. Wasmosy took refuge in the US embassy building. The following day, in a demonstration of popular support for Wasmosy, thousands rallied outside the presidential palace. Declarations of support were also issued by the Commanders of the Navy and the Air Force, and by the Congreso Nacional. External pressure for Wasmosy to resist the overthrow of democratic rule came from the USA, which immediately suspended military aid, and from neighbouring South American countries, and was sufficient to prompt Wasmosy to seek a compromise: in return for his retirement from military service, Oviedo was given the position of Minister of Defence. However, the measure was condemned by the legislature, which threatened to initiate impeachment proceedings against Wasmosy should Oviedo be appointed. Public opinion was also strongly opposed to the appointment, and on 25 April, following Oviedo's retirement from military service, Wasmosy withdrew the offer of the defence portfolio. Despite fears of an outright coup, Oviedo accepted the final outcome of the dispute.

In May 1996 Oviedo announced the creation of a new faction of the Partido Colorado, the Unión Nacional de Colorados Eticos (UNACE). In that month, in an effort to purge the armed forces of officers sympathetic to Oviedo, Wasmosy announced the retirement of some 20 high-ranking officers. In June Oviedo was placed under house arrest on charges of insurrection and insubordination with respect to the events of April. In the following month his detention was revised from house arrest to preventative imprisonment; the move was protested by Oviedo's supporters, who rallied outside the Congreso Nacional to demand his release. Wasmosy continued to reorganize the military hierarchy, replacing several senior officers. In August an appeal court acquitted Oviedo of the charge of insurrection on the grounds of insufficient evidence. In December 1996 Oviedo was acquitted of the lesser charge of insubordination.

Amid continuing divisions within the ruling party, in September 1997 Oviedo succeeded in securing the Partido Colorado's presidential nomination, defeating Wasmosy's preferred candidate, Carlos Facetti Masulli, and Argaña in the party's primary election. However, Argaña's faction, which effectively controlled the party's executive board, refused to accept the outcome of the ballot, claiming that it had been fraudulent, and presented a legal challenge to the result.

In October 1997 Wasmosy issued an executive order for the 'disciplinary arrest', for a period of 30 days, of Oviedo; the grounds for the detention was contempt of the President and Commander-in-Chief of the Armed Forces, after Oviedo had publicly accused Wasmosy of corruption. In December, following endorsement of the arrest order by the Supreme Court, Oviedo surrendered to the military authorities. After he had served his 30-day period of confinement, however, a special military tribunal, established by Wasmosy to investigate the events of the coup attempt led by Oviedo in April 1996, ordered that he be detained indefinitely pending the results of the inquiry. In March the tribunal found Oviedo guilty of crimes committed against the order and security of the armed forces, and also of sedition, and sentenced him to 10 years' imprisonment. The Supreme Court ratified the military tribunal's decision in the following month, and the Supreme Electoral Tribunal consequently annulled Oviedo's presidential candidacy. In accordance with the law, the candidacy of the Partido Colorado was assumed by Raúl Cubas Grau, hitherto the vice-presidential nominee; Argaña was to be the new candidate for the vice-presidency.

Election and impeachment of Cubas Grau, 1998–99

The presidential election of 10 May 1998 resulted in victory for Cubas Grau. Colorado candidates were also most successful at legislative elections and at elections for provincial administrators held concurrently. Cubas Grau's election campaign had emphasized his support for his long-time political ally, Oviedo. Prior to the inauguration of the new administration, in July Vice-President-elect Argaña (a staunch opponent of Oviedo) concluded an informal political pact involving his faction of the Partido Colorado and the opposition PLRA and PEN, effectively depriving Cubas Grau of a congressional majority, while in early August President Wasmosy implemented a comprehensive reorganization of the military high command, which promoted the interests of many of Oviedo's military opponents.

Cubas Grau duly took office on 15 August 1998, and a new Council of Ministers, largely composed of supporters of Oviedo, was sworn in on the same day. One of Cubas Grau's first acts as President was to issue a decree commuting Oviedo's prison sentence to time already served, a deliberate circumvention of a new law restricting presidential pardons. On the following day the Congreso Nacional voted to condemn the decree and to initiate proceedings to impeach the President for unconstitutional procedure. In December the Argaña faction-controlled central apparatus of the Partido Colorado expelled Oviedo from the party. While the Congreso Nacional was unable to muster the two-thirds' majority support necessary to impeach President Cubas Grau, the country remained in effective political deadlock.

In March 1999, however, the political impasse ended dramatically. On 23 March Vice-President Argaña was assassinated, prompting nation-wide speculation that Oviedo was behind the attack, and galvanizing the Congreso Nacional sufficiently to secure the support of the two-thirds' majority needed to initiate Cubas Grau's impeachment. Increasing tensions were exacerbated three days later by the killing of seven protesters who were demonstrating in Asunción in support of demands for the res-

PARAGUAY

ignation of the President, in the light of Argaña's assassination. On 28 March Cubas Grau resigned the presidency and sought refuge in Brazil, while Oviedo crossed the border to Argentina. (In February 2002 Cubas Grau surrendered to the Paraguayan authorities and was placed under house arrest until June 2003, when he was released without the charges against him having been dismissed.) In April the judicial authorities ordered the arrest of Oviedo for involvement in the death of Argaña, after three of his close collaborators were identified as the assassins. (In 2000 Maj.-Gen. Reinaldo Servin, Constantino Rodas and Pablo Vera Esteche were sentenced to long prison terms for their roles in the assassination.) However, the Argentine Government rejected Paraguay's request for extradition, resulting in a rapid deterioration in the relationship between the two countries. Oviedo left Argentina in December in order to avoid being extradited by the new Argentine Government of Fernando de la Rúa.

Presidency of González Macchi, 1999–2003

Meanwhile, in accordance with the terms of the Constitution, in the absence of the elected President and Vice-President, the President of the Congreso Nacional, the pro-Argaña Colorado senator Luis González Macchi, was swiftly installed as head of state. He announced the composition of a multi-party Government of National Unity at the end of March 1999. In April the Supreme Court ruled that González Macchi should serve the remainder of Cubas Grau's presidential term. The Court also ruled that an election to select a new Vice-President should be conducted. Hoping to consolidate the new Government, González Macchi announced that his own party would not present a vice-presidential candidate. However, prominent figures within the Partido Colorado decided to contest the election none the less, precipitating tension with the PLRA, which had effectively been promised the post. Meanwhile, factionalism within the PLRA placed increasing strains on the Government of National Unity. Events culminated in February 2000 when PLRA members voted to withdraw from the ruling coalition, depriving the Government of a legislative majority.

In May 1999 González Macchi forcibly retired more than 100 army officers, including several high-ranking supporters of Oviedo. By mid-November another 45 senior commanders, thought to be supporters of Oviedo, had been replaced. However, the reorganization did not prevent a coup attempt, in May 2000, by rebellious soldiers thought to be sympathetic to Oviedo. It was swiftly defeated by the Government, which declared a 30-day state of emergency, assuming extraordinary powers that resulted in the arrest of more than 70 people, mostly members of the security forces. Oviedo denied any involvement with the coup, but in June he was arrested in Brazil. In March 2001 the Brazilian Chief Prosecutor ruled that Oviedo could be extradited, but in December the Supreme Court rejected the ruling, stating that Oviedo was a victim of political persecution, and released him from imprisonment.

The initial popularity of the Government of National Unity collapsed as thousands of peasants, assembled by rural organizations, mobilized on several occasions during 1999 to protest against the Government's lack of action on rural issues. In response, in November the Government offered a US $168m. rescue package for the agricultural and livestock sector, mostly for debt-refinancing schemes. In March 2000 the Government announced a scheme to assist 250,000 small farmers. However, by the end of the month there were an estimated 10,000 smallholders camped outside the Congreso building. (The protest continued until March 2001, when government concessions were eventually secured.) Strikes were undertaken by power and telecommunications workers and by public sector workers during March and June 2000, respectively. However, the Government insisted it would continue with its 'state restructuring' programme. In mid-November the Congreso Nacional approved legislation allowing for the sale of the state railway, water and telecommunications companies.

At the vice-presidential election, which was finally held on 13 August 2000, the 53-year Colorado monopoly on power was ended when Félix Argaña, son of the late Vice-President, was narrowly defeated (by less than 1% of the votes cast) by the PLRA candidate, Julio César Franco. The election of Franco, whose candidacy was endorsed by Oviedo, increased the divisions within the Partido Colorado and resulted in the resignation of the Minister of National Defence, Nelson Argaña, another son of the late Vice-President.

A corruption scandal in May 2001 forced the President of the Central Bank, Washington Ashwell, to resign over his alleged involvement in the fraudulent transfer of US $16m. to a US bank account. An opposition attempt to impeach the President over his alleged involvement in the fraud was defeated by the Cámara de Diputados in August. In September several thousand protesters marched in Asunción to demand the resignation of González Macchi. In April 2002 González Macchi was formally charged with involvement in the corruption scandal.

In January 2002 the credibility of the Government was further undermined after two leaders of the left-wing party Movimiento Patria Libre (MPL) alleged that they had been illegally detained for 13 days and tortured by the police, with the knowledge of government ministers, as part of an investigation into a kidnapping case. In response to the allegations, in February the head of the national police force and his deputy, as well as the head of the judicial investigations department, were dismissed. Following sustained public and political pressure the Minister of the Interior and the Minister of Justice and Labour resigned soon afterwards, although both protested their innocence. In addition, the national intelligence agency, the Secretaría Nacional de Informaciones, was disbanded. The Cámara de Diputados issued a statement assigning some responsibility for the detention of the MPL leaders to the President and the Attorney-General, and describing the event as 'state terrorism'. In late 2002 the MPL was renamed the Partido Patria Libre (PPL) and registered as a political party.

Throughout 2002 an alliance of farmers, trade unions and left-wing organizations staged mass protests throughout the country to call for an end to the Government's free market policies and to protest at widely perceived government corruption. In response to the mounting opposition, in June the Government suspended its planned privatization of the state telecommunications company. Nevertheless, the protests continued as the economic situation worsened, prompting González Macchi to declare a state of emergency in July, which was lifted two days later after clashes between anti-Government protesters and security forces resulted in two fatalities.

In December 2002 the Cámara de Diputados voted in favour of the impeachment of President González Macchi on five charges of corruption. In an attempt to avoid the charges, González Macchi offered to resign early from office, immediately following the presidential election due in April 2003 (his term of office officially ended in August of that year). However, in February 2003 the Senado voted narrowly against impeachment. Proceedings began against González Macchi in mid-2004 on charges relating to the May 2001 embezzlement scandal; in February 2005 further charges were brought against him for misuse of public funds and irregularities connected to the sale of two state-owned banks. He was found guilty on charges of embezzlement and false testimony and, despite appealing against the verdict, was sentenced to eight years' imprisonment in December 2006.

Duarte's presidency, 2003–08

The presidential election of 27 April 2003 was won by the Colorado candidate, Nicanor Duarte Frutos. However, the Partido Colorado lost its majority in the Cámara de Diputados in the concurrently held legislative ballot. At his inauguration on 15 August, President Duarte reiterated his election pledges to reduce corruption, improve the public finances and restore the country's international credibility. A number of well-regarded technocrats were appointed to the Council of Ministers, notably including the new Minister of Finance, Dionisio Borda. On taking office, Duarte announced his intention to effect wide-ranging judicial reform; to this effect, in October the Congreso reached consensus on impeachment proceedings against six Supreme Court judges suspected of corruption. Four of the judges resigned during the impeachment process, which finally resulted in the indictment of the remaining two judges in December. However, despite hopes that political influence in the selection of new judges might be avoided, two of the six new Supreme Court judges appointed in March 2004 were Colorado supporters.

In June 2004 Oviedo returned voluntarily from Brazil and was immediately taken to a military prison to serve the remainder of his 10-year sentence for organizing the 1996 attempted coup. In October, however, Oviedo was provisionally acquitted of having organized the failed coup attempt of May 2000, and in January 2005 charges against him relating to a discovered arms cache were dismissed. In March the Supreme Court ruled that Oviedo would nevertheless have to serve out his prison sentence. Throughout the rest of 2005 demonstrations against his detention were staged by his supporters.

In October 2004 the kidnap and murder of an 11-year-old child provoked a vociferous public outcry against the perceived deterioration of security in Paraguay. In response, President Duarte dismissed the Minister of the Interior, Orlando Fiorotto Sánchez (who was replaced by Attorney-General Nelson Mora), and the head of the national police, Umberto Núñez. In February 2005 Mora was himself dismissed—in addition to some 50 senior members of the police force—following the discovery of the body of Cecilia Cubas under a house in a suburb of Asunción. Cubas, the daughter of former President Raúl Cubas Grau, had been kidnapped in the previous September. In advance of the police inquiry, President Duarte held the PPL responsible for the killing. Twelve of the 15 people charged with involvement in the kidnap and murder of Cecilia Cubas, all of whom were members or sympathizers of the PPL, were found guilty in November 2006.

Throughout 2003 and 2004 strikes, roadblocks, marches and illegal land occupations were organized by farmers and indigenous groups in protest at a range of government policies, including agrarian reform and privatizations. In response to the continuing civil unrest, in September 2004 the Government signed an agreement to distribute some 13,000 ha of land in six western departments to landless peasants; however, the main peasant grouping, the Federación Nacional Campesina (FNC), maintained its demand for the redistribution of some 100,000 ha of land. Illegal land occupations and other protests continued in late 2004 and 2005, resulting in the arrest of hundreds of protesters and several fatalities.

In November 2005 President Duarte announced plans to reform the Constitution in order to allow for presidential re-election. At that time, Duarte was also seeking re-election to the leadership of the Partido Colorado, which he had ceded on taking office as President. However, opposition groups argued that it was unconstitutional for the President to hold any additional public office, and in December a motion to impeach President Duarte was proposed by the opposition Patria Querida, although this was subsequently defeated. In January 2006 the Supreme Electoral Tribunal also rejected criminal charges against Duarte, brought by the leader of the Frente Colorado faction, Luis Talavera, for attempting to hold two public offices, although the Court ruled that it would be unconstitutional for Duarte to hold another office concurrently with the presidency of the Republic. Duarte won a convincing victory in the Partido Colorado leadership election, in March 2006, and in the same month the Supreme Court overturned the Supreme Electoral Tribunal's earlier ruling forbidding the President from holding an additional office. On assuming leadership of the party, the President proposed a referendum on allowing presidential re-election. In response to the Supreme Court ruling, opposition groups again initiated impeachment proceedings against Duarte, as well as against the five judges of the Court's Constitutional Panel. Faced with such resistance, the following day Duarte resigned from the party presidency.

In February 2007 a group of more than 30 social and labour organizations joined the principal opposition parties in signing an accord to form the Concertación Nacional (CN). The new coalition announced its intention to present a single candidate in the presidential election in 2008 in the hope of providing an effective challenge to the Partido Colorado. In July six of the eight political parties in the CN, including the PLRA and the PEN, announced their support for Fernando Lugo Méndez, a popular former Roman Catholic bishop known for his frequent pronouncements on social justice and his work with deprived communities. However, Patria Querida and UNACE rejected the nomination of Lugo, arguing that it contravened the February accord's requirement to hold a primary election to select the opposition candidate, and both parties subsequently withdrew from the CN. As a result, in September Lugo founded the Alianza Patriótica para el Cambio (APC) to support his candidacy. Earlier in September Oviedo was granted conditional release from gaol by a military tribunal. In the following month the Supreme Court acquitted Oviedo of involvement in the 1996 coup attempt, thereby making him eligible to stand for the presidency, and he was declared the UNACE candidate in January 2008. There was speculation that Oviedo's acquittal was a government tactic to divide the opposition.

Recent developments: the Lugo Méndez presidency

At the presidential election, held on 20 April 2008, Lugo won a comfortable victory, securing 40.9% of votes cast, against 30.6% for the Colorado candidate, Blanca Ovelar. Oviedo won 21.9% of votes, while Pedro Fadul, again representing Patria Querida, obtained just 2.4%. In the concurrent legislative elections the Partido Colorado narrowly retained its status as the largest party in both chambers of the Congreso Nacional, securing 30 of the 80 seats in the Cámara de Diputados and 15 out of 45 seats in the Senado. The PLRA (the largest party in Lugo's APC) obtained 27 seats in the lower house and 14 in the upper, while UNACE won 15 and nine seats, respectively. In order to achieve a working majority in the Congreso, Lugo secured the support of UNACE and the 'Nicanorista' faction of the Partido Colorado, the latter comprising supporters of President Duarte. However, the stability of the new legislature was threatened by a dispute regarding the fact that Duarte had been elected to a seat in the Senado, in apparent contravention of the Constitution (which granted former Presidents a non-voting seat for life in the chamber, but prohibited a serving President from exercising any additional public office).

President Lugo was inaugurated on 15 August 2008. His cabinet included four representatives of different factions of the PLRA (in addition to the Vice-President, Federico Franco Gómez) and a number of non-affiliated ministers, notably including Dionisio Borda as Minister of Finance, a position he had held from 2003–06. In the first month of Lugo's presidency the dispute over Duarte's senatorial seat continued to disrupt relations between the new Government and the Congreso Nacional. On 26 August an inquorate session of the Senado chaired by the chamber's pro-Duarte President, Enrique González Quintana of UNACE, swore Duarte into office as an elected senator, but later the same day the PLRA Vice-President of the Senado, in defiance of González Quintana, chaired a session dominated by anti-Duarte senators that swore the former President's nominated alternate, Jorge Céspedes, into the same seat. The impasse, which appeared to indicate an inability of Lugo's allies to co-operate, was ended in early September after Lugo publicly accused Duarte and Oviedo, along with González Quintana and other senior political figures, of plotting a coup to overthrow the new Government. Although Duarte and Oviedo both strongly denied the allegations, UNACE subsequently relinquished its support for Duarte; on 4 September Céspedes was legitimately sworn in as a senator and Duarte was afforded the honorary position of senator for life. However, in a controversial judgment, the Supreme Court in September 2010 authorized Duarte to assume his elective seat in the Senado, raising concerns that the dispute would be reignited.

One of Lugo's main campaign pledges was to initiate a process of land reform. In 2008 peasants organized by the Mesa Coordinadora Nacional de Organizaciones Campesinas staged a series of land invasions, demanding that the new President promise to carry out a comprehensive land redistribution programme. The demonstrations intensified in October, when one person was killed in a violent confrontation between police and peasants occupying an agricultural estate in Alto Paraná. In the same month the government body responsible for rural development, the Instituto Nacional del Desarrollo Rural y de la Tierra, declared that it would no longer allow foreigners to acquire land in Paraguay; the large proportion of land in foreign (especially Brazilian) ownership was a major source of tension between landowners and landless peasants. In late October the Government announced the purchase of some 22,000 ha from 11 Brazilian farmers in the department of San Pedro for redistribution to landless families; none the less, protests by peasants continued, and were countered in December with demonstrations by landowners. In January 2009 the Government announced the first stage of its land reform programme, which concentrated on rural development and did not include any redistributive measures. The FNC continued to demand a major programme of redistribution, and the federation's annual demonstration in Asunción in March was attended by some 10,000 people protesting against the slow pace of reform.

President Lugo carried out a cabinet reorganization in April 2009, replacing the Ministers of Industry and Commerce, Justice and Labour, Agriculture and Livestock, and Education and Culture. The appointment of the new ministers, all of whom were members of the PLRA, was interpreted as an attempt to ensure the continued support of that party for the Government's legislative programme. Later in April Héctor Lacognata was appointed Minister of Foreign Affairs in place of Alejandro Hamed Franco. Public confidence in Lugo's presidency was damaged in April by the President's admission that he was the father of a two-year-old son, made after the child's mother presented a paternity suit against him. Two other women subsequently alleged that Lugo had fathered children by them during his time as Bishop of San Pedro. However, while request-

PARAGUAY

ing forgiveness for any failings, Lugo insisted that he intended to remain in office. (Of the two remaining cases, one was dismissed in September 2010 after the results of a paternity test proved that Lugo was not the father, while legal proceedings regarding the other commenced in December.)

The APC's weak position in the Congreso Nacional impeded the passage of the Government's legislative proposals throughout 2009. In May, for example, the 'Castiglionista' and 'Nicanorista' factions of the Partido Colorado, UNACE and five PLRA senators supportive of Vice-President Franco united in the Senado to approve a postponement of the planned introduction of a personal income tax, overturning a presidential veto against such a delay; the postponement was confirmed by the Cámara de Diputados in June. As relations between the Government and the legislature continued to deteriorate, Lugo suggested in June that he might organize a referendum on the performance of the Congreso, which he accused of thwarting his efforts to fulfil his pre-election pledges. The PLRA threatened to withdraw from the APC in July, after smaller parties in the alliance voted with the Partido Colorado and Patria Querida in a leadership ballot in the Senado. In August representatives of the main parties in the Congreso signed a 'democratic accord', reaffirming their commitment to a political system based on representative democracy; the agreement, which Lugo refused to sign, was interpreted by observers as being a response to the President's referendum proposal.

Lugo replaced the Commanders of the Armed Forces, the Army, Air Force and Navy in November 2009, following rumours that some officers might be plotting a coup. Meanwhile, tensions between the Congreso and the President continued to intensify, as a number of senators threatened to initiate impeachment proceedings against Lugo on various grounds: an alleged failure to address security concerns, following the abduction in October of rancher Fidel Zavala by the Ejército del Pueblo Paraguayo (EPP, a small guerrilla group linked to the PPL); comments by Lugo that they claimed were an incitement to 'class warfare'; and alleged corruption related to the purchase of 22,000 ha of land in San Pedro for redistribution to landless families. In January 2010 Lugo ordered a military and police offensive against the EPP in San Pedro, shortly after the release of Zavala, whose family had complied with some of the group's demands, but little progress was made in suppressing the movement. A deadly attack by EPP guerrillas near the San Pedro–Concepión border in late April prompted Lugo to declare a state of emergency in five northern departments and to mobilize some 1,000 members of the security forces to bolster the operation against the rebels. The Congreso also temporarily granted extensive powers of arrest to the police in the affected departments and restricted the freedom of assembly. The state of emergency expired after 30 days, but the offensive was widely regarded as a failure. New anti-terrorism legislation came into effect in June, although the vague definition of what constituted terrorism generated considerable controversy, owing to fears that the new laws could be inappropriately used against legitimate demonstrators. Between July and September a number of suspected EPP leaders were arrested or killed by the security forces. Nevertheless, the Minister of National Defence, Gen. (retd) Luis Bareiro Spaini, was forced to resign in August after a dispute involving the theft of military weapons by alleged EPP members led to the initiation of impeachment proceedings against him; Spaini was replaced by Gen. (retd) Cecilio Pérez Bordón. In a further change to the leadership of the armed forces, in September Lugo replaced the commanders of each branch of the military (the fourth time that he had done so since taking office).

Meanwhile, the creation of a new organization in support of the President, the Movimiento 20 de Abril (after the date on which Lugo was elected in 2008), was announced in February 2010 by Miguel López Perito, the Secretary-General of the Presidency. In the following month Frente Guasú, a coalition of 22 political organizations and social movements supportive of Lugo, including the constituent parties of the APC, was also established. It was revealed in August that Lugo had been diagnosed with cancer. Although his prognosis was favourable, Lugo was forced to reduce his activities while undergoing chemotherapy treatment, which was successfully completed in December. Municipal elections were conducted on 7 November and resulted in victory for the opposition Partido Colorado, which secured a majority of the contested municipalities, including the key municipality of Asunción. Infighting within the APC—primarily resulting from ongoing tensions between Lugo's supporters and anti-Lugo elements in the PLRA centred around Vice-President Franco (who had organized a protest rally against the President, attended by 5,000 people, in April)—had undermined the ruling coalition's efforts to present a coherent challenge to the Partido Colorado. Confronted by continued opposition in the Congreso, Lugo had made little progress with his reform agenda during 2010, and, with clear divisions evident within his own coalition, a breakthrough in the near future seemed unlikely.

Foreign Affairs

In 1991 the Presidents and Ministers of Foreign Affairs of Argentina, Brazil, Uruguay and Paraguay signed a formal agreement in Asunción creating a common market of the 'Southern Cone' countries, the Mercado Común del Sur (Mercosur, see p. 425). The agreement allowed for the dismantling of trade barriers between the four countries, and entered into full operation in 1995.

Following Fernando Lugo's accession to the presidency in 2008, relations with Brazil were dominated by the new President's stated commitment to renegotiate the treaty governing the Itaipú hydroelectric project on the border between Brazil and Paraguay. The Treaty of Itaipú, signed in 1973 and due to expire in 2023, apportioned to each country one-half of the electricity produced by the project, and bound each country to sell to the other any surplus (in the case of Paraguay, some 95% of its share) at the cost of production. In July 2009 President Lugo and his Brazilian counterpart, Lula da Silva, signed an agreement tripling the amount paid by Brazil to Paraguay for surplus electricity from Itaipú and permitting Paraguay to sell energy direct to Brazilian utility companies, rather than solely through the state-controlled enterprise Centrais Elétricas Brasileiras, SA (Eletrobrás). Brazil also agreed to provide financing for various infrastructure projects in Paraguay, including the construction of an electrical transmission line from Itaipú to central Paraguay. However, the Brazilian Government refused to allow Paraguay to sell its surplus production to third parties.

In April 2009 President Lugo and Bolivian President Evo Morales signed an agreement on the demarcation of their joint border. However, reports in September that Morales intended substantially to increase defence expenditure provoked concern in Paraguay.

Paraguay's relations with the USA were strained in 2006 when the Government announced that US military personnel operating in that country would no longer enjoy immunity from prosecution. Unlike other Mercosur countries, Paraguay had signed an agreement with the USA in 2005 protecting US soldiers from extradition to the International Criminal Court. The decision by Paraguay not to renew this agreement prompted the USA to announce the withdrawal of humanitarian and medical services that it had been providing to people living in remote, rural areas of Paraguay.

CONSTITUTION AND GOVERNMENT

Under the 1992 Constitution, legislative power is held by the bicameral Congreso Nacional (National Congress), whose members serve for five years. The Senado (Senate) has 45 members, and the Cámara de Diputados (Chamber of Deputies) 80 members. Elections to the legislature are by universal adult suffrage. Executive power is held by the President, directly elected for a single term of five years at the same time as the legislature. The President of the Republic governs with the assistance of a Vice-President and an appointed Council of Ministers. Judicial power is exercised by the Supreme Court of Justice and by the tribunals. Paraguay is divided into 17 departments, each administered by an elected governor.

REGIONAL AND INTERNATIONAL CO-OPERATION

Paraguay is a member of the Inter-American Development Bank (see p. 333), of the Latin American Integration Association (see p. 359), of the Latin American Economic System (see p. 448), of the Mercado Común del Sur (Mercosur, see p. 425) and of the Organization of American States (see p. 391). In December 2004 Paraguay was one of 12 countries that were signatories to the agreement creating the South American Community of Nations, intended to promote greater regional economic integration. A constitutive treaty for the community—which was renamed the Union of South American Nations in April 2007—was signed in May 2008, with full functionality of economic union tentatively scheduled for 2019.

Paraguay was a founder member of the UN in 1945. As a contracting party to the General Agreement on Tariffs and

Trade, Paraguay joined the World Trade Organization (see p. 430) on its establishment in 1995.

ECONOMIC AFFAIRS

In 2009, according to estimates by the World Bank, Paraguay's gross national income (GNI), measured at average 2007–09 prices, was US $14,430m., equivalent to $2,270 per head (or $4,430 per head on an international purchasing-power parity basis). During 2000–09, it was estimated, the population increased at an average annual rate of 1.9%, while gross domestic product (GDP) per head increased, in real terms, by an average of 0.9% per year. Overall GDP increased, in real terms, at an average annual rate of 2.8% in 2000–09; GDP decreased by an estimated 3.8% in 2009, but increased, according to preliminary figures, by 14.5% in 2010.

Agriculture (including forestry, hunting and fishing) contributed 21.4% of GDP in 2009, according to preliminary figures. In October–December 2008 some 26.5% of the economically active population were employed in the sector. The principal cash crop is soybeans, which accounted for an estimated 35.1% of total export revenue in 2010. Other significant crops are sugar cane, cassava, sunflowers, cotton, wheat and maize. Timber and wood manufactures provided an estimated 2.2% of export revenues in 2010. The raising of livestock (particularly cattle and pigs) is also important. Meat accounted for an estimated 20.3% of export earnings in 2010. According to official preliminary figures, agricultural GDP increased at an average annual rate of 6.3% in 2000–10; real agricultural GDP decreased by 17.3% in 2009, but increased by 31.9% in 2010.

Industry (including mining, manufacturing, construction and power) contributed 23.5% of GDP in 2009, according to preliminary figures, and employed 18.9% of the working population in October–December 2008. According to official preliminary figures, industrial GDP increased by an average of 2.1% per year in 2000–10; the sector increased by 8.3% in 2010.

Paraguay has almost no commercially exploited mineral resources, and the mining sector, which employed only 0.3% of the labour force in October–December 2007, contributed just 0.2% of GDP in 2009, according to preliminary figures. Production is confined to gypsum, kaolin and limestone. According to official preliminary figures, mining GDP increased by an average of 2.1% per year in 2000–10; the sector increased by 5.3% in 2010.

Manufacturing contributed 14.4% of GDP in 2009, according to preliminary figures, and employed 11.8% of the working population in October–December 2007. The main branch of manufacturing (in terms of value added) was production of food and beverages. The other principal sectors were wood and wood products, handicrafts, paper, printing and publishing, hides and furs, and non-metallic mineral products. According to official preliminary figures, manufacturing GDP increased at an average annual rate of 1.4% in 2000–10; real GDP of the sector declined by 0.8% in 2009, but increased by 7.0% in 2010.

The construction sector contributed 7.3% of GDP in 2009, according to preliminary figures, and engaged 6.2% of the working population in October–December 2008. According to official preliminary figures, construction GDP increased by an average of 3.8% per year in 2000–10; the sector increased by 13.2% in 2010.

Energy is derived almost completely from hydroelectric power. Imports of mineral fuels comprised 11.4% of the value of total merchandise imports in 2010, according to preliminary figures. Ethyl alcohol (ethanol), derived from sugar cane, is widely used as a component of vehicle fuel.

The services sector contributed 55.1% of GDP in 2009, according to preliminary figures, and engaged 54.6% of the working population in October–December 2008. Paraguay traditionally serves as an entrepôt for regional trade. According to official preliminary figures, the GDP of the services sector increased by an average of 3.6% per year in 2000–10; the sector increased by 8.9% in 2010.

In 2009 Paraguay recorded a visible trade deficit of US $1,031.5m., and there was a deficit of $86.4m. on the current account of the balance of payments. According to preliminary figures, in 2010 the principal source of registered imports was the People's Republic of China (34.6%); other major suppliers in that year were Brazil and Argentina. Uruguay was the principal market for registered exports in that year (an estimated 22.0% of total exports); other notable purchasers were Argentina and Brazil. The principal exports in 2010 were, according to preliminary estimates, soybeans and meat and meat derivatives. The principal imports were motors, general industrial machinery equipment and parts, mineral fuels, chemical products, and transport equipment.

In 2009 there was a central government budget surplus of 45,000m. guaraníes (equivalent to 0.1% of GDP). Paraguay's general government gross debt was 12,758,060m. guaraníes in 2009, equivalent to 18.0% of GDP. Paraguay's total external debt was US $4,162.7m. at the end of 2008, of which $2,265.4m. was public and publicly guaranteed debt. In that year the cost of debt-servicing was equivalent to 4.8% of the total value of exports of goods, services and income. Annual inflation averaged 8.1% in 2000–09; consumer prices increased by an average of 2.7% in 2009. An estimated 6.4% of the labour force were unemployed in October–December 2009.

In the early 21st century the Government relied on external loans, particularly from the IMF, to keep the economy afloat. Government revenues increased significantly in 2005 and 2006 owing to improved tax collection and a widening of the tax base. However, government expenditure increased in 2007 and 2008 as a result of additional subsidies to the country's ailing cotton industry, increased spending on health, education and social security and a 20% wage increase for government employees. GDP growth of 5.8% in 2008 was driven by increased soy production, high soy prices and greater export demand for the crop, the latter in spite of a strongly performing currency against the US dollar. According to the IMF, the economy contracted by an estimated 3.8% in 2009 as the increasingly severe global economic crisis stifled demand for Paraguayan exports, the value of which declined by 25.6%. This was compounded by a drought in late 2008 and early 2009 which drastically curtailed soybean production. However, inflation declined significantly in 2009, while international reserves increased substantially. A bumper harvest, combined with a resurgence in demand and prices for the country's key exports (soybeans and beef), resulted in a strong economic recovery throughout 2010. The flourishing agricultural sector supported renewed growth in other parts of the economy, including services and construction, resulting in dramatic growth of 14.5% in that year. The IMF projected GDP growth of 4% in 2011, assuming that the clement weather conditions, which had precipitated the increase in agricultural production in 2010, continued.

PUBLIC HOLIDAYS

2012: 1 January (New Year's Day), 1 March (Heroes' Day), 5 April (Maundy Thursday), 6 April (Good Friday), 1 May (Labour Day), 15 May (Independence Day), 12 June (Peace of Chaco), 15 August (Founding of Asunción), 1 October (for Battle of Boquerón), 8 December (Immaculate Conception), 25 December (Christmas Day).

PARAGUAY

Statistical Survey

Sources (unless otherwise stated): Dirección General de Estadística, Encuestas y Censos, Naciones Unidas, esq. Saavedra, Fernando de la Mora, Zona Norte; tel. (21) 51-1016; fax (21) 50-8493; internet www.dgeec.gov.py; Banco Central del Paraguay, Avda Federación Rusa y Marecos, Casilla 861, Barrio Santo Domingo, Asunción; tel. (21) 61-0088; fax (21) 60-8149; e-mail ccs@bcp.gov.py; internet www.bcp.gov.py; Secretaría Técnica de Planificación, Presidencia de la República, Iturbe y Eligio Ayala, Asunción.

Area and Population

AREA, POPULATION AND DENSITY

Area (sq km)	406,752*
Population (census results)	
26 August 1992	4,152,588
28 August 2002	
Males	2,627,831
Females	2,555,249
Total	5,183,080
Population (official estimates at mid-year)	
2009	6,340,639
2010	6,451,122
2011	6,561,785
Density (per sq km) at mid-2011	16.1

* 157,048 sq miles.

POPULATION BY AGE AND SEX
(official estimates at mid-2010)

	Males	Females	Total
0–14	1,102,702	1,063,186	2,165,888
15–64	2,002,401	1,955,799	3,958,200
65 and over	155,120	171,914	327,034
Total	3,260,223	3,190,899	6,451,122

DEPARTMENTS
(official population estimates at mid-2009)

	Area (sq km)	Population	Density (per sq km)	Capital
Alto Paraguay (incl. Chaco)	82,349	11,413	0.1	Fuerte Olimpo
Alto Paraná	14,895	736,942	49.5	Ciudad del Este
Amambay	12,933	124,848	9.7	Pedro Juan Caballero
Asunción	117	518,507	4,431.7	—
Boquerón (incl. Nueva Asunción)	91,669	56,164	0.6	Doctor Pedro P. Peña
Caaguazú	11,474	478,612	41.7	Coronel Oviedo
Caazapá	9,496	150,910	15.9	Caazapá
Canindeyú	14,667	179,656	12.2	Salto del Guairá
Central	2,465	1998,994	811.0	Asunción
Concepción	18,051	190,322	10.5	Concepción
Cordillera	4,948	273,606	55.3	Caacupé
Guairá	3,846	196,130	51.0	Villarrica
Itapúa	16,525	529,358	32.0	Encarnación
Misiones	9,556	115,851	12.1	San Juan Bautista
Ñeembucú	12,147	83,504	6.9	Pilar
Paraguarí	8,705	239,050	27.5	Paraguarí
Presidente Hayes	72,907	101,656	1.4	Pozo Colorado
San Pedro	20,002	355,115	17.8	San Pedro
Total	406,752	6,340,639	15.6	—

PRINCIPAL TOWNS
(population at 2002 census, incl. rural environs)

Asunción (capital)	510,910	Lambaré		119,830
Ciudad del Este*	222,109	Fernando de la Mora		113,990
San Lorenzo	203,150	Caaguazú		100,132
Luque	185,670	Encarnación		97,000
Capiatá	154,520	Pedro Juan Caballero		88,530

* Formerly Puerto Presidente Stroessner.

Mid-2010 ('000, incl. suburbs, UN estimate): Asunción 2,030 (Source: UN, *World Urbanization Prospects: The 2009 Revision*).

BIRTHS, MARRIAGES AND DEATHS

	Live births Number	Rate (per 1,000)	Marriages Number	Rate (per 1,000)	Deaths Number	Rate (per 1,000)
2002	46,012	8.3	16,100	2.9	19,416	3.5
2003	45,669	8.0	17,717	3.1	19,593	3.4
2004	49,857	8.6	17,763	3.1	20,283	3.5
2005	51,444	8.7	19,826	3.4	17,360	2.9
2006	49,473	8.2	19,476	3.2	19,298	3.2
2007	49,879	8.2	19,726	3.2	21,049	3.4
2008	51,423	8.3	18,832	3.0	20,053	3.2

Note: Rates were derived from estimates of mid-year population.

Life expectancy (years at birth, WHO estimates): 74 (males 71; females 77) in 2008 (Source: WHO, *World Health Statistics*).

ECONOMICALLY ACTIVE POPULATION
(household survey, '000 persons aged 10 years and over, October–December unless otherwise indicated)

	2006*	2007	2008
Agriculture, hunting, forestry and fishing	797,677	800,577	745,248
Mining and quarrying		8,617	
Manufacturing	271,905	319,250	346,803
Electricity, gas and water	18,714	8,799	10,769
Construction	149,445	154,915	174,096
Trade, restaurants and hotels	584,255	639,523	673,821
Transport, storage and communications	98,931	101,453	118,415
Financing, insurance, real estate and business services	84,028	104,225	120,802
Community, social and personal services	548,057	578,426	619,950
Sub-total	2,553,012	2,715,785	2,809,904
Activities not adequately described	628	580	602
Total employed	2,553,640	2,716,365	2,810,506
Unemployed	182,006	161,165	170,620
Total labour force	2,735,646	2,877,530	2,981,126

* November 2006–February 2007.

PARAGUAY

Health and Welfare

KEY INDICATORS

Total fertility rate (children per woman, 2008)	3.0
Under-5 mortality rate (per 1,000 live births, 2008)	28
HIV/AIDS (% of persons aged 15–49, 2007)	0.6
Physicians (per 1,000 head, 2002)	1.1
Hospital beds (per 1,000 head, 2006)	1.3
Health expenditure (2007): US $ per head (PPP)	253
Health expenditure (2007): % of GDP	5.7
Health expenditure (2007): public (% of total)	42.4
Access to water (% of persons, 2008)	86
Access to sanitation (% of persons, 2008)	70
Total carbon dioxide emissions ('000 metric tons, 2007)	4,129.3
Carbon dioxide emissions per head (metric tons, 2007)	0.7
Human Development Index (2010): ranking	96
Human Development Index (2010): value	0.640

For sources and definitions, see explanatory note on p. vi.

Agriculture

PRINCIPAL CROPS
('000 metric tons)

	2007	2008	2009
Wheat	800	799	1,067
Rice, paddy	130	150	220
Maize	1,900	2,472	1,858
Sorghum	25*	27	26
Sweet potatoes*	166	166	173
Cassava (Manioc)	4,800	2,219	2,610
Sugar cane	4,100	5,080	4,800
Beans, dry	70	45	43
Soybeans (Soya beans)	6,000	6,312	3,855
Oil palm fruit*	143	143	152
Sunflower seed	190	191	194
Tomatoes	89*	40	44
Onions, dry*	29	30	30
Carrots and turnips	27*	8	11
Watermelons*	118	118	122
Cantaloupes and other melons*	29	30	30
Bananas	46*	58	59
Oranges	300*	225	226
Tangerines, mandarins, clementines and satsumas	19*	44	45
Grapefruit and pomelos*	39	39	40
Guavas, mangoes and mangosteens*	29	29	30
Pineapples	73*	54	56
Maté	88*	77	77

* FAO estimate(s).

Aggregate production ('000 metric tons, may include official, semi-official or estimated data): Total cereals 2,855 in 2007, 3,447 in 2008, 3,171 in 2009; Total roots and tubers 4,967 in 2007, 2,386 in 2008, 2,784 in 2009; Total vegetables (incl. melons) 344 in 2007, 279 in 2008, 291 in 2009; Total fruits (excl. melons) 586 in 2007, 529 in 2008, 539 in 2009.

Source: FAO.

LIVESTOCK
('000 head, year ending September)

	2007	2008	2009
Cattle	10,464	10,562	11,643
Horses	380*	284	285*
Pigs	1,200*	1,073	1,200*
Sheep	550*	365	400*
Goats	167*	130	n.a.
Chickens	20,000*	16,056	18,00*
Ducks	760	1,034	1,050*
Geese and guinea fowls*	110	115	n.a.
Turkeys	115*	179	n.a.

* FAO estimate(s).
Source: FAO.

LIVESTOCK PRODUCTS
('000 metric tons)

	2007	2008*	2009*
Cattle meat	265	276	315
Pig meat	149*	175	187
Chicken meat	28*	35	36
Cows' milk	375*	375	380
Hen eggs	120*	120	n.a.

* FAO estimate(s).
Source: FAO.

Forestry

ROUNDWOOD REMOVALS
('000 cubic metres, excluding bark, FAO estimates)

	2007	2008	2009
Sawlogs, veneer logs and logs for sleepers	3,515	3,515	3,515
Other industrial wood	529	529	529
Fuel wood	6,252	6,358	6,466
Total	10,296	10,402	10,510

Source: FAO.

SAWNWOOD PRODUCTION
('000 cubic metres, including railway sleepers)

	1995	1996	1997
Total (all broadleaved)	400	500	550

1998–2009: Annual production as in 1997 (FAO estimates).
Source: FAO.

Fishing

('000 metric tons, live weight, FAO estimates)

	2004	2005	2006
Capture	22.0	21.0	20.0
Characins	7.8	7.5	7.0
Freshwater siluroids	10.8	10.3	10.0
Other freshwater fishes	3.4	3.2	3.0
Aquaculture	2.1	2.1	2.1
Total catch	24.1	23.1	22.1

2007–08: Figures assumed to be unchanged from 2006 (FAO estimates).
Source: FAO.

Industry

SELECTED PRODUCTS
('000 metric tons)

	2007	2008	2009
Soya bean oil*†	260	265	265
Hydraulic cement‡§	600	600	600

* Unofficial figures.
† Data from FAO.
‡ Data from US Geological Survey.
§ Estimates.

Total sugars: 119 in 2006 (FAO estimate—Source: FAO).

PARAGUAY

Finance

CURRENCY AND EXCHANGE RATES

Monetary Units
100 céntimos = 1 guaraní (G).

Sterling, Dollar and Euro Equivalents (30 November 2010)
£1 sterling = 7,435.7 guaraníes;
US $1 = 4,788.6 guaraníes;
€1 = 6,224.2 guaraníes;
100,000 guaraníes = £13.45 = $20.88 = €16.07.

Average Exchange Rate (guaraníes per US dollar)
2007   5,030.3
2008   4,363.2
2009   4,965.4

BUDGET
(central government operations, '000 million guaraníes)

Revenue	2007	2008	2009
Taxation	7,019	8,656	9,207
Corporate taxes	1,229	1,531	2,193
Value-added tax	3,318	4,428	4,450
Import duties	853	1,058	977
Non-tax revenue and grants	3,794	4,063	4,422
Capital revenues	55	62	278
Total	10,868	12,781	13,907

Expenditure	2007	2008	2009
Current expenditure	7,964	8,962	10,606
Personal	4,456	5,263	6,079
Other	3,508	3,699	4,527
Capital expenditure	2,311	1,989	3,256
Total	10,275	10,950	13,862

INTERNATIONAL RESERVES
(excl. gold, US $ million at 31 December)

	2007	2008	2009
IMF special drawing rights	43.65	44.19	173.00
Reserve position in IMF	33.94	33.08	33.67
Foreign exchange	2,383.89	2,767.29	3,631.97
Total	2,461.47	2,844.56	3,838.64

2010: IMF special drawing rights 170.08; Reserve position in IMF 33.07.
Source: IMF, *International Financial Statistics*.

MONEY SUPPLY
('000 million guaraníes at 31 December)

	2008	2009	2010
Currency outside depository corporations	3,997.14	4,418.03	5,277.93
Transferable deposits	9,026.60	12,102.11	14,249.69
Other deposits	5,082.18	5,987.74	6,708.45
Securities other than shares	5,951.05	6,888.16	8,676.49
Broad money	24,056.97	29,396.04	34,912.55

Source: IMF, *International Financial Statistics*.

COST OF LIVING
(Consumer Price Index for Asunción; base: 2000 = 100)

	2007	2008	2009
Food (incl. beverages)	213.2	246.1	247.5
Housing (incl. fuel and light)	159.7	172.0	175.2
Clothing (incl. footwear)	141.5	146.0	150.6
All items (incl. others)	178.8	196.9	202.1

Source: ILO.

NATIONAL ACCOUNTS
('000 million guaraníes at current prices)

Expenditure on the Gross Domestic Product

	2007	2008*	2009*
Final consumption expenditure	52,849.9	64,147.3	63,312.4
Households†	46,450.7	57,027.4	54,954.4
General government	6,399.2	7,119.9	8,358.0
Gross capital formation	11,095.9	13,289.3	10,975.4
Gross fixed capital formation	10,695.3	12,977.8	10,726.1
Changes in inventories‡	400.6	311.6	249.3
Total domestic expenditure	63,945.8	77,436.6	74,287.8
Exports of goods and services	30,129.9	37,092.5	32,899.7
Less Imports of goods and services	32,564.0	40,907.4	36,482.1
GDP in purchasers' values	61,511.7	73,621.7	70,705.3
GDP at constant 1994 prices	17,451.6	18,468.4	17,758.0

* Preliminary figures.
† Including non-profit institutions serving households.
‡ Including acquisitions, less disposals, of valuables.

2010 (preliminary): GDP in purchasers' values 84,616.6; GDP at constant 1994 prices 20,341.7.

Gross Domestic Product by Economic Activity

	2007	2008*	2009*
Agriculture, hunting, forestry and fishing	13,533.4	17,379.3	13,657.7
Mining and quarrying	68.9	88.7	105.7
Manufacturing	7,901.7	9,241.4	9,186.7
Construction	3,269.5	4,498.0	4,625.1
Electricity and water	1,048.0	1,058.5	1,084.6
Trade	11,982.5	13,820.5	12,734.6
Transport and communications	4,863.5	5,167.6	5,164.4
Financial intermediation	1,540.0	2,365.2	2,505.7
Government services	5,640.0	6,238.7	7,205.7
Real estate, renting and business activities	2,073.3	2,344.3	2,607.6
Hotels and restaurants	659.0	777.2	789.4
Other services	3,263.4	3,719.2	4,118.9
Gross value added in basic prices	55,843.2	66,698.7	63,786.1
Net taxes on products	5,668.4	6,923.0	6,919.2
GDP in market prices	61,511.7	73,621.7	70,705.3

* Preliminary figures.

PARAGUAY

BALANCE OF PAYMENTS
(US $ million)

	2007	2008	2009
Exports of goods f.o.b.	5,652.1	7,798.2	5,805.2
Imports of goods f.o.b.	−6,185.0	−8,844.3	−6,836.7
Trade balance	−532.9	−1,046.1	−1,031.5
Exports of services	961.9	1,149.9	1,448.1
Imports of services	−463.3	−591.6	−537.3
Balance on goods and services	−34.4	−487.8	−120.8
Other income received	336.7	390.1	337.1
Other income paid	−491.4	−620.3	−648.9
Balance on goods, services and income	−189.0	−718.0	−432.5
Current transfers received	374.8	415.6	520.3
Current transfers paid	−1.5	−1.4	−1.4
Current balance	184.2	−303.8	86.4
Capital account (net)	28.0	33.0	55.0
Direct investment abroad	−7.2	−8.4	−8.0
Direct investment from abroad	206.3	278.7	204.7
Other investment assets	470.4	−97.8	284.0
Other investment liabilities	53.1	435.5	100.3
Net errors and omissions	−309.8	59.2	204.9
Overall balance	625.0	396.4	927.3

Source: IMF, *International Financial Statistics*.

External Trade

PRINCIPAL COMMODITIES
(US $ million)

Imports f.o.b.	2008	2009*	2010*
Food and live animals	337.8	293.4	361.9
Beverages and tobacco	198.8	220.0	309.7
Mineral fuels	1,301.7	909.5	1,072.8
Chemical products	840.1	527.2	682.1
Road vehicles	347.0	234.3	314.7
Transport equipment and accessories	590.8	391.5	677.2
Electrical appliances	317.0	204.0	344.4
Motors, general industrial machinery equipment and parts	2,388.8	1,835.2	2,851.7
Total (incl. others)	8,506.0	6,496.9	9,399.8

Exports f.o.b.	2008	2009*	2010*
Meat and derivatives	622.2	579.0	919.8
Cereals	373.0	456.9	549.2
Oleaginous seeds	1,485.3	787.2	1,590.8
Vegetable oil	586.9	260.8	275.6
Flour	545.8	378.7	349.2
Wood and wooden products	120.0	96.0	101.6
Cotton fibres	25.4	20.2	24.4
Total (incl. others)	4,463.3	3,167.0	4,533.8

* Preliminary figures.

PRINCIPAL TRADING PARTNERS
(US $ '000)

Imports f.o.b.	2005	2006*	2007*
Argentina	639,188	677,181	799,692
Brazil	883,944	959,795	1,587,833
Chile	38,208	56,744	70,586
China, People's Republic	667,440	1,196,593	1,566,789
Germany	50,683	64,514	102,091
Japan	93,401	187,087	238,744
Korea, Republic	35,453	86,575	68,079
Malaysia	30,540	65,134	57,654
Switzerland-Liechtenstein	136,981	176,183	48,056
Taiwan	53,711	64,613	49,661
USA	169,299	331,904	292,652
Uruguay	52,987	51,810	73,720
Venezuela	5,697	139,922	141,776
Total (incl. others)	3,251,429	4,488,972	5,576,794

Exports f.o.b.	2005	2006*	2007*
Argentina	107,304	168,499	551,785
Brazil	325,528	327,983	557,925
Cayman Islands	169,329	180,228	145,462
Chile	64,787	79,038	206,465
Germany	13,864	19,438	30,548
Italy	16,335	21,198	66,630
Japan	18,478	24,699	30,946
Netherlands	47,194	41,661	34,661
Russia	101,084	227,802	143,302
Switzerland-Liechtenstein	14,565	34,127	83,369
USA	51,561	62,376	66,570
Uruguay	479,290	420,243	264,221
Total (incl. others)	1,687,823	1,906,367	2,784,728

* Preliminary figures.

2008 (US $ '000): *Imports:* Argentina 1,216,223; Brazil 2,301,914; China, People's Republic 2,346,732; Uruguay 100,412; Total (incl. others) 8,505,982. *Exports:* Argentina 727,038; Brazil 628,108; China, People's Republic 95,520; Uruguay 780,214; Total (incl. others) 4,463,309.

2009 (US $ '000, preliminary): *Imports:* Argentina 1,037,348; Brazil 1,512,727; China, People's Republic 1,952,360; Uruguay 81,813; Total (incl. others) 6,496,912. *Exports:* Argentina 343,129; Brazil 655,501; China, People's Republic 33,650; Uruguay 534,109; Total (incl. others) 3,167,021.

2010 (US $ '000, preliminary): *Imports:* Argentina 1,460,163; Brazil 2,280,033; China, People's Republic 3,255,209; Uruguay 140,237; Total (incl. others) 9,399,843. *Exports:* Argentina 538,129; Brazil 660,501; China, People's Republic 34,067; Uruguay 995,707; Total (incl. others) 4,533,777.

Transport

RAILWAYS
(traffic)

	1988	1989	1990
Passengers carried	178,159	196,019	125,685
Freight (metric tons)	200,213	164,980	289,099

Source: UN, *Statistical Yearbook*.

Passenger-kilometres: 3.0 million per year in 1994–96.

Freight ton-kilometres: 5.5 million in 1994.

Source: UN Economic Commission for Latin America and the Caribbean.

ROAD TRAFFIC
(vehicles in use)

	1999	2000
Cars	267,587	274,186
Buses	8,991	9,467
Lorries	41,329	42,992
Vans and jeeps	134,144	138,656
Motorcycles	6,872	8,825

Source: Organización Paraguaya de Cooperación Intermunicipal.

PARAGUAY

SHIPPING

Merchant Fleet
(registered at 31 December)

	2007	2008	2009
Number of vessels	45	47	49
Total displacement ('000 grt)	49.3	53.6	54.3

Source: IHS Fairplay, *World Fleet Statistics*.

CIVIL AVIATION
(traffic)

	2007	2008	2009
Passengers carried ('000)	659.5	697.9	569.6
Freight carried ('000 metric tons)	15.8	16.4	15.0

Tourism

ARRIVALS BY NATIONALITY

	2006	2007	2008
Argentina	194,532	184,745	195,948
Brazil	98,480	126,592	134,985
Chile	14,238	12,707	9,517
Germany	9,324	10,362	10,467
Uruguay	10,295	10,623	9,327
USA	13,262	14,540	13,241
Total (incl. others)	388,465	415,702	428,215

Tourism receipts (US $ million, incl. passenger transport): 112 in 2006; 121 in 2007; 128 in 2008.

Source: World Tourism Organization.

Communications Media

	2007	2008	2009
Telephones ('000 main lines in use)	394.4	370.4	387.3
Mobile cellular telephones ('000 subscribers)	4,694.4	5,790.8	5,618.6
Internet users ('000)	686.8	890.1	1,104.7*
Broadband subscribers ('000)	51.7†	89.0	140.9

* Estimate.
† Broadband defined as 64 kbps or more.

Personal computers: 460,000 (77.9 per 1,000 persons) in 2005.

Television receivers ('000 in use): 1,200 in 1997.

Radio receivers ('000 in use): 925 in 1997.

Daily newspapers (estimates): 5 in 1996 (average circulation 213,000 copies).

Non-daily newspapers (estimates): 2 in 1988 (average circulation 16,000 copies).

Book production (estimates): 152 titles (incl. 23 pamphlets) in 1993.

Sources: UNESCO, *Statistical Yearbook*; UN, *Statistical Yearbook*; International Telecommunication Union.

Education

(2007/08 unless otherwise indicated)

	Institutions*	Teachers	Students
Pre-primary schools	4,071	6,304.5	157,707
Primary	7,456	32,998.2	872,906
Secondary	2,149	34,340.7	543,056
Tertiary: university level	111	1,844†	180,637‡

* 1999.
† 1999/2000.
‡ 2006/07.

Source: partly UNESCO Institute for Statistics.

Pupil-teacher ratio (primary education, UNESCO estimate): 26.5 in 2007/08 (Source: UNESCO Institute for Statistics).

Adult literacy rate (UNESCO estimates): 94.6% (males 95.7%; females 93.5%) in 2007 (Source: UNESCO Institute for Statistics).

Directory

The Government

HEAD OF STATE

President: Fernando Armindo Lugo Méndez (took office 15 August 2008).
Vice-President: Luis Federico Franco Gómez.

COUNCIL OF MINISTERS
(May 2011)

The Government is formed by a coalition, comprising members of the constituent parties of the Alianza Patriótica para el Cambio and of the Partido Liberal Radical Auténtico, and several independents.

Minister of the Interior: Rafael Filizzola.
Minister of Foreign Affairs: Jorge Lara Castro.
Minister of Finance: Dionisio Borda.
Minister of Industry and Commerce: Francisco José Rivas Almada.
Minister of Public Works and Communications: Pedro Efraín Alegre Sasiain.
Minister of National Defence: Gen. (retd) Cecilio Pérez Bordón.
Minister of Public Health and Social Welfare: Esperanza Martínez.
Minister of Justice and Labour: Humberto Blasco.
Minister of Agriculture and Livestock: Enzo Cardozo Jiménez.
Minister of Education and Culture: Luis Alberto Riart Montaner.

MINISTRIES

Office of the President: Palacio de los López, Asunción; tel. (21) 414-0200; internet www.presidencia.gov.py.

Ministry of Agriculture and Livestock: Edif. San Rafael, Yegros, entre 25 de Mayo y Cerro Corá 437, Asunción; tel. (21) 45-0937; fax (21) 49-7965; e-mail prensa@mag.gov.py; internet www.mag.gov.py.

Ministry of Education and Culture: 15 de Agosto, esq. Gral Díaz y Eduardo V. Haedo, Edif. del ex-BNT, Asunción; tel. (21) 44-3078; fax (21) 44-3919; internet www.mec.gov.py.

Ministry of Finance: Chile 252, entre Palma y Presidente Franco, Asunción; tel. (21) 44-0010; fax (21) 44-8283; e-mail info@hacienda.gov.py; internet www.hacienda.gov.py.

Ministry of Foreign Affairs: Edif. Benigno López, Palma, esq. 14 de Mayo, Asunción; tel. (21) 49-3872; fax (21) 49-3910; e-mail sistemas@mre.gov.py; internet www.mre.gov.py.

Ministry of Industry and Commerce: Avda Marescal López 3333, esq. Dr Wiss, Villa Morra, Casilla 2151, Asunción; tel. (21) 616-3012; fax (21) 616-3000; e-mail sprivada@mic.gov.py; internet www.mic.gov.py.

Ministry of the Interior: Chile 1002, esq. Manduvira, Asunción; tel. (21) 415-2000; fax (21) 44-6448; e-mail ministro@mdi.gov.py; internet www.mdi.gov.py.

PARAGUAY

Ministry of Justice and Labour: Avda Dr José Gaspar Rodríguez de Francia, esq. Estados Unidos, Asunción; tel. (21) 49-3209; fax (21) 20-8469; e-mail info@mjt.gov.py; internet www.mjt.gov.py.

Ministry of National Defence: Avda Mariscal López, esq. Vicepresidente Sánchez y 22 de Septiembre, Asunción; tel. (21) 21-0052; fax (21) 21-1815; e-mail ministro@mdn.gov.py; internet www.mdn.gov.py.

Ministry of Public Health and Social Welfare: Avda Pettirossi, esq. Brasil, Asunción; tel. (21) 20-4601; fax (21) 20-6700; internet www.mspbs.gov.py.

Ministry of Public Works and Communications: Oliva y Alberdi 411, Casilla 1221, Asunción; tel. (21) 414-9000; fax (21) 44-4421; e-mail comunicaciones@mopc.gov.py; internet www.mopc.gov.py.

President and Legislature

PRESIDENT

Election, 20 April 2008

Candidate	Votes	% of votes
Fernando Armindo Lugo Méndez (APC)	766,502	40.90
Blanca Ovelar de Duarte (ANR—PC)	573,995	30.63
Gen. (retd) Lino César Oviedo Silva (UNACE)	411,034	21.93
Pedro Nicolás Fadul Niella (PPQ)	44,060	2.35
Others	12,233	0.65
Total	**1,874,127***	**100.00**

*Including 38,485 blank and 27,818 invalid ballots.

CONGRESO NACIONAL
(National Congress)

President of the Senado and the Congreso Nacional: OSCAR ALBERTO GONZÁLEZ DAHER (ANR).

President of the Cámara de Diputados: VÍCTOR ALCIDES BOGADO GONZÁLEZ (ANR).

General Election, 20 April 2008

	Seats	
Party	Cámara de Diputados	Senado
Asociación Nacional Republicana—Partido Colorado	30	15
Partido Liberal Radical Auténtico	27	14
Unión Nacional de Ciudadanos Eticos	15	9
Partido Patria Querida	3	4
Others	5	3
Total	**80**	**45**

Election Commission

Tribunal Superior de Justicia Electoral (TSJE): Avda Eusebio Ayala 2759 y Santa Cruz de la Sierra, Casilla 1209, Asunción; tel. and fax (21) 618-0111; e-mail protocolo@tsje.gov.py; internet www.tsje.gov.py; f. 1995; Pres. ALBERTO RAMÍREZ ZAMBONINI.

Political Organizations

Alianza Patriótica para el Cambio (APC): República Argentina, esq. Fernando de la Mora, Asunción; tel. (21) 55-9400; f. 2007 to support the presidential campaign of Fernando Lugo Méndez; alliance of parties and other orgs; mems incl. Partido Encuentro Nacional, Partido Demócrata Cristiano, Partido Frente Amplio, Partido País Solidario and Partido Revolucionario Febrerista.

Asociación Nacional Republicana—Partido Colorado (ANR—PC): Casa de los Colorados, 25 de Mayo 842, Asunción; tel. (21) 45-2543; fax (21) 45-4136; internet www.anr.org.py; f. 19th century; factions include Movimiento Vanguardia Colorada, led by LUIS CASTIGLIONI; Pres. LILIAN SAMANIEGO.

Convergencia Popular Socialista (CPS): Avda Brasil 663, entre Azara y Herrera, Asunción; tel. (21) 21-2850; e-mail prensapcps@gmail.com; internet convergenciapopular.blogspot.com; f. 2009; Leader ELVIO BENÍTEZ; Sec.-Gen. OSCAR HUGO RICHER FLORENTIN.

Frente Guasú: Asunción; f. 2010; a coalition of 22 political orgs and social movts supportive of President Fernando Lugo Méndez, incl. the constituent parties of the APC.

Movimiento 20 de Abril: Asunción; f. 2010 by supporters of President Fernando Lugo Méndez; Leader MIGUEL ANGEL LÓPEZ PERITO; Sec.-Gen. LIZ TORRES.

Partido Comunista Paraguayo (PCP): Brasil 228, Asunción; internet www.pcparaguay.org; f. 1928; banned 1928–46, 1947–89; Leader ANANÍAS MAIDANA; Sec.-Gen. NAJEEB AMADO.

Partido Demócrata Cristiano (PDC): Dupuis 962, entre Montevideo y Colón, Asunción; tel. (21) 42-0434; e-mail info@pdc.org.py; internet www.pdc.org.py; f. 1960; 20,500 mems; Pres. ALBA ESPINOLA DE CRISTALDO.

Partido Democrático Progresista (PDP): Avda 25 de Mayo, entre Constitución y Brasil, Asunción; tel. (21) 22-5354; e-mail info@pdp.org.py; internet www.pdp.org.py; f. 2007; democratic socialist; Pres. DESIRÉE MASI.

Partido Encuentro Nacional (PEN): Fulgencio R. Moreno 1048, entre Estados Unidos y Brasil, Asunción; tel. (21) 60-3935; fax (21) 61-0699; e-mail parenac@pla.net.py; f. 1991 as Movimiento Encuentro Nacional; Pres. FERNANDO CAMACHO PAREDES.

Partido Frente Amplio: Antequera 764, esq. Fulgencio R. Moreno, Asunción; tel. (21) 44-1389; e-mail arevalovicente@hotmail.com; Gen. Sec. VÍCTOR BAREIRO ROA.

Partido Humanista Paraguayo: San Francisco 1318, San Antonio, Barrio Jara, Asunción; tel. (21) 23-3085; e-mail tere_notario@hotmail.com; f. 1985; recognized by the Tribunal Superior de Justicia Electoral in March 1989; campaigns for the protection of human rights and environmental issues; Sec.-Gen. SERGIO MARTÍNEZ.

Partido Liberal Radical Auténtico (PLRA): Iturbe 936, entre Manuel Domínguez y Teniente Fariña, Asunción; tel. (21) 49-8442; fax (21) 49-8443; e-mail prensa@plra.org.py; internet www.plra.org.py; f. 1978; centre party; 806,000 mems; Pres. BLAS ANTONIO LLANO RAMOS; Sec.-Gen. EMILIO GUSTAVO FERREIRA SAGGIORATO.

Partido del Movimiento al Socialismo (PMAS): 15 de agosto 1660, entre Nuestra Señora de la Asunción 4 y 5, Asunción; tel. (21) 39-1525; e-mail info@pmas.org.py; internet www.pmas.org.py; f. 2006; Sec.-Gen. ROCÍO CASCO.

Partido País Solidario: Avda 5, esq. Méjico, Asunción; tel. (21) 39-1271; e-mail presidencia@paissolidario.org.py; internet www.paissolidario.org.py; f. 2000; mem. of Socialist International; Pres. Dr CARLOS FILIZZOLA PALLARÉS; Exec. Sec. MARÍA TERESA FERREIRA.

Partido Patria Libre (PPL): 15 de Agosto 1939, Asunción; tel. (21) 37-2384; f. 1990 as Corriente Patria Libre; renamed Movimiento Patria Libre in 1992; renamed as above and regd as a political org. in 2002; Marxist.

Partido Patria Querida (PPQ): Padre Cardozo 469, Asunción; tel. 21-3300; e-mail comunicaciones@patriaquerida.org; internet www.patriaquerida.org; f. 2002; recognized by the Tribunal Superior de Justicia Electoral in March 2004; Leader PEDRO NICOLÁS FADUL NIELLA; Sec.-Gen. ARSENIO OCAMPOS VELÁZQUEZ.

Partido Popular Tekojojá: Carios, esq. Médicos del Chaco, Asunción; tel. and fax (21) 55-4104; e-mail tekojoja@tekojoa.org.py; internet www.tekojoja.org.py; f. 2006 to support the presidential campaign of Fernando Lugo Méndez; left-wing, mainly comprising social and indigenous groups; Pres. SIXTO PEREIRA; Sec. FIDELINA ROJAS.

Partido Revolucionario Febrerista (PRF): Casa del Pueblo, Manduvira 522, Asunción; tel. (21) 49-4041; e-mail partyce@mixmail.com; f. 1951; social democratic; mem. of Socialist International; Pres. EDGAR FERREIRA.

Partido Social Demócrata (PSD): 25 de Mayo, esq. Tacuarí, Asunción; tel. (21) 45-3293; e-mail partidosocialdemocrata.paraguay@gmail.com; f. 2007; Pres. MANUEL DOLDÁN DEL PUERTO.

Partido de los Trabajadores (PT): Hernandarias y Piribebuy 890, Asunción; tel. (21) 44-5009; e-mail info@ptparaguay.org; internet www.ptparaguay.org; f. 1989; Socialist; Pres. GLORIA BAREIRO.

Partido de la Unidad Popular (PUP): Palma 561, entre 14 de Mayo y 15 de Agosto, Planta Alta, Asunción; tel. (21) 21-5059; fax (21) 49-8018; e-mail j_acosta@tigo.com.py; recognized by the Tribunal Superior de Justicia Electoral in March 2004; Pres. JUAN DE DIOS ACOSTA MENA.

Unión Nacional de Ciudadanos Eticos (UNACE): Avda Mariscal López, Saturio Ríos, Asunción; tel. (21) 59-1900; e-mail loviedo@unace.org.py; internet www.unace.org.py; f. 1996 as Unión Nacional de Colorados Eticos, a faction of the Partido Colorado; f. 2002 as political party under current name; left-wing; Pres. Gen. (retd) LINO CÉSAR OVIEDO SILVA; Exec. Sec. HERMINIO CHENA VALDEZ.

PARAGUAY   *Directory*

Diplomatic Representation

EMBASSIES IN PARAGUAY

Argentina: Avda España, esq. Avda Perú, Casilla 757, Asunción; tel. (21) 21-2320; fax (21) 21-1029; e-mail contacto@embajada-argentina .org.py; internet www.embajada-argentina.org.py; Ambassador RAFAEL EDGARDO ROMÁ.

Bolivia: Campos Cervera 6421, Barrio Villa Aurelia, Asunción; tel. (21) 61-4984; fax (21) 60-1999; e-mail emboliviapy@tigo.com.py; Ambassador FREDDY MARCEL QUEZADA GAMBARTE.

Brazil: Coronel Irrazábal, esq. Eligio Ayala, Casilla 22, Asunción; tel. (21) 248-4000; fax (21) 21-2693; e-mail parbrem@embajadabrasil .org.py; internet www.embajadabrasil.org.py; Ambassador EDUARDO DOS SANTOS.

Chile: Capital Emilio Nudelman 351, esq. Campos Cervera, Asunción; tel. (21) 61-3855; fax (21) 66-2755; e-mail echilepy@tigo.com.py; Ambassador CRISTIÁN MAQUIEIRA ASTABURUAGA.

Colombia: Coronel Francisco Brizuela 3089, esq. Ciudad del Vaticano, Asunción; tel. (21) 22-9888; fax (21) 22-9703; e-mail easuncio@ cancilleria.gov.co; Ambassador MAURICIO GONZÁLEZ LÓPEZ.

Cuba: Luis Morales 757, esq. Luis de León y Luis de Granada, Barrio Jara, Asunción; tel. (21) 22-2108; fax (21) 21-3879; e-mail embajada@ embacuba.org.py; internet www.embacuba.org.py; Ambassador ROLANDO ANTONIO GÓMEZ GONZÁLEZ.

Dominican Republic: Edif. Asturias, 9°, Suite C, Avda Mariscal López, esq. Dr Pane 127, Asunción; tel. (21) 21-3143; e-mail embajadadominicanapy@hotmail.com; Ambassador RODOLFO RINCÓN MARTÍNEZ.

Ecuador: Dr Bestard 861, esq. Juan XXIII, Barrio Manorá, Casilla 13162, Asunción; tel. (21) 61-4814; fax (21) 61-4813; e-mail eecuparaguay@mmree.gov.ec; Ambassador JULIO CÉSAR PRADO ESPINOSA.

France: Avda España 893, esq. Padre Pucheu, Casilla 97, Asunción; tel. (21) 21-2449; fax (21) 21-1690; e-mail chancellerie@ambafran.gov .py; internet www.ambafrance-py.org; Ambassador GILLES BIENVENU.

Germany: Avda Venezuela 241, Casilla 471, Asunción; tel. (21) 21-4009; fax (21) 21-2863; e-mail info@asuncion.diplo.de; internet www .asuncion.diplo.de; Ambassador DIETMAR BLAAS.

Holy See: Ciudad del Vaticano 350, casi con 25 de Mayo, Casilla 83, Asunción (Apostolic Nunciature); tel. (21) 21-5139; fax (21) 21-2590; e-mail nunciatura@tigo.com.py; Apostolic Nuncio Most Rev. ELISEO ANTONIO ARIOTTI (Titular Archbishop of Vibiana).

Italy: Quesada 5871 con Bélgica, Asunción; tel. (21) 61-5620; fax (21) 61-5622; e-mail ambitalia@cmm.com.py; internet www .embajadadeitalia.org.py; Ambassador PIETRO PORCARELLI.

Japan: Avda Mariscal López 2364, Casilla 1957, Asunción; tel. (21) 60-4616; fax (21) 60-6901; e-mail embajaponpy@rieder.net.py; internet www.py.emb-japan.go.jp; Ambassador KAZUO WATANABE.

Korea, Republic: Avda Rep. Argentina Norte 678, esq. Pacheco, Casilla 1303, Asunción; tel. (21) 60-5606; fax (21) 60-1376; e-mail paraguay@mofat.go.kr; internet pry.mofat.go.kr; Ambassador PARK DONG-WON.

Lebanon: San Francisco 629, esq. República Siria y Juan de Salazar, Asunción; tel. (21) 22-9375; fax (21) 23-2012; e-mail embajadadelibano@tigo.com.py; Ambassador FARES EID.

Mexico: Avda España 1428, casi San Rafael, Casilla 1184, Asunción; tel. (21) 618-2000; fax (21) 618-2500; e-mail embamex@embamex .com.py; internet www.embamex.com.py; Ambassador ERNESTO CAMPOS TENORIO.

Panama: Carmen Soler 3912, esq. Radio Operadores del Chaco, Barrio Seminario, Asunción; tel. and fax (21) 21-1091; e-mail embapana@gmail.com.py; Ambassador SABRINA DEL CARMEN GARCÍA BARRERA.

Peru: Edif. Santa Teresa, Dept 8B, Avda Santa Teresa 2415, Aviadores del Chaco, Casilla 433, Asunción; tel. (21) 60-0226; fax (21) 60-0901; e-mail embperu@embperu.com.py; Ambassador JORGE ANTONIO LÁZARO GELDRES.

Russia: Edif. Las Palmas, Molas López, esq. Dr C. Caceres y Julio Correa, Barrio Las Lomas, Asunción; tel. (21) 62-3733; fax (21) 62-3735; e-mail reshchikov@inbox.ru; Ambassador IGOR I. EZHOV.

Spain: Edif. S. Rafael, 5° y 6°, Yegros 437, Asunción; tel. (21) 49-0686; fax (21) 44-5394; e-mail emb.asuncion@maec.es; internet www .mae.es/embajadas/asuncion; Ambassador MIGUEL ANGEL CORTIZO NIETO.

Switzerland: Edif. Parapití, 4°, Ofs 419–423, Juan E. O'Leary 409, esq. Estrella, Casilla 552, Asunción; tel. (21) 44-8022; fax (21) 44-5853; e-mail asu.vertretung@eda.admin.ch; internet www.eda .admin.ch/asuncion; Ambassador EMANUEL JENNI.

Taiwan (Republic of China): Avda Mariscal López 1133 y Vicepresidente Sánchez, Casilla 503, Asunción; tel. (21) 21-3362; fax (21) 21-2373; e-mail embroc01@rieder.net.py; internet www .taiwanembassy.org/py; Ambassador HUANG LIEN-SHENG.

USA: Avda Mariscal López 1776, Casilla 402, Asunción; tel. (21) 21-3715; fax (21) 21-3728; e-mail paraguayusembassy@state.gov; internet paraguay.usembassy.gov; Ambassador LILIANA AYALDE.

Uruguay: Edif. Maria Luisa, 3°, Avda Boggiani 5832, esq. Alas Paraguayas, Asunción; tel. (21) 66-4244; fax (21) 60-1335; e-mail uruasun@embajadauruguay.com.py; internet www .embajadauruguay.com.py; Ambassador JUAN ENRIQUE FISCHER.

Venezuela: Soldado Desconocido 348, Avda España, Barrio Manorá, Asunción; tel. (21) 66-4682; fax (21) 66-4683; e-mail despacho2@ embaven.org.py; internet www.embaven.org.py; Ambassador JAVIER ARRÚE DE PABLO.

Judicial System

The Corte Suprema de Justicia (Supreme Court of Justice) is composed of nine judges appointed on the recommendation of the Consejo de la Magistratura (Council of the Magistracy).

Corte Suprema de Justicia: Palacio de Justicia, Asunción; internet www.pj.gov.py; Ministers Dr LUIS MARÍA BENÍTEZ RIERA (President), Dr ANTONIO FRETES (First Vice-President), Dr MIGUEL O. BAJAC (Second Vice-President), Dr VÍCTOR MANUEL NÚÑEZ, Dr SINDULFO BLANCO, Dra ALICIA BEATRIZ PUCHETA DE CORREA, Dr CÉSAR ANTONIO GARAY ZUCCOLILLO, RAÚL TORRES KIRMSER, GLADYS ESTER BAREIRO DE MÓDICA.

Attorney-General: RUBÉN CANDIA AMARILLA.

Under the Supreme Court are the Courts of Appeal, the Tribunal of Jurors and Judges of First Instance, the Judges of Arbitration, the Magistrates (Jueces de Instrucción), and the Justices of the Peace.

Religion

The Roman Catholic Church is the established religion, although all sects are tolerated.

CHRISTIANITY

The Roman Catholic Church

For ecclesiastical purposes, Paraguay comprises one archdiocese, 11 dioceses and two Apostolic Vicariates. Some 91% of the population are Roman Catholics.

Bishops' Conference

Conferencia Episcopal Paraguaya, Calle Alberdi 782, Casilla 1436, 1209 Asunción; tel. (21) 49-0920; fax (21) 49-5115; e-mail cep@infonet .com.py; internet www.episcopal.org.py.

f. 1977, statutes approved 2000; Pres. Most Rev. EUSTAQUIO PASTOR CUQUEJO VERGA (Archbishop of Asunción).

Archbishop of Asunción: Most Rev. EUSTAQUIO PASTOR CUQUEJO VERGA, Arzobispado, Avda Mariscal López 130 esq. Independencia Nacional, Casilla 654, Asunción; tel. (21) 44-5551; fax (21) 44-4150; e-mail asa@pla.net.py.

The Anglican Communion

Paraguay constitutes a single diocese of the Iglesia Anglicana del Cono Sur de América (Anglican Church of the Southern Cone of America). The Presiding Bishop of the Church is the Bishop of Northern Argentina.

Bishop of Paraguay: Rt Rev. JOHN ELLISON, Iglesia Anglicana, Avda España casi Santos, Casilla 1124, Asunción; tel. (21) 20-0933; fax (21) 21-4328; e-mail iapar@sce.cnc.una.py.

The Baptist Church

Baptist Evangelical Convention of Paraguay: Casilla 1194, Asunción; tel. (21) 22-7110; fax (21) 21-0588; e-mail cebp@sce.cnc .una.py; internet www.ublaonline.org/paises/paraguay.htm; Exec. Sec. AUGUSTO VEGA.

BAHÁ'Í FAITH

National Spiritual Assembly of the Bahá'ís of Paraguay: Eligio Ayala 1456, Apdo 742, Asunción; tel. (21) 22-5747; e-mail bahai@ highway.com.py; internet www.bahai.org.py; Sec. MIRNA LLAMOSAS DE RIQUELME.

PARAGUAY

The Press

DAILIES

ABC Color: Yegros 745, Apdo 1421, Asunción; tel. (21) 49-1160; fax (21) 415-1310; e-mail azeta@abc.com.py; internet www.abc.com.py; f. 1967; independent; Propr ALDO ZUCCOLILLO; circ. 45,000.

La Nación: Avda Zavala Cué entre 2da y 3ra, Fernando de la Mora, Asunción; tel. (21) 51-2520; fax (21) 51-2535; e-mail redaccion@lanacion.com.py; internet www.lanacion.com.py; f. 1995; Dir ALEJANDRO DOMÍNGUEZ WILSON-SMITH; circ. 10,000.

Noticias: Avda Artigas y Avda Brasilia, Casilla 3017, Asunción; tel. (21) 29-2721; fax (21) 29-2716; e-mail alebluth@diarionoticias.com; f. 1985; independent; Dir ALEJANDRO BLUTH; circ. 20,000.

Popular: Avda Mariscal López 2948, Asunción; tel. (21) 60-3401; fax (21) 60-3400; e-mail popular@mm.com.py; internet www.diariopopular.com.py; Dir JAVIER PIROVANO PEÑA; circ. 28,000.

Ultima Hora: Benjamín Constant 658, Asunción; tel. (21) 49-6261; fax (21) 44-7071; e-mail ultimahora@uhora.com.py; internet www.ultimahora.com; f. 1973; independent; Dir OSCAR AYALA BOGARÍN; circ. 30,000.

PERIODICALS

Acción: CEPAG, Vicepresidente Sánchez 612, casi Azara, Asunción; tel. (21) 23-3541; e-mail revistaaccion@cepag.org.py; internet www.montoya.com.py/revista_accion.php; f. 1923; monthly; published by the Centro de Estudios Paraguayos Antonio Guasch (CEPAG—Jesuit org.); Dir JOSÉ MARÍA BLANCH.

Revista Zeta: Eligio Ayala 2002, esq. Gral Bruguez, Asunción; tel. (21) 61-3392; fax (21) 61-3393; e-mail zeta@revistazeta.com.py; internet www.revistazeta.com.py; f. 2000; monthly; general interest; Dir ZUNI CASTIÑEIRA.

TVO: Santa Margarita de Youville 250, Santa María, Asunción; tel. (21) 67-2079; fax (21) 21-1236; e-mail sugerencias@teveo.com.py; internet www.teveo.com.py; f. 1992; fmrly TeVeo; weekly; news and society; Commercial Dir MARTINA LECLERCQ.

NEWS AGENCY

Información Pública Paraguay (IP Paraguay): Palacio de los López, Asunción; e-mail ipparaguay@gmail.com; internet www.ipparaguay.com.py; f. 2009; attached to the Office of the President.

Jaku'éke Paraguay—Agencia Nacional de Noticias: Itapúa y Río Monday, Asunción; tel. (21) 29-7806; fax (21) 28-1950; internet www.jakueke.com; f. 2002; independent.

Publishers

Arandurā Editorial: Tte Fariña, Asunción; fax (21) 21-4295; e-mail arandura@tigo.com.py; internet www.arandura.pyglobal.com; f. 1991; poetry, literature, social history.

La Colmena, SA: Asunción; tel. (21) 20-0428; Dir DAUMAS LADOUCE.

Dervish SA, Editorial: Avda Mariscal López 1735, CP 1584, Asunción; tel. (21) 21-2062; fax (21) 22-2580; e-mail dervish@dervish.com.py; f. 1989; Co-ordinator JORGELINA MIGLIORISI; Vice-Pres. and Dir JANINE GIANI PATTERSON.

Ediciones Diálogo: Brasil 1391, Asunción; tel. (21) 20-0428; f. 1957; fine arts, literature, poetry, criticism; Man. MIGUEL ANGEL FERNÁNDEZ.

Ediciones Nizza: Eligio Ayala 1073, Casilla 2596, Asunción; tel. (21) 44-7160; medicine; Pres. Dr JOSÉ FERREIRA MARTÍNEZ.

Editorial Comuneros: Cerro Corá 289, Casilla 930, Asunción; tel. (21) 44-6176; fax (21) 44-4667; e-mail rolon@conexion.com.py; f. 1963; social history, poetry, literature, law; Man. OSCAR R. ROLÓN.

Editorial Servilibro: 25 de Mayo y México, Plaza Uruguaya, Asunción; fax (21) 44-4770; e-mail servilibro@gmail.com; internet www.servilibro.com.py; Dir-Gen. ELIZABETH BÁEZ.

Librería Intercontinental: Caballero 270, Calle Mariscal, Estigarribia, Asunción; tel. (21) 49-6991; fax (21) 44-8721; e-mail agatti@libreriaintercontinental.com.py; internet www.libreriaintercontinental.com.py; political science, law, literature, poetry; Dir ALEJANDRO GATTI VAN HUMBEECK.

R. P. Ediciones: Eduardo Víctor Haedo 427, Asunción; tel. (21) 49-8040; Man. (vacant).

Santillana: Avda Venezuela 276, Asunción; fax (21) 202-942; e-mail cls@santillana.com.py; internet www.santillana.com.py; educational books; Dir-Gen. JAVIER BARRETO.

Directory

ASSOCIATION

Cámara Paraguaya del Libro (CAPEL): Ayolas 129, esq. Benjamin Constant, Asunción; tel. (21) 497-352; fax (21) 44-7053; internet www.capel.org.py; Pres. EDGAR RUIZ DÍAZ.

Broadcasting and Communications

REGULATORY AUTHORITY

Comisión Nacional de Telecomunicaciones (CONATEL): Presidente Franco 780, esq. Ayolas, Asunción; tel. (21) 44-0020; fax (21) 49-8982; e-mail presidencia@conatel.gov.py; internet www.conatel.gov.py; Pres. JORGE ANTONIO SEALL SASIAIN.

TELECOMMUNICATIONS

Claro (AMX Paraguay, SA): Avda Mariscal López 1730, Asunción; tel. (21) 249-9000; fax (21) 249-9099; e-mail empresaspy@claro.com.py; internet www.claro.com.py; subsidiary of América Móvil, SA de CV (Mexico); fmrly CTI Móvil; mobile cellular telephone services.

Corporación Paraguaya de Comunicaciones, SA (COPACO): Edif. Morotí, 1°–2°, esq. Gen. Bruguez y Teodoro S. Mongelos, Casilla 2042, Asunción; tel. (21) 20-3800; fax (21) 20-3888; e-mail infoweb@copaco.com.py; internet www.copaco.com.py; fmrly Administración Nacional de Telecomunicaciones (ANTELCO); adopted current name in Dec. 2001 as part of the privatization process; privatization suspended in June 2002; Pres. MARIO ESQUIVEL BADO.

BROADCASTING

Radio

Radio Arapysandú: Avda Mariscal López y Capitán del Puerto San Ignacio, Misiones; tel. (82) 2374; fax (82) 2206; f. 1982; AM; Dir HECTOR BOTTINO.

Radio Asunción: Avda Artígas y Capitán Lombardo 174, Asunción; tel. and fax (21) 28-2662; fax (21) 28-2661; e-mail radioasuncion@cmm.com.py; internet www.radioasuncion.com.py; AM; Propr MIGUEL GERÓNIMO FERNÁNDEZ; Dir-Gen. BIBIANA LANDO MEYER.

Radio Cáritas: Kubitschek 661 y Azara, Asunción; tel. (21) 21-3570; fax (21) 20-4161; e-mail caritas@caritas.com.py; internet www.caritas.com.py; f. 1936; station of the Archdiocese of Asunción and the Universidad Católica Nuestra Señora de la Asunción; AM; Dir-Gen. JORGE BAZÁN; Dir of Operations PEDRO PORTILLO.

Radio Cardinal: Comendador Nicolás Bó 1334 y Guaraníes, Casilla 2532, Lambaré, Asunción; tel. (21) 31-0555; fax (21) 30-3089; e-mail info@cardinal.com.py; internet www.cardinal.com.py; f. 1991; AM and FM; Pres. ALFREDO CHENA; Man. ANDREA BITTAR.

Radio City: Edif. Líder III, Antequera 652, 9°, Asunción; tel. (21) 44-3324; fax (21) 44-4367; e-mail direccion@fmradiocity.com; internet www.fmradiocity.com; f. 1950; FM; Dir GREGORIO RAMAN MORALES.

Radio Concepción: Coronel Panchito López 241, entre Schreiber y Profesor Guillermo A. Cabral, Casilla 78, Concepción; tel. (31) 42318; fax (31) 42254; f. 1963; AM; Dir SERGIO E. DACAK.

Radio Emisoras del Paraguay, SRL: Teniente Martínez Ramella 1355, Calle Avda Eusebio Ayala, Asunción; tel. (21) 22-0132; e-mail administracion@emisorasparaguay.com.py; internet www.desdeparaguay.com/emisoras; FM; Dir FRANCISCO JAVIER BOSCARINO BÁEZ.

Radio Guairá: Presidente Franco 788 y Alejo García, Villarica; tel. (541) 42130; fax (541) 42385; e-mail administracion@fmguaira.com; internet www.fmguaira.com; f. 1950; AM and FM; Dir LÍDICE RODRÍGUEZ DE TRAVERSI.

Radio Itapiru SRL: Avda San Blás esq. Coronel Julián Sánchez, Ciudad del Este; tel. (61) 57-2207; fax (61) 57-2210; internet www.radioitapiru.com; f. 1969; AM and FM; Dir-Gen. FABIÁN ARANDA.

Radio La Voz de Amambay: 14 de Mayo y Cerro León, Pedro Juan Caballero, Amambay; tel. (36) 72537; f. 1959; AM and FM; Gen. Man. DANIEL ROLÓN DANTAS P.

Radio Nacional del Paraguay: Blas Garay 241, esq. Iturbe y Yegros, Asunción; tel. (21) 39-0374; fax (21) 39-0375; e-mail direccion@radionacionaldelparaguay.com.py; internet www.radionacionaldelparaguay.com.py; f. 1957; AM and FM; Dir JUDITH MARIA VERA.

Radio Ñandutí: Choferes del Chaco y Carmen Soler, Asunción; tel. (21) 60-4308; fax (21) 60-6074; e-mail prensaam@holdingderadio.com.py; internet www.nanduti.com.py; f. 1962; FM; Dir HUMBERTO LEÓN RUBÍN.

Radio Nuevo Mundo: Coronel Romero 1181 y Flórida, San Lorenzo, Asunción; tel. (21) 58-6258; fax (21) 58-2424; f. 1972; AM; Dir JULIO CÉSAR PEREIRA BOBADILLA.

PARAGUAY

Radio Primero de Marzo: Avda General Perón y Concepción, Casilla 1456, Asunción; tel. (21) 30-0380; fax (21) 33-3427; internet www.780am.com.py; AM and FM; Dir-Gen. ANGEL R. GUERREÑOS.

Radio Santa Mónica FM: Avda Boggiani y Herrera, 3°, Asunción; tel. (21) 50-7501; fax (21) 50-9494; f. 1973; FM; Dir RICARDO FACCETTI.

Radio Uno: Avda Mariscal López 2948, Asunción; tel. (21) 61-2151; internet www.radiouno.com.py; f. 1968 as Radio Chaco Boreal; AM; Dir JAVIER MARÍA PIROVANO SILVA.

Radio Venus: Avda República Argentina y Souza, Asunción; tel. (21) 61-0151; fax (21) 60-6484; e-mail 105.1@venus.com.py; internet www.venus.com.py; f. 1987; FM; Dir ANGEL AGUILERA.

Radio Ysapy: Independencia Nacional 1260, 1°, Asunción; tel. (21) 44-4037; e-mail info@radioysapy.com.py; internet www.radioysapy.com.py; FM; Dir JOSÉ TOMÁS CABRIZA SALVIONI.

Television

Paravision: Belgica 4498, casi Mariscal López, Asunción; tel. (21) 66-4380; e-mail info@paravision.com.py; internet www.paravision.com.py.

Red Guaraní (Canal 2): Complejo Textilia, General Santos 1024, casi Concordia, Asunción; tel. (21) 20-5444; e-mail oescobar@redguarani.com.py; internet www.redguarani.com.py; Exec. Dir Dr ARNOLDO WIENS; Gen. Man. OSCAR ESCOBAR.

Sistema Nacional de Televisión Cerro Corá—Canal 9 (SNT): Avda Carlos A. López 572, Asunción; tel. (21) 42-4222; fax (21) 48-0230; e-mail snt@snt.com.py; internet www.snt.com.py; f. 1965; commercial; Dir Gen. ISMAEL HADID.

Teledifusora Paraguaya—Canal 13: Comendador Nicolás Bó y Guaraníes, Lambaré, Asunción; tel. (21) 33-2823; fax (21) 33-2826; e-mail info@canal13.com.py; internet www.rpc.com.py; f. 1981; Pres. ALFREDO CHENA; Dir-Gen. GUSTAVO CUBILLA.

Telefuturo (TV Acción, SA): Andrade 1499 y O'Higgins, Asunción; tel. (21) 618-4000; fax (21) 618-4166; e-mail telefuturo@telefuturo.com.py; internet www.telefuturo.com.py; Gen. Man. MARCO GALANTI.

Finance

(cap. = capital; res = reserves; dep. = deposits; m. = million; brs = branches; amounts in guaraníes, unless otherwise indicated)

BANKING

Superintendencia de Bancos: Edif. Banco Central del Paraguay, Avda Federación Rusa y Avda Marecos, Barrio Santo Domingo, Asunción; tel. (21) 60-8148; fax (21) 419-2403; e-mail supban@bcp.gov.py; internet www.bcp.gov.py/supban; Supt EDGAR ANDRÉS LEGUIZAMON CARMONA.

Central Bank

Banco Central del Paraguay: Avda Federación Rusa y Cabo 1° Marecos, Casilla 861, Barrio Santo Domingo, Asunción; tel. (21) 60-8011; fax (21) 619-2328; e-mail informaciones@bcp.gov.py; internet www.bcp.gov.py; f. 1952; cap. 828,145m., res 454,695m., dep. 4,605,137m. (Dec. 2005); Pres. JORGE RAÚL CORVALÁN MENDOZA; Gen. Man. JORGE AURELIO VILLALBA LEGUIZAMON.

Development Banks

Banco Nacional de Fomento: Independencia Nacional, entre Cerro Cora y 25 de Mayo, Asunción; tel. (21) 44-4440; fax (21) 44-6056; e-mail correo@bnf.gov.py; internet www.bnf.gov.py; f. 1961 to take over the deposit and private banking activities of the Banco del Paraguay; cap. 293,585m., res −135,556m., dep. 1,849,758m. (Dec. 2008); Pres. AGUSTÍN SILVERA ORUE; Sec.-Gen. CÉSAR LEONARDO FURIASSE ROLÓN; 52 brs.

Crédito Agrícola de Habilitación (CAH): Caríos 362 y Willam Richardson, Asunción; tel. (21) 569-0100; fax (21) 55-4956; e-mail info@cah.gov.py; internet www.cah.gov.py; f. 1943; Pres. JOSÉ MARCELO BRUSTEIN ALEGRE.

Fondo Ganadero: Avda Mariscal López 1669 esq. República Dominicana, Asunción; tel. (21) 22-7288; fax (21) 22-7378; e-mail info@fondogan.gov.py; internet www.fondogan.gov.py; f. 1969; govt-owned; Pres. JUAN FERNANDO PERONI CAZAL RIBEIRO.

Commercial Banks

Banco Amambay, SA: Avda Aviadores del Chaco, entre San Martín y Pablo Alborno, Asunción; tel. (21) 60-8831; fax (21) 60-8813; e-mail bcoama@bancoamambay.com.py; internet www.bancoamambay.com.py; f. 1992; cap. US $10.9m., res $5.9m., dep. $125.7m. (Dec. 2008); Pres. and Gen. Man. HUGO JAVIER PORTILLO SOSA; 6 brs.

Banco Bilbao Vizcaya Argentaria Paraguaya, SA: Yegros 435, esq. 25 de Mayo, Casilla 824, Asunción; tel. (21) 417-6000; fax (21) 44-8103; e-mail info@bbva.com.py; internet www.bbva.com.py; f. 1961 as Banco Exterior de España, SA; present name adopted in 2000; cap. 40,052m., res 187,103m., dep. 3,327,164m. (Dec. 2008); Pres. VICENTE LUIS BOGLIOLO DEL RÍO; 5 brs.

Banco Continental, SAECA: Estrella 621, Calle 15 de Agosto, Casilla 021-442002, Asunción; tel. (21) 44-2002; fax (21) 44-2001; e-mail contil@connexion.com.py; internet www.bancontinental.com.py; f. 1980; cap. US $4.2m., res $2.5m., dep. $44.6m. (Dec. 2001); Pres. CARLOS ESPÍNOLA; 28 brs.

Interbanco, SA: Oliva 349, esq. Chile y Alberdi, Asunción; tel. (21) 617-1000; fax (21) 41-71372; e-mail sac@interbanco.com.py; internet www.interbanco.com.py; f. 1978; owned by Unibanco (Brazil); cap. 25,923m., res 330,969m., dep. 3,627,798m. (Dec. 2008); Pres. CLAUDIO YAMAGUTI; 17 brs.

Sudameris Bank, SAECA: Independencia Nacional y Cerro Corá, Casilla 1433, Asunción; tel. (21) 44-8670; fax (21) 44-4024; e-mail gerencia@sudameris.com.py; internet www.sudamerisbank.com.py; f. 1961; savings and commercial bank; cap. 42,991m., surplus and res 34,391m., dep. 970,480m. (Dec. 2007); Chair. CONOR MCENROY; Vice-Chair. and Gen. Man. JUAN LUIS KOSTNER; 8 brs.

Banking Associations

Asociación de Bancos del Paraguay: Jorge Berges 229, esq. Estados Unidos, Asunción; tel. (21) 214-9513; fax (21) 20-5050; e-mail abp.par@pla.net.py; mems: Paraguayan banks and foreign banks with brs in Asunción; Pres. PEDRO DANIEL MIRAGLIO.

Cámara de Bancos Paraguayos: 25 de Mayo, esq. 22 de Setiembre, Asunción; tel. (21) 22-2373; fax (21) 20-5050; Pres. MIGUEL ANGEL LARREINEGABE.

STOCK EXCHANGE

Bolsa de Valores y Productos de Asunción, SA: 15 de Agosto 640, esq. General Díaz y Víctor Haedo, Asunción; tel. (21) 44-2445; fax (21) 44-2446; internet www.bvpasa.com.py; f. 1977; Pres. RODRIGO CALLIZO LÓPEZ.

INSURANCE

Supervisory Authority

Superintendencia de Seguros: Edif. Banco Central del Paraguay, 1°, Federación Rusa y Sargento Marecos, Asunción; tel. (21) 619-2637; fax (21) 619-2542; e-mail dmarti@bcp.gov.py; internet www.bcp.gov.py; Supt DIEGO ARTURO MARTÍNEZ SÁNCHEZ.

Principal Companies

La Agrícola SA de Seguros Generales: Mariscal López 5377 y Concejal Vargas, Asunción; tel. (21) 60-9509; fax (21) 60-9606; e-mail sagricola@tigo.com.py; f. 1982; general; Pres. CARLOS ALBERTO LEVI SOSA.

ALFA SA de Seguros y Reaseguros: Yegros 944 esq. Tte Fariña, Asunción; tel. (21) 44-9992; fax (21) 44-9991; e-mail alfa.seg@conexion.com.py; Pres. NICOLÁS SARUBBI ZAYAS.

Aseguradora del Este SA de Seguros: Avda República Argentina 778, entre Pacheco y Souza, Asunción; tel. (21) 60-5015; e-mail dcespedes@aesaseguros.com.py; Pres. VÍCTOR ANDRÉS RIBEIRO ESPÍNOLA.

Aseguradora Paraguaya, SA (ASEPASA): Israel 309 esq. Rio de Janeiro, Casilla 277, Asunción; tel. (21) 21-5086; fax (21) 22-2217; e-mail asepasa@asepasa.com.py; internet www.asepasa.com.py; f. 1976; life and risk; Pres. and Gen. Man. GERARDO TORCIDA CONEJERO.

Aseguradora Yacyretá SA de Seguros y Reaseguros: Oliva 685, esq. Juan E. O'Leary y 15 de Agosto, Asunción; tel. (21) 45-2374; fax (21) 44-5070; e-mail spalomar@yacyreta.com.py; internet www.yacyretasa.com; f. 1980; Pres. OSCAR HARRISON JACQUET; Vice-Pres. NORMAN HARRISON PALEARI; Gen. Man. EDUARDO BARRIOS PERINI; 5 brs.

Atalaya SA de Seguros Generales: Independencia Nacional 565, 1°, esq. Azara y Cerro Corá, Asunción; tel. (21) 49-2811; fax (21) 49-6966; e-mail ataseg@telesurf.com.py; f. 1964; general; Pres. KARIN M. DOLL.

Cenit de Seguros, SA: Ayolas 1082, esq. Ibáñez del Campo, Asunción; tel. (21) 49-4972; fax (21) 44-9502; e-mail cenit@cenit.com.py; internet www.cenit.com.py; Pres. OSCAR CÁCERES CARDOZO.

Central SA de Seguros: Edif. Betón I, 1° y 2°, Eduardo Víctor Haedo 179, Independencia Nacional, Casilla 1802, Asunción; tel. (21) 49-4654; fax (21) 49-4655; e-mail censeg@conexion.com.py; f. 1977; general; Pres. MIGUEL JACOBO VILLASANTI; Gen. Man. Dr FÉLIX AVEIRO.

El Comercio Paraguayo SA Cía de Seguros Generales: Alberdi 453 y Oliva, Asunción; tel. (21) 49-2324; fax (21) 49-3562; e-mail elcomercioparaguayo@elcomercioparaguayo.com.py; internet www

PARAGUAY

.elcomercioparaguayo.com.py; f. 1947; life and risk; Dir Victoria Martínez de Elizeche.

La Consolidada SA de Seguros y Reaseguros: Chile 719 y Eduardo Víctor Haedo, Casilla 1182, Asunción; tel. (21) 49-5174; fax (21) 44-5795; internet www.consolidada.com.py; f. 1961; life and risk; Pres. Juan Carlos Delgadillo Echagüe.

Fénix SA de Seguros y Reaseguros: Iturbe 823 y Fulgencio R. Moreno, Asunción; tel. (21) 49-5549; fax (21) 44-5643; e-mail fenixsa@pla.net.py; internet www.fenixseguros.com.py; Pres. Víctor Martínez Yaryes.

Garantía SA de Seguros y Reaseguros: 25 de Mayo 640, Asunción; tel. (21) 44-3748; fax (21) 49-0678; e-mail garantia@rieder.net.py; Pres. Geraldo Cristaldo Jure.

Grupo General de Seguros y Reaseguros, SA: Edif. Grupo General, Jejuí 324 y Chile, 2°, Asunción; tel. (21) 49-7897; fax (21) 44-9259; e-mail general_de_seguros@ggeneral.com.py; Pres. Jorge Obelar Lamas.

La Independencia de Seguros y Reaseguros, SA: Edif. Parapatí, 1°, Juan E. O'Leary 409, esq. Estrella, Casilla 980, Asunción; tel. (21) 44-7021; fax (21) 44-8996; e-mail liseguros@laindependencia.com.py; f. 1965; general; Pres. Edmundo Emilio Richer Bécker.

Intercontinental SA de Seguros y Reaseguros: Iturbe 1047 con Teniente Fariña, Altos, Asunción; tel. (21) 49-2348; fax (21) 49-1227; e-mail intercontinentalseguros@flash.com.py; f. 1978; Pres. Dr Juan Módica Lucente; Gen. Man. Luis Santacruz.

Mapfre Paraguay, SA: Avda Mariscal López 910 y General Aquino, Asunción; tel. (21) 44-1983; fax (21) 49-7441; e-mail sac@mapfre.com.py; internet www.mapfre.com.py; Pres. Luis María Zubizarreta.

La Meridional Paraguaya SA de Seguros: Iturbe 1046, Teniente Fariña, Asunción; tel. (21) 49-8827; fax (21) 49-8826; e-mail meridian@conexion.com.py; Pres. Tito Livio Mujica Varela.

La Paraguaya SA de Seguros: Estrella 675, 7°, Asunción; tel. (21) 49-1367; fax (21) 44-8235; e-mail lps@laparaguaya.com.py; internet www.laparaguaya.com.py; f. 1905; life and risk; Pres. Juan Bosch Beynen.

Patria SA de Seguros y Reaseguros: General Santos 715 esq. Siria, Asunción; tel. (21) 22-5250; fax (21) 21-4001; e-mail patria@tigo.com.py; f. 1967; general; Pres. Dr Ernesto Goberman.

El Productor SA de Seguros y Reaseguros: Ind. Nacional 811 esq. Fulgencio R. Moreno, 8°, Asunción; tel. (21) 49-1577; fax (21) 49-1599; e-mail ncabanas@elproductor.com.py; Pres. Reinaldo Pavía Maldonado.

Regional SA de Seguros y Reaseguros: Roque González 390 y Dr Hassler, Asunción; tel. (21) 61-0692; fax (21) 22-4447; e-mail regisesa@itacom.com.py; Pres. Juan A. Diaz de Vivar Prieto.

Rumbos SA de Seguros: Estrella 851, Ayolas, Casilla 1017, Asunción; tel. (21) 44-9488; fax (21) 44-9492; e-mail rumbos@conexion.com.py; f. 1960; general; Pres. Miguel A. Larreinegabe Lesme; Man. Dir Roberto Gómez Verlangieri.

La Rural SA de Seguros: Avda Mariscal López 1082, esq. Mayor Bullo, Casilla 21, Asunción; tel. (21) 49-1917; fax (21) 44-1592; e-mail larural@larural.com.py; internet www.larural.com.py; f. 1920; general; Pres. Juan Carlos Maneglia; Gen. Man. Eduardo Barrios Perini.

Seguros Chaco SA de Seguros y Reaseguros: Mariscal Estigarribia 982, Casilla 3248, Asunción; tel. (21) 44-7118; fax (21) 44-9551; e-mail seguroschaco@pla.net.py; f. 1977; general; Pres. Emilio Velilla Laconich; Exec. Dir Alberto R. Zarza Taboada.

Seguros Generales, SA (SEGESA): Edif. SEGESA, 1°, Oliva 393 esq. Alberdi, Casilla 802, Asunción; tel. (21) 49-1362; fax (21) 49-1360; e-mail segesa@conexion.com.py; f. 1956; life and risk; Pres. César Avalos.

El Sol del Paraguay, Cía de Seguros y Reaseguros, SA: Cerro Corá 1031, Asunción; tel. (21) 49-1110; fax (21) 21-0604; e-mail elsol@elsol.com.py; internet www.elsol.com.py; f. 1978; Pres. Miguel Angel Berni Centurión; Vice-Pres. Carolina Vega de Onetto.

Universo de Seguros y Reaseguros, SA: Edif. de la Encarnación, 9°, 14 de Mayo esq. General Díaz, Casilla 788, Asunción; tel. (21) 44-8530; fax (21) 44-7278; f. 1979; Pres. Zenón Agüero Miranda.

Insurance Association

Asociación Paraguaya de Cías de Seguros: 15 de Agosto, esq. Lugano, Casilla 1435, Asunción; tel. (21) 44-6474; fax (21) 44-4343; e-mail apcs@activenet.com.py; f. 1963; Pres. Dr Emilio Velilla Laconich; Gen. Man. Rubén Rappenecker Coscia.

Trade and Industry

GOVERNMENT AGENCIES

Instituto Nacional de Desarrollo Rural y de la Tierra (INDERT): Tacuary 276, esq. Mariscal Estigarribia, Asunción; tel. and fax (21) 44-3161; internet www.indert.gov.py; f. 2003; land reform institute; Pres. Marciano Barreto Leiva.

Instituto Nacional de Tecnología, Normalización y Metrología (INTN): Avda General Artigas 3973 y General Roa, Casilla 967, Asunción; tel. (21) 29-0160; fax (21) 29-0873; e-mail intn@intn.gov.py; internet www.intn.gov.py; national standards institute; Dir-Gen. Mario Gustavo Leiva Enrique.

Instituto de Previsión Social: Edif. de la Caja Central, Constitución y Luis Alberto de Herrera, Casilla 437, Asunción; tel. (21) 22-3141; fax (21) 22-3654; e-mail secretaria_general@ips.gov.py; internet www.ips.gov.py; f. 1943; responsible for employees' welfare and health insurance scheme; Pres. Jorge Stevan Giucich Greenwood.

DEVELOPMENT ORGANIZATIONS

Alter Vida (Centro de Estudios y Formación para el Ecodesarrollo): Itapúa 1372, esq. Primer Presidente y Río Monday, Barrio Trinidad, Asunción; tel. (21) 29-8842; fax (21) 29-8845; e-mail info@altervida.org.py; internet www.altervida.org.py; f. 1985; ecological devt; Exec. Dir Víctor Benítez Insfrán.

Centro de Información y Recursos para el Desarrollo (CIRD): Avda Mariscal López 2029, esq. Acá Carayá, Casilla 1580, Asunción; tel. (21) 22-6071; fax (21) 21-2540; e-mail cird@cird.org.py; internet www.cird.org.py; f. 1988; information and resources for devt orgs; Exec. Pres. Agustín Carrizosa.

Centro de Cooperación Empresarial y Desarrollo Industrial (CEDIAL): Edif. UIP, 2°, Cerro Corá 1038, esq. Estados Unidos y Brasil, Asunción; tel. and fax (21) 23-0047; e-mail cedial@cedial.org.py; internet www.cedial.org.py; f. 1991; promotes commerce and industrial devt; Gen. Man. Hernán Ramírez.

Instituto de Biotecnología Agrícola (INBIO): Avda Brasilia 939, Calle Ciancio, Asunción; tel. (21) 23-3892; e-mail info@inbio-paraguay.org; internet www.inbio-paraguay.org; bio-technological research for agricultural devt; Pres. Ricardo Wollmeister; Sec. Humberto Páez.

Instituto Paraguayo de Artesanía (IPA): Asunción; tel. (21) 61-4896; fax (21) 60-0035; e-mail ipa@artesania.gov.py; internet www.artesania.gov.py; f. 2004; promotes handicraft industries; Pres. Freddy Gerardo Olmedo Colman.

Instituto Paraguayo del Indígena (INDI): Edif. Sudamérica, 2°, Iturbe 891, esq. Manuel Dominguez, Asunción; tel. (21) 44-5818; fax (21) 44-7154; e-mail informes@indi.gov.py; internet www.indi.gov.py; f. 1981; responsible for welfare of Indian population; Pres. Lida Acuña.

Red de Inversiones y Exportaciones (REDIEX): Avda Mariscal López 3333, CP 1892, Asunción; tel. (21) 616-3028; fax (21) 616-3034; e-mail info@rediex.gov.py; internet www.rediex.gov.py; replaced ProParaguay in 2007; responsible for promoting investment in Paraguay and the export of national products; Dir Oscar Stark Robledo.

Red Rural de Organizaciones Privadas de Desarrollo (Red Rural): Manuel Domínguez 1045, entre Brasil y Estados Unidos, Asunción; tel. (21) 22-9740; e-mail redrural@redrural.org.py; internet www.redrural.org.py; f. 1989; co-ordinating body for rural devt orgs; Gen. Co-ordinator Hermes García; Sec. José Larroza.

Secretaría Técnica de Planificación: Estrella 505, esq. 14 de Mayo, Asunción; tel. (21) 45-0422; fax (21) 49-6510; e-mail stp@stp.gov.py; internet www.stp.gov.py; govt body responsible for overall economic and social planning; Minister Bernardo Esquivel Vaesken; Co-ordinator Gen. Víctor Sebastián Uriarte.

CHAMBERS OF COMMERCE

Cámara Nacional de Comercio y Servicios de Paraguay: Estrella 540, esq. 14 de Mayo y 15 de Agosto, Asunción; tel. (21) 49-3321; fax (21) 44-0817; e-mail info@ccparaguay.com.py; internet www.ccparaguay.com.py; f. 1898; fmrly Cámara y Bolsa de Comercio; adopted current name 2002; Pres. Beltrán Macchi Salin; Gen. Man. Miguel Riquelme Olazar.

Cámara de Comercio Paraguayo-Americana (Paraguayan-American Chamber of Commerce): 25 de Mayo 2090, esq. Mayor Bullo, Asunción; tel. (21) 22-2160; fax (21) 22-1926; e-mail pamcham@pamcham.com.py; internet www.pamcham.com.py; f. 1981; Pres. Víctor González Acosta; Exec. Dir Gerald McCulloch; c. 120 mem. cos.

Cámara de Comercio Paraguayo-Argentina: Banco de la Nación Argentina, entre Palma y Alberdi (al lado del Consulado Argentino), Asunción; tel. (21) 49-7804; fax (21) 49-7805; e-mail administracion@

PARAGUAY

campyarg.org.py; internet www.campyarg.org.py; f. 1991; Pres. GERARDO DURÉ-PERONI; Man. MARCELA ESCOBAR.

Cámara de Comercio Paraguayo-Británica: Avda Boggiani 5848, Asunción; tel. (21) 61-2611; fax (21) 60-5007; e-mail britcham@conexion.com.py; Pres. GUILLERMO ALONSO.

Cámara de Comercio Paraguayo-Francesa (CCPF): Yegros 837, 1°, Of. 12, CP 3009, Asunción; tel. (21) 49-7852; fax (21) 44-6324; e-mail info@ccpf.com.py; internet www.ccpf.com.py; Pres. ANTONIO LUIS PECCI MILTOS; Man. IRIS FELIU DE FLEITAS.

Cámara de Industria y Comercio Paraguayo-Alemana: Independencia Nacional 811, Casilla 919, Asunción; tel. (21) 44-6594; fax (21) 44-9735; e-mail logistica@ahkasu.com.py; internet www.ahkparaguay.com; f. 1956; Pres. JAN HOECKLE; Gen. Man. HELMUT L. ZAGEL.

AGRICULTURAL, INDUSTRIAL AND EMPLOYERS' ORGANIZATIONS

Asociación de Empresas Financieras del Paraguay (ADEFI): Edif. Ahorros Paraguayos, Torre II, 6°, Of. 05, General Díaz 471, Asunción; tel. (21) 44-8298; fax (21) 49-8071; e-mail adefi@adefi.org.py; internet www.adefi.org.py; f. 1975; grouping of financial cos; Pres. SILVIA MURTO DE MÉNDEZ; Sec. MILCIADES FRETES RUBIANI.

Asociación Paraguaya de la Calidad: Eduardo Victor Haedo 680, O'Leary, Asunción; tel. (21) 44-7348; fax (21) 45-0705; e-mail apc@apc.org.py; internet www.apc.org.py; f. 1988; grouping of cos to promote quality of goods and services; Pres. JORGE MIGUEL BRUNOTTE; Sec. SANTIAGO LLANO CAVINA.

Asociación de Productores de Soja, Oleaginosas y Cereales del Paraguay (APS): Asunción; internet www.aps.org.py; soya and grain producers' asscn; Pres. REGIS MERELES.

Asociación Rural del Paraguay (ARP): Ruta Transchaco, Km 14, Mariano Roque Alonso; tel. (21) 75-4412; e-mail ania@arp.org.py; internet www.arp.org.py; grouping of agricultural cos and farmers; Pres. JUAN NÉSTOR NÚÑEZ; Exec. Dir EDUARDO RUIZ DÍAZ.

Cámara Paraguaya de Exportadores de Cereales y Oleaginosas (CAPECO): Avda Brasilia 840, Asunción; tel. (21) 20-8855; fax (21) 21-3971; internet www.capeco.org.py; f. 1980; grain exporters' asscn; Pres. ULRICH BAUER; Gen. Man. IGNACIO SANTIVIAGO.

Centro de Importadores del Paraguay (CIP): Avda Brasilia 1947, casi Artigas, Casillas 2609, Asunción; tel. (21) 29-9800; e-mail cip@cip.org.py; internet www.cip.org.py; f. 1939; importers' asscn; Pres. MAX HABER NEUMANN; Man. JULIO SÁNCHEZ LASPINA.

Federación de la Producción, Industria y Comercio (FEPRINCO): Edif. Union Club, Palma 751, 3°, esq. O'Leary y Ayolas, Asunción; tel. (21) 44-6634; fax (21) 44-6638; e-mail feprinco@quanta.com.py; org. of private-sector business execs; Pres. GERMÁN RUIZ.

Unión Industrial Paraguaya (UIP): Cerro Corá 1038, entre Estados Unidos y Brasil, Casilla 782, Asunción; tel. (21) 21-2556; fax (21) 21-3360; e-mail uip@uip.org.py; internet www.uip.org.py; f. 1936; org. of business entrepreneurs; Pres. GUSTAVO VOLPE; Sec. RAÚL HOECKLE.

UTILITIES

Electricity

Administración Nacional de Electricidad (ANDE): Avda España 1268, Casi Padre Cardozo, Asunción; tel. (21) 21-1001; fax (21) 21-2371; e-mail luis_rojas@ande.gov.py; internet www.ande.gov.py; f. 1949; national electricity board; Pres. GERMÁN FATECHA; Sec.-Gen. LUIS RAMÓN ROJAS IBARRA.

Entidad Binacional Yacyretá: General Díaz 831 esq. Ayolas y Montevideo, Edif. Héroes de Marzo, Asunción; tel. and fax (21) 44-5611; internet www.eby.gov.py; owned jtly by Paraguay and Argentina; operates the hydroelectric dam at Yacyretá on the Paraná river, completed in 1998; installed capacity of 3,200 MW; 14,673 GWh of electricity produced in 2007; Dir (Paraguay) ELBA RECALDE.

Itaipú Binacional: Centro Administrativo, Ruta Internacional Km 3.5, Avda Monseñor Rodríguez 150, Ciudad del Este, Depto Alto Paraná; tel. (61) 599-8989; e-mail itaipu@itaipu.gov.br; internet www.itaipu.gov.py; f. 1974; jtly owned by Paraguay and Brazil; hydroelectric power station on Brazilian–Paraguayan border; 85,970 GWh of electricity produced in 2010; Dir-Gen. (Paraguay) GUSTAVO CODAS FRIEDMANN.

Water

Empresa de Servicios Sanitarios del Paraguay, SA (ESSAP): José Berges 516, entre Brasil y San José, Asunción; tel. (21) 21-0330; fax (21) 21-2624; e-mail secretaria@essap.com.py; internet www.essap.com.py; fmrly Corporación de Obras Sanitarias (CORPOSANA); responsible for public water supply, sewage disposal and drainage; privatization plans suspended in 2002; Pres. EMILIANO INSFRÁN ROLÓN.

TRADE UNIONS

Central Nacional de Trabajadores (CNT): Piribebuy 1078, Asunción; tel. (21) 44-4084; fax (21) 49-2154; e-mail cnt@telesurf.com.py; Sec.-Gen. MIGUEL ZAYAS; 120,840 mems (2007).

Central Sindical de Trabajadores del Estado Paraguayo (Cesitep): Asunción; comprises public sector workers; Pres. REINALDO BARRETO MEDINA.

Central Unitaria de Trabajadores (CUT): San Carlos 836, Asunción; tel. (21) 44-3936; fax (21) 44-8482; f. 1989; Pres. JORGE ALVARENGA; Sec.-Gen. MIRTHA ARIAS.

Confederación Paraguaya de Trabajadores (CPT): Yegros 1309–33 y Simón Bolívar, Asunción; tel. 981878479 (mobile); e-mail cpt_paraguay@yahoo.com; f. 1951; Sec.-Gen. FRANCISCO BRITEZ RUIZ; 43,500 mems from 189 affiliated groups.

Coordinadora Agrícola de Paraguay (CAP): Juan B. Flores y Tacuary, Hernandarias; tel. (983) 52-7003; e-mail bhjca@tigo.com.py; farmers' org.; Pres. GERÓNIMO SÁNCHEZ; Sec. GERARDO BERTÓN.

Federación Nacional Campesina (FNC): Nangariry 1196, esq. Cacique Cará Cará, Asunción; tel. (21) 51-2384; grouping of peasants' orgs; Sec.-Gen. MARCIAL GÓMEZ.

Organización de Trabajadores de Educación del Paraguay (OTEP): Avda del Pueblo 845 con Ybyra Pyta, Barrio Santa Lucía, Lambaré; tel. and fax (21) 55-5525; e-mail otepsn@highway.com.py; Sec. GABRIELA ESPÍNOLA.

Transport

RAILWAYS

Ferrocarriles del Paraguay, SA (FEPASA): México 145, Casilla 453, Asunción; tel. (21) 44-6789; fax (21) 44-3273; e-mail cultura@ferrocarriles.com.py; internet www.ferrocarriles.com.py; f. 1854; state-owned since 1961; scheduled for privatization; 376 km of track; Pres. EDUARDO LATERZA RIVAROLA.

ROADS

In 2001 there were an estimated 29,500 km of roads, of which 14,986 km were paved. The Pan-American Highway runs for over 700 km in Paraguay and the Trans-Chaco Highway extends from Asunción to Bolivia. In 2011 the Government announced plans to spend US $170m. to improve some 5,150 km of roads and 189 bridges in the country's eastern region, under its national rural roads programme. In addition to $25.5m. in financing from the Government, the programme was to be funded through a $50m. loan from the Japan International Cooperation Agency, a $65.5m. loan from the Inter-American Development Bank and $29m. from OPEC's Fund for International Development.

SHIPPING

The rivers Paraguay and Paraná constitute the principal waterways for cargo transportation in the country. There are 3,100 km of navigable waterways. The country has six ports of which the port of Asunción is the most important.

Administración Nacional de Navegación y Puertos (ANNP) (National Shipping and Ports Administration): Colón y El Paraguayo Independiente, Asunción; tel. (21) 49-5086; fax (21) 49-7485; e-mail gciacomercial@annp.gov.py; internet www.annp.gov.py; f. 1965; responsible for ports services and maintaining navigable channels in rivers and for improving navigation on the Paraguay and Paraná rivers; Pres. ALBINO GONZÁLEZ VILLALBA.

Ocean Shipping

Compañía Paraguaya de Navegación de Ultramar, SA (Copanu): Presidente Franco 625, 2°, Casilla 77, Asunción; tel. (21) 49-2137; fax (21) 44-5013; f. 1963 to operate between Asunción, US and European ports; 10 vessels; Exec. Pres. ROBERT BOSCH B.

Navemar, SA: Avda Republica Argentina 1412, Casilla 273, Asunción; tel. (21) 61-2527; fax (21) 61-2526; e-mail navemar@navemar.com.py; internet www.navemar.com.py; f. 1969; shipping agency, stowage, fleet operations and management; 5 vessels.

Transporte Fluvial Paraguayo SACI: Edif. de la Encarnación, 13°, 14 de Mayo 563, Asunción; tel. (21) 49-3411; fax (21) 49-8218; e-mail tfpsaci@tm.com.py; Admin. Man. DANIELLA CHARBONNIER; 1 vessel.

CIVIL AVIATION

The major international airport, Aeropuerto Internacional Silvio Pettirossi, is situated 15 km from Asunción. A second international

PARAGUAY

airport, Aeropuerto Internacional Guaraní, 30 km from Ciudad del Este, was inaugurated in 1996.

National Airline

Transportes Aéreos del Mercosur (TAM Mercosur): Aeropuerto Internacional Silvio Pettirossi, Hangar TAM/ARPA, Luque, Asunción; tel. (21) 49-1039; fax (21) 64-5146; e-mail tammercosur@uninet.com.py; internet www.tam.com.py; f. 1963 as Líneas Aéreas Paraguayas (LAP); name changed as above in 1997; services to destinations within South America; 80% owned by TAM Linhas Aéreas (Brazil); Pres. Líbano Miranda Barroso.

Tourism

Tourism is undeveloped, but, with recent improvements in infrastructure, efforts were being made to promote the sector. Tourist arrivals in Paraguay in 2008 totalled 428,215 (of whom some 46% came from Argentina). In that year tourism receipts were US $128m.

Secretaría Nacional de Turismo: Palma 468, Asunción; tel. (21) 49-4110; fax (21) 49-1230; e-mail ministra@senatur.gov.py; internet www.senatur.gov.py; f. 1998; Exec. Sec. Liz Rosanna Crámer Campos.

Defence

As assessed at November 2010, Paraguay's armed forces numbered 10,650, of which 2,550 were conscripts. There was an army of 7,600 and an air force of 1,100. The navy, which is largely river-based, had 1,950 members, including 900 marines and a naval air force of 100. There is also a 14,800-strong paramilitary police force, including 4,000 conscripts. Military service, which is compulsory, lasts for 12 months in the army and for two years in the navy.

Defence Budget: 678,000m. guaraníes in 2010.

Commander-in-Chief of the Armed Forces: President of the Republic.

Commander of the Armed Forces: Gen. Benicio Melgarejo.

Commander of the Army: Brig.-Gen. Darío Martín Cáceres Snead.

Commander of the Air Force: Brig.-Gen. Miguel Christ Jacobs.

Commander of the Navy: Rear-Adm. Juan Carlos Benítez Formherz.

Education

Education is, where possible, compulsory for six years, to be undertaken between six and 12 years of age, but there are insufficient schools, particularly in the remote parts of the country. Primary education begins at the age of six and lasts for six years. Secondary education, beginning at 12 years of age, lasts for a further six years, comprising two cycles of three years each. In 2007 enrolment at primary schools included 90% of children in the relevant age-group, while enrolment at secondary schools included 58% of those in the relevant age-group. There are 12 universities in Paraguay. Public expenditure by all levels of government on education was equivalent to 10.0% of total government spending in 2004, according to UNESCO estimates.

PERU

Introductory Survey

LOCATION, CLIMATE, LANGUAGE, RELIGION, FLAG, CAPITAL

The Republic of Peru lies in western South America, bordered by Ecuador and Colombia to the north, by Brazil and Bolivia to the east, and by Chile to the south. Peru has a coastline of more than 2,300 km (1,400 miles) on the Pacific Ocean. The climate varies with altitude, average temperatures being about 11°C (50°F) lower in the Andes mountains than in the coastal plain. The rainy season is between October and April, with heavy rainfall in the tropical forests. Temperatures in Lima are usually between 13°C (55°F) and 28°C (82°F). The three official languages are Spanish, Quechua and Aymará. Almost all of the inhabitants profess Christianity, and the great majority are adherents of the Roman Catholic Church. The civil flag (proportions 2 by 3) has three equal vertical stripes, of red, white and red. The state flag additionally has the national coat of arms (a shield divided into three unequal segments: red, with a golden cornucopia spilling coins of yellow and white at the base, blue, with a yellow vicuña in the dexter chief, and white, with a green tree in the sinister chief; all surmounted by a green wreath, and framed by branches of palm and laurel, tied at the bottom with a red and white ribbon) in the centre of the white stripe. The capital is Lima.

CONTEMPORARY POLITICAL HISTORY

Historical Context

Following independence from Spain, declared in 1821 and finally achieved in 1824, Peruvian politics were characterized by alternating periods of civilian administration and military dictatorship. In the early 1920s opposition to the dictatorial regime of President Augusto Bernardino Leguía resulted in the creation of the Alianza Popular Revolucionaria Americana (APRA), Peru's oldest political party to command mass support. The party, founded as a nationalist revolutionary movement, was formally established in Peru as the Partido Aprista Peruano (PAP) in 1930, when Leguía was deposed and the party's founder (and its leader for more than 50 years), Dr Víctor Raúl Haya de la Torre, returned from enforced exile in Mexico. A long-standing tradition of hostility developed between the Apristas and the armed forces, and the party was banned in 1931–45, and again in 1948–56.

During 1945–63 political power shifted regularly between the armed forces and elected government. In 1948 Dr José Luis Bustamente y Rivera was deposed by Gen. Manuel Odría, following a right-wing military rebellion. Odría established a military junta which governed until 1950, when the General was elected unopposed to the presidency, and subsequently appointed a cabinet composed of military officers and civilians. In 1956 Odría was succeeded by Dr Manuel Prado y Ugartache (who had been President in 1939–45). An inconclusive presidential election in 1962 precipitated military intervention, and power was assumed by Gen. Ricardo Pérez Godoy, at the head of a military junta. In March 1963, however, Pérez was supplanted by his second-in-command, Gen. Nicolás Lindley López.

Fernando Belaúnde Terry, the joint candidate of his own Acción Popular (AP) party and the Partido Demócrata Cristiano, was elected President in June 1963. An increase in internal disturbances in predominantly Indian areas resulted in the temporary suspension of constitutional guarantees in 1965–66 and an intensive military campaign of counter-insurgency. Lack of congressional support for the Government contributed to a succession of ministerial crises which, together with continuing internal unrest, prompted renewed military intervention in October 1968, when Gen. Juan Velasco Alvarado assumed the presidency, dissolved Congress and appointed a military cabinet.

Despite the re-emergence of internal disturbances and dissension within the armed forces, Velasco retained power until August 1975, when he was overthrown and replaced by Gen. Francisco Morales Bermúdez. In July 1977 President Morales announced plans for the restoration of civilian rule. Accordingly, a national election was conducted in June 1978 to select the members of a constituent assembly, which was to draft a new constitution in preparation for presidential and congressional elections. In the election, PAP emerged as the largest party, and in July the assembly elected the 83-year-old Dr Haya de la Torre to be its President. The new Constitution, adopted in July 1979, provided for elections by universal adult suffrage, and extended the franchise to the sizeable illiterate population.

Domestic Political Affairs

The presidential contest of May 1980 was won decisively by Belaúnde. At the same time, the AP won an outright majority in the Cámara de Diputados (Chamber of Deputies) and also secured the greatest representation in the Senado (Senate). The new organs of state were inaugurated in July, when the new Constitution became fully effective. While Belaúnde sought to liberalize the economy, much of his term of office was dominated by the threat to stability posed by the emergence, in the early 1980s, of the Maoist rebel group Sendero Luminoso (SL—Shining Path). The situation deteriorated following the uncompromising response of the armed forces to terrorist activity in a designated emergency zone, which extended to 13 provinces (primarily in the departments of Ayacucho, Huancavelica and Apurímac) by mid-1984, and a dramatic increase in violent deaths and violations of human rights was reported.

At elections in April 1985 Alan García Pérez (the candidate for PAP) received 46% of the votes in the presidential poll, while PAP secured a majority in both houses (the Cámara and the Senado) of the Congreso (legislature). García's victory was ensured in May, prior to a second round of voting, when his closest opponent, Dr Alfonso Barrantes Lingán (of the left-wing Izquierda Unida coalition), withdrew his candidature. At his inauguration in July, García announced that his Government's priorities would be to arrest Peru's severe economic decline and to eradicate internal terrorism.

Widespread opposition to the Government's economic programme was manifested in a succession of well-supported general strikes in 1987–88. Government plans in 1987 for the nationalization of Peru's banks and private financial and insurance institutions encountered considerable opposition from the financial sector, and prompted the creation of Libertad, a 'freedom movement' expressing opposition to the plans (which were subsequently modified), established under the leadership of a well-known writer, Mario Vargas Llosa. The authority of the García administration was further undermined by persistent rumours of military unrest, by allegations of links between members of the Government and the right-wing paramilitary 'death squad', the Comando Rodrigo Franco, and by the continuing terrorist activities of the SL and a resurgence of activity by the Movimiento Revolucionario Túpac Amaru (MRTA) guerrilla group, in north-east Peru. In addition, the Government was criticized by international human rights organizations for its methods of combating political violence.

The Fujimori era

General elections took place in April 1990, despite the attempts of the SL to disrupt them. In the presidential poll Vargas Llosa, the candidate of the centre-right Frente Democrático (FREDEMO) alliance (established in 1988 by the AP, Libertad and the Partido Popular Cristiano), obtained the largest percentage of the votes cast, followed by a hitherto little-known agronomist, Alberto Fujimori, the candidate of the Cambio 90 group of independents. In a second round of voting, conducted in June, Fujimori emerged as the successful candidate, having attracted late support from left-wing parties and from PAP. Following his inauguration in July, Fujimori announced the composition of a new centre-left Council of Ministers, with Juan Carlos Hurtado Miller, a member of the AP, as President of the Council (prime minister) and Minister of Economy and Finance.

Subsidies for consumers were abolished in August 1990, thereby increasing prices by more than 3,000% for petrol and by as much as 600% for basic foods. Although these reforms secured Peru's rehabilitation within the international financial community, they provoked widespread opposition and industrial unrest (as well as the resignation of Hurtado). In November 1991, despite public and congressional dissent, Fujimori took advantage of a 150-day period of emergency legislative powers (granted to him in June in order that the country's potentially destabilizing economic and security problems might be addressed) to issue a series of decrees. Those represented a continuation of policies concerning the elimination of state monopolies of telecommunications, postal networks and railways, the opening to private investment of the power sector, the privatization of schools and a reform of the health and social security services.

On 5 April 1992 Fujimori announced the immediate suspension of the 1979 Constitution and the dissolution of the Congreso, pending a comprehensive restructuring of the legislature. The President maintained that the reform of the Congreso was essential in order to eradicate 'corruption and inefficiency', to enable him to implement a programme of 'pacification' of the nation by combating terrorism and drugs-trafficking, and also fully to implement free-market economic policies. In the interim an Emergency and National Reconstruction Government would govern the country, and legislative power would be exercised by the President, with the approval of the Council of Ministers. Fujimori also announced a reform of the judiciary. The constitutional coup (or 'autogolpe') was implemented with the full co-operation and support of the armed forces. On the following day the President of the Council of Ministers, Alfonso de los Heros Pérez Albela, resigned in protest, and was replaced by Oscar de la Puente; most government ministers, however, elected to remain in office. Members of the dissolved parliament declared Fujimori to be incapable of continuing in office, although an attempt to establish Máximo San Román, the First Vice-President, as the head of an alternative 'constitutional government' was undermined by a lack of domestic and international support. Moreover, while Fujimori's actions prompted outrage from politicians, the judiciary and the media, popular reaction to the 'autogolpe' was less hostile. Bolstered by demonstrations of public support for his actions, Fujimori dismissed 13 of Peru's 28 Supreme Court judges, whom he accused of corruption, and detained several prominent opposition party figures. The President of the central bank was also removed from office, as were 134 judges. The Organization of American States (OAS, see p. 391) deplored Fujimori's actions, and dispatched a mission to attempt to effect a reconciliation between the legislature and the executive. Later in April Fujimori announced that congressional elections would be conducted in February 1993.

The threat posed to Fujimori's programme of radical reform by economic constraints resulting from the suspension of international financial aid to Peru prompted the revision of the timetable for a return to democracy, and in June 1992 Fujimori confirmed that national elections would be conducted in October to a unicameral constituent congress, which would then draft a new constitution. The President also announced that, pending approval of a new document, the 1979 Constitution would be reinstated without certain articles that might 'impede the progress of the Government'.

A 'National Dialogue for Peace and Development', comprising a series of discussions with representatives of the political opposition and with the public, sought to identify important issues for future consideration by the new Congreso Constituyente Democrático (CCD). Elections to the CCD, conducted on 22 November 1992 and attended by OAS observers, were a qualified success for pro-Government parties. An electoral coalition of Cambio 90 and the Nueva Mayoría (a new independent party supported by many former cabinet ministers), headed by Fujimori's former Minister of Energy and Mines, Jaime Yoshiyama Tanaka (who was subsequently elected President of the CCD), secured 44 of the 80 congressional seats. The only significant opposition party not to boycott the elections, the Partido Popular Cristiano, took eight seats. In December, at the inaugural meeting of the CCD, Yoshiyama identified its immediate aims as the restoration of the autonomy of the judiciary, the eradication of terrorism, the generation of employment and of favourable conditions for foreign investment, and the projection of an enhanced national image abroad. In January 1993, having formally reinstated the 1979 Constitution, the CCD confirmed Fujimori as constitutional Head of State. Following the resignation of de la Puente's Government in July, Alfonso Bustamante y Bustamente was appointed prime minister in August.

The final text of the draft Constitution, which enhanced presidential powers and provided for the establishment of a unicameral legislature, was approved by the CCD in September 1993. Among the text's most controversial articles were the introduction of the death penalty for convicted terrorists and a provision permitting a President of the Republic to be re-elected for a successive five-year term of office. At a national referendum held on 31 October—the first occasion on which such popular consultation had been sought in Peru—the Constitution was narrowly approved, by 52% of the votes cast. The Constitution was promulgated on 29 December.

In a presidential election conducted on 9 April 1995, Fujimori secured an unexpected outright victory over his closest opponent, Javier Pérez de Cuéllar de la Guerra (the former UN Secretary-General and the candidate of the Unión por el Perú—UPP), obtaining 64% of the votes. In concurrent legislative elections, Fujimori's coalition movement, Cambio 90-Nueva Mayoría, also secured an absolute majority in the unicameral Congreso. The composition of the new Government, installed following Fujimori's inauguration in July, was largely unaltered. Efraín Goldenberg, who had succeeded Bustamente as prime minister in February 1994, was replaced by Dante Córdova Blanco.

In June 1995 legislation was approved by the Congreso granting an amnesty to all members of the military, police and intelligence forces who had been convicted of human rights violations committed since 1980 in the internal conflict against separatist violence. The legislation attracted criticism from opposition parties, and internationally. In August an international warrant was issued for the arrest of former President García, who had been accused of receiving bribes and other corrupt practices during his term of office.

In April 1996 the sudden resignation of the President of the Council of Ministers demonstrated the extent of disunity within the Government, particularly over economic policy. Alberto Pandolfi Arbulu was appointed premier, and the Government's privatization programme was accelerated. Meanwhile, Fujimori was attempting to formulate legislation that would allow him to stand for election for a third presidential term. A congressional committee approved a new 'interpretation' of the Constitution in August (on the grounds that Fujimori was first elected under the 1979 Constitution), and the legislation was approved by the Congreso later that month. In January 1997 the Constitutional Tribunal ruled the new interpretation of the Constitution to be invalid.

On 17 December 1996 MRTA activists launched an assault on the residence of the Japanese ambassador in Lima, and detained more than 500 people attending an evening reception. Among those taken hostage were the Peruvian Ministers of Foreign Affairs and of Agriculture, at least nine foreign ambassadors and other diplomatic personnel, leading police and security officials and representatives of the business community. The MRTA activists' demands included the release of all 458 MRTA prisoners in detention in Peru, safe passage to an area in Peru's central highlands, greater economic assistance to the country's poorest people and payment of a 'war tax'. On 27 December Fujimori declared a state of emergency in Lima. On 22 April 1997 Peruvian troops launched an unexpected assault on the ambassador's residence, ending the MRTA siege. Two soldiers and all 14 of the MRTA activists were killed in the operation, and one of the 72 remaining hostages died of heart failure; it was later alleged that some of the MRTA members might have been killed after having surrendered to army officers.

Ongoing concerns regarding the President's circumvention of the traditional role of the judiciary intensified in May 1998 when Fujimori introduced draconian anti-crime legislation by decree (subsequently approved by the Congreso) seeking to extend the extreme powers and penalties employed in recent successful anti-terrorism initiatives to other areas of criminal activity. Among the provisions of the new law were plans to increase the powers of military tribunals to try civilians. Despite appeals by international observers and opposition groups for greater judicial independence and respect for human rights, in December the Congreso voted to extend the period of judicial reorganization initiated by Fujimori's administration for a further two-year period.

As Fujimori's popularity waned during 1998, his attempts to consolidate his position and reassert his authority resulted in repeated changes to the Council of Ministers. In April 1999 the entire Council of Ministers resigned, amid a rift over corruption allegations against officials at the state customs authority. Another mass cabinet resignation followed in October, in accordance with the law requiring public officials intending to stand for election to resign their posts six months before the April 2000 polls. Alberto Bustamante Belaúnde was appointed to lead a new cabinet.

Meanwhile, Fujimori's continuing efforts to secure support for a third presidential term were encouraged by the defeat in the Congreso, in September 1998, of an opposition proposal to decide the question of Fujimori's eligibility by a national referendum. Opposition to Fujimori's possible re-election was vociferously expressed when a broad range of labour unions and political parties participated in April 1999 in a one-day general strike. However, this, together with a demonstration involving some 20,000 people in October, failed to prevent the announcement in December of Fujimori's candidature on behalf of the newly created Perú 2000 alliance. On 1 January 2000 the Jurado Nacional Electoral (JNE—National Electoral Board), which was dominated by Fujimori's supporters, ratified his candidacy in response to a legal challenge by the opposition. The election board's rationale was that although the Constitution did not permit a President to serve three terms, Fujimori had only served one term under the current Constitution, as amended in 1993. The ruling precipitated further street protests. Allegations of electoral fraud and campaign misconduct were widespread. Opposition plans to reach a consensus on a single candidate to challenge Fujimori did not materialize, and in January 2000 seven opposition candidates registered to contest the presidency.

The general election proceeded on 9 April 2000. During the vote count opposition candidates and international observers alleged that the ballot was marred by fraud. US officials issued increasingly strong statements stressing the need for a second round of voting as the only credible proof of legitimacy. Fujimori officially received 49.9% of the votes cast and Alejandro Toledo (the first presidential candidate of Amerindian descent) 40.2%. In the congressional elections Perú 2000 won 52 of the 120 seats, while Perú Posible (PP), which supported Toledo, won 29. The JNE resisted pressure for a postponement of the second round (scheduled for 28 May), in order to correct irregularities noted in the first round. In response, Toledo withdrew his candidature one week before the election and urged his supporters to spoil their votes in protest. Violent incidents, including the firebombing of the presidential palace, followed the JNE decision. The OAS and US-based Carter Center suspended monitoring of the election, citing difficulties with the computer system for tabulating votes. Amid further mass demonstrations, Fujimori contested the election effectively unopposed (although the JNE ruled that Toledo remained a candidate and refused to remove his name from the ballot papers), taking 51% of the total votes; Toledo received 18%. Excluding spoiled (30%) and blank (1%) papers, the incumbent was thus returned to office with 74% of the valid votes cast. The result was denounced as invalid by the opposition and by the US Government (though it later moderated its position, describing the outcome as imperfect). Fujimori's inauguration on 28 July was accompanied by violent protests in Lima.

In September 2000 a major political scandal erupted after the disclosure of a video that allegedly showed Vladimiro Montesinos, the head of the national intelligence service and a close ally of the President, bribing an opposition member of the Congreso. In response, Fujimori declared that new elections would be held, in which he would not participate. He also announced that the national intelligence service would be disbanded. At the same time, 10 Perú 2000 deputies defected to the opposition, thus depriving Fujimori of his majority in the legislature. Demonstrations, led by Toledo, demanded the immediate resignation of Fujimori and the arrest of Montesinos, who fled to Panama. On 5 October the Congreso approved OAS-mediated proposals paving the way for power to be transferred from Fujimori to his successor in mid-2001, as well as the disbandment of the Congreso to make way for a newly elected legislature. Later in the month Fujimori announced the replacement of the most senior commanders of the armed forces.

The political crisis deepened in late October 2000 when Montesinos returned from Panama, after failing to obtain political asylum there. His apparent impunity supported the widely held view that the armed forces were protecting him. At the same time, the first Vice-President, Francisco Tudela, resigned in protest against government attempts to make new elections conditional upon an amnesty for those in the armed forces accused of human rights violations. Further OAS-sponsored negotiations between opposition groups and the Government led to the announcement that new elections would be held on 8 April 2001, without any conditions attached. An investigation into Montesinos's activities was launched, with charges ranging from corruption to torture and murder. In mid-November the Congreso voted to replace its pro-Fujimori President, Martha Hildebrandt Pérez Treviño, with Valentín Paniagua Corazao, effectively giving the opposition control of the legislature. The following day Fujimori travelled to Japan, from where, on 20 November, he resigned the presidency. The Congreso, however, refused to accept the resignation, and instead voted to dismiss Fujimori.

On 22 November 2000 Paniagua was appointed interim President. A new cabinet was sworn in three days later, which included Javier Pérez de Cuéllar as prime minister and Minister of Foreign Affairs, and was to serve until 28 July 2001. Several days later the new Minister of Defence, Walter Ledesma Rebaza, announced the decision to retire 13 generals who were associates of Montesinos. A congressional commission, established to investigate the activities of Montesinos, uncovered hundreds of secret videotapes that seemed to compromise the integrity of judges, politicians, military officers, businessmen and bishops. In early December the commission's investigations were extended to Fujimori. In mid-December it was announced that Fujimori had taken up Japanese citizenship and was thus, in effect, protected from the threat of extradition from Japan. Nevertheless, in February 2001 corruption charges were formally filed against him. Furthermore, in August the Congreso voted unanimously to lift Fujimori's constitutional immunity and issued an international warrant for his arrest on the charge of dereliction of duty. Further charges of embezzlement and illicit enrichment were subsequently filed against the former President. However, the Japanese Government stated that it had no intention of allowing Fujimori's extradition. In June 2005 the Japanese authorities rejected a further extradition request for Fujimori, citing a lack of further evidence to justify its approval.

In June 2001 Montesinos was arrested in Venezuela. He was sent back to Peru and, in July 2002, sentenced to nine years' imprisonment on charges relating to 'usurpation of power'. However, investigating judges subsequently brought a further 80 indictments against him, including murder, bribery and the illegal sale of weapons and narcotics. Following his first public trial in February 2003, Montesinos was convicted on corruption charges and sentenced to a further five years' imprisonment. In June 2004 Montesinos was found guilty of bribing newspaper editors to support Fujimori's re-election attempt in 2000, and was sentenced to a further 15 years' imprisonment. (In January 2005 eight newspaper chiefs were sentenced to five years in gaol after being convicted of receiving payments from Montesinos.) In August 2005 the trial began of Montesinos and 56 alleged members of the Colina group on charges of involvement in the disappearances of 36 people under the administration of President Fujimori. In September 2006 Montesinos received another gaol term of 20 years after being convicted of arms-trafficking.

The election of Toledo

In January 2001, only a few days after corruption charges against him were ruled to have expired under the statute of limitations, former President Alan García Pérez returned to Peru to launch his campaign for the forthcoming presidential election. Toledo won 37% of the votes cast at the first round of the election, which was held on 8 April, while García attracted 26% of the ballot and Lourdes Flores Nano of the Unidad Nacional alliance 24%. In concurrently held elections to the 120-seat Congreso, no party secured a majority: PP took 45 seats, PAP 27 and the Unidad Nacional 17, while the right-wing Frente Independiente Moralizador (FIM) won 12 seats. In the second round of the presidential election, held on 3 June, Toledo won, with 53% of the vote. Toledo was inaugurated on 28 July. A broad-based, 15-member cabinet was appointed, headed by lawyer Roberto Dañino and with Pedro Pablo Kuczynski as Minister of Economy and Finance. The new Government promised to create more jobs, to reduce poverty and to put an end to the corruption of the Fujimori regime. In the previous month a congressional commission implicated 180 people in corruption scandals that took place during Fujimori's presidencies, including Gen. Walter Chacón Málaga, the recently appointed head of the armed forces.

However, the popularity of the Toledo Government declined sharply after only a few months in power, as high expectations were not matched by an increase in economic prospects. In September and October 2001 popular protests erupted throughout Peru as workers demanded more jobs and improvements to transport infrastructure and health care. Hundreds of former public sector workers protested in central Lima in January 2002 to demand their jobs back. The protests proliferated, and in June, following a week of violent demonstrations in protest at government plans to privatize two regional electricity companies in Arequipa, the Minister of the Interior, Fernando Rospigliosi Capurro, resigned and the privatization process was suspended indefinitely. An extensive cabinet reorganization was carried out in July, in which the Secretary-General of PP, Luis Solari, replaced Dañino as prime minister and Kuczynski was succeeded by Javier Silva Ruete. Nevertheless, popular dissatisfaction continued, and in January 2003 difficulties in the reform of the police service led to the resignation of the Minister of the Interior, Gino Costa Santolaya. In the same month the ruling party's congressional majority was reduced after five PP deputies resigned from the party.

In January 2003 the Constitutional Tribunal ruled that anti-terrorism legislation adopted by the Fujimori administration had violated the Constitution. In order to alleviate the potential pressure on the judiciary, and to prevent the release of large numbers of alleged terrorists, the Congreso granted President Toledo exceptional temporary powers to legislate by decree on security issues. In February the Government announced that all military sentences passed during Fujimori's presidency were to be annulled. The courts would have 60 days to decide whether to release convicted individuals or commit them for retrial. In March anti-terrorism legislation received congressional approval.

In February 2003 coca growers staged demonstrations to demand the suspension of the Government's coca-eradication policy. The demonstrations escalated after a coca growers' federation leader, Nelson Palomino La Serna, was imprisoned on terrorism charges. At the end of the month the Government announced that some US $3,000m. was to be invested in a coca-eradication plan by 2020. Following 11 days of protests, a temporary truce was declared between the coca growers and the Government, although the Government refused to release Palomino La Serna and pledged to continue with its eradication strategy. Following 20 days of further negotiations, the Government agreed to give $11m. in direct aid to farmers affected by the eradication efforts. In April thousands of coca growers began a protest march towards Lima to demand subsidies for alternative crops and an increase in the amount of coca that could legally be grown. Following a meeting with the coca leaders, on 23 April President Toledo signed into law a decree pledging that the eradication programme would be gradual and that the Government would discuss policy with the growers. Nevertheless, civil unrest continued; in May public sector workers began a series of demonstrations against salary levels and conditions. Outbreaks of violence during these demonstrations prompted the President to declare a state of emergency in 12 of the country's 25 regions.

In 2003–04 a rapid succession of government changes reflected President Toledo's deteriorating public credibility. Following the resignation of the entire Council of Ministers in June 2003, the President appointed Beatriz Merino Lucero, previously the head of the tax inspection service, as President of the Council. However, Merino Lucero was obliged to resign in December following reports of nepotistic practices during her previous career and opposition allegations relating to her personal life. Carlos Ferrero Costa, a former President of the Congreso, was appointed to succeed her. In February 2004 Ferrero Costa effected a wide-ranging cabinet reorganization, appointing a number of independent technocrats. A notable inclusion in the new cabinet was Pedro Pablo Kuczynski, who was reappointed Minister of Economy and Finance. The reallocation of portfolios removed members of the FIM from the Government; nevertheless, the FIM pledged to continue its legislative alliance with PP.

Throughout 2004 President Toledo, his family and his advisers were implicated in several major scandals. In January a purported recording was made public of his former legal adviser, César Almeyda, meeting with an associate of Vladimiro Montesinos. Almeyda was placed under house arrest at the end of January, but was cleared of any wrongdoing in June. Almeyda had been director of the national intelligence service until April 2003, when he had been forced to resign after being accused of authorizing the illegal use of surveillance technology. He was replaced by Adm. (retd) Alfonso Panizzo; however, in September Panizzo also tendered his resignation after it emerged that the intelligence agency had been spying on journalists investigating corrupt practices in public office. Panizzo's successor, Gen. (retd) Daniel Mora, held the post until March 2004, when the revelation that the agency had been compiling a dossier on Minister of the Interior, Fernando Rospigliosi Capurro, forced his resignation. In late March Toledo announced that the national intelligence agency was to be abolished. A government committee was formed to oversee the establishment of a successor body, the Agencia de Inteligencia Estratégica. In May Rospigliosi Capurro himself was forced to resign from the Government, having been held responsible for the authorities' inability to quell violent disturbances in the southern region of Puno, which had culminated in April in the lynching of a local mayor. Javier Reátegui was named as the new Minister of the Interior.

In July 2004 the President's sister, Margarita Toledo, was ordered by a judge not to leave the country pending investigations into an alleged large-scale forging of signatures in 1999 in order to register PP for the 2000 legislative elections. Toledo and her husband were placed under house arrest in January 2005. A special congressional commission was established to investigate the case. Meanwhile, in July 2004 President Toledo granted investigators authority to probe bank accounts held in Peru and abroad by himself and his wife, Eliane Karp, following media accusations that they had accepted bribes. In mid-July a general strike was held in protest at, *inter alia*, the perceived corruption of the Toledo administration and its failure to fulfil electoral promises, as well as at the proposed free trade agreement with the USA and the Government's failure to act upon the findings of the Truth Commission (see below). In early May 2005 a congressional committee concluded that Toledo and his associates had violated electoral law by forging signatures to register PP for the 2000 elections. However, on 20 May the Congreso decided, by 57 to 47 votes, not to impeach President Toledo. In February 2006 the Supreme Court issued a ruling ending Margarita Toledo's house arrest; however, the charges of electoral fraud against her remained. Having left office in July, former President Toledo was charged in December in connection with the forgery case; he denied all allegations against him.

Meanwhile, on 1 January 2005 about 200 members of an ultra-nationalist grouping, the Movimiento Etnocacerista (allied to the Movimiento Nacionalista Peruana), forcibly occupied a police station in the southern province of Andahuaylas, taking 21 people hostage. President Toledo declared a state of emergency in the province and troops were dispatched to the region. The uprising, which resulted in the death of seven people, including four police officers, was primarily intended to force the resignation of President Toledo, whom the group accused of incompetence, corruption, acquiescence to foreign interests and the debasement of the armed forces. On 3–4 January the insurgents and their leader, Maj. (retd) Antauro Igor Humala Tasso, surrendered to the police; all were arrested on terrorism charges. In response to public dissatisfaction with the authorities' handling of events, Reátegui resigned as Minister of the Interior; he was succeeded by Félix Murazzo, the former head of the national police.

In August 2005, following the resignation of the Minister of Foreign Affairs, Manuel Rodrígues Cuadros, President Toledo appointed the outspoken FIM leader, Fernando Olivera, to succeed him. However, Olivera's appointment caused dissent within the Council of Ministers (ostensibly over Olivera's approval of the legalization of coca cultivation for traditional use in the province of Cusco), and prompted the resignation of the prime minister, Ferrero Costa. Three days after his appointment, Olivera resigned as Minister of Foreign Affairs.

The criminal conviction of Fujimori

In November 2005 Fujimori was arrested on his arrival in Chile, where he had arrived unannounced from Japan via Mexico. It was believed that the former President, who had announced his intention to contest the presidential election scheduled for April 2006, had planned to conduct his election campaign from Chile. A petition for the extradition of Fujimori to Peru was formally submitted to the Chilean Government in January 2006. Fujimori was released on bail in May. In November a Peruvian judge issued a new international arrest warrant for Fujimori on the charge that he ordered the killing of 20 members of the SL during a prison riot in May 1992. In September 2007, following a ruling by the Chilean Supreme Court, Fujimori was extradited to Peru on seven charges. In December the former President went on trial before the Supreme Court in Lima on four of those charges: namely, responsibility for the killing of 15 civilians in Barrios Altos in 1991, and of nine students and a professor at Lima's La Canuta university in 1992, by an assassination squad known as the Colina group (see below); and the abductions of a journalist and a businessman, also in 1992. In April 2009 Fujimori was convicted of all four charges and sentenced to 25 years' imprisonment (upheld by the Supreme Court in January 2010). The trial, which was praised by international human rights organ-

The return of García

Presidential and legislative elections were held on 9 April 2006. A left-wing nationalist candidate, Lt-Col (retd) Ollanta Humala Tasso, who was the nominee of a coalition of his own party, the Partido Nacionalista Peruano (PNP), and the UPP, won the first round of the presidential ballot with 30.6% of valid votes, while former President García, representing PAP, secured 24.3%. The candidate of the conservative Unidad Nacional, Lourdes Flores Nano, came third with 23.8%. A high turn-out, of 88.7%, was recorded. In the concurrently held legislative elections the UPP emerged as the largest party in the new Congreso, winning 45 of the 120 seats, while PAP took 36 seats, the Unidad Nacional 17 and the Alianza por el Futuro (a coalition of Cambio 90 and Nueva Mayoría) 13. At a second round of presidential voting, held on 4 June, García defeated Humala, securing 52.6% of the votes cast. By portraying himself as a moderate who had learned from past errors, García had succeeded in attracting sufficient numbers of votes from those who had supported Flores in the first round, despite concerns regarding the policies he had pursued during his previous period in office (1985–90). Moreover, fears that Humala's intention to increase state control over Peru's natural resources would damage the economy had been heightened by the controversial endorsement of his candidacy by the Venezuelan President, Hugo Chávez Frías, which had provoked considerable diplomatic tensions (see below).

García took office on 28 July 2006. At his inauguration the new President focused on the need to reduce poverty, announcing plans to lower administrative expenses, including his own salary and those of members of the Congreso and other officials, and to invest some US $1,600m. in rural areas to improve public infrastructure and the provision of education and health care. Nine independents were appointed to the new 16-member Council of Ministers, including Luis Carranza Ugarte, a former director of the central bank, as Minister of Economy and Finance, and Antonio García Belaúnde, a senior diplomat, as Minister of Foreign Affairs. Jorge del Castillo Gálvez, a Secretary-General of PAP and a close ally of García, was designated President of the Council of Ministers.

Although the UPP-PNP coalition had secured the largest number of seats in the legislature, divisions within the alliance soon became apparent, with the UPP favouring the adoption of a less confrontational approach towards García's administration. In August the UPP announced that it had severed ties with Humala and the PNP, leaving PAP as the largest bloc in the Congreso. Humala suffered a further set-back in late August, when he was formally charged with human rights abuses based on allegations of murder and torture by counter-insurgency troops under his command at a military base in the department of San Martín in 1992; the former army officer denied any involvement in rights violations, claiming that the charges were a form of political persecution. In December Humala was also charged with rebellion in relation to his alleged involvement in the uprising at a police station in Andahuaylas in January 2005 (led by his imprisoned brother, Antauro).

In August 2006 the Congreso endorsed the Government's five-year programme, which was dominated by measures to alleviate poverty. A social welfare fund was to be established to finance projects in the High Andes and the Amazon (where Humala had received strong support in the presidential election), while, under the 'Sierra Exportadora' initiative, US $102m. was to be spent over five years on cultivating 150,000 hectares of land in the Andes, with the aim of producing 730,000 metric tons of agricultural goods for export and creating 300,000 jobs. However, critics expressed doubt about the viability of the 'Sierra Exportadora' project, questioning the agricultural capacity of the area concerned.

President García suffered his first congressional defeat in January 2007, when the legislature rejected his proposal to apply the death penalty to those convicted of terrorism. Although the Constitution provided for the death penalty to be imposed in cases of treason in times of war or of terrorism, the penal code did not allow capital punishment for acts of terrorism.

The Government's reputation was damaged by widespread social unrest in several of the country's regions in July 2007. An indefinite strike, initiated in early July by teachers protesting against the introduction of a controversial education law, later escalated into a two-day general strike organized by the Confederación General de Trabajadores del Perú (CGTP), during which one person was killed in Satipo. The army was mobilized to support the police in maintaining order.

Environmental issues and indigenous unrest

Civil unrest and violence continued in various parts of the country during 2008. In February a strike by farmers protesting against the Government's agricultural policies resulted in four deaths in Ayacucho. In June miners went on strike in Moquegua in protest at a new law that would have reduced the revenue received by the regional government from mining royalties; some 28 people were injured during the demonstrations, and a number of police officers were taken hostage by protesters while attempting to break up a roadblock. The 10-day strike was ended after the Government reached an agreement with the regional authorities regarding the distribution of mining revenues. A further one-day general strike was held in July in protest at the Government's economic policies and the rising cost of living. In August a state of emergency was declared in several provinces after members of 65 indigenous groups erected roadblocks and picketed energy installations in protest against two decrees, promulgated earlier in the month, relating to the sale of native land. The protesters claimed that the new laws, which allowed indigenous communities to sell their land if more than 50% of the community voted in favour of the sale (rather than a two-thirds' majority, as was previously the case), would have put large areas of the Amazon rainforest at risk of development by energy companies. Despite strong opposition from the Government, which argued that the exploitation of hydrocarbons in the Amazon basin would increase investment in rural areas, the controversial decrees were revoked by the Congreso in late August.

In October 2008 a series of tape recordings emerged that appeared to indicate that a senior official of Perupetro, the government agency responsible for the development of the petroleum industry, had accepted bribes in exchange for the awarding of exploration contracts to a small Norwegian company, Discover Petroleum. The Minister of Energy and Mines, Juan Valdivia Romero, resigned in response to the allegations, as did the head of the state oil company, Petroperú, César Gutiérrez, who was also implicated in the scandal. Three days later, on 10 October, the entire Council of Ministers tendered its resignation, following allegations that the prime minister, del Castillo, had been involved in the affair. The President of the northwestern region of Lambayeque, Yehude Simon Munaro, was appointed as prime minister. It was thought that the appointment of Simon, a left-winger who had been imprisoned under the Fujimori Government for supposed links to the MRTA (for which he was subsequently pardoned), would help to diminish tension between the Government and the regions in the wake of further strikes and protests in early October. Among the new cabinet appointments was Remigio Hernani Meloni as Minister of the Interior; however, Hernani was subsequently criticized for his confrontations with senior police officers, as well as for a number of perceived failures of the police force. In February 2009 he was replaced by a PAP congresswoman, Mercedes Cabanillas Bustamante, who immediately promised measures to reform the police. Meanwhile, in July 2008 Carranza had resigned as Minister of Economy and Finance for personal reasons, and had been replaced by Luis Valdivieso Montano; however, in January 2009 García dismissed Valdivieso and reappointed Carranza to his former role. Carranza continued in this role until December, when Mercedes Aráoz Fernández, hitherto Minister of Production, replaced him.

In June 2009 indigenous protests against the industrial development of the Amazon rainforest led to serious violent clashes in which many people were killed. Groups of indigenous people in the Amazonas region in Bagua province had gathered to protest against controversial legislation relating to the rainforest that had been agreed during negotiations on a free trade agreement with the USA. According to official reports, a total of 33 people were killed (including 24 police officers); however, indigenous groups claimed that at least 40 of their people had been massacred and their bodies dumped in an attempt to conceal the killings. The prime minister and Minister of the Interior narrowly avoided official censure in a motion to the Congreso immediately after the incident, amid calls for their resignations. One member of the cabinet, the Minister of Women and Social Development, Carmen Vildoso, resigned her post in protest at the Government's handling of the affair. In late June the Congreso repealed the two most controversial pieces of legislation, which allocated 45m. ha of the Amazonian rainforest (some 50% of the Peruvian Amazon) for development by international companies with mining, logging or mineral exploration interests and which allowed these operators to do so without the consent of local communities.

A series of strikes and demonstrations organized across the country in early July 2009, in support of the indigenous communities involved in the previous month's violence and in protest against the Government's economic and social policies, prompted Simon's resignation as prime minister. He was replaced by Javier Velásquez Quesquén, and a major cabinet reorganization was effected, which included the appointment of former national police chief Octavio Salazar as Minister of the Interior, replacing Cabanillas, who had faced intense criticism for the Government's handling of the crisis.

The Minister of Justice, Aurelio Pastor Valdivieso, was dismissed in March 2010, following controversy over his involvement in the decision in December 2009 to pardon José Enrique Crousillat, the former owner of América Televisión, who had been sentenced to eight years' imprisonment in 2006 after being convicted of accepting bribes from Montesinos to provide favourable coverage of former President Fujimori. Two days before dismissing Pastor, President García had revoked Crousillat's pardon, which had been granted on humanitarian grounds, after evidence emerged indicating that Crousillat was, in fact, in good health. Víctor García Toma, the former President of the Constitutional Tribunal, was appointed to replace Pastor. PAP was damaged in April 2010 by corruption scandals involving the party's joint Secretaries-General, former prime minister del Castillo and Omar Quesada Martínez, both of whom had been considered potential candidates for the presidential election scheduled for April 2011. Tape recordings emerged that appeared to indicate that del Castillo had lobbied in favour of Petrolera Monterrico, an oil company owned by an associate, during his premiership, while Quesada was accused of involvement in corrupt land sales made by a state agency he headed, the Organismo de Formalización de la Propiedad Informal (Cofopri). Quesada stood down as executive director of Cofopri and both men temporarily resigned from their party positions, although they denied the allegations against them. Several Cofopri officials were subsequently arrested.

Further demonstrations against government plans related to the mining and energy sectors took place during 2010. Five people were reportedly killed in Arequipa in April during clashes between police and protesters opposed to a recently approved decree that prohibited unregulated gold panning and dredging of rivers. In response to the unrest, prime minister Velásquez agreed to create a commission, including representatives of the informal mining sector, to discuss the decree. In May the Congreso adopted legislation requiring the state to consult indigenous communities on projects affecting their territories, but in June President García refused to promulgate the law in its current form on the grounds that it would impede national economic development. Velásquez declared a state of emergency in the Echarate district of Cusco at the beginning of August, following several days of violent protests against the exportation of natural gas, in which one person had died, with many more injured. The protests ended later that month, when the prime minister addressed concerns regarding domestic shortages of gas by guaranteeing that gas from one of the Camisea field's two blocs would be exclusively for domestic use; a new processing plant and pipeline would supply regional demand. In December a company exploring for gold in the Catac district of the northern region of Ancash had its licence revoked, following major demonstrations by indigenous groups in the regional capital, Huaraz.

A government reorganization was effected in mid-September 2010, following the resignation of Velásquez and other ministers who intended to contest the forthcoming presidential and legislative elections. José Antonio Chang Escobedo was appointed to succeed Velásquez as the President of the Council of Ministers, while retaining the post of Minister of Education. New appointees included Ismael Benavides as Minister of Economy and Finance, Fernando Barrios Ipenza as Minister of the Interior and Jaime Thorne León as Minister of Defence. Thorne replaced Rafael Rey Rey, who was reported to have been responsible for a controversial decree, issued earlier in September, which stated that the exemption of human rights abuses from the statute of limitations only applied to crimes committed after November 2003, when Peru signed the International Convention on Crimes against Humanity. Shortly afterwards, at President García's request, the Congreso repealed the decree, which had been widely condemned by human rights organizations. Barrios resigned as Minister of the Interior in November, following accusations in the media that he had improperly arranged to receive severance pay on leaving his previous post at the state-owned health agency; Gen. Miguel Hidalgo Medina, hitherto director of the national police force, was allocated the interior portfolio.

Regional elections held in October 2010 were marked by the success of local movements and the poor performance of the traditional, national parties; PAP secured just one of the 25 regional presidencies (compared with three in the 2006 polls). In concurrent municipal elections, Susana Villarán, of the centre-left Partido Decentralista Fuerza Social, was notably elected mayor of Lima, narrowly defeating the conservative Lourdes Flores Nano, who had unsuccessfully contested the presidential elections of 2001 and 2006.

Chang resigned as President of the Council of Ministers and as Minister of Education in March 2011, citing personal reasons. The Minister of Justice, Rosario Fernández, assumed the premiership for the remaining four months of President García's term in office.

Recent developments: 2011 elections

The first round of the presidential and legislative elections was held on 10 April 2011. There were 11 presidential candidates, while 13 political parties and alliances participated in the elections to the enlarged 130-seat Congreso. PAP notably did not contest the presidency, its representative, former Minister of Economy and Finance Mercedes Aráoz Fernández, having withdrawn her candidacy in January in protest at the inclusion on the party's list for the congressional elections of del Castillo, who remained under investigation in relation to the scandal that led to his resignation as prime minister in 2008. Ollanta Humala, the candidate of Gana Perú (a PNP-led alliance of left-wing parties), won 31.7% of the valid votes cast in the presidential ballot, while his closest rival, Keiko Fujimori, daughter of imprisoned former President Fujimori, who stood for the right-wing Fuerza 2011, took 23.6%. Pedro Pablo Kuczynski, President of the Council of Ministers in 2005–06, who was representing the Alianza por el Gran Cambio (a grouping of four centre-right parties, including the Partido Popular Cristiano), was placed third, with 18.5%, followed by former President Toledo, of PP, with 15.6%. The nationalist Humala, who conducted a far more moderate campaign than he had done in the 2006 vote, and Fujimori were to proceed to a second round, scheduled to take place on 5 June. Having previously emphasized her father's record in addressing Peru's economic and security difficulties, Keiko Fujimori appeared to distance herself from him during the campaign for the second round of the election as she sought to broaden her support base. In the legislative elections, preliminary indications were that Gana Perú would be the largest grouping in the new Congreso, followed by Fuerza 2011, and that no party would hold a majority of seats.

The Resurgence of Sendero Luminoso

In the early 1990s the SL intensified its attacks against government and military targets, strategic power installations, commercial enterprises and rural defence groups. Following Fujimori's 'autogolpe' of April 1992 (effected partly in response to continuing congressional opposition to his efforts to expand the role of the armed forces), considerable concern was expressed by human rights organizations that the security forces would be permitted an increasing degree of autonomy. In September 1992 government forces succeeded in capturing the SL's founder and leader, Abimael Guzmán Reynoso, together with 20 prominent SL members. Guzmán was tried by a military court, where he was found guilty of treason and sentenced to life imprisonment. The SL, however, remained highly active, and in early 1993 was held responsible for the assassination of 20 candidates campaigning in local elections, and for attacks on rural communities that had formed self-defence militia units. The Government actively pursued its offensive against terrorist organizations in the mid-1990s, and publicized the detention of leading members of the SL, the MRTA and the dissident SL 'Sendero Rojo' faction (which advocated a continuation of the armed struggle). In 1999 Oscar Ramírez Durand (alias 'Comrade Feliciano'), the leader of Sendero Rojo, was captured and sentenced to life imprisonment.

The SL emerged again in 2001, with at least 31 deaths attributed to the terrorist organization in that year. In March 2002, three days before the US President, George W. Bush, was due to visit Peru (the first such visit by a serving US head of state), a car bomb killed 10 people and injured at least 40 more near the US embassy in Lima. The attack was attributed to a radical wing of the SL, and did not herald an immediate return to a sustained campaign of terrorism. In June 2003 the Government attributed the abduction of 60 pipeline construction workers in the Ayacucho region to the remnants of the SL; the hostages were subsequently released unharmed. In November the kidnappers' alleged leader, Jaime Zuñiga Córdova, was captured by security forces. In November 2004 a retrial of Guzmán and 16 other SL militants began in a civilian court after the Constitutional Tribunal ruled that their convictions by military court in 1992 were invalid. The retrial was subsequently suspended for 30 days following the resignation, at the request of the state prosecutor, of two of the three judges. President Toledo's announcement in late November 2004, in advance of the verdict, that none of the defendants would go free also contributed to the collapse of the retrial soon afterwards. In September 2005, however, the retrial of Guzmán began anew. Guzmán and his former second-in-command, Elena Iparraguirre, were both sentenced to life imprisonment in October 2006, while the 10 other defendants being retried received prison sentences ranging between 24 and 35 years.

Meanwhile, in December 2005 13 police officers were killed in ambushes by SL guerrillas in rural provinces known to be centres of coca cultivation and cocaine production. It was believed that the SL was increasingly turning away from its ideological struggle in favour of protecting the illegal drugs trade, from which it allegedly derived a substantial part of its funding. In January 2006 President Toledo announced the establishment of a new police unit to combat the resurgence of the SL. Eight people, including five police officers, were killed in December in an ambush mounted against a coca eradication operation near the town of Machente in Ayacucho. The Government dispatched some 500 commandos to the area, and eight alleged SL rebels were subsequently arrested. A month earlier the Minister of Defence had announced the deployment of 1,500 special troops to combat terrorism and drugs-trafficking in the regions of Ayacucho and Huancayo, in co-ordination with military personnel already stationed at bases in that area. An attack on a police station in Ocobamba, Apurímac, by some 50–80 armed men in November 2007, which resulted in the death of a police officer, was blamed by the Government on SL members involved in the drugs trade. Increased military operations in the wake of the attack resulted in the killing, later that same month, of a senior SL commander, Mario Epifanio Espíritu Acosta. In August 2008 the army launched an offensive in the area of the Apurímac-Ene valley aimed at defeating the larger of the two remaining SL contingents in Peru; none the less, attacks by the guerrilla group in the area intensified. In October the SL inflicted its most deadly attack on the army in 11 years when it ambushed a military convoy in a coca-producing area in Huancavelica: it was reported that 13 soldiers from an anti-terrorist unit and at least three civilians were killed in the attack. Despite some apparent advances by the army during the following months, in April 2009 two co-ordinated ambushes by the SL in the Huanta province of Ayacucho resulted in the deaths of another 13 soldiers.

A series of small-scale attacks against military targets by the SL in late 2009 and early 2010 reinforced the belief that the organization was becoming more active. Moreover, leaked documents revealed in January 2010 appeared to provide evidence of growing links with the Colombian guerrilla organization Fuerzas Armadas Revolucionarias de Colombia (FARC). The murders of two coca eradication workers and a police officer in the Huallaga province of San Martín in April were attributed to the SL. In October the arrest in the region of Huánuco was reported of Edgar Mejia (alias 'Comrade Izula'), a senior SL commander who was alleged to have led attacks in which several police officers had died. Later that month a Peruvian soldier was killed in an attack on a military base in Huánuco. Landmines believed to have been laid by the SL caused a number of deaths in San Martín in November.

Human Rights Issues and the Illegal Drugs Trade

The Peruvian Government attracted criticism from human rights organizations for its methods in achieving the apparent subjugation of the terrorist movements in the 1990s. In July 1999 Peru withdrew from the jurisdiction of the Inter-American Court of Human Rights (IACHR, see p. 392), a branch of the OAS, after the court ruled the previous month that new trials should be held for four Chilean MRTA activists who were serving life sentences. However, in January 2001, apparently as part of its effort to improve the country's international image, the Congreso approved Peru's return to the jurisdiction of the IACHR. In March, one week after the IACHR ruled that a military amnesty law approved in 1995 was incompatible with the American Convention on Human Rights, two former intelligence generals were arrested on charges of involvement in the early 1990s with the right-wing Colina death squad. In September 2001 the Attorney-General charged Fujimori with responsibility for two mass killings by the Colina group that took place in the early 1990s, for which crimes he was subsequently tried and convicted (see above). In November 2006 the IACHR ruled that the Peruvian state was responsible for the killings of 41 suspected members of the SL during an assault by the security forces on a prison in 1992, and ordered the current Government to pay compensation totalling some US $20m. to relatives of the deceased and to survivors who were injured during the attack. President García later declared that the Government would challenge the ruling. In a separate case, the court also held the state responsible for the abduction and subsequent summary execution by Colina of 10 civilians at La Canuta university (which constituted one of the charges against Fujimori); compensation of $1.8m. was to be paid to the victims' relatives. The opposition PNP suggested that the President's efforts to restore the death penalty in early 2007 (see above) were intended to undermine the authority of the IACHR ahead of the court's ruling on human rights cases dating from García's first term in office (1985–90).

In January 2001 a Truth Commission, composed of church leaders and civil and military representatives, was established to investigate the impact of the campaign against the guerrilla groups in the 1980s and 1990s. The Commission conducted some 17,000 interviews, and initially secured the support of the Peruvian army (although the navy refused to co-operate). In August 2003 the body presented its findings, which estimated the number of deaths during the conflict at some 69,000, twice the previous official total, with some 6,000 individuals reported as 'disappeared'. Nevertheless, despite the report's conclusion that the SL was responsible for the greater part of the killings, its conclusions were criticized by elements of the Roman Catholic Church, the military and PAP. In November President Toledo publicly apologized for the state's actions during the period and announced a US $817m. plan to improve social conditions in the regions most affected by the violence.

In February 1990, in Cartagena, Colombia, the Presidents of Peru, Colombia, Bolivia and the USA signed the Cartagena Declaration, pledging the intensification of efforts to combat the consumption, production and trafficking of illegal drugs. However, commitments to fund subsequent anti-drugs schemes in Peru were suspended by the US Administration as a result of international criticism of the Peruvian Government's record on human rights and its flouting of accepted democratic processes. In January 1996 responsibility for combating the drugs trade was transferred from the military to the national police force, following a series of allegations that army officers had themselves been involved in illegal trafficking. A new bilateral agreement to combat the drugs trade was signed with the USA in July. Following the approval of the Andean Trade Promotion and Drug Eradication Act by the US Congress in August 2002, it was announced that Peru qualified for expanded US benefits and trade preferences. In March 2003 a new US $3,000m. development strategy for the regions of Peru affected by coca cultivation was announced; the plans envisaged the reforestation of 1m. hectares of arable land judged to be capable of producing coca, and the replanting of some 500,000 ha with alternative crops. The Government also envisaged that the new initiatives would lead to the creation of some 2.5m. jobs by 2020, with the complete elimination of coca in the area under illegal cultivation (which totalled approximately 24,600 ha). However, in February 2005 it was reported that US funding to the Andean region for drugs eradication would prioritize Colombia over Bolivia and Peru, which were to receive some 16% less in 2005 (Peru's funding would total some $115m. and $97m. in 2005 and 2006, respectively). There was speculation that the reduction of funding to Peru reflected the US Administration's disappointment with the lack of progress made by the Toledo Government in coca eradication. In that same month Nils Ericsson, head of the Comisión Nacional para el Desarrollo y Vida sin Drogas (Devida—Peru's anti-narcotics agency), announced that some 17,000 ha of coca had been planted in 2004, exceeding the quantities eradicated, and that cocaine production had increased by 13% in the previous year, to 160 metric tons. In October 2005 Ericsson announced that international funding for Peru's counter-narcotics operations in 2006 would be some $10m. less than in the previous year. In September 2006 Rómulo Pizarro Tomasio, Minister of the Interior under Toledo, replaced Ericsson as head of Devida. Pizarro announced that García's new Government intended to increase the state's presence in coca-producing areas and to extend crop-replacement programmes. However, US funding for drugs eradication continued to decline, with a total of only $66m. proposed for 2007/08. In March 2007, following protests in the province of Tocache by coca growers who claimed that crops destined for sale to the state coca company were being destroyed by the authorities, the Minister of Agriculture, Juan José Salazar, agreed to suspend coca eradication in the province for 10 days and provide compensation for those whose crops had been mistakenly destroyed. Salazar subsequently proposed a shift in Peru's counter-narcotics policy, to focus more on combating the production and smuggling of cocaine rather than the eradication of coca. Salazar provoked further controversy in May by signing an agreement with coca producers in the Cusco region that committed the Government to re-evaluating its membership of the Vienna Convention on Narcotic Drugs (ratified by Peru in November 1991, and which required that the authorities implement measures to control coca production). Following Salazar's resignation over the issue later that month, the new Minister of Agriculture, Ismael Benavides, signalled that his ministry would avoid involvement in coca eradication, stating that it was the sole responsibility of Devida.

Foreign Affairs
Meeting in Caracas, Venezuela, in May 1991, the Presidents of the five South American nations comprising the Andean Group (now the Andean Community of Nations, see p. 189) formalized their commitment to the full implementation of an Andean free trade area by the end of 1995, to be achieved by a gradual reduction in tariffs and other trade barriers. An agreement to restructure the Group into the Andean Community, thus strengthening regional integration, was signed in March 1996 in Trujillo. In June 1997 the Peruvian Government announced plans to abolish tariffs on some 2,500 goods entering Peru from within the Community (with immediate effect), and its intention to remove tariffs on a further 3,500 goods (including more than 600 deemed 'sensitive') by 2005. Peru was admitted as an associate member of the Southern Common Market (Mercosur—Mercado Común del Sur, see p. 425) in August 2003. The US Andean Trade Promotion and Drug Eradication Act (ATPDEA), which awarded Peru significant new tariff reductions on exports to the USA, including clothing and manufactures, came into operation in August 2002, but expired in February 2011. Peru concluded a free trade agreement with the USA in December 2005, in spite of vociferous opposition from left-wing and indigenous groups. Following ratification by the Peruvian Congreso in June 2006, and by the US House of Representatives and Senate in November and December 2007, respectively, the free trade agreement was enacted in January 2009. Panama signed a number of further free trade accords in 2009–10; with the People's Republic of China, which had become a major trading parter, in April 2009 (coming into effect in March 2010), with the European Union in May 2010, and with the Republic of Korea in November.

A long-standing border dispute with Ecuador over the Cordillera del Cóndor descended into armed conflict in January 1981. A cease-fire was declared a few days later, under the auspices of the guarantors (Argentina, Brazil, Chile and the USA) of the Rio de Janeiro Protocol of 1942, which had awarded the area, affording access to the Amazon river basin, to Peru. However, the Protocol had never been recognized by Ecuador, and, despite mutual efforts to achieve a constructive dialogue, the matter continued to be a source of tension and recurrent skirmishes between the two countries. In January 1995 serious fighting broke out. In February representatives of both countries, meeting in Brazil under the auspices of the Rio de Janeiro Protocol guarantors, approved a provisional cease-fire. Following further negotiations, on 17 February both countries signed the Itamaraty Peace Declaration. Foreign affairs ministers from both countries, meeting in Uruguay at the end of the month, signed the Montevideo Declaration, which ratified the Itamaraty agreement. The withdrawal of forces from the disputed border area was achieved by mid-May. None the less, reports of further armed clashes prompted requests from both countries for an extension of the observer mission. Agreement on the delimitation of a demilitarized zone in the disputed Cenepa river region came into effect on 1 August. In September Fujimori agreed to reopen the border with Ecuador for commercial purposes, and in November both countries agreed to pursue further confidence-building measures. In October 1996 the Ministers of Foreign Affairs of both countries, meeting in Chile under the auspices of the guarantor countries, signed the Santiago Agreement, which was to provide a framework for a settlement of the border issue.

Following further negotiations, in early 1998 a number of commissions were established to examine specific aspects of a potential agreement between Peru and Ecuador, including a trade and navigation treaty and the fixing of frontier markers on the ground in the Cordillera del Cóndor. Talks culminated in the signing of an accord in Brasília, Brazil, in October by the Ministers of Foreign Affairs of Peru and Ecuador in the presence of the two countries' Presidents and of six other regional leaders. The accord confirmed Peru's claim regarding the delineation of the border, but granted Ecuador navigation and trading rights on the Amazon and its tributaries and the opportunity to establish two trading centres in Peru (although this was not to constitute sovereign access). Moreover, Ecuador was given 1 sq km of territory, as private property, at Tiwintza in Peru, where many Ecuadorean soldiers, killed during the conflict in 1995, were buried. Both countries were committed to establishing ecological parks along the border, where military personnel would not be allowed access. Although considerable opposition to the accord was expressed in Peru, notably in the town of Iquitos, international reaction was very favourable and resulted in several offers of finance from multilateral agencies for cross-border development projects. The Presidents of Peru and Ecuador met in May 1999 at the Peru–Ecuador frontier to mark the placing of the last boundary stone on the border.

In January 1992 the Presidents of Peru and Bolivia concluded an agreement whereby Bolivia would be granted access to the Pacific Ocean via the Peruvian port of Ilo (which would be jointly developed as a free zone). In return, Bolivia agreed to help facilitate Peruvian access to the Atlantic Ocean (through Brazil) by way of the Bolivian town of Puerto Suárez. In August 2004, following negotiations on economic integration, the Presidents of Peru and Bolivia signed a declaration of intent to create a special zone in Ilo for the exportation of Bolivian gas. In October 2010 the Peruvian and Bolivian Presidents signed an agreement expanding the 1992 accord, by allowing Bolivia to construct docks, storage facilities and a naval academy in Ilo.

The support of President Chávez for Humala in the presidential election of 2006 severely strained Peru's relations with Venezuela. In late April Chávez threatened to sever diplomatic ties with Peru if García won the election. In response, President Toledo criticized Chávez for interfering in Peru's domestic affairs and withdrew Peru's ambassador from Venezuela, prompting Chávez to recall the Venezuelan ambassador from Peru a few days later. Full diplomatic relations were restored in February 2007, with the exchange of new ambassadors, following talks between Presidents García and Chávez in the previous month. The establishment in March 2008 of a congressional committee to investigate the 'Casas del Alba'—ostensibly humanitarian organizations founded in previous months by Peruvian supporters of Chávez—once again strained relations between the two countries. Venezuela strongly denied allegations by the Peruvian Government that the offices, named after Chávez's regional integration project, the Alternativa Bolivariana para las Américas (ALBA), were funded by the Venezuelan Government as a means of promoting 'Bolivarian' ideology in Peru. Nevertheless, in March 2009 a report published by the congressional committee concluded that both Venezuela and Bolivia, another ALBA member country, had interfered in Peru's internal affairs through the Casas del Alba; the report recommended that the Congreso close all 146 Casas del Alba and submit formal protests to the Governments of Venezuela and Bolivia. Relations with Venezuela were further impaired in April by the Peruvian Government's decision to grant asylum to the Venezuelan opposition leader and former presidential candidate, Manuel Rosales, who had taken refuge in Peru after being charged with corruption offences in his home country. Venezuela recalled its ambassador in response to the incident.

Peru's relations with Chile, which had been strained during Toledo's presidency, improved significantly after García took office in July 2006. In August the two countries agreed to expand the scope of a bilateral economic agreement reached in 1998 by including provisions related to cross-border investment and trade in services. It was hoped that this would eventually lead to the conclusion of a free trade agreement. García also urged the

Chilean Government to rejoin the Andean Community as an associate member (which it did in November 2006), and an agreement on military co-operation was reached in October. Notwithstanding these advances, an ongoing dispute over maritime boundaries was rekindled in August 2007 by the Peruvian Government's publication of an official map that restated the country's long-standing claim to some 37,900 sq km of the Pacific Ocean controlled by Chile. The move prompted the Chilean Government, which maintained that the issue had already been resolved by previous bilateral treaties, to recall its ambassador for consultations. In January 2008 Peru presented an application to the International Court of Justice (see p. 23) for adjudication on the disputed border.

REGIONAL AND INTERNATIONAL CO-OPERATION

Peru is a member of the Andean Community of Nations (see p. 189), the Inter-American Development Bank (IDB, see p. 333), the Southern Common Market (Mercosur—Mercado Común del Sur, see p. 425) and the Latin American Integration Association (ALADI, see p. 359), all of which encourage regional economic development, and of the Rio Group (formerly the Group of Eight, see p. 462), which attempts to reduce regional indebtedness. Peru became a member of the Asia-Pacific Economic Co-operation group (APEC, see p. 197) in 1998. In December 2004 Peru was one of 12 countries that were signatories to the agreement, signed in Cusco, creating the South American Community of Nations (which was inaugurated, as the Unión Suramericana de Naciones—UNASUR—in May 2008), intended to promote greater regional economic integration. The country is a member of the Organization of American States (OAS, see p. 391). Peru became a member of the UN in 1945. The country has been a member of the World Trade Organization (see p. 430) since January 1995. Peru is a member of the Group of 15 (G15, see p. 447) and the Group of 77 (G77, see p. 447) organization of developing states.

CONSTITUTION AND GOVERNMENT

A new Constitution, drafted by the Congreso Constituyente Democrático, was approved by a national referendum on 31 October 1993, and was promulgated on 29 December. Under the terms of the Constitution, executive power is vested in the President, who is elected for a five-year term by universal adult suffrage and is eligible for re-election for a successive term of office. Two Vice-Presidents are also elected. The President governs with the assistance of an appointed Council of Ministers. Legislative power is vested in a single chamber Congreso (removing the distinction in the 1979 Constitution of an upper and lower house) consisting of 130 members (increased from 120 following the 2011 elections, in accordance with a constitutional amendment adopted in September 2009). The members of the Congreso are elected for a five-year term by universal adult suffrage. For administrative purposes, Peru comprises 25 regions, which are subdivided into 195 provinces; the provinces are further subdivided into districts.

ECONOMIC AFFAIRS

In 2009, according to estimates by the World Bank, Peru's gross national income (GNI), measured at average 2007–09 prices, was US $120,911m., equivalent to $4,150 per head (or $8,140 per head on an international purchasing-power parity basis). During 2000–09, it was estimated, the population increased by an average of 1.3% per year, while gross domestic product (GDP) per head increased, in real terms, at an average annual rate of 4.0%. Overall GDP increased, in real terms, at an average annual rate of 5.3% in 2000–09; growth was 8.8% in 2010.

Agriculture (including forestry and fishing) contributed 7.3% of GDP in 2009, and the sector engaged 8.1% of the economically active population residing in urban areas in 2008. Rice, maize and potatoes are the principal food crops. The principal cash crop is coffee. Peru is the world's leading producer of coca, and the cultivation of this shrub, for the production of the illicit drug cocaine, reportedly generates revenue of US $1,500m.–$2,500m. per year. Undeclared revenue from the export of coca is believed to exceed revenue from legal exports. Fishing, particularly for the South American pilchard and the anchoveta, provides another important source of revenue, and the fishing sector contributed an estimated 0.7% of GDP in 2009. Fishing accounted for 1.9% of the total value of exports in 2009. During 2000–09 agricultural GDP (including fishing) increased at an average annual rate of 3.7%; the sector's GDP increased by 1.7% in 2009.

Industry (including mining, manufacturing, construction and power) provided 34.1% of GDP in 2009 and employed 20.8% of the working population in 2008. During 2000–09 industrial GDP increased by an average of 5.7% per year; industrial GDP increased by 10.1% in 2008, but declined by 2.4% in 2009.

Mining (including hydrocarbon extraction) contributed 10.6% of GDP and employed 1.0% of the urban working population in 2008. Production of natural gas rose sharply from 2005, following the opening of the Camisea natural gas export pipeline in 2004, reaching 255,609m. cu ft in 2010. Peru's first natural gas liquefaction plant was inaugurated in June 2010. Copper accounted for 14.7% of total export earnings in 2009. Zinc, gold, petroleum and its derivatives, lead and silver are also major mineral exports. During 2000–09 the GDP of the mining and petroleum sector increased at an average annual rate of 5.9%; real GDP growth in the sector was 0.6% in 2009.

Manufacturing contributed 14.0% of GDP in 2009 and employed 13.9% of the employed urban population in 2008. The principal branches of manufacturing, measured by gross value of output, were food products, petroleum refineries, non-ferrous metals, beverages, and textiles and clothing. During 2000–09 manufacturing GDP increased by an average of 4.9% per year. The sector's GDP increased by 9.1% in 2008, but declined by 7.2% in 2009.

Construction contributed 7.5% of GDP in 2009 and employed 5.4% of the employed urban population in 2008.

Energy is derived principally from domestic supplies of hydro-electric power (65.3% of total electricity production in 2007) and petroleum (6.0%). Imports of mineral fuels and lubricants comprised 14.1% of the value of merchandise imports in 2009.

The services sector contributed 58.6% of GDP in 2009 and employed 71.1% of the urban working population in 2008. Tourism is gradually emerging as an important source of foreign revenue (US $2,396m. in 2008). In 2000–09 the GDP of the services sector increased at an average annual rate of 5.4%. The sector's GDP grew by 2.9% in 2009.

In 2009 Peru recorded a visible trade surplus of US $5,873m., and there was a surplus of $247m. on the current account of the balance of payments. In 2009 the principal source of imports (19.8%) was the USA, which was also the principal market for exports (17.2%). Other major trading partners were the People's Republic of China and Brazil for imports, and China, Switzerland-Liechtenstein, Canada and Japan for exports. In February 2009 a free trade agreement with the USA came into effect. A free trade agreement with China was signed in April 2009 and took effect in March 2010. The principal exports in 2009 were crude materials (particularly copper and zinc), food and live animals, basic manufactures, mineral fuels and lubricants, and miscellaneous manufactured articles. The principal imports in the same year were machinery and transport equipment, basic manufactures, chemicals and related products, mineral fuels and lubricants, and food and live animals.

In 2010 there was a preliminary general budgetary deficit of 1,949m. new soles. In that year Peru's general government gross debt was 104,508m. new soles, equivalent to 27.4% of GDP. Peru's external debt at the end of 2008 was US $28,555m., of which $19,330m. was long-term public and publicly guaranteed debt. In that year the cost of debt-servicing was equivalent to 12.5% of the value of exports of goods, services and income. The annual rate of inflation averaged 2.5% in 2000–09. Consumer prices increased by an average of 2.9% in 2009. According to official figures, 7.8% of the labour force were unemployed in 2008. This figure was estimated to have increased to 9.6% in early 2010.

The election of the left-wing Government of Alan García (who had presided over a period of economic decline during 1985–90) in 2006 initially tempered investor confidence; however, the new President signalled that fiscal austerity would be adhered to, and measures were subsequently taken to improve private investment. The economy performed well in 2006–08, largely owing to high commodity prices, which significantly increased revenues from mineral exports and fuelled growth in the services sector (including commerce, transport and finance) involved in mining activities. Meanwhile, infrastructure projects benefited from strong investment, which, in turn, stimulated growth in the construction sector. Although Peru's financial services sector was well-placed to weather the global banking crisis in 2008, the faltering international economy engendered a steep decline in mineral prices, reducing the value of exports and levels of foreign investment. However, following a sharp deceleration to 0.9% in 2009, GDP growth

PERU

Statistical Survey

recovered to 8.8% in 2010, as private investment and domestic demand rose strongly and export revenue increased by some 31%, mainly as a result of higher mineral prices. In response to this potentially unsustainable growth, the central bank tightened monetary policy, increasing its interest rate from 1.25% in April 2010 to 4.00% by April 2011, and also intervened in the foreign exchange market to curb the appreciation of the currency. GDP growth of some 7% was forecast for 2011. There was a degree of uncertainty regarding the future direction of economic policy at May 2011, with two very different candidates due to contest a second round of presidential voting in the following month (see Domestic Political Affairs).

PUBLIC HOLIDAYS

2012: 1 January (New Year's Day), 5 April (Maundy Thursday), 6 April (Good Friday), 1 May (Labour Day), 24 June (Day of the Peasant, half-day only), 29 June (St Peter and St Paul), 28–29 July (Independence), 30 August (St Rose of Lima), 8 October (Battle of Angamos), 1 November (All Saints' Day), 8 December (Immaculate Conception), 25 December (Christmas Day).

Statistical Survey

Sources (unless otherwise stated): Banco Central de Reserva del Perú, Jirón Antonio Miró Quesada 441–445, Lima 1; tel. (1) 4267041; fax (1) 4275880; e-mail webmaster@bcrp.gob.pe; internet www.bcrp.gob.pe; Instituto Nacional de Estadística e Informática, Avda General Garzón 658, Jesús María, Lima; tel. (1) 2218990; fax (1) 4417760; e-mail infoinei@inei.gob.pe; internet www.inei.gob.pe.

Area and Population

AREA, POPULATION AND DENSITY
(excluding Indian jungle population)

Area (sq km)	
Land	1,280,086
Inland water	5,130
Total	1,285,216*
Population (census results)†‡	
11 July 1993	22,048,356
21 October 2007	
Males	13,626,717
Females	13,792,577
Total	27,419,294
Population (UN estimates at mid-year)§	
2009	29,164,883
2010	29,496,120
2011	29,831,820
Density (per sq km) at mid-2011	23.2

* 496,225 sq miles.
† Excluding adjustment for underenumeration, estimated at 2.35% in 1993.
‡ An additional census was compiled, according to different methodology, during 18 July–20 August 2005. The total population was recorded at 27,219,264 in that year, including adjustment for an estimated 3.92% underenumeration (when the enumerated total was 26,152,265).
§ Source: UN, *World Population Prospects: The 2008 Revision*.

POPULATION BY AGE AND SEX
(UN estimates at mid-2011)

	Males	Females	Total
0–14	4,483,565	4,319,710	8,803,275
15–64	9,632,090	9,574,559	19,206,649
65 and over	832,096	989,800	1,821,896
Total	14,947,751	14,884,069	29,831,820

Source: UN, *World Population Prospects: The 2008 Revision*.

REGIONS
(2007 census)

	Area (sq km)	Population	Density (per sq km)	Capital
Amazonas	39,249	375,993	9.6	Chachapoyas
Ancash	35,915	1,063,459	29.6	Huaraz
Apurímac	20,896	404,190	19.3	Abancay
Arequipa	63,345	1,152,303	18.2	Arequipa
Ayacucho	43,815	612,489	14.0	Ayacucho
Cajamarca	33,318	1,387,809	41.7	Cajamarca
Callao*	147	876,877	5,965.1	Callao
Cusco	71,987	1,171,403	16.3	Cusco (Cuzco)
Huancavelica	22,131	454,797	20.6	Huancavelica
Huánuco	36,849	762,223	20.7	Huánuco
Ica	21,328	711,932	33.4	Ica
Junín	44,197	1,232,611	27.9	Huancayo
La Libertad	25,500	1,617,050	63.4	Trujillo
Lambayeque	14,231	1,112,868	78.2	Chiclayo
Lima	34,802	8,445,211	242.7	Lima
Loreto	368,852	891,732	2.4	Iquitos
Madre de Dios	85,301	109,555	1.3	Puerto Maldonado
Moquegua	15,734	161,533	10.3	Moquegua
Pasco	25,320	280,449	11.1	Cerro de Pasco
Piura	35,892	1,676,315	46.7	Piura
Puno	71,999	1,268,441	17.6	Puno
San Martín	51,253	728,808	14.2	Moyabamba
Tacna	16,076	288,781	18.0	Tacna
Tumbes	4,669	200,306	42.9	Tumbes
Ucayali	102,411	432,159	4.2	Pucallpa
Total	**1,285,216**	**27,419,294**	**21.3**	—

* Province.

PRINCIPAL TOWNS
(population of towns and urban environs at 21 October 2007)

Lima (capital)	8,472,935*	Iquitos	370,962
Arequipa	749,291	Cusco (Cuzco)	348,935
Trujillo	682,834	Chimbote	334,568
Chiclayo	524,442	Huancayo	323,054
Callao	515,200†	Tacna	242,451
Piura	377,496	Ica	219,856

* Metropolitan area (Gran Lima) only.
† Estimated population of town, excluding urban environs, at mid-1985.

Mid-2010 ('000, incl. suburbs, UN estimate): Lima (capital) 8,940,555; Arequipa 789,490 (Source: UN, *World Urbanization Prospects: The 2009 Revision*).

PERU

BIRTHS AND DEATHS*

	Live births		Deaths	
	Number	Rate (per 1,000)	Number	Rate (per 1,000)
1996	656,435	27.1	160,045	6.6
1997	652,467	26.4	160,830	6.5
1998	648,075	25.8	161,615	6.4
1999	642,874	25.2	162,457	6.4
2000	636,064	24.5	163,263	6.3
2001	630,947	24.0	164,296	6.2
2002	626,714	23.4	165,467	6.2
2003	623,521	23.0	166,777	6.1

* Data are estimates and projections based on incomplete registration, but including an upward adjustment for under-registration.

2007 (registrations, assumed to be incomplete): Live births 508,384; Deaths 82,620 (Source: UN, *Population and Vital Statistics Report*).

2008 (registrations, assumed to be incomplete): Live births 457,033; Deaths 108,100 (Source: UN, *Population and Vital Statistics Report*).

Marriages: 89,162 in 2006 (marriage rate 3.2 per 1,000); 90,883 in 2007 (marriage rate 3.2 per 1,000); 94,971 in 2008 (marriage rate 3.3 per 1,000) (Source: UN, *Demographic Yearbook*).

Life expectancy (years at birth, WHO estimates): 76 (males 74; females 77) in 2008 (Source: WHO, *World Health Statistics*).

EMPLOYMENT
('000 persons aged 14 and over, urban areas)

	2006	2007	2008
Agriculture, hunting and forestry	857.3	698.5	710.7
Fishing	42.0	58.7	59.0
Mining and quarrying	94.2	97.2	98.8
Manufacturing	1,135.7	1,292.2	1,316.6
Electricity, gas and water	26.3	21.1	35.8
Construction	431.6	469.8	512.0
Wholesale and retail trade; repair of motor vehicles, motorcycles and personal and household goods	2,035.2	2,087.6	2,101.4
Hotels and restaurants	631.1	680.5	730.2
Transport, storage and communications	750.7	840.5	907.0
Financial intermediation	74.5	69.5	92.3
Real estate, renting and business activities	426.8	483.0	486.4
Public administration and defence; compulsory social security	396.5	437.6	423.2
Education	545.7	650.3	641.5
Health and social work	201.1	248.4	270.5
Other services	568.7	587.1	634.5
Private households	476.0	474.3	423.4
Extra-territorial organizations	0.7	1.5	2.2
Total employed	**8,694.0**	**9,197.8**	**9,445.5**

Source: ILO.

2007 (persons aged 14 years and over, census figures): Total employed 10,166,179 (males 6,563,384, females 3,602,795); Unemployed 474,464 (males 316,021, females 158,443); *Total labour force* 10,640,643 (males 6,879,405, females 3,761,238).

Health and Welfare

KEY INDICATORS

Total fertility rate (children per woman, 2008)	2.6
Under-5 mortality rate (per 1,000 live births, 2008)	24
HIV/AIDS (% of persons aged 15–49, 2007)	0.5
Physicians (per 1,000 head, 1999)	1.2
Hospital beds (per 1,000 head, 2004)	0.9
Health expenditure (2007): US $ per head (PPP)	327
Health expenditure (2007): % of GDP	4.3
Health expenditure (2007): public (% of total)	58.4
Access to water (% of persons, 2008)	82
Access to sanitation (% of persons, 2008)	68
Total carbon dioxide emissions ('000 metric tons, 2007)	42,953.1
Carbon dioxide emissions per head (metric tons, 2007)	1.5
Human Development Index (2010): ranking	63
Human Development Index (2010): value	0.723

For sources and definitions, see explanatory note on p. vi.

Agriculture

PRINCIPAL CROPS
('000 metric tons)

	2007	2008	2009
Wheat	181.6	206.9	223.1
Rice, paddy	2,435.1	2,775.8	2,989.6
Barley	177.5	186.0	213.2
Maize	1,368.2	1,480.9	1,544.1
Potatoes	3,388.0	3,578.9	3,716.7
Sweet potatoes	184.8	189.9	260.8
Cassava (Manioc)	1,158.0	1,171.8	1,221.3
Sugar cane	8,228.6	9,396.0	10,100.1
Beans, dry	81.8	86.1	98.3
Oil palm fruit	238.4	265.3*	265.3*
Cabbages	32.2	36.1	39.8
Asparagus	284.1	328.4	313.9
Tomatoes	173.3	210.7	220.4
Pumpkins, squash and gourds	121.6	121.6*	n.a.
Chillies and peppers, green*	10.0	10.0	n.a.
Onions, dry	634.4	641.5	602.0
Garlic	80.9	67.6	57.6
Peas, green	98.5	101.8	105.1
Broad beans, dry	61.3	64.3	69.5
Carrots and turnips	161.8	170.8	162.4
Maize, green	332.3	374.1	391.4
Plantains	1,834.5	1,792.9	1,854.2
Oranges	344.3	380.0	377.7
Tangerines, mandarins, clementines and satsumas	190.4	187.2	166.0
Lemons and limes	280.8	236.3	211.2
Apples	136.7	135.2	137.0
Grapes	196.6	223.4	264.5
Watermelons	77.7	97.1	106.9
Guavas, mangoes and mangosteens	294.4	322.7	165.6
Avocados	121.7	136.3	160.0
Pineapples	212.1	243.5	274.4
Papayas	157.8	167.4	174.9
Coffee, green	226.0	273.8	255.0

* FAO estimate(s).

Aggregate production ('000 metric tons, may include official, semi-official or estimated data): Total cereals 4,211.9 in 2007, 4,697.2 in 2008, 5,028.9 in 2009; Total roots and tubers 5,014.5 in 2007, 5,224.4 in 2008, 5,483.0 in 2009; Total vegetables (incl. melons) 2,421.8 in 2007, 2,596.1 in 2008, 2,598.8 in 2009; Total fruits (excl. melons) 4,132.2 in 2007, 4,206.1 in 2008, 4,159.5 in 2009.

Source: FAO.

PERU

LIVESTOCK
('000 head, year ending September)

	2007	2008	2009
Horses*	730	730	n.a.
Asses*	630	630	n.a.
Mules*	30	30	n.a.
Cattle	5,421	5,443	5,459
Pigs	3,116	3,151	3,257
Sheep	14,580	14,510	14,138
Goats	1,926	1,904	1,929
Chickens	120,228	131,179	137,838

* FAO estimates.
Source: FAO.

LIVESTOCK PRODUCTS
('000 metric tons)

	2007	2008	2009
Cattle meat	163.2	163.3	164.7
Sheep meat	33.8	33.4	33.5
Pig meat	114.5	115.2	114.7
Chicken meat	770.4	877.2	964.4
Cows' milk	1,455.8	1,565.5	1,652.1
Hen eggs	257.6	266.5	268.7
Wool, greasy	10.9	10.9	n.a.

Source: FAO.

Forestry

ROUNDWOOD REMOVALS
('000 cubic metres, excluding bark)

	2007	2008	2009
Sawlogs, veneer logs and logs for sleepers	1,810	1,542	1,192
Other industrial wood	161	240	155
Fuel wood*	7,454	7,337	7,343
Total	9,425	9,119	8,690

* FAO estimates.
Source: FAO.

SAWNWOOD PRODUCTION
('000 cubic metres, including railway sleepers)

	2007	2008	2009
Coniferous (softwood)	16*	13	7
Broadleaved (hardwood)	932	795	619
Total	948	808	626

* FAO estimate.
Source: FAO.

Fishing

('000 metric tons, live weight)

	2006	2007	2008
Capture	7,017.5	7,210.5	7,362.9
Chilean jack mackerel	277.6	254.4	169.5
Anchoveta (Peruvian anchovy)	5,935.3	6,159.8	6,256.0
Jumbo flying squid	434.3	427.6	533.4
Aquaculture	28.4	39.5	43.1
Total catch	7,045.9	7,250.1	7,406.0

Note: Figures exclude aquatic plants ('000 metric tons, all capture): 3.4 in 2006; 10.8 in 2007; 13.8 in 2008.
Source: FAO.

Mining

('000 metric tons, unless otherwise indicated, preliminary figures)*

	2006	2007	2008
Crude petroleum ('000 barrels)	42,187.2	41,562.2	43,930.4
Natural gas (million cubic feet)	62,691.1	94,485.5	119,955.8
Copper	818.5	952.8	1,036.7
Lead	288.4	303.0	317.7
Molybdenum	16.5	16.1	16.1
Tin	33.4	33.9	33.9
Zinc	1,029.9	1,236.1	1,371.5
Iron ore	4,861.2	5,185.3	5,243.3
Gold (kg)	197.0	165.4	174.7
Silver (kg)	3,263.0	3,291.9	3,465.4

* Figures for metallic minerals refer to metal content only.

2010 ('000 metric tons, unless otherwise indicated): Crude petroleum ('000 barrels) 57,363; Natural gas (million cubic feet) 255,609; Copper 1,023.9; Lead 241.1; Tin 29.4; Zinc 1,258.5; Iron ore 6,139.3; Gold (kg) 158.7; Silver (kg) 3,422.5.

Industry

SELECTED PRODUCTS
('000 metric tons, unless otherwise indicated)

	2005	2006	2007
Canned fish	55.5	107.3	84.3
Wheat flour	1,034	1,088	1,056
Raw sugar	695.0	805.1	910.1
Beer ('000 hectolitres)	7,916	9,634	10,535
Motor spirit (petrol, '000 barrels)*	8,968	12,777	13,948
Kerosene ('000 barrels)*	2,501	960	818
Distillate fuel oils ('000 barrels)*	15,287	17,598	19,018
Residual fuel oils ('000 barrels)*	20,740	14,713	14,669
Portland cement	4,535	5,052	5,335
Crude steel*†	750	750	750
Copper (refined)	189.5	205.7	188.4
Zinc (refined)	164.7	177.5	162.7
Electric energy (million kWh)	25,509.9	27,402.5	29,856.5

* Source: US Geological Survey.
† Estimates.

2008 ('000 barrels, unless otherwise indicated): Residual fuel oils 13,874; Motor spirit 13,355; Kerosene 598; Distillate fuel oils 19,519; Crude steel ('000 metric tons) 750 (Source: US Geological Survey).

2009 ('000 barrels, unless otherwise indicated, preliminary): Residual fuel oils 10,170; Motor spirit 9,063; Kerosene 150; Distillate fuel oils 27,747; Crude steel ('000 metric tons) 750 (Source: US Geological Survey).

Finance

CURRENCY AND EXCHANGE RATES

Monetary Units
100 céntimos = 1 nuevo sol (new sol).

Sterling, Dollar and Euro Equivalents (31 December 2010)
£1 sterling = 4.305 new soles;
US $1 = 2.809 new soles;
€1 = 3.740 new soles;
100 new soles = £23.23 = $35.61 = €26.74.

Average Exchange Rate (new soles per US $)
2008 2.9244
2009 3.0115
2010 2.8251

Note: On 1 February 1985 Peru replaced its former currency, the sol, by the inti, valued at 1,000 soles. A new currency, the nuevo sol (equivalent to 1m. intis), was introduced in July 1991.

PERU

Statistical Survey

CENTRAL GOVERNMENT BUDGET
(million new soles, preliminary figures)

Revenue	2008	2009	2010
Taxation	58,287	52,566	64,429
Taxes on income, profits, etc.	24,146	20,346	25,802
Taxes on imports (excl. VAT)	1,911	1,493	1,803
Value-added tax	31,583	29,519	35,536
Domestic	15,749	17,322	19,629
Imports	15,834	12,197	15,907
Excises	3,461	4,146	4,670
Fuel duty	1,457	2,255	2,410
Other taxes	4,371	4,400	4,566
Less Refunds	7,185	7,339	7,948
Other current revenue	9,716	8,265	10,283
Capital revenue*	394	444	747
Total	**68,397**	**61,275**	**75,459**

Expenditure	2008	2009	2010
Current non-interest expenditure	46,095	48,462	51,591
Compensation of employees	13,870	15,160	15,823
Goods and non-labour services	10,849	13,341	15,537
Transfers	21,375	19,962	20,230
Interest payments	5,128	4,867	4,766
Internal	1,814	1,801	1,875
External	3,314	3,066	2,891
Capital expenditure	8,882	14,537	19,048
Gross capital formation	6,966	9,878	13,452
Total	**60,104**	**67,867**	**75,405**

*Net of payments to the American International Group and the Perú-Alemania Agreement.

General Budget (million new soles, preliminary figures): *2008:* Total revenue 78,150 (current 77,755, capital 395); Total expenditure 70,116 (current non-interest 49,204, capital 15,163, interest payments 5,749). *2009:* Total revenue 71,385 (current 70,997, capital 388); Total expenditure 79,566 (current non-interest 52,869, capital 21,800, interest payments 4,898). *2010:* Total revenue 86,951 (current 86,205, capital 746); Total expenditure 88,900 (current non-interest 57,491, capital 26,417, interest payments 4,992).

INTERNATIONAL RESERVES
(US $ million at 31 December)

	2008	2009	2010
Gold	982.6	1,217.7	1,564.9
IMF special drawing rights	9.0	821.6	807.2
Foreign exchange	30,262.5	30,999.8	41,652.8
Total	**31,254.1**	**33,039.1**	**44,024.9**

Source: IMF, *International Financial Statistics*.

MONEY SUPPLY
(million new soles at 31 December)

	2007	2008	2009
Currency outside banks	14,985	17,508	19,497
Demand deposits at commercial and development banks	25,586	28,385	30,194
Total money (incl. others)	**43,983**	**48,594**	**50,511**

2010: Currency outside banks 24,449.

Source: IMF, *International Financial Statistics*.

COST OF LIVING
(Consumer Price Index, Lima metropolitan area; base: 2000 = 100)

	2005	2006	2007
Food (incl. beverages)	107.6	110.2	113.0
Rent	120.3	123.3	124.5
Electricity, gas and other fuels	129.7	132.5	132.9
Clothing (incl. footwear)	107.5	109.1	111.9
All items (incl. others)	**110.1**	**112.3**	**114.3**

2008: Food (incl. beverages) 123.3; All items (incl. others) 120.9.
2009: Food (incl. beverages) 128.5; All items (incl. others) 124.4.

Source: ILO.

NATIONAL ACCOUNTS
(million new soles at current prices)

Expenditure on the Gross Domestic Product

	2008	2009	2010
Government final consumption expenditure	33,312	39,452	42,271
Private final consumption expenditure	237,340	249,891	269,650
Gross capital formation	102,856	88,192	117,330
Total domestic expenditure	**373,508**	**377,535**	**429,251**
Exports of goods and services	102,831	92,462	112,827
Less Imports of goods and services	98,776	77,432	97,618
GDP in purchasers' values	**377,562**	**392,565**	**444,460**
GDP at constant 1994 prices	191,367	192,994	209,886

Gross Domestic Product by Economic Activity

	2007	2008	2009
Agriculture, hunting and forestry	19,342	22,352	23,945
Fishing	2,183	2,569	2,605
Mining and quarrying	38,413	39,267	38,354
Manufacturing	49,035	54,921	50,897
Electricity and water	6,011	6,539	7,413
Construction	20,395	24,112	27,082
Wholesale and retail trade	42,104	48,602	52,319
Restaurants and hotels	11,694	13,511	14,628
Transport and communications	28,622	32,210	34,811
Government services	21,630	23,922	27,108
Other services	68,584	76,633	83,484
Gross value added at basic prices	**308,012**	**344,640**	**362,646**
Import duties	26,129	31,012	28,426
Taxes on products	2,198	1,911	1,493
GDP in purchasers' values	**336,339**	**377,562**	**392,565**

BALANCE OF PAYMENTS
(US $ million)

	2007	2008	2009
Exports of goods f.o.b.	27,882	31,529	26,885
Imports of goods f.o.b.	−19,595	−28,439	−21,011
Trade balance	**8,287**	**3,090**	**5,873**
Exports of services	3,152	3,649	3,653
Imports of services	−4,343	−5,611	−4,765
Balance on goods and services	**7,095**	**1,128**	**4,761**
Other income received	1,587	1,837	1,432
Other income paid	−9,945	−10,611	−8,803
Balance on goods, services and income	**−1,263**	**−7,646**	**−2,609**
Current transfers received	2,636	2,929	2,863
Current transfers paid	−10	−7	−7
Current balance	**1,363**	**−4,723**	**247**
Capital account (net)	−136	−121	−78
Direct investment abroad	−66	−736	−396
Direct investment from abroad	5,491	6,924	4,760
Portfolio investment assets	−390	462	−3,590
Portfolio investment liabilities	4,030	−1	1,247
Other investment assets	−443	860	531
Other investment liabilities	534	1,510	169
Net errors and omissions	−38	−717	−986
Overall balance	**10,343**	**3,457**	**1,902**

Source: IMF, *International Financial Statistics*.

PERU

External Trade

PRINCIPAL COMMODITIES
(distribution by SITC, US $ million)

Imports c.i.f.	2007	2008	2009
Food and live animals	838.8	2,348.9	1,943.0
Cereals and cereal preparations	249.7	1,240.5	877.7
Vegetables and fruits	328.7	133.9	133.1
Mineral fuels, lubricants and related materials	0.6	5,467.5	3,085.6
Petroleum, petroleum products and related materials	0.6	5,125.5	2,974.5
Chemicals and related products	3,287.7	4,078.1	3,289.3
Medicinal and pharmaceutical products	3,033.9	458.3	520.8
Plastics in primary forms	0.0	1,136.3	745.9
Basic manufactures	795.1	4,915.6	3,470.1
Iron and steel	10.8	2,056.3	1,155.1
Machinery and transport equipment	4,335.4	10,095.0	7,617.8
Machinery specialized for particular industries	307.7	1,421.9	1,118.9
General industrial machinery, equipment, etc.	133.5	1,724.5	1,340.1
Office machines and automatic data processing machines	494.5	780.7	711.3
Telecommunications, sound recording and reproducing equipment	80.0	1,574.4	1,011.8
Road vehicles	2,828.6	2,767.4	1,901.5
Miscellaneous manufactured articles	7,417.2	1,724.2	1,533.5
Professional, scientific and controlling instruments	1,685.8	333.3	310.4
Total (incl. others)	20,464.2	29,952.8	21,869.7

Exports f.o.b.	2007	2008	2009
Food and live animals	3,571.8	4,497.3	4,278.4
Fish, crustaceans, molluscs and preparations thereof	488.3	609.5	510.6
Coffee	427.0	645.1	585.4
Crude materials	9,363.9	9,032.0	7,132.5
Iron ore and concentrates	285.4	385.1	297.7
Copper ores and concentrates	4,600.5	4,897.5	3,920.9
Lead ores and concentrates	649.4	801.3	895.1
Zinc ores and concentrates	2,318.6	1,294.0	1,123.1
Molybdenum ores and concentrates (excl. roasted)	984.1	1,079.4	275.9
Mineral fuels and lubricants	2,409.6	2,860.5	2,068.3
Petroleum, petroleum products and related materials	2,407.5	2,850.6	1,923.5
Basic manufactures	5,386.5	5,760.7	3,723.6
Non-ferrous metals	4,633.4	4,813.0	2,952.1
Copper	2,947.1	3,127.1	2,192.2
Miscellaneous manufactured articles	1,804.6	2,071.2	1,512.6
Total (incl. others)	27,800.1	31,288.2	26,738.3

Source: UN, *International Trade Statistics Yearbook*.

PRINCIPAL TRADING PARTNERS
(US $ million)

Imports c.i.f.	2007	2008	2009
Argentina	791.7	1,582.0	875.1
Brazil	1,236.2	2,417.8	1,682.9
Canada	284.6	436.1	410.4
Chile	149.6	1,183.4	997.3
China, People's Republic	467.1	4,069.5	3,268.8
Colombia	2,807.8	1,283.0	950.0
Ecuador	14.4	1,776.0	1,022.1
France (incl. Monaco)	101.3	266.8	205.9
Germany	558.5	857.4	715.4
India	672.1	504.1	311.0

Imports c.i.f.—continued	2007	2008	2009
Italy	1,494.0	731.1	392.8
Japan	547.6	1,277.0	930.2
Korea, Republic	685.7	780.0	667.9
Mexico	43.3	1,163.5	735.3
Nigeria	0.0	73.3	435.8
Spain	1,172.0	422.0	313.5
United Kingdom	126.5	174.8	143.8
USA	6,746.4	5,647.5	4,339.3
Venezuela	0.0	333.0	256.8
Total (incl. others)	20,464.2	29,952.8	21,869.7

Exports f.o.b.	2007	2008	2009
Belgium	558.3	411.8	381.9
Bolivia	223.9	350.9	321.8
Brazil	934.6	895.4	508.1
Canada	1,834.2	1,949.9	2,310.9
Chile	1,694.3	1,840.8	752.2
China, People's Republic	3,034.7	3,735.0	4,078.0
Colombia	616.6	708.7	643.8
Ecuador	379.1	504.1	576.5
Germany	928.5	1,028.0	1,042.4
Italy	817.3	927.2	607.5
Japan	2,181.6	1,860.0	1,376.5
Korea, Republic	887.9	552.0	749.6
Mexico	269.9	298.7	242.5
Netherlands	630.8	788.3	466.0
Panama	397.2	296.1	91.4
Spain	982.5	1,023.9	736.5
Switzerland-Liechtenstein	2,335.3	3,410.3	3,954.3
United Kingdom	229.6	377.5	229.0
USA	5,383.4	5,835.3	4,603.8
Venezuela	765.3	1,079.5	614.2
Total (incl. others)	27,800.1	31,288.2	26,738.3

Source: UN, *International Trade Statistics Yearbook*.

Transport

RAILWAYS
(traffic)*

	2003	2004	2005
Passenger-km (million)	103	119	126
Freight ton-km (million)	1,117	1,147	1,115

* Including service traffic.

Source: UN, *Statistical Yearbook*.

ROAD TRAFFIC
(motor vehicles in use)

	2002	2003	2004
Passenger cars	781,751	812,978	824,613
Buses and coaches	44,576	44,486	43,919
Lorries and vans	425,679	415,206	418,884
Motorcycles	231,148	248,395	268,125

2007 (motor vehicles in use): Passenger cars 917,110; Buses and coaches 44,401; Lorries and vans 480,876.

2008 (motor vehicles in use): Passenger cars 996,755; Buses and coaches 49,882; Lorries and vans 534,061.

Source: IRF, *World Road Statistics*.

SHIPPING

Merchant Fleet
(registered at 31 December)

	2007	2008	2009
Number of vessels	751	759	777
Total displacement ('000 grt)	272.5	285.1	356.1

Source: IHS Fairplay, *World Fleet Statistics*.

PERU

International Sea-borne Freight Traffic
('000 metric tons)

	2004*	2005*	2006
Goods loaded	6,600	6,800	6,329
Goods unloaded	10,100	8,900	9,490

* Approximate figures extrapolated from monthly averages.

Source: UN, *Monthly Bulletin of Statistics*.

CIVIL AVIATION
(traffic on scheduled services)

	2007	2008	2009
Kilometres flown (million)	60	83	88
Passenger-km (million)	6,472	8,720	8,765
Total ton-km (million)	236	222	107

Source: UN Economic Commission for Latin America and the Caribbean, *Statistical Yearbook*.

Tourism

ARRIVALS BY NATIONALITY

	2006	2007	2008
Argentina	69,256	82,722	97,478
Bolivia	85,365	87,399	86,619
Brazil	45,265	53,558	64,573
Canada	41,443	43,992	51,975
Chile	420,801	470,443	452,705
Colombia	54,505	62,825	76,559
Ecuador	112,100	119,471	128,063
France	54,311	59,781	63,920
Germany	43,760	50,445	52,173
Italy	33,872	34,622	39,825
Japan	36,827	39,864	46,059
Mexico	29,820	31,639	30,589
Spain	75,976	72,180	84,906
United Kingdom	60,277	67,067	66,455
USA	330,845	381,828	420,608
Total (incl. others)	1,720,746	1,916,400	2,057,620

Tourism receipts (US $ million, incl. passenger transport): 1,782 in 2006; 2,222 in 2007; 2,396 in 2008.

Source: World Tourism Organization.

Communications Media

	2007	2008	2009
Telephones ('000 main lines in use)	2,673.4	2,878.2	2,965.3
Mobile cellular telephones ('000 subscribers)	15,417.2	20,951.8	24,700.4
Internet users ('000)	7,000.0	8,815.4	9,157.8
Broadband subscribers ('000)	570.2	725.6	809.6

* Estimate.

Television receivers ('000 in use): 3,800 in 2000.
Radio receivers ('000 in use): 6,650 in 1997.
Book production (titles): 612 in 1996.
Daily newspapers: 73 in 2004.
Personal computers: 2,800,000 (100.6 per 1,000 persons) in 2005.

Sources: UNESCO, *Statistical Yearbook*; International Telecommunication Union.

Education

(2008 unless otherwise indicated, incl. adult education)

	Institutions	Teachers	Pupils
Nursery	19,055	52,448	971,715
Primary	35,893	191,738	3,803,453
Secondary	11,378	162,861	2,504,299
Higher: universities*	78	33,177	435,637
Higher: other tertiary	1,054	25,347	343,321
Special	429	3,351	20,472
Vocational	2,078	13,271	286,677

* Figures for 2000.

Source: Ministerio de Educación del Perú.

Pupil-teacher ratio (primary education, UNESCO estimate): 20.9 in 2007/08 (Source: UNESCO Institute for Statistics).

Adult literacy rate (UNESCO estimates): 89.6% (males 94.9%; females 84.6%) in 2007 (Source: UNESCO Institute for Statistics).

Directory

The Government

HEAD OF STATE

President: ALAN GABRIEL LUDWIG GARCÍA PÉREZ (took office 28 July 2006).
First Vice-President: LUIS ALEJANDRO GIAMPIETRI ROJAS.
Second Vice-President: LOURDES MENDOZA DEL SOLAR.

COUNCIL OF MINISTERS
(May 2011)

The Government was formed by the PAP, UPP, PNP and several independent members.

President of the Council of Ministers and Minister of Justice: ROSARIO FERNÁNDEZ FIGUEROA.
Minister of Foreign Affairs: JOSÉ ANTONIO GARCÍA BELAÚNDE.
Minister of Defence: JAIME THORNE LEÓN.
Minister of the Interior: Gen. MIGUEL HIDALGO MEDINA.
Minister of Education: VICTOR RAÚL DÍAZ.
Minister of Economy and Finance: ISMAEL BENAVIDES FERREYROS.
Minister of Labour and Employment: MANUELA ESPERANZA GARCÍA COCHAGNE.
Minister of International Trade and Tourism: EDUARDO FERREYROS KÜPPERS.
Minister of Transport and Communications: ENRIQUE JAVIER CORNEJO RAMÍREZ.
Minister of Housing, Construction and Sanitation: JUAN SARMIENTO SOTO.
Minister of Health: OSCAR UGARTE UBILLÚS.
Minister of Agriculture: JORGE ELISBAN VILLASANTE ARANÍBAR.
Minister of Energy and Mines: PEDRO SÁNCHEZ GAMARRA.
Minister of Production: LUIS NAVA GUIBERT.
Minister of Culture: JUAN OSSIO ACUÑA.
Minister of Women and Social Development: DORA BORRA TOLEDO.
Minister of the Environment: ANTONIO BRACK EGG.

MINISTRIES

Office of the President of the Council of Ministers: Jirón Carabaya, cuadra 1 s/n, Anexo 1105-1107, Lima; tel. (1) 7168600; fax (1) 4449168; e-mail atencionciudadana@pcm.gob.pe; internet www.pcm.gob.pe.

Ministry of Agriculture: Avda La Universidad 200, La Molina, Lima; tel. (1) 6135800; e-mail postmaster@minag.gob.pe; internet www.minag.gob.pe.

PERU

Directory

Ministry of Defence: Edif. Quiñones, Avda de la Peruanidad s/n, Jesús María, Lima 1; tel. (1) 6255959; e-mail webmaster@mindef.gob.pe; internet www.mindef.gob.pe.

Ministry of Economy and Finance: Jirón Junín 319, 4°, Circado de Lima, Lima 1; tel. (1) 3115930; e-mail postmaster@mef.gob.pe; internet www.mef.gob.pe.

Ministry of Education: Biblioteca Nacional del Perú, Avda de la Poesía 160, San Borja, Lima 41; tel. (1) 6155800; fax (1) 4370471; e-mail webmaster@minedu.gob.pe; internet www.minedu.gob.pe.

Ministry of Energy and Mines: Avda Las Artes Sur 260, San Borja, Lima 41; tel. (1) 6188700; e-mail webmaster@minem.gob.pe; internet www.minem.gob.pe.

Ministry of the Environment: Avda Javier Prado Oeste 1440, San Isidro, Lima; tel. (1) 6116000; fax (1) 2255369; e-mail minam@minam.gob.pe; internet www.minam.gob.pe.

Ministry of Foreign Affairs: Jirón Lampa 535, Lima 1; tel. (1) 2042400; e-mail informes@rree.gob.pe; internet www.rree.gob.pe.

Ministry of Health: Avda Salaverry 801, Jesús María, Lima 11; tel. (1) 3156600; fax (1) 6271600; e-mail webmaster@minsa.gob.pe; internet www.minsa.gob.pe.

Ministry of Housing, Construction and Sanitation: Avda Paseo de la República 3361, San Isidro, Lima; tel. (1) 2117930; e-mail webmaster@vivienda.gob.pe; internet www.vivienda.gob.pe.

Ministry of the Interior: Plaza 30 de Agosto 150 s/n, Urb. Córpac, San Isidro, Lima 27; tel. (1) 5180000; fax (1) 2242405; e-mail ministro@mininter.gob.pe; internet www.mininter.gob.pe.

Ministry of International Trade and Tourism: Calle Uno Oeste 50, Urb. Córpac, San Isidro, Lima 27; tel. (1) 5136100; fax (1) 2243362; e-mail webmaster@mincetur.gob.pe; internet www.mincetur.gob.pe.

Ministry of Justice: Scipión Llona 350, Miraflores, Lima 18; tel. (1) 4404310; fax (1) 4223577; e-mail webmaster@minjus.gob.pe; internet www.minjus.gob.pe.

Ministry of Labour and Employment: Avda Salaverry 655, cuadra 8, Jesús María, Lima 11; tel. (1) 6306000; fax (1) 6306060; e-mail webmaster@mintra.gob.pe; internet www.mintra.gob.pe.

Ministry of the Presidency: Plaza de Armas s/n, Lima 1; tel. (1) 3113900; internet www.presidencia.gob.pe.

Ministry of Production: Calle Uno Oeste 60, Urb. Córpac, San Isidro, Lima 27; tel. (1) 6162222; e-mail portal@produce.gob.pe; internet www.produce.gob.pe.

Ministry of Transport and Communications: Avda Jirón Zorritos 1203, Lima 1; tel. (1) 6187800; e-mail atencionalciudadano@mtc.gob.pe; internet www.mtc.gob.pe.

Ministry of Women and Social Development: Jirón Camaná 616, Lima 1; tel. (1) 6261600; fax (1) 4261665; e-mail postmaster@mimdes.gob.pe; internet www.mimdes.gob.pe.

Regional Presidents
(April 2011)

Amazonas: José Arista Arbildo.
Ancash: César Joaquín Alvarez Aguilar.
Apurímac: Elías Segovia Ruiz.
Arequipa: Juan Manuel Guillén Benavides.
Ayacucho: Wilfredo Oscorima Núñez.
Cajamarca: Gregorio Santos Guerrero.
Callao: Félix Moreno Caballero.
Cusco: Jorge Acurio Tito.
Huancavelica: Maciste Díaz.
Huánuco: Luis Raúl Picón Quedo.
Ica: Alonso Alberto Navarro Cabanillas.
Junín: Vladimir Cerrón Rojas.
La Libertad: José Humberto Murgia Zannier.
Lambayeque: Humberto Acuña Peralta.
Lima (Provincias): Jesús Alvarado Gonzáles del Valle.
Loreto: Yván Enrique Vásquez Valera.
Madre de Dios: José Luis Aguirre Pastor.
Moquegua: Martín Vizcarra Cornejo.
Pasco: Klever Meléndez.
Piura: Javier Atkins.
Puno: Mauricio Rodríguez Rodríguez.
San Martín: César Villanueva Arévalo.
Tacna: Tito Chocano.
Tumbes: Gerardo Fidel Viñas Dioses.
Ucayali: Jorge Velásquez Portocarrero.

President and Legislature

PRESIDENT
Election, first round, 10 April 2011*

Candidate	Valid votes cast	% of votes
Lt-Col (retd) Ollanta Moisés Humala Tasso (Gana Perú)	4,643,064	31.70
Keiko Sofía Fujimori Higuchi (Fuerza 2011)	3,449,562	23.56
Pedro Pablo Kuczynski Godard (Alianza por el Gran Cambio)	2,711,332	18.51
Alejandro Toledo Manrique (Perú Posible)	2,289,540	15.63
Luis Castañeda Lossio (Solidaridad Nacional)	1,440,242	9.83
Others	113,423	0.78
Total valid votes†	**14,647163**	**100.00**

* As no candidate received at least 50% of the votes cast, a run-off election between the two leading candidates was scheduled to be held on 5 June 2011.
† In addition, there were 1,477,696 blank votes and 574,875 invalid votes cast.

CONGRESO
President: César Alejandro Zumaeta Flores.

General Election, 10 April 2011, preliminary results

Parties	Valid votes cast	% of valid votes
Gana Perú	3,153,276	25.43
Fuerza 2011	2,840,358	22.91
Perú Posible	1,837,671	14.82
Alianza por el Gran Cambio	1,779,373	14.35
Solidaridad Nacional	1,263,089	10.19
Partido Aprista Peruano	801,295	6.46
Cambio Radical	332,592	2.68
Asociación Nacional de Fonavistas de los Pueblos del Perú	164,740	1.33
Others	227,371	1.83
Total*	**12,399,765**	**100.00**

* Excluding blank votes and spoiled votes.

Election Commission

Oficina Nacional de Procesos Electorales (ONPE): Jirón Washington 1894, Lima 1; tel. (1) 4170630; e-mail informes@onpe.gob.pe; internet www.onpe.gob.pe; f. 1995; independent; Nat. Dir Dra Magdalena Chú Villanueva.

Political Organizations

The following parties were active at a national level in 2011.

Acción Popular (AP): Paseo Colón 218, Lima 1; tel. and fax (1) 3321965; e-mail webmaster@accionpopular.pe; internet www.accionpopular.pe; f. 1956; 1.2m. mems; liberal; contesting the 2011 elections as part of the Perú Posible alliance; Pres. Javier Alva Orlandini; Sec.-Gen. Yonhy Lescano Ancieta.

Agrupación Independiente Sí Cumple (Sí Cumple): Jirón Lampa 974, Lima; tel. (1) 5392235; f. 2003; supporters of fmr President Fujimori; barred from contesting 2011 elections; Sec.-Gen. Carlos Orellana Quintanilla.

Alianza para la Alternativa de la Humanidad (APHU): f. 2010; indigenous grouping; not yet officially registered by the Oficina Nacional de Procesos Electorales; Leader Alberto Pizango.

Alianza por el Gran Cambio: Avda Salaverry 2007, Lima; tel. (1) 4710985; e-mail contacto@ppk.pe; internet www.ppk.pe; f. 2010; right-wing coalition formed to contest the 2011 elections; Presidential candidate Pedro Pablo Kuczyinski; comprises the following parties:

Alianza para el Progreso: Avda de la Policía 643, entre Cuadra 8 y 9 de Gregorio Escobedo, Jesús María, Lima; tel. (1) 4613197; e-mail app@app-peru.org.pe; internet www.app-peru.org.pe; f. 2001; Founder and Pres. César Acuña Peralta; Sec.-Gen. Juan Pablo Horna Santa Cruz; Nat. Exec. Sec. Gloria Edelmira Montenegro Figueroa.

PERU

Partido Humanista Peruano (PHP): Canaval y Moreyra 680, San Isidro, Lima; tel. (1) 2241243; e-mail contactenos@partidohumanista.org.pe; internet www.partidohumanista.org.pe; Pres. YEHUDÉ SIMÓN MUNARO; Sec.-Gen. ELSA VEGA FERNANDEZ.

Partido Popular Cristiano (PPC): Avda Alfonso Ugarte 1484, Breña, Lima; tel. (1) 4238722; fax (1) 4238721; e-mail estflores@terra.com.pe; internet www.ppc.pe; f. 1967; 250,000 mems; Pres. LOURDES FLORES NANO; Sec.-Gen. RAÚL CASTRO STAGNARO.

Restauración Nacional: Avda Arequipa 3750, San Isidro, Lima; tel. (1) 3117546; internet www.restauracionnacional.org; f. 2005; evangelical Christian party; Pres. HUMBERTO LAY SUN; Sec.-Gen. JUAN DAVID PERRY CRUZ.

APRA: see entry for PAP.

Asociación Nacional de Fonavistas de los Pueblos del Perú (ANFPP): Jirón Caylloma 824, Of. 102, Lima; tel. (1) 4242913; internet www.fonavistas.com; Pres. ANDRES AVELINO ALCANTARA PAREDES; Vice-Pres. LUIS LUZURIAGA GARIBOTTO.

Cambio Radical: Calle Victor Hugo G 16, La Calera de la Merced, Lima; tel. (1) 1028676; e-mail cambioradical.peru@gmail.com; internet www.cambioradicalperu.com; f. 2004; Pres. JOSÉ BARBA CABALLERO.

Despertar Nacional: Avda Benavides 2470, Miraflores, Lima 18; tel. (1) 3583657; e-mail comunicaciones@despertarnacional.com; internet www.despertarnacional.com; f. 1999; Leader RICARDO NORIEGA SALAVERRY.

Fuerza 2011: Paseo Colón 422, Cercado de Lima, Lima; tel. 999383300 (mobile); e-mail contacto@fuerza2011.com; internet www.fuerza2011.com; Pres. KEIKO SOFIA FUJIMORI HIGUCHI; Sec.-Gen. CLEMENTE JAIME YOSHIYAMA TANAKA.

Fuerza Nacional: Jíron Martín Alonzo de Meza 221, Pueblo Libre, Lima; f. 1998 as Movimiento Amplio País Unido; name changed as above in 2001; Leader Dr ANTONIO KETÍN VIDAL HERRERA; Sec.-Gen. TEODORO WALDIR VIDAL HERRERA.

Justicia, Tecnologia, Ecologia: Avda Arenales 2085, Of. 1, 2°, Lince; tel. (1) 4728743; e-mail juste2011@hotmail.com; internet juste2011.org; Leader HUMBERTO PINAZO.

Partido Aprista Peruano (PAP): Avda Alfonso Ugarte 1012, Breña, Lima 5; tel. (1) 4250218; internet www.apra.org.pe; f. in Mexico 1924, in Peru 1930; legalized 1945; democratic left-wing party; although legally known as PAP, the party is commonly known as APRA; Pres. ALAN GABRIEL LUDWIG GARCÍA PÉREZ; Secs-Gen. CARLOS ARANA VIVAR, OMAR QUEZADA MARTÍNEZ; 700,000 mems.

Partido Descentralista Fuerza Social: Jíron Cápac Yupanqui 1076, Jesús María, Lima; tel. (1) 4717895; e-mail central@fuerzasocial.pe; internet www.fuerzasocial.org; f. 2007; Pres. VLADIMIRO HUAROC PORTOCARRERO; Sec.-Gen. GUSTAVO GUERRA-GARCÍA PICASSO.

Partido Nacionalista Peruano (PNP): Avda Arequipa 3410, Lima 27; tel. (1) 4223592; internet www.partidonacionalistaperuano.com; f. 2005; contesting the 2011 elections a part of the Gana Perú alliance; Pres. Lt-Col (retd) OLLANTA MOISÉS HUMALA TASSO.

Partido Político Adelante: Jirón Ricardo Palma 120, San Isidro, Lima; tel. (1) 2212563; e-mail 2004adelante@gmail.com; internet www.adelante.org.pe; f. 2004; Sec.-Gen. RAFAEL BELAUNDE AUBRY.

Perú Posible (PP): Avda Faustino Sánchez Carrión 601, Jesús María, Lima 11; tel. (1) 4602493; fax (1) 2612418; e-mail sgpp@mixmail.com; internet www.peruposible.org.pe; f. 1994; contesting the 2011 elections in alliance with Acción Popular and Somos Perú; Leader ALEJANDRO TOLEDO MANRIQUE; Sec.-Gen. JAVIER REÁTEGUI ROSSELLÓ.

Renovación Nacional: Avda Camino Real 1206, 2°, San Isidro, Lima; tel. (1) 5673798; f. 1992; contesting the 2011 elections in alliance with the Fuerza 2011 party (q.v.); Pres. RAFAEL REY; Sec.-Gen. WILDER RUÍZ SILVA.

Solidaridad Nacional (SN): Amador Merino Reyna 140, San Isidro, Lima 27; tel. (1) 4213348; e-mail fsandoval@psn.org.pe; internet www.psn.org.pe; f. 1999; centre-left; Pres. LUIS CASTAÑEDA LOSSIO; Sec.-Gen. MARCO ANTONIO PARRA SÁNCHEZ.

Somos Perú (SP): Mariscal Las Heras 393, Lince, Lima 14; tel. (1) 4714484; e-mail postmaster@somosperu.org.pe; internet www.somosperu.org.pe; f. 1998; contesting the 2011 elections as part of the Perú Posible alliance; Pres. FERNANDO ANDRADE CARMONA; Sec.-Gen. YURI VILELA SEMINARIO.

Unión por el Perú (UPP): Avda Cuba 543, Jesús María, Lima; tel. (1) 4271941; e-mail ivega@partidoupp.org; internet www.partidopoliticoupp.org; f. 1994; ind. movt; Pres. EDUARDO ESPINOZA RAMOS; Sec.-Gen. JOSÉ VEGA ANTONIO.

ARMED GROUPS

Movimiento Nacionalista Peruano (MNP) (Movimiento Etnocacerista): Pasaje Velarde 188, Of. 204, Lima; tel. (1) 4338781; e-mail movnacionalistaperuano@yahoo.es; internet mnp.tripod.com.pe; ultra-nationalist paramilitary group; Pres. Dr ISAAC HUMALA NÚÑEZ; Leader of paramilitary wing Maj. (retd) ANTAURO IGOR HUMALA TASSO (arrested Jan. 2005 following an armed uprising in Andahuaylas).

Sendero Luminoso (SL) (Shining Path): f. 1970; began armed struggle 1980; splinter group of PCP; active in the Apurímac-Ene and Upper Huallaga valleys; advocated the policies of Mao Zedong in the People's Republic of China; from the mid-2000s it became increasingly involved in the illegal drugs trade; founder Dr ABIMAEL GUZMÁN REYNOSO (alias 'Chairman Gonzalo'—arrested Sept. 1992); leaders VÍCTOR QUISPE PALOMINO (alias 'Comrade José'—commander of the Apurímac-Ene contingent), 'COMRADE ARTEMIO' (identified as Filomeno Cerrón Cardoso—commander of the Upper Huallaga contingent).

Diplomatic Representation

EMBASSIES IN PERU

Algeria: Miguel de Cervantes 504–510, San Isidro, Lima; tel. (1) 4217582; fax (1) 4217580; e-mail embarg@embajadadeargelia.com; Ambassador MUHAMMAD BENSABRI.

Argentina: Avda Arequipa 121, Cercado de Lima, Lima 1; tel. (1) 4339966; fax (1) 4330769; e-mail contacto@embajadaargentinaenperu.org; internet www.embajadaargentinaenperu.org; Ambassador DARÍO PEDRO ALESSANDRO.

Australia: Torre Real 3, Of. 1301, Avda Victor Andres Belaunde 147, Via Principal 155, San Isidro, Lima; tel. (1) 2054000; fax (1) 2054012; Ambassador JOHN M. L. WOODS.

Austria: Edif. de las Naciones, Avda República de Colombia 643, 5°, San Isidro, Lima 27; tel. (1) 4420503; fax (1) 4428851; e-mail lima-ob@bmeia.gv.at; Ambassador ANDREAS LIEBMANN MEIÁN.

Belgium: Avda Angamos Oeste 380, Miraflores, Lima 18; tel. (1) 2417566; fax (1) 2416379; e-mail lima@diplobel.fed.be; internet www.diplomatie.be/lima; Ambassador BEATRIX VAN HEMELDONCK.

Bolivia: Los Castaños 235, San Isidro, Lima 27; tel. (1) 4402095; fax (1) 4402298; e-mail embajada@boliviaenperu.com; Ambassador FRANZ SOLANO CHUQUIMIA.

Brazil: Avda José Pardo 850, Miraflores, Lima; tel. (1) 5120830; fax (1) 4452421; e-mail embajada@embajadabrasil.org.pe; internet www.embajadabrasil.org.pe; Ambassador JORGE D'ESCRAGNOLLE TAUNAY FILHO.

Canada: Calle Bolognesi 228, Miraflores, Casilla 18-1126, Lima; tel. (1) 3193200; fax (1) 4464912; e-mail lima@international.gc.ca; internet www.canadainternational.gc.ca/peru-perou; Ambassador RICHARD LECOQ.

Chile: Avda Javier Prado Oeste 790, San Isidro, Lima; tel. (1) 7102211; fax (1) 7102223; e-mail contacto@chileabroad.gov.cl; internet chileabroad.gov.cl/peru; Ambassador FAVIO VIO UGARTE.

China, People's Republic: Jirón José Granda 150, San Isidro, Apdo 375, Lima 27; tel. (1) 2220841; fax (1) 4429467; e-mail chinaemb_pe@mfa.gov.cn; internet www.embajadachina.org.pe; Ambassador ZHAO WUYI.

Colombia: Avda J. Basadre 1580, San Isidro, Lima 27; tel. (1) 4410954; fax (1) 4419806; e-mail elima@cancilleria.gov.co; internet www.embajadaenperu.gov.co; Ambassador JORGE VISBAL MARTELO.

Costa Rica: Baltazar La Torre 828, San Isidro, Lima; tel. (1) 2642999; fax (1) 2642799; e-mail embcr.peru@gmail.com; Ambassador SARA FAIGENZICHT WEISLEDER.

Cuba: Coronel Portillo 110, San Isidro, Lima; tel. (1) 5123400; fax (1) 2644525; e-mail embacuba@pe.embacuba.cu; internet embacu.cubaminrex.cu/peru; Ambassador LUIS DELFÍN PÉREZ OSORIO.

Czech Republic: Baltazar La Torre 398, San Isidro, Lima 27; tel. (1) 2643374; fax (1) 2641708; e-mail lima@embassy.mzv.cz; internet www.mfa.cz/lima; Ambassador VLADIMIR EISENBRUK.

Dominican Republic: Calle Tudela y Varela 360, San Isidro, Lima 27; tel. (1) 4219765; fax (1) 4219763; e-mail embdomperu@speedy.com.pe; internet www.embajadadominicanaperu.org; Ambassador RAFAEL JULIÁN CEDANO.

Ecuador: Las Palmeras 356 y Javier Prado Oeste, San Isidro, Lima 27; tel. (1) 2124171; fax (1) 4220711; e-mail embajada@mecuadorperu.org.pe; internet www.mecuadorperu.org.pe; Ambassador DIEGO RIBADENEIRA ESPINOSA.

Egypt: Avda Jorge Basadre 1470, San Isidro, Lima 27; tel. (1) 4222531; fax (1) 4402369; e-mail egipto@sspeedy.com.pe; Ambassador HISHAM MUHAMMAD ABAS KHALIL.

PERU

Directory

El Salvador: Avda Javier Prado 2108, San Isidro, Lima 27; tel. (1) 4403500; fax (1) 2212561; e-mail embajadasv@terra.com.pe; Ambassador Raúl Soto-Ramírez.

Finland: Edif. Real Tres, Of. 502, 5°, Avda Víctor Andrés Belaúnde 147, San Isidro, Lima; tel. (1) 2224466; fax (1) 2224463; e-mail sanomat.lim@formin.fi; internet www.finlandia.org.pe; Ambassador Pekka Orpana.

France: Avda Arequipa 3415, Lima 27; tel. (1) 2158400; fax (1) 2158410; e-mail france.consulat@ambafrance-pe.org; internet www.ambafrance-pe.org; Ambassador Cécile Mouton-Brady de Pozzo di Borgo.

Germany: Avda Arequipa 4202–4210, Miraflores, Lima 18; tel. (1) 2125016; fax (1) 4226475; e-mail info@lima.diplo.de; internet www.lima.diplo.de; Ambassador Christoph Müller.

Greece: Avda Principal 190, Urb. Santa Catalina, La Victoria, Lima 13; tel. (1) 4761548; fax (1) 2232486; e-mail gremb.lim@mfa.gr; internet www.mfa.gr/lima; Ambassador Ionnis Papadopoulos.

Guatemala: Inca Ripac 309, Jesús María, Lima 11; tel. (1) 4602078; fax (1) 4635885; e-mail embperu@minex.gob.gt; Ambassador Gabriel Aguilera Peralta.

Holy See: Avda Salaverry, 6a cuadra, Lima 11 (Apostolic Nunciature); tel. (1) 7174897; fax (1) 7174896; e-mail nunciaturaperu@inbox.com; Apostolic Nuncio Most Rev. Bruno Musarò (Titular Archbishop of Abari).

Honduras: Calle Juan Dellepiani 231, 2°, San Isidro, Lima 27; tel. (1) 2644600; fax (1) 2640008; e-mail info@embhonpe.org; internet www.embhonpe.org; Ambassador Juán José Cueva Membreño.

India: Avda Salaverry 3006, San Isidro, Lima 27; tel. (1) 4602289; fax (1) 4610374; e-mail hoc@indembassy.org.pe; internet www.indembassy.org.pe; Ambassador Appunni Ramesh.

Indonesia: Avda Las Flores 334-336, San Isidro, Lima; tel. (1) 2220308; fax (1) 2222684; e-mail kbrilima@indonesia-peru.org.pe; internet www.indonesia-peru.org.pe; Ambassador Yosef Berty Fernandez.

Israel: Edif. El Pacifico, 6°, Plaza Washington, Natalio Sánchez 125, Santa Beatriz, Lima; tel. (1) 4180500; fax (1) 4180555; e-mail info@lima.mfa.gov.il; internet lima.mfa.gov.il; Ambassador Yoav Bar-on.

Italy: Avda Giuseppe Garibaldi 298, Apdo 0490, Lima 11; tel. (1) 4632727; fax (1) 4635317; e-mail ambasciata.lima@esteri.it; internet www.amblima.esteri.it; Ambassador Francesco Rausi.

Japan: Avda San Felipe 356, Apdo 3708, Jesús María, Lima 11; tel. (1) 2181130; fax (1) 4630302; e-mail cultjapon@embajadajapon.org.pe; internet www.pe.emb-japan.go.jp; Ambassador Shuichiro Megata.

Korea, Democratic People's Republic: Los Nogales 227, San Isidro, Lima; tel. (1) 4411120; fax (1) 4409877; e-mail embcorea@hotmail.com; Ambassador Ri Mun Gyu.

Korea, Republic: Avda Principal 190, 7°, Urb. Santa Catalina, La Victoria, Lima; tel. (1) 4760815; fax (1) 4760950; e-mail peru@mofat.go.kr; internet per.mofat.go.kr; Ambassador Park Hee-Kwon.

Malaysia: Avda Daniel Hernández 350, San Isidro, Lima 27; tel. (1) 4220297; fax (1) 2210786; e-mail mallima@kln.gov.my; internet www.kln.gov.my/perwakilan/lima; Ambassador Ahmad Izlam Bin Idris.

Mexico: Avda Jorge Basadre 710, esq. Los Ficus, San Isidro, Lima; tel. (1) 6121600; fax (1) 6121627; e-mail info@mexico.org.pe; internet www.mexico.org.pe; Ambassador Manuel Rodríguez Arriaga.

Morocco: Calle Tomás Edison 205, San Isidro, Lima; tel. (1) 4403117; fax (1) 4404391; e-mail sifa@embajadamarrueoslima.com; internet www.embajadamarrueoslima.com; Ambassador Oumama Aouad.

Netherlands: Torre Parque Mar, 13°, Avda José Larco 1301, Miraflores, Lima; tel. (1) 2139800; fax (1) 2139805; e-mail info@nlgovlim.com; internet www.nlgovlim.com; Ambassador Arjan Hamburger.

Nicaragua: Avda Alvarez Calderón 738, San Isidro, Lima 27; tel. (1) 4223892; fax (1) 4223895; e-mail embanic@telefonica.net.pe; Ambassador Tomás Wigberto Borge Martínez.

Panama: Avda Trinidad Morán 1426, Lince, Lima; tel. (1) 4228084; fax (1) 4227871; e-mail secretaria@panaembaperu.com.pe; internet www.panaembaperu.com.pe; Ambassador Carlos Luis Linares Brin.

Paraguay: Alcanfores 1286, Miraflores, Lima; tel. (1) 4474762; fax (1) 4442391; e-mail embaparpe@infonegocio.net.pe; Ambassador Modesto Luis Guiggiari Zavala.

Poland: Avda Salaverry 1978, Jesús María, Lima 11; tel. (1) 4713920; fax (1) 4714813; e-mail lima.amb.sekretariat@msz.gov.pl; internet www.lima.polemb.net; Ambassador Jarosław Spyra.

Portugal: Calle Antequera 777, 3°, San Isidro, POB 3692, Lima 100; tel. (1) 4409905; fax (1) 4215979; e-mail limaportugal@hotmail.com; Ambassador Nuno Bessa Lópes.

Romania: Avda Jorge Basadre 690, San Isidro, Lima; tel. (1) 4224587; fax (1) 4210609; e-mail ambrom@terra.com.pe; Ambassador Ştefan Costin.

Russia: Avda Salaverry 3424, San Isidro, Lima 27; tel. (1) 2640036; fax (1) 2640130; e-mail embrusa@infonegocio.net.pe; internet www.embajada-rusa.org; Ambassador Mikhail G. Troyanskii.

Serbia: Carlos Porras Osores 360, Apdo 18-0392, San Isidro, Lima 27; Apdo 0392, Lima 18; tel. (1) 4212423; fax (1) 4212427; e-mail serbiaembperu@rcp.com.pe; Ambassador Goran Mesić.

South Africa: Edif. Real Tres, Avda Víctor Andres Belaúnde 147, Of. 801, Lima 27; tel. (1) 6124848; fax 4223881; e-mail general.peru@dirco.gov.za; Ambassador Albert Leslie Manley.

Spain: Jorge Basadre 498, San Isidro, Lima 27; tel. (1) 2125155; fax (1) 4402020; e-mail embesppe@correo.mae.es; Ambassador Franciso Javier Sandomingo Núñez.

Switzerland: Avda Salaverry 3240, San Isidro, Lima 27; tel. (1) 2640305; fax (1) 2641319; e-mail lim.vertretung@eda.admin.ch; internet www.eda.admin.ch/lima; Ambassador Anne-Pascale Krauer Müller.

Thailand: Avda Los Incas 255-275, San Isidro, Lima 27; tel. (1) 2216442; fax (1) 4229895; e-mail thailim@mfa.go.th; Ambassador Udomphol Ninnad.

Ukraine: José Dellepiani 470, San Isidro, Lima; tel. (1) 2642884; fax (1) 2642892; e-mail emb_pe@mfa.gov.ua; internet www.mfa.gov.ua/peru; Chargé d'affaires a.i. Victor Kharaminskyi.

United Kingdom: Torre Parque Mar, 22°, Avda José Larco 1301, Miraflores, Lima; tel. (1) 6173000; fax (1) 6173100; e-mail belima@fco.gov.uk; internet www.ukinperu.fco.gov.uk; Ambassador James Dauris.

USA: Avda La Encalada 17, Surco, Lima 33; tel. (1) 6182000; fax (1) 6182397; internet lima.usembassy.gov; Ambassador Rose M. Likins.

Uruguay: José D. Anchorena 84, San Isidro, Lima 27; tel. (1) 7192550; fax (1) 7192865; e-mail uruinca@americatelnet.com.pe; Ambassador Juan José Arteaga Sáenz de Zumarán.

Venezuela: Avda Arequipa 298, Lima; tel. (1) 4334511; fax (1) 4331191; e-mail consulve@millicom.com.pe; Ambassador Arístides Medina (recalled in April 2009).

Judicial System

The Supreme Court consists of a President and 17 members. There are also Higher Courts and Courts of First Instance in provincial capitals. A comprehensive restructuring of the judiciary was implemented during the late 1990s.

SUPREME COURT

Corte Suprema
Palacio de Justicia, 2°, Avda Paseo de la República, Lima 1; tel. (1) 4284457; fax (1) 4269437; internet www.pj.gob.pe.
President: Dr César San Martín Castro.
Attorney-General: José Antonio Peláez Bardales.

Religion

CHRISTIANITY

The Roman Catholic Church

For ecclesiastical purposes, Peru comprises seven archdioceses, 19 dioceses, 10 territorial prelatures and eight Apostolic Vicariates. According to the latest census (2007), some 81% of the population are Roman Catholics.

Bishops' Conference
Conferencia Episcopal Peruana, Jirón Estados Unidos 838, Apdo 310, Lima 100; tel. (1) 4631010; fax (1) 4636125; e-mail sgc@iglesiacatolica.org.pe; internet www.iglesia.org.pe.
f. 1981; Pres. Héctor Miguel Cabrejos Vidarte (Archbishop of Trujillo).

Archbishop of Arequipa: Javier Augusto Del Rio Alba, Arzobispado, Moral San Francisco 118, Apdo 149, Arequipa; tel. (54) 234094; fax (54) 242721; e-mail arzobispadoaqp@planet.com.pe.

Archbishop of Ayacucho or Huamanga: Luis Abilio Sebastiani Aguirre, Arzobispado, Jirón 28 de Julio 148, Apdo 30, Ayacucho; tel. and fax (64) 812367; e-mail arzaya@mail.udep.edu.pe.

Archbishop of Cusco: Juan Antonio Ugarte Pérez, Arzobispado, Herrajes, Hatun Rumiyoc s/n, Apdo 148, Cusco; tel. (84) 225211; fax (84) 222781; e-mail arzobisp@terra.com.pe.

PERU

Archbishop of Huancayo: PEDRO RICARDO BARRETO JIMENO, Arzobispado, Jirón Puno 430, Apdo 245, Huancayo; tel. (64) 234952; fax (64) 239189; e-mail arzohyo@hotmail.com.

Archbishop of Lima: Cardinal JUAN LUIS CIPRIANI THORNE, Arzobispado, Jirón Carabaya, Plaza Mayor, Apdo 1512, Lima 100; tel. (1) 4275980; fax (1) 4271967; e-mail arzolim@terra.com.pe; internet www.arzobispadodelima.org.

Archbishop of Piura: JOSÉ ANTONIO EGUREN ANSELMI, Arzobispado, Libertad 1105, Apdo 197, Piura; tel. and fax (74) 327561; e-mail ocordova@upiura.edu.pe.

Archbishop of Trujillo: HÉCTOR MIGUEL CABREJOS VIDARTE, Arzobispado, Jirón Mariscal de Orbegozo 451, Apdo 42, Trujillo; tel. (44) 256812; fax (44) 231473; e-mail arztrujillo@terra.com.pe.

The Anglican Communion

The Iglesia Anglicana del Cono Sur de América (Anglican Church of the Southern Cone of America), formally inaugurated in April 1983, comprises seven dioceses, including Peru. The Presiding Bishop of the Church is the Bishop of Northern Argentina.

Bishop of Peru: Rt Rev. HAROLD WILLIAM GODFREY, Apdo 18-1032, Miraflores, Lima 18; tel. and fax (1) 4229160; e-mail diocesisperu@anglicanperu.org; internet www.peru.anglican.org.

The Methodist Church

There are an estimated 4,200 adherents of the Iglesia Metodista del Perú.

President: Rev. JORGE BRAZO CABALLERO, Baylones 186, Lima 5; Apdo 1386, Lima 100; tel. (1) 4245970; fax (1) 4318995; e-mail iglesiamp@computextos.com.pe; internet www.iglesiametodista.org.pe.

Other Protestant Churches

Among the most popular are the Iglesia Evangélica del Perú (accounting for some 12% of the population at the 2007 census), the Asamblea de Dios, the Iglesia del Nazareno, the Alianza Cristiana y Misionera and the Iglesia de Dios del Perú.

BAHÁ'Í FAITH

National Spiritual Assembly of the Bahá'ís of Peru: Horacio Urteaga 827, Jesús María, Apdo 11-0209, Lima 11; tel. (1) 4316077; fax (1) 4333005; e-mail bahai@pol.com.pe; mems resident in 220 localities.

The Press

DAILIES

Lima

El Bocón: Jirón Jorge Salazar Araoz 171, Urb. Santa Catalina, Apdo 152, Lima 1; tel. (1) 6908090; fax (1) 6908127; internet www.elbocon.com.pe; f. 1994; football; Editorial Dir JORGE ESTÉVES ALFARO; circ. 90,000.

El Comercio: Empresa Editora 'El Comercio', SA, Jirón Antonio Miró Quesada 300, Lima; tel. (1) 3116310; fax (1) 4260810; e-mail editorweb@comercio.com.pe; internet www.elcomercioperu.com.pe; f. 1839; morning; Editor JUAN CARLOS LUJÁN; Dir-Gen. FRANCISCO MIRÓ QUESADA G.; circ. 150,000 weekdays, 220,000 Sundays.

Expreso: Jirón Antonio Elizalde 753, Lima; tel. (1) 6124000; fax (1) 6124024; e-mail luis.garciamiro@expreso.com.pe; internet www.expreso.com.pe; f. 1961; morning; conservative; Dir LUIS GARCÍA MIRÓ; circ. 100,000.

Extra: Jirón Libertad 117, Miraflores, Lima; tel. (1) 4447088; fax (1) 4447117; e-mail extra@expreso.com.pe; f. 1964; evening edition of Expreso; Dir CARLOS SÁNCHEZ; circ. 80,000.

Gestión: Miró Quesada 247, 8°, Lima 1; tel. (1) 3116370; fax (1) 3116500; e-mail gestion2@diariogestion.com.pe; internet www.gestion.pe; f. 1990; Gen. Editor JULIO LIRA; Gen. Man. ERNESTO CORTES ROJAS; circ. 131,200.

Ojo: Jirón Jorge Salazar Araoz 171, Urb. Santa Catalina, Apdo 152, Lima; tel. (1) 4709696; fax (1) 4761605; internet www.ojo.com.pe; f. 1968; morning; Editorial Dir AGUSTÍN FIGUEROA BENZA; circ. 100,000.

Perú 21: Jirón Miró Quesada 247, 6°, Lima; tel. (1) 3116500; fax (1) 3116391; e-mail director@peru21.com; internet www.peru21.com; independent; Editors CLAUDIA IZAGUIRRE, MANUEL TUMI.

El Peruano (Diario Oficial): Avda Alfonso Ugarte 873, Lima 1; tel. (1) 3150400; fax (1) 4245023; e-mail gbarraza@editoraperu.com.pe; internet www.elperuano.com.pe; f. 1825; morning; official State Gazette; Dir DELFINA BECERRA GONZÁLEZ; circ. 27,000.

La República: Jirón Camaná 320, Lima 1; tel. (1) 7116000; fax (1) 2511029; e-mail otxoa@larepublica.com.pe; internet www.larepublica.pe; f. 1982; left-wing; Dir GUSTAVO MOHME SEMINARIO; circ. 50,000.

Arequipa

Arequipa al Día: Santa Marta 103, Arequipa; tel. (54) 215515; fax (54) 217810; internet www.ucsm.edu.pe/arequipa; f. 1991; Dir CARLOS MENESES CORNEJO; Editor-in-Chief ENRIQUE ZAVALA CONCHA.

Correo de Arequipa: Calle Bolívar 204, Arequipa; tel. (54) 235150; e-mail diariocorreo@epensa.com.pe; internet www.correoperu.com.pe; Dir ALDO MARIÁTEGUI; circ. 70,000.

El Pueblo: Sucre 213, Arequipa; tel. and fax (54) 205086; internet www.elpueblo.com.pe; f. 1905; morning; independent; Pres. DANIEL MACEDO GUTIÉRREZ; Dir CARLOS MENESES CORNEJO; circ. 70,000.

Chiclayo

La Industria: Tacna 610, Chiclayo; tel. (74) 237952; fax (74) 227678; f. 1952; Dir JULIO ALBERTO ORTIZ CERRO; circ. 20,000.

Cusco

El Diario del Cusco: Centro Comercial Ollanta, Avda El Sol 346, Cusco; tel. (84) 229898; fax (84) 229822; e-mail buzon@diariodelcusco.com; internet www.diariodelcusco.com; morning; independent; Exec. Pres. WASHINTON ALOSILLA PORTILLO; Gen. Man. JOSÉ FERNANDEZ NÚÑEZ.

Huacho

El Imparcial: Avda Grau 203, Huacho; tel. (34) 2392187; fax (34) 2321352; e-mail elimparcial1891@hotmail.com; f. 1891; evening; Dir ADÁN MANRIQUE ROMERO; circ. 5,000.

Huancayo

Correo de Huancayo: Jirón Cusco 337, Huancayo; tel. (64) 235792; fax (64) 233811; evening; Editorial Dir RODOLFO OROSCO.

La Opinión Popular: Huancayo; tel. (64) 231149; f. 1922; Dir MIGUEL BERNABÉ SUÁREZ OSORIO.

Ica

La Opinión: Avda Los Maestros 801, Apdo 186, Ica; tel. (56) 235571; f. 1922; evening; independent; Dir GONZALO TUEROS RAMÍREZ.

La Voz de Ica: Castrovirreyna 193, Ica; tel. and fax (56) 232112; e-mail lavozdeica1918@infonegocio.net.pe; f. 1918; Dir ATILIO NIERI BOGGIANO; Man. MARIELLA NIERI DE MACEDO; circ. 4,500.

Pacasmayo

Diario Ultimas Noticias: 2 de Mayo 33, Pacasmayo; tel. and fax (44) 523022; e-mail escribanos@ultimasnoticiasdiario.com; internet www.ultimasnoticiasdiario.com; f. 1973; morning; independent; Editor MARÍA DEL CARMEN BALLENA RAZURI; circ. 3,000.

Piura

Correo: Zona Industrial Manzana 246, Lote 6, Piura; tel. (74) 321681; fax (74) 324881; Editorial Dir ROLANDO RODRICH ARANGO; circ. 12,000.

El Tiempo: Ayacucho 751, Piura; tel. (74) 325141; fax (74) 327478; e-mail lmhelguero@eltiempo.com.pe; internet www.eltiempo.com.pe; f. 1916; morning; independent; Dir LUZ MARÍA HELGUERO; circ. 18,000.

Tacna

Correo: Jirón Hipólito Unanue 636, Tacna; tel. (54) 711671; fax (54) 713955; Editorial Dir RUBÉN COLLAZOS ROMERO; circ. 8,000.

Trujillo

La Industria: Gamarra 443, Trujillo; tel. (44) 295757; fax (44) 427761; e-mail phidalgo@laindustria.com; internet www.laindustria.com; f. 1895; morning; independent; Dir ERNESTO BARREDA ARIAS; circ. 8,000.

PERIODICALS

Business: Avda La Molina 1110, Of. 203, La Molina, Lima 12; tel. (1) 2500596; fax (1) 2500597; e-mail correo@businessperu.com.pe; internet www.businessperu.com.pe; f. 1994; monthly; Dir DANIEL VALERA LOZA.

Caretas: Jirón Huallaya 122, Portal de Botoneros, Plaza de Armas, Lima 1; Apdo 737, Lima 100; tel. (1) 4289490; fax (1) 4262524; e-mail info@caretas.com.pe; internet www.caretas.com.pe; weekly; current affairs; Dir MARCO ZILERI DOUGALL; circ. 90,000.

PERU

Cosas: Calle Recaveren 111, Miraflores, Lima 18; tel. (1) 2023000; fax (1) 4473776; internet www.cosasperu.com; weekly; society; Editor ELIZABETH DULANTO.

Debate Agrario: Avda Salaverry 818, Lima 11; tel. (1) 4336610; fax (1) 4331744; e-mail fegurenl@cepes.org.pe; f. 1987 by Centro Peruano de Estudios Sociales; every 4 months; rural issues; Dir FERNANDO EGUREN L.

Gente Peru: Calle Las Margaritas, San Eugenio, Lince, Lima 14; tel. (1) 2217997; fax (1) 4413646; internet www.genteinternacional.com; f. 1958; weekly; circ. 25,000; Dir HÉCTOR ESCARDÓ.

Industria Peruana: Los Laureles 365, San Isidro, Apdo 632, Lima 27; tel. (1) 6164444; fax (1) 6164412; e-mail industriaperuana@sni.org.pe; internet www.sni.org.pe/servicios/publicaciones; monthly publication of the Sociedad Nacional de Industrias; Dir BORIS ROMERO OJEDA.

Orbita: Parque Rochdale 129, Lima; tel. (1) 4610676; weekly; f. 1970; Dir LUZ CHÁVEZ MENDOZA.

Perú Económico: Apdo 671, Lima 100; tel. (1) 2425656; fax (1) 4455946; internet www.apoyopublicaciones.com/perueconomico; f. 1978; monthly.

The Peruvian Times: Paseo de la República 291, Of. 702, Lima 1; tel. (1) 4676609; e-mail egriffis@peruviantimes.com; internet www.peruviantimes.com; f. 1940, successor to West Coast Leader (f. 1912); refounded 2007 as an online publ; general news, analysis and features; English; daily; Editor RICK VECCHIO.

QueHacer: León de la Fuente 110, Lima 17; tel. (1) 6138300; fax (1) 6138308; e-mail qh@desco.org.pe; internet www.desco.org.pe/quehacer; f. 1979; 6 a year; supported by Desco research and devt agency; Editor-in-Chief MARTÍN PAREDES; Dir ABELARDO SÁNCHEZ-LEÓN; circ. 5,000.

Revista Agraria: Avda Salaverry 818, Lima 11; tel. (1) 4336610; fax (1) 4331744; internet www.cepes.org.pe/revista/agraria.htm; f. 1987 by Centro Peruano de Estudios Sociales; monthly review of rural problems; Dir FERNANDO EGUREN; circ. 100,000.

Semana Económica: Juan de la Fuente 625, Miraflores, Lima 18; tel. (1) 2130600; fax (1) 4445240; e-mail se@apoyopublicaciones.com; internet www.semanaeconomica.com; f. 1985; weekly; Exec. Dir GONZALO ZEGARRA MULANOVICH.

NEWS AGENCY

Andina—Agencia de Noticias Peruana: Jirón Quilca 556, Lima; tel. (1) 3306341; fax (1) 4312849; e-mail bbecerra@editoraperu.com.pe; internet www.andina.com.pe; f. 1981; state-owned; Pres. MARÍA DEL PILAR TELLO LEYVA; Dir of Media DELFINA BECERRA GONZÁLEZ.

PRESS ASSOCIATIONS

Asociación Nacional de Periodistas del Perú: Jirón Huancavélica 320, Apdo 2079, Lima 1; tel. (1) 4270687; fax (1) 4278493; internet www.anp.org.pe; f. 1928; 8,800 mems; Pres. ROBERTO MARCOS MEJÍA ALARCÓN.

Federación de Periodistas del Perú (FPP): Avda Abancay 173, 3°, Lima; tel. (1) 4261806; e-mail fpp@omco.org; internet www.omco.org/fpp; f. 1950; Pres. JESÚS GERMÁN LLANOS CASTILLO.

Publishers

Asociación Editorial Bruño: Avda Arica 751, Breña, Lima 5; tel. (1) 4237890; fax (1) 4240424; e-mail federico@brunoeditorial.com.pe; internet www.brunoeditorial.com.pe; f. 1950; educational; Man. FEDERICO DÍAZ TINEO.

Biblioteca Nacional del Perú: Avda de la Poesia 160, San Borja, Lima 41; tel. (1) 5136900; fax (1) 5137060; e-mail contactobnp@bnp.gob.pe; internet www.bnp.gob.pe; f. 1821; general non-fiction, directories; Dir RAMÓN ELÍAS MUJICA PINILLA.

Borrador Editores: Avda Fray Luis de León 39, San Borja; tel. (1) 2710192; e-mail borradoreditores@gmail.com; internet www.borradoreditores.blogspot.com; Man. PEDRO VILLA GAMARRA.

Ediciones del Hipocampo: Avda Alfredo Franco 195, Urb. Chama, Lima 33; tel. (1) 3586783; e-mail editor@hipocampo.com.pe; internet www.hipocampo.com.pe; f. 2000; travel literature; Gen. Man. JOSÉ MIGUEL HELFER ARGUEDAS.

Ediciones PEISA: Avda 2 de Mayo 1285, San Isidro, Lima; tel. and fax (1) 2215988; e-mail peisa@terra.com.pe; internet www.peisa.com.pe; f. 1968; fiction and scholarly; Dir GERMÁN CORONADO.

Ediciones SM: Calle Micaela Bastidas 125, San Isidro, Lima; tel. (1) 6148900; fax (1) 6148914; e-mail contacto@ediciones-sm.com.pe; internet www.ediciones-sm.com.pe; textbooks, education, children's literature; Gen. Man. SIMÓN BERNILLA CARRILLO.

Edigraber Editora Gráfica: Avda Tacna 685, 5°, Of. 54, Lima; tel. and fax (1) 4287073; e-mail info@edigraberperu.com; internet www.edigraberperu.com; Gen. Man. SIMÓN BERNILLA CARRILLO.

Editora Normas Legales, SA: Angamos Oeste 526, Miraflores, Lima; tel. and fax (1) 4861410; e-mail ventas@normaslegales.com; internet www.normaslegales.com; law textbooks; Man. JAVIER SANTA MARÍA SILVE.

Editorial Arkabas: Jirón Miraflores 291, Barranco, Lima; tel. (1) 6525350; internet www.arkabas.com; Gen. Man. DANIEL ZÚÑIGA-RIVERA.

Editorial Casatomada: Avda Mariátegui 1600, Of. 803, Jesús María, Lima; tel. (1) 6245992; e-mail ecasatomada@gmail.com; internet www.editorialcasatomada.com; f. 2005; fiction, folklore; Dir GABRIEL RIMACHI SIALER.

Editorial Cuzco, SA: Calle 5 Marzo, Jirón Lote 3, Urb. Las Magnolias, Surco, Lima; tel. (1) 4453261; e-mail ccuzco@camaralima.org.pe; law; Man. SERGIO BAZÁN CHACÓN.

Editorial Horizonte: Avda Nicolás de Piérola 995, Lima 1; tel. (1) 4279364; fax (1) 4274341; e-mail damonte@terra.com.pe; f. 1968; social sciences, literature, politics; Man. HUMBERTO DAMONTE.

Editorial Milla Batres, SA: Lima; f. 1963; history, literature, art, archaeology, linguistics and encyclopaedias on Peru; Dir-Gen. CARLOS MILLA BATRES.

Editorial Océano Peruana, SA: Ricardo Angulo 795, 5°, Urb. Corpac, San Isidro, Lima; tel. (1) 2230800; fax (1) 4219773; e-mail ocelibros@oceano.com.pe; general interest and reference; Gen. Man. JORGE A. DAVELOUIS SARTORI.

Editorial Salesiana: Avda Brasil 218, Apdo 0071, Lima 5; tel. (1) 4235225; internet www.libreriasalesiana.com; f. 1918; religious and general textbooks; Man. Dir Dr FRANCESCO VACARELLO.

Editorial San Marcos: Jirón Dávalos Lissón 135, Lima; tel. (1) 3311535; fax (1) 3302405; e-mail informes@editorialsanmarcos.com; internet www.editorialsanmarcos.com; educational, academic, legal; Gen. Man. ANÍBAL JESÚS PAREDES GALVÁN.

Editorial Santillana: Avda Primavera 2160, Santiago de Surco, Lima; tel. (1) 3134000; fax (1) 3134001; e-mail santillana@santillana.com.pe; internet www.gruposantillana.com.pe; literature, scholarly and reference; Man. ANA CECILIA HALLO.

Grijley: Jirón Lampa 1221, Lima; tel. (1) 4273147; e-mail info@grijley.com; internet www.grijley.com; law.

Grupo Editorial Mesa Redonda: Pasaje José Payán 141, Miraflores, Lima; tel. (1) 2212957; e-mail editoramesaredonda@gmail.com; internet www.editorialmesaredonda.com; f. 2003; literature, humanities; imprints incl. Mesa Redonda and Calcomanía; Dir JUAN MIGUEL MARTHANS.

Palestra Editores: Jirón Ica 435, Of. 201, Lima 1; tel. (1) 4261363; fax (1) 4271025; e-mail palestra@palestraeditores.com; internet www.palestraeditores.com; law; Gen. Man. PEDRO GRANDEZ CASTRO.

Pontificia Universidad Católica del Perú, Fondo Editorial: Avda Universitaria 1801, San Miguel, Lima 32; tel. (1) 6262650; fax (1) 6262913; e-mail feditor@pucp.edu.pe; internet www.pucp.edu.pe; Dir-Gen. ANA PATRICIA ARÉVALO MAJLUF.

Sociedad Bíblica Peruana, AC: Avda Petit Thouars 991, Apdo 14-0295, Lima 100; tel. (1) 4336608; fax (1) 4336389; internet www.casadelabiblia.org; f. 1821; Christian literature and bibles; Gen. Sec. PEDRO ARANA-QUIROZ.

Universidad Nacional Mayor de San Marcos: Of. General de Editorial, Avda República de Chile 295, 5°, Of. 508, Lima; tel. (1) 4319689; internet www.unmsm.edu.pe; f. 1850; textbooks, education; Man. Dir JORGE CAMPOS REY DE CASTRO.

PUBLISHING ASSOCIATIONS

Alianza Peruana de Editores (ALPE): Lima; tel. (1) 2759081; e-mail alianzaeditores@gmail.com; internet alpe.wordpress.com; f. 2007; independent publrs' asscn; Pres. GERMÁN CORONADO.

Cámara Peruana del Libro: Avda Cuba 427, esq. Jesús María, Apdo 10253, Lima 11; tel. (1) 4729516; fax (1) 2650735; e-mail cp-libro@amauta.rep.net.pe; internet www.cpl.org.pe; f. 1946; 102 mems; Pres. CARLOS A. BENVIDES AGUIJE; Exec. Dir LOYDA MORÁN BUSTAMANTE.

Vida y Espiritualidad: Avda Brasil 3029, Lima 17; tel. (1) 4637644; fax (1) 4617153; e-mail pvalera@vidayespiritualidad.org; internet vidayespiritualidad.org; Dir KLAUS BERCKHOLTZ BENAVIDES.

PERU

Broadcasting and Communications

TELECOMMUNICATIONS

Regulatory Authorities

Dirección General de Regulación y Asuntos Internacionales de Telecomunicaciones: Avda Jirón Zorritos 1203, Lima 1; tel. (1) 6157800; Dir-Gen. PATRICIA CARREÑO FERRÉ.

Instituto Nacional de Investigación y Capacitación de Telecomunicaciones (INICTEL): Avda San Luis 1771, esq. Bailetti, San Borja, Lima 41; tel. (1) 6261400; fax (1) 6261402; e-mail informes@inictel-uni.edu.pe; internet www.inictel-uni.edu.pe; Pres. MANUEL ADRIANZEN.

Organismo Supervisor de Inversión Privada en Telecomunicaciones (OSIPTEL): Calle de la Prosa 136, San Borja, Lima 41; tel. (1) 2251313; fax (1) 4751816; e-mail sid@osiptel.gob.pe; internet www.osiptel.gob.pe; f. 1993; established by the Peruvian Telecommunications Act to oversee competition and tariffs, to monitor the quality of services and to settle disputes in the sector; Pres. Dr GUILLERMO THORNBERRY VILLARÁN.

Major Service Providers

Claro Perú: Lima; internet www.claro.com.pe; f. 2005; owned by América Móvil, SA de SV (Mexico); mobile cellular telecommunications services; Gen. Dir HUMBERTO CHÁVEZ.

Telefónica MoviStar: Juan de Arona 786, San Isidro, Lima; tel. (1) 9817000; internet www.telefonicamoviles.com.pe; f. 1994; 98% bought by Telefónica Móviles, SA (Spain) in 2000; mobile telephone services; 1.8m. customers.

Telefónica del Perú, SA: Avda Arequipa 1155, Santa Beatriz, Lima 1; tel. (1) 2101013; fax (1) 4705950; e-mail mgarcia@tp.com.pe; internet www.telefonica.com.pe; Pres. ANTONIO CARLOS VALENTE.

Telmex: Torre Parque Mar, Avda Larco 1301, Miraflores, Lima; tel. (1) 6105555; internet www.telmex.com/pe.

BROADCASTING

Regulatory Authorities

Asociación de Radio y Televisión del Perú (AR&TV): Avda Roma 140, San Isidro, Lima 27; tel. (1) 4703734; Pres. HUMBERTO MALDONADO BALBÍN; Exec. Dir DANIEL LINARES BAZÁN.

Coordinadora Nacional de Radio: Avda Javier Prado Oeste 109, Magdalena del Mar; tel. (1) 2616257; fax (1) 4715808; e-mail prensa@cnr.org.pe; internet www.cnr.org.pe; f. 1978; Pres. HUGO RAMÍREZ HUAMÁN; Exec. Dir JORGE ACEVEDO ROJAS.

Instituto Nacional de Comunicación Social: Jirón de la Unión 264, Lima; Dir HERNÁN VALDIZÁN.

Unión de Radioemisoras de Provincias del Perú (UNRAP): Mariano Carranza 754, Santa Beatriz, Lima 1.

State Corporation

Instituto Nacional de Radio y Televisión Peruana (IRTP): Avda Paseo de la República 1110, Lima 1; tel. (1) 6190707; fax (1) 6190723; e-mail comercial@irtp.com.pe; internet www.irtp.com.pe; f. 1996; Exec. Pres. ALFONSO SALCEDO RUBIO; runs the following stations:

Radio Nacional del Perú: Avda Paseo de la Republica 1110, Santa Beatriz, Lima 1; tel. (1) 4331404; fax (1) 4338952; internet www.radionacional.com.pe; state broadcaster; Man. FELIPE TOMÁS GRANADOS VÁSQUEZ.

Televisión Nacional del Perú (TV Perú): Lima; tel. (1) 6190707; internet www.tnp.gob.pe; f. 1958 as Radio y Televisión Peruana; state broadcaster; 22 stations; Commercial Man. RODOLFO RUSCA LEVANO.

Radio

Radio Agricultura del Perú, SA—La Peruanísima: Casilla 625, Lima 11; tel. (1) 4246677; e-mail radioagriculturadelperu@yahoo.com; internet www.laperuanisima.com; f. 1963; Gen. Man. LUZ ISABEL DEXTRE NÚÑEZ.

Radio América: Montero Rosas 1099, Santa Beatriz, Lima 1; tel. (1) 2653841; fax (1) 2653844; f. 1943; Dir-Gen. KAREN CROUSILLAT.

Cadena Peruana de Noticias: Gral Salaverry 156, Miraflores, Lima; tel. (1) 4461554; fax (1) 4457770; e-mail webmastercpn@gestion.com.pe; internet www.cpnradio.pe; f. 1996; Pres. MANUEL ROMERO CARO; Gen. Man. OSCAR ROMERO CARO.

Radio Cutivalú, La Voz del Desierto: Jirón Ignacio de Loyola 300, Urb. Miraflores, Castilla, Piura; tel. (73) 343370; e-mail cutivalu630am@hotmail.com; internet www.radiocutivalu.org; f. 1986; Pres. FRANCISCO MUGUIRO IBARRA; Dir RODOLFO AQUINO RUIZ.

Directory

Emisoras Cruz del Perú: Jirón Victorino Laynes 1402, Urb. Elio, Lima 1; tel. (1) 3190240; fax (1) 3190244; e-mail info@emisorascruz.com.pe; internet www.emisorascruz.com.pe; Pres. FERNANDO CRUZ MENDOZA; Gen. Man. MARCO CRUZ MENDOZA.

Emisoras Nacionales: León Velarde 1140, Lince, Lima 1; tel. (1) 4714948; fax (1) 4728182; Gen. Man. CÉSAR COLOMA R.

Radio Inca del Perú: Pastor Dávila 197, Lima; tel. (1) 2512596; fax (1) 2513324; f. 1951; Gen. Man. ABRAHAM ZAVALA CHOCANO.

Radio Panamericana: Paseo Parodi 340, San Isidro, Lima 27; tel. (1) 4226787; fax (1) 4221182; internet www.radiopanamericana.com; f. 1953; Dir RAQUEL DELGADO DE ALCÁNTARA.

Radio Programas del Perú (GRUPORPP): Avda Paseo de la República 3866, San Isidro, Lima; tel. (1) 2150200; fax (1) 2150269; internet www.rpp.com.pe; Pres. HUGO DELGADO NACHTIGAL; Gen. Man. MANUEL DELGADO PARKER.

Radio Santa Rosa: Jirón Camaná 170, Apdo 206, Lima; tel. (1) 4277488; fax (1) 4269219; f. 1958; Dir P. JUAN SOKOLICH ALVARADO.

Sonograbaciones Maldonado: Mariano Carranza 754, Santa Beatriz, Lima; tel. (1) 4715163; fax (1) 4727491; Pres. HUMBERTO MALDONADO B.; Gen. Man. LUIS HUMBERTO MALDONADO.

Television

América Televisión, Canal 4: Jirón Montero Rosas 1099, Santa Beatriz, Lima; tel. (1) 4194000; fax (1) 2656979; e-mail web@americatv.com.pe; internet www.americatv.com.pe; CEO and Gen. Man. ERIC JURGENSEN.

ATV, Canal 9: Avda Arequipa 3570, San Isidro, Lima 27; tel. (1) 2118800; fax (1) 4427636; e-mail webmaster@atv.com.pe; internet www.tuteve.tv; f. 1983; Gen. Man. MARCELLO CÚNEO LOBIANO.

Frecuencia Latina, Canal 2: Avda San Felipe 968, Jesús María, Lima; tel. (1) 2191000; fax (1) 2656660; internet www.frecuencialatina.com.pe; Pres. BARUCH IVCHER.

Global Televisión, Canal 13: Gen. Orbegoso 140, Breña, Lima; tel. (1) 3303040; fax (1) 4238202; f. 1989; Pres. GENARO DELGADO PARKER; Gen. Man. RAFAEL LEGUÍA.

Nor Peruana de Radiodifusión, SA: Avda Arequipa 3520, San Isidro, Lima 27; tel. (1) 403365; fax (1) 419844; f. 1991; Dir FRANCO PALERMO IBARGUENGOITIA; Gen. Man. FELIPE BERNINZÓN VALLARINO.

Panamericana Televisión SA, Canal 5: Avda Alejandro Tirado 217, Santa Beatriz, Lima; tel. (1) 4113201; fax (1) 4703001; internet www.24horas.com.pe; Pres. RAFAEL RAVETTINO FLORES; Gen. Man. FEDERICO ANCHORENA VÁSQUEZ.

Cía Peruana de Radiodifusión, Canal 4 TV: Mariano Carranza y Montero Rosas 1099, Santa Beatriz, Lima; tel. (1) 4728985; fax (1) 4710099; f. 1958; Dir JOSÉ FRANCISCO CROUSILLAT CARREÑO.

RBC Televisión, Canal 11: Avda Manco Cápac 333, La Victoria, Lima; tel. (1) 6132929; fax (1) 4331237; internet www.rbctelevision.com; f. 1966; Pres. FERNANDO GONZÁLEZ DEL CAMPO; Gen. Man. JUAN SÁENZ MARÓN.

Cía de Radiodifusión Arequipa SA, Canal 9: Centro Comercial Cayma, R2, Arequipa; tel. (54) 252525; fax (54) 254959; f. 1986; Dir ENRIQUE MENDOZA NÚÑEZ; Gen. Man. ENRIQUE MENDOZA DEL SOLAR.

Uranio, Canal 15: Avda Arequipa 3570, 6°, San Isidro, Lima; e-mail agamarra@atv.com.pe; Gen. Man. ADELA GAMARRA VÁSQUEZ.

Finance

In April 1991 a new banking law was introduced, relaxing state control of the financial sector and reopening the sector to foreign banks (which had been excluded from the sector by a nationalization law promulgated in 1987).

BANKING

(cap. = capital; res = reserves; dep. = deposits; m. = million; brs = branches; amounts in new soles unless otherwise indicated)

Superintendencia de Banca y Seguros: Los Laureles 214, San Isidro, Lima 27; tel. (1) 2218990; fax (1) 4417760; e-mail mostos@sbs.gob.pe; internet www.sbs.gob.pe; f. 1931; Supt FELIPE TAM FOX; Sec.-Gen. NORMA SOLARI PRECIADO.

Central Bank

Banco Central de Reserva del Perú: Jirón Antonio Miró Quesada 441-445, Lima 1; tel. (1) 4267041; fax (1) 4273091; e-mail webmaster@bcrp.gob.pe; internet www.bcrp.gob.pe; f. 1922; refounded 1931; cap. 295.7m., res 110.3m., dep. 39,030.5m. (Dec. 2006); Chair. JULIO VELARDE FLORES; Gen. Man. RENZO ROSSINI MIÑÁN; 7 brs.

Other Government Banks

Banco de la Nación: Avda República de Panamá 3664, San Isidro, Lima 1; tel. (1) 5192164; fax (1) 5192217; e-mail dep_ccorporativa@bn.com.pe; internet www.bn.com.pe; f. 1966; cap. 866.5m., res 336.4m., dep. 10,928.0m. (Dec. 2006); conducts all commercial banking operations of official govt agencies; Exec. Pres. HUMBERTO ORLANDO MENESES ARANCIBIA; Gen. Man. JULIO DEL CASTILLO VARGAS; 391 brs.

Corporación Financiera de Desarrollo (COFIDE): Augusto Tamayo 160, San Isidro, Lima 27; tel. (1) 6154000; fax (1) 4423374; e-mail postmaster@cofide.com.pe; internet www.cofide.com.pe; f. 1971; also owners of Banco Latino; Pres. AURELIO LORET DE MOLA BÖHME; Gen. Man. MARCO CASTILLO TORRES; 11 brs.

Commercial Banks

Banco de Comercio: Avda Paseo de la República 3705, San Isidro, Lima; tel. (1) 5136000; fax (1) 4405458; e-mail postmaster@bancomercio.com.pe; internet www.bancomercio.com; f. 1967; fmrly Banco Peruano de Comercio y Construcción; cap. 54.6m., res 0.3m., dep. 548.8m. (Dec. 2005); Chair. WILFREDO JESÚS LAFOSSE QUINTANA; Gen. Man. CARLOS ALBERTO MUJICA CASTRO; 23 brs.

Banco de Crédito del Perú: Calle Centenario 156, Urb. Las Laderas de Melgarejo, Apdo 12-067, Lima 12; tel. (1) 3132000; internet www.viabcp.com; f. 1889; cap. 1,286.5m., res 1,037.9m., dep. 37,071.7m., total assets 43,713.7m. (Dec. 2007); Pres. and Chair. DIONISIO ROMERO SEMINARIO; Gen. Man. WALTER BAYLY; 217 brs.

Banco Interamericano de Finanzas, SA: Avda Rivera Navarrete 600, San Isidro, Lima 27; tel. (1) 6133000; fax (1) 2212489; e-mail gchang@bif.com.pe; internet www.bif.com.pe; f. 1991; cap. 156.3m., res 11.7m., dep. 2,813.1m. (Dec. 2007); Pres. FRANCISCO ROCHE; Gen. Man. and CEO JUAN IGNACIO DE LA VEGA; 37 brs.

BBVA Banco Continental: Avda República de Panamá 3055, San Isidro, Lima 27; tel. (1) 2111000; fax (1) 2111788; internet www.bbvabancocontinental.com; f. 1951; merged with BBVA of Spain in 1995; 92.01% owned by Holding Continental, SA; cap. 852.9m., res 369.6m., dep. 16,445.2m. (Dec. 2006); Pres. and Chair. PEDRO BRESCIA CAFFERATA; Gen. Man. JOSÉ ANTONIO COLOMER GUIU; 190 brs.

INTERBANK (Banco Internacional del Perú): Carlos Villarán 140, Urb. Santa Catalina, Lima 13; tel. (1) 2192347; fax (1) 2192336; e-mail krubin@intercorp.com.pe; internet www.interbank.com.pe; f. 1897; commercial bank; cap. 478.6m., res 117.6m., dep. 8,691.7m. (Dec. 2007); Chair. and Pres. CARLOS RODRÍGUEZ-PASTOR; Gen. Man. JORGE FLORES ESPINOZA; 90 brs.

Scotiabank Perú, SAA: Avda Dionisio Derteano 102, San Isidro, Apdo 1235, Lima; tel. (1) 2116060; fax (1) 4407945; e-mail scotiaenlinea@scotiabank.com.pe; internet www.scotiabank.com.pe; f. 2006 by merger of Banco Sudamericano (owned by Scotiabank, Canada) and Banco Wiese Sudameris; cap. 502.6m., res 1,353.6m., dep. 10,671.7m. (Dec. 2006); Chair. JIM MEEK; Vice-Pres. and CEO CARLOS GONZÁLEZ-TABOADA.

Banking Association

Asociación de Bancos del Perú: Calle 41, No 975, Urb. Córpac, San Isidro, Lima 27; tel. (1) 6123333; fax (1) 6123316; e-mail estudioseconomicos@asbanc.com.pe; internet www.asbanc.com.pe; f. 1929; refounded 1967; Pres. OSCAR JOSÉ RIVERA; Gen. Man. ENRIQUE ARROYO RIZO PATRÓN.

STOCK EXCHANGE

Bolsa de Valores de Lima: Pasaje Acuña 106, Lima 100; tel. (1) 6193333; fax (1) 4267650; internet www.bvl.com.pe; f. 1860; Pres. ROBERTO HOYLE.

Regulatory Authority

Comisión Nacional Supervisora de Empresas y Valores (CONASEV): Santa Cruz 315, Miraflores, Lima; tel. (1) 6106300; fax (1) 6106325; e-mail cendoc@conasev.gob.pe; internet www.conasev.gob.pe; f. 1968; regulates the securities and commodities markets; responsible to Ministry of Economy and Finance; Pres. NAHIL LILIANA HIRSH CARRILLO.

INSURANCE

ACE Seguros, SA: Avda Paseo de la República 3587, 10°, San Isidro, Lima; tel. (1) 4428228; fax (1) 422717; Chair. and CEO EVAN G. GREENBERG.

Interseguro Compañía de Seguros, SA: Avda Pardo y Aliaga 640, 2°, San Isidro, Lima; tel. (1) 6114712; fax (1) 6114725; e-mail juan.vallejo@interseguro.com.pe; internet www.interseguro.com.pe; f. 1998; life and non-life, annuities; owned by Intergroup Financial Services (IFS); Chair. FELIPE MORRIS GUERINONI; CEO JUAN CARLOS VALLEJO BLANCO.

Invita Seguros de Vida, SA: Torre Wiese, Canaval y Moreyra 532, San Isidro, Lima; tel. (1) 2222222; fax (1) 2211683; e-mail dcosta@invita.com.pe; internet www.invita.com.pe; f. 2000; life; fmrly Wiese Aetna, SA; Pres. CARIDAD DE LA PUENTE WIESE; Gen. Man. JAVIER FREYRE TRIVELLI.

Mapfre Perú Cía de Seguros: Avda 28 de Julio 873, Miraflores, Apdo 323, Lima 100; tel. (1) 2137373; fax (1) 2433131; e-mail fmarco@mapfreperu.com; internet www.mapfreperu.com; f. 1994; general; fmrly Seguros El Sol, SA; Pres. RENZO CALDA GIURATO.

Pacífico, Cía de Seguros y Reaseguros: Avda Juan de Arona 830, San Isidro, Lima 27; tel. (1) 5184000; fax (1) 5184295; e-mail arodrigo@pps.com.pe; internet www.pacificoseguros.com; f. 1943; general; Pres. DIONISIO ROMERO SEMINARIO; Gen. Man. DAVID SAETTONE WATMOUGH.

La Positiva Cía de Seguros y Reaseguros, SA: San Francisco 301, Arequipa; tel. (54) 214130; fax (54) 214939; e-mail jaimep@lapositiva.com.pe; internet www.lapositiva.com.pe; f. 1947; Pres. JUAN MANUEL PEÑA ROCA; Gen. Man. GUILLERMO ZARAK.

Rimac Internacional, Cía de Seguros: Las Begonias 475, 3°, San Isidro, Lima; tel. (1) 4218383; fax (1) 4210570; e-mail jortecho@rimac.com.pe; internet www.rimac.com.pe; f. 1896; acquired Seguros Fénix in 2004; Pres. Ing. PEDRO BRESCIA CAFFERATA; Gen. Man. PEDRO FLECHA ZALBA.

SECREX, Cía de Seguro de Crédito y Garantías: Avda Angamos Oeste 1234, Miraflores, Lima; Apdo 0511, Lima 18; tel. (1) 4424033; fax (1) 4423890; e-mail ciaseg@secrex.com.pe; internet www.secrex.com.pe; f. 1980; Pres. Dr RAÚL FERRERO COSTA; Gen. Man. JUAN A. GIANNONI MURGA.

Insurance Association

Asociación Peruana de Empresas de Seguros (APESEG): Arias Araguez 146, Miraflores, Lima 18; tel. (1) 4442294; fax (1) 4468538; e-mail rda@apeseg.org.pe; internet www.apeseg.org.pe; f. 1904; Pres. ALFREDO JOCHAMOWITZ STAFFORD; Gen. Man. RAÚL DE ANDREA DE LAS CARRERAS.

Trade and Industry

GOVERNMENT AGENCIES

Agencia de Promoción de la Inversión Privada (ProInversión): Avda Paseo de la República 3361, 9°, San Isidro, Lima 27; tel. (1) 6121200; fax (1) 2212941; e-mail contact@proinversion.gob.pe; internet www.proinversion.gob.pe; f. 2002 to promote economic investment; Exec. Dir JORGE LEÓN BALLÉN; Sec.-Gen. GUSTAVO VILLEGAS DEL SOLAR.

Empresa Nacional de la Coca, SA (ENACO): Avda Arequipa 4528, Miraflores, Lima; tel. (1) 4442292; fax (1) 4471667; e-mail jjara@enaco.com.pe; internet www.enaco.com.pe; f. 1949; agency with exclusive responsibility for the purchase and resale of legally produced coca and the promotion of its derivatives; Pres. JULIO BALTAZAR JARA LADRÓN DE GUEVARA; Gen. Man. RAÚL CAMPANA RAMOS.

Fondo Nacional de Cooperación para el Desarrollo Social (FONCODES): Avda Paseo de la República 3101, San Isidro, Lima; tel. (1) 4212102; fax (1) 4214128; e-mail jllacsahuache@foncodes.mimdes.gob.pe; internet www.foncodes.gob.pe; f. 1991; responsible for social devt and eradicating poverty; Exec. Dir JOSÉ EUDOCIO LLACSAHUACHE GARCÍA.

Instituto de Investigaciones de la Amazonía Peruana (IIAP): Avda Abelardo Quiñones Km 2.5, Apdo 784, Loreto; tel. (65) 265516; fax (65) 2265527; e-mail info@iiap.org.pe; internet www.iiap.org.pe; promotes sustainable devt of Amazon region; Pres. LUIS CAMPOS BACA.

Perúpetro, SA: Luis Aldana 320, San Borja, Lima; tel. (1) 6171800; fax (1) 6171801; e-mail mcobena@perupetro.com.pe; internet www.perupetro.com.pe; f. 1993; responsible for promoting investment in hydrocarbon exploration and exploitation; Chair. DANIEL SABA DE ANDREA; CEO ISABEL TAFUR MARÍN.

DEVELOPMENT ORGANIZATIONS

ACP Inversiones y Desarrollo: Avda Domingo Orue 165, 5°, Surquillo, Lima 34; tel. (1) 2220202; fax (1) 2224166; e-mail accion@accion.org.pe; f. 1969; fmrly Acción Comunitaria del Perú; promotes economic, social and cultural devt through improvements in service provision.

Asociación de Exportadores (ADEX): Avda Javier Prado Este 2875, San Borja, Lima 41; Apdo 1806, Lima 1; tel. (1) 6183333; fax (1) 6183355; e-mail prensa@adexperu.org.pe; internet www.adexperu.org.pe; f. 1973; exporters' asscn; Pres. JUAN MANUEL VARILIAS VELÁSQUEZ; Gen. Man. ALBERTO INFANTO ANGELES; 600 mems.

Asociación Kallpa para la Promoción Integral de la Salud y el Desarrollo: Pasaje Capri 140, Urb. Palomar Norte, La Victoria, Lima 13; tel. (1) 2243344; fax (1) 2429693; e-mail peru@kallpa.org.pe;

PERU

internet www.kallpa.org.pe; health devt for youths; Pres. ALEJANDRINA ZAMORA PARIONA.

Asociación Nacional de Centros de Investigación, Promoción Social y Desarrollo: Belisario Flores, Lince, Lima 14; tel. (1) 4728888; fax (1) 4728962; e-mail postmaster@anc.org.pe; internet www.anc.org.pe; umbrella grouping of devt orgs; Pres. FRANCISCO SOBERÓN GARRIDO; Exec. Sec. IRIS CASTRO ORDÓÑEZ.

Asociación para la Naturaleza y Desarrollo Sostenible (ANDES): Calle Ruinas 451, Casilla 567, Cusco; tel. (8) 4245021; fax (8) 4232603; e-mail andes@andes.org.pe; internet www.andes.org.pe; devt org. promoting the culture, education and environment of indigenous groups; Exec. Dir CÉSAR ARGUMEDO.

Sociedad Nacional de Industrias (SNI) (National Industrial Association): Los Laureles 365, San Isidro, Apdo 632, Lima 27; tel. (1) 6164444; fax (1) 6164433; e-mail sni@sni.org.pe; internet www.sni.org.pe; f. 1896; comprises permanent commissions covering various aspects of industry including labour, integration, fairs and exhibitions, industrial promotion; its Small Industry Cttee groups over 2,000 small enterprises; Pres. PEDRO OLAECHEA; Gen. Man. FEDERICO DE APARICI; 90 dirs (reps of firms); 2,500 mems; 60 sectorial cttees.

Centro de Desarrollo Industrial (CDI): Los Laureles 365, San Isidro, Lima; tel. (1) 2158888; fax (1) 2158877; e-mail cdi@sni.org.pe; internet www.cdi.org.pe; f. 1986; supports industrial devt and programmes to develop industrial cos; Exec. Dir LUIS TENORIO PUENTES.

CHAMBERS OF COMMERCE

Cámara de Comercio de Lima (Lima Chamber of Commerce): Avda Giuseppe Garibaldi 396, Jesús María, Lima 11; tel. (1) 4633434; fax (1) 2191674; e-mail secreceex@camaralima.org.pe; internet www.camaralima.org.pe; f. 1888; Pres. CARLOS DURAND CHAHUD; Gen. Man. JOSÉ ROSAS BERNEDO; 5,500 mems.

Cámara Nacional de Comercio, Producción y Servicios (PERUCAMARAS): Giuseppe Garibaldi 396, 6°, Jesús María, Lima 11; tel. (1) 2191580; fax (1) 2191586; e-mail cnadministracion@perucam.com; internet www.perucam.com; national asscn of chambers of commerce; Pres. GUILLERMO VEGA ALVEAR; Gen. Man. MÓNICA M. WATSON ARAMBURÚ.

There are also Chambers of Commerce in Arequipa, Cusco, Callao and many other cities.

EMPLOYERS' ORGANIZATIONS

Asociación Automotriz del Perú: Avda Dos de Mayo 299, Apdo 1248, San Isidro, Lima 27; tel. (1) 6403636; fax (1) 4428865; e-mail aap@aap.org.pe; internet www.aap.org.pe; f. 1926; asscn of importers of motor cars and accessories; 360 mems; Pres. ARMANDO NEGRI PIÉROLA; Gen. Man. ENRIQUE PRADO REY.

Asociación de Ganaderos del Perú (Agalep) (Association of Stock Farmers of Peru): Pumacahua 877, 3°, Jesús María, Lima; f. 1915; Gen. Man. HÉCTOR GUEVARA.

Confederación Nacional de Instituciones Empresariales Privadas (CONFIEP): Edif. Real Tres, Of. 401, Avda Victor Andrés Belaúnde 147, San Isidro, Lima; tel. (1) 4223311; e-mail postmaster@confiep.org.pe; internet www.confiep.org.pe; f. 1984; federation of 20 employers' orgs; Pres. RICARDO BRICEÑO VILLENA; Gen. Man. XIMENA ZAVALA LOMBARDI.

Consejo Nacional del Café: Lima; reps of govt and industrial coffee growers; Pres. ENRIQUE ALDAVE.

Sociedad Nacional de Minería y Petróleo: Francisco Graña 671, Magdalena del Mar, Lima 17; tel. (1) 2159250; fax (1) 4601616; e-mail postmaster@snmpe.org.pe; internet www.snmpe.org.pe; f. 1940; asscn of cos involved in mining, petroleum and energy; Pres. HANS FLURY ROYLE; Gen. Man. CATERINA PODESTÁ MEVIUS.

Sociedad Nacional de Pesquería (SNP): Avda Javier Prado Oeste 2442, San Isidro, Lima 27; tel. (1) 2612970; fax (1) 2617912; e-mail snpnet@terra.com.pe; internet www.snp.org.pe; f. 1952; private sector fishing interests; Pres. RAÚL ALBERTO SÁNCHEZ SOTOMAYOR; Gen. Man. RICHARD INURRITEGUI BAZÁN.

STATE HYDROCARBONS COMPANY

Petroperú (Petróleos del Perú, SA): Avda Enrique Canaval Moreyra 150, Lima 27; tel. (1) 2117800; fax (1) 6145000; internet www.petroperu.com; f. 1969; state-owned petroleum-refining co; Pres. LUIS REBOLLEDO SOBERÓN; Gen. Man. MIGUEL CELI RIVERA.

UTILITIES

Regulatory Authority

Gerencia Adjunta de Regulación Tarifaria (GART): Avda Canadá 1470, San Borja, Lima 41; tel. (1) 2240487; fax (1) 2240491; internet www2.osinerg.gob.pe/gart.htm; autonomous agency controlling tariffs.

Electricity

Distriluz: Edif. Torre el Pilar, 13°, Avda Camino Real 348, San Isidro, Lima 27; tel. (1) 2115500; e-mail central@distriluz.com.pe; internet www.distriluz.com.pe; operates 4 energy distribution cos: Enosa, Ensa, Hidrandina and Electrocentro; Dir GENARO VÉLEZ CASTRO; Gen. Man. MANUEL SUÁREZ MENDOZA.

Edegel (Empresa de Generación Eléctrica de Lima): Lima; e-mail comunicacion@edegel.com; internet www.edegel.com; privatized in 1995; generates electricity; Pres. BLANCO FERNÁNDEZ; Gen. Man. CARLOS ALBERTO LUNA CABRERA.

Electroperú: Prolongación Pedro Miotta 421, San Juan de Miraflores, Lima 29; tel. (1) 2170600; fax (1) 2170621; internet www.electroperu.com.pe; state-owned; Pres. LUIS ALEJANDRO BEDOYA WALLACE; Gen. Man. RAÚL TENGAN MATSUTAHARA.

EnerSur: Avda República de Panamá 3490, San Isidro, Lima 27; tel. (1) 6167979; fax (1) 6167878; e-mail contacto@enersur.com.pe; internet www.enersur.com.pe; f. 1996; part of Grupo GDF SUEZ; electricity generation and transmission; Gen. Man. PATRICK EECKELERS.

Sociedad Eléctrica del Sur-Oeste, SA (SEAL): Consuelo 310, Arequipa; tel. (54) 212946; fax (54) 213296; e-mail seal@seal.com.pe; internet www.seal.com.pe; f. 1905; Pres. MAURICIO CHIRINOS CHIRINOS; Gen. Man. JOSÉ OPORTO VARGAS.

Water

Autoridad Nacional del Agua: Calle Diecisiete 355, Urb. El Palomar, San Isidro, Lima; tel. (1) 2243298; fax (1) 2243298; e-mail comunicaciones@ana.gob.pe; internet www.ana.gob.pe; Dir FRANCISCO PALOMINO GARCÍA.

TRADE UNIONS

Central Unica de Trabajadores Peruanos (CUTP): Lima; f. 1992; Pres. JULIO CÉSAR BAZÁN; includes:

Confederación General de Trabajadores del Perú (CGTP): Plaza 2 de Mayo 4, Lima 1; tel. (1) 4242357; e-mail cgtp@cgtp.org.pe; internet www.cgtp.org.pe; f. 1968; Pres. CARMELA SIFUENTES INOSTROZA; Sec.-Gen. MARIO HUAMÁN RIVERA.

Confederación Intersectorial de Trabajadores Estatales (CITE) (Union of Public Sector Workers): Lima; tel. (1) 4245525; f. 1978; Sec.-Gen. ALAVARO COLE; Asst Sec. OMAR CAMPOS; 600,000 mems.

Confederación Nacional de Trabajadores (CNT): Avda Iquitos 1198, Lima; tel. (1) 4711385; affiliated to the PPC; c. 12,000 mems; Sec.-Gen. ANTONIO GALLARDO EGOAVIL.

Confederación de Trabajadores del Perú (CTP): Jirón Ayacucho 173, CP 3616, Lima 1; tel. (1) 4261310; e-mail ctp7319@hotmail.com; affiliated to PAP; Sec.-Gen. ELÍAS GRIJALVA ALVARADO.

Federación de Empleados Bancarios (FEB) (Union of Bank Employees): Jirón Miró Quesada 260, 7°, Lima; tel. (1) 7249570; e-mail febperu@terra.com.pe; Sec.-Gen. HÉCTOR PÉREZ PÉREZ.

Federación Nacional de Trabajadores Mineros, Metalúrgicos y Siderúrgicos (FNTMMS) (Federation of Peruvian Mineworkers): Jirón Callao 457, Of. 311, Lima; tel. (1) 4277554; Sec.-Gen. PEDRO ESCATE SULCA; 70,000 mems.

Movimiento de Trabajadores y Obreros de Clase (MTOC): Lima.

Sindicato de Estibadores: Callao; stevedores' union; Sec.-Gen. WILMER ESTÉVEZ.

Sindicato Unitario de los Trabajadores en la Educación del Perú (SUTEP) (Union of Peruvian Teachers): Camaná 550, Lima; tel. (1) 4276677; fax (1) 4268692; e-mail suteperu@yahoo.es; internet www.sutep.org.pe; f. 1972; Sec.-Gen. LUIS MUÑOZ.

Independent unions, representing an estimated 37% of trade unionists, include the Comité para la Coordinación Clasista y la Unificación Sindical, the Confederación de Campesinos Peruanos (CCP) and the Confederación Nacional Agraria (Pres. MIGUEL CLEMENTE ALEGRE).

Confederación Nacional de Comunidades Industriales (CONACI): Lima; co-ordinates worker participation in industrial management and profit-sharing.

The following agricultural organizations exist:

Confederación Nacional de Productores Agropecuarios de las Cuencas Cocaleras del Perú (CONPACCP): Lima; coca-growers' confederation; Sec.-Gen. NELSÓN PALOMINO.

Consejo Unitario Nacional Agrario (CUNA): f. 1983; represents 36 farmers' and peasants' orgs, including:

Confederación Campesina del Perú (CCP): radical left-wing; Pres. ANDRÉS LUNA VARGAS; Sec. HUGO BLANCO.

Organización Nacional Agraria (ONA): org. of dairy farmers and cattle breeders.

Transport

RAILWAYS

In 2010 there were some 2,020 km of track.

Ministry of Transport and Communications: see section on The Government (Ministries).

Consorcio Ferrocarriles del Perú: in July 1999, following the privatization of the state railway company, Empresa Nacional de Ferrocarriles (ENAFER), the above consortium won a 30-year concession to operate the following lines:

Empresa Minera del Centro del Perú SA—División Ferrocarriles (Centromín-Perú SA) (fmrly Cerro de Pasco Railway): Edif. Solgas, Avda Javier Prado Este 2175, San Borja, Apdo 2412, Lima 41; tel. (1) 4761010; fax (1) 4769757; acquired by Enafer-Perú in 1997; 212.2 km; Pres. HERNÁN BARRETO; Gen. Man. GUILLERMO GUANILO.

Ferrocarril Transandino, SA (Southern Railway): Avenida Tacna y Arica 200, Arequipa; tel. (54) 215350; fax (54) 231603; internet www.ferrocarriltransandino.com; 915 km open; operates Ferrocarril del Sur y Oriente; also operates steamship service on Lake Titicaca; Man. RÓMULO GUIDINO.

Ferrovías Central Andina, SA: Avda José Galvez Barrenechea 566, 5°, San Isidro, Lima; tel. (1) 2266363; e-mail ferroviasperu@fcca.com.pe; internet www.ferroviasperu.com.pe; f. 1999; operates Ferrocarril del Centro del Perú; Gen. Man. JAIME FERNANDO BLANCO RAVINA.

Tacna–Arica Ferrocarril (Tacna–Arica Railway): Avda Aldarracín 484, Tacna; 62 km open.

Ferrocarril Ilo–Toquepala–Cuajone: Apdo 2640, Lima; 219 km open, incl. five tunnels totalling 27 km; owned by the Southern Peru Copper Corpn for transporting copper supplies and concentrates only; CEO OSCAR GONZÁLEZ ROCHA; Gen. Dir, Operations MAURICIO PERÓ.

ROADS

There are 102,887 km of roads in Peru as estimated in 2007, of which approximately 23,838 km are highways and national roads. The most important highways are: the Pan-American Highway (3,008 km), which runs from the Ecuadorean border along the coast to Lima; Camino del Inca Highway (3,193 km) from Piura to Puno; Marginal de la Selva (1,688 km) from Cajamarca to Madre de Dios; and the Trans-Andean Highway (834 km), which runs from Lima to Pucallpa on the River Ucayali via Oroya, Cerro de Pasco and Tingo María. In 2010 plans were announced for the Linea Amarilla highway project in Lima, funded by the Inter-American Development Bank. The estimated total cost of the project was US $600m.

SHIPPING

Most trade is through the port of Callao, but there are 13 deep-water ports. There are river ports at Iquitos, Pucallpa and Yurimaguas, aimed at improving communications between Lima and Iquitos, and a further port is under construction at Puerto Maldonado.

Agencia Naviera Maynas, SA: Avda San Borja Norte 761, San Borja, Lima 41; tel. (1) 4752033; fax (1) 4759680; e-mail lima@navieramaynas.com.pe; internet www.peruvianamazonline.com.pe; f. 1970; owned by the Naviera Yacu Puma, SA; liner services to and from Amazon river ports and Gulf of Mexico; Pres. LUIS VARGAS V.; Gen. Man. ROBERTO MELGAR BARABINO.

Asociación Marítima del Perú: Avda Javier Prado Este 897, Of. 33, San Isidro, Apdo 3520, Lima 27; tel. and fax (1) 4221904; internet www.asmarpe.org.pe; f. 1957; asscn of 14 int. and Peruvian shipping cos; Pres. GUILLERMO ACOSTA RODRÍGUEZ.

Consorcio Naviero Peruano, SA: Avda República de Colombia 643, 7° y 8°, San Isidro, Lima 27; tel. (1) 4116500; fax (1) 4116599; e-mail cnp@cnpsa.com; internet www.cnpsa.com; f. 1959; Gen. Man. ALEJANDRO JOSÉ PEDRAZA MAC LEAN.

Empresa Nacional de Puertos, SA (Enapu): Avda Contralmirante Raygada 110, Callao; tel. (1) 4299210; fax (1) 4691010; e-mail enapu@inconet.net.pe; internet www.enapu.com.pe; f. 1970; govt agency administering all coastal and river ports; Pres. MARIO ARBULÚ MIRANDA; Gen. Man. JUAN ARRISUEÑO GOMEZ DE LA TORRE.

Naviera Humboldt, SA: Edif. Pacífico–Washington, 9°, Natalio Sánchez 125, Apdo 3639, Lima 1; tel. (1) 4334005; fax (1) 4330503; e-mail info@humboldt.com.pe; internet www.humboldt.com.pe; f. 1970; cargo services; Pres. AUGUSTO BEDOYA CAMERE; Gen. Man. ERNESTO FERRARO AMICO.

Naviera Universal, SA: Calle 41 No 894, Urb. Corpac, San Isidro, Apdo 10307, Lima 100; tel. (1) 4757020; fax (1) 4755233; Chair. HERBERT C. BUERGER.

Petrolera Transoceánica, SA (PETRANSO): Víctor Maútua 135, San Isidro, Lima 27; tel. (1) 5139000; fax (1) 5139321; e-mail petranso@petranso.com; internet www.petranso.com; f. 1956; privatized in 1993; CEO JUAN VILLARÁN; Exec. Vice-Pres. CHRISTIAN CSASZAR.

CIVIL AVIATION

Of Peru's 294 airports and airfields, the major international airport is Jorge Chávez Airport near Lima. Other important international airports are Coronel Francisco Secada Vignetta Airport, near Iquitos, Velasco Astete Airport, near Cusco, and Rodríguez Ballón Airport, near Arequipa.

Corporación Peruana de Aeropuertos y Aviación Comercial: Aeropuerto Internacional Jorge Chávez, Avda Elmer Faucett, Callao; tel. (1) 6301000; fax (1) 5745578; e-mail sugerencias@corpac.gob.pe; internet www.corpac.gob.pe; f. 1943; Pres. WALTER HUGO TELLO CASTILLO; Gen. Man. LUIS FELIPE VALLEJO LEIGH.

Domestic Airlines

Aero Cóndor: Juan de Arona 781, San Isidro, Lima; tel. (1) 4425215; fax (1) 2215783; domestic services; Pres. CARLOS PALACÍN FERNÁNDEZ.

LAN Perú, SA: Centro Comercial Real Plaza, Avda Garcilazo de la Vega 1337, Tienda 1001, Lima; tel. (1) 2138200; internet www.lan.com; f. 1999; operations temporarily suspended in Oct. 2004; CEO ENRIQUE CUETO P; Gen. Man. JORGE VILCHES.

StarPerú: Avda Comandante Espinar 331, Miraflores, Lima 18; tel. (1) 7059000; fax (1) 3324789; e-mail atencionalcliente@starperu.com; internet www.starperu.com; f. 1997; operates services to eight domestic destinations; Gen. Man. ROMÁN KASIANOV.

Tourism

Tourism is centred on Lima, with its Spanish colonial architecture, and Cusco, with its pre-Inca and Inca civilization, notably the 'lost city' of Machu Picchu. Lake Titicaca, lying at an altitude of 3,850 m above sea level, and the Amazon jungle region to the north-east are also popular destinations. In 2008 Peru received 2,057,620 visitors. Receipts from tourism generated an estimated US $2,396m. in the same year.

Comisión de Promoción del Perú (PromPerú): Edif. Mitinci, Calle Uno Oeste, 13°, Urb. Corpac, San Isidro, Lima 27; tel. (1) 2243279; fax (1) 2243323; e-mail postmaster@promperu.gob.pe; internet www.peru.info; f. 1993; Head of Tourism MARÍA DEL PILAR LAZARTE CONROY; Gen. Man. MARÍA M. SEMINARIO MARÓN.

Defence

As assessed at November 2010, Peru's armed forces numbered 115,000: army 74,000, navy 24,000, air force 17,000. Paramilitary police forces numbered 77,000. There were 188,000 army reserves. Military service was selective and lasted for two years.

Defence Budget: 3,140m. new soles for defence and domestic security in 2010.

President of the Joint Command of the Armed Forces: Gen. LUIS RICARDO HOWELL BALLENA.

Commander of the Army: Gen. PAÚL TITO DA SILVA GAMARRA.

Commander of the Air Force: Gen. CARLOS EDUARDO SAMAMÉ QUIÑONES.

Commander of the Navy: Adm. JORGE DE LA PUENTE RIBEYRO.

Education

Education in Peru is based on a series of reforms introduced after the 1968 revolution. The educational system is divided into three levels: the first level is for children up to six years of age in either nurseries or kindergartens. Basic education is provided at the second level. It is free and, where possible, compulsory between six and 15 years of age. Primary education lasts for six years. Secondary education, beginning at the age of 12, is divided into two stages, of two and three years, respectively. In 2008 enrolment at primary schools included 94% of pupils in the relevant age-group, while secondary enrolment included 75% of students in the relevant age-group. Higher education includes the pre-university and university levels. There were 78 universities in 2000. There is also provision for adult literacy programmes and bilingual education. Total central government expenditure on education was estimated at 2.9% of GDP in 2000. Budget proposals for 2005 allocated some US $2,600m. to education.

THE PHILIPPINES

Introductory Survey

LOCATION, CLIMATE, LANGUAGE, RELIGION, FLAG, CAPITAL

The Republic of the Philippines lies in the western Pacific Ocean, east of mainland South-East Asia. The island of Borneo is to the south-west, and New Guinea to the south-east. The principal islands of the Philippine archipelago are Luzon, in the north, and Mindanao, in the south. Between these two (which together account for 66% of the country's area) lie the 7,000 islands of the Visayas. The climate is maritime and tropical. It is generally hot and humid, except in the mountains. There is abundant rainfall, and the islands are frequently in the path of typhoons. At the 1995 census there were 102 languages; the most frequently used were Tagalog (by 29.3% of the population), Cebuano (21.2%), Ilocano (9.3%), Hiligaynon (Ilongo—9.1%) and Bicol (5.7%). Filipino, based on Tagalog, is the native national language. English is widely spoken, and Spanish is used in some communities. In 1991 94.2% of the population were Christians (84.1% Roman Catholics, 6.2% belonged to the Philippine Independent Church (Aglipayan) and 3.9% were Protestants). In 1990 an estimated 4.6% of the population were Muslims. The national flag (proportions 1 by 2) has two equal horizontal stripes, of blue and red, with a white triangle, enclosing a yellow 'Sun of Liberty' (with eight large and 16 small rays) and three five-pointed yellow stars (one in each corner), at the hoist. The capital is Manila, on the island of Luzon.

CONTEMPORARY POLITICAL HISTORY

Historical Context

The Philippines became a Spanish colony in the 16th century. During the Spanish–American War, the independence of the Philippines was declared on 12 June 1898 by Gen. Emilio Aguinaldo, leader of the revolutionary movement, with the support of the USA. Under the Treaty of Paris, signed in December 1898, Spain ceded the islands to the USA. A new Constitution, ratified by plebiscite in May 1935, gave the Philippines internal self-government and provided for independence after 10 years. During the Second World War the islands were occupied by Japanese forces from 1942, but, after Japan's surrender in 1945, US rule was restored. The Philippines became an independent republic on 4 July 1946, with Manuel Roxas as its first President. A succession of Presidents, effectively constrained by US economic interests and the Filipino land-owning class, did little to help the peasant majority or to curb disorder and political violence.

Domestic Political Affairs

At elections in November 1965 the incumbent President, Diosdado Macapagal of the Liberal Party (LP), was defeated by Ferdinand Marcos of the Nacionalista Party (NP). Rapid development of the economy and infrastructure followed. President Marcos was re-elected in 1969. His second term was characterized by civil unrest, economic difficulties and an increase in guerrilla activity (see Separatist Tensions and Militancy, below).

In September 1972, before completing the (then) maximum of two four-year terms of office, President Marcos declared martial law in order to deal with subversive activity and to introduce drastic reforms. The bicameral Congress was suspended, opposition leaders were arrested, the private armies of the landed oligarchs were disbanded, stringent press censorship was introduced, and Marcos began to rule by decree. In November a new Constitution was approved by a constitutional convention, and in January 1973 it was ratified by Marcos. It provided for a unicameral National Assembly and a Constitutional President, with executive power held by a Prime Minister, to be elected by the legislature. Transitional provisions gave the incumbent President the combined authority of the presidency (under the 1935 Constitution) and the premiership, without any fixed term of office. Under martial law, the definitive provisions of the new Constitution remained in abeyance.

A referendum in July 1973 approved Marcos's continuation in office beyond his elected term. Referendums in February 1975 and October 1976 approved the continuation of martial law and the adoption of constitutional amendments, including a provision for the formation of an interim assembly. In December 1977 a fourth referendum approved the extension of Marcos's presidential term.

Criticism of President Marcos became more widespread after November 1977, when a sentence of death was imposed by a military tribunal on the principal opposition leader, Benigno Aquino, Jr—a former senator and Secretary-General of the LP, who had been detained since 1972—for alleged murder, subversion and the possession of firearms. Marcos allowed a stay of execution, and conceded some relaxation of martial law in 1977. Elections to the interim National Assembly took place in April 1978. Opposition parties were allowed to participate, but the pro-Government Kilusang Bagong Lipunan (KBL—New Society Movement), founded in 1978 by Marcos and former members of the NP, won 151 of the Assembly's 165 elective seats. The Assembly was inaugurated in June, when Marcos was also confirmed as Prime Minister. Martial law remained in force, and Marcos retained the power to legislate by decree. Local elections held in January 1980 resulted in decisive victories for the KBL. In May Aquino was released from prison to undergo medical treatment in the USA.

In January 1981 martial law was ended, although Marcos retained most of his former powers. A referendum in April approved constitutional amendments that permitted Marcos to renew his presidential mandate by direct popular vote and to nominate a separate Prime Minister. In June, amid allegations of electoral malpractice, Marcos was re-elected President for a six-year term. In April 1982 the United Nationalist Democratic Organization (UNIDO), an alliance of opposition groups, formed an official coalition: it included Lakas ng Bayan (the People's Power Movement, founded by Benigno Aquino in 1978) and the Pilipino Democratic Party (PDP), which merged to form PDP-Laban in 1983.

In August 1983 Benigno Aquino, returning from exile in the USA, was shot dead on arrival at Manila airport. Rolando Galman, the alleged communist assassin, was killed immediately by military guards. A commission of inquiry, nominated by the Government, concluded that Aquino's murder had been a military conspiracy. However, the Supreme Court announced in December 1985 that the evidence submitted to the commission was inadmissible, acquitted the 26 military personnel who had been accused of conspiring to murder Aquino and upheld the Government's assertion that the assassin was Galman.

Benigno Aquino's death served to unite the opposition in its criticism of Marcos. At elections to the National Assembly in May 1984, public participation was high, and, after numerous accusations by the opposition of electoral fraud and corruption by Marcos, the opposition won 59 of the 183 elective seats.

In November 1985, in response to US pressure, Marcos announced that a presidential election would be held in February 1986, 18 months earlier than scheduled. Corazon Aquino, the widow of Benigno Aquino, was chosen as the UNIDO presidential candidate, in spite of her lack of political experience. More than 100 people were killed in violence during the election campaign. Vote-counting was conducted by the government-controlled National Commission on Elections (Comelec) and by the independent National Citizens' Movement for Free Elections (Namfrel). Allegations of electoral fraud and irregularities, apparently perpetrated by supporters of Marcos, were substantiated by international observers. The National Assembly declared Marcos the winner of the presidential election, with 10.8m. votes, compared with 9.3m. for Corazon Aquino, according to figures from Comelec. According to Namfrel figures (based on 69% of the total votes), Aquino was in the lead. Marcos immediately announced the resignation of the Cabinet, and declared his intention to establish a council of presidential advisers. Aquino rejected an offer to participate in the council.

Later in February 1986 Lt-Gen. (later Gen.) Fidel Ramos, the acting Chief of Staff of the Armed Forces, and Juan Ponce Enrile, the Minister of National Defense, along with about 300 troops, established a rebel headquarters in the Ministry of National Defense (later moving to the police headquarters), stating that they no longer accepted Marcos's authority and asserting that Corazon Aquino was the rightful President. Attempts by forces loyal to Marcos to attack the rebels were foiled by large unarmed crowds, which gathered to protect them at the instigation of the Catholic Archbishop of Manila, Cardinal Jaime Sin. Troops supporting Ramos subsequently secured control of the government broadcasting station. Rival ceremonies were held, at which both Marcos and Aquino were sworn in as President. However, later the same day, under pressure from the USA, Marcos agreed to withdraw, and left the Philippines for the US state of Hawaii.

President Aquino appointed her Vice-President, Salvador Laurel (the President of UNIDO), to be Prime Minister and Minister of Foreign Affairs, while Enrile retained the post of Minister of National Defense. Ramos was appointed Chief of Staff of the Armed Forces. At the end of February 1986 Aquino ordered the controversial release of all political prisoners, including communist leaders. In March the Government announced the restoration of habeas corpus, the abolition of press censorship and the suspension of local government elections (scheduled for May). The Government also secured the resignation of all Justices of the Supreme Court, as well as the resignation of Comelec members. Aquino announced that the 1973 Constitution was to be replaced by an interim document, providing for the immediate abolition of the National Assembly and for the inauguration of a provisional government, with the President being granted emergency powers. The post of Prime Minister was temporarily abolished, and in May a commission was appointed to draft a new constitution.

In March 1986 military leaders pledged their loyalty to President Aquino. The Government then began to implement a programme of military reform, in accordance with the demands of officers of the Rebolusyonaryong Alyansang Makabayan (RAM—Nationalist Revolutionary Alliance—also known as the Reform the Armed Forces Movement), who had supported the February revolution. In September the Supreme Court ordered the retrial of the members of the military who had earlier been acquitted of the murder of Benigno Aquino. In September 1990 a special court convicted 16 members of the armed forces of the murder of both Aquino and Galman.

In July 1986 an abortive coup took place in Manila, led by Arturo Tolentino, a former Minister of Foreign Affairs and Marcos's vice-presidential candidate, and a group of 300 pro-Marcos troops. One of the principal reasons for military dissatisfaction was the new Government's conciliatory attitude towards communist insurgents. In June the Government had announced that formal negotiations for a cease-fire agreement would begin with representatives of the National Democratic Front (NDF), a left-wing group that included the Communist Party of the Philippines (CPP) and the New People's Army (NPA, which was estimated to number 25,000–30,000 members; see Separatist Tensions and Militancy). In October, however, increasing pressure from Enrile and the RAM prompted President Aquino to threaten the insurgents with open warfare if a solution were not reached by the end of November. In late November a group of army officers attempted to gain control of several military camps and to replace Aquino with Nicanor Yniguez, a former Speaker of the National Assembly. The rebellion was quelled by Ramos and troops loyal to Aquino; Enrile was dismissed from the Cabinet. In January 1987 a further coup attempt by 500 disaffected soldiers was suppressed by forces loyal to the President, and an attempt by Marcos to return to the Philippines was thwarted by US officials.

In February 1987 a new Constitution was approved by 76% of voters in a national plebiscite. The new Constitution gave President Aquino a mandate to rule until 30 June 1992, and established an executive presidency (see Constitution and Government). All members of the armed forces swore an oath of allegiance to the new Constitution. An order followed disbanding all 'fraternal organizations' (such as the RAM) within the armed forces, because they 'encouraged divisiveness'. Elections to the bicameral Congress of the Philippines took place on 11 May 1987, at which more than 83% of the electorate participated. Aquino's Lakas ng Bayan coalition secured 180 of the 200 elective seats in the House of Representatives and 22 of the 24 seats in the Senate.

In August 1987 Ramos and troops loyal to Aquino averted a serious coup attempt, when rebel officers (led by Col Gregorio Honasan, an officer closely associated with Enrile) occupied the army headquarters, and captured a radio and television station. In the intense fighting that ensued in Manila and Cebu, 53 people were killed. Honasan and his supporters fled, successfully evading capture until December. (However, Honasan escaped from detention in April 1988.) In December 1990 a military court sentenced 81 members of the armed forces to prison terms of up to 32 years for their part in the rebellion.

In October 1988 former President Marcos and his wife, Imelda, were indicted in the USA and charged with the illegal transfer into the country of some US $100m. that had allegedly been obtained by embezzlement and racketeering. In November thousands of civilian supporters of Marcos entered Manila and distributed leaflets demanding a military rebellion to overthrow Aquino, before being dispersed by the armed forces. In February 1989 Laurel (who had formally dissociated himself from Aquino) began to campaign for Marcos to be permitted to return to the Philippines. In May Marcos's NP was revived, with Laurel as President and Enrile as Secretary-General.

In September 1989 the Philippine Government began the first of 35 planned civil suits against Marcos *in absentia* on charges of corruption. However, the former President died in Hawaii at the end of September. In July 1990, in New York, Imelda Marcos was acquitted of charges of fraud and of the illegal transfer of stolen funds to the USA.

In December 1989 an abortive coup was staged by members of two élite military units, in collusion with the now illicit RAM and officers loyal to Marcos. President Aquino subsequently addressed a rally of 100,000 supporters, accusing Laurel and Enrile (who were both included in an eight-member provisional junta named by the rebels) of involvement in the coup attempt. In August 1990 Aquino expressed willingness to hold discussions both with dissident troops (who had perpetrated a series of bombings of allegedly corrupt businesses owned by US interests or associated with the Aquino Government) and with communist rebels (who had unilaterally declared a cease-fire in Manila and in northern areas affected by an earthquake in July), in an effort to achieve a general reconciliation. Opposition leaders, including Enrile (who had been charged with rebellion), were also invited to attend. In September Aquino belatedly suspended offensives against the NPA in the affected areas. However, later in that month the NPA ended the truce. The dissident members of the armed forces also continued their campaign to destabilize the Government.

In July 1991 Ramos resigned as Secretary of National Defense in order to contest the presidential election (scheduled for 1992). Having failed to secure the nomination of the ruling party, Laban ng Demokratikong Pilipino (LDP—formed in 1988 by members of pro-Government parties), Ramos, with Aquino's endorsement, resigned from the LDP and registered a new party, EDSA-LDP, with the support of 25 former LDP members of Congress. (EDSA was the popular acronym for the Epifanio de los Santos Avenue, the main site of the February 1986 uprising.) The party, which subsequently altered its title to Lakas ng EDSA, formed an alliance with the National Union of Christian Democrats to become Lakas-NUCD.

In February 1992 Amnesty International published a report accusing the Aquino administration of acquiescence in violations of human rights by the armed forces, in which it claimed that 550 extrajudicial killings had taken place during 1988–91. The armed forces denied the report's findings. The NPA had killed 563 members of the armed forces between January and April 1991.

On 11 May 1992 elections took place to select the President, Vice-President, 12 senators, 200 members of the House of Representatives and 17,014 local officials. Fidel Ramos was elected to the presidency, winning 23.6% of the votes cast; his closest rivals were Miriam Defensor Santiago, a former Secretary of Agrarian Reform (with 19.7%), and Eduardo Cojuangco (Aquino's estranged cousin, whose wing of the NP had been renamed the Nationalist People's Coalition—NPC) (18.2%). The success of Ramos and the high level of support for Santiago was widely regarded as a rejection of traditional patronage party politics, since neither candidate was supported by a large-scale party organization. However, in the legislative elections the LDP (the only party that had local bases in every province) won 16 of the 24 seats in the Senate and 89 of the 200 elective seats in the House of Representatives. Despite his party's poor representation in Congress, Ramos, who was inaugurated on 30 June, managed to gain the support of the NPC, the LP and 55 defectors (now known as Laban) from the LDP, to form a 'rainbow coalition', comprising 145 of the 200 elected members of the House of Representatives. The Senate remained under the control of the LDP.

On assuming power, Ramos gave priority to persuading mutinous right-wing soldiers, communist insurgents and Muslim separatists to abandon their armed struggle (see Separatist Tensions and Militancy). In July 1992 Ramos formed the Presidential Anti-Crime Commission (PACC), headed by Vice-President Joseph Estrada, to combat organized crime, particularly the increase in abduction for ransom. It emerged that members of the Philippine National Police (PNP) were largely responsible for the abductions, and in August the Chief of Police resigned. In April 1993, following a review of the PNP, Ramos ordered the discharge of hundreds of personnel. There was also a serious decline in public respect for the judiciary, following allegations that seven Supreme Court judges were accepting bribes from drugs dealers and other criminal syndicates. In February Congress adopted legislation (which was signed into law in December) to reinstate the death penalty, which had been banned under the 1987 Constitution.

In December 1992 seven military renegades, including Honasan, emerged from hiding to sign a preliminary agreement to take part in talks with the Government. Discussions between the National Unification Commission (NUC—formed in August to consult rebel groups and formulate a viable amnesty programme) and representatives of the RAM and the Young Officers' Union (YOU—a progressive offshoot of the RAM, which was alleged to have played an important role in the December 1989 coup attempt) began in January 1993, but were subsequently suspended. In February 1994 it was announced that peace negotiations with the RAM and the YOU would remain suspended, pending the release of six military detainees. In the following month Ramos proclaimed a general amnesty for all rebels and for members of the security forces charged with offences committed during counter-insurgency operations, as recommended by the NUC; however, the amnesty did not include persons convicted of torture, arson, massacre, rape and robbery. The RAM rejected the amnesty on the grounds that it failed to address the causes of the rebellion, while Saturnino Ocampo of the NDF dismissed the proclamation as being biased against the communist rebels. Following agreement between the RAM and the Government during 1994 on certain government programmes and the issue of electoral reform, in 1995 formal negotiations resumed. In October the RAM and the YOU signed a peace agreement with the Government, which provided for the return of the rebels' military weapons within 90 days and the reintegration of members of the two organizations into the armed forces.

In September 1993 Imelda Marcos (who had returned to the Philippines in 1991, with Aquino's permission, to stand trial on charges of fraud and tax evasion) was convicted of corruption and sentenced to 18 years' imprisonment; she remained at liberty pending an appeal against the conviction. In February 1994 a court in Hawaii awarded US $2,000m. in punitive damages to 10,000 Filipinos tortured under President Marcos's administration, following a court ruling in October 1992 that victims of abuses of human rights under the Marcos regime could sue his estate for compensation. Imelda Marcos announced that she would appeal against the decision. Further charges of embezzlement were filed against her in April and June 1994 and in September 1995.

Prior to legislative and local elections held on 8 May 1995, in which an estimated 80% of all eligible voters participated, more than 80 people were killed in campaign violence. The ruling coalition won the vast majority (about 70%) of seats in the House of Representatives, and an electoral alliance between Lakas-NUCD and the LDP (Lakas-Laban) won nine of the 12 contested seats in the Senate. One of the three opposition seats was secured by Honasan, despite a campaign by Aquino against his candidacy. Imelda Marcos secured a seat in the House of Representatives, having been allowed to contest the election pending the outcome of her appeal, although she was not permitted to take her seat in Congress until November, following a ruling in her favour by the Supreme Court.

During 1995–97 Ramos's supporters campaigned to amend the constitutional stipulation that restricted the President to a single term of office; however, the Senate opposed the proposal. In September 1997 a rally organized by Cardinal Sin, to protest against any such constitutional change, was attended by more than 500,000 demonstrators and supported by Corazon Aquino. Prior to the rally Ramos finally stated categorically that he would not contest the presidential election.

The presidency of Joseph Estrada

The formation of an opposition grouping, the Laban ng Makabayang Masang Pilipino (LaMMP—Struggle of Nationalist Filipino Masses), to contest the elections scheduled for May 1998 was announced in June 1997. The LaMMP was composed of the Partido ng Masang Pilipino, led by Estrada, the LDP, led by Edgardo Angara (which had withdrawn from its alliance with Lakas-NUCD in February 1996), and the NPC, led by Ernesto Maceda. In December 1997 Estrada and Angara were formally endorsed as the LaMMP's presidential and vice-presidential candidates, respectively. The campaign was characterized by an emphasis on personalities and scandals and failed to address substantive policy issues.

Presidential, legislative and local elections took place on 11 May 1998; an estimated 80% of the electorate participated in the polls. Although an estimated 51 people were killed in pre-election violence (mostly in the southern province of Mindanao), the elections were considered relatively orderly and free. Estrada was elected to the presidency with 39.9% of the votes cast. His closest rival was the Lakas-NUCD candidate, Jose de Venecia (who was responsible for negotiations with both the Islamist separatists and the NDF), who secured 15.9% of the votes. The vice-presidency was won by Gloria Macapagal Arroyo (the daughter of former President Diosdado Macapagal), who had supported de Venecia's candidacy. According to Comelec, seven of the victorious senators were members of the LaMMP, while the other five were Lakas-NUCD candidates. However, Lakas-NUCD dominated the House of Representatives, winning 106 seats compared with only 66 for the LaMMP. In a development indicative of the weakness of the party system, many congressional members subsequently defected to Estrada's party, which was renamed Laban ng Masang Pilipino (Fight of the Filipino Masses).

Joseph Estrada was inaugurated as President at the end of June 1998. In his inaugural address he reiterated campaign pledges to eradicate poverty and corruption, but also assured the business sector that he would continue Ramos's programme of economic reform. His new Cabinet, which elicited widespread approval, comprised members from a wide political and social spectrum, including wealthy ethnic Chinese business executives, former associates of Marcos, and allies from Estrada's career as mayor and senator, as well as former activists from the communist movement and left-wing non-governmental organizations (NGOs). Five members of Lakas-NUCD were allocated portfolios and Ramos accepted a post as Senior Adviser. However, Estrada was criticized for appointing friends and relatives to lucrative and influential positions. Additional concerns about a reversion to the Marcos era of 'cronyism' were raised by the return to prominence of former Marcos associates, some of whom had made substantial financial contributions to Estrada's presidential campaign fund. The Marcoses' daughter, Imee, and their son, Ferdinand Jr, were elected to Congress and the governorship of Ilocos Norte, respectively.

In June 1998 the Solicitor-General, Romeo de la Cruz, recommended that the Supreme Court acquit Imelda Marcos of charges of corruption. A ruling by the Court in January had upheld her appeal against one charge of corruption but dismissed an appeal against her conviction in 1993 on a second corruption charge, which carried a sentence of up to 12 years' imprisonment. However, Ramos had dismissed de la Cruz and his appointed successor, and withdrew the Government's petition for acquittal. Marcos was, nevertheless, acquitted in October 1998, although numerous civil suits remained pending against her. In December Marcos announced plans to initiate a legal appeal to recover 500,000m. pesos in assets allegedly belonging to her late husband, claiming that he had entrusted the money to close associates who refused to return it. Estrada favoured a negotiated settlement with the Marcos family to resolve the dispute over funds misappropriated by the former President and also gave his support to the burial of Marcos in the National Heroes' Cemetery. However, popular outrage prompted Imelda Marcos to postpone the burial indefinitely in the national interest.

Meanwhile, in January 1998 the Swiss Supreme Court ruled that the total sum of US $560m. of Marcos's wealth in Swiss bank accounts be released (to be disbursed by the Philippine courts). The Swiss Supreme Court rejected an appeal by the Marcos family in April. Later in that month the Marcoses filed a new petition, requesting that the Swiss Federal Court review the case; this request was also rejected. In February 1999 the Marcos family agreed to pay a total of $150m. in damages to 9,539 victims of human rights abuses. In March the Philippines Supreme Court upheld a 1990 decision by the Bureau of Internal Revenue assessing the unpaid inheritance tax owed by the heirs of Ferdinand Marcos at 23,500m. pesos. (In July 2003 the Philippines Supreme Court ruled that the sum of approximately

$658m. that had been held by Ferdinand Marcos in several Swiss bank accounts should be released to the Philippine Government.)

In spite of widespread apprehension regarding his leadership abilities, Estrada was credited with several successes during his first year in office, including a dramatic reduction in kidnappings for ransom, facilitated by the creation in July 1998 of the Presidential Anti-Organized Crime Task Force. Estrada also effectively abolished 'pork barrel' funds (state funds from which congress members financed projects in their constituencies), which had led to corruption and the reinforcement of patronage politics.

In March 1999 the Senate Blue Ribbon Committee, which had been established to investigate anomalies in government, recommended the prosecution of former President Ramos and five members of his Cabinet for the misapplication of public funds to celebrate the centennial anniversary of Philippine independence in June 1998. Obliged to justify his actions before a newly formed Independent Citizens' Committee, Ramos claimed that the accusations were politically motivated and designed to distract attention from investigations into misconduct by Estrada's associates. The Committee's final report recommended the indictment for corruption of the former Vice-President, Salvador Laurel, who had led the centennial celebration committee, and fines for Ramos and his Secretary of Finance, Salvador Enrique, for failing to prevent Laurel's abuses.

In late 1999 President Estrada's hitherto excellent popularity ratings began to decline owing to his perceived failure to alleviate poverty and amid increasing concern about 'cronyism' and corruption in his administration. In August Aquino and Cardinal Sin mobilized 100,000 demonstrators in a Rally for Democracy to protest particularly against government plans to amend the 1987 Constitution. Estrada's stated aim in amending the Constitution was to extend economic deregulation by altering the provisions limiting to 40% foreign ownership of land and public utilities. While in any case opposed to these proposals, critics feared the potential removal from the Constitution of the stipulation limiting the President to a single term of office. Later in August 1999 Estrada relaunched the ruling coalition, restyling it the Lapian ng Masang Pilipino (LAMP—Party of the Filipino Masses).

Following a report by the World Bank in November 1999 claiming that 20% of the Philippine budget was lost to corruption, President Estrada pledged to intensify investigations of officials suspected of dishonesty. In the same month, in a further attempt to dispel criticism, Estrada established the EDSA People Power Commission to promote the ideals of the 1986 uprising; its 15 members included Aquino, Ramos and Estrada. However, these measures proved inadequate to reverse a trend that was compounded by the unexpected resignation of the respected Secretary of Finance, Edgardo Espiritu, in January 2000 and his subsequent accusations of undue influence exerted by unelected associates of Estrada. Estrada responded to growing public dissatisfaction by announcing the reform of his administration. He dismissed his informal advisers, replacing them with a six-member Economic Co-ordinating Council to promote coherence in economic affairs, and recruited five eminent business leaders to act as an economic advisory council. The proposed constitutional reforms were suspended and replaced by plans to achieve economic liberalization through legislation. Estrada's attempts to improve his popularity were swiftly undermined by the testimony in January of the Chairman of the Securities and Exchange Commission (SEC), Perfecto Yasay, to a Senate Committee investigating possible illegal share trading. Yasay alleged that Estrada had pressed him to exonerate Estrada's close associate, Dante Tan, who was suspected of illegally manipulating the share price of BW Resources Corporation. Estrada denied the intervention, although he admitted telephoning Yasay four times in relation to the investigation. Despite frequent rumours of an impending coup attempt and a request for Estrada's resignation by Teofisto Guingona, Jr, the President of Lakas-NUCD, an attempt to mobilize anti-Estrada sentiment in a mass protest in April received very little support.

Despite the President's denial in October 2000 of allegations that he had accepted large sums of money in bribes from illegal gambling businesses, opposition parties announced their intention to begin the process of impeaching him. Earlier in the month Vice-President Gloria Arroyo had announced her resignation from the Cabinet, in which she served as Secretary of Social Welfare and Development. However, she did not relinquish the vice-presidency, leading to speculation that she was preparing to succeed Estrada in the event of his departure from office, and she proceeded to establish an alliance of opposition parties.

In November 2000 the House of Representatives endorsed the impeachment of the President after more than one-third of its members signed a petition favouring this action. Supporters of Estrada condemned the impeachment proceedings as unconstitutional since they had not been submitted to a formal vote in the House of Representatives. (The Speaker of the House had ruled that such a vote was unnecessary because more than one-third of its members had signed the petition.) Estrada himself welcomed an impeachment trial in the Senate as an opportunity to prove his innocence, and he was formally summoned by the Senate. The legal action pursued by Estrada in order to force the Senate to dismiss the charges against him was unsuccessful, and in December he pleaded not guilty to charges of bribery, corruption, betrayal of public trust and violation of the Constitution. However, the impeachment trial in the Senate was adjourned indefinitely in January 2001 after prosecutors failed to obtain the disclosure of bank records as evidence against him. This effective acquittal of the President provoked mass demonstrations against him. Estrada had lost the support of many members of his Cabinet, the police and the armed forces, and, in response to a request by Vice-President Arroyo, the Supreme Court declared the presidency to be vacant.

President Arroyo's first term

Gloria Arroyo was sworn in as President on 20 January 2001, and the new administration acted quickly to prevent Estrada, members of his family and his associates from leaving the Philippines, insisting that the former President would be prosecuted. Estrada continued to assert that he remained the legitimate head of state, but in March the Supreme Court affirmed the legitimacy of Arroyo's office. In April Estrada was formally indicted for a number of alleged offences, including one of economic plunder, which was punishable by the death penalty. Estrada was arrested for the first time in mid-April and charged with corruption and perjury. At the beginning of May supporters of Estrada attempted to storm the presidential palace in Manila. Three members of the Senate were arrested for having allegedly conspired to bring down the Government, and President Arroyo declared a state of rebellion, which permitted her to deploy the armed forces to quell the unrest. Estrada, who had subsequently been rearrested, was removed to a detention centre outside Manila, having had his application for bail denied.

Legislative and local elections were held on 14 May 2001. Lakas-NUCD secured 87 seats in the House of Representatives, followed by the NPC with 62. The People Power Coalition (PPC—a coalition of Lakas-NUCD, the LP and several smaller parties, which had been formed by President Arroyo to contest the election) won eight seats in the Senate, while allies of the Laban ng Demokratikong Pilipino-Pwersa ng Masa (LDP-PnM—the opposition coalition formed to support Estrada) secured four. The remaining seat went to an independent candidate. President Arroyo thus succeeded in securing a majority in both chambers. As a result of violence throughout the election period, 83 people died. The elections were further marred by reports of widespread corruption.

In October 2001 Estrada's trial on charges of perjury and plunder finally commenced; he had refused to enter a plea to any of the charges against him. In November the Supreme Court rejected a legal challenge brought by Estrada against his trial and affirmed the constitutionality of the anti-plunder law under which he was being tried. After the suspension of two senior judges involved in the trial (one following complaints that cases under his remit were proceeding too slowly and the other following defence allegations that he lacked impartiality), the trial was adjourned and resumed in January 2002 in a special anti-graft court. In February Estrada instructed his entire legal team to resign in protest against what he alleged to be a prejudiced court. In July 2004 the court ruled that Estrada had not been guilty of money-laundering when he opened a bank account under a different name in 2000. A few days later the court approved Estrada's transfer from military detention to house arrest. In September 2007 Estrada was convicted of plunder, having misappropriated some US $80m. during his tenure of office, and sentenced to life imprisonment; he was found not guilty of the charge of perjury. He denounced the verdict as being a 'political decision'. However, after apparently agreeing not to seek political office, Estrada was pardoned by President Arroyo in October. The pardon, and in particular the swiftness with which it had been granted, provoked considerable controversy.

In October 2001 Jose Miguel Arroyo, the husband of the President, was investigated by the Senate over allegations that he had diverted funds from a state lottery in order to finance electoral campaigns for prospective senators. In the same month Imelda Marcos was rearrested on four charges of corruption, connected to the suspected plunder of the economy under the regime of her late husband, before being released on bail; she appeared in court in November and denied all the charges.

In June 2002 Senator John Osmeña defected to the opposition, depriving the PPC of its narrow majority in the Senate. Owing to the simultaneous absence abroad of another senator, proceedings in the Senate were suspended for almost two months. In October the Senate gave its assent to the Absentee Voting Bill, which rendered Filipino citizens living and working abroad eligible to vote in future legislative and presidential elections. The bill was enacted in February 2003. In November 2002 President Arroyo announced her intention to adopt a strict policy aimed at ending the corruption apparently endemic within the Government. In December the President announced that she did not intend to contest the presidential election scheduled to take place in 2004, claiming that she wished to spare the country further political division. She subsequently stated her intention to revive the Council of State, an advisory body originally established during the presidency of her father, while holding exploratory talks with leading members of the opposition with the possible aim of forming a 'government of national unity'.

In July 2003 approximately 350 disaffected members of the armed forces staged a mutiny, taking control of a shopping centre in the Manila commercial district of Makati. The rebels, who demanded the resignation of the President and Secretary of National Defense Angelo Reyes, finally surrendered peacefully. While the Government claimed that the mutiny constituted an attempted coup, those who had participated claimed that they were merely seeking a chance to air their grievances, which included, most notably, allegations that senior military personnel were guilty of systematic collusion with Muslim rebels in the south. Later in July the head of military intelligence, Brig.-Gen. Victor Corpus, who had been accused of misconduct by the rebels, resigned. In the aftermath of the mutiny President Arroyo declared a nation-wide state of rebellion, which was removed in August. In that month charges were filed against more than 1,000 people in connection with the mutiny. Senator Gregorio Honasan was charged with involvement, along with six of his associates. Meanwhile, Secretary of National Defense Reyes resigned, while denying the allegations of corruption; Eduardo Ermita was appointed as his successor in September. In November the criminal charges of planning a *coup d'état* that had been filed against 290 of those who had taken part in the July mutiny were abandoned; however, it was announced that the 31 officers believed to have led the mutiny would be tried by a civilian court. In addition, all 321 soldiers were to appear at a court martial on separate charges related to their involvement in the mutiny. Six of the leaders of the uprising publicly apologized to the President in September 2004.

In May 2005 the court martial sentenced 184 of the soldiers to one year's confinement with hard labour, demotion in rank and forfeiture of two-thirds of their basic salaries for three to six months; the soldiers had pleaded guilty to lesser offences in exchange for the withdrawal of a mutiny charge against them. Charges against a number of others had already been dismissed, while the court martial of a further 67 soldiers and 29 suspected leaders of the mutiny continued. In April 2007 54 soldiers, mostly junior officers, were sentenced to seven years and six months in prison for their involvement in the mutiny; their sentences were reduced to four years in June, and they were later dishonourably discharged from the armed forces, before being released in December. Charges against several other officers were dismissed. In August, having pleaded guilty, 12 of the 29 officers believed to have led the mutiny were convicted of the charge of conduct unbecoming an officer by the court martial and ordered to be discharged from service. A further five officers changed their plea before the court martial to guilty of conduct unbecoming an officer in April 2008, and were similarly ordered to be discharged; two of the officers were additionally sentenced to seven-and-a-half years' imprisonment for conduct prejudicial to good order and military discipline. In June 11 other officers reversed their pleas to guilty before the court martial. Meanwhile, the civilian trial of 20 of the 29 officers on separate charges of mounting a coup continued; in April, having changed their plea to guilty, two of the officers had been sentenced to life imprisonment, while seven received prison terms ranging from six to 12 years, although all nine were granted presidential pardons in May. (In November 2007 several of the defendants had briefly attempted to stage a further coup, but swiftly surrendered—see The elections of 2007 and subsequent events.)

In October 2003, in a reversal of her statement of December 2002, President Arroyo announced that she did intend to contest the next presidential election, scheduled to take place in May 2004. Vice-President Teofisto Guingona, Jr, resigned from Lakas-NUCD (which restyled itself as Lakas-Christian Muslim Democrats—Lakas-CMD—in 2003), in advance of the announcement, citing differences of principle, but he retained his cabinet position. In November 2003 Secretary of Finance Jose Isidro Camacho tendered his resignation; Under-Secretary Juanita Amatong was appointed to succeed him. In the same month two armed men occupied the air traffic control tower at the Ninoy Aquino International Airport in Manila, protesting against government corruption and prompting speculation concerning another coup attempt. Both men were shot dead by the police.

The elections of 2004 and subsequent events

In advance of the May 2004 legislative and presidential elections, Senator Edgardo Angara, President of the opposition LDP, announced that his party had merged with the PDP-Laban group and Estrada's Pwersa ng Masang Pilipino (PMP) to form the Koalisyon ng Nagkakaisang Pilipino (KNP—Coalition of the United Filipino). The KNP subsequently announced that it had nominated the film actor Fernando Poe, Jr, as its presidential candidate. Later in the same month, however, former chief of police Brig.-Gen. Panfilo Lacson stated his intention to stand as the official presidential candidate of the LDP, while former Secretary of Education, Culture and Sports Raul Roco, who had resigned in August 2002, secured the presidential nomination of Aksyon Demokratiko. The fifth presidential candidate to emerge was Eduardo Villanueva, the leader of the 'Jesus is Lord' Church, who was to represent the newly established Bangon Pilipinas (Rise Philippines). The incumbent President Gloria Arroyo formed a new coalition in support of her candidacy—the Koalisyon ng Katapatan at Karanasan sa Kinabukasan (K-4)—which consisted of Lakas-CMD, the LP, Reporma and Probinsya Muna Development Intiatives (PROMDI). The coalition replaced the PPC, which had effectively been disbanded following the withdrawal of its most important members.

Presidential, legislative and local elections were held as planned on 10 May 2004. Almost 100 people were killed as a result of violence during the campaign period, despite the deployment of some 230,000 police officers and troops at polling stations throughout the country. Arroyo won a narrow victory in the presidential election, receiving 40.0% of the votes cast, compared with Poe's 36.5%. Poe refused to accept the result, alleging widespread fraud. Noli de Castro, representing Lakas-CMD, was elected to the vice-presidency. Lakas-CMD also performed well in the legislative elections, securing 93 of the 212 elective seats in the House of Representatives, while the NPC won 54 seats and the LP 34. Seven candidates of the K-4 coalition, dominated by Lakas-CMD, were elected to the Senate, with the remaining five contested seats taken by the KNP.

Having secured an electoral mandate for her presidency, Arroyo was sworn in for a second term of office at the end of June 2004. During her inauguration speech she pledged to curb corruption, to improve basic services and to reform the economy, notably promising to create 6m. new jobs during her six-year term. On the day before the ceremony police had dispersed several thousand supporters of Poe who were demonstrating against the Government in Manila and, in a separate incident, arrested four Muslims suspected of planning a bomb attack in the capital during the inauguration. In July Angelo Reyes, a close ally of the President, returned to the Government as Secretary of the Interior and Local Government, following the resignation of Jose Lina from that position. Later in that month Poe and his defeated vice-presidential candidate, Loren Legarda, lodged separate complaints with the Supreme Court, demanding a recount of votes cast in more than 118,000 voting precincts on the grounds of electoral fraud. Poe died in December after suffering a stroke.

In August 2004 Arroyo announced a cabinet reorganization, in which former Executive Secretary Alberto Romulo succeeded Delia Domingo-Albert as Secretary of Foreign Affairs; Eduardo Ermita, hitherto Secretary of National Defense, replaced Romulo, and was in turn replaced by Avelino Cruz, the President's former chief legal adviser. The Government launched a medium-term development plan for 2004–10 in October. As well as setting various economic targets, the plan proposed a number of political reforms, some of which would require the amendment of the Constitution. Major changes envisaged included the introduction of a federal form of government and a unicameral parliamentary system; the revision of restrictive provisions on foreign ownership; and the reform of the electoral system.

In late 2004 and early 2005 a number of military officers were charged with corruption, notably Maj.-Gen. Carlos Garcia, the former comptroller of the armed forces, who was to answer charges relating to 143m. pesos in unexplained wealth that he had allegedly amassed. Garcia was tried by both a military court and the special anti-graft court in November 2004. He was sentenced to two years' hard labour by the military court in December 2005. In February 2009 the anti-graft court found him guilty of perjury and sentenced him to two years' imprisonment. Following a controversial plea bargain agreement sanctioned by the court in May 2010, the plunder charges against Garcia were dismissed in exchange for his pleading guilty to the lesser offences of bribery and money-laundering. Under the terms of the agreement, plunder and money-laundering charges against Garcia's wife and children, who had been extradited from the USA, were also dismissed, and they were released from detention.

Meanwhile, in January 2005 the Secretary of Finance, Juanita Amatong, and the Secretary of Energy, Vicente Perez, resigned from office. The finance portfolio was allocated to Cesar Purisima, hitherto Secretary of Trade and Industry, who was replaced by Juan Santos. Perez agreed to remain in the post until the end of March, when he was succeeded by Raphael Lotilla.

In June 2005 a major political scandal arose over the issue of a recording of a telephone conversation held between President Arroyo and an election official while votes in the 2004 presidential poll were still in the process of being counted. Arroyo acknowledged that she had made an 'error of judgement' by speaking with an election official at that time, but strenuously denied having tried to influence the outcome of the poll. Secretary of Agriculture Arthur Yap tendered his resignation from the Cabinet at the end of the month in order to focus his efforts on contesting tax evasion charges filed against him following the purchase of property in Pasig City (he was reappointed in October 2006). Further resignations from the Cabinet followed in July 2005, in protest against what the departing ministers, who included Secretary of Finance Purisima, perceived to be the illegality of Arroyo's presidency. Later in that month Arroyo announced that Purisima's position was to be assumed by Margarito Teves. In September Congress formally rejected three separate impeachment cases against Arroyo, deeming the complaints too weak to stand up to legislative scrutiny. In January 2006 the influential 120-member Catholic Bishops' Conference urged that investigations into the allegations of alleged malpractice against Arroyo be continued since previous efforts were perceived to have been undermined by 'acts of evasion and obstruction of truth'. In February the National Bureau of Investigation announced that it had concluded its own investigation into the episode, since (because the recording of the conversation had been adjudged to have been tampered with) there was no longer any sound basis for continuing with the proceedings. In the same month an estimated 20,000 people marched through the capital to demand Arroyo's resignation as they marked the 20th anniversary of the ousting of former President Marcos. In March it was reported that members of the opposition were compiling evidence with which to file another impeachment complaint against Arroyo, regarding not only the vote-manipulation allegations but also accusations concerning the mismanagement of a sum of 728m. pesos that had been intended to fund a fertilizer scheme, which, it was claimed, had been misappropriated by Arroyo and her allies to help fund her presidential election campaign in 2004. A fresh impeachment motion against Arroyo was defeated in the House of Representatives in August 2006. A Senate inquiry into the vote-manipulation allegations commenced in September 2007; however, in December 2008 the Supreme Court barred the Senate from continuing its investigations because the chamber had not published its rules of procedure before initiating the inquiry. In February 2009 the Senate Blue Ribbon Committee recommended the prosecution of former Under-Secretary of Agriculture Jocelyn Bolante and nine others in connection with the fertilizer scandal, but found no direct evidence to link Arroyo to the controversy.

Meanwhile, in February 2006 a minor explosion within the presidential palace compound at Malacañang led to rumours of a potential military coup. A statement purporting to be from a rebel military faction, the Young Officers' Union-new generation (YOUng), claimed responsibility for the explosion; however, the YOUng leadership distanced itself from the statement, and, furthermore, forensic tests revealed the blast to have been the result of an inadvertent chemical reaction, rather than of terrorist activity. In late February it was reported that an attempted military coup intended to displace the Arroyo Government had been averted after 14 junior army officers had confessed to their involvement in the plot. A few days later Arroyo issued Presidential Proclamation 1017, the declaration of a state of emergency, in response to the 'clear threat' to the nation, a decision that attracted considerable censure from the opposition, the media and civil liberties groups, which criticized Arroyo for infringing upon public freedoms. Under the terms of martial law, the authorities were granted the right to arrest people without warrant and to detain suspects without charge for an extended period of time; public protests were also prohibited. One week after the military's announcement that the threat had been successfully countered, Arroyo removed the state of emergency. A Supreme Court hearing into the legality of Proclamation 1017 commenced in March. Only days after the start of proceedings Solicitor-General Alfredo Benipayo tendered his resignation, effective from the beginning of April, amid rumours that Arroyo was dissatisfied with his efforts. In the same month a special task force, comprising élite army units, was created in order to counter any further threats to the Government. In April a total of 49 people, including members of the legislature and the military, were charged with rebellion for their alleged involvement in the February coup plot. In May the Supreme Court ruled that Arroyo's declaration of a state of emergency had been legal, but that several actions that had followed the declaration, including certain arrests, were unlawful. In June 2007 the Supreme Court dismissed charges of rebellion against six members of the legislature.

The Arroyo administration's campaign for constitutional amendments to transform the bicameral legislative system into a unicameral parliamentary system was the subject of intense debate during 2006. The Government chose to pursue reform through two possible channels: a people's initiative, involving the collection of signatures and the holding of a plebiscite; and the formation of a constituent assembly. In October, however, following Comelec's rejection of the people's initiative petition, the Supreme Court ruled that approach to be unconstitutional. Signalling the adoption of the alternative method of amending the Constitution, the Speaker of the House of Representatives, Jose de Venecia, proposed in November the adoption by the House of a resolution to become a constituent assembly, whereupon a new constitution would be approved by mid-December. The Speaker envisioned the postponement of elections from May 2007 to November and the completion of the transformation of the legislature after June 2010. The move encountered significant opposition from the Senate (which was effectively excluded from the reform process), the Catholic Bishops' Conference of the Philippines and large sections of the public, with plans for anti-Government demonstrations in several cities. Under considerable pressure, the reformists in the House of Representatives proposed the formation of a constitutional convention of elected delegates as an alternative means towards constitutional amendments, but, with the suspension of the original resolution and a loss of momentum, the initiative was abandoned.

In June 2006 President Arroyo ratified a law that abolished the death penalty. In February 2007 Congress approved the Human Security Act, anti-terrorism legislation giving security officials powers of detention for a period of up to three days in the absence of a warrant or charge, and allowing access to suspicious financial accounts. Critics, including human rights organizations, opposition politicians and the Roman Catholic Church, expressed concern that the Act could be used to suppress legitimate political dissent.

The increasing occurrence of extra-judicial killings and human rights violations was highlighted in 2006 and 2007 by several independent reports. In February 2007 the UN Special Rapporteur on extra-judicial, summary or arbitrary executions, Philip Alston, contended that, although the highest level of Government recognized the gravity of the situation, the army was 'in a state of almost total denial of its need to respond effectively and authentically to the significant number of killings which have been convincingly attributed to them'. Also in February, an inquiry supported by the Government and led by Jose

THE PHILIPPINES

Melo, a retired judge, found links between sections of the military and politically motivated murders. As part of efforts to address the issue, the armed forces and the national police established their own human rights offices, and in March the Chief Justice designated 99 special tribunals to try cases of political killings, with the intention of giving priority to such cases. In November Arroyo ordered the creation of a task force against political violence, comprising representatives of eight government departments and agencies. On the following day Alston's final report was released, in which he concluded that claims by the armed forces that extra-judicial killings of leftist activists were a result of internal purges within communist groups were 'strikingly unconvincing' and observed that no one had been convicted of these killings. Other victims identified by Alston included civil society leaders, human rights activists, trade unionists and advocates of land reform. While welcoming measures initiated by the Government to combat the problem, Alston noted that they had yet to succeed.

The elections of 2007 and subsequent events

Legislative and local elections held on 14 May 2007 were marred by numerous reports of fraud, voter intimidation and violence; some 120 people had been killed in election-related violence since the beginning of the year. Polling in 13 towns in the province of Lanao del Sur on Mindanao was postponed owing to the threat of violence, finally taking place on 26 May, amid heightened security. Moreover, six days before the elections at least eight people were killed in a bomb attack in the city of Tacurong, on Mindanao, which the security forces attributed to the regional militant organization Jemaah Islamiah (JI).

In the elections for 12 of the 24 seats in the Senate, the pro-Arroyo TEAM (Together Everyone Achieves More) Unity coalition—including Lakas-CMD, Kabalikat ng Malayang Pilipino (Kampi, founded in 1997 to support Arroyo) and the LDP—won three seats, while the Genuine Opposition (GO) coalition—including the LP, the PDP-Laban and the NP—won seven, giving a majority to opponents of President Arroyo. Notably elected for the GO was Antonio Trillanes IV, who remained in detention for his alleged role in the 2003 mutiny. The remaining two seats in the Senate were secured by independent candidates, one of whom was Gregorio Honasan, who was on bail accused of involvement in the same mutiny (the charges were dismissed in July 2007). None the less, supporters of Arroyo retained control of the House of Representatives, with parties belonging to TEAM Unity reportedly securing 168 elective seats compared with the GO's 44. Voter turn-out was estimated at 68% for the upper chamber and 70% for the lower chamber. Some 17,000 provincial and municipal posts, including 81 provincial governorships, were also contested on the same day.

Addressing the newly elected Congress in July 2007, Arroyo focused on her Government's economic achievements and pledged to allocate more resources to reducing poverty and to ending the insurgencies in the south of the country. As some 3,000 protesters participated in anti-Government demonstrations outside the legislative building, the President also urged Congress to adopt legislation aimed at curbing politically motivated killings and defended the Human Security Act, which came into force earlier in that month.

In September 2007 President Arroyo suspended a US $329m. contract signed by the Government and the Chinese ZTE Corporation in April for the provision of a national broadband telecommunications network, amid claims that Philippine officials brokering the agreement had both solicited and offered bribes. Testifying before a Senate investigation into the allegations earlier in that month, Jose de Venecia III (the son of the Speaker of the House of Representatives), whose company had unsuccessfully bid for the broadband contract, and the former Director-General of the National Economic and Development Authority, Romulo Neri, had both implicated the Chairman of Comelec, Benjamin Abalos, in the scandal. De Venecia III had also claimed that the President's husband, Jose Miguel Arroyo, had warned him not to pursue the project. Abalos and Jose Miguel Arroyo denied any wrongdoing. Meanwhile, additional troops were deployed in Manila after the Chief of Staff of the Armed Forces, Gen. Hermogenes Esperon, announced that several junior officers who were suspected of recruiting soldiers to join a plot to destabilize the Government had been suspended or reassigned. The contract with ZTE Corporation, the bid of which had been substantially higher than those of rival companies, was cancelled in early October. In November a new impeachment complaint against President Arroyo based on her alleged failure to act on the bribery accusations concerning Abalos, who had resigned in October, was dismissed owing to 'lack of substance'.

A bomb exploded outside the House of Representatives in mid-November 2007, killing four people, including Wahab Akbar, the suspected target, who represented the island of Basilan in the lower chamber. The attack was attributed to Abu Sayyaf, the Islamist secessionist group (see Separatist Tensions and Militancy) of which Akbar was allegedly a former member. Later in that month several military officers walked out of a court in Manila where they were being tried on charges of staging a coup in July 2003 (see President Arroyo's first term) and occupied a nearby hotel, from where, joined by other dissident soldiers, former Vice-President Teofisto Guingona, Jr, and a number of Catholic priests, among others, they appealed to the armed forces to withdraw support for President Arroyo. More than 1,000 heavily armed troops were deployed to quash the rebellion. Having failed to inspire a mass uprising, the leaders of the mutiny, Senator Antonio Trillanes IV and Brig.-Gen. Danilo Lim, surrendered to the authorities after several hours, claiming that they were doing so in order to avoid casualties. Most of the rebels were detained, although three reportedly managed to evade capture. Several journalists covering the incident were also detained, but later released, and an overnight curfew was imposed in Manila. In December 2007 Trillanes, Lim, Guingona and 33 others were charged with rebellion and incitement to rebellion; the charges against 18 civilians, including Guingona, were dismissed later in that month.

The controversy over the broadband contract with ZTE Corporation persisted in early 2008, as the Senate hearings into the affair continued, with further witnesses corroborating the bribery allegations. De Venecia was removed as Speaker of the House of Representatives in a vote in February, after accusing President Arroyo and the Government of corruption. Prospero Nograles was immediately elected to replace him. Once a close ally, de Venecia's relationship with Arroyo had recently been strained as a result of the allegations made by his son before the Senate inquiry. De Venecia resigned as President of Lakas-CMD in March; he was again succeeded in this post by Nograles. Meanwhile, in February an estimated 10,000 people participated in a demonstration in Manila to demand the resignation of Arroyo over the corruption scandal, while more than 50 former government officials issued a joint statement also urging the President to leave office. At the end of the month former Presidents Aquino and Estrada addressed an anti-Government rally attended by some 15,000 people in the capital, while smaller demonstrations were held in other towns. Yielding to considerable pressure, notably from the Catholic Bishops' Conference, in March Arroyo revoked a controversial executive order issued in September 2005 that prevented public officials from attending congressional hearings on alleged corruption in the Government unless permitted by the President. Meanwhile, it was announced that three alleged militants, believed to have links to Abu Sayyaf or JI, had been arrested on suspicion of plotting to bomb foreign embassies in Manila and to assassinate Arroyo. In July 2008 it was announced that a human rights lawyer and four former military officers had been arrested in connection with a new plot to oust President Arroyo; however, all five were acquitted of the charges against them in early 2009.

Juan Ponce Enrile, considered to be an ally of Arroyo, was elected as President of the Senate in November 2008, following the resignation of the incumbent, NP President Manuel Villar, who had recently been embroiled in controversy over the funding of a road extension project and had lost the support of the majority of senators. (In September Villar had declared his intention to contest the presidential election, due to be held in May 2010.) In December 2008 the House of Representatives rejected a fourth impeachment complaint against Arroyo, which detailed various accusations of corruption and human rights abuses under her administration. The President's husband came under considerable pressure in early 2009 to appear before a Senate inquiry into corruption involving World Bank-funded public works projects; allegations linked Jose Miguel Arroyo to claims of collusion between government officials and contractors in bids for road development contracts. The scandal had emerged in January, when three Philippine and four Chinese companies were barred from tendering for future World Bank-financed projects. In March the Office of the Ombudsman recommended that 17 former and current officials of the Department of Public Works and Highways, which was responsible for implementing the bidding process, be charged with corruption.

Constitutional reform was again under consideration in 2008–09. In April 2008 12 senators, led by Aquilino Pimentel, proposed a resolution on the formation of a constituent assembly to amend the Constitution by introducing a federal system of government, comprising 11 states and one administrative region centred on Manila, while retaining the presidency and a bicameral legislature; a concurrent resolution supporting Pimentel's initiative was filed in the House of Representatives in May. In August the President expressed her support for federalism as a means of achieving stability in Mindanao. However, later in that month the House of Representatives' committee on constitutional amendments deferred a planned vote on the need for constitutional change, instead approving a motion to conduct nationwide public consultations on the issue. Opposition politicians pledged to challenge efforts to reform the Constitution before the expiry of Arroyo's term of office in 2010, alleging that the President's supporters in the legislature intended to attempt to extend her tenure or to introduce a parliamentary system of government (under which she could assume the premiership); Arroyo's administration rejected these claims. Meanwhile, there was also considerable disagreement over the interpretation of the Constitution regarding the convening of a constituent assembly, with some claiming that the required approval of three-quarters of the members of Congress had to be secured in separate votes in both chambers, while others maintained that a joint vote in the combined Congress was sufficient; the latter approach (which Luis Villafuerte, the President of Kampi, was reportedly pursuing) would allow the House of Representatives to force through change, even if opposed by all 24 senators. In December 2008 all the members of the Senate signed a resolution stating that any attempt by the House to propose constitutional revisions unilaterally would be unconstitutional. Also that month several thousand opponents of constitutional reform, supported by former Presidents Aquino and Estrada, attended a rally in the Makati district of Manila. In February 2009 the House of Representatives' committee on constitutional amendments approved a resolution, drafted by Speaker Nograles, seeking to remove constitutional restrictions on foreign ownership of companies and land. Opponents of Nograles's proposal argued that, once the process of reforming the Constitution's economic provisions began, more controversial amendments might follow. In April Villafuerte filed a resolution to form a constituent assembly 'for the purpose of considering proposals to amend or revise the Constitution upon a vote of three-fourths of all members of Congress'. Despite Villafuerte subsequently withdrawing support for his own resolution, in May the House of Representatives' committee on constitutional amendments rejected a motion proposing to archive the resolution and thus end discussions on the matter. However, the death in August of former President Corazon Aquino, which provoked a period of national mourning during which tens of thousands of Filipinos took to the streets to pay their last respects to their erstwhile leader, appeared to diminish hopes of achieving charter change in the foreseeable future. Aquino had been vociferous in her objections to reform of the Constitution, which her administration had introduced in 1987, and several prominent politicians, including the then acting Executive Secretary and presidential adviser, Gabriel Claudio, urged members of the House of Representatives to refrain from demanding charter change out of deference to the late Aquino.

Meanwhile, Lakas-CMD and Kampi were merged in May 2009, thereby forming Lakas-Kampi-CMD, in a move that was deeply unpopular among significant factions within both Lakas-CMD and Kampi. In September a group comprising 50 Lakas-CMD officials, led by former Speaker Jose de Venecia and former President Fidel Ramos, denounced the merger as 'illegal and null and void', since a national assembly meeting had not been convened to approve it, and urged Comelec to proscribe the newly established party from using the name of Lakas. De Venecia filed a petition with the Supreme Court in November, seeking the cancellation, by Comelec, of Lakas-Kampi-CMD's registration and for Lakas-CMD to be reinstated as the ruling party. However, the Supreme Court upheld the legality of the merger in December, deeming Comelec's conduct to have been 'in accord with the facts and applicable laws and jurisprudence'. Meanwhile, in the President's State of the Nation address in July 2009, Arroyo publicly refuted ongoing claims that she was seeking to change the Constitution in order to secure a second six-year term of office.

The Maguindanao massacre

In mid-November 2009 some 57 people were killed when a convoy of supporters of local politician Ismael Mangudadatu was ambushed by a group of armed men on the island of Mindanao; the convoy had been on its way to file nomination papers for Mangudadatu, who had previously announced his intention to stand against local mayor Andal Ampatuan, Jr (son of the incumbent Governor of Maguindanao, Andal Ampatuan Sr, and a prominent member of the powerful provincial Ampatuan clan) in municipal polls due to be held, concurrently with legislative and presidential elections, in May 2010. It later emerged that Mangudadatu had sent the convoy to file his papers on his behalf, fearing that he might be attacked should he himself attempt to do so and believing that his female relatives would not be harmed. Witnesses described seeing the group of armed men, estimated to number some 100, shoot the victims at close range before burying their bodies in shallow graves; Mangudadatu's wife and two sisters, along with 30 journalists, were among the dead. Jesus Dureza, adviser to President Arroyo on Mindanao, denounced the attack as 'a gruesome massacre of civilians unequalled in recent history'; Arroyo, who pledged to spare no effort to bring those responsible to justice, declared a state of emergency in the region, upon Dureza's recommendation, in order to assist the authorities in their search for the perpetrators of the violence. Witnesses were reported to have identified Ampatuan, Jr, as the main assailant; shortly thereafter, he was expelled from the ruling Lakas-Kampi-CMD party, together with his brother, Zaldy Ampatuan, who was also suspended as Governor of the Autonomous Region of Muslim Mindanao (ARMM—see Separatist Tensions and Militancy), and his father, who was dismissed as Governor of Maguindanao. Ampatuan, Jr, surrendered to the authorities at the end of November but denied any involvement in the attack. At the beginning of December he was charged with 25 counts of murder, and he was subsequently charged with a further 16 of the 57 killings. A few days later martial law was imposed in Maguindanao, coinciding with the launch, by the police and armed forces, of a large-scale operation against militants in the region. Also in early December it was announced that the entire provincial police force, comprising some 1,092 police officers, was to be replaced by personnel from other regions in order to ensure an impartial investigation of the murders, without fear of relatives and supporters of the Ampatuan clan within the Maguindanao police force sabotaging the investigation.

Martial law was removed in mid-December 2009, following widespread criticism by the opposition that its implementation had been a disproportionate response. Following a preliminary court hearing, also in mid-December, Ampatuan, Jr formally pleaded not guilty on 41 charges of murder in January 2010. In February 196 people were charged with involvement in the attack, among them Andal Ampatuan, Sr, Zaldy Ampatuan and other prominent members of the clan. In mid-April the acting Secretary of Justice, Alberto Agra, directed prosecutors to dismiss multiple murder charges against Zaldy Ampatuan and his cousin, Akmad Ampatuan, the mayor of Mamasapano, owing to an apparent lack of evidence. (The two had filed a petition seeking a judicial review of the charges against them; similar petitions lodged by Andal Ampatuan, Jr, and his father were not granted.) In the following week the families of 43 of the victims filed a joint motion for reconsideration of Agra's directive, contending that it was merely a reflection of Arroyo's indebtedness to the Ampatuan clan, which had supported her throughout her presidency; the Government repudiated such claims. However, Agra reversed his decision in early May, citing the emergence of new evidence that appeared to incriminate both Zaldy and Akmad Ampatuan. In June the two men lodged separate petitions with the Court of Appeals seeking to nullify Agra's revocation of his initial directive on the grounds that their constitutionally guaranteed right to due process had been violated when Agra accepted as fact testimony submitted by a private prosecution lawyer without affording the accused an opportunity to provide counter-evidence. At mid-2011 the appeals process continued; Zaldy and Akmad Ampatuan remained in detention pending a final decision.

Meanwhile, the trial of 19 of the 196 people charged in connection with the massacre, including principal suspects Andal Ampatuan, Jr and his father, commenced at the beginning of September 2010. Given the naming of 200 witnesses by the prosecution and of a further 300 by the defence, the trial was not expected to be concluded rapidly. On the opening day of the trial, a former house servant of the Ampatuan family testified that

Ampatuan, Sr had asked members of his family how best to prevent Mangudadatu from filing his election candidacy papers six days before the massacre, in response to which Ampatuan, Jr had allegedly suggested the multiple killings. The former employee further alleged that on the day of the murders he had overheard Ampatuan, Sr recommending that the journalists accompanying the convoy of Mangudadatu's supporters be released unharmed, but that Ampatuan, Jr had overruled his father, insisting that sparing the lives of any witnesses to the ambush would pose a threat to the clan. With less than one-half of the 196 charged persons in custody by the time the trial opened, there were widespread reports of attempts to intimidate investigators and witnesses by supporters of the Ampatuan clan. At least five people known to have provided, or agreed to provide, incriminating testimony against the Ampatuans were reported to have been killed prior to the commencement of the trial.

A rift between the public prosecutors and the private lawyers of the victims' relatives became increasingly apparent as the trial progressed, and precipitated the resignation, in March 2011, of two public prosecutors, both of whom cited an 'intolerable' working environment. Meanwhile, a report published by international organization Human Rights Watch in November 2010 claimed that during the previous 20 years the Ampatuan clan had been responsible for at least 56 killings in addition to those of the Maguindanao massacre; the organization urged the Philippine Government to conduct a full investigation into the claims.

The elections of 2010

In late November 2009 President Arroyo announced that she would be standing for election to the Congress at the 2010 elections from her home province of Pampanga. Her decision was criticized by the opposition, which contended that it represented a calculated bid to hold on to power and to retain immunity from potential corruption charges. Observers also noted that a congressional seat could provide Arroyo with a platform from which to effect constitutional change in order to introduce a parliamentary system of government, whereby she might continue to govern the country in a newly created prime-ministerial position. As with similar allegations made against her in mid-2008 (see The elections of 2007 and subsequent events), Arroyo strenuously denied the claims.

In January 2010 it was announced that about 100,000 additional police officers and soldiers were to be deployed across the Philippines in advance of the elections, in order to help enforce a ban on all unlicensed weapons and to encourage private militias to disband. The announcement was widely interpreted as an attempt to reassure the public about security in the aftermath of the Maguindanao massacre. The Philippines' first-ever presidential election debate, in which eight candidates participated, was staged in February. Former President Joseph Estrada, standing as a candidate, was notably absent from the proceedings, citing 'bias' against him by the *Philippine Daily Inquirer*, which had organized the debate. Official campaigning for the presidential contest began on the following day. Opinion polls conducted in February had suggested that the leading candidates were NP President Manuel Villar and Benigno 'NoyNoy' Aquino, the son of former President Corazon Aquino, whose death in August 2009 had resulted in a significant surge in popular support for Benigno's presidential candidacy. In April Comelec approved the formation of an electoral alliance between the NP and NPC; the LP had contended that the NP-NPC alliance was a 'bogus' union, contrived to attract the status of 'dominant minority party' on account of it boasting the largest number of incumbent officials, one of the factors considered in accrediting a grouping with the status; securing that rank would entitle the NP-NPC to a copy of election returns from electronic ballot-counting machines.

Presidential, legislative and local elections, held according to schedule on 10 May 2010, were, as on previous occasions, marred by numerous reports of fraud and 'vote-buying'. Voters fled a polling station in the town of Datu Piang, in Maguindanao province close to the scene of the November 2009 massacre, to escape clashes between rival gangs and soldiers. Elections were postponed in several towns owing to security concerns; in Kabuntalan voting was suspended after two people died in a gun battle between two clans of rival candidates contesting the position of deputy mayor. At least 10 people were reported to have died in election-related violence, although polling in the majority of areas was generally conducted in a peaceful manner. However, the first national computerized election in the history of the Philippines was reported to have presented significant problems in both the casting and the counting of ballots. According to some sources, as many as 7m.–8m. people had been unable to cast their vote owing to the failure of numerous automated counting machines. Moreover, the discovery of a large cache of automated voting machines in a private residence two days after the polls prompted considerable speculation of serious electoral fraud. However, the Chairman of Comelec, Jose Melo, dismissed the incident as a routine relocation of machines in order to ensure their eventual safe return, and continued to insist that the fully computerized system made it impossible to counterfeit results without detectable irregularities appearing in the data. Melo contended that the allegations of electoral fraud had been contrived to delay the proclamation of the results, and demanded evidence from those who claimed that the elections had not been free and fair. According to an audit of the precinct count optical scan (PCOS) machines, which compared the vote tally transmitted by the machines with a manual count in selected precincts, the PCOS machines generated a 99.6% degree of accuracy in counting ballots, while a poll indicated that the percentage of Filipinos who believed that the counting of votes had been carried out in a free and fair manner increased to 83% (from just 55% at the 2007 election), with 65% of those surveyed identifying the new automated system as being primarily responsible for the increased legitimacy of the polls.

In the presidential election, according to the official results released by Comelec on 8 June 2010, Benigno Aquino received 15,208,678 votes, equivalent to 41.9% of the total cast. Joseph Estrada secured 9,487,837 votes (26.1%), Manuel Villar garnered 5,573,835 votes (15.4%) and the former Lakas-Kampi-CMD Chairman and Secretary of National Defense, Gilberto Teodoro, received 4,095,839 votes (11.3%). Despite Aquino's considerable margin, Estrada's second placing represented a far better performance than had been expected of the former President, who had been placed fourth by the opinion polls conducted in February, behind Villar, Aquino and Teodoro, the candidate endorsed by the outgoing Arroyo administration. (Prior to the election it had been claimed that Arroyo, realizing that Teodoro was unlikely to be elected, had been secretly supporting, and securing votes for, Villar; the allegations were adamantly refuted by her administration, which insisted that Arroyo had remained committed to Teodoro's electoral bid.) The election for the vice-presidency was narrowly won by Jejomar 'Jojo' Binay, leader of the PDP-Laban group and Estrada's running mate; Binay defeated Aquino's running mate, Manuel 'Mar' Roxas II of the LP (the grandson of the former President of the same name), by 14,645,574 votes to 13,918,490. Meanwhile, on 12 May Arroyo was proclaimed as the congressional representative of the second district of Pampanga, having defeated her three rivals by a significant margin.

Lakas-Kampi-CMD was subsequently reported to have won 105 of the 286 seats in the House of Representatives, the LP 42 and the NPC 31, with numerous seats apparently remaining undeclared some time after the polls. In the elections for 12 of the 24 seats in the Senate, the LP and the NP-NPC alliance won three seats each, Lakas-Kampi-CMD and the PMP secured two each, and the People's Reform Party (PRP) won one seat. The remaining seat was secured by an independent candidate. The newly elected Senators included PRP President Miriam Defensor Santiago, a candidate in the 1992 presidential poll, and Teofisto Guingona III, the son of former Vice-President Teofisto Guingona, Jr.

Recent developments: the administration of Benigno Aquino (2010–)

Benigno Aquino was sworn in as President on 30 June 2010. In his inauguration speech, the new President hailed the day as marking 'the end of a regime indifferent to the needs of the people'; Aquino also pledged to lessen the country's problems 'by wielding the tools of justice, social reform and equitable governance', and identified a number of priorities for his administration, including combating corruption, addressing the persistent budgetary deficit, reducing bureaucracy in order to render the country more attractive to potential investors, enhancing national infrastructure and improving the education system. On the previous day Aquino had announced the composition of his new Cabinet, which was dominated by members of the LP, technocrats and representatives of the business sector. Alberto Romulo retained the foreign affairs portfolio, while Voltaire Gazmin was appointed Secretary of National Defense; both men had been close allies of former President Corazon Aquino. Cesar Purisima, who had resigned from the post of Secretary of Finance in 2005 in protest against the perceived illegality of

Arroyo's presidency, resumed responsibility for the finance portfolio. Other notable members of the incoming Cabinet included Leila de Lima, hitherto Chairperson of the Commission on Human Rights of the Philippines, who became Secretary of Justice, an appointment that was well received by human rights and anti-corruption groups. Also on 29 June 2010 Aquino announced plans to create a 'truth commission', which was to investigate alleged anomalies from the Arroyo presidency.

On 1 July 2010 Arroyo filed a congressional resolution appealing for a constitutional convention to propose changes to the Constitution, furthering concerns among her critics that she was seeking the introduction of a parliamentary system of government with a view to returning to power in a prime-ministerial position. Some observers, while supportive of constitutional reform, questioned whether Arroyo was the right person to file the resolution, arguing that her unpopularity would likely result in the resolution being defeated, while others suggested that Arroyo's decision to file the resolution reflected an addiction to power on the part of the former President. A presidential spokesperson stated that constitutional change was 'not a priority' and that debates on the proposal would distract attention from the Aquino administration's primary objectives of combating poverty and corruption, while Feliciano Belmonte, who was elected Speaker of the House of Representatives in mid-July, argued that the issue of constitutional reform was 'time-consuming and divisive'. Aquino himself stated that he would not endorse proposals to reform the Constitution unless there was proof that such action was urgently required. At the end of July Aquino revoked by executive order some 977 'midnight appointments' authorized by the Arroyo administration during its final weeks, and formally established the Philippines Truth Commission of 2010. A small group of legislators, known allies of Arroyo, filed a petition with the Supreme Court in August seeking to nullify the Commission, claiming that it was unconstitutional and encroached upon the respective remits of the Department of Justice and the Office of the Ombudsman. In December the Court ruled that the Commission was unlawful since it 'singled out' an individual, Arroyo, which contravened the terms of the Constitution. Aquino expressed concern at the ruling, which he denounced as a set-back for anti-graft reform but vowed to continue his efforts undeterred. The Secretary of Justice dismissed the ruling as being politically motivated, an apparent reference to the fact that 14 of the 15 Supreme Court justices had been appointed by Arroyo, including the Chief Justice, Renato Corona, whose 'midnight appointment' in April had not been challenged by the incoming Aquino administration. In October a petition filed by Bai Omera Dianalan-Lucman appealing against the revocation of his 'midnight appointment' was upheld by the Supreme Court, prompting an angry response from Aquino, who urged the Court to reconsider its ruling, which, the President argued, would have 'far-reaching consequences' throughout the executive branch of government.

In October 2010 the Supreme Court upheld the constitutionality of the Human Security Act, which was known to have been invoked just twice since its implementation in July 2007. Several human rights groups and legislators had lodged separate petitions seeking to revoke the legislation, arguing that its definition of 'terrorism' was too broad-based and that it posed a significant threat to civil liberties. At mid-2011 both legislative chambers were debating controversial legislation, first introduced in 2005, seeking to promote awareness, and increase availability, of contraceptives, which, if approved, would require the Government to provide reproductive health education in schools. Critics of the Responsible Parenthood, Reproductive Health and Population and Development Bill argued that it would lead to an increase in the number of abortions and a decline in moral values. Tens of thousands of people attended a rally in Manila in March 2011 to protest against the draft legislation, which was due to be voted on later in the year. However, others contested that the legislation was necessary in order to reduce both the national population growth rate (and in turn the rate of poverty) and the incidence of medical complications arising from the practice of unsafe abortions (abortion being illegal in the Philippines).

Meanwhile, in early July 2010 Nicanor Faeldon voluntarily surrendered to the authorities 'in recognition of the legitimacy' of Aquino's presidency; Faeldon was one of several military officers who in November 2007 had walked out of court during their trial on charges of staging a coup in July 2003 and occupied a hotel in protest against the perceived illegitimacy of Arroyo's presidency. In October 2010 Aquino announced a presidential proclamation granting amnesty to rebel soldiers involved in the military uprisings of 2003 and 2006. Senator Antonio Trillanes IV was among those released from prison in December 2010, and was able to take up his seat in the Senate for the first time in January 2011. In February former cabinet minister Angelo Reyes, a close ally of Arroyo who had served as army chief of staff in 2000–01, committed suicide prior to a scheduled appearance before a congressional committee investigating allegations that he had embezzled more than US $1m. from state coffers upon his departure from his military post.

In January 2011 the US district court of Hawaii approved the disbursement of US $1,000 to each of 7,526 victims of human rights abuses perpetrated during the regime of former President Ferdinand Marcos; the compensation payments commenced in late February, and by mid-April some 6,500 victims had received their monies. The US court also held Imelda Marcos and Ferdinand Marcos, Jr in contempt for violating a court order requesting information on assets belonging to the Marcos estate, and fined them $353.6m., which was to fulfil in part the $2,000m. ruling against the Marcos estate in 1994.

In late February 2011 Albert del Rosario was appointed acting Secretary of Foreign Affairs, in place of Alberto G. Romulo. On the same day Edcel Lagman was elected as National Chairman of Lakas-Kampi-CMD, in place of Gloria Arroyo, while Ramon Bong Revilla, Jr was chosen as the party's National President.

Meanwhile, in early August 2010 an apparent suicide bombing at Zamboanga airport in the southern Philippines claimed the lives of two people, including the perpetrator, and injured 24 others, among them the Governor of Sulu, Sakur Tan. The US ambassador to the Philippines cancelled a scheduled visit to Zamboanga. The attack was believed to have been an attempt to assassinate Sakur Tan, who had spearheaded campaigns targeting members of the Abu Sayyaf grouping. Eight Hong Kong tourists were killed and a further seven injured when a bus was hijacked in Manila in mid-August by a former Filipino police officer, Rolando Mendoza, who had recently been dismissed on suspicion of extortion and brutality. An 11-hour siege was finally concluded when armed police officers approached the bus at close quarters and fatally shot Mendoza. The Aquino administration attracted criticism for its handling of the incident, with local police officers and government officials apparently having been left to tackle the situation without direct federal assistance. Aquino issued a public apology for the outcome of the affair and pledged to reprimand those found to be responsible. Witnesses stated that negotiation efforts appeared to have been leading to a peaceful resolution to the impasse when the authorities decided to approach the bus and that it was the advance of the police officers that had provoked Mendoza into opening fire on his hostages; the strategy had been intended to carry the element of surprise, but, unbeknown to the authorities, had been broadcast live on television and watched by Mendoza on a monitor aboard the bus. Of further embarrassment to the Philippine authorities was the revelation by Secretary of Justice de Lima in September that the Government was investigating the theory that some of the tourists killed might have been shot by the police officers trying to rescue them. In the same month investigators recommended that criminal charges be brought against 12 people deemed to have been responsible for the violent conclusion to the siege, including police officers, the mayor of Manila and two journalists; three national broadcasting networks, which had relayed live images of the police operation, were also identified as having been culpable.

Separatist Tensions and Militancy

During the early 1970s there was an increase in guerrilla activity, by the New People's Army (NPA), the armed wing of the outlawed (Maoist) Communist Party of the Philippines (CPP), in the north of the country, and by the Moro National Liberation Front (MNLF), a mainly Muslim separatist movement, in the south. The Philippines continued to be affected by regional instability during the years that followed, owing to the activities of these and other insurgent groups.

Upon his inauguration in June 1992, President Fidel Ramos gave priority to persuading the various factions to give up their armed struggle. In July two communist leaders were conditionally released, and Ramos submitted to Congress an amnesty proclamation for about 4,500 members of the NPA, the MNLF and renegade former members of the armed forces who had already applied for amnesty. In August, following the formation of the NUC (see above), Ramos ordered the temporary release from prison of more communist leaders, including the Commander of the NPA, Romulo Kintanar, and the NDF Spokesman, Saturnino Ocampo, and also of 16 rebel soldiers.

The NDF, the CPP and the NPA

In mid-August 1992 the Government began discussions with exiled representatives of the NDF in the Netherlands. In September President Ramos repealed anti-subversion legislation, in place since 1957, that proscribed the CPP. Nevertheless, the exiled leadership of the NDF pledged that the CPP would continue its armed struggle, although there was a widening division within the CPP over co-operation with the NUC.

In July 1993 the CPP's influential Metro Manila-Rizal regional committee publicly broke away from the CPP Central Committee led by Jose Maria Sison, a founder member of the CPP who had been based in the Netherlands since his release from prison in 1986, and who had assumed the party chairmanship in April 1992. This followed the attempted dissolution by Sison of the region's leading committee and its armed unit, the Alex Boncayao Brigade (ABB), accused of factionalism and military excesses. The Metro Manila-Rizal organization, which comprised about 40% of CPP members, was subsequently joined by the CPP regional committee of the Visayas. In October four communist leaders, including Kintanar, were expelled from the CPP and the NPA for refusing to recognize the authority of Sison.

Negotiations between the Government and the NDF in 1994–96 were marred by their failure to agree terms for the granting of immunity for NDF members and the arrest and subsequent release of a number of leading members of the organization. In March 1998 the Government and the NDF signed a Comprehensive Agreement on Respect for Human Rights and International Law, the first of four agreements that would complete the peace process.

Despite Joseph Estrada's inclusion of former communist activists in the Government upon his inauguration as President in June 1998, the leadership of the NDF-CPP-NPA condemned his administration. In July Estrada approved the human rights agreement that had been reached by the NDF and the Ramos administration, and invited the exiled leadership of the NDF to the Philippines to resume peace negotiations. In February 1999, however, Estrada suspended peace talks with the communists following the NPA's abduction of three hostages. The Government also suspended the Joint Agreement on Safety and Immunity Guarantees, exposing NDF-CPP-NPA members to the risk of arrest. A total of five hostages were released by the NPA in April, although the communists continued to reject other conditions for negotiations.

In May 1999 the NDF withdrew from peace negotiations in response to the Senate's ratification of a defence treaty with the USA (see below). Estrada subsequently adopted a position of outright hostility towards the movement. However, the NDF-CPP-NPA were recruiting increasing numbers of members, who were disillusioned with the Estrada administration. In an attempt to divide the communist movement, Estrada entered into negotiations with several breakaway factions, but failed to make substantial progress. In January 2000 the Government suspended military operations against the communists to facilitate the release of two NPA hostages. In December Estrada announced that a peace agreement had been concluded with the Revolutionary Proletarian Army (RPA)-ABB. The agreement, which applied only to the central Philippines, was accompanied by a presidential amnesty for some political prisoners whose death sentences had been upheld by the Supreme Court, and by the release of an additional 235 political detainees. In the same month the NPA rejected an offer by the Government of a truce.

In April 2001 the Government of President Gloria Arroyo held peace talks with the NDF in Oslo, Norway. The talks were reported to have made some progress, with both sides agreeing to undertake confidence-building measures, including the release of political prisoners. Further discussions were held in May, but were suspended in June when the NDF was implicated in the assassination of Congressman Rodolfo Aguinaldo. In November 28 people were killed on the island of Mindanao when fighting broke out between the NPA and government soldiers. However, despite the renewal of violence, exiled NDF members announced shortly afterwards that they had agreed to resume peace talks with the Government in Oslo in December. In the same month Arroyo announced a temporary cease-fire with the NDF, following its offer to suspend hostilities for one month if the Government made a reciprocal gesture. However, the arrival of US troops in the Philippines in 2002 (see below) threatened further peace negotiations, as the NDF continued to oppose any US involvement in the country. In May Arroyo called off further peace negotiations following a number of political assassinations.

In August 2002 the USA added the CPP and the NPA to its list of international terrorist organizations and requested that the Government of the Netherlands cease benefit payments to all group members resident there. In the same month government representatives met with members of the NDF in Quezon City, with the intention of resuming peace talks. However, Sison continued to oppose any negotiations between the CPP and the Government while Arroyo remained President. In October the Government formally designated the NDF a terrorist organization, while emphasizing that it remained willing to continue peace negotiations. In January 2003 police officials announced that they intended to charge Sison with involvement in several murders, including those of Aguinaldo and former NPA leader Romulo Kintanar (who was killed by unidentified gunmen in that month), and to seek his extradition to stand trial in the Philippines. In June fighting broke out between government troops and NPA rebels on the island of Samar, and in July, following continued hostilities by the NPA, the Government announced that it intended to launch a military offensive in order to quell the insurgency. In January 2004 NPA rebels attacked a power station near Manila, causing eight deaths.

Peace negotiations between the Government and the NDF finally recommenced in Oslo in February 2004, despite ongoing clashes between the two sides. A third round of talks took place in Oslo in June. Negotiations were scheduled to resume in August, but were suspended after the NDF claimed that the Government was failing to meet its demands, including the implementation of measures to secure the removal of the CPP and the NPA from the USA's list of international terrorist organizations. Sporadic violence continued, and at the end of 2004 the armed forces announced that a total of 182 NPA members had been killed in clashes with government troops in that year and a further 910 had surrendered or been captured. In February 2005 14 NPA rebels and two government soldiers were killed in skirmishes in the town of Compostela, some 930 km south-east of Manila. Negotiations between the NDF and the Government resumed during the first half of 2005, but were abandoned by the former in August in response to the political scandal surrounding President Arroyo (see Domestic Political Affairs). Discussions between the two sides resumed in September. However, hopes for a peaceable resolution to the ongoing conflict suffered a setback in November, when at least nine soldiers were killed and approximately 20 were injured in an ambush near Calinog, in the province of Iloilo, which was alleged to have been carried out by NPA members. Furthermore, in January 2006 a group of suspected NPA members conducted a raid on a prison in Barangay Cuta, Iloilo, during which they released 14 detainees. Later in that month it was reported that Philippine troops had killed at least 18 NPA rebels during fierce clashes in Santa Ignacia, north of Manila. In October Arroyo expressed her hope that the NPA movement would be largely defeated by the time that her term expired in May 2010.

In May 2007 five police officers were killed on the island of Mindoro by a landmine believed to have been planted by the NPA. In August Sison was arrested in the Netherlands, where he remained in exile, on suspicion of ordering the assassinations of former associates Romulo Kintanar and Arturo Tabara in 2003 and 2004, respectively; he was released in September owing to lack of evidence. (The Dutch prosecution service subsequently conducted further investigations into the case, before concluding in March 2009 that there was still insufficient evidence to prosecute Sison.) Meanwhile, at the beginning of September 2007 the Philippines military filed charges with the Commission on Human Rights accusing Sison and 18 other members of the CPP and the NPA of the murder or attempted murder of six people. Shortly afterwards, in an effort to restart the stalled peace negotiations, Arroyo signed a proclamation offering amnesty to communist rebels who relinquished their weapons. However, the NPA continued its activities, raiding a mining project of a Swiss company in January 2008. In March at least one government soldier and seven NPA rebels were killed in fighting after the NPA attacked an army base in the province of Surigao del Sur, on Mindanao. Also in that month the army claimed to have secured control of an NPA base in the north of the country, following a week of fighting in which two soldiers died. In May it was reported that Philippine troops had killed three NPA militants in clashes on Mindanao. Continued sporadic violence resulted in further fatalities on both sides in the following months. Little progress appeared to have been made at

THE PHILIPPINES

Introductory Survey

two rounds of informal talks between the Government and the NDF held in Oslo in May and November, with the NDF reportedly rejecting the Government's demand for an indefinite cease-fire as a condition for the resumption of formal peace negotiations. In December the military announced that five soldiers had been killed in an NPA attack on an army vehicle in the province of Surigao del Norte. Philippine troops captured an NPA base on Mindanao in February 2009, following fighting in which at least 11 rebels and five soldiers died. At least nine further rebels and one soldier were killed in December during a raid by Philippine troops on an NPA camp near the town of Valencia. Meanwhile, the Government and the CPP agreed in August 2009 to renew peace talks following the release by the Government of two senior CPP leaders; some observers interpreted the resumption of negotiations as a tactical move to enhance the popularity of both the CPP and of political allies of President Arroyo in advance of the 2010 elections. However, hopes of a resumption of formal talks were threatened by the arrest in February of that year of 43 people attending a health convention on suspicion of belonging to the NPA. The detainees denied any connection to the NPA and accused the authorities of fabricating incriminating evidence against them.

Upon assuming power in June 2010, the administration of President Benigno Aquino emphasized its commitment to concluding a peace settlement with the NDF, the NPA and the CPP. In July Aquino announced the formation of two government 'peace panels', one to facilitate negotiations with the NDF, the NPA and the CPP, and the other to focus on the peace process with the Moro Islamic Liberation Front (MILF—see The activities of the MILF). The NDF continued to appeal for the release of all political prisoners and meaningful land reform, while sporadic violent clashes were reported throughout 2010. In August NPA members killed a local official and eight police officers on Samar island. Following a meeting between the Government's chief negotiator, Alexander Padilla, and senior NDF leader Luis Jalandoni in Hong Kong in early December, it was announced that formal peace negotiations were to be convened in February 2011, under the auspices of the Norwegian Government. In the mean time, Padilla announced that safe passage and immunity from prosecution was to be restored to NDF negotiators. In mid-December 2010 Aquino ordered the release of the 43 people arrested at the health convention in February, declaring that their 'right to due process' had been denied during the full term of their detention. Also in mid-December 10 government soldiers were killed in an ambush by NPA rebels, just two days before the scheduled commencement of an 18-day cease-fire between government troops and the NPA, the longest cease-fire agreed in some 10 years. Nevertheless, the cease-fire appeared to be observed by both sides. Following its conclusion in early January 2011, senior NPA leader Tiro Alcantara (alias Ka or Comrade Bart) was arrested and charged with more than 20 counts of murder. Formal peace talks were convened as scheduled in February, and were reported to have been constructive, with both sides expressing their resolve to conclude a comprehensive settlement by June 2012.

The activities of the MNLF

During 1986 the Government of Corazon Aquino conducted negotiations to seek a solution to the conflict with Muslim separatists in the south. A cease-fire was established with the MNLF in September, following an announcement by the Government that it would grant legal and judicial autonomy to four predominantly Muslim provinces in Mindanao. Further talks ensued, under the auspices of the Organization of the Islamic Conference (OIC, see p. 400), and on 5 January 1987 the MNLF signed an agreement to relinquish demands for complete independence in Mindanao, and to accept autonomy. In February 1988, however, the MNLF resumed its offensive against the Government, which had attempted to prevent the MNLF from gaining membership of the OIC (which would imply that the MNLF was regarded as representing an independent state). The 1987 Constitution granted eventual autonomy to Muslim provinces in Mindanao, which had been promised by President Ferdinand Marcos in 1976. In November 1989 a referendum was held, in the country's 13 southern provinces and nine cities in Mindanao, on proposed legislation that envisaged the autonomy of these provinces and cities, with direct elections to a unicameral legislature in each province; this contrasted with the MNLF's demand for autonomy in 23 provinces, to be granted without a referendum. Four provinces (Lanao del Sur, Maguindanao, Tawi-Tawi and Sulu) voted in favour of the government proposal, and formed the ARMM.

In February 1990 the candidate favoured by Aquino, Zacaria Candao (formerly the legal representative of the MNLF), was elected to the governorship of Muslim Mindanao. In October the autonomous regional government was granted limited executive powers. The MNLF boycotted the election, on the grounds that the provisions for autonomy were more limited than those reached with Marcos in 1976. Under Ramos's programme of reconciliation, the MNLF participated in discussions with the NUC. In October 1992 the leader of the MNLF, Nur Misuari, agreed to return to the Philippines from exile in Libya to facilitate negotiations. In January 1993 talks were suspended, and violence in Mindanao escalated prior to the impending elections for the region's Governor and Assembly. At the elections, which took place on 25 March, a former ambassador, Lininding Pangandaman, was elected Governor, with the unofficial support of Ramos.

In April 1993 exploratory discussions in Jakarta, Indonesia, between Nur Misuari and representatives of the Philippine Government led to an agreement on the resumption of formal peace talks under the auspices of the OIC. Further exploratory talks took place in Saudi Arabia in June, prior to the first formal negotiations in October in Jakarta, where the MNLF demanded the creation of an autonomous Islamic state in the south, as agreed in 1976. In November 1993 the two sides signed a memorandum of understanding (MOU) and an interim cease-fire was agreed.

The second round of formal peace negotiations between the Government and the MNLF took place in Jakarta in April 1994. Agreement was subsequently reached on government administration in the proposed autonomous region, Islamic law, education and revenue-sharing between Manila and the autonomous zones. In August 1995 Misuari agreed for the first time to a referendum (which was required under the Constitution) prior to the establishment of an autonomous zone, but demanded the immediate establishment of a provisional MNLF government to ensure that the referendum was conducted fairly.

In June 1996 it was announced that the MNLF and the Government had finally reached agreement on a proposal by Ramos for the establishment of a transitional administrative council, to be known as the Southern Philippines Council for Peace and Development (SPCPD), which was to derive powers from the Office of the President. The five-member SPCPD, which was to be headed by Misuari, was to co-ordinate peace-keeping and development efforts in 14 provinces and 10 cities in Mindanao, with the assistance of an 81-member Consultative Assembly and a religious advisory council. After a period of three years a referendum was to be conducted in each province and city to determine whether it would join the existing ARMM (the MNLF had abandoned its demands for autonomy in 23 provinces in Mindanao). In July government officials announced that, under the peace agreement, Muslims were to be allocated one cabinet post, and were to be granted representation in state-owned companies and constitutional commissions. In addition, Ramos offered to support the candidacy of Misuari in the forthcoming gubernatorial election in the ARMM. In September the Government and the MNLF signed a final draft of the peace agreement in Jakarta. In the same month elections took place peacefully in the ARMM for the region's Governor and Assembly; Misuari, who, as agreed, contested the gubernatorial election with the support of Lakas-NUCD, was elected unopposed. In October it was announced that Misuari had been officially appointed Chairman of the SPCPD. In March 1997 more than 1,000 former MNLF members were integrated into the armed forces under the terms of the peace accord.

In August 2001, after some delay, the referendum was finally held. As a result, the city of Marawi and the province of Basilan elected to join the ARMM. However, 10 provinces and 13 cities rejected the offer of membership and the electoral turn-out was low. In November around 600 supporters of Governor Misuari (who had been dismissed from the leadership of the MNLF in April owing to his widespread unpopularity) led an armed uprising against military and police outposts on the island of Jolo, resulting in the deaths of more than 100 people. The violence was reportedly intended to prevent an election to the governorship of the ARMM, scheduled for late November, from taking place. By instigating the rebellion, Misuari had violated the terms of his five-year peace accord with the Government, although he claimed that by holding an election the Government was itself breaking the terms of the agreement. Shortly afterwards President Arroyo suspended Misuari from his post. Later in November Misuari and six of his supporters were arrested by the Malaysian authorities for attempting to gain illegal entry into the country. On 26 November polls to elect a new governor, vice-governor and 44 regional legislators for the province were conducted. The turn-out was low, a fact partly attributed to the escalating military presence in the region. The next day government forces launched air-strikes on MNLF insurgents who remained in Zamboanga City, killing 25 rebels and one civilian. As they attempted to flee, the rebels took several local residents hostage. The next day the hostages were released in return for the rebels' safe passage out of the city, thus bringing an end to the confrontation. In early December the President's favoured candidate, former MNLF member Farouk Hussein, was declared Governor. He immediately urged the establishment of peace in the troubled region and stated that he would seek to open a dialogue with the remaining followers of Misuari and other radical groups in the area, including Abu Sayyaf. In January 2002 Misuari was finally deported from Malaysia to stand trial in Manila on charges of inciting a rebellion; he subsequently refused to enter a plea to the charges against him. In January 2003 the four factions comprising the MNLF signed a declaration of unity in advance of the election of a new leadership; significantly, Misuari's name was excluded from the statement, preventing him from regaining the chairmanship of the group.

In February 2005 more than 500 MNLF rebels loyal to Misuari, led by Habier Malik, attacked government troops in several towns on the island of Jolo, in retaliation for a recent army assault, which military leaders insisted had been targeted at Abu Sayyaf (see below), rather than the MNLF; an estimated 30 soldiers and 70 MNLF fighters were killed in the ensuing clashes. Elections to the governorship and Regional Legislative Assembly of the ARMM took place in August; Zaldy Ampatuan, the candidate of Lakas-CMD, was elected Governor. At least nine MNLF rebels were killed in April 2007 during an offensive by government troops on a base commanded by Malik, who was believed to be responsible for a recent attack on an army outpost in which two soldiers and a child had died; some 8,000 people reportedly fled the violence. The OIC appealed for both sides to cease fighting and to abide by the 1996 peace agreement, but the Chief of Staff of the Armed Forces, Gen. Hermogenes Esperon, maintained that the operation was not targeted at the MNLF, but rather at Malik and his followers, who had allegedly aligned themselves with Abu Sayyaf. Misuari, who remained under house arrest near Manila but was yet to be convicted, contested the Sulu gubernatorial election in May 2007, but was overwhelmingly defeated. In August President Arroyo insisted that efforts would be made to maintain the cease-fire with the MNLF, despite the apparent involvement of members of the group in clashes between the armed forces and Abu Sayyaf (see The activities of Abu Sayyaf).

Tripartite talks involving the OIC, the Philippine Government and the MNLF were held in Jeddah, Saudi Arabia, in November 2007 with the aim of addressing complaints by the MNLF that the Government had failed fully to implement the 1996 agreement; a second round of discussions was held in Istanbul, Turkey, in February 2008. Meanwhile, there was disquiet among MNLF members over the accord being negotiated between the Government and the MILF (see The activities of the MILF), amid fears that it would violate the group's own peace agreement. The appointment by the MNLF Central Committee of Muslimin Sema, hitherto Secretary-General of the group, as its Chairman was rejected by Misuari loyalists in April, prompting the OIC to express concern at the internal divisions within the group. Misuari was released from house arrest on bail later in that month. In May leaders of various factions of the MNLF, meeting in Tripoli, Libya, agreed to form a 'transitional leadership and unification committee', comprising six members, including Misuari and Sema, with the aim of resolving their differences. However, it later appeared that Misuari, who had sent two representatives to the meeting rather than attending himself, was unwilling to accept this arrangement. A third round of tripartite discussions, which was scheduled to be held in Manila in late May, was postponed indefinitely, reportedly as a result of the uncertainty over the leadership of the MNLF. Gubernatorial and regional legislative elections were held in the ARMM on 11 August; Ampatuan was re-elected Governor of the region. Later in that month, following a meeting with Sema, the Secretary of the Interior and Local Government, Ronaldo Puno, announced that a total of 5,000 former MNLF fighters had been integrated into the armed forces, and a further 1,600 into the police force. The third round of tripartite talks finally took place in Manila in March 2009, at which the Government and the MNLF agreed to form a joint legal panel to propose amendments to the 1996 agreement; the MNLF delegation was reportedly headed by Misuari and also included Sema. Further talks were held in Damascus, Syria, in May 2009. In the same month skirmishes between MNLF and MILF rebels caused an estimated 2,000 families to flee from Maguindanao and Sultan Kudarat. Sporadic clashes between MNLF and government troops were reported to have resulted in the deaths of about 20 MNLF members and several government soldiers during the latter half of 2009. In April 2010 an MOU emphasizing the intention of both the MNLF and the Government to work towards 'just, meaningful and lasting peace and development in Mindanao' was signed in Libya, and in the following month arrangements for the Bangsamoro Development Assistance Fund were concluded in Surabaya, Indonesia. In December consensus points for proposed amendments to the 1996 ARMM peace accord were initialled by government and MNLF representatives meeting at the Indonesian embassy in Manila. A number of issues of contention remained, but both sides welcomed the initialling of consensus points as a sign of meaningful progress having been made. The fourth round of tripartite talks was held in Jeddah in February 2011; the formation of three panels of experts, which were to report to the OIC in June, was approved. Meanwhile, in January–February clashes between hundreds of rival MNLF and MILF members were reported to have killed at least 13 rebels and injured about a dozen others; some 3,000 local villagers were displaced by the violence.

The activities of the MILF

The MILF, an Islamist fundamentalist grouping demanding secession for Mindanao, which was formed as a breakaway movement from the MNLF in 1978, was covered by the government cease-fire agreed in January 1994 but was not a party to the peace talks. The grouping was widely suspected of having taken advantage of negotiations between the MNLF and the Government to strengthen its position, both by an accumulation of weapons and the recruitment of young militants disaffected with the compliance of the MNLF. In April 1996 the Government and the MILF agreed to a cease-fire in North Cotabato.

In August 1996, for the first time, MILF and government officials met in Davao City for preliminary peace discussions. The MILF had rejected the peace agreement with the MNLF and continued to demand separatism for 23 provinces in Mindanao. Alternating hostilities and short-term cease-fires, together with a high incidence of abductions by the rebels, characterized relations between the Government and the MILF between late 1996 and late 1997. In November 1997 a further cease-fire agreement was signed in which so-called terrorist acts (including abduction and arson) were banned as well as public executions based on Islamic (*Shari'a*) law. However, when the leader of the MILF, Hashim Salamat, returned to the Philippines (after living in Libya for 20 years) in December, he announced that public executions would continue in defiance of the government ban. Despite further clashes between the MILF and the Government in January 1998, with mutual accusations of violations of the cease-fire agreement, peace negotiations continued in February when the MILF demanded recognition of 13 MILF camps in Mindanao as 'legitimate territories'. In March the two sides agreed to create a 'quick response team' to resolve conflicts and confrontations before they escalated into serious clashes. In October the MILF and the Government agreed to disclose the location of their forces to prevent accidental encounters. However, in January 1999, following a statement by the MILF advocating independence for Mindanao, Estrada conducted successive offensives against the MILF, causing the collapse of the 1997 cease-fire agreement. Up to 60 people were estimated to have died in the ensuing fighting and 90,000 residents were displaced. A new cease-fire was implemented at the end of January 1999, and at the beginning of February the Presidential Adviser, Robert Aventajado, was sent to Mindanao to meet Salamat inside an MILF camp. They agreed to the resumption of peace negotiations and to a meeting between Salamat and Estrada to re-establish goodwill between the two sides. However, Estrada cancelled the meeting, as a result of a dispute over its location and security considerations. In March Salamat and Nur Misuari met for the first time in 20 years in an attempt to promote the peace process.

Estrada continued to vacillate between supporting the economic development of Mindanao to eradicate insurrection and threatening to eliminate the rebels through military action. Negotiations between the Government and the MILF took place in October 1999, despite MILF protests against continued government attacks on MILF camps in Mindanao. Clashes between the Government and the MILF continued despite reports of a renewed cease-fire agreement in November. Formal peace negotiations, originally scheduled for December, finally commenced in January 2000 but failed to achieve substantial progress. In that month Estrada announced a new anti-insurgency programme, the National Peace and Development Plan, which aimed to remove the causes of insurgency in Mindanao, including poverty, injustice and disease. Peace talks resumed in March after negotiations scheduled for February were suspended owing to escalating violence, during which the Government claimed to have captured an important MILF base, Camp Omar. Several incendiary devices planted on buses in Mindanao in February, which resulted in nearly 50 civilian deaths, were attributed by government sources to the MILF, but the MILF claimed that the bombings were perpetrated by government agents in an attempt to justify the intensification of the military campaign against the MILF. At further talks in March a protocol was signed with enhanced cease-fire provisions, whereby the Government agreed to recognize 39 MILF camps as 'safe areas' while the MILF representatives agreed to carry a government identity card during talks (which they had formerly claimed would represent a surrender of sovereignty). However, intense fighting took place between the MILF and government forces in March and April in Lanao del Norte and Maguindanao Provinces. The MILF, which captured a small town in Lanao del Norte, claimed the attacks were designed to pressure government forces into the immediate cessation of its offensive against the MILF in central Mindanao. The escalation of violence in Mindanao prompted Estrada to convene a meeting of the National Security Council in March.

In May 2000 the MILF was reported to have withdrawn from a section of the Narciso Ramos highway, a strategically significant route, which it had controlled for more than five years. The withdrawal appeared to augur well for the resumption of peace negotiations, although the Government held Islamist separatist movements responsible for bomb attacks in Manila and Mindanao in the same month. Peace negotiations between the Government and the MILF resumed later in May, and in June the MILF was reported to be assessing an improved offer of autonomy by the Government. However, the MILF subsequently rejected the extension of the deadline for its acceptance of this offer from 1 July to 15 December, owing to a stipulation that it should meanwhile abandon its pursuit of independence. In late June, following a major offensive, government forces captured the MILF's military headquarters at Abubakar. In December the MILF appeared to have resumed its armed struggle after an attack on government forces on Jolo island was attributed to the movement. Bomb explosions in Manila at the end of the month, in which 22 people died, were also blamed on the group. (In January 2009 three Muslim militants with alleged links to both the MILF and JI were sentenced to life imprisonment in connection with the bombings.)

The new Cabinet appointed by President Arroyo in January 2001 included two members who originated from Mindanao. The incoming President stated that she would seek to resume the peace negotiations with the MILF, and in February the Government's military campaign against the MILF ceased. The MILF welcomed the Government's offer to resume talks, although sporadic clashes between its forces and those of the Government continued throughout February. In late March the Government announced that it had reached an agreement with the MILF to resume peace negotiations, and appeared prepared to accept the MILF's condition that renewed talks should be held in an OIC member state. In April the MILF announced a unilateral cease-fire, declaring its intention to observe this until the conclusion of a peace agreement. In June government representatives initiated talks with the MILF in Libya, leading to the conclusion of a preliminary cease-fire agreement in July. Following a new round of peace talks, a further cease-fire agreement was signed in August. In the same month the MILF also reached an accord with the MNLF. In September sporadic fighting between the MILF and army troops on Mindanao, which led to the deaths of 15 rebels, threatened to undermine the peace process. However, in October the MILF signed a pact with the Government to safeguard the recent cease-fire agreement. In November the Pentagon Gang, formed in 2000 and mainly comprising renegade members of the MILF, kidnapped an Italian priest, Father Giuseppe Pierantoni, in northern Manila. The leader of the faction, Akiddin Abdusalem, was shot dead as he attempted to escape from custody after being captured by government troops. In January 2002 39 separatist MILF guerrillas surrendered to government forces and relinquished a large cache of weapons. In February the MILF announced that it was to hold a new series of discussions with the Government as the situation had been complicated by the arrival of US troops on the island of Basilan (see below). In April government troops finally secured the release of Father Pierantoni after conducting intensive operations against the Pentagon Gang.

In May 2002 the Government signed several new peace agreements with the MILF in Putrajaya, Malaysia. In December the MILF denied responsibility for an ambush on Mindanao that resulted in the deaths of 12 employees of a Canadian mining company, as well as for a bomb attack that killed 17 people in the same week; the group claimed that it continued to observe the cease-fire agreed upon in 2001. Meanwhile, President Arroyo succeeded in deterring the US Government from classifying the MILF as an international terrorist organization, citing concerns that the ongoing negotiation process might be undermined by such an action. In February 2003 peace negotiations broke down when government troops assumed control of the important MILF base of Pikit, on Mindanao, in violation of the cease-fire arrangement. The Government claimed that it had ordered the military action in an attempt to capture members of the Pentagon Gang, who it believed were being sheltered by the MILF. Although President Arroyo called a halt to the operation several days later and proposed a peace agreement, many rebels were believed to have been killed in the fighting that had resulted. Insurgency in the area continued to intensify, as the MILF refused to negotiate unless government troops withdrew from Pikit. A number of attacks occurred, the most serious of which took place in March when a bomb exploded near Davao Airport, resulting in the deaths of 23 people. Although the MILF denied responsibility for the attack, the police subsequently filed charges against 150 of its members; four of the group's leaders were charged with murder and warrants issued for their arrest. (Five alleged members of the MILF were arrested in late 2004 in connection with the bomb attack. One of those detained reportedly claimed to have been trained by a leader of JI.) In late March 2003 the MILF sent representatives for preliminary discussions with government officials in Malaysia, and in April the Government declared that formal peace negotiations would restart, although with the exclusion of those indicted in connection with the March attack on Davao Airport, including MILF leader Hashim Salamat. However, shortly afterwards the MILF was responsible for several further outbreaks of violence in the area and, in May, the Government abandoned peace talks and renewed its military offensive against the organization. Later in that month the MILF declared a 10-day unilateral cease-fire in order, it claimed, to prepare the way for the renewal of negotiations, but the Government rejected the offer following the perpetration of further attacks by the MILF during the cease-fire period. Nevertheless, at the request of the Malaysian Government, the MILF extended the cease-fire by a further 10 days in June and, later in that month, Salamat announced that the group had renounced terrorism, an important precondition for any peace agreement. Despite this, the Government continued to take military action against the organization. However, in July it was announced that the two sides had finally concluded a peace agreement. In August it was reported that Hashim Salamat had died as a result of a heart attack in the previous month; he was replaced as Chairman by Murad Ebrahim.

Following exploratory talks in February 2004, formal peace negotiations were to take place in April, but were postponed owing to the May elections (see Domestic Political Affairs). In late April the MILF protested against the arrest of four of its members on suspicion of collaborating with JI, claiming it contravened the cease-fire agreement. In July it was announced that the MILF had agreed to co-operate with the armed forces in operations against kidnapping gangs and JI elements based in Mindanao. A 60-member International Monitoring Team (IMT), led by Malaysia, was deployed in Mindanao in October to oversee the ongoing cease-fire between the government forces and the MILF. Further exploratory talks aimed at restarting the stalled formal peace negotiations were held in December; the two sides reportedly made progress on the contentious issue of ancestral domain. In January 2005 at least six government soldiers were killed in an attack on an army outpost by MILF rebels. The Government stated that it regarded the attack, which had not been sanctioned by the MILF leadership, as an isolated incident. Exploratory talks between the two sides were conducted between February and December.

In March 2005 the Government and the MILF finally agreed to resume formal peace negotiations in Malaysia, which commenced in February 2006 at Port Dickson, near Kuala Lumpur. ARMM Governor Zaldy Ampatuan urged the holding of a plebiscite to assist the efforts to resolve the contentious issue of ancestral domain. In early March, however, the Malaysian Government postponed the next round of talks, scheduled for 5–7 March, owing to the state of emergency imposed upon the Philippines by President Arroyo (see Domestic Political Affairs), although negotiations were resumed in late March following the removal of martial law. In the same month rumours circulated of a failed attempt to oust Murad Ebrahim from the MILF leadership, but senior MILF members denied such reports. Also in March it was reported that at least 50 suspected members of the MILF had surrendered to the army in advance of the resumption of peace talks with the Government; however, a spokesman for the organization disputed that those who had surrendered were in any way associated with the MILF, alleging that they were instead affiliated to the MNLF. In June a bomb explosion in Mindanao resulted in several fatalities and precipitated clashes between local paramilitaries and MILF rebels after the latter was accused of responsibility for the attack; in the following month, however, the two sides agreed to a cease-fire. The MILF denied perpetrating further bomb attacks in Mindanao in October, but suspicions were raised about the group's links to JI and Abu Sayyaf. Several MILF members were reported to be among at least 47 prisoners who escaped during an attack on a prison in Mindanao by a group of around 25 armed men in February 2007; the MILF denied any involvement in the incident. An Italian priest, Father Giancarlo Bossi, was kidnapped in June in his parish on Mindanao by suspected renegade members of the MILF. In July clashes between some 300 rebels and a group of marines who were searching for the priest on Basilan resulted in the deaths of 14 marines, 10 of whom were beheaded. The MILF claimed that it had ambushed the soldiers in self-defence, but denied beheading them. Father Bossi was released later in that month on Mindanao. There was speculation that Abu Sayyaf members might have been involved in the kidnapping or the fighting.

In November 2007 the Government announced that the latest round of peace negotiations with the MILF in Malaysia had resulted in agreement on the demarcation of the land and maritime boundaries of a proposed new autonomous area on Mindanao, to be known as the Bangsamoro Juridical Entity (BJE). Although no details of the borders were disclosed, it was reported that the BJE would cover a larger area than the ARMM. However, talks faltered in December over continued disagreement on ancestral domain, with the MILF opposed to the Government's position that any agreement should be implemented through the 'constitutional process', i.e. by conducting a plebiscite in the villages to be added to the ARMM to create the proposed BJE. Apparently frustrated at the lack of progress in the negotiations, Malaysia withdrew 28 of its cease-fire monitors from the IMT in May 2008. Finally, in July it was announced that the Government and the MILF had concluded a Memorandum of Agreement on Ancestral Domain (MOA-AD), which would be signed in a formal ceremony in Kuala Lumpur on 5 August. The accord envisaged the creation of the BJE by extending the ARMM to include a further 712 villages, subject to the approval of their residents in a plebiscite to be conducted within 12 months, and outlined the expanded political and economic powers to be devolved to the new entity. However, the MOA-AD provoked considerable controversy, particularly within predominantly Christian communities intended for inclusion in the BJE, and a protest against the accord held in Zamboanga City in early August was attended by an estimated 15,000 people. On 4 August, in response to a number of petitions challenging the constitutionality of the MOA-AD, the Supreme Court issued a temporary restraining order, preventing the signing ceremony from taking place on the following day.

Tensions in the south subsequently escalated, as MILF rebels reportedly occupied some 15 villages in North Cotabato, prompting renewed fighting with government troops, which led to the displacement of an estimated 160,000 people in the province and the deaths of at least two soldiers and more than 20 militants. By mid-August 2008 the armed forces had secured control of the occupied villages, and people began to return home. However, on 18 August brutal raids by MILF forces on several towns and villages in the provinces of Lanao del Norte and Sarangani left more than 30 civilians dead and forced thousands to flee the violence, while seven soldiers died in a MILF ambush of an army convoy in Lanao del Sur. The MILF leadership claimed that the three commanders held responsible for the attacks, Abdullah Macapaar, Umbra Kato and Aleem Pangalian, were 'renegades', but refused to surrender them to the armed forces. The Government declared the MOA-AD defunct a few days later, and in early September the President ordered the dissolution of the peace panel responsible for negotiating with the MILF and announced a new policy of promoting direct dialogue with local communities, stating that future negotiations with armed groups would focus on disarmament, demobilization and reintegration. The National Disaster Co-ordinating Council (NDCC) estimated that some 500,000 people had been displaced by the violence by the end of September. In October the Supreme Court ruled the MOA-AD to be unconstitutional (by a narrow margin of eight votes to seven), noting that its implementation would require constitutional amendments that the President did not have the authority to guarantee would be adopted and criticizing Esperon for failing to consult local government and communities about the proposed agreement. Malaysia withdrew altogether from the IMT in November, although monitors from Brunei, Libya and Japan were to continue their participation.

Despite the re-establishment of the government peace panel in December 2008, talks with the MILF remained in abeyance and sporadic fighting between MILF rebels and government troops continued during late 2008 and early 2009. The two sides agreed to a cease-fire in July 2009, by which month more than 1,000 people were reported to have been killed and nearly 750,000 people displaced by the conflict since the failure of peace talks in August 2008. (In July 2009 the MILF claimed to have killed more than 500 government troops during that period, although this was refuted by the Philippine military.) In February, meanwhile, more than 112,000 of those displaced in August–September 2008 remained in camps, according to the NDCC, while a further 200,000 were believed to be residing with friends or relatives.

In December 2009 the Government and the MILF reconvened for formal peace negotiations, held in Kuala Lumpur; the two sides agreed to revive an international monitoring team of cease-fire observers and announced that they hoped to reach a peace deal by April 2010. A second round of talks was held in January of that year, at which the Philippine Government submitted a draft power-sharing proposal; however, this was rejected by the MILF, which argued that the draft contained provisions that had not been discussed previously and did not offer sufficient autonomy. However, in what was welcomed by government negotiators as a positive development in the quest for peace, the MILF officially abandoned its demands for full independence and a separate Islamic state, instead envisaging, in the words of a prominent MILF negotiator, 'a real state and sub-state relationship where we can have real governance and control over our lives'.

While the objective of securing an agreement by April was not met, it was hoped that the election of Benigno Aquino as President in May 2010 would provide a boost to the peace process. One of Aquino's principal election pledges had been to intensify efforts to negotiate peace with the various separatist groups, and upon assuming office the new President reiterated his Government's commitment to resuming talks with the MILF by October. In September Aquino announced the formation of an advisory body to assist the Government's negotiating team and to facilitate 'greater transparency and accountability' during the forthcoming peace negotiations with the MILF. An attack by MILF rebels later that month on a military outpost on Mindanao, which resulted in an exchange of gunfire with government soldiers, was interpreted by some observers as an attempt by certain elements within the MILF to disrupt the peace process. Tensions as a result of the incident, together with a disagreement over the Malaysian facilitator, resulted in a delay in the resumption of the talks. The Philippine Government claimed that Othman Razak, who had been facilitating the peace talks between the Government and the MILF since 2003, was biased towards the latter, and demanded his replacement with an intermediary who would remain impartial; the MILF denied that Razak had demonstrated any such bias and insisted that he be allowed to continue as facilitator in order to ensure continuity in the talks. The arrest of a senior MILF leader, Abraham Yap Alonto, in October 2010 was condemned by the MILF leadership as 'a direct blow to the early resumption of the negotiations'. In the same month a bomb explosion on a bus in North Cotabato province in the southern Philippines, which claimed the lives of eight people and injured a further 10, was believed by the authorities to have been carried out by a splinter group of JI in an attempt further to delay the resumption of peace talks between the Government and the MILF. A bomb attack on a bus terminal in North Cotabato in November, which killed one person and injured two others, was similarly attributed to Islamist militants seeking to disrupt the peace process. In January 2011 a further bomb explosion on a bus, in Manila, killed five people and injured 13 others; no claim of responsibility was immediately issued, but the authorities stated that the device used in the bombing was similar to those used in recent attacks on Mindanao.

Despite the apparent efforts to impede the peace process, formal negotiations between the MILF and the Philippine Government were reconvened in Kuala Lumpur in February 2011, with both sides expressing confidence that a peace agreement could be concluded within 12 months. The MILF was reported to have presented its 'comprehensive compact' for peace, which the Government confirmed did not include the demand for independence. A second round of negotiations was scheduled to be held in late April, followed by a third round at which the Government was to present a draft of its proposed peace settlement. The Aquino Government stressed that it would not repeat the mistakes made by the Arroyo administration, pledging to consult all involved parties prior to finalizing its draft proposal. Meanwhile, shortly before the resumption of talks in February it was revealed that a splinter group of the MILF had been formed. Headed by Ustadz Ameril Umbra Kato, the so-called Bangsamoro Islamic Freedom Fighters (BIFF) was identified as a threat to the peace process by both the MILF and the Government; it was not certain whether the BIFF would respect the cease-fire agreed in July 2009. In April 2011 the MILF leadership announced that Kato had been expelled from the MILF after refusing to disband his armed grouping.

The activities of Abu Sayyaf

In early June 1994 the Government undertook a major offensive against Abu Sayyaf, which was held responsible for numerous attacks, principally on the islands of Jolo and Basilan, to the south of Mindanao. In retaliation for the capture by the armed forces of its base on Jolo, the group took a number of Christians hostage on Basilan, killing 15 of them. All but one of the remaining 21 hostages were released in mid-June, following the apparent payment of a ransom and the intercession of the MNLF. Later in June government troops captured the group's main headquarters in Basilan. In August the group's remaining hostage was released, and the authorities announced that Abu Sayyaf had been 'eliminated'. In April 1995, however, the group was believed to be responsible for an attack on the town of Ipil, in Mindanao, in which as many as 100 people were killed. Some of the assailants were also believed to belong to a splinter group of the MNLF, the Islamic Command Council. Some 14 hostages were reportedly killed as the army pursued the rebels in their retreat from Ipil. Despite intense counter-insurgency measures by government troops, Abu Sayyaf perpetrated a further assault in Tungawan, south of Ipil, in which six civilians were killed. In April 1996 two bomb explosions in Zamboanga City were widely attributed to Abu Sayyaf or to other groups opposed to the peace negotiations between the Government and the MNLF. Abu Sayyaf subsequently denounced the MNLF's peace agreement with the Government. In December 1998 the leader of Abu Sayyaf, Abdurajat Abubakar Janjalani, was killed in an exchange of fire with government security forces; he was subsequently replaced by his younger brother, Khadafi Janjalani.

Under the leadership of Khadafi Janjalani, Abu Sayyaf began to employ a new tactic of kidnapping hostages to use them as both a means of political bargaining and a source of financing, often demanding high ransoms from the families of those abducted. In April 2000 armed Abu Sayyaf troops abducted 21 people, including 10 foreign tourists, from the island resort of Sipadan in Malaysia, and held them hostage on Jolo. One month earlier members of a separate Abu Sayyaf group had seized a number of Filipino hostages on the island of Basilan where, demanding the release of convicted Islamist terrorists held in US prisons, they had at the end of April managed to evade capture by government forces by which they had been besieged. The Government's military response to the hostage crisis remained largely ineffective, and a stalemate lasting several months ensued, punctuated by both formal and informal negotiations and a partially successful intervention, involving the payment of ransoms, by Libyan mediators. Although sporadic releases were secured, some hostages were also killed by their captors. In April 2001 President Arroyo declared 'all-out war' against Abu Sayyaf.

In May 2001 Abu Sayyaf rebels abducted 20 people, including three US tourists, from a holiday resort off the western island of Palawan. President Arroyo immediately ordered a military response, although the group threatened to kill the hostages if it was attacked. In June the rebels succeeded in fleeing from a military siege; nine Filipino captives escaped as a result. Later in the same month the Government was forced to bring in a Malaysian mediator in order to avert the threatened execution of the three US hostages still being held. It was reported that one, Guillermo Sobero, had already been beheaded, although his body had not been found. In July two Filipino hostages were released, but Abu Sayyaf stated that it intended to continue attacking US and European citizens until government forces had been withdrawn from the southern Philippines. Nadzmie Sabtulah, the rebel leader alleged to have planned the May abductions, was arrested, together with three other members of the group. However, Abu Sayyaf activities continued, and in August a group of Abu Sayyaf guerrillas raided the town of Lamitan on the island of Basilan, taking at least 36 hostages and beheading 10. The next day 11 hostages were released and soon afterwards 13 more were freed, following an armed raid by government troops. However, the military failed to capture any members of the Abu Sayyaf leadership and 21 hostages remained in captivity, leading to allegations of collusion between Abu Sayyaf and the Philippine military. Soon afterwards three Chinese nationals were abducted as they tried to negotiate the release of a Chinese engineer who had been held by the group since June 2001. Two of the Chinese hostages were later killed following a clash between the kidnappers and government forces in Sultan Kudurat province.

In October 2001 Abu Sayyaf was responsible for two explosions in Zamboanga City. Meanwhile, government soldiers were reported to have cornered the kidnappers and their hostages following two days of fighting, which had resulted in the deaths of 21 guerrillas. Shortly afterwards the group threatened to behead its two US hostages—Martin and Gracia Burnham—prior to President Arroyo's scheduled November visit to the USA unless the military halted its offensive. In late October an explosion in Zamboanga, which killed six people, was attributed to the group. In the following month a Canadian man was abducted by men claiming to be Abu Sayyaf separatists. The group then released one hostage, followed a week later by a further seven. In December government troops succeeded in rescuing the Canadian man. Three hostages remained—the Burnhams and Ediborah Yap, a Filipino nurse. The military offensive against Abu Sayyaf was intensified by the arrival of US troops on Basilan in 2002. In April a series of bombs exploded in the southern city of General Santos, killing 15 people and prompting President Arroyo to declare a state of emergency in the area. The police later arrested five men in connection with the attacks. While the suspects were initially thought to be connected to the MILF, Abu Sayyaf claimed responsibility for the bombings. Shortly afterwards four men reported to be members of Abu Sayyaf were killed during a gun battle with police in the area. In June Gracia Burnham was rescued in a military operation, but her husband and Ediborah Yap were killed. Later in the same month it was reported that Aldam Tilao (alias Abu Sabaya), a senior member of the organization, had died during a gunfight at sea.

In July 2002 the joint US-Philippine military exercises that had been conducted on Basilan were formally concluded; President Arroyo subsequently ordered the redeployment of government forces to combat insurgency elsewhere in the country. Although it was thought that the exercises had achieved some success in defeating Abu Sayyaf, in August the group was responsible for the kidnapping of eight members of a Christian sect on Jolo; although two of the hostages were released, a further two were beheaded. Following the group's threat to perpetrate attacks in retaliation for the military offensive being conducted against it, in early October a bomb exploded in Zamboanga City, resulting in the deaths of three people, including a US soldier. Responsibility for the attack was attributed to Abu Sayyaf. Later in the same month two further explosions in Zamboanga, which led to the deaths of seven people, were also suspected to have been carried out by members of Abu Sayyaf, although there was speculation that JI members might also have been involved. The bombings followed the terrorist attack on the island of Bali, Indonesia, several days previously (see the chapter on Indonesia). Meanwhile, a bomb exploded on a bus in Manila, killing at least three people.

In January 2003 three government soldiers were killed during a battle with Abu Sayyaf rebels on the island of Jolo. In the following month further fighting broke out in advance of the resumption of counter-terrorism exercises between US and

THE PHILIPPINES

Philippine troops in the area. In late February President Arroyo imposed a 90-day deadline upon military commanders for the elimination of the threat posed by Abu Sayyaf. In May the final two members of the Christian sect captured in August 2002 were freed from captivity, and in June 2003 the last hostage to have been taken from Sipadan in April 2000 escaped. Meanwhile, the Government announced the establishment of a commission to investigate claims by former hostage Gracia Burnham that collusion had taken place between Abu Sayyaf and Philippine military forces during her time in captivity. In December 2003 it was announced that government forces had captured Galib Andang, alias 'Commander Robot', a senior Abu Sayyaf figure, following a gun battle in Sulu. Abu Sayyaf claimed responsibility for a bomb explosion in February 2004 that caused a fire on a passenger ferry in Manila Bay in which 116 were presumed to have died. In March the Government announced that it had apprehended six members of Abu Sayyaf, thought to have connections to JI, who were believed to have been planning a bomb attack on Manila; one of those detained also allegedly confessed to planting the bomb on the ferry. In April the armed forces claimed to have killed Hamsiraji Sali, a leading member of Abu Sayyaf for whose capture the USA had offered a reward of US $1m., following a gun battle on the island of Basilan. Also in April at least eight members of Abu Sayyaf were among 53 prisoners who escaped from a prison on Basilan, using smuggled firearms; within four days 34 of the prisoners had been killed or recaptured by the security forces. In August 17 members of Abu Sayyaf were sentenced to death, having been convicted of kidnapping Ediborah Yap, two other nurses and a general hospital worker in 2001; four of the defendants were among those who had escaped in April 2004 and were sentenced *in absentia*. Sitra Tilao, the sister of Aldam, was arrested in September for her alleged participation in the kidnapping operations of Abu Sayyaf. In October President Arroyo announced that six members of Abu Sayyaf had been charged with murder and attempted murder in connection with the ferry bombing in February; Redendo Dellosa and Alhamser Limbong had been arrested in March, but the other four remained at large. A bomb exploded in a market in General Santos in December, killing 16 people and injuring 52. The police arrested five men in connection with the attack, for which Abu Sayyaf was suspected of being responsible.

In January 2005 the armed forces commenced a major offensive against Abu Sayyaf. Some 30,000 people fled the heavy fighting that ensued in the following month on the island of Jolo between government troops and Abu Sayyaf members, joined by followers of former MNLF leader Nur Misuari. Meanwhile, in February Abu Sayyaf claimed responsibility for three co-ordinated bomb explosions, in Manila, General Santos and Davao City, in which 12 people were killed and some 150 injured. Amid fears of further attacks, the Government increased security at airports, seaports, bus terminals and shopping centres. In March the security forces quashed an uprising at a prison near Manila, killing at least 22 detainees, including the Abu Sayyaf leaders Nadzmie Sabtulah, Galib Andang and Alhamser Limbong, after the expiry of an ultimatum for the prisoners to surrender weapons that they had seized from guards. Abu Sayyaf subsequently threatened to retaliate for the deaths of its members.

In the southern Philippines in August 2005 three explosive devices were detonated in Zamboanga City, injuring 26 people. In the same month a bomb exploded on a ferry, injuring at least 30 people. The Philippine authorities attributed the attacks to Abu Sayyaf. In October two alleged Abu Sayyaf members were sentenced to death, together with a suspected member of JI, for their part in a bomb attack on a bus in Manila's financial district, which had killed four people in February. In November at least 23 alleged Abu Sayyaf members were killed, and dozens more wounded, in violent clashes with government troops on the island of Jolo. In February 2006, in another suspected Abu Sayyaf attack, an explosion near an army base that was being used by US troops killed one person and injured an estimated 28 others. In January 2007 the campaign against Abu Sayyaf seemed to have made significant progress when it was reported that Jainal Antel Sali, or Abu Sulaiman, a senior Abu Sayyaf leader wanted for his alleged involvement in the kidnapping of several tourists in 2001 (see above) and the bombing of a ferry in 2004, had been killed by government forces on Jolo island. In the same month DNA tests confirmed earlier reports that the leader of Abu Sayyaf, Khadafi Janjalani, had been killed in September 2006. Four Filipinos later received a US $10m. reward from the US authorities for providing information that led to the two killings. None the less, Abu Sayyaf militants remained active, decapitating seven Christians whom they had taken hostage on Jolo in April 2007, and sending the severed heads to military camps on the island. In June it emerged that Abu Sayyaf had chosen one of its founders, Yasser Igasan, to replace Janjalani as leader.

In August 2007 President Arroyo ordered the temporary transfer of the headquarters of the armed forces to Zamboanga City and announced that a major offensive had been launched against Abu Sayyaf on Jolo and Basilan, following clashes on Jolo in which 26 soldiers and an estimated 31 militants died. Rogue elements of the MNLF were also reported to be involved in the fighting, which prompted some 24,000 people to flee their homes. Later in that month the armed forces claimed to have killed 42 members of Abu Sayyaf in an attack on a camp on Basilan. Clashes continued in the following months, with further casualties reported on both sides. Abu Sayyaf was also held responsible for a bomb explosion outside the House of Representatives in Manila in November, in which four people died. In December 14 members of Abu Sayyaf were sentenced to life imprisonment for the May 2001 abduction of 20 people from a holiday resort off Palawan (see above). Later in that month government troops killed Mobin Abdurajak, a senior leader of Abu Sayyaf and brother-in-law of Khadafi Janjalani, who was wanted for the April 2000 abduction of 21 people from a Malaysian resort (see above). A Catholic priest who had reportedly been receiving death threats from Abu Sayyaf was abducted and killed on the island of Tawi-Tawi in January 2008. Two minor bomb explosions in Zamboanga City in April were attributed to Abu Sayyaf. A further bomb attack outside an air force base in Zamboanga City in late May killed two people and injured at least 22 others; the MILF rejected suggestions that its members had perpetrated the bombing jointly with Abu Sayyaf. In June three employees of the ABS-CBN Broadcasting Corporation and an academic were abducted on Jolo, allegedly by Abu Sayyaf militants, but were released within 10 days. It was announced in August that Ruben Pestano Lavilla, Jr, who was wanted for his alleged involvement in the ferry bombing in 2004, as well as several other bomb attacks, had been arrested in Bahrain and deported to the Philippines. Moreover, in November 2008 Sakirin Andalan Sali (alias Kirih-Kirih), an Abu Sayyaf commander suspected of involvement in the April 2000 abduction, was captured on Jolo, while Faidar Hadjadi (alias Abu Solomon), another senior member of the movement wanted for kidnapping, was killed during a gunfight with troops in Sulu.

Three aid workers from the International Committee of the Red Cross (ICRC) were abducted by members of Abu Sayyaf on Jolo in January 2009. In March 10 people were killed in fighting between troops and militants holding the three ICRC workers captive. Later in that month Abu Sayyaf threatened to behead one of the ICRC hostages if all troops had not been withdrawn from several villages on Jolo by 31 March. At least 800 of 1,000 soldiers subsequently retreated, although the Government insisted that a complete withdrawal would compromise the security of residents. At the end of that month, as the deadline imposed by the rebels approached, the Governor of Sulu imposed a state of emergency in the province. At the beginning of April one of the hostages was released; another hostage escaped from captivity later in that month, and the remaining hostage was released in July. Meanwhile, a Sri Lankan peace advocate kidnapped on Basilan in February was released in March. Clashes between Abu Sayyaf members and government troops on Basilan in August reportedly resulted in the deaths of more than 20 government soldiers and of at least 30 militants. The group was believed to be responsible for the kidnapping in October of a teacher on Jolo; in the following month the teacher was beheaded after his family refused to pay the ransom demanded by his kidnappers. A spokesperson for the President stated that Arroyo had ordered 'punitive action' to 'put an end to the Abu Sayyaf group's heinous and inhumane atrocities'.

In December 2009 the authorities announced the capture of a founding member of Abu Sayyaf, Abdul Basir Latip, who was alleged to have been involved in the kidnapping of foreigners and Christians. The killing by the security forces of Albader Parad, a senior Abu Sayyaf commander held responsible for the abduction of the three ICRC workers, during an operation on Jolo in February 2010 was thought to represent another significant loss for the group. Later that month at least 11 people were reported to have been killed when a group of about 70 Abu Sayyaf members attacked a village on Basilan, in an apparent act of revenge for the killing of Parad. In the following month it emerged that Khair Mundus, who was on the US Federal Bureau of Investigation (FBI)'s list of 'most wanted' terrorists, with a US $500,000 reward offered for information leading to his capture, had become Abu Sayyaf's leader on Basilan; it was feared that the prominent involvement of Mundus, who was reported to have links to Malaysian and Saudi financial sources, would result in a significant increase in the levels of foreign funding that Abu Sayyaf might be able to attract. Mundus and another senior Abu Sayyaf leader, Puruji Indama, were the intended targets of a security operation on Sakol island in March 2011; Indama, who was thought to have co-ordinated a number of kidnappings, was alleged to have links to Malaysian bomber Zulkifli bin Hir (alias Marwan), a prominent member of JI, for information leading to whose capture the FBI was offering a $5m. reward. However, both men escaped unharmed and were believed to have fled to Basilan. Meanwhile, at the end of August 2010 the Government filed a petition with a court on Basilan seeking to outlaw Abu Sayyaf as a terrorist organization under the terms of the controversial Human Security Act of 2007 (see Domestic Political Affairs); if approved, the petition would allow the Government to arrest members of Abu Sayyaf without them having committed any crime other than belonging to the group, and would enable the Government to seek assistance from foreign law enforcement agencies in order to freeze Abu Sayyaf's funding from external sources.

Foreign Affairs
Regional relations

The Philippines' engagement with the Association of Southeast Asian Nations (ASEAN, see p. 206) deepened during the administrations of Presidents Fidel Ramos and Joseph Estrada. At the ASEAN ministerial meeting in Manila in July 1998, Secretary of Foreign Affairs Domingo Siazon, Jr joined his Thai counterpart in expressing support for 'constructive intervention' in member countries' internal affairs, in marked contrast to ASEAN's policy of non-interference hitherto. In November 1999 an informal summit meeting took place of the leaders of ASEAN and of China, Japan and the Republic of Korea (collectively known as ASEAN + 3), at which it was formally agreed to hold annual East Asian summit meetings of all 13 nations and to strengthen present economic co-operation with the distant aim of forming an East Asian bloc, with a common market and monetary union. At the annual ASEAN summit meeting held in Laos in November 2004, it was agreed to transform the ASEAN + 3 summit meeting into the East Asia summit, with the long-term objective of establishing an East Asian Community. In January 2007 the Philippines hosted the 12th annual ASEAN summit meeting and the second East Asia summit in Cebu. In October 2008 the Philippines ratified the new ASEAN Charter, which codified the principles and purposes of the Association and came into effect in December of that year; President Gloria Arroyo had previously suggested that the Philippines would not ratify the new Charter while Myanma opposition leader Aung San Suu Kyi remained under house arrest. During 2009 and early 2010 the Philippines was outspoken in its appeals for Myanmar's first legislative election since 1990, due to be held before the end of 2010, to be genuinely inclusive, with the opposition able fully to participate in a free and fair contest. At an ASEAN summit meeting held in Hanoi, Viet Nam, in late October 2010, the Philippine delegation communicated the view of President Benigno Aquino's administration that the forthcoming election, which was held on 7 November, was 'a farce to democratic values', following recent developments that indicated that the poll would be neither free nor fair (see the chapter on Myanmar). Addressing the summit, Secretary of Foreign Affairs Alberto Romulo urged the Myanma Government to implement its own 'road map' to democracy, and appealed for the immediate and unconditional release of all political prisoners, including Suu Kyi, and the all-inclusive participation of all parties and sectors in the elections.

Relations with Malaysia were somewhat strained, owing to the Philippines' claim to the Malaysian state of Sabah, dating from 1962, before Sabah joined the Federation of Malaysia; attempts by both Presidents Ferdinand Marcos and Corazon Aquino to abandon the claim were thwarted by the Senate. In August 1993 the Philippine and Malaysian ministers responsible for foreign affairs signed a memorandum creating a commission to address bilateral issues, including the Philippines' claim to Sabah. In the latter half of 1998 bilateral relations were strained by Estrada's public condemnation of the arrest and mistreatment of the former Malaysian Deputy Prime Minister, Dato' Seri Anwar Ibrahim. Estrada's decision to hold a private meeting with Anwar's wife, Wan Azizah Wan Ismail, during her visit to the Philippines in May 1999 further displeased the Malaysian Government. In August 2001 President Arroyo visited Malaysia on her first overseas trip since assuming the presidency. In November, however, relations were jeopardized again when the Malaysian authorities detained rebel leader Nur Misuari for attempting to enter the country illegally. After some vacillation, Misuari was finally deported in January 2002 and relations remained cordial. However, in August the bilateral relationship deteriorated following the implementation of stringent new laws in Malaysia whereby all illegal immigrants remaining in the country risked harsh penalties and deportation. Many of those affected were Filipino workers. The Philippine Government filed a formal complaint against Malaysia over its treatment of the immigrants and sent an official delegation to investigate allegations of maltreatment. Malaysia subsequently suspended implementation of the legislation. In March 2009 Arroyo met with Malaysian Prime Minister Abdullah Badawi to request assistance in peace talks with the MILF (see Separatist Tensions and Militancy). Bilateral relations were threatened by the abduction of two Malaysian labourers in Sabah by a group of unidentified Philippine assailants in February 2010. However, the safe return of the pair was secured in December, and was welcomed by the Malaysian embassy in Manila as a 'reflection of the close co-operation' between the two countries' police forces.

In August 2001 Indonesian President Megawati Sukarnoputri visited the Philippines on her first overseas trip since assuming power. During her brief stay she met with President Arroyo, and the two leaders promised to assist each other in overcoming the separatist violence endemic in both their countries. In March 2002 bilateral relations threatened to become strained when the Philippine police filed charges against three Indonesian men who had been arrested at Manila Airport for illegal possession of explosives. One of those arrested was believed to be a member of the Majelis Mujahidin Indonesia (MMI—Indonesian Mujahidin Council), an extremist Islamist organization, and to have links to JI. The Indonesian Government was reported to have been angered by the arrests and stated that the detentions should not be used as a pretext to portray Indonesia as a haven for Islamist extremists. However, in early 2003 it was reported that Philippine rebels were engaged in smuggling weapons to militant groups in Indonesia, despite increased anti-terrorism co-operation between the two countries as a result of a trilateral security treaty signed by the Philippines, Indonesia and Malaysia in May 2002. In October Fathur Rohman al-Ghozi, believed to be a senior Indonesian member of JI, was shot dead by Philippine government forces on Mindanao three months after his escape from a prison in Manila, where he had been detained following his conviction for illegal possession of explosives. In November 2006 an additional security pact between the Philippines and Indonesia was signed, which was intended further to improve co-operation in combating transnational crime and terrorism.

Diplomatic relations were established with the People's Republic of China in 1975, at which time the Philippine Government recognized Taiwan as an 'inalienable' part of the People's Republic. However, conflicting claims to the Spratly Islands, in the South China Sea, were a source of tension between the Philippines and China. (Viet Nam, Brunei, Malaysia and Taiwan also claimed sovereignty over some or all of the islands.) Bilateral animosity was exacerbated by intermittent incidents during the early 1990s, including the occupation by the Chinese armed forces of Mischief Reef, which lay within the Philippines' 200-mile exclusive economic zone established by a UN Convention on the Law of the Sea. Following two days of consultations in August 1995, however, the Chinese Government agreed for the first time to settle disputes in the South China Sea according to international law, rather than insisting that historical claims should take precedence. The Chinese and Philippine Governments issued a joint statement agreeing on a code of conduct to reduce the possibility of a military confrontation in the area. A similar agreement was signed with Viet Nam in November 1995. In March 1996 the Philippines and China agreed to co-operate in combating piracy, which was also a source of tension between the two countries as pirate vessels in the area often sailed under Chinese flags. Despite these agreements, sporadic tension continued during 1996–98.

In January 1999 the National Security Council was convened for the first time in three years to discuss the Spratly Islands and Muslim unrest in Mindanao. China, which was opposed to any external intervention, rebuffed the Philippines' attempts to involve the UN through a meeting with the Secretary-General,

Kofi Annan, in the USA and threatened to leave the Asia-Europe meeting in Berlin, Germany, if the Spratly issue were discussed. A meeting in Manila achieved little progress, with the Chinese dismissing a Philippine proposal for joint use of the facility, owing to the allegedly aggressive behaviour of the Philippine armed forces. In April the Philippines and Viet Nam agreed to joint military operations and leisure activities to reduce the risk of confrontation. In October, however, the Philippines lodged a protest at the Vietnamese embassy, following an incident in which Vietnamese forces had fired on a Philippine aircraft patrolling in the area of the Spratly Islands.

In November 1999 ASEAN officials agreed on a regional code of conduct drafted by the Philippines to prevent conflicts in the Spratlys. In the same month the Chinese Premier, Zhu Rongji, visited the Philippines, and he and Estrada agreed to strengthen co-operation between the two countries. However, China rejected the proposed regional code of conduct. In early 2000 China proposed a new draft code omitting previous references to a ban on construction on islands or atolls and excluding the Paracel Islands, which China had seized from Viet Nam in 1974. However, China did meet with all the ASEAN representatives to discuss the draft, a departure from its previously exclusively bilateral approach. In May 2000 Estrada made a visit to China, where he met President Jiang Zemin and signed a joint statement on the framework for co-operation between China and the Philippines.

In mid-2002 relations with China were jeopardized when the Philippine Secretary of Justice, Hernando Perez, demanded that the Chinese ambassador be expelled from the country. His request marked the culmination of a dispute regarding the fate of more than 100 Chinese fishermen, who had been arrested over the preceding months and accused of fishing illegally in Philippine waters. Perez accused the ambassador of reneging on an agreement whereby the fishermen would be freed on condition that they entered guilty pleas and paid fines, claiming that the ambassador had attempted to coerce the Philippine Government into releasing the fishermen without penalty. However, Perez subsequently withdrew his expulsion demand and, shortly afterwards, the Chinese Minister of Defence paid a goodwill visit to the country. In November 2002 the improvement in bilateral relations was demonstrated when a senior delegation from the Chinese Communist Party arrived in the Philippines. Also in that month a 'declaration on the conduct of parties in the South China Sea' was signed by the ministers responsible for foreign affairs of China and the ASEAN member states. In September 2004, during a three-day state visit by President Arroyo to China, her first foreign trip since her election, the two countries signed five bilateral agreements, including one to conduct joint marine research in the South China Sea. It was also agreed to explore the possibility of defence co-operation. In March 2005 the national oil companies of the Philippines, China and Viet Nam signed a three-year agreement on undertaking joint research into petroleum resources in the South China Sea.

In March 2006 the Chinese Government granted the Philippine administration US $3m. with which to establish a Chinese-language military training programme, in return for the Philippines' continued adherence to the 'One China' policy, which recognized Taiwan as an integral part of the People's Republic of China. The Chinese Government also donated engineering equipment and invited the Philippines to participate in joint naval exercises. In January 2007 the Chinese Premier, Wen Jiabao, spent two days in Manila, after attending the 10th ASEAN-China summit and other ASEAN-related meetings in Cebu. During his visit several bilateral accords were signed, most notably a framework agreement on expanding economic and trade co-operation. President Arroyo visited China in October, shortly after suspending a telecommunications contract with China's ZTE Corporation, following allegations of bribery in the bidding process (see Domestic Political Affairs). In talks with the Chinese President, Hu Jintao, Arroyo sought to ensure that the cancellation of the contract did not adversely affect bilateral relations. However, Arroyo's administration was subsequently forced to defend the propriety of other economic agreements with China, amid criticism from Philippine opposition parties. Tension over sovereignty in the South China Sea re-emerged in February 2009, when the Philippines adopted legislation seeking to define the country's maritime boundaries: this referred to the disputed Kalayaan group of islands (more commonly known as the Spratly Islands and referred to as the Nansha Islands by China) and the Scarborough Shoal (or Huangyan) as being part of a 'regime of islands under the Republic of the Philippines'. The Chinese Government denounced the territorial claims as being illegal and invalid. However, in October the two countries signed the Philippines-China Joint Action Plan for Strategic Co-operation, which set out the direction of bilateral co-operation in the fields of, *inter alia*, politics, the economy, trade and investment, and tourism during 2010–15, and the Philippines-China Consular Agreement, which was the first consular accord that the Philippines had signed since the multilateral Vienna Convention on Consular Relations in 1963. On her final foreign visit as President, Arroyo travelled to the Chinese city of Shanghai in June 2010, on the 35th anniversary of the establishment of diplomatic relations between the two countries; a number of political, economic and cultural exchanges and events were held to commemorate the anniversary. Proposals to formulate a binding Code of Conduct for the Spratly Islands were espoused in October 2010, and discussions to this end continued in mid-2011.

However, relations with China were compromised by the killing of eight Hong Kong tourists in Manila in a bus hijacking in August 2010 (see Domestic Political Affairs). The affair also had a negative impact on relations with the Government of Hong Kong: Chief Executive Donald Tsang described the management of the incident by the Philippine authorities as 'disappointing', and his administration issued a warning against all travel to the Philippines. The Chinese Government demanded a thorough investigation into the handling of the incident, while the Chinese Minister of Foreign Affairs, Yang Jiechi, declared himself to be 'appalled' at the violent conclusion to the siege. Aquino conceded that the authorities' response to the incident had been unsatisfactory and pledged to improve standards within the police force.

Meanwhile, in September 2006 Arroyo and the Japanese Prime Minister, Junichiro Koizumi, signed an economic partnership agreement, which would eliminate tariffs on almost 95% of trade and provide for the entry of more Filipino workers to Japan. The agreement was approved by the Japanese legislature in December, but did not enter into force until two years later, in December 2008; its ratification by the Philippine Senate was delayed until October of that year, following considerable controversy over, *inter alia*, provisions apparently granting Japanese investors rights almost equal to those of Filipinos. Bilateral co-operation was expected further to be bolstered following the announcement by the Japanese Government in November 2010 that it was to invest some US $5,500m. in the Philippines.

Australia, along with the USA and Japan, was one of the Philippines' leading bilateral aid donors in the early 21st century; total assistance for 2009/10 was budgeted at $A123m., which was primarily to be disbursed on improving basic education, national stability and human security, and economic growth. Meanwhile, in May 2007 President Arroyo and the Australian Prime Minister, John Howard, signed a new security pact designed to assist the Philippines in its efforts to combat insurgents in the south of the country. Under the agreement, Australian special forces would train Philippine troops and joint counter-terrorism exercises would be organized. In June 2010 the Philippine ambassador to Australia hailed bilateral relations as 'vibrant and robust'.

The Philippines contributed 1,000 troops to a UN multinational force to restore peace and security in East Timor (which became Timor-Leste upon its accession to independence in May 2002), following the violence that erupted after the East Timorese voted in a referendum for independence from Indonesia. The two East Timorese independence leaders, José Alexandre (Xanana) Gusmão and José Ramos Horta, visited the Philippines in February 2000 and held a meeting with President Estrada. The Philippines also participated in subsequent UN missions in Timor-Leste, most recently the UN Integrated Mission in Timor-Leste (UNMIT), which was established in August 2006. A number of bilateral agreements were signed in August 2008, during Ramos Horta's first state visit to the Philippines since taking office as President of Timor-Leste in May 2007. During another visit to the Philippines in July 2010, Ramos Horta met separately with President Benigno Aquino and Vice-President Jejomar 'Jojo' Binay, expressing his belief that bilateral relations would be enhanced under the presidency of Benigno Aquino. The Timorese President voiced gratitude for the Philippine contribution to UNMIT, as a result of which, he declared, peace and stability had returned to Timor-Leste. Ramos Horta also appealed for greater Philippine investment in Timorese infrastructure development projects, and extended invitations to both Aquino and Binay to make reciprocal visits to Timor-Leste.

THE PHILIPPINES

Introductory Survey

Other external relations

The Philippines and the USA enjoy long-standing cordial relations and close military co-operation. In November 1991 the US military formally transferred management of the Clark Air Base to the Philippines, in accordance with the Philippine Constitution's stipulation that foreign military bases should not be allowed in the country after 1991. In December negotiations for an extended withdrawal period of US forces from Subic Bay naval base collapsed, owing principally to the USA's policy of refusing to confirm or deny the presence of nuclear weapons (prohibited from the Philippines under the 1987 Constitution) on board naval vessels. US personnel withdrew from Subic Naval Bay at the end of September 1992, and from the Cubi Point Naval Air Station towards the end of November.

Relations between the USA and the Philippines improved following the occupation, by the People's Republic of China, of a reef in the Spratly Islands claimed by the Philippines (see Regional relations). A joint naval exercise between US and Philippine forces took place in July 1995 about 100 km from the Spratly Islands. Owing to the intensification of the dispute with China over the Islands, the Philippines signed an agreement with the USA in October 1998 to allow for the formal resumption of joint military exercises. The first phase of such exercises, which took place in January 2000, provoked popular protests outside the US embassy in Manila against the return to the Philippines of US troops. Meanwhile, in February 1998 the Philippine and US Governments signed a Visiting Forces Agreement (VFA), which was intended as 'a mechanism for regulating the circumstances and conditions under which US forces may visit the Philippines for bilateral military exercises'; *inter alia*, the VFA allowed the US Government to retain jurisdiction over US military personnel accused of committing crimes in the Philippines, unless the crimes were of particular importance to the latter country, and authorized the unrestricted movement of US military aircraft and vessels within the Philippines. Despite significant opposition to the VFA, it was ratified by the Philippine Senate in May 1999.

Following the terrorist attacks on the USA, attributed to the al-Qa'ida Islamist network, in September 2001 (see the chapter on the USA), President Gloria Arroyo offered US President George W. Bush her unqualified support for the US campaign against terrorism. In October Arroyo stated that she had volunteered logistical and intelligence assistance, the use of Philippine airspace, and the former US military bases at Clark and Subic Bay to the US Government. An offer of combat troops had also been made, pending congressional approval. In November Arroyo left for the USA, where she addressed the UN General Assembly and held talks with Bush. In return for the ongoing support of the Philippines in the US anti-terrorist campaign, Bush promised the country US $100m. in military assistance and further development aid for Mindanao. The funds included $39m. to aid the Government in its continuing war against Abu Sayyaf, which had proven links to al-Qa'ida. However, President Arroyo declined an offer of direct US military involvement, limiting its role to the provision of technical and financial assistance for the offensive.

In January 2002 it was reported that the US Government had sent 660 soldiers to the southern Philippines to participate in joint training exercises with Philippine troops; however, they were not to engage in any direct combat as this would contravene the Constitution. The deployment marked the first significant extension of the US-led 'war on terror' beyond Afghanistan. Despite some popular opposition to the deployment, President Arroyo's stance was considerably strengthened when the National Security Council determined that it was authorized under the terms of the VFA. In February more than 20 people died following clashes in the city of Jolo between police and soldiers; a later bomb blast in the city killed a further five people. A second explosion in Zamboanga, which was serving as a temporary base for US service personnel, occurred on the same day. The incidents were attributed to opponents of the ongoing military exercises. Arroyo was also severely criticized by many members of Congress over her decision to allow the deployment, with several claiming that the exercises were intended to conceal a US offensive against Abu Sayyaf. Her most outspoken critic was the Vice-President and Secretary of Foreign Affairs, Teofisto Guingona, Jr, whose stance was a decisive factor in his resignation from the foreign affairs portfolio in July of that year. In April Arroyo sanctioned the deployment of hundreds more US troops to the region and extended the deadline for their departure, owing to the apparent success of the exercises in containing terrorist activities in the Philippines. The exercises were formally concluded at the end of July and the US troops left the Philippines in September; however, about 600 troops remained, forming the counter-insurgency Joint Special Operations Task Force-Philippines (JSOTF-P). (In July 2009 US Secretary of Defense Robert Gates had visited the Philippines to assist him in making a decision regarding the JSOTF-P's future, and in the following month he announced that the force was to remain in the country for the foreseeable future.)

In late 2002 the US Government signed a five-year military agreement with the Philippines, pledging to extend co-operation between the armed forces of the two countries and to facilitate the movement of heavy equipment and logistical supplies. In January 2003 an advance deployment of US Special Forces troops arrived in Zamboanga to commence anti-terrorism training exercises. In February the USA announced that it intended to send a new deployment of soldiers to the island of Jolo, a stronghold of Abu Sayyaf; it specified, controversially, that the troops would assume a combat role for the first time. However, the Philippine Government stressed later that US forces would play an entirely non-combative role in any counter-terrorism exercises. In March Arroyo stated that, owing to local opposition, military exercises would not be conducted on Jolo; in April it was announced that they were to take place in various alternative locations across the Philippines.

During a visit to the USA by President Arroyo in May 2003, US President Bush designated the Philippines as a Major Non-North Atlantic Treaty Organization (NATO) Ally (MNA), entitling it to increased US military co-operation and supplies of armaments. Later in that month the Government stated that it expected to receive a total of US $356m. in military assistance from the USA. In October Bush visited the Philippines during a tour of the region and thanked the country for its continued co-operation in the US-led 'war on terror'. Relations with the USA were strained in July 2004 by Arroyo's decision to withdraw the small Philippine contingent from the US-led coalition forces in Iraq a month ahead of schedule, in order to comply with the demands of militants who had taken a Filipino civilian hostage in the country. Nevertheless, joint US-Philippine military exercises continued during 2004–06. In December 2006 the USA threatened to cancel the joint exercises scheduled for the following year owing to a bilateral dispute that had arisen over the conviction, by a Philippine court, of a soldier on the charge of having raped a Filipino woman, which, the USA argued, was counter to the terms of the VFA signed in 1998; however, in January 2007 the USA announced that the exercises were to go ahead as planned. Meanwhile, in August 2005 bilateral trade discussions were held; issues discussed included agriculture, trade and investment, intellectual property rights and telecommunications, with both the Philippines and the USA affirming that the negotiations had generated mutually beneficial results. During a visit to the USA in June 2008, Arroyo was praised by Bush for her efforts to counter terrorism. Arroyo returned to the USA in February 2009, when she held discussions with the new US Secretary of State, Hillary Clinton, on issues such as the international economic downturn and the insurgency in the southern Philippines. In a further visit to the USA, in July, Arroyo met with Bush's successor as President, Barack Obama; in a joint press conference, Obama affirmed the significance of US-Philippine relations and emphasized the Philippines' importance as a vital link between the USA and Asia, expressing his gratitude for the 'strong voice' with which the Philippines had dealt with a variety of regional issues. In November Secretary of State Clinton visited Manila to show solidarity with the Philippine people in the aftermath of a series of destructive typhoons that had struck the country in previous weeks, killing several hundred people and causing extensive damage.

Following his inauguration at the end of June 2010, incoming President Benigno Aquino visited New York in September, his first overseas visit since assuming the presidency. Addressing the UN General Assembly, Aquino urged UN members to lend their support to the global fight against poverty. He also attended the second summit meeting of US and ASEAN leaders, at which the South China Sea dispute was among a number of issues discussed. Aquino and US President Obama held a brief bilateral discussion on the sidelines of the US-ASEAN summit, during which they agreed to hold more detailed talks in due course. During the seven-day visit, Aquino secured a number of agreements collectively worth an estimated US $2,800m., including a $434m. grant from the Millennium Challenge Corporation (a US aid agency), which was intended, *inter alia*, to improve tax revenues and enhance road infrastructure in the Philippines.

During a visit to St Petersburg, Russia, in June 2009, President Arroyo met with Russian President Dmitrii Medvedev and the two leaders signed a number of formal and informal agreements, including one that provided for the supply of Russian liquefied natural gas to the Philippines for the first time. Arroyo and Medvedev also agreed further to consolidate military co-operation. An air services agreement was signed between the two countries in December (replacing an existing agreement signed in 1992), which provided for the opening of direct scheduled flights between the Russian capital of Moscow and several locations within the Philippines, including Manila and Cebu; the new accord was expected to facilitate increased bilateral tourism, trade and investment.

CONSTITUTION AND GOVERNMENT

The Constitution, which was approved by a national referendum on 2 February 1987, provided for a bicameral Congress, comprising a Senate, with 24 members directly elected by universal suffrage (for a six-year term, with one-half of the membership being elected every three years), and a House of Representatives (with a three-year mandate), with a maximum of 250 members, one being directly elected from each legislative district: in addition, one-fifth of the total number of representatives was to be elected under a party list system from lists of nominees proposed by minority groups. The number of members in the House of Representatives was increased to 275 at the 2007 election.

The President is Head of State, Chief Executive of the Republic and Commander-in-Chief of the Armed Forces. The President is elected by the people for a six-year term, and is not eligible for re-election. The President cannot prevent the enactment of legislative proposals if they are approved by a two-thirds' majority vote in Congress. The President may declare martial law in times of national emergency, but Congress is empowered to revoke such actions at any time by a majority vote of its members. The President appoints a Cabinet and other officials, with the approval of the Commission on Appointments (drawn from members of both chambers of Congress).

Local government is by Barangays (citizens' assemblies), and autonomy is granted to any region where its introduction is endorsed in a referendum. The Autonomous Region of Muslim Mindanao (ARMM), granted autonomy in November 1989, has its own 24-seat Regional Legislative Assembly (RLA).

REGIONAL AND INTERNATIONAL CO-OPERATION

The Philippines is a member of the Association of Southeast Asian Nations (ASEAN, see p. 206), the Asia-Pacific Economic Co-operation (APEC, see p. 197) forum, the Asian Development Bank (ADB, see p. 202), the UN's Economic and Social Commission for Asia and the Pacific (ESCAP, see p. 37) and the Colombo Plan (see p. 446).

The Philippines became a member of the UN in 1945. As a contracting party to the General Agreement on Tariffs and Trade, the Philippines joined the World Trade Organization (WTO, see p. 430) on its establishment in 1995. The Philippines participates in the Group of 77 (G77, see p. 447) developing nations, and is also a member of the International Labour Organization (ILO, see p. 138) and the Non-aligned Movement (see p. 461).

ECONOMIC AFFAIRS

In 2009, according to estimates by the World Bank, the Philippines' gross national income (GNI), measured at average 2007–09 prices, was US $164,532m., equivalent to $1,790 per head (or $3,540 per head on an international purchasing-power parity basis). During 2000–09, it was estimated, the population increased at an average annual rate of 1.9%, while gross domestic product (GDP) per head increased, in real terms, by an average of 2.4% per year. According to figures from the World Bank, overall GDP increased, in real terms, at an average annual rate of 4.4% in 2000–09. According to the Asian Development Bank (ADB), GDP increased by 1.1% in 2009 and by 7.3% in 2010.

Agriculture (including hunting, forestry and fishing) contributed 14.8% of GDP in 2009 and engaged 34.3% of the employed labour force in the same year. Rice, maize and cassava are the main subsistence crops. None the less, the Philippines relies on substantial imports of rice to meet domestic demand. In April 2008 the Government announced a 43,700m. pesos programme of investment in the agricultural sector, aimed at improving general food security and achieving self-sufficiency in rice by 2013. The principal crops cultivated for export are coconuts, sugar cane, bananas and pineapples. Livestock (mainly pigs, buffaloes, goats and poultry) and fisheries are important. According to the World Bank, agricultural GDP increased at an average annual rate of 3.5% during 2000–09. According to the ADB, the agricultural sector recorded no discernible growth in 2009 and contracted by 0.5% in 2010.

Industry (including mining, manufacturing, construction and power) contributed 30.2% of GDP in 2009 and engaged 14.5% of the employed labour force in the same year. According to the World Bank, industrial GDP increased at an average annual rate of 3.3% in 2000–09. According to the ADB, industrial GDP increased by 12.1% in 2010, after declining by 0.9% in 2009.

Mining contributed 1.6% of GDP in 2009 and engaged 0.5% of the employed labour force in the same year. Copper is the Philippines' leading mineral product; gold, silver, chromium, nickel and coal are also extracted. Commercial production of crude petroleum began in 1979. Production from a substantial natural gas field and petroleum reservoir, off the island of Palawan, commenced in 2001. According to figures from the ADB, mining GDP increased at an average annual rate of 11.8% in 2000–09. The GDP of the mining sector expanded by 2.1% in 2008, and by 21.5% in 2009.

Manufacturing contributed 20.4% of GDP in 2009, and engaged 8.3% of the employed labour force in the same year. The most important branches of manufacturing include food products and beverages, electronic products and components (mainly telecommunications equipment), petroleum products and chemicals. According to the World Bank, the GDP of the manufacturing sector increased at an average annual rate of 3.0% in 2000–09, contracting by 6.2% in 2009. Manufacturing output increased by 12.3% in 2010, according to the ADB.

Construction contributed 5.1% of GDP in 2009 and engaged 5.4% of the employed labour force in the same year. According to ADB data, the GDP of the construction sector increased at an average annual rate of 1.2% in 2000–09; the sector's GDP increased by 9.8% in 2009. Construction activities were reported to have expanded by 10.5% in 2010, supported largely by demand for office accommodation.

The energy sector's reliance on imported petroleum has decreased significantly, as new sources of power have become available. In 2007 coal accounted for 28.2% of the total amount of electrical energy produced, natural gas for 32.6%, hydroelectric power for 14.4% and petroleum for 7.5%. In January 2009, as part of the Government's long-term programme to increase the contribution of renewable sources to the electricity supply, plans to construct five biomass plants on the islands were announced. In 2009 petroleum and its products accounted for 16.8% of the value of total merchandise imports. The Government hoped to complete the privatization of its various holdings in the power sector in 2011.

The services sector contributed 55.0% of GDP in 2009, and engaged 51.1% of the employed labour force in the same year. Although periodically affected by political unrest, tourism remains a significant sector of the economy, with receipts (including passenger transport) estimated at US $4,990m. in 2008. Foreign visitor arrivals rose from 1.9m. in 2003 to more than 3.5m. (including Filipinos resident overseas) in 2010. The provision of business process outsourcing facilities and attendant call-centre services has expanded rapidly, to become a significant sector of the economy. Revenue from these activities was estimated to have increased by 19% in 2009, in which year 450,000 workers were employed. According to the World Bank, the GDP of the services sector increased at an average annual rate of 5.6% in 2000–09. According to the ADB, the GDP of the services sector increased by 2.8% in 2009 and by 7.1% in 2010.

In 2009 the Philippines recorded a visible trade deficit of US $8,863m., while there was a surplus of $8,788m. on the current account of the balance of payments. Remittances from Filipino workers abroad make a vital contribution to the economy, rising to an estimated $18,800m. in 2010. In 2009 the principal source of imports was Japan (accounting for 12.6% of the total); other significant suppliers were the USA (12.0%), the People's Republic of China, Singapore, the Republic of Korea and Thailand. The principal market for exports in that year was the USA (17.7%); other major purchasers were Japan (16.2%), the Netherlands, Hong Kong, China, Germany and Singapore. The principal imports in 2009 were machinery and transport equipment (47.0%); other imports include mineral fuels, food and live animals, chemical products and basic manufactures. The prin-

THE PHILIPPINES

cipal exports in that year were machinery and transport equipment, which accounted for 69.3% of total exports, miscellaneous manufactured articles, basic manufactures and food and live animals.

The budget for 2010 projected revenue of 1,207,900m. pesos and expenditure of 1,522,400m. pesos, the resultant deficit expected to reach the equivalent of 3.6% of GDP. The general government gross debt was 3,754,460m. pesos in 2009, equivalent to 48.9% of GDP. According to the ADB, the Philippines' external debt totalled US $59,771m. at the end of 2010; in that year the cost of servicing the debt was equivalent to 8.7% of the value of exports of goods and services. The annual rate of inflation averaged 5.2% in 2000–10. According to official figures, consumer prices increased by 3.2% in 2009 and by 3.8% in 2010. In 2010, according to official figures, 7.3% of the labour force were unemployed (compared with 11.8% in 2004).

A major issue confronting President Benigno Aquino, who took office in June 2010, was the persistently high rate of unemployment, particularly among young Filipinos. In an attempt to reduce concomitant levels of poverty, therefore, the incoming administration aimed to improve business conditions and thereby create more job opportunities. The new Government also undertook to decrease government debt and to restrict the budget deficit to 2.0% of GDP by 2013. The 2011 budget placed greater emphasis on social welfare, while attempting to restrict other public expenditure. The Government of Benigno Aquino hoped to attract wider private investment in areas such as the development of the country's infrastructure. Having been severely curtailed by the decrease in global demand in 2009, the country's export revenues rose by almost 35% in 2010, with a particularly robust recovery being reported in sales of electronic items. Meanwhile, despite the unfavourable global situation of 2008–09, remittances from overseas workers (who were estimated to total almost 9m. in 2008) continued to rise. Such remittances were reported to have increased by more than 8% in dollar terms in 2010, in turn sustaining domestic demand. The surplus on the current account was also supported by the continued strength of the business outsourcing sector. In early 2011, however, the political unrest in the Middle East (a region in which many Filipino workers were employed) gave rise to some concern that remittances from overseas might henceforth be constrained. Furthermore, foreign direct investment was estimated to have declined from US $1,963m. in 2009 to $1,713m. in 2010. Investment inflows were expected to remain weak in 2011 in the aftermath of the tsunami disaster in Japan, a major provider of investment financing and also of development assistance to the Philippines. Although the appreciation of the peso helped to contain rising inflationary pressures in the latter months of 2010, the increase in global petroleum prices led to higher transport costs and to increased charges for utilities. In September 2010 the Government released its first issue of peso-denominated global bonds; subsequent sales of long-term government bonds were reported to be heavily oversubscribed. Following the acceleration in the GDP growth rate in 2010, expansion of 5.0% in 2011 was forecast by the ADB.

PUBLIC HOLIDAYS

2012 (provisional): 2 January (for New Year's Day, also Rizal Day), 28 February (EDSA Revolution Day), 5 April (Maundy Thursday), 6 April (Good Friday), 9 April (Bataan Day—Araw ng Kagitingan), 1 May (Labour Day), 12 June (Independence Day, anniversary of 1898 declaration), 25 June (for Araw ng Maynila)*, 20 August (for Quezon Day)†, 21 August (Ninoy Aquino Day), 29 August (National Heroes' Day), 1 November (All Saints' Day), 28 November (Bonifacio Day), 25 December (for Christmas Day), 31 December (Last Day of the Year).

* Observed only in Metro Manila.
† Observed only in Quezon City.

Statistical Survey

Source (unless otherwise stated): National Statistics Office, Solicarel 1, R. Magsaysay Blvd, Santa Mesa, 1008 Metro Manila; tel. (2) 7160807; fax (2) 7137073; internet www.census.gov.ph.

Area and Population

AREA, POPULATION AND DENSITY

Area (sq km)	300,000*
Population (census results)	
1 May 2000	
Males	38,524,266
Females	37,979,811
Total	76,504,077
1 August 2007†	88,566,732
Population (UN estimates at mid-year)‡	
2009	91,983,099
2010	93,616,853
2011	95,247,566
Density (per sq km) at mid-2011	317.5

* 115,831 sq miles.
† Includes 2,279 Filipinos in Philippine embassies, consulates and missions abroad.
‡ Source: UN, *World Population Prospects: The 2008 Revision*.

POPULATION BY AGE AND SEX
(UN estimates at mid-2011)

	Males	Females	Total
0–14	16,112,791	15,384,322	31,497,113
15–64	29,972,491	29,601,288	59,573,779
65 and over	1,887,431	2,289,243	4,176,674
Total	47,972,713	47,274,853	95,247,566

Source: UN, *World Population Prospects: The 2008 Revision*.

REGIONS
(population at 2007 census)

	Population
National Capital Region	11,566,325
Ilocos (Region I)	4,546,789
Cagayan Valley (Region II)	3,051,487
Central Luzon (Region III)	9,709,177
CALABARZON (Region IV-A)*	11,757,755
MIMAROPA (Region IV-B)*	2,559,791
Bicol (Region V)	5,106,160
Western Visayas (Region VI)	6,843,643
Central Visayas (Region VII)	6,400,698
Eastern Visayas (Region VIII)	3,915,140
Zamboanga Peninsula (Region IX)†	3,230,094
Northern Mindanao (Region X)	3,952,437
Davao (Region XI)‡	4,159,469
SOCCSKSARGEN (Region XII)§	3,830,500
Cordillera Administrative Region	1,520,847
Autonomous Region of Muslim Mindanao	4,120,795
Caraga	2,293,346
Total	88,566,732‖

* Southern Tagalog region prior to September 2001.
† Western Mindanao region prior to September 2001.
‡ Southern Mindanao region prior to September 2001.
§ Including area designated Central Mindanao region prior to September 2001.
‖ Total includes Filipinos in Philippine embassies, consulates and missions abroad (2,279 persons).

THE PHILIPPINES

PRINCIPAL TOWNS
(population at 2007 census)

Manila (capital)*	1,660,714	Bacolod City	499,497
Quezon City*	2,679,450	Muntinlupa City*	452,943
Caloocan City*	1,381,610	Marikina City	424,610
Davao City	1,366,153	Iloilo City	418,710
Cebu City	799,762	Pasay City*	403,064
Zamboanga City	774,407	Mandaue City	318,577
Pasig City*	627,445	Angeles City	317,398
Valenzuela City	568,928	Iligan City	308,046
Makati City*	567,349	Mandaluyong City*	305,576
Cagayan de Oro City	553,966	Baguio City	301,926
Parañaque City	552,660	Butuan City	298,378
Las Piñas City	532,330	Cotabato City	259,153
Gen. Santos City	529,542	Olongapo City	227,270

* Part of Metropolitan Manila.

BIRTHS, MARRIAGES AND DEATHS*

	Registered live births		Registered marriages		Registered deaths	
	Number	Rate (per 1,000)	Number	Rate (per 1,000)	Number	Rate (per 1,000)
1996	1,608,468	23.0	525,555	7.5	344,363	4.9
1997	1,653,236	23.1	562,808	7.9	339,400	4.7
1998	1,632,859	22.3	549,265	7.5	352,992	4.8
1999	1,613,335	21.6	551,445	7.4	347,989	4.7
2000	1,766,440	23.1	577,387	7.5	366,931	4.8
2001	1,714,093	22.0	559,162	7.2	381,834	4.9
2002	1,666,773	21.0	583,167	7.3	396,297	5.0
2003	1,669,442	20.6	593,553	7.3	396,331	4.9
2004	1,710,994	20.7	582,281	7.0	403,191	4.9

* Registration is incomplete. According to UN estimates, the average annual rates per 1,000 were: births 28.9 in 1995–2000, 26.4 in 2000–05, 25.0 in 2005–10; deaths 5.5 in 1995–2000, 5.0 in 2000–05, 4.8 in 2005–10 (Source: UN, *World Population Prospects: The 2008 Revision*).

2005: Registered live births 1,688,918 (20.1 per 1,000); Registered marriages 518,595 (6.2 per 1,000); Registered deaths 676,156 (5.1 per 1,000).

2006: Registered live births 1,663,029 (19.1 per 1,000); Registered marriages 492,666 (5.7 per 1,000).

Life expectancy (years at birth, WHO estimates): 70 (males 67; females 74) in 2008 (Source: WHO, *World Health Statistics*).

ECONOMICALLY ACTIVE POPULATION
('000 persons aged 15 years and over)

	2006	2007	2008
Agriculture, hunting and forestry	10,254	10,342	10,604
Fishing	1,428	1,444	1,426
Mining and quarrying	139	149	158
Manufacturing	3,053	3,059	2,926
Electricity, gas and water	128	135	130
Construction	1,677	1,778	1,834
Wholesale and retail trade; repair of motor vehicles, motorcycles and personal and household goods	6,202	6,354	6,446
Hotels and restaurants	887	907	953
Transport, storage and communications	2,483	2,599	2,590
Financial intermediation	344	359	368
Real estate, renting and business activities	783	885	953
Public administration and defence; compulsory social security	1,485	1,551	1,676

—continued	2006	2007	2008
Education	999	1,035	1,071
Health and social work	359	373	391
Other community, social and personal services	801	849	833
Private households with employed persons	1,612	1,740	1,729
Extra-territorial organizations and bodies	2	2	2
Total employed	32,636	33,560	34,089
Unemployed	2,829	2,653	2,716
Total labour force	35,465	36,213	36,805
Males	21,811	22,217	22,673
Females	13,653	13,996	14,131

Source: ILO.

2009 ('000 persons aged 15 years and over): Total employed 35,062; Unemployed 2,831; Total labour force 37,893.

2010 ('000 persons aged 15 years and over): Total employed 36,047; Unemployed 2,859; Total labour force 38,906.

Health and Welfare

KEY INDICATORS

Total fertility rate (children per woman, 2008)	3.1
Under-5 mortality rate (per 1,000 live births, 2008)	32
HIV/AIDS (% of persons aged 15–49, 2005)	<0.1
Physicians (per 1,000 head, 2004)	0.58
Hospital beds (per 1,000 head, 2006)	1.3
Health expenditure (2007): US $ per head (PPP)	130
Health expenditure (2007): % of GDP	3.9
Health expenditure (2007): public (% of total)	34.7
Access to water (% of persons, 2008)	91
Access to sanitation (% of persons, 2008)	76
Total carbon dioxide emissions ('000 metric tons, 2007)	70,858.1
Carbon dioxide emissions per head (metric tons, 2007)	0.8
Human Development Index (2010): ranking	97
Human Development Index (2010): value	0.638

For sources and definitions, see explanatory note on p. vi.

Agriculture

PRINCIPAL CROPS
('000 metric tons)

	2007	2008	2009
Rice, paddy	16,240	16,816	16,266
Maize	6,737	6,928	7,034
Potatoes	118	121	119
Sweet potatoes	574	573	600*
Cassava (Manioc)	1,871	1,942	2,044
Taro	114	116	120*
Yams	29	24	25*
Sugar cane	22,235	26,601	22,933
Beans, dry	29	30	28
Groundnuts, with shell	31	30	31
Coconuts	14,853	15,320	15,668
Oil palm fruit*	286	286	n.a.
Cabbages and other brassicas	123	129	125
Tomatoes	188	196	199
Pumpkins, squash and gourds	259	253	248
Aubergines (Eggplants)	210	200	201
Onions, dry	146	129	127
Watermelons	126	103	97

THE PHILIPPINES

—continued	2007	2008	2009
Bananas	7,484	8,688	9,013
Grapefruit and pomelos	38	37	40*
Guavas, mangoes and mangosteens	1,024	884	771
Avocados	25	24	25*
Pineapples	2,016	2,209	2,198
Papayas	164	183	177
Coffee, green	98	97	96
Ginger	28	28	27
Tobacco, unmanufactured	34	32	36
Natural rubber	404	411	391

* FAO estimate(s).

Aggregate production ('000 metric tons, may include official, semi-official or estimated data): Total cereals 22,977 in 2007, 23,744 in 2008, 23,301 in 2009; Total roots and tubers 2,779 in 2007, 2,850 in 2008, 2,983 in 2009; Total vegetables (incl. melons) 5,381 in 2007, 5,342 in 2008, 5,325 in 2009; Total fruits (excl. melons) 14,153 in 2007, 15,621 in 2008, 15,911 in 2009.

Source: FAO.

LIVESTOCK
('000 head, year ending 30 June)

	2007	2008	2009
Cattle	2,566	2,566	2,586
Pigs	13,459	13,070	13,596
Buffaloes	3,384	3,339	3,321
Horses*	232	235	240
Goats*	4,046	4,174	4,222
Sheep*	30	30	n.a.
Chickens	135,640	158,663	158,372
Ducks	10,162	10,508	10,577

* FAO estimates.
Source: FAO.

LIVESTOCK PRODUCTS
('000 metric tons)

	2007	2008	2009
Cattle meat	178	180	184*
Buffalo meat	110.2	99.2	100.0*
Pig meat	1,616.7	1,606.0	1,710.4*
Chicken meat	661.8	740.7	752.0*
Cows' milk	13.4	13.8	14.3
Hen eggs†	470	550	555
Other poultry eggs†	73.0	72.0	74.0

* Unofficial figure.
† FAO estimates.
Source: FAO.

Forestry

ROUNDWOOD REMOVALS
('000 cubic metres, excl. bark)

	2007	2008	2009
Sawlogs, veneer logs and logs for sleepers*	648	474	689
Pulpwood	227	338	109
Other industrial wood*	2,295	3,000	3,000
Fuel wood*	12,698	12,581	12,469
Total	15,868	16,393	16,267

* FAO estimates.
Source: FAO.

SAWNWOOD PRODUCTION
('000 cubic metres, incl. railway sleepers)

	2007	2008	2009
Total (all broadleaved)	362	358	300

Source: FAO.

Fishing
('000 metric tons, live weight)

	2006	2007	2008
Capture	2,319.0	2,499.7	2,561.2
Scads (Decapterus)	377.6	437.3	414.0
Sardinellas	303.8	313.1	369.2
Frigate and bullet tunas	175.3	191.5	156.3
Skipjack tuna	164.3	185.9	222.0
Yellowfin tuna	115.5	135.8	169.4
Indian mackerel	90.3	89.6	91.3
Aquaculture	623.4	709.7	741.1
Nile tilapia	160.5	180.1	188.1
Milkfish	315.1	349.7	350.8
Total catch	2,942.4	3,209.4	3,302.3

Note: Figures exclude aquatic plants ('000 metric tons): 1,469.2 (capture 0.3, aquaculture 1,468.9) in 2006; 1,505.5 (capture 0.4, aquaculture 1,505.1) in 2007; 1,667.0 (capture 0.4, aquaculture 1,666.6) in 2008.

Source: FAO.

Mining
('000 metric tons unless otherwise indicated)

	2006	2007	2008
Coal	2,529	3,401	3,610
Crude petroleum ('000 barrels)	181	184	965
Chromium ore (gross weight)	46.7	31.6	15.3
Copper ore*	17.2	22.9	21.2
Salt (unrefined)	418	438	510
Nickel ore*	64.7	91.4	83.9
Gold (metric tons)*	36.1	38.8	35.6
Silver (metric tons)*	23.5	27.8	12.7
Dolomite	1,083.3	1,092.7	1,150.0
Limestone†	21,888	26,419	31,528

* Figures refer to the metal content of ores and concentrates.
† Excludes limestone for road construction.
Source: US Geological Survey.

Industry

SELECTED PRODUCTS
('000 metric tons unless otherwise indicated)

	2005	2006	2007
Plywood ('000 cubic metres)	314	317	281
Mechanical wood pulp*	38	38	38
Chemical wood pulp	147	147	147
Paper and paperboard*	1,097	1,097	1,097
Jet fuels	665	714	729
Motor spirit—petrol	1,629	1,590	1,409
Kerosene	210	162	158
Distillate fuel oils	3,399	3,575	3,511
Residual fuel oils	3,463	3,057	3,093
Liquefied petroleum gas	322	327	250
Cement	15,494	12,033	13,048
Smelter (unrefined) copper	170	162	162
Electric energy (million kWh)	56,568	56,784	59,612

* Estimates.

2008 ('000 metric tons unless otherwise indicated): Electric energy (million kWh) 60,821; Plywood ('000 cubic metres) 235; Mechanical wood pulp 38 (FAO estimate); Chemical wood pulp 147; Paper and paperboard 5,000 (FAO estimate).

2009: Electric energy (million kWh) 61,379 (preliminary); Plywood ('000 cubic metres) 253; Mechanical wood pulp 38 (FAO estimate); Chemical wood pulp 147; Paper and paperboard 5,000 (FAO estimate).

Sources: FAO; UN Industrial Commodity Statistics Database; Asian Development Bank.

THE PHILIPPINES

Finance

CURRENCY AND EXCHANGE RATES

Monetary Units
100 centavos = 1 Philippine peso.

Sterling, Dollar and Euro Equivalents (31 December 2010)
£1 sterling = 68.70 pesos;
US $1 = 43.89 pesos;
€1 = 58.64 pesos;
1,000 Philippine pesos = £14.56 = $22.79 = €17.05.

Average Exchange Rate (pesos per US $)
2008 44.323
2009 47.680
2010 45.110

GENERAL BUDGET
(million pesos)

Revenue*	2003	2004	2005†
Tax revenue	537,684	596,408	677,707
Taxes on net income and profits	243,735	278,848	319,102
Taxes on property	712	798	914
Taxes on domestic goods and services	186,784	203,779	225,041
General sales tax	82,444	93,727	109,094
Excises on goods	56,865	51,433	50,699
Taxes on international trade	106,453	112,983	132,650
Non-tax revenue	87,748	79,491	80,239
Bureau of the Treasury income	56,657	40,735	45,369
Fees and charges	29,375	22,993	24,643
Privatization	1,716	1,000	500
Other non-tax revenue	—	14,763	9,726
Total	**625,432**	**675,898**	**757,945**

Expenditure‡	2003	2004	2005†
Economic services	169,881	155,585	159,158
Agriculture	32,932	25,262	25,941
Natural resources and the environment	6,752	6,776	6,803
Trade and industry	2,722	2,833	3,020
Tourism	1,182	1,200	1,412
Power and energy	1,099	1,999	1,512
Water resources, development and flood control	7,007	6,180	6,471
Transport and communications	67,149	54,908	54,949
Other economic services	1,688	7,077	5,982
Allotment to local government units	49,350	49,350	53,068
Social services	237,532	247,888	254,297
Education, culture and training	128,995	133,321	135,470
Health	12,400	12,880	12,927
Social security, welfare and employment	39,096	38,381	40,080
Housing and community development	3,019	2,577	1,739
Land distribution	907	4,284	4,422
Other social services	945	4,275	3,558
Allotment to local government units	52,170	52,170	56,101
Defence	44,439	43,847	44,193
General public services	141,233	137,278	140,650
General administration	43,442	42,254	40,143
Public order and safety	52,565	53,213	54,290
Other general public services	5,746	2,331	3,763
Allotment to local government units	39,480	39,480	42,454
Interest payments	226,408	271,531	301,692
Total	**819,493**	**856,129**	**899,990**

* Excluding grants received (million pesos): 1,198 in 2003; 511 in 2004; 527 in 2005 (forecast).
† Forecasts.
‡ Excluding net lending (million pesos): 5,620 in 2003; 5,500 in 2004; 7,600 in 2005 (forecast).

2006: *Revenue:* Tax revenue 859,857; Non-tax revenue 119,598; Total revenue 979,455 (excl. grants 183). *Expenditure:* Allotment to local government units 174,713; Interest payments 310,108; Subsidy 13,810; Equity 3,561; Tax expenditures 15,577; Others 526,529; Total expenditure 1,044,298 (excl. net lending 131).

2007: *Revenue:* Tax revenue 932,937; Non-tax revenue 203,473; Total revenue 1,136,410 (excl. grants 150). *Expenditure:* Allotment to local government units 193,712; Interest payments 267,800; Subsidy 27,336; Equity 3,729; Tax expenditures 24,984; Others 621,690; Total expenditure 1,139,251 (excl. net lending 9,750).

2008: *Revenue:* Tax revenue 1,049,179; Non-tax revenue 153,601; Total revenue 1,202,780 (excl. grants 125). *Expenditure:* Allotment to local government units 222,995; Interest payments 272,218; Subsidy 21,145; Equity 1,663; Tax expenditures 49,717; Others 679,895; Total expenditure 1,247,633 (excl. net lending 14,393).

INTERNATIONAL RESERVES
(US $ million at 31 December)

	2008	2009	2010
Gold*	4,358	5,460	7,010
IMF special drawing rights	11	1,141	1,121
Reserve position in IMF	135	138	251
Foreign exchange	33,047	37,504	53,989
Total	**37,551**	**44,243**	**62,371**

*Valued at market-related prices.

Source: IMF, *International Financial Statistics*.

MONEY SUPPLY
('000 million pesos at 31 December)

	2006	2007	2008
Currency outside depository corporations	305.42	344.80	432.98
Transferable deposits	496.46	596.44	651.32
Other deposits	2,983.83	3,208.70	3,393.10
Securities other than shares	18.68	19.88	111.09
Broad money	**3,804.39**	**4,169.82**	**4,588.48**

Source: IMF, *International Financial Statistics*.

COST OF LIVING
(Consumer Price Index; base: 2000 = 100)

	2008	2009	2010
Food (incl. beverages and tobacco)	152.3	161.2	166.1
Fuel, light and water	193.9	188.8	213.8
Clothing (incl. footwear)	130.1	133.4	136.0
Housing and repairs	139.6	143.6	146.1
Services	180.5	180.1	188.0
Miscellaneous	126.1	129.4	131.2
All items	**155.0**	**160.0**	**166.1**

NATIONAL ACCOUNTS
('000 million pesos at current prices)

Expenditure on the Gross Domestic Product

	2007	2008	2009
Government final consumption expenditure	653.8	697.7	809.7
Private final consumption expenditure	4,611.9	5,281.1	5,675.0
Gross fixed capital formation	977.2	1,090.5	1,130.1
Change in inventories	45.2	45.6	−5.4
Total domestic expenditure	**6,288.1**	**7,114.9**	**7,609.4**
Exports of goods and services	2,826.6	2,736.3	2,431.4
Less Imports of goods and services	2,810.2	2,842.0	2,364.8
Statistical discrepancy	342.8	400.2	3.0
GDP in purchasers' values	**6,647.3**	**7,409.4**	**7,678.9**
GDP at constant 1985 prices	**1,366.5**	**1,417.1**	**1,432.1**

THE PHILIPPINES

Gross Domestic Product by Economic Activity

	2007	2008	2009
Agriculture, hunting, forestry and fishing	943.3	1,102.5	1,138.3
Mining and quarrying	108.3	111.0	119.2
Manufacturing	1,459.1	1,654.6	1,566.7
Electricity, gas and water	230.9	235.6	242.5
Construction	299.9	346.6	390.4
Wholesale and retail trade, restaurants and hotels	981.5	1,088.2	1,115.4
Transport, storage and communications	478.4	508.8	514.3
Financial intermediation	362.0	404.9	443.5
Public administration	473.3	507.2	574.4
Other services	1,310.8	1,450.0	1,574.0
GDP in purchasers' values	6,647.3	7,409.4	7,678.9

Source: Asian Development Bank.

BALANCE OF PAYMENTS
(US $ million)

	2007	2008	2009
Exports of goods f.o.b.	49,512	48,253	37,610
Imports of goods f.o.b.	−57,903	−61,138	−46,473
Trade balance	−8,391	−12,885	−8,863
Exports of services	9,766	9,717	10,248
Imports of services	−7,517	−8,557	−8,698
Balance on goods and services	−6,142	−11,725	−7,313
Other income received	5,351	5,973	5,712
Other income paid	−6,250	−5,868	−5,684
Balance on goods, services and income	−7,041	−11,620	−7,285
Current transfers received	14,573	15,780	16,696
Current transfers paid	−420	−533	−623
Current balance	7,112	3,627	8,788
Capital account (net)	24	53	104
Direct investment abroad	−3,536	−259	−359
Direct investment from abroad	2,916	1,544	1,948
Portfolio investment assets	834	789	−1,865
Portfolio investment liabilities	3,922	−4,416	2,155
Financial derivatives assets	170	541	403
Financial derivatives liabilities	−458	−654	−371
Other investment assets	−4,840	4,305	−2,192
Other investment liabilities	4,645	−3,544	−934
Net errors and omissions	−2,082	−1,889	−1,265
Overall balance	8,707	97	6,411

Source: IMF, *International Financial Statistics*.

External Trade

PRINCIPAL COMMODITIES
(distribution by SITC, US $ million)

Imports c.i.f.	2007	2008	2009
Food and live animals	3,713.1	5,866.2	4,806.9
Mineral fuels, lubricants, etc.	9,883.0	12,803.6	7,654.2
Petroleum, petroleum products, etc.	8,834.3	11,582.0	6,635.5
Crude petroleum oils, etc.	5,832.0	7,683.6	3,354.6
Chemicals and related products	4,229.2	5,166.6	4,482.7
Basic manufactures	4,729.5	4,893.9	3,639.5
Textile yarn, fabrics, etc.	1,189.2	872.5	604.2
Machinery and transport equipment	31,706.1	27,896.9	21,540.8
Office machines and automatic data-processing equipment	5,204.5	4,757.6	3,989.4
Parts and accessories for office machines, etc.	4,915.0	4,435.4	3,663.6
Telecommunications and sound equipment	1,234.5	1,297.8	1,200.8
Other electrical machinery, apparatus, etc.	20,091.9	16,118.5	11,638.7
Thermionic valves, tubes, etc.	18,080.4	14,126.8	9,897.7
Electronic microcircuits	5,118.5	5,123.8	4,243.8
Parts for electronic microcircuits	12,675.2	8,693.4	5,434.7
Road vehicles and parts (excl. tyres, engines and electrical parts)	1,827.5	2,093.8	2,044.4
Miscellaneous manufactured articles	1,762.9	1,730.9	1,603.5
Total (incl. others)	57,995.7	60,419.7	45,877.7

Exports f.o.b.	2007	2008	2009
Food and live animals	2,021.1	2,340.6	2,079.5
Basic manufactures	3,746.2	3,958.3	2,678.1
Machinery and transport equipment	35,224.4	33,030.8	26,623.7
Office machines and automatic data-processing equipment	10,209.0	9,016.4	8,210.1
Automatic data-processing machines and units	7,941.3	6,852.0	5,753.1
Digital automatic data-processing machines and units thereof	1,250.0	1,447.1	1,397.2
Digital central storage units, separately consigned	2,082.6	1,651.4	1,106.0
Parts and accessories for data-processing machines	2,135.2	2,013.4	2,346.9
Telecommunications and sound equipment	996.8	1,061.9	841.5
Other electrical machinery, apparatus, etc.	21,156.6	19,741.5	14,710.8
Thermionic valves, tubes, etc.	17,672.5	15,572.7	11,066.7
Diodes, transistors, etc.	1,860.6	1,789.3	1,458.0
Electronic microcircuits	15,226.6	13,165.2	8,815.8
Road vehicles and parts (excl. tyres, engines and electrical parts)	1,808.1	2,213.6	1,567.3
Miscellaneous manufactured articles	4,442.9	4,090.5	3,381.0
Clothing and accessories (excl. footwear)	2,294.4	1,979.0	1,534.1
Total (incl. others)	50,465.7	49,077.5	38,435.8

Source: UN, *International Trade Statistics Yearbook*.

2010 (US $ million): Total imports 54,492.9; Total exports 51,431.7.

THE PHILIPPINES

PRINCIPAL TRADING PARTNERS
(US $ million)

Imports f.o.b.	2007	2008	2009
Australia	760.6	956.8	784.7
China, People's Republic	4,232.9	4,561.1	4,060.4
France (incl. Monaco)	626.9	821.3	546.4
Germany	1,291.9	1,148.4	1,008.0
Hong Kong	2,325.8	2,101.6	1,547.6
India	514.5	654.3	532.3
Indonesia	1,357.2	1,602.3	1,915.1
Iran	200.3	292.7	106.0
Ireland	1,435.0	644.2	185.4
Japan	7,219.1	7,121.9	5,764.9
Korea, Republic	3,403.9	3,128.5	3,160.9
Malaysia	2,370.1	2,583.2	1,787.1
Saudi Arabia	3,592.3	5,154.4	1,558.5
Singapore	6,411.3	6,217.9	3,931.1
Thailand	2,402.5	2,997.6	2,595.7
Viet Nam	906.5	1,800.7	1,401.7
United Arab Emirates	1,297.9	1,377.9	807.6
USA	8,115.3	7,738.1	5,488.2
Total (incl. others)	57,995.7	60,419.7	45,877.7

Exports f.o.b.	2007	2008	2009
Australia	528.4	470.8	296.3
Belgium	666.3	639.8	492.5
China, People's Republic	5,749.5	5,469.2	2,933.9
Germany	2,149.3	2,440.1	2,505.6
Hong Kong	5,803.5	4,987.5	3,213.3
Indonesia	524.5	602.7	382.7
Japan	7,304.1	7,707.1	6,208.4
Korea, Republic	1,783.7	2,522.5	1,828.2
Malaysia	2,506.7	1,957.6	1,359.9
Netherlands	4,149.5	3,708.4	3,743.5
Singapore	3,138.7	2,606.7	2,477.3
Thailand	1,403.0	1,509.0	1,236.1
United Kingdom	479.0	482.8	296.7
USA	8,601.4	8,216.4	6,797.1
Total (incl. others)	50,465.7	49,077.5	38,435.8

Source: UN, *International Trade Statistics Yearbook*.

2010 (US $ million): Total imports 54,492.9; Total exports 51,431.7.

Transport

RAILWAYS
(traffic)

	2002	2003	2004
Passenger-km (million)	93	83	84
Freight ton-km ('000)	63	69	76

Source: UN, *Statistical Yearbook*.

ROAD TRAFFIC
(registered motor vehicles)

	2008	2009	2010
Passenger cars	761,919	780,252	808,583
Utility vehicles	1,595,162	1,643,878	1,700,795
Sports utility vehicles (SUVs)	198,497	221,980	261,213
Buses	29,745	33,033	34,933
Trucks	296,276	311,582	317,903
Motorcycles and mopeds*	2,982,511	3,200,968	3,482,149
Trailers	27,162	28,740	29,279

* Including tricycles.

Source: Land Transportation Office, Manila.

SHIPPING
Merchant Fleet
(registered at 31 December)

	2007	2008	2009
Number of vessels	1,768	1,808	1,823
Total displacement ('000 grt)	5,066.2	5,029.2	5,219.3

Source: IHS Fairplay, *World Fleet Statistics*.

International Sea-borne Shipping
(freight traffic)

	1994	1995	1996
Vessels ('000 net registered tons):			
entered	53,453	61,298	n.a.
cleared	53,841	61,313	n.a.
Goods ('000 metric tons):			
loaded	14,581	16,658	15,687
unloaded	38,222	42,418	51,830

CIVIL AVIATION
(traffic on scheduled services)

	2004	2005	2006
Kilometres flown (million)	82	87	87
Passengers carried ('000)	7,388	8,057	8,305
Passenger-km (million)	15,739	17,123	16,800
Total ton-km (million)	1,929	2,085	2,040

Source: UN, *Statistical Yearbook*.

Tourism

TOURIST ARRIVALS

Country of residence	2006	2007	2008
Australia	101,313	112,466	121,514
Canada	80,507	91,308	102,381
China, People's Republic	133,585	157,601	163,689
Germany	51,402	55,894	55,303
Hong Kong	96,296	111,948	116,653
Japan	421,808	395,012	359,306
Korea, Republic	572,133	653,310	611,629
Singapore	81,114	94,008	100,177
Taiwan	114,955	112,206	118,782
United Kingdom	68,490	79,670	87,422
USA	567,355	578,983	578,246
Total (incl. others)*	2,843,345	3,091,993	3,139,422

* Including Philippine nationals permanently resident abroad.

Tourism receipts (US $ million, incl. passenger transport): 4,019 in 2006; 5,520 in 2007; 4,990 in 2008.

Source: World Tourism Organization.

2009 (foreign visitor arrivals by country of residence): Australia 132,330; Canada 99,012; China, People's Republic 155,019; Germany 55,912; Hong Kong 122,786; Japan 324,980; Korea, Republic 497,936; Malaysia 68,679; Singapore 98,305; Taiwan 102,274; United Kingdom 91,009; USA 582,537; Total (incl. others) 3,017,099. Note: Including Philippine nationals permanently resident abroad (Source: Department of Tourism, Manila).

2010 (foreign visitor arrivals by country of residence): Australia 40,928; Canada 106,345; China, People's Republic 187,446; Germany 58,725; Hong Kong 133,746; Japan 358,744; Korea, Republic 740,622; Malaysia 79,694; Singapore 121,083; Taiwan 142,455; United Kingdom 96,925; USA 600,165; Total (incl. others) 3,520,471. Note: Including Philippine nationals permanently resident abroad (Source: Department of Tourism, Manila).

THE PHILIPPINES

Communications Media

	2007	2008	2009
Telephones ('000 main lines in use)	3,940.1	4,076.1	6,783.4
Mobile cellular telephones ('000 subscribers)	57,344.8	68,117.2	92,226.6
Internet users ('000)	5,296.5	5,619.7	8,278.5
Broadband subscribers ('000)	496.2	1,045.7	1,722.4

Personal computers: 6,300,000 (72.3 per 1,000 persons) in 2006.

Radio receivers ('000 in use): 11,500 in 1997.

Television receivers ('000 in use): 13,500 in 2001.

Book production (titles, excluding pamphlets): 1,380 in 1999.

Daily newspapers: 82 (with average circulation of 6,514,102 copies) in 2004.

Non-daily newspapers: 498 (with average circulation of 971,220 copies) in 2004.

Sources: International Telecommunication Union; UN, *Statistical Yearbook*; UNESCO, *Statistical Yearbook*.

Education

(2009/10 unless otherwise stated, estimates)

	Institutions	Teachers	Pupils
Pre-primary	} 44,846	410,386	{ 1,474,644
Primary schools			13,934,172
Secondary schools	10,384	197,684	6,806,079
University and other tertiary education*	1,619	111,225	2,402,315

*2004/05 figures.

Sources: Department of Education; Commission on Higher Education.

Pupil-teacher ratio (primary education, UNESCO estimate): 33.7 in 2006/07 (Source: UNESCO Institute for Statistics).

Adult literacy rate (UNESCO estimates): 93.6% (males 93.3%; females 93.9%) in 2008 (Source: UNESCO Institute for Statistics).

Directory

The Government

HEAD OF STATE

President: BENIGNO AQUINO, III (assumed office 30 June 2010).
Vice-President: JEJOMAR BINAY.

CABINET
(May 2011)

The Cabinet comprises members of the Liberal Party and numerous unaffiliated representatives of the public and private sectors.

Executive Secretary: PAQUITO OCHOA, Jr.
Secretary of the Interior and Local Government: JESSE ROBREDO.
Secretary of Foreign Affairs: ALBERTO ROMULO.
Secretary of Finance: CESAR PURISIMA.
Secretary of Justice: LEILA L. DE LIMA.
Secretary of National Defense: VOLTAIRE GAZMIN.
Secretary of Education: Brother ARMIN A. LUISTRO.
Secretary of the Budget and Management: FLORENCIO ABAD.
Secretary of Agriculture: PROCESO V. ALCALA.
Secretary of Energy: JOSE RENE V. ALMENDRAS.
Secretary of the Environment and Natural Resources: RAMON PAJE.
Secretary of Health: Dr ENRIQUE T. ONA.
Secretary of Labor and Employment: ROSALINDA BALDOZ.
Secretary of Public Works and Highways: ROGELIO SINGSON.
Secretary of Science and Technology: Dr MARIO G. MONTEJO.
Secretary of Social Welfare and Development: CORAZON SOLIMAN.
Secretary of Tourism: ALBERTO A. LIM.
Secretary of Trade and Industry: GREGORY L. DOMINGO.
Secretary of Transportation and Communications: JOSE DE JESUS.
Secretary of Agrarian Reform: VIRGILIO DE LOS REYES.
Secretary of Presidential Communications Development and Strategic Planning: RAMON CARANDANG.
Secretary of the Presidential Communications Operations Office: HERMINIO COLOMA.
Director-General of the National Economic and Development Authority: CAYETANO L. PADERANGA, Jr.

There are a further 11 officials of cabinet rank.

MINISTRIES

Office of the President: New Exec. Bldg, Malacañang Palace Compound, J. P. Laurel St, San Miguel, Metro Manila; tel. (2) 7356201; fax (2) 9293968; e-mail opnet@ops.gov.ph; internet www.president.gov.ph.

Office of the Vice-President: PNB Financial Center, 7th Floor, President Diosdado Macapagal Blvd, Pasay City, 1300 Metro Manila; tel. (2) 8333311; fax (2) 8316676; e-mail vp@ovp.gov.ph; internet www.ovp.gov.ph.

Department of Agrarian Reform: DAR Bldg, Elliptical Rd, Diliman, Quezon City, Metro Manila; tel. (2) 9287031; fax (2) 9293088; e-mail info@dar.gov.ph; internet www.dar.gov.ph.

Department of Agriculture: DA Bldg, 4th Floor, Elliptical Rd, Diliman, Quezon City, Metro Manila; tel. (2) 9288741; fax (2) 9203987; e-mail usec.gonzales@da.gov.ph; internet www.da.gov.ph.

Department of the Budget and Management: DBM Bldg, Gen. Solano St, Malacañang, San Miguel, Metro Manila; tel. (2) 7354933; fax (2) 7354809; e-mail dbmtis@dbm.gov.ph; internet www.dbm.gov.ph.

Department of Education: DepED Complex, Meralco Ave, Pasig City, 1600 Metro Manila; tel. (2) 6321361; fax (2) 6388634; internet www.deped.gov.ph.

Department of Energy: Energy Center, Merritt Rd, Fort Bonifacio, Taguig, 1201 Metro Manila; tel. and fax (2) 8402278; e-mail info@doe.gov.ph; internet www.doe.gov.ph.

Department of the Environment and Natural Resources: DENR Bldg, Visayas Ave, Diliman, Quezon City, 1100 Metro Manila; tel. (2) 9296626; fax (2) 9204352; e-mail osec@denr.gov.ph; internet www.denr.gov.ph.

Department of Finance: DOF Bldg, BSP Complex, Roxas Blvd, 1004 Metro Manila; tel. (2) 5236051; fax (2) 5268474; e-mail hotline@dof.gov.ph; internet www.dof.gov.ph.

Department of Foreign Affairs: DFA Bldg, 2330 Roxas Blvd, Pasay City, 1330 Metro Manila; tel. (2) 8344000; fax (2) 8321597; e-mail webmaster@dfa.gov.ph; internet www.dfa.gov.ph.

Department of Health: San Lazaro Compound, Rizal Ave, Santa Cruz, 1003 Metro Manila; tel. (2) 7438301; fax (2) 7431829; e-mail ftduque@co.doh.gov.ph; internet www.doh.gov.ph.

Department of the Interior and Local Government: A. Francisco Gold Condominium II, Epifanio de los Santos Ave, cnr Mapagmahal St, Diliman, Quezon City, 1100 Metro Manila; tel. (2) 9250349; fax (2) 9250386; e-mail dilgmail@dilg.gov.ph; internet www.dilg.gov.ph.

Department of Justice: Padre Faura St, Ermita, 1000 Metro Manila; tel. (2) 5238481; fax (2) 5267643; e-mail info@doj.gov.ph; internet www.doj.gov.ph.

Department of Labor and Employment: DOLE Exec. Bldg, 7th Floor, Muralla Wing, Muralla St, Intramuros, 1002 Metro Manila; tel. (2) 5273000; fax (2) 5273494; e-mail osec@dole.gov.ph; internet www.dole.gov.ph.

Department of National Defense: DND Bldg, 3rd Floor, Camp Aguinaldo, Quezon City, 1110 Metro Manila; tel. (2) 9116402; fax (2) 9111651; e-mail webmaster@dnd.gov.ph; internet www.dnd.gov.ph.

Department of Public Works and Highways: DPWH Bldg, Bonifacio Dr., Port Area, Metro Manila; tel. (2) 3043000; fax (2) 5275635; e-mail bonoan.manuel@dpwh.gov.ph; internet www.dpwh.gov.ph.

THE PHILIPPINES

Department of Science and Technology: DOST Compound, Gen. Santos Ave, Bicutan, Taguig, 1631 Metro Manila; tel. (2) 8372071; fax (2) 8373161; e-mail efa@dost.gov.ph; internet www.dost.gov.ph.

Department of Social Welfare and Development: Batasang Pambansa, Constitution Hills, Quezon City, Metro Manila; tel. (2) 9318101; fax (2) 9318191; e-mail lfp@dswd.gov.ph; internet www.dswd.gov.ph.

Department of Tourism: T. F. Valencia Circle, T. M. Kalaw St, Rizal Park, Metro Manila; tel. (2) 5238411; fax (2) 5256538; e-mail amflor@tourism.gov.ph; internet www.wowphilippines.com.ph.

Department of Trade and Industry: Industry and Investments Bldg, 385 Sen. Gil J. Puyat Ave, Buendia, Makati City, 1200 Metro Manila; tel. (2) 7510384; fax (2) 8956487; e-mail mis@dti.dti.gov.ph; internet www.dti.gov.ph.

Department of Transportation and Communications: Columbia Tower, 17th Floor, Ortigas Ave, Mandaluyong City, 1555 Metro Manila; tel. (2) 7277960; fax (2) 7234925; e-mail webmaster@dotc.gov.ph; internet www.dotc.gov.ph.

National Economic and Development Authority (NEDA—Department of Socio-Economic Planning): NEDA-sa-Pasig Bldg, 12 St Josemaria Escriva Dr., Ortigas Center, Pasig City, 1605 Metro Manila; tel. (2) 6313747; fax (2) 6313282; e-mail info@neda.gov.ph; internet www.neda.gov.ph.

Philippine Information Agency (Office of the Press Secretary): PIA Bldg, Visayas Ave, Diliman, Quezon City, 1101 Metro Manila; tel. (2) 9204345; fax (2) 9204390; e-mail angie.villapando@gmail.com; internet www.pia.gov.ph.

President and Legislature

PRESIDENT

Election, 10 May 2010

Candidate	Votes	% of votes
Benigno Aquino III (Liberal Party—LP)	15,208,678	41.87
Joseph Estrada (Pwersa ng Masang Pilipino—PMP)	9,487,837	26.12
Manuel Villar (Nacionalista Party—NP)	5,573,835	15.35
Gilberto Teodoro (Lakas-Kampi-CMD)	4,095,839	11.28
Eduardo Villanueva (Bangon Pilipinas)	1,125,878	3.10
Richard Gordon (Bagumbayan-VNP)	501,727	1.38
Vetellano Acosta (Kilusang Bagong Lipunan—KBL)	181,985*	0.50
Nicanor Perlas (Independent)	54,575	0.15
Jamby Madrigal (Independent)	46,489	0.13
John Carlos de los Reyes (Ang Kapatiran)	44,244	0.12
Total	**36,321,087**	**100.00**

* Candidate was disqualified after ballot papers had been printed; all votes for Vetellano Acosta were therefore deemed invalid.

THE CONGRESS OF THE PHILIPPINES

Senate

President of the Senate: JUAN PONCE ENRILE.

Elections for 12 of the 24 seats were held on 10 May 2010. The LP and the NP-Nationalist People's Coalition (NPC) alliance both won three seats, while Lakas-Kampi-CMD and the PMP secured two seats each, and the People's Reform Party took one. The remaining seat was secured by an independent candidate.

House of Representatives

Speaker of the House: FELICIANO BELMONTE.

General Election, 10 May 2010, provisional results

	Seats
Lakas-Kampi-CMD	105
Liberal Party (LP)	42
Nationalist People's Coalition (NPC)	31
Nacionalista Party (NP)	25
Independents	7
Pwersa ng Masang Pilipino (PMP)	5
Others	46
Undeclared	25
Total	**286**

Note: The total includes 57 seats reserved for members of minority and cause-orientated groups allocated under the concurrent party list elections.

Autonomous Region

MUSLIM MINDANAO

The Autonomous Region of Muslim Mindanao (ARMM) originally comprised the provinces of Lanao del Sur, Maguindanao, Tawi-Tawi and Sulu. The Region was granted autonomy in November 1989. Elections took place in February 1990, and the formal transfer of limited executive powers took place in October of that year. In August 2001 a plebiscite was conducted in 11 provinces and 14 cities in Mindanao to determine whether or not they would become members of the ARMM. The city of Marawi and the province of Basilan subsequently joined the Region. The Regional Legislative Assembly was expanded to 24 seats, from 21 previously, at elections held on 8 August 2005. A total of six candidates contested the concurrent gubernatorial election; Zaldy Ampatuan, the candidate of Lakas ng EDSA-Christian Muslim Democrats (Lakas-CMD), won an estimated 63.7% of the votes cast, defeating Mahid Mutilan of the Ompia Party, a Muslim grouping, and Ibrahim Paglas of the Liberal Party, who received 24.3% and 11.8% of the votes respectively. Ampatuan was re-elected Governor on 11 August 2008. However, owing to his alleged involvement in the killing of 57 people on Mindanao in November 2009, Ampatuan was subsequently suspended from office and replaced by his deputy, Ansaruddin Adiong, in an acting capacity.

Governor: ANSARUDDIN ALONTO ADIONG (acting).

Vice-Governor: REJIE SAHALI-GENERALE (acting).

Election Commission

Commission on Elections (COMELEC): Postigo St, Intramuros, 1002 Metro Manila; tel. (2) 5275581; e-mail asd@comelec.gov.ph; internet www.comelec.gov.ph; f. 1940; Chair. SIXTO BRILLANTES, Jr.

Political Organizations

Akbayan (Citizens' Action Party): 36B Madasalin St, Teacher's Village West, Diliman, Quezon City, 1101 Metro Manila; tel. (2) 4336933; fax (2) 9252936; e-mail secretariat@akbayan.org; internet www.akbayan.org; f. 1998; left-wing party list; Chair. PERCIVAL CENDANA; Pres. RONALD LLAMAS; Sec.-Gen. CONRAD CASTILLO.

Aksyon Demokratiko (Democratic Action Party): 16th Floor, Strata 2000 Bldg, F. Ortigas Jr Rd, Ortigas Center, Pasig City, 1600 Metro Manila; tel. (2) 6385381; fax (2) 6343072; e-mail senator@raulroco.com; internet 203.115.161.138/library/raulroco/aksyond/aksyond.htm; f. 1997; est. to support presidential candidacy of RAUL ROCO; joined Alyansa ng Pag-asa in 2003 to contest 2004 elections; Chair. SONIA M. ROCO; Pres. JAIME GALVEZ-TAN; Sec.-Gen. LORNA KAPUNAN.

Bagumbayan-Volunteers for a New Philippines (Bagumbayan-VNP): Unit 3C, Classica Condominium I, H. V. Dela Costa St, Makati City, Metro Manila; tel. (2) 813-1257; e-mail join@bagumbayan-vnp.com; f. 2009; Chair. RICHARD GORDON; Pres. LEON B. HERRERA.

Bangon Pilipinas (Rise Philippines): 8th Floor, Dominion Bldg, 833 Arnaiz Ave, Legaspi Village, Makati City, 1200 Metro Manila; tel. (2) 8113355; fax (2) 8111110; e-mail feedback@bangonpilipinas.org; internet bangonpilipinas.com; Pres. CIELITO F. HABITO; Chair. EDUARDO VILLANUEVA.

Bayan Muna (People First): 153 Scout Rallos St, Kamuning, Quezon City, 1103 Metro Manila; tel. (2) 4251045; fax (2) 9213473; e-mail information@bayanmuna.net; internet www.bayanmuna.net; f. 1999; Pres. SATUR C. OCAMPO; Chair. Dr REYNALDO LESACA, Jr.

Kilusang Bagong Lipunan (KBL) (New Society Movement): Metro Manila; f. 1978 by Pres. MARCOS and fmr mems of the Nacionalista Party; Chair. FERDINAND 'BONG BONG' MARCOS, Jr.

Laban ng Demokratikong Pilipino (LDP) (Fight of Democratic Filipinos): 3-B, Osmena Bldg, 1991 A. Mabini St, Malate, Metro Manila; internet www.edangara.com; f. 1987; reorg. 1988 as an alliance of Lakas ng Bansa and a conservative faction of the PDP-Laban Party; mem. of Lapian ng Masang Pilipino (LAMP) until Jan. 2001; split into two factions, led by EDGARDO ANGARA and AGAPITO AQUINO, to contest 2004 elections; Angara faction joined Koalisyon ng Nagkakaisang Pilipino (KNP) in Dec. 2003 to support presidential candidacy of FERNANDO POE, Jr; Aquino faction supported presidential candidacy of PANFILO LACSON; Pres. EDGARDO ANGARA.

Lakas-Kampi-CMD: 6th Floor, CLMC Bldg, Greenhills East, Mandaluyong City; tel. (2) 7250872; fax (2) 7250736; f. 2009; est. by merger of Lakas ng EDSA-Christian Muslim Democrats (fmrly Lakas-National Union of Christian Democrats/Lakas-NUCD) and

THE PHILIPPINES

of Kabalikat ng Malayang Pilipino (Kampi); Nat. Chair. EDCEL LAGMAN; Nat. Pres. RAMON BONG REVILLA, Jr.

Liberal Party (LP): 2nd Floor, Matrinco Bldg, Chino Roces Ave, Makati City, 1231 Metro Manila; tel. (2) 8937483; fax (2) 8930218; e-mail liberalpartyphils@gmail.com; internet www.liberalparty.ph; f. 1946; represents centre-liberal opinion of the fmr Nacionalista Party, which split in 1946; joined Koalisyon ng Katapatan at Karanasan sa Kinabukasan (K-4) in Jan. 2004 to contest 2004 elections; Chair. FRANKLIN M. DRILON; Pres. MANUEL ROXAS, II.

Nacionalista Party (NP): 2nd Floor, Starmall EDSA, cnr Shaw Blvd, Mandaluyong City, 1552 Metro Manila; tel. (2) 7224727; fax (2) 7274223; e-mail secretariat@nacionalistaparty.com; internet www.nacionalistaparty.com; formed alliance with NPC in April 2010 to contest election in May; Pres. MANUEL VILLAR; Sec.-Gen. ALAN PETER CAYETANO.

Nationalist People's Coalition (NPC): 8 Bouganvilla St, cnr Balete Dr., Mariana, Quezon City, 1112 Metro Manila; tel. (2) 5847518; fax (2) 5847568; e-mail npcparty@gmail.com; internet npcparty.org; f. 1991; breakaway faction of the NP, with which it formed an alliance in April 2010, in advance of the legislative election in May; mem. of Lapian ng Masang Pilipino (LAMP) from 1997 until Jan. 2001; Chair. FAUSTINO DY, Jr; Pres. FRISCO SAN JUAN.

Partido Demokratiko Pilipino-Lakas Ng Bayan (PDP-Laban): 721 J. P. Rizal St, Makati City, Metro Manila; internet www.pdplaban.org; tel. (2) 8901792; fax (2) 8900858; f. 1983; est. following merger of Pilipino Democratic Party (f. 1982 by fmr mems of the Mindanao Alliance) and Laban (Lakas ng Bayan—People's Power Movement, f. 1978 and led by BENIGNO S. AQUINO, Jr, until his assassination in 1983); centrist; formally dissolved in Sept. 1988, following formation of the LDP, but a faction continued to function as a political movement; formed United Opposition (UNO) alliance with the PMP in advance of the May 2010 elections; Pres. JEJOMAR BINAY; Sec.-Gen. AQUILINO PIMENTEL, III.

Partido Demokratiko Sosyalista ng Pilipinas (PDSP) (Philippine Democratic Socialist Party): 45 Melchor St, Varsity Hills, Quezon City, Metro Manila; tel. and fax (2) 4161325; fax 9286678; e-mail secretariat@pdsp.net; internet pdsp.net; f. 1981; formed by mems of the Batasang Pambansa allied to the Nacionalista (Roy faction), Pusyon Visaya and Mindanao Alliance parties; joined People Power Coalition (PPC) in Feb. 2001; Chair. NORBERTO GONZALES.

Partido ng Manggagawang Pilipino (Filipino Workers' Party): e-mail pinoy_bolshevik@yahoo.com; internet manggagawang pilipino.tripod.com; f. 2002; est. by fmr supporters of the CPP.

Partido para sa Demokratikong Reporma: Chateau Bldg, Pasig City, Metro Manila; joined People Power Coalition (PPC) in Feb. 2001; Chair. RENATO DE VILLA; Sec.-Gen. RAFAEL COLET.

People's Reform Party (PRP): Narsan Bldg, 4th Floor, 3 West Fourth St, West Triangle Quezon Ave, Quezon City, Metro Manila; e-mail miriam@miriam.com; f. 1991; formed by MIRIAM DEFENSOR SANTIAGO to support her candidacy in the 1992 presidential election; Santiago re-elected to Senate for a third term in 2010; Pres. MIRIAM DEFENSOR SANTIAGO.

Probinsya Muna Development Initiatives (PROMDI): 7 Pasteur St, Lahug, Cebu City; tel. (32) 2326692; fax (32) 2313609; f. 1997; Leader EMILIO ('LITO') OSMEÑA.

Pwersa ng Masang Pilipino (PMP): 409 Shaw Bld, Mandaluyong City, Metro Manila; e-mail pmp_power@yahoo.com; formed United Opposition (UNO) alliance with PDP-Laban in advance of the May 2010 elections; Pres. JOSEPH EJERCITO ESTRADA; Sec.-Gen. JOSEPH VICTOR EJERCITO.

United Negros Alliance (UNA): Negros Occidental; formed alliance with the NPC in advance of the May 2010 elections; Chair. ALFREDO MARAÑON, Jr.

The following organizations are, or have been, in conflict with the Government:

Abu Sayyaf (Bearer of the Sword): Mindanao; radical Islamist group seeking the establishment of an Islamic state in Mindanao; breakaway grouping of the MILF; est. strength 1,500 (2000); Leader YASSER IGASAN.

Alex Boncayao Brigade (ABB): communist urban guerrilla group, fmrly linked to CPP; formed alliance with Revolutionary Proletarian Party in 1997; est. strength 500 (April 2001); Leader NILO DE LA CRUZ.

Islamic Command Council (ICC): Mindanao; splinter group of MNLF; Leader MELHAM ALAM.

Maranao Islamic Statehood Movement: Mindanao; f. 1998; armed grouping seeking the establishment of an Islamic state in Mindanao.

Mindanao Independence Movement (MIM): Mindanao; claims a membership of 1m; Leader REUBEN CANOY.

Moro Islamic Liberation Front (MILF): Camp Abubakar, Lanao del Sur, Mindanao; aims to establish an Islamic state in Mindanao; comprises a faction that broke away from the MNLF in 1978; its armed wing, the Bangsa Moro Islamic Armed Forces, has c. 12,500 armed regulars; Chair. Al-Haj MURAD EBRAHIM.

Moro Islamic Reform Group: Mindanao; breakaway faction from MNLF; est. strength of 200 in 2000.

Moro National Liberation Front (MNLF): internet mnlf.net; seeks autonomy for Muslim communities in Mindanao; signed a peace agreement with the Govt in Sept. 1996; its armed wing, the Bangsa Moro Army, comprised an est. 10,000 mems in 2000; Chair. and Pres. of Cen. Cttee Dr NUR MISUARI.

Moro National Liberation Front—Islamic Command Council (MNLF—ICC): Basak, Lanao del Sur; f. 2000; Islamist separatist movement committed to urban guerrilla warfare; breakaway faction from MNLF.

National Democratic Front (NDF): a left-wing alliance of 14 mem. groups; Chair. MARIANA OROSA; Spokesman GREGORIO ROSAL.

The NDF includes:

Communist Party of the Philippines (CPP): f. 1968; breakaway faction of the Partido Komunista ng Pilipinas (PKP, f. 1930); legalized Sept. 1992; in July 1993 the Metro Manila-Rizal and Visayas regional committees, controlling 40% of total CPP membership (est. 15,000 in 1994), split from the Central Committee; Chair. JOSE MARIA SISON; Gen. Sec. BENITO TIAMZON.

New People's Army (NPA): f. 1969; est. as the military wing of the CPP; based in central Luzon, but operates throughout the Philippines; est. strength 9,500; Leader JOVENCIO BALWEG; Spokesman GREGORIO ROSAL.

Revolutionary Proletarian Party: Metro Manila; f. 1996; comprises mems of the Metro Manila-Rizal and Visayas regional committees, which broke away from the CPP in 1993; has a front organization called the Buklaran ng Manggagawang Pilipino (Association of Filipino Workers); Leader ARTURO TABARA.

Rajah Solaiman Movement (RSM): Mindanao; f. 2002; radical Islamist group seeking to establish an Islamic state in the Philippines; predominantly composed of converts to Islam.

Workers and Peasants Party (WPP): Unit 113, Legaspi Suites, 11th Floor, 178 Salcedo St, Legaspi Village, Makati City, Metro Manila; fmrly known as Lapiang Mangagawa; Pres. JOSE MALVAR VILLEGAS, Jr; Sec.-Gen. FRANK PASION.

Diplomatic Representation

EMBASSIES IN THE PHILIPPINES

Argentina: 8th Floor, Liberty Center, 104 H. V. de la Costa St, Salcedo Village, Makati City, 1227 Metro Manila; tel. (2) 8453218; fax (2) 8453220; e-mail embarfil@eastern.com.ph; Ambassador ISMAEL MARIO SCHUFF.

Australia: 23rd Floor, Tower II, RCBC Plaza, 6819 Ayala Ave, Makati City, 1200 Metro Manila; tel. (2) 7578100; fax (2) 7578268; e-mail public-affairs-MNLA@dfat.gov.au; internet www.australia.com.ph; Ambassador ROD SMITH.

Austria: Prince Bldg, 4th Floor, 117 Rada St, Legaspi Village, POB 2411, Makati City, 1200 Metro Manila; tel. (2) 8179191; fax (2) 8134238; e-mail manila-ob@bmeia.gv.at; internet www.aussenministerium.at/manila; Ambassador WILHELM DONKO.

Bangladesh: Universal-Re Bldg, 2nd Floor, 106 Paseo de Roxas, Legaspi Village, Makati City, Metro Manila; tel. (2) 8175001; fax (2) 8164941; e-mail bdemb.manila@yahoo.com; Ambassador IKHTIAR MOMIN CHOWDHURY.

Belgium: Multinational Bancorporation Center, 9th Floor, 6805 Ayala Ave, Makati City, Metro Manila; tel. (2) 8451869; fax (2) 8452076; e-mail manila@diplobel.fed.be; internet www.diplomatie.be/manila; Ambassador CHRISTIAN MEERSCHMAN.

Brazil: 16th Floor, Liberty Center, 104 H. V. de la Costa St, Salcedo Village, Makati City, 1227 Metro Manila; tel. (2) 8453651; fax (2) 8453676; e-mail brascom@info.com.ph; internet www.brasemb.org.ph; Ambassador ALCIDES G. R. PRATES.

Brunei: Bank of the Philippine Islands Bldg, 11th Floor, Ayala Ave, cnr Paseo de Roxas, Makati City, 1227 Metro Manila; tel. (2) 8162836; fax (2) 8916646; Ambassador MALAI Hajah HALIMAH MALAI YUSSOF.

Cambodia: Unit 7A, 7th Floor, Country Space One Bldg, Sen. Gil J. Puyat Ave, Makati City, Metro Manila; tel. (2) 8189981; fax (2) 8189983; e-mail phnompenhpe@ezecom.com.kh; Ambassador IN MAY.

Canada: 6th–8th Floors, Tower 2, RCBC Plaza, 6819 Ayala Ave, POB 2098, Makati City, 1200 Metro Manila; tel. (2) 8579000; fax (2) 8431082; e-mail manil@dfait-maeci.gc.ca; internet www.canadainternational.gc.ca/philippines; Ambassador CHRISTOPHER THORNLEY.

THE PHILIPPINES

Chile: 17th Floor, Liberty Center, 104 H. V. de la Costa St, cnr Leviste St, Salcedo Village, Makati City, 1227 Metro Manila; tel. (2) 8433461; fax (2) 8431976; e-mail echileph@eastern.com.ph; internet www.embachileph.com; Ambassador OVID HARASICH.

China, People's Republic: 4896 Pasay Rd, Dasmariñas Village, Makati City, Metro Manila; tel. (2) 8443148; fax (2) 8452465; e-mail chinaemb_ph@mfa.gov.cn; internet ph.chineseembassy.org; Ambassador LIU JIANCHAO.

Cuba: 101 Aguirre St, cnr Trasierra St, Cacho-Gonzales Bldg Penthouse, Legaspi Village, Makati City, Metro Manila; tel. (2) 8171192; fax (2) 8164094; e-mail embacuba@pldtdsl.net; Ambassador JORGE REY JIMÉNEZ.

Czech Republic: 30th Floor, Rufino Pacific Tower, 6784 Ayala Ave, 1200 Makati City, Metro Manila; tel. (2) 8111155; fax (2) 8111020; e-mail manila@embassy.mzv.cz; internet www.mzv.cz/manila; Ambassador JOSEF RYCHTAR.

Egypt: 2229 Paraiso St, cnr Banyan St, Dasmariñas Village, Makati City, Metro Manila; tel. (2) 8439232; fax (2) 8439239; Ambassador SALWA MOUFID KAMEL MAGARIOUS.

Finland: 21st Floor, BPI Buendia Center, Sen. Gil J. Puyat Ave, POB 2447, MCPO, Makati City, 1264 Metro Manila; tel. (2) 8915011; fax (2) 8914107; e-mail sanomat.mni@formin.fi; internet www.finland.ph; Ambassador HEIKKI HANNIKAINEN.

France: Pacific Star Bldg, 16th Floor, Makati Ave, cnr Sen. Gil J. Puyat Ave, 1200 Makati City, Metro Manila; tel. (2) 8576900; fax (2) 8576951; e-mail consulat@ambafrance-ph.org; internet www.ambafrance-ph.org; Ambassador THIERRY BORJA DE MOZOTA.

Germany: 25th Floor, Tower 2, RCBC Plaza, 6819 Ayala Ave, Makati City, Metro Manila; tel. (2) 7023000; fax (2) 7023015; e-mail deboma@pldtdsl.net; internet www.manila.diplo.de; Ambassador CHRISTIAN-LUDWIG WEBER-LORTSCH.

Holy See: 2140 Taft Ave, POB 3364, 1099 Metro Manila (Apostolic Nunciature); tel. (2) 5210306; fax (2) 5211235; e-mail nuntiusp@info.com.ph; Apostolic Nuncio Most Rev. GIUSEPPE PINTO.

India: 2190 Paraiso St, Dasmariñas Village, POB 2123, Makati City, MCPO, Metro Manila; tel. (2) 8430101; fax (2) 8158151; e-mail info@embindia.org.ph; internet www.embindia.org.ph; Ambassador Shri RAJEET MITTER.

Indonesia: 185 Salcedo St, Legaspi Village, POB 1671, MCPO, Makati City, Metro Manila; tel. (2) 8925061; fax (2) 8925878; e-mail fungsipensosbud@yahoo.com.ph; internet www.kbrimanila.org.ph; Ambassador YOHANNES KRISTIARTO SOERYO LEGOWO.

Iran: 2224 Paraiso St, cnr Pasay Rd, Dasmariñas Village, Makati City, Metro Manila; tel. (2) 8884757; fax (2) 8884777; e-mail mrouzbehani@gmail.com; Ambassador ALI MOJTABA ROUZBEHANI.

Israel: Trafalgar Plaza, 23rd Floor, 105 H. V. de la Costa St, Salcedo Village, Makati City, 1227 Metro Manila; tel. (2) 8940441; fax (2) 8941027; e-mail info@manila.mfa.gov.il; internet manila.mfa.gov.il; Ambassador ZVI VAPNI.

Italy: Zeta II Bldg, 6th Floor, 191 Salcedo St, Legaspi Village, Makati City, Metro Manila; tel. (2) 8924531; fax (2) 8171436; e-mail informazioni.manila@esteri.it; internet www.ambmanila.esteri.it; Ambassador RUBENS ANNA FEDELE.

Japan: 2627 Roxas Blvd, Pasay City, 1300 Metro Manila; tel. (2) 5515710; fax (2) 5515780; e-mail jicc-mnl@japanembassy.ph; internet www.ph.emb-japan.go.jp; Ambassador TOSHINAO URABE.

Korea, Republic: 10th Floor, Pacific Star Bldg, Sen. Gil J. Puyat Ave, cnr Makati Ave, Makati City, 1226 Metro Manila; tel. (2) 8116139; fax (2) 8116148; e-mail philippines@mofat.go.kr; internet embassy_philippines.mofat.go.kr; Chargé d'affaires KIM YONG-HO.

Kuwait: 1230 Acacia Rd, Dasmariñas Village, POB 2033, Makati City, Metro Manila; tel. (2) 8876880; fax (2) 8876887; Ambassador BADER NASSER AL-HOUTI.

Laos: 34 Lapu-Lapu St, Magallanes Village, Makati City, Metro Manila; tel. and fax (2) 8525759; Ambassador LEUANE SOMBOUNKHAN.

Libya: 1644 Dasmariñas St, cnr Mabolo St, Dasmariñas Village, Makati City, Metro Manila; tel. (2) 8177331; fax (2) 8177337; e-mail lpbmanila@skynet.net; Chargé d'affaires a.i. SADEK A. S. OSMAN.

Malaysia: 107 Tordesillas St, Salcedo Village, Makati City, 1200 Metro Manila; tel. (2) 8640761; fax (2) 8640727; e-mail mwmanila@indanet.com; internet www.kln.gov.my/perwakilan/manila; Ambassador AHMAD RASIDI HAZIZI.

Mexico: 150 Legaspi St, G. C. Corporate Plaza, Legaspi Village, Makati City, Metro Manila; tel. (2) 8122211; fax (2) 8927635; e-mail embmxfil@info.com.ph; internet portal.sre.gob.mx/filipinaseng; Ambassador TOMAS JAVIER CALVILLO UNNA.

Myanmar: Gervasia Corporate Center, 8th Floor, 152 Amorsolo St, Legaspi Village, Makati City, Metro Manila; tel. (2) 8931944; fax (2) 8928866; e-mail myanila@mydestiny.net; Ambassador AUNG KHIN SOE (designate).

Netherlands: Equitable PCI Bank Tower, 26th Floor, 8751 Paseo de Roxas, Makati City, Metro Manila; tel. (2) 7866666; fax (2) 7866600; e-mail man@minbuza.nl; internet www.netherlandsembassy.ph; Ambassador ROBERT BRINKS.

New Zealand: BPI Buendia Center, 23rd Floor, Sen. Gil J. Puyat Ave, POB 3228, MCPO, Makati City, Metro Manila; tel. (2) 8915358; fax (2) 8915357; e-mail nzmanila@nxdsl.com.ph; internet www.nzembassy.com/philippines; Ambassador ANDREW MATHESON.

Nigeria: 2211 Paraiso St, Dasmariñas Village, POB 3174, Makati City, 1271 Metro Manila; tel. (2) 8439866; fax (2) 8439867; e-mail embassy@nigeriamanila.org; internet www.nigeriamanila.org; Chargé d'affaires a.i. NDUBUISI V. AMAKU.

Norway: Petron Mega Plaza Bldg, 21st Floor, 358 Sen. Gil J. Puyat Ave, Makati City, 1209 Metro Manila; tel. (2) 8863245; fax (2) 8863384; e-mail emb.manila@mfa.no; internet www.norway.ph; Ambassador KNUT SOLEM.

Pakistan: Alexander House, 6th Floor, 132 Amorsolo St, Legaspi Village, Makati City, Metro Manila; tel. (2) 8172776; fax (2) 8400229; e-mail pakrepmanila@yahoo.com; internet www.cpsctech.org/~pkembphil; Ambassador MUHAMMAD NAEEM KHAN.

Palau: Marbella Condominium II, Unit 101, Ground Floor, 2071 Roxas Blvd, Malate, Manila; tel. (2) 5221982; fax (2) 5210402; e-mail ropembassy-pi@pldtdsl.net; Ambassador RAMON RECHEBEI.

Panama: 10th Floor, MARC 2000 Tower, 1973 Taft Ave and San Andres St, cnr Quirino Ave, Malate, 1004 Metro Manila; tel. (2) 5212790; fax (2) 5215755; e-mail panamaph@pldtdsl.net; Ambassador JUAN FELIPE PITTY.

Papua New Guinea: 3rd Floor, Corinthian Plaza Condominium Bldg, cnr Paseo de Roxas and Gamboa St, Makati City, Metro Manila; tel. (2) 8113465; fax (2) 8113466; e-mail kundumnl@pngembmnl.com.ph; Ambassador CHRISTIAN ANTHONY VIHRURI.

Qatar: 1398 Cabellero St, cnr Lumbang St, Dasmariñas Village, Makati City, Metro Manila; tel. (2) 8874944; fax (2) 8876406; e-mail gemanila2000@yahoo.com; Ambassador ABDULLAH AHMED YOUSIF AL-MUTAWA.

Romania: 1216 Acacia Rd, Dasmariñas Village, Makati City, Metro Manila; tel. (2) 8439014; fax (2) 8439063; e-mail amarom@zpdee.net; Ambassador VALERIU GHEORGHE.

Russia: 1245 Acacia Rd, Dasmariñas Village, Makati City, Metro Manila; tel. (2) 8930190; fax (2) 8109614; e-mail RusEmb@i-manila.com.ph; internet www.philippines.mid.ru; Ambassador VITALII Y. VOROBIEV.

Saudi Arabia: Saudi Embassy Bldg, 389 Sen. Gil J. Puyat Ave Ext., Makati City, Metro Manila; tel. (2) 8564444; fax (2) 8953493; e-mail phemb@mofa.gov.sa; internet www.saudiembassy.com.ph; Ambassador MOHAMMAD AMEEN WALI.

Singapore: 505 Rizal Drive, Bonifacio, 1634 Taguig City, Metro Manila; tel. (2) 8569922; fax (2) 8569932; e-mail singemb_mnl@sgmfa.gov.sg; internet www.mfa.gov.sg/manila; Ambassador A. SELVERAJAH.

South Africa: 29th Floor, Yuchengco Tower, RCBC Plaza, 6819 Ayala Ave, Makati City, 1227 Metro Manila; tel. (2) 8899383; fax (2) 8899337; e-mail manila@foreign.gov.za; Ambassador PIETER VERMEULEN.

Spain: 27th Floor, Equitable Bank Tower, 8751 Paseo de Roxas, 1226 Metro Manila; tel. (2) 8176676; fax (2) 8174892; e-mail emb.manila@mae.es; Ambassador LUIS ARIAS ROMERO.

Sri Lanka: 7th Floor, G. C. Corporate Plaza, 150 Legaspi St, Legaspi Village, Makati City, Metro Manila; tel. (2) 8120124; fax (2) 8120126; e-mail slembmanila@pldtdsl.net; internet www.slembmanila.ph; Chargé d'affaires a.i. SIRIMEWAN DAWULAGALA.

Switzerland: Equitable Bank Tower, 24th Floor, 8751 Paseo de Roxas, Makati City, 1226 Metro Manila; tel. (2) 7579000; fax (2) 7573718; e-mail man.vertretung@eda.admin.ch; internet www.eda.admin.ch/manila; Ambassador IVO SIEBER.

Thailand: 107 Rada St, Legaspi Village, Makati City, 1229 Metro Manila; tel. (2) 8154220; fax (2) 8154221; e-mail infomnl@pldtdsl.net; internet www.thaiembassymnl.ph; Ambassador KULKUMUT SINGHARA NA AYUDHYA.

Timor-Leste: 17th Floor, Centerpoint Condominium, Rm 1703, cnr Julia Vargas Ave, Ortigas Center, Pasig City, 1605 Metro Manila; tel. (2) 637-9405; fax (2) 637-9408; e-mail timorlesteembassyinmanila@yahoo.com; Ambassador FRANCISCO CEPEDA.

Turkey: 2268 Paraiso St, Dasmariñas Village, Makati City, Metro Manila; tel. (2) 8439705; fax (2) 8439702; e-mail turkembm@info.com.ph; Ambassador ADNAN BASAGA.

United Arab Emirates: Renaissance Bldg, 2nd Floor, 215 Sakedo St, Legaspi Village, Makati City, Metro Manila; tel. (2) 8173906; fax (2) 8183577; Ambassador MUSA ABDUL WAHED ABDUL GHAFAR AL-KHAJA.

THE PHILIPPINES

United Kingdom: Locsin Bldg, 15th–17th Floors, 6752 Ayala Ave, cnr Makati Ave, Makati City, 1226 Metro Manila; tel. (2) 5808700; fax (2) 8197206; e-mail uk@info.com.ph; internet www.ukinthephilippines.fco.gov.uk; Ambassador STEPHEN LILLIE.

USA: 1201 Roxas Blvd, Ermita, 1000 Metro Manila; tel. (2) 3012000; fax (2) 3012399; internet manila.usembassy.gov; Ambassador HARRY THOMAS, Jr.

Venezuela: Unit 17A, Multinational Bancorporation Center, 6805 Ayala Ave, Makati City, Metro Manila 1226; tel. (2) 8452841; fax (2) 8452866; e-mail venezemb@info.com.ph; Chargé d'affaires a.i. MANUEL VICENTE PÉREZ ITURBE.

Viet Nam: 670 Pablo Ocampo St, Malate, Metro Manila; tel. (2) 5216843; fax (2) 5260472; e-mail vnembph@yahoo.com; internet www.vietnamembassy-philippines.org; Ambassador VU XUAN TRUONG.

Judicial System

The Philippine judicial system comprises the Supreme Court, the Court of Appeals, Regional Trial Courts, Metropolitan Trial Courts, Municipal Courts in Cities, Municipal Courts and Municipal Circuit Trial Courts. There is also a special court for trying cases of corruption (the Sandiganbayan). The Office of the Ombudsman (Tanodbayan) investigates complaints concerning the actions of public officials. Islamic *Shari'a* courts were established in the southern Philippines in July 1985 under a presidential decree of February 1977. They are presided over by three district magistrates and six circuit judges.

SUPREME COURT

The February 1987 Constitution provides for the establishment of a Supreme Court comprising a Chief Justice and 14 Associate Justices; the Court may sit *en banc* or in divisions of three, five or seven members. Justices of the Supreme Court are appointed by the President from a list of a minimum of three nominees prepared by a Judicial and Bar Council.

Chief Justice: RENATO CORONA, New Supreme Court Bldg Annex, 3rd Floor, Padre Faura St, Ermita, 1000 Metro Manila; tel. (2) 5225090; fax (2) 5268129; e-mail pio@sc.judiciary.gov.ph; internet sc.judiciary.gov.ph.

COURT OF APPEALS

Consists of a Presiding Justice and 68 Associate Justices.

Presiding Justice: ANDRES B. REYES, Jr, Maria y Orosa St, Ermita, 1000 Metro Manila; tel. (2) 524-1241; e-mail ca_manila@yahoo.com; internet ca.judiciary.gov.ph.

Religion

According to the results of the 2000 census, 81.1% of the population were Roman Catholics and 11.6% belonged to other Christian denominations. The Islamic community constituted 5% of the population, Buddhists accounted for 0.1%, while indigenous and other religious traditions comprised a further 1.7%. Atheists and persons who did not state a religious preference accounted for 0.5%.

CHRISTIANITY

Sangguniang Pambansa ng mga Simbahan sa Pilipinas (National Council of Churches in the Philippines): 879 Epifanio de los Santos Ave, West Triangle, Quezon City 1104, Metro Manila; tel. (2) 9293745; fax (2) 9267076; e-mail library@nccphilippines.org; internet www.nccphilippines.org; f. 1963; 10 mem. churches, 10 assoc. mems; Gen. Sec. REX R. B. REYES, Jr.

The Roman Catholic Church

For ecclesiastical purposes, the Philippines comprises 16 archdioceses, 55 dioceses, six territorial prelatures, one military ordinate and seven apostolic vicariates. At 31 December 2007 approximately 81.2% of the population were adherents.

Catholic Bishops' Conference of the Philippines (CBCP): 470 General Luna St, Intramuros, 1076 Metro Manila; tel. (2) 5274054; fax (2) 5279634; e-mail cbcp@info.com.ph; internet www.cbcponline.org; f. 1945; statutes approved 1952; Pres. Most Rev. ANGEL N. LAGDAMEO (Archbishop of Jaro).

Archbishop of Caceres: Most Rev. LEONARDO Z. LEGASPI, Archbishop's House, Elias Angeles St, POB 6085, 4400 Naga City; tel. (54) 4738483; fax (54) 4738383; e-mail chancerynaga@yahoo.com.

Archbishop of Cagayan de Oro: Most Rev. ANTONIO J. LEDESMA, Archbishop's Residence, POB 113, 9000 Misamis Oriental, Cagayan de Oro City; tel. (8822) 722375; fax (8822) 726304; e-mail acdo_chancery@yahoo.com.

Archbishop of Capiz: Most Rev. ONESIMO C. GORDONCILLO, Chancery Office, POB 44, 5800 Roxas City; tel. (36) 6215595; fax (36) 6211053.

Archbishop of Cebu: Most Rev. JOSÉ SEROFIA PALMA, Archbishop's Residence, cnr P. Gomez St and P. Burgos St, POB 52, 6000 Cebu City; tel. (32) 2541861; fax (32) 2530123; e-mail adelito@skynet.net.

Archbishop of Cotabato: Most Rev. ORLANDO B. QUEVEDO, Archbishop's Residence, 154 Sinsuat Ave, POB 186, 9600 Cotabato City; tel. (64) 4212918; fax (64) 4211446.

Archbishop of Davao: Most Rev. FERNANDO R. CAPALLA, Archbishop's Residence, 247 Florentino Torres St, POB 80418, 8000 Davao City; tel. (82) 2275992; fax (82) 2279771; e-mail bishopdavao@yahoo.com.

Archbishop of Jaro: Most Rev. ANGEL N. LAGDAMEO, Archbishop's Residence, Jaro, 5000 Iloilo City; tel. (33) 3294442; fax (33) 3293197; e-mail abpjaro@yahoo.com.

Archbishop of Lingayen-Dagupan: Most Rev. OSCAR V. CRUZ, Archbishop's House, Jovellanos St, 2400 Pangasinan, Dagupan City; tel. (75) 5235357; fax (75) 5221878; e-mail oscar@rezcom.com.

Archbishop of Lipa: Most Rev. RAMON C. ARGÜELLES, Archbishop's House, St Lorenzo Ruiz Rd, Lipa City, 4217 Batangas; tel. (43) 7562572; fax (43) 7560005; e-mail chancery@batangas.net.ph.

Archbishop of Manila: Most Rev. GAUDENCIO B. ROSALES, Arzobispado, 121 Arzobispo St, Intramuros, POB 132, 1099 Metro Manila; tel. (2) 5277631; fax (2) 5273956; e-mail aord-aom2004@yahoo.com; internet www.rcam.org.

Archbishop of Nueva Segovia: Most Rev. ERNESTO A. SALGADO, Archbishop's House, Vigan, 2700 Ilocos Sur; tel. (77) 7222018; fax (77) 7221591; e-mail nschancery@yahoo.com.ph.

Archbishop of Ozamis: Most Rev. JESUS A. DOSADO, Archbishop's House, POB 2760, Rizal Ave, Banadero, 7200 Ozamis City; tel. (65) 5212771; fax (65) 5211574.

Archbishop of Palo: Most Rev. JOSE S. PALMA, Archdiocesan Chancery, Palo, 6501 Leyte; POB 173, Tacloban City, 6500 Leyte; tel. (53) 3232213; fax (53) 3235607; e-mail rcap@mozcom.com.

Archbishop of San Fernando (Pampanga): Most Rev. PACIANO B. ANICETO, Chancery Office, San José, San Fernando, 2000 Pampanga; tel. (45) 9612819; fax (45) 9616772; e-mail rca@pamp.pworld.net.ph.

Archbishop of Tuguegarao: Most Rev. DIOSDADO A. TALAMAYAN, Archbishop's House, Rizal St, Tuguegarao, 3500 Cagayan; tel. (78) 8441663; fax (78) 8462822; e-mail chancerycat@lycos.com.

Archbishop of Zamboanga: Most Rev. ROMULO G. VALLES, Pastoral Centre, POB 1, Puerto del Sol, Gov. Camins Ave, 7000 Zamboanga City; tel. (62) 9927668; fax (62) 9932608; e-mail zambochancery-10@yahoo.com.

Other Christian Churches

Convention of Philippine Baptist Churches: POB 263, 5000 Iloilo City; tel. (33) 3290621; fax (33) 3290618; e-mail gensec@iloilo.net; f. 1935; Gen. Sec. Rev. Dr NATHANIEL M. FABULA; Pres. DONATO ENABE.

Episcopal Church in the Philippines: POB 10321, Broadway Centrum, Quezon City, 1102 Metro Manila; tel. (2) 7228481; fax (2) 7211923; e-mail ecpnational@yahoo.com.ph; internet www.episcopalchurchphilippines.org; f. 1901; six dioceses; Prime Bishop Most Rev. EDWARD MALECDAN.

Iglesia Evangélica Metodista en las Islas Filipinas (Evangelical Methodist Church in the Philippines): Beulah Land, Iemelif Center, Greenfields 1, Subdivision, Marytown Circle, Novaliches, Quezon City, 1123 Metro Manila; tel. (2) 9356519; fax (2) 4185017; e-mail admin@iemelif.org; internet www.iemelif.org; f. 1909; 40,000 mems (2003); Gen. Supt Bishop NATHANAEL P. LAZARO.

Iglesia Filipina Independiente (Philippine Independent Church): POB 2484, 1000 Metro Manila; tel. (2) 5212794; fax (2) 5213932; e-mail gensec@ifi.ph; internet www.ifi.ph; f. 1902; 34 dioceses; 6.0m. mems; Obispo Maximo (Supreme Bishop) Most Rev. GODOFREDO J. DAVID.

Iglesia ni Cristo: 1 Central Ave, New Era, Quezon City, 1107 Metro Manila; tel. (2) 9814311; fax (2) 9814333; f. 1914; 5m. mems; Exec. Minister Brother EDUARDO V. MANALO.

Lutheran Church in the Philippines: 4461 Old Santa Mesa, 1008 Metro Manila; POB 507, 1099 Metro Manila; tel. (2) 7157084; fax (2) 7142395; internet www.lutheranphilippines.org; f. 1946; Pres. Rev. JAMES CERDEÑOLA.

Union Church of Manila: cnr Legaspi St and Rada St, Legaspi Village, Makati City, Metro Manila; tel. (2) 8126062; fax (2) 8172386; e-mail ucmweb@unionchurch.ph; internet www.unionchurch.ph; Senior Pastor Rev. STEVE RUESTCHLE.

THE PHILIPPINES

United Church of Christ in the Philippines: 877 Epifanio de los Santos Ave, West Triangle, Quezon City, Metro Manila; POB 718, MCPO, Ermita, 1099 Metro Manila; tel. (2) 9240215; fax (2) 9240207; e-mail uccpnaof@manila-online.net; internet www.uccp.ph; f. 1948; 900,000 mems (1996); Gen. Sec. Rev. ELIEZER PASCUA (Bishop).

Among other denominations active in the Philippines are the Iglesia Evangélica Unida de Cristo and the United Methodist Church.

ISLAM

Some 14 different ethnic groups profess the Islamic faith in the Philippines. Mindanao and the Sulu and Tawi-Tawi archipelago, in the southern Philippines, are predominantly Muslim provinces, but there are 10 other such provinces, each with its own Imam, or Muslim religious leader. More than 500,000 Muslims live in the north of the country (mostly in, or near to, Manila).

Islamic Da'wah Council of the Philippines (IDCP): Suite 400, FUBC Bldg, Escolta, Metro Manila; tel. (2) 2458456; fax (2) 2415142; e-mail idcp@edsamail.com.ph; internet www.idcp-ph.org; f. 1982; federation of 95 mem. orgs; Pres. ABDUL RAHAM R. T. LINZAG.

BAHÁ'Í FAITH

National Spiritual Assembly: 1070 A. Roxas St, cnr Bautista St, Singalong Subdiv., Malate, 1004 Metro Manila; POB 4323, 1099 Metro Manila; tel. (2) 5240404; fax (2) 5232449; e-mail nsaphil@greendot.com.ph; mems resident in 129,949 localities; Chair. ALFREDO RAMIREZ; Sec.-Gen. MA ADORACION NEWMAN.

The Press

The Office of the President implements government policies on information and the media. Freedom of the press and freedom of speech are guaranteed under the Constitution.

METRO MANILA

Dailies

Abante: 167 Liberty Bldg, Roberto S. Oca St, Port Area, Metro Manila; tel. (2) 5276722; fax (2) 5280147; e-mail abante@abante-tonite.com; internet www.abante.ph; morning; Filipino and English; Man. Editor NICOLAS V. QUIJANO, Jr; circ. 417,000.

Abante Tonite: 167 Liberty Bldg, Roberto S. Oca St, Port Area, Metro Manila; tel. (2) 5276722; fax (2) 5279838; e-mail tonite@abante-tonite.com; internet www.abante-tonite.com; afternoon; Filipino and English; Man. Editor NICOLAS V. QUIJANO, Jr; circ. 277,000.

Balita: Liwayway Publishing Inc, 2249 Pasong Tamo, Makati City, Metro Manila; tel. (2) 5278121; fax (2) 4000095; e-mail balitamb@yahoo.com; f. 1972; morning; Filipino; Publr HERMOGENES P. POBRE; circ. 151,000.

BusinessMirror: Dominga Bldg (Annex), 2nd Floor, 2113 Chino Roces Ave, cnr De La Rosa St, Makati City, Metro Manila; tel. (2) 8179467; fax (2) 8137025; e-mail news@businessmirror.com.ph; internet www.businessmirror.com.ph; f. 2005; Editor-in-Chief LOURDES M. FERNANDEZ; Man. Editor VLADIMIR S. BUNOAN.

BusinessWorld: Raul L. Locsin Bldg I, 95 Balete Dr. Ext., New Manila, Quezon City, 1112 Metro Manila; tel. (2) 5359901; fax (2) 5359926; internet www.bworldonline.com; f. 1987; Exec. Editor ARNOLD E. BELLEZA; Man. Editor WILFREDO G. REYES; circ. 54,000.

Daily Tribune: Penthouse Suites, GLC Bldg, T. M. Kalaw St, cnr A. Mabini St, Ermita, Metro Manila; tel. (2) 5215584; fax (2) 5215522; e-mail nco@tribune.net.ph; internet www.tribune.net.ph; f. 2000; English; Publr and Editor-in-Chief NINEZ CACHO-OLIVARES.

Malaya Business Insight: Leyland Bldg, 20th St, cnr Railroad St, Port Area, Metro Manila; tel. (2) 3393324; fax (2) 5271839; e-mail malayanews@yahoo.com; internet www.malaya.com.ph; f. 1981; originally Filipino; English since 1983; Exec. Editor ENRIQUE P. ROMUALDEZ; Editor-in-Chief JOY DE LOS REYES; circ. 175,000.

Manila Bulletin: Bulletin Publishing Corpn, Muralla St, cnr Recoletos St, Intramuros, POB 769, 1002 Metro Manila; tel. (2) 5278121; fax (2) 5277510; e-mail bulletin@mb.com.ph; internet www.mb.com.ph; f. 1900; English; Publr HERMOGENES P. POBRE; Editor-in-Chief Dr CHRIS J. ICBAN, Jr; circ. 265,000.

Manila Standard Today: Leyland Bldg, 21st St, cnr Railroad St, Port Area, Metro Manila; tel. (2) 5278151; fax (2) 5246649; e-mail mst@manilastandardtoday.com; internet www.manilastandardtoday.com; f. 1987 as Manila Standard; name changed as above in 2005, following merger with rival newspaper *Today*; morning; English; Editor-in-Chief JOJO ROBLES; circ. 96,000.

Manila Times: 371A Bonifacio Dr., Port Area, Metro Manila; tel. (2) 5245664; fax (2) 3019552; e-mail newsboy1@manilatimes.net; internet www.manilatimes.net; f. 1945; morning; English; Publr and Editor-in-Chief FRED DELA ROSA.

People's Journal: Universal-Re Bldg, 6th Floor, 106 Paseo de Roxas, cnr Perea and Gallardo Sts, Legaspi Village, Makati City, Metro Manila; tel. (2) 5278421; fax (2) 5274627; internet www.journal.com.ph; English and Filipino; Editor AUGUST B. VILLANUEVA; circ. 219,000.

People's Taliba: 6th Floor, Universal-Re Bldg, 106 Paseo de Roxas, cnr Perea and Gallardo Sts, Legaspi Village, Makati City, Metro Manila; fax (2) 5274627; Filipino; Editor BENJAMIN DEFENSOR; circ. 229,000.

People's Tonight: 6th Floor, Universal-Re Bldg, 106 Paseo de Roxas, cnr Perea and Gallardo Sts, Legaspi Village, Makati City, Metro Manila; tel. (2) 5278421; fax (2) 5274627; f. 1978; English and Filipino; Editor FERDIE RAMOS; circ. 500,000.

Philippine Daily Inquirer: Philippine Daily Inquirer Bldg, Chino Roces Ave, cnr Mascardo and Yague Sts, Pasong Tamo, POB 2353, Makati City, 1263 Metro Manila; tel. (2) 8978808; fax (2) 8974793; e-mail feedback@inquirer.com.ph; internet www.inquirer.com.ph; f. 1985; English; Editor-in-Chief LETTY JIMENEZ-MAGSANOC; circ. 250,000.

Philippine Star: 202 Railroad St, cnr 13th St, Port Area, 1016 Metro Manila; tel. (2) 5276856; fax (2) 5276851; e-mail editor@philstar.com; internet www.philstar.com; f. 1986; Editor ISAAC BELMONTE; circ. 275,000.

Pilipino Star Ngayon: 202 Railroad St, cnr 13th St, Port Area, 1016 Metro Manila; tel. (2) 5272389; fax (2) 5272403; e-mail psngayon@philstar.net.ph; internet www.philstar.com; f. 1986; Filipino tabloid; Chief Editor ALFONSO G. PEDROCHE; circ. 286,452.

Tempo: Bulletin Publishing Corpn, Muralla St, cnr Recoletos St, Intramuros, POB 769, 1002 Metro Manila; tel. (2) 5278121; fax (2) 5277510; internet www.tempo.com.ph; f. 1982; English and Filipino; Editor-in-Chief BAMBANG HARYMURTI; circ. 230,000.

United Daily News: 812–818 Benavides St, Binondo, 1006 Metro Manila; tel. (2) 2447171; e-mail united_dailynews@yahoo.com; f. 1973; Chinese; Editor-in-Chief CHUA KEE; circ. 85,000.

Selected Periodicals

Weeklies

Bannawag: c/o Manila Bulletin Publishing Corpn, Muralla St, cnr Recoletos St, Intramuros, Metro Manila; tel. (2) 5278121; fax (2) 5277510; f. 1934; Ilocano; Editor DIONISIO S. BULONG; circ. 42,900.

Bisaya: c/o Manila Bulletin Publishing Corpn, Muralla St, cnr Recoletos St, Intramuros, Metro Manila; tel. (2) 5278121; fax (2) 5277510; f. 1934; Cebu-Visayan; Editor EDGAR S. GODIN; circ. 90,000.

Liwayway: c/o Manila Bulletin Publishing Corpn, Muralla St, cnr Recoletos St, Intramuros, Metro Manila; tel. (2) 5278121; fax (2) 5277510; f. 1922; Tagalog; circ. 102,400.

Panorama: Manila Bulletin Publishing Corpn, Muralla St, cnr Recoletos St, Intramuros, POB 769, Metro Manila; tel. and fax (2) 5277509; e-mail panorama@mb.com.ph; internet www.panorama.com.ph; f. 1968; English; Editor RANDY V. URLANDA; circ. 239,600.

Philippine Starweek: 13th St, cnr Railroad St, Port Area, Metro Manila; tel. (2) 5277901; fax (2) 5275819; e-mail feedback@philstar.net.ph; internet www.philstar.com; English; Editor JOSEPH NACINO; circ. 268,000.

SELECTED PROVINCIAL PUBLICATIONS

The Aklan Reporter: 1227 Rizal St, Kalibo, Panay, 5600 Aklan; tel. (36) 2684158; f. 1971; weekly; English and Aklanon; Editor SUNRA ROJO; circ. 1,000.

Baguio Midland Courier: 16 Kisad Rd, POB 50, Baguio City; tel. (74) 4422444; fax (74) 4439485; e-mail baguiomidlandcourier@yahoo.com; internet www.baguiomidlandcourier.com.ph; f. 1947; English; Publr CHARLES M. HAMADA; circ. 24,500.

Bayanihan Weekly News: Bayanihan Publishing Co, P. Guevarra Ave, Santa Cruz, Laguna; f. 1966; Mon.; Filipino and English; Editor ARTHUR A. VALENOVA; circ. 1,000.

Bohol Chronicle: 56 B. Inting St, Tagbilaran City, 6300 Bohol; tel. and fax (38) 5010077; fax (38) 4113100; e-mail editor@bolchronicle.com; internet www.boholchronicle.com; f. 1954; 2 a week; English and Cebuano; Editor and Publr ZOILO DEJARESCO; circ. 5,500.

The Bohol Times: 100 Gallares St, Tagbilaran City, 6300 Bohol; tel. (38) 4112961; fax (38) 4112656; e-mail boholtimes@yahoo.com; Publr Dr LILIA A. BALITE; Editor-in-Chief SALVADOR D. DIPUTADO.

The Ilocos Times: Barangay 23, M. H. del Pilar St, 2900 Laoag City; tel. (77) 7720976; fax (77) 7711378; e-mail publisher@ilocostimes.com; internet www.ilocostimes.com; f. 1920; weekly; publ. by Ilocos Publishing Corpn; English and Iluko; Publr and Editor EFREN S. RAMOS, Jr; circ. 5,000.

The Kapawa News: L. V. Moles and Jose Abad Santos Sts, Tangub, POB 365, 6100 Bacolod City; tel. and fax (34) 4441941; e-mail

LM-Kapawa@eudoramail.com; f. 1966; weekly; Sat.; Hiligaynon and English; Publr HENRY G. DOBLE; circ. 2,000.

Mindanao Post: Blk 16, Lot 3, SIR New Matina, Davao City, Mindanao; f. 1999; Editor-in-Chief DOMING ROSAL.

Mindanao Times: UMBN Bldg, Ponciano Reyes St, Davao City, Mindanao; tel. 2273252; e-mail editorial.mtimes@gmail.com; internet www.mindanaotimes.com.ph; daily; Editor-in-Chief AMALIA B. CABUSAO; circ. 5,000.

Pagadian Times: 0519 Alano St, 7016 Pagadian City; tel. (62) 2141721; fax (62) 2151504; e-mail pagtimes@mozcom.com; f. 1969; weekly; English; Publr PEDE G. LU; Editor REMAI ALEJADS; circ. 7,000.

Panay News: Panay News Complex, Q. Abeto St, Mandurriao, Iloilo City; tel. (33) 3212749; fax (33) 5094159; e-mail pnnews@panaynewsphilippines.com; internet www.panaynewsphilippines.com; Editor-in-Chief DANNY FAJARDO.

Sorsogon Today: 2903 Burgos St, East District, 4700 Sorsogon; tel. and fax (56) 4215306; fax (56) 2111340; e-mail sortoday@yahoo.com; f. 1977; weekly; Publr and CEO MARCOS E. PARAS, Jr; circ. 2,250.

Sun Star Cebu: Sun Star Bldg, 3rd Floor, cnr of P. del Rosario St and P. Cui St, Cebu City; tel. (32) 2546100; fax (32) 2537256; e-mail centralnewsroom@sunstar.com.ph; internet www.sunstar.com.ph/cebu; f. 1982; daily; English; Editor-in-Chief PACHICO A. SEARES; Gen. Man. JULIUS NERI.

Superbalita Davao: 5–6 Granland Business and Warehouse Center, R. Castillo St, Agdao, Davao City; tel. (82) 2351004; fax (82) 2351006; e-mail ssdavao@gmail.com; internet www.sunstar.com.ph/superbalitadavao; daily; Editor-in-Chief STELLA ESTREMERA.

The Tribune: Jarlego & Sons Bldg, Maharlika Highway, 2301 Cabanatuan City, Luzon; f. 1960; weekly; English and Filipino; Editor and Publr ORLANDO M. JARLEGO; circ. 8,000.

The Valley Times: Daang Maharlika, San Felipe, Ilagan, Isabela; f. 1962; weekly; English; Editor AUREA A. DE LA CRUZ; circ. 4,500.

The Visayan Tribune: 1973 Mezzanine Floor, Masonic Temple Bldg, Plaza Libertad 5000, Iloilo City; f. 1959; weekly; English; Editor HERBERT L. VEGO; circ. 5,000.

The Voice of Islam: Davao City; f. 1973; monthly; English and Arabic; official Islamic news journal; Editor and Publr NASHIR MUHAMMAD AL'RASHID AL HAJJ.

NEWS AGENCY

Philippines News Agency: PIA Bldg, 2nd Floor, Visayas Ave, Diliman, Quezon City, Metro Manila; tel. (2) 9206551; fax (2) 9206566; e-mail bert.panganiban@gmail.com; internet www.pna.gov.ph; f. 1973; Gen. Man. VITTORIO V. VITUG; Exec. Editor DANILO C. TAGUIBAO (acting).

PRESS ASSOCIATION

National Press Club of the Philippines: National Press Club Bldg, Magallanes Drive, Intramuros, 1002 Metro Manila; tel. (2) 3010521; fax (2) 5219300; e-mail ad-nationalpressclub@yahoo.com; f. 1952; Pres. BENNY ANTIPORDA; Vice-Pres. ROLLY GONZALO; 1,405 mems.

Publishers

Abiva Publishing House Inc: Abiva Bldg, 851 Gregorio Araneta Ave, Quezon City, 1113 Metro Manila; tel. (2) 7120245; fax (2) 7120486; e-mail mmrabiva@i-manila.com.ph; internet www.abiva.com.ph; f. 1937; reference and textbooks; Pres. JORGE GARCIA.

Ateneo de Manila University Press: Bellarmine Hall, Ateneo de Manila University, Katipunan Ave, Loyola Heights, Quezon City, Metro Manila; tel. (2) 4265984; fax (2) 4265909; e-mail unipress@admu.edu.ph; internet www.ateneopress.org; f. 1972; literary, textbooks, humanities, social sciences, reference books on the Philippines; Dir MARICOR E. BAYTION.

Bookman, Inc: 373 Quezon Ave, Quezon City, 1114 Metro Manila; tel. (2) 7124818; fax (2) 7124843; e-mail bookman@info.com.ph; f. 1945; textbooks, reference, educational; Pres. LINA PICACHE-ENRIQUEZ; Exec. Vice-Pres. MARIETTA PICACHE-MARTINEZ.

Capitol Publishing House, Inc: 13 Team Pacific Bldg, Jose C. Cruz St, cnr F. Legaspi St, Barrio Ugong, Pasig City, Metro Manila; tel. (2) 6712662; fax (2) 6712664; e-mail cacho@mozcom.com; f. 1947; Gen. Man. MANUEL L. ATIENZA.

Heritage Publishing House: 33 4th Ave, cnr Main Ave, Cubao, Quezon City, POB 3667, Metro Manila; tel. (2) 7216218; fax (2) 7220468; e-mail heritage@skydsl.com.ph; art, anthropology, history, political science; Pres. MARIO R. ALCANTARA; Man. Dir GEORGE B. ALCANTARA.

The Lawyers' Co-operative Publishing Co Inc: 1071 Del Pan St, Makati City, 1206 Metro Manila; tel. (2) 5634073; fax (2) 5642021; e-mail lawbooks@info.com.ph; f. 1908; law, educational; Pres. ELSA K. ELMA.

Mutual Books Inc: Rm 208, Jovan Condominium, 600 Shaw Blvd, Mandaluyong City, Metro Manila; tel. (2) 5329656; fax (2) 5342665; internet mutualbooks.com; f. 1959; textbooks on accounting, management and economics, computers and mathematics; Pres. ALFREDO S. NICDAO, Jr.

Reyes Publishing Inc: Mariwasa Bldg, 4th Floor, 717 Aurora Blvd, Quezon City, 1112 Metro Manila; tel. (2) 7221827; fax (2) 7218782; e-mail reyespub@skyinet.net; f. 1964; art, history and culture; Pres. LOUIE REYES.

SIBS Publishing House Inc: Phoenix Bldg, 927 Quezon Ave, Quezon City, Metro Manila; tel. (2) 3764041; fax (2) 3764034; e-mail sibsbook@sibs.com.ph; internet www.sibs.com.ph; f. 1996; science, language, religion, literature and history textbooks; Pres. CARMEN MIMETTE M. SIBAL.

Sinag-Tala Publishers Inc: GMA Lou-Bel Plaza, 6th Floor, Chino Roces Ave, cnr Bagtikan St, San Antonio Village, Makati City, 1203 Metro Manila; tel. (2) 8971162; fax (2) 8969626; e-mail stpi@info.com.ph; internet www.sinagtala.com; f. 1972; educational textbooks; business, professional and religious books; Man. Dir LUIS A. USON.

University of the Philippines Press: Epifanio de los Santos St, U. P. Campus, Diliman, Quezon City, 1101 Metro Manila; tel. (2) 9252930; fax (2) 9282558; e-mail mricana@eee.upd.edu.ph; f. 1965; literature, history, political science, sociology, cultural studies, economics, anthropology, mathematics; Dir MARIA LUISA T. CAMAGAY.

Vibal Publishing House, Inc: 1253 G. Araneta Ave, cnr Maria Clara St, Talayan, Quezon City, Metro Manila; tel. (2) 7122722; fax (2) 7118852; e-mail inquire@vibalpublishing.com; internet www.vibalpublishing.com; f. 1953; linguistics, social sciences, mathematics, religion; Pres. and Gen. Man. ESTHER A. VIBAL.

PUBLISHERS' ASSOCIATIONS

Philippine Educational Publishers' Assen: 84 P. Florentino St, Santa Mesa Heights, Quezon City, 1113 Metro Manila; tel. (2) 7402698; fax (2) 7115702; e-mail info@pepa.org.ph; internet www.pepa.org.ph; Pres. DOMINADOR D. BUHAIN.

Publishers' Association of the Philippines Inc: Unit 206 Cityland 8, 98 Sen. Gil Puyat Ave, Makati City 1200, Metro Manila; tel. (2) 8191215; fax (2) 8931690; e-mail papi@gawab.com; internet papiphilippines.org; f. 1974; more than 1,000 mems; Pres. JUAN P. DAYANG.

Broadcasting and Communications

TELECOMMUNICATIONS

National Telecommunications Commission (NTC): NTC Bldg, BIR Rd, East Triangle, Diliman, Quezon City, 1104 Metro Manila; tel. (2) 9244042; fax (2) 9244048; e-mail bsd@ntc.gov.ph; internet www.ntc.gov.ph; f. 1979; supervises and controls all private and public telecommunications services; Commr GAMALIEL A. CORDOBA.

BayanTel: Diliman Corporate Center, Bayan Bldg, Maginhawa St, cnr Malingap St, Teacher's Village East, Quezon City, 1101 Metro Manila; tel. (2) 4121212; fax (2) 4492174; e-mail bayanserve@bayantel.com.ph; internet www.bayantel.com.ph; 359,000 fixed lines (1999); Chair. OSCAR M. LOPEZ; Pres. and CEO EUGENIO L. LOPEZ III.

Bell Telecommunications Philippines (BellTel): Pacific Star Bldg, 3rd Floor, Sen. Gil J. Puyat Ave, cnr Makati Ave, Makati City, Metro Manila; tel. (2) 68002355; fax (2) 8915618; e-mail info@belltel.ph; internet www.belltel.ph; f. 1997; Pres. EDGARDO REYES.

Capitol Wireless Inc: Dolmar Gold Tower, 6th Floor, 107 Carlos Palanca, Jr, St, Legaspi Village, Makati City, Metro Manila; tel. (2) 8159961; fax (2) 8941141; Pres. EPITACIO R. MARQUEZ.

Digital Telecommunications Philippines Inc (DIGITEL): 110 Eulogio Rodriguez Jr Ave, Bagumbayan, Quezon City, 1110 Metro Manila; tel. and fax (2) 3978888; e-mail customerservice@digitel.ph; internet digitel.webready.ph; provision of fixed line telecommunications services; over 400,000 fixed lines; Pres. and CEO JAMES L. GO.

Digital Mobile Philippines Inc: 110 Eulogio Rodriguez Jr Ave, Bagumbayan, Quezon City, 1110 Metro Manila; tel. (2) 3958000; e-mail customerservice@digitel.ph; internet www.suncellular.com.ph; f. 2003; wireless services under the brand name Sun Cellular; CEO CHARLES LIM.

Domestic Satellite Philippines Inc (DOMSAT): Solid House Bldg, 4th Floor, 2285 Pasong Tamo Ext., Makati City, 1231 Metro Manila; tel. (2) 8105917; fax (2) 8671677; Pres. SIEGFRED MISON.

Globe Telecom (GMCR) Inc: Globe Telecom Plaza 1, 5th Floor, Pioneer St, cnr Madison St, 1552 Mandaluyong City, Metro Manila; tel. (2) 7301000; fax (2) 7390072; e-mail custhelp@globetel.com.ph; internet www.globe.com.ph; fixed line and mobile telecommunica-

THE PHILIPPINES

tion services; 23.2m. mobile telephone subscribers (2009); Chair. Jaime Augusto Zobel de Ayala; Pres. and CEO Ernest Cu.

Philippine Communications Satellite Corpn (PhilcomSat): 12th Floor, Telecoms Plaza, 316 Sen. Gil J. Puyat Ave, Makati City, Metro Manila; tel. (2) 8158406; fax (2) 8159287; internet philcomsat.com.ph; Pres. Manuel H. Nieto.

Philippine Global Communications, Inc (PhilCom): 8755 Paseo de Roxas, Makati City, 1259 Metro Manila; tel. (2) 8451101; fax (2) 8189720; e-mail helpdesk@philcom.com; internet www.philcom.com; Chair. Willy N. Ocier; CEO Salvador M. Castillo.

Philippine Long Distance Telephone Co (PLDT): Ramon Cojuangco Bldg, Makati Ave, POB 2148, Makati City, Metro Manila; tel. (2) 8168024; fax (2) 8446654; e-mail customercare@pldt.com; internet www.pldt.com.ph; f. 1928; monopoly on overseas telephone service until 1989; transferred to private sector in 2007; major fixed line and wireless services provider; 44.7m. subscribers (2010); Chair. Manuel V. Pangilinan; Pres. and CEO Napoleon L. Nazareno.

Smart Communications, Inc (SCI): SMART Tower, 6799 Ayala Ave, Makati City, 1226 Metro Manila; tel. (2) 8881111; fax (2) 8488830; e-mail customercare@smart.com.ph; internet www.smart.com.ph; 43.2m. subscribers (2010); Pres. and CEO Napoleon L. Nazareno.

Pilipino Telephone Corpn (Piltel): SMART Tower, 25th Floor, 6799 Ayala Ave, Makati City, 1200 Metro Manila; tel. (2) 8913888; fax (2) 8171121; subsidiary of Smart Communications, Inc; major cellular telephone provider; 400,000 subscribers (1999); Chair. Manuel V. Pangilinan; Pres. and CEO Napoleon L. Nazareno.

BROADCASTING

Radio

Bureau of Broadcast Services (BBS) (Philippine Broadcasting Service): Media Centre Bldg, 4th Floor, Visayas Ave, Diliman, Quezon City, 1100 Metro Manila; tel. (2) 9203968; fax (2) 9203961; e-mail pbs.inquiry@gmail.com; internet www.pbs.gov.ph; f. 1952; est. as Philippine Broadcasting Service; govt-operated; 32 radio stations; Dir John S. Manalili.

Cebu Broadcasting Co: Star City Complex, Vicente Sotto St, Roxal Blvd, Pasay City; tel. (2) 8326134; fax (2) 8326133; e-mail ed_montilla@hotmail.com; Chair. Hadrian Arroyo.

Far East Broadcasting Co Inc: 62 Karuhatan Rd, Karuhatan, Valenzuela City, 1441 Metro Manila; tel. (2) 2921152; fax (2) 2925790; e-mail info@febc.org.ph; internet www.febc.org.ph; f. 1948; 18 stations; operates a classical music station, eight domestic stations and an overseas service in 64 languages throughout Asia; Pres. Dan Andrew Cura.

Filipinas Broadcasting Network: Legaspi Towers 200, Room 306, Paseo de Roxas, Makati City, Metro Manila; tel. (2) 8176133; fax (2) 8177135; six stations; Gen. Man. Diana C. Gozum.

GMA Network Inc: GMA Network Center, EDSA cnr Timog Ave, Diliman, Quezon City, 1103 Metro Manila; tel. and fax (2) 9287021; e-mail investor_relations@gmanetwork.com; internet www.gmanetwork.com; f. 1950; fmrly Republic Broadcasting System Inc; 21 stations; Chair., Pres. and CEO Felipe L. Gozon; Exec. Vice-Pres. Gilberto R. Duavit, Jr.

Manila Broadcasting Co: Star City Complex, Vicente Sotto St, Roxas Blvd, Pasay City; tel. (2) 8326142; fax (2) 8326143; internet www.mbcsales.com.ph; f. 1946; affiliate of Philippine Broadcasting Service; 16 stations; Chair. Fred J. Elizalde; Pres. Ruperto Nicdao, Jr.

Nation Broadcasting Corpn: 8th–9th Floors, Jacinta Bldg 2, Edsa Guadalupe, Makati City; tel. (2) 8821622; fax (2) 8821400; e-mail radio@philexport.com; f. 1963; 13 stations; Pres. Manuel Pangilinan.

Newsounds Broadcasting Network Inc: 2406 Nobel, cnr Edison St, Makati City, 3117 Metro Manila; tel. (2) 8430116; fax (2) 8430122; 10 stations; Gen. Man. E. Billones; Office Man. Herman Basbano.

Pacific Broadcasting System: c/o Manila Broadcasting Co, Star City Complex, vicente Sotto St, Roxas Blvd, Metro Manila; tel. (2) 8326142; fax (2) 8326143; three stations; Pres. Ruperto Nicdao, Jr; Vice-Pres. Rudolph Jularbal.

PBN Broadcasting Network Inc: Ersan Bldg, 3rd Floor, 32 Quezon Ave, Quezon City, Metro Manila; tel. (2) 7120190; fax (2) 7438162; e-mail pbnbroadcasting@yahoo.com; internet www.pbnbicol.com; f. 1958; five radio stations, two TV stations; Chair. Jorge D. Bayona.

Philippine Federation of Catholic Broadcasters: 201 Sunrise Condominium, 226 Ortigas Ave, North Greenhills, San Juan, Metro Manila 1503; tel. (2) 7249850; fax (2) 7249962; e-mail cmnftd@cmn-ftd.org; internet www.catholicmedianetwork.org; f. 1965; operates under the brand name Catholic Media Network (CMN); all 51 radio stations are united by the Dream Satellite; Chair. Bishop Bernardino Cortez; Pres. Fr Francis Lucas.

Radio Philippines Network, Inc: Broadcast City, Capitol Hills, Diliman, Quezon City, Metro Manila; tel. (2) 9318618; fax (2) 4357403; e-mail dody_lacuna@yahoo.com; internet www.rpn9.com; f. 1969; 14 radio stations; Pres. Antonio Albano; Gen. Man. Felipe G. Medina.

Radio Veritas Asia: Buick St, Fairview Park, POB 2642, Quezon City, Metro Manila; tel. (2) 9390011; fax (2) 9381940; e-mail rveritas-asia@rveritas-asia.org; internet www.rveritas-asia.org; f. 1969; Catholic short-wave station; broadcasts in 14 languages; owned by Philippine Radio Educational and Information Center, Inc; Pres. and Chair. Cardinal Gaudencio B. Rosales; Gen. Man. Fr Roberto M. Ebisa (SVD).

UM Broadcasting Network: cnr P. Reyes and Palma Gil Sts, Davao City; tel. (82) 2279535; fax (82) 2217824; e-mail umbndvo@mozcom.com; internet www.umbn.com.ph; 14 stations; Exec. Vice-Pres. Willy Torres.

Vanguard Radio Network: Cityland Pasong Tamo Tower, Rm 520, Chino Roces Ave, Makati City; tel. (2) 7161233; fax (2) 7160899; Pres. Manuel Galvez.

Television

ABC Development Corpn: APMC Bldg, 136 Amorsolo St, cnr Gamboa St, Legaspi Village, Makati City, Metro Manila; tel. (2) 8923801; fax (2) 8128840; CEO Edward U. Tan.

ABS-CBN Broadcasting Corpn: ABS-CBN Broadcasting Center, Sgt E. Esguerra Ave, cnr Mother Ignacia Ave, Quezon City, 1103 Metro Manila; tel. (2) 9244101; fax (2) 4163567; e-mail feedback_web@abs-cbn.com; internet www.abs-cbn.com; Chair. Eugenio Lopez III; Pres. Rosario Santos-Concio.

AMCARA Broadcasting Network: ABS-CBN Broadcasting Centre, Mother Ignacia St, cnr Sgt Esguerra Ave, Quezon City, 1103 Metro Manila; tel. (2) 4152272; fax (2) 4121259; e-mail studio23@abs.pinoycentral.com; internet www.studio23.tv; Man. Dir Leonardo P. Katigbak.

Channel V Philippines: 89 Timog Ave, South Triangle, Quezon City; tel. (2) 9292151; e-mail feedback@channelv.ph; internet www.channelv.ph; Pres. Joel Jimenez; Gen. Man. Mon Alcaraz.

GMA Network, Inc: (see radio) transmits nation-wide through 46 VHF and 2 affiliate stations and in Asia, Australia and Hawaii through Measat-2 satellite.

Intercontinental Broadcasting Corpn: Broadcast City Complex, Capitol Hills, Diliman, Quezon City, Metro Manila; tel. (2) 9318781; fax (2) 9524002; e-mail ibcpres@ibc.com.ph; 5 stations; Pres. Roberto del Rosario.

National Broadcasting Network (NBN): Broadcast Complex, Visayas Ave, Quezon City, Metro Manila; tel. (2) 9204389; fax (2) 9204342; internet ptni.tv/nbn; f. 1992; public television network; fmrly People's Television Network (PTV4); CEO Jose S. Isabelo.

Radio Mindanao Network: State Condominium, 4th Floor, 1 Salcedo St, Legaspi Village, Makati City, Metro Manila; tel. (2) 8191073; fax (2) 8163680; e-mail sales@rmn.com.ph; f. 1952; 2 stations; Chair. Henry Canoy; Pres. Eric S. Canoy.

Radio Philippines Network, Inc: (see radio); operates 7 TV stations.

Rajah Broadcasting Network, Inc (RJ TV 29): Save a Lot Bldg, 3rd Floor, 2284 Pasong Tamo Ext., Makati City, Metro Manila; tel. (2) 8932360; fax (2) 8933404; e-mail rjofc@compass.com; f. 1993; Gen. Man. Bea J. Colamonici.

Southern Broadcasting Network, Inc: Suite 2902, Jollibee Plaza, 29th Floor, Ortigas Jr Rd, Ortigas Center, Pasig City, Metro Manila; tel. (2) 6363286; fax (2) 6363288; e-mail gemceo@sbnphilippines.net; four stations; Pres. and CEO Teofilo A. Henson; Vice-Pres. Germeline Dinopol.

United Broadcasting Network: FEMS Tower 1, 11th Floor, 1289 Zobel Roxas, cnr South Superhighway, Malate; tel. (2) 5216138; fax (2) 5221226; Gen. Man. Joseph Hodreal.

Broadcasting Association

Kapisanan ng mga Brodkaster sa Pilipinas (KBP) (Association of Broadcasters in the Philippines): LTA Bldg, 6th Floor, 118 Perea St, Legaspi Village, Makati City, 1226 Metro Manila; tel. (2) 8151990; fax (2) 8151993; e-mail info@kbp.org.ph; internet www.kbp.org.ph; f. 1973; est. in order to regulate the broadcasting industry, elevate standards, disseminate govt information and strengthen relations with advertising industry; Chair. Basbaño Herman; Pres. Ruperto Nicdao, Jr.

THE PHILIPPINES

Finance

(cap. = capital; res = reserves; dep. = deposits; m. = million; brs = branches; amounts in pesos, unless otherwise stated)

BANKING

In 1994 legislation providing for the establishment in the Philippines of additional foreign bank branches was enacted. By the end of 2008 the number of foreign banks had increased to 21; at that time some 38 principal commercial banks were operating in the Philippines.

Central Bank

Bangko Sentral ng Pilipinas (Central Bank of the Philippines): A. Mabini St, cnr Pablo Ocampo St, Malate, 1004 Metro Manila; tel. (2) 5247011; fax (2) 5236210; e-mail bspmail@bsp.gov.ph; internet www.bsp.gov.ph; f. 1993; cap. 10,000m., surplus and res 164,419.5m., dep. 661,015.1m. (Dec. 2007); Gov. AMANDO M. TETANGCO, Jr; 18 brs.

Principal Commercial Banks

Allied Banking Corpn: 6754 Allied Bank Centre, Ayala Ave, cnr Legaspi St, Makati City, 1200 Metro Manila; tel. (2) 8163311; fax (2) 8160921; e-mail info@alliedbank.com.ph; internet www.alliedbank.com.ph; f. 1977; cap. 3,302.4m., res 1,654.1m., dep. 152,543.6m. (Dec. 2009); Chair. DOMINGO T. CHUA; Pres. ANTHONY Q. CHUA; 285 brs.

Banco de Oro Unibank Inc: 7899 Makati Ave, Makati City, 0726 Metro Manila; tel. (2) 8407000; e-mail irandcorplan@bdo.com.ph; internet www.bdo.com.ph; f. 1996; fmrly known as Banco de Oro Universal Bank; name changed as above following merger with Equitable PCI Bank in 2007; acquired 1st e-Bank June 2003; cap. 23,096.6m., res 36,743.7m. (Dec. 2007), dep. 694,678m. (Dec. 2009); Chair. TERESITA T. SY; Pres. NESTOR V. TAN; 185 brs.

Bank of Commerce: Phil First Bldg, 6764 Ayala Ave, Makati City, 1226 Metro Manila; tel. (2) 8120000; fax (2) 8300651; e-mail mscallangan@bankcom.com.ph; internet www.bankcom.com.ph; f. 1983; fmrly Boston Bank of the Philippines; merged with Traders Royal Bank 2001; cap. 5,211.4m., res 2,264m., dep. 91,029m. (Dec. 2009); Chair. RAUL B. DE MESA; Pres. and CEO VIRGILIO MARTIN GOQUINGCO; 117 brs.

Bank of the Philippine Islands: BPI Bldg, 6768 Ayala Ave, Makati City, 1226 Metro Manila; tel. (2) 8185541; fax (2) 8910170; e-mail expressonline@bpi.com.ph; internet www.bpiexpressonline.com; f. 1851; merged with Far East Bank and Trust Co in April 2000; merged with DBS Bank Philippines, Inc, 2001; cap. 32,467m., res 1,171m., dep. 618,065m. (Dec. 2009); Pres. and Dir AURELIO R. MONTINOLA, III; Chair. JAIME ZOBEL DE AYALA, II; 896 local brs; 1 overseas br.

China Banking Corpn: CBC Bldg, 8745 Paseo de Roxas, cnr Villar St, Makati City, 1226 Metro Manila; tel. (2) 8855555; fax (2) 8920220; e-mail online@chinabank.com.ph; internet www.chinabank.ph; f. 1920; cap. 9,750.8m., res 20,350.1m., dep. 197,585m. (Dec. 2009); Chair. GILBERT U. DEE; Pres. and CEO PETER S. DEE; 206 brs.

ChinaBank Savings Inc (CBS): 6772 Ayala Ave, Makati City, 1226 Metro Manlia; tel. (2) 7516000; fax (2) 8645016; internet www.chinabank.ph; f. 1999; est. as Manila Banking Corpn; present name adopted following acquisition by China Banking Corpn in 2007; cap. 531m., res 2,288m., dep. 6,704m. (Dec. 2006); Pres. SAMUEL L. CHIONG; Chair. RICARDO R. CHUA; 6 brs.

Development Bank of the Philippines: DBP Bldg, Makati Ave, cnr Sen. Gil J. Puyat Ave, Makati City, 1200 Metro Manila; tel. (2) 8189511; fax (2) 8934311; e-mail info@dbp.ph; internet www.dbp.ph; f. 1947; est. as the Rehabilitation Finance Corpn; govt-owned; provides medium- and long-term loans for strategic devt projects; cap. 39,984m., dep. 124,015m. (Dec. 2009); Chair. JOSÉ A. NUÑEZ, Jr; Pres. and CEO FRANCISCO F. DEL ROSARIO, Jr; 81 brs.

East West Banking Corpn: PBCOM Tower, 20th Floor, 6795 Ayala Ave, cnr Herrera St, Salcedo Village, Makati City, 1226 Metro Manila; tel. (2) 8150233; fax (2) 3250412; e-mail service@eastwestbanker.com; internet www.eastwestbanker.com; f. 1994; Chair. JONATHAN T. GOTIANUN; Pres. and CEO ANTONIO C. MONCUPA, Jr; 89 brs.

Export and Industry Bank Inc (Exportbank): Exportbank Plaza, Chino Roces Ave, cnr Sen. Gil J. Puyat Ave, Makati City, 1200 Metro Manila; tel. (2) 8780190; fax (2) 8879969; e-mail expertinfo@exportbank.com.ph; internet www.exportbank.com.ph; merged with Urban Bank, Inc, 2002; cap. 4,787m., dep. 12,479m. (June 2007); Chair. JAIME GONZALEZ; Pres. JUAN VICTOR S. TANJUATCO; 50 brs.

Land Bank of the Philippines: POB 2284, Manila Central Post Office, Metro Manila; tel. (2) 5220000; fax (2) 5288580; e-mail landbank@mail.landbank.com; internet www.landbank.com; f. 1963; specialized govt bank with universal banking licence; cap. 11,971m., res 17,787.6m., dep. 428,715.1m. (Dec. 2009); Chair. CESAR V. PURISIMA; Pres. and CEO GILDA E. PICO; 324 brs.

Directory

Maybank Philippines Inc: Legaspi Towers 300, Pablo Ocampo St, cnr Roxas Blvd, Malate, 1004 Metro Manila; tel. (2) 5237777; fax (2) 5218514; e-mail mayphil@maybank.com.ph; internet www.maybank2u.com.my/philippines/index.shtml; f. 1961; cap. 4,542.2m., res 122.5m., dep. 20,174.7m. (Dec. 2009); Chair. Dato' MOHD SALEH Haji HARUN; Pres. and CEO ONG SEET JOON; 45 brs.

Metropolitan Bank and Trust Co (Metrobank): Metrobank Plaza, Sen. Gil J. Puyat Ave, Makati City, 1200 Metro Manila; tel. (2) 8988000; fax (2) 8176248; e-mail customercare@metrobank.com.ph; internet www.metrobank.com.ph; f. 1962; acquired Global Business Bank (Globalbank) 2002; cap. 36,145.4m., res 11,670m., dep. & bonds 649,556m. (Dec. 2008); Chair. ANTONIO S. ABACAN; Pres. ARTHUR TY, Jr; 700 local brs, 35 overseas brs.

Philippine Bank of Communications: PBCOM Tower, 6795 Ayala Ave, cnr V. A. Rufino St, Makati City, 1226 Metro Manila; tel. (2) 8307000; fax (2) 8182598; e-mail info@pbcom.com.ph; internet www.pbcom.com.ph; f. 1939; merged with AsianBank Corpn in 1999; cap. 8,259.9m., res 519.8m., dep. 35,978m. (Dec. 2009); Chair. ENRIQUE LUY; Pres. and CEO HENRY Y. UY; 66 brs.

Philippine National Bank (PNB): PNB Financial Center, President Diosdado Macapagal Blvd, Pasay City, 1300 Metro Manila; tel. (2) 5738888; fax (2) 5734580; e-mail customercare@pnb.com.ph; internet www.pnb.com.ph; f. 1916; partially transferred to the private sector in 1996 and 2000; 10.93% govt-owned; cap. 26,490m., res 3,939.5m., dep. 221,041m. (Dec. 2009); Chair. FLORENCIA G. TARRIELA; Pres. and CEO EUGENE ACEVEDO; 324 local brs, 5 overseas brs.

Philippine Veterans Bank: PVB Bldg, 101 V. A. Rufino St, cnr de la Rosa St, Legaspi Village, Makati City, Metro Manila; tel. (2) 9021600; fax (2) 9021700; e-mail corpcomm@veteransbank.com.ph; internet www.veteransbank.com.ph; cap. 4,200m., assets 29,600m. (Dec. 2006); Chair. EMMANUEL V. DE OCAMPO; Pres. and CEO RICARDO A. BALBIDO, Jr; 45 brs.

Philtrust Bank (Philippine Trust Co): Philtrust Bank Bldg, United Nations Ave, cnr San Marcelino St, Ermita, 1045 Metro Manila; tel. (2) 5249061; fax (2) 5217309; e-mail ptc@philtrustbank.com; internet www.philtrustbank.com; f. 1916; cap. 6,617m., res 263m., dep. 73,960m. (Dec. 2009); Pres. ANTONIO H. OZAETA; Chair. JAIME C. LAYA; 46 brs.

Rizal Commercial Banking Corpn: Yuchengco Tower, RCBC Plaza, 6819 Alaya Ave, Makati City, 0727 Metro Manila; tel. (2) 8949000; fax (2) 8949958; e-mail customercontact@rcbc.com; internet www.rcbc.com; f. 1960; cap. 10,112.5m., res 11,011.3m., dep. 236,895m. (Dec. 2009); Chair. HELEN Y. DEE; Pres. and CEO LORENZO V. TAN, Jr; 287 brs.

Security Bank Corpn: 6776 Ayala Ave, Makati City, 0719 Metro Manila; tel. (2) 8676788; fax (2) 8911079; e-mail ccad@securitybank.com.ph; internet www.securitybank.com; f. 1951; fmrly Security Bank and Trust Co; cap. 4,186.3m., res 3,136.5m., dep. 119,610.2m. (Dec. 2009); Pres. and CEO ALBERTO S. VILLAROSA; Chair. FREDERICK Y. DY; 125 brs.

Union Bank of the Philippines: Union Bank Plaza, Meralco Ave, cnr Onyx and Sapphire Sts, Ortigas Center, Pasig City, 1605 Metro Manila; tel. (2) 6676388; fax (2) 6325259; e-mail online@unionbankph.com; internet www.unionbankph.com; f. 1982; cap. 6,414.2m., res 24,866.1m., dep. 200,600.8m. (Dec. 2009); Chair. and CEO JUSTO A. ORTIZ; Pres. VICTOR B. VALDEPEÑAS; 111 brs.

United Coconut Planters Bank (UCPB): UCPB Bldg, 7907 Makati Ave, Makati City, 0728 Metro Manila; tel. (2) 8119000; fax (2) 8119706; e-mail crc@ucpb.com; internet www.ucpb.com; f. 1963; cap. 1,484.8m., res 9,661m., dep. 137,897.8m. (Dec. 2009); Chair. CARLOS C. EJERCITO; Pres. and CEO RAMON Y. SY; 178 brs.

United Overseas Bank Philippines: 17th Floor, Pacific Star Bldg, Sen. Gil J. Puyat Ave, cnr Makati Ave, Makati City, Metro Manila; tel. (2) 67008686; fax (2) 8115917; e-mail info@uob.com.ph; internet www.uob.com.ph; f. 1999; cap. 920m., res −725m., dep. 2,208.2m. (Dec. 2009); Pres. and CEO EMMANUEL MANGOSING; 67 brs.

Rural Banks

Small private banks have been established with the assistance of the Government in order to promote the rural economy. Their principal objectives are to provide credit facilities on reasonable terms and, in co-operation with other agencies of the Government, to give advice on management.

Thrift Banks

Thrift banks mobilize small savings and provide loans to lower-income groups. The thrift banking system comprises savings and mortgage banks, stock savings and loan associations, and private development banks.

THE PHILIPPINES

Development Bank

Pampanga Development Bank: MacArthur Highway, Dolores San Fernando, Pampanga, Luzon; tel. (45) 9612786; fax (45) 9633931; e-mail pdb@ag.triasia.net; originally Agribusiness Development Bank; name changed as above 1995; cap. 75.0m., res 4.3m., dep. 125.8m. (Dec. 2006); Pres. Jose Eriberto H. Suarez.

Islamic Bank

Al-Amanah Islamic Investment Bank of the Philippines: 4th Floor, DBP Bldg, Makati Ave, Makati City, Metro Manila; tel. (2) 8934350; fax (2) 8195249; e-mail info@al-amanahbank.com; internet www.al-amanahbank.com.ph; f. 1989; Chair. and CEO Enrique D. Bautista.

Banking Associations

Bankers Association of the Philippines: Sagittarius Cond. Bldg, 11th Floor, H. V. de la Costa St, Salcedo Village, Makati City, Metro Manila; tel. (2) 8103858; fax (2) 8103860; e-mail secretariat@bap.org.ph; Pres. Aurelio R. Montinola, III; Exec. Dir Cesar O. Virtusio.

Bankers Institute of the Philippines, Inc (BAIPhil): TRB Tower, 6th Floor, Unit 66, Paseo de Roxas, Makati City, Metro Manila; tel. (2) 8534457; fax (2) 8530889; e-mail secretariat@baiphil.org; internet www.baiphil.org; f. 1941; est. as Nat. Asscn of Auditors and Comptrollers; name changed to Bank Administration Institute in 1968, and as above in 2001; Pres. Emmanuel E. Barcena.

Chamber of Thrift Banks: Cityland 10 Condominium Tower 1, Unit 614, H. V. de la Costa St, Salcedo Village, Makati City, Metro Manila; tel. (2) 8126974; fax (2) 8127203; internet www.ctb.com.ph; Pres. Patrick D. Cheng.

Offshore Bankers' Association of the Philippines, Inc: MCPO 3088, Makati City, 1229 Metro Manila; tel. (2) 8103554; Chair. Teresita Malabanan.

Rural Bankers' Association of the Philippines: RBAP Bldg, A. Soriano Jr Ave, cnr Arzobispo St, Intramuros, Metro Manila; tel. (2) 5272968; fax (2) 5272980; e-mail info@rbap.org; internet www.rbap.org; Pres. Corazon L. Miller.

STOCK EXCHANGES

Securities and Exchange Commission: SEC Bldg, Epifanio de los Santos Ave, Greenhills, Mandaluyong City, Metro Manila; tel. (2) 5840923; fax (2) 5845293; e-mail mis@sec.gov.ph; internet www.sec.gov.ph; f. 1936; Chair. Teresita J. Herbosa.

Philippine Stock Exchange: Philippine Stock Exchange Center, Exchange Rd, Ortigas Center, Pasig City, 1605 Metro Manila; tel. (2) 6887600; fax (2) 6345113; e-mail pirs@pse.com.ph; internet www.pse.com.ph; f. 1994 following the merger of the Manila and Makati Stock Exchanges; 237 listed cos (Dec. 2005); Chair. Cornelio Peralta; Pres. Hans B. Sicat.

INSURANCE

At the end of 2000 a total of 156 insurance companies were authorized by the Insurance Commission to transact in the Philippines. Foreign companies were also permitted to operate in the country.

Principal Domestic Companies

Ayala Life Assurance Inc: Ayala Life-FGU Center, 14th–15th Floors, 6811 Ayala Ave, Makati City, Metro Manila; tel. (2) 8885433; fax (2) 8180171; e-mail customer.service@ayalalife.com.ph; internet www.ayalalife.com.ph; Chair. Xavier Loinaz.

BPI/MS Insurance Corpn: Ayala Life-FGU Center, 11th Floor, 6811 Ayala Ave, Makati City, 1226 Metro Manila; tel. (2) 8409000; fax (2) 8409099; e-mail insure@bpims.com; internet www.bpims.com; f. 2002; est. by merger of FGU Insurance Corpn and FEB Mitsui Marine Insurance Corpn; jt venture of Bank of the Philippine Islands and Sumitomo Insurance Co (Japan); cap. 731m. (2006), sales 2,140m.; Chair. Aurelio R. Montinola, III; Pres. Takaaki Ueda.

Central Surety & Insurance Co: 2nd Floor, Universal-Re Bldg, 106 Paseo de Roxas, Legaspi Village, Makati City, 1200 Metro Manila; tel. (2) 8174931; fax (2) 8170006; f. 1945; bonds, fire, marine, casualty, motor car; Pres. Fermin T. Castañeda.

Commonwealth Insurance Co: BDO Plaza, 10th Floor, 8737 Paseo de Roxas, Makati City, Metro Manila; tel. (2) 8187626; fax (2) 8138575; e-mail info@cic.com.ph; internet www.cic.com.ph; f. 1935; Pres. Mario Noche.

Co-operative Insurance System of the Philippines: CISP Bldg, 80 Malakas St, Diliman, Quezon City, Metro Manila; tel. (2) 4359100; fax (2) 4333211; e-mail cisplife@cisplife.com; internet www.cisplife.com; Chair. Leonida V. Chavez; Pres. Ambrosio M. Rodriguez.

Empire Insurance Co: Prudential Life Bldg, 2nd Floor, 843 Arnaiz Ave, Legaspi Village, Makati City, 1229 Metro Manila; tel. (2) 8159561; fax (2) 8152599; e-mail empire_ins_co@yahoo.com; f. 1949; fire, bonds, marine, accident, motor car, extraneous perils; Pres. and CEO Jose Ma G. Santos.

Equitable Insurance Corpn: Equitable Bank Bldg, 4th Floor, 262 Juan Luna St, Binondo, POB 1103, Metro Manila; tel. (2) 2430291; fax (2) 2415768; e-mail info@equitableinsurance.com.ph; internet www.equitableinsurance.com.ph; f. 1950; fire, marine, casualty, motor car, bonds; Pres. Nora T. Go; Exec. Vice-Pres. Antonio C. Ocampo.

Great Domestic Insurance Co of the Philippines: 5th Floor, Champ Bldg, Anda Circle, Bonifacio Drive, Port Area, Manila; tel. (2) 5273044; fax (2) 5273052; e-mail grdomic@intertasia.com.ph; internet www.greatdomesticph.com; f. 1946; cap. 10m.; Pres. and Chair. Mar S. Lopez.

Insular Life Assurance Co Ltd: Insular Life Corporate Center, Insular Life Drive, Filinvest Corporate City, Alabang, 1781 Muntinlupa City; tel. (2) 5821818; fax (2) 7711717; e-mail corplan@insular.com.ph; internet www.insularlife.com.ph; f. 1910; members' equity 14,000m. (Dec. 2009); Chair. and CEO Vicente R. Ayllón.

Makati Insurance Co Inc: BPI Buendia Center, 19th Floor, Sen. Gil J. Puyat Ave, Makati City, 1200 Metro Manila; tel. (2) 8459576; fax (2) 8915229; f. 1965; non-life; Pres. and Gen. Man. Jaime L. Darantinao; Chair. Octavio V. Espiritu.

Malayan Insurance Co Inc: Yuchengco Tower I, 4th Floor, 484 Quintin Paredes St, Binondo, 1099 Metro Manila; tel. (2) 2428888; fax (2) 2412188; e-mail malayan@malayan.com; internet www.malayan.com; f. 1949; cap. 100m.; insurance and bonds; Pres. Yvonne S. Yuchengco; Chair. Adelita Vergel de Dios.

Manila Surety & Fidelity Co Inc: 66 P. Florentino St, Quezon City, Metro Manila; tel. (2) 7122251; fax (2) 7124129; f. 1945; cap. p.u. 50m., members' equity 85m. (Dec. 2003); Pres. Maria Lourdes V. Peña; Vice-Pres. Maria Editha Peña-Lim; 4 brs.

Metropolitan Insurance Co: Ateneum Bldg, 3rd Floor, 160 L. P. Leviste St, Salcedo Village, Makati City, Metro Manila; tel. (2) 8672888; fax (2) 8162294; f. 1933; non-life; Pres. Jose M. Periquet, Jr; Exec. Vice-Pres. Roberto Abad.

National Life Insurance Co of the Philippines: National Life Insurance Bldg, 6762 Ayala Ave, Makati City, Metro Manila; tel. (2) 8100251; fax (2) 8178718; f. 1933; Pres. Benjamin L. de Leon; Sr Vice-Pres. Douglas McLaren.

National Reinsurance Corpn of the Philippines: AXA Life Center, 18th Floor, Sen. Gil J. Puyat Ave, cnr Tindalo St, Makati City, 1200 Metro Manila; tel. (2) 7595801; fax (2) 7595886; e-mail nrcp@nrcp.com.ph; internet www.nrcp.com.ph; f. 1978; Chair. Helen Y. Dee; Pres. and CEO Roberto B. Crisol.

Paramount Life and General Insurance Corpn: Sage House, 14th and 15th Floors, 110 V. A. Rufino St, Legaspi Village, Makati City, 1229 Metro Manila; tel. (2) 8127956; fax (2) 8131140; e-mail insure@paramount.com.ph; internet www.paramount.com.ph; f. 1950; fmrly Paramount General Insurance Corpn; name changed to Paramount Union Insurance Corpn in 2001; name changed as above in 2002; fire, marine, casualty, motor car; Chair. Patrick L. Go; Pres. George T. Tiu.

Philippine American Life and General Insurance Co (Philamlife): Philamlife Bldg, United Nations Ave, Metro Manila; POB 2167, 0990 Metro Manila; tel. (2) 5269404; fax (2) 5222863; e-mail philamwebmaster@aig.com; internet www.philamlife.com; Pres. Trevor Bull.

Philippine AXA Life Insurance Corpn: Philippine AXA Life Centre, Sen. Gil J. Puyat Ave, cnr Tindalo St, Makati City, Metro Manila; tel. (2) 5815292; fax (2) 8192631; e-mail customer.service@axa.com.ph; internet www.axa.com.ph; Pres. and CEO Severinus Hermans.

Philippine Charter Insurance Coprn: Skyland Plaza, Sen. Gil J. Puyat Ave, cnr Tindalo St, Makati City 1203; tel. (2) 5806800; fax (2) 8154797; e-mail customerservice@philcharter.com.ph; internet www.philcharter.com.ph; f. 1960; Chair. Bienvenido E. Laguesma; Pres. Melecio Mallillin.

Pioneer Insurance and Surety Corpn: Pioneer House Makati, 108 Paseo de Roxas, Legaspi Village, Makati City, 1229 Metro Manila; tel. (2) 8127777; fax (2) 8171461; e-mail info@pioneer.com.ph; internet www.pioneer.com.ph; f. 1954; cap. 5,441m. (2009); Pres. and CEO David C. Coyukiat.

Rizal Surety and Insurance Co: Prudential Life Bldg, 3rd Floor, 843 Arnaiz Ave, Legaspi Village, Makati City, Metro Manila; tel. (2) 8159561; fax (2) 8152599; e-mail rizalsic@mkt.weblinq.com; f. 1939; fire, bond, marine, motor car, accident, extraneous perils; Chair. and Pres. S. Corpus.

Standard Insurance Co Inc: Petron Mega Plaza Bldg, 28th Floor, Sen. Gil J. Puyat Ave, Makati City, Metro Manila; tel. (2) 9886388; f. 1958; Chair. Lourdes T. Echauz; Pres. Patricia Chilip.

Sterling Insurance Co: Zeta II Annex Bldg, 6th Floor, 191 Salcedo St, Legaspi Village, Makati City, Metro Manila; tel. (2) 8923794; fax

THE PHILIPPINES

Directory

(2) 8923794; f. 1960; fmrly Dominion Insurance Corpn; name changed as above Nov. 2001; fire, marine, motor car, accident, engineering, bonds; Pres. RAFAEL GALLAGA.

Tico Insurance Co Inc: Trafalgar Plaza, 7th Floor, 105 H. V. de la Costa St, Salcedo Village, Makati City, 1227 Metro Manila; tel. (2) 8140143; fax (2) 8140150; f. 1937; fmrly Tabacalera Insurance Co Inc; Chair. and Pres. CARLOS CATHOLICO.

UCPB General Insurance Co Inc: UCPB Bldg, 5th Floor, 7907 Makati Ave, Makati City; tel. (2) 8111788; fax (2) 2773333; e-mail ucpbgen@ucpbgen.com; internet www.ucpbgen.com; f. 1963; non-life; Pres. ISABELO P. AFRICA; Chair. JULITA S. MANAHAN.

Universal Reinsurance Corpn: Ayala Life Bldg, 9th Floor, 6786 Ayala Ave, Makati City, Metro Manila; tel. (2) 7514977; fax (2) 8173745; f. 1949; life and non-life; Chair. JAIME AUGUSTO ZOBEL DE AYALA II; Pres. HERMINIA S. JACINTO.

Regulatory Body

Insurance Commission: 1071 United Nations Ave, Metro Manila; tel. and fax (2) 5238461; e-mail pubassist_ic@yahoo.com.ph; internet www.insurance.gov.ph; regulates the private insurance industry by, among other things, issuing certificates of authority to insurance companies and intermediaries and monitoring their financial solvency; Commr EMMANUEL F. DOOC.

Trade and Industry

GOVERNMENT AGENCIES

Board of Investments: Industry and Investments Bldg, 385 Sen. Gil J. Puyat Ave, Makati City, 1200 Metro Manila; tel. (2) 8901332; fax (2) 8961166; e-mail nerbac@boi.gov.ph; internet www.boi.gov.ph; Chair. GREGORY L. DOMINGO.

Bureau of Domestic Trade (BDT): Trade and Industry Bldg, Ground Floor, 361 Sen. Gil J. Puyat Ave, Makati City, Metro Manila; tel. (2) 7513223; fax (2) 7513324; e-mail bdt@dti.gov.ph; Dir MEYNARD R. ORBETA.

Cagayan Economic Zone Authority: Westar Bldg, 7th Floor, 611 Shaw Blvd, Pasig City, 1603 Metro Manila; tel. (2) 6365774; fax (2) 6313997; e-mail info@ceza.gov.ph; internet ceza.gov.ph; Administrator and CEO JOSÉ MARI B. PONCE.

Clark Development Corpn: Bldg 2122, C. P. Garcia St, Clark Freeport Zone, Pampanga; tel. (45) 5999000; fax (45) 5992507; e-mail info@clark.com.ph; internet www.clark.com.ph; Pres. and CEO BENIGNO N. RICAFORT.

Industrial Technology Development Institute: DOST Compound, Gen. Santos Ave, Bicutan, Taguig, 1631 Metro Manila; tel. (2) 8372071; fax (2) 8373167; e-mail adiv@dost.gov.ph; internet itdibiz.com; Dir Dr NUNA E. ALMANZOR.

Maritime Industry Authority (MARINA): Parkview Plaza, 984 Taft Ave, cnr T. M. Kalaw St, Ermita, Manila; tel. (2) 5239078; fax (2) 5242746; e-mail oadm@marina.gov.ph; internet www.marina.gov.ph; f. 1974; development of inter-island shipping, overseas shipping, shipbuilding and repair, and maritime power; Administrator MARIA ELENA H. BAUTISTA, Jr.

National Tobacco Administration: NTA Bldg, Scout Reyes St, cnr Panay Ave, Quezon City, Metro Manila; tel. (2) 3743987; fax (2) 3742505; e-mail mis@nta.gov.ph; internet www.nta.da.gov.ph; f. 1987; Administrator CARLITOS S. ENCARNACION.

Philippine Coconut Authority (PCA): PCA Compound, Elliptical Rd, Diliman, Quezon City, 1100 Metro Manila; tel. (2) 9284501; fax (2) 9216173; e-mail pca_cpo@yahoo.com.ph; internet www.pca.da.gov.ph; f. 1973; Chair. ARTHUR C. YAP; Administrator OSCAR G. GARIN.

Philippine Council for Advanced Science and Technology Research and Development (PCASTRD): DOST Main Bldg, Gen. Santos Ave, Bicutan, Taguig, 1631 Metro Manila; tel. (2) 8377522; fax (2) 8373168; e-mail pcastrd@dost.gov.ph; internet www.pcastrd.dost.gov.ph; f. 1987; Exec. Dir Dr REYNALDO V. EBORA.

Philippine Economic Zone Authority: Roxas Blvd, cnr San Luis St, Pasay City, Metro Manila; tel. (2) 5513454; fax (2) 8916380; e-mail info@peza.gov.ph; internet www.peza.gov.ph; f. 1995; Dir-Gen. Dr LILIA B. DE LIMA.

Privatization and Management Office: Department of Finance, 104 Gamboa St, Legaspi Village, Makati City, 1229 Metro Manila; tel. (2) 8932383; fax (2) 8933453; e-mail pmo@eastern.com.ph; internet www.pmo.gov.ph; f. 2002; formed to handle the privatization of govt assets; succeeded Asset Privatization Trust; Chief Privatization Officer GUILLERMO N. HERNANDEZ.

Subic Bay Metropolitan Authority: Administration Bldg, 229 Waterfront Rd, Subic Bay Freeport Zone, 2222 Zambales; tel. (47) 2524000; fax (47) 2524216; e-mail webteam@sbma.com; internet www.sbma.com; Chair. FELICIANO G. SALONGA; CEO and Administrator ARMAND C. ARREZA.

DEVELOPMENT ORGANIZATIONS

Bases Conversion and Development Authority: Bonifacio Technology Center, 2nd Floor, 31st St, Cres. Park West, Bonifacio Global City, POB 42, Taguig, 1634 Metro Manila; tel. (2) 8166666; fax (2) 8160996; e-mail bcda@bcda.gov.ph; internet www.bcda.gov.ph; f. 1992; est. to facilitate the conversion, privatization and development of fmr military bases; Chair. ALOYSIUS R. SANTOS; Pres. and CEO NARCISO L. ABAYA.

Bureau of Land Development: DAR Bldg, Elliptical Rd, Diliman, Quezon City, Metro Manila; tel. (2) 9287031; fax (2) 9260971; Dir EUGENIO B. BERNARDO.

Capital Market Development Council (CMDC): Unit 1901, 19th Floor, 139 Corporate Center, Valero St, Salcedo Village, Makati City, Metro Manila; tel. (2) 8114052; fax (2) 8114185; e-mail cmdcphil@yahoo.com.ph; internet www.cmdc-phil.net; f. 1991; Chair. ABELARDO V. CORTEZ; Exec. Dir RESCINA BHAGWANI.

Cooperative Development Authority: CDA Bldg, Ground Floor, 827 Aurora Blvd, Immaculate Conception Village, Quezon City, Metro Manila; tel. (2) 3736894; fax (2) 3712077; e-mail cda.oed@gmail.com; internet www.cda.gov.ph; Chair. LECIRA V. JUAREZ; Exec. Dir NIEL A. SANTILLAN.

Micro, Small and Medium Enterprise Development Council: Oppen Bldg, 3rd Floor, 349 Sen. Gil J. Puyat Ave, Makati City, Metro Manila; tel. and fax (2) 8967916; e-mail bsmbd@mnl.sequel.net; f. 2008; est. to replace Small and Medium Enterprise Devt Council; initiates and implements programmes and projects addressing the specific needs of micro, small and medium enterprises in areas concerning entrepreneurship, institutional development, productivity improvement, organization, financing and marketing; chaired by Sec. of Trade and Industry; Vice-Chair. JOSE CONCEPCION, III.

Bureau of Micro, Small and Medium Enterprise Development (BMSMED): Trade and Industry Bldg, 5th Floor, 361 Sen. Gil J. Puyat Ave, Makati City, Metro Manila; tel. (02) 8971693; fax (02) 8967916; e-mail bmsmed@dti.gov.ph; f. 2008, to replace Bureau of Small and Medium Business Development; Secr. of the MSMED Council.

National Development Co (NDC): NDC Bldg, 8th Floor, 116 Tordesillas St, Salcedo Village, Makati City, 1227 Metro Manila; tel. (2) 8404838; fax (2) 8404862; e-mail info@ndc.gov.ph; internet www.ndc.gov.ph; f. 1919; govt-owned corpn engaged in the organization, financing and management of subsidiaries and corpns, incl. commercial, industrial, mining, agricultural and other enterprises assisting national economic devt; also jt industrial ventures with other ASEAN countries; Chair. PETER B. FAVILA; Gen. Man. LOURDES F. RUBUENO.

Philippine National Oil Co (PNOC): PNOC Bldg 6, Energy Center, Merritt Rd, Fort Bonifacio, Taguig City, Metro Manila; tel. (2) 7897662; internet www.pnoc.com.ph; f. 1973; state-owned energy devt agency mandated to ensure stable and sufficient supply of oil products and to develop domestic energy resources; Chair. ANGELO T. REYES; Pres. and CEO ANTONIO M. CAILAO.

Southern Philippines Development Authority: Basic Petroleum Bldg, 104 Carlos Palanca, Jr, St, Legaspi Village, Makati City, Metro Manila; fax (2) 8183907; Chair. ROBERTO AVENTAJADO; Manila Rep. GERUDIO 'KHALIQ' MADUENO.

CHAMBERS OF COMMERCE AND INDUSTRY

Cebu Chamber of Commerce and Industry (CCCI): CCCI Center, cnr 11th and 13th Ave, North Reclamation Area, 6000 Cebu City; tel. (32) 2321421; fax (32) 2321422; internet www.cebubusinesswebportal.com; f. 1913; Pres. SAMUEL L. CHIOSON.

Chamber of Mines of the Philippines: Rm 809, Ortigas Bldg, Ortigas Ave, Pasig City, 1605 Metro Manila; tel. (2) 6354123; fax (2) 6354160; e-mail info@chamberofmines.com.ph; internet www.chamberofmines.com.ph; f. 1975; Chair. ARTEMIO F. DISINI; Pres. BENJAMIN PHILIP G. ROMUALDEZ.

Federation of Filipino-Chinese Chambers of Commerce and Industry Inc: Federation Center, 6th Floor, Muelle de Binondo St, Binondo, POB 23, Metro Manila; tel. (2) 2419201; fax (2) 2422361; internet www.ffcccii.com.ph/main.html; f. 1954; Pres. TAN CHING.

Philippine Chamber of Coal Mines (Philcoal): Rm 1007, Princeville Condominium, S. Laurel St, cnr Shaw Blvd, 1552 Mandaluyong City, Metro Manila; tel. (2) 5330518; fax (2) 5315513; f. 1980; Exec. Dir BERTRAND GONZALES.

Philippine Chamber of Commerce and Industry (PCCI): 3rd Floor, ECC Bldg, 355 Sen. Gil Puyat Ave, Makati City, Metro Manila; tel. (2) 8964549; fax (2) 8991727; e-mail pcci@philippinechamber.com; internet www.philippinechamber.com; f. 1978; Chair. MIGUEL B. VARELA; Pres. EDGARDO G. LACSON.

FOREIGN TRADE ORGANIZATIONS

Bureau of Export Trade Promotion (BETP): New Solid Bldg, 6th Floor, 357 Sen. Gil J. Puyat Ave, Makati City, 1200 Metro Manila; tel. (2) 8904707; fax (2) 8904693; e-mail infobetp@dti.gov.ph; internet www.tradelinephil.dti.gov.ph; Dir FERNANDO P. CALA, II.

Bureau of Import Services (BIS): Tara Bldg, 3rd Floor, 389 Sen. Gil J. Puyat Ave, Makati City, Metro Manila; tel. (2) 8964431; fax (2) 8964430; e-mail bis@dti.gov.ph; Dir LUIS M. CATIBAYAN.

Garments and Textile Export Board (GTEB): New Solid Bldg, 2nd and 3rd Floors, 357 Sen. Gil J. Puyat Ave, Makati City, Metro Manila; tel. (2) 8978723; fax (2) 4904653; e-mail gtebebs@dti.gov.ph; manages and supervises the garment textile quota system; Exec. Dir FELICITAS R. AGONCILLO REYES.

Philippine International Trading Corpn (PITC): NDC Bldg, 5th Floor, 116 Tordesillas St, Salcedo Village, 1227 Metro Manila; tel. (2) 8189801; fax (2) 8920782; e-mail pitc@pitc.com.ph; internet www.pitc.gov.ph; f. 1973; state trading company to conduct international marketing of general merchandise, industrial and construction goods, raw materials, semi-finished and finished goods, and bulk trade of agri-based products; also provides financing, bonded warehousing, shipping, cargo and customs services; Chair. PETER B. FAVILA; Pres. and CEO JORGE MENDOZA JUDAN.

INDUSTRIAL AND TRADE ASSOCIATIONS

Beverage Industry Association of the Philippines: SMPC Bldg, 23rd Floor, St Francis St, Mandaluyong City, Metro Manila; tel. (2) 6346840; fax (2) 6318672; e-mail rbkmlo@mnl.sequel.net; f. 1988; Pres. HECTOR GUBALLA.

Chamber of Automotive Manufacturers of the Philippines (CAMPI): Suite 1206, 12th Floor, Jollibee Center, San Miguel Ave, Ortigas Center, Pasig City, 1600 Metro Manila; tel. (2) 6329733; fax (2) 6339941; e-mail campi@globelines.com.ph; internet www.campiauto.org; f. 1995; 13 mems; Pres. ELIZABETH H. LEE.

Construction Industry Authority of the Philippines (CIAP): Jupiter I Bldg, 4th Floor, Jupiter St, Makati City, Metro Manila; tel. (2) 8979336; e-mail pocb@skynet.net; Officer-in-Charge KATHERINE T. DELA CRUZ.

Cotton Development Administration (CODA): ATI Bldg, 1st Floor, Elliptical Rd, Diliman, Quezon City, 1100 Metro Manila; tel. (2) 9208878; fax (2) 9209238; e-mail coda@da.gov.ph; internet www.coda.da.gov.ph; f. 1998; Administrator Dr EUGENIO D. ORPIA, Jr.

Federation of Philippine Industries (FPI): Unit 701, Atlanta Center, 31 Annapolis St, Greenhills, San Juan City, Metro Manila; tel. (2) 7223409; fax (2) 7229737; e-mail fpi@fpi.ph; internet www.fpi.ph; f. 1991; 129 mems; Chair. MENELEO J. CARLOS, Jr; Pres. JESUS L. ARRANZA.

Fiber Industry Development Authority: Asiatrust Bank Annex Bldg, 1424 Quezon Ave, Quezon City, Metro Manila; tel. (2) 3737494; fax (2) 4944126; e-mail fida@pldtdsl.net; internet www.fida.da.gov.ph/home.html.html; f. 1977; Administrator CECILIA GLORIA J. SORIANO.

Philippine Association of Electrical Industries: Banks of the Philippines Bldg, Suite 702, Plaza Cervantes, Binondo, Metro Manila; tel. and fax (2) 2421144; Pres. RICARDO SY.

Philippine Fisheries Development Authority: PCA Annex Bldg, 2nd Floor, 1 Elliptical Rd, Diliman, Quezon City, 1109 Metro Manila; tel. (2) 9258472; fax (2) 9256444; e-mail oagm@pfda.gov.ph; internet www.pfda.da.gov.ph; f. 1976; Gen. Man. PETRONILO B. BUENDIA.

Philippine Liquefied Petroleum Gas Association: 218 San Vicente St, Binondo, Metro Manila; tel. (2) 2412668; fax (2) 6337781; f. 1966; Pres. JOSELITO ASENTERO.

Semiconductor and Electronic Industries in the Philippines (SEIPI): Unit 902, RCBC Plaza, Tower 2, Ayala Ave, cnr Sen. Gil J. Puyat Ave, Makati City, 1200 Metro Manila; tel. (2) 8449028; fax (2) 8449037; e-mail philippine.electronics@seipi.org.ph; internet www.seipi.org.ph; f. 1984; 226 mems; Pres. ERNESTO B. SANTIAGO.

EMPLOYERS' ORGANIZATIONS

Cement Manufacturers' Association of the Philippines (CeMAP): Corporal Cruz St, cnr E. Rodriguez Jr Ave, Bagong Ilog, Pasig City, Metro Manila; tel. and fax (2) 6717585; e-mail cementinfo@cemap.org.ph; internet www.cemap.org.ph; f. 1957; est. as Cement Institute of the Philippines; renamed in 1965 as Cement Asscn of the Philippines, in 1973 as Philippine Cement Corpn, and in 1980 as Philippine Cement Mfrs' Corpn; present name adopted in 2003; 14 mems; Chair. RENATO SUNICO; Pres. ERNESTO M. ORDOÑEZ.

Employers' Confederation of the Philippines (ECOP): ECC Bldg, 2nd Floor, 355 Sen. Gil J. Puyat Ave, Makati City, Metro Manila; tel. (2) 8904845; fax (2) 8958623; e-mail ecop@webquest.com; internet www.ecop.org.ph; f. 1975; Chair. MIGUEL B. VARELA; Pres. SERGIO ORTIZ-LUIS, Jr.

Filipino Shipowners' Association: Victoria Bldg, Rm 503, 429 United Nations Ave, Ermita, 1000 Metro Manila; tel. (2) 5227318; fax (2) 5243164; e-mail filiship@info.com.ph; internet www.filipinoshipowners.com.ph; f. 1950; 24 mems, incl. 6 assoc. mems; Chair. CARLOS C. SALINAS; Exec. Sec. AUGUSTO Y. ARREZA, Jr.

Philippine Coconut Producers' Federation, Inc: Wardley Bldg, 2nd Floor, 1991 Taft Ave, cnr San Juan St, Pasay City, 1300 Metro Manila; tel. (2) 5230918; fax (2) 5211333; e-mail cocofed@pworld.net.ph; Pres. MARIA CLARA L. LOBREGAT.

Philippine Retailers' Association (PRA): Unit 2610, Jollibee Plaza, F. Ortigas Jr Rd, Ortigas Center, Pasig City, Metro Manila; tel. (2) 6874180; fax (2) 6360825; e-mail philretailers@gmail.com; internet www.philretailers.com; f. 1976; est. as Chamber of Philippine Dept Stores and Retailers, Inc; present name adopted 1991; Pres. JORGE MENDIOLA.

Philippine Sugar Millers' Association Inc: 1402 Security Bank Centre, 6776 Ayala Ave, Makati City, 1226 Metro Manila; tel. (2) 8911138; fax (2) 8911144; e-mail psma@psma.com.ph; internet www.psma.com.ph; f. 1922; Chair. JULIO O. SY; Pres. PEDRO E. ROXAS.

Textile Mills Association of the Philippines, Inc (TMAP): Ground Floor, Alexander House, 132 Amorsolo St, Legaspi Village, Makati City, 1229 Metro Manila; tel. (2) 8186601; fax (2) 8183107; e-mail tmap@pacific.net.ph; f. 1956; 11 mems; Pres. HERMENEGILDO C. ZAYCO; Chair. JAMES L. GO.

Textile Producers' Association of the Philippines, Inc: Downtown Center Bldg, Rm 513, 516 Quintin Paredes St, Binondo, Metro Manila; tel. (2) 2411144; fax (2) 2411162; Pres. GO CUN UY; Exec. Sec. ROBERT L. TAN.

UTILITIES

Energy Regulatory Commission: Pacific Center Bldg, San Miguel Ave, Ortigas Center, Pasig City, 1600 Metro Manila; tel. (2) 9145000; fax (2) 6315818; e-mail info@erc.gov.ph; internet www.erc.gov.ph; f. 2001; Chair. and CEO ZENAIDA CRUZ-DUCUT; Exec. Dir FRANCIS SATURNINO C. JUAN.

Electricity

Davao Light and Power Co: 163–165 C. Bangoy Sr St, 8000 Davao City; tel. (82) 2293572; internet www.davaolight.com; f. 1929; the country's third largest electric utility.

Manila Electric Co (Meralco): Lopez Bldg, 2nd Floor, Meralco Center, Ortigas Ave, Pasig City, 0300 Metro Manila; tel. (2) 6312222; fax (2) 6315591; e-mail finplan.inv.relations@meralco.com.ph; internet www.meralco.com.ph; f. 1903; partially privatized in 1991; 34% govt-owned; supplies electric power to Manila and seven provinces in Luzon; largest electricity distributor, supplying 54% of total consumption in 2000; Chair. and CEO MANUEL M. LOPEZ; Pres. JOSE P. DE JESUS.

National Power Corpn (NAPOCOR): Quezon Ave, cnr BIR Rd, Quezon City, Metro Manila; tel. (2) 9213541; fax (2) 9212468; e-mail webmaster@napocor.gov.ph; internet www.napocor.gov.ph; f. 1936; state-owned corpn supplying electric and hydroelectric power throughout the country; partially privatized in 2007; Pres. FROILAN TAMPINCO.

Gas

First Gen Corpn: Benpres Bldg, 3rd Floor, Exchange Rd, cnr Meralco Ave, Pasig City, Metro Manila; tel. and fax (2) 4496400; fax (2) 6378366; e-mail info@firstgen.com.ph; internet www.firstgen.com.ph; f. 1998; major interests in power generation and distribution; Chair. OSCAR M. LOPEZ; Pres. FEDERICO R. LOPEZ.

Water

Regulatory Authority

Metropolitan Waterworks and Sewerage System: 4th Floor, Administration Bldg, MWSS Complex, 489 Katipunan Rd, Balara, Quezon City, 1105 Metro Manila; tel. (2) 9223757; fax (2) 9212887; e-mail info@mwss.gov.ph; internet www.mwss.gov.ph; govt regulator for water supply, treatment and distribution within Metro Manila; Administrator GERARDO ESQUIVEL (acting).

Distribution Companies

Davao City Water District: Km 5, Jose P. Laurel Ave, Bajada, 8000 Davao City; tel. (82) 2219400; fax (82) 2264885; e-mail dcwd@davao-water.gov.ph; internet www.davao-water.gov.ph; f. 1973; public utility responsible for the water supply of Davao City; Chair. EDUARDO A. BANGAYAN; Gen. Man. Eng. RODORA N. GAMBOA.

Manila Water: MWSS Administration Bldg, 489 Katipunan Rd, Balara, Quezon City, 1105 Metro Manila; tel. (2) 9267999; fax (2) 9818164; e-mail info@manilawater.com; internet www.manilawater.com; f. 1997 following the privatization of Metro Manila's water and wastewater services; responsible for water supply and wastewater

THE PHILIPPINES

services to Manila East until 2037; Pres. and CEO GERARDO C. ABLAZA, Jr.

Maynilad Water: MWSS Compound, 489 Katipunan Rd, Balara, Quezon City, 1105 Metro Manila; tel. (2) 9813333; fax (2) 9223759; e-mail customer.helpdesk@mayniladwater.com.ph; internet www.mayniladwater.com.ph; f. 1998; est. following the privatization of Metro Manila's water services; responsible for water supply, sewage and sanitation services for Manila West until 2021; Pres. ROGELIO SINGSON.

Metropolitan Cebu Water District: Magallanes St, cnr Lapulapu St, 6000 Cebu City; tel. (32) 2548434; fax (32) 2545391; e-mail mcwd@cvis.net.ph; internet www.mcwd.gov.ph; f. 1974; public utility responsible for water supply and sewerage of Cebu City and surrounding towns and cities; Chair. JUAN SAUL F. MONTECILLO; Gen. Man. ARMANDO H. PAREDES.

TRADE UNION FEDERATIONS

Katipunang Manggagawang Pilipino (KMP-TUCP) (Trade Union Congress of the Philippines): TUCP Training Center Bldg, TUCP-PGEA Compound, Masaya St, cnr Maharlika St, Diliman, Quezon City, 1101 Metro Manila; tel. (2) 9247551; fax (2) 9219758; e-mail secrtucp@tucp.org.ph; internet www.tucp.org.ph; f. 1975; 1.0m. mems; Pres. DEMOCRITO T. MENDOZA; Gen. Sec. ERNESTO F. HERRERA; 39 affiliates, incl.:

    Associated Labor Union for Metalworkers (ALU—METAL): TUCP-PGEA Compound, Diliman, Quezon City, 1101 Metro Manila; tel. (2) 9222575; fax (2) 9247553; e-mail alumla@info.com.ph; 29,700 mems; Pres. DEMOCRITO T. MENDOZA.

    Associated Labor Union for Textile Workers (ALU—TEXTILE): TUCP-PGEA Compound, Elliptical Rd, Diliman, Quezon City, 1101 Metro Manila; tel. (2) 9222575; fax (2) 9247553; e-mail alumla@info.com.ph; 41,400 mems; Pres. DEMOCRITO T. MENDOZA.

    Associated Labor Unions (ALU—TRANSPORT): 1763 Tomas Claudio St, Baclaran, Parañaque, Metro Manila; tel. (2) 8320634; fax (2) 8322392; 49,500 mems; Pres. ALEXANDER O. BARRIENTOS.

    Associated Labor Unions—Visayas Mindanao Confederation of Trade Unions (ALU-VIMCONTU): ALU Bldg, Quezon Blvd, Port Area, Elliptical Rd, cnr Maharlika St, Diliman, Quezon City, 1101 Metro Manila; tel. (2) 9222185; fax (2) 9247553; e-mail alumla@info.com.ph; f. 1954; 350,000 mems; Pres. DEMOCRITO T. MENDOZA.

    Associated Professional, Supervisory, Office and Technical Employees Union (APSOTEU): TUCP-PGEA Compound, Elliptical Rd, Diliman, Quezon City, 1101 Metro Manila; tel. (2) 9222575; fax (2) 9247553; e-mail alumla@info.com.ph; Pres. CECILIO T. SENO.

Association of Independent Unions of the Philippines: Vila Bldg, Mezzanine Floor, Epifanio de los Santos Ave, Cubao, Quezon City, Metro Manila; tel. (2) 9224652; Pres. EMMANUEL S. DURANTE.

Association of Trade Unions (ATU): Antwel Bldg, Room 1, 2nd Floor, Santa Ana, Port Area, Davao City; tel. (82) 2272394; 2,997 mems; Pres. JORGE ALEGARBES.

Confederation of Labor and Allied Social Services (CLASS): Doña Santiago Bldg, TUCP Suite 404, 1344 Taft Ave, Ermita, Metro Manila; tel. (2) 5240415; fax (2) 5266011; f. 1979; 4,579 mems; Pres. LEONARDO F. AGTING.

Federation of Agrarian and Industrial Toiling Hands (FAITH): Kalayaan Ave, cnr Masigla St, Diliman, Quezon City, Metro Manila; tel. (2) 9225244; 220,000 mems; Pres. RAYMUNDO YUMUL.

Federation of Consumers' Co-operatives in Negros Oriental (FEDCON): Bandera Bldg, Cervantes St, Dumaguete City; Chair. MEDARDO VILLALON.

Federation of Unions of Rizal (FUR): Suite 307, Buenavista Bldg, 3rd Floor, 82 Quirino Ave, cnr Rivera St, Parañaque City, Metro Manila; tel. and fax (2) 8320110; 10,853 mems; Pres. EDUARDO ASUNCION.

Lakas sa Industriya ng Kapatirang Haligi ng Alyansa (LIKHA): 32 Kabayanihan Rd Phase IIA, Karangalan Village, Pasig City, Metro Manila; tel. and fax (2) 6463234; e-mail jbvlikha@yahoo.com; Pres. JESUS B. VILLAMOR.

National Association of Free Trade Unions (NAFTU): Rm 404, San Luis Terrace, T. M. Kalaw St, Ermita, Metro Manila; tel. (2) 598705; 7,385 mems; Pres. JAIME RINCAL.

National Congress of Unions in the Sugar Industry of the Philippines (NACUSIP): 7431A Yakal St, Barangay San Antonio, Makati City, Metro Manila; e-mail nacusip@compass.com.ph; 32 affiliated unions and 57,424 mems; Nat. Pres. ZOILO V. DELA CRUZ, Jr.

National Mines and Allied Workers' Union (NAMAWU): Unit 201, A. Dunville Condominium, 1 Castilla St, cnr Valencio St, Quezon City, Metro Manila; tel. (2) 7265070; fax (2) 4155582; 13,233 mems; Pres. ROBERTO A. PADILLA.

Pambansang Kilusan ng Paggawa (KILUSAN): TUCP-PGEA Compound, Elliptical Rd, Diliman, Quezon City, 1101 Metro Manila; tel. (2) 9284651; 13,093 mems; Pres. AVELINO V. VALERIO; Sec.-Gen. IGMIDIO T. GANAGANA.

Philippine Agricultural, Commercial and Industrial Workers' Union (PACIWU): 5 7th St, Lacson, Bacolod City; fax (2) 7097967; Pres. ZOILO V. DELA CRUZ, Jr.

Philippine Federation of Labor (PFL): Metro Manila; fax (2) 5272838; 8,869 mems; Pres. ALEJANDRO C. VILLAVIZA.

Philippine Federation of Teachers' Organizations (PFTO): BSP Bldg, Rm 112, Concepcion St, Ermita, Metro Manila; tel. (2) 5275106; Pres. FEDERICO D. RICAFORT.

Philippine Government Employees' Association (PGEA): TUCP-PGEA Compound, Elliptical Rd, Diliman, Quezon City, Metro Manila; tel. (2) 9261573; fax (2) 6375764; e-mail eso_pgea@hotmail.com; f. 1945; 120,000 mems; Pres. ESPERANZA S. OCAMPO.

Philippine Integrated Industries Labor Union (PIILU): Mendoza Bldg, Rm 319, 3rd Floor, Pilar St, Zamboanga City; tel. (992) 2299; f. 1973; Pres. JOSE J. SUAN.

Philippine Labor Federation (PLF): ALU Bldg, Quezon Blvd, Port Area, Cebu City; tel. (32) 71219; fax (32) 97544; 15,462 mems; Pres. CRISPIN B. GASTARDO.

Philippine Seafarers' Union (PSU): TUCP-PGEA Compound, Elliptical Rd, cnr Maharlika Ave, Diliman, Quezon City, 1101 Metro Manila; tel. (2) 9222575; fax (2) 9247553; e-mail psumla@info.com.ph; internet www.psu.org.ph; f. 1984; 10,000 mems; Pres. DEMOCRITO T. MENDOZA; Gen. Sec. ERNESTO F. HERRERA.

Philippine Transport and General Workers' Organization (PTGWO—D): Cecilleville Bldg, 3rd Floor, Quezon Ave, Quezon City, Metro Manila; tel. (2) 4115811; fax (2) 4115812; f. 1953; 33,400 mems; Pres. VICTORINO F. BALAIS.

Port and General Workers' Federation (PGWF): Manila; Pres. FRANKLIN D. BUTCON.

Public Services Labor Independent Confederation (PSLINK): 15 Clarion Lily St, Congressional Ave, Quezon City, 1100 Metro Manila; tel. (2) 9244710; fax (2) 9281090; e-mail annie.geron@pslink.org; internet www.pslink.org; f. 1987; est. as Public Sector Labor Integrative Center; 35,108 mems; Pres. JARAH HAMJAH; Gen. Sec. ANNIE ENRIQUEZ-GERON.

United Sugar Farmers' Organization (USFO): SPCMA Annex Bldg, 3rd Floor, 1 Luzuriaga St, Bacolod City; Pres. BERNARDO M. REMO.

Workers' Alliance Trade Unions (WATU): Metro Manila; tel. (2) 9225093; fax (2) 975918; f. 1978; 25,000 mems; Pres. TEMISTOCLES S. DEJON, Sr.

INDEPENDENT LABOUR FEDERATIONS

The following organizations are not affiliated to the KMP-TUCP:

Associated Marine Officers and Seamen's Union of the Philippines (AMOSUP): Seaman's Centre, cnr Cabildo and Sta Potenciana Sts, Intramuros, Metro Manila; tel. (2) 5278491; fax (2) 5273534; e-mail s_center@amosup.org; internet www.amosup.org.ph; f. 1960; 23 affiliated unions with 55,000 mems; Pres. GREGORIO S. OCA.

Federation of Free Workers (FFW): FFW Bldg, 1943 Taft Ave, Malate, Metro Manila; tel. (2) 5219435; fax (2) 4006656; internet www.ffw.org.ph; f. 1950; affiliated to Int. Trade Union Confed. (ITUC); 300 affiliated local unions and 400,000 mems; Pres. ANTONIO ASPER.

Kilusang Mayo Uno (KMU): 63 Narra St, Barangay Claro, Quezon City, 1102 Metro Manila; tel. (2) 4210986; fax (2) 4210768; e-mail obrero@kilusangmayouno.org; internet www.kilusangmayouno.org; f. 1980; Chair. ELMER LABOG; Sec.-Gen. WILSON BALDONAZA.

Lakas ng Manggagawa Labor Center: Metro Manila; tel. and fax (2) 5280482; a grouping of 'independent' local unions; Chair. OSCAR M. ACERSON.

Manggagawa ng Komunikasyon sa Pilipinas (MKP): 22 Libertad St, Mandaluyong City, Metro Manila; tel. (2) 5313701; fax (2) 5312109; f. 1951; Pres. PETE PINLAC.

National Confederation of Labor: Suite 402, Carmen Bldg, Ronquillo St, cnr Evangelista St, Quiapo, Metro Manila; tel. and fax (2) 7334474; f. 1994 by fmr mems of Kilusang Mayo Uno; Pres. ANTONIO DIAZ.

Philippine Social Security Labor Union (PSSLU): Carmen Bldg, Suite 309, Ronquillo St, Quiapo, Metro Manila; f. 1954; Nat. Pres. ANTONIO B. DIAZ; Nat. Sec. OFELIA C. ALAVERA.

Samahang Manggagawang Pilipino (SMP-NATOW) (National Alliance of Teachers and Office Workers): 236 J. Romualdez St,

THE PHILIPPINES

Mandaluyong City, Metro Manila; tel. and fax 9176242569 (mobile); e-mail smpnatow@smpnatow.org; internet smpnatow.org; Pres. JOSEPH JOVELLANOS; Sec.-Gen. MILAGROS C. OGALINDA.

Solidarity Trade Conference for Progress: Rizal Ave, Dipolog City; tel. and fax (65) 2124303; Pres. NICOLAS E. SABANDAL.

Trade Unions of the Philippines and Allied Services (TUPAS): Med-dis Bldg, Suites 203–204, Solana St, cnr Real St, Intramuros, Metro Manila; tel. (2) 493449; affiliated to the World Fed. of Trade Unions; 280 affiliated unions and 75,000 mems; Nat. Pres. DIOSCORO O. NUÑEZ; Pres. VLADIMIR R. TUPAZ.

Transport

RAILWAYS

The railway network is confined mainly to the island of Luzon.

Light Rail Transit Authority (Metrorail): Adm. Bldg, LRTA Compound, Aurora Blvd, Pasay City, Metro Manila; tel. (2) 8530041; fax (2) 8316449; e-mail lrtamain@lrta.gov.ph; internet www.lrta.gov.ph; managed and operated by Light Rail Transit Authority (LRTA); electrically driven mass transit system; Line 1 (15 km, Baclaran to Monumento) began commercial operations in Dec. 1984; Line 2 (13.8 km, Santolan to Recto) became fully operational in Oct. 2004; Line 1 South Extension (12 km, Baclaran to Bacoot) planned; Administrator RAFAEL S. RODRIGUEZ.

Philippine National Railways: PNR Exec. Bldg, Mayhaligue St, Tondo, Metro Manila; tel. (2) 3190041; fax (2) 3190169; e-mail info@pnr.gov.ph; internet www.pnr.gov.ph; f. 1887; govt-owned; northern line services run from Manila to Caloocan, 6 km (although the track extends to San Fernando, La Union); southern line services run from Manila to Legaspi, Albay, 479 km; Chair. GERARD L. RABONZA; Gen. Man. MANUEL D. ANDAL.

ROADS

In 2009 there were 213,151 km of roads in the Philippines, of which 29,898 km were national roads and 183,253 km were covered by provincial, city, municipal and barangay roads; an estimated 53,596 km of the total network were paved. Bus services provided the most widely used form of inland transport.

Department of Public Works and Highways: Bonifacio Dr., Port Area, Metro Manila; tel. (2) 3043300; e-mail singson.rogelio@dpwh.gov.ph; internet www.dpwh.gov.ph; responsible for the construction and maintenance of roads and bridges; Sec. ROGELIO L. SINGSON.

Land Transportation Franchising and Regulatory Board: East Ave, Diliman, Quezon City, Metro Manila; tel. (2) 9257191; fax (2) 4262515; e-mail officeofthechairman@ltfrb.gov.ph; internet www.ltfrb.gov.ph; f. 1987; Chair. DANTE M. LANTIN.

Land Transportation Office (LTO): East Ave, Quezon City, 1100 Metro Manila; tel. (2) 9219072; fax (2) 9219071; e-mail ltombox@lto.gov.ph; internet www.lto.gov.ph; f. 1987; plans, formulates and implements land transport rules, regulations and safety measures; registration of motor vehicles; issues licences; Asst Sec. VIRGINIA TORRES; Exec. Dir RICARDO E. ALFONSO, Jr.

SHIPPING

In 2000 there were 102 national and municipal ports, 20 baseports, 58 terminal ports and 270 private ports. The eight major ports are Manila, Cebu, Iloilo, Cagayan de Oro, Zamboanga, General Santos, Polloc and Davao.

Pangasiwaan ng Daungan ng Pilipinas (Philippine Ports Authority): Bonifacio Dr., South Harbour, Port Area, 1018 Metro Manila; tel. (2) 5274856; fax (2) 5274853; e-mail info@ppa.com.ph; internet www.ppa.com.ph; f. 1977; supervises all ports within the Philippine Ports Authority port system; Gen. Man. JUAN C. SANTA ANA.

Philippine Shippers' Bureau (PSB): Trade and Industry Bldg, 2nd Floor, 361 Sen. Gil J. Puyat Ave, Makati City, Metro Manila; tel. and fax (2) 7513304; fax (2) 7513305; e-mail psb@dti.gov.ph; shipping facilitator for international and domestic trade; promotes and protects the interests of shippers, exporters, importers and domestic traders; Dir PEDRO VICENTE C. MENDOZA.

Domestic Lines

Aboitiz Transport System Corpn: 12th Floor, Times Plaza Bldg, United Nations Ave, cnr Taft Ave, Ermita, Metro Manila; tel. (2) 5287171; e-mail corporate_communications@atsc.com.ph; internet www.atsc.com.ph; f. 1996 following the merger of William Lines, Aboitiz Shipping and Carlos A. Gothong Lines; fmrly WG & A Philippines; passenger and cargo inter-island services; Chair. JON RAMON ABOITIZ; Pres. ENRIQUE M. ABOITIZ.

Albar Shipping and Trading Corpn: 2649 Molave St, cnr East Service Rd, United Hills Village, Parañaque, 1713 Metro Manila; tel. (2) 8232391; fax (2) 8233046; e-mail info@albargroup.com.ph; internet www.albargroup.com.ph; f. 1974; manning agency (maritime), trading, ship husbanding; Chair. AKIRA S. KATO; Pres. JOSE ALBAR G. KATO.

Candano Shipping Lines, Inc: Victoria Bldg, 6th Floor, 429 United Nations Ave, Ermita, 2802 Metro Manila; tel. (2) 5238051; fax (2) 5211309; f. 1953; inter-island and Far East chartering, cargo shipping; Pres. and Gen. Man. TRINIDAD CANDANO.

Delsan Transport Lines Inc: Magsaysay Center Bldg, 520 T. M. Kalaw St, Ermita, Metro Manila; tel. (2) 5219172; fax (2) 2889331; Pres. VICENTE A. SANDOVAL; Gen. Man. CARLOS A. BUENAFE.

Eastern Shipping Lines, Inc: ESL Bldg, 54 Anda Circle, Port Area, POB 4253, 2803 Metro Manila; tel. (2) 5277841; fax (2) 5273006; e-mail eastship@skyinet.net; f. 1957; services to Japan; Pres. ERWIN L. CHIONGBIAN; Exec. Vice-Pres. ROY L. CHIONGBIAN.

Loadstar Shipping Co Inc: Loadstar Bldg, 1294 Romualdez St, Paco, 1007 Metro Manila; tel. (2) 5238381; fax (2) 5218061; Pres. and Gen. Man. TEODORO G. BERNARDINO.

Lorenzo Shipping Corpn: 20th Floor, Times Plaza Bldg, United Nations Ave, cnr Taft Ave, Ermita, Metro Manila; tel. (2) 5672180; fax (2) 5672030; internet www.lorenzoshipping.com; Pres. ROBERTO UMALI.

Luzteveco (Luzon Stevedoring Corpn): Magsaysay Bldg, 520 T. M. Kalaw St, Ermita, Metro Manila; f. 1909; two brs; freight-forwarding, air cargo, world-wide shipping, broking, stevedoring, salvage, chartering and oil-drilling support services; Pres. JOVINO G. LORENZO; Vice-Pres. RODOLFO B. SANTIAGO.

National Shipping Corpn of the Philippines: Metro Manila; tel. (2) 473631; fax (2) 5300169; services to Hong Kong, Taiwan, Korea, USA; Pres. TONY CHOW.

Negros Navigation Co Inc: Pier 2, North Harbor, Metro Manila; tel. and fax (2) 5548777; fax (2) 5548717; e-mail gcabalo@negrosnavigation.ph; internet www.negrosnavigation.ph; Chair. and CEO SULFICIO O. TAGUD.

Philippine Pacific Ocean Lines Inc: Delgado Bldg, Bonifacio Drive, Port Area, POB 184, Metro Manila; tel. (2) 478541; Vice-Pres. C. P. CARANDANG.

Philippine President Lines, Inc: PPL Bldg, 1000–1046 United Nations Ave, POB 4248, Metro Manila; tel. (2) 5249011; fax (2) 5251308; trading world-wide; Chair. EMILIO T. YAP; Pres. ENRIQUE C. YAP.

Sulpicio Lines, Inc: Don Sulpicio Go Bldg, Sulpicio Go St, Reclamation Area, POB 137, 6000 Cebu City; tel. (32) 2325361; fax (32) 2321216; internet www.sulpiciolines.com; Chair. ENRIQUE S. GO; Man. Dir CARLOS S. GO.

Transocean Transport Corpn: Magsaysay Bldg, 8th Floor, 520 T. M. Kalaw St, Ermita, POB 21, Metro Manila; tel. (2) 506611; Pres. and Gen. Man. MIGUEL A. MAGSAYSAY; Vice-Pres. EDUARDO U. MANESE.

United Philippine Lines, Inc: Plaza Santiago Bldg, Santa Clara St, Intramuros, POB 127, Metro Manila; tel. (2) 5277491; fax (2) 3380087; e-mail mailadmin@uplines.net; internet www.uplines.net; services world-wide; Pres. FERNANDO V. LISING.

CIVIL AVIATION

In addition to the international airports in Metro Manila (Ninoy Aquino International Airport), Cebu (Mactan International Airport), Angeles City (Clark International Airport) and Olongapo City (Subic Bay International Airport), there are five alternative international airports: Laoag City, Ilocos Norte; Davao City; Zamboanga City; Gen. Santos (Tambler) City; and Puerto Princesa City, Palawan. There are also numerous domestic and private airports. By late 2006 the development of new airports in Silay City, Iloilo City and Bohol was under way.

Civil Aviation Authority: MIA Rd, Pasay City, Metro Manila; tel. (2) 8799104; fax (2) 8340143; e-mail information@mis.caap.gov.ph; internet www.caap.gov.ph; implements govt policies for the development and operation of a safe and efficient aviation network; Dir-Gen. ALFONSO G. CUSI.

Civil Aeronautics Board: CAB Bldg, Old MIA Rd, Pasay City, Metro Manila; tel. (2) 8537259; fax (2) 8516911; e-mail tmanalac@cab.gov.ph; internet cab.gov.ph; exercises general supervision and regulation of, and jurisdiction and control over, air carriers, their equipment facilities and franchise; Exec. Dir LEANDRO R. MENDOZA.

Manila International Airport Authority (MIAA): Metro Manila; tel. (2) 8322938; fax (2) 8331180; e-mail gm@miaa.gov.ph; internet www.miaa.gov.ph; Gen. Man. Maj.-Gen. (retd) JOSE ANGEL HONRADO.

Air Philippines: R1 Hangar, APC Gate 1, Andrews Ave, Nichols, Pasay City, Metro Manila; tel. (2) 8517601; fax (2) 8517922; e-mail info@airphilippines.com.ph; internet www.airphils.com; f. 1995; domestic and regional services; Chair. LUCIO TAN; Pres. DAVID LIM.

Cebu Pacific Air: Airlines Operations Center Bldg, Manila Domestic Airport Complex, Pasay City, Metro Manila; tel. (2) 2905271; fax (2) 8512871; e-mail customerservice@cebupacificair.com; internet www.cebupacificair.com; f. 1995; domestic and international services; Chair. RICARDO J. ROMULO; Pres. and CEO LANCE Y. GOKONGWEI.

Grand Air: Mercure Hotel, Philippines Village Airport Compound, 8th Floor, Pasay City, 1300 Metro Manila; tel. (2) 8313001; fax (2) 8917682; f. 1994; Pres. REBECCA PANLILI.

Philippine Airlines Inc (PAL): PNB Financial Center, Pres. Diosdado Macapagal Ave, CCP Complex, Pasay City, Metro Manila; tel. (2) 5562220; fax (2) 5562221; e-mail webmgr@pal.com.ph; internet www.philippineairlines.com; f. 1941; in Jan. 1992 67% of PAL was transferred to the private sector; operates domestic, regional and international services to destinations in the Far East, Australasia, the Middle East, the USA and Canada; Chair. and CEO LUCIO TAN; Pres. JAIME J. BAUTISTA.

Spirit of Manila Airlines: Roxas Sea Front Garden, Roxas Blvd, cnr Ortigas St, Pasay City; tel. (2) 7844888; fax (2) 5567377; e-mail sales@spiritofmanilaairlines.com; internet www.spiritofmanilaairlines.com; regional and international passenger services from Manila to destinations in Asia and Middle East; Pres. and CEO BASILIO P. REYES.

Zest Airways Inc: General Aviation Area, Pasay City; e-mail customerrelations@zestair.com.ph; internet www.zestair.com.ph; f. 1995; est. as Asian Spirit; following takeover by AMY Holdings, renamed as above 2008; operates services to about 20 domestic destinations, and international services to the Republic of Korea (South Korea); three aircraft; Chair. DONALD DEE; Pres. and CEO ALFREDO YAO.

Tourism

Although intermittently affected by political unrest, tourism remains an important sector of the economy. In 2009 visitor arrivals totalled 3,017,099 (including 197,921 Filipinos permanently resident overseas), compared with 3,139,422 in the previous year. According to provisional figures, tourist receipts, excluding passenger transport, totalled US $4,388m. in 2008.

Philippine Convention and Visitors' Corpn: Legaspi Towers, 4th Floor, 300 Roxas Blvd, 1004 Metro Manila; tel. (2) 5259318; fax (2) 5253314; e-mail pcvcnet@dotpcvc.gov.ph; internet www.dotpcvc.gov.ph; Chair. JOSEPH H. DURANO; Exec. Dir DANIEL G. CORPUZ.

Philippine Tourism Authority: Department of Tourism Bldg, T. M. Kalaw St, Teodoro F. Valencia Circle, Ermita, 1000 Metro Manila; tel. (2) 5247141; fax (2) 5218113; e-mail info@philtourism.gov.ph; internet www.philtourism.com; Gen. Man. and CEO MARK T. LAPID.

Defence

As assessed at November 2010, the total strength of the armed forces was estimated at 125,000: army 86,000, navy an estimated 24,000 (including 8,300 Marines), air force an estimated 15,000. Active paramilitary forces, comprising the Philippine National Police (under the Department of Interior and Local Government), numbered 40,500. The Citizen Armed Forces Geographical Units (CAFGU), which replaced the civil home defence force, numbered about 50,000. Military service is voluntary.

Defence Expenditure: Budgeted at an estimated 105,000m. pesos for 2011.

Chief of Staff of the Armed Forces: Lt-Gen. EDUARDO OBAN.

Chief of Staff (Army): Lt-Gen. ARTURO ORTIZ.

Chief of Staff (Navy): Rear-Adm. ALEXANDER PAMA.

Chief of Staff (Air Force): Lt-Gen. OSCAR RABENA.

Education

The 1987 Constitution commits the Government to provide free elementary and high school education; elementary education is compulsory. The organization of education is the responsibility of the Department of Education.

There were 44,846 pre-primary and primary schools in 2009/10. In that year there were 1,474,644 pupils enrolled at pre-primary schools and 13,934,172 pupils enrolled at primary schools. Total enrolment at pre-primary level in 2007/08 included 39% (males 39%; females 38%) of children in the relevant age-group. In the same year 92% (males 91%; females 93%) of all children in the relevant age-group were enrolled at primary schools. In 2009/10 there were a total of 10,384 secondary schools, at which 6,806,079 pupils were enrolled. In 2007/08 enrolment at secondary level included 61% (males 55.0%; females 66.0%). In 2009/10 there were a total of 1,619 tertiary level institutions, at which 2,402,315 pupils were enrolled. In 2005/06 total enrolment at tertiary level was equivalent to 28.0% (males 25%; females 32%) of the relevant age-group. Instruction is in both English and Filipino at elementary level, and English is the usual medium at the secondary and tertiary levels. The 2005 budget allocated 135,470m. pesos (15.1% of total national expenditure) to education, culture and training.

POLAND

Introductory Survey

LOCATION, CLIMATE, LANGUAGE, RELIGION, FLAG, CAPITAL

The Republic of Poland is situated in eastern Europe, bounded to the north by the Baltic Sea and an exclave of the Russian Federation (Kaliningrad Oblast), to the north-east by Lithuania, to the east by Belarus, to the south-east by Ukraine, to the west by Germany, and to the south by the Czech Republic and Slovakia. The climate is temperate in the west but continental in the east. Poland has short summers and cold, snowy winters. Temperatures in Warsaw are generally between −6°C (21°F) and 24°C (75°F). The official language is Polish, spoken by almost all of the population, and there is a small German-speaking community. Most of the inhabitants profess Christianity: more than 95% are adherents of the Latin-rite Catholic Church, but there are numerous other denominations. The national flag (proportions 5 by 8) has two equal horizontal stripes of white and red. The capital is Warsaw (Warszawa).

CONTEMPORARY POLITICAL HISTORY

Historical Context

Poland, partitioned since the 18th century, was declared an independent republic on 11 November 1918, at the end of the First World War. The country was ruled by a military regime from 1926 until 1939, when Poland was invaded by and partitioned between Germany and the USSR. After Germany declared war on the USSR in June 1941, its forces occupied the whole of Poland until they were expelled by Soviet troops in March 1945.

At the end of the Second World War a pro-communist 'Polish Committee of National Liberation', established under Soviet auspices in July 1944, was transformed into a Provisional Government. Under the Potsdam Agreement, signed by the major Allied powers in 1945, the former German territories lying east of the rivers Oder and Neisse (which now comprise one-third of Poland's total area) came under Polish sovereignty, while Poland's frontier with the USSR was shifted westward. These border changes were accompanied by a major resettlement of the population in the affected areas.

Non-communist political groups suffered severe intimidation during national elections in January 1947, in which the communist-led 'democratic bloc' claimed victory. In February a People's Republic, dominated by the Polish Workers' Party (PPR) of Władysław Gomułka was established. Gomułka's reluctance to implement the collectivization of agriculture demanded by the Soviet authorities led to his dismissal as First Secretary of the PPR in 1948. In December the PPR merged with the Polish Socialist Party to form the Polish United Workers' Party (PZPR). Two other parties, the United Peasants' Party (ZSL) and the Democratic Party (SD), were permitted to remain in existence, but were closely controlled by the PZPR, and Poland effectively became a one-party state.

In 1956 mass demonstrations, provoked by food shortages, were suppressed by security forces. In the ensuing political crisis, Gomułka was returned to office, despite Soviet opposition. In 1964–70 limited economic reforms were implemented. In December 1970 a sharp rise in food prices led to strikes and demonstrations in the Baltic port of Gdańsk and in other cities. Many demonstrators were killed or injured in clashes with the police and army, and Gomułka was forced to resign as First Secretary of the PZPR; he was succeeded by Edward Gierek.

In July 1980 an increase in meat prices prompted widespread labour unrest, and shipyard employees in the Baltic ports, notably at Gdańsk, demanded the right to form free trade unions. The Government finally granted permission for several self-governing trade unions to be established, under the guidance of Solidarity, the organization involved in the Gdańsk strike, which was led by a local worker, Lech Wałęsa. As labour unrest continued, Gierek was replaced as First Secretary of the PZPR by Stanisław Kania. Under the growing influence of Solidarity (which claimed an estimated 10m. members by 1981), strikes continued throughout the country, and in February Józef Pińkowski resigned as Chairman of the Council of Ministers. He was succeeded by Gen. Wojciech Jaruzelski, Minister of Defence (a post he retained) since 1968. Despite further concessions to Solidarity, the crisis persisted, forcing Kania's resignation in October; he was succeeded by Jaruzelski, who thus held the leading posts in both the PZPR and the Government.

On 13 December 1981 martial law was imposed throughout Poland. A governing Military Council of National Salvation, led by Jaruzelski, was established; all trade union activity was suspended, and Wałęsa and other Solidarity leaders were detained. Violent clashes between workers and security forces ensued, and thousands of protesters were arrested. Sporadic disturbances continued in 1982, particularly in response to legislation abolishing all trade unions. Wałęsa was released in November, and in December martial law was suspended and some prisoners were freed. (During 1982 about 10,000 people were detained, and at least 15 demonstrators killed.) In July 1983 martial law was formally ended; the Military Council of National Salvation was dissolved, and an amnesty was declared for most political prisoners and activists. In October Wałęsa was awarded the Nobel Peace Prize.

In July 1984, to mark the 40th anniversary of the establishment of the communist regime in Poland, some 35,000 detainees were granted amnesty. In August US sanctions (imposed following the declaration of martial law) were relaxed. However, the murder, in October, of Fr Jerzy Popiełuszko, a well-known pro-Solidarity Catholic priest, provoked renewed unrest. In February 1985 four officers from the Ministry of Internal Affairs were found guilty of the murder.

Legislative elections took place in October 1985. New regulations gave voters a choice of two candidates for 410 of the 460 seats in the Sejm (Assembly), the remaining 50 deputies being elected unopposed on a national list. Solidarity appealed for a boycott of the poll and disputed the Government's claim that 79% of the electorate had participated. In November Jaruzelski resigned as Chairman of the Council of Ministers, in order to become President of the Council of State (Head of State). He was succeeded by Prof. Zbigniew Messner.

In December 1986, in an effort to broaden the regime's support, Jaruzelski established a 56-member Consultative Council, comprising mainly non-PZPR members. Nevertheless, Solidarity activists attempted to disrupt the official May Day celebrations in several cities in 1987, and in June there were violent clashes between police and protesters during a visit by Pope John Paul II to his native country. Significant price rises were imposed in 1988, prompting widespread protests, and the May Day celebrations were again disrupted. In August a strike by coal workers rapidly spread to other sectors, leading to the most serious industrial unrest since 1981.

The Messner Government resigned in September 1988. Dr Mieczysław Rakowski, Deputy Chairman in 1981–85, was appointed Chairman of a new Council of Ministers, which included several non-PZPR and reformist politicians. However, the Government's announcement that the Lenin Shipyard in Gdańsk was to be closed provoked further strike action. By April 1989 agreement had been reached on the restoration of legal status to Solidarity, as well as on the holding of elections to a new, bicameral legislature, the Zgromadzenie Narodowe (National Assembly). Solidarity and other non-communist groups were to be permitted to contest all the seats in a new upper chamber, the Senat (Senate), which would have a limited right of veto over the lower chamber, the Sejm. Just 35% of the seats in the Sejm were to be subject to free elections, with the remainder open only to candidates of the PZPR and its associate organizations. A new post of executive President was also to be introduced. The necessary amendments to the Constitution were duly approved by the Sejm. In May the Catholic Church, which enjoyed widespread support and adherence among the population, was accorded legal status.

Elections to the new legislature took place on 4 and 8 July 1989. Some 62% of eligible voters participated in the first round, but only 25% in the second. In the elections to the Senat, the electoral wing of Solidarity, the Solidarity Citizens' Committee, secured all but one of the 100 seats. In the elections to the 460-

member Sejm, Solidarity secured all the 161 seats that it was permitted to contest, and the other 299 seats were divided between the PZPR (173 seats), its allied parties—the ZSL (76) and the SD (27)—and members of Catholic organizations (23). The new legislature narrowly elected Jaruzelski, unopposed, as executive President. He was replaced as First Secretary of the PZPR by Rakowski. Jaruzelski accepted Wałęsa's proposal of a coalition of Solidarity, the SD and the ZSL. The appointment of Tadeusz Mazowiecki, a newspaper editor and member of Solidarity, as Chairman of the Council of Ministers, was approved by the Sejm on 24 August 1989, thereby bringing an end to exclusively communist rule. A Solidarity-dominated administration was formed in September.

The new Government's programme of radical political and economic reforms emphasized the creation of democratic institutions and the introduction of a market economy. In December 1989 the legislature voted to rename the country the Republic of Poland, and the pre-communist national symbols were reintroduced. In January 1990 the PZPR was dissolved to allow the establishment of a new party, Social Democracy of the Republic of Poland (SdRP). Local elections held in May were the first entirely free elections in Poland for more than 50 years. Candidates of the Solidarity Citizens' Committee won more than 41% of the seats, while nominally independent candidates secured 38%. By mid-1990 tension had developed between Wałęsa, who advocated accelerated economic reform, and the more cautious Mazowiecki.

Domestic Political Affairs

In September 1990 Jaruzelski agreed to resign, to permit a direct presidential election to take place. In the first round, held on 25 November, Mazowiecki was placed third, behind Wałęsa and an émigré business executive, Stanisław Tymiński. These two candidates proceeded to a second round of voting on 9 December, when Wałęsa won 74.3% of the votes cast. Wałęsa resigned the chairmanship of Solidarity (he was replaced in February 1991 by Marian Krzaklewski), and in December 1990 was inaugurated as President for a five-year term. Jan Krzysztof Bielecki, a reformist economist, became Prime Minister. The new regime rapidly encountered challenges to its reform programme, including, in May 1991, a nation-wide day of strikes and demonstrations organized by Solidarity.

Legislative elections took place on 27 October 1991, with the participation of 43.2% of the electorate. Some 29 parties won representation in the Sejm. The party with the largest number of deputies (62) was Mazowiecki's Democratic Union (UD). The Democratic Left Alliance (SLD), an electoral coalition of the SdRP and the All Poland Trade Unions' Alliance, won 60 seats. The UD was also the largest single party in the Senat, with 21 seats, compared with Solidarity's 11. After Bronisław Geremek of the UD failed to form a government, Wałęsa nominated Jan Olszewski of the Centre Alliance (PC) as Prime Minister. An attempt by Olszewski to submit his resignation was rejected by the Sejm, which proceeded, in December, to approve a new centre-right Council of Ministers, incorporating members of the PC, the Peasant Alliance and the Christian-National Union (ZChN).

In June 1992, following controversy regarding government attempts to expose alleged communist conspirators, the Sejm approved a motion of no confidence in the Olszewski Government. After the failure of Waldemar Pawlak of the Polish People's Party (PSL) to form a government, the Sejm approved the appointment of Hanna Suchocka of the UD as Prime Minister. Her new Government, a seven-party coalition dominated by the UD and the ZChN, was immediately challenged by a month-long strike by 40,000 workers at a copper plant in Legnica. In December an interim 'Small Constitution' entered into effect, pending a comprehensive revision of the 1952 Constitution. A motion of no confidence in the Suchocka administration, proposed by the Solidarity group after the failure of negotiations between the Government and striking teachers and health workers, was narrowly approved by the Sejm in May 1993. However, Wałęsa refused to accept Suchocka's resignation; instead, he dissolved the Sejm, scheduling new elections to both houses of parliament for September. The electoral code was amended, in order to achieve greater political stability, with a new stipulation that a party (with the exception of organizations representing national minorities) must secure at least 5% of the total votes cast (8% in the case of an electoral alliance) in order to achieve parliamentary representation.

The legislative elections of September 1993

The general election held on 19 September 1993 resulted in victory for parties of the left, as voters demonstrated their dissatisfaction with the immediate consequences of recent reforms. The SLD and the PSL, both dominated by former communists and their allies, won, respectively, 171 and 132 seats in the Sejm (with, respectively, 20.4% and 15.4% of the votes cast), and 37 and 36 seats in the Senat. The UD took 74 seats in the Sejm (with 10.6% of the votes cast) and four in the Senat, while Solidarity won 10 seats in the Senat. Wałęsa's Non-Party Bloc for Reform, established in June, won 16 seats in the Sejm and two seats in the Senat. Almost 35% of the votes cast in elections to the Sejm were for parties that received fewer than 5% of the total votes, notably the PC and the ZChN, and therefore secured no representation; the rate of participation by voters was 52.1%. In October Pawlak formed a coalition Government, dominated by members of his PSL and the SLD. In early 1994 the Deputy Prime Minister and Minister of Finance, Marek Borowski (of the SLD), resigned. In February at least 20,000 people took part in a Solidarity-led demonstration in Warsaw, to demand increased government investment in the public sector and measures to combat unemployment. Solidarity began a nation-wide programme of strike action in March.

In January 1995 Wałęsa refused to endorse legislation to increase rates of personal income tax; however, after his actions were ruled to be unconstitutional, he was obliged to approve the legislation. Relations between the Government and the President deteriorated sharply in February, when Wałęsa threatened to dissolve parliament if the Prime Minister did not resign. Further conflict was averted by Pawlak's departure, and in March Józef Oleksy, a member of the SLD and hitherto Marshal (Speaker) of the Sejm, took office as Prime Minister.

The first round of the 1995 presidential election took place on 5 November. The two leading candidates, Aleksander Kwaśniewski, the Chairman of the SdRP (and formerly a leading member of the PZPR), and Wałęsa proceeded to a second round on 19 November, when Kwaśniewski achieved a narrow victory, with 51.7% of the votes cast. On taking office on 23 December, Kwaśniewski asserted his commitment to the further integration of Poland into Western institutions and to the continuation of policies of economic liberalization. Following Kwaśniewski's election, the ministers responsible for foreign affairs, internal affairs and national defence submitted their resignations. The outgoing Minister of Internal Affairs, Andrzej Milczanowski, claimed that Oleksy had acted on behalf of Soviet (and subsequently Russian) espionage agents since the 1980s; despite denying the charges, Oleksy resigned as Prime Minister in January 1996 (an official report, published in October, exonerated him of all charges). Oleksy was subsequently elected Chairman of the SdRP, replacing Kwaśniewski, who had resigned his party membership following his election as President. Włodzimierz Cimoszewicz of the SLD was appointed as Prime Minister in February.

In June 1996 some 25 centre-right political parties, including Solidarity, the PC and the ZChN, established a new electoral bloc, Solidarity Electoral Action (AWS). In September Cimoszewicz dismissed Jacek Buchacz as Minister of Foreign Economic Relations, prompting his party, the PSL, to withdraw for several weeks from government negotiations on proposed administrative reforms. Agreement was subsequently reached on the distribution of ministerial portfolios, whereby the PSL was accorded responsibility for the new Ministry of the Treasury, while the SLD secured the Ministry of Internal Affairs and Administration and the new Ministry of the Economy.

The 1997 legislative elections

On 2 April 1997 the legislature voted to adopt a new Constitution, which slightly reduced presidential powers and provided for the maintenance of a social market economy, pending its approval by national referendum. In the referendum, held on 25 May, some 52.7% of the votes cast were in support of the new text (42.9% of the electorate participated). Among the prominent opponents of the document were the AWS and the conservative Movement for the Reconstruction of Poland (ROP). The new Constitution came into force on 17 October.

In the general election of 21 September 1997, AWS secured 201 seats in the Sejm (with 33.8% of the valid votes cast) and 51 in the Senat, while the SLD won 164 seats in the Sejm (with 27.1% of the votes) and 28 in the Senat. The PSL retained only 27 seats in the Sejm and three in the Senat. The rate of voter participation was 48%. Krzaklewski, the leader of AWS, subsequently initiated coalition talks with the economically liberal Freedom Union (UW) and the ROP, which had won, respectively, 60 and six seats in the Sejm, and eight and five in the Senat. Jerzy Buzek of Solidarity was nominated as Prime Minister in mid-October. Following lengthy negotiations, AWS and the UW signed a coalition agreement later that month, despite some opposition from two members of the AWS alliance, the ZChN and the PC. A new Council of Ministers included Leszek Balcerowicz, leader of the UW, as Deputy Prime Minister, Minister of Finance and Chairman of the Economic Committee. In November the Sejm approved the new Government's programme, which prioritized rapid integration with the North Atlantic Treaty Organization (NATO, see p. 368) and the European Union (EU, see p. 270), and accelerated privatization and government reform. Shortly afterwards, the Social Movement of Solidarity Electoral Action, which was to replace Solidarity within AWS, applied for registration as a new political party.

In July 1998 a new structure of local and regional government was approved, reducing the number of voivodships (provinces) from 48 to 16. Local elections were held in the new voivodships in October. In nine voivodships, the opposition SLD was returned as the largest party, although the governing AWS-UW coalition won the largest number of seats overall, and secured control of the seven remaining voivodships. Meanwhile, the approval of the divestment of the Gdańsk shipyard (which was completed in September) prompted six AWS deputies to withdraw their support for the Government. (In preceding weeks nine other deputies had also left the ruling coalition.) In December a strike by coal miners over imminent changes to the pensions system spread to more than 50 mines, and resulted in government concessions; industrial unrest also affected the steel, armaments, agricultural and railway sectors.

In June 1998 the Sejm adopted a resolution (which was opposed by the SLD) condemning the communist regime imposed on post-war Poland by the USSR. In September the Sejm approved legislation granting access for Polish citizens to files compiled on them by the security services during the communist era. In February 1999 it was announced that the leader of the Self-Defence Trade Union (which had organized a series of protests by farmers in the previous year), Andrzej Lepper, was to stand trial for having organized illegal road blocks. During March the Prime Minister undertook a major government reorganization. The Secretary-General of the UW resigned in protest at two of the ministerial appointments.

In May 1999 farmers resumed their protests against agricultural policy. In June a protest in Warsaw by workers from a weapons factory in the central town of Radom resulted in violent clashes between the police and demonstrators. Farmers joined demonstrations against the low price of grain in August; an estimated 80 people were injured when violence erupted between police and farmers in northern Poland. Protests against the economic slowdown and the implementation of government reforms in education, health and pensions provision culminated, in September 1999, in a march through Warsaw by some 35,000 agricultural and industrial workers (as well as leaders from the opposition SLD and PSL parties).

In September 1999 the Deputy Prime Minister and Minister of Internal Affairs and Administration, Janusz Tomaszewski, announced his resignation. Following a minor government reorganization in October, AWS and the UW renewed their coalition agreement for a further two years. In late October the Government reached a compromise with miners' representatives from Solidarity regarding the restructuring of the industry. It was announced in December that Solidarity was to withdraw from political activities and become an 'organization of employees'. In January 2000 Lepper announced the formation of the Self-Defence Party of the Republic of Poland (SRP), a populist party opposed to Polish membership of the EU that incorporated elements of several farmers' organizations and trade unions, under his leadership.

In May 2000 the ruling coalition entered a serious crisis when the Prime Minister suspended the UW-SLD local government authorities of Warsaw's central commune and replaced it with an AWS-affiliated commissioner. At the end of the month the UW announced its withdrawal from the national governing coalition, in protest at the blocking of Balcerowicz's proposals for economic reform by AWS deputies. Negotiations on re-establishing the coalition collapsed in June, and Buzek went on to form a minority AWS Government.

In the presidential election, held on 8 October 2000, Kwaśniewski was re-elected with 53.9% of the valid votes cast, ahead of Andrzej Olechowski, an independent former foreign minister, who secured 17.3% of the votes; Krzaklewski obtained 15.6%, Lepper 3.1% and Wałęsa just 1.0%. The rate of participation by the electorate was 61.1%. Krzaklewski resigned as leader of AWS in January 2001, and was succeeded by Prime Minister Buzek. Meanwhile, Balcerowicz resigned the leadership of the UW in November 2000, and became President of the National Bank in December.

In January 2001 Olechowski, together with the Marshal of the Sejm, Maciej Plazyński of AWS, and a Vice-Marshal of the Senat, Donald Tusk of the UW, founded a new centre-right, economically liberal political movement, the Civic Platform (PO). Kwaśniewski signed a new electoral law at the end of April, introducing a new method for the calculation of voting under the system of proportional representation. Following the enactment of the law, legislative elections were scheduled for September. Thereafter, significant political realignment took place, and in May AWS was restructured as Solidarity Electoral Action of the Right (AWSP), in alliance with the ROP. At the end of May the conservative Catholic, nationalist League of Polish Families (LPR), which opposed Polish membership of the EU, was registered as a party. Also in May Lepper was sentenced to 16 months' imprisonment, after being found guilty of charges associated with the farmers' blockades of 1998–99. Lepper commenced an appeal against the sentence.

The 2001 legislative elections

The legislative elections took place on 23 September 2001, with a rate of voter participation of 46.3%. Neither AWSP nor the UW received the requisite 8% of the votes cast to obtain seats in the Sejm, although both parties contested the elections to the Senat as part of the Blok Senat 2001 (also comprising the PO, the ROP, and Law and Justice—PiS—a conservative party founded earlier in the year by former members of AWS, which won 15 of the 100 seats. Support for conservative parties was divided between PiS, which obtained 44 seats in the Sejm, and the LPR, which secured 38 seats in the Sejm and two in the Senat. Another party elected to the Sejm for the first time was the SRP, which obtained 53 seats in the Sejm and two in the Senat. An electoral coalition of the SLD and the Union of Labour (UP) won 216 seats in the Sejm and 75 seats in the Senat, falling short of an overall majority. The PO, which received 65 seats in the Sejm, rejected an initial proposal to form a coalition with the SLD-UP. Instead, on 9 October the SLD and the UP signed a coalition agreement with the PSL, which had obtained 42 seats in the elections to the Sejm and four seats in the Senat. The leader of the SLD, Leszek Miller, was sworn in as Prime Minister and Chairman of the European Integration Committee on 19 October; the PSL's leader, Jarosław Kalinowski, and the leader of the UP, Marek Pol, were appointed as Deputy Prime Ministers. Miller pledged to revive economic progress, and announced that a referendum on entry to the EU would be held in mid-2003.

In November 2001 Lepper was dismissed as a Vice-Marshal of the Sejm. In March 2002, on appeal, Lepper's prison sentence was reduced to a suspended one-year term. Government changes in July included the resignation of Marek Belka as Minister of Finance; Grzegorz Kołodko subsequently assumed the post, being appointed additionally as a Deputy Prime Minister, and in December he survived a vote of no confidence in the Sejm.

Meanwhile, on 27 October 2002 local elections were held, in which the ruling SLD-UP coalition won 33.7% of the votes cast; the SRP won 18.0% of the votes and the LPR secured 16.4%. A second round of voting took place on 10 November. In January 2003 the Prime Minister reorganized the Government, consolidating the Ministries of the Economy and of Labour into a new Ministry of the Economy, Labour and Social Policy, under Jerzy Hausner. On 1 March Miller expelled the PSL from the Government, after it voted with opposition deputies against new tax legislation in the Sejm. In mid-March the Sejm rejected a motion, proposed by the LPR, to dissolve parliament. The following day the SLD-UD coalition formed a parliamentary alliance with the Peasant Democratic Party (PLD), although it remained 13 seats short of a majority. Meanwhile, public dissatisfaction at the state of the economy and the high rate of unemployment was expressed by frequently violent demonstrations led by Solidarity.

In June 2003 Miller transferred responsibility for economic policy from the Ministry of Finance to Hausner's Ministry of the Economy, Labour and Social Policy, prompting the resignation of Kołodko from the Government. Hausner assumed Kołodko's former responsibilities as a Deputy Prime Minister (while retaining his previous portfolio), while Andrzej Raczko became Minister of Finance. The Government subsequently won a vote of confidence in the Sejm.

In January 2004, as part of a minor government reorganization, Miller appointed Deputy Chairman of the SLD and former premier Oleksy as Deputy Prime Minister and Minister of Internal Affairs and Administration. In late January the PLD withdrew its support for the ruling coalition, thereby reducing the Government's majority in parliament. In February Miller announced that he was to resign as Chairman of the SLD, but retain the premiership, to enable him to focus on Poland's planned accession to the EU on 1 May (see below). On 6 March Krzysztof Janik was elected as the new party Chairman, although later in the month more than 20 deputies, led by Borowski, announced that they were to defect from the SLD in order to establish a new party, Polish Social Democracy (SDPL); Borowski subsequently resigned as Marshal of the Sejm. On 26 March Miller acknowledged the loss of support for his leadership and announced that he would resign as Prime Minister on 2 May. Three days later President Kwaśniewski nominated former Minister of Finance Belka (latterly Director of Economic Policy in the US-led Coalition Provisional Authority in Iraq) to head a new government; Belka announced that he intended to retain key ministers, including Hausner, who had devised a controversial economic austerity programme for 2004–07. In late April Oleksy was elected as the new Marshal of the Sejm.

Miller resigned on 2 May 2004, as announced, and Belka's Government, principally composed of SLD members and independents, took office, pending approval by the Sejm. Isabela Jaruga-Nowacka, who had been recently elected leader of the UP, was appointed as a Deputy Prime Minister. In mid-May, however, the Sejm rejected the nomination to the premiership of Belka, forcing the resignation of the new Government. The Sejm failed to propose a new candidate within the requisite two weeks, and Kwaśniewski duly renominated Belka. In late June the Sejm approved Belka's appointment by 236 votes to 215, thus averting early elections. In order to secure the support of the SDPL, Belka agreed to hold a further confidence vote in October to confirm his mandate to govern. In July the Minister of Finance, Andrzej Raczko, resigned to become Poland's representative at the IMF; he was succeeded by Mirosław Gronicki. In August the Government abandoned some elements of its economic austerity programme in order to secure political support for the majority of its proposals. In September the Minister of Justice, Marek Sadowski, resigned, after media reports suggested that he had abused his official positions to avoid investigation into a road accident in which he had been involved in 1995.

In October 2004 Belka won the scheduled vote of confidence in the Sejm, by 234 votes to 218. Ahead of the vote Belka had announced to the lower chamber that Poland would begin reducing its 2,500-strong military contingent in Iraq (see below) from early 2005. Krzysztof Pater resigned as Minister of Social Policy in November, after the Sejm rejected austerity measures on corporate social insurance and pensions. Deputy Prime Minister Jaruga-Nowacka subsequently assumed additional responsibility for social policy.

In December 2004 Oleksy was elected Chairman of the SLD, defeating Krzysztof Janik. Shortly afterwards, Janik and his allies announced plans to form a faction within the party. A few days later, following several years of investigations, the Vetting Court ruled that Oleksy had concealed his collaboration with the communist-era military intelligence services; Oleksy, who strongly denied the charges against him, announced that he would appeal against the Court's verdict. In response to mounting pressure, Oleksy resigned as Marshal of the Sejm, and in January 2005 Włodzimierz Cimoszewicz, hitherto Minister of Foreign Affairs, was elected as his replacement. Adam Rotfeld assumed the foreign affairs portfolio.

In February 2005 Hausner resigned from the SLD, after the party's national council voted against holding early legislative elections in June. In March he also tendered his resignation as Deputy Prime Minister and Minister of the Economy and Labour, to which position Jacek Piechota was subsequently appointed. In late February Hausner and Władysław Frasyniuk, the leader of the UW, announced plans to create a new centrist political organization, the Democratic Party (PD), the founding congress of which was held in May. Amid speculation that he was to join the new party, in March Belka urged the Sejm to dissolve itself to allow early elections to take place, as the minority Government lacked sufficient legislative support for proposed budget reforms. However, the Sejm voted to reject three motions submitted by opposition parties for its dissolution, and President Kwaśniewski rejected Belka's resignation, tendered on 6 May, stating that the Government should remain in office until the forthcoming legislative elections. Meanwhile, Jaruga-Nowacka resigned from the leadership of the UP. In late May Wojciech Olejniczak was elected as Chairman of the SLD, succeeding Oleksy. In June Belka made public his police file, in response to allegations that he had collaborated with the communist security services.

The Lech Kaczyński presidency

In the legislative elections, held on 25 September 2005, and in which 40.5% of the electorate participated, PiS obtained the largest number of seats in both the Sejm (taking 155 of the 460 seats, with 27.0% of the votes) and the Senat (with 49 of the 100 seats). PO won 133 seats in the Sejm (with 24.1% of the votes) and 34 seats in the Senat, whereas the incumbent SLD received just 55 seats in the Sejm (with 11.3% of the votes cast). Two days later the leader of PiS, Jarosław Kaczyński, announced that he did not intend to lead the new government, and instead proposed Kazimierz Marcinkiewicz for the premiership, while Kaczyński's twin brother, Lech, the Mayor of Warsaw, was to contest the forthcoming presidential election for PiS.

After a first round of voting in the presidential election, conducted on 9 October 2005, PO leader Donald Tusk (who obtained 36.3% of the votes) and Lech Kaczyński (33.1%) progressed to a second round on 23 October. Kaczyński emerged as the winner in the run-off poll, with 54.0% of the votes. The rate of participation by the electorate was 49.7% in the first round and 51.0% in the second. Kaczyński was inaugurated as President on 23 December.

Meanwhile, although PiS and the more economically liberal PO, as the two principal parties of the centre-right, had been widely expected to negotiate a coalition government, the parties were unable to agree on the distribution of senior positions, and on 31 October 2005 Marcinkiewicz was appointed as Prime Minister of a minority Government, comprising nine members of PiS and eight independents. Stefan Meller, a career diplomatist, became Minister of Foreign Affairs, and other non-affiliated ministers were appointed to the treasury, finance and economy portfolios. Bogdan Borusewicz, an independent, was appointed Marshal of the Senat, and Marek Jurek of PiS became Marshal of the Sejm. On 10 November the Government won a motion of confidence in the Sejm, by 272 to 187 votes, with the support of several smaller, mostly right-wing, parties (the SRP, the LPR and the PSL).

In January 2006 the Minister of the Treasury, Andrzej Mikosz, resigned, following media allegations that his wife had been involved in financial misdemeanours in 2002; he was replaced by Wojciech Jasiński in February 2006. Also in January Teresa Lubinska was dismissed as Minister of Finance; she was succeeded by Zyta Gilowska, an independent (formerly aligned with PO), who also became Deputy Prime Minister. In late April PiS signed a coalition agreement with the SRP and the LPR. Stefan Meller subsequently resigned as Minister of Foreign Affairs, in protest at the Government's decision to co-operate with the populist SRP. Several new ministers were appointed to the Government on 5 May, giving the Government a majority in the Sejm for the first time. The leaders of both the SRP and the LPR were awarded with deputy prime ministerial positions, with Lepper additionally gaining responsibility for agriculture and rural development, while the leader of the LPR, Roman Giertych, also became the Minister of National Education.

In June 2006 Gilowska resigned from the Council of Ministers, following the opening of an investigation into claims that she had lied about collaborating with the secret services during the communist era. (Former members of the Soviet-backed secret services were eligible to hold public office, but falsely denying such links was considered a serious offence.) Gilowska was succeeded as Minister of Finance by Paweł Wojciechowski. In early July Marcinkiewicz tendered his resignation, reportedly owing to disagreements with the leader of his party, Jarosław Kaczyński, over economic policy, as a result of which the entire Government was constitutionally obliged to resign. Shortly afterwards President Kaczyński nominated his twin brother as Marcinkiewicz's replacement; this appointment was subsequently approved by the Sejm, and Jarosław Kaczyński was formally sworn into office on 14 July, together with his new Council of Ministers, to which only one change had been made—the replacement of Wojciechowski by Stanisław Kluza, hitherto Deputy Minister of Finance. However, in September, after she had been cleared of the accusations levied against her, Gilowska was reappointed as Deputy Prime Minister and Minister of

Finance, and Kluza left the Government. Also in September, following several policy disagreements, President Kaczyński dismissed Lepper. In response, the SRP withdrew from the ruling coalition, which thereby lost its parliamentary majority. However, in October, a few days prior to a planned parliamentary vote on an opposition-initiated motion for the legislature to dissolve itself, Lepper's dismissal was retracted and the alliance between PiS and the SRP revived.

Also in October 2006 both pro- and anti-Government rallies were held in Warsaw, following the broadcast in late September of a video purporting to show an aide of Prime Minister Kaczyński attempting to buy the support of a member of the opposition. The Prime Minister rejected demands that he resign and insisted that his aide had been engaged in legitimate political bargaining. In local elections held in November, PiS performed robustly overall, but crucially lost the mayoralty of Warsaw, which was secured by Hanna Gronkiewicz-Waltz of PO, a former Governor of the Central Bank, who defeated Marcinkiewicz.

In February 2007 the Minister of National Defence, Radosław Sikorski, tendered his resignation, following policy differences with the Prime Minister; he was succeeded by a former head of the presidential chancellery, Aleksander Szczygło. In the same month Ludwik Dorn resigned the internal affairs portfolio (while initially retaining the post of Deputy Prime Minister), owing to a disagreement with the Prime Minister. A former Prosecutor-General, Janusz Kaczmarek, became the new Minister of Internal Affairs and Administration. Andrzej Krawczyk, foreign policy adviser to the President, was dismissed in March, owing to his alleged collaboration with the communist-era secret services in 1982. (Although Krawczyk denied the accusation and was exonerated by a court in the same month, the President refused to rescind the dismissal.) In April Dorn was elected Marshal of the Sejm, after Marek Jurek resigned from that position in response to the chamber's failure to adopt a constitutional amendment that would have enforced stricter legislation on abortion. Jurek also resigned from PiS to form a new party, the Right of the Republic (PR), which was to emphasize pro-life and other traditionalist Catholic policies. In July Prime Minister Kaczyński again removed Lepper from his government post, on the grounds that he was under investigation for corrupt practice in the designation of agricultural land. The Minister of Sports was also dismissed, after allegations of corruption. Lepper announced that his SRP would provisionally remain in the Government, after deputies threatened to divide the party. However, on 13 August President Kaczyński dismissed the remaining SRP representatives and the LPR members from the Government, thereby ending the ruling coalition; they were replaced by PiS representatives on an interim basis, and it was announced that early legislative elections were to be organized.

Civic Platform assumes leadership in the Sejm

On 7 September 2007 the Sejm voted to dissolve itself. Elections to both parliamentary chambers were scheduled for 21 October. Prime Minister Kaczyński dismissed all 15 government ministers to prevent a motion of no confidence planned by the PO; they were subsequently reappointed on an interim basis. At the elections to the Sejm, conducted on 21 October, the PO obtained 209 seats, receiving 41.5% of the votes cast, with PiS receiving 166 seats (32.1% of the votes); an SLD-led coalition, known as Left and Democrats (LiD), secured 53 seats (13.2%), and the PSL 31 seats (8.9%). The rate of participation was 53.8% of the electorate. Neither the LPR (which had contested the elections in a coalition with the PR) nor the SRP obtained legislative representation. Later in October Giertych resigned from the leadership of the LPR. On 5 November Prime Minister Kaczyński submitted the resignation of his minority Government. On 9 November President Kaczyński nominated Tusk, as leader of PO, as Prime Minister. Tusk reached a coalition agreement with the PSL; together, the PO and the PSL held 240 seats in the 460-member Sejm. The new PO-PSL Government was approved by 238 of the votes cast in the Sejm. Although Jarosław Kaczyński won a vote of confidence in his leadership of PiS at a party congress in December, increasing divisions within the party became apparent with the defection of three deputies from the PiS faction in the Sejm.

In early September 2008 the trial began of Gen. (retd) Wojciech Jaruzelski and seven other former communist officials, on charges relating to the imposition of martial law in 1981. In the same month the Government announced a financial plan to prevent the bankruptcy of three major shipyards, situated at Gdynia, Gdańsk and Szczecin, following an investigation by the European Commission into use of state aid by the Polish authorities to support the shipyards, seemingly in a manner that contravened EU regulations. However, in November the European Commission issued a decision ordering the Government to sell the assets of the Gdynia and Szczecin shipyards by May 2009 (although this deadline was subsequently extended) in order to enable the Government to reimburse some €2,300m. in aid.

At elections to the European Parliament, held on 7 June 2009, the PO secured 44.4% of the votes cast and 25 of the 50 contested seats, while PiS won 27.4% of the votes and 15 seats, the SLD (in alliance with the UP) 12.3% of the votes and seven seats, and the PSL 7.0% of the votes and three seats; the rate of participation by voters was recorded at 24.5% of the electorate.

In October 2009 the parliamentary leader of the PO, Zbigniew Chlebowski, resigned from his post, after media allegations of his involvement in a corruption scandal. The parliamentarian was accused of offering assistance to the gambling industry by refusing to support proposed tax rises as part of a new gambling law. Three PO ministers subsequently left the Government in association with the scandal. The Deputy Prime Minister and Minister of Internal Affairs and Administration, Grzegorz Schetyna, the Minister of Justice, Andrzej Czuma, and the Minister of Sport and Tourism, Mirosław Drzewiecki, were replaced in mid-October. In early December the Minister of the Environment, Maciej Nowicki, announced his retirement.

At the end of March 2010 the Marshal of the Sejm, Bronisław Komorowski, was selected as the PO's candidate in the presidential election due to be held in late 2010, following primary elections based on the US model, in which he overwhelmingly defeated Sikorski, the Minister of Foreign Affairs.

The death of President Kaczyński

On 10 April 2010 Kaczyński was killed, with 96 others, in an air crash near Smolensk, Russia, while travelling to mark the 70th anniversary of the massacre of Poles by Soviet troops at Katyń. There were no survivors of the crash, which killed a large number of senior political and military figures, including the President of the National Bank of Poland, Sławomir Skrzypek, and the Chief of Staff of the Defence Forces, Gen. Franciszek Gągor, as well as the President's wife. In accordance with the Constitution, Komorowski, as the Marshal of the Sejm, was appointed acting President, and immediately declared a week of national mourning. A presidential election was to be held on 20 June. Komorowski was to stand as the PO candidate in the election, which was also to be contested by the deceased President's twin brother, Jarosław Kaczyński, as the candidate of PiS.

On 10 May 2010 some 2,500 people reportedly demonstrated outside the presidential palace in Warsaw to demand an independent international inquiry into the crash, expressing dissatisfaction with the ongoing, joint Russian-Polish inquiry. Reports emerged following the crash that Russian staff at the air traffic control centre had repeatedly warned the Polish pilots of poor weather conditions and dense fog, advising that attempts to land should be aborted. Nevertheless, the pilot made three failed attempts to land the aircraft before the fourth, fatal, attempt, prompting speculation that President Kaczyński had ordered the pilot to land the plane regardless of the weather conditions. Recordings of communications confirmed that Russian air traffic control staff, speaking in Russian (in breach of international protocols, which require the use of English for such communications), had advised against attempting to land at Smolensk.

A report by Russian aviation investigators, released in January 2011, found that there was no mechanical fault with the aircraft and that the air crash had been caused by pilot error. It confirmed that the crew on board the aircraft had failed to heed warnings to abort the landing and divert to an alternative airport. Flight deck recordings revealed that both the Polish Air Force commander and a senior official at the Ministry of Foreign Affairs had entered the flight deck during the approach to Smolensk, adding weight to concerns that the pilot had acquiesced to demands from those on board (possibly including the President) to land the aircraft despite warnings against so doing. The Minister of Internal Affairs and Administration, Jerzy Miller, accepted the findings but stated that Russian officials had also been at fault; it was suggested that the Russians should have closed the airport instead of permitting a potentially dangerous attempt to land. The late President's brother, however, rejected the conclusions of the report, claiming that there was insufficient evidence in support of claims that the late President had given orders to land, while many Poles deemed the findings unfair and made demands for an independent investigation into the incident.

Recent developments: Bronisław Komorowski elected President

Meanwhile, early elections were held on 20 June 2010, following the death of President Kaczyński. In the first round of voting Komorowski was placed first, with 41.5% of the votes cast. He and Jarosław Kaczyński (who received 36.5%) proceeded to a second round. The third-placed candidate was the SLD's Grzegorz Napieralski, who replaced the party's intended candidate Jerzy Szmajdziński, who had died in the Smolensk plane crash. In the run-off ballot, contested on 4 July, Komorowski was elected President, receiving 53.0% of the votes cast. Some 54.9% of citizens voted in the first round of polling, and 52.0% participated in the run-off vote. On 8 July Grzegorz Schetyna was elected to replace Komorowski as Marshal of the Sejm. Schetyna duly became acting President until Komorowski's inauguration ceremony on 6 August, where a minute's silence was observed to commemorate the late President and all those lost in the Smolensk crash.

Relations between Prime Minister Tusk and the late President Kaczyński had become increasingly strained. Thus, with the election of Komorowski, a founding member of Tusk's PO and the resulting consolidation of power, it was hoped that the Government could proceed with much-needed economic and political reforms. However, Komorowski's margin of victory was smaller than anticipated and, despite minor changes, including measures to combat the trade of semi-legal drugs, the implementation of extensive reforms in state administration, public finances and the labour market remained elusive. Legislative elections were due to be held no later than October 2011; by April of that year public opinion polls showed that the PO's lead over the PiS and a resurgent left-wing movement was diminishing.

Foreign Affairs

Regional relations

After 1991, close relations were retained with the Czech Republic, Hungary and Slovakia through the structures of the Visegrad Group and the Central European Free Trade Agreement, and also with other countries of the Baltic region. In 1991–92 Poland established diplomatic relations with the former republics of the USSR, developing particularly strong links with Ukraine. In May 1997 the Polish and Ukrainian Presidents signed a declaration of reconciliation, which included the condemnation of the killing of tens of thousands of Poles by Ukrainian nationalists in 1942–43, and of the 'Wisła Operation' of 1947, in which more than 100,000 Ukrainians were forcibly deported from their homes in south-east Poland.

All former Soviet combat troops were withdrawn from Poland by November 1992, and the last remaining Russian military presence was withdrawn in September 1994. Although relations between Poland and Russia deteriorated after Poland acceded to NATO in 1999, in July 2000 President Kwaśniewski became the first Polish head of state to pay an official visit to Moscow since the collapse of communist rule, and Russian President Vladimir Putin made an official visit to Poland in January 2002. The Polish Government continued to oppose Russia's plans to construct a natural gas pipeline to Slovakia through Poland, bypassing Ukraine, considering that the project threatened adversely to affect Polish-Ukrainian relations. In 2005 Poland expressed concern at plans to construct a North European Natural Gas Pipeline between Russia and Germany, under the Baltic Sea, effectively bypassing Poland.

In April 2010 President Lech Kaczyński died in an air crash while travelling to Russia for a ceremony to remember thousands of Poles killed by Soviet troops at Katyń (see Domestic Political Affairs). Having previously been accused of concealing evidence, in May Russia provided acting Polish President Bronisław Komorowski with historical documents relating to the 1940 massacre. Days before the Smolensk crash, the Russian premier Putin met with Polish Prime Minister Tusk at the site of the Katyń massacre as a symbol of improved relations between the two countries. In November 2010 Russia's Federal Assembly issued an historic declaration accepting that former Soviet leader Iosif Dzhugashvili (Stalin) had given the order for the massacre in 1940; it was only in 1990 that Russia ceased blaming Germany's Nazi regime for the Katyń atrocities. Reports also emerged in late 2010 that Putin was planning 'destalinization' measures, declassifying information and reminding Russians of crimes committed under Stalin's dictatorship.

Meanwhile, in July 2005 Poland recalled its ambassador to Belarus, and appealed to the EU for assistance in protecting the Polish minority there, after the main Polish-language newspaper in the country had been suppressed by the authorities, and the leadership of the Union of Poles in Belarus replaced and its offices sequestrated. The Polish ambassador returned to Belarus in October. In March 2006 Belarus briefly recalled its ambassador to Poland, after a number of Polish journalists and parliamentarians were refused entry to Belarus in advance of the presidential election there, and a former Polish ambassador to Belarus was imprisoned for 15 days after participating in an unauthorized protest. In February 2010 several members of the Union of Poles in Belarus were imprisoned, accused of organizing an unauthorized demonstration, prompting condemnation from Poland. Relations remained strained in 2011, following the re-election of Belarusian President Alyaksandr Lukashenka in December 2010 and the arrest, shortly after the election, of several of the opposition candidates. Poland appealed to other EU states to collectively impose or reimpose travel restrictions on Lukashenka's associates while facilitating travel abroad for Belarusian citizens.

In November 1990 Poland and Germany signed a border treaty confirming their post-1945 borders, and in June 1991 the two countries signed a treaty of 'good neighbourliness and friendly co-operation'. Poland welcomed the announcement made by the German Government in February 1999 of the establishment of a compensation fund for over 2m. Poles who were employed as forced labour in German companies during the Second World War. In December a compensation agreement was signed, whereby DM 10,000m. was to be paid by German companies into a compensation fund. The German Chancellor, Gerhard Schröder, attended a ceremony in Warsaw in August 2004 to mark the 60th anniversary of the city's failed uprising against the Nazi occupation, becoming the first German leader to participate in such an event. In January 2005 the German President, Horst Köhler, attended a ceremony in Poland to commemorate the 60th anniversary of the liberation of the Nazi concentration camp at Oświęcim (Auschwitz). In August an exhibition devoted to the expulsion of Germans from Eastern Europe in the aftermath of the Second World War provoked outrage in Poland, and the Polish Government argued that it sought to rewrite history by portraying Germany as the victim of the war; the acting Mayor of Warsaw, former Prime Minister Marcinkiewicz, cancelled a planned visit to Berlin in protest. In March 2007 German Federal Chancellor Angela Merkel met President Kaczyński during an official visit to Poland. As Prime Minister since November of that year, Donald Tusk has sought to forge closer relations with Merkel, seeing Poland's economic future as being closely aligned with a resurgent German power, whereas his predecessor emphasized the importance of maintaining a close relationship with the USA. In December 2010 Poland's Minister of Foreign Affairs, Radosław Sikorski, met with his German counterpart to discuss measures to ensure fair elections in Belarus (see above).

A national referendum on EU membership took place in June 2003, at which some 77% of the votes cast by 58.9% of the electorate were in favour of accession. In October, in preparation for its accession to the EU, Poland introduced visa requirements for Belarusian, Moldovan, Russian and Ukrainian citizens, in accordance with EU policy, although simplified visa arrangements were instituted for residents of the Russian exclave of Kaliningrad. Poland became a full member of the EU on 1 May 2004. In December 2007, following the approval of legislation in the Sejm in August, Poland, together with eight other nations, implemented the EU's Schengen Agreement on freedom of travel, effectively removing border controls between those states subject to the Agreement. On 9 April 2008 President Kaczyński approved a law allowing him to ratify the EU's Lisbon Treaty (signed in December 2007), after a compromise agreement securing the parliamentary support of PiS had permitted the Treaty's endorsement in both the Sejm and the Senat earlier that month. However, at the end of June, following a referendum in Ireland that resulted in rejection of the Treaty, Kaczyński indicated that he would suspend finalization of the ratification process until a resolution was reached in Ireland. Kaczyński finally ratified the Treaty in October 2009. Poland was due to assume the presidency of the Council of the EU in July 2011 and priorities were expected to focus on two areas: implementing EU directives pertaining to internal markets in an effort to increase the country's credibility as a strong economic partner within Europe; and strengthening regional relations, offering support to Balkan nations seeking accession to the EU. Poland was keen not to allow legislative elections, due in October, to distract it from its obligations to the EU, fearing that a weak EU presidency

POLAND

would threaten the country's position of growing credibility in Europe.

Other external relations

The Polish Government strongly supported the US-led military campaign to remove from power the regime of the Iraqi President, Saddam Hussain, in early 2003, and Poland was subsequently offered the opportunity to manage one of three reconstruction zones in Iraq, under overall US command. In September the USA transferred responsibility for security in an area of central Iraq to a 9,500-strong multinational force led by Poland, which contributed some 2,500 troops. In early 2005 Poland reduced its military contingent in Iraq to 1,700 troops. Following his installation as Prime Minister in November 2007, Donald Tusk announced the withdrawal of the remaining 900 Polish troops in Iraq, despite the continued opposition of President Kaczyński; the final Polish contingent left Iraq in October 2008. In March 2009 Tusk announced that the 1,600-member Polish force supporting the US-led coalition in Afghanistan would be reinforced by 400 troops, and by mid-2011 Polish troops numbered 2,600. However, Minister of National Defence Bogdan Klich announced in June 2010 that Polish troops should be withdrawn from Afghanistan by 2013, subject to several criteria being met, including the assumption of control by Afghan forces of the districts in the Ghazni province, where the majority of Poland's troops were deployed.

At a NATO summit meeting, which took place in Bucharest, Romania, in April 2008, member states endorsed US plans to position missile defence bases (forming part of its proposed National Missile Defence programme) in Poland and the Czech Republic. On 20 August a treaty was signed in Warsaw between Polish Minister of Foreign Affairs Radosław Sikorski and US Secretary of State Condoleezza Rice, providing for the installation of 10 US anti-missile interceptors, and guaranteeing the permanent stationing of US missiles, in Poland. The announcement prompted immediate protests by Russia: in early September the Russian Minister of Foreign Affairs, Sergei Lavrov, during a visit to Warsaw, reiterated that the missile installation presented a threat to Russian security (despite assurances by the US Administration that this was not so). Meanwhile, Russian President Dmitrii Medvedev announced that the Russian Government would respond by stationing short-range missiles in the bordering Russian exclave of Kaliningrad Oblast. However, following the election of US President Barack Obama in November, the new US Administration indicated in early 2009 that it would review security policy, including the planned missile defence system. On 17 September President Obama informed Tusk that the US Administration had cancelled plans for the permanent missile defence installation in Poland. Two days later the Russian Government announced that its proposal to deploy missiles to Kaliningrad had been abandoned. In October Poland reached agreement on the deployment of a much smaller-scale installation of US missile interceptors.

CONSTITUTION AND GOVERNMENT

Under the Constitution, which came into force in October 1997, legislative power is vested in the bicameral Zgromadzenie Narodowe (National Assembly), which is elected for a four-year term and comprises the 100-member Senat (Senate, upper chamber) and the 460-member Sejm (Assembly, lower chamber). The Senat reviews the laws adopted by the Sejm and may propose their rejection. Senators and deputies are elected by universal, direct suffrage. In the Sejm, deputies are elected under a system of proportional representation. Executive power is vested in the President of the Republic, who is directly elected (a second ballot being held if necessary) for a five-year term and may be re-elected only once, and in the appointed Council of Ministers, led by the Prime Minister. The Council of Ministers is responsible to the Sejm for its activities. The judiciary is independent. Poland is divided into 16 voivodships (provinces) and 308 powiats (districts).

REGIONAL AND INTERNATIONAL CO-OPERATION

Poland is a member of the European Bank for Reconstruction and Development (EBRD, see p. 265) and the Council of Europe (see p. 250). In May 2004 Poland became a full member of the European Union (EU, see p. 270).

Poland became a member of the UN in 1955. As a contracting party to the General Agreement on Tariffs and Trade, Poland joined the World Trade Organization (WTO, see p. 430) in 1995. Poland is also a member of the Organisation for Economic Co-operation and Development (OECD, see p. 376) and the North Atlantic Treaty Organization (NATO, see p. 368).

ECONOMIC AFFAIRS

In 2009, according to the World Bank, Poland's gross national income (GNI), measured at average 2007–09 prices, was US $467,545m., equivalent to $12,260 per head (or $18,440 per head on an international purchasing-power parity basis). During 2000–09 the population decreased by 0.1%, while gross domestic product (GDP) per head increased, in real terms, at an average annual rate of 4.0%. Overall GDP increased, in real terms, at an average annual rate of 3.9% in 2000–09; growth was 1.7% in 2009.

Agriculture contributed 3.6% of GDP and engaged 15.2% of the employed labour force in 2009. The principal crops are sugar beet, potatoes, wheat, barley and rye. Livestock production is important to the domestic food supply. According to World Bank estimates, during 2000–09 the GDP of the agricultural sector increased, in real terms, by an average annual rate of 1.7%; real agricultural GDP increased by 3.0% in 2009.

Industry (including mining, manufacturing, power and construction) accounted for 29.9% of GDP and engaged 27.2% of the employed labour force in 2009. According to World Bank estimates, during 2000–09 industrial GDP increased, in real terms, by an average of 4.9% per year; real industrial GDP increased by 4.4% in 2009.

Mining and quarrying contributed 2.5% of GDP and engaged 1.3% of the employed labour force in 2008. Poland is a significant producer of copper, silver and sulphur, and there are also considerable reserves of natural gas and coal. At the end of 2008 Poland's proven coal reserves stood at 7,502m. metric tons. During 1992–96 mining GDP declined at an average annual rate of 1.5%; the sector's GDP declined by an estimated 4.6% in 1998.

The manufacturing sector contributed 16.2% of GDP in 2009 and engaged 20.4% of the employed labour force in 2008. According to World Bank estimates, in 2000–09 manufacturing GDP increased, in real terms, at an average annual rate of 7.2%. Manufacturing GDP increased by 5.2% in 2009.

The construction sector contributed 7.8% of GDP in 2009 and engaged 7.8% of the employed labour force in 2008.

Energy is derived principally from coal, which satisfied 93.0% of the country's total energy requirements in 2007. In 1998 the Government announced plans to reduce Poland's dependence on coal: it was projected that by 2010 some 15% of power generation would be fuelled by imported natural gas. Mineral fuels and lubricants accounted for 11.3% of the value of merchandise imports in 2008; some 6.5% of electricity generated was exported in 2000.

The services sector contributed 66.5% of GDP and engaged 57.5% of the employed labour force in 2009. Services expanded rapidly from the early 1990s, with considerable growth in financial services, retailing, tourism and leisure. According to World Bank estimates, the GDP of the services sector increased, in real terms, by an average of 3.6% per year in 2000–09. Real services GDP increased by 1.8% in 2009.

In 2008 Poland recorded a visible trade deficit of US $4,355m., and there was a deficit of $9,598m. on the current account of the balance of payments. In 2008 the principal source of imports was Germany (accounting for 23.0%); other major suppliers were Russia, the People's Republic of China and Italy. Germany was also the principal market for exports (25.1%); other significant purchasers were France, Italy, the United Kingdom, the Czech Republic and Russia. The principal exports in 2008 were machinery and transport equipment (accounting for 41.2% of all exports), basic manufactures, miscellaneous manufactured articles, food and live animals, and chemicals and related products. The principal imports in that year were machinery and transport equipment (which accounted for 34.9% of total imports), basic manufactures, chemicals and related products, mineral fuels and lubricants, miscellaneous manufactured articles, and food and live animals.

According to estimates by the IMF, Poland's budgetary surplus for 2009 was some 42,456m. new złotys, equivalent to 3.0% of GDP. Poland's general government gross debt was 684,365m. new złotys in 2009, equivalent to 50.9% of GDP. Poland's external debt totalled US $218,022m. at the end of 2009, of which $43,426m. was public and publicly guaranteed debt. In 2009 the cost of debt-servicing was equivalent to 25.0% of the value of exports of goods, services and income. According to ILO estimates, the average annual rate of inflation was 2.8% in 2000–10.

Consumer prices increased by 2.6% in 2010. In 2008 7.1% of the labour force were registered as unemployed.

After the Government of Prime Minister Donald Tusk took office in late 2007, the need to reduce the budgetary deficit to less than 3% of GDP, prior to Poland's planned adoption of the euro, remained the most challenging element of economic policy. In late 2008 the global financial crisis led to a significant weakening of the national currency, the złoty, and in mid-2009 the IMF provided US $20,600m. of funding under a new flexible credit line, to support the economy in the event of further financial turmoil. Despite the economic downturn, Poland recorded GDP growth of 1.7% in 2009, according to the IMF, and this accelerated in 2010 to 3.8%. The IMF announced that Poland was the only EU country to have avoided recession in 2009, owing to its exchange-rate flexibility and a lack of reliance on export trade. However, the general government deficit increased, from less than 2% of GDP in 2007 to 7.9% in 2010. Despite further GDP growth of 3.8% predicted for 2011, in November 2010 it was reported that general debt had reached 750,000m. złoty, just under 55% of GDP forecast for that year. If debt were to exceed 55%, the Government would be obliged by law to reduce the budget deficit the following year. The election of President Komorowski in July 2010 (see Domestic Political Affairs) brought about a consolidation of power, with both the President and Prime Minister now being from the reformist PO, leading observers to believe that much-needed economic reforms, to which the late President Kaczyński had been opposed, could now be implemented. The IMF in October praised Poland's fiscal consolidation efforts and forecast a gradual erosion of the government deficit to 3% of GDP by 2013. In late 2009 the Government announced plans for a large-scale privatization programme, and intended to delay its adoption of the euro until at least 2015, particularly given widespread concern about the possible effects on other European countries of the debt crisis experienced by Greece at that time. The official budget for 2011 outlined austerity measures to reduce public spending and explore alternative means of generating revenue; the EU allocated €67,000m. in structural funds for the period 2007–13, some of which was to be used to develop the transport network in an attempt to encourage greater foreign investment.

PUBLIC HOLIDAYS

2012: 1 January (New Year's Day), 9 April (Easter Monday), 1 May (State Holiday), 3 May (Polish National Day, Proclamation of 1791 Constitution), 7 June (Corpus Christi), 15 August (Assumption), 1 November (All Saints' Day), 11 November (Independence Day), 25–26 December (Christmas).

Statistical Survey

Source (unless otherwise indicated): Główny Urząd Statystyczny (Central Statistical Office), 00-925 Warsaw, Al. Niepodległości 208; tel. (22) 6083161; fax (22) 6083869; internet www.stat.gov.pl.

Area and Population

AREA, POPULATION AND DENSITY

Area (sq km)	
Land	311,888
Inland water	791
Total	312,679*
Population (census results)†	
7 December 1988	37,879,105
20 May 2002	
Males	18,516,403
Females	19,713,677
Total	38,230,080
Population (official estimates at 31 December)†	
2007	38,115,641
2008	38,135,876
2009	38,167,329
Density (per sq km) at 31 December 2009	122.1

* 120,726 sq miles.
† Figures exclude civilian foreign nationals within the country and include civilian nationals temporarily outside the country.

POPULATION BY AGE AND SEX
(official estimates at 31 December 2009)

	Males	Females	Total
0–14	2,968,048	2,814,729	5,782,777
15–64	13,516,264	13,706,818	27,223,082
65 and over	1,944,430	3,217,040	5,161,470
Total	18,428,742	19,738,587	38,167,329

VOIVODSHIPS
(official estimates at 31 December 2009)

	Area (sq km)	Population ('000)	Density*	Principal city
Dolnośląskie	19,947	2,876.6	144.2	Wrocław
Kujawsko-Pomorskie	17,972	2,069.1	115.1	Bydgoszcz
Lubelskie	25,122	2,157.2	85.9	Lublin
Lubuskie	13,988	1,010.0	72.2	Gorzów Wlkp†
Łódzkie	18,219	2,541.8	139.5	Łódź
Małopolskie	15,183	3,298.3	217.2	Kraków
Mazowieckie	35,558	5,222.2	146.9	Warsaw
Opolskie	9,412	1,031.1	109.6	Opole
Podkarpackie	17,845	2,101.7	117.8	Rzeszów
Podlaskie	20,187	1,189.7	58.9	Białystok
Pomorskie	18,310	2,230.1	121.8	Gdańsk
Śląskie	12,333	4,640.7	376.3	Katowice
Świętokrzyskie	11,711	1,270.1	108.5	Kielce
Warmińsko-Mazurskie	24,174	1,427.1	59.0	Olsztyn
Wielkopolskie	29,826	3,408.2	114.3	Poznań
Zachodniopomorskie	22,892	1,693.2	74.0	Szczecin
Total	312,679	38,167.3	122.1	—

* Per sq km.
† Gorzów Wielkopolski.

POLAND

PRINCIPAL TOWNS
(official estimates at 31 December 2009)

Town	Population	Town	Population
Warszawa (Warsaw, the capital)	1,714,446	Olsztyn	176,457
Kraków	755,000	Bielsko-Biała	175,402
Łódź	742,387	Rzeszów	172,770
Wrocław	632,146	Ruda Śląska	143,394
Poznań	554,221	Rybnik	141,372
Gdańsk	456,591	Tychy	129,449
Szczecin	406,307	Dąbrowa Górnicza	127,686
Bydgoszcz	357,650	Płock	126,542
Lublin	349,440	Elbląg	126,419
Katowice	308,548	Opole	125,792
Białystok	294,685	Gorzów Wielkopolski	125,383
Gdynia	247,859	Wałbrzych	121,363
Częstochowa	239,319	Zielona Góra	117,503
Radom	223,397	Włocławek	117,402
Sosnowiec	219,300	Tarnów	115,158
Toruń	205,718	Chorzów	113,007
Kielce	204,835	Kalisz	107,019
Gliwice	196,167	Koszalin	106,987
Zabrze	187,674	Legnica	104,178
Bytom	182,749		

BIRTHS, MARRIAGES AND DEATHS

	Registered live births Number	Rate (per 1,000)	Registered marriages Number	Rate (per 1,000)	Registered deaths Number	Rate (per 1,000)
2002	353,765	9.3	191,935	5.0	359,486	9.4
2003	351,072	9.2	195,446	5.1	365,230	9.6
2004	356,131	9.3	191,824	5.0	363,522	9.5
2005	364,383	9.6	206,916	5.4	368,285	9.7
2006	376,035	9.8	226,181	5.9	369,686	9.7
2007	387,873	10.2	248,702	6.5	377,226	9.9
2008	414,499	10.9	257,744	6.8	379,399	9.9
2009	417,589	11.0	250,794	6.6	384,940	10.1

Life expectancy (years at birth, WHO estimates): 76 (males 71; females 80) in 2008 (Source: WHO, *World Health Statistics*).

IMMIGRATION AND EMIGRATION
('000)*

	2007	2008	2009
Immigrants	15.0	15.3	17.4
Emigrants	35.5	30.1	18.6

* Figures refer to immigrants arriving for permanent residence in Poland and emigrants leaving for permanent residence abroad.

ECONOMICALLY ACTIVE POPULATION*
('000 persons aged 15 years and over)

	2005	2006	2007
Agriculture, hunting and forestry	2,439	2,294	2,239
Fishing	13	10	8
Mining and quarrying	225	237	248
Manufacturing	2,831	2,988	3,162
Electricity, gas and water supply	228	223	218
Construction	843	925	1,054
Wholesale and retail trade; repair of motor vehicles, motorcycles, and personal and household goods	2,020	2,060	2,264
Hotels and restaurants	247	272	291
Transport, storage and communications	862	942	973
Financial intermediation	294	329	363
Real estate, renting and business activities	822	836	953
Public administration and defence; compulsory social security	892	917	937
Education	1,103	1,140	1,128

—continued	2005	2006	2007
Health and social work	820	871	871
Other community, social and personal service activities	459	534	511
Private households with employed persons	12	11	16
Sub-total	14,110	14,589	15,236
Activities not adequately defined and unallocated	5	5	5
Total employed	14,116	14,594	15,241
Unemployed	3,045	2,344	1,619
Total labour force	17,161	16,938	16,860
Males	9,362	9,283	9,234
Females	7,800	7,653	7,626

* Excluding regular military personnel living in barracks, and conscripts.

Note: Totals may not be equal to the sum of component parts, owing to rounding.

2008: Agriculture, forestry and fishing 2,206; Mining and quarrying 234; Manufacturing 3,228; Electricity, gas, steam, air conditioning and water supply 340; Construction 1,234; Wholesale and retail trade, repair of motor vehicles and motorcycles 2,326; Transport and storage 897; Accommodation and food service activities 307; Information and communications 295; Financial and insurance activities 340; Real estate activities 143; Professional, scientific and technical activities 411; Administrative and support service activities 363; Public administration, defence and compulsory social security 984; Education 1,184; Human health and social work activities 857; Arts, entertainment and recreation 197; Other service activities 225; Activities of households as employers 19; *Sub-total* 15,792; Not classified by economic activity 8; *Total employed* 15,800; Unemployed 1,211; *Total labour force* 17,011 (males 9,317, females 7,694).

Source: ILO.

Health and Welfare

KEY INDICATORS

Total fertility rate (children per woman, 2008)	1.3
Under-5 mortality rate (per 1,000 live births, 2008)	7
HIV/AIDS (% of persons aged 15–49, 2007)	0.1
Physicians (per 1,000 head, 2005)	2.0
Hospital beds (per 1,000 head, 2005)	5.2
Health expenditure (2007): US $ per head (PPP)	1,035
Health expenditure (2007): % of GDP	6.4
Health expenditure (2007): public (% of total)	70.9
Access to sanitation (% of total population, 2008)	90
Total carbon dioxide emissions ('000 metric tons, 2007)	317,119.2
Carbon dioxide emissions per head (metric tons, 2007)	8.3
Human Development Index (2010): ranking	41
Human Development Index (2010): value	0.795

For sources and definitions, see explanatory note on p. vi.

Agriculture

PRINCIPAL CROPS
('000 metric tons)

	2007	2008	2009
Wheat	8,317.3	9,274.9	9,789.6
Barley	4,008.1	3,619.5	3,983.9
Maize	1,722.3	1,844.4	1,706.6
Rye	3,125.7	3,448.6	3,712.9
Oats	1,462.3	1,262.4	1,415.4
Triticale (wheat-rye hybrid)	4,147.1	4,459.6	5,234.0
Mixed grain	4,257.4	3,672.9	3,884.1
Potatoes	11,791.1	10,462.1	9,702.8
Sugar beet	12,681.6	8,715.1	10,849.2
Rapeseed	2,129.9	2,105.8	2,496.8
Cabbages and other brassicas	1,389.2	1,256.5	1,337.3
Tomatoes	689.7	702.5	709.2
Cauliflowers and broccoli	282.4	274.9	291.1

POLAND

—continued

	2007	2008	2009
Cucumbers and gherkins	511.4	501.6	480.6
Onions, dry	752.5	618.2	707.8
Carrots and turnips	938.2	817.0	913.3
Mushrooms and truffles*	180.0	180.0	180.0
Apples	1,040.0	2,830.9	2,626.3
Pears	30.7	72.8	83.0
Sour (Morello) cherries	107.7	201.7	189.2
Plums and sloes	53.5	113.6	120.7
Strawberries	174.6	200.7	198.9
Currants	138.6	196.6	196.5

* FAO estimates.

Aggregate production ('000 metric tons, may include official, semi-official or estimated data): Total cereals 27,143 in 2007, 27,664 in 2008, 29,826 in 2009; Total roots and tubers 11,791 in 2007, 10,462 in 2008, 9,703 in 2009; Total vegetables (incl. melons) 6,014 in 2007, 5,507 in 2008, 5,786 in 2009; Total fruits (excl. melons) 1,731 in 2007, 3,880 in 2008, 3,687 in 2009.

Source: FAO.

LIVESTOCK
('000 head year ending September)

	2007	2008	2009
Horses	329	325	298
Cattle	5,696	5,757	5,700
Pigs	18,129	15,425	14,279
Sheep	332	324	286
Chickens	133,072	128,788	124,129
Geese and guinea fowls	3,814	3,881	4,039
Turkeys	8,019	7,745	8,065
Ducks	5,551	4,837	4,327

Source: FAO.

LIVESTOCK PRODUCTS
('000 metric tons)

	2007	2008	2009
Cattle meat	379.5	393.4	403.3
Pig meat	2,150.7	1,920.4	1,734.9
Horse meat	12.6	1.1	13.5
Game meat*	11.3	11.3	n.a.
Chicken meat	896.5	729.8	1,059.8
Duck meat*	17.0	17.0	17.0
Turkey meat*	60.0	60.0	60.0
Cows' milk	12,096.0	12,425.3	12,447.2
Hen eggs	546.7	581.7	605.0
Honey	15.0	14.0	14.0

* FAO estimates.

Source: FAO.

Forestry

ROUNDWOOD REMOVALS
('000 cubic metres, excl. bark)

	2007	2008	2009
Sawlogs, veneer logs and logs for sleepers	15,772	14,138	13,604
Pulpwood	14,800	14,610	15,385
Other industrial wood	1,889	1,721	1,486
Fuel wood	3,474	3,804	4,154
Total	35,935	34,273	34,629

Source: FAO.

SAWNWOOD PRODUCTION
('000 cubic metres, incl. railway sleepers)

	2007	2008	2009
Coniferous (softwood)	3,770	3,299	3,153
Broadleaved (hardwood)	647	487	441
Total	4,416	3,786	3,594

Source: FAO.

Fishing
('000 metric tons, live weight)

	2006	2007	2008
Capture	144.5	151.8	142.5
Freshwater fishes	21.4	21.7	21.1
European flounder	9.4	10.7	9.1
Atlantic cod	15.9	11.8	11.3
Atlantic herring	22.1	25.2	16.8
European sprat	55.9	60.2	55.6
Antarctic krill	6.4	7.4	8.0
Aquaculture	35.9	35.6*	36.8*
Common carp	15.6	15.7	17.2
Rainbow trout	17.0	16.7	16.5
Total catch	181.4	187.4*	179.3*

* FAO estimate.

Source: FAO.

Mining
('000 metric tons, unless otherwise indicated)

	2006	2007	2008
Hard coal	95,220	88,313	84,345
Brown coal (incl. lignite)	60,844	57,538	59,668
Crude petroleum	797	721	756
Salt (unrefined)	4,029	3,522	3,518
Native sulphur	800	834	762
Copper ore (metric tons)*	559,894	505,900	482,400
Lead ore (metric tons)*	82,800	104,200	108,000†
Magnesite ore—crude	63,000	65,000	65,000†
Silver (metric tons)*	1,270	1,244	1,220†
Zinc ore (metric tons)*	144,800	136,100	130,000†
Natural gas (million cu metres)	5,650	5,652	5,382

* Figures refer to the metal content of ores.
† Estimate.

Source: US Geological Survey.

Industry

SELECTED PRODUCTS
('000 metric tons, unless otherwise indicated)

	2007	2008	2009
Sausages and smoked meat	845	899	n.a.
Refined sugar	2,062	1,553	1,683
Margarine	345	341	363
Beer ('000 hl)	36,896	37,108	36,236
Wine, mead and other fermented beverages ('000 hl)	2,456	2,230	1,947
Cigarettes (million)	123,960	130,171	115,450
Leather footwear ('000 pairs)	15,154	13 377	11,418
Mechanical wood pulp*	65,354	48,875	20,290
Chemical wood pulp*	813,758	819,945	826,266
Newsprint*	204	170	166
Rubber tyres ('000)[1]	43,701	42,922	51,949
Sulphuric acid—100%	2,010	1,813	1,243
Caustic soda—96%	101	80	75
Soda ash—98%	1,132	1,140	n.a.
Nitrogenous fertilizers (a)[2]	5,087	4,825	4,472
Phosphate fertilizers (b)[2]	466	458	146
Motor spirit—Petrol[3]	4,035	4,128	4,283
Diesel oils	7,573	8,529	9,016
Coke-oven coke	7,906	7,653	5,305
Cement	17,120	17,207	15,537
Pig-iron[4]	5,804	4,934	2,984
Crude steel	10,631	9,727	7,128
Rolled steel products	8,011	7,610	6,232
Aluminium—unwrought[5]	37.2	29.5	10.3
Refined copper—unwrought	518	493	458

POLAND

—continued	2007	2008	2009
Refined lead—unwrought	59.9	62.2	49.4
Zinc—unwrought[5]	65	n.a.	n.a.
Radio receivers ('000)	33	22	18
Television receivers ('000)[6]	15,936	17,563	23,506
Merchant ships launched (gross reg. tons)	517	453	337
Passenger motor cars ('000)	695	842	819
Lorries and tractors (number)	88,528	90,890	52,213
Domestic washing machines ('000)	1,938	2,492	3,281
Domestic refrigerators and freezers ('000)	2,305	2,253	1,886
Electric energy (million kWh)	158,670	153,030	151,758

* Source: FAO.
[1] Tyres for passenger motor cars and commercial vehicles, including inner tubes and tyres for animal-drawn road vehicles, and tyres for non-agricultural machines and equipment.
[2] Fertilizer production is measured in terms of (a) nitrogen or (b) phosphoric acid. Phosphate fertilizers include ground rock phosphate.
[3] Including synthetic products.
[4] Including blast furnace ferro-alloys.
[5] Figures refer to both primary and secondary metal. Zinc production includes zinc dust and remelted zinc.
[6] Including monitors.

Finance

CURRENCY AND EXCHANGE RATES

Monetary Units
100 groszy (singular: grosz) = 1 new złoty.

Sterling, Dollar and Euro Equivalents (31 December 2010)
£1 sterling = 4.640 new złotys;
US $1 = 2.964 new złotys;
€1 = 3.961 new złotys;
100 new złotys = £21.55 = $33.74 = €25.25.

Average Exchange Rate (new złotys per US dollar)
2008   2.409
2009   3.120
2010   3.015

GOVERNMENT FINANCE
(general government transactions, non-cash basis, million new złotys)

Summary of Balances

	2007	2008	2009
Revenue	463,651	496,968	497,099
Less Expense	461,284	512,023	550,623
Net operating balance	2,367	−15,055	−53,524
Less Net acquisition of non-financial assets	22,840	32,867	42,456
Net lending/borrowing	−20,473	−47,922	−95,980

Revenue

	2007	2008	2009
Taxes	268,878	291,832	274,128
Taxes on income, profits and capital gains	93,515	102,529	93,083
Taxes on goods and services	153,437	165,851	158,124
Social contributions	140,422	144,337	152,085
Grants	5,841	7,826	12,743
Other revenue	48,510	52,973	58,143
Total	463,651	496,968	497,099

Expense/Outlays

Expense by economic type	2007	2008	2009
Compensation of employees	112,867	126,714	137,447
Use of goods and services	69,163	76,027	71,601
Consumption of fixed capital	22,191	22,513	24,252
Interest	24,145	30,491	34,863
Subsidies	6,389	7,306	7,541
Grants	11,477	13,529	14,291
Social benefits	190,261	206,659	228,715
Other expense	24,791	28,784	31,913
Total	461,284	512,023	550,623

Outlays by functions of government*	2007	2008	2009
General public services	60,804	69,530	77,841
Defence	18,815	20,560	12,468
Public order and safety	22,794	25,670	25,722
Economic affairs	48,634	61,535	70,430
Environmental protection	6,777	7,799	9,973
Housing and community amenities	8,833	10,785	12,299
Health	51,332	60,071	67,910
Recreation, culture and religion	12,734	15,596	17,653
Education	61,451	66,886	71,267
Social protection	191,950	206,458	227,516
Total	484,124	544,890	593,079

* Including net acquisition of non-financial assets.
Source: IMF, *Government Finance Statistics Yearbook*.

INTERNATIONAL RESERVES
(US $ million at 31 December)

	2008	2009	2010
Gold (national valuation)	2,862.1	3,652.9	4,666.4
IMF special drawing rights	108.7	2,099.5	2,006.5
Reserve position in IMF	265.9	430.3	497.9
Foreign exchange	58,931.0	73,393.6	86,317.4
Total	62,167.7	79,576.3	93,488.2

Source: IMF, *International Financial Statistics*.

MONEY SUPPLY
(million new złotys at 31 December)

	2008	2009	2010
Currency outside depository corporations	90,812	89,778	92,711
Transferable deposits	259,130	298,567	356,617
Other deposits	313,764	329,507	330,652
Securities other than shares	4,084	4,332	4,100
Broad money	667,790	722,184	784,080

Source: IMF, *International Financial Statistics*.

COST OF LIVING
(Consumer Price Index; base: 2000 = 100)

	2006	2007	2008
Food (incl. alcoholic beverages)	111.2	115.9	122.5
Electricity, gas and other fuels	138.1	143.2	157.5
Clothing (incl. footwear)	83.3	77.1	71.8
Rent	142.0	147.6	157.1
All items (incl. others)	115.7	118.6	123.6

2009: Food (incl. alcoholic beverages) 127.8; All items (incl. others) 127.9.
2010: Food (incl. alcoholic beverages) 131.1; All items (incl. others) 131.2.
Source: ILO.

POLAND

NATIONAL ACCOUNTS
(million new złotys at current prices)

Expenditure on the Gross Domestic Product

	2007	2008	2009
Government final consumption expenditure	211,027	236,103	247,753
Private final consumption expenditure	711,872	778,949	824,762
Changes in inventories	33,928	20,943	−11,081
Gross fixed capital formation	253,729	283,906	285,230
Total domestic expenditure	1,210,556	1,319,901	1,346,664
Exports of goods and services	479,606	508,888	530,278
Less Imports of goods and services	513,425	559,522	529,269
Statistical discrepancy	—	6,165	−4,016
GDP in market prices	1,176,737	1,275,432	1,343,657

Source: IMF, *International Financial Statistics*.

Gross Domestic Product by Economic Activity
(preliminary)

	2005	2006	2007
Agriculture, hunting, forestry and fishing	39,051	39,712	43,948
Construction	52,207	59,777	80,985
Other industry	213,836	231,402	236,983
Mining and quarrying	21,960	22,484	23,418
Manufacturing	160,374	176,406	179,339
Electricity, gas and water	31,502	32,512	34,226
Trade and repair	164,154	176,559	200,646
Other services	397,081	426,405	459,304
Gross value added in basic prices *	866,329	933,855	1,021,866
Taxes, *less* subsidies, on products	116,973	126,176	145,930
GDP in market prices	983,302	1,060,031	1,167,795

* Financial intermediation services indirectly measured (FISIM) is distributed to uses.

2007 (revised figures, provisional): Gross value added in basic prices 1,029,441.6 (Construction 73,459.2; Other industry 252,225.4; Market services 512,339.5; Non-market services 146,865.0); Taxes, less subsidies, on products 147,295.1; GDP in market prices 1,176,736.7.

2008 (revised figures, provisional): Gross value added in basic prices 1,116,476.4 (Construction 81,073.9; Other industry 271,035.6; Market services 560,353.3; Non-market services 162,316.9); Taxes, less subsidies, on products 158,955.9; GDP in market prices 1,275,432.3.

2009 Gross value added in basic prices 1,193,981.7 (Construction 87,545.0; Other industry 291,681.8; Market services 596,085.6; Non-market services 175,156.6); Taxes, less subsidies, on products 149,674.8; GDP in market prices 1,343,656.5.

2010 Gross value added in basic prices 1,246,823.0 (Construction 86,668.4; Other industry 308,089.8; Market services 625,896.6; Non-market services 182,082.9); Taxes, less subsidies, on products 165,961.2; GDP in market prices 1,412,784.2.

BALANCE OF PAYMENTS
(US $ million)

	2007	2008	2009
Exports of goods f.o.b.	145,337	178,427	142,085
Imports of goods f.o.b.	−162,394	−204,399	−146,440
Trade balance	−17,057	−25,972	−4,355
Exports of services	28,914	35,549	28,986
Imports of services	−24,156	−30,543	−24,191
Balance on goods and services	−12,299	−20,966	440
Other income received	10,140	11,126	7,304
Other income paid	−26,588	−23,970	−23,879
Balance on goods, services and income	−28,747	−33,810	−16,135
Current transfers received	15,244	16,633	15,336
Current transfers paid	−6,750	−8,377	−8,799
Current balance	−20,253	−25,554	−9,598
—*continued*	2007	2008	2009
Capital account (net)	4,771	6,115	7,040
Direct investment abroad	−5,664	−4,613	−5,100
Direct investment from abroad	23,651	14,978	13,796
Portfolio investment assets	−6,340	2,358	−264
Portfolio investment liabilities	925	−4,455	16,315
Financial derivatives liabilities	−2,046	−993	−1,692
Other investment assets	−1,771	5,217	5,275
Other investment liabilities	30,124	26,815	8,130
Net errors and omissions	−10,353	−21,825	−19,140
Overall balance	13,044	−1,957	14,761

Source: IMF, *International Financial Statistics*.

External Trade

PRINCIPAL COMMODITIES
(distribution by SITC, US $ million)

Imports c.i.f.	2006	2007	2008
Food and live animals	6,197.2	8,589.0	11,689.0
Crude materials (inedible) except fuels	3,764.6	4,836.6	6,313.4
Mineral fuels, lubricants, etc.	13,017.7	16,319.0	23,862.6
Chemicals and related products	16,690.9	20,980.7	26,839.6
Basic manufactures	25,676.9	34,093.6	38,618.5
Machinery and transport equipment	44,678.7	57,887.9	73,512.3
Miscellaneous manufactured articles	9,768.8	13,817.2	18,591.9
Total (incl. others)	125,645.3	164,172.5	210,478.5

Exports f.o.b.	2006	2007	2008
Food and live animals	9,130.0	11,519.1	14,206.7
Crude materials (inedible) except fuels	2,428.7	3,120.7	3,709.4
Mineral fuels, lubricants, etc.	4,909.9	5,222.4	7,296.7
Chemicals and related products	7,767.3	10,045.3	13,318.2
Basic manufactures	24,904.1	31,627.9	36,734.4
Machinery and transport equipment	43,870.3	56,661.0	70,736.1
Miscellaneous manufactured articles	14,254.0	17,460.3	21,035.1
Total (incl. others)	109,584.1	138,785.0	171,859.9

Source: UN, *International Trade Statistics Yearbook*.

PRINCIPAL TRADING PARTNERS
(US $ million)*

Imports c.i.f.	2006	2007	2008
Austria	2,146.3	2,733.6	3,611.1
Belgium	3,156.4	4,152.6	5,022.4
China, People's Republic	7,711.7	11,753.4	16,797.9
Czech Republic	4,380.8	5,673.8	7,532.2
Denmark	1,634.8	2,113.3	2,560.8
Finland	1,618.5	2,150.2	3,126.9
France (incl. Monaco)	6,883.6	8,380.5	9,946.8
Germany	30,144.5	39,399.7	48,514.0
Hungary	2,699.9	3,449.8	3,747.1
Italy	8,535.9	11,235.9	13,689.4
Japan	2,076.8	3,171.2	4,381.2
Korea, Republic	2,895.3	3,856.1	5,157.6
Netherlands	3,953.8	5,602.4	7,233.4
Norway	1,663.3	1,773.9	2,861.2
Russia	12,145.0	14,352.8	20,545.0
Slovakia	2,219.1	2,986.9	3,996.1
Spain	2,473.3	3,503.7	4,557.2
Sweden	2,770.0	3,622.3	4,367.9
Switzerland (incl. Liechtenstein)	1,282.1	1,628.6	2,091.3
Turkey	1,576.0	2,137.6	2,520.0
Ukraine	1,319.4	1,693.5	2,351.7
United Kingdom	3,600.4	5,107.0	5,968.3
USA	2,772.0	3,463.5	4,596.4
Total (incl. others)	125,645.3	164,172.5	210,478.5

POLAND

Exports f.o.b.	2006	2007	2008
Austria	2,008.2	2,609.3	3,366.6
Belgium	3,025.8	3,721.6	4,382.8
Czech Republic	6,066.9	7,683.8	9,803.7
Denmark	2,155.9	2,659.1	3,334.0
France (incl. Monaco)	6,823.1	8,443.1	10,668.0
Germany	29,701.3	35,901.2	43,104.5
Hungary	3,330.7	4,033.8	4,791.4
Italy	7,174.7	9,151.6	10,273.8
Lithuania	1,627.5	2,266.9	2,790.1
Netherlands	4,209.0	5,302.1	6,910.9
Norway	2,122.4	2,493.4	2,864.0
Romania	1,292.9	2,153.9	2,680.3
Russia	4,711.1	6,432.3	8,917.3
Slovakia	2,292.9	3,026.3	4,201.3
Spain	2,721.7	4,006.5	4,335.6
Sweden	3,512.8	4,464.6	5,465.4
Turkey	1,304.5	1,508.2	1,772.1
Ukraine	3,967.8	5,511.3	6,436.7
United Kingdom	6,254.0	8,238.0	9,900.6
USA	2,103.7	2,057.5	2,470.8
Total (incl. others)	109,584.1	138,785.0	171,859.9

* Imports by country of purchase; exports by country of sale.

Source: UN, *International Trade Statistics Yearbook*.

Transport

POLISH STATE RAILWAYS
(traffic)

	2007	2008	2009
Paying passengers ('000 journeys)	279,657	291,892	282,729
Passenger-km (million)	19,859	20,195	18,671
Freight carried ('000 metric tons)	245,346	248,860	201,226
Freight ton-km (million)	54,253	52,043	43,455

ROAD TRAFFIC
('000 motor vehicles registered at 31 December)

	2007	2008	2009
Passenger cars	14,589	16,080	16,495
Lorries and vans (incl. road tractors)	2,521	2,710	2,797
Buses and coaches	88	92	95
Motorcycles	825	909	975

INLAND WATERWAYS
(traffic, including coastal transport)

	2007	2008	2009
Passengers carried ('000)	1,490	1,791	1,671
Passenger-km (million)	33	35	30
Freight carried ('000 metric tons)	9,792	8,109	5,655
Freight ton-km (million)	1,338	1,274	1,020

SHIPPING

Merchant Fleet
(registered at 31 December)

	2007	2008	2009
Number of vessels	351	358	338
Displacement ('000 gross registered tons)	193.3	212.9	203.8

Source: IHS Fairplay, *World Fleet Statistics*.

Sea Transport
(by owned or leased ships)

	2001	2002	2003
Passengers carried ('000)	582	559	526
Passenger-kilometres (million)	154	150	137
Freight carried ('000 metric tons)	22,426	25,222	25,435
Freight ton-kilometres (million)	108,517	104,190	100,455

International Sea-borne Shipping at Polish Ports

	2001	2002	2003
Vessels entered ('000 net reg. tons)	39,594	41,563	50,794
Vessels entered (number)	32,299	30,212	29,771
Passengers ('000): arrivals	2,220	1,718	1,617
Passengers ('000): departures	2,197	1,587	1,572
Cargo ('000 metric tons): loaded*	31,526	33,168	35,848
Cargo ('000 metric tons): unloaded*	14,684	14,943	15,171

* Including ships' bunkers and transshipments.

Source: Centre of Maritime Statistics.

CIVIL AVIATION
(traffic on scheduled services)

	2004	2005	2006
Kilometres flown (million)	73	77	81
Passengers carried ('000)	3,493	3,554	3,701
Passenger-km (million)	5,861	6,223	6,720
Total ton-km (million)	654	687	735

Source: UN, *Statistical Yearbook*.

2007: Passengers carried ('000) 4,269.7 (Source: World Bank, World Development Indicators database).

2008: Passengers carried ('000) 4,634.8 (Source: World Bank, World Development Indicators database).

Tourism

FOREIGN TOURIST ARRIVALS
('000, including visitors in transit)

Country of residence	2008	2009	2010
Belarus	2,130	2,360	3,090
Czech Republic	7,820	8,180	9,240
Germany	34,630	26,070	25,860
Lithuania	1,930	2,640	2,690
Russia	1,290	1,210	1,530
Slovakia	3,740	5,040	6,010
Ukraine	3,320	3,820	5,030
Total (incl. others)	59,935	53,840	58,340

Source: Institute of Tourism.

Receipts from tourism (US $ million): 8,122 in 2006; 11,686 in 2007; 12,841 in 2008 (Source: World Tourism Organization).

Communications Media

	2006	2007	2008
Radio subscribers ('000)*	8,070	7,805	7,346
Television subscribers ('000)*	7,820	7,564	7,109
Telephones ('000 main lines in use)†	11,475.6	10,490.6	9,725.5
Mobile cellular telephones ('000 subscribers)†	36,745.5	41,388.8	43,926.4
Internet users ('000)†‡	17,012.9	18,532.2	20,244.7
Broadband subscribers ('000)†	2,911.2	4,174.0	4,440.8
Book production: titles§	24,640	25,226	28,248
Book production: copies (million)§	80.0	77.5	85.0
Daily and non-daily newspapers: number	n.a.	62	48
average circulation ('000 copies)	n.a.	5,450	4,711
Other periodicals: number	6,693	6,886	7,013
Other periodicals: average circulation ('000 copies)	n.a.	78,403	79,443

* At 31 December.
† Source: International Telecommunication Union.
‡ Estimates.
§ Including pamphlets.

2009: Telephones ('000 main lines in use) 9,587.1; Mobile cellular telephones ('000 subscribers) 44,806.6; Internet users ('000, estimate) 22,452.1; Broadband subscribers ('000) 4,921.4 (Source: International Telecommunication Union).

Personal computers: 6,456,000 (169.3 per 1,000 persons) in 2006 (Source: International Telecommunication Union).

Education

(2007/08 unless otherwise indicated)

	Institutions	Teachers*	Males	Females	Total
Pre-primary	17,337†	51,011	445.4	426.5	871.9
Primary	15,344‡	238,917	1,223.4	1,151.8	2,375.2
Secondary	17,825‡	279,408	1,585.1	1,499.9	3,085.0
Tertiary	400‡	100,500	918.8	1,247.2	2,166.0

Students ('000)*

* Data from UNESCO Institute for Statistics.
† 2001/02 figure.
‡ 2004/05 figure.

Pupil-teacher ratio (primary education, UNESCO estimate): 9.9 in 2007/08 (Source: UNESCO Institute for Statistics).

Adult literacy rate (UNESCO estimates): 99.5% (males 99.7%; females 99.3%) in 2008 (Source: UNESCO Institute for Statistics).

Directory

The Government

HEAD OF STATE

President: Bronisław Komorowski (elected 4 July 2010, assumed office 6 August 2010).

COUNCIL OF MINISTERS
(May 2011)

A coalition comprising the Civic Platform (PO), the Polish People's Party (PSL) and Independents.

Prime Minister: Donald Tusk (PO).
Deputy Prime Minister and Minister of the Economy: Waldemar Pawlak (PSL).
Minister of Internal Affairs and Administration: Jerzy Miller (Independent).
Minister of Foreign Affairs: Radosław Sikorski (PO).
Minister of National Defence: Bogdan Klich (PO).
Minister of the State Treasury: Aleksander Grad (PO).
Minister of Justice: Krzysztof Kwiatkowski (PO).
Minister of Science and Higher Education: Barbara Kudrycka (PO).
Minister of Labour and Social Policy: Jolanta Fedak (PSL).
Minister of National Education: Katarzyna Hall (PO).
Minister of Agriculture and Rural Development: Marek Sawicki (PSL).
Minister of Regional Development: Elżbieta Bieńkowska (Independent).
Minister of Culture and National Heritage: Bogdan Zdrojewski (PO).
Minister of Health: Ewa Kopacz (PO).
Minister of the Environment: Andrzej Kraszewski (Independent).
Minister of Finance: Jan (Jacek) Vincent-Rostowski (Independent).
Minister of Sport and Tourism: Adam Giersz (Independent).
Minister of Infrastructure: Cezary Grabarczyk (PO).
Minister, Member of the Council of Ministers: Michał Boni (Independent).

MINISTRIES

Chancellery of the President: 00-902 Warsaw, ul. Wiejska 10; tel. (22) 6952900; fax (22) 6952238; e-mail listy@prezydent.pl; internet www.prezydent.pl.

Chancellery of the Prime Minister: 00-583 Warsaw, Al. Ujazdowskie 1/3; tel. (22) 6946000; fax (22) 6252637; e-mail kontakt@kprm.gov.pl; internet www.kprm.gov.pl.

Ministry of Agriculture and Rural Development: 00-930 Warsaw, ul. Wspólna 30; tel. (22) 6231000; fax (22) 6232750; e-mail kanceleria@minrol.gov.pl; internet www.minrol.gov.pl.

Ministry of Culture and National Heritage: 00-071 Warsaw, ul. Krakowskie Przedmieście 15/17; tel. (22) 4210100; fax (22) 4210131; e-mail minister@mkidn.gov.pl; internet www.mkidn.gov.pl.

Ministry of the Economy: 00-507 Warsaw, pl. Trzech Krzyży 3/5; tel. (22) 6935000; fax (22) 6934048; e-mail mg@mg.gov.pl; internet www.mg.gov.pl.

Ministry of the Environment: 00-922 Warsaw, ul. Wawelska 52/54; tel. (22) 5792900; fax (22) 5792511; e-mail info@mos.gov.pl; internet www.mos.gov.pl.

Ministry of Finance: 00-916 Warsaw, ul. Świętokrzyska 12; tel. (22) 6945555; fax (22) 6944177; e-mail kancelaria@mf.gov.pl; internet www.mf.gov.pl.

Ministry of Foreign Affairs: 00-580 Warsaw, Al. Szucha 23; tel. (22) 5239000; fax (22) 6287819; e-mail dabw.sekretariat@msz.gov.pl; internet www.msz.gov.pl.

Ministry of Health: 00-952 Warsaw, ul. Miodowa 15; tel. (22) 6349600; fax (22) 6349213; e-mail kancelaria@mz.gov.pl; internet www.mz.gov.pl.

Ministry of Infrastructure: 00-928 Warsaw, ul. Chałubińskiego 4/6; tel. (22) 6301000; fax (22) 6301116; e-mail info@mi.gov.pl; internet www.mi.gov.pl.

Ministry of Internal Affairs and Administration: 02-591 Warsaw, ul. Stefana Batorego 5; tel. (22) 6014427; fax (22) 6227973; e-mail wp@mswia.gov.pl; internet www.mswia.gov.pl.

Ministry of Justice: 00-950 Warsaw, Al. Ujazdowskie 11; tel. (22) 5212888; fax (22) 6214986; e-mail bm@ms.gov.pl; internet www.ms.gov.pl.

Ministry of Labour and Social Policy: 00-513 Warsaw, ul. Nowogrodzka 1/3/5; tel. (22) 6610100; fax (22) 6611336; e-mail info@mpips.gov.pl; internet www.mps.gov.pl.

Ministry of National Defence: 00-911 Warsaw, Al. Niepodległości 218; tel. (22) 6840212; fax (22) 6840224; e-mail dpimon@wp.mil.pl; internet www.mon.gov.pl.

POLAND

Ministry of National Education: 00-918 Warsaw, Al. Szucha 25; tel. (22) 3474100; fax (22) 6283504; e-mail informacja@men.gov.pl; internet www.men.gov.pl.

Ministry of Regional Development: 00-926 Warsaw, ul. Wspólna 2/4; tel. (22) 4613000; fax (22) 4613275; internet www.mrr.gov.pl.

Ministry of Science and Higher Education: 00-529 Warsaw, ul. Wspólna 1/3; tel. (22) 5292718; fax (22) 6280922; e-mail sekretariat.minister@mnisw.gov.pl; internet www.nauka.gov.pl.

Ministry of Sport and Tourism: 00-921 Warsaw, ul. Senatorska 14; tel. (22) 2443142; fax (22) 2443255; e-mail kontakt@msport.gov.pl; internet www.msport.gov.pl.

Ministry of the State Treasury: 00-522 Warsaw, ul. Krucza 36; tel. (22) 6958000; fax (22) 6280872; e-mail minister@msp.gov.pl; internet www.msp.gov.pl.

President

Presidential Election, First Ballot, 20 June 2010

Candidates	Votes	%
Bronisław Komorowski	6,981,319	41.54
Jarosław Kaczyński	6,128,255	36.46
Grzegorz Napieralski	2,299,870	13.68
Janusz Korwin-Mikke	416,898	2.48
Waldemar Pawlak	294,273	1.75
Andrzej Olechowski	242,439	1.44
Marek Jurek	214,657	1.28
Andrzej Lepper	177,315	1.06
Others	51,144	0.31
Total	**16,806,170**	**100.00**

Second Ballot, 4 July 2010

Candidates	Votes	%
Bronisław Komorowski	8,933,887	53.01
Jarosław Kaczyński	7,919,134	46.99
Total	**16,853,021**	**100.00**

Legislature

The Zgromadzenie Narodowe (National Assembly) is bicameral, comprising the Sejm (Assembly), the lower chamber, and the Senat (Senate), the upper chamber.

Sejm
(Assembly)

00-902 Warsaw, ul. Wiejska 4/6; tel. (22) 6285927; e-mail zjablon@sejm.gov.pl; internet www.sejm.gov.pl.

Marshal: GRZEGORZ SCHETYNA.

Election, 21 October 2007

Parties and alliances	Votes	% of votes	Seats
Civic Platform (PO)	6,701,010	41.51	209
Law and Justice (PiS)	5,183,477	32.11	166
Left and Democrats (LiD)*	2,122,981	13.15	53
Polish People's Party (PSL)	1,437,638	8.91	31
German Minority (MN)	32,462	0.20	1
Self-Defence Party of the Republic of Poland (SRP)	247,335	1.53	—
League of Polish Families (LPR)	209,171	1.30	—
Others	208,128	1.29	—
Total	**16,142,202**	**100.00**	**460**

*A coalition of the Democratic Left Alliance (SLD), Polish Social Democracy (SDPL), the Democratic Party (PD) and the Union of Labour (UP).

Senat
(Senate)

00-902 Warsaw, ul. Wiejska 6; tel. (22) 6949265; fax (22) 6949428; internet www.senat.gov.pl.

Marshal: BOGDAN BORUSEWICZ.

Election, 21 October 2007

Parties and alliances	Seats
Civic Platform	60
Law and Justice	39
Independent	1
Total	**100**

Election Commission

Państwowa Komisja Wyborcza (PKW) (State Election Commission): 00-902 Warsaw, ul. Wiejska 10; tel. (22) 6250617; fax (22) 6293959; internet www.pkw.gov.pl; Pres. STEFAN JAN JAWORSKI.

Political Organizations

Civic Platform (PO) (Platforma Obywatelska): 00-159 Warsaw, ul. Andersa 21; tel. (22) 6357879; fax (22) 6357641; e-mail donald.tusk@sejm.pl; internet www.platforma.org; f. 2001 by independent presidential candidate and factions of the Freedom Union (UW) and Solidarity Electoral Action (AWS); conservative-liberal; Leader DONALD TUSK.

Democratic Left Alliance (SLD) (Sojusz Lewicy Demokratycznej): 00-419 Warsaw, ul. Rozbrat 44 A; tel. (22) 6210341; fax (22) 6216069; e-mail rk@sld.org.pl; internet www.sld.org.pl; f. 1999; contested 2007 legislative elections as mem. of Left and Democrats coalition; Chair. GRZEGORZ NAPIERALSKI.

Democratic Party (PD) (Partia Demokratyczna): 00-581 Warsaw, ul. Marszałkowska 2/4; tel. (22) 3355800; fax (22) 4651284; e-mail sekretariat@demokraci.pl; internet www.demokraci.pl; f. 2005 to replace Freedom Union (UW); contested 2007 legislative elections as mem. of Left and Democrats coalition; Leader BRYGIDA KUŹNIAK.

German Minority (Mniejszość Niemiecka—MN): 45-004 Opole, ul. M. Konopnickiej 6; tel. (77) 4021070; concerned with cultural and educational issues to help combat social problems; Chair. RASCH NORBERT.

Law and Justice (PiS) (Prawo i Sprawiedliwość): 02-018 Warsaw, ul. Nowogrodzka 84/86; tel. (22) 6215035; fax (22) 6216767; e-mail biuro@pis.org.pl; internet www.pis.org.pl; f. 2001; conservative; Pres. JAROSŁAW KACZYŃSKI.

League of Polish Families (LPR) (Liga Polskich Rodzin): 00-528 Warsaw, ul. Hoża 9; tel. (22) 6223648; fax (22) 6223138; e-mail info@lpr.pl; internet www.lpr.pl; f. 2001 as alliance comprising the National Party, All-Poland Youth, the Polish Accord Party, the Catholic National movement and the Peasant National Bloc; Roman Catholic, nationalist, anti-EU; Pres. WITOLD BAŁAŻAK.

Polish Labour Party (Polska Partia Pracy—PPP): 00-570 Warsaw, ul. Wyzwolenia 18; tel. (22) 3929180; e-mail bzietek@wzz.org.pl; internet www.partiapracy.pl; f. 2001; Chair. BOGUSŁAW ZIĘTEK.

Polish People's Party (PSL) (Polskie Stronnictwo Ludowe): 00-924 Warsaw, ul. Kopernika 36/40; tel. (22) 6206020; fax (22) 6543583; e-mail biuronkw@psl.org.pl; internet www.psl.pl; f. 1990 on basis of United Peasant Party (f. 1949) and Polish Peasant Party—Rebirth (f. 1989); centrist, advocates devt of agriculture and social market economy; Chair. WALDEMAR PAWLAK.

Polish Social Democracy (SDPL) (Socjaldemokracja Polski): 00-560 Warsaw, ul. Mokotowska 29A; tel. (22) 6213640; fax (22) 6215342; e-mail sdpl@sdpl.pl; internet www.sdpl.pl; f. 2004; contested 2007 legislative elections as mem. of Left and Democrats coalition; Chair. WOJCIECH FILEMONOWICZ.

Right of the Republic (PR) (Prawica Rzeczypospolitej): 00-687 Warsaw, ul. Wspólna 61/105; tel. (22) 3920554; e-mail lech.luczynski@prawicarzeczypospolitej.org; internet www.prawicarzeczypospolitej.org; f. 2007; opposed to abortion, euthanasia, and supportive of traditional Roman Catholic values; Leader MAREK JUREK.

Self-Defence Party of the Republic of Poland (SRP) (Partia Samoobrona Rzeczypospolitej Polskiej): 00-024 Warsaw, Al. Jerozolimskie 30; tel. (22) 6250472; fax (22) 6250477; e-mail samoobrona@samoobrona.org.pl; internet www.samoobrona.pl; agrarian, populist, anti-EU; Leader ANDRZEJ LEPPER.

Union of Labour (UP) (Unia Pracy): 00-513 Warsaw, ul. Nowogrodzka 4; tel. (22) 6256776; e-mail biuro@uniapracy.org.pl; internet www.uniapracy.org.pl; f. 1992; contested 2007 legislative elections as mem. of Left and Democrats coalition; Chair. WALDEMAR WITKOWSKI.

Women's Party (Partia Kobiet—PK): 00-278 Warsaw, ul. Kanonia 24/26; tel. (22) 644434; e-mail przewodniczaca@partiakobiet.org.pl;

internet www.polskajestkobieta.org; f. 2007; socially liberal; Chair. IWONA PIĄTEK.

Diplomatic Representation
EMBASSIES IN POLAND

Afghanistan: 02-954 Warsaw, ul. Goplańska 1; tel. (22) 8855410; fax (22) 8856500; e-mail warsaw@afghanembassy.com.pl; internet www.afghanembassy.com.pl; Ambassador ZIAUDDIN MOJADEDI.

Albania: 02-386 Warsaw, ul. Altowa 1; tel. (22) 8241427; fax (22) 8241426; e-mail embassy.warsaw@mfa.gov.al; Ambassador FLORENT ÇELIKU.

Algeria: 03-932 Warsaw, ul. Dąbrowiecka 21; tel. (22) 6175855; fax (22) 6160081; e-mail ambalggovdz@zigzag.pl; Ambassador ABDELKADER KHEMRI.

Angola: 02-635 Warsaw, ul. Balonowa 20; tel. (22) 6463529; fax (22) 8447452; e-mail embaixada@emb-angola.pl; Ambassador LIZETH NAWANGA SATUMBO PENA.

Argentina: 03-973 Warsaw, ul. Brukselska 9; tel. (22) 6176028; fax (22) 6177162; e-mail epolo@home.pl; Ambassador GERARDO MANUEL BIRITOS.

Armenia: 02-803 Warsaw, ul. Bekasów 50; tel. (22) 8990940; fax (22) 8990935; e-mail secretariat@armenia.internetdsl.pl; Ambassador ASHOT GALOYAN.

Australia: 00-513 Warsaw, ul. Nowogrodzka 11, 3rd Floor, Nautilus Bldg; tel. (22) 5213444; fax (22) 6273500; e-mail ambasada.australia@dfat.gov.au; internet www.poland.embassy.gov.au/wsaw/home.html; Ambassador RUTH LORRAINE PEARCE.

Austria: 00-748 Warsaw, ul. Gagarina 34; tel. (22) 8410081; fax (22) 8410085; e-mail warschau-ob@bmaa.gv.at; internet www.ambasadaaustrii.pl; Ambassador HERBERT KRAUSS.

Azerbaijan: 03-941 Warsaw, ul. Zwycięców 12; tel. (22) 6162188; fax (22) 6161949; e-mail warsaw@mission.mfa.gov.az; internet www.azembassy.pl; Ambassador HASAN AZIZ HASANOV.

Belarus: 02-952 Warsaw, ul. Wiertnicza 58; tel. (22) 7420990; fax (22) 7420980; e-mail poland@belembassy.org; internet www.belembassy.org/poland; Ambassador WIKTAR GAISENAK.

Belgium: 00-095 Warsaw, ul. Senatorska 34; tel. (22) 5512800; fax (22) 8285711; e-mail warsaw@diplobel.fed.be; internet www.diplomatie.be/warsawfr; Ambassador RAOUL ROGER DELCORDE.

Bosnia and Herzegovina: 00-789 Warsaw, ul. Humańska 10; tel. (22) 8569935; fax (22) 8481521; e-mail amb-bih.pl@poczta.internetdsl.pl; Ambassador KOVILJKA ŠPIRIĆ.

Brazil: 03-963 Warsaw, ul. Bajońska 15; tel. (22) 6174800; fax (22) 6178689; e-mail brasil@brasil.org.pl; internet www.brasil.org.pl; Ambassador CARLOS ALBERTO SIMAS MAGALHÃES.

Bulgaria: 00-540 Warsaw, Al. Ujazdowskie 33/35; tel. (22) 6294071; fax (22) 6282271; e-mail office@bgemb.com.pl; internet www.mfa.bg/en/57/pages/menu/501; Ambassador IVAN A. NAYDENOV.

Canada: 00-481 Warsaw, ul. Matejki 1/5; tel. (22) 5843100; fax (22) 5843190; e-mail wsaw@international.gc.ca; internet www.canada.pl; Ambassador DANIEL COSTELLO.

Chile: 02-925 Warsaw, ul. Okrężna 62; tel. (22) 8582330; fax (22) 8582329; e-mail embachile@onet.pl; internet www.embachile.pl; Ambassador JOSÉ MANUEL SILVA VIDAURRE.

China, People's Republic: 00-203 Warsaw, ul. Bonifraterska 1; tel. (22) 8313836; fax (22) 6354211; e-mail ambchina@pol.pl; internet www.chinaembassy.org.pl; Ambassador SUN YUXI.

Colombia: 03-936 Warsaw, ul. Zwycięzców 29; tel. (22) 6170973; fax (22) 6176684; e-mail embcol@medianet.pl; Ambassador JORGE ALBERTO BARRANTES ULLOA.

Croatia: 02-611 Warsaw, ul. Ignacego Krasickiego 25; tel. (22) 8442393; fax (22) 8444808; e-mail croemb.warszawa@mvpei.hr; internet pl.mvp.hr; Ambassador IVAN DEL VECHIO.

Cuba: 02-516 Warsaw, ul. Rejtana 15/8; tel. (22) 8481715; fax (22) 8482231; e-mail embacuba@medianet.pl; internet emba.cubaminrex.cu/polonia; Ambassador ROSARIO CRISTINA NAVAS MORATA.

Cyprus: 02-629 Warsaw, ul. Pilicka 4; tel. (22) 8444577; fax (22) 8442558; e-mail ambasada@ambcypr.pl; Ambassador KALLIOPI AVRAAM.

Czech Republic: 00-555 Warsaw, ul. Koszykowa 18; tel. (22) 5251850; fax (22) 5251898; e-mail warsaw@embassy.mzv.cz; internet www.mfa.cz/warsaw; Ambassador JAN SECHTER.

Denmark: 02-517 Warsaw, ul. Marszałkowska 142; tel. (22) 5652900; fax (22) 5652970; e-mail wawamb@um.dk; internet www.ambwarszawa.um.dk; Ambassador THOMAS ØSTRUP MILLER.

Ecuador: 02-516 Warsaw, ul. Rejtana 15/15; tel. (22) 8487230; fax (22) 8488196; e-mail eccupolonia@mmrree.gov.ec; Ambassador FABIÁN VALDIVIESO EGUIGUREN.

Egypt: 03-972 Warsaw, ul. Alzacka 18; tel. (22) 6176973; fax (22) 6179058; e-mail embassyofegypt@neostrada.pl; Ambassador FAHMY AHMED FAYED SALAMA.

Estonia: 02-639 Warsaw, ul. Karwińska 1; tel. (22) 8811810; fax (22) 8811812; e-mail embassy@estemb.pl; internet www.estemb.pl; Ambassador TAAVI TOOM.

Finland: 00-559 Warsaw, ul. Chopina 4/8; tel. (22) 5989500; fax (22) 6213442; e-mail sanomat.var@formin.fi; internet www.finland.pl; Ambassador VESA TAPANI HIMANEN.

France: 00-477 Warsaw, ul. Piękna 1; tel. (22) 5293000; fax (22) 5293001; e-mail presse@ambafrance-pl.org; internet www.ambafrance-pl.org; Ambassador FRANÇOIS BARRY MARTIN-DELONGCHAMPS.

Georgia: 03-976 Warsaw, ul. Berneńska 6; tel. (22) 6166221; fax (22) 6166226; e-mail warsaw.emb@mfa.gov.ge; internet www.poland.mfa.gov.ge; Ambassador NIKOLOZ NIKOLOZISHVILI.

Germany: 00-467 Warsaw, ul. Jazdów 12; tel. (22) 5841700; fax (22) 5841739; e-mail warszawa@wars.diplo.de; internet www.warschau.diplo.de; Ambassador RÜDIGER FREIHERR VON FRITSCH.

Greece: 00-432 Warsaw, ul. Górnośląska 35; tel. (22) 6229460; fax (22) 6229464; e-mail gremb.war@mfa.gr; internet www.greece.pl; Ambassador GABRIEL COPTSIDIS.

Holy See: 00-582 Warsaw, Al. J. Ch. Szucha 12, POB 163; tel. (22) 6288488; fax (22) 6284556; e-mail nuncjatura@episkopat.pl; Apostolic Nuncio Most Rev. CELESTINO MIGLIORE (Titular Archbishop of Canosa).

Hungary: 00-559 Warsaw, ul. Chopina 2; tel. (22) 6284451; fax (22) 6218561; e-mail mission.vao@kum.hu; internet www.mfa.gov.hu/kulkepviselet/PL/HU; Ambassador RÓBERT KISS.

India: 02-516 Warsaw, ul. Rejtana 15/2–7; tel. (22) 8495800; fax (22) 8496705; e-mail ambassador.office@indianembassy.pl; internet indembwarsaw.in; Ambassador DEEPAK VOHRA.

Indonesia: 03-903 Warsaw, ul. Estońska 3–5; tel. (22) 6175179; fax (22) 6174455; e-mail comwar@indonesianembassy.pl; internet www.indonesianembassy.pl; Ambassador DARMANSJAH DJUMALA.

Iran: 03-928 Warsaw, ul. Królowej Aldony 22; tel. (22) 6171585; fax (22) 6178452; e-mail iranemb@iranemb.warsaw.mfa.pl; internet www.iranemb.warsaw.pl; Ambassador SAMAD ALI LAKIZADEH.

Iraq: 03-932 Warsaw, ul. Dąbrowiecka 9A; tel. (22) 6175773; fax (22) 6177065; e-mail ambasada.irak@neostrada.pl; Ambassador Dr SAAD JAWAD QINDEEL.

Ireland: 00-496 Warsaw, ul. Mysia 5; tel. (22) 8496633; fax (22) 8498431; e-mail warsawembassy@dfa.ie; internet www.embassyofireland.pl; Ambassador EUGENE HUTCHINSON.

Israel: 02-078 Warsaw, ul. Krzywickiego 24; tel. (22) 5970500; fax (22) 8251607; e-mail ambass-sec@warsaw.mfa.gov.il; internet www.israel.pl; Ambassador ZVI RAV-NER.

Italy: 00-055 Warsaw, pl. Dąbrowskiego 6; tel. (22) 8263471; fax (22) 8278507; e-mail ambasciata.varsavia@esteri.it; internet www.ambvarsavia.esteri.it; Ambassador ALDO MANTOVANI.

Japan: 00-464 Warsaw, ul. Szwoleżerów 8; tel. (22) 6965000; fax (22) 6965001; e-mail info-cul@emb-japan.pl; internet www.pl.emb-japan.go.jp; Ambassador YUICHI KUSUMOTO.

Kazakhstan: 02-954 Warsaw, ul. Królowej Marysieńki 14; tel. (22) 6425388; fax (22) 6423427; e-mail kazdipmis@hot.pl; internet www.kazakhstan.pl; Ambassador ALEKSEI VOLKOV.

Korea, Democratic People's Republic: 00-728 Warsaw, ul. Bobrowiecka 1A; tel. (22) 8405813; fax (22) 8405710; e-mail korembpl@yahoo.com; Ambassador KIM PYONG IL.

Korea, Republic: 00-464 Warsaw, ul. Szwoleżerów 6; tel. (22) 5592900; fax (22) 5592905; e-mail koremb_waw@mofat.go.kr; Ambassador LEE JOON-JAE.

Kuwait: 00-486 Warsaw, ul. Franciszka Nullo 13; tel. (22) 6222860; fax (22) 6274314; e-mail embassy@kuwait-embassy.pl; Ambassador ADEL MUHAMMAD A. H. HAYAT.

Laos: 02-386 Warsaw, ul. Usypiskowa 8; tel. (22) 6686699; fax (22) 6686690; e-mail sotholaw@yahoo.com; Chargé d'affaires a.i. SIVIENGPHET PHETVORASACK.

Latvia: 03-928 Warsaw, ul. Królowej Aldony 19; tel. (22) 6171105; fax (22) 6171106; e-mail embassy.poland@mfa.gov.lv; internet www.latvia.pl; Ambassador EINARS SEMANIS.

Lebanon: 02-516 Warsaw, ul. Starościńska 1B/10–11; tel. (22) 8445065; fax (22) 6460030; e-mail embassy@lebanon.com.pl; internet www.lebanon.com.pl; Ambassador HIKMAD AOUAD.

Lithuania: 00-478 Warsaw, Al. Ujazdowskie 14; tel. (22) 6253368; fax (22) 6253440; e-mail amb.pl@urm.lt; internet www.lietuva.pl; Ambassador LORETTA ZAKAREVIČIENÉ.

Luxembourg: 00-789 Warsaw, ul. Słoneczna 15; tel. (22) 5078650; fax (22) 5078661; e-mail varsovie.amb@mae.etat.lu; Ambassador CONRAD BRUCH.

POLAND

Macedonia, former Yugoslav republic: 02-954 Warsaw, ul. Królowej Marysieńki 40; tel. (22) 6517291; fax (22) 6517292; e-mail ambrmwar@zigzag.pl; Ambassador FATMIR XHELADINI.

Malaysia: 03-902 Warsaw, ul. Gruzińska 3; tel. (22) 6174413; fax (22) 6176256; e-mail mwwarsaw@poczta.neostrada.pl; internet www.kln.gov.my/web/pol; Ambassador ROSMIDAH BINTE ZAHID.

Malta: 02-520 Warsaw, ul. Wiśniowa 40/4; tel. (22) 6464639; fax (22) 6464685; e-mail maltaembassy.warsaw@gov.mt; Ambassador GODWIN MONTANARO.

Mexico: 02-017 Warsaw, Al. Jerozolimskie 123, 20th Floor; tel. (22) 6468800; fax (22) 6464222; e-mail embamex@embamex.pl; internet www.sre.gob.mx/polonia; Ambassador (vacant).

Moldova: 02-710 Warsaw, ul. Imielińska 1; tel. and fax (22) 6462099; e-mail embassy@moldova.pl; internet www.polonia.mfa.md; Ambassador LURIE BODRUG.

Mongolia: 02-516 Warsaw, ul. Rejtana 15/16; tel. and fax (22) 8499391; e-mail mongamb@ikp.atm.com.pl; internet www.ambasadamongolii.pl; Ambassador OTGON DAMBIINYAM.

Montenegro: Warsaw, Al. Ujazdowskie 41; tel. 531208600 (mobile); e-mail dragica.ponorac@mfa.gov.me; Chargé d'affaires a.i. DRAGICA PONORAC.

Morocco: 02-516 Warsaw, ul. Starościńska 1/11–12; tel. (22) 8496341; fax (22) 8481840; e-mail info@moroccoembassy.org.pl; Ambassador MOHA OUALI TAGMA.

Netherlands: 00-468 Warsaw, ul. Kawalerii 10; tel. (22) 5591200; fax (22) 8402638; e-mail war@minbuza.nl; internet www.nlembassy.pl; Ambassador MARCEL KURPERSHOEK.

New Zealand: 00-536 Warsaw, Al. Ujazdowskie 51; tel. (22) 5210500; fax (22) 5210510; e-mail nzwsw@nzembassy.pl; internet www.nzembassy.com/poland; Chargé d'affaires a.i. PAUL WILLIS.

Nigeria: 02-516 Warsaw, ul. Starościńska 1B/17; tel. (22) 5424117; fax (22) 5424113; e-mail info@nigeriaembassy.pl; internet www.embassyofnigeria.pl; Ambassador ASALINA RAYMOND MAMUNO.

Norway: 00-559 Warsaw, ul. Chopina 2A; tel. (22) 6964030; fax (22) 6280938; e-mail emb.warsaw@mfa.no; internet www.amb-norwegia.pl; Ambassador ENOK NYGAARD.

Pakistan: 02-516 Warsaw, ul. Starościńska 1/1–2; tel. (22) 8494808; fax (22) 8491160; e-mail parepwarsaw@wp.pl; internet www.mofa.gov.pk/poland; Ambassador MURAD ALI.

Panama: 02-946 Warsaw, ul. Biedronki 13A; tel. (22) 6422143; fax (22) 6517616; e-mail panamaembassy@neostrada.pl; Ambassador BERNARDO DÍAZ DE ICAZA.

Peru: 02-516 Warsaw, ul. Starościńska 1/3; tel. (22) 6468806; fax (22) 6468617; e-mail embperpl@atomnet.pl; internet www.perupol.pl; Ambassador MARTHA CHAVARRI DUPUY.

Philippines: 00-956 Warsaw, ul. Lentz 11; tel. (22) 4902025; fax (60) 2541012; e-mail pe.warsaw@gmail.com; Chargé d'affaires a.i EDGARDO MANUEL.

Portugal: 03-905 Warsaw, ul. Francuska 37; tel. (22) 5111010; fax (22) 5111013; e-mail embaixada@embport.internetdsl.pl; internet www.ambasadaportugalii.pl; Ambassador JOSÉ DUARTE SEQUEIRA E SERPA.

Qatar: 00-493 Warsaw, ul. Prusa 2/271; tel. (22) 6222288; fax (22) 6225566; e-mail qtrembassypl@yahoo.com; Ambassador HADI NASER MANSOUR AL-HAJRI.

Romania: 00-559 Warsaw, ul. Chopina 10; tel. (22) 6215983; fax (22) 6285264; e-mail gpredescu@roembassypl.org; internet varsovia.mae.ro; Ambassador GHEORGHE PREDESCU.

Russia: 00-761 Warsaw, ul. Belwederska 49; tel. (22) 6213453; fax (22) 6253016; e-mail embassy@rusemb.pl; internet www.poland.mid.ru; Ambassador ALEKSANDER ALEKSEYEV.

Saudi Arabia: 00-739 Warsaw, ul. Stępińska 55; tel. (22) 8400000; fax (22) 8405636; e-mail info@saudiembassy.pl; internet www.saudiembassy.pl; Ambassador WALEED TAHER RADWAN.

Serbia: 02-729 Warsaw, Al. Rolna 175A–B; tel. (22) 6285161; fax (22) 6297173; e-mail embassy.warsaw@mfa.rs; internet warsaw.mfa.rs; Ambassador RADOJKO BOGOJEVIĆ.

Slovakia: 00-581 Warsaw, ul. Litewska 6; tel. (22) 5258110; fax (22) 5258122; e-mail emb.warsaw@mzv.sk; internet www.mzv.sk/varsava; Ambassador VASIL GRIVNA.

Slovenia: 02-516 Warsaw, ul. Starościńska 1/23–24; tel. (22) 8498282; fax (22) 8484090; e-mail vvr@gov.si; Ambassador MARJAN SETINC.

South Africa: 00-675 Warsaw, ul. Koszykowa 54, 6th Floor; tel. (22) 6256228; fax (22) 6256270; e-mail warsaw.political@foreign.gov.za; internet www.southafrica.pl; Ambassador L.S. TED PEKANE.

Spain: 00-459 Warsaw, ul. Myśliwiecka 4; tel. (22) 5834000; fax (22) 6225408; e-mail embesppl@mail.mae.es; Ambassador FRANCISCO FERNÁNDEZ FÁBREGAS.

Sri Lanka: 02-665 Warsaw, Al. Wilanowska 313A; tel. (22) 8538896; fax (22) 8435348; e-mail lankaemb@medianet.pl; internet www.srilankaembassy.com.pl; Ambassador PAMELA J. DEEN.

Sweden: 00-585 Warsaw, ul. Bagatela 3; tel. (22) 6408900; fax (22) 6408983; e-mail ambassaden.warszawa@foreign.ministry.se; internet www.swedenabroad.com/warsaw; Ambassador DAG FILIP HARTELIUS.

Switzerland: 00-540 Warsaw, Al. Ujazdowskie 27; tel. (22) 6280481; fax (22) 6210548; e-mail var.vertretung@eda.admin.ch; internet www.eda.admin.ch/warsaw; Ambassador BÉNÉDICT DE CERJAT.

Syria: 02-610 Warsaw, ul. Goszczyńskiego 30; tel. (22) 8484809; fax (22) 8489178; e-mail embsyria@palmyra.neostrada.pl; internet www.syrian-embassy.com; Chargé d'affaires a.i. Dr WISSAL ISSA.

Thailand: 00-790 Warsaw, ul. Willowa 7; tel. (22) 8496414; fax (22) 8492630; e-mail thaiemb@thaiemb.internetdsl.pl; internet www.thaiembassy.pl; Ambassador AKRASID AMATAYAKUL.

Tunisia: 00-459 Warsaw, ul. Myśliwiecka 14; tel. (22) 6286330; fax (22) 6216295; e-mail at.varsovie@ambtun.pl; Ambassador ALI IDOUDI.

Turkey: 02-622 Warsaw, ul. Malczewskiego 32; tel. (22) 6464321; fax (22) 6463757; e-mail turkemb@zigzag.pl; internet warsaw.emb.mfa.gov.tr; Ambassador REŞIT UMAN.

Ukraine: 00-580 Warsaw, Al. J. Ch. Szucha 7; tel. (22) 6293446; fax (22) 6298103; e-mail kancelaria@ukraine-emb.pl; internet www.mfa.gov.ua/poland; Ambassador MARKIYAN Z. MALSKY.

United Kingdom: 00-556 Warsaw, ul. Kawalerii 12; tel. (22) 3110000; fax (22) 3110311; e-mail info@britishembassy.pl; internet ukinpoland.fco.gov.uk; Ambassador DAMIAN RODERIC (RIC) TODD.

USA: 00-540 Warsaw, Al. Ujazdowskie 29/31; tel. (22) 5042000; fax (22) 5042688; e-mail publicwrw@state.gov; internet poland.usembassy.gov; Ambassador LEE ANDREW FEINSTEIN.

Uruguay: 02-516 Warsaw, ul. Rejtana 15/12; tel. (22) 8495040; fax (22) 6466887; e-mail urupol@urupol.ikp.pl; Ambassador JULIO GIAMBRUNO VIANA.

Uzbekistan: 02-804 Warsaw, ul. Kraski 21; tel. (22) 8946230; fax (22) 8946231; e-mail uzembassy@gmail.com; internet www.uzbekistan.pl; Chargé d'affaires a.i. UTKUR TURAEV.

Venezuela: 02-516 Warsaw, ul. Rejtana 15/20–21; tel. (22) 6468760; fax (22) 6468761; e-mail embajada@embavenez.pl; Chargé d'affaires a.i. JESÚS MIGUEL CRUZ GUEVARA.

Viet Nam: 02-956 Warsaw, ul. Resorowa 36; tel. (22) 6516098; fax (22) 6516095; e-mail office@ambasadawietnamu.org; internet www.vietnamembassy-poland.org; Ambassador NGUYEN VAN XUONG.

Yemen: 02-956 Warsaw, ul. Królewicza Jakuba 54; tel. (22) 6176025; fax (22) 6176022; e-mail biuro@ambasada-jemenu.pl; Ambassador ALI ALI ABD AL-AZIZ AQLAN.

Judicial System

Supreme Court (Sąd Najwyższy Rzeczpospolitej Polskiej): 00-951 Warsaw, pl. Krasińskich 2/4/6; tel. (22) 5308000; fax (22) 5309100; e-mail pp@sn.pl; internet www.sn.pl; the highest judicial organ; exercises supervision over the decision-making of all other courts; justices are appointed by the President of the Republic on motions of the National Council of Judiciary and serve until the age of retirement. The First President of the Supreme Court is appointed from among the Supreme Court Justices by the President of the Republic, and serves a six-year term. The First President is also the Chairman of the Tribunal of State (Trybunał Stanu), before which certain, constitutionally determined, high state positions are accountable for violations of the Constitution or statutes; First Pres. STANISŁAW DĄBROWSKI.

Supreme Administrative Court (Naczelny Sąd Administracyjny): 00-013 Warsaw, ul. Jasna 6; tel. (22) 5516000; fax (22) 8267531; e-mail informacje@nsa.gov.pl; internet www.nsa.gov.pl; f. 1980; examines complaints concerning the legality of administrative decisions; 11 regional brs; Pres. ROMAN HAUSER.

Constitutional Tribunal (Trybunał Konstytucyjny): 00-918 Warsaw, Al. J. Ch. Szucha 12A; tel. and fax (22) 6295526; e-mail prasainfo@trybunal.gov.pl; internet www.trybunal.gov.pl; comprises 15 judges, each appointed by the Sejm for a nine-year term; supervises compliance of legislation with the Constitution; Pres. ANDRZEJ RZEPLIŃSKI.

Religion

CHRISTIANITY

The Roman Catholic Church

The Roman Catholic Church was granted full legal status in May 1989, when legislation guaranteeing freedom of worship was approved. The Church was also permitted to administer its own affairs, and to operate schools, hospitals and other charitable organizations. A Concordat, agreed by the Polish Government and the Holy See in 1993, was ratified in January 1998.

For ecclesiastical purposes, Poland comprises 15 archdioceses (including one for the Catholics of the Byzantine-Ukrainian rite) and 28 dioceses (including one for the Catholics of the Byzantine-Ukrainian rite), an Ordinariate for the faithful of the Oriental rite, and a Military Ordinariate. There were some 34.3m. adherents in Poland (96.1% of the population) at 31 December 2008.

Bishops' Conference: 01-015 Warsaw, Skwer Kardynała Stefana Wyszyńskiego 6; tel. (22) 5304800; fax (22) 8380967; Pres. Most Rev. JÓZEF MICHALIK (Latin Rite Archbishop of Przemyśl).

Latin Rite

Archbishop of Białystok: Most Rev. EDWARD OZOROWSKI, 15-087 Białystok, Pl. Jana Pawła II 1; tel. (85) 7416473; fax (85) 7322213; e-mail sekretariat@bialystok.opoka.org.pl.

Archbishop of Częstochowa: Most Rev. STANISŁAW NOWAK, 42-200 Częstochowa, Al. Najśw. Maryi Panny 54; tel. (34) 3241044; fax (34) 3651182; e-mail kuria@czestochowa.opoka.org.pl.

Archbishop of Gdańsk: Most Rev. SŁAWOJ LESZEK GŁÓDŹ, 80-330 Gdańsk-Oliwa, ul. Biskupa Edmunda Nowickiego 1; tel. (58) 5520051; fax (58) 5522775; e-mail kuria@diecezja.gda.pl.

Archbishop of Gniezno, Primate of Poland: Most Rev. JÓZEF KOWALCZYK, 62-200 Gniezno, ul. Kanclerza Jana Łaskiego 7; tel. (61) 4262102; fax (61) 4262105; e-mail kuriagni@gniezno.opoka.org.pl.

Archbishop of Katowice: Most Rev. DAMIAN ZIMOŃ, 40-043 Katowice, ul. Jordana 39; tel. (32) 2512160; fax (32) 2514830; e-mail kancelaria@kuria.katowice.pl.

Archbishop of Kraków: Cardinal STANISŁAW DZIWISZ, 31-004 Kraków, ul. Franciszkańska 3; tel. (12) 6288100; fax (12) 4294617; e-mail kuria@diecezja.krakow.pl.

Archbishop of Łódź: Most Rev. WŁADYSŁAW ZIÓŁEK, 90-458 Łódź, ul. Ks Ignacego Skorupki 1; tel. (42) 6648700; fax (42) 6648796; e-mail kuria@archidiecezja.lodz.pl.

Archbishop of Lublin: (vacant), 20-950 Lublin, ul. Ks Prymasa Stefana Wyszyńskiego 2; tel. (81) 5321058; fax (81) 5346141; e-mail kanclerz@kuria.lublin.pl.

Archbishop of Poznań: Most Rev. STANISŁAW GĄDECKI, 61-109 Poznań, ul. Ostrów Tumski 2; tel. (61) 8512800; fax (61) 8512814; e-mail kuria@archpoznan.org.pl.

Archbishop of Przemyśl (Latin Rite): Most Rev. JÓZEF MICHALIK, 37-700 Przemyśl, pl. Katedralny 4A; tel. (16) 6786694; fax (16) 6782674; e-mail kuria@przemysl.opoka.org.pl.

Archbishop of Szczecin-Kamień: Most Rev. ANDRZEJ DZIĘGA, 71-459 Szczecin, ul. Papieża Pawła VI 4; tel. (91) 4542292; fax (91) 4536908; e-mail kuria@szczecin.opoka.org.pl.

Archbishop of Warmia: Most Rev. WOJCIECH ZIEMBA, 10-006 Olsztyn, ul. Pieniężnego 22; tel. (89) 5272280; fax (89) 5355172; e-mail kuria@olsztyn.opoka.org.pl.

Archbishop of Warsaw: Cardinal KAZIMIERZ NYCZ, 00-246 Warsaw, ul. Miodowa 17/19; tel. (22) 5317200; fax (22) 6354324; e-mail kanclerz@mkw.pl; internet www.spp.episkopat.pl.

Archbishop of Wrocław: Most Rev. MARIAN GOŁĘBIEWSKI, 50-328 Wrocław, ul. Katedralna 13; tel. (71) 3271111; fax (71) 3228269; e-mail kuria@archidiecezja.wroc.pl.

Byzantine-Ukrainian Rite

Archbishop of Przemyśl-Warsaw: Most Rev. IVAN MARTYNIAK, 37-700 Przemyśl, ul. Basztowa 13; tel. and fax (16) 6787868; e-mail kuria@przemyslgr.opoka.pl.

The Orthodox Church

Polish Autocephalous Orthodox Church (Polski Autokefaliczny Kościół Prawosławny): 03-402 Warsaw, Al. Solidarności 52; tel. (22) 6190886; fax (22) 6192996; e-mail kancelaria@orthodox.pl; internet www.orthodox.pl; comprises six dioceses, seven archbishoprics and three bishoprics; 509,500 mems (2001); Archbishop of Warsaw and Metropolitan of All Poland Sawa MICHAŁ HRYCUNIAK.

Protestant Churches

In 1999 there were an estimated 148,738 Protestants in Poland.

Evangelical Augsburg (Lutheran) Church in Poland (Kościół Ewangelicko-Augsburski czyli Luterański w Polsce): 00-246 Warsaw, ul. Miodowa 21; tel. (22) 8870200; fax (22) 8870218; e-mail biskup@luteranie.pl; internet www.luteranie.pl; 75,000 mems, 134 parishes (2007); Bishop and Pres. of Consistory JERZY SAMIEC.

Pentecostal Church in Poland (Kościół Zielonoświątkowy w Polsce): 00-825 Warsaw, ul. Sienna 68/70; tel. and fax (22) 5951820; e-mail sekretariat@kz.pl; internet www.kz.pl; f. 1910; 20,000 mems (2000); Chief Presbyter Bishop MIECZYSŁAW CZAJKO.

There are also several other small Protestant churches, including the Church of Christ, the Church of Evangelical Christians, the Evangelical Christian Church, the Jehovah's Witnesses, the Pentecostal Church, the Seventh-day Adventist Church and the United Methodist Church.

ISLAM

In 1999 there were about 5,125 Muslims, principally of Tatar origin, in Białystok Voivodship (Prefecture), in eastern Poland, and smaller communities in Warsaw, Gdańsk and elsewhere.

Religious Union of Muslims in Poland (Muzułmański Związek Religijny): 15-426 Białystok, Rynek Kosciuszki 26/2; tel. (85) 414970; Chair. STEFAN MUCHARSKI.

JUDAISM

The overwhelming majority of the Jewish population of Poland were killed during the occupation by Nazi Germany in the Second World War (1939–45). In the mid-2000s there were believed to be between 10,000 and 20,000 Jews in Poland.

Union of Jewish Communities in Poland (Związek Gmin Wyznaniowych Żydowskich w Rzeczypospolitej Polskiej): 00-950 Warsaw, ul. Twarda 6; tel. (22) 6204324; fax (22) 6201037; e-mail union@jewish.org.pl; 14 synagogues and about 2,500 registered mems; Pres. PIOTR KADLČIK.

The Press

In 2008 there were 48 newspapers in Poland, with a total circulation of 4,711,000. In that year there were 7,013 periodicals, with a combined circulation of 79.4m. copies.

Axel Springer Polska Sp. z o.o.: 02-672 Warsaw, ul. Domaniewska 52; tel. (22) 2320000; fax (22) 2325534; e-mail asp@axelspringer.pl; internet axelspringer.pl; subsidiary of Axel Springer AG (Germany); publishes two major dailies, *Dziennik* and *Fakt*, and is the country's second largest magazine publisher, printing women's, fiction, computer, food, economics, news and motoring magazines; CEO ANDREAS TILK.

WARSAW DAILIES

Dziennik (Daily): 02-672 Warsaw, ul. Domaniewska 52; tel. (22) 2320519; fax (22) 2325550; e-mail dziennik@dziennik.pl; internet www.dziennik.pl; f. 2006; Mon.–Sat; publ. by Axel Springer Polska; Editor-in-Chief ROBERT KRASOWSKI; circ. 77,750 (Nov. 2008).

Fakt (Fact): 02-672 Warsaw, ul. Domaniewska 52; tel. (22) 6085554; fax (22) 6085508; e-mail redakcja@efakt.pl; internet www.efakt.pl; f. 2003; owned by Axel Springer Polska Sp. z o.o.; Editor KATARZYNA SIELICKA; circ. 410,756 (Nov. 2010).

Gazeta Wyborcza: 00-732 Warsaw, ul. Czerska 8/10; tel. (22) 5556000; fax (22) 5557990; e-mail redakcja_portalu@agora.pl; internet www.wyborcza.pl; f. 1989; non-party; national edn and 20 local edns; weekend edn: *Gazeta Świateczna*; special supplements; Editor-in-Chief ANDRZEJ OLEJNICZAK; circ. 411,192 (2008).

Nasz Dziennik (Our Daily): 04-476 Warsaw, ul. Żeligowskiego 16/20; tel. (22) 5157777; fax (22) 5157778; e-mail redakcja@naszdziennik.pl; internet www.naszdziennik.pl; national; Editor-in-Chief EWA NOWINA KONOPKA; circ. 250,000.

Polska Zbrojna (Military Poland): 00-909 Warsaw, Al. Jerozolimskie 97; tel. (22) 6845365; fax (22) 6845503; e-mail sekretariat@zbrojni.pl; internet www.polska-zbrojna.pl; f. 1943; Editor KATARZYNA PIETRASZEK; circ. 50,000.

Przegląd Sportowy (Sports Review): 02-672 Warsaw, Al. Domaniewska 52; tel. (22) 2320503; fax (22) 2325523; e-mail redakcja@przeglad.com.pl; internet www.sports.pl; f. 1921; Editor MARCIN KALITA; circ. 64,332 (2008).

Rzeczpospolita (The Republic): 00-838 Warsaw, ul. Prosta 51; tel. (22) 6283401; fax (22) 6280588; e-mail p.aleksandrowicz@rzeczpospolita.pl; internet www.rp.pl; f. 1982; 51% owned by Orkla (Norway); Editor-in-Chief PAWEŁ LISICKI; circ. 157,136 (2008).

Super Express: 00-939 Warsaw, ul. Jubilerska 10; tel. (22) 5159100; fax (22) 5159010; e-mail internet@se.com.pl; internet www.se.pl; f. 1991; popular; Editor-in-Chief SŁAWOMIR JASTRZĘBOWSKI; circ. 183,976 (Nov. 2010).

POLAND
Directory

Życie Warszawy (Warsaw Life): 00-838 Warsaw, Prosta 51; tel. (22) 6530433; fax (22) 4630011; e-mail sekretariat@zw.com.pl; internet www.zw.com.pl; f. 1944; independent; Editor-in-Chief TOMASZ SOBIECKI; circ. 3,753 (2009).

REGIONAL DAILIES

Dziennik Bałtycki (Baltic Newspaper): 80-894 Gdańsk, Targ Drzewny 9/11; tel. (58) 3003300; fax (58) 3003303; e-mail internet@prasa.gda.pl; internet www.dziennikbaltycki.pl; f. 1945; non-party; Editor-in-Chief GRZEGORZ POPŁAWSKI; circ. 41,330 (Nov. 2010).

Dziennik Łódzki (Łódz Daily): 90-532 Łódź, ul. Ks. Skorupki 17/19; tel. (42) 6659100; fax (42) 6659101; e-mail dziennik@dziennik.lodz.pl; internet www.dziennik.lodz.pl; f. 1945; non-party; Editor ROBERT SAKOWSKI; circ. 38,376 (Nov. 2010).

Dziennik Polski (Polish Daily): 31-072 Kraków, ul. Wielopole 1; tel. (12) 6199200; fax (12) 6199275; e-mail redakcja@dziennik.krakow.pl; internet www.dziennik.krakow.pl; f. 1945; Mon.–Sat; Editor PIOTR LEGUTKO; circ. 39,145 (Nov. 2010).

Dziennik Wschodni (Eastern Daily): 20-081 Lublin, ul. Staszica 20; tel. (81) 4626800; fax (81) 4626801; e-mail redakcja@dziennikwschodni.pl; internet www.dziennikwschodni.pl; Chief Editor KRZYSZTOF WIEJAK; circ. 13,084 (Nov. 2010).

Dziennik Zachodni (Western Daily): 41-203 Sosnowiec, ul. Baczyńskiego 25A; tel. (32) 6342200; fax (32) 1538196; e-mail redakcja@dz.com.pl; internet www.dz.com.pl; f. 1945; absorbed Trybuna Śląska in 2004; non-party; Editor-in-Chief MAREK TWARÓG; circ. 69,600 (Nov. 2010).

Echo Dnia (Echo of the Day): 25-520 Kielce, ul. Targowa 18; tel. (41) 3495353; fax (41) 3682218; e-mail redakcja@echodnia.eu; internet www.echodnia.eu; f. 1971; Chief Editor STANISŁAW WRÓBEL; circ. 37,573 (Nov. 2010).

Gazeta Krakowska (Kraków Gazette): 31-548 Kraków, Al. Pokoju 3; tel. (12) 6888000; fax (12) 6888109; e-mail sekretariat@gk.pl; internet www.gk.pl; f. 1949; Editor-in-Chief TOMASZ LACHOWICZ; circ. 26,652 (Nov. 2010).

Gazeta Lubuska: 65-042 Zielona Góra, Al. Niepodległości 25, POB 120; tel. (68) 3248800; fax (68) 3248875; e-mail ar@gazetalubuska.pl; internet www.gazetalubuska.pl; f. 1952; independent; Chief Editor IWONA ZIELIŃSKA; circ. 40,193 (Nov. 2010).

Gazeta Olsztyńska (Olsztyn Gazette): 10-364 Olsztyn, ul. Tracka 5; tel. (89) 5397700; e-mail internet@gazetaolsztynska.pl; internet gazetaolsztynska.wm.pl; f. 1886; Editor-in-Chief EWA BARTNIKOWSKA; circ. 24,293 (Nov. 2010).

Gazeta Pomorska: 85-063 Bydgoszcz, ul. Zamoyskiego 2; tel. (52) 3263100; fax (52) 3221542; e-mail gp.redakcja@pomorska.pl; internet www.pomorska.pl; f. 1948; independent; Editor-in-Chief WOJCIECH POTOCKI; circ. 66,512 (Nov. 2010).

Gazeta Wrocławska (Wrocław Gazette): 53-611 Wrocław, ul. Strzegomska 42A; tel. (71) 3748151; fax (71) 3748175; e-mail redakcja@gazeta.wroc.pl; internet www.gazetawroclawska.pl; Editor-in-Chief ARKADIUSZ FRANAS; circ. 26,945 (Nov. 2010).

Gazeta Współczesna: 15-419 Białystok, POB 193, ul. Św. Mikołaja 1; tel. (85) 7487400; fax (85) 7487401; e-mail gazeta@wspolczesna.pl; internet www.wspolczesna.pl; f. 1951; Editor KONRAD KRUSZEWSKI; circ. 14,033 (Nov. 2010).

Głos Pomorza (Voice of Pomerania): 76-200 Słupsk, ul. Pobożnego 19; tel. (59) 8488100; fax (59) 8488104; e-mail akcja@gp24.pl; internet www.gp24.pl; f. 1952; Chief Editor KRZYSZTOF NAŁĘCZ; circ. 43,952 (Nov. 2010).

Głos Szczeciński (Szczecin Voice): 71-875 Szczecin, ul. Nowy Rynek 3; tel. (91) 4813300; fax (91) 4334864; e-mail akcja@gs24.pl; internet www.gs24.pl; f. 1947; Chief Editor KRZYSZTOF NAŁĘCZ; circ. 30,000 (weekdays), 100,000 (weekends).

Głos Wielkopolski (Voice of Wielkopolska): 60-782 Poznań, ul. Grunwaldzka 19; tel. (61) 8694100; fax (61) 8606115; e-mail redakcja@glos.com; internet www.glos.com; f. 1945; independent; Editor-in-Chief ADAM PAWŁOWSKI; circ. 45,534 (Nov. 2010).

Kurier Lubelski (Lublin Courier): 20-002 Lublin, Krakowskie Przedmieście 10/1; tel. (81) 4462800; fax (81) 4462830; e-mail redakcja@kurierlubelski.pl; internet www.kurierlubelski.pl; f. 1830; independent; evening; Editor-in-Chief DARIUSZ KOTLARZ; circ. 7,322 (Nov. 2010).

Kurier Szczeciński (Szczecin Courier): 70-550 Szczecin, pl. Hołdu Pruskiego 8; tel. (91) 4429101; fax (91) 4429105; e-mail t.kowalczyk@kurier.szczecin.pl; internet www.24kurier.pl; Editor-in-Chief TOMASZ KOWALCZYK; circ. 20,054 (Nov. 2010).

NoWiny 24 (News): 35-016 Rzeszów, ul. Kraszewskiego 2; tel. (17) 8672210; fax (17) 8672201; e-mail online@nowiny24.pl; internet www.nowiny24.pl; f. 1949; evening; Editor-in-Chief STANISŁAW SOWA; circ. 100,000.

Nowa Trybuna Opolska (New Opole Tribune): 45-086 Opole, ul. Powstańców Śląskich 9; tel. (77) 4432500; fax (77) 4432515; e-mail nto@nto.pl; internet www.nto.pl; f. 1952; independent; Editor KRZYSZTOF ZYZIK; circ. 27,112 (Nov. 2010).

PERIODICALS

Computerworld Polska: 04-204 Warsaw, ul. Jordanowska 12, POB 73; tel. (22) 32178103217800; fax (22) 3217888; e-mail cw@idg.com.pl; internet www.computerworld.pl; weekly; Editor-in-Chief ANDRZEJ GONTARZ; circ. 3,695 (2009).

Dobre Rady (Good Advice): 00-034 Wrocław, ul. Warecka 11A; tel. (71) 3517758; fax (71) 3737288; e-mail dobrerady@burdamedia.pl; internet www.dobrerady.pl; f. 2002; publ. by Burda Polska; Editor-in-Chief ANNA MANDES-TARASSOV; circ. 508,844 (2009).

Dom i Wnętrze (Home and Interior): 00-480 Warsaw, ul. Wiejska 19; tel. (22) 5842200; fax (22) 5842591; e-mail info@domiwnetrze.pl; internet www.domiwnetrze.pl; f. 1991; illustrated monthly; Editor-in-Chief EWA MIERZEJEWSKA; circ. 20,945 (2009).

Dziecko (Child): 00-732 Warsaw, ul. Czerska 8/10; tel. (22) 5556882; fax (22) 5556669; e-mail dziecko@agora.pl; internet www.edziecko.pl; f. 1995; monthly; women's magazine concerning children's affairs; Editor JUSTYNA DĄBROWSKA; circ. 65,984 (Mar. 2010).

Dziewczyna (Girl): 02-672 Warsaw, ul. Domaniewska 52, Axel Springer Polska; tel. (22) 2320750; e-mail redakcja@dziewczyna.pl; internet www.dziewczyna.pl; f. 2000; monthly; lifestyle magazine for young women; Publr DONATA CIESLIK; Editor-in-Chief ANDRZEJ GUMULAK; circ. 94,211 (2009).

Les Echos de Pologne: 02-530 Warsaw, ul. Kielecka 42/14; tel. (22) 4030870; fax (22) 4030872; e-mail echos@echos.pl; internet www.echos.pl; f. 2003; fortnightly; in French; Editor-in-Chief KRYSTYNA KOCERBA.

Gazeta Bankowa (Banking Gazette): 00-140 Warsaw, Al. Solidarności 117; tel. (22) 6525914; fax (22) 6525910; e-mail redakcja@wtrendy.pl; internet www.gb.pl; f. 1988; weekly; business and finance; Editor-in-Chief ANDRZEJ S. NARTOWSKI.

Głos Nauczycielski (Teachers' Voice): 00-389 Warsaw, ul. J. Smulikowskiego 6/8; tel. (22) 3189260; fax (22) 8281355; e-mail glos@glos.pl; internet www.glos.pl; f. 1917; weekly; organ of the Polish Teachers' Union; Chief Editor JAKUB RZEKANOWKSI; circ. 40,000.

Lubie Gotować (I Love Cooking): 00-732 Warsaw, ul. Czerska 8/10; tel. (22) 5556606; fax (22) 5556668; e-mail lubiegotowac@agora.pl; internet www.lubiegotowac.pl; f. 1997; monthly; cookery; Editor-in-Chief JOANNA NOWICKA; circ. 31,314 (2009).

Nie (No): 00-789 Warsaw, ul. Słoneczna 25; tel. (22) 8488448; fax (22) 8497258; e-mail nie@redakija.nie.com.pl; internet www.nie.com.pl; f. 1990; satirical; weekly; Editor JERZY URBAN; circ. 500,000.

Nowa Fantastyka (New Fantasy): 02-651 Warsaw, ul. Garażowa 7; tel. (22) 6077790; fax (22) 8482266; e-mail nowafantastyka@fantastyka.pl; internet www.fantastyka.pl; f. 1982; monthly; science fiction and fantasy; Editor-in-Chief JAKUB WINIARSKI; circ. 9,889 (2009).

Nowe Życie Gospodarcze (New Economic Life): 00-549 Warsaw, ul. Piękna 24/26; tel. (22) 6280628; fax (22) 6288392; e-mail nzg@nzg.pl; e-mail sekretariat@nzg.pl; internet www.nzg.pl; f. 1945 as *Życie Gospodarcze* (Economic Life); weekly; economic; Chair. and Editor-in-Chief JERZY DZIĘCIOŁOWSKI; circ. 35,700.

Państwo i Prawo (State and Law): 00-330 Warsaw, ul. Nowy Świat 72; tel. (22) 6288296; e-mail panstwoiprawo@wolterskluwer.pl; internet www.panstwoiprawo.pl; f. 1946; monthly organ of the Polish Academy of Sciences; publ. by Wolters Kluwer Polska; Chief Editor Dr LESZEK KUBICKI; circ. 3,000.

Polityka (Politics): 02-309 Warsaw, ul. Słupecka 6, POB 13; tel. (22) 4516133; fax (22) 4516135; e-mail polityka@polityka.com.pl; internet www.polityka.pl; f. 1957; weekly; political, economic, cultural; Editor JERZY BACZYŃSKI; circ. 144,894 (2009).

Poradnik Gospodarski (Farmers' Guide): 60-163 Poznań, ul. Sieradzka 29; tel. and fax (61) 8685492; e-mail poradnik.gospodarsk@wodr.poznan.pl; internet www.poradnik.wodr.poznan.pl; f. 1889; monthly; agriculture; Editor-in-Chief TADEUSZ SZALCZYK; circ. 10,000.

Przekrój (Review): 00-695 Warsaw, ul. Nowogrodzka 47A; tel. (22) 2842533; fax (22) 5259988; e-mail redakcja@przekroj.pl; internet www.przekroj.pl; f. 1945; weekly; illustrated; cultural; Chief Editor KATARZYNA JANOWSKA; circ. 52,657 (2009).

Przyjaciółka (Girlfriend): 00-480 Warsaw, ul. Wiejska 19; tel. (22) 5842438; fax (22) 5842436; e-mail info@przyjaciolka.pl; internet www.przyjaciolka.pl; f. 1948; weekly; women's magazine; Editor-in-Chief URSZULA ZUBCZYŃSKA; circ. 476,571 (2009).

Res Publica Nowa (The New Republic): 00-362 Warsaw 1, ul. Gałczyńskiego 5; tel. (22) 8260566; fax (22) 3430833; e-mail redakcja@res.publica.pl; internet www.publica.pl; f. 1987; monthly; political and cultural; Editor WOJCIECH PRZYBYLSKI; circ. 5,000.

Sprawy Międzynarodowe (International Affairs): Polish Institute of International Affairs, 00-950, Warsaw, ul. Warecka 1A, POB 1010; tel. (22) 5568000; fax (22) 5568099; e-mail sprawy@pism.pl; internet www.sprawymiedzynarodowe.pl; f. 1948; quarterly; publ. by Polish Institute of International Affairs; Editor-in-Chief HENRYK SZLAJFER; circ. 800.

Świat Nauki (World of Science): 02-651 Warsaw, ul. Garażowa 7; tel. (22) 6077811; fax (22) 8482266; e-mail swiatnauki@proszynskimedia.pl; internet www.swiatnauki.pl; f. 1991; monthly; Polish edn of *Scientific American*; Editor-in-Chief ELŻBIETA WIETESKA; circ. 18,746 (2009).

Szpilki (Needles): Warsaw; tel. (22) 6280429; f. 1935; weekly; illustrated; satirical; Editor JACEK JANCZARSKI; circ. 100,000.

Tygodnik Solidarność (Solidarity Weekly): 02-390 Warsaw, ul. Grójecka 186, POB 613; tel. and fax (22) 8822796; e-mail redakcja@tygodniksolidarnosc.com; internet www.tygodniksolidarnosc.com; f. 1981; reactivated 1989; weekly; Editor-in-Chief JERZY KŁOSIŃSKI; circ. 60,000.

The Warsaw Voice: 01-452 Warsaw, ul. Księcia Janusza 64; tel. (22) 3359700; fax (22) 3359710; e-mail voice@warsawvoice.pl; internet www.warsawvoice.pl; f. 1988; weekly; political, social, cultural and economic; in English; Editor ANDRZEJ JONAS; circ. 10,500.

Wiedza i Życie (Knowledge and Life): 02-651 Warsaw, ul. Garażowa 7; tel. (22) 6077753; fax (22) 8482266; e-mail wiedzaizycie@proszynskimedia.pl; internet www.wiz.pl; f. 1926; monthly; popular science; Editor ELŻBIETA WIETESKA; circ. 35,677 (2009).

Wprost (To The Point): 02-672 Warsaw, ul. Domaniewska 39A, Horizon Plaza; tel. (22) 5291100; fax (22) 4299101; e-mail redakcja@wprost.pl; internet www.wprost.pl; f. 1982; weekly; news and comment; Publr TOMASZ PLATA; Editor-in-Chief TOMASZ LIS; circ. 98,549 (2009).

NEWS AGENCY

Polska Agencja Prasowa (PAP) (Polish Press Agency): 00-502 Warsaw, ul. Bracka 6/8; tel. (22) 5092222; fax (22) 5092234; e-mail newsroom@pap.pl; internet www.pap.com.pl; f. 1944; brs in 22 Polish towns and 13 foreign capitals; 240 journalist and photojournalist mems; Pres. KRZYSZTOF HOFMAN.

PRESS ASSOCIATION

Stowarzyszenie Dziennikarzy Polskich (SDP) (Polish Journalists' Association): 00-366 Warsaw, ul. Foksal 3/5; tel. and fax (22) 8278720; e-mail sdp@sdp.pl; internet www.sdp.pl; f. 1951; dissolved 1982, legal status restored 1989; 2,500 mems; Pres. KRYSTYNA MOKROSIŃSKA; Gen. Sec. STEFAN TRUSZCZYŃSKI.

Publishers

Bertelsmann Media Sp. z o.o.: 02-786 Warsaw, ul. Rosoła 10; tel. (22) 6458200; fax (22) 6484732; e-mail poczta@swiatksiazki.com.pl; internet www.swiatksiazki.com.pl; f. 1994 as Bertelsmann Publishing Świat Książki Sp. z o.o.; *belles lettres*, science fiction, popular science, albums, books for children and teenagers; Pres. ANDRZEJ KOSTARCZYK; Editor-in-Chief BOGUSŁAW DĄBROWSKI.

Dom Wydawniczy ABC Sp. z o.o.: 01-231 Warsaw, ul. Płocka 5A; tel. (22) 5358000; fax (22) 5358001; e-mail info@abc.com.pl; internet www.abc.com.pl; f. 1989; legal, business and financial books; part of Polskie Wydawnictwa Profesjonalne Sp. z o.o; owned by Wolters Kluwer (Netherlands); Owners WŁODZIMIERZ ALBIN, KRZYSZTOF BRZESKI.

Dom Wydawniczy Bellona: 00-844 Warsaw, ul. Grzybowska 77; tel. (22) 6204291; fax (22) 6522695; e-mail bellona@bellona.pl; internet www.bellona.pl; f. 1947; fiction, history and military; Pres. Col JÓZEF SKRZYPIEC; Dir ZBIGNIEW CZERWIŃSKI.

Dom Wydawniczy Rebis Sp. z o.o.: 60-171 Poznań, ul. Żmigrodzka 41/49; tel. (61) 8678140; fax (61) 8673774; e-mail rebis@rebis.com.pl; internet www.rebis.com.pl; f. 1990; historical fiction, history of art; Pres. and Man. Dir TOMASZ SZPONDER.

Drukarnia i Księgarnia św. Wojciecha (St Adalbert—Wojciech Printing and Publishing Co): 60-967 Poznań, pl. Wolności 1; tel. (61) 8529186; fax (61) 8523746; e-mail wydawnictwo@ksw.com.pl; internet www.ksw.com.pl; f. 1895; textbooks and Catholic publications; Dir Rev. BOGDAN REFORMAT; Editor-in-Chief BOŻYSŁAW WALCZAK.

Egmont Sp. z o.o.: 01-029 Warsaw, ul. Dzielna 60; tel. (22) 8384100; fax (22) 8384200; e-mail kluby@egmont.pl; internet www.egmont.pl; f. 1990; books and comics for children and teenagers; Man. Dir JACEK BEŁDOWSKI; Editor-in-Chief HANNA BALTYN.

Instytut Wydawniczy Pax (Pax Publishing Institute): 00-390 Warsaw, ul. Wybrzeże Kościuszkowskie 21A; tel. (22) 6253398; fax (22) 6251378; e-mail iwpax@wpax.com.pl; internet sklep.iwpax.com.pl; f. 1949; theology, philosophy, religion, history, literature; Dir KRZYSZTOF PRZESTRZELSKI; Editor-in-Chief ZBIGNIEW BOROWIK.

Muza SA: 00-590 Warsaw, ul. Marszałkowska 8; tel. (22) 6211776; fax (22) 6292349; e-mail muza@muza.com.pl; internet www.muza.com.pl; f. 1991; albums, encyclopedias, lexicons, handbooks, dictionaries, *belles lettres*, books for children and youth; Man. Dir MARCIN GARLINSKI.

Oficyna Wydawnicza Volumen: 00-354 Warsaw, ul. Dynasy 2A; tel. and fax (60) 7678936; e-mail volumen@owvolumen.pl; f. 1984 (working clandestinely as WERS), 1989 officially; science, popular history, anthropology and socio-political sciences; Dir MIROSLAWA LATKOWSKA.

Pallottinum—Wydawnictwo Stowarzyszenia Apostolstwa Katolickiego: 60-959 Poznań, Al. Przybyszewskiego 30, POB 23; tel. (61) 8675233; fax (61) 8675238; e-mail pallottinum@pallottinum.pl; internet www.pallottinum.pl; f. 1947; religious and philosophical books; Dir STEFAN DUSZA.

Państwowe Wydawnictwo Rolnicze i Leśne (State Agricultural and Forestry Publishers): 02-272 Warsaw, ul. Malownicza 14; tel. and fax (22) 8684529; e-mail pwril@pwril.com; internet www.pwril.com; f. 1947; professional publications on agriculture, forestry, health and veterinary science; Dir and Editor-in-Chief JOLANTA KUCZYŃSKA.

Państwowy Instytut Wydawniczy (State Publishing Institute): 00-372 Warsaw, ul. Foksal 17; tel. (22) 8260201; fax (22) 8261536; e-mail piw@piw.pl; internet www.piw.pl; f. 1946; Polish and foreign classical and contemporary literature, fiction, literary criticism, biographies, performing arts, culture, history, popular science, and fine arts; Dir and Editor-in-Chief RAFAŁ SKĄPSKI.

Pierwszy Wybór Profesjonalisty: 01-231 Warsaw, ul. Płocka 5A; tel. (22) 5358000; fax (22) 5358001; e-mail obsluga.klienta@wolterskluwer.pl; internet www.pwp.pl; country's largest legal publisher; Pres. ALBIN WŁODZIMIERZ.

Polskie Przedsiębiorstwo Wydawnictw Kartograficznych im. E. Romera (E. Romer Polish Cartographical Publishing House): 02-389 Warsaw, Al. Bohaterów Września 9; tel. (22) 5851800; fax (22) 5851801; e-mail ppwk@ppwk.com.pl; internet www.ppwk.com.pl; f. 1951; maps, atlases, travel guides, books on geodesy and cartography; Man. Dir JACEK BŁASCZYŃSKI.

Polskie Wydawnictwo Muzyczne (Polish Publishing House for Music): 31-111 Kraków, Al. Krasińskiego 11A; tel. (12) 4227044; fax (12) 4220174; e-mail pwm@pwm.com.pl; internet www.pwm.com.pl; f. 1945; music and books on music; Chair. and Man. Dir Dr SŁAWOMIR J. TABKOWSKI; Editor-in-Chief ANDRZEJ KOSOWSKI.

Prószyński i S-ka Publishing House: 02-651 Warsaw, ul. Garazowa 7; tel. (22) 6077700; fax (22) 6077704; e-mail wydawnictwo@proszynski.pl; internet www.proszynski.pl; f. 1990; poetry, fiction, non-fiction, educational text and reference books, popular science, etc.; Pres. MIECZYSŁAW PRÓSZYŃSKI; 110 employees.

Spółdzielnia Wydawnicza Czytelnik ('Reader' Co-operative Publishing House): 00-490 Warsaw, ul. Wiejska 12A; tel. (22) 5831407; fax (22) 6283178; e-mail sekretariat@czytelnik.pl; internet www.czytelnik.pl; f. 1944; general, especially fiction and contemporary Polish literature; Pres. MAREK ŻAKOWSKI; Editor-in-Chief JANUSZ DRZEWUCKI.

Spółdzielnia Wydawniczo-Handlowa 'Książka i Wiedza' ('Books and Knowledge' Trade Co-operative Publishing House): 00-375 Warsaw, ul. Smolna 13; tel. (22) 8275401; fax (22) 8279423; e-mail publisher@kiw.com.pl; internet www.kiw.com.pl; f. 1948; philosophy, religion, linguistics, literature and history; Chair. WŁODZIMIERZ GAŁĄSKA; Editor-in-Chief ELŻBIETA KONECKA.

Wydawnictwa Naukowo-Techniczne (Scientific-Technical Publishers): 00-048 Warsaw, ul. Mazowiecka 2/4, POB 359; tel. (22) 8267271; fax (22) 8268293; e-mail wnt@pol.pl; internet www.wnt.com.pl; f. 1949; scientific and technical; Man. Dir and Editor Dr ANIELA TOPULOS.

Wydawnictwa Szkolne i Pedagogiczne (WSiP) (School and Pedagogical Publishers): 00-965 Warsaw, Al. Jerozolimskie 136; tel. (22) 5762510; fax (22) 5762509; e-mail wsip@wsip.com.pl; internet www.wsip.pl; f. 1945; school textbooks and popular science books, scientific literature for teachers, visual teaching aids, periodicals for teachers and youth; Chair. (vacant).

Wydawnictwo Arkady: 00-344 Warsaw, ul. Dobra 28, POB 137; tel. (22) 8269316; fax (22) 8274194; e-mail arkady@arkady.com.pl; internet www.arkady.com.pl; f. 1957; publications on building, town planning, architecture and art; Dir and Pres. JANINA KRYSIAK.

Wydawnictwo C. H. Beck.: 01-518 Warsaw, ul. Gen. Zajączka 9; tel. (22) 3377600; fax (22) 3377601; e-mail redakcja@beck.pl; internet www.beck.pl; f. 1993; law and economics; Man. Dir PAWEŁ ESSE.

POLAND

Wydawnictwo Dolnośląskie Sp. z o.o.: 50-010 Wrocław, ul. Podwale 62; tel. (71) 7859040; fax (71) 7859066; e-mail sekretariat@wd.wroc.pl; internet www.wd.wroc.pl; f. 1986; *belles lettres*, essays, memoirs, translations, general non-fiction; Pres. of Bd ANDRZEJ ADAMUS.

Wydawnictwo Iskry (Sparks Publishing House Ltd): 00-375 Warsaw, ul. Smolna 11; tel. and fax (22) 8279415; e-mail iskry@iskry.com.pl; internet www.iskry.com.pl; f. 1952; travel, Polish and foreign fiction, science fiction, essays, popular science, history, memoirs; Chair. Dr WIESŁAW UCHAŃSKI; Editor-in-Chief MAGDALENA SŁYSZ.

Wydawnictwo Kurpisz: 01-341 Poznań, ul. Przemysława 46; tel. (61) 8331517; fax (61) 8351294; e-mail kurpisz@kurpisz.pl; internet www.kurpisz.pl; f. 1991; *belles lettres*, reprints, dictionaries, encyclopedias, periodicals; Dir KAZIMIERZ GRZESIAK.

Wydawnictwo Lekarskie PZWL (PZWL Medical Publishers): 02-672 Warsaw, ul. Domaniewska 41; tel. and fax (22) 6954033; e-mail promocja@pzwl.pl; internet www.pzwl.pl; f. 1945; medical literature and manuals, lexicons, encyclopedias; Pres. KRYSTYNA REGULSKA.

Wydawnictwo Literackie (Literary Publishing House): 31-147 Kraków, ul. Długa 1; tel. (12) 4232254; fax (12) 4225423; e-mail redakcja@wl.net.pl; internet www.wl.net.pl; f. 1953; works of literature and *belles lettres*; Dir BARBARA DRWOTA; Editor-in-Chief MAŁGORZATA NYCZ.

Wydawnictwo Nasza Księgarnia (Our Booksellers' Publishing House): 02-868 Warsaw, ul. Sarabandy 24c; tel. (22) 6439389; fax (22) 6437028; e-mail naszaksiegarnia@nk.com.pl; internet www.nk.com.pl; f. 1921; books and periodicals for children and young readers; Pres. AGNIESZKA TOKARCZYK; Editor JOLANTA SZTUCZYŃSKA.

Wydawnictwo Naukowe PWN (PWN Scientific Publishers): 02-676 Warsaw, ul. Postepu 18; tel. (22) 6954180; fax (22) 6954288; e-mail international@pwn.com.pl; internet www.pwn.pl; f. 1951; reference, academic, incl. multimedia; Pres. BARBARA JOZWIAK.

Wydawnictwo Nowa Era: 02-305 Warsaw, Al. Jerozolimskie 146D; tel. (22) 5702580; fax (22) 5702581; e-mail nowaera@nowaera.com.pl; internet www.nowaera.com.pl; school textbooks; Chair. MARIUSZ KOPER.

Wydawnictwo Ossolineum (Ossolineum Publishing House): 50-062 Wrocław, pl. Solny 14A; tel. (71) 3436961; fax (71) 3448103; e-mail wydawnictwo@ossolineum.pl; internet www.ossolineum.pl; f. 1817; publishing house of the Polish Academy of Sciences; academic publications in humanities and sciences; Man. Dir WOJCIECH KARWACKI; Editor-in-Chief STANISŁAW ROŚCICKI.

Wydawnictwo Prawnicze LexisNexis—LexPolonia (LexPolonia—LexisNexis Legal Publishing House): Warsaw; tel. (22) 5729500; fax (22) 5729508; e-mail biuro@lexisnexis.pl; internet www.lexisnexis.pl; f. 1952; present name adopted 2003; Exec. Dir OLGA DYMKOWSKA-PULCHNY.

Wydawnictwo Publicat: 61-003 Poznań, ul. Chlebowa 24; tel. (61) 8679546; fax (61) 6529200; internet www.najlepszyprezent.pl; f. 1990 as Wydawnictwo Podsiedlik-Raniowski Sp. z o.o.; popular and children's literature, poetry, prose, classical works, educational books; Pres. MICHAŁ KAIK.

Wydawnictwo Śląsk Sp. z o.o. (Silesia Publishing House Ltd): 40-161 Katowice, Al. W. Korfantego 51; tel. (32) 580756; fax (32) 583229; e-mail biuro@slaskwn.com.pl; internet www.slaskwn.com.pl; f. 1952; social, popular science, technical, and regional literature; Chair. and Editor-in-Chief Dr TADEUSZ SIERNY.

Wydawnictwo W.A.B. (WAB Publishers): 02-502 Warsaw, ul. Łowicka 31; tel. (22) 6460510; fax (22) 6460511; e-mail wab@wab.com.pl; internet www.wab.com.pl; f. 1991; contemporary Polish fiction, historical and cultural essays, and literature for children.

Wydawnictwo Wam (For You Publishers): 31-501 Kraków, ul. Kopernika 26; tel. (12) 6293200; fax (12) 4295003; e-mail wam@wydawnictwowam.pl; internet www.wydawnictwowam.pl; f. 1872; Roman Catholic textbooks, encyclopedias, non-fiction, fiction and children's books; Dir HENRYK PIETRAS.

Wydawnictwo Wiedza Powszechna (General Knowledge Publishers): 00-054 Warsaw, ul. Jasna 26; tel. and fax (22) 8270799; e-mail info@wiedza.pl; internet www.wiedza.pl; f. 1952; popular science books, Polish and foreign language dictionaries, foreign language textbooks, encyclopedias and lexicons; Dir TERESA KORSAK.

Wydawnictwo Zysk i S-ka (Zysk Publishers): 61-744 Poznań, ul. Wielka 10; tel. (61) 8532767; fax (61) 8526326; e-mail sekretariat@zysk.com.pl; internet www.zysk.com.pl; f. 1994; *belles lettres*, popular, scientific and religious literature; Pres. TADEUSZ ZYSK.

Znak Społeczny Instytut Wydawniczy (Znak Social Publishing Institute): 30-105 Kraków, ul. Kościuszki 37; tel. (12) 6199500; fax (12) 6199502; internet www.znak.com.pl; f. 1959; religion, philosophy, *belles lettres*, essays, history; Chief Exec. HENRYK WOŹNIAKOWSKI; Editor-in-Chief JERZY ILLG.

Broadcasting and Communications

TELECOMMUNICATIONS

Regulatory Authority

Office of Electronic Communications (Urząd Komunikacji Elektronicznej—UKE): 01-211 Warsaw, ul. Kasprzaka 18/20; tel. (22) 5349190; fax (22) 5349162; e-mail uke@uke.gov.pl; internet www.uke.gov.pl; f. 2001; formerly the Office of Telecommunications and Post Regulation (URTIP); reorganized Jan. 2006; Chair. ANNA STREŻYŃSKA.

Service Providers

Polkomtel: 02-676 Warsaw, ul. Postępu 3; tel. (22) 6071000; fax (22) 4260103; internet www.polkomtel.com.pl; f. 1996; provides mobile cellular telecommunications services under the brand names Plus GSM, SimplusTeam and mixPlus; 3G network commenced operations Sept. 2004; Pres. WŁADYSŁAW BARTOSZEWICZ.

Polska Telefonia Cyfrowa (PTC) (Polish Digital Telephone): 02-222 Al. Jerozolimskie 181, Warsaw; tel. (22) 4136000; fax (22) 4134949; e-mail biznes@era.pl; internet www.era.pl; f. 1996; provides mobile cellular telecommunications under the brand names Era, Heyah and Blue Connect; 70.5% owned by T-Mobile Deutschland GmbH; 22.5% owned by T-Mobile Poland Holding B.V.; Chair. Dr KLAUS HARTMANN.

PTK Centertel (Polish Cellular Telecommunications Co 'Centertel'): 01-230 Warsaw, ul. Skierniewicka 10A; tel. (22) 6342882; fax (22) 5887883; e-mail info@idea.pl; internet www.orange.pl; f. 1998; provides mobile cellular telecommunications services under the brand name Orange; 66% owned by TP, 34% by France Telecom (France).

TP—Telekomunikacja Polska (Polish Telecommunications): 00-105 Warsaw, ul. Twarda 18; tel. (22) 5270000; internet www.tp.pl; f. 1992; mem. of France Telecom group (France); Chair. MACIEJ WITUCKI.

BROADCASTING

Regulatory Authority

National Broadcasting Council (Krajowa Rada Radiofonii i Telewizji—KRRiTV): 00-015 Warsaw, Skwer Kardinala Wyszyńskiego, Prymasa Polski 9; tel. (22) 5973001; fax (22) 5973054; internet www.krrit.gov.pl; f. 1993; Chair. ELŻBIETA KRUK.

Radio

Polskie Radio (Polish Radio): 00-977 Warsaw, Al. Niepodległości 77/85; tel. (22) 6459259; fax (22) 6455924; internet www.polskieradio.pl; home service comprises four national channels, broadcasting 24 hours a day; foreign service broadcasts in Polish, English, German, Russian, Belarusian, Ukrainian and Hebrew; Pres. KRZYSZTOF CZABAŃSKI.

Radio Maryja: 87-100 Toruń, ul. Żwirki i Wigury 80; tel. (56) 6552361; fax (56) 6552362; e-mail radio@radiomaryja.pl; internet www.radiomaryja.pl; traditionalist Catholic; Dir TADEUSZ RYDZYK.

Radio Musyka Fakty (RMF FM): 30-204 Kraków, Al. Waszyngtona 1, Kopiec Kosciuszki; tel. (12) 4219696; fax (12) 4217895; e-mail redakcja@rmf.pl; internet www.rmf.pl; Pres. STANISŁAW TYCZYNSKI; Dir JOLANTA WIŚNIEWSKA.

Radio Zet: 00-503 Warsaw, ul. Żurawia 8; tel. (22) 5833382; fax (22) 5833356; e-mail radiozet@radiozet.com.pl; internet www.radiozet.com.pl; f. 1990; independent; 24 hours; national broadcasts commenced 1994; wholly owned by the Eurozet media group; Pres. and Editor-in-Chief ROBERT KOZYRA.

Television

Telewizja Polska (Polish Television): 00-999 Warsaw, ul. J. P. Woronicza 17, POB 211; tel. (22) 5474450; fax (22) 5477719; e-mail pr@tvp.pl; internet www.tvp.pl; f. 1952; Chair. BRONISŁAW WILDSTEIN.

PolSat: 04-028 Warsaw, Al. Stanów Zjednoczonyck 53; tel. (22) 5104001; fax (22) 5134295; internet www.polsat.com.pl; f. 1992; satellite broadcasts; Propr ZYGMUNT SOLORZ.

TVN: 02-952 Warsaw, ul. Wiertnicza 166; tel. (22) 8566060; fax (22) 8566666; e-mail widzowie@tvn.pl; internet www.tvn.pl; f. 1997; Pres. PIOTR WALTER.

POLAND

Finance

(cap. = capital; res = reserves; dep. = deposits; m. = million; amounts in new złotys, unless otherwise indicated; brs = branches)

BANKING

Foreign banks were permitted to operate freely in the country from 1997. In early 2010 there were 49 domestic commercial banks and 20 branches of credit institutions operating in Poland.

Supervisory Authority

Polish Financial Supervision Authority (PFSA) (Komisja Nadzoru Finansowego): 00-950 Warsaw, Plac Powstańców Warszawy 1; tel. (22) 3326600; fax (22) 3326602; e-mail knf@knf.gov.pl; internet www.knf.gov.pl; f. 2008 to succeed Financial Supervision Commission; Chair. STANISŁAW KLUZA.

National Bank

Narodowy Bank Polski—NBP (National Bank of Poland): 00-919 Warsaw, ul. Świętokrzyska 11/21, POB 1011; tel. (22) 6531000; fax (22) 6208518; e-mail listy@nbp.pl; internet www.nbp.pl; f. 1945; cap. 1,500.0m., res 969.3m., dep. 83,920.9m. (Dec. 2007); Pres. MAREK BELKA; 16 brs.

Other Banks

Bank BPH SA: 31-548 Kraków, Al. Pokoju 1; tel. (12) 5318095; fax (12) 5073152; e-mail bank@bphpbk.pl; internet www.bph.pl; f. 1989; fmrly Bank Przemysłowo-Handlowy PBK SA; present name adopted 2004; 52.1% owned by Bank Austria Creditanstalt AG (HVB Group, Austria); cap. 143.5m., res 1,171.3m., dep. 11,564.5m. (Dec. 2008); Pres. JÓZEF WANCER; 201 brs.

Bank Gospodarki Żywnościowej—BGZ (BGZ) (Bank of Food Economy): 01-211 Warsaw, ul. Kasprzaka 10/16; tel. (22) 8604000; fax (22) 8605000; e-mail info@bgz.pl; internet www.bgz.pl; f. 1919; present name adopted 1994; universal commercial bank; finances agriculture, forestry and food-processing; 37.3% state-owned; 44.5% owned by Rabobank (Netherlands); cap. 43.1m., res 2,022.0m., dep. 21,322.6m. (Dec. 2008); Exec. Pres. JACEK BARTKIEWICZ; 256 brs.

Bank Gospodarstwa Krajowego—BGK (National Economy Bank): 00-955 Warsaw, Al. Jerozolimskie 7, POB 41; tel. (22) 5229105; fax (22) 6270378; e-mail bgk@bgk.com.pl; internet www.bgk.com.pl; f. 1924; 100% state-owned; cap. 980.0m., res 5,612.4m., dep. 19,698.1m. (Dec. 2007); Pres. of Bd DOMINIK RADZIWIŁŁ; 20 brs.

Bank Millennium: 02-593 Warsaw, Stanisława Żaryna 2A; tel. (22) 5981565; fax (22) 5981563; e-mail wojciech.kaczorowski@bankmillennium.pl; internet www.bankmillennium.pl; f. 1989 as Bank Inicjatyw Gospodarczych (BIG); present name adopted 2003; 65.0% owned by Banco Comercial Português SA (Portugal); cap. 849.2m., res 512.5m., dep. 42,805.2m. (Dec. 2008); Chair. of Bd BOGUSŁAW KOTT; 410 brs.

Bank Ochrony Środowiska—BOS (Environmental Protection Bank): 00-950 Warsaw 1, Al. Jana Pawła II 12, POB 150; tel. (22) 8508720; fax (22) 8508891; e-mail bos@bosbank.pl; internet www.bosbank.pl; f. 1991; 77.2% by Polish National Fund for the Protection of the Environment and Water; cap. 446.8m., res –9.1m., dep. 10,135.2m. (Dec. 2008); Pres. of Exec. Bd MARIUSZ KLIMCZAK; 48 brs.

Bank Polska Kasa Opieki—Bank Pekao: 00-950 Warsaw, ul. Grzybowska 53/57; tel. (22) 6560000; fax (22) 6560004; e-mail info@pekao.com.pl; internet www.pekao.com.pl; f. 1929; universal bank; 52.9% owned by UniCredito Italiano SpA (Italy); cap. 262.2m., res 12,194.5m., dep. 113,904.6m. (Dec. 2008); CEO ALICJA KORNASIEWICZ; Chair. JERZY WOZNICKI; 720 brs and sub-brs.

Bank Polskiej Spóldzielczości: 01-231 Warsaw, ul. Plocka 9/11B; tel. (22) 5395100; fax (22) 5395222; e-mail pr@bankbps.pl; internet www.bankbps.pl; f. 1992; present name adopted 2002; cap. 133.2m., res 224.2m., dep. 10,524.4m. (Dec. 2008); Pres. MIROSŁAW POTULSKI.

Bank Zachodni WBK (Western Bank): 50-950 Wrocław, Dolnośląskie Rynek 9/11; tel. (71) 3701000; fax (71) 3702771; e-mail press.office@bzwbk.pl; internet www.bzwbk.pl; f. 1989; present name adopted 2001; 70.5% owned by AIB European Investments Ltd (Ireland); cap. 729.6m., res 2,881.7m., dep. 49,903.9m. (Dec. 2008); Pres. MATEUSZ MORAWIECKI; 433 brs.

BNP Paribas Bank Polska: 02-676 Warsaw, ul. Suwak 3; tel. (22) 5669300; fax (22) 5669079; internet www.bnpparibas.pl; f. 1990; fmrly Fortis Bank Polska; present name adopted 2011; 99.1% owned by BNP Paribas (France); cap. 503.1m., res 635.5m., dep. 17,824.2m. (Dec. 2008); CEO ALEXANDER PAKLONS; Chair. CAMILLE FOHL.

BRE Bank: 00-950 Warsaw, ul. Senatorska 18, POB 728; tel. (22) 8290000; fax (22) 8290033; e-mail info@brebank.pl; internet www.brebank.com.pl; f. 1987; present name adopted 1999; 70.3% owned by Commerzbank AG (Germany); specializes in corporate banking; cap. 118.7m., res 2,675.8m., dep. 65,102.8m. (Dec. 2008); Pres. and CEO MARIUSZ GRENDOWICZ; 172 brs.

Citibank Handlowy: 00-923 Warsaw, ul. Senatorska 16; tel. (22) 6904000; fax (22) 6925023; e-mail relacjeinwestorskie@citi.com; internet www.citibankhandlowy.pl; f. 1870; trade and finance bank; specializes in corporate and investment banking; fmrly Bank Handlowy w Warszawie (Trade Bank in Warsaw); 89.3% owned by Citibank Overseas Investment Corpn (USA); cap. 522.6m., res 4,371.1m., dep. 35,180.4m. (Dec. 2007); Pres. SŁAWOMIR SIKORA; Chair. STANISŁAW SOŁTYSIŃSKI; 149 brs.

Deutsche Bank PBC: 00-609 Warsaw, Al. Armii Ludowej 26; tel. (22) 5799800; fax (22) 5799801; e-mail info@db-pbc.pl; internet www.deutsche-bank-pbc.pl; f. 1991; fmrly Bank Wspolpracy Regionalnej SA w Krakowie; present name adopted 2003; 99.7% owned by Deutsche Bank Privat- und Geschäftskunden Aktiengesellschaft (Germany); cap. 581.7m., res 277.7m., dep. 14,206.8m. (Dec. 2008); Chair. of Supervisory Bd GUIDO HEUVELDOP; Pres. LESZEK NIEMYCKI.

Deutsche Bank Polska: 00-609 Warsaw, Al. Armii Ludowej 26; tel. (22) 5799000; fax (22) 5799001; e-mail public.relations@db.com; internet www.db-polska.pl; f. 1995; 100% owned by Deutsche Bank AG (Germany); corporate banking; cap. 230.0m., res 194.5m., dep. 5,513.0m. (Dec. 2007); Chair. of Bd PETER TILS; Chair. KRZYSZTOF KALICKI.

Getin Noble Bank SA: 02-675 Warsaw, ul. Domaniewska 39 B; tel. (32) 2008500; fax (32) 2008685; e-mail marketing@getinbank.pl; internet www.getinbank.pl; f. 1990; fmrly Górnośląski Bank Gospodarczy; renamed Getin Bank in 2004; present name adopted 2010 after merger with Noble Bank; cap. 336.3m., res 1,239.7m., dep. 21,083.8m. (Dec. 2008); Pres. MICHAŁ HANDZLIK; Chair. KRZYSZTOF ROSIŃSKI; 146 brs.

ING Bank Śląski: 40-086 Katowice, ul. Sokolska 34; tel. (32) 3570069; fax (32) 3577507; e-mail mampytanie@ingbank.pl; internet www.ing.pl; f. 1989; 75% owned by ING Bank NV (Netherlands); cap. 130.1m., res 936.8m., dep. 64,728.2m. (Dec. 2008); Chair. ANNA FORNALCZYK; Pres. MAŁGORZATA KOŁAKOWSKA; 350 brs and sub-brs.

Kredyt Bank: 01-211 Warsaw, ul. Kasprzaka 2/8, POB 93; tel. (22) 6345400; fax (22) 6345335; internet www.kredytbank.com.pl; f. 1997; 80% owned by KBC Bank NV (Belgium); cap. 1,358.3m., res 919.8m., dep. 35,482.8m. (Dec. 2008); Chair. ANDRZEJ WITKOWSKI; Pres. MACIEJ BARDAN; 75 brs.

Nordea Bank Polska: 81-303 Gdynia, ul. Kielecka 2, POB 11; tel. (58) 6691111; fax (58) 6691110; e-mail nordea@nordea.com; internet www.nordea.pl; f. 1991; 98.9% owned by Nordea Bank AB (Sweden); cap. 227.5m., res 695.9m., dep. 14,333.8m. (Dec. 2008); Pres. WLODZIMIERZ KICINSKI; Chair. WOJCIECH RYBOWSKI.

PKO Bank Polski—Powszechna Kasa Oszczędności Bank Państwowy—PKO (State Savings Bank): 00-975 Warsaw, ul. Pulawska 15, POB 183; tel. (22) 5218440; fax (22) 5218029; internet www.pkobp.pl; f. 1919; 51.5% state-owned; cap. 1,000.0m., res 9,618.7m., dep. 113,709.5m. (Dec. 2008); Pres. of Management Bd ZBIGNIEW JAGIEŁŁO; Chair. of Supervisory Bd CEZARY BANASIŃSKI; 1,153 brs and sub-brs.

Polski Bank Przedsiebiorczosci: 02-672 Warsaw, ul. Domaniewska 39A; tel. (22) 6530604; fax (22) 2082640; e-mail westlb@westlb.pl; internet www.westlb.pl; f. 1995; renamed WestLB Bank Polska in 2003; current name adopted Jan. 2011; cap. 183.6m., res 60.9m., dep. 2,197.2m. (Dec. 2007); Chair. and Gen. Man. MACIEJ STANCZUK.

Raiffeisen Bank Polska: 00-549 Warsaw, ul. Piekna 20, POB 53; tel. (22) 5852000; fax (22) 5852585; internet www.raiffeisen.pl; f. 1991; present name adopted 2000; 100% owned by Raiffeisen International Bank Holding AG (Austria); cap. 998.0m., res 956.7m., dep. 26,150.1m. (Dec. 2008); Pres. PIOTR CZARNECKI; Chair. HERBERT STEPIC; 37 brs.

STOCK EXCHANGE

The Warsaw Stock Exchange was re-established in April 1991. In January 1998 a derivatives market was launched. At the end of 2008 the Stock Exchange's shareholders included 35 entities, comprising banks, brokerage firms, an Exchange company and the State Treasury (which held a share of 98.8%).

Warsaw Stock Exchange: 00-498 Warsaw, ul. Książęca 4; tel. (22) 6283232; fax (22) 6281754; e-mail wse@wse.com.pl; internet www.wse.com.pl; opened for trading in 1991; Pres. and Chief Exec. Dr LUDWIK SOBOLEWSKI.

INSURANCE

In late 2009 there were 30 insurance companies operating in Poland.

Allianz Życie Polska: 02-685 Warsaw, ul. Rodziny Hiszpańskich 1; tel. (22) 5294000; fax (22) 5294040; internet www.allianz.pl; f. 1997; Pres. PAWEŁ DANGEL.

Amplico Life: 00-450 Warsaw, ul. Przemysłowa 26; tel. (22) 6271000; fax (22) 6271010; e-mail lifeinfo@amplico.pl; internet www.amplicolife.pl; f. 1990; Pres. ŁUKASZ KALINOWSKI.

POLAND   Directory

Aviva Towarzystwo Ubezpieczeń na Życie: 00-838 Warsaw, ul. Prosta 70; tel. (22) 5574050; fax (22) 5574075; e-mail bok@aviva.pl; internet www.aviva.pl; f. 1991; Pres. MACIEJ JANKOWSKI.

Axa Życie Towarzystwo Ubezpieczeń: 00-867 Warsaw, ul. Budynek 51, Warsaw Trade Tower Bldg; tel. (22) 5550050; fax (22) 5550052; e-mail ubezpieczenia@axa-polska.pl; internet www.axa-polska.pl; f. 1993; Pres. MACIEJ SZWARC.

Benefia Towarzystwo Ubezpieczeń na Życie: 01-793 Warsaw, ul. Rydygiera 21; tel. (22) 5441400; fax (22) 5441451; e-mail bok.infolinia@benefia.pl; internet www.benefia.pl/benefiazycie; f. 1994; Pres. TOMASZ TELEJKO.

Commercial Union Polska—Towarzystwo Ubezpieczeń na Życie: 00-838 Warsaw, ul. Prosta 70; tel. (22) 5574050; fax (22) 5574075; e-mail bok@cu.com.pl; internet www.cu.com.pl; f. 1991; owned by Aviva Group (United Kingdom); pensions, life insurance; Pres. ZBIGNIEW ANDRZEJEWSKI.

Grupa Powszechny Zakład Ubezpieczeń (PZU) (Polish National Insurance Group): 00-133 Warsaw, Al. Jana Pawła II 24; tel. (22) 3084940; fax (22) 3084942; internet www.pzu.pl; f. 1803; insurance group comprising two principal companies dealing in various areas of insurance (PZU SA—property insurance, and PZU Życie SA—life insurance), and six support companies; 55% state-owned; further privatization scheduled; Pres. ANDRZEJ KLESYK; 400 brs; 14,000 employees.

ING Towarzystwo Ubezpieczeń na Życie: 00-406 Warsaw, ul. Ludna 2; tel. (22) 5220000; fax (22) 5221111; e-mail info@ing.pl; internet www.ing.pl; f. 1994; Pres. JAROSŁAW JAMKA.

Nordea Polska Towarzystwo Ubezpieczeń na Życie: 00-867 Warsaw, Al. Jana Pawła II/27; tel. (22) 5410100; fax (22) 5410101; e-mail zycie@nordeapolska.pl; internet www.nordeazycie.pl; f. 1994; Pres. MARIUSZ SOBIECH.

TU EUROPA SA: 53-333 Wrocław, ul. Powstańców Śląskich 2–4; tel. (71) 3341800; fax (71) 3341808; e-mail sekretariat@tueuropa.pl; internet www.europa-tu.com.pl; f. 2002; Pres. JACEK PODOBA.

UNIQA Towarzystwo Ubezpieczeń na Życie: 90-520 Łódź, ul. Gdańska 132; tel. (42) 6344700; fax (42) 6377687; e-mail zycie@uniqa.pl; internet www.uniqa.pl; f. 1994; Pres. JAROSŁAW PARKOT.

Warta—Towarzystwo Ubezpieczeń i Reasekuracji Warta (Warta Insurance and Reinsurance Co): 00-805 Warsaw, ul. Chmielna 85/87; tel. (22) 5810100; fax (22) 5811375; e-mail info@warta.pl; internet www.warta.pl; f. 1920; marine, air, motor, fire, luggage and credit; Chair. of Bd JOHN HOLLOWS; 25 brs.

Trade and Industry

GOVERNMENT AGENCIES

Agency for the Restructuring and Modernization of Agriculture (Agencja Restrukturyzacji i Modernizacji Rolnictwa): 00-175 Warsaw, Al. Jana Pawła II 70; fax (22) 3185330; e-mail info@arimr.gov.pl; internet www.arimr.gov.pl; f. 1994; Pres. Prof. GRZEGORZ SPYCHALSKI.

Agricultural Market Agency (Agencja Rynku Rolnego): 00-400 Warsaw, ul. Nowy Świat 6/12; tel. (22) 6617272; fax (22) 6289353; e-mail tpi@arr.gov.pl; internet www.eng.arr.gov.pl; f. 1991; implements selected schemes under the Common Agricultural Policy of the European Union; Pres. STANISŁAW GRZEGORZ KAMIŃSKI.

Polish Agency for Enterprise Development (PARP) (Polska Agencja Rozwoju Przedsiębiorczości): 00-834 Warsaw, ul. Pańska 81/83; tel. (22) 4328080; fax (22) 4328620; e-mail biuro@parp.gov.pl; internet www.parp.gov.pl; f. 2000; manages funds assigned from the state budget and the European Union for the support of entrepreneurship and devt of human resources, particularly concerning small and medium-sized enterprises; Chief Exec. DANUTA JABŁOŃSKA.

Polish Information and Foreign Investment Agency (Polska Agencja Informacji i Inwestycji Zagranicznych): 00-585 Warsaw, ul. Bagatela 12; tel. (22) 3349800; fax (22) 3349999; e-mail post@paiz.gov.pl; internet www.paiz.gov.pl; f. 2003; Pres. ANDRZEJ KANTHAK.

DEVELOPMENT AGENCY

Industrial Development Agency (Agencja Rozwoju Przemysłu): 02-675 Warsaw, ul. Wołoska 7, Budynek Mars, Klatka A; tel. (22) 4603636; fax (22) 4603637; e-mail lucyna.stepien@arp.com.pl; internet www.arp.com.pl; Pres. PAWEŁ BRZEZICKI.

CHAMBERS OF COMMERCE

Polish Chamber of Commerce (National Economic Chamber—Krajowa Izba Gospodarcza): 00-074 Warsaw, ul. Trębacka 4, POB 361; tel. (22) 6309600; fax (22) 8274673; e-mail kig@kig.pl; internet www.kig.pl; f. 1990; Pres. ANDRZEJ ARENDARSKI; Sec.-Gen. MAREK KŁOCZKO; 145 mems.

Foreign Investors' Chamber of Industry and Trade in Poland (Izba Przemysłowo-Handlowa Inwestorów Zagranicznych—IPHIZ): 00-834 Warsaw, ul. Pańska 73; tel. (22) 3147575; fax (22) 3147576; e-mail biuro@iphiz.com.pl; internet www.iphiz.com.pl; f. 1989; Pres. ZDZISŁAW JAGODZIŃSKI.

UTILITIES

Energy Regulatory Authority (Urząd Regulacji Energetyki): 00-872 Warsaw, ul. Chłodna 64; tel. (22) 6616107; fax (22) 6616152; e-mail ure@ure.gov.pl; internet www.ure.gov.pl; Pres. Dr LESZEK JUCHNIEWICZ.

Electricity

The electricity sector has been reorganized into separate generation, transmission and distribution entities.

Koncern Energetyczny ENERGA: 80-557 Gdańsk, ul. Marynarki Polskiej 130; tel. (58) 3473013; fax (58) 3010152; internet www.energa.pl; f. 2004; renamed as above 2005; group of eight regional electricity distributors in central and northern Poland, known as G8; partial privatization suspended in 2004; Chief Exec. WALDEMAR BARTELIK; 7,500 employees.

PGE Polska Grupa Energetyczna: 00-496 Warsaw, ul. Mysia 2; tel. (22) 6931580; fax (22) 6285964; internet www.pgesa.pl; national transmission-system operator; fmrly Polskie Sieci Elektroenergetyczne (PSE); Chair. of Bd TOMASZ ZADROGA.

National Atomic Energy Agency (Państwowa Agencja Atomistyki): 00-522 Warsaw, ul. Krucza 36; tel. (22) 6282722; fax (22) 6290164; e-mail niewodniczanski@paa.gov.pl; internet www.paa.gov.pl; f. 1982; central govt organ concerned with issues of nuclear safety and radiological protection; Pres. Prof. JERZY NIEWODNICZAŃSKI.

STOEN Stołeczny Zakład Energetyczny (STOEN Capital-City Power Distribution Co): 00-347 Warsaw, Wybrzeże Kopciuszkowskie 41; tel. (22) 8214646; fax (22) 8214647; e-mail stoen@stoen.pl; internet www.stoen.pl; f. 1993; transmits and distributes electric energy; privatized in 2002; 85% owned by RWE Energie AG (Germany); 15% state-owned; Chief Exec. HARRY SCHUR; Chair. of Supervisory Bd Dr ANDREAS RADMACHER.

Gas

EuRoPol GAZ: 04-028 Warsaw, Al. Stanów Zjednoczonych 61; tel. (22) 5174000; fax (22) 5174040; e-mail konto@europolgaz.com.pl; internet www.europolgaz.com.pl; f. 1993; jt venture between PGNiG and Gazprom (Russia); Pres. KAZIMIERZ ADAMCZYK.

Polish Oil and Gas Co (Polskie Górnictwo Naftowe i Gazownictwo—PGNiG): 00-537 Warsaw, ul. Krucza 6/14; tel. (22) 5835000; fax (22) 5835856; e-mail pr@pgnig.pl; internet www.pgnig.pl; f. 1982; divided into six regional distribution subsidiaries in 2003; state-owned natural gas producer and supplier; scheduled for partial privatization; Pres. of Bd KRZYSZTOF GLOGOWSKI; 47,300 employees.

TRADE UNIONS

All-Poland Alliance of Trade Unions (Ogólnopolskie Porozumienie Związków Zawodowych—OPZZ): 00-924 Warsaw, ul. Kopernika 36/40; tel. (22) 5515500; fax (22) 5515501; e-mail inter@opzz.org.pl; internet www.opzz.org.pl; f. 1984; Pres. JAN GUZ.

Independent Self-governing Trade Union—Solidarity (NSZZ Solidarność): 80-855 Gdańsk, ul. Wały Piastowskie 24; tel. (58) 3016737; fax (58) 3010143; e-mail zagr@solidarnosc.org.pl; internet www.solidarnosc.org.pl; f. 1980; outlawed 1981–89; Chair. JANUSZ SNIADEK.

Transport

RAILWAYS

At the end of 2002 there were 21,073 km of railway lines making up the state network, of which 12,207 km were electrified.

Office for Railway Transport (Urząd Transportu Kolejowego): 00-928 Warsaw, ul. Chałubinskiego 4/6; tel. (22) 6301950; fax (22) 6301892; e-mail utk@utk.gov.pl; internet www.utk.gov.pl; fmrly General Railway Inspectorate; reorganized in July 2003; Pres. WIESŁAW JAROSIEWICZ; Dir-Gen. LIDIA OSTROWSKA.

Polish State Railways (Polskie Koleje Państwowe—PKP): 00-973 Warsaw, ul. Szcześliwicka 62; tel. (22) 4749000; fax (22) 4749102; e-mail biuro.zarzadu@pkp.pl; internet www.pkp.pl; f. 1926; freight and passenger transport; PKP Group comprises 12 cos; from 2004 Regional Services (WKD), a principal subsidiary, has been operated by local govts; Polskie Koleje Państwowe Polskie Linie Kolejowe (PKP PLK) operates the railway network; Pres. ANDRZEJ WACH; Gen. Dir MACIEJ MECLEWSKI; 125,000 employees.

ROADS

In 2003 there were 423,997 km of roads, of which 484 km were motorways; 69.7% of the road network was paved. Poland launched a road construction scheme in mid-2002, partly funded by the European Union (EU), which aimed to enhance the country's position as a major transit route between western and eastern Europe. The EU was, additionally, to provide funding of €19,000m. for road construction in Poland in 2007–13.

General Directorate of Public Roads and Motorways (Generalna Dyrekcja Dróg Krajowych i Autostrad): 00-848 Warsaw, ul. Żelazna 59; tel. (22) 3758888; fax (22) 3758763; e-mail kancelaria@gddkia.gov.pl; internet www.gddkia.gov.pl; Dir ZBIGNIEW KOTLAREK.

INLAND WATERWAYS

Poland has 6,850 km of waterways, of which 3,640 km were navigable in 2002. The main rivers are the Wisła (Vistula), Odra (Oder), Bug, Warta and San. There are some 5,000 lakes. In addition, there is a network of canals.

SHIPPING

Poland has three large harbours on the Baltic Sea: Gdynia, Gdańsk and Szczecin. At 31 December 2008 the Polish merchant fleet comprised 358 vessels, with a total displacement of 212,940 grt.

Authority of Szczecin and Świnoujście Authority Co: 70-603 Szczecin, ul. Bytomska 7; tel. (91) 4308240; fax (91) 4624842; e-mail info@port.szczecin.pl; internet www.port.szczecin.pl; f. 1950; Pres. and Man. Dir JANUSZ CATEWICZ.

Port of Gdańsk Authority Co: 80-955 Gdańsk, ul. Zamknięta 18; tel. (58) 7379100; fax (58) 7379485; e-mail info@portgdansk.pl; internet www.portgdansk.pl; f. 1997; management of land and port infrastructure; Pres. of Bd STANISŁAW CORA.

Port of Gdynia Authority Co: 81-337 Gdynia, ul. Rotterdamska 9; tel. (58) 6274002; fax (58) 6203191; e-mail marketing@port.gdynia.pl; internet www.port.gdynia.pl; f. 1922; Pres. JANUSZ JAROSIŃSKI.

Principal Shipping Companies

Polska Żegluga Bałtycka—Polferries (Polish Baltic Shipping Co—POLFERRIES): 78-100 Kołobrzeg, ul. Portowa 41; tel. (94) 3552102; fax (94) 3552208; internet www.polferries.pl; f. 1976; operates three ferries on four routes between Denmark and Sweden; also serves as travel agency and tour operator.

Polska Żegluga Morska (PZM) (Polish Steamship Co—Polsteam): 70-419 Szczecin, Pl. Rodła 8; tel. (91) 3594333; fax (91) 3594288; e-mail pzmmanagement@polsteam.com.pl; internet www.polsteam.com.pl; f. 1951; state-owned; world-wide tramping; operates 75 vessels totalling 2m. dwt, incl. four liquid sulphur carriers; largest dry bulk carrier in Europe; operates ferry service between Poland and Sweden (Unity Line); Gen. Dir PAWEŁ SZYNKARUK; 2,800 employees.

Polskie Linie Oceaniczne (PLO) (Polish Ocean Lines): 81-364 Gdynia, ul. 10 Lutego 24; tel. (58) 6900670; fax (58) 6900672; e-mail pol@pol.com.pl; internet www.pol.com.pl; f. 1951; holding co for six shipping cos operating within PLO group; tonnage operated by the POL-Levant Shipping Lines; Pres. of Bd ANDRZEJ OSIECIMSKI.

CIVIL AVIATION

Fryderyk Chopin–Okęcie international airport is situated near Warsaw. In addition, international flights serve a number of other airports, including those at Bydgoszcz, Gdańsk, Katowice, Kraków, Łódź, Poznań, Rzeszów, Szczecin and Wrocław.

Civil Aviation Office (Urząd Lotnictwa Cywilnego): 00-848 Warsaw, ul. Żelazna 59; tel. (22) 5207200; fax (22) 5207300; e-mail kancelaria@ulc.gov.pl; internet www.ulc.gov.pl; Pres. GRZEGORZ KRUSZYŃSKI.

LOT—Polskie Linie Lotnicze (Polish Airlines): 00-906 Warsaw, ul. 17 Stycznia 39; tel. (22) 6066111; fax (22) 8460909; e-mail lot@lot.com; internet www.lot.com; f. 1929; 67.97% state-owned; domestic and international services; operates low-cost subsidiary Eurolot (f. 1996) providing domestic scheduled and international scheduled and charter services; Pres. SEBASTIAN MIKOSZ (acting).

Tourism

Poland is rich in historic cities, such as Gdańsk, Wrocław, Kraków, Poznań and Warsaw. There are numerous health and climatic resorts, while the mountains, forests and rivers provide splendid scenery and excellent facilities for touring and sporting holidays. In 2010 Poland was visited by some 58.3m. foreign tourists. Receipts from tourism amounted to US $12,841m. in 2008.

Polish Tourist Organization (Polska Organizacja Turystyczna—POT): 00-613 Warsaw, ul. Chałubińskiego 8, XIX piętro; tel. (22) 5367070; fax (22) 5367004; e-mail pot@pot.gov.pl; internet www.pot.gov.pl; Pres. TOMASZ WILCZAK.

Defence

As assessed at November 2010, the Poland's active armed forces numbered 100,000, comprising an army of 47,300, a navy of 8,000, air forces of 17,500, special forces of 1,650 and joint forces of 25,550. The 21,400 paramilitary forces comprised border guards (14,100) and interior ministry units (7,300). Compulsory military service was abolished with effect from February 2009. Poland joined the 'Partnership for Peace' military co-operation programme of the North Atlantic Treaty Organization (NATO) in 1994 and became a full member of the alliance in 1999.

Defence Expenditure: Budgeted at 25,300m. new złotys for 2011.
Chief of Staff of the Defence Forces: Gen. MIECZYSŁAW CIENIUCH.

Education

Education is free and compulsory for nine years. Before the age of seven, children may attend crèches and kindergartens. Compulsory basic schooling begins at seven years of age with primary school. Primary education lasts for six years, divided into two equal cycles. Lower secondary education (at the gimnazjum) is compulsory for three years. In 2006/07 net enrolment at primary schools included 95.5% of children in the relevant age-group. In the same year enrolment in secondary schools included 93.8% of children in the relevant age-group. Three years of education at general secondary schools commence at the age of 16 years, for pupils who successfully complete the entrance examination; there are general secondary schools, vocational technical schools and basic vocational schools. The last provide courses consisting of three days' theoretical and three days' practical training per week, and in addition some general education is given. New post-secondary schools were introduced in 1999 to prepare students from technical and vocational schools for skilled jobs. Curriculums are standardized throughout Poland. In 2004/05 there were 400 higher education establishments, including 17 universities and 22 technical universities. In 2007/08 there were 2.2m. students of higher education. In 2009 state budgetary expenditure on education amounted to 71,267m. new złotys (12.0% of total spending).

PORTUGAL

Introductory Survey

LOCATION, CLIMATE, LANGUAGE, RELIGION, FLAG, CAPITAL

The mainland portion of the Portuguese Republic lies in Western Europe, on the Atlantic side of the Iberian peninsula, bordered by Spain to the north and east. The country also includes two archipelagos in the Atlantic Ocean, the Azores (Açores) and the Madeira Islands. The climate is mild and temperate, with an annual average temperature of 16°C (61°F). In the interior the weather is drier and hotter. Almost all of the inhabitants speak Portuguese and are adherents of the Roman Catholic Church. The national flag (proportions 2 by 3) has two vertical stripes, of green and red, the green occupying two-fifths of the total area; superimposed on the stripes (half on the green, half on the red) is the state coat of arms: a white shield, containing five small blue shields (each bearing five white roundels) in the form of an upright cross, with a red border containing seven yellow castles, all superimposed on a yellow armillary sphere. The capital is Lisbon (Lisboa).

CONTEMPORARY POLITICAL HISTORY

Historical Context

The monarchy that had ruled Portugal from the 11th century was overthrown in 1910, when the King was deposed in a bloodless revolution, and a republic was proclaimed. A period of great instability ensued until a military coup installed the regime of the Estado Novo (New State) in 1926. Dr António de Oliveira Salazar became Minister of Finance in 1928 and Prime Minister in 1932, establishing a right-wing dictatorial regime, influenced by Italian Fascism. A new Constitution, establishing a corporate state, was adopted in 1933. Only one political party was authorized, and suffrage was limited. Portugal remained neutral during the Second World War. The Government strove to achieve international acceptance, but Portugal was not admitted to the UN until 1955. Unlike the other European colonial powers, Portugal insisted on maintaining its overseas possessions, regarding them as 'inalienable'. In 1961 Portuguese enclaves in India were successfully invaded by Indian forces, and in the same year a rebellion against Portuguese rule began in Angola. Similar rebellions followed, in Portuguese Guinea (1963) and Mozambique (1964), and protracted guerrilla warfare ensued in the three African provinces. Salazar remained in power until illness forced his retirement in September 1968. He was succeeded by Dr Marcello Caetano, who had been Deputy Prime Minister in 1955–58. Caetano pursued slightly more liberal policies. Opposition parties were legalized for elections to the Assembléia Nacional in October 1969, but the União Nacional, the government party, won all 130 seats. Immediately after the elections, the opposition groups were outlawed again. The government party, renamed Acção Nacional Popular in February 1970, also won every seat at the next elections to the Assembléia, in October 1973, following the withdrawal of all opposition candidates.

The drain on Portugal's economy by the long wars against nationalist forces in the overseas provinces contributed to the overthrow of Caetano in a bloodless coup on 25 April 1974, initiated by the Movimento das Forças Armadas (MFA), a group of young army officers. Gen. António Ribeiro de Spínola, head of the Junta da Salvação Nacional (Junta of National Salvation) that assumed power, became President in May and promised liberal reforms. The new Government recognized the right of Portugal's overseas territories to self-determination. The independence of Guinea-Bissau (formerly Portuguese Guinea), proclaimed in September 1973, was recognized by Portugal in September 1974. The remaining African territories were all granted independence in 1975. Portugal also withdrew from Portuguese Timor (Timor-Leste) in that year.

Following a split between the Junta's right and left wings, President Spínola resigned in September 1974 and was replaced by Gen. Francisco da Costa Gomes. An abortive counter-coup by senior officers in March 1975 resulted in a move to the left. All existing organs of the MFA were dissolved, a Supreme Revolutionary Council (SRC) was created, and six of the country's political parties agreed that the SRC would stay in power for five years. On 25 April a general election was held for a Constituent Assembly. Of the 12 parties contesting the election, the Partido Socialista (PS) obtained the largest share of the votes cast and won 116 of the Assembly's 250 seats. However, disputes between Socialists and Communists provoked withdrawals from the new coalition Government, and the Prime Minister, Gen. Vasco Gonçalves, was dismissed. Adm. José Pinheiro de Azevedo became Prime Minister in August. In September a new Government of 'united action' was formed, including members of the armed forces, the PS, the Partido Popular Democrático (PPD) and the Partido Comunista Português (PCP). In November the Government suspended its activities, owing to a lack of support from the armed forces. An abortive leftist military coup resulted from the political turmoil. Changes took place within the SRC, and in December the armed forces announced a plan to reduce their political power.

Domestic Political Affairs

A new Constitution, committing Portugal to make a transition to socialism, took effect on 25 April 1976. The SRC was renamed the Council of the Revolution, becoming a consultative body, headed by the President, with powers to delay legislation and the right of veto in military matters. At the general election for the new Assembléia da República (Assembly of the Republic), the PS won 107 of the Assembléia's 263 seats. In June the Army Chief of Staff, Gen. António Ramalho Eanes, a non-party candidate supported by the PS, the PPD and the Centro Democrático Social (CDS), was elected President. He took office in July, when a minority Socialist Government was formed under Dr Mário Lopes Soares, who had been Minister of Foreign Affairs in 1974–75. The Government resigned in December 1977, but the President again invited Soares to take office as Prime Minister. A new PS-CDS coalition was established in January 1978, but it collapsed after only six months. A new Government was formed in November under Prof. Carlos Mota Pinto, but he resigned in July 1979. President Eanes appointed Dr Maria de Lourdes Pintasilgo to head a provisional Government.

The centre-right alliance, Aliança Democrática (AD), which included the Partido Social Democrata (PSD, formerly the PPD) and the CDS, won a majority in the Assembléia da República in an early general election held in December 1979. Dr Francisco Sá Carneiro, the leader of the PSD, was appointed Prime Minister. At the general election held in October 1980, the AD increased its parliamentary majority. In December Sá Carneiro and his Minister of Defence, Adelino Amaro da Costa, were killed in an apparent air accident. (In 2004 tests revealed that a bomb had exploded on board the aircraft, and the eighth commission of inquiry into the crash cited Amaro da Costa's attempt to stop the illegal sale of arms to Iran as a possible motive for the bombing.) The presidential election took place as planned, however, and Eanes was re-elected. Dr Francisco Pinto Balsemão, co-founder of the PSD, was appointed Prime Minister. In March 1981 the offices of the President of the Republic and the Chief of Staff of the Armed Forces were formally separated.

In August 1982 the Assembléia da República approved the final draft of the new Constitution, which completed the transition to full civilian government. Following divisions within the PSD, and losses at local elections in December, Balsemão resigned as Prime Minister. In addition, the Deputy Prime Minister and leader of the CDS, Prof. Diogo Freitas do Amaral, resigned from all party and political posts. In February 1983 Mota Pinto became leader of the PSD. At an early general election, held in April, the PS won 101 of the 250 seats. Soares formed a coalition Government with the PSD (the AD having been dissolved).

In February 1985 Mota Pinto resigned as leader of the PSD, and subsequently as Deputy Prime Minister and Minister of Defence, and was replaced by Rui Machete, the Minister of Justice. In May Machete was replaced as party leader by Prof. Aníbal Cavaco Silva, a former Minister of Finance. In June, on the day after Portugal signed its treaty of accession to the European Community (EC, now European Union—EU, see

PORTUGAL

p. 270), the PS-PSD coalition disintegrated. Eanes called a general election for October, at which the PSD won 88 seats, while the PS won 57 seats and the Partido Renovador Democrático (PRD, a new party founded in early 1985 by supporters of President Eanes) won 45 seats. Cavaco Silva was able to form a minority PSD-led Government.

During the mid-1980s a number of terrorist attacks were perpetrated by the radical left-wing group Forças Populares 25 de Abril (FP-25) and other groups. Targets including both Portuguese and foreign business interests, installations of the North Atlantic Treaty Organization (NATO, see p. 368) and the US embassy in Lisbon. In July 1985 the trial opened of more than 70 alleged members of FP-25—including Lt-Col Otelo Saraiva de Carvalho, the former revolutionary commander—but was adjourned owing to the fatal shooting of a key prosecution witness. The trial later resumed and, in May 1987, Saraiva de Carvalho was found guilty of subversion and sentenced to 15 years' imprisonment (subsequently increased to 18 years). In March 1996, following a personal initiative by President Soares, the Assembléia da República approved a pardon for Saraiva de Carvalho and other members of FP-25.

Four candidates contested the January 1986 presidential election. As no candidate achieved the requisite 50% majority, a second round of voting was held in February: Mário Soares narrowly defeated Freitas do Amaral, former leader of the CDS, to become Portugal's first civilian President for 60 years, taking office in March.

Cavaco Silva's minority Government encountered difficulties in securing the adoption of reformist legislation. In April 1987 the Prime Minister resigned, following his defeat in a motion of censure. At an early general election in July the PSD secured 148 seats in the Assembléia da República, becoming the first party since 1974 to win an absolute majority. The PS won 60 seats, and the Coligação Democrático Unitária (CDU, a new left-wing coalition comprising the PCP and the ecologist Partido Ecologista 'Os Verdes' and also known as the PCP-PEV) won 31 seats. Cavaco Silva was reappointed as Prime Minister and announced a programme of radical economic reform, which included the partial privatization of state-owned companies. A controversial bill to reform the restrictive labour laws was approved by the Assembléia da República in April, despite mass public protests; in the following month, however, the Constitutional Court ruled that the new legislation violated the Constitution. The legislation was approved by President Soares in February 1989, although labour unrest persisted. Having secured the approval of both the Assembléia and the President, amendments removing Marxist elements from the Constitution entered into force in August.

Soares was decisively re-elected President at an election held in January 1991. At legislative elections in October the PSD renewed its absolute majority, winning 135 of the 230 seats (reduced from 250) in the Assembléia da República. The PS secured 72 seats, the CDU 17 and the CDS five. A new Government was appointed in late October. During 1992 tension between President Soares and Cavaco Silva became more evident, owing to the President's increasingly frequent use of his power of veto in order to obstruct the passage of legislation.

The Government of António Guterres: 1995–2002

At legislative elections held in October 1995 the PS won 112 of the 230 seats in the Assembléia da República. The PSD won 88 seats, the Centro Democrático Social-Partido Popular (CDS-PP—formerly the CDS) 15 and the CDU also 15. The Secretary-General of the PS, António Guterres, was appointed Prime Minister, leading a minority administration that incorporated several non-party ministers. At the presidential election held in January 1996, Cavaco Silva was defeated by Jorge Sampaio, the former Mayor of Lisbon and erstwhile leader of the PS, who took office in March.

In August 1996 Guterres announced proposals for radical reform of the country's political system. The opening of electoral lists to independent citizens (thus ending the monopoly of the major parties) and provision for the holding of referendums on issues of national interest were among the changes envisaged. In early 1997 the ruling PS and the opposition PSD reached a broad consensus on these proposals, also agreeing upon the gradual establishment of a professional army and a reduction in compulsory military service. In September the Assembléia da República gave its approval to the various constitutional reforms.

In February 1997, in a free vote, the Assembléia da República narrowly rejected proposals to liberalize the country's abortion law. The issue aroused bitter controversy, and created a deep division within the PS. In February 1998 the legislature voted by a narrow margin to relax the law on abortion. At a referendum in June 51% of those casting a vote favoured the liberalization of the law; however, the result was declared null and void, owing to the low rate of participation. Guterres suffered a setback in November when another referendum, on the question of regional devolution, resulted in an overwhelming rejection (by 64% of participants) of the Government's proposals to divide mainland Portugal into eight administrative regions, each with a proposed elected local assembly and regional president. However, owing to the high abstention rate, the result of this referendum was also declared invalid.

At the general election in October 1999 the PS secured 115 of the 230 seats in the Assembléia da República, while the PSD won 81 seats and the CDU 17 seats (including two seats allocated to the ecologist PEV). The recently established Bloco de Esquerda (BE), a militant left-wing grouping, unexpectedly obtained two seats. Thus, one seat short of an absolute majority, Guterres was returned to office and a new Council of Ministers was appointed. In November the incoming Government announced a programme of reforms aimed at narrowing the disparity between Portugal and the more developed member states of the EU. At a presidential election in January 2001 Sampaio was re-elected for a second term, obtaining 55.8% of the votes cast and defeating four other candidates.

Following municipal elections held in December 2001, at which the PS suffered significant losses, Guterres resigned both as Prime Minister and as leader of the PS. The poor electoral results were widely attributed to a decline in the economy, as well as to discontent with public services, which had been adversely affected by reductions in government expenditure. Guterres was replaced as Secretary-General of the PS in January 2002 by Eduardo Ferro Rodrigues. At an early general election in March the PSD, whose campaign had featured reductions in corporate taxation and public expenditure and the privatization of state services, emerged victorious, winning 105 seats in the Assembléia da República, although without an overall majority. The PS secured 96 seats, the CDS-PP 14 seats, the CDU alliance 12 seats and the BE three seats. The leader of the PSD, José Manuel Durão Barroso, was appointed Prime Minister and formed a centre-right coalition Government with the CDS-PP.

PSD-led Government: 2002–05

Durão Barroso's Government announced its intention to introduce austerity measures to counter the large public deficit, which contravened the country's obligations under the regulations for the European single currency. In July 2002 the Government proposed a new labour code designed to combat low productivity by increasing the ease of recruitment and dismissal of staff and limiting the power of the unions. In November and December two public sector one-day general strikes, involving up to 500,000 workers, were organized to protest against the introduction of the labour legislation and other recent austerity measures.

In May 2003 Paolo Pedroso, the deputy leader and parliamentary spokesman of the PS, was arrested in connection with a child abuse scandal surrounding the Casa Pia children's homes. Several other establishment figures had been arrested earlier that year. Throughout his custody Pedroso maintained that the allegations against him were part of a PSD plot to discredit him. He was charged in December (with nine other prominent figures) on 23 counts of sexual abuse, although the charges against him were later dropped. (In September 2008 Pedroso was awarded damages of around €100,000, following a civil court case in which the judge ruled that his arrest and subsequent imprisonment constituted a 'grave error'.) Seven defendants in the Casa Pia case went on trial in late November 2004; they were all found guilty in September 2010. Meanwhile, the Government established a tribunal to consider compensation claims brought by victims of abuse at Casa Pia orphanages, which in March 2006 awarded a total of more than €50m. to 44 claimants.

In June 2004 Durão Barroso was unexpectedly invited to take over the role of President of the European Commission in October. In order to accept this appointment, Durão Barroso resigned as leader of the PSD, and subsequently as Prime Minister on 5 July; the populist Mayor of Lisbon and Secretary-General of the PSD, Pedro Santana Lopes, was elected as his successor. President Sampaio invited Santana Lopes to form a new Government, which was inaugurated on 17 July. Ferro Rodrigues subsequently resigned as Secretary-General of the PS, claiming that Sampaio had betrayed the party's interests by not holding

PORTUGAL

early legislative elections. José Sócrates Carvalho, a moderate and a former Minister of the Environment, was elected Secretary-General of the PS in September.

In November 2004 directors and a prominent newscaster resigned from the state broadcasting company, Radiotelevisão Portuguesa (RTP), in protest at perceived pressure from the Government, and the state media authority criticized the Government for attempting to limit RTP's freedom. A series of cabinet reorganizations took place, culminating in the resignation of Henrique Chaves, formerly a close associate of the Prime Minister, as Minister for Youth and Sport. Chaves, who had been moved from the position of Minister in Assistance to the Prime Minister days earlier, cited Santana Lopes's disloyalty. At the end of November President Sampaio informed Santana Lopes of his decision to dissolve parliament and call legislative elections. Prior to the dissolution, the President permitted time for the adoption of the 2005 budget. However, the expansionary budget, which was approved by the Assembléia da República in early December, proved controversial as it contained tax reductions and increases in the state pension that were likely to cause Portugal to breach the budget deficit limit (equivalent to 3% of gross domestic product—GDP) specified in the EU's Stability and Growth Pact. Sampaio formally dissolved the legislature on 10 December, citing a loss of confidence in the Government.

At the elections, which took place on 20 February 2005, the PS, which during the campaign had advocated institutional reform and policies to increase economic growth, won an outright majority, securing 121 seats in the Assembléia da República, with 45.0% of the votes cast; the CDU and the BE also performed well at the expense of the right. The PSD won 75 seats, while its junior partner in the previous Government, the CDS-PP, won 12 seats. Santana Lopes and Portas resigned as leader of the PSD and the CDS-PP, respectively. In April Luís Marques Mendes was elected leader of the PSD, while José Ribeiro e Castro became President of the CDS-PP.

The first Government of José Sócrates: 2005–09

A new 16-member Council of Ministers, headed by Sócrates, took office in March 2005. It included an equal number of members of the PS and independents, most notably former CDS leader Freitas do Amaral, who had been an outspoken critic of the US-led invasion of Iraq in 2003, as Minister of Foreign Affairs. Another independent, and former deputy governor of the Banco de Portugal, Luís Campos e Cunha, was allocated the finance portfolio.

On taking office the new Government adopted a policy of strict economic austerity in an effort to reduce the budget deficit, which was forecast to be considerably higher than the EU limit of 3% of GDP. Disagreements arose between Campos e Cunha and Sócrates, however, and the Minister of Finance resigned in July 2005; he was replaced by Fernando Teixeira dos Santos of the PS. Plans to increase value-added tax (VAT) and reduce government expenditure, notably on social security, led to a series of protests and strikes by public sector employees. A one-day general strike in July, observed by an estimated 500,000 workers, was followed, in September and October, by protests and industrial action staged by employees in various sectors. In November, and again in February 2006, public sector workers participated in large-scale protests against the reduction in social welfare benefits, a wage freeze and the raising of the retirement age.

Six candidates contested the presidential election on 22 January 2006, including former President Soares and former Prime Minister Cavaco Silva. (Sampaio was not eligible to stand for a third term.) Cavaco Silva narrowly won an overall majority (with 50.5% of the valid votes cast), and took office on 9 March, the first centre-right President since the coup of 1974. In June Freitas do Amaral resigned as Minister of Foreign Affairs, for health reasons, and was replaced by Luís Amado, hitherto Minister of National Defence.

In November 2006 the draft budget for 2007 was approved in the Assembléia da República with the sole support of the PS. All other parties opposed the budget, which included significant reductions in public expenditure, to be largely financed by a reform of public administration. The public sector trade unions organized a two-day strike to coincide with the passage of the legislation, in protest against cuts in wages and pensions for public sector workers. General discontent with government policies had also been manifested in a demonstration organized by one of the principal trade union federations, the Confederação Geral dos Trabalhadores Portugueses-Intersindical Nacional (CGTP—General Confederation of Portuguese Workers) in October. In January 2007 the Government began negotiations with trade unions over the reform of labour legislation, which was to be implemented in 2008. The trade unions expressed vehement opposition to the proposals, which were likely to entail significant reductions in the number of civil servants.

In a referendum held in February 2007, 59.2% of those voting approved plans to legalize abortion (hitherto permitted only in restricted circumstances) for all women up to the 10th week of pregnancy; however, only 43.6% of the electorate voted, below the 50% needed to make the result legally binding. None the less, Sócrates declared that the result represented a mandate for reform. Legislation providing for decriminalization was adopted by the Assembléia da República in March and, after receiving presidential approval in April, entered into force in July.

The Government's reform programme continued to provoke labour unrest in mid-2007, with a one-day general strike called by the CGTP causing significant disruption to public services in late May. In June the Government approved a new system of remuneration and career progression for civil servants, despite ongoing opposition from the CGTP. In November the three principal public sector unions organized a one-day strike in protest against a 2.1% pay increase for civil servants for 2008. The unions had demanded rises of between 3.5% and 5.8%. None the less, the Government appeared to be succeeding in its efforts to reduce the budget deficit, despite the unpopularity of its reforms.

In September 2007 Luís Filipe Menezes was elected leader of the PSD, narrowly defeating the incumbent, Marques Mendes, with 54.1% of the votes cast. However, Menezes resigned in April 2008 after only seven months in the post, citing criticism of his performance by a number of senior party members and ongoing disagreements within the PSD. Manuela Ferreira Leite, the Minister of State and of Finance in 2002–04, was elected to succeed him as party leader in May.

Relations between the two main parties deteriorated in early 2009 as the PS and the PSD began preparations for the forthcoming general election. In January the Prime Minister accused his opponents of seeking to discredit him, following media reports linking him with an ongoing investigation into alleged financial improprieties related to the redesignation, in 2002, of land in an environmental protection zone in Alcochete, near Lisbon, for the construction of a shopping centre; Sócrates, who was Minister of the Environment and Territorial Planning at the time of the redesignation, denied any impropriety. In February 2009 he was re-elected unopposed as Secretary-General of the PS, with 96.4% of the votes cast.

In July 2009 Manuel Pinho was forced to resign as Minister of the Economy and Innovation, after he had caused outrage by making an offensive gesture towards a PCP deputy during a debate in the Assembléia da República. Teixeira dos Santos was appointed to take over Pinho's portfolio (in addition to his existing role of Minister of State and of Finance) pending the general election.

The re-election of Sócrates in 2009

At the general election held on 27 September 2009 the PS remained the largest party in the Assembléia da República, but lost its majority, winning 97 of the 230 seats with 37.7% of the votes cast. The other parties all increased their representation: the PSD won 30.0% of the votes and took 81 seats, while the CDS-PP emerged with 21 seats, the BE 16 and the CDU 15. On 12 October, following local elections held on the previous day (at which the PS won the largest number of votes cast), President Cavaco Silva asked Sócrates to form a new government. Later in October, after negotiations with other parties on the formation of a coalition had failed to produce agreement, Sócrates announced the composition of his new, minority administration, which, like the previous Government, contained an equal number of PS members and independents. Most of the senior ministers remained in their posts, although Augusto Santos Silva, hitherto Minister of Parliamentary Affairs, was appointed Minister of National Defence, while Dr Alberto Martins (a former minister under Guterres) became Minister of Justice. Also in October, in response to her party's poor performance in the general and local elections, Ferreira Leite announced that she would resign the PSD leadership in March 2010; in that month Pedro Passos Coelho was elected to succeed her.

On taking office for a second term, Sócrates declared that his administration would continue its policy of public investment in order to counteract the effects of the global economic crisis, confirming plans to invest some €60,000m. in infrastructure over the following decade. However, by early 2010 concerns in inter-

PORTUGAL

national financial markets over the size of Portugal's budget deficit (which was equivalent to 9.4% of GDP in 2009) had forced the Government to emphasize measures to reduce public spending. In early February the Government was defeated in the Assembléia da República over amendments to a regional finance bill proposed by the opposition that would allow the autonomous regional governments of the Azores and Madeira to increase their levels of debt. Although the Minister of Finance, Teixeira dos Santos, maintained that the measures would undermine efforts to reduce the deficit and damage Portugal's international financial credibility, the Government ceased its opposition to the amendments later in February after storms and flooding caused severe damage on the island of Madeira. In March public sector workers took part in a one-day strike in protest at austerity measures in the proposed budget, including a freeze on salaries. None the less, the budget received parliamentary approval later in the month after the PSD abstained.

Meanwhile, in February 2010 the Assembléia da República approved legislation to allow persons of the same sex to marry, while preventing married homosexual couples from adopting children. In January, at the bill's first reading, the legislature had rejected demands by the PSD that the question be decided by a referendum. In March President Cavaco Silva, who had made known his opposition to the bill on moral grounds, referred it to the Constitutional Court, which in April ruled that the legislation did not violate the Constitution. Despite speculation that the President might refuse to sign the bill (thus sending it back to the Assembléia, which would be able to overturn a presidential veto), in May Cavaco Silva signed it into law, stating that he did not wish to distract the legislature's attention from the economic crisis. Portugal thus became the sixth country to legalize same-sex marriage.

Recent developments: the EU and IMF bail-out

In May 2010 the Government proposed new austerity measures, aiming to reduce the budget deficit to the equivalent of 7.3% of GDP in 2010: the measures included increases in VAT, income tax and corporate tax. Planned major infrastructure improvements, including a new Lisbon airport, were postponed. The PSD agreed to support the necessary legislation, and later in May a motion of censure proposed by the PCP, in protest at the plans, was defeated. Nevertheless, in the course of the year there was persistent speculation that Portugal would become the third member of the euro area (after Greece, in May, and Ireland, in November) to require emergency assistance from the EU and the IMF in order to avoid defaulting on its debts. This was repeatedly denied by the Government, which pointed out that its budgetary deficit and state debt were not as large as those of Greece and Ireland, and that, unlike in Ireland, there had been no crisis in the Portuguese banking sector, requiring massive government support. However, the international financial markets' lack of confidence in the Portuguese economy meant that the cost of borrowing reached record levels by the end of the year. In October, in its budget for 2011, the Government proposed a third set of austerity measures, aiming to reduce the budget deficit to the equivalent of 4.5% of GDP in 2011, through tax increases (including raising VAT to 23%) and further reductions in public spending, notably on public sector pay, state pensions and family benefits. After some of its demands for less extensive tax increases had been met, the PSD agreed to abstain in the legislative vote on the budget, which was duly adopted at the end of November, a few days after a one-day general strike organized by the CGTP in protest at the proposals and at the resulting likelihood of an increase in the record levels of unemployment.

At the presidential election on 23 January 2011 Cavaco Silva was elected for a second term, winning 53.0% of the valid votes cast, while his nearest rival, Manuel Alegre of the PS, secured 19.8%: only 46.5% of the electorate participated. In the same month the Bank of Portugal predicted that, despite stronger than expected growth in Portugal's GDP in 2010, the economy would again fall into recession in 2011. The cost to Portugal of borrowing on the international markets increased to levels that were widely regarded as unsustainable. In March the Government proposed yet more reductions in public spending, without first consulting the opposition parties (as it had done on previous occasions), and the proposals were defeated in the Assembléia da República. On 23 March Sócrates resigned, but remained as a caretaker Prime Minister, pending an early general election, which was subsequently announced for 5 June. At the end of March it was announced that the budget deficit for 2010 had been equivalent to 8.6% of GDP, compared with the Government's target of 7.3%. On 7 April 2011 Portugal finally made a formal request for financial assistance from the EU and the IMF, which was approved in May. Portugal was to receive emergency loans of €78,000m., of which about one-third was to be provided by the IMF. The three-year agreement was conditional upon the imposition of even more extensive economic austerity measures, including the reform of the country's health care system and public administration, and the implementation of an extensive privatization programme.

Foreign Affairs

Regional relations

Portugal became a member of the European Community (EC, now European Union—EU, see p. 270) in January 1986, and participated in the introduction of the European single currency, the euro, on 1 January 1999. The EU Treaty establishing a Constitution for Europe was signed by the EU heads of state and of government in October 2004. In March 2005 the new PS administration announced its intention to hold a referendum on the EU constitutional treaty in October, after seeking the necessary constitutional amendment. However, following the rejection of the treaty in referendums in France and the Netherlands, in June 2005 the Portuguese Government postponed its own national referendum. The constitutional treaty was subsequently abandoned and, shortly after Portugal assumed the six-month rotating Presidency of the Council of the European Union, an Intergovernmental Conference was convened in Lisbon in July 2007 to draft a replacement. The resulting Treaty of Lisbon amending the Treaty on European Union and the Treaty establishing the European Community, which retained many of the provisions of the constitutional treaty (although it amended existing treaties rather than replacing them), was signed by EU leaders in December. In January 2008 Sócrates announced that the treaty was to be ratified by parliamentary vote in Portugal, rather than by a national referendum, as had been promised for the constitutional treaty. It was speculated that the Prime Minister had come under pressure from other European leaders who feared that a referendum in Portugal might jeopardize the ratification process in their own countries. The treaty was ratified by the Assembléia da República in April and received presidential approval in May; it entered into force in December 2009 following ratification by all 27 EU member states. In May 2011 Portugal became the third member of the euro area (after Greece and Ireland) to receive emergency assistance under the EU's financial stability mechanism, in order to avoid defaulting on its debts.

Other external relations

Negotiations with the People's Republic of China on the question of the Portuguese overseas territory of Macao commenced in June 1986, and in April 1987 Portugal and China signed an agreement whereby Portugal would transfer the administration of Macao to China in December 1999. On 19 December 1999 the sovereignty of Macao was duly transferred (see chapter on Macao). In November 2010, during a state visit to Portugal by the Chinese President, Hu Jintao, China agreed to purchase Portuguese government bonds, and the two countries undertook to increase mutual trade and to conduct joint ventures, particularly in Portugal's former colonies of Angola and Mozambique.

The former Portuguese territory of Timor-Leste (East Timor) was unilaterally annexed by Indonesia in 1976. UN-sponsored negotiations between Portugal and Indonesia began in 1983, but proved inconclusive. Under UN auspices, talks between Portugal and Indonesia on the Timor-Leste issue were resumed in December 1992, but again ended without agreement. In January 1995 Portugal and Indonesia agreed to the holding of discussions, under UN auspices, between the factions of Timor-Leste. In August 1998, following President Suharto's replacement in May and the subsequent implementation of a series of Indonesian troop withdrawals from the disputed region, the UN Secretary-General announced that Portugal and Indonesia had agreed to hold discussions on the possibility of autonomy for Timor-Leste. In March 1999 it was announced that Portugal and Indonesia had reached an accord providing for the holding of a referendum in the territory on the question of either autonomy or independence. The referendum finally proceeded in August, and resulted in an overwhelming endorsement of proposals for full independence for Timor-Leste. The announcement of the result, however, precipitated a rapid decline in the security situation, leading to the declaration of martial law in the territory. In mid-September a multinational peace-keeping force, led by Australia, was deployed in the territory. Following the restoration of order in

PORTUGAL

Timor-Leste and the Indonesian Government's acceptance of the result of the referendum, in December 1999 Portugal and Indonesia resumed full diplomatic relations, which had been severed in 1975, and in January 2001 a new Indonesian ambassador to Portugal was appointed. Meanwhile, Portugal committed an initial 700 troops to the UN peace-keeping force that replaced the Australian-led multinational force in early 2000. The Portuguese Government also pledged an annual sum of US $75m. towards the reconstruction of Timor-Leste. Official diplomatic relations with Timor-Leste were established with the creation of an embassy in Lisbon in 2002. In June 2006 120 members of the National Republican Guard were dispatched to Timor-Leste, following an upsurge in violence in that country. Portugal also contributed police and military liaison officers to the UN Integrated Mission in Timor-Leste, which was established in August.

Portugal played a significant role in the peace process in Angola, a former Portuguese overseas possession. Several meetings between representatives of the Angolan Government and the União Nacional para a Independência Total de Angola (UNITA) rebel group were held in Lisbon, culminating in the signing of a peace accord in 1991. In June 1993, following the resumption of hostilities in January, UNITA rejected Portugal's status as an observer in the new peace process; however, in May 1994 a UNITA spokesman welcomed the possibility of further Portuguese mediation. A new peace agreement was signed in November of that year. In early 1995, however, the neutrality of the Portuguese Government was impugned by allegations that it had given technical assistance to the Angolan Government. In July 1998, following renewed hostilities in Angola, Portugal requested the intervention of the UN Secretary-General. In August UNITA severed its links with Portugal and the other observers in the peace process, accusing them of bias towards the Angolan Government. In March 2000 tensions between Angola and Portugal increased, following comments by the Angolan Minister of Social Communication, accusing the former Portuguese President, Mario Soares, and his son, João, of benefiting from UNITA's illegal trade in diamonds. The allegations were strongly denied by UNITA. However, in May it was announced that military co-operation between Portugal and the government forces was to be increased. Following the cessation of hostilities in Angola in April 2002, Portugal was one of three states with representatives observing the peace process according to the Lusaka Protocol. Portugal was to continue with military support, including overseeing the integration of UNITA soldiers into new armed forces and the establishment of a military academy.

Portugal was also involved in attempts to reach a peace settlement in Mozambique. Relations with Mozambique deteriorated in March 1989, however, when a Mozambican diplomat was expelled from Portugal, following his implication in the assassination, in April 1988, of a Mozambican resistance leader. Nevertheless, in January 1992 Portugal received a formal invitation to attend the peace talks as an observer, and in October a peace treaty was signed in Italy.

In July 1996 Portugal hosted the inaugural meeting of the Comunidade dos Países de Língua Portuguesa (CPLP, see p. 459), a grouping of lusophone countries (including Angola, Brazil, Mozambique and Guinea-Bissau), which aimed to promote closer political and economic co-operation. In late 1998, as part of a CPLP initiative, Portugal played a major role in the implementation of a peace agreement in Guinea-Bissau, ending several months of conflict between government and rebel forces in the former colony. In the aftermath of a coup in May 1999, the deposed President of Guinea-Bissau, João Vieira, was granted asylum in Portugal. Following the bloodless coup in Guinea-Bissau in September 2003, the Portuguese Government provided US $1.5m. in aid to the new Government. New Portuguese legislation on immigration, which entered into force in August 2007, was aimed, *inter alia*, at integrating foreign workers by facilitating the granting of residence permits to undocumented migrants, the majority of whom came from Brazil and lusophone African countries.

Support for the proposed US-led military campaign to remove the regime of Saddam Hussain in Iraq by the Prime Minister, Durão Barroso, provoked strong opposition from rival politicians, including President Sampaio, and public disapproval in early 2003. In January the Government authorized the USA to use the Lajes airbase in the Azores in the event of war. In March Durão Barroso affirmed his Government's support for the proposed military action in Iraq, with or without a UN mandate, and later that month he hosted an emergency summit between the leaders of the USA, the United Kingdom and Spain. However, following the rejection by the UN Security Council of a resolution endorsing military action against Iraq, a compromise on Portugal's stance was announced by President Sampaio: Portuguese troops would not participate in the conflict, although transit facilities would be made available for use by coalition forces. The Government defeated motions of censure submitted to the Assembléia da República in March by the four left-wing opposition parties and, in April, the Prime Minister indicated Portugal's willingness to deploy troops in Iraq for humanitarian and peace-keeping purposes. The proposed deployment gained the conditional support of opposition parties, who insisted that any such mission should take place under UN auspices. In November some 120 members of the paramilitary National Republican Guard were sent to Iraq. The contingent returned to Portugal in February 2005, following democratic elections in Iraq, although six troops remained in Iraq. Following an agreement between the Portuguese and Iraqi Governments, the contingent of six troops completed its mission and returned to Portugal in January 2009.

In mid-2005 Portuguese troops were deployed in Afghanistan as part of the NATO-led International Security Assistance Force (ISAF). Although Portuguese forces in Afghanistan were gradually reduced in 2008, in December 2009 Portugal agreed to contribute a further 150 troops to ISAF. In March 2011 there were 114 Portuguese troops stationed in the country.

CONSTITUTION AND GOVERNMENT

A new Constitution, envisaging the construction of a socialist society in Portugal, was promulgated in 1976 and revised in 1982, when ideological elements were diminished. Subsequent revisions included the provision in 1997 for the holding of referendums on issues of national interest. The organs of sovereignty are the President, the Assembléia da República and the Government. The President, elected by popular vote for a five-year term, appoints the Prime Minister and, on the latter's proposal, other members of the Government, principally the Council of Ministers. The Council of State (Conselho de Estado) is a consultative body. The unicameral Assembléia has 230 members, including four representing Portuguese citizens abroad, elected by universal adult suffrage for four years (subject to dissolution). The mainland comprises 18 administrative districts. The Azores and Madeira (integral parts of the Portuguese Republic) were granted autonomy in 1976.

REGIONAL AND INTERNATIONAL CO-OPERATION

Portugal is a member of the European Union (EU, see p. 270), the Council of Europe (see p. 250) and the Organization for Security and Co-operation in Europe (OSCE, see p. 385).

Portugal joined the UN in 1955; it was elected as a non-permanent member of the Security Council for the period 2011–12. As a contracting party to the General Agreement on Tariffs and Trade, it joined the World Trade Organization (WTO, see p. 430) on its establishment in 1995. Portugal was a founding member of the North Atlantic Treaty Organization (NATO, see p. 368) and is a member of the Organisation for Economic Co-operation and Development (OECD, see p. 376) and the Comunidade dos Países de Língua Portuguesa (CPLP, see p. 459), which has its headquarters in Lisbon.

ECONOMIC AFFAIRS

In 2009, according to estimates by the World Bank, Portugal's overall gross national income (GNI), measured at average 2007–09 prices, was US $222,649m., equivalent to $20,940 per head (or $22,870 on an international purchasing-power parity basis). During 2000–09, it was estimated, the population increased at an average rate of 0.4% per year, while gross domestic product (GDP) per head increased, in real terms, by an average of 0.1% per year. Overall GDP expanded, in real terms, at an average annual rate of 0.5% in 2000–09. According to provisional official figures, GDP declined by 2.5% in 2009, but increased by 1.3% in 2010.

Agriculture (including forestry and fishing) contributed an estimated 2.3% of GDP in 2010, and engaged 11.5% of the employed labour force in 2008. The principal crops are grapes, tomatoes, potatoes, maize, sugar beet, olives, wheat, apples and oranges. The production of wine, particularly port, is significant. The fishing industry is important; the sardine catch, at 90,900 metric tons in 2009, being by far the largest. According to World Bank figures, agricultural GDP decreased, in real terms, by 0.1% per year during 2000–08, although agricultural GDP increased by 4.3% in 2008.

Industry (comprising mining, manufacturing, construction and power) contributed an estimated 23.7% of GDP in 2010 and engaged 29.3% of the employed labour force in 2008. The GDP of the industrial sector remained almost unchanged, in real terms, during 2000–08; however, industrial GDP decreased by 2.7% in 2008. The mining and quarrying industry makes a minimal contribution to GDP, engaging just 0.3% of the employed labour force in 2008. Limestone, granite, marble, copper pyrites, gold and uranium are the most significant products.

Manufacturing provided 13.1% of GDP in 2010, and engaged 17.6% of the employed labour force in 2008. Manufacturing GDP remained almost unchanged in 2000–06. The textile industry is the most important branch of manufacturing. Basic manufactures accounted for 21.8% of total export earnings in 2009. Other significant manufactured products include cork items, chemicals, electrical appliances, ceramics and paper pulp.

Construction provided 6.5% of GDP in 2010, and engaged 10.7% of the employed labour force in 2008.

In 2007 26.4% of electricity production was derived from coal, 28.0% from natural gas, 21.5% from hydroelectric power and 10.4% from petroleum. In 2009 imports of mineral fuels accounted for 12.8% of total import costs. Portugal's heavy dependence on petroleum was reduced in 1997 when a pipeline carrying natural gas from Algeria (via Morocco and Spain) was inaugurated. Investment in renewable energy sources has increased significantly during recent years, in accordance with the Government's aim to produce some 60% of Portugal's energy from renewable sources by 2020. In January 2007 the construction of an 11-MW solar power plant was completed in Serpa, some 200 km south-east of Lisbon; a photovoltaic plant under construction at Moura, in the southern region of Alentejo, which was to be the largest in the world, was connected to the grid at the end of 2008. The use of wind power expanded the 2000s. In addition, a commercial wave-energy project was under way off the coast of northern Portugal. In February 2009 an agreement was signed between Energias de Portugal and the US-based Principle Power to generate electricity from wind turbines off the Portuguese coast.

Services provided 74.0% of GDP in 2010 and engaged 59.3% of the employed labour force in 2008. The tourism industry remained a significant source of foreign exchange earnings in 2008, when receipts (including passenger transport) totalled an estimated US $14,047m. In 2008 there were around 7.0m. tourist arrivals in Portugal. Emigrants' remittances are also important to the Portuguese economy, reaching €1,277m. in 2005. The GDP of the services sector increased, in real terms, by an estimated average of 1.7% per year during 2000–08; services GDP increased by 1.4% in 2008.

In 2009 Portugal recorded a visible trade deficit of US $24,410m., and there was a deficit of $23,952m. on the current account of the balance of payments. Most of Portugal's trade is with other members of the European Union (EU, see p. 270). In 2009 Spain (provided 31.5% of total imports) was the main source of imports; other major suppliers were Germany, France (including Monaco), Italy, and the Netherlands. The principal export market was also Spain (which contributed 26.2% of the total exports) in that year; other major purchasers were Germany, France (including Monaco), Angola and the United Kingdom. The main exports in 2009 were machinery and transport equipment, basic manufactures, miscellaneous manufactured articles, chemicals and related products, food and live animals, and mineral fuel and lubricants. The principal imports were machinery and transport equipment, basic manufactures, mineral fuels, chemicals and related products, food and live animals, and miscellaneous manufactured articles.

The central government budget deficit for 2009 was estimated at €15,426m., equivalent to 9.2% of GDP. In 2009 Portugal's general gross government debt was estimated at €127,908m., equivalent to 76.3% of GDP. In 2000–09 the annual rate of inflation averaged 2.5%. The average rate of deflation was 0.8% in 2009, but consumer prices rose by an average of 1.4% in 2010. The unemployment rate averaged 9.5% in 2009.

Following a period of strong growth during the late 1990s, the economy slowed considerably in the early 2000s. By 2005 the budget deficit had increased to the equivalent of 6.1% of GDP, exceeding the 3% stipulated in the EU's Stability and Growth Pact. The Government achieved some progress in its programme of fiscal and administrative reforms during 2005–07, most notably reducing benefit payments and raising the minimum age of retirement for public sector workers from 60 to 65 years, and the budget deficit decreased to 2.6% in 2007 and an estimated 2.2% in 2008. However, the Portuguese economy officially entered recession at the end of 2008, owing to the effects of the global economic crisis. GDP declined by 2.7% in 2009, following negligible growth in 2008. The budget deficit and general government debt increased significantly in 2009, reaching an estimated 9.4% and 76.8% of GDP, respectively, owing to the effects of the downturn and the impact of a fiscal stimulus package to encourage growth. The state budget approved in March 2010 included measures aimed at reducing the deficit to the equivalent of 2.8% of GDP by 2013, including below-inflation increases in public sector salaries and the postponement of planned investment in transport infrastructure. Further measures, adopted in May 2010, envisaged increases in corporate tax (from 25% to 27.5% on annual profits above €2m.), income tax (by up to 1.5%) and value-added tax (VAT, from 20% to 21%), aiming to reduce the budget deficit to the equivalent of 7.3% of GDP in 2010 and 4.6% in 2011, while the Government's budget proposals for 2011, adopted in November 2010, included new restrictions on public sector pay and pensions, limits on eligibility for family benefits, and a further VAT increase, to 23%. These unpopular measures failed to reduce the budget deficit to the hoped-for level: it was equivalent to 9.1% of GDP in 2010. Uncertainty on the international financial markets as to whether Portugal would be capable of paying its debts led to successive downgradings of its sovereign credit rating, and the cost of borrowing consequently increased during 2010, so that by early 2011 government bond yields (i.e. the interest on debt) were in excess of 8%, regarded as an unsustainable level. In April, following the rejection by the legislature of yet more austerity measures, and the resignation of the Prime Minister, the caretaker Government was finally obliged to request emergency assistance from the EU and the IMF. A three-year programme of loans valued at €78,000m., approved by the EU and IMF in May, was conditional upon the adoption of new economic adjustment measures, including an extensive programme of privatization. Portugal's GDP increased by 1.3% in 2010, partly owing to an increase of 9% in the value of exports, but a contraction in GDP of 2% was forecast in 2011 and 2012, as a result of constraints on economic growth caused by austerity measures, with the rate of unemployment likely to exceed 13%.

PUBLIC HOLIDAYS

2012: 1 January (New Year's Day), 21 February (Carnival Day)*, 6 April (Good Friday), 25 April (Liberty Day), 1 May (Labour Day), 7 June (Corpus Christi), 10 June (Portugal Day), 13 June (St Anthony—Lisbon only)*, 24 June (St John the Baptist—Oporto only)*, 15 August (Assumption), 5 October (Proclamation of the Republic), 1 November (All Saints' Day), 1 December (Restoration of Independence), 8 December (Immaculate Conception), 25 December (Christmas Day).

* Optional.

Statistical Survey

Source (unless otherwise stated): Instituto Nacional de Estatística (INE), Av. António José de Almeida 2, 1000-043 Lisbon; tel. (21) 8426100; fax (21) 8426380; e-mail ine@ine.pt; internet www.ine.pt.

Area and Population

AREA, POPULATION AND DENSITY

Area (sq km)	
Land	91,906
Inland water	439
Total	92,345*
Population (census results)	
15 April 1991	9,862,540
1 March 2001	
Males	5,000,141
Females	5,355,976
Total	10,356,117
Population (official estimates at 31 December)	
2007	10,617,575
2008	10,627,250
2009	10,637,713
Density (per sq km) at 31 December 2009	115.2

* 35,655 sq miles.

POPULATION BY AGE AND SEX
(official estimates at 31 December 2009)

	Males	Females	Total
0–14	828,733	787,884	1,616,617
15–64	3,526,058	3,593,885	7,119,943
65 and over	793,412	1,107,741	1,901,153
Total	5,148,203	5,489,510	10,637,713

REGIONS
(official estimates at 31 December 2009)

	Area (sq km)*	Population	Density (per sq km)
Continental Portugal	88,796	10,144,940	114.2
Norte	21,278	3,745,575	176.0
Centro	23,668	2,381,068	100.6
Lisboa e Vale do Tejo	11,931	2,830,867	237.3
Alentejo	26,931	753,407	28.0
Algarve	4,988	434,023	87.0
Autonomous Regions	3,109	492,773	158.5
Os Açores (Azores)	2,330	245,374	105.3
Madeira	779	247,399	317.6
Total	91,905	10,637,713	115.7

* Excluding river estuaries (439 sq km).

PRINCIPAL TOWNS
(population at 2001 census)

Lisboa (Lisbon, the capital)	564,657		Vila Nova de Gaia	69,698
Porto (Oporto)	263,131		Guimarães	63,058
			Algueirão-Mem Martins	62,557
Amadora	151,486		Parede	61,821
Braga	112,039		Odivelas	53,449
Coimbra	104,489		Amora	50,991
Funchal	103,961		Leiria	50,167
Setúbal	96,776			
Agualva-Cacém	81,845			

Source: Thomas Brinkhoff, *City Population* (internet www.citypopulation.de).

Mid-2006: (UN estimates) Lisboa (Lisbon) 514,773; Porto (Oporto) 230,628; Amadora 175,000 (Source: UN, *Demographic Yearbook*).

Mid-2010 (incl. suburbs, UN estimates): Lisboa (Lisbon) 2,823,965; Porto (Oporto) 1,354,688 (Source: UN, *World Urbanization Prospects: The 2009 Revision*).

BIRTHS, MARRIAGES AND DEATHS

	Registered live births		Registered marriages		Registered deaths	
	Number	Rate (per 1,000)	Number	Rate (per 1,000)	Number	Rate (per 1,000)
2002	114,456	11.0	56,457	5.4	106,690	10.2
2003	112,589	10.8	53,735	5.1	109,148	10.4
2004	109,356	10.4	49,178	4.7	102,371	9.7
2005	109,399	10.4	48,671	4.6	107,462	10.2
2006	105,449	10.0	47,857	4.5	101,990	9.6
2007	102,492	9.7	46,329	4.4	103,512	9.8
2008	104,594	9.8	43,228	4.1	104,280	9.8
2009	99,491	9.4	40,391	3.8	104,434	9.8

Life expectancy (years at birth, WHO estimates): 79 (males 76; females 83) in 2008. (Source: WHO, *World Health Statistics*).

ECONOMICALLY ACTIVE POPULATION
(ISIC major divisions, '000 persons aged 15 years and over)

	2006	2007	2008
Agriculture, hunting and forestry	587.7	584.3	577.7
Fishing	16.2	17.1	17.9
Mining and quarrying	17.6	19.3	18.0
Electricity, gas and water supply	26.1	33.7	32.4
Manufacturing	980.5	954.0	916.9
Construction	553.0	570.8	553.6
Wholesale and retail trade; repair of motor vehicles, motorcycles and personal and household goods	751.2	750.2	777.3
Hotels and restaurants	280.0	288.8	319.4
Transport, storage and communications	239.6	223.7	224.9
Financial intermediation	90.1	95.7	96.1
Real estate, renting and business activities	294.5	325.4	336.3
Public administration and defence; compulsory social security	354.3	327.0	341.9
Education	318.7	306.7	343.7
Health and social work	329.8	340.2	305.4
Other community, social and personal service activities*	164.9	162.4	158.8
Private households with employed persons	152.4	167.5	175.5
Sub-total	5,156.6	5,166.9	5,195.7
Unallocated	2.9	2.8	2.1
Total employed*	5,159.5	5,169.7	5,197.8
Unemployed	427.8	448.6	427.1
Total labour force	5,587.3	5,618.3	5,624.8
Males	2,984.5	2,986.1	2,991.4
Females	2,602.9	2,632.2	2,633.4

* Including regular members of the armed forces, but excluding persons on compulsory military service.

Source: partly ILO.

PORTUGAL

Health and Welfare

KEY INDICATORS

Total fertility rate (children per woman, 2008)	1.4
Under-5 mortality rate (per 1,000 live births, 2008)	4
HIV/AIDS (% of persons aged 15–49, 2006)	0.5
Physicians (per 1,000 head, 2005)	3.4
Hospital beds (per 1,000 head, 2005)	3.7
Health expenditure (2007): US $ per head (PPP)	2,284
Health expenditure (2007): % of GDP	10.0
Health expenditure (2007): public (% of total)	70.6
Total carbon dioxide emissions ('000 metric tons, 2007)	58,063.4
Carbon dioxide emissions per head (metric tons, 2007)	5.5
Human Development Index (2010): ranking	40
Human Development Index (2010): value	0.795

For sources and definitions, see explanatory note on p. vi.

Agriculture

PRINCIPAL CROPS
('000 metric tons)

	2007	2008	2009
Wheat	136	203	110
Rice, paddy	156	151	159
Barley	74	100	76
Maize	647	700	594
Rye	24	22	18
Oats	48	92	67
Triticale (wheat-rye hybrid)	25	42	33
Potatoes	639	567	519
Sweet potatoes*	26	27	27
Sugar beet	254	137	137
Olives	212	346	363
Sunflower seeds	17	16	14
Cabbages and other brassicas*	150	161	163
Lettuce and chicory*	100	101	102
Tomatoes	1,236	1,148	1,347
Cauliflower and broccoli*	40	40	n.a.
Onions, dry*	117	120	n.a.
Broad beans, horse beans, dry*	18	19	19
Beans, green*	17	17	n.a.
Carrots and turnips*	150	180	n.a.
Carobs*	20	20	n.a.
Chestnuts	22	22	21
Bananas*	30	30	n.a.
Oranges	201	177	202
Tangerines, mandarins, clementines and satsumas	56	64	64
Apples	247	239	280
Pears	141	195	249
Peaches and nectarines	53	50	54
Grapes	825	763	488
Cantaloupes and other melons*	22	22	n.a.

* FAO estimates.

Aggregate production ('000 metric tons, may include official, semi-official or estimated data): Total cereals 1,109 in 2007, 1,310 in 2008, 1,057 in 2009; Total roots and tubers 668 in 2007, 596 in 2008, 549 in 2009; Total vegetables (incl. melons) 2,544 in 2007, 2,500 in 2008, 2,703 in 2009; Total fruits (excl. melons) 1,685 in 2007, 1,653 in 2008, 1,503 in 2009.

Source: FAO.

LIVESTOCK
('000 head, year ending September)

	2007	2008	2009
Horses*	19	19	n.a.
Asses*	125	125	n.a.
Cattle	1,407	1,443	1,439
Pigs	2,295	2,374	2,340
Sheep	3,549	3,356	3,145
Goats	509	496	485*
Chickens	37,000*	38,000	39,000*
Turkeys*	7,500	7,500	7,500

* FAO estimate(s).
Source: FAO.

LIVESTOCK PRODUCTS
('000 metric tons)

	2007	2008	2009
Cattle meat	91	109	103
Sheep meat	24	22*	18*
Pig meat	364	381	373
Chicken meat	223	237	247
Cows' milk	1,909	1,961	1,939
Sheep's milk	92	89	82
Goats' milk	27	27	27
Hen eggs	122	124	n.a.

* Unofficial figure.
Source: FAO.

Forestry

ROUNDWOOD REMOVALS
('000 cubic metres, excluding bark)

	2007	2008	2009
Sawlogs, veneer logs and logs for sleepers	2,674	2,368	2,554
Pulpwood	7,369	7,020	6,230
Other industrial wood	179	180	180
Fuel wood	600	600	600
Total	10,822	10,168	9,564

Source: FAO.

SAWNWOOD PRODUCTION
('000 cubic metres, including railway sleepers)

	2007	2008	2009
Coniferous (softwood)	910	909	958
Broadleaved (hardwood)	101	101	135
Total	1,011	1,010	1,093

Source: FAO.

Fishing

('000 metric tons, live weight)

	2006	2007	2008
Capture	229.1	238.4	240.2
Atlantic redfishes	12.8	11.7	8.3
European pilchard (sardine)	74.1	78.9	82.6
Atlantic horse mackerel	17.3	11.7	12.8
Chub mackerel	17.8	22.8	25.4
Blue shark	9.4	12.0	11.6
Octopuses	7.8	10.0	15.1
Aquaculture	7.9	7.4	6.4
Total catch	237.0	245.8	246.7

Note: Figures exclude aquatic plants ('000 metric tons): 0.8 in 2006; 0.5 in 2007; 0.2 in 2008. Also excluded are aquatic mammals, recorded by number rather than weight. The number of whales and porpoises caught was: 1 in 2006; nil in 2007–08.

Source: FAO.

PORTUGAL

Mining

('000 metric tons)

	2007	2008	2009*
Iron ore: gross weight†	14.0	14.0	14.0
Iron ore: metal content†	10.0	10.0	10.0
Copper ore‡	90.2	89.5	86.5
Tungsten ore (metric tons)‡	846	982	823
Silver ore (metric tons)‡	24.2	28.8	22.5
Marble	741	578	n.a.
Kaolin	183.6	231.3	270.5
Salt (rock)	590.6	606.5	576.7
Gypsum and anhydrite	418.0	372.7	n.a.
Talc (metric tons)	12,367	11,220	11,567

* Preliminary.
† Estimates.
‡ Figures refer to the metal content of ores.

Granite (crushed and ornamental): 27.5 in 2006.

Source: US Geological Survey.

Industry

SELECTED PRODUCTS
('000 metric tons, unless otherwise indicated)

	2004	2005	2006
Frozen fish	37.1	43.0	45.4
Tinned fish	48.8	51.2	38.9
Wheat flour	645	664	662
Refined sugar	394	391	402
Prepared animal feeds	4,134	3,916	3,481
Distilled alcoholic beverages ('000 hl)	249	267	221
Wine ('000 hl)	5,207	5,251	4,906
Beer ('000 hl)	7,712	7,702	8,337
Cigarettes (million units)	26,415	27,013	26,608
Cotton yarn (other than sewing thread)	62.5	51.8	47.8
Woven cotton fabrics (million sq m)	140.4	93.0	88.6
Woven woollen fabrics (million sq m)	10.0	2.5	2.8
Knitted fabrics	26.1	35.7	23.8
Footwear, excl. rubber ('000 pairs)	60,790	55,197	53,786
Wood pulp (sulphate and soda)	647	699	709
Caustic soda (Sodium hydroxide)	81	72	74
Soda ash (Sodium carbonate)*	150	150	150
Nitrogenous fertilizers	496	547	437
Jet fuels	779	854	856
Motor spirit (petrol)	2,551	2,466	2,750
Naphthas	1,175	1,188	1,037
Distillate fuel oils	4,703	4,906	5,102
Residual fuel oils	2,969	3,062	2,920
Liquefied petroleum gas	365	391	406
Cement	8,839	8,427	8,327
Pig-iron*†	100	100	100
Crude steel (ingots)*	730	1,400	1,400
Refrigerators for household use ('000)	399	166	208
Radio receivers ('000)	7,805	9,487	10,592
Electric energy (million kWh)	45,105	46,575	49,041

* Source: US Geological Survey.
† Estimates.

2007 ('000 metric tons, estimates): Wheat flour 680; Knitted fabrics 23.9; Wood pulp (sulphate and soda) 1,955; Soda ash (Sodium carbonate) 150 (estimate); Jet fuels 745; Motor spirit (petrol) 2,591; Naphthas 1,071; Distillate fuel oils 4,634; Residual fuel oils 2,622; Liquefied petroleum gas 366; Pig-iron 100 (estimate); Crude steel (ingots) 1,400 (estimate); Electric energy (million kWh) 47,253.

2008 ('000 metric tons, estimates): Soda ash (Sodium carbonate) 150; Pig-iron 100; Crude steel (ingots) 1,400 (Source: US Geological Survey).

2009 (preliminary): Soda ash 150; Pig-iron 100; Crude steel (ingots) 1,400 (Source: US Geological Survey).

Source: mainly UN Industrial Commodity Statistics Database.

Finance

CURRENCY AND EXCHANGE RATES

Monetary Units
100 cent = 1 euro (€).

Sterling and Dollar Equivalents (31 December 2010)
£1 sterling = 1.172 euros;
US $1 = 0.748 euros;
€10 = £8.54 = $13.36.

Average Exchange Rate (euros per US dollar)
2008   0.6827
2009   0.7198
2010   0.7550

Note: The national currency was formerly the Portuguese escudo. From the introduction of the euro, with Portuguese participation, on 1 January 1999, a fixed exchange rate of €1 = 200.482 escudos was in operation. Euro notes and coins were introduced on 1 January 2002. The euro and local currency circulated alongside each other until 28 February, after which the euro became the sole legal tender.

BUDGET
(€ million)*

Revenue	2008	2009
Current revenue	70,419.7	66,624.3
Taxes on income and wealth	16,516.5	14,998.0
Taxes on production and imports	24,291.1	21,365.7
Social contributions	21,551.6	22,446.5
Other current revenue	8,060.5	7,814.3
Capital revenue	1,558.6	1,481.3
Total	**71,978.3**	**68,105.7**

Expenditure	2008	2009
Current expenditure	71,964.3	77,049.9
Wages and salaries	21,435.8	22,424.1
Social transfers	33,190.3	36,436.2
Intermediate consumption	7,240.9	7,632.2
Interest payments	4,834.5	4,648.6
Subsidies	1,969.5	2,336.7
Other current expenditure	3,293.3	3,572.0
Capital expenditure	4,718.6	6,481.4
Gross capital formation	3,773.2	3,979.8
Other	945.3	2,501.6
Total	**76,682.9**	**83,531.3**

* Figures refer to the consolidated accounts of the central Government, excluding assets and liabilities.

Source: Direcção-Geral do Orçamento, Ministério das Finanças.

INTERNATIONAL RESERVES
(US $ million at 31 December)

	2008	2009	2010
Gold (Eurosystem valuation)	10,639	13,577	17,343
IMF special drawing rights	123	1,306	1,283
Reserve position in IMF	165	337	356
Foreign exchange	1,022	811	2,013
Total	**11,949**	**16,031**	**20,995**

Source: IMF, *International Financial Statistics*.

PORTUGAL

MONEY SUPPLY
(incl. shares, depository corporations, national residency criteria, € '000 million at 31 December)

	2008	2009	2010
Currency issued	17.75	19.13	19.91
Banco de Portugal	2.07	1.19	0.87
Demand deposits	52.09	53.29	51.68
Other deposits	134.80	144.62	167.04
Securities other than shares	54.36	79.73	83.14
Money market fund shares	0.02	0.01	0.05
Shares and other equity	45.25	53.56	57.09
Other items (net)	−21.86	−26.82	−35.96
Total	282.41	323.52	342.95

Source: IMF, *International Financial Statistics*.

COST OF LIVING
(Consumer Price Index; base: 2000 = 100)

	2007	2008	2009
Food and beverages	117.0	121.1	116.9
Clothing	106.3	108.1	102.3
Electricity, gas and other fuels	128.7	134.4	n.a.
Rent	123.7	n.a.	n.a.
All items (incl. others)*	123.3	126.4	125.2

*Excluding rent.
Source: ILO.

All items (Consumer Price Index; base: 2005 = 100): 108.4 in 2008; 107.5 in 2009; 109.0 in 2010 (Source: IMF, *International Financial Statistics*).

NATIONAL ACCOUNTS
(€ million at current prices)

Composition of the Gross National Income

	2008	2009	2010
Gross domestic product at market prices	172,021.9	168,073.8	172,836.8
Primary incomes received from abroad	14,491.9	10,615.9	12,482.1
Less Primary incomes paid abroad	20,418.9	17,136.0	17,968.3
Gross national income	166,094.9	161,553.7	167,350.6
Less Consumption of fixed capital	29,865.1	29,613.9	30,817.0
Net national income	136,229.8	131,939.8	136,533.6
Current transfers from abroad	4,900.2	4,549.9	4,754.3
Less Current transfers paid abroad	3,086.7	3,393.9	3,486.3
Net national disposable income	138,043.3	133,095.8	137,801.6

Expenditure on the Gross Domestic Product

	2008	2009	2010
Final consumption expenditure	149,665.5	147,774.3	153,240.0
Households and non-profit institutions serving households	115,704.4	111,948.6	116,032.7
General government	33,961.1	35,825.7	37,207.3
Gross capital formation	39,674.8	33,150.4	32,182.8
Total domestic expenditure	189,340.3	180,924.7	185,422.8
Exports of goods and services	55,861.2	47,017.5	53,333.1
Less Imports of goods and services	73,179.6	59,868.4	65,919.1
GDP in market prices	172,021.9	168,073.8	172,836.8

Gross Domestic Product by Economic Activity

	2008	2009	2010
Agriculture, hunting, forestry and fishing	3,449.0	3,448.3	3,553.5
Electricity, gas and water	5,105.7	5,582.8	6,097.9
Industry	20,942.0	19,313.0	20,062.1
Construction	11,095.6	9,807.1	9,976.7
Trade, restaurants and hotels	27,721.1	27,883.4	29,057.9
Transport, storage and communications	12,817.6	12,021.1	12,309.3
Finance, insurance and real estate	23,928.8	23,554.8	24,064.4
Other services	44,733.2	46,397	47,480.7
Gross value added in basic prices	149,792.8	148,007.5	152,602.5
Taxes on products (net)	22,662.5	19,479.5	21,056.2
Statistical discrepancy	−433.4	586.8	−821.9
GDP in market prices	172,021.9	168,073.8	172,836.8

BALANCE OF PAYMENTS
(US $ million)

	2007	2008	2009
Exports of goods f.o.b.	52,801	57,871	44,494
Imports of goods f.o.b.	−79,251	−91,659	−68,904
Trade balance	−26,450	−33,787	−24,410
Exports of services	23,308	26,299	22,774
Imports of services	−14,315	−16,566	−14,356
Balance on goods and services	−17,458	−24,054	−15,992
Other income received	17,149	18,403	11,063
Other income paid	−26,781	−29,845	−22,015
Balance on goods, services and income	−27,090	−35,496	−26,944
Current transfers received	8,705	9,423	8,931
Current transfers paid	−5,131	−5,779	−5,939
Current balance	−23,516	−31,852	−23,952
Capital account (net)	2,889	3,869	1,922
Direct investment abroad	−5,465	−2,774	−1,245
Direct investment from abroad	2,970	4,681	2,808
Portfolio investment assets	−10,731	−17,149	−22,708
Portfolio investment liabilities	24,712	39,990	40,816
Financial derivatives assets	11,513	33,180	27,425
Financial derivatives liabilities	−11,277	−32,965	−27,276
Other investment assets	−15,795	14,626	−203
Other investment liabilities	22,990	−11,440	2,829
Net errors and omissions	750	−50	679
Overall balance	−962	115	1,095

Source: IMF, *International Financial Statistics*.

PORTUGAL

External Trade

PRINCIPAL COMMODITIES
(US $ million)

Imports c.i.f.	2007	2008	2009
Food and live animals	7,890.0	8,860.7	7,653.3
Fish, crustaceans and molluscs	1,840.1	1,875.4	1,582.2
Cereal and cereal preparations	1,312.0	1,662.3	1,270.1
Mineral fuels, lubricants and related materials	10,924.3	15,139.2	9,033.6
Petroleum and petroleum products	8,471.0	11,371.8	6,631.5
Chemicals and related products	8,415.9	9,383.7	8,182.4
Medicinal and pharmaceutical products	2,579.3	2,931.9	3,011.6
Basic manufactures	13,069.2	13,501.0	9,235.2
Paper, paperboard and articles thereof	1,424.3	1,526.3	1,278.1
Textile yarn, fabrics and related products	2,007.7	1,921.9	1,441.6
Machinery and transport equipment	23,633.3	25,897.7	19,881.0
General industrial machinery and equipment	2,468.2	2,775.1	2,144.9
Office machines and data processing machines	1,726.4	1,960.9	1,535.3
Telecommunications and sound recording equipment	2,533.1	2,660.6	2,224.4
Miscellaneous manufactured articles	7,850.9	8,500.9	7,261.1
Articles of clothing and clothing accessories	2,110.5	2,244.4	2,029.0
Total (incl. others)	78,325.6	90,105.6	69,985.0

Exports f.o.b.	2007	2008	2009
Food and live animals	2,574.4	3,188.6	2,916.4
Vegetables and fruit	679.5	855.3	832.9
Beverages and tobacco	1,625.6	1,776.1	1,679.2
Wine	827.2	856.8	767.2
Crude materials (inedible), except fuels	2,076.0	2,148.5	1,760.9
Metalliferous ore and metal scrap	977.1	930.9	604.5
Mineral fuels, lubricants and related materials	2,280.9	3,274.5	2,202.0
Petroleum and petroleum products	2,072.4	2,754.8	2,047.1
Chemicals and related products	3,611.0	3,820.9	3,094.2
Organic chemicals	843.0	794.0	382.6
Basic manufactures	11,109.9	11,639.3	9,469.9
Cork and wood manufactures	1,640.0	1,599.9	1,236.9
Cork manufacture	1,039.2	1,033.5	852.4
Textile yarn, fabrics and related products	1,949.5	1,867.6	1,540.3
Non-metallic mineral manufactures	1,885.0	2,037.8	1,633.8
Iron and steel	1,390.9	1,481.2	897.1
Manufactures of metal	1,872.6	2,096.1	1,599.0
Machinery and transport equipment	16,074.8	16,810.0	11,632.5
General industrial machinery and equipment	1,996.0	2,229.5	1,644.0
Telecommunications and sound recording equipment	1,592.8	1,548.1	1,331.7
Electrical machinery and appliances	4,250.3	4,371.3	2,227.0
Road vehicles	6,058.6	6,283.0	4,795.0
Miscellaneous manufactured articles	8,186.0	8,381.7	7,118.4
Total (incl. others)	51,517.0	55,940.7	43,396.5

Source: UN, *International Trade Statistics Yearbook*.

PRINCIPAL TRADING PARTNERS
(US $ million)

Imports c.i.f.	2007	2008	2009
Algeria	789.1	1,040.9	384.3
Belgium	2,184.7	2,303.7	1,942.0
Brazil	1,872.7	1,986.1	1,217.4
China, People's Repub.	1,437.8	1,956.5	1,545.4
France (incl. Monaco)	6,534.5	7,164.1	5,982.9
Germany	10,034.0	10,401.4	8,668.3
Ireland	629.1	838.1	676.0
Italy	4,096.1	4,407.1	3,871.0
Japan	774.8	858.6	382.5
Libya	1,085.0	1,457.5	464.3
Netherlands	3,521.0	3,881.6	3,663.4
Nigeria	1,381.8	2,549.4	1,737.1
Norway	933.1	1,019.4	813.9
Russia	752.5	586.8	738.0
Saudi Arabia	592.1	987.4	562.7
Spain	23,100.1	26,033.2	22,066.8
Sweden	826.1	1,082.7	727.5
United Kingdom	2,692.8	2,738.3	2,243.9
USA	1,288.8	1,498.7	1,189.1
Total (incl. others)	78,325.6	90,105.6	69,985.0

Exports f.o.b.	2007	2008	2009
Angola	2,302.1	3,339.1	3,126.7
Belgium	1,250.3	1,310.9	1,045.3
Brazil	351.6	468.2	401.3
Denmark	340.5	366.2	315.8
Finland	284.5	340.0	183.1
France (incl. Monaco)	6,160.3	6,098.2	5,236.8
Germany	6,446.7	6,878.6	5,643.9
Italy	1,978.3	1,930.0	1,614.4
Malaysia	545.4	550.0	33.0
Netherlands	1,402.5	1,605.5	1,551.1
Poland	326.5	389.2	361.9
Singapore	969.4	1,271.5	114.7
Spain	13,774.1	14,116.8	11,390.0
Sweden	573.5	618.1	507.6
Switzerland (incl. Liechtenstein)	340.8	420.1	378.2
Turkey	253.2	263.9	210.5
United Kingdom	2,974.9	2,902.3	2,401.0
USA	2,318.9	1,874.0	1,312.0
Total (incl. others)	51,517.0	55,940.7	43,396.5

Source: UN, *International Trade Statistics Yearbook*.

Transport

RAILWAYS
(traffic)

	2002	2003	2004
Passenger journeys (million)	161	151	153
Passenger-km (million)	3,926	3,585	3,693
Freight ('000 metric tons)	10,739	8,718	11,151
Freight ton-km (million)	2,583	2,073	2,589

Passenger journeys (million): 151 in 2005; 155 in 2006; 157 in 2007; 158 in 2008.

ROAD TRAFFIC
(motor vehicles registered at 31 December)

	2001	2002	2003
Light and heavy vehicles	7,361,572	7,690,019	7,910,572
Motorcycles	371,114	390,209	402,759
Tractors	309,775	322,283	329,761
Trailers and semi-trailers	363,722	376,719	377,552

PORTUGAL

SHIPPING

Merchant Fleet
(registered at 31 December)

	2007	2008	2009
Number of vessels	469	472	482
Total displacement (grt)	1,070,055	1,095,708	1,287,560

Source: IHS Fairplay, *World Fleet Statistics*.

International Sea-borne Freight Traffic
(Figures exclude the Azores)

	2007	2008	2009
Vessels entered ('000 gross registered tons)	151,816	157,056	148,719
Goods loaded ('000 metric tons)	21,174	21,795	19,802
Goods unloaded ('000 metric tons)	47,055	44,862	41,911

CIVIL AVIATION
(million)

	2001	2002	2003
Passenger-km	12,857	14,244	16,421
Freight ton-km	218	206	217
Mail ton-km	20	20	21

2004: 18,591m. passenger-km.

Tourism

FOREIGN TOURIST ARRIVALS BY COUNTRY OF RESIDENCE*

Country of origin	2006	2007	2008
Belgium	144,300	158,292	169,913
Brazil	200,709	246,190	306,228
France	535,099	594,259	665,737
Germany	718,964	722,084	736,200
Ireland	148,237	166,453	168,705
Italy	394,040	401,994	380,226
Japan	76,821	66,446	63,486
Netherlands	325,748	331,005	363,215
Spain	1,345,724	1,423,034	1,365,372
Sweden	102,406	99,136	104,870
United Kingdom	1,166,933	1,245,914	1,261,871
USA	248,393	259,849	227,068
Total (incl. others)	6,349,449	6,787,797	6,961,707

* Arrivals at all accommodation establishments.

Receipts from tourism (US $ million, incl. passenger transport): 10,438 in 2006; 12,917 in 2007, 14,047 in 2008.

Source: World Tourism Organization.

Communications Media

	2007	2008	2009
Telephones ('000 main lines in use)	4,203.8	4,110.5	4,254.9
Mobile cellular telephones ('000 subscribers)	13,477.4	14,953.2	15,929.4
Internet users ('000)	4,478.8	4,711.8	5,168.3
Broadband subscribers ('000)	1,512.4	1,635.4	1,865.1

Personal computers: 1,938,455 (182.5 per 1,000 persons) in 2008.

Source: International Telecommunication Union.

Radio receivers ('000 in use): 3,020 in 1997.

Television receivers ('000 in use): 6,319 in 2000.

Books published (titles): 2,186 in 1998.

Daily newspapers (number of titles): 28 (total distribution 1,026,000) in 2000; 27 in 2004.

Non-daily newspapers: 242 (average circulation 1,152,000) in 1999; 596 in 2004.

Sources: mainly UN, *Statistical Yearbook*; UNESCO Institute for Statistics; UNESCO, *Statistical Yearbook*.

Education

(public and private, 2008/09)

	Institutions	Teachers	Students
Pre-school	6,981	18,242	274,628
Basic: 1st cycle	5,865	34,361	488,114
Basic: 2nd cycle	1,163	34,069	271,924
Basic: 3rd cycle	1,526	91,325	523,155
Secondary	947		498,327
Higher	301	35,380	373,002

Pupil-teacher ratio (primary education, UNESCO estimate): 11.3 in 2007/08 (Source: UNESCO Institute for Statistics).

Adult literacy rate (UN estimates): 94.6% (males 96.5%; females 92.9%) in 2008 (Source: UNESCO Institute for Statistics).

Directory

The Government

HEAD OF STATE

President: ANÍBAL CAVACO SILVA (took office 9 March 2006; re-elected 23 January 2011).

COUNCIL OF MINISTERS
(May 2011)

The interim Government comprises members of the Partido Socialista (PS) and independents (Ind.).

On 23 March 2011 the Prime Minister, José Sócrates, resigned following the rejection of proposed austerity measures by the Chamber of Deputies. Sócrates continued as Caretaker Prime Minister in an administration with limited powers, pending a general election, which was to be held on 5 June.

Caretaker Prime Minister: JOSÉ SÓCRATES CARVALHO PINTO DE SOUSA (PS).

Minister of State and of Foreign Affairs: LUÍS FILIPE MARQUES AMADO (PS).

Minister of State and of Finance: FERNANDO TEIXEIRA DOS SANTOS (PS).

Minister of the Presidency: MANUEL PEDRO CUNHA DA SILVA PEREIRA (PS).

Minister of National Defence: AUGUSTO SANTOS SILVA (PS).

Minister of Internal Administration: RUI CARLOS PEREIRA (Ind.).

Minister of Justice: Dr ALBERTO MARTINS (PS).

Minister of the Economy, Innovation and Development: JOSÉ ANTÓNIO FONSECA VIEIRA DA SILVA (PS).

Minister of Agriculture, Rural Development and Fisheries: Prof. Dr ANTÓNIO MANUEL SOARES SERRANO (Ind.).

Minister of Public Works, Transport and Communications: Prof. Dr ANTÓNIO AUGUSTO DA ASCENSÃO MENDONÇA (Ind.).

PORTUGAL

Minister of the Environment and Territorial Planning: Dulce dos Prazeres Fidalgo Alvaro Pássaro (Ind.).
Minister of Labour and Social Solidarity: Dra Maria Helena dos Santos André (Ind.).
Minister of Health: Ana Maria Teodoro Jorge (PS).
Minister of Education: Dra Isabel Alçada (Ind.).
Minister of Science, Technology and Higher Education: José Mariano Rebelo Pires Gago (Ind.).
Minister of Culture: Maria Gabriela da Silveira Ferreira Canavilhas (Ind.).
Minister of Parliamentary Affairs: Dr Jorge Lacão Costa (PS).

MINISTRIES

Office of the President: Presidência da República, Palácio de Belém, Calçada da Ajuda 11, 1349-022 Lisbon; tel. (21) 3614600; fax (21) 3636603; e-mail belem@presidencia.pt; internet www.presidencia.pt.

Office of the Prime Minister, Presidency of the Council of Ministers: Rua da Imprensa à Estrela 4, 1200-888 Lisbon; tel. (21) 3923500; fax (21) 3951616; e-mail pm@pm.gov.pt; internet www.portugal.gov.pt.

Ministry of Agriculture, Rural Development and Fisheries: Praça do Comércio, 1149-010 Lisbon; tel. (21) 3234600; fax (21) 3234601; e-mail geral@min-agricultura.pt; internet www.min-agricultura.pt.

Ministry of Culture: Palácio Nacional da Ajuda, 1300-018 Lisbon; tel. (21) 3614500; fax (21) 3649872; e-mail gmc@mc.gov.pt; internet www.culturaonline.pt.

Ministry of the Economy, Innovation and Development: Rua da Horta Seca 15, 1200-221 Lisbon; tel. (21) 3245400; fax (21) 3245440; e-mail gmei@mei.gov.pt; internet www.min-economia.pt.

Ministry of Education: Av. 5 de Outubro 107, 1069-018 Lisbon; tel. (21) 7811800; fax (21) 7811835; e-mail gme@me.gov.pt; internet www.min-edu.pt.

Ministry of the Environment and Territorial Planning: Rua de O Século 51, 1200-433 Lisbon; tel. (21) 3232500; fax (21) 3232531; e-mail gsea@maotdr.gov.pt; internet www.maotdr.gov.pt.

Ministry of Finance and Public Administration: Av. Infante D. Henrique 1, 1149-009 Lisbon; tel. (21) 8816800; fax (21) 8816819; e-mail gab.mf@mf.gov.pt; internet www.min-financas.pt.

Ministry of Foreign Affairs: Palácio das Necessidades, Largo do Rilvas, 1399-030 Lisbon; tel. (21) 3946000; fax (21) 3946070; e-mail ministro@mne.gov.pt; internet www.mne.gov.pt.

Ministry of Health: Av. João Crisóstomo 9, 1049-062 Lisbon; tel. (21) 3305000; fax (21) 3305175; e-mail info_portal@sg.min-saude.pt; internet www.portaldasaude.pt.

Ministry of Internal Administration: Praça do Comércio, 1149-015 Lisbon; tel. (21) 3233000; fax (21) 3468031; e-mail dirp@sg.mai.gov.pt; internet www.mai.gov.pt.

Ministry of Justice: Praça do Comércio, 1149-019 Lisbon; tel. (21) 3222300; fax (21) 3479208; e-mail gmj@mj.gov.pt; internet www.mj.gov.pt.

Ministry of Labour and Social Solidarity: Praça de Londres 2, 16°, 1049-056 Lisbon; tel. (21) 8424100; fax (21) 8424108; e-mail gmtss@mtss.gov.pt; internet www.mtss.gov.pt.

Ministry of National Defence: Av. Ilha da Madeira 1, 1400-204 Lisbon; tel. (21) 3010001; fax (21) 3020284; e-mail gcrp@sg.mdn.gov.pt; internet www.mdn.gov.pt.

Ministry of Parliamentary Affairs: Palácio de São Bento, 1249-068 Lisbon; tel. (21) 3920500; fax (21) 3920515; e-mail map@map.gov.pt.

Ministry of the Presidency: Rua Prof. Gomes Teixeira, 1399-265 Lisbon; tel. (21) 3923600; fax (21) 3927860; e-mail gab.mp@mp.gov.pt; internet www.mp.gov.pt.

Ministry of Public Works, Transport and Communications: Palácio do Conde de Penafiel, Rua de São Mamede (ao Caldas) 21, 1149-050 Lisbon; tel. (21) 8815100; fax (21) 8867622; e-mail gmoptc@moptc.gov.pt; internet www.moptc.pt.

Ministry of Science, Technology and Higher Education: Palácio das Laranjeiras, Estrada das Laranjeiras 197–205, 1649-018 Lisbon; tel. (21) 7231000; fax (21) 7271457; e-mail mctes@mctes.gov.pt; internet www.mctes.pt.

COUNCIL OF STATE

The Council of State (Conselho de Estado) is the political consultative organ of the President of the Republic. It is presided over by the President and comprises the President of the Assembleia da República (Assembly of the Republic), the Prime Minister, the President of the Constitutional Court, the Superintendent of Justice, the Presidents of the Regional Governments, certain former Presidents of the Republic, five citizens nominated by the President of the Republic and five citizens elected by the Assembly.

President

Election, 23 January 2011

Candidate	Votes	% of votes
Aníbal Cavaco Silva (PSD) (CDS-PP)	2,231,603	52.95
Manuel Alegre (PS) (BE)	832,637	19.76
Fernando Nobre (Ind.)	594,068	14.10
Francisco Lopes (CDU—PCP-PEV)	300,921	7.14
José Coelho (PND)	189,091	4.49
Defensor Moura (Ind.)	66,112	1.57
Total	**4,214,432***	**100.00**

*Excluding 191,284 blank and 86,581 spoiled votes.

Legislature

Assembleia da República
(Assembly of the Republic)

Palácio de São Bento, 1249-068 Lisbon; tel. (21) 3919267; fax (21) 3917434; e-mail correio.geral@ar.parlamento.pt; internet www.parlamento.pt.

President: Jaime José Matos da Gama.

General Election, 27 September 2009

Party	Votes	% of votes	Seats
Partido Socialista (PS)	2,077,695	37.73	97
Partido Social Democrata (PSD)	1,654,777	30.05	81
Centro Democrático Social-Partido Popular (CDS-PP)	592,997	10.77	21
Bloco de Esquerda (BE)	558,062	10.13	16
Coligação Democrática Unitária (PCP-PEV)	446,994	8.12	15
Others	176,258	3.20	—
Total	**5,506,783**	**100.00**	**230**

Autonomous Regions

Following the promulgation of a new Constitution in 1976, the mid-Atlantic archipelagos of the Azores and Madeira were officially designated as Autonomous Regions of the Portuguese Republic. Each region is afforded a degree of political and administrative autonomy, as well as the power to raise funds through taxation. Members of the Legislative Assemblies are elected by universal suffrage for a term of four years, according to a system of proportional representation. Executive functions are vested in a Regional Government. The state is represented in each region by a Minister of the Republic, who appoints both the President of the Regional Government and its members.

OS AÇORES
(The Azores)

President of the Regional Government: Carlos Manuel Martins do Vale César (PS).

Assembleia Legislativa da Região Autónoma dos Açores
Rua Marcelino Lima, 9901 858 Horta, Azores; tel. (292) 207600; fax (292) 293798; e-mail secgeral@alra.pt; internet www.alra.pt.

President of the Assembly: Francisco Coelho.

Election, 19 October 2008

Party	Seats
Partido Socialista (PS)	30
Partido Social Democrata (PSD)	18
Centro Democrático Social-Partido Popular (CDS-PP)	5
Bloco de Esquerda (BE)	2
Coligação Democrática Unitária (PCP/PEV)	1
Partido Popular Monárquico (PPM)	1
Total	**57**

PORTUGAL   *Directory*

MADEIRA

President of the Regional Government: Dr ALBERTO JOÃO JARDIM (PSD).

Assembleia Legislativa da Região Autónoma da Madeira
Av. do Mar e das Comunidades Madeirenses, 9004 506 Funchal, Madeira; tel. (291) 210500; fax (291) 232977; e-mail info@alram.pt; internet www.alram.pt.
President of the Assembly: JOSÉ MIGUEL JARDIM D'OLIVAL DE MENDONÇA.

Election, 6 May 2007

Party	Seats
Partido Social Democrata (PSD)	33
Partido Socialista (PS)	7
Coligação Democrática Unitária (PCP/PEV)	2
Centro Democrático Social-Partido Popular (CDS-PP)	2
Bloco de Esquerda (BE)	1
Partido da Terra (MPT)	1
Nova Democrácia (PND)	1
Total	**47**

Election Commission

Comissão Nacional de Eleições (CNE): Av. D. Carlos I 128, 7°, 1249-065 Lisbon; tel. (21) 3923800; fax (21) 3953543; e-mail cne@cne.pt; internet www.cne.pt; Pres. appointed by the judiciary, other mems by the Assembleia da República and the Govt; Pres. Dr FERNANDO COSTA DE SOARES.

Political Organizations

Bloco de Esquerda (BE) (Left Bloc): Rua da Palma 268, 1100-394 Lisbon; tel. (21) 3510510; fax (21) 3510519; e-mail bloco.esquerda@bloco.org; internet www.bloco.org; f. 1999 by several left-wing groups; Leader FRANCISCO LOUÇÃ.

Centro Democrático Social-Partido Popular (CDS-PP) (Social Democratic Centre-Popular Party): Largo Adelino Amaro da Costa 5, 1149-063 Lisbon; tel. (21) 8814700; fax (21) 8860454; e-mail cds-pp@cds.pt; internet www.cds.pt; f. 1974 as Centro Democrático Social; present name adopted 1993; centre-right; mem. of International Democrat Union; supports social market economy and reduction of public sector intervention in the economy; defended revision of 1976 Constitution; Pres. PAULO SACADURA CABRAL PORTAS.

Coligação Democrática Unitária (CDU): coalition of left-wing parties, led by PCP:

Partido Comunista Português (PCP) (Portuguese Communist Party): Rua Soeiro Pereira Gomes 3, 1600-196 Lisbon; tel. (21) 7813800; fax (21) 7969824; e-mail internacional@pcp.pt; internet www.pcp.pt; f. 1921; legalized 1974; theoretical foundation is Marxism-Leninism; aims are the defence and consolidation of the democratic regime and the revolutionary achievements, and ultimately the building of a socialist society in Portugal; Sec.-Gen. JERÓNIMO DE SOUSA.

Partido Ecologista 'Os Verdes' (PEV) (The Greens): Rua da Boavista 83, 3° dto, 1200-066 Lisbon; tel. (21) 3960291; fax (21) 3960424; e-mail pev@osverdes.pt; internet www.osverdes.pt; f. 1982; ecological party.

Movimento Esperança Portugal (MEP) (Movement for Hope): Travessa das Pedras Negras 1, 4°, r/c, 1100-404 Lisbon; tel. (21) 8844180; fax (21) 8877666; e-mail secretariado@mep.pt; internet www.mep.pt; f. 2008; centrist; Leader RUI MARQUES.

Nova Democracia (PND): Rua da Trinidade 36, 1200-302 Lisbon; tel. (21) 3247020; fax (21) 3247029; e-mail partidonovademocracia@gmail.com; internet www.pnd.pt; f. 2003 by disaffected mems of the CDS-PP; right-wing, nationalist and Eurosceptic; Pres. MANUEL MONTEIRO; Sec.-Gen. JOEL VIANA.

Partido Comunista dos Trabalhadores Portugueses/Movimento Revolucionário Português do Proletariado (PCTP/MRPP) (Communist Workers' Party/Proletarian Portuguese Revolutionary Movement): Rua da Palma 159, 2°A dto, 1100-391 Lisbon; tel. (21) 8880780; fax (21) 8884036; e-mail pctp@pctpmrpp.org; internet www.pctpmrpp.org; f. 1970 as Movimento Reorganizativo do Partido do Proletariado; present name adopted 1976; Leader LUÍS FRANCO.

Partido Nacional Renovador (PNR) (National Renewal Party): Apartado 2130, 1103-001 Lisbon; tel. 964378225; internet www.pnr.pt; extreme nationalist; f. 2000 by fmr mems of Movimento de Acção Nacional and Partido Renovador Democrático; Leader JOSÉ PINTO-COELHO.

Partido Popular Monárquico (PPM) (Popular Monarchist Party): Travessa da Pimenteira 2, r/c esq., 1300-460 Lisbon; tel. and fax (21) 3622153; e-mail ppm.geral@sapo.pt; internet www.ppm.pt; f. 1974; advocates a system of constitutional monarchy; Pres. PAULO ESTÉVÃO.

Partido Social Democrata (PSD) (Social Democratic Party): Rua de São Caetano 9, 1249-087 Lisbon; tel. (21) 3918500; fax (21) 3976967; e-mail psd@psd.pt; internet www.psd.pt; f. 1974 as Partido Popular Democrático; present name adopted 1976; centre-right; aims to promote market economy, taking into account the welfare of the community; encourages European integration; Leader PEDRO PASSOS COELHO; Sec.-Gen. MIGUEL RELVAS.

Partido Socialista (PS) (Socialist Party): Largo do Rato 2, 1269-143 Lisbon; tel. (21) 3822000; fax (21) 3822022; e-mail portal@ps.pt; internet www.ps.pt; f. 1973 from fmr Acção Socialista Portuguesa (Portuguese Socialist Action); affiliate of the Socialist International and Party of European Socialists; advocates a society of greater social justice and co-operation between public, private and co-operative sectors, while respecting public liberties and the will of the majority attained through free elections; Pres. ANTÓNIO DE ALMEIDA SANTOS; Sec.-Gen. JOSÉ SÓCRATES CARVALHO PINTO DE SOUSA.

Partido da Terra (MPT) (The Earth Party): Rua da Beneficência 111, 1°, Apartado 43050, 1601-301 Lisbon; tel. (96) 9640021; fax (21) 8438029; e-mail mpt@mpt.pt; internet www.mpt.pt; f. 1993; contested 2005 election in coalition with PSD; Pres. PAULO NORONHA TRANCOSO.

Diplomatic Representation

EMBASSIES IN PORTUGAL

Algeria: Rua Duarte Pacheco Pereira 58, 1400-140 Lisbon; tel. (21) 3041520; fax (21) 3010393; e-mail embaixada-argelia@clix.pt; internet www.emb-argelia.pt; Ambassador FATIHA SELMANE.

Andorra: Rua do Possolo 76, 2°, 1350-251 Lisbon; tel. (21) 3913740; fax (21) 3913749; e-mail embaixada@andorra.pt; Ambassador JULIÀ VILA.

Angola: Av. da República 68, 1069-213 Lisbon; tel. (21) 7961830; fax (21) 7971238; e-mail embaixadadeangola@mail.telepac.pt; internet www.embaixadadeangola.org; Ambassador JOSÉ MARCOS BARRICA.

Argentina: Av. João Crisóstomo 8, r/c esq., 1000-178 Lisbon; tel. (21) 7959223; fax (21) 7959225; e-mail embargpi@mail.telepac.pt; Ambassador JORGE MARCELO FAURIE.

Australia: Av. da Liberdade 200, 2°, 1250-147 Lisbon; tel. (21) 33101500; fax (21) 3101555; e-mail austemb.lisbon@dfat.gov.au; internet www.portugal.embassy.gov.au; Ambassador PATRICK LAWLESS.

Austria: Av. Infante Santo 43, 4°, 1399-046 Lisbon; tel. (21) 3943900; fax (21) 3958224; e-mail lissabon-ob@bmeia.gv.at; Ambassador BERNHARD WRABETZ.

Belgium: Praça Marquês de Pombal 14, 6°, 1269-024 Lisbon; tel. (21) 3170510; fax (21) 3561556; e-mail lisbon@diplobel.fed.be; internet www.diplomatie.be/lisbon; Ambassador JEAN-MIGUEL VERANNE-MANDE WATERVLIET.

Brazil: Quinta de Mil Flores, Estrada das Laranjeiras 144, 1649-021 Lisbon; tel. (21) 7248510; fax (21) 7267623; e-mail geral@embaixadadobrasil.pt; internet www.embaixadadobrasil.pt; Ambassador MÁRIO VILALVA.

Bulgaria: Rua do Sacramento à Lapa 31, 1200-792 Lisbon; tel. (21) 3976364; fax (21) 3979272; e-mail ebul@mail.telepac.pt; internet www.mfa.bg/lisbon; Ambassador IVAN PETROV IVANOV.

Canada: Av. da Liberdade 198–200, 3°, 1269-121 Lisbon; tel. (21) 3164600; fax (21) 3164693; e-mail lsbon@international.gc.ca; internet www.canadainternational.gc.ca/portugal; Ambassador ANNE-MARIE BOURCIER.

Cape Verde: Av. do Restelo 33, 1449-025 Lisbon; tel. (21) 3041440; fax (21) 3041466; e-mail info@embcv.pt; internet www.embcv.pt; Ambassador ARNALDO ANDRADE RAMOS.

Chile: Av. Miguel Bombarda 5, 1°, 1000-207 Lisbon; tel. (21) 3148054; fax (21) 3150909; e-mail embachile@net.novis.pt; internet www.emb-chile.pt; Ambassador LUIS FERNANDO AYALA GONZÁLEZ.

China, People's Republic: Rua do Pau de Bandeira 11–13, 1200-756 Lisbon; tel. (21) 3928430; fax (21) 3928431; e-mail chinaemb_pt@mfa.gov.cn; internet pt.china-embassy.org/pot; Ambassador ZHANG BEISAN.

Colombia: Palácio Sottomayor, 6°, Av. Fontes Pereira de Melo 16, 1050-021 Lisbon; tel. (21) 3188480; fax (21) 3188499; e-mail embajada@embaixadadacolombia.pt; internet www

PORTUGAL

.embaixadadacolombia.pt; Ambassador GERMÁN SANTAMARÍA BARRAGÁN.

Congo, Democratic Republic: Av. Fontes Pereira de Melo 31, 7°, 1050-117 Lisbon; tel. and fax (21) 3522895; e-mail ambalisbonne@minaffecirde.cd; Chargé d'affaires a.i. MBULA KELE-KELE.

Croatia: Rua D. Lourenço de Almeida 24, 1400-126 Lisbon; tel. (21) 3021033; fax (21) 3021251; e-mail croemb.lisboa@mvpei.hr; Ambassador ŽELJKO VUKOSAV.

Cuba: Rua Pero da Covilhã 14 (Restelo), 1400-297 Lisbon; tel. (21) 3041860; fax (21) 3011895; e-mail embaixada.cuba@netcabo.pt; Ambassador EDUARDO CARLOS GONZÁLEZ LERNES.

Cyprus: Av. da Liberdade 229, 1°, 1250-142 Lisbon; tel. (21) 3194180; fax (21) 3194189; e-mail chipre@netcabo.pt; internet www.mfa.gov.cy/embassylisbon; Ambassador GEORGE ZODIATES.

Czech Republic: Rua Pêro de Alenquer 14, 1400-294 Lisbon; tel. (21) 3010487; fax (21) 3010629; e-mail czechembassylisbon@gmail.com; internet www.mfa.cz/lisbon; Ambassador MARKÉTY SARBOCHOVÁ.

Denmark: Rua Castilho 14c, 3°, 1269-077 Lisbon; tel. (21) 3512960; fax (21) 3554615; e-mail lisamb@um.dk; internet www.amblissabon.um.dk; Ambassador HANS KOFOED-HANSEN.

Dominican Republic: Av. Campo Grande 35, 12° A, 1700-087 Lisbon; tel. (21) 7811120; fax (21) 7811129; e-mail embajadom@mail.ptprime.pt; Ambassador ANA SILVIA REYNOSO DE ABUD.

Egypt: Av. D. Vasco da Gama 8, 1400-128 Lisbon; tel. (21) 3018301; fax (21) 3017909; e-mail egyptianembassyportugal@net.novis.pt; Ambassador HAMDI LOZA.

Estonia: Rua Filipe Folque 10J, 2° esq., 1050-113 Lisbon; tel. (21) 3194150; fax (21) 3194155; e-mail embassy.lisbon@mfa.ee; internet www.embest.pt; Ambassador MARIN MÕTTUS.

Finland: Rua do Possolo 76, 1°, 1350-251 Lisbon; tel. (21) 3933040; fax (21) 3904758; e-mail sanomat.lis@formin.fi; internet www.finlandia.org.pt; Ambassador ASKO NUMMINEN.

France: Rua de Santos-o-Velho 5, 1249-079 Lisbon; tel. (21) 3939100; fax (21) 3939151; e-mail ambafrance@hotmail.com; internet www.ambafrance-pt.org; Ambassador PASCAL TEIXEIRA DA SILVA.

Germany: Campo dos Mártires da Pátria 38, 1169-043 Lisbon; tel. (21) 8810210; fax (21) 8853846; e-mail info@lissabon.diplo.de; internet www.lissabon.diplo.de; Ambassador HELMUT ELFENKÄMPER.

Greece: Rua do Alto do Duque 13, 1449-026 Lisbon; tel. (21) 3031260; fax (21) 3011205; e-mail gremb.lis@mfa.gr; Ambassador VASSILIOS COSTIS.

Guinea-Bissau: Rua de Alcolena 17, 1400-004 Lisbon; tel. and fax (21) 3009081; Ambassador FALI EMBALÓ.

Holy See: Av. Luís Bivar 18, 1069-147 Lisbon; tel. (21) 3171130; fax (21) 3171149; e-mail nunciatura@netcabo.pt; Apostolic Nuncio Most Rev. RINO PASSIGATO (Titular Archbishop of Nova Caesaris).

Hungary: Calçada de Santo Amaro 85, 1349-042 Lisbon; tel. (21) 3630395; fax (21) 3632314; e-mail mission.lis@kum.hu; internet www.mfa.gov.hu/emb/lisbon; Ambassador NORBERT KONKOLY.

India: Rua Pêro da Covilhã 16, 1400-297 Lisbon; tel. (21) 3041090; fax (21) 3016576; e-mail hoc@indembassy-lisbon.org; internet www.indembassy-lisbon.org; Ambassador PRIMROSE SHARMA.

Indonesia: Rua Miguel Lupi 12, 1°, 1249-080 Lisbon; tel. (21) 3932070; fax (21) 3932079; e-mail info@embaixada-indonesia.pt; Ambassador ALBERT MATONDANG.

Iran: Rua do Alto do Duque 49, 1400-009 Lisbon; tel. (21) 3041850; fax (21) 3010777; e-mail iranembassy@emb-irao.pt; internet www.emb-irao.pt; Ambassador SAYED RASUL.

Iraq: Rua do Arriaga à Lapa 9, 1200-608 Lisbon; tel. (21) 3933310; fax (21) 3977052; e-mail iraqemblis@yahoo.com; Ambassador HUSSEIN SINJARI.

Ireland: Rua da Imprensa à Estrela 1–4, 1200-684 Lisbon; tel. (21) 3929440; fax (21) 3977363; e-mail lisbon@dfa.ie; internet www.embassyofireland.pt; Ambassador DECLAN O'DONOVAN.

Israel: Rua António Enes 16, 4°, 1050-025 Lisbon; tel. (21) 3553640; fax (21) 3553658; e-mail israemb@lisboa.mfa.gov.il; internet lisbon.mfa.gov.il; Ambassador EHUD GOL.

Italy: Largo Conde de Pombeiro 6, 1150-100 Lisbon; tel. (21) 3515320; fax (21) 3154926; e-mail ambasciata.lisbona@esteri.it; internet www.amblisbona.esteri.it; Ambassador LUCA DEL BALZO DI PRESENZANO.

Japan: Av. da Liberdade 245,6°, 1269-033 Lisbon; tel. (21) 3110560; fax (21) 3537600; e-mail cultural@embjapao.pt; internet www.pt.emb-japan.go.jp; Ambassador NOBUTAKA SHINOMIYA.

Korea, Republic: Edif. Presidente, Av. Miguel Bombarda 36, 7°, 1051-802 Lisbon; tel. (21) 7937200; fax (21) 7977176; e-mail embpt@mofat.go.kr; internet prt.mofat.go.kr; Ambassador KANG DAE-HYUN.

Latvia: Rua Sacramento à Lapa 50, 1200-794, Lisbon; tel. (21) 3407170; fax (21) 3469045; e-mail embassy.portugal@mfa.gov.lv; Ambassador ARTIS BERTULIS.

Libya: Av. das Descobertas 24, 1400-092 Lisbon; tel. (21) 3016301; fax (21) 302921; e-mail bureau.popular.libia@clix.pt; Sec. of the People's Bureau (vacant).

Lithuania: Av. 5 de Outubro 81, 1° esq., 1050-050 Lisbon; tel. (21) 7990110; fax (21) 7996363; e-mail amb.pt@urm.lt; internet pt.mfa.lt; Ambassador ALGIMANTAS RIMKŪNAS.

Luxembourg: Rua das Janelas Verdes 43, 1200-690 Lisbon; tel. (21) 3931940; fax (21) 3901410; e-mail lisbonne.amb@mae.etat.lu; internet lisbonne.mae.lu; Ambassador PAUL SHMIT.

Malta: Av. da Liberdade 49, 5° esq., 1250-139 Lisbon; tel. (21) 3405470; fax (21) 3405479; e-mail maltaembassy.lisbon@gov.mt; Ambassador Dr JOSEPH CASSAR.

Mexico: Estrada de Monsanto 78, 1500-462 Lisbon; tel. (21) 7621290; fax (21) 7620045; e-mail embamex.port@mail.telepac.pt; internet www.sre.gob.mx/portugal; Chargé d'affaires a.i. FRANCISCO JAVIER PATIÑO OLAVARRÍA.

Moldova: Rua Gonçalo Velho Cabral 31A, 1400-188 Lisbon; tel. (21) 3009060; fax (21) 3009067; e-mail moldembportugal@sapo.pt; internet www.embaixada-moldova.pt; Ambassador VALERIU TUREA.

Morocco: Rua Alto do Duque 21, 1400-099 Lisbon; tel. (21) 3020842; fax (21) 3020935; e-mail sifmar@emb-marrocos.pt; internet www.emb-marrocos.pt; Ambassador KARIMA BENYAICH.

Mozambique: Av. de Berna 7, 1050-036 Lisbon; tel. (21) 7971994; fax (21) 7932720; e-mail embamoc.portugal@minec.gov.mz; Ambassador MIGUEL DA COSTA MKAIMA.

Netherlands: Av. Infante Santo 43, 5°, 1399-011 Lisbon; tel. (21) 3914900; fax (21) 3966436; e-mail nlgovlis@netcabo.pt; internet www.emb-paisesbaixos.pt; Ambassador HENK J. W. SOETERS.

Nigeria: Av. D. Vasco da Gama 3, 1400-127 Lisbon; tel. (21) 3016189; fax (21) 3018152; e-mail nigerieemblisbon@portugal.pt; Ambassador EMMANUEL MBANEFO OBIAKO.

Norway: Av. D. Vasco da Gama 1, 1400-127 Lisbon; tel. (21) 3015344; fax (21) 3016158; e-mail emb.lisbon@mfa.no; internet www.noruega.org.pt; Ambassador INGA MAGISTAD.

Pakistan: Rua António Saldanha 46, 1400-021 Lisbon; tel. (21) 3009070; fax (21) 3013514; e-mail parep.lisbon.1@mail.telepac.pt; Ambassador GUL HANEEF.

Panama: Av. Helen Keller 15, Lote C, 4° esq., 1400-197 Lisbon; tel. (21) 3644576; fax (21) 3644589; e-mail panemblisboa@netcabo.pt; Ambassador FREDERICO HUMBERT.

Paraguay: Av. Campo Grande 4, 7° dto, 1700-092 Lisbon; tel. (21) 7965907; fax (21) 7965905; e-mail embaparlisboa@net.novis.pt; Ambassador LUIS ANTONIO FRETES CARRERAS.

Peru: Rua Castilho 50, 4° dto, 1250-071 Lisbon; tel. (21) 3827470; fax (21) 3827479; e-mail info@embaixadaperu.pt; Ambassador FELIPE U. BERÚN.

Poland: Av. das Descobertas 2, 1400-092 Lisbon; tel. (21) 3012350; fax (21) 3041429; e-mail recepcao.embpol@mail.telepac.pt; internet www.lizbona.polemb.net; Ambassador KATARZYNA SKÓRZYŃSKA.

Romania: Rua de São Caetano à Lapa 5, 1200-828 Lisbon; tel. (21) 3968812; fax (21) 3960984; e-mail ambrom@mail.telepac.pt; internet lisabona.mae.ro; Chargé d'affaires a.i. DIANA RADU.

Russia: Rua Visconde de Santarém 57, 1000-286 Lisbon; tel. (21) 8462423; fax (21) 8463008; e-mail mail@embaixadarussia.pt; internet www.portugal.mid.ru; Ambassador PAVEL F. PETROVSKII.

São Tomé and Príncipe: Edif. EPAC 6°, Av. Gago Coutinho 26A, 1000-017 Lisbon; tel. (21) 8461917; fax (21) 8461895; e-mail embaixada@emb-saotomeprincipe.pt; Ambassador DAMIÃO ALMEIDA.

Saudi Arabia: Av. do Restelo 42, 1400-315 Lisbon; tel. (21) 3041750; fax (21) 3014209; e-mail saudiembassy@netcabo.pt; Ambassador HISHAM BIN SULTAN AL-ZAFER AL-QAHTANI.

Senegal: Rua António Pedro 46, 2°, 1000-039 Lisbon; tel. (21) 3160180; fax (21) 3162530; e-mail ambassenelisbonne@mail.telepac.pt; Ambassador MAYMOUNA DIOP SY.

Serbia: Av. das Descobertas 12, 1400-092 Lisbon; tel. (21) 3015311; fax (21) 3015313; e-mail serviaemba@netcabo.pt; Ambassador DUŠKO LOPANDIĆ.

Slovakia: Av. Fontes Pereira de Melo 19, 7° D, 1050-116 Lisbon; tel. (21) 3583300; fax (21) 3583309; e-mail emb.lisbon@mzv.sk; Ambassador JAROSLAV JARÚNEK.

Slovenia: Av. da Liberdade 49, 6° esq., 1250-139 Lisbon; tel. (21) 3423301; fax (21) 3423305; e-mail vli@gov.si; Ambassador BERNARDA GRADIŠNIK.

South Africa: Av. Luís Bivar 10, 1069-024 Lisbon; tel. (21) 3192200; fax (21) 3535713; e-mail embsa@embaixada-africadosul.pt; internet www.embaixada-africadosul.pt; Ambassador KEITUMETSE MATTHEWS.

PORTUGAL

Directory

Spain: Rua do Salitre 1, 1296-052 Lisbon; tel. (21) 3472381; fax (21) 3472384; e-mail emb.lisboa@mae.es; internet www.maec.es/embajadas/lisboa; Ambassador Francisco Villar.

Sweden: Rua Miguel Lupi 12, 2°, 1249-077 Lisbon; tel. (21) 3942260; fax (21) 3942261; e-mail ambassaden.lissabon@foreign.ministry.se; internet www.swedenabroad.com/lissabon; Ambassador Bengt Lundborg.

Switzerland: Travessa do Jardim 17, 1350-185 Lisbon; tel. (21) 3944090; fax (21) 3955945; e-mail lis.vertretung@eda.admin.ch; internet www.eda.admin.ch/lisbon; Ambassador Rudolf Schaller.

Thailand: Rua de Alcolena 12, 1400-005 Lisbon; tel. (21) 3014848; fax (21) 3018181; e-mail thai.lis@mail.telepac.pt; internet www.thaiembassy.org/lisbon; Ambassador Kasivat Paruggamanont.

Timor-Leste: Largo dos Jerónimos 3, 1°, Santa Maria de Belém, 1400-209 Lisbon; tel. (21) 3933730; fax (21) 3933739; e-mail embaixada.rdtl@mail.telepac.pt; Ambassador Natália Carrascalão.

Tunisia: Rua Rodrigo Rebelo 16, 1400-318 Lisbon; tel. (21) 3010330; fax (21) 3016817; e-mail at.lisbonne@netcabo.pt; Ambassador Mahmud Karoui.

Turkey: Av. das Descobertas 22, 1400-092 Lisbon; tel. (21) 3003110; fax (21) 3017934; e-mail info-turk@mail.telepac.pt; Ambassador Ali Savut.

Ukraine: Av. das Descobertas 18, 1400-092 Lisbon; tel. (21) 3010043; fax (21) 3010059; e-mail emb_pt@mfa.gov.ua; internet www.mfa.gov.ua/portugal; Ambassador Oleksandr Nykonenko.

United Kingdom: Rua de São Bernardo 33, 1249-082 Lisbon; tel. (21) 3924000; fax (21) 3924178; e-mail ppa.lisbon@fco.gov.uk; internet ukinportugal.fco.gov.uk; Chargé d'affaires a.i. Joanna O'Sullivan.

USA: Av. das Forças Armadas (Sete Rios), 1600-081 Lisbon; Apdo 43033, 1601-301 Lisbon; tel. (21) 7273300; fax (21) 7269109; e-mail reflisbon@state.gov; internet portugal.usembassy.gov; Ambassador Allan J. Katz.

Uruguay: Rua Sampaio Pina 16, 2°, 1070-249 Lisbon; tel. (21) 3889265; fax (21) 3889245; e-mail urulusi@sapo.pt; Ambassador Jóse Ignacio Korzeniak.

Venezuela: Av. Duque de Loulé 47, 4°, 1050-086 Lisbon; tel. (21) 3573803; fax (21) 3527421; e-mail embavenezlisboacentral@gmail.com; internet www.embavenezuela.pt; Ambassador Lucas Enrique Rincón Romero.

Judicial System

The judicial system of the Portuguese Republic comprises several categories of courts which, according to the Constitution, are sovereign bodies. The country is divided into four judicial districts, which are, in turn, divided into 37 judicial circuits. The principle of habeas corpus is recognized. Citizens who have been unjustly convicted are entitled to a review of their sentence and to compensation. The death penalty is prohibited by the Constitution. The jury system, reintroduced for certain types of crime in 1976, operates only at the request of the Public Prosecutor or defendant.

Judges are appointed for life and are irremovable. Practising judges may not hold any other office, whether public or private, except a non-remunerated position in teaching or research in the legal field. The Conselho Superior da Magistratura controls their appointment, transfer and promotion and the exercise of disciplinary action.

PUBLIC PROSECUTION

The state is represented in the courts by the Public Prosecution, whose highest organ is the Procuradoria-Geral da República (Attorney-General's Office).

Procuradoria-Geral da República: Rua da Escola Politécnica 140, 1269-269 Lisbon; tel. (21) 3921900; fax (21) 3975255; e-mail mailpgr@pgr.pt; internet www.pgr.pt; Attorney-General Dr Fernando José Matos Pinto Monteiro.

SUPREME COURT

Supremo Tribunal de Justiça

Praça do Comércio, 1149-012 Lisbon; tel. (21) 3218900; fax (21) 3474919; e-mail correio@lisboa.stj.pt; internet www.stj.pt.

The highest organ of the judicial system; consists of 60 judges, incl. the President.

President: Luís António Noronha do Nascimento.

COURTS OF SECOND INSTANCE

There are five Courts of Second Instance (or Courts of Appeal):

Tribunal da Relação de Coímbra: Palácio da Justiça, Rua da Sofia, 3004-501 Coimbra; tel. (239) 852950; fax (239) 838985; e-mail coimbra.tr@tribunais.org.pt; internet www.trc.pt; 46 judges, incl. the President; Pres. António Joaquim Piçarra.

Tribunal da Relação de Évora: Palácio Barahona, Rua da República 141–143, 7004-501 Évora; tel. (266) 758800; fax (266) 701529; e-mail evora.tr@tribunais.org.pt; internet www.tre.pt; 39 judges, incl. the President; Pres. Manuel Cipriano Nabais.

Tribunal da Relação de Guimarães: Largo João Franco 248, 4810-269 Guimarães; tel. (253) 439900; fax (253) 439999; e-mail guimaraes.tr@tibunais.org.pt; internet www.trg.mj.pt; 31 judges, incl. the President; Pres. Dr António da Silva Gonçalves.

Tribunal da Relação de Lisboa: Rua Arsenal, Letra G, 1100-038 Lisbon; tel. (21) 3222900; fax (21) 3479844; e-mail lisboa.tr@tribunais.org.pt; internet www.trl.pt; 108 judges, incl. the President; Pres. Dr Luís Maria Vaz das Neves.

Tribunal da Relação do Porto: Campo Mártires de Pátria, 4099-012 Porto; tel. (22) 2008531; fax (22) 2000715; e-mail porto.tr@tribunais.org.pt; internet www.trp.pt; 91 judges, incl. the President; Pres. Dr José António de Sousa Lameira.

COURTS OF FIRST INSTANCE

There are 258 Courts of First Instance within Portuguese territory: 195 *comarca* courts hear cases of a general nature, while 46 labour courts hear specific matters. There are five family courts and two courts for the enforcement of sentences. Circuit Courts total 33.

CONSTITUTIONAL COURT

Tribunal Constitucional

Palácio Ratton, Rua de O Século 111, 1249-117 Lisbon; tel. (21) 3233600; fax (21) 3233649; e-mail tribunal@tribconstitucional.pt; internet www.tribunalconstitucional.pt.

Rules on matters of constitutionality according to the terms of the Constitution of the Portuguese Republic; exercises jurisdiction over all Portuguese territory; consists of 13 judges, incl. the President.

President: Rui Manuel Gens de Moura Ramos.

SUPREME ADMINISTRATIVE COURT

Supremo Tribunal Administrativo

Rua de S. Pedro de Alcântara 75–79, 1269-137 Lisbon; tel. (21) 3216200; fax (21) 3466129; e-mail correio@lisboa.sta.mj.pt; internet www.stadministrativo.pt.

The highest organ of the administrative system; has jurisdiction over metropolitan Portugal, the Azores and Madeira; there is also a Supremo Tribunal Administrativo Norte and Sul; consists of 37 judges, incl. the President.

President: Lúcio Alberto de Assunção Barbosa.

Religion

There is freedom of religion in Portugal. The dominant Christian denomination is Roman Catholicism. In the 2001 census, of the 8,699,515 respondents to the question regarding religion, 7,353,548 identified themselves as Roman Catholic, 17,443 as Orthodox Christian, 48,301 as Protestant and 122,745 as other Christian. A further 1,773 were Jewish, 12,014 were Muslim and 13,882 followed another religion.

CHRISTIANITY

The Roman Catholic Church

For ecclesiastical purposes, Portugal comprises 17 dioceses, grouped into three metropolitan sees (the patriarchate of Lisbon and the archdioceses of Braga and Évora). At 31 December 2006 some 9,058,788 Portuguese were adherents of the Roman Catholic Church, representing 86.4% of the population.

Bishops' Conference

Conferência Episcopal Portuguesa, Quinta do Cabeço, Porta D, 1885-076 Moscavide, Lisbon; tel. (21) 8855460; fax (21) 8855461; e-mail cep.sgeral@ecclesia.pt; internet www.ecclesia.pt.

f. 1932; Pres. Most Rev. Jorge Ferreira da Costa Ortiga (Archbishop of Braga); Sec. Fr Manuel Morujão.

Patriarch of Lisbon: Cardinal José da Cruz Policarpo, Casa Patriarcal, Quinta do Cabeço, 1800-076 Moscavide, Lisbon; tel. (21) 9457310; fax (21) 9457329; e-mail gab.patriarca@patriarcado-lisboa.pt; internet www.patriarcado-lisboa.pt.

Archbishop of Braga: Most Rev. Jorge Ferreira da Costa Ortiga, Paço Arquiepiscopal, Rua de Santa Margarida 181, 4710-306 Braga; tel. (253) 203189; fax (253) 203191.

PORTUGAL

Archbishop of Évora: Most Rev. José Francisco Sanches Alves, Cúria Arquidiocesana, Largo Marquês de Marialva, 7000-809 Évora; tel. (266) 748850; fax (266) 748851; e-mail diocese@diocese-evora.pt; internet www.diocese-evora.pt.

Other Christian Churches and Organizations

Associação de Igrejas Baptistas Portuguesas (Assen of Portuguese Baptist Churches): Rua da Escola 18, Maceira, 2715 Pero Pinheiro; tel. (21) 9271150; f. 1955; Pres. Rev. João S. Regueiras.

Conselho Português de Igrejas Cristãs (COPIC) (Portuguese Council of Christian Churches): Apto 392, 4430-003 Vila Nova de Gaia; tel. (22) 3754018; fax (22) 3752016; e-mail igreja@lusitana.org; f. 1971; mems include the Igreja Lusitana Católica Apostólica Evangélica, the Igreja Evangélica Metodista Portuguesa and the Igreja Evangélica Presbiteriana de Portugal; Pres. Rt Rev. Fernando Luz Soares.

Convenção Baptista Portuguesa (Portuguese Baptist Convention): Rua Luís Simões 7, 1°, Apdo 3085, 2745 Queluz; tel. (21) 4343370; fax (21) 4343379; e-mail geral@acampamentobaptista.com.pt; f. 1920; Pres. Pastor António Pires; Sec. Maria Hercília Melo; 4,338 mems (2003).

Igreja Evangélica Metodista Portuguesa (Portuguese Evangelical Methodist Church): Praça Coronel Pacheco 23, 4050-453 Porto; tel. (22) 2007410; fax (22) 2086961; e-mail sede-geral@igreja-metodista.pt; internet www.igreja-metodista.pt; Bishop Sifredo Teixeira.

Igreja Evangélica Presbiteriana de Portugal (Presbyterian Church of Portugal): Rua Tomás da Anunciação, 56, 1° dto, 1350-328 Lisbon; tel. (21) 3974959; fax (21) 3956326; e-mail office@iepp.org; internet www.iepp.org; f. 1952; Pres. José Salvador; Gen. Sec. David Valente.

Igreja Lusitana Católica Apostólica Evangélica—Comunhão Anglicana (Lusitanian Catholic Apostolic Evangelical Church—Anglican Communion): Rua de Afonso Albuquerque 86, Apdo 392, 4431-905 Vila Nova de Gaia; tel. (22) 3754018; fax (22) 3752016; e-mail comunicacao@igreja-lusitana.org; internet www.igreja-lusitana.org; f. 1880; extraprovincial diocese of the Anglican Communion under the metropolitan authority of the Archbishop of Canterbury (United Kingdom) since 1980; Bishop Rt Rev. Fernando Luz Soares.

ISLAM

Comunidade Islamica de Lisboa: Mesquita Central de Lisboa, Av. José Malhoa, 1070 Lisbon; tel. (21) 3874142; fax (21) 3872230; e-mail info@comunidadeislamica.pt; internet www.comunidadeislamica.pt; f. 1968; Pres. Abdul Majid Karim Vakil.

JUDAISM

There are Jewish communities in Lisbon, Oporto, Belmonte and Portimão.

Comunidade Israelita de Lisboa: Rua do Monte Olivete 16, r/c, 1200-280 Lisbon; tel. (21) 3931130; fax (21) 3931139; e-mail administrativo@cilisboa.org; internet www.cilisboa.org; Pres. Dr José Oulman Carp.

Comunidade Israelita do Porto: Rua Guerra Junqueiro 340, 4150-186 Oporto; tel. (93) 3192747; e-mail direccao@comunidade-israelita-porto.org; internet comunidade-israelita-porto.org; f. 1923.

The Press

PRINCIPAL DAILIES
(circulation figures refer to Oct.–Dec. 2007, unless otherwise indicated)

Aveiro

Diário de Aveiro: Av. Dr Lourenço Peixinho 15, 5°, 3800-801 Aveiro; tel. (234) 000030; fax (234) 000033; e-mail diarioaveiro@diarioaveiro.pt; internet www.diarioaveiro.pt; f. 1985; morning; Dir Adriano Callé Lucas; circ. 4,073.

Braga

Diário do Minho: Rua de Santa Margarida 4, 4710-306 Braga; tel. (253) 609460; fax (253) 609465; e-mail redaccao@diariodominho.pt; internet www.diariodominho.pt; f. 1919; morning; Dir José Miguel Pereira; circ. 5,033.

Coímbra

Diário as Beiras: Rua 25 de Abril, Apdo 44, 3040-935 Taveiro, Coímbra; tel. (239) 980280; fax (239) 983574; e-mail beirastexto@asbeiras.pt; internet www.asbeiras.pt; Dir António Abrantes; circ. 7,959.

Diário de Coímbra: Rua Adriano Lucas, 3020-264 Coímbra; tel. (239) 492133; fax (239) 492128; e-mail redac@diariocoimbra.pt; internet www.diariocoimbra.pt; f. 1930; morning; *Domingo* publ. on Sun. (f. 1974; circ. 8,000); Dir Adriano Mário da Cunha Lucas; circ. 10,079.

Évora

Diário do Sul: Estrada de Arraiolos, Évora; tel. (266) 730410; fax (266) 730411; internet www.diariodosul.com.pt; f. 1969; morning; Dir Manuel Madeira Piçarra; circ. 5,520.

Leiria

Diário de Leiria: Edif. Maringá, Rua S. Franciso 7, 4° esq., 2400-232 Leiria; tel. (244) 000031; fax (244) 000032; e-mail diarioleiria@diarioleiria.pt; internet www.diarioleiria.pt; f. 1987; morning; Dir Adriano Callé Lucas; circ. 2,267.

Lisboa
(Lisbon)

A Bola: Travessa da Queimada 23, 2°D r/c esq., 1294 Lisbon; tel. (21) 3463981; fax (21) 3432275; internet www.abola.pt; f. 1945; sport; Dir Victor Serpa.

Correio da Manhã: Av. João Crisóstomo 72, 1069-043 Lisbon; tel. (21) 3185200; fax (21) 3156146; e-mail geral@correiomanha.pt; internet www.correiomanha.pt; f. 1979; morning; independent; Dir Octávio Ribeiro; circ. 112,116.

Diário Económico: Rua de Oliveira ao Carmo 8, 1249-111 Lisbon; tel. (21) 3236800; fax (21) 3236775; e-mail deconomico@economicasgps.com; internet diarioeconomico.sapo.pt; Dir André Macedo; circ. 14,639.

Diário de Notícias: Av. da Liberdade 266, 1250-149 Lisbon; tel. (21) 3187500; fax (21) 3187515; e-mail webmaster@dn.pt; internet dn.sapo.pt; f. 1864; morning; Dir João Marcelino; circ. 35,932.

i (informação): Taguspark, Edif. Tecnologia I, Corpo 1, 2740-257 Oeiras; tel. (21) 0434000; fax (21) 0434011; e-mail info@ionline.pt; internet www.ionline.pt; f. 2009; morning; Dir Manuel Queiroz; circ. 15,030 (Oct.–Dec. 2009).

Público: Rua Viriato 13, 1069-315 Lisbon; tel. (21) 0111000; fax (21) 0111006; internet www.publico.pt; f. 1990; morning; Dir Bárbara Reis; circ. 40,913.

Record: Av. Conde Valbom 30, 4-5°, 1050-068 Lisbon; tel. (21) 0124900; fax (21) 3476279; e-mail record@record.pt; internet www.record.pt; f. 1949; sport; Dir Alexandre Pais; circ. 70,436.

Porto
(Oporto)

O Jogo: Rua de Gil Vicente 129, 1°, 4000-814 Porto; tel. (22) 5071900; fax (22) 5504550; e-mail ojogo@mail.telepac.pt; internet www.ojogo.pt; sporting news; Dir Manuel Tavares; circ. 32,741.

Jornal de Notícias: Rua Gonçalo Cristóvão 195–219, 4049-011 Porto; tel. (22) 2096111; fax (22) 2096140; e-mail noticias@jn.pt; internet www.jn.pt; f. 1888; morning; Dir José Leite Pereira; circ. 89,480.

O Primeiro de Janeiro: Rua Coelho Neto 65, 4000 Porto; tel. (22) 0109100; fax (22) 5103291; e-mail geral@oprimeirodejaneiro.pt; internet www.oprimeirodejaneiro.pt; f. 1868; independent; morning; Dir Nassalete Miranda; circ. 20,200.

Setúbal

Correio de Setúbal: Rua Camilo Castelo Branco 163 F–H, Apdo 549, 2900-450 Setúbal; tel. (265) 538810; fax (265) 538813; e-mail correiodesetubal@sado2000.pt; internet www.cs.publ.pt.

Viseu

Diário Regional de Viseu: Rua Alexandre Herculano 198, 1° esq., 3510-033 Viseu; tel. (232) 000031; fax (232) 000032; e-mail diarioviseu@diarioregional.pt; internet www.diarioregional.pt; Dir Adriano Callé Lucas; circ. 1,839.

Notícias de Viseu: Av. do Convento 1, Apdo 3115, 3511-689 Viseu; tel. (232) 410410; fax (232) 410418; e-mail geral@noticiasdeviseu.com; internet www.noticiasdeviseu.com; f. 1974; Dir Fernando Abreu.

Os Açores
(The Azores)

Açoriano Oriental: Rua Dr Bruno Tavares Carreiro 36, 9500-055 Ponta Delgada; tel. (296) 202800; fax (296) 202826; e-mail pub.ao@acorianooriental.pt; internet www.acorianooriental.pt; f. 1835; morning; Dir Paolo Simões; circ. 4,226.

PORTUGAL

Correio dos Açores: Rua Dr João Francisco de Sousa 14, 9500 Ponta Delgada; tel. (296) 201060; fax (296) 286119; f. 1920; morning; Dir AMÉRICO NATALINO VIVEIROS.

Diário dos Açores: Rua Dr João Francisco de Sousa 16, 9500-187 Ponta Delgada; tel. (296) 284355; fax (296) 284840; e-mail jornal@diariodosacores.pt; internet www.diariodosacores.pt; f. 1870; morning; Dir PAULO HUGO VIVEIROS.

Diário Insular: Av. Infante D. Henrique 1, 9700-098 Angra do Heroísmo, Terceira; tel. (295) 401050; fax (295) 214246; e-mail diarioins@mail.telepac.pt; internet www.diarioinsular.com; f. 1946; morning; Dir JOSÉ LOURENÇO.

O Telégrafo: Rua Conselheiro Medeiros 30, 9902 Horta; tel. and fax (292) 22245; f. 1893; morning; Dir RUBEN RODRIGUES.

Madeira

Diário de Notícias: Rua Dr Fernão de Ornelas 56, 3°, 9054-514 Funchal; tel. (291) 202300; fax (291) 202306; e-mail dnmad@dnoticias.pt; internet www.dnoticias.pt; f. 1876; morning; independent; Dir JOSÉ BETTENCOURT DA CÂMARA; circ. 13,677.

Jornal da Madeira: Rua Dr Fernão de Ornelas 35, 4°, 9001-905 Funchal; tel. (291) 210400; fax (291) 210401; e-mail editorial@jornaldamadeira.pt; internet www.jornaldamadeira.pt; f. 1927; morning; Catholic; Dir JOÃO AFONSO DE ALMEIDA.

PRINCIPAL PERIODICALS

Activa: Rua Calvet de Magalhães 242, Laveiras, 2770-022 Paço de Arcos; tel. (21) 4143078; fax (21) 4107050; internet activa.aeiou.pt; f. 1991; monthly; for women; Editor ROSÁRIA BARRETO; circ. 70,800 (2010).

Africa Hoje: Rua Joaquim António de Aguiar 45, 5° esq., 1070 Lisbon; tel. (21) 557175; fax (21) 3557667; e-mail geral@lucidus.pt; f. 1985; monthly; African affairs; Dir ALBÉRICO CARDOSO; circ. 30,000 (2007).

Anglo-Portuguese News: Apdo 113, 2766-902 Estoril, Lisbon; tel. (21) 4661471; fax (21) 4660358; e-mail apn@mail.telepac.pt; f. 1937; Thurs.; English language newspaper; Publr and Editor NIGEL BATLEY; circ. 30,000 (2007).

Autosport: Edif. São Francisco de Sales, Rua Calvet de Magalhães 242, 2770-022 Paço de Arcos; tel. (21) 4698197; fax (21) 4698552; e-mail autosport@autosport.pt; internet www.autosport.pt; weekly; motoring; Dir RUI FREIRE; circ. 15,523 (2010).

Avante: Av. Almirante Gago Coutinho 121, 1700-029 Lisbon; tel. (21) 7817190; fax (21) 7817193; e-mail avante.pcp@mail.telepac.pt; internet www.avante.pt; weekly; organ of the Portuguese Communist Party; Dir JOSÉ CASANOVA.

Brotéria—Revista de Cultura: Rua Maestro António Taborda 14, 1249-094 Lisbon; tel. (21) 3961660; fax (21) 3956629; e-mail geral@broteria.pt; internet www.broteria.pt; f. 1902; monthly; review of culture; Dir ANTÓNIO VAZ PINTO; circ. 1,400 (2007).

Casa & Jardim: Rua da Misericórdia 137, s/loja, 1249-037 Lisbon; tel. (21) 3472127; fax (21) 3421490; e-mail direccao@casajardim.pt; f. 1978; monthly; home, interior and exterior design, fine arts, exhibitions and antique fairs; Dir EDUARDO FORTUNATO DE ALMEIDA; circ. 14,486 (2006).

Colóquio/Letras: Av. de Berna 45, 1067-001 Lisbon; tel. (21) 7823567; fax (21) 7823631; e-mail coloquioletras@gulbenkian.pt; internet www.coloquio.gulbenkian.pt; f. 1971; 3 a year; literary; Dir Prof. NUNO JÚDICE; circ. 2,000.

Correio da Madeira: Rua do Carmo 19, 3° dto, 9000 Funchal; tel. (291) 20738; f. 1987; weekly newspaper; Dir JOSÉ CAMPOS; circ. 5,000.

Eles e Elas: Rua de São Bento 311, 3° esq., 1269-083 Lisbon; tel. (21) 3224660; fax (21) 3224679; e-mail gabinete1@gabinete1.pt; internet www.gabinete1.pt; f. 1983; monthly; fashion, culture, social events; Dir MARIA DA LUZ DE BRAGANÇA.

Elle: Rua Filipe Folque 40, 4°, 1050 Lisbon; tel. (21) 3156907; fax (21) 3164205; e-mail elle@hachette.pt; f. 1988; monthly; women's magazine; Dir FÁTIMA COTTA; circ. 44,533 (2010).

Expresso: Edif. S. Francisco de Sales, Rua Calvet de Magalhães 242, 2770-022 Paço de Arcos; tel. (21) 4544000; fax (21) 4435349; e-mail director@expresso.pt; internet www.expresso.pt; weekly newspaper; Dir HENRIQUE MONTEIRO; circ. 104,131 (2010).

Gente e Viagens: Rua Joaquim António de Aguiar 45, 1099-058 Lisbon; tel. (21) 3839810; fax (21) 862746; e-mail lucidus@mail.telepac.pt; internet genteviagens.sapo.pt; f. 1980; monthly; tourism; circ. 30,000.

Guia—Revista Prática: Av. Almirante Gago Coutinho 113, 1749-087 Lisbon; tel. (21) 8474410; fax (21) 8474396; e-mail mpcorreia@tvguia.pt; weekly; fashion and housekeeping; Dir MARGARIDA PINTO CORREIA; Editor-in-Chief PALMIRA SIMÕES; circ. 40,000.

JL (Jornal de Letras, Artes e Ideias): Rua Calvet de Magalhães 242, Laveiras, 2770-022 Paço de Arcos; tel. (21) 574520; e-mail jcvasconcelos@edimpresa.pt; internet aeiou.visao.pt/jornal-de-letras; f. 1981; fortnightly; Dir JOSÉ CARLOS DE VASCONCELOS; circ. 7,679 (2010).

Manchete: Rua de São Bento 311, 3° esq., 1269-083 Lisbon; tel. (21) 3224660; fax (21) 3224679; e-mail gabinete1@gabinete1.pt; internet www.gabinete1.pt; f. 1992; monthly; national and international events; Dir MARIA DA LUZ DE BRAGANÇA.

Maria: Av. Miguel Bombarda 33, 2745 Queluz; tel. 4364401; fax 4365001; internet www.impala.pt; f. 1977; weekly; women's magazine; Dir JACQUES RODRIGUES; Editor-in-Chief PAULA RODRIGUES; circ. 204,451 (2010).

Máxima: Av. João Crisóstomo 72, 3°, 1069-043 Lisbon; tel. (21) 3309400; fax (21) 3540410; e-mail lauratorres@maxima.cofina.pt; internet www.maxima.pt; f. 1989; women's magazine; Dir LAURA LUZES TORRES; circ. 68,459 (2006).

Moda & Moda: Rua Braamcamp 12, r/c esq., 1250-050 Lisbon; tel. (21) 3862426; fax (21) 3862426; e-mail modaemoda@netcabo.pt; f. 1984; 5 a year; fashion, beauty and art; Dir MARIONELA GUSMÃO; circ. 20,000 (2007).

Mulher Moderna: Rua da Impala 33A, 2710-070 Sintra; tel. (21) 9238218; fax (21) 9238463; internet www.impala.pt; f. 1988; weekly; women's magazine; Dir JACQUES RODRIGUES; Editor-in-Chief PAULA RODRIGUES; circ. 16,512 (2006).

Nova Gente: Rua da Impala 33A, 2710-070 Sintra; tel. (21) 9238130; fax (21) 9238197; internet www.impala.pt; f. 1979; weekly; popular; Dir JACQUES RODRIGUES; Editor-in-Chief ANTÓNIO SIMÕES; circ.117,564 (2010).

Portugal Socialista: Largo do Rato 2, 1269-143 Lisbon; tel. (21) 3822000; f. 1967; quarterly; organ of the Socialist Party; Dir AUGUSTO SANTOS SILVA; circ. 5,000.

Povo Livre: Rua S. Caetano 9, 1249-087 Lisbon; tel. (21) 3918500; fax (21) 3976967; e-mail povolivre@psd.pt; weekly; organ of the Social Democratic Party; Dir JORGE MANUEL FERRAZ DE FREITAS NETO.

Revista ACP: Rua Rosa Araújo 24, 1250-195 Lisbon; tel. (21) 3180100; fax (21) 3180170; e-mail apoio.socio@acp.pt; internet www.acp.pt; f. 1908; monthly; motoring and tourism; Propr Automóvel Club de Portugal; Editor ANTÓNIO RAPOSO DE MAGALHÃES; circ. 184,887 (2010).

Revista Exame: Rua Calvet de Magalhães 242, Laveiras, 2770-022 Paço de Arcos; tel. (21) 4698000; fax (21) 4698500; e-mail icanha@edimpresa.pt; internet www.exame.pt; monthly; finance; Dir ISABEL CANHA; circ. 21,074 (2010).

Segredos de Cozinha: Edif. do Grupo Impala, Ranholas, 2710-460 Sintra; tel. (21) 9298033; fax (21) 9238044; e-mail gracamorais@impala.pt; internet www.impala.pt; f. 1985; weekly; cookery; Dir GRAÇA MORAIS; Editor-in-Chief PAULA RODRIGUES; circ. 12,271 (2010).

Selecções do Reader's Digest: Lagoas Park, Edif. 11-1°, 2740-270 Porto Salvo; tel. (21) 3810000; fax (21) 3859203; e-mail clientes.portugal@seleccoes.pt; internet www.seleccoes.pt; monthly magazine; Dir ISABEL BIVAR; circ. 103,690 (Oct.–Dec. 2007).

Semanário Económico: Rua da Oliveira ao Carmo 8, 5°, 1249-111 Lisbon; tel. (21) 3236774; fax (21) 3237603; e-mail seconomico@economicasgps.com; internet www.semanarioeconomico.com; weekly; economy, business and finance; Dir INÊS SERRA LOPES; circ. 10,616 (Oct.–Dec. 2007).

Sol: Rua de São Nicolau 120, 1100-550 Lisbon; tel. (21) 3246500; fax (21) 3246540; e-mail geral@sol.pt; internet sol.sapo.pt; f. 2006; weekly newspaper; Sat.; publ. by O Sol é Essencial; Dir JOSÉ ANTÓNIO SARAIVA; circ. 49,046 (Oct.–Dec. 2007).

TV Guia: Av. Almirante Gago Coutinho 113, 1749-087 Lisbon; tel. (21) 8474410; fax (21) 8474395; e-mail jgobern@tvguia.pt; weekly; TV programmes and general features; Dir JOÃO GOBERN; circ. 73,275 (2010).

TV 7 Dias: Av. Miguel Bombarda 33, 2745 Queluz; tel. 4364401; fax 4365001; internet www.tv7dias.pt; f. 1985; weekly; television magazine; Dir JOSÉ PAULO CANELAS; Editor-in-Chief FREDERICO VALARINHO; circ. 151,770 (2010).

Vida Económica: Rua Gonçalo Cristovão 111, 5°–7°, 4049-037 Porto; tel. (22) 3399400; fax (22) 2058098; e-mail ve@vidaeconomica.pt; internet www.vidaeconomica.pt; weekly; financial; Dir JOÃO PEIXOTO DE SOUSA; Editor-in-Chief JOÃO LUÍS DE SOUSA; circ. 12,202 (2010).

Visão: Rua Calvet de Magalhães 242, Laveiras, 2770-022 Paço de Arcos; tel. (22) 4698000; fax (22) 8347557; e-mail visao@impresa.pt; internet www.visaoonline.pt; f. 1993; weekly magazine; Dir-Gen. PEDRO CAMAHO; circ. 99,771 (2010).

NEWS AGENCY

Lusa (Agência de Notícias de Portugal, SA): Rua Dr João Couto, Lote C, 1500 Lisbon; tel. (21) 7116500; fax (21) 7116531; e-mail agencialusa@lusa.pt; internet www.lusa.pt; f. 1987; Pres. JOSÉ MANUEL DOS REIS BARROSO; News Editor LUÍS MIGUEL VIANA.

PORTUGAL

PRESS ASSOCIATIONS

Associação Portuguesa da Imprensa (APIMPRENSA) (Portuguese Press Association): Rua Gomes Freire 183, 4° esq., 1169-041 Lisbon; tel. (21) 3555092; fax (21) 3142191; e-mail geral@apimprensa.pt; internet www.apimprensa.pt; f. 1961; represents 600 publications, both local and national; Pres. JOÃO PALMEIRO; Sec.-Gen. JOANA RAMADA CURTO.

Associação da Imprensa Diária (Association of the Daily Press): Rua de Artilharia Um 69, 2°, 1250-138 Lisbon; tel. (21) 3857584; fax (21) 3873541; e-mail associacao.imprensa.diaria@gmail.com; f. 1938; 6 mems; Pres. FERNANDO ALVES MONTEIRO; Sec. ADRIANO CALLE LUCAS.

Associação da Imprensa Estrangeira em Portugal (AIEP): Sala da Imprensa, Palácio Foz, Praça dos Restauradores, 1250-187 Lisbon; fax (21) 3464145; e-mail belenchurg@yahoo.com; internet www.aiep.eu; f. 1976; Pres. BELÉN RODRIGO; Exec. Sec. ANNE GOVERNO.

Publishers

Âncora Editora: Av. Infante Santo 52, 3° esq., 1350-179 Lisbon; tel. (21) 3951223; fax (21) 3951222; e-mail ancora.editora@ancora-editora.pt; internet www.ancora-editora.pt; f. 1998; Portuguese literature and culture, factual and educational works.

Areal Editores: Rua da Torrinha 228H, 3°, 4050-610 Porto; tel. (22) 3393900; fax (22) 2005708; e-mail areal@arealeditores.pt; internet www.arealeditores.pt; educational.

Assírio & Alvim: Rua Passos Manuel 67B, 1150-258 Lisbon; tel. (21) 3583030; fax (21) 3583039; e-mail assirio@assirio.com; internet www.assirio.pt; f. 1972; poetry, fiction, essays, gastronomy, photography, art, children's literature, history, social science; Man. VASCO DAVID.

Bertrand Editora, SA: Rua Prof. Jorge da Silva Horta 1, 1500-499 Lisbon; tel. (21) 0305590; fax (21) 7607149; e-mail info@bertrand.pt; internet www.bertrand.pt; literature, arts, humanities, educational; Man. MARIO CORREIA.

Casa das Letras: Rua Cidade de Córdova 2, 2610-038 Alfragide; tel. (21) 0417410; fax (21) 4717737; e-mail servicocliente@leya.com; internet www.casadasletras.leya.com; fiction, politics, religion, history, economics, management, biographies, dictionaries, memoirs.

Circulo de Leitores: Rua Prof. Jorge da Silva Horta 1, 1500-499 Lisbon; tel. (21) 7626000; fax (21) 7607149; e-mail correio@circuloleitores.pt; internet www.circuloleitores.pt; f. 1971; fiction and non-fiction.

Coímbra Editora, Lda: Rua do Armado, Apdo 101, 3001-951 Coímbra; tel. (239) 8526540; fax (239) 852651; e-mail info@coimbraeditora.pt; internet www.coimbraeditora.pt; f. 1920; law, education, linguistics; Man. Dr JOÃO CARLOS A. OLIVEIRA SALGADO.

Edições Afrontamento, Lda: Rua de Costa Cabral 859, 4200-225 Porto; tel. (22) 5074220; fax (22) 5074229; e-mail editorial@edicoesafrontamento.pt; internet www.edicoesafrontamento.pt; f. 1963; fiction, poetry, cinema, children's books, history, sociology, philosophy, economics, politics, etc.; Dirs J. SOUSA RIBEIRO, A. SOUSA LUÍS.

Edições Almedina, SA: Rua Fernandes Tomás 76–80, 3000-167 Coimbra; tel. (239) 851903; e-mail editora@almedina.net; internet www.almedina.net; law, education; Dir JOAQUIM MACHADO.

Edições Asa: Rua Cidade de Córdova 2, 2610-038 Alfragide; tel. (22) 6166030; fax (21) 5322831; e-mail edicoes@asa.pt; internet www.asa.pt; f. 1951; literature, arts, schoolbooks, children's books, educational equipment; Gen. Man. AMÉRICO A. AREAL.

Edições Caixotim: Rua dos Clérigos 23, 4050-205 Porto; tel. (22) 3390831; fax (22) 3390819; e-mail edicoescaixotim@caixotim.pt; internet www.caixotim.pt; f. 2001; literature, history, criticism, essays, art, etc.; Publr and Editorial Dir PAULO SAMUEL.

Edições 70, Lda: Av. Fernão de Magalhães 584, 5°, 3000-174 Coimbra; tel. (21) 3190240; fax (21) 3190249; e-mail geral@edicoes70.pt; internet www.edicoes70.pt; f. 1970; history, linguistics, anthropology, philosophy, psychology, education, art, architecture, science, reference books; Dir CARLOS PINTO.

Editora Educação Nacional, Lda: Rua do Almada 125, 4018-001 Porto; tel. (22) 2005351; fax (22) 2080742; e-mail contacto@editoraeducnacional.pt; internet www.editoraeducnacional.pt; school textbooks and review, *Educação Nacional*.

Editora Livros do Brasil, SA: Estrada da Outurela 121, 2794-051 Carnaxide; tel. (21) 3462621; fax (21) 3428487; e-mail geral@livrosdobrasil.com; internet www.livrosdobrasil.com; f. 1944; literature, history, politics, science, management, health, children's books; Dir ANTÓNIO LUIS DE SOUZA PINTO.

Editora Pergaminho, Lda: Rua de Alegria 486A, Amoreira, 2645-167 Cascais; tel. (21) 4646110; fax (21) 4674008; e-mail info@editorapergaminho.pt; internet www.editorapergaminho.pt; f. 1991; cinema, music, humour, fiction; Dir MÁRIO MENDES DE MOURA.

Editora Portugalmundo, Lda: Rua Gonçalves Crespo 47, r/c, 1150-184 Lisbon; tel. (21) 3304685; fax (21) 3590420; e-mail editoraportugalmundo@gmail.com; internet www.editoraportugalmundo.com; f. 1976; children's books, poetry, biographies, law, music, fiction, theatre; Dir MARIA ALEXANDRA SANTOS.

Editora Replicação, Lda: Rua Pedro Sintra 26A, 1400-277 Lisbon; tel. (21) 3021583; fax (21) 3021584; e-mail replic@mail.telepac.pt; f. 1982; textbooks, children's books, dictionaries, language materials; Dir JOSÉ CARLOS ANAIA CRISTO.

Editorial Bizancia, Lda: Largo Luis Chaves 11–11A, 1600-487 Lisbon; tel. (21) 7550228; fax (21) 7520072; e-mail bizancio@editorial-bizancio.pt; internet www.editorial-bizancio.pt; f. 1998; general fiction and non-fiction.

Editorial Confluência: Calçada do Combro 99, 1200-112 Lisbon; tel. and fax (21) 3466917; e-mail livroshorizonte@mail.telepac.pt; f. 1945; dictionaries; Man. ROGÉRIO MENDES DE MOURA.

Editorial Estampa, Lda: Rua da Escola do Exército 9, r/c dto, 1169-090 Lisbon; tel. (21) 3555663; fax (21) 3141911; e-mail estampa@estampa.pt; internet www.estampa.pt; f. 1960; sociology, economics, occult, fiction, sport, history, art, alternative medicine, children's; Dir ANTÓNIO CARLOS MANSO PINHEIRO.

Editorial Futura: Rua General Morais Sarmento 9, c/v esq., 1500-310 Lisbon; tel. and fax (21) 7155848; e-mail editorialfutura@netcabo.pt; literature, comics.

Editorial Minerva: Rua Luz Soriano 33, 1200-246 Lisbon; tel. (21) 3224950; fax (21) 3224952; e-mail minerva-beta@sapo.pt; internet www.editorialminerva.com; f. 1927; literature, politics, children's; Man. NARCISA FERNANDES.

Editorial Nova Ática, SA: Calçado Nova de S. Francisco, 10, 1° esq., 1200-300 Lisbon; tel. (21) 3420557; fax (21) 3420305; e-mail editorialnovaatica@sapo.pt; f. 1935; poetry, literature, essays, theatre, history, philosophy; Chief Execs VASCO SILVA, JOSÉ RODRIGUES.

Editorial Presença, Lda: Estrada das Palmeiras 59, Queluz de Baixo, 2730-132 Barcarena; tel. (21) 4347000; fax (21) 4346502; e-mail info@presenca.pt; internet www.presenca.pt; f. 1960; social sciences, fiction, textbooks, computer books, business, leisure, health, children's books, etc.; Dir FRANCISCO ESPADINHA.

Editorial Verbo SA: Av. António Augusto de Aguiar 148, 2B, 1069-019 Lisbon; tel. (21) 3801100; fax (21) 3861122; e-mail comerciais@editorialverbo.pt; internet www.editorialverbo.pt; f. 1958; imprints include Editora Ulisseia; encyclopaedias, dictionaries, reference, history, general science, textbooks, education and children's books; Dir FERNANDO GUEDES.

Europress—Editores e Distribuidores de Publicações, Lda: Rua João Saraiva 10A, 1700–249 Lisbon; tel. (21) 8444340; fax (21) 8492061; e-mail europress@mail.telepac.pt; internet www.europress.pt; f. 1982; academic, children's, law, poetry, health, novels, history, social sciences, medicine, etc.; Man. ANTÓNIO BENTO VINTÉM.

FCA (Editora de Informática, Lda): Rua D. Estefânia 183, r/c esq., 1000-154 Lisbon; tel. (21) 3532735; fax (21) 3577827; e-mail fca@fca.pt; internet www.fca.pt; f. 1991; computer science.

Gradiva—Publicações, Lda: Rua Almeida e Sousa 21, r/c esq., 1399-041 Lisbon; tel. (21) 3974067; fax (21) 3953471; e-mail geral@gradiva.mail.pt; internet www.gradiva.pt; f. 1981; philosophy, education, history, fiction, science, social sciences, children's books, cartoons; Man. Dir GUILHERME VALENTE.

Guimarães Editores, Lda: Rua da Misericórdia 68–70, 1200-273 Lisbon; tel. (21) 3243120; fax (21) 3243129; e-mail geral@guimaraes-ed.pt; internet www.guimaraes-ed.pt; f. 1899; literature, philosophy, history, etc.

Imprensa Nacional—Casa da Moeda, SA (INCM): Edif. Casa da Moeda, Av. António de José de Almeida, 1000-042 Lisbon; tel. (21) 7810700; fax (21) 7810754; e-mail incm@incm.pt; internet www.incm.pt; f. 1972 as Imprensa Nacional—Casa da Moeda, EP; changed status as above in 1999; Portuguese literature, arts, philosophy, history, geography, sociology, economics, encyclopaedias, dictionaries, and the *Diário da República*; Dir Dr HELENA ESTEVES FELGAS.

Lello Editores, Lda: Rua Dom João de Castro 539, 4435-674 Baguim do Monte; tel. (22) 3326084; fax (22) 3326086; e-mail joselello@lelloeditores.com; internet www.lelloeditores.com; fiction, poetry, history, reference, biography, religion; Dir-Gen. JOSÉ MANUEL BERNARDES PEREIRA LELLO.

Lidel Edições Técnicas, Lda: Rua D. Estefânia 183, r/c dto, 1049-057 Lisbon; tel. (21) 3511440; fax (21) 3577827; e-mail lidel@lidel.pt; internet www.lidel.pt; f. 1963; Portuguese as a foreign language, management, technology, computer science; Man. Dir FREDERICO CARLOS DA SILVA ANNES.

Lisboa Editora, Lda: Av. dos Estados Unidos da América 1B, 1700-163 Lisbon; tel. (21) 8430910; fax (21) 8430911; e-mail geral@

PORTUGAL

lisboaeditora.pt; internet www.lisboaeditora.pt; textbooks; Editorial Dirs MARIA DE LOURDES PAIXÃO, BRIGITTE THUDICHUM.

Livraria Civilização Editora: Rua Alberto Aires de Gouveia 27, 4050-023 Porto; tel. (22) 6050917; fax (22) 6050999; e-mail info@civilizacao.pt; internet www.civilizacao.pt; f. 1920; social sciences, politics, economics, history, art, medicine, fiction, children's; Man. Dir MOURA BESSA.

Livraria Editora Figueirinhas, Lda: Rua do Freixo 643, 4300-217 Porto; tel. (22) 5309026; fax (22) 5309027; e-mail correio@liv-figueirinhas.pt; f. 1898; literature, school textbooks; Dir FRANCISCO GOMES PIMENTA.

Livraria Multinova: Av. Santa Joana Princesa 12E, 1700-357 Lisbon; tel. (21) 8421820; fax (21) 8483436; e-mail geral@multinova.pt; internet www.multinova.pt; f. 1970; school books, general, religion, Brazilian works; Dir CARLOS SANTOS.

Livraria Romano Torres: Rua Marcos Portugal 20A, 1200-258 Lisbon; tel. (21) 3880430; fax (21) 3040818; e-mail info@estudodidactico.pt; f. 1885; fiction; Dir FRANCISCO NORONHA DE ANDRADE.

Livros Cotovia: Rua Nova da Trindade 24, 1200-303 Lisbon; tel. (21) 3471447; fax (21) 3470467; e-mail geral@livroscotovia.pt; internet www.livroscotovia.pt; f. 1988; literature, drama, poetry, etc.

Livros Horizonte, Lda: Rua das Chagas 17, 1° dto, 1200-106 Lisbon; tel. (21) 3466917; fax (21) 3159259; e-mail geral@livroshorizonte.pt; internet www.livroshorizonte.pt; f. 1953; art, education, history, social sciences; Dir CLAUDIA MOURA.

Lusodidacta (Sociedade Portuguesa de Materia Didáctico, Lda): Rua Darío Cannas 5A, 2670-427 Loures; tel. (21) 9839840; fax (21) 9839847; e-mail loures1@lusodidacta.pt; internet www.lusodidacta.pt; f. 1976; textbooks, dictionaries, medicine.

McGraw-Hill de Portugal: Edif. Castilho 5, r/c A, Rua Barata Salgueiro, 51A, 1250-043 Lisbon; tel. (21) 3553180; fax (21) 3553189; e-mail servico_clientes@mcgraw-hill.com; scientific, technical and medical; Gen. Man. ANTÓNIO DE MARCO.

PAULUS Editora: Rua Dom Pedro de Cristo 10, 1749-092 Lisbon; tel. (21) 8437620; fax (21) 8437629; e-mail editor@paulus.pt; internet www.paulus.pt; religion, theology, psychology, etc.; Dir DARLEI ZANON.

Plátano Editora, SARL: Av. de Berna 31, 2° esq., 1069-054 Lisbon; tel. (21) 7979278; fax (21) 7954019; e-mail geral@platanoeditora.pt; internet www.platanoeditora.pt; f. 1972; literature, educational, science, technical, dictionaries, etc.; Dir FRANCISCO PRATA GINJA.

Porto Editora, Lda: Rua da Restauração 365, 4099-023 Porto; tel. (22) 6088300; fax (22) 6088301; e-mail secretariado@portoeditora.pt; internet www.portoeditora.pt; f. 1944; general literature, school books, dictionaries, children's books, multimedia; Dirs VASCO TEIXEIRA, JOSÉ ANTÓNIO TEIXEIRA, ROSÁLIA TEIXEIRA.

Publicações Dom Quixote: Rua Cidade de Córdova 2, 2610-038 Alfragide; tel. (21) 4272200; fax (21) 4272201; e-mail info@dquixote.pt; internet www.dquixote.pt; f. 1965; general fiction, poetry, history, philosophy, psychology, politics, didactics and sociology; university textbooks; children's books.

Publicações Europa-América, Lda: Rua Francisco Lyon de Castro 2, Apdo 8, 2725-397 Mem Martins; tel. (21) 9267700; fax (21) 9267771; e-mail secretariado@europa-america.pt; internet www.europa-america.pt; f. 1945; imprints include Edições CETOP, Editorial Inquerito, Livros de Vida Editores, Lyon Edições and Publicações Alfa; fiction, current affairs, economics, reference, history, technical, children's; Dir TITO LYON DE CASTRO.

Quimera Editores, Lda: Rua do Vale Formoso 37, 1949-013 Lisbon; tel. (21) 8455950; fax (21) 8455951; e-mail quimera@quimera-editores.com; internet www.quimera-editores.com; f. 1987; literature, art, history, photography, etc.; Dirs JOSÉ ALFARO, LUÍS VEIGA.

Rés—Editora, Lda: Praça Marquês de Pombal 78, 4000-390 Porto; tel. (22) 5024174; fax (22) 5026098; e-mail res-editora@res-editora.pt; internet www.res-editora.pt; f. 1975; economics, philosophy, law, sociology; Dir REINALDO DE CARVALHO.

Texto Editora, Lda: Rua Cidade de Córdova 2, 2610-038 Alfragide; tel. (21) 4272200; fax (21) 4272201; e-mail info@texto.pt; internet pt.textoeditores.com; f. 1977; school textbooks, management, pedagogy, health, beauty, cooking, children's books, multimedia; Man. Dir MANUEL JOSÉ DO ESPÍRITO SANTO FERRÃO.

PUBLISHERS' ASSOCIATION

Associação Portuguesa de Editores e Livreiros (Portuguese Association of Publishers and Booksellers): Av. dos Estados Unidos da América 97, 6° esq., 1700-167 Lisbon; tel. (21) 8435180; fax (21) 8489377; e-mail geral@apel.pt; internet www.apel.pt; f. 1927; Pres. PAULO TEIXEIRA PINTO; Sec.-Gen. MIGUEL FREITAS DA COSTA.

Broadcasting and Communications

REGULATORY AUTHORITY

Autoridade Nacional de Comunicações (ANACOM): Av. José Malhoa 12, 1009-017 Lisbon; tel. (21) 7211000; fax (21) 7211001; e-mail info@anacom.pt; internet www.anacom.pt; formerly known as the Instituto das Comunicações de Portugal (ICP); Pres. JOSÉ MANUEL AMADO DA SILVA.

TELECOMMUNICATIONS

Portugal Telecom, SA (PT): Av. Fontes Pereira de Melo 40, 1069-300 Lisbon; tel. (21) 5002000; fax (21) 5000902; e-mail geral@telecom.pt; internet www.telecom.pt; f. 1994; by merger of 3 regional telecommunications operators; state holding reduced to 25% in 1997; relinquished monopoly on fixed-line operations in Jan. 2000; Chair. HENRIQUE GRANADEIRO; CEO ZEINAL BAVA.

AR Telecom, SA: Edif. Diogo Cão, Doca de Alcântara Norte, 1350-352 Lisbon; tel. and fax (21) 0301030; e-mail 16300@artelecom.pt; internet www.artelecom.pt; f. 2000 as Jazztel Portugal, SA; renamed as above in 2005; subsidiary of Grupo SGC; fixed-line operator.

Oni Communications, SA: Edif. Qualidade A1 e A2, Tagus Park, Av. Prof. Dr Cavaco Silva, 2740-269 Porto Salvo; tel. (21) 1154300; fax (21) 1154399; e-mail geral@oni.pt; internet www.oni.pt; f. 1998; fixed-line operator; CEO XAVIER RODRÍGUEZ-MARTÍN.

Optimus Telecomunicações, SA: Apartado 52121, 1721-501 Lisbon; tel. (21) 7233600; fax (21) 7546275; e-mail 1693@optimus.pt; internet www.optimus.pt; f. 1998; provides mobile telephone services; CEO MIGUEL ALMEIDA.

Sonaecom-Serviços de Comunicações, SA: Rua Henrique Pousão 432, 7°, 4460-191 Senhora da Hora; tel. (93) 1002000; fax (22) 0111850; e-mail comunicacao@sonae.com; internet www.sonae.com; fixed-line operator; merged with Optimus Telecomunicações, SA in 2007.

TMN (Telecomunicações Móveis Nacionais), SA: Av. Álvaro Pais 2, 1649-041 Lisbon; tel. (21) 7914400; fax (21) 7914500; e-mail tmn.comunica@tmn.pt; internet www.tmn.pt; f. 1991; part of Portugal Telecom; Pres. ZEINAL ABEDIN MAHOMED BAVA.

UZO: Av. Álvaro Pais 2, 1649-041 Lisbon; e-mail info@uzo.pt; internet www.uzo.pt; f. 2005; part of Portugal Telecom; mobile operator; Exec. Dir JOÃO MENDES.

Vodafone Portugal—Comunicações Pessoais, SA: Parque das Nações, Av. D. João II, Lote 1.04.01, 1998-017 Lisbon; tel. (21) 0915000; fax (21) 0952899; e-mail press.pt@vodafone.com; internet www.vodafone.pt; f. 1991; fmrly Telecel-Comunicações Pessoais; subsidiary of Vodafone Group PLC (United Kingdom); provides mobile and fixed-line telephone services; Chief Exec. ANTÓNIO COIMBRA.

Other fixed-line operators include Cabovisão, Coltel, Refer Telecom, Telemilénio, TV Cabo and TVTEL.

BROADCASTING

In 2006 there were around 350 radio stations in operation.

Radio
State-controlled Radio

Radiodifusão Portuguesa, SA (RDP): Av. Marechal Gomes da Costa 37, 1849-030 Lisbon; tel. (21) 7947000; fax (21) 7947570; internet www.rtp.pt; f. 1975; part of Radio e Televisão de Portugal SA (see below); Dir of Programmes RUI FERNANDES PÊGO.

Domestic Services:

Antena 1: tel. (21) 7947000; fax (21) 3873972; e-mail antena1.programas@rtp.pt; internet www.rtp.pt/antena1; broadcasts 24 hours daily on medium-wave and FM; news, sport, music, etc.; Dir JOÃO COELHO.

Antena 2: tel. (21) 3820000; fax (21) 3820199; e-mail rdp.antena2@rtp.pt; internet tv1.rtp.pt/antena2; broadcasts classical music 24 hours daily on FM; Dep. Dir JOÃO ALMEIDA.

Antena 3: tel. (21) 3820000; fax (21) 3820017; e-mail antena3@programas.rdp.pt; internet tv1.rtp.pt/antena3; broadcasts 24 hours daily on FM; music and entertainment for young people; Dir JOSÉ MARINO CORREIA.

Commercial and Private Radio

Cidade FM: Rua Sampaio e Pina 24–26, 1099-044 Lisbon; tel. (21) 3821500; fax (21) 3821589; internet cidadefm.clix.pt; one FM transmitter; broadcasts 24 hours a day; Dir-Gen. JORDI JORDÀ; Dir of Programmes NUNO GONÇALVES.

Orbital FM: Travessa do Olival 6, 2685 Sacavém; tel. (21) 9401019; fax (21) 9427757; e-mail orbital@orbital.pt; internet www.orbital.pt; one FM transmitter; broadcasts 24 hours a day in Lisbon region.

PORTUGAL

Rádio Capital: Rua Viriato 25, 4° dto, 1050-234 Lisbon; tel. (21) 0105760; fax (21) 2740781; e-mail geral@radiocapital.fm; internet www.radiocapital.fm; one FM transmitter; broadcasts 24 hours a day in Lisbon and Oporto.

Rádio Clube: Rua Sampaio e Pina 24, 1099-044 Lisbon; tel. (21) 3821500; fax (21) 3821589; e-mail internet@radiocomercial.pt; f. 1992; fmrly Radio Nostalgia; broadcasts music 24 hours daily on FM; Head LUÍS MONTEZ; Dir of Programmes MIGUEL CRUZ.

Rádio Comercial, SA: Rua Sampaio e Pina 24/26, 1000 Lisbon; tel. (21) 3821500; fax (21) 3821559; e-mail geral@radiocomercial.pt; internet www.radiocomercial.pt; f. 1979 as RDP-3; transferred to private ownership in 1993; broadcasts music, news and sport 24 hours daily on Rádio Comercial: (FM); and since March 1998 on Rádio Nacional on MW to central and southern Portugal, also music, news and sport; Head PEDRO RIBEIRO; Dir of Programmes MIGUEL CRUZ.

Rádio Europa Lisboa: Rua Latino Coelho 50, 1°, 1050-137 Lisbon; tel. (21) 3510580; fax (21) 3510598; e-mail programas@radioeuropa.fm; internet www.radioeuropa.fm; fmrly Rádio Paris Lisboa; present name adopted 2006; one FM transmitter; broadcasts 24 hours a day; Dir ANTONIETA LOPES DA COSTA.

Rádio Juventude: Edif. Plátano, Loja A, Rua Prof. Hugo Correia Pardal, 6000-267 Castelo Branco; tel. (272) 341758; fax (272) 347660; e-mail radio.juventude@netvisao.pt; internet juventude.radios.pt; one FM transmitter; broadcasts 24 hours a day.

Rádio Viriato: Complexo Conventurispress, Orgens, Apdo 3115, 3511-689 Viseu; tel. (232) 410416; fax (232) 410418; e-mail inforadio@viriato.fm.com; f. 1987; one FM transmitter; broadcasts 24 hours a day; Dir ANABELA ABREU.

RR (Rádio Renascença): Rua Ivens 14, 1249-108 Lisbon; tel. (21) 3239200; fax (21) 3239299; e-mail mail@rr.pt; f. 1937; Roman Catholic station; broadcasts 24 hours a day on Rádio Renascença (FM, medium-wave and satellite; internet www.rr.pt), on RFM (FM and satellite; internet www.rfm.pt; Dir ANTÓNIO MENDES) and on MEGA FM (FM and satellite; internet www.mega.fm.pt; Dir NELSON CUNHA); Chair. FERNANDO MAGALHÃES CRESPO.

TSF—Rádio Jornal: Edif. Altejo, Sala 301, Rua 3 da Matinha, 1900-823 Lisbon; tel. (21) 8612500; fax (21) 8612510; e-mail tsf@tsf.pt; internet www.tsf.pt; broadcasts news and sport 24 hours daily on FM; Pres. JOAQUIM OLIVEIRA.

Television

State-controlled Television

Radio e Televisão de Portugal, SA (RTP): Av. Marechal Gomes da Costa 37, 1849-030 Lisbon; tel. (21) 7947000; fax (21) 7947570; e-mail rtp@rtp.pt; internet www.rtp.pt; f. 1956; nationalized in 1975; became jt-stock co (with 100% public capital) in 1992; 12 studios incl. Lisbon, Oporto, Ponta Delgada and Funchal; Pres. GUILHERME COSTA; Dir of Programmes JOSÉ MANUEL FRAGOSO.

Regional Centres:

RTP/Porto: Rua Conceição Fernandes, Apdo 174, 4402 Vila Nova de Gaia; tel. (22) 7156000; fax (22) 7110963; Dir DJALME NEVES.

RTP/Açores: Rua Castelo Branco, 9500-062 Ponta Delgada; tel. (296) 201100; fax (296) 201120; e-mail rtpa@rtp.pt; internet www.rtp.pt; Dir PEDRO BICUDO.

RTP—Madeira: Caminho Santo António 145, 9020-002 Funchal; tel. (291) 709100; fax (291) 741859; e-mail rtp.madeira@rtp.pt; Dir Dr MARTIM FIGUEIROA GOMES SANTOS.

RTP/Internacional (RTPi): e-mail rtpi@rtp.pt; internet rtpi.rtp.pt; commenced satellite transmissions in June 1992; broadcasts in Portuguese 24 hours a day; Dir FERNANDO BALSINHA.

RTP/Africa: commenced transmissions to lusophone countries of Africa in 1997; broadcasts 24 hours a day; Dir JORGE GONÇALVES.

Cable, Commercial and Private Television

Bragatel—Companhia de Televisão por Cabo de Braga, SA: Av. 31 de Janeiro 177, Apdo 17, 4715-052 Braga; tel. (253) 616600; fax (253) 616998; e-mail mail@bragatel.pt; internet www.zon.pt/bragatel; f. 1993; authorized to operate in Braga, Barceios and Espsende.

Cabo TV Açoreana: Av. Antero de Quental 9C, 1°, 9500-160 Ponta Delgada; tel. (296) 302401; fax (296) 302405; e-mail cliente@zon-acores.pt; internet www.cabotva.net.

Cabovisão—Sociedade de Televisão por Cabo, SA: Lugar de Poços, Vale de Touros, 2950-425 Palmela; tel. (21) 0801080; fax (21) 0801000; e-mail info@cabovisao.pt; internet www.cabovisao.pt; authorized to operate in 156 municipalities (4.5m. homes).

Pluricanal Leiria: Av. General Humberto Delgado 2, 2400 Leiria; tel. (244) 824925; fax (244) 824943.

Pluricanal Santarém: Edif. Ribatel, Estrada Nacional 3, S. Pedro, 2000 Santarém; tel. (244) 824925; fax (244) 824943.

SIC (Sociedade Independente de Comunicação, SA): Estrada da Outurela, Carnaxide, 2795 Linda-a-Velha; tel. 4173111; fax 4173118; e-mail atendimento@sic.pt; internet www.sic.pt; commenced transmissions in 1992; news and entertainment; Head FRANCISCO PINTO BALSEMÃO; Dir of Programmes NUNO SANTOS.

TV Cabo: Rua Adelina Abranches Ferrão 10, 1600 Lisbon; tel. 808 200400; e-mail cliente@netcabo.pt; internet www.tvcabo.pt; offers subscription-based television services, also broadband internet access and fixed-line telecommunications; operates 17 regional companies; Chair. RODRIGO JORGE LUÍS DE ARAÚJO COSTA.

TVI (Televisão Independente, SA): Rua Mário Castelhano 40, 2734-502 Barcarena; tel. (21) 4347500; fax (21) 4347654; internet www.tvi.pt; commenced transmissions in 1993; Pres. MANUEL POLANCO; Gen. Man. JOSÉ EDUARDO MONIZ.

TVTEL Comunicações, SA: Rua Delfim Ferreira 383, 4100-201 Porto; tel. (22) 0325800; fax (22) 6154949; e-mail info@tvtel.pt; internet www.tvtel.pt.

Zon Cabo TV Madeirense: Av. Estados Unidos da América, Nazaré, 9000-090 Funchal; tel. (291) 700800; fax (291) 766132; e-mail tvcabo@cabotvm.pt; internet www.cabotvm.pt; 78% owned by ZON Multimedia; CEO NUNO AGUIAR.

Zon Multimédia—Serviços de Telecomunicações e Multimédia, SGPS, SA: Av. 5 de Outubro 208, 1069-203, Lisbon; tel. (21) 7824721; fax (21) 7824910; e-mail ir@pt-multimedia.pt; internet www.pt-multimedia.pt; fmrly PT Multimédia; renamed as above in 2008; Chair. RODRIGO JORGE LUÍS DE ARAÚJO COSTA; 1.7m. customers.

Finance

(cap. = capital; res = reserves; dep. = deposits; m. = million; brs = branches; amounts in euros)

BANKING

Central Bank

Banco de Portugal: Rua do Ouro 27, 1100-150 Lisbon; tel. (21) 3213200; fax (21) 3464843; e-mail info@bportugal.pt; internet www.bportugal.pt; f. 1846; reorganized 1931 with the sole right to issue notes; nationalized in 1974; cap. 1m., res 6,017m., dep. 5,406m. (Dec. 2008); Gov. CARLOS DA SILVA COSTA; also maintains br. in Oporto.

Principal Banks

Banco Activobank (Portugal), SA (ActivoBank7): Rua Augusta 84, 1149-023 Lisbon; tel. (21) 4232673; fax (21) 0066883; e-mail ab7_dop@activobank7.pt; internet www.activobank7.pt; f. 1969 as Sociedade Financeira Portuguesa; nationalized 1975; privatized 1991 and name changed to Banco Mello, SA; name changed to above in 2001; owned by Banco Comercial Português, SA; Chair. PAULO TEIXEIRA PINTO.

Banco Bilbao Vizcaya Argentaria (Portugal), SA: Av. da Liberdade 222, 1250-148 Lisbon; tel. (21) 3117200; fax (21) 3117500; e-mail helpdesk@bbva.pt; internet www.bbva.pt; f. 1991 as Banco Bilbao Vizcaya; name changed 2000; cap. 220m., res –6m., dep. 6,424m. (Dec. 2008); Man. Dir ALBERTO CHARRO; 100 brs.

Banco BPI, SA: Rua Tenente Valadim 284, 4100-476 Porto; tel. (22) 2075000; fax (22) 6002954; e-mail dirint@bpi.pt; internet www.bancobpi.pt; f. 1998 following the absorption of Banco Fonsecas e Burnay and Banco Borges e Irmão by Banco de Fomento e Exterior; cap. 900m., res 448m., dep. 36,985m. (Dec. 2008); Chair. FERNANDO ULRICH; 700 brs.

Banco Comercial Português (Millennium BCP): Praça D. João I 28, 4000-295 Porto; tel. (22) 7502424; fax (22) 2064139; internet www.millenniumbcp.pt; f. 1985; cap. 4,695m., res 1,957m., dep. 84,060m. (Dec. 2009); Chair., Exec. Bd CARLOS JORGE RAMALHO DOS SANTOS FERREIRA; 1,000 brs.

Banco Efisa, SA: Av. António Augusto de Aguiar 134, 4°, 1050-020 Lisbon; tel. (21) 3117800; fax (21) 3117915; e-mail dcb@bancoefisa.pt; f. 1994 by merger; nationalized in Nov. 2008; cap. 22m., res 4m., dep. 420m. (Dec. 2007); Man. Dir JOSÉ AUGUSTO OLIVEIRA COSTA.

Banco Espírito Santo, SA: Av. da Liberdade 195, 1250-142 Lisbon; tel. (21) 3501000; fax (21) 8557491; e-mail info@bes.pt; internet www.bes.pt; f. 1884; nationalized 1975; transfer to private sector completed 1992; 40% owned by BESPAR SGPS Lisbon, 10.8% owned by Crédit Agricole SA (France); cap. 2,500m., res 1,597m., dep. 66,130m. (Dec. 2008); Pres. and CEO RICARDO ESPÍRITO SANTO SILVA SALGADO; 457 brs.

Banco Finantia, SA: Rua General Firmino Miguel 5, 1600-100 Lisbon; tel. (21) 7201200; fax (21) 7202030; e-mail finantia@finantia.com; internet www.finantia.com; f. 1987; investment bank; 50% owned by Finantipar SGPS, SA; cap. 115m., res 229m., dep. 3,362m. (Dec. 2008); Pres. ANTÓNIO MANUEL AFONSO GUERREIRO; also br. in Oporto.

PORTUGAL

Banco Itaú BBA International, SA: Centro Comercial Amoreiras, Torre 3, 11°, Rua Tierno Galvan, 1099-048 Lisbon; tel. (21) 3811000; fax (21) 3887219; e-mail bie.global@itaueuropa.pt; internet www.itaueuropa.pt; f. 1994; owned by Itaúsa Portugal SGPS, Lisbon; cap. 383m., res 72m., dep. 4,061m. (Dec. 2008); Pres. and Chair. ROBERTO EGYDIO SETÚBAL; CEO ALMIR VIGNOTO.

Banco Popular Portugal, SA: Rua Ramalho Ortigão 51, 1099-090 Lisbon; tel. (21) 0071000; fax (21) 0071996; e-mail s.mercados@bancopopular.pt; internet www.bancopopular.pt; f. 1991 as Banco Nacional de Crédito; present name adopted 2005; cap. 376m., res 293m., dep. 7,461m. (Dec. 2008); owned by Banco Popular Español (Spain); CEO RUI MANUEL MORGANHO SEMEDO; 174 brs.

Banco Privado Português, SA: Rua Mouzinho da Silveira 12, 1250-167 Lisbon; tel. (21) 3137000; fax (21) 3137092; internet www.bpp.pt; f. 1996; cap. 150m., res 79m., dep. 1,193m. (Dec. 2008); CEO FERNANDO ADÃO DA FONSECA.

Banco Santander Totta: Rua do Ouro 88, 1100-063 Lisbon; tel. (21) 3262000; fax (21) 3262271; e-mail santandertotta@santandertotta.pt; internet www.santandertotta.pt; f. 2004 by merger of Banco Totta & Açores, Banco Santander Portugal and Crédito Predial Português; owned by Banco Santander (Spain); cap. 590m., res 910m., dep. 36,892m. (Dec. 2008); CEO NUNO MANUEL DA SILVA AMADO; 640 brs.

Banif—Banco Internacional do Funchal SA: Rua de João Tavira 30, 9000-509 Funchal, Madeira; tel. (291) 207731; fax (291) 230221; e-mail info@banif.pt; internet www.banif.pt; f. 1988; cap. 290m., res 41m., dep. 8,832m. (Dec. 2008); absorbed Banco Banif e Comercial dos Açores in 2008; Chair. HORÁCIO DA SILVA ROQUE; CEO Dr JOAQUIM FILIPE MARQUES DOS SANTOS.

BPN—Banco Português de Negócios, SA: Edif. Fronteira, Av. António Augusto de Aguiar 132, 1050-020 Lisbon; tel. (21) 3598000; fax (21) 3191622; e-mail marketing@banco.bpn.pt; internet www.bpn.pt; f. 1993; nationalized in Nov. 2008; cap. 380m., res –1,626m., dep. 8,413m. (Dec. 2008); Chair. FRANCISCO MANUEL MARQUES BANDEIRA; 213 brs.

Caixa-Banco de Investimento, SA (CaixaBI): Rua Barata Salgueiro 33, 1269-057 Lisbon; tel. (21) 3137300; fax (21) 3526327; e-mail caixabi@caixabi.pt; internet www.caixabi.pt; f. 1984 as Manufacturers Hanover Trust Co; present name adopted 2000; 99.7% owned by Caixa Geral de Depósitos, SA; cap. 81m., res 127m., dep. 1,564m. (Dec. 2009); Pres. and Chair. Dr JOSÉ LOURENÇO SOARES; CEO JORGE HUMBERTO CORREIA TOMÉ; 3 brs.

Caixa Central de Crédito Agrícola Mútuo, CRL (Crédito Agrícola): Rua Castilho 233–233A, 1099-004 Lisbon; tel. (21) 3809900; fax (21) 3860996; e-mail dint.cccam@creditoagricola.pt; internet www.creditoagricola.com; f. 1984; co-operative bank; cap. 680.7m., res 61.6m., dep. 9,174.6m. (Dec. 2007); Chair. and Pres. CARLOS COURELAS; CEO JOÃO ANTÓNIO MORAIS DA COSTA PINTO; 670 brs.

Caixa Económica Montepio Geral (Montepio Geral): Rua Áurea 219–241, POB 2882, 1100-062 Lisbon; tel. (21) 3248000; fax (21) 3248228; internet www.montepio.pt; f. 1844 as Caixa Económica de Lisboa; present name adopted 1991; cap. 660m., res 130m., dep. 15,510m. (Dec. 2008); Pres. ANTÓNIO TOMÁS CORREIA; 55 brs.

Caixa Geral de Depósitos, SA (CGD): Av. João XXI 63, 1000-300 Lisbon; tel. (21) 7953000; fax (21) 7905050; e-mail cgd@cgd.pt; internet www.cgd.pt; f. 1876; state-owned; grants credit for agriculture, industry, building, housing, energy, trade and tourism; dep. 98,957m., total assets 120,985m. (Dec. 2009); Pres. and Chair. FERNANDO MANUEL BARBOSA FARIA DE OLIVEIRA; 768 brs.

Deutsche Bank (Portugal), SA: Rua Castilho 20, 1250-069 Lisbon; tel. (21) 3186845; fax (21) 3106803; e-mail dbonline.dbp@db.com; internet www.deutsche-bank.pt; f. 1990 as Deutsche Bank de Investimento; name changed 1999; owned by Deutsche Bank AG (Germany); cap. 80m., res 29m., dep. 4,105m. (Dec. 2007); Pres., Exec. Cttee FILIPE SILVA; 49 brs.

Finibanco, SA: Av. de Berna 10, 5°, 1050-040 Lisbon; tel. (21) 7902800; fax (21) 7902801; e-mail comunicacao@finibanco.pt; internet www.finibanco.pt; f. 1993; cap. 120m., res 17m., dep. 2,546m. (Dec. 2008); CEO HUMBERTO DA COSTA LEITE; 158 brs.

Banking Association

Associação Portuguesa de Bancos (APB): Av. da República 35, 5°, 1050-186 Lisbon; tel. (21) 3510070; fax (21) 3579533; e-mail apbancos@apb.pt; internet www.apb.pt; f. 1984; Pres. Prof. ANTÓNIO DE SOUSA; Sec.-Gen. Dr JOÃO MENDES RODRIGUES; 28 mems.

STOCK EXCHANGE

Euronext Lisbon: Av. da Liberdade 196, 7°, 1250-147 Lisbon; tel. (21) 7900000; fax (21) 7952021; internet www.euronext.com; f. 1769 as Bolsa de Valores de Lisboa e Porto; merged with Euronext in 2002 and adopted current name; merged with New York Stock Exchange in 2007 to form NYSE Euronext; Chair. MIGUEL ATHAYDE MARQUES.

Regulatory Authority

Comissão do Mercado de Valores Mobiliários (CMVM): Av. da Liberdade 252, 1056-801 Lisbon; tel. (21) 3177000; fax (21) 3537077; e-mail cmvm@cmvm.pt; internet www.cmvm.pt; f. 1991; independent securities exchange commission; Pres. Dr CARLOS TAVARES.

INSURANCE

At the end of 2009 there were 46 insurance companies based in Portugal, of which 16 specialized in life insurance. In that year 40 foreign-owned companies were operating in Portugal.

Principal Companies

AXA-Portugal—Companhia de Seguros, SA: Rua Gonçalo Sampaio 39, 4002-001 Porto; tel. (22) 6081100; fax (22) 6081136; e-mail contacto@axa-seguros.pt; internet www.axa.pt; non-life; net profits 27.3m. (2005); Pres. Dr JOÃO LEANDRO.

AXA-Portugal—Companhia de Seguros de Vida, SA: Praça Marquês de Pombal 14, Apdo 1953, 1250-162 Lisbon; tel. (21) 3506000; fax (21) 3506136; e-mail contacto@axa-seguros.pt; internet www.axa.pt; life and pension funds; Pres. Dr CARLOS PEDRO BRANDÃO DE MELO DE SOUSA E BRITO.

BPI Vida—Companhia de Seguros de Vida, SA: Rua Braamcamp 11, 6°, 1250-049 Lisbon; tel. (21) 3111020; fax (21) 3111082; e-mail bpi.vida.reportes@bancobpi.pt; internet www.bpiinvestimentos.pt; f. 1991; life and pension funds; owned by Banco BPI; net profits 10.1m. (2006); Pres. Dr FERNANDO MARIA COSTA DUARTE ULRICH.

Companhia de Seguros Açoreana, SA: Largo da Matriz 45–52, 9501-908 Ponta Delgada; tel. (296) 201400; fax (296) 201483; e-mail info@csanet.pt; internet www.acornet.pt; f. 1892; life and non-life; net profits 17.7m. (2006); Pres. Dr HORÁCIO DA SILVA ROQUE.

Companhia de Seguros Allianz Portugal, SA: Rua Andrade Corvo 32, 1069-014 Lisbon; tel. (21) 3165300; fax (21) 3165570; e-mail info@allianz.pt; internet www.allianz.pt; f. 1907; fmrly Allianz Portugal; life, non-life and pension funds; net profits 21.4m. (2004); CEO IVÁN JOSÉ DE LA SOTA DUÑABEITIA.

Companhia de Seguros Fidelidade–Mundial, SA: Largo do Calhariz 30, 1249-001 Lisbon; tel. (21) 3238000; fax (21) 3238001; e-mail apoiocliente@fidelidademundial.pt; internet www.fidelidademundial.pt; f. 1980 from merger of 4 cos; life, non-life and pension funds; net profits 95.4m. (2005); Pres. Dr JORGE MANUEL MAGALHÃES CORREIA.

Companhia de Seguros Tranquilidade, SA: Av. da Liberdade 242, 1250-149 Lisbon; tel. (21) 3503500; fax (21) 8553051; e-mail infogeral@tranquilidade.pt; internet www.tranquilidade.pt; f. 1871; non-life; net profits 32.5m. (2006); 100% privatized in 1990; Pres. PEDRO DE BRITO E CUNHA.

Companhia de Seguros Tranquilidade Vida, SA (T-Vida): Av. da Liberdade 230, 1250-148 Lisbon; tel. (21) 3167500; fax (21) 3153194; e-mail correio@tranquilidade-vida.pt; internet www.tranquilidade.pt; life and pension funds; net profits 34.2m. (2005); Pres. Dr LUÍS FREDERICO REDONDO LOPES.

Cosec (Companhia de Seguro de Créditos, SA): Av. da República 58, 1069-057 Lisbon; tel. and fax (21) 7913700; fax (21) 7913720; e-mail cosec@cosec.pt; internet www.cosec.pt; f. 1969; domestic and export credit insurance; bond insurance; net profits 5.5m. (2007); Chair. JOSÉ MIGUEL GOMES DA COSTA.

Crédito Agrícola Vida, SA: Rua Castilho 233A, 1050-185 Lisbon; tel. (21) 3805660; fax (21) 3859695; e-mail linhadirecta@creditoagricola.pt; internet www.credito-agricola.pt; life; net profits 3.4m. (2004); Pres. JOAQUIM DA SILVA BERNARDO.

Eurovida, SA: Rua Rua Ramalho Ortigão 51, 1099-090 Lisbon; tel. (21) 7924700; fax (21) 7924701; e-mail seguros@eurovida.pt; internet www.eurovida.pt; net profits 1.9m. (2004); Pres. Dr LUÍS EDUARDO DA SILVA BARBOSA.

Global—Companhia de Seguros, SA: Av. Duque de Avila 171, 1069-031 Lisbon; tel. (21) 3137500; fax (21) 3554021; e-mail globalseguros@global-seguros.pt; internet www.global-seguros.pt; non-life; net profits 12.1m. (2006); Exec. Pres. ALBERTINO SILVA.

GroupAMA Seguros: Av. de Berna 24D, 1069-170 Lisbon; tel. (21) 7923100; fax (21) 7923232; e-mail groupama@groupama.pt; internet www.groupama.pt; life and non-life; cap. 31.0m. (2004).

Império Bonança—Companhia de Seguros, SA: Rua Alexandre Herculano 53, 1269-152 Lisbon; tel. (21) 3702000; fax (21) 3702835; e-mail apoiocliente@imperiobonanca.pt; internet www.imperiobonanca.pt; f. by merger of Companhia de Seguros Bonança, SA and Companhia de Seguros Império, SA; net income 29.0m. (2006); Chair. Dr JORGE MANUEL BAPTISTA MAGALHÃES CORREIA.

Liberty Seguros, SA: Av. Fontes Pereira de Melo 6, 1069-001 Lisbon; tel. (21) 3124300; fax (21) 3553300; e-mail geral@libertyseguros.pt; internet www.libertyseguros.pt; f. 1922; life and

PORTUGAL
Directory

non-life; fmrly Companhia Europeia de Seguros, SA; net profits 9.6m. (2006); CEO José António Sousa.

Lusitânia—Companhia de Seguros, SA: Rua São Domingos à Lapa 35–41, 1249-130 Lisbon; tel. (21) 3926900; fax (21) 3973099; e-mail cdirectos@lusitania.pt; internet www.lusitania-cs.pt; non-life; net profits 2.3m. (2006); Pres. Dr José da Silva Lopes.

MAPFRE Seguros Gerais, SA: Rua Castilho 52, 1250-071 Lisbon; tel. (21) 3819700; fax (21) 3819799; e-mail marketing@mapfre.pt; internet www.mapfre.pt; f. 1998; non-life; net profits 5.5m., cap. 33.1m. (2007); CEO António Manuel Cardoso Belo (acting).

Real Seguros, SA: Edif. Capitólio, Av. de França 316, 2°, 4050-276 Porto; tel. (22) 8330100; fax (22) 8330149; e-mail info@realseguros.pt; internet www.realseguros.pt; f. 1988; non-life; net profits 7.3m. (2006); Pres. Fernando Soares Ferreira.

Santander Totta Seguros—Companhia de Seguros de Vida, SA: Rua da Mesquita 6, Torre A, S. S. Pedreira, Lisbon; tel. (21) 3704000; fax (21) 3705878; e-mail ermelinda.martins@santander.pt; internet www.santandertotta.pt; life; net profits 10.9m. (2006); Pres. Pedro Aires Coruche de Castro e Almeida.

Victoria—Seguros de Vida, SA/Victoria—Seguros, SA: Edif. Victoria, Av. da Liberdade 200, 1250-147 Lisbon; tel. (21) 3134100; fax (21) 3134700; e-mail victoria@victoria-seguros.pt; internet www.victoria-seguros.pt; f. 1930/1981; transferred to private sector in 1993; life and pensions; non-life; total net profits 7.0m. (2006); Pres. Bernd Knof.

Zurich—Companhia de Seguros, SA/Zurich—Companhia de Seguros Vida, SA: Rua Barata Salgueiro 41, 1269-058 Lisbon; tel. (21) 3133100; fax (21) 3133111; e-mail lisboa@zurich.com; internet www.zurichportugal.com; f. 1918; fmrly Companhia de Seguros Metrópole; net profits (non-life) 25.7m., (life) 5.8m. (2006); Pres. Dr Nuno Maria Serra Soares da Fonseca; Chief Exec. José M. Coelho.

Mutual Companies

Mútua dos Armadores da Pesca do Arrasto: Av. António Augusto de Aguiar 7, 1°, 1069-117 Lisbon; tel. (21) 3515970; fax (21) 3515999; e-mail info@mutuamar.com; f. 1942; marine and workers' compensation, personal accident, sickness, fire, etc.; Pres. Dr António Alberto Carvalho da Cunha.

Mútua dos Pescadores—Mútua dos Seguros, C.R.L.: Av. Santos Dumont 57, 6°, 1050-202 Lisbon; tel. (21) 3936300; fax (21) 3936310; e-mail geral@mutuapescadores.pt; internet www.mutuapescadores.pt; f. 1942; co-operative; personal accident, marine, fire, workers' compensation, etc.; net profits 0.5m. (2007); Dir-Gen. Jerónimo Teixeira.

Supervisory Authority

Instituto de Seguros de Portugal (ISP): Av. da República 76, 1600-205 Lisbon; tel. (21) 7903100; fax (21) 7938568; e-mail isp@isp.pt; internet www.isp.pt; f. 1982; office in Oporto; Pres. Fernando Dias Nogueira.

Insurance Association

Associação Portuguesa de Seguradores (APS): Rua Rodrigo da Fonseca 41, 1250-190 Lisbon; tel. (21) 3848100; fax (21) 3831422; e-mail aps@apseguradores.pt; internet www.apseguradores.pt; f. 1982; Pres. Pedro Rogério de Azevedo Seixas Vale.

Trade and Industry

GOVERNMENT AGENCIES

AICEP Portugal Global: Av. 5 de Outubro 101, 1050-051 Lisbon; tel. (21) 7909500; fax (21) 7935028; e-mail aicep@portugalglobal.pt; internet www.portugalglobal.pt; f. 2007; fmrly Agência para o Investimento e Comércio Externo de Portugal; promotes internationalization of the Portuguese economy; Chair. and Chief Exec. Basílio Horta.

Autoridade de Segurança Alimentar e Económica (ASAE): Av. Conde de Valbom 98, 1050-185 Lisbon; tel. (21) 7983600; fax (21) 7983654; e-mail correio.asae@asae.pt; internet www.asae.pt; f. 2005; regulatory authority for food safety and economic activities (Ministry of the Economy, Innovation and Development); Inspector-Gen. Dr António Nunes.

Gabinete de Estratégia e Estudos (GEE): Av. da República 79, 1050-243 Lisbon; tel. (21) 7998150; fax (21) 7998154; e-mail gee@gee.min-economia.pt; internet www.gee.min-economia.pt; advises on economic policy and strategy (Ministry of the Economy, Innovation and Development); Dir João Reis Leão.

Instituto de Apoio às Pequenas e Médias Empresas e a Inovação (IAPMEI): Edif. A, Estrada do Paço do Lumiar, 1649-038 Lisbon; tel. (21) 3836000; fax (21) 3836283; internet www.iapmei.pt; financial and technical support to small and medium-sized enterprises (Ministry of the Economy, Innovation and Development); Pres. Jaime Serrão Andrez.

Instituto de Financiamento da Agricultura e Pescas (IFAP): Rua Castilho 45–51, 1269-163 Lisbon; tel. (21) 3846000; fax (21) 3846170; e-mail ifap@ifap.pt; internet www.ifap.min-agricultura.pt; f. 2007; provides loans for agriculture and fisheries, acts as intermediary with the European Agricultural Guarantee Fund (EAGF), the European Agricultural Fund for Rural Development (EAFRD) and the European Fisheries Fund (EFF).

Instituto Nacional de Engenharia Tecnologia e Inovação (INETI): Estrada do Paço do Lumiar, 1649-038 Lisbon; tel. (21) 0924900; fax (21) 7160901; e-mail atendimento@ineti.pt; internet www.ineti.pt; f. 1977; industrial and technological research (Ministry of the Economy, Innovation and Development); Pres. Prof. Maria Teresa Costa Pereira da Silva Ponce de Leão.

Instituto Português de Apoio ao Desenvolvimento (IPAD): Av. da Liberdade 192, 2°, 1250-147 Lisbon; tel. (21) 3176700; fax (21) 3147897; e-mail cooperacao.portuguesa@ipad.mne.gov.pt; internet www.ipad.mne.gov.pt; f. 2003; part of Ministry of Foreign Affairs; supports international devt; Pres. Augusto Manuel Correia.

Instituto Português da Qualidade (IPQ): Rua António Gião 2, 2829-513 Caparica; tel. (21) 2948100; fax (21) 2948101; e-mail ipq@mail.ipq.pt; internet www.ipq.pt; manages and develops the Portuguese Quality System (Ministry of the Economy, Innovation and Development); Pres. José Manuel Diogo Marques dos Santos.

DEVELOPMENT ORGANIZATIONS

Centro para o Desenvolvimento e Inovação Tecnológicos (CEDINTEC): Rua de São Domingos à Lapa 117, 2° dto, 1200-834 Lisbon; tel. (21) 3955302; fax (21) 3961203; e-mail geral@cedintec.pt; internet www.cedintec.pt; f. 1982; supports the creation of technological infrastructures; Pres. Eng. João Pedro de Saldanha Verschneider Gonçalves.

Cotec Portugal: Rua de Salazares 842, 4149-002 Porto; tel. (22) 6192910; fax (22) 6192919; e-mail secretariado@cotec.pt; internet www.cotec.pt; f. 2003; co-ordinates research and innovation between public and private bodies; Pres. Dr Artur Santos Silva; Dir-Gen. Daniel Bessa.

Instituto do Vinho do Douro e do Porto (IVDP): Rua dos Camilos 90, 5050–272 Peso da Régua; tel. (25) 4320130; fax (25) 4320149; e-mail ivdp@ivdp.pt; internet www.ivdp.pt; an official body dealing with quality control and the promotion of port and Douro wines; also gives technical advice to exporters; Pres. Luciano Vilhena Pereira.

Sociedade de Desenvolvimento da Madeira (SDM): Rua da Mouraria 9, 1°, 9000-047 Funchal, Madeira; tel. (291) 201333; fax (291) 201399; e-mail sdm@sdm.pt; internet www.sdm.pt; concessionaire of Madeira's International Business Centre; Chair. Dr Francisco Costa.

Sociedade Nacional de Empreendimentos e Desenvolvimento Económico, SA (SNEDE): Av. Fontes Pereira de Melo 35, 19A, 1050-118 Lisbon; tel. and fax (21) 3139889; e-mail snede@mail.telepac.pt; internet www.snede.pt; f. 1976; private consultancy co in economy and management; Pres. Dr Alfredo Gonzalez Esteves Belo.

CHAMBERS OF COMMERCE AND TRADE ASSOCIATIONS

Associação Comercial e Industrial do Funchal/Câmara de Comércio e Indústria da Madeira (ACIF/CCIM): Rua dos Aranhas 24–26, 9000-044 Funchal; tel. (291) 206800; fax (291) 206868; e-mail geral@acif-ccim.pt; internet www.acif-ccim.pt; f. 1836; Pres. Duarte Nuno Ferreira Rodrigues.

Associação Comercial de Lisboa/Câmara de Comércio e Indústria Portuguesa (ACL/CCIP): Palácio do Comércio, Rua das Portas de Santo Antão 89, 1169-022 Lisbon; tel. (21) 3224050; fax (21) 3224051; e-mail geral@port-chambers.com; internet www.port-chambers.com; f. 1834; Pres. Bruno Bobone; Sec.-Gen. Dr Pedro Madeira Rodrigues; 2,100 mems.

Associação Comercial do Porto/Câmara de Comércio e Indústria do Porto (ACP/CCIP): Palácio da Bolsa, Rua Ferreira Borges, 4050-253 Porto; tel. (22) 3399000; fax (22) 3399090; e-mail correio@cciporto.pt; internet www.cciporto.com; f. 1834; Chair. Dr Rui Moreira; 800 mems.

Associação Industrial Portuguesa—Câmara de Comércio e Indústria (AIP-CCI): Praça das Indústrias, Apdo 3200, EC Junqueira, 1301-918 Lisbon; tel. (21) 3601000; fax (21) 3641301; e-mail info@aip.pt; internet www.aip.pt; f. 1837; privately owned; Chief Exec. Manuel Duarte Oliveira; 4,500 mems (2010).

Câmara de Comércio e Indústria de Ponta Delgada/Associação Empresarial das Ilhas de São Miguel e Santa Maria (CCIPD): Rua Ernesto do Canto 13–15, 9504-531 Ponta Delgada, Azores; tel. (296) 305000; fax (296) 305050; e-mail ccipd@ccipd.pt;

PORTUGAL

internet www.ccipd.pt; f. 1979; Pres. Mário Fortuna; Dir Carlos Alberto da Costa Martins; 800 mems.

OTHER INDUSTRIAL AND TRADE ASSOCIATIONS

Associação dos Comerciantes e Industriais de Bebidas Espirituosas e Vinhos (ACIBEV): Largo do Carmo 15, 1°, 1200-092 Lisbon; tel. (21) 3462318; fax (21) 3427517; e-mail acibevmail@acibev.pt; internet www.acibev.org; f. 1975; spirit and wine traders and manufacturers; Pres. Dr António Soares Franco.

Associação Empresarial de Portugal: Av. da Boavista 2671, 4100-135 Porto; tel. (22) 6158500; fax (22) 6176840; e-mail mjmagalhaes@aeportugal.com; internet www.aeportugal.pt; f. 1849; represents industry in northern Portugal in all sectors; organizes trade fairs, exhibitions, congresses, etc.; Pres. Angelo Ludgero Marques; 2,500 mems.

Associação Nacional de Comerciantes e Industriais de Produtos Alimentares (ANCIPA): Largo de São Sebastião da Pedreira 31, 1050-205 Lisbon; tel. (21) 3528803; fax (21) 3154665; e-mail geral@ancipa.pt; internet www.ancipa.pt; f. 1975; national asscn of food products manufacturers and traders; Pres. Manuel Fulgéncio Tarré Fernandes.

Associação Nacional das Indústrias de Vestuário e Confecção (ANIVEC/APIV): Av. da Boavista 3523, 7°, 4100-139 Porto; tel. (22) 6165470; fax (22) 6168714; e-mail geral@anivec.com; internet www.anivec.com; clothing manufacturers' asscn; Pres. Alexandre Monteiro Pinheiro.

Associação Portuguesa da Indústria de Cerâmica (APICER): Edif. C, Rua Col Veiga Simão, 3020-053 Coimbra; tel. (239) 497600; fax (239) 497601; e-mail info@apicer.pt; internet www.apicer.pt; ceramics asscn; Pres. Maria Paula da Graça Cardoso.

Associação Portuguesa de Cortiça (APCOR) (Portuguese Cork Association): Av. Comendador Henrique Amorim 580, 4536-904 Sta Maria de Lamas; tel. (22) 7474040; fax (22) 7474049; e-mail info@apcor.pt; internet www.apcor.pt; f. 1956; asscn of cork manufacturers and exporters; Pres. António Rios de Amorim.

Associação Portuguesa dos Industriais de Calçado, Componentes, e Artigos de Pele e seus Sucedâneos (APICCAPS): Rua Alves Redol 372, 4011-001 Porto; tel. (22) 5074150; fax (22) 5074179; e-mail apiccaps@mail.telepac.pt; internet www.apiccaps.pt; f. 1975; footwear and leather goods manufacturers' asscn; Pres. Fortunato Frederico.

Associação Têxtil e Vestuário de Portugal (ATP): Edif. do Citeve, Rua Fernando Mesquita 2785, 4760-034 Vila Nova de Famalicão; tel. (252) 303030; fax (252) 303039; e-mail atp@atp.pt; internet www.atp.pt; textile and ready-to-wear clothing industries; Pres. Dr Joao Costa.

Confederação dos Agricultores de Portugal (CAP): Av. do Colégio Militar, Lote 1786, 1549-012 Lisbon; tel. (21) 7100000; fax (21) 7166122; e-mail cap@cap.pt; internet www.cap.pt; farmers' confederation; Pres. João Pedro Gorjão Cyrillo Machado.

Confederação do Comércio e Serviços de Portugal (CCP): Av. D. Vasco da Gama 29, 1449-032 Lisbon; tel. (21) 3031380; fax (21) 3031401; e-mail ccp@ccp.pt; internet www.ccp.pt; f. 1976; Pres. Dr João Manuel Lança Vieira Lopes; c. 100 mem. trade asscns.

Confederação da Indústria Portuguesa (CIP): Av. 5 de Outubro 35, 1°, 1069-193 Lisbon; tel. (21) 3164700; fax (21) 3579986; e-mail geral@cip.org.pt; internet www.cip.org.pt; f. 1974; represents employers; Pres. António Saraiva; over 35,000 mems.

UTILITIES

In 2006 Spain and Portugal began operating an integrated electricity market, the Mercado Ibérico de Electricidade (MIBEL).

Regulatory Authority

Entidade Reguladora dos Serviços Energéticos (ERSE): Rua Dom Cristovão da Gama 1, 3°, 1400-113 Lisbon; tel. (21) 3033200; fax (21) 3033201; e-mail erse@erse.pt; internet www.erse.pt; regulator of electricity and natural gas in Portugal; Pres. Prof. Vítor Manuel da Silva Santos.

Electricity

Rede Eléctrica Nacional, SA (REN): Av. Estados Unidos da América 55, 1749-061 Lisbon; tel. (21) 0013500; fax (21) 0013310; e-mail secretariaren@ren.pt; internet www.ren.pt; f. 1994; subsidiary of Redes Energéticas Nacionais, SGPS, SA; concessionaire of the Portuguese transmission grid and transmission system operator in mainland Portugal; Pres. José Rodrigues Pereira dos Penedos; Chair. and CEO Rui Manuel Janes Cartaxo.

Energias de Portugal—EDP, SA: Praça Marquês de Pombal 12, 1250-162 Lisbon; tel. (21) 0012500; fax (21) 0021403; internet www.edp.pt; fmrly Electricidade de Portugal; production, purchase, transport, distribution and sale of electrical energy in Portugal and Spain (via Hidrocantábrico); partially privatized in 2004; CEO António Mexia.

EDP Comercial—Comercialização de Energia, SA: Rua Castilho 165, 4°, 1050-045 Lisbon; tel. (21) 0024321; fax (21) 0014330; Pres. Eng. Jorge Cruz Morais.

EDP Distribuição—Energia, SA: Praça Marquês de Pombal 12, 1250-162 Lisbon; tel. (21) 0012500; fax (21) 0021403; internet www.edp.pt; electricity distribution.

EDP Produção—Gestãoda Produção de Energia, SA: Praça Marquês de Pombal 12, 1250-162 Lisbon; tel. (21) 0012500; fax (21) 0021403; e-mail geral@edpproducao.edp.pt; internet www.edp.pt; production and sale of electrical energy; in 2005 the Govt reduced its stake from 30% to 10%; Pres. Eng. João Talone; Vice-Pres. Eng. Jorge Ribeirinho Machado.

Gas

REN Gasodutos, SA: Av. Estados Unidos da América 55, 1749-061 Lisbon; tel. (21) 0013500; fax (21) 0013950; e-mail secretariaren@ren.pt; internet www.ren.pt; f. 2006; subsidiary of Redes Energéticas Nacionais, SGPS, SA; concessionaire of the national gas transmission network; Pres. José Rodrigues Pereira dos Penedos.

Galp Energia, SGPS, SA: Edif. Galp Energia, Rua Tomás de Fonseca, 1600-209 Lisbon; tel. (21) 7242500; fax (21) 7240573; e-mail comunicacao@galpenergia.com; internet www.galpenergia.com; f. 1999; partially privatized in 2000; also comprises Petróleos de Portugal (Petrogal), SA, a petroleum refining co, and Gás de Portugal (GDP), SA, a gas distribution co; Chair. Francisco Luís Murteira Nabo; CEO Manuel Ferreira de Oliveira.

Lisboagás GDL—Sociedade Distribuidora de Gás Natural de Lisboa, SA: Rua Tomás da Fonseca, Torre C, 4°, 1600-209 Lisbon; tel. (21) 7242500; fax (21) 8681161; e-mail lisboagas@galpenergia.com; f. 1995; regional natural gas distribution; there are 8 other regional distributors operating in Portugal: Beiragás, Dianagás, Duriensegás, Lusitaniagás, Medigás, Paxgás, Setgás and Tagusgás; Pres. Dr João Carlos Fevereiro Ferreira de Lima; Man. Dir Carlos Augusto.

Water

Aguas de Portugal, SGPS, SA (AdP): Rua Visconde de Seabra 3, 1700-421 Lisbon; tel. (21) 2469500; fax (21) 2469501; e-mail info@adp.pt; internet www.adp.pt; f. 1993; Chair. Pedro Eduardo Passos da Cunha Serra.

TRADE UNIONS

National Confederations

Confederação Geral dos Trabalhadores Portugueses-Intersindical Nacional (CGTP-IN) (General Confederation of Portuguese Workers): Rua Victor Cordon 1, 2°, 1249-102 Lisbon; tel. (21) 3236500; fax (21) 3236695; e-mail cgtp@cgtp.pt; internet www.cgtp.pt; f. 1970; reorganized 1974; 107 affiliated unions; Sec.-Gen. Manuel Carvalho da Silva.

União Geral dos Trabalhadores de Portugal (UGT) (General Union of Portuguese Workers): Av. Almirante Gago Coutinho 132, 1700-033 Lisbon; tel. (21) 3931200; fax (21) 3974612; e-mail ugt@mail.telepac.pt; internet www.ugt.pt; f. 1978; pro-socialist; comprises 58 unions and 2 feds; Pres. João Dias da Silva; Sec.-Gen. João Proença.

Principal Federations and Unions

Federação Intersindical das Indústrias Metalúrgica, Química, Farmacêutica, Eléctrica, Energia e Minas (FIEQUIMETAL) (Metal, Chemical, Pharmaceutical, Electrical, Energy and Mining): Rua dos Douradores 160, 1100-207 Lisbon; tel. (21) 8818500; fax (21) 8818555; e-mail mail@fiequimetal.pt; internet www.fiequimetal.pt; f. 2007 by merger of Fequimetal and Federação das Indústrias Eléctricas; affiliated to CGTP-IN.

Federação Nacional dos Médicos (FNAM) (Doctors): Praça da República 28, 2°, 3000 Coimbra; tel. (239) 827737; e-mail fnam@fnam.pt; internet www.fnam.pt; f. 1988; non-affiliated; Pres. Mário Jorge Neves.

Federação Nacional de Professores (FENPROF) (Teachers): Rua Fialho de Almeida 3, 1070-128 Lisbon; tel. (21) 3819190; fax (21) 3819198; e-mail fenprof@fenprof.pt; internet www.fenprof.pt; non-affiliated; Sec.-Gen. Mário Nogueira.

Federação Nacional dos Sindicatos da Educação (FNE): Rua Costa Cabral 1035, 4200-226 Oporto; tel. (22) 5073880; fax (22) 5092906; e-mail secretariado@fne.pt; internet www.fne.pt; f. 1982; affiliated to UGT; Sec.-Gen. Prof. João Dias da Silva.

Federação Nacional dos Sindicatos da Função Pública (FNSFP): Rua Rodrigues Sampaio 138, 3°, 1150-282 Lisbon; tel. (21) 3172480; fax (21) 3172489; e-mail fnsfp@fnsfp.pt; internet www.fnsfp.pt; represents public sector workers; affiliated to CGTP-IN.

PORTUGAL

Federação Portuguesa dos Sindicatos da Construção, Ceramica e Vidro (FEVICCOM): Rua dos Douradores 160, 1100–207 Lisbon; tel. (21) 8818585; fax (21) 8818599; e-mail feviccom@mail.sitepac.pt; affiliated to CGTP-IN.

Federação dos Sindicatos da Agricultura, Alimentação, Bebidas, Hotelaria e Turismo de Portugal (FESAHT): Páteo do Salema 4, 3°, 1150-062 Lisbon; tel. (21) 8873844; fax (21) 8870510; e-mail fesaht@fesaht.pt; internet www.fesaht.pt; affiliated to CGTP-IN.

Federação dos Sindicatos do Sector da Pesca (Fisheries): Av. Elias Garcia 123, 2° dto, 1050-098 Lisbon; tel. (21) 7802250; fax (21) 7802259; e-mail fpescas@mail.telepac.pt; affiliated to CGTP-IN; Pres. FREDERICO PEREIRA.

Federação dos Sindicatos dos Trabalhadores Têxteis, Lanifícios, Vestuário, Calçado e Peles de Portugal (FESETE) (Textiles, Wool, Clothing, Shoes, Leather): Av. da Boavista 583, 4100–127 Oporto; tel. (22) 6002377; fax (22) 6002164; e-mail fesete@netcabo.pt; internet www.fesete.pt; f. 1976; affiliated to CGTP-IN; Sec.-Gen. MANUEL FREITAS.

Federação dos Sindicatos dos Transportes e Comunicações (FECTRANS) (Transport and Communications): Av. António José de Almeida 22, 1049–009 Lisbon; tel. (21) 8453466; fax (21) 8453469; e-mail fectrans@fectrans.pt; affiliated to CGTP-IN; Sec.-Gen. VÍTOR PEREIRA.

Federação dos Trabalhadores do Comércio, Escritórios e Serviços de Portugal (CESP): Rua Almirante Barroso 3, 1049-023 Lisbon; tel. (21) 3583350; fax (21) 3583339; e-mail cesplisboa@mail.telepac.pt; internet www.cesp.pt; f. 1998; represents workers in commercial, administrative and service sectors; affiliated to CGTP-IN; 51,998 mems (2006).

Sindicato Democrático da Energia, Química, Têxtil e Indústrias Diversas (SINDEQ) (Energy, Chemicals, Textiles and Industry): Rua Padre Luís Aparicio 9, 1° esq, 1150-248 Lisbon; tel. (21) 3300920; fax (21) 3300929; e-mail reglisboa@sindeq.pt; internet www.sindeq.pt; affiliated to UGT; Sec.-Gen. FRANCISCO AFONSO NEGRÕES.

Sindicato Democrático dos Trabalhadores das Comunicações e dos Média (SINDETELCO) (Communications and Media): Rua Bernardim Ribeiro 52, 1° and 2°, 1150-073 Lisbon; tel. (21) 3148620; fax (21) 3145826; e-mail sindetelco@netcabo.pt; internet www.sindetelco.pt; f. 1981; affiliated to UGT; Sec.-Gen. MANUEL DA SILVA.

Transport

RAILWAYS

In 2006 the total length of the rail track totalled 3,614.8 km, of which 1,436.2 km was electrified. In 2005 the Government announced plans to develop high-speed rail links connecting Lisbon and Oporto with the Spanish capital, Madrid, and Vigo in north-west Spain. The Lisbon–Madrid link was scheduled to open in 2013. However, construction of the Lisbon–Oporto–Vigo line was postponed.

Rede Ferroviária Nacional—REFER, E.P.: Estação de Santa Apolónia, Largo dos Caminhos de Ferro, 1100-105 Lisbon; tel. (21) 1022000; fax (21) 1022439; internet www.refer.pt; f. 1997; assumed responsibility for rail infrastructure in 1999; Pres. LUÍS FILIPE MELO E SOUSA PARDAL.

Comboios de Portugal (CP): Calçada do Duque 20, 1249-109 Lisbon; tel. (21) 1023000; fax (21) 3474468; e-mail webmaster@mail.cp.pt; internet www.cp.pt; f. 1856; nationalized in 1975 as Caminhos de Ferro Portugueses; incorporated Sociedade Estoril Caminhos de Ferro from Cais do Sodré to Cascais in 1977; renamed as above in 2004; Pres. FRANCISCO JOSÉ CARDOSO DOS REIS.

Metropolitano de Lisboa, EP (ML): Av. Fontes Pereira de Melo 28, 1069-095 Lisbon; tel. (21) 7980600; fax (21) 7980605; e-mail relacoes.publicas@metrolisboa.pt; internet www.metrolisboa.pt; opened 1959; operates the underground system, consisting of 46 stations and 4 lines covering 37.7 km (2007); Pres. JOAQUIM JOSÉ DE OLIVEIRA REIS.

ROADS

In 2006 there were 12,890 km of roads in continental Portugal, of which 2,545 km were motorway.

Brisa (Auto-Estradas de Portugal, SA): Edif. Brisa, Quinta da Torre da Aguilha, 2785-599 São Domingos de Rana; tel. (21) 4448500; fax (21) 4448672; e-mail ir@brisa.pt; internet www.brisa.pt; f. 1972; responsible for construction, maintenance and operation of motorways; Pres. VASCO MARIA GUIMARÃES JOSÉ DE MELLO.

Estradas de Portugal (EP): Praça da Portagem, 2809-013 Almada; tel. (21) 2879000; fax (21) 2951997; e-mail ep@estradasdeportugal.pt; internet www.estradasdeportugal.pt; f. 1999 as Instituto de Estradas de Portugal; merged with Instituto para a Conservação e Exploração da Rede Rodoviária (ICERR) and Instituto para a Construção Rodoviária (ICOR) in 2002; present name adopted 2004; road infrastructure policy, construction and maintenance of the road network; Pres. ALMERINDO DA SILVA MARQUES.

SHIPPING

The principal Portuguese ports are Aveiro, Lisbon, Leixões (Oporto), Setúbal, Sines, and Funchal (Madeira). The ports of Portimão (Algarve) and the Azores regularly receive international cruise liners. At December 2009 Portugal's registered merchant fleet comprised 482 vessels, totalling 1.1m. grt.

Principal Shipping Companies

Portline (Transportes Marítimos Internacionais, SA): Av. Infante D. Henrique 332, 3°, 1849-025 Lisbon; tel. (21) 8391800; fax (21) 8376680; e-mail mail@portline.pt; internet www.portline.pt; f. 1984; marine transport; Gen. Man. MANUEL PINTO DE MAGALHÃES.

Sacor Marítima, SA: Rua do Açúcar 86, 1950-010 Lisbon; tel. (21) 3585100; fax (21) 3585195; e-mail sacor.maritima@petrogal.pt; tanker transport; owned by Petrogal SA, subsidiary of Galp Energia; Chair. LUÍS MARTINS CARNEIRO.

CIVIL AVIATION

There are international airports at Lisbon, Oporto, Faro, Funchal (Madeira), Santa Maria and São Miguel (both Azores). Construction of a second international airport serving Lisbon was expected to be completed by 2017.

TAP Portugal: Aeroporto de Lisboa, CP 50194, 1704-801 Lisbon; tel. (21) 8415000; fax (21) 8415881; e-mail gcrp.com@tap.pt; internet www.flytap.com; f. 1945; state-owned; national airline serving destinations in Europe, Africa, North, Central and South America; scheduled, international, domestic, passenger and cargo services; joined Star Alliance in 2005; Chair., Supervisory Bd MANUEL PINTO BARBOSA; CEO FERNANDO PINTO.

Portugália Airlines (PGA): Edif. 70, Aeroporto de Lisboa, Rua C, 1749-078 Lisbon; tel. (21) 8938070; fax (21) 8938049; f. 1988; subsidiary of TAP Portugal; regional airline operating scheduled and charter, international and domestic flights from Lisbon.

SATA (Air Açores—Serviço Açoreano de Transportes Aéreos—EP): Av. Infante D. Henrique 55, 9505-528 Ponta Delgada, São Miguel, 9500 Azores; tel. (296) 209727; fax (296) 209722; e-mail pdlsd@sata.pt; internet www.sata.pt; f. 1941; owned by the regional govt of the Azores; inter-island services in the Azores archipelago; Pres. and Chief Exec. ANTÓNIO GOMES DE MENEZES.

Tourism

Portugal is popular with visitors because of its mild and clement weather. Apart from Lisbon and the Algarve on the mainland, Madeira and the Azores are much favoured as winter resorts. In 2008 the number of tourist arrivals at accommodation establishments totalled 7.0m.; revenue from tourism (including passenger transport) totalled US $14,047m. in that year.

Turismo de Portugal: Rua Ivone Silva 6, 1050-124 Lisbon; tel. (21) 7808800; fax (21) 7937537; e-mail info@turismodeportugal.pt; internet www.turismodeportugal.pt; f. 2007 to replace the Direcção-Geral do Turismo, the Instituto de Formação Turística and the Instituto de Turismo de Portugal; an agency of the Ministry of the Economy, Innovation and Development; Pres. LUÍS MANUEL DOS SANTOS SILVA PATRÃO.

Defence

Portugal is a member of the North Atlantic Treaty Organization (NATO, see p. 368) and of Western European Union (WEU, see p. 463). The total strength of the armed forces, as assessed at November 2010, was 44,340: army 26,700, navy 10,540 and air force 7,100. There were reserves of 210,900. The paramilitary National Republican Guard and the Public Security Police totalled 26,100 and 21,600, respectively. Compulsory military service was abolished in 2004. At November 2010 a total of 705 US troops were stationed in Portugal, mainly at the air force base at Lajes in the Azores. In November 2004 Portugal confirmed its participation in one of a number of European Union (EU, see p. 270) 'battlegroups' (with Italy, Spain and Greece). The battlegroups, two of which were to be ready for deployment to a crisis area at any one time, following a rotational schedule, reached full operational capacity from 1 January 2007. Portugal subsequently agreed to participate in a second EU battlegroup, led by Spain and also involving Germany and France.

PORTUGAL

Defence Budget: €2,420m. in 2011.
General Chief of Staff of the Armed Forces: Gen. LUÍS EVANGE-LISTA ESTEVES DE ARAÚJO.
Army Chief of Staff: Gen. JOSÉ LUÍS PINTO RAMALHO.
Navy Chief of Staff: Adm. FERNANDO JOSÉ RIBEIRO DE MELO GOMES.
Air Force Chief of Staff: Gen. JOSÉ ANTÓNIO DE MAGALHÃES ARAÚJO PINHEIRO.

Education

The Ministry of Education is responsible for providing education in Portugal. Formal education at all levels is provided at both public and private institutions. Pre-school education, for children aged from three to five years, is not compulsory and is available free of charge. Education is compulsory for 12 years, between the ages of six and 18 years, and is provided free of charge in public schools. Primary education is divided into two cycles: the first lasts for four years, the second for two years. Lower secondary and upper secondary education each last for three years. Entry to the second cycle of primary education and to lower and upper secondary education is dependent on the successful completion of the previous cycle. In 2006/07 98.9% of children in the relevant age-group were enrolled in primary schools, while 87.7% of children in the relevant age-group were enrolled in secondary schools. At the non-tertiary level, above the age of 18 years, students can enrol for a *Cursos de Especialização Tecnológica* (CET, specialized technological course). Higher education comprises university and polytechnic education. Fees are set by the institution depending on the course. Universities award the following academic degrees: the *licenciatura*, after four to six years of study; the *mestrado*, after one or two years of study and research work; and the *doutoramento*. Regional polytechnic institutes, grouping technical, management, educational and fine arts schools, offer three-year courses leading to the *bacharel* and specialized studies leading to a diploma after one to two years. In 2008/09 a total of 373,002 students were enrolled in higher education. Expenditure on education in 2004 was €7,132m (representing 15.9% of general government expenditure).

QATAR

Introductory Survey

LOCATION, CLIMATE, LANGUAGE, RELIGION, FLAG, CAPITAL

The State of Qatar occupies a peninsula, projecting northwards from the Arabian mainland, on the west coast of the Persian (Arabian) Gulf. It is bordered, to the south, by Saudi Arabia and the United Arab Emirates. The archipelago of Bahrain lies to the north-west. On the opposite side of the Gulf lies Iran. The climate is exceptionally hot in the summer, when temperatures may reach 49°C (120°F), with high humidity on the coast; conditions are relatively mild in the winter. Rainfall is negligible. The official language is Arabic. Almost all of the inhabitants are adherents of Islam, although an influx of guest workers in recent years has precipitated official recognition of Christian denominations. Native Qataris, who comprise less than one-quarter of the total population, belong mainly to the strictly orthodox Wahhabi sect of Sunni Muslims. The national flag (proportions 11 by 28) is maroon, with a broad vertical white stripe at the hoist, the two colours being separated by a serrated line. The capital is Doha.

CONTEMPORARY POLITICAL HISTORY

Historical Context

Qatar was formerly dominated by the Al Khalifa family of Bahrain. The peninsula became part of Turkey's Ottoman Empire in 1872, but Turkish forces evacuated Qatar at the beginning of the First World War (1914–18). The United Kingdom recognized Sheikh Abdullah Al Thani as Ruler of Qatar, and in 1916 made a treaty with him, providing British protection against aggression in return for supervision of Qatar's external affairs. A 1934 treaty extended fuller British protection to Qatar.

In October 1960 Sheikh Ali Al Thani, Ruler of Qatar since 1949, abdicated in favour of his son, Sheikh Ahmad. In 1968 the British Government announced its intention to withdraw British forces from the Persian (Arabian) Gulf area by 1971. Qatar thus attempted to associate itself with Bahrain and Trucial Oman (now the United Arab Emirates—UAE) in a proposed federation. In April 1970 Sheikh Ahmad announced a provisional Constitution, providing for a partially elected Consultative Assembly, although he retained effective power. In May the Deputy Ruler, Sheikh Khalifa Al Thani (a cousin of Sheikh Ahmad), was appointed Prime Minister. After the failure of attempts to agree terms for union with neighbouring Gulf countries, Qatar became fully independent on 1 September 1971, whereupon the Ruler took the title of Amir. The 1916 treaty was replaced by a new treaty of friendship with the United Kingdom.

In February 1972 Sheikh Ahmad was deposed in a bloodless coup by Sheikh Khalifa, who proclaimed himself Amir, while retaining the premiership. The new Amir adopted a policy of wide-ranging social and economic reform, and the previous extravagance and privileges of the royal family were curbed. In accordance with the 1970 Constitution, the Amir appointed an Advisory Council in April 1972 to complement the ministerial Government. The Council was expanded from 20 to 30 members in 1975 and to 35 members in 1988. Its term has been extended at regular intervals since its establishment, most recently, for a period of three years, in 2010.

Domestic Political Affairs

Accession of Sheikh Hamad

On 27 June 1995 the Deputy Amir, Heir Apparent, Minister of Defence and Commander-in-Chief of the Armed Forces, Maj.-Gen. Sheikh Hamad bin Khalifa Al Thani, deposed his father in a bloodless coup. Sheikh Hamad proclaimed himself Amir, claiming the support of the royal family and the Qatari people. Sheikh Khalifa, who was in Switzerland at the time of the coup, immediately denounced his son's actions, and vowed to return to Qatar. Although Sheikh Khalifa had effectively granted Sheikh Hamad control of the emirate's affairs (with the exception of the treasury) in 1992, a power struggle was reported to have emerged between the two in the months prior to the coup: Sheikh Khalifa was particularly opposed to his son's independent foreign policy (notably the strengthening of relations with both Iran and Iraq, and with Israel), and had attempted to regain influence in policy-making. Sheikh Hamad, however, reputedly enjoyed widespread support both nationally and internationally, and his domestic reforms were perceived as having contributed to Qatar's stability at a time when social unrest and Islamist extremism were emerging in the region. The United Kingdom, the USA and Saudi Arabia swiftly recognized the new Amir. In July 1995 Sheikh Hamad reorganized the Council of Ministers and appointed himself Prime Minister, while retaining the posts of Minister of Defence and Commander-in-Chief of the Armed Forces.

In January 1996 it was confirmed that Sheikh Khalifa had gained control of a substantial part of Qatar's financial reserves. In the following month security forces in Qatar were reported to have foiled an attempted coup. As many as 100 people were arrested, and a warrant was issued for the arrest of Sheikh Hamad bin Jasim bin Hamad Al Thani, a former government minister and a cousin of the Amir. Sheikh Khalifa denied any involvement, although he was quick to imply that the alleged plot indicated popular support for his return. In July legal proceedings were initiated in Qatar, Europe and the USA in an attempt to recover some US $3,000m.–$8,000m. in overseas assets that were asserted by the new Amir to have been amassed by his father from state oil and investment revenues. In October, however, it was reported that Sheikh Hamad and Sheikh Khalifa had been reconciled and had reached an out-of-court settlement regarding the return of state funds. By early 1997 all lawsuits issued against the former Amir had been withdrawn.

In October 1996 Sheikh Hamad named the third of his four sons, Sheikh Jasim bin Hamad bin Khalifa Al Thani, as Heir Apparent. The Amir subsequently appointed his younger brother, Sheikh Abdullah bin Khalifa Al Thani (the Minister of the Interior), as Prime Minister. Further to the ending of media censorship earlier in the year, the post of Minister of Information and Culture was abolished. (The relevant ministry was dissolved in March 1998.) In November 1996 Sheikh Hamad announced the creation of a new Defence Council, over which he would preside. The Council, to be comprised of senior ministers and armed forces and security personnel, was expected to function in an advisory and consultative capacity. It was also reported that the Amir had appointed the Gulf region's first female member of government (as Under-Secretary of State for Education and Culture).

Elections to Qatar's new 29-member Central Municipal Council (CMC), held by universal suffrage on 8 March 1999, were the first in the country's history. Announced by Sheikh Hamad in November 1997 and provided for by law in July 1998, the CMC was to have a consultative role in the operations of the Ministry of Municipal Affairs and Agriculture. The rate of participation by voters reportedly exceeded 90% in Doha, and was estimated at 60%–70% of the registered electorate in rural areas. However, only about 22,000 voters of an eligible 40,000 actually participated in the elections.

The draft constitution

In July 1999 a 32-member constitutional committee was established to draft a permanent constitution; this was to include provision for the creation of a new National Assembly. The committee produced a draft constitution in July 2002, which provided for a separation of the executive, the judiciary and the legislature, but which would retain executive power in the hands of the Amir and the Council of Ministers. The draft constitution also guaranteed freedom of expression, religion and association, and provided for the establishment of an independent judiciary and of a new 45-member Consultative Council (to replace the Advisory Council), comprising 30 elected and 15 appointed members. Under the proposed constitution, the Amir would be obliged to provide reasons for rejecting draft laws adopted by the Council. The Amir would be required to approve such legislation sent to him a second time by the Council with two-thirds' majority support, although he would have a discretionary right to halt implementation of laws in question on a temporary basis if he deemed this to be in the greater interests of the country. The parliament was to have a four-year mandate, and suffrage was to be extended to all citizens, including women, aged 18 years and above. In a referendum held on 29 April 2003, an overwhelming majority (96.6%) of the 71,406 voters approved the new Constitution, and it was expected that the affirmative vote would lead to legislative elections being conducted in 2004. However, the planned elections were repeatedly postponed and by early 2011 a date had yet to be announced (see Recent developments).

Meanwhile, Sheikh Hamad bin Jasim bin Hamad Al Thani was arrested in July 1999 for his alleged role in the coup plot of 1996. The trial of those accused of involvement in the coup (which began in November 1997) ended in February 2000, with the former minister and 32 co-defendants sentenced to life imprisonment; 85 others were acquitted. Appeal proceedings were subsequently lodged by all 33 who had been convicted. In May 2001 the Court of Appeal overruled the previous sentences of life imprisonment, sentencing to death 19 of the defendants (including Sheikh Hamad bin Jasim bin Hamad); the court was also reported to have sentenced 26 defendants to terms of life imprisonment, and acquitted two others.

In January 2002 it was reported that a group styling itself the General Congress of the Qatari Opposition had emerged to demand that the Amir stand down in favour of his son, Crown Prince Jasim. The group, which claimed to include former members of the armed forces, tribal chiefs, businessmen, students and officials who had served under the previous regime, accused the Amir of pursuing 'reckless' policies, of corruption and of alienating Qatar's Gulf neighbours. This last charge was interpreted as possibly referring not only to Qatar's pursuit of an increasingly independent foreign policy but also to the activities of Al Jazeera, a satellite television station linked to the Al Thani family with a wide audience throughout the region. Al Jazeera's reporting style and scope of coverage had caused several governments to threaten to restrict its freedom to operate in their countries. In January 2005 it was announced that Al Jazeera was to be privatized; the proposed sale was regarded as a means of distancing the Qatari Government from Al Jazeera's more controversial broadcasts and was a further indication of the closeness of the relationship between Qatar and the US Administration, which had allegedly been critical of the station for its broadcasting of videos purportedly featuring senior operatives of the militant Islamist organization al-Qa'ida. However, by early 2011 no significant announcements had been made regarding the privatization of the channel

The 2003 and 2007 elections to the Central Municipal Council

The second elections to the CMC were held on 7 April 2003. A turn-out of about 35% was estimated for the country as a whole, but the rate of participation was reportedly as low as 25% of the registered electorate at several polling stations, including in the largest constituency, al-Kharitaat. A female candidate, Sheikha al-Jufairi, was elected unopposed after the competing candidates stood aside, and thus became the first woman in the Gulf region to hold elected office, but none of the five other women who contested the elections was successful. Three further candidates were also elected unopposed, and the remaining 25 seats were contested by 85 candidates, including 18 incumbents. In May Sheikha bint Ahmad al-Mahmoud became the first woman to join the Council of Ministers when she was appointed Minister of Education. In August Sheikh Jasim was replaced as Heir Apparent by Sheikh Tamim bin Hamad bin Khalifa Al Thani, the Amir's fourth-eldest son. In December Sheikh Muhammad bin Ahmad bin Jasim Al Thani replaced Sheikh Hamad bin Faisal Al Thani as Minister of Economy and Commerce.

Meanwhile, in February 2004 the Government approved an anti-terrorism law, which included the provision of the death penalty for anyone who killed 'through a terror act' and for anyone 'founding, organizing or managing a group or organization to commit a terror act'. In addition, the crime of assisting a terrorist group was to be punishable by a life sentence. In May a law permitting the formation of trade unions was approved. In addition, the legislation granted workers the right to strike, banned children aged under 16 years from employment and set a maximum eight-hour working day.

In April 2005 the Amir removed from their posts his Chief of Staff, Abdullah bin Muhammad bin Sa'ud Al Thani, and two recently appointed ministers—Muhammad bin Abd al-Latif bin Abd al-Rahman al-Mana, the Minister of Awqaf (Religious Endowments) and Islamic Affairs, and Muhammad bin Isa Hamad al-Mehannadi, the Minister of State for Council of Ministers' Affairs—amid allegations that three cabinet members and several businessmen had been questioned by officials over their connections to fraudulent activities relating to the sale of the state-owned Qatar Gas Transport Co (Nakilat) in early 2005. Faisal bin Abdullah al-Mahmud was awarded the religious affairs portfolio, Sultan bin Hassan al-Dhabit al-Dousary, the Minister of Municipal Affairs and Agriculture, received the position of Minister of State for Council of Ministers' Affairs in addition to his existing responsibilities, and Sheikh Abd al-Rahman bin Sa'ud Al Thani was appointed as the new Chief of Staff.

A bomb exploded outside a theatre frequented by Western expatriates in Doha in March 2005. One British citizen was killed in the suicide attack and 12 people were injured. The bomber was reported to be an Egyptian citizen, Omar Ahmad Abdullah Ali, and Jund al-Sham (the Army of the Levant), a previously little-known militant grouping, claimed responsibility for the attack. Although the bombing was the first of its kind in Qatar, Western embassies had previously issued warnings to expatriates that the threat from terrorism in the emirate was high.

In March 2006 the Minister of Economy and Commerce, Sheikh Muhammad, was unexpectedly dismissed from the Council of Ministers. No official explanation was given for his removal; however, the decision was widely believed to have been prompted by a recent crash on the Doha Securities Market. The ministerial portfolio was added to the responsibilities of the Minister of Finance, Yousuf Hussain Kamal.

The third elections to the CMC, contested by 118 candidates, took place on 1 April 2007. Turn-out, although relatively low, exceeded expectations, at 51.1% of the electorate, compared with an estimated 35% in the 2003 polls. Of the three female candidates standing for election, only one was successful: Sheikha al-Jufairi was re-elected, securing 800 of the 879 votes cast in the Old Airport constituency—the highest proportion of votes achieved by any candidate. A few days later it was announced that the Prime Minister, Sheikh Abdullah, had resigned, but no explanation was offered for his decision. Sheikh Hamad, hitherto First Deputy Prime Minister and Minister of Foreign Affairs, replaced him, while retaining the foreign affairs portfolio.

Administrative reorganizations, 2008–10

In July 2008 the Amir effected a major reorganization of the Council of Ministers. Seven new ministerial portfolios were created—including those of culture, arts and heritage, business and trade, environment, and international co-operation—bringing the number of members of the Council of Ministers to 20, in addition to the Amir himself. A new Minister of Public Health, Sheikha Ghalia bint Muhammad bin Hamad Al Thani, was appointed, increasing the number of female ministers to two. However, Sheika Ghalia and the Minister of Education and Higher Education, Sheikha bint Ahmad al-Mahmoud, were replaced in April 2009, following a minor reallocation of cabinet portfolios.

Following the death of Sheikh Fahd bin Jassem Al Thani, the Minister of Business and Trade, in a road traffic accident in May 2009, the Amir effected a minor cabinet reorganization in June. Dr Khalid bin Muhammad al-Attiya, the Minister of State for International Co-operation, was accorded responsibility for the business and trade portfolio in an acting capacity, in addition to his existing responsibilities; Sheikha bint Ahmad al-Mahmoud was appointed Minister of State without Portfolio.

Sheikh Tamim, the Heir Apparent, took a more active role in government affairs from the second half of 2009, overseeing a major reorganization of Qatar's administrative structure in August, under which several ministries were restructured and numerous, formerly autonomous state agencies were reintegrated into cabinet ministries. Notable developments included: the assignment of the Civil Aviation Authority and the Qatar Tourism Authority to the Ministry of Business and Trade; the reallocation of the Public Works Authority to the Ministry of Municipal Affairs and Urban Planning; and the division of the Ministry of Foreign Affairs into two separate departments, responsible for foreign affairs and international co-operation, respectively. Furthermore, Sheikh Tamim was accorded direct responsibility for the General Secretariat for Development Planning (GSDP), the agency responsible for co-ordination of the National Development Strategy, which was intended to facilitate efforts to meet the objectives of the National Vision 2030—a long-term development programme launched under the supervision of the GSDP in October 2008, which aims to promote and manage Qatar's ambitious economic and social development programme while protecting its culture, traditions and environment. The National Development Strategy was initially expected to be launched in mid-2010; however, by early 2011 it still awaited formal implementation.

Meanwhile, in October 2008 the international Doha Centre for Media Freedom commenced operations, under the direction of Robert Ménard, founder of the Paris (France)-based advocacy group Reporters Sans Frontières. Heralded as the first body of its kind in the region, the Doha Centre had been established by the Amir, under the patronage of his wife, Sheikha Mozah bint Nasser al-Misnad, in December 2007. In addition to promoting media freedom, the centre was to provide refuge for journalists under threat of persecution. In February 2009 the centre published a report detailing government restrictions on the media in Qatar and the biased nature of Al Jazeera's coverage of Qatari events. Ménard subsequently attracted strong criticism from some conservative newspapers in Qatar, which accused him of promoting media content that they considered insulting to Muslims. In June Ménard resigned as Director-General, alleging that certain Qatari officials were obstructing the centre's operations and compromising its independent status. None the less, Qatar's international reputation in the field of human rights received a boost in May, with the opening in Doha of the UN Human Rights Training and Documentation Centre for South-West Asia and the Arab Region. The centre, which benefited from a US $1m. donation from the Qatari Government, was established to promote the development and documentation of human rights in the region.

Recent developments

It was hoped that a new electoral law approved by the Advisory Council in May 2008 would facilitate the organization of long-awaited elections to the Consultative Council provided for in the Constitution. The extension of the Advisory Council's term for a further two years in July 2008 had prompted speculation that legislative elections might take place in mid-2010; however, the Council's term was subsequently extended once again, until 2013, indicating the likelihood that elections would not be staged until that year. Questioned about the reasons for the delay, the Amir declared in November 2010 that Qatar was 'not yet ready' to stage its first legislative poll, stating that only three-quarters of the necessary legislation had been implemented. At early 2011 the electoral law approved by the Advisory Council in 2008 still awaited ratification by the Amir. Meanwhile, according to the preliminary results of a national census conducted in April 2010, the Qatari population more than doubled between 2004 and early 2010, increasing to nearly 1.7m.

In November 2010 the Amir announced that the Council of Ministers was reviewing the status of Qatar's foreign worker sponsorship system, by which employers sponsor foreign workers' residency; the Bahraini Government had abolished a similar system in 2009. The controversial system was widely regarded as an affront to workers' rights and as allowing employers excessive control over their workers: under its provisions, an employer had the authority, inter alia, to deny a worker's request to change jobs, and there were widespread reports of employers confiscating workers' passports. Human rights groups welcomed the Qatari Prime Minister's announcement, urging the Government to take firm action on the issue. However, the sponsorship system remained in place in early 2011.

In January 2011 the Amir announced the appointment of Abdullah bin Hamad al-Attiya, hitherto Deputy Prime Minister and Minister of Energy and Industry, to the position of Chairman of the Emiri Diwan. Al-Attiya, who had headed the energy portfolio since 1992, retained the deputy premiership and was replaced as Minister of Energy and Industry by his deputy, Muhammad Saleh al-Sada. A government spokesperson stated that the changes were not indicative of any revision of the country's oil policy.

Qatar's Role as a Regional Mediator

In June 2007, and again in February 2008, Qatari negotiators played a leading role in brokering peace agreements between the Government of Yemen and rebels loyal to the late Shi'a cleric Hussain al-Houthi, who had been engaged in a sporadic civil war in Saada province since 2004. Although the Qatari-brokered accords ultimately failed to end the hostilities, they demonstrated the gulf state's willingness and capability to act as an independent mediator in regional conflicts. In May 2008 Qatari diplomats brokered a deal in Doha to resolve an 18-month-long political stalemate between rival factions in Lebanon (see the chapter on Lebanon). The agreement, which provided for the formation of a power-sharing government, the election of a President and the drafting of a new electoral law, was widely believed to have averted the threat of civil war. Qatar's success in brokering the Lebanese accord was attributed to its independent foreign policy and lack of vested interests in the region, and significantly bolstered its reputation as a regional mediator. Amid an escalation in political tensions in Lebanon (q.v.), the Amir made an unexpected visit to the Lebanese capital, Beirut, in November 2010, whereupon he met with Lebanese President Gen. Michel Suleiman, shortly before Suleiman left for a two-day state visit to Doha. Following the collapse of the national unity coalition Government on 12 January 2011, Sheikh Hamad and the Turkish Minister of Foreign Affairs, Prof. Dr Ahmet Davutoğlu, chaired negotiations between the rival Lebanese factions in an attempt to secure an end to the impasse; however, Qatar and Turkey announced a suspension of their mediation efforts on 19 January 'owing to certain reservations'. Meanwhile, further confirmation of Qatar's growing stature in regional affairs was provided by the emirate's presence at a four-nation summit, also involving Syria, France and Turkey, in Damascus, Syria, in September 2008.

Qatari mediators were also involved in efforts during 2008 to conclude a peace agreement between participants in the conflict in Darfur, Sudan. Talks between Darfur-based rebel group the Sudan Justice and Equality Movement (JEM) and the Government of Sudan, which were sponsored by the African Union (AU, see p. 183) and the League of Arab States (the Arab League, see p. 361), were held in Doha in February 2009 and resulted in the signing of a confidence-building agreement intended to lead to broader peace negotiations. Furthermore, negotiations between the Governments of Sudan and Chad, aimed at resolving a bilateral dispute arising from the conflict in the Darfur, commenced in Doha in April. The negotiations, which were sponsored by Qatar and Libya, resulted in the signing of a framework agreement on the normalization of bilateral relations in May. Meanwhile, talks between the JEM and Sudan's Government resumed in Doha in April and, following several rounds of negotiations during 2009, culminated in the signing of a provisional cease-fire and power-sharing agreement in February 2010. The Qatari Government pledged US $1,000m. for reconstruction efforts in Darfur. Following Qatari-chaired negotiations intended to resolve a protracted border dispute between Djibouti and Eritrea in mid-2010, Prime Minister Sheikh Hamad announced in early June that Eritrea had withdrawn its troops from contested border areas. A few days later an agreement was signed by Djibouti and Eritrea in Doha, under the terms of which the two countries agreed to entrust to Qatar the role of mediating in efforts to draft a 'final and binding resolution' to the bilateral dispute. Qatar's offer of mediation in the dispute was welcomed by many within the international community, including the UN Security Council, which pledged its 'full support' to Qatari efforts.

Foreign Affairs
Regional relations

Qatar's relations with Bahrain have long been impeded by a protracted dispute over sovereignty of the Hawar islands (which had been awarded to Bahrain in 1939 by a British judgment) and the shoals of Fasht al-Dibal and Qit'at Jaradah (over which the British had recognized Bahrain's 'sovereign rights' in 1947). In February 1995 the International Court of Justice (ICJ) declared that it would have authority to adjudicate in the dispute (despite Bahrain's refusal to accept the principle of an ICJ ruling), while Saudi Arabia also proposed to act as mediator between the two countries. Qatar subsequently indicated its willingness to withdraw the case from the ICJ if Saudi arbitration proved successful. Bilateral relations subsequently deteriorated, and in December 1996 Bahrain boycotted the annual summit meeting of the Co-operation Council for the Arab States of the Gulf (Gulf Co-operation Council—GCC, see p. 243), which took place in Doha. The meeting none the less decided to establish a quadripartite committee, comprising those GCC countries not involved in the dispute, to mediate between Qatar and Bahrain. The committee's efforts achieved a degree of success, and meetings between senior Qatari and Bahraini representatives in London, United Kingdom, and Manama, Bahrain, in early 1997 resulted in the announcement that diplomatic relations at ambassadorial level were to be established. In September, however, Bahrain challenged the authenticity of documents presented to the ICJ by Qatar in support of its territorial claim; the ICJ subsequently directed Qatar to produce a report on the authenticity of the documents by September 1998. Following the submission of the report, in which four experts differed in their opinion of the documents, Qatar announced its decision to disregard them, to enable the case to proceed.

In December 1999 the Amir made his first official visit to Manama, during which it was agreed that a joint committee, headed by the Crown Princes of Bahrain and Qatar, would be established to encourage bilateral co-operation. Qatar also agreed to withdraw its petition from the ICJ in the event of the joint committee reaching a solution to the territorial disputes. A second senior-level meeting was held in January 2000, when the new Amir of Bahrain made his first visit to Qatar. The two countries agreed to expedite the opening of embassies in Manama and Doha. In February, following the first meeting of the Bahrain-Qatar Supreme Joint Committee, it was announced that the possibility of constructing a causeway to link the two states was to be investigated. In May Bahrain announced its decision to suspend the activities of the Supreme Joint Committee pending the ICJ ruling on the dispute. The ICJ's final verdict, issued in March 2001, was virtually identical to the British judgment of 1939: Bahrain was found to have sovereignty over the Hawar islands and Qit'at Jaradah, while Qatar held sovereignty over Zubarah, Janan island and the low-tide elevation of Fasht al-Dibal; the Court drew a single maritime boundary between the two states. Both Qatar and Bahrain accepted the ICJ ruling, and declared that their territorial dispute was ended.

In August 2002 a Danish consortium completed a feasibility study for the construction of the planned causeway linking Qatar to Bahrain (the Friendship Bridge). Both Governments had approved the project by May 2004, and international companies were invited to present bids for the contract in late 2004. By this time Bahrain and Qatar were reportedly also discussing co-operation on gas projects and other economic issues. Following extensive negotiations, a US $3,000m. contract to design and build the causeway was signed in May 2008 by a consortium led by VINCI Construction, a French company, and the Qatar-Bahrain Causeway Foundation. However, substantial revisions to the design were required after a decision, in late 2008, to incorporate a railway line into the project; the rail link was expected to add up to $1,000m. to the cost of the project. Construction had been expected to commence in 2010, with completion scheduled for 2015. However, at early 2011 work on the causeway had yet to commence, with the construction workers reportedly in the process of demobilizing and the project appearing to have stalled amid elevated bilateral tensions. Relations had been damaged when a Bahraini fisherman was seriously injured by Qatari coastguards in a 'naval incident' in May 2010, which resulted in a renewal of hostilities over ownership of the Hawar islands. Tensions were further exacerbated later that month following the broadcasting by Al Jazeera of a television programme on poverty and the treatment of foreign labourers in Bahrain; the programme was widely interpreted as a public criticism of the Bahraini Government, which promptly announced a suspension of Al Jazeera's operations in Bahrain, citing a 'breach of press and publishing regulations'.

Following the multinational military operation to liberate Kuwait from Iraqi occupation in early 1991, Qatar resumed tentative contact with Iraq in 1993. In March 1995, during the first official visit to the country by a senior Iraqi official since the Gulf War, Iraq's Minister of Foreign Affairs met with his Qatari counterpart to discuss the furtherance of bilateral relations; the Qatari Minister subsequently indicated Qatar's determination to pursue a foreign policy independent from that of its GCC neighbours when he announced his country's support for the ending of UN sanctions against Iraq. In early 1998, as the crisis deepened regarding UN weapons inspections in Iraq (see the chapter on Iraq), Qatar urged a diplomatic solution, and appealed to Iraq to comply with all pertinent UN Security Council resolutions. With Qatar continuing to advocate an end to sanctions against Iraq, in December 2001 a meeting took place in Doha between the new Iraqi Minister of Foreign Affairs, Naji Sabri, and Qatari and Omani officials. In June 2003, after the removal of Saddam Hussain's regime by the US-led coalition, Qatar Airways became the first airline for 12 years to operate commercial air services to Iraq, after the scheduling of a bi-weekly service to Basra. Meanwhile, in September the US-appointed interim Cabinet in Iraq voted to expel Al Jazeera reporters for one month, pending a review of their broadcasts, after the station was accused of inciting violence against US and Iraqi authorities. Despite official announcements in 2004 that the Government planned to cancel most of the estimated US $4,000m. worth of debt owed to Qatar by Iraq, by early 2011 significant Iraqi debt relief had yet to be authorized.

In September 1992 tension arose with Saudi Arabia (with which Qatar had previously enjoyed close ties) when Qatar accused Saudi forces of attacking a Qatari border post, killing two border guards and capturing a third in the process. In protest, in October Qatar suspended a 1965 border agreement with Saudi Arabia (which had never been fully ratified) and temporarily withdrew its 200-strong contingent from the Saudi-based GCC 'Peninsula Shield' force (at the time stationed in Kuwait). The Saudi Government denied the involvement of its armed forces, claiming that the incident had been caused by fighting between rival Bedouin tribes within Saudi territory. Relations between the two countries reportedly improved as a result of Kuwaiti mediation, and the Qatari hostage was released later in October 1992. In December, after mediation by Egypt, Sheikh Khalifa and King Fahd of Saudi Arabia signed an agreement whereby a committee was to be established formally to demarcate the border between the two states. In November 1994, however, Qatar boycotted a GCC ministerial meeting in Saudi Arabia, in protest against what it alleged to have been armed incidents on the border with Saudi Arabia in March and October. Bilateral relations appeared to improve in August 1995, when the new Amir held talks with King Fahd in Saudi Arabia. In December, nevertheless, Qatar boycotted the closing session of the annual GCC summit, following the appointment of a Saudi national as the next GCC Secretary-General (in preference to a Qatari candidate). In March 1996 the dispute was reported to have been settled, after mediation by Oman, and in April Qatar and Saudi Arabia agreed to establish a joint committee to complete the demarcation of their mutual border. In March 2001, at a ceremony in Doha, Saudi and Qatari officials signed an apparently final agreement concerning the land and maritime demarcation of their joint border.

In October 2002 relations between Saudi Arabia and Qatar worsened, however, when the Saudi ambassador to Qatar was recalled following the airing of a television programme via the Al Jazeera network that was deemed to be critical of the Saudi regime. Relations had already been strained by the expansion of US military facilities in Qatar and by the relocation, in April, of the main US air operations in the Gulf region from Saudi Arabia to Doha (see the chapter on Saudi Arabia). Furthermore, Saudi Arabia subsequently reopened the border dispute, despite the 2001 agreement, threatening in July 2007 to block a US $3,500m. gas pipeline between Qatar and the UAE on the grounds that sections of the undersea pipeline ran through what it claimed to be Saudi territory. A visit to Jeddah, Saudi Arabia, undertaken by Sheikh Hamad in September 2007 engendered optimism for an improvement in bilateral ties, however, with the announcement of a number of agreements arising from the Amir's dialogue with King Abdullah: Sheikh Hamad gave an assurance that Al Jazeera would not broadcast material that could be regarded as defamatory in respect of Saudi Arabia, in return for which Al Jazeera would be permitted to establish a presence in the kingdom. Saudi Arabia also confirmed the return of its diplomatic envoy to Qatar, and King Abdullah agreed to attend the forthcoming GCC summit in Doha (an invitation he had refused in 2002, when Qatar had last hosted a meeting of the organization). Saudi objections to the Qatar-UAE gas pipeline were also resolved. The new Saudi ambassador to Qatar acceded to his position in March 2008, and relations were further bolstered in that month by an official visit to the emirate by Saudi Crown Prince Sultan ibn Abd al-Aziz as-Sa'ud for talks with the Amir on the countries' bilateral relations and other international issues. In July the Qatari and Saudi Governments agreed to resolve the issue of border demarcation and to establish a Joint Co-ordination Council to encourage co-operation in military, industrial, agricultural and energy affairs. A Land and Maritime Border Delimitation Agreement was signed in December, together with various other agreements on bilateral co-operation, at the first meeting of the Saudi-Qatari Joint Coordination Council, and was registered with the UN in March 2009. Following the eighth meeting of the joint Qatari-Saudi technical committee for the demarcation of land and maritime borders, in Doha in January 2010, a French company was awarded the contract for the completion of the land border demarcation, and the defining of the maritime border beyond Khor Al-Udaid, in south-west Qatar. Relations were strengthened further in February when Sheikh Hamad visited the Saudi capital, Riyadh, for talks with King Abdullah on bilateral relations and regional affairs. The summit was preceded by the inaugural meeting of the Saudi-Qatari Joint Businessmens' Forum in Riyadh, which was attended by more than 150 Qatari businessmen and entrepreneurs. In May the Amir, reportedly in response to a request by King Abdullah, granted a pardon to a number of Saudi nationals who had been convicted in connection with the thwarted plot to overthrow the regime in 1996 (see Domestic Political Affairs); the group returned to Saudi Arabia a few days later.

In September 1994 Qatar, along with the other GCC states, revoked aspects of the economic boycott of Israel. In November 1995 Israel signed a memorandum of intent to purchase Qatari liquefied natural gas (LNG). Relations between the two countries were consolidated further in April 1996, when Shimon Peres made the first official visit to Qatar by an Israeli Prime Minister. However, in late 1996 Israel declared that the memorandum of intent had expired, although negotiations would continue, and in November Qatar stated that any deal would be dependent on progress in the Middle East peace process. In March 1998 the Qatari Government stated that it was reviewing its relations with Israel, given the severe difficulties in the peace process. Nevertheless, Qatar was criticized by other Arab states in September 2000 following a meeting in New York, USA, at the UN Millennium Summit between the Amir and the Israeli Prime Minister, Ehud Barak. Prior to the ninth conference of the Organization of the Islamic Conference (OIC, see p. 400), held in Doha in November, several Islamic states (notably Saudi Arabia and Iran) threatened to boycott the summit unless Qatar agreed to sever its low-level diplomatic relations with Israel. (Arab and Islamic states were keen to demonstrate support for the Palestinians in their renewed uprising against Israeli occupation from late September.) The Qatari leadership apparently bowed to regional pressure when, in November, it announced that the Israeli trade office in Doha was to be closed, although the office continued to function until January 2009 (see below), exacerbating tensions with Saudi Arabia in particular. In March 2002 Qatar's Minister of Foreign Affairs travelled to the Palestinian territories for talks with the leader of the Palestinian (National) Authority (PA), Yasser Arafat, who at that time remained under Israeli siege in Ramallah. In October 2006 the Secretary-General of the GCC, Abd al-Rahman al-Attiya, praised Qatar's mediation efforts between the two rival Palestinian movements, the Islamic Resistance Movement (Hamas) and Fatah, singling out in particular the endeavours of Sheikh Hamad.

Delegations from both Israel and Qatar attended the 62nd UN General Assembly in New York in September 2007. At a meeting with the Israeli Vice-Prime Minister and Minister of Foreign Affairs, Tzipi Livni, initiated by Sheikh Hamad, Livni reiterated the importance of the involvement of 'moderate' Arab states in regional discussions towards promoting political negotiations with the Palestinians, and appealed for greater solidarity with Israel against the emergence of extremist elements in the region. Despite Qatar's unprecedented, and isolated, invitation to Iran to attend the GCC's annual summit meeting, held in Doha in December (see below), Livni maintained Israeli dialogue with Qatar and subsequently embarked on a series of diplomatic visits to the country in early 2008, including attendance at the Doha Forum on Democracy, Development and Free Trade in April. While Qatar, together with other GCC members, strongly condemned Israel's renewed military offensive in the Gaza Strip in January 2008 (see the chapters on Israel and the Palestinian Autonomous Areas), in February the country pledged its willingness to facilitate a cease-fire agreement between Israel and Hamas. However, Qatar's accommodation of the Israeli Minister of Foreign Affairs precipitated the withdrawal from the conference of several other participants, notably members of the Hezbollah-led opposition in Lebanon.

In response to the military offensive launched by Israel against Hamas targets in the Gaza Strip in late December 2008, Sheikh Hamad sought to convene an emergency summit of the Arab League (see p. 361)in Doha to formulate a unified Arab response to the crisis. It was subsequently claimed by Palestinian sources that more than 1,400 Palestinians had been killed and some 5,000 wounded in the Israeli offensive. However, the proposed Doha summit on Gaza was resisted by several countries, notably Saudi Arabia and Egypt, which were strongly opposed to any measures that would offer support to Hamas. Thirteen Arab states agreed to attend the summit, including Algeria, Lebanon, Syria and the UAE; however, this was two fewer than the quorum of 15 required to grant the meeting official status. Delegates at the summit, which was convened on 16 January 2009, including the President of Iran, Mahmoud Ahmadinejad, proposed the suspension of the Arab League peace initiative originally conceived in 2002 and an end to all relations with Israel, and denounced Israel's actions as war crimes. The presence of Khalid Meshaal, the Syria-based head of Hamas's political bureau, and the absence of Mahmud Abbas, the Executive President of the PA, underlined the partisan nature of the gathering. During the summit the Qatari Government announced the closure of Israel's trade office in Doha and the suspension of diplomatic ties. The Doha summit failed in its stated aim of developing a united Arab response to the Israeli aggression in Gaza. Instead, it highlighted regional divisions over the Palestinian issue, exemplified by the emergence of two opposing blocs: one broadly supportive of Hamas and open to Iranian influence, the other supportive of the Fatah-led PA and generally aligned with the USA. Meanwhile, Sheikh Hamad attended an emergency GCC summit on Gaza in Riyadh on 15 January 2009, which focused on seeking an end to the hostilities and on the provision of aid. The Amir also attended the Arab Economic, Social and Development Summit in Kuwait on 19–20 January and argued strongly for Arab reconciliation. On the sidelines of the summit, King Abdullah of Saudi Arabia hosted a private meeting with the leaders of Qatar, Egypt, Kuwait and Syria, which was heralded as achieving substantial progress towards Arab unity. However, despite the plethora of high-level meetings during January, a unified Arab political response to the Gaza crisis failed to be agreed. A Qatari offer to resume diplomatic and economic ties in return for an easing of the Israeli blockade of Gaza (see the chapter on the Palestinian Autonomous Areas), so as to allow the import into Gaza of construction materials in order to facilitate rebuilding efforts within the territory, was rejected by Israel in May 2010. Senior Israeli government officials stated that construction materials could fall into the possession of Hamas and be used for military purposes.

Despite maintaining significant military co-operation with the USA, Qatar has established outwardly strong relations with Iran, and has publicly supported Iran's right to pursue civil nuclear technology. The two states' shared ownership of the world's largest non-associated gasfield, Qatar's North Field and Iran's South Pars field, in the Persian (Arabian) Gulf, underlines the strategic importance of stable political and commercial relations. In December 2007 the Amir extended an unprecedented invitation to Iran's President, Mahmoud Ahmadinejad, to attend the 28th GCC summit in Doha. In October 2008 Qatar, Iran and Russia, the holders of the world's largest gas reserves, announced the formation of a strategic trilateral alliance to promote co-operation in the sector. Sheikh Hamad visited Iran in March 2009, and again in November, for discussions on bilateral relations and regional affairs with President Ahmadinejad. In February 2010 a memorandum of understanding on defence co-operation, encompassing joint training and counter-terrorism operations, was signed by Maj.-Gen. Hamad bin Ali al-Attiya, Chief of Staff of Qatar's Armed Forces, and the Iranian Minister of Defence and Armed Forces Logistics, Brig.-Gen. Ahmad Vahidi. During a visit to Doha in November 2010 Iran's First Vice-President, Muhammad Reza Rahimi, met with Sheikh Hamad and Sheikh Tamim, whereupon both sides pledged further to enhance bilateral relations, and signed several agreements intended to bolster commerce, trade and customs co-operation. However, despite the appearance of friendly co-operation, relations have in recent years been widely suspected of being characterized by mutual mistrust. This view appeared to be confirmed by the publication by the WikiLeaks organization in late 2010 of a series of leaked US diplomatic cables. In one such communiqué, the Amir was reported to have told US Senator John Kerry that Iran 'will give you 100 words; trust only one of the 100'. Another cable indicated that the Qatari Government had secretly agreed in principle to allow the USA to launch an attack against Iran from Qatari territory if it were to receive security guarantees from the US Administration in return, and that Qatar had also demanded US assistance in retaining Qatari sovereignty over the North Field gasfield at the Qatari–Iranian border. (Iran's ambassador to Qatar had announced in January 2010 that a provisional agreement had been reached on demarcation of the two countries' maritime border; however, a final agreement had yet to be reached by early 2011.)

Following the signing of a memorandum of understanding between Qatar and Turkey in October 2009 that was intended to bolster energy co-operation and facilitate the eventual supply of

Qatari LNG to Turkey, in May 2010 Qatar was reported to be in talks with Turkey, as well as Lebanon, about the potential sale of LNG. However, by early 2011 an agreement had yet to be reached.

Doha hosted the annual summit of the GCC in December 2007, when, *inter alia*, consensus was reached upon the establishment of a common market—which became effective on 1 January 2008—which permitted the free movement of both capital and citizens of GCC member countries for the purposes of travel, residency and employment, and served to enhance regional integration and co-operation.

Other external relations

An emergency summit meeting of the OIC was convened in Doha in October 2001, in response to the previous month's suicide attacks against New York and Washington, DC, and the subsequent commencement of US-led military action against targets in Afghanistan linked to the Taliban regime and to the al-Qa'ida organization of Osama bin Laden, the Saudi-born fundamentalist Islamist held principally responsible for the attacks in the USA.

Despite Qatar's active support for an end to UN sanctions against Iraq, and its pursuit of contacts with the incumbent regime of Saddam Hussain (see above), by the time US Vice-President Dick Cheney visited Qatar in March 2002—as part of a tour of the Gulf aimed at garnering support for a potential extension of the US-led 'war on terror' to target the Iraqi regime—Qatar was apparently alone among the Gulf states in indicating that it would allow the use of its territory as a base for action against Saddam Hussain. During the decade after the Gulf War the Government had signed a number of defence agreements with the USA, and there was reported to have been a significant increase in the amount of US military personnel and equipment positioned in Qatar since September 2001. Furthermore, the construction of a major air facility at the Al-Udaid military base enhanced its strategic importance within the US military network in the region; in December 2002 the US Department of Defense dispatched more than 600 personnel from the US military command centre to the base, which was to act as the main US command post in the Gulf. None the less, Qatar, concerned about the popular reaction to a US-led war in Iraq and the regional implications such a conflict might have, continued to advocate a diplomatic solution to the crisis. By the time of the commencement of hostilities in March 2003, the USA had stationed some 3,000 air force personnel and 36 tactical jets at Al-Udaid. In January 2007 US Secretary of Defense Robert Gates visited Doha as part of a tour of the Middle East, the focus of which was the situation in Iraq. During his stay he met with the Amir to discuss the further improvement of bilateral relations. In March the Qatari Government announced that it would not allow from its soil the launch by the USA of any military action against Iran, and strongly advocated a peaceful resolution to the ongoing impasse between the US and Iranian Governments. However, a US diplomatic cable published by WikiLeaks in late 2010 appeared to indicate that the Qatari and US Governments had previously reached a covert agreement by which the USA would be able to launch a future attack against Iran from Qatari soil, in exchange for security assurances (see Regional relations).

The Ethiopian authorities accused Qatar of promoting instability in the Horn of Africa in April 2008, alleging that Qatar's relationship with Eritrea was a threat to Ethiopia's national security. Ethiopia broke off diplomatic relations, while Qatar strongly denied the allegations.

During a state visit to the People's Republic of China by the Qatari Prime Minister and Minister of Foreign Affairs, Sheikh Hamad, in April 2008, economic relations were augmented through an agreement for Qatar, as the largest producer of LNG globally, to supply 2m. metric tons per year (t/y) of LNG to the China National Offshore Oil Corporation (CNOOC). A separate contract, incorporating the purchase of 3m. t/y of LNG from Qatar Liquefied Gas Co (Qatargas) by PetroChina over a period of 25 years, was also signed between the two companies and Royal Dutch Shell (Netherlands/United Kingdom) during Sheikh Hamad's discussions with Chinese President Hu Jintao as part of enhanced Qatari-Chinese investment and co-operative initiatives. Qatargas signed two further deals in November 2009, under the terms of which it was to provide CNOOC with a further 3m. t/y of LNG from 2013 and PetroChina with an additional 2m. t/y during 2010–15. In May 2010 Qatar Petroleum, PetroChina and Royal Dutch Shell signed a 30-year gas exploration and production-sharing agreement providing for the joint exploration in Qatar's Block D concession, which spans an area of more than 8,000 sq km on shore and off shore close to the north-eastern city of Ras Laffan. Under the terms of the deal, Shell was to operate the block with a 75% stake, with PetroChina accounting for the remaining 25% share. Qatar Petroleum also stated its intention to launch additional exploration tenders in 2011–12.

Relations between Qatar and India have strengthened considerably in recent years. Sheikh Hamad visited India in 2005, followed by Prime Minister Sheikh Abdullah in 2006. Between 2004 and 2007 the volume of trade between the two countries increased three-fold; by 2008 Qatar was the largest supplier of LNG to India, exporting around 5m. metric tons annually, while there were an estimated 300,000 Indians living and working in Qatar. During an official visit to Doha by Indian Prime Minister Manmohan Singh in November 2008 two security co-operation agreements were signed, covering matters such as maritime security, intelligence sharing and law enforcement.

The selection in early December 2010 of Qatar as the host of the 2022 football World Cup, the first time that the right to host the event had been awarded to a Middle Eastern country, was widely expected to boost Qatar's international profile. The cost of construction work to implement the necessary stadia, tourism infrastructure and transport links in advance of the tournament was expected to total some US $6,000m.

CONSTITUTION AND GOVERNMENT

According to the provisional Constitution that took effect in 1970, Qatar is an absolute monarchy, with full powers vested in the Amir as head of state. Executive power is exercised by the Council of Ministers, appointed by the head of state. An Advisory Council was formed in April 1972, with 20 nominated members (expanded to 30 in 1975 and to 35 in 1988). The Advisory Council's constitutional entitlements include the power to debate legislation drafted by the Council of Ministers before ratification and promulgation. It also has the power to request ministerial statements on matters of general and specific policy, including the draft budget. In March 1999 elections took place, by universal adult suffrage, for a 29-member Central Municipal Council, which was to have a consultative role in the operations of the Ministry of Municipal Affairs and Agriculture; further elections were held in April 2003 and April 2007. The Amir formally adopted a new Constitution following its approval at a referendum held on 29 April 2003. Under the Constitution, the Amir is to remain head of the executive, while a 45-member unicameral parliament, of which two-thirds are to be directly elected (the remainder being appointed by the Amir), is to have the powers, *inter alia*, to legislate, review the state budget and monitor government policy. However, elections to the new legislature, after which the Advisory Council was to be abolished, were repeatedly postponed, most recently owing to the need to introduce an appropriate legal framework. A new electoral law was duly adopted by the Advisory Council in May 2008 and was awaiting ratification by the Amir in early 2011.

REGIONAL AND INTERNATIONAL CO-OPERATION

Qatar is a member of the Co-operation Council for the Arab States of the Gulf (GCC, see p. 243). GCC member states created a unified regional customs tariff in January 2003. The economic convergence criteria for the proposed monetary union were agreed at a heads of state meeting in Abu Dhabi, the UAE, in December 2005, and in January 2008 the GCC launched its common market. The country is also a member of the League of Arab States (Arab League, see p. 361) and the Organization of Arab Petroleum Exporting Countries (OAPEC, see p. 397).

Qatar joined the UN on 21 September 1971, having gained independence earlier that month. The country became a member of the World Trade Organization (WTO, see p. 430) in 1996. It also participates in the Organization of the Petroleum Exporting Countries (OPEC, see p. 405) and the Organization of the Islamic Conference (OIC, see p. 400).

ECONOMIC AFFAIRS

In 1997, according to estimates by the World Bank, Qatar's gross national income (GNI), measured at average 1995–97 prices, was US $11,627m., equivalent to $22,147 per head. According to unofficial sources, GNI totalled $17,150m. in 2001 and $17,490m. in 2002 (equivalent to some $28,300 per head). According to the World Bank, during 2000–09, it was estimated, the population increased at an average annual rate of 9.6%, while gross domestic product (GDP) per head increased, in real terms, by an average of 0.3% per year during 2000–06. Non-Qataris accounted for some

80% of the total population by the beginning of the 21st century. Overall GDP was estimated to have increased, in real terms, at an average rate of 10.4% per year in 2000–07; according to official figures, real GDP growth was estimated at 8.7% in 2009, compared with some 25.4% in 2008.

Agriculture (including fishing) contributed an estimated 0.1% of GDP in 2009, and according to the 2010 census, the sector engaged some 1.3% of the employed population. All agricultural land is owned by the Government, and most farm managers are immigrants employing a largely expatriate work-force. The main crops are cereals (principally barley), vegetables and dates. Qatar is self-sufficient in winter vegetables and nearly self-sufficient in summer vegetables. Some vegetables are exported to other Gulf countries. The Government has prioritized education in agricultural techniques and experimentation with unconventional methods of cultivation (including the use of sea water and solar energy to produce sand-based crops). Livestock-rearing and fishing are also practised. The GDP of the agricultural sector was estimated to have increased by an average annual rate of 0.7% during 2004–09. Real agricultural GDP declined by 5.7% in 2008, but increased by an estimated 1.9% in 2009.

Industry (including mining, manufacturing, construction and power) contributed an estimated 61.3% of GDP in 2009, and in 2010 the sector engaged 54.9% of the employed population. Industrial GDP was estimated to have increased by an average of 14.6% per year in 2004–09. According to official figures, growth in the sector's real GDP was estimated at 0.7% in 2009, compared with some 27.7% in 2008.

The mining and quarrying sector (comprising principally the extraction and processing of petroleum and natural gas) provided an estimated 45.4% of GDP in 2009, and engaged just 6.7% of the employed population. Proven recoverable petroleum reserves at the end of 2009 were 26,833m. barrels, sufficient to maintain production for just over 54 years at 2009 levels—averaging some 1,345,000 barrels per day (b/d). As a member of the Organization of the Petroleum Exporting Countries (OPEC, see p. 405), Qatar is subject to production quotas agreed by the Organization's Conference. Proven gas reserves were 25,370,000m. cu m at the end of 2009 (representing 13.5% of known world reserves at that date—behind only Russia and Iran), primarily located in the North Field, the world's largest gas reserve not associated with petroleum. The real GDP of the mining and quarrying sector was estimated to have increased at an average annual rate of 15.0% in 2004–09. According to official figures, growth in the sector was an estimated 7.7% in 2009, compared with 23.1% in 2008.

Manufacturing contributed an estimated 7.8% of GDP in 2009 (excluding activities related to petroleum and natural gas), and the sector engaged 7.9% of the employed population. The principal manufacturing activities are linked to the country's oil and gas resources—petroleum-refining and the production of liquefied natural gas (LNG—developed as part of the North Field project), together with industrial chemicals (particularly fertilizers) and steel production. Manufacturing GDP (excluding hydrocarbons) was estimated to have increased by an average of 0.4% per year in 2004–09. According to official figures, the sector's real GDP declined by an estimated 10.3% in 2009, following an increase of 0.8% in 2008.

Construction contributed an estimated 7.1% of GDP in 2009, while the sector engaged 39.8% of the employed population. According to official figures, the sector's GDP increased by an average of 29.3% per year in 2004–09. Construction GDP was estimated to have declined by 21.8% in 2009, compared with an increase of some 77.0% in the previous year.

Electrical energy is derived almost exclusively from Qatar's natural gas resource. Solar energy is being developed in conjunction with desalination.

The services sector contributed an estimated 38.6% of GDP in 2009, and engaged 43.8% of the employed population. The establishment in March 2005 of the Qatar Financial Centre, which was to provide a hub for the emirate's financial services sector, had reportedly proved popular with investors by early 2006 and was expected to stimulate further activity in the sector. The GDP of the services sector was estimated to have increased by an average of 22.7% per year in 2004–09. According to official figures, services GDP increased by 20.6% in 2008 and by an estimated 26.0% in 2009.

According to official figures for 2009, Qatar recorded a visible trade surplus of QR 87,264m., while there was a surplus of QR 30,542m. on the current account of the balance of payments. In 2008 the principal source of imports (9.6% of the total value) was Japan; other important suppliers in that year were the USA, Germany, Italy, the People's Republic of China, the United Arab Emirates (UAE), and the Republic of Korea (South Korea). In the same year Japan took 33.8% of Qatar's exports by value (excluding re-exports); South Korea, Singapore and India were also significant markets for exports in 2008. The principal exports are petroleum and gas and their derivatives, and chemical products. The principal imports in 2008 were machinery and electrical equipment, base metals and their articles, and vehicles, vessels, aircraft and other transport equipment.

In the financial year ending 31 March 2010 Qatar recorded a preliminary budget surplus of QR 46,589m. Qatar's gross government debt was QR 131,340m. in 2009, equivalent to 34.2% of GDP (compared with just 11.9% in 2008). According to ILO data, the annual rate of inflation averaged 7.2% in 2000–09; consumer prices increased by an average of 15.2% in 2008, but declined by an average of 4.9% in 2009 and again, by 2.5%, in 2010. The Qatari economy is heavily dependent on immigrant workers, owing to a shortage of indigenous labour; according to the 2010 census, some 94.4% of the employed population were non-Qataris.

The generation of income through sales of LNG since 1997 must be considered Qatar's most notable achievement in recent years. The emirate has become the largest exporter of LNG, with exports in 2008 valued at US $17,640m., while production capacity increased from 30m. metric tons per year (t/y) in 2008 to some 77m. t/y at mid-December 2010. From 2008 the combined value of exports of LNG and other associated and non-associated gas products has exceeded that of crude petroleum, hitherto Qatar's principal export. Efforts have also been made to expand petroleum production capacity (which reached an estimated 1m. b/d by the end of 2009—considerably in excess of Qatar's recent OPEC production quotas). In 2010 efforts to boost the capacity of Qatar's petrochemicals industry were impeded by the withdrawal of foreign investors from major projects. Honam Petrochemical of South Korea abandoned a joint venture agreement with Qatar Petroleum (QP) to build a $2,600m. petrochemicals complex in Umm Said (Mesaieed) in April, while in August the US company ExxonMobil withdrew from a $6,000m. joint venture project with QP in Ras Laffan. However, the industry's outlook was improved in the final quarter of 2010, with the opening in November of a 700,000-t/y plant in Mesaieed, and the signing in December of a memorandum of understanding between QP and Royal Dutch Shell (United Kingdom/the Netherlands), providing for the joint development of a plant in Ras Laffan. Total Qatari petrochemicals production of 28m. t/y was targeted for 2014. Since the 2000/01 financial year successive fiscal surpluses have been recorded, and by 2008 external debt had been reduced to an estimated 35.3% of GDP, from some 90% of GDP at the end of 2002. The nation's increased wealth was accompanied by higher inflation, with consumer prices rising by an annual average of 15% in 2008, the highest in the region. However, following a decline in commodity prices stemming from the global economic slowdown, the rate of inflation declined in the following two years; the IMF projected an increase of 4.2% in 2011. The state budget for 2010–11 projected spending of $9,700m. on infrastructure projects, of total budgeted expenditure of $32,000m. Following Qatar's successful bid to host the 2022 football World Cup (see Foreign Affairs), some 40% of budgetary spending was expected to be allocated to infrastructure projects through to 2016. In early 2011 major projects under development included the construction of a new international airport, a new port in Doha and a national rail network. It was hoped that the introduction, effective from January 2010, of a flat, 10% corporate tax rate for foreign-owned businesses, compared with a progressive rate ranging from 10% to 35%, would render the economy more attractive to foreign investors. In its Regional Outlook for the Middle East, published in April 2011, the IMF indicated GDP growth of 16.3% in 2010. Growth was projected to accelerate further, to 20.0%, in 2011, buoyed by a robust performance by the natural gas sector.

PUBLIC HOLIDAYS

2012: 16 June* (Leilat al-Meiraj, Ascension of the Prophet), 27 June (Anniversary of the Amir's Accession), 19 July* (Ramadan begins), 18 August* (Id al-Fitr, end of Ramadan), 25 October* (Id al-Adha, Feast of the Sacrifice), 14 November* (Muharram, Islamic New Year), 18 December* (National Day).

*These holidays are dependent on the Islamic lunar calendar and may differ by one or two days from the dates given.

QATAR
Statistical Survey

Statistical Survey

Sources (unless otherwise stated): Dept of Economic Policies, Qatar Central Bank, POB 1234, Doha; tel. 4456456; fax 4413650; e-mail elzainys@qcb.gov.qa; internet www.qcb.gov.qa; Qatar Statistics Authority, POB 7283, Doha; tel. 4958888; fax 4839999; e-mail customer_services@planning.gov.qa; internet www.qsa.gov.qa.

Area and Population

AREA, POPULATION AND DENSITY

Area (sq km)	11,493*
Population (census results)†	
1 March 2004	744,029
20 October 2010	
Males	1,284,739
Females	414,696
Total	1,699,435
Density (per sq km) at 2010 census	147.9

* 4,437 sq miles.
† Including resident workers from abroad.

POPULATION BY AGE AND SEX
(population at 2010 census*)

	Males	Females	Total
0–14	119,140	113,444	232,584
15–64	1,157,450	295,584	1,453,034
65 and over	8,149	5,668	13,817
Total	1,284,739	414,696	1,699,435

* Including resident workers from abroad.

PRINCIPAL TOWNS
(population of municipalities at 2010 census)

Al Dawhah (Doha)	796,947	Umm Salal	60,509
Al-Rayyan	455,623	Al Daayen	43,176
Al-Khawr (Al-Khor)	193,983	Al-Shamal	7,975
Al-Wakrah	141,222		

BIRTHS, MARRIAGES AND DEATHS

	Registered live births Number	Rate (per 1,000)	Registered marriages Number	Rate (per 1,000)	Registered deaths Number	Rate (per 1,000)
2002	12,200	17.9	2,351	3.4	1,220	1.8
2003	12,856	17.9	2,550	3.6	1,311	1.8
2004	13,190	17.5	2,649	3.5	1,341	1.8
2005	13,401	16.8	2,734	3.4	1,545	1.9
2006	14,120	16.8	3,019	3.6	1,750	2.1
2007	15,681	12.8	3,206	2.6	1,776	1.5
2008	17,210	11.9	3,235	2.2	1,942	1.3
2009	18,351	11.2	3,153	1.9	2,008	1.2

Life expectancy (years at birth, WHO estimates): 76 (males 76; females 76) in 2008 (Source: WHO, *World Health Statistics*).

ECONOMICALLY ACTIVE POPULATION
(population aged 15 years and over, 2010 census)

	Qatari	Non-Qatari	Total
Agriculture, hunting, forestry and fishing	46	17,070	17,116
Mining and quarrying	5,076	80,659	85,735
Manufacturing	783	99,882	100,665
Electricity, gas and water	1,663	3,333	4,996
Construction	621	505,816	506,437
Wholesale and retail trade; repair of motor vehicles, motorcycles and personal and household goods	1,874	141,085	142,959
Hotels and restaurants	44	28,963	29,007
Transport and storage	701	33,300	34,001
Information and communications	2,251	6,898	9,149
Financial intermediation	2,486	7,930	10,416

—*continued*	Qatari	Non-Qatari	Total
Real estate, renting and business activities	496	8,138	8,634
Public administration	42,055	30,165	72,220
Professional, scientific and technical activities	311	20,084	20,395
Administrative and support service activities	395	38,809	39,204
Education	8,277	18,319	26,596
Health and social work	3,414	15,711	19,125
Arts, entertainment and recreation	883	4,352	5,235
Other community, social and personal service activities	118	5,310	5,428
Private households with employed persons	60	132,410	132,470
Extra-territorial organizations and bodies	19	1,645	1,664
Total employed	71,573	1,199,879	1,271,452
Unemployed	2,514	2,005	4,519
Total labour force	74,087	1,201,884	1,275,971
Males	46,979	1,071,697	1,118,676
Females	27,108	130,187	157,295

Health and Welfare

KEY INDICATORS

Total fertility rate (children per woman, 2008)	2.4
Under-5 mortality rate (per 1,000 live births, 2008)	8
Physicians (per 1,000 head, 2005)	2.6
Hospital beds (per 1,000 head, 2006)	2.5
Health expenditure (2007): US $ per head (PPP)	3,075
Health expenditure (2007): % of GDP	3.8
Health expenditure (2007): public (% of total)	75.6
Total carbon dioxide emissions ('000 metric tons, 2007)	63,002.5
Carbon dioxide emissions per head (metric tons, 2007)	55.4
Human Development Index (2010): ranking	38
Human Development Index (2010): value	0.803

For sources and definitions, see explanatory note on p. vi.

Agriculture

PRINCIPAL CROPS
('000 metric tons)

	2005	2006	2007
Barley	4.9	4.9	5.0*
Cauliflowers and broccoli	1.1	1.2	1.2*
Pumpkins, squash and gourds	1.3	2.8	4.0
Aubergines (Eggplants)	3.1	2.5	2.9
Chillies and peppers, green	0.3*	0.7	0.9
Onions, dry	3.0	2.6	3.7
Tomatoes	5.3	8.0	11.9
Cantaloupes and other melons	4.3*	0.7	4.3*
Dates	19.8	21.6	21.6

* FAO estimate.

2008: Production assumed to be unchanged from 2007 (FAO estimates). Note: No data were available for individual crops in 2009.

Aggregate production ('000 metric tons, may include official, semi-official or estimated data): Total cereals 7.1 in 2005–06, 7.7 in 2007–08, 7.8 in 2009; Total fruits (excl. melons) 20.9 in 2005, 22.6 in 2006–09; Total vegetables (incl. melons) 22.8 in 2005; 35.0 in 2006, 52.8 in 2007–09.

Source: FAO.

QATAR

LIVESTOCK
('000 head, year ending September)

	2005	2006	2007
Horses	2.0	4.8	2.1*
Cattle	6.6	7.4	8.0*
Camels	13.8	23.2	32.4
Sheep	111.6	134.7	145.2
Goats	152.7	131.9	160.0*
Chickens*	4,500	4,500	4,500

* FAO estimate(s).

2008: Figures assumed to be unchanged from 2007 (FAO estimates).

2009 (FAO estimates): Camels 34.0; Sheep 148.0.

Source: FAO.

LIVESTOCK PRODUCTS
('000 metric tons)

	2005	2006	2007
Camel meat*	1.1	1.1	1.1
Sheep meat*	4.0	4.1	4.1
Chicken meat*	4.9	5.0	5.0
Cows' milk*	4.5	4.8	5.1
Camels' milk*	4.5	4.6	4.6
Goats' milk*	5.7	5.7	6.0
Hen eggs	4.1	4.2*	4.2*

* FAO estimate(s).

2008: Figures assumed to be unchanged from 2007 (FAO estimates).

2009 (FAO estimate): Sheep meat 4.1.

Source: FAO.

Fishing

('000 metric tons, live weight)

	2006	2007	2008
Capture	16.4	15.2	17.7
Groupers	1.7	1.6	2.3
Grunts and sweetlips	1.0	1.0	1.0
Emperors (Scavengers)	5.5	4.1	5.0
Narrow-barred Spanish mackerel	2.0	1.8	2.6
Aquaculture	0.0	0.0	0.0
Total catch	16.4	15.2	17.7

Source: FAO.

Mining

	2007	2008	2009
Crude petroleum ('000 metric tons)	53,605	60,843	57,868
Natural gas (million cu m)*	63,200	76,974	89,300

* Excluding gas flared or recycled.

Source: BP, *Statistical Review of World Energy*.

Industry

SELECTED PRODUCTS
('000 metric tons unless otherwise indicated)

	2004	2005	2006
Ammonia (for fertilizer)	1,737.2	2,133.8	2,170.2
Urea (for fertilizer)	2,238.7	2,978.8	2,908.9
Organic fertilizers	24	42	57
Cement	1,202	1,182	2,169
'Super' petrol (motor spirit—gasoline)	801.0	754.6	889.4
'Premium' petrol (motor spirit—gasoline)	857.9	901.7	1,004.7
Jet fuel (incl. kerosene)	957.7	905.5	1,087.1
Gas diesel (distillate fuel) oils	995.1	925.6	997.9
Residual fuel oils	250.7	418.3	614.6
Liquefied petroleum gas	127.6	131.0	217.0
Natural gas condensate	1,545.1	1,556.1	1,667.9
Butane	963.0	1,075.4	1,151.8
Propane	1,242.6	1,403.1	1,576.2
Electric energy (million kWh)	12,992.6	14,395.9	14,983.2

Finance

CURRENCY AND EXCHANGE RATES

Monetary Units
100 dirhams = 1 Qatar riyal (QR).

Sterling, Dollar and Euro Equivalents (31 December 2010)
£1 sterling = 5.698 riyals;
US $1 = 3.640 riyals;
€1 = 4.864 riyals;
100 Qatar riyals = £17.55 = $27.47 = €20.56.

Average Exchange Rate.

Note: Since June 1980 the official mid-point rate has been fixed at US $1 = QR 3.64.

BUDGET
(QR million, year ending 31 March)

Revenue	2007/08	2008/09	2009/10*
Petroleum and natural gas	70,748	80,009	69,445
Investments	30,343	33,271	53,874
Other	16,775	27,712	31,355
Total	117,866	140,992	154,674

Expenditure	2007/08	2008/09	2009/10*
Current expenditure	52,316	65,817	72,176
Wages and salaries	16,003	18,661	20,533
Interest payments	1,855	2,100	3,656
Supplies and services	6,387	9,153	6,586
Other	28,071	35,903	41,401
Development expenditure	33,934	33,478	35,909
Total	86,250	99,295	108,085

* Preliminary.

INTERNATIONAL RESERVES
(US $ million at 31 December)

	2008	2009	2010
Gold (national valuation)	348.1	436.0	566.5
IMF special drawing rights	45.2	420.4	413.2
Reserve position in IMF	51.3	80.4	96.0
Foreign exchange	9,553.0	17,868.9	30,111.6
Total	9,997.6	18,805.7	31,187.3

Source: IMF, *International Financial Statistics*.

QATAR

MONEY SUPPLY
(QR million at 31 December)

	2008	2009	2010
Currency outside depository corporations	5,368	5,653	6,095
Transferable deposits	61,938	65,740	81,484
Other deposits	116,699	143,689	177,137
Broad money	184,005	215,082	264,716

Source: IMF, *International Financial Statistics*.

COST OF LIVING
(Consumer Price Index; base: 2006 = 100)

	2008	2009	2010
Food, beverages and tobacco	128.8	130.4	133.3
Clothing and footwear	125.9	120.2	118.6
Rent, fuel and energy	154.7	136.1	119.1
Transport and communication	111.4	106.6	109.2
All items (incl. others)	130.9	124.5	121.4

NATIONAL ACCOUNTS
(QR million at current prices)

Expenditure on the Gross Domestic Product

	2007	2008	2009
Government final consumption expenditure	63,522	75,140	88,239
Private final consumption expenditure	52,757	71,064	74,741
Increase in stocks	4,000	4,355	-1,500
Gross fixed capital formation	106,423	157,865	140,812
Total domestic expenditure	226,702	308,424	302,292
Exports of goods and services	166,026	212,348	167,288
Less Imports of goods and services	98,795	117,779	111,720
GDP in purchasers' values	293,933	402,993	357,860
GDP at constant 2004 prices	186,539	233,966	254,194

Source: IMF, *International Financial Statistics*.

Gross Domestic Product by Economic Activity

	2007	2008	2009
Agriculture and fishing	270	305	315
Mining and quarrying*	166,642	215,053	165,325
Manufacturing	26,001	37,946	28,363
Electricity, gas and water	3,179	4,348	3,913
Construction	21,625	32,507	25,781
Trade, restaurants and hotels	15,480	20,674	23,946
Transport and communications	13,539	21,199	22,696
Finance, insurance, real estate and business services	27,309	38,106	43,374
Government services	20,828	32,755	44,652
Social services	1,820	2,860	2,865
Other services	1,515	2,991	2,974
Sub-total	298,208	408,744	364,204
Import duties	2,703	3,316	4,088
Less Imputed bank service charge	6,978	9,067	10,432
GDP in purchasers' values	293,933	402,993	357,860

* Including services incidental to mining of petroleum and natural gas.

BALANCE OF PAYMENTS
(QR million)

	2007	2008	2009
Exports of goods f.o.b.	152,951	199,880	160,000
Crude petroleum	69,820	93,769	42,580
Natural gas liquids	53,859	82,012	89,882
Imports of goods f.o.b.	-72,158	-91,492	-72,736
Trade balance	80,793	108,388	87,264
Exports of services	13,075	12,468	7,288
Imports of services	-26,637	-26,287	-20,638
Balance on goods and services	67,231	94,569	73,914
Other income received	4,978	5,646	3,594
Other income paid	-20,408	-30,260	-25,719
Balance on goods, services and income	51,801	69,955	51,789
Current transfers (net)	-13,779	-18,270	-21,247
Expatriates' remittances	-16,264	-19,034	-25,338
Current balance	38,022	51,685	30,542
Capital account (net)	-4,118	-4,949	-6,538
Financial account (net)	-25,849	-35,416	8,735
Net errors and omissions	6,090	-9,697	-2,481
Overall balance	14,145	1,623	30,258

External Trade

PRINCIPAL COMMODITIES
(distribution by HS, QR million)

Imports	2006*	2007*	2008
Live animals; animal products	1,080.5	1,367.6	2,083.2
Mineral products	1,720.5	2,572.7	3,662.7
Chemical products, etc.	2,517.6	3,255.1	4,703.7
Base metals and articles of base metal	11,764.1	16,158.7	20,012.2
Articles of iron and steel	9,001.8	12,343.7	14,478.7
Machinery and electrical equipment	21,593.5	31,599.9	37,996.7
Boilers, machinery and mechanical appliances and other apparatus (such as nuclear reactors)	14,121.8	21,232.1	24,065.3
Electrical machinery and equipment; sound and television recorders and reproducers	7,471.7	10,367.8	13,931.4
Vehicles, vessels, aircraft and other transport equipment	9,448.7	11,027.0	14,941.0
Vehicles other than trains, vessels and air and spacecraft	8,825.9	9,580.4	12,744.1
Total (incl. others)	59,841.4	80,097.0	101,556.3

Exports†	2006	2007	2008
Mineral products	111,292.1	137,080.9	184,952.4
Mineral fuels and oils, and products thereof	111,206.4	136,916.4	184,509.5
Chemical products, etc.	5,530.6	7,247.9	11,083.5
Plastics, rubber and articles thereof	4,101.6	4,974.8	5,285.3
Plastics and articles thereof	4,101.4	4,974.6	5,284.8
Total (incl. others)	122,401.7	151,025.2	202,846.9

* Preliminary figures.
† Excluding re-exports (QR million): 1,546.7 in 2006; 1,927.5 in 2007; 3,150.3 in 2008.

QATAR

PRINCIPAL TRADING PARTNERS
(QR million)

Imports	2006	2007	2008
Australia	757.8	917.9	883.3
Belgium	881.0	818.1	828.1
Brazil	543.9	488.3	1,058.8
China, People's Republic	3,482.8	4,974.8	7,326.6
France	2,311.6	3,024.5	3,733.9
Germany	5,581.0	6,619.8	8,527.1
India	1,642.0	2,419.2	3,282.0
Indonesia	475.2	816.2	554.4
Italy	5,543.3	8,855.4	7,473.6
Japan	7,182.8	8,596.8	9,785.1
Korea, Republic	3,278.4	5,182.8	5,577.3
Malaysia	857.6	1,207.1	1,311.7
Saudi Arabia	3,054.9	4,162.7	4,954.4
Singapore	583.8	1,273.9	823.6
Spain	580.9	938.8	1,607.6
Switzerland	883.2	1,154.6	1,599.2
Thailand	935.7	1,145.5	1,510.4
Turkey	1,217.0	1,749.2	3,827.0
United Arab Emirates	3,606.5	5,961.0	6,727.6
United Kingdom	2,985.0	4,140.9	4,773.4
USA	5,899.6	9,561.1	9,168.6
Total (incl. others)	59,845.9	85,283.5	101,556.3

Exports*	2006	2007	2008
Belgium	338.7	2,179.1	4,975.5
China, People's Republic	1,444.3	1,213.3	2,064.1
India	5,995.2	9,696.6	10,378.5
Japan	51,382.6	62,033.0	68,609.7
Korea, Republic	17,197.9	26,694.2	43,521.8
Pakistan	1,361.5	1,710.4	1,426.2
Singapore	11,679.8	17,267.4	23,345.0
Spain	3,041.9	3,406.3	4,927.7
Taiwan	1,943.4	1,849.7	2,554.9
Thailand	3,386.5	7,001.3	7,390.2
United Arab Emirates	4,798.3	4,982.7	2,082.3
USA	492.3	993.0	221.0
Total (incl. others)	122,401.7	151,025.2	202,846.9

* Excluding re-exports (QR million): 1,546.7 in 2006; 1,927.5 in 2007; 3,150.3 in 2008.

Transport

ROAD TRAFFIC
(registered vehicles)

	2004	2005	2006
Private cars	265,609	293,355	337,056
Other private transport	114,115	126,541	148,436
Heavy equipment	11,162	13,262	17,438
Motorcycles and mopeds	4,420	4,698	5,048
Total (incl. others)	406,626	451,388	525,795

SHIPPING
Merchant Fleet
(vessels registered at 31 December)

	2007	2008	2009
Number of vessels	84	90	100
Total displacement ('000 grt)	619.5	902.7	1,016.4

Source: IHS Fairplay, *World Fleet Statistics*.

INTERNATIONAL SEA-BORNE FREIGHT TRAFFIC
(2003)

	Traffic
Doha Port	
Vessels entered and cleared	751
Containers	272
Capacity ('000 grt)	1,258
Umm Said (Mesaieed) Port	
Vessels entered and cleared	1,557
Tankers	633
Containers	604
Capacity ('000 grt)	53,189
Halul Port	
Vessels entered and cleared	109
Tankers	109
Capacity ('000 grt)	15,881
Ras Laffan Port	
Vessels entered and cleared	617
Tankers	342
Capacity ('000 grt)	36,675
Total	
Vessels entered and cleared	3,034
Tankers	1,084
Containers	876
Capacity ('000 grt)	118,324

CIVIL AVIATION
(Doha International Airport)

	2004	2005	2006
Aircraft arrivals	49,614	60,828	67,472
Passenger arrivals ('000)*	2,790	3,654	4,424
Passengers in transit ('000)	1,589	2,185	4,573
Cargo and mail received (metric tons)	102,455	127,042	161,759
Cargo and mail dispatched (metric tons)	61,047	83,554	105,760

* Excluding private aircraft.

Tourism

TOURIST ARRIVALS
(arrivals of non-resident tourists in hotels and similar establishments)

Region of residence	2006	2007	2008
Asia	180,543	203,465	216,742
Europe	201,187	265,965	329,059
Middle East	413,523	361,139	628,440
Total (incl. others)	945,970	963,573	1,404,850

Tourism receipts (US $ million, excl. passenger transport): 498 in 2004; 760 in 2005; 874 in 2006.

Source: World Tourism Organization.

Communications Media

	2007	2008	2009
Telephones ('000 main lines in use)	237.4	263.4	285.3
Mobile cellular telephones ('000 in use)	1,264.4	1,683.0	2,472.1
Internet users ('000)	420.9	499.5	563.8
Broadband subscribers ('000)	87.0	115.0	145.8

Personal computers: 157,000 (156.9 per 1,000 persons) in 2006.

Source: International Telecommunication Union.

Newspapers: *Daily:* 5 titles in 2004; total circulation 90,000 in 1996. *Weekly:* 2 titles in 2001; total circulation 7,000 in 1995 (Source: UNESCO).

Book Production: 209 titles in 1996 (Source: UNESCO).

Education
(2007/08)

	Institutions	Teachers	Males	Females	Total
Government schools	141	5,790	16,654	22,461	39,115
Primary	71	2,984	9,032	10,545	19,577
Preparatory	37	1,260	3,224	5,371	8,595
General secondary*	33	1,546	4,398	6,545	10,943
Private schools†	338	5,107	46,097	38,631	84,728
Pre-primary	137	1,169	10,536	9,686	20,222
Primary	85	1,708	21,539	17,792	39,331
Preparatory	69	1,058	8,069	6,454	14,523
General secondary	47	1,172	5,953	4,699	10,652
Independent schools	88	3,341	21,551	19,630	41,181
Pre-primary	12	145	703	958	1,661
Primary	35	1,501	8,955	9,669	18,624
Preparatory	23	962	6,860	5,369	12,229
General secondary*	18	733	5,033	3,634	8,667
Total	567	14,238	84,302	80,722	165,024
Pre-primary	149	1,314	11,239	10,644	21,883
Primary	191	6,193	39,526	38,006	77,532
Preparatory	129	3,280	18,153	17,194	35,347
General secondary*	98	3,451	15,384	14,878	30,262
University of Qatar	—	535‡	2,110	6,419	8,529

* Including specialized secondary schools.
† Including the Qatar Foundation for Education, Science and Community Development (including the Qatar Academy and the Qatar Leadership Academy and Learning Centre) and the Academy for Sports Excellence (Aspire).
‡ Excluding teaching assistants and administrators.

Pupil-teacher ratio (primary education, UNESCO estimate): 11.2 in 2008/09 (Source: UNESCO Institute for Statistics).

Adult literacy rate (UNESCO estimates): 93.1% (males 93.8%; females 90.4%) in 2007 (Source: UNESCO Institute for Statistics).

Directory

The Government

HEAD OF STATE

Amir and Commander-in-Chief of the Armed Forces: Maj.-Gen. Sheikh HAMAD BIN KHALIFA AL THANI (assumed power 27 June 1995).

Heir Apparent and Deputy Commander-in-Chief of the Armed Forces: Sheikh TAMIM BIN HAMAD BIN KHALIFA AL THANI.

COUNCIL OF MINISTERS
(May 2011)

Amir and Minister of Defence: Maj.-Gen. Sheikh HAMAD BIN KHALIFA AL THANI.

Prime Minister and Minister of Foreign Affairs: Sheikh HAMAD BIN JASIM BIN JABER AL THANI.

Deputy Prime Minister and Chairman of the Emiri Diwan: ABDULLAH BIN HAMAD AL-ATTIYA.

Minister of Energy and Industry: MUHAMMAD SALEH AL-SADA.

Minister of Economy and Finance: YOUSUF HUSSAIN KAMAL.

Minister of Business and Trade: Sheikh JASSIM BIN ABD AL-AZIZ BIN JASSIM BIN HAMAD AL THANI.

Minister of the Interior: Sheikh ABDULLAH BIN KHALID AL THANI.

Minister of Awqaf (Religious Endowments) and Islamic Affairs: Dr GHAITH BIN MUBARAK BIN IMRAN AL-KUWARI.

Minister of Municipal Affairs and Urban Planning: Sheikh ABD AL-RAHMAN BIN KHALIFA BIN ABD AL-AZIZ AL THANI.

Minister of the Environment: ABDULLAH BIN MUBARAK BIN ABOUD AL-MIDHADHI.

Minister of Justice: HASSAN BIN ABDULLAH AL-GHANEM.

Minister of Education and Higher Education: SAAD BIN IBRAHIM AL-MAHMOUD.

Minister of Social Affairs and Acting Minister of Labour: NASSER BIN ABDULLAH AL-HAMIDI.

Minister of Public Health: ABDULLAH BIN KHALID AL-QAHTANI.

Minister of Culture, Arts and Heritage: Dr HAMAD BIN ABD AL-AZIZ AL-KAWARI.

Minister of State for Foreign Affairs: AHMAD BIN ABDULLAH AL-MAHMOUD.

Minister of State for the Interior: Sheikh ABDULLAH BIN NASSER BIN KHALIFA AL THANI.

Minister of State for International Co-operation: Dr KHALID BIN MUHAMMAD AL-ATTIYA.

Minister of State for Cabinet Affairs: Sheikh NASSER BIN MUHAMMAD ABD AL-AZIZ AL THANI.

Ministers of State without Portfolio: Sheikh MUHAMMAD BIN KHALID AL THANI, Sheikha BINT AHMAD AL-MAHMOUD.

MINISTRIES

Ministry of Awqaf (Religious Endowments) and Islamic Affairs: POB 422, Doha; tel. 44470777; fax 44470700; e-mail awqaf@awqaf.gov.qa; internet www.islam.gov.qa.

Ministry of Business and Trade: POB 1968, Doha; tel. 44945555; fax 44932111; e-mail pru@mbt.gov.qa; internet www.mbt.gov.qa.

Ministry of Culture, Arts and Heritage: POB 23700, Doha; tel. 44668777; fax 44670363; e-mail info@nccah.com; internet www.moc.gov.qa.

Ministry of Defence: Qatar Armed Forces, POB 37, Doha; tel. 44614111.

Ministry of Economy and Finance: POB 83, Doha; tel. 44414944; fax 44435370; e-mail qatfin@mof.gov.qa; internet www.mof.gov.qa.

Ministry of Education and Higher Education: POB 80, al-Waqf Tower, al-Dafna, Doha; tel. 44941111; fax 44941445; e-mail e.alhorr@moe.edu.qa; internet www.moe.edu.qa.

QATAR

Ministry of Energy and Industry: POB 2599, Doha; tel. 44846444; fax 44832024; e-mail did@mei.gov.qa; internet www.mei.gov.qa.

Ministry of the Environment: tel. 44207777; fax 44415246; e-mail moe@qatarenv.org.qa; internet www.moe.gov.qa.

Ministry of Foreign Affairs: POB 250, Doha; tel. 44334334; fax 44324131; e-mail webmaster@mofa.gov.qa; internet www.mofa.gov.qa.

Ministry of the Interior: POB 115, Doha; tel. 44330000; fax 44322927; e-mail info@moi.gov.qa; internet www.moi.gov.qa.

Ministry of Justice: POB 917, Doha; tel. 44842222; fax 44832875; e-mail info@moj.gov.qa; internet www.moj.gov.qa.

Ministry of Labour: POB 36, Doha; tel. 44841111; fax 44841441; e-mail customerservice@mol.gov.qa; internet www.mol.gov.qa.

Ministry of Municipal Affairs and Urban Planning: POB 22332, Main Bldg, Corniche St, Doha; tel. 44413331; fax 44430239; e-mail info@baladiya.gov.qa; internet www.baladiya.gov.qa.

Ministry of Public Health: POB 42, Doha; tel. 44070000; fax 44446294; e-mail info@nha.org.qa; internet www.nha.org.qa.

Ministry of Social Affairs: POB 36, Doha; tel. 44841137; fax 44841959; e-mail mosa@mosa.gov.qa; internet www.mosa.gov.qa.

Advisory Council

POB 2034, Doha; tel. 44416292; fax 44221222; e-mail fahad@shura.gov.qa.

The Advisory or *Shura* Council was established in 1972, with 20 nominated members. It was expanded to 30 members in 1975, and to 35 members in 1988. Under the terms of the new Constitution, promulgated in 2003, the Advisory Council was to be replaced by a 45-member unicameral parliament, of which two-thirds of the members were to be directly elected.

Speaker: MUHAMMAD BIN MUBARAK AL-KHOLAIFI.

Political Organizations

There are no political organizations in Qatar.

Diplomatic Representation

EMBASSIES IN QATAR

Afghanistan: POB 22104, Isteolal St, West Bay, Doha; tel. 44930821; fax 44930819; e-mail doha@afghanistan-mfa.net; Ambassador KHALID AHMAD ZEKRIYA.

Albania: POB 22659, Doha; tel. and fax 44953522; e-mail embassy.doha@mfa.gov.al; Ambassador RIDI KURTEZI.

Algeria: POB 2494, Doha; tel. 44831186; fax 44836452; Ambassador ABD AL-FATTAH ZAYYANI.

Azerbaijan: POB 23900, Doha; tel. 44932450; fax 44931755; e-mail azembassy@qatar.net.qa; Ambassador ELDAR N. SALIMOV.

Bahrain: al-Dafna St, Area 66, POB 24888, Doha; tel. 44839360; fax 44831018; e-mail doha.mission@mofa.gov.bh; Chargé d'affaires ABDULLA RABEAH SAEED RABEAH.

Bangladesh: POB 2080, 77 Mussab bin Omair St, Doha; tel. 44671927; fax 44671190; e-mail bdootqat@qatar.net.qa; internet www.bdembassydoha.com; Ambassador MUHAMMAD SHAHADAT HUSSAIN.

Belgium: POB 24418, al-Sanaa St, District 64, Doha; tel. 44931542; fax 44930151; e-mail doha@diplobel.fed.be; internet www.diplomatie.be/doha; Ambassador LUC DEVOLDER.

Benin: Doha; tel. 44930128; fax 44115713; e-mail ambabenin-doha@hotmail.com; Ambassador SAIDOU BAKU BUKHARI.

Bosnia and Herzegovina: POB 876, Doha; tel. 44670194; fax 44670595; e-mail info@bosnianembassyqatar.org; internet www.bosnianembassyqatar.org; Ambassador NAJIM RITSA.

Brazil: POB 23122, Doha; tel. 44838227; fax 44838087; e-mail brasil@brasembdoha.com.qa; internet www.brasembdoha.com.qa; Ambassador ANUAR NAHES.

Brunei: POB 22772, Doha; tel. 44831956; fax 44836798; e-mail bruemb@qatar.net.qa; Chargé d'affaires Haji ALI HASSAN Haji MUHAMMAD SALLEH.

China, People's Republic: POB 17200, Doha; tel. 44934203; fax 44934201; e-mail chinashi@qatar.net.qa; internet qa.china-embassy.org; Ambassador ZHANG ZHILIANG.

Cuba: POB 12017, Saha 76, New Dafna, West Bay Lagoon, Doha; tel. 44110713; fax 44110387; e-mail embacuba@qatar.net.qa; internet www.embacubaqatar.com; Ambassador ARMANDO VERGARA BUENO.

Cyprus: POB 24482, 3 Saba Saha 12 St, District 63, West Bay, Doha; tel. 44934390; fax 44933087; e-mail kyprosdoha@qatar.net.qa; internet www.mfa.gov.cy/embassydoha; Ambassador PANICOS KYRIACOU.

Djibouti: POB 23796, Doha; tel. 44838461; fax 44839245; e-mail mahamadeali@hotmail.com; Ambassador MOHAMMEDI ALI MOHAMMEDI.

Dominican Republic: POB 23545, Doha; tel. 44113868; fax 44113267; e-mail dominicanrepembassydoha@hotmail.com; internet www.domrepemb-qatar.com; Ambassador HUGO GUILIANI CURY.

Egypt: POB 2899, Doha; tel. 44832555; fax 44832196; e-mail eg.emb_doha@mfa.gov.eg; Ambassador MAHMOUD FAWZI ABU DINA.

El Salvador: POB 23031, Saha 72, Doha; tel. 44110195; fax 44110962; e-mail esvq@rree.gob.sv; Ambassador VICTOR MANUEL LAGOS PIZZATI.

Eritrea: POB 4309, D-Ring Rd 14, Doha; tel. 44667934; fax 44664139; Ambassador ALI IBRAHIM AHMED.

France: POB 2669, West Bay, Diplomatic Area, Doha; tel. 44832283; fax 44832254; e-mail ambadoha@qatar.net.qa; internet www.ambafrance-qa.org; Ambassador GILLES BONNAUD.

The Gambia: POB 22377, Doha; tel. 44651429; fax 44651705; Ambassador ANSUMANA JAMMEH.

Germany: POB 3064, 6 al-Jazeera al-Arabiya St, Doha; tel. 44082300; fax 44082333; e-mail germany@qatar.net.qa; internet www.doha.diplo.de; Ambassador ANNE ROTH HERKES.

Hungary: POB 23525, Area 66, West Bay, Doha; tel. 44932531; fax 44932537; e-mail mission.doh@kum.hu; internet www.mfa.gov.hu/kulkepviselet/qu; Ambassador LÁSZLÓ SZABÓ.

India: POB 2788, Doha; tel. 44255777; fax 44670488; e-mail indembdh@qatar.net.qa; internet www.indianembassy.gov.qa; Ambassador DEEPA GOPALAN WADHWA.

Indonesia: POB 22375, al-Maheed St, Doha; tel. 44657945; fax 44657610; e-mail inemb@qatar.net.qa; internet www.kbridoha.com; Chargé d'affaires ANDANG PRAMANA SOSODORO.

Iran: POB 1633, Doha; tel. 44835300; fax 44831665; e-mail embiriqr@qatar.net.qa; internet www.iranembassy.org.qa; Ambassador ABDULLAH SOHRABI.

Iraq: POB 1526, Doha; tel. 44672237; fax 44673347; e-mail dohemb@iraqmofamail.net; Ambassador Dr JAWAD AL-HINDAWI.

Italy: POB 4188, St 913, Plot 83, Doha; tel. 44831828; fax 44831909; e-mail ambasciata.doha@esteri.it; internet sedi.esteri.it/doha; Ambassador ANDREA FERRARI.

Japan: POB 2208, Diplomatic Area, West Bay, Doha; tel. 44840888; fax 44832178; e-mail eojqatar@eoj.com.qa; internet www.qa.emb-japan.go.jp; Ambassador KENJIRO MONJI.

Jordan: POB 2366, Doha; tel. 44832202; fax 44832173; e-mail jordand@qatar.net.qa; internet www.jordanembassy.com.qa; Ambassador AHMAD AL-MEFLEH.

Kazakhstan: POB 25513, Doha; tel. 44128015; fax 44128014; e-mail embassykz@qatar.net.qa; Ambassador AZAMAT R. BERDYBAI.

Kenya: POB 23091, West Bay, Zone 66, St 840, Doha; tel. 44931870; fax 44831730; Ambassador GALMA MUKHE BORU.

Korea, Democratic People's Republic: POB 799, Doha; tel. 44417614; fax 44424735; Ambassador HO JONG.

Korea, Republic: POB 3727, Diplomatic Area, West Bay, Doha; tel. 44832238; fax 44833264; e-mail koemb_qa@mofat.go.kr; internet qat.mofat.go.kr; Ambassador CHANG SEE-JEONG.

Kuwait: POB 1177, Doha; tel. 44832111; fax 44832042; e-mail aldoha@mofa.gov.kw; Ambassador ALI SALMAN AL-HAIFI.

Lebanon: POB 2411, 63 United Nations St, al-Haditha Area, Doha; tel. 44933330; fax 44933331; e-mail embleb@qatar.net.qa; Ambassador HASSAN SAAD.

Libya: POB 574, Doha; tel. 44429546; fax 44429548; Ambassador HASSONA AL-LAFI AL-SHAWISH.

Macedonia, former Yugoslav republic: POB 24262, Villa 28, al-Ithar St, Diplomatic Area, al-Dafna, Doha; tel. 44931374; fax 44831572; e-mail doha@mfa.gov.mk; Ambassador FUAD HASANOVIC.

Malaysia: POB 23760, Lusail St, West Bay, Doha; tel. 44836463; fax 44836453; e-mail maldoha@kln.gov.my; internet www.kln.gov.my/perwakilan/doha; Ambassador AHMAD JAZRI BIN MUHAMMAD JOHAR.

Mauritania: POB 3132, Doha; tel. 44836003; fax 44836015; Ambassador MUHAMMAD FAL OULD BILAL.

Morocco: POB 3242, Doha; tel. 44831885; fax 44833416; e-mail moroccoe@qatar.net.qa; Ambassador ABD AL-AZIM AL-TABER.

Nepal: POB 23002, St No. 810, Doha; tel. 44675681; fax 44675680; e-mail nembdoha@qatar.net.qa; internet www.nembdoha.org.qa; Ambassador Dr SURYA NATH MISHRA.

QATAR

Netherlands: POB 23675, 6th Floor, al-Mirqab Tower, al-Dafna, Corniche, Doha; tel. 44954700; fax 44836340; e-mail doh@minbuza.nl; internet qatar.nlembassy.org; Ambassador J. C. M. GROFFEN.

Oman: POB 1525, 41 Ibn al-Qassim St, Villa 7, Doha; tel. 44931514; fax 44932278; e-mail doha@mofa.gov.om; Ambassador MUHAMMAD BIN NASSER HAMAD AL-WIHAIBI.

Pakistan: POB 334, Diplomatic Area, Plot 30, West Bay, Doha; tel. 44832525; fax 44832227; e-mail parepqat@qatar.net.qa; internet www.pakmissiondoha.com; Ambassador MUHAMMAD ASGHAR AFRIDI.

Philippines: POB 24900, Doha; tel. 44831585; fax 44831595; e-mail dohape@qatar.net.qa; Ambassador CRESCENTE RELACION.

Poland: POB 23380, al-Qutaifiya 66, West Bay, Doha; tel. 44113230; fax 44110307; e-mail doha@ct.futuro.pl; internet www.doha.polemb.net; Ambassador ROBERT ROSTEK.

Romania: POB 22511, Doha; tel. 44934848; fax 44934747; e-mail romamb@qatar.net.qa; internet www.romaniaemb.com.qa; Ambassador ADRIAN MĂCELARU.

Russia: POB 15404, Doha; tel. 44836231; fax 44836243; e-mail rusemb@qatar.net.qa; internet www.qatar.mid.ru; Ambassador VLADIMIR I. TITORENKO.

Saudi Arabia: POB 1255, Doha; tel. 44832030; fax 44832720; Ambassador AHMAD BIN ALI AL-QAHTANI.

Senegal: Ibn Almoutas St, House 65, al-Dafna, Doha; tel. 44837644; fax 44838872; Ambassador ADAMA SARR.

Singapore: POB 24497, New West Bay Area, Doha; tel. 44128082; fax 44128180; e-mail singemb_doh@sgmfa.gov.sg; internet www.mfa.gov.sg/doha; Chargé d'affaires a.i. UMEJ SINGH BHATIA.

Somalia: POB 1948, Doha; tel. 44832771; fax 44834568; Ambassador OMAR IDRIS.

South Africa: POB 24744, Doha; tel. 44857111; fax 44835961; e-mail doha.admin@foreign.gov.za; Ambassador Dr VINCENT TINIZA ZULU.

Spain: POB 24616, Lusail St, West Bay, Doha; tel. 44835886; fax 44835887; e-mail emb.doha@mae.es; Ambassador JUAN JOSÉ SANTOS AGUADO.

Sri Lanka: 4 al-Kharja St, POB 19705, Doha; tel. 44677627; fax 44674788; e-mail lankaemb@qatar.net.qa; Ambassador VIJAYASIRI PADUKKAGE.

Sudan: POB 2999, Doha; tel. 44831474; fax 44833031; e-mail suemdoha@yahoo.com; Ambassador IBRAHIM ABDULLAH FAKIRI.

Syria: POB 1257, Doha; tel. 44831844; fax 44832139; Ambassador Dr RIAD ISMAT.

Thailand: POB 22474, Doha; tel. 44934426; fax 44930514; e-mail thaidoh@qatar.net.qa; internet www.thaiembqatar.com; Ambassador PANYARAK POOLTHUP (designate).

Tunisia: POB 2707, Doha; tel. 44128188; fax 44128938; e-mail at.doha@qatar.net.qa; Ambassador AHMED ELQADIDI.

Turkey: POB 1977, al-Istiqlal St, Doha; tel. 44951300; fax 44951320; e-mail tcdohabe@qatar.net.qa; internet www.doha.emb.mfa.gov.tr; Ambassador HAKKI EMRE YUNT.

United Arab Emirates: POB 3099, 22 al-Markhiyah St, Diplomatic Area, Khalifa Northern Town, Doha; tel. 44838880; fax 44836186; e-mail embassyofuae@gmail.com; Chargé d'affaires a.i. SALEM AL-ZAABI.

United Kingdom: POB 3, West Bay, Doha; tel. 44962000; fax 44962086; e-mail embassy.qatar@fco.gov.uk; internet ukinqatar.fco.gov.uk; Ambassador JOHN HAWKINS.

Uruguay: POB 23237, Doha; tel. 44113540; fax 44113833; e-mail uruqatar@uruguayembassy.org.qa; Ambassador JOSÉ LUIS REMEDI.

USA: POB 2399, 22nd February St, al-Luqta District, Doha; tel. 44884101; fax 44884298; e-mail pasdoha@state.gov; internet qatar.usembassy.gov; Ambassador JOSEPH EVAN LEBARON.

Venezuela: POB 24470, Doha; tel. 44932730; fax 44932729; e-mail venezuela@embavenqatar.com.qa; internet www.embavenqatar.com.qa; Ambassador JUAN ANTONIO HERNÁNDEZ.

Yemen: POB 3318, Doha; tel. 44432555; fax 44429400; Ambassador ABD AL-MALIK SAID.

Judicial System

The independence of the judiciary was guaranteed by the provisional Constitution and further augmented in the Constitution formally adopted by the Amir in April 2003. All aspects pertaining to the civil judiciary are supervised by the Ministry of Justice, which organizes courts of law through its affiliated departments. The *Shari'a* judiciary hears all cases of personal status relating to Muslims, other claim cases, doctrinal provision and crimes under its jurisdiction. Legislation adopted in 1999 unified all civil and *Shari'a* courts in one judicial body, and determined the jurisdictions of each type of court. The law also provided for the establishment of a court of cassation; this was to be competent to decide on appeals relating to issues of contravention, misapplication and misinterpretation of the law, and on disputes between courts regarding areas of jurisdiction. In addition, the law provided for the establishment of a supreme judiciary council, to be presided over by the head of the court of cassation and comprising, *inter alia*, the heads of the *Shari'a* and civil courts of appeal. The legislation came into effect in 2003. An Amiri decree published in June 2002 provided for the establishment of an independent public prosecution system. A Supreme Constitutional Court was established in 2008 to adjudicate on the constitutionality of laws and to arbitrate in disputes between different branches of the judiciary.

Presidency of Shari'a Courts: POB 232, Doha; tel. 44452222; Pres. Sheikh ABD AL-RAHMAN BIN ABDULLAH AL-MAHMOUD.

Public Prosecution Office: POB 705, Doha; tel. 4843333; fax 44843211; e-mail info@pp.gov.qa; internet www.pp.gov.qa; Attorney-Gen. Dr ALI BIN FITAISE AL-MERRI.

Supreme Judiciary Council: POB 9673, Doha; tel. 44859222; fax 44833939; e-mail sjc@sjc.gov.qa; internet www.sjc.gov.qa; f. 2003; Pres. MASOUD MUHAMMAD AL-AMRI.

Religion

The indigenous population are Muslims of the Sunni sect, most being of the strict Wahhabi persuasion. In March 2008 the first official Christian church (of the Roman Catholic branch) was consecrated in Doha; open worship among adherents of Christianity had previously been prohibited.

CHRISTIANITY

The Anglican Communion

Within the Episcopal Church in Jerusalem and the Middle East, Qatar forms part of the diocese of Cyprus and the Gulf. The Anglican congregation in Qatar is entirely expatriate. The Bishop in Cyprus and the Gulf is resident in Cyprus, while the Archdeacon in the Gulf is resident in Bahrain.

The Roman Catholic Church

An estimated 100,000 adherents in Qatar, mainly expatriates, form part of the Apostolic Vicariate of Northern Arabia. The Vicar Apostolic is resident in Kuwait.

The Press

NEWSPAPERS

Al-'Arab (The Arabs): POB 22612, Doha; tel. 44997333; fax 44677879; e-mail alarab@alarab.com.qa; internet www.alarab.com.qa; f. 1972; ceased publication in 1996, but recommenced following relaunch in Nov. 2007; daily; Arabic; publ. by Dar al-Ouroba Printing and Publishing; Editor-in-Chief Prof. ABD AL-AZIZ IBRAHIM AL-MAHMOUD.

Gulf Times: POB 2888, Doha; tel. 44350478; fax 44350474; e-mail edit@gulf-times.com; internet www.gulf-times.com; f. 1978; daily and weekly edns; English; political; publ. by Gulf Publishing and Printing Co; Man. Editor NEIL COOK; circ. 20,000 (daily).

The Peninsula: POB 3488, Doha; tel. 44557777; fax 44557746; e-mail editor@thepeninsulaqatar.com; internet www.thepeninsulaqatar.com; f. 1995; daily; English; political; publ. by Dar al-Sharq Printing, Publishing and Distribution; Chair. Sheikh THANI BIN ABDULLAH AL THANI; Man. Editor RACHEL MORRIS; circ. 8,000.

Qatar Tribune: POB 23493, Doha; tel. 44422077; fax 44416790; e-mail editor-in-chief@qatar-tribune.com; internet www.qatar-tribune.com; f. 2006; daily; English; Editor-in-Chief Dr HASSAN MUHAMMAD AL-ANSARI; circ. 10,000.

Al-Rayah (The Banner): POB 3464, Doha; tel. 44466636; fax 44320080; e-mail edit@raya.com; internet www.raya.com; f. 1979; daily and weekly edns; Arabic; political; publ. by Gulf Publishing and Printing Co; Editor NASSER AL-OTHMAN; circ. 25,000.

Al-Sharq (The Orient): POB 3488, Doha; tel. 44662444; fax 44662450; e-mail jaber.alharmi@gmail.com; internet www.al-sharq.com; f. 1985; daily; Arabic; political; publ. by Dar al-Sharq Printing, Publishing and Distribution; Editor-in-Chief ABD AL-LATIF AL-MAHMOUD; Dep. Editor JABER AL-HARMI; circ. 45,018.

Al-Watan: POB 22345, Doha; tel. 44652244; fax 44654482; e-mail alwatan@qatar.net.qa; internet www.al-watan.com; f. 1995; daily; Arabic; political; publ. by Dar al-Watan Printing, Publishing and Distribution; Editor-in-Chief AHMAD ALI AL-ABDULLAH; circ. 25,000.

QATAR
Directory

PERIODICALS

Glam: POB 3272, Doha; tel. 44672139; fax 44550982; e-mail contact@omsqatar.com; internet www.omsqatar.com/glam; monthly; English; fashion and lifestyle; publ. by Oryx Advertising Co; f. 2008; Editor-in-Chief YOUSUF JASSEM AL-DARWISH.

Al-Jawhara (The Jewel): POB 2531, Doha; tel. 44414575; fax 44671388; f. 1977; monthly; Arabic; magazine covering watches and jewellery; publ. by al-Ahd Establishment for Journalism, Printing and Publications Ltd; Editor-in-Chief ABDULLAH YOUSUF AL-HUSSAINI; circ. 8,000.

Al-Ouroba (Arabism): POB 663, Doha; tel. 44325874; fax 44429424; f. 1970; weekly; Arabic; political; publ. by Dar al-Ouroba Printing and Publishing; Editor-in-Chief YOUSUF NAAMA; circ. 12,000.

Qatar Al-Yom: POB 3272, Doha; tel. 44672139; fax 44550982; e-mail contact@omsqatar.com; internet www.omsqatar.com/qatar-al-yom; f. 2005; Arabic; news, business and lifestyle; publ. by Oryx Advertising Co; Editor-in-Chief YOUSUF JASSEM AL-DARWISH; circ. 22,000.

Qatar Today: POB 3272, Doha; tel. 44672139; fax 44550982; e-mail qtoday@omsqatar.com; internet www.omsqatar.com/qatar-today; f. 1978; monthly; English; news, business and lifestyle; publ. by Oryx Advertising Co; Editor-in-Chief YOUSUF JASSEM AL-DARWISH; circ. 27,000.

Al-Tarbiya (Education): POB 9865, Doha; tel. 44941709; fax 44838890; e-mail netcom@qatar.net.qa; f. 1971; quarterly; publ. by Qatar Nat. Comm. for Education, Culture and Science; Editor-in-Chief MUHAMMAD SIDDIQ; circ. 2,000.

Al-Tijara Wal A'amal: POB 272, Doha; tel. 44478042; fax 44478063; e-mail info@mashaheermedia.com; internet www.mashaheermedia.com; f. 2003; English; business and industry; publ. by Mashaheer Media Qatar.

Al-Ufuq: POB 3488, Doha; tel. 44602844; fax 44601294; e-mail alsharqpp@qatar.net.qa; f. 2002; monthly; Arabic; business; publ. by Dar al-Sharq Printing, Publishing and Distribution.

Al-Ummah: POB 893, Doha; tel. 44447300; fax 44447022; e-mail m_dirasat@islam.gov.qa; f. 1982; bi-monthly; Islamic thought and affairs, current cultural issues, book serializations.

Woman Today: POB 3272, Doha; tel. 44672139; fax 44550982; e-mail wtoday@omsqatar.com; internet www.omsqatar.com/woman-today; f. 2005; monthly; English; magazine aimed at working women; publ. by Oryx Advertising Co; Editor-in-Chief YOUSUF JASSEM AL-DARWISH; circ. 20,500.

NEWS AGENCY

Qatar News Agency (QNA): POB 3299, Doha; tel. 44450321; fax 44438316; e-mail info@qnaol.com; internet www.qnaol.net; f. 1975; affiliated to Ministry of Foreign Affairs; Dir and Editor-in-Chief AHMAD JASSIM AL-HUMAR.

Publishers

Ali bin Ali Printing and Publishing: POB 75, Doha; tel. 44423481; fax 44432045; e-mail publishing@alibinali.com; internet www.alibinali.com; part of Ali bin Ali Group; publrs of *Qatar Telephone Directory* and *Yellow Pages*; Chair. and Pres. ADEL ALI BIN ALI; Gen. Man. MUHAMMAD MUSTAFA.

Bloomsbury Qatar Foundation Publishing: POB 5825, Villa 3, Qatar Education City, Doha; tel. 44542431; fax 44542438; e-mail bqfp@qf.org.qa; internet www.bqfp.com.qa; f. 2009; publr of fiction and non-fiction in English and Arabic, including educational, academic, reference and children's books; owned by the Qatar Foundation; Dir KATHY ROONEY.

Dar al-Sharq Printing, Publishing and Distribution: POB 3488, Doha; tel. 44557866; fax 44557871; e-mail alsharqpp@qatar.net.qa; internet www.al-sharq.com/DarAlSharq.aspx; publrs of *Al-Sharq* and *The Peninsula* newspapers, and *Al-Ufuq* magazine; distributor for various foreign newspapers; Gen. Man. ABD AL-LATIF AL-MAHMOUD.

Gulf Publishing and Printing Co: POB 533, Doha; tel. 44350475; fax 44350474; e-mail gm@gulftimes.com; internet www.gulf-times.com; f. 1978; publrs of *Gulf Times* and *Al-Rayah*; Chair. ABDULLAH BIN KHALIFA AL-ATTIYA.

Oryx Advertising Co WLL: POB 3272, Doha; tel. 44672139; fax 44550982; e-mail contact@omsqatar.com; internet www.omsqatar.com; publs include *Qatar Today*, *Qatar Al-Yom*, *Glam* and *Woman Today*; Publr and Editor-in-Chief YOUSUF JASSEM AL-DARWISH.

Qatar National Printing Press: POB 355, Doha; tel. 44448452; fax 44449550; e-mail qnppgm@gmail.com; Man. ABD AL-KARIM DEEB.

Broadcasting and Communications

TELECOMMUNICATIONS

Supreme Council for Communications and Information Technology (ictQATAR): POB 23264, al-Mirqab Tower, al-Corniche St, Doha; tel. 44995333; fax 44935913; e-mail info@ict.gov.qa; internet www.ict.gov.qa; f. 2004 to oversee deregulation of telecommunications sector; Chair. Crown Prince Sheikh TAMIM BIN HAMAD BIN KHALIFA AL THANI; Sec.-Gen. Dr HESSA SULTAN AL-JABER.

Qatar Telecommunications Corpn—Qatar Telecom (Q-Tel): POB 217, Doha; tel. 44830000; fax 44476231; e-mail customer.service@qtel.com.qa; internet www.qtel.com.qa; f. 1987; majority state-owned; provides telecommunications services within Qatar; Chair. Sheikh ABDULLAH BIN MUHAMMAD AL THANI; CEO Dr NASSER MARAFIH.

Vodafone Qatar QSC: POB 74057, Unit 207, Level 2, Tech 2, Qatar Science & Technology Park, Doha; tel. 44096666; internet www.vodafone.com.qa; f. 2008; majority shareholders Vodafone Group PLC (United Kingdom) and Qatar Foundation for Education, Science and Community Devt; initial public offering for Qatari nationals of 40% of shares conducted in April 2009; awarded Qatar's second mobile telephone operating licence in June 2008; Chair. Sheikh ABD AL-RAHMAN BIN SAUD AL THANI; CEO JOHN TOMBLESON (acting).

BROADCASTING

Regulatory Authority

Qatar Radio and Television Corpn (QRTC): POB 1414, Doha; tel. 44894444; fax 44882888; e-mail ksaid@rtc.gov.qa; f. 1997; autonomous authority reporting direct to the Council of Ministers; Dir-Gen. ABD AL-RAHMAN OBEIDAN.

Radio

Qatar Broadcasting Service (QBS): POB 3939, Doha; tel. 44894444; fax 44882888; f. 1968; govt service transmitting in Arabic, English, French and Urdu; programmes include Holy Quran Radio and Doha Music Radio; Dir ALI NASSER AL-KUBAISI.

Sout al-Khaleej: POB 1414, Doha; tel. 44888334; fax 44879999; e-mail info@soutalkhaleej.fm; internet www.soutalkhaleej.fm; f. 2002; Arabic arts broadcasting.

Television

Al Jazeera Satellite Network: POB 23123, Doha; tel. 44896044; fax 44873577; e-mail imr@aljazeera.net; internet www.aljazeera.net; f. 1996; 24-hr broadcasting of news and current affairs in Arabic; English-language service launched Nov. 2006; documentary channel launched Jan. 2007; Dir-Gen. WADAH KHANFAR; Chief Editor AHMED SHEIKH.

Qatar Television Service (QTV): POB 1944, Doha; tel. 44894444; fax 44874170; f. 1970; operates two channels (of which one broadcasts in English); 24-hr broadcasting; Dir MUHAMMAD AL-KUWARI; Asst Dir ABD AL-WAHAB MUHAMMAD AL-MUTAWA'A.

Finance

(cap. = capital; res = reserves; dep. = deposits; m. = million; brs = branches; amounts in Qatar riyals, unless otherwise indicated)

STATE FINANCIAL AUTHORITIES

In March 2005 the Government established the Qatar Financial Centre (QFC), which was intended to attract international financial institutions and multinational corporations to Qatar, 'to establish business operations in a best-in-class international environment'. The QFC comprised the QFC Authority and the QFC Regulatory Authority (QFCRA—see below), as well as two legal bodies—the QFC Regulatory Tribunal and the QFC Civil and Commercial Court—which were charged with upholding the rule of law and ensuring the transparency of QFC transactions. In July 2007 plans were announced for the creation of a single, integrated, fully independent financial regulatory authority, which would merge the regulatory activities of the QFCRA, the Qatar Financial Markets Authority and the Qatar Central Bank, and oversee all banking, insurance, securities, asset management and other financial services. The new body was expected to become operational in 2011.

Qatar Financial Centre Authority (QFCA): POB 23245, Doha; tel. 44967777; fax 44967676; e-mail info@qfc.com.qa; internet www.qfc.com.qa; f. 2005; charged with promoting Qatar as an attractive location for international banking, insurance and financial services; Chair. YOUSUF HUSSAIN KAMAL (Minister of Economy and Finance); CEO SHASHANK SRIVASTAVA (acting).

Qatar Financial Centre Regulatory Authority (QFCRA): POB 22989, Level 14, Qatar Financial Centre Tower, Doha; tel. 44956888;

QATAR

Directory

fax 44835031; e-mail info@qfcra.com; internet www.qfcra.com; f. 2005; charged with the regulation and supervision of a wide range of financial activities, incl. banking, insurance, asset management and financial advisory services; Chair. and CEO PHILLIP THORPE.

Qatar Financial Markets Authority: POB 25552, Doha; tel. 44289999; fax 44441221; e-mail info@qfma.org.qa; internet www.visionwmg.com/qfma/website; f. 2007 to supervise the stock exchange and securities industry; Chair. YOUSUF HUSSAIN KAMAL (Minister of Economy and Finance); Chief Exec. NASSER AHMAD SHAIBI.

BANKING
Central Bank

Qatar Central Bank: POB 1234, Doha; tel. 44456456; fax 44414190; e-mail webmaster@qcb.gov.qa; internet www.qcb.gov.qa; f. 1966 as Qatar and Dubai Currency Bd; became Qatar Monetary Agency in 1973; renamed Qatar Cen. Bank in 1993; state-owned; cap. and res 9,982.5m., total assets 44,458.5m., currency in circulation 6,912.8m. (Dec. 2008); Gov. ABDULLAH BIN SAUD AL THANI.

Commercial Banks

Ahlibank QSC: POB 2309, Suhmin bin Hamad St, al-Sadd Area, Doha; tel. 44232222; fax 44232323; e-mail info@ahlibank.com.qa; internet www.ahlibank.com.qa; f. 1984 as Al-Ahli Bank of Qatar QSC; name changed as above in 2004; cap. 613m., res 1,314m., dep. 15,998m. (Dec. 2009); Chair. Sheikh FAISAL BIN ABD AL-AZIZ BIN JASIM AL THANI; CEO SALAH JASSIM MURAD; 9 brs.

Commercial Bank of Qatar QSC (CBQ): POB 3232, Grand Hamad Ave, Doha; tel. 44900000; fax 44490070; e-mail info@cbq.com.qa; internet www.cbq.com.qa; f. 1975; cap. 2,165m., res 9,709m., dep. 33,662m. (Dec. 2009); Man. Dir HUSSAIN IBRAHIM AL-FARDAN; Group CEO ANDREW C. STEVENS; 23 brs.

Doha Bank: POB 3818, Grand Hamad Ave, Doha; tel. 44456600; fax 44410625; e-mail international@dohabank.com.qa; internet www.dohabank.com.qa; f. 1979; cap. 2,177.2m., res 3,567.0m., dep. 38,379.2m. (Dec. 2009); Chair. Sheikh FAHAD BIN MUHAMMAD BIN JABER AL THANI; CEO R. SEETHARAMAN; 35 brs in Qatar, 3 abroad.

International Bank of Qatar QSC (IBQ): POB 2001, Suhaim bin Hamad St, Doha; tel. 44473700; fax 44473745; e-mail qatarenq@ibq.com.qa; internet www.ibq.com.qa; f. 2000 as Grindlays Qatar Bank QSC; previously a branch of ANZ Grindlays Bank (f. 1956); name changed as above in 2004, after Nat. Bank of Kuwait SAK assumed management of the bank; announced plans to merge with Al-Khalij Commercial Bank in mid-2010; cap. 1,000m., res 1,631m., dep. 19,940m. (Dec. 2009); Chair. Sheikh HAMAD BIN JASIM BIN JABER AL THANI (Prime Minister and Minister of Foreign Affairs); Man. Dir GEORGE NASRA.

Al-Khalij Commercial Bank (QSC) (al-Khaliji): POB 28000, Doha; tel. 44996000; fax 44996020; e-mail info@alkhaliji.com; internet www.alkhaliji.com; f. 2007; announced plans to merge with Int. Bank of Qatar in mid-2010; cap. 3,600.0m., res 1,042.8m., dep. 12,376.2m. (Dec. 2009); Chair. and Man. Dir HAMAD BIN FAISAL BIN THANI AL THANI; CEO ROBIN MCCALL (acting).

Masraf Al Rayan: POB 28888, Doha; tel. 44253333; fax 44253312; e-mail info@alrayan.com; internet www.alrayan.com; f. 2006; offers *Shari'a*-compliant banking services; cap. 4,124m., res 1,820m., dep. 17,831m. (Dec. 2009); Chair. Dr HUSSAIN ALI AL-ABDULLA; CEO ADEL MUSTAFAWI; 5 brs.

Qatar Development Bank (QDB): POB 22789, Doha; tel. 44596666; fax 44350433; e-mail contact@qdb.org.qa; internet www.qidb.com.qa; f. 1996 as Qatar Industrial Devt Bank; inaugurated Oct. 1997; relaunched under above name in April 2007 with expanded capital provision to facilitate private sector involvement in national economic devt; state-owned; provides long-term low-interest industrial loans; finances wide range of industrial and social projects; broadened consultancy services following relaunch; cap. 200m., total assets 392.0m. (Dec. 2006); Chair. Sheikh ABDULLAH BIN SA'UD AL THANI; CEO MANSOUR IBRAHIM AL-MAHMOUD.

Qatar First Investment Bank: POB 28028, Suhaim bin Hamad St, Doha; tel. 44483333; fax 44483560; e-mail information@qfib.com.qa; internet www.qfib.com.qa; f. 2008; offers *Shari'a* -compliant investment banking services; Chair. ABDULLA BIN FAHAD BIN GHORAB AL-MARRI; CEO EMAD MANSOUR.

Qatar International Islamic Bank: POB 664, Grand Hamad St, Doha; tel. 44385555; fax 44444101; e-mail qiibit@qiib.com.qa; internet www.qiib.com.qa; f. 1990; cap. 1,387m., res 2,381m., dep. 11,575m. (Dec. 2009); Chair. and Man. Dir KHALID BIN THANI BIN ABDULLAH AL THANI; CEO ABD AL-BASIT AL-SHAIBEI; 5 brs.

Qatar Islamic Bank SAQ (QIB): POB 559, Grand Hamad St, Doha; tel. 44409409; fax 44412700; e-mail info@qib.com.qa; internet www.qib.com.qa; f. 1982; cap. 2,067.5m., res 6,937.5m., dep. 29,051.9m. (Dec. 2009); Chair. Sheikh JASIM BIN HAMAD BIN JASIM BIN JABER AL THANI; CEO AHMAD MESHARI (acting); 25 brs.

Qatar National Bank SAQ: POB 1000, Doha; tel. 44407777; fax 44413753; e-mail ccsupport@qnb.com.qa; internet www.qnb.com.qa; f. 1964; owned 50% by Govt of Qatar and 50% by Qatari nationals; cap. 3,011m., res 14,330m., dep. 148,752m. (Dec. 2009); Chair. YOUSUF HUSSAIN KAMAL (Minister of Economy and Finance); CEO ALI SHAREEF AL-EMADI; 32 brs in Qatar, 3 abroad.

SOVEREIGN WEALTH FUND

Qatar Investment Authority (QIA): POB 23224, Doha; tel. 44995900; fax 44995991; e-mail info@qia.qa; internet www.qia.qa; f. 2005 to develop, invest and manage state reserve funds; Chair. Sheikh TAMIM BIN HAMAD BIN KHALIFA AL THANI; CEO Sheikh HAMAD BIN JASIM BIN JABER AL THANI (Prime Minister and Minister of Foreign Affairs).

STOCK EXCHANGE

Qatar Exchange (QE): POB 22114, Grand Hamad St, Doha; tel. 44333666; fax 44319233; e-mail dsm@dsm.com.qa; internet www.dsm.com.qa; f. 2009 to replace fmr Doha Securities Market (f. 1997); 80% stake owned by Qatar Holding, 20% owned by NYSE Euronext; 42 cos listed in June 2009; Chair. Dr KHALID BIN MUHAMMAD AL-ATTIYA; CEO ANDRE WENT.

INSURANCE

Doha Insurance Co: POB 7171, Doha; tel. 44335000; fax 44657777; e-mail dohainsco@qatar.net.qa; internet www.dicqatar.com; f. 1999 as public shareholding co; cap. 127.2m., total assets 518.3m. (Dec. 2007); Chair. Sheikh NAWAF BIN NASSER BIN KHALID AL THANI; Gen. Man. BASSAM HUSSAIN.

Al-Khaleej Insurance and Reinsurance Co QSC (SAQ): POB 4555, Doha; tel. 44414151; fax 44430530; e-mail alkhalej@qatar.net.qa; internet www.alkhaleej.com; f. 1978; cap. and res 568.4m. (2007); all classes except life; Chair. ABDULLAH BIN MUHAMMAD JABER AL THANI; Gen. Man. KARAM AHMAD MAHMOUD.

Qatar General Insurance and Reinsurance Co SAQ: POB 4500, A Ring Rd, al-Asmakh Area, Doha; tel. 44282222; fax 44437302; e-mail qgirc-tec@qatar.net.qa; internet www.qgirco.com; f. 1979; total assets 1,729.7m. (2007); all classes; Chair. and Man. Dir Sheikh NASSER BIN ALI AL THANI; Gen. Man. GHAZI ABU NAHL.

Qatar Insurance Co SAQ: POB 666, Tamin St, West Bay, Doha; tel. 44962222; fax 44831569; e-mail qatarins@qic.com.qa; internet www.qatarinsurance.com; f. 1964; cap. 424.7m., total assets 5,860.7m. (Dec. 2007); all classes; the Govt has a majority share; Chair. and Man. Dir Sheikh KHALID BIN MUHAMMAD ALI AL THANI; Pres. and CEO KHALIFA A. AL-SUBAY'I; brs in Doha and Khalifa Town, Dubai and Abu Dhabi (UAE), Saudi Arabia, Kuwait, Oman and Malta.

Qatar Insurance Services LLC (Qatarlyst): 12th Floor, QFC Tower, POB 23245, Doha; tel. 44968301; e-mail enquiries@qatarlyst.com; internet www.qatarlyst.com; f. 2008 by the QFCA, with the aim of establishing Qatar as a regional hub for the insurance industry; launched internet-based insurance-trading and -processing service (Qatarlyst) June 2009; CEO JAMES SUTHERLAND; Chair. ABD AL-RAHMAN AHMAD AL-SHAIBI.

Qatar Islamic Insurance Co: POB 22676, Doha; tel. 44658888; fax 44550111; e-mail qiic@qatar.net.qa; internet www.qiic.net.qa; f. 1993; cap. 150.0m., res 137.0m. (Dec. 2007); Chair. Sheikh ABDULLAH BIN THANI AL THANI; Gen. Man. JASSIM A. AL-SADI.

Trade and Industry

DEVELOPMENT ORGANIZATIONS

Department of Industrial Development: POB 2599, Doha; tel. 44846444; fax 44832024; e-mail did@mei.gov.qa; a div. of the Ministry of Energy and Industry; conducts research, licensing, devt and supervision of new industrial projects; Dir-Gen. SAID MUBARAK AL-KUWAIRI.

General Secretariat for Development Planning: POB 1588, Doha; tel. 44958888; e-mail webmaster@planning.gov.qa; internet www.gsdp.gov.qa; f. 2006; responsible for co-ordination of the emirate's long-term devt strategy; monitors progress of Qatar's Nat. Vision 2030 and Nat. Strategy; Sec.-Gen. Dr IBRAHIM AL-IBRAHIM; Dir-Gen. Sheikh HAMAD BIN JASIM BIN JABER AL THANI.

Public Works Authority (Ashghal): POB 22188, Doha; tel. 44950000; fax 44950999; e-mail info@ashghal.gov.qa; internet www.ashghal.com; f. 2004; responsible for the management and devt of public infrastructure projects; Chair. Sheikh ABD AL-RAHMAN BIN KHALIFA BIN ABD AL-AZIZ AL THANI (Minister of Municipal Affairs and Urban Planning); Pres. NASSER ALI ABDULLAH AL-MAWLAWI.

Urban Planning and Development Authority: POB 22423, Doha; tel. 44955549; fax 44955594; e-mail general@up.org.qa; internet www.up.org.qa; f. 2005; planning, co-ordination and man-

QATAR

agement of urban devt projects; oversees devt of the Master Plan for the State of Qatar; Dir-Gen. ALI ABDULLAH AL-ABDULLAH.

CHAMBER OF COMMERCE

Qatar Chamber of Commerce and Industry: POB 402, Doha; tel. 44559111; fax 44661693; e-mail info@qcci.org; internet www.qcci.org; f. 1963; 17 elected mems; Chair. Sheikh KHALIFA BIN JASIM BIN MUHAMMAD AL THANI; Gen. Man. KHALID AL-HAJRI.

STATE HYDROCARBONS COMPANIES

Qatar International Petroleum Marketing Co (Tasweeq): POB 24183, Doha; tel. 44976111; fax 44976276; e-mail info@tasweeq.com.qa; internet www.tasweeq.com.qa; f. 2007 to take sole responsibility for all exports of natural gas and oil products; wholly govt-owned; CEO ALI AL-HAMADI.

Qatar Petrochemical Co SAQ (QAPCO): POB 756, Doha; tel. 44242444; fax 44324700; e-mail information@qapco.com.qa; internet www.qapco.com.qa; f. 1974; 80% owned by Industries Qatar, 20% by Total Petrochemicals (France); total assets QR 5,090.7m. (2006); operation of petrochemical plant at Mesaieed; produced 549,928 metric tons of ethylene, 359,460 tons of low-density polyethylene, and 32,297 tons of solid sulphur in 2007; Chair. HAMAD RASHID AL-MOHANNADI; Gen. Man. MUHAMMAD YOUSUF AL-MULLA; 879 employees (2004).

Qatofin Co Ltd: POB 55013, Doha; tel. 44242555; fax 44325936; e-mail info@qatofin.com.qa; internet www.qatofin.com.qa; f. 2009; 63% owned by Qatar Petrochemical Co, 36% by Total and 1% by Qatar Petroleum; capacity to produce 450,000 metric tons of low-density polyethylene; Chair. HAMAD RASHID AL-MOHANNADI; Vice-Chair. MUHAMMAD YOUSUF AL-MULLA.

Qatar Petroleum (QP): POB 3212, Doha; tel. 44402000; fax 44831125; e-mail webmaster@qp.com.qa; internet www.qp.com.qa; f. 1974 as Qatar Gen. Petroleum Corpn (QGPC), name changed 2001; total assets QR 137,851m. (2006); sales QR 2,243m. (2006); oil production 850,000 b/d (2006); the State of Qatar's interest in cos active in petroleum and related industries has passed to QP; has responsibility for all phases of oil and gas industry both on shore and off shore, incl. exploration, drilling, production, refining, transport and storage, distribution, sale and export of oil, natural gas and other hydrocarbons; Oryx gas to liquids (GTL) plant became operational in 2006, with capacity for 34,000 b/d of GTL products; Chair. and Man. Dir MUHAMMAD SALEH AL-SADA (Minister of Energy and Industry); Dep. Chair. HAMAD RASHID AL-MOHANNADI; 5,500 employees.

Qatar Liquefied Gas Co (Qatargas): POB 22666, Doha; tel. 44736000; fax 44736666; e-mail infos@qatargas.com.qa; internet www.qatargas.com; f. 1984 to develop the North Field of unassociated gas; cap. QR 500m.; 65% owned by Qatar Petroleum, 10% each by ExxonMobil (USA) and Total, and 7.5% each by Marubeni Corpn and Mitsui & Co of Japan; expansion plans to supply 42m. metric tons of LNG to European, Asian and North American markets scheduled for completion by 2010; Chair. MUHAMMAD SALED AL-SADA (Minister of Energy and Industry); CEO KHALID BIN KHALIFA AL-THANI.

Ras Laffan LNG Co Ltd (RasGas): POB 24200, Doha; tel. 44738000; fax 44738480; e-mail site-admin@rasgas.com.qa; internet www.rasgas.com; f. 1993; 70% owned by Qatar Petroleum, 30% by ExxonMobil; operates five LNG trains, which had a production capacity of 20.7m. metric tons per year in 2007; CEO HAMAD RASHID AL-MOHANNADI.

Qatar Petroleum also wholly or partly owns: Industries Qatar (IQ) and its subsidiaries, Qatar Gas Transport Co (Nakilat), Gulf Helicopters Co Ltd (GHC), Qatar Vinyl Co (QVC), Qatar Chemical Co (Q-Chem), Qatar Clean Energy Co (QACENCO), Qatar Electricity and Water Co (QEWC), Qatar Shipping Co (Q-Ship), Arab Maritime Petroleum Transport Co (AMPTC), Arab Petroleum Pipelines Co (SUMED), Arab Shipbuilding and Repair Yard Co (ASRY), Arab Petroleum Services Co (APSC) and Arab Petroleum Investments Corpn (APICORP).

UTILITIES

Qatar General Electricity and Water Corpn (Kahramaa): POB 41, Doha; tel. 44845555; fax 44845496; e-mail kmcontact@km.com.qa; internet www.km.com.qa; f. 2000; state authority for planning, implementation, operation and maintenance of electricity and water sectors; Chair. ISSA HILAL AL-KUWARI.

Qatar Electricity and Water Co (QEWC): POB 22046, Doha; tel. 44858585; fax 44831116; e-mail welcome@qewc.com; internet www.qewc.com; f. 1990; 57% privately owned; devt and operation of power generation and water desalination facilities; Chair. ABDULLAH BIN HAMAD AL-ATTIYA (Deputy Prime Minister and Chair. of the Emiri Diwan); Gen. Man. FAHAD HAMAD AL-MOHANNADI.

Transport

A Transportation Master Plan for Qatar, intended to provide a comprehensive framework for the development of the transport infrastructure over a 20-year period, was implemented in late 2007. Government expenditure on infrastructure projects was projected at US $9,700m. for the 2010/11 fiscal year, equivalent to 30.1% of total budgeted expenditure.

RAILWAYS

There are no railways in Qatar; however, in November 2009 the Qatar Railways Development Co, a joint venture comprising Qatari Diar Real Estate Investment Co and Deutsche Bahn AG (Germany), was established to supervise the development of a national rail network, which would be linked to a regional rail network, connecting Qatar with member countries of the Co-operation Council for the Arab States of the Gulf (Gulf Co-operation Council—GCC).

ROADS

The total road network in 2006 was estimated to be 7,790 km. A 105-km road from Doha to Salwa was completed in 1970, and joins one leading from Hufuf in Saudi Arabia. A 418-km highway, built in conjunction with Abu Dhabi (United Arab Emirates), links both states with the Gulf network. A major upgrading of the national road network was planned for the first years of the 21st century. Work on the QR 8,000m., 13-phase Doha Expressway project, which involves the construction of a dual carriageway linking the north and south of the country and a Doha ring-road, commenced in late 2007; several stretches of the Expressway had been opened to the public by mid-2010. A project to construct a causeway (the Friendship Bridge) linking Qatar with Bahrain was approved by both Governments in 2004. After protracted discussions and numerous delays, in May 2008 the contract to design and build the causeway, at a cost of some US $3,000m., was awarded to a France-based consortium. The decision, in late 2008, to incorporate a railway line into the project necessitated substantial design revisions that were expected to add up to $1,000m. to the cost of the causeway. Construction had yet to commence at early 2011.

SHIPPING

Doha Port has nine general cargo berths of 7.5 m–9.0 m depth. The total length of the berths is 1,699 m. In addition, there is a flour mill berth, and a container terminal (with a depth of 12.0 m and a length of 600 m) with a roll-on roll-off (ro-ro) berth at the north end currently under construction. Cold storage facilities exist for cargo of up to 500 metric tons. At Umm Said Harbour, the Northern Deep Water Wharves consist of a deep-water quay 730-m long with a dredged depth alongside of 15.5 m, and a quay 570-m long with a dredged depth alongside of 13.0 m. The General Cargo Wharves consist of a quay 400-m long with a dredged depth alongside of 10.0 m. The Southern Deep Water Wharves consist of a deep-water quay 508-m long with a dredged depth alongside of 13.0 m. The North Field gas project has increased the demand for shipping facilities. A major new industrial port was completed at Ras Laffan in 1995, providing facilities for LNG and condensate carriers and ro-ro vessels. Qatar Petroleum initiated a US $1,000m. expansion of Ras Laffan port in mid-2005. Further expansion plans at Ras Laffan, to accommodate the shipping requirements of the burgeoning LNG and associated industries, were finalized in early 2008; completion of the project would render Ras Laffan the largest man-made harbour in the world, bounded by 26 km of breakwaters. In October 2007 Sheikh Hamad issued a decree announcing that the New Doha Port development would be located at Mesaieed industrial city. On completion of its first phase (scheduled for 2014), at a projected cost of some $5,500m., the port was expected to have annual handling capacity of 2m. 20-ft equivalent units (TEUs), with capacity projected to increase to 6m. TEUs by 2025. Capacity at Doha's existing port, which was to be decommissioned on completion of the new port, was some 400,000 TEUs, with 340,000 TEUs handled in 2007.

Port Authority

Customs and Ports General Authority (CPGA): POB 81, Doha; tel. 44457457; fax 44414959; e-mail comments@customs.gov.qa; internet www.customs.gov.qa; Chair. AHMAD ALI MUHAMMAD AL-MOHANNADI.

Principal Shipping Companies

Qatar Gas Transport Co Ltd (Nakilat): POB 22271, Doha; tel. 44998111; fax 44326788; e-mail info@qgtc.com.qa; internet www.nakilat.com.qa; f. 2004; 50% owned by private Qatari investors, 15% by Qatar Shipping Co, 15% by Qatar Navigation, 5% by Qatar Petroleum and 15% by other Qatari cos; specializes in the shipment of LNG, LPG and petroleum products; owns 54 vessels; Chair. HAMAD RASHID AL-MOHANNADI; Man. Dir MUHAMMAD AL-GHANIM; 220 employees.

QATAR

Qatar Navigation QSC: POB 153, 60 al-Tameen St, West Bay, Doha; tel. 44468666; fax 44468777; e-mail info@qatarnavigation.com; internet www.qatarnav.com; f. 1957 as Qatar Nat. Navigation and Transport Co Ltd; acquired Qatar Shipping Co in 2010; 100% owned by Qatari nationals; shipping agents, stevedoring, chandlers, forwarding, shipowning, repair, construction, etc.; Chair. Sheikh HAMAD BIN SUHAIM AL THANI; CEO KHALIFA BIN ALI AL-HITMI.

Qatar Shipping Co QSC (Q-Ship): POB 22180, al-Muntazah St, Doha; tel. and fax 44191760; e-mail rahul@qship.com; internet www.qship.com; f. 1992; subsidiary of Qatar Navigation QSC; oil and bulk cargo shipping; wholly owns 7 vessels; Chair. and Man. Dir SALEM BIN BUTTI AL-NAIMI; CEO K. K. KOTHARI.

CIVIL AVIATION

Doha International Airport is equipped to receive all types of aircraft. In 2001 some 2.7m. passengers used the airport. In 2004 Bechtel, a US engineering company, won the contract to manage the redevelopment of the airport (to be known upon completion of the project as New Doha International Airport), 4 km to the east of the existing site. Phase one of the project, which was expected to cost some QR 9,500m., involved the construction of two runways and a new terminal building and was set to increase annual passenger-handling capacity to 24m. After delays to the original schedule, phase one were expected to be completed in March 2012. Upon completion of phase three of the expansion, scheduled for 2015, passenger-handling capacity was to reach 50m.

Civil Aviation Authority: POB 3000, Doha; tel. 44557333; fax 44557105; e-mail info@caa.gov.qa; internet www.caa.gov.qa; Chair. and Man. Dir ABD AL-AZIZ MUHAMMAD AL-NOAIMI.

Doha International Airport: POB 22550, Doha; tel. 44622999; fax 44622044; e-mail diainfo@qatarairways.com.qa; internet www.dohaairport.com; CEO AKBAR AL-BAKER.

Gulf Helicopters Co Ltd (GHC): POB 811, Doha; tel. 44333888; fax 44411004; e-mail enquiries@gulfhelicopters.com; internet www.gulfhelicopters.com; f. 1974; owned by Qatar Petroleum; Chair. SAEED MUBARAK AL-MOHANNADI; CEO MUHAMMAD AL-MOHANNADI.

Qatar Airways: POB 22550, Qatar Airways Tower, Airport Rd, Doha; tel. 44496666; fax 44621792; e-mail infodesk@qatarairways.com; internet www.qatarairways.com; f. 1993; state-owned; services to more than 80 international destinations; operated a fleet of 87 aircraft at August 2010; planned fleet expansion to 110 aircraft by 2013; CEO AKBAR AL-BAKER.

Tourism

Since 2000 the tourism industry has been undergoing a programme of expansion and development, and Qatar's reputation as a venue for international conferences and sporting events has grown. The 15th Asian Games, held in Doha in December 2006, provided a substantial impetus for increased hotel construction from 2004. In December 2010 Qatar was awarded the right to host the 2022 football World Cup, a development that was expected to promote extensive development of the country's tourism infrastructure. A new Museum of Islamic Art opened in Doha in 2008, and several other new museums and cultural establishments were planned. Notable tourist attractions outside the capital include the historic forts and archaeological sites at al-Zubarah, and the natural beauty of the Khor al-Udaid, or Inland Sea, region. There were 1,404,850 tourist arrivals in 2008; receipts from tourism totalled US $874m. in 2006.

Qatar National Hotels Co: POB 2977, Doha; tel. 44237777; fax 44270707; internet www.qnhc.com; f. 1993; develops and manages hotels and other tourist facilities; govt-owned; Chair. Sheikh NAWAF BIN JASIM BIN JABER AL THANI; CEO JAN POUL N. DE BOER.

Qatar Tourism Authority (QTEA): POB 24624, Doha; tel. 44997499; fax 44991919; e-mail soha@qatartourism.gov.qa; internet www.qatartourism.gov.qa; f. 2000; affiliated with the Ministry of Business and Trade; Chair. AHMED ABDULLAH AL-NUAIMI; Head of Promotions SOHA MOUSSA.

Defence

Chief of Staff: Maj.-Gen. HAMAD BIN ALI AL-ATTIYA.
Estimated Defence Budget (2010): QR 9,100m.
Total armed forces (as assessed at November 2010): 11,800: army 8,500; navy 1,800 (incl. marine police); air force 1,500.

Education

All education within Qatar is provided free of charge, although it is not compulsory, and numerous scholarships are awarded for study overseas. In the academic year 2007/08 there were 78,635 students at primary, intermediate and secondary levels of government-funded, regular education in Qatar; there were 64,506 students in private schools in the same year. In 2007/08 there were 21,883 children enrolled in pre-primary education. Primary schooling begins at six years of age and lasts for six years. In 2007/08 state primary schools were attended by 19,577 pupils. The next level of education, beginning at 12 years of age, is divided between a three-year preparatory stage and a further three-year secondary stage, with a total of 19,538 pupils at government schools in 2007/08. In 2007/08 there were 88 independent schools, which were attended by 18,624 pupils at primary level and 20,896 at preparatory and secondary levels. There are specialized religious, industrial, commercial and technical secondary schools for boys; the technical school admitted its first students in 1999/2000, as did two scientific secondary schools (one for girls). In 2008/09 93% of all children in the relevant age-group were enrolled at primary schools; the comparable ratio for secondary enrolment was 77%. The University of Qatar was established in 1977. In 2007/08 there were 8,529 students enrolled at the university. The Qatar Foundation for Education, Science and Community Development, established in 1995, is involved in various programmes to develop educational and research facilities, including through partnerships with international institutions. Education City Qatar, the foundation's flagship project, which opened in October 2003, hosts branch campuses of five US universities and numerous other educational and research institutions. In 2006/07 government expenditure on education amounted to QR 3,062.7m., equivalent to 12.9% of total government spending.

ROMANIA

Introductory Survey

LOCATION, CLIMATE, LANGUAGE, RELIGION, FLAG, CAPITAL

Romania lies in south-eastern Europe, bounded to the north and east by Ukraine, to the north-east by Moldova, to the north-west by Hungary, to the south-west by Serbia and to the south by Bulgaria. The south-east coast is washed by the Black Sea. Romania has hot summers and cold winters, with moderate rainfall. The average summer temperature is 23°C (73°F) and the winter average is −3°C (27°F). The official language is Romanian, although minority groups speak Hungarian (Magyar), German and other languages. Most of the inhabitants profess Christianity, and about 87% of the population are adherents of the Romanian Orthodox Church. The national flag (proportions 3 by 5) consists of three equal vertical stripes, of blue, yellow and red. The capital is Bucharest (Bucureşti).

CONTEMPORARY POLITICAL HISTORY

Historical Context

Formerly part of Turkey's Ottoman Empire, Romania became an independent kingdom in 1881. During the dictatorship of the Fascist 'Iron Guard' movement, Romania entered the Second World War as an ally of Nazi Germany. However, Soviet forces entered Romania in 1944, when the pro-Nazi regime was overthrown. Under Soviet pressure, King Michael (Mihail) I accepted the appointment of a communist-led coalition Government in March 1945. At elections in November 1946 a communist-dominated bloc claimed 89% of the votes cast, but the results were widely believed to have been fraudulent. In 1947 the small Romanian Communist Party (RCP) merged with the Social Democratic Party to become the Romanian Workers' Party (RWP). King Michael was forced to abdicate on 30 December 1947, when the Romanian People's Republic was proclaimed. The republic's first Constitution was adopted in 1948, and in the same year the nationalization of the main industrial and financial institutions was begun. In 1949 private landholdings were expropriated and amalgamated into state and collective farms. The implementation of Soviet-style economic policies was accompanied by the establishment of full political control by the RWP.

In 1952, following a purge of the RWP membership, a new Constitution, closer to the Soviet model, was adopted. Gheorghe Gheorghiu-Dej, the First Secretary of the RWP, became Romania's unchallenged leader and proceeded to implement large-scale plans for industrialization. Gheorghiu-Dej died in 1965; he was succeeded as First Secretary of the RWP by Nicolae Ceauşescu, a Secretary of the RWP Central Committee since 1954. In June 1965 the RWP again became the RCP, and Ceauşescu's post of First Secretary was restyled General Secretary. A new Constitution, adopted in August, changed the country's name to the Socialist Republic of Romania.

Ceauşescu continued his predecessor's relatively independent foreign policy, criticizing the invasion of Czechoslovakia by troops of the Warsaw Pact (the defence grouping of the Soviet bloc) in 1968, and establishing links with Western states and institutions. However, the use of foreign loans for investment led to severe economic problems by the early 1980s. In order to strengthen his position, Ceauşescu (who had become President of the Republic in 1974) implemented frequent changes in the RCP leadership and the Government. In March 1980 his wife, Elena, became a First Deputy Chairman of the Council of Ministers, and numerous other family members held government and party posts.

In late 1985 an energy crisis resulted in a declaration of a state of emergency in the electric power industry and the dismissal of ministers and senior officials. In November 1987 thousands of people marched through the city of Braşov and stormed the local RCP headquarters, protesting against declining living standards and working conditions. Hundreds of arrests were made, and similar protests followed in other cities. In March 1988 Ceauşescu announced details of a rural urbanization programme, to entail the demolition of some 8,000 villages, and the resettlement of their residents (mostly ethnic Hungarians) in new 'agro-industrial centres'. Despite domestic and international criticism, Ceauşescu maintained that the programme would raise living standards and ensure social equality.

In December 1989 there was unrest in the western city of Timişoara as supporters of László Tőkés, a Protestant clergyman (an ethnic Hungarian who had repeatedly criticized the Government's policies), demonstrated their opposition to his eviction from his church. A further protest was attended by thousands of local residents. Security forces opened fire on the crowd, reportedly killing several hundred people. There were reports of protests in other towns, and the country's borders were closed.

On 21 December 1989 President Ceauşescu attended a mass rally in Bucharest, intended to demonstrate popular support. Instead, his address was interrupted by hostile chanting, and anti-Government demonstrations followed later in the day, leading to clashes between protesters and members of the Securitate (the secret police force), during which many civilians were killed. The disturbances quickly spread to other parts of the country, and on the following day Ceauşescu declared a state of emergency; however, soldiers of the regular army declared their support for the protesters. Nicolae and Elena Ceauşescu escaped from the RCP Central Committee headquarters by helicopter as demonstrators stormed the building. The Ceauşescus were captured near Târgovişte and, on 25 December, after a summary trial, were executed by firing squad. Fighting continued for several days, mainly between Securitate forces and regular soldiers.

Meanwhile, a 145-member National Salvation Front (NSF) was formed, and a provisional Government was established. Ion Iliescu, a former Secretary of the RCP Central Committee, became interim President, and Petre Roman, an academic, was appointed Prime Minister. The new Government immediately decreed an end to the RCP's constitutional monopoly of power, and cancelled the rural urbanization programme. The RCP was banned, it was announced that free elections would be held in 1990, and the designation of Socialist Republic was abandoned. By early January 1990 the army had restored order, and the Securitate was abolished. According to official figures, 689 people were killed during the revolution.

Special military tribunals were established to try Ceauşescu's former associates. In February 1990 four senior RCP officials were found guilty of responsibility for the shootings in Timişoara and Bucharest and were sentenced to life imprisonment. Numerous other former government and RCP members were similarly charged. In September Ceauşescu's son, Nicu, who was found to have ordered security forces to open fire on demonstrators in Sibiu in December 1989, received a 20-year prison sentence. (He was released in 1992 on the grounds of ill health, and died in 1996.) Gen. Iulian Vlad, the former head of the Securitate, was sentenced to 12 years' imprisonment in 1991; in January 1994, however, he was released as part of a general amnesty. In December 1991 eight associates of the former President were sentenced to prison terms of up to 25 years for their part in the shootings in Timişoara.

Domestic Political Affairs

Despite the widespread jubilation that followed the downfall of Ceauşescu, the NSF did not enjoy total public support. Many citizens believed that the Front's leadership was too closely linked with the Ceauşescu regime, and were particularly critical of the NSF's control of the media. Furthermore, the NSF's announcement, in January 1990, that it was to contest the forthcoming elections, and its reversal of the prohibition of the RCP, increased fears that members of the disgraced regime were attempting to regain power. In January the offices of two opposition parties, the National Liberal Party (NLP) and the National Peasants' Party, were attacked by NSF supporters. In February, after negotiations among representatives of 29 political parties, the NSF agreed to share power with the opposition, pending the elections, in a 180-member Provisional National Unity Council (PNUC). Each of the political parties represented in the talks was allocated three seats on the Council, and the PNUC was subsequently expanded to 253 members to permit representation by other political parties; nevertheless, NSF members and supporters occupied 111 seats in the Council. The PNUC elected an Executive Bureau, with Iliescu as its President. Opposition to the NSF persisted, particularly in the armed forces. The Minister of National Defence was replaced in compliance with demands from within the military, but shortly afterwards thousands of anti-Government demonstrators demanded the resignation of Iliescu, and some 250 protesters forcibly entered the NSF headquarters.

As the elections approached, there were mass anti-communist demonstrations in Bucharest. The election campaign was acrimonious, and there were widespread accusations of systematic intimidation and harassment of the NSF's opponents. At the presidential and legislative elections, held on 20 May 1990, Iliescu won 85.1% of the valid votes cast in the presidential poll. In the elections to the bicameral legislature, the NSF won 65% of the votes cast, securing 263 of the 387 seats in the Camera Deputaților (Chamber of Deputies) and 91 of the 119 seats in Senatul (the Senate).

Unrest continued, and in June 1990 a protest in Bucharest was forcibly broken up by the police. The brutal treatment of the demonstrators provoked renewed clashes, in which the armed forces opened fire on rioters. Following an appeal for support by Iliescu, some 7,000 miners and other workers were transported to the capital, where they swiftly seized control of the streets. The disturbances resulted in several deaths and hundreds of injuries. Following President Iliescu's inauguration in late June, Roman was reappointed Prime Minister, and a new Council of Ministers was formed, in which nearly all the members of the interim administration were replaced. In the following months, as popular discontent at the deteriorating economic situation intensified, there was widespread strike action. In October Roman announced extensive economic reforms. In the following month price increases led to demonstrations in Bucharest, including a protest march by some 100,000 people, organized by a new opposition grouping, the Civic Alliance. Nevertheless, the Government proceeded with its (slightly modified) reform programme. In April 1991 Roman allocated three government portfolios to opposition politicians.

In September 1991 miners, by this time opposed to President Iliescu, began a strike in support of demands for pay increases and the resignation of the Government. Thousands of miners travelled to Bucharest, where they attacked government offices and ransacked the parliament building. Four people were killed and hundreds injured during violent clashes with the security forces, as a result of which the Council of Ministers was obliged to resign. Theodor Stolojan, a former Minister of Finance, was appointed as Prime Minister, leading a coalition Government formed in October, comprising members of the NSF, the NLP, the Agrarian Democratic Party of Romania (ADPR) and the Romanian Ecological Movement.

A new Constitution, enshrining a multi-party system, a free-market economy and guarantees of the respect of human rights, was approved by the legislature in November 1991 and was endorsed by some 77.3% of voters in a referendum in December. The results of local elections, which took place between February and April 1992, confirmed the decline in support for the NSF. Many seats were won by the centre-right Democratic Convention of Romania (DCR), an alliance of 18 parties and organizations, including the Christian-Democratic National Peasants' Party (CDNPP) and the Party of the Civic Alliance. The NSF divided into two factions, and in April the faction loyal to Iliescu, which favoured only limited reforms, was registered as the Democratic National Salvation Front (DNSF).

Against a background of renewed labour unrest, legislative and presidential elections took place on 27 September 1992. The DNSF won 117 of the 328 elective seats in the Camera Deputaților and 49 of the 143 seats in Senatul, making it the largest party in the new Parlamentul (Parliament). Its closest rival was the DCR, with 82 seats in the Camera Deputaților and 34 in Senatul. The NSF secured only 43 and 18 seats, respectively. In the presidential election, the two leading candidates, Iliescu and Emil Constantinescu, representing the DCR, proceeded to a second round of voting on 11 October, at which Iliescu won 61.4% of the votes cast. In November Nicolae Văcăroiu, an economist with no professed political party affiliation, formed a Government comprising equal numbers of DNSF members and independents.

The abolition of price subsidies for many basic commodities and services, from May 1993, precipitated renewed labour unrest. The Government's position was also undermined by successive confidence motions. Meanwhile, the DNSF had changed its name to the Party of Social Democracy of Romania (PSDR) in July and absorbed three other parties. In May, in an apparently similar attempt to distance itself from the events of 1989–90, Roman's NSF renamed itself the Democratic Party—National Salvation Front (DP—NSF). By late 1993 Văcăroiu's administration appeared increasingly unstable. In November a protest march in Bucharest, demanding rapid economic reforms, was the largest public demonstration in the country since the overthrow of the Ceaușescu regime. A government reorganization in March continued the pattern of single-party (PSDR) rule supplemented by independent 'technocrats' (although later in the year two members of the Romanian National Unity Party—RNUP—were appointed to the Council of Ministers). In November 1995 Iliescu approved legislation providing for the restitution of property confiscated by the communist regime in the late 1940s and 1950s.

In May 1996 the PSDR terminated its parliamentary co-operation with the RNUP. Although the PSDR secured the largest number of mayoral and council seats at the local elections in June, the results indicated a decline in support for the party. The DCR and the Social Democratic Union (SDU), formed by the DP—NSF and the Romanian Social Democratic Party (RSDP) in January, won control of many major cities, including Bucharest. In September the RNUP ministers were dismissed from the Government: the breakdown in relations with the PSDR had been exacerbated by the RNUP's opposition to the signing of a treaty with Hungary (see Minority Ethnic Groups).

The legislative and presidential elections of 1996

Legislative and presidential elections took place on 3 November 1996. The DCR won the largest number of parliamentary seats, with 122 of the 328 seats in the Camera Deputaților and 53 of the 143 seats in Senatul. The PSDR took 91 and 41 seats in the respective chambers, and the SDU 53 and 23. The DCR and the SDU subsequently reached agreement on political co-operation. In the first round of the presidential election, which was contested by 16 candidates, Iliescu won 32.3% of the valid votes cast, and Constantinescu took 28.2%. With the support of nearly all the opposition parties, Constantinescu, who had asserted his commitment to the integration of Romania into Western political, economic and defence institutions, was duly elected in a second round on 17 November, with 54.4% of the votes cast. At the end of November Victor Ciorbea of the DCR, the Mayor of Bucharest, was nominated as Prime Minister, and in mid-December a new coalition Government, comprising the DCR, the SDU and the Democratic Alliance of Hungarians in Romania (DAHR), took office.

Despite protests from opposition parties, the Government restored citizenship to former King Michael, who visited Romania in February 1997. Meanwhile, in January a National Council for Action against Corruption and Organized Crime, headed by Constantinescu, was established; a number of leading bankers were subsequently arrested, principally on charges of fraud, and several senior members of the security forces were dismissed. The arrest, in February, of Miron Cozma, the leader of the miners' demonstrations in Bucharest in June 1990 and September 1991, prompted protests from miners and their trade union leaders.

Several prominent members of the PSDR resigned from the party in June 1997, and formed a new party, the Alliance for Romania (AFR). A government reorganization in December, which included the appointment of a number of technocrats to principal portfolios, failed to ease mounting tensions within the coalition, and the DAHR temporarily suspended its participation in the Government.

Adrian Severin, Minister of State and Minister of Foreign Affairs, and a member of the DP (as the DP—NSF had been renamed), resigned in December 1997, after a judicial investigation failed to confirm his allegations that certain political leaders and newspaper editors were working with foreign intelligence services. In January 1998 the resignation of the Minister of Transport, Traian Băsescu of the DP, owing to his criticism of Ciorbea's Government, led the DP to demand his reinstatement, and DP ministers eventually withdrew from the Government.

In March 1998, in response to increasing pressure within the coalition, Ciorbea and his Government resigned. Radu Vasile, the Secretary-General of the CDNPP and a Deputy Chairman of Senatul, was designated Prime Minister in April. A new Council of Ministers was endorsed by Parlamentul in mid-April. As Romania's economic situation worsened, the Minister of Finance, Daniel Dăianu, was dismissed in September; he was replaced by Decebal Traian Remes. In October Sorin Dimitriu resigned as Minister of Privatization and head of the State Ownership Fund. Meanwhile, in September, after the DAHR threatened to leave the ruling coalition unless Parlamentul adopted legislation providing for the establishment of a minority-language university, the Government agreed to create an independent university in Cluj-Napoca for Hungarian and German minorities.

In January 1999 a strike by miners escalated when Vasile refused to negotiate with Cozma, who had been released from prison in mid-1998, after serving an 18-month sentence for the possession of firearms and ammunition. Encouraged by nationalist politicians (notably from the Greater Romania Party—GRP), 10,000–20,000 miners marched towards Bucharest, and in Costeşti, some 190 km north-west of Bucharest, violent clashes broke out with the security forces. Following emergency talks between the Prime Minister and miners' leaders, a temporary agreement was reached. The Minister of the Interior, Gavril Dejeu, resigned, amid severe criticism of the security forces' failure to halt the march; he was replaced by Constantin Dudu Ionescu. In February the Supreme Court of Justice sentenced Cozma, *in absentia*, to 18 years' imprisonment for undermining state authority. In protest, approximately 2,000–4,000 miners, led by Cozma, again marched towards Bucharest. The miners were stopped by the security forces some 160 km west of Bucharest, where more than 100 people were injured and one miner died during the violence that ensued; Cozma and several hundred miners were arrested. (In June 2002 Cozma was sentenced to an additional 12 years' imprisonment—to be served concurrently—for his involvement in the 1999 violence; in January 2007, however, it was reported that he had been granted early release.)

In early June 1999 the Camera Deputaţilor approved amendments to the electoral law, increasing the threshold for parliamentary representation from 3% to 5%, with alliances required to secure a further 3% for each member party. Later that month the Camera Deputaţilor voted in favour of providing public access to the files of the Securitate (although many documents were believed to have been destroyed); the President promulgated the legislation in December. In July Gen. Victor Stănculescu and Gen. Mihai Chiţac were sentenced to 15 years' imprisonment, having been found guilty of the murders of 72 people, by ordering the security forces to open fire on protesters during the Timişoara uprising in December 1989. The ruling was severely criticized by Victor Babiuc, the Minister of National Defence, whose ministry was ordered to pay damages to those wounded in the shootings and the relatives of the dead. (Babiuc resigned from the Government and from his party several months later.)

In November 1999 students undertook strike action, and some 10,000 trade union members participated in protest rallies to demand the resignation of the Government. In mid-December, as labour unrest continued, Constantinescu dismissed Vasile, after all seven CDNPP government ministers, followed by the three NLP ministers, resigned from the Government. Constantinescu nominated Mugur Isărescu, hitherto Governor of the National Bank of Romania (and without affiliation to any political party), as Prime Minister. The legislature subsequently approved the appointment of Isărescu and his Council of Ministers, which remained largely unchanged, although Roman joined the new Government as Minister of State and Minister of Foreign Affairs. Vasile was expelled from the CDNPP later that month.

In local elections, held on 4 June 2000, the PSDR won the largest proportion of the votes cast (36.7%). Băsescu left the Government, after being elected as Mayor of Bucharest. In July President Constantinescu unexpectedly announced that he would not stand for re-election at the forthcoming presidential election. In September the RSDP withdrew from the governing coalition, announcing that it was to merge with the main opposition party, the PSDR.

The legislative and presidential elections of 2000

Legislative and presidential elections took place concurrently on 26 November 2000. The PSDR secured 155 seats in the Camera Deputaţilor and 65 in Senatul, while the GRP obtained 84 and 37 seats, respectively. The rate of voter participation was the lowest recorded since the collapse of communism, at 57.5%. Representatives of the PSDR and the GRP were also the principal candidates in the presidential election, in which the former President, Iliescu, obtained 36.4% of the votes cast and Corneliu Vadim Tudor of the GRP won 28.3%. As neither candidate secured an overall majority, a 'run-off' election was held on 10 December, in which Iliescu won 66.8% of the votes cast. The increased support for the extreme nationalists was thought to reflect popular disillusionment with economic hardship and high unemployment.

In December 2000 President Iliescu nominated Adrian Năstase of the PSDR as Prime Minister. Năstase subsequently signed a joint statement on priorities for the development of Romania with the leaders of the DAHR, the NLP and the DP. Although Năstase insisted that the declaration did not represent a coalition agreement, the support of those parties enabled the PSDR to form a minority Government, and ensured the isolation of the GRP. The new, expanded Council of Ministers was sworn in on 28 December.

In February 2001 President Iliescu endorsed a law, which provided for the return of some 300,000 properties nationalized during the communist era to their original owners; it superseded legislation on the restitution of property that had been approved in 1995. In mid-June the PSDR and the RSDP formally merged, creating the Social Democratic Party (SDP), under the leadership of Prime Minister Năstase. In November some 15,000 people took part in a demonstration in Bucharest against poverty and the Government's austerity programme. A further large-scale protest took place in December.

In March 2002 attempts to tackle corruption led the Government to announce the establishment, with effect from September, of a new National Anti-corruption Prosecution Office. Also in March the Government sought to moderate the power of labour organizations through the signature of a 'social pact' with three of the five largest trade unions, which provided for an increased minimum wage and the creation of 10,000 jobs. In September Senatul approved a new law on political parties, which required all parties to re-register by 31 December, and to be composed of a minimum of 10,000 members from at least 21 of Romania's 41 administrative sub-divisions. On 10 November local elections took place in 21 counties, in which the SDP was the most successful party. In early 2003 a number of prominent CDNPP members were expelled from the party after participating in the foundation of the new Popular Action civic movement, led by former President Constantinescu; in February it was confirmed that the movement was to become a political party.

In June 2003 Năstase reorganized the Council of Ministers, reducing the number of portfolios from 23 to 14. In a referendum held on 18–19 October some 90% of votes cast by 55.7% of the electorate approved 79 proposed amendments to the Constitution, which aimed to bring it into conformity with EU requirements (by, *inter alia*, guaranteeing the right to private property, strengthening legal rights for ethnic minorities and limiting the powers of the executive branch of government). The revised Constitution entered into force on 29 October.

In March 2004 Năstase announced the appointment of three new Ministers of State (effectively deputy prime ministers). Three existing ministers also assumed the additional positions of Ministers of State. In August charges of abuse of office and embezzlement were brought against 79 people, including Băsescu (in his former capacity as Minister of Transport in 1991–92 and 1997–2000), relating to the alleged illegal sale of 16 ships from the national maritime fleet in 1991–2000. Some commentators suggested that the charge was an attempt to discredit the opposition prior to national legislative and presidential elections; Băsescu had been re-elected as Mayor of Bucharest two months earlier. In local elections held on 6 and 20 June 2004 the SDP received the greatest number of mayoral mandates, closely followed by the NLP. In September 2004 the SDP and the Humanist Party of Romania (HPR) formed an electoral alliance, the National Union. Meanwhile, the NLP and the DP announced their intention to contest the forthcoming legislative elections as the Justice and Truth Alliance.

The legislative and presidential elections of 2004

Legislative and presidential elections were held on 28 November 2004. The National Union emerged as the largest bloc in both chambers, with 132 seats (of a total of 332) in the Camera Deputaţilor and 57 (of a total of 137) in Senatul. The Justice and Truth Alliance received 112 seats in the Camera Deputaţilor and 49 in Senatul. The representation of the GRP was markedly reduced in both chambers, to 48 deputies in the lower chamber, and 21 senators. In the presidential ballot no candidate secured an absolute majority of votes cast, and Năstase (with 40.9%) and Traian Băsescu (with 33.9%) proceeded to a second round of voting on 12 December. In the 'run-off' election, Băsescu achieved a narrow victory, with 51.2% of the votes cast. Băsescu was inaugurated as President on 20 December (thus gaining immunity from prosecution). Năstase was elected as Chairman of the Camera Deputaţilor, and Văcăroiu, a Deputy Chairman of the SDP, was elected as Chairman of Senatul in a vote that was boycotted by senators of the Justice and Truth Alliance and the DAHR.

Băsescu nominated Călin Popescu-Tăriceanu to form a government. The HPR was persuaded to abandon its electoral partner, the SDP, to form a coalition with the NLP, the DP and the DAHR, although the parties only held one more seat than the requisite quorum in the bicameral legislature. On 28 December 2004 the new coalition Council of Ministers was approved by both chambers of the legislature. In February 2005 Popescu-Tăriceanu was elected as President of the NLP.

The HPR was renamed the Conservative Party (CP) in May 2005. In June Iliescu reportedly became the subject of an investigation into the deaths of six people during the demonstrations by miners in 1990 (see above); however, as a member of Senatul and a former Head of State, Iliescu was immune from prosecution. In late June Emil Boc was elected President of the DP. In early July the Constitutional Court rejected the Government's programme for judicial reform, prompting Popescu-Tăriceanu to announce that he intended to submit the resignation of his administration, in an attempt to precipitate early elections; in mid-July, however, an extraordinary session of Parlamentul approved amendments to the legislation, to accommodate the Court's objections. Popescu-Tăriceanu subsequently announced that his Government would remain in place in order to respond to severe flooding in central and eastern parts of the country. In August Popescu-Tăriceanu reorganized the Council of Ministers.

In October 2005 the EU Commissioner responsible for Enlargement, Olli Rehn, warned Romania that its planned accession to the European Union (EU, see p. 270) in 2007 could be subject to delay if measures were not taken to combat corruption and accelerate the pace of judicial reform. In early 2006 a number of political figures duly came under investigation as a result of allegations of fraud, and in January Năstase resigned from the leadership of the SDP, following concerns about the legitimacy of an inheritance received by his wife. In February Năstase was indicted on charges of bribery pertaining to the acquisition of land in 1998. Năstase resigned as Chairman of the Camera Deputaţilor in March, following a vote of no confidence by the SDP; he was succeeded by Bogdan Olteanu of the NLP. In December the CP announced its withdrawal from the coalition Government, prompting the resignation of two ministers and ending the parliamentary majority commanded by Popescu-Tăriceanu.

In January 2007 Băsescu accused Popescu-Tăriceanu of attempting to influence a criminal investigation against a close associate accused of financial misconduct. In February Mihai Ungureanu resigned as Minister of Foreign Affairs at the request of Popescu-Tăriceanu, after he had failed to inform the Government about the detention of two Romanian nationals by US forces in Iraq; Băsescu subsequently refused to endorse the Prime Minister's nomination of an NLP representative, Adrian Cioroianu, to the post. At the beginning of April Popescu-Tăriceanu accused Băsescu of provoking dissension within the Government and ended his party's coalition with the DP, thereby removing eight DP ministers. He formed a new minority Government, comprising 13 representatives of the NLP and four of the DAHR, which was approved by Parlamentul, with the support of the SDP, on 3 April (and endorsed by Băsescu on the following day). Cioroianu became Minister of Foreign Affairs, while Tudor Chiuariu of the NLP, who had hitherto headed the anti-corruption department in the Office of the Prime Minister, was appointed Minister of Justice. On 19 April a motion initiated by the SDP to suspend Băsescu from office on grounds of unconstitutional conduct (by creating political instability, pressurizing the judiciary and interfering in government affairs) was approved by Parlamentul, after receiving the support of the ruling coalition deputies. On 9 May, in accordance with EU requirements, Senatul approved legislation providing for the creation of a national agency to monitor the activities of civil servants, including parliamentary deputies, in an effort to prevent corruption. At a national referendum, held on 19 May, Băsescu's removal from office was opposed by about 74.5% of those who voted. Băsescu was officially reinstated as President on 23 May.

On 25 November 2007 elections (postponed since May) to 35 seats in the European Parliament (see below) were conducted. The DP won 13 seats and the SDP 10 seats, while the NLP secured six seats and its coalition partner, the DAHR, two seats; the Liberal Democratic Party (formed in late 2006 by breakaway members of the NLP, and led by Theodor Stolojan) won three seats, and the remaining seat was obtained by an independent. In December the DP merged with the Liberal Democratic Party to form the Democratic Liberal Party (DLP), under the continued leadership of Boc.

In December 2007 Chiuariu resigned as Minister of Justice, following the initiation of a criminal investigation into his alleged abuse of office. In January 2008 Băsescu refused to endorse Popescu-Tăriceanu's selected candidate, demanding that the new minister be a representative of a party other than the NLP. After the Constitutional Court ruled in support of Băsescu, in March Cătălin Marian Predoiu, a lawyer with no political affiliation, was appointed as the new Minister of Justice. Following the failure of a referendum held simultaneously with the legislative elections in November 2007, on the adoption of a single-mandate voting system, in March 2008 Senatul adopted legislation providing for the introduction of compromise electoral reforms: rather than the existing party list system, candidates were to be directly elected by an absolute majority of votes in single-member constituencies, while the overall distribution of seats in each chamber was to be determined by proportional representation among parties securing a minimum of 5% of votes cast nationally. Prior to local elections, Constantinescu's Popular Action party merged with the NLP. Local, county and municipal elections were conducted on 1 June, with a second round of voting held in mayoral elections, where required, on 15 June. Notably, Sorin Oprescu, an independent candidate who, none the less, was closely affiliated with the SDP (and had represented the party in Senatul in 2000–08), was elected as Mayor of Bucharest. In August the Camera Deputaţilor voted against the official prosecution of Năstase on charges of bribery. However, later that month Senatul voted in favour of investigating Paul Păcuraru, the Minister of Labour, the Family and Equal Opportunities, who was alleged to have accepted bribes. Năstase was finally indicted in May 2010.

The legislative and presidential elections of 2008–09

Elections to the bicameral legislature were conducted under the new, mixed-member system of proportional representation on 30 November 2008. The DLP marginally secured the greatest representation in both chambers, with 115 of the total 334 seats in the Camera Deputaţilor (and 32.4% of the votes cast), and 51 of 137 seats in Senatul (and 33.6% of the votes cast); the SDP, allied with the CP, won 114 seats (33.1% of votes) in the Camera Deputaţilor and 49 seats (34.2%) in Senatul, and the NLP 65 seats (18.6%) in the Camera Deputaţilor and 28 seats (18.7%) in Senatul. In early December Băsescu invited former Prime Minister Stolojan, of the DLP, to establish a new administration; however, Stolojan unexpectedly ceded the nomination to Boc. Following a coalition agreement between the DLP and the SDP, a new Government comprising members of both parties was approved by the legislature on 22 December. The Vice-President of the SDP, Dan Nica, became Deputy Prime Minister; the DLP and the SDP were each allocated nine ministries, while Predoiu retained the justice portfolio. In January 2009 the first SDP representative appointed as Minister of Administration and the Interior resigned, after attracting censure from the party for his nomination of a former associate of Băsescu as head of the intelligence service. In early February the candidate appointed to succeed him, Liviu Dragnea, also tendered his resignation after only 12 days in the post (reportedly after nominations he made were also rejected), citing an inadequate budget and tensions within the governing coalition. Nica additionally assumed the post of Minister of Administration and the Interior. Crin Antonescu was elected President of the NLP at a party congress in March, defeating the incumbent, Popescu-Tăriceanu.

At elections to the European Parliament, conducted on 7 June 2009, the SDP-CP alliance secured 11 of the country's 33 seats. The DLP obtained 10 seats, the NLP five seats, and the DAHR and the GRP three seats each. One independent candidate, Elena Băsescu, the daughter of the President, was elected. Some 27.7% of the electorate participated in voting.

Nica was dismissed from the Government in late September 2009, following comments he made regarding the potential for fraud in the presidential election due to take place in November, prompting the SDP to withdraw from the ruling coalition at the beginning of October. The DLP remained in office as a minority Government, with the party's ministers assuming temporary responsibility for the portfolios previously allocated to the SDP. In mid-October, however, Parlamentul approved a motion of no confidence in Boc's Government, marking the first time during the post-communist period that a Government had been dismissed by the legislature. The SDP, the NLP and the DAHR subsequently agreed to nominate Klaus Iohannis, the Mayor of Sibiu and leader of the Democratic Forum of Germans in Romania, to the premiership, but Băsescu instead designated economist Lucian Croitoru, an adviser to the National Bank of Romania, as Prime Minister. The SDP, the NLP and the DAHR refused to support Croitoru, whose proposed Council of Ministers was consequently rejected by Parlamentul in early November. Two days later Băsescu designated the Mayor of Bucharest's third administrative sector, Liviu Negoiță of the DLP, as Prime Minister, but his cabinet was not approved prior to the election. In late November the Court of Appeals ruled that Nica's dismissal from the Government in September had been illegal.

The first round of the presidential election, which was conducted on 22 November 2009 and contested by 12 candidates, was inconclusive: Băsescu secured 32.4% of the votes cast, followed by Mircea Geoană, the President of the SDP, with 31.2%, and NLP leader Antonescu, with 20.0%. A rate of voter participation of 54.4% was recorded. In a concurrently held referendum, in which 50.9% of the electorate participated, 77.8% of voters endorsed a proposal by Băsescu for the legislature to be restructured into a single chamber, while 88.8% supported a reduction in the number of legislators from 471 to 300. Băsescu narrowly defeated Geoană in a second round of presidential voting on 6 December, securing 50.3% of the votes cast; 58.0% of the electorate participated in the ballot. The SDP and the CP challenged the results, alleging that electoral violations had taken place, but the Constitutional Court rejected their appeal for an annulment. On 17 December Băsescu nominated acting Prime Minister Boc to form a new government; two days earlier Negoiță had stood down as Prime Minister-designate.

Băsescu was inaugurated to serve a second term as President on 21 December 2009. On 23 December Parlamentul approved Boc's new Council of Ministers, which comprised nine members of the DLP, four members of the DAHR and four independents. The President of the DAHR, Markó Béla, was appointed Deputy Prime Minister.

Recent developments: the second Government of Emil Boc

The coalition Government's most immediate challenge was to secure the adoption of austerity measures demanded by the IMF and other donors (see Economic Affairs). In early February 2010, however, an estimated 45,000 workers participated in a two-hour 'warning' strike in protest against plans to reduce salaries and employment in the public sector. Victor Ponta was elected President of the SDP at a party congress later that month, defeating Geoană.

In early March 2010 the Government decided to publish nearly 8,000 hitherto secret documents relating to the overthrow of the Ceaușescu regime in December 1989. In April, just one month after the European Commission had criticized Romania over its lack of progress in combating corruption, the Constitutional Court made a decision to limit the powers of the National Integrity Agency (established in 2007 on the recommendation of the EU to increase the accountability of public officials), declaring its main functions to be unconstitutional. The decision was opposed by democracy activists, and Boc announced that he intended to reverse the Court's decision by means of an emergency decree. The European Commission subsequently urged the Romanian Government to resolve the issue.

On 21 April 2010 Boc's administration adopted a draft proposal on reducing the size of the legislature from 471 seats to 300, as approved by the 2009 referendum. In May 2010 the Camera Deputaților passed legislation prohibiting former high-ranking communists from standing for public office for five years. On 15 June the Government secured a narrow victory (with 228 votes cast in favour, and 197 against) in a no confidence vote in parliament, over proposed austerity measures. Opposition parties subsequently appealed to the Constitutional Court, which ruled in late June that the proposed reduction of 15% in pensions was unconstitutional. On the same day demonstrators attempted to storm the presidential palace.

In July 2010, in a report issued by the European Commission, Romania was criticized for demonstrating insufficient commitment to the eradication of corruption and fraud and was urged to implement judicial reforms. On 2 September Prime Minister Boc replaced six members of the cabinet, including those responsible for finance and the economy, prompting demands for Boc's resignation from within the DLP. At the end of the month the Minister of Administration and the Interior, Vasile Blaga, resigned his post following a protest by police against the proposed austerity measures. In late October a proposed vote of no confidence by opposition parties failed to secure the requisite number of votes in Parlamentul. In early December Parlamentul finally adopted a pensions law, which set the retirement age at 63 years for women and 65 years for men; this was subsequently approved by the Constitutional Court. None the less, opposition parties continued their campaign against austerity measures; Boc subsequently survived two further votes of no confidence in Parlamentul. Meanwhile, in mid-December Geoană was suspended from the SDP for six months, after accusing Victor Ponta of advising him to give false information during his 2009 presidential campaign. It was agreed, however, that Geoană would retain support from the party in his role as Chairman of Senatul.

In February 2011 the European Commission published a report stating that Romania had made 'significant progress' in combating corruption, but urging the country to continue to pursue high-level corruption cases. Also in February the head of the National Authority for Customs was indicted by anti-corruption prosecutors on charges of accepting bribes, and dismissed; his dismissal formed part of a large-scale operation against border corruption, which resulted in the arrests of some 200 police officers and customs officials on the country's borders with Ukraine, Serbia and Moldova during that month. In mid-March a no confidence motion against Boc was defeated in Parlamentul. The vote was linked to the implementation of a labour law introducing contracts for temporary workers and increasing penalties for illegal employment, as required by Romania's international creditors. While several thousand protesters gathered in front of the parliament building and demanded Boc's resignation, opposition parties announced their intention to challenge the legislation in the Constitutional Court.

In April 2011 the Minister of Labour, the Family and Social Welfare, Ioan Boțis, resigned following an inquiry into the Minister's assets, and claims of a conflict of interest involving his wife's involvement as an adviser for an EU-funded programme.

Minority Ethnic Groups

Romania experienced frequent occurrences of ethnic unrest after the fall of Ceaușescu. In 1991 there were organized attacks on Roma (Gypsy) communities throughout Romania, resulting in the emigration of many Roma to Germany. In September 1992 Germany repatriated 43,000 Romanian refugees, more than one-half of whom were Roma, having agreed to provide financial assistance for their resettlement in Romania. In January 2002 the Council of Europe (see p. 250) published a report condemning police brutality and widespread discrimination against Roma communities in Romania, and the EU made the improvement of the treatment of the Roma minority a requirement for Romania to be declared eligible to accede to the Union. In February 2005 Romania was one of eight countries in the region to announce its adherence to a World Bank-financed 10-year plan to assist the Roma community. In December 2010 the introduction of a bill in Parlamentul proposing to change the official name of the Roma to 'Țigan', a term often considered pejorative, was opposed by activists within the Roma minority. In March 2011 President Băsescu signed a law designating 20 February an official holiday in Romania to commemorate the abolition of slavery of the Roma population in 1856.

Following the overthrow of Ceaușescu, ethnic Hungarians (a sizeable minority, numbering more than 7% of the total population at the 1992 census) sought to increase their cultural and linguistic autonomy in Transylvania. In March 1990 demonstrations by ethnic Hungarians demanding such rights were attacked by Romanian nationalists in Târgu Mureș. Tanks and troops were deployed to quell the unrest, in which several people were killed, and a state of emergency was declared in the town. In mid-1992 there was renewed tension when the Mayor of Cluj-Napoca, Gheorghe Funar (later head of the right-wing RNUP), ordered the removal of Hungarian-language street signs in the city, and ethnic Hungarian prefects in Covasna and Harghita were replaced by ethnic Romanians. The Government attempted to calm the situation by appointing 'parallel' prefects of ethnic Hungarian background, but further controversy was caused by the removal, in September, of the only ethnic Hungarian State Secretary in the Government. An agreement on Hungarian minority rights was signed in July 1993, which included guarantees for the training of Hungarian-speaking schoolteachers and bilingual street signs in areas with Hungarian populations of at least 30%. In May Romania ratified the

Framework Convention of the Council of Europe on the general protection of national minorities. In September 1996 Romania and Hungary signed a treaty of friendship, as a result of which Romania agreed to safeguard the rights of ethnic Hungarians, and Hungary relinquished any claim to territory in Transylvania. In December two DAHR leaders were appointed to the new Government. Relations between Romania and Hungary improved further in February 1997 with the signature of a defence co-operation agreement. Proposals to amend legislation on education, in favour of ethnic minorities, provoked controversy in Romania in 1997 and 1998, although the amendments were finally approved in June 1999.

In January 2001 the Camera Deputaţilor approved a new public administration law, which made compulsory bilingual place names and signs, and the use of a given minority's language in local administration, in towns where that minority formed at least 20% of the population. In June the Government condemned Hungary's intention to introduce a new 'status law', which was to grant education, employment and medical rights to ethnic Hungarians living in neighbouring countries (including Romania) from January 2002. In December 2001 the Prime Ministers of the two countries signed a memorandum of understanding, which extended the short-term employment rights offered to ethnic Hungarians under the terms of the status law to all Romanian citizens. Finally, in September 2003 Prime Minister Năstase and his Hungarian counterpart, Péter Medgyessy, signed a bilateral agreement on the implementation of the status law in Romania. Hungary proved to be a staunch supporter of Romania's candidacy for EU membership. In October 2005 the first joint Romanian-Hungarian inter-governmental meeting was held in Bucharest, at which a treaty was concluded on the border regime, co-operation and mutual assistance.

Foreign Affairs

Regional relations

Diplomatic relations with the former Soviet republic of Moldova (much of which formed part of Romania in 1918–40, and where a majority of the population are ethnic Romanians) were established in August 1991, and some political groups began to advocate the unification of the two states. The Romanian leadership opposed unification, but encouraged the development of closer cultural and economic ties with Moldova. In March 1994 a plebiscite was held in Moldova on the question of reunification with Romania; more than 95% of those who took part in the referendum voted for an independent state, effectively signalling the demise of the pro-unification movement. In 2000, as formal negotiations on Romania's accession to the EU commenced, hundreds of Moldovans applied for Romanian citizenship, in anticipation of the eventual tightening of border regulations. After Romania's accession to the EU on 1 January 2007 necessitated the possession of entry visas for Moldovan citizens wishing to visit Romania, the Moldovan Government strongly criticized Romania for granting Romanian citizenship to large numbers of Moldovan nationals, and in March reversed a decision to allow Romania to open two new consulates in the country. In December Moldova expelled two Romanian diplomats, who had allegedly supplied funds to opposition newspapers. Violent protests in Moldova, which erupted in April 2009 following legislative elections, precipitated a breach in relations with Romania. The Moldovan President, Vladimir Voronin, accused the Romanian Government of organizing a coup attempt (since many of the protesters had exhibited pro-Romanian sentiments) and expelled the Romanian ambassador, recalled the Moldovan envoy in Bucharest and introduced visa requirements for Romanians (thereby refusing a number of Romanian journalists entry to Moldova). Romania demanded an EU investigation into alleged abuses by the Moldovan authorities. Băsescu subsequently pledged that the Romanian Government would expedite the process of granting Romanian citizenship to Moldovans, claiming that some 1m. applications had been received. Bilateral relations improved in September, following Voronin's resignation as President of Moldova and the formation of a pro-Western Government in that country; the new acting Moldovan President, Mihai Ghimpu, swiftly abolished the visa requirements imposed on Romanians in April. In November, moreover, the Romanian and Moldovan Prime Ministers signed a Convention on Small-Scale Border Traffic, allowing Moldovan citizens residing within 50 km of the joint border (an estimated 1.2m. people) to travel within an equivalent area in Romania without requiring a visa. The signature of the Convention, which entered into force in February 2010, had been repeatedly delayed owing to the Moldovan Government's previous unwillingness to sign the document prior to the conclusion of a border treaty. In April Băsescu and his Moldovan counterpart signed a joint declaration urging a strategic partnership between the two countries to assist with Moldova's objective of accession to the EU. In November the border treaty was finally signed.

A basic treaty between Romania and Ukraine, signed in June 1997, guaranteed the inviolability of their joint border, and provided for separate treaties to be established regarding the administration of the frontier and the disputed ownership of the Black Sea continental shelf. In June 2003 President Iliescu and President Leonid Kuchma of Ukraine signed an accord confirming the mutual land border of the two countries, as it was delineated in 1961, with the exception of the continental shelf. No further progress was made in resolving the disagreement over the disputed maritime area (comprising an islet, known as Serpents' Island, and surrounding waters, which were believed to have significant petroleum and gas reserves). In 2004 both states agreed to refer the issue to the International Court of Justice (ICJ, see p. 23). In February 2009 the ICJ finally issued a ruling awarding some 79% of the maritime area under dispute to Romania.

An association agreement with the European Community (now EU) was signed in February 1993; in June 1995 Romania formally applied for full membership of the EU. In October 1993 Romania was admitted to the Council of Europe. In December 1999 Romania was one of six countries invited to begin negotiations on possible entry to the EU, and formal accession talks commenced in February 2000. In December the EU decided to impose conditions on Romania before granting its citizens the right to visa-free travel in Europe, partly in response to Romania's failure to combat illegal immigration. In December 2004 Romania concluded accession negotiations, but with a cautionary clause whereby the country's accession could be delayed by one year if it failed to meet its reform commitments. In April 2005 members of the European Parliament voted to approve 2007 as the anticipated accession date for Romania. Formal accession agreements were signed by both Bulgaria and Romania on 25 April 2005. In May both chambers of the legislature unanimously ratified the EU accession treaty.

In May 2006 the European Commission announced that a final decision on Romania's scheduled date of accession to the EU was to be postponed until October, and emphasized the need to implement further reform measures. In a report issued at the end of September, the European Commission confirmed that Romania was sufficiently prepared to meet the accession criteria by 1 January 2007, but also identified issues requiring further attention; the Co-operation and Verification Mechanism (CVM) was to be established to further progress in the areas of judicial reform and measures against corruption. Romania's accession to the EU on 1 January 2007 was welcomed with mass celebrations in Bucharest. In January 2011 the admission of Romania (and Bulgaria) to the EU's Schengen area (which provides for free movement between EU member states and the strengthening of border controls with non-members), hitherto anticipated to take place in March, was postponed, owing to concern from some EU countries, particularly France and Germany, about the readiness of the two Balkan countries.

Other external relations

In early 1997 Romania appealed directly to member countries of the North Atlantic Treaty Organization (NATO, see p. 368) to support its candidacy for admittance to the Alliance. Following the large-scale suicide attacks against the USA on 11 September 2001, attributed by the USA to the Saudi-born Islamist fundamentalist Osama bin Laden (see the chapter on the USA), Romania immediately pledged full co-operation with US anti-terrorism efforts and opened its airspace to US military flights to and from Afghanistan, the Taliban regime of which was harbouring militants of bin Laden's al-Qa'ida organization. Romania made available basing facilities in the port city of Constanţa, and offered the USA the use of its air bases. The Romanian intelligence services were restructured in January 2002, and Romania secured an invitation to join NATO at a summit meeting held in Prague, Czech Republic, in November, after which US President George W. Bush paid a visit to the country. Romania supported US-led military action in Iraq in early 2003, opening its airspace and offering other resources to the coalition. Romania was officially admitted to NATO on 29 March 2004, together with six other countries. In December 2005 the US Secretary of State signed an agreement with the Romanian Minister of Foreign

ROMANIA

Affairs, granting US troops access to military bases under the command of the Romanian army. Romania hosted a NATO summit meeting in Bucharest on 2–4 April 2008. In January 2010 the Romanian Supreme Defence Council decided to reinforce the 1,020-member Romanian contingent deployed in Afghanistan by a further 600 troops. In the following month the Council approved the deployment in Romania of elements of a proposed US missile defence system (prompting criticism from the Russian Government); negotiations were to be conducted on a detailed plan for the establishment, by 2015, of interceptors on Romanian territory, which would require the approval of Parlamentul.

CONSTITUTION AND GOVERNMENT

Under the Constitution of 1991 (and as subsequently modified, most substantially in 2003), legislative power is vested in the bicameral Parlamentul (Parliament), comprising the Camera Deputaților (Chamber of Deputies, lower house) and Senatul (the Senate, upper house). Parlamentul is elected by universal adult suffrage for a term of four years. Executive power is vested in the President of the Republic, who may serve a maximum of two five-year terms and who is directly elected by universal adult suffrage. The President appoints the Prime Minister, who in turn appoints the Council of Ministers. Judicial power is exercised by the High Court of Cassation and Justice, as well as county and local courts.

For administrative purposes, Romania comprises 40 administrative divisions (counties) and the municipality of Bucharest.

REGIONAL AND INTERNATIONAL CO-OPERATION

Romania is a member of the European Bank for Reconstruction and Development (EBRD, see p. 265), of the Council of Europe (see p. 250) and of the Organization of the Black Sea Economic Co-operation (see p. 398). In 2007 Romania acceded to the European Union (see p. 270).

Romania became a member of the UN in 1955 and, as a contracting party to the General Agreement on Tariffs and Trade, joined the World Trade Organization (see p. 430) on its establishment in 1995. In 2004 Romania joined the North Atlantic Treaty Organization (see p. 368).

ECONOMIC AFFAIRS

In 2009, according to the World Bank, Romania's gross national income (GNI), measured at average 2007–09 prices, totalled US $178,900m., equivalent to $8,330 per head (or $14,460 per head on an international purchasing-power parity basis). During 2000–09, it was estimated, the population decreased at an average annual rate of 0.5%, while gross domestic product (GDP) per head increased, in real terms, at an average annual rate of 5.2%. Overall GDP increased, in real terms, by an average of 4.7% annually during 2000–09. Real GDP increased by 9.4% in 2008, but declined by 8.5% in 2009.

Agriculture (including hunting, forestry and fishing) contributed 6.7% of GDP in 2010 and the sector employed 28.8% of the employed labour force in 2008. The principal crops are maize, wheat, potatoes, sunflower seeds, barley and grapes. Wine production plays a significant role. Forestry, the cropping of reeds (used as a raw material in the paper and cellulose industry) and the breeding of fish are also important. By 1999, according to the IMF, some 97.2% of agricultural land was privately owned. During 2000–09, according to the World Bank, agricultural GDP increased, in real terms, by an average of 8.0% per year. Real agricultural GDP increased by 5.9% in 2009.

Industry (including mining, manufacturing, construction, power and water) accounted for 39.7% of GDP in 2010 and employed 31.4% of the working population in 2008. According to the World Bank, industrial GDP increased, in real terms, by an average of 6.0% annually in 2000–09. Real industrial GDP increased by 5.9% in 2009.

The mining sector employed 1.1% of the employed labour force in 2008. Lignite (brown coal), hard coal, salt, iron ore, bauxite, copper, lead and zinc are mined. Onshore production of crude petroleum began to increase in the early 1990s. At the end of 2007 Romania had proven reserves of 500m. barrels of petroleum, remaining the largest producer in central and eastern Europe, despite a dramatic decline in production. IMF figures indicated that mining output declined by 0.3% in 2005.

Manufacturing accounted for 21.6% of GDP in 2009, according to the World Bank, and engaged 20.6% of the employed labour force in the previous year. The sector is based mainly on the metallurgical, mechanical engineering, chemical and timber-processing industries. However, many industries (particularly iron and steel) have been hampered by shortages of electricity and raw materials. According to the World Bank, manufacturing GDP increased, in real terms, by an average of 5.5% annually in 2005–09. Real sectoral GDP increased by some 5.0% in 2009.

In 2010 construction accounted for 10.0% of GDP and employed 8.0% of the working population.

According to the World Bank, in 2007 some 41.0% of gross electricity production was derived from coal, 25.9% from hydroelectric power, 18.7% from natural gas and 12.5% from nuclear power. The initial unit of Romania's first nuclear power station, at Cernavoda, became operational in December 1996; the second (700 MW) unit entered into operation in 2008. A further two units at the site were expected to commence operations by around 2016. A natural gas pipeline to connect the country with Hungary, and ultimately with a 'corridor' between Austria and Turkey (the Nabucco project), was under construction. In April 2008 Romania signed an agreement with Croatia and Serbia on a project that envisaged the construction of a pipeline linking the Romanian port city of Constanța with Trieste, Italy, via Croatia, Serbia and Slovenia. According to official data, 36.1% of energy resources were imported in 2005. In that year mineral fuels accounted for 14.0% of total imports. In 2009 mineral fuels comprised 9.3% of total imports.

According to official figures, the services sector contributed 53.6% of GDP in 2010, and engaged 39.8% of the labour force in 2008. The GDP of the services sector increased, in real terms, by an average of 5.3% per year in 2000–09; the real GDP of the sector increased by 6.4% in 2009.

In 2009 Romania recorded a visible trade deficit of US $9,482m., and there was a deficit of $7,298m. on the current account of the balance of payments. In 2009 the principal source of imports was Germany, which provided 17.3% of the total. Other major suppliers were Italy, Hungary and France. Germany was also the main market for exports in that year (accounting for 18.8% of the total); other important purchasers were Italy and France. In 2009 the principal imports were machinery and transport equipment (32.9%), basic manufactures, chemical products, mineral fuels and lubricants, miscellaneous manufactured articles and food and live animals. The major exports in that year were machinery and transport equipment (42.6%), miscellaneous manufactured articles, basic manufactures, mineral fuels, and chemical products.

In 2010, according to the IMF, the overall budget deficit was estimated at 33,125m. new lei. Romania's general government gross debt was 146,938m. new lei in 2009, equivalent to 29.9% of GDP. Romania's total external debt in 2008 was US $104,943m., of which $14,988m. was public and publicly guaranteed debt. In that year the cost of debt-servicing was equivalent to 25.3% of the value of exports of goods, services and income. The annual rate of inflation averaged 12.8% in 2000–09; the rate of inflation was 7.8% in 2008 and 5.6% in 2009. In 2008 some 5.8% of the labour force were unemployed.

Romania's progress towards the development of a market economic system was considerably slower than that of many other post-communist states of Central and Eastern Europe. None the less, the Romanian economy demonstrated considerable growth prior to EU accession on 1 January 2007. However, the increasing severity of the global economic crisis challenged the implementation of the Government's economic plans from late 2008, and in March 2009 multilateral financial assistance amounting to €19,900m. was announced for Romania to support an IMF-supervised programme of reforms. Political instability in late 2009 (see Domestic Political Affairs) impeded the implementation of structural reforms demanded by the IMF, which had contributed €12,900m. in the form of a two-year stand-by loan. The new Government, formed in December, envisaged a budget deficit for 2010 equivalent to 5.9% of GDP; this was revised to 6.8% in June 2010. Austerity measures introduced to meet IMF demands included a 25% reduction in public-sector wages and a 5% increase in value-added tax (VAT), to 24%. In December Parlamentul (Parliament) finally approved the proposed reforms to the pension system and the raising of the retirement age to 65. Although these measures satisfied the requirements of international institutions, Romania continued to experience recession, as declining demand affected industrial production. GDP contracted by an estimated 2.0% in 2010, while foreign direct investment declined by 25.6%, according to the central bank. The rate of inflation reached 8% in December 2010, the highest level recorded in

ROMANIA

more than two years, while the rate of unemployment was some 9%. None the less, economic growth, of around 1.5%, was anticipated for 2011. The budget deficit for 2011 was projected to represent some 4.4% of GDP. GDP contracted by an estimated 2.0% in 2010, while foreign direct investment declined by 25.6%, according to the central bank.

PUBLIC HOLIDAYS

2012: 1–2 January (New Year), 6 January (Epiphany), 15–16 April (Orthodox Easter), 1 May (Labour Day), 4 June (Pentecost Monday), 15 August (Dormition of the Virgin Mary), 1 December (National Day), 25–26 December (Christmas).

Statistical Survey

Source (unless otherwise indicated): Institutul National de Statistică (National Institute of Statistics), 050706 Bucharest, Bd. Libertății 16; tel. (21) 3124875; fax (21) 3124873; e-mail romstat@insse.ro; internet www.insse.ro/cms/rw/pages/index.ro.do.

Area and Population

AREA, POPULATION AND DENSITY

Area (sq km)	238,391*
Population (census results)	
7 January 1992	22,810,035
18–27 March 2002	
Males	10,568,741
Females	11,112,233
Total	21,680,974
Population (official estimates at 1 January)	
2008	21,528,627
2009	21,498,616
2010†	21,462,186
Density (per sq km) at 1 January 2010	90.0

* 92,043 sq miles.
† Preliminary.

POPULATION BY AGE AND SEX
(official estimates at 1 January 2010)

	Males	Females	Total
0–14	1,669,453	1,582,665	3,252,118
15–64	7,483,671	7,519,989	15,003,660
65 and over	1,297,969	1,908,439	3,206,408
Total	10,451,093	11,011,093	21,462,186

POPULATION BY ETHNIC GROUP
(2002 census)

	Number	% of total
Romanian	19,399,597	89.5
Hungarian	1,431,807	6.6
Gypsy (Roma)	535,140	2.5
Others and unknown	314,430	1.5
Total	21,680,974	100.0

ADMINISTRATIVE DIVISIONS
(estimates at 1 January 2010)

	Area (sq km)	Population	Density (per sq km)	Administrative capital
Counties				
Alba	6,242	373,134	59.8	Alba Iulia
Arad	7,754	455,477	58.7	Arad
Argeș	6,826	640,484	93.8	Pitești
Bacău	6,621	716,260	108.2	Bacău
Bihor	7,544	592,957	78.6	Oradea
Bistrița-Năsăud	5,355	317,316	59.3	Bistrița
Botoșani	4,986	448,749	90.0	Botoșani
Brăila	4,766	359,119	75.4	Brăila
Brașov	5,363	598,208	111.5	Brașov
Buzău	6,103	481,694	78.9	Buzău
Călărași	5,088	312,697	61.5	Călărași
Caraș-Severin	8,520	322,060	37.8	Reșița
Cluj	6,674	692,339	103.7	Cluj-Napoca
Constanța	7,071	723,696	102.3	Constanța
Covasna	3,710	222,481	60.0	Sfântu Gheorghe
Dâmbovița	4,054	530,332	130.8	Târgoviște
Dolj	7,414	704,436	95.0	Craiova
Galați	4,466	609,398	136.5	Galați
Giurgiu	3,526	280,959	79.7	Giurgiu
Gorj	5,602	376,916	67.3	Târgu Jiu
Harghita	6,639	325,127	49.0	Miercurea-Ciuc
Hunedoara	7,063	463,102	65.6	Deva
Ialomița	4,453	287,678	64.6	Slobozia
Iași	5,476	824,780	150.6	Iași
Ilfov*	1,593	317,247	199.2	Bucharest
Maramureș	6,304	511,093	81.1	Baia Mare
Mehedinți	4,933	292,231	59.2	Drobeta-Turnu Severin
Mureș	6,714	580,672	86.5	Târgu Mureș
Neamț	5,896	563,392	95.6	Piatra Neamț
Olt	5,498	465,019	84.6	Slatina
Prahova	4,716	814,689	172.8	Ploiești
Sălaj	3,864	241,417	62.5	Zalău
Satu Mare	4,418	364,597	82.5	Satu Mare
Sibiu	5,432	424,796	78.2	Sibiu
Suceava	8,553	708,109	82.8	Suceava
Teleorman	5,790	400,431	69.2	Alexandria
Timiș	8,697	678,795	78.0	Timișoara
Tulcea	8,499	246,785	29.0	Tulcea
Vâlcea	5,765	407,431	70.7	Râmnicu Vâlcea
Vaslui	5,318	451,106	84.8	Vaslui
Vrancea	4,857	390,526	80.4	Focșani
Capital City				
Bucharest*	228	1,944,451	8,528.3	Bucharest
Total	238,391	21,462,186	90.0	

* Although Bucharest is a separate administrative division, the city is also the capital of the surrounding Ilfov County. The area and population given for Ilfov County do not include data for Bucharest.

PRINCIPAL TOWNS
(at 1 January 2009)

București (Bucharest, the capital)	1,944,367	Arad	166,003
Timișoara	311,586	Sibiu	154,548
Iași	308,843	Târgu Mureș	145,151
Cluj-Napoca	306,474	Baia Mare	139,154
Constanța	302,171	Buzău	132,210
Craiova	298,928	Botoșani	116,110
Galați	291,354	Satu Mare	112,705
Brașov	278,048	Râmnicu Vâlcea	110,901
Ploiești	229,285	Piatra Neamț	107,504
Brăila	212,501	Suceava	106,934
Oradea	204,477	Drobeta-Turnu Severin	106,507
Bacău	177,087	Focșani	98,467
Pitești	166,893		

ROMANIA

BIRTHS, MARRIAGES AND DEATHS

	Registered live births Number	Rate (per 1,000)	Registered marriages Number	Rate (per 1,000)	Registered deaths Number	Rate (per 1,000)
2002	210,529	9.7	129,018	5.9	269,666	12.4
2003	212,459	9.8	133,953	6.2	266,575	12.3
2004	216,261	10.0	143,304	6.6	258,890	11.9
2005	221,020	10.2	141,832	6.6	262,101	12.1
2006	219,483	10.2	146,637	6.8	258,094	12.0
2007	214,728	10.0	189,240	8.8	251,965	11.7
2008	221,900	10.3	149,439	6.9	253,202	11.8
2009	222,388	10.3	134,275	6.2	257,213	12.0

Life expectancy (years at birth, WHO estimates): 73 (males 70; females 77) in 2008 (Source: WHO, *World Health Statistics*).

ECONOMICALLY ACTIVE POPULATION
(labour force surveys, '000 persons aged 15 years and over)

	2006	2007	2008
Agriculture, hunting and forestry	2,840.3	2,756.7	2,689.9
Fishing*	3.1	5.3	4.3
Mining and quarrying	119.7	109.2	107.2
Manufacturing	1,978.5	1,973.8	1,929.8
Electricity, gas and water	197.5	175.9	161.4
Construction	557.6	678.6	746.4
Wholesale and retail trade; repair of motor vehicles, motorcycles, and personal and household goods	1,049.3	1,151.4	1,178.2
Hotels and restaurants	143.0	136.6	154.2
Transport, storage and communications	491.8	488.7	508.5
Financial intermediation	92.0	97.2	110.4
Real estate, renting and business services	281.6	282.0	298.3
Public administration	507.5	468.4	476.1
Education	410.6	400.2	396.9
Health and social assistance	378.3	375.4	396.0
Other services	262.5	253.9	211.5
Total employed	9,313.3	9,353.3	9,369.1
Unemployed	728.4	641.0	575.5
Total labour force	10,041.7	9,994.3	9,944.6
Males	5,526.4	5,515.0	5,526.6
Females	4,515.3	4,479.3	4,418.0

*Figures obtained as residuals.

Source: ILO.

Health and Welfare

KEY INDICATORS

Total fertility rate (children per woman, 2008)	1.3
Under-5 mortality rate (per 1,000 live births, 2008)	13
HIV/AIDS (% of persons aged 15–49, 2007)	0.1
Physicians (per 1,000 head, 2006)	1.9
Hospital beds (per 1,000 head, 2006)	6.5
Health expenditure (2007): US $ per head (PPP)	369
Health expenditure (2007): % of GDP	4.7
Health expenditure (2007): public (% of total)	80.3
Access to water (% of persons, 2006)	88
Access to sanitation (% of persons, 2008)	72
Total carbon dioxide emissions ('000 metric tons, 2007)	94,106.2
Carbon dioxide emissions per head (metric tons, 2007)	4.4
Human Development Index (2010): ranking	50
Human Development Index (2010): value	0.767

For sources and definitions, see explanatory note on p. vi.

Agriculture

PRINCIPAL CROPS
('000 metric tons)

	2007	2008	2009
Wheat	3,044.5	7,181.0	5,202.5
Barley	531.4	1,209.4	1,182.1
Maize	3,853.9	7,849.1	7,973.3
Rye	20.6	31.4	33.0
Oats	251.6	382.0	295.8
Potatoes	3,712.4	3,649.0	4,004.0
Sugar beet	748.8	706.7	816.8
Beans, dry	18.0	25.2	22.3
Peas, dry	17.3	36.3	29.9
Walnuts, with shell	25.5	32.3	38.3
Soybeans (Soya beans)	136.1	90.6	84.3
Sunflower seed	546.9	1,169.9	1,098.0
Rapeseed	361.5	673.0	569.6
Cabbages and other brassicas	899.2	967.6	1,004.2
Lettuce and chicory	6.8	1.7	1.9
Tomatoes	640.8	814.4	755.6
Pumpkins, squash and gourds	62.1	52.4	96.5
Cucumbers and gherkins	119.8	173.6	176.5
Chillies and peppers, green	184.9	238.7	245.7
Onions, dry	325.0	395.6	378.1
Garlic	49.9	72.3	63.2
Beans, green	45.5	61.6	55.9
Peas, green	16.3	25.4	20.5
Watermelons	374.5	508.5	602.8
Cantaloupes and other melons	33.4	53.8	50.0
Apples	475.4	459.0	517.5
Pears	62.9	52.6	66.1
Cherries	65.2	67.7	67.9
Apricots	27.6	32.1	32.5
Plums and sloes	372.6	475.3	533.7
Grapes	873.2	996.0	990.2
Tobacco, unmanufactured	1.1	2.4	1.6

Aggregate production ('000 metric tons, may include official, semi-official or estimated data): Total cereals 7,806.6 in 2007, 16,811.1 in 2008, 14,849.8 in 2009; Total roots and tubers 3,712.4 in 2007, 3,649.0 in 2008, 4,004.0 in 2009; Total vegetables (incl. melons) 3,119.0 in 2007, 3,821.5 in 2008, 3,904.1 in 2009; Total fruits (excl. melons) 1,959.2 in 2007, 2,195.3 in 2008, 2,321.9 in 2009.

Source: FAO.

LIVESTOCK
('000 head, year ending September)

	2007	2008	2009
Horses	805	862	820
Cattle	2,934	2,819	2,684
Pigs	6,815	6,565	6,174
Sheep	7,678	8,469	8,882
Goats	727	865	898
Chickens	84,991	82,036	84,373

Source: FAO.

LIVESTOCK PRODUCTS
('000 metric tons)

	2007	2008	2009
Cattle meat	164.6	149.7	155.2
Sheep meat	50.4	46.7	70.7
Goat meat	4.4	4.2	4.4
Pig meat	470.2	439.0	470.5
Horse meat*	9.4	9.4	9.5
Chicken meat	312.1	316.0	371.4
Cows' milk	5,652.1	5,468.2	5,208.7
Sheep's milk	637.7	656.8	600.4
Hen eggs	311.3	333.6	297.3
Other poultry eggs	14.8	11.3	13.3
Honey	16.8	19.8	19.9
Wool, greasy*	21.0	17.7	n.a.

*FAO estimates.

Source: FAO.

ROMANIA

Forestry

ROUNDWOOD REMOVALS
('000 cubic metres, excluding bark)

	2007	2008	2009
Sawlogs, veneer logs and logs for sleepers	9,777	8,255	7,222
Pulpwood	1,248	601	489
Other industrial wood	547	661	877
Fuel wood	3,769	4,150	3,969
Total	15,341	13,667	12,557

Source: FAO.

SAWNWOOD PRODUCTION
('000 cubic metres, including railway sleepers)

	2007	2008	2009
Coniferous (softwood)	2,159	2,202	2,087
Broadleaved (hardwood)	1,984	1,592	1,510
Total	4,143	3,794	3,597

Source: FAO.

Fishing

(metric tons, live weight)

	2006	2007	2008
Capture	6,663	6,183	5,410
Freshwater bream	1,278	1,090	988
Goldfish	2,507	2,907	1,642
Pontic shad	220	167	601
European sprat	491	228	234
Aquaculture	8,088	10,312*	12,532*
Common carp	3,136	3,544	3,977
Goldfish	1,268	1,653	1,462
Silver carp	2,091	1,695	2,959
Bighead carp	894	2,056	2,228
Rainbow trout	111	187	268
Total catch	14,751	16,495*	17,942*

* FAO estimate.

Source: FAO.

Mining

('000 metric tons unless otherwise indicated)

	2007	2008	2009
Brown coal (incl. lignite)*	32,500	35,000	30,000
Crude petroleum	5,086	4,798	4,494
Iron ore†	45*	—	—
Copper concentrates‡	2.2	2.0	1.0
Lead concentrates‡	0.8	—	—
Zinc concentrates‡	1.0	—	—
Salt (unrefined)	2,475	2,450*	2,040*
Natural gas (million cu metres)	12,245	11,400*	10,859

* Estimate(s).
† Figures refer to gross weight.
‡ Figures refer to the metal content of concentrates.

Source: US Geological Survey.

Industry

SELECTED PRODUCTS
('000 metric tons, unless otherwise indicated)

	2004	2005	2006
Meat and meat products	464	555	652
Refined sugar	523	514	605
Margarine	60.9	65.8	61.3
Wine ('000 hectolitres)	7,071	2,602	5,014
Beer ('000 hectolitres)	14,406	15,295	17,484
Tobacco products	35	33	30
Cotton yarn—pure and mixed	32	28	29
Cotton fabrics—pure and mixed (million sq metres)	201	112	114
Woollen yarn—pure and mixed	24	22	24
Woollen fabrics—pure and mixed (million sq metres)	12	15	18
Silk fabrics—pure and mixed (million sq metres)*	31	23	21
Flax and hemp yarn—pure and mixed	4	2	2
Linen, hemp and jute fabrics—pure and mixed (million sq metres)	2	1	1
Chemical filaments and fibres	21	16	13
Footwear (million pairs)	75	72	69
Chemical wood pulp	237	134	108
Paper and paperboard	521	411	434
Synthetic rubber	12	12	2
Rubber tyres ('000)	12,408	14,208	15,330
Sulphuric acid	28	11	0
Caustic soda (sodium hydroxide)	414	443	477
Soda ash (sodium carbonate)	398	346	453
Nitrogenous fertilizers (a)†	1,104	1,580	1,061
Phosphatic fertilizers (b)†	86	76	61
Pesticides	3	3	2
Motor spirit (petrol)	4,292	4,956	4,888
Kerosene and white spirit	429	455	461
Distillate fuel oils	3,947	4,542	4,484
Residual fuel oils	1,560	1,707	1,303
Petroleum bitumen (asphalt)	203	157	242
Liquefied petroleum gas	366	658	677
Coke	1,675	1,891	1,790
Cement	6,239	7,043	8,253
Pig-iron	4,244	4,098	3,946
Crude steel	6,076	6,280	6,266
Aluminium—unwrought	229	258	277
Television receivers ('000)	76	32	43
Merchant ships launched ('000 deadweight tons)	222	103	155
Passenger motor cars ('000)	99	175	202
Motor tractors, lorries and dump trucks (number)	277	171	530
Buses ('000)	2	—	5
Domestic refrigerators ('000)	700	826	1,169
Domestic washing and drying machines ('000)	42	25	23
Domestic vacuum cleaners ('000)	112	318	393
Domestic cookers ('000)	737	855	825
Electric energy (million kWh)	56,482	59,413	62,696

* Including fabrics of artificial silk.
† Production in terms of (a) nitrogen or (b) phosphoric acid.

Electric energy (million kWh): 61,673 in 2007; 64,956 in 2008.

ROMANIA

Finance

CURRENCY AND EXCHANGE RATES

Monetary Units
100 bani (singular: ban) = 1 Romanian leu (plural: lei).

Sterling, Dollar and Euro Equivalents (31 December 2010)
£1 sterling = 5.017 lei;
US $1 = 3.205 lei;
€1 = 4.282 lei;
100 Romanian lei = £19.93 = $31.21 = €23.35.

Average Exchange Rate (lei per US $)
2008   2.5189
2009   3.0493
2010   3.1779

Note: On 1 July 2005 the leu was revalued at a rate of 10,000 old lei = 1 new leu.

STATE BUDGET
(hundred million new lei)

Revenue	2004*	2005*	2006†
Tax revenue	610.6	698.3	782.3
Value-added tax	138.1	151.0	160.2
Social security taxes	228.2	257.7	276.6
Profits tax	48.8	55.5	59.3
Income tax	73.2	86.1	98.4
Excise taxes	62.0	83.2	118.7
Customs duties	9.0	9.4	10.1
Other indirect taxes	51.3	55.4	59.0
Non-tax revenue	32.5	27.0	26.5
Capital revenue (incl. grants)	0.9	0.9	1.0
Total	**644.0**	**726.2**	**809.8**

Expenditure	2004*	2005*	2006†
Public authorities	36.8	38.6	40.9
Defence	41.5	47.7	52.9
Public order and safety	40.4	42.2	43.9
Education	86.7	98.8	108.8
Health	78.4	82.6	83.9
Social security and welfare	216.2	235.5	249.9
Community services, public development and housing	47.5	50.3	52.6
Recreational, cultural and religious affairs	11.3	12.1	12.7
Agriculture and forestry	24.9	28.9	31.4
Industry	16.5	18.4	19.1
Transport and communications	77.1	81.9	85.2
Other economic affairs and services	14.4	16.1	18.1
National debt expenditure	48.0	40.9	42.4
Other	8.4	9.8	11.4
Loans	1.6	1.7	1.7
Total	**749.7**	**805.5**	**854.9**

* Estimates.
† Forecasts.
Source: Ministry of Public Finance, Bucharest.

Government finance (general government operations on cash basis, '000 million new lei): Total revenue 128.9 (Taxes 76.4) in 2007, 157.3 (Taxes 95.4) in 2008, 156.1 (Taxes 88.2) in 2009, 167.9 (Taxes 93.0) in 2010; Total expenditure 125.2 in 2007, 159.3 in 2008, 166.3 in 2009; 173.3 in 2010 (Source: IMF, *International Financial Statistics*).

INTERNATIONAL RESERVES
(US $ million at 31 December)

	2008	2009	2010
Gold (national valuation)	2,882	3,680	4,704
IMF special drawing rights	121	1,412	1,058
Foreign exchange	36,747	39,344	42,303
Total	**39,750**	**44,436**	**48,065**

Source: IMF, *International Financial Statistics*.

MONEY SUPPLY
('000 million new lei at 31 December)

	2008	2009	2010
Currency outside depository corporations	25.32	23.97	26.79
Transferable deposits	67.30	55.40	54.81
Other deposits	81.12	108.65	117.98
Securities other than shares	0.35	1.80	3.18
Broad money	**174.09**	**189.81**	**202.77**

Source: IMF, *International Financial Statistics*.

COST OF LIVING
(Consumer Price Index; base: 2000 = 100)

	2006	2007	2008
Food	222.0	230.6	251.9
Fuel and light	388.2	417.1	460.1
Clothing	188.7	194.9	201.4
Rent	216.7	372.2	469.7
All items (incl. others)	246.9	258.8	279.1

2009: Food 260.1; All items (incl. others) 294.7.
Source: ILO.

NATIONAL ACCOUNTS
(million new lei at current prices)

Expenditure on the Gross Domestic Product

	2008	2009	2010
Total final consumption	420,917.5	402,246.0	405,422.4
Changes in inventories	–3,382.5	–4,566.2	19,127.5
Gross fixed capital formation	164,279.4	130,602.6	116,793.1
Total domestic expenditure	**581,814.4**	**528,282.4**	**541,343.0**
Exports of goods and services	156,629.3	153,349.8	183,832.6
Less Imports of goods and services	223,743.7	183,624.7	211,534.8
GDP in purchasers' values	**514,700.0**	**498,007.5**	**513,640.8**

Gross Domestic Product by Economic Activity

	2008	2009	2010
Agriculture, hunting, forestry and fishing	34,126.3	31,734.9	30,728.6
Construction	54,628.2	49,350.0	45,481.9
Other industry*	11,848.6	121,842.5	135,472.0
Trade; hotels and restaurants; transport, storage and communications	114,762.5	107,556.2	108,502.3
Financial intermediation; real estate transactions, renting and business activities	68,622.0	68,265.8	71,473.4
Other services	67,910.5	69,097.8	64,265.9
Gross value added in basic prices	**458,535.5**	**447,847.2**	**455,924.1**
Taxes on products	57,607.9	51,366.1	58,807.7
Less Subsidies on products	1,443.4	1,205.8	1,091.0
GDP in market prices	**514,700.0**	**498,007.5**	**513,640.8**

* Comprising mining and quarrying, manufacturing, electricity, gas and water.

ROMANIA

BALANCE OF PAYMENTS
(US $ million)

	2007	2008	2009
Exports of goods f.o.b.	40,555	49,760	40,713
Imports of goods f.o.b.	−65,121	−77,942	−50,195
Trade balance	**−24,566**	**−28,182**	**−9,482**
Exports of services	9,439	12,856	9,778
Imports of services	−8,909	−11,905	−10,275
Balance on goods and services	**−24,036**	**−27,231**	**−9,979**
Other income received	3,321	3,330	1,614
Other income paid	−8,983	−8,702	−4,582
Balance on goods, services and income	**−29,698**	**−32,603**	**−12,947**
Current transfers received	9,867	13,074	9,212
Current transfers paid	−3,249	−4,190	−3,563
Current balance	**−23,080**	**−23,719**	**−7,298**
Capital account (net)	1,145	912	774
Direct investment abroad	−278	−277	−224
Direct investment from abroad	9,925	13,883	6,310
Portfolio investment assets	142	−310	−236
Portfolio investment liabilities	481	−412	1,017
Financial derivatives assets	338	889	593
Financial derivatives liabilities	−753	−1,276	−587
Other investment assets	−1,173	−841	−3,623
Other investment liabilities	20,851	13,371	−1,291
Net errors and omissions	−1,319	−2,065	−1,804
Overall balance	**6,279**	**155**	**−6,369**

Source: IMF, *International Financial Statistics*.

External Trade

PRINCIPAL COMMODITIES
(distribution by SITC, US $ million)

Imports c.i.f.	2007	2008	2009
Food and live animals	3,567.1	4,746.9	4,113.0
Crude materials (inedible) except fuels	1,786.0	2,237.5	1,223.9
Mineral fuels, lubricants, etc.	7,523.6	10,460.6	5,059.2
Petroleum, petroleum products, etc.	5,251.7	7,374.4	4,013.2
Gas, natural and manufactured	1,492.6	2,048.4	722.4
Chemicals and related products	6,997.6	8,798.0	7,437.2
Medicinal and pharmaceutical products	2,005.6	2,649.4	2,649.7
Basic manufactures	15,821.6	17,768.4	11,326.6
Textiles and textile articles	3,685.8	3,524.1	2,634.4
Iron and steel	3,554.1	4,650.0	2,089.3
Manufactures of metals	2,773.1	3,179.2	2,201.3
Machinery and transport equipment	26,093.3	29,147.8	17,850.6
Machinery specialized for particular industries	2,637.7	2,928.8	1,629.0
General industrial machinery and parts	3,614.9	4,058.9	2,587.1
Telecommunications, sound recording and reproducing equipment	2,273.0	3,132.1	2,951.8
Electric machinery, apparatus, etc.	4,941.8	5,724.9	4,422.7
Road vehicles	8,832.1	9,323.5	3,335.5
Miscellaneous manufactured articles	5,927.8	7,055.6	4,978.9
Total (incl. others)	69,946.2	82,965.0	54,256.3

Exports f.o.b.	2007	2008	2009
Crude materials (inedible) except fuels	2,097.8	2,783.2	2,236.0
Cork and wood	689.0	653.2	632.1
Mineral fuels, lubricants, etc.	3,044.4	4,535.0	2,394.3
Petroleum, petroleum products, etc.	2,740.3	3,971.3	2,046.7
Chemicals and related products	2,283.7	2,996.4	2,029.0
Basic manufactures	8,667.2	9,488.2	6,146.5
Iron and steel	3,267.0	3,603.5	1,591.8
Non-ferrous metals	1,068.2	1,013.9	497.9
Machinery and transport equipment	13,460.0	17,539.7	17,308.6
Telecommunications, sound recording and reproducing equipment	405.7	1,098.8	2,399.2
Electrical machinery, apparatus, etc.	4,300.6	5,366.7	4,469.0
Road vehicles	3,243.6	4,081.6	4,910.6
Miscellaneous manufactured articles	8,771.6	8,890.6	7,114.3
Furniture and parts	1,525.4	1,612.1	1,394.0
Clothing and accessories (excl. footwear)	4,315.2	4,090.7	3,041.6
Footwear	1,782.5	1,749.2	1,359.8
Total (incl. others)	40,264.7	49,538.9	40,620.9

Source: UN, *International Trade Statistics Yearbook*.

PRINCIPAL TRADING PARTNERS
(US $ million)*

Imports c.i.f.	2007	2008	2009
Austria	3,395.8	4,045.8	2,581.5
Belgium	1,376.4	1,649.0	1,129.3
China, People's Republic	2,284.5	3,505.1	2,646.1
Czech Republic	1,703.8	2,076.2	1,285.5
France (incl. Monaco)	4,375.4	4,738.3	3,339.6
Germany	12,029.4	13,573.4	9,411.0
Greece	1,072.3	1,186.8	820.8
Hungary	4,856.7	6,131.8	4,548.2
Italy	8,899.4	9,438.7	6,382.5
Japan	425.3	442.7	260.1
Kazakhstan	1,357.7	3,800.9	1,910.5
Korea, Republic	820.7	765.3	478.2
Netherlands	2,536.8	3,091.6	2,087.9
Poland	2,380.6	2,843.2	1,934.7
Russia	4,417.2	4,950.3	2,094.6
Slovakia	895.7	1,232.7	752.4
Spain	1,421.4	1,622.7	1,044.8
Turkey	3,763.8	4,081.0	2,024.8
Ukraine	785.0	771.5	325.9
United Kingdom	1,351.9	1,616.3	1,202.8
USA	936.3	1,201.4	690.3
Total (incl. others)	69,946.2	82,965.0	54,256.3

ROMANIA

Exports f.o.b.	2007	2008	2009
Austria	1,033.8	1,123.2	958.4
Belgium	642.6	812.2	725.7
Bulgaria	1,302.6	2,062.6	1,534.5
Czech Republic	557.1	775.1	671.3
France (incl. Monaco)	3,117.1	3,656.4	3,338.4
Germany	6,827.6	8,176.0	7,641.9
Greece	687.7	898.9	768.9
Hungary	2,248.3	2,530.6	1,765.5
India	449.1	310.2	256.9
Italy	6,866.9	7,658.8	6,237.5
Moldova	632.5	824.4	520.9
Netherlands	831.8	1,430.4	1,329.8
Poland	870.1	986.7	901.5
Russia	582.8	897.7	716.3
Serbia	434.8	700.6	576.9
Spain	933.1	1,144.1	1,224.7
Turkey	2,819.1	3,276.0	2,008.7
Ukraine	741.5	1,220.2	487.2
United Arab Emirates	452.8	462.3	241.7
United Kingdom	1,660.7	1,628.2	1,364.0
USA	808.3	838.5	475.7
Total (incl. others)	40,264.7	49,538.9	40,620.9

* Imports by country of production; exports by country of last consignment.

Source: UN, *International Trade Statistics Yearbook*.

Transport

RAILWAYS
(traffic)

	2006	2007	2008
Passenger journeys (million)	94	88	78
Passenger-km (million)	8,093	7,476	6,958
Freight transported (million metric tons)	68	69	67
Freight ton-km (million)	16,000	16,000	15,000

ROAD TRAFFIC
('000 motor vehicles in use at 31 December)

	2006	2007	2008
Passenger cars	3,221	3,541	4,027
Buses and coaches	33	34	42
Lorries and vans	457	502	645
Motorcycles and mopeds	43	56	72

INLAND WATERWAYS
(traffic)

	2006	2007	2008
Passenger journeys ('000)	500	500	500
Passenger-km (million)	13	23	21
Freight transported (million metric tons)	15	15	15
Freight ton-km ('000 million)	5	5	5

SHIPPING
Merchant Fleet
(registered at 31 December)

	2007	2008	2009
Number of vessels	192	188	177
Total displacement ('000 grt)	269.5	261.8	246.0

Source: IHS Fairplay, *World Fleet Statistics*.

International Sea-borne Freight Traffic
('000 metric tons)

	2006	2007	2008
Goods loaded	22,150	20,298	20,857
Goods unloaded	24,559	28,630	29,601

CIVIL AVIATION
(traffic)

	2006	2007	2008
Passengers carried ('000)	2,000	3,000	4,000
Passenger-km (million)	2,618	3,984	4,347
Freight transported ('000 metric tons)	6	5	5
Freight ton-km (million)	7	7	8

Tourism

FOREIGN VISITOR ARRIVALS
('000)*

Country of origin	2006	2007	2008
Austria	151.5	218.0	210.1
Bulgaria	399.3	818.0	1,114.1
France	129.5	184.5	183.4
Germany	342.7	473.4	521.7
Hungary	1,366.7	1,743.1	1,950.4
Italy	277.9	397.6	433.2
Moldova	1,489.7	1,109.9	1,428.6
Poland	74.6	191.0	276.5
Serbia and Montenegro	166.8	171.2	183.8
Turkey	219.1	284.2	302.5
Ukraine	433.4	720.2	729.8
USA	130.2	139.4	137.3
Total (incl. others)	6,037.0	7,721.7	8,862.1

* Figures refer to arrivals at frontiers of visitors from abroad, including same-day visitors (excursionists).

Tourism receipts (US $ million, incl. passenger transport): 1,676 in 2006; 2,065 in 2007; 2,627 in 2008.

Source: World Tourism Organization.

Communications Media

	2006	2007	2008
Radio users ('000 subscribers)	5,095	5,106	n.a.
Television users ('000 subscribers)	5,478	5,532	n.a.
Telephones ('000 main lines in use)	4,198.0	4,416.0	5,209.0
Mobile cellular telephones ('000 subscribers)	15,991.0	20,400.0	24,500.0
Internet users ('000)*	5,312.0	6,070.4	6,925.3
Broadband subscribers ('000)	1,090.0	1,949.0	2,490.0
Book production (incl. pamphlets):			
titles	14,373	15,566	13,700
copies ('000)	9,720	11,028	10,210
Daily newspapers	81	80	75
Other periodicals	2,180	2,320	2,615

* Estimates.

Personal computers: 4,144,000 (192.3 per 1,000 persons) in 2007.

2009: Telephones ('000 main lines in use) 5,323.0; Mobile cellular telephones ('000 subscribers) 25,400.0; Internet users ('000, estimate) 7,786.6; Broadband subscribers ('000) 2,800.0.

Source: partly International Telecommunication Union.

Education

(2009/10 unless otherwise indicated)

	Institutions*	Teachers ('000)	Pupils ('000)
Kindergartens	1,731	38	666
Primary and gymnasium schools	4,737	135	1,720
Secondary schools	1,426	60	838
Vocational schools	147	3	115
Specialized technical schools	83	1	63
Higher education	106	31	775

* 2007/08 figures.

Pupil-teacher ratio (primary education, UNESCO estimate): 16.5 in 2005/06 (Source: UNESCO Institute for Statistics).

Adult literacy rate (UNESCO estimates): 97.6% (males 98.3%; females 96.9%) in 2008 (Source: UNESCO Institute for Statistics).

Directory

The Government

HEAD OF STATE

President: TRAIAN BĂSESCU (elected 12 December 2004; inaugurated 14 December 2004; re-elected 6 December 2009).

COUNCIL OF MINISTERS
(May 2011)

A coalition of the Democratic Liberal Party (DLP), the Democratic Alliance of Hungarians in Romania (DAHR) and Independents (Ind.).

Prime Minister: EMIL BOC (DLP).
Deputy Prime Minister: MARKÓ BÉLA (DAHR).
Minister of Administration and the Interior: TRAIAN IGAŞ (DLP).
Minister of Public Finance: GHEORGHE IALOMIŢIANU (DLP).
Minister of the Economy, Trade and the Business Environment: ION ARITON (DLP).
Minister of Foreign Affairs: TEODOR BACONSCHI (DLP).
Minister of Transport and Infrastructure: ANCA-DANIELA BOAGIU (PDL).
Minister of the Environment and Forestry: LÁSZLÓ BORBÉLY (DAHR).
Minister of Regional Development and Tourism: ELENA GABRIELA UDREA (DLP).
Minister of National Defence: GABRIEL OPREA (Ind.).
Minister of Culture and National Heritage: KELEMEN HUNOR (DAHR).
Minister of Justice: CĂTĂLIN MARIAN PREDOIU (Ind.).
Minister of Communications and the Information Society: VALERIAN VREME (DLP).
Minister of Labour, the Family and Social Welfare: EMIL BOC (DLP) (acting).
Minister of Education, Research, Youth and Sport: DANIEL PETRU FUNERIU (DLP).
Minister of Health: CSEKE ATTILA (DAHR).
Minister of Agriculture and Rural Development: VALERIU TABĂRĂ (DLP).

MINISTRIES

Office of the President: 060116 Bucharest 5, Palatul Cotroceni, Str. Geniuliu 1–3; tel. (21) 4100581; fax (21) 4103858; e-mail procetatean@presidency.ro; internet www.presidency.ro.

Office of the Prime Minister: 011791 Bucharest 1, Piaţa Victoriei 1; tel. (21) 3143400; fax (21) 3139846; e-mail drp@guv.ro; internet www.guv.ro.

Ministry of Administration and the Interior: 010086 Bucharest 1, Piaţa Revoluţiei 1A; tel. (21) 3037080; fax (21) 3103072; e-mail petitii@mai.gov.ro; internet www.mai.gov.ro.

Ministry of Agriculture and Rural Development: 020921 Bucharest 3, Bd. Carol I 24, POB 37; tel. (21) 3072300; fax (21) 3078554; e-mail relatii.publice@madr.ro; internet www.madr.ro.

Ministry of Communications and the Information Society: 050706 Bucharest 5, Bd. Libertăţii 14; tel. (21) 4001190; fax (21) 3114131; e-mail office@mcsi.ro; internet www.mcsi.ro.

Ministry of Culture and National Heritage: 011374 Bucharest 1, Şos. Kiseleff 30; tel. (21) 2244665; fax (21) 2228320; e-mail ministru@cultura.ro; internet www.cultura.ro.

Ministry of the Economy, Trade and the Business Environment: 010096 Bucharest 1, Calea Victoriei 152; tel. (21) 2025399; fax (21) 2025108; e-mail dezbateri_publice@minind.ro; internet www.minind.ro.

Ministry of Education, Research, Youth and Sport: 010168 Bucharest 1, Str. Gen. Berthelot 28–30; tel. (21) 4056200; fax (21) 3124719; e-mail public@min.edu.ro; internet www.edu.ro.

Ministry of the Environment and Forestry: 040129 Bucharest 5, Bd. Libertăţii 12; tel. (21) 3160215; fax (21) 3166138; e-mail srp@mmediu.ro; internet www.mmediu.ro.

Ministry of Foreign Affairs: 011822 Bucharest, Al. Alexandru 31; tel. (21) 3192108; fax (21) 3196862; e-mail mae@mae.ro; internet www.mae.ro.

Ministry of Health: 010024 Bucharest 1, Str. Cristian Popişteanu 1–3; tel. (21) 3072690; fax (21) 3124916; e-mail ministru@ms.ro; internet www.ms.ro.

Ministry of Justice: 050741 Bucharest 5, Str. Apolodor 17; tel. (37) 2041046; fax (37) 2041226; e-mail relatiipublice@just.ro; internet www.just.ro.

Ministry of Labour, the Family and Social Welfare: 010026 Bucharest 1, Str. Demetru I. Dobrescu 2–4; tel. and fax (21) 3136267; e-mail presa@mmuncii.ro; internet www.mmuncii.ro.

Ministry of National Defence: 050561 Bucharest 5, Str. Izvor 3–5; tel. (21) 4023400; fax (21) 3195698; e-mail drp@mapn.ro; internet www.mapn.ro.

Ministry of Public Finance: 050741 Bucharest 5, Str. Apolodor 17; tel. (21) 3199759; fax (21) 3122509; e-mail publicinfo@mfinante.gov.ro; internet www.mfinante.gov.ro.

Ministry of Regional Development and Tourism: 050741 Bucharest 5, Str. Apolodor 17; tel. (37) 2111409; fax (37) 2111630; e-mail info@mdrt.ro; internet www.mdlpl.ro.

Ministry of Transport and Infrastructure: 010873 Bucharest 1, Bd. Dinicu Golescu 38; tel. (21) 3196124; fax (21) 3138869; e-mail relpub@mt.ro; internet www.mt.ro.

ROMANIA

President

Presidential Election, First Ballot, 22 November 2009

Candidates	Votes	%
Traian Băsescu (Democratic Liberal Party)	3,153,640	32.45
Mircea Dan Geoană (Social Democratic Party-Conservative Party alliance)	3,027,838	31.15
Crin Antonescu (National Liberal Party)	1,945,831	20.02
Corneliu Vadim Tudor (Greater Romania Party)	540,380	5.56
Hunor Kelemen (Democratic Alliance of Hungarians in Romania)	372,764	3.84
Sorin Mircea Oprescu (Independent)	309,764	3.19
Gheorghe Becali (New Generation—Christian Democratic Party)	186,390	1.92
Others	182,233	1.88
Total	**9,718,840**	**100.00**

Second Ballot, 6 December 2009

Candidates	Votes	%
Traian Băsescu (Democratic Liberal Party)	5,275,808	50.33
Mircea Dan Geoană (Social Democratic Party-Conservative Party alliance)	5,205,760	49.67
Total	**10,481,568**	**100.00**

Legislature

PARLAMENTUL ROMÂNIEI
(The Romanian Parliament)

The bicameral Parlamentul României comprises the 334-member lower chamber, the Camera Deputaților (Chamber of Deputies), and the 137-member upper chamber, Senatul (the Senate). Members of both chambers are directly elected, for a term of four years.

Camera Deputaților
(Chamber of Deputies)

050563 Bucharest, Palatul Parlamentului, Str. Izvor 2–4, Sector 5; tel. (21) 3160300; fax (21) 4022149; e-mail secretar.general@cdep.ro; internet www.cdep.ro.

Chairman: ROBERTA ALMA ANASTASE.

General Election, 30 November 2008

Parties	Votes	% of votes	Seats
Democratic Liberal Party	2,228,860	32.36	115
Social Democratic Party-Conservative Party alliance	2,279,449	33.10	114
National Liberal Party	1,279,063	18.57	65
Democratic Alliance of Hungarians in Romania	425,008	6.17	22
Parties representing minority ethnic groups*	199,871	2.90	18
Greater Romania Party	217,595	3.16	—
New Generation—Christian Democratic Party	156,901	2.28	—
Others	100,047	1.45	—
Total	**6,886,794**	**100.00**	**334**

*One deputy was elected from each of the following parties: the Albanian League Association of Romania; the Armenian Union of Romania; the Bulgarian Union of the Banat-Romania; the Croat Union of Romania; the Cultural Union of Ruthenians of Romania; the Democratic Forum of Germans of Romania; the Democratic Turkish Union of Romania; the Democratic Union of Slovaks and Czechs of Romania; the Democratic Union of Turkic-Muslim Tatars of Romania; the Federation of Jewish Communities of Romania; the Greek Union of Romania; the Italian Association of Romania; the Macedonian Association of Romania; the Polish Union of Romania; the Pro-Europe Roma Party; the Rusyn-Lipovan Community of Romania; the Serb Union of Romania; and the Ukrainian Union of Romania.

Senatul
(The Senate)

050711 Bucharest 5, Calea 13 Septembrie 1–3; tel. (21) 4021111; fax (21) 3121184; e-mail csava@senat.ro; internet www.senat.ro.

Chairman: MIRCEA DAN GEOANĂ.

General Election, 30 November 2008

Parties	Votes	% of votes	Seats
Democratic Liberal Party	2,312,358	33.57	51
Social Democratic Party-Conservative Party alliance	2,352,968	34.16	49
National Liberal Party	1,291,029	18.74	28
Democratic Alliance of Hungarians in Romania	440,449	6.39	9
Greater Romania Party	245,930	3.57	—
New Generation—Christian Democratic Party	174,519	2.53	—
Others	70,802	1.03	—
Total	**6,888,055**	**100.00**	**137**

Election Commission

Central Electoral Office (Biroul Electoral Central): Bucharest 1, Str. Ion Câmpineanu 28; tel. (21) 3188641; fax (21) 3188642; Pres. OCTAVIAN OPRIȘ.

Political Organizations

Christian-Democratic National Peasants' Party (CDNPP) (Partidul Național Țărănesc Creștin Democrat): 7000 Bucharest 2, Bd. Carol I 24; tel. and fax (21) 2641460; e-mail pntcdsecretargeneral@yahoo.com; internet www.pntcd.eu; f. 1989 by merger of centre-right Christian Democratic Party and traditional National Peasant Party, as revival of party originally founded in 1869 and banned in 1947; absorbed the Union for the Reconstruction of Romania in March 2005; supports pluralist democracy and the restoration of peasant property; Pres. RADU SARBU.

Conservative Party (CP) (Partidul Conservator—PC): 010093 Bucharest, Str. Muzeul Zambaccian 17, Sector 1; tel. (21) 4251100; fax (21) 2304776; e-mail secretariat@partidulconservator.ro; internet www.partidulconservator.ro; f. 1991 as the Humanist Party of Romania; contested legislative and presidential elections in 2004 in alliance with the SDP, as the National Union; renamed in May 2005; absorbed the Romanian National Unity Party in Feb. 2006; Pres. DANIEL CONSTANTIN.

Democratic Alliance of Hungarians in Romania (DAHR) (Uniunea Democrată Maghiară din România/Romániai Magyar Demokrata Szövetség—UDMR/RMDSZ): 024015 Bucharest, Str. Avram Iancu 8; tel. (21) 3144356; fax (21) 3144583; e-mail elhivbuk@rmdsz.ro; internet www.rmdsz.ro; f. 1990; supports the rights of ethnic Hungarians in Romania; Pres. KELEMEN HUNOR.

Democratic Liberal Party (DLP) (Partidul Democrat Liberal—PD-L): 011825 Bucharest, Al. Modrogan 1; tel. (21) 2303701; fax (21) 2301625; e-mail office@pd.ro; internet www.pd-l.ro; f. 1993; fmrly Democratic Party—National Salvation Front, then Democratic Party; present name adopted 2008, following merger with Liberal Democratic Party; contested legislative and presidential elections in 2004 in alliance with the NLP, as the Justice and Truth Alliance; Pres. EMIL BOC; Sec.-Gen. VASILE BLAGA.

Greater Romania Party (GRP) (Partidul România Mare—PRM): 010296 Bucharest, Str. G. Clemenceau 8–10; tel. (21) 3130967; fax (21) 3126182; e-mail prm@prm.org.ro; internet www.prm.org.ro; f. 1991; known as the Popular Greater Romania Party (under the chairmanship of Corneliu Ciontu) in March–June 2005; nationalist; splinter group formed under Ciontu in mid-2005 (People's Party), which subsequently merged with the New Generation—Christian Democratic Party; Chair. CORNELIU VADIM TUDOR.

National Liberal Party (NLP) (Partidul Național Liberal—PNL): 011866 Bucharest, Bd. Aviatorilor 86; tel. (21) 2310795; fax (21) 2310796; e-mail dre@pnl.ro; internet www.pnl.ro; f. 1990 as revival of party originally founded in 1869 and banned in 1947; merged with Liberal Party in 1993, and with Party of the Civic Alliance and Liberal Party of Romania in 1998, absorbed Alliance for Romania in 2002 and the Union of Rightist Forces in 2003; supports the integration of Romania into the European Union and the North Atlantic Treaty Organization, advocates freedom of expression and religion, a market economy and the decentralization of state powers; contested legislative and presidential elections in 2004 in alliance with the Democratic Party, as the Justice and Truth Alliance; Pres. GEORGE CRIN LAURENȚIU ANTONESCU; Sec.-Gen. RADU STROE.

New Generation—Christian Democratic Party (Partidul Noua Generatie—Crestin Democrat—PNG): 030061 Bucharest 3, Str. Blănari 21–23; tel. (21) 3149360; fax (21) 3149361; e-mail

ROMANIA

secretariat@png.ro; internet www.png.ro; f. 2003; Chair. GHEORGHE BECALI.

Social Democratic Party (SDP) (Partidul Social Democrat—PSD): 011346 Bucharest 1, Şos. Kiseleff 10; tel. (21) 2222953; fax (21) 2223272; internet www.psd.ro; f. 2001 by the merger of the Romanian Social Democratic Party and the Party of Social Democracy of Romania; contested legislative and presidential elections in 2004 in alliance with the Humanist Party of Romania, as the National Union; Pres. VICTOR PONTA; Sec.-Gen. LIVIU DRAGNEA.

Diplomatic Representation

EMBASSIES IN ROMANIA

Albania: 712012 Bucharest, Str. Duiliu Zamfirescu 7, Sector 1; tel. (21) 2119829; fax (21) 2108039; e-mail embassy.bucharest@mfa.gov.al; Ambassador DASHNOR DERVISHI.

Algeria: 010663 Bucharest, Bd. Lascăr Catargiu 29, Sector 1; tel. (21) 2124185; fax (21) 2115695; e-mail ambalgerie@roumanie.eunet.ro; Ambassador HAMRAOUI HABIB CHAWKI.

Argentina: 010031 Bucharest, Union International Centre, Str. Ion Campineanu 11, 3rd Floor, Rm 101; tel. (21) 3122626; fax (21) 3120116; e-mail eruma@mrecic.gov.ar; Ambassador CLAUDIO PÉREZ PALADINO.

Armenia: 014136 Bucharest, Str. Poiana 27, Sector 1; tel. (21) 2332452; fax (21) 2332725; e-mail armembro@cinor.ro; Ambassador HAMLET GASPARIAN.

Austria: 020461 Bucharest, Str. Dumbrava Roşie 7, Sector 2; tel. (21) 2015612; fax (21) 2100885; e-mail bukarest-ob@bmeia.gv.at; internet www.aussenministerium.at/bukarest; Ambassador MICHAEL SCHWARZINGER.

Azerbaijan: 014132 Bucharest 1, Str. Grigore Gafencu 10, Sector 1; tel. (21) 2332484; fax (21) 2332465; e-mail azsefroman@azembassy.ro; internet www.azembassy.ro; Ambassador ELDAR HASANOV.

Belarus: 011411 Bucharest, Str. Tuberozelor 6, Sector 1; tel. (21) 2231776; fax (21) 2231763; e-mail romania@belembassy.org; internet www.romania.belembassy.org; Chargé d'affaires a.i. SERGEI MOLUNOV.

Belgium: 020061 Bucharest, Bd. Dacia 58, Sector 2; tel. (21) 2102970; fax (21) 2102803; e-mail bucharest@diplobel.org; internet www.diplobel.org/bucharest; Ambassador LEO D'AES.

Bosnia and Herzegovina: 011786 Bucharest 1, Str. Stockholm 12; tel. (21) 4092601; fax (21) 4092603; e-mail amb.bukurest@mvp.gov.ba; Ambassador BRANKO T. NEŠKOVIĆ.

Brazil: 011863 Bucharest, Bd. Aviatorilor 40, Sector 1; tel. (21) 2301130; fax (21) 2301599; e-mail braembuc@starnets.ro; Ambassador VITOR CANDIDO PAIM GOBATO.

Bulgaria: 011835 Bucharest, Str. Rabat 5; tel. (21) 2302159; fax (21) 2307654; e-mail bulembassy@rdsmail.ro; internet www.bgembassy-romania.org; Ambassador VALENTIN RADOMIRSKI.

Canada: 011411 Bucharest, Str. Tuberozelor 1–3, Sector 1; tel. (21) 3075000; fax (21) 3075010; e-mail bucst@international.gc.ca; internet www.canadainternational.gc.ca/romania-roumanie; Ambassador PHILIPPE BEAULNE.

Chile: 010732 Bucharest, Calea Griviţei 24; tel. (21) 3127239; fax (21) 3127246; e-mail info@chile.ro; internet chileabroad.gov.cl/rumania; Ambassador MARÍA ELIANA CUEVAS.

China, People's Republic: 014103 Bucharest, Şos. Nordului 2, Sector 1; tel. (21) 2328858; fax (21) 2330684; e-mail chinaemb_ro@mfa.gov.cn; internet www.chinaembassy.org.ro; Ambassador LIU ZENGWEN.

Congo, Democratic Republic: 010517 Bucharest, Str. Mihai Eminescu 50–54/15, Sector 1; tel. (21) 2105498; e-mail ambardcbuc@yahoo.fr; Chargé d'affaires a.i. PHOBA-KI-KUMBU.

Croatia: 024031 Bucharest, Str. Dr Burghelea 1, Sector 2; tel. (21) 3130457; fax (21) 3130384; e-mail croemb.bucharest@mvp.hr; internet ro.mfa.hr; Ambassador ANDREA GUSTOVIĆ ERCEGOVAC.

Cuba: 010516 Bucharest, Str. Mihai Eminescu 44–48, 2nd Floor, Rm 5; tel. (21) 2118739; fax (21) 2118916; e-mail embacuba@embacuba.ro; Ambassador MARÍA CARIDAD FAJARDO PALET.

Cyprus: 011406 Bucharest, Str. Petofi Sandor 2; tel. (21) 2230455; fax (21) 2230456; e-mail cypemb@cyprusembassy.ro; Ambassador SPYROS ATTAS.

Czech Republic: 030045 Bucharest, Str. Ion Ghica 11, Sector 3; tel. (21) 3039230; fax (21) 3122539; e-mail bucharest@embassy.mzv.cz; internet www.mzv.cz/bucharest; Ambassador PETR DOKLÁDAL.

Denmark: 024031 Bucharest, Str. Dr Burghelea 3, Sector 2; tel. (21) 3000800; fax (21) 3120358; e-mail buhamb@um.dk; internet www.ambbukarest.um.dk; Ambassador MICHAEL STERNBERG.

Egypt: 010407 Bucharest 1, Bd. Dacia 67, Sector 1; tel. (21) 2110938; fax (21) 2100337; e-mail embassy.bucharest@mfa.gov.eg; Ambassador SANAA ESMAIL ATALLAH ESMAIL.

Finland: 011832 Bucharest, Str. Atena 2 bis; tel. (21) 2307504; fax (21) 2307505; e-mail sanomat.buk@formin.fi; internet www.finland.ro; Ambassador IRMELI MUSTONEN.

France: 010392 Bucharest, Str. Biserica Amzei 13–15, Sector 1; tel. (21) 3031000; fax (21) 3031090; e-mail chancellerie.bucarest-amba@diplomatie.gouv.fr; internet www.ambafrance-ro.org; Ambassador HENRI PAUL.

Georgia: 011981 Bucharest 1, Str. Herăstrău 16, Sector 1; tel. (21) 2100602; fax (21) 2113999; e-mail bucuresti.emb@mfa.gov.ge; internet www.romania.mfa.gov.ge; Ambassador LEVAN METREVELI.

Germany: 011849 Bucharest, Str. Capt. Aviator Gh. Demetriade 6–8, Sector 1; tel. (21) 2029830; fax (21) 2305846; e-mail info@bukarest.diplo.de; internet www.bukarest.diplo.de; Ambassador ANDREAS VON METTENHEIM.

Greece: 021403 Bucharest, Bd. Pache Protopopescu 1–3, Sector 2; tel. (21) 2094170; fax (21) 2094175; e-mail gremb.buc@mfa.gr; internet www.grembassy.ro; Ambassador GEORGIOS POUKAMISSAS.

Holy See: 010187 Bucharest, Str. Pictor Stahi 5–7; tel. (21) 3123883; fax (21) 3120316; e-mail nuntius@clicknet.ro; Apostolic Nuncio Monsignor FRANCISCO-JAVIER LOZANO (Titular Archbishop of Penafiel).

Hungary: 020034 Bucharest, Str. Dimitrie Gerotă 63–65; tel. (21) 3111987; fax (21) 6204326; e-mail mission.buc@kum.hu; internet www.mfa.gov.hu/kulkepviselet/RO; Ambassador OSZKÁR LÁSZLÓ FÜZES.

India: 020078 Bucharest, Str. Mihai Eminescu 183, Sector 2; tel. (21) 2115451; fax (21) 2110614; e-mail office@embassyofindia.ro; internet www.embassyofindia.ro; Ambassador DEBASHISH CHAKRAVARTI.

Indonesia: 010488 Bucharest 1, Str. Orlando 10, Sector 1; tel. (21) 3120742; fax (21) 3120214; e-mail indobuch@indonezia.ro; internet www.indonezia.ro; Ambassador MARIANNA SUTADI.

Iran: 010633 Bucharest, Bd. Lascăr Catargiu 39, Sector 1; tel. (21) 3120495; fax (21) 3120496; e-mail iranembassyro@gmail.ro; internet www.iranembassy.ro; Ambassador BAHADOR AMINIAN JAZI.

Iraq: 011834 Bucharest 1, Str. Venezuela 6–8, Sector 1; tel. (21) 2339008; fax (21) 2339007; e-mail iraqbuchrest@yahoo.com; Ambassador MOHAMMED SAED AL-SHAKARCHY.

Ireland: 011015 Bucharest 1, Str. Buzeşti 50–52, 3rd Floor; tel. (21) 3102131; fax (21) 3102181; e-mail bucharestembassy@dfa.ie; internet www.embassyofireland.ro; Ambassador JOHN MORAHAN.

Israel: 040231 Bucharest 4, Bd. Dimitrie Cantemir 1, tronson 2 & 3, B2, 5th Floor; tel. (21) 3189416; fax (21) 3189402; e-mail info@bucharest.mfa.gov.il; internet bucharest.mfa.gov.il; Ambassador DAN BEN-ELIEZER.

Italy: 010667 Bucharest, Str. Henri Coandă 7–9, Sector 1; tel. (21) 3052100; fax (21) 3120422; e-mail ambasciata.bucarest@esteri.it; internet www.ambbucarest.esteri.it; Ambassador MARIO COSPITO.

Japan: 011141 Bucharest 1, Şos. Nicolae Titulescu 4–8, Sector 1; tel. (21) 3191890; fax (21) 3191895; e-mail embassy@embjpn.ro; internet www.ro.emb-japan.go.jp; Ambassador NATSUO AMEMIYA.

Jordan: 020461 Bucharest 2, Str. Dumbrava Roşie 1; tel. (21) 2104705; fax (21) 2100320; e-mail jordan.embassy@pcnet.ro; Ambassador RASSEM YAQOUB HASHEM.

Kazakhstan: 020225 Bucharest, Str. Giuseppe Garibaldi 26 bis, Sector 2; tel. (21) 2300865; fax (21) 2300866; e-mail dipmissionkz@zappmobile.ro; Chargé d'affaires a.i. KAIRAT AMAN.

Korea, Democratic People's Republic: 014103 Bucharest, Şos. Nordului 6, Sector 1; tel. (21) 2321994; fax (21) 2321992; e-mail ambasadarpdc@yahoo.com; Ambassador KIM SON GYONG.

Korea, Republic: 012013 Bucharest, Bd. Mircea Eliade 14; tel. (21) 2307198; fax (21) 2307629; e-mail romania@mofat.go.kr; internet rou.mofat.go.kr; Ambassador IM HAN-TAEK.

Kuwait: 011751 Bucharest 1, Str. Louis Blanc 19A-B; tel. (21) 3154444; fax (21) 3159992; e-mail kuwaitstampa@tiscalinet.it; internet www.kuwaitembassy.ro; Ambassador FAHD HAJAR SHAOUF AL-MUTAIRI.

Lebanon: 011817 Bucharest 1, Str. Andrei Mureşanu 16, Sector 1; tel. (21) 2308175; fax (21) 2308179; e-mail ambasada.liban@gmail.com; Ambassador MUHAMMAD EL-DIB.

Lithuania: 011973 Bucharest 1, Bd. Primăverii 51/2, Sector 1; tel. (21) 3115997; fax (21) 3115919; e-mail amb.ro@urm.lt; internet ro.mfa.lt; Ambassador VLADIMIR JARMOLENKO.

Macedonia, former Yugoslav Republic: 020083 Bucharest, Str. Mihai Eminescu 144, Sector 2; tel. (21) 2100880; fax (21) 2117295; e-mail ammakbuk@rdsmail.ro; Ambassador LJUPČO ARSOVSKI.

Malaysia: 020521 Bucharest, Str. Drobeta 11, Sector 2; tel. (21) 2113801; fax (21) 2100270; e-mail mwbucrst@itcnet.ro; internet

ROMANIA

www.kln.gov.my/web/rou; Ambassador Datin Paduka Halimah Abdullah.

Mexico: 020082 Bucharest, Str. Mihai Eminescu 124c /13–14, Sector 2; tel. (21) 2104577; fax (21) 2104713; e-mail embamex@xnet.ro; internet www.embamex.ro; Chargé d'affaires a.i. María Cristina de la Garza Sandoval.

Moldova: 712732 Bucharest 1, Al. Alexandru 40, Sector 1; tel. (21) 2300474; fax (21) 2307790; e-mail bucuresti@mfa.md; internet www.romania.mfa.gov.md; Ambassador Iurie Reniță.

Morocco: 010459 Bucharest 1, Str. Dionisie Lupu 78, Sector 1; tel. (21) 3174124; fax (21) 3174144; e-mail ambamarbuc@ambasadamaroc.ro; internet www.ambasadamaroc.ro; Ambassador Ahmed Sendague.

Netherlands: 011832 Bucharest, Al. Alexandru 20; tel. (21) 2086030; fax (21) 2307620; e-mail bkr@minbuza.nl; internet www.olanda.ro; Ambassador Maria Wilhelmina Josepha Antonia van Gool.

Nigeria: 010449 Bucharest, Str. Orlando 9, POB 1-305, Sector 1; tel. (21) 3128685; fax (21) 3120622; e-mail nigeremb@canad.ro; Ambassador Mba Ama Mba.

Norway: 011832 Bucharest, Str. Atena 18; tel. (21) 3069800; fax (21) 3069890; e-mail emb.bucharest@mfa.no; internet www.norvegia.ro; Ambassador Øystein Hovdkinn.

Pakistan: 011352 Bucharest 1, Str. Barbu Delavrancea 22, Sector 1; tel. (21) 3187873; fax (21) 3187874; e-mail parepbucharest@live.com; internet www.mofa.gov.pk/romania; Ambassador Rab Nawaz Khan.

Peru: 020372 Bucharest, Bd. Lacul Tei 29/4, Sector 2; tel. (21) 2111816; fax (21) 2111818; e-mail embajadaperu.bk_ro@yahoo.com; Ambassador Ernesto Pinto Bazurco Rittler.

Philippines: 050453 Bucharest 5, Str. Carol Davila 105–107, 5th Floor, Rm 10–11; tel. (21) 3198252; fax (21) 3198253; e-mail bucharestpe@rdsmail.ro; Chargé d'affaires a.i. Maria Pangilian.

Poland: 011821 Bucharest 1, Al. Alexandru 23, Sector 1; tel. (21) 3082200; fax (21) 2307832; e-mail ambasada@bukareszt.ro; internet www.bukareszt.polemb.net; Chargé d'affaires a.i. Magdalena Bogdziewicz.

Portugal: 011815 Bucharest 1, Str. Paris 55, POB 63-91; tel. (21) 2304136; fax (21) 2304117; e-mail secretariat@embportugal.ro; internet www.embportugal.ro; Ambassador António Antas de Campos.

Qatar: 011834 Bucharest, Str. Venezuela 10a, Sector 1; tel. (21) 2304741; fax (21) 2305446; e-mail qtr_embassy@b.astral.ro; internet www.qatarembassy.ro; Ambassador Salem Abdullah Sultan al-Jaber.

Russia: 011341 Bucharest 1, Şos. Kiseleff 6, Sector 1; tel. (21) 2223170; fax (21) 2229450; e-mail rab@mb.roknet.ro; internet www.romania.mid.ru; Ambassador Aleksandr A. Churilin.

Saudi Arabia: 010501 Bucharest 1, Str. Polonă 6, Sector 1; tel. (21) 2109109; fax (21) 2107093; e-mail ksa_embassy@yahoo.com; Ambassador Abd al-Rahman bin Ibrahim al-Resi.

Serbia: 010573 Bucharest 1, Calea Dorobanților 34, Sector 1; tel. (21) 2119871; fax (21) 2100175; e-mail mail@ambserbia.ro; internet www.ambserbia.ro; Ambassador Zoran S. Popović.

Slovakia: 020977 Bucharest 2, Str. Oțetari 3, Sector 2; tel. (21) 3006100; fax (21) 3006101; e-mail emb.bucharest@mzv.sk; internet www.bucharest.mfa.sk; Ambassador Dagmar Repčeková.

Slovenia: 011995 Bucharest, Str. Puşkin 10, Sector 1; tel. (21) 3002780; fax (21) 3150927; e-mail vbk@gov.si; internet www.bukaresta.veleposlanistvo.si; Chargé d'affaires a.i. Marcel Koprol.

South Africa: 010113 Bucharest, Str. Ştirbei Vodă 26–28, Sector 1; tel. (21) 3133725; fax (21) 3133795; e-mail saembassy.bucharest@yahoo.com; Ambassador Pieter Andries Swanepoel.

Spain: 011822 Bucharest, Str. Al. Alexandru 43, Sector 1; tel. (21) 3181080; fax (21) 3181072; e-mail emb.bucharest@maec.es; internet www.maec.es/embajadas/bucarest; Ambassador Estanislao de Grandes Pascual.

Sudan: 011941 Bucharest 1, Str. Barajul Argeş 6, Sector 1; tel. (21) 2339181; fax (21) 2339188; e-mail sudanbuc@sudanembassy.ro; internet www.sudanembassy.ro; Ambassador Ajing Adiang Marik.

Sweden: 011343 Bucharest, Şos. Kiseleff 43, Sector 1; tel. (21) 4067100; fax (21) 4067124; e-mail ambassaden.bucharest@foreign.ministry.se; internet www.swedenabroad.com/bukarest; Ambassador Anders Bengtcén.

Switzerland: 010626 Bucharest, Str. Grigore Alexandrescu 16–20, Sector 1; tel. (21) 2061600; fax (21) 2061620; e-mail buc.vertretung@eda.admin.ch; internet www.eda.admin.ch/bucarest; Ambassador Livio Hürzeler.

Syria: 010673 Bucharest, Bd. Lascăr Catargiu 50, Sector 1; tel. (21) 3192467; fax (21) 3129554; e-mail syrambro@yahoo.com; Ambassador Dr Walid Ali Osman.

Thailand: 020953 Bucharest, Str. Vasile Conta 12, Sector 2; tel. (21) 3110031; fax (21) 3110044; e-mail thaibuh@speedmail.ro; Ambassador Chantipha Phutrakul.

Tunisia: 010517 Bucharest 1, Str. Mihai Eminescu 50–54/10; tel. (21) 2101197; fax (21) 2101114; e-mail at.bucarest@b.astral.ro; Ambassador Saloua Bahri.

Turkey: 010575 Bucharest, Calea Dorobanților 72, Sector 1; tel. (21) 2063700; fax (21) 2063737; e-mail turkemb.bucharest@mfa.gov.tr; internet bucharest.emb.mfa.gov.tr; Ambassador Ömür Şölendil.

Turkmenistan: 012582 Bucharest, Str. Crinului 5, Sector 1; tel. (21) 3169066; fax (21) 3169047; Ambassador Shohrat Jumayev.

Ukraine: 010572 Bucharest, Bd. Aviatorilor 24, Sector 1; tel. (21) 2303660; fax (21) 2303661; e-mail emb_ro@mfa.gov.ua; internet www.ucraina.ro; Ambassador Markiyan Z. Kulyk.

United Arab Emirates: 011825 Aleea Modrogan 4; tel. (21) 2317676; fax (21) 2315588; e-mail uae@zappmobile.ro; Ambassador Yacub Yusuf al-Hosani.

United Kingdom: 010463 Bucharest, Str. Jules Michelet 24, Sector 1; tel. (21) 2017200; fax (21) 2017299; e-mail press@bucharest.mail.fco.gov.uk; internet ukinromania.fco.gov.uk; Ambassador Martin Harris.

USA: 020942 Bucharest, Str. Tudor Arghezi 7–9; tel. (21) 2003300; fax (21) 2003442; internet romania.usembassy.gov; Ambassador Mark Henry Gitenstein.

Uruguay: 011952 Bucharest, Str. Maxim Gorki 22/1, Sector 1; tel. and fax (21) 3138129; e-mail ururumania@embadeuruguay.ro; internet www.embadeuruguay.ro; Ambassador Pedro Mo Amaro.

Venezuela: 011396 Bucharest 1, Str. Pictor Mirea 18, Sector 1; tel. (21) 2225874; fax (21) 2225073; e-mail embavero@pcnet.ro; Chargé d'affaires a.i. Margot July Márquez García.

Viet Nam: 020011 Bucharest, Str. C. A. Rosetti 35; tel. (21) 3110334; fax (21) 3121626; e-mail vnemb.ro@mofa.gov.vn; internet www.vietnamembassy-romania.org; Ambassador Nguyen Quang Chien.

Judicial System

In preparation for its entry into the European Union on 1 January 2007, Romania implemented a programme of judicial reform, with a particular emphasis on guaranteeing the independence of the judiciary.

High Court of Cassation and Justice
(Înalte Curte de Casație și Justiție a României)

020936 Bucharest 2, Str. Batişte 2; tel. (21) 3137656; fax (21) 3137655; internet www.scj.ro.

The High Court of Cassation and Justice, which was reorganized in June 2004, exercises control over the judicial activity of all courts. It ensures the correct and uniform application of the law. The Court includes sections dealing with: civil and intellectual property law; criminal law; commercial law; and administrative and fiscal regulations.

President: Livia Doina Stanciu.

Constitutional Court of Romania (Curtea Constituțională a României): 050725 Bucharest, Palatul Parlamentului, Calea 13 Septembrie 2, Sector 5; tel. (21) 4022121; fax (21) 3124359; e-mail ccr@ccr.ro; internet www.ccr.ro; f. 1992; Pres. Ioan Vida.

Office of the Prosecutor-General: 050706 Bucharest 5, Bd. Libertății 14; tel. (21) 4102727; fax (21) 3113939; e-mail pg@kappa.ro; Prosecutor-General Laura Codruta Kovesi.

COUNTY COURTS AND LOCAL COURTS

The judicial organization of courts at the county and local levels was established by Law 92 of 4 August 1992. In each of the 40 counties, there is a county court and between three and six local courts. The county courts also form 15 circuits of appeal courts, where appeals against sentences passed by local courts are heard, which are generally considered courts of first instance. There is also a right of appeal from the appeal courts to the Supreme Court. In both county courts and local courts, the judges are professional magistrates.

Religion

In Romania there are 15 religious denominations and more than 400 religious associations recognized by the state. According to census figures, about 87% of the population belonged to the Romanian Orthodox Church in January 1992.

State Secretariat for Religious Affairs: 020962 Bucharest, Str. Nicolae Filipescu 40; tel. (21) 2118116; fax (21) 2109471; e-mail ssc@mediasat.ro; f. 1990; State Sec. Laurențiu Tănase.

CHRISTIANITY

The Romanian Orthodox Church

The Romanian Orthodox Church is the major religious organization in Romania (with more than 19m. believers) and is organized as an autocephalous patriarchate, led by the Holy Synod and headed by a patriarch. The Patriarchate comprises five metropolitanates, 10 archdioceses and 13 dioceses.

Romanian Patriarchate
(Patriarhia Română)

040163 Bucharest, Al. Dealul Mitropoliei 25; tel. (21) 3374035; fax (21) 3370097; e-mail externe@patriarhia.ro; internet www.patriarhia.ro.

Patriarch, Metropolitan of Muntênia and Dobrogea and Archbishop of Bucharest: DANIEL (CIOBOTEA), 040161 Bucharest, Str. Patriarhiei 21; tel. (21) 3372776.

Metropolitan of Banat and Archbishop of Timişoara and Caransebeş: Dr NICOLAE (CORNEANU), 300021 jud. Timiş, Timişoara, Bd. Constantin Diaconovici Loga 7; tel. (256) 190960; internet www.mitropolia-banatului.home.ro.

Metropolitan of Cluj, Alba, Crişana and Maramureş and Archbishop of Vad, Feleac and Cluj: BARTOLOMEU (ANANIA), 400117 jud. Cluj, Cluj-Napoca, Piaţa Avram Iancu 18; tel. (264) 593944; fax (264) 595184; e-mail bartolomeu@arhiepiscopia-ort-cluj.org; internet www.arhiepiscopia-ort-cluj.org.

Metropolitan of Moldova and Bucovina and Archbishop of Iaşi: TEOFAN (SAVU), 700064 jud. Iaşi, Iaşi, Bd. Ştefan cel Mare şi Sfânt 16; tel. (232) 214771; fax (232) 212656; e-mail iecum@mail.dntis.ro; internet www.mmb.ro.

Metropolitan of Oltenia and Archbishop of Craiova: IRINEU (POPA), 200381 jud. Dolj, Craiova, Str. Mitropolit Firmilian 3; tel. (251) 415054; fax (251) 418369; e-mail secretariat@m-ol.ro; internet www.mitropoliaolteniei.ro.

Metropolitan of Transylvania and Archbishop of Sibiu: LAURENŢIU, 550179 jud. Sibiu, Sibiu, Str. Mitropoliei 24; tel. (269) 412867.

The Roman Catholic Church

Catholics in Romania include adherents of the Armenian, Latin and Romanian (Byzantine) Rites.

Bishops' Conference: 010804 Bucharest, via Popa Tatu 68; tel. (21) 3111289; fax (21) 3111591; e-mail b_cazmir@pcnet.ro; internet www.catholica.ro; f. 1990; Pres. Most Rev. IOAN ROBU (Archbishop of Bucharest).

Latin Rite

There are two archdioceses (including one directly subordinate to the Holy See) and four dioceses. At 31 December 2007 there were 1,106,783 adherents of the Latin Rite (about 5.1% of the total population).

Archbishop of Alba Iulia: Most Rev. GYÖRGY-MIKLÓS JAKUBÍNYI, 510010 jud. Alba, Alba Iulia, Str. Mihai Viteazul 21; tel. (258) 811689; fax (258) 811454; e-mail albapress@gyrke.uab.ro.

Archbishop of Bucharest: Most Rev. IOAN ROBU, 010164 Bucharest, Str. Gen. Berthelot 19; tel. (21) 3158349; fax (21) 3121208; e-mail secretariat@arcb.ro.

Romanian Rite

There is one archbishopric-major and four dioceses. At 31 December 2007 there were 718,341 adherents of the Romanian Rite (about 3.3% of the total population).

Archbishop-Major of Făgăraş and Alba Iulia: Most Rev. LUCIAN MUREŞAN, 515400 jud. Alba, Blaj, Str. Petru Pavel Aron 2; tel. (258) 712057; fax (258) 713602; e-mail mitropolia@bru.ro.

Armenian Rite

There were 803 adherents of the Armenian Rite in Romania at 31 December 2007, represented by an Ordinariate.

Reformed (Calvinist) Church

The Reformed (Calvinist) Church has some 700,000 members. There are two bishoprics.

Bishop of Oradea: 410210 jud. Bihor, Oradea, Str. J. Calvin 1; tel. (259) 431710; e-mail krekpht@partium.ro; internet www.kiralyhagomellek.ro; Bishop LÁSZLÓ TŐKÉS.

Bishop of the Transylvanian Reformed Church District: 400079 jud. Cluj, Cluj-Napoca, Str. I. C. Brătianu 51; tel. (264) 597472; fax (264) 595104; e-mail office@reformatus.ro; internet portal.reformatus.ro; Bishop Rev. Dr GÉZA PAP.

Other Protestant Churches

Evangelical Church of the Augsburg Confession in Romania: 550185 Sibiu, Str. Gen. Magheru; tel. and fax (269) 217864; e-mail bischofsamt@evlk.artelecom.net; internet www.evang.ro; 13,271 mems (2010); Bishop REINHART GUIB.

Evangelical-Lutheran Church in Romania: 400105 jud. Cluj, Cluj-Napoca, Bd. 21 Decembrie 1989 1; tel. (264) 596614; fax (264) 593897; internet www.lutheran.ro; 30,720 mems (2010); Superintendent Bishop ZOLTÁN ADORJANI DEZSŐ.

Romanian Evangelical Church (Biserica Evanghelica România): 050454 Bucharest, Str. Carol Davila 48; tel. (21) 4119622; fax (21) 4103652; e-mail ber@rdsmail.ro; internet www.ber.ro.

Unitarian Church in Transylvania: 400105 jud. Cluj, Cluj-Napoca, Str. 21 Decembrie 1989 9; tel. (264) 593236; fax (264) 595927; e-mail ekt@unitarius.com; internet www.unitarius.com; f. 1568; comprises about 75,000 mems, principally of Hungarian ethnicity; 125 churches and 30 fellowships; Bishop ÁRPÁD SZABÓ.

Other Christian Churches

Belaya Krinitsa Old Believers' Orthodox Church: 810140 jud. Brăila, Brăila, Str. Zidari 5; tel. (239) 647023; Metropolitan LEONTY IZOTOV.

Pentecostal Church: 050453 Bucharest, Str. Carol Davila 81; tel. (21) 2126419; fax (21) 2204303; e-mail cuvadev@fx.ro; f. 1922; 2,455 churches, 525 pastors (Dec. 2001); 450,000 mems; Pres. Rev. RIVIS TIPEI PAVEL; Gen. Sec. Rev. IOAN GURĂU.

Seventh-day Adventist Church: 077190 jud. Ilfov, Voluntari, Str. Erou Iancu Nicolae 38; tel. (21) 4908590; fax (21) 4908570; e-mail communicatii@adventist.ro; internet www.adventist.ro; f. 1920; 67,000 mems; Pres. of the Union Rev. ADRIAN BOCANEANU; Sec.-Gen. TEODOR HUTANU.

ISLAM

There are an estimated 55,000 Muslims in Romania, mostly of Turkish or Tatar origin.

Muftiatul Cultului Musulman din Romania: Grand Mufti OSMAN NEGEAT, 900742 jud. Constanţa, Constanţa, Bd. Tomis 41; tel. (241) 611390.

JUDAISM

In 1999 there were about 14,000 Jews, organized in some 70 communities, in Romania.

Federation of Jewish Communities (Federatia Comunitatilor Evreiesti din Romania): 030202 Bucharest 3, Str. Sf. Vineri 9–11; tel. (21) 3132538; fax (21) 3120869; e-mail vainer@jewish.ro; internet www.jewish.ro; Pres. AUREL VAINER; Chief Rabbi MENACHEM HACOHEN.

The Press

The Romanian press is highly regionalized. In 2008 there were 75 daily newspapers and 2,615 periodicals in circulation. In 2002 some 10 newspapers and 207 periodicals were published in the languages of minority ethnic groups in Romania, including Hungarian, German, Serbian, Ukrainian, Armenian and Yiddish.

The publications listed below are in Romanian, unless otherwise indicated.

PRINCIPAL DAILY NEWSPAPERS

Adevărul (The Truth): 013701 Bucharest, Piaţa Presei Libere 1; tel. (21) 2240067; fax (21) 2243612; e-mail redactia@adevarul.kappa.ro; internet www.adevarul.ro; f. 1888; daily except Sun.; independent; Editor-in-Chief GRIGORE CARTIANU; circ. 91,006 (Jan. 2011).

Azi (Today): 010062 Bucharest, Calea Victoriei 39A, CP 45–49; tel. (21) 3141998; fax (21) 3144378; e-mail redactie@azi.ro; internet www.azi.ro; f. 1990; independent; Editor RUXANDRA NEGREA.

Cotidianul (The Daily): 020922 Bucharest 2, Bd. Carol I 34–36; tel. (21) 3173192; fax (21) 3173124; e-mail office@cotidianul.ro; internet www.cotidianul.ro; f. 1927; revived in 1991; daily except Sun.; online only; 50% owned by Academia Caţavencu; Editorial Dir DORU BUŞCU; Editor-in-Chief CORNEL NISTORESCU; circ. 120,000.

Cronica Română: 013701 Bucharest 1, POB 33, Piaţa Presei Libere 1, corp. C, etaj 1, camera 31; tel. (21) 3179165; fax (21) 3179169; e-mail cronica@rdsmail.ro; internet www.cronicaromana.ro; f. 1992; daily; Editor-in-Chief IULIAN BADEA; circ. 29,000.

Curierul Naţional (The National Courier): 010024 Bucharest, Str. Cristian Popişteanu 2–4; tel. (21) 5995500; fax (21) 3121300; e-mail office@curierulnational.ro; internet www.curierulnational.ro; f. 1991; Man. Editor ADRIAN VOINEA; circ. 3,206 (Sept. 2010).

ROMANIA

Economistul (The Economist): 010702 Bucharest 1, Calea Grivitei 21, 8th Floor; tel. (21) 3122248; fax (21) 3129717; e-mail eredactie@economistul.ro; internet www.economistul.ro; f. 1990; daily; Editor-in-Chief OCTAVIAN DRAGOMIR JORA.

Evenimentul Zilei (The Event of the Day): 020337 Bucharest 2, Bd. Dimitrie Pompeiu 6; tel. (21) 2022099; fax (21) 2022001; e-mail online@evz.ro; internet www.evz.ro; f. 1991; owned by Ringier (Switzerland); tabloid; Bucharest, Transylvania and western regional editions; Editor-in-Chief VLAD MACOVEI; circ. 20,003 (Sept. 2010).

Gândul (The Thought): 020097 Bucharest, Str. Aurel Vlaicu 62–64, Sector 2; tel. (31) 8257125; fax (31) 8257188; e-mail redactia@gandul.info; internet www.gandul.info; f. 2005; independent; Editor-in-Chief CLAUDIU PĂNDARU; circ. 12,238 (Jan. 2011).

Gazeta Sporturilor (Sports Gazette): 051431 Bucharest 1, Șos. Dionisie Lupu 64–66; tel. (21) 4066507; fax (21) 2087484; e-mail contact@gsp.ro; internet www.gsp.ro; f. 1924; daily except Sun.; independent; Editor-in-Chief CĂTĂLIN TOLONTAN; circ. 44,524 (Jan. 2011).

Jurnalul National (The National Journal): 013701 Bucharest 1, Piața Presei Libere 1, Corp. D, etaj 8; tel. (21) 3182029; fax (21) 3182027; e-mail dan.constantin@jurnalul.ro; internet www.jurnalul.ro; f. 1993; Editor-in-Chief DAN CONSTANTIN; circ. 46,074 (Jan. 2011).

Libertatea (Freedom): 020337 Bucharest, Bd. Dimitrie Pompeiu 6, Sector 2; tel. (21) 2030804; fax (21) 2030832; internet www.libertatea.ro; f. 1989; owned by Ringier (Switzerland); daily; Sunday edition, *Libertatea de Duminica*, launched in 2002; tabloid; morning paper; Editor-in-Chief ANA NITA; circ. 126,475 (Jan. 2011).

ProSport: 020337 Bucharest 2, Bd. Dimitrie Pompeiu 6, Novo Parc; tel. (21) 2030803; fax (21) 2030836; e-mail contact@prosport.ro; internet www.prosport.ro; f. 1997; owned by Ringier (Switzerland); sports news; circ. 39,039 (Jan. 2011).

România Libera (Free Romania): 031041 Bucharest 3, Str. Nerva Traian 3/101M, etaj 4; tel. (21) 2028290; fax (21) 2028143; e-mail redactia@romanialibera.ro; internet www.romanialibera.ro; f. 1877; daily except Sun.; independent; Editor-in-Chief DAN CRISTIAN TRUTURICĂ; circ. 40,308 (Jan. 2011).

Ziarul Financiar: 020097 Bucharest, Str. Aurel Vlaicu 62-64, Sector 2; tel. (31) 8256288; fax (31) 8256285; e-mail zf@zf.ro; internet www.zf.ro; Editor SORIN PISLARU; circ. 12,223 (Jan. 2011).

DISTRICT NEWSPAPERS

Adevărul (The Truth): 310130 jud. Arad, Arad, Bd. Revoluției 81; tel. (257) 281802; fax (257) 280904; e-mail adevarul@arad.ro; internet www.adevarul.arad.ro; f. 1989; independent; daily; Dir DOREL ZAVOIANU; circ. 25,900.

Adevărul Harghitei (Harghita Truth): 530190 jud. Harghita, Miercurea-Ciuc, Str. Leliceni 45; tel. (266) 371805; fax (266) 172065; f. 1990; independent; daily; Editor-in-Chief MIHAI GROZA.

Argeșul Liber (Free Argeș): 110177 jud. Argeș, Pitești, Str. Republicii 88; tel. (24) 8217704; fax (24) 8210060; e-mail argesul@gmail.com; internet www.ziarulargesul.ro; f. 1990; independent; daily; Editor-in-Chief GABRIEL LIXANDRU.

Bună Ziua Brașov (Good Afternoon Brașov): 500090 jud. Brașov, Brașov, Str. Mihai Kogalniceanu 19, etaj 7; tel. (268) 547780; fax (268) 547780; e-mail bzb@bzb.ro; internet www.bzb.ro; f. 1995; Dir MIRELA LEONTICĂ; circ. 30,000.

Ceahlăul: 610263 jud. Neamț, Piatra-Neamț, Al. Tiparului 14; tel. (233) 225282; fax (233) 225282; e-mail redactie@ziarulceahlaul.ro; internet www.ziarulceahlaul.ro; f. 1989; daily; Editor-in-Chief CORNELIU LĂMĂTIC; circ. 20,000.

Crai nou: 720059 jud. Suceava, Suceava, Str. Mihai Viteazul 32; tel. (230) 215996; fax (230) 214723; e-mail redactie@crainou.ro; internet www.crainou.ro; f. 1990; daily; Editor-in-Chief L D. CLEMENT.

Cuget Liber (Free Thinking): 900711 jud. Constanța, Constanța, Șos. I. C. Brătianu 5; tel. (241) 582100; fax (241) 619524; e-mail office@cugetliber.ro; internet www.cugetliber.ro; f. 1989; independent; daily; Editor-in-Chief COSMIN ZAPOROJAN.

Curierul de Vâlcea (Courier of Vâlcea): 240591 jud. Vâlcea, Râmnicu Vâlcea, Carol I/19; tel. (250) 732325; fax (250) 732326; e-mail office@curierul.ro; internet www.curierul.ro; f. 1990; independent; daily except Mon.; commerce; Editor-in-Chief MARIUS CIUTACU.

Cuvântul Liber (The Free Word): 540015 jud. Mureș, Târgu Mureș, Str. Gh. Doja 9; tel. and fax (265) 266629; internet www.cuvantul-liber.ro; f. 1989; independent; daily; Editor-in-Chief LAZĂR LADARIU; circ. 10,000 (2009).

Cuvântul Libertății (The Word of Liberty): 200020 jud. Dolj, Craiova, Str. Nicolăescu Plopșor. 22A; tel. (251) 412457; fax (251) 414141; e-mail mediafax@cvl.homeip.net; internet www.cvlpress.ro; f. 1989; daily except Sun.; Editor-in-Chief MIRCEA CANȚAR; circ. 10,000 (2010).

Cuvântul nou (The New Word): 520064 jud. Covasna, Sfântu Gheorghe, Str. Pieței 8A; tel. and fax (240) 2311388; e-mail cuvnou@znet.ro; f. 1968; new series 1990; daily except Mon.; Editor-in-Chief DUMITRU MĂNOLĂCHESCU.

Dâmbovița: 130082 jud. Dâmbovița, Târgoviște, Bul. Unirii 32; tel. and fax (245) 634017; e-mail ziar_dambovita@yahoo.com; internet www.ziardambovita.ro; f. 1990; independent; Editor-in-Chief ALEXANDRU ILIE.

Datina (Tradition): 220016 jud. Mehedinți, Drobeta-Turnu Severin, Str. Tabla-Buții 74 A; tel. (252) 311995; fax (252) 326052; f. 1990; independent; Editor-in-Chief GHEORGHE BUREȚEA.

Delta (The Delta): 820180 jud. Tulcea, Tulcea, Str. Spitalului 4; tel. (2405) 12406; fax (2405) 16616; f. 1885; new series 1990; daily except Mon.; Editor-in-Chief NECULAI AMIHULESEI.

Deșteptarea (The Awakening): 600010 jud. Bacău, Bacău, Str. Vasile Alecsandri 41; tel. (234) 511272; fax (234) 523515; e-mail redactie@desteptarea.ro; internet www.desteptarea.ro; f. 1989; Editor-in-Chief DORIAN POCOVNICU; circ. 50,000.

Erdélyi Napló: 400009 jud. Kolozsvár, Str. Gen. Eremia Grigorescu 52, POB 1320; tel. (36) 4142301; fax (36) 4109836; e-mail office@erdelyinaplo.ro; internet www.hhrf.org/erdelyinaplo; in Hungarian; weekly; Man. Editor JÓZSEF MAKKAY.

Evenimentul: 700497 jud. Iași, Iași, Str. Crișan 14; tel. (232) 246000; fax (232) 246002; e-mail contact@evenimentul.ro; internet www.evenimentul.ro; f. 1991; daily; Editor-in-Chief DAN N. DOBOȘ; circ. 3,868 (Jan. 2011).

Făclia de Cluj (Cluj Torch): 401050 jud. Cluj, Cluj-Napoca, Str. Napoca 16; tel. (264) 591681; fax (264) 592828; e-mail redactia@ziarulfaclia.ro; internet www.ziarulfaclia.ro; f. 1989; fmrly *Adevărul de Cluj* (Cluj Truth); present name adopted 2007; independent; Editor-in-Chief ILIE CĂLIAN; circ. 200,000.

Gazeta de Transilvania (Transylvanian Gazette): 500030 jud. Brașov, Brașov, Str. M. Sadoveanu 3; tel. (268) 472099; fax (268) 475604; e-mail gazeta.transilvania@brasovia.ro; internet www.gtbv.ro; f. 1838; ceased publication 1946, re-established 1989; daily except Mon.; independent; Editor-in-Chief ADRIAN TEACĂ.

Gorjanul: 210192 jud. Gorj, Târgu Jiu, Str. Constantin Brâncuși 15; tel. (253) 217464; fax (253) 212072; e-mail redactie@gorjeanul.ro; internet www.gorjeanul.ro; f. 1990; Editor-in-Chief ANAMARIA STOICA.

Graiul Maramureșului (The Voice of Maramureș): 430051 jud. Maramureș, Baia Mare, Bd. București 25; tel. (262) 221017; fax (262) 224871; e-mail graiul@graiul.ro; internet www.graiul.ro; f. 1989; independent; daily except Sun.; Editor-in-Chief AUGUSTIN COZMUȚA; circ. 10,000.

Graiul Sălajului (Voice of Sălaj): 450042 jud. Sălaj, Zalău, Str. Mihai Viteazul 14; tel. (260) 611320; fax (260) 612479; e-mail graiulsj@unisys.ro; internet www.graiulsalajului.ro; f. 1990; Editor-in-Chief DANIEL MUNTEANU.

Hargita Népe (People of Hargita): 530190 jud. Harghita, Miercurea-Ciuc, Str. Leliceni 45; tel. (266) 372633; e-mail office@hargitanepe.ro; internet www.topnet.ro/hargitanepe; daily; in Hungarian; Dir ISTVÁN CSONGOR ISAN; circ. 7,691 (Jan. 2011).

Háromszék (Three Chairs): 520003 jud. Covasna, Sfântu Gheorghe, Str. Gábor Áron 2; tel. (267) 351504; fax (367) 405264; e-mail hpress@3szek.ro; internet www.3szek.ro; f. 1989; socio-political; daily; in Hungarian; Editor-in-Chief BOTOND FARCÁDI.

Mesagerul de Bistrița-Năsăud: 420074 jud. Bistrița-Năsăud, Bistrița, Str. Ursului 14; tel. (402) 63234688; fax (402) 63234689; e-mail mesagerul@mesagerul.ro; internet www.mesagerul.ro; daily.

Milcovul Liber (Free Milcov): 620095 jud. Vrancea, Focșani, Bd. Unirii 18; tel. (237) 614579; fax (237) 613588; f. 1989; weekly; Dir OVIDIU BUTUC.

Monitorul de Botoșani: 710210 jud. Botoșani, Botoșani, Str. Mihail Kogălniceanu 4; tel. (231) 515053; fax (231) 515130; e-mail monitorul@monitorulbt.ro; internet www.monitorulbt.ro; Editor-in-Chief CĂTĂLIN MORARU; circ. 6,685 (Jan. 2011).

Monitorul de Iași (Iași Monitor): 700237 jud. Iași, Iași, Șos. Națională 45; tel. (332) 430806; fax (332) 430807; e-mail redactia@monitorul.com.ro; internet www.monitorul.com.ro; f. 1991; daily; Editor-in-Chief LAURA MUSINA.

Népújság (People's Journal): 540015 jud. Mureș, Târgu Mureș, Str. Gh. Doja 9; tel. (265) 266780; fax (265) 266270; e-mail nepujsag@e-nepujsag.ro; internet www.hhrf.org/nepujsag; f. 1990; daily; in Hungarian; Editor-in-Chief MIKLÓS NAGY KUND.

Opinia (Opinion): 120024 jud. Buzău, Buzău, Str. Str. Chiristigii 3; tel. (238) 711063; fax (238) 412764; e-mail opinia@buzau.ro; internet ziarul.opiniabuzau.ro; f. 1990; independent; daily; Editor-in-Chief GABRIEL COSTIANU.

Pământul (Free Earth): 991048 jud. Călărași, Călărași, Str. București 187; tel. (2911) 15840; fax (2911) 313630; f. 1990; socio-political; weekly; Editor-in-Chief GHEORGHE FRANGULEA.

ROMANIA

Prahova: 100066 jud. Prahova, Ploiești, Bd. Republicii 2; tel. (244) 515691; fax (244) 407399; e-mail edprahova@asesoft.ro; internet www.ziarulprahova.ro; f. 1870; Editor-in-Chief LUIZA RADULESCU-PINTILIE; circ. 17,000.

Renașterea Bănățeană (The Banat Renaissance): 300024 jud. Timiș, Timișoara, Bd. Revoluției 1989 8; tel. (256) 490145; fax (256) 490370; e-mail renasterea@renasterea.ro; internet www.renasterea.ro; f. 1990; daily; independent; tabloid; Editor-in-Chief OCTAVIAN ROȘA; circ. 11,623 (Jan. 2011).

Szabadság (Freedom): 400009 jud. Cluj, Cluj-Napoca, Str. Napoca 16, POB 340; tel. (264) 596408; fax (264) 597206; e-mail office@szabadsag.ro; internet www.szabadsag.ro; f. 1989; organ of Minerva Cultural Asscn (non-governmental org.); daily except Sun.; in Hungarian; online edition in parallel since 1995 (up to 5,000 readers); covers five counties; Editor-in-Chief ILDIKÓ ÚJVÁRI; circ. 10,000.

Szatmári Friss Újság: 440026 jud. Satu Mare, Satu Mare, Str. Mihai Viteazul 32; tel. (261) 714654; fax (261) 712024; e-mail marta.antal@informmedia.ro; internet www.frissujsag.ro; f. 1990; daily except Sun.; in Hungarian; Editor-in-Chief ELEK ANIKÓ; circ. 7,509 (Jan. 2011).

Szilágyaság (Word from Sălaj): 450042 jud. Sălaj, Zalău, Piața Libertății 9, POB 68; tel. (299) 633736; e-mail szilagysag@zappmobile.ro; f. 1990; organ of Hungarian Democratic Union of Romania; weekly; Editor-in-Chief JÁNOS KUI.

Teleormanul Liber (Free Teleorman): 140033 jud. Teleorman, Alexandria, Str. Ion Creangă 63; tel. (247) 311950; fax (247) 323871; e-mail etl@starnets.ro; f. 1990; daily; Editor-in-Chief GHEORGHE FILIP.

Timișoara: 300012 jud. Timiș, Timișoara, Str. Bredicanu 37A; tel. (256) 264546; fax (256) 146170; e-mail timisoara@rdstm.ro; internet www.cotidianultimisoara.ro; f. 1990; daily; Editor-in-Chief OSCAR BERGER.

Tribuna: 550013 jud. Sibiu, Sibiu, Str. Gheorghe Coșbuc 38; tel. (269) 211318; fax (269) 214141; e-mail red@tribuna.ro; internet www.tribuna.ro; f. 1884; daily; independent; Man. Editor FLORIN STAICU; circ. 17,000.

Tribuna Ialomiței (Ialomița Tribune): 920033 jud. Ialomița, Slobozia, Str. Dobrogeanu-Gherea 2; f. 1969; weekly; Editor-in-Chief TITUS NIȚU.

Unirea (The Union): 510093 jud. Alba, Alba Iulia, Str. Decebal 27; tel. (258) 811419; fax (258) 812464; e-mail unirea@unirea-pres.ro; internet www.ziarulunirea.ro; f. 1891; independent; daily except Sun.; Gen. Man. GHEORGHE CIUL; Editor-in-Chief MARIA LUCIA MUNTEANU; circ. 17,577 (Jan. 2011).

Viața Libera (Free Life): 800215 jud. Galați, Galați, Str. Domnească 68; tel. (23) 460620; fax (23) 471028; e-mail katia@viata-libera.ro; internet www.viata-libera.ro; f. 1989; independent; daily; Editor-in-Chief KATIA NANU; circ. 7,648 (Jan. 2011).

Ziarul de Iași: 700399 jud. Iași, Iași, Str. Smârdan 5; tel. (232) 271333; fax (232) 270415; e-mail redactie@ziaruldeiasi.ro; internet www.ziaruldeiasi.ro; daily; Editor-in-Chief TONI HRITAC; circ. 5,798 (Jan. 2011).

PRINCIPAL PERIODICALS

22: 010093 Bucharest, Calea Victoriei 120; tel. (21) 3112208; fax (21) 3141776; e-mail redactia@revista22.ro; internet www.revista22.ro; f. 1990; weekly; Editor-in-Chief RODICA PALADE; circ. 10,000 (2008).

Academia Cațavencu (Cațavencu Academy): 030016 Bucharest 2, Bd. Regina Elisabeta 7–9, et. 6; tel. (21) 3140235; fax (21) 3140258; e-mail office@catavencu.ro; internet www.catavencu.ro; f. 1991; weekly; satirical; Dir MARCELA PETRACHE; circ. 22,111 (Jan. 2011).

Bursa: 010804 Bucharest 1, Str. Popa Tatu 71; tel. (21) 3154356; fax (21) 3124556; e-mail marketing@bursa.ro; internet www.bursa.ro; f. 1990; finance; Editor-in-Chief FLORIAN GOLDSTEIN; circ. 35,000.

Capital: 020337 Bucharest 2, Bd. Dimitrie Pompeiu 6, Novo Park; tel. (21) 2030802; fax (21) 2030902; e-mail secretariat@capital.ro; internet www.capital.ro; f. 1992; owned by Ringier (Switzerland); weekly; economic and financial magazine; Editor-in-Chief IULIAN BORTOS; circ. 12,250 (Jan. 2011).

Contemporanul—Ideea Europeană (The Contemporary—The European Idea): 014780 Bucharest 1, Piața Amzei, Asociația Contemporanul, POB 113, Of. p. 22; tel. (21) 2125692; fax (21) 3106618; e-mail office@contemporanul.ro; internet www.ideeaeuropeana.ro/revista-contemporanul.php; f. 1881; monthly; cultural, political and scientific review; published by the European Idea Cultural Foundation; Editor-in-Chief AURA CHRISTI.

Cronica: 700037 jud. Iași, Iași, Str. I. C. Brătianu 22; tel. and fax (232) 262140; e-mail cronica_iasi@yahoo.com; internet www.revistacronica.wordpress.com; f. 1966; monthly; cultural review; Editor-in-Chief VALERIU STANCU; circ. 5,000.

Erdélyi Figyelö (Transylvanian Observer): 540026 jud. Mureș, Târgu Mureș, Str. Primăriei 1; tel. (265) 166910; fax (265) 168688; f. 1958; fmrly Uj Élet; quarterly; illustrated magazine; in Hungarian; Editor-in-Chief JÁNOS LÁZOK.

Femeia Moderna (Modern Woman): 011013 Bucharest, Buzesti 85, et. 4, Sector 1; tel. (31) 2258700; fax (31) 2258715; e-mail revistafemeia@sanomahearst.ro; internet www.femeia.ro; f. 1868; monthly; Editor-in-Chief LUANA MURESAN; circ. 15,164 (Jan. 2011).

Flacăra (The Flame): 013701 Bucharest 1, Piața Presei Libere 1; tel. (21) 3179142; fax (21) 3179143; e-mail office@publicatiileflacara.ro; internet www.revistaflacara.ro; f. 1911; monthly; Editor-in-Chief LILIANA PETRUȘ; circ. 1,847 (Jan. 2011).

Jurnalul Afacerilor (Romanian Business Journal): 013701 Bucharest 1, Piața Presei Libere 1, Corp. 3, 3rd Floor, Rm 317–321; tel. (21) 2246897; fax (21) 2246896; e-mail rbj@euroweb.ro; f. 1990; Dir MARCEL BARBU; circ. 25,000.

Korunk (Our Time): 400304 jud. Cluj, Cluj-Napoca, Str. Gen. Eremia Grigorescu 52; tel. (264) 375035; fax (264) 375093; e-mail korunk@gmail.com; internet www.korunk.org; f. 1926; monthly; social review; in Hungarian; Editor-in-Chief IMRE JÓZSEF BALÁZS; circ. 1,500 (2006).

Magazin istoric (Historical Magazine): 010155 Bucharest, Piața Valter Mărăcineanu 1–3, POB 15-702; tel. (21) 3126877; fax (21) 3150991; e-mail mistoric@gmail.com; internet www.magazinistoric.ro; f. 1967; monthly; review of historical culture; Chief Editor DORIN MATEI; circ. 20,000 (2010).

Napsugár (Sun Ray): 400462 jud. Cluj, Constantin Brâncuși 202/101, POB 137; tel. and fax (264) 418001; e-mail naps.sziv@napsugar.ro; internet www.napsugar.ro; f. 1956; monthly; illustrated literary magazine for children aged 7–12 years; in Hungarian; Editor-in-Chief EMESE ZSIGMOND; circ. 13,500 (2011).

Orizont (Horizon): 300085 jud. Timiș, Timișoara, Piața St Gheorghe 3; tel. and fax (256) 294893; e-mail fundatia@3europe.org; internet www.revistaorizont.ro; f. 1949; monthly; review of the Writers' Union (Timișoara br.); Editor-in-Chief MIRCEA MIHĂIEȘ.

Panoramic Radio-TV: 011964 Bucharest, Str. Jean Baptiste Molière dramaturg 2–4; tel. (21) 2307501; fax (21) 156992; e-mail micara.dumutrescu@tvr.ro; f. 1990; weekly; Dir STEFAN DIMITRIU; Editor-in-Chief ADRIAN IONESCU; circ. 50,000.

PC World Romania: 011455 Bucharest, Pl. Independentei 202A, Sector 1; tel. (21) 3144102; fax (21) 3144120; e-mail pcworld@idg.ro; internet www.pcworld.ro; f. 1993; monthly; computing; Editor-in-Chief STEFANIA MIHALCEA; circ. 15,000.

Practic in bucătărie: 020912 Bucharest, Str. Carol I 31–33, Complexul Asirom, Sector 2; tel. (37) 2106000; fax (37) 2106055; e-mail publicitate@burda.ro; owned by Hubert Burda Media (Germany); monthly; cookery and kitchen-design magazine; Man. Editor VALENTIN IORDACHE; circ. 178,389 (Jan. 2011).

Revista Română de Statistică (Romanian Statistical Review): 050706 Bucharest, Bd. Libertății 16; tel. and fax (21) 3171110; e-mail rrs@insse.ro; internet www.revistadestatistica.ro; f. 1952; monthly; organ of Romanian National Institute of Statistics.

România Literară (Literary Romania): 010071 Bucharest, Calea Victoriei 133, Sector 1; tel. (21) 2127981; fax (21) 2127981; e-mail revistaromanialiterara@gmail.com; internet www.romlit.ro; f. 1968; weekly; literary, artistic and political magazine; published by the Fundation România Literară (Writers' Union); Dir NICOLAE MANOLESCU; Gen. Editor IONELA STANCIU.

România Mare (Greater Romania): 010062 Bucharest, Calea Victoriei 39A; tel. (21) 6156093; fax (21) 3125396; internet www.romare.ro; f. 1990; weekly; nationalist; Editor-in-Chief CORNELIU VADIM TUDOR; circ. 90,000.

Super Magazin: 013701 Bucharest, Piața Presei Libere 1; tel. (21) 2223323; fax (21) 2226382; f. 1993; Editor-in-Chief GHEORGHE VOICU; circ. 200,000.

Szivárvány (Rainbow): 400462 jud. Cluj, Cluj-Napoca, Bd.Constantin brancusi 202/101; tel. and fax (264) 418001; e-mail naps.sziv@napsugar.ro; internet www.napsugar.ro; f. 1980; monthly; illustrated literary magazine for children aged 3–6 years; in Hungarian; Editor-in-Chief EMESE ZSIGMOND; circ. 16,000 (2011).

Tehnium: 013701 Bucharest, Piața Presei Libere 1; tel. (21) 2223374; f. 1970; monthly; hobbies; Editor-in-Chief ILIE MIHĂESCU; circ. 100,000.

Tribuna: 400091 jud. Cluj, Cluj-Napoca, Str. Universității 1; tel. (264) 117548; f. 1884; weekly; cultural review; Editor-in-Chief AUGUSTIN BUZURA.

Tribuna economică (Economic Tribune): 010336 Bucharest, Bd. Magheru 28–30, Sector 1; tel. (21) 3165544; fax (21) 3103833; e-mail tribunae@tribuneconomica.ro; internet www.tribuneconomica.ro; f. 1899; weekly; Editor-in-Chief Dr GH. N. IOSIF; circ. 10,000.

ROMANIA

Vânătorul şi Pescarul Român (The Romanian Hunter and Angler): 020882 Bucharest, Calea Moşilor 128; tel. (21) 3133363; fax (21) 3136804; f. 1948; monthly review; Editor-in-Chief Gabriel Cheroiu.

NEWS AGENCIES

Agerpres (Agenţia Română de Presă): 013701 Bucharest, Piaţa Presei Libere 1; tel. (21) 2076110; fax (21) 3170707; e-mail office@ agerpres.ro; internet www.agerpres.ro; f. 1889; renamed as Rompress in 1989, and as above in 2008; provides news and photo services; in English and French; Dir-Gen. Ioan Rosca.

Mediafax: 020097 Bucharest 2, Str. Aurel Vlaicu 62–64; tel. (31) 8256100; fax (31) 8256140; e-mail credactie.online@mediafax.ro; internet www.mediafax.ro; f. 1995; general and business news; Chief Exec. Cristian Dimitriu.

PRESS ASSOCIATION

Society of Romanian Journalists—Federation of All Press Unions (Societatea Ziariştilor din România—Federaţia Sindicatelor din Întreaga Presă): 013701 Bucharest, Piaţa Presei Libere 1; tel. (21) 2228351; fax (21) 3179796; e-mail szrpress@moon.ro; f. 1990; affiliated to International Organization of Journalists and to International Federation of Journalists; Pres. Cornelius Popa; 5,000 mems.

Publishers

Editura Academiei Române (Publishing House of the Romanian Academy): 050711 Bucharest, Calea 13 Septembrie 13; tel. (21) 4119008; fax (21) 4103983; e-mail edacad@ear.ro; internet www .ear.ro; f. 1948; books and periodicals on original scientific work; 80 periodicals in Romanian and foreign languages; Gen. Man. Dumitru Radu Popescu.

Editura Albatros: 013701 Bucharest, Piaţa Presei Libere 1, Of. 33; tel. and fax (21) 2228493; f. 1969; Romanian literature and culture; Editor-in-Chief Georgeta Dimisiano.

Editura Artemis (Artemis Publishing House): 013701 Bucharest, Piaţa Presei Libere 1; tel. (21) 2226661; f. 1991; fine arts, fiction, children's literature, history; Dir Mirella Acsente.

Editura Cartea Românească (Publishing House of the Romanian Book): 010071 Bucharest 1, Calea Victoriei 115; tel. (21) 2315237; fax (21) 2244829; e-mail ecr@cartearomaneasca.ro; internet www .cartearomaneasca.ro; f. 1969; Romanian contemporary literature; Dir Dan Cristea.

Editura Ceres: 013701 Bucharest, Piaţa Presei Libere 1; tel. (21) 2224836; f. 1953; books on agriculture and forestry; Dir Maria Damian.

Editura Dacia (Dacia Publishing House): 400660 jud. Cluj, Cluj-Napoca, Str. Ospatariei 4; tel. and fax (264) 429675; e-mail office@ edituradacia.ro; internet www.edituradacia.ro; f. 1969; classical and contemporary literature, science fiction, academic, technical, philosophical and scientific books; in Romanian and Hungarian; Gen. Man. Ioan Vădan.

Editura Didactică şi Pedagogică (Educational Publishing House): 010176 Bucharest, Str. Spiru Haret 12; tel. and fax (21) 3122885; internet www.edituradp.ro; f. 1951; school, university, technical and vocational textbooks, pedagogic literature and methodology, teaching materials; Gen. Man. Prof. Mihaela Zărnescu-Enceanu.

Editura Eminescu (Eminescu Publishing House): 020982 Bucharest 2, Str. Sfantul Spiridon 8; tel. and fax (21) 2123588; e-mail info@edituraeminescu.ro; internet www.edituraeminescu.ro; f. 1969; contemporary original literary works and translations of world literature; Dir Silvia Cinca.

Editura Enciclopedică (Encyclopedia Publishing House): 013701 Bucharest, Piaţa Presei Libere 1; tel. and fax (21) 3179035; e-mail enciclopedica2006@yahoo.com; f. 1968; encyclopedias, dictionaries, monographs, reference books and children's books; Dir Marcel Popa.

Editura Humanitas (Humanitas Publishing House): 013701 Bucharest, Piaţa Presei Libere 1; tel. (21) 3171819; fax (21) 3171824; e-mail secretariat@humanitas.ro; internet www .humanitas.ro; f. 1990; philosophy, religion, political and social sciences, economics, history, fiction, textbooks, art, literature, practical books; Dir Gabriel Liiceanu.

Editura Litera Internaţional (International Letter Publishing House): 011422 Bucharest, Str. Emanoil Porumbaru 31a, et. 1, ap. 3; tel. (21) 3196393; fax (21) 3196390; e-mail info@litera.ro; internet www.litera.ro; f. 1989; original literature; Dir-Gen. Dan Vidrascu.

Editura Medicală SA (Medical Publishing House): 021411 Bucharest 2, Bd. Protopopescu Pache 131; tel. (21) 2525188; fax (21) 2525189; e-mail office@ed-medicala.ro; internet www.ed-medicala .ro; f. 1954; medical literature; Dir Prof. Al C. Oproiu.

Directory

Editura Militară (Military Publishing House): 061353 Bucharest 6, Drumul Taberei 7–9; tel. and fax (21) 3149161; e-mail adrian .pandea@edituramilitara.ro; internet www.edituramilitara.ro; f. 1950; military history, theory, science, technics, medicine and fiction; Dir Adrian Pandea.

Editura Muzicală (Musical Publishing House): 010071 Bucharest, Calea Victoriei 141; tel. and fax (21) 3129867; e-mail em@ edituramuzicala.ro; internet www.edituramuzicala.ro; f. 1957; books on music, musicology and musical scores; Dir Marius Vasileanu.

Editura Polirom: 700505 jud. Iaşi, Iaşi, Bd. Carol I 4, etaj 4, POB 266; tel. (232) 214100; fax (232) 214111; e-mail office@polirom.ro; internet www.polirom.ro; f. 1995; Dir Silviu Lupescu.

Editura Tehnică (Technical Publishing House): 024056 Bucharest 2, Str. Olari 213; tel. (21) 2522366; fax (21) 2525077; e-mail tehnica@ edituratehnica.ro; internet www.edituratehnica.ro; f. 1950; technical and scientific books, technical dictionaries; Dir Roman Chirilă.

Editura Univers: 010209 Bucharest, Str. Mircea Vulcănescu 2; tel. (21) 3153307; fax (21) 3153308; e-mail office@edituraunivers.ro; internet www.edituraunivers.ro; f. 1961; translations from world literature, criticism, essays, literary history, philosophy of culture, educational; Man. Dir Sergiu Crupenschi.

Editura de Vest (Publishing House of the West): 300085 jud. Timiş, Timişoara, Piaţa Sfântul Gheorghe 2; tel. and fax (256) 434382; f. 1972 as Editura Facla; socio-political, technical, scientific and literary works; in Romanian, Hungarian, German and Serbian; Dir Vasile Popovici.

PUBLISHERS' ASSOCIATION

Romanian Publishers' Asscn (Asociaţia Editorilor din România): 010326 Bucharest, Bd. Magheru 35, 4th Floor, ap. 42; tel. (21) 2125162; fax (21) 2125178; e-mail info@aer.ro; internet www.aer .ro; f. 1993; 57 mems; Pres. Gabriel Liiceanu.

Broadcasting and Communications

TELECOMMUNICATIONS

Regulatory Authority

National Regulatory Authority for Communications (Autoritatea Naţională de Reglementare in Comunicaţii—ANRC): 050706 Bucharest 5, Bd. Libertăţii 14; tel. (21) 3075400; fax (21) 3075402; e-mail anrc@anrc.ro; internet www.anrc.ro; f. 2002.

Service Providers

Cosmote Romanian Mobile Telecommunications SA: 011141 Bucharest 1, Şos. Nicolae Titulescu 4–8; tel. (21) 4041234; fax (21) 4137530; e-mail info@cosmote.ro; internet www.cosmote.ro; f. 2000; fmrly CosmoROM; owned by COSMOTE (Greece); mobile cellular telecommunications services; Chief Exec. Nikolaos Tsolas.

Orange Romania SA: 010665 Bucharest 1, Bd. Lascar Catargiu 51–53, Europe House; tel. (21) 2033030; fax (21) 2033413; e-mail infocorporate@orange.ro; internet www.orange.ro; f. 1996; fmrly Mobil-Rom; owned by Orange (France); mobile cellular telecommunications services; Exec. Dir Pierre Mattei; 5m. subscribers (2005).

Romtelecom SA: 050706 Bucharest 5, Bd. Libertăţii 14–16; tel. (21) 4001212; fax (21) 4105581; e-mail contact@romtelecom.ro; internet www.romtelecom.ro; f. 1933; fmr state monopoly; 54% owned by Hellenic Telecommunications Organization (Greece); Dir-Gen. Georgios Ioannidis.

Telemobil SA (Zapp): 077015 jud. Ilfov, Baloteşti, Str. Bucureşti 2 bis; tel. (21) 4024444; fax (21) 4024456; internet www.telemobil.ro; f. 1999; operates mobile cellular telephone network; Man. Dir and Chief Exec. Diwaker Singh.

Vodafone Romania: 061344 Bucharest 6, Bd. Vasile Milea 4a; tel. (21) 3021111; fax (21) 3021413; e-mail contact@connex.ro; internet www.vodafone.ro; fmrly Connex (Mobifon); operates mobile cellular telephone network and third-generation (GSM) services, and provides internet services; 99% owned by Vodafone Group PLC (United Kingdom); Pres. Al Tolstoy.

BROADCASTING

Radio

Societatea Româna de Radiodifuziune (SRR) (Romanian Radio Corpn): 010171 Bucharest, Str. Gen. Berthelot 60–64, POB 63-1200; tel. (21) 3031432; fax (21) 3121057; e-mail mesaje@rornet.ro; internet www.srr.ro; f. 1928; 39 transmitters on medium-wave, 69 transmitters on VHF; 114 relays; operates the Radio Romania and Radio Romania International stations: news, cultural, youth and music programmes, plus two local and six regional programmes; foreign broadcasts on one medium-wave and eight short-wave transmitters

ROMANIA

in Arabic, Bulgarian, Chinese, English, German, Greek, Hungarian, Italian, Portuguese, Romanian, Russian, Serbian, Spanish, Turkish and Ukrainian; Pres. MARIA TOGHINA.

Kiss FM: 060022 Bucharest 6, Spl. Independenței 202A; tel. (21) 3188000; fax (21) 3125346; e-mail kissfm@kissfm.ro; internet www.kissfm.ro; owned by SBS Broadcasting S.a.r.l.

Pro FM: 021409 Bucharest 2, Bd. Protopopescu Pache 109, etaj 6; tel. (21) 2501430; internet www.profm.ro; f. 1993; owned by Central European Media Enterprises Ltd (Bermuda); Gen. Dir ADRIAN SARBU.

Radio Europa FM: 010541 Bucharest 1, Intr. Camil Petrescu 5; tel. (21) 2010500; fax (21) 2010519; e-mail europafm@europafm.ro; internet www.europafm.ro; Gen. Dir ILIE NĂSTASE.

Radio Nord-Est: 700479 jud. Iași, Iași, Str. Codrescu 1; tel. and fax (232) 211570; e-mail rneiasi@dntis.ro; f. 1992; independent; Man. MIHAI GRETY.

Societatea Națională de Radiocommunicații, SA (National Radiocommunications Co): 050706 Bucharest 5, Bd. Libertății 14; tel. (21) 3073007; fax (21) 3149798; e-mail info@snr.ro; internet www.snr.ro; f. 1991 through the reorganization of Rom Post Telecom; state-owned; radio and television broadcasting (including digital), high-speed internet and broadband services, satellite communications; 2,445 employees.

Television

Televiziunea Română (TVR) (Romanian Television): 015089 Bucharest, Calea Dorobanților 191, POB 63-1200; tel. (21) 2312704; fax (21) 2307514; e-mail tvr@tvr.ro; internet www.tvr.ro; f. 1956; state-owned; public broadcasting service; four channels broadcasting 24 hours; Pres. and Dir-Gen. GIURGIU TUDOR.

Antena 1: 013682 Bucharest, Șos. București-Ploiești 25–27; tel. (21) 2121844; internet www.antena1.ro; f. 1993; independent commercial television station.

Prima TV: 040204 Bucharest 4, Calea Serban Voda 95–101; tel. (21) 3359341; e-mail focus@primatv.ro; internet www.primatv.ro; f. 1997; owned by SBS Broadcasting SA.

Pro TV: 021409 Bucharest 2, Bd. Pache Protopopescu 109, etaj 6; tel. (21) 2505063; fax (21) 2501951; e-mail info@protv.ro; internet www.protv.ro; f. 1995; owned by Central European Media Enterprises Ltd (CME), Bermuda; commercial station; Gen. Dir ADRIAN SARBU.

Finance

(cap. = capital; res = reserves; dep. = deposits; m. = million; brs = branches; amounts in new lei, unless otherwise indicated)

BANKING

Central Bank

National Bank of Romania (Banca Națională a României): 030031 Bucharest 3, Str. Lipscani 25; tel. (21) 3130410; fax (21) 3123831; e-mail info@bnro.ro; internet www.bnro.ro; f. 1880; central bank and bank of issue; manages monetary policy; supervises commercial banks and credit business; cap. 30.0m., res 12,885.5m., dep. 24,593.2m. (Dec. 2008); Gov. MUGUR CONSTANTIN ISĂRESCU; 22 brs.

Other Banks

Alpha Bank Romania SA: 010566 Bucharest 1, Calea Dorobanților 237B; tel. (21) 2092100; fax (21) 2316570; e-mail info@alphabank.ro; internet www.alphabank.ro; f. 1994; present name adopted 2000; 99.9% owned by Alpha Bank AE (Greece); cap. 694.7m., res 362.8m., dep. 15,853.2m. (Dec. 2008); Pres. SERGIU BOGDAN OPRESCU.

Banca Comercială Carpatica SA (BCC): 550135 jud. Sibiu, Sibiu, Str. Autogarii 1; tel. (269) 233985; fax (269) 233371; e-mail centrala@carpatica.ro; internet www.carpatica.ro; f. 1999; cap. 201.2m., res 57.2m., dep. 1,728.9m. (Dec. 2008); Pres. and Chair. NICOLAE SURDU.

Banca Comercială Română SA—BCR (Romanian Commercial Bank): 030016 Bucharest 3, Bd. Regina Elisabeta 5; tel. (21) 3126185; fax (21) 3122096; internet www.bcr.ro; f. 1990; 69.2% owned by Erste Bank (Austria); cap. 2,119.7m., res 936.5m., dep. 56,980.8m. (Dec. 2008); Pres. ANDREAS TREICHL; 372 brs and sub-brs.

Banca de Export-Import a României (Eximbank Romania): 050092 Bucharest 5, Str. Splaiul Independenței 15; tel. (21) 4053132; fax (21) 3192999; e-mail bucuresti@eximbank.ro; internet www.eximbank.ro; f. 1992; 93.4% state-owned; cap. 1,694.3m., res −780.0m., dep. 1,863.8m. (Dec. 2008); CEO IONUȚ MIRCEA COSTEA; 7 brs.

Banca Românească SA (Romanian Bank): 030822 Bucharest 3, Bd. Unirii 35, Bloc A3; tel. (21) 3059300; fax (21) 3059191; e-mail office@brom.ro; internet www.brom.ro; f. 1993; 88.7% owned by National Bank of Greece SA (NBG); cap. 479.9m., dep. 6,013.0m. (Dec. 2007); Vice-Pres. AGIS LEOPOULOS.

Banca Transilvania SA (Transylvanian Bank): 400027 jud. Cluj, Cluj-Napoca, Str. G. Baritiu 8; tel. (264) 407150; fax (264) 407179; e-mail piatacapital@bancatransilvania.ro; internet www.bancatransilvania.ro; f. 1994; cap. 1,149.5m., res 230.6m., dep. 15,076.8m. (Dec. 2007); Chair. HORIA CIORCILA; Dir-Gen. ROBERT C. REKKERS; 55 brs, 341 agencies.

Bancpost SA: 020337 Bucharest 3, Dimitrie Pompeiu 6A; tel. (21) 3084666; fax (21) 3233868; e-mail suportcomercianti@bancpost.ro; internet www.bancpost.ro; f. 1991; 93.3% owned by EFG Eurobank Ergasias SA (Greece); cap. 619.6m., res 169.4m., dep. 13,541.4m. (Dec. 2008); CEO MIHAI BOGZA; Gen. Man. MANUELA PLAPCIANU.

BRD-Groupe Société Générale SA (Romanian Bank for Development): 011171 Bucharest 1, Bd. Ion Mihalache 1–7; tel. (21) 3014000; fax (21) 3014004; e-mail vocalis@brd.ro; internet www.brd.ro; f. 1990 to replace Investment Bank of Romania (f. 1923); present name adopted 2004; financial and banking services and operations to individuals and private and small cos; 58.3% owned by Société Générale (France); cap. 2,515.6m., res −9.9m., dep. 36,947.0m. (Dec. 2008); Pres. and CEO GUY POUPET; 191 brs.

CEC Bank SA: 030022 Bucharest 3, Calea Victoriei 11–13; tel. (21) 3111119; fax (21) 3125425; e-mail office@cec.ro; internet www.cec.ro; f. 1864; fmrly Casa de Economii și Consemnațiuni; present name adopted 2008; state-owned; scheduled for privatization; handles private savings, loans for the inter-banking market and mortgages; cap. 649.7m., res 569.9m., dep. 8,489.4m. (Dec. 2007); Chair. and Chief Exec. RADU GRATIAN GHETEA; 42 brs.

Citibank Romania SA: 011742 Bucharest 1, Str. Calea Victoriei 145; tel. (21) 2035550; fax (21) 2035565; internet www.citibank.ro; f. 1996; 99.6% owned by Citigroup Overseas Investment Corpn (USA); cap. 70.5m., res 248.1m., dep. 3,253.5m. (Dec. 2007); Dir-Gen. SHAHMIR KHALIQ; 40 brs.

Credit Europe Bank (Romania) SA: 061331 Bucharest 6, Timișoara 26z, Clădirea Anchor Plaza; tel. (21) 4064000; fax (21) 3172066; e-mail office@crediteurope.ro; internet www.crediteurope.ro; f. 1993; fmrly Finansbank (Romania) in 2000; present name adopted 2007; 94.41% owned by Credit Europe Bank NV; cap. 675.0m., res 30.3m., dep. 7,491.8m. (Dec. 2008); CEO OMER TETIK; 86 brs.

Marfin Bank (Romania) SA: 010775 Bucharest 1, Str. Emanoil Porumbaru 90-92, BP 22-155; tel. (21) 2064200; fax (21) 2064281; e-mail office@marfinbank.ro; internet www.marfinbank.ro; f. 1998; fmrly Egnatia Bank (Romania); present name adopted 2008; 98.98% owned by Marfin Egnatia Bank SA (Greece); dep. €539.7m., total assets €589.2m. (Dec. 2008); Gen. Man. STYLIANOS SOFIANOS.

MKB Romexterra Bank SA: Bucharest 5, Str. Elefterie 18, Elefterie Business Center; tel. (21) 4051754; fax (21) 3178217; e-mail info@romexterro.ro; internet www.romexterra.ro; f. 1993; 75.49% owned by MKB Bank Nyrt (Hungary); present name adopted 2007; cap. 200.0m., res 49.5m., dep. 1,928.7m. (Dec. 2007); CEO DAN SANDU; 68 brs.

OTP Bank Romania SA: 011017 Bucharest 3, Str. Buzesti 66–68; tel. (21) 3075700; fax (21) 3075730; e-mail office@otpbank.ro; internet www.otpbank.ro; f. 1995; present name adopted 2005; 99.99% owned by OTP Bank Ltd (Hungary); cap. 432.9m., res 42.8m., dep. 2,811.6m. (Dec. 2008); Chair. of Bd Dr ANTAL PONGRACZ.

Piraeus Bank Romania SA: 011132 Bucharest, Șos. Nicolae Titulescu 29-31, Sector 1; tel. (21) 3036969; fax (21) 3036968; e-mail office@piraeusbank.ro; internet www.piraeusbank.ro; f. 1995; present name adopted 2000; 88.0% owned by Piraeus Bank (Greece); cap. 916.5m., res 24.1m., dep. 4,924.4m. (Dec. 2007); CEO CĂTĂLIN PARVU; 3 brs.

Raiffeisen Bank SA: 011857 Bucharest 1, Piața Charles de Gaulle 15; tel. (21) 3061000; fax (21) 2300700; e-mail centrala@rzb.ro; internet www.raiffeisen.ro; f. 1968; present name adopted 2002; 99.5% owned by Raiffeisen International Beteiligungs AG (Austria); cap. 1,196.3m., res 64.2m., dep. 16,262.3m. (Dec. 2008); Pres. STEVEN VAN GRONIGEN; 329 brs.

UniCredit Tiriac Bank SA: 014106 Bucharest, Str. Ghetarilor 23–25, Sector 1; tel. (21) 2002020; fax (21) 2002022; e-mail office@unicredit.ro; internet www.unicredit-tiriac.ro; f. 1991; present name adopted 2007; cap. 1,101.6m., res 150.7m., dep. 14,925.6m. (Dec. 2008); Chair. CORNELIU DAN PASCARIU; Chief Exec. CĂTĂLIN RASVAN RADU; 50 brs.

Volksbank România SA: 021323 Bucharest 2, Șos. Mihai Bravu 171; tel. (21) 2094400; fax (21) 2094490; e-mail marketing@volksbank.com.ro; internet www.volksbank.com.ro; f. 2000; 97.9% owned by Volksbank International AG (Austria); cap. 341.1m., res 575.1m., dep. 11,153.3m. (Dec. 2007); Pres. GERALD SCHREINER.

BANKING ASSOCIATION

Romanian Banking Association (Asociația Română a Băncilor): 030205 Bucharest 3, Aleea Negru Voda 4–6, Bloc C3; tel. (21) 3212078; fax (21) 3212095; e-mail arb@arb.ro; internet www.arb

ROMANIA

.ro; f. 1991; 39 mems; Chair. RADU GRAȚIAN GHEȚEA; Sec.-Gen. RADU NEGREA.

STOCK EXCHANGE

Bucharest Stock Exchange (Bursa de Valori București): 020922 Bucharest 2, Bd. Carol I 34–36, 14th Floor; tel. (21) 3079500; fax (21) 3079519; e-mail bvb@bvb.ro; internet www.bvb.ro; f. 1882; reopened 1995 (ceased operations 1948); 73 listed cos; Chair. VALENTIN IONESCU; CEO ANCA DUMITRU.

COMMODITIES EXCHANGE

Romanian Commodities Exchange (Bursa Română de Mărfuri): 013701 Bucharest 1, Piața Presei Libere 1; tel. (21) 2244560; fax (21) 2242878; e-mail bursa@brm.ro; internet www.brm.ro; Pres. and CEO GABRIEL PURICE.

INSURANCE

In 2003 there were 46 insurance companies.

Allianz-Tiriac Asigurări: 010616 Bucharest, Str. Căderea Bastiliei 80–84; tel. (21) 2082222; fax (21) 2082211; e-mail relatii.publice@ allianztiriac.ro; internet www.allianztiriac.ro; CEO CRISTIAN CONSTANTINESCU.

Asigurarea Românească SA (ASIROM) (Romanian Insurance): 020912 Bucharest 2, Bd. Carol I 31–33; tel. (21) 6011289; fax (21) 6011288; internet www.asirom.com.ro; f. 1991; life and non-life; Chair. of Bd PETER HÖFINGER; 41 brs.

Astra SA: 031041 Bucharest 3, Str. Nerva Traian 3/101M; tel. (21) 3188080; fax (21) 3188074; e-mail office@astrasig.ro; internet www.astrasig.ro; f. 1991; Pres. RADU MUSTATEA.

ING Asigurări de Viață SA: 050552 Bucharest 3, Str. Costache Negri 1–5, Opera Centre; tel. (21) 4028391; fax (21) 4028581; e-mail asigurari@ing.ro; internet www.ingasigurari.ro; f. 1997; life; CEO CORNELIA AURELIA COMAN.

Omniasig SA: 011862 Bucharest 1, Bd. Aviatorilor 28; tel. (21) 2315040; fax (21) 2315029; e-mail secretary@omniasig.ro; internet www.omniasig.ro; f. 1994; insurance and reinsurance co; 98.9% owned by Vienna Insurance Group (Austria); Chair. CONSTANTIN TOMA.

Unita: 010413 Bucharest 1, Bd. Dacia 30; tel. (21) 2120882; fax (21) 2120843; e-mail unita@unita.ro; internet www.unita.ro; f. 1990; mem. of Uniqa Group (Austria); Dir IULIAN DUMITRU.

Insurance Association

Uniunea Națională a Societăților de Asigurare și Reasigurare din România (National Association of Insurance and Re-insurance Companies of Romania): 040129 Bucharest 4, Bd. Libertății 12, Bloc 114, sc. 3, 4th Floor, ap. 68; tel. (31) 4057328; fax (21) 3177832; e-mail office@unsar.ro; internet www.unsar.ro; f. 1994; 26 mems; Pres. CRISTIAN CONSTANTINESCU; Dir-Gen. FLORENTINA ALMAJANU.

Trade and Industry

GOVERNMENT AGENCIES

Agency for Small and Medium Enterprises and Co-operatives (Agenția Națională pentru Întreprinderi Mici și Mijlocii și Cooperație): 040263 Bucharest 4, Str. Poterași 11; tel. (21) 3352620; fax (21) 3361843; e-mail mariana.spranceana@mimmc.ro; internet www.mimmc.ro; Pres. (vacant).

Authority for the Recovery of State Assets (Autoritatea pentru Valorificarea Activelor Statului—AVAS): 715151 Bucharest 1, Str. Capt. A. Șerbănescu 50; tel. (21) 3036122; fax (21) 3036680; e-mail infopublic@avas.gov.ro; internet www.avas.gov.ro; created by merger of the Banking Assets Resolution Agency (AVAB) and the Authority for Privatization and Management of State Ownership (APAPS); successor org. to the State Ownership Fund; Pres. TEODOR ATANASIU.

Romanian Agency for Foreign Investment: 011974 Bucharest 1, Bd. Primaverii 22; tel. (21) 2339103; fax (21) 2339104; e-mail aris@ arisinvest.ro; internet www.arisinvest.ro; f. 2002; Sec.-Gen. FLORIN VASILACHE.

Romanian Trade Promotion Centre (Centrul Român pentru Promovarea Comertului—CRPC): 050741 Bucharest 5, Str. Apolodor 17, POB 1/756; tel. (21) 3185050; fax (21) 3111491; e-mail office@ traderom.ro; internet www.traderom.ro; f. 1995; Dir-Gen. SANDOR NEMES.

CHAMBER OF COMMERCE

Chamber of Commerce and Industry of Romania: 030982 Bucharest 3, Bd. Octavian Goga 2; tel. (21) 3229536; fax (21) 3229542; e-mail ccir@ccir.ro; internet www.ccir.ro; f. 1868; Pres. GHEORGHE COJOCARU.

EMPLOYERS' ASSOCIATIONS

Alliance of Employers' Confederations of Romania (ACPR) (Alianța Confederațiilor Patronale din România): 030982 Bucharest 3, Str. Octavian Goga 2, floor 10; tel. (21) 3211381; fax (21) 3211443; internet www.acpr.ro; f. 2004; includes the National Confederation of Romanian Employers (CNPR), the Employer Confederation of Romanian Industry (CONPIROM) and four others; Pres. GHEORGHE COPOS.

National Confederation of Romanian Employers (Confederația Națională a Patronatului Român—CNPR): 020982 Bucharest 3, Bd. Octavian Goga 2; tel. (21) 3212074; fax (21) 3212075; e-mail cnpr@untrr.ro; internet www.cnpr.org.ro; Pres. DINU PATRICIU; Dir-Gen. CRISTIAN PARVAN.

Romanian Private Farmers' Federation (Federația agricultorilor privatizați din România): 010043 Bucharest 1, Bd. Nicolae Bălcescu 17–19; tel. (21) 6131869; fax (21) 6133043; f. 1991; represents 4,000 farming co-operatives and 41 district unions; Pres. GHEORGHE PREDILA.

Union of Romanian Employers (Uniunea Patronatelor din România—UPR): 020361 Bucharest 2, Str. Luigi Galvani 17–19, c/o Romanian Employers' Organization (PR); tel. (21) 2111246; fax (21) 2103075; e-mail office@patronatulroman.ro; internet www.patronatulroman.ro; f. 2004; consists of 6 nationally representative employers' organizations; Pres. OVIDIU TENDER.

UTILITIES

Regulatory Authorities

National Energy Regulatory Authority (Autoritatea Națională de Reglementare in domeniul Energiei—ANRE): 020995 Bucharest 2, Str. Constantin Nacu 3; tel. (21) 3112244; fax (21) 3124365; internet www.anre.ro; f. 1999; Pres. NICOLAE OPRIS.

National Regulatory Authority for the Natural Gas Sector (Autoritatea Națională de Reglementare în domeniul Gazelor Naturale—ANRGN): 060114 Bucharest 6, Șos. Cotroceni 4; tel. (21) 3033800; fax (21) 3033808; e-mail anrgn@anrgn.ro; internet www.anrgn.ro; f. 2000; Pres. STEFAN COSMEANU.

Electricity

Electrica SA: 010621 Bucharest, Str. Grigore Alexandrescu 9, Sector 1; tel. (21) 2085999; fax (21) 2085998; internet www.electrica.ro; f. 2002; electricity distributor and supplier; 3 regional generating and 4 regional distribution branches, based in Cluj-Napoca (Transilvania Nord), Transilvania Sud (Brașov), Muntenia Nord (Ploiești) and Muntenia (Bucharest), 1 national servicing branch; Chair. CRISTIAN ISTODORESCU.

Hidroelectrica SA: 020995 Bucharest, Str. Constantin Nacu 3, Sector 2; tel. (21) 3112231; fax (21) 3111174; e-mail generala@ hidroelectrica.ro; internet www.hidroelectrica.ro; state-owned; administers 120 hydropower plants and 4 pumping stations through 10 regional subsidiaries; Gen. Man. EUGEN PENA.

Nuclearelectrica SA: 010494 Bucharest 1, POB 22–102, Str. Polonă 65; tel. (21) 2038200; fax (21) 3169400; e-mail office@ nuclearelectrica.ro; internet www.nuclearelectrica.ro; f. 1998; electrical and thermal power generation; production of nuclear fuel; Gen. Dir Dr POMPILIU BUDULAN; 2,308 employees (2003).

Transelectrica SA: 021012 Bucharest 2, Str. Armand Calinescu 2–4; tel. (21) 3035611; fax (21) 3035820; e-mail office@transelectrica.ro; internet www.transelectrica.ro; f. 2000; 73.7% state-owned; transmission system operator; includes 9 brs and 6 subsidiaries; Chair. and Gen. Dir ADRIAN BAICUSI; 2,188 employees.

Gas

E.ON Gaz România: 540069 jud. Mureș, Tirgu Mureș, Justiției 12; tel. (365) 403836; fax (365) 403807; e-mail office@eon-gaz-romania .ro; internet www.eon-gaz-romania.ro; f. 1975; fmrly DistriGaz Nord SA; 51% owned by E.ON Ruhrgas (Germany); natural gas distributor; Dir-Gen. VIRGIL METEA; 500 employees.

GDF SUEZ Energy România SA: 040254 Bucharest 4, Bd. Mărășești 4–6; tel. (21) 9366; fax (21) 3012116; e-mail contact@gdfsuez .ro; internet www.gdfsuez-energy.ro; privatized 2004/05; a subsidiary of GDF Suez (France); natural gas distributor.

SNTGN Transgaz SA (Societății Naționale de transport Gaze Naturale Transgaz SA): 551130 jud. Sibiu, Mediaș, Piața Constantin I. Moțaș 1; tel. (269) 803333; fax (269) 839031; e-mail cabinet@ transgaz.ro; internet www.transgaz.ro; 75.5% state-owned; exploration, transmission and distribution of natural gas; Gen. Dir IOAN RUSU.

TRADE UNIONS

Cartel Alfa National Trade Union Confederation (Confederația Națională Sindicală Cartel Alfa—CNS Cartel Alfa): 060041 Bucharest 6, Spl. Independenției 202A, 2nd Floor; tel. (21) 3171045; fax (21) 3123481; e-mail alfa@cartel-alfa.ro; internet www.cartel-alfa.ro; f. 1990; 750,000 mems (2008); 46 professional affiliations; Pres. BOGDAN IULIU HOSSU.

Confederation of Democratic Trade Unions of Romania (Confederația Sindicatelor Democratice din România—CSDR): 010155 Bucharest 1, Piața Walter Maracineanu 1–3; tel. (21) 3156542; e-mail csdr@b.astral.ro; f. 1994; 20 professional federations; 101,000 mems (2007); Pres. IACOB BACIU.

Frăția (Brotherhood) National Confederation of Free Trade Unions of Romania (Confederația Națională a Sindicatelor Libere din România Frăția—CNSLR Frăția): 010024 Bucharest 1, Str. Cristian Popisteanu 1–3; tel. and fax (21) 3151632; e-mail biroupresa@cnslr-fratia.ro; internet www.cnslr-fratia.ro; merged with the National Trade Union Bloc (Blocul Național Sindical—f. 1991) in 2004; 520,000 mems (2007); 44 professional federations; Pres. MARIUS PETCU.

Meridian National Trade Union Confederation (MNTUC) (Confederația Sindicala Națională Meridian): 010366 Bucharest 1, Str. D. I. Mendeleev 36–38; tel. (21) 3168017; fax (21) 3168018; e-mail csnmeridian@csnmeridian.ro; internet www.csnmeridian.ro; f. 1994; 27 br. federations; Pres. ION POPESCU.

Transport

RAILWAYS

In 2003 there were 11,077 km of track in operation (of which 3,965 km were electrified).

Romanian Railway Authority (Autoritatea Feroviara Româna—AFER): 010719 Bucharest 1, Calea Grivitei 393; tel. (21) 3077900; fax (21) 2241832; e-mail secretariat@afer.ro; internet www.afer.ro; f. 1998; under the jurisdiction of the Ministry of Transport and Infrastructure; Gen. Dir VASILE BELIBOU.

National Freight Railway Transport Co (Societatea Națională de Transport Feroviar de Marfă) (CFR Marfă SA): 010873 Bucharest, Bd. Dinicu Golescu 38; tel. (21) 2249336; fax (21) 3124700; e-mail vtulbure@marfa.cfr.ro; internet www.cfrmarfa.cfr.ro; f. 1998 after the reorganization of the SNCFR; main railway freight transport operator in Romania; Gen. Man. LIVIU BOBAR.

National Passenger Railway Transport Co (Societatea Națională de Transport Feroviar de Călători—CFR Călători SA): 010873 Bucharest, Bd. Dinicu Golescu 38; tel. (21) 3190322; fax (21) 4112054; e-mail marketing.calatori@cfr.ro; internet www.cfr.ro/calatori; f. 1998; divided into eight regional administrations since 1999; reorganized in Feb. 2001 and merged with eight regional companies; operates all local, regional, long-distance and international passenger rail services; Chair. and Chief Exec. ALEXANDRU NOAPTES.

National Railways Company (CFR SA): 010873 Bucharest, Bd. Dinicu Golescu 38; tel. (21) 3192400; fax (21) 3192401; e-mail virgil.daschievici@cfr.ro; internet www.cfr.ro; f. 1998; management of railway infrastructure; Gen. Dir VIOREL SCURTU.

City Underground Railway

The Bucharest underground railway network totals 63.5 km in length.

Metrorex SA—Societatea Comercială de Transport cu Metroul București: 010873 Bucharest 1, Bd. Dinicu Golescu 38; tel. (21) 2248975; fax (21) 3125149; e-mail contact@metrorex.ro; internet www.metrorex.ro; f. 1977; Gen. Man. MARIUS IONEL LĂPĂDAT.

ROADS

In 2004 the total length of the national road network was 198,817 km, of which only 30.2% was paved; there were 14,809 km of highways and 36,010 km of secondary roads.

National Administration of Roads (Administrația Națională a Drumurilor RA—AND): Ministerul Transporturilor, 010873 Bucharest 1, Bd. Dinicu Golescu 38; tel. (21) 2232606; fax (21) 3120984; e-mail and@andnet.ro; internet www.andnet.ro; Gen. Dir MIHAI GRECU.

INLAND AND OCEAN SHIPPING

The Danube–Black Sea Canal was officially opened to traffic in 1984, and has an annual handling capacity of 80m. metric tons. Romania's principal ports are at Constanța, on the Black Sea; and Tulcea, Galați, Brăila and Giurgiu, on the Danube. In 2009 Romania's merchant fleet had 177 vessels, with a combined aggregate displacement of 246,000 grt.

Administration of Navigable Canals SH (Administrația Canalelor Navigabile SA): 907015 jud. Constanța, Agigea, Str. Ecluzei nr 1; tel. (241) 702705; fax (241) 737711; e-mail compania@acn.ro; internet www.acn.ro; f. 1984; Gen. Man. ZEICU ILIE VALENTIN.

Maritime Port Administration of Constanța SA (NC MPA SA): 900900 jud. Constanța, Constanța, Portului Incinta, Gara Maritima; tel. (241) 611540; fax (241) 619512; e-mail apmc@constantza-port.ro; internet www.portofconstantza.com; f. 1991; also administrates Midia and Mangalia ports, and Tomis marina; Gen. Man. IOAN BALAN.

National Co for the Administration of Maritime Ports on the Danube (CN APDM SA) (CN Administrația Porturilor Dunării Maritime SA–Galați): 800025 jud. Galați, Galați, Str. Portului 34; tel. (236) 460660; fax (236) 460140; e-mail apdm@apdm.galati.ro; internet apdm.galati.ro; f. 1998; manages ports at Galați, Brăila, Tulcea, Chilia, Sulina and Sf. Gheorghe; Gen. Man. CARMEN COSTACHE.

National Co for the Administration of River Ports on the Danube (CN Administrația Porturilor Dunării Fluviale SA—APDF SA): 080011 jud. Giurgiu, Giurgiu, Șos. Portului 1; tel. (246) 213003; fax (21) 3110521; internet www.apdf.ro; f. 1998; Gen. Man. CRISTIAN NEMTESCU.

NAVROM—Romanian River Navigation Co (Compania de Navigatie Fluviala Romana SA—NAVROM): 800025 jud. Galați, Galați, Str. Portului 34; tel. (236) 460706; fax (236) 460190; e-mail navrom@rls.roknet.ro; fleet of over 400 barges and tugs on the River Danube.

Petromin Shipping Co (CNM Petromin SA): 900125 jud. Constanța, Constanța, Portului Incinta, Poarta 2; tel. (241) 617802; fax (241) 619690; e-mail office@petromin.cunet.ro; undergoing privatization; merchant fleet of 30 ships and tankers; Chair. ANDREI CARAIANI.

River Administration of the Lower Danube–Galați (Administrația Fluvială a Dunării de Jos RA–Galați): 800025 jud. Galați, Galați, Str. Portului 28–30; tel. (236) 460812; fax (236) 460847; e-mail secretariat@afdj.ro; internet www.afdj.ro; 2 brs and 3 agencies; Gen. Man. MIHAI OCHIALBESCU.

CIVIL AVIATION

There are two international airports at Bucharest: Aurel Vlaicu International (Băneasa) and the larger Henri Coandă International (Otopeni). There are other international airports at Constanța (M. Kogălniceanu), Timișoara, Sibiu and Cluj-Napoca. Domestic airports include those at Arad, Bacău, Iași and Oradea.

Romanian Civil Aeronautic Authority (Regia Autonomă Autoritatea Aeronautică Civilă Română): 715621 Bucharest, District 1, Șos. București-Ploiești 38–40; tel. (21) 2081508; fax (21) 2081572; e-mail dir.gen@caa.ro; internet www.caa.ro; f. 1993; Dir-Gen. CLAUDIA VIRLAN.

Blue Air Transport Aerian: 013695 Bucharest, Șos. București–Ploiești 40, Aeroport București-Băneasa-Aurel Vlaicu International; tel. (21) 2088686; e-mail info@blue-air.ro; internet www.blueairweb.com; f. 2004; low-cost flight co operating flights to domestic and European destinations; Gen. Dir GHEORGHE RACARU.

Carpatair: 307201 jud. Timiș, Timișoara, Timișoara International Airport; tel. (256) 306933; fax (256) 306962; e-mail timisoara@carpatair.com; internet www.carpatair.ro; f. 1999 as Veg Air; assumed present name in 1999; scheduled domestic and international flights; Pres. NICOLAE PETROV.

Tarom—Compania Națională de Transporturi Aeriene Române SA (TAROM): 013697 Bucharest, Șos. București–Ploiești, km 16.5, Henri Coandă International (Otopeni) Airport; tel. (21) 2322494; fax (21) 3125686; e-mail secrgen@tarom.ro; internet www.tarom.ro; f. 1954; joint-stock co; services throughout Europe, the Middle East, Asia, the USA and domestically; Pres. GHEORGHE RACARU.

Tourism

The Carpathian Mountains, with their numerous painted monasteries, the Danube delta and the Black Sea resorts (Mamaia, Eforie, Mangalia and others) are the principal attractions. There were 8.9m. foreign tourist arrivals in 2008, when receipts from tourism (including passenger transport) totalled US $2,627m.

National Tourism Authority: 010873 Bucharest 1, Bd. Dinicu Golescu 38; tel. (21) 3149957; fax (21) 3149960; e-mail promovare@mturism.ro; internet www.romaniatravel.com; govt org.; Pres. IULIU MARIAN OVIDIU.

ROMANIA

Defence

As assessed at November 2010, active forces totalled 71,745: army 42,500, navy 7,345, air force 8,400 and a joint force of 13,500. Reserves totalled 45,000. There were also 22,900 border guards and a gendarmerie of an estimated 57,000 (under the control of the Ministry of Administration and the Interior). Conscription was officially abolished in October 2006. In January 1994 Romania became the first former Warsaw Pact state to join the North Atlantic Treaty Organization's (NATO) 'Partnership for Peace' programme, and became a full member of NATO on 29 March 2004.

Defence Expenditure: Budgeted at an estimated 7,160m. lei in 2011.

Chief of Staff of the Army: Maj.-Gen. ȘTEFAN DĂNILĂ.

Education

Education is free and compulsory between the ages of six and 16 years. Before reaching the age of six years, children may attend crèches (creșe) and kindergartens (grădinițe de copii); in 2002/03 76.5% of pre-school age children were attending kindergarten. Between the ages of six and 16 years children attend the general education school (școală de cultură generală de zece ani). In 2005 primary enrolment included 92.6% of children in the relevant age-group, while the comparable ratio for secondary education was 80.4%. The general secondary school (liceul), for which there is an entrance examination, provides a specialized education suitable for preparation of students for admission to university or college. There are also specialized secondary schools, where the emphasis is on industrial, agricultural and teacher training, and art schools, which correspond to secondary schools, but cover several years of general education. Vocational secondary schools (școli profesionale de ucenici) train pupils for a particular career. Tuition in minority languages, particularly Hungarian and German, is available. In June 1999 legislation providing for the establishment of a minority-language university was approved. In 2007/08 there were 106 higher educational institutes in Romania. In 2006 the state budget allocated an estimated 10,880m. new lei to education, equivalent to 12.7% of total expenditure in that year.

THE RUSSIAN FEDERATION

Introductory Survey

LOCATION, CLIMATE, LANGUAGE, RELIGION, FLAG, CAPITAL

The Russian Federation, or Russia, constituted the major part of the USSR, providing some 76% of its area and approximately 51% of its population in 1989. It is bounded by Norway, Finland, Estonia and Latvia to the north-west, and by Belarus and Ukraine to the west. The southern borders of European Russia are with the Black Sea, Georgia, Azerbaijan, the Caspian Sea and Kazakhstan. The Siberian and Far Eastern regions have southern frontiers with the People's Republic of China, Mongolia and the Democratic People's Republic of Korea. The eastern coastline is on the Sea of Japan, the Sea of Okhotsk, the Pacific Ocean and the Barents Sea, and the northern coastline is on the Arctic Ocean. The region around Kaliningrad (formerly Königsberg in East Prussia), on the Baltic Sea, became part of the Russian Federation in 1945. Separated from the rest of Russia by Lithuania and Belarus, it borders Poland to the south, Lithuania to the north and east, and has a coastline on the Baltic Sea. The climate of Russia is extremely varied, ranging from extreme Arctic conditions in northern areas and much of Siberia to generally temperate weather in the south. The average temperature in Moscow in July is 19°C (66°F); the average for January is −9°C (15°F). Average annual rainfall in Moscow is 575 mm (23 ins). The official language is Russian, but many other languages are also used. Christianity is the major religion, with the Russian Orthodox Church (Moscow Patriarchate) the largest denomination. The main concentrations of adherents of Islam are among the Tatar, Bashkir and Chuvash peoples of the middle Volga, and the peoples of the northern Caucasus, including the Chechen, Ingush, Kabardins and the peoples of Dagestan. Buddhism is the main religion of the Buryats, the Tyvans and the Kalmyks. The large pre-1917 Jewish population has been depleted by war and emigration, but some 230,000 Jews remained in the Russian Federation in 2002, according to census results. The national flag (proportions 2 by 3) consists of three equal horizontal stripes of (from top to bottom) white, blue and red. The capital is Moscow (Moskva).

CONTEMPORARY POLITICAL HISTORY

Historical Context

By the late 19th century the Russian Empire extended throughout vast territories in eastern Europe, and included much of northern and central Asia, a result of the territorial expansionism of the Romanov dynasty, which had ruled Russia as an autocracy since 1613. Growing dissatisfaction with economic conditions in urban areas, combined with the adverse effect of defeats in the Russo–Japanese War (1904–05), led Tsar Nicholas (Nikolai) II (1894–1917) to issue a manifesto in October 1905, which promised respect for civil liberties and the introduction of some constitutional order, although the ensuing attempt at reforms failed to placate the increasingly restive workers and peasants. In 1917 there were strikes and demonstrations in the capital, Petrograd (as St Petersburg had been renamed in 1914). In March 1917 the Tsar was forced to abdicate and a liberal Provisional Government, composed mainly of landowners, took power. However, most real authority lay with the soviets (councils), composed largely of workers and soldiers, which were attracted to socialist ideas.

The inability of the Provisional Government, led first by Prince Georgii Lvov and then by the moderate socialist Aleksandr Kerenskii, to implement land reforms, or to effect a withdrawal from the First World War, allowed more extreme groups, such as the Bolshevik faction of the Russian Social Democratic Labour Party (RSDLP) led by Vladimir Ulyanov (Lenin), to attain prominence. On 7 November 1917 (25 October in the Old Style calendar, which remained in use until February 1918) the Bolsheviks, who had come to dominate the Petrograd Soviet, seized power in the capital, with minimal use of force, and proclaimed the Russian Soviet Federative Socialist Republic (RSFSR or Russian Federation). The Bolsheviks subsequently adopted the name All-Russian Communist Party (Bolsheviks).

The Bolsheviks asserted that they would respect the self-determination of the former Empire's many nations. Poland, Finland, and the Baltic states of Estonia, Latvia and Lithuania achieved independence, but other independent states established in 1917–18 were forced, militarily, to declare themselves Soviet Republics. These were proclaimed as independent republics, in alliance with the RSFSR, but the laws, Constitution and Government of the Federation were supreme in all of them. However, in 1922 the RSFSR joined the Belarusian, Ukrainian and Transcaucasian republics as constitutionally equal partners in a Union of Soviet Socialist Republics (USSR, or Soviet Union), and institutions of the RSFSR were re-formed as institutions of the new Union. The USSR eventually numbered 15 constituent Soviet Socialist Republics (SSRs). Moscow, the RSFSR's seat of government since 1918, became the capital of the USSR.

The RSFSR, in common with the other republics, experienced hardship as a result of the collectivization campaign of the early 1930s and the widespread repression under Iosif Dzhugashvili (Stalin), who established a brutal dictatorship after the death of Lenin in 1924. The Five-Year Plans, introduced in the late 1920s, effected rapid industrialization, a process that was reinforced by the removal of strategic industries from the west of the republic to the Ural regions during the Second World War (or 'Great Patriotic War'), which the USSR was drawn into in 1941. Under the Nazi German-Soviet Treaty of Non-Aggression (the 'Molotov-Ribbentrop Pact') of August 1939, the USSR annexed the Baltic states as well as other territories. Victory in the war in 1945 led to further territorial gains for the Russian Federation. In the west it gained part of East Prussia around Königsberg (now Kaliningrad) from Germany, a small amount of territory from Estonia and Latvia, and those parts of Finland annexed during the Soviet–Finnish War (1939–40). In the east it acquired the Kurile Islands from Japan. The nominally independent People's Republic of Tuva (Tyva), situated between the USSR and Mongolia, was annexed in 1944. In 1954 the peninsula of Crimea was ceded by the Russian Federation to the Ukrainian SSR.

Shortly after the death of Stalin in 1953, Nikita Khrushchev became First Secretary of the Communist Party of the Soviet Union (CPSU—as the Communist Party had been renamed in 1952), and gradually assumed predominance over his rivals. The most brutal aspects of the regime were ended, and in 1956 Khrushchev admitted the existence of large-scale repression under Stalin. Khrushchev was dismissed in 1964. He was replaced as First Secretary (later General Secretary) of the CPSU by Leonid Brezhnev. During the 1970s relations with the West, which had, since the late 1940s, been generally characterized by the intense mutual hostility of the 'Cold War', experienced a considerable *détente*; however, this was ended by the Soviet invasion of Afghanistan in 1979. Brezhnev's successor as CPSU General Secretary, following his death in 1982, was Yurii Andropov. He was succeeded upon his death, in February 1984, by Konstantin Chernenko, who, in turn, died in March 1985.

Chernenko's successor as General Secretary was Mikhail Gorbachev. A policy of glasnost (openness) provided a greater degree of freedom for the mass media. In November 1987, however, supporters of perestroika (restructuring), as Gorbachev's reform programme was known, seemed to suffer a reverse, with the dismissal from the Politburo (the executive committee of the CPSU) of Boris Yeltsin. In June 1988 Gorbachev announced plans for the introduction of a two-tier legislature, elected largely by competitive elections. In elections to the new USSR Congress of People's Deputies, held in March 1989, many reformist politicians, including Yeltsin, were successful in achieving election. In May the Congress elected Gorbachev to the new post of executive President of the USSR.

Within the USSR, the RSFSR was clearly pre-eminent, both economically and politically, and ethnic Russians dominated the Soviet élite. However, this prominence meant that Russia developed few autonomous institutions. The initial stage in the process of instituting Russian sovereignty was the election of the RSFSR Congress of People's Deputies in March 1990 by largely free and competitive elections. In May the Congress

THE RUSSIAN FEDERATION

elected Yeltsin to the highest state post in the RSFSR, the Chairman of the Supreme Soviet (the permanent working body of the Congress). On 12 June the Congress adopted a declaration asserting the sovereignty of the RSFSR in which the federation laws had primacy over all-Union legislation. In March 1991, when a referendum was held in nine republics to determine whether a restructured USSR should be retained, voters in the RSFSR also approved an additional question on the introduction of a Russian presidency. A direct presidential election, held in June, was won by Yeltsin and his Vice-President, Aleksandr Rutskoi, with 57.3% of the votes cast.

Domestic Political Affairs

On 19 August 1991, one day before the new union treaty was due to be signed, the conservative communist 'State Committee for the State of Emergency' (SCSE), led by the Soviet Vice-President, Gennadii Yanayev, seized power in Moscow, taking advantage of Gorbachev's absence from the city. The attempted coup collapsed within three days, and Yeltsin asserted control over all-Union bodies, appointing RSFSR ministers to head central institutions.

In October 1991 Yeltsin announced a programme of radical economic reforms. In November a new Government was announced, with Yeltsin as Chairman (Prime Minister). The CPSU was banned. In the same month the Congress granted Yeltsin special powers for one year, including the right to issue decrees with legislative force and to appoint government ministers without parliamentary approval, and elected Ruslan Khasbulatov, hitherto First Deputy Chairman of the Supreme Soviet, to succeed Yeltsin as Chairman.

On 8 December 1991 the leaders of Belarus, Ukraine and Russia announced the annulment of the 1922 Union Treaty creating the USSR; the Commonwealth of Independent States (CIS, see p. 238), defined as a co-ordinating organization, was created in its place. The CIS was formally established by the Almaty (Alma-Ata) Declaration, signed on 21 December 1991. Of the former Soviet republics, only Georgia, Estonia, Latvia and Lithuania remained outside the new body. (Georgia joined the CIS in December 1993.) On 25 December 1991 Gorbachev resigned as President of the USSR, and the Russian Supreme Soviet formally changed the name of the RSFSR to the Russian Federation.

In June 1992 Yeltsin appointed Yegor Gaidar, an advocate of radical economic reform, as acting Chairman, and in the same month the Supreme Soviet adopted legislation permitting large-scale privatization. In December the Congress of People's Deputies refused to endorse Gaidar's nomination, and Yeltsin was forced to appoint a new, substantially less reformist, premier, Viktor Chernomyrdin. Following the annulment, in March 1993, of an agreement on constitutional reform by the Congress, Yeltsin announced that he would rule by decree prior to the holding of a referendum on a draft constitution, which was held on 25 April 1993. A question on confidence in Yeltsin as President received a positive response from 57.4% of voters, while 53.7% of voters expressed support for Yeltsin's socio-economic policies. Support for an early presidential election was only 49.1%, but 70.6% of voters favoured early elections to the Congress of People's Deputies.

In July 1993 the Constitutional Conference approved a draft that provided for a presidential system with a bicameral parliament—the Federalnoye Sobraniye (Federal Assembly)—comprising a lower chamber (Gosudarstvennaya Duma—State Duma) and an upper chamber (Sovet Federatsii—Federation Council); however, the Congress of People's Deputies rejected this draft. The long-standing impasse between the presidential administration and the legislature eventually resulted in violent confrontation. On 21 September Yeltsin suspended the Congress of People's Deputies and the Supreme Soviet, and scheduled elections to the Federalnoye Sobraniye for December. The Supreme Soviet consequently voted to dismiss Yeltsin as President, announcing the appointment of Rutskoi in his place; an emergency session of the Congress of People's Deputies confirmed this appointment, and voted to impeach Yeltsin. On 27 September government troops surrounded the parliament building: some 180 deputies remained inside, with armed supporters. Conflict erupted in early October, as supporters of the rebel deputies attempted to seize control of strategic buildings in Moscow, and Yeltsin declared a state of emergency in the capital. On 4 October army tanks bombarded the parliament building, forcing the surrender of the rebels. The leaders of the rebellion were imprisoned and charged with inciting mass disorder. According to official figures, 160 people were killed in the fighting.

Introductory Survey

The new draft constitution, which strengthened the powers of the President, was submitted to a referendum on 12 December 1993, held concurrently with elections to the Federalnoye Sobraniye. Of the 54.8% of the registered electorate that participated in the plebiscite, 58.4% endorsed the draft. In the elections to the Gosudarstvennaya Duma, Vladimir Zhirinovskii's nationalist Liberal Democratic Party of Russia (LDPR) secured a total of 64 seats, the largest number obtained by any single party or alliance. (Of the 450 members of the lower chamber, 225 were elected by proportional representation on the basis of party lists, and 225 within single-member constituencies.) Russia's Choice, an alliance of pro-reform groups, led by Gaidar, secured 58 seats. The Communist Party of the Russian Federation (CPRF), which had been founded earlier in the year, took 48 seats, while the Agrarian Party of Russia (APR) won 33 seats. With the ensuing alignment of parties and the 130 independents into parliamentary factions, Russia's Choice emerged as the largest group in the Duma, although no coherent pro-Government majority was established. The Sovet Federatsii was to comprise two representatives from each of Russia's 89 federal subjects (as the constituent territories of the Federation were known), although in December representatives were not elected in the separatist republics of Tatarstan and Chechnya, owing to a voter boycott. The majority of the Council's members were non-partisan republican or regional leaders. A new Government was appointed in January 1994. In February the Duma voted in favour of granting amnesties to Rutskoi, Khasbulatov and other leaders of the 1993 rebellion, as well as to the SCSE.

In October 1994 a sudden decline in the value of the rouble prompted the resignation or dismissal of government members and the Chairman of the Central Bank, Viktor Gerashchenko. In November the reformist Anatolii Chubais, who had hitherto been responsible for the privatization programme, was promoted to the post of First Deputy Chairman, although other government appointments appeared to advance those opposed to further economic liberalization.

In late 1994 Russia commenced military intervention in the separatist Chechen Republic (Chechnya); an apparent lack of progress there, together with the continued deterioration of the economy, were instrumental in the approval by the Duma, in June 1995, of a motion expressing no confidence in the Government. Yeltsin subsequently dismissed a number of ministers, and in July a second vote of no confidence (as required by the Constitution) failed to secure the necessary majority.

Elections to the Duma took place on 17 December 1995. In accordance with a new electoral law, which introduced a minimum requirement of 5% of the votes cast for seats allocated on the basis of party lists, only four parties—the CPRF, the LDPR, Chernomyrdin's Our Home is Russia (OHR) and the liberal Yabloko—secured representation on this basis, while an additional 10 parties and 77 independent candidates obtained seats through voting in single-member constituencies. The CPRF emerged as the largest single party in the Duma, with 157 of the 450 deputies. OHR won 55 seats, the LDPR 51 and Yabloko 45.

In January 1996 Yeltsin dismissed Chubais as First Deputy Chairman. In the same month the Duma elected Gennadii Seleznev, a CPRF deputy, as its Chairman. In the first round of presidential voting, held on 16 June, and contested by 10 candidates, Yeltsin, with 35.8% of the votes cast, narrowly defeated Gennadii Zyuganov (of the CPRF), with 32.5%. Gen. Aleksandr Lebed, who had until recently commanded Russian forces in the separatist Transnistria (Pridnistrovie) region of Moldova, was placed third, with 14.7%. Since neither had received the 50% of the votes required for outright victory, Yeltsin and Zyuganov proceeded to a second round of voting. Yeltsin subsequently appointed Lebed as Secretary of the Security Council and National Security Adviser, and granted him particular responsibility for resolving the crisis in Chechnya. Despite increasingly infrequent public appearances, apparently a result of poor health, Yeltsin was re-elected as President in the second ballot, on 3 July, with 54% of the total votes cast. Chernomyrdin was subsequently reappointed as premier, and Chubais was promoted to head the Presidential Administration. Despite the successful negotiation of a cease-fire agreement in Chechnya in August, in October Yeltsin dismissed Lebed. In November Yeltsin underwent heart surgery, reassuming full presidential duties in December, although he was again hospitalized shortly afterwards, and there was growing pressure for his resignation.

Although Yeltsin delivered a vehement criticism of the Government in his annual address to the Federalnoye Sobraniye in March 1997, in a subsequent government reorganization Chernomyrdin retained his post, thereby avoiding the need to seek parliamentary approval of the new, broadly reformist, cabinet. Chubais was appointed First Deputy Chairman and Minister of Finance, and Boris Nemtsov was appointed as First Deputy Chairman, with responsibility for dismantling state monopolies, particularly in the areas of fuel and energy. In November Nemtsov lost the fuel and energy portfolio, and Chubais was dismissed as Minister of Finance, although both retained their posts as First Deputy Chairmen.

In March 1998 Yeltsin removed Chernomyrdin from office. The Duma confirmed the appointment of Sergei Kiriyenko, hitherto Minister of Fuel and Energy, as Chairman in mid-April. Several ministers, including Nemtsov, retained their portfolios in the new Government formed during April–May. Chubais, meanwhile, was appointed Chairman of the electricity monopoly, Unified Energy System of Russia. An attempt by the CPRF to initiate impeachment charges against Yeltsin was ruled unconstitutional by a parliamentary commission in late July. In mid-August, however, the Duma succeeded in approving a resolution demanding the voluntary resignation of Yeltsin.

In August 1998 mounting political instability was exacerbated by severe economic difficulties. Yeltsin dismissed Kiriyenko and his Government, reappointing Chernomyrdin as Chairman. However, Chernomyrdin's candidacy to the premiership was twice rejected by the Duma. In mid-September Yeltsin (aware that should his candidate be rejected for a third time he would be constitutionally obliged to dissolve the Duma) nominated Yevgenii Primakov (Minister of Foreign Affairs since 1996, and a former Director of the Foreign Intelligence Service) as Chairman, a candidacy that was endorsed by a large majority.

In May 1999 Yeltsin dismissed Primakov. Sergei Stepashin, hitherto First Deputy Chairman and Minister of Internal Affairs, was appointed as Chairman, and a new Government was formed later in the month. However, Yeltsin dismissed Stepashin in August. Later in the month the Duma endorsed his replacement by Vladimir Putin, a former colonel in the Soviet Committee for State Security (KGB), First Deputy Chairman of St Petersburg City Government in 1994–96, and hitherto head of the Federal Security Service (FSB) and Secretary of the Security Council.

Following a number of incursions by Chechen militants into the neighbouring Republic of Dagestan in August 1999, tensions resurfaced relating to the unresolved status of Chechnya and the emergence there, from the mid-1990s, of militant Islamist groups. Moreover, Putin attributed to Chechen militant groups a series of bomb explosions in Moscow, in Dagestan and in Rostov Oblast, which took place in August–September, killing more than 300 people. Citing the threat posed by militants in the separatist republic, Putin announced that military action was to recommence, and, prior to the large-scale deployment of ground troops, the aerial bombardment of Chechnya began on 23 September 1999.

In the months preceding Duma elections in December 1999 several new political alliances were formed; in August Fatherland-All Russia (FAR) was formed by the merger of the centrist party of the Mayor of Moscow, Yurii Luzhkov, with a grouping of regional governors. In September a pro-Government bloc, Unity, was formed under the leadership of Sergei Shoigu, the civil defence and emergencies minister, while Kiriyenko and Nemtsov were among the leaders of a new pro-market bloc, the Union of Rightist Forces (URF).

Some 29 parties and blocs contested the elections to the Gosudarstvennaya Duma on 19 December 1999, in which 62% of the electorate participated. Six parties obtained representation on the basis of party lists; a further eight parties and blocs, and 106 independent candidates, secured representation from single-member constituency ballots. The CPRF, with 24.3% of the votes, again won the largest number of seats, with 113. Unity, which received 23.3% of the votes cast, was the second largest party in the Duma, with 72 seats; FAR won 67, the URF 29, Yabloko 21 and the Zhirinovskii bloc (chiefly comprising the LDPR) 17.

On 31 December 1999 Boris Yeltsin unexpectedly resigned as President. Putin assumed the presidency in an acting capacity. He granted Yeltsin immunity from prosecution, and removed from office principal members of Yeltsin's administration. When the new Duma convened in mid-January 2000, the CPRF and Unity factions formed an alliance; thus, for the first time since the dissolution of the USSR, pro-Government forces held a majority in the legislature.

Vladimir Putin is elected President

Putin received 52.9% of the votes cast in the presidential election held on 26 March 2000, having received the support of FAR, as well as Unity. His closest rival was Zyuganov, of the CPRF, with 29.2%. Putin was inaugurated as President on 7 May. In mid-May Mikhail Kasyanov, hitherto First Deputy Chairman and Minister of Finance, was approved as Chairman of the Council of Ministers. A new Government was appointed shortly afterwards.

Concerns regarding the freedom of the media in Russia were heightened following the presidential approval in September 2000 of a new information doctrine and by the severe restrictions imposed over coverage of the conflict in Chechnya. Meanwhile, Vladimir Gusinskii, the owner of the Mediya-Most holding company (which included Russia's only wholly independent national television broadcaster, NTV), was arrested in June and charged with fraud. Although all charges were withdrawn in July, Gusinskii fled to Spain. In September the state-controlled gas monopoly, Gazprom (to which Mediya-Most was heavily indebted), brought charges of criminal embezzlement against Mediya-Most's management. Gusinskii lost control of the company in November, and the deal reached with Alfred Kokh, the head of a Gazprom subsidiary, Gazprom-Mediya, effectively gave the state a controlling stake in all Mediya-Most enterprises, with the exception of NTV. In December the Moscow fiscal authorities demanded that Mediya-Most be closed, on grounds of insolvency. In the same month Gusinskii was detained in Spain. Following the refusal of the Spanish authorities to extradite Gusinskii to Russia, in April 2001 he took up residence in Israel (where he held dual citizenship). None the less, Russia issued a fresh warrant for Gusinskii's arrest, on charges of money-laundering. In October 2003, following Gusinskii's arrest in Greece, a Greek court ruled against his extradition to Russia.

Meanwhile, other prominent businessmen were subjected to examinations of their business affairs, in what was interpreted as an attempt by the Government to reduce the powers of the 'oligarchs', as a number of wealthy businessmen, who in many cases had acquired control of formerly nationalized industries in the 1990s, were widely known. In July 2000 Boris Berezovskii, a prominent business executive and former Deputy of the Security Council and Executive Secretary of the CIS (who had played a major role in promoting Putin's candidacy as President), relinquished his seat in the Duma and, therefore, his immunity from prosecution, accusing Putin of having adopted an increasingly authoritarian style of governance. In September Berezovskii announced his intention to relinquish his 49% of shares in the state-controlled television station, ORT, claiming that he had received an ultimatum that he should surrender his holding to the state or risk imprisonment; the sale finally took place in February 2001. None the less, a warrant for Berezovskii's arrest was issued in November 2000, after he failed to return to Russia from France to answer questions relating to charges of money-laundering and illegal entrepreneurship in a case that had recently been reopened.

Putin introduced significant changes to regional governance during 2000. In May, as part of measures intended to promote structures of 'vertical power', seven Federal Okrugs (Districts) were created, each of which was headed by a presidential appointee, to whom regional governments and governors were to be answerable. A new consultative body, the State Council, comprising the heads of the federal subjects, was created by presidential decree in September.

In March 2001 Putin implemented a minor ministerial reorganization, appointing Boris Gryzlov, the head of the Unity faction in the Duma, as Minister of Internal Affairs, and Sergei Ivanov (hitherto Secretary of the Security Council and a former deputy head of the FSB) as Minister of Defence. In April it was announced that the Unity faction in the Duma was, henceforth, to form an alliance with FAR, in preference to the CPRF.

NTV was acquired by Gazprom-Mediya in April 2001. Following the dismissal of NTV's management, Yevgenii Kiselyev, the company's former Director-General and Editor-in-Chief, was appointed to head a small television channel owned by Berezovskii, TV6, to which the majority of the former NTV journalists transferred. Later in the year Berezovskii, who remained outside Russia, formed a political party, Liberal Russia. Meanwhile, in July the legislature approved a law banning foreign citizens, as well as Russians holding dual citizenship, from acquiring a majority stake in Russian television channels.

THE RUSSIAN FEDERATION

Introductory Survey

In July 2001 Putin signed a law imposing new conditions on political parties; henceforth, parties would be required to have a minimum of 10,000 members, including no fewer than 100 members in at least 50 of the 89 federal subjects, in order to be permitted to participate in elections. At the beginning of December the first congress of Unity and Fatherland-United Russia (subsequently known simply as United Russia—UR), formed by the merger of FAR and Unity, marked the formal establishment of the party, which held a majority of seats in both parliamentary houses. Although not a member of that party or of any other, Putin attended the founding congress.

In January 2002 TV6 ceased transmissions, following a court case brought by a minority shareholder, a subsidiary of the state-controlled petroleum company LUKoil, which had demanded the television company's liquidation on the grounds of unprofitability. In March it was announced that a new, non-profit organization, Mediya-Sotsium, associated with Primakov, had been awarded the contract to broadcast formerly held by TV6; Kiselyev and many TV6 journalists transferred to the new channel, which commenced operations as TVS. Meanwhile, Berezovskii presented a video-recording in London, United Kingdom, which purported to demonstrate the FSB's involvement, and Putin's acquiescence, in the bombings of mid-1999.

A new session of the Sovet Federatsii, chaired by Sergei Mironov, an ally of Putin, opened in January 2002, with a reformed composition. In place of regional leaders and chairmen of regional legislative assemblies, the Council comprised their full-time appointees; the formation of political factions and groups in the Council was to be prohibited.

In October 2002 Berezovskii was charged, *in absentia*, with defrauding the state. (Berezovskii was arrested in the United Kingdom, where he was resident, in March 2003 in response to an extradition request from the Russian authorities, but was granted political asylum in September, and the extradition proceedings were dismissed.) Meanwhile, in mid-October 2002, following the publication of an interview in a nationalist journal in which Berezovskii appeared to support the formation of a united opposition front by liberal and left-wing forces, he was suspended from Liberal Russia; one week later the Ministry of Justice agreed to register the party, which had hitherto been denied registration on several occasions, and which had obtained only negligible public support.

In late October 2002, following the deaths of at least 129 people as the result of an armed siege at a Moscow theatre by heavily armed militants linked to Chechen extremists (see Chechnya), the Government implemented a number of personnel changes in Chechnya. In mid-November Stanislav Ilyasov, hitherto the Prime Minister of Chechnya, was appointed to the federal Government as Minister without Portfolio, responsible for the Social and Economic Development of the Chechen Republic.

In March 2003 presidential decrees provided for the transfer of powers from various other organs of state to the FSB and to the Ministry of Internal Affairs. In April one of the co-chairmen of Liberal Russia, Sergei Yushenkov, was assassinated in Moscow (another deputy of the party, Vladimir Golovlev, had been murdered in August 2002); in June 2003 a party member, Mikhail Kodanev, was arrested on suspicion of involvement in the killing of Yushenkov, along with three others. (In March 2004 Kodanev was sentenced to 20 years' imprisonment for organizing the assassination; the three other suspects each received custodial sentences of between 11 and 20 years.) In June the Ministry of the Press, Broadcasting and Mass Media ordered the closure of TVS, purportedly as a result of financial difficulties experienced by the station, the broadcasts of which were replaced by a newly established, state-controlled sports channel.

On 18 June 2003 the Duma failed to approve a motion of no confidence in the Government that had been presented by the CPRF and Yabloko factions. Meanwhile, attacks against civilian targets by militants associated with Chechen separatist, or Islamist, rebels continued to occur, particularly in regions of southern Russia near Chechnya and in Moscow. In July at least 18 people were killed following two suicide bombings at a music festival near Moscow. A suicide bombing, in early December, on a train in southern Russia killed at least 42 people, and injured some 200 others. On 9 December, two days after the legislative elections (see below), a suicide bombing in central Moscow resulted in at least six deaths. In early February 2004 at least 39 people were killed and more than 100 injured in a further bomb attack on a train on the Moscow Metro.

During the latter half of 2003 several court cases and judicial investigations were instigated against senior officials of the prominent privately owned petroleum company Yukos, and its subsidiary companies. The chief executive of the company, Mikhail Khodorkovskii (who was reported to be the wealthiest person in Russia), had recently announced that he was providing financial support to Yabloko and the URF. On 25 October Khodorkovskii was arrested by FSB officers; he was subsequently charged with tax evasion and fraud, and imprisoned pending further investigations.

Elections to the Duma, held on 7 December 2003, were contested by 32 parties and blocs. Only four of these groupings received the minimum 5% share of votes cast required to obtain representation on the basis of federal party lists: UR won an absolute majority of seats in the new legislature, with 226 seats, while the representation of the CPRF was substantially reduced, to 53 seats. The LDPR secured 38 seats, while a recently formed electoral bloc, Motherland—People's Patriotic Union (Motherland), which comprised several communist and nationalist groups, received 37 seats. Nine other groups and 57 independent deputies achieved representation in the new Duma on the basis of constituency voting. The failure of the URF and Yabloko to obtain representation on the basis of proportional representation (the two parties received around 8% of the votes between them, and a total of seven seats) was regarded as a serious reverse for pro-Western reformists. The URF, Yabloko and the CPRF alleged that electoral fraud had been perpetrated, and electoral observers of the Organization for Security and Co-operation in Europe (OSCE, see p. 385) expressed concern that UR, which had become increasingly identified with the presidential administration, had benefited from the use of state administrative resources in support of the party. Moreover, several government members held senior positions in UR, in apparent defiance of a constitutional clause prohibiting ministers from holding membership of political parties, and the party had effectively received the endorsement of Putin on several occasions. Gryzlov, the Chairman of the Supreme Council of UR, was elected as the Chairman of the Duma on 24 December. He was succeeded as Minister of Internal Affairs by Col-Gen. Rashid Nurgaliyev.

Putin re-elected for a second presidential term

Campaigning for the presidential election held on 14 March 2004 was characterized by an absence of prominent or credible challengers to Putin, who contested the election as an independent candidate, and refused to participate in televised debates with other candidates. In place of their leaders, who had contested the presidential elections in 1996 and 2000, the CPRF and LDPR nominated relatively obscure figures, Nikolai Kharitonov and Oleg Malyshkin, respectively, as their candidates. The URF's refusal to endorse the candidacy of one of its leading members, Irina Khakamada, obliged her to campaign as an independent candidate; Khakamada and Nemtsov both subsequently resigned from the URF. Meanwhile, the candidacy of Sergei Glazyev, an economist who had been regarded as the principal instigator of the Motherland electoral bloc, failed to obtain the support of any of its constituent parties, and he therefore contested the election as an independent candidate. Mironov contested the election as the candidate of his party, the Russian Party of Life (RPL), but none the less expressed support for Putin. (A further candidate, Ivan Rybkin, an ally of Berezovskii, withdrew his candidacy in early March 2004, after he had apparently been taken hostage in Ukraine for several days.) Meanwhile, the leader of Yabloko, Grigorii Yavlinskii, announced that his party was to boycott the presidential election. On 24 February Putin dismissed the Government, and on 1 March Putin announced the nomination of Mikhail Fradkov, hitherto the permanent representative of Russia to the European Communities, as the new Chairman of the Government. The appointment of Fradkov, widely regarded as a 'technocrat', without significant political support of his own, was subsequently approved by the Duma, and on 9 March the formation of a new Government was announced; the number of ministers was significantly reduced, to 17, compared with 31 in the outgoing administration. Although most of the principal positions within the Government remained unchanged, a new Minister of Foreign Affairs, Sergei Lavrov, hitherto ambassador to the UN, was appointed.

On 14 March 2004 Putin was re-elected, as had been widely anticipated, for a second, and under the terms of the Constitution final, term of office, receiving 71.3% of the votes cast. His nearest rival, Kharitonov, took 13.7%. The rate of participation was 64.4%. Putin's inauguration took place on 7 May.

Violent attacks on Russian civilians, attributed to extremist Chechen separatists, culminated in a series of incidents in mid-

2004, which intensified following the assassination of the President of Chechnya in May. On 24 August two passenger planes, both flying from Moscow's Domodedovo airport, crashed, killing all 89 people on board. Both crashes were subsequently attributed to Chechen suicide bombers. On 1 September, the first day of the school year, armed militants occupied a school in Beslan, in the Republic of North Osetiya—Alaniya, taking at least 1,100 children, parents and teachers hostage. On 3 September troops stormed the building, reportedly in reaction to a series of explosions. Some 350 hostages, including 186 children, died in the ensuing battle, according to official figures. The militant Chechen leader, Shamil Basayev, subsequently claimed responsibility for the hostage-taking operation.

Apparently in reaction to this event, President Putin proposed a series of political reforms, chief among which was the introduction of a system whereby all regional governors would be appointed by the federal President, subject to the approval of the regional legislature. (Directly elected governors had become almost universal across the subjects of the Russian Federation in the second half of the 1990s.) Putin signed legislation to this end on 12 December 2004, following its approval by both chambers of the Federalnoye Sobraniye. The final scheduled gubernatorial election in the Federation took place in February 2005, and henceforth all regional governors were appointed in accordance with the new system. Putin also announced proposals that all 450 members of the Duma be elected on the basis of proportional representation and party lists. Moreover, the minimum membership required of a political party for it to be eligible for registration was to be increased from 10,000 to 50,000, with effect from January 2006. The quota for representation in the Duma on the basis of federal party lists was also to be increased from 5% of the total votes cast to 7%.

Meanwhile, in June 2004 the trial of Khodorkovskii and his business associate, Platon Lebedev, the Chairman of the Menatep financial group, began in Moscow, on seven charges, including tax evasion, forgery and fraud. While the trial was in progress, the state authorities presented Yukos with a series of demands for unpaid taxes for 2000–03, totalling some US $27,500m., and demanded that the principal production subsidiary of Yukos, Yuganskneftegaz, be brought to auction. In December Yuganskneftegaz was sold for $9,350m. to a previously unknown company, Baikalfinansgrup, which was acquired by the state-owned petroleum company Rosneft shortly after the auction. In May 2005 Khodorkovskii and Lebedev were each sentenced to nine years' imprisonment. (In December 2010 Khodorkovskii and Lebedev were found guilty on further charges of embezzlement and money-laundering at the conclusion of a court case that had commenced in 2009; they were each sentenced to 14 years' imprisonment, although this was to run concurrently with the sentences that they had begun serving in 2005.) In July 2005 a criminal investigation, on charges of corruption related to the illicit acquisition of a state property, was opened against former premier Kasyanov, amid widespread speculation that the charges were politically motivated. Meanwhile, liberal democratic and pro-Western opposition to the Putin administration was increasingly expressed by a grouping known as the United Civil Front, led by the former international chess champion Garri Kasparov.

On 14 November 2005 President Putin announced a government reorganization. Dmitrii Medvedev, the Chairman of the Board of Directors of Gazprom and hitherto Chief of the Presidential Staff, was appointed to the newly created post of First Deputy Chairman (while retaining his post at Gazprom). Sergei Ivanov, while retaining the defence portfolio, was also to serve as one of two Deputy Chairmen of the Government.

A major focus of parliamentary activity during the second half of 2005 was the development of measures intended to result in greater government supervision and regulation of civil society and non-governmental organizations (NGOs), at least in part in response to apparent concern that the so-called 'colour revolutions' that had taken place in Georgia in 2003, Ukraine in 2004 and Kyrgyzstan earlier in 2005 had been, to a certain extent, facilitated by externally financed NGOs. After several months of discussions, new legislation that, inter alia, permitted the authorities to close NGOs deemed to infringe Russia's sovereignty, unity or cultural heritage was signed into law by President Putin in January 2006. On 12 March, after the restrictions on party registration entered into effect on 1 January, the first 'unified election day' (for elections to various levels of government, or to certain local and regional assemblies in the Federation) took place. (Henceforth, the overwhelming majority of such elections were to take place in March and October each year.) UR won control of the overwhelming majority of regional assemblies to which elections were conducted (a pattern that was repeated at subsequent unified election days), although the rate of voter participation was relatively low. In June Putin nominated the Minister of Justice, Yurii Chaika, to serve as Prosecutor-General; Chaika was succeeded as Minister of Justice by Vladimir Ustinov, the previous Prosecutor-General. In October Motherland, the RPL and the Russian Pensioners' Party united to form a new political party, A Just Russia (AJR). Mironov was elected as Chairman of AJR (which absorbed another small party, the People's Party, in April 2007).

In October 2006 a journalist of the independent newspaper *Novaya Gazeta*, Anna Politkovskaya, a leading critic of the Russian military campaigns in Chechnya and the official Chechen leadership, was shot dead at her apartment building in Moscow. Her death attracted international attention, amid widespread speculation that the Chechen authorities may have been implicated in her killing. (According to independent estimates, at least 13 journalists had been murdered in Russia since 2000; a substantially greater number of journalists had been killed in suspicious circumstances during the 1990s.) In November Aleksandr Litvinenko, a former officer in the FSB and exile to the United Kingdom, died in a London hospital as a result of radiation-poisoning, having publicly accused Putin of responsibility for his sickness. Medical tests concluded that Litvinenko had been exposed to the radioactive substance Polonium-210. Police investigations into the killing of Litvinenko, who had been a close associate of Berezovskii, and had published a book accusing elements within the FSB of committing the apartment bombings of September 1999 (see Chechnya), commenced in both the United Kingdom and Russia. The Russian authorities subsequently refused to accede to a request by the British Government for the extradition of the principal suspect, Andrei Lugovoi, who had met with Litvinenko in London around the time of his poisoning, on the grounds that it contravened the Constitution. (In December 2007 Lugovoi was elected to the Gosudarstvennaya Duma, thereby securing immunity from prosecution within Russia.)

In early December 2006 Putin signed into law further amendments to electoral legislation, including the abolition of the minimum voter turn-out requirement for elections at every level. At the end of that month the Chairman of the Central Electoral Commission (CEC), Aleksandr Veshnyakov, announced that the forthcoming presidential election would take place on 9 March 2008, on the expiry of Putin's second four-year term. On 15 February 2007 Putin reorganized the Government, appointing Sergei Ivanov to the office of First Deputy Chairman (thereby granting him equal status to Medvedev). Anatolii Serdyukov, hitherto the head of the Federal Tax Service, replaced Ivanov as Minister of Defence, becoming the first appointee to that position not to have a background in the military or security services. Putin also appointed the President of the Chechen Republic, Maj.-Gen. Alu Alkhanov, to the post of deputy justice minister in the federal Government, enabling the controversial Prime Minister of Chechnya, Ramzan Kadyrov, to become acting republican President. In early March a mass opposition rally was organized in St Petersburg by Another Russia, a coalition of both left- and right-wing groups opposing Putin; leaders of Another Russia included Kasparov, Kasyanov and the leader of the extremist and prohibited National Bolshevik Party, Eduard Limonov. The subsequent removal of Veshnyakov from the post of Chairman of the CEC was attributed in the Russian media to his public criticism of the pro-Government parties and the amendments to the electoral legislation.

In April 2007, after Berezovskii declared to the British newspaper *The Guardian* that he planned the forcible ousting of the Putin administration, Minister of Foreign Affairs Lavrov reiterated demands for his extradition from the United Kingdom and announced further criminal proceedings against him. The insistence of the British authorities that Berezovskii was immune from extradition, owing to his political asylum status, further exacerbated tensions between the two countries. (In November Berezovskii was sentenced *in absentia* by a Moscow district court to six years' imprisonment for embezzlement; in June 2009 he was convicted *in absentia* on a further charge of embezzlement from car manufacturer AvtoVAZ in 1994 and received a term of 13 years' imprisonment.) In mid-April 2007 Another Russia organized anti-Government demonstrations in Moscow and St Petersburg, which were violently suppressed by troops associated with the Ministry of Internal Affairs (OMON). Some 350 protesters, including Kasparov and Kasyanov, were briefly detained in Moscow.

On 14 September 2007, following the resignation of Fradkov and his Government, the Gosudarstvennaya Duma approved Putin's nomination of Viktor Zubkov, hitherto head of the Federal Financial Monitoring Service, as Chairman. Later that month Putin announced a government reorganization; three new ministers were appointed, while the Minister of Finance, Aleksei Kudrin, also became a Deputy Chairman. In October Putin announced, in a statement made at UR's party congress, that he would head the party's list of candidates in the forthcoming legislative elections on 2 December and that he viewed favourably a proposal by delegates that he, eventually, become Chairman of the Government. Popular support for Putin's continued leadership increased during campaigning, and a number of regional organizations that had staged rallies in favour of a third presidential term for him grouped in November to form a 'For Putin' movement. In the same month Another Russia organized demonstrations in Moscow and St Petersburg, which resulted in the temporary detention of opposition leaders, including Kasparov. In November the Office for Democratic Institutions and Human Rights (ODIHR) of the OSCE announced the abandonment of plans to monitor the elections, after Russia imposed restrictions on the number of observers who would be invited; however, the Parliamentary Assemblies of the OSCE and Council of Europe (see p. 250) dispatched small monitoring missions.

At the elections to the Gosudarstvennaya Duma on 2 December 2007, UR won a substantial majority, securing 64.3% of the votes cast, according to official results, and 315 seats; the CPRF received 11.6% of votes and 57 seats, the LDPR 8.1% and 40 seats, and AJR 7.7% and 38 seats. Voter turn-out was 63.7% of the electorate. Reports emerged that students and public sector workers had been placed under considerable pressure by the authorities to vote for UR. The Russian Government dismissed a subsequent joint statement by the OSCE and the Council of Europe that the conduct of the elections had failed to meet international standards for democracy, following widespread allegations of media bias in favour of UR and voting irregularities. (A report by CIS observers upheld the organization of the elections.) On 10 December Putin announced his support for the nomination by UR and three other parties of Medvedev as a candidate in the forthcoming presidential election on 2 March 2008.

The presidency of Dmitrii Medvedev and premiership of Putin

In January 2008 the CEC rejected the presidential candidacy of Kasyanov, ruling that a number of the signatures collected in his support were invalid; he subsequently urged a boycott of the poll. In February the ODIHR again announced that it would not dispatch a monitoring mission to Russia, on the grounds that a stipulation by the Russian authorities that 70 observers be invited only three days before the poll would prevent adequate monitoring of the elections. On 2 March, as widely anticipated, Medvedev (following his endorsement by Putin) was elected to the presidency, with some 70.3% of the votes cast, according to final official results; Zyuganov of the CPRF received 17.7% of the votes, and Zhirinovskii of the LDPR about 9.4%. The official rate of participation by the electorate was estimated at 69.8%. Observers from the Parliamentary Assembly of the Council of Europe acknowledged popular support for Medvedev, but reported that aspects of the electoral campaign had failed to meet democratic principles. At a UR congress in April, Putin formally accepted an invitation to assume the new post of Chairman of the party, although it was confirmed that he would not become a member of the party. Medvedev was inaugurated as President on 7 May (when Putin, on relinquishing the presidency, officially became Chairman of UR). Shortly afterwards Medvedev nominated Putin as Chairman of the Government; on 8 May the Gosudarstvennaya Duma approved his nomination to the office by an overwhelming majority (with only CPRF deputies opposing it). On 12 May Putin announced a government reorganization, in which an additional three ministries were created. Zubkov became First Deputy Chairman, and was to assume particular responsibility for the agricultural sector, while a senior presidential aide, Igor Shuvalov, was also accorded the post of First Deputy Chairman. Igor Sechin, the Chairman of Rosneft and hitherto deputy head of the presidential administration, was appointed to the Government as a Deputy Chairman and was to supervise industrial development programmes. Ivanov remained in the new administration as a Deputy Chairman; other principal ministers, including Kudrin, Lavrov and Serdyukov, retained their posts.

In October 2008 Dmitrii Kozak, hitherto Minister of Regional Development, was appointed as a Deputy Chairman of the Government. In his first annual address on 5 November, Medvedev announced proposed amendments to the Constitution that principally extended the term of office of the President from four to six years and that of the deputies of the Gosudarstvennaya Duma from four to five years. The constitutional amendments were adopted by both parliamentary chambers later in November. On 12 December opposition leaders from many organizations, including Nemtsov and Kasparov, officially established an opposition movement, Solidarity. Marches of dissent were organized by Another Russia in Moscow and St Petersburg, in protest against the Government's failure to address the economic crisis (see Economic Affairs) and against the extension of the presidential and legislative mandates. Demonstrations were also staged in Vladivostok, the administrative centre of the far-eastern Maritime (Primorskii) Krai, and some 30 other cities later in December, in protest against government plans to increase tariffs on imported cars; the rally in Vladivostok was violently suppressed by OMON forces. With the incidence of racially motivated attacks increasing, in December seven extreme nationalist 'skinheads', who had killed at least 20 people in a series of racist attacks in Moscow, were sentenced to terms of between six and 20 years' imprisonment. The constitutional amendments (which had been approved by all 83 regional legislatures) were signed into law by Medvedev on 30 December.

In January 2009 a prominent human rights lawyer, Stanislav Markelov, who had represented the relatives of a Chechen woman murdered by a Russian officer in 2000, and a journalist were shot and killed in Moscow. (In November 2009 two members of an extreme nationalist group were arrested on suspicion of their killings, which were allegedly motivated by Markelov's representation of anti-fascist activists.) In February three suspects charged with involvement in the killing of Anna Politkovskaya in 2006 (of whom two were Chechen nationals and one was a former police officer) were acquitted by a Moscow court. A former FSB officer, who was widely believed to have ordered Politkovskaya's murder, was acquitted of a related charge. Also in February 2009 the Minister of Agriculture, Aleksei Gordeyev, was transferred to the post of Governor of Voronezh Oblast; he was replaced by the head of a state agro-industrial company, Yelena Skrynnik, in early March. In April Medvedev dismissed the head of the Main Intelligence Directorate, Gen. Valentin Korabelnikov (who had been appointed to the post in 1997), on grounds of old age, and also removed a further two senior defence officials. In May acute economic difficulties in the town of Pikalevo, near St Petersburg, including mass unemployment resulting from the closure of three local factories, and the suspension of power supplies to the town, led to substantial civil disorder there. As local unrest continued, Putin visited Pikalevo and, publicly rebuking the owner of one of the closed factories, the prominent 'oligarch' Oleg Deripaska, ordered that production be resumed at the factory. In June the Supreme Court overturned the acquittal of the two Chechens and the former police officer charged with killing Politkovskaya, on grounds of procedural irregularities, and ordered a retrial. In early September the Supreme Court additionally ordered a further investigation into the murder of Politkovskaya, reversing an earlier decision by a lower military court.

On 11 October 2009 elections were conducted to local and municipal authorities in 76 federal subjects, together with elections to three regional legislatures (including that of Moscow City); UR won decisively in nearly every poll. Opposition leaders accused the authorities of mass falsification of the elections; notably in Moscow City. Deputies belonging to the AJR, CPRF and LDPR temporarily suspended participation in the State Duma, in an unprecedented protest against alleged widespread electoral malpractice on the part of the authorities. In his annual address to the federal legislature in November, Medvedev pledged to continue efforts to suppress the insurgency in the North Caucasus and announced the appointment of a special presidential envoy for the region; he also notably proposed that the number of time zones in Russia be reduced (two of the 12 time zones then existing within the Federation were abolished with effect from April 2010). Later in November 2009 the bombing of an express train travelling from Moscow to St Petersburg was widely perceived to have been directed against prominent St Petersburg officials; some 26 people were killed, including a former Deputy Governor of the city, Sergei Tarasov, and the head of the federal agency for state reserves. In an internet statement, the Chechen militant leader, Doku Umarov (see Chechnya), claimed responsibility for the attack. In January 2010 Medvedev announced the creation of a new North Caucasus Federal Okrug in a restructuring of regional government, as part of efforts to strengthen federal control over the North Caucasus region. The Presidential Representative of the new district, Aleksandr Khloponin, was also appointed as a Deputy Chairman of the Government, with responsibility primarily for co-ordinating the economic development of the North Caucasus. Later in January marches of dissent (which had taken place on several occasions during 2009) were again organized by opposition leaders in Moscow and St Petersburg; a large protest (of some 10,000–12,000 people) was also staged in Kaliningrad, where it reflected popular discontent over economic conditions in the exclave.

In February 2009 Medvedev dismissed two deputy internal affairs ministers and 16 senior police officials, as part of extensive measures to reduce corruption in law enforcement bodies. On a further 'unified election day' on 14 March, local, municipal and regional elections took place in 76 federal subjects. An independent monitoring organization, GOLOS, reported widespread irregularities in many polls, particularly in municipal voting in Yekaterinburg, the principal city in Sverdlovsk Oblast, and attacks on independent journalists. The election results demonstrated a decline in support in some regions for UR, which had, unusually, secured less than 50% of votes cast to four of eight contested regional legislatures and lost two mayoral polls in Irkutsk Oblast, in Siberia. In late March unauthorized demonstrations demanding the resignation of Putin, in response to continuing economic difficulties, took place in cities across Russia, and were violently suppressed in Moscow. (In addition, opposition groups had, from July 2009, organized 'Strategy 31' marches nationwide on the last day of every month with 31 days, in reference to Article 31 of the Russian Constitution that allows peaceful demonstrations.)

On 29 March 2010 some 40 people were killed and more than 100 injured in two suicide bomb attacks on the Moscow Metro (the first explosion occurring at a station located beneath FSB headquarters). Umarov subsequently released a video recording in which he stated that the bombings had been undertaken on his orders, in response to the killing by federal security forces of a group of Chechen civilians near the village of Arshty, on the Chechen–Ingushetiyan border, in early February, and that more attacks would follow. International observers suggested that the Metro bomb attacks had been staged in retaliation for the killing of two senior militant commanders in FSB operations in the North Caucasus in March. Putin announced that two suicide bomb attacks staged in Dagestan at the end of March 2010, in which 14 people, including nine police officers, were killed, were related to the Metro bombings (which, it was reported, were perpetrated by natives of Dagestan). In April, following the announcement of a new anti-terrorism strategy, Medvedev established an inter-agency group, which was principally to investigate acts of terrorism and attacks against officials. In May the head of the FSB officially announced that three organizers of the Metro bombings had been shot dead by security agents during an attempt to arrest them.

From July 2010 a prolonged drought and unusually high temperatures resulted in thousands of forest fires breaking out across the country, destroying many villages, and causing a noxious smog in Moscow and other cities to the east of the capital. By mid-August the fires had killed 54 people and left thousands homeless. On 2 August President Medvedev declared a state of emergency in several central regions, and ordered an investigation into the fires. Later that month the head of the Federal Forestry Agency was replaced. Putin pledged that compensation would be paid and housing restored; following the destruction of some one-third of the country's grain harvest, the premier subsequently announced a ban on grain exports (which was subsequently extended until the end of 2011). In early September 2010 a car bomb exploded in the city of Vladikavkaz, the capital of North Osetiya, in the North Caucasus region, killing at least 17 people.

Recent developments: apparent dissent between the President and premier

On 28 September 2010 President Medvedev dismissed Luzhkov, who had been Mayor of Moscow since 1992 and a close ally of Putin, stating that he had lost the confidence of the President. Luzhkov's removal (which followed that of many long-serving regional leaders) had apparently been prompted by a newspaper article, written by him earlier that month, criticizing Medvedev's decision to suspend a construction project for a new highway between Moscow and St Petersburg that would have destroyed important forestland. Prior to his dismissal, Luzhkov had been subject to criticism in a series of broadcasts on state-controlled television accusing him of corruption and extreme incompetence, and had resisted pressure that he resign. Luzhkov also resigned from UR, complaining that the party had failed to support him. (In February 2011 the state Audit Chamber announced that investigations into the finances of the Moscow City Government under Luzhkov had revealed violations in 2009 and 2010 amounting to 230,000m. roubles. A further investigation by the Ministry of the Interior was under-way into an alleged malpractice scheme that involved several companies associated with Luzhkov, including the Bank of Moscow, and the construction company owned by Luzhkov's wife, Inteko.)

On 10 October 2010 local and municipal elections took place in 77 territories, together with elections to three regional legislatures: UR secured about 60% of votes cast overall. GOLOS again noted widespread violations, both during the electoral campaign and the voting process. On 21 October Sergei Sobyanin, a hitherto Deputy Chairman of the federal Government and Head of the Government Staff, was inaugurated as Mayor of Moscow, after the Municipal Duma voted, earlier on the same day, in support of his nomination by President Medvedev. A Deputy Speaker of the State Duma, Vyacheslav Volodin, was appointed to succeed Sobyanin in his government posts. Sobyanin immediately relaxed the stance of the municipal authorities towards the holding of opposition protests in the capital, granting permission for a limited 'Strategy 31' demonstration to be staged in central Moscow at the end of October (reportedly with the support of the newly appointed head of the Presidential Human Rights Council, Mikhail Fedotov), although large numbers of participants in 'Strategy 31' gatherings in other major cities were again arrested. The opposition groups represented in 'Strategy 31' became divided, with human rights activists Lyudmila Alekseyeva and Lev Ponomaryov henceforth organizing limited, officially authorized, protests, and Limonov continuing to stage unauthorized rallies.

In early December 2010 clashes erupted between extreme nationalists and police in Moscow, after a rally, organized to protest against the killing earlier in the month of a football supporter during a fight with a group of men from the North Caucasus. After the crowds were dispersed, disturbances continued across Moscow, and numerous people originating from Central Asia and the Caucasus were attacked; at least two people from minority ethnic groups died as a result. Nationalist demonstrations and protests subsequently spread to other cities across Russia. The state prosecutor initiated a criminal investigation into the release of suspects in the killing, following criticism from both Putin and Medvedev. Meanwhile, on 21 December the State Duma approved legislation, to enter into effect in 2015, prohibiting regional leaders from using the designation 'President' (as used by the leaders of several republics within the Federation). At the end of December 2010 some 60 people were arrested during a 'Strategy 31' rally in Moscow, despite it having been officially authorized. Nemtsov, who was among those detained, was sentenced to 15 days' imprisonment, prompting further protests by his supporters.

On 24 January 2011 a suicide bomb attack was carried out at Domodedovo international airport in Moscow, killing 36 people and injuring a further 168. The Federal Investigative Committee stated that the bombing had been primarily intended to kill foreign nationals. In early February Umarov released a video recording claiming direct responsibility for the attack. The authorities announced that they had identified the perpetrator of the attack, who was from Ingushetiya, and named a further six suspects also from Ingushetiya, of whom three were arrested. On 18 February five tourists from Moscow were attacked as they were travelling to a ski resort in the Mount Elbrus area of the Kabardino-Balkar Republic; three were killed and two injured. In March, following an investigation, Umarov was officially charged with organizing the suicide bombing at Domodedovo airport.

Elections conducted to local and municipal authorities in 74 federal subjects, together with elections to 12 regional legislatures, on 13 March 2011 were viewed as a gauge of public opinion prior to the federal parliamentary elections in December. Although UR secured an estimated 68% of the contested legislative seats, according to preliminary results, it received only about 46% of the votes cast overall (significantly lower than in the 2007 federal elections). Opposition parties complained of numerous electoral violations, particularly in the regions of Adygeya and Dagestan. Later in March 2011 speculation of dissent between Medvedev and Putin increased, when the President publicly rebuked Putin for denouncing a UN Security Council resolution authorizing military intervention in the civil conflict in Libya (see the chapter on Libya); Medvedev openly favoured the resolution, which Russia had consequently not opposed in the Security Council. (Putin stated that his remarks, likening the proposed military action to medieval crusades, had reflected his personal opinion, rather than Russia's official position.) Medvedev subsequently dismissed the Russian ambassador in Libya, Vladimir Chamov, who had accused Medvedev of jeopardizing Russian interests in Libya (with which Russia had significant armaments agreements) by supporting the action against Libyan leader Col Muammar al-Qaddafi, and declared his approval of Putin's rejection of the UN response. A prominent member of the UR central executive committee, Aleksei Chadayev, was subsequently ordered to resign, following his criticism of government support for the UN Security Council resolution. At the end of March Medvedev officially announced that government officials were to be replaced as directors of state companies, thereby reducing considerably state influence (and, in particular, that of close allies of Putin) on the business sector. Accordingly, in early April Sechin (who was considered the most senior of the so-called *siloviki*, politicians whose background was in the security services) resigned from the chairmanship of Rosneft; Zubkov and Kudrin, among other officials, were also expected to relinquish posts in state banks. Meanwhile, indications given by Medvedev in a media interview that he envisaged contesting the 2012 presidential election further increased speculation over his relationship with Putin.

Regional Government
In the early 1990s the Russian Federation encountered difficulties in attempting to satisfy the aspirations of its many minority ethnic groups for self-determination. In March 1992 some 18 of Russia's 20 nominally autonomous republics signed a federation treaty. The two dissenters, both predominantly Islamic and petroleum-producing regions, were Tatarstan, which had voted for self-rule earlier in the month, and the Checheno-Ingush Republic, which had declared independence from Russia in November 1991 (as the Chechen Republic—Chechnya). The new treaty granted the republics greater authority, including control of natural resources and formal borders, and allowed them to conduct their own foreign trade. An agreement signed with the Russian Government in February 1994 accorded Tatarstan a considerable measure of sovereignty. Other power-sharing agreements, granting varying degrees of sovereignty, were eventually signed by some 42 of the 89 federal subjects during Yeltsin's presidency; however, from 2000 President Putin implemented a number of measures intended to curtail the power of regional governors, which led to the rescission of the vast majority of the power-sharing treaties by mid-2002. In May 2000 the Gosudarstvennaya Duma approved legislation according the President the right to dismiss regional governors. As a result of legislation approved in December 2004, regional governors (the election of whom had become almost universal across the Federation by the late 1990s) were appointed by the federal President, subject to the approval of regional legislatures, from early 2005. In the mid-2000s the negotiation of new power-sharing treaties between the federal authorities and Chechnya and Tatarstan was undertaken. However, the Chechen authorities subsequently expressed opposition to the signature of any such document, while the treaty agreed with Tatarstan, ratified by the federal legislature in mid-2007, granted only limited privileges to the Republic.

In December 2009 President Medvedev proposed amendments to federal law regarding the numbers of seats in regional legislatures in order to stipulate a minimum and maximum number of deputies according to the size of the population in the region. On 19 January 2010 Medvedev announced the restructuring of the system of federal okrugs. A new North Caucasus Federal Okrug was created, comprising seven territories (six of which were ethnically defined republics formerly included within the Southern Federal Okrug). Aleksandr Khloponin, hitherto the Governor of Krasnoyarsk Krai in Siberia, was appointed as the Presidential Representative to the new federal district.

Chechnya
In March 1992, in response to the unilateral declaration of independence by Chechnya, the Ingush inhabitants of the former Checheno-Ingush Republic demanded the establishment of a separate republic. The formation of the new republic, Ingushetiya, was approved by the federal Supreme Council in June. Additionally, Ingush activists claimed territories in neighbouring North Osetiya, which had formed part of the Ingush Republic prior to the Second World War, when the Ingush (and Chechens, in common with several other nationalities of the USSR) were deported *en masse* to Central Asia. In October 1992 violent conflict broke out in the disputed Prigorodnyi district in North Osetiya. By November more than 300 people had died in the conflict and some 50,000 Ingush had fled the region. In September 1997, following mediation by Yeltsin, a treaty on normalizing relations was signed by the republican Governments of North Osetiya and Ingushetiya.

In late 1993 armed hostilities commenced in Chechnya between forces loyal to the republican authorities and those of the separatist leader, Gen. Dzhokhar Dudayev (who had been elected President of the Republic in October 1991, following a coup against the republic's communist Government, led by Doku Zavgayev). Chechnya boycotted the Russian general election and referendum of December 1993; in August 1994 an unsuccessful attempt to overthrow the Dudayev regime was reputedly aided by the federal security services. Following the defeat of a further offensive in November, federal troops entered Chechnya in December. The troops rapidly gained control of the lowland area of northern Chechnya. Dudayev's forces, estimated to number some 15,000 irregular troops, were concentrated in the Chechen capital, Groznyi, a city upon which federal troops launched an assault in late December, following heavy bombardment from the air. Despite sustaining significant casualties, federal troops gradually took control of the city and seized the presidential palace (the headquarters of Dudayev's forces) in January 1995. Groznyi suffered great devastation during the assault, and there were reported to be thousands of civilian casualties. In June Chechen gunmen engaged local security forces in Budennovsk, some 200 km from the border with Chechnya, and took hostage more than 1,000 people in the city hospital. The rebels demanded that the Russian Government initiate talks with Dudayev on the immediate withdrawal of troops from Chechnya. Following the failure of attempts by federal army units to free the hostages, telephone negotiations were conducted between the rebel leader, Shamil Basayev, and federal premier Chernomyrdin, by which time some 100 people had reportedly been killed. Subsequently, as a cease-fire took effect in Chechnya, the rebels began gradually to release hostages. Peace talks between a delegation from the federal Government and the Chechen leadership commenced in Groznyi in late June, and a cease-fire agreement was formalized in July.

In October 1995, following an assassination attempt on the commander of the federal forces in Chechnya, the federal Government announced a temporary suspension of the July agreement. In response, the Chechen leadership announced its complete rejection of the accord. In December elections took place in Chechnya, to both the republican Duma and presidency. Zavgayev was elected republican President, reportedly receiving some 93% of the votes cast in elections that Dudayev rejected as invalid.

In January 1996 Chechen militants seized about 2,000 civilians in Kizlyar, Dagestan, and held them hostage in a hospital. Following negotiations, most were released, and the rebels departed, accompanied by some 150 hostages, for Chechnya. Federal troops halted the rebels in the border village of Pervomaiskoye and demanded the release of the remaining hostages. After further negotiations failed, federal forces attacked and captured the village. Although the rebels' leader, Salman Raduyev, escaped to Chechnya with some of his forces and around 40 hostages, some 150 rebels, and a number of their captives, were reportedly killed in the assault. In April Dudayev was killed in a missile attack. He was succeeded as leader of the separatists by Zemlikhan Yandarbiyev, who subsequently developed an association with the Islamist Taliban regime in Afghanistan. Sporadic fighting persisted, but a new cease-fire agreement between the federal authorities and Yandarbiyev was reached in May. A formal military agreement, concluded in June, envisaged a withdrawal of the federal troops by the end of August and the disarmament of the separatist fighters. In August separatist forces, led by Basayev, launched a sustained offensive against Groznyi. Yeltsin granted Gen. Lebed, the recently appointed Secretary of the Security Council, extensive powers to co-ordinate federal operations in the republic and to conduct a negotiated settlement. Following discussions involving Yandarbiyev and the Chechen military leader, Gen. Khalid ('Aslan') Maskhadov, a fresh cease-fire was brokered in mid-August. Following further negotiations, the withdrawal of troops commenced, and on 31 August Lebed and Maskhadov signed a conclusive peace agreement (the Khasavyurt Accords) in Dagestan, according to which any decision regarding Chechnya's future political status was to be deferred until December 2001. The withdrawal of federal troops and the exchange of prisoners of war began, and the cease-fire was largely respected. In September 1996 a Chechen Government was created, with Maskhadov as Prime Minister, and Yandarbiyev as Chairman of the cabinet. Nevertheless, sporadic violence continued: by early 1997 it was estimated that the conflict had caused some 80,000 deaths, and resulted in the displacement of 415,000 civilians.

All federal troops were withdrawn before the republican presidential and legislative elections, held on 27 January 1997. Maskhadov was elected President, with some 59.3% of the total votes cast. Of the 12 remaining candidates, Basayev won 23.5% of the votes, and Yandarbiyev 10.1%. The rate of voter participation was reported to be 79.4%, and international observers reported no serious discrepancies in the electoral process. Maskhadov declined his seat in the Sovet Federatsii, and affirmed his support for Chechen independence. Elections to the Chechen legislature were inconclusive, and, after a second round of voting, only 45 of the 63 seats had been filled; further rounds were held in May and June. On 12 May Yeltsin and Maskhadov signed a formal peace treaty, defining the principles of future relations between Chechnya and the Russian Federation, and renouncing the use of violence as a means of resolving differences. The treaty, however, did not address the issue of Chechnya's constitutional status and, moreover, was refused ratification by the Gosudarstvennaya Duma.

Attacks and, in particular, hostage-taking continued to be perpetrated by rebels opposed to the peace agreement. Meanwhile, Chechnya's introduction of elements of *Shari'a* (Islamic religious) law in 1997, in particular the holding of public executions, was strongly opposed by the federal authorities. In January 1998 Maskhadov dismissed his cabinet and reappointed First Deputy Prime Minister Basayev (who had been indicted by the federal authorities on charges of terrorism), as acting Prime Minister, entasked with the formation of a new government. In late March the republican parliament announced that the territory was henceforth to be known as the 'Chechen Republic of Ichkeriya'. Increasing lawlessness and militancy was reported in the republic. In May Chechen rebels kidnapped Yeltsin's special representative to Chechnya, Vladimir Vlasov; he was freed in November by interior ministry troops. As disorder increased, Maskhadov dismissed the entire Chechen administration in October, and declared a further state of emergency in December. It became apparent that militant Islamist groups, including a faction led in Chechnya by Omar ibn al-Khattab (believed to be of Saudi or Jordanian origin), were increasingly implicated in the violence in Chechnya.

From August 1999 Islamist factions associated with Basayev launched a series of attacks on Dagestan, with the aim of protecting and extending the jurisdiction of a 'separate Islamic territory' in Dagestan, over which rebels had obtained control in the previous year. (The territory was returned to federal rule in mid-September.) A series of bomb explosions in August and September in Moscow, Dagestan and Volgodonsk (Rostov Oblast), including two that destroyed entire apartment blocks, officially attributed by the Government to Chechen separatists, killed almost 300 people, prompting the redeployment of federal armed forces in the republic from late September; the recently inaugurated premier, Putin, described the deployment as an 'anti-terrorist operation'. Allegations persisted that sources associated with the FSB had ordered the attacks, in order to justify a renewed military campaign in Chechnya; notably, the discovery of an apparent attempt to initiate a further bombing in an apartment block in Ryazan heightened concerns of FSB involvement, although the authorities insisted that the incident was simply an exercise designed to ensure a heightened state of public vigilance. (In January 2004 two men were sentenced to life imprisonment for their part in the attacks.) In February 2000, following concerted air and ground offensives, federal forces obtained control of Groznyi and proceeded to destroy much of the capital; many republican and federal administrative bodies were relocated to Gudermes, Chechnya's second city.

In May 2000 President Putin decreed that, henceforth, Chechnya would be governed federally. Akhmad haji Kadyrov, a former senior mufti, was inaugurated as administrative leader (Governor) of the republic in June. Kadyrov, a former ally of Maskhadov, was to be directly responsible to the federal authorities. In January 2001 Putin signed a decree transferring control of operations in Chechnya from the Ministry of Defence to the FSB, and announced the intention of withdrawing the majority of the 80,000-strong federal forces from the region, leaving a 15,000-strong infantry division and 7,000 interior ministry troops. The local administration in Chechnya was restructured, and Stanislav Ilyasov, a former Governor of Stavropol Krai, was appointed as the Chechen premier. Despite claims that federal military operations had effectively ended, guerrilla attacks showed no sign of abating, and concern escalated among international human rights organizations about the conduct of 'cleansing' operations by federal troops, in which entire towns or areas were searched for rebels. In early 2001 a number of violent incidents outside Chechnya were staged by rebels, with the intention of drawing attention to the ongoing conflict. In May the continuing disorder in Chechnya was demonstrated by the announcement that the planned withdrawal of troops from the province had been halted.

In November 2001 the first direct negotiations between the warring factions since the renewal of hostilities in 1999, held in Moscow between the presidential representative to the Southern Federal Okrug, Col-Gen. Viktor Kazantsev, and Maskhadov's deputy, Akhmed Zakayev, reached no substantive agreement, and no further high-level meetings took place. In December Raduyev, the only prominent Chechen rebel leader to have been captured by federal forces, was sentenced to life imprisonment, having been found guilty of 10 charges, including murder, terrorism and hostage-taking. (Raduyev died in prison in December 2002.)

In April 2002 Khattab was killed by federal forces. Rebel activity increased markedly in the months that followed; although the political authority of Maskhadov had dwindled, his military leadership of what was known as the State Defence Committee became increasingly prominent as a focus for resistance to the federal troops. In July it was reported that Basayev had been appointed to a senior position on the Committee. In August federal forces experienced their single largest loss of life since the recommencement of operations in 1999, when a military helicopter was shot down by rebels in Groznyi, killing some 118 troops.

On 23–26 October 2002 over 40 heavily armed rebels held captive more than 800 people in a Moscow theatre, and demanded the withdrawal of federal troops from the republic. The siege ended when élite federal forces stormed the theatre, having initially filled the building with an incapacitating gas. The rebels were killed, and it subsequently emerged that at least 129 hostages had also died, in almost all cases owing to the toxic effects of the gas. Maskhadov issued a statement condemning the rebels' use of terrorist methods, but, despite denials by the rebel Chechen leadership of their involvement in the incident, Zakayev was arrested in late October, reportedly on the orders of the federal Government, in Denmark. In December the Danish authorities refused to extradite Zakayev to Russia, citing a lack of credible evidence of his involvement in terrorist activities. Zakayev's presence in Denmark resulted in the relocation to Brussels, Belgium, of the European Union (EU, see p. 270)-Russia summit that had been scheduled to take place in Copenhagen, Denmark, in November. Zakayev subsequently fled to the United Kingdom, where, in November 2003, he was granted political asylum, following the dismissal of a Russian request for his extradition.

In mid-November 2002 Ilyasov was transferred from his position as Prime Minister of Chechnya and appointed as a minister in the federal Government, in which capacity he was to be responsible for the social and economic development of Chechnya; Ilyasov was succeeded as the premier of Chechnya by Capt. (retd) Mikhail Babich, who had previously held senior positions in two regional administrations elsewhere in Russia. In late November Ilyasov announced that a referendum on a new draft Chechen constitution, which would, *inter alia*, determine the status of the republic within the Russian Federation, was to be held in March 2003. At the end of December 2002 at least 83 people died, and more than 150 others were injured, when suicide bombers detonated bombs in two vehicles stationed outside the headquarters of the republican Government in Groznyi. (Basayev subsequently claimed responsibility for the attack.) By late December 2002 federal losses during the campaign, according to official figures, were put at 4,572 dead and 15,549 wounded, with 29 missing, although Chechen estimates were considerably higher. (It was also estimated that more than 14,000 rebel fighters had been killed since September 1999.) In late January 2003 Babich resigned as premier. On 10 February Anatolii Popov, the hitherto deputy chairman of the state commission for the reconstruction of Chechnya, was appointed as the new republican premier.

The referendum on the draft constitution for Chechnya, describing the republic (which was to be renamed the Chechen—Nokchi Republic) as both a sovereign entity, with its own citizenship, and as an integral part of the Russian Federation, proceeded, as scheduled, on 23 March 2003, despite concerns that the instability of the republic would prevent the poll from being free and fair. The draft constitution also provided for the holding of fresh elections to a strengthened republican presidency and legislature. According to the official results, some 88.4% of the electorate participated in the plebiscite, of whom 96.0% supported the draft constitution. Two further questions, on the method of electing the President and the Parliament of Chechnya, were supported by 95.4% and 96.1% of participants, respectively. However, independent observers challenged the results, reporting that the rate of participation by the electorate had been much lower than officially reported.

Political violence continued to dominate Chechen affairs after the referendum. In early May 2003 at least 59 people were killed when suicide bombers attacked government offices in the north of Chechnya. Two days later another suicide bombing at a religious festival attended by Kadyrov resulted in at least 14 deaths, although Kadyrov escaped unhurt; Basayev claimed responsibility for the organization of both attacks. On 21 June Kadyrov inaugurated an interim legislative body, the State Council, comprising the head of, and an appointed representative of, each administrative district. In July Putin announced that a presidential election in Chechnya would be held in October. None the less, clashes continued, and in August at least 50 people were killed in an attack on a military hospital in neighbouring North Osetiya.

From 1 September 2003 control of military operations in Chechnya was transferred from the FSB to the federal Ministry of Internal Affairs; such operations were no longer regarded as having an 'anti-terrorist' character but were, rather, to form part of an 'operation to protect law and constitutional order'. Meanwhile, campaigning for the presidential election commenced, and by mid-August 11 candidates had registered. However, the subsequent withdrawal of Aslanbek Aslakhanov, a representative of Chechnya in the Gosudarstvennaya Duma, and the debarring of a business executive, Malik Saidullayev, effectively removed any major challenges to Kadyrov's candidacy. As had been widely anticipated, on 5 October Kadyrov was elected as President, receiving 87.7% of the votes cast, according to official figures. The rate of participation by the electorate was stated to be 82.6%. In mid-December at least 12 people were killed in clashes that followed incursions by heavily armed Chechen rebels into Dagestan, resulting in the imposition of a state of emergency in the region. An explosion in a Moscow Metro train on 6 February 2004, which resulted in the deaths of at least 39 people, was attributed to Chechen militants.

In February 2004 Yandarbiyev was killed by a car bomb in Doha, Qatar. (Two Russian intelligence agents were subsequently sentenced to life imprisonment for Yandarbiyev's murder by a Qatari court; however, they were returned to Russia to serve out their sentences in December, and in early 2005 it was reported that they were no longer being held in detention.) In early March 2004 another influential rebel leader, Ruslan Gelayev, was reported to have been killed in clashes with federal troops in Dagestan. In mid-March Popov was formally dismissed as premier of Chechnya, following a period of ill health; he was replaced by Sergei Abramov, who had previously worked in the republican Ministry of Finance.

An explosion in Groznyi on 9 May 2004, at a celebration to mark 'Victory Day', resulted in the deaths of several senior officials, including Kadyrov and Khusain Isayev, the head of the republican legislature. (Basayev subsequently claimed responsibility for the attack.) Abramov assumed presidential responsibilities in an acting capacity, pending an election, while Ramzan Kadyrov, the son of the assassinated President and the leader of the presidential security service (often known as the *Kadyrovtsi* and which was widely believed to have been implicated in several unexplained 'disappearances'), was appointed as First Deputy Prime Minister. Chechen militants were suspected of involvement in a series of raids on interior ministry targets in the neighbouring republic of Ingushetiya, which took place in June. In the presidential election held on 29 August, Maj.-Gen. Alu Alkhanov, an officer in the interior ministry troops, and generally acknowledged to be the candidate favoured by the federal Government, was elected President, receiving 73.5% of the votes cast, according to official figures, which evaluated the rate of participation at 85.2%. The Council of Europe described the elections as undemocratic. Alkhanov retained Abramov as Prime Minister, while Ramzan Kadyrov was retained both as First Deputy Prime Minister and as head of the presidential security service. In the period immediately before and after the election, attacks on Russian civilians, attributed to extremist Chechen separatists, intensified, with the destruction, apparently by suicide bombers, of two passenger planes, the explosion of a bomb outside a Moscow Metro station, and the occupation of a school in Beslan, in the Republic of North Osetiya—Alaniya, on 1–3 September (see Domestic Political Affairs). Basayev subsequently released a statement claiming that the attacks had occurred under his orchestration, and describing the demands of the Beslan hostage-takers as the complete withdrawal of federal troops from Chechnya and the resignation of President Putin.

In February 2005 Maskhadov announced that he had ordered separatist fighters to observe a unilateral one-month cease-fire, in what he described as a 'goodwill gesture' towards the Russian authorities. On 8 March he was killed during a special operation by FSB forces north of Groznyi. Maskhadov was replaced as leader of the State Defence Committee by his chosen successor, Abdul-Khalim Sadulayev. Sadulayev, like Maskhadov before him, announced his willingness to enter into negotiations with the federal authorities, but maintained that the use of force was legitimate in the absence of such negotiations. In June Sadulayev issued a decree appointing Doku Umarov, a rebel commander believed to be a close associate of Basayev (who had, earlier in the year, stated that Chechen militants would launch large-scale operations in other regions of Russia as part of a so-called 'Caucasus Front'), as vice-president of the rebel leadership, and issued a statement threatening military operations in other regions of Russia, in vengeance for the actions of federal forces in Chechnya. In mid-August Sadulayev dismissed the rebel Chechen 'parliament-in-exile' and a network of 'ambassadors', which he collectively accused of financial malpractice and incompetence; he also appointed a new rebel 'Government' at the end of the month, to which, notably, Basayev was appointed as 'First Deputy Prime Minister', while Zakayev was appointed to represent the rebel authorities internationally. In early October a co-ordinated series of attacks by some 100 militants against law-enforcement bodies in Nalchik, the capital of the Kabardino-Balkar Republic, in the western North Caucasus, resulted in the deaths of at least 130 people; Basayev claimed responsibility for the organization of the attack. An Islamist group active in the Kabardino-Balkar Republic, the Yarmuk Jamaat, also claimed to have participated in the attacks, as part of the 'Caucasus Front'. Meanwhile, tensions between Chechens and the most numerous ethnic group in neighbouring Dagestan, the Avars, were also heightened on several occasions from the first half of 2005, as a result of security forces associated with the Chechen authorities (most notably members of the *Kadyrovtsi*) making incursions into Dagestan, apparently in response to Chechen rebels taking refuge there. Clashes were also reported between those troops loyal to Ramzan Kadyrov and those loyal to the federal authorities.

On 27 November 2005 elections were held in Chechnya to a new, bicameral legislature, comprising the 18-seat Council of the Republic (the upper chamber) and the 40-seat People's Assembly (the lower chamber). The federal Government cited the ballot as evidence that normality was returning to Chechnya, although no candidates advocating Chechen independence were allowed to stand. The rate of participation by the electorate was estimated as some 60%, well above the 25% required to validate the election; however, international observers expressed doubt that the vote was free and fair. As predicted, the majority of deputies in the new parliament (33 out of 58) were from UR. Thus, the position of Kadyrov, a member of UR and for a long time perceived as de facto leader of the Chechen Government, was consolidated; furthermore, Kadyrov at this time held the position of acting premier, after Abramov sustained injuries in an automobile accident earlier in the month.

On 28 February 2006 Abramov resigned as Prime Minister of Chechnya. On 4 March the republican legislature unanimously approved the appointment of Kadyrov as his successor. Although this appointment effectively confirmed the distribution of power that had been in place in the Republic for several months, it was not without controversy. As acting Prime Minister, Kadyrov had spoken in favour of permitting men to marry up to four women, although this would be in clear breach of the family code, and had expressed support for other Islamist causes. In June Sadulayev was killed in an operation by special forces in Chechnya. He was succeeded as leader of the separatist Chechen rebels by Umarov, who appointed Basayev as his deputy. In July Basayev was killed, in an explosion in Ingushetiya (for which the FSB claimed responsibility). In October Kadyrov reached 30 years of age (the minimum age for eligibility to serve as Chechen President). On 15 February 2007 Putin's transferral of Alkhanov to the federal Government (see Domestic Political Affairs) allowed Kadyrov, as Chairman of the republican Government, to assume the duties of President, in an acting capacity. Later in the month it was confirmed that he was the federal authorities' preferred nominee to become President; his appointment was endorsed by the republican legislature on 2 March.

On 21 June 2007 the Chechen Constitutional Assembly approved amendments to the republican Constitution, proposed by Kadyrov, which included the replacement of the bicameral legislature with a 41-member unicameral Parliament, the abolition of direct elections to the republican presidency, the extension of the presidential term from four to five years, and the adoption of Chechen as a state language, in addition to Russian; the changes were endorsed by 96.9% of the votes cast in a referendum in December. Meanwhile, in October Umarov issued a statement proclaiming himself emir of 'the Caucasus Emirate', which sought to establish an Islamic state across the North Caucasus, thereby precipitating a split in the separatist movement between Islamist and nationalist elements. In November the rebel Chechen 'parliament-in-exile' announced that Umarov's powers as 'President' of the 'Chechen Republic of Ichkeriya' had been formally removed. The rebel 'Minister of Foreign Affairs' based in London, United Kingdom, Zakayev, condemned Umarov's statement, and subsequently received the support of senior rebel commanders. The chairman of the 'parliament-in-exile' issued a decree appointing Zakayev as 'Prime Minister', although this appointment was not recognized by supporters of Umarov.

Legislative elections were conducted in Chechnya on 12 October 2008; according to official results, UR secured some 88.4% of the votes cast and 37 of the 41 seats in the reconstituted unicameral Parliament. Following the completion of the post-conflict reconstruction of much of Groznyi, in April 2009 Medvedev issued a decree formally ending the counter-terrorism operation in Chechnya and providing for the withdrawal of some 20,000 of the 50,000 Russian troops deployed in the republic at that time. However, the federal military authorities rapidly reinstated special security measures in five southern districts of Chechnya, in response to renewed rebel activity. In mid-July an employee of human rights organization Memorial, Natalya Estemirova, was discovered dead in Ingushetiya, after her abduction in Groznyi. Estemirova had been an outspoken critic of the Chechen authorities and in March 2008 had been summoned to a meeting with Kadyrov during which he had allegedly threatened her. The Chairman of Memorial subsequently accused Kadyrov of responsibility for her death, causing him to threaten legal action against the organization. Following her killing, Memorial suspended its activities in Chechnya. In August 2009 a further two prominent human rights activists were discovered dead in Groznyi. Meanwhile, a sharp increase in suicide bomb attacks was reported in the North Caucasus region, notably including an attack in Nazran, Ingushetiya, in June, in which the President of the Republic, Yunus-bek Yevkurov, was severely injured. On 10 October direct elections to municipal authorities took place in Chechnya (and in Ingushetiya) for the first time since 1990. In the mayoral poll in Groznyi, the incumbent Head of the City Administration, who was a close ally of Kadyrov, was returned to the post, with 87.4% of votes cast.

In January 2010 Chechnya became part of a new North Caucasus Federal Okrug (also comprising Dagestan, Ingushetiya and four other territories), which was created by Medvedev in an effort to strengthen federal control over the region. Also in January Umarov issued a statement that Islamist separatist forces under his control would stage attacks in Russian cities. He subsequently declared that he had personally ordered two suicide bomb attacks on the Moscow Metro in March (see Domestic Political Affairs), having also claimed responsibility for the bombing of an express train travelling from Moscow to St Petersburg in November 2009, in an apparent revival of the terrorist strategy pursued in Russia in the early 2000s under the command of Basayev. Nevertheless, in March 2010 Kadyrov announced that he had issued a request to the federal authorities to end the deployment in Chechnya of police and FSB personnel from elsewhere in Russia. At the end of March the Chechen republican parliament adopted a statement strongly critical of the Presidential Representative of the new Federal Okrug, Aleksandr Khloponin, particularly for his delay in the establishment of an economic reform team. In April Arkadii Yedelov, a former federal Deputy Minister of Internal Affairs who had been involved in anti-insurgent operations in the North Caucasus since 2001 and was a close associate of Kadyrov, was appointed as a deputy to Khloponin. On 1 August 2010 it was reported that, for health reasons, Umarov was to resign his position as leader of the 'North Caucasus Emirate', although this decision was rescinded several days later. Speculation regarding a division in the insurgent leadership was confirmed later in August, when numerous Chechen field commanders announced that they had withdrawn their support for Umarov, instead pledging allegiance to another Chechen militant leader, Khusein Gakayev (Emir Hussein). In the same month the Chechen parliament voted to change Kadryov's title to 'Head of the Republic', with effect from 2 September. In October at least six people were killed as the result of an attack on the Chechen parliamentary building. In February 2011 Umarov claimed responsibility for a suicide bomb attack perpetrated at Domodedovo international airport in Moscow.

Foreign Affairs
Regional relations

Following the dissolution of the USSR in December 1991, Russia's most immediate foreign policy concerns were with the other former Soviet republics, generally referred to in Russia as the 'near abroad'. Relations with Ukraine were, initially, dominated by a dispute over the division of the former Soviet Black Sea Fleet, based mainly in Sevastopol, on the Crimean peninsula (Ukraine). Russia and Ukraine signed an agreement on the division of the Fleet in June 1995, but Russia subsequently refused to implement the accord, owing to continued disagreement concerning the status of Sevastopol. In May 1997 an agreement was concluded with Ukraine, whereby Russia was to lease part of the city's naval base for 20 years, and was to provide financial compensation for ships and equipment received from Ukraine. (Upon expiry, the treaty could be renewed for five years, should both parties agree, but would then be subject to renegotiation.) A Treaty on Friendship, Co-operation and Partnership was signed by the two countries in that month. In January 2003 a treaty delineating the land boundary between Russia and Ukraine (which remained largely unmarked and unregulated) was signed by Putin and President Leonid Kuchma of Ukraine, although discussions on the status of the Sea of Azov, which lies between the two countries, remained unresolved. Work on the construction of a dam in the Sea, which commenced, apparently at the instigation of the regional authorities in Krasnodar Krai, in September, precipitated considerable controversy, and raised concerns that the territorial integrity of Ukraine was being violated. In December the Presidents of the two countries signed an agreement on the use of the Sea of Azov, the entirety of which was defined as comprising the internal waters of both countries. Agreement was also reached on the maritime state boundary of Russia and Ukraine in the region.

Relations with Ukraine were damaged by the circumstances of the disputed 2004 presidential election in that country (see the chapter on Ukraine), as Putin openly supported the candidacy of the incumbent Prime Minister, Viktor Yanukovych, whose reported victory in the second round was subsequently overturned following large public protests over the conduct of the poll. Notably, Putin visited Ukraine twice during the campaign, appearing publicly with Yanukovych on both occasions, and telephoned Yanukovych to congratulate him on his victory before the official (and later discredited) results had been announced. Putin also described the protests that led to the election being repeated, and which became known as the 'orange revolution', as a violation of constitutional order. In a move widely interpreted as acknowledging the necessity of continued co-operation between the two countries (and reflecting the substantial ethnic Russian and Russian-speaking population of Ukraine), the newly elected President, Viktor Yushchenko, visited Moscow the day after his inauguration in January 2005. However, relations between the two countries were again strained later in 2005, following the announcement by the Russian state-controlled company Gazprom that it intended to charge Ukraine market prices for the supply of natural gas, which had hitherto been supplied at a subsidized rate. After failing to negotiate new terms, on 1 January 2006 Gazprom halted supplies to Ukraine, a measure that resulted in a reduced output of gas in several countries in central and western Europe supplied by pipelines crossing Ukraine. Supplies were restored on 4 January, following agreement on new terms of supply less favourable to Ukraine. In October 2007 Gazprom threatened again to suspend natural gas supplies to Ukraine, stating that it was owed US $1,300m.; a few days later it was announced that a compromise agreement had been reached. In February 2008 Gazprom warned that it would reduce supplies to Ukraine, in response to debts incurred during the previous month. After further discussions, in April the Ukrainian Government announced that a new payment scheme had been agreed; at the insistence of the Russian authorities, the Swiss-registered RosUkrEnergo was to remain the intermediary trading company in gas supplies to Ukraine, operating within Russia.

A further acrimonious dispute over the price Ukraine would pay for Russian gas and the level of transit fees to be paid by Gazprom during 2009 resulted in Russia's suspension of gas supplies to Ukraine on 1 January. After accusing Ukraine of abstracting gas flowing through its pipelines intended for export to Europe, Russia also halted supplies to Europe via Ukraine on 7 January (during a period of extremely cold weather). Following intensive EU mediation and emergency discussions between Gazprom and Ukrainian state utility Naftogaz, on 19 January Putin and the Ukrainian Prime Minister, Yuliya Tymoshenko, signed an agreement in Moscow, whereby Ukraine would pay an average price for Russian gas in 2009 that would be 20% lower than the European price, while the transit price would remain unchanged; Ukraine was obliged to purchase 40,000m. cu m of Russian gas in that year. Gas supplies to Europe were finally restored on 21 January. Gazprom was reported to have lost US $1,500m. in revenue by the end of January as a result of the dispute, and European energy officials urged measures to address the EU's over-dependence on Russian gas. Following further discussions between Putin and Tymoshenko in Moscow at the end of April, it was agreed that Gazprom would not penalize Ukraine for failure to accept the contracted amount of gas in 2009 and would assist in payment of the transit fee to ensure supply, while Russia was invited to participate in an EU-supported programme to modernize Ukraine's gas transportation system.

In a highly critical open letter to President Yushchenko in August 2009, Medvedev accused his counterpart of pursuing 'anti-Russian' policies and of supplying Ukrainian weapons to Georgian forces in the previous year's conflict (see below), as well as attributing responsibility to the Ukrainian Government for the periodic disruption of Russian gas supplies to Europe via Ukraine. Medvedev also stated that he would delay sending a new Russian ambassador to Ukraine (the previous ambassador, former Russian premier Chernomyrdin, having been recalled in June). Following the overwhelming defeat of Yushchenko in a presidential election in Ukraine in early 2010, and his replacement by Viktor Yanukovych, the new Ukrainian President pledged to restore cordial relations between Ukraine and Russia and to end the recurrent disputes over gas supplies. In mid-February Medvedev, who also predicted an improvement in bilateral relations, invited Yanukovych to Moscow. In late March the new Ukrainian Prime Minister, Mykola Azarov, met Putin and Gazprom officials for discussions in Moscow, when Putin consented to conduct further negotiations on gas prices. In April Medvedev and Yanukovych, meeting in Kharkiv, Ukraine, reached an agreement whereby Russia was to grant Ukraine a significant discount on the price of Russian gas, while Ukraine was to extend the lease on the base of the Black Sea Fleet in the Crimean peninsula (due to expire in 2017) for a further 25 years. (The agreement was ratified by the State Duma on 27 April.) However, in April 2011 it was reported that the Ukrainian Government had failed to respond to an invitation, extended by Putin during a visit to Ukraine, to join Russia's customs union with Belarus and Kazakhstan (see below).

In April 1996 Russia and Belarus signed an agreement creating a 'Community of Russia and Belarus', according to which the two countries would pursue economic integration and close co-ordination of foreign and defence policies. In May 1997 a 'Charter of the Union of Belarus and Russia' was concluded, which, while promoting greater co-operation between the two countries, moved away from advocating full union, although in June the first official session of the Union's joint Parliamentary Assembly was convened. During 1998 the Union was strengthened by the decision to grant joint citizenship to residents, and the establishment of a joint legislative and representative body to deal with union issues. A treaty on unification entered into force on 26 January 2000, when the President of Belarus, Alyaksandr Lukashenka, was appointed Chairman of the High State Council of the Union. A union budget was approved at a session of the Parliamentary Assembly (established under the 1996 Treaty, and comprising 36 members from the legislature of each country) in May. In early February 2009 it was announced that Belarus and Russia had signed an official treaty providing for the creation of a joint air defence system. Although bilateral relations deteriorated from 2009, owing in part to Lukashenka's failure to extend recognition to the separatist regions of Abkhazia and South Ossetia (see the chapter on Belarus), Belarus (and Kazakhstan) agreed to enter into a customs union with Russia. Despite a subsequent dispute between Russia and Belarus, which objected to Russia's continued imposition of export duties on petroleum, the customs union entered into force in July 2010. Relations with Belarus again deteriorated in mid-2010, and a Russian state-owned television channel broadcast a series of programmes portraying Lukashenka in extremely unfavourable terms, prompting speculation that Russia might provide support for an alterative candidate at the next presidential election in Belarus. However, in December (shortly before a pre-term presidential election in Belarus), Lukashenka visited Medvedev in Moscow, and terms were agreed on a reduction in the duties paid by Belarus on imports of Russian petroleum, and for Belarus to pay to Russia the duties that it received from re-exporting Russian oil products.

Concern at the treatment and status of ethnic Russians in Estonia and Latvia remained a particular source of tension, and the demarcation of mutual frontiers also created difficulties. In the early 2000s Russia expressed particular concern for its citizens in the Russian exclave of Kaliningrad, which is separated from the remainder of the Russian Federation by Belarus and Lithuania. Russian premier Kasyanov attempted to ensure that residents of the exclave would be exempted from visa requirements that were to be imposed by Lithuania and Poland prior to the two countries' accession to the EU (which took effect from 1 May 2004). In November 2002, at an EU-Russia summit meeting, held in Brussels, Russia finally agreed to an EU proposal for simplified visa arrangements. According to the compromise accord, multiple-transit travel documentation would be made available to residents of the exclave travelling by motor vehicle; the new regulations came into effect on 1 July 2003. In 2006 President Putin inaugurated a railway ferry service, initially servicing only cargo, connecting the exclave to metropolitan Russia.

Following the dissolution of the USSR, Russia maintained significant political and military influence in many former Soviet republics, especially in those areas involved in civil or ethnic conflicts. Russian troops were deployed in Tajikistan to support the Tajikistani Government against rebel forces during the civil war of 1992–97, and remained thereafter to ensure the security of the Tajikistani–Afghan border. In 2004 it was announced that Russian troops were to transfer responsibility for border security to the Tajikistani military; in October, meanwhile, it was announced that Russia had been formally granted a permanent military base in Tajikistan. In October 2003 a Russian military base commenced operations in Kyrgyzstan, the first to be established outside Russia subsequent to the dissolution of the USSR; the base was intended to meet the requirements of the Collective Security Treaty Organization (CSTO, see p. 459), inaugurated in April to succeed the CIS Collective Security Treaty. In November 2005 Putin and President Islam Karimov of Uzbekistan signed a defence pact, which provided for mutual support in the event that one of the countries came under attack. Russia, together with Belarus, Kazakhstan, Kyrgyzstan and Tajikistan, was a founding member of the Eurasian Economic Community (EURASEC, see p. 447), which was formally established in 2001. In October 2007 EURASEC leaders approved the legal basis for the establishment of a new customs union that was initially to comprise Belarus, Kazakhstan and Russia. In early June Putin announced that Russia was withdrawing its long-standing application for membership of the World Trade Organization (WTO,

THE RUSSIAN FEDERATION

see p. 430) in order to pursue joint accession with Belarus and Kazakhstan. In November the Presidents of Russia, Kazakhstan and Belarus signed agreements finalizing plans for the establishment of a customs union, which fully entered into effect in July 2010. (However, the member states of the customs union subsequently agreed to apply separately to the WTO.) In April Prime Minister Putin strenuously denied any Russian involvement in a popular uprising in Kyrgyzstan, which resulted in the de facto overthrow of Kyrgyzstani President Kurmanbek Bakiyev (who went into exile in Belarus) and the establishment of an opposition Interim Government of National Trust. Some 150 Russian troops were dispatched to Kyrgyzstan to protect the Russian air base and military personnel based in the Kyrgyzstani town of Kant. Putin, who had met Kyrgyzstani opposition leaders shortly before the coup, rapidly indicated recognition of the legitimacy of the interim administration, which was expected to seek further Russian support. The Russian Minister of Finance subsequently declared that the Government was prepared to allocate US $20m. in aid to Kyrgyzstan and to provide a loan of $30m. to support agriculture in the country.

Separatist Conflicts in Moldova and Georgia

Considerable controversy arose from the 1990s because of the Russian Government's provision of support for separatist factions in Moldova and Georgia. In 1999 it was announced that all Russian troops in the separatist Transnistria region of Moldova were to be withdrawn by the end of 2002; however, this was subsequently postponed, and in February 2004 the Russian Minister of Defence, Sergei Ivanov, indicated that Russia intended to maintain a military presence in the region. Meanwhile, in December 1998 Russia and Georgia signed an agreement that provided for the incremented transfer of the control of their mutual frontiers, from Russian to Georgian guards. (Control of the frontier was, however, complicated by the existence of separatist and rebel-controlled regions on both sides of the border—Chechnya within Russia, and Abkhazia and South Ossetia within Georgia). In November 1999 it was agreed that two of the four Russian bases on Georgian territory would be closed by mid-2001. Russian troops had left the two bases in Georgia by November 2001. (An agreement signed between Russia and Georgia in March 2006 provided for a Russian withdrawal from the military base that it maintained at Akhalkalaki and headquarters at Tbilisi by the end of 2007, and from the second base at Batumi in 2008; in the event, the withdrawal of Russian forces from the military bases was completed in November 2007, earlier than scheduled.) In September 2002 the Russian authorities accused Georgia of permitting Chechen rebels to operate from bases within its territory, and declared that Russia reserved the right to instigate 'pre-emptive' military action, in self-defence, should the situation persist. However, in early October tensions abated somewhat, when Russia and Georgia agreed to commence joint patrols of their common border. Putin attended talks in Moscow with the newly inaugurated President of Georgia, Mikheil Saakashvili, in February 2004.

In October 2006 Russia temporarily withdrew its ambassador and closed all transport, postal and banking communications with Georgia, following the detention, in late September, of four Russian military officers in Georgia, on charges of espionage. In subsequent weeks large numbers of Georgian citizens residing illegally in Russia were deported. In August 2007 the Georgian authorities protested against an alleged incident, in which two military jets had entered Georgia's airspace from Russia and launched a missile on its territory, near South Ossetia. Shortly after the declaration of independence of Kosovo from Serbia in February 2008 (see below), which prompted international concern regarding other secessionist regions, Russia stated that it upheld the territorial integrity of Georgia and Moldova. In April, however, a Russian presidential decree providing for increased co-operation in trade and culture with Abkhazia and South Ossetia, and protection to Russian citizens living in those regions, was strongly criticized by the international community. Also in April, following the resumption of direct air links with Georgia in March, the Russian authorities announced the restoration of postal services between the two countries and envisaged the removal of other sanctions. Tension between the two countries increased later in April, after a Georgian reconnaissance aeroplane was shot down over Abkhazia, allegedly by a Russian military aircraft; although Russia denied involvement in the incident, the Georgian Government condemned it as an act of aggression. Meanwhile, at a summit meeting of the North Atlantic Treaty Organization (NATO, see p. 368), which was convened in Bucharest, Romania, on 2 April, leaders indicated that Ukraine and Georgia would be offered Membership Action Plans in the future; Russia's permanent representative at NATO had criticized US support for the aspirations towards NATO accession of those countries.

On 8 August 2008, following an offensive by Georgia against the Russian-supported separatist region of South Ossetia (see the chapter on Georgia), Russia launched an intensive counter-attack, dispatching large numbers of troops through the Roki tunnel to South Ossetia, where they engaged in hostilities with Georgian forces at Tskhinvali; the Russian Government stated that it sought to protect its citizens and peace-keeping troops present in the region, and alleged that Georgia intended to commit 'genocide' against the South Ossetian population. (Many South Ossetians had been issued with Russian passports by the separatist authorities since the mid-2000s.) Russian aircraft commenced bombardment of Georgian targets beyond the separatist territory, including the port of Poti and the military base at Senaki. Russian forces rapidly gained control of Tskhinvali, expelling the Georgian troops, and also advanced into the other separatist region of Abkhazia. On 12 August President Medvedev ordered an end to Russia's military operation in Georgia, claiming that its aims had been achieved. Georgia and Russia agreed to a peace plan, mediated by French President Nicolas Sarkozy (on behalf of the EU), providing for an immediate cease-fire, humanitarian assistance, and the withdrawal of Russian troops to pre-conflict positions. On 19 August, after Russia failed to implement fully the withdrawal of troops as stipulated, NATO foreign ministers decided to suspend meetings of the NATO-Russia Council (see Other external relations) until Russia was considered to have observed the terms of the peace plan. Two days later Russia announced its suspension of military co-operation with NATO. On 26 August President Medvedev endorsed a resolution, which had been approved in both chambers of the Russian legislature, officially recognizing South Ossetia and Abkhazia as independent, sovereign states. Georgia, the USA and the EU condemned the decision. (Nicaragua was the only other country to have recognized the two regions as independent states.) On 29 August Georgia formally suspended diplomatic relations with Russia, in protest against the continued Russian occupation of South Ossetia and Abkhazia, and against the establishment of security zones around the two regions.

In early September 2008, following further negotiations with an EU delegation led by President Sarkozy in Moscow, Russia agreed on additional measures for the implementation of the August cease-fire plan, principally the withdrawal of all remaining forces from Georgian territory (apart from South Ossetia and Abkhazia) within 10 days of the deployment of EU monitors (scheduled for 1 October). On 17 September Russia signed friendship and co-operation treaties with the leaders of South Ossetia and Abkhazia, pledging to support the two regions militarily; the treaties also formalized economic co-operation between Russia and the regions. EU monitors were deployed in Georgia, and the withdrawal of the remaining Russian troops from areas adjacent to South Ossetia and Abkhazia was verified by 10 October, as scheduled. However, the Georgian Government claimed that Russia continued to be in violation of the cease-fire agreement until it reduced the number of troops it deployed within South Ossetia and Abkhazia to pre-conflict levels and also withdrew from areas previously held by Georgian forces. (Russia had confirmed its intention to maintain a total of at least 7,600 troops within the two separatist regions, and to establish military bases there.) From October a series of discussions between Russian and Georgian delegations, which were also attended by South Ossetian and Abkhazian officials, were held in Geneva, Switzerland, under the aegis of the UN, the EU and the OSCE, but failed to result in any further agreement. At the end of December the mandate of the OSCE mission in Georgia (deployed in South Ossetia since 1992) expired, owing to Russia's refusal to approve a further extension.

On 5 March 2009 NATO decided to restore relations with Russia, despite the Russian Government's unchanged policy regarding South Ossetia and Abkhazia. NATO resumed formal discussions with Russia at ambassadorial level on 29 April; however, later that day NATO ordered the expulsion of two Russian diplomats (one of whom was the son of Russia's ambassador to the EU) attached to the Russian mission at NATO headquarters on suspicion of espionage. (NATO's action followed the imprisonment in February of the head of the security department at the Estonian Ministry of Defence during 2000–06, Herman Simm, who had been convicted of having passed classified Estonian, and later NATO, military documents to the Russian Foreign Intelligence Service over a period of more than 10 years.) The Russian Government disputed the accusations of espionage against the two diplomats, and protested vehemently against their expulsion; Lavrov subsequently announced that he would not attend a planned ministerial meeting of the NATO-Russia Council. On 30 April Medvedev signed agreements with the leaders of the separatist authorities of South Ossetia and Abkhazia, under which Russia was to assist in securing and patrolling the borders of the two regions with Georgia for an initial period of five years, pending the establishment of their own border services. In early May Russia expelled two Canadian diplomats based at NATO's office in Moscow, on grounds of espionage. NATO strongly criticized the agreements signed by Russia with South Ossetia and Abkhazia as being in contravention of the Russian Government's commitments under the EU-mediated peace agreements. On 6 May NATO commenced military exercises in Georgia, involving more than 1,000 troops, which were denounced by the Russian Government.

In mid-May 2009 the separatist authorities of Abkhazia granted management rights over the territory's airport and railways to Russia for a period of 10 years. Later that month the Government of Abkhazia signed a five-year agreement according Rosneft the right to prospect for petroleum and natural gas off the territory's Black Sea coast. In mid-June Russia vetoed the extension of the mandate of the UN Observer Mission in Georgia, which had been created in 1993 for deployment in Abkhazia. On 27 June, at the first ministerial meeting of the NATO-Russia Council to take place since the conflict, it was agreed to resume military co-operation, despite continued differences over South Ossetia and Abkhazia. At the end of June Russia commenced several days of large-scale military exercises near the Georgian border; the Georgian Government denounced the manoeuvres, involving 8,500 troops, as provocation. In late August it was announced that Russia had reduced the number of its troops in Abkhazia and South Ossetia to 1,700 in each. In mid-September the Russian Government signed further defence agreements with Abkhazia and South Ossetia, allowing it to maintain military bases in the territories for an initial period of 49 years (with the subsequent possibility of five-year renewals). The first high-level military meeting between representatives of NATO and Russia since the conflict was held in Brussels in late January 2010. In August Russia announced that it had deployed anti-aircraft missiles in Abkhazia, and that an air defence system had also been established in South Ossetia. In November Russia refuted allegations by the Georgian Government that a number of people arrested on suspicion of subversive activity, including four Russian nationals, were members of a Russian espionage network. The internationally mediated negotiations, which were attended by Abkhaz and South Ossetian delegations, continued in Geneva but resulted in little progress.

Other external relations

After December 1991 the Russian Federation was recognized as the successor to the USSR. It was granted the USSR's permanent seat on the UN Security Council and, additionally, was to be responsible for the receipt and destruction of all nuclear weapons of the former USSR located in other newly independent republics (Belarus, Kazakhstan and Ukraine), a process that was successfully completed by the mid-1990s. In January 1993 Russia and the USA signed the second Strategic Arms Reduction Treaty (START II), which envisaged a reduction in the strategic nuclear weapons of both powers. The Russian legislature ratified START II in April 2000; however, enactment of the treaty was contingent on the continuation of the Anti-Ballistic Missile (ABM) treaty (signed with the USSR in 1972). In December 2001 US President George W. Bush announced the USA's withdrawal from the ABM Treaty after a six-month notice period.

Russia offered assistance and gave support to the USA in its attempts to form a global coalition against militant Islamist terrorism, after the suicide air attacks against the USA of 11 September 2001 (see the chapter on the USA). Although Russia refused to commit troops to participate in the military campaign against targets of the Taliban regime in Afghanistan, which commenced in October, it provided military intelligence, and allowed access to its airspace. Russia also increased logistical and military support to the anti-Taliban forces of the United Islamic Front for the Salvation of Afghanistan.

In November 2001, at a meeting in Texas, USA, Bush and Putin announced that significant reductions would be made to their countries' nuclear arsenals over the following decade. In May 2002 Russia and the USA announced that agreement had been reached on the reduction of their nuclear arsenals by approximately two-thirds, and a nuclear accord and a declaration on strategic partnership were duly signed by Presidents Putin and Bush on 24 May. The USA withdrew from the ABM treaty on 13 June, and the following day Russia withdrew from START II, which had been superseded by the treaty signed with the USA in the previous month.

The Russian Government consistently condemned intermittent US-led missile attacks on Iraq during the 1990s and early 2000s; additionally, in 1996, in contravention of a UN embargo, Russia concluded an agreement with Iraq on the development of oilfields in that country. In late 1997, following Iraq's refusal to permit weapons inspectors of the UN Special Commission (UNSCOM) access to contentious sites, the Russian Government intervened in an attempt to avert a renewal of hostilities, and the conclusion of an agreement between the UN and Iraq in late February 1998 was regarded by Russia as a significant diplomatic success. Russia resumed scheduled flights to Iraq in late 2000, in contravention of UN sanctions. In mid-2001 Russia, which supported Iraq in its demands that the sanctions regime in force since 1990 should be revoked, effectively obstructed a British-drafted proposal before the Security Council for the introduction of a new, US-advocated, programme of 'smart' sanctions. As the US Administration of George W. Bush, from the second half of 2002, utilized increasingly bellicose rhetoric against Iraq, Russia urged the USA to avoid the use of unilateral force, and encouraged Iraq's compliance with UN demands regarding weapons inspections, so as to facilitate the lifting of sanctions. Although Russia voted to support UN Security Council Resolution 1441, approved in November 2002, which provided for the expedited return of weapons inspectors to Iraq under the auspices of the UN Monitoring, Verification and Inspection Commission (UNMOVIC), it was a leading opponent of attempts, led by the USA and the United Kingdom in February–March 2003, to approve a further Security Council resolution explicitly to endorse military action in Iraq, and President Putin described the conflict, which commenced in mid-March, as a 'political mistake'. Observers speculated that Russia's commitment to renew exports of nuclear fuel to Iran in early 2005 (see below), and seeming pursuit of closer ties with Syria (with reports in 2005 suggesting that Russia was to sell missiles to Syria), could be harmful to relations with the USA, the foreign policy of which was notably hostile towards those countries. In April 2009 Iraqi Prime Minister Nuri Kamal al-Maliki met President Medvedev in Moscow (the first visit by an Iraqi political leader to Russia since 1981); it was reported that the restoration of Russian contracts that had been suspended after the military action against Iraq in 2003 was under discussion.

In early 2007 the Russian Government declared emphatically its opposition to the establishment of a radar installation in the Czech Republic and missile interceptors in Poland by 2011–12 as part of the USA's proposed National Missile Defence programme, despite repeated US assurances that the plan was not intended to threaten Russian interests. Russia warned that it would take retaliatory measures against the US programme, including withdrawal from the Conventional Forces in Europe (CFE) Treaty, prompting the Czech and Polish Governments to demand security and legal guarantees from the USA and further exacerbating strained relations with the West. At a conference on security policy, held in Munich, Germany, in February 2007, President Putin strongly criticized the US Administration for its stance on defence, which he described as being against the fundamental principles of international law. Legislation providing for Russia's suspension of the CFE Treaty was formally adopted by both parliamentary chambers in November, and, after its endorsement by Putin, entered into effect in December. At a NATO summit meeting in April 2008, member states endorsed US plans to position missile defence bases in the Czech Republic and Poland (a previous suggestion by Putin that bases in Azerbaijan be used having been rejected by the USA). A formal treaty signed between Poland and the USA in August, providing for the installation of 10 US anti-missile interceptors, and guaranteeing the permanent stationing of missiles on Polish territory, prompted strenuous protests by the Russian Government. (A provisional accord providing for the installation of a US anti-missile radar system in the Czech Republic had also been signed in July.) However, following the election of US President Barack Obama in November, the new US Administration indicated in early 2009 that it would review security policy, including the planned missile defence system. In January the Russian authorities announced that plans to deploy missiles in Kaliningrad (bordering Poland), in response to the US deployment in Poland and the Czech Republic, had been suspended. Lavrov and US Secretary of State Hillary Clinton, meeting in Geneva, Switzerland, in early March, affirmed commitment to the revision of US-Russian relations. Lavrov declared the adoption of a successor agreement to the START I nuclear treaty (which had entered into force in 1994 and was due to expire at the end of 2009) to be a priority, and urged the US Administration to consider Russian concerns in the review of its planned missile defence system. Medvedev and Obama met for the first time at a summit of the heads of state and of government of the Group of 20 (G20) leading economies, which took place in London, United Kingdom, on 2 April, and issued a joint statement agreeing to replace START I with a new treaty.

On 19 May 2009 arms control negotiations between Russian and US delegations officially began in Moscow, subsequently continuing in Geneva. On 6 July Medvedev and Obama, meeting in Moscow, signed a joint understanding to negotiate a new nuclear arms control treaty before the expiry of START I at the end of 2009. The two Presidents also agreed to create a bilateral presidential commission, comprising several working groups charged with advancing co-operation in areas including nuclear energy, counter-terrorism activities, drugs-trafficking and civil society. In addition, Russian and US officials signed a new strategic framework for military co-operation, which had been suspended since August 2008, and an agreement to allow the USA to transport military personnel and equipment across Russia to support its operations in Afghanistan. In September 2009 Medvedev welcomed a decision by Obama to revise US defence system plans, thereby abandoning the initiative of the Bush Administration to establish missile defence facilities in the Czech Republic and Poland. A series of formal negotiations between Russian and US officials failed to result in agreement by the expiry of START I on 5 December. Following further negotiations in Geneva in early 2010 and a meeting between Lavrov and Clinton in Moscow in March, the Russian and US Governments announced on 26 March that agreement had been reached on a new treaty limiting strategic offensive weapons. On 8 April Medvedev and Obama, meeting in the Czech capital, Prague, signed the new START treaty, whereby both states, within seven years of its ratification by their respective legislatures, were each to reduce their operationally deployed nuclear warheads to 1,550, while the number of deployed ballistic missiles and heavy bombers on each side was to be restricted to 700, and the number of deployed and non-deployed launchers and heavy bombers equipped for nuclear armaments to 800 each. (At that time Russia was believed to have 2,600 and the USA 2,252 nuclear warheads.) A bilateral body was to be established to oversee the implementation of the treaty. Following its approval by the US and Russian legislatures, and ratification by Medvedev on 28 January 2011, the new START treaty entered into force on 5 February.

In June 2010 Medvedev visited the USA, meeting Obama in Washington, DC, and attending discussions in the high-technology business centre of 'Silicon Valley' in California. Later that month, however, the US Administration announced the detention, as a result of the findings of the Federal Bureau of Investigation, of 10 suspected Russian agents, who had been resident in the USA since the 1990s. The 10 suspects were officially charged with failing to register as agents of a foreign government, and with money-laundering. In early July the 10 defendants pleaded guilty in a New York court to the charges of conspiring to act as unregistered agents; they were immediately deported to Russia, in exchange for the pardoning and release of four Russian nationals, three of whom had been convicted and imprisoned on espionage charges. In March 2011 US Vice-President Joe Biden made an official visit to Moscow, where he confirmed US support for Russia's accession to the WTO.

Continuing strains in Russia's relations with the United Kingdom, principally following the death of Aleksandr Litvinenko in London in November 2006 (see Domestic Political Affairs) and attempts by the Russian authorities to close British Council offices in Russia in early 2008, intensified when a British Member of Parliament confirmed in December 2010 that his Russian aide had been detained and served with a deportation order. Tensions between Russia and the United Kingdom increased with the expulsion of a Russian diplomat from London for alleged espionage, which was followed by the reciprocal expulsion of a British diplomat from Moscow the following day. In February 2011 Russian Minister of Foreign Affairs Lavrov visited the United Kingdom for discussions with Prime Minister David Cameron and senior ministers, in en effort to improve bilateral relations.

In February 2010 premier Putin invited his Polish counterpart, Donald Tusk, to attend a ceremony in Russia marking the 70th anniversary of a massacre of some 20,000 Polish officers by Soviet secret police at Katyń during the Second World War. (While the Soviet administration under Gorbachev had, belatedly, admitted Soviet responsibility for the massacre in 1990, the issue continued to strain relations between Russia and Poland.) For the first time, a joint ceremony to commemorate the massacre, attended by the Russian and Polish premiers, took place at Katyń, near Smolensk, on 7 April, and was regarded as significant in furthering good bilateral relations. On 10 April Polish President Lech Kaczyński and 95 other senior Polish government, military and cultural personnel, who had been travelling to Katyń to attend a further anniversary ceremony of the massacre, were killed when their aeroplane crashed in adverse weather conditions near Smolensk airport. Putin, who visited the crash site with Tusk, was appointed by Medvedev to supervise a special commission to investigate the crash. (Following the crash, a Russian state-controlled federal TV channel broadcast a Polish film about the Katyń massacre, giving unprecedented prominence in Russia to the announcement of Soviet responsibility for the killings.) Later in April the Polish interim President, Bronisław Komorowski, accepted an invitation from Medvedev to attend ceremonies in Moscow in early May for the 65th anniversary of the victory of the Allied forces in the Second World War. In November the State Duma formally acknowledged that Stalin had directly ordered the Katyń massacre. In December Medvedev made an official visit to Warsaw, where he signed agreements intended to strengthen bilateral co-operation. However, further tensions developed in January 2011, after the Russian Interstate Aviation Committee released a final report attributing responsibility for the air crash to the Polish pilots, concluding that they had violated safety procedures owing to perceived pressure to land at Smolensk. The Polish Government, with the support of Polish public opinion, protested that the report should also cite the contributory responsibility of the Russian air traffic controllers. The replacement of a memorial plaque at the crash site with one that failed to mention the Katyń massacre also attracted fierce criticism from Poland; in April 2011, following discussions in Smolensk between Medvedev and his Polish counterpart, Bronisław Komorowski, on the anniversary of the air crash, it was announced that the design of a new plaque would be agreed by both sides.

Following Kosovo's unilateral declaration of independence from Serbia on 17 February 2008, Russia, in continued strong support of Serbia, opposed Kosovo's sovereignty, and subsequently obstructed the deployment of an EU mission (see the chapter on Kosovo). Meanwhile, in January 2008 relations between Russia and Serbia were consolidated with the signature of an agreement whereby Serbia was to join Russia's 'South Stream' pipeline project (see Economic Affairs), and Gazprom acquired a 51% share in the Serbian state-owned petroleum enterprise, Naftna Industrija Srbije. (The sale of the majority share in Naftna Industrija Srbije was completed in February 2009; contractual agreements on the 'South Stream' project were signed with Italy, Bulgaria, Serbia and Greece in Sochi on 15 May.) In October President Medvedev visited Serbia, where he met Serbian President Boris Tadić for discussions and signed a number of bilateral agreements.

In April 2010 the Governments of Russia and Norway reached agreement on a protracted territorial dispute over a region of the Barents Sea, in the Arctic. On 15 September Russian Minister of Foreign Affairs Lavrov and his Norwegian counterpart signed a treaty in Murmansk, in northern Russia, that delineated the disputed maritime border, thereby ending a moratorium on the development of oil- and gas-fields in the region. (The border agreement with Norway was ratified by both chambers of the Russian legislature in March 2011.)

In June 1994 Russia joined NATO's 'Partnership for Peace' (see p. 371) programme of military co-operation with former Eastern bloc states. A 'Founding Act on Mutual Relations, Co-operation and Security between NATO and the Russian Federation' was signed in May 1997. The Act provided for enhanced Russian participation in all NATO decision-making activities, equal status in peace-keeping operations and representation at the Alliance headquarters at ambassadorial level. A NATO-Russian Permanent Joint Council was established. Russia's relations with NATO became increasingly strained in 1999, in particular after the situation in the province of Kosovo, in the

THE RUSSIAN FEDERATION

Republic of Serbia, then Yugoslavia, precipitated the aerial bombardment of Yugoslav targets by NATO forces in late March (see the chapter on Serbia). Russia condemned the air offensive, and suspended its relations with the Alliance. Following the capitulation of Yugoslav forces in mid-June, and their withdrawal from Kosovo, Russian troops were the first to enter the province, before NATO forces. Contacts were resumed between Russia and NATO in February 2000. In July 2001 Putin appealed for a pan-European security pact to be established in place of NATO, to incorporate Russia. On 28 May 2002 Putin and the heads of state and of government of the 19 NATO member states, meeting in Italy, signed the Rome Declaration, inaugurating a new NATO-Russia Council to replace the Permanent Joint Council. The new Council would enable Russia to enter into negotiations with its members on a range of issues, including terrorism, non-proliferation, defence and peace-keeping. Although Russia had expressed concern at the expansion of NATO to include seven eastern European countries, including the three Baltic states, from early 2004, Putin emphasized that the expansion would not have negative consequences for the Alliance's relations with Russia. At the NATO summit meeting in April 2008, Russia demonstrated strenuous opposition to the aspirations of Georgia and Ukraine for NATO membership. NATO suspended relations with Russia in August, in response to Russian military action in Georgia; relations were formally restored in March 2009, but remained strained. In April 2011 Russian Minister of Foreign Affairs Lavrov criticized NATO for exceeding the UN Security Council mandate for military intervention in Libya, and urged a political settlement to the conflict (see the chapter on Libya).

In January 1996 Russia was admitted as a member of the Council of Europe. As a condition of membership, Russia was to abolish the death penalty by the end of February 1999. However, the Duma has yet to approve its abolition, although capital punishment has been subject to a moratorium since Russia's admission to the organization. Russia's voting rights were suspended between April 2000 and January 2001, as a result of allegations of human rights abuses committed during its renewed military campaign in Chechnya. In February 2005 the European Court of Human Rights (ECHR, a subsidiary institution of the Council of Europe), in a ruling on cases brought by six Chechen citizens, concluded that serious human rights abuses had been committed by the Russian military in Chechnya and ordered the Russian Government to pay compensation to the victims' relatives. In June 2010 the ECHR, finding Russia to be in violation of the European Convention on Human Rights, ordered the authorities to pay a total of €473,800 to the families of eight Chechen men who had disappeared in 2001 and 2002. In the same month a resolution by the Parliamentary Assembly of the Council of Europe urging Russia to co-operate in implementing ECHR rulings relevant to the North Caucasus was for the first time approved by the Russian delegation to the Council of Europe.

Russia's relations with Iran in the late 1990s and early 2000s were a cause of concern for the USA. In mid-1997 Iran and Russia held discussions on nuclear co-operation, primarily focusing on the development of a nuclear power plant in Bushehr, Iran. In December 2000 Igor Sergeyev, the Russian Minister of Defence, paid the first official visit to Iran by a Russian official since the Islamic Revolution in that country of 1979, with a view to increasing military and technical co-operation. In March 2001, during a visit to Moscow by the Iranian President, Muhammad Khatami, Russia agreed to resume the sale of conventional weapons to Iran and to assist with the construction of the Bushehr power plant; an agreement for arms sales worth some US $300m., the first such agreement between the two countries since 1995, was signed in October. Although in December 2002 it was announced that Russia was to increase its nuclear co-operation with Iran, the Russian Minister of Foreign Affairs, Igor Ivanov, reiterated that this co-operation was of a civilian nature and that Russia remained opposed to Iran's potential development of nuclear weapons. In mid-2003 Russia announced that it was to suspend exports of nuclear fuel to Iran; however, in February 2005 a new agreement was reached between the two countries on the provision of nuclear fuel (which would, however, be returned to Russia, once it was spent). In February 2006 Russia was one of 27 countries represented on the 35-member Board of Governors of the International Atomic Energy Agency (IAEA) to vote in favour of Iran's referral to the UN Security Council, after it was discovered not to have complied with the conditions of an agreement reached with the IAEA; none the less, Russia remained opposed to the use of military force against Iran to bring it into compliance. In October 2007 Putin visited the Iranian capital, Tehran, to attend a summit meeting of the five Caspian state leaders. The declaration adopted by the parties at the end of the summit postponed settlement of territorial issues, but asserted that each country would not allow its territory to be used by other states for the purposes of a military attack against another state.

Relations with Japan were complicated by a continuing dispute over the status of the Kurile Islands (in Sakhalin Oblast, and known in Japan as the Northern Territories), which became part of the USSR at the end of the Second World War; Japan maintained its long-standing demand that four of the islands be returned to Japanese sovereignty. Discussions on the territorial dispute between the leaderships of Russia and Japan were ongoing from the late 1990s, but resulted in little progress. Despite Russian President Vladimir Putin's repudiation of Japan's claim to any of the islands during his first official visit to Tokyo in September 2000, Russia subsequently offered to abide by a 1956 declaration that it would relinquish two of the islands after the signature of a peace treaty, but Japan rejected this partial solution. In August 2006 Russian security troops killed one Japanese fisherman and detained three others who had allegedly been fishing illegally in Russian waters; the captain of the Japanese vessel subsequently received a fine for intrusion into Russian waters and poaching. The revocation, in the following month, of an environmental permit associated with the Sakhalin-2 natural gas project, and the subsequent enforced reduction of the share held in the project by Japanese companies, was a further cause of heightened tensions between Russia and Japan. In April 2008, during an official visit by Japanese Prime Minister Yasuo Fukuda to Russia, he and President Putin agreed that further discussions would be conducted, in an effort to resolve the territorial dispute; pledges for increased bilateral co-operation were also made. However, in July the Russian Government criticized Japanese plans to introduce school textbooks depicting the Kurile Islands as part of Japanese territory. In January 2010 Japan formally protested to Russia, after two Japanese fishing vessels were shot at by Russian coastal guards near the disputed islands; Russian media reports stated that the vessels had been suspected of operating illegally in Russia's economic zone.

Relations with the People's Republic of China improved significantly during the 1990s. In 1999 several agreements on bilateral economic and trade co-operation, and a final accord on the demarcation of a common border between the two countries, were signed. Meanwhile, negotiations in the mid-1990s that initially focused on defining the mutual borders of China, Kazakhstan, Kyrgyzstan, Russia and Tajikistan appeared to be instrumental in bringing about closer co-operation between these countries, which in 1996 formed the so-called Shanghai Five group. The group subsequently broadened its areas of activity to include trade, cultural, military and security co-operation; in June 2001 Uzbekistan joined the grouping, which was renamed the Shanghai Co-operation Organization (see p. 462). In September 2003 the Organization announced its intention to establish a joint anti-terrorism centre, to be located in Tashkent, Uzbekistan, and a secretariat, in the Chinese capital, Beijing. Kasyanov visited Beijing in August 2002, to discuss strategic issues, and Putin visited China in December, when he met President Jiang Zemin and his appointed successor, Hu Jintao. The two countries issued a joint declaration on a number of global strategic issues, particularly urging a peaceful resolution to the USA's diplomatic crisis with Iraq. Russia also participated in multilateral negotiations in China in mid-2003, attended by representatives of the Governments of China, the Democratic People's Republic of Korea (DPRK—North Korea), Japan, the Republic of Korea (South Korea) and the USA, which were intended to encourage the DPRK to abandon its nuclear weapons programme. In October 2004 a treaty was signed by Presidents Putin and Hu settling a long-standing dispute over the border between the two states. In 2005 Russia and China conducted joint military manoeuvres for the first time. In August 2010 a section of a new oil pipeline linking Siberia to China's north-eastern border was inaugurated.

CONSTITUTION AND GOVERNMENT

Under the Constitution of December 1993, the Russian Federation is a democratic, federative, multi-ethnic republic, in which state power is divided between the legislature, executive and judiciary, which are independent of one another. The President

THE RUSSIAN FEDERATION

Introductory Survey

of the Russian Federation is Head of State and Commander-in-Chief of the Armed Forces, and also holds broad executive powers. The President, who is elected for a term of six years, renewable once, by universal direct suffrage, appoints the Chairman of the Government (Prime Minister). Supreme legislative power is vested in the bicameral Federalnoye Sobraniye (Federal Assembly). The upper chamber is the Sovet Federatsii (Federation Council), which comprises two representatives from each of the country's federal territorial units (appointed by the legislature and the executive in each region); its lower chamber is the 450-member Gosudarstvennaya Duma (State Duma), which is elected by direct universal suffrage for a period of five years. The Supreme Court is the highest judicial authority on civil, criminal, administrative and other cases within the jurisdiction of the common plea courts. The Supreme Arbitration Court is the highest authority in settling economic and other disputes within the jurisdiction of the courts of arbitration. The judges of the three higher courts (including the Constitutional Court) are appointed by the Federation Council on the recommendation of the President. Judges of other federal courts are appointed by the President. The majority of Russia's regions introduced jury trials, in many cases only for the most serious crimes, during 2003. The Russian Federation comprises 83 territorial 'subjects', comprising 21 republics, nine krais (provinces), 46 oblasts (regions), two cities of federal status, one autonomous oblast and four autonomous okrugs (districts). The republics and the autonomous oblast and okrugs are nominally representative of ethnic groups, and the administrative oblasts and krais of geographic regions. These territories are grouped into eight federal okrugs, each of which is headed by a Presidential Representative.

REGIONAL AND INTERNATIONAL CO-OPERATION

Russia is a founder member of the Commonwealth of Independent States (CIS, see p. 238), and a member of the Collective Security Treaty Organization (CSTO, see p. 459), the Eurasian Economic Community (EURASEC, see p. 447), the Asia-Pacific Economic Co-operation forum (APEC, see p. 197), the Shanghai Co-operation Organization (see p. 462), the Organization of the Black Sea Economic Co-operation (BSEC, see p. 398), the Council of the Baltic Sea States (see p. 248), the Organization for Security and Co-operation in Europe (OSCE, see p. 385), the Council of Europe (see p. 250) and the Organization of the Petroleum Exporting Countries (OPEC, see p. 405). The customs union of Belarus, Russia and Kazakhstan entered into effect in July 2010.

Russia is a member of the UN and permanent member of the UN Security Council (having been recognized as the successor to the USSR, a founder member of the UN). Russia participates in the Group of Eight major industrialized nations (G8, see p. 460) and the Group of 20 major industrialized and systemically important emerging market nations (G20).

ECONOMIC AFFAIRS

In 2009, according to estimates by the World Bank, Russia's gross national income (GNI), measured at average 2007–09 prices, was US $1,329,670m., equivalent to $9,370 per head (or $18,390 per head on an international purchasing-power parity basis). In 2000–09, it was estimated, the population declined at an average annual rate of 0.3%, while gross domestic product (GDP) per head increased, in real terms, at an average annual rate of 5.2%. According to the World Bank, overall GDP increased, in real terms, at an average annual rate of 4.8% in 2000–09. Real GDP increased by 5.6% in 2008, but decreased by 7.9% in 2009.

Agriculture (including forestry and fishing) contributed 4.7% of GDP in 2009. In 2008, according to ILO, 8.6% of the employed labour force were engaged in the agricultural sector. The principal agricultural products are grain, potatoes and livestock. In 1990 the Russian Government began a programme to encourage the development of private farming, to replace the state and collective farms. Legislation to permit the sale and purchase of agricultural land from 2003 was approved by the Gosudarstvennaya Duma in June 2002. According to World Bank estimates, real agricultural GDP increased at an average annual rate of 8.5% in 2000–08; the GDP of the sector increased by 2.6% in 2007 and by 8.5% in 2008.

Industry contributed 33.8% of GDP in 2009. In 2008 the industrial sector (including mining, manufacturing, construction and utilities) provided 28.9% of employment. According to estimates by the World Bank, industrial GDP increased, in real terms, at an average annual rate of 5.4% in 2000–08. Industrial GDP increased by 5.4% in 2007 and by 3.1% in 2008.

Mining and quarrying contributed 8.9% of GDP in 2009, and employed 1.9% of the employed labour force in 2008. Russia has considerable reserves of energy-bearing minerals, including one-third of the world's natural gas reserves and substantial deposits of petroleum, coal and peat. It also has large supplies of palladium, platinum and rhodium. Other minerals exploited include bauxite, cobalt, copper, diamonds, gold, iron ore, mica, nickel and tin.

The manufacturing sector contributed 14.6% of GDP in 2009, and provided 16.4% of employment in 2008.

The construction sector contributed 6.2% of GDP in 2009, and provided 7.6% of employment in 2008.

Electric energy is derived from petroleum-, gas- and coal-fired power stations, nuclear power stations, and hydroelectric installations. In 2007 nuclear reactors supplied some 15.8% of total electricity generation, while coal accounted for some 16.7% of Russia's generating capacity; hydroelectric power accounted for 17.5% of electricity production, and 48.0% of the country's generating capacity originated from natural gas. Russia is a major exporter of natural gas and crude petroleum, and Russia's largest company, Gazprom, is also the world's largest producer of natural gas. Since the early 2000s Russia has also consistently been, with Saudi Arabia, one of the two largest producers of oil. From the late 1990s Russia sought to increase its exports of mineral fuels, particularly to central and western Europe. The construction of the 'Blue Stream' pipeline, which was to carry natural gas from Novorossiisk, Krasnodar Krai, in southern Russia, to Ankara, Turkey, was completed in 2002. In early 2005 it was announced that a pipeline would be constructed from eastern Siberia to Nakhodka on the Pacific Coast, enabling exports to Japan and the wider Pacific region. In November 2007 Gazprom and Italian energy company Eni signed an agreement creating the 'South Stream' joint venture for the construction of a pipeline to transport Russian natural gas to Italy; Bulgaria, Hungary, Serbia and Greece subsequently agreed to participate in the project. Work on the pipeline was scheduled to be completed by 2015. Imports of fuel comprised just 1.3% of the value of Russia's total merchandise imports in 2007.

The services sector contributed 61.5% of GDP in 2009, and provided 62.4% of employment in 2008. According to estimates by the World Bank, the GDP of the services sector increased, in real terms, at an average annual rate of 7.1% in 2000–08. The GDP of the sector increased by 9.9% in 2007 and by 6.9% in 2008.

In 2009 Russia recorded a visible trade surplus of US $111,585m., and there was a surplus of $49,365m. on the current account of the balance of payments. In 2009 the most significant source of imports was the People's Republic of China (accounting for 13.6% of the total), followed by Germany, the USA, Ukraine and France. The largest market for Russian exports in that year was the Netherlands (accounting for 12.0% of total exports), followed by Italy, Germany, Belarus, China and Turkey. The principal exports in 2009 were mineral fuels (accounting for 67.3% of total exports), followed by metals and precious stones, and machinery, vehicles and transport equipment. The principal imports in that year were machinery, vehicles and transport equipment (accounting for 43.3% of total imports), followed by foodstuffs and agricultural raw materials, excluding textiles, chemical products and rubber, and metals and precious stones.

In 2009 Russia recorded a deficit on the federal budget of 2,322,300m. roubles, equivalent to 6.0% of GDP. Russia's general government gross debt was 4,253,700m. roubles in 2009, equivalent to 10.9% of GDP. At the end of 2008 the country's total external debt was US $402,453.4m., of which $103,246.2m. was public and publicly guaranteed debt. In that year the cost of debt-servicing was equivalent to 11.5% of the value of exports of goods, services and income. Following the collapse of the rouble in 1998, the rate of inflation was 85.7% in 1999, but it declined thereafter. In 2000–08 the average annual rate of inflation was 13.3%, according to estimates by ILO. The rate of inflation was 13.3% in 2008 and 8.8% in 2009. According to the IMF, in 2010 the rate of consumer price inflation was 6.9%. In November 2009 some 6.2m. people (8.2% of the labour force) were unemployed.

After the dissolution of the USSR, a programme of economic reforms was initiated to effect the transition to a market-orientated system. Following a financial crisis in mid-1998, Russia recorded sustained growth, largely attributable to high international prices for petroleum, natural gas and metals, Russia's principal exports. The dismantling, in late 2004, of the privately

THE RUSSIAN FEDERATION

owned petroleum company Yukos, and the effective renationalization of its most productive subsidiary, Yuganskneftegaz, through its effective acquisition by the state-owned petroleum company Rosneft (see Domestic Political Affairs), and the approval in 2005 of legislation that limited the degree of involvement permitted to foreign companies in the exploitation of natural resources, demonstrated a reverse from the free market principles. Meanwhile, Russia began to expand its network of international pipelines to east Asia and eastern, northern and southern Europe. Concerns persisted that the successes of the fossil fuel sector were obscuring the relative lack of innovation in the wider economy. This view was compounded when prices for crude oil began to decrease sharply amid the US banking crisis in September 2008. In April 2009 the budget was revised to include a large fiscal stimulus, the resultant widening budget deficit being supported by the Oil Reserve Fund. The international economic crisis of 2008–09 caused factories to institute widespread reductions in working hours and delay the payment of wages, thereby increasing social unrest, particularly in *monogorods* (cities with a single industry), where the closure of the main factory would result in mass localized unemployment. In September the Government announced plans for an extensive programme of privatization of state-owned enterprises, including in the banking sector, which would raise funds to cover projected high budget deficits, while also enabling investment in infrastructure. In April 2010 the Government's first sovereign Eurobond issue for 12 years generated US $5,500m. In June President Dmitrii Medvedev officially announced that zero-rate taxation on capital gains would be introduced from January 2011 for companies working on long-term investments in the country. In August widespread forest fires (following severe drought conditions) resulted in the destruction of large areas of arable land and loss of about one-third of the crop; the Government announced a ban on grain exports (which was subsequently extended until the end of 2011), and pledged some $1,150m. in emergency assistance for farmers. Meanwhile, Russia's customs union with Belarus and Kazakhstan entered into force in July 2010. In December the IMF urged Russia to reduce the non-oil budget deficit (then equivalent to about 13% of GDP); further measures to strengthen the supervisory framework of the banking system were deemed essential. Following a GDP contraction of 7.9% in 2009 (the largest recorded in any major emerging market), the IMF projected growth of 3.7% for 2010, on the basis of a recovery in the latter part of that year. However, political uncertainties related to the 2012 presidential election were believed to have contributed to high capital outflows during 2010. A proposed Arctic joint venture and $16,000m. share exchange between Rosneft and British group BP, agreed in January 2011, was delayed by legal action by BP's Russian partners. The Government's extensive privatization programme began in February, with the sale of a share in VTB Bank. In March Medvedev ordered that government officials be removed from the board of directors of state companies; this was expected to have the consequence of markedly reducing the influence of certain state officials on the business sector.

PUBLIC HOLIDAYS

2012: 1–8 January (New Year and Orthodox Christmas), 23 February (Defenders of the Fatherland Day), 8 March (International Women's Day), 1–2 May (Spring Holiday and Labour Day), 9 May (Victory Day), 11 June (Russia Day), 28 June (Baptism of Rus'), 4 November (National Unity Day).

Statistical Survey

Source (unless otherwise indicated): Federal Service of State Statistics, 103450 Moscow, ul. Myasnitskaya 39; tel. (495) 207-49-02; fax (495) 207-40-87; e-mail stat@gks.ru; internet www.gks.ru.

Area and Population

AREA, POPULATION AND DENSITY

Area (sq km)	17,098,200*
Population (census results)	
9–16 October 2002	145,166,731
14–25 October 2010 (preliminary)	
Males	66,205,000
Females	76,700,200
Total	142,905,200
Density (per sq km) at 2010 census	8.4

* 6,601,652 sq miles.

POPULATION BY AGE AND SEX
(official estimates at 1 January 2010)

	Males	Females	Total
0–14	10,968,117	10,432,495	21,400,612
15–64	48,944,851	53,278,380	102,223,231
65 and over	5,726,412	12,564,254	18,290,666
Total	65,639,380	76,275,129	141,914,509

Note: Estimates do not take account of preliminary results of 2010 census.

POPULATION BY ETHNIC GROUP
(census of 9–16 October 2002)

	'000	%
Russian*	115,889.1	79.83
Tatar†	5,554.6	3.83
Ukrainian	2,943.0	2.03
Bashkir	1,673.4	1.15
Chuvash	1,637.1	1.13
Chechen‡	1,360.2	0.94
Armenian	1,130.5	0.78
Mordovian§	843.4	0.58
Avar‖	814.5	0.56
Belarusian	808.0	0.56
Others¶	12,512.9	8.62
Total	145,166.7	100.00

* Including Cossacks and Pomors.
† Including Astrakhan Tatars, Kryashens (Christian Tatars) and Siberian Tatars, but excluding Crimean Tatars.
‡ Including Chechen-akkintsy.
§ Including Erzya-Mordovians and Moksha-Mordovians.
‖ Including Akhvakhtsy, Andiitsy, Bezhtintsy, Didoitsy, Karatintsy, and nine other ethnic groups with a declared population of under 1,000 each.
¶ Including 1,460,751 respondents (1.01% of the total) who did not state their nationality or ethnic group.

THE RUSSIAN FEDERATION

Statistical Survey

ADMINISTRATIVE DIVISIONS
(2010 census, preliminary)

Federal territory	Area ('000 sq km)	Population ('000)	Density (per sq km)	Capital (with population, '000)
Central Federal Okrug	650.2	38,438.6	59.1	Moscow
Moscow City	1.1	11,514.3	10,467.5	Moscow (11,514.3)
Belgorod Oblast	27.1	1,532.7	56.6	Belgorod (356.4)
Bryansk Oblast	34.9	1,278.1	36.6	Bryansk (415.6)
Ivanovo Oblast	21.4	1,062.6	49.7	Ivanovo (409.3)
Kaluga Oblast	29.8	1,011.6	33.9	Kaluga (325.2)
Kostroma Oblast	60.2	667.5	11.1	Kostroma (268.6)
Kursk Oblast	30.0	1,126.5	37.6	Kursk (414.6)
Lipetsk Oblast	24.0	1,172.8	48.9	Lipetsk (508.1)
Moscow Oblast	45.8	7,092.9	154.9	Moscow*
Orel Oblast	24.7	787.2	31.9	Orel (317.9)
Ryazan Oblast	39.6	1,154.2	29.1	Ryazan (525.1)
Smolensk Oblast	49.8	985.5	19.8	Smolensk (326.9)
Tambov Oblast	34.5	1,092.4	31.7	Tambov (280.5)
Tula Oblast	25.7	1,553.9	60.5	Tula (501.1)
Tver Oblast	84.2	1,353.5	16.1	Tver (403.7)
Vladimir Oblast	29.1	1,444.6	49.6	Vladimir (345.6)
Voronezh Oblast	52.2	2,335.8	44.7	Voronezh (890.0)
Yaroslavl Oblast	36.2	1,272.5	35.2	Yaroslavl (591.5)
North-Western Federal Okrug	1,687.0	13,583.8	8.1	St Petersburg
St Petersburg City	1.4	4,848.7	3,463.4	St Petersburg (4,848.7)
Republic of Kareliya	180.5	645.2	3.6	Petrozavodsk (263.5)
Republic of Komi	416.8	901.6	2.2	Syktyvkar (235.0)
Archangel Oblast	589.9	1,228.1	2.1	Archangel (348.7)
Nenets Autonomous Okrug	176.8	42.7	0.2	Naryn-Mar (19.8)†
Kaliningrad Oblast	15.1	941.5	62.4	Kaliningrad (431.5)
Leningrad Oblast	83.9	1,712.7	20.4	St Petersburg*
Murmansk Oblast	144.9	796.1	5.5	Murmansk (307.7)
Novgorod Oblast	54.5	634.1	11.6	Velikii Novgorod (218.7)
Pskov Oblast	55.4	673.5	12.2	Pskov (203.3)
Vologda Oblast	144.5	1,202.3	8.3	Vologda (301.6)
Southern Federal Okrug	420.9	13,856.7	32.9	Rostov-on-Don
Republic of Adygeya	7.8	440.4	56.5	Maikop (144.2)
Republic of Kalmykiya	74.7	289.4	3.9	Elista (103.7)
Krasnodar Krai	75.5	5,225.8	69.2	Krasnodar (744.9)
Astrakhan Oblast	49.0	1,010.7	20.6	Astrakhan (520.7)
Rostov Oblast	101.0	4,279.2	42.4	Rostov-on-Don (1,089.9)
Volgograd Oblast	112.9	2,611.2	23.1	Volgograd (1,021.2)
North Caucasus Federal Okrug	170.4	9,496.8	55.7	Pyatigorsk (142.4)
Chechen (Nokchi) Republic	15.6	1,269.1	81.4	Groznyi (271.6)
Republic of Dagestan	50.3	2,977.4	59.2	Makhachkala (578.0)
Republic of Ingushetiya	3.6	413.0	114.7	Magas (0.5)†
Kabardino-Balkar Republic	12.5	859.8	68.8	Nalchik (240.1)
Karachai-Cherkess Republic	14.3	478.5	33.5	Cherkessk (121.4)
Republic of North Osetiya—Alaniya	8.0	712.9	89.1	Vladikavkaz (311.6)
Stavropol Krai	66.2	2,786.1	42.1	Stavropol (398.3)
Volga Federal Okrug	1,037.0	29,900.4	28.8	Nizhnii Novgorod
Republic of Bashkortostan	142.9	4,072.1	28.5	Ufa (1,062.3)
Chuvash Republic	18.3	1,251.6	68.4	Cheboksary (453.6)
Republic of Marii-El	23.4	696.3	29.8	Yoshkar-Ola (248.7)
Republic of Mordoviya	26.1	834.8	32.0	Saransk (297.4)
Republic of Tatarstan	67.8	3,786.4	55.8	Kazan (1,143.6)
Udmurt Republic	42.1	1,522.7	36.2	Izhevsk (628.1)
Perm Krai	160.2	2,635.8	16.5	Perm (991.5)
Kirov Oblast	120.4	1,341.3	11.1	Kirov (473.7)
Nizhnii Novgorod Oblast	76.6	3,310.6	43.2	Nizhnii Novgorod (1,250.6)
Orenburg Oblast	123.7	2,032.9	16.4	Orenburg (547.0)
Penza Oblast	43.4	1,386.2	31.9	Penza (517.1)
Samara Oblast	53.6	3,215.7	60.0	Samara (1,164.9)
Saratov Oblast	101.2	2,521.8	24.9	Saratov (837.8)
Ulyanovsk Oblast	37.2	1,292.2	34.7	Ulyanovsk (613.8)
Urals Federal Okrug	1,818.5	12,082.7	6.6	Yekaterinburg
Chelyabinsk Oblast	88.5	3,478.6	39.3	Chelyabinsk (1,130.3)
Kurgan Oblast	71.5	910.9	12.7	Kurgan (333.6)
Sverdlovsk Oblast	194.3	4,298.0	22.1	Yekaterinburg (1,350.1)
Tyumen Oblast	1,464.2	3,395.2	2.3	Tyumen (581.8)
Khanty-Mansii Autonomous Okrug—Yugra	534.8	1,532.0	2.9	Khanty-Mansiisk (75.9)†
Yamalo-Nenets Autonomous Okrug	769.3	522.8	0.7	Salekhard (43.5)†

THE RUSSIAN FEDERATION

Statistical Survey

Federal territory—continued	Area ('000 sq km)	Population ('000)	Density (per sq km)	Capital (with population, '000)
Siberian Federal Okrug	5,145.0	19,254.3	3.7	Novosibirsk
Altai Republic	92.6	206.2	2.2	Gorno-Altaisk (56.0)†
Republic of Buryatiya	351.3	972.7	2.8	Ulan-Ude (404.4)
Republic of Khakasiya	61.6	532.3	8.6	Abakan (165.2)
Republic of Tyva	168.6	307.9	1.8	Kyzyl (109.9)
Altai Krai	168.0	2,419.4	14.4	Barnaul (612.1)
Krasnoyarsk Krai	2,366.8	2,828.2	1.2	Krasnoyarsk (973.9)
Transbaikal Krai	431.9	1,106.6	2.6	Chita (323.9)
Irkutsk Oblast	774.8	2,428.7	3.1	Irkutsk (587.2)
Kemerovo Oblast	95.7	2,763.4	28.9	Kemerovo (532.9)
Novosibirsk Oblast	177.8	2,665.9	15.0	Novosibirsk (1,473.7)
Omsk Oblast	141.1	1,977.5	14.0	Omsk (1,154.0)
Tomsk Oblast	314.4	1,045.5	3.3	Tomsk (522.9)
Far Eastern Federal Okrug	6,169.3	6,291.9	1.0	Khabarovsk
Republic of Sakha (Yakutiya)	3,083.5	958.3	0.3	Yakutsk (269.5)
Kamchatka Krai	464.3	321.8	0.7	Petropavlovsk-Kamchatskii (179.5)
Khabarovsk Krai	787.6	1,344.2	1.7	Khabarovsk (577.7)
Maritime (Primorskii) Krai	164.7	1,956.4	11.9	Vladivostok (592.1)
Amur Oblast	361.9	829.2	2.3	Blagoveshchensk (214.4)
Magadan Oblast	462.5	157.0	0.3	Magadan (106.3)†
Sakhalin Oblast	87.1	497.9	5.7	Yuzhno-Sakhalinsk (181.7)
Jewish Autonomous Oblast	36.3	176.6	4.9	Birobidzhan (75.4)†
Chukot Autonomous Okrug	721.5	50.5	0.1	Anadyr (11.8)†
Russian Federation	17,098.2	142,905.2	8.4	Moscow

* Although Moscow and St Petersburg are the administrative centres of Moscow and Leningrad Oblasts, respectively, the cities themselves do not form part of the oblasts.
† Population estimates at 1 January 2010; estimates not adjusted to take account of 2010 census results.

PRINCIPAL TOWNS
(population in '000, 2010 census, preliminary)

Moskva (Moscow, the capital)	11,514.3	Tomsk	522.9
Sankt-Peterburg (St Petersburg)	4,848.7	Astrakhan	520.7
Novosibirsk	1,473.7	Penza	517.1
Yekaterinburg	1,350.1	Naberezhnye Chelnyi	513.2
Nizhnii Novgorod	1,250.6	Lipetsk	508.1
Samara	1,164.9	Tula	501.1
Omsk	1,154.0	Kirov	473.7
Kazan	1,143.6	Cheboksary	453.6
Chelyabinsk	1,130.3	Kaliningrad	431.5
Rostov-na-Donu (Rostov-on-Don)	1,089.9	Bryansk	415.6
Ufa	1,062.3	Kursk	414.6
Volgograd	1,021.2	Ivanovo	409.3
Perm	991.5	Magnitogorsk	408.4
Krasnoyarsk	973.9	Ulan-Ude	404.4
Voronezh	890.0	Tver	403.7
Saratov	837.8	Stavropol	398.3
Krasnodar	744.9	Nizhnii Tagil	361.9
Tolyatti	719.5	Belgorod	356.4
Izhevsk	628.1	Arkhangelsk (Archangel)	348.7
Ulyanovsk	613.8	Vladimir	345.6
Barnaul	612.1	Sochi	343.3
Vladivostok	592.1	Kurgan	333.6
Yaroslavl	591.5	Smolensk	326.9
Irkutsk	587.2	Kaluga	325.2
Tyumen	581.8	Chita	323.9
Makhachkala	578.0	Orel	317.9
Khabarovsk	577.7	Volga	314.4
Novokuznetsk	547.9	Cherepovets	312.3
Orenburg	547.0	Vladikavkaz	311.6
Kemerovo	532.9	Murmansk	307.7
Ryazan	525.1	Surgut	306.7

BIRTHS, MARRIAGES AND DEATHS

	Registered live births Number	Rate (per 1,000)	Registered marriages Number	Rate (per 1,000)	Registered deaths Number	Rate (per 1,000)
2002	1,396,967	9.7	1,019,762	7.1	2,332,272	16.2
2003	1,477,301	10.2	1,091,778	7.6	2,365,826	16.4
2004	1,502,477	10.4	979,667	6.8	2,295,402	16.0
2005	1,457,376	10.2	1,066,366	7.5	2,303,935	16.1
2006	1,479,637	10.4	1,113,562	7.8	2,166,703	15.2
2007	1,610,122	11.3	1,262,500	8.9	2,080,445	14.6
2008	1,713,947	12.1	1,179,007	8.3	2,075,954	14.6
2009	1,761,687	12.4	1,199,446	8.5	2,010,543	14.2

Life expectancy (years at birth, WHO estimates): 68 (males 62; females 74) in 2008 (Source: WHO, *World Health Statistics*).

IMMIGRATION AND EMIGRATION

	2007	2008	2009
Immigrants	286,956	281,614	279,907
Emigrants	47,013	39,508	32,458

ECONOMICALLY ACTIVE POPULATION
(sample surveys, '000 persons aged 15 to 72 years, at November, excl. Chechen Republic)

	2006	2007	2008
Agriculture, hunting and forestry	6,691	6,155	5,994
Fishing	176	192	141
Mining and quarrying	1,198	1,324	1,350
Manufacturing	12,472	12,324	11,663
Electricity, gas and water supply	2,063	2,017	2,116
Construction	4,462	4,933	5,413
Wholesale and retail trade; repair of motor vehicles and motorcycles and personal and household goods	10,599	11,096	10,774
Restaurants and hotels	1,392	1,344	1,467
Transport, storage and communications	6,211	6,573	6,560
Financial intermediation	1,060	1,249	1,316

THE RUSSIAN FEDERATION

—continued	2006	2007	2008
Real estate, renting and business activities	4,148	4,410	4,448
Public administration and defence; compulsory social security	4,876	4,903	5,409
Education	6,198	6,420	6,442
Health and social work	4,896	5,177	5,243
Other community, social and personal service activities	2,388	2,439	2,580
Private households with employed persons	21	16	43
Extra-territorial organizations and bodies	4	—	5
Total employed	68,855	70,570	70,965
Unemployed	5,312	4,588	4,791
Total labour force	74,167	75,158	75,756
Males	37,506	38,103	38,681
Females	36,661	37,056	37,076

Source: ILO.

2009 (sample surveys, '000 persons aged 15 to 72 years, at November, incl. Chechen Republic): Total employed 69,362; Unemployed 6,162; Total labour force 75,524 (males 38,501, females 37,023).

Health and Welfare

KEY INDICATORS

Total fertility rate (children per woman, 2008)	1.4
Under-5 mortality rate (per 1,000 live births, 2008)	11
HIV/AIDS (% of persons aged 15–49, 2007)	1.1
Physicians (per 1,000 head, 2006)	4.3
Hospital beds (per 1,000 head, 2006)	9.7
Health expenditure (2007): US $ per head (PPP)	797
Health expenditure (2007): % of GDP	5.4
Health expenditure (2007): public (% of total)	64.2
Access to water (% of persons, 2008)	96
Access to sanitation (% of persons, 2008)	87
Total carbon dioxide emissions ('000 metric tons, 2007)	1,536,099.0
Carbon dioxide emissions per head (metric tons, 2007)	10.8
Human Development Index (2010): ranking	65
Human Development Index (2010): value	0.719

For sources and definitions, see explanatory note on p. vi.

Agriculture

PRINCIPAL CROPS
('000 metric tons)

	2007	2008	2009
Wheat	49,370.0	63,765.1	61,739.8
Rice, paddy	704.5	738.3	913.0
Barley	15,559.1	23,148.5	17,880.8
Maize	3,798.0	6,682.3	3,963.4
Rye	3,909.4	4,505.1	4,333.1
Oats	5,383.5	5,834.9	5,401.2
Millet	417.4	711.0	264.7
Buckwheat	1,004.4	924.1	564.0
Potatoes	36,784.2	28,874.2	31,134.0
Sugar beet	28,836.2	28,995.3	24,892.0
Peas, dry	862.6	1,256.8	1,348.9
Soybeans (Soya beans)	650.2	746.0	943.7
Sunflower seed	5,671.4	7,350.2	6,454.3
Rapeseed	630.3	752.2	666.8
Cabbages and other brassicas	2,661.7	3,169.9	3,312.1
Tomatoes	1,791.0	1,938.7	2,170.4
Cucumbers and gherkins	1,001.3	1,129.9	1,132.7
Onions, dry	1,318.0	1,712.5	1,601.6

—continued	2007	2008	2009
Garlic	249.0	226.7	227.3
Carrots and turnips	1,347.0	1,530.2	1,518.7
Watermelons	853.4	1,382.5	1,419.0
Apples*	2,333	1,467	1,596
Sweet cherries*	100	63	69
Sour (Morello) cherries*	250	157	170
Plums and sloes*	183	115	125
Strawberries*	230.4	145.0	158.0
Currants*	456.9	288.6	314.0
Grapes	315.0	267.9	298.7

* Unofficial figures.

Aggregate production ('000 metric tons, may include official, semi-official or estimated data): Total cereals 80,207.5 in 2007, 106,391.9 in 2008, 95,079.5 in 2009; Total roots and tubers 36,784.2 in 2007, 28,874.2 in 2008, 31,134.0 in 2009; Total primary oilcrops 2,714.2 in 2007, 3,479.3 in 2008, 3,115.1 in 2009; Total pulses 1,302.1 in 2007, 1,812.1 in 2008, 1,547.0 in 2009; Total vegetables (incl. melons) 12,367.9 in 2007, 14,349.1 in 2008, 14,826.9 in 2009; Total fruits (excl. melons) 4,357.9 in 2007, 2,811.5 in 2008, 3,066.8 in 2009.

Source: FAO.

LIVESTOCK
('000 head at 1 January)

	2007	2008	2009
Horses	1,304	1,321	1,353
Cattle	21,515	21,546	21,038
Pigs	15,919	16,340	16,162
Sheep	17,508	19,290	19,602
Goats	2,167	2,213	2,168
Chickens	358,260	351,058	366,282
Turkeys	9,107	12,426	12,400*

* FAO estimate.

Source: FAO.

LIVESTOCK PRODUCTS
('000 metric tons)

	2007	2008	2009
Cattle meat	1,689.6	1,768.7	1,740.6
Sheep meat	149.6	156.2	164.5
Pig meat	1,872.7	2,042.1	2,169.5
Chicken meat	1,868.9	2,000.7	2,313.4
Cows' milk	31,914.9	32,099.7	32,325.8
Goats' milk	259.7	245.8	234.9
Hen eggs*	2,103.3	2,118.5	2,194.5
Honey	53.7	57.4	53.6
Wool, greasy	52.0	53.5	54.7

* Unofficial figures.

Source: FAO.

Forestry

ROUNDWOOD REMOVALS
('000 cubic metres, excl. bark; figures are rounded)

	2007	2008	2009
Sawlogs, veneer logs and logs for sleepers	82,700	78,200	62,800
Pulpwood	60,600	42,700	38,100
Other industrial wood	18,700	15,800	12,000
Fuel wood	45,000	44,700	38,500
Total	207,000	181,400	151,400

Source: FAO.

THE RUSSIAN FEDERATION

SAWNWOOD PRODUCTION
('000 cubic metres, incl. railway sleepers)

	2007	2008	2009
Coniferous (softwood)	21,347	19,579	17,069
Broadleaved (hardwood)	2,911	2,039	1,905
Total	24,258	21,618	18,974

Source: FAO.

Fishing

('000 metric tons, live weight)

	2006	2007	2008
Capture	3,284.3	3,454.2	3,383.7
Pink (humpback) salmon	202.3	263.5	164.2
Atlantic cod	207.5	189.9	194.6
Alaska (Walleye) pollock	1,021.7	1,218.5	1,318.7
Blue whiting (Poutassou)	329.4	252.3	225.2
Atlantic herring	131.1	171.5	202.2
Pacific herring	222.3	169.6	158.1
Aquaculture	105.5	105.5	115.4
Total catch	3,389.8	3,559.7	3,499.1

Note: Figures exclude seaweeds and other aquatic plants ('000 metric tons): 12.4 (capture 11.6, aquaculture 0.8) in 2006; 8.6 (capture 8.3, aquaculture 0.3) in 2007; 10.5 (capture 10.2, aquaculture 0.3) in 2008. Also excluded are aquatic mammals, recorded by number rather than weight. The number of whales caught was: 139 in 2006; 126 in 2007; 147 in 2008. The number of seals (incl. walrus) caught was: 23,176 in 2006; 12,895 in 2007; 17,623 in 2008.

Source: FAO.

Mining

('000 metric tons unless otherwise indicated)

	2006	2007	2008
Iron ore: gross weight	102,000	105,000	99,900
Copper ore*†	725	740	750
Nickel ore†	277	280	277*
Bauxite	6,399	6,777	6,300*
Lead ore*†	34.0	50.0	60.0
Zinc ore*†	190	185	204
Tin (metric tons)*†	3,000	2,500	1,500
Manganese ore*†	2.4	9.0	9.2
Chromium ore	966.1	776.7	750.0*
Tungsten concentrates (metric tons)*†	2,800	3,300	3,000
Molybdenum (metric tons)*	3,100	3,300	3,600
Cobalt ore (metric tons)*†	5,500	3,800	2,500
Mercury (metric tons)*	50	50	50
Silver (metric tons)*†	1,250	1,200	1,300
Uranium concentrate (metric tons)†	3,262	3,413	3,521
Gold (metric tons)†	159.3	157.0	176.3
Platinum (metric tons)*	29	27	23
Palladium (metric tons)*	98	97	88
Kaolin (concentrate)*	1,000	1,000	1,000
Magnesite*	1,200	1,200	1,200
Phosphate rock (Apatite)*‡	4,040	4,120	3,800
Potash§	6,610*	7,275	6,730
Native sulphur*	50	50	50
Fluorspar (concentrate)*	210	180	269
Barite (Barytes)*	63	63	63

—continued	2006	2007	2008
Salt (unrefined)	2,800	2,200	2,200*
Diamonds: gems ('000 metric carats):			
gem	23,400*	23,300*	21,925
industrial*	15,000	15,000	15,000
Gypsum (crude)*	2,200	2,300	2,300
Asbestos	925*	1,025	1,017
Mica*	100	100	100
Talc*	160	170	160
Feldspar*	160	160	160
Peat (horticulture and fuel use)	1,300	1,300	1,300

* Estimated production.
† Figures refer to the metal content of ores.
‡ Figures refer to the phosphoric acid content. The data exclude sedimentary rock (estimates, '000 metric tons): 118 in 2006, 120 in 2007 and 120 in 2008.
§ Figures refer to the potassium oxide content.

Source: US Geological Survey.

Crude petroleum (million metric tons): 469,986 in 2005; 480,529 in 2006; 491,306 in 2007; 488,487 in 2008; 494,247 in 2009 (Source: BP, *Statistical Review of World Energy*).

Natural gas (excl. flared or recycled, million cu m): 580,090 in 2005; 595,154 in 2006; 592,036 in 2007; 601,719 in 2008; 527,511 in 2009 (Source: BP, *Statistical Review of World Energy*).

Coal (commercial solid fuels only, million metric tons): 298.3 in 2005; 309.9 in 2006; 313.5 in 2007; 328.6 in 2008; 298.1 in 2009 (Source: BP, *Statistical Review of World Energy*).

Industry

SELECTED PRODUCTS
('000 metric tons, unless otherwise indicated)

	2007	2008	2009
Flour	12,500	13,500	n.a.
Granulated sugar	6,112	5,873	5,023
Cotton fabrics (million sq m)	2,108	1,915	1,477
Woollen fabrics (million sq m)	28.7	23.9	18.1
Linen fabrics (million sq m)	141	114	91
Footwear, excl. rubber footwear ('000 pairs)	54,200	56,500	57,500
Plywood ('000 cu m)	2,777	2,592	2,128
Particle board ('000 cu m)	5,501	5,751	4,600
Newsprint	1,979	1,987	2,006
Cardboard	3,498	3,696	3,458
Paper	4,084	4,007	3,937
Sulphuric acid	9,700	9,100	8,500
Soda ash (sodium carbonate)	2,939	2,820	2,322
Mineral fertilizers	17,300	16,211	14,640
Synthetic ammonia	13,200	12,700	n.a.
Gasoline	35.1	35.6	35.8
Rubber tyres ('000)	43,309	38,373	28,327
Rubber footwear ('000 pairs)	21,000	22,000	21,500
Cement	59,900	53,500	44,300
Pig-iron	51,523	48,300	44,000
Steel	72,370	68,711	59,362
Steel pipes	8,706	7,800	6,600
Rolled metal products	59,612	56,664	50,799
Tractors (number)	13,500	n.a.	n.a.
Refrigerators and freezers ('000)	3,539	3,728	2,750
Domestic washing machines ('000)	2,713	2,694	2,260
Televisions ('000)	6,823	7,028	4,825
Electric vacuum cleaners ('000)	649	1,252	222
Passenger motor cars ('000)	1,294	1,470	600
Electric energy (million kWh)	1,015,000	1,040,000	992,000

THE RUSSIAN FEDERATION

Finance

CURRENCY AND EXCHANGE RATES

Monetary Units
100 kopeks = 1 Russian rubl (ruble or rouble).

Sterling, Dollar and Euro Equivalents (31 December 2010)
£1 sterling = 47.712 roubles;
US $1 = 30.477 roubles;
€1 = 40.723 roubles;
1,000 roubles = £20.96 = $32.81 = €24.56.

Average Exchange Rate (roubles per US dollar)
2008   24.8529
2009   31.7404
2010   30.3679

Note: On 1 January 1998 a new rouble, equivalent to 1,000 of the former units, was introduced. Figures in this Survey are expressed in terms of new roubles, unless otherwise indicated.

FEDERAL BUDGET
('000 million roubles)

Revenue	2007	2008	2009
Tax revenue	4,604.1	5,199.0	3,863.9
Profit tax	641.3	761.1	195.4
Value-added tax	2,261.5	2,132.2	2,050.0
Excise duties	135.0	160.5	101.5
Social tax revenues	405.0	506.8	509.8
Other	1,161.3	1,638.4	1,007.2
Non-tax revenue	2,736.7	3,847.2	3,168.1
Customs duties	2,408.3	3,584.9	2,683.3
Other non-tax revenue	328.4	262.3	484.8
Total (incl. others)	7,781.1	9,275.9	7,337.8

Expenditure	2007	2008	2009
General government	815.7	839.4	853.1
Debt service	143.1	153.3	176.2
National defence and national security and militia	1,498.9	1,876.5	2,192.7
National economy	692.6	1,025.0	1,650.7
Fuel and electric power	8.3	9.8	34.9
Agriculture and fishing	27.8	58.0	83.1
Transport	172.6	296.3	444.1
Communication and informatics	14.1	18.7	26.9
Other	409.0	568.3	986.9
Housing and communal utilities	294.9	129.5	151.6
Social and cultural activities	776.1	1,015.7	1,205.5
Transfers to non-budget funds	1,043.9	1,580.0	2,113.2
Total (incl. others)	5,986.6	7,570.9	9,660.1

Source: Ministry of Finance, Moscow.

INTERNATIONAL RESERVES
(US $ million at 31 December)

	2008	2009	2010
Gold (national valuation)	14,533.4	22,797.7	35,788.1
IMF special drawing rights	0.8	8,896.9	8,744.0
Reserve position in IMF	1,053.4	1,927.0	1,893.4
Foreign exchange	410,695.4	405,824.9	432,948.5
Total	426,283.0	439,446.5	479,374.0

Source: IMF, *International Financial Statistics*.

MONEY SUPPLY
('000 million roubles at 31 December)

	2008	2009	2010
Currency outside depository corporations	3,794.8	4,038.0	5,062.8
Transferable deposits	3,796.6	4,256.5	5,795.6
Other deposits	9,183.3	11,225.6	13,094.2
Broad money	16,774.7	19,520.1	23,952.6

Source: IMF, *International Financial Statistics*.

COST OF LIVING
(Consumer Price Index; base: previous year = 100)

	2007	2008	2009
Food and beverages	115.6	116.5	106.1
Other consumer goods	106.5	108.0	109.7
Services	113.3	115.9	111.6
All items	111.9	113.3	108.8

All items (Consumer Price Index; base: 2005 = 100): 136.4 in 2008; 152.3 in 2009; 162.8 in 2010 (Source: IMF, *International Financial Statistics*).

NATIONAL ACCOUNTS
('000 million roubles at current prices)

Expenditure on the Gross Domestic Product

	2007	2008	2009
Final consumption expenditure	21,968.6	27,543.5	29,351.2
Households	16,031.7	19,967.0	20,979.9
Non-profit institutions serving households	185.9	216.7	217.0
General government	5,751.0	7,359.8	8,154.3
Gross capital formation	8,034.1	10,526.1	7,340.4
Gross fixed capital formation. Acquisitions, less disposals, of valuables	6,980.4	9,200.8	8,530.7
Changes in inventories	1,053.7	1,325.3	−1,190.3
Total domestic expenditure	30,002.7	38,069.6	36,691.6
Exports of goods and services	10,028.8	12,923.6	10,896.8
Less Imports of goods and services	7,162.2	9,111.0	7,954.3
Sub-total	32,869.3	41,882.2	39,634.1
Statistical discrepancy*	378.2	−617.3	−836.9
GDP in market prices	33,247.5	41,264.9	38,797.2
GDP at constant 2003 prices	17,676.5	18,604.2	17,150.4

* Referring to the difference between the sum of the expenditure components and official estimates of GDP, compiled from the production approach.

Gross Domestic Product by Economic Activity

	2007	2008	2009
Agriculture, hunting and forestry	1,194.8	1,486.4	1,513.0
Fishing	61.6	62.7	80.9
Mining and quarrying	2,865.5	3,284.6	3,007.8
Manufacturing	5,025.2	6,163.5	4,925.6
Electricity, gas and water supply	855.9	1,033.9	1,387.9
Construction	1,633.9	2,225.2	2,107.0
Wholesale and retail trade; repair of motor vehicles, motorcycles and personal and household goods	5,745.0	7,137.6	6,104.1
Hotels and restaurants	286.3	357.5	350.1
Transport, storage and communications	2,750.9	3,258.2	3,238.4
Financial intermediation	1,253.8	1,537.7	1,723.4
Real estate, renting and business activities	3,102.8	3,949.1	4,087.4
Public administration and defence; compulsory social security	1,466.4	1,884.4	2,201.7
Education	769.9	970.7	1,138.3
Health and social work	950.5	1,197.8	1,360.5
Other community, social and personal services	522.1	621.5	589.1
Sub-total	28,484.5	35,170.8	33,814.9
Taxes, *less* subsidies, on products	4,763.0	6,094.2	4,982.3
GDP in market prices	33,247.5	41,264.9	38,797.2

THE RUSSIAN FEDERATION

Statistical Survey

BALANCE OF PAYMENTS
(US $ million)

	2007	2008	2009
Exports of goods f.o.b.	354,401	471,603	303,388
Imports of goods f.o.b.	−223,486	−291,861	−191,803
Trade balance	130,915	179,742	111,585
Exports of services	39,257	51,132	41,546
Imports of services	−58,145	−75,468	−61,429
Balance on goods and services	112,027	155,406	91,702
Other income received	47,397	61,778	34,012
Other income paid	−78,149	−110,758	−73,487
Balance on goods, services and income	81,275	106,426	52,227
Current transfers received	8,423	10,969	8,908
Current transfers paid	−11,929	−13,734	−11,770
Current balance	77,768	103,661	49,365
Capital account (net)	−10,224	496	−11,869
Direct investment abroad	−45,916	−55,594	−44,494
Direct investment from abroad	55,073	75,002	36,751
Portfolio investment assets	−9,992	−7,843	−10,375
Portfolio investment liabilities	15,545	−27,594	8,195
Financial derivatives assets	2,762	9,117	9,890
Financial derivatives liabilities	−2,430	−10,487	−13,134
Other investment assets	−60,062	−177,649	5,959
Other investment liabilities	139,751	63,239	−25,201
Net errors and omissions	−13,347	−11,268	−1,725
Overall balance	148,928	−38,919	3,363

Source: IMF, *International Financial Statistics*.

External Trade

PRINCIPAL COMMODITIES
(US $ '000 million)

Imports	2007	2008	2009
Foodstuffs and agricultural raw materials (excl. textiles)	27.6	35.2	30.1
Mineral products	4.7	8.3	4.1
Chemical products and rubber	27.5	35.2	27.9
Leather, fur, and articles thereof	0.7	1.0	0.8
Wood, pulp and paper products	5.3	6.5	5.1
Textiles, textile articles and footwear	8.6	11.7	9.6
Metals, precious stones, and articles thereof	16.4	19.3	11.3
Machinery, vehicles and transport equipment	102.0	141.0	72.6
Other	7.2	9.1	6.0
Total	199.8	267.1	167.5

Exports	2007	2008	2009
Foodstuffs and agricultural raw materials (excl. textiles)	9.1	9.3	10.0
Mineral products	228.4	326.0	203.0
Chemical products and rubber	20.8	30.3	8.7
Leather, fur, and articles thereof	0.3	0.4	0.2
Wood, pulp and paper products	12.3	11.6	8.4
Textiles, textile articles and footwear	1.0	0.9	0.7
Metals, precious stones, and articles thereof	56.0	61.8	38.7
Machinery, vehicles and transport equipment	19.7	22.8	17.9
Other	4.4	4.5	3.8
Total	351.9	467.6	301.7

PRINCIPAL TRADING PARTNERS
(US $ million)

Imports	2007	2008	2009
Austria	2,458	3,115	2,059
Belarus	8,879	10,552	6,714
Belgium	3,187	4,062	2,539
Brazil	4,109	4,672	3,510
China, People's Republic	24,424	34,780	22,840
Czech Republic	2,451	3,614	2,317
Denmark	1,596	1,829	1,373
Finland	5,026	6,639	3,954
France	7,766	10,015	8,425
Germany	26,534	34,115	21,231
Hungary	2,602	3,685	2,629
India	1,310	1,707	1,524
Italy	8,537	10,002	7,884
Japan	12,717	18,586	7,252
Kazakhstan	4,623	6,380	3,685
Korea, Republic	8,838	10,594	4,865
Netherlands	3,857	4,817	3,583
Poland	4,631	7,060	4,212
Spain	3,200	4,269	2,274
Sweden	3,112	4,533	2,036
Turkey	4,180	6,146	3,215
Ukraine	13,330	16,254	9,121
United Kingdom	5,645	7,616	3,534
USA	9,471	13,790	9,174
Uzbekistan	1,471	1,300	843
Total (incl. others)	199,754	267,101	167,457

Exports	2007	2008	2009
Austria	2,735	2,303	1,625
Belarus	17,205	23,507	16,717
Belgium	2,810	4,618	4,044
China, People's Republic	15,895	21,142	16,669
Cyprus	4,831	1,254	792
Czech Republic	4,656	7,250	4,435
Finland	10,751	15,741	9,159
France	8,684	12,201	8,723
Germany	26,346	33,164	18,711
Greece	2,628	4,306	2,290
Hungary	6,121	9,220	3,831
India	4,012	5,230	5,937
Israel	2,049	2,034	1,047
Italy	27,530	41,999	25,060
Japan	7,665	10,327	7,263
Kazakhstan	11,920	13,299	9,147
Korea, Republic	6,168	7,789	5,689
Netherlands	42,879	56,973	36,291
Poland	13,298	20,194	12,500
Romania	3,211	4,166	1,558
Slovakia	5,151	6,565	2,981
Spain	4,325	5,061	2,892
Sweden	3,009	4,123	3,200
Switzerland	13,523	9,557	6,349
Taiwan	907	1,036	792
Turkey	18,534	27,665	16,385
Ukraine	16,425	23,567	13,780
United Kingdom	11,030	14,884	9,073
USA	8,335	13,357	9,219
Total (incl. others)	351,930	467,581	301,745

Transport

RAILWAYS
(traffic)

	2007	2008	2009
Paying passengers ('000 journeys)	1,282,000	1,296,000	1,137,000
Freight carried ('000 metric tons)	1,345,000	1,304,000	1,109,000
Passenger-km (million)	174,100	175,900	151,500
Freight ton-km (million)	2,090,000	2,116,000	1,865,000

THE RUSSIAN FEDERATION

ROAD TRAFFIC
(motor vehicles in use)

	2005	2006	2007
Passenger cars	25,569,700	26,793,500	29,249,000
Buses and coaches	792,100	824,200	861,000
Lorries and vans	4,848,500	4,928,600	4,730,000

Motorcycles and mopeds: 7,165,900 in 1998; 6,328,600 in 1999.

Source: IRF, *World Road Statistics*.

SHIPPING
Merchant Fleet
(registered at 31 December)

	2007	2008	2009
Number of vessels	3,481	3,444	3,465
Total displacement ('000 grt)	7,587.3	7,527.0	7,650.0

Source: IHS Fairplay, *World Fleet Statistics*.

International Sea-borne Freight Traffic
('000 metric tons, rounded data)

	2004	2005	2006
Goods loaded	8,200	9,100	7,700
Goods unloaded	1,100	700	400

Note: Annual data extrapolated from monthly averages.
Source: UN, *Monthly Bulletin of Statistics*.

CIVIL AVIATION
(traffic on scheduled services)

	2007	2008	2009
Passengers carried ('000)	47,000	51,000	47,000
Freight carried (million metric tons)	1.0	1.0	1.0
Passenger-km (million)	111,000	122,600	112,500
Freight ton-km (million)	3.4	3.7	3.6

Kilometres flown (million): 680 in 2005; 749 in 2006. (Source: UN, *Statistical Yearbook*).

Tourism

FOREIGN VISITOR ARRIVALS
('000, incl. excursionists)

Country of origin	2006	2007	2008
Azerbaijan	935.5	993.9	989.5
China, People's Republic	765.3	765.1	815.5
Estonia	438.2	390.6	662.9
Finland	1,078.2	975.6	1,000.2
Germany	553.7	613.9	636.3
Kazakhstan	2,598.6	2,895.7	2,732.1
Kyrgyzstan	409.0	512.2	552.7
Latvia	380.7	398.7	423.1
Lithuania	980.5	742.5	680.5
Moldova	925.9	1,042.8	1,167.3
Poland	1,149.0	957.5	779.8
Tajikistan	600.8	737.5	900.7
Ukraine	6,447.0	6,421.8	6,415.4
Uzbekistan	958.9	1,184.8	1,556.2
Total (incl. others)	22,486.0	22,908.6	23,676.1

Total arrivals ('000): 20,605 in 2007 (revised); 21,566 in 2008; 19,420 in 2009 (preliminary).

Receipts from tourism (US $ million, excl. passenger transport): 9,447 in 2007; 11,819 in 2008; 9,297 in 2009 (provisional).

Source: World Tourism Organization.

Communications Media

	2007	2008	2009
Telephones ('000 main lines in use)	45,218.2	45,539.3	45,379.6
Mobile cellular telephones ('000 subscribers)	171,200	199,522	230,500
Internet users ('000)	35,002.7	37,936.1	40,853.4
Broadband subscribers ('000)	4,900	9,280	12,900

Source: International Telecommunication Union.

Television receivers ('000 in use): 79,000 in 2000.

Radio receivers ('000 in use): 61,500 in 1997.

Book production (including pamphlets): 36,237 titles in 1996 (421,387,000 copies).

Daily newspapers: 250 in 2004 (average circulation 13,280,000 copies).

Non-daily newspapers: 7,267 in 2004 (average circulation 164,070,000 copies).

Other periodicals: 2,751 in 1996 (average circulation 387,832,000 copies).

Personal computers: 19.0m. (133.3 per 1,000 persons) in use in 2006.

Sources: UNESCO, *Statistical Yearbook*; and UN, *Statistical Yearbook*.

Education

(2009/10)

	Institutions	Students*	Teachers*
Pre-primary	45,346	5,228,200	600,800
Primary and general secondary	51,657	13,330,000	1,308,000
Vocational secondary	2,866	2,142,000	146,200
Higher	1,114	7,419,000	397,500

*Rounded figures.

Pupil-teacher ratio (primary education, UNESCO estimate): 17.4 in 2007/08 (Source: UNESCO Institute for Statistics).

Adult literacy rate (UNESCO estimates): 99.5% (males 99.7%; females 99.4%) in 2008 (Source: UNESCO Institute for Statistics).

THE RUSSIAN FEDERATION

Directory

The Government

HEAD OF STATE

President of the Russian Federation: DMITRII A. MEDVEDEV (elected 2 March 2008; inaugurated 7 May).

THE GOVERNMENT
(May 2011)

Chairman: VLADIMIR V. PUTIN.
First Deputy Chairman: VIKTOR A. ZUBKOV.
First Deputy Chairman: IGOR I. SHUVALOV.
Deputy Chairman: ALEKSANDR D. ZHUKOV.
Deputy Chairman: SERGEI B. IVANOV.
Deputy Chairman: DMITRII N. KOZAK.
Deputy Chairman: IGOR I. SECHIN.
Deputy Chairman, Minister of Finance: ALEKSEI L. KUDRIN.
Deputy Chairman, Head of the Government Staff: VYACHESLAV V. VOLODIN.
Deputy Chairman, Presidential Representative to the North Caucasus Federal Okrug: ALEKSANDR G. KHLOPONIN.
Minister of Agriculture: YELENA B. SKRYNNIK.
Minister of Civil Defence, Emergencies and Clean-up Operations: Col-Gen. SERGEI K. SHOIGU.
Minister of Communications and the Mass Media: IGOR O. SHCHEGOLEV.
Minister of Culture: ALEKSANDR A. AVDEYEV.
Minister of Defence: ANATOLII E. SERDYUKOV.
Minister of Economic Development: ELVIRA S. NABIULLINA.
Minister of Education and Science: ANDREI A. FURSENKO.
Minister of Energy: SERGEI I. SHMATKO.
Minister of Foreign Affairs: SERGEI V. LAVROV.
Minister of Health and Social Development: TATYANA A. GOLIKOVA.
Minister of Industry and Trade: VIKTOR B. KHRISTENKO.
Minister of Internal Affairs: Col-Gen. RASHID G. NURGALIYEV.
Minister of Justice: ALEKSANDR V. KONOVALOV.
Minister of Natural Resources and Ecology: YURII P. TRUTNEV.
Minister of Regional Development: VIKTOR F. BASARGIN.
Minister of Sport, Tourism and Youth Policy: VITALII L. MUTKO.
Minister of Transport: IGOR YE. LEVITIN.

MINISTRIES

Office of the President: 103132 Moscow, Staraya pl. 4; tel. (495) 625-35-81; fax (495) 606-07-66; e-mail president@gov.ru; internet www.kremlin.ru.

Office of the Government: 103274 Moscow, Krasnopresnenskaya nab. 2; tel. (495) 605-53-29; fax (495) 605-52-43; e-mail duty_press@aprf.gov.ru; internet www.government.ru.

Ministry of Agriculture: 107139 Moscow, Orlikov per. 1/11; tel. (495) 607-80-00; fax (495) 607-83-62; e-mail info@gov.mcx.ru; internet www.mcx.ru.

Ministry of Civil Defence, Emergencies and Clean-up Operations: 109012 Moscow, Teatralnyi prozeyd 3; tel. (495) 449-99-99; fax (495) 624-19-46; e-mail info@mchs.gov.ru; internet www.mchs.gov.ru.

Ministry of Communications and the Mass Media: 125375 Moscow, ul. Tverskaya 7; tel. (495) 771-81-00; fax (495) 771-87-10; e-mail office@minsvyaz.ru; internet www.minsvyaz.ru.

Ministry of Culture: 125993 Moscow, M. Gnezdnikovskii per. 7/6; tel. (495) 629-20-08; fax (495) 629-72-69; e-mail info@mkrf.ru; internet www.mkrf.ru.

Ministry of Defence: 119160 Moscow, ul. Znamenka 19; tel. and fax (495) 696-84-37; internet www.mil.ru.

Ministry of Economic Development: 125993 Moscow, ul. 1-ya Tverskaya-Yamskaya 1/3; tel. and fax (495) 694-03-53; e-mail mineconom@economy.gov.ru; internet www.economy.gov.ru.

Ministry of Education and Science: 125993 Moscow, ul. Tverskaya 11; tel. and fax (495) 629-70-62; internet www.mon.gov.ru.

Ministry of Energy: 109074 Moscow, Kitaigorodskii proyezd 7; tel. and fax (495) 710-55-00; e-mail minenergo@minenergo.gov.ru; internet minenergo.gov.ru.

Ministry of Finance: 109097 Moscow, ul. Ilinka 9; tel. and fax (495) 987-91-01; internet www.minfin.ru.

Ministry of Foreign Affairs: 119200 Moscow, Smolenskaya-Sennaya pl. 32/34; tel. and fax (495) 244-16-06; e-mail ministry@mid.ru; internet www.mid.ru.

Ministry of Health and Social Development: 127994 Moscow, Rakhmanovskii per. 3; tel. and fax (495) 628-44-53; internet www.minzdravsoc.ru.

Ministry of Industry and Trade: 109074 Moscow, Kitaigorodskii proyezd 7; tel. and fax (495) 710-55-00; e-mail info_admin@minprom.gov.ru; internet www.minprom.gov.ru.

Ministry of Internal Affairs: 119049 Moscow, ul. Zhitnaya 16; tel. (495) 667-45-79; fax (495) 667-57-33; e-mail mvd12@mvdrf.ru; internet www.mvd.ru.

Ministry of Justice: 119991 Moscow, ul. Zhitnaya 14; tel. (495) 955-59-99; fax (495) 955-57-79; e-mail pst@minjust.ru; internet www.minjust.ru.

Ministry of Natural Resources and Ecology: 123995 Moscow, ul. B. Gruzinskaya 4/6; tel. and fax (495) 254-48-00; e-mail admin@mnr.gov.ru; internet www.mnr.gov.ru.

Ministry of Regional Development: 127994 Moscow, ul. Sadovaya-Samotechnaya 10/23/1; tel. and fax (495) 980-25-47; e-mail info@minregion.ru; internet www.minregion.ru.

Ministry of Sport, Tourism and Youth Policy: 105064 Moscow, ul. Kazakova 18; tel. and fax (495) 601-91-20; e-mail minsportturism@mail.ru; internet www.minstm.gov.ru.

Ministry of Transport: 109012 Moscow, ul. Rozhdestvenka 1/1; tel. and fax (495) 626-10-00; e-mail info@mintrans.ru; internet www.mintrans.ru.

President

Presidential Election, 2 March 2008

Candidates	Votes	%
Dmitrii A. Medvedev (United Russia)	52,530,712	70.28
Gennadii A. Zyuganov (Communist Party of the Russian Federation)	13,243,550	17.72
Vladimir V. Zhirinovskii (Liberal Democratic Party of Russia)	6,988,510	9.36
Andrei V. Bogdanov (Independent)	968,344	1.30
Total*	74,746,649	100.00

* Including 1,005,533 invalid votes, equivalent to 1.34% of the total.

Legislature

The Federalnoye Sobraniye (Federal Assembly) is a bicameral legislative body, comprising the Sovet Federatsii (Federation Council) and the Gosudarstvennaya Duma (State Duma).

Sovet Federatsii
(Federation Council)

103426 Moscow, ul. B. Dmitrovka 26; tel. (495) 692-11-50; fax (495) 692-43-05; e-mail post_sf@gov.ru; internet www.council.gov.ru.

The Sovet Federatsii is the upper chamber of the Federalnoye Sobraniye. It comprises two deputies appointed from each of the constituent members (federal territorial units) of the Russian Federation, representing the legislative and executive branches of power in each republic and region.

Chairman: ALEKSANDR P. TORSHIN (acting).

Gosudarstvennaya Duma
(State Duma)

103265 Moscow, Okhotnyi ryad 1; tel. (495) 692-80-00; fax (495) 203-42-58; e-mail stateduma@duma.ru; internet www.duma.gov.ru.

Chairman: BORIS V. GRYZLOV.

THE RUSSIAN FEDERATION
Directory

General Election, 2 December 2007

Parties and blocs	Votes	%	Seats
United Russia	44,714,241	64.30	315
Communist Party of the Russian Federation	8,046,886	11.57	57
Liberal Democratic Party of Russia	5,660,823	8.14	40
A Just Russia: Motherland/Pensioners/Life	5,383,639	7.74	38
Others	5,731,476	8.24	—
Total*	69,537,065	100.00	450

* Excluding 759,929 invalid votes.

Election Commission

Central Electoral Commission of the Russian Federation (Tsentralnaya izbiratelnaya komissiya Rossiiskoi Federatsii): 109012 Moscow, B. Cherkassii per. 9; tel. (495) 606-79-57; e-mail info@cikrf.ru; internet www.cikrf.ru; Chair. VLADIMIR YE. CHUROV.

Political Organizations

Legislation approved in 2004 required each political party to have at least 50,000 members, including no fewer than 500 members resident in at least one-half of the subjects (territorial units) of the Federation, with at least 250 members in each of the remaining regions, in order to register and to function legally. Based on the requirements of the amended legislation, only 11 parties were officially registered to contest elections to the Gosudarstvennaya Duma in December 2007. The following were the principal parties to be officially registered in mid-2010:

Communist Party of the Russian Federation (CPRF) (Kommunisticheskaya partiya Rossiiskoi Federatsii—KPRF): 103051 Moscow, per. M. Sukharevskii 3/1; tel. (495) 628-04-90; fax (495) 692-87-44; e-mail kprf2005@yandex.ru; internet www.kprf.ru; f. 1993; claims succession to the Russian Communist Party, which was banned in 1991; Chair. of Central Committee GENNADII A. ZYUGANOV; 184,181 mems (2006).

A Just Russia (AJR) (Spravedlivaya Rossiya): 123104 Moscow, ul. Tverskaya 13/1; tel. (495) 787-85-15; fax (495) 787-85-20; e-mail info@spravedlivo.ru; internet www.spravedlivo.ru; f. 2006 by merger of Motherland, Russian Party of Life and Russian Pensioners' Party; absorbed People's Party of the Russian Federation in Apr. 2007; statist, patriotic party; Chair. of Council and Leader ; Chair. NIKOLAI V. LEVICHEV.

Liberal Democratic Party of Russia (LDPR) (Liberalno-demokraticheskaya partiya Rossii): 103045 Moscow, Lukov per. 9; tel. (495) 624-08-69; fax (495) 692-92-42; e-mail pressldpr@rambler.ru; internet www.ldpr.ru; f. 1988; nationalist; Chair. VLADIMIR V. ZHIRINOVSKII; 180,000 mems (2008).

Patriots of Russia (Patrioty Rossii): 119121 Moscow, Smolenskii bulv. 11/2; tel. (495) 604-42-71; fax (495) 692-15-50; e-mail patriot-rus@bk.ru; internet www.patriot-rus.ru; f. 2002; fmrly Russian Party of Labour; Leader GENNADII YU. SEMIGIN.

The Right Cause (Pravoye Delo): 101000 Moscow, ul. Myasnitskaya 16; tel. (495) 620-96-81; fax (495) 229-32-11; e-mail party@pravoedelo.ru; internet www.pravoedelo.ru; f. 2008, registered 2009 by fmr mems of Union of Rightist Forces, Civic Force and the Democratic Party of Russia; economically liberal; Leader MIKHAIL D. PROKHOROV; 56,000 mems (2009).

United Russia (UR) (Yedinaya Rossiya): 129110 Moscow, Pereyaslavskii per. 4; tel. (495) 786-82-89; fax (495) 975-30-78; e-mail portalrss@edinros.ru; internet www.er.ru; f. 2001 as Unity and Fatherland—United Russia, on the basis of Unity (f. 1999, incorporating Our Home is Russia), Fatherland (f. 1999, and led by Mayor of Moscow YURII LUZHKOV) and the All Russia grouping of regional governors; pragmatic centrist grouping that promotes moderate economic reforms and a strong state; absorbed Agrarian Party of Russia in Oct. 2008; Chair. VLADIMIR V. PUTIN; Chair. of Supreme Council BORIS V. GRYZLOV; 659,654 mems (2006).

Yabloko Russian United Democratic Party (Rossiiskaya obyedinennaya demokraticheskaya partiya 'Yabloko'): 119017 Moscow, ul. Pyatnitskaya 31/2; tel. (495) 780-30-10; fax (495) 780-30-12; e-mail info@yabloko.ru; internet www.yabloko.ru; f. 1993 on the basis of the Yavlinskii-Boldyrev-Lukin electoral bloc; present name adopted 2008; democratic, politically and socially liberal; Chair. SERGEI S. MITROKHIN; 60,440 mems (2006).

Diplomatic Representation

EMBASSIES IN RUSSIA

Afghanistan: 121069 Moscow, ul. Povarskaya 42; tel. and fax (495) 290-01-46; e-mail safarat_moscow@yahoo.com; Ambassador AZIZULLAH KARZAI.

Albania: 119049 Moscow, ul. Mytnaya 3/8; tel. (495) 982-38-52; fax (495) 982-38-54; e-mail embassy.moscow@mfa.gov.al; Ambassador SOKOL GJOKA.

Algeria: 103051 Moscow, Krapivinskii per. 1A; tel. (495) 937-46-00; fax (495) 937-46-25; e-mail algamb@ntl.ru; internet www.algerianembassy.ru; Ambassador SMAIL CHERGUI.

Angola: 119590 Moscow, ul. U. Palme 6; tel. (499) 143-63-24; fax (495) 956-18-80; e-mail angomosc@col.ru; internet www.angolarussia.ru; Ambassador SAMUEL TITO ARMANDO.

Argentina: 119017 Moscow, ul. B. Ordynka 72; tel. (495) 502-10-20; fax (495) 755-58-00; e-mail efrus@co.ru; Ambassador (vacant).

Armenia: 101990 Moscow, Armyanskii per. 2; tel. (495) 625-73-05; fax (495) 624-45-35; e-mail info@armenianembassy.ru; internet www.armenianembassy.ru; Ambassador OLEG YESAIAN.

Australia: 109028 Moscow, Podkolokolnyi per. 10A/2; tel. (495) 956-60-70; fax (495) 956-61-70; e-mail austembmos@dfat.gov.au; internet www.russia.embassy.gov.au; Ambassador MARGARET EILEEN TWOMEY.

Austria: 119034 Moscow, Starokonyushennyi per. 1; tel. (495) 780-60-66; fax (495) 937-42-69; e-mail moskau-ob@bmeia.gv.at; internet www.aussenministerium.at/moskau; Ambassador Dr MARGOT KLESTIL-LÖFFLER.

Azerbaijan: 125009 Moscow, Leontyevskii per. 16; tel. (495) 629-43-32; fax (495) 202-50-72; e-mail embassy@azembassy.msk.ru; internet www.azembassy.ru; Ambassador POLAD BÜLBÜLOĞLU.

Bahrain: 109017 Moscow, ul. B. Ordynka 18/1; tel. (495) 953-00-22; fax (495) 953-74-74; e-mail moscow.mission@mofa.gov.bh; Chargé d'affaires AHMED ABDULLA ALHARMASI ALHAJERI.

Bangladesh: 119121 Moscow, Zemledelcheskii per. 6; tel. (499) 246-78-04; fax (499) 248-31-85; e-mail bdoot.moscow@mail.ru; internet www.bangladeshembassy.ru; Ambassador S. M. SAIFUL HOQUE.

Belarus: 101990 Moscow, ul. Maroseika 17/6; tel. (495) 777-66-44; fax (495) 777-66-33; e-mail mail@embassybel.ru; internet www.embassybel.ru; Ambassador VASILY DOLGOLEV.

Belgium: 121069 Moscow, ul. M. Molchanovka 7; tel. (495) 780-08-31; fax (495) 780-08-42; e-mail moscow@diplobel.org; internet www.diplomatie.be/moscow; Ambassador GUY TROUVEROY.

Benin: 127006 Moscow, Uspenskii per. 7; tel. (495) 699-23-60; fax (495) 694-02-26; e-mail amba_beninmos@yahoo.fr; Ambassador VISSINTO AYI D'ALMEIDA.

Bolivia: 115191 Moscow, ul. Serpukhovskii val 8/135–137; tel. (495) 954-06-30; fax (495) 958-07-55; e-mail embolrus@online.ru; internet www.emborus.com; Ambassador MARÍA LUISA RAMOS URZAGASTE.

Bosnia and Herzegovina: 119590 Moscow, ul. Mosfilmovskaya 50/1; tel. (495) 147-64-88; fax (495) 147-64-89; e-mail embassybih@mail.ru; Ambassador ŽELJKO JANJETOVIĆ.

Brazil: 121069 Moscow, ul. B. Nikitskaya 54; tel. (495) 363-03-66; fax (495) 363-03-67; e-mail brasrus@brasemb.ru; internet www.brasemb.ru; Ambassador CARLOS ANTONIO DA ROCHA PARANHOS.

Brunei: 121059 Moscow, Berezhkovskaya nab. 2, Radisson-Slavyanskaya Hotel, kom. 413, 440–441; tel. (495) 941-82-15; fax (495) 941-82-14; e-mail moscow.russia@mfa.gov.bn; Ambassador Haji EMRAN BAHAR.

Bulgaria: 119590 Moscow, ul. Mosfilmovskaya 66; tel. (495) 143-90-22; fax (495) 232-33-02; e-mail bulemrus@bolgaria.ru; internet www.mfa.bg/bg/60/; Ambassador PLAMEN I. GROZDANOV.

Burundi: 119049 Moscow, Kaluzhskaya pl. 1/226–227; tel. (495) 230-25-64; fax (495) 230-20-09; e-mail bdiamb@yahoo.fr; Ambassador GUILLAUME RUZOVIYO.

Cambodia: 121002 Moscow, Starokonyushennyi per. 16; tel. (495) 637-47-36; fax (495) 956-65-73; e-mail cambemoscow@stream.ru; Ambassador VANNA THAY.

Cameroon: 121069 Moscow, ul. Povarskaya 40; tel. (495) 690-65-49; fax (495) 690-00-63; e-mail ambacamos@yahoo.fr; Ambassador MAHAMAT PABA SALE.

Canada: 119002 Moscow, Starokonyushennyi per. 23; tel. (495) 925-60-00; fax (495) 925-60-25; e-mail mosco@international.gc.ca; internet www.canadainternational.gc.ca/russia-russie; Ambassador JOHN C. SLOAN.

Central African Republic: 117571 Moscow, ul. 26-i Bakinskikh Kommissarov 9/124–125; tel. (495) 434-45-20; fax (495) 933-28-99; Ambassador (vacant).

THE RUSSIAN FEDERATION

Chad: 117393 Moscow, ul. Akademika Pilyugina 14, korp. 3/895–896; tel. (495) 936-17-63; fax (495) 936-11-01; e-mail ambatchamo@yahoo.fr; Ambassador DJIBRINE ABDOUL.

Chile: 119002 Moscow, Denezhnii per. 7, str. 1; tel. (499) 241-01-45; fax (499) 241-68-67; e-mail echile@col.ru; internet www.embachilerusia.ru; Ambassador JUAN EDUARDO EGUIGUREN.

China, People's Republic: 117330 Moscow, ul. Druzhby 6; tel. (495) 938-20-06; fax (495) 956-11-69; e-mail chiemb@microdin.ru; internet ru.china-embassy.org; Ambassador LI HUI.

Colombia: 119121 Moscow, ul. Burdenko 20/2; tel. (495) 248-30-73; fax (495) 248-30-25; e-mail emrusia@colombia.ru; Ambassador DIEGO JOSÉ TÓBON ECHEVERRI.

Congo, Democratic Republic: 117556 Moscow, Simferopolskii bulv. 7A/49–50; tel. and fax (499) 613-83-48; e-mail amba_rdc_moscow@yahoo.fr; Ambassador MOÏSE KABAKU MUTSHALL.

Congo, Republic: 119049 Moscow, ul. Korovii val 7/1/10–12; tel. (495) 236-33-68; fax (495) 236-41-16; e-mail ambacoru@yahoo.fr; Ambassador JEAN-PIERRE LOUYÉBO.

Costa Rica: 121615 Moscow, Rublevskoye shosse 26/1/150–151; tel. (495) 415-40-14; fax (495) 415-40-42; e-mail embaric2@rol.ru; Ambassador MANUEL ANTONIO BARRANTES RODRÍGUEZ.

Côte d'Ivoire: 119034 Moscow, Korobeinikov per. 14/9; tel. (495) 637-24-00; fax (495) 637-21-57; e-mail ambacimow@hotmail.com; internet ambaci-russie.org; Ambassador GNAGNO PHILIBERT FAGNIDI.

Croatia: 119034 Moscow, Korobeinikov per. 16/10; tel. (495) 637-38-68; fax (495) 637-46-24; e-mail crorus@mvpei.hr; internet ru.mvp.hr; Ambassador NEBOJŠA KOHAROVIĆ.

Cuba: 119017 Moscow, ul. B. Ordynka 66; tel. and fax (495) 933-79-57; e-mail rusiadespacho@embacuba.ru; internet emba.cubaminrex.cu/rusia; Ambassador JUAN VALDÉS FIGUEROA.

Cyprus: 121069 Moscow, ul. Povarskaya 9; tel. (495) 744-29-44; fax (495) 744-29-45; e-mail moscowembassy@mfa.gov.cy; internet www.mfa.cy/embassymoscow; Ambassador PETROS KESTORAS.

Czech Republic: 123056 Moscow, ul. Yu. Fuchika 12/14; tel. (495) 276-07-01; fax (045) 250-15-23; e-mail moscow@embassy.mzv.cz; internet www.mfa.cz/moscow; Ambassador PETR KOLAR.

Denmark: 119034 Moscow, Prechistenskii per. 9; tel. (495) 642-68-00; fax (495) 775-01-91; e-mail mowamb@um.dk; internet www.ambmoskva.um.dk; Ambassador TOM RISDAHL JENSEN.

Dominican Republic: 121615 Moscow, Rublevskoye shosse 26, korp. 1, podyezd 4, of. 211; tel. (495) 415-25-96; fax (495) 415-36-01; Ambassador JORGE LUIS PÉREZ ALVARADO.

Ecuador: 103064 Moscow, Gorokhovskii per. 12; tel. (499) 261-55-27; fax (499) 267-70-79; e-mail embajada@embajada-ecuador.ru; internet www.embajada-ecuador.ru; Ambassador PATRICIO ALBERTO CHÁVEZ ZAVALA.

Egypt: 119034 Moscow, Kropotkinskii per. 12; tel. (495) 246-02-34; fax (495) 246-10-64; e-mail egyemb_moscow@yahoo.com; Ambassador MUHAMMAD ALAA ELDIN A. SHAWKY AL-HADIDI.

Equatorial Guinea: 119017 Moscow, Pogorelskii per. 7/1; tel. (495) 953-27-66; fax (495) 953-20-84; e-mail embajada1968@mail.ru; Ambassador CIPRIANO TOMO NGUEMA.

Eritrea: 119049 Moscow, ul. Kirovii val 7/31; tel. (499) 238-30-25; fax (499) 238-18-68; e-mail erembassy@yandex.ru; Ambassador TEKLAY MINASSIE ASGEDOM.

Estonia: 125009 Moscow, M. Kislovskii per. 5; tel. (495) 737-36-40; fax (495) 737-36-46; e-mail embassy.moskva@mfa.ee; internet www.estemb.ru; Ambassador SIIMU TIIK.

Ethiopia: 129041 Moscow, Orlovo-Davydovskii per. 6; tel. (495) 680-16-16; fax (495) 680-66-08; e-mail eth-emb@col.ru; Ambassador MELES KASAHUN DENDER.

Finland: 119034 Moscow, Kropotkinskii per. 15/17; tel. (495) 787-41-74; fax (495) 247-33-80; e-mail sanomat.mos@formin.fi; internet www.finland.org.ru; Ambassador MATTI KALERVO ANTTONEN.

France: 119049 Moscow, ul. B. Yakimanka 45; tel. (495) 937-15-00; fax (495) 937-14-46; e-mail amba@ambafrance.ru; internet www.ambafrance.ru; Ambassador JEAN DE GLINIASTY.

Gabon: 119002 Moscow, Denezhnyi per. 16; tel. (499) 241-00-80; fax (499) 241-15-85; e-mail ambgab_ru@mail.ru; Ambassador RENÉ MAKONGO.

The Gambia: 115035 Moscow, Kadashevskaya nab. 32/2/3; tel. and fax 258-36-82; Ambassador MOSES BENJAMIN JALLOW.

Germany: 119285 Moscow, ul. Mosfilmovskaya 56; tel. (495) 937-95-00; fax (495) 938-23-54; e-mail germanmo@aha.ru; internet www.moskau.diplo.de; Ambassador ULRICH BRANDENBURG.

Ghana: 121069 Moscow, Skatertnyi per. 14; tel. (495) 690-19-69; fax (495) 690-21-98; e-mail embghmos@astelit.ru; Ambassador Dr SETH KORANGTENG.

Greece: 103009 Moscow, Leontiyevskii per. 4; tel. (495) 290-14-46; fax (495) 771-65-10; e-mail gremb.mow@mfa.gr; Ambassador MIHALIS SPINELLIS.

Guatemala: 119049 Moscow, ul. Korovii val 7/98; tel. (499) 238-22-14; fax (499) 238-14-46; e-mail embrusia@minex.gob.gt; Ambassador ARTURO ROMEO DUARTE ORTIZ.

Guinea: 119049 Moscow, ul. Korovii val 7/1/101–102; tel. (499) 238-10-85; fax (499) 238-97-68; e-mail ambaguineemoscou@yahoo.fr; Ambassador Lt-Col AMARA BANGOURA.

Guinea-Bissau: 117556 Moscow, Simferopolskii bulv. 7A/180; tel. and fax (495) 317-95-82; Ambassador ROGERIO ARAUJO ADOLPHO HERBERT.

Holy See: 127055 Moscow, Vadkovskii per. 7/37; tel. (495) 726-59-30; fax (495) 726-59-32; e-mail nuntius@inbox.ru; Apostolic Nuncio Most Rev. IVAN JURKOVIČ (Titular Archbishop of Corbavia).

Hungary: 119285 Moscow, ul. Mosfilmovskaya 62; tel. (495) 796-93-70; fax (495) 796-93-80; e-mail mission.mow@kum.hu; internet www.mfa.gov.hu/emb/moscow; Ambassador ISTVÁN IJGYÁRTÓ.

Iceland: 121069 Moscow, Khlebnyi per. 28; tel. (495) 956-76-04; fax (495) 956-76-12; e-mail icemb.moscow@utn.sthr.is; internet www.iceland.org/ru; Ambassador BENEDIKT ASGEIRSSON.

India: 101000 Moscow, ul. Vorontsovo Pole 6–8; tel. (495) 783-75-35; fax (495) 917-22-85; e-mail indambru@com2com.ru; internet www.indianembassy.ru; Ambassador AJAI MALHOTRA (designate).

Indonesia: 109017 Moscow, ul. Novokuznetskaya 12; tel. (495) 951-95-50; fax (495) 230-64-31; e-mail kbrimos@rol.ru; Ambassador HAMID AWALUDDIN.

Iran: 101000 Moscow, Pokrovskii bulv. 7; tel. (495) 917-72-82; fax (495) 230-96-83; e-mail info@iranembassy.ru; internet www.iranembassy.ru; Ambassador SAYED MAHMOUD REZA SAJJADI.

Iraq: 119121 Moscow, ul. Pogodinskaya 12; tel. (499) 246-55-07; fax (499) 246-27-34; e-mail mosemb@iraqmofamail.net; Ambassador FAEK FAREEK ABD AL-AZIZ NEROYI.

Ireland: 115127 Moscow, Grokholskii per. 5; tel. (495) 937-59-11; fax (495) 680-06-23; e-mail moscowembassy@dfa.ie; internet www.embassyofireland.ru; Ambassador PHILIP MCDONAGH.

Israel: 119017 Moscow, ul. B. Ordynka 56; tel. (495) 660-27-00; fax (495) 660-27-68; e-mail info@moscow.mfa.gov.il; internet moscow.mfa.gov.il; Ambassador DORIT GOLENDER.

Italy: 121002 Moscow, Denezhnyi per. 5; tel. (495) 796-96-91; fax (495) 253-92-89; e-mail embitaly.mosca@esteri.it; internet www.ambmosca.esteri.it; Ambassador ANTONIO ZANARDI LANDI.

Japan: 129090 Moscow, Grokholskii per. 27; tel. (495) 229-25-50; fax (495) 229-25-55; e-mail japan-info@japan.ru; internet www.ru.emb-japan.go.jp; Ambassador TIKAHITO HARADA.

Jordan: 123001 Moscow, Mamonovskii per. 3; tel. (495) 699-12-43; fax (495) 699-43-54; e-mail emjordan@umail.ru; Ambassador AHMAD S. AL-HASSAN.

Kazakhstan: 101000 Moscow, Chistoprudnyi bulv. 3A; tel. (495) 627-18-12; fax (495) 608-26-50; e-mail kazembassy@kazembassy.ru; internet www.kazembassy.ru; Ambassador ZAUTBEK TURISBEKOV.

Kenya: 119034 Moscow, Lopukhinskii per. 5; tel. (495) 637-21-86; fax (495) 637-54-63; e-mail kenemb@kenemb.ru; internet www.kenemb.ru; Ambassador PAUL KIBIWOTT KURGAT.

Korea, Democratic People's Republic: 107140 Moscow, ul. Mosfilmovskaya 72; tel. (499) 143-62-31; fax (499) 143-63-12; Ambassador KIM YONG JAE.

Korea, Republic: 131000 Moscow, ul. Plyushchikha 56/1; tel. (495) 783-27-27; fax (495) 783-27-77; e-mail embru@mofat.go.kr; internet rus-moscow.mofat.go.kr; Ambassador LEE YUNHO.

Kuwait: 119285 Moscow, ul. Mosfilmovskaya 44A; tel. (495) 147-00-40; fax (495) 956-60-32; e-mail kuwaitmoscow@yahoo.com; internet kuwaitembassy-russia.com; Ambassador NASSER Haji IBRAHIM AL-MUZAYYAN.

Kyrgyzstan: 119017 Moscow, ul. B. Ordynka 64; tel. (495) 237-48-82; fax (495) 951-60-62; e-mail embassy@embas-kyrg.msk.ru; internet www.kyrgyzembassy.ru; Ambassador ULUKBEK K. CHINALIEV.

Laos: 121069 Moscow, ul. M. Nikitskaya 18; tel. (495) 690-25-60; fax (495) 203-49-24; e-mail post@laoembassy.ru; internet www.laoembassy.ru; Ambassador SOMPHONE SICHALEUNE.

Latvia: 105062 Moscow, ul. Chaplygina 3; tel. (495) 232-97-60; fax (495) 232-97-50; e-mail embassy.russia@am.gov.lv; internet www.am.gov.lv/lv/moscow; Ambassador EDGARS SKUJA.

Lebanon: 115127 Moscow, ul. Sadovaya-Samotechnaya 14; tel. (495) 694-13-20; fax (495) 694-32-22; e-mail leb.emb.moscow@mtu-net.ru; Ambassador (vacant).

Libya: 131940 Moscow, ul. Mosfilmovskaya 38; tel. (495) 143-03-54; fax (495) 938-21-62; e-mail libyanbureau@mail.ru; Ambassador AMIR AL-ARABI ALI GHARIB.

THE RUSSIAN FEDERATION

Lithuania: 121069 Moscow, Borisoglebskii per. 10; tel. (495) 785-86-05; fax (495) 785-86-00; e-mail amb.ru@urm.lt; internet ru.mfa.lt; Chargé d'affaires a.i. ANDRIUS PULOKAS.

Luxembourg: 119034 Moscow, Khrushchevskii per. 3; tel. (495) 786-66-63; e-mail moscou.amb@mae.etat.lu; Ambassador GASTON PIERRE JEAN STRONCK.

Macedonia, former Yugoslav republic: 117292 Moscow, ul. D. Ulyanova 16, korp. 2/509–510; tel. (495) 124-33-57; fax (495) 982-36-34; e-mail mkambmos@mail.tascom.ru; Ambassador ILIJA ISAJLOVSKI.

Madagascar: 119034 Moscow, Kursovoi per. 5; tel. (495) 695-28-92; fax (495) 695-28-54; e-mail info@ambamadagascar.ru; internet www.ambamadagascar.ru; Ambassador ELOI ALPHONSE MAXIME DOVO.

Malaysia: 119192 Moscow, ul. Mosfilmovskaya 50; tel. (499) 147-15-14; fax (495) 937-96-02; e-mail malmoscow@kln.gov.my; Ambassador ZAINOL ABIDIN BIN OMAR.

Mali: 113184 Moscow, ul. Novokuznetskaya 11; tel. (495) 951-06-55; fax (495) 951-27-84; e-mail amaliru@mail.ru; Ambassador Gen. BRAHIMA COULIBALY.

Malta: 119049 Moscow, ul. Korovii val 7/219; tel. (495) 237-19-39; fax (495) 237-21-58; e-mail maltaembassy.moscow@gov.mt; Ambassador Dr CARAMEL INGUANEZ.

Mauritania: 119121 Moscow, B. Sabbinskii per. 21; tel. (495) 245-11-76; fax (495) 246-25-19; e-mail mauritanie@redline.ru; Ambassador SIDI MOHAMED OULD TALEB AMAR.

Mauritius: 109240 Moscow, ul. Nikolo-Yamskaya 8; tel. (495) 915-76-17; fax (495) 915-76-65; Ambassador MAHENDR DOSIEAH.

Mexico: 119034 Moscow, B. Levshinskii per. 4; tel. (495) 969-28-79; fax (495) 969-28-77; e-mail info@embamex.ru; internet portal.sre.gob.mx/rusia; Ambassador ALFREDO ROGERIO PÉREZ BRAVO.

Moldova: 107031 Moscow, ul. Kuznetskii most 18; tel. (495) 624-53-53; fax (495) 624-95-90; e-mail info@moldembassy.ru; internet www.moldembassy.ru; Ambassador ANDREI NEGUȚA.

Mongolia: 121069 Moscow, Borisoglebskii per. 11; tel. (495) 290-67-92; fax (495) 291-46-36; e-mail moscow@mfat.gov.mn; internet www.mongolianembassy.ru; Ambassador DOLOONJINGIIN IDEVKHTEN.

Montenegro: 119049 Moscow, ul. Mytnaya 3/23–25; tel. (499) 230-18-65; fax (499) 230-18-86; e-mail ambasadacg@ya.ru; Ambassador SLOBODAN BACKOVIĆ.

Morocco: 121069 Moscow, ul. B. Nikitskaya 51; tel. (495) 291-17-62; fax (495) 609-94-93; e-mail sifmamos@xrus.ru; internet www.ambmaroc.ru; Ambassador ABDELKADER LECHEHEB.

Mozambique: Moscow, ul. Krutitskii Val 3; tel. (495) 786-30-05; fax (495) 786-30-07; e-mail embamocru@hotmail.com; Ambassador BERNARDO MARCELINO CHERINDA.

Myanmar: 119049 Moscow, ul. B Nikitskaya 41; tel. (495) 291-56-14; fax (495) 956-18-78; e-mail mofa.aung@mptmail.net.mm; Ambassador MIN THEIN.

Namibia: 113096 Moscow, 2-i Kazachii per. 7; tel. (495) 230-32-75; fax (495) 230-22-74; e-mail namembrf@online.ru; Ambassador NDALI CHE KAMATI.

Nepal: 119121 Moscow, 2-i Neopalimovskii per. 14/7; tel. (499) 252-82-15; fax (499) 252-80-00; e-mail nepalemb@mtu-net.ru; Ambassador SURYA KIRAN GURUNG.

Netherlands: 115127 Moscow, Kalashnyi per. 6; tel. (495) 797-29-00; fax (495) 797-29-04; e-mail mos@minbuza.nl; internet www.netherlands-embassy.ru; Ambassador RON KELLER.

New Zealand: 121069 Moscow, ul. Povarskaya 44; tel. (495) 956-35-79; fax (495) 956-35-83; e-mail nzembmos@umail.ru; internet www.nzembassy.com/russia; Ambassador IAN ALEXANDER HILL.

Nicaragua: 117330 Moscow, ul. Mosfilmovskaya 50, korp. 1; tel. (495) 938-20-09; fax (495) 938-27-01; e-mail embanicaragua@hotmail.com; Ambassador LUIS ALBERTO MOLINA CUADRA.

Nigeria: 121069 Moscow, ul. M. Nikitskaya 13; tel. (495) 690-37-83; fax (495) 956-28-25; e-mail info@nigerianembassy.ru; internet www.nigerianembassy.ru; Ambassador TIMOTHY MAI SHELPIDI.

Norway: 131940 Moscow, ul. Povarskaya 7; tel. (495) 933-14-10; fax (495) 933-14-14; e-mail emb.moscow@mfa.no; internet www.norvegia.ru; Ambassador KNUT HAUGE.

Oman: 109180 Moscow, Staromonetnyi per. 14, str. 1; tel. (495) 230-15-87; fax (495) 230-15-44; e-mail moscow@mofa.gov.om; Ambassador MUHAMMAD BIN AWAD BIN ABD AL-RAHMAN AL-HASSAN.

Pakistan: 123001 Moscow, ul. Sadovaya-Kudrinskaya 17; tel. (495) 251-49-24; fax (495) 956-90-97; e-mail parepmoscow@yahoo.com; internet www.pakistanembassy.ru; Ambassador MOHAMMAD KHALID KHATTAK.

Panama: 119590 Moscow, ul. Mosfilmovskaya 50, korp. 1; tel. (495) 956-07-29; fax (495) 956-07-30; e-mail empanrus@aha.ru; Ambassador JULIO ERNESTO CORDOBA DE LEON.

Paraguay: 119049 Moscow, ul. Korovii val 7/142; tel. and fax (499) 230-18-10; e-mail embajada@embapar.ru; Ambassador MARCIAL BOBADILLA GUILLEN.

Peru: 121002 Moscow, Smolenskii bulv. 22/14/15; tel. (499) 248-77-38; fax (499) 248-00-72; e-mail leprumoscu@mtu-net.ru; Ambassador MARTA ELENA TOLEDO-OCAMPO UREN.

Philippines: 121099 Moscow, Karmanitskii per. 6; tel. (499) 241-05-63; fax (499) 241-26-30; e-mail moscowpe@stream.ru; Ambassador VICTOR G. GARCIA, III.

Poland: 123557 Moscow, ul. Klimashkina 4; tel. (495) 231-15-00; fax (495) 231-15-15; e-mail embassy@polandemb.ru; internet www.moskwa.polemb.net; Ambassador WOJCIECH JACEK ZAJĄCZKOWSKI.

Portugal: 129010 Moscow, Botanicheskii per. 1; tel. (495) 981-34-10; fax (495) 981-34-16; e-mail embptrus@moscovo.dgaccp.pt; Ambassador PEDRO NUNO DE ABREU E MELO BÁRTOLO.

Qatar: 117049 Moscow, ul. Korovii Val 7/196–198; tel. (495) 980-69-18; fax (495) 980-69-17; e-mail moscow@mofa.gov.qa; Ambassador AHMAD SAIF KHALAF AL-MIDHADI.

Romania: 119590 Moscow, ul. Mosfilmovskaya 64; tel. (499) 143-04-24; fax (499) 143-04-49; e-mail ambasada@orc.ru; internet moscova.mae.ro; Ambassador CONSTANTIN MIHAIL GRIGORIE.

Saudi Arabia: 119121 Moscow, 3-i Neopalimovskii per. 3; tel. (495) 245-23-10; fax (495) 246-94-71; e-mail saudiemb@msk.org.ru; internet www.saudiarabiaembassy.ru; Ambassador ALI HASSAN JAAFAR.

Senegal: 119049 Moscow, ul. Korovii val 7/1/193–194; tel. (495) 230-21-02; fax (495) 230-20-63; internet www.ambassen.ru; Ambassador MAMADOU SALIOU DIOUF.

Serbia: 119285 Moscow, ul. Mosfilmovskaya 46; tel. (499) 988-66-45; fax (499) 988-66-46; e-mail ambasada.moskva@mfa.rs; internet www.moskva.mfa.rs; Ambassador JELICA KURJAK.

Sierra Leone: 121615 Moscow, Rublevskoye shosse 26, korp. 1/58–59; tel. (495) 415-41-66; fax (495) 415-41-24; e-mail slembassymoscow@yahoo.com; Ambassador Dr JOHN YAMBASU.

Singapore: 121099 Moscow, per. Kamennoi slobody 5; tel. (499) 241-39-14; fax (499) 241-78-95; e-mail sinembmow@co.ru; Ambassador SIMON TENSING DE CRUZ.

Slovakia: 123056 Moscow, ul. Yu. Fuchika 17/19; tel. (495) 956-49-20; fax (495) 250-15-91; e-mail emb.moscow@mzv.sk; internet www.mzv.sk/moskva; Ambassador Dr JOZEF MIGAŠ.

Slovenia: 127006 Moscow, ul. M. Dmitrovka 14/1; tel. (495) 737-33-98; fax (495) 694-15-68; e-mail vmo@gov.si; internet moscow.embassy.si; Ambassador ADA FILIP-SLIVNIK.

Somalia: 117556 Moscow, Simferopolskii bulv. 7A/145; tel. and fax (499) 317-06-22; e-mail somembassy@nabad.org; Ambassador MOHAMED MOHAMOUD HANDULLE.

South Africa: 123001 Moscow, Granatnyi per. 1, str. 9; tel. (495) 926-11-77; fax (495) 926-11-78; e-mail moscow.ambassador@foreign.gov.za; internet saembassy.ru; Ambassador MANDISI BONGANI MABUTO MPAHLWA.

Spain: 121069 Moscow, ul. B. Nikitskaya 50/8; tel. (495) 690-29-93; fax (495) 291-91-71; e-mail embespru@mail.mae.es; internet www.maec.es/embajadas/moscu; Ambassador JUAN ANTONIO MARCH PUJOL.

Sri Lanka: 129090 Moscow, ul. Shchepkina 24; tel. (495) 688-16-20; fax (495) 688-17-57; e-mail lankaemb@com2com.ru; internet www.srilankaembassy.org; Ambassador UDAYANGA WEERATUNGA.

Sudan: 127006 Moscow, Uspenskii per. 4A; tel. (495) 699-54-61; fax (495) 699-33-42; e-mail sudmos@cityline.ru; Ambassador MUHAMMAD HASSAN HUSSEIN ZARUG.

Sweden: 119590 Moscow, ul. Mosfilmovskaya 60; tel. (495) 937-92-00; fax (495) 937-92-02; e-mail moscow.sweinfo@foreign.ministry.se; internet www.swedenabroad.com/moscow; Ambassador LARS PETER TOMAS BERTELMAN.

Switzerland: 101000 Moscow, per. Ogorodnoi slobody 2/5; tel. (495) 258-38-30; fax (495) 621-21-83; e-mail mos.vertretung@eda.admin.ch; internet www.eda.admin.ch/moscow; Ambassador WALTER BRUNO GYGER.

Syria: 119034 Moscow, Mansurovskii per. 4; tel. (499) 766-95-28; fax (495) 956-31-91; Ambassador HASSAN RISHEH.

Tajikistan: 103001 Moscow, Granatnyi per. 13; tel. (495) 290-38-46; fax (495) 291-89-98; e-mail info@tajembassy.ru; internet www.tajembassy.ru; Ambassador ABDULMAJID S. DOSTIYEV.

Tanzania: 109017 Moscow, ul. Pyatnitskaya 33; tel. (495) 953-82-21; fax (495) 953-07-85; e-mail info@tanzania.ru; internet www.tanzania.ru; Ambassador JAKA MGWABI MWAMBI.

Thailand: 129090 Moscow, ul. B. Spasskaya 9; tel. (495) 608-08-17; fax (495) 290-96-59; e-mail thaiemb@nnt.ru; internet www.thaiembassymoscow.com; Ambassador CHALERMPOL THANCHITT.

THE RUSSIAN FEDERATION

Tunisia: 113105 Moscow, ul. M. Nikitskaya 28/1; tel. (495) 691-28-58; fax (495) 691-75-88; e-mail atmos@post.ru; Ambassador KHEMAIES JHINAOUI.

Turkey: 119121 Moscow, 7-i Rostovskii per. 12; tel. (495) 994-48-08; fax (495) 956-55-97; e-mail turemb@viprt.ru; internet www.moscow.emb.mfa.gov.tr; Ambassador AYDIN ADNAN SEZGIN.

Turkmenistan: 119019 Moscow, Filippovskii per. 22; tel. (495) 291-66-36; fax (495) 291-09-35; e-mail turkmen@dol.ru; internet www.turkmenembassy.ru; Ambassador KHALNAZAR A. AGAKHANOV.

Uganda: 119049 Moscow, ul. Korovii val 7, str. 1/3; tel. (499) 230-22-76; fax (499) 230-21-31; e-mail info@uganda.ru; internet www.uganda.ru; Ambassador Dr MOSES EBUK.

Ukraine: 103009 Moscow, Leontiyevskii per. 18; tel. (495) 629-35-42; fax (495) 629-46-81; e-mail tem_rf@mail.ru; internet www.mfa.gov.ua/russia; Ambassador VLADIMIR YELCHENKO.

United Arab Emirates: 101000 Moscow, ul. U. Palme 4; tel. (499) 234-40-60; fax (495) 234-40-70; e-mail uaemirates@mtu-net.ru; Ambassador OMAR SAIF GHOBASH.

United Kingdom: 121099 Moscow, Smolenskaya nab. 10; tel. (495) 956-72-00; fax (495) 956-72-01; e-mail moscow@britishembassy.ru; Ambassador Dame ANNE PRINGLE.

USA: 121099 Moscow, B. Devyatinskii per. 8; tel. (495) 728-50-00; fax (495) 728-50-90; e-mail consulmo@state.gov; internet moscow.usembassy.gov; Ambassador JOHN ROSS BEYRLE.

Uruguay: 119049 Moscow, ul. Mytnaya 3/16; tel. (495) 230-77-65; fax (495) 230-29-49; Ambassador JORGE ALBERTO MEYER LONG.

Uzbekistan: 109017 Moscow, Pogorelskii per. 12; tel. (495) 230-00-76; fax (495) 238-89-18; e-mail info@uzembassy.ru; internet www.uzembassy.ru; Ambassador ZIYADULLA S. PULATXOJAYEV.

Venezuela: 115127 Moscow, B. Karetnyi per. 13/15; tel. (495) 699-40-42; fax (495) 956-61-08; Ambassador HUGO JOSÉ GARCIA HERNÁNDEZ.

Viet Nam: 119021 Moscow, ul. B. Pirogovskaya 13; tel. (495) 245-09-25; fax (495) 246-31-21; e-mail dsqvn@com2com.ru; Ambassador BUI DINH DINH.

Yemen: 119121 Moscow, 2-i Neopalimovskii per. 6; tel. (499) 246-15-40; fax (495) 246-17-98; Ambassador MUHAMMAD SALEH AHMED AL-HELALI.

Zambia: 129041 Moscow, pr. Mira 52A; tel. (495) 688-50-01; fax (499) 763-12-92; e-mail zambiamoscow@yahoo.com; Ambassador PATRICK NAILOBI NINYINZA.

Zimbabwe: 119121 Moscow, per. Serpov 6; tel. (499) 248-43-67; fax (499) 248-15-75; e-mail zimbabwe@rinet.ru; Ambassador (vacant).

Judicial System

In January 1995 the first section of a new code of civil law came into effect. It included new rules on commercial and financial operations, and on ownership issues. The second part of the code was published in January 1996. The Constitutional Court rules on the conformity of government policies, federal laws, international treaties and presidential enactments with the Constitution. The Supreme Arbitration Court rules on disputes between commercial bodies. The Supreme Court (which was relocated from Moscow to St Petersburg in 2008) oversees all criminal and civil law, and is the final court of appeal from lower courts. A system of Justices of the Peace, to deal with certain civil cases, and with criminal cases punishable by a maximum of two years' imprisonment, was established in 1998. The majority of Russia's regions introduced jury trials, in many cases only for the most serious crimes, during 2003.

Constitutional Court of the Russian Federation (Konstitutsionnyi Sud Rossiiskoi Federatsii): 190000 St Petersburg, pl. Dekabristov 1; tel. (812) 404-33-11; e-mail ksrf@krsf.ru; internet www.ksrf.ru; f. 1991; Chair. VALERII D. ZORKIN; Sec.-Gen. YELENA V. KRAVCHENKO.

Office of the Prosecutor-General: 125993 Moscow, ul. B. Dmitrovka 15A; tel. (495) 692-26-82; fax (495) 292-88-48; internet www.genproc.gov.ru; Prosecutor-Gen. YURII YA. CHAIKA.

Supreme Arbitration Court of the Russian Federation (Vysshii Arbitrazhnyi Sud Rossiiskoi Federatsii): 101000 Moscow, M. Kharitonevskii per. 12; tel. (495) 208-11-19; fax (495) 208-11-62; internet www.arbitr.ru; f. 1993; Chair. ANTON A. IVANOV.

Supreme Court of the Russian Federation (Verkhovnyi Sud Rossiiskoi Federatsii): 103289 Moscow, ul. Ilinka 7/3; tel. (495) 924-23-47; fax (495) 202-71-18; e-mail gastello@ilinka.supcourt.ru; internet www.supcourt.ru; Chair. VYACHESLAV M. LEBEDEV.

Religion

The majority of the population of the Russian Federation are adherents of Christianity, but there are significant Islamic, Buddhist and Jewish minorities.

In 1997 legislation restricted the operation of religious groups to those that were able to prove that they had been established in Russia for a minimum of 15 years. Russian Orthodoxy, Islam, Buddhism and Judaism, together with some other Christian denominations, were deemed to comply with the legislation. Religious organizations failing to satisfy this requirement were, henceforth, obliged to register annually for 15 years, before being permitted to publish literature, hold public services or invite foreign preachers into Russia. Moreover, foreign religious groups were additionally obliged to affiliate themselves to Russian organizations.

CHRISTIANITY

The Russian Orthodox Church (Moscow Patriarchate)

The Russian Orthodox Church (Moscow Patriarchate) is the dominant religious organization in the Russian Federation, with an estimated 75m. adherents. In 2004 there were 12,638 parishes operating under the auspices of the Patriarchate in Russia.

Moscow Patriarchate: 115191 Moscow, Danilov Monastery, ul. Danilovskii Val 22; tel. (495) 954-04-54; fax (495) 633-72-81; e-mail cs@mospatr.ru; internet www.mospat.ru; Patriarch of Moscow and all Rus KIRILL (GUNDYAYEV).

The Roman Catholic Church

At 31 December 2007 there were an estimated 774,500 Catholics in the Russian Federation. In 1991 administrative structures of the Catholic Church in Russia were restored. The organization of the Church in Russia comprises one archdiocese, three dioceses, one apostolic prefecture, and an apostolic exarchate for adherents of the Byzantine Rite.

Conference of Catholic Bishops of the Russian Federation: 101031 Moscow, ul. Petrovka 19/5/35; tel. and fax (495) 923-16-97; e-mail ostastop@glasnet.ru; internet www.catholic.ru; f. 1999; Pres. Most. Rev. JOSEPH WERTH (Bishop of the Diocese of the Transfiguration at Novosibirsk).

Archbishop of the Archdiocese of the Mother of God at Moscow: Most Rev. PAOLO PEZZI, 123557 Moscow, ul. M. Gruzinskaya 27/2; tel. (495) 785-54-34; fax (495) 785-54-70; e-mail p.pezzi@fscb.org.

Apostolic Prefect of Yuzhno-Sakhalinsk and Bishop of St Joseph at Irkutsk: Most Rev. CYRYL KLIMOWICZ, 664074 Irkutsk, ul. Gryboyedova 110, POB 4; tel. (3952) 41-03-10; fax (3952) 41-04-14; e-mail curiocat@curiocat.irk.ru.

Apostolic Exarch for Catholics of the Byzantine Rite In Russia: (vacant).

Protestant Churches

Russian Church of Christians of the Evangelical Faith: 123363 Moscow, ul. Fabritsiusa 31A; tel. (495) 493-57-88; internet hve.ru; f. 1907, re-established 1990; fmrly known as Union of Christians of the Evangelical Faith-Pentecostalists in Russia; 1,600 parishes and more than 300,000 adherents in 2005; Elder NAZAR P. RESHCHIKOVETS.

Russian Union of Evangelical Christians-Baptists: 117015 Moscow, Varshavskoye shosse 29/2; tel. (495) 958-13-36; fax (495) 975-23-67; e-mail bapt.un@g23.relcom.ru; internet baptist.org.ru; affiliated to the Euro-Asiatic Federation of Evangelical Christians-Baptists; Exec. Sec. YURII APATOV.

Other Christian Churches

Armenian Apostolic Church: 123022 Moscow, ul. S. Makeyeva 10; tel. (495) 255-50-19.

Russian Autonomous Orthodox Church: 125212 Moscow, Church of the New Martyrs and Confessors of Russia, Golovinskoye shosse 13 A; tel. (495) 152-50-76; formally established in 1990 as the Free Russian Orthodox Church; re-registered in 1998 under above name following opposition by local, 'catacomb' priests to moves of reconciliation between the Russian Orthodox Church Abroad and the Moscow Patriarchate; 100 parishes in 2001; First Hierarch Metropolitan of Suzdal and Vladimir VALENTIN (RUSANTSOV).

Russian Orthodox Old Belief (Old Ritual) Church (Russkaya Pravoslavnaya Staroobryadcheskaya Tserkov): 109052 Moscow, ul. Rogozhskii pos. 1B/3; tel. (495) 361-51-92; e-mail mitropolia@mail.ru; internet rpsc.ru; f. 1666 by separation from the Moscow Patriarchate; some 300 groups registered in 2005; divided into two main branches: the *popovtsi* (which have priests) and the *bespopovtsi* (which reject the notion of ordained priests and the use of all sacraments, other than that of baptism). Both branches are further divided into various groupings. The largest group of *popovtsi* are those of the Belokri-

THE RUSSIAN FEDERATION

nitskii Concord, under the Archbishop of Novozybkov, Moscow and All Rus, KORNILII (TITOV); c. 250 parishes, seven bishops in Russia, Ukraine and Moldova; a further significant group of *popovtsi* Old Believers are those of the Beglopopovtsyi Concord.

ISLAM

Most Muslims in the Russian Federation are adherents of the Sunni sect. Islam is the predominant religion among many peoples of the North Caucasus, such as the Chechens, the Ingush and many smaller groups, and also in the Central Volga region, among them the Tatars, Chuvash and Bashkirs.

Central Muslim Spiritual Board for Russia and European Countries of the CIS: 450057 Bashkortostan, Ufa, ul. Tukaya 50; tel. (3472) 50-80-86; f. 1789; 27 regional branches in the Russian Federation, and one branch in Ukraine; Chair. (vacant).

Council of Muftis of Russia: 129090 Moscow, per. Vypolzov 7; tel. and fax (495) 681-49-04; e-mail mufty@muslim.ru; internet www.muslim.ru; Chair. Mufti Sheikh RAVIL KHAZRAT GAINUTDIN.

JUDAISM

At the beginning of the 20th century approximately one-half of the world's Jews lived in the Russian Empire. Although many Jews emigrated from the USSR in the 1970s and 1980s, there is still a significant Jewish population (230,000 in late 2002, according to the official results of the census, although some estimates were considerably higher) in the Russian Federation.

Congress of Jewish Religious Communities and Organizations of Russia: 101000 Moscow, B. Spasoglinishevskii per. 10, Moscow Choral Synagogue; tel. (495) 917-95-92; fax (495) 740-12-18; e-mail keroor@mail.ru; f. 1996; co-ordinates activities of 120 Jewish communities throughout Russia; Chief Rabbi ADOLF SHAYEVICH; Dir ZINOVY KOGAN.

Federation of the Jewish Communities of Russia: 121099 Moscow, ul. Novyi Arbat 36/9/2; tel. (495) 290-75-18; fax (495) 290-86-49; e-mail office@fjc.ru; internet www.fjc.ru; unites 179 communities in Russia; affiliated to Federation of the Jewish Communities of the CIS and the Baltic States; Chief Rabbi of Russia, Chair. of Rabbinical Alliance of Russia and the CIS BEREL LAZAR.

Russian Jewish Congress: 101000 Moscow, B. Spasoglinishchevskii per. 9/1/936; tel. (495) 780-61-00; fax (495) 780-60-90; e-mail rjc@rjc.ru; internet www.rjc.ru; Pres. VYACHESLAV KANTOR.

BUDDHISM

Buddhism (established as an official religion in Russia in 1741) is most widespread in the Republic of Buryatiya, where the Traditional Buddhist Sangkha of Russia has its seat, in the Republics of Kalmykiya and Tyva, in Transbaikal Krai (formerly Chita Oblast), and in Irkutsk Oblast.

Buddhist Traditional Sangkha of Russia (Buddiiskaya Traditsionnaya Sangkha Rossii): 670000 Buryatiya, Ulan-Ude, Ivolginskii datsan; e-mail buddhism@buryatia.ru; internet buddhism.buryatia.ru; Head Pandito Khambo Lama DAMBA AYUSHEYEV.

The Press

In 2004 there were 46,000 officially registered printed media, including some 26,000 newspapers. However, the number of titles in circulation was only around one-half of the total. The total print run of Russian newspapers in that year was 8,500m. copies, and that of magazines was around 600m. copies. At that time *Moskovskii Komsomolets*, with a circulation of 2.2m., was the best-selling daily, while the weekly *Argumenty i Fakty*, which had a circulation of 2.9m. in 2007, was the best-selling newspaper overall.

REGULATORY AUTHORITY

Federal Agency for the Press and the Mass Media (Federalnoye Agentstvo po pechati i massovym kommunikatsiyam): 127994 Moscow, Strastnoi bulv. 5; tel. (495) 650-39-86; fax (495) 650-52-03; e-mail info@fapmc.ru; internet www.fapmc.ru; f. 2004; Chair. MIKHAIL V. SESLAVINSKII.

PRINCIPAL NEWSPAPERS

Moscow

Argumenty i Fakty (Arguments and Facts): 101000 Moscow, ul. Myasnitskaya 42; tel. (495) 735-44-47; e-mail n-boris@aif.ru; internet www.aif.ru; f. 1978; weekly; Editor-in-Chief NIKOLAI ZYATKOV; circ. 2.9m. (2007).

Gazeta (Newspaper): 123242 Moscow, ul. Zoologicheskaya 4; tel. (495) 787-39-99; fax (495) 787-39-98; e-mail info@gzt.ru; internet www.gzt.ru; f. 2001; Editor-in-Chief PAVEL V. SUKHOV; circ. 726,000 (2005).

Gazeta.ru: 121059 Moscow, Berezhkovskaya nab. 16A/2; tel. (495) 980-80-28; fax (495) 980-90-73; internet www.gazeta.ru; online only; has no assen with *Gazeta* newspaper; Editor-in-Chief ALEKSANDR PISAREV.

Grani.ru: Moscow; tel. (495) 585-84-11; e-mail info@grani.ru; internet grani.ru; f. 2000; online only; Dir-Gen. YULIYA BEREZOVSKAYA; Editor-in-Chief VLADIMIR KORSUNSKII.

Gudok (The Horn): 105066 Moscow, ul. Staraya Basmannaya 38/2/3; tel. (495) 262-26-53; fax (495) 624-78-53; e-mail gudok@css-rzd.ru; internet www.gudok.ru; f. 1917 as newspaper of railway workers; daily; Editor-in-Chief ALEKSANDR RETYUNIN; circ. 214,000 (2007).

Izvestiya (News): 127994 Moscow, ul. Tverskaya 18/1, POB 4; tel. (495) 209-05-81; fax (495) 933-64-52; e-mail izv@izvestia.ru; internet www.izvestia.ru; f. 1917; 50.19% owned by Gazprom Mediya, 49.81% by Prof-Mediya; Editor VITALY ABRAMOV; circ. 130,000 (2007).

Kommersant (Businessman): 125080 Moscow, ul. Vrubelya 4/1; tel. (499) 943-97-71; fax (499) 943-97-28; e-mail kommersant@kommersant.ru; internet www.kommersant.com; f. 1989; daily; Chief Editor AZER MURSALIYEV; circ. 119,322 (2007).

Komsomolskaya Pravda (Young Communist League Truth): 103287 Moscow, Staryi Petrovsko-Razumovskii proyezd 1/23/1; tel. (495) 777-02-84; fax (495) 200-22-93; e-mail kp@kp.ru; internet www.kp.ru; f. 1925; fmrly organ of the Lenin Young Communist League (Komsomol); independent; weekly supplements *KP-Tolstushka* (KP-Fat volume), *KP-Ponedelnik* (KP-Monday); managed by Prof-Mediya; Chair. OLEG RUDNOV; Editor-in-Chief VLADIMIR SUNGORKIN; circ. 700,000.

Krasnaya Zvezda (Red Star): 123007 Moscow, Khoroshevskoye shosse 38; tel. (495) 941-21-58; fax (495) 941-40-57; e-mail mail@redstar.ru; internet www.redstar.ru; f. 1924; organ of the Ministry of Defence; Editor N. N. YEFIMOV; circ. 80,000 (2000).

The Moscow News: 119021 Moscow, Zubovskii bulv. 4; tel. (495) 645-64-03; fax (495) 637-27-46; e-mail info@mnweekly.ru; internet www.mnweekly.ru; f. 1930; twice a week; in English; democratic, liberal; Editor-in-Chief TIM WALL; circ. c. 75,000 (2010).

Moscow Times: 127018 Moscow, ul. Polkovaya 3/1; tel. (495) 232-47-74; fax (495) 232-65-28; e-mail moscowtimes.editors@imedia.ru; internet www.themoscowtimes.com; f. 1992; daily; in English; Publr MAXINE MATERS; Editor ANDREW MCCHESNEY.

Moskovskaya Pravda (The Moscow Truth): 123846 Moscow, ul. 1905 Goda 7, POB D-22; tel. (495) 259-82-33; fax (495) 259-63-60; e-mail newspaper@mospravda.ru; internet www.mospravda.ru; f. 1918; fmrly organ of the Moscow city committee of the CPSU and the Moscow City Council; 5 a week; independent; Editor-in-Chief SHOD S. MULADZHANOV; circ. 400,000 (2007).

Moskovskii Komsomolets (MK): 123995 Moscow, ul. 1905 Goda 7; tel. (495) 250-72-72; fax (495) 259-46-39; e-mail info@mk.ru; internet www.mk.ru; f. 1919 as *Moskovskii Komsomolets* (The Moscow Young Communist); 6 a week; independent; Editor-in-Chief PAVEL GUSEV; circ. 800,000 in Moscow, 2.2m. nation-wide (2004).

Nezavisimaya Gazeta (NG) (Independent Newspaper): 101000 Moscow, ul. Myasnitskaya 13; tel. (495) 645-54-28; e-mail info@ng.ru; internet www.ng.ru; f. 1990; 5 a week; regular supplements include *NG-Nauka* (NG-Science), *NG-Regiony* (NG-Regions), *NG-Politekonomiya* (NG-Political Economy), *NG-Dipkuryer* (NG-Diplomatic Courier); Gen. Man. and Editor-in-Chief KONSTANTIN REMCHUKOV; circ. 53,000 (2005).

Novaya Gazeta (New Newspaper): 101990 Moscow, Potapovskii per. 3; tel. and fax (495) 623-68-88; e-mail pr@novayagazeta.ru; internet www.novayagazeta.ru; f. 1993; weekly; Editor DMITRII A. MURATOV; circ. 60,437 (March 2010).

Novye Izvestiya (New News): 107076 Moscow, ul. Elektrozavodskaya 33; tel. (495) 783-06-36; fax (495) 783-06-37; e-mail webmaster@newizv.ru; internet www.newizv.ru; f. 2003 following the closure of the fmr *Novye Izvestiya* (f. 1997); daily; Editor-in-Chief VALERII YAKOV.

Parlamentskaya Gazeta (Parliamentary Newspaper): 125993 Moscow, ul. 1-ya Yamskogo Polya 28; tel. (495) 257-50-90; fax (495) 257-50-82; e-mail pg@pnp.ru; internet www.pnp.ru; f. 1998; 5 a week; organ of the Federalnoye Sobraniye; Editor-in-Chief ANDREI B. FEDOTKIN; circ. 50,000 (2005).

Polit.ru: 101000 Moscow, Krivokolennyi per. 10/6A; tel. (495) 624-80-09; e-mail edit@polit.ru; internet www.polit.ru; f. 1998; independent; online only; Editor-in-Chief ANDREI LEVKIN.

Pravda (Truth): 125993 Moscow, ul. Pravdy 24; tel. and fax (499) 257-11-08; e-mail pravda2@cnt.ru; internet www.gazeta-pravda.ru; f. 1912; fmrly organ of the Cen. Cttee of the CPSU; independent; communist; Editor-in-Chief VALENTIN S. SHURCHANOV; circ. 100,300 (2007).

Pravda.ru: Moscow, ul. Staraya Basmannaya 16/1 A; 105066 Moscow, POB 26; tel. (495) 287-41-69; fax (495) 287-41-69; e-mail home@pravda.ru; internet pravda.ru; f. 1999; online only, in Russian,

THE RUSSIAN FEDERATION

English and Portuguese; has no asscn with the newspaper *Pravda*; Dir-Gen. INNA S. NOVIKOVA.

Rossiiskaya Gazeta (Russian Newspaper): 125993 Moscow, ul. Pravdy 24, POB 40; tel. (499) 257-56-50; fax (495) 973-22-56; e-mail office@rg.ru; internet www.rg.ru; f. 1990; organ of the Russian Govt; 6 a week; Gen. Man. ALEKSANDR N. GORBENKO; Editor-in-Chief VLADISLAV A. FRONIN; circ. 373,820 (2004).

Rossiiskiye Vesti (Russian News): 105086 Moscow, ul. Bakuninskaya 74–76; tel. and fax (495) 641-04-57; e-mail rosvesty@yandex.ru; internet www.rosvesty.ru; f. 1991; weekly; Editor-in-Chief MIKHAIL PALIEVSKY; circ. 2,500 (2009).

Russkii Zhurnal (Russian Journal): 125009 Moscow, per. M. Gnezdnikovskii 9/8/3A; tel. and fax (495) 745-22-25; e-mail russ@russ.ru; internet www.russ.ru; f. 1997; online only; culture, politics, society; Editor-in-Chief and Publr GLEB PAVLOVSKII.

Selskaya Zhizn (Country Life): 125993 Moscow, ul. Pravdy 24; tel. (495) 257-51-51; fax (495) 257-58-39; e-mail sg@sgazeta.ru; internet www.sgazeta.ru; f. 1918 as *Bednota* (Poverty), present name adopted in 1960; 2 a week; fmrly organ of the Cen. Cttee of the CPSU; independent; Editor-in-Chief and Gen. Man. SHAMUN M. KAGERMANOV; circ. 94,500.

Tribuna (Tribune): 127015 Moscow, Bumazhnii proyezd 14/1; tel. (499) 257-59-13; fax (499) 257-07-04; e-mail tribuna@tribuna.ru; internet www.tribuna.ru; f. 1969; national industrial daily; Editor-in-Chief OLEG KUZIN; circ. 57,500 (2010).

Trud (Labour): 125993 Moscow, ul. Pravdy 24/5; tel. (495) 735-44-46; e-mail letter@trud.ru; internet www.trud.ru; f. 1921; 5 a week; Editor-in-Chief VLADISLAV VDOVIN.

Vechernyaya Moskva (Evening Moscow): 123995 Moscow, ul. 1905 Goda 7, POB 5/22; tel. (499) 259-81-87; fax (499) 259-55-50; e-mail post@vm.ru; internet www.vm.ru; f. 1923; Chair. VLADIMIR V. ZUBKOV.

Vedomosti (Gazette): 127018 Moscow, ul. Polkovaya 3/1; tel. (495) 956-34-58; fax (495) 956-07-16; e-mail lys@vedomosti.ru; internet www.vedomosti.ru; f. 1999; independent business newspaper, publ. jointly with the *Financial Times* (United Kingdom) and *The Wall Street Journal* (USA); Editor-in-Chief LYSOVA TATIANA.

Vremya Novosti (News Time): 115326 Moscow, ul. Pyatnitskaya 25; tel. (495) 231-18-77; e-mail info@vremya.ru; internet www.vremya.ru; f. 2000; Editor-in-Chief VLADIMIR S. GUREVICH.

Zhizn (Life): 125212 Moscow, ul. Vyborgskaya 16/1; tel. (495) 510-29-84; fax (495) 510-29-81; e-mail info@zhizn.ru; internet www.zhizn.ru; weekly; Editor-in-Chief RUSLAN SAGAYEV; circ. 2.2m. within Russia (2007).

St Petersburg

Novosti Peterburga (Petersburg News): 197101 St Petersburg, ul. B. Monetnaya 16; tel. (812) 313-82-26; e-mail info@novostispb.ru; internet www.novostispb.ru; f. 1997; independent; Editor-in-Chief BORIS SUDAKOV.

Peterburgskii Chas Pik (Petersburg Rush Hour): 191040 St Petersburg, Nevskii pr. 81; tel. (812) 579-25-65; fax (812) 579-19-12; e-mail nabor@chaspik.spb.ru; internet www.chaspik.spb.ru; f. 1988; weekly; owned by Gazprom-Mediya; Editor-in-Chief LARISA AFONINA; circ. 30,000 (2010).

Sankt-Peterburgskiye Vedomosti (St Petersburg Gazette): 191025 St Petersburg, ul. Marata 25; tel. (812) 325-31-00; fax (812) 764-48-40; e-mail post@spbvedomosti.ru; internet www.spbvedomosti.ru; f. 1991 as revival of 1728–1917 title; Editor-in-Chief and Gen. Man. SERGEI A. SLOBODSKOI.

Smena (The Rising Generation): 191119 St Petersburg, ul. Marata 69; tel. (812) 315-04-76; fax (812) 315-03-53; e-mail info@smena.ru; internet www.smena.ru; f. 1919; 6 a week; controlled by Sistema Mass-Mediya; Editor-in-Chief LEONID DAVYDOV; circ. 80,000 (2002).

The St Petersburg Times: 190000 St Petersburg, Isaakevskaya pl. 4; tel. and fax (812) 325-60-80; e-mail letters@sptimes.ru; internet www.sptimes.ru; f. 1993; 2 a week; in English; independent; Editor TOBIN AUBER.

Vechernii Peterburg (Evening Petersburg): 197101 St Petersburg, ul. Mira 34; tel. (812) 334-35-64; fax (812) 314-31-05; e-mail gazeta@vspb.spb.ru; internet vppress.ru; f. 1917; Editor-in-Chief KONSTANTIN V. MIKOV.

REGIONAL NEWSPAPERS

Chelyabinskii Rabochii (The Chelyabinsk Worker): 454091 Chelyabinsk, ul. Pushkina 12; tel. and fax (351) 263-26-22; e-mail common@chelrabochy.ru; internet www.chelrabochy.ru; f. 1908; 5 a week; Editor-in-Chief BORIS N. KIRSHIN; circ. 23,000 (2010).

Dagestanskaya Pravda (The Dagestan Truth): 367018 Dagestan, Makhachkala, pr. Petra I 61; tel. (8722) 65-00-10; fax (8722) 65-00-12; e-mail pravda@dagpravda.ru; internet www.dagpravda.ru; f. 1918; daily; Editor-in-Chief RADZHAB M. IDRISOV; circ. 22,000 (2003).

Kaliningradskaya Pravda (The Kaliningrad Truth): 236000 Kaliningrad, ul. Karla Marksa 18; tel. (4012) 21-14-87; fax (4012) 21-77-33; e-mail info@kaliningradka.ru; internet www.kaliningradka.ru; f. 1946; 5 a week; Editor-in-Chief DAMIR BATYRSHIN; circ. 13,066 (July 2010).

Kommuna (The Commune): 394036 Voronezh, ul. Komissarzhevskoi 4A; tel. and fax (4732) 51-24-87; e-mail mail@kommuna.ru; internet www.communa.ru; f. 1917; social-political; 4 a week; Editor-in-Chief VIKTOR G. RUDENKO; circ. 17,300 (June 2009).

Krasnoyarskii Rabochii (The Krasnoyarsk Worker): 660075 Krasnoyarsk, ul. Respubliki 51; tel. and fax (391) 211-77-17; e-mail redaktor@krasrab.krsn.ru; internet www.krasrab.com; f. 1905; 5 a week; Editor-in-Chief VLADIMIR YE. PAVLOVSKII; circ. 11,000 (2010).

Krasnyi Sever (The Red North): 160001 Vologda, ul. Maltseva 52/4; tel. (8202) 72-00-33; fax (8202) 72-04-61; e-mail reklama@krassever.ru; internet www.krassever.ru; f. 1917; 3 a week; publishes official documentation on behalf of the Governor and Legislative Assembly of Vologda Oblast on Tuesdays and Saturdays, and a full-colour edn, with various supplements, on Thursdays covering politics, culture, sport, etc.; daily; Editor-in-Chief NADEZHDA A. KUZMINSKAYA; circ. 42,100 (Thursdays, 2010).

Kubanskiye Novosti (Kuban News): 350000 Krasnodar, ul. Pashkovskaya 2; tel. (861) 259-30-49; fax (861) 259-60-27; e-mail redaktor@kubnews.ru; internet www.kubnews.ru; f. 1991; organ of the Governor and Legislative Assembly of Krasnodar Krai; 4 a week; Editor-in-Chief YEVGENII V. KHOMUTOV; circ. 55,000 (2010).

Mestnoye Vremya (Local Time): 614000 Perm, ul. Lenina 38/307; tel. (342) 200-01-53; fax (342) 200-01-57; e-mail vremyan@permv.ru; internet www.permv.ru; f. 1992; socio-political, weekly; Editor-in-Chief YELENA V. TRETYAKOVA; circ. 250,000 (2010).

Nizhegorodksaya Pravda (The Nizhnii Novgorod Truth): 603006 Nizhnii Novgorod, ul. Varvarskaya 32, POB 417; tel. (831) 419-63-11; internet www.pravda-nn.ru; f. 1918; organ of the Governor and Legislative Assembly of Nizhnii Novgorod Oblast; 3 a week; Editor-in-Chief TATYANA V. METELKINA; circ. 17,000 (2007).

Novaya Sibir (Molodaya Sibir—Novaya Sibir) (New Siberia—A Young Siberia Is A New Siberia): 630048 Novosibirsk, ul. N. Danchenko 104; tel. (383) 335-60-06; e-mail newsib2005@yandex.ru; internet www.newsib.net; f. 1993; socio-political; weekly; Editor-in-Chief VYACHESLAV DOSYCHEV.

Oblastnaya Gazeta (Regional Newspaper): 620004 Sverdlovsk obl., Yekaterinburg, ul. Malysheva 101; tel. (343) 355-29-46; e-mail reklama@oblgazeta.ru; internet www.oblgazeta.ru; f. 1990; 5 a week; organ of the Governor and Legislative Assembly of Sverdlovsk Oblast; circ. 71,000 (2010).

Pravda Severa (Truth of the North): 163002 Archangel, Novgorodskii pr. 32/507; tel. (8182) 20-37-98; fax (8182) 29-15-33; e-mail info@pravdasevera.ru; internet www.pravdasevera.ru; f. 1917; 3 a week; Editor SVETLANA N. LOICHENKO; circ. 8,000 (Tuesdays and Saturdays, 2010), 20,050 (Wednesdays, 2010).

Respublika Tatarstan (Republic of Tatarstan): 420066 Tatarstan, Kazan, ul. Dekabristov 2, POB 41; tel. (843) 562-11-02; fax (843) 292-37-00; e-mail info@rt-online.ru; internet www.rt-online.ru; f. 1917; organ of the Government and Parliament of the Republic of Tatarstan; 5 a week; Editor-in-Chief ALEKSANDR N. LATYSHEV; circ. 31,000 (2007).

Severnyi Kavkaz (The North Caucasus): 360000 Kabardino-Balkar Rep., Nalchik, ul. Molodogvardeiskaya 17; tel. (8662) 77-49-50; internet www.sknews.ru; f. 1990; independent; news coverage of various regions of the North Caucasus, and also the countries of the South Caucasus, and Turkey, Iran and Lebanon; weekly; Editor-in-Chief ALI M. KAZIKHANOV.

Sloboda: 300026 Tula, pr. Lenina 116, 1st Floor; tel. (4872) 35-14-51; fax (4872) 23-55-99; e-mail info@myslo.ru; internet www.tula.rodgor.ru; f. 1994; weekly; Editor-in-Chief TATYANA ALEKSEEVA; circ. 102,000 (2002).

Stavropolskaya Pravda (The Stavropol Truth): 355035 Stavropol, ul. Spartaka 8; tel. (8652) 94-05-09; fax (8652) 94-17-08; e-mail gazeta@stapravda.ru; internet www.stapravda.ru; f. 1917; 5 a week; Editor-in-Chief MIKHAIL L. TSYBULKO; circ. 20,135 (Jan. 2007).

Tyumenskaya Pravda (The Tyumen Truth): 625002 Tyumen, ul. Osipenko 81; tel. (3452) 22-74-12; fax (3452) 22-73-93; e-mail redaktortp@yandex.ru; internet pravda.port72.ru; f. 1963; social-political; 5 a week; Editor-in-Chief LARISA N. VOKHMINA.

Vladivostok: 690014 Maritime Krai, Vladivostok, ul. Narodnyi pr. 13, POB 35–47; tel. (4232) 41-56-00; fax (4232) 41-56-15; e-mail salova@vladnews.ru; internet vladnews.ru; f. 1992; daily; Editor-in-Chief YELENA V. VLADIMIROVNA.

THE RUSSIAN FEDERATION

PRINCIPAL PERIODICALS

Agriculture, Forestry, etc.

Ekologiya i Promlyshlennost Rossii (The Ecology and Industry of Russia): 119049 Moscow, Leninskii pr. 4; tel. (495) 913-80-94; e-mail info@kalvis.ru; internet www.ecip-kalvis.ru; f. 1996; monthly; environmental protection; Editor-in-Chief Prof. Dr V. D. KALNER.

Zashchita i Karantin Rastenii (Plant Protection and Quarantine): 107140 Moscow, Krasnoselskii per. 21; tel. and fax (495) 607-39-30; e-mail fitopress@ropnet.ru; internet www.z-i-k-r.ru; f. 1932; monthly; Editor-in-Chief YURII N. NEIPERT; circ. 5,000 (2009).

For Children

Koster (Campfire): 193024 St Petersburg, ul. Mytninskaya 1/20; tel. (812) 274-15-72; fax (812) 274-46-26; e-mail root@kostyor.spb.org; internet www.kostyor.ru; f. 1936; monthly; journal of the International Union of Children's Organizations (UPO-FCO); fiction, poetry, sport, reports and popular science; for ages 10–14 years; Editor-in-Chief N. B. KHARLAMPIYEV; circ. 7,500 (2000).

Murzilka: 127015 Moscow, ul. Novodmitrovskaya 5A; tel. and fax (495) 685-18-81; e-mail red-murzilka@yandex.ru; internet www.murzilka.org; f. 1924; monthly; illustrated; for first grades of school; Editor TATYANA ANDROSENKO; circ. 85,000 (2010).

Pionerskaya Pravda (Pioneers' Truth): 127994 Moscow, ul. Sushchevskaya 21; tel. and fax (495) 787-62-43; e-mail info@pionerka.ru; internet www.pionerka.ru; f. 1925; 4 a week; Editor MIKHAIL N. BARANNIKOV.

Yunyi Naturalist (Young Naturalist): 125015 Moscow, ul. Novodmitrovskaya 5A; tel. (495) 685-39-31; e-mail unnat1@mail.ru; internet www.unnaturalist.ru; f. 1928; monthly; popular science for children of fourth–10th grades, who are interested in biology; Editor L. V. SAMSONOVA.

Yunyi Tekhnik (Young Technician): 125015 Moscow, ul. Novodmitrovskaya 5A; tel. (495) 685-44-80; fax (495) 787-35-58; e-mail yut.magazine@gmail.com; internet www.utechnik.org; f. 1956; monthly; popular science for children and youth; Chief Editor ALEKSANDR A. FIN.

Culture and Arts

Ex Libris-NG: 113935 Moscow, ul. Myasnitskaya 13; tel. (495) 928-48-50; fax (495) 975-23-46; e-mail exlibris@ng.ru; internet exlibris.ng.ru; weekly; literature; Editor-in-Chief IGOR ZOTOV.

Iskusstvo Kino (The Art of the Cinema): 125319 Moscow, ul. Arbat 35; tel. (499) 248-28-22; fax (499) 241-08-52; e-mail filmfilm@yandex.ru; internet www.kinoart.ru; f. 1931; monthly; journal of the Russian Film-makers' Union; Editor DANIIL B. DONDUREI; circ. 5,000 (2004).

Knizhnoye Obozreniye (Literary Review): 115054 Moscow, ul. Pyatnitskaya 71/5/2/9; tel. and fax (495) 955-79-70; e-mail all@knigoboz.ru; internet www.knigoboz.ru; f. 1966; weekly; summaries of newly published books; Editor-in-Chief ALEKSANDR M. NABOKOV; circ. 10,500 (2003).

Kultura (Culture): 101484 Moscow, ul. Novoslobodskaya 73; tel. (495) 685-06-40; fax (496) 685-31-50; e-mail kultura@dol.ru; internet www.kulturagz.ru; f. 1929; controlled by Sistema Mass-Mediya; weekly; Editor-in-Chief YURII I. BELYAVSKII; circ. 30,000 (2008).

Literaturnaya Gazeta (Literary Newspaper): 109028 Moscow, Khokhlovskii per. 10/6; tel. and fax (499) 788-02-10; e-mail litgazeta@lgz.ru; internet www.lgz.ru; f. 1831; publ. restored 1929; weekly; literature, politics, society; controlled by Sistema Mass-Mediya; Editor-in-Chief YU. M. POLYAKOV.

Literaturnaya Rossiya (Literary Russia): 103051 Moscow, Tsvetnoi bulv. 32/3; tel. (495) 694-03-65; fax (495) 694-50-10; e-mail litrossia@litrossia.ru; internet www.litrossia.ru; f. 1958; weekly; essays, verse, literary criticism; Editor VYACHESLAV OGRYZKO; circ. 10,000 (2010).

Nash Sovremennik (Our Contemporary): 127051 Moscow, Tsvetnoi bulv. 32/2; tel. (495) 621-48-71; fax (495) 200-24-12; e-mail n-sovrem@yandex.ru; internet www.nash-sovremennik.ru; f. 1956; monthly; publ. by the Union of Writers of Russia; contemporary prose and 'patriotic polemics'; Editor STANISLAV KUNAYEV; circ. 9,000 (2010).

Snob (Snob): 105064 Moscow, Nizhnii Susalnyi per. 5/19; tel. and fax (495) 785-65-85; e-mail snob@snob.ru; internet www.snob.ru; f. 2009; 10 a year; history, literature, culture, intended for élite international audience; Chief Editor VLADIMIR YAKOVLEV.

Znamya (Banner): 103001 Moscow, ul. B. Sadovaya 2/46; tel. (495) 299-52-38; e-mail info@znamlit.ru; internet magazines.russ.ru/znamia; f. 1931; monthly; independent; novels, poetry, essays; Editor-in-Chief SERGEI I. CHUPRININ; circ. 5,300 (2004).

Economics and Finance

Chelovek i Trud (Man and Labour): 105064 Moscow, Yakovoapostolskii per. 6/3; tel. and fax (495) 917-76-36; e-mail chelt@yandex.ru; internet www.chelt.ru; monthly; f. 1956 as *Sotsialisticheskii trud* (Socialist Labour); present name adopted 1992; employment issues, unemployment, social policy, pensions, personnel management; Editor-in-Chief M. A. BARINOVA; circ. 10,000 (2005).

Dengi (Money): 125080 Moscow, ul. Vrubelya 4/1; tel. (499) 943-97-71; fax (499) 943-97-28; e-mail dengi@kommersant.ru; internet www.kommersant.ru/money; weekly; publ. by the Kommersant Publishing House; Chief Editor SERGEI YAKOVLEV.

Ekonomika i Zhizn (Economics and Life): 125319 Moscow, ul. Chernyakhovskogo 16; tel. and fax (499) 152-68-65; e-mail eg@ekonomika.ru; internet www.eg-online.ru; f. 1918; weekly; fmrly *Ekonomicheskaya gazeta*; news and information about the economy and business; Editor TATYANA A. IVANOVA; circ. 150,000 (2005).

Ekspert (Expert): 125866 Moscow, ul. Pravdy 24, Novyi Gazetnyi kor., POB 33; tel. (495) 789-44-65; fax (495) 228-00-78; e-mail ask@expert.ru; internet www.expert.ru; f. 1995; weekly; business and economics; financial and share markets; policy and culture; regional edns: *Ekspert Severo-Zapad* (St Petersburg and North-Western Russia), *Ekspert Sibir* (Siberia), *Ekspert Ural* (Urals), *Ekspert Volga* (The Volga region), *Ekspert Yug* (Southern Russia), and edns for Kazakhstan and Ukraine; Editor-in-Chief VALERII FADEYEV.

Finansovaya Gazeta (Financial Newspaper): 101000 Moscow, ul. Tkatskaya 5D/3/202, POB 589; tel. and fax (499) 166-03-95; e-mail fingazeta@fingazeta.ru; internet www.fingazeta.ru; f. 1991; accounting, auditing, taxation and finance; official publ. of the Ministry of Finance (q.v.).

Finansy (Finance): 125009 Moscow, ul. Tverskaya 22B; tel. (495) 699-44-27; fax (495) 699-96-16; e-mail finance-journal@mail.ru; internet www.finance-journal.ru; f. 1926; monthly; theory and information on finance; compilation and execution of the state budget, insurance, lending, taxation, etc.; Editor YU. M. ARTEMOV; circ. 10,000 (2004).

Glavukh (Chief Accountant): 127015 Moscow, ul. Novodmitrovskaya 5A/8, POB 100; tel. (495) 788-53-16; fax (495) 788-53-17; e-mail glavred@glavbukh.ru; internet www.glavbukh.ru; f. 1994; taxation and accounting; Editor-in-Chief DMITRII A. VOLOSHIN; circ. 162,000.

Kompaniya (The Firm): 109544 Moscow, ul. B. Andronyevskaya 17; tel. (495) 745-84-10; e-mail ko@idr.ru; internet www.ko.ru; f. 1997; weekly; politics, economics, finance; Editor-in-Chief ALEKSANDR ZOTIKOV; circ. 63,400 (2010).

Rossiiskii Ekonomicheskii Zhurnal (Russian Economic Journal): 109542 Moscow, Ryazanskii pr. 99; tel. and fax (495) 377-25-56; internet www.e-rej.ru; f. 1958; monthly; economics; Editor A. YU. MELENTEV; circ. 6,100 (2004).

Voprosy Ekonomiki (Questions of Economics): 117218 Moscow, Nakhimovskii pr. 32; tel. and fax (499) 124-52-28; e-mail mail@vopreco.ru; internet www.vopreco.ru; f. 1929; monthly; journal of the Institute of Economics of the Russian Academy of Sciences; theoretical problems of economic devt, market relations, social aspects of transition to a market economy, international economics, etc.; Editor LEONID I. ABALKIN; circ. 5,300 (2009).

International Affairs

Ekho Planety (Echo of the Planet): 103860 Moscow, Tverskoi bulv. 12; tel. (499) 791-04-04; fax (499) 791-04-09; e-mail ekho@ekhoplanet.ru; internet www.ekhoplanet.ru; f. 1988; weekly; publ. by ITAR—TASS; international affairs, economic, social and cultural; Editor-in-Chief VALENTIN VASILETS.

Mezhdunarodnaya Zhizn (International Life): 105064 Moscow, Gorokhovskii per. 14; tel. (499) 265-37-81; fax (499) 265-37-71; e-mail journal@interaffairs.ru; internet www.interaffairs.ru; f. 1954; monthly; Russian and English; publ. by the Pressa Publishing House; foreign policy and diplomacy; Editor-in-Chief O. G. OGANEYAN; circ. 70,000.

Novoye Vremya—The New Times: 125009 Moscow, Tverskoi bulv. 14/1; tel. (495) 648-07-60; fax (495) 648-07-61; e-mail info@newtimes.ru; internet www.newtimes.ru; f. 1943; weekly; foreign and Russian affairs; Editor-in-Chief IRENA LESNEVSKAYA.

Russkii Reporter (Russian Reporter): 125866 Moscow, Bumazhnyi proyezd 14/1; tel. (495) 609-66-74; e-mail reporter@expert.ru; internet www.rusrep.ru; f. 2007; monthly; domestic and international affairs and culture; Chief Editor VITALII LEIBIN.

Leisure, Sport and General

Afisha (Poster): 103009 Moscow, B. Gnezdnikovskii per. 7/28/1; tel. (495) 785-17-00; fax (495) 785-12-00; e-mail info@afisha.ru; internet www.afisha.ru; f. 1999; every 2 weeks; listings and reviews of events; 3 edns, for Moscow, St Petersburg, and the rest of Russia; Chief Editor ILYA KRASILSHIK.

THE RUSSIAN FEDERATION

Bolshoi Gorod (Big City): 125009 Moscow, Bersenevskaya nab. 2/1; tel. (495) 744-01-77; fax (495) 785-17-01; e-mail info@bg.ru; internet www.bg.ru; f. 2001; every 2 weeks; Moscow and St Petersburg edns; culture, travel, technology; Chief Editor FILIPP DZYADKO.

Moya Lyubimaya Dacha (My Favourite Cottage): 105082 Moscow, ul. Bakuninskaya 71/10, POB 5; tel. (495) 775-14-35; fax (495) 775-14-36; internet www.ldacha.ru; publ. by Edipress-Konliga; monthly; gardening, landscape designing; Chief Editor YELENA FESTA.

Ogonek (Beacon): c/o Kommersant, 125080 Moscow, ul. Vrubelya 4 D; tel. (495) 960-31-18; fax (499) 973-14-30; e-mail ogoniok@kommersant.ru; internet www.kommersant.ru/ogoniok; f. 1899; weekly; politics, popular science, economics, literature; Editor VIKTOR LOSHAK; circ. 69,000 (2007).

Rossiiskaya Okhotnichya Gazeta (Russian Hunters' Magazine): 123995 Moscow, ul. 1905 Goda 7; tel. (495) 250-72-72; e-mail rog@mk.ru; internet www.gusevhunting.ru; weekly; hunting, shooting, fishing; Editor-in-Chief PAVEL GUSEV.

Russkii Vestnik (Russian Herald): 115035 Moscow, Chernigovskii per. 19/13; tel. (495) 953-70-10; fax (495) 953-68-36; e-mail rusvest@rv.ru; internet www.rv.ru; f. 1991; socio-political; every 2 weeks; Editor-in-Chief ALEKSEI SENIN.

Sovetskii Sport (Soviet Sport): 125993 Moscow, Staryi Petrovsko-Razumovskii proyezd 1/23/1; tel. (495) 637-64-33; fax (495) 637-64-24; e-mail info@sovietsport.ru; internet www.sovsport.ru; f. 1924; weekly; Editor-in-Chief IGOR KOTS.

Speed-Info: 125284 Moscow, POB 42; tel. (495) 255-02-99; fax (495) 252-09-20; e-mail s-info@si.ru; internet www.s-info.ru; f. 1991; two a month; popular; Editor-in-Chief OLGA BELAN; Gen. Dir IGOR SAZONOV; circ. 850,000 (2008).

Sport Ekspress (Sport Express): 123056 Moscow, ul. Krasina 27/2; tel. (495) 254-47-87; fax (495) 733-93-08; e-mail sport@sport-express.ru; internet www.sport-express.ru; f. 1991; daily; sport; Editor-in-Chief VLADIMIR TITORENKO; circ. in Moscow and St Petersburg 190,000 (2004).

Vokrug Sveta (Around the World): 125362 Moscow, ul. Mescheriakova 5/1; tel. (495) 490-56-55; fax (495) 491-18-28; e-mail vokrugsveta@vokrugsveta.ru; internet www.vokrugsveta.ru; f. 1861; monthly; geographical, travel and adventure; illustrated; Chief Editor YELENA KNYAZEVA (acting).

History, Politics and Military Affairs

Nezavisimoye Voyennoye Obozreniye (Independent Military Review): 101000 Moscow, ul. Myasnitskaya 13/10; tel. (495) 645-54-28; e-mail nvo@ng.ru; internet nvo.ng.ru; f. 1990; Editor KONSTANTIN REMCHUKOV; circ. 20,140 (2004).

Rodina (Motherland): 127025 Moscow, ul. Novyi Arbat 19; tel. (495) 203-75-98; fax (495) 203-47-45; e-mail istrodina@mail.ru; internet www.istrodina.com; f. 1989 as revival of 1879–1917 publication; monthly; publ. by Administration of the President of the Russian Federation and Government of the Russian Federation; popular historical; supplement *Istochnik* (Source), every 2 months, documents state archives; Chief Editor YURII BORISENOK; circ. 20,000 (2003).

Rodnaya Gazeta (Native Gazette): 119121 Moscow, Smolenskii bulv. 11/2; tel. and fax (499) 248-42-36; e-mail mail@rodgaz.ru; internet www.rodgaz.ru; f. 2003; weekly; politics, culture, nationalist, left-wing; Dir-Gen. and Chief Editor KONSTANTIN PATRIN.

Rossiiskaya Federatsiya Segodnya (The Russian Federation Today): 127994 Moscow, ul. M. Dmitrovka 3/10; tel. (495) 933-54-79; fax (495) 933-54-74; e-mail rfs@russia-today.ru; internet www.russia-today.ru; f. 1994; journal of the Gosudarstvennaya Duma; Editor YURII A. KHRENOV.

Rossiya v Globalnoi Politike/ Russia in Global Affairs: 125009 Moscow, Zubovskii bulv. 4; tel. (495) 980-73-53; fax (495) 937-76-11; e-mail info@globalaffairs.ru; internet www.globalaffairs.ru; f. 2002; co-founded by the Russian Union of Industrialists and Entrepreneurs, the Council for Foreign and Defence Politics and the newspaper *Izvestiya*, in collaboration with the US journal, *Foreign Affairs*; 6 a year (Russian); 4 a year (English); online edns in Czech and Polish; Chair. of Editorial Bd SERGEI A. KARAGANOV; Editor-in-Chief FEDOR A. LUKYANOV.

Russia Profile: 119021 Moscow, Zubovskii bulv. 4; tel. (495) 981-64-86; fax (495) 201-30-71; e-mail info@russiaprofile.org; internet www.russiaprofile.org; f. 1966; monthly; in English; publ. by Independent Media for RIA-Novosti in association with the International Relations and Security Network (Zurich, Switzerland) and the Center for Defense Information (Washington, DC, USA); Editor ANDREI ZOLOTOV, Jr.

Shchit i Mech (Shield and Sword): 127434 Moscow, Ivanovskii pr. 18; tel. (495) 976-66-44; fax (495) 619-80-90; e-mail gazeta@simech.ru; internet www.simech.ru; f. 1989; weekly; military, security, geopolitical concerns; publ. by the Ministry of Internal Affairs; Editor-in-Chief VALERII KULIK; circ. 50,000 (2004).

Vlast (Power): 125080 Moscow, ul. Vrubelya 4/1; tel. (499) 195-96-36; fax (499) 943-97-28; e-mail vlast@kommersant.ru; internet www.kommersant.ru/k-vlast; f. 1997; weekly; Chief Editor MAKSIM KOVALSKII.

Yezhenedelnyi Zhurnal (Weekly Magazine): 129110 Moscow, Pereyaslavskii per. 4; tel. (495) 785-82-50; fax (495) 785-82-51; e-mail info@ej.ru; internet www.ej.ru; f. 2001; Editor-in-Chief ALEKSANDR RYKLIN.

Zavtra (Tomorrow): 119146 Moscow, Frunzenskaya nab. 18/60; tel. (495) 726-54-83; e-mail zavtra@zavtra.ru; internet www.zavtra.ru; extreme left, nationalist; Editor-in-Chief ALEKSANDR A. PROGANOV; circ. 100,000.

Popular Scientific

Meditsinskaya Gazeta (Medical Gazette): 129090 Moscow, B. Sukharevskaya pl. 1/2; tel. (495) 608-86-95; fax (495) 208-69-80; e-mail mggazeta@post.ru; internet www.mgzt.ru; f. 1938; 2 a week; professional international periodical; Editor ANDREI POLTORAK.

Nauka i Zhizn (Science and Life): 101990 Moscow, ul. Myasnitskaya 24; tel. (495) 624-18-35; fax (495) 625-05-90; e-mail mail@nkj.ru; internet www.nkj.ru; f. 1890, resumed 1934; monthly; recent developments in all branches of science and technology; Editor-in-Chief YELENA LOZOVSKAYA; circ. 44,000 (2009).

PC Week: 109047 Moscow, ul. Marksistskaya 34/10; tel. (495) 974-22-60; fax (495) 974-22-63; e-mail editorial@pcweek.ru; internet www.pcweek.ru; f. 1995; 48 a year; Editor-in-Chief ALEKSEI MAKSIMOV.

Tekhnika-Molodezhi (Engineering Is For Youth): 127055 Moscow, ul. Lesnaya 39/307; tel. ((499) 972-63-11; fax (495) 628-34-79; e-mail real@tm-magazin.ru; internet www.tm-magazin.ru; f. 1933; monthly; engineering and science; Editor A. N. PEREVOZCHIKOV.

Vestnik Svyazi (Herald of Communications): 101000 Moscow, Krivokolennyi per. 14/1; tel. (495) 625-42-57; fax (495) 621-27-97; e-mail vs@vestnik-sviazy.ru; internet www.vestnik-sviazy.ru; f. 1917; monthly; telecommunications; Editor E. B. KONSTANTINOV.

Zdorovye (Health): 127994 Moscow, Bumazhnyi proyezd 14/1; tel. and fax (499) 257-32-51; e-mail zdorovie@zdr.ru; internet www.zdr.ru; f. 1955; monthly; Editor TATYANA YEFIMOVA; circ. 170,000 (2006).

Religion

Foma (Thomas): 123242 Moscow, ul. Druzhinnikovskaya 15, POB 46; tel. (495) 775-73-61; e-mail info@foma.ru; internet www.foma.ru; f. 1998; Orthodox and the relation of Orthodoxy to social and cultural life; monthly; Chief Editor VLADIMIR R. LEGOIDA; circ. 30,000.

Mezhdunarodnaya Yevreyskaya Gazeta (International Jewish Newspaper): 107005 Moscow, Pleteshkovskii per. 3A; tel. and fax (495) 265-08-69; e-mail info@jig.ru; internet www.jig.ru; f. 1989; weekly; Editor YELENA SATAROVA; circ. 15,000 (2002).

NG-Religii (The Independent-Religions): 101000 Moscow, ul. Myasnitskaya 13; tel. (495) 923-42-40; fax (495) 921-58-47; e-mail ngr@ng.ru; internet religion.ng.ru; f. 1997; analysis of religious affairs and their domestic and global social and political implications; 2 a month; Editor-in-Chief MAKSIM SHEVCHENKO.

Tserkovnyi Vestnik (Church Herald): 119435 Moscow, ul. Pogodinskaya 20/2; tel. and fax (495) 246-01-65; e-mail info03@rop.ru; internet www.e-vestnik.ru; f. 1989; 24 a year; organ of the Russian Orthodox Church (Moscow Patriarchate); Editor-in-Chief Protohierarch VLADIMIR SILOVYEV; circ. 20,000 (2007).

Yevreiskoye Slovo (The Jewish Word): 127018 Moscow, 2-i Vysheslavtsev per. 5A; tel. (495) 710-99-48; e-mail redaktor@e-slovo.ru; internet www.e-slovo.ru; f. 2000; Editor-in-Chief VLADIMIR DYNKIN.

Zhurnal Moskovskoi Patriarkhii (Journal of the Moscow Patriarchate): 119435 Moscow, ul. Pogodinskaya 20/2; tel. (499) 246-98-48; fax (499) (499) 246-01-65; e-mail info03@rop.ru; internet www.rop.ru; f. 1934; monthly; official publication of the Russian Orthodox Church (Moscow Patriarchate); Editor Archpriest VLADIMIR SILOVYEV.

Women's Interest

Cosmopolitan Beauty: 127018 Moscow, ul. Polkovaya 3/1; tel. (495) 232-32-00; fax (495) 232-17-61; internet www.cosmobeauty.ru; f. 2003; quarterly; health and beauty; Editor-in-Chief NATALIYA SHERSTYUK; circ. 195,000.

Domashnii Ochag (The Domestic Hearth): 127018 Moscow, ul. Polkovaya 3D/1; tel. (495) 232-32-00; e-mail goodhouse@imedia.ru; internet www.goodhouse.ru; fashion; Editor-in-Chief MARIYA VINOGRADOVA.

Domovoi (House-Sprite): 109544 Moscow, ul. B. Andronyevskaya 17; tel. (495) 745-84-43; fax (495) 678-52-05; e-mail domovoy@idr.ru; internet www.domovoy.ru; f. 1993; monthly; Chief Editor ANASTASIYA RAKHLINA; circ. 105,000.

Elle: 115162 Moscow, ul. Shabolovka 31B; tel. (495) 891-39-10; fax (495) 981-39-11; e-mail editor@elle.ru; internet www.elle.ru; f. 1996; monthly; fashion; Editor-in-Chief YELENA SOTNIKOVA.

Krestyanka (Peasant Woman): 127994 Moscow, ul. B. Andronyevskaya 17; tel. (495) 257-39-39; fax (495) 257-39-63; e-mail mail@krestyanka.ru; f. 1922; monthly; popular; Chief Editor TAMARA VIRKUNEN; circ. 85,000 (2004).

NEWS AGENCIES

ANP—Agentstvo novostei i prognozy (News and Forecasting Agency): 103009 Moscow, Kalashnyi per. 10/2; tel. (495) 782-33-71; fax (495) 153-57-45; e-mail aninons@online.ru; f. 2001 on basis of ANI News and Information Agency (f. 1991); Editor-in-Chief ALEKSEI SHCHAVELEV.

Interfax: 127006 Moscow, ul. 1-aya Tverskaya-Yamskaya 2; tel. (495) 250-98-40; fax (495) 250-97-27; e-mail info@interfax.ru; internet www.interfax.ru; f. 1989; independent information agency; Chief Exec. MIKHAIL KOMISSAR.

ITAR—TASS (Information Telegraphic Agency of Russia—Telegraphic Agency of the Sovereign Countries): 125993 Moscow, Tverskoi bulv. 10/12; tel. (495) 202-29-81; fax (495) 202-54-74; e-mail worldmarket@itar-tass.com; internet www.itar-tass.com; f. 1904 as St Petersburg Telegraph Agency, renamed as TASS (Telegraph Agency of the Soviet Union) in 1925; present name adopted 1992; state information agency; 74 bureaux in Russia and the states of the former USSR, 65 foreign bureaux outside the former USSR; Dir-Gen. VITALII N. IGNATENKO.

Prima Human Rights News Agency: 111399 Moscow, POB 5; tel. and fax (495) 455-30-11; e-mail prima@prima-news.ru; internet www.prima-news.ru; f. 2000; Editor-in-Chief ALEKSANDR PODRABINEK.

RIA—Novosti (Russian Information Agency—News): 119021 Moscow, Zubovskii bulv. 4; tel. (495) 637-24-24; fax (495) 201-45-45; e-mail marketing@rian.ru; internet www.rian.ru; f. 1961 as Agenstvo Pechati 'Novosti' (APN); present name adopted 1991; network covers over 45 countries; provider of Russian news features and photographs; Dir-Gen. NIKOLAI BIRYUKOV; Editor-in-Chief SVETLANA MIRONYUK.

RosBalt Information Agency: 190000 St Petersburg, Konnogvardeiskii bulv. 7; tel. (812) 320-50-30; fax (812) 320-50-31; e-mail rosbalt@rosbalt.ru; internet www.rosbalt.ru; news coverage of European Russia and other countries in northern Europe; Chair. NATALIYA CHERKESOVA.

Rossiiskoye Informatsionnoye Agentstvo 'Oreanda' (RIA 'Oreanda'): 117342 Moscow, POB 21; tel. (495) 330-98-50; fax (495) 23-04-39; e-mail info@oreanda.ru; internet www.oreanda.ru; f. 1994.

PRESS ASSOCIATIONS

Russian Guild of Publishers of Periodical Press: 125047 Moscow, ul. Lesnaya 20/6-211; tel. and fax (495) 978-41-89.

Union of Journalists of Russia: 119021 Moscow, Zubovskii bulv. 4; tel. (495) 201-51-01; fax (495) 201-35-47; f. 1991; Sec.-Gen. IGOR YAKOVENKO.

Publishers

Ad Marginem-Ad Patres: 105082 Moscow, Perevedenovskii per. 18; tel. and fax (495) 988-15-32; e-mail info@admarginem.ru; internet admarginem.ru; f. 1993; fiction, philosophy, artistic and literary criticism; Dir ALEKSANDR IVANOV.

AST: 129085 Moscow, Zvezdnyi bulv. 21; tel. (495) 215-01-01; fax (495) 215-51-10; e-mail astpub@aha.ru; internet www.ast.ru; original and translated fiction and non-fiction, children's and schoolbooks.

Azbuka (Alphabet): 191014 St Petersburg, ul. Chekhova 9, POB 192; tel. (812) 327-04-55; fax (812) 327-01-60; e-mail assistant@azbooka.spb.ru; internet www.azbooka.ru; f. 1995; literary fiction, including translations; Dir-Gen. GENNADII MOLCHANOV.

Bolshaya Rossiiskaya Entsiklopediya (The Great Russian Encyclopedia): 109028 Moscow, Pokrovskii bulv. 8; tel. (495) 917-90-00; fax (495) 916-01-22; e-mail secretar@greatbook.ru; internet www.greatbook.ru; f. 1925; encyclopedias and reference; Dir-Gen. NIKOLAI S. ARTEMOV.

Drofa: 127018 Moscow, ul. Sushchevskii Val 49; tel. (495) 795-05-50; fax (495) 795-05-44; e-mail info@drofa.ru; internet www.drofa.ru; f. 1991; school textbooks, children's fiction; Dir-Gen. ALEKSANDR F. KISELEV.

Ekonomika (Economy): 123955 Moscow, Berezhkovskaya nab. 6; tel. (499) 240-58-18; fax (499) 240-48-178; e-mail info@economizdat.ru; internet www.economizdat.ru; f. 1963; various aspects of economics, management and marketing; Dir YELIZABETA V. POLIYEVKTOVA.

Eksmo: 127299 Moscow, ul. K. Tsetkina 18/5; tel. and fax (495) 411-68-86; e-mail info@eksmo.ru; internet www.eksmo.ru; f. 1991; fiction; Gen. Dir OLEG YE. NOVIKOV.

Finansy i Statistika (Finance and Statistics): 101000 Moscow, ul. Pokrovka 7; tel. (495) 625-47-08; fax (495) 625-09-57; e-mail mail@finstat.ru; internet www.finstat.ru; f. 1924; education, economics, tourism, finance, statistics, banking, insurance, accounting, computer science; Dir Dr ALEVTINA N. ZVONOVA.

Forum: 101000 Moscow, Kolpachnyi per. 9A; tel. and fax (495) 625-52-43; e-mail mail@forum-books.ru; internet www.forum-books.ru; f. 2001; general and professional educational textbooks; Gen. Man. SVETLANA P. SILVANOVICH.

Galart: 125319 Moscow, ul. Chernyakhovskogo 4; tel. and fax (495) 151-25-02; e-mail galart@m9com.ru; internet www.galart-moscow.ru; f. 1969; fmrly Sovetskii Khudozhnik (Soviet Artist); art reproduction, art history and criticism; Gen. Dir A. D. SARABYANOV.

INFRA-M: 127282 Moscow, ul. Polyarnara 31B; tel. and fax (495) 363-42-60; e-mail books@infra-m.ru; internet www.infra-m.ru; f. 1992; economics, law, computing, history, reference works, encyclopedias; Man. Dir VADIM D. SINYANSKII.

Khimiya (Chemistry): 107976 Moscow, ul. Strominka 21/2; tel. (495) 268-29-76; f. 1963; chemistry and the chemical industry; Dir BORIS S. KRASNOPEVTSEV.

Khudozhestvennaya Literatura (Fiction): 107078 Moscow, ul. Novobasmannaya 19; tel. (499) 261-88-65; fax (499) 261-83-00; fiction and works of literary criticism, history of literature, etc.; Dir A. N. PETROV; Editor-in-Chief V. S. MODESTOV.

Kompozitor (Composer): 119034 Moscow, M. Levshinskii per. 7/2; tel. (495) 955-19-66; fax (495) 209-54-98; e-mail komp@kompubl.com; internet www.idk.su; f. 1957; music and music criticism; Dir GRIGORII A. VORONOV.

Meditsina (Medicine): 101838 Moscow, Petroverigskii per. 6/8; tel. (495) 924-87-85; fax (495) 928-60-03; e-mail meditsina@iname.com; internet www.medlit.ru; f. 1918; state-owned; imprint of Association for Medical Literature; books and journals on medicine and health; Dir A. M. STOCHIK.

Mezhdunarodnye Otnosheniya (International Relations): 107078 Moscow, ul. Sadovaya-Spasskaya 18/709; tel. (495) 207-67-93; fax (495) 200-22-04; e-mail info@inter-rel.ru; internet www.inter-rel.ru; f. 1957; international relations, economics and politics of foreign countries, foreign trade, international law, foreign-language textbooks and dictionaries, translations and publications for the UN and other international organizations; Dir B. P. LIKHACHEV.

Moscow M. V. Lomonosov State University Press: 119899 Moscow, ul. Khokhlova 11; tel. (495) 939-33-23; fax (495) 203-66-71; e-mail kd_mgu@rambler.ru; internet www.msu.ru/depts/MSUPubl2005/; f. 1756; scientific, educational and reference, books and journals; Dir YURIY YU. PETRUNIN.

Muzyka (Music): 127051 Moscow, ul. Petrovka 26; tel. (495) 921-51-70; fax (495) 928-33-04; e-mail muz-sekretar@yandex.ru; f. 1861; sheet music, music scores and related literature; Dir MARK ZILBERQUIT.

Mysl (Thought): 117071 Moscow, Leninskii pr. 15; tel. (495) 955-04-58; f. 1963; science, popular science, philosophy, history, political science, geography; Dir YEVGENYI A. TIMOFEYEV.

Nauka (Science): 117997 Moscow, ul. Profsoyuznaya 90; tel. (495) 334-71-51; fax (495) 420-22-20; e-mail secret@naukaran.ru; internet www.naukaran.ru; f. 1923; publishing house of the Academy of Sciences; general and social science, mathematics, physics, chemistry, biology, earth sciences, oriental studies, books in foreign languages, university textbooks, scientific journals, translation, export, distribution, typesetting and printing services; Dir-Gen. V. VASILIYEV.

Nauka i Tekhnologiya (Science and Technology): 107076 Moscow, Stromynskii per. 4; tel. (495) 164-47-74; fax (495) 164-47-74; e-mail admin@nait.ru; internet www.nait.ru; f. 2000; journals on chemistry, electronics and telecommunications; Gen. Dir MAKSIM A. KOVALEVSKII.

Nedra Biznestsentr (Natural Resources Business Centre): 125047 Moscow, pl. Tverskoi Zastavy 3; tel. (495) 251-31-77; fax (495) 250-27-72; e-mail business@nedrainform.ru; internet www.nedrainform.ru; f. 1964; geology, natural resources, mining and coal industry, petroleum and gas industry; Dir V. D. MENSHIKOV.

Nezavisimaya Gazeta ('Independent Newspaper' Publishing House): 101000 Moscow, ul. Myasnitskaya 13/10; tel. and fax (495) 981-61-53; e-mail ngbooks@ng.ru; internet www.ng.ru/izdatelstvo; f. 1991; books on history, literary essays, poetry, history of literature and of art, biography, dictionaries, encyclopedias; Dir VIKTOR A. OBUKHOV.

THE RUSSIAN FEDERATION

Pedagogika Press (Pedagogy Press): 119034 Moscow, Smolenskii bulv. 4; tel. and fax (495) 246-59-69; f. 1969; scientific and popular books on pedagogics, didactics, psychology, developmental physiology; young people's encyclopaedias, dictionaries; Dir I. Kolesnikova.

Pressa (The Press): 127137 Moscow, ul. Pravdy 24; tel. (499) 257-46-22; fax (499) 257-09-38; e-mail adm@media-pressa.ru; internet www.media-pressa.ru; f. 1934 as Pravda (Truth) Publishing House; booklets, newspapers and periodicals; Dir I. V. Poltavtsev.

Profizdat (Professional Publishers): 101000 Moscow, ul. Myasnitskaya 13/18; tel. (495) 924-57-40; fax (495) 975-23-29; e-mail profizdat@profizdat.ru; f. 1930; books and magazines; Gen. Dir Vladimir Solovyev.

Prosveshcheniye (Enlightenment): 127521 Moscow, 3-i proyezd Maryinoi roshchi 41; tel. (495) 789-30-40; fax (495) 789-30-41; e-mail prosv@prosv.ru; internet www.prosv.ru; f. 1930; school textbooks, dictionaries, atlases, reference and scientific books, educational materials; Dir Aleksandr M. Kondakov.

Raduga (Rainbow): 129090 Moscow, Grokholskii per. 32/2; tel. and fax (495) 680-12-39; e-mail radugarel@sumail.ru; internet www.raduga-publ.ru; f. 1982; translations of Russian fiction into foreign languages and of foreign authors into Russian; Gen. Dir Kseniya Atarova.

Respublika (Republic): 125811 Moscow, Miusskaya pl. 7; tel. and fax (495) 656-09-70; e-mail respublik@dataforce.net; internet www.republik.ru; f. 1918; fmrly Politizdat (Political Publishing House); dictionaries, books on politics, human rights, philosophy, history, economics, religion, fiction, arts, reference; Dir Vladimir V. Akimov.

Rosmen (Rosman): 127018 Moscow, ul. Oktyabrskaya 4/2; tel. (495) 933-70-70; fax (495) 933-71-36; e-mail rosman@rosman.ru; internet www.rosman.ru; children's literature, general, popular science; Dir-Gen. Oleg V. Zhivykh.

Rosspen Publishing House—Russian Political Encyclopedia: 117393 Moscow, ul. Profsoyuznaya 82; tel. and fax (495) 334-81-62; e-mail rosspen@rosspen.su; internet www.rosspen.su; f. 1992; politics, history, other academic and reference publishing; Dir-Gen. A. K. Sorokin.

Shkola-Press (School-Press): 127254 Moscow, ul. Sh. Rustaveli 10/3; tel. and fax (495) 219-83-80; e-mail marketing@schoolpress.ru; internet www.schoolpress.ru; books on psychology, pedagogy, magazines.

Slovo (Word): 109147 Moscow, Vorontsovskaya 41; tel. and fax (495) 911-61-33; internet www.slovo-online.ru; f. 1989; illustrated books on art, world literature in translation; Dir-Gen. Nataliya Avetisyan.

Stroyizdat (Construction Publishing House): 101442 Moscow, ul. Kalyayevskaya 23a; tel. (495) 251-69-67; f. 1932; building, architecture, environmental protection, fire protection and building materials; Dir V. A. Kasatkin.

Tekst (Text): 127299 Moscow, ul. Kosmonavta Volkova 7; tel. and fax (495) 150-0472; e-mail textpubl@yandex.ru; internet www.textpubl.ru; f. 1988; foreign poetry and prose fiction in translation, Russian poetry and prose, children's literature, social sciences, history, law; Dir Olget M. Libkin.

Vagrius: 125993 Moscow, ul. Nikoloyamskaya 1; tel. (495) 221-61-80; fax (495) 510-56-10; e-mail vagrius@vagrius.com; internet www.vagrius.ru; f. 1992; fiction, politics, history; Pres. and Dir-Gen. Gleb Uspenskii.

Ves Mir (The Whole World): 117342 Moscow, ul. Butlerova 17 b/338; tel. (495) 739-09-71; fax (495) 334-85-91; e-mail info@vesmirbooks.ru; internet www.vesmirbooks.ru; f. 1994; university textbooks, scholarly works in social sciences and humanities; Dir Dr Oleg A. Zimarin.

Vysshaya Shkola (Higher School): 127994 Moscow, ul. Neglinnaya 29/14; tel. (495) 200-04-56; fax (495) 200-34-86; e-mail info_vshkola@mail.ru; internet www.vshkola.ru; f. 1939; textbooks for higher-education institutions; Dir Mikhail L. Zorin.

Yuridicheskaya Literatura (Legal Literature): 121069 Moscow, ul. M. Nikitskaya 14; tel. (495) 203-83-84; fax (495) 291-98-83; internet www.jurizdat.ru; f. 1917; legal; official publishers of enactments of the Russian President and Govt; Dir Ivan A. Bunin.

Znaniye (Knowledge): 101835 Moscow, proyezd Serova 4; tel. (495) 928-15-31; f. 1951; popular books and brochures on politics and science; Dir V. K. Belyakov.

Broadcasting and Communications

TELECOMMUNICATIONS

Golden Telecom: 115114 Moscow, Kozhevnicheskii proyezd 1; tel. (495) 797-93-00; fax (495) 797-93-32; e-mail publicrelations@gldn.net; internet www.goldentelecom.ru; f. 1994; operates mobile cellular telecommunications network in cities across the Russian Federation, and in Almatı (Kazakhstan) and Kyiv (Ukraine); Chief Exec. Jean-Pierre Vandromme.

Megafon: 119435 Moscow, Savvinskaya nab. 15; tel. (495) 504-50-20; fax (495) 504-50-21; e-mail aklimov@megafon.ru; internet www.megafon.ru; f. 2002; operates mobile cellular communications networks across Russia; 6 regional cos; 15.6m. subscribers (March 2005); Gen. Dir Sergei Soldatenkov.

Mobilnye TeleSistemi/Mobile TeleSystems (MTS): 109147 Moscow, ul. Marksistskaya 4; tel. (495) 766-01-77; e-mail info@mts.ru; internet www.mts.ru; f. 1993; provides mobile cellular telecommunications in 82 regions of Russia; majority-owned by Sistema Telecom; 35.1% owned by Deutsche Telekom (Germany); over 85m. subscribers, incl. subsidiary cos in Armenia, Belarus, Ukraine and Uzbekistan (2008); Pres. Leonid A. Melamed.

Moscow City Telephone Network (MGTS—Moskovskaya Gorodskaya Telefonnaya Set): 103051 Moscow, Petrovskii bulv. 12/3; tel. (495) 950-00-00; fax (495) 950-06-18; e-mail mgts@mgts.ru; internet www.mgts.ru; f. 1882; provides telecommunications services in Moscow City; Gen. Man. Nikolai A. Maksimenka.

Petersburg Telephone Network (PTS—Peterburgskaya Telefonnaya Set): 119186 St Petersburg, ul. B. Morskaya 24; tel. (812) 314-15-50; fax (812) 110-68-34; e-mail office@ptn.ru; internet www.ptn.ru; f. 1993; Dir Igor N. Samylin.

Rostelekom (Rostelecom): 125047 Moscow, ul. 1-aya Tverskaya-Yamskaya 14; tel. (495) 787-28-49; fax (495) 972-82-83; e-mail info@rostelecom.ru; internet www.rt.ru; 50.7% owned by Svyazinvest; dominant long-distance and international telecommunications service provider; 7 regional cos based in St Petersburg, Samara, Novosibirsk, Yekaterinburg, Khabarovsk, Moscow and Rostov-on-Don; Dir Dmitrii Yerokhin.

Svyazinvest: 119121 Moscow, ul. Plyushchikha 55/2; tel. (495) 248-24-71; fax (495) 248-24-53; e-mail dms@svyazinvest.ru; internet www.sinvest.ru; f. 1995; 75% state-owned; holds controlling stakes in 7 'mega-regional' telecommunications operators, 1 international and domestic long-distance operator, and 2 local telecommunications cos, and non-controlling stakes in 2 city telecommunications cos; Chair. Leonid D. Reiman.

VympelKom-Bilain (Vympelcom-Beeline): 127006 Moscow, ul. Krasnoproletarskaya 4; tel. (495) 725-07-00; fax (495) 991-79-03; e-mail info@beeline.ru; internet www.beeline.ru; operates mobile cellular telecommunications in 78 regions of Russia, and in Armenia, Georgia, Kazakhstan, Tajikistan, Ukraine and Uzbekistan; 26.6% owned by Telenor (Norway); Chief Exec. Aleksandr V. Izosimov.

BROADCASTING

Pervyi Kanal (First Channel), operated by Public Russian Television (ORT), is received throughout Russia and many parts of the CIS. The All-Russian State Television Company (VGTRK) broadcasts Telekanal 'Rossiya', which reaches some 92% of the Russian population, and Telekanal 'Kultura' and Telekanal 'Sport'. In addition to the nation-wide television channels, there are local channels, and the NTV (Independent Television) channel (65% owned by the gas utility Gazprom, in which the Government holds a majority stake) is broadcast in most of Russia. In the regions, part of Rossiya's programming is devoted to local affairs, with broadcasts in minority languages. A state-supported, international, English-language TV station, Russia Today, commenced broadcasts in 2006. In mid-2005 there were four nation-wide radio stations, as well as 11 urban radio networks and more than 200 regional stations. At that time Radio Rossiya had more listeners than any other state-run channel, but the commercial music station Russkoye Radio, established in 1995, was the most popular station overall.

Association of Regional State Television and Radio Broadcasters: 113326 Moscow, ul. Pyatnitskaya 25/226; tel. and fax (495) 950-60-28; e-mail fstratyv@rzn.rosmail.com; Chair. of Bd Aleksandr N. Levchenko.

Regulatory Authority

Russian Television and Radio Broadcasting Network: 113326 Moscow, ul. Pyatnitskaya 25; tel. (495) 233-66-03; fax (495) 233-28-93; f. 2001; Gen. Man. Gennadii I. Sklyar.

Radio

All-Russian State Television and Radio Broadcasting Company (VGTRK): 125040 Moscow, ul. 5-aya Yamskogo Polya 19/21; tel. (495) 745-39-78; fax (495) 975-26-11; e-mail rtrinterdep@rfn.ru; internet www.tvradio.ru; f. 1991; broadcasts 'Rossiya', 'Kultura', 'Sport' and 'Zvezda' television channels, 89 regional television and radio cos, and national radio stations 'Radio Rossiya', 'Radio Mayak' and 'Radio Nostalzhi'; Chair. Oleg Dobrodeyev.

Radio Mayak (Radio Beacon): 113326 Moscow, ul. Pyatnitskaya 25; tel. (495) 950-67-67; fax (495) 959-42-04; e-mail inform@radiomayak.ru; internet www.radiomayak.ru; f. 1964; state-owned; Chair. IRINA A. GERASIMOVA.

Radio Nostalzhi (Radio Nostalgia): 113162 Moscow, ul. Shabolovka 37; tel. (495) 955-84-00; e-mail nostalgie@vimain.vitpc.com; f. 1993; Gen. Man. IRINA A. GERASIMOVA.

Radio Rossiya (Radio Russia): 125040 Moscow, ul. 5-aya Yamskogo Polya 19/21; tel. (495) 234-85-94; fax (495) 730-42-77; e-mail direction@radiorus.ru; internet www.radiorus.ru; f. 1990; broadcasts information, social, political, musical, literary and investigative programming; Dir-Gen. ALEKSEI V. ABAKUMOV.

Ekho Moskvy (Moscow Echo): 119992 Moscow, ul. Novyi Arbat 11; tel. (495) 202-92-29; e-mail info@echo.msk.ru; internet www.echo.msk.ru; f. 1990; stations in Moscow, St Petersburg, Rostov-on-Don and Vologda; also broadcasts from Moscow to Chelyabinsk, Krasnoyarsk, Novosibirsk, Omsk, Perm, Saratov and Yekaterinburg; 66% owned by Gazprom-Mediya, 34% staff-owned; Gen. Man. YURII FEDUTINKOV.

Golos Rossii (The Voice of Russia): 115326 Moscow, ul. Pyatnitskaya 25; tel. (495) 950-63-31; fax (495) 951-20-17; e-mail voiceofrussia@ruvr.ru; internet www.vor.ru; fmrly Radio Moscow International; international broadcasts in 34 languages; Man. Dir ARMEN G. OGANESIAN.

Russkoye Radio (Russian Radio): 105064 Moscow, ul. Kazakova 16; tel. (495) 232-16-36; fax (495) 956-13-60; internet www.rusradio.ru; f. 1995; owned by Russkaya Mediyagruppa (Russian Media Group); nation-wide commercial music station; broadcasts to more than 700 towns in Russia, Ukraine, Kazakhstan, Moldova, Kyrgyzstan, the Baltic Republics and the USA; also *Russkoye Radio 2*, principally news and talk programming, broadcast to Moscow; Dir-Gen. SERGEI KOZHEVNIKOV.

Serebryanyi Dozhd (Silver Rain): 127083 Moscow, Petrovsko-Razumovskaya alleya 12A; tel. (495) 925-10-01; internet www.silver.ru; f. 1995; commercial station broadcasting information and entertainment programming; broadcasts to 98 cities in Russia and the 'near abroad'; Dir-Gen. DMITRII SAVITSKII.

Yevropa Plyus (Europa Plus): 127427 Moscow, ul. Akademika Koroleva 19; tel. (495) 217-82-57; fax (495) 956-35-08; e-mail main@europaplus.ru; internet www.europaplus.ru; FM station, broadcasting music, entertainment and information programmes to 500 cities; Pres. ZHORZH POLINSKI.

Television

All-Russian State Television and Radio Broadcasting Company (VGTRK): 125040 Moscow, ul. 5-aya Yamskogo Polya 19/21; tel. (495) 745-39-78; fax (495) 975-26-11; e-mail rtrinterdep@rfn.ru; internet www.tvradio.ru; f. 1991; broadcasts 'Rossiya', 'Kultura', 'Sport' and 'Zvezda' television channels, 89 regional television and radio cos, and national radio stations 'Radio Rossiya', 'Radio Mayak' and 'Radio Nostalzhi'; Chair. OLEG DOBRODEYEV.

Telekanal 'Kultura' (Television Channel 'Culture'): 123995 Moscow, ul. M. Nikitskaya 24; e-mail kultura@tvkultura.ru; internet www.tvkultura.ru; f. 1997; Gen. Dir ALEKSANDR S. PONOMAREV.

Telekanal 'Rossiya' (Television Channel 'Russia'): 115162 Moscow, ul. Shabolovka 37; tel. (495) 924-63-74; fax (495) 234-87-71; e-mail info@rutv.ru; internet www.rutv.ru; fmrly RTR-TV; name changed as above in 2002; Dir-Gen. ALEKSANDR S. PONAMAREV.

Telekanal 'Sport' (Television Channel 'Sport'): 115162 Moscow, ul. Shabolovka 37; e-mail reception@sport.vgtek.com; internet sportbox.ru; f. 2003; Dir-Gen. VASILII KIKNADZE.

Telekanal 'Zvezda' (Television Channel 'Star'): 129110 Moscow, Suvorovskaya pl. 2; tel. (495) 631-58-83; internet www.tvzvezda.ru; f. 2005; Gen. Dir SERGEI V. SABUSHKIN.

NTV—Independent Television: 127427 Moscow, ul. Akademika Koroleva 12; tel. (495) 725-54-03; fax (495) 725-54-01; e-mail info@ntv.ru; internet www.ntv.ru; f. 1993; 65% owned by Gazprom-Mediya; also NTV World (NTV Mir), broadcasting to Russian communities in Israel, Europe and the USA; Dir-Gen. NIKOLAI YU. SENKEVICH.

Pervyi Kanal—First Channel (Channel One): 127427 Moscow, ul. Akademika Koroleva 12; tel. (495) 617-73-87; fax (495) 215-82-47; e-mail ort_int@ortv.ru; internet www.1tv.ru; f. 1995; fmrly ORT—Public Russian Television; name changed as above in 2002; 51% state-owned; 49% owned by private shareholders; Chair. MIKHAIL PYATKOVSKII; Dir-Gen. KONSTANTIN ERNST.

Ren-TV Network: 119843 Moscow, Zubovskii bulv. 17/510; tel. (495) 246-25-06; fax (495) 245-09-98; e-mail site@rentv.dol.ru; internet www.ren-tv.com; f. 1991; network of more than 100 television stations in the Russian Federation and 60 stations in republics of the CIS; Chair. MIKHAIL KONTSEREV.

STS—Network of Television Stations: 123298 Moscow, ul. 3-aya Khoroshevskaya 12; tel. (495) 797-41-73; fax (495) 797-41-01; e-mail www@ctc-tv.ru; internet www.ctc-tv.ru; f. 1996; owned by StoryFirst Communications (USA); broadcasts programmes of popular entertainment to 350 cities in Russia; Dir-Gen. ALEKSANDR YE. RODNYANSKII.

TNT—Territory of Our Viewers—TV Network: 127427 Moscow, ul. Akademika Koroleva 19; tel. (495) 217-81-88; fax (495) 748-14-90; e-mail info@tnt-tv.ru; internet www.tnt-tv.ru; f. 1997; cable television network broadcasting to 582 cities in Russia; Chief Exec. ALEKSANDR DYBAL; Dir-Gen. ROMAN PETRENKO.

TV-Tsentr (TVTs—TV-Centre): 113184 Moscow, ul. B. Tatarskaya 33/1; tel. (495) 959-39-87; fax (495) 959-39-66; e-mail info@tvc.ru; internet www.tvc.ru; f. 1997; broadcasting consortium for terrestrial cable and satellite television; receives funding from Govt of Moscow City; Dir-Gen. ALEKSANDR S. PONOMAREV.

Finance

(cap. = capital; res = reserves; dep. = deposits; m. = million; brs = branches; amounts in new roubles, unless otherwise stated)

BANKING

Central Bank

Bank Rossii—Central Bank of the Russian Federation: 107016 Moscow, ul. Neglinnaya 12; tel. (495) 771-91-00; fax (495) 621-64-65; e-mail webmaster@www.cbr.ru; internet www.cbr.ru; f. 1990; cap. 3,000m., res 1,899,352m., dep. 10,250,052m. (Dec. 2008); Chair. SERGEI M. IGNATIYEV; 79 brs.

Major Banks

AK BARS Bank: 420066 Tatarstan, Kazan, ul. Dekabristov 1; tel. (843) 519-39-99; fax (843) 519-39-75; e-mail mail@akbars.ru; internet www.akbars.ru; f. 1993; cap. 25,244.0m., res 349.6m., dep. 153,917.8m. (Dec. 2008); Chair. of Bd ROBERT MINNEGALIYEV; 22 brs.

Alfa-Bank: 107078 Moscow, ul. Kalanchevskaya 27; tel. (495) 974-25-15; fax (495) 788-03-89; e-mail mail@alfabank.ru; internet www.alfabank.ru; f. 1990; cap. US $944.8m., res −$350.8m., dep. $23,444.5m. (Dec. 2008); Chair. of Exec. Bd RUSHAN KHVESYUK; Pres. PETR AVEN.

Bank of Moscow (Bank Moskvy): 107996 Moscow, ul. Rozhdestvenka 8/15/3; tel. (495) 925-80-00; fax (495) 795-26-00; e-mail info@mmbank.ru; internet www.mmbank.ru; f. 1995; present name adopted 2004; 60% owned by Govt of Moscow City; cap. 16,212.7m., res 21,714.3m., dep. 724,102.6m. (Dec. 2008); Pres. MIKHAIL KUZOVLEV.

Bank Petrocommerce (Bank Petrokommerts): 127051 Moscow, ul. Petrovka 24; tel. (495) 411-64-11; fax (495) 623-36-07; e-mail welcome@pkb.ru; internet www.pkb.ru; f. 1992; cap. 7,752.5m., res 1,330.5m., dep. 141,357.7m. (Dec. 2008); Pres. and Chair. of Bd VLADIMIR N. NIKITENKO.

Bank Sankt-Peterburg/Bank Saint Petersburg: 191167 St Petersburg, Nevskii pr. 178A; tel. (812) 329-50-50; fax (812) 329-50-70; e-mail cc@bspb.ru; internet www.bspb.ru; f. 1990; cap. 3,629.5m., res 17,742.6m., dep. 200,256.4m. (Dec. 2009); Chair. ALEKSANDR SAVELIYEV.

Bank Soyuz: 127055, Moscow, ul. Sushchevskaya 27/1; tel. (495) 729-55-55; fax (495) 729-55-05; e-mail info@banksoyuz.ru; internet www.banksoyuz.ru; f. 1993; cap. 5,389m., res 158m., dep. 75,177m. (Dec. 2007); Chair. ANDREI A. KHANDRUYEV.

Bank Uralsib: 119048 Moscow, ul. Yefremova 8; tel. and fax (495) 705-90-39; e-mail rum_vk@uralsib.ru; internet www.uralsib.ru; f. 1993; cap. 32,607m., res 8,725m., dep. 376,157m. (Dec. 2008); Chair. ILDAR R. MUSLIMOV.

Bank Vozrozhdeniye—V-Bank: 101999 Moscow, per. Luchnikov 7/4/1, POB 9; tel. (495) 620-19-35; fax (495) 620-90-65; e-mail vbank@co.voz.ru; internet www.vbank.ru; f. 1991; cap. 250m., res 7,358m., dep. 117,609m. (Dec. 2008); Chair. of Man. Bd DMITRII L. ORLOV; 170 brs.

Bank VTB 24: 101000 Moscow, ul. Myasnitskaya 35; tel. (495) 777-24-24; fax (495) 980-46-66; e-mail info@vtb24.ru; internet www.vtb24.ru; f. 1991; present name adopted 2006; cap. 38,523.8m., res 15,256.9m., dep. 510,167.2m. (Dec. 2008); Chair. of Bd ANDREI L. KOSTIN; 44 brs.

Bank VTB Severo-Zapad (Bank VTB North-West): 197022 St Petersburg, ul. L. Tolstogo 9/10; tel. (812) 329-84-54; fax (812) 310-61-73; e-mail lider@vtb-sz.ru; internet www.vtb-sz.ru; f. 1870 as Volga-Kama Bank; fmrly Industry and Construction Bank; present name adopted 2007; cap. 1,932.4m., res 2,164.4m., dep. 181,145.1m. (Dec. 2008); Chair. VLADIMIR SKATIN; 54 brs.

THE RUSSIAN FEDERATION

Bank Zenit: 129110 Moscow, Bannyi per. 9; tel. (495) 937-07-37; fax (495) 777-57-06; e-mail info@zenit.ru; internet www.zenit.ru; f. 1994; 24.6% owned by Tatneft; cap. 12,698.1m., res −178.9m., dep. 162,930.2m. (Dec. 2008); Chair. of Bd ALEKSEI A. SOKOLOV; 4 brs.

Gazprombank: 117420 Moscow, ul. Nametkina 16/1; tel. (495) 913-74-74; fax (495) 913-73-19; e-mail mailbox@gazprombank.ru; internet www.gazprombank.ru; f. 1990; 41.7% owned by Gazprom; cap. 31,836m., res 26,044m., dep. 1,522,818m. (Dec. 2008); Chair. of Management Bd ANDREI I. AKIMOV; 32 brs.

Home Credit & Finance Bank (Khoum Kredit end Finans Bank): 125040 Moscow, ul. Pravdy 8/1; tel. (495) 785-82-22; fax (495) 785-82-18; e-mail info@homecredit.ru; internet www.homecredit.ru; f. 1990; present name adopted 2003; cap. 4,405.7m., res 9,630.5m., dep. 91,157.6m. (Dec. 2008); Chair. JIŘÍ SMEJC.

ING Bank (Eurasia): 127473 Moscow, ul. Krasnoproletarskaya 36; tel. (495) 755-54-00; fax (495) 755-54-99; e-mail mail.russia@ingbank.com; internet www.ing.ru; f. 1993; 99.9% owned by ING Bank NV (Netherlands); cap. 3,749.7m., res 10,359.3m., dep. 142,328.3m. (Dec. 2008); Dir-Gen. HENDRIK WILLEM TEN BOSCH.

Khanty-Mansiiskii Bank: 628012 Tyumen obl., Khanty-Mansii AOk—Yugra, Khanty-Mansiisk, ul. Mira 38; tel. (34671) 302-10; fax (34671) 302-19; e-mail hmbank@khmb.ru; internet www.khmb.ru; f. 1992; cap. 7,782.3m., res 2,509.0m., dep. 101,190.3m. (Dec. 2008); Pres. DMITRII MIZGULIN; 16 brs.

MDM Bank: 630004, Novosibirsk, ul. Lenina 18; tel. and fax (383) 227-75-99; fax (383) 325-04-42; e-mail info@mdm.ru; internet www.mdm.ru; f. 1993; merged with URSA Bank in 2009; cap. 4,207m., res 35,493m., dep. 326.810m. (Dec. 2009); Dir IGOR KIM.

Mezhdunarodnyi Promyshlennyi Bank (International Industrial Bank): 125009 Moscow, ul. B. Dmitrovka 23/1; tel. (495) 626-44-46; fax (495) 692-82-84; e-mail mail@iib.ru; internet www.iib.ru; f. 1992; cap. 25,000.0m., res 36.7m., dep. 114,486.7m. (Dec. 2008); Chair. ALEKSANDR A. DIDENKO; 5 brs.

Moscow Bank for Reconstruction and Development (Moskovskii Bank Rekonstruktsii i Razvitiya): 119034 Moscow, Yeropkinskii per. 5; tel. (495) 921-28-00; fax (495) 232-27-54; e-mail mbrd@mbrd.ru; internet www.mbrd.ru; 58.44% owned by Sistema; cap. 1,360.9m., res 11,562.9m., dep. 145,983.8m. (Dec. 2008); Chair. of Bd FELIKS V. YEVTUSHENKOV.

Nomos-Bank: 109240 Moscow, ul. Verkhnyaya Radishchevskaya 3/1; tel. (495) 721-80-80; fax (495) 797-32-50; e-mail info@nomos.ru; internet www.nomos.ru; f. 1992; cap. 5,982.3m., res 13,331.1m., dep. 233,999.8m. (Dec. 2008); Pres. DMITRII SOKOLOV.

Nordea Bank: 125040 Moscow, ul. 3-aya Yamskogo Polya 19/1; tel. (495) 777-34-77; fax (495) 921-25-03; e-mail all@nordea.ru; internet www.nordea.ru; f. 1994; fmrly Orgresbank; renamed as above in March 2009; cap. 7,381.6m., dep. 151,807.5m. (Dec. 2008); Chair. IGOR BULANTSEV.

Promsvyazbank: 109052 Moscow, ul. Smirnovskaya 10/22; tel. (495) 727-10-20; fax (495) 727-10-21; e-mail info@psbank.ru; internet www.psbank.ru; f. 1995; cap. 10,062.5m., res 16,729.8m., dep. 399,296.8m. (Dec. 2009); Chair. of Bd of Dirs ALEKSEI ANANIYEV; Pres. ALEKSANDR A. LEVKOVSKII; 11 brs.

Raiffeisenbank ZAO: 129090 Moscow, ul. Troitskaya 17/1; tel. (495) 721-99-00; fax (495) 721-99-01; e-mail info@raiffeisen.ru; internet www.raiffeisen.ru; f. 1996; owned by Raiffeisenbank (Austria); cap. 43,268.8m., res 2,111.1m., dep. 329,754.0m. (Dec. 2008); Chair. of Man. Bd PAVEL GOURINE; 7 brs and sub-brs.

Rosbank: 107078 Moscow, ul. M. Poryvayevoi 11, POB 208; tel. (495) 921-01-01; fax (495) 725-05-11; e-mail mailbox@rosbank.ru; internet www.rosbank.ru; f. 1993; 50% owned by Société Générale (France); cap. 9,270.9m., res 23,388.9m., dep. 443,033.7m. (Dec. 2008); Chair. of Bd of Dirs JEAN-LOUIS MATTEI; Chief Exec. VLADIMIR YE GOLUBKOV; 68 brs.

RosselkhozBank (Russian Agricultural Bank): 119034 Moscow, Gagarinskii per. 3; tel. (495) 363-02-90; fax (495) 363-02-76; e-mail office@rshb.ru; internet www.rhsb.ru; f. 2000; wholly state-owned; cap. 106,973m., res 856m., dep. 435,047m. (Dec. 2009); Chair. of Bd and Chief Exec. YURII V. TRUSHIN.

Russkii Standart Bank: 105187 Moscow, ul. Tkacka 36; tel. (495) 748-07-48; fax (495) 797-84-40; e-mail bank@bank.rs.ru; internet www.rs.ru; f. 1993; cap. 1,739m., res 829m., dep. 168,284m. (Dec. 2008); Chair. RUSTAM V. TARIKO; Chief Exec. DMITRII O. LEVIN.

Sberbank—Savings Bank of the Russian Federation: 117997 Moscow, ul. Vavilova 19; tel. (495) 500-55-50; fax (495) 957-57-31; e-mail sbrf@sbrf.ru; internet www.sbrf.ru; f. 1841 as a deposit-taking institution, reorganized as a joint-stock commercial bank in 1991; 60.6% owned by Bank Rossii—Central Bank of the Russian Federation; cap. 87,742m., res 286,486m., dep. 5,617,417m. (Dec. 2009); Chair. of Bd and Chief Exec. GERMAN O. GREF; 17 regional head offices, 823 brs and 19,307 sub-brs.

Svyaz-Bank (Interregional Bank for Settlements of the Telecommunications and Postal Services): 125375 Moscow, ul. Tverskaya 7; tel. (495) 771-32-60; fax (495) 771-32-76; e-mail sviaz-bank@sviaz-bank.ru; internet www.sviaz-bank.ru; f. 1991; absorbed Russian Industrial Bank in 2008; 90.0% owned by Vneshekonombank; cap. 5,131.4m., res 6,909.0m., dep. 111,617.5m. (Dec. 2008); Chair. of Bd of Dirs ANATOLII V. TIKHONOV.

TransKreditBank (TransCreditBank): 105066 Moscow, ul. N. Basmannaya 37A/1; tel. (495) 788-08-80; fax (495) 788-08-79; e-mail info@bnk.ru; internet www.tcb.ru; f. 1992; 55.1% owned by Russian Railways; cap. 3,973.5m., res 4,043.7m., dep. 217,777.0m. (Dec. 2008); Pres. YURII V. NOVOZHILOV.

UniCredit Bank ZAO: 119034 Moscow, Prechistenskaya nab. 9; tel. (495) 258-72-00; fax (495) 258-72-72; e-mail unicredit@unicreditgroup.ru; internet www.unicreditbank.ru; f. 1989; fmrly International Moscow Bank; present name adopted 2007; 100% owned by UniCredit Bank Austria AG (Austria); cap. 24,413.8m., res −161.3m., dep. 539,107.8m. (Dec. 2008); Chair. of Bd MIKHAIL ALEKSEEV; 22 brs.

Vneshekonombank (State Corporation Bank for Development and Foreign Economic Affairs): 107996 Moscow, pr. Sakharova 9; tel. (499) 721-18-63; fax (499) 975-21-43; e-mail info@veb.ru; internet www.veb.ru; f. 1924; wholly state-owned; res −8,315.7m., dep. 1,284.7m. (Dec. 2008); Chair. VLADIMIR A. DMITRIYEV; Chair. of Supervisory Bd VLADIMIR V. PUTIN (Chairman of the Government).

VTB Bank: 190000 St Petersburg, ul. B. Morskaya 29; tel. (495) 739-77-99; fax (495) 258-47-81; e-mail info@vtb.ru; internet www.vtb.ru; f. 1990; fmrly Bank for Foreign Trade; present name adopted 2007; 77.5% owned by Govt of Russian Federation; cap. US $3,084m., res $7,489m., dep. $69,797m. (Dec. 2008); Chair. of Bd and Chief Exec. ANDREI L. KOSLIN.

Bankers' Association

Association of Russian Banks (Assostiatsiya Rossiiskikh Bankov): 121069 Moscow, Skatertnyi per. 20/1; tel. (495) 291-66-30; fax (495) 291-66-66; e-mail arb@arb.ru; internet www.arb.ru; f. 1991; 755 mem. orgs, incl. 576 credit orgs (2007); Pres. GAREGIN A. TOSUNYAN.

INSURANCE

Agroinvest Insurance Co: 127422 Moscow, ul. Timiryazevskaya 26; tel. (495) 976-94-56; fax (495) 977-05-88; health, life and general insurance services; Pres. YURII I. MORDVINTSEV.

AIG Insurance and Reinsurance Co (AIG strakhovaya i perestrakhovochnaya kompaniya—ZAO Chartis): 125009 Moscow, ul. Tverskaya 16/1; tel. (495) 935-89-50; fax (495) 935-89-52; e-mail tverskaya.moscow@aig.com; internet www.aigirc.ru; f. 1994; wholly owned subsidiary of AIG Europe (France); fmrly AIG Russia; present name adopted 2009; personal and business property insurance, also marine, life, financial, etc.; Pres. E. J. STUKANOVA.

Allianz Insurance Co: 127473 Moscow, 3-i Samotechnii per. 3; tel. (495) 937-69-96; fax (495) 937-69-80; e-mail allianz@allianz.ru; internet www.allianz.ru; engineering, professional liability, life, medical, property, marine and private; Man. Dir MICHAEL HERGESELL.

Ingosstrakh Insurance Co: 115998 Moscow, ul. Pyatnitskaya 12/2; tel. (495) 956-55-55; fax (495) 959-44-05; e-mail ingos@ingos.ru; internet www.ingos.ru; f. 1947; undertakes all kinds of insurance and reinsurance; Chair. ALEKSANDR V. GRIGORYEV; Gen. Dir YEVGENII TUMANOV.

Medstrakh—Medical Insurance Fund of the Russian Federation: 107076 Moscow, pl. Preobrazhenskaya 7A/1; tel. (495) 964-84-27; fax (495) 964-84-21; e-mail mz@mcramn.ru; internet www.medstrah.ru; f. 1991; health, life, property, travel, liability; also provides compulsory medical insurance; Pres. PETR KUZNETSOV.

RESO-Garantiya Insurance Co: 117105 Moscow, Nagornyi pr. 6; tel. (495) 730-30-00; fax (495) 956-25-85; e-mail mail@reso.ru; internet www.reso.ru; f. 1991; Dir-Gen. DMITRII G. RAKOVSHCHIK.

Rosgosstrakh—Russian State Insurance: 127994 Moscow, ul. Novoslobodskaya 23; tel. (495) 781-24-00; fax (495) 978-27-64; e-mail pr@rgs.ru; internet www.gosstrah.ru; majority state-owned; 49% stake transferred to private ownership in 2001; undertakes domestic insurance; subsidiary cos in 80 federal subjects (territorial units) of the Russian Federation; Chair. VLADISLAV REZNIK; Gen. Dir D. E. MARKAROV.

ROSNO—Russian National Society Insurance Co: 115184 Moscow, Ozerkovskaya nab. 30; tel. (495) 232-33-33; fax (495) 232-00-14; e-mail info@rosno.ru; internet www.rosno.ru; f. 1992; 100 brs and 186 agencies; 47% owned by AFK Sistema; 45.3% owned by Allianz AG (Germany); CEO HANNES SHARIPUTRA CHOPRA.

Russkiye Strakhovye Traditsii (Russian Traditions Insurance Co): 129110 Moscow, pr. Mira 69/1; tel. and fax (495) 730-55-33; e-mail info@rustrad.ru; internet www.rustrad.ru; f. 1992; Pres. IVAN I. DAVYDOV.

THE RUSSIAN FEDERATION

SOGAZ—Insurance Co of the Gas Industry: 142770 Moscow obl., Leninskii raion, pos. Gazoprovod, Biznes-Tsentr; 115035 Moscow, ul. Bolotnaya 16/1; tel. (495) 428-57-27; fax (495) 739-21-40; e-mail sogaz@sogaz.ru; internet www.sogaz.ru; f. 1993; owned by gas industry interests; Chair. of Management Bd VADIM E. YANOV.

Soglasiye (Agreement) Insurance Co: 109017 Moscow, M. Tolmachevskii per. 8–11/3; tel. (495) 739-01-01; e-mail official@soglasie.ru; internet www.soglasie.ru; f. 1993 as Interros-Soglasiye; owned by Interros; Dir-Gen. LYUBOV YELTSOVA.

STOCK EXCHANGES

Moscow Stock Exchange (MSE) (Moskovskaya Fondovaya Birzha): 127422 Moscow, ul. Vsevoloda Vishnevskogo 4; tel. (495) 771-35-80; fax (495) 771-35-81; e-mail mse@mse.ru; internet www.mse.ru; f. 1997; Pres. ALEKSEI RYZHKOV.

RTS—Russian Trading System: 125009 Moscow, ul. Vozdvizhenka 4/7; tel. (495) 705-90-31; fax (495) 733-95-15; e-mail international@rts.ru; internet www.rts.ru; f. 1995; Chief Exec. ROMAN YU. GORYUNOV.

Siberian Stock Exchange: 630104 Novosibirsk, ul. Frunze 5, POB 233; tel. (3832) 21-60-67; fax (3832) 21-06-90; e-mail sibex@sibex.nsk.su; f. 1991; Pres. ALEKSANDR V. NOVIKOV.

COMMODITY EXCHANGES

Asiatic Commodity Exchange: 670000 Buryatiya, Ulan-Ude, ul. Sovetskaya 23/37; tel. and fax (3012) 22-26-81; f. 1991; Chair. ANDREI FIRSOV.

European-Asian Exchange (EAE): 101000 Moscow, ul. Myasnitskaya 26; tel. and fax (495) 787-58-93; e-mail info@eae.ru; internet www.eae.ru; f. 2000; Chair. of Council TATYANA S. SOKOLOVA; Gen. Man. ALEKSANDR B. YEREMIN.

Khabarovsk Commodity Exchange (KhCE): 680000 Khabarovsk; tel. and fax (4212) 33-65-60; f. 1991; Pres. YEVGENII V. PANASENKO.

Komi Commodity Exchange (KoCE): 167610 Komi, Syktyvkar, Oktyabrskii pr. 16; tel. (8212) 22-32-86; fax (8212) 23-84-43; f. 1991; Pres. PETR S. LUCHENKOV.

Kuzbass Commodity and Raw Materials Exchange (KECME): 650090 Kemerovo, ul. Novgorodskaya 19; tel. (3842) 23-45-40; fax (3842) 23-49-56; f. 1991; Gen. Man. FEDOR MASENKOV.

Moscow Commodity Exchange (MCE): 129223 Moscow, pr. Mira, Russian Exhibition Centre, Pavilion 69 (4); tel. (495) 187-86-14; fax (495) 187-88-76; f. 1990; organization of exchange trading (cash, stock and futures market); Pres. and Chair. of Bd YURII MILYUKOV.

Petrozavodsk Commodity Exchange (PCE): 185028 Kareliya, Petrozavodsk, ul. Krasnaya 31; tel. and fax (8142) 7-80-57; f. 1991; Gen. Man. VALERII SAKHAROV.

Russian Commodity Exchange of the Agro-Industrial Complex (RosAgroBirzha): 125080 Moscow, Volokolamskoye shosse 11; tel. (495) 209-52-25; f. 1990; Chair. of Exchange Cttee ALEKSANDR VASILIYEV.

Russian Exchange (RE): 101000 Moscow, ul. Myasnitskaya 26; tel. (495) 787-84-34; fax (495) 262-57-57; e-mail ic@ci.re.ru; internet www.re.ru; f. 1990; Pres. PAVEL PANOV.

St Petersburg Exchange: 199026 St Petersburg, Vasilyevskii Ostrov, 26-aya liniya 15; tel. (812) 322-44-11; fax (812) 322-73-90; e-mail spbex@spbex.ru; internet www.spbex.ru; f. 1991; Pres. and Chief Exec. VIKTOR V. NIKOLAYEV.

Udmurt Commodity Universal Exchange (UCUE): 426075 Udmurt Rep., Izhevsk, ul. Soyuznaya 107; tel. (3412) 37-08-88; fax (3412) 37-16-57; e-mail iger@udmnet.ru; f. 1991; Pres. N. F. LAZAREV.

Yekaterinburg Commodity Exchange (UCE): 620012 Sverdlovsk obl., Yekaterinburg, pr. Kosmonavtov 23; tel. (343) 234-43-01; fax (343) 251-53-64; f. 1991; Chair. of Exchange Cttee KONSTANTIN ZHUZHLOV.

Trade and Industry

GOVERNMENT AGENCY

Russian Federal Property Fund (Rossiiskii Fond Federalnogo Imushchestva): 119049 Moscow, Leninskii pr. 9; tel. (495) 236-71-15; fax (495) 956-27-80; e-mail rffi@dol.ru; internet www.fpf.ru; f. 1992 to ensure consistency in the privatization process and to implement privatization legislation; Chair. YURII A. PETROV.

NATIONAL CHAMBER OF COMMERCE

Chamber of Commerce and Industry of the Russian Federation (Torgovo-Promyshlennaya Palata RF): 109012 Moscow, ul. Ilinka 6; tel. (495) 929-00-09; fax (495) 929-03-60; e-mail dios-inform@tpprf.ru; internet www.tpprf.ru; f. 1991; Pres. YEVGENII M. PRIMAKOV.

REGIONAL CHAMBERS OF COMMERCE

In early 2011 there were 173 regional chambers of commerce. The following are among the most important:

Astrakhan Chamber of Commerce: 414040 Astrakhan, ul. Zhelyabova 50; tel. (8512) 25-58-44; fax (8512) 28-14-42; e-mail cci@mail.astrakhan.ru; internet astrcci.astrakhan.ru; f. 1992; Pres. ALEKSEI D. KANTEMIROV.

Bashkortostan Chamber of Commerce: 450007 Bashkortostan, Ufa, ul. Vorovskogo 22; tel. (3472) 23-23-80; fax (3472) 51-70-79; e-mail office@tpprb.ru; internet www.tpprb.ru; f. 1990; Chair. BORIS A. BONDARENKO.

Central Siberian Chamber of Commerce: 660049 Krasnoyarsk, ul. Kirova 26; tel. (3912) 23-96-13; fax (3912) 23-96-83; e-mail cstp@mail.ru; internet www.cstpp.ru; f. 1985; Chair. VALERII A. KOSTIN.

East Siberian Chamber of Commerce: 664003 Irkutsk, ul. Sukhe-Batora 16; tel. (3952) 33-50-60; fax (3952) 33-50-66; e-mail info@ccies.ru; internet www.ccies.ru; f. 1974; Pres. KONSTANTIN S. SHAVRIN.

Far East Chamber of Commerce: 680670 Khabarovsk, ul. Sheronova 113; tel. (4210) 30-47-70; fax (4210) 30-54-58; e-mail dvtpp@fecci.khv.ru; f. 1970; Pres. MIKHAIL V. KRUGLIKOV.

Kaliningrad Chamber of Commerce and Industry: 236010 Kaliningrad, ul. Vatutina 20; tel. (4012) 95-68-01; fax (4012) 95-47-88; e-mail kaliningrad_cci@baltnet.ru; internet www.kaliningrad-cci.ru; f. 1990; Pres. IGOR V. TSARKOV.

Kamchatka Chamber of Commerce: 683000 Kamchatka Krai, Petropavlovsk-Kamchatskii, ul. Leninskaya 38/208; tel. and fax (4152) 12-35-10; e-mail kamtpp@iks.ru; Pres. ALLA V. PARKHOMCHUK.

Krasnodar Chamber of Commerce: 350063 Krasnodar, ul. Kommunarov 8; tel. and fax (861) 268-22-13; e-mail tppkk@tppkuban.ru; internet www.tppkuban.ru; f. 1969; Chair. YURII N. TKACHENKO.

Kuzbass Chamber of Commerce: 650099 Kemerovo, pr. Sovetskii 63/407; tel. and fax (3842) 58-77-64; e-mail ktpp@mail.kuzbass.net; internet city.info.kuzbass.net/ktpp; f. 1991; Pres. TATYANA O. IVLEVA.

Maritime (Primorskii) Krai Chamber of Commerce: 690600 Maritime Krai, Vladivostok, Okeanskii pr. 13A; tel. (4232) 26-96-30; fax (4232) 22-72-26; e-mail palata@online.vladivostok.ru; internet www.ptpp.ru; f. 1964; Pres. VLADIMIR B. BREZHNEV.

Moscow Chamber of Commerce: 117393 Moscow, ul. Akademika Pilyugina 22; tel. (495) 132-07-33; fax (495) 132-75-03; e-mail extern@mtpp.org; internet www.mtpp.org; f. 1991; Chair. YURII I. KOTOV; Pres. LEONID V. GOVOROV.

Nizhnii Novgorod Chamber of Commerce: 603005 Nizhnii Novgorod, pl. Oktyabrskaya 1; tel. (8312) 19-42-10; fax (8312) 19-40-09; e-mail tpp@rda.nnov.ru; internet www.tpp.nnov.ru; f. 1990; Pres. GENNADII M. KHODYRYEV.

Northern Chamber of Commerce and Industry: 183766 Murmansk, per. Rusanova 10; tel. (8152) 47-29-99; fax (8152) 47-39-78; e-mail ncci@online.ru; internet www.ncci.ru; f. 1990; Pres. ANATOLII M. GLUSHKOV.

Novosibirsk Chamber of Commerce: 630064 Novosibirsk, pr. K. Marksa 1; tel. and fax (383) 346-41-50; e-mail org@ntpp.ru; internet www.ntpp.ru; f. 1991; Chair. BORIS V. BRUSILOVSKII; 315 mems (2002).

Omsk Chamber of Commerce: 644007 Omsk, ul. Gertsena 51/53; tel. (3812) 25-43-50; fax (3812) 23-45-80; e-mail omtpp@omsknet.ru; internet www.omsktpp.ru; f. 1992; Pres. TATYANA A. KHOROSHAVINA.

Rostov Chamber of Commerce: 344022 Rostov-on-Don, ul. Pushkinskaya 176; tel. and fax (836) 264-45-47; e-mail tpp@rost.ru; internet www.tpp.tis.ru; f. 1992; Pres. NIKOLAI I. PRISYAZHNYUK.

Sakha (Yakutiya) Chamber of Commerce: 677000 Sakha (Yakutiya), Yakutsk, ul. Lenina 22/214; tel. (4112) 26-64-96; e-mail palata91@mail.ru; f. 1991; Chair. SERGEI G. BAKULIN.

Samara Chamber of Commerce: 443099 Samara, ul. A. Tolstogo 6; tel. (8462) 32-11-59; fax (8462) 70-48-96; e-mail ccisr@samara.ru; internet www.cci.samara.ru; f. 1988; Pres. BORIS V. ARDALIN.

Saratov Regional Chamber of Commerce and Industry: 410600 Saratov, ul. B. Kazachya 30; tel. (8452) 27-70-78; fax (8452) 27-70-82; e-mail srcci@sgtpp.ru; internet www.sgtpp.ru; f. 1986; Pres. MAKSIM A. FATEYEV.

Smolensk Chamber of Commerce: 214000 Smolensk, ul. Bakunina 10A; tel. and fax (481) 238-74-50; e-mail smolenskcci@keytown.com; internet www.smolcci.keytown.com; f. 1993; Pres. VLADIMIR P. ARKHIPENKOV.

South Urals Chamber of Commerce: 454080 Chelyabinsk, ul. S. Krivoi 56; tel. (351) 266-18-16; fax (351) 265-41-53; e-mail mail@

THE RUSSIAN FEDERATION

uralreg.ru; internet www.uralreg.ru; f. 1992; Pres. FEDOR L. DEGTYAREV; 550 mems (2007).

St Petersburg Chamber of Commerce: 191123 St Petersburg, ul. Chaikovskogo 46–48; tel. and fax (812) 273-48-96; e-mail spbcci@spbcci.ru; internet www.spbcci.ru; f. 1921; Pres. VLADIMIR I. KATENEV.

Stavropol Chamber of Commerce and Industry: 355003 Stavropol, ul. Lenina 384; tel. (8652) 94-53-34; fax (8652) 34-05-10; e-mail stcci@statel.stavropol.ru; f. 1991; Pres. VITALII S. NABATNIKOV.

Tatarstan Republic Chamber of Commerce and Industry: 420111 Tatarstan, Kazan, ul. Pushkina 18; tel. (843) 264-62-07; fax (843) 236-09-66; e-mail tpprt@tpprt.ru; internet www.tpprt.ru; f. 1992; Gen. Dir SHAMIL R. AGEYEV; 1,200 mems (2007).

Ulyanovsk Chamber of Commerce: 432063 Ulyanovsk, ul. Engelsa 19; tel. (8422) 41-03-61; fax (8422) 41-02-31; e-mail info@ultpp.ru; f. 1992; Pres. YEVGENII S. BALANDIN.

Urals Chamber of Commerce and Industry: 620027 Sverdlovsk obl., Yekaterinburg, ul. Vostochnaya 6; tel. (343) 353-04-49; fax (343) 353-58-63; e-mail ucci@ucci.ur.ru; internet ucci.ur.ru; f. 1959; Pres. YURII P. MATUSHKIN.

Volgograd Chamber of Commerce: 400005 Volgograd, ul. 7-aya Gvardeiskaya 2; tel. (8442) 93-61-35; fax (8442) 34-22-02; e-mail cci@volgogradcci.ru; internet www.volgogradcci.ru; f. 1990; Pres. ALEKSANDR D. BELITSKII.

Vologda Chamber of Commerce and Industry: 160000 Vologda, ul. Lermontova 15; tel. and fax (8172) 72-46-87; e-mail grant@vologda.ru; internet www.vologdatpp.ru; f. 1992; Pres. GALINA D. TELEGINA.

Voronezh Chamber of Commerce: 394030 Voronezh, 'Voronezhvnesh-servis', POB 63; tel. and fax (473) 252-49-38; e-mail mail@oootpp.vm.ru; f. 1991; fmrly Central-Black Earth Chamber of Commerce and Industry; Pres. VYACHESLAV A. KONDRATYEV.

EMPLOYERS' ORGANIZATIONS

Co-ordinating Council of Employers' Unions of Russia (Koordinatsionnyi Sovet Obyedinenii Rabotodatelei Rossii—KSORR): 109017 Moscow, per. M. Tolmachevskii 8–11; tel. (495) 232-55-77; fax (495) 959-46-06; e-mail official@ksorr.ru; internet www.ksorr.ru; f. 1994; co-ordinates and represents employers in relations with government bodies and trade unions, and represents Russian employers in the International Labour Organization (ILO) and the International Organization of Employers (IOE); Chair. OLEG V. YEREMEYEV; Gen. Dir SERGEI V. LUKONIN; unites 35 major employers' unions, incl. the following:

Agro-Industrial Union of Russia: 107139 Moscow, POB 139; tel. (495) 204-41-04; fax (495) 207-83-62; e-mail sva@gvs.aris.ru; Pres. VASILII A. STARODUBTSEV.

All-Russian Social Organization of Small and Medium-sized Businesses (OPORA Rossii) (Obshcherossiiskaya Obshchestvennaya Organizatsiya Malogo i Srednego Predprinimatelstva): 125047 Moscow, ul. 4-ya Tverskaya-Yamskaya 21/22/3; tel. (495) 775-81-11; fax (495) 775-81-91; internet www.opora.ru; f. 2002; Pres. SERGEI BORISOV.

Russian Union of Industrialists and Entrepreneurs (Employers) (RSPPR) (Rossiiskii Soyuz Promyshlennikov i Predprinimatelei): 103070 Moscow, Staraya pl. 10/4; tel. (495) 748-42-37; fax (495) 206-11-29; e-mail pr_dep@rspp.net; internet www.rspp.ru; f. 1991; Pres. ALEKSANDR SHOKHIN; Exec. Sec. NIKOLAI TONKOV.

UTILITIES

Electricity

Federal Energy Commission: 103074 Moscow, Kitaigorodskii proyezd 7; tel. (495) 220-40-15; fax (495) 206-81-08; e-mail fecrf@orc.ru; regulatory authority for natural energy monopolies; sole responsibility for establishing tariff rates for energy, transportation, shipping, postal and telecommunications industries in the Russian Federation from Sept. 2001; Chair. ANDREI ZADERNYUK.

Irkutskenergo (Irkutsk Energy Co): 664000 Irkutsk, ul. Sukhe-Batora 3; tel. (3952) 21-73-00; fax (3952) 21-78-99; e-mail idkan@irkutskenergo.ru; internet www.irkutskenergo.ru; f. 1954; generation and transmission of electrical and thermal energy; Dir-Gen. VLADIMIR V. KOLMOGOROV.

Mosenergo (Moscow Energy Co): 113035 Moscow, Raushskaya nab. 8; tel. (495) 957-35-30; fax (495) 957-34-70; e-mail press-centre@mosenergo.ru; internet www.mosenergo.ru; f. 1887; 49% owned by Unified Energy System of Russia; power generator and distributor; Chair. YURII A. UDALTSOV.

Rosenergoatom (Russian Atomic Energy Concern): 119017 Moscow, ul. B. Ordynka 24/26; tel. (495) 239-24-22; fax (495) 239-46-03; e-mail npp@rosatom.ru; internet www.rosenergoatom.ru; f. 1992; electricity-generating co, manages Russia's 10 nuclear reactors; Dir-Gen. SERGEI OBOZOV.

Sverdlovenergo (Sverdlovsk Energy Co): 620219 Sverdlovsk obl., Yekaterinburg, pr. Lenina 38; tel. (343) 259-13-99; fax (343) 259-12-22; e-mail post@energo.pssr.ru; internet www.po.pssr.ru; f. 1942; Chair. of Bd ALEKSANDR V. CHIKUNOV; Gen. Man. VLADIMIR V. KALSIN.

Uralenergo (Ural Energy): 454006 Chelyabinsk, ul. Rossiiskaya 17; tel. (3512) 67-59-54; fax (3512) 67-59-48; e-mail info@uralenergo.com; internet www.uralenergo.com; manages 22 joint-stock cos; oversees 55 thermal power stations and 6 hydroelectric stations; total installed capacity of over 28,500m. kW; Dir ALEKSANDR S. NEMTSEV.

Gas

Gazprom: 117997 Moscow, ul. Nametkina 16; tel. (495) 719-30-01; fax (495) 719-83-33; e-mail gazprom@gazprom.ru; internet www.gazprom.ru; f. 1989 from assets of Soviet Ministry of Oil and Gas; became independent joint-stock co in 1992, privatized in 1994; 51% state-owned; Chair. of Bd of Dirs VIKTOR A. ZUBKOV; Chair. of Management Bd and Deputy Chair. of Bd of Dirs ALEKSEI B. MILLER.

Mezhregiongaz (Interregional Gas Supply Company): 142770 Moscow obl., Leninskii raion, p/o Kommunarkap. Gazoprovod; tel. (495) 719-55-55; fax (495) 719-52-10; e-mail pr@mrg.gazprom.ru; internet www.mrg.ru; f. 1996; gas-marketing co; subsidiary of Gazprom; brs in more than 65 federal subjects; Dir-Gen. KIRILL SELEZNEV.

Water

Mosvodokanal: 105005 Moscow, per. Pleteshkovskii 2; tel. (499) 763-34-34; fax (495) 265-22-01; e-mail post@mosvodokanal.ru; internet www.mosvodokanal.ru; f. 1937; state-owned; provides water and sewerage services to Moscow and the surrounding region; Dir-Gen. STANISLAV KHRAMENKOV.

Vodokanal: 191015 St Petersburg, ul. Kavalergardskaya 42; tel. (812) 274-16-79; fax (812) 274-13-61; e-mail office@vodokanal.spb.ru; internet www.vodokanal.spb.ru; water and sewerage utility; Gen. Man. FELIKS V. KARMAZINOV.

TRADE UNIONS

In 1990 several branch unions of the All-Union Central Council of Trade Unions (ACCTU) established the Federation of Independent Trade Unions of the Russian Federation (FITUR), which took control of part of the property and other assets of the ACCTU. The ACCTU was re-formed as the General Confederation of Trade Unions of the USSR, which was, in turn, renamed the General Confederation of Trade Unions—International Organization in 1992.

Principal Trade Union Coalitions

All-Russian Labour Confederation: 103031 Moscow, ul. Rozhdestvenka 5/7; tel. (495) 785-21-30; fax (495) 915-83-67; e-mail vktrussia@online.ru; internet www.trud.org/guide/VKT.htm; f. 1995; unites five national trade unions and 40 regional orgs with 1,270,900 mems; Pres. ALEKSANDR N. BUGAYEV.

Federation of Independent Trade Unions of Russia (FITUR) (Federatsiya Nezavisimykh Profsoyuzov Rossii—FNPR): 119119 Moscow, Leninskii pr. 42; tel. (495) 938-73-12; fax (495) 137-06-94; e-mail korneev@fnpr.ru; internet www.fnpr.ru; f. 1990; unites 48 national trade unions and 78 regional orgs (with c. 40m. mems); affiliated to General Confederation of Trade Unions (q.v.); Pres. MIKHAIL V. SHMAKOV.

General Confederation of Trade Unions (VKP): 119119 Moscow, Leninskii pr. 42; tel. (495) 938-01-12; fax (495) 938-21-55; e-mail inter@vkp.ru; internet www.vkp.ru; f. 1992 to replace General Confederation of Trade Unions of the USSR; co-ordinating body for trade unions in CIS member states; unites 10 national and 30 regional industrial orgs with 50m. mems; publishes *Profsoyuzy* (Trade Unions), weekly, *Vestnik profsoyuzov* (Herald of the Trade Unions), every two weeks, and *Inform-Contact*, in English and French, quarterly; Pres. MIKHAIL SHMAKOV; Sec.-Gen. VLADIMIR SCHERBAKOV.

Moscow Trade Unions Federation: 121205 Moscow, ul. Novyi Arbat 36/9; tel. (495) 290-82-62; fax (495) 202-92-70; e-mail main@mtuf.ru; f. 1990; largest regional branch of FITUR (q.v.); Chair. MIKHAIL D. NAGAITSEV; 2.2m. mems.

Transport

RAILWAYS

At the end of 2006 the total length of railway track in use was 84,821 km, around one-half of which was electrified.

Russian Railways OAO (RZhD) (Rossiiskiye zheleznyye dorogi): 107174 Moscow, ul. Novobasmannaya 2; tel. (495) 262-16-28; fax

THE RUSSIAN FEDERATION

(495) 975-24-11; e-mail info@rzd.ru; internet www.rzd.ru; f. 2003; Pres. VLADIMIR YAKUNIN.

City Underground Railways

Moscow Metro: 129110 Moscow, pr. Mira 41/2; tel. (495) 622-10-01; fax (495) 631-37-44; e-mail info@mosmetro.ru; internet www.mosmetro.org; f. 1935; 12 lines (301 km) with 182 stations in 2010; Gen. Man. DMITRII V. GAYEV.

Nizhnii Novgorod Metro: 603002 Nizhnii Novgorod, pl. Revolutsii 7; tel. (8312) 44-17-60; fax (8312) 44-20-86; e-mail metro@sandy.ru; f. 1985; 15 km with 13 stations; Gen. Man. A. KUZMIN.

Novosibirsk Metro: 630099 Novosibirsk, ul. Serebrennikovskaya 34; tel. (3832) 90-81-10; fax (3832) 46-56-82; e-mail nsk@metro.snt.su; internet www.nsk.su/~metro; f. 1986; 2 lines (13.2 km) with 11 stations, and a further 6 km under construction; Gen. Man. V. I. DEMIN.

St Petersburg Metro: 190013 St Petersburg, Moskovskii pr. 28; tel. (812) 251-66-68; fax (812) 316-14-41; e-mail np@metro.spb.ru; internet www.metro.spb.ru; f. 1955; 4 lines (106 km) with 60 stations; Gen. Man. VLADIMIR A. GARYUGIN.

Short underground railways began to operate in Samara, Yekaterinburg and Kazan in 1987, 1991 and 2005, respectively. In 2010 the construction of underground railways was under way in Chelyabinsk, Krasnoyarsk and Omsk, and a light railway was scheduled to open in Sochi, prior to the holding of the Winter Olympics there in 2014.

ROADS

At the end of 2006 the total length of roads was 597,421 km, and 85.2% of roads were paved. In Siberia and the Far East, there are few roads, and they are often impassable in winter, while the *rasputitsa*, or spring thaw, notoriously impedes rural road traffic, even in European Russia.

SHIPPING

The seaports of the Russian Federation provide access to the Pacific Ocean, in the east, the Baltic Sea and the Atlantic Ocean, in the west, and the Black Sea, in the south. Major eastern ports are at Vladivostok, Nakhodka, Vostochnyi, Magadan and Petropavlovsk. In the west, St Petersburg and Kaliningrad provide access to the Baltic Sea, and the northern ports of Murmansk and Archangel (Arkhangelsk) have access to the Atlantic Ocean, via the Barents Sea. Novorossiisk and Sochi are the principal Russian ports on the Black Sea.

Principal Ship-owning Companies

Baltic Shipping Co: 198035 St Petersburg, Mezhevoi kanal 5; tel. (812) 251-33-97; fax (812) 186-85-44; freight and passenger services; Chair. MIKHAIL A. ROMANOVSKII.

Baltic Transport Systems: 199106 St Petersburg, pl. Morskoi Slavy 1; tel. (812) 303-99-14; fax (812) 380-34-76; e-mail bts@baltics.ru; internet www.baltics.ru; f. 1994; freight and passenger services; Gen. Man. ALEKSEI E. SHUKLETSOV.

Far Eastern Shipping Co: 690019 Maritime (Primorskii) Krai, Vladivostok, ul. Aleutskaya 15; tel. (4232) 41-14-32; fax (4232) 52-15-51; e-mail 41401@41.fesco.ru; internet www.fesco.ru; f. 1880; Gen. Man. YEVGENII N. AMBROSOV.

Kamchatka Shipping Co: 683600 Kamchatka Krai, Petropavlovsk-Kamchatskii, ul. Radiosvyazi 65; tel. (41522) 2-82-21; fax (41522) 2-19-60; f. 1949; freight services; Pres. NIKOLAI M. ZABLOTSKII.

Murmansk Shipping Co: 183038 Murmansk, ul. Kominterna 15; tel. (8152) 48-10-48; fax (8152) 48-11-48; e-mail postmaster@msco.ru; f. 1939; shipping and ice-breaking services; Gen. Dir VYACHESLAV RUKSHA.

Northern Shipping Co (NSC Arkhangelsk) (Severnoye morskoye parokhodstvo OAO—SMP): 163000 Archangel, nab. Severnoi Dviny 36; tel. (8182) 63-72-03; fax (8182) 63-71-95; e-mail nsosnina@ansc.ru; internet www.ansc.ru; f. 1870; dry cargo-shipping, liner services; Gen. Dir VIKTOR A. IZBITSKII.

Novorossiisk Shipping Co: 353900 Krasnodar Krai, Novorossiisk, ul. Svobody 1; tel. (8617) 25-31-26; fax (8617) 25-11-43; e-mail novoship@novoship.ru; internet www.novoship.ru; f. 1992; Chair. V. I. YAKUNIN.

Primorsk Shipping Corpn: 692900 Maritime (Primorskii) Krai, Nakhodka-4, Administrativnyi Gorodok; tel. (4236) 69-45-05; fax (4236) 69-45-75; e-mail psc@prisco.ru; internet www.prisco.ru; f. 1972; tanker shipowner; Dir-Gen. ALEKSANDR MIGUNOV.

Sakhalin Shipping Co: 694620 Sakhalin obl., Kholmsk, ul. Pobedy 16; tel. (42433) 6-62-07; fax (42433) 6-60-20; e-mail chief@sasco.sakhalin.ru; internet www.sasco.org; f. 1945; ship-owners and managers, carriage of cargo and passengers; Pres. YAKUB ZH. ALEGEDPINOV.

Directory

Sovfrakht: 127944 Moscow, Rakhmanovskii per. 4, Morskoi Dom; tel. (495) 258-27-41; fax (495) 230-26-40; e-mail general@sovfracht.ru; internet www.sovfracht.ru; f. 1929; jt-stock co; chartering and broking of tanker, cargo and other ships; forwarding, booking and insurance agency; ship management; Dir-Gen. D. YU. PURIM; 120 employees (2003).

White Sea and Onega Shipping Co (Belomorsko-Onezhskoye parokhodstvo): 185005 Kareliya, Petrozavodsk, ul. Rigachina 7; tel. (8142) 71-12-01; fax (8142) 71-12-67; e-mail dir@bop.onego.ru; internet bop.onego.ru; f. 1940; cargo-shipping, cargo ship construction and repair; Gen. Dir STANISLAV ROZOLINSKII; Pres. ALEKSANDR LYALLYA.

CIVIL AVIATION

Until 1991 Aeroflot—Soviet Airlines was the only airline operating on domestic routes in the former USSR. In 1992–94 some 300 different independent airlines emerged on the basis of Aeroflot's former regional directorates. Several small private airlines were also established. In 2003 there were 451 airports in Russia.

Aeroflot-Don: 344009 Rostov-on-Don, pr. Sholokhova 272; tel. (863) 276-78-11; fax (863) 252-11-78; e-mail avia1@aeroflot-don.ru; internet www.aeroflot-don.ru; f. 1925; present name adopted 2000; 100% owned by Aeroflot—Russian Airlines; operates scheduled and chartered passenger and cargo flights to various domestic and international destinations (incl. Armenia, Austria, Egypt, Germany, Israel, Turkey, Ukraine, United Arab Emirates) from Rostov-on-Don, Moscow and Sochi, and between Moscow and Groznyi; Dir-Gen. MIKHAIL S. KRITSKII.

Aeroflot—Russian Airlines: 125167 Moscow, Leningradskii pr. 37/9; tel. and fax (495) 223-55-55; e-mail presscentr@aeroflot.ru; internet www.aeroflot.ru; f. 1923; 51% state-owned; operates flights to 94 destinations in 49 countries; Chair. IGOR YE. LEVITIN; Gen. Dir VALERII M. OKULOV.

Gazpromavia: 117997 Moscow, ul. Novocheremushkinskaya 71/32; tel. (495) 719-18-32; fax (495) 719-11-85; e-mail gazpromavia@gazprom.ru; internet www.gazpromavia.ru; f. 1995; Dir-Gen. ANDREI S. OVCHARENKO.

KD Avia: 238315 Kaliningrad obl., Guryevskii raion, Khrabrovo, Aeroport; tel. (401) 235-51-75; e-mail info@kdavia.ru; internet www.kdavia.ru; f. 1945; present name adopted 2005; international and domestic flights from Kaliningrad; Dir-Gen. VALERII MIKHAILOV.

Kuban Airlines (Kubanskiye Avialinii): 350026 Krasnodar, Krasnodar—Pashkovskaya Airport; tel. (861) 237-06-00; fax (861) 237-38-11; e-mail info@kuban-airlines.com; internet www.kuban-airlines.de; f. 1932; regional and international flights.

Rossiya—Russian Airlines: 191025 St Petersburg, Nevskii pr. 61; tel. (812) 333-22-22; fax (812) 333-22-44; internet www.rossiya-airlines.ru; f. 1992; merged with Pulkovo Airlines in 2006; state-owned; operates scheduled and charter passenger flights from St Petersburg and Moscow to domestic and international destinations; Gen. Dir SERGEI MIKHALIENKO.

S7 Airlines (Siberia Airlines): 633115 Novosibirsk obl., gorod Ob-4; tel. (3832) 59-90-11; fax (3832) 59-90-64; e-mail pr@s7.ru; internet www.s7.ru; fmrly Sibir Airlines; scheduled and charter flights to domestic, Asian, European and Middle Eastern destinations; Gen. Dir VLADISLAV FILEV.

SkyExpress: 119027 Moscow, Vnukovo, ul. Tsentralnaya 2/2; tel. (495) 648-93-60; fax (495) 980-74-61; e-mail info@skyexpress.ru; internet www.skyexpress.ru; f. 2006; 'low cost' airline operating passenger flights between Moscow (Vnukovo) and Murmansk, and Rostov-on-Don and Sochi (Krasnodar Krai); also international charter flights; Chief Exec. MARINA BUKALOVA.

Transaero Airlines: 127083 Moscow, Mishina 56/3; tel. (495) 788-80-80; fax (495) 937-84-64; e-mail info@transaero.ru; internet www.transaero.ru; f. 1991; Russia's largest privately owned airline; operates scheduled and charter passenger services to Europe, Asia and Central America; CEO OLGA PLESHAKOVA.

Ural Airlines (Uralskiye Aviyalinii): 620910 Sverdlovsk obl., Yekaterinburg, ul. Sputnikov 6; tel. (343) 226-81-26; fax (343) 226-82-49; e-mail margarita@uralairlines.ru; internet www.uralairlines.ru; f. 1993; flights from Yekaterinburg to domestic and international destinations; Gen. Dir SERGEI SKURATOV.

Vladivostok Avia: 692756 Maritime (Primorskii) Krai, Artem, ul. Portovaya 41, Vladivostok Airport; tel. (4232) 30-73-33; fax (4232) 30-73-43; e-mail office@vladavia.ru; internet www.vladavia.ru; f. 1994; freight and scheduled passenger services from Vladivostok and Moscow to domestic and international destinations; Gen. Dir VLADIMIR SAIBEL.

THE RUSSIAN FEDERATION

Tourism

In 2009 there were an estimated 19,420,000 tourist arrivals in Russia, and receipts from tourism, according to provisional data, totalled US $9,297m.

Intourist: 129366 Moscow, pr. Mira 150; tel. (495) 730-19-19; fax (495) 956-42-02; e-mail info@intourist.ru; internet www.intourist.ru; f. 1929; brs throughout Russia and abroad; Chair. VYACHESLAV KOPIEV.

Defence

In May 1992 the Russian Federation established its own armed forces, on the basis of former Soviet forces on the territory of the Russian Federation, and former Soviet forces outside its territory not subordinate to other former republics of the USSR. As assessed at November 2010, the total Russian active armed forces numbered an estimated 1,046,000, comprising 360,000 members of the army, 35,000 airborne troops, a navy of 161,000, 80,000 members of the Strategic Defence Forces and 250,000 command and support troops. There were an estimated 20,000,000 reserves. There were a further estimated 449,000 paramilitary troops, including 160,000 members of the Federal Border Guard Service, which is directly subordinate to the President, 200,000 troops of the Ministry of Internal Affairs, and an estimated 4,000 active (armed) members of the Federal Security Service. Compulsory military service (for males over the age of 18 years) lasts for a period of one year.

Defence Expenditure: Budgeted at 1,520,000m. roubles in 2011.
Chief of the General Staff, First Deputy Minister of Defence: Gen. NIKOLAI YE. MAKAROV.
Chief of Staff of the Internal Troops: Col-Gen. SERGEI BUNIN.
Commander-in-Chief of the Army: Col-Gen. ALEKSANDR POSTNIKOV.
Commander-in-Chief of the Navy: Adm. VLADIMIR S. VYSOTSKII.
Chief of Staff of the Air Force: Col-Gen. ALEKSANDR N. ZELIN.

Education

Education is compulsory for nine years, to be undertaken between the ages of six and 15 years. State education is generally provided free of charge, although in 1992 some higher education establishments began charging tuition fees. Students of selected courses in higher education receive a small stipend from the state. Primary education usually begins at six years of age and lasts for four years. Secondary education, beginning at 10 years of age, lasts for seven years, comprising a first cycle of five years and a second of two years. In 2006/07 enrolment at primary schools was equivalent to 96% of children in the appropriate age group, while the comparable ratio for secondary enrolment was 84%.

In 2009/10 7.4m. students were enrolled at institutes of higher education. Although Russian is the principal language used in educational establishments, a number of local languages are also in use. Budgetary expenditure on education (excluding scientific research and technology) in 2005 was an estimated 1,665,500m. roubles (representing 11.9% of total expenditure).

In 2008/09 there were 691 independent primary and general secondary schools, 249 independent vocational secondary schools, and 474 independent higher education institutions.

RWANDA
Introductory Survey

LOCATION, CLIMATE, LANGUAGE, RELIGION, FLAG, CAPITAL

The Rwandan Republic is a land-locked country in eastern central Africa, just south of the Equator, bounded by the Democratic Republic of the Congo to the west, by Uganda to the north, by Tanzania to the east and by Burundi to the south. The climate is tropical, although tempered by altitude. It is hot and humid in the lowlands, but cooler in the highlands. The average annual rainfall is 785 mm (31 ins). The main rainy season is from February to May. The population is composed of three ethnic groups: Hutu (85%), Tutsi (14%) and Twa (1%). French, English and Kinyarwanda, the native language, are all in official use, and Kiswahili is widely spoken. About one-half of the population adhere to animist beliefs. Most of the remainder are Christians, mainly Roman Catholics. There are Protestant and Muslim minorities. The national flag (proportions 1 by 2) has three unequal horizontal stripes, of blue, yellow and green, with a blue-ringed, yellow disc (framed by 24 yellow rays) depicted near the fly end of the top stripe. The capital is Kigali.

CONTEMPORARY POLITICAL HISTORY

Historical Context

Rwanda, with the neighbouring state of Burundi, became part of German East Africa in 1899. In 1916, during the First World War, it was occupied by Belgian forces from the Congo. From 1920 Rwanda was part of Ruanda-Urundi, administered by Belgium under a League of Nations mandate and later as a UN Trust Territory. Long-standing dissension between the majority Hutu tribe and their former overlords, the Tutsi, caused a rebellion and the proclamation of a state of emergency in 1959. In September 1961 it was decided by referendum to abolish the monarchy and to establish a republic. Full independence followed on 1 July 1962. Serious tribal conflict erupted in December 1963, and massacres (of an estimated 20,000) were perpetrated by the Hutu against the Tutsi. During 1964–65 large numbers of displaced Rwandans were resettled in neighbouring countries. In 1969 Grégoire Kayibanda, the new Republic's first President, was re-elected, and all 47 seats in the legislature were retained by the governing party, the Mouvement démocratique républicain (MDR).

Tension between Hutu and Tutsi escalated again at the end of 1972 and continued throughout February 1973. In July the Minister of Defence and head of the National Guard, Maj.-Gen. Juvénal Habyarimana, led a bloodless coup against President Kayibanda, proclaimed a Second Republic and established a military administration. In August a new Council of Ministers, with Habyarimana as President, was formed. All political activity was banned until July 1975, when a new ruling party, the Mouvement révolutionnaire national pour le développement (MRND), was formed.

A national referendum in December 1978 approved a new Constitution, which was intended to return the country to democratically elected government (in accordance with an undertaking made by Habyarimana in 1973 to end the military regime within five years). Elections to the legislature, the Conseil national de développement (CND), took place in December 1981 and in December 1983; also in December 1983 Habyarimana was re-elected President. In December 1988 Habyarimana was again elected (unopposed) to the presidency, securing 99.98% of the votes cast. Elections to the CND were conducted in the same month.

Domestic Political Affairs

In September 1990 a Commission was appointed to compile recommendations for a draft national charter, which was to provide for the establishment of a multi-party system. In April 1991, following the CND's revision of the Commission's proposals, a draft constitution was presented to an extraordinary congress of the MRND, at which the party was renamed the Mouvement républicain national pour la démocratie et le développement (MRNDD). On 10 June the reforms were promulgated by Habyarimana, and legislation regulating the formation of political parties was adopted; parties were to be non-tribal and independent, while members of the security forces and the judiciary were to be banned from political activity. (By June 1992 15 parties, among them the MRNDD and a revived MDR, had officially registered.) In October 1991 Sylvestre Nsanzimana, hitherto Minister of Justice, was appointed to the new post of Prime Minister, and in December he formed a transitional Government, in which all but two portfolios (assigned to the Parti démocrate chrétien—PDC) were allocated to members of the MRNDD. Opposition parties, which had been excluded from participation in the transitional Government for their rejection of an MRNDD Prime Minister, organized anti-Government demonstrations in late 1991 and early 1992, demanding the removal of Nsanzimana and the convening of a national conference. A series of negotiations between the Government and the major opposition parties was initiated in February 1992, and in April a protocol agreement was signed, providing for the establishment of a new transitional administration, with Dismas Nsengiyaremye of the MDR as Prime Minister. Habyarimana announced that multi-party elections would be conducted within one year of the installation of the new Government.

Relations with neighbouring Uganda were frequently strained, owing mainly to the presence of some 250,000 Rwandan refugees in Uganda (mainly members of Rwanda's Tutsi minority), who had fled their homeland following successive outbreaks of persecution by the Hutu regime in 1959, 1963 and 1973. In October 1990 rebel forces, based in Uganda, invaded northern Rwanda, occupying several towns. The 4,000-strong rebel army, known as the Front patriotique rwandais (FPR), which mainly comprised Rwandan Tutsi refugees, aimed to overthrow the Habyarimana regime and secure the repatriation of all Rwandan refugees. The Rwandan Government accused the Ugandan leadership of supporting the rebel forces (many of whom had served in the Ugandan armed forces), although this accusation was strenuously denied. With the assistance of French, Belgian and Zairean troops, the Rwandan army succeeded in repelling the FPR before it could reach Kigali. In late October the Government declared a cease-fire, although hostilities continued in northern Rwanda.

Unsuccessful negotiations took place during 1991 and early 1992, but further talks held in Arusha, Tanzania, in July resulted in an agreement on the implementation of a new cease-fire, effective from the end of that month, and the creation of a military observer group (GOM), sponsored by the Organization of African Unity (OAU—now the African Union—AU, see p. 183), to comprise representatives from both sides, together with officers from the armed forces of Nigeria, Senegal, Zimbabwe and Mali. However, subsequent negotiations failed to resolve outstanding problems concerning the creation of a proposed 'neutral zone' between the Rwandan armed forces and the FPR, the incorporation of the FPR in a future combined Rwandan national force, the repatriation of refugees, and FPR demands for full participation in a transitional government and legislature.

A resurgence in violence followed the breakdown of negotiations in February 1993. An estimated 1m. civilians fled the advancing FPR forces into neighbouring Uganda and Tanzania. France dispatched reinforcements to join a small military contingent that had been stationed in Kigali since October 1990 to protect French nationals. Meanwhile, the commander of the 50-member GOM declared that the group had inadequate manpower and resources to contain the FPR, and requested the deployment of an additional 400 troops from the OAU. In late February 1993 the Government accepted FPR terms for a cease-fire, in return for an end to attacks against FPR positions and Tutsi communities, and the withdrawal of foreign troops. Although fighting continued with varying intensity, fresh peace negotiations were convened in Arusha in March, and France subsequently began to withdraw its troops. Negotiations conducted during April failed to produce a solution to the crucial issue of the structure of a future single armed Rwandan force. In the same month the five participating parties in the ruling coalition agreed to a three-month extension of the Government's mandate, in order to facilitate the successful conclusion of a peace accord. Significant progress was made during renewed talks between the Government and the FPR during May, when a timetable for the demobilization of the 19,000-strong security forces was agreed. In June the UN Security Council approved the creation of the UN Observer Mission Uganda-Rwanda (UNOMUR), to be deployed on the Ugandan side of the border, for an initial period of six months, in order to prevent the maintenance of a military supply line for the FPR.

In July 1993 President Habyarimana met with delegates from those political parties represented in the Government to seek a further extension of the coalition's mandate. However, the Prime Minister's insistence that the FPR should be represented in any new government exacerbated existing divisions within the MDR, prompting Habyarimana to conclude the agreement with a conciliatory group of MDR dissidents, including the Minister of Education, Agathe Uwilingiyimana, who was elected to the premiership.

In August 1993 a peace accord was formally signed in Arusha by Habyarimana and Col Alex Kanyarengwe of the FPR. A new transitional government, to be headed by a mutually approved Prime Minister, would be installed, and multi-party elections would be conducted after a 22-month period. In October the UN Security Council adopted Resolution 872, providing for the establishment of the UN Assistance Mission to Rwanda (UNAMIR), to be deployed in Rwanda for an initial period of six months, with a mandate to monitor observance of the cease-fire, to contribute to the security of the capital and to facilitate the repatriation of refugees. UNAMIR, which was to incorporate UNOMUR and GOM and to comprise some 2,500 personnel, was formally inaugurated on 1 November. In December the UN expressed the opinion that conditions had been sufficiently fulfilled to allow the inauguration of the transitional institutions.

On 5 January 1994 Habyarimana was invested as President of a transitional administration, for a 22-month period, under the terms of the Arusha accord. The inauguration of the transitional government and legislature was, however, repeatedly delayed, owing to political opposition to the proposed Council of Ministers, and to the insistence of Habyarimana that the list of proposed legislative deputies, presented in March, should be modified to include representatives of additional political parties, including the reactionary Coalition pour la défense de la République (CDR). Meanwhile, political frustration had erupted into violence in February, with the murder of the Minister of Public Works and Energy, Félicien Gatabazi of the Parti social-démocrate (PSD), who had been a prominent supporter of the Arusha accord and of the transitional administration. Within hours the CDR leader, Martin Bucyana, was killed in a retaliatory attack by PSD supporters, and a series of violent confrontations ensued.

Collapse of civil order and genocide

On 6 April 1994 the presidential aircraft was fired on, above Kigali airport, and exploded, killing all 10 passengers, including Habyarimana. (The President of Burundi, Cyprien Ntaryamira, two Burundian cabinet ministers and the Chief of Staff of the Rwandan armed forces were among the other victims.) In Kigali the presidential guard immediately initiated a campaign of retributive violence against Habyarimana's political opponents, although it remained unclear who had been responsible for the attack on the aircraft. As politicians and civilians fled the capital, the brutality of the political assassinations was compounded by attacks on the clergy, UNAMIR personnel and members of the Tutsi tribe. Many Hutu civilians were reportedly forced to murder their Tutsi neighbours, and the mobilization of the Interahamwe unofficial militias (allegedly affiliated to the MRNDD and the CDR), committed to the massacre of Tutsi civilians and opponents of the Government, was encouraged by the presidential guard (with support from some factions of the armed forces) and by inflammatory radio broadcasts. The Prime Minister, the President of the Constitutional Court and the Ministers of Labour and Social Affairs and of Information were among the prominent politicians murdered (or declared missing and presumed dead) within hours of Habyarimana's death. On 8 April the Speaker of the CND, Dr Théodore Sindikubwabo, announced that he had assumed the office of interim President of the Republic, in accordance with the provisions of the 1991 Constitution. The five remaining participating political parties and factions of the Government selected a new Prime Minister, Jean Kambanda, and a new Council of Ministers (drawn largely from the MRNDD) from among their ranks. The legality of the new administration was immediately challenged by the FPR, which claimed that the terms of the Constitution regarding succession had been superseded by the terms of the Arusha accord. The legitimacy of the Government was subsequently rejected by several political parties and factions.

In mid-April 1994 the FPR resumed operations from its northern stronghold, with the stated aim of relieving its beleaguered battalion in Kigali, restoring order there and halting the massacre of civilians. Belgium's UNAMIR contingent of more than 400 troops was also withdrawn, having encountered increasing hostility as a result of persistent rumours of Belgian complicity in the attack on President Habyarimana's aircraft, and accusations that Belgian troops were providing logistical support to the FPR.

As the violent campaign initiated by the presidential guard and the estimated 30,000 Interahamwe gathered national momentum, the militia's identification of all Tutsi as political opponents of the State provoked tribal polarization and an effective pogrom. Reports of mass Tutsi graves and of unprovoked attacks on fleeing Tutsi refugees and those sheltering in schools, hospitals and churches provoked unqualified international outrage, and promises were made of financial and logistical aid for an estimated 2m. displaced Rwandans. By late May 1994 attempts to assess the full scale of the humanitarian catastrophe in Rwanda were complicated by reports that the FPR (which claimed to control more than one-half of the territory) was perpetrating retaliatory atrocities against Hutu civilians.

In view of the deteriorating security situation, in late April 1994 the UN Security Council approved a resolution to reduce UNAMIR to just 270 personnel. This was condemned by the Rwandan authorities, and in mid-May, following intense international pressure and the disclosure of the vast scale of the humanitarian crisis in the region, the Security Council approved Resolution 917, providing for the eventual deployment of some 5,500 UN troops with a revised mandate, including the protection of refugees in designated 'safe areas'. In early June the UN Security Council extended the mandate of what was designated UNAMIR II until December. However, the UN Secretary-General continued to encounter considerable difficulty in securing equipment and armaments requested by those countries that had agreed to participate.

By mid-June 1994 the emergence of confirmed reports of retributive murders committed by FPR members and the collapse of an OAU-brokered truce prompted the French Government to announce its willingness to lead an armed police action, endorsed by the UN, in Rwanda. Despite French insistence that its force (expected to total 2,000 troops) would maintain strict political neutrality, and operate in a purely humanitarian capacity pending the arrival of a multinational UN force, the FPR was vehemently opposed to its deployment, citing political bias. The UN Secretary-General welcomed the French initiative; however, the OAU expressed serious reservations as to the appropriateness of the action. In late June a first contingent of 150 French marine commandos launched 'Operation Turquoise', entering the western town of Cyangugu, in preparation for a large-scale operation to protect refugees in the area. An estimated 1m. Rwandans sought refuge in the Zairean border town of Goma, while a similar number attempted to cross the border elsewhere in the south-west. The FPR, meanwhile, swiftly secured all major cities and strategic territorial positions, but halted its advance several kilometres from the boundaries of the French-controlled neutral zone, requesting the apprehension and return for trial of those responsible for the recent atrocities. (In early July the UN announced the creation of a commission of inquiry to investigate allegations of genocide, following an initial report that as many as 500,000 Rwandans had been killed since April.)

Refugee crisis

On 19 July 1994 Pasteur Bizimungu, a Hutu, was inaugurated as President for a five-year term. On the same day the FPR announced the composition of a new Government of National Unity, with the leader of the MDR moderate faction, Faustin Twagiramungu, as Prime Minister. The majority of cabinet posts were assigned to FPR members (including the FPR military chief, Maj.-Gen. Paul Kagame, who became Minister of Defence and also assumed the newly created post of Vice-President), while the remainder were divided among the MDR, the PSD, the Parti libéral (PL) and the Parti démocrate chrétien (PDC). The new administration urged all refugees to return to Rwanda, and issued assurances that civilian Hutus could return safely to their homes. The new Government declared its intention to honour the terms of the Arusha accord within the context of an extended period of transition. The claims to legitimacy of the exiled former administration were seriously undermined by recognition by the European Union (EU, see p. 270) of the new Government of National Unity in September.

Amid persistent rumours that the Rwandan armed forces were attempting to regroup and rearm in Zaire, in preparation for a counter-offensive against the FPR, in late August 1994 the UN initiated the deployment of some 2,500 UNAMIR II forces in the security zone (redesignated 'zone four'). French troops began to withdraw from the area (the final contingent departed in late September), prompting hundreds of thousands of internally displaced Hutu refugees within the zone to move to Zairean border areas. An estimated 500,000 refugees remained at camps in the former security zone at the end of August. The UNAMIR II mandate was extended for a further six months. (In June 1995, at the request of the Rwandan Government, the six-month mandate of the force, which was reduced from 5,586 to 2,330 personnel, was again renewed.)

In November 1994 a number of amendments to the terms of the August 1993 Arusha accord were adopted under a multi-party protocol of understanding. The most notable of the new provisions was the exclusion from the legislative process of those parties implicated in alleged acts of genocide during 1994. A 70-member Transitional National Assembly was formally inaugurated in December, with a composition including five representatives of the armed forces and one member of the national police force. On 5 May 1995 this legislature adopted a new Constitution, which was based on selected articles of the 1991 Constitution, the terms of the Arusha accord, the FPR's victory declaration of July 1994 and the November multi-party protocol.

In late 1994 Hutu refugees within Rwanda and in neighbouring countries were continuing to resist the exhortations of the UN and the new Rwandan administration to return to their homes, despite the deteriorating security situation in many camps (which had, moreover, forced the withdrawal of a number of relief agencies). Hutu militias were reported to have assumed control of several camps, notably Katale in Zaire and Benaco in Tanzania. The reluctance of many refugees to return to their homes was also attributed to persistent allegations that the Tutsi-dominated FPR armed forces (the Armée patriotique rwandaise—APR) were conducting a systematic campaign of reprisal attacks against returning Hutus.

A political crisis emerged in August 1995, after the Prime Minister expressed dissatisfaction with the Government's lack of adherence to the provisions of the Arusha accord regarding power-sharing, and with the security forces' repeated recourse to violence in their management of the refugee crisis. Twagiramungu and four other disaffected ministers were subsequently replaced. Pierre Célestin Rwigyema of the MDR, also Hutu and the former Minister of Primary and Secondary Education, was named as the new Prime Minister at the end of the month. The new Council of Ministers included representatives of both major ethnic groups and four political parties.

Also in August 1995, in response to requests made by the Rwandan Government, the UN Security Council voted to suspend the arms embargo to Rwanda (imposed in May 1994) for one year, in order to allow the Government to safeguard against the threat of a military offensive by Hutu extremists encamped in neighbouring countries. Meanwhile, the security situation in refugee camps along the Zairean border had deteriorated to such an extent that the Zairean Government initiated a programme of forcible repatriation, attracting widespread international concern. Despite a formal agreement between the office of the UN High Commissioner for Refugees (UNHCR) and the Zairean Government for a more regulated approach to the refugee crisis, APR attacks near the border with Zaire further deterred refugees. At a conference of the Great Lakes countries, convened in Cairo, Egypt, in late November President Mobutu Sese Seko of Zaire indicated that the forcible return of remaining refugees in early 1996 was no longer a realistic objective. The conference also accepted the Rwandan President's assertion that the participation of UNAMIR forces in peace-keeping operations in Rwanda was no longer necessary, but urged the Rwandan Government to accept the extension of a revised, three-month mandate for the forces to provide assistance in the refugee repatriation process. (A three-month mandate for a 1,200-strong force was thus renewed in December 1995, and the mission was formally terminated in April 1996.)

Post-genocide justice

In February 1995 the UN Security Council adopted Resolution 977, whereby Arusha was designated the seat for the International Criminal Tribunal for Rwanda (ICTR), which was to investigate allegations made against some 400 individuals of direct involvement in the planning and execution of crimes against humanity perpetrated in Rwanda during 1994. The six-member Tribunal, to be headed by a Senegalese lawyer, Laïty Kama, was inaugurated in June 1995 for a four-year term.

The ICTR began formal proceedings in November 1995. The first court session of the ICTR was convened in September 1996, but hearings concerning the first two (of 21) individuals indicted on charges of crimes against humanity were almost immediately postponed. Tribunal officials attributed the virtual collapse of proceedings to the escalating conflict in eastern Zaire, but widespread concern was expressed at the high number of administrative errors committed. In contrast, in January 1997 regional courts within Rwanda passed death sentences on five individuals accused of acts of genocide. (Whereas capital punishment would not be invoked by the ICTR, legislation published by the Rwandan authorities in September 1996 regarding penalties for crimes committed during 1994 made provision for the application of the death penalty.) In July 1997 former Prime Minister Jean Kambanda, two senior armed forces officers and a former government minister were arrested in Kenya and transferred for trial to Arusha.

Some 300 genocide suspects were tried by Rwandan courts during 1997, and an estimated 125,000 defendants were in detention awaiting trial; arrests reportedly continued at a rate of 1,000 per month. In late 1997, in an attempt to address the problem of severe overcrowding in prisons, the release was authorized of elderly, infirm or juvenile detainees. (This policy was denounced by organizations representing survivors of the 1994 massacres, and there were reports of attacks on freed genocide suspects.) The announcement that 23 people convicted of acts of genocide were to be publicly executed provoked international condemnation. Amnesty International and other human rights organizations expressed serious concerns that those convicted had been denied adequate opportunity to prepare a defence. The Rwandan authorities refuted such claims, and dismissed pleas for clemency. The public executions proceeded in April 1998.

Meanwhile, in August 1996, during a visit to Kigali by the Zairean Prime Minister, a bilateral agreement for the organized and unconditional repatriation of all Rwandan refugees in Zaire was concluded (without the participation of UNHCR officials). During September, however, relations between the two countries were placed under renewed strain, when the attempts of the Interahamwe and the Zairean armed forces to displace large numbers of Zairean Banyamulenge (ethnic Tutsis) from eastern Zaire encountered large-scale armed resistance from the Banyamulenge, resulting in Zairean accusations of Rwandan support for the Banyamulenge, and culminating in a cross-border exchange of fire later that month.

There was renewed international concern for the estimated 1m. refugees previously encamped in eastern Zaire, following reports that the regional conflict had resulted in the sudden exodus of some 250,000 refugees, and the interruption of food aid distribution. The rebel army in Zaire (the Alliance des forces démocratiques pour la libération du Congo-Zaïre—AFDL) declared a cease-fire for returning refugees and announced the creation of a humanitarian corridor to the Rwandan border. The large-scale return of refugees was finally prompted by an AFDL attack on Interahamwe units operating from the camp. In April 1997 the AFDL leader, Laurent-Désiré Kabila, demanded that the UN complete full repatriation of the refugees within 60 days, after which time their return would be undertaken unilaterally by the rebels. The Rwandan authorities, meanwhile, expressed concern that the UN was delaying the rapid repatriation of refugees from eastern Zaire. (By the end of May the AFDL had gained control of most of Zaire, which was renamed the Democratic Republic of the Congo—DRC, and Kabila assumed power as Head of State.) Continuing ethnic unrest and violence, particularly in north-west Rwanda, throughout 1997 were exacerbated by the return from the DRC of large numbers of Hutus (see also the chapter on the DRC). An extensive demobilization programme was undertaken from September, with the aim of reintegrating former combatants into civil society; some 57,500 personnel were to be demobilized over a three-year period.

The trial of genocide suspects continued in 1998, both in Rwanda and at the ICTR, and in early September the ICTR reached its first verdict. A former mayor of Taba, Jean-Paul Akayesu, was convicted and sentenced to life imprisonment; Kambanda, who had pleaded guilty to six charges of genocide and crimes against humanity, was also given a life sentence. Rwandan courts convicted and sentenced some 1,000 genocide suspects during 1998 (the authorities had aimed to hear 5,000 cases during the year). By June about 5,000 suspects in Rwandan prisons had pleaded guilty to acts of genocide in order to lessen their sentences, apparently in response to the public executions in April. In October some controversy was caused by the decision to release at least 10,000 genocide suspects owing to lack of evidence against them. It was announced in November that 34,000 suspects had been freed since 1994.

In June 1998 the Transitional National Assembly approved draft legislation establishing a commission that was to prepare a new constitution and the period of political transition, originally set at five years in 1994, was extended by a further four years. Legislation establishing a national police force (which was to unify the existing national gendarmerie, and the communal and judicial police) was adopted in August 1998.

During 1999 a number of prominent Hutu, including three former government ministers, were arrested on suspicion of involvement in the 1994 genocide and extradited to the ICTR. In May 1999 a former Rwandan mayor (the first Rwandan to be tried abroad for genocide) was convicted by a Swiss court on charges of inciting the killing of Tutsi civilians, and sentenced to life imprisonment. In June Navanethem Pillay succeeded Kama as President of the ICTR, and in September Carla del Ponte became UN Chief Prosecutor.

Kagame appointed President

In February 2000 the National Assembly voted in favour of investigating alleged abuses of power by Rwigyema. On 28 February he resigned from the office of Prime Minister, citing differences with the legislature. Bernard Makuza, hitherto the Rwandan ambassador in Germany, was appointed Prime Minister in March, and subsequently announced a government reorganization, in which six ministers were replaced. The new Government was the first since 1994 in which the parties were not represented in accordance with the 1993 Arusha peace accords. At its inauguration, Kagame (who remained Vice-President and Minister of Defence and National Security) failed to swear allegiance to the President. On 23 March 2000 Bizimungu resigned from office, owing to disagreement over the composition of the new Government, and Kagame was subsequently appointed interim President by the Supreme Court. On 17 April he was formally elected President of Rwanda by members of the Transitional National Assembly and the Government, securing 81 of 86 votes cast. He was inaugurated on 22 April (becoming the first Tutsi Head of State since 1959).

In July 2000 Rwigyema was removed from the leadership of the MDR by the party's political bureau, which accused him of acting contrary to its interests. In April 2001 an international warrant was issued for the arrest of Rwigyema, who had taken refuge in the USA, on suspicion of participating in the genocide of 1994. In December 2001 a new national flag, emblem and anthem officially replaced those adopted at independence in 1962.

By late 2001, with the number of prisoners awaiting trial having increased to some 115,000, those suspected of lesser crimes relating to the genocide were henceforth to be tried by a traditional system of justice, known as *gacaca* (on the grass). In April 2002 the trial of Col Theoneste Bagosora, who was considered to be the principal organizer of the genocide, commenced at the ICTR. Bagosora, who had been in custody since his arrest in Cameroon in 1996, had allegedly planned the massacre of Tutsi civilians by the militia and had personally ordered the assassination of prominent politicians. He, and a further three former senior army officers on trial, refused to attend the initial session of the ICTR, on the grounds that their right to defence had been violated. Later in April 2002 security forces arrested former President Bizimungu (who had attempted to form an opposition political party in May 2001), and searched his residence. The authorities subsequently announced that Bizimungu had continued to engage in illegal political activity, and would be charged with endangering state security.

In early August 2002 Gen. Augustin Bizimungu, the army Chief of Staff in 1994, who had been indicted by the ICTR jointly with four other former military commanders, was arrested in Angola and transferred to the Tribunal. Later that month he pleaded not guilty to 10 charges, including that of genocide. In November 2002 trials by the *gacaca* court system officially commenced in large parts of the country.

In January 2003, in an effort to reduce numbers in prisons, Kagame issued a decree providing for the provisional release of some 40,000 of those held in detention, including many who had pleaded guilty to charges related to the 1994 genocide. Although the Ministry of Justice maintained that legal proceedings against the released prisoners would continue, organizations representing survivors of the genocide criticized the measure. Most of the prisoners due for release were to be dispatched to 'solidarity camps', where they were to be prepared for reintegration into society. (By the end of 2003 some 25,000 suspects had been released.)

A new Constitution, providing for the establishment of a bicameral legislature (comprising an 80-member Chamber of Deputies and a 26-member Senate) and a President, who was to be elected by universal suffrage, was approved by 93.4% of the electorate at a national referendum, which took place on 26 May 2003. The new Constitution entered into effect on 4 June; under its provisions, political associations formed on the basis of ethnicity, tribal or regional affiliation, religion or any other grounds for discrimination were prohibited. (Some existing political organizations were restructured to end such affiliations.) The presidential election was subsequently scheduled for 25 August, and was to be followed by legislative elections in late September. Kagame announced his intention to seek re-election, while former Prime Minister Twagiramungu returned to Rwanda from exile in Belgium in order to contest the presidency.

Kagame's second term

The first presidential election to take place in Rwanda since the single candidate poll of 1988 was conducted on 25 August 2003 (thereby marking the end of the nine-year transitional period). Kagame was returned to power, with 95.1% of votes cast, while Twagiramungu won 3.6%, and Jean-Népomuscène Nayinzira 1.3% of the votes. Kagame was officially inaugurated on 12 September. Four political parties subsequently agreed to contest the forthcoming legislative elections in alliance with the FPR. Following the dissolution of the MDR, many of its former members joined the newly emerged Parti du progrès et de la concorde. In addition to the FPR-led coalition, the PSD, the PL and a number of independent candidates registered to contest the legislative elections. Elections to the Chamber of Deputies commenced on 29 September, with voting for seats allocated to one disabled and two youth representatives. The poll for the 53 seats contested by political parties and independent candidates followed on 30 September; the FPR-led coalition, with 73.8% of votes cast, secured 40 seats, while the PSD (12.3% of votes) won seven seats, and the PL (10.6%) six seats. The remaining 24 female representatives were selected at provincial level on 2 October. Kagame formed a new Council of Ministers on 19 October; Makuza was reappointed to the office of Prime Minister and most principal ministers retained their portfolios. Twagiramungu left the country in early November, after claiming that he faced detention owing to his opposition to Kagame's Government.

In September 2003 a Gambian judge, Hassan Bubacar Jallow, was appointed Chief Prosecutor of the ICTR, replacing del Ponte. In December the owners of Radio Télévision Libre des Mille Collines and the Hutu extremist newspaper *Kangura* were sentenced to life imprisonment at the ICTR, on charges relating to public incitement to commit genocide. By February 2004 the ICTR had convicted 18 and acquitted three defendants and in that month the Rwandan authorities urged those prisoners awaiting trial in connection with the genocide to qualify for a general amnesty by confessing to the charges against them. Meanwhile, at the ongoing trial of Bagosora at the ICTR, the testimony of a principal witness, a former Canadian UN commander, Gen. (retd) Romeo Dallaire, implicated French forces in failing to prevent the genocide.

In June 2004 former President Bizimungu (who had remained in detention since April 2002) was sentenced to a term of 15 years' imprisonment, after being convicted of corruption, inciting civil disobedience and criminal association; he was, however, acquitted of the principal charge of endangering state security through anti-Government activities. In July 2004 the Minister of Finance of the 1994 Government, Emmanuel Ndindabahizi, who had been arrested in Belgium in July 2001, received a sentence of life imprisonment at the ICTR on charges of genocide and two counts of crimes against humanity for his participation in the massacre of Tutsi refugees during that period. Proceedings for some of the large number of cases to be transferred from the ICTR to the *gacaca* courts commenced in early 2005. In February the Minister of Family and Women's Affairs of the 1994 Government became the first woman to be charged with genocide in connection with organized killings in the Butare prefecture. At the end of March the serving Minister of Defence, Gen. Marcel Gatsinzi, appeared before a *gacaca* court, where he pleaded not guilty to charges of failing to prevent troops under his command from perpetrating massacres in Butare.

In early October 2005 the trial began of Protais Zigiranyirazo (who had been extradited to the ICTR in October 2001); he pleaded not guilty to all charges relating to the genocide. (By late 2005 it was reported that some 4,162 cases, including those of several former officials, had been tried by the *gacaca* system.) In July 2006 phase two of the *gacaca* system began. While those charged with crimes related to the genocide were in prison in Rwanda, many of those suspected of issuing the orders had fled and were living in exile. However, an announcement was made in October that France, Belgium and the Netherlands had agreed to seek those who had taken up residence in those countries and bring them to trial. Frustrated at the slow progress being made by the ICTR—since 1997 only 29 of those responsible for the genocide had been convicted—the Rwandan Government wanted suspects transferred to face trial in Rwanda. Since the country maintained the death penalty suspects could not be extradited, but in July 2007 legislation to abolish this was officially promulgated; it was reported that those who had been sentenced to death would instead be subjected to terms of life imprisonment. Proceedings began in August to seek extradition orders.

Meanwhile, in October 2005 both legislative chambers approved a number of constitutional amendments, which principally provided for the reorganization of local government structures (reducing the number of provinces, formerly prefectures, from 12 to five) to allow greater decentralization; the territorial reforms entered into effect at the beginning of 2006. In February the Supreme Court upheld the 15-year sentence imposed on Bizimungu (who had submitted an appeal against the charges in October 2005). Also in February 2006 the Rwandan Government denied a request by Jallow for the transfer of the trial of a suspected Interahamwe military leader to Norway. In April 2007 Bizimungu received a presidential pardon and was released from prison.

In 2003 the UN Security Council had mandated the ICTR to complete the first instance trials of genocide suspects by December 2008, and all appeals proceedings were to be completed by 2010. However, there were concerns that the trials would not be completed before the expiry of the ICTR's mandate and that too few of the suspected key perpetrators of the genocide had been prosecuted. In May 2008 the USA announced that it was to re-establish a programme offering large financial rewards for information leading to the arrest of 13 genocide suspects still at large before the ICTR ceased operations, while in June legislation was approved granting *gacaca* courts the jurisdiction to try up to 90% of those suspects who would otherwise be required to be brought before the ICTR. In November the ICTR concluded the trial of several high-profile suspects: Bagosora received a life sentence for genocide, war crimes and crimes against humanity and Zigiranyirazo was sentenced to 20 years in prison. In July 2009, when the ICTR had concluded only 44 cases, the mandate of the ICTR was extended by the UN Security Council until December 2010. This was later extended further until December 2012. However, the ICTR received criticism for failing to prosecute members of the FPR for their crimes committed during the conflict.

In October 2009 former Hutu rebel leader Salfe Bizimungu Mahoro was convicted of genocide and related charges, and sentenced to life imprisonment; several more suspects were found and detained in France, Germany, Italy and Uganda. The Rwandan authorities had succeeded in reducing the number of people detained on charges of crimes committed during the genocide from some 83,000 in 2003 to fewer than 39,000 in 2009. In November the ICTR overturned Zigiranyirazo's conviction and acquitted him of all charges, on the grounds that several inconsistencies in the trial and sentencing procedures had emerged. The Rwandan Government condemned the decision.

Meanwhile, in a major governmental reorganization in March 2008, the number of full cabinet positions was increased to 22 from 19, while the number of ministers of state was reduced from 11 to six. Charles Murigande, hitherto Minister of Foreign Affairs and Co-operation, became Minister of Cabinet Affairs at the newly created ministry; Rosemary Museminari replaced Murigande, one of four women to enter the cabinet.

The 2008 legislative elections

On 15 September 2008, in only the second legislative elections to be held since the genocide of 1994, the FPR secured a resounding victory with 78.8% of the votes cast and winning 42 of the 53 directly elected seats; the PSD took seven seats and the PL four. It was the first time that women outnumbered men in the legislature, occupying some 56% of the seats. Turn-out for the elections was estimated at over 98%. The following month Rose Mukantantabana was nominated as Speaker of the Chamber of Deputies, the first woman to hold that position in the country's history.

It was announced in September 2009 that a presidential election would be held in August 2010. President Kagame, who confirmed his intention to seek re-election to the presidency, was criticized by the opposition for making it difficult for parties to register their candidates. The Parti socialiste rwandais and the FPR both subsequently announced that they would not be presenting candidates in the election. President Kagame effected a cabinet reorganization in December 2009, appointing John Rwangombwa to replace James Musoni as Minister of Finance and Economic Planning; Louise Mushikiwabo replaced Rosemary Museminari as Minister of Foreign Affairs.

In January 2010 the findings of a two-year investigation into the assassination of President Habyarimana, which was carried out by the Rwandan Committee of Independent Experts under the chairmanship of Jean Mutsinzi, a Rwandan judge and the President of the African Court on Human and Peoples' Rights, were made public. Although some 600 witnesses had been interviewed during the investigation, the conclusions revealed little new information (and broadly agreed with those of UNAMIR), but maintained that Hutu extremists led by Bagosora, who were opposed to Habyarimana's intention to implement the Arusha accord, were responsible for the attack and that the missiles that brought down the aircraft had been launched from the Kanombe military camp where members of the presidential guard were based. It was also stated that there appeared to be widespread knowledge that an assassination attempt on Habyarimana was imminent, and that there had been significant French involvement in the incident.

A major reorganization of senior defence staff was implemented by President Kagame in April 2010. The Minister of Defence, Gen. Marcel Gatsinzi, was replaced in that position by the hitherto Chief of Defence Staff, Gen. James Kabarebe, while the Chief of Staff of the Army, Lt-Gen. Charles Kayonga succeeded Kabarebe. Gatsinzi was appointed Minister of Disaster Preparedness and Refugee Affairs, and Lt-Gen. Caesar Kayizari assumed the role of Army Chief of Staff. Days later the former Chief of Staff of the Air Force and another senior general were suspended from office and arrested following allegations of corruption and misuse of office and immoral conduct, respectively. There were reports in the Rwandan press that the arrests were connected to a series of bomb attacks in Kigali in February and March in which over 30 people were injured and at least one person was killed. Also in April the publication of two independent newspapers, *Umuseso* and *Umuvugizi*, was suspended by the authorities.

Recent developments: the 2010 presidential election

The campaign period prior to the presidential election was marred by further grenade attacks, attributed to the Interahamwe, in Kigali and increased FPR measures against opposition politicians, journalists and dissident military officials. In April 2010 Victoire Ingabire, the leader of the Forces démocratiques unifiées—Inkingi party and Kagame's main prospective presidential opponent, was arrested and imprisoned on charges of genocide denial and of collaborating with Hutu rebels in the DRC. In May her US lawyer, Peter Erlinder, was also arrested in Rwanda on charges of genocide denial (shortly after the US Administration had expressed concerns over the human rights situation in the country prior to the presidential election). Violent incidents included the murders of the editor of suspended publication *Umuvugizi*, Jean-Léonard Rugambage (who had claimed to have knowledge of government responsibility for the shooting of a former army chief of staff in South Africa), in June and of André Kagwa Rwisereka, Vice-President of the opposition Parti démocratique vert, in July; the FPR was widely suspected of involvement in the killings. The presidential election was conducted on 9 August: according to official results released by the National Electoral Commission, Kagame, secured an overwhelming victory, winning 93.1% of the votes cast. The second placed candidate, Dr Jean Damascene

Ntawukuriryayo of the PSD, took only 5.2% of the votes. Some 97.5% of the registered electorate participated in the poll. Although the European Commission welcomed the successful organization of the election, the US National Security Council expressed concern at the incidents in the preceding period. A final report by the Commonwealth Observer Group concluded that the poll had proceeded peacefully, but cited a lack of transparency of the results consolidation, an absence of critical opposition and problems faced by some media outlets. On 6 September Kagame was inaugurated for a second seven-year term. His Government was reappointed unchanged on 14 September.

At the beginning of October 2010 the UN released a report listing the violations of human rights and international humanitarian law committed in the DRC in 1993–2003, which had been significantly modified after a leaked draft of the text prompted the Rwandan Government to threaten to withdraw its peacekeeping troops from all UN missions upon its publication. Nevertheless, the Government denounced the report, which implicated the Rwandan armed forces in massacres of Hutu refugees. Later in October Ingabire was again arrested, and charged with forming a terrorist organization; Human Rights Watch expressed concern at her detention and the hospitalization of another opposition leader, Bernard Ntaganda, who had staged a hunger strike after his arrest in June. In January 2011 the High Military Court sentenced two former senior army officers to 24 years' imprisonment *in absentia* and a further two former officials in Kagame's administration to 20 years *in absentia* for threatening state security, after they issued a document in September 2010 denouncing Kagame's Government as authoritarian, corrupt and repressive. Meanwhile, with 52 cases completed and nine trials (involving 21 suspects) in progress and one pending in early 2011, the ICTR was expected to complete all trials by the end of 2011, with appeals to be completed in 2013; 10 indictees remained at large. In December 2010 the UN Security Council established the International Residual Mechanism for Criminal Tribunal, which was to begin operations in July 2012 and was to conclude the remaining tasks of the ICTR following its closure.

In May 2011 Augustin Bizimungu was sentenced to 30 years' imprisonment by the ICTR for his role in the genocide of 1994. The former head of the paramilitary police, Augustin Ndindiliyimana, was also convicted of genocide and crimes against humanity, but was released from detention having already served 11 years in gaol.

Foreign Affairs
Regional relations

At the end of July 1998 Laurent-Désiré Kabila (the President of the DRC since 31 May 1997) announced that military co-operation with both Rwanda and Uganda was to end, and demanded that all foreign forces leave the DRC. Relations between Rwanda and the DRC subsequently deteriorated. Kabila claimed that a rebellion, which commenced in the east of the DRC in August, constituted a Rwandan invasion; the Rwandan Government denied any involvement, but in late 1998 conceded that Rwandan troops were present in the DRC to provide logistical support to the rebel-led action. The Rwandan Government participated in a series of regional peace negotiations, at which Kabila refused to negotiate directly with the rebels. Rwanda later denied reports that it was maintaining a joint military command with Uganda in the DRC (see also the chapter on the DRC).

Rwandan action in the DRC continued in 1999, although Rwanda's alliance with Uganda became increasingly unstable during that year. At the end of April Uganda temporarily recalled its ambassador to Rwanda, following an incident in the DRC, in which Rwandan troops killed a number of members of the Ugandan armed forces. A split within the rebel movement in the DRC, the Rassemblement congolais pour la démocratie (RCD), resulted in the creation of two factions, one supported by Rwanda and one by Uganda. Following further clashes in the DRC between Rwandan and Ugandan troops in Kisangani in August, both armies agreed to leave the city. In June the DRC instituted proceedings against Burundi, Rwanda and Uganda at the International Court of Justice (ICJ) in The Hague, Netherlands, accusing these countries of acts of armed aggression. (In early February 2001, however, the DRC abandoned proceedings against Burundi and Rwanda.)

In May 2000 Rwandan and Ugandan forces again clashed in the town of Kisangani (despite a cease-fire agreement, which had been reached by all forces involved in the conflict in April). After meeting a UN Security Council delegation, the Rwandan and Ugandan contingents agreed to the demilitarization of the town, and its transfer to the control of the UN Mission in the Democratic Republic of the Congo (MONUC, see p. 94) deployed in the country. Despite further fighting, it was confirmed at the end of June that all Rwandan and Ugandan forces had withdrawn from Kisangani. In December, however, the principal RCD faction, supported by Rwandan troops, succeeded in gaining control of the south-eastern town of Pweto. The Rwandan Government denied any involvement in the assassination of Kabila in January 2001 (see the chapter on the DRC). In February Kagame met the new DRC President, Joseph Kabila (the son of Laurent-Désiré), in Washington, DC, USA, to discuss the ongoing conflict. Later that month the groups involved in the conflict, under the aegis of the UN Security Council, agreed to a disengagement of their forces by mid-March, followed by a complete withdrawal of foreign troops from the DRC by mid-May. Although some military disengagement of forces took place accordingly in March, factions subsequently refused to continue until MONUC guaranteed security in the region. In April the Governments of Burundi, Rwanda and Uganda rejected the claims of a UN report that the forces of these countries had exploited the natural resources of the DRC. In June it was reported that Interahamwe militia, led by former members of the Rwandan army, had intensified incursions into north-western Rwanda from the DRC. Despite continued pressure from the UN Security Council, in August Kagame insisted that Kabila fulfil pledges to demobilize the Interahamwe (who were supporting DRC government forces), as a precondition to the withdrawal of Rwandan forces from the DRC.

At the end of July 2002, after further discussions mediated by the South African Government, a peace agreement was signed by Kabila and Kagame in Pretoria, South Africa. Under the accord, Kabila pledged to arrest and disarm the Interahamwe militia in the DRC, while the Rwandan Government agreed to withdraw all troops from the country. In October it was announced that all 23,400 Rwandan troops had been withdrawn from the DRC. The Rwandan authorities denied reports that they planned to redeploy forces in the DRC, in response to the continued Ugandan involvement in hostilities there. In September 2003 the Governments of Rwanda and the DRC agreed to re-establish diplomatic links, and the improvement in relations between the two countries was further demonstrated by the visit to Rwanda of the DRC Minister of Foreign Affairs in October. In May 2009 diplomatic ties were established with the DRC: Amandin Rugira was appointed ambassador to that country while Norbert Nkulu Kilombo was later named envoy to Rwanda. In early August President Kabila met with President Kagame for the first bilateral negotiations in 13 years. Talks were held at a hotel near the border under tight security, during which both parties pledged to increase economic and security co-operation. Joint projects for extracting natural gas from sources under Lake Kivu, situated between the two countries, were also discussed.

In November 2001 Kagame and the Ugandan Head of State, Lt-Gen. Yoweri Kaguta Museveni, met in London, United Kingdom, in an effort to resolve the increasing tension between the two nations, following the repeated clashes in the DRC. The Ugandan Government had accused Rwanda of supporting dissidents who intended to overthrow Museveni's administration, while Kagame claimed that Ugandan troops were amassing on the joint border between the two countries. In February 2002 further discussions between Kagame and Museveni, with mediation by the British Secretary of State for International Development, were conducted in Uganda. It was agreed that both Governments would urge the dissidents based in their respective countries to take refuge elsewhere, and the adoption of a mutual extradition treaty was envisaged. In July 2003 the Rwandan Government signed a tripartite agreement with the Ugandan authorities and UNHCR, providing for the voluntary repatriation of some 26,000 Rwandans resident in refugee camps in western Uganda. (Similar accords were signed between Rwanda and the Governments of Malawi, Togo, Zambia and Tanzania.) In February 2004 an improvement in diplomatic relations between Rwanda and Uganda was demonstrated by a bilateral agreement to strengthen co-operation in several fields.

In October 2008 the DRC accused Rwanda of military incursions into Nord-Kivu to support Laurent Nkunda's Tutsi rebels; UN peace-keepers intervened to investigate the claims and relations between Rwanda and the DRC deteriorated. However, an unexpected accord was concluded between Presidents Kagame and Kabila in January 2009, and on 22 January

RWANDA

Rwandan forces detained Nkunda as he attempted to cross the border into Rwandan territory. Although it had appeared that Nkunda and Rwanda shared the common goal of overpowering the Hutu militia, responsible for the genocide, intense diplomacy was believed to have been behind the tentative allegiance between Rwanda and the DRC. In early 2011 Nkunda remained under house arrest in Rwanda.

Other external relations

Since 1994 the role of the international community in failing to avert the genocide has come under frequent scrutiny. In late 1997 the report of a Belgian Senate investigation concluded that the international community, and more specifically the UN and the Belgian authorities, was directly or indirectly responsible for certain aspects of the developments arising from the political violence from April 1994. Testifying before the ICTR in February 1998, the former UNAMIR commander stated that he had warned the UN in early 1994 of the impending ethnic catastrophe in Rwanda, but that the international community had lacked the will to intervene adequately. Suggestions that Kofi Annan, the head of UN peace-keeping operations at the time of the conflict, had failed to respond to such warnings prompted tensions between the UN Secretary-General (as Annan had subsequently become) and the Rwandan authorities in May 1998, as government officials refused to receive the Secretary-General in the course of a visit to Rwanda. Meanwhile, in February the OAU announced the establishment of a committee to investigate the genocide; the committee held its first meeting in October. In December a French parliamentary committee, established in March, presented its report on French involvement in events prior to and at the time of the genocide. (Despite evidence to the contrary, the French authorities have persistently denied allegations that France continued to supply military equipment and support to Rwanda after the imposition of the UN arms embargo in May 1994.) The report cleared France of any direct complicity in the genocide, although it conceded that 'Operation Turquoise' both delayed the accession to power of the FPR, and facilitated the escape of Hutu extremist forces into the DRC. The report attributed responsibility for the genocide to the international community as a whole, particularly to the USA (which had failed to support UN peace-keeping operations in Rwanda).

In March 1999 the UN Security Council approved a proposal for the establishment of a commission of inquiry into the actions of the UN prior to and during the genocide. The three-member commission of inquiry presented its report in December after a six-month investigation. The report criticized the UN for failing in its mission to prevent the genocide and for ignoring the warnings of the head of the peace-keeping mission. It also cited the UN Security Council's failure to deploy sufficient peace-keepers at the end of 1993. Following the report, Kofi Annan issued a personal apology for UN inaction at the time. In March a Canadian newspaper published a UN memorandum, stating that the FPR was responsible for the attack on the aircraft on 6 April 1994, which killed President Juvénal Habyarimana, and that Kagame had been in overall command of the force that carried out the attack. Kagame subsequently dismissed the allegations, claiming that the report was part of a UN attempt to absolve itself of blame for the genocide of 1994.

In August 2001 the French Minister of Foreign Affairs made an official visit to Rwanda (the first by a senior French official since 1994), in an effort to normalize bilateral relations. (Diplomatic links were restored in 2002.) In March 2002 the French Government (which, within the UN Security Council, had placed increasing pressure on Rwanda to withdraw forces from the DRC) protested that Rwandan troops had launched a major offensive in the east of that country. In March 2004 the results of an official French investigation into the destruction of President Habyarimana's aircraft alleged that Kagame, as leader of the FPR, had ordered the missile attack. Kagame again denied any responsibility, and claimed that French forces had, by training and arming the Hutu militia, supported the mass killings. In early April the French Secretary of State for Foreign Affairs curtailed his visit to Rwanda, after Kagame repeated these accusations at an official ceremony in Kigali commemorating the 10th anniversary of the genocide. On the following anniversary in April 2005 the Rwandan Government reiterated demands that the UN instigate legal proceedings against French officials for complicity in the genocide. In December a French military tribunal began to investigate claims by survivors of the genocide that French forces had facilitated attacks against Tutsi in 1994 (by failing to prevent massacres and then by allowing the perpetrators of the genocide to evade capture).

In November 2006 Rwanda severed diplomatic relations with France, recalling the ambassador to that country and closing the French embassy. The move followed the order by the French judiciary to issue international arrest warrants against President Kagame and nine high-ranking Rwandan officials. In September 2007, for the first time since the severance of diplomatic ties, a delegation of French officials visited Kigali with the aim of making progress towards the restoration of normal relations. Despite the abolition of the death penalty in Rwanda in July 2007, the French Government had refused to extradite genocide suspects; however, in November a French court approved the extradition of one of the suspects currently resident in France. In January 2008 French Minister of Foreign and European Affairs Bernard Kouchner met briefly with President Kagame to resume dialogue with Rwanda, and in a press conference Kouchner admitted that France had made a political mistake in its response to the 1994 genocide; nevertheless, he denied any military responsibility. Relations between the two countries had been improving since a meeting between the two Heads of State at a summit in Lisbon, Portugal, in December 2007. However, in August 2008 a Rwandan commission of inquiry issued a report accusing high-ranking French officials of involvement in the genocide; among those mentioned were former President François Mitterrand and former Prime Minister Dominique de Villepin. Rwanda demanded that the French officials named be brought to trial and submitted the findings of the report as the basis for issuing arrest warrants. France denied all accusations made by Rwanda but reiterated its commitment to rebuilding a relationship with the African country. In November Rose Kabuye, a senior presidential aide and former guerrilla fighter with the now ruling FPR, was detained in Frankfurt, Germany, and extradited to France on charges of involvement in the attack on President Habyarimana's aircraft. Kabuye denied the accusations against her and was subsequently released from custody under a supervision order. Relations between Rwanda and Germany were severed as a result of the arrest, but were restored in January 2009.

In November 2009 it was announced that, following extensive consultations and negotiations between the two countries, Rwanda and France were to restore diplomatic relations. In early January 2010 Laurent Contini, hitherto the French ambassador to Zimbabwe, was appointed ambassador to Rwanda and days later Kouchner visited Kigali for further discussions regarding the normalization of relations between the two countries. Rwanda officially reopened its embassy in Paris in late February immediately prior to the visit of President Nicolas Sarkozy to Kigali, during which he admitted that France had made a number of 'serious errors of judgement' (although again no admission of responsibility was forthcoming) in the period following the assassination of President Habyarimana, and pledged to bring any person suspected of involvement in the genocide resident in France to justice. The decision taken the previous month by the French authorities to create a special investigative unit as part of the Tribunal de Grande Instance in Paris to expedite the prosecution of genocide crimes was welcomed by the Rwandan Government. In September 2010 a trial against the Belgian state and three Belgian army officers formerly belonging to UNAMIR, who were accused of failing to protect refugees during the 1994 genocide, began in the Belgian capital, Brussels, following a case brought by two survivors of a massacre of more than 2,000 Tutsis in April 1994.

CONSTITUTION AND GOVERNMENT

Under the terms of the Constitution, which entered into force on 4 June 2003, executive power is exercised by the President (Head of State), assisted by an appointed Council of Ministers. The President is elected by universal suffrage for a seven-year term, and is restricted to two mandates. Legislative power is vested in a bicameral Parliament, comprising a Chamber of Deputies and a Senate. The Chamber of Deputies has 80 deputies, who are elected for a five-year term. In addition to 53 directly elected deputies, 27 seats are allocated, respectively, to two youth representatives, one disabilities representative, and 24 female representatives, who are indirectly elected. The Senate comprises 26 members, of whom 12 are elected by local government councils in the 12 provinces, and two by academic institutions, while the remaining 12 are nominated (eight by the President and four by a regulatory body, the Parties' Forum). Members of the Senate serve for eight years.

RWANDA

Following territorial reforms, which entered into effect at the beginning of 2006, the country is divided into five provinces and subdivided into 30 districts, each administered by an elected mayor.

REGIONAL AND INTERNATIONAL CO-OPERATION

Rwanda is a member of the African Union (see p. 183), and, with Burundi and the DRC, is a founding member of the Economic Community of the Great Lakes Countries (see p. 447) and of the Common Market for Eastern and Southern Africa (see p. 228). Rwanda joined the East African Community (EAC, see p. 447) in 2007 and was admitted to the Commonwealth in 2009.

Rwanda became a member of the UN in 1962 and was admitted to the World Trade Organization (WTO, see p. 430) in 1996. Rwanda participates in the Group of 77 (G77, see p. 447) developing countries. Rwanda is also a member of the International Coffee Organization (see p. 443).

ECONOMIC AFFAIRS

In 2009, according to estimates by the World Bank, Rwanda's gross national income (GNI), measured at average 2007–09 prices, was US $4,628m., equivalent to $460 per head (or $1,060 per head on an international purchasing-power parity basis). During 2000–09, it was estimated, the population increased at an average annual rate of 2.6%, while gross domestic product (GDP) per head rose, in real terms, by an average of 4.4% per year. Overall GDP increased, in real terms, at an average annual rate of 7.1% in 2000–09; growth of 5.3% was recorded in 2009.

Agriculture (including forestry and fishing) contributed 36.1% of GDP in 2009 according to official figures. According to FAO estimates, 89.3% of the employed labour force were engaged in the sector (mainly at subsistence level) at mid-2011. The principal food crops are plantains, sweet potatoes, cassava, dry beans and sorghum. The principal cash crops are coffee (which contributed 18.2% of total export earnings in 2009) and tea (14.5%). Pyrethrum and quinquina are also cultivated for export. Goats and cattle are traditionally the principal livestock raised. According to official figures, agricultural GDP increased by an average of 5.5% per year during 2000–09; sectoral GDP increased by 7.6% in 2009.

Industry (including mining, manufacturing, power and construction) accounted for 15.4% of GDP in 2009, and the industrial sector engaged 2.8% of the employed labour force in 2002. According to official figures, industrial GDP increased at an average annual rate of 9.6% during 2000–09; the GDP of the industrial sector increased by 1.3% in 2009.

Mining and quarrying contributed just 0.6% of GDP in 2009. Cassiterite (a tin-bearing ore) is Rwanda's principal mineral resource. Exports of tin ores and concentrates contributed 16.0% of the value of total merchandise exports in 2009. There are also reserves of wolframite (a tungsten-bearing ore), columbo-tantalite, gold and beryl, and work is under way to exploit natural methane gas reserves, estimated to total at least 55,000m. cu m, beneath Lake Kivu. Mining GDP increased at an estimated average annual rate of 11.9% in 2000–09, according to official figures. However, mining GDP decreased by 18.8% in 2008, and by 15.4% in 2009.

Manufacturing accounted for 6.8% of GDP in 2009, while production activities engaged 1.3% of the employed labour force in 2002. The principal branches of manufacturing are beverages and tobacco, food products and basic consumer goods, including soap, textiles and plastic products. According to official figures, manufacturing GDP increased by an average of 8.0% per year during 2000–09; the GDP of the sector increased by 3.2% in 2009.

The construction sector contributed 7.8% of GDP in 2009, and engaged 1.3% of the employed labour force in 2002. According to official figures, the GDP of the construction sector increased at an average annual rate of 11.7% during 2000–09; growth in the construction sector was 1.3% in 2009.

Output of electricity is insufficient to meet domestic needs, and the rate of connection is low. In 1999 Rwanda imported 35.5% of its electricity, but subsequently benefited from the completion of the Ruzizi-II plant (a joint venture with Burundi and the Democratic Republic of the Congo—DRC). In March 2009 the Government of Rwanda signed an agreement with a US-based company for the development of an integrated extraction and generation facility to supply methane gas-fired electricity from the Lake Kivu resource to Rwanda and the East Africa region. (Rwanda's first pilot methane gas plant was inaugurated in late 2008, and subsequently began supplying the national grid.) Projects such as the Nyabarongo hydroelectric dam, construction of which was under way in the late 2000s, and other planned 'micro-dams', are expected to reduce Rwanda's reliance on thermal energy sources. Imports of fuels and lubricants comprised 7.8% of the total value of merchandise imports in 2009.

The services sector contributed 48.6% of GDP in 2009, and engaged 8.6% of the employed labour force in 2002. According to official figures, the GDP of the services sector increased at an average annual rate of 10.3% during 2000–09; growth in the services sector was 5.7% in 2009.

In 2009 Rwanda recorded a visible trade deficit of US $768m., and there was a deficit of $379m. on the current account of the balance of payments. In 2009 the principal source of imports was Kenya, which supplied 17.3% of merchandise imports in that year; other major suppliers were Uganda, Tanzania, the People's Republic of China and the United Arab Emirates. In the same year Kenya was also the principal market for exports (15.1%); other significant purchasers were Belgium, Swaziland, Hong Kong and Switzerland-Liechtenstein. The principal exports in 2009 were metalliferous ores and metal scrap, coffee and tea. The main imports in that year were road vehicles, medicinal and pharmaceutical products, petroleum and petroleum products, and iron and steel.

An overall budgetary deficit of 49.4m. Rwanda francs was recorded in 2009. Rwanda's general government gross debt was 598,437m. Rwanda francs in 2009, equivalent to 20.2% of GDP. At the end of 2008 Rwanda's external debt totalled US $679m., of which $645m. was public and publicly guaranteed debt. The cost of debt-servicing in 2007 was equivalent to 4.0% of the value of exports of goods, services and income. In 2000–09 the average annual rate of inflation was 8.6%. Consumer prices increased by 11.2% in 2009.

By the late 2000s, through a sustained programme of donor-funded assistance, the Government of Rwanda had achieved considerable success in its efforts towards economic recovery and restructuring. Strong annual growth rates were based principally on expansion in the services, manufacturing and construction sectors. As a result of relief under the heavily indebted poor countries and multilateral debt relief initiatives (for which Rwanda qualified in 2005 and 2006, respectively), Rwanda's external debt declined from the equivalent of 71.6% of GNI at the end of 2005 to 16.9% in 2006. The Government's Economic Development and Poverty Reduction Strategy, inaugurated in late 2007, aimed to address inadequacies in key areas of infrastructure, such as education, health, energy, roads, the financial sector, and information and communications technology; to enhance agricultural development and trade; and to promote business development and private sector activity. It was planned to increase the country's revenue-to-GDP ratio by 0.2% annually over the medium term by means of fiscal reform. In mid-2009 Rwanda adopted the July–June fiscal year used across the East African Community (EAC). Rwanda gained full membership of the EAC customs union in July, requiring adjustments to the country's external tariff rates, moving from band four to band three. A stimulus package was also put in place to help stabilize the economy during the global economic crisis, which had resulted in a decline in export revenue and slowdown in economic activity. A common market protocol, allowing the free movement of goods, services, people and capital within the EAC, was signed by member states in November and entered into force in July 2010. After the IMF completed the sixth and final review of a Poverty Reduction and Growth Facility (PRGF) in July 2009, a new three-year economic programme supported by the IMF's Policy Support Instrument was approved in June 2010. Following a decline to 4.1% in 2009 from 11.2% in 2008, according to IMF estimates, real GDP growth for 2010 was projected to reach 6.5%, generated by a recovery in exports (reflecting a resurgence in international prices and strong volumes of main exports) and growth in the services sector.

PUBLIC HOLIDAYS

2012: 1 January (New Year), 28 January (Democracy Day), 7 April (National Mourning Day), 9 April (Easter Monday), 17 May (Ascension Day), 1 May (Labour Day), 1 July (Independence Day), 1 August (Harvest Festival), 15 August (Assumption), 8 September (Culture Day), 25 September (Kamarampaka Day, anniversary of 1961 referendum), 1 October (Armed Forces Day), 1 November (All Saints' Day), 25 December (Christmas).

Statistical Survey

Source (unless otherwise stated): National Institute of Statistics of Rwanda (NISR); tel. 250571037; e-mail info@statistics.gov.rw; internet www.statistics.gov.rw.

Area and Population

AREA, POPULATION AND DENSITY

Area (sq km)	26,338*
Population (census results)	
15 August 1991	7,142,755
16 August 2002†	
Males	3,879,448
Females	4,249,105
Total	8,128,553
Population (UN estimate at mid-year)‡	
2009	9,997,614
2010	10,277,212
2011	10,560,142
Density (per sq km) at mid-2011	400.9

* 10,169 sq miles.
† Provisional results.
‡ Source: UN, *World Population Prospects: The 2008 Revision*.

POPULATION BY AGE AND SEX
(UN estimates at mid-2011)

	Males	Females	Total
0–14	2,220,450	2,259,905	4,480,355
15–64	2,797,185	3,024,084	5,821,269
65 and over	103,619	154,899	258,518
Total	5,121,254	5,438,888	10,560,142

Source: UN, *World Population Prospects: The 2008 Revision*.

PREFECTURES
(1991 census)

	Area (sq km)	Population*	Density (per sq km)
Butare	1,830	765,910	418.5
Byumba	4,987	779,365	159.2
Cyangugu	2,226	517,550	232.5
Gikongoro	2,192	462,635	211.1
Gisenyi	2,395	728,365	304.1
Gitarama	2,241	849,285	379.0
Kibungo	4,134	647,175	156.5
Kibuye	1,320	472,525	358.0
Kigali	3,251	921,050	355.2
Kigali-Ville		233,640	
Ruhengeri	1,762	765,255	434.3
Total	26,338	7,142,755	271.2

* Source: UN, *Demographic Yearbook*.

PRINCIPAL TOWNS
(population at 1978 census)

Kigali (capital)	117,749	Ruhengeri	16,025
Butare	21,691	Gisenyi	12,436

Mid-2010 (incl. suburbs, UN estimate): Kigali 939,425 (Source: UN, *World Urbanization Prospects: The 2009 Revision*).

BIRTHS AND DEATHS
(annual averages, UN estimates)

	1995–2000	2000–05	2005–10
Birth rate (per 1,000)	40.3	41.0	41.0
Death rate (per 1,000)	22.2	16.8	14.7

Source: UN, *World Population Prospects: The 2008 Revision*.

Life expectancy (years at birth, WHO estimates): 58 (males 56; females 59) in 2008 (Source: WHO, *World Health Statistics*).

ECONOMICALLY ACTIVE POPULATION
(persons aged 14 years and over, at census of August 2002)

	Males	Females	Total
Agriculture	1,218,181	1,731,411	2,949,592
Fishing	3,374	94	3,468
Industrial activities	3,692	1,636	5,328
Production activities	32,994	10,649	43,643
Electricity and water	2,390	277	2,667
Construction	41,641	1,244	42,885
Trade reconstruction	56,869	32,830	89,699
Restaurants and hotels	4,525	2,311	6,836
Transport and communications	29,574	1,988	31,562
Financial intermediaries	1,560	840	2,400
Administration and defence	22,479	5,585	28,064
Education	22,688	17,046	39,734
Health and social services	7,521	7,054	14,575
Sub-total	1,447,488	1,812,965	3,260,453
Activities not adequately defined	69,042	39,458	108,500
Total employed	1,516,530	1,852,423	3,368,953

Source: IMF, *Rwanda: Selected Issues and Statistical Appendix* (December 2004).

Mid-2011 (estimates in '000): Agriculture, etc. 4,337; Total labour force 4,858 (Source: FAO).

Health and Welfare

KEY INDICATORS

Total fertility rate (children per woman, 2008)	5.4
Under-5 mortality rate (per 1,000 live births, 2008)	112
HIV/AIDS (% of persons aged 15–49, 2007)	2.8
Physicians (per 1,000 head, 2004)	0.05
Hospital beds (per 1,000 head, 2007)	1.6
Health expenditure (2007): US $ per head (PPP)	95
Health expenditure (2007): % of GDP	10.3
Health expenditure (2007): public (% of total)	47.0
Access to water (% of persons, 2008)	65
Access to sanitation (% of persons, 2008)	54
Total carbon dioxide emissions ('000 metric tons, 2007)	714.5
Carbon dioxide emissions per head (metric tons, 2007)	0.1
Human Development Index (2010): ranking	152
Human Development Index (2010): value	0.385

For sources and definitions, see explanatory note on p. vi.

RWANDA

Agriculture

PRINCIPAL CROPS
('000 metric tons)

	2007	2008	2009
Maize	102.0	167.0	150.0*
Sorghum	164.0	144.0	150.0*
Potatoes	967.0	1,162.0	1,200.0*
Sweet potatoes	841.0	826.0	850.0*
Cassava (Manioc)	779.0	978.5	980.0*
Taro (Cocoyam)	125.0*	110.6	n.a.
Sugar cane	97.0	63.0	63.0*
Beans, dry	329.0	308.0	300.0*
Peas, dry	14.0	14.3	n.a.
Groundnuts, with shell	10.0*	11.5	n.a.
Pumpkins, squash and gourds*	215.0	215.0	n.a.
Plantains	2,686.0	2,604.0*	2,600.0
Coffee, green	14.7	20.7	28.0†
Tea	20.5	20.0	20.0*

* FAO estimate(s).
† Unofficial figure.

Aggregate production ('000 metric tons, may include official, semi-official or estimated data): Total cereals 355 in 2007, 417 in 2008, 404 in 2009; Total roots and tubers 2,716 in 2007, 3,080 in 2008, 3,144 in 2009; Total pulses 343 in 2007, 322 in 2008, 314 in 2009; Total vegetables (incl. melons) 421 in 2007, 434 in 2008, 434 in 2009; Total fruits (excl. melons) 2,870 in 2007, 2,801 in 2008, 2,798 in 2009.

Source: FAO.

LIVESTOCK
('000 head, year ending September)

	2006	2007*	2008
Cattle	1,200*	1,300*	1,549
Pigs	340.0*	330.0*	310.8
Sheep*	470	470	470
Goats	1,500.0*	1,600.0*	1,736.2
Chickens	1,776	2,000	2,000*

* FAO estimate(s).
Source: FAO.

LIVESTOCK PRODUCTS
('000 metric tons, FAO estimates)

	2006	2007	2008
Cattle meat	28.6	31.2	36.9
Goat meat	5.3	5.6	6.1
Pig meat	6.3	6.1	5.7
Chicken meat	2.0	2.2	2.4
Game meat	12.3	12.5	12.5
Cows' milk	120.0	120.0	118.8
Sheep's milk	2.3	2.3	2.3
Goats' milk	26.8	26.8	26.8
Hen eggs	2.5	2.6	2.8

2009: Production assumed to be unchanged from 2008 (FAO estimates).
Source: FAO.

Forestry

ROUNDWOOD REMOVALS
('000 cubic metres, excluding bark, FAO estimates)

	2007	2008	2009
Sawlogs, veneer logs and logs for sleepers	245	961	962
Other industrial wood	250	250	250
Fuel wood	9,503	1,675	1,865
Total	9,998	2,886	3,077

Source: FAO.

SAWNWOOD PRODUCTION
('000 cubic metres, including railway sleepers)

	2007	2008	2009
Coniferous (softwood)	22	40	50
Non-coniferous (hardwood)	57	81	85
Total	79	121	135

Source: FAO.

Fishing

(metric tons, live weight)

	2005*	2006*	2007
Capture	7,800	8,400	9,050
Nile tilapia	3,100	3,500	3,950
Aquaculture	386	400	388*
Nile tilapia	340	340	300*
Total catch	8,186	8,800	9,438*

* FAO estimate(s).
2008: Catch assumed to be unchanged from 2007 (FAO estimates).
Source: FAO.

Mining

(metric tons unless otherwise indicated)

	2006	2007	2008*
Tin concentrates†	470*	899	1,100
Tungsten concentrates†	820	1,700	1,700
Columbo-tantalite‡	188	490	490

* Estimate(s).
† Figures refer to the metal content of ores and concentrates.
‡ Figures refer to the estimated production of mineral concentrates. The metal content (metric tons, estimates) was: Niobium (Columbium) 62 in 2006, 160 in 2007, 160 in 2008 (estimate); Tantalum 38 in 2006, 100 in 2007, 100 in 2008 (estimate).

Source: US Geological Survey.

Industry

SELECTED PRODUCTS

	2001	2002	2003
Beer ('000 hectolitres)	479	539	412
Soft drinks ('000 hectolitres)	228	n.a.	n.a.
Cigarettes (million)	278	391	402
Soap (metric tons)	7,056	5,571	4,456
Cement (metric tons)	83,024	100,568	105,105

Source: IMF, *Rwanda: Statistical Annex* (August 2002) and IMF, *Rwanda: Selected Issues and Statistical Appendix* (December 2004).

Cement ('000 metric tons): 101.1 in 2005; 102.6 in 2006; 103.0 in 2007; 103.2 in 2008 (Source: US Geological Survey).

Electric energy (million kWh): 112.8 in 2005; 170.7 in 2006; 169.1 in 2007 (Source: UN Industrial Commodity Statistics Database).

Finance

CURRENCY AND EXCHANGE RATES

Monetary Units
100 centimes = 1 franc rwandais (Rwanda franc).

Sterling, Dollar and Euro Equivalents (29 October 2010)
£1 sterling = 941.488 Rwanda francs;
US $1 = 591.313 Rwanda francs;
€1 = 819.382 Rwanda francs;
10,000 Rwanda francs = £10.62 = $16.91 = €12.20.

Average Exchange Rate (Rwanda francs per US $)
2007   546.955
2008   546.849
2009   568.281

Note: Since September 1983 the currency has been linked to the IMF special drawing right (SDR). Until November 1990 the mid-point exchange rate was SDR 1 = 102.71 Rwanda francs. In November 1990 a new rate of SDR 1 = 171.18 Rwanda francs was established. This remained in effect until June 1992, when the rate was adjusted to SDR 1 = 201.39 Rwanda francs. The latter parity was maintained until February 1994, since when the rate has been frequently adjusted. In March 1995 the Government introduced a market-determined exchange rate system.

BUDGET
('000 million Rwanda francs)

Revenue*	1999	2000	2001†
Tax revenue	60.4	65.3	79.5
Taxes on income and profits	15.2	17.9	23.9
Company profits tax	7.4	10.0	14.4
Individual income tax	6.1	7.5	9.0
Domestic taxes on goods and services	33.6	35.2	41.0
Excise taxes	17.9	18.8	14.2
Turnover tax	12.9	13.8	24.2
Road fund	2.7	2.5	2.6
Taxes on international trade	11.0	11.6	14.0
Import taxes	8.4	9.3	11.1
Non-tax revenue	3.2	3.3	6.7
Total	**63.6**	**68.7**	**86.2**

Expenditure‡	1999	2000	2001†
Current expenditure	86.0	89.2	107.4
General public services	31.5	35.7	53.7
Defence	27.0	25.8	28.6
Social services	21.9	30.5	36.2
Education	17.2	24.0	29.8
Health	3.3	3.8	5.1
Economic services	2.6	2.1	4.9
Energy and public works	0.7	0.4	2.3
Interest on public debt	4.0	1.8	2.8
Adjustment	−1.1	−6.7	−18.8
Capital expenditure	40.8	42.0	50.0
Sub-total	**126.8**	**131.2**	**157.5**
Adjustment for payment arrears§	2.0	−1.2	31.7
Total	**128.8**	**130.0**	**189.2**

* Excluding grants received ('000 million Rwanda francs): 38.5 in 1999; 63.7 in 2000; 63.3† in 2001.
† Estimates.
‡ Excluding lending minus repayments ('000 million Rwanda francs): −0.4 in 1999; 0.5 in 2000; 0.6 in 2001†.
§ Minus sign indicates increase in arrears.

Source: IMF, *Rwanda: Statistical Annex* (August 2002).

2002 (estimates, '000 million Rwanda francs): *Revenue:* Tax revenue 94.6; Non-tax revenue 6.6; Total 101.2 (excl. grants received 70.8). *Expenditure:* Current 123.7; Capital 56.4; Total 180.1 (excl. net lending 11.5) (Source: IMF, *Rwanda: First Review Under the Three-Year Arrangement Under the Poverty Reduction and Growth Facility and Request for Waiver of Nonobservance of Performance Criteria—Staff Report; Staff Statement; Press Release on the Executive Board Discussion; and Statement by the Executive Director for Rwanda*—June 2003).

2005 ('000 million Rwanda francs): *Revenue:* Tax revenue 162.6; Non-tax revenue 17.7; Total 180.3 (excl. grants received 169.1). *Expenditure:* Current 214.9; Capital 121.4; Total 336.3 (excl. net lending 4.4) (Source: IMF, *Rwanda: Third Review Under the Three-Year Arrangement Under the Poverty Reduction and Growth Facility and Request for Waiver of Non-observance of Performance Criterion—Staff Report; Staff Supplement; Press Release on the Executive Board Discussion; and Statement by the Executive Director for Rwanda*—March 2008).

2006 ('000 million Rwanda francs): *Revenue:* Tax revenue 193.6; Non-tax revenue 14.6; Total 208.2 (excl. grants received 167.8). *Expenditure:* Current 254.1; Capital 118.7; Total 372.9 (excl. net lending 9.6) (Source: IMF, *Rwanda: Third Review Under the Three-Year Arrangement Under the Poverty Reduction and Growth Facility and Request for Waiver of Non-observance of Performance Criterion—Staff Report; Staff Supplement; Press Release on the Executive Board Discussion; and Statement by the Executive Director for Rwanda*—March 2008).

2007 ('000 million Rwanda francs): *Revenue:* Tax revenue 237.8; Non-tax revenue 15.1; Total 252.9 (excl. grants received 183.8). *Expenditure:* Current 312.6; Capital 159.9; Total 472.5 (excl. net lending -8.1) (Source: IMF, *Rwanda: 2008 Article IV Consultation, Fifth Review Under the Three-Year Arrangement Under the Poverty Reduction and Growth Facility, and Request for Waiver of Nonobservance of Performance Criterion—Staff Report; Staff Supplement and Statement; Public Information Notice and Press Release on the Executive Board Discussion; and Statement by the Executive Director for Rwanda*—February 2009).

2008 ('000 million Rwanda francs): *Revenue:* Tax revenue 328.7; Non-tax revenue 52.3; Total 381.0 (excl. grants received 279.8). *Expenditure:* Current 368.9; Capital 267.8; Total 636.7 (excl. net lending -13.5) (Source: African Development Bank).

2009 ('000 million Rwanda francs): *Revenue:* Tax revenue 360.3; Non-tax revenue 56.0; Total 416.3 (excl. grants received 133.3). *Expenditure:* Current 357.9; Capital 258.7; Total 616.6 (excl. net lending -17.6) (Source: African Development Bank).

INTERNATIONAL BANK RESERVES
(US $ million at 31 December)

	2008	2009	2010
IMF special drawing rights	31.42	130.92	128.55
Foreign exchange	564.86	611.82	684.21
Total	**596.28**	**742.74**	**812.76**

Source: IMF, *International Financial Statistics*.

RWANDA

MONEY SUPPLY
(million Rwanda francs at 31 December)

	2003	2004	2005
Currency outside banks	29,246	36,512	46,277
Demand deposits at deposit money banks	52,220	62,604	82,524
Total money (incl. others)	82,305	99,941	129,326

2006: Currency outside banks 52,620.

Source: IMF, *International Financial Statistics*.

COST OF LIVING
(Consumer Price Index for Kigali; base: 2000 = 100)

	2007	2008	2009
Food (incl. non-alcoholic beverages)	185.0	215.2	248.3
Clothing	119.2	n.a.	n.a.
Rent	200.6	n.a.	n.a.
All items	164.2	189.5	210.8

2010 Food (incl. non-alcoholic beverages) 254.4; All items (incl. others) 214.0.

Source: ILO.

NATIONAL ACCOUNTS
('000 million Rwanda francs at current prices)

Expenditure on the Gross Domestic Product

	2007	2008	2009
Government final consumption expenditure	338	378	434
Private final consumption expenditure	1,637	2,022	2,433
Changes in inventories			
Gross fixed capital formation	369	585	645
Total domestic expenditure	2,345	2,985	3,511
Exports of goods and services	224	372	347
Less Imports of goods and services	523	778	866
GDP in purchasers' values	2,046	2,579	2,992
GDP in constant 2006 prices	1,849	2,064	2,187

Gross Domestic Product by Economic Activity

	2007	2008	2009
Agriculture, hunting, forestry and fishing	729	834	1,012
Mining and quarrying	21	25	16
Manufacturing	125	159	190
Electricity, gas and water	8	5	6
Construction	132	194	219
Wholesale and retail trade, restaurants and hotels	289	415	449
Finance, insurance, real estate and business services	230	301	351
Transport and communications	145	197	223
Public administration and defence	97	112	128
Education	95	108	140
Health	30	36	44
Other personal services	27	30	30
Sub-total	1,926	2,414	2,807
Less Imputed bank service charges	31	40	41
Indirect taxes, less subsidies	151	204	226
GDP in purchasers' values	2,046	2,579	2,992

BALANCE OF PAYMENTS
(US $ million)

	2007	2008	2009
Exports of goods f.o.b.	184	257	193
Imports of goods f.o.b.	–637	–880	–961
Trade balance	–452	–623	–768
Exports of services	179	408	341
Imports of services	–272	–521	–519
Balance on goods and services	–545	–736	–946
Other income received	48	28	15
Other income paid	–63	–62	–52
Balance on goods, services and income	–560	–771	–983
Current transfers received	435	558	655
Current transfers paid	–22	–40	–51
Current balance	–147	–252	–379
Capital account (net)	161	210	200
Direct investment abroad	13	—	—
Direct investment from abroad	67	103	119
Portfolio investment assets	—	–19	—
Other investment assets	–13	–88	–19
Other investment liabilities	–32	—	143
Net errors and omissions	4	–5	–2
Overall balance	53	–51	63

Source: IMF, *International Financial Statistics*.

External Trade

PRINCIPAL COMMODITIES
(US $ million)

Imports c.i.f.	2007	2008	2009
Food and live animals	67.0	73.7	104.8
Cereals and cereal preparations	33.6	34.2	56.7
Rice	7.5	4.8	11.8
Vegetables and fruit	2.2	1.4	7.7
Sugar, sugar preparations and honey	17.9	19.2	23.8
Crude materials, inedible, except fuels	30.6	52.6	43.7
Textile fibres and their wastes	11.5	22.0	14.0
Mineral fuels, lubricants and related materials	60.3	75.7	98.1
Petroleum, petroleum products and related materials	59.8	74.8	97.2
Animal and vegetable oils, fats and waxes	21.5	30.8	35.7
Chemicals and related products	105.5	146.1	191.7
Medicinal and pharmaceutical products	57.1	48.2	81.1
Basic manufactures	133.5	248.2	225.5
Iron and steel	40.7	91.2	57.2
Machinery and transport equipment	213.8	412.5	448.6
Telecommunications, sound recording and reproducing equipment	28.4	86.2	88.9
Electric machinery, apparatus and appliances, and parts	12.5	3.5	2.4
Road vehicles	89.7	127.7	109.8
Miscellaneous manufactured articles	58.3	95.5	100.5
Total (incl. others)	696.9	1,145.6	1,257.6

RWANDA

Statistical Survey

Exports f.o.b.	2007	2008	2009
Coffee, tea, cocoa, spices, and manufactures thereof	62.7	180.8	69.5
Coffee	32.4	55.3	38.6
Tea	30.3	125.5	30.8
Crude materials, inedible, except fuels	90.5	142.7	71.9
Metalliferous ores and metal scrap	83.1	138.0	68.1
Tin ores and concentrates	39.5	80.2	33.8
Ores and concentrates of other non-ferrous base metals	22.1	38.0	20.4
Ores of molybdenum, niobium and titanium	20.8	17.1	11.0
Total (incl. others)	183.5	398.3	211.9

Source: UN, *International Trade Statistics Yearbook*.

PRINCIPAL TRADING PARTNERS
(US $ million)

Imports	2007	2008	2009
Belgium	43.9	67.5	59.4
China	43.2	95.9	92.7
Denmark	4.6	11.4	39.4
Egypt	11.9	12.3	13.7
France (incl. Monaco)	38.8	30.2	23.3
Germany	28.5	39.4	38.2
India	24.8	39.7	45.7
Italy	8.4	6.9	8.9
Japan	14.6	16.4	16.7
Kenya	123.8	183.7	217.0
Netherlands	12.5	13.7	21.8
Saudi Arabia	1.3	7.8	2.9
South Africa	25.4	75.9	61.6
Switzerland-Liechtenstein	10.2	6.0	11.5
Tanzania	47.1	53.5	94.1
Uganda	97.3	165.7	165.8
UAE	54.6	96.3	80.2
United Kingdom	12.1	22.5	25.9
USA	24.9	39.0	37.9
Total (incl. others)	696.9	1,145.6	1,257.6

Exports	2007	2008	2009
Belgium	25.6	66.0	29.1
Burundi	7.3	6.2	5.6
China	0.9	5.8	7.6
France (incl. Monaco)	1.2	0.6	0.6
Germany	1.3	8.3	3.3
Hong Kong	23.0	26.0	15.8
Italy	1.3	3.7	1.1
Kenya	34.3	127.0	31.9
Netherlands	0.8	1.0	1.1
Pakistan	0.0	0.1	n.a.
South Africa	4.3	12.4	5.5
Swaziland	5.9	20.3	23.6
Switzerland-Liechtenstein	13.3	18.3	12.7
Tanzania	0.5	1.1	4.0
Uganda	3.2	7.0	6.5
United Kingdom	34.4	13.6	4.7
USA	9.5	5.0	4.3
Total (incl. others)	183.5	398.3	211.9

Source: UN, *International Trade Statistics Yearbook*.

Transport

ROAD TRAFFIC
(motor vehicles in use at 31 December, estimates)

	1995	1996
Passenger cars	12,000	13,000
Lorries and vans	16,000	17,100

2008 (motor vehicles in use at 31 December): Passenger cars 22,251; Buses and coaches 4,776; Vans and lorries 10,827; Motorcycles and mopeds 24,013.

Source: IRF, *World Road Statistics*.

CIVIL AVIATION
(traffic on scheduled services)

	2006	2007	2008
Passengers carried	179,447	234,408	276,115
Freight carried (metric tons)	4,562	4,924	8,544

Tourism

(by country of residence)

	2000	2001*
Africa	93,058	99,928
Burundi	20,972	9,455
Congo, Democratic Republic	10,450	28,514
Kenya	2,050	2,243
Tanzania	18,320	18,697
Uganda	38,897	38,472
Americas	2,250	2,785
Europe	6,412	8,395
Belgium	1,866	2,057
Total (incl. others)	104,216	113,185

* January–November.

Tourism receipts (US $ million, excl. passenger transport, unless otherwise indicated): 23 in 2000; 25 in 2001; 31 in 2002; 30 in 2003; 44 in 2004; 49 in 2005; 31 in 2006; 66 in 2007 (incl. passenger transport).

Source: World Tourism Organization.

Communications Media

	2007	2008	2009
Telephones ('000 main lines in use)	23.1	16.8	33.5
Mobile cellular telephones ('000 subscribers)	635.1	1,322.6	2,429.3
Internet users ('000)	200.0	300.0	450.0
Broadband subscribers ('000)	2.5	4.2	8.4

Personal computers: 28,000 (3.0 per 1,000 persons) in 2006.

Radio receivers ('000 in use): 601 in 1997.

Daily newspapers: 1 in 1998.

Non-daily newspapers: 25 in 2004.

Sources: International Telecommunication Union; UN, *Statistical Yearbook*; UNESCO, *Statistical Yearbook*.

Education

(2008/09 unless otherwise indicated)

		Students		
	Teachers	Males	Females	Total
Pre-primary	552*	74,797	75,203	150,000
Primary	33,158	1,114,253	1,150,419	2,264,672
Secondary	10,715†	176,392	170,126	346,518
Tertiary	1,231	31,174	24,039	55,213

* 2001/02.
† 2007/08.

Source: UNESCO Institute for Statistics.

Pupil-teacher ratio (primary education, UNESCO estimate): 68.3 in 2008/09 (Source: UNESCO Institute for Statistics).

Adult literacy rate (UNESCO estimates): 70.3% (males 74.8%; females 66.1%) in 2008 (Source: UNESCO Institute for Statistics).

Directory

The Government

HEAD OF STATE

President: Maj.-Gen. PAUL KAGAME (took office 22 April 2000; re-elected 25 August 2003 and 9 August 2010).

COUNCIL OF MINISTERS
(May 2011)

Prime Minister: BERNARD MAKUZA.
Minister of Agriculture and Animal Resources: Dr AGNES KALIBATA.
Minister of the East African Community: MONIQUE MUKARULIZA.
Minister of Health: Dr AGNES BINAGWAHO.
Minister of Internal Security: MUSSA FAZIL HERERIMANA.
Minister of Defence: Gen. JAMES KABAREBE.
Minister of Lands, Environment, Forestry and Mines: STANISLAS KAMANZI.
Minister of Finance and Economic Planning: JOHN RWANGOMBWA.
Minister of Disaster Preparedness and Refugee Affairs: Gen. MARCEL GATSINZI.
Minister of Local Government: JAMES MUSONI.
Minister in the Office of the Prime Minister, in charge of Gender and Family Promotion: ALOYSIA INYUMBA.
Minister of Youth, Sports and Culture: PROTAIS MITALI KABANDA.
Minister of Justice and Attorney-General: THARCISSE KARUGARAMA.
Minister in the Office of the President: VENANTIA TUGIREYEZU.
Minister of Education: PIERRE DAMIEN HABAMUREMYI.
Minister of Public Service and Labour: ANASTASE MUREKEZI.
Minister of Foreign Affairs: LOUISE MUSHIKIWABO.
Minister in the Office of the President, in charge of ICT: Dr IGNACE GATARE.
Minister in the Office of the Prime Minister, in charge of Cabinet Affairs: PROTAIS MUSONI.
Minister of Trade and Industry: FRANCOIS KANIMBA.
Minister of Infrastructure: ALBERT NSENGIYUMVA.
Minister of State in the Ministry of Local Government, in charge of Social Affairs and Community Development: CHRISTINE NYATANYI.
Minister of State in the Ministry of Infrastructure, in charge of Energy and Water: COLETA RUHAMYA.
Minister of State in the Ministry of Education, in charge of Primary and Secondary Education: Dr MATHIAS HABAMUNGU.

MINISTRIES

Office of the President: BP 15, Kigali; tel. 59062000; fax 572431; e-mail info@presidency.gov.rw; internet www.presidency.gov.rw.
Office of the Prime Minister: Kigali; tel. 250585444; fax 250583714; e-mail primature@gov.rw; internet www.primature.gov.rw.
Ministry of Agriculture and Animal Resources: BP 621, Kigali; tel. 250585008; fax 250585057; e-mail info@minagri.gov.rw; internet www.minagri.gov.rw.
Ministry of Defence: BP 23, Kigali; tel. 250577942; fax 250576969; e-mail info@mod.gov.rw; internet www.mod.gov.rw.
Ministry of the East African Community: BP 267, Kigali; tel. 250599122; internet www.mineac.gov.rw.
Ministry of Education: BP 622, Kigali; tel. 250583051; fax 250582161; e-mail info@mineduc.gov.rw; internet www.mineduc.gov.rw.
Ministry of Finance and Economic Planning: blvd de la Révolution, opp. Kigali City Council, BP 158, Kigali; tel. 250576701; fax 250577581; e-mail mfin@minecofin.gov.rw; internet www.minecofin.gov.rw.
Ministry of Foreign Affairs: blvd de la Révolution, pl. de l'Indépendance, BP 179, Kigali; tel. 250575386; fax 250573797; e-mail info@minaffet.gov.rw; internet www.minaffet.gov.rw.
Ministry of Forestry and Mines: BP 3052, Kigali; tel. 250582628; fax 250582629; e-mail info@minirena.gov.rw; internet www.minirena.gov.rw.
Ministry of Gender and Family Promotion: Kigali; tel. 250577626; fax 250577543; internet www.migeprofe.gov.rw.
Ministry of Health: BP 84, Kigali; tel. 250577458; fax 250576853; e-mail info@moh.gov.rw; internet www.moh.gov.rw.
Ministry of Information: Kigali; e-mail ikabagambe@yahoo.com.
Ministry of Infrastructure: BP 24, Kigali; tel. 250585503; fax 250585755; e-mail info@mininfra.gov.rw; internet www.mininfra.gov.rw.
Ministry of Internal Affairs: BP 446, Kigali; tel. 250586708; e-mail sec_cent@mininter.gov.rw; internet www.mininter.gov.rw.
Ministry of Justice: BP 160, Kigali; tel. 250586561; fax 250586509; e-mail mjust@minijust.gov.rw; internet www.minijust.gov.rw.
Ministry of Lands and Environment: BP 3052, Kigali; tel. 250582628; fax 250582629; e-mail info@minirena.gov.rw; internet www.minirena.gov.rw.
Ministry of Local Government: BP 790, Kigali; tel. 250585406; fax 250582228; e-mail webmaster@minaloc.gov.rw; internet www.minaloc.gov.rw.
Ministry of Public Service and Labour: BP 403, Kigali; tel. 250585714; fax 250583621; e-mail mifotra@mifotra.gov.rw; internet www.mifotra.gov.rw.
Ministry of Sports and Culture: BP 1044, Kigali; tel. 250583531; fax 250583518; e-mail info@minispoc.gov.rw; internet www.minispoc.gov.rw.
Ministry of Trade and Industry: BP 73, Kigali; tel. 250599103; fax 250599101; e-mail albert.bizimana@minicom.gov.rw; internet www.minicom.gov.rw.
Ministry of Youth: BP 3738, Kigali; tel. 250522730; e-mail info@miniyouth.gov.rw; internet www.miniyouth.gov.rw.

President and Legislature

PRESIDENT

Presidential Election, 9 August 2010

Candidate	Votes	% of votes
Paul Kagame	4,638,560	93.08
Jean Damascene Ntawukuriryayo	256,488	5.15
Prosper Higiro	68,235	1.37
Alivera Mukabaramba	20,107	0.40
Total	**4,983,390**	**100.00**

CHAMBER OF DEPUTIES

Speaker: ROSE MUKANTANTABANA.

General Election, 15 September 2008

Party	Votes	% of votes	Seats
Front patriotique rwandais*	3,655,956	78.76	42
Parti social-démocrate	609,327	13.12	7
Parti libéral	348,186	7.5	4
Independent	27,848	0.6	—
Total	**4,641,317**	**100.00**	**80†**

*Contested the elections in alliance with the Parti démocrate chrétien, the Parti démocratique islamique, the Union démocratique du peuple rwandais, the Parti de prospérité et de solidarité and the Parti socialiste rwandais.
† In addition to the 53 directly elected deputies, 27 seats are allocated, respectively, to two youth representatives, one disabilities representative and 24 female representatives, who are indirectly elected.

SENATE

Speaker: Dr VINCENT BIRUTA.

The Senate comprises 26 members, of whom 12 are elected by local government councils in the 12 provinces and two by academic institutions, while the remaining 12 are nominated (eight by the President and four by a regulatory body, the Parties' Forum).

Election Commission

National Electoral Commission: BP 6449, Kigali; tel. 250597800; fax 250597851; e-mail comelena@rwanda1.com; internet www.comelena.gov.rw; f. 2000; independent; Chair. Prof. CHRYSOLOGUE KARANGWA.

RWANDA

Political Organizations

Under legislation adopted in June 2003, the formation of any political organization based on ethnic groups, religion or sex was prohibited.

Democratic Green Party: BP 6334, Kigali; tel. 788563039 (mobile); e-mail info@rwandagreendemocrats.org; internet www.rwandagreendemocrats.org; f. 2009; Pres. FRANK HABINEZA.

Front patriotique rwandais (FPR): internet www.rpfinkotanyi.org; f. 1990; also known as Inkotanyi; comprises mainly Tutsi exiles, but claims multi-ethnic support; commenced armed invasion of Rwanda from Uganda in Oct. 1990; took control of Rwanda in July 1994; Chair. Maj.-Gen. PAUL KAGAME; Vice-Chair. CHRISTOPHE BAZIVAMO; Sec.-Gen. FRANÇOIS NGARAMBE.

Parti démocrate chrétien (PDC): BP 2348, Kigali; tel. 250576542; fax 250572237; f. 1990; Chair. AGNES MUKABARANGA.

Parti démocratique islamique (PDI): Tresor Bldg, 2nd Floor, Kigali; f. 1991; Leader SHEIKH HARERIMANA MUSSA FAZIL.

Parti démocratique rwandais (Pader): Kigali; f. 1992; Sec. JEAN NTAGUNGIRA.

Parti libéral (PL): BP 1304, Kigali; tel. 252577916; fax 252577838; f. 1991; restructured 2003; Chair. PROSPER HIGIRO; Sec.-Gen. Dr ODETTE NYIRAMIRIMO.

Parti du progrès et de la concorde (PPC): f. 2003; incl. fmr mems of Mouvement démocratique républicain; Leader Dr CHRISTIAN MARARA.

Parti progressiste de la jeunesse rwandaise (PPJR): Kigali; f. 1991; Leader ANDRÉ HAKIZIMANA.

Parti de prospérité et de solidarité (PSP): Kigali.

Parti républicain rwandais (Parerwa): Kigali; f. 1992; Leader AUGUSTIN MUTAMBA.

Parti social-démocrate (PSD): Kigali; f. 1991 by a breakaway faction of fmr Mouvement révolutionnaire national pour le développement; Leader Dr VINCENT BIRUTA.

Parti Social Imberakuri (PS Imberakuri): Nyamirambo, Kigali; tel. 788307145 (mobile); e-mail ntagandab@yahoo.fr; internet www.imberakuri.org; f. 2009; Pres. BERNARD NTAGANDA; Sec.-Gen. THEOBALD MUTARAMBIRWA.

Parti socialiste rwandais (PSR): BP 827, Kigali; tel. 252576658; f. 1991; workers' rights; Chair. JEAN-BAPTISTE RUCIBIGANGO.

Rassemblement travailliste pour la démocratie (RTD): BP 1894, Kigali; tel. 250575622; fax 250576574; f. 1991; Leader EMMANUEL NIZEYIMANA.

Union démocratique du peuple rwandais (UDPR): Kigali; f. 1992; Leader ADRIEN RANGIRA.

Other political organizations have been formed by exiled Rwandans and operate principally from abroad; these include:

Rassemblement républicain pour la démocratie au Rwanda (RDR): Postbus 3124, 2280 GC, Rijswijk, Netherlands; tel. (31) 623075674; fax (31) 847450374; e-mail info@rdrwanda.org; internet www.rdrwanda.org; f. 1995; prin. opposition party representing Hutu refugees in exile; Pres. VICTOIRE UMUHOZA INGABIRE.

Union du peuple rwandais (UPR): Brussels, Belgium; f. 1990; Hutu-led; Pres. SILAS MAJYAMBERE; Sec.-Gen. EMMANUEL TWAGILIMANA.

Diplomatic Representation

EMBASSIES IN RWANDA

Belgium: rue Nyarugenge, BP 81, Kigali; tel. 250575551; fax 250573995; e-mail kigali@diplobel.fed.be; internet www.diplomatie.be/kigali; Ambassador IVO GOEMANS.

Burundi: rue de Ntaruka, BP 714, Kigali; tel. 250575010; Ambassador Col REMY SINKAZI.

China, People's Republic: BP 1345, 44 blvd de la Revolution, Kigali; tel. 250570843; fax 250570848; e-mail chinaemb_rw@mfa.gov.cn; internet rw.chineseembassy.org; Ambassador SHU ZHAN.

Congo, Democratic Republic: 504 rue Longue, BP 169, Kigali; tel. 250575289; Ambassador NORBERT NKULU KILOMBO.

Egypt: BP 1069, Kigali; tel. and fax 28082686; e-mail egypt@rwanda1.com; Ambassador KHALED ABD AL-RAHMAN.

France: rue du Député Kamunzinzi, BP 53, Kigali; tel. 252551800; fax 252551820; e-mail ambafrance.kigali-amba@diplomatie.gouv.fr; Ambassador LAURENT CONTINI.

Germany: 10 ave Paul VI, BP 355, Kigali; tel. 250575141; fax 502087; e-mail info@kigali.diplo.de; internet www.kigali.diplo.de; Ambassador ELMAR TIMPE.

Holy See: 49 ave Paul VI, BP 261, Kigali (Apostolic Nunciature); tel. 252575293; fax 252575181; e-mail na.rwanda@diplomat.va; internet www.vatican.va; Apostolic Nuncio Most Rev. IVO SCAPOLO (Titular Archbishop of Tagaste).

Japan: 1236, Kacyiru South Gasabo, BP 874, Kigali; tel. 250500884; internet www.rw.emb-japan.go.jp; Ambassador KUNIO HATANAKA.

Kenya: BP 1215, Kigali; tel. 250583332; fax 250510919; e-mail kigali@mfa.go.ke; High Commissioner ROSE MAKENA MUCHIRI.

Korea, Democratic People's Republic: Kigali; Ambassador KIM PONG GI.

Libya: BP 1152, Kigali; tel. 250576470; Secretary of the People's Bureau MOUSTAPHA MASAND EL-GHAILUSHI.

Russia: 19 ave de l'Armée, BP 40, Kigali; tel. 250575286; fax 250503322; e-mail ambruss@rwandatel1.rwanda1.com; internet www.rwanda.mid.ru; Ambassador MIRGAYAS M. SHIRINSKII.

South Africa: 1370 blvd de l'Umuganda, POB 6563, Kacyiru-Sud, Kigali; tel. 250583185; fax 250583191; e-mail saemkgl@rwanda1.com; internet www.saembassy-kigali.org.rw; High Commissioner GLADSTONE DUMISANI GWADISO (recalled July 2010).

Sweden: Aurore House, Kacyiru, 1st Floor, Kigali; tel. 252597400; fax 252597459; e-mail ambassaden.kigali@sida.se; internet www.swedenabroad.com/kigali; Ambassador ANN DISMORR.

Uganda: 31 ave de la Paix, BP 656, Kigali; tel. and fax 250503537; e-mail embassy@ugandaembassy.rw; internet www.ugandaembassy.rw; High Commissioner RICHARD KABONERO.

United Kingdom: Parcelle 1131, Blvd de l'Umuganda, Kacyiru, BP 576, Kigali; tel. 250584098; fax 250582044; e-mail embassy.kigali@fco.gov.uk; internet ukinrwanda.fco.gov.uk/en; High Commissioner BENEDICT LLEWELLYN-JONES.

USA: 2657 ave de la Gendarmerie, Kacyiru, BP 28, Kigali; tel. 252596400; fax 252596771; e-mail irckigali@state.gov; internet rwanda.usembassy.gov; Ambassador W. STUART SYMINGTON.

Judicial System

The judicial system is composed of the Supreme Court, the High Court of the Republic, and provincial, district and municipal Tribunals. In addition, there are specialized judicial organs, comprising *gacaca* and military courts. The *gacaca* courts were established to try cases of genocide or other crimes against humanity committed between 1 October 1990 and 31 December 1994. Trials for categories of lesser genocide crimes were to be conducted by councils in the communities in which they were committed, with the aim of alleviating pressure on the existing judicial system. Trials under the *gacaca* court system formally commenced on 25 November 2002. Military courts (the Military Tribunal and the High Military Court) have jurisdiction in military cases. The President and Vice-President of the Supreme Court and the Prosecutor-General are elected by the Senate.

Supreme Court

BP 2197, Kigali; tel. 252517649; fax 252582276; e-mail info@supremecourt.gov.rw; internet www.supremecourt.gov.rw.

The Supreme Court comprises five sections: the Department of Courts and Tribunals; the Court of Appeals; the Constitutional Court; the Council of State; and the Revenue Court.

President of the Supreme Court: ALOYSIA CYANZAIRE.

Vice-President: Prof. SAM RUGEGE.

Prosecutor-General: MARTIN NGOGAEU.

Religion

AFRICAN RELIGIONS

About one-half of the population hold traditional beliefs.

CHRISTIANITY

Union des Eglises Rwandaises: BP 79, Kigali; tel. 28085825; fax 28083554; f. 1963; fmrly Conseil Protestant du Rwanda.

The Roman Catholic Church

Rwanda comprises one archdiocese and eight dioceses. About 49% of the total population is Roman Catholic.

Bishops' Conference

Conférence Episcopale du Rwanda, BP 357, Kigali; tel. 250575439; fax 250578080; e-mail cerwanda@rwanda1.com.

f. 1980; Pres. Rt Rev. ALEXIS HABIYAMBERE (Bishop of Nyundo).

Archbishop of Kigali: Most Rev. THADDÉE NTIHINYURWA, Archevêché, BP 715, Kigali; tel. 250575769; fax 250572274; e-mail kigarchi@yahoo.fr.

RWANDA

The Anglican Communion
The Church of the Province of Rwanda, established in 1992, has nine dioceses.
Archbishop of the Province and Bishop of Kigali: Most Rev. EMMANUEL MUSABA KOLINI, BP 61, Kigali; tel. and fax 250576340; e-mail ek@rwanda1.com.
Provincial Secretary: Rev. EMMANUEL GATERA, BP 61, Kigali; tel. and fax 250576340; e-mail egapeer@yahoo.com.

Protestant Churches
Eglise Baptiste: Nyantanga, BP 59, Butare; Pres. Rev. DAVID BAZIGA; Gen. Sec. ELEAZAR ZIHERAMBERE.
Eglise Luthérienne du Rwanda: BP 3099, Kigali; tel. 755110035 (mobile); fax 250519734; e-mail luthchurchlcr@yahoo.com; Bishop GEORGE W. KALIISA; 40,000 mems (2010).
There are about 250,000 other Protestants, including a substantial minority of Seventh-day Adventists.

BAHÁ'Í FAITH
National Spiritual Assembly: BP 652, Kigali; tel. 250572550.

ISLAM
There is a small Islamic community.

The Press

REGULATORY AUTHORITY
Haut Conseil de la Presse (HCP): Revolution Ave, POB 6929, Kigali; tel. 250570333; fax 250570334; e-mail hcp@terramail.rw; internet www.hcp.gov.rw; f. 2002; Pres. DOMINIQUE KAREKEZI PADIRI; Exec. Sec. PATRICE MULAMA.

DAILY
The New Times: BP 4953, Kigali; tel. 788301166; fax 250574166; e-mail editorial@newtimes.co.rw; internet www.newtimes.co.rw; f. 1995; daily; English; CEO and Editor-in-Chief JOSEPH BIDERI.

PERIODICALS
Bulletin Agricole du Rwanda: OCIR—Café, BP 104, Kigali-Gikondo; f. 1968; quarterly; French; Pres. of Editorial Bd Dr AUGUSTIN NZINDUKIYIMANA; circ. 800.
L'Ere de Liberté: BP 1755, Kigali; fortnightly.
Etudes Rwandaises: Université Nationale du Rwanda, Rectorat, BP 56, Butare; f. 1977; quarterly; pure and applied science, literature, human sciences; French; Pres. of Editorial Bd CHARLES NTAKIRUTINKA; circ. 1,000.
Hobe: BP 761, Kigali; f. 1955; monthly; children's interest; circ. 95,000.
Inkingi: BP 969, Kigali; tel. 250577626; fax 250577543; monthly.
Inkoramutima: Union des Eglises Rwandaises, BP 79, Kigali; quarterly; religious; circ. 5,000.
Kinyamateka: 5 blvd de l'OUA, BP 761, Kigali; tel. 250576164; e-mail km@rwanda1.com; internet www.kinyamateka.org.rw; f. 1933; fortnightly; economics; circ. 11,000; Dir Fr PIERRE CLAVER NKUSI.
La Nouvelle Relève: Office Rwandais d'Information, BP 83, Kigali; tel. 250575735; e-mail lnr2020@yahoo.fr; internet www.orinfor.gov .rw; f. 1976; weekly; politics, economics, culture; French; Dir GÉRARD RUGAMBWA; circ. 1,700.
Nouvelles du Rwanda: Université Nationale du Rwanda, BP 117, Butare; every 2 months.
Nyabarongo—Le Canard Déchaîné: BP 1585, Kigali; tel. 250576674; monthly.
Le Partisan: BP 1805, Kigali; tel. 250573923; fortnightly.
La Patrie—Urwatubyaye: BP 3125, Kigali; tel. 250572552; monthly.
Revue Dialogue: BP 572, Kigali; tel. 250574178; f. 1967; bi-monthly; Christian issues; Belgian-owned; circ. 2,500.
Revue Médicale Rwandaise: Ministry of Health, BP 84, Kigali; tel. 250576681; f. 1968; quarterly; French.
Revue Pédagogique: Ministry of Education, BP 622, Kigali; quarterly; French.
Rwanda Herald: Kigali; f. Oct. 2000; owned by Rwanda Independent Media Group.
Rwanda Libération: BP 398, Kigali; tel. 250577710; monthly; Dir and Editor-in-Chief ANTOINE KAPITENI.
Rwanda Renaître: BP 426, Butare; fortnightly.

Rwanda Rushya: BP 83, Kigali; tel. 250572276; fortnightly.
Le Tribun du Peuple: BP 1960, Kigali; bi-monthly; Owner JEAN-PIERRE MUGABE.
Umucunguzi: Gisenyi; f. 1998; Kinyarwanda and French; Chief Editor EMILE NKUMBUYE.
Umuhinzi-Mworozi: OCIR—Thé, BP 1334, Kigali; tel. 250514797; fax 250514796; f. 1975; monthly; circ. 1,500.
Umusemburo—Le Levain: BP 117, Butare; monthly.
Umuseso: Kigali; independent; weekly; Kinyarwanda; publ. suspended in April 2010; Editor CHARLES KABONERO.
Urunana: Grand Séminaire de Nyakibanda, BP 85, Butare; tel. 250530793; e-mail wellamahoro@yahoo.fr; f. 1967; 3 a year; religious; Pres. WELLAS UWAMAHORO; Editor-in-Chief DAMIEN NIYOYIREMERA.

NEWS AGENCIES
Agence Rwandaise d'Information (ARI): BP 453, Kigali; tel. 250587215; fax 250587216; internet www.ari-rna.co.rw; f. 1975.
Office Rwandais d'Information (Orinfor): BP 83, Kigali; tel. 250575735; fax 250576539; internet www.orinfor.gov.rw; f. 1973; Dir JOSEPH BIDERI.

Publishers

Editions Rwandaises: Caritas Rwanda, BP 124, Kigali; tel. 250575786; fax 250574254; e-mail caritas1@rwanda1.com; Man. Dir Abbé CYRIAQUE MUNYANSANGA; Editorial Dir ALBERT NAMBAJE.
Implico: BP 721, Kigali; tel. 250573771.
Imprimerie de Kabgayi: BP 66, Gitarama; tel. 250562252; fax 250562345; e-mail imprikabgayi@yahoo.fr; f. 1932; Dir Abbé CYRILLE UWIZEYE.
Imprimerie de Kigali, SARL: 1 blvd de l'Umuganda, BP 956, Kigali; tel. 250582032; fax 250584047; e-mail impkig@rwandatel1 .rwanda1.com; f. 1980; Dir LÉONCE NSENGIMANA.
Imprimerie URWEGO: BP 762, Kigali; Dir JEAN NSENGIYUNVA.
Pallotti-Presse: BP 863, Kigali; tel. 250574084.

GOVERNMENT PUBLISHING HOUSES
Imprimerie Nationale du Rwanda: BP 351, Kigali; tel. 250576214; fax 250575820; f. 1967; Dir JUVÉNAL NDISANZE.
Régie de l'Imprimerie Scolaire (IMPRISCO): BP 1347, Kigali; e-mail imprisco@rwandatel1.rwanda1.com; f. 1985; Dir JEAN DE DIEU GAKWANDI.

Broadcasting and Communications

TELECOMMUNICATIONS
MTN Rwandacell: BP 264, MTN Centre, Nyarutarama, Kigali; tel. 250586863; fax 250586865; internet www.mtn.co.rw; f. 1998; provides mobile cellular telephone services; CEO KHALED MIKKAWI.
Rwanda Utilities Regulatory Agency: POB 7289, Kigali; tel. 252584562; fax 252584563; e-mail info@rura.gov.rw; internet www .rura.gov.rw; f. 2001; regulatory authority; also responsible for regulation of electricity, water, sanitation, gas and transportation sectors; Chair. EUGENE KAZIGE; Dir-Gen. DIOGNE MUDENGE.
Rwandatel: ECOBANK Bldg, 7th Floor, ave de La Paix, BP 1332, Kigali; tel. 75100; e-mail info@rwandatel.rw; internet www .rwandatel.rw; national telecommunications service; privatized 2007.
Tigo Rwanda: 9801, Nyarutarama, POB 6979, Kigali; tel. 722000100 (mobile); internet www.tigo.co.rw; provides mobile cellular telephone and internet services; CEO TOM GUTJAHR.

BROADCASTING

Radio
Radio Rwanda: BP 83, Kigali; tel. 250575665; fax 250576185; f. 1961; state-controlled; daily broadcasts in Kinyarwanda, Swahili, French and English; Dir of Programmes DAVID KABUYE.
Deutsche Welle Relay Station Africa: Kigali; daily broadcasts in German, English, French, Hausa, Swahili, Portuguese and Amharic.

Television
Télévision rwandaise (TVR): Kigali; fax 250575024; f. 1992; transmissions reach more than 60% of national territory; broadcasts for 10 hours daily in Kinyarwanda, French and English.

RWANDA

Finance

(cap. = capital; res = reserves; dep. = deposits; m. = million; brs = branches; amounts in Rwanda francs)

BANKING

In 2010 there were 12 banks in Rwanda.

Central Bank

Banque Nationale du Rwanda: ave Paul VI, BP 531, Kigali; tel. 250575282; fax 250572551; e-mail info@bnr.rw; internet www.bnr.rw; f. 1964; bank of issue; cap. 7,000m., res 21,183.0m., dep. 297,242.9m. (Dec. 2009); Gov. CLAVER GATETE.

Commercial Banks

Following the privatization of two commercial banks, government control of the banking section was reduced from 45% in 2003 to 22% in 2005, although the three largest banks continued to control two-thirds of the system's assets, valued at US $365m. (equivalent to 34% of GDP).

Access Bank (Rwanda) Ltd: 3rd Floor, UTC Bldg, 1232 ave de la Paix, BP 2059, Kigali; tel. 250500091; fax 250575761; e-mail bancor@rwanda1.com; internet www.accessbankplc.com/rw/; f. 1995 as Banque à la Confiance d'Or; fmrly Bancor SA; name changed as above in 2009 when acquired by private investors; 75% owned by Access Bank (Nigeria); cap. and res 3,417.1m., total assets 34,549.3m. (Dec. 2005); Chair. NICHOLAS WATSON.

Banque Commerciale du Rwanda, SA: BP 354, 11 blvd de la Revolution, Kigali; tel. 250595200; fax 250573395; e-mail bcr@rwanda1.com; internet www.bcr.co.rw; f. 1963; privatized Sept. 2004; cap. 5,000m., res 749m., dep. 74,559m. (Dec. 2009); Chair. Dr NKOSANA MOYO; Man. Dir DAVID KUWANA; 6 brs.

Banque de l'Habitat du Rwanda: ave de la Justice, BP 1034, Kigali; tel. 250573843; fax 250572799; e-mail bhr@rwanda1.com; internet www.bhr.co.rw; f. 1975 as Caisse Hypothécaire du Rwanda; name changed as above in 2005; 56% state-owned; cap. 778.2m., total assets 6,966.8m. (Dec. 2003); Pres. FRANÇOIS RUTISHASHA; Dir-Gen. GERVAIS NTAGANDA.

Banque de Kigali, SA: 63 ave du Commerce, BP 175, Kigali; tel. 250593100; fax 250573461; e-mail bk@bk.rw; internet www.bk.rw; f. 1966; cap. 5,005.0m., res 10,892.3m., dep. 124,586.8m. (Dec. 2009); Chair. LADO GURGENIDZE; Man. Dir JAMES GATERA; 7 brs.

Compagnie Générale de Banque: blvd de l'Umuganda, BP 5230, Kigali; tel. 250597500; fax 250503336; e-mail cogebank@cogebank.com; internet www.cogebank.com; f. 1999; cap. and res 1,210.8m., total assets 7,297.4m. (Dec. 2003); Pres. ANDRÉ KATABARWA; 13 brs.

Ecobank Rwanda: ave de la Paix, BP 3268, Kigali; tel. 250503580; fax 250501319; e-mail contact@ecobank.com; internet www.ecobank.com; cap. and res 3,158.4m., total assets 45,950.9m. (Dec. 2003); Man. Dir DANIEL SACKEY.

Fina Bank SA: 20 blvd de la Révolution, BP 331, Kigali; tel. 250598600; fax 250573486; e-mail info@finabank.co.rw; internet www.finabank.com; f. 1983 as Banque Continentale Africaine (Rwanda); name changed 2005; cap. 5,000.6m., res 634.6m., dep. 40,885.6m. (Dec. 2009); privatized; Chair. ROBERT BINYON; Man. Dir STEPHEN CALEY; 5 brs.

Development Banks

Banque Rwandaise de Développement, SA (BRD): blvd de la Révolution, BP 1341, Kigali; tel. 250575079; fax 250573569; e-mail brd@brd.com.rw; internet www.brd.com.rw; f. 1967; 56% state-owned; cap. and res 4,104.6m., total assets 13,920.7m. (Dec. 2003); Man. Dir JACK NKUSI KAYONGA (acting).

Banques Populaires du Rwanda (Banki z'Abaturage mu Rwanda): BP 1348, Kigali; tel. 250573559; fax 250573579; e-mail info@bpr.rw; internet www.bpr.rw; f. 1975; cap. and res 1,180.5m., total assets 20,433.8m. (Dec. 2002); Pres. MANASSÉ TWAHIRWA; CEO BEN KALKMAN; 145 brs.

INSURANCE

In 2010 there were five insurance companies in Rwanda.

Compagnie Générale d'Assurances et de Réassurances au Rwanda (COGEAR): ave de l'Armée, BP 2753, Kigali; tel. 250576041; fax 250576082; Dir-Gen. ANASTASE MUNYANDAMUTSA.

Société Nationale d'Assurances du Rwanda (SONARWA): 2417 blvd de la Révolution, BP 1035, Kigali; tel. 250572101; fax 250572052; e-mail sonarwa@rwandatel1.rwanda1.com; internet www.sonarwa.co.rw; f. 1975; 35% owned by Industrial and General Insurance Co Ltd (Nigeria); cap. 500m.; Pres. FRANÇOIS NGARAMBE; Dir-Gen. HOPE MURERA.

Société Rwandaise d'Assurances, SA (SORAS): blvd de la Révolution, BP 924, Kigali; tel. 250573712; fax 250573362; e-mail info@soras.co.rw; internet www.soras.co.rw; f. 1984; cap. 1,002m. (2007); Pres. CHARLES MHORANYI; Dir-Gen. MARC RUGENERA.

Trade and Industry

GOVERNMENT AGENCIES

Rwanda Agricultural Development Authority (RADA): BP 538, Kigali; tel. 755102618 (mobile); e-mail infos@rada.gov.rw; internet www.rada.gov.rw; f. 2006; contributes towards the growth of agricultural production through the development of appropriate technologies, providing advisory, outreach and extension services to stakeholders in agriculture; Acting Dir-Gen. NORBERT SENDEGE.

Rwanda Investment and Export Promotion Agency: Kimihurura, ave du Lac Muhazi, POB 6239, Kigali; tel. 250510248; fax 250510249; e-mail info@rwandainvest.com; internet www.rwandainvest.com; f. 1998 as Rwanda Investment Promotion Agency; Dir-Gen. FRANCIS GATARE.

Rwanda Public Procurement Authority: ave de la Paix, POB 4276, Kigali; tel. 250501403; fax 250501402; e-mail rppa1@rwanda1.com; internet www.rppa.gov.rw; f. 2008 to replace the Nat. Tender Bd (f. 1998); organizes and monitors general public procurement; Chair. DAMIEN MUGABO; Dir AUGUSTUS SEMINEGA.

Rwanda Revenue Authority (RRA): ave du Lac Muhazi, POB 3987, Kimihurura, Kigali; tel. 250595520; fax 250578488; e-mail cg@rra.gov.rw; internet www.rra.gov.rw; f. 1998 to maximize revenue collection; Commissioner-Gen. MARY BAINE.

DEVELOPMENT ORGANIZATIONS

Coopérative de Promotion de l'Industrie Minière et Artisanale au Rwanda (COOPIMAR): BP 1139, Kigali; Dir DANY NZARAMBA.

Institut de Recherches Scientifiques et Technologiques (IRST): BP 227, Butare; tel. 250530395; fax 250530939; e-mail irst@irst.ac.rw; internet www.irst.ac.rw; Dir-Gen. Dr JEAN BAPTISTE NDUWAYEZU.

Institut des Sciences Agronomiques du Rwanda (ISAR): 47 rue du Député Kamunzinzi, POB, 5016 Kigali; tel. 250530642; fax 250530644; e-mail info@isar.rw; internet www.isar.rw; for the devt of subsistence and export agriculture; Dir DAPHROSE GAHAKWA; 12 centres.

Office National pour le Développement de la Commercialisation des Produits Vivriers et des Produits Animaux (OPROVIA): BP 953, Kigali; privatization pending; Dir DISMAS SEZIBERA.

Régie d'Exploitation et de Développement des Mines (REDEMI): BP 2195, Kigali; tel. 250573632; fax 250573625; e-mail ruzredem@yahoo.fr; f. 1988 as Régie des Mines du Rwanda; privatized in 2000; state org. for mining tin, columbo-tantalite and wolfram; Man. Dir JEAN-RUZINDANA MUNANA.

Rwanda Coffee Development Authority (RCDA): BP 104, Kigali; tel. 250575600; fax 250573992; e-mail ocircafe@rwanda1.com; internet www.rwandacafe.com; f. 1978; devt of coffee and other new agronomic industries; operates a coffee stabilization fund; Dir-Gen. ALEX KANYANKORE.

Rwanda Development Board: Gishushu, Nyarutarama Rd, POB 6239, Kigali; tel. 250580804; e-mail info@rdb.rw; internet www.rdb.rw; f. 2008 to replace eight govt agencies (RIEPA, ORTPN, Privatization Secretariat, Rwanda Commercial Registration Services Agency, Rwanda Information and Technology Authority, Centre for Support to Small and Medium Enterprises, Human Resource and Institutional Capacity Development Agency, and Rwanda Environmental Management Authority); CEO JOHN GARA.

Rwanda Tea Authority (RTA): BP 1344, Kigali; tel. 250514797; fax 250514796; e-mail info@rwandatea.com; internet www.rwandatea.com; devt and marketing of tea; Man. Dir ANTHONY BUTERA.

Société de Pyrèthre au Rwanda (SOPYRWA): BP 79, Ruhengeri; tel. and fax 250546364; e-mail info@sopyrwa.com; internet www.sopyrwa.com; f. 1978; cultivation and processing of pyrethrum; post-war activities resumed in Oct. 1994; current production estimated at 80% pre-war capacity; Dir SYLVAIN NZABAGAMBA.

INDUSTRIAL ASSOCIATIONS

Association des Industriels du Rwanda: BP 39, Kigali; tel. and fax 250575430; Pres. YVES LAFAGE; Exec. Sec. MUGUNGA NDOBA.

Private Sector Federation (PSF): Gikonda Magerwa, POB 319, Kigali; tel. 250583541; fax 250583574; e-mail info@rpsf.org.rw; internet psf.org.rw; f. 1999 to replace the Chambre de Commerce et d'Industrie de Rwanda; promotes and represents the interests of the Rwandan business community; Dir JEAN BOSCO KABAGEMBE; Sec.-Gen. EMMANUEL HATEGEKA.

RWANDA

UTILITIES

Rwanda Utilities Regulatory Agency: see Telecommunications.

Rwanda Electricity Corpn and Rwanda Water and Sanitation Corpn (RECO & RWASCO): POB 537, Kigali; tel. 252598400; e-mail fgatanazi@electrogaz.co.rw; internet www.electrogaz.co.rw; f. 1976 as Electrogaz; changed name as above in 2009 after company was split, although it is managed as one institution; state-owned water and electricity supplier; Man. Dir YVES MUYANGE; Dir of Electricity CHARLES KANYAMIHIGO; Dir of Water THEONESTE MINANI.

TRADE UNIONS

Centrale d'Education et de Coopération des Travailleurs pour le Développement/Alliance Coopérative au Rwanda (CECOTRAD/ACORWA): BP 295, Kigali; f. 1984; Pres. ELIE KATABARWA.

Centrale Syndicale des Travailleurs du Rwanda: BP 1645, Kigali; e-mail cestrav@rwandatel1.rwanda1.com; Sec.-Gen. FRANÇOIS MURANGIRA.

Transport

RAILWAYS

There are no railways in Rwanda, although plans exist for the construction of a line linking Kigali and Isaka in Tanzania, with possible extensions to Bujumbura in Burundi and the Democratic Republic of the Congo. Rwanda has access by road to the Tanzanian railways system.

ROADS

In 2004 there were an estimated 14,008 km of roads, of which 2,662 km were paved. There are road links with Uganda, Tanzania, Burundi and the Democratic Republic of the Congo. Internal conflict during 1994 caused considerable damage to the road system and the destruction of several important bridges.

Office National des Transports en Commun (ONATRACOM): BP 619, Kigali; tel. 250575411; fax 250576126; e-mail onatraco@rwanda1.com; f. 1978; Dir-Gen. ESDRAS NKUNDUMUKIZA.

INLAND WATERWAYS

There are services on Lake Kivu between Cyangugu, Gisenyi and Kibuye, including two vessels operated by ONATRACOM.

CIVIL AVIATION

The Kanombe international airport at Kigali can process up to 500,000 passengers annually. There is a second international airport at Kamembe, near the border with the Democratic Republic of the Congo. Bugesera International Airport, currently under construction, was expected to receive its first flight in 2015. There are airfields at Butare, Gabiro, Ruhengeri and Gisenyi, servicing internal flights.

Rwandair: Kigali Int. Airport Bldg, Top Floor, BP 7275, Kigali; tel. 250503687; fax 250503686; e-mail info@rwandair.com; internet www.rwandair.com; f. 1998; privately owned; international services; Chair. and CEO JOHN MIRENGE.

Tourism

Attractions for tourists include the wildlife of the national parks (notably mountain gorillas), Lake Kivu and fine mountain scenery. Since the end of the transitional period in late 2003, the Government has increased efforts to develop the tourism industry. In 1998 there were only an estimated 2,000 foreign visitors to Rwanda, but by 2001 the number of tourist arrivals had increased to 113,185. Total receipts from tourism were estimated at US $66m. in 2007.

Office Rwandais du Tourisme et des Parcs Nationaux (ORTPN): blvd de la Révolution 1, BP 905, Kigali; tel. 250576514; fax 250576515; e-mail info@rwandatourism.com; internet www.rwandatourism.com; f. 1973; govt agency; Dir-Gen. ROSETTE RUGAMBA.

Defence

As assessed at November 2010, the total strength of the Rwandan armed forces was estimated at 33,000, comprising an army of 32,000 and an air force of 1,000. In addition, there were an estimated 2,000 local defence forces. A programme to restructure the army, which was expected to be reduced in size to number about 25,000, was planned and a Rwanda Demobilization and Reintegration Commission was mandated to facilitate the reintegration of discharged military personnel into civilian life.

Defence Expenditure: Budgeted at 43,600m. Rwanda francs in 2010.

Chief of Defence Staff: Lt-Gen. CHARLES KAYONGA.

Chief of Staff, Land Forces: Lt-Gen. CAESAR KAYIZARI.

Chief of Staff of the Air Force: JOSEPH DEMALI (acting).

Education

Primary education, beginning at seven years of age and lasting for six years, is officially compulsory. Secondary education, which is not compulsory, begins at the age of 14 and lasts for a further six years, comprising two equal cycles of three years. In 2003, however, the Government announced plans to introduce a nine-year system of basic education, including three years of attendance at lower secondary schools. Schools are administered by the state and by Christian missions. In 2007/08 96% of children in the relevant age-group (males 95%, females 97%) were enrolled in primary schools, according to UNESCO estimates, while secondary enrolment in 2006/07 was equivalent to only 13.4% of children in the appropriate age-group (males 14.2%, females 12.7%) in 2004/05. The Ministry of Education established 94 new secondary schools in 2003, and a further 58 in 2005. Rwanda has a university, with campuses at Butare and Ruhengeri, and several other institutions of higher education, but some students attend universities abroad, particularly in Belgium, France or Germany. In 2008/09 the number of students in tertiary education (there are six public higher education institutions and seven private higher institutions) was 55,213. At the beginning of the 2011 school year, English became the language of instruction in all public Rwandan educational establishments. In 2008 spending on education represented 20.4% of total budgetary expenditure.

SAINT CHRISTOPHER* AND NEVIS

Introductory Survey

LOCATION, CLIMATE, LANGUAGE, RELIGION, FLAG, CAPITAL

The Federation of Saint Christopher and Nevis is situated at the northern end of the Leeward Islands chain of the West Indies, with Saba and St Eustatius (both in the Netherlands Antilles) to the north-west, Barbuda to the north-east and Antigua to the south-east. Nevis lies about 3 km (2 miles) to the south-east of Saint Christopher, separated by a narrow strait. The tropical heat, varying between 17°C (62°F) and 33°C (92°F), is tempered by constant sea winds, and annual rainfall averages 1,400 mm (55 ins) on Saint Christopher and 1,220 mm (48 ins) on Nevis. English is the official language. The majority of the population are Christians of the Anglican Communion, and other Christian denominations are represented. The national flag (proportions 2 by 3) comprises two triangles, one of green (with its base at the hoist and its apex in the upper fly) and the other of red (with its base in the fly and its apex in the lower hoist), separated by a broad, yellow-edged black diagonal stripe (from the lower hoist to the upper fly) bearing two five-pointed white stars. The capital is Basseterre, on Saint Christopher.

CONTEMPORARY POLITICAL HISTORY

Historical Context

Saint Christopher, settled in 1623, was Britain's first colony in the West Indies. The French settled part of the island a year later, and conflict over possession continued until 1783, when Saint Christopher was eventually ceded to Britain under the Treaty of Versailles. Nevis was settled by the British in 1628, and remained one of the most prosperous of the Antilles until the middle of the 19th century. The island of Anguilla was first joined to the territory in 1816. The St Kitts-Nevis-Anguilla Labour Party, formed in 1932, campaigned for independence for the islands. In 1958 Saint Christopher-Nevis-Anguilla became a member of the West Indies Federation, remaining so until the Federation's dissolution in 1962. A new Constitution, granted to each of the British territories in the Leeward Islands in 1960, provided for government through an Administrator and an enlarged Legislative Council. After an abortive attempt to form a smaller East Caribbean Federation, Saint Christopher-Nevis-Anguilla attained Associated Statehood in February 1967, as part of an arrangement that gave five of the colonies full internal autonomy, while the United Kingdom retained responsibility for defence and foreign relations. The House of Assembly replaced the Legislative Council, the Administrator became Governor, and the Chief Minister, Robert Bradshaw, leader of the Labour Party, became the state's first Premier. Three months later Anguilla rebelled against government from Saint Christopher, and in 1971 reverted to being a de facto British dependency. Anguilla was formally separated from the other islands in 1980.

Domestic Political Affairs

A general election in 1971 returned Robert Bradshaw to the premiership. In the 1975 election the Labour Party again won the largest number of seats, while the Nevis Reformation Party (NRP) once more took both the Nevis seats. Bradshaw died in May 1978 and was succeeded as Premier by Paul Southwell, hitherto Deputy Premier (and a former Chief Minister). Southwell died in May 1979, and was replaced by the party's leader, Lee L. Moore.

In February 1980 the Labour Party was removed from government for the first time in nearly 30 years: although the Labour Party had won 58% of the popular vote, a coalition Government comprising the People's Action Movement (PAM) and the NRP was formed under PAM leader Dr Kennedy A. Simmonds. The change of government led to the suspension of a timetable for independence, which had been scheduled for June 1980. In 1982 proposals for a greater degree of autonomy for Nevis and for independence for the whole state were approved by the House of Assembly, although the Labour Party opposed the plans, arguing that the coalition Government did not have a mandate for its independence policy. Disagreements concerning the content of the proposed independence constitution led to civil disturbances in 1982 and 1983. Nevertheless, Saint Christopher and Nevis became an independent state, under a federal Constitution, on 19 September 1983. The Labour Party denounced the special provisions for Nevis in the Constitution (see below) as giving the island a powerful role in government that was disproportionate to its size and population. Elections to the Nevis Island Assembly were held in August, at which the NRP, led by Simeon Daniel, won all five elective seats.

Early elections to an enlarged National Assembly (now with 11 elective seats) took place in June 1984, at which the ruling PAM-NRP coalition was returned to power. At an election to the Nevis Island Assembly in December 1987, the NRP retained four seats and the Concerned Citizens' Movement (CCM) secured one. At the general election of March 1989, however, the CCM took one of the three Nevis seats from the NRP. Moore resigned as leader of the Labour Party and was succeeded by Denzil Douglas. The electoral success of the coalition Government under the leadership of Simmonds was attributed to its economic policies, and was achieved despite persistent rumours of official connivance in drugs-trafficking activities on the islands.

The CCM secured a majority in the Nevis Island Assembly at an election in June 1992. The party's leader, Vance Amory, became Premier of the Island Administration.

At a general election in November 1993 neither the PAM nor the Labour Party managed to secure a legislative majority. Following the refusal of Amory to form a coalition government with either the PAM or the Labour Party, the Governor-General invited Simmonds to form a minority government with the support of the NRP. Douglas protested against the decision and appealed for a general strike to support his demands for a further general election. Serious disturbances ensued, and in early December the Governor-General declared a 21-day state of emergency. Meanwhile, Simmonds withdrew from negotiations with Douglas, although an initial agreement to hold a further general election had been reached, in protest at Douglas's premature public revelation of the agreement.

In October 1994 six people were charged in connection with the murder, in Basseterre, of the head of the Saint Christopher special investigations police unit, Jude Matthew, who had been conducting an investigation into the recent disappearances of William Herbert, the country's Permanent Representative to the UN, and Vincent Morris, a son of the Deputy Prime Minister Sidney Morris. Preliminary investigations suggested that these events were connected to the discovery, at the same time as Morris's disappearance, of a large consignment of cocaine in Saint Christopher. In November Sidney Morris resigned, following the arrest of two other sons on charges related to drugs and firearms offences.

Dominance of the Labour Party

A 'forum for national unity' was convened in November 1994, at which representatives of all political parties, church organizations, and tourism, trade, labour and law associations agreed to seek closer political co-operation in the months preceding an early general election, in order to halt the advance of drugs-related crime and the attendant erosion of investor confidence in the islands. None the less, fierce electoral campaigning culminated, in June 1995, in a violent clash between rival PAM and Labour Party supporters, which resulted in a number of serious injuries. The general election, conducted on 3 July, was won decisively by the Labour Party, and Denzil Douglas became Prime Minister. Simmonds was among prominent PAM politicians who lost their seats. Douglas resolved to address promptly the problems of increasingly violent crime and of deteriorating prison conditions. The Prime Minister also announced plans to draft proposals for constitutional reform that would provide for the establishment of separate governments for the two islands.

In July 1997 the National Assembly approved legislation to restore a full-time defence force, to include the coastguard, with the principal aim of strengthening the islands' anti-drugs operations. (The Simmonds administration had disbanded the army

---

*While this island is officially called Saint Christopher as part of the state, the name is usually abbreviated to St Kitts.

in 1981.) The Nevis administration and the PAM accused the Labour Government of seeking to enhance its authority by recruiting party loyalists to the force. In July 1998 a convicted murderer was executed—the first implementation of the death penalty in the country since 1985. The Attorney-General, Delano Bart, defended the reintroduction of capital punishment, against criticism from the Roman Catholic Church and the human rights organization Amnesty International, as part of the Government's strategy to reduce crime rates.

In March 1999 a Constitutional Task Force, chaired by former Governor Sir Fred Phillips, began work on the drafting of a new constitution. In August the Task Force submitted its report to the Prime Minister, who appointed a seven-member select committee, comprising representatives of all the major parties, to review its recommendations and to draft proposals for constitutional change.

At a general election in March 2000 the Labour Party won all eight seats available on Saint Christopher, gaining the seat previously held by the PAM. There was no change in the position on Nevis, where the CCM retained its two seats and the NRP its one. In October Lindsay Grant, a lawyer, was elected the new leader of the PAM, replacing Simmonds.

The new Government again sought to address the increasing crime rate on the islands, which was affecting the tourism industry. In February 2001 a curfew for all children under 15 was introduced in an effort to reduce youth crime, and in June the Government sought to persuade the US Navy to relocate one of its bases to Saint Christopher. Douglas stated his hope that the country would derive 'economic, social and financial' benefits from the US presence. The per-head murder rate in 2007 (33 murders per 100,000 people) was one of the highest in the Caribbean. On 19 December 2008 a convicted murderer was hanged in Basseterre, the first execution to be carried out in the territory for 10 years. In January 2009 the Government engaged the services of former US Federal Bureau of Investigation chief Mark Mershon to devise a crime reduction strategy.

The Labour Party was returned to office for a third consecutive term at a general election held on 25 October 2004. The incumbent administration, which campaigned on its social development record, won seven of the eight seats on Saint Christopher; the PAM, whose leader, Lindsay Grant, narrowly failed to get elected, secured the other seat. The balance of power remained the same on Nevis, where the CCM secured two seats and the NRP secured one. Turn-out on Saint Christopher was 62.2%, but was less than 50% overall, reflecting the dissatisfaction of many Nevisians with the current system. Although the voter registration process was regarded as imperfect, the team of observers from the Caribbean Community and Common Market (CARICOM, see p. 219) monitoring the election reported the contest to be generally free and fair.

Remarks made by Commonwealth and CARICOM observers of the 2004 general election precipitated governmental discussions from that year towards electoral reform in an effort to achieve a more comprehensive and democratic system of voting and greater regulation of campaign practices. Amendments submitted to the National Assembly in August 2006 included: the supervision of campaign spending; the consideration of constitutional revisions to provide for more inclusive consultations, particularly with political organizations without parliamentary representation; and a review and possible redefinition of constituency boundaries to achieve more proportional representation of the electorate. It was also suggested that a national registration scheme be conducted to ensure that records of eligible voters were current and accurate, and proposals for a voter identification card initiative, first advanced by the Labour Party in 2000, were also resurrected. The Electoral Reform Consultative Committee conducted a public consultation and submitted a report of its findings on 1 February 2007. The Government began to implement new legislation in early 2008 when the National Identification Card was introduced for registered voters, who were to receive the card on re-registering at an electoral office. The opposition expressed dissatisfaction, claiming there were a number of discrepancies with the process, including the opportunity for voters to confirm their addresses in multiple constituencies.

Recent developments: the 2010 election

A general election was held on 25 January 2010. The Labour Party won an unprecedented fourth term in office, albeit with a slightly reduced majority. The ruling party secured six of the 11 elected seats in the National Assembly (all in St Kitts constituencies), while the opposition CCM retained two seats (both on Nevis). The PAM increased its parliamentary representation to two deputies (one on each island) and the NRP held onto its single Nevis seat. The PAM launched legal challenges to the outcome of ballots in three constituencies, including one where its leader, Lindsay Grant, had failed to secure election. The party claimed that its earlier challenges to changes to constituency boundaries had not received sufficient hearing by the National Advisory Electoral Reform and Boundaries Committee. A preliminary report by election observers from the Organization of American States recommended that outstanding boundary issues should be addressed as soon as possible, but declared itself satisfied with the election process. Leader Denzil Douglas was reappointed Prime Minister. A new Cabinet was sworn in in early February, which included NRP member Patrice Nisbett as Attorney-General and Minister of Justice and Legal Affairs, an appointment Douglas claimed proved the federal Government's intention to promote closer bonds with Nevis.

In October 2010 the Government implemented a closed circuit television scheme, with 70 security cameras installed in high-crime areas of Basseterre and Charlestown (the capital of Nevis). However, the country's crime problems came under international scrutiny in the following month, when a tourist bus was ambushed by armed thieves; two cruise lines diverted their vessels to neighbouring Antigua in response. Douglas emphasized that combating crime was the Government's main priority and boosted funding for the ministry responsible for national security in the 2011 budget. A controversial bill granting the authorities permission to intercept telecommunications transmissions was approved by the National Assembly in February 2011; the Government argued that the new legislation would form an important part of its strategy to address crime. The murder rate declined from a record 27 in 2009 to 20 in 2010.

Autonomy for Nevis?

In June 1996 Amory announced that the Nevis Island Assembly was initiating proceedings (as detailed in the Constitution—see below) for the secession of Nevis from the federation with Saint Christopher. The announcement was made as plans proceeded for the establishment of a federal government office on Nevis (which Amory considered to be unconstitutional) and as the National Assembly considered a financial services bill that proposed referring all potential investors in Nevis to the federal administration for approval. The Nevis Island Assembly was reported to have interpreted both measures as serious infringements of its administrative rights. Despite the prompt intervention of a number of regional diplomatic initiatives to preserve the federation, a secession bill for Nevis received its preliminary reading in the National Assembly in July. In October the NRP, while supportive of the right to secede, expressed concern at the precipitant nature of Amory's secession timetable, and in November the NRP representative in the National Assembly boycotted a second reading of the bill, forcing a postponement of the debate.

At elections to the Nevis Island Assembly in February 1997 Amory's CCM retained three of the five elective seats, while the NRP retained the remaining two. In October the Nevis Assembly voted unanimously in favour of secession; a referendum on the issue was held in August 1998, in which 61.7%, less than the two-thirds' majority required by the Constitution, voted for autonomy. The leaders of the two islands immediately announced that they would work to improve relations, and Douglas pledged to implement the principal recommendations of a constitutional review commission intended to augment inter-island affairs.

In elections to the Nevis Island Assembly in September 2001 the CCM strengthened its control of the legislature, gaining a total of four elective seats. The NRP, under the leadership of Joseph Parry, took the remaining seat.

In October 2002 Douglas, pronouncing on the recurring issue of greater autonomy for Nevis, said that, while he supported the constitutional right of Nevis to secede from the federation, the federal Government was willing to discuss ways to increase the autonomy of the Nevis Island Administration and Assembly. Amory, however, remained convinced that full autonomy and separate membership of the Organisation of Eastern Caribbean States (OECS, see p. 462) would be a better option for Nevis. In January 2004 an OECS Heads of Government meeting urged the Nevis administration to review its intention to campaign for independence in favour of preserving the status quo. CARICOM (see p. 219), in 2003, and the US Administration, earlier in January 2004, also indicated their support for the existing federation.

The NRP emerged from 15 years in opposition to secure a legislative majority at an election to the Nevis Island Assembly in July 2006. The party captured three of the five elective seats, while the CCM won the remaining two seats. Parry took office as Nevis Island Premier later in the same month. The issue of secession was again foregrounded, with the participating parties presenting opposing stances on a move towards greater autonomy; the outgoing CCM had campaigned for independence from Saint Christopher, while the NRP indicated a preference for constitutional reform. In January 2007 Prime Minister Douglas encouraged the pursuit of greater collaboration between the two islands; by this time the possibility of an imminent referendum on Nevis, promulgated by the former CCM Government, seemed, once again, to have receded.

Foreign Affairs

Regional relations

In the late 1980s regional discussions were held on the issue of political unity in the East Caribbean. Saint Christopher and Nevis expressed interest in political unity only if the proposed merger included its Leeward Island neighbours and the Virgin Islands, where an estimated 10,000 Kittitians and Nevisians reside. From January 1990 the OECS agreed to relax restrictions on travel between member states. Moreover, in February 2002 it was agreed, with effect from March, to allow nationals of member states to travel freely within the OECS area and to remain in the territory of any other member state for up to six months. A Caribbean Community and Common Market (CARICOM, see p. 219) passport, designed to enhance a sense of community and facilitate intra- and extra-regional travel for citizens of participating nations, was launched in January 2005 and implemented by Saint Christopher and Nevis in October of that year. On 6 July 2006 the Government—together with those of five other Caribbean states—signed a declaration of participation in CARICOM's Caribbean Single Market and Economy (CSME), which was established by six founding member states on 1 January. The CSME was intended to enshrine the free movement of goods, services and labour throughout the CARICOM region.

Other external relations

In September 2005 Douglas reiterated the Government's commitment to its lucrative diplomatic relationship with Taiwan. Saint Christopher and Nevis, along with Saint Vincent and the Grenadines, remained the only Caribbean countries still to recognize the statehood of Taiwan, which was losing a contest of so-called 'dollar diplomacy' in the region with the People's Republic of China. In January 2008 Saint Christopher and Nevis opened an embassy in Taiwan, the first embassy of a Caribbean country to be located in Asia. However, relations were briefly strained in April when the Government of Saint Christopher and Nevis failed to send a congratulatory message to the winner of Taiwan's presidential election, Ma Ying-jeou, until some two weeks after the ballot. Vice-President Annette Lu Hsu-lien claimed that diplomatic relations were fragile, but the Chargé d'affaires of Saint Christopher and Nevis in Taiwan, Jasmine Huggins, denied the pronouncement and claimed that her message had not been sent earlier owing to personal problems.

CONSTITUTION AND GOVERNMENT

Saint Christopher and Nevis is a constitutional monarchy. Executive power is vested in the British monarch, as Head of State, and is exercised locally by the monarch's personal representative, the Governor-General, who acts in accordance with the advice of the Cabinet. Legislative power is vested in Parliament, comprising the monarch and the National Assembly. The National Assembly is composed of the Speaker, three (or, if a nominated member is Attorney-General, four) nominated members, known as Senators (two appointed on the advice of the Premier and one appointed on the advice of the Leader of the Opposition), and 11 elected members (Representatives), who are chosen from single-member constituencies for up to five years by universal adult suffrage. The Cabinet comprises the Prime Minister, who must be able to command the support of the majority of the members of the National Assembly, the Attorney-General (ex officio) and four other ministers. The Prime Minister and the Cabinet are responsible to Parliament.

The Nevis Island legislature comprises the Nevis Island Assembly and the Nevis Island Administration, headed by the British monarch (who is represented on the island by the Deputy Governor-General). It operates similarly to the Saint Christopher and Nevis legislature but has power to secede from the federation, subject to certain restrictions (see Constitution, below).

REGIONAL AND INTERNATIONAL CO-OPERATION

Saint Christopher and Nevis is a member of the Caribbean Community and Common Market (CARICOM, see p. 219), of the Organisation of Eastern Caribbean States (OECS, see p. 462), of the Organization of American States (see p. 391), and the Association of Caribbean States (see p. 445). The Eastern Caribbean Central Bank (see p. 451), of which Saint Christopher is a member, is based in Basseterre. In 2001 a regional stock exchange, the Eastern Caribbean Securities Exchange, opened in Basseterre. On 18 June 2010 Saint Christopher and Nevis was a signatory to the Revised Treaty of Basseterre, establishing an Economic Union among OECS member states. The Economic Union, which involved the removal of barriers to trade and the movement of labour as a step towards a single financial and economic market, came into effect on 21 January 2011.

Saint Christopher and Nevis joined the UN upon independence in 1983. It acceded to the World Trade Organization (see p. 430) in 1996. Upon independence, Saint Christopher and Nevis became a full member of the Commonwealth (see p. 230). The country is a party to the Cotonou Agreement (see p. 327), the successor agreement to the Lomé Convention, signed in June 2000 between the European Union (see p. 270) and a group of developing countries. The country is a member of the Group of 77 (see p. 447) organization of developing states and acceded to the Non-aligned Movement in 2006.

ECONOMIC AFFAIRS

In 2009, according to estimates by the World Bank, Saint Christopher and Nevis's gross national income (GNI), measured at average 2007–09 prices, was US $501m., equivalent to $10,100 per head (or $13,660 per head on an international purchasing-power parity basis). During 2000–09 the population increased by an average of 1.3% per year, while over the same period, it was estimated, gross domestic product (GDP) per head increased, in real terms, at an average annual rate of 1.0%. Overall GDP increased, in real terms, by an average of 3.8% annually in 2001–08; according to the Eastern Caribbean Central Bank (ECCB, see p. 451), growth was 4.6% in 2008.

Agriculture (including forestry and fishing) contributed 2.5% of GDP in 2008. According to FAO estimates, some 21.7% of the working population would be employed in the agriculture sector (including sugar-manufacturing) in mid-2011. Major crops include coconuts and sea-island cotton, although some vegetables are also exported. Sugar and sugar products had dominated the economy since the 1960s, but the industry, which had accumulated a debt of US $141.5m., closed after the 2005 harvest. In spite of a guaranteed European Union (see p. 270) sugar price, which was well above world market levels, the sugar industry had survived only as a result of generous government subsidies. Large areas formerly used for sugar have been redesignated for tourism, and the Government was expected to make provision for the retraining of sugar industry employees. Other important crops include yams, sweet potatoes, groundnuts, onions, sweet peppers, cabbages, carrots and bananas. Fishing is an increasingly important commercial activity. According to ECCB estimates, agricultural GDP increased at an average annual rate of 1.1% in 2001–08. The real value of agricultural GDP increased by 14.3% in 2008.

Industry (including mining, manufacturing, construction and public utilities) provided 23.8% of GDP in 2008. Excluding sugar manufacturing, the sector employed 21.0% of the working population in 1994. According to ECCB estimates, real industrial GDP increased at an average annual rate of 0.2% in 2001–08. In 2008 the GDP of the sector expanded by an estimated 2.6%.

Manufacturing provided 7.9% of GDP in 2008, and the sector (excluding sugar-manufacturing) employed 7.8% of the working population in 1994. The principal manufactured products are garments, electrical components, food products, beer and other beverages. The sector recorded average annual growth of 0.1% during 2001–08. In 2008, according to the ECCB, real manufacturing GDP increased by 2.7%.

Construction contributed 13.5% of GDP in 2008, according to ECCB figures, and employed 10.5% of the working population in 1994. The sector grew by 0.3% in 2001–08; growth was 2.6% in 2008.

The islands are dependent upon imports of fuel and energy (8.1% of total imports in 2008) for their energy requirements. In September 2005 the Government became one of 13 Caribbean administrations to sign the PetroCaribe accord, under which Saint Christopher and Nevis was allowed to purchase petroleum from Venezuela at reduced prices. From 2008 the Government took steps to explore alternative energy sources and to thereby decrease its dependency on costly fuel imports; to this end a wind farm was inaugurated on Nevis in June 2010, producing up to 10,000 MW of electricity per year.

The services sector contributed 73.7% of GDP in 2008, and employed 64.4% of the working population in 1994. Tourism is a major contributor to the economy, although the sector declined from the mid-2000s. In 2009 tourism generated some EC $225.4m. in receipts. In the same year total visitor arrivals stood at 547,561, a 2.7% increase on the previous year's total. However, this increase was mainly owing to a rise in cruise ship passengers rather than in stop-over tourists (who traditionally spend more money). Stop-over numbers fell from 127,705 in 2008 to 93,081 in 2009. The real GDP of the services sector increased at an average annual rate of 5.0% in 2001–08; growth was an estimated 4.0% in 2008.

In 2010 Saint Christopher and Nevis recorded a trade deficit of EC $546.24m. and there was a deficit of some $464.35m. on the current account of the balance of payments. The USA was the islands' principal trading partner in 2008, supplying 61.0% of imports and purchasing 83.6% of exports. Trade with the United Kingdom and with other Caribbean states is also important. Electrical machinery was the country's leading export (accounting for 45.9% of total export revenues in 2008), and the principal imports were machinery and transport equipment, basic manufactures, and food and live animals.

In 2009 the central Government of Saint Christopher and Nevis recorded a budgetary surplus of EC $9.5m., according to preliminary figures from the ECCB. Saint Christopher and Nevis' general government gross debt was EC $2,779m. in 2009, equivalent to 184.7% of GDP. The country's total external debt was estimated to be US $258m. at the end of 2008, of which US $257m. was long-term public and publicly guaranteed debt. In 2007 the cost of debt-servicing was equivalent to 17.3% of the value of exports of goods and services. According to IMF estimates, the annual rate of inflation averaged 4.0% in 2003–09; consumer prices decreased by 0.8% in 2009. The rate of unemployment, reported to be around 10% in early 2003, is mitigated by mass emigration, particularly from Nevis; remittances from abroad provide an important source of revenue.

Following the closure of the sugar industry, the most rapidly developing industry has been tourism, which was forecast by the World Travel and Tourism Council to provide some 28.2% of the country's GDP and 26.7% of employment in 2011. The development of light manufacturing, particularly of electronic components and textiles, has also helped to broaden the islands' economic base. In addition, a small 'offshore' financial sector on Nevis has been developed. The global economic downturn negatively affected the tourism and construction sectors, and the Government estimated that GDP contracted by a dramatic 9.6% in 2009. The Labour Government that was returned to office for an historic fourth term in early 2010 set out its economic priorities as increasing employment and business opportunities on the islands. It pledged to continue with the diversification of the economy through expansion of the tourism, finance and telecommunications sectors, but not at the expense of agriculture and manufacturing. The economy remained depressed throughout 2010, with the IMF projecting a further GDP contraction of 1.5% in that year. The slow economic recovery in the country's key tourist markets of the USA and the United Kingdom contributed to continuing stagnation within the industry in 2010, although the reopening in December of the Four Seasons Resort Nevis (the island's largest hotel, which had been closed since October 2008 after suffering damage from Hurricane Omar) was a positive development. In an attempt to boost tax receipts, in August 2010 the National Assembly approved the implementation of a 17% value added tax (10% for the tourism sector), which came into effect in November, replacing the existing inefficient system. The IMF forecast negligible real GDP growth of 1.5% in 2011.

PUBLIC HOLIDAYS

2012: 2 January (for New Year's Day), 3 January (Carnival Last Lap), 6 April (Good Friday), 9 April (Easter Monday), 1 May (May Day), 28 May (Whit Monday), 2 August (Culturama Last Lap), 6 August (Emancipation Day), 16 September (Heroes' Day), 19 September (Independence Day), 25–26 December (Christmas).

Statistical Survey

Source (unless otherwise stated): St Kitts and Nevis Information Service, Government Headquarters, Church St, POB 186, Basseterre; tel. 465-2521; fax 466-4504; e-mail skninfo@caribsurf.com; internet www.stkittsnevis.net.

AREA AND POPULATION

Area (sq km): 269.4 (Saint Christopher 176.1, Nevis 93.3).

Population: 40,618 (males 19,933, females 20,685) at census of 12 May 1991; 45,841 (males 22,784, females 23,057) at census of 14 May 2001. *2009:* 51,967 (mid-year estimate). Sources: UN, *Population and Vital Statistics Report* and Eastern Caribbean Central Bank.

Density (mid-2009): 192.9 per sq km.

Population by Age and Sex (at mid-2000): *0–14:* 12,390 (males 6,390, females 6,000); *15–64:* 24,450 (males 12,340, females 12,110); *65 and over:* 3,570 (males 1,670, females 1,900); *Total* 40,410 (males 20,400, females 20,010) (Source: UN, *Demographic Yearbook*).

Principal Town (estimated population incl. suburbs, mid-2009): Basseterre (capital) 12,847. Source: UN, *World Urbanization Prospects: The 2009 Revision.*

Births and Deaths (2001): Registered live births 803 (birth rate 17.4 per 1,000); Registered deaths 352 (death rate 7.6 per 1,000). *2010:* Crude birth rate 14.2 per 1,000; Crude death rate 7.1 per 1,000 (Source: Pan American Health Organization).

Life Expectancy (years at birth, WHO estimates): 73 (males 70; females 76) in 2008. Source: WHO, *World Health Statistics.*

Employment (labour force survey, 1994): Sugar cane production/manufacturing 1,525; Non-sugar agriculture 914; Mining and quarrying 29; Manufacturing (excl. sugar) 1,290; Electricity, gas and water 416; Construction 1,745; Trade (except tourism) 1,249; Tourism 2,118; Transport and communications 534; Business and general services 3,708; Government services 2,738; Other statutory bodies 342; *Total* 16,608 (Saint Christopher 12,516, Nevis 4,092). Source: IMF, *St Kitts and Nevis: Recent Economic Developments* (August 1997).

HEALTH AND WELFARE
Key Indicators

Total Fertility Rate (children per woman, 2010): 1.8.

Under-5 Mortality Rate (per 1,000 live births, 2008): 15.

Physicians (per 1,000 head, 2000): 1.1.

Hospital Beds (per 1,000 head, 2009): 6.0.

Health Expenditure (2007): US $ per head (PPP): 863.

Health Expenditure (2007): % of GDP: 6.0.

Health Expenditure (2007): public (% of total): 57.8.

Access to Sanitation (% of persons, 2008): 96.

Total Carbon Dioxide Emissions ('000 metric tons, 2007): 249.2.

Carbon Dioxide Emissions Per Head (metric tons, 2007): 5.1.

Human Development Index (2007): ranking: 62.

Human Development Index (2007): value: 0.838.

Source: partly Pan American Health Organization; for other sources and definitions, see explanatory note on p. vi.

AGRICULTURE, ETC.

Principal Crops ('000 metric tons, 2008 unless otherwise indicated, FAO estimates): Sugar cane 111.0; Coconuts 1.3. Note: No data were available for individual crops in 2009. *Aggregate Production* ('000 metric tons, may include official, semi-official or estimated data, 2009): Roots and tubers 1.3; Vegetables (incl. melons) 0.9; Fruits (excl. melons) 1.4.

Livestock ('000 head, 2008, FAO estimates): Cattle 7.0; Sheep 7.0; Goats 9.0; Pigs 6.0. Note: No data were available for 2009.

SAINT CHRISTOPHER AND NEVIS

Livestock Products ('000 metric tons, 2009 unless otherwise indicated, FAO estimates): Pig meat 0.1; Chicken meat 0.2; Cattle meat 0.1; Hen eggs 0.2 (2008).

Fishing (metric tons, live weight, 2008, FAO estimates): Groupers 25; Snappers 70; Grunts, sweetlips 15; Goatfishes, red mullets 80; Parrotfishes 45; Surgeonfishes 40; Triggerfishes, durgons 20; Caribbean spiny lobster 40; Stromboid conchs 90; *Total catch* (incl. others) 450.

Source: FAO.

INDUSTRY

Production: Raw sugar 10,700 metric tons in 2005; Electric energy 223.4 million kWh in 2009. Sources: IMF, *St Kitts and Nevis: Statistical Appendix* (April 2008) and Eastern Caribbean Central Bank.

FINANCE

Currency and Exchange Rates: 100 cents = 1 Eastern Caribbean dollar (EC $). *Sterling, US Dollar and Euro Equivalents* (31 December 2010): £1 sterling = EC $4.227; US $1 = EC $2.700; €1 = EC $3.608; EC $100 = £23.66 = US $37.04 = €27.72. *Exchange Rate*: Fixed at US $1 = EC $2.70 since July 1976.

Budget (EC $ million, 2009, preliminary): *Revenue:* Revenue from taxation 380.7 (Taxes on income 134.9, Taxes on property 9.0, Taxes on domestic goods and services 71.2, Taxes on international trade and transactions 165.4); Other current revenue 140.5; Capital revenue 26.5; Foreign grants 59.3; Total 606.9. *Expenditure:* Current expenditure 521.7 (Personal emoluments and wages 219.9, Goods and services 130.3, Interest payments 117.3, Transfers and subsidies 54.2); Capital expenditure and net lending 75.7; Total 597.4. Source: Eastern Caribbean Central Bank.

International Reserves (US $ million at 31 December 2010): Reserve position in IMF 0.13; IMF special drawing rights 13.07; Foreign exchange 155.63; Total 168.83. Source: IMF, *International Financial Statistics*.

Money Supply (EC $ million at 31 December 2010): Currency outside depository corporations 101.05; Transferable deposits 574.26; Other deposits 1,629.51; *Broad money* 2,304.82. Source: IMF, *International Financial Statistics*.

Cost of Living (Consumer Price Index; base: 2005 = 100): All items 110.1 in 2007; 118.5 in 2008; 117.6 in 2009. Source: IMF, *International Financial Statistics*.

Gross Domestic Product (EC $ million at constant 1990 prices): 800.78 in 2006; 817.01 in 2007; 854.87 in 2008. Source: Eastern Caribbean Central Bank.

Expenditure on the Gross Domestic Product (EC $ million at current prices, 2008): Government final consumption expenditure 263.20; Private final consumption expenditure 1,149.43; Gross capital formation 627.00; *Total domestic expenditure* 2,039.63; Exports of goods and services 591.60; *Less* Imports of goods and services 1,091.85; *GDP at market prices* 1,539.38. Source: Eastern Caribbean Central Bank.

Gross Domestic Product by Economic Activity (EC $ million at current prices, 2008): Agriculture, hunting, forestry and fishing 34.57; Mining and quarrying 2.72; Manufacturing 110.56; Electricity and water 30.00; Construction 188.18; Wholesale and retail trade 163.10; Restaurants and hotels 103.31; Transport 155.75; Communications 60.37; Finance and insurance 226.63; Real estate and housing 28.12; Government services 228.84; Other community, social and personal services 59.72; *Sub-total* 1,391.87; *Less* Financial intermediation services indirectly measured 128.21; *Total in basic prices* 1,263.66; Taxes, less subsidies, on products 275.72; *GDP at market prices* 1,539.38. Source: Eastern Caribbean Central Bank.

Balance of Payments (EC $ million, 2010): Exports of goods 137.90; Imports of goods –684.14; *Trade balance* –546.24; Services (net) 59.30; *Balance on goods and services* –486.94; Other income received (net) –56.16; *Balance on goods, services and income* –543.10; Current transfers received (net) 78.75; *Current balance* –464.35; Capital account (net) 16.51; Direct investment (net) 380.78; Portfolio investment (net) –30.52; Other investment (net) 96.24; Net errors and omissions –1.41; *Overall balance* –2.75. Source: Eastern Caribbean Central Bank.

EXTERNAL TRADE

Principal Commodities (US $ million, 2008): *Imports c.i.f.:* Food and live animals 48.7; Mineral fuels, lubricants, etc. 26.2 (Refined petroleum products 22.4); Chemicals 21.1; Basic manufactures 57.9 (Iron and steel manufactures 9.6); Machinery and transport equipment 73.5 (Road vehicles 20.2); Total (incl. others) 324.8. *Exports f.o.b.:* Food and live animals 0.8; Beverages and tobacco 3.8; Basic manufactures 0.4 (Metal manufactures 0.3); Machinery and transport equipment 41.3 (Electrical machinery 23.8); Miscellaneous manufactures 3.2 (Printed matter 1.9); Total (incl. others) 51.8. Source: UN, *International Trade Statistics Yearbook*.

Principal Trading Partners (US $ million, 2008): *Imports:* Antigua and Barbuda 0.8; Barbados 5.4; Canada 6.7; China, People's Rep. 3.7; Denmark 2.2; Dominican Republic 5.7; France 1.6; Germany 0.4; Grenada 2.0; Jamaica 3.4; Japan 9.8; Netherlands Antilles 6.2; Trinidad and Tobago 37.5; United Kingdom 14.6; USA 198.1; Total (incl. others) 324.8. *Exports* (excl. re-exports): Antigua and Barbuda 0.8; Dominica 0.2; Netherlands Antilles 1.2; Trinidad and Tobago 0.2; United Kingdom 2.3; USA 43.3; Total (incl. others) 51.8. Source: UN, *International Trade Statistics Yearbook*.

TRANSPORT

Road Traffic (registered motor vehicles): 11,352 in 1998; 12,432 in 1999; 12,917 in 2000.

Shipping: *Arrivals* (2000): 1,981 vessels. *International Sea-borne Freight Traffic* ('000 metric tons, 2000): Goods loaded 24.7; Goods unloaded 234.2. *Merchant Fleet* (vessels registered at 31 December 2009): Number 258; Total displacement 898,925 grt (Source: IHS Fairplay, *World Fleet Statistics*).

Civil Aviation (aircraft arrivals): 24,800 in 1998; 23,500 in 1999; 19,400 in 2000.

TOURISM

Visitor Arrivals: 379,473 (123,062 stop-over visitors, 5,177 excursionists, 1,911 yacht passengers, 249,323 cruise ship passengers) in 2007; 533,353 (127,705 stop-over visitors, 3,920 excursionists, 812 yacht passengers, 400,916 cruise ship passengers) in 2008; 547,561 (93,081 stop-over visitors, 3,718 excursionists, 209 yacht passengers, 450,553 cruise ship passengers) in 2009. *Stop-over Visitors by Country* (2009): Canada 6,413; Caribbean 22,410; United Kingdom 6,496; USA 54,410; Other 3,352.

Tourism Receipts (EC $ million): 336.92 in 2007; 297.17 in 2008; 225.41 in 2009.

Source: Eastern Caribbean Central Bank.

COMMUNICATIONS MEDIA

Radio Receivers ('000 in use, 1997): 28.

Television Receivers ('000 in use, 1999): 10.

Telephones ('000 main lines in use, 2009): 20.5.

Mobile Cellular Telephones (subscribers, 2009): 83,000.

Personal Computers: 11,000 (234.1 per 1,000 persons) in 2004.

Internet Users (2009): 17,000.

Broadband Subscribers (2009): 13,000.

Non-daily Newspapers (2004, unless otherwise indicated): Titles 4; Circulation 34,000 (1996).

Sources: mainly UNESCO, *Statistical Yearbook*; UN, *Statistical Yearbook*; International Telecommunication Union.

EDUCATION

Pre-primary (2008/09 unless otherwise indicated): 77 schools (2003/04); 102 teachers; 1,605 pupils.

Primary (2008/09 unless otherwise indicated): 23 schools (2003/04); 443 teachers; 6,334 pupils.

Secondary (2008/09 unless otherwise indicated): 7 schools (2003/04); 441 teachers; 4,270 pupils.

Tertiary (2007/08 unless otherwise indicated): 1 institution; 79 teachers (2003/04); 859 students.

Pupil-teacher Ratio (primary education, UNESCO estimate): 14.3 in 2008/09.

Adult Literacy Rate: 97.8% in 2004 (Source: UN Development Programme, *Human Development Report*).

Source: mostly UNESCO Institute for Statistics.

Directory

The Government

HEAD OF STATE

Queen: HM Queen Elizabeth II.
Governor-General: Sir Cuthbert Montroville Sebastian (took office 1 January 1996).

CABINET
(May 2011)

The Cabinet consists of members of the St Kitts-Nevis Labour Party and one member of the Nevis Reformation Party.

Prime Minister and Minister of Finance, Sustainable Development and Human Resource Development: Dr Denzil Llewellyn Douglas.
Deputy Prime Minister and Minister of Foreign Affairs, National Security, Labour, Immigration and Social Security: Sam Terrence Condor.
Minister of International Trade, Industry, Commerce, Agriculture, Marine Resources, Consumer Affairs and Constituency Empowerment: Dr Timothy Sylvester Harris.
Minister of Public Works, Housing, Energy and Utilities: Dr Earl Asim Martin.
Attorney-General and Minister of Justice and Legal Affairs: Patrice Nisbett (NRP).
Minister of Health, Social Services, Community Development, Culture and Gender Affairs: Marcella Liburd.
Minister of Youth Empowerment, Sports, Information Technology and Telecommunications and Post: Glen Phillip.
Minister of Education: Nigel Alexis Carty.
Minister of Tourism and International Transport: Richard Oliver Skerritt.

MINISTRIES

Office of the Governor-General: Government House, Basseterre; tel. 465-2315.
Government Headquarters: Church St, POB 186, Basseterre; tel. 465-2521; fax 466-4505; e-mail infocom@sisterisles.kn; internet www.gov.kn.
Prime Minister's Office: Government Headquarters, Church St, POB 186, Basseterre; tel. 465-9698; fax 465-9997; e-mail sknpmpresssec@cuopm.com; internet www.cuopm.org.
Attorney-General's Office and Ministry of Justice and Legal Affairs: Church St, POB 164, Basseterre; tel. 465-2521; fax 465-5040; e-mail attorneygeneral@gov.kn.
Ministry of Education: Church St, POB 333, Basseterre; tel. 465-2521.
Ministry of Finance, Sustainable Development and Human Resource Development: Church St, POB 186, Basseterre; tel. 465-2521; fax 465-0198; e-mail adminskbmof@caribsurf.com.
Ministry of Foreign Affairs, National Security, Labour, Immigration and Social Security: Church St, POB 186, Basseterre; tel. 465-2521; fax 465-5202; e-mail foreigna@sisterisles.kn; internet www.mofa.gov.kn.
Ministry of Health, Social Services, Community Development, Culture and Gender Affairs: Church St, POB 186, Basseterre; tel. 465-2521.
Ministry of International Trade, Industry, Commerce, Agriculture, Marine Resources, Consumer Affairs and Constituency Empowerment: Basseterre.
Ministry of Public Works, Housing, Energy and Utilities: Basseterre.
Ministry of Tourism and International Transport: Basseterre.
Ministry of Youth Empowerment, Sports, Information Technology and Telecommunications and Post: Basseterre.

NEVIS ISLAND ADMINISTRATION

Premier: Joseph W. Parry.
There are also two appointed members.

Administrative Centre: Main St, POB 689, Charlestown, Nevis; tel. 469-1469; fax 469-0039; e-mail nevfin@caribsurf.com; internet www.gisnevis.com.

Legislature

NATIONAL ASSEMBLY

Speaker: Curtis Martin.
Elected members: 11. Nominated members: 3. Ex officio members: 1.

Election, 25 January 2010

Party	Seats
St Kitts-Nevis Labour Party	6
Concerned Citizens' Movement	2
People's Action Movement	2
Nevis Reformation Party	1
Total	**11**

NEVIS ISLAND ASSEMBLY

Elected members: 5. Nominated members: 3.

Elections to the Nevis Island Assembly took place in July 2006. The Nevis Reformation Party took three seats and the Concerned Citizens' Movement secured the remaining two seats.

Political Organizations

Concerned Citizens' Movement (CCM): Charlestown, Nevis; tel. 469-3519; e-mail partyorganiser@myccmparty.com; internet myccmparty.com; f. 1986; Leader Vance W. Amory; Sec. Livingstone Herbert.
Nevis Reformation Party (NRP): Government Rd, POB 480, Charlestown, Nevis; tel. 469-0630; e-mail JosephParry@VoteNRP.com; internet www.votenrp.com; f. 1970; Pres. Joseph W. Parry; Gen. Sec. Llewelyn Parris.
People's Action Movement (PAM): POB 1294, Basseterre; tel. 466-2726; fax 466-3854; e-mail pamdemocrat@pamdemocrat.org; internet www.pamdemocrat.org; f. 1965; Political Leader Lindsay Grant; Deputy Leaders Shawn Richards, Eugene Hamilton.
St Kitts-Nevis Labour Party (SKNLP): Masses House, Church St, POB 239, Basseterre; tel. 465-5347; fax 465-8328; e-mail wanda.connor@sknlabourparty.com; f. 1932; socialist party; Chair. Dr Timothy Harris; Leader Dr Denzil Llewellyn Douglas.

Diplomatic Representation

EMBASSIES IN SAINT CHRISTOPHER AND NEVIS

Brazil: St Kitts Marriott, Suite 17-206, 858 Frigate Bay Rd, Frigate Bay, Basseterre; tel. 465-1054; fax 465-2015; e-mail central@brazilskn.org; internet www.brazilskn.org; Ambassador Miguel Junior França Chaves de Magalhãse.
Cuba: 34 Bladen Housing Devt, POB 600, Basseterre; tel. 466-3374; fax 465-8072; e-mail embacubask@sisterisles.kn; Ambassador Jorge Desiderio Payret Zurbiaur.
Taiwan (Republic of China): Taylor's Range, POB 119, Basseterre; tel. 465-2421; fax 465-7921; e-mail rocemb@caribsurf.com; Ambassador Miguel Tsao.
Venezuela: Delisle St, POB 435, Basseterre; tel. 465-2073; fax 465-5452; e-mail frontado@caribsurf.com; Ambassador Cruz de Jesús Bello.

Diplomatic relations with other countries are maintained at consular level, or with ambassadors and high commissioners resident in other countries of the region, or directly with the other country.

Judicial System

Justice is administered by the Eastern Caribbean Supreme Court (ECSC), based in Saint Lucia and consisting of a Court of Appeal and a High Court. Two judges of the High Court are responsible for Saint Christopher and Nevis and preside over the Court of Summary Jurisdiction. One of two ECSC Masters, chiefly responsible for procedural and interlocutory matters, is also resident in Saint Kitts. The Magistrates' Courts deal with summary offences and civil offences involving sums of not more than EC $5,000.

High Court Judges: Ianthea Leigertwood-Octave (acting), Errol Thomas (acting).
Master: Pearletta Lanns.

SAINT CHRISTOPHER AND NEVIS

Registrar: CLAUDETTE JENKINS.
Magistrates' Office: Losack Rd, Basseterre; tel. 465-2170.

Religion

CHRISTIANITY

St Kitts Christian Council: Victoria Rd, POB 48, Basseterre; tel. 465-2167; e-mail stgeorgessk@hotmail.com; Chair. Archdeacon VALENTINE HODGE.

The Anglican Communion

Anglicans in Saint Christopher and Nevis are adherents of the Church in the Province of the West Indies. The islands form part of the diocese of the North Eastern Caribbean and Aruba. The Bishop is resident in The Valley, Anguilla.

The Roman Catholic Church

The diocese of Saint John's-Basseterre, suffragan to the archdiocese of Castries (Saint Lucia), includes Anguilla, Antigua and Barbuda, the British Virgin Islands, Montserrat and Saint Christopher and Nevis. The Bishop participates in the Antilles Episcopal Conference (currently based in Port of Spain, Trinidad and Tobago).

Bishop of Saint John's-Basseterre: (vacant), POB 836, St John's, Antigua; e-mail djr@candw.ag.

Other Churches

There are also communities of Methodists, Moravians, Seventh-day Adventists, Baptists, Pilgrim Holiness, the Church of God, Apostolic Faith and Plymouth Brethren.

The Press

The Democrat: Cayon St, POB 30, Basseterre; tel. 466-2091; fax 465-0857; e-mail thedemocrat@caribsurf.com; internet www.pamdemocrat.org/Newspaper; f. 1948; weekly (Sat.); organ of PAM; Man. Editor DENIECE ALLEYNE; circ. 3,000.

The Labour Spokesman: Masses House, Church St, POB 239, Basseterre; tel. 465-2229; fax 466-9866; e-mail sknunion@sisterisles.kn; internet www.labourspokesman.com; f. 1957; Wed. and Sat.; organ of St Kitts-Nevis Trades and Labour Union; Editor DAWUD ST LLOYD BYRON; Man. WALFORD GUMBS; circ. 6,000.

The Leewards Times: Pinneys Industrial Site, POB 146, Nevis; tel. 469-1049; fax 469-0662; e-mail hbramble@caribsurf.com; internet www.leewardstimes.net; weekly (Fri.); Editor HOWELL BRAMBLE.

The St Kitts and Nevis Observer: Cayon St, POB 657, Basseterre; tel. 466-4994; fax 466-4995; e-mail observsk@caribsurf.com; internet www.thestkittsnevisobserver.com; weekly (Fri.); independent; Publr and Editor-in-Chief KENNETH A. WILLIAMS.

Publishers

Caribbean Publishing Co (St Kitts-Nevis) Ltd: Dr William Herbert Complex, Frigate Bay Rd, POB 745, Basseterre; tel. 465-5178; fax 466-0307; e-mail sbrisban@caribpub.com; internet stkittsyp.com.

MacPennies Publishing Co: 10A Cayon St East, POB 318, Basseterre; tel. 465-2274; fax 465-8668; e-mail mcpenltd@macpennies.com; internet www.macpennies.com; f. 1969.

St Kitts-Nevis Publishing Association Ltd: 1 Observer Plaza, Observer Dr., POB 510, Charlestown, Nevis; tel. 469-5907; fax 469-5891; e-mail observnv@sisterisles.kn; internet www.thestkittsnevisobserver.com; f. 1994; Publr and Editor-in-Chief KENNETH A. WILLIAMS.

Broadcasting and Communications

TELECOMMUNICATIONS

Regulatory Authority

Eastern Caribbean Telecommunications Authority: Miriam House, Lozack Rd, POB 450, Basseterre; tel. 465-2900; fax 465-1147; e-mail ectel@ectel.int; internet www.ectel.int; f. 2000; based in Castries, Saint Lucia; regulates telecommunications in Saint Christopher and Nevis, Dominica, Grenada, Saint Lucia and Saint Vincent and the Grenadines; Dir (Saint Christopher and Nevis) JASON HAMILTON.

Service Providers

Caribbean Cable Communications (CCC): Charlestown, Nevis; tel. 469-5601; e-mail customersupport@caribcable.com; internet ccc2.caribcable.com; provides internet and cable television services to Nevis; nationalized by Nevis Island Assembly in 2009 and ownership transferred to Nevis Cable Communications Corpn.

Digicel St Kitts and Nevis: Wireless Ventures (Saint Kitts and Nevis) Ltd, Bldg 16, Of. 4, POB 1033, Basseterre; tel. 762-4000; fax 466-4194; e-mail customercarestkittsandnevis@digicelgroup.com; internet www.digicelstkittsandnevis.com; acquired Cingular Wireless' Caribbean operations and licences in 2005; owned by an Irish consortium; Chair. DENIS O'BRIEN; Gen. Man. (St Kitts and Nevis) SEAN LATTY.

LIME (St Kitts and Nevis): Cayon St, POB 86, Basseterre; tel. 465-1000; fax 465-1106; e-mail support@cw.kn; internet www.time4lime.com; f. 1985 as St Kitts and Nevis Telecommunications Co Ltd (SKANTEL); fmrly Cable & Wireless St Kitts and Nevis; name changed as above 2008; CEO DAVID SHAW; Exec. Vice-Pres. (Leeward Islands) DAVIDSON CHARLES.

BROADCASTING

Radio

Radio One (SKNBC): Bakers Corner, POB 1773, Basseterre; tel. 466-0941; fax 465-1141; e-mail radio1941fm@yahoo.com; internet www.radioone941fm.com; owned by St Kitts & Nevis Broadcasting Corpn; music and commentary; Man. Dir GUS WILLIAMS.

Radio Paradise: Bath Plains, POB 508, Charlestown, Nevis; tel. 469-1994; fax 469-1642; e-mail info@radioparadiseonline.com; internet www.radioparadiseonline.com; owned by Trinity Broadcasting Network (USA); Christian; Gen. Man. ANDRE GILBERT.

Sugar City Roc FM: Greenlands, Basseterre; tel. 466-1113; e-mail sugarcityroc903fm@hotmail.com; internet sugarcityscr903.com; Gen. Man. VAL THOMAS.

Voice of Nevis (VON) Radio 895 AM: Bath Plains, POB 195, Charlestown, Nevis; tel. 469-1616; fax 469-5329; e-mail gmanager@vonradio.com; internet www.vonradio.com; f. 1988; owned by Nevis Broadcasting Co Ltd; Gen. Man. EVERED (WEBBO) HERBERT.

WINN FM: Unit C24, The Sands, Newtown Bay Rd, Basseterre; tel. 466-9586; fax 466-7904; e-mail info@winnfm.com; internet www.winnfm.com; owned by Federation Media Group; Chair. MICHAEL KING.

ZIZ Radio and Television: Springfield, POB 331, Basseterre; tel. 465-2622; fax 465-5624; e-mail info@zizonline.com; internet www.zizonline.com; f. 1961; television from 1972; commercial; govt-owned; Gen. Man. WINSTON MCMAHON.

Television

ZIZ Radio and Television: see Radio.

Finance

(cap. = capital; res = reserves; dep. = deposits; brs = branches)

BANKING

Central Bank

Eastern Caribbean Central Bank (ECCB): Headquarters Bldg, Bird Rock, POB 89, Basseterre; tel. 465-2537; fax 465-9562; e-mail info@eccb-centralbank.org; internet www.eccb-centralbank.org; f. 1965 as East Caribbean Currency Authority; expanded responsibilities and changed name 1983; responsible for issue of currency in Anguilla, Antigua and Barbuda, Dominica, Grenada, Montserrat, Saint Christopher and Nevis, Saint Lucia and Saint Vincent and the Grenadines; res EC $248.3m., dep. EC $1,302.5m., total assets EC $2,383.0m. (March 2009); Gov. and Chair. Sir K. DWIGHT VENNER; Country Dir WENDELL LAWRENCE.

Other Banks

Bank of Nevis Ltd: Main St, POB 450, Charlestown, Nevis; tel. 469-5564; fax 469-5798; e-mail info@thebankofnevis.com; internet www.thebankofnevis.com; dep. EC $0.3m., total assets EC $0.4m. (Dec. 2006); Chair. RAWLINSON ISAAC; Gen. Man. L. EVERETTE MARTIN.

FirstCaribbean International Bank (Barbados) Ltd: The Circus, POB 42, Basseterre; tel. 465-2449; fax 465-1041; internet www.firstcaribbeanbank.com; f. 2002 following merger of Caribbean operations of Barclays Bank PLC and CIBC; Barclays relinquished its stake to CIBC in 2006; res EC $0.8m. (March 2006); Exec. Chair. MICHAEL MANSOOR; CEO JOHN D. ORR.

RBTT Bank (SKN) Ltd: Chappel St, POB 60, Charlestown, Nevis; tel. 469-5277; fax 469-1493; internet www.rbtt.com; f. 1955 as Nevis Co-operative Banking Co Ltd; acquired by Royal Bank of Trinidad and Tobago (later known as RBTT) in 1996; Group Chair. PETER J. JULY.

St Kitts-Nevis-Anguilla National Bank Ltd: Central St, POB 343, Basseterre; tel. 465-2204; fax 466-1050; e-mail webmaster@sknanb.com; internet www.sknanb.com; f. 1971; Govt of St Kitts and Nevis owns 51%; cap. EC $81.0m., res EC $325.5m., dep. EC $1,380.3m. (June 2008); Chair. WALFORD GUMBS; Man. Dir Sir EDMUND W. LAURENCE; 5 brs.

Development Bank

Development Bank of St Kitts and Nevis: Church St, POB 249, Basseterre; tel. 465-2288; fax 465-4016; e-mail info@skndb.com; internet www.skndb.com; f. 1981; cap. EC $10.8m., res EC $5.8m., dep. EC $34.0m. (Dec. 2007); Chair. ELVIS NEWTON; Gen. Man. LENWORTH HARRIS.

STOCK EXCHANGE

Eastern Caribbean Securities Exchange: Bird Rock, POB 94, Basseterre; tel. 466-7192; fax 465-3798; e-mail info@ecseonline.com; internet www.ecseonline.com; f. 2001; regional securities market designed to facilitate the buying and selling of financial products for the eight member territories—Anguilla, Antigua and Barbuda, Dominica, Grenada, Montserrat, Saint Christopher and Nevis, Saint Lucia and Saint Vincent and the Grenadines; Chair. Sir K. DWIGHT VENNER; Gen. Man. TREVOR E. BLAKE.

INSURANCE

National Caribbean Insurance Co Ltd: Central St, POB 374, Basseterre; tel. 465-2694; fax 465-3659; internet www.nci-biz.com; f. 1973; subsidiary of St Kitts-Nevis-Anguilla National Bank Ltd; Gen. Man. JUDITH ATTONG.

St Kitts-Nevis Insurance Co Ltd (SNIC): Central St, POB 142, Basseterre; tel. 465-2845; fax 465-5410; e-mail snic@tdcltd.com; internet www.tdclimited.com/snic; subsidiary of St Kitts Nevis Anguilla Trading & Devt Co Ltd (TDC); Chair. DENNIS MICHAEL ARTHUR MORTON; Gen. Man. AUSTIN DA SILVA.

Several foreign companies also have offices in Saint Christopher and Nevis.

Trade and Industry

GOVERNMENT AGENCIES

Central Marketing Corpn (CEMACO): Pond's Pasture, POB 375, Basseterre; tel. 465-2628; fax 465-7823; Man. VERNA HERBERT.

Frigate Bay Development Corporation (FBDC): Frigate Bay, POB 315, Basseterre; tel. 465-8339; fax 465-4463; promotes tourist and residential devts; Chair. JANET HARRIS; Man. Dir RANDOLPH MORTON.

Nevis Investment Promotion Agency (NIPA): Charlestown, Nevis; f. 2008.

St Kitts Investment Promotion Agency: Pelican Mall, Bay Rd, POB 132, Basseterre; tel. 465-4040; fax 465-6968; f. 1987.

Social Security Board: Robert Llewellyn Bradshaw Bldg, Bay Rd, POB 79, Basseterre; tel. 465-2535; fax 465-5051; e-mail pubinfo@socialsecurity.kn; internet www.socialsecurity.kn; f. 1977; Dir SEPHLIN LAWRENCE.

CHAMBER OF COMMERCE

St Kitts-Nevis Chamber of Industry and Commerce: Horsford Rd, Fortlands, POB 332, Basseterre; tel. 465-2980; fax 465-4490; e-mail sknchamber@sisterisles.kn; internet www.stkittsnevischamber.org; incorporated 1949; 137 mems (2006); Pres. FRANKLIN BRAND; Exec. Dir WENDY PHIPPS.

EMPLOYERS' ORGANIZATIONS

Building Contractors' Association: Anthony Evelyn Business Complex, Paul Southwell Industrial Park, POB 1046, Basseterre; tel. 465-6897; fax 465-5623; e-mail sknbca@caribsurf.com; Pres. ANTHONY E. EVELYN.

Nevis Cotton Growers' Association Ltd: Charlestown, Nevis; Pres. IVOR STEVENS.

Small Business Association: Anthony Evelyn Business Complex, Paul Southwell Industrial Park, POB 367, Basseterre; tel. 465-8630; fax 465-6661; e-mail sb-association@caribsurf.com; Pres. EUSTACE WARNER.

UTILITIES

Nevis Electricity Company Ltd (Nevlec): POB 852, Charlestown, Nevis; tel. 469-7245; fax 469-7249; e-mail info@nevlec.com; internet www.nevlec.com; owned by the Nevis Island Administration; Gen. Man. CARTWRIGHT FARRELL.

West Indies Power (Nevis) Ltd: POB 368, Charlestown, Nevis; tel. 662-4032; fax 469-0792; e-mail l.diaz@westindiespower.com; internet www.westindiespower.com; subsidiary of West Indies Power Holdings (Bonaire); devt of geothermal energy; CEO KERRY MCDONALD; Man. (Nevis) RAWLINSON A. ISAAC.

TRADE UNIONS

Nevis Teachers' Union: POB 559, Charlestown, Nevis; tel. 469-8465; fax 469-5663; e-mail nevteach@caribsurf.com; Pres. WAKELY DANIEL; Gen. Sec. BERNELLA CAINES HAMILTON.

St Kitts-Nevis Trades and Labour Union (SKTLU): Masses House, Church St, POB 239, Basseterre; tel. 465-2229; fax 466-9866; e-mail sknunion@caribsurf.com; f. 1940; affiliated to Caribbean Maritime and Aviation Council, Caribbean Congress of Labour, International Federation of Plantation, Agricultural and Allied Workers, and International Trade Union Confederation; associated with St Kitts-Nevis Labour Party; Pres. CLIFFORD THOMAS; Gen. Sec. BATUMBA TAK; c. 3,000 mems.

St Kitts Teachers' Union: Green Tree Housing Devt, POB 545, Basseterre; tel. 465-1921; e-mail stkittsteachersunion@hotmail.com; Pres. CLYDE CHRISTOPHER; Gen. Sec. CARLENE HENRY-MORTON.

Transport

RAILWAYS

There are 58 km (36 miles) of narrow-gauge light railway on Saint Christopher, serving the sugar plantations. The railway, complete with new trains and carriages, was restored and developed for tourist excursions and opened in late 2002.

St Kitts Scenic Railway: Sands Unit A6, Bay Rd, POB 191, Basseterre; tel. 465-7263; fax 466-4815; e-mail scenicreservations@sisterisles.kn; internet www.stkittsscenicrailway.com; f. 2002; Exec. Vice-Pres. and Gen. Man. THOMAS A. WILLIAMS.

ROADS

In 2000 there were 320 km (199 miles) of road in Saint Christopher and Nevis, of which approximately 136 km (84 miles) were paved. In 2009 the Caribbean Development Bank approved a loan of US $6.29m. to the Government for the West Basseterre Bypass Road (WBBR) project.

SHIPPING

The Government maintains a commercial motorboat service between the islands, and numerous regional and international shipping lines call at the islands. A deep-water port, Port Zante, was opened at Basseterre in 1981. In 2003 the Government of Kuwait provided a loan of EC $15m. for the development of cruise ship facilities at Port Zante. In addition, there is the Basseterre Deep Water (Cargo) Port and Ferry Dock. There are three ports in Nevis, at Charlestown, Long Point Port and New Castle. A ferry service operates between Charlestown and Basseterre.

Nevis Air and Sea Ports Authority: Nisbett Bldg, Main St, POB 741, Charlestown; tel. 469-2001; fax 469-2006; e-mail nevports@sisterisles.kn; internet www.nevisports.com; f. 1995; Chair. LAURIE LAWRENCE; Gen. Man. SPENCER HANLEY; Airport Man. STEPHEN HANLEY; Sea Port Man. EVERETTE MASON.

St Christopher Air and Sea Ports Authority: Bird Rock, POB 963, Basseterre; tel. 465-8121; fax 465-8124; e-mail info@scaspa.com; internet www.scaspa.com; f. 1993 to combine St Kitts Port Authority and Airports Authority; Chair. LINKON MAYNARD; CEO and Gen. Man. TERRENCE GROSSMAN; Airport Man. DENZIL JONES; Sea Port Man. ROSEVELT TROTMAN.

Shipping Companies

Delisle Walwyn and Co Ltd: Liverpool Row, POB 44, Basseterre; tel. 465-2631; fax 465-1125; e-mail info@delislewalwyn.com; internet www.delislewalwyn.com; f. 1951; Chair. KISHU CHANDIRAMANI; Man. Dir DENZIL V. CROOKE.

Tony's Ltd: Main St, POB 564, Charlestown, Nevis; tel. 469-5413.

CIVIL AVIATION

Robert Llewellyn Bradshaw (formerly Golden Rock) International Airport, 4 km (2.5 miles) from Basseterre, is equipped to handle jet aircraft and is served by scheduled links with most Caribbean destinations, the United Kingdom, the USA and Canada. A US $17m. expansion and development project at the airport, financed by Taiwan and the St Kitts-Nevis-Anguilla National Bank Ltd, was completed in 2006. A further expansion, to construct a private jet facility, was scheduled to begin in early 2011. Saint Christopher and Nevis is a shareholder in the regional airline, LIAT (see chapter on Antigua and Barbuda), which began operating a joint flight schedule with its troubled rival, Caribbean Star Airlines (also headquartered in Antigua and Barbuda) in February 2007; LIAT's full acquisition of Caribbean Star was completed in October 2007. Vance W. Amory International Airport (formerly Newcastle Airfield), 11 km (7 miles) from Charlestown, Nevis, has regular scheduled services to St Kitts and other islands in the region. A new airport, Castle Airport, was opened on Nevis in 1998.

Nevis Air and Sea Ports Authority: see Shipping.

St Christopher Air and Sea Ports Authority: see Shipping.

Private Airlines

Air St Kitts-Nevis: Vance W. Amory International Airport, Newcastle, Nevis; tel. 465-8571; fax 496-9241.

LIAT (1974) Ltd: Robert Llewellyn Bradshaw International Airport; tel. 465-5491; fax 465-7042; e-mail customerrelations@liatairline.com; internet www.liatairline.com; f. 1956 as Leeward Islands Air Transport Services, jtly owned by 11 regional Govts; privatized in 1995; shares are held by the Govts of Antigua and Barbuda, Montserrat, Grenada, Barbados, Trinidad and Tobago, Jamaica, Guyana, Dominica, Saint Lucia, Saint Vincent and the Grenadines and Saint Christopher and Nevis (30.8%), Caribbean Airlines (29.2%), LIAT employees (13.3%) and private investors (26.7%); merger negotiations with Caribbean Star Airlines were finalized in March 2007; deal was abandoned in July in favour of a buyout arrangement in which LIAT would acquire all remaining shares in Caribbean Star; scheduled passenger and cargo services to 19 destinations in the Caribbean; charter flights are also undertaken; Chair. JEAN STEWART HOLDER; CEO BRIAN CHALLENGER (acting); Country Man. AVENICE JEFFERS-THOMPSON.

Tourism

The introduction of regular air services to the US cities of Miami and New York has opened up the islands as a tourist destination. Visitors are attracted by the excellent beaches and the historical Brimstone Hill Fortress National Park on Saint Christopher, the spectacular mountain scenery of Nevis and the islands' associations with Lord Nelson and Alexander Hamilton. Many hotels and other tourist accommodation were constructed or refurbished in advance of the 2007 Cricket World Cup, hosted by several Caribbean nations, including Saint Christopher and Nevis. In 2009 there were 450,553 cruise ship passengers and 93,081 stop-over visitors. Receipts from tourism were EC $225.41m. in 2009.

Nevis Tourism Authority: Main St, POB 917, Charlestown, Nevis; tel. 469-7550; fax 469-7551; e-mail info@nevisisland.com; internet www.nevisisland.com; f. 2001; Chair. RICHARD LUPINACCI; CEO JOHN HANLEY.

Nevis Tourism Bureau: Main St, Charlestown, Nevis; tel. 469-1042; fax 469-1066; e-mail nevtour@caribsurf.com; Dir ELMEADER BROOKES.

St Kitts-Nevis Hotel and Tourism Association: Liverpool Row, POB 438, Basseterre; tel. 465-5304; fax 465-7746; e-mail stkitnevhta@caribsurf.com; f. 1972; Pres. KISHU CHANDIRAMANI; Man. MICHAEL HEAD.

St Kitts Tourism Authority: Pelican Mall, Bay Rd, POB 132, Basseterre; tel. 465-4040; fax 465-8794; e-mail ceo@stkittstourism.kn; internet www.stkittstourism.kn; Chair. RICHARD OLIVER SKERRITT; CEO ROSECITA JEFFERS.

Defence

The small army was disbanded by the Government in 1981, and its duties were absorbed by the Volunteer Defence Force and a special tactical unit of the police. Saint Christopher and Nevis participates in the US-sponsored Regional Security System, comprising police, coastguards and army units, which was established by independent Eastern Caribbean states in 1982. According to the 2008 budget address, the Ministry of National Security, Immigration and Labour was to receive an allocation of EC $40.3m. in that year.

Education

Education is compulsory for 12 years between five and 17 years of age. Primary education begins at the age of five, and lasts for seven years. Secondary education, from the age of 12, generally comprises a first cycle of four years, followed by a second cycle of two years. In 2004/05 enrolment at primary schools included 93.4% of children in the relevant age-group, according to UNESCO estimates, while comparable enrolment at secondary schools included 86.1% of pupils. There are 30 state, eight private and five denominational schools. There is also a technical college. In September 2000 a privately financed 'offshore' medical college, the Medical University of the Americas, opened in Nevis with 40 students registered. The Ross University School of Veterinary Medicine and the International University of Nursing also operated on Saint Christopher. Budgetary expenditure on education, training and youth development by the central Government in 2008 was projected to total EC $72.6m. A Basic Education Project funded by the Caribbean Development Bank was, in 2003, complemented by a EC $18.8m. Secondary Education Project, which was to include the construction of a new school in Saddlers.

SAINT LUCIA

Introductory Survey

LOCATION, CLIMATE, LANGUAGE, RELIGION, FLAG, CAPITAL

Saint Lucia is the second largest of the Windward Islands group of the West Indies, lying 40 km (25 miles) to the south of Martinique and 32 km (20 miles) to the north-east of Saint Vincent, in the Caribbean Sea. The island is volcanic, with spectacular mountain scenery; the Pitons, the island's twin, jungle-clad volcanic mountains, were designated a UNESCO (see p. 153) World Heritage Site in June 2004. The average annual temperature is 26°C (79°F), with a dry season from January to April, followed by a rainy season from May to August. The average annual rainfall is 1,500 mm (60 ins) in the low-lying areas, and 3,500 mm (138 ins) in the mountains. The official language is English, although a large proportion of the population speak a French-based patois. Almost all of the island's inhabitants profess Christianity, and 68% are adherents of the Roman Catholic Church. The national flag (proportions 1 by 2) is blue, bearing in its centre a white-edged black triangle partly covered by a gold triangle rising from a common base. The capital is Castries.

CONTEMPORARY POLITICAL HISTORY

Historical Context

British settlers made an unsuccessful attempt to colonize the island (originally inhabited by a Carib people) in 1605. A further British party arrived in 1638 but were killed by the indigenous Carib population. France claimed sovereignty in 1642, and fighting between French and Caribs continued until 1660, when a peace treaty was signed. Control of Saint Lucia was transferred 14 times before it was ceded by the French and became a British colony in 1814. It remained under British rule for the next 165 years.

Representative government was introduced in 1924. The colony was a member of the Windward Islands, under a federal system, until December 1959. It joined the newly formed West Indies Federation in January 1958, and remained a member until the Federation's dissolution in May 1962. From January 1960 Saint Lucia, in common with other British territories in the Windward Islands, was given a new Constitution, with its own Administrator and an enlarged Legislative Council.

Domestic Political Affairs

In 1951 the first elections under adult suffrage were won by the Saint Lucia Labour Party (SLP), which retained power until 1964, when John (later Sir John) Compton, of the newly formed conservative United Workers' Party (UWP), became Chief Minister. In 1967 Saint Lucia became one of the West Indies Associated States, gaining full autonomy in internal affairs, with the United Kingdom retaining responsibility for defence and foreign relations only. The Legislative Council was replaced by a House of Assembly, the Administrator was designated Governor, and the Chief Minister became Premier.

In 1975 the Associated States agreed that they would seek independence individually. After three years of negotiations, Saint Lucia became independent on 22 February 1979, remaining within the Commonwealth. Compton became the country's first Prime Minister.

A general election in July 1979 returned the SLP to government with a clear majority, and its leader, Allan Louisy, succeeded Compton as Prime Minister. In February 1980 a new Governor-General, Boswell Williams, was appointed. This led to disputes within the Government and contributed to a split in the SLP. The controversy continued until April 1981, when Louisy was forced to resign after Deputy Prime Minister George Odlum and three other SLP members of the House voted with the opposition against the Government's budget. In May Winston Cenac took office as Prime Minister. In September the Cenac administration narrowly defeated a motion of no confidence, introduced jointly by UWP and Progressive Labour Party (PLP—formed by Odlum) members of the House, who accused the Government of political and economic mismanagement. In January 1982 a government proposal to alter legislation regarding the expenses of members of Parliament produced widespread accusations of corruption. Demands for the Government's resignation increased from all sectors of the community, culminating in a general strike. Cenac resigned, and an all-party interim administration was formed, under the deputy leader of the PLP, Michael Pilgrim. At an election in May the UWP was returned to power, and John Compton was re-elected Prime Minister. In December Sir Allen Lewis was reappointed Governor-General, following the dismissal of Boswell Williams because of his previous close association with the SLP.

In 1984 the opposition parties began to reorganize in order to present a more effective opposition to the UWP Government. The UWP won a one-seat majority at a general election in April 1987; a further election took place at the end of the month, in the hope of a more decisive result, but the distribution of seats remained unchanged. In June the UWP's majority was increased to three seats, when Cenac defected from the SLP. He was subsequently appointed Minister of Foreign Affairs.

The UWP won a further term in office at a general election in April 1992. The SLP attributed its defeat largely to a redefinition of constituency boundaries by the Government prior to the election.

The SLP in power

In August 1995 the report of a commission of inquiry into allegations of the Government's involvement in the misappropriation, for electoral purposes, of some US $100,000 in UN contributions concluded that the former Permanent Representative to the UN, Charles Flemming, had been the sole perpetrator of the fraud. Flemming, who insisted that he had acted with the knowledge and endorsement of senior members of the UWP (including the Prime Minister), failed to return from a visit to the USA undertaken during the commission's hearings. The Minister of State with Responsibility for Financial Services and the National Development Corporation, Rufus Bousquet (who claimed to have been an unwitting recipient of the funds), had been dismissed in May, after he publicly questioned whether it was appropriate that the Government remain in office pending investigation of the affair.

The UWP, in January 1996, appointed Vaughan Lewis, the former Director-General of the Organisation of Eastern Caribbean States (OECS, see p. 462), to the vacancy created by the Prime Minister's retirement from the party leadership. Lewis won the Central Castries parliamentary by-election in February, and was subsequently appointed Minister without Portfolio. SLP leader Julian Hunte resigned later in the month; Kenny Anthony, a former SLP education and culture minister, replaced him. In March Compton resigned the premiership, and was succeeded in April by Lewis.

A general election in May 1997 was won decisively by the SLP, which was returned to power after 15 years, securing 16 of the 17 seats in the House of Assembly. Kenny Anthony was sworn in as the new Prime Minister. Among the nine ministers in his first Cabinet was George Odlum, who had rejoined the SLP in July 1996. Following his electoral defeat Lewis announced his intention to resign the leadership of the UWP; Sir John Compton (as he had become), the former UWP leader and former Prime Minister, replaced him in June 1998.

In August 1997 the Governor-General, Sir George Mallet, resigned. His appointment, in June 1996, had been opposed by the SLP, on the grounds that the post's tradition of neutrality would be compromised: Mallet had previously been Deputy Prime Minister, and his portfolio had included several influential ministries. Saint Lucia's first female Governor-General, Dr Pearlette Louisy, was appointed in September 1997.

In September 1997 the inquiry into allegations of corruption under the UWP, which had been promised by the SLP Government after its election, began. However, legal challenges to the impartiality of the sole commissioner, Monica Joseph, effectively stalled proceedings and she withdrew from the inquiry in March 1998. Sir Louis Blom-Cooper, a prominent British jurist, was appointed in her place. In August 1999 Blom-Cooper submitted his report to the Government. The report cleared Compton and

Lewis of corruption, but noted instances of impropriety and a 'high degree of maladministration' in their Governments.

In January 2001, following an increase in tourist cancellations, Prime Minister Anthony announced a series of measures intended to reduce the crime rate in Saint Lucia. These included the establishment of a National Anti-Crime Commission, the creation of a 10-member police 'rapid response unit', a review of the penal code, and reforms to the police service. In June Anthony announced the creation of four more rapid response units, a special task force to target known criminals, plans for more severe penalties for gun crimes, an increase in police patrols and an amnesty for holders of illegal firearms. A special joint session of Parliament convened in the following month to debate the increase in violent crime.

In March 2001 the Minister of Foreign Affairs and International Trade, George Odlum, left the Government and the SLP to join a new opposition grouping, the National Alliance (NA), founded by former premier Sir John Compton and UWP leader Morella Joseph. Julian Hunte, a former Permanent Representative to the UN, replaced Odlum as foreign minister.

In October 2001 the NA's assembly elected Compton to head the party. However, Odlum rejected the decision and claimed the voting process was flawed. Later the same month the UWP withdrew from the Alliance and announced it would contest the elections as a single party. Odlum chose to retain the National Alliance name for his group.

As expected, the ruling SLP achieved another convincing victory at the December 2001 general election, winning 14 of the 17 parliamentary seats. The remaining seats were taken by the UWP. Joseph and Odlum, leaders of the UWP and the NA, respectively, both lost their seats. Joseph resigned as UWP leader and was replaced by Vaughan Lewis. Meanwhile, in the same month, Prime Minister Anthony announced a new 15-member Cabinet.

In July 2003 Parliament approved a constitutional amendment abolishing the oath of allegiance to the British monarch; instead, elected members were to pledge loyalty to the Saint Lucian people. In November the Government announced the establishment of a Constitutional Review Commission. The development, which was supported by the opposition, was designed to expand public participation in Saint Lucia's democracy. Meanwhile, also in November the Government adopted a new Criminal Code, which included two particularly controversial clauses. The first, Section 361, provided for a two-year prison sentence for anyone convicted of spreading 'false news'. The clause provoked consternation among local media representatives and the UWP, whose parliamentary members absented themselves from the vote. The second controversial element of the Code, Section 166, allowed for the legalization of abortion, previously illegal in all circumstances, in cases of rape, incest and medical danger to the mother. The law prompted trenchant criticism from anti-abortion and religious groups, and in January 2004 led to the dismissal of Sarah Flood-Beaubrun from her post as Minister of Home Affairs and Gender Relations; she resigned from the SLP in March and later established a new political party, the Organization for National Empowerment.

Flood-Beaubrun's dismissal from the Government was part of a wider cabinet realignment in early 2004, which included the appointment of Calixte George as head of a new Ministry of Home Affairs and Internal Security. The new department was to oversee the police service, previously the responsibility of the Attorney-General's Office, and was charged with finding a solution to the island's spiralling crime rate. In November 2005 an Interception of Communication bill, which granted extra powers to law enforcement authorities and attracted emphatic criticism from opposition parties, received senate approval. Despite the recruitment of 10 British police officers in November 2006 and renewed pledges by the Government for more rigorous anti-crime initiatives and deterrents, the murder rate escalated to a record 39 by the end of that year.

Recent developments: a UWP Government

The UWP celebrated an unprecedented and decisive victory in the 11 December 2006 general election: the party secured 11 of the 17 parliamentary seats contested (equivalent to 51.4% of votes cast), while the incumbent SLP secured the remaining six seats (with 48.2% of the vote). Turn-out by the electorate was preliminarily put at approximately 60%, and election monitors from the Organization of American States (see p. 391) declared the ballot free and fair. Compton, who had replaced Lewis as party leader in the previous year, was sworn in as premier on 15 December.

Mindful of the significant public debt burden requiring the new Government's urgent attention, Compton announced in January 2007 that an audit commission was to be established to investigate considerable ministerial overspending on public sector projects. The inquiry followed reports of widespread financial irregularities and unexplained delays in implementation. The new UWP administration also confirmed in January that proposals by the previous Government to grant an amnesty to Caribbean Community and Common Market (CARICOM, see p. 219) nationals residing illegally in Saint Lucia would be sustained, offering those concerned the opportunity to 'regularize' their citizenship status upon payment of a stipulated fee. It was estimated that approximately 1,000 Guyanese, in addition to Jamaican, Trinidadian and other CARICOM nationals would benefit from the agreement.

Compton suffered a series of minor strokes in April 2007. Stephenson King, the Minister of Health and UWP Chairman, was appointed acting Prime Minister in his absence. Compton died on 7 September. The remaining 10 elected members of the UWP designated King as Compton's permanent successor, and he was duly sworn in as Prime Minister. The new premier announced his Cabinet on 12 September, in which he assumed the portfolios for finance, external affairs, home affairs and national security.

In May 2008 Minister of Economic Affairs, Economic Planning, National Development and Public Service Ausbert d'Auvergne tendered his resignation following criticism from UWP colleagues over an alleged business relationship with convicted criminals. His departure prompted King to execute a reallocation of cabinet portfolios. Notable in the reorganization was the reappointment of Rufus Bousquet to the Government, as trade and industry minister. Bousquet had been dismissed from the Cabinet in the previous June, reportedly after he re-established diplomatic relations with Taiwan (see below) without the knowledge of Compton. At the end of the year Bousquet was allocated the external affairs portfolio, in addition to his existing duties.

A Commission of Inquiry was appointed in early 2009 to investigate claims of mismanagement of public funds by the Anthony Government. Among the allegations to be examined was the authorization of a loan for the construction of the Hyatt Hotel in 1997. The High Court in 2003 had ruled the refinancing 'void and illegal', in part because the SLP administration had not sought parliamentary approval for the project. The Commission's report, published in late October, found instances of irregularities and mismanagement by the Anthony Government, but no criminal activity. It recommended, *inter alia*, proper management, financial and accounting systems be put in place when awarding government contracts and an end to the time limit put on the recovery of public funds.

Fears over rising crime rates prompted the Government in early 2009 to announce its intention to resume capital punishment of convicted murderers. Although the law allowed for capital punishment, the last execution in Saint Lucia occurred in 1995. In August 2010 the high-security Bordelais Correctional Facility came under attack from a group of armed men, who freed three prisoners, including two Venezuelan drugs-traffickers. A large mobilization of police officers failed to recapture the escapees. Confronted by SLP demands for the dismissal of George Guy Mayers, the Minister for Home Affairs and National Security, the Government quickly initiated an inquiry into the incident. However, further embarrassment was caused in the following month when another prisoner escaped from the same gaol. In 2010 there were a record 48 murders in Saint Lucia, compared with 25 in 2007. Between January and February 2011 a further 15 unlawful killings were committed, indicating a worrying rise in gang-related violence. In response, Prime Minister King announced in February that Israeli authorities would be helping the police force to develop its surveillance and intelligence capabilities, and that a request for US technical support had also been made.

Meanwhile, Attorney-General and Minister for Justice Nicholas Frederick was replaced in July 2010 by Lorenzo Rudolph Francis. Press reports suggested that Frederick's dismissal had resulted from his involvement in the approval of controversial duty-free concessions for a property belonging to Keith Mondesir, the minister responsible for health.

King declared a state of emergency on 2 November 2010 following the widespread damage to infrastructure, housing and agriculture caused by Hurricane Tomas in late October. Reconstruction costs were estimated at US $336m., and at least

14 people lost their lives in the disaster. The Prime Minister of Trinidad and Tobago, Kamla Persad-Bissessar, generated considerable controversy by initially implying that assistance to Saint Lucia (and other Caribbean nations affected by Hurricane Tomas) would come only if companies in Trinidad and Tobago would benefit financially from reconstruction contracts.

The Banana Sector

In October 1993 a three-day strike was organized by a new pressure group, the Banana Salvation Committee (BSC), in support of demands for an increase in the minimum price paid to local producers for bananas and for the dismissal of the board of directors of the Saint Lucia Banana Growers' Association (SLBGA). Following recommendations made by a government-appointed committee, the Government implemented price increases and dismissed the board of directors of the SLBGA. An announcement by the Government that the SLBGA was to be placed into receivership provoked a strike by the BSC in March 1994. The BSC organized further strikes by banana farmers that year and in 1995 in support of demands for an extraordinary meeting of the SLBGA, and for an inquiry into the deaths of two demonstrators during the October 1993 strike. Further industrial action was undertaken by the BSC in February 1996, in protest at the monopoly on banana exports exercised by the state-run Windward Islands Banana Development and Exporting Co (Wibdeco). In September the House of Assembly approved legislation revising the selection procedure for members of the SLBGA and the responsibilities of its general manager. The new legislation effectively transferred control of the association from the Government to the banana growers, who would henceforth elect six members of the board of directors (while the Government would continue to nominate the remaining five). In October the BSC co-ordinated industrial action by banana growers in support of renewed demands for an end to the Wibdeco monopoly, and for reform of the industry's management and payment systems. Attempts by a number of farmers who opposed the strike to transport produce to ports resulted in violent clashes. Subsequent negotiations with a parliamentary review committee and with the Government (which promised to transfer some responsibility for the industry to the private sector) failed to appease the farmers.

In September 1997 the directors of the SLBGA resigned, at Anthony's request: the Government was reportedly concerned that divisions at boardroom level were damaging the association's operations. Such divisions became increasingly pronounced as plans proceeded for the privatization of the SLBGA, one of the stated aims of the SLP Government. The Concerned Farmers Group (CFG), formed in December and led by the ousted Chairman, Rupert Gajadhar, which grouped larger farmers, expressed concern that the more numerous smaller producers in the BSC (whose secretary, Patrick Joseph, was also a government senator) would unduly dominate the new company, since decision-making was to be on the basis of 'one member, one vote'. Members of the CFG threatened to establish their own company unless their concerns were addressed.

In July 1998 the SLBGA was privatized and the Saint Lucia Banana Corpn (SLBC) was created in its place. The Government agreed to assume the debts incurred by the dissolved SLBGA, equivalent to EC $44m. The CFG, which had refused to participate in the process, subsequently established a rival company, the Tropical Quality Fruit Co (TQF). In October a court judgment ruled that the SLBC did not enjoy monopoly rights in the banana trade. This ruling followed complaints from the TQF that Wibdeco had been refusing to accept its fruit for shipment. The TQF alleged that this refusal was owing to pressure exerted by the SLBC Chairman, Patrick Joseph, in his capacity as a member of the Wibdeco board.

In January 1999 the SLBC announced that it had incurred losses of EC $6m. in 1998 and would therefore be forced to reduce the price paid to farmers. The SLBC blamed its operating deficit primarily on the fact that, because banana production had been underestimated, Wibdeco had failed to obtain sufficient European Union (EU, see p. 270) licences, meaning that much of the fruit produced did not reach high-paying markets. The TQF also announced a deficit, but claimed that its lower operating costs had reduced its losses. The TQF further suggested that the SLBC had damaged its own profitability by keeping prices deliberately high in an attempt to force the TQF out of business.

In July 1999 the Government founded a Banana Industry Trust, which was to oversee the improvement of farming practices in the banana sector and manage the financial resources available to the industry, including EC $21m. in funds provided by the EU. In the same month the Government announced that it was to loan $7m. to the SLBC and $1.9m. to the TQF. In August Wibdeco agreed to finance a temporary subsidy on prices in order to alleviate hardship among growers. In late 1999, however, the company encountered increasing pressure from the SLBC and from the Government to deliver increased returns to farmers, and in January 2000, following the expiry of its agreement to sell through Wibdeco, the SLBC announced plans to sell direct to Geest Bananas, despite criticism from its other regional partners in Wibdeco.

The SLBC entered into a dispute with Wibdeco when, in February 2008, the latter announced plans to terminate its contract with the SLBC as it had not been certified by the Fairtrade Labelling Organization of the United Kingdom. The Chairman of the SLBC, Eustace Monrose, claimed that the company had not been given adequate notice to achieve fair trade status and instructed Wibdeco to withdraw its notice of termination. However, in March Wibdeco signed a sales and purchase agreement with two other companies, one of which was the Windward Islands Farmers' Association, in order to bring the supply chain of the island's bananas into line with fair trade regulations. The SLBC, now faced with the threat of closure, was subsequently granted a court injunction preventing Wibdeco from effecting its termination notice. Instability within the SLBC continued into May after Monrose stepped down as Chairman.

Saint Lucia's most important export market is the United Kingdom, which receives most of the banana crop under the terms of the Cotonou Agreement (see p. 327). In July 1993 new regulations came into effect governing the level of imports of bananas by the European Community (now EU, of which the United Kingdom is a member). The regulations were introduced to protect traditional producers from competition from the expanding Latin American producers. At the instigation of the Latin American producers, consecutive dispute panels were appointed by the General Agreement on Tariffs and Trade (GATT, which was succeeded by the World Trade Organization—WTO, see p. 430) to rule on whether the EU's actions contravened GATT rules. Although the disputes panel ruled in favour of the Latin American producers, the rulings were not enforceable. In February 1996 the USA renewed consultations with the WTO concerning the EU's banana import quota regime. A WTO interim report in 1997 appeared to uphold many of the charges of unfair discrimination brought by the plaintiffs. The WTO Appellate Body rejected representations by the EU against the ruling in September, and ruled that the EU must formulate a new system for banana imports by early 1998; new arrangements were duly proposed by the EU, under which it would apply a system of quotas and tariffs to both groups of producers, while retaining an import-licensing system.

The EU's new banana import regime was implemented on 1 January 1999 in compliance with the WTO ruling, though the USA criticized the reforms as negligible. Further discussions on the issue broke down in late January 1999 when Saint Lucia, backed by other countries, objected to any discussion of US demands for sanctions on EU goods. On 1 February the USA introduced punitive import duties on various EU goods, and in March the WTO disputes panel was asked to consider whether the EU had done enough to amend its import regime and whether the USA could legally impose retaliatory import tariffs. In retaliation, the banana-exporting countries threatened to withdraw their co-operation with the US campaign against drugs-trafficking, while banana producers warned that they might switch to growing marijuana if they were forced out of business. On 6 April WTO arbitrators awarded damages against the EU, although at a lower level than the USA had been claiming, and a week later delivered a ruling criticizing aspects of the EU banana-importing regime, which gave the USA permission to impose retaliatory tariffs on certain European goods. In April 2001 the USA agreed to suspend these sanctions from July, after the dispute was resolved: following a transition period, a new, tariff-only regime was introduced from January 2006. Despite substantial government and EU assistance, augmented by the efforts of a Banana Emergency Recovery Unit and the Banana Industry Trust, the Saint Lucian banana industry continued to exhibit decline. Agreement on the structure of the tariff-only regime was finally reached in December 2009. Saint Lucia would continue to enjoy tariff-free access to the EU market, but tariffs imposed on Latin American producers would be reduced over the following seven years. The EU pledged some €200m. in compensation to Caribbean producers, to be disbursed in 2010–14.

SAINT LUCIA

Nevertheless, the sector was expected to contract further following the final resolution of the dispute.

Foreign Affairs
Regional relations

Saint Lucia is a member of the OECS, and, since May 1987, has been a prominent advocate of the creation of a unitary East Caribbean state. In 1988, however, Antigua and Barbuda expressed opposition to political union, thereby discouraging any participation by Montserrat or Saint Christopher and Nevis. The four English-speaking Windward Islands countries (Saint Lucia, Dominica, Grenada, and Saint Vincent and the Grenadines) thus announced plans to proceed independently towards a more limited union. In 1990 the leaders of the four countries established a Regional Constituent Assembly. Following a series of discussions, the Assembly issued its final report in 1992, in which it stated that the four countries were committed to the establishment of economic and political union under a federal system.

Together with 12 other Caribbean administrations, in September 2005 the Government signed the PetroCaribe accord, under which Saint Lucia would be allowed to purchase petroleum from Venezuela at reduced prices. However, owing to very limited storage facilities in the region, many of the signatories—including Saint Lucia—were unable to proceed further in accepting fuel shipments. Furthermore, the UWP Government that came to power in December 2006 indicated that implementation of the PetroCaribe initiative would not be a priority and the enterprise was abandoned indefinitely.

In November 2003 Parliament approved legislation enabling the Government to pledge US $2.5m. towards the establishment of the Caribbean Court of Justice (CCJ), to be headquartered in Trinidad. The CCJ, which was to replace the Privy Council in the United Kingdom as the region's highest court, was inaugurated in April 2005; however, in 2011 Saint Lucia's final court of appeal remained the Privy Council.

Other external relations

In August 1997 the new SLP Government effected a significant reorientation of foreign policy when it was announced that diplomatic relations were to be established with the People's Republic of China. Taiwan subsequently severed relations with Saint Lucia. By 2004 it was estimated that China had provided Saint Lucia with funds worth US $100m. throughout the seven years of their association. In late 2005 Prime Minister Anthony accused the UWP of jeopardizing Saint Lucia's profitable relationship with China after allegations emerged that Sir John Compton had secretly met the President of Taiwan and sought to develop a relationship between the UWP and Taiwan. Such fears were partly allayed with the signing of a technical co-operation agreement between the premier and the Chinese Minister of Foreign Affairs, Li Zhaoxing, in September 2006. In February 2007 the new foreign affairs minister, Rufus Bousquet, reiterated his Government's intention to maintain links with China, but in April he announced that the country would resume diplomatic relations with Taiwan; China subsequently suspended ambassadorial relations with Saint Lucia. During an official state visit to the island in January 2008, Taiwan's President Chen Shui-bian stated his commitment to provide aid and investment, including US $100,000 for repairs to an earthquake-damaged school and funds for the redevelopment of a hospital. The opposition SLP accused the Taiwanese ambassador on the island of interfering in political affairs in March 2009 after it emerged that Taiwan was funding the establishment of a computer-literacy centre in the constituency headquarters of a prominent UWP politician (the centre was subsequently moved to a more neutral location). A similar accusation of political interference was made in August 2010, when the SLP claimed that the Taiwanese ambassador had provided funding to a UWP constituency group for a sports programme. This allegation was rejected by the Government and by the Taiwanese embassy.

CONSTITUTION AND GOVERNMENT

The Constitution came into force at the independence of Saint Lucia in February 1979. Saint Lucia is a constitutional monarchy. Executive power is vested in the British monarch, as Head of State, and is exercisable by the Governor-General, who represents the monarchy and is appointed on the advice of the Prime Minister. Legislative power is vested in Parliament, comprising the monarch, the 17-member House of Assembly, elected from single-member constituencies for up to five years by universal adult suffrage, and the Senate, composed of 11 members appointed by the Governor-General, including six appointed on the advice of the Prime Minister and three on the advice of the Leader of the Opposition. Government is effectively by the Cabinet. The Governor-General appoints the Prime Minister and, on the latter's recommendation, the other Ministers. The Prime Minister must have majority support in the House, to which the Cabinet is responsible. Judicial power is vested in the Eastern Caribbean Supreme Court.

REGIONAL AND INTERNATIONAL CO-OPERATION

Saint Lucia is a member of the Caribbean Community and Common Market (CARICOM, see p. 219). The country became a signatory to CARICOM's Caribbean Single Market and Economy (CSME) on 3 July 2006. The CSME, which was established by six founding member states on 1 January 2006, was to enshrine the free movement of goods, services and labour throughout most of the CARICOM region. An intra-regional CARICOM passport initiative, regarded as an integral component in the advance towards economic union and designed to facilitate travel for citizens of participating nations, was implemented in Saint Lucia on 16 January 2007. Saint Lucia is a party to the Caribbean Basin Initiative (CBI). The country is a member of the Organisation of Eastern Caribbean States (OECS, see p. 462), of the Organization of American States (see p. 391), the Association of Caribbean States (see p. 445), and the Eastern Caribbean Central Bank (see p. 451). On 18 June 2010 Saint Lucia was a signatory to the Revised Treaty of Basseterre, establishing an Economic Union among OECS member states. The Economic Union, which involved the removal of barriers to trade and the movement of labour as a step towards a single financial and economic market, came into effect on 21 January 2011, although by early March Saint Lucia had still not ratified the Treaty.

Saint Lucia joined the UN soon after independence in 1979. As a contracting party to the General Agreement on Tariffs and Trade, Saint Lucia joined the World Trade Organization (see p. 430) on its establishment in 1995. Upon independence, Saint Lucia became a full member of the Commonwealth (see p. 230). Saint Lucia is a party to the Cotonou Agreement (see p. 327), the successor agreement to the Lomé Convention, signed in June 2000 between the European Union (see p. 270) and a group of developing countries. The country is a member of the Group of 77 (see p. 447) organization of developing states and acceded to the Non-aligned Movement in 2006.

ECONOMIC AFFAIRS

In 2009, according to estimates by the World Bank, Saint Lucia's gross national income (GNI), measured at average 2007–09 prices, was US $890m., equivalent to $5,170 per head (or $8,880 per head on an international purchasing-power parity basis). During 2000–09, it was estimated, the population increased at an average annual rate of 1.1%, while gross domestic product (GDP) per head rose by 0.5% per year during the same period. Overall GDP increased, in real terms, at an average annual rate of 1.6% in 2000–09; real GDP declined by 3.8% in 2009.

Agriculture (including hunting, forestry and fishing) accounted for 4.4% of GDP in 2008. The sector employed some 12.2% of the active working population in 2007. Despite the decline in the banana industry, the fruit remains Saint Lucia's principal cash crop, although in 2008 it accounted for 13.3% of the total value of merchandise exports, compared with 49.9% in 2002. Other important crops include coconuts, mangoes, citrus fruit, cocoa and spices. Commercial fishing was being developed. During 2001–08 real agricultural GDP decreased at an average annual rate of 2.0%, largely as a result of an average annual decline of 3.5% in the banana sector over 2001–07. The agriculture sector's GDP grew by 20.5% in 2008, largely owing to a 30.0% increase in the banana sector in that year.

Industry (including mining, manufacturing, public utilities and construction) accounted for 16.3% of GDP in 2008, and the sector engaged an estimated 19.9% of the active working population in 2007. During 2001–08 industrial GDP increased at an average annual rate of 0.2%. However, in 2008 the sector's real GDP declined by 9.8%.

Manufacturing accounted for 5.4% of GDP in 2008, and employed 6.1% of the employed population in 2007. The principal manufacturing industries, which have been encouraged by the establishment of 'free zones', include the processing of agricultural products, the assembly of electronic components and the

SAINT LUCIA

production of garments, plastics, paper and packaging (associated with banana production), and beer, rum and other beverages. During 2001–08 the sector's real GDP increased at an average annual rate of 3.6%. Real manufacturing GDP declined by 5.4% in 2008.

Construction contributed 6.0% to GDP in 2008, and engaged 13.1% of the employed labour force in 2007. The sector's GDP decreased at an average annual rate of 0.6% in 2001–08. Construction GDP contracted by 14.4% in 2008.

Energy is traditionally derived from imported hydrocarbon fuels (mineral fuels and lubricants comprised an estimated 25.9% of total imports in 2008). There is a petroleum storage and transshipment terminal on the island. Saint Lucia was a signatory to the PetroCaribe accord, introduced in 2005, under which the country was allowed to purchase petroleum from Venezuela at reduced prices, although implementation of the initiative was postponed after the United Workers' Party was returned to power in December 2006.

The services sector contributed 79.3% of GDP in 2008, and engaged an estimated 68.0% of those employed in 2007. Tourism is the most important of the service industries, and in 2009 tourist receipts totalled EC $799.7m. Total visitor arrivals increased by 7.1% in 2009; however, this was largely as a result of a 12.8% increase in cruise ship passengers in that year. The more lucrative stop-over visitor total declined by 5.8% in 2009. The real GDP of the hotels and restaurants sector decreased by 7.4% in 2007. However, the sector recovered in 2008, growing by 2.2%. During 2001–08 the real GDP of the services sector increased at an average annual rate of 4.1%. Sectoral GDP increased by 2.9% in 2008.

In 2009 Saint Lucia recorded an estimated visible trade deficit of EC $791.36m., and a deficit of some EC $378.51m. on the current account of the balance of payments. The principal source of imports in 2008 was the USA (42.6% of the total); other important markets in that year were Trinidad and Tobago and Japan. The principal market for exports in 2008 was also the USA (34.0% of the total); other major export markets were Trinidad and Tobago and the United Kingdom. The Caribbean states accounted for 30.9% of imports in 2008 and 43.5% of exports in 2008. Miscellaneous manufactured articles were the principal export commodity in 2008, ahead of refined petroleum, machinery and transport equipment, food and live animals (comprising mainly bananas sent to the United Kingdom), and beverages and tobacco (mainly beer). The principal imports in that year were mineral fuels and lubricants, machinery and transport equipment, and food and live animals.

In 2009 there was an overall budgetary deficit of EC $91.1m. Saint Lucia's general government gross debt was EC $1,975m. in 2009, equivalent to 74.7% of GDP. Saint Lucia's total external debt at the end of 2008 was US $831m., of which US $317m. was public and publicly guaranteed debt. In 2007 the cost of debt-servicing was equivalent to 7.7% of the value of exports of goods services and income. The annual rate of inflation averaged 3.3% in 2003–09; inflation averaged 1.3% in 2009. In 2007 the average rate of unemployment was 14.6%.

The Saint Lucian economy, which traditionally relied on the production of bananas for export, underwent considerable structural change at the end of the 20th century, with the emergence of service industries as the most important sectors of the economy, while investment in the island's infrastructure also benefited the tourism industry, which became the principal source of foreign exchange. In 2011 the World Travel and Tourism Council (WTTC) estimated that the tourism sector accounted for about 46% of Saint Lucia's GDP and employment. However, the tourism sector declined by an estimated 11.6% in 2009, according to the WTTC, owing to the global downturn. The agricultural sector, nevertheless, remained a significant source of employment, and the loss of Saint Lucia's preferential access to European markets was of considerable concern. The tourism industry recovered during 2010, although the economy as a whole remained sluggish, and the IMF projected growth of just 1.1% in that year. The agricultural sector was badly affected by Hurricane Tomas, which completely destroyed the banana crop along with most of the island's other crops in late October 2010, and the industry was not expected to recover until mid-2011. Tourism activity was also disrupted while damaged roads and bridges were repaired. The IMF released US $8.2m. in funding in January 2011 to support the country's reconstruction programme, the cost of which (an estimated $336m.) had led to a rise in the fiscal deficit. Nevertheless, a further recovery in tourist numbers was expected to contribute to growth of 2.3% in 2011.

PUBLIC HOLIDAYS

2012: 1–2 January (New Year), 22 February (Independence Day), 6 April (Good Friday), 9 April (Easter Monday), 1 May (Labour Day), 27 May (Whit Monday), 7 June (Corpus Christi), 1 August (Emancipation Day), 1 October (Thanksgiving Day), 13 December (Saint Lucia Day), 25–26 December (Christmas).

Statistical Survey

Source (unless otherwise indicated): St Lucian Government Statistics Department, Block A, Government Bldgs, Waterfront, Castries; tel. 452-7670; fax 451-8254; e-mail statsdept@candw.lc; internet www.stats.gov.lc.

AREA AND POPULATION

Area: 616.3 sq km (238 sq miles).

Population: 135,685 (males 65,988, females 69,697) at census of 12 May 1991; 162,982 (males 79,877, females 83,105) at census of 22 May 2001 (including estimate for underenumeration). *2006:* 166,838 (mid-year estimate). *By District* (estimates at mid-2006): Castries 68,209; Anse La Raye 6,468; Canaries 1,920; Soufrière 8,037; Choiseul 6,376; Laborie 7,705; Vieux Fort 15,942; Micoud 16,794; Dennery 13,458; Gros Islet 21,929. *Mid-2011* (UN estimate): 175,663 (Source: UN, *World Population Prospects: The 2008 Revision*).

Density (at mid-2011): 285.0 per sq km.

Population by Age and Sex (UN estimates at mid-2011): *0–14:* 44,584 (males 22,469, females 22,115); *15–64:* 119,137 (males 58,244, females 60,893); *65 and over:* 11,942 (males 5,256, females 6,686); *Total* 175,663 (males 85,969, females 89,694) (Source: UN, *World Population Prospects: The 2008 Revision*).

Principal Town (population incl. suburbs, mid-2006): Castries (capital) 14,509. *Mid-2009* (estimates): Castries 15,395. Source: UN, *World Urbanization Prospects: The 2009 Revision*.

Births, Marriages and Deaths (2005, provisional): Registered live births 2,904 (birth rate 19.0 per 1,000); Registered marriages 655; Registered deaths 941 (death rate 6.0 per 1,000). *2010:* Crude birth rate 14.8 per 1,000; Crude death rate 6.9 per 1,000 (Source: Pan American Health Organization).

Life Expectancy (years at birth, WHO estimates): 75 (males 71; females 78) in 2008. Source: WHO, *World Health Statistics*.

Economically Active Population (persons aged 15 years and over, labour survey for October–December 2007): Agriculture, hunting and forestry 7,670; Fishing 600; Manufacturing 4,160; Electricity, gas and water 420; Construction 8,940; Wholesale and retail trade, repair of motor vehicles, motorcycles and personal and household goods 11,210; Hotels and restaurants 8,870; Transport, storage and communications 4,370; Financial intermediation 1,090; Real estate, renting and business activities 2,950; Public administration and compulsory social security 12,200; Education 890; Health and social work 280; Other community, social and personal service activities 2,080; Private households with employed persons 2,280; *Sub-total* 68,010; Activities not adequately defined 420; Not reported 4,350; *Total employed* 72,780; Unemployed 12,480; *Total labour force* 85,260 (males 45,510, females 39,750).

HEALTH AND WELFARE

Key Indicators

Total Fertility Rate (children per woman, 2010): 1.8.

Under-5 Mortality Rate (per 1,000 live births, 2010): 15.

Physicians (per 1,000 head, 2009): 0.8.

SAINT LUCIA

Hospital Beds (per 1,000 head, 2009): 1.4.
Health Expenditure (2007): US $ per head (PPP): 608.
Health Expenditure (2007): % of GDP: 6.3.
Health Expenditure (2007): public (% of total): 54.2.
Access to Water (% of persons, 2008): 98.
Access to Sanitation (% of persons, 2004): 89.
Total Carbon Dioxide Emissions ('000 metric tons, 2007): 381.1.
Carbon Dioxide Emissions Per Head (metric tons, 2007): 2.3.
Human Development Index (2007): ranking: 69.
Human Development Index (2007): value: 0.821.

Source: partly Pan American Health Organization; for other sources and definitions, see explanatory note on p. vi.

AGRICULTURE, ETC.

Principal Crops ('000 metric tons, 2008, FAO estimates): Cassava 1.0; Yams 0.5; Coconuts 14.0; Bananas 54.0; Plantains 0.8; Citrus fruits 2.2. Note: No data were available for individual crops in 2009. *Aggregate Production* ('000 metric tons, 2009, may include official, semi-official or estimated data): Roots and tubers 4.2; Vegetables (incl. melons) 2.6; Fruits (excl. melons) 53.4.

Livestock ('000 head, 2008, FAO estimates): Cattle 11.0; Sheep 13.0; Goats 9.0; Pigs 20.0; Horses 1.1; Poultry 450. Note: No data were available for 2009.

Livestock Products ('000 metric tons, 2009 unless otherwise indicated, FAO estimates): Pig meat 1.4; Chicken meat 1.6; Cows' milk 1.1 (2008); Hen eggs 1.2 (2008).

Fishing (metric tons, live weight, 2008): Capture 1,713 (Wahoo 180; Skipjack tuna 168; Blackfin tuna 179; Yellowfin tuna 106; Common dolphinfish 341; Stromboid conchs 40); Aquaculture 0; Total catch 1,713. Figures exclude aquatic plants.

Source: FAO.

INDUSTRY

Production (2006, unless otherwise indicated): Electric energy 355.9 million kWh (2009); Copra 1,094 metric tons (2004); Coconut oil (unrefined) 1.2m. litres; Coconut oil (refined) 88,700 litres; Coconut meal 499,300 kg; Rum 191,900 proof gallons (Source: partly Eastern Caribbean Central Bank).

FINANCE

Currency and Exchange Rates: 100 cents = 1 Eastern Caribbean dollar (EC $). *Sterling, US Dollar and Euro Equivalents* (31 December 2010): £1 sterling = EC $4.227; US $1 = EC $2.700; €1 = EC $3.608; EC $100 = £23.70 = US $37.03 = €27.72. *Exchange Rate:* Fixed at US $1 = EC $2.70 since July 1976.

Budget (EC $ million, 2009): *Revenue:* Tax revenue 724.0 (Taxes on income and profits 226.3; Taxes on property 4.2; Taxes on domestic goods and services 107.4; Taxes on international trade and transactions 386.1); Other current revenue 29.7; Capital revenue 0.1; Total 753.9 (excl. grants 25.9). *Expenditure:* Current expenditure 644.8 (Personal emoluments 309.0; Goods and services 117.9; Interest payments 89.8; Transfers and subsidies 127.9); Capital expenditure and net lending 200.2; Total 845.0. Source: Eastern Caribbean Central Bank.

International Reserves (US $ million at 31 December 2010): IMF special drawing rights 23.92; Reserve position in IMF 0.01; Foreign exchange 182.33; Total 206.26. Source: IMF, *International Financial Statistics*.

Money Supply (EC $ million at 31 December 2010): Currency outside depository corporations 151.53; Transferable deposits 658.32; Other deposits 2,196.48; *Broad money* 3,006.33. Source: IMF, *International Financial Statistics*.

Cost of Living (Consumer Price Index; base: 2005 = 100): All items 105.5 in 2007; 114.1 in 2008; 115.2 in 2009. Source: IMF, *International Financial Statistics*.

Gross Domestic Product (EC $ million at constant 1990 prices): 1,699.37 in 2006; 1,735.96 in 2007; 1,750.63 in 2008. Source: Eastern Caribbean Central Bank.

Expenditure on the Gross Domestic Product (EC $ million at current prices, 2008): Government final consumption expenditure 508.87; Private final consumption expenditure 2,490.06; Gross capital formation 695.51; *Total domestic expenditure* 3,694.44; Exports of goods and services 1,355.09; *Less* Imports of goods and services 2,387.13; *GDP at market prices* 2,662.40. Source: Eastern Caribbean Central Bank.

Gross Domestic Product by Economic Activity (EC $ million in current prices, 2008): Agriculture, hunting, forestry and fishing 103.38; Mining and quarrying 7.22; Manufacturing 126.93; Electricity and water 110.09; Construction 142.01; Wholesale and retail trade 299.67; Restaurants and hotels 292.48; Transport 267.69; Communications 180.45; Banking and insurance 244.70; Real estate and housing 204.53; Government services 323.71; Other services 67.29; *Sub-total* 2,370.15; *Less* Imputed bank service charge 198.61; *Total in basic prices* 2,171.54; Taxes, less subsidies, on products 490.86; *GDP at market prices* 2,662.40. Source: Eastern Caribbean Central Bank.

Balance of Payments (EC $ million, 2010): Exports of goods 471.60; Imports of goods –1,262.96; *Trade balance* –791.36; Services (net) 538.10; *Balance on goods and services* –253.26; Other income received (net) –165.42; *Balance on goods, services and income* –418.68; Current transfers received (net) 40.17; *Current balance* –378.51; Capital account (net) 50.03; Direct investment (net) 267.45; Portfolio investment (net) –22.48; Other investment 103.25; Net errors and omissions 29.68; *Overall balance* 49.41. Source: Eastern Caribbean Central Bank.

EXTERNAL TRADE

Principal Commodities (US $ million, 2008): *Imports c.i.f.:* Food and live animals 108.6 (Meat and preparations thereof 25.0; Cereals and preparations thereof 22.1); Beverages and tobacco 27.7 (Beverages 23.5); Mineral fuels, lubricants, etc. 169.9 (Refined petroleum products 169.9); Chemicals 40.7; Basic manufactures 88.3 (Metal manufactures 17.4); Machinery and transport equipment 127.1 (Telecommunications equipment 8.5; Road vehicles 60.3); Miscellaneous manufactured articles 78.4; Total (incl. others) 655.7. *Exports f.o.b.* (incl. re-exports): Food and live animals 26.6 (Bananas 21.8); Beverages and tobacco 20.4 (Beer 13.4); Mineral fuels, lubricants, etc. 31.2 (Refined petroleum products 31.2); Basic manufactures 11.4 (Paper products 5.7); Machinery and transport equipment 27.3 (Telecommunications equipment 5.0; Electric machinery, etc. 3.1; Road vehicles 3.9); Miscellaneous manufactured articles 32.8; Total (incl. others) 164.0. Source: UN, *International Trade Statistics Yearbook*.

Principal Trading Partners (US $ million, 2008): *Imports c.i.f.:* Barbados 23.1; Canada 11.9; China, People's Repub. 0.1; Finland 0.4; France (incl. Monaco) 8.4; Germany 5.9; Japan 28.2; Netherlands 7.0; Panama 8.8; Saint Vincent and the Grenadines 5.4; Thailand 11.4; Trinidad and Tobago 156.0; United Kingdom 26.8; USA 279.1; Total (incl. others) 655.7. *Exports f.o.b.* (excl. re-exports): Antigua and Barbuda 3.7; Barbados 13.9; Dominica 4.6; France (incl. Monaco) 1.9; Grenada 3.0; Saint Vincent and the Grenadines 4.9; Trinidad and Tobago 38.1; United Kingdom 24.8; USA 55.8; Total (incl. others) 164.0. Source: UN, *International Trade Statistics Yearbook*.

TRANSPORT

Road Traffic (registered motor vehicles, 2002): Goods vehicles 9,554; Taxis and hired vehicles 1,880; Motorcycles 797; Private vehicles 21,421; Passenger vans 3,439; Total (incl. others) 38,572.

Shipping: *Arrivals* (2006): 1,557 vessels. *International Sea-borne Freight Traffic* (at Castries and Vieux Fort, metric tons, 2010): Goods loaded 101,478; Goods unloaded 526,754. Source: Saint Lucia Air and Sea Ports Authority.

Civil Aviation (traffic at George F. L. Charles and Hewanorra airports, 2009): Aircraft movements 36,883; Passenger departures 400,127; Passenger arrivals 391,146; Cargo loaded (metric tons) 1,284.0; Cargo unloaded (metric tons) 1,738.7. Source: Saint Lucia Air and Sea Ports Authority.

TOURISM

Visitor Arrivals: 931,685 (287,518 stop-over visitors, 7,841 excursionists, 26,163 yacht passengers, 610,163 cruise ship passengers) in 2007; 947,445 (295,761 stop-over visitors, 9,582 excursionists, 22,422 yacht passengers, 619,680 cruise ship passengers) in 2008; 1,014,761 (278,491 stop-over visitors, 4,967 excursionists, 31,997 yacht passengers, 699,306 cruise ship passengers) in 2009. *Stop-over Visitors by Country* (2009): USA 98,685; United Kingdom 71,853; Caribbean 60,179; Canada 28,563; Other 19,211.

Tourism Receipts (EC $ million): 814.5 in 2007; 839.7 in 2008; 799.7 in 2009.

Source: Eastern Caribbean Central Bank.

COMMUNICATIONS MEDIA

Radio Receivers ('000 in use, 1997): 111.
Television Receivers ('000 in use, 1999): 56.

SAINT LUCIA

Telephones ('000 main lines in use, 2009): 41.0.
Mobile Cellular Telephones ('000 subscribers, 2009): 176.0.
Personal Computers: 26,000 (160.1 per 1,000 persons) in 2004.
Internet Users ('000 subscribers, 2009): 18.6.
Broadband Subscribers (2009, estimate): 18.6.
Non-daily Newspapers (2004 unless otherwise indicated): Titles 5; Circulation 34,000 (1996).

Sources: UN, *Statistical Yearbook*; UNESCO, *Statistical Yearbook*; International Telecommunication Union; Eastern Caribbean Telecommunications Authority, *Annual Telecommunications Sector Review 2006*.

EDUCATION

Pre-primary (state institutions only, 2005/06): 148 schools; 480 teachers; 5,062 pupils.
Primary (state institutions only, 2007/08): 75 schools; 922 teachers; 20,164 pupils.
General Secondary (state institutions only, 2007/08): 23 schools; 924 teachers; 15,630 pupils.
Special Education (state institutions only, 2007/08): 4 schools; 47 teachers; 227 students.
Adult Education (state institutions only, 2006/07 unless otherwise indicated): 13 centres; 70 facilitators; 1,395 learners.
Tertiary (state institutions, including part-time, 2000/01): 127 teachers; 1,403 students.

Source: partly Caribbean Development Bank, *Social and Economic Indicators*.

Pupil-teacher Ratio (primary education, UNESCO estimate): 20.0 in 2008/09. Source: UNESCO Institute for Statistics.
Adult Literacy Rate (UNESCO estimate): 94.8% in 2004. Source: UN Development Programme, *Human Development Report*.

Directory

The Government

HEAD OF STATE

Queen: HM Queen ELIZABETH II.
Governor-General: Dame PEARLETTE LOUISY (took office 17 September 1997).

CABINET
(May 2011)

The Government is formed by the United Workers' Party.

Prime Minister and Minister for Finance (International Financial Services), and for Economic Affairs, Economic Planning and National Development: STEPHENSON KING.
Minister for Social Transformation, Public Service, Human Resource Development, Youth and Sports: LENARD SPIDER MONTOUTE.
Minister for Health Wellness, Family Affairs, National Mobilisation, Human Services and Gender Relations: Dr KEITH MONDESIR.
Minister for Physical Development, Housing, Urban Renewal, Local Government and the Environment: RICHARD FREDERICK.
Minister for Education and Culture: ARSENE VIGIL JAMES.
Minister for Agriculture, Lands, Fisheries, and Forestry: EZECHIEL JOSEPH.
Minister for Home Affairs and National Security: GEORGE GUY MAYERS.
Minister for External Affairs, International Trade and Investment: RUFUS GEORGE BOUSQUET.
Minister for Communications, Works, Transport and Public Utilities: GUY EARDLEY JOSEPH.
Minister for Tourism and Civil Aviation: ALLEN M. CHASTANET.
Minister for Labour, Information and Broadcasting: EDMUND ESTEPHANE.
Minister of Commerce, Industry and Consumer Affairs: CHARLOTTE ELIZABETH THERESA TESSA MANGAL.
Attorney-General and Minister for Justice: LORENZO RUDOLPH FRANCIS.
Minister in the Ministry of Education and Culture: GASPARD PETER DAVID CHARLEMAGNE.

MINISTRIES

Office of the Prime Minister: Greaham Louisy Administrative Bldg, 5th Floor, Waterfront, Castries; tel. 468-2111; fax 453-7352; e-mail admin@pm.gov.lc; internet www.pm.gov.lc.
Attorney-General's Office and Ministry of Justice: Francis Compton Bldg, 2nd Floor, Waterfront, Castries; tel. 468-3200; fax 458-1131; e-mail atgen@gosl.gov.lc.
Ministry of Agriculture, Lands, Fisheries and Forestry: Sir Stanislaus James Bldg, 4th and 5th Floor, Waterfront, Castries; tel. 468-4104; fax 453-6314; e-mail adminag@candw.lc; internet www.maff.egov.lc.
Ministry of Commerce, Industry and Consumer Affairs: Ives Heraldine Rock Bldg, 4th Floor, Block B, Waterfront, Castries; tel. 468-4202; fax 453-7347; e-mail mitandt@candw.lc; internet www.commerce.gov.lc.
Ministry of Communications, Works, Transport and Public Utilities: Williams Bldg, Bridge St, Castries; tel. 468-4300; fax 453-2769; e-mail min_com@gosl.gov.lc.
Ministry of Economic Affairs, Economic Planning and National Development: American Drywall Bldg, POB 929, Vide Boutielle, Castries; tel. 468-2180; fax 451-9706; e-mail projects@candw.lc.
Ministry of Education and Culture: Francis Compton Bldg, 4th Floor, Waterfront, Castries; tel. 468-5203; fax 453-2299; e-mail mineduc@candw.lc; internet www.education.gov.lc.
Ministry of External Affairs, International Trade and Investment: Conway Business Centre, 7th Floor, Waterfront, Castries; tel. 468-4501; fax 452-7427; e-mail foreign@candw.lc.
Ministry of Finance (International Financial Services): Financial Centre, 2nd Floor, Bridge St, Castries; tel. 468-5500; fax 451-9231; e-mail minfin@gosl.gov.lc.
Ministry of Health Wellness, Family Affairs, National Mobilisation, Human Services and Gender Relations: Sir Stanislaus James Bldg, 2nd Floor, Castries; tel. 468–5300; fax 452-5655; e-mail health@candw.lc.
Ministry of Home Affairs and National Security: Sir Stanislaus James Bldg, 1st Floor, Waterfront, Castries; tel. 468-3600; fax 456-0228; e-mail pshans@gosl.gov.lc.
Ministry of Housing, Urban Renewal and Local Government: Cox Bldg, 2nd Floor, Jeremie St, POB 602, Castries; tel. 468-2600; fax 453-1530; e-mail minphul@gosl.gov.lc.
Ministry of International Trade and Investment: Heraldine Rock Bldg, 4th Floor, Waterfront, Castries; tel. 468-4202; fax 451-6986.
Ministry of Labour, Information and Broadcasting: Conway Business Centre, 5th Floor, Waterfront, Castries; tel. 468-2701; fax 453-7347; e-mail agencyadmin@gosl.gov.lc.
Ministry of Physical Development and the Environment: Greaham Lousiy Administrative Bldg, 3rd Floor, Waterfront, Castries; tel. 468-4419; fax 452-2506; internet www.planning.gov.lc.
Ministry of Social Transformation, Public Service, Human Resource Development, Youth and Sports: Greaham Louisy Administrative Bldg, 2nd and 4th Floors, Waterfront, Castries; tel. 468-5101; fax 453-7921; e-mail most@gosl.gov.lc; e-mail minpet@candw.lc (Public Service).
Ministry of Tourism and Civil Aviation: Heraldine Rock Bldg, 4th Floor, Waterfront, Castries; tel. 453-6644; fax 451-7414; e-mail psmot@gosl.gov.lc.

Legislature

PARLIAMENT

Senate

The Senate has nine nominated members and two independent members.

President: LEONNE THEODORE-JOHN.

SAINT LUCIA   *Directory*

House of Assembly
Speaker: Dr HILDA ROSE MARIE HUSBANDS-MATHURIN.
Clerk: KURT THOMAS.
Election, 11 December 2006

Party	Seats
United Workers' Party	11
Saint Lucia Labour Party	6
Total	**17**

Election Commission

Election Commission: St Lucia Electoral Dept, 23 High St, POB 1074, Castries; tel. 452-3725; fax 451-6513; e-mail info@electoral.gov.lc; internet www.electoral.gov.lc; Election Commr CARSON RAGGIE.

Political Organizations

Lucian People's Movement: Castries; internet www.lpmnow.org; f. 2010; Co-Chairs THEROLD PRUDENT, FRANKLIN MCDONALD, S. JULIAN BEST (acting).

Organization for National Empowerment (ONE): POB 1496, Castries; tel. 484-9424; fax 452-9574; e-mail aziea99@yahoo.com; f. 2004; Leader PETER ALEXANDER; Chair. ROSEMUND CLERY.

Saint Lucia Labour Party (SLP): Tom Walcott Bldg, 2nd Floor, Jeremie St, POB 427, Castries; tel. 451-8446; fax 451-9389; e-mail slp@candw.lc; internet www.stlucialabourparty.org; f. 1946; socialist party; Leader Dr KENNY DAVIS ANTHONY; Chair. JULIAN HUNTE; Gen. Sec. LEO CLARKE.

United Workers' Party (UWP): 9 Coral St, POB 1550, Castries; tel. 451-9103; fax 451-9207; e-mail unitworkers@netscape.net; f. 1964; right-wing; Chair. and Leader STEPHENSON KING; Gen. Sec. GERTRUDE GEORGE.

Diplomatic Representation

EMBASSIES AND HIGH COMMISSION IN SAINT LUCIA

Brazil: 1 Bella Rosa Rd, 3rd Floor, POB 6136, Gros Islet; tel. 450-1671; fax 450-4733; e-mail brasemb.castries@itamaraty.gov.br; Ambassador JOÃO BATISTA CRUZ.

Cuba: Rodney Heights, Gros Islet, POB 2150, Castries; tel. 458-4665; fax 458-4666; e-mail embacubasantalucia@candw.lc; internet embacu.cubaminrex.cu/santaluciaing; Ambassador LYDIA GONZÁLEZ NAVARRO.

France: French Embassy to the OECS, GPO Private Box 937, Vigie, Castries; tel. 455-6060; fax 455-6056; e-mail frenchembassy@candw.lc; internet www.ambafrance-lc.org; Ambassador MICHEL PROM.

Mexico: Nelson Mandela Dr., POB 6096, Vigie, Castries; tel. 453-1250; fax 451-4252; e-mail mexicanembassy@candw.lc; internet www.sre.gob.mx/santalucia; Ambassador GERARDO LOZANO ARREDONDO.

Taiwan (Republic of China): Reduit Beach Ave, Rodney Bay; tel. 452-8105; fax 452-0441; e-mail luciaemb@gmail.com; internet www.taiwanembassy.org/lc; Ambassador TOM CHOU.

United Kingdom: Francis Compton Bldg, Waterfront, POB 227, Castries; tel. 452-2484; fax 453-1543; e-mail postmaster.castries@fco.gov.uk; High Commissioner PAUL BRUMMELL.

Venezuela: Casa Santa Lucía, POB 494, Castries; tel. 452-4033; fax 453-6747; e-mail vembassy@candw.lc; Ambassador EDUARDO ALFONZO BARRANCO HERNÁNDEZ.

Judicial System

SUPREME COURT

Eastern Caribbean Supreme Court: Heraldine Rock Bldg, Block B, Waterfront, POB 1093, Castries; tel. 452-7998; fax 452-5475; e-mail appeal@candw.lc; the West Indies Associated States Supreme Court was established in 1967 and was known as the Supreme Court of Grenada and the West Indies Associated States from 1974 until 1979, when it became the Eastern Caribbean Supreme Court. Its jurisdiction extends to Anguilla, Antigua and Barbuda, the British Virgin Islands, Dominica, Grenada (which rejoined in 1991), Montserrat, Saint Christopher and Nevis, Saint Lucia and Saint Vincent and the Grenadines. It is composed of the High Court of Justice and the Court of Appeal. The High Court is composed of the Chief Justice, who is head of the judiciary, and 16 High Court Judges, three of whom are resident in Saint Lucia. The Court of Appeal is itinerant and presided over by the Chief Justice and three other Justices of Appeal. Additionally, there are two Masters whose principal responsibilities extend to procedural and interlocutory matters. Jurisdiction of the High Court includes fundamental rights and freedoms, membership of the parliaments, and matters concerning the interpretation of constitutions. The Caribbean Court of Justice, inaugurated in April 2005, was intended to replace the Judicial Committee of the Privy Council, based in the United Kingdom, as Saint Lucia's final court of appeal, although by 2011 only Barbados, Guyana and Belize were officially under the jurisdiction of the new regional court.

Chief Justice: HUGH ANTHONY RAWLINS.
Justices of Appeal: OLA MAE EDWARDS, JANICE MESADIS GEORGE-CREQUE, DAVIDSON BAPTISTE.
Managing Judge: ESBON ANTHONY ROSS.
Chief Registrar: KIMBERLY CENAC PHULGENCE.
High Court Judges resident in Saint Lucia: KENNETH ANDREW CHARLES BENJAMIN, FRANCIS BELL, ROSALYN E. WILKINSON, EPHRAIM FRANCIS GEORGES (acting).
Registrar: CYBELLE CENAC-MARAGH.

Religion

CHRISTIANITY

The Roman Catholic Church

Saint Lucia forms a single archdiocese. The Archbishop participates in the Antilles Episcopal Conference (currently based in Port of Spain, Trinidad and Tobago). According to the latest census (2001), some 68% of the population are Roman Catholics

Archbishop of Castries: ROBERT RIVAS, Archbishop's House, Nelson Mandela Dr., POB 267, Castries; tel. 452-2416; fax 452-3697; e-mail secretaries@archdioceseofcastries.org; internet www.archdioceseofcastries.org.

The Anglican Communion

Anglicans in Saint Lucia are adherents of the Church in the Province of the West Indies, comprising eight dioceses. The Archbishop of the West Indies is the Bishop of Nassau and the Bahamas. Saint Lucia forms part of the diocese of the Windward Islands (the Bishop is resident in Kingstown, Saint Vincent). Some 2% of the population are Anglicans, according to the 2001 census.

Other Christian Churches

According to the 2001 census, 9% of the population are Seventh-day Adventists, 6% are Pentecostalists, 2% are Evangelical Christians and 2% are Baptists.

Seventh-day Adventist Church: St Louis St, POB 117, Castries; tel. 452-4408; e-mail khansamuel@hotmail.com; internet www.tagnet.org/cacoasda; Pastor THEODORE JARIA.

Trinity Evangelical Lutheran Church: Gablewoods Mall, POB 858, Castries; tel. 458-4638; e-mail spiegelbergs@candw.lc; Pastor Rev. TOM SPIEGELBERG.

The Press

The Catholic Chronicle: POB 778, Castries; f. 1957; monthly; Editor Rev. PATRICK A. B. ANTHONY; circ. 3,000.

The Crusader: 19 St Louis St, Castries; tel. 452-2203; fax 452-1986; f. 1934; weekly (Sat.); circ. 4,000.

The Mirror: Bisee Industrial Estate, POB 1782, Castries; tel. 451-6181; fax 451-6197; e-mail webmaster@stluciamirror.com; internet www.stluciamirroronline.com; f. 1994; weekly (Fri.); Man. Editor GUY ELLIS; circ. 3,900.

One Caribbean: POB 852, Castries; e-mail dabread@candw.lc; weekly; Editor D. SINCLAIR DABREO.

She Caribbean: Rodney Bay Industrial Estate, Massade, Gros Islet, POB 1146, Castries; tel. 450-7827; fax 450-8694; e-mail shanna.h@stluciastar.com; internet www.shecaribbean.com; quarterly; Publr and Editor-in-Chief MAE WAYNE.

The Star: Rodney Bay Industrial Estate, Gros Islet, POB 1146, Castries; tel. 450-7827; fax 450-8694; e-mail shanna.h@stluciastar.com; internet www.stluciastar.com; f. 1987; 3 a week (Mon., Wed. and weekend edns); circ. 8,000; Propr RICK WAYNE; Man. Editor NICOLE MCDONALD.

SAINT LUCIA

Tropical Traveller: Rodney Bay Industrial Estate, Massade, Gros Islet, POB 1146, Castries; tel. 450-7827; fax 450-8694; e-mail infostar@stluciastar.com; internet www.tropicaltraveller.com; f. 1989; monthly; Editorial Dir MAE WAYNE; Man. Editor NANCY ATKINSON.

Visions of St Lucia Island Guide: 7 Maurice Mason Ave, Sans Soucis, POB 947, Castries; tel. 453-0427; fax 452-1522; e-mail visions@candw.lc; internet www.visionsofstlucia.com; f. 1989; official tourist guide; publ. by Island Visions Ltd; annual; Chair. and Man. Dir ANTHONY NEIL AUSTIN; circ. 120,000.

The Weekend Voice: Odessa Bldg, Darling Rd, POB 104, Castries; tel. 452-2590; fax 453-1453; weekly (Sat.); circ. 8,000.

PRESS ORGANIZATION

Eastern Caribbean Press Council (ECPC): Castries; f. 2003; independent, self-regulating body designed to foster and maintain standards in regional journalism, formed by 14 newspapers in the Eastern Caribbean and Barbados; Chair. Lady MARIE SIMMONS.

NEWS AGENCY

Caribbean Media Corporation: Bisee Rd, Castries; tel. 453-7162; e-mail admin@cmccaribbean.com; internet www.cananews.com; f. 2000 by merger of Caribbean News Agency and Caribbean Broadcasting Union.

Publishers

Caribbean Publishing Co Ltd: American Drywall Bldg, Vide Bouteille Hwy, POB 104, Castries; tel. 452-3188; fax 452-3181; e-mail publish@candw.lc; internet stluciayp.com; f. 1978; publr of telephone directories and magazines; Chair. RANDY FRENCH.

Crusader Publishing Co Ltd: 19 St Louis St, Castries; tel. 452-2203; fax 452-1986.

Island Visions Ltd: 7 Maurice Mason Ave, Sans Soucis, POB 947, Castries; tel. 453-0472; fax 452-1522; e-mail visions@candw.lc; internet www.visionsofstlucia.com; f. 1989; Chair. and Man. Dir ANTHONY NEIL AUSTIN.

Mirror Publishing Co Ltd: Bisee Industrial Estate, POB 1782, Castries; tel. 451-6181; fax 451-6503; e-mail mirror@candw.lc; f. 1994; Man. Editor GUY ELLIS.

Star Publishing Co: Rodney Bay Industrial Estate, Massade, Gros Islet, POB 1146, Castries; tel. 450-7827; fax 450-8694; e-mail infostar@stluciastar.com; internet www.stluciastar.com; Propr RICK WAYNE.

Voice Publishing Co Ltd: Odessa Bldg, Darling Rd, POB 104, Castries; tel. 452-2590; fax 453-1453; e-mail gordonm@candw.lc; internet www.thevoiceslu.com; Man. Dir MICHAEL BRUCE GARNET GORDON.

Broadcasting and Communications

TELECOMMUNICATIONS

Regulatory Authorities

Eastern Caribbean Telecommunications Authority (ECTEL): Vide Bouteille, POB 1886, Castries; tel. 458-1701; fax 458-1698; e-mail ectel@ectel.int; internet www.ectel.int; f. 2000 to regulate telecommunications in Saint Lucia, Dominica, Grenada, Saint Christopher and Nevis and Saint Vincent and the Grenadines; Chair. ISAAC SOLOMON; Man. Dir EMBERT CHARLES.

National Telecommunications Regulatory Commission (NTRC): Global Tile Bldg, Bois D'Orange, POB GM 690, Castries; tel. 458-2035; fax 453-2558; e-mail ntrc_slu@candw.lc; internet www.ntrc.org.lc; f. 2000; regulates the sector in conjunction with ECTEL; Chair. ELMA GENE ISAAC.

Major Service Providers

Digicel St Lucia: Rodney Bay, Gros Islet, POB GM 791, Castries; tel. 456-3400; fax 450-3872; e-mail customercare.stlucia@digicelgroup.com; internet www.digicelstlucia.com; f. 2003; owned by an Irish consortium; acquired operations of Cingular Wireless in Saint Lucia in 2006; Chair. DENIS O'BRIEN; Eastern Caribbean States (South) CEO GERALDINE PITT.

LIME: Bridge St, POB 111, Castries; tel. 453-9720; fax 453-9700; e-mail talk2us@candw.lc; internet www.time4lime.com; fmrly Cable & Wireless St Lucia; name changed as above 2008; provides fixed-line, mobile, internet and cable television services; CEO DAVID SHAW.

Saint Lucia Boatphone Ltd: Gros Islet, POB 2136, Castries; tel. 452-0361; fax 452-0394; e-mail boatphone@candw.lc; wholly owned subsidiary of Cable & Wireless Caribbean Cellular.

BROADCASTING

Radio

Radio Caribbean International: 11 Mongiraud St, POB 121, Castries; tel. 452-2636; fax 452-2637; e-mail rci@candw.lc; internet www.rcistlucia.com; operates Radio Caraïbes; English and Creole services; broadcasts 24 hrs; Station Mans PETER EPHRAIM, PET GIBSON.

Saint Lucia Broadcasting Corporation: Morne Fortune, POB 660, Castries; tel. 452-2337; fax 453-1568; govt-owned; Man. KEITH WEEKES.

    Radio 100-Helen FM: Morne Fortune, POB 621, Castries; tel. 451-7260; fax 453-1737; e-mail radio@htsstlucia.com; internet www.htsstlucia.com; Gen. Man. STEPHENSON ANIUS.

    Radio Saint Lucia Co Ltd (RSL): Morne Fortune, POB 660, Castries; tel. 452-2337; fax 453-1568; e-mail info@rslonline.com; internet www.rslonline.com; f. 1972; English and Creole services; Chair. LINDELL GUSTAVE; Man. Dir MARY POLIUS.

Television

Cablevision: George Gordon Bldg, Bridge St, POB 111, Castries; tel. 453-9311; fax 453-9740.

Catholic Broadcasting TV Network (CBTN): Micoud St, Castries; tel. 452-7050.

Daher Broadcasting Service Ltd (DBS): Vigie, POB 1623, Castries; tel. 453-2705; fax 452-3544; e-mail dbstv@candw.lc; internet dbstelevision.com; Man. Dir LINDA DAHER.

Helen Television System (HTS): National Television Service of St Lucia, POB 621, The Morne, Castries; tel. 452-2693; fax 454-1737; e-mail hts@candw.lc; internet www.htsstlucia.com; f. 1967; commercial station; Gen. Man. STEPHENSON ANIUS.

National Television Network (NTN): Castries; f. 2001; operated by the Government Information Service; provides information on the operations of the public sector.

Finance

(cap. = capital; dep. = deposits; m. = million; brs = branches)

BANKING

The Eastern Caribbean Central Bank, based in Saint Christopher, is the central issuing and monetary authority for Saint Lucia.

Eastern Caribbean Central Bank—Saint Lucia Office: Colony House, Unit 5, John Compton Hwy, POB 295, Castries; tel. 452-7449; fax 453-6022; e-mail eccbslu@candw.lc; internet www.eccb-centralbank.org; Country Dir ISAAC ANTHONY; Rep. GREGOR FRANKLIN.

Local Banks

1st National Bank Saint Lucia Ltd: 21 Bridge St, POB 168, Castries; tel. 455-7000; fax 453-1630; e-mail manager@1stnationalbankslu.com; internet www.1stnationalbankonline.com; inc. 1937 as Saint Lucia Co-operative Bank Ltd; name changed as above Jan. 2005; commercial bank; share cap. EC $5m., asset base EC $221.4m. (Dec. 2004); Chair. and Pres. CHARMAINE GARDNER; Man. Dir G. CARLTON GLASGOW; 4 brs.

Bank of Saint Lucia Ltd: Financial Centre, 5th Floor, 1 Bridge St, POB 1860, Castries; tel. 456-6000; fax 456-6702; e-mail info@bankofsaintlucia.com; internet www.bankofsaintlucia.com; f. 2001 by merger of National Commercial Bank of St Lucia Ltd and Saint Lucia Devt Bank; total assets EC $1,600m. (Dec. 2007); 35% state-owned; parent co is East Caribbean Financial Holding Co Ltd; Chair. VICTOR A. EUDOXIE; Gen. Man. RYAN DEVEAUX; 7 brs.

FirstCaribbean International Bank (Barbados) Ltd: Bridge St, POB 335, Castries; tel. 456-2422; fax 452-3735; internet www.firstcaribbeanbank.com; f. 2002 following merger of Caribbean operations of Barclays Bank PLC and CIBC; CIBC acquired Barclays' 43.7% stake in 2006; Exec. Chair. MICHAEL MANSOOR; CEO JOHN D. ORR.

RBTT Bank Caribbean Ltd: 22 Micoud St, POB 1531, Castries; tel. 452-2265; fax 452-1668; e-mail rbttslu.isd@candw.lc; internet www.rbtt.com; f. 1985 as Caribbean Banking Corpn Ltd, name changed as above in March 2002; owned by R and M Holdings Ltd; Chair. PETER JULY; Country Man. EARL P. CRICHTON; 4 brs.

SAINT LUCIA   *Directory*

STOCK EXCHANGE

Eastern Caribbean Securities Exchange: based in Basseterre, Saint Christopher and Nevis; tel. 869-466-7192; fax 869-465-3798; e-mail info@ecseonline.com; internet www.ecseonline.com; f. 2001; regional securities market designed to facilitate the buying and selling of financial products for the eight member territories—Anguilla, Antigua and Barbuda, Dominica, Grenada, Montserrat, Saint Christopher and Nevis, Saint Lucia and Saint Vincent and the Grenadines; Chair. Sir K. DWIGHT VENNER; Gen. Man. TREVOR E. BLAKE.

INSURANCE

Local companies include the following:

Caribbean General Insurance Ltd: Laborie St, POB 290, Castries; tel. 452-2410; fax 452-3649.

Eastern Caribbean Insurance Ltd: Laborie St, POB 290, Castries; tel. 452-2410; fax 452-3393; e-mail cgi.ltd@candw.lc.

Saint Lucia Insurances Ltd: 48 Micoud St, POB 1084, Castries; tel. 452-3240; fax 452-2240; e-mail sl.ins@candw.lc; principal agents of Alliance Insurance Co Ltd.

Saint Lucia Motor and General Insurance Co Ltd: 38 Micoud St, POB 767, Castries; tel. 452-3323; fax 452-6072.

Trade and Industry

DEVELOPMENT ORGANIZATION

National Development Corporation (NDC): 1st Floor, Heraldine Rock Bldg, The Waterfront, POB 495, Castries; tel. 452-3614; fax 452-1841; e-mail info@investstlucia.com; internet www.investstlucia.com; f. 1971 to stimulate, facilitate and promote investment opportunities for foreign and local investors and to promote the economic devt of Saint Lucia; owns and manages seven industrial estates; br. in Miami, FL, USA; Exec. Chair. VERN GILL; CEO WAYNE VITALIS.

CHAMBER OF COMMERCE

Saint Lucia Chamber of Commerce, Industry and Agriculture: American Drywall Bldg, 2nd Floor, Vide Bouteille, POB 482, Castries; tel. 452-3165; fax 453-6907; e-mail info@stluciachamber.org; internet www.stluciachamber.org; f. 1884; Pres. CHESTER HINKSON; Exec. Dir BRIAN LOUISY; 150 mems.

INDUSTRIAL AND TRADE ASSOCIATIONS

Saint Lucia Banana Corporation (SLBC): 7 Manoel St, POB 197, Castries; tel. 452-2251; f. 1998 following privatization of Saint Lucia Banana Growers' Asscn (f. 1967); Chair. EUSTACE MONROSE; Sec. DURAND DORSEIDE.

Saint Lucia Industrial and Small Business Association: , POB 585, La Panse, Castries; tel. 452-7616; fax 453-1023; e-mail slisbaslu@gmail.com; internet www.slisbastlucia.com; Pres. FLAVIA CHERRY.

Small Enterprise Development Unit (SEDU): Ministry of Commerce, Industry and Consumer Affairs, Heraldine Rock Bldg, 4th Floor, Waterfront, Castries; tel. 468-4220; fax 453-2891; f. 2000; Dir PETER LORDE.

EMPLOYERS' ASSOCIATIONS

Saint Lucia Agriculturists' Association Ltd: Mongiraud St, POB 153, Castries; tel. 452-2494; fax 453-2693; distributor and supplier of agricultural, industrial and organic products; exporter of cocoa; Chair. CUTHBERT PHILLIPS; CEO KERDE M. SEVERIN.

Saint Lucia Coconut Growers' Association Ltd: Palmiste Rd, POB 269, Castries; tel. 459-7227; fax 459-7216; e-mail slcga1@candw.lc; f. 1939; Gen. Man. GERALD MORRIS.

Saint Lucia Employers' Federation: c/o The Morgan Bldg, L'Anse Rd, POB 160, Castries; tel. 452-2190; fax 452-7335; e-mail slefslu@candw.lc; internet www.slef-slu.org; Pres. CALLISTUS VERN GILL.

Saint Lucia Fish Marketing Corpn: POB 891, Sans Souci, Castries; tel. 452-1341; fax 451-7073; e-mail slfmc@candw.lc; Gen. Man. GREGORY ST HELENE.

Saint Lucia Marketing Board (SLMB): Conway, POB 441, Castries; tel. 452-3214; fax 453-1424; e-mail slmb@candw.lc; Gen. Man. THERESA DESIR (acting).

Windward Islands Banana Development and Exporting Co (Wibdeco): Manoel St, POB 115, Castries; tel. 452-2411; fax 453-1638; e-mail wibdeco@candw.lc; internet www.wibdeco.com; f. 1994 in succession to the Windward Islands Banana Growers' Asscn (WINBAN); regional org. dealing with banana devt and marketing; jtly owned by the Windward govts and island banana asscns; CEO BERNARD CORNIBERT.

UTILITIES

Electricity

Caribbean Electric Utility Services Corpn (CARILEC): Desir Ave, Sans Soucis, POB CP 5907, Castries; tel. 452-0140; fax 452-0142; e-mail info@carilec.org; internet www.carilec.com; f. 1989; Exec. Dir NIGEL HOSEIN.

St Lucia Electricity Services Ltd (LUCELEC): Sans Soucis, POB 230, Castries; tel. 457-4400; fax 457-4409; e-mail lucelec@candw.lc; internet www.lucelec.com; f. 1964; Canadian energy co Emera acquired a 19% share in LUCELEC in Jan. 2007; Chair. MARIUS ST ROSE; Man. Dir TREVOR LOUISY.

Water

Water and Sewerage Company (WASCO): L'Anse Rd, POB 1481, Castries; tel. 452-5344; fax 452-6844; e-mail wasco@candw.lc; f. 1999 as the Water and Sewerage Authority (WASA); planned privatization under review; Chair. GORDON CHARLES; Man. Dir JOHN C. JOSEPH.

TRADE UNIONS

National Workers' Union (NWU): Bour Bon St, POB 713, Castries; tel. 452-3664; fax 453-2896; e-mail natwork3@hotmail.com; f. 1973; represents daily-paid workers; affiliated to World Federation of Trade Unions; Pres.-Gen. TYRONE MAYNARD; Sec.-Gen. GEORGE GODDARD, Jr; 3,200 mems (2005).

Saint Lucia Civil Service Association: Sans Soucis, POB 244, Castries; tel. 452-3903; fax 453-6061; e-mail csa@candw.lc; internet www.csastlucia.org; f. 1951; Pres. MARY ISAAC; Gen. Sec. SIMONIA ALTINOR; 2,381 mems.

Saint Lucia Medical and Dental Association: POB 691, Castries; tel. 451-8441; fax 458-1147; e-mail slmdaoffice@gmail.com; internet www.slmda.org; f. 1969; Pres. Dr TANYA DESTANG-BEAUBRUN; Gen. Sec. Dr KIMBERLY JOHNNY.

Saint Lucia Nurses' Association: Victoria Hospital, Nurses' Home, 2nd Floor, POB 819, Castries; tel. 452-1403; fax 456-0121; e-mail slna1970@gmail.com; internet www.stlucianursesassociation.org; f. 1947; Pres. ALICIA BAPTISTE; Gen. Sec. LYDIA LEONCE.

Saint Lucia Seamen, Waterfront and General Workers' Trade Union: L'Anse Rd, POB 166, Castries; tel. 452-1669; fax 452-5452; e-mail seamen@candw.lc; f. 1945; affiliated to Int. Trade Union Confed., Int. Transport Fed. and Caribbean Congress of Labour; Pres. ESTHER ST MARIE (acting); Sec. CELICA ADOLPH; 1,000 mems.

Saint Lucia Teachers' Union: La Clery, POB 821, Castries; tel. 452-4469; fax 453-6668; e-mail sltu@candw.lc; f. 1934; Pres. JULIAN MONROSE; Gen. Sec. WAYNE CUMBERBATCH.

Saint Lucia Trade Union Federation: c/o Saint Lucia Teachers' Union, La Clery, POB 821, Castries; tel. 452-4469; fax 453-6668; e-mail cumbatch42@gmail.com; f. 2005; comprises nine trade unions of Saint Lucia, including the Saint Lucia Civil Service Asscn, Saint Lucia Teachers' Union, Saint Lucia Medical and Dental Asscn, Saint Lucia Nurses' Asscn, Saint Lucia Seamen and Waterfront General Workers' Union, National Farmers' Asscn, Police Welfare Asscn, Saint Lucia Fire Service Asscn and Vieux Fort General and Dock Workers' Union; Pres. JULIAN MONROSE; Gen. Sec. WAYNE CUMBERBATCH.

Saint Lucia Workers' Union: Reclamation Grounds, Conway, Castries; tel. 452-2620; f. 1939; affiliated to International Trade Union Confederation; Pres. GEORGE LOUIS; Sec. TITUS FRANCIS; 1,000 mems.

Vieux Fort General and Dock Workers' Union: New Dock Rd, POB 224, Vieux Fort; tel. 454-5128; e-mail dockworkersunion@hotmail.com; f. 1954; Pres. ATHANATIUS DOLOR; Gen. Sec. CLAUDIA AUGUSTE (acting); 846 mems (1996).

Transport

RAILWAYS

There are no railways in Saint Lucia.

ROADS

In 2000 there was an estimated total road network of 910 km, of which 150 km were main roads and 127 km were secondary roads. In that year only 5.2% of roads were paved. The main highway passes through every town and village on the island. The construction of a coastal highway, to link Castries with Cul de Sac Bay, was completed in 2000. Improvements to the road infrastructure outlined in the 2010/11 budget address included the 22 km West Coast Road Overlay

SAINT LUCIA

between Roseau and Soufriere and the rehabilitation of 60 small road and bridge projects around the island. The total allocation for the Ministry of Communications, Works, Transport and Public Utilities was EC $84.8m. in that financial year, of which $48.1m. was set aside for various road infrastructure projects.

SHIPPING

The ports at Castries and Vieux Fort have been fully mechanized. Castries has six berths with a total length of 2,470 ft (753 m). The two dolphin berths at the Pointe Seraphine cruise ship terminal have been upgraded to a solid berth of 1,000 ft (305 m) and one of 850 ft (259 m). The port of Soufrière has a deep-water anchorage, but no alongside berth for ocean-going vessels. There is a petroleum trans-shipment terminal at Cul de Sac Bay. In 2009 699,306 cruise ship passengers called at Saint Lucia. Regular services are provided by a number of shipping lines, including ferry services to neighbouring islands. In 2007 plans for substantial upgrade work to enhance facilities and operations at the marina at Rodney Bay were announced. There were also plans to develop the waterfront area at Castries in order for it to become a dedicated cruise ship port; the port at Vieux Fort was also to be expanded in order to handle all commercial cargo.

Saint Lucia Air and Sea Ports Authority (SLASPA): Manoel St, POB 651, Castries; tel. 452-2893; fax 452-2062; e-mail info@slaspa.com; internet www.slaspa.com; f. 1983; Chair. ISAAC ANTHONY; Gen. Man. SEAN MATTHEW; Dir of Airports PETER FERGUSON JEAN; Dir of Sea Ports ADRIAN HILAIRE (acting).

Saint Lucia Marine Terminals Ltd (SLMTL): POB VF 355, Vieux Fort; tel. 454-8738; fax 454-8745; e-mail info@slmtl.com; internet www.slmtl.com; f. 1995; wholly owned subsidiary of the Saint Lucia Air and Sea Ports Authority; private port management co; manages Port Vieux Fort; Chair MICHAEL CHITOLIE; Gen. Man. LENIUS LENDOR.

CIVIL AVIATION

There are two airports in use: Hewanorra International (formerly Beane Field near Vieux Fort), 64 km (40 miles) from Castries, which is equipped to handle large jet aircraft, and George F. L. Charles Airport, which is at Vigie, in Castries, and which is capable of handling medium-range jets. Saint Lucia is served by scheduled flights to the USA, Canada, Europe and most destinations in the Caribbean. The country is a shareholder in the regional airline LIAT (see chapter on Antigua and Barbuda).

Saint Lucia Air and Sea Ports Authority: see Shipping.

American Eagle Airlines: George F. L. Charles Airport, POB GM655, Castries; tel. 452-1820; fax 451-7941.

LIAT Airlines: Brazil St, POB 416, Castries; tel. 452-3051; fax 453-6563; e-mail slu@liatairline.com; internet www.liatairline.com; Country Dir MARIO REYES.

Tourism

Saint Lucia possesses spectacular mountain scenery, a tropical climate and sandy beaches. Historical sites, rich birdlife and the sulphur baths at Soufrière are other attractions. Visitor arrivals totalled 1,014,761 in 2009. Tourism receipts in that year were EC $799.7m. The USA is the principal market (35.4% of total stop-over visitors in 2009), followed by the United Kingdom (with 25.8%).

Saint Lucia Hotel and Tourism Association (SLHTA): John Compton Hwy, POB 545, Castries; tel. 452-5978; fax 452-7967; e-mail slhta@candw.lc; internet www.slhta.org; f. 1963; Pres. KAROLIN TROUBETZKOY; Exec. Gen. Man. SILVANIUS FONTENARD.

Saint Lucia Tourist Board: Sureline Bldg, Top Floor, Vide Bouteille, POB 221, Castries; tel. 452-4094; fax 453-1121; e-mail slutour@candw.lc; internet www.stlucia.org; f. 1981; 5 brs overseas; Chair. LAURIE BARNARD; Dir LOUIS LEWIS.

Defence

The Royal Saint Lucia Police Force, which numbers about 300 men, includes a Special Service Unit for purposes of defence. This Unit was increased to 100 men in 2006, with a further 60 cadets in training. Saint Lucia participates in the US-sponsored Regional Security System, comprising police, coastguards and army units, which was established by independent East Caribbean states in 1982. There are also two patrol vessels for coastguard duties. Some EC $69.0m. (equivalent to 9.9%) of total planned recurrent expenditure was allocated to the Ministry of Home Affairs and National Security in the 2007/08 budget.

Education

Education is compulsory for 10 years between five and 15 years of age. Primary education begins at the age of five and lasts for seven years. Secondary education, beginning at 12 years of age, lasts for five years, comprising a first cycle of three years and a second cycle of two years. Enrolment at primary schools in 2007/08 included 91% of children in the relevant age-group, while comparable enrolment in secondary level education, according to UNESCO estimates, included 80% of pupils in the relevant age category. Free education is provided in more than 90 government-assisted schools. Facilities for industrial, technical and teacher-training are available at the Sir Arthur Lewis Community College at Morne Fortune, which also houses an extra-mural branch of the University of the West Indies. The Community College was being upgraded to a university in time for the 2011/12 academic year. Some EC $127.2m. of government recurrent expenditure was allocated to the Ministry of Education and Culture in the 2007/08 budget (equivalent to 18.3% of total planned recurrent expenditure).

SAINT VINCENT AND THE GRENADINES

Introductory Survey

LOCATION, CLIMATE, LANGUAGE, RELIGION, FLAG, CAPITAL

Saint Vincent and the Grenadines is situated in the Windward Islands group, approximately 160 km (100 miles) west of Barbados, in the West Indies. The nearest neighbouring countries are Saint Lucia, some 34 km (21 miles) to the northeast, and Grenada, to the south. As well as the main volcanic island of Saint Vincent, the state includes the 32 smaller islands and cayes known as the Saint Vincent Grenadines, the northerly part of an island chain stretching between Saint Vincent and Grenada. The principal islands in that part of the group are Bequia, Canouan, Mustique, Mayreau, Isle D'Quatre and Union Island. The climate is tropical, with average temperatures of between 18°C and 32°C (64°F–90°F). Annual rainfall ranges from 1,500 mm (60 ins) in the extreme south, to 3,750 mm (150 ins) in the mountainous interior of the main island. English is the official language. Most of the inhabitants profess Christianity. The national flag (proportions 2 by 3) has three unequal vertical stripes, of blue (at the hoist), yellow and green (at the fly), with three lozenges in green, in a 'V' formation, superimposed on the broad central yellow stripe. The capital is Kingstown, on the island of Saint Vincent.

CONTEMPORARY POLITICAL HISTORY

Historical Context

The islands were first settled by an Arawak people, who were subsequently conquered by the Caribs. The arrival of shipwrecked and escaped African slaves resulted in the increase of a so-called 'Black Carib' population, some of whose descendants still remain. Under the collective name of Saint Vincent, and despite the opposition of the French and the indigenous population, the islands finally became a British possession during the 18th century. With other nearby British territories, the Governor of the Windward Islands administered Saint Vincent, under a federal system, until December 1959. The first elections under universal adult suffrage took place in 1951. The islands participated in the West Indies Federation from its foundation in January 1958 until its dissolution in May 1962. From January 1960, Saint Vincent, in common with the other Windward Islands, had a new Constitution, with its own Administrator and an enlarged Legislative Council.

Domestic Political Affairs

After the failure of negotiations to form a smaller East Caribbean Federation, most of the British colonies in the Leeward and Windward Islands became Associated States, with full internal self-government, in 1967. This change of status was delayed in Saint Vincent because of local political differences. At controversial elections to the Legislative Council in 1966, the ruling People's Political Party (PPP) was returned with a majority of only one seat. Further elections took place in May 1967, when the Saint Vincent Labour Party (SVLP) secured a majority in the Council. Milton Cato, leader of the SVLP, became Chief Minister. On 27 October 1969, despite objections from the PPP, Saint Vincent became an Associated State, with the United Kingdom retaining responsibility for defence and foreign relations only. The Legislative Council was renamed the House of Assembly, the Administrator was designated Governor, and the Chief Minister became Premier.

Elections were held in April 1972 for an enlarged, 13-seat House of Assembly. The PPP and the SVLP each obtained six seats, while James Mitchell, formerly a minister in the SVLP Government and standing as an independent, secured the remaining one. The PPP agreed to form a Government with Mitchell as Premier. In September 1974 a motion expressing no confidence in Mitchell's Government was approved, and the House was dissolved. In the ensuing election in December the SVLP secured a majority of seats. Cato became Premier again, at the head of a coalition with the PPP, and committed his Government to attaining full independence from the United Kingdom.

After a constitutional conference in September 1978, the colony became fully independent, within the Commonwealth, on 27 October 1979. The Governor became Governor-General, while Cato took office as the country's first Prime Minister.

Cato's position was reinforced in the general election of December 1979, when the SVLP obtained a majority of seats. In 1982 the leader of the opposition United People's Movement (UPM), Dr Ralph Gonsalves, resigned, accusing the UPM of harbouring Marxist tendencies, and founded a new party, the Movement for National Unity (MNU). In June 1984 Cato announced an early general election, hoping to take advantage of divisions within the opposition. However, scandals surrounding the Government, and the economic and taxation policies of the SVLP, contributed to an unexpected victory for the centrist New Democratic Party (NDP) at the election in July. The NDP leader, James Mitchell, became Prime Minister.

At a general election in May 1989 the NDP won all 15 elective seats in the newly enlarged House of Assembly. Mitchell remained as Prime Minister and formed a new Cabinet. The NDP secured its third consecutive term of office at a general election in February 1994. In September the MNU and the SVLP formally merged to form the Unity Labour Party (ULP).

Opposition charges that the Government had failed to address problems presented by a marked decline in banana production, a crisis in the health and education sectors and persistent allegations that drugs-related activities were being conducted on the islands culminated in the defeat of a motion of no confidence in the Government in August 1994. The execution, by hanging, of three convicted murderers in February 1995 provoked outrage from international human rights organizations, which expressed concern at the alacrity and secrecy with which the sentences had been implemented.

At a general election in June 1998 the NDP suffered a reverse, attributed to voter dissatisfaction with the state of the economy. Although the ULP had obtained around 55% of the vote, Mitchell claimed that the result was a mandate for his Government to undertake a record fourth term of office. The ULP leader, Vincent Beache, called on the NDP to hold fresh elections within nine months, and not to govern on the basis of a minority vote. The ULP also claimed to have obtained evidence of irregularities during the elections. In July, at the opening of the first session of the House of Assembly, several hundred protesters demonstrated against the new Government and two ministers were attacked.

In November 1998 members of the public and of the opposition demonstrated outside government offices to demand the resignation of Mitchell and Arnhim Eustace, the Minister of Finance and Public Services. The protests followed the announcement of the details of an agreement reached by the Government with the Government of Italy and a consortium of European financial institutions on the repayment of US $67m., incurred because the Government had guaranteed a loan of $50m. made to a company of Italian developers that subsequently went into liquidation. The loan had been made to finance the failed Ottley Hall marina and shipyard project, valued at only $5m. The new agreement stipulated that the shipyard should be sold and that repayments of $32m. of debt should begin immediately.

In late November 1998 marijuana growers demonstrated outside the Prime Minister's office against plans to use regional and US troops to destroy the marijuana crop in the highlands of Saint Vincent. Mitchell refused to meet representatives of the protesters, telling them to take advantage of government schemes to promote economic diversification. In December US marines and troops provided by the Regional Security System destroyed crops during a two-week operation, despite opposition from growers. Mitchell subsequently warned the USA that, if Saint Vincent's banana producers were bankrupted by the US initiative to challenge the preferential treatment accorded by the

SAINT VINCENT AND THE GRENADINES

European Union (EU, see p. 270) to banana exports from Caribbean and African states, it was likely that producers would turn instead to the cultivation of marijuana. In March 1999 Saint Vincent and the Grenadines was one of a number of Caribbean states to warn that, if the USA continued to threaten their economic stability by pursuing its case against the EU banana import regime at the World Trade Organization (see p. 430), they would withdraw co-operation with US-sponsored anti-drugs initiatives. (See the Saint Lucia chapter for further details of the trade dispute over bananas between the USA and the EU.) In December, nevertheless, a large-scale marijuana eradication exercise took place in Saint Vincent with backing from US marines.

In December 1999 a proposed increase in salaries of members of the House of Assembly was opposed by the ULP. The Government's subsequent introduction in April 2000 of legislation increasing the salaries and benefits of legislative members provoked protests throughout the islands. The ULP and public sector trade unions accused the Government of 'disregard and contempt' for ordinary workers. There were several days of public demonstrations at the end of April, culminating in a mass rally in Kingstown. In early May the Government and the workers reached an agreement, the Grand Beach accord, whereby fresh legislative elections were to be called before March 2001; the accord also allowed for a national dialogue on constitutional reform.

In October 2000 Arnhim Eustace succeeded Mitchell as Prime Minister, following the latter's retirement as head of government. Mitchell remained in the Cabinet as Senior Minister.

The ULP in power

The ULP secured an overwhelming victory in the general election of 28 March 2001, winning 12 of the 15 parliamentary seats. The NDP, which had been in power since 1984, secured the remaining three seats. The new Government took office in mid-April, led by Dr Ralph Gonsalves. In December 2002 Gonsalves established a 25-member Constitutional Review Commission, the first report of which was presented in March 2004. Among the issues to be addressed were local government organization and finance, civil service reform and the electoral system.

In March 2004 the opposition boycotted the House of Assembly and established an 'alternative parliament' at the NDP's headquarters; Eustace claimed that the parliamentary Speaker, Hendrick Alexander, had consistently demonstrated a pro-Government bias. The opposition again boycotted the House of Assembly and re-established its 'alternative parliament' in March 2005. On this occasion, the NDP was particularly unhappy about constituency boundaries and the registration of voters before the next elections, which were due by March 2006.

Despite the concerns of the opposition, Gonsalves' Government maintained its popularity; however, during its first term in office violent crime became an increasingly prominent issue and it was widely held that the Government had devoted insufficient funds to attempting to resolve the problem. Moreover, Saint Vincent remained one of the largest cultivators of marijuana in the region. In November 2004 Gonsalves, who had previously expressed severe reservations about capital punishment, claimed that the use of the death penalty was necessary to reduce the influence of criminal gangs in the country. The comments were made in the House of Assembly, during the passage of the Firearm Amendment Act, which was to introduce stricter penalties for illegal possession of weapons.

At legislative elections, held on 7 December 2005, the ULP again secured 12 of the 15 seats in the House of Assembly. The NDP secured the remaining three legislative seats. Registered votes were cast by 63.7% of the electorate. Monitoring teams from various international organizations described the contest as free and fair. Following his party's re-election, Gonsalves pledged to introduce constitutional reform after popular consultation via referendums. In addition, the Prime Minister announced his intention to ask the House of Assembly to approve legislation making the Caribbean Court of Justice (CCJ—which had been inaugurated in Trinidad and Tobago in April 2005) the country's senior court of appeal, in place of the Privy Council in the United Kingdom.

Prime Minister Gonsalves and his ULP Government suffered a significant threat in February 2007 when the NDP marshalled a demonstration in Kingstown demanding the removal of the premier from office and requisitioning a general election. Public and opposition unrest had escalated during the preceding months following increased public concerns over crime, despite the fact that the overall crime rate had declined during that year and that a sustained decline had been recorded from 2001. The early release of a convicted drugs offender caused particular disquiet. The NDP contested that Gonsalves' endorsement of the decision had severely compromised the Government's integrity and had undermined public confidence. Eustace further suggested that the increasing prevalence of drugs-related and violent crime in the country was directly attributable to Gonsalves' inadequate enforcement of penal law, and that the Government was implicated in the alleged engagement of drugs magnates in the financing of political campaigns.

Tensions between the Government and opposition parties intensified during 2007 and early 2008. An inquiry into the failed Ottley Hall marina and shipyard development project, begun in 2003, remained stalled; the losses incurred under the scheme, according to some reports, accounted for more than one-quarter of Saint Vincent's total external debt. The NDP attempted to increase its popularity by challenging government plans to introduce a value added tax, and in January 2008 it accused Gonsalves of misleading teachers in a 'reclassification' exercise of the public sector pay structure. In the same month more than 1,000 teachers went on strike in protest at the changes, supported by the Saint Vincent and the Grenadines Teachers' Union.

A referendum on adopting a new constitution was held on 25 November 2009. The proposed new constitution would increase autonomy in the country, replacing the Queen as Head of State with an indirectly elected president, introducing electoral reform, and superceding the Privy Council as the country's final appellate body with the Trinidad-based CCJ. This last proposal, argued Gonsalves, would allow Saint Vincent greater power in carrying out death sentences without what he regarded as undue interference from the London-based appeal court. Although the opposition NDP supported Saint Vincent becoming a republic, the party campaigned against the new bill of rights, claiming that it did not reduce enough the powers of the Prime Minister, and that the House of Assembly, rather than the public, would be given more influence. Some 43.7% of voters were in favour of the Government's proposals, far short of the two-thirds' majority necessary, while 56.3% voted against them. The NDP claimed the result was an indication of voters' dissatisfaction with the ruling ULP.

Recent developments: the 2010 election

The ULP secured a narrow victory at the general election held on 13 December 2010, attracting 51.1% of the valid votes cast. Although the party secured a third term in office, the ULP's number of parliamentary seats fell to eight (from 12). The NDP gained 48.7% of the votes and the remaining seven legislative seats (up from three). Turn-out was 62.3%. Observers from the Organization of American States declared the election free and fair, although Eustace claimed that there had been extensive voting irregularities. After being sworn in as Prime Minister on 15 December, Gonsalves effected a cabinet reorganization. Most notably, Girlyn Miguel became Deputy Prime Minister, while retaining responsibility for education, and Douglas Slater was appointed as Minister of Foreign Affairs, Foreign Trade, and Consumer Affairs.

Gonsalves announced in January 2010 that police had foiled an alleged plot by 'two major drugs-trafficking and money-laundering entities' to assassinate him. Gonsalves claimed that these criminal organizations targeted him because of his uncompromising stance on the illegal drugs trade. He also made vague intimations that the NDP might have been involved in the alleged conspiracy, a charge vehemently denied by Eustace.

Foreign Affairs
Regional relations

There was some public unease over Saint Vincent and the Grenadines' burgeoning economic relations with Venezuela. Specific protest was made against a memorandum of understanding, signed by Gonsalves in February 2007, subscribing to the principles of President Hugo Chávez's Bolivarian Alternative for the Americas (Alternativa Bolivariana para las Américas—ALBA), an economic integration initiative to rival the stagnant Free Trade Areas of the Americas proposed by the USA. Eustace cautioned that the accord conspicuously aligned the country with Venezuela at the possible expense of its diplomatic relationship with the USA. Gonsalves maintained that relations with these respective nations were not mutually exclusive and emphasized the importance of Venezuela's influence

SAINT VINCENT AND THE GRENADINES

upon the progress of national development, citing the benefits of the recently implemented PetroCaribe initiative (under which the country could purchase petroleum from Venezuela at discounted prices) and the Venezuelan Government's contribution to the construction of an international airport. In April 2009 Saint Vincent and the Grenadines was accepted as a member of ALBA; Eustace criticized the Government's failure to explain to the public what membership of the bloc would involve.

In 1992 the islands established diplomatic relations with Cuba. The two countries signed accords pledging further co-operation in a number of areas, including health and education, in 2001 and 2002.

Other external relations

In 2001 Libya granted the islands, in common with other eastern Caribbean countries, access to a US $2,000m. development fund. It was also reported that Libya had agreed to provide Saint Vincent and the Grenadines with a grant of $4.5m. (including an immediate disbursement of $1.5m.), following Gonsalves' controversial visit to the Libyan capital, Tripoli, earlier in the month. In February 2011, with international outrage growing at the deadly suppression of anti-Government protests in Libya, the opposition NDP condemned as 'blood money' US $250,000 of aid provided by the Libyan authorities in the aftermath of Hurricane Tomas, which had caused extensive damage to the islands in October 2010. Gonsalves attempted to justify his Government's acceptance of the funds by arguing that the financing had been arranged prior to the outbreak of violence in Libya.

Further controversy arose in 2001 after Japan pledged to provide $6m. for the construction of a fish market. It was claimed that, in return for Japanese financial aid, Saint Vincent and the Grenadines would support the pro-whaling bloc at meetings of the International Whaling Commission (IWC); Gonsalves refuted the allegation. However, the controversy re-emerged at the IWC meeting in June 2006 when Saint Vincent and the Grenadines endorsed Japan's proposal to end a 20-year moratorium on commercial whaling, invoking the vehement criticism of prominent international trading partners and creating a potential threat to the region's crucial tourism industry. Moreover, the subsequent announcement of a new EC $33m. fisheries complex to be financed by the Japanese Government provoked allegations of diplomacy motivated by economic incentive.

Taiwan and Saint Vincent and the Grenadines celebrated 25 years of diplomatic relations in 2006; in the same year the Taiwanese Government announced the donation of US $15m. and extension of a $10m. loan towards the construction of an international airport on the islands, while reiterating its commitment to assisting in Saint Vincent's infrastructural and human resource development. Following a visit to the Taiwanese capital, Taipei, in mid-2008, Gonsalves announced that the Taiwanese Government had agreed to increase funding for development projects in Saint Vincent and the Grenadines.

It was announced in August 2008 that Saint Vincent and the Grenadines was to establish diplomatic relations with Iran, with Iran providing US $7m. in development loans and grants for the airport construction project. The US Ambassador to the Eastern Caribbean expressed concern at the decision at a time when there were US anxieties at Iran's nuclear activities.

CONSTITUTION AND GOVERNMENT

The Consitution came into force at independence, in October 1979. Saint Vincent and the Grenadines is a constitutional monarchy. Executive power is vested in the British monarch, as Head of State, and is exercisable by the Governor-General, who represents the British monarch locally and who is appointed on the advice of the Prime Minister. Legislative power is vested in Parliament, comprising the Governor-General and the House of Assembly (composed of 21 members: six nominated Senators and 15 Representatives (17 from 2010), elected for up to five years by universal adult suffrage). Senators are appointed by the Governor-General: four on the advice of the Prime Minister and two on the advice of the Leader of the Opposition. Government is effectively by the Cabinet. The Governor-General appoints the Prime Minister and, on the latter's recommendation, selects the other Ministers. The Prime Minister must be able to command the support of the majority of the House, to which the Cabinet is responsible. Judicial power is invested in the Eastern Caribbean Supreme Court, based in Saint Lucia. The country's final appellate body is the Privy Council, based in the United Kingdom.

REGIONAL AND INTERNATIONAL CO-OPERATION

Saint Vincent and the Grenadines is a member of the Caribbean Community and Common Market (CARICOM, see p. 219) and of the Organisation of Eastern Caribbean States (OECS, see p. 462). On 18 June 2010 Saint Vincent and the Grenadines was a signatory to the Revised Treaty of Basseterre, establishing an Economic Union among OECS member states. The Economic Union, which involved the removal of barriers to trade and the movement of labour as a step towards a single financial and economic market, came into effect on 21 January 2011. Saint Vincent and the Grenadines implemented CARICOM's intra-regional common passport initiative, regarded as an integral component in the advance towards economic union, in April 2006. Saint Vincent and the Grenadines, together with five other Caribbean states, became a signatory to CARICOM's Caribbean Single Market and Economy (CSME) in July, which had been established by six founding member states on 1 January of that year. The CSME was intended to enshrine the free movement of goods, services and labour throughout the CARICOM region. Two phases of implementation were to ensue: the first would be consolidation of the single market and initiation of the single economy by 1 January 2009; while the second phase, spanning 2010–15, would define and institute the single economy and regional monetary union.

Saint Vincent and the Grenadines became a member of the UN in 1980, shortly after independence. As a contracting party to the General Agreement on Tariffs and Trade, Saint Vincent and the Grenadines joined the World Trade Organization (see p. 430) on its establishment in 1995. Upon independence, Saint Vincent became a full member of the Commonwealth (see p. 230). The country is a signatory of the Cotonou Agreement (see p. 327), the successor agreement to the Lomé Convention. In February 2003 Saint Vincent and the Grenadines was admitted to the Non-Aligned Movement (see p. 461).

ECONOMIC AFFAIRS

In 2009, according to estimates by the World Bank, Saint Vincent and the Grenadines' gross national income (GNI), measured at average 2007–09 prices, was US $558m., equivalent to $5,110 per head (or $8,840 per head on an international purchasing-power parity basis). During 2000–09, it was estimated, the population increased at an average annual rate of 0.1%, while gross domestic product (GDP) per head increased, in real terms, by an average of 4.3% per year. Overall GDP increased, in real terms, at an average annual rate of 4.9% in 2001–08; according to the Eastern Caribbean Central Bank (ECCB, see p. 451), real GDP increased by 1.1% in 2008.

Agriculture (including forestry and fishing) contributed 6.8% of GDP in 2008. The sector employed an estimated 20.4% of the working population in 2009, according to FAO, and agricultural products account for the largest share of export revenue. Despite the decline in the sector, the principal cash crop is still bananas, which contributed an estimated 15.9% of the value of total exports in 2008. Other important crops are arrowroot, sweet potatoes, tannias, taro, plantains and coconuts. According to the ECCB, during 2001–08 real agricultural GDP increased at an annual average rate of 1.2%. Sectoral GDP declined by 6.5% in 2008.

Industry (including mining, manufacturing, electricity, water and construction) employed 21.1% of the working population in 1991, and contributed 23.5% of GDP in 2008. During 2001–08 real industrial GDP increased at an average annual rate of 4.1%, according to the ECCB; the sector's GDP declined by 1.7% in 2008.

The manufacturing sector contributed 3.9% of GDP in 2008, and engaged 8.5% of the employed labour force in 1991. Apart from a garment industry and the assembling of electrical components, the most important activities involve the processing of agricultural products, including flour- and rice-milling, brewing, rum distillation, and processing dairy products. During 2001–08 real manufacturing GDP decreased by an average annual rate of 1.0%, according to ECCB figures. The sector's GDP declined by 9.7% in 2008.

Construction employed 10.6% of the working population in 1991, and contributed 14.3% of GDP in 2008. During 2001–08 construction GDP increased at an average annual rate of 6.6%, according to the ECCB; the sector's GDP expanded by 1.4% in 2008.

Energy is derived principally from the use of hydrocarbon fuels (mineral fuels and lubricants accounted for around 18.1% of total imports in 2009). The islands imported most of their energy

SAINT VINCENT AND THE GRENADINES

requirements. There is, however, an important hydroelectric plant in Cumberland. In 2005 the Government became one of 13 Caribbean administrations to sign the PetroCaribe accord, under which the country would be allowed to purchase petroleum from Venezuela at reduced prices.

The services sector contributed an estimated 69.7% of GDP in 2008 and engaged 53.8% of the employed population at the time of the 1991 census. Tourism is the most important activity within the sector, but is smaller in scale than in most other Caribbean islands. Although total arrivals increased in 2009 by 14.9%, this was primarily owing to a 40% growth in the number of cruise ship passengers, traditionally a less lucrative sector than stop-over visitors (totals for which fell by 13.6%). Tourism generated EC $236m. in revenue in 2009, compared with $259m. in the previous year. Aside from tourism, a small 'offshore' financial sector also contributes to the services sector. Following its inclusion, in 2009, on the Organisation for Economic Co-operation and Development's (OECD) so-called 'grey list' of territories that had yet substantially to implement reform of the sector, the country made significant efforts to reach international standards, signing 16 tax information sharing agreements with other jurisdictions. As a result, in March 2010 OECD declared itself satisfied with the measures Saint Vincent had effected. During 2001–08 the real GDP of the services sector as a whole increased by an average annual rate of 5.0%, according to the ECCB; there was a negligible decline in the sector in 2008.

In 2010 Saint Vincent and the Grenadines recorded an estimated visible trade deficit of EC $708.71m., while there was a deficit of $575.89m. on the current account of the balance of payments. The principal source of imports is the USA (accounting for an estimated 35.0% of the total in 2009). Other important suppliers in that year were Trinidad and Tobago and the United Kingdom. Trinidad and Tobago is the principal market for exports (accounting for an estimated 20.5% of total exports in 2009). Other important markets in that year were Saint Lucia, Barbados, the United Kingdom, and the USA. The principal exports in 2009 were vegetables and fruits (46.8%), while the principal imports were food and live animals (19.4%), followed by machinery and transport equipment, and mineral fuels and lubricants.

In 2008 there was an estimated overall budget deficit of EC $11.8m., equivalent to 0.8% of GDP. Saint Vincent and the Grenadines' general government gross debt was EC $1,156m. in 2009, equivalent to 75.0% of GDP. Saint Vincent and the Grenadines' total external debt was US $207m. at the end of 2008, of which US $206m. was public and publicly guaranteed debt. The cost of debt-servicing was equivalent to 10.3% of the value of exports of goods, services and income in 2007. The average annual rate of inflation was 4.2% in 2003–09, and consumer prices decreased by an average of 1.6% in 2009, but increased by 1.0% in 2010. At the 1991 census 20.0% of the labour force were unemployed. In 2002 the IMF estimated that the rate of unemployment remained at a similar level.

Two of Saint Vincent and the Grenadines' most important economic sectors—bananas and tourism—suffered reverses in the late 2000s. The banana sector had been declining from the 1990s and, more recently, the erosion of the islands' preferential access to European markets, together with lower prices and poor climatic conditions proved disastrous for the sector. The increasingly important tourism sector was affected by the global economic downturn from 2008. Expansion of this sector had been inhibited by the absence of an international airport, but construction of such a facility at Argyle began in mid-2008, partially financed by the Governments of Venezuela, Cuba and Taiwan. It was hoped that the new facility would increase overall capacity and attract a greater number of stop-over arrivals, a more lucrative market than cruise ship passengers. The airport was scheduled for completion in 2013. Activity in the tourism and construction sectors remained sluggish in 2010, while agricultural output was undermined by drought and disease. The agricultural sector was also severely affected by Hurricane Tomas, which completely destroyed the banana crop along with most of the country's other crops in late October 2010. The Government put the cost of damage to the sector at some US $25m. With extensive devastation to infrastructure and housing also reported, reconstruction spending placed added pressure on the already strained fiscal account. To support the country's reconstruction programme, the World Bank approved a $5m. credit in January 2011 and the IMF released $3.3m. in the following month. The IMF projected modest economic expansion of 0.5% and 2.0% in 2010 and 2011, respectively.

PUBLIC HOLIDAYS

2012: 1 January (New Year's Day), 14 March (National Heroes' Day), 6 April (Good Friday), 9 April (Easter Monday), 1 May (Labour Day), 27 May (Whit Monday), 2 July (CARICOM Day), 3 July (Carnival Tuesday), 1 August (Emancipation Day), 27 October (Independence Day), 25–26 December (Christmas).

Statistical Survey

Source (unless otherwise stated): Statistical Office, Ministry of Finance and Economic Planning, Administrative Centre, Bay St, Kingstown; tel. 456-1111; e-mail statssvg@vincysurf.com.

AREA AND POPULATION

Area: 389.3 sq km (150.3 sq miles). The island of Saint Vincent covers 344 sq km (133 sq miles).

Population: 97,914 at census of 12 May 1980; 106,499 (males 53,165, females 53,334) at census of 12 May 1991; 109,202 at preliminary census count of May 2001. *Mid-2011* (UN estimate): 109,339. Source: UN, *World Population Prospects: The 2008 Revision*.

Density (at mid-2011): 317.8 per sq km.

Population by Age and Sex (UN estimates at mid-2011): *0–14:* 28,595 (males 14,437, females 14,158); *15–64:* 73,435 (males 37,432, females 36,003); *65 and over:* 7,309 (males 3,323, females 3,986); *Total* 109,339 (males 55,192, females 54,147) (Source: UN, *World Population Prospects: The 2008 Revision*).

Principal Town: Kingstown (capital) population 13,526 at preliminary census count of May 2001. *Mid-2009* (population incl. suburbs, UN estimate): Kingstown 28,199. Source: UN, *World Urbanization Prospects: The 2009 Revision*.

Births, Marriages and Deaths (registrations, 2005): Live births 1,779 (birth rate 17.1 per 1,000); Marriages 576 (marriage rate 5.6 per 1,000); Deaths 813 (death rate 7.8 per 1,000). Source: UN, *Demographic Yearbook*.

Life Expectancy (years at birth, WHO estimates): 71 (males 66; females 76) in 2008. Source: WHO, *World Health Statistics*.

Economically Active Population (persons aged 15 years and over, 1991 census): Agriculture, hunting, forestry and fishing 8,377; Mining and quarrying 98; Manufacturing 2,822; Electricity, gas and water 586; Construction 3,535; Trade, restaurants and hotels 6,544; Transport, storage and communications 2,279; Financing, insurance, real estate and business services 1,418; Community, social and personal services 7,696; *Total employed* 33,355 (males 21,656, females 11,699); Unemployed 8,327 (males 5,078, females 3,249); *Total labour force* 41,682 (males 26,734, females 14,948). Source: ILO, *Yearbook of Labour Statistics*.

HEALTH AND WELFARE

Key Indicators

Total Fertility Rate (children per woman, 2010): 1.9.

Under-5 Mortality Rate (per 1,000 live births, 2010): 25.

Physicians (per 1,000 head, 2009): 0.6.

Hospital Beds (per 1,000 head, 2007): 3.0.

Health Expenditure (2007): US $ per head (PPP): 474.

Health Expenditure (2007): % of GDP: 5.4.

Health Expenditure (2007): public (% of total): 61.3.

Access to Water (% of persons, 2000): 93.

Access to Sanitation (% of persons, 2000): 96.

Total Carbon Dioxide Emissions ('000 metric tons, 2007): 201.5.

Carbon Dioxide Emissions Per Head (metric tons, 2007): 1.8.

Human Development Index (2007): ranking: 91.

SAINT VINCENT AND THE GRENADINES

Human Development Index (2007): value: 0.772.

Source: partly Pan American Health Organization; for other sources and definitions, see explanatory note on p. vi.

AGRICULTURE, ETC.

Principal Crops ('000 metric tons, 2008, FAO estimates): Maize 0.7; Cassava 0.8; Sweet potatoes 2.3; Yams 2.3; Sugar cane 20.0; Coconuts 4.7; Bananas 51.0; Plaintains 2.5; Oranges 1.7; Lemons and limes 1.3; Apples 1.3; Mangoes 1.6. Note: No data were available for individual crops in 2009. *Aggregate Production* ('000 metric tons, 2009, may include official, semi-official or estimated data): Roots and tubers 17.0; Vegetables (incl. melons) 4.9; Fruits (excl. melons) 60.2.

Livestock ('000 head, year ending September 2008, FAO estimates): Cattle 5.1; Sheep 13.0; Goats 7.3; Pigs 9.2; Chickens 230. No data were available for 2009.

Livestock Products ('000 metric tons, 2009, unless otherwise indicated, FAO estimates): Pig meat 0.6; Chicken meat 0.5; Cows' milk 13.0; Hen eggs 0.7 (2008).

Fishing (capture production, metric tons, live weight, 2008): Albacore 201; Skipjack tuna 83; Wahoo 24; Yellowfin tuna 2,547; Other tuna-like fishes 124; Other marine fishes 600; *Total catch* (incl. others) 3,828.

Source: FAO.

INDUSTRY

Selected Products ('000 metric tons, 2005 unless otherwise stated): Copra 2 (FAO estimate); Raw sugar 1.6 (2002); Rum 9,000 hectolitres (2003); Electric energy 143.3 million kWh (2009). Sources: FAO, Eastern Caribbean Central Bank and UN Industrial Commodity Statistics Database.

FINANCE

Currency and Exchange Rates: 100 cents = 1 Eastern Caribbean dollar (EC $). *Sterling, US Dollar and Euro Equivalents* (31 December 2010): £1 sterling = EC $4.227; US $1 = EC $2.700; €1 = EC $3.608; EC $100 = £23.66 = US $37.04 = €27.72. *Exchange Rate:* Fixed at US $1 = EC $2.70 since July 1976.

Budget (EC $ million, 2008): *Revenue:* Revenue from taxation 448.0 (Taxes on income 110.4, Taxes on goods and services 245.8, Taxes on property 2.2, Taxes on international trade and transactions 89.5); Other current revenue 41.6; Capital revenue 15.7; Foreign grants 45.2; Total 550.5. *Expenditure:* Current expenditure 431.3 (Personal emoluments 206.8, Other goods and services 91.0, Interest payments 46.8, Transfers and subsidies 86.7); Capital expenditure and net lending 131.0; Total 562.3. *2009* (EC $ million, provisional figures): Total revenue 522.5; Total expenditure 571.5. Source: Eastern Caribbean Central Bank.

International Reserves (US $ million at 31 December 2010): IMF special drawing rights 1.14; Reserve position in IMF 0.77; Foreign exchange 110.79; Total 112.70. Source: IMF, *International Financial Statistics*.

Money Supply (EC $ million at 31 December 2010): Currency outside depository corporations 50.61; Transferable deposits 369.45; Other deposits 811.88; *Broad money* 1,231.94. Source: IMF, *International Financial Statistics*.

Cost of Living (Consumer Price Index; base: 2005 = 100): All items 123.4 in 2008; 121.4 in 2009; 122.6 in 2010. Source: IMF, *International Financial Statistics*.

Gross Domestic Product (EC $ million at constant 1990 prices): 1,028.51 in 2007; 1,040.03 in 2008. Source: Eastern Caribbean Central Bank.

Expenditure on the Gross Domestic Product (EC $ million at current prices, 2008): Government final consumption expenditure 300.91; Private final consumption expenditure 1,346.95; Gross capital formation 555.35; *Total domestic expenditure* 2,203.21; Exports of goods and services 552.74; *Less* Imports of goods and services 1,185.3; *GDP at market prices* 1,570.65. Source: Eastern Caribbean Central Bank.

Gross Domestic Product by Economic Activity (EC $ million at current prices, 2008): Agriculture, hunting, forestry and fishing 91.31; Mining and quarrying 3.09; Manufacturing 52.49; Electricity and water 69.42; Construction 192.70; Wholesale and retail trade 256.18; Restaurants and hotels 24.21; Transport 159.43; Communications 72.94; Banking and insurance 127.51; Real estate and housing 24.12; Government services 251.48; Other services 26.86; *Subtotal* 1,351.74; *Less* Financial intermediation services indirectly measured 109.59; *Total in basic prices* 1,242.15; Taxes, less subsidies, on products 328.50; *GDP at market prices* 1,570.65. Source: Eastern Caribbean Central Bank.

Balance of Payments (EC $ million, 2010): Exports of goods 105.90; Imports of goods –814.62; *Trade balance* –708.71; Services (net) 131.86; *Balance on goods and services* –576.85 Other income received (net) –31.73; *Balance on goods, services and income* –608.58; Current transfers (net) 32.69; *Current balance* –575.89; Capital account (net) 142.45; Direct investment (net) 247.97; Portfolio investment (net) 1.75; Other investment (net) 154.27; Net errors and omissions 1.47; *Overall balance* –27.99. Source: Eastern Caribbean Central Bank.

EXTERNAL TRADE

Principal Commodities (US $ million, 2009): *Imports c.i.f.:* Food and live animals 64.8; Beverages and tobacco 11.6; Crude materials 10.3; Mineral fuels, lubricants, etc. 60.5; Chemicals and related products 27.3; Basic manufactures 60.9; Machinery and transport equipment 61.4; Total (incl. others) 333.5. *Exports f.o.b.:* Food and live animals 29.3 (Rice 4.3, Vegetables and fruit 13.7); Beverages and tobacco 3.0; Basic manufactures 5.3 (Iron and steel 1.9); Machinery and transport equipment 8.4; Miscellaneous manufactured articles 1.8; Total (incl. others) 49.1. Source: UN, *International Trade Statistics Yearbook*.

Principal Trading Partners (US $ million, 2009): *Imports c.i.f.:* Barbados 11.1; Brazil 3.8; Canada 6.8; China, People's Rep. 9.9; France (incl. Monaco) 3.3; Germany 2.5; Guyana 3.1; Italy 7.5; Japan 9.0; Trinidad and Tobago 85.5; United Kingdom 21.1; USA 116.7; Total (incl. others) 333.5. *Exports f.o.b.:* Antigua and Barbuda 3.9; Barbados 4.7; Dominica 2.1; Jamaica 0.7; Saint Lucia 9.1; Trinidad and Tobago 10.1; United Kingdom 3.7; USA 2.9; Total (incl. others) 49.1. Source: UN, *International Trade Statistics Yearbook*.

TRANSPORT

Road Traffic (motor vehicles in use, 2008): Private cars 9,247; Buses and coaches 122; Lorries and vans 12,897; Motorcycles 1,217. Source: International Road Federation, *World Road Statistics*.

Shipping: *Arrivals* (2000): Vessels 1,007. *International Sea-borne Freight Traffic* ('000 metric tons, 2000): Goods loaded 54; Goods unloaded 156. *Merchant Fleet* (vessels registered at 31 December 2009): Number 1,043; Total displacement 5,152,120 grt (Source: IHS Fairplay, *World Fleet Statistics*).

Civil Aviation (visitor arrivals): 99,657 in 2004; 104,432 in 2005; 106,466 in 2006 (estimate). Source: IMF, *St Vincent and the Grenadines: Statistical Appendix* (April 2009).

TOURISM

Visitor Arrivals: 283,161 (89,532 stop-over visitors, 6,797 excursionists, 42,277 yacht passengers, 144,555 cruise ship passengers) in 2007; 249,868 (84,101 stop-over visitors, 5,781 excursionists, 43,277 yacht passengers, 116,709 cruise ship passengers) in 2008; 287,118 (72,632 stop-over visitors, 7,137 excursionists, 44,009 yacht passengers, 163,340 cruise ship passengers) in 2009. *Stop-over Visitors by Country* (2009): Canada 6,810; Caribbean 25,358; United Kingdom 13,087; USA 19,069; Other 8,308.

Tourism Receipts (EC $ million): 297.0 in 2007; 259.3 in 2008; 236.4 in 2009.

Source: Eastern Caribbean Central Bank.

COMMUNICATIONS MEDIA

Radio Receivers ('000 in use, 2000): 100.

Television Receivers ('000 in use, 2000): 50.

Telephones ('000 main lines in use, 2009): 23.0.

Mobile Cellular Telephones (subscribers, 2009): 121,100.

Personal Computers: 16,500 (151.8 per 1,000 persons) in 2005.

Internet Users ('000, 2009): 76.

Broadband Subscribers ('000, 2009): 11.5.

Daily Newspapers (2005): Titles 3.

Non-daily Newspapers (2000): Titles 8; Circulation 50,000.

Sources: mainly UNESCO, *Statistical Yearbook*; UN, *Statistical Yearbook*; and International Telecommunication Union.

EDUCATION

Pre-primary (2008/09 unless otherwise indicated): 97 schools (1993/94); 378 teachers; 2,925 pupils.

Primary (2008/09 unless otherwise indicated): 60 schools (2000); 879 teachers; 14,909 pupils.

Secondary (2008/09 unless otherwise indicated): 21 schools (2000); 886 teachers; 11,425 pupils.

Teacher Training (2000): 1 institution; 10 teachers; 107 students.
Technical College (2000): 1 institution; 19 teachers; 187 students.
Community College (2000): 1 institution; 13 teachers; 550 students.
Nursing College (2000): 1 institution; 6 teachers; 60 students.

Pupil-teacher Ratio (primary education, UNESCO estimate): 17.0 in 2008/09.

Sources: partly Caribbean Development Bank, *Social and Economic Indicators*, and UNESCO Institute for Statistics.

Adult Literacy Rate: 88.1% in 2004. Source: UN Development Programme, *Human Development Report*.

Directory

The Government

HEAD OF STATE

Queen: HM Queen ELIZABETH II.
Governor-General: Sir FREDERICK NATHANIEL BALLANTYNE (took office 2 September 2002).

CABINET
(May 2011)

The Government was formed by the Unity Labour Party.

Prime Minister and Minister of Finance, National Security, Grenadines Affairs and Legal Affairs: Dr RALPH E. GONSALVES.
Deputy Prime Minister and Minister of Education: GIRLYN MIGUEL.
Minister of Foreign Affairs, Foreign Trade and Consumer Affairs: DOUGLAS SLATER.
Minister of Housing, Informal Human Settlements, Physical Planning, and Lands and Surveys: CLAYTON BURGIN.
Minister of Agriculture, Forestry, Fisheries and Rural Transformation: MONTGOMERY DANIEL.
Minister of Tourism and Industry: SABOTO CEASAR.
Minister of National Reconciliation, Public Service, Information, Labour and Ecclesiastical Affairs: MAXWELL CHARLES.
Minister of Health, Wellness and the Environment: CECIL MCKEE.
Minister of Transport, Works, Urban Development and Local Government: JULIAN FRANCIS.
Minister of National Mobilization, Social Development, the Family, Persons with Disabilities, Gender Affairs, Youth, Sports and Culture: FREDERICK STEPHENSON.
Attorney-General: JUDITH S. JONES-MORGAN.

MINISTRIES

Office of the Governor-General: Government House, Kingstown; tel. 456-1401; fax 457-9701.
Office of the Prime Minister: Administrative Bldg, 4th Floor, Bay St, Kingstown; tel. 456-1703; fax 457-2152; e-mail pmo.svg@caribsurf.com.
Office of the Attorney-General and Ministry of Legal Affairs: New Methodist Church Bldg, 3rd Floor, Granby St, Kingstown; tel. 456-1762; fax 457-2848; e-mail att.gen.chambers@caribsurf.com.
Ministry of Agriculture, Forestry, Fisheries and Rural Transformation: Richmond Hill, Kingstown; tel. 456-1410; fax 457-1688; e-mail office.agriculture@mail.gov.vc; internet www.agriculture.gov.vc.
Ministry of Education: Halifax St, Kingstown; tel. 457-1104; fax 457-1114; e-mail office.education@mail.gov.vc; internet www.education.gov.vc.
Ministry of Finance and Economic Planning: Halifax St, Kingstown; tel. 456-1111; fax 457-2943.
Ministry of Foreign Affairs, Foreign Trade and Consumer Affairs: Administrative Bldg, 3rd Floor, Bay St, Kingstown; tel. 456-2060; fax 456-2610; e-mail office.foreignaffairs@mail.gov.vc; internet www.foreign.gov.vc.
Ministry of Health, Wellness and the Environment: Ministerial Bldg, 1st Floor, Bay St, Kingstown; tel. 456-1111; fax 457-2684; e-mail office.health@mail.gov.vc; internet www.health.gov.vc.
Ministry of Housing, Informal Human Settlements, Physical Planning, and Lands and Surveys: Methodist Church Bldg, Granby St, Kingstown; tel. 456-2050; e-mail minister.housing@mail.gov.vc; internet www.housing.gov.vc.
Ministry of National Mobilization, Social Development, the Family, Persons with Disabilities, Gender Affairs, Youth, Sports and Culture: Halifax St, Kingstown; tel. 450-0395; fax 457-2476; e-mail mohesvg@vincysurf.com.
Ministry of National Reconciliation, Public Service, Information, Labour and Ecclesiastical Affairs: Ministerial Bldg, 2nd Floor, Halifax St, Kingstown; tel. 451-2707; fax 451-2820; e-mail natrecon@gov.vc; internet www.reconciliation.gov.vc.
Ministry of National Security: Ministerial Bldg, 3rd Floor, Halifax St, Kingstown; tel. 451-2707; fax 451-2820; e-mail office.natsec@mail.gov.vc.
Ministry of Tourism and Industry: NIS Bldg, 2nd Floor, Upper Bay St, POB 834, Kingstown; tel. 456-6222; fax 451-2425; e-mail office.tourism@mail.gov.vc; internet www.tourism.gov.vc.
Ministry of Transport, Works, Urban Development and Local Government: Halifax St, Kingstown; tel. 457-2039; fax 456-2168; e-mail office.transport@mail.gov.vc; internet www.transport.gov.vc.

Legislature

HOUSE OF ASSEMBLY

Senators: 6.
Elected Members: 15.
Speaker: HENDRICK ALEXANDER.
Clerk: NICOLE HERBERT, House of Assembly, Court House, Halifax St, Kingstown; tel. 457-1872; fax 457-1825; internet www.assembly.gov.vc.

Election, 13 December 2010

Party	Valid votes	% of votes	Seats
Unity Labour Party	32,099	51.11	8
New Democratic Party	30,568	48.67	7
Saint Vincent and the Grenadines Green Party	138	0.22	—
Total	62,805	100.00	15

Election Commission

Electoral Office: Glenville St, Kingstown; tel. 457-1762; fax 485-6844; e-mail electoraloffice@gov.vc; Supervisor of Elections SYLVIA FINDLAY SCRUBB.

Political Organizations

New Democratic Party (NDP): Democrat House, Murray Rd, POB 1300, Kingstown; tel. 451-2845; fax 457-2647; e-mail ndp@caribsurf.com; f. 1975; democratic party supporting political unity in the Caribbean, social devt and free enterprise; Chair. LINTON LEWIS; Leader ARNHIM ULRIC EUSTACE; Gen. Sec. DANIEL E. CUMMINGS; 7,000 mems.

Saint Vincent and the Grenadines Green Party: POB 1707, Kingstown; tel. and fax 456-9579; e-mail mail@svggreenparty.org; internet www.svggreenparty.org; f. 2005; Leader IVAN O'NEAL; Gen. Sec. ORDAN O. GRAHAM.

Unity Labour Party (ULP): Tennis Court Cnr, Murrays Rd, POB 1651, Kingstown; tel. 457-2761; fax 457-1292; e-mail info@voteulp.com; internet voteulp.com; f. 1994 by merger of Movement for National Unity and the Saint Vincent Labour Party; moderate, social-democratic party; Chair. EDWIN SNAGG; Political Leader Dr RALPH E. GONSALVES; Gen. Sec. JULIAN FRANCIS.

SAINT VINCENT AND THE GRENADINES

Diplomatic Representation

EMBASSIES IN SAINT VINCENT AND THE GRENADINES

Brazil: Hotel-Beaccombers, Kingstown; tel. and fax 457-4021; Ambassador RENATO XAVIER.
Cuba: Ratho Mill, Kingstown; tel. 458-5844; fax 456-9344; e-mail embajador@vc.embacuba.cu; internet www.embacu.cubaminrex.cu/sanvicente; Ambassador PABLO ANTONIO RODRÍGUEZ VIDAL.
Taiwan (Republic of China): Murray Rd, POB 878, Kingstown; tel. 456-2431; fax 456-2913; e-mail rocemsvg@caribsurf.com; Ambassador WEBER SHIH.
Venezuela: Baynes Bros Bldg, Granby St, POB 852, Kingstown; tel. 456-1374; fax 457-1934; e-mail embavenezsanvicente@vincysurf.com; Ambassador YOEL PÉREZ MARCANO.

Judicial System

Justice is administered by the Eastern Caribbean Supreme Court, based in Saint Lucia and consisting of a Court of Appeal and a High Court. Three High Court Judges are resident in Saint Vincent and the Grenadines. There are five Magistrates, including the Registrar of the Supreme Court, who acts as an additional Magistrate.

High Court Judges: FREDERICK VICTOR BRUCE-LYLE, GERTEL THOM, MONICA JOSEPH (acting).
Registrar: TAMARA GIBSON-MARKS.

Religion

CHRISTIANITY

Saint Vincent Christian Council: Melville St, POB 445, Kingstown; tel. 456-1408; f. 1969; four mem. churches; Chair. Mgr RENISON HOWELL.

The Anglican Communion

Anglicans in Saint Vincent and the Grenadines are adherents of the Church in the Province of the West Indies, comprising eight dioceses. The Archbishop of the West Indies is the Bishop of Nassau and the Bahamas, and is resident in Nassau. The diocese of the Windward Islands includes Grenada, Saint Lucia and Saint Vincent and the Grenadines.

Bishop of the Windward Islands: Rt Rev. CALVERT LEOPOLD FRIDAY, Bishop's Court, POB 502, Kingstown; tel. 456-1895; fax 456-2591; e-mail diocesewi@vincysurf.com.

The Roman Catholic Church

Saint Vincent and the Grenadines comprises a single diocese (formed when the diocese of Bridgetown-Kingstown was divided in October 1989), which is suffragan to the archdiocese of Castries (Saint Lucia). The Bishop participates in the Antilles Episcopal Conference, currently based in Port of Spain, Trinidad and Tobago. Some 13% of the population are Roman Catholics.

Bishop of Kingstown: (vacant), Bishop's Office, POB 862, Edinboro, Kingstown; tel. 457-2363; fax 457-1903; e-mail rcdok@caribsurf.com.

Other Christian Churches

The Methodists, Seventh-day Adventists, Baptists and other denominations also have places of worship.

BAHÁ'Í FAITH

National Spiritual Assembly: POB 1043, Kingstown; tel. 456-4717.

The Press

SELECTED WEEKLIES

The News: Frenches Gate, POB 1078, Kingstown; tel. 456-2942; fax 456-2941; e-mail thenews@caribsurf.com; weekly; Man. Dir SHELLEY CLARKE.
Searchlight: Interactive Media Ltd, POB 152, Kingstown; tel. 456-1558; fax 457-2250; e-mail search@caribsurf.com; internet www.searchlight.vc; weekly on Fri.; Chair. CORLITA OLLIVERRE; CEO and Acting Man. Editor CLAIRE KEIZER.
The Vincentian: St George's Pl., Kingstown; tel. 456-1123; fax 457-2821; e-mail info@thevincentian.com; internet www.thevincentian.com; f. 1919; weekly; owned by the Vincentian Publishing Co; Man. Dir EGERTON M. RICHARDS; Editor-in-Chief TERRANCE PARRIS; circ. 6,000.
The Westindian Crusader: Kingstown; tel. 458-0073; fax 456-9315; e-mail crusader@caribsurf.com; weekly; Editor ELSEE CARBERRY; Man. Editor LINA CLARKE.

SELECTED PERIODICALS

Caribbean Compass: POB 175, Bequia; tel. 457-3409; fax 457-3410; e-mail tom@caribbeancompass.com; internet www.caribbeancompass.com; marine news; monthly; free distribution in Caribbean from Puerto Rico to Panama; circ. 11,000; Man. Dir TOM HOPMAN; Editor SALLY ERDLE.
Government Gazette: Govt Printery, Campden Park St, POB 12, Kingstown; tel. 457-1840; fax 453-3240; e-mail govprint@vincysurf.com; f. 1844; Govt Printer OTHNIEL WHITE; circ. 492.
Unity: Middle and Melville St, POB 854, Kingstown; tel. 456-1049; fortnightly; organ of the Unity Labour Party.

Publishers

CJW Communications: POB 1078, Frenches Gate, Kingstown; tel. 456-2942; fax 456-2941.
Interactive Media Ltd: Lower Kingstown Park, POB 152, Kingstown; tel. 456-1558; fax 457-2250; e-mail search@vincysurf.com; internet searchlight.vc; f. 1995; Chair. CORLETHA OLLIVIERRE; CEO CLARE KEIZER (acting).
SVG Publishers Inc.: Campden Park Industrial Estate, POB 1609, Kinstown; tel. 453-3166; fax 453-3538; e-mail info@svgpublishers.com; internet www.svgpublishers.com.
The Vincentian Publishing Co Ltd: St George's Pl., Kingstown; tel. 456-1123; fax 457-2821; e-mail info@thevincentian.com; internet www.thevincentian.com; Man. Dir EGERTON M. RICHARDS.

Broadcasting and Communications

TELECOMMUNICATIONS

Regulatory Authorities

Eastern Caribbean Telecommunications Authority (ECTEL): based in Castries, Saint Lucia; f. 2000 to regulate telecommunications in Saint Vincent and the Grenadines, Dominica, Grenada, Saint Christopher and Nevis and Saint Lucia.
National Telecom Regulatory Commission (NTRC): NIS Bldg, 2nd Floor, Upper Bay St, Kingstown; tel. 457-2279; fax 457-2834; e-mail ntrc@ntrc.vc; internet www.ntrc.vc; f. 2001 by the Telecommunications Act to regulate the sector in collaboration with ECTEL (q.v.); Chair K. DOUGLAS.

Major Service Providers

Digicel: Suite KO59, cnr Granby and Sharpe Sts, Kingstown; tel. 453-3000; fax 453-3010; e-mail customercaresvg@digicelgroup.com; internet www.digicelsvg.com; f. 2003; mobile cellular phone operator; owned by an Irish consortium; Chair. DENIS O'BRIEN; Eastern Caribbean CEO KEVIN WHITE.
LIME: Halifax St, POB 103, Kingstown; tel. 457-1901; fax 457-2777; e-mail support@vincysurf.com; internet www.time4lime.com; fmrly Cable & Wireless (St Vincent and the Grenadines) Ltd; name changed as above 2008; CEO DAVID SHAW; Exec. Vice-Pres. (Windward Islands) MICHAEL IAN BLANCHARD.

BROADCASTING

National Broadcasting Corporation of Saint Vincent and the Grenadines (NBC): Richmond Hill, POB 705, Kingstown; tel. 457-1111; fax 456-2749; e-mail nbcsvgadmin@nbcsvg.com; internet www.nbcsvg.com; govt-owned; Chair. ELSON CRICK; Gen. Man. CORLITA OLLIVERRE.

Radio

NBC Radio: National Broadcasting Corpn, Richmond Hill, POB 705, Kingstown; tel. 457-1111; fax 456-2749; e-mail nbcsvgadmin@nbcsvg.com; internet www.nbcsvg.com; commercial; broadcasts BBC World Service (United Kingdom) and local programmes.
Nice Radio FM: BDS Company Ltd, Dorsetshire Hill, POB 324, Kingstown; tel. 458-1013; fax 456-5556; e-mail bdsnice@caribsurf.com; internet www.niceradio.org; Man. Dir DOUGLAS DE FREITAS.

SAINT VINCENT AND THE GRENADINES

Television

National Broadcasting Corporation of Saint Vincent and the Grenadines: see above.

SVG Television (SVGTV): Dorsetshire Hill, POB 617, Kingstown; tel. 456-1078; fax 456-1015; e-mail svgbc@vincysurf.com; internet www.svgbc.com/svgtv.htm; f. 1980; broadcasts local, regional and international programmes; Man. Dir R. PAUL MACLEISH.

Television services from Barbados can be received in parts of the islands.

Finance

(cap. = capital; res = reserves; dep. = deposits; m. = million; br. = branch)

BANKING

The Eastern Caribbean Central Bank, based in Saint Christopher, is the central issuing and monetary authority for Saint Vincent and the Grenadines.

Eastern Caribbean Central Bank—Saint Vincent and the Grenadines Office: Frenches House, POB 839, Frenches; tel. 456-1413; fax 456-1412; e-mail eccbsvg@vincysurf.com; Country Dir ELRITHA DICK.

Regulatory Authority

International Financial Services Authority (IFSA): Upper Bay St, POB 356, Kingstown; tel. 456-2577; fax 457-2568; e-mail info@svgifsa.com; internet www.svgifsa.com; f. 1996; Chair. CLAUDE SAMUEL; Exec. Dir SHARDA SINANAN-BOLLERS.

Financial Intelligence Unit (FIU): POB 1826, Kingstown; tel. 451-2070; fax 457-2014; e-mail svgfiu@vincysurf.com; internet www.svgifsa.com/fin_intl_unit.htm; f. 2002; Dir GRENVILLE WILLIAMS.

Local Banks

Bank of Nova Scotia Ltd (Canada): 76 Halifax St, POB 237, Kingstown; tel. 457-1601; fax 457-2623; e-mail bruce.sali@scotiabank.com; Man. BRUCE SALI.

Bank of St Vincent and the Grenadines Ltd: Cnr Halifax and Egmont Sts, POB 880, Kingstown; tel. 457-1844; fax 456-2612; e-mail natbank@caribsurf.com; internet www.svgncb.com; f. 1977 as National Commercial Bank (SVG) Ltd, name changed 2010; govt-owned until 2010 when 51% stake sold to East Caribbean Financial Holding Ltd (St Lucia); sale of a further 29% stake planned for 2011; share cap. EC $14.0m., res EC $19.1m., dep. EC $520.7m. (June 2006); CEO PHILIP H. HERNANDEZ; Chair. DESMOND MORGAN.

FirstCaribbean International Bank (Barbados) Ltd: Lower Halifax St, POB 212, Kingstown; tel. 457-1587; e-mail Earl.Crichton@firstcaribbeanbank.com; internet www.firstcaribbeanbank.com; f. 2002 following merger of Caribbean operations of Barclays Bank PLC and CIBC; CIBC acquired Barclays' 43.7% stake in 2006; Exec. Chair. MICHAEL MANSOOR; CEO JOHN D. ORR; Man. EARL CRICHTON.

RBTT Bank Caribbean Ltd: 81 South River Rd, POB 81, Kingstown; tel. 456-1501; fax 456-2141; internet www.rbtt.com; f. 1985 as Caribbean Banking Corpn Ltd, name changed as above in 2002; Chair. PETER J. JULY.

'OFFSHORE' FINANCIAL SECTOR

Legislation permitting the development of an 'offshore' financial sector was introduced in 1976 and revised in 1996 and 1998. International banks are required to have a place of business on the islands and to designate a licensed registered agent. International Business Companies registered in Saint Vincent and the Grenadines are exempt from taxation for 25 years. Legislation also guarantees total confidentiality. In 2009 the 'offshore' financial sector comprised 8,855 International Business Companies, 149 trusts and four banks.

Saint Vincent Trust Service: Trust House, 112 Bonadie St, POB 613, Kingstown; tel. 457-1027; fax 457-1961; e-mail info@st-vincent-trust.com; internet www.jeeves-group.com; br. in Liechtenstein; Pres. BRYAN JEEVES.

'Offshore' Banks

European Commerce Bank: The Financial Services Centre, Paul's Ave, POB 1822, Kingstown; tel. 456-1460; fax 456-1455; e-mail info@eurocombank.com; internet www.eurocombank.com.

Loyal Bank Ltd: Cedar Hill Crest, POB 1825, Kingstown; tel. 485-6705; fax 451-2757; e-mail ceo@loyalbank.com; internet www.loyalbank.com; f. 1997; owned by Ost West Stiftung; CEO ADRIAN BARON.

Safe Harbor Bank Ltd: Nanton's Bldg, Egmont St, POB 2630, Kingstown; tel. 451-2030; fax 451-2031; e-mail info@safeharborbank.com; internet www.safeharborbank.com; f. 2000; Contact GRAHAME BOLLERS.

Trend Bank Ltd: The Financial Services Centre, Paul's Ave, POB 1823, Kingstown; tel. 457-0548; fax 451-2672; internet www.trendb.com; Pres. ADOLPHO J. SILVA MELLO NETO.

STOCK EXCHANGE

Eastern Caribbean Securities Exchange: based in Basseterre, Saint Christopher and Nevis; tel. (869) 466-7192; fax (869) 465-3798; e-mail info@ecseonline.com; internet www.ecseonline.com; f. 2001; regional securities market designed to facilitate the buying and selling of financial products for the eight mem. territories—Anguilla, Antigua and Barbuda, Dominica, Grenada, Montserrat, Saint Christopher and Nevis, Saint Lucia, and Saint Vincent and the Grenadines; Chair. Sir K. DWIGHT VENNER; Gen. Man. TREVOR E. BLAKE.

INSURANCE

A number of foreign insurance companies have offices in Kingstown. Local companies include the following:

Abbott's Insurance Co: Cnr Sharpe and Bay St, POB 124, Kingstown; tel. 456-1511; fax 456-2462.

BMC Agencies Ltd: Sharpe St, POB 1436, Kingstown; tel. 457-2041; fax 457-2103.

Durrant Insurance Services: South River Rd, Kingstown; tel. 457-2426.

Haydock Insurances Ltd: Granby St, POB 1179, Kingstown; tel. 457-2903; fax 456-2952.

Metrocint General Insurance Co Ltd: St George's Pl., POB 692, Kingstown; tel. 456-1821.

Saint Hill Insurance Co Ltd: Bay St, POB 1741, Kingstown; tel. 457-1227; fax 456-2374.

Saint Vincent Insurances Ltd: Lot 69, Grenville St, POB 210, Kingstown; tel. 456-1733; fax 456-2225; e-mail vinsure@caribsurf.com.

Trade and Industry

DEVELOPMENT ORGANIZATIONS

Invest SVG: POB 608, Kingstown; tel. 457-2159; fax 456-2688; e-mail info@investsvg.com; internet www.investsvg.com; f. 2003 as National Investment Promotions Inc; assumed DEVCO's (q.v.) responsibilities for investment promotion and foreign direct investment; reports to the Office of the Prime Minister; board mems appointed from both public and private sectors by the Cabinet; Exec. Dir CLEO HUGGINS; Chair. EDMOND A. JACKSON.

Saint Vincent Development Corporation (DEVCO): Grenville St, POB 841, Kingstown; tel. 457-1358; fax 457-2838; e-mail devco@caribsurf.com; f. 1970; finances industry, agriculture, fisheries, tourism; Chair. SAMUEL GOODLUCK; Man. CLAUDE M. LEACH.

CHAMBER OF COMMERCE

Saint Vincent and the Grenadines Chamber of Industry and Commerce (Inc): Corea's Bldg, 3rd Floor, Halifax and Hillsborough Sts, POB 134, Kingstown; tel. 457-1464; fax 456-2944; e-mail svgchamber@svg-cic.org; internet svg-cic.org; f. 1925; Pres. ANGUS STEELE; Exec. Dir SHAFIA LONDON.

INDUSTRIAL AND TRADE ASSOCIATION

Saint Vincent Marketing Corporation: Upper Bay St, POB 873, Kingstown; tel. 457-1603; fax 456-2673; e-mail svmc@caribsurf.com; f. 1959; CEO SONNY WILLIAMS.

EMPLOYERS' ORGANIZATIONS

Saint Vincent Arrowroot Industry Association: Upper Bay St, POB 70, Kingstown; tel. 457-1511; fax 457-2151; e-mail info@svgarrowroot.com; f. 1930; producers, manufacturers and sellers; 186 mems; Chair. GEORGE O. WALKER.

Saint Vincent Banana Growers' Association: Sharpe St, POB 10, Kingstown; tel. 457-1605; fax 456-2585; f. 1955; over 7,000 mems; Chair. LESLINE BEST; Gen. Man. HENRY KEIZER.

Saint Vincent Employers' Federation: Corea's Bldg, 3rd Floor, Middle St, POB 348, Kingstown; tel. 456-1269; fax 457-2777; e-mail svef@caribsurf.com; Pres. NOEL DICKSON; Exec. Dir PHYLLIS JOHN-PRIMUS.

Windward Islands Farmers' Association (WINFA): Paul's Ave, POB 817, Kingstown; tel. 456-2704; fax 456-1383; e-mail winfa@

SAINT VINCENT AND THE GRENADINES

Directory

winfacaribbean.org; internet www.winfacaribbean.org; f. 1982; Chair. JULIUS POLIUS; Co-ordinator RENWICK ROSE.

UTILITIES
Electricity

Saint Vincent Electricity Services Ltd (VINLEC): Paul's Ave, POB 865, Kingstown; tel. 456-1701; fax 456-2436; e-mail vinlec@vinlec.com; internet www.vinlec.com; 100% state-owned; country's sole electricity supplier; Chair. DOUGLAS COLE; CEO THORNLEY O. A. O. MYERS; 275 employees.

Water

Central Water and Sewerage Authority (CWSA): New Montrose, POB 363, Kingstown; tel. 456-2946; fax 456-2552; e-mail cwsa@vincysurf.com; internet www.cwsasvg.com; f. 1961; Chair. RICHARD MACLEISH; Gen. Man. GARTH SAUNDERS.

CO-OPERATIVES

There are 26 Agricultural Credit Societies, which receive loans from the Government, and five Registered Co-operative Societies.

TRADE UNIONS

Commercial, Technical and Allied Workers' Union (CTAWU): Lower Middle St, POB 245, Kingstown; tel. 456-1525; fax 457-1676; e-mail ctawu@vincysurf.com; f. 1962; affiliated to CCL, ICFTU and other international workers' orgs; Pres. CHERYL BACCHUS; Gen. Sec. LLOYD SMALL; 2,500 mems.

National Labour Congress: POB 875, Kingstown; tel. 457-1801; fax 457-1705; five affiliated unions; Pres. NOEL JACKSON.

National Workers' Movement: Burkes Bldg, Grenville St, POB 1290, Kingstown; tel. 457-1950; fax 456-2858; e-mail natwok@karicable.com; Gen. Sec. NOEL C. JACKSON.

Public Services Union of Saint Vincent and the Grenadines: McKie's Hill, POB 875, Kingstown; tel. 457-1950; fax 456-2858; e-mail psuofsvg@caribsurf.com; f. 1943; Pres. AUBREY BURGIN; Gen. Sec. ELROY BOUCHER; 738 mems.

Saint Vincent and the Grenadines Teachers' Union: McKies Hill, POB 304, Kingstown; tel. 457-1062; fax 456-1098; e-mail svgtu@caribsurf.com; f. 1952; Pres. ELVIS CHARLES; Gen. Sec. JOY MATTHEWS; 1,250 mems.

Transport

RAILWAYS

There are no railways in the islands.

ROADS

In 2009 there was an estimated total road network of 1,033 km (642 miles), of which 70% were paved. The first stage of a three-phase project to link Troumaca with Fergusson Gap was completed in 2007, at a cost of EC $2.5m. A government plan to extend and rehabilitate the Windward Highway was scheduled to be completed by 2010 and the South Leeward Highway Rehabilitation Project was expected to begin in 2011. In the 2010 budget EC $3m. was allocated for road and bridge improvement.

SHIPPING

The deep-water harbour at Kingstown can accommodate two ocean-going vessels and about five motor vessels. There are regular motor-vessel services between the Grenadines and Saint Vincent. Geest Industries, formerly the major banana purchaser, operated a weekly service to the United Kingdom. Numerous shipping lines also call at Kingstown harbour. Some exports are flown to Barbados to link up with international shipping lines. A new dedicated Cruise Terminal opened in 1999, permitting two cruise ships to berth at the same time.

Saint Vincent and the Grenadines Port Authority: Upper Bay St, POB 1237, Kingstown; tel. 456-1830; fax 456-2732; e-mail pkirby@svgpa.com; internet www.svgpa.com; Port Man. BISHEN JOHN.

CIVIL AVIATION

There is a civilian airport, E. T. Joshua Airport, at Arnos Vale, situated about 3 km (2 miles) south-east of Kingstown, that does not accommodate long-haul jet aircraft. Construction of an international airport at Argyle, 13 miles east of Kingstown, began in 2008 and was due to be completed in 2013. The new airport would be able to accomodate international jet services and would have facilities for 1.4m. passengers per year, more than five times the capacity at the existing airport. The project was estimated to cost EC $589m. The island of Canouan has a small airport with a recently upgraded runway and passenger terminal; construction of a jet airport was completed in May 2008, at a reported cost of US $21.5m. In March 2009 LIAT began scheduled flights from Grenada and Barbados to Canouan. Other airports include the J. F. Mitchell Airport in Bequia, Union Island Airport and one in Mustique island, which has a landing strip for light aircraft only.

Leeward Islands Air Transport (LIAT): tel. 456-6333; fax 456-6111; e-mail pattersond@liatairline.com; internet www.liatairline.com; f. 2009; Station Man. DOMINIQUE PATTERSON; Dir ISAAC SOLOMON.

Mustique Airways: POB 1232, E. T. Joshua Airport, Arnos Vale; tel. 458-4380; fax 456-4586; e-mail info@mustique.com; internet www.mustique.com; f. 1979; charter and scheduled flights; Chair. JONATHAN PALMER.

Saint Vincent and the Grenadines Air Ltd (SVG Air): POB 39, Arnos Vale; tel. 457-5124; fax 457-5077; e-mail info@svgair.com; internet www.svgair.com; f. 1990; charter and scheduled flights; CEO MARTIN BARNARD.

Tourism

The island chain of the Grenadines is the country's main tourism asset. There are superior yachting facilities, but the lack of major air links with countries outside the region has resulted in a relatively slow development for tourism. In 2009 Saint Vincent and the Grenadines received 163,340 cruise ship passengers and 72,632 stop-over tourists. Tourism receipts totalled EC $236.4m. in 2009.

Saint Vincent and the Grenadines Hotel and Tourism Association (SVGHTA): E. T. Joshua International Airport, Arnos Vale; tel. 458-4379; fax 456-4456; e-mail office@svghotels.com; internet www.svghotels.com; f. 1968 as Saint Vincent Hotel Asscn; renamed as above in 1999; non-profit org.; mem. of the Caribbean Hotels Asscn; Pres. LEROY LEWIS; Exec. Dir DAWN SMITH; 71 mems.

St Vincent and the Grenadines Tourism Authority (SVGTA): NIS Bldg, Upper Bay St, POB 834, Kingstown; tel. 456-6222; fax 485-6020; e-mail svgta@discoversvg.com; internet www.discoversvg.com; f. 2009.

Defence

Saint Vincent and the Grenadines participates in the US-sponsored Regional Security System, comprising police, coastguards and army units, which was established by independent Eastern Caribbean states in 1982. Since 1984, however, the paramilitary Special Service Unit has had strictly limited deployment. The recurrent budget for 2008 allocated some 10.3% of total expenditure (projected at EC $423m.) for defence purposes.

Education

Free primary education, beginning at five years of age and lasting for seven years, is available to all children in government schools, although it is not compulsory and attendance is low. There are 61 government, and five private, primary schools. Secondary education, beginning at 12 years of age, comprises a first cycle of five years and a second, two-year cycle. However, government facilities at this level are limited, and much secondary education is provided in schools administered by religious organizations, with government assistance. There are also a number of junior secondary schools. Enrolment at primary schools during the 2008/09 academic year included 95% of children in the relevant age-group, while comparable enrolment in secondary schools in 2007/08 included 90% of pupils. There is a teacher-training college and a technical college. Total budgetary expenditure on education by the central Government was a projected EC $126.5m. in 2008 (17% of the total budget). The Government announced in 2005 that it had achieved its objective of instituting universal secondary education.

SAMOA

Introductory Survey

LOCATION, CLIMATE, LANGUAGE, RELIGION, FLAG, CAPITAL

The Independent State of Samoa (formerly Western Samoa) lies in the southern Pacific Ocean, about 2,400 km (1,500 miles) north of New Zealand. Its nearest neighbour is American Samoa, to the east. The country comprises two large and seven small islands, of which five are uninhabited. The climate is tropical, with temperatures generally between 23°C (73°F) and 30°C (86°F). The rainy season is from November to April. The languages spoken are Samoan (a Polynesian language) and English. Almost all of the inhabitants profess Christianity, and the major denominations are the Congregational, Roman Catholic and Methodist Churches. The national flag (proportions 1 by 2) is red, with a rectangular dark blue canton, containing five differently sized white five-pointed stars in the form of the Southern Cross constellation, in the upper hoist. The capital is Apia.

CONTEMPORARY POLITICAL HISTORY

Historical Context

The islands became a German protectorate in 1899. During the First World War (1914–18) they were occupied by New Zealand forces, who overthrew the German administration. In 1919 New Zealand was granted a League of Nations mandate to govern the islands. In 1946 Western Samoa (as it was known until July 1997) was made a UN Trust Territory, with New Zealand continuing as the administering power. From 1954 measures of internal self-government were gradually introduced, culminating in the adoption of an independence Constitution in October 1960. This was approved by a UN-supervised plebiscite in May 1961, and the islands became independent on 1 January 1962. The office of Head of State was held jointly by two traditional rulers but, upon the death of his colleague in April 1963, Malietoa Tanumafili II became sole Head of State for life, performing the duties of a constitutional monarch.

Fiame Mata'afa Mulinu'u, Prime Minister since 1959, lost the general election in 1970, and a new Cabinet, led by Tupua Tamasese Lealofi, was formed. Mata'afa regained power in 1973, following another general election, and remained in office until his death in May 1975. He was again succeeded by Tamasese, who, in turn, lost the general election in March 1976 to his cousin, Tupuola Taisi Efi. The previously unorganized opposition members formed the Human Rights Protection Party (HRPP) in 1979, and won the elections in February 1982, taking 24 of the 47 seats in the Fono (Legislative Assembly). Va'ai Kolone was appointed Prime Minister, but in September he was removed from office as a result of previous electoral malpractice. His successor, Tupuola Efi, with much popular support, sought to nullify an earlier agreement between Kolone and the New Zealand Government which, in defiance of a ruling by the British Privy Council, denied automatic New Zealand citizenship to all Western Samoans except those already living in New Zealand. However, Tupuola Efi resigned in December 1982, after the Fono had rejected his budget, and was replaced by the new HRPP leader, Tofilau Eti Alesana.

Domestic Political Affairs

At elections in February 1985 the HRPP won 31 of the 47 seats, increasing its majority in the Fono from one to 15 seats; the newly formed Christian Democratic Party (CDP), led by Tupuola Efi, obtained the remaining 16 seats. In December Tofilau Eti resigned, following the rejection of the proposed budget by the Fono and the Head of State's refusal to call another general election. Va'ai Kolone, with the support of a number of CDP members and HRPP defectors, was appointed Prime Minister of a coalition Government in January 1986.

At the February 1988 general election the HRPP and an alliance composed of independents and the CDP (later known as the Samoa National Development Party—SNDP) both initially gained 23 seats, with votes in the remaining constituency being tied. After two recounts proved inconclusive, a judge from New Zealand presided over a third and declared the CDP candidate the winner. However, before a new government could be formed, a newly elected member of the Legislative Assembly defected from the SNDP alliance to the HRPP. In April Tofilau Eti was re-elected Prime Minister, and a new Government, composed of HRPP members, was appointed.

In early 1990 proposed legislation to permit local village councils to fine, or to impose forced labour or exile on, individuals accused of offending communal rules was widely perceived as an attempt by the Government to ensure the support of the Matai (elected clan chiefs) at the next general election. Of the 47 seats in the Fono, 45 were traditionally elected by holders of Matai titles. However, the political importance of the Matai had been increasingly diminished by the procurement of Matai titles by those seeking to be elected to the Fono. This practice was believed to have undermined the system of chief leadership to such an extent that universal suffrage would have to be introduced to decide all of the seats in the Fono. A referendum was conducted in October 1990, at which voters narrowly accepted government proposals for the introduction of universal suffrage. A second proposal, to create an upper legislative chamber composed of the Matai, was rejected. A bill to implement universal adult suffrage was approved by the Fono in December 1990, despite strong opposition from the SNDP.

Tofilau Eti Alesana's final term as Prime Minister

A general election, scheduled for February 1991 was postponed to April, owing to the need to register an estimated 80,000 newly enfranchised voters. In the weeks following the poll petitions were filed with the Supreme Court against 11 newly elected members of the Fono who were accused of corrupt or illegal electoral practices. Moreover, subsequent political manoeuvring resulted in the HRPP increasing its parliamentary representation from an initial 26 to 30 seats, while the SNDP ultimately secured only 16 seats in the Fono, and the remaining seat was retained by an independent. At the first meeting of the new Fono, convened in May, Tofilau Eti was re-elected for what, he later announced, would be his final term of office as Prime Minister. In November the Fono approved legislation to increase the parliamentary term from three to five years and to create an additional two seats in the Fono. These seats were contested in early 1992 and won by the HRPP.

The introduction of a value-added tax on goods and services in January 1994 (which greatly increased the price of food and fuel in the country) provoked a series of demonstrations and protest rallies, as well as demands for the resignation of the Prime Minister. In March, therefore, the Government agreed to amend the most controversial aspects of the tax. Meanwhile, four members of the Fono (including three recently expelled HRPP members), who had opposed the financial reforms, established a new political organization, the Samoa Liberal Party, under the leadership of the former Speaker, Nonumalo Leulumoega Sofara.

Protests against the value-added tax on goods and services continued in early 1995, following the Government's decision to charge two prominent members of the Tumua ma Pule group of traditional leaders and former members of the Fono with sedition, for organizing demonstrations against the tax during 1994. In March 1995 3,000 people delivered a petition to the Prime Minister, bearing the signatures of 120,000 people (some 75% of the population), which demanded that the tax be revoked. The Prime Minister questioned the authenticity of the signatures and appointed a 14-member committee to investigate the matter. In late June the case against the two members of Tumua ma Pule, which had attracted attention from several international non-governmental organizations (including the World Council of Churches and Amnesty International), was dismissed on the grounds of insufficient evidence.

In December 1995 the HRPP unanimously re-elected Tofilau Eti as the leader of the party. In March 1996 one of the two female members of the Fono, Matatumua Naimoaga, left the HRPP in order to form the Samoa All-People's Party. The formation of the new party, in preparation for the forthcoming general election, was reportedly a result of dissatisfaction with the Government's alleged mismanagement of public assets, together with concern over corruption. Legislation introduced in April attempted to distinguish between the traditional Samoan practice of exchanging gifts and acts of bribery, amid numerous reports that voters were demanding gifts and favours from electoral candidates in return for their support.

A general election took place on 26 April 1996. The opposition was highly critical of the protracted counting of votes, claiming that the delay allowed the HRPP to recruit successful independent candidates in an attempt to gain a majority of seats in the Fono. It was eventually announced in mid-May that the HRPP had secured a total of 28 seats (with the recruitment of several independent members to their ranks), the SNDP had won 14 seats and independent candidates had secured seven. Tofilau Eti was subsequently re-elected as Prime Minister, defeating the Leader of the Opposition, Tuiatua Tupua Tamasese, by 34 votes to 14.

In May 1997 the Prime Minister proposed a constitutional amendment in the Fono to change the country's name to Samoa. (The country has been known simply as Samoa at the UN since its admission to the organization in 1976.) In July the Fono voted by 41 votes to one to approve the change, which took effect on the next day. However, the neighbouring US territory of American Samoa expressed dissatisfaction with the change (which was believed to undermine the Samoan identity of its islands and inhabitants), and in September introduced legislation to prohibit recognition of the new name within the territory. In March 1998 the House of Representatives in American Samoa voted against legislation that proposed not to recognize Samoan passports (thereby preventing Samoans from travelling to the territory), but decided to continue to refer to the country as Western Samoa and to its inhabitants as Western Samoans. Nevertheless, in January 2000 Samoa and American Samoa signed a memorandum of understanding (MOU), increasing co-operation in areas including health, trade and education.

A series of reports in *The Samoa Observer*, an independent newspaper, in mid-1997 alleged that a serious financial scandal involving the disappearance of some 500 blank passports, and their subsequent sale to Hong Kong Chinese purchasers for up to US $26,000 each, had occurred. The Government refused to comment on the newspaper's allegations, beyond confirming that several senior immigration officials had been suspended pending the outcome of an investigation into the affair. Moreover, the Government subsequently brought charges of defamatory libel against the editor, Savea Sano Malifa, for publishing a letter criticizing the Prime Minister (who was reported to have told the Fono of his intention to change legislation governing business licences, such that publications could have their licences withdrawn for publishing dissenting material). The regional Pacific Islands News Association also condemned the Prime Minister's comments as an attack on freedom of information and expression. The continued existence of the newspaper was placed in jeopardy when Savea Sano Malifa was found guilty of defaming the Prime Minister in two libel cases in July and September 1998, and was ordered to pay a total of some $17,000 in costs. The newspaper had alleged that public funds had been used to construct a hotel owned by the Prime Minister and had criticized the allocation of $0.25m. in the 1998 budget to Tofilau Eti's legal costs. The Government's increasingly autocratic style, its apparent intolerance of dissent and the perceived lack of accountability of its members, coupled with its poor economic record, resulted in frequent expressions of popular discontent during 1997. A series of protest marches in late 1997 and early 1998, organized by the Tumua ma Pule group of chiefs and attended by several thousand people, aimed to increase pressure on the Prime Minister to resign.

A long-standing dispute over land rights near Faleolo airport appeared to be the cause of violent activity in June 1998, when villagers shot a government official, burned buildings and slaughtered or stole hundreds of cattle on a government estate. However, it was subsequently revealed that the incidents had been perpetrated by members of a gang styling themselves as Japanese Ninja warriors, who were believed to be involved in the cultivation of marijuana and cattle theft. Some 38 men, thought to be members of the gang, were later arrested. The dispute, which originated in a land survey carried out in 1871, re-emerged in January 2003 when villagers presented the Government with a petition and a list of demands relating to land rights and revenue from the airport. In July 2005 the Government stated that it wanted all families living on the disputed land to vacate the area (covering about 22 acres) and move to a nearby, larger plot of government land, ostensibly in order to comply with health and safety regulations. However, the villagers resolved to resist the Government's request, restating their original demand for the return of 6,000 acres close to the airport, which they claimed had been wrongfully taken from them at the end of the 19th century. They were led in their resistance by senior Matai and the former Minister of Civil Aviation, Toalepaiali'i Toeolesulusulu Suafaiga Siueva Pose Salesa III.

The premiership of Tuila'epa Sailele Malielegaoi

In November 1998 Tofilau Eti resigned as Prime Minister, owing to ill health. He was replaced by the Deputy Prime Minister, Tuila'epa Sailele Malielegaoi, and the Cabinet was reorganized. In July 1999 the Minister of Public Works, Luagalau Levaula Kamu, was shot dead while attending an event commemorating the 20th anniversary of the foundation of the ruling HRPP. Speculation followed that the killer's intended target had been the Prime Minister, but this was denied both by Tuila'epa Sailele and by New Zealand police officers sent to the island to assist in the investigation. In August Altise Leafa, the son of the Minister of Women's Affairs, Leafa Vitale, was convicted of the murder and sentenced to death (subsequently commuted to a life sentence). In April 2000 Leafa Vitale and the former Minister of Telecommunications, Toi Akuso, were found guilty of murdering Luagalau and were sentenced to death, which was similarly commuted to life imprisonment. It later emerged that Luagalau had been killed in an attempt to prevent him from uncovering cases of corruption and bribery in which the two ministers had become involved. Toi Akuso died in prison in April 2009. Alatise Leafa and Leafa Vitale were granted parole and released in May and June 2010, respectively.

Meanwhile, in November 1999 the ruling HRPP increased its number of seats in the Fono to 34 (out of a possible 49) following the defection of an independent candidate to the HRPP. By-elections for the two imprisoned former ministers' seats were held in June 2000, and HRPP candidates were successful in both constituencies. In August 2000 a supreme court ruling ordered the Government to allow opposition politicians access to the state-controlled media, which for several years had been denied.

At a general election on 2 March 2001 the HRPP won 22 seats, the SNDP secured 13 seats and independent candidates took 14 seats. On 16 March Tuila'epa Sailele won 28 votes in the Fono, after securing the support of six independents, to be re-elected Prime Minister. However, the opposition mounted a number of legal challenges to his election. In August charges of electoral malpractice against eight elected members of the Fono, including the Deputy Prime Minister, the Minister of Health and the Minister of Internal Affairs, Women's Affairs and Broadcasting, were brought to the Supreme Court. None of the cabinet ministers was found guilty. By-elections for the vacant parliamentary seats were held in October and November, all four of which were won by the HRPP.

An Electoral Commission, established shortly after the elections of March 2001, published its recommendations in October, urging the replacement of the two Individual Voters Roll seats with two Urban Seats and that government employees who wished to stand for election to the Fono should first be obliged to resign from their offices.

In mid-2003 concerns were raised with regard to the increasing numbers of qualified medical staff choosing to emigrate or to leave the profession. It was estimated that one-third of Samoa's nurses had left the profession between 2002 and 2003, while half of all doctors' positions remained vacant. In September 2005 Samoan doctors went on strike in protest against low rates of pay and working conditions. When doctors refused to return to work, the Government was forced to recruit temporary staff from overseas. In late November some 1,500 people marched through the streets of Apia in support of 23 doctors who had resigned in protest. A petition was presented to the Prime Minister's Department, whereupon two cabinet ministers stated that the issue would be addressed. A commission of inquiry made recommendations for changes, to which the Government then agreed, but no increase in doctors' starting salaries, as demanded by protesters, was forthcoming. By January 2006 four of the doctors involved in the protests had relocated overseas; 11 others returned to government employment.

Concern was expressed in early 2005 that the proliferation of Matai titles was leading to the making of hasty and undesirable decisions by village councils. A senior village chief and member of the Fono, Leva'a Sauaso, claimed that many of the new title-holders were lacking in knowledge and experience of village affairs and that these clan leaders were consequently making decisions that were detrimental to Samoan society.

The general election held on 31 March 2006 was contested by a total of 211 candidates, including 18 women. The ruling HRPP regained power, securing 33 of the 49 parliamentary seats, thus decisively defeating the Samoa Democratic United Party (SDUP, formed upon the merger of the SNDP and the Samoa Independent Party), which won 10 seats. The remaining seats were taken by independent candidates. However, violence ensued when it was declared that the Minister for Public Works, Faumui Liuga, had defeated Letagaloa Pita, a senior-ranking Matai, in the constituency of Savai'i. In late August the opposition SDUP announced the appointment of a new leader, Asiata Sale'imoa Va'ai. The party's long-standing leader, Lemamea Mualia, initially disputed his replacement but formally resigned in late September, subsequently sitting as an independent member of the Fono. Following other departures from the party, the SDUP was unable to command the requisite eight seats for continued recognition in the chamber, and by the end of 2006 all SDUP members of the Fono had become independent legislators.

The Samoan Head of State, Malietoa Tanumafili II, died in May 2007 at the age of 95. He had served as sole Head of State, for life, since 1963. His funeral was attended by regional leaders, including the King of Tonga and the New Zealand Prime Minister. In June 2007 the Fono unanimously elected former Prime Minister Tuiatua Tupua Tamasese Efi as Head of State, for a term of five years.

Concerns with regard to the issue of press freedom re-emerged in October 2008, when Savea Sano Malifa, the editor and publisher of *The Samoa Observer,* criticized the imposition of 'guidelines' in relation to the reporting of the proceedings of a public commission of inquiry into the conduct of the islands' Commissioner of Police.

Recent developments

In May 2009 nine members of the Fono were disqualified by the Speaker on account of their formation in 2008 of a new political organization, the Tautua Samoa Party (TSP). Electoral law prohibited legislators from transferring allegiance from one party to another during the course of the parliamentary term. Among the nine legislators was Paluesalue Faapo, a former cabinet minister, who had left the HRPP in 2008 (as did one other HRPP member of the Fono) as a result of his disagreement with the Government's controversial plan for Samoan drivers to switch to using the left-hand side of the road (see below). In July 2009, however, the Supreme Court overruled the Speaker's decision, and the nine opposition members were reinstated in the Fono. In response to the ruling, the Government introduced legislation to amend the electoral law, which was approved in October, followed by the requisite revision of the Constitution in February 2010. In protest against the Government's use of intimidatory tactics, in March three opposition members resigned from the Fono, having deliberately refused to dissociate themselves from the TSP, thus prompting the need to hold by-elections. In May, with one TSP legislator being returned unopposed, polling was held for the other two seats, one of which was taken by the HRPP.

A state of disaster was declared at the end of September 2009, when Samoa was devastated by a tsunami. The disaster resulted in 143 deaths in Samoa and displaced thousands of islanders. Substantial damage was sustained, estimated to be in the region of US $38m. Hundreds of homes were destroyed, and tourist accommodation was seriously damaged. Emergency assistance and relief supplies were provided by Australia and New Zealand. In May 2010 concern was raised by reports that a number of those whose homes had been destroyed were still awaiting permanent shelter some eight months after the tsunami. The Prime Minister announced in the following month that the UN had agreed to delay Samoa's scheduled transition from the UN list of Least Developed Countries to that of Developing Countries as a result of the set-backs posed by the post-tsunami recovery efforts. It was announced in September that the transition, which was scheduled to have been effected during 2011, was to take place on 1 January 2014. In October 2010 a report broadcast on New Zealand television claimed that up to $45m. tsunami recovery funding had been misappropriated, a claim that was strongly refuted by the Prime Minister, who argued that of the $80m. pledged by foreign donors Samoa had received just $15m. to date.

Meanwhile, following an unsuccessful lawsuit against the decision, the Government's plan for vehicles to drive on the left side of Samoa's roads, instead of the right as hitherto, was implemented in September 2009. The switch was apparently intended to encourage expatriate Samoans resident in Australia and New Zealand to dispatch used right-hand-drive cars to their families in Samoa, thereby reducing the country's need to import costly left-hand-drive vehicles from the USA and allowing more Samoans to own a motor vehicle. In September 2010 Prime Minister Tuila'epa Sailele Malielegaoi stated that the Government's objectives in initiating the transition had been achieved and that an anticipated increase in the number of automobile accidents, the principal reason for the considerable opposition to the change, had not transpired.

The Prime Minister announced in October 2010 that parliament was to be dissolved in January 2011 in advance of legislative elections to be held in March. In December 2010 it was revealed that an alleged plot to assassinate both the Prime Minister and the Chief Justice of the Supreme Court, Patu Tiava'asu'e Falefatu, was being investigated; the apparent plot was reported to be linked to the assassination in 1999 of Minister of Public Works Luagalau Levaula Kamu (see The premiership of Tuila'epa Sailele Malielegaoi). Also in December 2010 Papalii Panoa Tavita Moala resigned as Leader of the TSP; Va'ai Papu was elected to replace him later in the month. Deputy Prime Minister Misa Telefoni Retzlaff announced in February 2011 that he would not seek re-election in the forthcoming election. Later in that month the Supreme Court disqualified three electoral candidates (two TSP members and an independent candidate), owing to a provision in legislation requiring electoral nominations to secure the approval of Matai on the basis of service to the community. The decision was received with concern by many observers, and the TSP pledged to revoke the provision should it be elected to power.

The legislative election, held on 4 March 2011, was contested by a total of 158 candidates, of whom 102 were members of the HRPP, 47 represented the TSP and 32 were independent candidates. As a result of the disqualifications by the Supreme Court, Prime Minister Tuila'epa Sailele Malielegaoi secured re-election to his seat uncontested. Turn-out was recorded at 87.1%. The HRPP secured 29 of the 44 parliamentary seats, but was bolstered by the election of seven nominally independent candidates who supported the ruling party. Notably, three cabinet ministers lost their seats: the Ministers of Justice, of Communications, and of Education, Sports and Culture. The TSP increased its representation to 13 seats. A new Cabinet, comprising eight new ministers, was inaugurated in mid-March.

Following the polls, 10 petitions challenging election results were lodged with the Supreme Court, including petitions against the Ministers of Education, Sport and Culture, of Finance, and of Works, Transport and Infrastructure; two of the 10 complaints were subsequently withdrawn. The Court began hearing the petitions in mid-April 2011. The first ruling was handed down in late April: the accused was found guilty on three allegations of vote-buying; however, the petitioner (of the HRPP) was found to have committed five acts of vote-buying himself. The Court declared the seat vacant and both men were disqualified from participating in elections for five years; a by-election was to be held later in the year. In May, having been found guilty of bribery and thus disqualified from holding his parliamentary seat, Va'ai Papu was replaced as Leader of the TSP by Palusalue Faapo.

In May 2011 the Government announced plans to transfer the country to the western side of the international dateline in a bid to facilitate the conduct of business with Australia and New Zealand (increasingly Samoa's most significant trading partners). The transition—following which Samoa would be three hours ahead of, rather than 21 hours behind, the Australian business and financial hub of Sydney—was scheduled to take effect on 29 December and would reverse an earlier transfer, in 1892, to the eastern side of the dateline.

Foreign Affairs
Regional relations

Samoa maintains strong links with New Zealand, where many Samoans live and many more receive secondary and tertiary education. In June 2002 New Zealand formally apologized for injustices that it had committed against its former colony during its administration between 1914 and 1962. These included allowing the 1918 influenza pandemic to kill 22% of Samoa's population (the virus having been brought in on a ship from New Zealand); the murder of a Samoan paramount chief and independence leader, Tupua Tamasese Lealofi III, and the killing of nine other supporters of the pacifist Mau movement during a non-violent protest in 1929; and the banishment of native leaders, who were also stripped of their chiefly titles. The apology, while accepted, drew mixed reactions from Samoans, many of whom were more concerned with the issue of the restoration of their rights to New Zealand citizenship (which had been severely curtailed by the Citizenship Western Samoa Act of 1982). In March 2003 large protest marches took place in Samoa and New Zealand demanding the repeal of the 1982 law. In May 2004 a parliamentary select committee rejected a 100,000-signature petition seeking a repeal of the law and upheld the principles of the 1982 ruling. The number of Samoans applying for New Zealand citizenship under a quota scheme increased by more than 50% in 2004 to reach 8,600. Bilateral ministerial consultations continued on a regular basis. In February 2009 the recently appointed Minister of Foreign Affairs of New Zealand, Murray McCully, embarked upon his first official visit to Samoa, where he had meetings with the Prime Minister and other senior government officials. In a reflection of New Zealand's fresh approach to its provision of foreign aid, renewed emphasis was to be placed on sustainable development. As part of plans to promote the private sector (see Economic Affairs), McCully also had discussions with local business leaders. McCully revisited Samoa in July. New Zealand Prime Minister John Key visited Samoa in the same month, during which he pledged to increase New Zealand development aid to Samoa; the funding was to be focused on education, health, and public and private sector development. Development aid to Samoa was further increased in 2010/11 (see Economic Affairs).

In April 2009 Samoa and Australia signed a new MOU to renew their bilateral Defence Co-operation Programme. Following the tsunami that caused widespread damage in Samoa in September 2009 (see Domestic Political Affairs), Australia donated US $24m. to the Samoan Government to assist in clean-up and recovery operations. In February 2010, as part of the Samoa-Australia Partnership for Development, the Australian Government provided $A1.15m., the first allocation within a six-year programme of support for the purposes of addressing the impact of climate change on health, agriculture and food security in the islands. During a visit to Samoa in October, Australia's Parliamentary Secretary for Pacific Island Affairs, Richard Marles, commended the Samoan Government for the manner in which it had deployed Australian aid and the results achieved in so doing, and announced the provision of US $700,000 to help Samoa establish, train and equip an emergency response team to deal with natural disasters akin to the tsunami in the previous year. Along with New Zealand, Australia was also providing support for the introduction of free education in Samoa.

In September 2004 the Samoan Government announced that it was seeking to formalize its maritime boundary with American Samoa, owing to a number of recent, unspecified incidents. Discussions began in Apia in March 2005. In January 2006 the Samoan Government announced that it was to open a consulate in the American Samoan capital of Pago Pago.

In May 2007 Samoa hosted a regional meeting attended by ministers from countries including New Zealand, Solomon Islands and Tonga, in order to discuss maritime issues. In April 2009 Samoa and six neighbouring Pacific countries formed the South Pacific Cruise Group, the priority of which was to attract higher levels of cruise ship visitors to the countries.

Other external relations

Samoa hosted the 13th South Pacific Games in August–September 2007, in which 22 Pacific island nations participated. The Government of the People's Republic of China financed much of the cost of Samoa's preparations, including a US $12.7m. aquatic centre and the reconstruction of Apia Park Stadium, at a cost of $6.9m. However, the total cost was estimated at approximately $92m., and in September Deputy Prime Minister Misa Telefoni acknowledged that preparations for the event had left Samoa in debt. The Chinese Government was also financing the construction of buildings for the legislature and the judiciary in 2007; the latter was inaugurated in January 2010. Other projects financed by China included new sports facilities. Meanwhile, burgeoning relations were reflected in the opening of a Samoan embassy in China in January 2009. (Samoa also opened an embassy in Japan in the same month.) Under the terms of an agreement signed in May 2010, trade duties were to be exempted on 472 of Samoa's exports to China, about 60% of its total exports to the East Asian country; eventually, some 95% of Samoa's exports to China were to be tariff-free. A visit to Samoa by a Chinese delegation headed by Jia Qinglin, Chairman of the National Committee of the Chinese People's Political Consultative Conference, the senior-most political advisory body in the People's Republic, attracted considerable attention in April 2011; Jia was the highest-ranking Chinese official ever to visit Samoa. During the visit, Jia held talks with Prime Minister Tuila'epa Sailele Malielegaoi and Head of State Tuiatua Tupua Tamasese Efi, expressing gratitude for Samoa's continued 'firm support' of the 'one China policy'. A bilateral MOU pertaining to the provision of broadband internet services was signed, together with a separate agreement providing for $6.1m. in Chinese financial assistance to Samoa.

Following her visit to New Zealand in July 2008, the US Secretary of State, Condoleezza Rice, travelled on to Samoa, for a brief meeting with the country's Prime Minister. She also had discussions with her regional counterparts, meeting the ministers responsible for foreign affairs of the member countries of the Pacific Islands Forum (see p. 413). The Samoan Government announced in September 2010 that it was engaged in negotiations concerning the possible opening of a US-owned telecommunications call centre in Samoa, which, if confirmed, would lead to the creation of hundreds of local jobs.

The European Union (EU, see p. 270) has supported development programmes in Samoa since the 1970s, latterly focusing primarily on water and waste services. In May 2010 the EU allocated the sum of €16.7m. over the period 2010–13 for the purposes of upgrading water and sanitation facilities in the islands. In March 2011 the EU allocated €5.5m. to Samoa's budgetary support programme for 2011/12, to support measures intended to engender a recovery from the global financial crisis of 2008–09. Also in March 2011 the EU granted an additional €3m. for Samoa's Civil Society Support Programme, a four-year programme intended to help eradicate poverty and hardship among the Samoan population through sustainable development.

Samoa has sought to establish diplomatic relations with a number of new countries in recent years. Diplomatic relations were established with Brunei in February 2006, with Cuba in October 2007, with Estonia in January 2009, with Bosnia and Herzegovina in March 2009, with Georgia and Botswana both in March 2010, with the United Arab Emirates in May 2010, and with Morocco in February 2011.

CONSTITUTION AND GOVERNMENT

The country's Constitution, which took effect in 1962, provides for the Head of State to be elected by the Legislative Assembly for a term of five years. Until 2007 the Head of State held office for life. The Legislative Assembly is composed of 49 members, all of whom are elected by universal suffrage. A total of 47 members are elected from among holders of Matai titles (elected clan chiefs), and two are selected from non-Samoan candidates. Members hold office for five years. Executive power is held by the Cabinet, comprising the Prime Minister and other selected members of the Assembly. The Prime Minister is appointed by the Head of State with the necessary approval of the Assembly. Judicial power is exercised by two district courts, the Land and Titles Court, the Supreme Court and the Court of Appeal.

REGIONAL AND INTERNATIONAL CO-OPERATION

Samoa is a member of the Pacific Islands Forum (see p. 413), the Pacific Community (see p. 410), the Asian Development Bank (ADB, see p. 202) and the UN's Economic and Social Commission for Asia and the Pacific (ESCAP, see p. 37). It is also a signatory to the Lomé Conventions and the successor Cotonou Agreement (see p. 327) with the European Union.

Samoa joined the UN in 1976. The country is a member of the Commonwealth.

ECONOMIC AFFAIRS

In 2009, according to estimates by the World Bank, Samoa's gross national income (GNI), measured at average 2007–09 prices, was US $508m., equivalent to $2,840 per head (or $4,270 per head on an international purchasing-power parity basis). During 2000–09, it was estimated, the population increased at an average annual rate of 0.1%, while during the same period gross domestic product (GDP) per head increased, in real terms, by an average of 3.0% per year. Overall GDP increased, in real terms, at an average annual rate of 3.2% in 2000–09. According to official estimates, real GDP declined by 5.1% in the fiscal year ending 30 June 2009, but registered only negligible decline in 2009/10.

Agriculture (including hunting, forestry and fishing) accounted for 11.0% of GDP in fiscal 2009/10, and the sector engaged some 35.7% of the employed labour force at the 2006 census. The principal cash crops are coconuts and taro (also the country's primary staple food). Breadfruit, yams, maize, passion fruit, papaya, pineapples and mangoes are also cultivated, some of which are exported. Pigs, cattle, poultry and goats are raised, mainly for local consumption. The country's commercial fishing industry expanded considerably from the late 1990s; revenue from exports of fresh fish totalled 20.0m. tala in 2007. Exports of food and live animals earned 23.2m. tala (18.8% of total export receipts) in 2009. Between 2000 and 2009, according to figures from the ADB, the GDP of the entire agricultural sector decreased, in real terms, at an average annual rate of 2.4%. In real terms, agricultural GDP decreased by 4.5% in the fiscal year ending 30 June 2010, according to official figures.

Industry (comprising manufacturing, mining, construction and power) employed 25.9% of the employed labour force at the 2006 census, and the sector provided 27.2% of GDP in fiscal 2009/10. According to ADB figures, between 2000 and 2009 industrial GDP increased, in real terms, at an average annual rate of 3.3%. The GDP of the industrial sector increased by 3.2%, in real terms, in the fiscal year ending 30 June 2010, according to official figures.

Manufacturing (including handicrafts) provided 9.5% of GDP in fiscal 2009/10 and, including mining, engaged 19.7% of the employed labour force at the 2006 census. The manufacturing sector expanded considerably in the early 1990s with the establishment of a Japanese-owned factory producing electrical components for road vehicles. The Yazaki EDS Samoa factory, which assembles wire harnessing systems for export to car-manufacturing plants, is the major employer in the private sector. Other products of the manufacturing sector include beverages. Beer accounted for 8.6% of exports in 2007. Soft drinks are also manufactured, mainly for local consumption. A major water-bottling plant, which hoped to sell its product to the US market, opened in 2008. Coconut-based products and cigarettes are also produced. Between 2000 and 2009, according to figures from the ADB, manufacturing GDP decreased, in real terms, at an average annual rate of 1.7%. However, the GDP of the manufacturing sector increased by 6.3%, in real terms, in the fiscal year ending 30 June 2010, according to official figures.

Construction employed 4.6% of the employed labour force at the 2006 census, and the sector provided 12.8% of GDP in fiscal 2009/10. According to ADB figures, between 2000 and 2009 construction GDP increased, in real terms, at an average annual rate of 9.5%. The GDP of the sector declined by 7.3% in fiscal 2008/09, but increased by 0.6% in 2009/10, according to official figures.

Energy is derived principally from hydroelectric power and thermal power stations. A programme for the generation of electricity from coconut oil commenced in early 2009. The construction of a 5-MW solar power station, with assistance from the Chinese Government, was also under consideration. Imports of fuel accounted for 18.6% of the value of total imports in 2009. In 2005 a US company announced plans to begin conducting exploration activity in Samoan waters, hoping to find new sources of petroleum and natural gas.

The services sector provided 61.8% of GDP in fiscal 2009/10 and engaged 36.9% of the employed labour force in 2006. Between 2000 and 2009, according to ADB figures, the sector's GDP increased at an average annual rate of 4.5%. Despite steady growth in recent years, in fiscal 2009/10 the GDP of the services sector declined, in real terms, by 0.6%, according to official figures, largely as a result of a significant reduction in revenues from hotels and restaurants. Tourism makes a significant contribution to the economy, with revenue from this source (including passenger transport) rising to an estimated 304.3m. tala in 2009. Tourist arrivals were reported to total 129,487 in 2010. 'Offshore' banking was introduced to the islands in 1989, and by July of that year more than 30 companies had registered in Apia. A large proportion of the islands' revenue is provided by remittances from nationals working abroad, which reached the equivalent of 24.8% of GDP in 2008.

In 2009 the country recorded a visible trade deficit of 182.8m. tala, and a deficit of 0.6m. tala on the current account of the balance of payments. In 2009, when imports totalled 620.7m. tala and exports reached 123.7m. tala, New Zealand was Samoa's principal supplier of imports, providing 35.8% of the total, other important suppliers were Australia, the USA, Japan and the People's Republic of China. Australia was the dominant buyer of Samoan goods, accounting for 68.9% of exports. New Zealand was also an important trading partner in that year, accounting for 18.3% of imports. The principal exports, excluding re-exports to Australia, are machinery and transport equipment (accounting for 71.9% of the total) and food and live animals. The main imports are food and live animals, basic manufactures, mineral fuels, machinery and transport equipment, chemicals and miscellaneous manufactured articles.

The large budget deficits of the early 2000s reflected an increase in development spending financed by external borrowing and a decrease in lending to the domestic banking system. Deficits were financed by means of concessionary loans, with the remainder being provided through the issuance of government securities. In the fiscal year ending 30 June 2010 an overall budget deficit, including external funding, of 112.9m. tala was recorded, the deficit being equivalent to 7.9% of GDP in the 2009 calendar year to December, as estimated by the ADB. In response to the tsunami disaster of September 2009, a supplementary budget, envisaging expenditure of 78m. tala, was announced. Aid from Australia and New Zealand is a major source of finance. An estimated $A26.4m. was to be provided by Australia in 2010/11, with $NZ16.0m. to be supplied by New Zealand in 2010/11. Assistance from China is of increasing significance (see Foreign Affairs). The European Union (EU) has also provided substantial aid for various development projects. The EU provided €5.5m. for the purposes of budgetary support in 2011/12. At the end of 2009 the country's total external debt was estimated by the ADB at US $214m. The cost of debt-servicing in that year was equivalent to 78.6% of the value of exports of goods and services. In 2000–08 the annual rate of inflation (excluding rents) averaged 6.2%. According to the ADB, consumer prices increased by 6.6% in 2009 and by 1.3% in 2010. The rate of unemployment was 1.3% of the labour force at the 2006 census, although ADB estimates for the same year were higher, at 4.0%.

The economy of Samoa has remained vulnerable to external factors, notably fluctuations in world commodity prices and variations in global demand for Samoa's export items. Furthermore, the global recession of 2008/09 led to a reduction in remittances (a vital source of income for many) from Samoan workers employed overseas. In 2009/10 remittances were reported to have decreased by more than 5%, to US $149m. Following its recovery from the tsunami disaster of September 2009, the tourism sector attracted increasing numbers of visitors. However, with spending per head declining, tourist receipts decreased by 6% in 2009/10, in which year they totalled $130m. Although inflationary pressures eased somewhat during 2009, these were reported to be reappearing in the latter part of 2010, largely owing to the higher costs of imported fuel and foodstuffs. Following three consecutive years of weak economic performance, the ADB projected GDP growth of 2.1% in 2010/11. The Strategy for the Development of Samoa (2008–12), supported by Australia and New Zealand, placed particular emphasis on the development of the private sector; initiatives included the creation of the Private Sector Support Fund (co-financed by the UN Development Programme) and the establishment of the Small Business Enterprise Centre. The 2008–12 plan also envisaged the expansion of the agricultural sector and the development of tourism, along with the improvement of health and education facilities. However, the Samoan economy was seriously affected by the tsunami of September 2009. To assist the country's recovery from the disaster, in November the World Bank announced that it was to double its aid to Samoa, to US $40m., and in December the IMF approved the release of SDR5.8m. The Government's supplementary budget, announced in the latter month, provided for additional expenditure on relief measures and reconstruction work. In April 2011 it was reported that the working hours of more than 800 employees of the Yazaki automotive parts plant were to be temporarily reduced, by as much as 50%, in response to the tsunami catastrophe in March in Japan (the base of the parent company) and to the decrease in demand for wire harnessing from Toyota Australia.

PUBLIC HOLIDAYS

2012 (provisional): 2–3 January (for New Year), 6–9 April (Easter), 7 May (Mother's Day), 1 June (Independence Celebrations), 13 August (Father's Day), 15 October (Monday after Lotu a Tamaiti, Children's Day), 2 November (Arbor Day), 25–26 December (Christmas).

Statistical Survey

Source (unless otherwise indicated): Samoa Bureau of Statistics, Ministry of Finance, Government Building (MFMII), POB 1151, Apia; tel. 24384; fax 24675; e-mail info.stats@sbs.gov.ws; internet www.sbs.gov.ws.

AREA AND POPULATION

Area: Savai'i and adjacent small islands 1,708 sq km; Upolu and adjacent small islands 1,123 sq km; Total 2,831 sq km (1,093 sq miles).

Population: 176,710 at census of 5 November 2001; 180,741 (males 93,677, females 87,064) at census of 5 November 2006. *By Island* (2006 census): Savai'i 43,142; Upolu 137,599 (Apia Urban Area 37,708, North West Upolu 56,122, Rest of Upolu 43,769). *Mid-2011* (Secretariat of the Pacific Community estimate): 183,617 (Source: Pacific Regional Information System).

Density (at mid-2011): 64.7 per sq km.

Population by Age and Sex (Secretariat of the Pacific Community estimates at mid-2011): *0–14:* 69,441 (males 36,165, females 33,276); *15–64:* 104,899 (males 55,073, females 49,825); *65 and over:* 9,277 (males 4,199, females 5,078); *Total* 183,617 (males 95,437, females 88,180) (Source: Pacific Regional Information System).

Principal Towns (population at 2006 census, provisional results): Apia (capital) 37,237 (urban area); Vaitele 6,294; Faleasi'u 3,548; Vailele 3,174; Le'auva'a 3,015. *Mid-2009:* Apia (capital) 36,000 (Source: UN, *World Urbanization Prospects: The 2009 Revision*).

Births, Marriages and Deaths (registrations, 2001): Live births 3,516; Marriages 821; Deaths 339. *2004:* Live births 1,679; Deaths 547. Note: Registration is incomplete. *2005–10* (annual averages, UN estimates): Birth rate 23.8 per 1,000; Death rate 5.3 per 1,000 (Source: UN, *World Population Prospects: The 2008 Revision*).

Life Expectancy (years at birth, WHO estimates): 68 (males 66; females 70) in 2008. Source: WHO, *World Health Statistics*.

Economically Active Population (persons aged 15 years and over, 2006 census): Agriculture, hunting and forestry 17,196; Fishing 1,903; Manufacturing and handicrafts (incl. mining) 10,548; Electricity, gas and water supply 872; Construction 2,476; Wholesale and retail trade; repair of motor vehicles, motorcycles and personal and household goods 3,947; Hotels and restaurants 2,018; Transport, storage and communications 3,255; Financial intermediation 967; Real estate, renting and business activities 472; Public administration and defence; compulsory social security 2,706; Education 2,842; Health and social work 833; Other community, social and personal service activities 2,437; Private households with employed persons 811; Extra-territorial organizations and bodies 279; *Sub-total* 53,562; Activities not adequately defined 366; *Total employed* 53,928 (males 36,478, females 17,450); Unemployed 707 (males 418, females 289); *Total labour force* 54,635 (males 36,896, females 17,739).

HEALTH AND WELFARE
Key Indicators

Total Fertility Rate (children per woman, 2008): 4.0.

Under-5 Mortality Rate (per 1,000 live births, 2008): 26.

Physicians (per 1,000 head, 2003): 0.3.

Hospital Beds (per 1,000 head, 2005): 1.0.

Health Expenditure (2007): US $ per head (PPP): 237.

Health Expenditure (2007): % of GDP: 5.0.

Health Expenditure (2007): public (% of total): 84.5.

Total Carbon Dioxide Emissions ('000 metric tons, 2007): 161.2.

Carbon Dioxide Emissions Per Head (metric tons, 2007): 0.9.

Human Development Index (2007): ranking 94.

Human Development Index (2007): value 0.771.

For sources and definitions, see explanatory note on p. vi.

AGRICULTURE, ETC.

Principal Crops ('000 metric tons, 2008 unless otherwise indicated, FAO estimates): Taro 20 (2009); Yams 3.0 (2009); Other roots and tubers 3.0; Coconuts 155; Bananas 23.0; Papayas 3.8; Pineapples 4.6; Guavas, mangoes and mangosteens 4.0; Avocados 1.2; Other fruits 1.8; Vegetables 1.0; Cocoa beans 0.5.

Livestock ('000 head, year ending September 2008, FAO estimates): Pigs 202; Cattle 30; Horses 1.9; Chickens 620. Note: No data were available for 2009.

Livestock Products (metric tons, 2008, FAO estimates): Cattle meat 1,100; Pig meat 4,000; Chicken meat 584; Cows' milk 1,500; Hen eggs 360; Honey 400. Note: No data were available for 2009.

Forestry ('000 cubic metres, 2006): *Roundwood Removals* (excl. bark): Sawlogs and veneer logs 3; Other industrial roundwood 3; Fuel wood 70; Total 76. *Sawnwood Production* (incl. sleepers): 1. *2006–2009* (FAO estimates): Annual output as in 2006.

Fishing (metric tons, live weight, 2008): Albacore 2,342; Yellowfin tuna 300 (FAO estimate); Other marine fishes 534 (FAO estimate); Marine crustaceans 203 (FAO estimate); Marine molluscs 200 (FAO estimate); Sea-urchins and other echinoderms 212 (FAO estimate); Total capture (incl. others) 3,800 (FAO estimate); Aquaculture 3 (FAO estimate); Total catch 3,803 (FAO estimate).

Source: FAO.

INDUSTRY

Electric Energy (million kWh): 113.5 in 2006; 119.6 in 2007; 109.9 in 2008. Note: Figures relate only to government-owned power schemes. Source: Treasury Department of Samoa. *2009:* 108 million kWh (Source: Asian Development Bank).

FINANCE

Currency and Exchange Rates: 100 sene (cents) = 1 tala (Samoan dollar). *Sterling, US Dollar and Euro Equivalents* (30 November 2010): £1 sterling = 3.761 tala; US $1 = 2.422 tala; €1 = 3.148 tala; 100 tala = £26.59 = US $41.29 = €31.77. *Average Exchange Rate* (tala per US $): 2.6166 in 2007; 2.6442 in 2008; 2.7308 in 2009.

Budget (million tala, year ending 30 June 2006): *Revenue:* Tax revenue 273.1 (Income tax 47.2; Excise tax 69.0; Taxes on international trade 40.9; Value-added gross receipts and services tax 108.6); Other revenue 42.2; Total 315.4, excl. external grants received (71.8). *Expenditure:* Current expenditure 281.9 (General administration 69.5, Law and order 20.2, Education 55.3, Health 47.3, Social security and pensions 14.0, Agriculture 11.7, Public works 29.6, Natural resources 12.4, Other economic services 2.6, Interest on public debt 4.3, Other purposes 29.7, *Less* Value-added gross receipts and services tax payable by government 14.7); Development expenditure 86.1; Total 368.0, excl. net lending (23.7) (Source: IMF, *Samoa: Selected Issues and Statistical Appendix*—June 2007). *2008/09* (million tala): Total revenue 492.0 (Domestic receipts 381.4, External grants 110.7); Total expenditure 551.0 (Domestically financed 356.7). *2009/10* (million tala): Total revenue 533.2 (Domestic receipts 380.4, External grants 152.8); Total expenditure 646.1 (Domestically financed 367.3). (Source: Ministry of Finance, *Quarterly Economic Review*).

International Reserves (US $ million at 31 December 2010): IMF special drawing rights 19.41; Reserve position in IMF 1.07; Foreign exchange 188.97; *Total* 209.45. Source: IMF, *International Financial Statistics*.

Money Supply (million tala at 31 December 2009): Currency outside banks 55.21; Transferable deposits 168.61; Other deposits 481.42. *Broad money* 705.24. Source: IMF, *International Financial Statistics*.

Cost of Living (Consumer Price Index, excluding rent; base: 2005 = 100): All items 122.1 in 2008; 129.7 in 2009; 131.0 in 2010. Source: IMF, *International Financial Statistics*.

Gross Domestic Product (million tala at constant 2002 prices, fiscal year ending 30 June): 1,116.8 in 2007/08; 1,059.8 in 2008/09; 1,059.6 in 2009/10.

Expenditure on the Gross Domestic Product (million tala in current prices, fiscal year ending 30 June 2010): Final consumption expenditure 1,466.8 (Households 1,050.9, Non-profit institutions serving households 69.3, General government 346.6); Gross fixed capital formation 393.1; Changes in inventories 29.7; *Total domestic expenditure* 1,889.6; Exports of goods and services 471.2; *Less* Imports of goods and services 762.6; Statistical discrepancy –151.6; *GDP in market prices* 1,446.6.

Gross Domestic Product by Economic Activity (million tala in current prices, fiscal year ending 30 June 2010): Agriculture and fishing 160.8; Manufacturing 138.8; Electricity, gas and water 73.2; Construction 187.1; Trade 290.8; Hotels and restaurants 50.9; Transport and communications 203.4; Finance and business services 125.8; Public administration 125.5; Ownership of dwellings 48.4; Other services 60.8; *Sub-total* 1,465.5; *Less* Financial intermediation services indirectly measured 18.9; *Total* 1,446.6.

Balance of Payments (US $ million, 2009): Exports of goods f.o.b. 25.1; Imports of goods f.o.b. –207.9; *Trade balance* –182.8; Exports of services 149.2; Imports of services –78.2; *Balance on goods and services* –111.8; Other income received 7.8; Other income paid –26.7;

SAMOA

Balance on goods, services and income –130.8; Current transfers received 138.3; Current transfers paid –8.1; *Current balance* –0.6; Capital account (net) 46.8; Direct investment from abroad 3.0; Portfolio investment assets –1.3; Portfolio investment liabilities 0.0; Other investments assets –11.4; Other investment liabilities 1.6; Net errors and omissions 10.1; *Overall balance* 48.2. Source: IMF, *International Financial Statistics*.

EXTERNAL TRADE

Principal Commodities (million tala, 2009): *Imports c.i.f.:* Food and live animals 151.2; Crude materials (excl. fuels) 16.6; Mineral fuels, etc. 115.4; Chemicals 44.9; Basic manufactures 116.6; Machinery and transport equipment 107.9; Miscellaneous manufactured articles 44.8; Total (incl. others) 620.7. *Exports (incl. re-exports) f.o.b.:* Food and live animals 23.2; Beverages and tobacco 1.0; Basic manufactures 1.2; Machinery and transport equipment 89.0; Total (incl. others) 123.7.

Principal Trading Partners (million tala, 2009): *Imports:* Australia 131.1; China, People's Republic 32.8; Japan 33.7; New Zealand 222.0; USA 75.1; Total (incl. others) 620.7. *Exports (incl. re-exports):* Australia 85.2; New Zealand 22.6; USA 4.4; Total (incl. others) 123.7.

TRANSPORT

Road Traffic (motor vehicles registered, 2007): Private cars 5,189; Pick-ups 4,136; Taxis 1,916; Trucks 2,375; Buses 251; Motorcycles 104; Tractors 45; Total (incl. others) 16,215.

International Shipping (freight traffic, '000 metric tons, 2009): Goods loaded 207.2; Goods unloaded 45.6. *Merchant Fleet* (at 31 December 2009): Vessels 10; Total displacement ('000 grt) 10.5 (Source: IHS Fairplay, *World Fleet Statistics*).

Civil Aviation (traffic on scheduled services, 2006): Kilometres flown 6 million; Passengers carried 288,000; Passenger-kilometres 384 million; Total ton-kilometres 36 million. Source: UN, *Statistical Yearbook*.

TOURISM

Visitor Arrivals: 122,352 in 2007; 122,163 in 2008; 129,238 in 2009.

Visitor Arrivals by Country (2009): American Samoa 24,285; Australia 24,497; Fiji 2,537; New Zealand 54,574; USA 9,247; Total (incl. others) 129,238.

Tourism Receipts (million tala, incl. passenger transport): 262.5 in 2007; 288.4 in 2008; 304.3 in 2009.

COMMUNICATIONS MEDIA

Telephones (2009): 31,900 main lines in use*.
Personal Computers: 4,200 (23.5 per 1,000 persons) in 2006*.
Internet Users (2009): 9,000*.
Broadband Subscribers (2009): 200*.
Mobile Cellular Telephones (2009): 151,000 subscribers*.
Radio Receivers (1997): 410,000 in use†.
Television Receivers (2001): 26,000 in use*.
Daily Newspapers (2004): 2†.
Non-daily Newspapers (1988): 5 (estimated circulation 23,000)†.

* Source: International Telecommunication Union.
† Source: UNESCO, *Statistical Yearbook*.

EDUCATION

Pre-primary (2008/09): 299 teachers; 4,080 pupils.
Primary (2008/09 unless otherwise indicated): 167 schools (2005); 936 teachers; 29,663 pupils.
Secondary (2008/09): 1,206 teachers; 25,429 pupils.
Universities and other Higher (2001): 140 teachers; 1,179 students.

Source: mainly UNESCO Institute for Statistics.

Pupil-teacher Ratio (primary education, UNESCO estimate): 31.7 in 2008/09. Source: UNESCO Institute for Statistics.

Adult Literacy Rate (UNESCO estimates): 98.7% (males 99.0%; females 98.5%) in 2008. Source: UNESCO Institute for Statistics.

Directory

The Government

HEAD OF STATE

O le Ao o le Malo: TUIATUA TUPUA TAMASESE EFI (elected by the Fono 15 June 2007).

CABINET
(May 2011)

The Government is formed by the Human Rights Protection Party.

Prime Minister and Minister of Foreign Affairs, Trade and Tourism: TUILA'EPA SAILELE MALIELEGAOI.
Deputy Prime Minister and Minister of Commerce, Industry and Labour: FONOTOE PIERRE LAUOFO.
Minister of Women, Community and Social Development: TOLOFUAIVALELEI FALEMOE LEI'ATAUA.
Minister of Police and Prisons: SALA FATA PINATI.
Minister of Works, Transport and Infrastructure: MANU'ALESAGALALA POSALA ENOKATI.
Minister of Natural Resources and Environment: FA'AMOETAULOA FA'ALE TU'UMALI'I.
Minister of Finance: FAUMUINA TIATIA LIUGA.
Minister of Customs and Revenue: TUILOMA PULE LAMEKO.
Minister of Health: Dr TUITAMA TALALELEI TUITAMA.
Minister of Communications and Information Technology: TUISUGALETAUA SOFARA AVEAU.
Minister of Education, Sports and Culture: MAGELE MAUILIU MAGELE.
Minister for Justice and Courts Administration: FIAME NAOMI MATA'AFA.
Minister of Agriculture and Fisheries: LE MAMEA ROPATI.

MINISTRIES

Prime Minister's Department: POB L 1861, Apia; tel. 63222; fax 21339; e-mail presssecretariat@samoa.ws; internet www.govt.ws.
Ministry of Agriculture and Fisheries: POB 1874, Apia; tel. 22561; fax 21865; e-mail tai.matatumua@maf.gov.ws; internet www.maf.gov.ws.
Ministry of Commerce, Industry and Labour: Apia; tel. 20441; fax 20443; e-mail mpal@mcil.gov.ws; internet www.mcil.gov.ws.
Ministry of Communications and Information Technology: Private Bag, Apia; tel. 26117; fax 24671; e-mail mcit@mcit.gov.ws; internet www.mcit.gov.ws.
Ministry of Education, Sports and Culture: POB 1869, Apia; tel. 21911; fax 21917; e-mail samoamesc@lesamoa.net; internet www.mesc.gov.ws.
Ministry of Finance: Private Bag, Apia; tel. 34333; fax 21312; e-mail information@mof.gov.ws; internet www.mof.gov.ws.
Ministry of Foreign Affairs and Trade: POB L 1859, Apia; tel. 21171; fax 21504; e-mail mfat@mfat.gov.ws; internet www.mfat.gov.ws.
Ministry of Health: Private Bag, Apia; tel. 68100; fax 24496; e-mail moh@health.gov.ws; internet www.health.gov.ws.
Ministry of Justice and Courts Administration: POB 49, Apia; tel. 22671; fax 21050; e-mail ceojustice@samoa.ws; internet www.mjca.gov.ws.
Ministry of Natural Resources and Environment: Private Bag, Apia; tel. 23800; fax 23176; e-mail info@mnre.gov.ws; internet www.mnre.gov.ws.
Ministry of Police: Apia; tel. 28055; fax 21319; e-mail anisi.tua@police.gov.ws; internet www.police.gov.ws.
Ministry for Revenue: POB 1877, Apia; tel. 20411; fax 20414; e-mail info_services@revenue.gov.ws; internet www.revenue.gov.ws.

SAMOA

Ministry of Women, Community and Social Development: Private Bag, Apia; tel. 20854; fax 23665; internet www.mwcsd.gov.ws.

Ministry of Works, Transport and Infrastructure: Private Bag, Apia; tel. 21611; fax 21990; e-mail enquiries@mwti.gov.ws; internet www.mwti.gov.ws.

Election Commission

Office of the Electoral Commissioner: POB 219, Apia; tel. 25967; fax 24309; internet www.oec.gov.ws; Electoral Commr TANUVASA ISITOLO LEMISIO.

Legislature

FONO
(Legislative Assembly)

The Assembly has 47 Matai members, representing 41 territorial constituencies, and two individual members. Elections are held every five years. A total of 158 candidates contested the general election of 4 March 2011. The ruling Human Rights Protection Party (HRPP) was returned to office, winning the support of 36 newly elected legislators, including seven independent members of the Fono. The Tautua Samoa Party took 13 seats.

Speaker: LA'AULIALEMALIETOA LEUATEA POLATAIVAO FOSI.

Political Organizations

Human Rights Protection Party (HRPP): c/o The Fono, Apia; f. 1979; Western Samoa's first formal political party; Leader TUILA'EPA SAILELE MALIELEGAOI; Gen. Sec. LAULU DAN STANLEY.

The People's Party (TPP): f. 2008; Leader SOLOMONA TOAILOA.

Samoa Christian Party: Leader TUALA TIRESA MALIETOA.

Samoa Democratic United Party (SDUP): POB 1233, Apia; tel. 23543; fax 20536; f. 1988; est. as Samoa National Development Party (SNDP); coalition party comprising Christian Democratic Party (CDP) and several independents; assumed present name after 2001 election, following merger of SNDP and Samoa Independent Party; Leader (vacant); Sec. VALASI TAFITO.

Samoa Progressive Political Party: Leader TOEOLESULUSULU SIUEVA.

Tautua Samoa Party (TSP): Apia; f. 2008; Leader PALUSALUE FAAPO.

Diplomatic Representation

EMBASSIES AND HIGH COMMISSIONS IN SAMOA

Australia: Beach Rd, POB 704, Apia; tel. 23411; fax 23159; internet www.samoa.embassy.gov.au; High Commissioner Dr STEPHEN HENNINGHAM.

China, People's Republic: Private Bag, Vailima, Apia; tel. 22474; fax 21115; e-mail TCE@SAMOA.NET; Ambassador ZHAO WEIPING.

New Zealand: Beach Rd, POB 1876, Apia; tel. 21711; fax 20086; e-mail nzhcapia@samoa.ws; High Commissioner NICK HURLEY.

USA: POB 3430, Matafele, Apia; tel. 21631; fax 22030; e-mail AmEmbApia@state.gov; internet samoa.usembassy.gov; Ambassador Dr DAVID HUEBNER (resident in New Zealand).

Judicial System

The Supreme Court, which is composed of six local judges and presided over by the Chief Justice, has full jurisdiction for both criminal and civil cases. Appeals lie with the Court of Appeal, which sits twice a year and is presided over by three overseas judges. The Magistrates' Court was replaced by two District Courts in 1998. The Land and Titles Court has jurisdiction in respect of disputes over land ownership and Samoan titles. It consists of the President and two Samoan judges appointed by the President.

Attorney-General: MING LEUNG WAI.

Chief Justice of the Supreme Court: PATU TIAVA'ASU'E FALEFATU SAPOLU.

President of the Court of Appeal: WILLIAM DAVID BARAGWANATH (non-resident).

District Court Judges: VAEMOA VAAI, TAUILIILI HARRY SCHUSTER.

President of the Land and Titles Court: TAGALOA KERSLAKE.

Religion

Almost all of Samoa's inhabitants profess Christianity.

CHRISTIANITY

Fono a Ekalesia i Samoa (Samoa Council of Churches): POB 574, Apia; f. 1967; four mem. churches; Sec. Rev. EFEPAI KOLIA.

The Anglican Communion

Samoa lies within the diocese of Polynesia, part of the Church of the Province of New Zealand. The Bishop of Polynesia is resident in Fiji, while the Archdeacon of Tonga and Samoa is resident in Tonga.

Anglican Church: POB 16, Apia; tel. 20500; fax 24663; Rev. PETER E. BENTLEY.

The Roman Catholic Church

The islands of Samoa constitute the archdiocese of Samoa-Apia. At 31 December 2007 there were an estimated 40,500 adherents in the country. The Archbishop participates in the Catholic Bishops' Conference of the Pacific, based in Fiji.

Archbishop of Samoa-Apia: Cardinal ALAPATI L. MATA'ELIGA, Archbishop's House, Fetuolemoana, POB 532, Apia; tel. 20400; fax 20402; e-mail archdiocese@samoa.ws.

Other Churches

Church of Jesus Christ of Latter-day Saints (Mormon): Samoa Apia Mission, POB 1865, Apia; tel. 64210; fax 64222; f. 1888; Pres. RENDAL V. BROOMHEAD; f. 1888; 65,000 mems.

Congregational Christian Church in Samoa: Tamaligi, POB 468, Apia; tel. 22279; fax 20429; e-mail cccsgsec@lesamoa.net; f. 1830; 100,000 mems; Gen. Sec. Rev. MAONE F. LEAUSA.

Congregational Church of Jesus in Samoa: 505 Borie St, Honolulu, HI 96818, USA; Rev. NAITULI MALEPEAI.

Methodist Church in Samoa (Ekalesia Metotisi i Samoa): POB 1867, Apia; tel. 22283; fax 22203; e-mail afereti@samoa.ws; f. 1828; 37,000 mems; Pres. Rev. AFERETI SAMUELU; Gen. Sec. Rev. TUPU FOLASA.

Seventh-day Adventist Church: POB 600, Apia; tel. 20451; f. 1895; covers Samoa and American Samoa; 5,000 mems; Pres. Pastor SAMUELU AFAMASAGA; Sec. UILI SOLOFA.

BAHÁ'Í FAITH

National Spiritual Assembly: POB 1117, Apia; tel. 23348; fax 21363.

The Press

Newsline: POB 2441, Apia; tel. 24216; fax 23623; twice a week; Editor PIO SIOA.

Samoa News: POB 1160, Apia; daily; merged with the weekly *Samoa Times* (f. 1967) in Sept. 1994; Publr RHONA ANNESLEY.

The Samoa Observer: POB 1572, Apia; tel. 21099; fax 21195; e-mail samoaobserver@yahoo.com; internet www.samoaobserver.ws; f. 1979; 5 a week; independent; English and Samoan; also publ. in New Zealand twice a week; Editor-in-Chief SAVEA SANO MALIFA; Editor KENI LESA; circ. 4,500.

Samoa Weekly: Saleufi, Apia; f. 1977; weekly; independent; bilingual; Editor LANCE POLU; circ. 4,000.

Savali: POB L 1861, Apia; tel. 26938; fax 21339; e-mail savalinews@samoa.ws; publ. of Lands and Titles Court; monthly; govt-owned; Samoan edn f. 1904; Editor FALESEU L. FUA; circ. 6,000; English edn f. 1977; circ. 500; bilingual commercial edn f. 1993; circ. 1,500; Editor TUPUOLA TERRY TAVITA.

South Seas Star: POB 800, Apia; tel. 23684; weekly.

PRESS ASSOCIATION

Journalists' Association of Samoa (JAWS): Apia; tel. 7773776; e-mail jawsexec@yahoo.com; internet jawsamoa.blogspot.com; f. 1980; Pres. UALE PAPALII TAIMALELAGI.

Broadcasting and Communications

TELECOMMUNICATIONS

Digicel Samoa Ltd: Vaimea, Apia; fax 28005; e-mail customercaresamoa@digicelgroup.com; internet www.digicelsamoa.com; f. 2006; est. following acquisition of Telecom Samoa by Digicel

SAMOA

Group; 90% owned by Digicel Group, 10% govt-owned; CEO PEPE CHRISTIAN FRUEAN.

SamoaTel: Maluafou, Private Bag, Apia; tel. 67846; fax 24000; internet www.samoatel.ws; corporatized in 1999; in process of privatization in 2011; 70% stake sold to Blue Sky (American Samoa) in Jan; telecommunications and postal services provider; Chair. Rev. IUTISONE SALEVAO; CEO MIKE JOHNSTONE.

Samoa.ws: Lotemau Centre, Apia; tel. 20926; e-mail helpdesk@samoa.ws; internet www.samoa.ws; locally owned internet service provider.

BROADCASTING
Radio and Television

Samoa Broadcasting Corpn: Apia; tel. 21420; fax 21072; f. 1948; govt-controlled, with commercial sponsorship; operates SBC Radio 1 and SBC Television 1; CEO FAIASEA LEI SAM MATAFEO.

Graceland Broadcasting Network: POB 3444, Apia; tel. 20197; fax 25487; e-mail gbn@lesamoa.net; internet www.welcome.to/gbn; f. 1992; telecommunications, television and radio.

Magik 98 FM: POB 762, Apia; tel. 25149; fax 25147; e-mail magic98fm@samoa.net; f. 1989; privately owned; operates on FM wavelengths 98.1 and 99.9 MHz; Man. COREY KEIL.

Star Television: Apia; f. 2009; Man. Dir APULU LANCE POLU.

Finance

(cap. = capital; res = reserves; dep. = deposits; m. = million; brs = branches; amounts in tala, unless otherwise indicated)

BANKING
Central Bank

Central Bank of Samoa: Private Bag, Apia; tel. 34100; fax 20293; e-mail centralbank@cbs.gov.ws; internet www.cbs.gov.ws; f. 1984; cap. 10.0m., res 18.0m. (Nov. 2009); Gov. LEASI PAPALI'I TOMMY SCANLAN.

Commercial Banks

ANZ Bank (Samoa) Ltd: Beach Rd, POB L 1885, Apia; tel. 69999; fax 69972; e-mail samoa@anz.com; internet www.anz.com/samoa; f. 1959; est. as Bank of Western Samoa, name changed 1997; 100% owned by ANZ Funds Pty Ltd; cap. 1.5m., res 28.4m., dep. 246.1m. (Sept. 2001); CEO STEPHEN ROGERS; 1 br.

National Bank of Samoa: ACB Bldg, 1st Floor, Beach Rd, Apia 00685; tel. 26766; fax 23477; internet www.nbs.ws; f. 1995; owned by consortium of private interests in Samoa, American Samoa and the USA; Chair. SALA EPA TUIOTI; CEO MALCOLM JOHNSTON; 15 agencies; 5 brs.

Samoa Commercial Bank: POB L 602, Apia; tel. 31233; fax 30250; e-mail info@scbl.ws; internet www.scbl.ws; f. 2003; CEO RAY AH LIKI.

Westpac Bank Samoa Ltd: Beach Rd, POB 1860, Apia; tel. 20000; fax 22848; e-mail westpacsamoa@westpac.com.au; internet www.westpac.com.ws; f. 1977; est. as Pacific Commercial Bank Ltd, current name adopted 2001; first independent bank; 93.5% owned by Westpac Banking Corpn (Australia); cap. 1.2m., res 1.1m., dep. 215.7m. (Sept. 2009); Chair. ALAN WALTER; Gen. Man. JASON GREEN; 3 brs.

Development Bank

Development Bank of Samoa: POB 1232, Apia; tel. 22861; fax 23888; e-mail dbs@dbsamoa.ws; internet www.dbsamoa.ws; f. 1974; est. by Govt to foster economic and social development; Chair. TUPAIMATUNA LULAI LAVEA; CEO TUIASAU SAUMANI WONGSIN.

INSURANCE

National Pacific Insurance Ltd: DBS Bldg, Level 5, Beach Rd, Apia; tel. 20481; fax 23374; e-mail NationalPacificInsurance@npisamoa.ws; internet www.nationalpacificinsurance.com; f. 1977; Gen. Man. DARRYL WILLIAMSON.

Progressive Insurance Company: POB 620, Lotemau Centre, Apia; tel. 26110; fax 26112; e-mail progins@samoa.ws; f. 1993; Gen. Man. I. O. FILEMU.

Samoa Life Assurance Corporation: POB 494, Apia; tel. 23360; fax 23024; e-mail info@samoalife.ws; internet www.samoalife.ws; f. 1977; Gen. Man. A. S. CHAN TING.

Trade and Industry
CHAMBER OF COMMERCE

Samoa Chamber of Commerce and Industry: 1st Floor, Le Sanalele Complex, Saleufi, POB 2014, Apia; tel. 31090; fax 31089; e-mail chamber@samoa.ws; internet www.samoachamber.ws; f. 1938; represents the interests of the private sector; Pres. NAMULAUULU SAMI LEOTA.

INDUSTRIAL AND TRADE ASSOCIATIONS

Samoa Coconut Products: Apia.

Samoa Forest Corporation: Apia.

UTILITIES
Electricity

Electric Power Corporation: POB 2011, Apia; tel. 65246; fax 23748; e-mail fepuleait@epc.ws; internet www.epc.ws; f. 1972; autonomous govt-owned corpn; part of Public Works Dept, known as Electric Power Scheme, until 1972; Gen. Man. MUAAUSA JOSEPH WALTER.

Water

Samoa Water Authority: POB 245, Apia; tel. 20409; fax 21298; e-mail taputoa@swa.gov.ws; internet www.swa.gov.ws; Chair. AFIOGA TUISUGALETAUA AVEAU SOFARA AVEAU.

TRADE UNIONS

Samoa Association of Manufacturers and Exporters (SAME): POB 3428, Apia; tel. 23377; fax 26895; e-mail info@same.org.ws; internet www.same.ws; f. 1981; Pres. EDDIE WILSON.

Samoa Nurses' Association (SNA): POB 3491, Apia; tel. 24439; fax 26976; e-mail sna@lesamoa.ne; internet www.samoanursing.ws; Pres. FAAMANATU NIELSEN; 252 mems.

Samoa Trade Union Congress (STUC): POB 1515, Apia; tel. 24134; fax 20014; f. 1981; affiliate of ITUC; Pres. FALEFATA TUANIU PETAIA; Dir MATAFEO R. MATAFEO; 5,000 mems.

Transport

Public Works Department: Private Bag, Apia; tel. 20865; fax 21927; e-mail pwdir@lesamoa.net; Dir of Works ISIKUKI PUNIVALU.

ROADS

In 1999 there were 790 km of roads on the islands, of which some 42% were paved. In 2004 the Government announced a programme of road-building, including new roads from Apia to the airport and to the inter-island wharves.

SHIPPING

There are deep-water wharves at Apia and Asau. Regular cargo services link Samoa with Australia, New Zealand, American Samoa, Fiji, New Caledonia, Solomon Islands, Tonga, US Pacific coast ports and various ports in Europe.

Samoa Ports Authority: POB 2279, Apia; tel. 64400; fax 25870; e-mail spa@spasamoa.ws; internet www.spasamoa.ws; f. 1999; Gen. Man. TOLEAFOA ELON BETHAM.

Samoa Shipping Corporation Ltd: Private Bag, Shipping House Matautu-tai, Apia; tel. 20935; fax 22352; e-mail info@samoashipping.com; internet www.samoashipping.com; Man. Dir PAPALI'I WILLIE NANSEN.

Samoa Shipping Services Ltd: POB 1884, Apia; tel. 20790; fax 20026; e-mail sss@lesamoa.net; internet www.sssl.ws.

CIVIL AVIATION

There is an international airport at Faleolo, about 35 km from Apia, and an airstrip at Fagali'i, 4 km east of Apia Wharf, which receives light aircraft from American Samoa.

Polynesian Blue: internet www.polynesianblue.com; f. 2005; 49% owned by the Samoan Govt, 49% owned by Virgin Blue, 2% owned by independent Samoan shareholder; flies between Samoa, Australia and New Zealand; replaced the services of Polynesian Airlines upon that carrier's cessation of international operations in 2005; CEO JOHN BARTLETT.

Polynesian Ltd: 2nd Floor, SNPF Bldg, Beach Rd, POB 599, Apia; tel. 21261; fax 20023; e-mail enquiries@polynesianairlines.com; internet www.polynesianairlines.com; f. 1959; 100% govt-owned; operates service to American Samoa and offers charter services between the islands of Upolu and Savai'i; Chair. TUILA'EPA SAILELE MALIELEGAOI; CEO TAUA FATU TIELU.

Tourism

The principal attractions are the scenery and the pleasant climate. Samoa has traditionally maintained a cautious attitude towards tourism, fearing that the Samoan way of life might be disrupted by an influx of foreign visitors. Tourist arrivals were reported to have risen from 122,163 in 2008 to 128,804 in 2009, partly owing to an increase in cruise-ship visits, rising to an estimated 129,487 in 2010. Most visitors come from New Zealand, American Samoa, Australia and the USA. Tourist receipts (including passenger transport) totalled an estimated 304.3m. tala in 2009.

Samoa Tourism Authority: POB 2272, Apia; tel. 63500; fax 20886; e-mail info@samoa.travel; internet www.samoa.travel; f. 1986; CEO MATATAMALI'I SONJA HUNTER.

Samoa Hotel Association: POB 3973, Apia; tel. 30160; fax 30161; e-mail info@samoa-hotels.ws; internet www.samoa-hotels.ws; f. 1999; owned by Asscn of Accommodation Providers; Pres. STEVE YOUNG.

Defence

In August 1962 Western Samoa (as it was then known) and New Zealand signed a Treaty of Friendship, whereby the New Zealand Government, on request, acts as the sole agent of the Samoan Government in its dealings with other countries and international organizations. In April 2009 Samoa and Australia renewed a bilateral programme of defence co-operation. In the year ending June 2008 expenditure on defence amounted to 26.8m. tala (equivalent to 7.0% of total budgetary expenditure).

Education

The education system is divided into pre-primary, primary, intermediate and secondary and is based on the New Zealand system. In 2008/09 there were 4,080 pupils at pre-primary schools and 29,663 pupils at primary schools. In the same year 25,429 pupils were undergoing secondary-level education. Teaching staff at primary level numbered 936 in 2008/09; in the same year there were 299 pre-primary teachers and 1,206 secondary-school teachers. There are also a trades training institute, a teacher-training college and a college for tropical agriculture. About 99% of the adult population are literate. The National University of Samoa was founded in 1988, and had an initial intake of 328 students. By 2001 some 1,179 students were enrolled in university and other higher education. Samoa joined other governments in the region in establishing the University of the South Pacific, based in Fiji, in 1977. Current government expenditure on education in the year ending 30 June 2008 was an estimated 106.1m. tala (27.7% of total current expenditure). With support from Australia and New Zealand, the Government was in the process of implementing a programme of free education in 2009/10.

SAN MARINO

Introductory Survey

LOCATION, CLIMATE, LANGUAGE, RELIGION, FLAG, CAPITAL

The Republic of San Marino is in southern Europe, entirely surrounded by Italy. The country is situated on the slopes of Mount Titano, in the Apennines, bordered by the central Italian region of Emilia-Romagna to the north, and the Marches region to the south. San Marino has cool winters and warm summers, with temperatures generally between −2°C (28°F) and 30°C (86°F). Average annual rainfall totals 880 mm (35 ins). The language is Italian. Almost all of the inhabitants profess Christianity, and the state religion is Roman Catholicism. The civil flag (proportions 3 by 4) has two equal horizontal stripes, of white and light blue. The state flag has, in addition, the national coat of arms (a shield, framed by a yellow cartouche, bearing three green mountains—each with a white tower, surmounted by a stylized ostrich feather, at the summit—the shield being surmounted by a bejewelled crown and framed by branches of laurel and oak, and surmounting a white ribbon bearing, in black, the word 'libertas') in the centre. The capital is San Marino.

CONTEMPORARY POLITICAL HISTORY

San Marino evolved as a city-state in the early Middle Ages and is the sole survivor of the numerous independent states that existed in Italy prior to its unification in the 19th century. A treaty of friendship and co-operation with Italy was signed in 1862, renewed in March 1939 and revised in September 1971.

From 1945 to 1957 San Marino was ruled by a left-wing coalition of the Partito Comunista Sammarinese (PCS) and the Partito Socialista Sammarinese (PSS). Defections from the PCS in 1957 led to a bloodless revolution, after which a coalition of the Partito Democratico Cristiano Sammarinese (PDCS) and the Partito di Democrazia Socialista came to power. In early 1973 an internal dispute over economic policy led to the resignation of the Government, and a new Government was formed by an alliance between the PDCS and the PSS. The PSS withdrew from the coalition in November 1975, resulting in the collapse of the Government. The Captains-Regent took over the administration until March 1976, when a new coalition between the PDCS and the PSS was formed. This Government collapsed in late 1977 but continued in an interim capacity until a new administration was formed. Attempts by the PCS to form a government were frustrated by the lack of a clear majority in the unicameral legislature, the Great and General Council (Consiglio Grande e Generale). Eventually the Council agreed to a dissolution and elections were held in May 1978, when the PDCS secured 26 of the 60 seats. However, they were still unable to form an administration and the three left-wing parties, the PCS, PSS and the Partito Socialista Unitario, which together held 31 seats, agreed to form a coalition Government led by the PCS. San Marino thus became the only Western European country with a communist-led government. A left-wing coalition again formed the administration following the May 1983 elections.

In 1986 a political crisis, resulting from a financial scandal which allegedly involved several prominent PSS members, led to the formation of a new coalition Government, the first to be composed of the PDCS and the PCS. The coalition was renewed in June 1988, following a general election in May. In 1990 the PCS was renamed the Partito Progressista Democratico Sammarinese (PPDS). In 1992 the PDCS negotiated the formation of a coalition Government with the PSS.

At the general election of May 1993 the PDCS and the PSS obtained 26 and 14 seats, respectively. The election was regarded as a defeat for the PPDS, which secured only 11 seats, and was also notable for the success of three recently formed parties, the Alleanza Popolare dei Democratici Sammarinese (known as the Alleanza Popolare—AP), the Movimento Democratico and the Rifondazione Comunista Sammarinese (RCS). In June the PDCS and the PSS agreed to form a coalition Government. The PDCS and the PSS were again dominant at the general election of 31 May 1998, winning 25 and 14 seats, respectively. The PPDS won 11 seats, the AP six, and the RCS two. The remaining two seats were secured by a new grouping, Socialisti per le Riforme, which had been founded in 1997. A coalition Government was formed by the PDCS and the PSS in July 1998. In February 2000 the PSS left the Government, and in March a new coalition Government was formed, with six members of the PDCS, three members of the PPDS and one member of the Socialisti per le Riforme; it also had parliamentary support from Idee in Movimento (as the Movimento Democratico had been renamed in 1998). In March 2001 the Partito dei Democratici Sammarinese (PdD) was formed, following an alliance between Idee in Movimento, the PPDS and the Socialisti per le Riforme; the PPDS Secretary-General, Claudio Felici, was appointed as the PdD's Secretary-General.

At legislative elections held in June 2001 the PDCS won 25 seats and the PSS obtained 15. The two parties subsequently formed a coalition Government. The PdD won 12 seats, while the AP secured five, the RCS two and the Alleanza Nazionale Sammarinese one.

In June 2002 the PDCS-PSS coalition Government collapsed after the PSS withdrew its support, ending the long-term domination of Sammarinese politics by the PDCS. A new coalition Government was formed later in June, incorporating five members of the PSS, three of the PdD and two members of the AP. By December, however, the alliance between the PSS and the PDCS had been renewed, and a new coalition Government was instituted on 17 December, with five members from each party. In January 2003 a new political party, Sammarinesi per la Libertà, was formed. In December the coalition Government collapsed owing to disagreements between the two ruling parties, and a new coalition comprising four PDCS members and two each from the PSS and the PdD was installed. In early 2005 the PSS and the PdD merged to form the Partito dei Socialisti e dei Democratici (PSD). Former members of the PSS founded a new party, the Nuovo Partito Socialista, in November.

At a general election in June 2006 the PDCS won 21 of the 60 seats in the Great and General Council. However, the PSD, which secured 20 seats, subsequently formed a coalition Government with the AP and the Sinistra Unita (SU, an alliance of the RCS and Zona Franca), which received seven and five seats, respectively. The new Government, comprising six members of the PSD and two each from the AP and the SU, took office in July. However, in October the coalition collapsed after a government bill regarding judicial reform was narrowly rejected by the Great and General Council. In November a new four-party coalition was formed, comprising the PSD (five members), the AP, the SU (each two) and a new party, the Democratici di Centro (DdC), which had been formed by disaffected former members of the PDCS and which took the remaining post.

In June 2008 the coalition once again collapsed due to disagreements between the AP and the other ruling parties; an early general election was subsequently held on 9 November. Under the terms of new regulations approved earlier in the year, which had aligned the country's electoral system more closely to that of the Italian model, the parties contested the elections in two major coalitions: the Patto per San Marino (a right-wing coalition that included the PDCS, the AP, the Lista della Libertà, Europopolari per San Marino, Arengo e Libertà and the Unione Sammarinesi dei Moderati); and Riforme e Libertà (a left-wing coalition including the PSD, Sammarinesi per la Libertà, the SU and the DdC). The Patto per San Marino won 54.2% of the valid votes cast and 35 seats, while Riforme e Libertà won 45.8% of the votes and 25 seats. The rate of participation by eligible voters was 68.5%. A new coalition Government was sworn in at the beginning of December, comprising three members of the PDCS, two each from the AP and the Lista della Libertà, and a sole representative each from the Unione Sammarinesi dei Moderati and Arengo e Libertà.

San Marino's tradition of banking secrecy has given rise to concerns (expressed particularly by its neighbour, Italy) that the country's banks might be used for tax avoidance, money-laundering and the financing of terrorism. An Italian judicial investigation into money-laundering, involving San Marino's largest bank, the Cassa di Risparmio della Repubblica de San Marino, and an Italian subsidiary, resulted in the arrest of five senior executives in May 2009. An investigation by the Italian Guardia di Finanzia (financial police) into value-added tax (VAT) fraud revealed that large quantities of goods, particularly computers and other electronic equipment, were being traded between San Marino and Italy without payment of VAT: under the investigation, by February 2010 42 companies had been charged with tax evasion, involving unpaid VAT amounting to some €125m. By early 2010 San Marino was listed by the Organisation for Economic Co-operation and Development (OECD, see p. 376) as conforming to the OECD's international standards for the exchange of financial information, allowing the disclosure of account details to the relevant authorities where fraud or tax evasion were suspected. By June San Marino had concluded bilateral tax information exchange agreements with 25 countries. However, an agreement with Italy concerning taxation, signed in 2002, had still not been ratified by either country in April 2011; as a result, under a 'tax amnesty' announced by the Italian Government in July 2009, repatriation of funds was the only way that Italians wishing to declare deposits held in San Marino could avail themselves of the amnesty, and by mid-2010 about €5,000m., or more than one-third of total deposits, had been withdrawn from San Marino banks. The withdrawal contributed to the economic recession experienced by San Marino in 2009 and 2010, accompanied by increasing unemployment. Budgetary constraints led to a temporary 'freeze' on state spending in July 2010. In December local trade unions organized a one-day general strike and demonstrations against the budget for 2011, which envisaged a 'one-off' increase in income tax of 15%, a tax on higher pensions and the non-replacement of retiring public sector employees; it also, controversially, imposed extra taxation on Italian cross-border workers in San Marino, who numbered about 6,000.

CONSTITUTION AND GOVERNMENT

The *Leges Statutae Sancti Marini* date back to 1600 and outline the main administrative posts and legal basis of the republic. Electoral legislation dates from 1926. Legislative power is vested in the unicameral Great and General Council (Consiglio Grande e Generale), with 60 members elected by universal adult suffrage, under a system of proportional representation, for five years (subject to dissolution). The Council elects two of its members to act jointly as Captains-Regent (Capitani Reggenti), with the functions of Head of State and Government, for six months at a time (ending in March and September). Executive power is held by the Congress of State (Congresso di Stato), with 10 members elected by the Council for the duration of its term. The Congress is presided over by the Captains-Regent.

San Marino is divided into nine 'Castles' (Castelli) corresponding to the original parishes of the Republic. Each 'Castle' is governed by a Castle Captain (Capitano di Castello), who holds office for two years, and a Castle Board (Giunta di Castello), which holds office for five years.

REGIONAL AND INTERNATIONAL CO-OPERATION

San Marino is a member of the Council of Europe (see p. 250) and the Organization for Security and Co-operation in Europe (OSCE, see p. 385). It joined the UN in 1990. San Marino is closely linked to the European Union (EU, see p. 270) through a Co-operation and Customs Union Agreement, originally concluded in 1991, and an agreement on monetary relations, concluded in 2000, which allowed San Marino to adopt the single European currency, the euro.

ECONOMIC AFFAIRS

San Marino's gross national product (GNP) was €824m. in 2009, equivalent to €24,990 per head. According to the World Bank, annual gross domestic product (GDP) growth averaged 3.2% in 2000–08. According to official figures, GDP decreased by 1.1% in 2008 and by a further 13.0% in 2009.

Agriculture contributed only 0.1% of GDP in 2009 and engaged 0.2% of the employed population (excluding the self-employed) in that year. The principal crops are wheat, barley, maize, olives and grapes. Livestock-rearing and dairy farming are also significant. Olive oil and wine are produced for export.

Industry (including manufacturing and construction) contributed 39.2% of GDP in 2009 and engaged 35.6% of the employed population (excluding the self-employed) in that year. Stone-quarrying is the only mining activity in San Marino, and is an important export industry. Manufacturing contributed 33.3% of GDP and engaged 28.7% of the employed population (excluding the self-employed) in 2009. The most important branches of manufacturing are the production of cement, synthetic rubber, leather, textiles and ceramics. The sector is largely export-orientated, owing to integration with firms in Italy.

Energy is derived principally from gas (more than 75%). San Marino is dependent on the Italian state energy companies for much of its energy requirements.

The services sector contributed 60.7% of GDP and engaged 64.2% of the employed population (excluding the self-employed) in 2008. Tourism is a significant source of government revenue. In 2004 the number of visitor arrivals was 2,127,573; however, of that number, only 41,546 stayed at least one night. Total visitor arrivals numbered 1,976,481 in 2010. The sale of coins and postage stamps, mainly to foreign collectors, is also a significant source of foreign exchange. San Marino was granted special dispensation to mint its own euro coins in 2002, with a view to providing for this specialist market. The sale of uncirculated minted coins to collectors plays a significant role in San Marino's economy and it was permitted to continue to mint gold scudi as a legal tender for San Marino only. The financial sector is increasingly important, with the credit and insurance sectors contributing 17.6% of GDP in 2009.

In 2002, according to official figures, San Marino recorded a trade deficit of €96.2m. In the same year, according to the IMF, there was a deficit of €302.5m. on the current account of the balance of payments. Data concerning imports and exports are included in those of Italy, with which San Marino maintains a customs union. A customs union is also maintained with the European Union (EU, see p. 270). The principal source of imports (estimated at 87%) is Italy, upon which the country is dependent for its supply of raw materials. The major exports are wine, woollen goods, furniture, ceramics, building stone and artisan- and hand-made goods.

San Marino receives a subsidy from the Italian Government, under the *Canone Doganale*, amounting to about €11m. annually, in exchange for the Republic's acceptance of Italian rules concerning exchange controls and the renunciation of customs duties. The European single currency, the euro, became the sole currency in circulation at the start of 2002.

No consolidated general government accounts are published by San Marino, and separate accounts and budgets are prepared by the central administration, the Social Security Institute, and each of the public enterprises, on an accrual basis. Figures published by the IMF, on a cash basis, for the budget of the central administration indicated a deficit equivalent to some 3.4% of GDP in 2009. The annual rate of inflation averaged 2.4% in 2003–10; consumer prices increased by 2.6% in 2010. In 2008 808 people were unemployed—equivalent to 3.9% of the total labour force (excluding the self-employed). An increasingly large proportion of the work-force (31.0% of the employed labour force, excluding the self-employed, in 2005, compared with 10.8% in 1991) are cross-border workers, mainly Italians from the surrounding regions.

San Marino's economy is linked to that of its neighbour, Italy, with which it shares a monetary and customs union. Owing to its size, it is extremely vulnerable to economic developments in Italy and the wider EU. Although traditionally manufacturing was the principal sector of the economy, its contribution to GDP has declined and the financial sector, which benefited from alternative taxation and regulation structures, has become increasingly significant. Tourism and commerce are also important. Growth in the financial sector was stimulated by advantageous banking confidentiality, which aroused some concern from the Organisation for Economic Co-operation and Development (OECD, see p. 376) that this would encourage tax fraud, money-laundering and the possible financing of terrorism. The Italian Government expressed particular concern that San Marino was being used as an illegal tax haven (see Contemporary Political History). New legislation was adopted in 2008 in relation to combating money-laundering and the financing of terrorism, in accordance with EU directives, and agreements were signed with a number of countries (25 by mid-2010) on the exchange of tax information. From late 2008 the international financial crisis placed severe strains on the financial sector and on the economy as a whole, which entered into recession at the end of the year; GDP contracted by 1.1% in 2008, by 13% in 2009, and by an estimated 1% in 2010, according to the IMF. The Government allocated significant funds in the 2009 budget to mitigate the effects of the downturn and encourage economic diversification, including increased investment in infrastructure projects and renewable energy sources. The budget deficit was equivalent to 3.4% of GDP in 2009, rising to 6.1% (according to IMF estimates) in 2010. Tax

SAN MARINO

reforms and reductions in public sector employment were envisaged in order to reduce the deficit. The IMF forecast slight growth, of less than 1%, in 2011.

PUBLIC HOLIDAYS

2012: 1 January (New Year's Day), 6 January (Epiphany), 5 February (Liberation Day), 19 March (St Joseph's Day), 25 March (Anniversary of the Arengo), 1 April (Investiture of the new Captains-Regent), 9 April (Easter Monday), 28 May (Labour Day), 7 June (Corpus Christi), 28 July (Fall of Fascism), 15 August (Assumption), 3 September (San Marino Day and Republic Day), 1 October (Investiture of the new Captains-Regent), 1 November (All Saints' Day), 2 November (Commemoration of the Dead), 8 December (Immaculate Conception), 25 December (Christmas Day), 26 December (St Stephen's Day).

Statistical Survey

Source (unless otherwise stated): Ufficio Programmazione Economica e Centro Elaborazione Dati e Statistica, Viale Antonio Onofri 109, 47890 San Marino; tel. 0549 885150; fax 0549 885154; e-mail statistica.upeceds@pa.sm; internet www.upeceds.sm.

AREA AND POPULATION

Area: 61.2 sq km (23.6 sq miles).

Population: 31,888 (males 15,651, females 16,237) at 1 January 2011 (*of whom* Sammarinese 27,001, Others 4,887).

Density (at 1 January 2011): 521.0 per sq km.

Population by Age and Sex (official estimates at 31 December 2010): *0–14:* 6,395 (males 3,362, females 3,033); *15–64:* 21,445 (males 10,551, females 10,894); *65 and over:* 4,047 (males 1,739, females 2,308); *Total* 31,887 (males 15,652, females 16,235).

Principal Towns (population at 1 January 2011): Serravalle 10,394; Borgo Maggiore 6,377; San Marino (capital) 4,296.

Births, Marriages and Deaths (registrations, 2010): Live births 334 (birth rate 10.5 per 1,000); Marriages 213 (marriage rate 6.7 per 1,000); Deaths 222 (death rate 7.0 per 1,000).

Life Expectancy (years at birth, official estimates, 2010): Males 80.9; females 86.0.

Migration (2010): Immigrants 314; Emigrants 171.

Economically Active Population (2010): Agriculture 31; Manufacturing 5,737; Construction 1,374; Trade and hospitality 3,297; Communication and transport 601; Finance 1,072; Real estate, information technology and business services 2,345; Health 191; Education 43; Public sector 4,196; Other services 1,071; *Sub-total* 19,955; Activities not adequately defined 1; *Total employed* 19,959 (males 11,248, females 8,711); Unemployed 808 (males 282, females 526); *Total labour force* 20,764 (males 11,530, females 9,237). Note: Figures exclude self-employed (1,950).

HEALTH AND WELFARE

Key Indicators

Total Fertility Rate (children per woman, 2008): 1.5.

Under-5 Mortality Rate (per 1,000 live births, 2008): 2.

Physicians (per 1,000 head, 1990): 47.35.

Hospital Beds (per 1,000 head, 1990): 7.2.

Health Expenditure (2007): US $ per head (PPP): 2,810.

Health Expenditure (2007): % of GDP: 7.1.

Health Expenditure (2007): public (% of total): 85.5.

For sources and definitions, see explanatory note on p. vi.

FINANCE

Currency and Exchange Rates: Italian currency: 100 cent = 1 euro (€). *Sterling and Dollar Equivalents* (31 December 2010): £1 sterling = 1.172 euros; US $1 = 0.748 euros; €10 = £8.54 = $13.36. *Average Exchange Rates* (euros per US $): 0.6827 in 2008; 0.7198 in 2009; 0.7550 in 2010. Note: The local currency was formerly the Italian lira (plural = lire). From the introduction of the euro, with Italian participation, on 1 January 1999, a fixed exchange rate of €1 = 1,936.27 lire was in operation. Euro notes and coins were introduced on 1 January 2002. The euro and local currency circulated alongside each other until 28 February, after which the euro became the sole legal tender.

General Budget (€ million, 2006): *Revenue:* Tax revenue 262.0 (Taxation on individuals 100.3; Taxes on goods and services 123.2); Social contributions 123.2; Grants 14.6; Other revenue 147.2; Total revenue 547.0. *Expenditure:* Compensation of employees 160.5; Use of goods and services 98.7; Consumption of fixed capital 14.9; Interest 11.0; Subsidies 15.5; Grants 1.6; Social benefits 143.8; Other expense 11.3; Total expenditure 457.3. Source: IMF, *Government Finance Statistics Yearbook*.

International Reserves (excl. gold, US $ million at 31 December 2009): IMF special drawing rights 26.16; Reserve position in IMF 6.43; Foreign exchange 757.68; *Total* 790.27. *2010* (US $ million at 31 December): IMF special drawing rights 25.72; Reserve position in IMF 6.32. Source: IMF, *International Financial Statistics*.

Money Supply (€ '000 at 31 December 2009): Demand deposits at banks 1,536,146. Source: IMF, *International Financial Statistics*.

Cost of Living (Consumer Price Index; base: 2003 = 100): All items 112.6 in 2008; 115.0 in 2009; 118.0 in 2010. Source: ILO.

Gross Domestic Product (€ million at constant 1995 prices): 948 in 2007; 938 in 2008; 816 in 2009.

Expenditure on the Gross Domestic Product (€ million at current prices, 2009): Final consumption expenditure 601; Increase in stocks −35; Gross fixed capital formation 272; *Total domestic expenditure* 838; Exports of goods and services 2,362; *Less* Imports of goods and services 2,098; *GDP in purchasers' values* 1,102.

Gross Domestic Product by Economic Activity (€ million at current prices, 2009): Agriculture 1.1; Manufacturing 367.0; Construction 65.0; Services 668.9 (Trade 148.8, Transport and communications 26.4, Finance and insurance 194.0, Public sector 149.8, Other services 149.9); Total 1,102.0.

Balance of Payments (US $ million, 1996, estimates): Merchandise exports f.o.b. 1,741,9; Merchandise imports c.i.f. −1,719.3; *Trade balance* 22.6; Exports of services 120.4; Imports of services −102.2; *Balance on goods and services* 40.9; Interest payments 63.5; Net labour income −57.9; Other capital income −45.5; *Balance on goods, services and income* 1.0; Net transfers 9.7; *Current balance* 10.7; Capital account (net) 218.5; Errors and omissions −219.8; *Overall balance* 9.4. Source: IMF, *San Marino: Recent Economic Developments* (April 1999).

EXTERNAL TRADE

Data concerning imports and exports are included in those of Italy, with which San Marino maintains a customs union.

TRANSPORT

Road Traffic (registered motor vehicles, 2005): Motorcycles 10,268; Passenger cars 31,747; Buses and coaches 3,421; Agricultural vehicles 1,015; Total (incl. others) 47,876.

TOURISM

Visitor Arrivals (incl. excursionists): 2,111,736 in 2008; 2,055,705 in 2009; 1,976,481 in 2010.

Tourist Arrivals (staying at least one night): 45,508 in 2002; 40,686 in 2003; 41,546 in 2004.

COMMUNICATIONS MEDIA

Radio Receivers (1998): 35,100 in use.

Television Receivers (1999): 23,000 in use.

Telephones (2009): 21,500 main lines in use.

Mobile Cellular Telephones (subscribers, 2009): 24,000.

Internet Users (2009): 17,000.

Broadband Subscribers (2009): 10,000.

Daily Newspapers (2004, unless otherwise indicated): 2 titles; 2,000 copies circulated (1998).

Non-Daily Newspapers (1998): 8 titles; 12,000 copies circulated.

SAN MARINO

Periodicals (1998): 17 titles; 10,000 copies circulated.

Personal Computers: 24,470 (800.2 per 1,000 persons) in 2007.

Sources: Direzione Generale Poste e Telecomunicazioni; International Telecommunication Union.

EDUCATION

Pre-primary (2009/10 unless otherwise indicated): 14 schools; 142 teachers (2008/09); 1,033 pupils.

Primary (2009/10): 14 schools; 252 teachers; 1,577 pupils.

Secondary (Scuola Media) (2009/10): 3 schools; 161 teachers; 933 pupils.

Secondary and Vocational (Scuola Secondaria Superiore e Formazione Professionale): 4 schools (2004/05); 90 teachers (2009/10); 691 pupils (2009/10—a further 710 pupils were studying outside San Marino).

University (2009/10): 1 university, 43 students (a further 832 students were attending courses outside San Marino).

Pupil-teacher Ratio (primary education, UNESCO estimate): 6.2 in 2008/09 (Source: UNESCO Institute for Statistics).

Directory

The Government

HEADS OF STATE

Capitani Reggenti (Captains-Regent): MARIA LUISA BERTI (Noi Sammarinesi), FILIPPO TAMAGNINI (PDCS) (1 April 2011–1 October 2011).

CONGRESSO DI STATO
(Congress of State)
(May 2011)

A coalition of the Partito Democratico Cristiano Sammarinese (PDCS), the Alleanza Popolare (AP), the Lista della Libertà (LdL), Arengo e Libertà, the Europopolari per San Marino (EPS) and the Unione Sammarinese dei Moderati (USM).

Secretary of State for Foreign and Political Affairs, Telecommunications and Transport: ANTONELLA MULARONI (AP).

Secretary of State for Internal Affairs and Civil Protection: VALERIA CIAVATTA (AP).

Secretary of State for Finance, the Budget and Relations with the Azienda Autonoma di Stato Filatelica e Numismatica (AASFN): PASQUALE VALENTINI (PDCS).

Secretary of State for Education, Culture and the University: ROMEO MORRI (USM).

Secretary of State for Health, Social Security, Welfare, Family and Social Affairs and Equal Opportunities: CLAUDIO PODESCHI (PDCS).

Secretary of State for Territory, Environment, Agriculture and Relations with the Azienda Autonoma di Stato di Produzione (AASP): GIANCARLO VENTURINI (PDCS).

Secretary of State for Labour, Co-operation and the Postal Service: FRANCESCO MUSSO (EPS).

Secretary of State for Industry, Handicrafts and Trade: MARCO ARZILLI (LdL).

Secretary of State for Justice, Information, Research and Relations with the Castle Boards: AUGUSTO CASALI (LdL).

Secretary of State for Tourism, Sport, Economic Planning and Relations with the Azienda Autonoma di Stato per i Servizi Pubblici (AASS): FABIO BERARDI (Arengo e Libertà).

MINISTRIES

Secretariat of State for Education, Culture and the University: Contrada Omerelli, 47890 San Marino; tel. 0549 882548; fax 0549 882301; e-mail segreteria.ic@gov.sm; internet www.educazione.sm.

Secretariat of State for Finance, the Budget and Relations with the Azienda Autonoma di Stato Filatelica e Numismatica (AASFN): Palazzo Begni, Contrada Omerelli, 47890 San Marino; tel. 0549 882661; fax 0549 882244; e-mail lbeccari@finanze.sm; internet www.finanze.sm.

Secretariat of State for Foreign and Political Affairs: Palazzo Begni, Contrada Omerelli, 47890 San Marino; tel. 0549 882312; fax 0549 882814; e-mail segreteriadistato@esteri.sm; internet www.esteri.sm.

Secretariat of State for Health, Social Security, Welfare, Family and Social Affairs and Equal Opportunities: Via V. Scialoia, 47895 Cailungo; tel. 0549 883040; fax 0549 883044; e-mail segretario.particolare.sanita@gov.sm; internet www.sanita.sm.

Secretariat of State for Industry, Handicrafts and Trade: Palazzo Mercuri, Contrada del Collegio, 47890 San Marino; tel. 0549 882528; fax 0549 882529.

Secretariat of State for Internal Affairs: Parva Domus, Piazza della Libertà, 47890 San Marino; tel. 0549 882425; fax 0549 885080; e-mail segreteria.interni@gov.sm; internet www.interni.segreteria.sm.

Secretariat of State for Justice, Information, Research and Relations with the Castle Boards: Via A. di Superchio 16, 47893 Borgo Maggiore; tel. 0549 883777; fax 0549 883766; e-mail info.giustizia@gov.sm; internet www.giustizia.sm.

Secretariat of State for Labour, Co-operation and the Postal Service: Palazzo Mercuri, Contrada del Collegio 38, 47890 San Marino; tel. 0549 882532; fax 0549 882535; e-mail info.seglavoro@gov.sm.

Secretariat of State for Territory, Environment, Agriculture and Relations with the Azienda Autonoma di Stato di Produzione (AASP): Contrada Omerelli, 47890 San Marino; tel. 0549 882470; fax 0549 882473; e-mail segr.territorio@omniway.sm.

Secretariat of State for Tourism, Sport, Economic Planning and Relations with the Azienda Autonoma di Stato per i Servizi Pubblici (AASS): Palazzo del Turismo, Contrada Omagnano, 47890 San Marino; tel. 0549 885397; fax 0549 885399; e-mail corrispondenza.turismo@gov.sm; internet www.visitsanmarino.com.

Legislature

Consiglio Grande e Generale
(Great and General Council)

Palazzo Pubblico, Piazza della Libertà, 47890 San Marino; tel. 0549 882273; fax 0549 882389; e-mail info.segristituzionale@pa.sm; internet www.consigliograndeegenerale.sm.

Election, 9 November 2008

Party	Votes	% of votes	Seats
Patto per San Marino	11,371	54.22	35
Partito Democratico Cristiano Sammarinese (PDCS)/ Europopolari per San Marino (EPS)/Arengo e Libertà	6,692	31.91	22
Alleanza Popolare (AP)	2,415	11.52	7
Lista della Libertà (LdL)	1,317	6.28	4
Unione Sammarinesi dei Moderati (USM)	874	4.17	2
Riforme e Libertà	9,601	45.78	25
Partito dei Socialisti e dei Democratici (PSD)/Sammarinesi per la Libertà	6,702	31.91	18
Sinistra Unita (SU)	1,797	8.57	5
Democratici di Centro (DdC)	1,037	4.94	2
Total	**20,972**	**100.00**	**60**

Political Organizations

Alleanza Nazionale Sammarinese (ANS) (San Marino National Alliance): Via Cà Bartoletto 26, 47893 Borgo Maggiore; tel. 0549 907815; fax 0549 875203; e-mail anrsm@omniway.sm; right-wing; formed a coalition, the Unione Sammarinese dei Moderati, with the Popolari Sammarinesi in early 2008 in order to contest the Nov. 2008 general election; Pres. ENNIO VITTORIO PELLANDRA; Political Sec. GLAUCO SANSOVINI.

Alleanza Popolare (AP) (Popular Alliance): Via Luigi Cibrario 25, 47893 Cailungo; tel. 0549 907080; fax 0549 907082; e-mail ap@alleanzapopolare.net; internet www.alleanzapopolare.net; f. 1993 as

SAN MARINO

Alleanza Popolare Democratici Sammarinesi; advocates a constitution and institutional reform; Pres. MARIO VENTURINI; Co-ordinator STEFANO PALMIERI.

Arengo e Libertà (Arengo and Freedom): Via XXVIII Luglio 99, 47893 Borgo Maggiore; tel. 0549 801818; fax 0549 942830; e-mail info@arengoeliberta.sm; internet www.arengoeliberta.sm; f. 2008 by fmr mems of the Partito dei Socialisti e dei Democratici; social democratic; Leader FABIO BERARDI.

Democratici di Centro (DdC) (Democrats of the Centre): Via Cà Franceschino 2, 47893 Borgo Maggiore; tel. 0549 909884; fax 0549 972855; e-mail gruppo.dc@omniway.sm; internet www.democraticidicentro.sm; f. 2007 by fmr mems of the Partito Democratico Cristiano Sammarinese; Pres. ORAZIO MAZZA; Co-ordinator GIOVANNI LONFERNINI.

Europopolari per San Marino (EPS) (European People for San Marino): Via dei Pini 1, 47895 Domagnano; tel. 0549 906622; fax 0549 902431; e-mail europopolari@omniway.sm; internet www.europopolari.sm; f. 2007 by fmr mems of the Partito Democratico Cristiano Sammarinese; Pres. GIAN MARCO MARCUCCI; Political Sec. LORENZO LONFERNINI.

Lista della Libertà (LdL) (Freedom List): e-mail info@listadellaliberta.com; internet listadellaliberta.com; f. Aug. 2008 to contest the Nov. 2008 general election; comprising Noi Sammarinesi and Nuovo Partito Socialista.

Noi Sammarinesi (We Sammarinese): Via XXVIII Luglio 160, 47893 Borgo Maggiore; tel. and fax 0549 907101; e-mail info@noisammarinesi.com; internet www.sammarinesi.com; f. 2006; contested Nov. 2008 general election as part of Lista della Libertà; Spokesman MARCO ARZILLI.

Nuovo Partito Socialista (NPS) (New Socialist Party): Via de Boschetti 57, 47893 Borgo Maggiore; tel. 0549 980093; fax 0549 902212; e-mail nuovopartitosocialista@omniway.sm; internet www.nuovopartitosocialista.sm; f. 2005 by fmr mems of the Partito Socialista Sammarinese; contested Nov. 2008 general election as part of Lista della Libertà; Pres. ANTONIO VOLPINARI; Political Sec. AUGUSTO CASALI.

Partito Democratico Cristiano Sammarinese (PDCS) (San Marino Christian Democrat Party): Via delle Scalette 6, 47890 San Marino; tel. 0549 991193; fax 0549 992694; e-mail pdcs@omniway.sm; internet www.pdcs.sm; f. 1948; Pres. TEODORO LONFERNINI; Political Sec. MARCO GATTI; 2,400 mems.

Partito dei Socialisti e dei Democratici (PSD) (Party of Socialists and Democrats): Via Ordelaffi 46, 47893 Borgo Maggiore; tel. 0549 903806; fax 0549 906438; e-mail info@democratici.sm; internet www.socialistiedemocratici.sm; f. 2005 by merger of the Partito dei Democratici and the Partito Socialista Sammarinese; Pres. DENISE BRONZETTI; Sec.-Gen. GERARDO GIOVAGNOLI.

Partito Socialista Riformista Sammarinese: Via XXVIII Luglio 212, 47893 Borgo Maggiore; tel. 0549 808008; fax 0549 808009; e-mail info@psrs.sm; internet www.psrs.sm; f. 2009 by fmr mems of Partito dei Socialisti e dei Democratici (PSD); Pres. PARIDE ANDREOLI; Sec. SIMONE CELLI.

Patto per San Marino (Pact for San Marino): internet www.pattopersanmarino.sm; f. mid-2008 to contest the Nov. 2008 general election; centre-right coalition, comprising the Partito Democratico Cristiano Sammarinese, Europopolari per San Marino, Arengo e Libertà, Alleanza Popolare, Noi Sammarinesi, Nuovo Partito Socialista, and Unione Sammarinese dei Moderati (comprising Alleanza Nazionale Sammarinese and the Popolari Sammarinesi).

Popolari Sammarinesi (PS) (Sammarinese People): Via Cà Bartoletto 26, 47893 Cailungo; tel. 0549 907776; fax 0549 944431; e-mail info@popolarisammarinesi.sm; formed a coalition, the Unione Sammarinese dei Moderati, with the Alleanza Nazionale Sammarinese in early 2008 in order to contest the Nov. 2008 general election; Pres. ANTONIO PUTTI; Political Sec. ANGELA VENTURINI.

Riforme e Libertà (Reform and Freedom): e-mail info@riformeeliberta.sm; internet www.riformeeliberta.sm; coalition formed to contest the Nov. 2008 general election; comprising Democratici di Centro, Partito dei Socialisti e dei Democratici, Sammarinesi per la Libertà and Sinistra Unita.

Sammarinesi per la Libertà (Sammarinese for Liberty): Via Ranco Mauro 16, 47891 Dogana; tel. 0549 908400; fax 0549 905970; e-mail info@sammarinesiperlaliberta.sm; internet www.sammarinesiperlaliberta.sm; f. 2002; Leader MONICA BOLLINI.

Sinistra Unita (SU) (United Left): Via delle Tamerici 1, 47895 Domagnano; tel. 0549 907656; fax 0549 944397; e-mail sinistraunita@omniway.sm; internet www.sxun.org; f. 2006; left-wing coalition, comprising Rifondazione Comunista Sammarinese and Zona Franca, formed to contest 2006 general election.

    Rifondazione Comunista Sammarinese (RCS) (San Marino Communist Refoundation): Strada delle Tamerici 1, 47895 Domagnano; tel. and fax 0549 907656; e-mail rcs@omniway.sm; f. 1992; communist.

Unione Sammarinese dei Moderati (USM) (Sammarinese Union of Moderates): coalition formed in early 2008 by the Alleanza Nazionale Sammarinese and Popolari Sammarinesi in order to contest the Nov. 2008 general election.

Diplomatic Representation

By December 2010 San Marino had established full diplomatic relations with 100 countries.

EMBASSIES IN SAN MARINO

Holy See: Domus Plebis 1, 47890 San Marino; tel. 0549 992448; Apostolic Nuncio Most Rev. GIUSEPPE BERTELLO (Titular Archbishop of Urbisaglia) (resident in Rome, Italy).

Italy: Viale Antonio Onofri 117, 47890 San Marino; tel. 0549 991146; fax 0549 992229; e-mail ambasciata.sanmarino@esteri.it; internet www.ambsanmarino.esteri.it; Ambassador GIORGIO MARINI.

Judicial System

The administration of justice is entrusted to foreign judges, with the exception of the Justice of the Peace, who must be of San Marino nationality, and who judges minor civil suits. The major judicial institutions are as follows:

Tribunale Commissariale Civile e Penale (Civil and Criminal Commissionary Tribunal): Via Luglio 28, 47893 Borgo Maggiore; tel. 0549 882626; fax 0549 8825980; e-mail tribunale@omniway.sm.

Commissario della Legge (Law Commissioner): deals with civil and criminal cases where the maximum sentence does not exceed three years' imprisonment.

Giudice Penale di Primo Grado (Criminal Judge of the Primary Court of Claims): deals with criminal cases that are above the competence of the Law Commissioner.

Giudice Amministrativo di Appello (Court of Appeal): two judges, who deal with civil and criminal proceedings.

Consiglio dei XII (Council of Twelve): has authority as a Supreme Court of Appeal, for civil proceedings only.

Religion

CHRISTIANITY

The Roman Catholic Church

Roman Catholicism is the official state religion of San Marino. The Republic forms part of the diocese of San Marino-Montefeltro (comprising mainly Italian territory), suffragan to the archdiocese of Ravenna-Cervia.

Bishop of San Marino-Montefeltro: Rt Rev. LUIGI NEGRI, Curia Vescovile, Piazza Giovanni Paolo II 1, 61016 Pennabilli, Pesaro, Italy; tel. (0541) 913720; fax (0541) 928832; e-mail vescovo.negri@diocesi-sanmarino-montefeltro.it; internet www.diocesi-sanmarino-montefeltro.it.

The Press

Argomenti: c/o CSdL, Via V Febbraio 17, Fiorina C-3, 47895 Domagnano; tel. 0549 962060; fax 0549 962075; organ of the Confederazione Sammarinese del Lavoro (CSdL); periodical; Dir ANDREA LEARDINI; circ. 5,000.

Corriere di Informazione Sammarinese: Via Piana, 47890 San Marino; tel. 0549 995147; fax 0549 879021; e-mail corriere@rimini.com; daily.

Il San Marino: Via delle Scalette 6, 47890 San Marino; tel. 0549 991193; fax 0549 992694; e-mail info@pdcs.sm; internet www.pdcs.sm; periodical; organ of the PDCS; quarterly; Dir TEODORO LONFERNINI.

San Marino Fixing: Via G. Giacomini 37, 47890 San Marino; tel. 0549 991719; fax 0549 879049; e-mail fixing@omniway.sm; internet www.sanmarinofixing.com; weekly; economics and politics; Dir LORIS PIRONI.

La Tribuna Sammarinese: Via Gino Giacomini 86A, 47890 San Marino; tel. 0549 990420; fax 0549 990398; e-mail redazione@latribunasammarinese.net; internet www.latribunasammarinese.net; daily; Dir DAVIDE GRAZIOSI.

SAN MARINO

Publishers

AIEP Editore: Via Rancaglia 25, 47899 Serravalle; tel. 0549 941457; fax 0549 973164; e-mail info@aiepeditore.net; internet www.aiepeditore.net; f. 1980; general book publishing; Man. GIUSEPPE MARIA MORGANTI.

Guardigli Editore: Via Istriani 94, 47890 San Marino; tel. 0549 995144; fax 0549 990454; e-mail guardiglieditore@omniway.sm; f. 1991; book publishing; Man. Dir PIER PAOLO GUARDIGLI.

Broadcasting and Communications

TELECOMMUNICATIONS

Direzione Generale Poste e Telecomunicazioni: Contrada Omerelli 17, 47890 San Marino; tel. 0549 882555; fax 0549 992760; e-mail telecomunicazioni.dirposte@pa.sm; state body responsible for telecommunications; Dir-Gen. Dott. ROSA ZAFFERANI.

San Marino Telecom: Piazza Tini 20, 47891 San Marino; tel. 0549 941502; fax 0549 942768; e-mail info@smt.sm; internet www.smt.sm; mobile services; Pres. SIMON MURRAY.

Telecom Italia San Marino, SpA: Strada degli Angariari 3, 47891 Falciano; tel. 0549 886111; fax 0549 886188; e-mail secretary@telecomitalia.sm; internet www.telecomitalia.sm; f. 1992; provides international telecommunications services; CEO CESARE PISANI.

Telefonia Mobile Sammarinese, SpA (TMS): Via XXVIII Luglio 148, 47893 Borgo Maggiore; tel. 0549 980222; fax 0549 980044; e-mail info@tms.sm; internet www.tms.sm; f. 1999; mobile services.

BROADCASTING

In addition to the broadcasts of San Marino RTV, San Marino receives radio and television broadcasts from Italy.

San Marino RTV (Radiotelevisione della Repubblica di San Marino): Viale Kennedy 13, 47890 San Marino; tel. 0549 882000; fax 0549 882840; e-mail redazione@sanmarinortv.sm; internet www.sanmarinortv.sm; f. 1991; began broadcasting in 2003; jointly owned by the Italian state broadcaster, Rai—Radiotelevisione Italiana, and Ente per la Radiodiffusione Sammarinese; operates 1 television station and 2 radio stations, Radio San Marino and Radio San Marino Classic; Pres. STEFANO VALENTINO PIVA; Dir-Gen. Dott. CARMEN LASORELLA.

Finance

(cap. = capital; res = reserves; dep. = deposits; m. = million; brs = branches; amounts in euros)

In August 2010 there were 12 banks operating in San Marino.

BANKING

Central Bank

Banca Centrale della Repubblica di San Marino: Via del Voltone 120, 47890 San Marino; tel. 0549 882325; fax 0549 882328; e-mail info@bcsm.sm; internet www.bcsm.sm; f. 2003; formed by a merger between the Istituto di Credito Sammarinese and the Ispettorato per il Credito e le Valute; cap. 12.9m., res 11.8m., dep. 464.2m. (Dec. 2008); Chair. RENATO CLARIZIA; Vice-Chair. ORIETTA BERARDI; Dir-Gen. MARIO GIANNINI.

Commercial Banks

Banca Agricola Commerciale della Repubblica di San Marino SpA: Piazza Marino Tini 26, 47891 Dogana; tel. 0549 871111; fax 0549 871222; internet www.bac.sm; f. 1920; cap. 16.9m., res 88.0m., dep. 1,804.1m (Dec. 2008); Pres. LUIGI LONFERNINI; Dir-Gen. PIER PAOLO FABBRI; 8 brs.

Banca Commerciale Sammarinese: Via Cinque Febbraio 17, 47895 Domagnano; tel. 0549 904280; fax 0594 901356; e-mail info@bcs.sm; internet www.bcs.sm; Pres. Dott. EMILIO DELLA BALDA; Dir-Gen. Dott. PAOLO DROGHINI.

Banca di San Marino, SpA: Strada della Croce 39, 47896 Faetano; tel. 0549 873411; fax 0549 873401; e-mail info@bsm.sm; internet www.bsm.sm; f. 1920 as Cassa Rurale Depositi e Prestiti di Faetano, Scrl; changed name as above in 2001; cap. 114.6m., res 40.5m., dep. 1,723.7m. (Dec. 2008); Chair. FAUSTO MULARONI; Dir-Gen. Prof. VINCENZO TAGLIAFERRO; 9 brs.

Cassa di Risparmio della Repubblica di San Marino: Piazzetta del Titano 2, 47890 San Marino; tel. 0549 872301; fax 0549 872700; e-mail info@carisp.sm; internet www.carisp.sm; f. 1882; cap. 350m., res 72.7m., dep. 3,366.6m. (Dec. 2008); Pres. and CEO LEONE SIBANI; 16 brs.

Credito Industriale Sammarinese SpA: Piazza Bertoldi 8, 47899 Serravalle; tel. 0549 874115; fax 0549 874116; e-mail info@cis.sm; internet www.cis.sm; f. 1933; owned by Banca Carim (Italy); cap. 35.0m., res 52.1m., dep. 406.9m. (Dec. 2009); Chair. LORENZO STANGHELLINI; CEO ALBERTO MOCCHI; 4 brs.

Euro Commercial Bank SpA: Strada dei Censiti 21, 47891 Rovereta; tel. 0549 943711; fax 0549 943737; e-mail info@ecb.sm; internet www.ecb.sm; f. 2000; cap. and res 26.9m., total assets 242.1m. (2006); Dir-Gen. GIUSEPPE GUIDI; 2 brs.

Istituto Bancario Sammarinese SpA: Via III Settembre 99, 47891 Dogana; tel. 0549 872011; fax 0549 872050; e-mail info@ibs.sm; internet www.ibs.sm; f. 2000 as Merchant Bank di San Marino SpA; changed name in 2001 following expansion into commercial banking; cap. 20.0m., res 1.4m., dep. 653.3m. (Dec. 2008); Pres. and Man. Dir ALBERTAZZI FABIO; 7 brs.

INSURANCE

Several major Italian insurance companies have agencies in San Marino.

Trade and Industry

GOVERNMENT AGENCIES

Azienda Autonoma di Stato Filatelica e Numismatica (AASFN): Piazza Garibaldi 5, 47890 San Marino; tel. 0549 882365; fax 0549 885179; e-mail aasfn@omniway.sm; internet www.aasfn.sm; autonomous public enterprise; responsible for production and distribution of postage stamps and coins; Pres. PIGNATTA ORAZIO; Dir-Gen. GIOIA GIARDI.

Azienda Autonoma di Stato di Produzione (AASP): Via Ventotto Luglio 50, 47031 Borgo Maggiore; tel. 0549 883600; fax 0549 883600; e-mail aasp@omniway.sm; civil engineering works, road works, land reclamation; Pres. PAOLO RONDELLI; Dir FABIO BERARDI.

Azienda Autonoma di Stato per la gestione della Centrale del Latte: Strada Genghe di Atto 71, 47031 Acquaviva; tel. 0549 999207; fax 0549 999606; operates state monopoly in production and distribution of dairy products; Pres. TIZIANO CANINI; Dir PAOLO MUSCI.

CHAMBER OF COMMERCE

Camera di Commercio, Industria, Artigianato e Agricoltura di San Marino (CCIAA): Strada di Paderna 2, 47895 San Marino; tel. 0549 980380; fax 0549 944554; e-mail info@cc.sm; internet www.cc.sm; f. 2004; Pres. SIMONA MICHELOTTI; Gen. Man. Dott. MASSIMO GHIOTTI.

INDUSTRIAL AND TRADE ASSOCIATIONS

Associazione Nazionale dell'Industria Sammarinese (ANIS) (National Association for Industry): Via Gino Giacomini 39, 47890 San Marino; tel. 0549 873911; fax 0549 992832; e-mail anis@omniway.sm; internet www.anis.sm; Pres. PAOLO RONDELLI; Sec.-Gen. CARLO GIORGI.

Associazione Sammarinese Coltivatori Diretti, Affittuari e Mezzadri (ASCDAM): San Marino; tel. 0549 998222; farmers' association.

Associazione Sammarinese Produttori Agricoli (ASPA): Serrabolino 42, 47893 Borgo Maggiore; tel. 0549 902617; agricultural producers' association.

Consorzio San Marino 2000 srl: Via Piana 103, 47890 San Marino; tel. 0549 995031; fax 0549 990573; e-mail info@sanmarino2000.sm; internet www.sanmarino2000.sm; f. 1998; fmrly Unione Sammarinese Operatori Turistici (USOT); hotels and restaurants association.

Organizzazione Sammarinese degli Imprenditori (OSLA): Via N. Bonaparte 75, 47890 San Marino; tel. 0549 992885; fax 0549 992620; e-mail ufficiosegreteria@osla.sm; internet www.osla.sm; f. 1985; organization for the self-employed; Pres. MARIA TERESA VENTURINI.

Unione Nazionale Artigiani di San Marino (UNAS): Piazzale M. Giangi 2, San Marino; tel. 0549 992148; e-mail info@unas.sm; f. 1968; artisans' association; Pres. PIER MARIMO BEDETTI.

Unione Sammarinese Commercianti (USC): Via Piana 111, 47890 San Marino; tel. 0549 992892; shopkeepers' association; Pres. MARCO ARZILLI.

UTILITIES

All utilities are imported from Italy.

Azienda Autonoma di Stato per i Servizi Pubblici (AASS): Via Andrea di Superchio 16, 47031 Cailungo; tel. 0549 883782; fax 0549 883720; e-mail info@aass.sm; internet www.aass.sm; f. 1981; autonomous state service company; distributes electricity, gas and water

SAN MARINO

within San Marino; Pres. Matteo Lonfernini; Dir-Gen. Emanuele Valli.

TRADE UNIONS

Centrale Sindacale Unitaria (CSU): Via V Febbraio 17, 47895 Domagnano; tel. 0549 962011; fax 0549 962055; e-mail amministrazione@csu.sm; f. 1976; Pres. Giuliano Tamagnini Marco Tura.

Confederazione Democratica dei Lavoratori Sammarinesi (CDLS): Via V Febbraio 17, 47895 Domagnano; tel. 0549 962080; fax 0549 962095; e-mail info@cdls.sm; internet www.cdls.sm; f. 1957; affiliated to ITUC and ETUC; Sec.-Gen. Marco Beccari; 4,960 mems.

Confederazione Sammarinese del Lavoro (CSdL): Via 5 Febbraio 17, 47895 Domagnano; tel. 0549 962060; fax 0549 962075; e-mail info@csdl.sm; internet www.csdl.sm; f. 1943; Sec.-Gen. Giuliano Tamagnini; 5 mem. feds; 5,200 individual mems.

Unione Sammarinese dei Lavoratori (USL): Via Ventotto Luglio 212, Centro Uffici Tavolucci, 47893 Borgo Maggiore; tel. 0549 907031; fax 0549 908978; e-mail segreteria@usl.sm; internet www.usl.sm; f. 2008; affiliated to the Unione Italiana del Lavoro; Sec.-Gen. Francesco Biordi.

Transport

The capital, San Marino, is connected with Borgo Maggiore, about 1.5 km away, by funicular. There is also a bus service, and a highway down to the Italian coast at Rimini, about 24 km away. San Marino has an estimated 220 km of roads. The nearest airport to the Republic is at Rimini. There are no frontier or customs formalities.

Azienda Autonoma di Stato per i Servizi Pubblici (AASS): (see Utilities); numerous responsibilities include public transport and funicular railway.

Tourism

The mild climate attracts many visitors to San Marino each year, as do the contrasting scenery and well-preserved medieval architecture. In 2010 San Marino received approximately 2.0m. visitors (including excursionists).

Ufficio di Stato per il Turismo (State Tourist Board): Contrada Omagnano 20, 47890 San Marino; tel. 0549 882914; fax 0549 882575; e-mail info@visitsanmarino.com; internet www.visitsanmarino.com; Dir Antonio Macina.

Defence

There are combined Voluntary Military Forces, comprising the military police (Gendarmeria), a uniformed militia (Compagnia Uniformata delle Milizie) and two bodies of institutional guards (Guardia del Consiglio Grande e Generale and Guardia di Rocca). There is no obligatory military service but citizens aged between 16 and 55 years may be enlisted, in certain circumstances, to defend the state.

High Commandant of the Militia: Gen. Rosolino Martelli.

Education

Education is compulsory for 10 years between the ages of six and 16 years. Primary education begins at six years of age and lasts for five years. Secondary education begins at the age of 11 and may last for up to eight years: a first cycle of three years, a second of two years and a third, non-compulsory, cycle of three years. There is one, state-run, university, the University of the Republic of San Marino. In 2009/10 1,033 pupils were attending pre-primary schools and 1,577 were attending primary schools, while 2,334 were undertaking secondary and vocational education (710 of whom were studying outside San Marino). In that year 43 university students were studying in San Marino, with a further 832 attending courses outside the country. In 2004, according to official figures, spending on education was €35.1m., equivalent to 8.1% of public spending.

SÃO TOMÉ AND PRÍNCIPE

Introductory Survey

LOCATION, CLIMATE, LANGUAGE, RELIGION, FLAG, CAPITAL

The Democratic Republic of São Tomé and Príncipe lies in the Gulf of Guinea, off the west coast of Africa. There are two main islands, São Tomé and Príncipe, and the country also includes the rocky islets of Caroço, Pedras and Tinhosas, off Príncipe, and Rôlas, off São Tomé. The climate is warm and humid, with average temperatures ranging between 22°C (72°F) and 30°C (86°F). The rainy season extends from October to May, and average annual rainfall varies from 500 mm (20 ins) in the southern highlands to 1,000 mm (39 ins) in the northern lowlands. Portuguese is the official language and native dialects are widely spoken. Almost all of the inhabitants profess Christianity, and the overwhelming majority (some 72.3%) are adherents of the Roman Catholic Church. The national flag (proportions 1 by 2) has three horizontal stripes, of green, yellow (one-half of the depth) and green, with a red triangle at the hoist and two five-pointed black stars on the yellow stripe. The capital is the town of São Tomé, on São Tomé island.

CONTEMPORARY POLITICAL HISTORY

Historical Context

A former Portuguese colony, São Tomé and Príncipe became an overseas province of Portugal in 1951 and received local autonomy in 1973. A nationalist group, the Comissão de Libertação de São Tomé e Príncipe, was formed in 1960 and became the Movimento de Libertação de São Tomé e Príncipe (MLSTP) in 1972, under the leadership of Dr Manuel Pinto da Costa. Based in Libreville, Gabon, the MLSTP was recognized by the Organization of African Unity (now the African Union—AU, see p. 183) in 1973.

Following the military coup in Portugal in April 1974, the Portuguese Government recognized the right of the islands to independence. Negotiations began in November, at which Portugal recognized the MLSTP as the sole representative of the people. On 12 July 1975 independence was achieved, with da Costa as the country's first President and Miguel dos Anjos da Cunha Lisboa Trovoada as Prime Minister. In December a legislative Assembleia Popular Nacional (National People's Assembly) was elected.

Worsening economic conditions, following a severe drought in 1982, prompted the Government to review the country's close ties with communist regimes and its consequent isolation from major Western aid sources. In late 1984 da Costa declared São Tomé and Príncipe to be politically non-aligned.

Domestic Political Affairs

In October 1987 the Central Committee of the MLSTP announced major constitutional reforms, including the election by universal adult suffrage of the President of the Republic and of members of the Assembleia Popular Nacional. The amended Constitution also allowed 'independent' candidates to contest legislative elections, although the President of the MLSTP, chosen by the MLSTP Congress from two candidates proposed by the Central Committee, would continue to be the sole candidate for the presidency of the Republic. In January 1988 the premiership was restored, and Celestino Rochas da Costa, hitherto Minister of Education, Labour and Social Security, was appointed as Prime Minister.

In March 1990 a joint meeting of the Assembleia Popular Nacional and the MLSTP Central Committee approved a new draft constitution, which provided for the establishment of a multi-party system, limited the President's tenure of office to two five-year terms, and permitted independent candidates to participate in legislative elections. On 22 August, in a national referendum, 72% of the electorate endorsed the new Constitution. In the following month new legislation on the formation of political parties came into effect. Delegates to the MLSTP Congress in October voted to replace da Costa as party President, appointing Carlos Alberto Monteiro Dias da Graça to the new post of Secretary-General. The party's name was amended to the Movimento de Libertação de São Tomé e Príncipe—Partido Social Democrata (MLSTP—PSD).

In January 1991 elections to the new Assembleia Nacional resulted in defeat for the MLSTP—PSD, which secured only 21 seats in the 55-member legislature, while the Partido de Convergência Democrática—Grupo de Reflexão (PCD—GR) won 33 seats. The Partido Democrático de São Tomé e Príncipe—Coligação Democrático da Oposição (PDSTP—CODO) took the remaining seat. In February a transitional Government, headed by the Secretary-General of the PCD—GR, Daniel Lima dos Santos Daio, was installed. In the same month President da Costa announced that he would not be contesting the presidential election, to be held in March. The MLSTP—PSD did not present an alternative candidate. In late February two of the three remaining presidential candidates withdrew from the election. Miguel Trovoada, who stood as an independent candidate (with the support of the PCD—GR), was thus the sole contender, and on 3 March he was elected President with the support of 81% of those who voted. He took office on 3 April.

In April 1992, following demonstrations demanding the resignation of the Daio Government due to the unpopular imposition of stringent austerity measures, Trovoada dismissed the Daio administration. The PCD—GR was invited to designate a new Prime Minister, and in May Norberto Costa Alegre (hitherto Minister of Economy and Finance) was chosen as Prime Minister. A new Government was named shortly afterwards.

Meanwhile, relations between the Government and the presidency deteriorated, and in April 1994 Trovoada publicly dissociated himself from government policy. Political tension increased in June, when the PCD—GR accused Trovoada of systematic obstruction of the government programme. In July Trovoada dismissed the Alegre Government and appointed Evaristo do Espírito Santo de Carvalho (the Minister of Defence and Security in the outgoing administration) as Prime Minister. The PCD—GR, refusing to participate in an administration formed on presidential initiative, subsequently expelled Carvalho from the party. An interim Government, comprising principally technocrats and senior civil servants, was appointed. Shortly afterwards Trovoada dissolved the Assembleia Nacional, thus preventing the PCD—GR from using its parliamentary majority to declare the new Government unconstitutional.

Legislative elections were held on 2 October 1994, at which the MLSTP—PSD secured 27 seats, one short of an absolute majority. The PCD—GR and Acção Democrática Independente (ADI) each obtained 14 seats; da Graça was subsequently appointed Prime Minister. Despite initial efforts to involve opposition parties in a government of national unity, his Council of Ministers was dominated by members of the MLSTP—PSD.

In March 1995 the first elections to a new seven-member regional assembly and five-member regional government were conducted on Príncipe, which had been granted local autonomy by the Assembleia Nacional in 1994. The elections resulted in an absolute majority for the MLSTP—PSD; the ADI and the PCD—GR did not present candidates, supporting instead a local opposition group. The new regional Government began functioning in April 1995.

In mid-August 1995 a group of some 30 soldiers, led by five junior officers, seized control of the presidential palace in a bloodless coup. Trovoada was detained at the headquarters of the armed forces and da Graça was placed under house arrest. The legislature was disbanded, the Constitution suspended and a curfew imposed. Following talks mediated by an Angolan delegation, the insurgents and the Government signed a 'memorandum of understanding', providing for the reinstatement of Trovoada and the restoration of constitutional order. In return, the Government gave an undertaking to restructure the armed forces, and the Assembleia Nacional granted a general amnesty to all those involved in the coup.

The 1996 presidential election

In late December 1995 Armindo Vaz d'Almeida was appointed Prime Minister, by presidential decree, to head a Government of National Unity. The new administration included six members

SÃO TOMÉ AND PRÍNCIPE

of the MLSTP—PSD, four members of the ADI and one of the PDSTP—CODO. The three parties had signed a political pact, with the aim of ensuring political stability. In February 1996, at the request of the Comissão Eleitoral Nacional (National Electoral Commission), the forthcoming presidential election, which had been set for March, was postponed, pending the satisfactory completion of the electoral rolls. The date of the election was subsequently rescheduled for 30 June. In March Pinto da Costa was selected as the presidential candidate of the MLSTP—PSD and Francisco Fortunato Pires was appointed Secretary-General of the party, replacing the more moderate da Graça. In April Trovoada declared his candidacy for the presidential election, supported by the ADI and the PDSTP—CODO.

At the presidential election of 30 June 1996 no candidate secured an absolute majority. The two leading candidates thus proceeded to a second round of voting on 21 July, at which Trovoada won 52.7% of the votes, defeating Pinto da Costa. Although he did not command majority support in the Assembleia Nacional, Trovoada dismissed the possibility of new legislative elections, announcing instead his intention to seek a broadly based government of national consensus. Vaz d'Almeida remained as Prime Minister in an interim capacity until November, when Raul Wagner da Conceição Bragança Neto, Assistant Secretary-General of the MLSTP—PSD, was appointed Prime Minister. A new coalition Government, including five members of the MLSTP—PSD, three members of the PCD—GR and one independent, was inaugurated later that month.

At an extraordinary congress of the MLSTP—PSD in May 1998, Pinto da Costa was elected unopposed as President of the party. (The ruling party of Angola, the Movimento Popular de Libertação de Angola (MPLA), had made the resumption of financial support for the MLSTP—PSD conditional on da Costa's election; following his defeat in the 1996 presidential election, the MPLA had ceased payments, creating serious problems for the MLSTP—PSD.) New party statutes were approved, creating the position of party President, together with three vice-presidential posts.

At legislative elections held on 8 November 1998 the MLSTP—PSD secured a majority, with 31 seats, while the ADI won 16 seats and the PCD—GR obtained the remaining eight seats. In December Guilherme Pósser da Costa (a Vice-President of the MLSTP—PSD and former Minister of Foreign Affairs and Co-operation) was appointed Prime Minister. A new Council of Ministers was installed in January 1999.

A presidential election took place on 29 July 2001. Among the five candidates to succeed Trovoada were former President Manuel Pinto da Costa, the leader of the MLSTP—PSD, and Fradique de Menezes, a businessman representing the ADI. In the event, de Menezes was elected to the presidency, winning 56.3% of the votes cast, while da Costa secured 38.7%. De Menezes was inaugurated as President on 3 September. A new Government of 'presidential initiative', which did not include any members of the MLSTP—PSD, was appointed in late September. The new Council of Ministers, led by Evaristo de Carvalho as Prime Minister, was composed of members of the ADI, the PCD (which had voted to remove the suffix Grupo de Reflexão from its official name at a recent congress) and one independent. In early December de Menezes dissolved the Assembleia Nacional and announced that legislative elections would be held in March 2002, after which a new, more broadly based Government would be formed, according to an agreement reportedly signed by the President and representatives of political parties. In January 2002 the PCD formed an electoral alliance with the Movimento Democrático Força da Mudança (MDFM), which had been created in December by supporters of de Menezes.

At legislative elections held on 3 March 2002 no party obtained an absolute majority in the Assembleia Nacional. Provisional results indicated that the MLSTP—PSD and the MDFM-PCD alliance had each secured 23 of the 55 seats, while the remaining nine seats had been won by Uê Kédadji (UK), an alliance of the ADI and four minor parties. However, following a re-run of voting in one district, the MLSTP—PSD secured an extra seat, to the cost of the UK alliance, and was proclaimed victorious. Gabriel da Costa, the former ambassador to Portugal, was subsequently appointed as the nominally independent Prime Minister, and in April a new coalition Government of National Unity, which included representatives of the MLSTP—PSD, the MDFM-PCD and UK, as well as a number of independents, was installed.

Introductory Survey

In late September 2002 da Costa's Government was dismissed by de Menezes, who appointed Maria das Neves de Souza, of the MLSTP—PSD, hitherto Minister of Trade, Industry and Tourism, as Prime Minister in early October. A new Government of National Unity, with six representatives from the MLSTP—PSD, five from the MDFM-PCD alliance, two from the UK alliance and one independent, was formed. In December the first MDFM congress elected Tomé Vera Cruz as Secretary-General of the party.

Constitutional reform

Meanwhile, in November 2002 the Assembleia Nacional approved a resolution for constitutional reform, altering the structure of the semi-presidential system to reduce presidential power. However, the draft revisions caused a political crisis over President de Menezes' delays in their promulgation and his repeated threats to veto them, according to powers vested in him by the Constitution of 1990. An apparent consensus was reached in December 2002, but the situation deteriorated further in early 2003, and in mid-January the President vetoed the new draft constitution on the grounds that it should be endorsed by public referendum before coming into force. De Menezes dissolved the Assembleia Nacional by presidential decree later that month and called early elections for 13 April. However, Prime Minister das Neves vowed to continue working and transferred the Government of National Unity to the island of Príncipe. Following negotiations between the Government and the President, de Menezes reversed his decree, reinstating the Government, and a 'memorandum of understanding' was signed by de Menezes and the Assembleia Nacional, which provided for the immediate promulgation of the new Constitution.

The new Constitution, which took effect in March 2003, provided for the establishment of an advisory Council of State and a Constitutional Tribunal, with jurisdiction over issues of constitutionality. The President's right to veto constitutional amendments was removed. The changes were regarded as significantly reducing the executive power of the President, although maintaining a semi-presidential system pending the referendum.

On 16 July 2003, while de Menezes was in Nigeria, Maj. Fernando Pereira 'Cobo', together with Sabino dos Santos and Alércio Costa, the leaders of a small political party, the Frente Democrata Cristã (FDC), took power in a bloodless *coup d'état*. They formed a Junta Militar de Salvação Nacional and detained government ministers. The coup was condemned by the international community, which demanded a return to civilian rule. Following successful regional mediation efforts, co-ordinated by Rodolphe Adada, the Republic of the Congo's Minister of Foreign Affairs, Co-operation and Francophone Affairs, on 22 July de Menezes returned to São Tomé. On the same day de Menezes, Pereira and Adada signed a 'memorandum of understanding', which provided for the restoration of de Menezes to the presidency, an amnesty for the coup leaders, a more transparent system of government finance, and the formation of a new government. In accordance with the conditions of the memorandum, Prime Minister das Neves resigned. She was subsequently reappointed by de Menezes to head a new Government of National Unity, comprising representatives of the MLSTP—PSD, the MDFM and the ADI. Vera Cruz was appointed to the increasingly significant post of Minister of Natural Resources and the Environment, and Lt-Col Oscar Sousa, an independent reportedly with close ties to de Menezes, became Minister of Defence and Internal Affairs.

In March 2004 tension increased between das Neves and de Menezes. Das Neves had repeatedly requested the dismissal of Vera Cruz and of Mateus Rita, the Minister of Foreign Affairs and Co-operation, claiming that she had not been appropriately consulted by either minister on government decisions. The subsequent resignations of Rita and Vera Cruz—both members of the MDFM—prompted the remaining two MDFM ministers, responsible for health and justice, to resign in protest. Agreements that Vera Cruz had signed with Canadian and South African mining companies were subsequently annulled. Later that month members of the ADI were appointed to head the ministries of health and of natural resources and the environment, while Elsa Pinto of the MLSTP—PSD became Minister of Justice, State Reform and Public Administration, and an independent, Ovídio Manuel Barbossa Pequeno, was appointed Minister of Foreign Affairs and Co-operation. In April 2004 Leonel Mário d'Alva was elected President of the PCD, while later that month Vera Cruz was re-elected as Secretary-General of the MDFM, which was restyled the MDFM—Partido Liberal, although it subsequently reverted to its original name.

SÃO TOMÉ AND PRÍNCIPE

In early September 2004 a report issued by the Auditor-General, Adelino Pereira, accused the das Neves Government of the embezzlement of funds provided by foreign donors and also revealed a series of financial irregularities during 2001–04, including illicit transfers of funds to the Ministry of Finance. Following requests by the MDFM and UK (the latter resigned from the Government in mid-September) for the removal of the das Neves Government, President de Menezes held a series of meetings with the main political parties in an attempt to establish a consensus. Das Neves and her Council of Ministers were dismissed in September, and Damião Vaz de Almeida, hitherto Minister of Labour, Employment and Security and Vice-President of the MLSTP—PSD, was asked to form a new administration. The new 14-member Government was a coalition of the MLSTP—PSD, the ADI and independents and comprised six members of the previous administration.

In late September 2004 Diógenes Moniz, the former Director of the Gabinete de Gestão das Ajudas (GGA—a department attached to the Ministry of Trade, Industry and Tourism responsible for the administration of food aid counterpart funds) was arrested on charges of embezzlement. In October das Neves was among a number of former ministers questioned by the Public Prosecutor about their involvement with the GGA.

In January 2005 an attempt by de Menezes to sue das Neves for libel was rejected by the Assembleia Nacional, on the grounds that das Neves enjoyed parliamentary immunity. (In September 2004, following her dismissal from the premiership, she had accused de Menezes and other members of the Government of corruption.) However, in February 2005 the Assembleia voted to remove parliamentary immunity from the former Prime Minister, Pósser da Costa, in order that he be questioned regarding an alleged assault on Pereira in November 2004. (Pósser da Costa received a suspended sentence in March 2005.) A further four members of the Assembleia, including das Neves, also had their immunity lifted, thus providing for the possibility of them being tried in connection with the GGA case. In May das Neves and Arzemiro dos Prazeres, a former Minister of Trade, Industry and Tourism, were charged with embezzlement. Meanwhile, in late February Pósser da Costa was elected President of the MLSTP—PSD.

In April 2005 trade unions representing public sector workers demanded a significant increase in the minimum salaries of their members. The Government, however, citing budgetary constraints, was unable to accede to the unions' demands and in late May the unions commenced a five-day general strike. Following declarations by de Menezes that the Government was responsible for the action, Prime Minister Vaz de Almeida abruptly resigned, accusing the President of a lack of institutional solidarity with the Government. On 9 June a new MLSTP—PSD Council of Ministers, led by Maria do Carmo Silveira, hitherto the Governor of the central bank, took office, and in late July the Assembleia Nacional approved the new Government's budget and a preliminary agreement on a pay rise for public sector workers was reached. Relations between de Menezes and the Government remained strained, however.

Voting in the legislative elections began as scheduled on 26 March 2006; however, owing to boycotts and protests against continuing poor living conditions, voting at 26 polling stations was rescheduled for 2 April when it proceeded without incident. According to results released by the Constitutional Court on 18 April, the renewed MDFM-PCD alliance won 23 seats in the Assembleia Nacional, the MLSTP—PSD took 20 and the ADI 11, while a newly formed party, the Novo Rumo, secured the remaining seat. The Secretary-General of the MDFM, Tomé Vera Cruz, was subsequently appointed Prime Minister (also assuming the media and regional integration portfolios) while Maria dos Santos Tebús Torres of the PCD became Deputy Prime Minister, with responsibility for finance and planning. The new 12-member Government took office on 21 April.

De Menezes re-elected

De Menezes was re-elected to the presidency on 30 July 2006, after securing 60.6% of the votes cast in a presidential election. His nearest rival, Patrice Emery Trovoada, of the ADI, received 38.8%. International observers deemed the election, at which voter turn-out was 64.9%, to have been transparent and fair. In late August, at the first local elections to be held on the islands since 1992, the MDFM-PCD alliance won six of the seven constituencies on São Tomé and secured an absolute majority in five of the six local assemblies. Supported by the ruling MDFM-PCD, the União para a Mudança e Progresso do Príncipe (UMPP) won all seven seats in the Assembleia Regional on Príncipe.

At an extraordinary party congress in February 2007, the MLSTP—PSD elected Joaquim Rafael Branco as party President; he defeated António Quintas by 675 votes to 221. Prime Minister Vera Cruz was re-elected Secretary-General of the MDFM at a convention in May; at the same time President de Menezes was elected Chairman of that party, despite a provision in the Constitution preventing the Head of State from accepting other public roles. De Menezes stated that he would not assume the role publicly while he remained President.

Vera Cruz announced his resignation as Prime Minister on 7 February 2008, after the Assembleia Nacional failed to approve his Government's budget for 2008. He was replaced by Patrice Emery Trovoada, who was sworn in on 14 February. Trovoada's ADI had agreed to form a coalition government with the MDFM-PCD on the condition that his party was awarded, *inter alia*, the premiership and the natural resources and environment portfolio. Trovoada named a Council of Ministers, which included Raúl Cravid as Minister of Planning and Finance, while both Pequeno and Carvalho retained the portfolios assigned to them in November 2007.

Although a revised national budget for 2008 was eventually approved by the Assembleia Nacional, in May the MLSTP—PSD presented a motion of no confidence against Trovoada's administration. The motion was adopted with the support of members of the PCD, who were critical of Trovoada, and the Government was dissolved. Following several weeks of negotiations, in late June Branco was sworn in as Prime Minister at the head of a new Council of Ministers (comprising members of the MLSTP—PSD, the PCD and the MDFM), in which Carlos Tiny assumed responsibility for the foreign affairs, co-operation and communities portfolio, Elsa Pinto became the country's first female Minister of National Defence, and Cravid was appointed Minister of the Interior, Territorial Administration and Civil Protection. Minister of Natural Resources, Energy and the Environment Agostinho Rita was dismissed in October and was replaced by Carlos Fernandes Marques. After a series of electricity outages during late 2008, believed to be the result of a power generating deficit, Marques resigned in November, citing health concerns. Marques was succeeded by Cristina Dias, hitherto a senior official at the Agência Nacional do Petróleo de São Tomé e Príncipe.

An attempted coup was staged in February 2009, believed to have been led by a group of South African former mercenaries. It was subsequently announced that a number of the group had been arrested and detained, including Alércio Costa of the FDC, and that 11 suspects had been released under supervision orders. In August a further 15 suspects were released and it was announced that those who remained in detention would be placed on trial, commencing in September. In November Costa was sentenced to five years' imprisonment, but in January 2010 he received a presidential pardon and was released.

In December 2009 de Menezes was re-elected as Chairman of the MDFM, prior to forthcoming legislative elections (which were subsequently postponed from February 2010 until August). In early January de Menezes withdrew the four members of the MDFM who held government portfolios from the Council of Ministers, following criticism by the other parties represented in the coalition at his continued chairmanship of the MDFM while he remained national President. In the new Government formed by Prime Minister Branco, the Minister of Defence and Internal Order, Elsa Pinto (of the MLSTP—PSD), also assumed responsibility for the justice and parliamentary affairs portfolio, while the Minister of Agriculture, Rural Development and Fishing, Xavier Mendes (PCD), took on the natural resources and energy portfolio. An additional PCD member, Carlos Gomes, was appointed Minister of Labour, Solidarity and Family, while an independent, António Paquete, became Minister of the Interior, Territorial Administration and Civil Protection. Two days later, de Menezes unexpectedly retracted his acceptance of the MDFM leadership, but denied that his decision had been influenced by political pressure. In March President de Menezes announced that local elections (which had originally been scheduled for August 2009 but had been postponed, allegedly owing to a lack of funding) would be held on 25 July and would be followed by the legislative elections on 1 August.

Recent developments: the 2010 legislative elections

In the local elections, which were conducted on 25 July 2010, the MLSTP—PSD obtained a majority in the four district councils of Lobata, Lembá, Cantagalo and Caué, while the ADI gained the majority in the two principal district councils of Água Grande (with the capital São Tomé) and Mé-Zóchi. The UMPP, led by José Cardoso Cassandra, won all seven seats of the Regional

SÃO TOMÉ AND PRÍNCIPE

Assembly of Príncipe. The ADI, with 42.2% of votes cast and 26 seats, secured the greatest representation in the legislative elections on 1 August (but failed to obtain an absolute majority in the Assembleia Nacional). The MLSTP—PSD of Branco, with 32.1% of votes, won 21 seats, while the PCD secured 13.6% of votes and seven seats. The MDFM of President de Menezes received only 7.1% of votes and one seat, compared with 12 in the previous legislative elections. Trovoada was again appointed Prime Minister on 10 August. On 14 August de Menezes approved the installation of a new minority Government, comprising 10 ministers and one secretary of state, and which included a number of independents in addition to ADI members.

In April 2011 it was announced that a presidential election was to be held on 17 July.

Foreign Affairs
Regional relations

São Tomé and Príncipe has important trade links with the nearby mainland states of Gabon, Cameroon and Equatorial Guinea. In November 1999 São Tomé and Príncipe was a founder of the seven-member Gulf of Guinea Commission to assist in solving inter-state conflicts within the region.

In 2000 São Tomé and Príncipe and Nigeria agreed to establish a joint development zone (JDZ) for the exploitation of petroleum resources. A further accord, on the joint exploitation of a variety of mineral resources, was signed in February 2001; Nigeria was to receive 60% of revenues and São Tomé and Príncipe 40%. In January 2002 the Presidents of both countries inaugurated a development authority to oversee the affairs of the JDZ. Disagreements developed during 2002, however, over Nigeria's commitment to provide São Tomé and Príncipe with 60,000 barrels of petroleum per day (reduced to 40,000 in September, and to 10,000 in October) and the relative lack of Santomean representation in the development authority. In November de Menezes refused to continue with the proposed sale of oil blocks until the issue was resolved; he was supported in this by a report from the World Bank, which suggested that the division of profits was unfair to São Tomé and Príncipe. By 2003, however, issues had been resolved sufficiently for bids for exploration rights in the first nine of the 25 blocks in the JDZ to open in October. In December 2009 a bilateral military commission was established jointly by the Nigerian and Santomean authorities to provide, *inter alia*, security for oil companies operating within the JDZ. Nigeria also agreed to collaborate with São Tomé and Príncipe by providing assistance in agricultural research and exchange of information and agricultural materials.

Other external relations

São Tomé and Príncipe maintains cordial relations with the other former Portuguese African colonies and with Portugal. In July 1996 São Tomé and Príncipe was among the five lusophone African countries that, together with Portugal and Brazil, formed the Comunidade dos Países de Língua Portuguesa (CPLP, see p. 459), a Portuguese-speaking commonwealth seeking to achieve collective benefits from co-operation in technical, cultural and social matters. In February 2004 Angola and São Tomé and Príncipe signed an agreement on the creation of a permanent joint commission on parliamentary co-operation.

CONSTITUTION AND GOVERNMENT

Under the Constitution adopted on 4 March 2003, legislative power is vested in the Assembleia Nacional, which comprises 55 members, elected by universal adult suffrage for a term of four years. No limit is placed on the number of political parties permitted to operate. Executive power is vested in the President of the Republic, who is Head of State, and who governs with the assistance of an appointed Council of Ministers, led by the Prime Minister. The Council of State acts as an advisory body to the President, who is elected by universal suffrage for a term of five years. The President's tenure of office is limited to two successive terms. The Prime Minister, who is appointed by the President, is, in theory, nominated by the deputies of the Assembleia Nacional. Judicial power is exercised by the Supreme Court and all other competent tribunals and courts. The Supreme Court is the supreme judicial authority and is accountable only to the Assembleia Nacional. Its members are appointed by the Assembleia Nacional. The right to a defence is guaranteed.

In 1994 the Assembleia Nacional granted political and administrative autonomy to the island of Príncipe. Legislation was adopted establishing a seven-member Assembleia Regional and a five-member regional government; both are accountable to the Government of São Tomé and Príncipe.

REGIONAL AND INTERNATIONAL CO-OPERATION

São Tomé and Príncipe is a member of the African Union (see p. 183) and of the Communauté économique des états de l'Afrique centrale (see p. 446).

São Tomé and Príncipe became a member of the UN in 1975 and has observer status at the World Trade Organization (WTO, see p. 430). São Tomé and Príncipe participates in the Group of 77 (G77, see p. 447) developing countries and is a member of the International Cocoa Organization (see p. 443).

ECONOMIC AFFAIRS

In 2009, according to estimates by the World Bank, São Tomé and Príncipe's gross national product (GNI), measured at average 2007–09 prices, was US $185m., equivalent to $1,140 per head (or $1,850 per head on an international purchasing-power parity basis). During 2000–09, it was estimated, the population increased at an average annual rate of 1.7%, while gross domestic product (GDP) per head, in real terms, increased at an average annual rate of 0.8% in 1995–2005. Overall GDP increased, in real terms, at an average annual rate of 3.5% in 1998–2005; growth of 5.8% was recorded in 2008.

Agriculture (including fishing) contributed an estimated 24.5% of GDP in 2008 according to the African Development Bank (AfDB), and accounted for an estimated 56.9% of the labour force in mid-2011, according to FAO estimates. The principal cash crop is cocoa, which accounted for 87.1% of export earnings in 2008. Secondary cash crops include coconuts and coffee. Staple crops for local consumption include bananas, taro and cassava. Agricultural production is principally concentrated on export commodities, although smallholder agriculture has become increasingly important. An agricultural policy charter, the Carta de Política e Desenvolvimento Rural, which was introduced in 2000, aimed to emphasize private sector involvement and diversification into areas such as ylang ylang, pepper, vanilla, fruits, vegetables and flowers. Fishing is also a significant activity. The sale of fishing licences to foreign fleets is an important source of income. According to the World Bank, agricultural GDP increased at an average annual rate of 3.6% in 1995–2005, while growth in the sector was 5.4% in 2008, according to the AfDB.

Industry (including mining, manufacturing, construction and power) contributed an estimated 13.9% of GDP in 2008, and employed 17.0% of the employed population in 2001. According to the World Bank, industrial GDP increased by an average of 2.8% per year in 1995–2003; growth in 2003 was 4.6%.

In 2008 mining contributed an estimated 0.1% of GDP. There are no mineral resources on the islands, but offshore prospecting for hydrocarbons resulted in the discovery of significant quantities of petroleum in 1998, including an estimated 4,000m. barrels in the joint development zone (JDZ) with Nigeria (see Contemporary Political History), as well as higher-risk resources in São Tomé's exclusive economic zone (EEZ). More than 20 companies lodged bids for exploration rights in the first nine of the 25 blocks in the JDZ in October 2003. In February 2005 a consortium led by ChevronTexaco was awarded a concession to exploit the first section of the JDZ. That company signed a production sharing agreement with the Joint Development Authority responsible for overseeing activities in the JDZ in 2005 and began drilling activities in January 2006. Inquiries into the subsequent award of a further five blocks to the Environmental Remedial Holding Corp (ERHC), resulted in the Attorney-General concluding that the procedures used in selecting petroleum companies were flawed. He recommended a restructuring of the procedures for future bidding rounds that would conform to international standards. The Attorney-General's report also demanded the re-examination of ERHC's preferential rights for Blocks 2–6 within the JDZ.

The manufacturing sector consists solely of small processing factories, producing soap, soft drinks, textiles and beer. Manufacturing contributed an estimated 3.4% of GDP in 2008, according to the AfDB. According to the World Bank, manufacturing GDP increased at an average annual rate of 2.4% in 1995–2003. According to the AfDB, the sector grew by 3.8% in 2008.

According to the AfDB, the construction sector contributed 9.6% of GDP in 2008 and grew by 3.7% in that year.

In 2000 some 74% of electricity generation was derived from thermal sources and 26% from hydroelectric sources. Imports of petroleum products comprised 15.5% of the value of merchandise imports in 2009. In late 2004 the national utility company was

SÃO TOMÉ AND PRÍNCIPE

privatized. In early 2006 it was announced that a thermal power plant, which would increase São Tomé's energy production by 70%, was to be built by a Nigerian company.

The services sector contributed an estimated 61.6% of GDP in 2008, and engaged 51.5% of the employed population in 2001. According to the World Bank, the GDP of the services sector increased by an average of 2.3% per year in 1995–2003; growth in 2003 was 4.4%.

In 2009 São Tomé and Príncipe recorded a trade deficit of US $74.56m. and a deficit of $78.75m. on the current account of the balance of payments. In 2009 the principal source of imports was Portugal (56.4%); the other major suppliers were Angola and Brazil. The principal market for exports in that year was also Portugal (32.3%); other significant purchasers were the Netherlands and Belgium,. The principal export in 2009 was cocoa. The principal imports in that year were foodstuffs, petroleum and petroleum products, machinery, transport equipment, beverages and construction materials.

In 2009 there was a projected budgetary surplus of 540,000m. dobras. São Tomé's general government gross debt was 2,024.60m. dobras in 2009, equivalent to 65.8% of GDP. São Tomé's total external debt was US $178m. at the end of 2008, of which $155m. was public and publicly guaranteed debt. In 2007 the cost of debt-servicing was equivalent to 39.2% of the total value of exports of goods, services and income. Annual inflation averaged 16.6% in 2000–09. Consumer prices increased by an average 17.3% in 2009. According to official figures, 14.2% of the labour force were unemployed in 2006.

São Tomé and Príncipe's economy has traditionally been dominated by cocoa production and is therefore vulnerable to adverse weather conditions and to fluctuations in international prices for that commodity. While the discovery of petroleum in Santomean waters was a welcome development, concerns were raised by international institutions regarding the lack of transparency and accountability in the petroleum sector. Thus, in mid-2004 the Government agreed to establish a National Petroleum Fund into which all petroleum earnings were to be deposited, and which was to be subject to annual independent audits; it was also announced that 65% of the total revenue from petroleum was to be allocated to the upgrading of infrastructure and to improvements in the health care and education sectors. Despite ongoing investigations into the misappropriation of donor funds, São Tomé and Príncipe continued to be a major recipient of external assistance. Following a series of missions since the suspension of the Poverty Reduction and Growth Facility (PRGF) arrangement in 2000, the IMF announced a new three-year PRGF, worth US $4.3m., which the country successfully completed in June 2008. In early 2009 the Fund approved a further three-year $3.8m. credit arrangement to support the authorities' economic programme. The authorities aimed to combat the country's poor revenue levels with the introduction of new legislation to simplify and modernize the tax system and encourage tax compliance. According to the IMF, GDP growth was estimated to have slowed to 4.0% in 2009, largely owing to a sharp decline in foreign direct investment as a result of the global economic crisis. In February 2010 the IMF completed its first review of the country's economic performance under the extended credit facility and, granting a waiver for the non-observance of certain criteria following a shortfall in tax revenue attributed to the effects of the global crisis, approved a disbursement of $570,000. A new Government, which was installed following legislative elections in August, pledged commitment to the objectives of the IMF-supported economic programme. Although foreign investment continued to decline in 2010, an increase in externally financed public investment projects stimulated economic activity, and a modest recovery in GDP growth in that year was estimated.

PUBLIC HOLIDAYS

2012: 1 January (New Year), 4 January (King Amador Day), 3 February (Martyrs' Day), 1 May (Labour Day), 12 July (Independence Day), 6 September (Armed Forces Day), 30 September (Agricultural Reform Day), 21 December (São Tomé Day), 25 December (Christmas Day).

Statistical Survey

Source (unless otherwise stated): Instituto Nacional de Estatística, CP 256, São Tomé; tel. 221982; internet www.ine.st.

AREA AND POPULATION

Area: 1,001 sq km (386.5 sq miles); São Tomé 859 sq km (331.7 sq miles), Príncipe 142 sq km (54.8 sq miles).

Population: 117,504 at census of 4 August 1991; 137,599 (males 68,236, females 69,363) at census of September 2001; 160,821 (males 79,027, females 81,794) at mid-2009 (official estimate).

Density (mid-2009): 160.7 per sq km.

Population by Age and Sex (UN estimates at mid-2011): *0–14:* 67,149 (males 33,924, females 33,225); *15–64:* 94,615 (males 46,604, females 48,011); *65 and over:* 6,338 (males 2,723, females 3,615); *Total* 168,102 (males 83,251, females 84,851) (Source: UN, *World Population Prospects: The 2008 Revision*).

Population by District (2006): Água-Grande 56,492, Mé-Zochi 38,668, Cantagolo 14,681, Caué 6,324, Lembá 11,759, Lobata 17,251, Pagué (Príncipe) 6,737; Total 151,912.

Principal Towns (population at census of 1991): São Tomé (capital) 42,300; Trindade 11,400; Santana 6,200; Santo Amaro 5,900; Neves 5,900. Source: Stefan Helders, *World Gazetteer* (internet www.world-gazetteer.com). *Mid-2009* (incl. suburbs): São Tomé (capital) 59,851 (Source: UN, *World Urbanization Prospects: The 2009 Revision*).

Births, Marriages and Deaths (2006): Registered live births 5,072 (birth rate 33.40 per 1,000); Registered marriages 171 (marriage rate 1.2 per 1,000) (2003); Registered deaths 1,111 (death rate 7.3 per 1,000). *2009:* Birth rate 31.5 per 1,000; Death rate 7.3 per 1,000 (Source: African Development Bank).

Life Expectancy (years at birth, WHO estimates): 61 (males 60; females 62) in 2008. (Source: WHO, *World Health Statistics*).

Economically Active Population (census of 2001): Agriculture and fishing 13,518; Industry, electricity, gas and water 2,893; Public works and civil construction 4,403; Trade, restaurants and hotels 8,787; Transport, storage and communications 792; Public administration 3,307; Health 776; Education 1,373; Other activities 7,088; Total employed 42,937. *2006:* Total employed 53,725 (males 28,729, females 24,996); Unemployed 8,894 (males 4,276, females 4,618); Total labour force 62,619 (males 33,005, females 29,614). *Mid-2011* ('000, estimates): Agriculture, etc. 33; Total labour force 58 (Source: FAO).

HEALTH AND WELFARE
Key Indicators

Total Fertility Rate (children per woman, 2008): 3.8.

Under-5 Mortality Rate (per 1,000 live births, 2008): 97.

Physicians (per 1,000 head, 2004): 0.5.

Hospital Beds (per 1,000 head, 2003): 3.2.

Health Expenditure (2007): US $ per head (PPP): 183.

Health Expenditure (2007): % of GDP: 11.2.

Health Expenditure (2007): public (% of total): 47.1.

Access to Water (% of persons, 2008): 89.

Access to Sanitation (% of persons, 2008): 26.

Total Carbon Dioxide Emissions ('000 metric tons, 2007): 128.2.

Carbon Dioxide Emissions Per Head (metric tons, 2007): 0.8.

Human Development Index (2010): ranking: 127.

Human Development Index (2010): value: 0.488.

For sources and definitions, see explanatory note on p. vi.

AGRICULTURE, ETC.

Principal Crops (metric tons, 2008, FAO estimates): Bananas 32,000; Maize 3,000; Cassava (Manioc) 6,500; Taro 28,000; Yams 1,600; Cocoa beans 2,000; Coconuts 28,000; Oil palm fruit 15,000; Coffee, green 30; Cinnamon 30. Note: No data were available for 2009.

SÃO TOMÉ AND PRÍNCIPE

Statistical Survey

Livestock (head, 2008, FAO estimates): Cattle 4,800; Sheep 3,000; Goats 5,200; Pigs 2,620; Chickens 420,000. Note: No data were available for 2009.

Livestock Products (metric tons, 2009, unless otherwise indicated, FAO estimates): Cattle meat 128 (2008); Pig meat 97 (2008); Sheep meat 6; Goat meat 19; Chicken meat 704; Hen eggs 490; Cows' milk 147.

Forestry ('000 cubic metres, 1988): Roundwood removals 9; Sawnwood production 5. *1989–2009:* Annual output assumed to be unchanged since 1988.

Fishing (metric tons, live weight, 2008, FAO estimates): Total catch 4,250 (Croakers and drums 165; Pandoras 190; Threadfins and tasselfishes 130; Wahoo 76; Little tunny 179; Atlantic sailfish 384; Flyingfishes 790; Jacks and crevalles 170; Sharks, rays and skates 132).

Source: FAO.

INDUSTRY

Production (metric tons, unless otherwise indicated): Bread and biscuits 3,768 (1995); Soap 261.1 (1995); Beer (litres) 529,400 (1995); Coconut oil 224 (2008, FAO estimate); Palm oil 3,000 (2008, FAO estimate); Electric energy (million kWh) 43 (2007). Sources: IMF, *Democratic Republic of São Tomé and Príncipe: Selected Issues and Statistical Appendix* (September 1998, February 2002, April 2004 and September 2006); UN Industrial Commodity Statistics Database; FAO.

FINANCE

Currency and Exchange Rates: 100 cêntimos = 1 dobra (Db). *Sterling, Dollar and Euro Equivalents* (31 August 2010): £1 sterling = 29,939.2 dobras; US $1 = 19,436.0 dobras; €1 = 24,644.8 dobras; 100,000 dobras = £3.34 = $5.15 = €4.06. *Average Exchange Rate* (dobras per US $): 13,536.8 in 2007; 14,695.2 in 2008; 16,208.5 in 2009.

Budget ('000 million dobras, 2008): *Revenue:* Taxation 411; Non-tax revenue 40; Grants 765; Total 1,216. *Expenditure:* Current expenditure 569 (Personnel costs 219, Goods and services 164, Interest on external debt 23, Transfers 124, Other current expenditure 39); Capital expenditure 219; HIPC-related social expenditure 53; Total 841. *2009* (projections): Total revenue and grants 1,808; Total expenditure 1,268. Source: IMF, *Democratic Republic of São Tomé and Príncipe: First Review Under the Three Year Arrangement Under the Extended Credit Facility Arrangement, and Request for Waivers of Performance Criteria—Staff Report; Staff Supplement; and Press Release on the Executive Board Discussion* (April 2010).

International Reserves (US $ million at 31 December 2007): IMF special drawing rights 0.01; Foreign exchange 39.32; Total 39.33. *IMF Special Drawing Rights* (US $ million at 31 December): 0.03 in 2008; 10.16 in 2009; 5.82 in 2010. Source: IMF, *International Financial Statistics*.

Money Supply ('000 million dobras at 31 December 2009): Currency outside depository corporations 149.1; Transferable deposits 718.1; Other deposits 266.2; Broad money 1,133.3. Source: IMF, *International Financial Statistics*.

Cost of Living (Consumer Price Index; base: 2000 = 100): 252.7 in 2007; 318.7 in 2008; 373.9 in 2009. Source: African Development Bank.

Gross Domestic Product ('000 million dobras at current prices): 1,952 in 2007; 2,361 in 2008; 2,739 in 2009. Source: Banco Central de São Tomé e Príncipe.

Expenditure on the Gross Domestic Product ('000 million dobras at current prices, 2008): Government final consumption expenditure 1,268.3; Private final consumption expenditure 1,668.3; Gross capital formation 1,392.7; *Total domestic expenditure* 4,329.3; Exports of goods and services 923.9; *Less* Imports of goods and services 2,898.3; *GDP in purchasers' values* 2,354.9. Source: African Development Bank.

Gross Domestic Product by Economic Activity ('000 million dobras at current prices, 2008): Agriculture 387.1; Mining and quarrying 1.5; Manufacturing 54.0; Electricity, gas and water 12.7; Construction 151.3; Trade, restaurants and hotels 209.6; Finance, insurance and real estate 26.5; Transport and communications 208.5; Public administration and defence 529.4; *GDP at factor cost* 1,580.7; Taxes on products 774.2; *GDP at market prices* 2,354.9. Note: Deduction for imputed bank service charge assumed to be distributed at origin. Source: African Development Bank.

Balance of Payments (US $ million, 2009): Exports of goods f.o.b. 9.21; Imports of goods f.o.b. −83.76; *Trade balance* −74.56; Exports of services 10.44; Imports of services −18.99; *Balance on goods and services* −83.11; Other income received 1.64; Other income paid −1.93; *Balance of goods, services and income* −83.39; Current transfers received 11.27; Current transfers paid −6.63; *Current balance* −78.75; Capital account (net) 39.89; Direct investment abroad −0.30; Direct investment from abroad 7.50; Other investment assets −12.53; Other investment liabilities 34.08; Net errors and omissions −4.51; *Overall balance* 8.94. Source: IMF, *International Financial Statistics*.

EXTERNAL TRADE

Principal Commodities (US $ million, 2009): *Imports f.o.b.:* Foodstuffs 28.9; Beverages 7.4; Petroleum and petroleum products 15.9; Machinery 13.8; Transport equipment 9.9; Construction materials 6.5; Total (incl. others) 102.3. *Exports f.o.b.:* Cocoa 5.4; Coconuts 0.1; Total (incl. others) 6.2.

Principal Trading Partners (US $ million, 2009): *Imports c.i.f.:* Angola 15.1; Belgium 1.9; Brazil 10.7; Gabon 2.8; Japan 4.5; Portugal 57.7; Total (incl. others) 102.3. *Exports f.o.b.:* Angola 0.1; Belgium 1.2; France 0.2; Netherlands 1.7; Portugal 2.0; Total (incl. others) 6.2. Source: Banco Central de São Tomé e Príncipe.

TRANSPORT

Road Traffic (registered vehicles, 2007, estimates): Passenger cars 305; Lorries and vans 37. Source: IRF, *World Road Statistics*.

Shipping: *International Freight Traffic* (estimates, metric tons, 1992): Goods loaded 16,000; Goods unloaded 45,000. *Merchant Fleet* (registered at 31 December 2009): Number of vessels 28; Total displacement 22,025 grt (Source: IHS Fairplay, *World Fleet Statistics*).

Civil Aviation (traffic on scheduled services, 2005): Kilometres flown (million) 1; Passengers carried ('000) 43; Passenger-km (million) 18; Total ton-km (million) 2. Source: UN, *Statistical Yearbook*.

TOURISM

Foreign Tourist Arrivals: 10,576 in 2004; 15,746 in 2005; 12,266 in 2006.

Arrivals by Country of Residence (2006): Angola 999; Brazil 248; Cape Verde 432; France 1,186; Gabon 351; Germany 467; Nigeria 468; Portugal 5,138; Spain 395; USA 277; Total (incl. others) 12,266.

Tourism Receipts (US $ million, excl. passenger transport): 7.3 in 2005; 6.5 in 2006; 4.9 in 2007; 7.7 in 2008.

Source: World Tourism Organization.

COMMUNICATIONS MEDIA

Radio Receivers (1998): 45,000 in use. Source: UNESCO, *Statistical Yearbook*.

Television Receivers (1999): 33,000 in use. Source: UNESCO, *Statistical Yearbook*.

Newspapers and Periodicals (2000, unless otherwise indicated): Titles 14 (1997); Average circulation 18,500 copies.

Telephones ('000 main lines, 2009): 7.8 in use. Source: International Telecommunication Union.

Mobile Cellular Telephones ('000 subscribers, 2009): 64.0. Source: International Telecommunication Union.

Personal Computers: 6,000 (39.3 per 1,000 persons) in 2005.

Internet Users (2009): 26,700. Source: International Telecommunication Union.

Broadband Subscribers (2009): 2,000. Source: International Telecommunication Union.

EDUCATION

Pre-primary (2009/10): 6,309 pupils (males 3,046, females 3,263); 330 teachers.

Primary (2009/10): 33,982 pupils (males 17,203, females 16,779); 1,265 teachers.

Secondary (2009/10 unless otherwise indicated): 10,045 pupils (males 5,008, females 5,037); 375 teachers (males 328, females 47) (2005/06).

Tertiary (2000/01 unless otherwise indicated): 1 polytechnic; 29 teachers; 766 pupils (2009/10).

Source: UNESCO Institute for Statistics; *Carta Escolar de São Tomé e Príncipe*, Ministério de Educação de Portugal.

Pupil-teacher Ratio (primary education, UNESCO estimate): 26.9 in 2009/10. Source: UNESCO Institute for Statistics.

Adult Literacy Rate (UNESCO estimates): 88.3% (males 93.5; females 83.3) in 2008. Source: UNESCO Institute for Statistics.

Directory

The Government

HEAD OF STATE

President and Commander-in-Chief of the Armed Forces: FRADIQUE DE MENEZES (took office 3 September 2001; re-elected 30 July 2006).

COUNCIL OF MINISTERS
(May 2011)

The Government comprises members of the Acção Democrática Independente (ADI) and independents.

Prime Minister: PATRICE EMERY TROVOADA (ADI).
Minister of Foreign Affairs and Communities: MANUEL SALVADOR DOS RAMOS (Ind.).
Minister of Defence and Public Security: CARLOS OLÍMPIO STOCK (ADI).
Minister of Justice and State Reform: ELÍSIO OSVALDO D'ALVA TEIXEIRA (ADI).
Minister of Parliamentary Affairs and Decentralization: ARLINDO RAMOS (ADI).
Minister, Secretary-General of the Government: AFONSO DA GRAÇA VARELA DA SILVA (Ind.).
Minister of Finance and International Co-operation: AMÉRICO D'OLIVEIRA DOS RAMOS (Ind.).
Minister of Planning and Development: AGOSTINHO QUARESMA DOS SANTOS FERNANDES (ADI).
Minister of Public Works and Natural Resources: CARLOS MANUEL VILA NOVA (Ind.).
Minister of Health and Social Affairs: ÂNGELA DOS SANTOS JOSÉ DA COSTA PINHEIRO (ADI).
Minister of Education, Culture and Vocational Training: OLINTO DA SILVA DE SOUSA DAIO (Ind.).
Secretary of State of Youth and Sports: ABNILDO D'OLIVEIRA (ADI).

Provisional Government of the Autonomous Region of Príncipe
(May 2011)

President: JOSÉ CARDOSO CASSANDRA.
Secretary for Social and Cultural Affairs: FELÍCIA FONSECA DE OLIVEIRA E SILVA.
Secretary for Economic and Financial Affairs: HÉLIO LAVRES.
Secretary for Infrastructure and the Environment: TIAGO ROSAMONTE.
Secretary for Political, Organizational and Institutional Affairs: (vacant).

MINISTRIES

Office of the President: Palácio Presidêncial, São Tomé; internet www.presidencia.st.
Office of the Prime Minister: Rua do Município, CP 302, São Tomé; tel. 223913; fax 224679; e-mail gpm@cstome.net.
Ministry of Defence and Public Security: Av. 12 de Julho, CP 427, São Tomé; tel. 222041; e-mail midefesa@cstome.net.
Ministry of Education, Culture and Vocational Training: Rua Misericórdia, CP 41, São Tomé; tel. 222861; fax 221466; e-mail mineducal@cstome.net.
Ministry of Finance and International Co-operation: São Tomé.
Ministry of Foreign Affairs and Communities: Av. 12 de Julho, CP 111, São Tomé; tel. 222309; fax 223237; e-mail minecoop@cstome.net; internet www.mnecc.gov.st.
Ministry of Health and Social Affairs: Av. Patrice Lumumba, CP 23, São Tomé; tel. 241200; fax 221306; e-mail msaude@cstome.net; internet saude.gov-stp.net.
Ministry of Justice and State Reform: Av. 12 de Julho, CP 4, São Tomé; tel. 222318; fax 222256; e-mail emilioma@cstome.net.
Ministry of Parliamentary Affairs and Decentralization: São Tomé.
Ministry of Planning and Development: Largo Alfândega, CP 168, São Tomé; tel. 224173; fax 222683; e-mail mpfc@cstome.net.
Ministry of Public Works and Natural Resources: São Tomé.
Ministry of Youth and Sports: Rua Misericórdia, CP 41, São Tomé; tel. 222861; fax 221466.

President and Legislature

PRESIDENT

Presidential Election, 30 July 2006

Candidate	Votes	% of votes
Fradique de Menezes	34,859	60.58
Patrice Emery Trovoada	22,339	38.82
Nilo de Oliveira Guimarães	340	0.59
Total	57,538	100.00

There were, in addition, 1,640 blank and other invalid votes.

ASSEMBLEIA NACIONAL

Assembleia Nacional: Palácio dos Congressos, CP 181, São Tomé; tel. 222986; fax 222835; e-mail romao.couto@parlamento.st; internet www.parlamento.st.
President: EVARISTO CARVALHO.

General Election, 1 August 2010

Party	Seats
Acção Democrática Independente	26
Movimento de Libertação de São Tomé e Príncipe—Partido Social Democrata	21
Partido de Convergência Democrática	7
Movimento Democrático Força da Mudança	1
Total	55

Election Commission

Comissão Eleitoral Nacional (CEN): Av. Amílcar Cabral, São Tomé; tel. 225497; fax 224116; e-mail censtome@cstome.net; Pres. JOSÉ CARLOS BARREIROS.

Political Organizations

Acção Democrática Independente (ADI): Av. Marginal 12 de Julho, Edif. C. Cassandra, São Tomé; tel. 222201; f. 1992; Sec.-Gen. PATRICE TROVOADA.
Frente Democrata Cristã—Partido Social da Unidade (FDC—PSU): São Tomé; f. 1990; Pres. ARLÉCIO COSTA; Vice-Pres. SABINO DOS SANTOS.
Geração Esperança (GE): São Tomé; f. 2005; Leader EDMILZA BRAGANÇA.
Movimento Democrático Força da Mudança (MDFM): São Tomé; f. 2001; Pres. FRADIQUE DE MENEZES; Sec.-Gen. RAUL CRAVID.
Movimento de Libertação de São Tomé e Príncipe—Partido Social Democrata (MLSTP—PSD): Estrada Riboque, Edif. Sede do MLSTP, São Tomé; tel. 222253; f. 1972 as MLSTP; adopted present name in 1990; sole legal party 1972–90; Pres. JOAQUIM RAFAEL BRANCO; Sec.-Gen. JOSÉ VIEGAS.
Novo Rumo: São Tomé; f. 2006 by citizens disaffected by current political parties; Leader JOÃO GOMES.
Partido de Coligação Democrática (CÓDÓ): São Tomé; f. 1990 as Partido Democrático de São Tomé e Príncipe—Coligação Democrática da Oposição; renamed as above June 1998; Leader MANUEL NEVES E SILVA.
Partido de Convergência Democrática (PCD): Av. Marginal 12 de Julho, CP 519, São Tomé; tel. and fax 223257; f. 1990 as Partido de Convergência—Grupo de Reflexão; formed alliance with MDFM to contest legislative elections in 2006; Pres. ALBERTINO BRAGANÇA; Sec.-Gen. DELFIM SANTIAGO DAS NEVES.
Partido Popular do Progresso (PPP): São Tomé; f. 1998; Leader FRANCISCO SILVA.
Partido de Renovação Democrática (PRD): São Tomé; tel. 903109; e-mail prd100@hotmail.com; f. 2001; Pres. ARMINDO GRAÇA.
Partido Social Renovado (PSR): São Tomé; f. 2004; Leader HAMILTON VAZ.
Partido Social e Liberal (PSL): São Tomé; f. 2005; promotes devt and anti-corruption; Leader AGOSTINHO RITA.

SÃO TOMÉ AND PRÍNCIPE

Partido Trabalhista Santomense (PTS): CP 254, São Tomé; tel. 223338; fax 223255; e-mail pascoal@cstome.net; f. 1993 as Aliança Popular; Leader ANACLETO ROLIN.

União para a Democracia e Desenvolvimento (UDD): São Tomé; f. 2005; Leader MANUEL DIOGO.

União Nacional para Democracia e Progresso (UNDP): São Tomé; f. 1998; Leader PAIXÃO LIMA.

The União para a Mudança e Progresso do Príncipe (UMPP) led by JOSÉ CARDOSO CASSANDRA operates on the island of Príncipe and there is also a local civic group, O Renascimento de Agua Grande, in the district of Agua Grande, which includes the city of São Tomé.

Diplomatic Representation

EMBASSIES IN SÃO TOMÉ AND PRÍNCIPE

Angola: Av. Kwame Nkrumah 45, CP 133, São Tomé; tel. 222400; fax 221362; e-mail embrang@cstome.net; Ambassador (vacant).

Brazil: Av. Marginal de 12 de Julho 20, São Tomé; tel. 226060; fax 226895; e-mail brasembsaotome@cstome.net; Ambassador ARTHUR VIVACQUA CORREA MEYER.

Equatorial Guinea: Av. Kwame Nkrumah, São Tomé; tel. 225427; Ambassador ANTÓNIO EBADE AYINGONO.

Gabon: Rua Damão, CP 394, São Tomé; tel. 224434; fax 223531; e-mail ambagabon@cstome.net; Ambassador BEKALÉ MICHEL.

Nigeria: Av. Kwame Nkrumah, CP 1000, São Tomé; tel. 225404; fax 225406; e-mail nigeria@cstome.net; Ambassador SUNDAY DOGONYARO OON.

Portugal: Av. Marginal de 12 de Julho, CP 173, São Tomé; tel. 221130; fax 221190; e-mail eporstp@cstome.net; Ambassador FERNANDO JOSÉ RODRIGUES RAMOS MACHADO.

South Africa: Av. da Independencia, No. 7 Representanção da República da Africa de Sul, CP 555, São Tomé; tel. 227568; e-mail consuafricasul@cstome.net; Chargé d'affaires a.i. T. E. MAMUREMI.

Taiwan (Republic of China): Av. Marginal de 12 de Julho, CP 839, São Tomé; tel. 223529; fax 221376; e-mail rocstp@cstome.net; Ambassador JOHN-C. CHEN.

Judicial System

Judicial power is exercised by the Supreme Court of Justice and the Courts of Primary Instance. The Supreme Court is the ultimate judicial authority. There is also a Constitutional Court, which rules on election matters.

Supremo Tribunal de Justiça: Av. Marginal de 12 de Julho, CP 04, São Tomé; tel. 222615; fax 222329; e-mail info@stj.st; internet www.stj.st; Pres. SILVESTRE LEITE.

Religion

According to the 2001 census more than 80% of the population are Christians, almost all of whom are Roman Catholics.

CHRISTIANITY

The Roman Catholic Church

São Tomé and Príncipe comprises a single diocese, directly responsible to the Holy See. An estimated 72% of the population were adherents. The bishop participates in the Episcopal Conference of Angola and São Tomé (based in Luanda, Angola).

Bishop of São Tomé and Príncipe: Rt Rev. MANUEL ANTÓNIO MENDES DOS SANTOS, Centro Diocesano, CP 104, Rua P. Pinto da Rocha 1, São Tomé; tel. 223455; fax 227348; e-mail diocese@cstome.net.

Other Churches

Igreja Adventista do 7° Dia (Seventh-Day Adventist Church): Rua Barão de Água Izé, São Tomé; tel. 223349; e-mail sdastp@gmail.com; Pres. JOSÉ MARQUES.

Igreja Evangélica: Rua 3 de Fevereiro, São Tomé; tel. 221350.

Igreja Evangélica Assembléia de Deus: Rua 3 de Fevereiro, São Tomé; tel. and fax 222442; e-mail iead@cstome.net.

Igreja Maná: Av. Amílcar Cabral, São Tomé; tel. and fax 224654; e-mail imana@cstome.net.

Igreja do Nazareno: Vila Dolores, São Tomé; tel. 223943; e-mail nszst@cstome.net.

Igreja Nova Apostólica: CP 220, Vila Maria, São Tomé; tel. and fax 222797; e-mail j.cunha@ina-stp.org; internet ina-stp.org.

Igreja Universal do Reino de Deus: Travessa Imprensa, São Tomé; tel. 224047.

The Press

Correio da Semana: Av. Amílcar Cabral 382, São Tomé; tel. 225299; e-mail correiodasemana@cstome.net; f. 2005; weekly; Dir JUVENAL RODRIGUES; circ. 3,000.

Diário da República: Cooperativa de Artes Gráficas, Rua João Devs, CP 28, São Tomé; tel. 222661; internet dre.pt/stp; f. 1836; official gazette; Dir OSCAR FERREIRA.

Jornal Maravilha: São Tomé; tel. 911690; f. 2006; Dir NELSON SIGNO.

Jornal Tropical: Rua Padre Martinho Pinto da Rocha, São Tomé; tel. 923140; e-mail jornaltropical06@hotmail.com; internet www.jornaltropical.st; Dir OCTÁVIO SOARES.

O Parvo: CP 535, São Tomé; tel. 221031; f. 1994; weekly; Publr AMBRÓSIO QUARESMA; Editor ARMINDO CARDOSO.

Téla Nón: Largo Água Grande, Edif. Complexo Técnico da CST, São Tomé; tel. 225099; e-mail diario_digital@cstome.net; internet www.cstome.net/diario; f. 2000; provides online daily news service; Chief Editor ABEL VEIGA.

Online newspapers include the Jornal de São Tomé e Príncipe (www.jornal.st) and Jornal Horizonte (www.cstome.net/jhorizonte) and Vitrina (www.vitrina.st).

PRESS ASSOCIATION

Associação Nacional de Imprensa (ANI): São Tomé; Pres. MANUEL BARRETO.

NEWS AGENCY

STP-Press: Av. Marginal de 12 de Julho, CP 112, São Tomé; tel. 223431; fax 221973; e-mail stp_press@cstome.net; internet www.cstome.net/stp-press; f. 1985; operated by the radio station in asscn with the Angolan news agency ANGOP; Dir MANUEL DÊNDE.

Broadcasting and Communications

TELECOMMUNICATIONS

Companhia Santomense de Telecomunicações, SARL (CST): Av. Marginal 12 de Julho, CP 141, São Tomé; tel. 222226; fax 222500; e-mail webmaster@cstome.net; internet www.cstome.net; f. 1989 by Govt of São Tomé (49%) and Grupo Portugal Telecom (Portugal, 51%) to facilitate increased telecommunications links and television reception via satellite; in March 1997 CST introduced internet services; Rádio Marconi's shares subsequently assumed by Portugal Telecom SA; introduced mobile cellular telephone service in 2001; Pres. FELISBERTO AFONSO L. NETO; Sec. JORGE LIMA D'ALVA TORRES.

BROADCASTING

Portuguese technical and financial assistance in the establishment of a television service was announced in May 1989. Transmissions commenced in 1992 and the service currently broadcasts seven days a week. In 1995 Radio France Internationale and Rádio Televisão Portuguesa Internacional began relaying radio and television broadcasts, respectively, to the archipelago. In 1997 Voice of America, which had been broadcasting throughout Africa since 1993 from a relay station installed on São Tomé, began local transmissions on FM. In 2004 there were plans for Televisão Pública de Angola to begin transmitting by the end of the year. The liberalization of the sector was approved by the Government in early 2005 and Rádio Jubilar, Rádio Tropicana (operated by the Roman Catholic Church) and Rádio Viva FM subsequently began broadcasting. The French television channel TV5 began broadcasting in December 2007.

Radio

Rádio Nacional de São Tomé e Príncipe: Av. Marginal de 12 de Julho, CP 44, São Tomé; tel. 223293; fax 221973; e-mail rnstp@cstome.net; f. 1958; state-controlled; home service in Portuguese and Creole; Dir MÁXIMO CARLOS.

Rádio Jubilar: Av. Kwam Kruman-Edifício da Catequese, CP 104, São Tomé; tel. 223868; e-mail radiojubilar@cstome.net; f. 2005; operated by the Roman Catholic Church; Dir LEONEL PEREIRA.

Rádio Tropicana: Travessa João de Deus, CP 709, São Tomé; tel. 226856; f. 2005; Dir AGUINALDO SALVATERRA.

SÃO TOMÉ AND PRÍNCIPE

Television

Televisão Santomense (TVS): Bairro Quinta de Santo António, CP 393, São Tomé; tel. 221041; fax 221942; state-controlled; Dir MATEUS FERREIRA.

Finance

(cap. = capital; res = reserves; dep. = deposits; m. = million; br(s). = branch(es); amounts in dobras, unless otherwise indicated)

BANKING

Central Bank

Banco Central de São Tomé e Príncipe (BCSTP): Praça da Independência, CP 13, São Tomé; tel. 243700; fax 222777; e-mail bcstp@bcstp.st; internet www.bcstp.st; f. 1992 to succeed fmr Banco Nacional de São Tomé e Príncipe; bank of issue; cap. 108,721.2m., res 175,726.5m., dep. 1,286,443.2m. (Dec. 2009); Gov. MARIA DO CARMO SILVEIRA.

Commercial Banks

Afriland First Bank/STP: Praça da Independência, CP 202, São Tomé; tel. 226749; fax 226747; e-mail stp@afrilandfirstbank.com; internet www.afrilandfirstbank.com; f. 2003; private bank; owned by Afriland First Bank, SA, Cameroon; cap. US $1.8m.; Gen. Man. AUGUSTIN DIAYO; Administrator-Delegate JOSEPH TINDJOU.

Banco Equador SARL: Rua de Moçambique 3B, CP 361, São Tomé; tel. 226150; fax 226149; e-mail be@bancoequador.st; internet www.bancoequador.st; f. 1995 as Banco Comercial do Equador; restructured and name changed to above in 2004; owned by Monbaka, Angola (40%) and Grupo António Mbakassi (40%); cap. US $3m.; Pres. DIONÍSIO MENDONÇA; Gen. Man. RUI MENDONÇA; 1 br.

Banco Internacional de São Tomé e Príncipe (BISTP) (International Bank of São Tomé and Príncipe): Praça da Independência 3, CP 536, São Tomé; tel. 243100; fax 222427; e-mail bistp@cstome.net; internet www.bistp.st; f. 1993; 48% govt-owned, 27% by Caixa Geral de Depósitos (Portugal), 25% by Banco Africano de Investimentos SARL (Angola); cap. 12,546.0m., res 201,953.5m., dep. 689,557.5m. (2009); CEO JOÃO CARLOS AGUIAR CRISTÓVÃO; 3 brs.

Commercial Bank—São Tomé e Príncipe: Av. Marginal 12 de Julho, CP 1109, São Tomé; tel. 227678; fax 227676; e-mail cobstp@cstome.net; internet www.cbc-bank.com; f. 2005; 42% owned by Groupe FOTSO (Cameroon); cap. US $3m. (2005); Chair. YVES MICHEL FOTSO; Gen. Man. JAQUES PAUL WOUENDJI.

Ecobank São Tomé: Edifício HB, Traversa de Pelorinho, CP 316, São Tomé; tel. 222141; fax 222672; e-mail ecobankstp@cstome.net; f. 2007; cap. US $1.5m.

Island Bank, SA: Rua de Guiné, CP 1044, São Tomé; tel. 227484; fax 227490; e-mail ceo@islandbanksa.com; internet www.islandbanksa.com; f. 2005; cap. US $1.8m. (2005); Pres. MARC WABARA; Man. Dir EDWIN F. B. KRUKRUBO.

Oceanic Bank STP: Rua Dr Palma Carlos, CP 1175, São Tomé; tel. 222689; fax 222641; f. 2008; cap. US $5.0m. (Dec. 2008); Dir PETER NWACHUKWU.

INSURANCE

Instituto de Segurança Social: Rua Soldado Paulo Ferreira, São Tomé; tel. 221382; e-mail inss@cstome.net; f. as Caixa de Previdência dos Funcionários Públicos, adopted present name 1994; insurance fund for civil servants; Pres. of Admin. Bd ALBINO GRAÇA DA FONSECA; Dir JUVENAL DO ESPÍRITO SANTO.

NICON Seguros STP: Av. 12 de Julho 997, CP556, São Tomé; tel. and fax 227057; e-mail niconseguros@cstome.net; f. 2008; cap. US $1.3m.; Dir TOWOJO PIUS AGBOOLA.

SAT INSURANCE: Av. Amilcar Cabral, CP 293, São Tomé; tel. 226161; fax 226160; e-mail satinsuran@cstome.net; f. 2001; general insurance; cap. US $1.0m.; Dir MICHEL SOBGUI.

Trade and Industry

GOVERNMENT AGENCIES

Agência Nacional do Petróleo de São Tomé e Príncipe (ANP—STP): Av. Nações Unidas, CP 1048, São Tomé; tel. 226940; fax 226937; e-mail anp_geral@cstome.net; internet www.anp-stp.gov.st; f. 2004; manages and implements govt policies relating to the petroleum sector; Exec. Dir LUÍS PRAZERES.

Nigeria-São Tomé and Príncipe Joint Development Authority (JDA): Plot 1101, Aminu Kano Cres., Wuse II, Abuja, Nigeria; Praça da UCCLA, São Tomé; tel. (234) 95241069; fax (234) 95241061; e-mail enquiries@nigeriasaotomejda.com; internet www.nigeriasaotomejda.com; f. 2002; manages devt of petroleum and gas resources in Joint Development Zone; Exec. Dir Dr JORGE PEREIRA DOS SANTOS.

DEVELOPMENT ORGANIZATION

Instituto para o Desenvolvimento Económico e Social (INDES): Travessa do Pelourinho, CP 408, São Tomé; tel. 222491; fax 221931; e-mail indes@cstome.net; f. 1989 as Fundo Social e de Infrastructuras; adopted present name 1994; channels foreign funds to local economy; Dir HOMERO JERÓNIMO SALVATERRA.

CHAMBER OF COMMERCE

Câmara do Comércio, Indústria, Agricultura e Serviços (CCIAS): Av. Marginal de 12 de Julho, CP 527, São Tomé; tel. 222723; fax 221409; e-mail ccias@cstome.net; internet www2.cciastp.org; Pres. ABÍLIO AFONSO HENRIQUES.

UTILITIES

Electricity and Water

Empresa de Água e Electricidade (EMAE): Av. Água Grande, CP 46, São Tomé; tel. 222096; fax 222488; e-mail emae@cstome.net; f. 1979; Synergie Investments (UK); state electricity and water co; privatized in 2004; Dir-Gen. Lt-Col ÓSCAR SOUSA.

TRADE UNIONS

Federação Nacional dos Pequenos Agricoltores (FENAPA): Rua Barão de Água Izé, São Tomé; tel. 224741; Pres. TEODORICO CAMPOS.

Organização Nacional de Trabalhadores de São Tomé e Príncipe (ONTSTP): Rua Cabo Verde, São Tomé; tel. 222431; e-mail ontstpdis@cstome.net; Sec.-Gen. JOÃO TAVARES.

Sindicato de Jornalistas de São Tomé e Príncipe (SJS): São Tomé; Pres. AMBRÓSIO QUARESMA.

Sindicato dos Trabalhadores do Estado (STE): São Tomé; Sec.-Gen. AURÉLIO SILVA.

União Geral dos Trabalhadores de São Tomé e Príncipe (UGSTP): Av. Kwame Nkrumah, São Tomé; tel. 222443; e-mail ugtdis@cstome.net; Sec.-Gen. COSTA CARLOS.

Transport

RAILWAYS

There are no railways in São Tomé and Príncipe.

ROADS

In 1999 there were an estimated 320 km of roads, of which 218 km were asphalted. In 2005 the European Union granted €930,000 towards upgrading the road network.

SHIPPING

The principal ports are at São Tomé city and at Neves on São Tomé island. At December 2009 São Tomé and Príncipe's registered merchant fleet comprised 28 vessels, totalling 22,025 grt.

Companhia Santomense de Navegação, SA (CSN): CP 49, São Tomé; tel. 222657; fax 221311; e-mail csn@setgrcop.com; shipping and freight forwarding.

Empresa Nacional de Administração dos Portos (ENAPORT): Largo Alfândega, CP 437, São Tomé; tel. 221841; fax 224949; e-mail enaport@cstome.net; internet www.enaport.st; Pres. DEODATO GOMES RODRIGUES.

Navetur-Equatour: CP 277, Rua Viriato da Cruz, São Tomé; tel. 223781; fax 222122; e-mail navequatur@cstome.net; internet www.navetur-equatour.st; Dir-Gen. LUÍS BEIRÃO.

Transportes e Serviços, Lda (TURIMAR): Rua Patrice Lumumba, CP 48, São Tomé; tel. 221869; fax 222162; e-mail turimar@cstome.net; internet www.turimar-stp.com; Man. ALBERTO PEREIRA.

CIVIL AVIATION

The international airport is at São Tomé.

Empresa Nacional de Aeroportos e Segurança Aérea (ENASA): Aeroporto, CP 703, São Tomé; tel. 221878; fax 221154; e-mail enasa@cstome.net; Dir ARISTIDES BAROS.

Linhas Aéreas São-tomenses (LAS): Rua Santo António do Príncipe, São Tomé; tel. 227282; fax 227281; e-mail hba.saotome@gmail.com; f. 2002; owned by Aerocontractors, Nigeria; Dir ANTÓNIO AGUIAR.

SCD-Aviation: Omali Lodge Luxury Hotel, São Tomé; tel. 222350; fax 221814.

SÃO TOMÉ AND PRÍNCIPE

STP-Airways: Av. Marginal 12 de Julho, São Tomé; tel. 221160; fax 223449; e-mail stp-airways@cstome.net; internet www.stpairways.st; f. 2006; 35% govt-owned; Dir Felisberto Neto.

Tourism

The islands benefit from spectacular mountain scenery, unspoilt beaches and unique species of flora and wildlife. Although still largely undeveloped, tourism is currently the sector of the islands' economy attracting the highest level of foreign investment. However, the high level of rainfall during most of the year limits the duration of the tourist season, and the expense of reaching the islands by air is also an inhibiting factor. There were 12,266 tourist arrivals in 2006, and receipts totalled some US $7.7m. in 2008.

Defence

In early 2005 the armed forces were estimated to number some 300. Military service, which is compulsory, lasts for 30 months. There is also a presidential guard numbering some 160. In 2000 Portugal and São Tomé renewed the military agreement for the stationing of the 'Aviocar' and a crew of the Portuguese Air Force in the country. Since April 1988 the aeroplane has provided humanitarian emergency flights from Príncipe to São Tomé, as well as rescue operations for local fishermen along the coast. In 2004 a paramilitary unit, trained by the Angolan Government and comprising 200 men, was created. In mid-2006 army recruitment was broadened to include women.

Defence Expenditure: Budgeted at 1,100m. dobras (excl. capital expenditure) in 2000.

Commander-in-Chief of the Armed Forces: Fradique de Menezes.

Chief of General Staff of the Armed Forces: Lt-Col Idalécio Pachire.

Education

Primary education is officially compulsory between six and 14 years of age. Secondary education lasts for a further seven years, comprising a first cycle of four years and a second cycle of three years. According to UNESCO estimates, in 2009/10 enrolment at primary schools included 99% of children in the relevant age-group, while the comparable ratio for secondary enrolment in 2006/07 was 32% (males 30%; females 35%). The country's first university, Universidade Lusíada, was inaugurated in October 2006. In 2000 public investment in education (including culture and sport) amounted to US $1.3m., equivalent to 6.7% of total public investment. The budget for 2005 allocated 13.4% of total government expenditure to education.

SAUDI ARABIA

Introductory Survey

LOCATION, CLIMATE, LANGUAGE, RELIGION, FLAG, CAPITAL

The Kingdom of Saudi Arabia occupies about four-fifths of the Arabian peninsula, in south-western Asia. It is bordered by Jordan, Iraq and Kuwait to the north, by Yemen to the south, by Oman to the south and east, and by Qatar and the United Arab Emirates to the north-east. Saudi Arabia has a long western coastline on the Red Sea, facing Egypt, Sudan and Eritrea, and a shorter coastline (between Kuwait and Qatar) on the Persian (Arabian) Gulf, with the Bahrain archipelago (to which Saudi Arabia is connected via a causeway) just off shore and Iran on the opposite coast. Much of the country is arid desert, and some places are without rain for years. In summer average temperatures in coastal regions range from 38°C to 49°C, and humidity is high. Temperatures sometimes reach 54°C in the interior. Winters are mild, except in the mountains. Annual rainfall averages between 100 mm and 200 mm in the north, and is even lower in the south. The official language is Arabic, which is spoken by almost all of the population. Except for the expatriate community (estimated to represent some 27% of the total population in 2009), virtually all of the inhabitants are adherents of Islam, the official religion. About 85% of the population are Sunni Muslims, and most of the indigenous inhabitants belong to the strictly orthodox Wahhabi sect. About 15% of the population are Shi'a Muslims, principally in the east of the country. The national flag (proportions 2 by 3) is green and bears, in white, an Arabic inscription ('There is no God but Allah and Muhammad is the Prophet of Allah') above a white sabre. The capital is Riyadh.

CONTEMPORARY POLITICAL HISTORY

Historical Context

The whole of the Arabian peninsula became part of Turkey's Ottoman Empire in the 16th century. Under the suzerainty of the Ottoman Sultan, the local tribal rulers enjoyed varying degrees of autonomy. The Wahhabi movement, dedicated to the reform of Islam, was launched in the Najd (Nejd) region of central Arabia in the 18th century. A Wahhabi kingdom, ruled by the House of Sa'ud from its capital at Riyadh, quickly expanded into the Hedjaz region on the west coast of Arabia. In 1890 the rival Rashidi family seized control of Riyadh, but in 1902 a member of the deposed Sa'udi family, Abd al-Aziz ibn Abd al-Rahman, expelled the Rashidi dynasty and proclaimed himself ruler of Najd. In subsequent years he recovered and consolidated the outlying provinces of the kingdom, defeating Turkish attempts to subjugate him. Having restored the House of Sa'ud as a ruling dynasty, Abd al-Aziz became known as Ibn Sa'ud. In order to strengthen his position, he instituted the formation of Wahhabi colonies, known as Ikhwan ('Brethren'), throughout the territory under his control.

During the First World War, in which Turkey was allied with Germany, the Arabs under Ottoman rule rebelled. In 1915 the United Kingdom signed a treaty of friendship with Ibn Sa'ud, who was then master of central Arabia, securing his co-operation against Turkey. Relations subsequently deteriorated as a result of the British Government's decision to support Hussein ibn Ali, who proclaimed himself King of the Hedjaz in 1916, as its principal ally in Arabia. Hussein was also Sharif of Mecca (the holiest city of Islam), which had been governed since the 11th century by his Hashimi (Hashemite) family, rivals of the House of Sa'ud. At the end of the war, following Turkey's defeat, the Ottoman Empire was dissolved. Continuing his conquests, Ibn Sa'ud successfully campaigned against the rulers of four Arabian states (the Hedjaz, Asir, Hayil and Jauf) between 1919 and 1925. In September 1924 his forces captured Mecca, forcing Hussein to abdicate, and in 1925 they overran the whole of the Hedjaz. In January 1926 Ibn Sa'ud was proclaimed King of the Hedjaz and Sultan of Najd. On 23 September 1932 the dual monarchy ended when the two areas were merged as the unified Kingdom of Saudi Arabia.

Commercially exploitable deposits of petroleum (the basis of Saudi Arabia's modern prosperity) were discovered in the Eastern Province in 1938, and large-scale exploitation of the kingdom's huge reserves of petroleum began after the Second World War. Petroleum royalties were used to develop and modernize the country's infrastructure and services.

Ibn Sa'ud remained in power until his death in November 1953; all subsequent rulers of Saudi Arabia have been sons of his. The kingdom has remained an absolute monarchy and a traditional Islamic society. The King is the supreme religious leader as well as the Head of State, and governs by royal decree. In foreign affairs, Saudi Arabia has historically allied itself with the USA and other Western countries.

Domestic Political Affairs

Ibn Sa'ud was succeeded by the Crown Prince, Sa'ud ibn Abd al-Aziz. Another of the late King's sons, Faisal ibn Abd al-Aziz, replaced Sa'ud as Crown Prince and Prime Minister. In 1958, bowing to pressure from the royal family, King Sa'ud conferred on Crown Prince Faisal full powers over foreign, internal and economic affairs. In March 1964 King Sa'ud relinquished power to Crown Prince Faisal, and in November was forced by the royal family to abdicate in his favour. The new King Faisal retained the post of Prime Minister, and appointed his half-brother, Khalid ibn Abd al-Aziz, to be Crown Prince in 1965. In the Six-Day War of June 1967 Saudi Arabian forces collaborated with Iraqi and Jordanian troops in action against Israel. As a result of the Arab–Israeli War of October 1973, Saudi Arabia led a movement by Arab oil producers to exert pressure on Western countries by reducing supplies of crude petroleum.

In March 1975 King Faisal was assassinated by one of his nephews, and was immediately succeeded by Crown Prince Khalid. The new King also became Prime Minister, and appointed his brother, Fahd ibn Abd al-Aziz (Minister of the Interior since 1962), as Crown Prince and First Deputy Prime Minister.

The religious fervour that the Middle East experienced in the wake of the Iranian Revolution also arose in Saudi Arabia in late 1979, when an armed group of about 250 Sunni Muslim extremists attacked and occupied the Grand Mosque in Mecca, the most important centre of pilgrimage for Muslims. There was also a riot by Shi'a Muslims in the Eastern Province. In response to the unrest, Crown Prince Fahd announced in early 1980 that a consultative assembly would be formed to act as an advisory body, although the assembly was not inaugurated until December 1993 (see below).

The reign of King Fahd

King Khalid died in June 1982 and was succeeded by Crown Prince Fahd, who, following precedent, became Prime Minister and appointed a half-brother, Abdullah ibn Abd al-Aziz (Commander of the National Guard since 1962), to be Crown Prince and First Deputy Prime Minister.

As a result of its position as the world's leading exporter of petroleum, Saudi Arabia is a dominant member of the Organization of the Petroleum Exporting Countries (OPEC, see p. 405) and one of the most influential countries in the Arab world. In May 1981 the kingdom joined five neighbouring states in establishing the Co-operation Council for the Arab States of the Gulf (the Gulf Co-operation Council—GCC, see p. 243).

In July 1988, after the US Congress had refused to sanction an agreement to supply military equipment to Saudi Arabia (following the delivery of an unspecified number of medium-range missiles from the People's Republic of China to Saudi Arabia earlier that year), the Government signed a large-scale defence procurement agreement with the United Kingdom, which as a result superseded the USA as Saudi Arabia's main supplier of military equipment.

Widely held misgivings regarding national defence capabilities, and fears of Iraqi expansionist policy (a pact of non-aggression was signed with Iraq in March 1989), were exacerbated in August 1990, when Iraq invaded and annexed Kuwait and proceeded to deploy armed forces along the Kuwaiti–Saudi Arabian border. King Fahd requested that US forces be deployed in Saudi Arabia, as part of a multinational force, in order to deter a possible attack by Iraq. The dispatch of US combat troops and aircraft to Saudi Arabia signified the beginning of 'Operation Desert Shield' for the defence of Saudi Arabia, in accordance with

Article 51 of the UN Charter. By the beginning of 1991 some 30 countries had contributed ground troops, aircraft and warships to the US-led multinational force based in Saudi Arabia and the Gulf region. The entire Saudi Arabian armed forces (numbering about 67,500 men) were mobilized. In January, following the failure of international diplomatic efforts to secure Iraq's withdrawal from Kuwait, the multinational force launched a military campaign ('Operation Desert Storm') to liberate Kuwait. As part of its response to the initial aerial bombardment, Iraq launched Scud missiles against targets in Saudi Arabia. However, fighting on Saudi Arabian territory was confined to a few minor incidents. In February Iraq formally severed diplomatic relations with Saudi Arabia.

Following the liberation of Kuwait in February 1991, the ministers responsible for foreign affairs of the GCC met their Syrian and Egyptian counterparts in Damascus, Syria, in March in order to discuss regional security issues. The formation of an Arab peace-keeping force, comprising mainly Egyptian and Syrian troops, was subsequently announced. In May, however, following the endorsement by the GCC member states of US proposals for an increased Western military presence in the Gulf region, Egypt announced its decision to withdraw all of its forces from the region, casting doubt on the future of joint Arab regional security arrangements. Diplomatic relations between Saudi Arabia and Iran were re-established in March, and Iranians resumed attendance of the *Hajj* (pilgrimage) to Mecca, their numbers regulated in accordance with the quota system.

In March 1992 King Fahd announced by royal decree the imminent creation of an advisory Consultative Council (Majlis al-Shoura), with 60 members to be selected by the King every four years. Two further decrees provided for the establishment of regional authorities, and a 'basic law of government', equivalent to a written constitution. In September Sheikh Muhammad al-Jubair, hitherto Minister of Justice, was appointed Chairman of the Majlis. The Majlis was inaugurated by King Fahd at the end of 1993. (Its membership was increased to 90 in July 1997, to 120 in May 2001 and to 150 in April 2005—see below.)

In May 1993 the Saudi authorities disbanded the Committee for the Defence of Legitimate Rights (CDLR), recently established by a group of six prominent Islamist scholars and lawyers. The organization's founders were also dismissed from their positions, and their spokesman, Muhammad al-Masari, was arrested. In April 1994 members of the CDLR, including al-Masari (who had recently been released from custody), relocated their organization to the United Kingdom.

More than 1,000 people, including clerics and academics, were reportedly detained in September 1994, after most of them had attended a demonstration in Buraidah, north-west of Riyadh, to protest at the arrest of two religious leaders who had allegedly been agitating for the stricter enforcement of *Shari'a* (Islamic) law. The Government announced in October that only 157 people had been arrested in September, 130 of whom had since been released. Also in October the King approved the creation of a Higher Council for Islamic Affairs, in a measure apparently aimed at limiting the influence of militant clerics and at diminishing the authority of the powerful 18-member Council of Senior Ulama (Saudi Arabia's most senior Islamic authority). In mid-1995 King Fahd replaced six of the seven university chancellors and more than one-half of the members of the Council of Senior Ulama, in an attempt to counter the perceived spread of Islamist fundamentalism.

In June 1995 an opposition activist, Abdullah Abd al-Rahman al-Hudaif, was sentenced to 20 years' imprisonment for his part in an attack on a security officer and for maintaining links with the CDLR in the United Kingdom. In August al-Hudaif was reported to have been executed. A further nine opposition activists reportedly received prison sentences ranging from three to 18 years; according to prominent human rights organization Amnesty International, as many as 200 'political suspects' remained in detention in Saudi Arabia.

In August 1995 the King announced the most far-reaching reorganization of the Council of Ministers for two decades, although no changes were made to the portfolios held by members of the royal family. The strategic portfolios of finance and national economy and of petroleum and mineral resources were allocated to younger, though highly experienced, officials.

A Supreme Economic Council, established by royal decree, convened for the first time in October 1997 under the chairmanship of the Crown Prince. A Supreme Petroleum and Minerals Council was established by royal decree in January 2000. The Government declared in May that ministers were to lose their right to hold company posts while in office, with the exception of employees of the state-owned Saudi Aramco petroleum corporation. In June the inaugural session was held of the newly formed Royal Family Council, an officially apolitical body to be chaired by Crown Prince Abdullah.

Saudi Arabia's human rights record has for many years been the focus of international scrutiny, particularly regarding the use of public beheading in the Saudi judicial system. A report issued by Amnesty International in March 2000 alleged that Saudi Arabia was guilty of widespread human rights abuses, including the use of torture and refusal to allow prisoners access to family members and lawyers. In another document, published in September, Amnesty accused the Saudi authorities of widespread discrimination against women and cited serious abuses of their human rights, including arbitrary detention and torture. The organization also reiterated its criticism of the Saudi judiciary for failing to conduct trials in compliance with internationally recognized standards. However, it was reported in late 2000 that Saudi Arabia had agreed to sign the UN Convention on the Elimination of All Forms of Discrimination against Women, although it stated that it would lodge reservations regarding any section deemed to contravene *Shari'a* law.

King Fahd announced a restructured 27-member Council of Ministers in April 2003; this was only the third reorganization of the Government in almost 30 years. Reformists were disappointed that most of the key positions were unchanged, and that all the senior ministers belonging to the ruling Al Sa'ud family remained in post.

Following recent reports that the Saudi Government intended to follow the example of Bahrain and hold elections to the Majlis al-Shoura in 2005, in October 2003, at a human rights conference in Riyadh, the Government disclosed plans to create municipal councils and hold local elections by October 2004. The decision by the authorities to introduce a degree of democracy to the kingdom came amid huge pressure both from inside and outside the country to implement social, economic, political and constitutional reforms. However, Saudi reformists noted that one-half of the councillors would be centrally appointed and that there had been no suggestion in the official announcement that suffrage would be extended to women. The human rights conference was Saudi Arabia's first such meeting, although Western human rights bodies were not invited to attend. Several hundred protesters took part in an illegal demonstration, organized by the British-based Movement for Islamic Reform, outside the conference, demanding widespread reforms including the removal of the House of Sa'ud. Reports indicated that around 150 people were arrested the following day in connection with the demonstration. In November 2003 King Fahd issued a decree widening the legislative power of the Majlis. Under the new regulations, the Majlis was to be allowed to propose new laws and amendments to existing legislation without first asking permission from the King. In addition, the Council of Ministers was to be obliged to return laws to the Majlis for amendment should there be disagreement on an issue. (Under the previous system, whereby the Majlis was a purely advisory body, the matter would be resolved by the King.) In April 2005 a royal decree increased the membership of the Majlis to 150; the expansion prompted renewed demands for the introduction of a partially elected membership. In May the Government announced the establishment of a human rights supervision body, headed by Turki ibn Khalid al-Sudairi, who would be given the equivalent rank to that of a government minister.

The first stage of the elections for 178 municipal authorities in all 13 of the kingdom's provinces took place on 10 February 2005 in Riyadh, having been postponed from September 2004; however, suffrage was not extended to women. In excess of 1,800 candidates stood for the 592 contested seats in the 178 councils; reportedly only about one-quarter of eligible voters in the capital had registered for the elections. The second phase of the elections took place in the Eastern, Aseer, Jazan, Najran and al-Baha provinces on 3 March 2005. According to the local chamber of commerce, only around 12% of the local male population in the Eastern province had registered to vote. The final phase, in the northern border provinces, was held on 21 April. Nationally, Islamist candidates secured a comfortable majority of the council seats. Later in the year women were allowed to campaign openly for elected positions on the 18-member board of the Jeddah Chamber of Commerce and Industry; two women secured seats on the board. In December a female candidate secured an elected position on the 10-member board of the Saudi Engineers' Council.

SAUDI ARABIA

Accession of King Abdullah

On 1 August 2005 it was announced that King Fahd had died. He was succeeded by his half-brother, Crown Prince Abdullah, also aged 84, who had been the de facto ruler of the kingdom since King Fahd suffered a stroke in 1995. The Second Deputy Prime Minister, Minister of Defence and Civil Aviation and Inspector General, Prince Sultan ibn Abd al-Aziz, a full brother of King Fahd and also in his eighties, was named as the new Crown Prince. The Council of Ministers remained essentially unchanged; in accordance with the Constitution, King Abdullah assumed the role of Prime Minister and the Crown Prince was appointed Deputy Prime Minister. No replacement was named for the position of Second Deputy Prime Minister, which increased speculation surrounding the succession to the throne after Crown Prince Sultan. In October 2005 a National Security Council, chaired by King Abdullah, was established, with the power to: declare states of emergency and war; control diplomatic relations; and combat public corruption and mismanagement.

The Ministry of the Interior announced in May 2006 that the authority of the national religious police force (the *mutawwa'in*)—under the control of the Commission for the Promotion of Virtue and the Prevention of Vice—was to be reduced: those arrested on suspicion of moral offences were henceforth to be tried by a public prosecutor. On 20 October a constitutional amendment—first proposed by King Abdullah while he was still Crown Prince—was adopted that removed the monarch's power to choose his successor. Following the forthcoming accession to the throne of Crown Prince Sultan, subsequent heirs were to be elected by the Bay'ah Council (comprising senior members of the royal family). In May 2007 the Crown Prince stated that in the future it was intended that one-third of Saudi government posts would be allocated to women. Following Saudi Arabia's accession to the World Trade Organization (WTO, see p. 430) in December 2005, in October 2007 King Abdullah issued a royal decree allowing for the creation of a supreme court in Riyadh and special tribunals intended to settle commercial and labour grievances, as well as the introduction of appeal courts in each of the country's 13 regions, which were to be granted the legal authority to overrule the judgments of lower courts. The new Judiciary Law also included provision for the modernization of the judicial system.

In February 2007 nine political activists, who were believed to be preparing to launch a reformist political party, were arrested and subsequently held without trial. One of three reformists pardoned in October 2005, Abdullah al-Hamed, received a six-month prison sentence in November 2007, having been convicted of encouraging women to demonstrate against the arrest of their relatives in 2004, as part of a large security operation by the authorities against alleged Islamist militants in the kingdom. In May 2008 Matruk al-Faleh, another of the pardoned reformists, was arrested on unknown charges, while acting as legal representative for al-Hamed. After almost eight months in custody without being charged, al-Faleh was released in January 2009. An author of a popular pro-reform website, Fouad al-Farhan, who had written about the issue of political prisoners, was released without charge in April 2008 after five months' imprisonment. These cases provoked persistent protests from domestic and foreign human rights activists during 2008. Meanwhile, in April of that year a report by the US-based Human Rights Watch urged the Saudi authorities to reform their policies of sex segregation and male guardianship over women, noting that Saudi women required the consent of a male guardian in order to work, travel, receive health care or avail of public services. In its annual report for 2010 the organization noted that the Saudi authorities had not adhered to a pledge made to the UN Human Rights Council in 2009 regarding reform of the system of male guardianship.

King Abdullah's patronage of several inter-faith and inter-cultural forums in 2008 was regarded by some observers as evidence of his commitment to gradual social and political reform. In June the King inaugurated the International Islamic Conference for Dialogue in Mecca. The conference, organized by the Muslim World League and attended by some 600 senior Muslim clerics and world leaders, was established to foster co-operation and understanding between Muslims world-wide, including between Sunnis and Shi'as. In a conciliatory gesture, King Abdullah (a Sunni Muslim) entered the opening ceremony hand-in-hand with the former Iranian President, Ali Akbar Hashemi Rafsanjani (a Shi'a Muslim). Then, in July, the King hosted a three-day inter-faith conference in Madrid, Spain, attended by almost 300 religious, political and cultural leaders from 50 countries, including Jews, Muslims, Christians, Hindus and Buddhists. King Abdullah also sponsored a UN 'Culture of Peace' conference in November, in New York, USA, which was attended by numerous world leaders. The stated aim of the conference was to promote understanding and communication between different cultures and religions, and thereby facilitate the resolution of political conflicts. In one of the meeting's more significant speeches, Israeli President Shimon Peres addressed King Abdullah directly and praised his contribution to the Middle East peace process.

In September 2008 Human Rights Watch published a report criticizing the 'systematic discrimination' experienced by Saudi Arabia's significant Shi'a minority, particularly in the areas of government employment, the judicial system, education and religious freedom. Evidence of sectarian tensions within the kingdom surfaced in February 2009, when violence broke out between Shi'a pilgrims from the Eastern Province and members of the *mutawwa'in* near the tomb of the Prophet Muhammad in Medina. Sporadic clashes occurred over several days, leading to numerous injuries and the arrest of several pilgrims. While each side accused the other of provoking the violence, two rallies protesting against the treatment of the pilgrims were held near Qatif in the Eastern Province. In March, after receiving a delegation of Shi'a leaders, King Abdullah announced the release from custody of 38 Shi'a detainees.

Social and political reform under King Abdullah

King Abdullah implemented an extensive government reorganization in February 2009—his first since acceding to the throne in 2005—effecting wide-ranging changes at senior level throughout the kingdom's administrative, legal and education systems. Dr Abdullah ibn Muhammad ibn Ibrahim al-Sheikh, hitherto Minister of Justice, was appointed Chairman of the Majlis al-Shoura, while Dr Muhammad ibn Abd al-Karim ibn Abd al-Aziz al-Eissa was accorded the justice portfolio. Prince Faisal ibn Abdullah ibn Muhammad Al Sa'ud became Minister of Education; Dr Hamad ibn Abdullah al-Mane was succeeded as Minister of Health by renowned surgeon Dr Abdullah ibn Abd al-Aziz al-Rabea; and Dr Abd al-Aziz ibn Mohi el-Din Khoja, hitherto ambassador to Lebanon, assumed responsibility for the culture and information portfolio. In a move that gained widespread international media coverage, Nora bint Abdullah al-Fayez was appointed Deputy Minister for Girls' Education, the first ever ministerial-rank appointment for a woman in the kingdom. The outgoing Chairman of the Majlis, Dr Salih ibn Humayd, was installed as the new Chairman of the Supreme Council of Justice, the most senior post in the judiciary, replacing Sheikh Salih bin Muhammad al-Luhaidan, who had held the post since the mid-1980s. Sheikh al-Luhaidan, a staunchly conservative religious cleric who was extremely influential in Saudi society, had provoked domestic and international dismay when he issued a *fatwa* (edict) in September 2008 that described as lawful the killing of the owners of satellite television channels that broadcast 'depraved' programmes, such as soap operas and game shows, during Ramadan; channels targeted by his disapproval included those owned by members of the Saudi royal family. In another notable change to the conservative establishment, Sheikh Ibrahim al-Ghaith, President of the Commission for the Promotion of Virtue and the Prevention of Vice, was replaced by a more moderate scholar, Sheikh Abd al-Aziz al-Humayun. Several clerics were appointed to a restructured Council of Senior Ulama, which, for the first time, included representatives of all four schools of Sunni religious thought; however, Shi'ite clerics were still excluded. Among other appointments, most of which were expected to facilitate the King's programme of gradual reform and modernization, were: a new Governor at the Saudi Arabian Monetary Agency; a new Commander of Land Forces; and several new advisers at the Royal Court.

In March 2009 the King appointed his half-brother Prince Nayef ibn Abd al-Aziz Al Sa'ud, Minister of the Interior since 1975, as Second Deputy Prime Minister—a post which had been vacant since King Abdullah's accession in 2005. Observers suggested that the appointment had been precipitated by concerns about the ailing health of Crown Prince Sultan, now First Deputy Prime Minister, Minister of Defence and Civil Aviation and Inspector General, who was reported to have left Saudi Arabia in November 2008 to receive medical treatment in the USA. Following a period of recuperation in Morocco, the Crown Prince returned to the kingdom in December 2009.

Evidence of the gradual reform of the conservative religious establishment emerged in April 2009, with reports that several members of the *mutawwa'in* had been investigated, and

SAUDI ARABIA

subsequently indicted, for an alleged assault on a young woman in Tabuk. Such forceful intervention by civil authorities into the activities of the religious police was considered unprecedented; observers also noted the freedom with which the case had been reported in national newspapers. In late April 2010 the dismissal was announced of Sheikh Ahmad Qassim al-Ghamdi, a senior cleric of the Commission for the Promotion of Virtue and the Prevention of Vice in Mecca, who had advocated removing the prohibition on men and women mixing in public and in private prayer. Within hours, the official Saudi Press Agency released a statement cancelling the announcement of his dismissal and instructing the Saudi media to disregard the information. In the same month, as part of the ongoing modernization of the country's judicial system (initiated in 2007), the Council of Senior Ulama endorsed a further reform initiated by King Abdullah, which involved the codification of the *Shari'a*; however, the reform of the legal system was proceeding slowly, partly owing to the lack of support from Saudi Arabia's religious conservatives. Moreover, in mid-August 2010, as a growing number of clerics and religious scholars were issuing their own *fatwas*, the King decreed that henceforth only members of the Council would be allowed to declare *fatwas*. Sheikh al-Ghamdi caused further controversy at the end of November, when he stated at a conference on women's participation in Saudi Arabia's development that there was no reason under *Shari'a* law for the country to maintain its ban on women driving and that they should not be obliged to wear the *niqab* (veil).

Meanwhile, in mid-August 2010 the Minister of Labour, Dr Ghazi al-Gosaibi, died; he was replaced by Eng. Adel bin Muhammad Abd al-Kader Fakieh. In mid-November King Abdullah appointed one of his sons, Prince Mitab ibn Abdullah Al Sa'ud, as Minister of State and Commander of the National Guard (the élite military force charged with protecting the royal family), after standing down from the post he had held since 1962. King Abdullah also requested that the First Deputy Prime Minister assume responsibility for supervising the annual *Hajj*, traditionally a role for the Saudi monarch. There was considerable speculation that the decision of the King to relinquish some of his duties to other family members indicated a deterioration in his health.

Recent developments: response to domestic protests and unrest in the Middle East and North Africa

As political and social unrest spread across large parts of the Middle East and North Africa in the early months of 2011, a number of illegal street protests were held in Saudi Arabia. However, these were relatively small demonstrations initially held mainly in the Shi'a Eastern Province, which lies adjacent to Bahrain, by protesters demanding the release of political prisoners who they claimed were being held without trial. In response, the authorities warned that they would not tolerate any actions that posed a threat to Saudi Arabia's security and stability. Nevertheless, in late February King Abdullah—returning to the kingdom after a three-month absence to receive medical treatment in the USA and then to convalesce in Morocco—promised to increase social welfare payments by US $37,000m. and to raise the salaries of public sector workers by 15%. In the second week of February nine pro-reform campaigners sought the permission of the monarch to register a political party, the Islamic Umma Party, despite political organizations being illegal in Saudi Arabia. In early March a small number of demonstrators in Riyadh and other cities defied a government ban on holding public protests to take part in rallies demanding political reforms; this led the Government to warn that the security forces had been granted permission to take 'all measures needed' to maintain law and order. On 9–10 March in Qatif, hundreds of Shi'a demanded the release of nine prisoners who had been held without charge for at least 14 years on suspicion of involvement in the 1996 al-Khobar bombing (see Militant Islamism). Security forces were reported to have fired rubber bullets to disperse the protesters, and some attending the rallies described having witnessed beatings. Meanwhile, a group of young Saudis used a social networking website to urge people to join a 'day of rage' on 11 March 2011. One reason for the planned rally was said to be the arrest by the authorities in February of a Shi'a cleric, Sheikh Tawfiq al-Amer, who had advocated the transformation of Saudi Arabia into a constitutional monarchy; al-Amer was released in the week before 11 March in an apparent attempt to appease the demonstrators. In the event, the number of people who attended protests on the 'day of rage' was relatively small, apparently owing to the significant presence of Saudi security forces. Nevertheless, protests did continue in the east of the country: in mid-March police detained more than 100 Shi'a demonstrators, many of whom were protesting against Saudi Arabia's recent military intervention in Bahrain (see Regional relations). Meanwhile, after the Tunisian revolution of January 2011 (see the chapter on Tunisia), ousted President Zine al-Abidine Ben Ali fled the country and was given refuge in Saudi Arabia.

King Abdullah gave a rare speech on Saudi television on 18 March 2011, in which he again warned those protesters who threatened national security. However, a number of royal decrees were subsequently announced which included pledges to: raise the minimum wage for public sector employees; improve benefits for students and the unemployment; expand the provision of affordable housing; and establish an anti-corruption commission which would report directly to the Saudi monarch. Muhammad bin Abdullah al-Sharif was appointed as President of the National Commission to Combat Corruption, with the rank of government minister. In addition to King Abdullah's promised welfare payments, which amounted to an estimated US $91,000m., he also declared that the *mutawwa'in* was to be expanded, and that 60,000 new security posts were to be created within the Ministry of the Interior. Towards the end of March a new Ministry of Housing was created; Shuwaish al-Duwaihi was to assume responsibility for the portfolio. However, despite these changes, pro-reform campaigners were angered that the King made no announcement regarding reform of Saudi Arabia's political system.

Nevertheless, a political concession was made in late March 2011, when officials from the Ministry of Municipal and Rural Affairs declared that voter registration for municipal elections postponed from October 2009—in order to consider whether to extend participation to Saudi women—would commence on 23 April; the actual elections were to take place on 22 September. However, it was reported in mid-April 2011 that the National Society for Human Rights, the organization charged with monitoring the forthcoming elections, had decided to withdraw its participation from the polls in protest at the failure of the Government to include female voters in the process.

Militant Islamism

From the mid-1990s numerous bombings and other terrorist attacks, often targeted against foreign civilians, took place in Saudi Arabia. In November 1995 a car bomb exploded outside the offices of the National Guard in Riyadh, which was being used by US civilian contractors to train Saudi personnel. Seven foreign nationals (including five US citizens) were killed in the explosion, responsibility for which was claimed by several organizations, including the Islamic Movement for Change, which earlier in the year had warned that it would initiate attacks if non-Muslim Western forces did not withdraw from the Gulf region. In May 1996 four Saudi nationals were executed, having been convicted of involvement in the attack.

In June 1996 19 US military personnel were killed, and as many as 400 others (mostly Saudi, Bangladeshi and US citizens) were injured, when an explosive device attached to a petroleum tanker was detonated outside a military housing complex in al-Khobar, near Dhahran. By late 1996 there was speculation that the investigating authorities were holding Saudi Shi'a groups with possible links to Iran responsible for the atrocity, rather than the Sunni extremist factions that were widely blamed for the November 1995 bombing. The Iranian Government, however, repeatedly denied any involvement in the incident. In March 1997 the Canadian intelligence service announced the detention of Hani Abd al-Rahim al-Sayegh, a Saudi Shi'a Muslim implicated in the al-Khobar attack, who was alleged to have links with the militant Saudi Hezbollah. Al-Sayegh was extradited from Canada to stand trial in the USA, but in September US officials announced that there was insufficient evidence to secure a conviction. In May 1998 Saudi Arabia's Minister of the Interior stated that there was no indication of a foreign role in the bombing, despite continuing US assertions of Iranian involvement. In October 1999 al-Sayegh was extradited from the USA to Saudi Arabia, shortly after the Saudi Minister of the Interior stated that the country's security services possessed information regarding his involvement in the attack. Several Saudi nationals were arrested in January 2001 in connection with the bombing. In June US investigators indicted 14 individuals on charges relating to the explosion, although three of them remained at large in June 2002 when the Saudi authorities announced that sentences had been imposed on a number of the detainees. Meanwhile, al-Sayegh remained in custody in Saudi Arabia.

SAUDI ARABIA

Introductory Survey

Following the murders of a British defence contractor in February 2003 and of two North Americans in March, fears of intensified attacks against Westerners proved well-founded when a series of co-ordinated suicide attacks on an expatriate housing compound in Riyadh killed 34 people on 12 May. The Minister of Foreign Affairs indicated that 19 people, including 17 Saudis, were believed to have been responsible for the attacks. The bombings, widely held to be the work of the al-Qa'ida network, provoked further US criticism of Saudi security measures, and led to the withdrawal of most of the US diplomats stationed in the kingdom. It emerged after the attacks that the Saudi authorities had made an unsuccessful attempt to apprehend the perpetrators in the week prior to 12 May. The Saudi leadership responded to the bombings by acknowledging more openly that the threat presented by al-Qa'ida was indeed serious, and pledged to take effective action against members and sympathizers of the organization. Between 12 May and late October at least 600 suspected militant Islamists were arrested, 70–90 of whom were charged, and more than 2,000 people were interrogated. In addition, in June some 1,000 Muslim clergy were suspended and ordered to undergo retraining aimed at eliminating Islamist militancy from the profession. However, despite these measures, on 8 November al-Qa'ida apparently struck again when 17 people were killed and more than 120 others injured in a suicide attack on a housing complex, mostly populated by Arab expatriates, in Riyadh. In December the Government stated that, according to DNA evidence, two Saudi nationals had carried out the latest suicide bombing.

On 21 April 2004 a car bomb exploded close to one of the headquarters of Riyadh's security services, killing five people and wounding up to 150. A militant Islamist group called the al-Haramain Brigades (alleged to have links to al-Qa'ida) claimed responsibility for the attack, which was regarded as the first direct assault on the Saudi regime. On 1 May gunmen in the Red Sea port of Yanbu killed at least one Saudi and five Western petroleum industry workers. On 29 May an attack by militants against a compound housing oil workers at al-Khobar resulted in the deaths of three Saudis and 19 expatriate workers. The compound was eventually surrounded by Saudi police, which resulted in a 25-hour siege. Despite an attempt by security forces to storm the compound, three of the attackers managed to escape. It was alleged that the militants had agreed a deal with police officers sympathetic to al-Qa'ida, an accusation that was vehemently denied by the Saudi authorities. In early June two of those responsible for the atrocity were reported to have been killed by Saudi forces near Mecca. One of the men was believed to be Abd al-Rahman Muhammad Yazji, one of the kingdom's most wanted militants. In late June, during a public address broadcast on Saudi television, the Crown Prince announced that a dozen named individuals with alleged ties to al-Qa'ida would not face the death penalty should they surrender to the security forces within one month. The Saudi authorities were particularly keen to obtain the surrender of Saleh Muhammad al-Oufi, regarded as the overall leader of al-Qa'ida in the kingdom following the death of Abd al-Aziz al-Muqrin in a police raid in that month. It was, however, reported in November that al-Qa'ida had appointed Saud bin Hamoud al-Otaibi as the new leader of its Saudi network; some commentators presumed that this confirmed suspicions that al-Oufi had been killed by security forces in July. In February 2005 the Government launched a national awareness campaign to mobilize people against militant activity. In December seven expatriates and five Saudis died when gunmen attacked the US consulate in Jeddah.

Significant militant activity continued into 2006, leading the Saudi security forces to kill or detain a large number of suspected al-Qa'ida operatives. In August it was announced that more than 700 alleged al-Qa'ida sympathizers had been released after undergoing a 'correction' programme intended to uproot their belief in Islamist fundamentalism. In October the Deputy Minister of the Interior announced that trials of suspected Islamist militants in Islamic courts had commenced and that many defendants had already been sentenced and 'finished with'; it was unclear as to whether this meant that some had been executed. In February 2007 three French nationals were shot dead near the town of Tabuk, reportedly while travelling on a pilgrimage to Mecca; a fourth died later in hospital from injuries sustained in the ambush. In the same month Saudi police detained several people on suspicion of fund-raising on behalf of foreign terrorist organizations, and in April a further 172 people were arrested for allegedly plotting attacks against public figures, oil refineries and military targets in Saudi Arabia and other neighbouring countries. It was revealed in August that the Government had begun to establish an Industrial Security Force of some 35,000 personnel specifically charged with providing security at the country's petroleum facilities; by mid-November an estimated 9,000 members had been deployed, and a further 8,000 were expected to be deployed each year. In late November the Ministry of the Interior declared that 208 suspected al-Qa'ida-affiliated militants (including a number of other Arab nationals) had been detained in recent months, again for allegedly planning attacks against various Saudi targets. A reported 28 people, most of whom were Saudi citizens, were arrested in late December, on suspicion of preparing terrorist actions in the holy cities of Mecca and Medina during the *Hajj*. The detainees were alleged members of an organization taking its instructions from Ayman al-Zawahiri, believed to be the deputy leader of al-Qa'ida; by March 2008 Saudi security forces had reportedly dismantled the unit. The Ministry of the Interior announced in June that 701 suspected militants had been arrested thus far that year (although 181 had later been released owing to a lack of evidence), and in October that 991 detainees had been charged with involvement in more than 30 terrorist attacks in the kingdom over the preceding five years, in which 164 had been killed and more than 1,000 injured. During 2007–08 the frequency of violent attacks was clearly declining, and the Government's strategy of combining stronger security measures with the retraining of clerics and the re-education of convicted militants appeared to be having some success.

However, despite the apparent effectiveness of domestic counter-terrorism measures, the activities of Saudi militants outside the kingdom remained a source of considerable concern. In January 2009 two Saudi nationals appeared in a video posted on a jihadist website that announced the merger of al-Qa'ida's Saudi Arabian and Yemeni operations, forming an entity known as al-Qa'ida in the Arabian Peninsula (AQAP). Both men were former detainees at the US detention camp at Guantánamo Bay, Cuba, who had been released in 2007 and, despite undergoing the Saudi rehabilitation programme, had absconded to Yemen and allegedly resumed their jihadist activities. Saeed al-Shihri, who was suspected of involvement in the bombing of the US embassy in the Yemeni capital, San'a, in September 2008 (see the chapter on Yemen), was described in the video as the deputy leader of al-Qa'ida in Yemen; Muhammad al-Oufi was described as a field commander. In February 2009 the Saudi authorities released a list of 85 wanted alleged militants living abroad; 83 were Saudi nationals, two were Yemeni, and all were suspected of illegal activities with various al-Qa'ida-affiliated groups abroad and of plotting attacks against targets within Saudi Arabia. The list, which was subsequently distributed by the International Criminal Police Organization (INTERPOL), included several former Guantánamo detainees. Later that month al-Oufi reportedly surrendered to the security forces in Yemen and was handed over to the Saudi authorities.

In July 2009, following the conclusion of the first mass trial of suspected Islamist militants indicted on terrorism charges in October 2008, 330 suspects were convicted of membership of 'the deviant group', the customary Saudi term for al-Qa'ida; one suspect was sentenced to death, while the remaining 329 received sentences that ranged from house arrest to life imprisonment. In mid-August 2009 the Ministry of the Interior announced the arrest of a network of 44 suspected militants and the seizure of several caches of armaments, following a series of operations in Riyadh and Qassim. None of those arrested had been included on the list of 85 wanted militants issued in February. Later that month Prince Muhammad ibn Nayef, the Deputy Minister of the Interior and the kingdom's chief counter-terrorism official, narrowly survived a suicide bomb attack at his home in Jeddah. Responsibility for the bombing, which was the first direct attack on a member of the royal family in decades, was subsequently claimed by AQAP. In October militants launched a gun attack on security officers at a checkpoint in the south-western Jazan province; two militants and a security officer were killed during the clash.

In late March 2010 security officials arrested 113 suspected Islamist militants, including 55 foreign nationals from countries including Yemen, Somalia and Eritrea, who, as members of three separate cells, had allegedly been planning attacks against oil facilities in the Eastern Province. Evidence of direct links between the cells and AQAP militants in Yemen was reported by the authorities. The Government declared towards the end of November that a further 149 alleged militants—124 Saudis and 25 foreign nationals, most of whom were members of al-Qa'ida—

SAUDI ARABIA

had been detained since March. The Ministry of the Interior claimed that by detaining the suspected militants, one of whom was reported to be female, 19 terrorist cells had been prevented from carrying out attacks against senior officials and journalists in Saudi Arabia.

Foreign Affairs

Relations with the USA

Saudi Arabia severed diplomatic relations with the Taliban regime in Afghanistan in September 2001, in response to the suicide attacks on New York and Washington, DC. Saudi Arabia was one of only three countries (along with Pakistan and the United Arab Emirates—UAE) to have recognized the Taliban administration in Afghanistan. Although the USA's principal suspect in the attacks, Osama bin Laden (who was at that time based in Afghanistan), was born to a wealthy Saudi Arabian family, the Saudi authorities emphasized that bin Laden had been exiled since 1991 and his nationality revoked because of his subversive activities against the royal family. It was later revealed that 15 of the 19 hijackers were also of Saudi descent (although many of the identities were forged or stolen). Visiting Washington, DC, shortly after the attacks, Saudi Arabia's Minister of Foreign Affairs stated that he had conveyed to the US Secretary of State, Colin Powell, the support of the Saudi people for efforts to eliminate terrorism. Saudi Arabia also agreed to investigate alleged Saudi funding of bin Laden's al-Qa'ida network, said to be raised through certain charitable organizations and individual donations. However, the Saudi regime, under pressure from internal Islamist groups implacably opposed to the US military presence on Saudi territory and to any military action against another Islamic state, subsequently refused permission for the use of its airbases for military action against Afghanistan (although an air 'command and control' base in the kingdom was made available to support the military operation).

Following the launch of military attacks against Afghanistan by the US-led 'coalition against terror' in October 2001, the USA briefly closed its embassy in Saudi Arabia because of fear of reprisals. Later that month Crown Prince Abdullah accused the US media of conspiring to damage Saudi Arabia's reputation, following the publication of articles highly critical of Saudi Arabia's perceived lack of co-operation after the September attacks. Although official statements by the US Administration continued to praise the Saudi regime, rumours of a deterioration in their relationship persisted. In January 2002 the Saudi authorities asked for the return of all Saudi citizens (reported to number more than 100 detainees), captured in Afghanistan while apparently fighting for the Taliban, who were imprisoned at Guantánamo Bay. This request was denied by the US authorities, but in June a delegation of Saudi government officials was reported to have been allowed access to the Saudi prisoners.

Relations between Saudi Arabia and the USA were placed under renewed strain in August 2002, after a group representing 900 relatives of victims of the September 2001 attacks filed a civil suit in Washington, DC, USA, against senior Saudi ministers and institutions (and the Government of Sudan) seeking compensation amounting to US $1,000,000m. for their alleged funding of al-Qa'ida activities. Saudi investors reacted angrily to the suit, threatening to withdraw from the USA some $750,000m. in Saudi investments. In late 2002 Saudi Arabia was criticized by the USA for ignoring the funding of alleged terrorist organizations by Saudi nationals, and in November US media reports claimed that a charitable donation from the Saudi royal family had assisted two hijackers responsible for the suicide attacks on the USA. The allegations were strenuously denied by the Saudi authorities, and the US Administration was swift to defend the role Saudi Arabia had played in President George W. Bush's 'war on terror'.

Despite the Saudi–US tensions, in September 2002, following intense pressure from the USA and the United Kingdom, the Saudi Minister of Foreign Affairs indicated that Saudi Arabia might be prepared to approve the use of military bases in Saudi Arabia for a future US-led attack on the regime of Saddam Hussain in Iraq. However, he emphasized that Saudi cooperation would only be forthcoming if the Iraqi authorities continued to reject UN resolutions demanding the unconditional return of weapons inspectors to Iraq and if such a military undertaking was to be conducted under UN auspices. It was established in December that the highly equipped Prince Sultan airbase would be made available to the US military, and that, although combat aircraft would not be allowed to fly offensive missions from the base with the primary aim of bombing Iraqi targets, aircraft launched from Saudi soil would be permitted to open fire or release bombs in self-defence. In January 2003 Saudi Arabia attempted to secure support for a plan to persuade Saddam Hussain to relinquish power and go into exile in order to avert a US-led war to oust his regime. In the following month, however, as conflict appeared increasingly inevitable, the Saudi authorities deployed warships, troops and military helicopters to Kuwait, in order to strengthen the emirate's defences. In late April, after most of the USA's principal military objectives in Iraq had been achieved, it was announced that all but 400 of the 5,000 US military personnel in the country were to be withdrawn from Saudi Arabia by the end of August. Those troops that remained were to assist in training the Saudi armed forces. The Saudi authorities attempted to improve relations with the USA during 2004; in July, during a visit by Powell to Jeddah, Crown Prince Abdullah raised the possibility of the kingdom taking a leading role in the formation of a Muslim security force for Iraq. Meanwhile, Saudi Arabia and Iraq announced that their embassies in Baghdad and Riyadh, respectively, would be reopened for the first time since 1990.

In February 2006, following the victory of the Islamic Resistance Movement (Hamas) in the Palestinian legislative elections of the previous month, the Saudi Government incurred US displeasure when it refused to support a US-led plan to deny regional aid to the new Hamas-led administration in the West Bank and Gaza Strip. During a tour of the Middle East in January 2008, US President Bush visited Riyadh, where he reiterated his intention to pursue a controversial arms agreement with the Saudi Government, at an estimated cost of US $20,000m.; the deal formed part of a broader package of US military aid to its allies in the Gulf region aimed at countering any increased Iranian military strength. Bush's visit to Riyadh was, however, marred by Saudi demands that the US Administration hand over to the kingdom 13 of its citizens currently being held at Guantánamo Bay.

Saudi Arabia's status as a key regional ally of the USA was emphasized in June 2009, when US President Barack Obama, who had been inaugurated in January, began his first visit to the Middle East in Riyadh, where he held talks on regional affairs with King Abdullah. During a visit to the USA in June 2010, the King emphasized to President Obama that Saudi Arabia refused to normalize relations with Israel in the absence of 'genuine progress' in the Middle East peace process. It was confirmed in late October that the US Congress was examining the terms of a massive weapons agreement between the US Government and its Saudi counterpart, reportedly involving the purchase by Saudi Arabia of some US $60,000m.-worth of advanced weaponry (including fighter planes and helicopters) from the USA over a period of 15–20 years. In early December the content of a series of leaked confidential US diplomatic cables published by the WikiLeaks organization apparently indicated that the US Administration remained extremely concerned about the private funding of international Sunni terrorist organizations, including al-Qa'ida, by certain Saudi individuals.

Regional relations

In December 1994 Yemen accused Saudi Arabia of erecting monitoring posts and constructing roads on Yemeni territory. In January 1995 the two countries failed to renew the 1934 Ta'if agreement (renewable every 20 years), delineating their de facto frontier. Following military clashes between Saudi and Yemeni forces, and intense mediation by Syria, the two sides undertook to halt all military activity in the disputed border area. In February the Saudi and Yemeni Governments signed a memorandum of understanding that reaffirmed their commitment to the legitimacy of the Ta'if agreement and provided for the establishment of six joint committees to delineate the land and sea borders and to develop economic and commercial ties. A border security agreement was signed in July 1996. In May 1998, however, Saudi Arabia invaded the disputed island of Huraym in the Red Sea and was reported to have sent a memorandum to the UN stating that it did not recognize the 1992 border agreement between Yemen and Oman, claiming that parts of the area involved were Saudi Arabian territory. The Saudi objection to the accord was widely believed to be related to its attempts to gain land access to the Arabian Sea, via a corridor between Yemen and Oman, which it had thus far been denied in its negotiations with Yemen.

Yemen submitted a memorandum to the Arab League in July 1998, refuting the Saudi claim to the land and stating that the Saudi protests contravened the Ta'if agreement signed by that country. Further clashes were reported close to the land and sea

SAUDI ARABIA

border between Yemen and Saudi Arabia in June, and in July three Yemeni troops were killed during fighting with a Saudi border patrol on the disputed island of Duwaima in the Red Sea; Saudi Arabia claimed its actions there were in self-defence and that, under the Ta'if agreement, three-quarters of the island was Saudi territory. In January 2000 both countries denied further reports of armed confrontations in the border area, and a meeting of a joint military committee began in San'a in February. In June, during a visit to Saudi Arabia by Yemeni President Ali Abdullah Saleh, a final agreement delineating land and sea borders was signed. As part of the accord, which incorporated the 1934 Ta'if agreement and much of the 1995 memorandum of understanding, both sides agreed to promote economic, commercial and cultural relations, and each undertook not to permit on its territory activities against the other by opposition groups. The agreement did not demarcate sections of the eastern border, however, and in August 2000 three Saudi border guards and one Yemeni soldier were reportedly killed in border clashes. Nevertheless, the first meeting of the Saudi-Yemeni Co-ordination Council for more than a decade took place in December. It was also reported that the withdrawal from the border region of troops of both countries, in accordance with the border agreement, was almost complete. However, relations deteriorated again in early 2004, after the Saudi Government began construction of a 'security fence' along the border that risked violating the border demarcation treaty signed in June 2000. The construction of the barrier reflected a profound lack of trust on the part of the Saudi authorities in Yemen's ability to prevent weapons smugglers from infiltrating Saudi territory. In June 2006 the Saudi and Yemeni ministers responsible for internal affairs signed an agreement on the final demarcation of their shared border.

Following the formation of AQAP in early 2009 (see above), the Saudi Arabian authorities became increasingly concerned about the concentration of militant Islamist activity in ungoverned areas of Yemen. The growing lawlessness in Yemen's northern border region, exacerbated by a violent conflict between government forces and the Shi'ite al-Houthi movement, led to a significant expansion of Saudi military capacity in the region. In early November, following an exchange of gunfire between al-Houthi militants and Saudi border guards, Saudi Arabia launched a campaign of air-strikes and ground offensives against rebel targets in the Saudi–Yemeni border region (for more detailed information on the conflict with the al-Houthi movement, see the chapter on Yemen). The Saudi authorities insisted that their operations were limited to clearing al-Houthi 'infiltrators' from its territory. However, the Saudi Deputy Minister of Defence revealed that the kingdom's forces aimed to drive the rebels 'tens of kilometres inside their border', appearing to confirm reports of Saudi air-strikes inside Yemeni territory. Al-Houthi sources claimed that 54 civilians had been killed in one air-strike. Although Saudi Arabia announced the end of major combat operations in late December, stating that full control of the border region had been regained, sporadic fighting between Saudi forces and al-Houthi militants continued. In late January 2010 the al-Houthi rebels, in preparation for cease-fire negotiations with the Yemeni Government, offered a truce to the Saudi authorities, stating that all fighters had been withdrawn from the kingdom's territory. At that time, 133 Saudi troops had been killed in the recent military campaign. Meanwhile, in December 2009 King Abdullah announced plans for the construction of 10,000 new homes to accommodate Saudi citizens displaced by the conflict. Following a meeting of the Saudi-Yemeni Co-ordination Council in Riyadh in March 2010, a number of agreements were signed concerning Saudi-funded energy, health, education and humanitarian projects in Yemen. After a series of anti-Government demonstrations had been held in Yemen since February 2011 (see the chapter on Yemen), with protesters demanding the removal from office of President Saleh and government troops using considerable force against them, Saudi Arabia played a key role in efforts to formulate a GCC plan designed to end the increasingly violent situation in that country. At the start of May, by which time at least 135 people were reported to have been killed, it appeared that Saleh would not sign a proposed deal between the ruling party and opposition whereby the Yemeni leader would be given 30 days' immunity from prosecution if he agreed to step down, hand over power to his deputy and accept the staging of a presidential election two months later.

In September 1992 Qatar accused a Saudi force of attacking a Qatari border post, killing two border guards and capturing a third. As a result, Qatar suspended a 1965 border agreement with Saudi Arabia, which had never been fully ratified. In December 1992, following mediation by President Hosni Mubarak of Egypt, the Amir of Qatar, Sheikh Khalifa Al Thani, signed an agreement in Medina with King Fahd to establish a committee to demarcate the disputed border. In June 1999 officials of the two countries met in Riyadh to sign maps defining their joint border, and an apparently final land and maritime demarcation agreement was signed in Doha in March 2001. The border agreement provided for a joint Saudi-Qatari committee, charged with ensuring full implementation of the 1965 accord. In October 2002 the Saudi ambassador to Qatar was recalled, apparently following broadcasts by the Qatari television news channel Al-Jazeera that were deemed to be critical of the Saudi regime. Despite the 2001 agreement, the border dispute was revived in July 2007, when Saudi Arabia threatened to block a US $3,500m. gas pipeline between Qatar and the UAE, claiming that sections of the undersea pipeline ran through Saudi territory. In September the Qatari Amir, Sheikh Hamad bin Khalifa Al Thani, during a visit to Jeddah, gave an assurance that Al-Jazeera would not broadcast material that could be regarded as defamatory in respect of Saudi Arabia; in return, Al-Jazeera would be permitted to establish a presence in the kingdom. Saudi Arabia confirmed the return of its diplomatic envoy to Qatar, and King Abdullah agreed to attend the forthcoming GCC summit in Doha (an invitation he had refused in 2002, when Qatar had last hosted a meeting of the organization). Saudi objections to the Qatar–UAE gas pipeline were also resolved. The new Saudi ambassador to Qatar acceded to his position in March 2008, and relations were further bolstered in that month by an official visit to Qatar by Crown Prince Sultan. In July the Qatari and Saudi Governments agreed to resolve the issue of border demarcation and to establish a Joint Co-ordination Council to encourage co-operation in military, industrial, agricultural and energy affairs. A definitive Land and Maritime Border Delimitation Agreement was signed in December, together with various other agreements on bilateral co-operation, at the first meeting of the Saudi-Qatari Joint Co-ordination Council, and was registered with the UN in March 2009. In June the UAE Government lodged an official complaint to the UN concerning the signing of the Saudi-Qatari agreement, claiming that it ran contrary to a border accord it had signed with Qatar in 1969, as well as to a 2004 agreement between the UAE and Qatar concerning the Dolphin gas pipeline.

Officials from Saudi Arabia and Oman signed documents to demarcate their joint border in July 1995. In March 1999 Saudi Arabia held talks with Iran in an effort to mediate in its dispute with the UAE over the Tunb islands. Following a statement by the GCC condemning both Iran's recent military exercises near the islands and its claim to them and emphasizing UAE sovereignty of the islands, the Iranian President cancelled a planned visit to Saudi Arabia (the visit proceeded in May). Saudi Arabia's rapprochement with Iran had resulted in a deterioration in its relations with the UAE, and in March the UAE boycotted a meeting of GCC ministers responsible for petroleum production in protest at Saudi exploration of an oilfield in disputed territory prior to an agreement being reached. In September 2000 the Saudi Government approved an agreement, signed in July, which ended the long-standing dispute with Kuwait regarding their mutual sea border. Final maps delineating that border were signed by officials from both sides in January 2001.

In 2005 relations deteriorated between Saudi Arabia and three of its Gulf neighbours: Bahrain, Oman and the UAE. Bahrain and Oman had signed free trade agreements with the USA in September 2004 and October 2005, respectively, and in April 2006 the UAE was involved in negotiations with a view to signing a similar accord. Saudi Arabia, which argued that the GCC should negotiate a trade deal as a single body, claimed that the agreements contravened the GCC's external tariff treaty. In December relations with the UAE were further strained by a border dispute relating to the Shaybah oilfield in the Rub al-Khali desert region, which dated back to the 1970s and which formed the focal point of discussions between the UAE President, Sheikh Khalifa bin Zayed Al Nahyan, and the Saudi Minister of the Interior, Prince Nayef ibn Abd al-Aziz Al Sa'ud, in June 2006. In mid-March 2011 Saudi Arabia sent 1,000 of its armed forces to Bahrain as part of a GCC 'Peninsula Shield' force (500 UAE police officers were also deployed) to assist that country's military in preventing the escalating pro-democracy protests there from turning into a full-scale rebellion against the ruling Sunni monarchy. Bahrain's Shi'a opposition described the deployment as an 'overt occupation'.

In September 2000 Iraq accused Saudi Arabia and Kuwait of inflicting (through the maintenance of the sanctions regime) suffering on the Iraqi population, and alleged that Saudi Arabia was appropriating Iraqi petroleum transported under the oil-for-food programme. Nevertheless, Saudi Arabia, encouraged by the mediation of the League of Arab States (Arab League, see p. 361), indicated at the beginning of 2002 that it was ready for a cautious rapprochement with Iraq. In October the border crossing from Saudi Arabia to Iraq was reopened, providing a fifth land route for Iraqi trade under the UN oil-for-food arrangement. Following the US-led military campaign to remove Saddam Hussain's regime in Iraq in 2003 (see above), Saudi Arabia announced its intention to reopen its embassy in Baghdad. (Diplomatic relations between Iraq and Saudi Arabia had been severed in 1991, following Iraq's invasion of Kuwait.) In March 2007 King Abdullah publicly emphasized Saudi opposition to foreign intervention in Iraqi domestic affairs, insisting that Iraq's sovereignty and independence must be safeguarded. However, by early 2011 a Saudi embassy had yet to be opened in Baghdad, with the kingdom's authorities citing security concerns as the reason for the continuing delay. Meanwhile, a contract to construct a 900-km 'security fence' along Saudi Arabia's border with Iraq, at a cost of some US $900m., was awarded to a joint Saudi-European consortium in June 2008. The fence, which would incorporate sophisticated surveillance equipment, represented the first phase of a planned 6,500-km barrier along all the kingdom's borders. The contract for the second phase of the project, which would complete the barrier, was awarded to the same consortium in February 2009 and was estimated to be worth $2,200m.

Relations between Saudi Arabia and Iran, which were particularly strained by suspicions of Iranian involvement in the 1996 al-Khobar bombing (see Militant Islamism), improved considerably following the election of Muhammad Khatami to the Iranian presidency in 1997. Co-operation was notably strengthened following the September 2001 attacks on New York and Washington, DC, as Saudi Arabia and Iran sought to counter the emergence of anti-Islamic sentiment in the West. The election of Mahmoud Ahmadinejad to the Iranian presidency in June 2005 proved somewhat damaging to bilateral relations, however, with the Saudi Government becoming increasingly concerned by what it perceived to be Ahmadinejad's destabilizing effect on the region. Nevertheless, in January 2007 the two states were reported to be conducting negotiations to seek an end to the political impasse in Lebanon (q.v.). Furthermore, President Ahmadinejad was unexpectedly granted an audience with King Abdullah in Riyadh in March, which was widely seen as an implicit snub by the Saudi monarch of the US policy of exclusion towards Iran. The two leaders concurred that the greatest danger facing Muslims world-wide was the deliberate exacerbation by unnamed aggressors of divisions between the Sunni and Shi'ite factions. However, despite an exchange of public expressions of goodwill between King Abdullah and Ahmadinejad, the visit did not appear to have resulted in the establishment of any joint initiatives. Ahmadinejad returned to Saudi Arabia in December to participate, at the King's invitation, in the *Hajj* to Mecca, becoming the first Iranian President to do so.

Notwithstanding public displays of harmony, Saudi-Iranian relations remained somewhat adversarial throughout 2008 and early 2009. In May 2008 Saudi Minister of Foreign Affairs Prince Sa'ud al-Faisal, referring to Iran's support for the militant Lebanese organization Hezbollah's recent military clashes with government forces in that country, accused Iran of inciting sectarian conflict and interfering in the affairs of an independent state. In March 2009, at a meeting of Arab foreign ministers, Prince al-Faisal appealed for a unified Arab strategy in dealing with what he described as the 'Iranian challenge'. Meanwhile, President Ahmadinejad, in January 2009, appeared to accuse Saudi Arabia of complicity in the killing of Palestinians in the Israeli military operation in Gaza in late December 2008 and early January 2009 (see below), alleging that the kingdom was silent in the face of Israel's aggression and urging Saudi Arabia to end its trade ties with the Jewish state. Saudi Arabia's decision to assist the Bahraini Government in quelling popular unrest by sending 1,000 troops to Bahrain in mid-March 2011 led to a deterioration in relations with Iran, which had issued a formal complaint to the UN regarding the tough measures being taken by the Bahrain security forces against anti-Government demonstrators. Many in the Saudi establishment viewed the popular uprising in Bahrain, where the population is predominantly Shi'a, as being orchestrated in Iran, despite the fact that Sunni Bahrainis were also venting their frustration at their economic situation and what they perceived as the slow pace of political reform. In March and April Iranian students protested against the deployment of forces outside the Saudi embassy in Tehran and a Saudi consulate building in Mashhad. In mid-April, following a meeting of the GCC in Riyadh, member states urged the UN Security Council to prevent Iran's 'interference, provocation and threats', which they said risked destabilizing the entire Gulf region.

In February 2002 Crown Prince Abdullah put forward a proposal, based on the 1981 'Fahd Plan', to end the escalating conflict between Israel and the Palestinians based on the principle of 'land for peace'. In return for a collective Arab recognition of the State of Israel, the plan insisted on Israel's complete withdrawal from Arab territories occupied since 1967. The Crown Prince also urged the US Administration to exert pressure on Israel to withdraw its forces from the West Bank. The Saudi peace initiative was unanimously endorsed at a summit conference of the Arab League Council held in March 2002 in Beirut, Lebanon, but was rejected by Israel. In March 2007 Riyadh hosted the annual summit meeting of the Arab League Council, at which negotiations were dominated by the Israeli-Palestinian conflict, as well as by the situations in Iraq and Lebanon. The Council reaffirmed its endorsement of the 'land-for-peace' proposal, which had been amassing increasing levels of support, and which Israeli Prime Minister Ehud Olmert had conceded might provide an initial basis for the renewal of formal peace discussions with Arab leaders. A proposed military pact to assist the 22 member states to resolve regional conflicts without the need for external intervention was also discussed. Saudi Arabia participated in the US-sponsored international peace meeting held at Annapolis, Maryland, in November, at which negotiations towards a resolution of the Israeli-Palestinian conflict were officially relaunched.

In response to the military offensive launched by Israel against Hamas targets in the Gaza Strip in late December 2008 (see the chapters on Israel and the Palestinian Autonomous Areas), King Abdullah hosted an emergency GCC summit in Riyadh on 15 January 2009, which focused on seeking an end to the hostilities and on the provision of aid. Meanwhile, Sheikh Hamad of Qatar planned to convene an emergency Arab League summit in the Qatari capital, Doha, to formulate a unified Arab response to the conflict in Gaza, which by mid-January had reportedly resulted in more than 1,400 Palestinians deaths, with some 5,000 wounded. However, the Saudi King did not send a delegation to the Doha meeting, which was held on 16 January, stating his preference for the forthcoming Arab Economic, Social and Development Summit in Kuwait as a forum for pan-Arab discussions. As a result of the absence of Saudi Arabia, Egypt and others, the Doha summit failed to attain the quorum required to grant the meeting official status. The disagreement over Doha highlighted regional divisions on the Israeli-Palestinian conflict, with Saudi Arabia and Egypt committed to the principles of the existing peace process and broadly aligned with the USA, while Iran, Qatar and Syria offered support to Hamas and appealed for the severing of ties with Israel. During the scheduled summit in Kuwait, on 19–20 January, King Abdullah hosted a private meeting with the leaders of Egypt, Kuwait, Qatar and Syria, which was heralded as achieving substantial progress towards greater Arab unity.

Following the transfer of its ambassador in Damascus to Doha in early 2008, Saudi Arabia declined to appoint a new ambassador to Syria, demonstrating its disapproval at Syria's role in the ongoing political crisis in Lebanon. Saudi relations with Syria remained strained throughout 2008, and the two countries' conflicting interests in the region were highlighted by their divergent responses to the Israeli military offensive in Gaza launched in December 2008 (see above). However, there were hopes of a rapprochement after Syria and other Arab states held private talks with King Abdullah during the Arab Economic, Social and Development Summit in Kuwait in January 2009. In early March Saudi Minister of Foreign Affairs Prince Sa'ud al-Faisal held talks with Syrian President Bashar al-Assad in Damascus on Arab reconciliation and other regional issues; both sides described the discussions in positive terms. On 11 March the King hosted a one-day summit on regional affairs, which was attended by Assad (on his first visit to Saudi Arabia for four years), President Mubarak of Egypt and the Kuwaiti Amir, Sheikh Sabah al-Ahmad al-Jaber al-Sabah. Foremost among the objectives of the summit were the promotion of Arab unity and support for Egyptian-brokered reconciliation talks between the rival Palestinian factions, Fatah and Hamas.

The appointment, in July 2009, of a new Saudi ambassador to Syria confirmed the positive trend in bilateral relations. In September President Assad attended the inauguration ceremony of the new King Abdullah University of Science and Technology in Jeddah, after which he held discussions with King Abdullah. In October the Saudi monarch, accompanied by a senior-level ministerial delegation, completed his first official visit to Syria since acceding to the throne in 2005. The leaders held two rounds of talks on bilateral relations and regional issues, and an agreement on taxation was signed by the respective Ministers of Finance. Analysts regarded the summit as highly significant, given the important, and often antagonistic, influence exerted by both powers in the region. At the summit's conclusion King Abdullah and President Assad issued a statement confirming their joint support for: the establishment of a government of national unity in Lebanon; joint Arab measures in support of the Palestinian cause; and the safeguarding of stability and national unity in Yemen. President Assad made a reciprocal visit to Riyadh in mid-January 2010, during which discussions continued on a range of key regional issues. A Lebanese national unity administration had been formed in November 2009. At the end of July 2010 King Abdullah and President Assad held a tripartite summit meeting with the Lebanese President, Michel Suleiman, in Beirut, in an effort to prevent the tensions between Lebanon's rival Sunni and Shi'ite factions from descending into violence. This was the first visit to Lebanon by a Saudi monarch since 1957. The meeting was convened amid reports that the UN Special Tribunal established to investigate the 2005 assassination of former premier Rafiq Hariri was likely to implicate members of the Shi'ite Hezbollah—part of the governing coalition—in the crime. However, in mid-January 2011, with the first tribunal indictments expected to be issued later that month, the Lebanese Government collapsed, following the withdrawal of Hezbollah-allied ministers. The previous day the Saudi and Syrian Governments were reported to have failed in their efforts to secure a compromise agreement for Lebanon.

Other external relations

King Abdullah visited the People's Republic of China in January 2006—the first such visit by a Saudi monarch since the formal establishment of diplomatic relations in 1990—whereupon he signed a bilateral agreement to co-operate in the petroleum and natural gas sectors. With the deterioration in Saudi–US relations, the kingdom was keen to diversify its international trade, and China, as the world's second largest petroleum consumer, was an ideal candidate for partnership. In the same month Abdullah also became the first Saudi monarch to visit India since 1955. In February 2006 a visit to Pakistan further bolstered traditionally strong bilateral relations, with the signing of five agreements aimed at increasing co-operation on the economy, education, investment, science and technology. In April Crown Prince Sultan embarked upon a tour of the Far East, visiting Japan, Singapore and China. This 'look east' policy was adopted principally for economic gain, but it also served as a demonstration of Saudi independence from the USA.

In August 2006 Saudi Arabia reached agreement with the United Kingdom regarding the purchase of 72 *Eurofighter Typhoon* military aircraft as part of efforts to establish 'a greater partnership to modernize the Saudi Arabian armed forces'; the deal was confirmed by the Saudi authorities in September 2007. King Abdullah, accompanied by a large delegation of senior Saudi officials, began a high-profile state visit to the United Kingdom in October, during which protests were held by those angered at what they deemed to be Saudi Arabia's poor record on human rights and curbing Islamist extremism. In the following month King Abdullah undertook a landmark visit to the Vatican City, where he became the first Saudi monarch to hold discussions with a Supreme Pontiff of the Roman Catholic Church; the talks with Pope Benedict XVI were reported to have focused on how to promote peace between Christians, Muslims and Jews world-wide and to achieve a just solution to the Israeli–Palestinian conflict. In March 2008 discussions were said to be ongoing between Saudi and Vatican officials concerning the possibility of the first Catholic church being built in the kingdom; however, no agreement had been reached on the issue by early 2011.

CONSTITUTION AND GOVERNMENT

Saudi Arabia is an absolute monarchy, with no legislature or political parties. Constitutionally, the King rules in accordance with the *Shari'a*, the sacred law of Islam. He appoints and leads a Council of Ministers, which serves as the instrument of royal authority in both legislative and executive matters. Decisions of the Council are reached by majority vote, but require royal sanction. A Consultative Council (Majlis al-Shoura) was officially inaugurated in December 1993. Members of the Majlis are chosen by the King. Membership of the Majlis was increased from 60 to 90 in July 1997, to 120 in May 2001 and to 150 in April 2005.

The organs of local government are the General Municipal Councils and the tribal and village councils. A General Municipal Council is established in the towns of Mecca, Medina and Jeddah. Its members are proposed by the inhabitants and must be approved by the King. Functioning concurrently with each General Municipal Council is a General Administration Committee, which investigates ways and means of executing resolutions passed by the Council. Every village and tribe has a council with the power to enforce regulations; it is composed of the presiding sheikh, his legal advisers and two other prominent personages. A system of provincial government was announced in late 1993 by royal decree: this defined the nature of government for 13 newly created regions, as well as the rights and responsibilities of their governors, and appointed councils of prominent citizens for each region to monitor development and advise the government. Each council was to meet four times a year under the chairmanship of a governor, who would be an emir with ministerial rank. A royal decree, issued in April 1994, further divided the 13 regions into 103 governorates. In October 2003 it was announced that new municipal councils, of which one-half of the membership would be elected by universal suffrage and one-half appointed by the central Government, would be introduced. Municipal elections took place in early 2005 (for further details, see Contemporary Political History).

REGIONAL AND INTERNATIONAL CO-OPERATION

Saudi Arabia is a member of the Co-operation Council for the Arab States of the Gulf (the Gulf Co-operation Council—GCC, see p. 243), which created a unified regional customs tariff in January 2003 and agreed to establish a single market and currency. The economic convergence criteria for the proposed monetary union were agreed at a heads of state meeting in Abu Dhabi, the United Arab Emirates, in December 2005, and in January 2008 the GCC launched its common market. However, the introduction of a single currency, originally scheduled for 1 January 2010, was subsequently postponed until at least 2015. Saudi Arabia is also a member of the League of Arab States (Arab League, see p. 361), and the Organization of Arab Petroleum Exporting Countries (OAPEC, see p. 397).

The kingdom was a founder member of the UN on that organization's establishment in October 1945, and acceded to the World Trade Organization (WTO, see p. 430) in December 2005. Saudi Arabia also participates in the Organization of the Petroleum Exporting Countries (OPEC, see p. 405). The Organization of the Islamic Conference (OIC, see p. 400) maintains its permanent headquarters in Jeddah.

ECONOMIC AFFAIRS

In 2008, according to estimates by the World Bank, Saudi Arabia's gross national income (GNI), measured at average 2006–08 prices, was US $439,021m., equivalent to $17,700 per head (or $24,000 per head on an international purchasing-power parity basis). During 2000–09, it was estimated, the population increased at an average annual rate of 2.3%, while gross domestic product (GDP) per head increased, in real terms, by an average of 0.8% per year. Overall GDP increased, in real terms, at an average annual rate of 3.2% in 2000–09. According to official figures, real GDP increased by a preliminary 0.6% in 2009.

Agriculture (including forestry and fishing) contributed 2.9% of GDP in 2009, according to preliminary official figures. The sector employed 4.8% of the economically active population in 2008, according to the International Labour Organization (ILO). The principal crop is wheat, the production of which depends almost entirely on irrigation. Saudi Arabia has exported a large wheat surplus since the late 1980s; however, the kingdom planned gradually to reduce output of the crop (with production scheduled to cease entirely by 2016), owing to the increasing scarcity of water resources. Sorghum, barley, potatoes, tomatoes, watermelons and dates are also significant crops. Saudi Arabia is self-sufficient in many dairy products, and in eggs and broiler chickens. Agricultural GDP increased by an average of

SAUDI ARABIA

1.2% per year in 2000–09; the sector's GDP increased by an estimated 0.6% in 2009.

Industry (including mining, manufacturing, construction and power) provided 59.7% of GDP in 2009, according to preliminary figures. The sector employed 18.0% of the active labour force in 2008, according to ILO. During 2000–09, it was estimated, industrial GDP increased at an average annual rate of 2.6%; the sector expanded by 4.4% in 2008, but declined by an estimated 2.8% in 2009.

Mining and quarrying contributed 43.4% of GDP in 2009, according to preliminary figures, while it engaged only 1.4% of the employed population in 2008, according to ILO. The sector is dominated by petroleum and natural gas, which provided a preliminary 43.1% of GDP in that year. Saudi Arabia was the world's second largest petroleum producer in 2009, and mineral products provided 84.6% of total export revenue in that year. At the end of 2009 Saudi Arabia's proven recoverable reserves of petroleum were 264,590m. barrels, equivalent to 19.8% of the world's proven oil reserves. Crude petroleum production averaged 9.7m. barrels per day (b/d) in 2009. As a member of the Organization of the Petroleum Exporting Countries (OPEC, see p. 405), Saudi Arabia is subject to production quotas agreed by the Organization's Conference. By 2010 the Ministry of Petroleum and Mineral Resources had met its target of increasing oil production capacity to 12.5m. b/d, and it appeared that the Government had no plans significantly to increase capacity further. However, in late February 2011, after the popular uprising and subsequent conflict in Libya had virtually halted that country's oil production, the Saudi authorities agreed to increase oil output by 700,000 b/d in order to make up the shortfall. It has been conjectured by some observers that information pertaining to Saudi Arabia's recoverable reserves has been inaccurate and, moreover, that the country might not possess sufficient petroleum to meet demand in the long term; this was denied by the Saudi Government. Gas reserves, mostly associated with petroleum, totalled 7,919,000m. cu m at the end of 2009. In 2002 the world's largest natural gas plant was opened at Hawiya; the plant, which was the first Saudi project to produce gas not associated with petroleum, was expected to increase the country's production of gas by more than 30%. Further non-associated gas reserves are yet to be fully exploited. Other minerals produced include limestone, gypsum, marble, clay and salt, while there are substantial deposits of phosphates, bauxite, gold and other metals. The GDP of the mining sector increased at an average annual rate of 0.8% in 2000–09; the rate of growth increased by 4.2% in 2008, before declining by an estimated 7.9% in 2009.

Manufacturing contributed 10.4% of GDP in 2009, according to preliminary figures. The sector provided 6.4% of employment in 2008, according to ILO. The most important activity is the refining of petroleum, which contributed a preliminary 3.3% of GDP in 2009. The production of petrochemicals, fertilizers, construction materials (particularly steel and cement), and food- and drink-processing are also important activities. Manufacturing GDP increased by an average of 5.4% per year in 2000–09; the GDP of the sector increased by an estimated 2.3% in 2009.

According to preliminary figures, construction contributed 5.0% of GDP in 2009, while it engaged 9.4% of the employed labour force in 2008, according to ILO. Construction GDP increased by an average of 4.2% per year in 2000–09; the GDP of the sector increased by an estimated 4.7% in 2009.

Electrical energy is generated by thermal power stations, using Saudi Arabia's own petroleum resources, although an increasing amount of electricity is now produced in association with sea water desalination. Electricity expansion projects were being planned in 2010 to satisfy domestic demand, which was increasing by around 8% per year. In addition to building new electric power stations, the Government was also reported to be planning a civil nuclear energy programme. A regional electricity grid, linking countries of the Co-operation Council for the Arab States of the Gulf (the Gulf Co-operation Council, see p. 243) was expected to be fully operational during 2011–12, and eventually to achieve regional self-sufficiency up to 2058.

The services sector contributed 37.4% of GDP in 2009, according to preliminary figures. The sector engaged 77.2% of the employed labour force 2008, according to ILO. The GDP of the services sector increased by an average of 4.1% per year in 2000–09; the rate of growth was an estimated 4.0% in 2009.

In 2009 Saudi Arabia recorded a visible trade surplus of US $105,206m., and a surplus of $22,765m. on the current account of the balance of payments. In 2009, according to official provisional figures, the principal source of imports (14.3%) was the USA; other important suppliers were the People's Republic of China, Germany and Japan. Japan was the principal market for exports (15.1%) in that year; other major markets were the USA, China, the Republic of Korea (South Korea) and India. In 2009 the dominant exports were mineral products (particularly crude petroleum) and chemical products. The principal imports in that year were machinery and transport equipment, food and live animals, basic manufactures, and chemicals and related products.

A budgetary deficit of SR 70,000m. was forecast for 2010, and revised figures for 2009 indicated a deficit of SR 86,629m. Saudi Arabia's general government gross debt was SR 225,100m. in 2009, equivalent to 16.0% of GDP. According to ILO figures, consumer prices increased by an annual average of 2.3% in 2000–09, and by 5.1% in 2009. The overall unemployment rate was 5.4% in 2009, although for Saudi nationals the rate was higher, at 10.5%. In 2009 non-Saudi nationals comprised an estimated 50.2% of the total labour force, according to official figures. The Government approved legislation in 2005 to reduce the number of foreign workers to 20% of the population by 2015; the new law was also to provide maternity leave rights and childcare facilities, in order to encourage greater female participation in the work-force. Women, including non-Saudi nationals, comprised an estimated 14.9% of the total labour force in 2009, with Saudi women comprising only 8.2% of the total.

Saudi Arabia's prosperity is based on exploitation of its petroleum reserves. Although in 2009 the country was overtaken as the world's largest oil producer by Russia, Saudi Arabia remained the biggest exporter of oil world-wide and it continued to play a crucial role in determining OPEC production levels and thus world prices. Nevertheless, the decline in the price of petroleum in the early 1990s caused the Government to seek alternative sources of revenue. Since 2000 the Saudi authorities have aimed to increase private investment and growth in the private and non-oil sectors, and sought to expand employment opportunities and housing provision for the rapidly expanding Saudi population, most of whom reside in urban areas. The construction of the new King Abdullah Economic City, situated on the west coast between Jeddah and Rabigh, commenced in 2006 and was projected to be fully completed by 2025, with a new seaport expected to be inaugurated in 2012. A further five 'economic cities' were planned for other regions of the kingdom, as its huge petroleum revenues were utilized to increase private sector growth, establish new industries and create at least 1.3m. jobs by 2020. From mid-2008 the international price of petroleum fell sharply, and in 2009 the kingdom recorded its first fiscal deficit since 2002, equivalent to 6.1% of GDP (following a record surplus of 32.5% of GDP in 2008), which was explained by lower petroleum revenues and high public expenditure. In its Regional Outlook published in April 2011, the IMF estimated a return to fiscal surplus, equivalent to 7.7% of GDP, in 2010. Strong public spending, extensive foreign reserves and a sound regulatory framework enabled the Saudi economy to withstand the adverse effects of the global financial crisis from late 2008. Owing to the resultant global economic slowdown, the inflation rate declined from 9.9% in 2008 to 5.1% in 2009. The IMF expected consumer prices to rise by 5.4% in 2010 and by 6.0% in 2011. Real GDP grew by 0.6% in 2009 and by 3.8% in 2010, according to provisional official figures. The IMF forecast real GDP growth of some 7.5% in 2011. In October 2010 the Council of Ministers endorsed the Ninth Development Plan for 2010–14, which sought to continue the process of economic diversification and to base growth on the principal of sustainable development; around one-half of expenditure under the Plan was allocated to the education and training sector. Amid rare street protests in parts of Saudi Arabia in early 2011, caused in part by frustration over rising food prices and high youth unemployment (around 39% of 15–24 year-olds), in February and March the King announced a range of economic measures—including the introduction of unemployment benefit and the creation of additional public sector jobs (see Contemporary Political History).

PUBLIC HOLIDAYS

2012: 12–22 August* (Id al-Fitr, end of Ramadan), 23 September (National Day), 20–28 October* (Id al-Adha, Feast of the Sacrifice).

* These holidays are dependent on the Islamic lunar calendar and may vary by one or two days from the dates given.

SAUDI ARABIA

Statistical Survey

Sources (unless otherwise indicated): Central Department of Statistics, Ministry of Economy and Planning, POB 358, University St, Riyadh 11182; tel. (1) 401-3333; fax (1) 401-9300; e-mail info@cds.gov.sa; internet www.cdsi.gov.sa; Saudi Arabian Monetary Agency, *Annual Report* and *Statistical Summary*.

Area and Population

AREA, POPULATION AND DENSITY

Area (sq km)	2,240,000*
Population (census results)	
27 September 1992	16,948,388†
15 September 2004	
Males	12,557,240
Females	10,121,022
Total	22,678,262
Population (official estimates at mid-year)	
2007	24,242,578
2008	24,807,273
2009	25,373,512‡
Density (per sq km) at mid-2009	11.3

* 864,869 sq miles.
† Of the total population at the 1992 census, 12,310,053 (males 6,215,793, females 6,094,260) were nationals of Saudi Arabia, while 4,638,335 (males 3,264,180, females 1,374,155) were foreign nationals.
‡ Population comprised an estimated 18,543,246 Saudi nationals and 6,830,266 foreign nationals.

Saudi Arabia-Iraq Neutral Zone: The Najdi (Saudi Arabian) frontier with Iraq was defined in the Treaty of Mohammara in May 1922. Later a Neutral Zone of 7,044 sq km was established adjacent to the western tip of the Kuwait frontier. No military or permanent buildings were to be erected in the zone and the nomads of both countries were to have unimpeded access to its pastures and wells. A further agreement concerning the administration of this zone was signed between Iraq and Saudi Arabia in May 1938. In July 1975 Iraq and Saudi Arabia signed an agreement providing for an equal division of the diamond-shaped zone between the two countries, with the border following a straight line through the zone.

Saudi Arabia-Kuwait Neutral Zone: A Convention signed at Uqair in December 1922 fixed the Najdi (Saudi Arabian) boundary with Kuwait. The Convention also established a Neutral Zone of 5,770 sq km immediately to the south of Kuwait in which Saudi Arabia and Kuwait held equal rights. The final agreement on this matter was signed in 1963. Since 1966 the Neutral Zone, or Partitioned Zone as it is sometimes known, has been divided between the two countries and each administers its own half, in practice as an integral part of the State. However, the petroleum deposits in the Zone remain undivided and production from the onshore oil concessions in the Zone is shared equally between the two states' concessionaires.

POPULATION BY AGE AND SEX
(official demographic survey, 2007)

	Males	Females	Total
0–14	3,926,920	3,856,076	7,782,996
15–64	9,024,995	6,496,928	15,521,923
65 and over	349,254	326,661	675,915
Total	13,301,169	10,679,665	23,980,834

ADMINISTRATIVE REGIONS
(demographic survey for 2007)*

Aseer	1,756,625	Makkah	6,097,077
Al-Baha	387,717	Najran	449,186
Eastern	3,545,644	Northern Borders	294,896
Ha'il	551,523	Qassim	1,077,068
Jazan	1,253,089	Riyadh	5,835,613
Al-Jouf	382,070	Tabouk	735,682
Al-Madinah	1,614,644	**Total**	23,980,834

* Islamic year AH 1428, which corresponds to the period 20 January 2007 to 9 January 2008 in the Gregorian calendar.

PRINCIPAL TOWNS
(population at 2004 census)

Riyadh (royal capital)	4,087,152	Al-Mobarraz	285,067
Jeddah (administrative capital)	2,801,481	Ha'il (Hayil)	267,005
Makkah (Mecca)	1,294,168	Naijran	246,880
Al-Madinah (Medina)	918,889	Hafar al-Batin	231,978
Dammam	744,321	Jubail	222,544
Al-Ta'if	521,273	Abha	201,912
Tabouk	441,351	Al-Kharj	200,958
Buraidah	378,422	Al-Thuqbah	191,826
Khamis-Mushait	372,695	Yanbu	188,430
Hufuf	287,841	Al-Khubar	165,799

Source: UN, *Demographic Yearbook*.

Mid-2010 ('000, incl. suburbs, UN estimates): Riyadh 4,848; Jeddah 3,234; Mecca 1,484; Medina 1,104; Dammam 902 (Source: UN, *World Urbanization Prospects: The 2009 Revision*).

BIRTHS AND DEATHS
(UN estimates, annual averages)

	1995–2000	2000–05	2005–10
Birth rate (per 1,000)	29.5	26.5	23.6
Death rate (per 1,000)	4.0	3.8	3.6

Source: UN, *World Population Prospects: The 2008 Revision*.

Life expectancy (years at birth, WHO estimates): 72 (males 69; females 75) in 2008 (Source: WHO, *World Health Statistics*).

ECONOMICALLY ACTIVE POPULATION
(persons aged 15 years and over at April 2008)

	Males	Females	Total
Agriculture, hunting, forestry and fishing	381,854	518	382,372
Mining and quarrying	107,061	627	107,688
Manufacturing	498,491	10,353	508,844
Electricity, gas and water	66,902	—	66,902
Construction	743,518	2,256	745,774
Wholesale and retail trade	1,249,601	8,340	1,257,941
Restaurants and hotels	274,132	4,996	279,128
Transport and communications	359,675	2,234	361,909
Financial intermediation	81,448	4,555	86,003
Real estate, renting and business activities	305,851	7,618	313,469
Public administration and defence	1,469,825	33,088	1,502,913
Education	534,115	398,392	932,507
Health and social work	282,037	83,422	365,459
Other community and personal services	157,313	5,737	163,050
Private households with employed persons	319,794	556,802	876,596
Extra-territorial organizations	5,623	654	6,277
Total employed	6,837,240	1,119,592	7,956,832
Unemployed	250,402	167,660	418,062
Total labour force	7,087,642	1,287,252	8,374,894

Source: ILO.

SAUDI ARABIA

Health and Welfare

KEY INDICATORS

Total fertility rate (children per woman, 2008)	3.1
Under-5 mortality rate (per 1,000 live births, 2008)	21
Physicians (per 1,000 head, 2004)	1.4
Hospital beds (per 1,000 head, 2005)	2.3
Health expenditure (2007): US $ per head (PPP)	768
Health expenditure (2007): % of GDP	3.4
Health expenditure (2007): public (% of total)	79.5
Total carbon dioxide emissions ('000 metric tons, 2007)	402,120.3
Carbon dioxide emissions per head (metric tons, 2007)	16.6
Human Development Index (2010): ranking	55
Human Development Index (2010): value	0.752

For sources and definitions, see explanatory note on p. vi.

Agriculture

PRINCIPAL CROPS
('000 metric tons)

	2006	2007	2008
Wheat	2,630	2,558	1,986
Barley	31	28	24
Maize	126	135	163
Millet	7	6	6*
Sorghum	249	233	252
Potatoes	469	463	447
Tomatoes	480	478	522
Pumpkins, squash and gourds	124	116	116*
Cucumbers and gherkins	242	260	260
Aubergines (Eggplants)	71	66	52
Onions, dry	58	54	45
Carrots and turnips	52	48	81
Okra	58	55	52
Watermelons	384	393	364
Cantaloupes and other melons	216	209	236
Grapes	136	144	162
Dates	977	983	986

* FAO estimate.

Note: No data were available for individual crops in 2009.

Aggregate production ('000 metric tons, may include official, semi-official or estimated data): Total cereals 3,043 in 2006, 2,960 in 2007, 2,431 in 2008–09; Total roots and tubers 469 in 2006, 463 in 2007, 447 in 2008–09; Total vegetables (incl. melons) 2,090 in 2006, 2,085 in 2007, 2,134 in 2008–09; Total fruits (excl. melons) 1,641 in 2006, 1,664 in 2007, 1,685 in 2008–09.

Source: FAO.

LIVESTOCK
('000 head, year ending September)

	2005	2006	2007*
Asses*	100	100	100
Camels	268†	260*	260
Cattle	352	369	421
Sheep†	8,230	8,010	7,847
Goats	2,230†	2,200*	2,200
Chickens*	141,000	142,000	145,000

* FAO estimate(s).
† Unofficial figure(s).

2008: Figures assumed to be unchanged from 2007 (FAO estimates).
2009: Sheep 8,000 (FAO estimate).

Source: FAO.

LIVESTOCK PRODUCTS
('000 metric tons)

	2005	2006	2007
Cattle meat	22.4	20.8*	29.0*
Sheep meat*	81.4	79.2	77.6
Goat meat*	15.0	14.7	24.9
Chicken meat†	537.0	548.0	559.0
Camel meat	41.0	41.0	41.0*
Cows' milk	940.0	1,300.0	1,670.0
Sheep's milk*	96.0	82.5	82.5
Goats' milk*	70.0	76.5	76.5
Camels' milk*	90.0	90.0	90.0
Hen eggs	169.5	158.1	170.6
Wool, greasy*	12.5	10.8	10.8

* FAO estimate(s).
† Unofficial figures.

2008: Production assumed to unchanged from 2007 (FAO estimates).
2009: Sheep meat 79.0 (FAO estimate).

Source: FAO.

Fishing

(metric tons, live weight)

	2006	2007	2008
Capture	65,476	66,092	68,000*
Pink ear emperors	2,574	2,683	2,760*
Emperors (Scavengers)	4,011	4,503	4,650*
Spinefeet (Rabbitfishes)	2,393	1,984	2,050*
Narrow-barred Spanish mackerel	5,386	4,961	5,100*
Indian mackerel	3,226	4,081	4,200*
Green tiger prawns	7,488	8,643	8,900*
Aquaculture	15,586	18,497	22,253
Nile tilapia	3,402	3,606	3,673
Indian white prawn	11,615	14,528	17,912
Total catch	**81,062**	**84,589**	**90,253***

* FAO estimate.

Source: FAO.

Mining

('000 metric tons, unless otherwise indicated)

	2007	2008	2009
Crude petroleum (million barrels)*	3,218	3,366	2,987
Silver (kilograms)†	9,028	8,232	9,500‡
Gold (kilograms)†	4,440	4,527	5,500‡
Salt (unrefined)	1,507	1,600	1,600‡
Gypsum (crude)	2,100	2,300	2,100‡
Pozzolan	784	810	800‡

* Including 50% of the total output of the Neutral (Partitioned) Zone, shared with Kuwait (Source: Saudi Arabian Monetary Agency).
† Figures refer to the metal content of concentrate and bullion.
‡ Estimate.

Source: mainly US Geological Survey.

Natural gas (excluding flared and recycled, million cu m): 74,420 in 2007; 80,440 in 2008; 77,450 in 2009 (Source: BP, *Statistical Review of World Energy*).

SAUDI ARABIA

Industry

SELECTED PRODUCTS
(including 50% of the total output of the Neutral Zone; estimates, '000 barrels, unless otherwise indicated)

	2007	2008	2009
Phosphatic fertilizers ('000 metric tons)*†	300	300	300
Motor spirit (petrol) and naphtha	188,644	200,606	194,983
Jet fuel and kerosene	67,282	69,677	63,502
Gas-diesel (distillate fuel) oils	238,496	247,438	227,686
Residual fuel oils	174,385	174,381	181,613
Petroleum bitumen (asphalt)	15,041	17,960	17,035
Liquefied petroleum gas	11,521	11,303	12,692
Cement ('000 metric tons)	30,369	31,823	40,000†
Crude steel ('000 metric tons)	4,600	4,670	4,700†
Electric energy (million kWh sold)	169,303	181,097	193,472

* Production in terms of phosphoric acid.
† Estimate(s).

Sources: Saudi Arabian Monetary Agency; US Geological Survey.

Finance

CURRENCY AND EXCHANGE RATES

Monetary Units:
100 halalah = 20 qurush = 1 Saudi riyal (SR).

Sterling, Dollar and Euro Equivalents (31 December 2010):
£1 sterling = 5.871 riyals;
US $1 = 3.750 riyals;
€1 = 5.011 riyals;
100 Saudi riyals = £17.03 = $26.67 = €19.96.

Exchange Rate: Since June 1986 the official mid-point rate has been fixed at US $1 = 3.75 riyals.

BUDGET ESTIMATES
(million riyals)

Revenue	2008	2009	2010
Petroleum revenues	370,000	320,000	400,000
Other revenues	80,000	90,000	70,000
Total	450,000	410,000	470,000

Expenditure	2008	2009	2010
Human resource development	104,600	121,942	137,440
Transport and communications	12,143	14,642	16,442
Economic resource development	16,317	21,692	29,288
Health and social development	34,426	40,426	46,600
Infrastructure development	6,384	7,762	8,438
Municipal services	14,954	16,509	18,748
Defence and security	143,336	154,752	169,667
Public administration and other government spending	63,031	79,148	92,017
Government lending institutions*	479	524	596
Local subsidies	14,329	17,602	20,764
Total	410,000	475,000	540,000

* Including transfers to the Saudi Fund for Development (SFD).

2007 (revised figures, million riyals): Total revenue 642,800 (Petroleum revenue 562,186, Other revenue 80,614); Total expenditure 466,248.

2008 (revised figures, million riyals): Total revenue 1,100,993 (Petroleum revenue 983,369, Other revenue 117,624); Total expenditure 520,069.

2009 (revised figures, million riyals): Total revenue 509,805 (Petroleum revenue 434,420, Other revenue 75,385); Total expenditure 596,434.

INTERNATIONAL RESERVES
(US $ million in December)

	2008	2009	2010
Gold*	415	415	415
IMF special drawing rights	735	10,928	10,646
Reserve position in IMF	1,384	2,017	1,981
Foreign exchange	440,479	396,748	432,094
Total	443,013	410,108	445,136

* Valued at US $40 per troy ounce at 31 December 2010.

Source: IMF, *International Financial Statistics*.

MONEY SUPPLY
('000 million riyals in December)

	2008	2009	2010
Currency outside banks	83.01	88.40	95.52
Demand deposits at commercial banks	343.01	433.48	530.39
Total money	426.02	521.88	625.91

Source: IMF, *International Financial Statistics*.

COST OF LIVING
(Consumer Price Index for all cities; base: 1999 = 100)

	2007	2008	2009
Food and beverages	120.1	137.0	139.7
Housing, fuel and water	109.2	128.3	146.4
Textiles and clothing (incl. footwear)	85.6	85.9	86.3
House furnishing	96.4	103.8	112.6
Medical care	107.0	112.4	113.2
Transport and communications	88.1	88.3	89.2
Entertainment and education	98.9	101.0	102.3
All items (incl. others)	106.0	116.5	122.4

NATIONAL ACCOUNTS
(million riyals at current prices)

Expenditure on the Gross Domestic Product

	2007	2008	2009*
Government final consumption expenditure	322,086	345,098	348,469
Private final consumption expenditure	421,233	496,951	537,414
Increase in stocks	13,965	47,950	20,764
Gross fixed capital formation	295,401	348,011	347,510
Total domestic expenditure	1,052,685	1,238,010	1,254,157
Exports of goods and services	934,321	1,210,701	757,363
Less Imports of goods and services	544,434	662,568	602,396
GDP in purchasers' values	1,442,572	1,786,143	1,409,124
GDP at constant 1999 prices	802,211	836,133	841,184

Gross Domestic Product by Economic Activity

	2007	2008	2009*
Agriculture, forestry and fishing	40,154	41,136	41,419
Mining and quarrying:			
crude petroleum and natural gas	729,361	1,021,714	610,100
other	3,292	3,455	3,590
Manufacturing:			
petroleum refining	46,691	45,975	46,874
other	89,818	101,898	99,799
Electricity, gas and water	12,419	13,095	13,722
Construction	65,017	68,099	71,092
Trade, restaurants and hotels	73,990	81,263	85,261

SAUDI ARABIA

—continued	2007	2008	2009*
Transport, storage and communications	45,934	52,752	56,858
Finance, insurance, real estate and business services:			
ownership of dwellings	54,776	58,915	63,545
other	56,661	60,148	63,419
Government services	200,306	209,278	225,867
Other community, social and personal services	30,631	32,301	33,889
Sub-total	1,449,052	1,790,029	1,415,436
Import duties	11,801	14,940	12,987
Less Imputed bank service charge	18,280	18,825	19,299
GDP in purchasers' values	1,442,572	1,786,143	1,409,124

* Provisional.

BALANCE OF PAYMENTS
(US $ million)

	2007	2008	2009
Exports of goods f.o.b.	233,330	313,481	192,307
Imports of goods f.o.b.	−82,597	−101,454	−87,101
Trade balance	150,732	212,027	105,206
Exports of services	15,989	9,373	9,656
Imports of services	−62,682	−75,231	−73,538
Balance on goods and services	104,039	146,169	41,325
Other income received	15,138	21,498	19,725
Other income paid	−8,742	−12,333	−11,113
Balance on goods, services and income	110,436	155,334	49,937
Current transfers (net)	−17,043	−23,012	−27,172
Current balance	93,392	132,322	22,765
Direct investment abroad	135	−3,498	−2,148
Direct investment from abroad	24,335	39,456	10,499
Portfolio investment assets	−5,476	−3,847	−19,747
Portfolio investment liabilities	—	2,217	−5
Other investment assets	−16,849	−2,562	−9,792
Other investment liabilities	−24	2,963	2,244
Net errors and omissions	−15,695	−30,008	−36,454
Overall balance	79,819	137,043	−32,638

Source: IMF, *International Financial Statistics*.

External Trade

PRINCIPAL COMMODITIES
(distribution by SITC, US $ million)

Imports c.i.f.	2007	2008	2009
Food and live animals	10,604.9	11,475.7	9,645.7
Cereals and cereal preparations	3,620.9	5,361.1	3,627.4
Chemicals and related products	8,022.0	3,828.1	3,996.6
Medicinal and pharmaceutical products	2,230.3	1,777.6	2,380.7
Basic manufactures	18,508.1	10,824.4	6,697.3
Iron and steel	7,612.1	5,561.4	2,019.8
Machinery and transport equipment	42,376.1	27,676.2	23,286.6
General industrial machinery equipment and parts	9,009.5	3,368.5	1,943.6
Electrical machinery, apparatus, etc.	4,677.0	964.4	1,070.3
Road vehicles and parts	12,017.6	12,357.8	10,189.3
Passenger motor cars (excl. buses)	7,761.9	9,016.9	7,449.2
Miscellaneous manufactured articles	7,076.5	2,105.4	2,531.1
Total (incl. others)	90,214.0	115,133.9	95,552.2

Exports f.o.b.	2007	2008	2009
Mineral fuels, lubricants, etc.	206,996.9	280,623.5	162,726.4
Petroleum, petroleum products and related materials	198,157.3	270,337.2	157,474.3
Crude petroleum (bituminous)	180,030.4	247,097.2	142,194.2
Natural gas, manufactured	8,839.0	10,286.3	5,252.1
Chemicals and related products	14,258.9	14,651.6	12,239.8
Organic chemicals	5,662.2	5,756.5	4,776.0
Basic manufactures	4,231.7	1,993.9	1,778.3
Machinery and transport equipment	5,643.8	4,333.9	4,224.1
Total (incl. others)	234,950.8	313,462.2	192,314.1

Source: UN, *International Trade Statistics Yearbook*.

PRINCIPAL TRADING PARTNERS
(US $ million)

Imports c.i.f.	2007	2008	2009
Australia	1,946.8	2,473.1	1,668.5
Austria	843.0	1,127.2	1,172.6
Bahrain	831.6	1,181.1	941.3
Belgium	1,096.3	1,509.3	1,348.9
Brazil	1,751.4	2,893.6	2,390.6
Canada	956.5	1,812.4	1,378.4
China, People's Republic	8,716.0	12,677.7	10,827.9
Finland	1,285.5	1,208.8	688.9
France (incl. Monaco)	3,068.8	4,065.5	3,826.6
Germany	8,010.9	8,545.9	7,620.0
India	3,076.3	4,803.1	3,492.2
Italy	4,104.3	4,610.3	3,533.7
Japan	7,888.5	9,400.2	7,238.5
Korea, Republic	4,045.7	5,124.8	4,248.7
Malaysia	860.5	1,220.4	942.5
Netherlands	1,214.5	1,461.0	1,198.5
Spain	1,181.9	1,350.3	1,232.8
Sweden	1,272.4	1,561.0	1,403.0
Switzerland (incl. Liechtenstein)	1,420.4	2,065.4	1,677.5
Thailand	1,489.4	2,088.5	2,070.6
United Arab Emirates	2,251.2	2,883.9	2,877.5
United Kingdom	3,514.1	4,060.0	3,424.9
USA	12,253.1	15,774.3	13,626.6
Total (incl. others)	90,214.0	115,133.9	95,552.2

Exports (incl. re-exports)	2005	2006	2007*
Bahrain	4,974.4	6,065.9	1,205.7
Belgium	2,276.3	2,869.5	905.4
China, People's Republic	10,814.9	13,232.7	2,667.3
Egypt	2,046.2	2,755.7	2,818.7
France (incl. Monaco)	4,297.7	4,117.7	2,922.1
India	10,739.7	12,956.1	3,387.4
Indonesia	2,447.6	3,066.6	683.6
Italy	5,377.0	5,169.3	3,376.6
Japan	28,180.5	34,811.5	62,970.9
Korea, Republic	15,312.1	19,377.8	1,624.2
Netherlands	6,488.1	6,497.0	3,855.1
Singapore	9,472.2	9,988.1	2,889.0
South Africa	3,065.9	3,220.3	694.1
Spain	2,971.9	3,582.7	2,826.0
Thailand	3,207.2	3,541.8	604.7
United Arab Emirates	4,811.7	6,805.9	8,404.7
USA	27,958.5	31,842.2	41,033.0
Total (incl. others)	180,737.2	211,305.8	234,950.8

* Data for many countries assumed to exclude petroleum exports.

2008: Total exports 313,462.2.

2009: Total exports 192,314.1.

Source: UN, *International Trade Statistics Yearbook*.

SAUDI ARABIA

Statistical Survey

Transport

RAILWAYS
(traffic)

	2005	2006	2007
Passenger journeys ('000)	1,169	1,071	1,107
Passenger-km (million)	378	343	347
Freight carried ('000 metric tons)	2,458	2,640	3,258
Net freight ton-km (million)	1,171	1,257	1,604

ROAD TRAFFIC
(motor vehicles in use at 31 December)

	1989	1990	1991
Passenger cars	2,550,465	2,664,028	2,762,132
Buses and coaches	50,856	52,136	54,089
Goods vehicles	2,153,297	2,220,658	2,286,541
Total	4,754,618	4,936,822	5,103,205

2005 (motor vehicles in use at 31 December): Passenger cars 3,206,000; Buses and coaches 113,073; Vans and lorries 1,127,900; Motorcycles and mopeds 16,250; Total (incl. others) 4,446,973 (Source: IRF, *World Road Statistics*).

SHIPPING

Merchant Fleet
(vessels registered at 31 December)

	2007	2008	2009
Oil tankers:			
vessels	21	25	29
displacement ('000 grt)	88	189	437
Others:			
vessels	290	297	301
displacement ('000 grt)	854	1,161	1,274
Total vessels	311	322	330
Total displacement ('000 grt)	942	1,350	1,711

Source: IHS Fairplay, *World Fleet Statistics*.

International Sea-borne Freight Traffic
('000 metric tons)*

	1988	1989	1990
Goods loaded	161,666	165,989	214,070
Goods unloaded	42,546	42,470	46,437

* Including Saudi Arabia's share of traffic in the Neutral or Partitioned Zone.

Source: UN, *Monthly Bulletin of Statistics*.

2006 ('000 metric tons, excluding crude oil): Goods loaded 81,318; Goods unloaded 51,575.

2007 ('000 metric tons, excluding crude oil): Goods loaded 82,264; Goods unloaded 51,769.

CIVIL AVIATION
(traffic on scheduled services)

	2003	2004	2005
Kilometres flown (million)	125	135	141
Passengers carried ('000)	13,822	14,943	15,933
Passenger-kilometres (million)	20,801	22,557	23,793
Total ton-km (million)	2,739	3,000	3,174

Source: UN, *Statistical Yearbook*.

2006 (Saudi Arabian airlines): Passengers carried ('000) 17,800; Number of flights 141,964; Cargo carried ('000 metric tons) 296.

2007 (Saudi Arabian airlines): Passengers carried ('000) 18,200; Number of flights 132,637; Cargo carried ('000 metric tons) 326.

2008 (Saudi Arabian airlines): Passengers carried ('000) 17,700; Number of flights 157,944; Cargo carried ('000 metric tons) 345.

2009 (Saudi Arabian airlines): Passengers carried ('000) 18,300; Number of flights 165,253; Cargo carried ('000 metric tons) 308.

Tourism

Country of nationality	2006	2007	2008
Bahrain	389,513	483,410	594,188
Bangladesh	92,088	177,369	34,187
Egypt	609,831	1,622,320	1,853,663
India	345,431	613,347	601,922
Indonesia	373,027	296,469	501,758
Iran	387,556	435,977	349,848
Jordan	322,548	495,105	501,269
Kuwait	1,681,843	1,660,464	2,589,988
Pakistan	510,449	642,562	817,550
Qatar	501,157	596,468	808,072
Sudan	111,961	311,889	398,607
Syria	605,150	785,759	708,034
Turkey	266,072	184,133	248,500
United Arab Emirates	800,059	955,320	1,613,574
Yemen	200,260	331,494	197,652
Total (incl. others)	8,620,465	11,530,834	14,757,444

Tourism receipts (US $ million, incl. passenger transport): 5,204 in 2006; 6,768 in 2007; 7,227 in 2008.

Source: World Tourism Organization.

PILGRIMS TO MECCA FROM ABROAD

	2007*	2008†	2009‡
Total	1,707,814	1,729,841	1,613,965

* Figures for Islamic year 1428 (20 January 2007 to 9 January 2008).
† Figures for Islamic year 1429 (10 January 2008 to 28 December 2008).
‡ Figures for Islamic year 1430 (29 December 2008 to 17 December 2009).

Communications Media

	2007	2008	2009
Telephones ('000 main lines in use)	3,996	4,100	4,171
Mobile cellular telephones ('000 subscribers)	28,400	36,000	44,864
Internet users ('000)	7,404.1	9,072.2	9,773.8
Broadband subscribers ('000)	623.1	1,048.1	1,342.8

Personal computers: 17,200,000 (697.9 per 1,000 persons) in 2008.

1996: 185 non-daily newspapers.

1997: 6,250,000 radio receivers in use; Book titles published 3,780.

2004: 12 daily newspapers.

Sources: UNESCO, *Statistical Yearbook*; International Telecommunication Union.

Education

(2007/08, projections)

	Institutions	Teachers	Students
Pre-primary	1,650	11,125	125,433
Primary	13,993	215,625	2,694,161
Intermediate	7,175	106,856	1,175,409
Secondary (general)	3,861	73,509	916,872
Special	673	6,658	22,834
Adult education	4,446	11,570	84,298

Source: Ministry of Education, Riyadh.

Pupil-teacher ratio (primary education, UNESCO estimate): 11.4 in 2008/09 (Source: UNESCO Institute for Statistics).

Adult literacy rate (UNESCO estimates): 85.5% (males 89.5%; females 80.2%) in 2008 (Source: UNESCO Institute for Statistics).

Directory

The Government

HEAD OF STATE

King: HM King ABDULLAH IBN ABD AL-AZIZ AL SA'UD (acceded to the throne 1 August 2005).

COUNCIL OF MINISTERS
(May 2011)

Prime Minister: King ABDULLAH IBN ABD AL-AZIZ AL SA'UD.
First Deputy Prime Minister, Minister of Defence and Civil Aviation and Inspector General: Crown Prince SULTAN IBN ABD AL-AZIZ AL SA'UD.
Second Deputy Prime Minister and Minister of the Interior: Prince NAYEF IBN ABD AL-AZIZ AL SA'UD.
Minister of Municipal and Rural Affairs: Prince MANSOUR IBN MUTAIB IBN ABD AL-AZIZ AL SA'UD.
Minister of Foreign Affairs: Prince SA'UD AL-FAISAL AL SA'UD.
Minister of Petroleum and Mineral Resources: Eng. ALI IBN IBRAHIM AL-NUAIMI.
Minister of Labour: Eng. ADEL BIN MUHAMMAD ABD AL-KADER FAKIEH.
Minister of Social Affairs: Dr YOUSUF ABDULLAH AL-OTHMAN.
Minister of Agriculture: Dr FAHD IBN ABD AL-RAHMAN IBN SULAIMAN BALGHUNAIM.
Minister of Water and Electricity: ABDULLAH IBN ABD AL-RAHMAN AL-HUSSEIN.
Minister of Education: Prince FAISAL IBN ABDULLAH IBN MUHAMMAD AL SA'UD.
Minister of Higher Education: Dr KHALID IBN MUHAMMAD AL-ANGARI.
Minister of Communications and Information Technology: MUHAMMAD IBN JABIL IBN AHMAD MULLA.
Minister of Finance: Dr IBRAHIM IBN ABD AL-AZIZ AL-ASSAF.
Minister of Economy and Planning: KHALED IBN MUHAMMAD AL-QUSAIBI.
Minister of Culture and Information: Dr ABD AL-AZIZ IBN MOHI EL-DIN KHOJA.
Minister of Commerce and Industry: ABDULLAH IBN AHMAD ZAINAL ALIREZA.
Minister of Justice: Dr MUHAMMAD IBN ABD AL-KARIM IBN ABD AL-AZIZ AL-EISSA.
Minister of Pilgrimage (Hajj) Affairs: FOUAD IBN ABD AL-SALAM IBN MUHAMMAD AL-FARSI.
Minister of Awqaf (Religious Endowments), Dawa, Mosques and Guidance Affairs: SALEH IBN ABD AL-AZIZ MUHAMMAD IBN IBRAHIM AL-SHEIKH.
Minister of Health: Dr ABDULLAH IBN ABD AL-AZIZ AL-RABEA.
Minister of the Civil Service: Dr MUHAMMAD IBN ALI AL-FAYEZ.
Minister of Transport: Dr JUBARAH IBN EID AL-SURAISERI.
Minister of Housing: SHUWAISH AL-DUWAIHI.
Minister of State and Commander of the National Guard: Prince MITAB IBN ABDULLAH AL SA'UD.
Minister of State for Foreign Affairs: NIZAR IBN UBAYD MADANI.
Minister of State for Consultative Council Affairs: Dr SAUD IBN SAEED IBN ABD AL-AZIZ AL-MATHAMI.
Ministers of State: Dr MUTLIB IBN ABDULLAH AL-NAFISA, Dr MUSAID IBN MUHAMMAD AL-AYBAN, Prince ABD AL-AZIZ IBN FAHD AL SA'UD.

MINISTRIES

Most ministries have regional offices in Jeddah.

Council of Ministers: Murabba, Riyadh 11121; tel. (1) 488-2444.
Ministry of Agriculture: Airport Rd, Riyadh 11195; tel. (1) 401-6666; fax (1) 403-1415; e-mail pubrel@moa.gov.sa; internet www.moa.gov.sa.
Ministry of Awqaf (Religious Endowments), Dawa, Mosques and Guidance Affairs: Riyadh 11232; tel. (1) 473-0401; fax 477-2938; internet www.al-islam.com.
Ministry of the Civil Service: POB 18367, Riyadh 11114; tel. (1) 402-6900; fax (1) 405-6258; e-mail mcswebmaster@mcs.gov.sa; internet www.mcs.gov.sa.
Ministry of Commerce and Industry: POB 1774, Airport Rd, Riyadh 11162; tel. (1) 401-2222; fax (1) 403-8421; e-mail info@commerce.gov.sa; internet www.commerce.gov.sa.
Ministry of Communications and Information Technology: Intercontinental Rd, Riyadh 11112; tel. (1) 452-2222; fax (1) 452-2220; e-mail info@mcit.gov.sa; internet www.mcit.gov.sa.
Ministry of Culture and Information: Intercontinental Rd, Riyadh 11112; tel. (1) 401-4440; fax (1) 402-3570; internet www.moci.gov.sa.
Ministry of Defence and Civil Aviation: POB 26731, Airport Rd, Riyadh 11165; tel. (1) 478-9000; fax (1) 401-1336; internet www.moda.gov.sa.
Ministry of Economy and Planning: POB 358, 44 University St, Riyadh 11182; tel. (1) 401-1444; fax (1) 404-9473; e-mail minister@planning.gov.sa; internet www.mep.gov.sa.
Ministry of Education: POB 3734, Airport Rd, Riyadh 11148; tel. (1) 404-2888; fax (1) 401-2365; internet www.moe.gov.sa.
Ministry of Finance: Airport Rd, Riyadh 11177; tel. (1) 405-0000; fax (1) 403-3130; e-mail info@mof.gov.sa; internet www.mof.gov.sa.
Ministry of Foreign Affairs: POB 55937, Riyadh 11544; tel. (1) 405-5000; fax (1) 403-0645; e-mail info@mofa.gov.sa; internet www.mofa.gov.sa.
Ministry of Health: Airport Rd, Riyadh 11176; tel. (1) 401-2220; fax (1) 402-9876; e-mail f_otaibi@moh.gov.sa; internet www.moh.gov.sa.
Ministry of Higher Education: POB 225085, Riyadh 11324; tel. (1) 441-5555; fax (1) 441-9004; e-mail contact@mohe.gov.sa; internet www.mohe.gov.sa.
Ministry of Housing: Riyadh.
Ministry of the Interior: POB 2933, Airport Rd, Riyadh 11134; tel. (1) 401-1111; fax (1) 403-3125; internet www.moi.gov.sa.
Ministry of Justice: POB 7775, University St, Riyadh 11137; tel. (1) 405-7777; fax (1) 405-5399; internet www.moj.gov.sa.
Ministry of Labour: POB 21110, King Abd al-Aziz Rd, Riyadh 11475; tel. (1) 200-6666; fax (1) 478-9175; e-mail info@mol.gov.sa; internet www.mol.gov.sa.
Ministry of Municipal and Rural Affairs: POB 955, Nasseriya St, Riyadh 11136; tel. (1) 456-9999; fax (1) 456-3196; e-mail info@momra.gov.sa; internet www.momra.gov.sa.
Ministry of Petroleum and Mineral Resources: POB 247, Al Ma'ather St, Riyadh 11191; tel. (1) 478-1661; fax (1) 479-3596; e-mail info@mopm.gov.sa; internet www.mopm.gov.sa.
Ministry of Pilgrimage (Hajj) Affairs: al-Maazar St, Riyadh 11183; tel. (1) 404-3003; fax (1) 402-2555; internet www.hajinformation.com.
Ministry of Social Affairs: Riyadh 11167; tel. (1) 477-8888; fax (1) 477-7336; e-mail info@mosa.gov.sa; internet www.mosa.gov.sa.
Ministry of Transport: Airport Rd, Riyadh 11178; tel. (1) 404-3000; fax (1) 403-5743; e-mail info@mot.gov.sa; internet www.mot.gov.sa.
Ministry of Water and Electricity: King Fahd Rd, Riyadh 11233; tel. (1) 205-6666; fax (1) 205-2749; e-mail info@mowe.gov.sa; internet www.mowe.gov.sa.

Majlis al-Shoura (Consultative Council)

Al-Yamamh Palace, Riyadh 11212; tel. (1) 4821666; fax (1) 4816985; e-mail webmaster@shura.gov.sa; internet www.shura.gov.sa.

In March 1992 King Fahd issued a decree to establish a Consultative Council of 60 members, whose powers include the right to summon and question ministers. The composition of the Council was announced by King Fahd in August 1993, and it was officially inaugurated in December. Each member serves a term of four years. The Council's membership was increased to 90 when its second term began in July 1997; it was increased further, to 120, in May 2001, and to 150 in April 2005. King Fahd issued a decree extending the legislative powers of the Council in November 2003, including the right to propose new legislation.

Chairman: Dr ABDULLAH IBN MUHAMMAD IBN IBRAHIM AL-SHEIKH.
Vice-Chairman: Dr BANDAR IBN MUHAMMAD HAMZAH HAJJAR.
Secretary-General: Dr MUHAMMAD IBN ABDULLAH AL-GHAMDI.

Political Organizations

There are no political organizations in Saudi Arabia.

Diplomatic Representation

EMBASSIES IN SAUDI ARABIA

Afghanistan: POB 93337, Riyadh 11673; tel. (1) 480-3459; fax (1) 480-3451; e-mail afgembriyad@hotmail.com; Ambassador (vacant).

Albania: POB 94004, Riyadh 11693; tel. (1) 470-4217; fax (1) 470-4214; e-mail embassy.riyadh@mfa.gov.al; Ambassador Admirim Banaj.

Algeria: POB 94388, Riyadh 11693; tel. (1) 488-7171; fax (1) 482-1703; Ambassador Dr Habib Adami.

Argentina: POB 94369, Riyadh 11693; tel. (1) 465-2600; fax (1) 465-3057; e-mail earab@nesma.net.sa; Ambassador Jaime Sergio Cerda.

Australia: POB 94400, Riyadh 11693; tel. (1) 488-7788; fax (1) 488-7973; internet www.saudiarabia.embassy.gov.au; Ambassador Kevin Magee.

Austria: POB 94373, Riyadh 11693; tel. (1) 480-1217; fax (1) 480-1526; e-mail riyadh-ob@bmeia.gv.at; internet www.bmeia.gv.at/riyadh; Ambassador Dr Johannes Wimmer.

Azerbaijan: 59 al-Worood Quarter St, off Amir Failsal bin Sa'ud Abd al-Rahman, Aloroba Rd, Riyadh; tel. (1) 419-2382; fax (1) 419-2260; e-mail info@azembriyadh.org; Ambassador Tofiq Abdullayev.

Bahrain: POB 94371, Riyadh 11693; tel. (1) 488-0044; fax (1) 488-0208; e-mail riyadh.mission@mofa.gov.bh; Ambassador Muhammad Saleh al-Sheikh.

Bangladesh: POB 94395, Riyadh 11693; tel. (1) 419-5300; fax (1) 419-3555; e-mail info@bangladeshembassy.org.sa; internet www.bangladeshembassy.org.sa; Ambassador Muhammad Fazlul Karim.

Belgium: POB 94396, Riyadh 11693; tel. (1) 488-2888; fax (1) 488-2033; e-mail riyadh@diplobel.fed.be; internet www.diplomatie.be/riyadh; Ambassador Marc Vinck.

Bosnia and Herzegovina: POB 94301, Riyadh 11693; tel. (1) 456-7914; fax (1) 454-4360; e-mail baembsaruh@awalnet.net.sa; Ambassador Razim Čolić.

Brazil: POB 94348, Riyadh 11693; tel. (1) 488-0018; fax (1) 488-1073; e-mail embaixada@brazemb-ksa.org; internet www.brazemb-ksa.org; Ambassador Sergio Luiz Canaes.

Brunei: POB 94314, al-Warood, Area 29, al-Fujairah St, Riyadh 11693; tel. (1) 456-0814; fax (1) 456-1594; e-mail riyadh.arabsaudi@mfa.gov.bn; Ambassador Pengiran Haji Jabaruddin bin Pengiran Haji Muhammad Salleh.

Burkina Faso: POB 94330, Riyadh 11693; tel. (1) 465-2244; fax (1) 465-3397; e-mail burkinafaso.ksa@arab.net.sa; Ambassador Oumar Diawara.

Cameroon: POB 94336, Riyadh 11693; tel. (1) 488-0022; fax (1) 488-1463; e-mail ambacamriyad@ifrance.com; internet www.ambacamriyad.org.sa; Ambassador Iya Tidjani.

Canada: POB 94321, Riyadh 11693; tel. (1) 488-2288; fax (1) 488-1997; e-mail ryadh@international.gc.ca; internet www.canadainternational.gc.ca/saudi_arabia-arabie_saoudite; Ambassador David Chatterson.

Chad: POB 94374, Riyadh 11693; tel. and fax (1) 465-7702; Ambassador Saqr Yousuf Anto.

China, People's Republic: POB 75231, Riyadh 11578; tel. (1) 483-2126; fax (1) 281-2070; e-mail chinaemb_sa@mfa.gov.cn; internet www.chinaembassy.org.sa; Ambassador Yang Honglin.

Comoros: Riyadh; tel. (1) 293-4697; fax (1) 293-4797; Ambassador Assiandi Abdou Rahmane Amir.

Côte d'Ivoire: POB 94303, Riyadh 11693; tel. (1) 482-5582; fax (1) 482-9629; e-mail acisa@ambaci-riyadh.org; Ambassador Lancina Dosso.

Denmark: POB 94398, Riyadh 11693; tel. (1) 488-0101; fax (1) 488-1366; e-mail ruhamb@um.dk; internet www.ambriyadh.um.dk; Ambassador Christian Kønigsfeldt.

Djibouti: POB 94340, Riyadh 11693; tel. (1) 454-3182; fax (1) 456-9168; e-mail dya_bamakhrama@hotmail.com; Ambassador Dya-Eddine Said Bamakhrama.

Egypt: POB 94333, Riyadh 11693; tel. (1) 481-0464; fax (1) 481-0463; internet www.mfa.gov.eg/Missions/ksa/riyadh/embassy/en-gb/; Ambassador Mahmoud Muhammad Ouf.

Eritrea: POB 94002, Riyadh; tel. (1) 480-1726; fax (1) 482-7537; Ambassador Mohammed Omar Mahmoud.

Ethiopia: POB 94341, Riyadh 11693; tel. (1) 482-3919; fax (1) 483-3281; e-mail ethiopian@awalnet.net.sa; Ambassador Dr Muhammad Kebira.

Finland: POB 94363, Riyadh 11693; tel. (1) 488-1515; fax (1) 488-2520; e-mail sanomat.ria@formin.fi; internet www.finland.org.sa; Ambassador Jarno Syrjälä.

France: POB 94367, Riyadh 11693; tel. (1) 488-1255; fax (1) 488-2882; e-mail diplomatie@ambafrance.org.sa; internet www.ambafrance-sa.org; Ambassador Bertrand Besancenot.

Gabon: POB 94325, Riyadh 11693; tel. (1) 456-7171; fax (1) 453-6121; e-mail ambagabonriyad@yahoo.com; Ambassador Onunja Yubigi.

The Gambia: POB 94322, Riyadh 11693; tel. (1) 205-2158; fax (1) 456-2024; e-mail gamextriyadh@yahoo.com; Ambassador Omar Gibril Sallah.

Germany: POB 94001, Riyadh 11693; tel. (1) 488-0700; fax (1) 488-0660; e-mail info@riad.diplo.de; internet www.riad.diplo.de; Ambassador Volkmar Wenzel.

Ghana: POB 94339, Riyadh 11693; tel. (1) 454-5122; fax (1) 450-9819; e-mail ghanaemb@naseej.com; internet www.ghanaembassyksa.com; Ambassador Alhaji Abdulai Salifu.

Greece: POB 94375, Riyadh 11693; tel. (1) 480-1975; fax (1) 480-1969; e-mail gremb.ria@mfa.gr; Ambassador Dimitrios Letsios.

Guinea: POB 94326, Riyadh 11693; tel. (1) 488-1101; fax (1) 482-6757; e-mail riydambagunee@yahoo.fr; Ambassador el-Hadj Candido Rivas.

Hungary: POB 94014, al-Waha District, Ahmad Tonsy St 23, Riyadh 11693; tel. (1) 454-6707; fax (1) 456-0834; e-mail mission.ryd@kum.hu; e-mail www.mfa.gov.hu/emb/riyadh; Ambassador László Fodor.

India: POB 94387, Riyadh 11693; tel. (1) 488-4144; fax (1) 488-4189; e-mail info@indianembassy.org.sa; internet www.indianembassy.org.sa; Ambassador Talmiz Ahmad.

Indonesia: POB 94343, Riyadh 11693; tel. (1) 488-2800; fax (1) 488-2966; e-mail contact@kbri-riyadh.org.sa; internet www.riyadh.kemlu.go.id; Ambassador Gatot Abdullah Mansyur.

Iran: POB 94394, Riyadh 11693; tel. (1) 488-1916; fax (1) 488-1890; Ambassador Javad Rasouli Mahallati.

Iraq: Riyadh; tel. (1) 480-6514; e-mail rydemt@iraqmfamail.com; Ambassador Dr Ghanim Alwan Jawad al-Jumaili.

Ireland: POB 94349, Riyadh 11693; tel. (1) 488-2300; fax (1) 488-0927; e-mail riyadhembassy@dfa.ie; internet www.embassyofireland.org.sa; Ambassador Dr Niall Holohan.

Italy: POB 94389, Riyadh 11693; tel. (1) 488-1212; fax (1) 480-6964; e-mail segreteria1.riad@esteri.it; internet www.ambriad.esteri.it; Ambassador Dr Valentino Simonetti.

Japan: POB 4095, Riyadh 11491; tel. (1) 488-1100; fax (1) 488-0189; e-mail info@jpn-emb-sa.com; internet www.ksa.emb-japan.go.jp; Ambassador Shigeru Endo.

Jordan: POB 94316, Riyadh 11693; tel. (1) 488-0051; fax (1) 488-0072; e-mail jordan.embassy@nesma.net.sa; Ambassador Qaftan Majali.

Kazakhstan: POB 94012, Riyadh 11693; tel. (1) 470-1839; fax (1) 454-7304; e-mail office@kazembgulf.net; internet www.kazembgulf.net; Ambassador Lama-Sharif.

Kenya: POB 94358, Riyadh 11693; tel. (1) 488-1238; fax (1) 488-2629; e-mail kenya@shaheer.net.sa; Ambassador Mahmoud Ali Saleh.

Korea, Republic: POB 94399, Riyadh 11693; tel. (1) 488-2211; fax (1) 488-1317; e-mail emsau@mofat.go.kr; internet sau.mofat.go.kr/eng/index.jsp; Ambassador Kim Jong-Yong.

Kuwait: POB 94304, Riyadh 11693; tel. (1) 488-3201; fax (1) 488-3682; Ambassador Sheikh Hamad Jaber al-Ali al-Sabah.

Kyrgyzstan: POB 94383, Riyadh 11693; tel. (1) 229-3272; fax (1) 229-3274; e-mail info@kyrgyzembarabia.org; internet www.kyrgyzembarabia.org; Ambassador Yousef Sharif.

Lebanon: POB 94350, Riyadh 11693; tel. (1) 480-4060; fax (1) 480-4703; e-mail embassy@lebanon.org.sa; internet www.lebanon.org.sa; Ambassador Marwan Zein.

Libya: POB 94365, Riyadh 11693; tel. (1) 488-9757; fax (1) 488-3252; e-mail libianembassy@yahoo.com; Ambassador Muhammad Sa'id al-Qashat.

Malaysia: POB 94335, Riyadh 11693; tel. (1) 488-7100; fax (1) 482-4177; e-mail malriyadh@kln.gov.my; internet www.kln.gov.my/perwakilan/riyadh; Ambassador Dato' Syed Omar Muhammad al-Saggaf.

Maldives: 8 Abu El Izzu El Kharasaani Lane, al-Jauf St, al-Sulaimaniya District, Riyadh; tel. (1) 462-6787; fax (1) 464-3725; e-mail adhanu@gmail.com; Ambassador Adam Hassan.

Mali: POB 94331, Riyadh 11693; tel. (1) 464-5640; fax (1) 419-5016; e-mail consulat@sbm.net.sa; Ambassador Muhammad Mahmoud Ben Labat.

Malta: POB 94361, Riyadh 11693; tel. (1) 463-2345; fax (1) 463-3993; e-mail maltaembassy.riyadh@gov.mt; internet www.foreign.gov.mt/saudi_arabia; Ambassador Frank Galea.

SAUDI ARABIA

Mauritania: POB 94354, Riyadh 11693; tel. (1) 464-6749; fax (1) 465-8355; Ambassador MUHAMMAD MAHMOUD OULD ABDULLAH.
Mexico: POB 94391, Riyadh 11693; tel. (1) 480-8822; fax (1) 480-8833; e-mail embasaudita@sre.gob.mx; internet www.embamex.org.sa; Ambassador ARTURO TREJO.
Morocco: POB 94392, Riyadh 11693; tel. (1) 481-1858; fax (1) 482-7016; e-mail ambassaderiyad@maec.gov.ma; Ambassador EL-MUSTAPHA BELHAJ.
Myanmar: Villa No 5, al-Kadi St, King Fahd Area, Riyadh; tel. (1) 229-3306; e-mail meriyadh@gmail.com; Ambassador KHIN ZAW WIN.
Nepal: POB 94384, Riyadh 11693; tel. (1) 461-1108; fax (1) 464-0690; e-mail info@neksa.org; internet www.neksa.org; Chargé d'affaires a.i. PARAS GHIMIRE.
Netherlands: POB 94307, Riyadh 11693; tel. (1) 488-0011; fax (1) 488-0544; e-mail riy@minbuza.nl; internet www.mfa.nl/riy-en; Ambassador RONALD G. STRIKKER.
New Zealand: POB 94397, Riyadh 11693; tel. (1) 488-7988; fax (1) 488-7911; e-mail info@nzembassy.org.sa; internet www.nzembassy.com/saudiarabia; Ambassador ROD HARRIS.
Niger: POB 94334, Riyadh 11693; tel. and fax (1) 470-8698; e-mail ambassadeduniger_riyadh@yahoo.com; Ambassador HASSANE MOULAYE.
Nigeria: POB 94386, Riyadh 11693; tel. (1) 482-3024; fax (1) 482-4134; e-mail nigeria@nigeriariyadh.com; internet www.nigeria.org.sa; Ambassador ALHAJI A. GARBA AMINCI.
Norway: POB 94380, Riyadh 11693; tel. (1) 488-1904; fax (1) 488-0854; e-mail emb.riyadh@mfa.no; internet www.al-norwige.org.sa; Ambassador CARL SCHIÖTZ WIBYE.
Oman: POB 94381, Riyadh 11693; tel. (1) 482-3120; fax (1) 482-3738; e-mail riyadh@mofa.gov.om; Ambassador Dr SAEED AHMAD BIN HILAL BIN SAUD AL-BUSAIDI.
Pakistan: POB 94007, Riyadh 11693; tel. (1) 488-4111; fax (1) 488-7953; e-mail parep_riyadh@yahoo.com; Ambassador UMAR KHAN ALI SHERZAI.
Philippines: POB 94366, Riyadh 11693; tel. (1) 482-0507; fax (1) 488-3945; e-mail filembry@sbm.net.sa; Chargé d'affaires a.i. EZZEDIN H. TAGO.
Poland: POB 94016, Riyadh 11693; tel. (1) 454-9274; fax (1) 454-9089; e-mail riyadh@msz.gov.pl; internet www.rijad.polemb.net; Ambassador WITOLD SMIDOWSKI.
Portugal: POB 94328, Riyadh 11693; tel. (1) 482-9042; fax (1) 482-6981; e-mail portriade@nesma.net.sa; Ambassador (vacant).
Qatar: POB 94353, Riyadh 11461; tel. (1) 482-5544; fax (1) 482-5394; e-mail riyadh@mofa.gov.qa; Ambassador ALI ABDULLAH AL-MAHMOUD.
Romania: POB 94319, Riyadh 11693; tel. (1) 263-0456; fax (1) 456-9985; e-mail office@embrom.org.sa; Ambassador ION DOBRECI.
Russia: POB 94308, Riyadh 11693; e-mail springmail@arab.net.sa; tel. (1) 481-1875; fax (1) 481-1890; Ambassador OLEG OZEROV.
Rwanda: POB 94383, Riyadh 11693; tel. (1) 454-0808; fax (1) 456-1769; Ambassador SIMON INSONERE.
Senegal: POB 94352, Riyadh 11693; tel. (1) 488-0146; fax (1) 488-3804; Ambassador MOUHAMADOU DOUDOU LO.
Sierra Leone: POB 94329, Riyadh 11693; tel. (1) 465-6204; fax (1) 464-3662; e-mail slembrdh@zajil.net; Ambassador Alhaji WUSU MUNU.
Singapore: POB 94378, Riyadh 11693; tel. (1) 480-3855; fax (1) 483-0632; e-mail singemb_ruh@sgmfa.gov.sg; internet www.mfa.gov.sg/riyadh; Ambassador WONG KWOK PUN.
Somalia: POB 94372, Riyadh 11693; tel. (1) 464-3456; fax (1) 464-9705.
South Africa: POB 94006, Riyadh 11693; tel. (1) 442-9716; fax (1) 442-9708; e-mail riyadh.info@foreign.gov.za; Ambassador JOHN A. DAVIES.
Spain: POB 94347, Riyadh 11693; tel. (1) 488-0606; fax (1) 488-0420; e-mail embespas@nesma.net.sa; Ambassador DON PABLO BRAVO LOZANO.
Sri Lanka: POB 94360, Riyadh 11693; tel. (1) 460-8689; fax (1) 460-8846; e-mail contact@lankaemb-riyadh.org; internet www.lankaemb-riyadh.org; Ambassador AHMED A. JAWAD.
Sudan: POB 94337, Riyadh 11693; tel. (1) 488-7979; fax (1) 488-7729; Ambassador ABD AL-HAFEZ IBRAHIM MUHAMMAD.
Sweden: POB 94382, Riyadh 11693; tel. (1) 488-3100; fax (1) 488-0604; e-mail ambassaden.riyadh@foreign.ministry.se; internet www.swedenabroad.se/riyadh; Ambassador JAN THESLEFF.
Switzerland: POB 94311, Riyadh 11693; tel. (1) 488-1291; fax (1) 488-0632; e-mail rya.vertretung@eda.admin.ch; internet www.eda.admin.ch/riad; Ambassador PETER REINHARDT.
Syria: POB 94323, Riyadh 11693; tel. (1) 482-6191; fax (1) 482-6196; Ambassador MAHDI DAKHLALLAH.
Tanzania: POB 94320, Riyadh 11693; tel. (1) 454-2839; fax (1) 454-9660; e-mail tzriyad@deltasa.com; Ambassador KHALID AMIR MOSWAMI.
Thailand: POB 94359, Riyadh 11693; tel. (1) 488-1174; fax (1) 488-1179; e-mail thaiemryadsl@awalnet.net.sa; internet riyadh.thaiembassy.org; Chargé d'affaires a.i. CHARN JULLAMON.
Tunisia: POB 94368, Riyadh 11693; tel. (1) 488-7900; fax (1) 488-7641; e-mail amb.tunisie@saudi.net.sa; Ambassador NAJIB AL-MUNIF.
Turkey: POB 94390, Riyadh 11693; tel. (1) 482-0101; fax (1) 488-7823; e-mail vtn.riyad.be@mfa.gov.tr; internet riyadh.emb.mfa.gov.tr; Ambassador AHMET MUHTAR GÜN.
Turkmenistan: POB 94019, Riyadh 11693; tel. (1) 205-4898; fax (1) 205-2990; e-mail info@turkmenemb-sa.org; internet www.turkmenemb-sa.org; Ambassador MUKHAMED ABALAKOV.
Uganda: POB 94344, Riyadh 11693; tel. (1) 454-4910; fax (1) 454-9264; e-mail ugariyadh@hotmail.com; Ambassador AZIZ KALUNGI KASUJJA.
Ukraine: 6 Hassan al-Badr St, Salah al-Din, Riyadh; tel. (1) 450-8536; fax (1) 450-8534; e-mail emb_sa@mfa.gov.ua; internet www.mfa.gov.ua/saudiarabia; f. 1996; Ambassador PETRO KOLOS.
United Arab Emirates: POB 94385, Riyadh 11693; tel. (1) 488-1227; fax (1) 482-7504; e-mail uaer@cyberia.net.sa; Ambassador MUHAMMAD SAEED MUHAMMAD AL-DHAHIRI.
United Kingdom: POB 94351, Riyadh 11693; tel. (1) 488-0077; fax (1) 488-1209; e-mail PressOffice.Riyadh@fco.gov.uk; internet ukinsaudiarabia.fco.gov.uk; Ambassador TOM PHILLIPS.
USA: POB 94309, Riyadh 11693; tel. (1) 488-3800; fax (1) 488-7360; e-mail usembriyadhwebsite@state.gov; internet riyadh.usembassy.gov; Ambassador JAMES B. SMITH.
Uruguay: POB 94346, Riyadh 11693; tel. (1) 462-0739; fax (1) 462-0648; e-mail ururia@nesma.net.sa; Ambassador RODOLFO INVERNIZZI ARENA.
Uzbekistan: POB 94008, Riyadh 11693; tel. (1) 263-5223; fax (1) 263-5105; Ambassador ALISHER QADIROV.
Venezuela: POB 94364, Riyadh 11693; tel. (1) 480-7141; fax (1) 480-0901; e-mail embvenar@embvenar.org.sa; Ambassador JOSEBA ACHUTEGUI.
Yemen: POB 94356, Riyadh 11693; tel. (1) 488-1769; fax (1) 488-1562; Ambassador MUHAMMAD ALI MOHSEN AL-AHWAL.

Judicial System

Judges are independent and governed by the rules of Islamic *Shari'a*. A new Judicial Law approved in May 2007 provided for a number of significant changes to the courts system. The new legislation called for the establishment of appeal courts, criminal courts and specialized courts. A Supreme Court was to be established in Riyadh, and new appeals courts were planned for each of the kingdom's 13 regions. There were to be general courts to deal with all conflicts except labour, commercial and family disputes, and criminal courts to address crimes. Family and personal conflicts were to be handled by civil courts. However, by early 2011 few of these proposed amendments had yet to be implemented and the following courts remained in operation:

Supreme Judicial Council: comprises 11 mems; supervises work of the courts; reviews legal questions referred to it by the Minister of Justice and expresses opinions on judicial questions; reviews sentences of death, cutting and stoning; Chair. Dr SALIH IBN HUMAYD.

Court of Cassation: consists of Chief Justice and an adequate number of judges; includes department for penal suits, department for personal status and department for other suits.

General (Public) Courts: consist of one or more judges; sentences are issued by a single judge, with the exception of death, stoning and cutting, which require the decision of three judges.

Summary Courts: consist of one or more judges; sentences are issued by a single judge.

Specialized Courts: the setting up of specialized courts is permissible by Royal Decree on a proposal from the Supreme Council of Justice.

Religion

ISLAM

Arabia is the centre of the Islamic faith, and Saudi Arabia includes the holy cities of Mecca and Medina. Except in the Eastern Province, where a large number of people follow Shi'a rites, the majority of the population are Sunni Muslims, and most of the indigenous inhabitants belong to the strictly orthodox Wahhabi sect. The Wahhabis originated in the 18th century, but first became unified and influential under Abd al-Aziz (Ibn Sa'ud), who became the first King of Saudi Arabia. They are now the keepers of the holy places and control the pilgrimage to Mecca. In 1986 King Fahd adopted the title of Custodian of the Two Holy Mosques; the title passed to King Abdullah upon his accession to the throne in August 2005. The country's most senior Islamic authority is the Council of Senior Ulama.

Mecca: Birthplace of the Prophet Muhammad, seat of the Grand Mosque and Shrine of Ka'ba, visited by 1,613,965 Muslims from abroad in the Islamic year 1430 (2008/09).

Medina: Burial place of Muhammad, second sacred city of Islam.

Grand Mufti and Chairman of Council of Senior Ulama: Sheikh ABD AL-AZIZ IBN ABDULLAH AL-SHEIKH.

CHRISTIANITY

The Roman Catholic Church

A small number of adherents, mainly expatriates, form part of the Apostolic Vicariate of Northern Arabia. The Vicar Apostolic is resident in Kuwait.

The Anglican Communion

Within the Episcopal Church in Jerusalem and the Middle East, Saudi Arabia forms part of the diocese of Cyprus and the Gulf. The Anglican congregations in the country are entirely expatriate. The Bishop in Cyprus and the Gulf is resident in Cyprus, while the Archdeacon in the Gulf is resident in Bahrain.

Other Denominations

The Greek Orthodox Church is also represented.

The Press

Since 1964 most newspapers and periodicals have been published by press organizations, administered by boards of directors with full autonomous powers, in accordance with the provisions of the Press Law. These organizations, which took over from small private firms, are privately owned by groups of individuals experienced in newspaper publishing and administration (see Publishers).

There are also a number of popular periodicals published by the Government and by the Saudi Arabian Oil Co, and distributed free of charge. The press is subject to no legal restriction affecting freedom of expression or the coverage of news.

DAILIES

Arab News: POB 10452, SRP Bldg, Madinah Rd, Jeddah 21433; tel. (2) 639-1888; fax (2) 639-3223; e-mail arabnews@arabnews.com; internet www.arabnews.com; f. 1975; English; publ. by Saudi Research and Publishing Co; Editor-in-Chief KHALED AL-MAEENA; circ. 110,000.

Al-Bilad (The Country): POB 6340, Jeddah 21442; tel. (2) 672-3000; fax (2) 671-2545; internet www.albilad-daily.com; f. 1934; Arabic; publ. by Al-Bilad Publishing Org; Editor-in-Chief QUINAN AL-GHOMDI; circ. 66,210.

Al-Eqtisadiah: POB 10452, Jeddah 21433; tel. (2) 651-1333; fax (2) 667-6212; internet www.aleqt.com; f. 1992; business and finance; publ. by Saudi Research and Publishing Co; Editor-in-Chief ABD AL-WAHAB FAYEZ; circ. 81,000.

Al-Jazirah (The Peninsula): POB 354, Riyadh 11411; tel. (1) 487-0911; fax (1) 487-1063; e-mail ccs@al-jazirah.com.sa; internet www.al-jazirah.com; f. 1972; Arabic; publ. by Al-Jazirah Corpn for Press, Printing and Publishing; Dir-Gen. ABD AL-LATIF BIN SAAD; Editor-in-Chief KHALID BIN HAMAD AL-MALIK; circ. 110,000.

Al-Madina al-Munawara (Medina—The Enlightened City): POB 807, Makkah Rd, Jeddah 21421; tel. (2) 671-2100; fax (2) 671-1877; e-mail webmaster@al-madina.com; internet al-madina.com; f. 1937; Arabic; publ. by Al-Madina Press Establishment; Chief Editor FAHD HASSAN AL-AQRAN; circ. 46,370.

Al-Nadwah (The Council): POB 5803, Jarwal Sheikh Sayed Halabi Bldg, Mecca; tel. (2) 520-0111; fax (2) 520-3055; e-mail info@al-nadwah.com; internet www.alnadwah.com.sa; f. 1958; Arabic; publ. by Makkah Printing and Information Establishment; Editor AHMAD BIN SALEH BAYUSUF; circ. 35,000.

Okaz: POB 1508, Seaport Rd, Jeddah 21441; tel. (2) 672-7621; fax (2) 672-4297; e-mail 104127.266@compuserve.com; internet www.okaz.com.sa; f. 1948; Arabic; publ. by Okaz Org. for Press and Publication; Editor-in-Chief MUHAMMAD AL-TUNISI; circ. 110,000.

Al-Riyadh: POB 2943, Riyadh 11476; tel. (1) 487-1000; fax (1) 441-7417; internet www.alriyadh.com; f. 1965; Arabic; publ. by Al-Yamama Press Establishment; Editor TURKI A. AL-SUDARI; circ. 150,000 (Sat.–Thur.), 90,000 (Fri.).

Saudi Gazette: POB 5576, Jeddah 21432; tel. (2) 676-0000; fax (2) 672-7621; e-mail news@saudigazette.com.sa; internet www.saudigazette.com.sa; f. 1976; English; publ. by Okaz Org. for Press and Publication; Editor-in-Chief MUHAMMAD NASIR SHOUKANI; circ. 15,000.

Al-Watan: POB 15156, Airport Road, Abha; tel. (7) 227-3333; fax (7) 227-3756; e-mail editor@alwatan.com.sa; internet www.alwatan.com.sa; f. 1998; publ. by Assir Establishment for Press and Publishing; Dir-Gen. HATEM HAMID; circ. 150,000.

Al-Yaum (Today): POB 565, Dammam 31421; tel. (3) 858-0800; fax (3) 858-8777; e-mail mail@alyaum.com; internet www.alyaum.com; f. 1965; publ. by Dar al-Yaum Press, Printing and Publishing Ltd; Dir-Gen. SALEH ALI HAMID; Editor-in-Chief MUHAMMAD ABDULLAH AL-WAEEL; circ. 40,000.

WEEKLIES

Al-Muslimoon (The Muslims): POB 13195, Jeddah 21493; tel. (2) 669-1888; fax (2) 669-5549; f. 1985; Arabic; cultural and religious affairs; publ. by Saudi Research and Publishing Co; Editor-in-Chief Dr ABDULLAH AL-RIFA'E; circ. 68,665.

Saudi Economic Survey: POB 1989, Jeddah 21441; tel. (2) 657-8551; fax (2) 657-8553; e-mail info@saudieconomicsurvey.com; internet www.saudieconomicsurvey.com; f. 1967; English; review of Saudi Arabian economic and business activity; Publr SAIFUDDIN A. ASHOOR; Gen. Man. WALID S. ASHOOR.

Sayidaty (My Lady): POB 4556, Madina Rd, Jeddah 21412; tel. (2) 639-1888; fax (2) 669-5549; internet www.sayidaty.net; f. 1981; publ. in Arabic and English edns; women's magazine; publ. by Saudi Research and Publishing Co; Editor-in-Chief MUHAMMAD FAHAD AL-HARTHI.

Al-Shams (The Sun): Riyadh; internet shms.pressera.com; f. 2005; tabloid format; sports, culture, entertainment; publishing licence revoked by the Govt in Feb. 2006, but restored after some six weeks; Editor-in-Chief KHALAF AL-HARBI.

Al-Yamama: POB 851, Riyadh 11421; tel. (1) 442-0000; fax (1) 441-7114; f. 1952; literary magazine; Editor-in-Chief ABDULLAH AL-JAHLAN; circ. 35,000.

OTHER PERIODICALS

Ahlan Wasahlan (Welcome): POB 8013, Jeddah 21482; tel. (2) 686-2349; fax (2) 686-2006; internet pr.sv.net/aw; monthly; flight journal of Saudi Arabian Airlines; Gen. Man. and Editor-in-Chief YARUB A. BALKHAIR; circ. 150,000.

Al-Daragh: POB 2945, Riyadh 11461; tel. (1) 401-1999; fax (1) 401-3597; e-mail info@aldarahmagazine.com; internet aldarahmagazine.com; history journal; publ. by King Abd al-Aziz Foundation for Research and Archives.

Al-Faysal: POB 3, Riyadh 11411; tel. (1) 465-3027; fax (1) 464-7851; monthly; f. 1976; Arabic; culture, education, health, interviews; Man. Editor ABDULLAH Y. AL-KOWAILEET.

Majallat al-Iqtisad wal-Idara (Journal of Economics and Administration): King Abd al-Aziz University, POB 9031, Jeddah 21413; twice a year; Chief Editor Prof. ABD AL-AZIZ A. DIYAB.

Al-Manhal (The Spring): POB 2925, Jeddah; tel. (2) 643-2124; fax (2) 642-8853; e-mail info@manhalmagazine.com; f. 1937; monthly; Arabic; cultural, literary, political and scientific; Editor ZUHAIR N. AL-ANSARI.

The MWL Journal: Press and Publications Department, Rabitat al-Alam al-Islami, POB 537, Mecca; fax (2) 544-1622; e-mail info@themwl.org; internet www.themwl.org; monthly; English; Dir MURAD SULAIMAN IRQISOUS.

Al-Rabita: POB 537, Mecca; tel. (2) 560-0919; fax (2) 543-1488; e-mail info@themwl.org; internet www.themwl.org; Arabic; Chief Editor Dr OSMAN ABUZAID.

Saudi Review: POB 4288, Jeddah 21491; tel. (2) 651-7442; fax (2) 653-0693; f. 1966; English; monthly; newsletter from Saudi newspapers and broadcasting service; publ. by Int. Communications Co; Chief Editor SAAD AL-MABROUK; circ. 5,000.

Al-Sharkiah-Elle (Oriental Elle): POB 6, Riyadh; monthly; Arabic; women's magazine; Editor SAMIRA M. KHASHAGGI.

Al-Soqoor (Falcons): POB 2973, Riyadh 11461; tel. (1) 476-6566; f. 1978; 2 a year; air force journal; cultural activities; Editor HAMAD A. AL-SALEH.

Al-Tadhamon al-Islami (Islamic Solidarity): Ministry of Pilgrimage (Hajj) Affairs, Omar bin al-Khatab St, Riyadh 11183; monthly; Editor Dr MUSTAFA ABD AL-WAHID.

SAUDI ARABIA

Al-Tijarah (Commerce): POB 1264, Jeddah 21431; tel. (2) 651-5111; fax (2) 651-7373; e-mail jcci@mail.gcc.com.bh; f. 1960; monthly; publ. by Jeddah Chamber of Commerce and Industry; Chair. Sheikh Ismail Abu Daud; circ. 8,000.

NEWS AGENCIES

International Islamic News Agency (IINA): POB 5054, Jeddah 21422; tel. (2) 665-2056; fax (2) 665-9358; e-mail iina@islamicnews.org.sa; internet www.islamicnews.org.sa; f. 1972; operates under the auspices of the Org. of the Islamic Conference; Dir-Gen. Abd al-Wahab Kashif.

Saudi Press Agency (SPA): POB 7186, King Fahd Rd, Riyadh 11171; tel. (1) 419-5485; fax (1) 419-5685; e-mail wass@spa.gov.sa; internet www.spa.gov.sa; f. 1970; the Govt planned to transform the SPA into a public corpn; Dir-Gen. Abdullah bin Fahd al-Hussain.

Publishers

Assir Establishment for Press and Publishing: POB 15156, Abha; tel. (7) 227-3333; fax (7) 227-3590; f. 1998; publishes *Al-Watan*; cap. SR 200m.; Chair. Fahd al-Harithi.

Al-Bilad Publishing Organization: POB 6340, al-Sahafa St, Jeddah 21442; tel. (2) 672-3000; fax (2) 671-2545; publishes *Al-Bilad* and *Iqra'a*; Dir-Gen. Amin Abdullah al-Qarqouri.

Dar al-Maiman Publishers and Distributors: POB 90020, Riyadh 11613; tel. and fax (1) 4880806.

Dar al-Shareff for Publishing and Distribution: POB 58287, Riyadh 11594; tel. (1) 403-4931; fax (1) 405-2234; f. 1992; fiction, religion, science and social sciences; Pres. Ibrahim al-Hazemi.

Dar al-Yaum Press, Printing and Publishing Ltd: POB 565, Dammam 31421; tel. (3) 858-0800; fax (3) 858-8777; e-mail mail@alyaum.com; internet www.alyaum.com; f. 1964; publishes *Al-Yaum*; Chair. Abd al-Aziz Muhammad al-Hugail; Gen. Man. Salih Ali al-Humaidan.

International Publications Agency (IPA): POB 70, Dhahran 31942; tel. and fax (3) 895-4925; publishes material of local interest; Man. Said Salah.

Al-Jazirah Corpn for Press, Printing and Publishing: POB 354, Riyadh 11411; tel. (1) 441-9999; fax (1) 441-2536; e-mail ccs@al-jazirah.com; internet www.al-jazirah.com.sa; f. 1964; 42 mems; publishes *Al-Jazirah* daily newspaper; Chair. Mutlaq bin Abdullah al-Mutlaq; Editor-in-Chief Khalid el-Malek.

Al-Madina Press Establishment: POB 807, Jeddah 21421; tel. (2) 671-2100; fax (2) 671-1877; f. 1937; publishes *Al-Madina al-Munawara*; Gen. Man. Ahmad Salah Jamjoum.

Makkah Printing and Information Establishment: POB 5803, Jarwal Sheikh Sayed Halabi Bldg, Mecca; tel. (2) 542-7868; publishes *Al-Nadwah* daily newspaper; Chair. Muhammad Abdou Yamani.

Okaz Organization for Press and Publication: POB 1508, Jeddah 21441; tel. (2) 672-2630; fax (2) 672-8150; publishes *Okaz* and *Saudi Gazette*; Chair. Saeed al-Harthi.

Al-Rushd Publishers: POB 17522, Riyadh 11494; tel. (1) 459-3451; fax (1) 457-3381; e-mail alrushd@alrushdryh.com; internet www.rushd.com.sa; scientific and academic publs.

Saudi Publishing and Distributing House: Umm Aslam District, nr Muslaq, POB 2043, Jeddah 21451; tel. (2) 629-4278; fax (2) 629-4290; e-mail info@spdh-sa.com; internet www.spdh-sa.com; f. 1966; publishers, importers and distributors of English and Arabic books; Chair. Muhammad Salahuddin.

Saudi Research and Publishing Co: POB 478, Riyadh 11411; tel. (1) 441-9933; fax (1) 442-9555; internet www.srpc.com; publs include *Arab News*, *Asharq al-Awsat*, *Al-Majalla*, *Al-Muslimoon* and *Sayidati*; Chair. Prince Faisal bin Salman bin Abd al-Aziz; Gen. Man. Azzam al-Dakhil.

Al-Yamama Press Establishment: POB 2943, Riyadh 11476; tel. (1) 442-0000; fax (1) 441-7116; publishes *Al-Riyadh* and *Al-Yamama*; Dir-Gen. Sakhal Maidan.

Broadcasting and Communications

TELECOMMUNICATIONS

Regulatory Authority

Communications and Information Technology Commission (CITC): POB 75606, Riyadh; tel. (1) 461-8000; fax (1) 461-8002; internet www.citc.gov.sa; f. 2001 under the name Saudi Communications Comm.; present name adopted 2003; independent regulatory authority; Gov. Abd al-Rahman bin Ahmad al-Jaafari.

Principal Operators

Ettihad Etisalat: POB 9979, Riyadh 11423; tel. (1) 211-8015; fax (1) 211-8029; e-mail info@mobily.com.sa; internet www.mobily.com.sa; f. 2004; owned by consortium led by Emirates Telecommunications Corpn (United Arab Emirates); awarded the second licence to provide mobile telephone services in 2004; operates under the brand name *Mobily* (launched 2005); 14.8m. subscribers (Dec. 2008); Chair. Abd al-Aziz bin Saleh al-Sughayir; CEO Khalid al-Kaf.

Saudi Telecommunications Co—Saudi Telecom (STC): POB 87912, Riyadh 11652; tel. (1) 215-3030; fax (1) 215-2734; e-mail contactus@stc.com.sa; internet www.stc.com.sa; f. 1998; partially privatized in 2002; provides telecommunications services in Saudi Arabia; cap. SR 12,000m.; Chair. Dr Muhammad bin Suliman al-Jaser; Pres. Eng. Sa'ud bin Majid al-Daweesh.

Zain Saudi Arabia: POB 295814, Riyadh 11351; tel. (1) 216-1800; e-mail corporate.communications@sa.zain.com; internet www.sa.zain.com; f. 2007; wholly owned by Mobile Telecommunications Co KSC (Zain Kuwait); awarded the third licence to provide mobile telephone services in 2007; Chair. Prince Hussam ibn Sa'ud ibn Abd al-Aziz Al Sa'ud; CEO Saad al-Barrak.

In February 2008 three further fixed-line licences were awarded to Etihad Atheeb Telecom, Al-Mutakamilah Consortium and Optical Communications Co.

BROADCASTING

Radio

Saudi Arabian Broadcasting Service: c/o Ministry of Information and Culture, POB 60059, Riyadh 11545; tel. (1) 401-4440; fax (1) 403-8177; e-mail saudi-radio@saudiradio.net.sa; internet www.saudiradio.net; 24 medium- and short-wave stations, incl. Jeddah, Riyadh, Dammam and Abha, broadcast programmes in Arabic and English; 23 FM stations; overseas service in Bengali, English, Farsi, French, Hausa, Indonesian, Somali, Swahili, Turkestani, Turkish and Urdu; Dir-Gen. Muhammad al-Mansoor.

Saudi Aramco FM Radio: Bldg 3030 LIP, Dhahran 31311; tel. (3) 876-1845; fax (3) 876-1608; f. 1948; English; private; for employees of Saudi Aramco; Man. Essam Z. Tawfiq.

Television

Saudi Arabian Government Television Service: POB 7971, Riyadh 11472; tel. (1) 401-4440; fax (1) 404-4192; e-mail satepjeng@moci.gov.sa; began transmission 1965; 112 stations, incl. six main stations at Riyadh, Jeddah, Medina, Dammam, Qassim and Abha, transmit programmes in Arabic and English; operates four channels: Channel 1 (Arabic); Channel 2 (English and French); Channel 3 (sport); Al-Ekhbariya (news); Dir-Gen. Abd al-Aziz al-Hassan (Channel 1).

Finance

(cap. = capital; res = reserves; dep. = deposits; m. = million; br(s) = branch(es); amounts in Saudi riyals unless otherwise stated)

BANKING

Central Bank

Saudi Arabian Monetary Agency (SAMA): POB 2992, Riyadh 11169; tel. (1) 463-3000; fax (1) 466-2966; e-mail info@sama.gov.sa; internet www.sama.gov.sa; f. 1952; functions include stabilization of currency, administration of monetary reserves, regulation of banking and insurance sectors, and issue of notes and coins; dep. 962,808m., total assets 1,393,080m. (June 2009); Gov. Dr Muhammad ibn Sulayman al-Jasser; 10 brs.

National Banks

Alinma Bank: POB 66674, al-Anoud Tower, King Fahad Rd, Riyadh 11586; e-mail info@alinma.com; internet www.alinma.com; f. 2006; cap. 15,000m., res 151m., dep. 1,501m. (Dec. 2009); Chair. Abd al-Aziz Abdullah al-Zamil; 15 brs.

National Commercial Bank (NCB): POB 3555, King Abd al-Aziz St, Jeddah 21481; tel. (2) 649-3333; fax (2) 644-6468; e-mail contact@alahli.com; internet www.alahli.com; f. 1950; 69.3% govt-owned; cap. 15,000m., res 11,209m., dep. 220,781m. (Dec. 2009); Chair. Sheikh Abdullah Salim Bahamdan; 258 domestic brs, 2 abroad.

Al-Rajhi Banking and Investment Corpn (Al-Rajhi Bank): POB 28, al-Akariya Bldg, Oleya St, Riyadh 11411; tel. (1) 211-6000; fax (1) 460-0922; e-mail contactus@alrajhibank.com.sa; internet www.alrajhibank.com.sa; f. 1988; operates according to Islamic financial principles; cap. 15,000.0m., res 12,996.6m., dep. 128,963.9m. (Dec. 2009); Chair. Sheikh Sulayman bin Abd al-Aziz al-Rajhi; CEO and Man. Dir Abdullah Sulaiman al-Rajhi; 700 brs.

SAUDI ARABIA

Directory

Riyad Bank Ltd: POB 22601, King Abd al-Aziz St, Riyadh 11416; tel. (1) 401-3030; fax (1) 404-1255; internet www.riyadbank.com.sa; f. 1957; cap. 15,000m., res 12,722m., dep. 143,314m. (Dec. 2009); Chair. RASHED A. AL-RASHED; Pres. and CEO TALAL I. AL-QUDAIBI; 201 domestic brs, 1 abroad.

Specialist Bank

Arab Investment Co SAA (TAIC): POB 4009, King Abd al-Aziz St, Riyadh 11491; tel. (1) 476-0601; fax (1) 476-0514; e-mail taic@taic.com; internet www.taic.com; f. 1974 by 17 Arab countries for investment and banking; cap. US $600m., res $150m., dep. $1,687m. (Dec. 2009); Chair. YOUSUF IBN IBRAHIM AL-BASSAM; Chief Exec. Dr SALIH AL-HUMAIDAN; 1 br.

Banks with Foreign Interests

Arab National Bank (ANB): POB 56921, King Faisal St, North Murabba, Riyadh 11564; tel. (1) 402-9000; fax (1) 402-7747; e-mail info@anb.com.sa; internet www.anb.com.sa; f. 1980; Arab Bank PLC, Jordan, 40%, Saudi shareholders 60%; cap. 6,500m., res 5,603m., dep. 93,081m. (Dec. 2009); Chair. ABD AL-LATIF HAMAD AL-JABR; Man. Dir Dr ROBERT EID; 117 domestic brs, 1 abroad.

Bank al-Jazira: POB 6277, Khalid bin al-Waleed St, Jeddah 21442; tel. (2) 651-8070; fax (2) 653-2478; e-mail info@baj.com.sa; internet www.baj.com.sa; 94.17% Saudi-owned; cap. 3,000m., res 1,458m., dep. 24,833m. (Dec. 2009); Chair. TAHA ABDULLAH AL-KUWAIZ; 23 brs.

Banque Saudi Fransi (Saudi French Bank): POB 56006, Ma'ather Rd, Riyadh 11554; tel. (1) 404-2222; fax (1) 289-9999; e-mail communications@alfransi.com.sa; internet www.alfransi.com.sa; f. 1977; present name adopted 2002; Saudi shareholders 68.9%, Calyon, Paris La Défense 31.1%; cap. 7,232m., res 7,631m., dep. 96,068m. (Dec. 2009); Chair. Dr SALEH A. AL-OMAIR; Man. Dir JEAN MARION; 79 brs.

SAMBA Financial Group: POB 833, Riyadh 11421; tel. and fax (1) 477-4770; e-mail sambacare@samba.com; internet www.samba.com.sa; f. 1980; merged with United Saudi Bank in 1999; 96.4% owned by Saudi nationals; cap. 9,000m., res 7,096m., dep. 156,321m. (Dec. 2009); Chair. EISA AL-EISA; 66 domestic brs, 2 abroad.

Saudi British Bank (SABB): POB 9084, Prince Abd al-Aziz bin Mossaid bin Jalawi St, Riyadh 11413; tel. (1) 405-0677; fax (1) 405-0660; e-mail sabb@sabb.com; internet www.sabb.com.sa; f. 1978; 60% owned by Saudi nationals, 40% by HSBC Holdings BV; cap. 7,500.0m., res 4,850.5m., dep. 108,689.5m. (Dec. 2009); Chair. KHALED SULIMAN OLAYAN; Man. Dir DAVID DEW; 78 domestic brs, 1 abroad.

Saudi Hollandi Bank (Saudi Dutch Bank): POB 1467, Head Office Bldg, al-Dhabab St, Riyadh 11431; tel. (1) 406-7888; fax (1) 403-1104; e-mail csc@shb.com.sa; internet www.shb.com.sa; f. 1977 to assume activities of Algemene Bank Nederland NV in Saudi Arabia; jt stock co; ABN AMRO Bank (Netherlands) 40%, Saudi citizens 60%; cap. 3,307m., res 2,097m., dep. 50,583m. (Dec. 2009); Chair. Sheikh MUBARAK ABDULLAH AL-KHAFRAH; Man. Dir BERND VAN LINDER; 40 brs.

Saudi Investment Bank (SAIB): POB 3533, Riyadh 11481; tel. (1) 478-6000; fax (1) 477-6781; e-mail info@saib.com.sa; internet www.saib.com.sa; f. 1976; provides a comprehensive range of traditional and specialized banking services; cap. 4,500m., res 2,088m., dep. 41,459m. (Dec. 2009); Chair. Dr ABD AL-AZIZ O'HALI; Gen. Man. MUSAED AL-MINEEFI; 30 brs.

Government Specialized Credit Institutions

Real Estate Development Fund (REDF): POB 5591, Riyadh 11139; tel. (1) 479-2222; fax (1) 479-0148; f. 1974; provides interest-free loans to Saudi individuals and cos for private or commercial housing projects; loans granted amounted to 5,264m. in 2002; Chair. Dr IBRAHIM IBN ABD AL-AZIZ AL-ASSAF (Minister of Finance); Dir Gen. HASAN AL-ATTAS (acting); 24 brs.

Saudi Arabian Agricultural Bank (SAAB): POB 1811, Riyadh 11126; tel. (1) 402-3911; fax (1) 402-2359; f. 1963; provides loans to farmers for industry-specific use; loans disbursed amounted to 1,320.0m. in 2002; Controller-Gen. ABDULLAH SAAD AL-MENGASH; Gen. Man. ABD AL-AZIZ MUHAMMAD AL-MANQUR; 70 brs.

Saudi Credit Bank: POB 3401, Riyadh 11471; tel. (1) 402-9128; f. 1973; provides interest-free loans for specific purposes to Saudi citizens of moderate means; loans disbursed amounted to 348.0m. in 2002; Man. IBRAHIM AL-HINAISHIL; 25 brs.

STOCK EXCHANGE

The Electronic Securities Information System (ESIS) was formed in 1990 and operated by the Saudi Arabian Monetary Agency (see Central Bank). The ESIS was superseded by a new market system, Tadawul, in 2001. Since 2003 Tadawul has been supervised by the Capital Market Authority. A total of 57,269m. shares were traded in 2009, amounting to SR 1,262,148.8m.

Saudi Stock Exchange (Tadawul): NCCI Bldg, North Tower, King Fahd Rd, POB 60612, Riyadh 11555; tel. (1) 218-9999; e-mail webinfo@tadawul.com.sa; internet www.tadawul.com.sa; f. 2001; restructured as a jt stock co in 2007; 134 listed cos in 2009; Chair. TAHA A. AL-KUWAIZ.

Regulatory Authority

Capital Market Authority: Faisaliah Tower, King Fahd Rd, POB 220022, Riyadh 11311; fax (1) 279-7770; e-mail info@cma.org.sa; internet www.cma.org.sa; f. 2003 to regulate and develop the Saudi Arabian capital market; Chair. Dr ABD AL-RAHMAN A. AL-TUWAIJRI.

INSURANCE

A new Co-operative Insurance Law, promulgated in 2004, required all companies operating in the kingdom to be locally registered and brought the sector under the supervision of the Saudi Arabian Monetary Agency (see Central Bank). In March 2009 29 insurance companies were operating in Saudi Arabia.

Ace Arabia Insurance Co Ltd (E.C.): 7th and 8th Floors, Southern Tower, Khobar Business Gate, King Faisal Bin Abd al-Aziz St (Coastal Rd), al-Khobar; tel. (3) 849-3633; fax (3) 849-3660; e-mail ace@ace-arabia.com; internet www.ace-arabia.com; f. 1974; cap. US $1m.; Chair. Sheikh ABD AL-KARIM EL-KHEREIJI; CEO BRUCE C. AITKEN.

Allied Cooperative Insurance Group: POB 7076, Jeddah 21462; tel. (2) 663-3222; fax (2) 661-7421; e-mail csc@acig.com.sa; internet www.acig.com.sa; Chair. MUHAMMAD HANI ABD AL-KADER AL-BAKRI; CEO Dr OMAR Z. HAFIZ.

Bank Al-Jazira Takaful Ta'awuni: POB 6277, Jeddah 21442; tel. and fax (2) 683-6364; e-mail infotakaful@baj.com.sa; internet www.takaful.com.sa; Islamic life insurance; Gen. Man. DAWOOD Y. TAYLOR.

Mediterranean and Gulf Cooperative Insurance and Reinsurance Co (MEDGULF): POB 2302, Riyadh 11451; tel. (1) 405-5550; fax (1) 478-9219; e-mail riyadh@medgulf.com; internet www.medgulf.com.sa; Chair. SALEH A. S. AL-SAGRI; Exec. Pres. and Man. Dir LUTFI F. EL-ZEIN.

Al-Rajhi Co for Co-operative Insurance: Platinum Centre, 3rd Floor, Setteen St, POB 67791, Riyadh 11517; tel. (1) 475-2211; fax (1) 475-5017; e-mail info@alrajhitakaful.com; internet www.alrajhiinsurance.com.sa; f. 1990 as Al-Rajhi Insurance Co; renamed as above 2006; cap. 200m.; Chair. ABDULLAH SULAIMAN AL-RAJHI; CEO ABD AL-AZIZ M. AL-SEDEAS.

Red Sea Insurance Group of Cos: POB 5627, Jeddah 21432; tel. (2) 660-3538; fax (2) 665-5418; e-mail redsea@anet.net.sa; f. 1974; insurance, devt and reinsurance; Chair. KHALDOUN B. BARAKAT.

RSA Saudi Arabia—Al-Alamiya: 1st Floor, Obekan Bldg, Prince Sultan St, POB 2374, Jeddah 21451; tel. (2) 692-7085; fax (2) 692-7125; e-mail alamiya.insurance@sa.rsagroup.com; internet www.alamiyainsurance.com.sa; part of the Royal & Sun Alliance (RSA) Group; total assets US $73.0m. (2002); CEO STUART PURDY.

SABB Takaful Co: POB 9086, Riyadh 11413; tel. (1) 403-0087; fax (1) 402-5832; internet www.sabbtakaful.com; f. 2007; 32.5% owned by Saudi British Bank (SABB), 32.5% by HSBC, 35% by private investors; cap. 100m.; Chair. FOUAD ABD AL-WAHAB BAHRAWI; Man. Dir DAVID ROBERT HUNT.

Sanad Cooperative Insurance and Reinsurance Co: 3rd Floor, Dareen Centre, Alahsa St, POB 27477, Riyadh 27477; tel. and fax (1) 292-7111; fax 292-7888; e-mail info@sanad.com.sa; internet www.sanad.com.sa; Chair. AHMAD AL-ABDULLAH AL-AKEIL; CEO GRAEME EVANS.

Saudi IAIC Cooperative Insurance Co (SALAMA): POB 122392, Jeddah 21332; tel. (2) 664-7877; fax (2) 664-7387; e-mail customers.relation@salama.com.sa; internet www.salama.com.sa; Chair. Dr SALEH J. MALAIKAH.

Saudi National Insurance Co (E.C.): POB 5832, Jeddah 21432; tel. (2) 660-6200; fax (2) 667-4530; e-mail snic@eajb.com.sa; internet www.snic.com.sa; f. 1974; Chair. Sheikh HATEM ALI JUFFALI; Gen. Man. OMAR S. BILANI.

Tawuniya (NCCI): POB 86959, Riyadh 11632; tel. and fax (1) 218-0100; e-mail info@tawuniya.com.sa; internet tawuniya.com.sa; f. 1985 by royal decree as Nat. Co for Co-operative Insurance; name changed as above 2007; owned by three govt agencies; proposed privatization approved by the Supreme Economic Council in May 2004; initial public offering of shares in Dec. 2004; auth. cap. 500m.; Chair. SULAYMAN AL-HUMMAYYD; Man. Dir and Gen. Man. ALI A. AL-SUBAIHIN; 13 brs.

United Cooperative Assurance Co (UCA): POB 5019, Medina Rd, Jeddah 21422; tel. (2) 653-0068; fax (2) 651-1936; e-mail jeddah@uca.com.sa; internet www.uca.com.sa; f. 1974 as United Commercial Agencies Ltd; name changed as above 2007; all classes of insurance; cap. 200m.; Chair. HASSAN M. MAHASSINI; CEO MACHAAL A. KARAM.

SAUDI ARABIA

Wala'a Insurance: POB 31616, al-Khobar 31952; tel. (3) 865-1866; fax (3) 865-1944; e-mail khobar@walaa.com; internet www.walaa.com; f. 1976; fmrly Saudi United Insurance; operated by Saudi United Cooperative Insurance Co; provides all classes of insurance for businesses and govt agencies; majority shareholding held by Ahmad Hamad al-Gosaibi & Bros; cap. US $5m.; Chair. SULAYMAN AL-KADI; CEO ABDULLAH AL-OTHMAN (acting); 6 brs.

Trade and Industry
(Figures for weight are in metric tons)

DEVELOPMENT ORGANIZATIONS

Arab Petroleum Investments Corpn: POB 9599, Dammam 31423; tel. (3) 847-0444; fax (3) 847-0011; e-mail apicorp@apicorp-arabia.com; internet www.apicorp-arabia.com; f. 1975; affiliated to the Org. of Arab Petroleum Exporting Countries; specializes in financing petroleum and petrochemical projects and related industries in the Arab world and in other developing countries; shareholders: Kuwait, Saudi Arabia and the United Arab Emirates (17% each), Libya (15%), Iraq and Qatar (10% each), Algeria (5%), Bahrain, Egypt and Syria (3% each); auth. cap. US $1,200m.; cap. $550m. (Dec. 2006); Chair. ABDULLAH A. AL-ZAID; Gen. Man. and CEO AHMAD BIN HAMAD AL-NUAIMI.

National Agricultural Development Co (NADEC): POB 2557, Riyadh 11461; tel. (1) 404-0000; fax (1) 405-5522; e-mail info@nadec.com.sa; internet www.nadec.com.sa; f. 1981; interests include six dairy farms, two dairy processing plants and 40,000 ha of land for cultivation of wheat, barley, forage and vegetables and processing of dates; the Govt has a 20% share; chief agency for agricultural devt; cap. SR 400m.; Chair. SULAYMAN ABD AL-AZIZ AL-RAJHI; CEO ABD AL-AZIZ AL-BABTAIN.

Public Investment Fund: POB 6847, Riyadh 11452; tel. (1) 477-4488; fax (1) 474-2693; e-mail info@mof.gov.sa; internet www.mof.gov.sa/en/docs/ests/sub_invbox.htm; f. 1971 to facilitate devt of the nat. economy; 100% state-owned; under the control of the Ministry of Finance; provides the Govt's share of capital to mixed capital cos; has managed Sanabil al-Saudia, a sovereign wealth fund with cap. of US $5,300m., since 2008; Chair. Dr IBRAHIM IBN ABD AL-AZIZ AL-ASSAF (Minister of Finance); Sec.-Gen. MANSOUR AL-MAIMAN.

Saudi Arabian General Investment Authority (SAGIA): POB 5927, Riyadh 11432; tel. (1) 203-5555; fax (1) 263-2894; e-mail marketing_dept@sagia.gov.sa; internet www.sagia.gov.sa; f. 2000 to promote foreign investment; Gov. AMR BIN ABDULLAH AL-DABBAGH.

Saudi Fund for Development (SFD): POB 50483, Riyadh 11523; tel. (1) 464-0292; fax (1) 464-7450; e-mail info@sfd.gov.sa; internet www.sfd.gov.sa; f. 1974 to help finance projects in developing countries; state-owned; had financed 417 projects by 2007; total commitments amounted to SR 27,728.36m.; Chair. Dr IBRAHIM IBN ABD AL-AZIZ AL-ASSAF (Minister of Finance); Vice-Chair. and Man. Dir E. YOUSUF I. AL-BASSAM.

Saudi Industrial Development Fund (SIDF): POB 4143, Riyadh 11149; tel. (1) 477-4002; fax (1) 479-0165; e-mail sidf@sidf.gov.sa; internet www.sidf.gov.sa; f. 1974; supports and promotes local industrial devt, providing medium-term interest-free loans; also offers marketing, technical, financial and administrative advice; loans disbursed amounted to SR 8,544m. in 2007; cap. SR 20,000m. (2007); Chair. YOUSUF BIN IBRAHIM AL-BASSAM; Dir-Gen. ABDULLAH MUHAMMAD AL-OBOUDI.

TASNEE: POB 26707, Riyadh 11496; tel. (1) 476-7166; fax (1) 477-0898; e-mail general@tasnee.com; internet www.tasnee.com; f. 1985 as Nat. Industrialization Co to promote and establish industrial projects in Saudi Arabia; cap. SR 785m.; 100% owned by Saudi nationals; Chair. MUBARAK BIN ABDULLAH AL-KHAFRAH; CEO MOAYYED BIN ISSA AL-QURTAS.

CHAMBERS OF COMMERCE

Council of Saudi Chambers of Commerce and Industry: POB 16683, Riyadh 11474; tel. (1) 218-2222; fax (1) 218-2111; e-mail council@saudichambers.org.sa; internet www.saudichambers.org.sa; comprises one delegate from each of the chambers of commerce in the kingdom; Chair. MUHAMMAD ABD AL-QADER AL-FADEL; Sec.-Gen. Dr FAHD AL-SULTAN.

Abha Chamber of Commerce and Industry: POB 722, Abha; tel. (7) 227-1818; fax (7) 227-1919; e-mail info@abhacci.org.sa; internet www.abhacci.org.sa; Pres. ABDULLAH SAID AL-MOBTY; Sec.-Gen. Dr HAMDI ALI AL-MALIKI.

Al-Ahsa Chamber of Commerce and Industry: POB 1519, al-Ahsa 31982; tel. (3) 582-0458; fax (3) 587-5274; internet www.hcci.org.sa; Pres. SULAYMAN A. AL-HAMAAD.

Ar'ar Chamber of Commerce and Industry: POB 440, Ar'ar; tel. (4) 662-6544; fax (4) 662-4581; Sec.-Gen. THANI B. AL-ANEZI.

Al-Baha Chamber of Commerce and Industry: POB 311, al-Baha; tel. (7) 727-0291; fax (7) 828-0146; Pres. ABDULLAH M. AL-MOAGEB; Sec.-Gen. YAHYA AL-ZAHRANI.

Eastern Province Chamber of Commerce and Industry (Asharqia Chamber): POB 719, Dammam 31421; tel. (3) 857-1111; fax (3) 857-0607; e-mail info@chamber.org.sa; internet www.chamber.org.sa; f. 1952; Pres. ABD AL-RAHMAN RASHID AL-RASHID; Sec.-Gen. IBRAHIM ABDULLAH AL-OLAYAN.

Federation of Gulf Co-operation Council Chambers (FGCCC): POB 2198, Dammam 31451; tel. (3) 826-5943; fax (3) 826-6794; e-mail fgccc@zajil.net; internet www.fgccc.org; Pres. SALIM H. ALKHALILI; Sec.-Gen. MUHAMMAD A. AL-MULLA.

Ha'il Chamber of Commerce and Industry: POB 1291, Ha'il; tel. (6) 532-1060; fax (6) 533-1366; e-mail hussa_mk@yahoo.com; internet www.hcc.org.sa; Pres. KHALID A. AL-SAIF.

Jeddah Chamber of Commerce and Industry: POB 1264, Jeddah 21431; tel. (2) 651-5111; fax (2) 651-7373; e-mail customerservice@jcci.org.sa; internet www.jcci.org.sa; f. 1946; 26,000 mems; Chair. Sheikh SALEH KAMEL; Sec.-Gen. Dr HANI M. ABURAS.

Jizan Chamber of Commerce and Industry: POB 201, Jizan; tel. (7) 322-5155; fax (7) 322-3635; Pres. Eng. FAHD A. QALM.

Al-Jouf Chamber of Commerce and Industry: POB 585, al-Jouf; tel. (4) 624-9060; fax (4) 624-0108; Pres. MARZOUK S. AL-RASHID; Sec.-Gen. AHMAD KHALIFA AL-MUSALLAM.

Al-Majma' Chamber of Commerce and Industry: POB 165, al-Majma' 11952; tel. (6) 432-0268; fax (6) 432-2655; Pres. FAHD MUHAMMAD AL-RABIAH; Sec.-Gen. ABDULLAH IBRAHIM AL-JAAWAN.

Mecca Chamber of Commerce and Industry: POB 1086, Mecca; tel. (2) 534-3838; fax (2) 534-2904; f. 1947; Pres. ADEL ABDULLAH KA'AKI; Sec.-Gen. YASSER ABDULLAH AWAN.

Medina Chamber of Commerce and Industry: POB 443, King Abd al-Aziz Rd, Medina; tel. (4) 838-8909; fax (4) 838-8905; e-mail info@mcci.org.sa; internet www.mcci.org.sa; Pres. MUHAMMAD AL-GHAMDI; Sec.-Gen. Dr AMIR ABDULLAH SLEHM.

Najran Chamber of Commerce and Industry: POB 1138, Najran; tel. (7) 522-2216; fax (7) 522-3926; e-mail ywadidi@najcci.org.sa; internet www.najcci.org.sa; Pres. ALI BIN HAMAD HAMROUR AL-ABAAS; Sec.-Gen. ALI BIN SALEH AL-QUMAISH.

Al-Qassim Chamber of Commerce and Industry: POB 444, Buraydah, al-Qassim 51411; tel. (6) 381-4000; fax (6) 381-2231; e-mail info@qcc.org.sa; internet www.qcc.org.sa; Sec.-Gen. Dr FAISAL AL-KHAMIS.

Al-Qurayat Chamber of Commerce and Industry: POB 416, al-Qurayat; tel. (4) 642-6200; fax (4) 642-3172; Pres. OTHMAN ABDULLAH AL-YOUSUF; Sec.-Gen. JAMAL ALI AL-GHAMDI.

Riyadh Chamber of Commerce and Industry: POB 596, Riyadh 11421; tel. (1) 404-0044; fax (1) 402-1103; e-mail info@rdcci.org.sa; internet www.riyadhchamber.org.sa; f. 1961; acts as arbitrator in business disputes, information centre; Pres. ABD AL-RAHMAN ALI AL-JERAISY; Sec.-Gen. HUSSEIN ABD AL-RAHMAN AL-AZAL; 70,000 mems.

Tabouk Chamber of Commerce and Industry: POB 567, Tabouk; tel. (4) 422-2736; fax (4) 422-7387; internet www.tcci.org.sa; Pres. MUHAMMAD H. AL-WABSI; Sec.-Gen. AWADH AL-BALAWI.

Ta'if Chamber of Commerce and Industry: POB 1005, Ta'if; tel. (2) 736-6800; fax (2) 738-0040; e-mail info@taifchamber.org.sa; internet www.taifcci.com; Pres. NAIF A. AL-ADWANI; Sec.-Gen. Eng. YOUSUF MUHAMMAD AL-SHAFI.

Yanbu Chamber of Commerce and Industry: POB 58, Yanbu; tel. (4) 322-7878; fax (4) 322-6800; f. 1979; publishes quarterly magazine; 5,000 members; Pres. Dr MANSOUR M. AL-ANSARI; Sec.-Gen. KHALED SALMAN AL-SAHALI.

STATE HYDROCARBONS COMPANIES

Saudi Arabian Oil Co (Saudi Aramco): POB 5000, Dhahran 31311; tel. (3) 872-0115; fax (3) 873-8190; e-mail webmaster@aramco.com.sa; internet www.saudiaramco.com; f. 1933; previously known as Arabian-American Oil Co (Aramco); in 1993 incorporated the Saudi Arabian Marketing and Refining Co (SAMAREC, f. 1988) by merger of operations; holds the principal working concessions in Saudi Arabia; operates five wholly owned refineries (at Jeddah, Rabigh, Ras Tanura, Riyadh and Yanbu); Pres. and CEO KHALID A. AL-FALIH; Sr Vice-Pres. (Engineering and Project Management) SALIM S. AL-AYDH.

Aramco Gulf Operations Co (AGOC): POB 688, Khafji City 31971; tel. (3) 766-4024; fax (3) 767-5514; e-mail alsultanbf@kjo.com.sa; internet www.agoc.com.sa; f. 2000; wholly owned by Saudi Aramco; holds concession for offshore exploitation of Saudi Arabia's half-interest in the Saudi Arabia-Kuwait Neutral Zone; Pres. and CEO MUHAMMAD A. AL-SHAMMARY.

Petromin Corporation (Petromin Oils): POB 1432, Jeddah 21431; tel. (2) 215-7000; fax (2) 215-7111; e-mail info@petromin.com; internet www.petromin.com; f. 1968; 71% owned by Saudi Aramco, 29% by Mobil; manufacture and marketing of lubricating oils and other related products; production 140m. litres (2002); cap. 110m. riyals; Exec. Dir WAHEED A. SHAIKH; Pres. and CEO SAMIR M. NAWAR.

Rabigh Refining and Petrochemical Co (Petro Rabigh): POB 666, Rabigh 21911; tel. (2) 425-1855; fax (2) 425-2732; internet www.petrorabigh.com; f. 2005; jt venture between Saudi Aramco and Sumitomo Chemical (Japan); operation of integrated oil-refining and petrochemical production facilities at Rabigh; initial public offering of 20% of shares announced in Jan. 2008; Chair. ABD AL-AZIZ F. AL-KHAYYAL; Pres. and CEO SAAD FAHAD AL-DOSARI.

Saudi Aramco Lubricating Oil Refining Co (LUBEREF): POB 5518, Jeddah 21432; tel. (2) 427-5497; fax (2) 636-6933; e-mail webmaster@luberef.com; internet www.luberef.com; f. 1975; owned 70% by Saudi Aramco and 30% by Jadwa Industrial Investment Co; Pres. and CEO ABDULLAH O. AL-BAIZ.

Saudi Aramco Mobil Refinery Co Ltd (SAMREF): POB 30078, Yanbu; tel. (4) 396-4443; fax (4) 396-0942; e-mail amrihh@samref.com.sa; internet www.samref.com.sa; f. 1981; operation of oil-refining facilities at Yanbu; operated by Saudi Aramco and Mobil, capacity 360,000 b/d; Pres. and CEO FAWWAZ I. NAWWAB.

Saudi Aramco Shell Refinery Co (SASREF): POB 10088, Madinat al-Jubail, al-Sinaiyah 31961; tel. (3) 357-2000; fax (3) 357-2525; e-mail info@sasref.com.sa; internet www.sasref.com.sa; operation of oil-refining facilities at Jubail; operated by Saudi Aramco and Shell; capacity 300,000 b/d; exports began in 1985; Chair. HAMID T. AL-SAUDOON.

Saudi Basic Industries Corpn (SABIC): POB 5101, Riyadh 11422; tel. (1) 225-8000; fax (1) 225-9000; e-mail info@sabic.com; internet www.sabic.com; f. 1976 to foster the petrochemical industry and other hydrocarbon-based industries through jt ventures with foreign partners, and to market their products; 70% state-owned; production 55m. tons (2007); Chair. Prince SA'UD BIN THUNAYAN AL SA'UD; Vice-Chair. and CEO MUHAMMAD AL-MADY.

Projects include:

Arabian Petrochemical Co (Petrokemya): POB 10002, Jubail 31961; tel. (3) 358-7000; fax (3) 358-4480; e-mail petrokemya@petrokemya.sabic.com; f. 1981; wholly owned subsidiary of SABIC; produced 2.4m. tons of ethylene, 135,000 tons of polystyrene, 100,000 tons of butene-1, 570,000 tons of propylene, 100,000 tons of butadiene and 150,000 tons of benzene in 2001; owns 50% interest in ethylene glycol plant producing 610,000 tons per year of monoethylene glycol, 65,000 tons per year of diethylene glycol and 3,900 tons per year of triethylene glycol; Pres. SAMI A. AL-SUWAIGH.

Eastern Petrochemical Co (Sharq): POB 10035, Jubail 31961; tel. (3) 357-5000; fax (3) 358-0383; e-mail sharq@sharq.sabic.com; f. 1981 to produce linear low-density polyethylene, ethylene glycol; a SABIC jt venture with Japanese cos led by Mitsubishi Corpn; total capacity 660,000 tons of ethylene glycol and 280,000 tons of polyethylene per year; Chair. ABD AL-AZIZ AL-JARBOOA.

Al-Jubail Petrochemical Co (Kemya): POB 10084, Jubail 31961; tel. (3) 357-6000; fax (3) 358-7858; e-mail kemya@kemya.sabic.com; f. 1980; began production of linear low-density polyethylene in 1984, of high-density polyethylene in 1985, and of high alfa olefins in 1986, capacity of 330,000 tons per year of polyethylene; jt venture with Exxon Corpn (USA) and SABIC; Chair. HOMOOD AL-TUWAIJRI; Pres. ABD AL-AZIZ SULAYMAN AL-HAMAAD.

National Industrial Gases Co (Gas): POB 10110, Jubail 31961; tel. (3) 357-5738; fax (3) 358-8880; e-mail hussainaa@gas.sabic.com; 70% SABIC-owned jt venture with Saudi private sector; total capacity of 876,000 tons of oxygen and 492,750 tons of nitrogen per year; Pres. ALI AL-GHAMDI.

National Plastic Co (Ibn Hayyan): POB 10002, Jubail 31961; tel. (3) 358-7000; fax (3) 358-4736; f. 1984; 86.5% owned by SABIC; produces 390,000 tons per year of vinylchloride monomer and 324,000 tons per year of polyvinylchloride; Pres. KHALED AL-RAWAF.

Saudi-European Petrochemical Co (Ibn Zahr): POB 10330, Jubail 31961; tel. (3) 341-5060; fax (3) 341-2966; e-mail info@ibnzahr.sabic.com; f. 1985; annual capacity 1.4m. tons of methyl-tertiary-butyl ether (MTBE), 0.3m. tons of propylene; SABIC has an 80% share, Ecofuel and APICORP each have 10%; Chair. Dr ABD AL-RAHMAN S. AL-UBAID.

Saudi Kayan Petrochemical Co: POB 10302, Jubail Industrial City 31961; tel. (3) 359-3000; fax (3) 359-3111; e-mail shares@saudikayan.sabic.com; internet www.saudikayan.com; f. 2006; jt venture between SABIC and Al-Kayan Petrochemical Co; initial public offering of 45% of shares in 2008; production of ethylene, propylene, polypropylene, ethylene glycol, butene-1 and specialized products incl. aminomethyls, dimethylformamide and choline chloride; Chair. MUTLAQ HAMAD AL-MORISHED.

Saudi Methanol Co (ar-Razi): POB 10065, Jubail Industrial City 31961; tel. (3) 357-7800; fax (3) 358-5552; e-mail arrazi@arrazi.sabic.com; f. 1979; jt venture with a consortium of Japanese cos; capacity of 3.2m. tons per year of chemical-grade methanol; total methanol exports in 2001 were 3.2m. tons; Pres. NABIL A. MANSOURI; Exec. Vice-Pres. H. MIZUNO.

Saudi Petrochemical Co (Sadaf): POB 10025, Jubail 31961; tel. (3) 357-3000; fax (3) 357-3343; e-mail info@sadaf.sabic.com; f. 1980 to produce ethylene, ethylene dichloride, styrene, crude industrial ethanol, caustic soda and methyl-tertiary-butyl-ether (MTBE); total capacity of 4.3m. tons per year; Shell Chemicals Arabia has a 50% share; Pres. MOSAED S. AL-OHALI.

Saudi Yanbu Petrochemical Co (Yanpet): POB 30333, Yanbu 21441; tel. (4) 396-5000; fax (4) 396-5006; e-mail info@yanpet.sabic.com; f. 1980 to produce 820,000 tons per year of ethylene, 600,000 tons per year of high-density polyethylene and 340,000 tons per year of ethylene glycol; total capacity 1.7m. tons per year by 1990; ExxonMobil and SABIC each have a 50% share; Pres. SULAYMAN AL-HUSSAIN.

Yanbu National Petrochemical Co (Yansab): POB 31396, Yanbu Industrial City 21477; tel. (4) 325-9000; fax (4) 325-6666; e-mail shares@yansab.sabic.com; internet www.yansab.com.sa; f. 2006; 55% owned by SABIC; projected total capacity of over 4.0m. tons per year, incl. 1.3m. tons of ethylene; Chair. MUTLAQ HAMAD AL-MORISHED.

Foreign Concessionaire

Saudi Arabian Chevron: POB 363, Riyadh; tel. (1) 462-7274; fax (1) 464-1992; internet www.sachevron.com; also office in Kuwait; f. 1928; fmrly Getty Oil Co; renamed Saudi Arabian Texaco Inc. 1993, renamed as above 2007; holds concession (5,200 sq km at Dec. 1987) for exploitation of Saudi Arabia's half-interest in the Saudi Arabia-Kuwait Neutral (Partitioned) Zone; Pres. AHMAD AL-OMAR.

UTILITIES

Power and Water Utility Company for Jubail and Yanbu (MARAFIQ): POB 11133, Jubail 31961; tel. (3) 340-1111; fax (3) 340-1168; e-mail marafiqworld@marafiq.com.sa; internet www.marafiq.com.sa; f. 2003; equal ownership held by the Royal Comm. for Jubail and Yanbu, Saudi Aramco, Saudi Basic Industries Corpn and the Public Investment Fund; operation and devt of utility services; Chair. Prince SA'UD IBN ABDULLAH IBN THUNAYAN AL SA'UD; CEO THAMIR S. AL-SHARHAN.

Water and Electricity Co: POB 300091, Riyadh 11372; tel. (1) 211-3362; fax (1) 211-3313; e-mail info@wec.com.sa; internet www.wec.com.sa; f. 2003; jointly owned by Saline Water Conversion Corpn and Saudi Electricity Co; responsible for managing supply and demand of electricity and water; Chair. FAHID AL-SHARIF; CEO OMAR AL-GHAMDI.

Electricity

Electricity and Co-generation Regulatory Authority (ECRA): PO Box 4540, Riyadh 11412; tel. (1) 201-9045; e-mail public@ecra.gov.sa; internet www.ecra.gov.sa; f. 2001 to regulate the power industry and to recommend tariffs for the sector; Gov. Dr FAREED M. ZEDAN.

ACWA Power International: POB 22616, Riyadh 11416; tel. (1) 473-4400; fax (1) 474-9215; e-mail info@acwapower.com; internet www.acwapowerprojects.com; f. 2008; develops privately financed power and water projects; Exec. Chair. MUHAMMAD ABUNAYYAN.

Saudi Electricity Co (SEC): POB 57, Riyadh 11411; tel. (1) 403-2222; fax (1) 405-1191; internet www.se.com.sa; f. 1999 following merger of 10 regional cos, to organize the generation, transmission and distribution of electricity into separate operating cos; jt stock co; cap. SR 33,758m.; Chair. Dr SALEH HUSSEIN AL-AWAJI.

Water

National Water Co: POB 676, Riyadh 11421; tel. (1) 211-3014; fax (1) 211-3016; e-mail info@nwc.com.sa; internet www.nwc.com.sa; f. 2008 to consolidate all govt-run water and wastewater management services and to facilitate the gradual privatization of the sector; Chair. ABDULLAH IBN ABD AL-RAHMAN AL-HUSSEIN (Minister of Water and Electricity); CEO LOAY A. AL-MUSALLAM.

Saline Water Conversion Corpn (SWCC): POB 4931, 21412 Jeddah; tel. (2) 682-1240; fax (2) 682-0415; e-mail computerdirector@swcc.gov.sa; internet www.swcc.gov.sa; f. 1974; provides desalinated water; 24 plants; Gov. FAHID AL-SHARIF; Dir-Gen. ABD AL-AZIZ OMAR NASSIEF.

TRADE UNIONS

Trade unions are illegal in Saudi Arabia.

SAUDI ARABIA

Transport

RAILWAYS

Saudi Arabia has the only rail system in the Arabian peninsula. The Saudi Government Railroad comprises 719 km of single and 157 km of double track. In addition, the total length of spur lines and sidings is 348 km. The main line, which was opened in 1951, is 570 km in length and connects Dammam port, on the Gulf coast, with Riyadh, via Dhahran, Abqaiq, Hufuf, Harad and al-Kharj. A 310-km line, linking Hufuf and Riyadh, was inaugurated in May 1985. New 950-km and 115-km lines, connecting Riyadh with Jeddah and Dammam with Jubail, respectively, known as the Saudi Landbridge Project, were planned. The revamped network was to connect the Red Sea with the Persian (Arabian) Gulf and was to be closely linked with Jeddah Islamic Port and King Abd al-Aziz Port (at Dammam). Bidding for the build-operate-transfer contract was opened in February 2008 but was subsequently delayed owing to subsequent developments in the global economic climate; a decision regarding the contract was expected to be announced in 2011. In August 2009 it was announced that the Public Investment Fund, controlled by the Saudi Ministry of Finance, was to finance the project on an EPC basis. Concessions to build a 450-km line connecting the west coast centres of Mecca, Medina and Jeddah, and providing a passenger service for millions of *Umrah* and *Hajj* pilgrims every year, were tendered in 2006. In March 2009 a SR 6,900m. contract was awarded for the part one of the first phase of the Haramain High-Speed Rail Project, a proposed 450-km line that would connect the west coast centres of Mecca, Medina and Jeddah, and provide a passenger service for millions of *Umrah* and *Hajj* pilgrims every year. Contracts for part two were awarded to eight companies, including Saudi Binladin Group and Saudi Oger Ltd, in February 2011. Completion of the entire project was anticipated by the end of 2012. The concession for a 2,400-km North–South line, connecting Riyadh, Qassim, Ha'il, al-Zubayrah and al-Jalamid, to be mainly utilized for transporting minerals, was tendered, in several stages, from September 2007. The fourth and final construction contract was awarded to a Saudi consortium in September 2009. An 18-km elevated metro system linking the holy sites in Mecca was opened in November 2010. Plans for the construction of a metro system in Jeddah, with 200 stations, at a cost of some $5,600m., were announced in April 2009, while construction work on a two-line urban light-rail system in Riyadh was reportedly under way in early 2011. A total of 1.1m. passengers travelled by rail in the kingdom in 2009.

Saudi Railway Co (SAR): Diplomatic Quarter Bldg S-24, POB 64447, Riyadh 11452; tel. (1) 250-1111; fax (1) 480-7517; e-mail info@sar.com.sa; internet www.sar.com.sa; f. 2006; manages North–South Railway project; CEO RUMAIH AL-RUMAIH; Chair. MANSOUR IBN SALEH AL-MAYMAN.

Saudi Railways Organization (SRO): POB 36, Dammam 31241; tel. (3) 871-3000; fax (3) 827-1130; e-mail sro@sro.org.sa; internet www.saudirailways.org; scheduled for privatization; Pres. ABD AL-AZIZ BIN MUHAMMAD AL-HOQAIL.

ROADS

Asphalted roads link Jeddah to Mecca, Jeddah to Medina, Medina to Yanbu, al-Ta'if to Mecca, Riyadh to al-Kharj, and Dammam to Hufuf, as well as the principal communities and certain outlying points in Saudi Aramco's area of operations. The trans-Arabian highway links Dammam, Riyadh, al-Ta'if, Mecca and Jeddah. In February 2006 a long-considered project to build a causeway between Saudi Arabia and Egypt across the Straits of Tiran was revived. In 2005 there were 221,372 km of roads, of which 13,596 km were main roads (including motorways) and 33,924 km were secondary roads. Metalled roads link all the main population centres.

Saudi Public Transport Co (SAPTCO): POB 10667, Riyadh 11443; tel. (1) 454-5000; fax (1) 454-2100; e-mail info@saptco.com.sa; internet www.saptco.com.sa; f. 1979; operates a public bus service throughout Saudi Arabia and to neighbouring countries; the Govt holds a 30% share; Chair. ABDULLAH AL-MUGHBIL; CEO Dr ABD AL-AZIZ AL-OHALY.

SHIPPING

On average over 95% of Saudi Arabia's imports and exports pass through the country's sea ports. In 2009 the eight major sea ports received 11,055 vessels; the total cargo handled in that year, excluding crude petroleum, was 142.3m. metric tons, compared with 68.2m. tons in 1990/91, and some 1,168,673 passengers were processed. Responsibility for the management, operation and maintenance of a number of ports, including the commercial ports of Jeddah, Dammam, Jubail, Yanbu, Dhiba and Jizan, and the King Fahd Industrial Ports of Jubail and Yanbu, began to be transferred to the private sector from 1997, but all ports remain subject to regulation and scrutiny by the Ports Authority. In January 2008 the Ports Authority announced the signing of a US $586m. contract with the China Harbour Engineering Co Ltd to build a new port at Ras Azzawr.

Jeddah is the principal commercial port and the main point of entry for pilgrims bound for Mecca. It has 58 berths for general cargo, container traffic, roll-on roll-off (ro-ro) traffic, livestock and bulk grain shipments, with draughts ranging from 8 m to 16 m. The port also has a 200-metric ton floating crane, cold storage facilities and a fully equipped ship-repair yard. In 2009 a total of 4,383 vessels called at Jeddah Islamic Port. In that year some 40.9m. tons of cargo, excluding crude petroleum, were handled, and 340,441 passengers were processed. A new deep-water terminal, the Red Sea Gateway, with draughts of up to 18 m and a handling capacity of 1.5m. 20-ft equivalent units, became operational in late 2009.

Dammam is the second largest commercial port and has general cargo, container, ro-ro, dangerous cargo and bulk grain berths. Draughts range from 8 m to 13.5 m. It has a 200-metric ton floating crane and a fully equipped ship-repair yard. In 2009 a total of 2,289 vessels called at King Abd al-Aziz Port in Dammam; some 19.3m. tons of cargo, excluding crude petroleum, were handled in that year.

Jubail has one commercial and one industrial port. The commercial port has general cargo, container, ro-ro and bulk grain berths, and a floating crane. Draughts range from 12 m to 14 m. In 2009 a total of 428 vessels called at Jubail Commercial Port, and 3.2m. metric tons of goods, excluding crude petroleum, were handled. The industrial port has bulk cargo, refined and petrochemical and ro-ro berths, and an open sea tanker terminal suitable for vessels up to 300,000 dwt. Draughts range from 6 m to 30 m. In 2009 a total of 1,665 vessels called at King Fahd Industrial Port in Jubail; 43.1m. tons of cargo, excluding crude petroleum, were handled in that year.

Yanbu, which comprises one commercial and one industrial port, is Saudi Arabia's nearest major port to Europe and North America, and is the focal point of the most rapidly growing area, in the west of Saudi Arabia. The commercial port has general cargo, ro-ro and bulk grain berths, with draughts ranging from 10 m to 12 m. It also has a floating crane, and is equipped to handle minor ship repairs. In 2009 a total of 162 vessels called at Yanbu Commercial Port. In that year 1.5m. metric tons of cargo, excluding crude petroleum, were handled, and 69,136 passengers were processed. The industrial port has berths for general cargo, containers, ro-ro traffic, bulk cargo, crude petroleum, refined and petrochemical products and natural gas liquids, and a tanker terminal on the open sea. In 2009 a total of 1,270 vessels called at King Fahd Industrial Port in Yanbu; the port handled 33.0m. tons of cargo, excluding crude petroleum, in that year. The third phase of a project to increase the port's handling capacity was announced in November 2008.

Jizan is the main port for the southern part of the country. It has general cargo, ro-ro, bulk grain and container berths, with draughts ranging from 8 m to 11 m. It also has a 200-metric-ton floating crane. In 2009 a total of 131 vessels called at Jizan Port, and 0.8m. tons of cargo, excluding crude petroleum, were handled.

Port Authorities

Saudi Ports Authority: POB 5162, Riyadh 11422; tel. (1) 405-0005; fax (1) 405-3508; e-mail info@ports.gov.sa; internet www.ports.gov.sa; f. 1976; regulatory authority; Pres. Dr ABD AL-AZIZ BIN MUHAMMAD AL-TUWAIJRI; Chair. Dr JUBARAH IBN EID AL-SURAISERI (Minister of Transport).

Dammam: POB 28062, Dammam 31188; tel. (3) 858-3199; fax (3) 857-1727; Dir-Gen. NAEEM IBRAHIM AL-NAEEM.

Dhiba: POB 190, Dhiba; tel. (4) 432-1060; fax (4) 432-2679; Dir-Gen. MAHMOUD AL-HARBI (acting).

Jeddah: POB 9285, Jeddah 21188; tel. (2) 647-1200; fax (2) 647-7411; Dir-Gen. SAHIR M. TAHLAWI.

Jizan: POB 16, Jizan; tel. (7) 317-1000; fax (7) 317-0777; Dir-Gen. ALI HAMOUD BAKRI.

Jubail Commercial Port: POB 276, Jubail; tel. (3) 362-0600; fax (3) 362-3340; e-mail dir-jubail@ports.gov.sa; Dir-Gen. FAHD A. AL-AMER.

Jubail Industrial Port: POB 547, Jubail 31951; tel. (3) 357-8000; fax (3) 357-8011; Dir-Gen. ABDULLAH NASIR AL-TWAIJRI.

Yanbu Commercial Port: POB 1019, Yanbu; tel. (4) 322-2100; fax (4) 322-7643; Dir-Gen. ABDULLAH BIN AWAD AL-ZAIMI.

Yanbu Industrial Port: POB 30325, Yanbu; tel. (4) 396-7000; fax (4) 396-7037; Dir-Gen. Dr HUMOOD SAADI.

Principal Shipping Companies

Arabian Establishment for Trade and Shipping (AET): POB 832, Al-Matbouli Plaza, Jeddah 21421; tel. (2) 652-5500; fax (2) 657-1148; e-mail aetjed@aetshipping.com; internet www.aetshipping.com; f. 1963; shipping agency; Gen. Man. ANTHONY ROBINSON.

Arabian Petroleum Supply Co Ltd: POB 1408, Al-Qurayat St, Jeddah 21431; tel. (2) 608-1171; fax (2) 637-0966; e-mail marine@apsco-ksa.com; internet www.apsco.com.sa; f. 1961; Chair. Sheikh MUHAMMAD YOUSSUF ALI AL-REZA; Man. Dir MUHAMMAD ALI IBRAHIM ALIREZA.

SAUDI ARABIA

Directory

Baaboud Trading and Shipping Agencies: POB 7262, Jeddah 21462; tel. (2) 627-0000; fax (2) 627-1111; e-mail info@baaboud.net; internet www.baaboud.net; Chair. AHMAD M. BAABOUD; Man. Dir AHAD ABOUD BAABOUD.

Bakri Navigation Co Ltd: POB 3757, Jeddah 21481; tel. (2) 652-4298; fax (2) 652-4297; e-mail info@bakrinavigation.com; internet www.bakrinavigation.com; f. 1973; owns and operates a fleet of oil tankers, tug boats and utility vessels; Chair. Sheikh A. K. AL-BAKRY; Man. Dir G. A. K. AL-BAKRY.

National Shipping Co of Saudi Arabia (NSCSA): POB 8931, Riyadh 11492; tel. (1) 478-5454; fax (1) 477-8036; e-mail info@nscsa.com.sa; internet www.nscsa.com; f. 1979; transportation of crude petroleum and petrochemical products; routes through Red Sea and Mediterranean to USA and Canada; operates a fleet of 34 ships; Chair. ABDULLAH SULAIMAN AL-RUBAIAN; CEO SALEH AL-JASSER.

Saudi Shipping and Maritime Services Co Ltd (TRANSHIP): POB 7522, Jeddah 21472; tel. (2) 642-4255; fax (2) 643-2821; e-mail saudishipping@transhipsa.com; Chair. Prince SA'UD IBN NAYEF IBN ABD AL-AZIZ; Man. Dir Capt. MUSTAFA T. AWARA.

Shipping Corpn of Saudi Arabia Ltd: POB 1691, Arab Maritime Center, Malik Khalid St, Jeddah 21441; tel. (2) 647-1137; fax (2) 647-8222; e-mail arablines@arabjeddah.com; Pres. and Man. Dir ABD AL-AZIZ AHMAD ARAB.

CIVIL AVIATION

There are 27 commercial airports, which handled some 42m. passengers in 2008. Plans to privatize the kingdom's airports, which were first announced in 2003, had yet to be realized by 2010; however, in 2008 concessions were awarded to two foreign companies for the management of the three main airports—King Abd al-Aziz International Airport (KAIA, in Jeddah), King Khalid International Airport (KKIA, in Riyadh) and King Fahd International Airport (KFIA, in the Eastern Province, near Dammam). KAIA, which was opened in 1981, has three terminals, one of which is specifically designed to cope with the needs of the many thousands of pilgrims who visit Mecca and Medina each year. Construction of a new passenger terminal, with an annual passenger capacity of 30m., commenced in February 2011 and was expected to be completed by 2013 or 2014. A further two expansion phases, which would increase annual passenger capacity to about 80m. by 2035, were also planned. Prince Muhammad Bin Abd al-Aziz Airport in Medina, which opened in 1972, began handling international flights in 2006. Some 2.5m. passengers used the airport in 2008. Plans to build two new terminals and increase capacity to around 12m. passengers per year by 2019 were at an advanced planning stage in early 2011.

General Authority of Civil Aviation (GACA): POB 887, Jeddah 21165; tel. (2) 640-5000; fax (2) 640-1477; e-mail gaca-info@gaca.gov.sa; internet www.gaca.gov.sa; fmrly the Presidency of Civil Aviation; regulatory authority; Pres. FAISAL IBN HAMAD AL-SUGAIR.

National Air Services (NAS): POB 18118, 2nd Floor, Al-Jirasi Bldg, Madinah Rd, Jeddah 21415; tel. (2) 6910122; fax (2) 6520394; e-mail info@nasaviation.com; internet www.nasaviation.com; f. 1998; privately owned; cap. 60m. riyals; also operates low-cost air carrier, Nas Air; CEO SULAIMAN AL-HAMDAN.

Sama Airlines: POB 361662, Riyadh 11313; tel. (1) 263-9500; fax (1) 454-8720; e-mail contact@flysama.com; internet www.flysama.com; f. 2006; low-cost airline providing domestic and regional services; Chair. Prince BANDAR BIN KHALID AL FAISAL; CEO BRUCE ASHBY.

Saudi Arabian Airlines: POB 620, Jeddah 21231; tel. (2) 686-4588; fax (2) 686-4587; e-mail webmaster@saudiairlines.com.sa; internet www.saudiairlines.com; f. 1945; began operations in 1947; carried 15.4m. passengers in 2004; regular services to 25 domestic and 52 international destinations; catering and cargo divisions part-privatized in 2008; further divestment of shares in technical services and training divisions finalized in March 2010; Chair. Prince SULTAN IBN ABD AL-AZIZ; Dir-Gen. KHALID ABDULLAH AL-MULHIM.

Tourism

The vast majority of devout Muslims try to make at least one visit to the holy cities of Medina, the burial place of Muhammad, and Mecca, his birthplace. In 2000 the Government decided to issue tourist visas for the first time. A Supreme Commission for Tourism (now Saudi Commission for Tourism and Antiquities—SCTA) was subsequently established to develop the tourism industry in Saudi Arabia. According to the SCTA, at the end of 2008 there were 1,006 hotels operating in the kingdom, providing more than 270,000 hotel rooms. It was reported in 2008 that the SCTA planned to invest almost US $40,000m. to develop 19 tourism resorts on the Red Sea coast. Tourist numbers increased to 14.8m. in 2008 (compared with 7.3m. in 2003). Receipts from tourism were estimated at $7,227m. in 2008. An estimated 1.6m. foreign pilgrims visited Mecca in 2009.

Saudi Commission for Tourism and Antiquities (SCTA): POB 66680, Riyadh 11586; tel. (1) 880-8855; fax (1) 880-8844; internet www.scta.gov.sa; f. 2001 as Supreme Comm. for Tourism, renamed as above 2008; Pres. Prince SULTAN IBN SALMAN IBN ABD AL-AZIZ AL SA'UD.

Saudi Hotels and Resort Areas Co (SHARACO): POB 5500, Riyadh 11422; tel. (1) 481-6666; fax (1) 480-1666; e-mail info@saudi-hotels.com.sa; internet www.saudi-hotels.com.sa; f. 1975; construction and management of hotels, resorts and other tourism facilities; Saudi Govt has a 40% interest; Chair. MUSAAD AL-SENANY; Dir-Gen. ABD AL-AZIZ AL-AMBAR.

Defence

Chief of the General Staff: Gen. SALEH IBN ALI AL-MUHAYA.
Director-General of Public Security Forces: Brig.-Gen. ABDULLAH IBN AL-SHEIKH.
Commander of Land Forces: Lt-Gen. ABD AL-RAHMAN IBN ABDULLAH AL-MURSHID.
Commander of Air Force: Lt-Gen. MUHAMMAD IBN ABDULLAH AL-AYISH.
Commander of the Navy: Lt-Gen. DHAKHAIL ALLAH BIN AHMAD BIN MUHAMMAD AL-WAQDANI.
Defence Budget (2010): SR 170,000m.
Military Service: voluntary.
Total Armed Forces (as assessed at November 2010): 233,500 (army 75,000; navy 13,500; air force 20,000; air defence forces 16,000); national guard 100,000 (75,000 active personnel; 25,000 tribal levies); industrial security force 9,000.
Paramilitary Forces (as assessed at November 2010): 10,500 frontier force; 4,500 coastguard; and 500 special security force.

Education

The educational system in Saudi Arabia resembles that of other Arab countries. Educational institutions are administered mainly by the Government. The private sector plays a significant role at the first and second levels, but its total contribution is relatively small compared with that of the public sector.

Pre-elementary education is provided on a small scale, mainly in urban areas. Elementary or primary education is of six years' duration and the normal entrance age is six. The total number of pupils at this stage in 2008/09 was estimated at 3,255,244, with 215,712 teachers. Intermediate education begins at 12 and lasts for three years. The total number of pupils at this stage in 2008/09 was estimated at 1,518,391, with teachers numbering 110,141. Secondary education begins at 15 and extends for three years. After the first year, successful pupils branch into science or arts groups. The total number of pupils at this stage in 2008/09 was estimated at 1,363,551, with 91,606 teachers. According to UNESCO estimates, enrolment of children in the primary age-group increased from 32% in 1970 to 86% in 2008/09. Between 1970 and 2006/07 enrolment at the secondary level rose from 9% to 73%. The proportion of females enrolled in Saudi Arabian schools increased from 25% of the total number of pupils in 1970 to 47.7% in 2007. Vocational and technical education programs can be entered after completion of the intermediate stage. In 2008/09 a total of 86,675 students attended 97 technical and vocational institutes, including 35 technological colleges and 62 vocational training institutes.

In 2008/09 an estimated 706,869 students were enrolled in higher education. In that year the number of new students admitted to universities increased to 242,835, compared with 68,000 in 2003. In 2006 tertiary institutions included 110 university colleges and 87 colleges exclusively for women. The country's first private university, King Faisaliyah University, in partnership with a US technology institute, was under construction in 2007, and expansion of the Imam Muhammad bin Sa'ud Islamic University to include five female colleges was also under way. Early in 2006 the Ministry of Higher Education announced that foreign universities would be permitted to establish campuses in the kingdom for the first time. The Government's budget for 2010 envisaged expenditure on education of SR 137,600m., equivalent to 25.5% of total expenditure.

SENEGAL

Introductory Survey

LOCATION, CLIMATE, LANGUAGE, RELIGION, FLAG, CAPITAL

The Republic of Senegal lies on the west coast of Africa, bordered to the north by Mauritania, to the east by Mali, and to the south by Guinea and Guinea-Bissau. In the southern part of the country The Gambia forms a narrow enclave extending some 320 km (200 miles) inland. The climate is tropical, with a long dry season followed by a short wet season—from June to September in the north, and from June to October in the south. Average annual temperatures range from 22°C (72°F) to 28°C (82°F). French is the official language; the most widely spoken national languages at the time of the 1988 census were Wolof (spoken by 49.2% of the population), Peul (22.2%), Serer (12.8%) and Diola (5.1%). At the 1988 census almost 94% of the population were Muslims, and some 4% Christians, mostly Roman Catholics; a small number followed traditional beliefs. The national flag (proportions 2 by 3) has three equal vertical stripes, of green, yellow and red, with a five-pointed green star in the centre of the yellow stripe. The capital is Dakar. In July 2005 the Assemblée nationale approved legislation providing for the creation of a new administrative capital, near Kébèmer, on the Atlantic littoral.

CONTEMPORARY POLITICAL HISTORY

Historical Context

After 300 years as a French colony, Senegal became a self-governing member of the French Community in November 1958. The Mali Federation, linking Senegal with Soudan (later the Republic of Mali), had only two months of independence before being dissolved when Senegal seceded, to become a separate independent state, on 20 August 1960. The Republic of Senegal was proclaimed on 5 September, with Léopold Sédar Senghor, leader of the Union progressiste sénégalaise (UPS), as the country's first President.

In late 1962, following the discovery of a coup attempt led by the Prime Minister, Mamadou Dia, Senghor assumed the premiership; other political parties were gradually absorbed into the UPS or outlawed, effectively creating a one-party state by 1966. In 1970 the office of Prime Minister was restored and assigned to a provincial administrator, Abdou Diouf, who in 1976 was made Senghor's constitutional successor. In 1973 Senghor, the sole candidate, was re-elected President. Senghor amended the Constitution in March 1976 to allow three parties to contest elections—the UPS, renamed the Parti socialiste (PS), the Parti démocratique sénégalais (PDS) and the Parti africain de l'indépendance (PAI). The first national elections under the three-party system took place in February 1978; the PS won 83 of the 100 seats in the Assemblée nationale, the remainder being won by the PDS. In the concurrent presidential election, Senghor overwhelmingly defeated the leader of the PDS, Abdoulaye Wade.

Domestic Political Affairs

Senghor was succeeded as President by Diouf in January 1981. An amnesty was declared for political dissidents, and the Constitution was amended to allow the existence of an unlimited number of political parties. At elections in February 1983 Diouf received 83.5% of the presidential vote (compared with 14.8% for his nearest rival, Wade), while in legislative elections the PS won 111 of the 120 seats. In April Diouf abolished the post of Prime Minister, which had latterly been held by Habib Thiam.

When preliminary results of the February 1988 presidential and legislative elections indicated clear victories for both Diouf and the PS, opposition parties alleged fraud on the part of the ruling party, and, following the outbreak of rioting in Dakar, a state of emergency was imposed. According to the official results of the presidential election, contested by four candidates, Diouf obtained 73.2% of the votes cast and Wade 25.8%. In the legislative elections, the PS won 103 seats and the PDS the remaining 17.

In March 1991 the legislature approved several amendments to the Constitution, notably the restoration of the post of Prime Minister, to which post Thiam was again named in the following month. Thiam's Government included four representatives of the PDS (including Wade, as Minister of State, effectively the most senior post in the Government other than the Prime Minister). In September the Assemblée nationale adopted amendments to the electoral code. Presidential elections would henceforth take place, in two rounds if necessary (to ensure that the President would be elected by an absolute majority of votes cast), every seven years, with a mandate that would be renewable only once.

In October 1992 Wade and his three PDS colleagues resigned from the Council of Ministers, protesting that they had been excluded from the governmental process. Eight candidates contested the presidential election, which took place in February 1993. The opposition denounced the preliminary results, which indicated that Diouf had won a clear majority. In March the Constitutional Council announced that Diouf had been re-elected with 58.4% of the votes cast (51.6% of the electorate had voted); Wade secured 32.0% of the votes.

Elections to the Assemblée nationale took place in May 1993; the PS won 84 of the 120 elective seats and the PDS 27. The rate of participation by voters was 40.7%. Shortly after the announcement of the results the Vice-President of the Constitutional Council, Babacar Sèye, was assassinated. Wade and three other PDS leaders were detained for three days in connection with the killing, and in October Wade was charged with complicity in the assassination; Wade's wife and a PDS deputy were also charged in connection with the killing. In November Ousmane Ngom, the PDS parliamentary leader, and Landing Savané, the leader of And Jëf—Parti africain pour la démocratie et le socialisme (AJ—PADS), were among those detained following a protest in Dakar to demand the cancellation of austerity measures. Ngom, Savané and some 87 others were convicted of participating in an unauthorized demonstration, and received suspended prison sentences.

Following the devaluation of the CFA franc in January 1994, emergency measures were adopted to offset the immediate adverse economic effects. In February a demonstration in Dakar to denounce the devaluation degenerated into serious rioting, as a result of which eight people were killed. Wade and Savané were among those subsequently charged in association with the unrest. Charges against Wade and his opposition associates in connection with the murder of Sèye were dismissed in May 1994, although Wade and Savané remained in custody until July, in connection with the post-devaluation violence. In October three of Sèye's alleged assassins were convicted and sentenced to 18–20 years' imprisonment.

Five members of the PDS, including Wade, as Minister of State at the Presidency, were appointed to a new Council of Ministers in March 1995. Djibo Kâ, a long-serving government member who had been associated with the legal proceedings against Wade and other opposition leaders, left the Government. In January 1996 Diouf announced that a second legislative chamber, the Sénat, was to be established.

In February 1998 Wade appealed to the Constitutional Council to reject an amendment to the electoral code whereby the number of deputies in the Assemblée nationale was to be increased to 140; later in the month the Council annulled the proposed increase, the first occasion on which the Council had ruled against a decision of the legislature. In March, however, the Assemblée nationale again voted to increase the number of deputies. In April Kâ resigned from the PS to present his own list of candidates, as the Union pour le renouveau démocratique (URD).

Some 18 parties and coalitions contested the legislative elections on 24 May 1998. The PS obtained 93 seats in the enlarged assembly, while the number of PDS deputies was reduced to 23; Kâ's URD, in alliance with the Alliance pour le progrès et la justice—Jëf-Jël (APJ—JJ), secured 11 seats. Voter turn-out was 39% of the registered electorate. In July Thiam resigned as Prime Minister, and was replaced by Mamadou Lamine Loum. A new Council of Ministers was named shortly afterwards, in which Serigne Diop, the leader of the Parti démocratique sénégalais—Rénovation (which had broken away from the PDS in 1997), was the only non-PS member.

In August 1998 the Assemblée nationale voted to revise the Constitution to remove the clause restricting the Head of State to a maximum of two terms of office, thus permitting Diouf to contest the next presidential election, in 2000. A requirement that the President be elected by more than 25% of all registered voters was also abandoned. The opposition parties, condemning the amendments, boycotted the vote.

The PS won all 45 elective seats in the first, indirect, elections to the Sénat in January 1999; these 45 members were chosen by an electoral college of deputies, local, municipal and regional councillors. Only the PS, the Parti libéral du Sénégal (formed in 1998 by Ngom, leading a breakaway movement from the PDS), and a coalition of the Parti de l'indépendance et du travail (PIT) and AJ—PADS contested the elections; the PDS and other opposition parties were opposed to the introduction of an additional parliamentary chamber. A further 12 senators were appointed by the President of the Republic, including two opposition figures, and three were elected by Senegalese resident abroad. One of the 12 senators nominated by Diouf, Abdoulaye Diack, a prominent member of the PS, was elected President of the new body.

In March 1999 an alliance of AJ—PADS, the PIT, the PDS and the Ligue démocratique—Mouvement pour le parti du travail (LD—MPT) agreed to nominate Wade, who had resigned from the Assemblée nationale in mid-1998, as their joint candidate in the presidential election scheduled for 2000. In June 1999 former Minister of Foreign Affairs Moustapha Niasse announced his intention of contesting the presidential election, and published a document accusing Diouf and the PS of corruption; Niasse was consequently expelled from the PS and subsequently formed the Alliance des forces de progrès (AFP).

Although Diouf won the largest proportion of the votes cast (41.3%) at the election, held on 27 February 2000, his failure to secure an absolute majority of the votes cast necessitated a second round of voting, between Diouf and Wade (who had secured 31.0% of the votes cast). Of the remaining candidates, Niasse received 16.8% of the votes cast, while Kâ took 7.1%. Prior to the second round of voting, Wade received the endorsement of the majority of the candidates defeated in the first round, with the notable exception of Kâ. At the second round, on 19 March, Wade won 58.5% of the total votes cast, thus taking the presidency from the PS for the first time. Turn-out in the second round was estimated at 60.1%, marginally lower than in the first round.

The new Constitution

Wade was sworn in as President on 1 April 2000 and named Niasse as Prime Minister. The new Council of Ministers incorporated several other opposition leaders, including Savané of AJ—PADS and Abdoulaye Bathily of the LD—MPT. Wade announced that he did not envisage governing alongside an Assemblée nationale dominated by the PS, and that he therefore intended to hold fresh legislative elections, following a constitutional referendum. Among the proposed changes, the President would gain the power to dissolve the Assemblée nationale, while other presidential powers would be transferred to the Prime Minister, and the presidential mandate would again be reduced from seven to five years, renewable only once. Furthermore, the Sénat was to be abolished.

The constitutional referendum was held on 7 January 2001. Some 94.0% of the votes cast in the plebiscite supported the new Constitution; 65.8% of the registered electorate voted. Most provisions of the Constitution, including the abolition of the Sénat and the Economic and Social Council, took immediate effect, with only those sections relating to the legislature necessitating new elections before their implementation. Future presidential mandates would be reduced from seven to five years, and the number of deputies in the Assemblée nationale was reduced from 140 to 120.

The President dissolved the Assemblée nationale in February 2001 and announced that the new legislature, which was to be elected in April, would consist of 65 seats elected by majority voting in departments and 55 by proportional representation using national lists. In March Wade appointed Mame Madior Boye, a politically unaffiliated magistrate, and hitherto Minister of Justice, as Prime Minister. In the ensuing reshuffle Niasse and other members of the AFP were removed from office, in what was regarded as an attempt by Wade to create a more unified Government, which incorporated greater representation for the PDS and its allies, prior to the legislative elections.

Legislative elections duly took place on 29 April 2001, contested by 25 parties. The pro-Wade Sopi (Change) coalition won 89 of the 120 seats in the Assemblée nationale, the AFP 11 and the PS only 10. The rate of electoral participation was 67.5%. Boye was reappointed as Prime Minister on 10 May. The new 24-member Government comprised 11 members of the PDS (which obtained most principal posts), nine representatives of civil society, and two members each of AJ—PADS and the LD—MPT.

Following the elections, nine parties, including the AFP, the APJ—JJ and the URD, announced that they were to join the PS in an informal opposition alliance. In August 2001 some 25 parties, led by the PDS, formed a pro-presidential electoral alliance, the Convergence des actions autour du Président en perspective du 21ème siècle (CAP-21), in advance of local and municipal elections; meanwhile, opposition groups also formed an electoral alliance, the Cadre permanent de concertation. In February 2002 the three men convicted of the assassination of Babacar Sèye in 1993 were granted presidential pardons and subsequently released from prison, provoking renewed controversy about the case. In the local and municipal elections, which were held on 12 May 2002, CAP-21 won control of nine of the 11 regional governments, as well as a majority of municipal and communal seats.

The sinking of a state-owned passenger ferry, the MV *Joola*, in September 2002, en route from Ziguinchor, the principal city of Casamance, to Dakar led to a national political crisis, even before the final death toll of the accident, subsequently enumerated at more than 1,800 people, became apparent. In early October the Minister of Equipment and Transport, Youssouph Sakho, and the Minister of the Armed Forces, Yoba Sambou, resigned in response to the tragedy, as it became clear that the vessel had been severely overloaded; only 64 survivors were reported. Later in the month the head of the navy was dismissed, and Wade announced that the Government accepted responsibility for the disaster. In early November Wade dismissed Boye and her Government; the dismissal was widely believed to have been prompted by the Government's response to the disaster. Shortly after Boye's dismissal, an inquiry into the incident found that safety regulations had been widely violated on the *Joola*, and that the dispatch of rescue equipment and staff to the ship by the armed forces had been inexplicably delayed. Idrissa Seck, the Mayor of Thiès, a close ally of Wade and previously a senior official in the PDS, was appointed as the new Prime Minister. In August 2003 the Chief of Staff of the Armed Forces and the Chief of Staff of the Air Force were dismissed as a result of disciplinary action related to the response to the sinking of the *Joola*.

Political tensions intensified in early 2004 as several parties that had supported Wade's candidacy in the presidential election of 2000 and had ministerial representation in the Government, including the LD—MPT and AJ—PADS, declined to participate in celebrations organized to mark the fourth anniversary of Wade's accession to power. In April Wade dismissed Seck's Government, appointing Macky Sall, hitherto Minister of State, Minister of the Interior and Local Communities, Government Spokesperson, as Prime Minister. Although the allocation of most strategic portfolios in the new Council of Ministers remained largely unchanged, Cheikh Sadibou Fall was accorded the post of Minister of the Interior. In November Wade reorganized the Government, dismissing Fall as Minister of the Interior and replacing him with Ngom (who had been appointed as Minister of Trade in July).

In March 2005 Wade effected a further government reorganization, replacing two members of the LD—MPT with affiliates of the PDS, leaving AJ—PADS as the only party (other than the PDS) to retain ministerial representation from the alliance that supported Wade's presidential candidacy in 2000. The dismissals followed several months of discord between the PDS and the LD—MPT over the latter's criticism of Wade's presidency. Amid ongoing tensions within the PDS, a further reorganization of the Government in May 2005 was interpreted as an attempt to strengthen support for the President. Wade appointed members to a new Commission électorale nationale autonome (CENA) in June; however, the opposition expressed concern at the composition of the body.

Seck was questioned by police in July 2005, after he was accused by President Wade of overspending on work to upgrade roads in Thiès, where he served as mayor. The former Prime Minister, whose house had been attacked in May, refuted any suggestion that he had embezzled government funds from the project. Later in July Seck was formally charged with endangering national security; there was no immediate explanation of the charges, which Seck's defence lawyers claimed to be politically motivated. In September the Assemblée nationale ruled that Seck should be brought to trial on charges of embezzlement at the High Court of Justice, which was reserved for cases concerning crimes committed by members of the Government in the exercise of their duties. Meanwhile, the Assemblée nationale adopted legislation providing for the eventual creation of a new administrative and political capital some 150 km northeast of Dakar, near Kébèmer (rather than at Mékhé-Pékesse, which had been the location proposed in December 2002).

In December 2005 the Assemblée nationale approved legislation, supported by President Wade, that delayed the legislative elections, which had been scheduled for mid-2006, until February 2007, when they were to be held concurrently with presidential voting. Wade justified this postponement (which was condemned by the parliamentary opposition) on financial grounds. (The legislative elections were later postponed further until June 2007.)

Seck was released from detention in February 2006, following the partial dismissal of the charges of corruption and embezzlement against him (some minor charges remained against him, however); the charges of endangering state security had been dropped in the previous month.

In November 2006, prior to the forthcoming presidential election, the Assemblée nationale adopted new legislation ending the obligation for a candidate to receive votes from one-quarter of the total registered electorate to be elected in the first round. Under the new law it became possible for a candidate to secure victory in the first round by obtaining a majority of more than 50% of recorded votes.

Recent developments: Wade's second term

The presidential election took place on 25 February 2007. President Wade secured a second term of office in the first round, winning 55.9% of the votes cast; his closest rival, with 14.9% of the votes, was Seck. Two days after the election five ministers resigned and a government reorganization was implemented. Those who left the Government were members of AJ—PADS, hitherto an ally of the ruling PDS, and cited changes in the relationship with the ruling party as reasons for their resignations.

Legislative elections were held on 3 June 2007, at which President Wade's Sopi Coalition (comprising some 40 parties and movements, led by the PDS) secured 131 of the 150 available seats. However, many of the principal opposition parties chose to boycott the ballot when their demands for the establishment of an independent electoral commission were not met, and voter turn-out was estimated at just 34.7%. Later that month Prime Minister Sall resigned and was replaced by Cheikh Hadjibou Soumaré, hitherto Minister-delegate at the Office of the Minister of State of the Economy and Finance, responsible for the Budget. Soumaré subsequently named a new Government, which included 13 new appointees, eight of whom were women; the key portfolios remained unaltered.

Meanwhile, in May 2007 the Assemblée nationale voted to reinstate the Sénat, which had been dissolved in 2001 by President Wade owing to financial constraints. Opposition members who had contested the inauguration of the second chamber in 1999 accused President Wade of proposing contradictory policies. On 19 August 2007 parliamentarians and local officials elected 35 of the 100 senators; 34 of those seats were secured by PDS members. President Wade appointed the remaining 65 members, prompting concern that balance in the newly restored chamber would weigh in favour of the ruling party. The Sénat was officially installed in September; Pape Diop was elected President of that body and was replaced as President of the Assemblée nationale by former Prime Minister Sall.

In May 2008 President Wade proposed an amendment to the Constitution, approved by the Council of Ministers, that would result in the extension of the presidential term of office from five to seven years. Wade suggested that the current mandate did not allow sufficient time to develop long-term policies, although it was stated that the new legislation would not be applicable to the current presidency, and would only enter into force after the next presidential election, which was due to be held in 2012. Wade promulgated the amendment in October 2008. Also that month the Sénat approved the amendment of the mandate of the President of the Assemblée nationale, from five years to a renewable term of one year. The move was regarded as preparation for removing Sall from office and the following month he was dismissed; Mamadou Seck, a former finance minister, was appointed in Sall's place. Sall subsequently announced that he had left the PDS to establish his own party, the Alliance pour la République (APR—Yaakaar).

In April 2009 Prime Minister Soumaré tendered his resignation and that of the Government. The announcement followed local elections, held the previous month, in which opposition parties had secured the majority of the seats available for the first time since 2000. In May 2009 President Wade nominated Souleymane Ndéné Ndiaye, hitherto Minister of State, Minister of the Maritime Economy, Maritime Transport, Fisheries and Fishbreeding, as Prime Minister and a new Council of Ministers was announced. Although the key portfolios remained unchanged, Karim Wade, son of the President, entered the administration as Minister of State, Minister of International Co-operation, Land Settlement, Air Transport and Infrastructure. Countering speculation that Wade was opening the way for his son to stand in the next presidential election, in August Abdoulaye Wade confirmed that he would be the party's presidential candidate in 2012.

In October 2009 President Wade carried out a ministerial reorganization in which the Minister of State, Minister of Foreign Affairs, Cheikh Tidiane Gadio, who had been in office since Wade came to power, was replaced by Madické Niang, hitherto Minister of State, Minister of Justice. It was widely believed that Niang had been appointed in order to mediate in a diplomatic crisis caused by Wade's support of the junta leader, Capt. Moussa Dadis Camara, in neighbouring Guinea. The interior and defence portfolios were allocated to new appointees, with both new ministers coming from Casamance, where renewed unrest had been experienced (see Separatism in Casamance). Wade effected a series of minor changes to the composition of the Council of Ministers in December, most notably appointing El Hadji Amadou Sall to the position of Minister of State, Minister of Justice and Keeper of the Seals, in place of Prof. Moustapha Sourang.

In January 2010, following criticism from both the Muslim and Christian communities of his New Year's message and support for the construction of a so-called 'Monument to the African Renaissance', which was deemed to be idolatrous by some imams, President Wade appointed within his office an adviser on religious affairs with the aim of facilitating inter-faith accord. Later in the month Wade appointed close ally and former magistrate Doudou Ndir as President of the CENA, following the resignation of the incumbent, Mamadou Moustapha Touré, apparently at Wade's request. In June Sall was replaced as Minister of State, Minister of Justice and Keeper of the Seals, after only six months in office, by another associate of the President, Cheikh Tidjane Sy, who had formerly occupied the post in 2005–08. Wade further reorganized his Government later that month, notably dismissing the Minister of Agriculture and the Minister of Telecommunications, Information and Communication Technology, and Road and Rail Transport, the latter portfolio being divided into three; a number of additional women entered the Council of Ministers, including Innocence Ntap as Minister of State, Minister of Labour and Professional Organizations, bringing their number to 12 out of 41 ministers.

In August 2010 the opposition denounced a move to appoint further presidential allies to strategic posts ahead of the 2012 elections, when Wade nominated Cheikh Tidiane Diakhaté as President of the Constitutional Council, the body that would be responsible for considering any challenge to the legality of a third presidential mandate for Wade should he formally register his candidacy. In September 2010 three ministerial portfolios were reshuffled: Ngom, hitherto Minister of Mines, Industry, Agro-industry and Small and Medium-sized Enterprises became Minister of the Interior, replacing Bécaye Diop, who was appointed as Minister of the Armed Forces, succeeding Abdoulaye Baldé, who was allocated the mines portfolio; all three retained the rank of Minister of State. Meanwhile, there had been angry protests in Dakar against recurring power cuts, and in late September an IMF mission noted that electricity outages were one of the major factors negatively affecting economic growth. In response, in October President Wade dismissed the Minister of State, Minister of Energy, Samuel Sarr, and ordered an audit of the state electricity company, the Société nationale d'électricité. Karim Wade assumed additional responsibility for energy, becoming Minister of State, Minister of International Co-operation, Air Transport, Infrastructure and Energy, ceding the land settlement portfolio to the Minister of Road and Rail Transport, Nafissatou Diouf Ngom. In November President Wade issued a decree scheduling the presidential election for 26 February 2012, and a few days later a committee of the ruling PDS endorsed his candidacy, rejecting claims from the opposition that such a move was unconstitutional. Revision of the electoral lists began in January 2011. In May Wade carried out a minor reorganization of the Council of Ministers.

Separatism in Casamance

Long-standing resentment against the Government of Senegal in the southern province of Casamance (which is virtually cut off from the rest of the country by the enclave of The Gambia) was embodied from the early 1980s by the separatist Mouvement des forces démocratiques de la Casamance (MFDC). The announcement in May 1991 of the imminent release of more than 340 detainees (including the Secretary-General and executive leader of the MFDC, Fr Augustin Diamacouné Senghor) who had been arrested in connection with unrest in Casamance facilitated the conclusion, shortly afterwards in Guinea-Bissau, of a cease-fire agreement by representatives of the Senegalese Government and of the MFDC. An amnesty was approved by the Assemblée nationale later in June, and some 400 detainees were released. A period of relative calm ensued.

In January 1992 a peace commission, comprising government representatives and members of the MFDC, was established, with mediation by Guinea-Bissau. A resurgence of violence in Casamance from July prompted the Government to redeploy armed forces in the region, giving rise to MFDC protests that the 'remilitarization' of Casamance contravened the truce. Contradictory statements made by MFDC leaders regarding their commitment to the peace accord evidenced a split within the movement. The 'Front nord' and the MFDC Vice-President, Sidi Badji, appealed to the rebels to lay down their arms, while the 'Front sud', led by Diamacouné Senghor (who was now based in Guinea-Bissau), appeared determined to continue the armed struggle. After an escalation of the conflict in late 1992 and early 1993, a new round of negotiations resulted in the signing, in July 1993, of a cease-fire agreement, known as the Ziguinchor Accord, between the Government and Diamacouné Senghor (who had returned to Ziguinchor in March). Guinea-Bissau was to act as a guarantor of the agreement, and the Government of France was to be asked to submit an historical arbitration regarding the Casamance issue. In December France issued its judgment that Casamance had not existed as an autonomous territory prior to the colonial period, and that independence for the region had been neither demanded nor considered at the time of decolonization.

In September 1995 a Commission nationale de paix (CNP) was established and members of the commission reportedly sought a dialogue with Diamacouné Senghor and the MFDC's four other political leaders (all of whom remained under house arrest). During October renewed rebel attacks on government forces were accompanied by a major army offensive in the south-west. By the end of November it was reported that about 150 separatists and 15 members of the armed forces had been killed in clashes.

While both the Senegalese authorities and the MFDC leadership appeared committed to reviving the peace process, the deaths of 25 soldiers in August 1997 near Ziguinchor prompted fears of a revival of the conflict. In September the armed forces launched a new offensive, in which rebel forces were reported to have sustained heavy losses. A further armed forces offensive in October involved as many as 3,000 troops and resulted in the deaths of 12 soldiers and 80 rebels in clashes near the border with Guinea-Bissau, according to Senegalese military sources. Salif Sadio, the MFDC's military leader, stated that the organization remained committed to the peace process, but maintained that its forces were justified in defending themselves against armed attack.

In January 1998 Diamacouné Senghor appealed for a cease-fire, indicating that his organization would be prepared to abandon its demand for independence, subject to the Government instituting measures to ensure greater economic and social development in Casamance. Nevertheless, rebel violence continued intermittently throughout the second half of 1998.

In June 1999 talks between several MFDC factions began in Banjul, The Gambia, although several leaders of military and exiled factions of the MFDC did not attend, claiming that Diamacouné Senghor was effectively a hostage of the Senegalese Government. At the meeting, Léopold Sagna was confirmed as the head of the armed forces of the MFDC, replacing Sadio, who was reportedly less prepared to compromise with government demands. The Senegalese authorities subsequently acceded to the MFDC's demand that Diamacouné Senghor be released from house arrest; his movements were, however, to remain restricted.

In November 1999 Diamacouné Senghor agreed to recommence negotiations with the Senegalese Government, demanding, however, that the safety of MFDC negotiators be guaranteed, and that representatives of Casamançais civil society be included in the negotiations. At the meeting, held in Banjul in December, the Senegalese Government and the MFDC agreed to an immediate cease-fire and to create the conditions necessary to bring about lasting peace; the Governments of The Gambia and of Guinea-Bissau were to monitor the situation in the region. In February 2000 a joint mission of the Senegalese Government and the MFDC was established to oversee the cease-fire. Following his election as President in March, Abdoulaye Wade announced that he was to continue the process of negotiations, but that his preference was to conduct direct dialogue with the MFDC. Wade further announced that Diamacouné Senghor would be permitted total freedom of movement.

In November 2000 members of a peace commission, headed by the Minister of the Interior, Maj.-Gen. Mamadou Niang, and by Diamacouné Senghor, signed a joint statement that envisaged a series of official meetings between the Senegalese Government and the MFDC, the first of which would convene on 16 December. The Government simultaneously warned that full legal action would be taken against any person promoting or distributing speeches in favour of separatism. The discussions in December were boycotted by representatives of the Front sud of the MFDC, which was now led by Ali Badji. However, a senior MFDC official present at the onset of negotiations, Alexandre Djiba (who had long been resident outside Senegal), subsequently reportedly met Ali Badji's representatives in Guinea-Bissau.

The overwhelming support in Casamance for the new Constitution, which was endorsed by 96% of voters in the region at the referendum in January 2001, prompted Wade to announce that Casamance had definitively voted to remain part of Senegal. In mid-January the Guinea-Bissau armed forces reportedly destroyed all the Casamance rebel bases in that country, in response to clashes between rival MFDC factions there. Continued unrest in the region south-west of Ziguinchor further delayed the signature of a cease-fire agreement, originally intended to take place at the meeting of mid-December 2000, which had been rescheduled to occur in Dakar in early February 2001.

In February 2001 Diamacouné Senghor announced that, in order to accelerate the peace process in Casamance, several senior members of the MFDC, including Sidi Badji and Djiba, had been removed from their positions. However, Sidi Badji, who had served as Military Affairs Adviser to Diamacouné Senghor, rejected the legitimacy of his dismissal. Also in mid-February, in what was reportedly the most serious attack on civilian targets in Casamance for several years, separatist rebels killed some 13 civilians in an ambush. Both Sidi Badji and Diamacouné Senghor denied any knowledge of their supporters' involvement and condemned the attack, into which Wade announced the opening of a judicial inquiry.

In mid-March 2001 Minister of the Interior Mamadou Niang and Diamacouné Senghor signed a cease-fire agreement at a meeting in Ziguinchor, which provided for the release of detainees, the return of refugees, the removal of landmines (which had been utilized in the region since 1998) and for economic aid to reintegrate rebels and to ameliorate the infrastructure of Casamance. Some 16 prisoners were released several days after the accord was signed. The Gambian Government issued a communiqué in mid-March, in which it promised to prevent armed rebel groups from operating on Gambian territory; it was suspected that the renewed violence had been co-ordinated by groups based in The Gambia. Later in March Niang and Diamacouné Senghor signed a further agreement, which provided for the disarmament of rebel groups and the confinement to barracks of military forces in Casamance. In April Wade and Minister of the Armed Forces Yoba Sambou participated in negotiations with Diamacouné Senghor, at which other MFDC leaders, including Sidi Badji, were also present.

As a result of the renewed conflict, Diamacouné Senghor announced, in May 2001, that a proposed reconciliation forum, intended to unite the various factions of the MFDC, had been postponed indefinitely, and a number of members of the movement, including Djiba, were reportedly expelled. Nonetheless, Diamacouné Senghor and Sidi Badji attended a meeting convened by the Gambian Government in Banjul in early June, in an attempt to overcome the impasse. As tensions between factions within the MFDC intensified, with further clashes reported in

June and July, Diamacouné Senghor was removed from the position of Secretary-General of the MFDC in August, at the much-delayed reconciliation forum, and appointed as honorary President. Jean-Marie François Biagui, who had previously been involved in the French-based section of the MFDC, became Secretary-General and de facto leader. Sidi Badji, who continued to question the tactics of Diamacouné Senghor, was appointed as the organization's head of military affairs. Biagui not only demonstrated considerable reluctance to play a leadership role, but was also apparently unable to prevent Sidi Badji, who was reputed to have support from the authorities in The Gambia, from becoming the dominant force in the movement.

Despite these personnel changes within the MFDC, President Wade met Diamacouné Senghor at the presidential palace in Dakar in September 2001; both leaders reiterated the importance of implementing the cease-fire agreement. In response to this meeting, it was reported that the new leadership of the MFDC had suspended all further negotiations with the Government. Following further attacks by rebels, Biagui resigned as Secretary-General of the MFDC in early November. Sidi Badji was announced as Biagui's successor, in an acting capacity, although Diamacouné Senghor rejected this appointment, and reappointed Biagui as Secretary-General. In December Diamacouné Senghor's position was further undermined, when an episcopal conference declared that his leadership of a movement that was using armed struggle to attain its ends was incompatible with his role as a Roman Catholic priest.

In August 2002, following a joint declaration signed by Diamacouné Senghor and Sidi Badji urging the resumption of peace talks between the rebels and the Government, Wade appointed an official delegation, chaired by the Second Vice-President of the Assemblée nationale and President of Ziguinchor Regional Council, Abdoulaye Faye, and including among its membership Niang and Sambou, to undertake negotiations with the MFDC. Meanwhile, the holding of an intra-Casamance conference, in early September, appeared to indicate a decline in support for separatist aspirations, as the conference produced a declaration, signed by representatives of 10 ethnic groups resident in the region, in favour of a 'definitive peace in Casamance', and which referred to the region as 'belonging to the great and single territory of Senegal'. However, the absence from the meeting of the MFDC faction loyal to Sidi Badji appeared to refute reports that the various wings of the MFDC had effectively reunited. In late September five civilians, including the brother of Sambou, were killed in an attack attributed to separatist rebels north of Ziguinchor. The internal disunity of the MFDC was emphasized in October, when Biagui, announcing that the conflict had definitively ended, publicly demanded forgiveness from the people of Casamance and Senegal for the actions of the organization; this statement was emphatically rejected by Sidi Badji.

In May 2003 President Wade announced that several substantive measures towards the normalization of the political and economic situation in Casamance were to be implemented, notably major infrastructure projects and the rehabilitation of damaged villages. Wade also announced that the Government intended to accede to a further MFDC demand, by dismissing those implicated in the failed attempt to rescue the passengers of the stricken *Joola* ferry in September 2002 (see Domestic Political Affairs), and arranging the provision of a replacement for the vessel, which had provided a key transport link between the Casamance region and Dakar. Reports suggested that the apparent death of Salif Sadio, regarded as a leading opponent of compromise within the MFDC, had been a major factor in facilitating the improved relationship between the organization and the Government. (However, no clear proof of Sadio's death was presented.)

In May 2003 Diamacouné Senghor announced that an MFDC convention, comprising 460 participants from the various factions of the organization, was to be held in Guinea-Bissau in June. Following the death of Sidi Badji, from natural causes, in late May, the convention was postponed, initially to July. However, the Guinea-Bissau authorities announced that they would be unable to provide sufficient guarantees of security for participants, and the meeting was again postponed, until October, when the gathering was held in Ziguinchor. On this occasion both Diamacouné Senghor and Biagui issued statements confirming that the conflict had ended, and announced that what was termed the emancipation of Casamance did not, as a matter of course, necessarily entail its independence from Senegal. Following the restoration of peace in Casamance, it was anticipated that some 15,000 displaced persons would return to their home villages in the Ziguinchor administrative region, while demining operations commenced in July 2004.

In September 2004 it was reported that an extraordinary general assembly of the MFDC had dismissed Diamacouné Senghor as the organization's leader and, as in 2001, appointed him Honorary President, while Biagui was reappointed Secretary-General and de facto leader. Biagui subsequently announced that the MFDC intended to transform itself into a legitimate political party and contest national elections; however, his status as leader was rejected by the MFDC's military wing, which issued a statement declaring its continuing recognition of Diamacouné Senghor as the movement's leader, while also reaffirming its commitment to full independence for Casamance. (The Senegalese Government was also reported to regard Diamacouné Senghor as remaining the MFDC's legitimate leader for the purposes of negotiations.) Following talks in Paris, France, between representatives of the Government and the external wing of the MFDC, plans were announced for the signing of a cease-fire between the two parties in December 2004, to be followed by detailed negotiations towards a peaceful political settlement, although the Government's representatives insisted that there would be no concessions offered on the issue of independence for the region. Concerns persisted, however, over internal divisions within the MFDC: Diamacouné Senghor's appeal for a general assembly of the movement in November, intended to reconcile the various factions in advance of the signing of the cease-fire, was reportedly rejected by his rivals in the movement's political wing, while Abdoulaye Diédhiou, leader of the military wing Atika ('arrow'), insisted that independence remained the MFDC's primary aim and criticized Diamacouné Senghor for making excessive concessions to the Senegalese Government.

On 30 December 2004 a 'General Peace Accord' was signed in Ziguinchor by the Minister of the Interior, on behalf of the Government, and Diamacouné Senghor, representing the MFDC. President Wade also signed the accord, which was, however, rejected by several factions of the MFDC, including Atika, the Front nord and elements of the movement's international wing. Negotiations aimed at achieving a definitive resolution of the conflict in Casamance were opened by Prime Minister Sall on 1 February 2005 in the town of Foundiougne, some 160 km south-east of Dakar, but were boycotted by Biagui and Diédhiou, who reportedly favoured further dialogue within the MFDC before engaging in talks with the Government. Both sides agreed to establish joint technical commissions to address reconstruction, economic and social development, and disarmament, demobilization and demining. Meanwhile, Diamacouné Senghor appointed Ansoumana Badji, formerly the MFDC's representative in Portugal, as Secretary-General of the movement; Badji stated that he aimed to persuade as many MFDC members as possible to join the peace process. Biagui rejected the legitimacy of Badji's appointment.

Since the signing of the 2004 peace agreement, outbreaks of violence had been sporadic. However, in August 2006 violent incidents between the Senegalese armed forces and the MFDC in Casamance began to escalate and by mid-August fighting had resumed in earnest. Although the fighting spread north towards The Gambia, there were no reports of the conflict crossing the border. Nevertheless, many civilians fled to that country, seeking refuge and medical treatment. By October the violence began to subside as the army took control of the rebels' base. However, many civilians refused to return to the region until the security forces had departed. In 2007 small-scale operations were conducted to clear the region of landmines and the people of Casamance slowly began to return to their homes. However, having been empty for over a decade, many of the villages were uninhabitable. Tensions persisted between the MFDC and the Government and a rebel faction of the MFDC was blamed for sabotaging demining efforts. Minor conflicts continued and in December the presidential envoy to the region was killed, an incident that threatened to destabilize the reconstruction process.

Renewed violence was reported in Casamance in 2009 at the beginning of the grain-planting season as armed groups to the north-west of Ziguinchor attacked Senegalese military positions along the Gambian border. In September, in retaliation for the killing of a government soldier, a Senegalese military jet bombed MFDC bases. At least 600 people fled their homes on the outskirts of Ziguinchor, according to human rights organizations. In mid-March 2010 Senegalese troops shelled MDFC positions in Casamance, just days after capturing two rebel combatants. Earlier that month hostilities had again escalated, following the killing of a Senegalese soldier in an MFDC rocket attack.

In December 2010, on the anniversary of the beginning of the rebellion in 1982, renewed violence broke out in Casamance. Senegalese military forces that had been dispatched to deal with armed robberies in the area around the town of Bignona faced strong resistance and were forced to retreat. Seven Senegalese soldiers were killed in an ambush some 35 km from Ziguinchor, while unconfirmed reports suggested that there had also been casualties on the side of the rebels. A MFDC council that had been due to meet in January 2011 to harmonize the different rebel positions was postponed, and more than 1,000 women marched on Ziguinchor, demanding an immediate end to violence and a resumption of peace negotiations. A further three government soldiers were killed and six injured in February, when MFDC rebels reportedly attacked a Senegalese military convoy some 75 km north of Ziguinchor.

Foreign Affairs

Regional relations

From 1989 Senegal's regional relations underwent a period of considerable strain. A long-standing border dispute with Mauritania, which also involved ethnic and economic rivalries, was exacerbated by the deaths, in April of that year, of two Senegalese farmers, who had been involved in a dispute regarding grazing rights with Mauritanian livestock-breeders. Mauritanian nationals residing in Senegal were attacked, and their businesses looted, while Senegalese nationals in Mauritania suffered similar aggression. By early May it was believed that several hundred people, mostly Senegalese, had been killed. Operations to repatriate nationals of both countries commenced, with international assistance. Diplomatic relations, which had been suspended in August 1989, were fully restored in April 1992, and the process of reopening the border began in May, although the contentious issues that had hitherto impeded the normalization of relations remained largely unresolved. In December 1994, however, the Governments of Senegal and Mauritania agreed new co-operation measures, including efforts to facilitate the free movement of goods and people between the two countries.

In January 1995 the Governments of Senegal, Mauritania and Mali undertook to co-operate in resolving joint border issues and in combating extremism, arms-smuggling and drugs-trafficking. In July the office of the UN High Commissioner for Refugees (UNHCR) began a census of Mauritanian refugees in Senegal, estimated to number some 66,000, as part of initiatives for their eventual repatriation. In May 1998 the Ministers of the Interior of Mauritania, Mali and Senegal met to discuss border security, following reports of increased cross-border banditry, particularly in eastern Senegal. The unrest in the region was blamed by the Senegalese press on the continued presence there of Mauritanian refugees; in September it was reported that the Senegalese authorities had ceased to issue the refugees with travel documents. In May 1999 the two countries signed a further agreement on the joint exploitation of fisheries. In mid-2000, however, a dispute over water rights resulted in a period of substantial tension between Senegal and Mauritania. Following renewed negotiations, the visit of President Taya of Mauritania to Dakar in April, as the guest of honour at a ceremony to commemorate the 41st anniversary of the independence of Senegal, was widely regarded as indicating an improvement in relations between the countries. Presidents Taya and Wade met again in July 2003, when negotiations were conducted on a range of bilateral and international issues; Wade reiterated his support for Taya's administration, following an attempted coup in Mauritania in the previous month. The extradition of one of the suspected coup plotters from Senegal to Mauritania was also interpreted as an indication of improved relations between the countries, as was the Mauritanian Government's decision to accord 270 temporary fishing licences to Senegalese fishermen in June 2004. Around 21,300 UNHCR-assisted Mauritanian refugees were estimated to remain in Senegal in 2010.

In October 1993 Senegal and Guinea-Bissau signed an agreement regarding the joint exploitation and management of fishing and petroleum resources in their maritime zones. This treaty was ratified in December 1995, to the effect that fishing resources were to be shared equally between the two countries, while Senegal was to benefit from an 85% share of revenue obtained from petroleum deposits. During bilateral contacts in 1995–97 Senegal and Guinea-Bissau pledged co-operation in matters of joint defence and security. It was hoped that the movement of refugees from the conflict in Casamance to Guinea-Bissau, which began, under the auspices of UNHCR, in February 1996, would expedite efforts to restore security in the border region between the countries. In January 1998 it was announced that the authorities in Guinea-Bissau had intercepted a consignment of armaments destined for MFDC rebels and that some 15 officers of the Guinea-Bissau armed forces had been arrested and suspended from duty, including the head of the armed forces, Brig. (later Gen.) Ansumane Mané. In June, however, troops loyal to Mané rebelled against President Commdr João Vieira of Guinea-Bissau, and civil war broke out in that country. Senegalese troops intervened in support of the armed forces loyal to Vieira. By the end of the month refugees from the conflict were crossing into Casamance, exacerbating security concerns in the province, while it was also reported that members of the MFDC were fighting alongside the rebels against the Government of Guinea-Bissau and Senegalese forces. From December, as a result of a peace-keeping agreement brokered by the Economic Community of West African States (ECOWAS, see p. 257), Senegalese troops began to depart from Guinea-Bissau, but strengthened their presence in the border area, while the ECOWAS peace-keeping force, ECOMOG (see p. 261), assumed positions on the Guinea-Bissau side of the frontier with Casamance.

In May 1999 fighting again broke out in Guinea-Bissau, and Vieira was overthrown (although he returned from exile in 2005 to secure victory in democratic elections). Tensions between Guinea-Bissau and Senegal resurfaced in April 2000, when an armed group, reportedly composed of members of the MFDC operating from within Guinea-Bissau, attacked a Senegalese border post, killing three soldiers, and later that month the border between the two countries was temporarily closed. In August the terms of the agreement concerning the joint exploitation of maritime resources by the two countries was revised; henceforth, Guinea-Bissau was to receive 20% rather than 15% of the revenue generated from petroleum deposits. In early September, following clashes near the border in Guinea-Bissau, attributed to an armed faction of the MFDC, the Senegalese Government closed all border posts between the two countries. Following the killing of Mané in November 2000, during an attempted coup, relations between Senegal and Guinea-Bissau improved significantly.

In March 2009, following the assassination of both the Guinea-Bissau army chief of staff and of President Vieira, the country became severely destabilized and there were fears that violence would again be renewed in the Casamance region in Senegal, where peace had been largely dependent on political stability in Guinea-Bissau. In October Guinea-Bissau placed its troops on alert following a renewed border dispute over the allocation by Senegalese authorities of plots of land along the coast between Cabrouse (a Senegalese town in southern Casamance) and Tcheda in Guinea-Bissau. The area, which has potential to be developed for tourism, is claimed by Guinea-Bissau as an integral part of its territory.

In August 1989 Diouf announced the withdrawal of Senegalese troops from The Gambia, in protest at a request by President Jawara of that country that The Gambia be accorded more power within the confederal agreement of Senegambia that had been formed by the two countries in 1982. Diouf subsequently stated that, in view of The Gambia's reluctance to proceed towards full political and economic integration with Senegal, the functions of the Confederation would be suspended. The Confederation was dissolved in September. In January 1991 the two countries signed a bilateral treaty of friendship and co-operation. Senegal's abrupt decision to close the Senegalese–Gambian border in September 1993, apparently to reduce smuggling between the two countries, again strained relations, although subsequent negotiations sought to minimize the adverse effects of the closure on The Gambia's regional trading links. Since the coup in The Gambia in July 1994 Senegal has fostered cordial relations with the Government of President Jammeh and in June 1996 the two countries agreed to adopt joint measures to combat insecurity, illegal immigration, arms-trafficking and drugs-smuggling. In early 1998 Jammeh offered to act as a mediator between the Senegalese Government and the MFDC, and subsequently held regular meetings with MFDC representatives. None the less, intermittent disputes relating to transportation issues between the two countries have occurred, and tensions between the two countries again heightened in mid-2005, following a 100% increase in transportation fees on the ferry across the Gambia

SENEGAL

river by the Gambian port authorities. Senegalese trade unionists blockaded border crossings between Senegal and The Gambia to protest at the increase, and the Senegalese Government granted fuel subsidies to drivers who used a longer, alternative route between the southern and northern parts of Senegal, avoiding The Gambia. Although tensions lessened later in the year, when the port authority reduced the ferry charges by 15%, in what was described as a gesture of goodwill, there was increasing speculation that the Senegalese authorities were considering the construction of a tunnel to link the southern and northern parts of Senegal. Bilateral relations were again strained in March 2006 following allegations of Senegalese complicity in an abortive coup in The Gambia. One of those arrested in connection with the plot reportedly claimed to have been instructed by the alleged leader of the coup (who was believed to have fled to Senegal) to liaise with the Senegalese embassy in The Gambia. The Senegalese Government denied any involvement in the plot, which it condemned, and recalled its ambassador to The Gambia for consultations; a new ambassador was appointed in June. In February 2011 Senegal and The Gambia agreed to establish a boundary management commission to address matters relating to their common border.

Since his election in March 2000, President Wade has on several occasions promoted greater democratization in other West African countries and encouraged an expansion in the international political engagement of African countries. Notably, Wade's well-publicized condemnation, at an international conference on racism and xenophobia held under the auspices of the office of the UN High Commissioner for Human Rights in Dakar in January 2001, of the increasing importance of ethnically based politics in Côte d'Ivoire prompted violent demonstrations across Côte d'Ivoire. At the UN World Conference against Racism, Racial Discrimination, Xenophobia and Related Intolerance, held in Durban, South Africa, in August–September, Wade, notably among African leaders, condemned the notion that reparations should be paid by Western nations to the descendants of slaves. In February 2010 Wade was appointed by ECOWAS to mediate in the ongoing Nigerien political crisis, while in April he was also invited to participate in attempts to resolve the continued deadlock between the Government and the Forces nouvelles in Côte d'Ivoire. In early November, however, Côte d'Ivoire recalled its ambassador from Dakar, accusing the Senegalese Government of seeking to interfere in the forthcoming second round of its presidential election, after Wade met with the opposition candidate, Alassane Ouattara.

President Wade was one of the four African leaders most closely involved in the initial development of the New Partnership for Africa's Development (NEPAD, see p. 184), a long-term plan for socio-economic recovery in Africa that was launched in October 2001 in accordance with a decision of the Organization of African Unity (OAU, now the African Union—AU, see p. 183) summit of heads of state and government held in Lusaka, Zambia, in July of that year.

Other external relations

Relations with France have remained particularly strong since independence, and the existing defence arrangements between France and Senegal remained substantially unaltered following the major restructuring of the French armed forces undertaken by the administration of Jacques Chirac in the late 1990s and early 2000s. However, in April 2010, on the occasion of Senegal's 50th anniversary of independence from France, President Wade declared that Senegal would commence the reclamation of all military bases in the country previously held by France. The two countries had agreed in February to reduce the number of French troops stationed in Dakar from 1,200 to just 300 by the end of the year, and Wade indicated in his speech that discussions would swiftly commence regarding the logistics of the handover.

In late 2005 Senegal announced that it was to terminate its diplomatic relations with Taiwan in order to resume relations with the People's Republic of China. The respective embassies in Dakar and Beijing were reopened, and ambassadors were exchanged between the two countries in early 2006.

Senegal's previously strong relations with Iran were strained from October 2010, when an Iranian ship en route to Gambia docked at the port of Lagos, Nigeria, and was found to be carrying 13 containers of arms, including rocket launchers and grenades. It was widely suspected that the weapons were intended for Casamance separatist rebels (see Separatism in Casamance). The Senegalese ambassador to Iran was recalled in December, but in January 2011, following mediation by Turkey, President Wade held talks with the Iranian Minister of Foreign Affairs, Ali Akbar Salehi, in Dakar and subsequently reinstated his envoy to Iran. Investments in Senegal worth US $200m. were announced by Salehi during his visit. In February, however, the Senegalese Government again severed diplomatic relations with Iran, citing further evidence that MFDC rebels were in possession of arms supplied by that country.

Senegal is an active participant in regional and international peace-keeping operations. In February 1998 Senegal, with Mali and Mauritania, was among the principal participants in multinational military exercises conducted in eastern Senegal under the auspices of the UN and the OAU, as part of efforts to establish a regional crisis-intervention force. The exercise was organized by France and involved almost 3,500 troops from eight West African countries, as well as units from the USA, the United Kingdom and Belgium. Senegal is a member of the Accord de non-agression et d'assistance en matière de défense, which in April 1999 adopted a draft protocol on the setting up of a peace-keeping force in the region. In September a Senegalese contingent joined the international peace-keeping operation in the Kosovo and Metohija province of Yugoslavia (now Serbia and Montenegro). In April 2001 more than 500 Senegalese soldiers joined UN observer missions in the Democratic Republic of the Congo. In early 2003 it was announced that Senegal was to contribute some 650 troops to the ECOWAS military mission in Côte d'Ivoire (ECOMICI); Senegalese troops were also expected to play a prominent role in the UN Operation in Côte d'Ivoire (UNOCI, see p. 93) that assumed the responsibilities of ECOMICI from April 2004. Meanwhile, in August 2003 some 260 Senegalese troops were dispatched to serve in the ECOWAS Mission in Liberia (ECOMIL), which was replaced by the UN Mission in Liberia (UNMIL, see p. 91) in October. More recently, in 2007 Senegal agreed to contribute 1,600 peace-keeping troops to the AU/UN Hybrid Operation in Darfur, which was deployed in Sudan.

CONSTITUTION AND GOVERNMENT

The Constitution of the Republic of Senegal was promulgated following its approval by popular referendum on 7 January 2001, and entered into force thereafter, with the exception of those sections relating to the Assemblée nationale and the relations between the executive and legislative powers, which took effect following legislative elections on 29 April 2001. Executive power is held by the President, who is directly elected for a mandate of seven years (with effect from the election due in 2012), which is renewable only once. Legislative power rests with the Assemblée nationale, with 120 members elected for five years by universal adult suffrage. The judiciary is independent of the legislature and the executive. The formation of parties on an ethnic, religious or geographical basis is prohibited. The President appoints the Prime Minister, who, in consultation with the President, appoints the Council of Ministers. Senegal comprises 11 regions, each with an appointed governor, an elected local assembly and a separate budget.

REGIONAL AND INTERNATIONAL CO-OPERATION

Senegal is a member of the African Union (see p. 183), of the Economic Community of West African States (ECOWAS, see p. 257) and of the West African organs of the Franc Zone (see p. 332). Senegal is also a member of the African Groundnut Council (see p. 442), of the Africa Rice Center (see p. 442), of the Gambia River Basin Development Organization (see p. 447) and of the Organisation pour la mise en valeur du fleuve Sénégal (see p. 449).

Senegal became a member of the UN in 1960. As a contracting party to the General Agreement on Tariffs and Trade, Senegal joined the World Trade Organization (WTO, see p. 430) on its establishment in 1995. Senegal participates in the Group of 15 (G15, see p. 447) and the Group of 77 (G77, see p. 447) developing countries.

ECONOMIC AFFAIRS

In 2009, according to estimates by the World Bank, Senegal's gross national income (GNI), measured at average 2007–09 prices, was US $12,949m., equivalent to $1,030 per head (or $1,790 on an international purchasing-power parity basis). During 2000–09, it was estimated, the population increased at an average annual rate of 2.7%, while gross domestic product (GDP) per head increased by an average of 1.3% per year. Overall GDP increased, in real terms, at an average annual rate of 4.0% per year in 2000–09; growth in 2009 was 2.2%.

Agriculture (including forestry and fishing) contributed 15.5% of GDP in 2009, according to the African Development Bank (AfDB). The sector engaged 39.8% of the employed labour force in 2006. The principal cash crops are groundnuts and cotton. Senegal also exports fruit and vegetables to European markets. Groundnuts, millet, sorghum, rice, maize and vegetables are produced for domestic consumption, although Senegal has yet to achieve self-sufficiency in basic foodstuffs. The fishing sector makes an important contribution to both the domestic food supply and export revenue: fish and fish products are one of Senegal's principal export commodities, contributing 12.6% of export earnings in 2009. The sale of fishing licences to the European Union (EU, see p. 270) has been an important source of revenue. However, despite the inclusion of safeguards intended to preserve stocks, the Senegalese Government and the domestic fishing industry have expressed concerns regarding the impact of fishing by EU vessels on supplies in easily attainable waters, and negotiations for a new agreement with the EU, following the expiry of the 2002–06 accord, remained suspended in 2011. According to the World Bank, during 2000–09 agricultural GDP increased by an average of 2.0% per year; agricultural GDP rose by 7.2% in 2009.

According to the AfDB, industry (including mining, manufacturing, construction and power) contributed 23.1% of GDP in 2009. Some 17.5% of the employed labour force were engaged in the sector in 2006. During 2000–09, according to the World Bank, industrial GDP increased at an average annual rate of 3.4%. Industrial GDP decreased by 3.2% in 2008, but grew by 4.6% in 2009.

Mining contributed just 1.1% of GDP in 2009, according to the AfDB, and the sector engaged only 0.5% of the employed labour force in 2006. The principal mining activity is the extraction of calcium phosphates (aluminium phosphates are also mined in smaller quantities). Deposits of salt, fuller's earth (attapulgite), clinker, petroleum and natural gas are also exploited, and investigations are under way into the feasibility of mining copper, alluvial diamonds, uranium and iron ore. Explorations at Sabodala, in the south-east, have revealed gold reserves estimated at 30 metric tons; the first gold pour was made in March 2009. According to the AfDB, mining GDP decreased by 6.6% in 2008, but rose by 13.6% in 2009.

Manufacturing contributed 13.9% of GDP in 2009, according to the AfDB. The sector engaged 9.2% of the employed labour force in 2006. The most important manufacturing activities are food-processing (notably fish, groundnuts and sugar), chemicals, textiles and petroleum-refining (using imported crude petroleum). Exports of petroleum products contributed 23.3% of the value of total exports in 2009. According to the World Bank, manufacturing GDP increased at an average annual rate of 2.0% in 2000–09; GDP of the sector decreased by 5.1% in 2008, but increased by 6.5% in 2009.

Construction contributed 5.4% of GDP in 2009, according to the AfDB. Some 7.0% of the employed labour force were engaged in the sector in 2006. According to the AfDB, construction GDP increased by 0.2% in 2008, but decreased by 1.2% in 2009.

In 2007 Senegal derived 83.1% of its electrical energy from petroleum sources. Senegal also receives supplies from the Manantali hydroelectric power installation (constructed under the auspices of the Organisation pour la mise en valeur du fleuve Sénégal): 10.8% of Senegal's electricity was derived from hydropower in the same year. Imports of fuels (including petroleum for refining) accounted for 23.2% of the value of merchandise imports in 2009.

The services sector contributed 61.4% of GDP in 2009, according to the AfDB. Some 42.6% of the employed labour force were engaged in the sector in 2006. Tourism is a major source of foreign exchange, with receipts totalling US $622m. in 2007. Dakar's port is of considerable importance as a centre for regional trade. According to the World Bank, the GDP of the services sector increased by an average of 5.5% per year in 2000–09. The GDP of the sector increased by 6.0% in 2008, but declined by 0.2% in 2009.

In 2008 Senegal recorded a visible trade deficit of US $3,400m., and there was a deficit of $1,883.7m. on the current account of the balance of payments. In 2009 the principal source of imports was France, which supplied 20.0% of total imports; other major suppliers were Nigeria, the People's Republic of China and Thailand. Mali was the principal market for exports in that year, taking 19.3% of the total; Switzerland, India and France were also important purchasers. The principal exports in 2009 were petroleum products, fish and fish products, hydraulic cement and phosphoric acid. The principal imports in that year were agricultural and industrial machinery, petroleum and petroleum products, and rice.

Senegal's overall fiscal deficit was estimated at 304,000m. francs CFA in 2009 (equivalent to 5.0% of GDP). Senegal's general government gross debt was 1,924,960m. francs CFA in 2009, equivalent to 32.0% of GDP. Total external debt in 2008 was US $2,861m., of which $2,419m. was public and publicly guaranteed debt. In 2007 the cost of debt-servicing was equivalent to 4.4% of the value of exports of goods, services and income. The average annual rate of inflation in 2000–09 was 2.2%. Consumer prices increased by an average of 5.8% in 2008, but decreased by 1.1% in 2009. Some 10.0% of the economically active population were unemployed in 2006.

The attainment of sustained economic growth has been impeded by Senegal's dependence on revenue from a narrow export base, and by its consequent vulnerability to fluctuations in international prices for its principal commodities. Continued commitment to the programme of infrastructural development through public investment was considered essential to the maintenance of economic activity and promotion of employment, and the 2010 budget was aimed at inviting substantial private investment to provide further stimulus. Plans were announced to make Senegal a regional hub and encourage foreign partnerships, with the AfDB providing finance for three major projects: a new international airport near Ndiass (expected to be completed in 2011), the extension of the Dakar seaport, and a toll highway from Dakar linking the main economic centres. Local investment was also encouraged, with a new national airline under majority (64%) national private ownership inaugurated in January 2011. Recurrent electricity shortages were considered to be the main impediment to economic development. The Société nationale d'electricité du Sénégal continued its policy of rationing electricity in 2010, exacerbating a long-standing shortfall of national capacity and provoking protests. In early 2011 the Minister of State, Minister of International Co-operation, Air Transport, Infrastructure and Energy, Karim Wade, initiated Plan Takkal, a three-year programme aimed at addressing the power shortages by restructuring the energy sector. Meanwhile, a Saudi Arabian conglomerate acquired a 34% share in the national petroleum refinery, Société africaine de raffinage, in April 2010; the expansion of the refinery's capacity from 27,000 barrels per day to 130,000, at a cost of €350m., was planned. The Republic of Korea also agreed to increase its investment in Senegal, particularly in the energy sector, most notably through the construction of a coal-fired power plant with a capacity of 250 MW. The overall rate of economic growth slowed to 2.2% in 2009 from an already depressed 3.3% in 2008. However, the IMF projected a recovery in real GDP growth to 4.0% in 2010 and 4.4% in 2011.

PUBLIC HOLIDAYS

2012: 1 January (New Year's Day), 4 February* (Mouloud, Birth of the Prophet), 4 April (National Day), 6 April (Good Friday), 9 April (Easter Monday), 1 May (Labour Day), 17 May (Ascension Day), 28 May (Whit Monday), 14 July (Day of Association), 15 August (Assumption), 18 August* (Korité, end of Ramadan), 26 October* (Tabaski, Feast of the Sacrifice), 1 November (All Saints' Day), 24 November* (Ashoura), 25 December (Christmas).

* These holidays are determined by the Islamic lunar calendar and may vary by one or two days from the dates given.

SENEGAL

Statistical Survey

Source (unless otherwise stated): Agence nationale de la Statistique et de la Démographie, blvd de l'Est, Point E, BP 116, Dakar; tel. 33-824-0301; fax 33-824-9004; e-mail statsenegal@yahoo.fr; internet www.ansd.sn.

Area and Population

AREA, POPULATION AND DENSITY

Area (sq km)	197,722*
Population (census results)†	
27 May 1988	6,896,808
8 December 2002	
Males	4,846,126
Females	5,009,212
Total	9,855,338
Population (UN estimates at mid-year)‡	
2009	12,534,228
2010	12,860,717
2011	13,190,062
Density (per sq km) at mid-2011	66.9

* 75,955 sq miles.
† Figures for 1988 and 2002 refer to the *de jure* population. The de facto population at the 1988 census was 6,773,417, and at the 2002 census was 9,552,442.
‡ Source: UN, *World Population Prospects: The 2008 Revision*.

POPULATION BY AGE AND SEX
(UN estimates at mid-2011)

	Males	Females	Total
0–14	2,867,712	2,814,064	5,681,776
15–64	3,523,536	3,671,260	7,194,796
65 and over	144,864	168,626	313,490
Total	6,536,112	6,653,950	13,190,062

Source: UN, *World Population Prospects: The 2008 Revision*.

POPULATION BY ETHNIC GROUP
(at 1988 census)

Ethnic group	Number	%
Wolof	2,890,402	42.67
Serere	1,009,921	14.91
Peul	978,366	14.44
Toucouleur	631,892	9.33
Diola	357,672	5.28
Mandingue	245,651	3.63
Rural-Rurale	113,184	1.67
Bambara	91,071	1.34
Maure	67,726	1.00
Manjaag	66,605	0.98
Others	320,927	4.74
Total	6,773,417	100.00

Source: UN, *Demographic Yearbook*.

REGIONS
(population estimates, 2009)

	Area (sq km)	Population	Density (per sq km)
Dakar	546	2,536,959	4,646.4
Diourbel	4,862	1,315,200	270.5
Fatick	7,049	722,343	102.5
Kaffrine*	11,041	540,733	49.0
Kaolack	5,265	771,227	146.5
Kedougou*	16,825	125,763	7.5
Kolda	13,721	585,159	42.6
Louga	25,644	831,309	32.4
Matam	28,852	524,942	18.2
Saint-Louis	18,981	865,058	45.6
Sedhiou*	7,346	417,812	56.9
Tambacounda	42,638	630,247	14.8
Thiès	6,597	1,610,052	244.1
Ziguinchor	7,355	694,460	94.4
Total	196,722	12,171,264	61.9

* Region created in March 2008.

PRINCIPAL TOWNS
(2002 census, provisional results)

Dakar (capital)	955,897	Mbour	153,503
Pikine	768,826	Diourbel	95,984
Rufisque	284,263	Louga	73,662
Guediawaye	258,370	Tambacounda	67,543
Thiès	237,849	Kolda	53,921
Kaolack	172,305	Mbacké	51,124
Saint-Louis	154,555		

Note: Data given pertain to communes, except for Dakar, Pikine, Rufisque and Guediawaye, where the population figure given is that of the département.
Mid-2010 (incl. suburbs, UN estimate): Dakar 2,862,879 (Source: UN, *World Urbanization Prospects: The 2009 Revision*).

BIRTHS AND DEATHS
(annual averages, UN estimates)

	1995–2000	2000–05	2005–10
Birth rate (per 1,000)	41.4	39.6	38.8
Death rate (per 1,000)	12.4	11.6	11.0

Source: UN, *World Population Prospects: The 2008 Revision*.

2006: Birth rate 39.1 per 1,000; Death rate 11.2 per 1,000 (Source: African Development Bank).
2007: Birth rate 38.8 per 1,000; Death rate 11.0 per 1,000 (Source: African Development Bank).
2008: Birth rate 38.4 per 1,000; Death rate 10.8 per 1,000 (Source: African Development Bank).
2009: Birth rate 38.0 per 1,000; Death rate 10.6 per 1,000 (Source: African Development Bank).

Life expectancy (years at birth, WHO estimates): 59 (males 58; females 61) in 2008 (Source: WHO, *World Health Statistics*).

SENEGAL

Statistical Survey

ECONOMICALLY ACTIVE POPULATION
('000 persons, 2006)

	Males	Females	Total
Agriculture, hunting and forestry	631.9	354.6	986.5
Fishing	66.5	10.4	76.9
Mining and quarrying	11.5	2.6	14.1
Manufacturing	203.7	41.7	245.4
Electricity, gas and water supply	18.5	3.3	21.8
Construction	179.7	6.9	186.6
Wholesale and retail trade; repair of motor vehicles, motorcycles and personal household goods	388.0	397.9	785.9
Hotels and restaurants	12.2	16.4	28.6
Transport, storage and communication	135.9	5.8	141.7
Financial intermediation	11.8	4.9	16.7
Public administration and defence; compulsory social security; education; health and social work	118.7	39.0	157.7
Extra-territorial organizations and bodies	3.3	3.7	7.0
Sub-total	1,781.7	887.2	2,668.9
Not classified by economic activity	266.5	217.5	484.0
Total	2,048.1	1,104.8	3,152.9
Unemployed	174.5	176.8	351.4
Total labour force	2,222.6	1,281.6	3,504.3

Source: ILO.

Mid-2011 (estimates in '000): Agriculture, etc. 4,062; Total labour force 5,811 (Source: FAO).

Health and Welfare

KEY INDICATORS

Total fertility rate (children per woman, 2008)	5.0
Under-5 mortality rate (per 1,000 live births, 2008)	108
HIV/AIDS (% of persons aged 15–49, 2007)	1.0
Physicians (per 1,000 head, 2004)	0.06
Hospital beds (per 1,000 head, 2007)	0.1
Health expenditure (2007): US $ per head (PPP)	99
Health expenditure (2007): % of GDP	5.7
Health expenditure (2007): public (% of total)	56.0
Access to water (% of persons, 2008)	69
Access to sanitation (% of persons, 2008)	51
Total carbon dioxide emissions ('000 metric tons, 2007)	5,474.0
Carbon dioxide emissions per head (metric tons, 2007)	0.5
Human Development Index (2010): ranking	144
Human Development Index (2010): value	0.411

For sources and definitions, see explanatory note on p. vi.

Agriculture

PRINCIPAL CROPS
('000 metric tons)

	2007	2008	2009
Rice, paddy	193.4	408.2	502.1
Maize	158.3	397.3	328.6
Millet	318.8	678.2	810.1
Sorghum	100.7	251.5	225.0
Cassava (Manioc)	308.3	920.9	265.5
Sugar cane	836.0*	836.0*	n.a.
Cashew nuts	5.0*	5.1*	n.a.
Groundnuts, with shell	331.2	731.2	1,032.7
Oil palm fruit	71*	71*	n.a.
Tomatoes	178.6	43.8	45.0*
Onions, dry	142.0	150.0	165.0*
Watermelons	150.5	327.3	190.6
Oranges	40.0*	40.0*	n.a.
Guavas, mangoes and mangosteens	95.0	100.0	105.0*

* FAO estimate.

Aggregate production ('000 metric tons, may include official, semi-official or estimated data): Total cereals 772.2 in 2007, 1,739.7 in 2008, 1,868.9 in 2009; Total pulses 60.1 in 2007, 126.7 in 2008, 86.9 in 2009; Total roots and tubers 356.3 in 2007, 963.7 in 2008, 308.5 in 2009; Total vegetables (incl. melons) 629.6 in 2007, 699.7 in 2008, 586.1 in 2009; Total fruits (excl. melons) 192.6 in 2007, 203.6 in 2008, 209.1 in 2009.

Source: FAO.

LIVESTOCK
('000 head, year ending September)

	2006	2007	2008
Cattle	3,137	3,163	3,208
Sheep	4,996	5,109	5,241
Goats	4,263	4,353	4,471
Pigs	318	319	326
Horses	518	518	522
Asses	415	438	441
Camels	4	5	5
Chickens	30,646	34,928	39,407

2009 (FAO estimates): Cattle 3,300, Sheep 5,400, Chickens 44,000.

Source: FAO.

LIVESTOCK PRODUCTS
('000 metric tons)

	2007	2008	2009
Cattle meat	49.3	65.9	59.7*
Sheep meat	22.3	20.9	21.5*
Goat meat	13.4	13.7	n.a.
Pig meat	11.1	10.6	7.1*
Horse meat*	7.2	7.2	7.2
Chicken meat	37.0	41.1	45.7*
Cows' milk	118.1	125.6	n.a.
Sheep's milk	8.2	8.8	8.8*
Goats' milk	11.0	11.7	n.a.
Hen eggs	32*	36*	n.a.

* FAO estimate(s).

Source: FAO.

SENEGAL

Forestry

ROUNDWOOD REMOVALS
('000 cubic metres, excl. bark, FAO estimates)

	2007	2008	2009
Sawlogs, veneer logs and logs for sleepers*	40	40	40
Other industrial wood†	754	754	754
Fuel wood	5,336	5,366	5,396
Total	6,130	6,160	6,190

* Annual output assumed to be unchanged since 1986 (FAO estimates).
† Annual output assumed to be unchanged since 1999 (FAO estimates).
Source: FAO.

SAWNWOOD PRODUCTION
('000 cubic metres, incl. railway sleepers)

	1989	1990	1991
Total (all broadleaved)	15	22	23

1992–2009: Annual production assumed to be unchanged from 1991 (FAO estimates).
Source: FAO.

Fishing

('000 metric tons, live weight)

	2006	2007	2008
Capture	391.9*	435.5*	447.8
Freshwater fishes	48.4*	49.5*	13.0
Sea catfishes	11.7	11.3	10.2
Round sardinella	101.9	127.2	165.1
Madeiran sardinella	95.6	109.4	86.0
Bonga shad	18.9	19.5	23.5
Octopuses	3.0	5.2	3.7
Aquaculture*	0.2	0.2	0.2
Total catch*	392.1	435.7	448.0

* FAO estimate(s).
Source: FAO.

Mining

('000 metric tons, unless otherwise stated)

	2007	2008	2009
Crude petroleum ('000 barrels)	317	99	249
Gold (kg)	600*	600*	5,354
Cement, hydraulic	3,152	3,084	3,327
Calcium phosphates	691	645	948
Aluminium phosphates	4†	4	4†
Fuller's earth (attapulgite)	150†	167	200†
Salt (unrefined)	212	241	222

* Government estimates of unreported production of artisanal gold.
† Estimate.
Source: US Geological Survey.

Industry

PETROLEUM PRODUCTS
('000 metric tons)

	2005	2006	2007
Jet fuels	89	31	48
Motor gasoline (petrol)	118	46	94
Kerosene	19	5	5
Gas-diesel (distillate fuel) oils	356	115	342
Residual fuel (Mazout) oils	279	111	187
Lubricating oils	5	n.a.	n.a.
Liquefied petroleum gas	3	n.a.	n.a.

Source: UN, *Industrial Commodity Statistics Yearbook* and Database.

SELECTED OTHER PRODUCTS
('000 metric tons, unless otherwise indicated)

	2001	2002	2003
Raw sugar	95.0*	95.0†	95.0†
Sugar cubes	27.2	19.8	23.2
Tobacco products (tons)	2,132	2,245	2,218
Groundnut oil—crude	125.3	98.1	39.2
Vegetable oil—refined	70.6	78.5	75.7
Canned tuna	12.1	10.7	6.9
Footwear (million pairs)	0.6	n.a.	n.a.
Cotton yarn (tons)	411	n.a.	n.a.
Soap	38.6	34.8	33.4
Paints and varnishes	4.6	4.3	4.6
Cement	1,539.0	1,653.2	1,693.9
Metal cans (million)	113.2	185.2	182.2
Electricity (million kWh)	1,651.2	1,557.3	1,855.5

* Unofficial figure.
† FAO estimate.
Source: mainly IMF, *Senegal: Selected Issues and Statistical Appendix* (May 2005).

Nitrogenous fertilizers (nitrogen content, '000 metric tons, unofficial figures): 38.8 in 1998; 24.5 in 1999; 19.4 in 2000 (Source: FAO).

Phosphate fertilizers (phosphoric acid content, '000 metric tons, unofficial figures): 67.5 in 1998; 45.0 in 1999; 32.4 in 2000 (Source: FAO).

Cement ('000 metric tons): 3,152 in 2007; 3,084 in 2008; 3,327 (estimate) in 2009 (Source: US Geological Survey).

Electric energy (million kWh): 2,171.9 in 2005; 2,159.5 in 2006; 2,296.0 in 2007.

Finance

CURRENCY AND EXCHANGE RATES

Monetary Units
100 centimes = 1 franc de la Communauté financière africaine (CFA).

Sterling, Dollar and Euro Equivalents (31 December 2010)
£1 sterling = 768.523 francs CFA;
US $1 = 490.912 francs CFA;
€1 = 655.957 francs CFA;
10,000 francs CFA = £13.01 = $20.37 = €15.24.

Average Exchange Rate (francs CFA per US $)
2008   447.81
2009   472.19
2010   495.28

Note: An exchange rate of 1 French franc = 50 francs CFA, established in 1948, remained in force until January 1994, when the CFA franc was devalued by 50%, with the exchange rate adjusted to 1 French franc = 100 francs CFA. This relationship to French currency remained in effect with the introduction of the euro on 1 January 1999. From that date, accordingly, a fixed exchange rate of €1 = 655.957 francs CFA has been in operation.

SENEGAL

Statistical Survey

BUDGET
('000 million francs CFA)

Revenue*	2008	2009†	2010‡
Tax revenue	1,088	1,084	1,210
Income tax	273	287	326
Taxes on goods and services (excl. petroleum)	616	615	705
Taxes on petroleum products	199	182	180
Non-tax revenue	65	37	43
Total	**1,153**	**1,121**	**1,253**

Expenditure§	2008	2009†	2010‡
Current expenditure	979	997	1,011
Wages and salaries	348	364	397
Other operational expenses	593	587	554
Transfers and subsidies	333	286	250
Goods and services	239	292	277
Capital expenditure	595	607	687
Domestically financed	314	369	424
Externally financed	281	237	263
Total	**1,574**	**1,604**	**1,698**

* Excluding grants received ('000 million francs CFA): 140 in 2008; 182 in 2009 (estimate); 150 in 2010 (projection).
† Estimates.
‡ Projections.
§ Excluding net lending ('000 million francs CFA): 5 in 2008; 3 in 2009 (estimate); 8 in 2010 (projection).

Source: IMF, *Senegal: Sixth Review Under the Policy Support Instrument, Request for a Three-Year Policy Support Instrument and Cancellation of Current Policy Support Instrument—Staff Report; Debt Sustainability Analysis; Press Release; Executive Director Statement* (December 2010).

INTERNATIONAL RESERVES
(excluding gold, US $ million at 31 December)

	2007	2008	2009
IMF special drawing rights	0.1	0.2	204.4
Reserve position in IMF	2.6	2.6	2.7
Foreign exchange	1,657.3	1,599.4	1,916.1
Total	**1,660.0**	**1,602.2**	**2,123.2**

Source: IMF, *International Financial Statistics*.

MONEY SUPPLY
('000 million francs CFA at 31 December)

	2007	2008	2009
Currency outside banks	483.6	474.3	494.8
Demand deposits at deposit money banks	759.7	763.4	856.6
Checking deposits at post office	22.7	13.9	14.6
Total money (incl. others)	**1,266.6**	**1,252.7**	**1,366.9**

Source: IMF, *International Financial Statistics*.

COST OF LIVING
(Consumer Price Index; base: 2000 = 100)

	2006	2007	2008
Food (incl. tobacco)	116.0	124.5	136.4
Clothing	85.9	88.4	86.3
Electricity, gas and other fuels	112.0	123.2	n.a.
Rent	108.2	119.1	120.8
All items (incl. others)	**110.0**	**116.4**	**123.1**

2009: Food (incl. tobacco) 132.3; All items (incl. others) 121.8.
Source: ILO.

NATIONAL ACCOUNTS
(million francs CFA at current prices)

Expenditure on the Gross Domestic Product

	2007	2008	2009
Government final consumption expenditure	743,375	786,915	891,673
Private final consumption expenditure	4,278,835	4,695,227	4,800,365
Gross fixed capital formation	1,410,591	1,578,537	1,596,316
Changes in inventories	183,243	178,739	−263,815
Total domestic expenditure	**6,616,044**	**7,239,418**	**7,024,539**
Exports of goods and services	1,376,220	1,484,031	1,541,355
Less Imports of goods and services	2,587,630	2,779,456	2,580,617
GDP at purchasers' values	**5,404,633**	**5,943,992**	**5,985,277**

Gross Domestic Product by Economic Activity

	2007	2008	2009
Agriculture, hunting, forestry and fishing	643,696	826,126	820,740
Mining and quarrying	52,430	47,651	56,353
Manufacturing	681,587	757,193	736,204
Electricity, gas and water	137,456	150,719	146,318
Construction	265,865	271,733	288,900
Trade, restaurants and hotels	936,570	1,021,135	976,484
Finance, insurance and real estate	456,223	486,473	537,564
Transport and communications	591,772	662,009	618,757
Public administration and defence	743,375	786,915	681,632
Other services	260,590	314,838	442,559
Sub-total	**4,769,564**	**5,324,792**	**5,305,511**
Indirect taxes	742,873	731,228	823,583
Less imputed bank service charge	107,804	112,028	143,817
GDP at purchasers' values	**5,404,633**	**5,943,992**	**5,985,277**

Source: African Development Bank.

BALANCE OF PAYMENTS
(US $ million)

	2006	2007	2008
Exports of goods f.o.b.	1,594.0	1,673.8	2,206.0
Imports of goods f.o.b.	−3,193.7	−4,163.8	−5,606.0
Trade balance	**−1,599.7**	**−2,489.9**	**−3,400.0**
Exports of services	807.1	1,200.9	1,294.1
Imports of services	−841.7	−1,238.4	−1,414.5
Balance on goods and services	**−1,634.4**	**−2,527.4**	**−3,520.4**
Other income received	121.3	138.2	235.4
Other income paid	−184.7	−212.1	−283.3
Balance on goods, services and income	**−1,697.8**	**−2,601.2**	**−3,568.3**
Current transfers received	973.7	1,557.5	1,985.9
Current transfers paid	−137.0	−268.0	−301.3
Current balance	**−861.2**	**−1,311.7**	**−1,883.7**
Capital account (net)	2,291.1	332.7	239.5
Direct investment abroad	−9.9	−24.7	−126.3
Direct investment from abroad	220.3	297.4	397.6
Portfolio investment assets	−53.3	6.4	51.6
Portfolio investment liabilities	−13.6	24.7	20.9
Financial derivatives assets	−0.1	—	0.2
Financial derivatives liabilities	0.1	25.6	−0.2
Other investment assets	−34.3	84.4	147.7
Other investment liabilities	−1,689.7	421.7	599.7
Net errors and omissions	28.3	12.8	−13.5
Overall balance	**−122.4**	**−130.8**	**−566.5**

Source: IMF, *International Financial Statistics*.

SENEGAL

External Trade

PRINCIPAL COMMODITIES
('000 million francs CFA)

Imports c.i.f.	2007	2008	2009
Rice	174.8	235.0	163.9
Animal and vegetable oils and fats	77.2	95.5	68.6
Crude petroleum	193.2	343.3	186.7
Other petroleum products	267.0	146.3	214.2
Pharmaceutical products	62.0	63.4	64.8
Artificial plastic materials	76.1	77.4	73.6
Common metals	89.3	113.7	86.2
Agricultural and industrial machinery	269.0	349.3	312.0
Vehicles	64.5	74.5	69.7
Total (incl. others)	2,123.6	2,534.2	2,141.7

Exports f.o.b.	2007	2008	2009
Fresh fish	86.5	59.0	73.5
Crustaceans, molluscs and other shellfish	54.4	27.1	33.2
Frozen fish	6.1	3.8	5.8
Peanut oil	32.4	7.9	18.1
Hydraulic cement	43.5	55.0	70.6
Petroleum products	142.5	309.2	207.6
Phosphoric acid	47.0	106.9	69.8
Total (incl. others)	702.5	893.6	890.7

PRINCIPAL TRADING PARTNERS
('000 million francs CFA)

Imports c.i.f.	2007	2008	2009
Argentina	42.6	63.3	45.6
Belgium-Luxembourg	57.2	66.3	49.9
Brazil	91.8	87.3	80.8
China, People's Republic	128.2	165.3	192.0
Côte d'Ivoire	54.9	72.1	63.3
France (incl. Monaco)	498.9	455.5	427.4
Germany	62.5	83.4	75.9
India	77.7	71.1	47.5
Ireland	29.4	28.3	10.8
Italy	53.0	63.3	69.6
Japan	38.1	52.2	39.0
Morocco	25.4	39.3	37.9
Netherlands	87.5	56.7	61.7
Nigeria	196.6	345.5	197.4
South Africa	35.3	40.6	42.3
Spain	68.3	73.8	92.6
Thailand	113.4	153.1	116.9
Turkey	28.8	31.6	27.7
Ukraine	37.2	40.9	22.4
United Kingdom	50.3	55.2	40.1
USA	48.7	57.7	64.4
Viet Nam	12.7	18.5	33.5
Total (incl. others)	2,123.6	2,534.2	2,141.7

Exports f.o.b.	2007	2008	2009
Benin	8.6	5.8	5.8
Burkina Faso	11.1	8.0	10.1
Cameroon	15.8	5.5	7.8
Côte d'Ivoire	20.2	21.8	26.8
France (incl. Monaco)	70.9	56.7	51.7
The Gambia	36.9	38.0	33.4
Greece	13.4	10.4	12.1
Guinea	20.6	33.0	28.3
Guinea-Bissau	19.3	23.0	21.5
India	49.7	121.2	73.2
Italy	37.6	17.1	24.5
Japan	5.7	3.1	1.5
Mali	160.0	213.3	171.6
Mauritania	19.2	25.1	25.9
Netherlands	10.4	12.3	13.5
Spain	37.1	21.6	20.7
Switzerland	21.3	2.9	74.1
Togo	9.8	10.7	8.8
United Arab Emirates	8.3	12.0	13.0
Total (incl. others)	702.5	893.6	890.7

Transport

RAILWAYS
(traffic)

	2002	2003	2004
Passenger-km (million)	105	129	122
Net ton-km (million)	345	375	358

Passengers ('000): 4,789 in 1999.
Freight carried ('000 metric tons): 2,017 in 1999.

ROAD TRAFFIC
(motor vehicles in use)

	2006	2007	2008
Passenger cars	178,977	187,838	205,704
Buses and coaches	14,787	14,110	15,982
Lorries and vans	27,948	33,212	56,795
Trucks	13,022	17,822	19,983
Motorcycles and mopeds	9,201	10,656	13,403

Source: IRF, *World Road Statistics*.

SHIPPING

Merchant Fleet
(vessels registered at 31 December)

	2007	2008	2009
Number of vessels	186	186	189
Total displacement ('000 grt)	46.4	46.5	47.3

Source: IHS Fairplay, *World Fleet Statistics*.

International Sea-borne Freight Traffic
('000 metric tons)

	2006	2007	2008
Goods loaded	2,279	2,322	2,232
Goods unloaded	7,651	8,787	8,358

Source: Port Autonome de Dakar.

SENEGAL

CIVIL AVIATION
(traffic on scheduled services)*

	2004	2005	2006
Kilometres flown (million)	8	9	10
Passengers carried ('000)	416	450	501
Passenger-km (million)	767	851	937
Total ton-km (million)	69	77	94

* Including an apportionment of the traffic of Air Afrique.

Source: UN, *Statistical Yearbook*.

Tourism

FOREIGN TOURIST ARRIVALS BY NATIONALITY*

	2005	2006	2007
African states	87,565	106,396	97,398
Belgium, Luxembourg and the Netherlands	21,712	23,896	17,717
East Asian and Pacific states	3,837	3,846	3,620
France	191,580	184,376	171,452
Germany	9,615	8,708	6,973
Italy	11,493	13,705	13,953
Spain	15,353	17,021	19,039
United Kingdom	4,380	5,582	5,416
USA	11,080	12,404	20,482
Total (incl. others)	386,565	405,827	386,793

* Figures refer to arrivals at hotels and similar establishments.

Receipts from tourism (US $ million, incl. passenger transport): 334 in 2005; 329 in 2006; 622 in 2007.

Source: World Tourism Organization.

Communications Media

	2007	2008	2009
Telephones ('000 main lines in use)	269.1	237.8	278.8
Mobile cellular telephones ('000 subscribers)	3,630.8	5,389.1	6,901.5
Internet users ('000)	915.8	1,294.4	1,817.5
Broadband subscribers ('000)	38.1	47.4	58.7

Personal computers: 250,000 (22.2 per 1,000 persons) in 2005.

Television receivers ('000 in use): 380 in 2000.

Radio receivers ('000 in use): 1,240 in 1997.

Daily newspapers: 1 (average circulation 45,000 copies) in 1996; 13 in 2004.

Non-daily newspapers: 6 (average circulation 37,000 copies) in 1995.

Sources: mainly International Telecommunication Union; UNESCO, *Statistical Yearbook*, UNESCO Institute for Statistics.

Education

(2008/09, unless otherwise indicated)

	Institutions*	Teachers	Males	Females	Total
Pre-primary	1,725	4,983	59.8	66.6	126.4
Primary	7,939	47,685	816.3	836.3	1,652.6
Secondary	1,122	15,394†	326.7‡	255.4‡	582.1‡
Tertiary	n.a.	n.a.	59.5	34.9	94.4

Students ('000)

* 2008/09 (Source: Ministry of Education, Dakar).
† 2004/05.
‡ 2007/08.

Source: UNESCO Institute for Statistics.

Pupil-teacher ratio (primary education, UNESCO estimate): 34.7 in 2008/09 (Source: UNESCO Institute for Statistics).

Adult literacy rate (UNESCO estimates): 42.6% (males 53.1%; females 32.3%) in 2007 (Source: UNESCO Institute for Statistics).

Directory

The Government

HEAD OF STATE

President: ABDOULAYE WADE (took office 1 April 2000; re-elected 25 February 2007).

COUNCIL OF MINISTERS
(May 2011)

Prime Minister: SOULEYMANE NDÉNÉ NDIAYE.
Minister of State, Minister of Foreign Affairs: MADICKÉ NIANG.
Minister of State, Minister of the Economy and Finance: ABDOULAYE DIOP.
Minister of State, Minister of Justice and Keeper of the Seals: CHEIKH TIDJANE SY.
Minister of State, Minister of the Interior: OUSMANE NGOM.
Minister of State, Minister of the Armed Forces: BÉCAYE DIOP.
Minister of State, Minister of Culture and Gender Equality: AWA NDIAYE.
Minister of State, Minister of the Environment and the Protection of Nature: DJIBO LEYTI KÂ.
Minister of State, Minister of Housing, Construction and Hydraulics: OUMAR SARR.
Minister of State, Minister of International Co-operation, Air Transport, Infrastructure and Energy: KARIM WADE.
Minister of State, Minister of Mines, Industry, Agro-industry and Small and Medium-sized Enterprises: ABDOULAYE BALDÉ.
Minister of State, Minister of the Family and Female Groupings: AÏDA MBODJ.
Minister of State, Minister of the Civil Service and Employment: ABDOULAYE MAKHTAR DIOP.
Minister of State, Minister of Early Childhood: NDÈYE KHADY DIOP.
Minister of the Maritime Economy: KHOURÏCHI THIAM.
Minister of Higher Education, Universities and Scientific Research: Prof. AMADOU TIDIANE BÂ.
Minister of Agriculture: KHADIM GUEYE.
Minister of Nursery, Primary and Middle School Education and National Languages: KALIDOU DIALLO.
Minister of Health and Preventive Medicine: MODOU DIAGNE FADA.
Minister of Decentralization and Local Communities: Dr ALIOU SOW.
Minister of Labour and Professional Organizations: SADA NDIAYE.
Minister of Youth and Leisure: MAMADOU LAMINE KEITA.
Minister of Handicrafts, Tourism and Relations with the Private and Informal Sectors: THIERNO LÔ.
Minister of Town Planning and Redevelopment, and Public Hygiene and Living Conditions: ADAMA SALL.
Minister of Livestock-rearing: OUMOU KHAIRY GUÈYE SECK.
Minister of Road and Rail Transport and Land Settlement: NAFISSATOU DIOUF NGOM.
Minister of Technical and Professional Training: MOUSSA SAKHO.

SENEGAL

Minister of Trade: AMADOU NIANG.
Minister of Communication and Telecommunications, in charge of Information and Communication Technologies, Government Spokesperson: MOUSTAPHA GUIRASSY.
Minister of Senegalese Nationals Abroad: NGONÉ NDOYE.
Minister of Sport: FAUSTIN DIATTA.
Minister of Social Affairs and National Solidarity: THÉRÈSE COUMBA DIOP.
Minister in charge of Relations with the Institutions: AMINATA LO.
Minister of Female Entrepreneurship and Micro-finance: SEYNABOU LY MBACKÉ.
Minister in charge of Eco-villages, Reservoirs, Artificial Lakes and Pisciculture: BABACAR NDAO.
Minister of Renewable Energy: LOUIS SECK.
Minister-delegate to the Minister of the Economy and Finance, in charge of the Budget: ABDOULAYE DIOP.
Minister-delegate to the Minister of International Co-operation, Air Transport, Infrastructure and Energy, in charge of Energy: IBRAHIMA SAR.

MINISTRIES

Office of the President: ave Léopold Sédar Senghor, BP 168, Dakar; tel. 33-880-8080; internet www.presidence.sn.
Office of the Prime Minister: Bldg Administratif, 9e étage, ave Léopold Sédar Senghor, BP 4029, Dakar; tel. 33-889-6969; fax 33-823-4479; internet www.gouv.sn.
Ministry of Agriculture: Bldg Administratif, 3e étage, BP 4005, Dakar; tel. 33-849-7000; fax 33-823-3268; internet www.agriculture.gouv.sn.
Ministry of the Armed Forces: Bldg Administratif, 8e étage, ave Léopold Sédar Senghor, BP 4041, Dakar; tel. 33-849-7612; fax 33-823-6338; internet www.forcesarmees.gouv.sn.
Ministry of the Civil Service and Employment: Bldg Administratif, 1er étage, BP 4007, Dakar; tel. 33-849-7000; fax 33-823-7429; e-mail mineladiallo@yahoo.fr; internet www.fonctionpublique.gouv.sn.
Ministry of Communication and Telecommunications: 58 blvd de la République, Dakar; tel. 33-823-1065; fax 33-821-4504; internet www.telecom.gouv.sn.
Ministry of Culture and Leisure: Bldg Administratif, 3e étage, ave Léopold Sédar Senghor, BP 4001, Dakar; tel. 33-822-4303; fax 33-822-1638; internet www.culture.gouv.sn.
Ministry of Decentralization and Local Communities: Dieuppeul Derklé, rue DD, 142 BP 4002, Dakar; tel. 33-869-4700; fax 33-869-4713.
Ministry of the Economy and Finance: ave Carde, Bâtiment CEPOD, Dakar; tel. 33-823-3427; fax 33-821-8312; e-mail i_diouf@minfinances.sn; internet www.finances.gouv.sn.
Ministry of Eco-villages, Reservoirs, Artificial Lakes and Pisciculture: Bldg Administratif, 4e étage, BP 4021, Dakar; tel. 33-823-8716; fax 33-823-4470.
Ministry of the Environment and the Protection of Nature: Bldg Administratif, 2e étage, BP 4055, Dakar; tel. 33-889-0234; fax 33-822-2180; e-mail ministereenvironnement@gmail.com; internet www.environnement.gouv.sn.
Ministry of the Family, Female Groupings and Early Childhood: Bldg Administratif, 6e étage, BP 4050, Dakar; tel. 33-849-7000; fax 33-822-9490; e-mail communication@famille.gouv.sn; internet www.famille.gouv.sn.
Ministry of Female Entrepreneurship and Micro-finance: Bldg Administratif, ave Léopold Sédar Senghor, Dakar.
Ministry of Foreign Affairs: pl. de l'Indépendance, BP 4044, Dakar; tel. 33-889-1300; fax 33-825-5496; e-mail maeuase@senegal.diplomatie.sn; internet www.diplomatie.gouv.sn.
Ministry of Gender and Relations with African and International Women's Organizations: Bldg Administratif, Dakar.
Ministry of Handicrafts, Tourism and Relations with the Private and Informal Sectors: 23 rue Calmette, BP 4049, Dakar; tel. 33-822-7366; fax 33-822-9413.
Ministry of Health and Preventive Medicine: Fann Résidence, rue Aimé Césaire, BP 4024, Dakar; tel. 33-869-4242; fax 33-869-4269; e-mail mdseck@minsante.sn; internet www.sante.gouv.sn.
Ministry of Higher Education, Universities and Scientific Research: rue Docteur Calmette, BP 4025, Dakar; tel. 33-849-7556; fax 33-822-4563; internet www.recherche.gouv.sn.
Ministry of Housing, Construction and Hydraulics: blvd Dial Diop, pl. de l'ONU, BP 2372, Dakar; tel. 33-869-1526; fax 33-864-5932; internet www.habitat.gouv.sn.
Ministry of Information and Communication Technologies: Bldg Administratif, 6e étage, BP 4027, Dakar; tel. 33-849-7271; fax 33-823-6673; internet www.telecom.gouv.sn.
Ministry of the Interior: pl. Washington, BP 4002, Dakar; tel. 33-889-9100; fax 33-821-0542; e-mail mint@primature.sn; internet www.interieur.gouv.sn.
Ministry of International Co-operation, Air Transport, Infrastructure and Energy: Bldg Administratif, Dakar; tel. 33-849-8843; fax 33-849-8815.
Ministry of Justice: Bldg Administratif, 7e étage, ave Léopold Sédar Senghor, BP 4030, Dakar; tel. 33-849-7000; fax 33-823-2727; e-mail justice@justice.gouv.sn; internet www.justice.gouv.sn.
Ministry of Labour and Professional Organizations: Bldg Administratif, Dakar.
Ministry of Livestock-rearing: VDN, blvd du Koweit, BP 45677, Dakar; tel. 33-859-0630; fax 33-864-6311.
Ministry of the Maritime Economy: Bldg Administratif, 4e étage, BP 4050, Dakar; tel. 33-849-5073; fax 33-823-8720; e-mail abdoumbodj@yahoo.fr; internet www.ecomaritime.gouv.sn.
Ministry of Mines, Industry and Small and Medium-sized Enterprises: 122 bis ave André Peytavin, BP 4037, Dakar; tel. 33-822-9994; fax 33-822-5594; e-mail mindpme@msn.com; internet www.industrie.gouv.sn.
Ministry of Nursery, Primary and Middle School Education and National Languages: 56 ave Lamine Gueye, Dakar; tel. 33-849-5402; fax 33-821-8930; internet www.education.gouv.sn.
Ministry of Public Hygiene and Living Conditions: Bldg Administratif, Dakar.
Ministry of Relations with the Institutions: Bldg Administratif, ave Léopold Sédar Senghor, BP 49, Dakar; tel. 33-821-8060; fax 33-821-8850; e-mail mmbodj@sentoo.sn; internet www.mri.gouv.sn.
Ministry of Renewable Energy: Dakar.
Ministry of Road and Rail Transport and Land Settlement: Bldg Administratif, Dakar; tel. 33-849-7000; fax 33-842-0292.
Ministry of Senegalese Nationals Abroad: VDN, rue 50 X 23, Villa 23 bis, BP 45510, Dakar; tel. 33-867-0171; fax 33-867-0183; internet www.senex.gouv.sn.
Ministry of Social Affairs and National Solidarity: Point E X ave Dial Diop, BP 25555, Dakar; tel. 33-869-1601; fax 33-864-0771.
Ministry of Sport: Bldg Administratif, Dakar.
Ministry of Technical and Professional Training: Bloc 23, rue Calmette, Dakar; tel. 33-822-9523; fax 33-821-7196.
Ministry of Town Planning and Redevelopment: 54 ave Georges Pompidou X Raffenel, Immeuble Plazza, 1er étage, Dakar; tel. 33-889-0730.
Ministry of Trade: Bldg Administratif, Dakar; tel. 33-822-9542; fax 33-822-4669.
Ministry of Youth: Rue C X 100, Zone B, Dakar; tel. 33-859-3877; fax 33-829-2428; internet www.jeunesse.gouv.sn.

President and Legislature

PRESIDENT

Presidential Election, 25 February 2007

Candidate	Votes	% of valid votes
Abdoulaye Wade	1,914,403	55.90
Idrissa Seck	510,922	14.92
Ousmane Tanor Dieng	464,287	13.56
Moustapha Niasse	203,129	5.93
Robert Sagna	88,446	2.58
Abdoulaye Bathily	75,797	2.21
Landing Savané	70,780	2.07
Others	97,162	2.84
Total	**3,424,926**	**100.00**

LEGISLATURE

Assemblée nationale

pl. Soweto, BP 86, Dakar; tel. 33-823-1099; fax 33-823-6708; e-mail assnat@assemblee-nationale.sn; internet www.assemblee-nationale.sn.

President: MAMADOU SECK.

SENEGAL

General Election, 3 June 2007

Party	Votes	% of votes	Seats
Sopi Coalition*	1,190,609	69.21	131
Takku Defaraat Sénégal Coalition	86,621	5.04	3
And Defar Sénégal Coalition	84,998	4.94	3
Waar Wi Coalition	74,919	4.35	3
Rassemblement pour le peuple (RP)	73,083	4.25	2
Front pour le socialisme et la démocratie—Benno Jubël (FSD—BJ)	37,427	2.18	1
Alliance Jëf-Jël	33,297	1.94	1
Convergence pour le renouveau et la citoyenneté (CRC)	30,658	1.78	1
Parti socialiste authentique (PSA)	26,320	1.53	1
Union nationale patriotique (UNP)	22,271	1.29	1
Mouvement de la réforme pour le développement social (MRDS)	20,041	1.16	1
Rassemblement des écologistes du Sénégal (RES)	17,267	1.00	1
Parti social-démocrate—Jant Bi (PSD—JB)	15,968	0.93	1
Rassemblement patriotique sénégalais—Jammi Rewmi (RPS—JR)	6,847	0.40	—
Total	**1,720,326**	**100.00**	**150**

* A coalition of some 40 parties and movements, led by the PDS.

Sénat

President: PAPE DIOP.
Election, 19 August 2007

Party	Seats
Parti démocratique sénégalais (PDS)	34
And Jëf—Parti africain pour la démocratie et le socialisme (AJ—PADS)	1
Total	**100***

* The remaining 65 members are appointed by the President.

Election Commission

Commission électorale nationale autonome (CENA): BP 28900, Dakar; internet www.cena.sn; f. 2005; Pres. DOUDOU NDIR.

Political Organizations

In early 2011 there were 73 political parties registered in Senegal, of which the following were among the most important:

Alliance des forces de progrès (AFP): rue 1, angle rue A, point E, BP 5825, Dakar; tel. 33-869-7595; fax 33-825-7770; e-mail afp.net@yahoo.fr; internet www.afp-senegal.org; f. 1999; mem. of opposition Bennoo Senegal; Sec.-Gen. MOUSTAPHA NIASSE.

Alliance Jëf-Jël: Villa 5, rue 1, Castors Front de Terre, Dakar; tel. 77-652-2232; e-mail tallasylla@hotmail.com; f. 1997; mem. of opposition; Pres. TALLA SYLLA.

Alliance pour la République (APR—Yaakaar): Dakar; f. 2008; Leader MACKY SALL.

And Defar Sénégal Coalition: Kolda; Leader LANDING SAVANÉ.

And Jëf—Parti africain pour la démocratie et le socialisme (AJ—PADS): Villa 1, Zone B, BP 12136, Dakar; tel. and fax 33-864-4130; e-mail webmaster@ajpads.org; internet ajpads.com; f. 1992; Sec.-Gen. LANDING SAVANÉ.

Bloc des centristes Gaïndé (BCG): Villa 734, Sicap Baobabs, Dakar; tel. 33-825-3764; e-mail issa_dias@sentoo.sn; f. 1996; Pres. and Sec.-Gen. JEAN-PAUL DIAS.

Convergence pour le renouveau et la citoyenneté (CRC): 7 ave Bourguiba, Industrial Zone, Sodida, Dakar; tel. 33-824-4900; e-mail info@crc-sn.org; internet www.crc-sn.org; Sec.-Gen. ALIOU DIA.

Front pour le socialisme et la démocratie—Benno Jubël (FSD—BJ): contested 2001 election as mem. of Sopi Coalition; Sec.-Gen. BAMBA DIÈYE.

Ligue démocratique—Mouvement pour le parti du travail (LD—MPT): ave Bourguiba, Dieuppeul 2, Villa 2566, BP 10172, Dakar Liberté; tel. 33-825-6706; fax 33-827-4300; e-mail jallarbi@sentoo.sn; internet www.ldmpt.sn; regd 1981; social-democrat; Sec.-Gen. ABDOULAYE BATHILY.

Mouvement pour la démocratie et le socialisme—Naxx Jarinu (MDS—NJ): Unité 20, Parcelles Assainies, Villa 528, Dakar; tel. 33-869-5049; f. 2000; Leader OUMAR KHASSIMOU DAI.

Mouvement de la réforme pour le développement social (MRDS): HLM 4, Villa 858, Dakar; tel. 77-644-3170; e-mail sgmrds@mrds.sn; internet www.mrds.sn; f. 2000; Pres. IMAM MBAYE NIANG; Sec.-Gen. Imam IYANE SOW.

Mouvement pour le socialisme et l'unité (MSU): HLM 1, Villa 86, Dakar; tel. 33-825-8544; f. 1981 as Mouvement démocratique populaire; mem. of opposition Cadre permanent de concertation (f. 2001); National Co-ordinator-Gen. MOUHAMADOU BAMBA N'DIAYE.

Mouvement républicain sénégalais (MRS): Résidence du Cap-Vert, 10e étage, 5 pl. de l'Indépendance, BP 4193, Dakar; tel. 33-822-0319; fax 33-822-0700; e-mail agaz@omnet.sn; Sec.-Gen. DEMBA BA.

Parti africain de l'indépendance (PAI): Maison du Peuple, Guediewaye, BP 820, Dakar; tel. 33-837-0136; f. 1957; reorg. 1976; Marxist; Sec.-Gen. MAJMOUT DIOP.

Parti démocratique sénégalais (PDS): blvd Dial Diop, Immeuble Serigne Mourtada Mbacké, Dakar; tel. 33-823-5027; fax 33-823-1702; e-mail cedobe@aol.com; internet www.sopionline.com; f. 1974; liberal democratic; Sec.-Gen. Me ABDOULAYE WADE.

Parti de l'indépendance et du travail (PIT): route front de terre, BP 10470, Dakar; tel. 33-827-2907; fax 33-820-9000; regd 1981; Marxist-Leninist; mem. of opposition Cadre permanent de concertation (f. 2001); Sec.-Gen. AMATH DANSOKHO.

Parti libéral sénégalais (PLS): 13 ave Malick Sy, BP 28277, Dakar; tel. and fax 33-823-1560; f. 1998 by breakaway faction of PDS; Leader Me OUSMANE NGOM.

Parti populaire sénégalais (PPS): Quartier Escale, BP 212, Diourbel; tel. 33-971-1171; regd 1981; populist; mem. of opposition Cadre permanent de concertation (f. 2001); Sec.-Gen. Dr OUMAR WANE.

Parti pour le progrès et la citoyenneté (PPC): Quartier Merina, Rufique; tel. 33-836-1868; absorbed Rassemblement pour le progrès, la justice et le socialisme in 2000; Sec.-Gen. Me MBAYE JACQUES DIOP.

Parti pour la renaissance africaine—Sénégal (PARENA): Sicap Dieuppeul, Villa 2685/B, Dakar; tel. 77-636-8788; fax 33-823-5721; e-mail mariamwane@yahoo.fr; f. 2000; Sec.-Gen. MARIAM MAMADOU WANE LY.

Parti de la renaissance et de la citoyenneté: Liberté 6, Villa 7909, Dakar; tel. 33-827-8568; f. 2000; supports Pres. Wade; Sec.-Gen. SAMBA DIOULDÉ THIAM.

Parti social-démocrate—Jant Bi (PSD—JB): Leader MAMOUR CISSE.

Parti socialiste authentique (PSA): internet psa-senegal.org; Leader SOUTY TOURRE.

Parti socialiste du Sénégal (PS): Maison du Parti Socialiste Léopold Sédar Senghor, Colobane, BP 12010, Dakar; tel. and fax 33-824-7744; e-mail senegalpartisocialiste@gmail.com; internet www.partisocialiste.sn; f. 1958 as Union progressiste sénégalaise; reorg. 1978; social-democrat; First Sec. OUSMANE TANOR DIENG.

Rassemblement des écologistes du Sénégal—Les verts (RES): rue 67, angle rue 52, Gueule Tapée, BP 25226, Dakar-Fann; tel. and fax 33-842-3442; f. 1999; Sec.-Gen. OUSMANE SOW HUCHARD.

Rassemblement national démocratique (RND): Sacré-Coeur III, Villa no 9721, Dakar; tel. 765808617 (mobile); f. 1976; legalized 1981; mem. of opposition Bennoo Siggil Senegal (f. 2009); Sec.-Gen. MADIOR DIOUF.

Rassemblement patriotique sénégalais—Jammi Rewmi (RPS—JR): Leader ELY MADIODO FALL FALL.

Rassemblement des travailleurs africains—Sénégal (RTA—S): Immeuble Seydou Nourou Tall, Apt. B6, 2ème étage, 12 rue 14 angle P, BP 13725, Derklé, Grand-Yoff, Dakar; tel. 33-827-1579; e-mail rtas@rtasenegal.org; internet www.rtasenegal.org; f. 1997; Co-ordinator BOCAR LY.

Takku Defaraat Sénégal Coalition: VDN à côté de la Poste; tel. 33-860-5019; fax 33-860-5020; f. 2000; Leader ROBERT SAGNA.

Union nationale patriotique (UNP): Leader NDÈYE FATOU TOURÉ.

Union pour le renouveau démocratique (URD): Bopp Villa 234, rue 7, Dakar; tel. 33-864-7431; fax 33-820-7317; e-mail urd@urdsenegal.sn; internet www.urdsenegal.sn; f. 1998 by breakaway faction of PS; mem. of opposition Cadre permanent de concertation (f. 2001); Sec.-Gen. DJIBO LEÏTY KÂ.

The **Mouvement des forces démocratiques de la Casamance (MFDC)** was founded in 1947; it had paramilitary and political

SENEGAL

wings and formerly sought the independence of the Casamance region of southern Senegal. The MFDC is not officially recognized as a political party (the Constitution of 2001 forbids the formation of parties on a geographic basis) and waged a campaign of guerrilla warfare in the region from the early 1980s. Representatives of the MFDC have participated in extensive negotiations with the Senegalese Government on the restoration of peace and the granting of greater autonomy to Casamance, and in December 2004 a cease-fire agreement was signed between the two sides, pending further peace negotiations. The Honorary President of the MFDC, Fr AUGUSTIN DIAMACOUNÉ SENGHOR, died in January 2007; the post of Secretary-General was disputed between JEAN-MARIE FRANÇOIS BIAGUI and ANSOUMANA BADJI.

Diplomatic Representation

EMBASSIES IN SENEGAL

Algeria: 5 rue Mermoz, Plateau, POB 3233, Dakar; tel. 33-849-5700; fax 33-849-5701; e-mail ambalgdak@orange.sn; f. 1963; Ambassador ABDERRAHMANE BENGUERAH.

Austria: 18 rue Emile Zola, BP 3247, Dakar; tel. 33-849-4000; fax 33-849-4370; e-mail dakar-ob@bmaa.gv.at; Ambassador Dr GERHARD DEISS.

Belgium: ave des Jambaars, BP 524, Dakar; tel. 33-889-4390; fax 33-889-4398; e-mail dakar@diplobel.fed.be; internet www.diplomatie.be/dakar; Ambassador GEORGES S. GODART (recalled Jan. 2011).

Brazil: Immeuble Fondation Fahd, 4e étage, blvd Djily Mbaye, angle rue Macodou Ndiaye, BP 136, Dakar; tel. 33-823-1492; fax 33-823-7181; e-mail embdakar@sentoo.sn; Ambassador MARIA ELISA THÉOFILO DE LUNA.

Burkina Faso: Sicap Sacré Coeur III, Extension VDN No. 10628B, BP 11601, Dakar; tel. 33-864-5824; fax 33-864-5823; e-mail ambabf@sentoo.sn; Ambassador SALAMATA SAWADOGO.

Cameroon: 157–9 rue Joseph Gomis, BP 4165, Dakar; tel. 33-849-0292; fax 33-823-3396; Ambassador EMMANUEL MBONJO-EJANGUE.

Canada: rue Galliéni angle rue Amadou Cissé Dia, BP 3373, Dakar; tel. 33-889-4700; fax 33-889-4720; e-mail dakar@international.gc.ca; internet www.canadainternational.gc.ca/senegal; Ambassador PERRY CALDERWOOD.

Cape Verde: 3 blvd El-Hadji Djilly M'Baye, BP 11269, Dakar; tel. 33-822-4285; fax 33-821-0697; e-mail acvc.sen@metissacana.sn; Ambassador FRANCISCO PEREIRA DA VEIGA.

China, People's Republic: rue 18 prolongée, Fann Résidence, BP 342, Dakar; tel. 33-864-7775; fax 33-864-7780; Ambassador GONG YUANXING.

Congo, Democratic Republic: 16 rue Léo Frobénus, Fann Résidence, Dakar; tel. 33-824-6574; fax 33-864-6576; Chargé d'affaires a.i. FATAKI NICOLAS LUNGUELE MUSAMBYA.

Congo, Republic: Statut Mermoz, Pyrotechnie, BP 5242, Fann Résidence, Dakar; tel. 33-824-8398; fax 33-825-7856; Ambassador VALENTIN OLLESSONGO.

Côte d'Ivoire: ave Birago Diop, BP 359, Dakar; tel. 33-869-0270; fax 33-825-2115; e-mail cmrci@ambaci-dakar.org; internet www.ambaci-dakar.org; Ambassador COLETTE LAMBIN (recalled Nov. 2010).

Cuba: 43 rue Aimé Césaire, BP 4510, Fann Résidence, Dakar; tel. 33-869-0240; fax 33-864-1063; e-mail embacubasen@sentoo.sn; Ambassador VILMA REYES VALDESPINO.

Egypt: 22 ave Brière de l'Isle, Plateau, BP 474, Dakar; tel. 33-889-2474; fax 33-821-8993; e-mail ambegydk@telecomplus.sn; Ambassador MUHAMMAD GAMAL EL-DEIN MUHAMMAD ELISH.

Ethiopia: 18 blvd de la République, BP 379, Dakar; tel. 33-821-9896; fax 33-821-9895; e-mail ethembas@sentoo.sn; Ambassador ATO HASSEN ABDULKADIK.

France: 1 rue El Hadj Amadou Assane Ndoye, BP 4035, Dakar; tel. 33-839-5100; fax 33-839-5181; internet www.ambafrance-sn.org/france_senegal/spip.php?rubrique1; Ambassador NICOLAS NORMAND.

Gabon: ave Cheikh Anta Diop, cnr Fann Résidence, BP 436, Dakar; tel. 33-865-2234; fax 33-864-3145; e-mail ambgabon@refer.sn; Ambassador VINCENT BOULE.

The Gambia: 11 rue Elhadji Ismaïla Guèye (Thiong), BP 3248, Dakar; tel. 33-821-4416; fax 33-821-6279; e-mail gambit.high.commission@gmail.com; Ambassador GIBRIL SEMAN JOOF.

Germany: 20 ave Pasteur, angle rue Mermoz, BP 2100, Dakar; tel. 33-889-4884; fax 33-822-5299; e-mail info@daka.diplo.de; internet www.dakar.diplo.de; Ambassador CHRISTIAN CLAGES.

Ghana: Lot 27, Parcelle B, Almadies, BP 25370, Dakar; tel. 33-869-1990; fax 33-820-1950; e-mail info@ghembsen.org; Ambassador ABDULAI YAKUBU.

Directory

Guinea: rue 7, angle B&D, point E, BP 7123, Dakar; tel. 33-824-8606; fax 33-825-5946; Ambassador HADJA KOUMBA DIAKITÉ.

Guinea-Bissau: rue 6, angle B, point E, BP 2319, Dakar; tel. 33-823-0059; fax 33-825-2946; Ambassador MÁRIO CABRAL.

Holy See: rue Aimé Césaire, angle Corniche-Ouest, BP 5076, Dakar; tel. 33-824-2674; fax 33-824-1931; e-mail vatemb@orange.sn; Apostolic Nuncio Most Rev. LUIS MARIANO MONTEMAYOR (Titular Archbishop of Illici).

India: 5 rue Carde, BP 398, Dakar; tel. 33-849-5875; fax 33-822-3585; e-mail indiacom@orange.sn; internet www.ambassadeinde.sn; Ambassador M. K. J. FRANCIS.

Indonesia: ave Cheikh Anta Diop, BP 5859, Dakar; tel. 33-825-7316; fax 33-825-5896; e-mail kbri@sentoo.sn; Ambassador SUKARNI SIKAR.

Iran: 17 ave des Ambassadeurs, Fann Résidence, BP 735, Dakar; tel. 33-825-2528; fax 33-824-2314; e-mail ambiiran@telecomplus.sn; Ambassador JAHAN BAKHSHE HASANZADE.

Iraq: point E, rue 6, angle B, à coté de la Croix Rouge Internationale, BP45448, Dakar; tel. 33-869-7799; fax 33-824-0909; e-mail dkremb@iraqmfamail.com; Ambassador MOHAMMED HAKIM AL-ROBAI'EE.

Italy: rue Alpha Achamiyou Tall, BP 348, Dakar; tel. 33-889-2636; fax 33-821-7580; e-mail ambasciata.dakar@esteri.it; internet www.ambdakar.esteri.it; Ambassador GIUSEPPE CALVETTA.

Japan: blvd Martin Luther King, Corniche-Ouest, BP 3140, Dakar; tel. 33-849-5500; fax 33-849-5555; Ambassador HIROSHI FUKADA.

Korea, Republic: Villa Hamoudy, rue Aime Cesaire, Fann Résidence, BP 5850, Dakar; tel. 33-824-0672; fax 33-824-0695; e-mail senegal@mofat.go.kr; internet sen.mofat.go.kr; Ambassador KIM HYUNG-KUK.

Kuwait: blvd Martin Luther King, Dakar; tel. 33-824-1723; fax 33-825-0899; e-mail q8embassydkr@sentoo.sn; Ambassador MUHAMMAD AZ-ZUWAIKH.

Lebanon: 56 ave Jean XXIII, BP 6700 Dakar-Etoile, Dakar; tel. 33-822-0255; fax 33-823-5899; e-mail ambaliban@orange.sn; internet www.ambaliban.org; Ambassador MICHEL HADDAD.

Liberia: 146 Ouest-Foire, BP 5845, Dakar-Fann; tel. 33-869-4019; fax 33-820-8223; e-mail libembdkr1@yahoo.com; Ambassador JOHNNY A. MCCLAIN.

Libya: route de Ouakam, Dakar; tel. 33-824-5710; fax 33-824-5722; Ambassador AL HADY SALEM HAMMAD.

Madagascar: Immeuble rue 2, angle Ellipse, Point E, BP 25395, Dakar; tel. 33-825-2666; fax 33-864-4086; e-mail ambamad@sentoo.sn; internet www.ambamad.sn; Ambassador RICHARD AUGUSTE PARAIN.

Malaysia: 7 Extension VDN, Fann Mermoz, BP 15057, Dakar; tel. 33-825-8935; fax 33-825-4719; e-mail maldakar@kln.gov.my; Ambassador Dato' JAMAIYAH MOHAMED YUSOF.

Mali: Fann Résidence, Corniche-Ouest, rue 23, BP 478, Dakar; tel. 33-824-6252; fax 33-825-9471; e-mail ambamali@sentoo.sn; Ambassador N'TJI LAÏCO TRAORÉ.

Mauritania: 37 blvd Charles de Gaulle, Dakar; tel. 33-823-5344; fax 33-823-5311; Ambassador MOHAMMED VALL OULD BELLAL.

Morocco: 73 ave Cheikh Anta Diop, BP 490, Dakar; tel. 33-824-6927; fax 33-825-7021; e-mail ambmadk@sentoo.sn; Ambassador TALEB BERRADA.

Netherlands: 37 rue Jaques Bugnicourt, BP 3262, Dakar; tel. 33-849-0360; fax 33-821-7084; e-mail dak@minbuza.nl; internet www.nlambassadedakar.org; Ambassador GERBEN DE JONG.

Nigeria: 8 ave Cheikh Anta Diop, BP 3129, Dakar; tel. 33-869-8600; fax 33-825-8136; e-mail info@nigeriandakar.sn; internet www.nigeriandakar.sn; Ambassador AZUKA CECILIA UZOKA-EMEJULU.

Oman: Villa 7062, Stéle Mermoz, BP 2635, Dakar; tel. 33-824-6136; e-mail dakar@mofa.gov.om; Ambassador AHMED BARAKAT ABDULLAH AL-IBRAHIM.

Pakistan: Stèle Mermoz, Villa 7602, BP 2635, Dakar; tel. 33-824-6135; fax 33-824-6136; e-mail parepdakar@gmail.com; internet www.mofa.gov.pk/senegal; Ambassador RIZWAN AHMED SHEIKH.

Portugal: 6 Villa Martha, Fann Résidence, BP 281, Dakar; tel. 33-864-0317; fax 33-864-0322; e-mail ambportdakar@sentoo.sn; Ambassador RUI ALBERTO MANUPPELLA TERENO.

Qatar: 25 blvd Martin Luther King, BP 5150, Dakar; tel. 33-820-9559; fax 33-869-1012; Ambassador ALI ABDUL LATIF AHMED AL-MASALAMANI.

Romania: rue A prolongée, point E, BP 3171, Dakar; tel. 33-825-2068; fax 33-824-9190; e-mail romania.consul@orange.sn; internet dakar.mae.ro; Ambassador SIMONA CORLAN-IOAN.

Russia: ave Jean Jaurès, angle rue Carnot, BP 3180, Dakar; tel. 33-822-4821; fax 33-821-1372; e-mail ambrus@orange.sn; internet www.senegal.mid.ru; Ambassador VALERY NESTERUSHKIN.

SENEGAL — Directory

Saudi Arabia: 10 route de Ngor n° 10, BP 15150, Dakar; tel. 33-869-8390; fax 33-820-6553; e-mail snemb@mofa.gov.sa; Ambassador HAMAD SAEED AL-ZAABI.

South Africa: Memoz SUD, Lotissement Ecole de Police, BP 21010, Dakar-Ponty; tel. 33-865-1959; fax 33-864-2359; e-mail ambafsud@orange.sn; internet www.saesenegal.info; Ambassador S. S. KOTANE.

Spain: 18–20 ave Nelson Mandela, BP 2091, Dakar; tel. 33-821-1178; fax 33-821-6845; e-mail emb.dakar@mae.es; Ambassador JORGE TOLEDO ALBIÑANA.

Sudan: 31 route de la Pyrotechnie, Mermoz, Fann-Résidence, BP 15033, Dakar; tel. 33-824-9853; fax 33-824-9852; e-mail sudembse@sentoo.sn; Ambassador MAHMOUD HASSAN EL-AMIN.

Switzerland: rue René N'Diaye, angle rue Seydou, BP 1772, Dakar; tel. 33-823-0590; fax 33-822-3657; e-mail dak.vertretung@eda.admin.ch; internet www.eda.admin.ch/dakar; Ambassador MURIEL BERSET.

Syria: rue 1, point E, angle blvd de l'Est, BP 498, Dakar; tel. 33-824-6277; fax 33-824-9007; e-mail syrdak@orange.sn; Ambassador (vacant).

Thailand: 10 rue Léon Gontran Damas, Angle F, Fann Résidence BP 3721, Dakar; tel. 33-869-3290; fax 33-824-8458; e-mail thaidkr@sentoo.sn; internet www.mfa.go.th/web/2366.php; Ambassador KANYA CHAIMAN.

Tunisia: rue Alpha Hachamiyou Tall, BP 3127, Dakar; tel. 33-823-4747; fax 33-823-7204; e-mail at.dakar@sentoo.sn; Ambassador CHOUKRI HERMASSI.

Turkey: ave des Ambassadeurs, Fann Résidence, BP 6060, Etoile, Dakar; tel. 33-869-2542; fax 33-825-6977; e-mail trambdkr@sentoo.sn; Ambassador ASLI UĞDÜL.

United Kingdom: 20 rue du Dr Guillet, BP 6025, Dakar; tel. 33-823-7392; fax 33-823-2766; e-mail britembe@orange.sn; internet ukinsenegal.fco.gov.uk; Ambassador CHRISTOPHER JOHN TROTT.

USA: ave Jean XXIII, angle rue Kleber, BP 49, Dakar; tel. 33-829-2100; fax 33-822-2991; e-mail usadakar@state.gov; internet dakar.usembassy.gov; Ambassador MARCIA STEPHENS BLOOM BERNICAT.

Zimbabwe: rue de Louga, angle rue 31, Point E, BP 25342, Fann, Dakar; tel. 33-825-4131; fax 33-825-4016; e-mail zimdakar@yahoo.com; Ambassador TRUDY STEVENSON.

Judicial System

The Supreme Court was re-established in 2008, replacing the Court of Cassation and the Council of State. The Supreme Court is the highest court of appeal, and regulates the activities of subordinate courts and tribunals. It also judges complaints brought against the Executive and resolves electoral disputes. The Constitutional Council verifies that legislation and international agreements are in accordance with the Constitution; decides disputes between the Executive and the Legislature. The Revenue Court supervises the public accounts.

Supreme Court: blvd Martin Luther King, Dakar; tel. 33-889-1010; fax 33-823-7894; f. 2008; Pres. PAPE OMAR SAKHO.

Constitutional Council: BP 45732, Dakar; tel. 33-822-5252; fax 33-822-8187; e-mail magou_51@hotmail.com; internet www.gouv.sn/institutions/conseil_const.html; 5 mems; Pres. CHEIKH TIDIANE DIAKHATÉ.

Revenue Court (Cour des Comptes): 15 ave Franklin Roosevelt, BP 9097, Peytavin, Dakar; tel. 33-849-4001; fax 33-849-4362; e-mail amdjibgueye@courdescomptes.sn; internet www.courdescomptes.sn; f. 1999; Pres. ABDOU BAME GUEYE; Sec.-Gen. El Hadji ABDOUL MADJIB GUEYE; Pres. of Chambers ABBA GOUDIABY, MAMADOU TOURE, MAMADOU HADY SARR; Chief Administrator ABDOURAHMANE DIOUKNANE.

High Court of Justice: Dakar; competent to try the Prime Minister and other members of the Government for crimes committed in the exercise of their duties; The President of the Republic may only be brought to trial in the case of high treason; mems elected by the Assemblée nationale.

Religion

At the time of the 1988 census almost 94% of the population were Muslims, while some 5% professed Christianity (the dominant faith being Roman Catholicism); a small number, mostly in the south, followed traditional beliefs.

ISLAM

There are four main Islamic brotherhoods active in Senegal: the Tidjanes, the Mourides, the Layennes and the Qadiriyas.

Association pour la coopération islamique (ACIS): Dakar; f. 1988; Pres. Dr THIERNAO KÂ.

Grande Mosquée de Dakar: Dakar; tel. 33-822-5648; Grand Imam El Hadj BAYE DAME DIÈNE.

CHRISTIANITY

The Roman Catholic Church

Senegal comprises one archdiocese and six dioceses. Roman Catholics represented about 5% of the total population.

Bishops' Conference

Conférence des Evêques du Sénégal, de la Mauritanie, du Cap-Vert et de Guinée-Bissau, BP 941, Dakar; tel. 33-836-3309; fax 33-836-1617; e-mail archevchedkr@sentoo.sn.

f. 1973; Pres. Most Rev. JEAN-NOËL DIOUF (Bishop of Tambacounda).

Archbishop of Dakar: Cardinal THÉODORE-ADRIEN SARR, Archevêché, ave Jean XXIII, BP 1908, Dakar; tel. 33-889-0600; fax 33-823-4875; e-mail archevechedkr@sentoo.sn.

The Anglican Communion

The Anglican diocese of The Gambia, part of the Church of the Province of West Africa, includes Senegal and Cape Verde. The Bishop is resident in Banjul, The Gambia.

Protestant Church

Église Luthérienne du Senegal: BP 9, Fatick, Niakhar; tel. 33-949-1171; fax 33-949-1385; e-mail elsfk@orange.sn; Pres. Rev. ABDOU THIAM.

Eglise Protestante du Sénégal: 65 rue Wagane Diouf, BP 22390, Dakar; tel. 33-821-5564; fax 33-821-7132; f. 1862; Pastor ETITI YOMO DJERIWO.

BAHÁ'Í FAITH

National Spiritual Assembly: Point E, rue des Ecrivains, impasse 2 à droite après la Direction de la statistique, BP 1662, Dakar; tel. 33-824-2359; e-mail bahai@sentoo.sn; internet www.sn.bahai.org; regd 1975; Sec. ABOUBAKRINE BA.

The Press

DAILY NEWSPAPERS

L'Actuel: route du Front de Terre, angle ave Bourguiba, Immeuble Dramé, BP 11874, Dakar; tel. 33-864-2601; fax 33-864-2602; e-mail lactuel@sentoo.sn; Editor-in-Chief ABDOURAHMANE SY.

Dakar Soir: Point Presse Sarl, 3e étage, 108 Hann Maristes, BP 21548, Dakar; tel. and fax 33-832-1093; f. 2000; Editor-in-Chief ALAIN NDIAYE.

L'Evénement du Soir: Fann Résidence, rue A, angle rue 4, point E, BP 16060, Dakar; tel. 33-864-3430; fax 33-864-3600; evenings.

Frasques Quotidiennes: 51 rue du Docteur Thèze, BP 879, Dakar; tel. 33-842-4226; fax 33-842-4277; e-mail frasques@arc.sn.

L'Info 7: Sicap rue 10, BP 11357, Dakar; tel. and fax 33-864-2658; e-mail comsept@sentoo.sn; f. 1999.

Le Matin: route de l'Aéroport Léopold Sédar Senghor, Yoff, BP 6472, Dakar; tel. 33-869-1270; fax 33-820-1181; e-mail lematin@metissacana.sn; internet www.lematindelafrique.com; daily; independent; Editor-in-Chief ALIOUNE FALL.

L'Observateur: Immeuble Elimane Ndour, rue 15, angle Corniche, Dakar; tel. 33-849-1644; fax 33-849-1645; e-mail info@futursmedias.net; internet www.lobservateur.sn; Editor-in-Chief SERIGNE SALIOU SAMB.

L'Office: 9 rue de Thann, Dakar; tel. 33-824-2115; fax 33-824-2108; e-mail loffice@loffice.sn; internet www.loffice.sn; Editor-in-Chief LAMINE NDOUR.

Le Populaire: 114 ave Peytavin, Immeuble Serigne Massamba Mbacké, Dakar; tel. 33-822-7977; fax 33-822-7927; f. 2000; Editor-in-Chief DAOUDA DIARRA.

Le Quotidien: 12 Cité Adama Diop, Yoff Routes de Cimétieres, BP 25221, Dakar; tel. 33-869-8484; fax 33-820-7297; e-mail lequotidien@lequotidien.sn; internet www.lequotidien.sn; f. 2003; Dir MAMADOU BIAYE.

Le Soleil: Société sénégalaise de presse et de publications, route du Service géographique, Hann, BP 92, Dakar; tel. 33-859-5959; fax 33-832-0886; e-mail lesoleil@lesoleil.sn; internet www.lesoleilmultimedia.com; f. 1970; Editors-in-Chief HABIB DEMBA FALL, SIDY DIOP; circ. 25,000 (2009).

Sud Quotidien: Amitié II, angle blvd Bourguiba, BP 4130, Dakar; tel. 33-824-3306; fax 33-824-3322; e-mail info@sudonline.sn; internet

SENEGAL

www.sudonline.sn; independent; Dir ABDOULAYE NDIAGA SYLLA; circ. 30,000.

Tract: 13 rue de Thann, BP 3683, Dakar; tel. and fax 33-823-4725; e-mail tract.sn@laposte.net; f. 2000.

Wal Fadjri/L'Aurore (The Dawn): Sicap Sacré-Coeur 8542, BP 576, Dakar; tel. 33-824-2343; fax 33-824-2346; e-mail walf@walf.sn; internet www.walf.sn; f. 1984; Exec. Dir MBAYE SIDY MBAYE; circ. 15,000.

24 Heures Chrono: Sacré coeur 3, Villa 10595; tel. 77-576-0358; internet www.24sn.com; Editor SAMBA BIAGUI.

PERIODICALS

Afrique Médicale: 10 rue Abdou Karim Bourgi, BP 1826, Dakar; tel. 33-823-4880; fax 33-822-5630; f. 1960; 11 a year; review of tropical medicine; Editor P. CORREA; circ. 7,000.

Afrique Nouvelle: 9 rue Paul Holle, BP 283, Dakar; tel. 33-822-5122; f. 1947; weekly; devt issues; Roman Catholic; Dir RENÉ ODOUN; circ. 15,000.

Le Cafard Libéré: 10 rue Tolbiac, angle Autoroute, Soumédioune, BP 7292, Dakar; tel. 33-822-4383; fax 33-822-0891; f. 1987; weekly; satirical; Editor PAPE SAMBA KANE; circ. 12,000.

Construire l'Afrique: Dakar; tel. 33-823-0790; fax 33-824-1961; f. 1985; 6 a year; African business; Dir and Chief Editor CHEIKH OUSMANE DIALLO.

Le Courrier du Sud: BP 190, Ziguinchor; tel. 33-991-1166; weekly.

Démocratie: Liberté V, 5375 M, 71 rue du rond-point Liberté V et VI, Dakar; tel. 33-824-8669; fax 33-825-1879.

Eco Hebdo: rue 22, Médina, BP 11451, Dakar; tel. and fax 33-837-1414; weekly.

L'Equipe Sénégal: Dakar; tel. 33-824-0013; e-mail lequipesenegal@yahoo.fr; weekly; sports.

Ethiopiques: BP 2035, Dakar; tel. 33-849-1414; fax 33-822-1914; e-mail senghorf@orange.sn; internet www.refer.sn/ethiopiques; f. 1974; literary and philosophical review; publ. by Fondation Léopold Sédar Senghor; Editor BASSIROU DIENG.

Le Journal de l'Economie: 15 rue Jules Ferry, BP 2851, Dakar; tel. 33-823-8733; fax 33-823-6007; e-mail lejeco@sentoo.sn; weekly.

Journal Officiel de la République du Sénégal: Rufisque; tel. 33-849-1817; internet www.jo.gouv.sn; f. 1856; weekly; govt journal.

Nord Ouest: Immeuble Lonase, BP 459, Louga; tel. 76-680-7943; e-mail lenordouest@yahoo.fr; f. 2000; regional monthly; Dir of Publication PAPE MOMAR CISSÉ.

Nouvel Horizon: Liberté II, Villa 1589, BP 10037, Dakar; tel. 33-864-1152; fax 33-864-1150; e-mail nh-thiof@sentoo.sn; weekly; Editor-in-Chief ISSA SALL.

Nuit et Jour: Rocade Fann Bel-Air, Immeuble Seynabou Cissé, Dakar; tel. 33-832-1570; weekly.

Le Politicien: 8123 Terminus Liberté VI, BP 11018, Dakar; tel. and fax 33-827-6396; f. 1977; weekly; satirical.

Promotion: BP 1676, Dakar; tel. 33-825-6969; fax 33-825-6950; e-mail giepromo@telecomplus.sn; f. 1972; fortnightly; Dir BOUBACAR DIOP; circ. 5,000.

République: BP 21740, Dakar; tel. 33-822-7373; fax 33-822-5039; e-mail republike@yahoo.fr; f. 1994; weekly.

Sénégal d'Aujourd'hui: Dakar; monthly; publ. by Ministry of Culture; circ. 5,000.

Sopi (Change): 5 blvd Dial Diop, Dakar; tel. 33-824-4950; fax 33-824-4700; f. 1988; weekly; publ. by PDS; Editor CHEIKH KOUREYSSI BA.

Le Témoin: Gibraltar II, Villa 310, Dakar; tel. 33-822-3269; fax 33-821-7838; f. 1990; weekly; Editor-in-Chief MAMADOU OUMAR NDIAYE; circ. 5,000.

Unir Cinéma: 1 rue Neuville, BP 160, Saint Louis; tel. 33-861-1027; fax 33-861-2408; f. 1973; quarterly African cinema review; Editor PIERRE SAGNA.

Vive La République: Sicap Amitié III, Villa 4057, Dakar; tel. 33-864-0631; weekly.

Xareli (Struggle): BP 12136, Dakar; tel. 33-822-5463; fortnightly; publ. by AJ—PADS; circ. 7,000.

NEWS AGENCIES

Agence Panafricaine d'Information—PANA-Presse SA: ave Bourjuiba, BP 4056, Dakar; tel. 33-869-1234; fax 33-824-1390; e-mail marketing@panapress.com; internet www.panapress.com; f. 1979 as Pan-African News Agency (under the auspices of the Organization of African Unity), restructured as 75% privately owned co in 1997; Dir-Gen. BABACAR FALL.

Agence de Presse Sénégalaise: 58 blvd de la République, BP 117, Dakar; tel. 33-823-1667; fax 33-822-0767; e-mail aps@aps.sn; internet www.aps.sn; f. 1959; govt-controlled; Dir-Gen. MAMADOU KOUMÉ.

PRESS ORGANIZATION

Syndicat des Professionnels de l'Information et de la Communication du Sénégal (SYNPICS): BP 21722, Dakar; tel. 33-842-4256; fax 33-842-0269; e-mail synpics@yahoo.fr; Sec.-Gen. DIATA CISSÉ.

Publishers

Africa Editions: BP 1826, Dakar; tel. 33-823-4880; fax 33-822-5630; f. 1958; general, reference; Man. Dir JOËL DECUPPER.

Agence de Distribution de Presse: km 2.5, blvd du Centenaire de la Commune de Dakar, BP 374, Dakar; tel. 33-832-0278; fax 33-832-4915; e-mail adpresse@telecomplus.sn; f. 1943; general, reference; Man. Dir PHILIPPE SCHORP.

Centre Africain d'Animation et d'Echanges Culturels Editions Khoudia: BP 5332, Dakar-Fann; tel. 33-821-1023; fax 33-821-5109; f. 1989; fiction, education, anthropology; Dir AISSATOU DIA.

Editions Clairafrique: 2 rue El Hadji Mbaye Guèye, BP 2005, Dakar; tel. 33-822-2169; fax 33-821-8409; f. 1951; politics, law, sociology, anthropology, literature, economics, devt, religion, school books.

Editions des Ecoles Nouvelles Africaines: ave Cheikh Anta Diop, angle rue Pyrotechnie, Stèle Mermoz, BP 581, Dakar; tel. 33-864-0544; fax 33-864-1352; e-mail eenas@sentoo.sn; youth and adult education, in French.

Editions Juridiques Africaines (EDJA): 18 rue Raffenel, BP 22420, Dakar-Ponty; tel. 33 821-6689; fax 33 823-2753; e-mail edja.ed@orange.sn; internet www.edja.sn; f. 1987; law; Dir NDÉYE NGONÉ GUÉYE.

Editions des Trois Fleuves: blvd de l'Est, angle Cheikh Anta Diop, BP 123, Dakar; tel. 33-825-7923; fax 33-825-5937; f. 1972; general non-fiction; luxury edns; Dir GÉRARD RAZIMOWSKY; Gen. Man. BERTRAND DE BOISTEL.

Enda—Tiers Monde Editions (Environmental Development Action in the Third World): 54 rue Carnot, BP 3370, Dakar; tel. 33-822-9890; fax 33-823-5157; e-mail editions@enda.sn; internet www.enda.sn; f. 1972; Third-World environment and devt; Dir RAPHAËL NDIAYE; Exec. Sec. JOSÉPHINE OUÉDRAOGO.

Grande imprimerie africaine (GIA): 9 rue Amadou Assane Ndoye, Dakar; tel. 33-822-1408; fax 33-822-3927; f. 1917; law, administration; Man. Dir CHEIKH ALIMA TOURÉ.

Institut fondamental d'Afrique noire (IFAN)—Cheikh Anta Diop: BP 206, Campus universitaire, Dakar; tel. 33-825-9890; fax 33-824-4918; internet www.afrique-ouest.auf.org; f. 1936; scientific and humanistic studies of Black Africa, for specialist and general public.

Nouvelles éditions africaines du Sénégal (NEAS): 10 rue Amadou Assane Ndoye, BP 260, Dakar; tel. 33-822-1580; fax 33-822-3604; e-mail neas@telecomplus.sn; f. 1972; literary fiction, schoolbooks; Dir-Gen. SAYDOU SOW.

Per Ankh: BP 2, Popenguine; e-mail perankheditions@arc.sn; internet www.perankhbooks.com; history.

Société africaine d'édition: 16 bis rue de Thiong, BP 1877, Dakar; tel. 33-821-7977; f. 1961; African politics and economics; Man. Dir PIERRE BIARNES.

Société d'édition 'Afrique Nouvelle': 9 rue Paul Holle, BP 283, Dakar; tel. 33-822-3825; f. 1947; information, statistics and analyses of African affairs; Man. Dir ATHANASE NDONG.

Société nationale de Presse, d'édition et de publicité (SONA-PRESS): Dakar; f. 1972; Pres. OBEYE DIOP.

Sud-Communication: BP 4100, Dakar; operated by a journalists' co-operative; periodicals.

Xamal, SA: BP 380, Saint-Louis; tel. 33-961-1722; fax 33-961-1519; general literature, social sciences, in national languages and in French; Dir ABOUBAKAR DIOP.

GOVERNMENT PUBLISHING HOUSE

Société sénégalaise de presse et de publications—Imprimerie nationale (SSPP): route du Service géographique, BP 92, Dakar; tel. 33-832-4692; fax 33-832-0381; f. 1970; 62% govt-owned; Dir SALIOU DIAGNE.

SENEGAL

Broadcasting and Communications

TELECOMMUNICATIONS

Regulatory Authority

Agence de Régulation des Télécommunications et des Postes (ARTP): route des Almadies Angle Dioulikayes, BP 14130, Dakar-Peytavin; tel. 33-869-0369; fax 33-869-0370; e-mail contact@artp.sn; internet www.artp.sn; f. 2001; Pres. Prof. ABDOULAYE SAKHO; Dir-Gen. NDONGO DIAO.

Service Providers

Excaf Telecom: Domaine Industriel SODIDA, rue 14 Prolongée, BP 1656, Dakar; tel. 33-824-2424; fax 33-824-2191; e-mail dunyaa@excaf.com; internet www.excaf.com; f. 1972 as L'Agence Africaine de Commercialisation Artistique; name changed as above in 1992; Pres. and Dir-Gen. IBRAHIMA DIAGNE.

Expresso Sénégal: Dakar; internet www.expressotelecom.com; Dir-Gen. EMMANUEL HAMEZ.

Société Nationale des Télécommunications du Sénégal (SONATEL): 46 blvd de la République, BP 69, Dakar; tel. 33-839-1118; fax 33-823-6037; internet www.sonatel.sn; f. 1985; 52.2% owned by France Câbles et Radio (France Télécom, France), 27.67% owned by Govt; Pres. MICHEL HIRSCH; Man. Dir CHEIKH TIDIANE MBAYE; 2,340 employees (2007).

Orange Sénégal: 46 ave de la République, BP 2352, Dakar; tel. 33-839-1771; fax 33-839-1754; internet www.orange.sn; f. 1996 as Sonatel Mobiles; fmrly known as Alizé.

Télécom Plus SARL: 20 rue Amadou Assane Ndoye, BP 21100, Dakar; tel. 33-839-9700; fax 33-823-4632; telecommunications products and services.

Tigo: 15 route de Ngor, BP 146, Dakar; tel. 33-869-7420; fax 33-820-6788; internet www.tigo.sn; fmrly Sentel Sénégal GSM; name changed as above in 2005; mobile cellular telephone operator in Dakar, most western regions, and in selected localities nation-wide; 75% owned by Millicom International Cellular (Luxembourg), 25% by Senegalese private investors; Gen. Man. YOUVAL ROSH; 250,000 subscribers (2003).

BROADCASTING

Regulatory Authority

Haut Conseil de l'Audiovisuel: Immeuble Fahd, Dakar; tel. and fax 33-823-4784; f. 1991; Pres. AMINATA CISSÉ NIANG.

Radio

Société nationale de la Radiodiffusion-Télévision Sénégalaise (RTS): Triangle sud, angle ave Malick Sy, BP 1765, Dakar; tel. 33-849-1212; fax 33-822-3490; e-mail rts@rts.sn; internet www.rts.sn; f. 1992; state broadcasting co; broadcasts 2 national and 8 regional stations; Dir-Gen. BABACAR DIAGNE.

Radio Sénégal Internationale: Triangle sud, angle ave El Hadj Malick Sy, BP 1765, Dakar; tel. 33-849-1212; fax 33-822-3490; f. 2001; broadcasts news and information programmes in French, English, Arabic, Portuguese, Spanish, Italian, Soninké, Pulaar and Wolof from 14 transmitters across Senegal and on cable; Dir CHÉRIF THIAM.

RST1: Triangle sud, angle ave El Hadj Malick Sy, BP 1765, Dakar; tel. 33-849-1212; fax 33-822-3490; f. 1992; broadcasts in French, Arabic and 6 vernacular languages from 16 transmitters across Senegal; Dir MANSOUR SOW.

JDP FM (Jeunesse, Développement, Paix): Dakar; tel. 33-991-4813; e-mail abdousarr@orange.sn; Dir ABDOU SARR.

Oxy-Jeunes: Fojes BP 18303, Pikine, Dakar; tel. 33-834-4919; fax 33-827-3215; e-mail cheikh_seck@eudoramail.com; f. 1999; youth and community radio station supported by the World Asscn of Community Radio Stations and the Catholic Organization for Development and Peace.

Radio Nostalgie Dakar: BP 21021, Dakar; tel. 33-821-2121; fax 33-822-2222; e-mail nostafric@globeaccess.net; f. 1995; music; broadcasts in French and Wolof; Gen. Man. SAUL SAVIOTE.

Radio PENC-MI: BP 51, Khombole; tel. 33-957-9103; fax 33-824-5898; e-mail rdoucoure@oxfam.org.uk.

Radio Rurale FM Awagna de Bignona: BP 72, Bignona; tel. 33-994-1021; fax 33-994-1909; e-mail mksonko2000@yahoo.fr.

Sud FM: Immeuble Fahd, 5e étage, BP 4130, Dakar; tel. 33-865-0888; fax 33-822-5290; e-mail info@sudonline.sn; internet www.sudfm.net; f. 1994; operated by Sud-Communication; regional stations in Saint-Louis, Kaolack, Louga, Thiès, Ziguinchor and Diourbel; Dir-Gen. OUMAR-DIOUF FALL.

Wal Fadjri FM: Sicap Sacré-Coeur no 8542, BP 576, Dakar; tel. 33-824-2343; fax 33-824-2346; internet www.walf.sn/radio; f. 1997; Islamic broadcaster; Exec. Dir MBAYE SIDY MBAYE.

Television

Radiodiffusion-Télévision Sénégalaise (RTS): see Radio; Dir of Television BABACAR DIAGNE.

Canal Horizons Sénégal: 31 ave Albert Sarrault, BP 1390, Dakar; tel. 33-889-5050; fax 33-823-3030; e-mail infos@canalhorizons.sn; internet www.canalhorizons.com; f. 1990; private encrypted channel; 18.8% owned by RTS and Société Nationale des Télécommunications du Sénégal, 15% by Canal Horizons (France); Man. Dir BÉNÉDICTE CHENUET.

Réseau MMDS-EXCAF Télécom: rue 14 prolongée, HLM 1, Domaine Industriel SODIDA, BP 1656, Dakar; tel. 33-824-2424; fax 33-824-2191; broadcasts selection of African, US, European and Saudi Arabian channels.

The French television stations, France-2, TV5 and Arte France, are also broadcast to Senegal.

Finance

(cap. = capital; res = reserves; dep. = deposits; m. = million; br(s). = branch(es); amounts in francs CFA)

BANKING

In 2009 there were 18 commercial banks and three other financial institutions in Senegal.

Central Bank

Banque centrale des états de l'Afrique de l'ouest (BCEAO): blvd du Général de Gaulle, angle rue 11, BP 3159, Dakar; tel. 33-889-4545; fax 33-823-5757; e-mail akangni@bceao.int; internet www.bceao.int; f. 1962; bank of issue for mem. states of the Union économique et monétaire ouest africaine (UEMOA, comprising Benin, Burkina Faso, Côte d'Ivoire, Guinea-Bissau, Mali, Niger, Senegal and Togo); cap. 134,120m., res 1,474,195m., dep. 2,124,051m. (Dec. 2009); Interim Gov. JEAN-BAPTISTE MARIE PASCAL COMPAORÉ; Dir in Senegal FATIMATIOU ZAHRA DIOP; brs at Kaolack and Ziguinchor.

Commercial Banks

Bank of Africa—Sénégal: Résidence Excellence, 4 ave Léopold Sédar Senghor, BP 1992, Dakar; tel. 33-849-6240; fax 33-842-1667; e-mail information@boasenegal.com; internet www.boasenegal.com; f. 2001; cap. 2,750m., res 82,011m., dep. 48,703m. (Dec. 2007); Pres. PAUL DERREUMAUX; Dir-Gen. FAUSTIN AMOUSSOU; 8 brs.

Banque Internationale pour le Commerce et l'Industrie du Sénégal (BICIS): 2 ave Léopold Sédar Senghor, BP 392, Dakar; tel. 33-839-0390; fax 33-823-0737; e-mail bicis@africa.bnpparibas.com; internet www.bicis.sn; f. 1962; 54.11% owned by Groupe BNP Paribas (France); cap. 5,000m., res 21,473m., dep. 272,099m. (Dec. 2008); Chair. LANDING SANÉ; Dir-Gen. AMADOU KANE; 17 brs.

CBAO Groupe Attijariwafa bank: 1 pl. de l'Indépendance, BP 129, Dakar; tel. 33-33-849-9696; fax 33-823-2005; e-mail cbao@cbao.sn; internet www.cbao.sn; fmrly Compagnie Bancaire de l'Afrique Occidentale (CBAO), name changed as above in 2008 following merger with Attijari bank Sénégal; 100% owned by Attijariwafa Bank Group (Morocco); cap. 11,450m., res 48,171m., dep. 551,272m. (Dec. 2008); Pres. BOUBKER JAÏ; Dir-Gen. ABDELKRIM RAGHNI.

Citibank Senegal SA: Immeuble SDIH, 4e étage, 2 pl. de l'Indépendance, BP 3391, Dakar; tel. 33-849-1104; fax 33-823-8817; e-mail thioro.ba@citicorp.com; f. 1975; wholly owned subsidiary of Citibank NA (USA); cap. 1,626m., total assets 84,864m. (Dec. 2001); Pres. JOHN REED; Man. KEVIN A. MURRAY; 1 br.

Compagnie Ouest Africaine de Crédit Bail (LOCAFRIQUE): Immeuble Coumaba Castel, 11 rue Galandou Diouf, BP 292, Dakar; tel. 33-849-8100; fax 33-822-0894; e-mail locafrique@arc.sn; f. 1977; cap. 579m., total assets 1,241m. (Dec. 2003); Dir-Gen. AMADOU SY.

Crédit National du Sénégal (CNS): 7 ave Léopold Sédar Senghor, BP 319, Dakar; tel. 33-823-3486; fax 33-823-7292; f. 1990 by merger; 87% state-owned; cap. 1,900m., total assets 2,032m. (Dec. 1996); Pres. ABDOU NDIAYE.

Crédit du Sénégal (CLS): blvd El Hadji Djily Mbaye, angle rue Huart, BP 56, Dakar; tel. 33-849-0000; fax 33-823-8430; e-mail cl_senegal@creditdusenegal.com; internet www.creditdusenegal.com; f. 1989 by acquisition of USB by Crédit Lyonnais (France); name changed as above in 2007 following merger with Crédit Agricole (France); 95% owned by Attijariwafa Bank Group (Morocco); cap. 2,000m., res 9,099m., dep. 107,497m. (Dec. 2009); Pres. and Chair. BOUBKER JAÏ; Dir-Gen. MOHAMED EL-GHAZI; 5 brs.

SENEGAL

Ecobank Sénégal: 8 ave Léopold Sédar Senghor, BP 9095, Dakar; tel. 33-849-2000; fax 33-823-4707; e-mail ecobanksn@ecobank.com; internet www.ecobank.com; 41.45% owned by Ecobank Transnational Inc (Togo, operating under the auspices of the Economic Community of West African States), 17.0% by Ecobank Bénin, 12.43% by Ecobank Côte d'Ivoire, 4.56% by Ecobank Niger, 4.56% by Ecobank Togo; cap. 10,463m., res 3,351m., dep. 229,122m. (Dec. 2009); Pres. MAHENTA BIRIMA FALL; Dir-Gen. BOATIN KWASI.

International Commercial Bank (Senegal) SA: 18 ave Léopold Sédar Senghor, BP 32310, Dakar; tel. 33-823-5647; fax 33-842-2585; e-mail mail@icbank-senegal.com; internet www.icbank-senegal.com; f. 2006; CEO S. GANESH KUMAR; 1 br.

Société Générale de Banques au Sénégal (SGBS): 19 ave Léopold Sédar Senghor, BP 323, Dakar; tel. 33-839-5500; fax 33-823-9036; e-mail sgbs@sentoo.sn; internet www.sgbs.sn; f. 1962; 57.72% owned by Société Générale (France), 35.23% owned by private Senegalese investors; cap. 4,527m., res 28,301m., dep. 366,361m. (Dec. 2006); Pres. PAPA-DEMBA DIALLO; Dir-Gen. DANIEL TERUIN; 30 brs and sub-brs.

Development Banks

Banque de l'Habitat du Sénégal (BHS): 69 blvd du Général de Gaulle, BP 229, Dakar; tel. 33-839-3333; fax 33-823-8043; e-mail bdld10@calva.com; internet www.bhs.sn; f. 1979; cap. and res 19,661.0m., total assets 132,554.6m. (Dec. 2003); Pres. AHMED YÉRO DIALLO; Dir-Gen. BOCAR SY; 5 brs in Senegal and 5 brs abroad.

Caisse Nationale de Crédit Agricole du Sénégal (CNCAS): pl. de l'Indépendance, Immeuble ex-Air Afrique, 31–33 rue El Hadji Asmadou Assane Ndoye, angle ave Colbert, BP 3890, Dakar; tel. 33-839-3636; fax 33-821-2606; e-mail cncas@cncas.sn; internet www.cncas.sn; f. 1984; 23.8% state-owned; cap. 5,500m., res 2,065m., dep. 101,944m. (Dec. 2009); Pres. ABDOULAYE DIACK; Dir-Gen. ARFANG BOUBACAR DAFFE; 13 brs.

Société Financière d'Equipement (SFE): 2e étage, Immeuble Sokhna Anta, rue Dr Thèze, BP 252, Dakar; tel. 33-823-6626; fax 33-823-4337; 59% owned by Compagnie Bancaire de l'Afrique Occidentale; cap. and res 388m., total assets 6,653m. (Dec. 1999); Pres. ARISTIDE ORSET ALCANTARA; Dir-Gen. MOHAMED A. WILSON.

Islamic Bank

Banque Islamique du Sénégal (BIS): Immeuble Abdallah Fayçal, rue Huart, angle rue Amadou Ndoye, BP 3381, 18524 Dakar; tel. 33-849-6262; fax 33-822-4948; e-mail contact@bis-bank.com; internet www.bis-bank.com; f. 1983; 44.5% owned by Dar al-Maal al-Islami (Switzerland), 33.3% by Islamic Development Bank (Saudi Arabia), 22.2% state-owned; cap. 2,706m., res 1,335m., dep. 44,798m. (Dec. 2007); Pres. of Bd of Administration BADER EDDINE NOUIOUA; Dir-Gen. AZHAR S. KHAN; 4 brs.

Banking Association

Association Professionnelle des Banques et des Etablissements Financiers du Sénégal (APBEF): 5 rue Calmette, angle A. Assane Ndoye, BP 6403, Dakar; tel. 33-823-6093; fax 33-823-8596; e-mail apbef@orange.sn; Pres. ARFANG BOUBACAR DAFFÉ.

STOCK EXCHANGE

Bourse Régionale des Valeurs Mobilières (BRVM): BP 22500, Dakar; tel. 33-821-1518; fax 33-821-1506; e-mail nksy@brvm.org; internet www.brvm.org; f. 1998; national branch of BRVM (regional stock exchange based in Abidjan, Côte d'Ivoire, serving the member states of UEMOA); Man. NDÈYE KHADY SY.

INSURANCE

In 2010 the insurance sector comprised 22 companies: 13 non-life insurance companies, seven life insurance companies, one reinsurance company and one agricultural insurance company.

Allianz Sénégal Assurances: rue de Thann, angle ave Abdoulaye Fadiga, BP 2610, Dakar; tel. 33-849-4400; fax 33-823-1078; e-mail allianz.senegal@allianz-sn.com; internet www.allianz-senegal.com; name changed as above in 2009; Dir-Gen. OLIVIER MALÂTRE; also **Allianz Sénégal Assurances Vie**; life insurance.

AMSA Assurances: 43 ave Hassan II, BP 225, Dakar; tel. 33-839-3600; fax 33-823-3701; e-mail amsa-sn@amsa-group.com; internet amsa-group.com; f. 1977; fmrly Assurances Générales Sénégalaises (AGS); cap. 2,990m.; Dir-Gen. AÏDA DJIGO WANE; also **AMSA Assurances Vie**; life insurance.

Assurances La Sécurité Sénégalaise (ASS): BP 2623, Dakar; tel. 33-849-0599; fax 33-821-2581; e-mail ass.dk@orange.sn; internet ass-assurances.com; f. 1984; cap. 1,000m. (2007); Pres. MOUSSA SOW; Man. Dir MBACKÉ SENE.

AXA Assurances Sénégal: 5 pl. de l'Indépendance, BP 182, Dakar; tel. 33-849-1010; fax 33-823-4672; internet www.axa.sn; e-mail info@axa.sn; f. 1977; fmrly Csar Assurances; 51.5% owned by AXA (France); cap. 1,058m. (Mar. 2004); Pres. MOUSTAPHA CISSÉ; Dir-Gen. ALIOUNE NDOUR DIOUF.

Compagnie d'Assurances-Vie et de Capitalisation (La Nationale d'Assurances-Vie): 7 blvd de la République, BP 3853, Dakar; tel. 33-822-1181; fax 33-821-2820; f. 1982; cap. 80m.; Pres. MOUSSA DIOUF; Man. Dir BASSIROU DIOP.

Compagnie Générale d'Assurances (CGA): 10 ave Léopold Sédar Senghor, angle rue Félix Faure, BP 50184, Dakar; tel. 33-889-6200; fax 33-821-3363; e-mail cgasen@orange.sn; internet www.cga.sn; f. 2007; Pres. MAMADOU LAMINE LOUM; Dir-Gen. MAMADOU MOUSTAPHA NOBA.

Compagnie Nationale d'Assurance Agricole du Sénégal: BP 15297, Dakar; tel. 33-869-7800; fax 33-860-6880; e-mail cnaas@cnaas.sn; internet www.cnaas.sn; f. 2008; agricultural insurance; Dir-Gen. AMADOU NDIAYE.

Compagnie Nationale d'Assurance et de Réassurance des Transporteurs: Rocade Fann Bel-Air, pl. Bakou, BP 22545, Dakar; tel. 33-831-0606; fax 33-832-1205; e-mail cnart@cnart.sn; internet www.cnart.sn; f. 2000; Dir-Gen. MOR ADJ.

Compagnie Sénégalaise d'Assurances et de Réassurances (CSAR): 5 pl. de l'Indépendance, BP 182, Dakar; tel. 33-823-2776; fax 33-823-4672; f. 1972; cap. 945m.; 49.8% state-owned; Pres. MOUSTAPHA CISSÉ; Man. Dir MAMADOU ABBAS BA.

Gras Savoye Sénégal: Immeuble Isocèle au Point E, rue de Diourbel, angle Rond-Point de l'Ellipse, BP 9, Dakar; tel. 33-859-4051; fax 33-824-9392; e-mail gs.senegal@sn.grassavoye.com; affiliated to Gras Savoye (France); Man. THIERRY LABBÉ.

Intercontinental Life Insurance Co (ILICO): 16 rue de Thing, angle rue Moussé Diop, BP 1359, Dakar; tel. 33-889-8787; fax 33-822-0449; e-mail dakar@ilico.sn; internet www.ilico.sn; f. 1993; life insurance; fmrly American Life Insurance Co; Dir-Gen. YACINE DIOP DJIBO.

Mutuelles Sénégalaises d'Assurance et de Transport (MSAT): Dakar; tel. 33-822-2938; fax 33-823-4247; f. 1981; all branches; Dir MOR ATJ.

La Nationale d'Assurances: 5 ave Albert Sarrault, BP 3328, Dakar; tel. 33-822-1027; fax 33-821-2820; f. 1976; fire, marine, travel and accident insurance; privately owned; Pres. AMSATA DIOUF; also **La Nationale d'Assurances—Vie**; life insurance.

Nouvelle Société Interafricaine d'Assurances Sénégal (NSIA): 18–20 ave Léopold Sédar Senghor, BP 18524, Dakar; tel. 33-889-6060; fax 33-842-6464; e-mail nsiasenegal@orange.sn; f. 2002; Dir-Gen. SIDY FAYE; also **Nouvelle Société Interafricaine d'Assurances Vie Sénégal**; Dir-Gen. RAMATOULAYE NDIAYE.

Salama Assurances Sénégal: 67 blvd de la République, BP 21022, Dakar; tel. 33-849-4800; fax 33-822-9446; e-mail salama@orange.sn; internet www.salama.sn; f. 1987; fmrly Sosar al amane, name changed as above in 2008; Dir-Gen. MAMADOU FAYE.

Société Africaine d'Assurances: Dakar; tel. 33-823-6475; fax 33-823-4472; f. 1945; cap. 9m.; Dir CLAUDE GERMAIN.

Société Nationale d'Assurance Mutuelle Vie (SONAM Vie): 6 ave Léopold Sédar Senghor, angle Carnot, BP 210, Dakar; tel. 33-889-8900; fax 33-823-6315; e-mail sonam@sonam.sn; f. 1973; Dir-Gen. SOULEYMANE NIANE; also **Société Nationale d'Assurance Mutuelle Assurances**; Dir-Gen. MAMADOU DIOP.

Société Sénégalaise de Courtage et d'Assurances (SOSECODA): 16 ave Léopold Sédar Senghor, BP 9, Dakar; tel. 33-823-5481; fax 33-821-5462; f. 1963; cap. 10m.; 55% owned by SONAM; Man. Dir A. AZIZ NDAW.

Société Sénégalaise de Réassurances SA (SENRE): 39 ave Georges Pompidou, BP 386, Dakar; tel. 33-822-8089; fax 33-821-5652; e-mail moussadiaw@senre.sn; internet www.senre.sn; cap. 600m; Pres. MAREME MBENGUE; Dir-Gen. MOUSSA DIAW.

Union des Assurances du Sénégal Vie (UASen-Vie): 4 ave Léopold Sédar Senghor, BP 182, Dakar; tel. 33-889-0040; fax : 33-823-1108; e-mail uasenvie@uasen.com; Dir-Gen. ADJARATOU KHADY N'DAW SY.

Insurance Association

Fédération Sénégalaise des Sociétés d'Assurances (FSSA): 43 ave Hassan II, BP 1766, Dakar; tel. 33-889-4864; fax 33-821-4954; e-mail fssa@orange.sn; internet www.fssa.sn; f. 1967; fmrly Comité des Sociétés d'Assurances du Sénégal; Pres. MOR ADJ; Sec.-Gen. VADIOUROU DIALLO; 24 mems.

SENEGAL

Trade and Industry

GOVERNMENT AGENCIES

Agence de Développement et d'Encadrement des Petites et Moyennes Entreprises (ADEPME): 9 Fenêtre Mermoz, ave Cheikh Anta Diop, BP 333, Dakar-Fann; tel. 33-869-7071; fax 33-860-1363; e-mail adepme@orange.sn; internet www.adepme.sn; f. 2001; assists in the formation and operation of small and medium-sized enterprises; Dir-Gen. MARIE THÉRÈSE DIEDHIOU.

Agence nationale chargée de la promotion de l'investissement et des grands travaux (APIX): 52–54 rue Mohamed V, BP 430, 18524 Dakar; tel. 33-849-0555; fax 33-823-9489; e-mail contact@apix.sn; internet www.investinsenegal.com; f. 2000; promotes investment and major projects; Dir-Gen. AMINATA NIANE.

Agence Sénégalaise de Promotion des Exportations (ASEPEX): Ancienne piste 143, Sotrac Mermoz, BP 14709, Dakar; tel. 33-869-2021; fax 33-869-2022; e-mail asepex@asepex.sn; internet www.asepex.sn; f. 2005; promotes exports; Dir-Gen. SAGAR DIOUF TRAORÉ.

Société de Développement Agricole et Industriel (SODAGRI): Immeuble King Fahd, 9e étage, BP 222, Dakar; tel. 33-821-0426; fax 33-822-5406; e-mail contats@sodagri.net; internet www.sodagri.net; f. 1974; cap. 120m. francs CFA; agricultural and industrial projects; Dir-Gen. BOUBACAR SY.

Société de Gestion des Abattoirs du Sénégal (SOGAS): BP 14, Dakar; tel. 33-854-0740; fax 33-834-2365; e-mail sogas@sentoo.sn; f. 1962; cap. 619.2m. francs CFA; 28% state-owned; livestock farming; Dir-Gen. TALLA CISSÉ.

Société Nationale d'Aménagement et d'Exploitation des Terres du Delta du Fleuve Sénégal et des Vallées du Fleuve Sénégal et de la Falémé (SAED): 200 ave Insa Coulibaly-Sor, BP 74, Saint-Louis; tel. 33-961-1533; fax 33-961-1463; e-mail saed@orange.sn; internet www.saed.sn; f. 1965; cap. 2,500m. francs CFA; 100% state-owned; controls the agricultural devt of more than 40,000 ha around the Senegal river delta; Dir-Gen. MAMOUDOU DEME.

Société Internationale des Etudes de Développement en Afrique (SONED—AFRIQUE): Parc à Mazout, Immeuble Ndiaga Diop, Colobane, BP 2084, Dakar; tel. 33-825-8801; fax 33-825-8881; e-mail sonedaf@telecomplus.sn; internet www.soned-afrique.org; f. 1974; cap. 150m. francs CFA; Pres. ABDOUL EL MAZIDE NDIAYE.

DEVELOPMENT ORGANIZATIONS

Agence Française de Développement (AFD): 15 ave Nelson Mandela, BP 475, Dakar; tel. 33-849-1999; fax 33-823-4010; e-mail afddakar@groupe-afd.org; internet www.afd.fr; Country Dir DENIS CASTAING.

Centre International du Commerce Extérieur du Sénégal (CICES): route de l'Aéroport, BP 8166, Dakar-Yoff, Dakar; tel. 33-827-5414; fax 33-827-5275; e-mail cices@sn.ecobiz.ecowas.com; internet cicesfidak.com; Pres. MATAR GUEYE; Dir-Gen. BAÏDY SOULEYMANE NDIAYE.

Conseil des Investisseurs Européens au Sénégal (CIES): 2 pl. de l'Indépendance, BP 130, Dakar; tel. 33-823-6272; fax 33-823-8512; e-mail cies@orange.sn; f. 1993; Pres. GÉRARD SENAC.

France Volontaires: BP 1010, route de la VDN, Sacré coeur 3, Villa no 8908, Dakar; tel. 33-824-5295; fax 33-824-5390; e-mail afvp.dn@sentoo.sn; internet www.france-volontaires.org; f. 1972; name changed as above in 2009; Regional Delegate for Senegal, Cape Verde, Guinea, Guinea-Bissau, Mali and Mauritania JEAN-LOUP CAPDEVILLE; Nat. Delegate MAMADOU NDOUR CAMARA.

Groupements Economiques du Sénégal (GES): 21 ave Faidherbe, BP 282, Dakar; tel. 33-822-2821; Pres. MOR MATY SARR.

Service de Coopération et d'Action Culturelle: BP 2014, Dakar; tel. 33-839-5100; fax 33-839-5359; administers bilateral aid from France; fmrly Mission Française de Coopération et d'Action Culturelle; Dir JEAN-LUC LE BRAS.

CHAMBERS OF COMMERCE

Union Nationale des Chambres de Commerce, d'Industrie et d'Agriculture du Sénégal: 1 pl. de l'Indépendance, BP 118, Dakar; tel. 33-823-7169; fax 33-823-9363; f. 1888; restructured 2002; Pres. MAMADOU LAMINE NIANG.

Chambre de Commerce, d'Industrie et d'Agriculture de Dakar (CCIAD): 1 pl. de l'Indépendance, BP 118, Dakar; tel. 33-823-7189; fax 33-823-9363; e-mail cciad@orange.sn; internet www.cciad.sn; f. 1888; Pres. MAMADOU LAMINE NIANG; Sec.-Gen. ALY MBOUP.

Chambre de Commerce, d'Industrie et d'Agriculture de Diourbel: 744 ave Léopold Sédar Senghor, BP 7, Diourbel; tel. 33-971-1203; fax 33-971-3849; e-mail mamandiaye@hotmail.com; f. 1969; Pres. MOUSTAPHA CISSÉ LO; Sec.-Gen. MAMADOU NDIAYE.

Chambre de Commerce, d'Industrie et d'Agriculture de Fatick: BP 66, Fatick; tel. and fax 33-949-1425; e-mail ccfatick@cosec.sn; Pres. BABOUCAR BOP; Sec.-Gen. SEYDOU NOUROU LY.

Chambre de Commerce, d'Industrie et d'Agriculture de Kaolack: BP 203, Kaolack; tel. 33-941-2052; fax 33-941-2291; e-mail cciak@netcourrier.com; internet www.cciak.fr.st; Pres. IDRISSA GUÈYE; Sec.-Gen. SALIMATA S. DIAKHATÉ.

Chambre de Commerce d'Industrie et d'Agriculture de Kolda: BP 23, Quartier Escale, Kolda; tel. 33-996-1230; fax 33-996-1068; Pres. AMADOU MOUNIROU DIALLO; Sec.-Gen. YAYA CAMARA.

Chambre de Commerce, d'Industrie et d'Agriculture de Louga: 2 rue Glozel, BP 26, Louga; tel. 33-967-1114; fax 33-967-0825; e-mail ccial@orange.sn; Pres. CHEIKH MACKÉ FAYE; Sec.-Gen. CHEIKH SENE.

Chambre de Commerce, d'Industrie et d'Agriculture de Matam: BP 95, Matam; tel. and fax 33-966-6591; Pres. MAMADOU NDIADE; Sec.-Gen. BOCAR BA.

Chambre de Commerce, d'Industrie et d'Agriculture de Saint-Louis: 10 rue Blanchot, BP 19, Saint-Louis; tel. 33-961-1088; fax 33-961-2980; f. 1879; Pres. El Hadj ABIBOU DIEYE; Sec.-Gen. MOUSSA NDIAYE.

Chambre de Commerce, d'Industrie et d'Agriculture de Tambacounda: 120 blvd Diogoye, BP 127, Tambacounda; tel. 33-981-1014; fax 33-981-2995; Pres. DJIBY CISSÉ; Sec.-Gen. TENGUELLA BA.

Chambre de Commerce, d'Industrie et d'Agriculture de Thiès: 96 ave Lamine Guèye, BP 3020, Thiès; tel. 33-951-1002; fax 33-951-1397; e-mail ccthies@cosec.sn; f. 1883; 38 mems; Pres. ATTOU NDIAYE; Sec.-Gen. ABDOULKHADRE CAMARA.

Chambre de Commerce, d'Industrie et d'Agriculture de Ziguinchor: rue du Gen. de Gaulle, BP 26, Ziguinchor; tel. 33-991-1310; fax 33-991-5238; f. 1908; Pres. JEAN PASCAL EHEMBA; Sec.-Gen. MAMADOU LAMINE SANE.

EMPLOYERS' ASSOCIATIONS

Association des Industries et Prestataires de Services de la Zone Franche Industrielle de Dakar: km 18, route de Rufisque, BP 3857, Dakar; tel. 33-839-8484; fax 33-821-2609; Pres. MANSOUR GUEYE.

Chambre des Métiers de Dakar: route de la Corniche-Ouest, Soumbedioune, Dakar; tel. 33-821-7908; e-mail dakarmetiers@orange.sn; Pres. MAGATTE MBOW; Sec.-Gen. MBAYE GAYE.

Confédération Nationale des Employeurs du Sénégal: 5 ave Carde, Rez de Chaussée, BP 3819, Dakar; tel. 33-823-0974; fax 33-822-9658; e-mail cnes@sentoo.sn; internet www.cnes.sn; Pres. MANSOUR CAMA.

Conseil National du Patronat du Sénégal (CNP): 70 rue Jean Mermoz, BP 3537, Dakar; tel. 33-889-6565; fax 33-822-2842; e-mail cnp@orange.sn; internet www.cnp.sn; Pres. BAÏDY AGNE; Sec.-Gen. HAMIDOU DIOP.

Groupement Professionnel de l'Industrie du Pétrole au Sénégal (GPP): rue 6, km 4.5, blvd du Centenaire de la Commune de Dakar, BP 479, Dakar; tel. 33-849-3115; fax 33-832-5212; e-mail noeljp@orange.sn; Pres. BRUNO VINCENT; Sec.-Gen. JEAN-PIERRE NOËL.

Organisation des Commerçants, Agriculteurs, Artisans et Industriels: 52 rue Paul Holl, angle rue Tolbiac, Dakar; tel. 33-823-6794; fax 33-823-6550; Pres. ALASSANE SECK.

Rassemblement des Opérateurs Economiques du Sénégal (ROES): BP 5001/2, Dakar; tel. 33-825-5717; fax 33-825-5713; Pres. KHADIM BOUSSO.

Syndicat des Commerçants Importateurs, Prestataires de Services et Exportateurs de la République du Sénégal (SCIMPEX): 2 rue Parent, angle ave Abdoulaye Fadiga, BP 806, Dakar; tel. 33-821-3662; fax 33-842-9648; e-mail scimpex@orange.sn; f. 1943; Pres. PAPA ALSASSANE DIENG; Sec.-Gen. MAURICE SARR.

Syndicat Patronal de l'Ouest Africain des Petites et Moyennes Entreprises et des Petites et Moyennes Industries: BP 3255, 41 blvd Djily M'Baye, Dakar; tel. 33-821-3510; fax 33-823-3732; e-mail mactarniang@yahoo.fr; f. 1937; Pres. BABACAR SEYE; Sec.-Gen. MACTAR NIANG.

Syndicat Professionnel des Entrepreneurs de Bâtiments et de Travaux Publics du Sénégal: ave Abdoulaye Fadiga, BP 1520, Dakar; tel. 33-832-4708; fax 33-832-5071; f. 1930; 130 mems; Pres. OUMAR SOW.

Syndicat Professionnel des Industries du Sénégal (SPIDS): BP 593, Dakar; tel. 33-823-4324; fax 33-822-0884; e-mail spids@spids.sn; internet www.spids.sn; f. 1944; 110 mems; Pres. CHRISTIAN BASSE.

SENEGAL

Union des Entreprises du Domaine Industriel de Dakar: BP 10288, Dakar-Liberté; tel. 33-825-0786; fax 33-825-0870; e-mail snisa@orange.sn; Pres. ARISTIDE TINO ADEDIRAN.

Union Nationale des Chambres de Métiers: Domaine Industriel SODIDA, ave Bourguiba, BP 30040, Dakar; tel. 33-825-0588; fax 33-824-5432; e-mail uncm@orange.sn; internet www.artisanat-senegal.org; f. 1981; Pres. El Hadj SEYNI SECK; Sec.-Gen. BABOUCAR DIOUF.

Union Nationale des Commerçants et Industriels du Sénégal (UNACOIS): ave Cheikh Ahmadou Bamba 3780, BP 3698, Dakar; tel. 33-821-6080; fax 33-822-0185; e-mail unacois.as@orange.sn; internet www.unacois.org; Pres. IDY THIAM; Sec.-Gen MAME BOU DIOP.

UTILITIES
Electricity

Société Nationale d'Electricité (SENELEC): 28 rue Vincent, BP 93, Dakar; tel. 33-839-3030; fax 33-823-1267; e-mail webmaster@senelec.sn; internet www.senelec.sn; f. 1983; 100% state-owned; Pres. SERIGNE BABACAR DIOP; Dir-Gen. SEYDINA KANE.

Water

Société Nationale des Eaux du Sénégal (SONES): route de Front de Terre, BP 400, Dakar; tel. 33-839-7800; fax 33-832-2038; e-mail sones@sones.sn; internet www.sones.sn; f. 1995; water works and supply; state-owned; Pres. ABDOUL ALY KANE; Dir-Gen. Dr IBRAHIMA DIALLO.

Sénégalaise des Eaux (SDE): Centre de Hann-Route du Front de Terre, BP 224, Dakar; tel. 33-839-3737; fax 33-839-3705; e-mail eau@sde.sn; internet www.sde.sn; f. 1996; subsidiary of Groupe Saur International (France); water distribution services; Pres. ABDOULAYE BOUNA FALL; Dir-Gen. MAMADOU DIA.

TRADE UNIONS

Confédération Nationale des Travailleurs du Sénégal (CNTS): 7 ave du Président Laminé Gueye, BP 937, Dakar; tel. 33-821-0491; fax 33-821-7771; e-mail cnts@orange.sn; internet cnts-senegal.net; f. 1969; affiliated to PS; Sec.-Gen. MODY GUIRO.

Confédération Nationale des Travailleurs du Sénégal—Forces de Changement (CNTS—FC): Dakar; f. 2002 following split from CNTS; Sec.-Gen CHEIKH DIOP; 31 affiliated asscns.

Confédération des Syndicats Autonomes (CSA): BP 10224, Dakar; tel. 33-835-0951; fax 33-893-5299; e-mail csasenegal@yahoo.com; organization of independent trade unions; Sec.-Gen. MAMADOU DIOUF.

Union Démocratique des Travailleurs du Sénégal (UDTS): BP 7124, Médina, Dakar; tel. 33-835-3897; fax 33-854-1070; 18 affiliated unions; Sec.-Gen. MALAMINE NDIAYE.

Union Nationale des Syndicats Autonomes du Sénégal (UNSAS): BP 10841, HLM, Dakar; fax 33-824-8013; Sec.-Gen. MADEMBA SOCK.

Transport

RAILWAYS

There are 922 km of main line, including 70 km of double track. One line runs from Dakar north to Saint-Louis (262 km), and the main line runs to Bamako (Mali). All the locomotives are diesel-driven. In 2009 plans were announced for the construction of a 10,000-km transcontinental railway linking Dakar with Port Sudan (Sudan).

Société Nationale des Chemins de Fer du Sénégal (SNCS): BP 175A, Thiès; tel. 33-939-5300; fax 33-951-1393; f. 1905; state-owned; operates passenger and freight services on Dakar–Thiès and Djourbel-Kaoulack lines, following transfer of principal Dakar–Bamako (Mali) line to private management in 2003; suburban trains operate on Dakar–Thiès route as 'Le Petit Train Bleu'; Pres. DRAME ALIA DIENE; Man. Dir DIOUF MBAYE.

ROADS

In 2007 there were 14,600 km of roads, of which some 4,200 km were paved. A 162.5-km road between Dialakoto and Kédougou, the construction of which (at a cost of some 23,000m. francs CFA) was largely financed by regional donor organizations, was inaugurated in 1996. The road was to form part of an eventual transcontinental highway linking Cairo (Egypt) with the Atlantic coast, via N'Djamena (Chad), Bamako (Mali) and Dakar. In 1999 new highways were completed in the east of Senegal, linking Tambacounda, Kidira and Bakel.

Comité Executif des Transports Urbains de Dakar (CETUD): Résidence Fann, route du Front de Terre Hann, BP 17265 Dakar; tel. 33-859-4720; fax 33-832-5686; e-mail cetud@cetud.sn; internet www.cetud.sn; f. 1997; regulates the provision of urban transport in Dakar; Pres. OUSMANE THIAM.

Dakar-Bus: Dakar; f. 1999; operates public transport services within the city of Dakar; owned by RATP (France), Transdev (France), Eurafric-Equipment (Senegal), Mboup Travel (Senegal) and Senegal Tours (Senegal).

Dakar Dem Dikk: km 4.5, ave Cheikh Anta Diop, Dakar; tel. 33-865-1555; fax 33-860-3193; internet www.demdikk.com; f. 2001; Dir-Gen. MOUSSA DIAGNE.

INLAND WATERWAYS

Senegal has three navigable rivers: the Senegal, navigable for three months of the year as far as Kayes (Mali), for six months as far as Kaédi (Mauritania) and all year as far as Rosso and Podor, and the Saloun and the Casamance. Senegal is a member of the Organisation de mise en valeur du fleuve Gambie and of the Organisation pour la mise en valeur du fleuve Sénégal, both based in Dakar. These organizations aim to develop navigational facilities, irrigation and hydroelectric power in the basins of the Gambia and Senegal rivers, respectively.

SHIPPING

The port of Dakar is the second largest in West Africa, after Abidjan (Côte d'Ivoire), and the largest deepwater port in the region, serving Senegal, Mauritania, The Gambia and Mali. It handled more than 10m. metric tons of international freight in 2008. The port's facilities include 40 berths, 10 km of quays, and also 53,000 sq m of warehousing and 65,000 sq m of open stocking areas. In addition, there is a container terminal with facilities for vessels with a draught of up to 11 m. In March 2005 the Governments of Mauritania, Morocco and Senegal agreed that a shipping line linking the three countries and to transport merchandise was to commence operations, following the completion of a tendering process.

Compagnie Sénégalaise de Navigation Maritime (COSENAM): Dakar; tel. 33-821-5766; fax 33-821-0895; f. 1979; 26.1% state-owned, 65.9% owned by private Senegalese interests, 8.0% by private French, German and Belgian interests; river and ocean freight transport; Pres. ABDOURAHIM AGNE; Man. Dir SIMON BOISSY.

Conseil Sénégalais des Chargeurs (COSEC): BP 1423, Dakar; tel. 33-849-0707; fax 33-823-1144; e-mail cosec@cyg.sn; Dir-Gen. AMADOU KANE DIALLO.

Dakarnave: blvd du Centenaire de la Commune, 2POB 438, Dakar; tel. 33-849-1001; fax 33-823-8399; e-mail commercial@dakarnave.sn; internet dakarnaveshipyard.com; responsible for Senegalese shipyards; owned by Chantier Navals de Dakar, SA (Dakarnave), a subsidiary of Lisnave International, Portugal; CEO FREDERICO J. SPRANGER.

Maersk Sénégal: route de Rufisque, BP 3836, Dakar; tel. 33-859-1111; fax 33-832-1331; e-mail senmkt@maersk.com; internet www.maersksealand.com/senegal; f. 1986.

SDV Sénégal: 47 ave Albert Sarrault, BP 233, Dakar; tel. 33-839-0000; fax 33-839-0069; e-mail sdv.shipping@sn.dti.bollore.com; f. 1936; 51.6% owned by Groupe Bolloré (France); shipping agents, warehousing; Pres. ANDRÉ GUILLABERT; Dir-Gen. BERNARD FRAUD.

Société pour le Développement de l'Infrastructure de Chantiers Maritimes du Port de Dakar (Dakar-Marine): Dakar; tel. 33-823-3688; fax 33-823-8399; f. 1981; privately controlled; operates facilities for the repair and maintenance of supertankers and other large vessels; Man. YORO KANTE.

Société Maritime de l'Atlantique (SOMAT): c/o Port Autonome de Dakar, BP 3195, Dakar; internet www.somat.sn; f. 2005; 51% owned by Compagnie Marocaine de Navigation, COMANAV (Morocco), 24.5% by Conseil Sénégalais des Chargeurs, COSEC, 24.5% by Société Nationale de Port Autonome de Dakar, PAD; operates foot passenger and freight ferry service between Dakar and Ziguinchor (Casamance).

Société Nationale de Port Autonome de Dakar (PAD): 21 blvd de la Libération, BP 3195, Dakar; tel. 33-823-4545; fax 33-823-3606; e-mail pad@portdakar.sn; internet www.portdakar.sn; f. 1865; state-owned port authority; Pres. and Dir-Gen. BARA SADY.

SOCOPAO-Sénégal: BP 233, Dakar; tel. 33-823-1001; fax 33-823-5614; e-mail socopao@sn.dti.bollore.com; f. 1926; warehousing, shipping agents, sea and air freight transport; Man. Dir GILLES CUCHE.

TransSene: 1 blvd de l'Arsenal, face à la gare ferroviaire, Dakar; tel. 33-823-0290; fax 33-821-1431; e-mail transsene@transsene.com; internet www.transsene.com; f. 1978; CEO CHEIKH DIOP.

Yenco Shipping: Fondation Fahd, blvd Djily Mbaye, Dakar; tel. 33-821-2726; fax 33-822-0781; e-mail yencoshi@sentoo.sn; f. 1988; Dir of Finance M. DIANKA; Dir of Shipping M. DIOKHANE.

CIVIL AVIATION

The international airport is Dakar-Léopold Sédar Senghor. There are other major airports at Saint-Louis, Ziguinchor and Tambacounda, in addition to about 15 smaller airfields. The construction of a new international airport, near Ndiass, some 45 km south-east of Dakar, was expected to be completed in 2011.

Agence nationale de l'aviation civile du Sénégal (ANACS): BP 8184, Dakar; fax 33-820-0403; internet www.anacs.sn; civil aviation authority; Dir-Gen. MATHIACO BESSANE.

Aeroservices: Dakar; f. 1996; charter flights; Sec.-Gen. El Hadj OMAR BA.

African West Air: Dakar; tel. 33-822-4538; fax 33-822-4610; f. 1993; services to western Europe and Brazil; Man. Dir J. P. PIEDADE.

Sénégal Airlines: Immeuble La Rotonde, rue Amadou Assane Ndoye, Dakar; e-mail contact@senegalairlines.aero; internet www.senegalairlines.aero; f. 2010; 36% state-owned; domestic and regional services; Dir-Gen. EDGARDO BADIALI.

Tourism

Senegal's attractions for tourists include six national parks (one of which, Djoudj, is listed by UNESCO as a World Heritage Site) and its fine beaches. The island of Gorée, near Dakar, is of considerable historic interest as a former centre for the slave trade. In 2007 some 386,793 visitor arrivals were recorded; receipts from tourism in that year were US $622m.

Ministry of Handicrafts, Tourism and Relations with the Private and Informal Sector: rue Calmette, BP 46510, Dakar; tel. 33-822-7366; fax 33-822-9413; internet www.tourisme.gouv.sn.

Defence

As assessed at November 2010, Senegal's active armed forces comprised a land army of 11,900, a navy of 950, and an air force of 770. There was also a 5,000-strong paramilitary gendarmerie. Military service is by selective conscription and lasts for two years. France and the USA provide technical and material aid. In April 2010 President Abdoulaye Wade announced that Senegal was to reclaim all military bases held by France, although in November of that year 761 French troops remained in Senegal, despite Wade's assertion that this number would be reduced to just 300.

Defence Expenditure: Estimated at 98,700m. francs CFA in 2010.

Chief of Staff of the Armed Forces: Gen. ABDOULAYE FALL.

Education

Primary education, which usually begins at seven years of age, lasts for six years and is officially compulsory. In 2008/09 primary enrolment included 73% of children in the relevant age-group (males 72%; females 74%), according to UNESCO estimates. Secondary education usually begins at the age of 13, and comprises a first cycle of four years (also referred to as 'middle school') and a further cycle of three years. According to UNESCO estimates, in 2006/07 secondary enrolment included only 23% of children in the relevant age-group (males 25%; females 20%). There are three universities in Senegal: the Université Cheikh Anta Diop and the Université du Sahel in Dakar, and the Université Gaston Berger in Saint-Louis. Some 94,400 students were enrolled in tertiary education in 2008/09. Since 1981 the reading and writing of national languages has been actively promoted, and is expressly encouraged in the 2001 Constitution. In 2005 spending on education represented 18.9% of total budgetary expenditure.

SERBIA

Introductory Survey

LOCATION, CLIMATE, LANGUAGE, RELIGION, FLAG, CAPITAL

The Republic of Serbia (formerly part of the State Union of Serbia and Montenegro, and prior to that the Federal Republic of Yugoslavia—FRY) is situated in the central Balkan Peninsula, in south-eastern Europe, and is landlocked. There are western borders (from south to north) with Montenegro, Bosnia and Herzegovina, and Croatia, a border with Hungary to the north, with Romania and Bulgaria to the east, and with the former Yugoslav republic of Macedonia to the south. Kosovo (a former Serbian autonomous province, which made a declaration of independence in February 2008) also lies to the south. Serbia includes the Autonomous Province of Vojvodina. The climate is continental, with steady rainfall throughout the year. The average summer temperature in Belgrade is 22°C (71°F), the winter average being 0°C (32°F). The official language is Serbian, which is officially written in the Cyrillic script. Orthodox Christianity is predominant, the Serbian Orthodox Church being the largest denomination. Roman Catholicism is especially strong in Vojvodina. There is a small Jewish community. The national flag (proportions 1 by 2) has three equal horizontal stripes, of blue, white and red. The capital is Belgrade (Beograd).

CONTEMPORARY POLITICAL HISTORY

Historical Context

A pact between Serbia (which was under Ottoman Turkish rule until the 19th century) and the other South Slavs was signed in July 1917, declaring the intention to merge all the territories in a united state under the Serbian monarchy. Accordingly, when the First World War ended and Austria-Hungary was dissolved, the Kingdom of Serbs, Croats and Slovenes was proclaimed on 4 December 1918.

Prince Aleksandar, Regent of Serbia since 1914, accepted the regency of the new state, becoming King in August 1921. Following bitter disputes between Serbs and Croats, King Aleksandar assumed dictatorial powers in January 1929. He formally changed the country's name to Yugoslavia in October. Aleksandar's regime was Serb-dominated, and in October 1934 he was assassinated in France by Croat extremists. His brother, Prince Pavle, assumed power as Regent on behalf of King Petar II. An anti-Government group, the Communist Party of Yugoslavia (CPY), had been officially banned in 1921, but continued to operate clandestinely. In 1937 the CPY appointed a new General Secretary, Josip Broz (Tito).

In March 1941 the increasingly pro-German regime of Prince Pavle was overthrown in a coup, and a Government that supported the Allied Powers was installed, with King Petar II as Head of State. In April, however, German and Italian forces invaded, forcing the royal family and Government into exile. Resistance to the occupation forces was initially divided between two rival groups. The Yugoslav Army of the Fatherland (Cetniks) operated mainly in Serbia and represented the exiled Government, while the National Liberation Army (Partisans), led by the CPY, under Gen. (later Marshal) Tito, recruited supporters from Bosnia, Croatia, Montenegro and Slovenia. Rivalry between the two groups led to civil war, eventually won by the communist Partisans. On 29 November 1943 the Partisans proclaimed their own government in liberated areas. King Petar II was deposed in 1944.

After the war ended, elections were held, under communist supervision, for a Provisional Assembly. The Federative People's Republic of Yugoslavia was proclaimed on 29 November 1945, with Tito as Prime Minister. A Soviet-style Constitution, establishing a federation of six republics (Serbia, Montenegro, Croatia, Slovenia, Macedonia, and Bosnia and Herzegovina) and two autonomous provinces, both within Serbia (Kosovo and Metohija—with a substantial Albanian population, but also the location of the seat of the Serbian Orthodox Patriarchate—and Vojvodina, with a large Hungarian population), was adopted in January 1946.

In 1948 Yugoslavia was expelled from the Soviet-dominated Cominform (the official forum of the international communist movement). The CPY was renamed the League of Communists of Yugoslavia (LCY) in November 1952, by which time it had established exclusive political control. A new Constitution was adopted in January 1953, with Tito becoming President of the Republic. Another Constitution, promulgated in April 1963, changed the country's name to the Socialist Federal Republic of Yugoslavia (SFRY). Links with the USSR were resumed in 1955, but Yugoslavia largely pursued a policy of non-alignment, the first conference of the Non-aligned Movement (see p. 461) being held in the Serbian and federal capital, Belgrade, in 1961.

In July 1971 President Tito introduced a system of collective leadership and regular rotation of personnel between posts, in an attempt to unify the various nationalities. A collective Federal Presidency, headed by Tito, was established. According to amendments incorporated in a new Constitution introduced in February 1974, the two autonomous provinces within Serbia obtained substantially the same powers, with regard to representation at federal level, as the six republics, as a result of which three of the eight members of the rotating collective presidency represented Serbia and its provinces. The new Constitution granted Tito the Federal Presidency for an unlimited term of office, and in May he became Life President of the LCY. Tito died in 1980, and his responsibilities were transferred to the collective Federal Presidency and to the Presidium of the LCY.

Inter-ethnic tensions, largely suppressed during Tito's period in power, became increasingly evident in various regions of Yugoslavia. The most serious tensions were experienced in Kosovo, where a state of emergency was declared in 1981, following widespread demonstrations by ethnic Albanian nationalists, who supported the province being granted the status of a republic within the SFRY. Tensions were exacerbated in April 1987, when thousands of Serbs and Montenegrins protesting at Kosovo Polje (the site of a famous battle between Serbian forces and Osmanlı/Ottoman Turkish troops in 1389) against alleged harassment by the Albanian majority population clashed violently with the security forces. The perceived failure of the Serbian and federal leadership to curb Albanian nationalism led to the dismissal in September of the First Secretary of the League of Communists of Serbia (LCS—the Serbian branch of the LCY), Ivan Stambolić. His replacement, Slobodan Milošević, had denounced the Serbian leadership's policy on Kosovo (which was regarded as being too sympathetic to the demands of ethnic Albanians) and promised to reverse the emigration of Serbs from the area and halt the activities of Albanian nationalists.

During 1988 and 1989 ethnic unrest increased. Proposals to amend the Serbian Constitution to reduce the level of autonomy of Vojvodina and Kosovo were supported by regular demonstrations by Serbs. Protests against the local party leadership were organized by Milošević and his supporters in Vojvodina. In October 1988 rallies attended by some 100,000 demonstrators in Novi Sad, the administrative centre of Vojvodina, forced the resignation of the Presidium of the League of Communists of Vojvodina, which had opposed some of the proposed constitutional amendments. Tension between the respective party leaderships of Kosovo and Serbia increased, and in November, following the resignation of several members of the Kosovo leadership, some 100,000 ethnic Albanians demonstrated in Prishtina (Prishtinë/Priština—the administrative capital of Kosovo) to demand their reinstatement. In Belgrade a further mass rally was staged by Serbs in protest against alleged discrimination by the ethnic Albanian population in Kosovo. Public demonstrations in Kosovo were banned in late November. In Montenegro continuing unrest resulted in the resignations of the members of the Montenegrin Presidency and of the republican party leadership in January 1989, and their replacement by leaders more sympathetic to Milošević. In May 1989 Milošević, who had become increasingly associated with the cause of Serbian nationalism, particularly with regard to Kosovo, was elected President of the Serbian Presidency.

In January 1989 Ante Marković, a member of the Croatian Presidency, was appointed to head a new Federal Government. In September the Slovenian Assembly voted to adopt radical amendments to the Constitution of Slovenia, affirming its sovereignty and its right to secede from the SFRY. In early December Serbia imposed economic sanctions on Slovenia. In January 1990 the abolition of the LCY's constitutional monopoly of power and the introduction of a multi-party system were formally approved. In May, under the system of rotating leadership, Dr Borisav Jović of Serbia replaced Janez Drnovšek of Slovenia as President of the Federal Presidency. Jović promised to uphold Yugoslav territorial integrity and advocated the introduction of a stronger federal constitution. In June the Kosovo Provincial Assembly and Government were dissolved by the Serbian authorities. In response, a group of 114 ethnic Albanian deputies to the disbanded Assembly attempted to declare Kosovo's independence from Serbia. A new Serbian Constitution, which entered into effect in September, included provisions removing the autonomous status of the provinces of Kosovo (which was officially renamed Kosovo and Metohija, the name the territory had held in 1946–74) and Vojvodina. Unrest continued, and in the same month a general strike was organized to protest against the mass dismissals of ethnic Albanian officials by the Serbian authorities. Criminal charges were brought against more than 100 former members of the Kosovo Provincial Assembly, and several former ministers in the Government of Kosovo were charged with establishing an illegal separatist organization. During November and December multi-party elections were held in four republics. In Serbia, amid allegations of widespread irregularities, Milošević was re-elected President, overcoming a challenge by Vuk Drašković of the nationalist and anti-communist Serbian Renewal Movement (SRM). In the Narodna skupština Republike Srbije (National Assembly of the Republic of Serbia—as the republican legislature had been renamed) 194 of the 250 seats were won by the Socialist Party of Serbia (SPS—led by Milošević), which had been formed in July by the LCS and a smaller left-wing faction.

In October 1990 Croatia and Slovenia had proposed the transformation of the Yugoslav federation into a looser confederation, in which constituent republics would have the right to maintain armed forces and enter into diplomatic relations with other states. Serbia and Montenegro, however, advocated a centralized federal system, while Macedonia and Bosnia and Herzegovina supported the concept of a federation of sovereign states. Tension increased in December, when Croatia adopted a new Constitution, giving the republic the right to secede from Yugoslavia, while in Slovenia a majority voted in favour of secession at a referendum. In January 1991 Macedonia declared its sovereignty and right to secede from the SFRY.

In March 1991 mass demonstrations, led by Drašković's SRM, demanding the resignation of Milošević, were violently suppressed by the security forces. Jović resigned as President of the Federal Presidency, following his failure to secure approval from other members of the collective Presidency for emergency measures; his resignation was withdrawn following an appeal from the Narodna skupština Republike Srbije.

Meanwhile, in February 1991 Slovenia formally initiated its process of 'dissociation' from Yugoslavia, and Croatia asserted the primacy of its Constitution and laws over those of the federation. Later that month the self-proclaimed 'Serb Autonomous Region (SAR) of Krajina' (which subsequently formed part of a self-styled 'Republic of the Serb Krajina'—RSK) declared its separation from Croatia and its intention to unite with Serbia. In Croatia, in May the population voted in favour of independence at a referendum that was largely boycotted by the Serb minority, and armed clashes between Serbs and Croats ensued. Relations between Serbia and Croatia deteriorated further in that month, when Serbian representatives in the Federal Presidency refused to sanction the scheduled transfer of the leadership of the Presidency to Stipe Mesić of Croatia. On 25 June Slovenia and Croatia declared independence. In response, federal troops (largely Serb-dominated) attacked a number of targets in Slovenia, including Ljubljana airport, resulting in 79 deaths, according to official figures. A cease-fire agreement, mediated by the European Community (EC—now European Union—EU, see p. 270), resulted in Serbia's acceptance of Mesić as President of the Federal Presidency. In early July agreement was reached on the immediate cessation of hostilities and on a three-month suspension in the implementation of dissociation by Croatia and Slovenia. The withdrawal of federal troops from Slovenia (which had a negligible Serb population) began almost immediately, but fighting intensified in Croatia, where federal troops increasingly identified openly with local Serb forces. By September Serb forces controlled almost one-third of Croatia's territory, and successive cease-fire agreements failed to end the conflict. In the same month, at a referendum in Macedonia, voters approved the establishment of an independent republic.

In late September 1991 the UN Security Council adopted Resolution 713, which imposed an armaments embargo on all governments within the territories that had formed part of the SFRY and urged that all hostilities end immediately. However, sporadic fighting continued in Croatia. In October Croatia and Slovenia formally ended their association with Yugoslavia, the moratoriums on independence (agreed in July) having expired. In the same month the Assembly of Bosnia and Herzegovina declared the republic's sovereignty, despite the objections of ethnic Serb deputies. The Federal Prime Minister, Ante Marković, resigned, having been defeated in a vote of no confidence in the bicameral Savezna skupština (Federal Assembly, comprising the directly elected Veće građana—Chamber of Citizens—and the indirectly elected Veće Republika—Chamber of Republics). In December, declaring that Yugoslavia had ceased to exist, Stipe Mesić resigned as President of the Federal Presidency. In January 1992 Slovenia and Croatia were recognized as independent states by the members of the EC; numerous other countries followed.

After the independence of Croatia and Slovenia

Following the international recognition of the independence of Croatia and Slovenia, Serbia and Montenegro agreed to uphold the Yugoslav state. Macedonia's representative to the Federal Presidency had resigned in January 1992, but EC recognition of Macedonian independence was delayed, owing to opposition from Greece (see the chapter on the former Yugoslav republic of Macedonia). In March Bosnia and Herzegovina declared its independence from the SFRY, the decision having been approved in a referendum. However, later that month the 'Serb Republic (Republika Srpska) of Bosnia and Herzegovina' was proclaimed, and a severe escalation in the Bosnian conflict ensued, as troops from Republika Srpska launched military action against Bosniaks and besieged several cities, including the capital of Bosnia and Herzegovina, Sarajevo.

In April 1992 the Savezna skupština adopted a new Constitution, formally establishing the Federal Republic of Yugoslavia (FRY), which comprised Serbia (including the provinces of Kosovo and Metohija and Vojvodina) and Montenegro, thereby effectively acknowledging the secession of the four other former SFRY republics. (The Constitution was formally promulgated on 28 September.) In May elections to the Savezna skupština were held, the SPS enjoying considerable success as a result of an opposition boycott. In June Dobrica Ćosić became President of the FRY, and the collective Federal Presidency ceased to exist. In that month an alliance of opposition parties formed the Democratic Movement of Serbia (Depos), led by Drašković.

In May 1992 elections, declared to be illegal by the Serbian authorities, were held in Kosovo to establish a provincial 'Assembly', which described itself as the legislature of the self-proclaimed 'Republic of Kosovo'. In July Milan Panić was elected Federal Prime Minister by the Savezna skupština. At a conference on the former Yugoslavia, which took place in London, United Kingdom, in August, Panić condemned the policy of 'ethnic cleansing', following the discovery of Serb-run concentration camps in Bosnia and Herzegovina, and reiterated the claim that there was no federal military involvement in the republic. In an attempt to force Milošević's removal from office, presidential and legislative elections were scheduled for December. In October Milošević retaliated by using Serbian police forces to seize control of the federal police headquarters in Belgrade, blockading the building for several weeks. In November Panić narrowly survived a second vote of no confidence in the Savezna skupština. The Federal Minister of Foreign Affairs resigned in September, in protest against Panić's policies; in November three more federal ministers resigned.

Presidential and parliamentary elections, at both federal and republican levels, took place on 20 December 1992. Ćosić was re-elected Federal President, with some 85% of the votes cast. Milošević was re-elected President of Serbia, receiving 57.5% of the votes cast, and the SPS secured 47 of the 138 seats in the Veće građana. Panić was removed from the office of Federal Prime Minister on 29 December, after losing a third vote of no confidence. The SPS won 101 seats in the 250-member Narodna skupština Republike Srbije, while the extreme nationalist Serbian Radical Party (SRP) secured 73. In February 1993 a new Federal Government, comprising the SPS and the Democratic Party of Socialists of Montenegro (DPMS), was established, with Radoje Kontić as Federal Prime Minister. In the same month the SPS formed a new Serbian Government, headed by Nikola

SERBIA

Šainović. Depos, which had obtained 49 seats in the Narodna skupština, commenced a legislative boycott, claiming that the elections had been fraudulent.

On 1 June 1993 Ćosić (who was accused of conspiring with army generals to overthrow Milošević) was removed from office by a vote of no confidence in the Savezna skupština. Ćosić's dismissal was followed by a large anti-Government demonstration in Belgrade. In late June the Savezna skupština appointed Zoran Lilić of the SPS, regarded as sympathetic to Milošević, as Federal President, and a reorganization of the Serbian Government followed in July. In August it was announced that the Supreme Defence Council was to assume responsibility for all military and defence duties. By the second half of 1993 it appeared that the co-operation between Milošević and the SRP had ended; in October an attempt by the SRP to force a parliamentary vote expressing no confidence in the Šainović Government prompted Milošević to dissolve the Narodna skupština Republike Srbije.

In the elections to the Narodna skupština Republike Srbije, which took place on 19 December 1993, the SPS increased its representation to 123 deputies, winning 36.7% of the votes cast. Depos secured 45 seats, and the SRP took 39. In February 1994 a new Serbian Government was formed, with the support of the six members of the New Democracy (ND) party. Mirko Marjanović, a pro-Milošević business executive, was appointed Prime Minister, replacing Šainović, who became a Deputy Prime Minister in the Federal Government. In September a new Federal Government, in which Kontić remained Prime Minister, was appointed. The results of the elections in Serbia and the defection of the ND to the Government permitted Milošević to distance himself further from his erstwhile allies in the nationalist opposition, notably the SRP, and to consolidate his political control in the FRY. The position of the already controversial SRP leader Dr Vojislav Šešelj was further damaged when he was sentenced to a term of imprisonment in September for assaulting the parliamentary Speaker.

In August 1995, in a military offensive, Croatian troops took control of the RSK. The Yugoslav leadership protested strongly against the Croatian action, demanding UN intervention and a withdrawal of Croatian troops from the area. However, President Milošević also blamed the leadership of the RSK, criticizing its reluctance to comply with international peace proposals. The Croatian offensive against the RSK resulted in the exodus of some 150,000 Serb refugees to Yugoslavia and Serb-controlled areas of Bosnia and Herzegovina. Many were settled in Vojvodina, prompting protests from ethnic Hungarians in that region.

In early November 1995 peace negotiations were convened in Dayton, Ohio, USA, with the aim of resolving the conflict in the former Yugoslavia. The conference, at which Milošević represented not only Yugoslavia, but also the Bosnian Serbs, resulted in an agreement on the future territorial and constitutional structure of Bosnia and Herzegovina, including the recognition of Republika Srpska as one of two constituent entities within Bosnia and Herzegovina. All UN sanctions against the FRY were suspended in late November. The SRP denounced the Dayton agreement, which was also criticized by the Democratic Party (DP), the Democratic Party of Serbia (DPS—founded in 1992 by former members of the DP) and the increasingly nationalist leadership of the Serbian Orthodox Church. However, the SRM supported the agreement. In June 1996 the Serbian Government was reorganized. All the new ministers appointed were members of the increasingly influential Yugoslav United Left (YUL), led by Milošević's wife, Mirjana Marković.

A number of new coalitions were formed in advance of elections held in late 1996, notably a grouping known as Together (Zajedno), which comprised the SRM, the DP, the DPS and the Civic Alliance of Serbia. The SPS established an alliance with the YUL and the ND, which became known as the United List. On 3 November municipal elections, and elections to the Veće građana and the Skupština Republike Crne Gore (the Republican Assembly in Montenegro) were held. At the elections to the Veće građana (which were boycotted by many Kosovo Albanians), the United List secured 64 seats, Together took 22, the DPMS 20 and the SRP 16; of the 138 elected deputies, 108 were from Serbia and 30 from Montenegro. Following a second round of voting in the Serbian municipal elections, provisional results indicated that Together had obtained control of 14 principal towns, including Belgrade. After the SPS challenged the results, however, most of the opposition victories were annulled by (SPS-dominated) municipal courts and electoral commissions, precipitating mass demonstrations.

In December 1996 daily demonstrations (which had developed into general protests against the Milošević Government) continued in Belgrade and other towns. Milošević denied government involvement in electoral malpractice and condemned the protests. In late December the demonstrations degenerated into violent clashes with members of the security forces in Belgrade; it was reported that two people had been killed and 58 injured. The Ministry of Internal Affairs subsequently ordered a ban on demonstrations; nevertheless, anti-Government rallies continued. At the end of December a delegation from the Organization for Security and Co-operation in Europe (OSCE, see p. 385) issued a report upholding the results of the municipal elections. The international community exerted pressure on Milošević to comply with the OSCE ruling. In early February 1997 the violent suppression of anti-Government demonstrations attracted further international criticism. On 11 February the Narodna skupština Republike Srbije voted in favour of reinstating the annulled results (with deputies from the opposition and extreme nationalist parties boycotting the session); Together consequently obtained control of the municipal assemblies in Belgrade and 13 other towns. At the same time seven ministers were replaced in a reorganization of the Serbian Government. Later in February Zoran Đinđić, the leader of the DP, was elected Mayor of Belgrade by Together members, who controlled 69 of the 110 seats in the city's municipal council.

In June 1997 it was announced that the SRM had withdrawn from the Together coalition. The SPS nominated Milošević as a candidate for the Federal Presidency. Later that month a DPMS committee declared its support for Milošević's candidature. On 25 June Lilić relinquished office; the Speaker of the Veće Republika, Srđan Božović, was to act as interim President, pending an election. In July supporters of the Prime Minister of Montenegro, Milo Đukanović, within the DPMS voted to remove Momir Bulatović, President of Montenegro since 1990, from the party leadership. In mid-July Milošević was elected to the Federal Presidency by the Savezna skupština. Opposition deputies boycotted the vote in the Veće građana, which they subsequently declared to be invalid. On 23 July Milošević formally resigned from the office of President of Serbia and was inaugurated as Federal President.

In September 1997 students demonstrated in Belgrade in support of Đinđić, who, following the dissolution of Together, urged a boycott of the forthcoming Serbian presidential and legislative elections, on the grounds that they would be biased in favour of the incumbent administration. At the elections to the Narodna skupština Republike Srbije, held on 21 September, the United List coalition won 110 seats (failing to secure an outright majority); the SRP increased its representation to 82 seats and the SRM obtained 45 seats. In the concurrent presidential election, Lilić (the candidate of the United List) received 35.7% of the votes cast, while Šešelj, who contested the election on behalf of the SRP, won 27.3% of the votes and Drašković 20.6%. Some 62% of the electorate participated in the first round of presidential voting. In early October SPS and SRP councillors in the Belgrade municipal assembly voted in support of an SRM initiative to remove Đinđić from the office of Mayor of Belgrade. Security forces subsequently suppressed protests in Belgrade by supporters of the DP, who demanded that further legislative and municipal elections be conducted. In the second round of voting in the presidential election on 5 October, Šešelj won 49.1% and Lilić 47.9% of the votes cast. However, since less than 50% of the electorate had participated, the poll was declared to be invalid, and a new presidential election was scheduled.

Following his appointment as a Federal Deputy Prime Minister in November 1997, Lilić withdrew his candidacy to the Serbian presidency. In the new Serbian presidential election, contested by seven candidates on 7 December, the United List coalition was represented by the Federal Minister of Foreign Affairs, Milan Milutinović, who secured 43.7% of the votes cast; Šešelj received 32.2% of the votes. In the second round, which took place on 21 December, Milutinović won 59.2% of the votes cast, defeating Šešelj. The Serbian Electoral Commission announced that about 50.1% of the electorate had participated. However, Šešelj claimed that the Serbian authorities had perpetrated electoral malpractice, particularly in Kosovo, where ethnic Albanians had again boycotted the polls. OSCE observers reported that severe irregularities had taken place. None the less, on 29 December Milutinović was inaugurated as President of Serbia.

In February 1998 Milutinović reappointed Marjanović as Serbian Prime Minister. The SPS formed an alliance with the SRP in March. Marjanović subsequently formed a new coalition Government, comprising 15 representatives of the SRP (including Šešelj, who became a Deputy Prime Minister), 13 representatives of the SPS, and four of the YUL. In May the Savezna skupština adopted a motion expressing no confidence in the Federal Prime Minister, Kontić, which had apparently been initiated by DPMS deputies. Milošević's subsequent nomination of Bulatović to the office was approved by the Savezna skupština, and a new Federal Government was established. Đukanović, however, declared Bulatović's Government to be illegitimate. In June the Montenegrin legislature (in which supporters of Đukanović had obtained a majority in elections the previous month) withdrew the 20 deputies representing Montenegro from the Veće Republika and replaced them with members of Đukanović's coalition, to ensure that Milošević would not command the requisite two-thirds' majority for constitutional amendments. (Milošević, however, refused to allow deputies from Đukanović's coalition to assume seats in the Veće Republika.) In August a new Montenegrin Government, headed by Filip Vujanović of the DPMS, announced that it had suspended links with the Federal Government until Bulatović agreed to resign from the office of Prime Minister in favour of a supporter of Đukanović.

During 1998 and early 1999 inter-ethnic hostilities in Kosovo intensified, frequently resulting in violence, and, following the failure of internationally sponsored negotiations, culminated in the aerial bombardment of military, and subsequently certain civilian, targets in Serbia and Montenegro in March–June 1999 by North Atlantic Treaty Organization (NATO, see p. 368) forces, which sought to defend Kosovo Albanians from the Serbian security forces (see below). In late April Drašković was dismissed as Deputy Prime Minister of the FRY, after he publicly opposed Milošević's refusal to comply with NATO demands.

In May 1999 the International Criminal Tribunal for the former Yugoslavia (ICTY, see p. 20) indicted Milošević, together with Milutinović, Šainović, the former Serbian Minister of the Interior, Vlajko Stojiljković, and the Yugoslav Army Chief of Staff, Gen. (retd) Dragoljub Ojdanić, for crimes against humanity. In June SRP ministers and legislative deputies temporarily suspended participation in the Serbian Government, in protest against Milošević's acceptance of the peace plan for Kosovo, whereby NATO peace-keeping forces were to be deployed in the province (see below). From July a series of demonstrations was conducted by a loose grouping of opposition associations, known as Alliance for Change, in support of Milošević's resignation. In August Milošević reorganized the Federal Government. Also in August the Montenegrin Government presented proposals for the dissolution of the FRY, and its replacement with an 'Association of States of Serbia and Montenegro', and announced that a referendum on independence for the republic would be conducted if Milošević failed to agree to the demands. In September the Alliance for Change initiated a campaign against Milošević; however, Drašković refused to endorse the protests. In January 2000, following inter-party discussions, leaders of the Alliance for Change presented unified demands for elections to be conducted in Serbia by the end of April.

In mid-January 2000 a notorious Serbian paramilitary leader and war crimes suspect, Željko Ražnatović ('Arkan'), was shot and killed in Belgrade. In February the Federal Minister of Defence, Pavle Bulatović, was also killed. Milošević subsequently appointed Ojdanić to the post. In July the Savezna skupština approved constitutional amendments removing limits on the President's tenure of office, providing for direct election to the presidency and the Veće Republika, and reducing Montenegro's status within the FRY. The Skupština Republike Crne Gore subsequently voted to reject the amendments, which Vujanović condemned as an attempt by Milošević to retain power. At the end of July Milošević announced that federal presidential and legislative elections were to take place on 24 September. The Montenegrin Government announced that the republic would not participate in the forthcoming elections, in protest against the amendments. In early August an alliance of 18 opposition parties, the Democratic Opposition of Serbia (DOS), presented the leader of the DPS, Dr Vojislav Koštunica, as their joint candidate to oppose Milošević in the presidential election.

Domestic Political Affairs

Numerous allegations of electoral malpractice and intimidation emerged, both prior to and following the elections to the Federal presidency and legislature on 24 September 2000. Preliminary results, released by the Federal Election Commission, indicated that Koštunica had won about 48% of the votes cast, compared with the 40% of the votes received by Milošević, and thereby failed to obtain the 50% majority required to secure the presidency. Milošević subsequently insisted that a second round of voting be conducted on 8 October, while Koštunica rejected the results, claiming to have won the election outright. The international community declared its support for Koštunica and urged Milošević to accept defeat. The Yugoslav Army announced that it would not intervene on Milošević's behalf, while the SRP and Serbian parties in Montenegro also acknowledged Koštunica's victory. Opposition supporters commenced a campaign of peaceful protest in Serbia (including a widely observed general strike), in an effort to compel Milošević to resign. On 5 October protesters, who had gathered to stage a mass rally in Belgrade, overpowered security forces and seized control of the parliament building, the state television station and the official news agency, declaring Koštunica to be the elected President. On the following day, amid increasing international pressure, Milošević finally relinquished the presidency. Koštunica was officially inaugurated as President on 7 October. According to the final official results, Koštunica received 51.7% of the votes cast and Milošević 38.2%; in the concurrent legislative elections, the DOS secured 58 seats in the 138-member Veće građana, and the SPS 44. After the DOS negotiated an agreement with the SPS in mid-October, the Narodna skupština Republike Srbije was dissolved, and a transitional Government, in which the SPS retained the premiership, was installed, pending legislative elections, which were brought forward to December. Since only about 30% of the Montenegrin electorate had participated in the voting, as a result of Đukanović's boycott, Koštunica was obliged to form an administration with the Socialist People's Party of Montenegro (Socijalistička narodne partija Crne Gore—SNP, which was led by Predrag Bulatović and was the only Montenegrin party to be represented in the legislature). A member of that party, Zoran Žižić, was nominated to the post of Prime Minister, and a new Federal Government, comprising representatives of the DOS and the SNP, was established in early November. The normalization of relations between the FRY and the international community proceeded rapidly thereafter, and the country was formally admitted to the UN (from which it had been absent since the dissolution of the SFRY) on 1 November. In December Koštunica reorganized the armed forces, removing officers loyal to Milošević.

In the elections to the 250-member Narodna skupština Republike Srbije, held on 23 December 2000, the DOS secured a substantial majority, with 176 seats, while the SPS won 37 seats and the SRP 23. Later that month Đukanović announced proposals that the FRY become a loose union of two separate, internationally recognized states. At the end of December the People's Party of Montenegro, which supported a continued federation, withdrew from the governing coalition in Montenegro. Đukanović subsequently announced that elections to the Skupština Republike Crne Gore would take place in April 2001. In January Đinđić was elected to the Serbian premiership, and a new Serbian Government, comprising members of the DOS, was installed later that month.

In early 2001 the Federal Government came under increasing pressure from the EU and USA to arrest Milošević and other war crimes suspects; Koštunica maintained that their extradition would contravene the Constitution. Following a warning by the USA that it would end financial aid to the FRY unless the new administration fully co-operated with the ICTY by the end of March 2001, Milošević was taken into custody on 1 April. The federal Public Prosecutor issued a series of charges against Milošević for abuses of power during his term of office (principally extensive embezzlement from state funds, and involvement in political assassinations, electoral malpractice and organized crime). Later that month Milošević, who was in detention in Belgrade, received the ICTY indictment. At the end of April Serbian courts authorized the extension of Milošević's period of detention for a further two months, despite an appeal that he be released on grounds of ill health. Koštunica, however, refused to comply with international demands that Milošević be dispatched for trial at the ICTY (apparently owing to concern that his extradition might prompt political unrest). Meanwhile, at the elections to the expanded 78-member Skupština Republike Crne Gore, which were conducted on 22 April, the pro-independence alliance, led by the DPMS, won 36 seats. Đukanović announced that he would pursue his aim of organizing a referendum on Montenegrin independence.

Milošević extradited to The Hague

In June 2001, following continued international pressure, the Serbian Government approved a decree providing for the extradition of Milošević and other indicted war criminals to the ICTY; supporters of Milošević subsequently staged a large demonstration in Belgrade. On 29 June (shortly before an important international donor conference was to take place) Milošević was extradited to the ICTY. On the following day Žižić resigned from the office of Federal Prime Minister, in protest against the extradition (which had been strongly opposed by the SNP). In July Koštunica appointed Dragiša Pešić, also a member of the SNP and hitherto Federal Minister of Finance, to the post. Later that month a reorganized Federal Government, proposed by Pešić, was approved in the legislature. In August the division between Koštunica and Đinđić resulting from the Serbian Government's decision to extradite Milošević was further exacerbated by the killing in Belgrade of a security agent, who had reportedly been investigating alleged connections of state officials to organized crime. Koštunica accused Đinđić's administration of failing to address widespread crime, and withdrew the DPS ministers from the Government.

In October 2001 the initial indictment against Milošević relating to Kosovo was amended, henceforth alleging that he had organized security-force operations against Kosovo Albanians, which had resulted in the expulsion of 80,000 civilians from the province. Also in October Milošević was further indicted in connection with war crimes perpetrated in Croatia in 1991–92; he was accused of ordering the forcible removal of the majority of the non-Serb population from one-third of the territory of Croatia, with the aim of incorporating the region into a Serb-dominated state. Four former naval officers were indicted for participation in an offensive against Dubrovnik, in Croatia, in late 1991. The former Commander of the Yugoslav Navy, Pavle Strugar, surrendered to the ICTY later in October 2001. (He was sentenced to eight years' imprisonment in January 2005, but was released owing to ill health in February 2009.) In November 2001 Milošević (hitherto indicted for crimes against humanity, breaches of the 1949 Geneva Convention, and violations of the laws or customs of war) was charged with genocide, in connection with the atrocities perpetrated by Serb forces in Bosnia and Herzegovina in 1992–95. He continued to refuse to recognize the authority of the ICTY, and 'not guilty' pleas were submitted on his behalf for all three indictments. The trial of Milošević, who had decided to conduct his own defence, officially commenced on 12 February 2002.

In December 2001 the Speaker of the Narodna skupština Republike Srbije, Dragan Maršićanin, who was the deputy leader of the DPS and a close associate of Koštunica, resigned, having accused parties belonging to the DOS coalition of electoral malpractice. In January 2002 the Federal Minister of Finance also tendered his resignation. In that month the Narodna skupština Republike Srbije voted in favour of partially restoring the autonomous status of Vojvodina. In March one of the Serbian deputy prime ministers, Momčilo Perišić, was arrested, and subsequently resigned, after military intelligence sources claimed to have evidence that he had given classified information to a US diplomat. Đinđić rejected demands by Koštunica that he submit his resignation over the issue, and requested the dismissal of the head of the military security service responsible for Perišić's arrest. Perišić claimed that the charges had been fabricated, in an attempt to cause the dissolution of Đinđić's Government. In June the DPS withdrew from the Narodna skupština Republike Srbije, in protest against the expulsion of 21 DPS deputies. (The party was formally expelled from the ruling DOS coalition in the following month.) The Serbian Government was reorganized in the same month.

Following protracted negotiations on the issue of Montenegro's independence (which were mediated by the EU from November 2001), the government leaders of the FRY and the two republics signed a framework agreement on 14 March 2002, providing for the establishment of a State Union of Serbia and Montenegro. Under the accord, the two republics were to maintain separate economies, but have joint foreign and defence ministries, and elect a new, joint presidency and legislature. Montenegro was to retain the right to refer the issue of independence to a referendum after a period of three years. Later in March the Liberal Alliance of Montenegro (LAM) withdrew from Đukanović's coalition (thereby ending its narrow majority in the Skupština Republike Crne Gore), in protest against the agreement.

Meanwhile, the USA renewed pressure on the Federal Government to demonstrate co-operation with the ICTY. Following the expiry of a deadline for Yugoslav compliance with these demands, economic aid to the FRY was suspended at the end of March 2002. In April the Savezna skupština finally approved legislation providing for the extradition of indicted war crimes suspects, and the issue of arrest warrants for those who did not surrender to the ICTY. Shortly afterwards Stojiljković (the former Serbian Minister of the Interior who had been indicted in May 1999) committed suicide. Of 10 former Yugoslav state officials indicted, six (including Ojdanić and Sainoyić) agreed to surrender to the Tribunal. In early May 2002 Sainović was voluntarily transferred to the ICTY.

In late May 2002 the Savezna skupština officially approved the agreement on the creation of a State Union (which had been ratified by the legislatures of both republics in April). In July Lilić was arrested and extradited to the ICTY, having been subpoenaed as a prosecution witness in the trial of Milošević. He refused to testify unless he was guaranteed immunity from prosecution. It was announced that the presidential election in Serbia would be brought forward to 29 September, to allow the extradition of Milutinović to the ICTY.

At the Serbian presidential election, held on 29 September 2002, Koštunica won some 30.9% of the votes cast, while Miroljub Labus (the incumbent federal Deputy Prime Minister and Minister of Foreign Trade, who was supported by Đinđić) received 27.4% and Sešelj 23.2%; some 55.5% of the registered electorate voted. A second round of voting took place on 13 October between Koštunica and Labus, at which Koštunica secured some 68.4% of the votes cast. However, the election was declared invalid, owing to the participation of only 44.0% of the electorate, lower than the required minimum level of 50%.

State Union of Serbia and Montenegro

On 6 December 2002 a 27-member commission on constitutional reform, comprising representatives of the principal parties of the two republics, submitted a draft of the new Constitutional Charter for the proposed State Union. A third presidential poll in Serbia on 8 December (in which Koštunica won just 57.7% of the votes) was again annulled, owing to a rate of participation of just 45.0%. On 30 December Milutinović was replaced, on an interim basis, by the President of the Narodna skupština Republike Srbije, Nataša Mićić. (Đukanović's pro-independence coalition, by now known as Democratic List for a European Montenegro, had obtained an overall majority in the republican legislature at elections held in Montenegro in late October, although a presidential election in the republic, held on 22 December, was invalidated as a result of an insufficient level of participation by the electorate; a further vote was similarly declared invalid in mid-February 2003.)

In January 2003 Milutinović was voluntarily transferred to the ICTY, where he pleaded not guilty to charges relating to the 1999 conflict in Kosovo. In February 2003 Sešelj surrendered to the ICTY, where he was charged in connection with the forcible removal of the non-Serb population from various regions of Bosnia and Herzegovina, Croatia and Serbia (Vojvodina) in 1991–95. Meanwhile, the new Constitutional Charter, which provided for the creation of the State Union of Serbia and Montenegro, was approved by the Narodna skupština Republike Srbije on 27 January 2003 and by the Skupština Republike Crne Gore on 29 January. On 4 February both chambers of the Savezna skupština approved the Constitutional Charter, thereby officially replacing the FRY with the State Union of Serbia and Montenegro. On 25 February, in accordance with the Charter, the existing federal and republican legislatures elected a 126-member Skupština Srbije i Crne Gore (Assembly of Serbia and Montenegro), comprising 91 Serbian and 35 Montenegrin deputies. On 7 March a former Speaker of the Montenegrin legislature, Svetozar Marović, was elected unopposed as President of Serbia and Montenegro by the Skupština Srbije i Crne Gore. The President was also to chair a five-member Council of Ministers (with portfolios that included foreign affairs, defence, and human and minority rights), which was approved by the Skupština Srbije i Crne Gore on 18 March.

On 12 March 2003 Đinđić, having survived an apparent assassination attempt in February, was shot dead outside government buildings in Belgrade. Mićić immediately imposed a state of emergency in Serbia. The DP's nomination of former Federal Minister of Internal Affairs Zoran Živković to replace Đinđić as Serbian Prime Minister was approved by the Narodna skupština Republike Srbije on 18 March. At the end of March security forces discovered the remains of Ivan Stambolić, who had been abducted in August 2000. The Serbian authorities issued an international arrest warrant for Mirjana Marković and her son (who were in hiding in Russia), in connection with the killing of Stambolić; Milošević was subsequently also charged. In mid-April the Skupština Srbije i Crne Gore voted in favour of extending the state's co-operation with the ICTY, ending a stipulation that all war crimes suspects indicted by the Tribunal from that month be tried by domestic courts. Later that month the state of emergency in Serbia was ended.

In May 2003 Filip Vujanović was elected as President of Montenegro, following the abolition of the requirement that 50% of the electorate participate in polling; he subsequently pledged to hold a referendum on Montenegrin independence within three years. In September the Serbian Government announced that Milošević would be arraigned at a special court on charges of ordering the killing of Stambolić. In October the ICTY issued indictments against four senior Serbian military and security officials, including the former Chief of General Staff of the Yugoslav Army, Col-Gen. (retd) Nebojša Pavković (who had been removed from his post by Koštunica in June 2002), for war crimes perpetrated against the civilian population of Kosovo in 1998–99.

In November 2003, following long-standing dissension within the DOS, two small parties withdrew from the coalition, thereby ending its parliamentary majority. The DOS subsequently dissolved, and Živković scheduled fresh elections to the Narodna skupština Republike Srbije. Meanwhile, on 16 November a further presidential poll in Serbia (at which the acting leader of the SRP, Tomislav Nikolić, secured 47.9% of the votes cast) was declared invalid, owing to a rate of electoral participation of only 38.8%. In December the trial began of 36 suspects charged in connection with Đinđić's assassination (15 of them, including Milorad 'Legija' Ulemek—the leader of an organized criminal group and a prominent member of a paramilitary unit of Milošević's regime—in absentia). At the elections to the Narodna skupština Republike Srbije, held on 28 December, the SRP, with 28.0% of the votes cast, secured 82 seats, the DPS (18.0%) 53 seats, the DP (12.8%) 37 seats, a newly emerged reformist grouping known as G17 Plus (11.6%) 34 seats, an alliance of the SRM and New Serbia (NS—7.8%) 22 seats, and the SPS (7.7%) 22 seats. Candidates contesting parliamentary seats notably included four indicted war crimes suspects, two of whom (Milošević and Šešelj) were in detention at the ICTY. Following lengthy inter-party discussions, the DPS formed a minority coalition with G17 Plus and the SRM-NS alliance, which was also, to the concern of the international community, reliant on the support of the SPS. On 4 February 2004 the DPS Vice-President, Maršićanin, was elected President of the Narodna skupština Republike Srbije (from which position he had resigned in December 2001), thereby replacing Mićić as the Republic's acting President. In that month the Narodna skupština voted to abolish the minimum rate of participation for elections to the republican presidency, as a means of ending the protracted political impasse. A new Serbian Council of Ministers, headed by Koštunica, was formed in March; owing to Maršićanin's inclusion in the administration as Minister of the Economy, he was replaced as President of the Narodna skupština Republike Srbije (and therefore acting President of Serbia) by the hitherto deputy speaker, Predrag Marković. In mid-April the Skupština Srbije i Crne Gore approved a reorganization of the State Union's Council of Ministers; Drašković received the foreign affairs portfolio, Prvoslav Davinić of G17 Plus replaced Boris Tadić as Minister of Defence, and Predrag Ivanović of the DPMS became Minister of Foreign Economic Relations. Ulemek surrendered to the Serbian authorities in early May.

Tadić elected President

Some 15 candidates contested the election to the presidency of Serbia, held on 13 June 2004. Nikolić secured 30.1% of the votes cast, and Tadić, the candidate (and leader) of the DP, won 27.7% of the votes. Bogoljub Karić, a prominent businessman, won 18.5% of the votes, and Maršićanin (having resigned his ministerial post, and contesting the election for a coalition of parties led by the DPS) 13.5%. Nikolić's narrow victory in the first round was attributed to the failure of the reformist parties to agree on a common candidate. A second round between Nikolić and Tadić was conducted on 27 June; Tadić, who benefited from the transferred support of the governing coalition parties, was elected to the presidency, receiving 54.0% of the votes. At his inauguration on 17 July, Tadić pledged commitment to the continuation of economic reforms and for the eventual integration of Serbia into the EU.

In December 2004 a former Yugoslav Army officer, Gen. (retd) Dragoljub Milošević, surrendered to the Serbian authorities and was extradited to the ICTY, where he was charged with crimes relating to the blockade and bombardment of Sarajevo in 1994. In January 2005, however, the USA expressed dissatisfaction with the failure of Serbia and Montenegro to co-operate with the ICTY, and announced a reduction in financial aid and the withdrawal of US technical advisers from Serbian ministries. Representatives of the international community repeatedly accused the Serbian authorities of aiding the continuing evasion from the Tribunal of former Bosnian Serb military commander Gen. (retd) Ratko Mladić (who had originally been indicted in 1995 on a number of counts, including two of genocide), and cited his extradition as essential for Serbia and Montenegro's accession to NATO's Partnership for Peace' (PfP) programme. In February 2005 one of those indicted, a former military commander in Prishtina, Gen. (retd) Vladimir Lazarević, agreed to surrender to the ICTY after meeting with Koštunica, and was subsequently extradited.

Amid increasing concern over the future of the State Union, in February 2005 Koštunica and Đukanović met for discussions on the scheduling of elections to the Skupština Srbije i Crne Gore. On 7 April, following mediation by the EU High Representative for Common Foreign and Security Policy, Javier Solana Madriaga, the Prime Ministers agreed that the election of representatives to the Skupština Srbije i Crne Gore would take place concurrently with elections to the two republican legislatures; the Constitutional Charter was to be amended to allow the extension of the mandates of the incumbent deputies. The Montenegrin Government favoured the organization of a referendum on independence prior to elections, while supporters of the continuation of the State Union insisted that such a measure would require adherence to EU conditions and arbitration. Solana welcomed the agreement and commended Serbia's improved co-operation with the ICTY (following the transfer, between late 2004 and mid-2005, of 13 Serbian and Bosnian Serb war crime suspects, in surrenders reportedly mediated by the Koštunica Government, including that of Pavković in April 2005). Shortly afterwards the European Commission indicated that sufficient progress had been made for Serbia and Montenegro to commence negotiations on a Stabilization and Association Agreement (SAA) with the EU. (In February 2006 the Montenegrin Government and opposition agreed that the planned referendum on Montenegrin's secession from the State Union would take place on 21 May.)

In July 2005 Milorad Ulemek was sentenced to 40 years' imprisonment and the head of Milošević's secret service, Radomir Marković, to a 15-year term for the killing of Stambolić in August 2000; six former secret service officers also received custodial terms. In September 2005 a further international arrest warrant was issued for Mirjana Marković, who had failed to fulfil pledges to return from exile in Russia. On 10 October negotiations on the SAA officially commenced between the Government of Serbia and Montenegro and the EU.

On 11 March 2006 Milošević (whose trial had repeatedly been adjourned on grounds of ill health) died while in custody at the ICTY. Preliminary autopsy results concluded that the cause of death was a heart attack, but supporters of Milošević immediately criticized the medical treatment that he had received in detention and the Tribunal's refusal in late February to grant a request for his transfer to hospital in Russia. The Serbian authorities refused to organize a state funeral, and members of Milošević's family, including Mirjana Marković (despite the temporary suspension of the international arrest warrant against her), failed to attend the ceremony, which took place at his family residence in the Serbian town of Pozarevac; although there were scenes of public mourning, former nationalist supporters at the funeral were reported to number only a few hundred. In April an independent investigation by Dutch pathologists confirmed that Milošević's death was the result of a heart attack.

In early 2006 the Serbian authorities came under increasing pressure from the EU to effect Mladić's extradition to the ICTY. In March the ICTY Prosecutor, Carla Del Ponte, visited Belgrade, with the aim of securing assurances that Mladić would be apprehended. Negotiations on the SAA were, however, suspended on 3 May, after the Serbian Government failed to meet a deadline, of 30 April, for Mladić's extradition. Labus resigned from the post of Deputy Prime Minister of Serbia in protest at the failure of the authorities to apprehend Mladić, and subsequently also resigned from the leadership of G17 Plus, after the party refused to withdraw other representatives from the Government. Ivana Dulić-Marković (hitherto Minister of Agriculture) was appointed Deputy Prime Minister in June.

Montenegro's secession

At the referendum held in Montenegro on 21 May 2006, some 55.5% of votes were cast in favour of independence, narrowly exceeding the minimum requirement of 55% stipulated by the EU. Following Montenegro's subsequent declaration of independence on 3 June, the Narodna skupština Republike Srbije officially declared Serbia to be the successor state to the State Union of Serbia and Montenegro on 5 June. The Serbian Government announced that the central administration and other organs of the former State Union had ceased to exist. In mid-June the Serbian Government adopted a decision recognizing Montenegro's independence, and the Ministers of Foreign Affairs of the two countries signed a protocol on the establishment of diplomatic relations on 22 June. At the end of that month Tadić became the first Head of State to make an official visit to independent Montenegro.

In July 2006 the trial of six senior Serbian officials who had served under Milošević began at the ICTY: Milutinović, Šainović, Ojdanić, Pavković, Lazarević, and Gen. (retd) Sreten Lukić (the former head of police in Kosovo) were charged with crimes relating to human rights violations committed against ethnic Albanians in Kosovo during 1998–99. On 30 September 2006 the Narodna skupština Republike Srbije adopted a new draft Constitution by a unanimous vote (with 242 deputies attending). The new Constitution, which included increased provisions for the guarantee of human and minority rights, and notably referred to Kosovo and Metohija as an integral part of the Republic of Serbia, was approved by 53.0% of votes cast at a national referendum on 29 October and entered into effect on 8 November. At the end of November NATO invited Serbia (together with Bosnia and Herzegovina and Montenegro) to join the PfP programme; Del Ponte strongly criticized Serbia's admission to the programme (which officially took place on 14 December), in view of the authorities' continued failure to extradite Mladić to the ICTY. In December an SPS congress elected a former presidential candidate, Ivica Dačić, to replace Milošević as party leader. Two ethnic Albanian parties from the Preševo region established an alliance to contest the legislative elections, ending a boycott after the new Constitution no longer required minority parties to secure a minimum of 5% of the votes in order to obtain parliamentary representation.

At the elections to the Narodna skupština Republike Srbije, contested by 20 political parties and alliances on 21 January 2007, the SRP, with 29.1% of votes cast, obtained the largest number of seats (81), while the DP secured 23.1% of the votes (64 seats), and an alliance led by the DPS 16.8% of the votes (47 seats). The representation of G17 Plus, which received 6.9% of votes cast, declined to 19 seats, and that of the SPS, with 5.7% of the votes, to 16 seats, while a new reformist alliance led by the Liberal Democratic Party won 5.4% of the votes and 15 seats. (The SRM, having undergone internal dissension, failed to secure any parliamentary representation.) After smaller parliamentary parties declared reluctance to enter into a minority administration with the SRP, Tadić engaged in consultations with party leaders regarding the establishment of a new coalition government. EU officials urged the establishment of a new administration in favour of democratic reforms, indicating that this would allow negotiations on an SAA to proceed (thereby abandoning the previous stipulation for the prior extradition of Mladić). However, the expected formation of a coalition between the DP and DPS was impeded by ideological differences between the two parties, compounded by resistance to a UN proposal for supervised independence for Kosovo (see below).

On 8 May 2007 Nikolić was elected President of the Narodna skupština Republike Srbije, after Koštunica instructed DPS deputies to support his nomination. Nikolić's appointment prompted international consternation (which coincided with Serbia's assumption of the rotational chairmanship of the Council of Europe), and EU officials offered Serbia strong incentives to form a pro-democracy government. On 11 May Tadić announced that a coalition agreement had been reached between the DP, the DPS and New Serbia alliance, and G17 Plus, and that he had nominated Koštunica for a second term as Prime Minister. On 13 May Nikolić tendered his resignation from his new post. On 15 May, shortly before the expiry of the constitutional deadline, a coalition Government was approved by 133 votes in the Narodna skupština Republike Srbije; notably, the Government included the new position of a Minister of Kosovo and Metohija.

In May 2007 Milorad Ulemek and 11 others (five in absentia) were convicted by the Belgrade Special Court for Organized Crime for the assassination of Đinđić; Ulemek received a further sentence of 40 years' imprisonment. On 7 June the President of the European Commission invited Serbia to resume negotiations on an SAA, citing improved co-operation with the ICTY, following the arrest in Republika Srpska of a former Bosnian Serb army officer, Zdravko Tolimir, believed to be a close associate of Mladić and to be assisting his evasion of capture. Negotiations officially recommenced on 13 June; the EU (at the particular insistence of the Netherlands and Belgium) emphasized that conclusion of the Agreement continued to be conditional on full co-operation with the ICTY, resulting in the arrest and transfer of all ICTY indictees, including Mladić.

In early December 2007 several laws, including legislation on the election of the President in accordance with the new Constitution, were adopted in the Narodna skupština Republike Srbije, allowing a pre-term presidential election to be scheduled for early 2008. At the first round of the election, which was contested by nine candidates on 20 January, Nikolić won 40.0% of the votes cast and Tadić 35.4%. Koštunica failed to transfer support to Tadić in the second round of the presidential election, after Tadić rejected his demand to pledge not to sign an SAA with the EU if the EU deployed a mission in Kosovo without UN authorization. Nevertheless, at the second round, which was conducted on 3 February, Tadić was re-elected to the presidency, narrowly defeating Nikolić with about 50.3% of the votes cast, according to official figures. The rate of participation by the electorate was estimated at some 67%. EU officials welcomed the election results, which were widely viewed as an endorsement of Tadić's policy of favouring rapid EU integration. Tadić was inaugurated on 15 February.

Kosovo's declaration of independence

In early February 2008 Koštunica rejected the proposed political agreement with the EU (which had been supported by Tadić), owing to his strenuous opposition to the EU's decision to establish EULEX Kosovo, a police and justice mission for Kosovo. Kosovo's declaration of independence on 17 February 2008, which was rapidly recognized by a number of EU nations (see below), presented a further obstacle to prospects for EU integration, since the United Kingdom, France and Germany (principal supporters of Kosovo's independence) indicated that Serbia would be required to relinquish its territorial claim on Kosovo for accession. In early March Koštunica declared support for a draft resolution, proposed in the Narodna skupština Republike Srbije by the SRP, which made further progress towards EU accession conditional on the rejection of Kosovo's independence by the Union. However, on 8 March Koštunica resigned from the premiership, citing irreconcilable differences within the ruling coalition over Kosovo and EU integration. On 13 March Tadić dissolved the Narodna skupština, at the request of the Government, and scheduled legislative elections for 11 May (when local elections and elections to the Vojvodina Assembly were also due to be conducted). In April EU foreign ministers reached a decision to sign the SAA with Serbia, an offer that was widely perceived as an effort to strengthen popular support for reformist parties contesting the forthcoming elections and to prevent nationalist groups from gaining ascendancy. On 29 April the EU signed the SAA; however, its implementation was to be suspended until EU member states agreed unanimously on Serbia's full co-operation with the ICTY.

At the legislative elections on 11 May 2008, an electoral coalition of parties supporting EU integration formed by Tadić, known as For a European Serbia—Boris Tadić, won 38.4% of the votes cast, according to official results, increasing the DP and its allied parties' strength in the Narodna skupština Republike Srbije to 102 seats. The SRP secured 29.4% of the votes and 78 seats, and the alliance between the DPS and New Serbia 11.6% of votes and 30 seats; a coalition comprising the SPS, the Party of United Pensioners of Serbia and United Serbia increased its joint representation in the chamber to 20 seats, with 7.6% of the votes cast. The participation rate (including Serbs voting in Kosovo) was recorded at 60.1%. (Following a number of complaints submitted by the SRP, voting was repeated in three constituencies on 18 May, owing to irregularities.) At the concurrent poll in Vojvodina on 11 May (which was followed by a second round on 25 May), For a European Vojvodina secured 64 seats and the SRP 24 seats in the 120-member Assembly. The EU and the USA welcomed the election results (which had followed predictions of success for the SRP) and urged the rapid formation of a new administration. On 23 June, following lengthy discussions, SPS leader Dačić announced that the party's council had overwhelmingly decided to enter into a coalition agreement with For a European Serbia—Boris Tadić. On 7 July a new Government, comprising representatives of For a European Serbia—Boris Tadić and the SPS-led alliance, narrowly secured approval in the Narodna skupština Republike Srbije. A former Minister of Finance, Mirko Cvetković (a member of Tadić's DP), became Prime Minister, while Dačić became First Deputy Prime Minister and Minister of Internal Affairs. Meanwhile, in June the Supreme Court (in a third retrial) sentenced Radomir Marković and Milorad Ulemek to 40 years' imprisonment, and imposed lengthy custodial terms on five former state security and special police officers, for the attempted assassination of Vuk Drašković and the killing of four of his associates in 1999. On 21 July 2008 Tadić released a statement announcing that the former Bosnian Serb leader Radovan Karadžić, the most senior war crimes suspect indicted by the ICTY, had been located and apprehended in an operation by Serbian security officers. The unexpected arrest of Karadžić (who was transferred to the War Crimes Panel of the Belgrade District Court and subsequently extradited to the ICTY) was strongly welcomed by the international community.

In September 2008 the Narodna skupština Republike Srbije ratified the SAA; its implementation remained conditional on full co-operation with the ICTY, specifically the arrest of Mladić and the other remaining major war crimes suspect, Croatian Serb Goran Hadžić ('President' of the RSK in 1992–94), who had been indicted by the ICTY in 2004. Nikolić, who had accepted ratification of the SAA, was obliged to resign from the post of acting leader of the SRP, owing to opposition to the Agreement from Šešelj, who was supported by more traditionalist elements of the party; Nikolić subsequently formed a breakaway organization, the Serbian Progressive Party (SPP). In October 2008 the trial began at the ICTY of Momčilo Perišić, the Chief of the General Staff of the Yugoslav Army in 1993–98, who had surrendered to the Tribunal in March 2005 after being indicted on 13 counts relating to crimes committed in Sarajevo, the Croatian capital Zagreb and the Bosnian town of Srebrenica in 1993–95. In February 2009 the ICTY sentenced Šainović, Pavković and Milan Lukić to 22 years' imprisonment, while Lazarević and Ojdanić each received a term of 15 years, on charges relating to the killing and forced deportation of Kosovo Albanian civilians; Milutinović was acquitted (on the grounds that he had not been directly responsible for the command of forces). In the same month the ongoing trial of Šešelj (who had repeatedly staged hunger strikes in protest at the proceedings) was suspended, owing to prosecution claims of witness intimidation. In June the war crimes chamber of Belgrade district court sentenced three former members of the 'Scorpions' Serb paramilitary unit to 20 years' imprisonment, and another member to 15 years, for killing a number of ethnic Albanian civilians at Podujevo, in northern Kosovo, in March 1999. In July 2009 the ICTY convicted Šešelj of contempt of the Tribunal, sentencing him to 15 months' imprisonment for disclosing the name and other personal details of three protected witnesses in a book he had written and posted on his internet site. In September the ICTY convicted a journalist and former spokesperson to Carla del Ponte, Florence Hartmann, of contempt of the Tribunal for disclosing, in a book published in 2007, the existence of two confidential appellate rulings to withhold evidence relating to Serbia's involvement in the Bosnian conflict, including the massacre of some 8,000 Muslim males in Srebrenica in 1995; she was sentenced to pay a fine of €7,000.

Recent developments: EU membership application

At the end of November 2009 it was announced that Serbia (together with the former Yugoslav republic of Macedonia—FYRM and Montenegro) had met EU requirements for the abolishment of visa requirements, which were thereby removed with effect from late December. In early December the EU ended restrictions on the interim trade agreement with Serbia (which had been signed together with the SAA), after the Netherlands withdrew previous objections in recognition of the Serbian Government's efforts to apprehend Mladić. On 22 December Serbia submitted an official application to join the EU. At the end of March 2010 the Narodna skupština Republike Srbije adopted (with the support of 127 deputies) a resolution, which had been submitted by the government coalition parties, strongly condemning the massacre of Bosniaks by Bosnian Serb forces in Srebrenica in 1995. (At the reported insistence of the SPS, the term 'genocide' was not included in the resolution.) On 14 June 2010 the EU agreed to begin implementing the SAA with Serbia, following a favourable assessment of Serbia's co-operation with the ICTY.

In mid-2010 tensions increased in the majority Bosniak/Muslim region of Sandžak, at Serbia's border with Montenegro. In June the Bosniak Cultural Community (BCA), led by the head of the Islamic Community of Serbia, Mufti Muamer Zukorlić, secured 17 of 35 seats in elections to the Bosniak National Council. In August, after the Serbian Minister of Human and Minority Rights, Svetozar Čiplić, refused to recognize the Council (claiming that electoral regulations had been contravened), Zukorlić issued demands for the autonomy of the Sandžak region. In early September a protest organized by the Islamic Community of Serbia in the predominantly Bosniak town of Novi Pazar resulted in violent clashes with police; the Bosniak National Council subsequently urged the EU to dispatch monitors to Sandžak, claiming human rights violations against the Bosniak community. Čiplić rejected all demands for autonomy and accused Zukorlić of seeking to destabilize the region. Following continuing dissent between the BCA and the other two main Bosniak parties represented in the Council, the Serbian Government demanded that elections to the Council be repeated, although Zukorlić declared that his association would boycott a further vote. In January 2011 Čiplić announced that further elections to the Council would take place on 17 April. However, at the end of May the new Minister of Human and Minority Rights, Milan Marković, announced the decision to postpone the elections, after consultations with representatives of the three Bosniak organizations.

Meanwhile, on 25 October 2010 the EU Council agreed to recommend Serbia's application for EU membership to the European Commission, but, reportedly at the insistence of the Netherlands, stipulated that further progress on the application was dependent on Serbia's full co-operation with the ICTY. In a progress report in early November, the European Commission stated that Serbia had undertaken important measures towards regional reconciliation and in combating organized crime, but that greater co-operation towards independent Kosovo and commitments to the implementation of judicial and administrative reforms were required. The European Commission was expected to announce its decision on Serbia's candidacy application by the end of 2011.

In February 2011 Mlađan Dinkić, the leader of G17 Plus and the United Regions of Serbia (URS—a political grouping established in May 2010), was dismissed as Deputy Prime Minister and Minister of the Economy, after strongly criticizing dissent within the ruling coalition and Cvetković's leadership. Tomica Milosavljević, a member of G17 Plus, subsequently resigned as Minister of Health. Following popular protests against government economic policies, Cvetković announced an extensive reorganization of the Government, which was approved by the Narodna skupština Republike Srbije on 14 March. Notably, the number of ministries was reduced from 24 to 17, with Cvetković additionally assuming the finance portfolio; Verica Kalanović replaced Dinkić as Deputy Prime Minister, while Nebojša Ćirić was appointed Minister of the Economy and Regional Development. In April the URS began a public petition in support of extensive government decentralization; Dinkić anticipated that it would be submitted to the Narodna skupština by the end of May, after the requisite number of signatures had been secured. Also in April President Tadić rejected demands by Nikolić's SPP that early legislative elections be scheduled.

Kosovo

In early 1996 an ethnic Albanian paramilitary movement, the Kosovo Liberation Army (KLA), emerged and began to launch attacks against Serbian special forces operating in the province. In early 1998 the USA and EU issued statements condemning the violent measures taken by the Serbian security forces in Kosovo to suppress the activities of the KLA, while also criticizing the violence employed by the movement, which had announced its intention to achieve independence for the province through armed resistance. The US Government announced that it was to withdraw the concessions that it had granted to the FRY in February, and threatened possible military intervention in Kosovo. A 'Contact Group', comprising the United Kingdom, France, Germany, Italy, Russia and the USA, was convened in London; member nations envisaged the imposition of further sanctions against the FRY, including an embargo on armaments, unless the Serbian authorities acceded to a number of demands, including the withdrawal of security forces from Kosovo and the initiation of negotiations regarding the future status of the province. At the end of March the UN Security Council officially imposed an embargo on armaments against the FRY. The members of the Contact Group (apart from Russia) announced in April that Yugoslav assets abroad were to be frozen and in May imposed a ban on foreign investment in Serbia.

In July 1998 Milošević agreed that diplomatic observers from the EU, the USA and Russia would be allowed access to all regions of Kosovo to report on the activities of Serbian security forces. The Contact Group, which met in Bonn, Germany, to discuss a peace settlement for Kosovo, recognized for the first time that it would be necessary to include KLA representatives in future negotiations on the province. In September the UN Security Council adopted Resolution 1199, which demanded the immediate cessation of hostilities in Kosovo, the withdrawal of Serbian forces from the province, unrestricted access for humanitarian aid organizations, and the continuation of negotiations to determine the status of the province. NATO subsequently authorized its Supreme Allied Commander, Gen. Wesley Clark, to request member states to provide forces for possible military intervention. Despite an announcement by Serbian Prime Minister Marjanović at the end of September that hostilities against the KLA had been suspended, intensive fighting south of Prishtina (Prishtinë/Priština) was reported. NATO officially approved air bombardments against the FRY, and issued an ultimatum to Milošević that attacks would commence unless he complied with UN demands by a stipulated date later that month. (Russia continued to oppose military intervention against the FRY and had indicated that it would veto a further Security Council resolution authorizing such action.) Following intensive discussions with the US special envoy, Richard Holbrooke, Milošević agreed to the presence in Kosovo of a 2,000-member OSCE 'verification force', and to NATO surveillance flights in FRY airspace, to monitor the implementation of the Security Council's demands. It was subsequently reported that the majority of federal army units had been withdrawn from Kosovo, but that some 11,600 members of the special Serbian security forces remained in the province. NATO urged further progress in the withdrawal of Serbian forces from Kosovo, but at the end of October suspended indefinitely the implementation of military action against the FRY.

In November 1998 the deployment of OSCE observers in Kosovo commenced; however, intermittent violations of the cease-fire were reported. Following the outbreak of heavy fighting between the KLA and Serbian forces in northern Kosovo in December, it became evident that the OSCE monitoring force was inadequate (and had no mandate) for peace-keeping operations. A 2,300-member NATO 'extraction force' was deployed in the FYRM, near the border with Kosovo, to effect the evacuation of the OSCE monitors in the event of attacks against them. In early January 1999 further clashes between Serbian and KLA forces were reported. In mid-January the discovery that some 45 ethnic Albanian civilians had been killed at the village of Reçak (Račak) prompted international condemnation of the Serbian authorities. OSCE observers dismissed claims by the Federal Government that those killed had been members of the KLA. At the end of January the Contact Group, meeting in London, decided that a peace conference should be convened at the French town of Rambouillet in early February, with the participation of the KLA.

In early February 1999 the peace conference was convened in Rambouillet, as scheduled. Under the Contact Group's proposed peace plan, the Serbian authorities would be required to withdraw most of the 14,000 armed and security forces from Kosovo, while the KLA would be required to disarm within a period of three months. It was envisaged that NATO troops would be deployed in Kosovo to enforce the peace agreement. At the end of February the ethnic Albanian delegation, including the KLA representatives, agreed, in principle, to accept the peace plan. Meanwhile, in early March it was reported that Serbian troops had forced several thousand ethnic Albanian civilians to flee from southern Kosovo, amid continued heavy fighting in the province. The peace conference was reconvened at Rambouillet in mid-March. The ethnic Albanian representatives signed the agreement; however, the Serbian delegation continued to present objections and proposed amendments to the peace plan, which were rejected by the Contact Group. It was subsequently reported that the Federal Government had deployed a further 30,000 Serbian forces in, or near, Kosovo. NATO reiterated threats of imminent air bombardments, despite continued opposition from the Russian Government, which attempted unsuccessfully to persuade Milošević to accept the peace plan. In the absence of a negotiated settlement to the conflict, the NATO Secretary-General ordered the commencement of air attacks against the FRY, in a campaign, codenamed Operation Allied Force, which was designed to force Milošević's capitulation to the demands of the Contact Group.

On 24 March 1999 NATO forces commenced an aerial bombardment of air defences and military installations across Serbia and Montenegro, notably in Belgrade, Novi Sad, Prishtina and Podgorica. The Federal Government declared a state of war (which, however, the Montenegrin administration refused to recognize), suspended diplomatic relations with the USA, France, Germany and the United Kingdom (the countries directly involved in the attacks), and ordered foreign journalists to leave the country. The People's Republic of China and Russia immediately condemned the air offensive (which NATO justified on humanitarian grounds, despite the lack of endorsement by a UN Security Council resolution). Serbian security forces in Kosovo subsequently intensified the campaign of mass expulsions and large-scale massacres of the ethnic Albanian civilian population, precipitating a continued exodus of refugees from the province. By early April some 140,000 ethnic Albanians had fled to the FYRM, 300,000 to Albania, and 32,000 to Montenegro. Some 12,000 NATO troops were stationed at the FYRM border with Kosovo, after the reinforcement of the extraction force.

During April 1999 the NATO air offensive intensified, with the extension of targets to include those of political and economic significance, including the Serbian state television station. The increasing number of civilian casualties was condemned by opponents of the air offensive; notably, NATO aircraft bombarded a convoy of ethnic Albanian refugees in Kosovo in mid-April, killing about 64, apparently owing to confusion over Serbian military targets. The Russian special envoy to the Balkans (and former premier), Viktor Chernomyrdin, became engaged in intensive mediation efforts with the Federal Government, while urging a suspension of the NATO air offensive. NATO, however, continued to demand the full withdrawal of Serbian forces from Kosovo, and the return of refugees with an international military presence, as a precondition to the suspension of air attacks. In early May the Group of Eight (G8—comprising seven Western industrialized nations and Russia), meeting in Bonn, agreed on general principles for a political solution to the conflict (which was referred to the UN Security Council), although differences over the composition of the international military force for Kosovo remained. Shortly afterwards, apparently owing to faulty military information, NATO forces bombarded the embassy of the People's Republic of China in Belgrade. Violent anti-NATO protests ensued in the Chinese capital, Beijing, and the Chinese Government, supported by Russia, demanded a cessation of the air offensive as a precondition to the discussion of the settlement at the UN Security Council. At mid-May it was estimated that the NATO air campaign had resulted in the deaths of 1,200 civilians; about 600,000 ethnic Albanian refugees from Kosovo had fled to neighbouring countries.

In early 1999 the Federal Government announced that it had accepted the G8 principles for a solution to the conflict. On 3 June, following mediation by the President of Finland, Martti Ahtisaari, the Narodna skupština Republike Srbije formally approved a peace plan presented to the Federal Government by EU and Russian envoys. The peace agreement provided for the withdrawal of Serbian forces from Kosovo, and the deployment of a joint NATO-Russian peace-keeping force of about 50,000 personnel. Ethnic Albanian refugees were to be allowed to return to Kosovo, and the province was to be granted some autonomy under an interim administration. On 9 June, following discussions in the FYRM between NATO and Yugoslav military commanders in the FYRM, a Military Technical Agreement, providing for the complete withdrawal of Serbian forces within 11 days, was signed. On the following day the UN Security Council adopted Resolution 1244 approving the peace plan for Kosovo, and NATO announced the suspension of the air offensive, after it had been verified that the withdrawal of Serbian forces had commenced. NATO formally approved the establishment of a Kosovo Force (KFOR), and divided the province into five sectors (which were to be under the respective control of the United Kingdom, Germany, France, the USA and Italy). Shortly before NATO troops commenced deployment in Kosovo, however, about 200 Russian forces unexpectedly entered the province, and assumed control of the airport at Prishtina. An agreement was subsequently reached whereby a Russian contingent, numbering about 3,600, would participate in KFOR (without controlling a separate sector as the Russian Government had previously demanded). Under the terms of the UN Resolution, the UN Interim Administration Mission in Kosovo (UNMIK, see p. 88) was established as the supreme legal and executive authority in Kosovo, with responsibility for civil administration, and for facilitating the reconstruction of the province as an autonomous region. A 3,100-member international police unit (which constituted part of UNMIK) was to supervise the creation of a new security force in Kosovo. The OSCE was allocated primary responsibility for installing democratic institutions, organizing elections and monitoring human rights in the province. On 20 June 1999 NATO announced that the air campaign had officially ended, following the completion of the withdrawal of Serbian forces from Kosovo. The KLA subsequently signed an agreement with NATO, whereby the paramilitary organization was to disarm within a period of 90 days. On 24 June the Narodna skupština Republike Srbije formally ended the state of war in Serbia. Meanwhile, following the deployment of KFOR troops, nearly one-half of the ethnic Albanian refugees in neighbouring countries had returned to Kosovo by the end of the month, while an estimated 70,000 Serbian civilians had fled from the province, after reprisal attacks from KLA forces and members of the returning Albanian community. Investigators from the ICTY discovered increasing forensic evidence of large-scale massacres perpetrated by the Serbian forces against ethnic Albanian civilians during the conflict. Under a programme to establish partial provisional self-government in the province, elections to a Kosovo Assembly (Kuvendi i Kosovës/Skupština Kosova) were conducted in 2001 (see the chapter on Kosovo).

The process towards an agreement on a future status for Kosovo was problematic, since the authorities of Serbia and Montenegro strongly favoured conditions of increased autonomy, but less than total independence, while the Kosovo Albanian population insisted on unconditional independence; any final settlement was also to exclude any partition or border changes. In June 1995 UN Secretary-General Kofi Annan appointed the Norwegian ambassador to NATO, Kai Eide, as the special envoy responsible for assessing standards in Kosovo; he was given the task of undertaking a comprehensive review of the provincial Government's commitment to democracy, good governance and human rights. In September delegations from the Governments of Serbia and Kosovo met in Vienna, Austria, for preliminary discussions on decentralization and other technical issues. On 24 October, after Eide submitted a favourable review on Kosovo, the UN Security Council endorsed the initiation of final status negotiations on Kosovo. In November the Serbian Government adopted a unanimous resolution rejecting any eventual proclamation of independence by Kosovo, while the Kosovo Assembly approved a motion stating that it would accept only independence as the final status of the territory. Later that month former Finnish President Martti Ahtisaari, who had been appointed by Annan as the Special Envoy for the negotiations of Kosovo's future status, commenced separate discussions with Serbian and Kosovo leaders.

The first round of final status negotiations on Kosovo was conducted in Vienna in February 2006. After Montenegro's secession from the State Union of Serbia and Montenegro on 3 June (see above), the Serbian Government continued to resist strongly full independence for Kosovo, while agreeing to 'essential autonomy' for the province. At the instigation of Ahtisaari, direct high-level discussions, the first to involve the Presidents and Prime Ministers of Serbia and Kosovo since 1999, were conducted in Vienna in July 2006; the Kosovo delegation reiterated demands for full independence for the province by the end of that year, while the Serbian Prime Minister maintained that Serbia would not accept a loss of territory. The Kosovo delegation remained opposed to increased decentralization (including a Serbian proposal that a number of new Serb municipalities with autonomous powers be created), owing to concern that an effectively autonomous Serb polity would be established within the province. By the end of 2006 the two delegations had failed to reach any agreement on Kosovo's future status.

A new Serbian Constitution, which entered into effect in early November 2006, reaffirmed that Kosovo (again referred to as Kosovo and Metohija) was an integral part of the territory of Serbia, but one that was entitled to substantial autonomy. Following a subsequent announcement by the Serbian authorities that early legislative elections would take place on 21 January 2007, Ahtisaari declared that a proposed resolution for Kosovo's status (previously expected by the end of 2006) would be postponed until after the poll. Protests were subsequently staged in Kosovo, notably by supporters of an extreme ethnic Albanian movement, who attacked official buildings. The province's authorities indicated that they envisaged a unilateral declaration of independence in the absence of a diplomatic resolution. On 2 February 2007 Ahtisaari presented his proposal for the future status of Kosovo to the Serbian and Kosovo authorities and invited the delegations to engage in consultations on the draft in Vienna. The discussions, which commenced on 21 February, ended on 10 March, with a meeting of the Serbian and Kosovo government leaders; Ahtisaari concluded that, in view of the failure of the delegations to compromise on previously stated positions, there was no further prospect of achieving a negotiated agreement. On 26 March Ahtisaari submitted to the UN Security Council the finalized Comprehensive Proposal for the Kosovo Status Settlement, which recommended independence, to be supervised and supported for an initial period by an international military and civilian presence. On 3 April, at the beginning of a debate in the UN Security Council, Prime Minister Koštunica declared that Serbia rejected the Proposal (following a vote in the Serbian legislature in February), and requested that a new mediator be appointed. On 5 April Ahtisaari's plan was approved by 100 of 101 votes cast in the Kosovo Assembly. In August, after Russia obstructed the adoption of a resolution based on Ahtisaari's plan at the UN Security Council, a further series of negotiations began between Serbian and Kosovo delegations, with mediation by the USA, the EU and Russia. However, on 7 December it was announced that the negotiations had failed to result in an agreement.

In January 2008 Hashim Thaçi, the former leader of the KLA who had become Prime Minister of Kosovo, announced his intention to achieve independence for the territory. On 17 February the Kosovo Assembly adopted a declaration establishing the province as the Republic of Kosovo (Kosova), a sovereign state independent from Serbia, the resolution being based on Ahtisaari's Comprehensive Proposal for the Kosovo Status Settlement and in accordance with UN Security Council Resolution 1244 of 1999. Serbia, with the continued support of Russia, immediately protested that the declaration of independence contravened international law and demanded that it be annulled. On the following day the Serbian Ministry of the Interior issued arrest warrants against Thaçi and other Kosovo government officials for treason. KFOR reinforced the border between Kosovo and Serbia, after the destruction of two border posts by Serb protesters and reports that Serbian security forces had entered northern Kosovo. Several nations, including Albania, France, the USA and the United Kingdom, extended recognition to Kosovo on 18 February 2008, followed by many others; Serbia immediately recalled its ambassadors based in those countries. On 21 February Serb protesters rioted in Belgrade, attacking several embassies, including those of the United Kingdom and the USA. In March the Serbian Government announced that it intended to submit a legal challenge against Kosovo's declaration of independence at the ICJ and would also apply for international support at the UN General Assembly. After elections were conducted in predominantly Serb municipalities in Kosovo on 11 May, a parallel 'Assembly of the Community of Municipalities of the Autonomous Province of Kosovo and Metohija', unrecognized by the Kosovo Government, was established in June.

A new Constitution entered into effect in Kosovo on 15 June 2008, when UNMIK was scheduled to be replaced by an EU Rule of Law Mission in Kosovo (EULEX). However, the deployment of EULEX failed to proceed as envisaged, owing to the refusal of Kosovo Serbs and the Serbian Government (which was supported by Russia) to accept an EU mission. In July the Serbian Government announced its decision to return its ambassadors to the EU nations that had recognized Kosovo, in order to further the country's EU integration aspirations. In October it was announced that the remaining ambassadors were to return to the countries from where they had been withdrawn (notably including the USA). On 8 October the UN General Assembly adopted a Serbian resolution requesting that the ICJ arbitrate on the validity under international law of Kosovo's unilateral declaration of independence from Serbia. Representatives of 77 countries (including the five of the 27 EU nations that had not recognized Kosovo) voted in favour of the Serbian resolution, while six opposed it and 74 abstained. Following the continued refusal of Kosovo Serbs to accept the deployment of EULEX, in early November the UN Secretary-General presented an amended six-point plan on the reconfiguration of the international presence in Kosovo, under which officials in the Serb-majority areas would receive directives from UNMIK, while those in Albanian-majority areas would be the responsibility of EULEX. On 26 November the UN Security Council unanimously endorsed the six-point plan under the stipulated terms; deployment of EULEX throughout Kosovo began in early December.

In March 2009 the Serbian War Crimes Prosecutor announced that he intended to request that the Albanian Government reinvestigate Serbia's claims that some 300 Serbs had been abducted and killed during the Kosovo conflict in connection with an international organ-trafficking group based in Albania. In June former Prime Minister of Kosovo Agim Çeku was arrested in Bulgaria, under an international warrant issued by Serbia for alleged war crimes committed while he was a KLA military commander. The Serbian Government subsequently requested Çeku's extradition; however, he was released on the order of a Bulgarian court and at the end of June returned to Kosovo, after the Bulgarian prosecution decided not to appeal against the court's ruling. In December proceedings officially began at the ICJ to consider Serbia's challenge to the legality of Kosovo's declaration of independence. In January 2010 Serbia's Minister of Kosovo and Metohija, Goran Bogdanović, was expelled from Kosovo, shortly before meeting local Serb representatives, on the grounds that he had intended to conduct illicit political activities; the incident prompted the Serbian Government to protest to Western ambassadors. The Serbian Government continued to urge the Serb community in Kosovo to boycott elections and supported the organization of a poll in northern Kosovo in May (which Kosovo government leaders and the EU denounced as illegal). On 22 July the ICJ issued a non-binding, advisory opinion that Kosovo's declaration of independence on 17 February 2008 had not breached international law, Security Council Resolution 1244 or the constitutional framework. Serbia subsequently reaffirmed its intention to continue to withhold recognition of independence for Kosovo. In August 2010 the Kosovo Minister of the Interior accused Serbian government officials of encouraging the Kosovo Serb 'Assembly' to draft a declaration of independence in reprisal for the ICJ ruling. In September the UN General Assembly adopted a resolution, supported by Serbia and the EU member states, urging a direct dialogue between Serbia and Kosovo on ensuing issues.

Foreign Relations
Regional relations

On 27 February 2006 a case submitted to the ICJ at The Hague, Netherlands, in 1993 by Bosnia and Herzegovina against the FRY (represented by Serbia, as the successor state to the FRY and Serbia and Montenegro), claiming reparations for acts of genocide perpetrated against the Bosniak population in 1992–95, finally commenced. On 26 February 2007 the ICJ ruled that the Serbian state was not directly responsible for genocide or complicity in genocide in Bosnia and Herzegovina in 1992–95. However, the Court declared that Serbia was in violation of its obligation under international law by having failed to prevent the 1995 massacre in Srebrenica and to co-operate fully with the ICTY. In May 2007 the newly appointed Serbian Minister of Foreign Affairs, Vuk Jeremić, met his Bosnian counterpart for discussions in Sarajevo, in an effort to improve bilateral relations. In December 2009 direct rail connections between Belgrade and Sarajevo were restored. In February 2010 it was announced that, following Turkish mediation, Serbia had accepted the appointment of a new Bosnian ambassador (the post having remained vacant since 2007 owing to Serbia's rejection of the ambassadors nominated). On 1 March 2010 Ejup Ganić, the former President of the Federation of Bosnia and Herzegovina, was arrested at an airport in the British capital, London, in response to a request issued by Serbia for his extradition on war crimes charges related to an attack on a Yugoslav army convoy near Sarajevo in May 1992. In July 2010 a court in London rejected the Serbian authorities' attempt to extradite Ganić from the United Kingdom, describing it as being politically motivated. In April Serbian President Boris Tadić met the Chairman of the Bosnian collective Presidency, Haris Silajdžić, in Istanbul, Turkey, with the mediation of the Turkish President, Abdullah Gül, after which Tadić and Silajdžić signed a declaration pledging to improve relations and resolve outstanding disputes. However, the Republika Srpska Government rejected the declaration, on the grounds that Silajdžić had failed to consult with the other members of the Bosnian presidency; the close relations between Serbia and Republika Srpska were also believed to have been strained following a resolution in March by the Serbian legislature condemning the Srebrenica massacre (see above). Despite Tadić's support for Republika Srpska's secessionist premier, Milorad Dodik, prior to his election as President of the entity in October, in April 2011 he refused to endorse Dodik's plans to organize a referendum on legislation imposed by Bosnia's High Representative.

During a visit to Zagreb for a regional energy summit meeting in June 2007 President Tadić issued an unprecedented apology to the Croatian people for atrocities committed by Serbs during the war. However, Croatia's relations with Serbia became strained after the Croatian Government recognized Kosovo's independence in March 2008. In November the ICJ ruled that it had jurisdiction to hear Croatia's case of genocide against Serbia, pertaining to crimes allegedly committed by Yugoslav forces in Croatia in 1991–95, which had been referred to the Court in 1999. In January 2010 Serbia submitted a genocide counter-case against Croatia for alleged war crimes committed during Operation Storm in 1995. Following his election in January 2010, the Croatian President, Ivo Josipović, indicated that Croatia might be prepared to abandon its case against Serbia at the ICJ if the Serbian Government met conditions for negotiations on missing persons, war crimes trials and the return of cultural artefacts. Nevertheless, Tadić refused to attend Josipović's inauguration in February, owing to the presence of the Kosovo President at the ceremony. In April Josipović met Tadić and the Hungarian President for trilateral discussions in Budapest, Hungary, and subsequently visited Vojvodina; following the improvement in relations between Serbia and Croatia, it was reported that Tadić and Josipović favoured an out-of-court settlement of the two countries' reciprocal genocide cases submitted to the ICJ. In June the Serbian and Croatian Ministers of Defence signed a military co-operation agreement in Zagreb.

The decision of the FYRM and Montenegro in October 2008 to extend recognition to Kosovo prompted strong protests from the Serbian Government, which expelled the ambassadors of both countries (but in November invited the appointment of new envoys). In May 2009 Montenegrin President Filip Vujanović visited Belgrade, in an effort to improve bilateral relations, while President Tadić made a reciprocal visit to Montenegro in June. In October Serbia finally accepted the Montenegrin Government's nomination of a new ambassador. In January 2010 Serbia recalled its ambassador, in protest against Montenegro's decision to establish diplomatic relations with Kosovo; however, the Serbian ambassador returned to the Montenegrin capital of Podgorica in February.

Other external relations

Relations between Russia and Serbia were consolidated in early 2008, with the signature of an agreement (approved by the Serbian legislature in September) whereby Serbia was to join Russia's 'South Stream' pipeline project and Russian state-controlled energy producer Gazprom acquired a 51% share in the Serbian state-owned petroleum enterprise, Naftna Industrija Srbije. The sale of the majority share in Naftna Industrija Srbije was completed in February 2009; agreements with Serbia, together with Italy, Bulgaria and Greece, were signed in Sochi, Russia, in May. In October Russian President Dmitrii Medvedev made an official visit to Serbia (the first by a Russian Head of State); he approved a loan of US $1,500m. to support Serbia's economy and signed a number of bilateral agreements with President Tadić, including an accord providing for the establishment of a joint company to manage the construction of the Serbian section of the 'South Stream' gas pipeline. In March 2011 Russian Prime Minister Vladimir Putin made an official visit to Serbia, during which he reiterated his commitment to the joint energy projects, and issued an offer to lend the Serbian Government $3,000m. for the purchase of Russian fighter aircraft and air defence systems.

In December 2007 the Serbian legislature approved a resolution urging the Serbian Government to 'reconsider' diplomatic relations with any Western country that recognized Kosovo as independent. Having recalled all ambassadors from states that extended recognition to Kosovo following its declaration of independence in February 2008, the Serbian Government in July announced its decision to return its ambassadors to the EU member nations that had recognized Kosovo; the remaining Serbian ambassadors (including the ambassador to the USA) returned in October. Serbian Minister of Foreign Affairs Vuk Jeremić engaged in intensive diplomatic activity, visiting numerous states to urge their respective governments to withhold recognition of Kosovo. Following the arrest of former Bosnian Serb leader Radovan Karadžić in July, Serbia's relations with the EU and USA improved significantly. In May 2009

US Vice-President Joe Biden visited Serbia and neighbouring states; after meeting Tadić, he declared support for Serbia's aspirations for EU integration. In July Serbia presented an application to host the 50th anniversary summit of the Non-aligned Movement (see p. 461) in 2011. In August 2009 Tadić made an official seven-day visit to the People's Republic of China (the first by a Serbian Head of State since independence), where he and Chinese President Hu Jintao signed a strategic partnership agreement, pledging to increase political, economic and trade co-operation between the two countries. US Secretary of State Hillary Clinton visited Serbia in October 2010, and reiterated US support for the Government's objective of EU integration.

CONSTITUTION AND GOVERNMENT

On 5 June 2006 the Serbian legislature officially declared the Republic of Serbia to be the successor state to the State Union of Serbia and Montenegro (following Montenegro's declaration of independence on 3 June). Under the terms of a new Constitution, which officially entered into effect on 8 November, legislative power continued to be vested in the 250-member Narodna skupština Republike Srbije (National Assembly of the Republic of Serbia), which is directly elected for a period of four years. The President of the Republic, who is directly elected for a term of five years, nominates the Prime Minister for approval by the Narodna skupština. Executive power is vested in the Council of Ministers, which is proposed to the Narodna skupština by the designated Prime Minister. The Narodna skupština is to be dissolved if it fails to appoint a new Council of Ministers within 90 days of its inaugural session. The 11-member High Judicial Council ensures the independence of courts and judges, and is empowered to nominate or remove judges. Serbia formally comprises 24 administrative regions, including the seven regions of the province of Vojvodina, in the north of Serbia; the administrative regions are themselves divided into 170 municipalities.

REGIONAL AND INTERNATIONAL CO-OPERATION

Serbia is a member of the Organization for Security and Co-operation in Europe (OSCE, see p. 385) and the Council of Europe (see p. 250). In 2006 the North Atlantic Treaty Organization (NATO, see p. 368) invited Serbia to join its 'Partnership for Peace' programme. Serbia joined the Central European Free Trade Agreement (CEFTA, see p. 446) in 2007 and held its rotating chairmanship in 2010. On 22 December 2009 Serbia submitted an official application to join the EU.

Following Montenegro's achievement of independence on 3 June 2006, the membership of Serbia and Montenegro in the UN was inherited by Serbia as the successor state.

ECONOMIC AFFAIRS

In 2009, according to estimates by the World Bank, the gross national income (GNI) of Serbia, measured at 2007–09 prices, was US $43,834m., equivalent to $5,990 per head (or $11,420 per head on an international purchasing-power parity basis). During 2000–09, it was estimated, the population declined at an average annual rate of 0.3%, while gross domestic product (GDP) per head increased, in real terms, by an average of 4.8% per year. Overall GDP grew, in real terms, at an average annual rate of 4.5% in 2000–09; according to official figures, GDP increased by 5.5% in 2008, but declined by 3.1% in 2009.

Agriculture (including hunting, forestry and fishing) contributed 9.4% of GDP in 2009. In that year some 24.0% of the employed labour force were engaged in the sector. Serbia's principal crops are maize, wheat, sugar beet and potatoes. The cultivation of fruit and vegetables is also important. Agricultural GDP increased at an average annual rate of 0.1% during 2005–09, according to official figures; sectoral GDP rose by 8.6% in 2008, but by only 0.7% in 2009.

Industry (including mining, manufacturing, construction and power) contributed 27.1% of GDP in 2009, and the sector engaged 25.1% of the employed labour force in the same year. Industrial GDP decreased at an average annual rate of 0.3% in 2005–09; sectoral GDP grew by 2.0% in 2008, but declined by 12.0% in 2009.

The mining and quarrying sector contributed 1.6% of GDP in 2009, and engaged 1.1% of the employed labour force in that year. The principal minerals extracted are coal (mainly brown coal), copper ore and bauxite. Iron ore, crude petroleum, lead, zinc ore and natural gas are also produced. The GDP of the mining and quarrying sector increased at an average annual rate of 1.1% in 2005–09; mining GDP expanded by 4.5% in 2008, but declined by an estimated 4.7% in 2009.

The manufacturing sector contributed 15.8% of GDP in 2009, and engaged 17.0% of the employed labour force in the same year. Manufacturing GDP decreased at an average annual rate of 1.3% in 2005–09; the sector expanded by 1.2% in 2008, but declined by a huge 15.3% in 2009.

The construction sector contributed 4.8% of GDP in 2009, and the sector engaged 5.2% of the employed labour force in that year. Construction GDP increased at an average annual rate of 1.7% in 2005–09; the sector grew by 4.6% in 2008, but declined by 14.3% in 2009.

Energy in Serbia (including Montenegro) is derived principally from coal (which provided about 70.2% of total electricity generated in 2007) and hydroelectric power (27.5%). Imports of mineral fuels accounted for 17.8% of the value of total imports in 2010.

Services contributed 63.5% of GDP in 2009. Some 50.9% of the employed labour force were engaged in the sector in that year. Total foreign tourist arrivals in Serbia rose from 339,000 in 2003 to 646,000 in 2008. Services GDP increased at an average annual rate of 6.6% in 2005–09; sectoral GDP grew by 7.2% in 2008 and by only 0.8% in 2009.

In 2009 Serbia recorded a trade deficit of US $6,663.3m., and there was a deficit of $2,412.3m. on the current account of the balance of payments. In 2010 the principal source of imports to Serbia was Russia (accounting for 12.9% of the total); other major sources were Germany, Italy and the People's Republic of China. The principal market for exports in that year was Italy (taking 11.4% of all exports); other important purchasers were Bosnia and Herzegovina, Germany, Montenegro, Romania and Russia. (These figures excluded trade to or from Kosovo.) The main exports in 2010 were basic manufactures, food and live animals, machinery and transport equipment, miscellaneous manufactured articles and chemicals. The principal imports in that year were basic manufactures, machinery and transport equipment, mineral fuels and lubricants, chemicals, miscellaneous manufactured articles, and food and live animals.

In 2009 Serbia recorded an overall budgetary deficit of 121,000m. dinars (equivalent to 4.3% of GDP). Serbia's general government gross debt was €1,033,480m. in 2009, equivalent to 35.6% of GDP. At the end of 2008 the total external debt of Serbia was US $30,918.3m., of which $8,475.3m. was public and publicly guaranteed debt. In that year the cost of debt-servicing of Serbia was equivalent to 13.9% of the value of exports of goods, services and income. In 2000–09, according to the International Labour Organization (ILO), the annual rate of inflation in Serbia averaged 19.0%. Consumer prices increased by an annual average of 7.8% in 2009. The rate of unemployment in Serbia was an estimated 16.6% in October 2009.

In February 2006 the IMF approved the completion of its extended three-year stand-by credit arrangement with Serbia and Montenegro, allowing the country to secure a final cancellation of outstanding debt, under the terms of an agreement made with the 'Paris Club' of international creditors in 2001. Serbia resumed negotiations with the European Union (EU, see p. 270) on a Stabilization and Association Agreement (SAA) in June 2007, and began to receive EU financial aid under the instrument for pre-accession assistance; an Agreement was signed in April 2008. However, implementation of the SAA (and the associated interim trade agreement) was suspended until EU member states agreed unanimously that Serbia was co-operating fully with the International Criminal Tribunal for the former Yugoslavia (ICTY, see p. 20, see Domestic Political Affairs). In May 2009 the Government announced a number of stimulus measures (at a cost of some 40,000m. dinars) to counteract the adverse effects of the international economic crisis, including provisions for lower rates for business loans. Also in May the IMF confirmed that it was to increase its support to Serbia in a stand-by credit arrangement (initially approved in January) to some US $4,200m. over a period of 27 months; an immediate disbursement of funds was to strengthen state currency reserves. Meanwhile, the involvement of Serbia in Russia's 'South Stream' gas pipeline project (which was to supply natural gas from Russia to various countries in southern and eastern Europe) was expected to provide economic advantages to Serbia; under an agreement on Serbia's association with the project, a 51% share in the Serbian state-owned petroleum enterprise, Naftna Industrija Srbije, was sold to the Russian state-controlled energy producer Gazprom in February 2009. On 22 December Serbia submitted an official application to join the EU. In June 2010 the EU agreed to

SERBIA

begin implementation of the SAA with Serbia (following the adoption of the interim trade agreement in December 2009), in response to a favourable assessment of Serbia's co-operation with the ICTY. In October 2010 the EU Council submitted Serbia's EU membership application for the approval of the European Commission, which was expected to announce its decision on the candidacy by the end of 2011. In April 2011 the Government reached an agreement with the World Bank, under which it was able to draw funds of US $200m. each year for a four-year period. In the same month the IMF issued its final review of Serbia's economic performance under the stand-by credit arrangement and approved a further disbursement of funds amounting to $509m. (bringing total disbursements under the programme to about $2,200m.). Following the implementation of pension reforms, the Government was urged to lower the number of public sector employees as part of an agreed progressive reduction in public expenditure, and to improve the business environment. GDP, which had contracted by 3.1% in 2009 (after strong growth in the preceding five years), rose by an estimated 1.8% in 2010, demonstrating a slow recovery.

PUBLIC HOLIDAYS

2012: 1–2 January (New Year), 7–8 January (Christmas), 15 February (National Day), 13–16 April (Orthodox Easter), 1–2 May (Labour Day).

Statistical Survey

Source (unless otherwise indicated): Statistical Office of the Republic of Serbia, 11000 Belgrade, Milana Rakića 5; tel. (11) 2412922; fax (11) 2411260; internet webrzs.stat.gov.rs/axd/en/index.php.

Note: Except where otherwise stated, figures in this survey exclude data for Kosovo, which declared independence from Serbia on 17 February 2008. Certain figures pertain to the former Federal Republic of Yugoslavia, comprising Serbia and Montenegro, or to the State Union of those two republics that succeeded it from 2003 to 2006, when Montenegro achieved independence.

Area and Population

AREA, POPULATION AND DENSITY

Area (sq km)	77,498*
Population (census results)	
31 March 1991	7,576,837
31 March 2002	
Males	3,645,930
Females	3,852,071
Total	7,498,001
Population (official estimates at mid-year)	
2007	7,381,579
2008	7,350,222
2009	7,320,807
Density (per sq km) at mid-2009	94.5

* 29,922 sq miles, according to 2002 census.

2010 (official estimate of population at 1 January): 7,306,677.

POPULATION BY AGE AND SEX
(official estimates at mid-2009)

	Males	Females	Total
0–14	573,146	541,859	1,115,005
15–64	2,459,454	2,495,530	4,954,984
65 and over	527,448	723,370	1,250,818
Total	3,560,048	3,760,759	7,320,807

POPULATION BY ETHNIC GROUP
(2002 census)

Ethnic group	Population ('000)	%
Serbs	6,213	82.9
Hungarians	293	3.9
Bosniaks	136	1.8
Roma	108	1.4
Yugoslavs	81	1.1
Croats	71	0.9
Montenegrins	69	0.9
Others	527	7.0
Total	7,498	100.0

ADMINISTRATIVE DIVISIONS
(2002 census)

	Area (sq km)	Population ('000)	Density (per sq km)	Principal city
Capital				
Belgrade	3,224	1,576,124	488.9	—
Okruzi (Districts)				
Bor	3,507	146,551	41.8	Bor
Braničevo	3,865	200,503	51.9	Požarevac
Jablanica	2,769	240,923	87.0	Leskovac
Kolubara	2,474	192,204	77.7	Valjevo
Mačva	3,268	329,625	100.9	Šabac
Moravica	3,016	224,772	74.5	Čačak
Nišava	2,729	381,757	139.9	Niš
Pčinja	3,520	227,690	64.7	Vranje
Pirot	2,761	105,654	38.3	Pirot
Podunavlje	1,248	210,290	168.5	Smederevo
Pomoravlje	2,614	227,435	87.0	Jagodina
Rasina	2,668	259,441	97.2	Kruševac
Raška	3,918	291,230	74.3	Kraljevo
Šumadija	2,387	298,778	125.2	Kragujevac
Toplica	2,231	102,075	45.8	Prokuplje
Zaječar	3,623	137,561	38.0	Zaječar
Zlatibor	6,140	313,396	51.0	Užice
Province				
Vojvodina	21,536	2,031,992	94.4	Novi Sad
Okruzi (Districts) within the Province of Vojvodina				
Central Banat	3,256	208,456	64.0	Zrenjanin
North Bačka	1,784	200,140	112.2	Subotica
North Banat	2,329	165,881	71.2	Kikinda
South Bačka	4,016	593,666	147.8	Novi Sad
South Banat	4,245	313,937	74.0	Pančevo
Srem	3,486	335,901	96.4	Sremska Mitrovica
West Bačka	2,420	214,011	88.4	Sombor
Total	77,498	7,498,001	96.8	—

PRINCIPAL TOWNS
(population at 30 June 2009)

Beograd (Belgrade, the capital)	1,630,582	Šabac	118,720
Novi Sad	327,175	Čačak	115,612
Niš	255,479	Smederevo	108,046
Kragujevac	174,318	Novi Pazar	96,597
Leskovac	149,279	Valjevo	93,117
Subotica	144,540	Sombor	89,314
Kruševac	127,551	Vranje	86,753
Zrenjanin	125,391	Loznica	82,749
Pančevo	124,362	Sremska Mitrovica	81,613
Kraljevo	118,959	Užice	79,601

SERBIA

BIRTHS, MARRIAGES AND DEATHS

	Registered live births Number	Rate (per 1,000)	Registered marriages Number	Rate (per 1,000)	Registered deaths Number	Rate (per 1,000)
2002	78,101	10.4	41,947	5.6	102,785	13.7
2003	79,025	10.6	41,914	5.6	103,946	13.9
2004	78,186	10.5	42,030	5.6	104,320	14.0
2005	72,180	9.7	38,846	5.2	106,771	14.3
2006	70,997	9.6	39,756	5.4	102,884	13.9
2007	68,102	9.2	41,083	5.6	102,805	13.9
2008	69,083	9.4	38,285	5.2	102,711	14.0
2009	70,299	9.6	36,853	5.0	104,000	14.2

Life expectancy (years at birth, WHO estimates): 74 (males 71; females 76) in 2008 (Source: WHO, *World Health Statistics*).

ECONOMICALLY ACTIVE POPULATION
(labour force survey, persons aged 15 years and over, October 2009)

	Males	Females	Total
Agriculture, forestry, fishing and water works	366,711	255,474	622,185
Mining and quarrying	22,349	5,377	27,726
Manufacturing	293,798	147,674	441,472
Electricity, gas and water	40,320	5,664	45,984
Construction	119,380	16,098	135,478
Wholesale and retail trade	176,728	184,598	361,326
Hotels and restaurants	34,829	41,304	76,133
Transport, storage and communications	120,395	34,250	154,646
Financial intermediation	22,063	33,263	55,326
Real estate and property	48,963	40,294	89,257
Public administration and social security	71,552	56,113	127,665
Education	57,626	92,895	150,522
Health and social work	33,064	143,268	176,332
Other community, social and personal services	64,991	53,700	118,691
Households with employed persons	707	5,321	6,028
Extra-territorial organizations and bodies	538	877	1,415
Total employed	1,474,017	1,116,171	2,590,188
Unemployed	266,427	250,942	517,369
Total labour force	1,740,444	1,367,113	3,107,557

Health and Welfare

KEY INDICATORS
(data for Serbia only, unless otherwise indicated)

Total fertility rate (children per woman, 2008)	1.6
Under-5 mortality rate (per 1,000 live births, 2008)	8
HIV/AIDS (% of persons aged 15–49, 2007, Serbia and Montenegro)	0.1
Physicians (per 1,000 head, 2006)	2.0
Hospital beds (per 1,000 head, 2006)	5.4
Health expenditure (2007): US $ per head (PPP)	769
Health expenditure (2007): % of GDP	9.9
Health expenditure (2007): public (% of total)	61.8
Access to water (% of persons, 2008)	99
Access to sanitation (% of persons, 2008)	92
Human Development Index (2010): ranking	60
Human Development Index (2010): value	0.735

For sources and definitions, see explanatory note on p. vi.

Agriculture

PRINCIPAL CROPS
('000 metric tons; incl. Kosovo)

	2007	2008	2009
Wheat	1,863.8	2,095.4	2,067.6
Barley	259.0	344.1	302.5
Maize	3,904.8	6,158.1	6,396.3
Oats	76.9	95.6	73.6
Potatoes	743.3	843.5	898.3
Sugar beet	3,206.4	2,299.8	2,797.6
Beans, dry	60.0*	42.2	n.a.
Soybeans (Soya beans)	304.0	350.9	349.2
Sunflower seed	294.5	454.3	377.5
Cabbages and other brassicas	280.2	300.5	326.2
Tomatoes	152.0	176.5	189.4
Chillies and peppers, green	150.3	151.3	171.4
Onions, dry	116.0	141.4	131.2
Carrots and turnips	56.7	66.2	67.8
Watermelons	205.4	256.0	230.1
Apples	245.2	235.6	281.9
Pears	60.5	61.9	67.8
Sour (Morello) cherries	99.9	89.7	105.4
Peaches and nectarines	65.6	62.7	77.2
Plums and sloes	680.6	606.8	662.6
Raspberries and other berries	77.0	84.3	87.0
Grapes	353.3	373.0	431.3
Tobacco, unmanufactured	11.1	10.8	9.9

* FAO estimate.

Aggregate production ('000 metric tons, may include official, semi-official or estimated data): Total cereals 6,138.7 in 2007, 8,730.2 in 2008, 8,876.1 in 2009; Total roots and tubers 743.3 in 2007, 843.5 in 2008, 898.3 in 2009; Total vegetables (incl. melons) 1,146.7 in 2007, 1,285.3 in 2008, 1,316.4 in 2009; Total fruits (excl. melons) 1,683.2 in 2007, 1,619.1 in 2008, 1,827.4 in 2009.

Source: FAO.

LIVESTOCK
('000 head, year ending 30 September; incl. Kosovo)

	2007	2008	2009
Horses	18	17	14
Cattle	1,087	1,057	1,002
Pigs	3,832	3,594	3,631
Sheep	1,606	1,605	1,504
Goats	149	155	143
Chickens	15,708	16,684	22,399

Source: FAO.

LIVESTOCK PRODUCTS
('000 metric tons; incl. Kosovo)

	2007	2008	2009
Cattle meat	95	99	100
Sheep meat	20	23	25
Pig meat	643*	558*	528†
Chicken meat	70	76	80
Cows' milk	1,620	1,580	1,509*
Sheep's milk	14	14	14*
Hen eggs	69	60*	52*
Honey	4	3	5

* Unofficial figure.
† FAO estimate.

Source: FAO.

SERBIA
Statistical Survey

Forestry

ROUNDWOOD REMOVALS
('000 cubic metres, excl. bark; incl. Kosovo)

	2007	2008	2009
Sawlogs, veneer logs and logs for sleepers	1,292	1,410	1,175
Pulpwood	91	99	93
Other industrial roundwood	44	106	91
Fuel wood	1,554	1,571	1,778
Total	2,981	3,186	3,137

Source: FAO.

SAWNWOOD PRODUCTION
('000 cubic metres, including railway sleepers; incl. Kosovo)

	2007	2008	2009
Coniferous (softwood)	146	167	146
Non-coniferous (hardwood)	456	505	428
Total	602	672	574

Source: FAO.

Fishing

(data for Serbia and Montenegro, incl. Kosovo)

('000 metric tons, live weight)

	2003	2004	2005
Capture	1.8	2.4	2.5*
Freshwater fishes	1.0	1.6	1.7
Common carp	0.1	0.2	0.1*
Aquaculture	3.2	4.6	4.6*
Rainbow trout	2.6	4.0	n.a.
Total catch	5.0	7.0	7.0*

* FAO estimate.
Note: Figures exclude marine shells (metric tons): 3.1 in 2003; 3.0 in 2004; n.a. in 2005.
Source: FAO.

Mining

('000 metric tons, unless otherwise indicated)

	2007	2008	2009
Coal	37,073	38,585	38,897
Lignite	36,803	38,284	38,071
Crude petroleum	639	636	663
Natural gas (million cubic metres)	274	282	283
Lead and zinc ore	198	202	225
Copper ore	6,867	8,680	10,014
Clay and kaolin	190	190	161

Source: partly US Geological Survey.

Industry

SELECTED PRODUCTS
('000 metric tons, unless otherwise indicated)

	2007	2008	2009
Refined vegetable oils	123.4	101.8	136.9
Fruit and vegetable juices	233.6	262.1	240.3
Beer ('000 hectolitres)	6,547	6,470	5,436
Cigarettes (million)	21,304	20,873	20,482
Cotton yarn (metric tons)	580	1,584	804
Wool yarn (metric tons)	300	212	265
Hosiery ('000 pairs)	101,090	101,846	191,087
Underwear ('000 units)	7,609	7,442	12,449
Leather footwear ('000 pairs)	3,481	3,327	2,225
Parquet wooden flooring and blinds ('000 sq metres)	274.6	278.5	180.9
Paper and cardboard	120.8	95.2	101.0
Newsprint	49.8	56.5	45.2
Cement	2,676	2,843	2,232
Motor spirit (gasoline)*	624	n.a.	n.a.
Gas-diesel (distillate fuel) oil*	1,091	n.a.	n.a.
Residual fuel oil*	796	n.a.	n.a.
Nitrogenous fertilizers	534.9	251.9	220.7
Rubber tyres for vehicles ('000)	14,089	14,146	10,263
Pig-iron	1,377.5	1,516.1	964.6
Flat-rolled steel products	2,431.4	2,393.4	1,556.0
Electric light bulbs ('000)	1,722	2,277	n.a.
Alternating current motors (units)	58,000	41,226	29,993
Tractors (number)	1,949	1,826	3,625
Passenger cars (number)	9,403	7,748	16,512
Kitchen wooden furniture ('000 units)	75.9	39.7	66.2
Electric energy (million kWh)	36,652	37,393	38,376

* Source: UN Industrial Commodity Statistics Database.

Finance

CURRENCY AND EXCHANGE RATES

Monetary Units
100 para = 1 Serbian dinar.

Sterling, Dollar and Euro Equivalents (31 December 2010)
£1 sterling = 124.113 dinars;
US $1 = 79.280 dinars;
€1 = 105.934 dinars;
1,000 Serbian dinars = £8.06 = $12.61 = €9.44.

Average Exchange Rate (dinars per US $)
2008   55.724
2009   67.581
2010   77.734

CONSOLIDATED BUDGET
('000 million dinars; incl. Kosovo)

Revenue*	2009	2010†	2011‡
Tax revenue	1,000	1,061	1,052
Personal income tax	133	142	137
Social security contributions	319	336	322
Corporate income tax	31	24	32
Retail sales tax; value-added tax	297	325	321
Excises	135	148	150
Taxes on international trade and operations	48	44	43
Other taxes	37	43	47
Non-tax revenue	139	145	156
Total	1,140	1,206	1,208

SERBIA

Expenditure	2009	2010†	2011‡
Current expenditure	1,155	1,206	1,220
Wages and salaries	302	313	310
Expenditure on goods and services	211	213	226
Interest payments	22	39	34
Subsidies and other current transfers	619	641	650
Capital expenditure	93	111	112
Lending minus repayments	20	26	30
Total	1,268	1,344	1,362

* Excluding grants received ('000 million dinars): 7 in 2009; 2 in 2010 (budget forecast); 6 in 2011 (projection).
† Budget forecasts.
‡ Projections.

Source: IMF, *Republic of Serbia: Sixth Review Under the Stand-By Arrangement* (January 2011).

INTERNATIONAL RESERVES
(US $ million at 31 December; incl. Kosovo)

	2008	2009	2010
Gold (national valuation)	354.1	465.7	594.9
IMF special drawing rights	2.2	19.3	3.0
Foreign exchange	11,120.7	14,749.9	12,711.7
Total	11,477.0	15,234.9	13,309.6

Source: IMF, *International Financial Statistics*.

MONEY SUPPLY
(million dinars at 31 December)

	2008	2009	2010
Currency outside depository corporations	89,956	95,522	91,803
Transferable deposits	259,325	288,661	304,809
Other deposits	643,251	819,797	964,913
Broad money	992,533	1,203,980	1,361,525

Source: IMF, *International Financial Statistics*.

COST OF LIVING
(Consumer Price Index at January; base: 2006 = 100)

	2009	2010	2011
Food and non-alcoholic beverages	136.9	136.7	154.9
Tobacco and beverages	162.0	179.7	207.7
Clothing (incl. footwear)	114.3	122.1	129.4
Rent and fuels	110.5	115.2	124.6
All items (incl. others)	125.4	131.4	146.2

NATIONAL ACCOUNTS
('000 million dinars at current prices)

Expenditure on the Gross Domestic Product

	2007	2008	2009
Final consumption expenditure	2,206.2	2,584.5	2,708.3
Households	1,714.0	2,023.6	2,143.2
Non-profit institutions serving households	24.2	26.5	25.2
General government	290.1	346.6	361.9
Collective consumption expenditure	177.8	187.8	178.0
Gross fixed capital formation	552.3	632.4	510.2
Changes in inventories	107.1	158.9	−26.3
Acquisitions less disposals of valuables	0.3	0.4	0.5
Total domestic expenditure	2,865.9	3,376.2	3,192.7
Exports of goods and services	697.0	835.3	801.0
Less Imports of goods and services	1,286.0	1,550.2	1,280.2
Gross domestic product at market prices	2,276.9	2,661.4	2,713.2

Gross Domestic Product by Economic Activity

	2007	2008	2009
Agriculture, hunting, forestry and fishing	195.4	237.5	217.8
Mining and quarrying	27.3	32.9	36.3
Manufacturing	321.2	373.6	368.4
Electricity, gas and water	86.8	96.0	114.8
Construction	99.2	125.7	111.3
Wholesale and retail trade, and repairs	230.2	277.8	255.8
Restaurants and hotels	23.9	25.6	27.6
Transport, storage and communications	193.3	228.6	240.3
Financial intermediation	62.9	77.9	85.1
Real estate, renting and business activities	343.3	413.1	434.0
Public administration and defence; compulsory social security	91.5	91.6	90.5
Education	95.4	114.8	119.4
Health and social work	121.3	144.3	150.0
Other community, social and personal services	39.6	47.7	72.8
Private households with employed persons	2.4	2.6	2.5
Sub-total	1,933.8	2,289.9	2,326.5
Less Financial intermediation services indirectly measured	43.6	59.9	68.7
Gross value added in basic prices	1,890.2	2,230.0	2,257.8
Taxes on products	426.9	482.6	489.6
Less Subsidies on products	40.3	51.3	34.2
GDP in market prices	2,276.9	2,661.4	2,713.2

BALANCE OF PAYMENTS
(US $ million; incl. Kosovo)

	2007	2008	2009
Exports of goods f.o.b.	8,776.5	10,948.9	8,367.8
Imports of goods c.i.f.	−17,916.1	−22,077.5	−15,031.1
Trade balance	−9,139.6	−11,128.6	−6,663.3
Exports of services	3,168.3	4,030.2	3,490.5
Imports of services	−3,516.1	−4,295.8	−3,454.5
Balance on goods and services	−9,487.5	−11,394.1	−6,627.3
Other income received	710.0	830.4	692.1
Other income paid	−1,539.0	−2,185.4	−1,402.4
Balance on goods, services and income	−10,316.6	−12,749.1	−7,337.6
Current transfers received	4,285.4	4,150.3	5,269.8
Current transfers paid	−315.0	−407.0	−344.5
Current balance	−6,346.2	−9,005.8	−2,412.3
Capital account (net)	−407.6	20.3	2.6
Direct investment abroad	−943.2	−277.2	−55.3
Direct investment from abroad	3,447.8	2,993.2	1,921.4
Portfolio investment assets	−4.7	−41.1	−9.8
Portfolio investment liabilities	920.5	−94.9	−58.6
Financial derivatives liabilities	1.6	1.9	−2.2
Other investment assets	−2,300.8	−2,000.1	77.4
Other investment liabilities	6,572.0	6,287.1	2,368.2
Net errors and omissions	323.1	−230.0	−48.8
Overall balance	1,262.6	−2,346.7	1,782.6

Source: IMF, *International Financial Statistics*.

SERBIA

External Trade

PRINCIPAL COMMODITY GROUPS
(US $ million, distribution by SITC)

Imports c.i.f.	2008	2009	2010
Food and live animals	1,106.7	750.6	774.2
Beverages and tobacco	178.7	116.5	116.5
Crude materials (inedible) except fuels	896.0	461.1	647.9
Mineral fuels, lubricants, etc.	4,671.2	2,382.9	2,980.2
Chemicals and related products	3,165.3	2,036.1	2,088.7
Basic manufactures	4,542.8	2,646.4	3,036.5
Machinery and transport equipment	6,227.4	3,239.2	2,987.4
Miscellaneous manufactured articles	2,012.4	1,314.9	1,224.9
Total (incl. others)	**22,872.5**	**16,055.6**	**16,734.4**

Exports f.o.b.	2008	2009	2010
Food and live animals	1,483.8	1,509.0	1,768.1
Crude materials (inedible) except fuels	456.6	291.2	464.6
Mineral fuels, lubricants, etc.	373.5	390.1	500.5
Chemicals and related products	1,111.2	661.0	877.6
Basic manufactures	3,606.6	2,182.1	2,841.1
Machinery and transport equipment	1,901.3	1,477.1	1,590.0
Miscellaneous manufactured articles	1,540.8	1,336.2	1,233.6
Total (incl. others)	**10,971.4**	**8,344.3**	**9,794.5**

PRINCIPAL TRADING PARTNERS
(US $ million)

Imports c.i.f.	2008	2009	2010
Austria	572.9	534.4	511.6
Bosnia and Herzegovina	644.4	448.2	556.3
Bulgaria	746.5	397.9	580.9
China, People's Republic	1,719.0	1,135.4	1,202.5
Croatia	553.7	427.4	429.5
Czech Republic	368.3	269.2	317.2
France (incl. Monaco)	741.2	522.1	481.8
Germany	2,701.7	1,964.5	1,767.7
Greece	287.5	231.1	228.0
Hungary	815.2	645.9	808.0
Italy	2,182.1	1,549.8	1,431.7
Macedonia, former Yugoslav republic	379.3	230.9	272.2
Romania	630.9	525.1	596.6
Russia	3,492.5	1,969.9	2,157.1
Slovenia	627.0	526.0	508.5
Sweden	242.3	173.3	190.7
Turkey	436.6	293.8	324.9
Ukraine	661.0	256.8	285.2
USA	498.5	356.3	255.4
Total (incl. others)	**22,872.5**	**16,055.6**	**16,734.4**

Exports f.o.b.	2008	2009	2010
Austria	458.1	290.8	338.4
Bosnia and Herzegovina	1,338.6	1,015.6	1,089.0
Bulgaria	251.3	198.7	241.1
Croatia	434.4	278.7	307.1
France (incl. Monaco)	346.4	249.3	276.7
Germany	1,141.9	870.7	1,008.2
Greece	211.1	135.7	182.1
Hungary	324.8	255.5	303.4
Italy	1,128.4	820.8	1,118.5
Macedonia, former Yugoslav republic	492.9	429.1	476.8
Montenegro	1,287.1	836.2	803.8
Romania	397.8	482.3	650.7
Russia	550.9	349.4	534.7
Slovenia	501.9	343.8	425.9
Total (incl. others)	**10,971.4**	**8,344.3**	**9,794.5**

Transport
(data include Kosovo)

RAILWAYS
(traffic)

	2007	2008	2009
Passengers carried ('000)	5,974	5,618	5,358
Passenger-kilometres (million)	687	583	522
Freight carried ('000 metric tons)	14,902	14,130	10,419
Freight ton-kilometres (million)	4,551	4,339	2,967

ROAD TRAFFIC
(motor vehicles in use)

	2007	2008	2009
Passenger cars	1,476,642	1,486,608	1,641,352
Buses and coaches	8,887	8,557	8,853
Goods vehicles	129,877	139,331	148,252
Special-purpose passenger vehicles	14,574	13,574	13,475
Special-purpose goods vehicles	25,802	24,169	23,552
Road tractors	7,263	7,387	7,376
Trailers and semi-trailers	103,859	27,686	28,597
Motorcycles and mopeds	24,897	31,803	34,497

INLAND WATERWAYS

Traffic
('000 metric tons, national and international traffic at river ports, excl. transit)

	2007	2008	2009
Goods loaded	5,975	5,691	3,115
Goods unloaded	8,540	8,353	4,007

CIVIL AVIATION
(scheduled and non-scheduled services)

	2007	2008	2009
Kilometres flown (million)	19	19	16
Passengers carried ('000)	1,312	1,350	1,054
Passenger-kilometres (million)	1,395	1,445	1,123
Cargo carried (metric tons)	4,091	3,379	2,487
Total ton-kilometres (million)	4.6	4.0	2.7

Tourism

FOREIGN TOURIST ARRIVALS
('000 at accommodation establishments)

Country of origin	2006	2007	2008
Bosnia and Herzegovina	54	63	65
Bulgaria	18	24	23
Croatia	34	39	38
Germany	28	36	37
Greece	27	24	24
Italy	28	37	40
Macedonia, former Yugoslav republic	26	28	28
Montenegro	n.a.	112	93
Slovenia	54	65	46
Total (incl. others)	**469**	**696**	**646**

Tourism receipts (Serbia and Montenegro, US $ million, incl. passenger transport): 398 in 2006; 1,011 in 2007; 1,113 in 2008.
Source: World Tourism Organization.

Communications Media
(data includes Kosovo)

	2007	2008	2009
Telephones (fixed network, '000 subscribers)	2,864.2	3,084.9	2,969.7
Mobile cellular telephones ('000 subscribers)	8,452.6	8,796.0	9,912.3

Personal computers: 1,900,000 (258.5 per 1,000 persons) in 2008 (Source: International Telecommunication Union).

2009: Telephones ('000 main lines in use) 3,105.7; Mobile cellular telephones ('000 subscribers) 9,912.3; Internet users ('000, estimate) 4,107.4; Broadband subscribers ('000) 590.6 (Source: International Telecommunication Union).

Education
(2008/09)

	Institutions	Teachers	Students
Pre-primary	2,391	21,410	183,651
Regular primary	3,529	49,290	596,396
Special primary	249	1,764	7,092
Primary education of adults	17	255	2,833
Regular secondary	495	29,490	283,412
Special secondary	44		1,628
Accessory	100	n.a.	20,484
Higher	193	9,097	235,940

Pupil-teacher ratio (primary education, UNESCO estimate): 16.2 in 2008/09 (Source: UNESCO Institute for Statistics).

Adult literacy rate (UNESCO estimates): 97.6% (males 99.1%; females 96.2%) in 2008 (Source: UNESCO Institute for Statistics).

Directory

The Government

HEAD OF STATE

President: BORIS TADIĆ (elected 27 June 2004; re-elected 3 February 2008; inaugurated 15 February 2008).

COUNCIL OF MINISTERS
(May 2011)

A coalition Government, comprising representatives of an alliance led by the Democratic Party, For a European Serbia—Boris Tadić, and an alliance of the Socialist Party of Serbia, the Party of United Pensioners of Serbia and United Serbia.

Prime Minister and Minister of Finance: MIRKO CVETKOVIĆ.
First Deputy Prime Minister and Minister of Internal Affairs: IVICA DAČIĆ.
Deputy Prime Minister: BOŽIDAR ĐELIĆ.
Deputy Prime Minister: JOVAN KRKOBABIĆ.
Deputy Prime Minister: VERICA KALANOVIĆ.
Minister of Defence: DRAGAN ŠUTANOVAC.
Minister of the Economy and Regional Development: NEBOJŠA ĆIRIĆ.
Minister of Foreign Affairs: VUK JEREMIĆ.
Minister of Justice: SNEŽANA MALOVIĆ.
Minister of Agriculture, Trade, Forestry and Water Management: DUSAN PETROVIĆ.
Minister of Infrastructure and Energy: MILUTIN MRKONJIĆ.
Minister of Labour and Social Affairs: RASIM LJAJIĆ.
Minister of the Environment, Mining and Spatial Planning: OLIVER DULIĆ.
Minister of Education and Science: ŽARKO OBRADOVIĆ.
Minister of Youth and Sports: SNEŽANA SAMARDŽIĆ-MARKOVIĆ.
Minister of Culture, Media and Information Society: PREDRAG MARKOVIĆ.
Minister of Health: ZORAN STANKOVIĆ.
Minister of Religion and the Diaspora: SRĐAN SREĆKOVIĆ.
Minister of Kosovo and Metohija: GORAN BOGDANOVIĆ.
Minister of Human and Minority Rights, Public Administration and Local Self-Government: MILAN MARKOVIĆ.
Minister without Portfolio: SULEJMAN UGLJANIN.
Secretary-General of the Government: TAMARA STOJČEVIĆ.

MINISTRIES

Office of the President: 11000 Belgrade, Andrićev venac 1; tel. (11) 3043068; fax (11) 3030868; e-mail kontakt.predsednik@predsednik.rs; internet www.predsednik.rs.

Office of the Prime Minister: 11000 Belgrade, Nemanjina 11; tel. (11) 3617719; fax (11) 3617609; e-mail predsednikvladesrbije@gov.rs; internet www.srbija.gov.rs.

Ministry of Agriculture, Trade, Forestry and Water Management: 11000 Belgrade, Nemanjina 22–26; tel. (11) 3065038; fax (11) 3616272; e-mail office@minpolj.gov.rs; internet www.minpolj.gov.rs.

Ministry of Culture, Media and Information Society: 11000 Belgrade, Vlajkovićeva 3; tel. (11) 3398172; fax (11) 3032112; e-mail kabinet@kultura.gov.rs; internet www.kultura.gov.rs.

Ministry of Defence: 11000 Belgrade, Birčaninova 5; tel. (11) 3006311; fax (11) 3006062; e-mail info@mod.gov.rs; internet www.mod.gov.rs.

Ministry of the Economy and Regional Development: 11000 Belgrade, bul. Kralja Aleksandra 15; tel. (11) 2855008; fax (11) 2855097; e-mail kabinet@merr.gov.rs; internet www.merr.gov.rs.

Ministry of Education and Science: 11000 Belgrade, Nemanjina 22–26; tel. (11) 3616489; fax (11) 3616491; e-mail kabinet@mp.gov.rs; internet www.mp.gov.rs.

Ministry of the Environment, Mining and Spatial Planning: 11000 Belgrade, Nemanjina 11; tel. (11) 3617717; fax (11) 3617722; e-mail info@ekoplan.gov.rs; internet www.ekoplan.gov.rs.

Ministry of Finance: 11000 Belgrade, Kneza Miloša 20; tel. (11) 3614007; fax (11) 3618961; e-mail kabinet@mfin.gov.rs; internet www.mfin.gov.rs.

Ministry of Foreign Affairs: 11000 Belgrade, Kneza Miloša 24–26; tel. (11) 3616333; fax (11) 3618366; e-mail mfa@mfa.rs; internet www.mfa.gov.rs.

Ministry of Health: 11000 Belgrade, Nemanjina 22–26; tel. (11) 3613734; fax (11) 2656548; internet www.zdravlje.gov.rs.

Ministry of Human and Minority Rights, Public Administration and Local Government: 11000 Belgrade, bul. Mihaila Pupina 2; tel. (11) 3112410; fax (11) 3113929; e-mail kabinet@ljudskaprava.gov.rs; internet www.ljudskaprava.gov.rs.

Ministry of Infrastructure and Energy: 11000 Belgrade, Nemanjina 22–26; tel. (11) 3619833; fax (11) 3617632; e-mail mrkonjicm@mi.gov.rs; internet www.mi.gov.rs.

Ministry of Internal Affairs: 11000 Belgrade, bul. Mihaila Pupina 2; tel. (11) 3062000; fax (11) 3617814; e-mail muprs@mup.gov.rs; internet www.mup.gov.rs.

Ministry of Justice: 11000 Belgrade, Nemanjina 22–26; tel. (11) 3620458; fax (11) 3616419; e-mail kabinet@mpravde.gov.rs; internet www.mpravde.gov.rs.

Ministry of Kosovo and Metohija: 11000 Belgrade, bul. Mihaila Pupina 2; tel. (11) 3117081; fax (11) 3617693; e-mail kabinet@kim.gov.rs; internet www.kim.gov.rs.

Ministry of Labour and Social Affairs: 11000 Belgrade, bul. Nemanjina 22–24; tel. (11) 3617498; fax (11) 3114650; e-mail ministar@minrzs.gov.rs; internet www.minrzs.gov.rs.

Ministry of Religion and the Diaspora: 11000 Belgrade, Vase Čarapića 20; tel. (11) 3202900; fax (11) 2636815; e-mail info@mzd.gov.rs; internet www.mzd.gov.rs.

Ministry of Youth and Sports: 11070 Belgrade, bul. Mihaila Pupina 2; tel. (11) 3130912; fax (11) 3130915; e-mail tamara.mg@mos.gov.rs; internet www.mos.gov.rs.

SERBIA

President

Presidential Election, First Ballot, 20 January 2008

Candidate	Votes	% of votes
Tomislav Nikolić (Serbian Radical Party)	1,646,172	39.99
Boris Tadić (Democratic Party)	1,457,030	35.39
Velimir Ilić (New Serbia)	305,828	7.43
Milutin Mrkonjić (Socialist Party of Serbia)	245,889	5.97
Čedomir Jovanović (Liberal Democratic Party)	219,689	5.34
Others	163,765	3.69
Total*	4,116,844	100.00

*Including invalid votes.

Second Ballot, 3 February 2008

Candidate	Votes	% of votes
Boris Tadić (Democratic Party)	2,304,467	50.31
Tomislav Nikolić (Serbian Radical Party)	2,197,155	47.97
Total*	4,580,428	100.00

*Including invalid votes.

Legislature

Narodna skupština Republike Srbije (National Assembly of the Republic of Serbia)

11000 Belgrade, Kralja Milana 14; tel. (11) 3222001; e-mail webmaster@parlament.gov.rs; internet www.parlament.gov.rs.
President: Prof. SLAVICA ĐUKIĆ-DEJANOVIĆ.
Election, 11 May 2008

Parties	% of votes	Seats
For a European Serbia—Boris Tadić*	38.44	102
Serbian Radical Party	29.36	78
Democratic Party of Serbia-New Serbia	11.59	30
Socialist Party of Serbia-Party of United Pensioners of Serbia-United Serbia	7.60	20
Liberal Democratic Party	5.24	13
Hungarian Coalition—Ištvan Pásztor†	1.83	4
Bosniak List for a European Sandžak—Dr Sulejman Ugljanin‡	0.92	2
Albanian Coalition from the Preševo Valley	0.39	1
Strength of Serbia Movement	0.54	—
Others	1.86	—
Total§	100.00	250

* Coalition, principally comprising the Democratic Party, G17 Plus, the Serbian Renewal Movement, the League of Social-Democrats of Vojvodina and the Sandžak Democratic Party.
† Coalition of the Alliance of Vojvodina Hungarians, the Democratic Fellowship of Vojvodina Hungarians and the Democratic Party of Vojvodina Hungarians.
‡ Coalition of five parties from the Sandžak region.
§ Including invalid votes.

Election Commission

Electoral Commission of the Republic of Serbia: 11000 Belgrade, Kralja Milana 14; tel. (11) 3222001; fax (11) 3617839; e-mail rik@parlament.gov.rs; internet www.rik.parlament.gov.rs; Chair. PREDRAG GRGIĆ.

Political Organizations

A total of 342 political parties were registered in 2008. New requirements took effect from early 2010, in accordance with which political parties needed 10,000 members (or 1,000 members in the case of those representing minority ethnic groups) to obtain registration. Existing parties were required to re-register. At late April 2011 there were 77 registered parties in the country, 43 of them representing minority ethnic groups.

Alliance of Vojvodina Hungarians (Vajdasági Magyar Szövetség/ Savez Vojvođanskih Mađara): 24000 Subotica, Age Mamužića 11/I; tel. and fax (24) 553801; e-mail office@vmsz.org.rs; internet www.vmsz.org.rs; f. 1994; supports autonomous status for Vojvodina; contested legislative elections in May 2008 as part of the Hungarian Coalition—Ištvan Pásztor; Chair. IŠTVAN PÁSZTOR.

Democratic Party (DP) (Demokratska Stranka—DS): 11000 Belgrade, Krunska 69; tel. (11) 3443003; fax (11) 2444864; e-mail redakcija@ds.org.rs; internet www.ds.org.rs; f. 1990; led For a European Serbia—Boris Tadić coalition in legislative elections in May 2008; Pres. BORIS TADIĆ.

Democratic Party of Serbia (DPS) (Demokratska stranka Srbije—DSS): 11000 Belgrade, Pariska 13; tel. (11) 3204719; fax (11) 3204743; e-mail info@dss.rs; internet www.dss.rs; f. 1992 following split from Democratic Party; Leader Dr VOJISLAV KOŠTUNICA.

G17 Plus: 11000 Belgrade, trg Republike 5; tel. (11) 3210355; fax (11) 3284054; e-mail office@g17plus.rs; internet www.g17plus.rs; f. 2003; contested legislative elections in May 2008 as part of the For a European Serbia—Boris Tadić coalition; Pres. MLAĐAN DINKIĆ.

League of Social-Democrats of Vojvodina (LSV) (Liga Socijaldemokrata Vojvodine): 21000 Novi Sad, trg Mladenaca 10; tel. (21) 529139; fax (21) 420628; e-mail infolsv@eunet.rs; internet www.lsv.org.rs; Pres. NENAD ČANAK.

Liberal Democratic Party (LDP) (Liberalno-demokratska Stranka—LDS): 11000 Belgrade, Simina 41; tel. (11) 3208300; fax (11) 3208301; e-mail predsednik@ldp.rs; internet www.ldp.rs; f. 2005 by fmr mems of the Democratic Party; Pres. ČEDOMIR JOVANOVIĆ.

New Serbia (Nova Srbija): 11000 Belgrade, Obilićev venac 4/1; tel. (11) 3284766; fax (11) 2631748; e-mail nscentrala@gmail.com; internet www.nova-srbija.org; Pres. VELIMIR ILIĆ.

Party of United Pensioners of Serbia (PUPS) (Partija Ujedinjenih Penzionera Srbije): 7800 Banja Luka, Grčka 19; tel. and fax (51) 213198; e-mail office@pups.org.rs; internet www.pups.org.rs; Pres. JOVAN KRKOBABIĆ.

Roma Party (Romska Partija): represents Roma ethnic minority; Leader ŠAJN SRĐAN.

Roma Union of Serbia (Unija Roma Srbije): 11000 Belgrade, Sarajevska 11; tel. and fax (11) 2681693; e-mail unijaromasrbije@hotmail.com; internet www.unijaromasrbije.org.rs; f. 2004; represents Roma ethnic minority; Pres. Dr RAJKO ĐURIĆ.

Serbian Radical Party (SRP) (Srpska Radikalna Stranka—SRS): 11080 Belgrade, Zemun, Magistratski trg 3; tel. (11) 3164621; e-mail info@srpskaradikalnastranka.rs; internet www.srpskaradikalnastranka.org.rs; f. 1991; extreme nationalist; advocates a 'Greater Serbian' state of territories inhabited by Serbs within and outside Serbia; leader Dr Vojislav Šešelj in detention at the International Criminal Tribunal for the former Yugoslavia; Leader Dr VOJISLAV ŠEŠELJ; Vice-Pres. DRAGAN TODOROVIĆ.

Serbian Renewal Movement (SRM) (Srpski pokret obnove—SPO): 11000 Belgrade, Kneza Mihailova 48; tel. (11) 3283620; fax (11) 2628170; e-mail vuk@spo.rs; internet www.spo.rs; f. 1990; nationalist; Pres. VUK DRAŠKOVIĆ.

Social Democratic Party (SDP) (Socijaldemokratska Partija): 11000 Belgrade, Ruzveltova 45; tel. (11) 3290820; fax (11) 3294507; internet www.sdp.org.rs; f. 1997; Pres. Dr RASIM LJAJIĆ.

Social Democratic Union (Socijaldemokratska Unija): 11000 Belgrade, Kralja Milana 34/1; tel. (11) 3613649; fax (11) 3620862; e-mail info@sdu.org.rs; internet www.sdu.org.rs; f. 1996; Pres. ŽARKO KORAĆ.

Socialist Party of Serbia (SPS) (Socijalistička partija Srbije): 11000 Belgrade, Studentski trg 15; tel. (11) 3282713; fax (11) 2627170; e-mail glavniodbor@sps.org.rs; internet www.sps.org.rs; f. 1990 by merger of League of Communists of Serbia and Socialist Alliance of Working People of Serbia; Pres. IVICA DAČIĆ.

Strength of Serbia Movement (Pokret snaga Srbije): 11040 Belgrade, bul. Kneza Aleksandra Karađorđevića 49; tel. (11) 2651978; fax (11) 2651976; e-mail pokret@snagasrbije.com; internet www.snagasrbije.com; f. 2004; Leader BOGOLJUB KARIĆ.

United Serbia: 35000 Jagodina, Lole Ribara br. 14; tel. (81) 35233104; fax (81) 35852443; e-mail info@jedinstvenasrbija.org.rs; internet www.jedinstvenasrbija.org.rs; Pres. DRAGAN MARKOVIĆ.

Diplomatic Representation

EMBASSIES IN SERBIA

Albania: 11000 Belgrade, bul. Kneza Aleksandra Karađorđevića 25A; tel. (11) 3066642; fax (11) 2665439; e-mail embassy.belgrade@mfa.gov.al; Ambassador SHPËTIM ÇAUSHI.

Algeria: 11000 Belgrade, Maglajska 26 B; tel. (11) 3671211; fax (11) 2668200; e-mail ambalgerie-serbie@eunet.rs; internet www.ambalgserbia.rs; Ambassador ABDELKADER MESDOUA.

SERBIA

Angola: 11000 Belgrade, Vase Pelagića 32; tel. (11) 3690241; fax (11) 3690191; e-mail ambasada.angole@sbb.co.rs; internet www.angolaembassy.org.rs; Ambassador Toko Diakenga Serão.

Argentina: 11000 Belgrade, Kneza Mihajlova 24/I; tel. (11) 2623569; fax (11) 2622630; e-mail argentinabg@nadlanu.com; Ambassador Mario Eduardo Bossi de Ezcurra.

Australia: 11070 Novi Belgrade, Vladimira Popovića 38–40, 8th floor; tel. (11) 3303400; fax (11) 3303409; e-mail belgrade.embassy@dfat.gov.au; internet www.serbia.embassy.gov.au; Ambassador Dr Helena Studdert.

Austria: 11000 Belgrade, Kneza Sime Markovića 2; tel. (11) 3336500; fax (11) 2635606; e-mail belgrade-ob@bmeia.gv.at; internet www.aussenministerium.at/belgrad; Ambassador Clemens Koja.

Belarus: 11000 Belgrade, Deligradska 13; tel. (11) 3616938; fax (11) 3616836; e-mail sam@belembassy.org; internet www.serbia.belembassy.org; Chargé d'affaires a.i. Siarhei Chichuk.

Belgium: 11000 Belgrade, Krunska 18; tel. (11) 3230018; fax (11) 3244394; e-mail belgrade@diplobel.fed.be; Ambassador Alain Kundycki.

Bosnia and Herzegovina: 11000 Belgrade, Krunska 9; tel. (11) 3241170; fax (11) 3241057; e-mail bihambasada@sbb.rs; Ambassador Boriša Arnaut.

Brazil: 11000 Belgrade, Krunska 14; tel. (11) 3239781; fax (11) 3230653; e-mail brasbelg@eunet.rs; internet www.ambasadabrazila.org.rs; Ambassador Alexandre Addor-Neto.

Bulgaria: 11000 Belgrade, Birčaninova 26; tel. (11) 3613980; fax 3611136; internet wwww.mfa.bg/bg/105; Ambassador Georgi Dimitrov.

Canada: 11000 Belgrade, Kneza Miloša 75; tel. (11) 3063000; fax (11) 3063042; e-mail bgrad@international.gc.ca; internet www.canadainternational.gc.ca/serbia-serbie; Ambassador John Arthur Morrison.

China, People's Republic: 11000 Belgrade, Augusta Cesarca 2v; tel. (11) 3695057; fax (11) 3066001; e-mail chinaemb_yu@mail.mfa.gov.cn; internet rs.chineseembassy.org; Ambassador Wei Jinghua.

Congo, Democratic Republic: 11000 Belgrade, Moravska 5; tel. and fax (11) 3446431; e-mail ambardcbelgrade@yahoo.fr; Ambassador Dr Paul-Emile Tshinga Ahuka.

Croatia: 11000 Belgrade, Kneza Miloša 62; tel. (11) 3610535; fax (11) 3610032; e-mail crobg@mvpei.hr; internet rs.mvp.hr; Ambassador Željko Kuprešak.

Cuba: 11000 Belgrade, Vukovarska 3; tel. (11) 3692441; fax (11) 3692442; e-mail ambasada@ambasadakube.org.rs; internet www.ambasadakube.org.rs; Ambassador Mercedes Martínez Valdés.

Cyprus: 11000 Belgrade, Generala Save Grujića 18; tel. (11) 3620002; fax (11) 3621122; e-mail belgradeembassy@mfa.gov.cy; Ambassador Charalambos Hadjisawas.

Czech Republic: 125108 Belgrade, bul. Kralja Aleksandra 22; tel. (11) 3336200; fax (11) 3236448; e-mail belgrade@embassy.mzv.cz; internet www.mzv.cz/belgrade; Ambassador Hana Hubáčková.

Denmark: 11040 Belgrade, Neznanog Junaka 9A; tel. (11) 3679500; fax (11) 3679502; e-mail begamb@um.dk; internet www.ambbeograd.um.dk; Ambassador Mette Kjuel Nielsen.

Egypt: 11000 Belgrade, Andre Nikolića 12; tel. (11) 2650585; fax (11) 2652036; e-mail embassy.belgrade@mfa.gov.eg; Ambassador Aly Galal Bassiouny.

Finland: 11001 Belgrade, Birčaninova 29, POB 926; tel. (11) 3065400; fax (11) 3065375; e-mail sanomat.belgrade@formin.fi; internet www.finska.co.rs; Ambassador Kari Johannes Veijalainen.

France: 11000 Belgrade, Pariska 11, POB 283; tel. (11) 3023500; fax (11) 3023510; internet www.ambafrance-srb.org; Ambassador François-Xavier Deniau.

Germany: 11000 Belgrade, Kneza Miloša 74–76; tel. (11) 3064300; fax (11) 3064303; e-mail germany@sbb.rs; internet www.belgrad.diplo.de; Ambassador Wolfram Josef Maas.

Ghana: 11000 Belgrade, Đorđa Vajferta 50; tel. (11) 3440856; fax (11) 3440071; e-mail ghana@ghanaemb.rs; internet www.ghanaembelgrade.com; Ambassador Samuel Valis-Akyianu.

Greece: 11000 Belgrade, Francuska 33; tel. (11) 3226523; fax (11) 3344746; e-mail office@greekemb.rs; internet www.mfa.gr/belgrade; Ambassador Dimosthenis Stoidis.

Guinea: 11000 Belgrade, Ohridska 4; tel. (11) 2451391; fax (11) 3444870; Ambassador El Hadj Muhammad Issiaga Kourouma.

Holy See: 11000 Belgrade, Svetog Save 24; tel. (11) 3085356; fax (11) 3085216; e-mail nunbel@an.org.rs; Apostolic Nuncio Most Rev. Orlando Antonini.

Hungary: 11000 Belgrade, Krunska 72; tel. (11) 2440472; fax (11) 3441876; e-mail mission.blg@kum.hu; internet www.mfa.gov.hu/emb/belgrade; Ambassador Nikowitz Oszkár.

India: 11040 Belgrade, Ljutice Bogdana 8; tel. (11) 2661029; fax (11) 3674209; e-mail ssindemb@eunet.rs; internet www.embassyofindiabelgrade.org; Ambassador Nengcha Lhouvum Mukhopadhaya.

Indonesia: 11040 Belgrade, bul. Kneza Aleksandra Karađorđevića 18; tel. (11) 3674062; fax (11) 3672984; e-mail kombeojo@eunet.yu; internet www.indonesia-bgd.org; Ambassador Semuel Samson.

Iran: 11000 Belgrade, Ljutice Bogdana 40; tel. (11) 3674360; fax (11) 3674363; e-mail iran-emb@bitsyu.net; Ambassador Abolqasem Dalafi.

Iraq: 11000 Belgrade, Neznanog Junaka 27A; tel. (11) 2662681; fax (11) 2668068; e-mail bgremb@iraqmofamail.net; Ambassador Falah Abdul Hassan Abdul Sada.

Israel: 11000 Belgrade, bul. Kneza Aleksandra Karađorđevića 47; tel. (11) 3643500; fax (11) 3670304; e-mail info@belgrade.mfa.gov.il; internet belgrade.mfa.gov.il; Ambassador Arthur Koll.

Italy: 11000 Belgrade, ul. Birčaninova 11; tel. (11) 3066100; fax (11) 3249413; e-mail segreteria.belgrado@esteri.it; internet www.ambbelgrado.esteri.it; Ambassador Armando Varricchio.

Japan: 11070 Novi Belgrade, Vladimira Popovića 6; tel. (11) 3012800; fax (11) 3118258; internet www.yu.emb-japan.go.jp; Ambassador Toshio Tsunozaki.

Korea, Republic: 11070 Belgrade, Užička 32; tel. (11) 3674225; fax (11) 3674229; e-mail mail@koreanemb.org.rs; Ambassador Dr Kim Jong-Hee.

Lebanon: 11000 Belgrade, Diplomatska kolonija 5; tel. (11) 3675153; fax (11) 3675156; e-mail ambaleb@sbb.co.rs; Chargé d'affaires a.i. Ali al-Ghazzawi.

Libya: 11000 Belgrade, Sime Lozanića 8; tel. (11) 2663445; fax (11) 3670805; e-mail libyaamb@eunet.rs; Chargé d'affaires a.i. Giuma A. S. Alghali.

Macedonia, former Yugoslav republic: 11000 Belgrade, Gospodar Jevremova 34; tel. (11) 3284924; fax (11) 3285076; e-mail belgrade@mfa.gov.mk; Ambassador Ljubiša Georgievski.

Malaysia: 11040 Belgrade, Krajiška 2; tel. (11) 2662736; fax (11) 3679080; e-mail malbelgrade@sbb.co.rs; internet www.kln.gov.my/web/srb_belgrade; Chargé d'affaires a.i. Amizal Fadzli Bin Rajali.

Mexico: 11040 Belgrade, Ljutice Bogdana 5; tel. (11) 3674170; fax (11) 3675013; Ambassador Mercedes Felicitas Ruiz Zapata.

Montenegro: Belgrade, Užička 1; tel. (11) 2662300; fax (11) 3699546; e-mail emb.belgrade@mfa.gov.me; Ambassador Igor Jovović.

Morocco: 11000 Belgrade, Sanje Živanović 4; tel. (11) 3691866; fax (11) 3690499; Chargé d'affaires a.i. Muhammad Bouasria.

Myanmar: 11000 Belgrade, Kneza Miloša 72; tel. (11) 3617165; fax (11) 3614968; e-mail myanbel@sezampro.rs; Ambassador Soe Nwe.

Netherlands: 11000 Belgrade, Simina 29; tel. (11) 2023900; fax (11) 2023999; e-mail bel@minbuza.nl; internet www.nlembassy.rs; Ambassador Laurent Stokvis.

Norway: 11000 Belgrade, Užička 43; tel. (11) 3670404; fax (11) 3690158; e-mail emb.belgrade@mfa.no; internet www.norveska.org.rs; Ambassador Nils Ragnar Kamsvåg.

Pakistan: 11000 Belgrade, bul. Kneza Aleksandra Karađorđevića 62; tel. (11) 2661676; fax (11) 2661667; Ambassador Muhammad Nawaz Chaudhry.

Poland: 11000 Belgrade, Kneza Miloša 38; tel. (11) 2065318; fax (11) 3617576; e-mail belgrad.amb.sekretariat@msz.gov.pl; internet www.belgrad.polemb.net; Ambassador Andrzej Edward Jasionowski.

Portugal: 11040 Belgrade, Vladimira Gaćinovića 4; tel. (11) 2662894; fax (11) 2662892; Ambassador Caetano Luís Pequito de Almeida Sampaio.

Romania: 11000 Belgrade, Užička 10; tel. (11) 3675772; fax (11) 3675771; e-mail embassy@romania.org.rs; internet www.belgrad.mae.ro; Ambassador Ion Macovei.

Russia: 11000 Belgrade, ul. Deligradska 32; tel. (11) 3611090; fax (11) 3611900; e-mail ambarusk@nadlanu.com; internet www.ambasadarusije.org.rs; Ambassador Aleksandr V. Konuzin.

San Marino: 11000 Belgrade, Makedonska 24/25; tel. (11) 3223509; fax (11) 3374144; Ambassador Ubaldo Livolsi.

Slovakia: 11070 Belgrade, bul. Umetnosti 18; tel. (11) 2223800; fax (11) 2223820; e-mail embassy@belehrad.mfa.sk; internet www.belehrad.mfa.sk; Ambassador Ján Varšo.

Slovenia: 11000 Belgrade, Pariska 15; tel. (11) 3038477; fax (11) 3288657; e-mail vbg@gov.si; internet beograd.veleposlanistvo.si; Ambassador Franci But.

Spain: 11000 Belgrade, Prote Mateje 45; tel. (11) 3440231; fax (11) 3444203; e-mail emb.belgrado@mae.es; internet www.maec.es/subwebs/embajadas/belgrado; Ambassador Iñigo de Palacio España.

SERBIA

Sweden: 11040 Belgrade, Ledi Pedzet 2; tel. (11) 2069200; fax (11) 2069250; e-mail ambassaden.belgrad@foreign.ministry.se; internet www.swedenabroad.se/belgrad; Ambassador CHRISTER ASP.

Switzerland: 11000 Belgrade, Birčaninova 27; tel. (11) 3065820; fax (11) 2657253; e-mail bel.vertretung@eda.admin.ch; internet www.eda.admin.ch/belgrade; Ambassador ERWIN HELMUT HOFER.

Syria: 11000 Belgrade, Aleksandra Stamboliskog 13; tel. (11) 2666124; fax (11) 2660221; Ambassador Dr MAJED SHADOUD.

Tunisia: 11000 Belgrade, Vase Pelagića 19; tel. (11) 3691961; fax (11) 2651848; e-mail at.belgrade@sbb.rs; Chargé d'affaires a.i. RABII ZENATI.

Turkey: 11000 Belgrade, Krunska 1; tel. (11) 3232400; fax (11) 3332433; e-mail turem@eunet.rs; internet belgrade.emb.mfa.gov.tr; Ambassador ALI RIZA ÇOLAK.

Ukraine: 11040 Belgrade, ul. Paje Adamova 4; tel. (11) 3672411; fax (11) 3672413; e-mail emb_sm@mfa.gov.ua; internet www.mfa.gov.ua/serbia; Ambassador VIKTOR NEDOPAS.

United Kingdom: 11000 Belgrade, Resavska 46; tel. (11) 3060900; fax (11) 2659651; e-mail belgrade.ppd@fco.gov.uk; internet ukinserbia.fco.gov.uk; Ambassador MICHAEL DAVENPORT.

USA: 11000 Belgrade, Kneza Miloša 50; tel. (11) 3619344; fax (11) 3615489; internet serbia.usembassy.gov; Ambassador MARY BURCE WARLICK.

Judicial System

The judicial system in the Republic of Serbia comprises the courts of regular competence (138 municipal courts, 30 district courts and the Supreme Court of Serbia) and courts of special competence (17 commercial courts and the High Commercial Court). A new Constitution, which entered into effect on 8 November 2006, provided for an 11-member independent High Judicial Council, which was to guarantee the independence and autonomy of courts and judges. The legislature was to elect judges on the proposal of the High Judicial Council, while the High Judicial Council was to elect permanent judges. The Constitutional Court, comprising 15 judges, was to protect constitutionality and legality, as well as human and minority rights and freedoms.

Constitutional Court (Ustavni Sud Srbije): 11000 Belgrade, Nemanjina 26; tel. (11) 3616372; fax (11) 2658970; e-mail informacija@ustavni.sud.rs; internet www.ustavni.sud.rs; f. 1963; Pres. DRAGISA B. SLIJEPČEVIĆ.

Supreme Court (Vrhovni Sud Srbije): 11000 Belgrade, Resavska 42; tel. (11) 3634207; fax (11) 3619376; e-mail vss@vrh.sud.rs; internet www.vrh.sud.rs; Pres. NATA MESAROVIĆ.

Office of the Public Prosecutor of Serbia: 11000 Belgrade, Nemanjina 22-26; tel. (11) 3613702; fax (11) 3616305; e-mail kabinetrjt@rjt.gov.rs; internet www.rjt.gov.rs; Public Prosecutor ZAGORKA DOLOVAC.

Religion

Most of the inhabitants of Serbia are, at least nominally, Christian, but there is a significant Muslim minority. The main Christian denomination is Eastern Orthodox, but there is a strong Roman Catholic presence. There are also small minorities of Old Catholics, Protestants and Jews.

CHRISTIANITY

The Eastern Orthodox Church

Serbian Orthodox Church (Srpska Pravoslavna Crkva): 11001 Belgrade, Kralja Petra 5, POB 182; tel. (11) 3025112; e-mail info@spc.rs; internet www.spc.rs; 11m. adherents; Patriarch of Serbia, Archbishop of Peć and Metropolitan of Belgrade-Karlovci IRINEJ.

The Roman Catholic Church

Serbia comprises one archdiocese and three dioceses, including one, Srijem, responsible to the Croatian hierarchy. There is also an apostolic exarchate of Serbia and Montenegro for Catholics of the Byzantine rite. There were an estimated 446,028 adherents of the Latin Rite in Serbia, representing about 5.5% of the total population of Serbia. There were additionally an estimated 22,513 adherents of the Byzantine Rite in Serbia and Montenegro.

International Bishops' Conference of SS Cyril and Methodius: 11000 Belgrade, Višegradska 23; tel. (11) 3032246; fax (11) 3032248; f. 2006; membership comprises Bishops of Montenegro and Serbia; Pres. Most Rev. STANISLAV HOČEVAR (Archbishop of Belgrade).

Archbishop of Belgrade: Most Rev. STANISLAV HOČEVAR, 11000 Belgrade, Svetozara Markovića 20; tel. (11) 3032246; fax (11) 3032248; e-mail nadbiskupija@kc.org.rs; internet www.kc.org.rs.

Apostolic Exarch to Serbia and Montenegro for Catholics of the Byzantine Rite: ĐURA DŽUDŽAR (Titular Archbishop of Acrasso), 21000 Novi Sad, D. Magaraševića 18; tel. (21) 6371609; fax (21) 6371613; 22,653 adherents (2006).

Protestant Churches

Christian Reformed Church: 24323 Feketić, Bratsva 26; tel. and fax (24) 738070; f. 1919; 22,000 mems; Bishop ISTVAN CSETE-SZEMESI.

Evangelical Christian Church of the Augsburg (Lutheran) Confession in Serbia-Vojvodina: 24000 Subotica, Braće Radića 17; tel. and fax (24) 527778; e-mail lutheran@stcable.net; internet www.lutheran.org.rs; Superintendent DOLINSZKY ÁRPÁD.

Slovak Evangelical Church of the Augsburg (Lutheran) Confession: 21000 Novi Sad, Karadžićeva 2; tel. (21) 6611882; 50,000 mems (2002); Bishop Dr SAMUEL VRBOVSKY.

Union of Baptist Churches in Serbia: 11000 Belgrade, Slobodanke D. Savić 33; tel. and fax (11) 410964; f. 1992; Gen. Sec. Rev. AVRAM DEGA.

ISLAM

There are ethnic Slav Muslims (Bosniaks) in the part of Sandžak located in south-west Serbia, in particular in and around the town of Novi Pazar. Most Muslims in the country are Sunni.

Islamic Community of Serbia: Belgrade, G. Jevremova 11; tel. (11) 2622428; e-mail reis@rijaset.rs; internet www.rijaset.rs; Reis-ul-ulema ADEM EF. ZILKIĆ.

Islamic Community of Vojvodina: 21000 Novi Sad, Futoška 61; tel. and fax (21) 6619444; internet www.islamvojvodina.com; Chair. ZIJA ZEKIR.

JUDAISM

Federation of Jewish Communities in Serbia: 11000 Belgrade, Kralja Petra 71 A/III, POB 512; tel. (11) 2624359; fax (11) 2621837; e-mail office@savezscg.net; f. 1919, revived 1944; Pres. ALEKSANDAR NEĆAK.

The Press

PRINCIPAL DAILIES

Blic: 11000 Belgrade, Žorža Klemansoa 19; tel. (11) 3334559; fax (11) 3334556; e-mail redakcija@blic.rs; internet www.blic.rs; f. 1996; Editor-in-Chief VESLIN SIMONOVIĆ; circ. 230,000.

Borba: 11000 Belgrade, trg Nikole Pašića 7; tel. (11) 3398137; e-mail redakcija@borba.rs; internet www.borba.rs; f. 1922; morning; Editor-in-Chief OLIVERA ZEKIĆ.

Dnevnik (Daily News): 21000 Novi Sad, bul. Oslobođenja 81; tel. (21) 4806802; fax (21) 423761; e-mail redakcija@dnevnik.rs; internet www.dnevnik.rs; f. 1942 as *Slobodna Vojvodina* (Free Vojvodina); morning; Editor-in-Chief ALEKSANDAR DJIVULJSKIJ.

Glas Javnosti (Voice of the Public): 11000 Belgrade, Vlajkovićeva 8; tel. (11) 3240551; fax (11) 3240550; e-mail redakcija@glas-javnosti.rs; internet www.glas-javnosti.rs; f. 1874; Editor SONJA LAKIĆ.

Narodne Novine (The People's News): 18000 Niš, Gen. Bože Jankovića 9; tel. (18) 527595; fax (18) 527603; e-mail nn.edit@pogled.net; internet www.narodne.com; morning; Editor-in-Chief TIMOŠENKO MILOSAVLJEVIĆ.

Politika: 11000 Belgrade, Makedonska 29; tel. (11) 3301682; fax (11) 3373419; e-mail redakcija@politika.rs; internet www.politika.rs; f. 1904; Dir-Gen. MIRA GLISIĆ-SIMIĆ; Editor-in-Chief DRAGAN BUJOŠEVIĆ; circ. 110,000.

Pregled: 11030 Belgrade, Jasenova 5; tel. (11) 2395089; fax (11) 2519106; e-mail pregled@pregled.com; internet www.pregled.com; f. 1950; business and economics; Dir and Chief Editor ALEKSANDAR JOVANOVIĆ.

Večernje novosti (Evening News): 11000 Belgrade, trg Nikole Pašića 7; tel. (11) 3028000; e-mail redakcija@novosti.rs; internet www.novosti.rs; f. 1953; Gen. Dir and Editor-in-Chief MANOJLO MANJO VUKOTIĆ; circ. 270,000.

PERIODICALS

Ekonomist: Belgrade, Kosovska 1/IV; tel. (11) 3284034; internet www.emportal.rs; f. 1948; quarterly; journal of the Yugoslav Association of Economists; Editor Dr HASAN HADŽIOMEROVIĆ.

Ekonomska Politika (Economic Policy): 11000 Belgrade, trg Nikole Pašića 7; tel. (11) 3398298; fax (11) 3398300; f. 1952; weekly; Dir ČEDOMIR ŠOŠKIĆ; Editor-in-Chief SLAVKA KOVAČ.

SERBIA

Ilustrovana Politika: 11000 Belgrade, Makedonska 35; tel. (11) 3301442; fax (11) 3373346; e-mail ilustrovana@politika-ad.com; internet www.ilustrovana.com; f. 1958; weekly illustrated review; Gen. Dir MILORAD GUŠAVAC; Editor-in-Chief SRĐJAN JAKANOVIĆ; circ. 90,000.

Jisa Info: 11000 Belgrade, Zmaj Jovina 4; tel. (11) 2620374; fax (11) 2626576; e-mail jisa@jisa.rs; internet www.jisa.rs; f. 1993; publ. by Jisa (Jedinstveni informatički savez Srbije—Union of ICT Societies of Serbia); computing, technology; Pres. ĐORĐE DUKIĆ.

Letopis Matice Srpske: 21000 Novi Sad, Matice srpske 1; tel. (21) 6613864; fax (21) 528901; e-mail letopis@maticasrpska.org.rs; internet www.maticasrpska.org.rs/pages/izdanja/letopis.htm; f. 1824; monthly; literary review; Editor-in-Chief IVAN NEGRISORAC.

Međunarodni Problemi/International Problems: 11000 Belgrade, Institute of International Politics and Economics, Makedonska 25; tel. (11) 3373633; fax (11) 3373835; e-mail iipe@diplomacy.bg.ac.rs; internet www.diplomacy.bg.ac.rs/mpro.htm; f. 1949; quarterly; in Serbian and English; Editor BRANA MARKOVIĆ; circ. 1,000.

Mikro/PC World: 11030 Belgrade, Požeška 81A; tel. (11) 3055010; fax (11) 3058034; internet www.mikro.rs; f. 1997; 11 a year; computing; Editorial Dir ALEKSANDAR SPASIĆ; circ. 23,000 (2007).

Nezavisna Svetlost: 34000 Kragujevac, Branka Radičevića 9; tel. (34) 336176; fax (34) 335218; e-mail urednik@svetlost.rs; internet www.svetlost.rs; f. 1995; weekly news; Dir and Editor-in-Chief RANKO MILOSAVLJEVIĆ.

NIN—Nedeljne informativne novine (Weekly Informative News): 11000 Belgrade, Zorza Klemansoa 19; tel. (11) 3373171; fax (11) 3334658; e-mail redakcija@nin.co.rs; internet www.nin.co.rs; f. 1935; politics, economics, culture; Dir JELENA DRAKULIĆ-PETROVIĆ; Editor-in-Chief NEBOJŠA SPASIĆ; circ. 35,000.

Odbrana (Defence): 11002 Belgrade, Brace Jugovića 19; tel. (11) 3201808; fax (11) 3241363; e-mail redakcija@odbrana.mod.gov.rs; internet www.odbrana.mod.gov.rs; f. 2005 to replace *Vojska* (Soldier); two a month; publ. by Ministry of Defence; Editor-in-Chief RADENKO MUTAVDŽIĆ.

Ošišani Jež (Trimmed Hedgehog): 11000 Belgrade, Resavska 28; tel. (11) 3232211; fax (11) 3232423; f. 1935 as *Jež* (Hedgehog); fortnightly; satirical; Editor RADIVOJE BOJČIĆ; circ. 50,000.

Politikin Zabavnik: 11001 Belgrade, Cetinska 1; tel. (11) 3301452; fax (11) 3373319; e-mail politikin.zabavnik@politika-ad.com; internet www.politikin-zabavnik.rs; f. 1939; weekly; comic; Editor-in-Chief ZEFIRINO GRASI; circ. 41,000.

Pravoslavlje (Orthodoxy): 11000 Belgrade, Kralja Petra 5; tel. (11) 3025116; fax (11) 3282588; e-mail pravoslavljespc@gmail.com; internet www.pravoslavlje.rs; f. 1967; fortnightly; Orthodox Christian; Editor-in-Chief ALEKSANDAR ĐAKOVAĆ.

Pregled Republika Srbija/Survey—Republic of Serbia: 11000 Belgrade, Dečanska 8, POB 677; tel. (11) 3233610; fax (11) 3240291; e-mail info@pregled-rs.rs; internet www.pregled-rs.rs; f. 1957 as *Jugoslovenski pregled/Yugoslav Survey*, renamed *Pregled SCG/Survey Serbia & Montenegro* in 2003, present name adopted 2006; quarterly; general reference publication of basic documentary information about Serbia; Serbian and English edns; Editor-in-Chief ILE KOVAČEVIĆ.

Viva: 11000 Belgrade, Cetinjska 1v; tel. (11) 3301501; fax (11) 3373099; e-mail viva@politika.rs; internet www.vivamagazin.info; monthly; health; Editor-in-Chief Dr GRADIMIR JOKSIMOVIĆ; circ. 25,000.

Vreme (Time): 11000 Belgrade, Mišarska 12–14; tel. (11) 3234774; fax (11) 3238662; e-mail redakcija@vreme.com; internet www.vreme.com; weekly; Editor-in-Chief DRAGOLJUB ŽARKOVIĆ.

NEWS AGENCIES

Beta Press News Agency: 11000 Belgrade, Kraljana Milana 4; tel. (11) 3602400; fax (11) 2642551; e-mail plasman@beta.co.rs; internet www.beta.co.rs; f. 1992; regional independent news service; Dir LJUBICA MARKOVIĆ; Editor-in-Chief IVAN CVEJIĆ.

Tanjug News Agency (Novinska Agencija Tanjug): 11001 Belgrade, Obilićev Venac 2, POB 439; tel. (11) 3281608; fax (11) 3282766; e-mail direkcija@tanjug.rs; internet www.tanjug.rs; f. 1943; press and information agency; in Serbian, English, French and Spanish; Dir BRANKA ĐUKIĆ.

PRESS ASSOCIATIONS

Association of Journalists of Serbia (Udruženje novinara Srbije): 11000 Belgrade, Resavska 28/I; tel. (11) 3236337; fax (11) 3236493; e-mail ljiljana.smajlovic@uns.rs; internet www.uns.org.rs; f. 1881; Pres. LJILJANA SMAJLOVIĆ; Gen. Sec. NINO BRAJOVIĆ.

Independent Association of Journalists of Serbia (Nezavisno udruženje novinara Srbije): 11000 Belgrade, Resavska 28/II; tel. (11) 3343255; fax (11) 3343136; e-mail sekretar@nuns.rs; internet www.nuns.rs; Pres. VUKAŠIN OBRADOVIĆ.

Publishers

Alfa-Narodna (Alfa-People's Books) Publishing House: 11000 Belgrade, Višegradska 1A; tel. and fax (11) 3660349; internet www.narodnaknjigaskola.com; f. 1955; fiction, non-fiction, children's books and dictionaries; Gen. Man. MILIČKO MIJOVIĆ.

BIGZ (Beogradski izdavačko-grafički zavod) Publishing a.d. (Belgrade Publishing and Graphics Co): 11000 Belgrade, bul. Vojvode Mišića 17/III; tel. (11) 3691259; fax (11) 3690519; e-mail bigz@bigz-publishing.co.rs; internet www.bigz-publishing.co.rs; f. 1831; privately owned; literature and criticism, children's books, pocket books, popular science, philosophy, politics; Dir MIRJANA MILORADOVIĆ.

Dečje novine: 32300 Gornji Milanovac, T. Matijevića 4; tel. (32) 711195; fax (32) 711248; general literature, children's books, science, science fiction, textbooks; Gen. Dir MIROSLAV PETROVIĆ.

Forum Publishing Institute: 21000 Novi Sad, Vojvode Mišića 1, POB 200; tel. (21) 457216; fax (21) 457216; e-mail direktor@forumliber.rs; internet www.forumliber.rs; f. 1957; books and periodicals in Hungarian; Dir FERENC NEMET.

Gradevinska Knjiga (Citizens' Books) Publishing House: 11000 Belgrade, trg Nikole Pašića 8/II; tel. (11) 3233565; fax (11) 3233563; f. 1948; technical, scientific and educational textbooks; Dir LJUBINKO ANDELIĆ.

Jugoslovenska knjiga (Yugoslav Books) Publishing House: 11000 Belgrade, trg Republike 5, POB 36; tel. (11) 621992; fax (11) 625970; art, economics and culture; Dir ZORAN NIKODIJEVIĆ.

Vuk Karadžič Publishing House: 11000 Belgrade, Kraljevića Marka 9, POB 762; tel. (11) 628066; fax (11) 623150; scientific and academic literature, popular science, children's books, general; Gen. Man. VOJIN ANČIĆ.

Matice srpske Publishing House: 21000 Novi Sad, Matice Srpske 1; tel. (21) 527622; fax (21) 528901; e-mail ms@maticasrpska.org.rs; internet www.maticasrpska.org.rs; f. 1826; domestic and foreign fiction and humanities; Man. Dir MILORAD GRUJIĆ.

Medicinska knjiga (Medical Books) Publishing House: 11001 Belgrade, Mata Vidakovića 24–26; tel. (11) 458165; f. 1947; medicine, pharmacology, stomatology, veterinary; Dir MILE MEDIĆ.

Minerva Publishing House: 24000 Subotica, trg 29 Novembra 3; tel. (24) 25712; fax (24) 23208; novels and general; Dir LADISLAV ŠEBEK.

Naučna knjiga (Scientific Books) Publishing House: 11000 Belgrade, Uzun Mirkova 5; tel. (11) 637220; f. 1947; school, college and university textbooks, publications of scientific bodies; Dir Dr BLAŽO PEROVIĆ.

Nolit: 11000 Belgrade, Terazije 27; tel. (11) 3245017; fax (11) 627285; f. 1928; belles-lettres, philosophy and fine art; scientific and popular literature; Dir-Gen. RADIVOJE NEŠIĆ; Editor-in-Chief RADIVOJE MIKIĆ.

Prosveta (Education) Publishing House: 11000 Belgrade, Čika Ljubina 1; tel. (11) 2629843; fax (11) 2627465; e-mail prosveta@prosveta.co.rs; internet www.prosveta.co.rs; f. 1944; general literature, art books, dictionaries, encyclopaedias, science, music; Dir ZOVICA MIŠIĆ.

Rad Publishing House: 11000 Belgrade, Dečanska 12; tel. (11) 3715090; fax (11) 3715001; e-mail vanja.tomic@ips.rs; f. 1949; politics, economics, sociology, psychology, literature, biographies; Man. Dir VANJA TOMIĆ; Editor-in-Chief DANKO JESIĆ.

Savremena administracija (Contemporary Administration) Publishing House: 11000 Belgrade, Crnotravska 7–9; tel. (11) 667633; fax (11) 667277; e-mail m.jovic@savremena-ad.com; internet www.savremena-ad.com; f. 1954; economy, law, science university textbooks, encyclopaedias and dictionaries; Dir MILUTIN PEJČIĆ.

Srpska književna zadruga (Serb Publishing Collective): 11000 Belgrade, Srpskih Vladara 19/I; tel. (11) 330305; fax (11) 626224; f. 1892; works of classical and modern Serb writers, and translations of works of foreign writers; Pres. RADOVAN SAMARDŽIĆ; Editor RADOMIR RADOVANAĆ.

Tehnička Knjiga (Technical Books) Publishing House: 11000 Belgrade, Vojvode Stepe 89; tel. (11) 468596; fax (11) 473442; f. 1948; technical works, popular science, reference books, hobbies; Dir RADIVOJE GRBOVIĆ.

Zavod za udžbenike i nastavna sredstva (Institute for School Books and Teaching Aids): 11000 Belgrade, Obilićev Venac 5; tel. (11) 2637433; fax (11) 2637426; internet www.zavod.co.rs; f. 1957; textbooks and teaching aids; Dir and Editor-in-Chief MILOLJUB ALBIJANIĆ.

SERBIA

PUBLISHERS' ASSOCIATIONS

Asscn of Publishers and Booksellers of Serbia (Udruženje izdavača i knjižara Srbije): 11000 Belgrade, Kneza Miloša 25, POB 570; tel. (11) 642533; fax (11) 646339; f. 1954; organizes Belgrade International Book Fair; Dir OGNJEN LAKIĆEVIĆ; 116 mem. organizations.

Asscn of Publishers and Booksellers of Vojvodina (Poslovno udruženje izdavača i knjižara Vojvodine): 21000 Novi Sad; tel. and fax (21) 4720452; e-mail info@knjigavoj.co.rs; internet www.knjigavoj.co.rs; f. 2001; Dir ROMAN VEHOVEĆ; Chair. of Council ĐEZE BORDAS.

Broadcasting and Communications

TELECOMMUNICATIONS

Telekom Srbija (Telecom Serbia): 11000 Belgrade, Takovska 7; tel. (11) 3229991; internet www.telekomsrbija.com; 20% owned by OTE (Greece); provides fixed-line and mobile cellular telecommunications services in Serbia; Dir-Gen. BRANKO RADUJKO.

Telenor d.o.o.: 11070 Belgrade, Omladinskih Brigada 90; e-mail pr@telenor.rs; internet www.telenor.co.rs; f. 1994 as Mobtel Srbija; present name adopted 2006, following acquisition by Telenor Group (Norway); provides mobile cellular telecommunications in Serbia; additionally granted license to operate fixed-line telephony services in 2010; CEO KJELL-MORTEN JOHNSEN.

BROADCASTING

Association of Independent Electronic Media: 11000 Belgrade, Maršala Birjuzova 13A; tel. and fax (11) 2622467; e-mail anem@anem.org.rs; internet www.anem.org.rs; f. 1993; comprises 16 television and 28 radio stations, and 60 affiliated orgs; Chair. SAŠA MIRKOVIĆ.

Radiotelevizija Srbije (RTS) (Radio-Television of Serbia): 11000 Belgrade, Takovska 10; tel. (11) 3212200; fax (11) 3212211; internet www.rts.rs; f. 1929; comprises Radiotelevizija Beograd (Radio-Television of Belgrade); Dir-Gen. ALEKSANDAR TIJANIĆ.

Radiotelevizija Vojvodina (RTV) (Radio-Television of Vojvodina): 21000 Novi Sad, Ignjata Pavlasa 3; tel. (21) 425588; fax (21) 423348; e-mail pr@rtv.rs; internet www.rtv.rs; f. 2006 to replace Radiotelevizija Novi Sad; Gen. Dir BLAŽO POPOVIĆ; Dir of TV ALEKSANDR DOTLIĆ.

Radio

Međunarodni Radio Srbija (International Radio Serbia): 11000 Belgrade, Hilandarska 2, POB 200; tel. (11) 3244455; fax (11) 3232014; e-mail radioyu@bitsyu.net; internet www.glassrbije.org; f. 1951; fmrly Radio Jugoslavija (Radio Yugoslavia); state-owned short-wave station; broadcasts daily in Serbian, English, French, German, Russian, Spanish, Hungarian, Chinese, Albanian, Greek, Italian and Arabic; Dir MILENA JOKIĆ.

Radio B92: 11000 Belgrade, bul. Avnoja 64; tel. (11) 3012000; fax (11) 3012001; internet www.b92.net; f. 1989; independent; Dir VERAN MATIĆ; Dir of Radio Programming GORICA NEŠOVIĆ.

Radio JAT: 11000 Belgrade, Svetog Save 1/XVI; tel. (11) 2440142; e-mail radio_jat@jat.com.

Radiotelevizija Košava: 11000 Belgrade, Aleksandra Dubčeka 14; tel. (11) 3061491; fax (11) 3612135; internet www.kosava.co.rs; f. 1994; radio station broadcasting popular music and talk programmes to most regions of Serbia; Editor-in-Chief MILOMIR MARIĆ.

Radio TV Bajina Basta: 31250 Bajina Basta, Svetosavska 34; tel. (31) 851688; fax (31) 853162; e-mail office@bajinabasta.org; internet www.bajinabasta.org; f. 1986; independent radio and television station; Dir BOBAN TOMIĆ.

Television

B92 Televizija: 11000 Belgrade, bul. Avnoja 64; tel. (11) 3012000; fax (11) 3012001; internet www.b92.net; f. 2000; independent; Dir VERAN MATIĆ; Dir of Programming IVA IVANIŠEVIĆ.

BK Telecom (BK): 11070 Belgrade, Nikole Tesle 42A; tel. (11) 3013555; fax (11) 3013526; internet www.bktv.com; f. 1994; independent television station; Dir-Gen. Dr TIMOHIR SIMIĆ; Editor-in-Chief MILOMIR MARIĆ.

RTV Pink: 11000 Belgrade, Neznanog Junaka 1; tel. (11) 3063400; fax (11) 3063500; internet www.rtvpink.com; f. 1993; Pres. and CEO ŽELJKO MITROVIĆ.

Finance

(cap. = capital; res = reserves; dep. = deposits; m. = million; amounts in Serbian dinars, unless otherwise stated; brs = branches)

BANKING

Central Banking System

In 2003, following the reconstitution of the Federal Republic of Yugoslavia as the State Union of Serbia and Montenegro, the National Bank of Yugoslavia became Serbia's central bank, and was renamed the National Bank of Serbia. In May 2009 there were 34 banks in Serbia, 21 of which were in majority foreign ownership, 10 in majority domestic private ownership and three in majority state ownership.

National Bank of Serbia (Narodna banka Srbije): 11000 Belgrade, Kralja Petra 12, POB 1010; tel. (11) 3027100; fax (11) 3027394; e-mail kabinet@nbs.rs; internet www.nbs.rs; f. 1884; present name adopted 2003; cap. 14,751m., res 7,692m., dep. 705,635m. (Dec. 2007); Gov. RADOVAN JELAŠIĆ; 6 brs.

Other Banks

Alpha Bank Srbija a.d.: 11000 Belgrade, Kralja Milana 11; tel. (11) 3234931; fax (11) 3246840; e-mail alphabankserbia@alphabankserbia.com; internet www.alphabankserbia.com; f. 1956; 100% owned by Alpha Bank AE (Greece); present name adopted 2006; cap. 16,589.0m., res 741.9m., dep. 34,685.0m. (Dec. 2008); Chair. SPYROS N. FILARETOS; 23 brs.

Banca Intesa a.d. Beograd: 11070 Belgrade, Vladimira Popovića 8; tel. (11) 3108888; fax (11) 3108855; e-mail bi@bancaintesabeograd.com; internet www.bancaintesabeograd.com; f. 1991; present name adopted 2005; 90% owned by Intesa Holding International SA (Luxembourg); absorbed Panonska Banka a.d. in Jan. 2008; cap. 28,446.3m., res 9,581.8m., dep. 141,980.8m. (Dec. 2008); Chief Exec. DRAGINJA ĐURIĆ; 150 brs.

Erste Bank a.d. Novi Sad: 21000 Novi Sad, bul. Oslobođenja 5; tel. (21) 4873510; fax (21) 4890651; e-mail info@erstebank.rs; internet www.erstebank.rs; f. 1864 as Novosadska Banka a.d.; present name adopted 2005; 99.9% owned by Erste Bank Group AG (Austria); cap. 10,174.8m., res 15.6m., dep. 31,361.4m. (Dec. 2008); Pres. SLAVKO CARIĆ.

Hypo Alpe-Adria-Bank a.d. Beograd: 11070 Novi Beograd, bul. Mihaila Pupina 6; tel. (11) 2226000; fax (11) 2226555; e-mail office@hypo-alpe-adria.rs; internet www.hypo-alpe-adria.rs; f. 1991 as Depositno-Kreditna Banka; merged with Hypo Alpe-Adria-Bank 2002; cap. 12,225.6m., res 4,849.5m., dep. 97,593.7m. (Dec. 2007); Chair. VLADIMIR ČUPIĆ.

Komercijalna Banka a.d. Beograd: 11000 Belgrade, Svetog Save 14; tel. (11) 3080100; fax (11) 3441335; e-mail posta@kombank.com; internet www.kombank.com; f. 1970; 40.3% state-owned, 25.0% owned by European Bank for Reconstruction and Development (United Kingdom); cap. 17,062.5m., res 5,333.8m., dep. 132,903.4m. (Dec. 2008); Pres. IVICA SMOLIĆ.

NLB Banka a.d. Beograd: 11070 Novi Beograd, bul. Mihaila Pupina 165v; tel. (11) 2225100; fax (11) 2225194; e-mail info@nlb.rs; internet www.nlb.rs; f. 1991; fmrly NLB Continental Banka a.d. Novi Sad, renamed as above after merger with NLB LHB Banka Beograd a.d. in Jan. 2010; 92% owned by Nova Ljubljanska banka d.d. (Slovenia); cap. 6,320.9m., res 1,537.0m., dep. 25,807.2m. (Dec. 2008); Chair. ANDREJ HAZABENT.

OTP Banka a.d. Novi Sad: 21000 Novi Sad, bul. Oslobođenja 80; tel. (21) 4800000; fax (21) 4800032; e-mail office@otpbanka.rs; internet www.otpbanka.rs; f. 2007 by merger of Niška Banka a.d. Niš, Kulska Banka a.d. Novi Sad and Zepter banka a.d. Beograd; 91.4% owned by OTP Bank (Hungary); cap. 6,950.2m., res 4,224.5m., dep. 21,924.5m. (Dec. 2008); Pres. of Exec. Bd SZABOLCS HORVÁTH.

ProCredit Bank a.d. Beograd: 11000 Belgrade, bul. Milutina Milankovića 17; tel. (11) 2077906; fax (11) 2077905; e-mail info@procreditbank.rs; internet www.procreditbank.rs; f. 2001; 66.7% owned by ProCredit Holding AG (Germany); cap. 3,663.0m., res 4,433.9m., dep. 33,628.5m. (Dec. 2008); Chair. of Exec. Bd DÖRTE WEIDIG.

Raiffeisenbank a.d. Beograd: 11000 Belgrade, bul. Zorana Đinđića 64A; tel. (11) 3202100; fax (11) 2207080; e-mail info@raiffeisenbank.rs; internet www.raiffeisenbank.rs; f. 2001; 100% owned by Raiffeisenbank International Bank-Holding AG (Austria); cap. 27,466.1m., dep. 78.9m. (Dec. 2008); Chair. and Gen. Man. OLIVER ROEGL.

UniCredit Bank Srbija a.d.: 11000 Belgrade, Rajićeva 27–29; tel. (11) 3204500; fax (11) 3342200; e-mail office@unicreditgroup.rs; internet www.unicreditbank.co.rs; f. 2001; present name adopted 2007; 99.5% owned by Bank Austria Creditanstalt AG (Austria); cap. 13,419.7m., res 4,381.4m., dep. 56,169.7m. (Dec. 2008); Chair. of Management Bd KLAUS PRIVERSCHEK.

SERBIA

Vojvodjanska Banka, a.d. Novi Sad: 21000 Novi Sad, POB 391, trg Slobode 7; tel. (21) 4886600; fax (21) 6624859; e-mail office@voban.groupnbg.com; internet www.voban.co.rs; f. 1962; 100% owned by National Bank of Greece SA (Greece); cap. 16,337.5m., res 4,770.6m., dep. 55,291.0m. (Dec. 2008); Pres. Marinis Stratopoulos.

Banking Association

Association of Serbian Banks (Udruženje banaka Srbije): 11000 Belgrade, bul. Kralja Aleksandra 86; tel. (11) 3020760; fax (11) 3370179; e-mail ubs@ubs-asb.com; internet www.ubs-asb.com; f. 1955; association of business banks; works on improving inter-bank co-operation, organizes agreements of mutual interest for banks, gives expert assistance, establishes co-operation with foreign banks, other financial institutions and their associations, represents banks in relations with the Government and the National Bank of Serbia; Sec.-Gen. Veroljub Dugalić.

STOCK EXCHANGE

Belgrade Stock Exchange (Beogradska Berza): 11070 Belgrade, Omladinskih brigada 1, POB 50; tel. (11) 3115328; fax (11) 138242; e-mail info@belex.rs; internet www.belex.co.rs; Chair. of Bd Gordana Dostanić.

INSURANCE

AMS Osiguranje (AMS Insurance): 11000 Belgrade, Ruzveltova 16; tel. (11) 3084900; e-mail info@ams.co.rs; internet www.ams.co.rs; f. 1998; non-life; Gen. Dir Dragoljub Radojević.

DDOR Novi Sad: 21000 Novi Sad, bul. Mihaila Pupina 8; tel. (21) 4886000; internet www.ddor.co.rs; f. 1990; life and non-life insurance and reinsurance; Chair. of Exec. Bd Christian Otto Neu.

Delta Generali Osiguranje: 11070 Novi Beograd, Milentija Popovića 7b; tel. (11) 2220555; fax (11) 2011727; e-mail kontakt@deltagenerali.rs; internet www.deltagenerali.rs; life and non-life insurance and reinsurance.

Dunav Osiguranje (Danube Insurance): 11000 Belgrade, Makedonska 4, POB 624; tel. (11) 3221214; fax (11) 3344936; e-mail info@dunav.com; internet www.dunav.com; f. 1974; life and non-life insurance and reinsurance; Gen. Dir Mirko Petrović.

Sava osiguranje: 11000 Belgrade, Bulevar vojvode Mišića 51; tel. (11) 3644888; fax (11) 3644899; e-mail info@sava-osiguranje.rs; internet www.sava-osiguranje.rs; subsidiary of Sava Re (Slovenia); Chair. of Managing Bd Duško Jovanović.

SIM Osiguranje (SIM Insurance): 11000 Belgrade, Oblakovska 28; tel. and fax (11) 3690110.

Uniqa Osiguranje: 11070 Belgrade, Milutina Milankovića 134g; tel. (11) 2024100; e-mail info@uniqa.rs; internet www.uniqa.rs; fmrly Zepter Osiguranje; present name adopted 2006, following acquisition by Uniqa (Austria); life and non-life insurance; Gen. Dir Konstantin Klijen.

Trade and Industry

GOVERNMENT AGENCIES

Foreign Trade Institute (Institut za Spoljnu Trgovinu): 11000 Belgrade, Moše Pijade 8; tel. (11) 3235391; fax (11) 3235306; Dir Dr Slobodan Mrkša.

Investment and Export Promotion Agency of the Republic of Serbia (Agencija za strana ulaganja i promociju izvoza Republike Srbije—SIEPA): 11000 Belgrade, Vlajkovićeva 3; tel. (11) 3398550; fax (11) 3398814; e-mail office@siepa.gov.rs; internet www.siepa.gov.rs; f. 2001; Dir Vesna Perić.

CHAMBER OF COMMERCE

Chamber of Commerce of Serbia (Privredna Komora Srbije): 11000 Belgrade, Resavska 13–15; tel. (11) 3300900; fax (11) 3230949; internet pks.komora.net; Pres. Miloš Bugarin.

UTILITIES

Electricity

Elektroprivreda Srbije (EPS) (Serbia Electricity Corpn): 11000 Belgrade, Balkanska 13; tel. (11) 3610580; fax (11) 3611908; e-mail dragomir.markovic@eps.rs; internet www.eps.rs; state-owned; production, transmission and distribution of electric power in Serbia (incl. Kosovo); Chair. Petar Knežević; Gen. Man. Dragomir Marković.

Gas

Naftna Industrija Srbije—NIS a.d. Novi Sad (Oil Industry of Serbia): 21000 Novi Sad, Narodnog fronta 12; tel. (21) 4811111; fax (21) 4814321; e-mail office@nis.rs; internet www.nis.rs; four principal subsidiaries: NIS-Naftagas (NIS Oil and Gas); NIS-Petrol Jugpetrol (NIS Petrol); NIS-TNG (liquid petroleum gas); NIS-Ogostiteljstvo i turizam (Hospitality and Tourism); owns oil refineries at Pančevo and Novi Sad; 51% owned by Gazprom (Russia); Pres. Dr Petar Škundrić; Gen. Dir Kiril Kravčenko; 13,900 employees (2009).

Srbijagas: 21000 Novi Sad, Narodnog fronta 12; tel. (11) 4812703; fax (11) 4814305; internet www.srbijagas.com; f. 2005; transportation and distribution of natural gas and liquid petrol gas, civil engineering; Dir-Gen. Dušan Bajatović.

TRADE UNIONS

Association of Free and Independent Trade Unions: 11000 Belgrade, Karađorđeva 71; tel. and fax (11) 2623671; e-mail asns@asns.org.rs; internet www.asns.org.rs; Pres. Ranka Savić.

Confederation of Autonomous Trade Unions of Serbia (Savez Samostalnih Sindikata Srbije): 11000 Belgrade, trg Nikole Pašić 5; tel. (11) 3230922; fax (11) 3241911; 600,000 mems.

Transport

RAILWAYS

In 2009 there were 3,809 km of railway track in use in Serbia, excluding Kosovo, of which 1,196 km were electrified. A major infrastructure project for the relocation of the central railway station in Belgrade has been repeatedly delayed; the rehabilitation of the capital's rail system is also under way.

Železnice Srbije (Serbian Railways): 11000 Belgrade, Nemanjina 6; tel. (11) 3614811; fax (11) 3616722; internet www.zeleznicesrbije.com; Pres. Zoran Anđelković; Dir-Gen. Milovan Marković.

ROADS

In 2001 there were an estimated 44,993 km of roads in Serbia and Montenegro, of which 28,031 km were paved.

INLAND WATERWAYS

About 5.4m. metric tons of freight were carried on inland water transport in Serbia and Montenegro in 2007.

SHIPPING

Jugoagent Pomorska-rečna Agencija (Yugo Maritime and Rivers Shipping Agency): 11070 Belgrade, bul. Mihaila Pupina 165a, POB 210; tel. (11) 2018700; fax (11) 3112070; e-mail office@jugoagent.net; internet www.jugoagent.net; f. 1947; fmrly Jugoslovenska Pomorska Agencija (Yugoslav Maritime Agency); charter services, liner and container transport, port agency, passenger service, air cargo service; Gen. Man. Zoran Netković.

CIVIL AVIATION

There is an international airport at Belgrade and several domestic airports.

Jat Airways: 11070 Belgrade, bul. Umetnosti 16; tel. (11) 3114222; fax (11) 3112853; e-mail pr@jat.com; internet www.jat.com; f. 1927 as Aeroput; fmrly Jugoslovenski Aerotransport (JAT—Yugoslav Airlines); 51% owned by Govt; flights between Serbia and destinations in Central, Western, Eastern and Southern Europe and the Middle East; Chair. of Management Bd and Acting Dir-Gen. Saša Vlaisavljević.

Tourism

Serbia's tourism industry is considered to have considerable potential for development, with notable attractions including the mountain scenery, traditional thermal spas, historic cultural cities, and the heritage of monuments and monasteries. In 2008 tourist arrivals (excluding Kosovo) totalled some 646,000. Receipts from tourism to Serbia and Montenegro amounted to US $1,113m. in that year.

National Tourism Organization of Serbia (Turistička Organizacija Srbije): 11000 Belgrade, POB 433, Dečanska 8; tel. (11) 3232586; fax (11) 3221068; e-mail office@serbia.travel; internet www.serbia.travel; f. 1994; produces information and conducts market research and promotion in the field of tourism; Dir Gordana Plamenac.

Defence

Compulsory military service was abolished with effect from 1 January 2011. Voluntary military service for women was introduced in 1983. As assessed at November 2010, the estimated total strength of the armed forces was 29,125, of which the army accounted for 12,260 (including 1,800 conscripts) and the air force 4,262. Reserves totalled 50,171 personnel. In December 2006 Serbia was admitted to the 'Partnership for Peace' programme of the North Atlantic Treaty

SERBIA

Organization (NATO). The budget for 2010 allocated 70,700m. dinars to defence.

Chief of Staff of the Military: Lt-Gen. MILOJE MILETIĆ.
Commander of the Ground Forces: Maj.-Gen. LJUBIŠA DIKOVIĆ.
Commander of the Air Forces and Air Defence Forces: Brig.-Gen. RANKO ŽIVAK.

Education

Elementary education is free and compulsory for all children between the ages of seven and 15, when children attend the 'eight-year school'. Various types of secondary education are available to all who qualify, but the vocational and technical schools are the most popular. Alternatively, children may attend a general secondary school (gymnasium) where they follow a four-year course, prior to university entrance. At the secondary level, there are also a number of art schools, apprentice schools and teacher-training schools. In 2006/07 some 95.1% of children in the appropriate age-group were enrolled in primary schools, while enrolment in secondary education in the same year was equivalent to 87.9% of the relevant age-group. In 2008/09 some 235,940 students were enrolled in state and private higher education faculties. Serbia had seven state universities, including the University of Belgrade, which was established in 1863, and seven private universities.

SEYCHELLES

Introductory Survey

LOCATION, CLIMATE, LANGUAGE, RELIGION, FLAG, CAPITAL

The Republic of Seychelles comprises about 115 islands, widely scattered over the western Indian Ocean. Apart from the Seychelles archipelago, the country includes several other island groups, the southernmost being about 210 km (130 miles) north of Madagascar. The climate is tropical, with small seasonal variations in temperature and rainfall. The average temperature in Victoria is nearly 27°C (80°F) and average annual rainfall 236 cm (93 ins). In 1981 Seselwa, a creole spoken by virtually all Seychellois, replaced English and French as the official language. Almost all of the inhabitants are Christians, of whom more than 85% belong to the Roman Catholic Church. The national flag (proportions 1 by 2) has five rays, extending from the lower hoist corner, of blue, yellow, red, white and green. The capital is Victoria, on the island of Mahé.

CONTEMPORARY POLITICAL HISTORY

Historical Context

Seychelles was uninhabited until colonized by France in 1770. It was ceded to the United Kingdom in 1814 and administered as a dependency of Mauritius until 1903, when it became a Crown Colony. A ministerial system of government was introduced in 1970, and Seychelles proceeded to full independence, as a sovereign republic within the Commonwealth, on 29 June 1976, under a coalition Government with James (later Sir James) Mancham as President and Albert René, the leader of the Seychelles People's United Party (SPUP), as Prime Minister. Under the independence agreement, the United Kingdom returned to Seychelles the islands of Aldabra, Farquhar and Desroches, detached in 1965 to form part of the British Indian Ocean Territory (q.v.) and subsequently leased to the USA.

In June 1977 the SPUP staged an armed coup while Mancham was absent from the islands. René was declared President, the National Assembly was dissolved and the Constitution suspended. In May 1978 the SPUP was renamed the Seychelles People's Progressive Front (SPPF). A new Constitution, proclaimed in March 1979, established a one-party state. René was re-elected to the presidency in 1979, 1984 and again in 1989 as sole candidate, for a third term of office, the maximum period permitted under the 1979 Constitution. During this period opponents of René's socialist Government made a number of attempts to overthrow the regime. The most serious assault took place in November 1981, when about 50 mercenaries, mainly South Africans posing as tourists, flew to join insurgents already on the islands. When the rebellion collapsed, most of the mercenaries escaped to South Africa, where several of their number were later tried and imprisoned. Further plots, discovered in October 1982 and November 1983, were ascribed to the same Seychellois exiles who had planned the 1981 coup attempt.

Domestic Political Affairs

Until the early 1990s exiled opposition to René remained split among a number of small groups based principally in London, United Kingdom. In July 1991 five of these parties formed a coalition, the United Democratic Movement (UDM), under the leadership of Dr Maxime Ferrari, a former political associate of René, while ex-President Mancham established a 'Crusade for Democracy'. René, meanwhile, came under increasing pressure from France and the United Kingdom, the islands' principal aid donors, to restore a democratic political system. Internally, open opposition to the SPPF was fostered by the newly formed Parti Seselwa, or Parti Seychellois (PS), led by an Anglican clergyman, Wavel Ramkalawan. In August 1991 Ferrari returned from exile to organize support for the UDM, and in November the Government invited all political dissidents to return to the islands.

In December 1991 the SPPF agreed to surrender the party's monopoly of power. It was announced that, from January 1992, political groups numbering at least 100 members would be granted official registration, and that multi-party elections would take place in July for a constituent assembly, whose proposals for constitutional reform would be submitted to a national referendum, with a view to holding multi-party parliamentary elections before the end of 1992. In April Mancham returned from exile to lead the New Democratic Party (NDP). At the July elections for the 20-seat constitutional commission, the SPPF secured 11 representatives, while the NDP took eight. The PS was the only other political party to gain representation on the commission, obtaining the remaining seat.

The commission completed its work in October 1992; however, following publication of the draft Constitution, the Democratic Party (DP, as the NDP had been restyled) challenged the proposed voting arrangements for a new National Assembly, whose members were to be elected on a basis of one-half by direct vote and one-half by proportional representation. The latter formula was to reflect the percentage of votes obtained by the successful candidate in a presidential election, and was intended to ensure a legislative majority for the President's party. Other sections of the proposed Constitution, relating to social issues, were strongly opposed by the Roman Catholic Church, to which more than 90% of the islanders at that time belonged.

The draft Constitution, which required the approval of at least 60% of voters, was endorsed by only 53.7% at a referendum held in November 1992. A second constitutional commission, whose meetings were opened to the public, began work in January 1993 on proposals for submission to a further referendum, unanimously agreeing on a new draft Constitution, in which a compromise plan was reached on the electoral formula for a new National Assembly. With the joint endorsement of René and Mancham, the draft document was submitted to a national referendum in June, approved by 73.9% of voters. At the presidential election that followed in July, René, who under the new Constitution was eligible to stand for a further three five-year terms, received 59.5% of the votes, against 36.7% for Mancham. In the concurrently held legislative elections, the SPPF secured 21 of the 22 directly elective seats, and the DP one seat. Of the 11 additional seats allocated on a proportional basis, the SPPF received a further seven seats, the DP three seats and the PS one seat. The new Government began to promote a gradual transition from socialism to free-market policies, aimed at maximizing the country's potential as an 'offshore' financial and business centre. State-owned port facilities were transferred to private ownership in 1994, when plans were also announced for the creation of a duty-free International Trade Zone to provide transshipment facilities.

In early 1995 tensions developed within the opposition DP, whose only directly elected deputy, Christopher Gill, sought to remove Mancham from the party leadership, on the grounds that he had failed to oppose strenuously the policies of the René Government. Gill was suspended from the DP in June, and subsequently formed a breakaway 'New Democratic Party' with the aim of restructuring the DP under a new leader. The official registration of active political organizations, affording them corporate status, led to the formal amalgamation of several opposition parties as the United Opposition (UO), under the leadership of Ramkalawan.

In July 1996 the SPPF introduced a series of constitutional amendments, creating the post of Vice-President, to which James Michel, the Minister of Finance, Communications and Defence and a long-standing political associate of René, was appointed in the following month. The constitutional changes also provided for revisions in constituency boundaries, which were generally interpreted as favouring SPPF candidates in future parliamentary elections, and an increase in the number of seats in the National Assembly (see Constitution and Government).

The outcome of the elections of March 1998 provided the SPPF with a decisive victory. René obtained 66.7% of the presidential ballot, while his party secured 30 of the 34 seats in the enlarged National Assembly. Ramkalawan received 19.5% of the votes cast in the presidential election, while Mancham received only 13.8%. In the National Assembly the UO increased its representation from one to three seats, with the DP losing three of the four seats previously held. Since the 1993 elections, effective opposition to the Government had increasingly been led by Ramkalawan's

UO, as the DP opted to pursue a policy of 'reconciliation' with the SPPF. In mid-1998 the UO changed its name to the Seychelles National Party (SNP).

In July 2001 René declared a presidential election almost two years early, claiming that this was in order to reassure investors about the long-term stability of the country. On 31 August–2 September René was re-elected as President, but with a reduced mandate, securing 54.2% of the valid votes cast. Ramkalawan, the SNP candidate, won 45.0% of the votes, but refused to accept the result, claiming serious irregularities in the electoral process, and subsequently filed a formal complaint with the Constitutional Court. Legislative elections, which were due in 2003, took place early, on 4–6 December 2002. The SPPF retained its majority in the National Assembly, but with a reduced margin, securing 23 of the 34 seats, while the SNP won the remaining 11 seats. In March 2003 René indicated during the congress of the SPPF that he would progressively relinquish control of certain presidential duties to Vice-President Michel, who was also designated as the party's candidate for the next presidential election.

The Michel presidency

On 14 April 2004 President René formally retired, having spent almost 27 years in office. He was succeeded by Vice-President Michel, who was inaugurated as President on the same day. Joseph Belmont was subsequently appointed Vice-President, retaining responsibility for tourism and transport.

In the weeks prior to the 2006 presidential election, tensions increased between supporters of the leading political parties contesting the vote, and there were reports of numerous violent incidents. Nevertheless, the election proceeded as scheduled on 28–30 July, when Michel secured victory with 53.7% of the valid votes cast; Ramkalawan received 45.7%. A voter turn-out of 88.7% was recorded. In mid-August a new Government, which included three new ministers, was installed. In October several high-ranking SNP officials, including Ramkalawan, were injured by security forces, after protesting outside the parliamentary building. The incident followed a speech made by Ramkalawan at the National Assembly denouncing a proposal to ban all political parties from establishing private radio stations. Ramkalawan was among three members of the SNP who were subsequently charged with attending an illegal demonstration. They were brought to trial that month; however, President Michel later suspended the charges in an attempt to quell rising violence among the political parties and their supporters. An independent inquiry into the incident was launched in March 2007, and in February 2008 the Government accepted responsibility for injuries caused during the protests.

Meanwhile, the SNP (which continued to stage a boycott of the National Assembly) also threatened to boycott the parliamentary elections, scheduled to be held by the end of 2007, unless certain demands were met. In March President Michel dissolved the National Assembly and announced that early elections would be organized. At the legislative elections, which were conducted on 10–12 May, the SPPF retained 23 seats and its majority in the National Assembly, securing 56.2% of the votes cast. An alliance of the SNP and the DP received 43.8% of the votes, and took the 11 remaining seats. International observers praised the conduct of the elections, at which 85.9% of the registered electorate participated. In July President Michel reduced the number of government ministries from 10 to eight. Although the key ministers retained their positions, the Ministry of Finance was henceforth to encompass three separate departments, while the Ministry of Health became the Ministry of Social Development and Health.

The ruling SPPF and the opposition DP both adopted new names in June 2009: the former was restyled the Parti Lepep (People's Party) and the latter, no longer in alliance with the SNP, became the New Democratic Party (NDP). Michel, hitherto Secretary-General of the SPPF, was elected President of the Parti Lepep (René being accorded the title Founding President), while Ralph Volcere was confirmed as leader of the NDP, having assumed the leadership of the DP in March, following the resignation of Paul Chow.

Meanwhile, in April 2008 President Michel established an 11-member committee, chaired by former Attorney-General Francis Chang-Sam, to review the Constitution; the committee held its first meeting in June, and in December 2009 presented its findings to the President. In March 2010 Michel confirmed that the review's conclusions had been considered, and requested that the Attorney-General, Ronny Govinden, commence the process of revising the Constitution.

Recent developments: government reorganization

President Michel announced a reorganization of the Council of Ministers in June 2010, prompted by the imminent retirement of Vice-President Belmont and by the resignation of the Minister of Social Development and Health, Marie-Pierre Lloyd. The changes included the appointment of three new ministers to the Government: Jean-Paul Adam, previously Secretary of State in the Office of the President, as Minister of Foreign Affairs; Erna Athanasius as Minister of Health; and Peter Sinon, hitherto an Executive Director at the African Development Bank, as Minister of Investment, Natural Resources and Industry, a newly created post. Danny Faure, the Minister of Finance, succeeded Belmont as Vice-President on 1 July, retaining the finance portfolio and assuming additional responsibility for trade, information technology and public administration.

In February 2011 it was announced that a presidential election would take place on 19–21 May. The election duly took place on those dates and, according to official results, Michel was re-elected to the presidency having secured 55.5% of the total votes cast. Ramkalawan again finished in second place, with 41.4%, while the independent candidate Philippe Boullé and Volcere, representing the NDP, took just 1.7% and 1.5%, respectively.

Foreign Affairs

Seychelles has traditionally pursued a policy of non-alignment in international affairs, and supports movements for the creation of a 'zone of peace' in the Indian Ocean area. Until 1983 all naval warships wishing to dock at Seychelles had to provide a guarantee that they were not carrying nuclear weapons. The British and US Governments refused to agree to this condition, and their respective naval fleets were therefore effectively banned from using Seychelles port facilities. This requirement was withdrawn in September 1983, although Seychelles continued, in theory, to refuse entry to ships carrying nuclear weapons.

Since the late 1980s Seychelles has expanded the scope of its formal diplomatic contacts. Relations have been established with the Comoros and with Mauritius, and agreements have been made with the latter for co-operation in health and economic development matters. In 1989 diplomatic relations were established with Morocco, Madagascar and Côte d'Ivoire, and in 1990 with Kenya. During 1992 formal relations were established with Israel and South Africa, and in 1998 Seychelles proposed to establish a diplomatic mission in Malaysia to expand its relations in Asia and Oceania. Libya opened a diplomatic mission in Seychelles in January 2000, and diplomatic ties were established with Sudan in October. Following years of minimal interaction between France and Seychelles, owing to Seychelles' accumulated debt to the Agence Française de Développement, the French Minister for Co-operation was the first minister in over four years to visit Seychelles in February 2001. It was hoped that a resolution to the situation could be found and a new schedule for repayments negotiated. In 2001 relations were restored with Japan, which granted a subsidy for fishery development to Seychelles; this was said to be a consequence of the reversal of Seychelles' whaling policy. President Michel paid a state visit to Mauritius in March 2005, as guest of honour at that country's annual celebration of independence; various economic and co-operative agreements between the two countries were also signed. In December, as a result of the seventh session of the Seychelles-Mauritius Commission on Bilateral Co-operation, a further agreement was signed on the sharing of expertise in a wide range of fields. The Government also strengthened relations with the People's Republic of China, following a state visit to that country by Michel in November 2006.

CONSTITUTION AND GOVERNMENT

Under the 1993 Constitution, executive power is vested in the President, who is Head of State and Commander-in-Chief of the Armed Forces. The President, who is elected by direct popular vote, appoints and leads the Council of Ministers, which acts in an advisory capacity to him. The President also appoints the holders of certain public offices and the judiciary. The President may hold office for a maximum period of three five-year terms. The legislature is the unicameral National Assembly, presently comprising 34 members, of whom 25 are directly elected for five years and nine allocated on a proportional basis. Constitutional changes, introduced in July 1996, provide for an enlargement to 35 members: 25 directly elected and a maximum of 10 allocated on a proportional basis. A review of the Constitution was ongoing in 2010 (see Contemporary Political History).

SEYCHELLES

Introductory Survey

REGIONAL AND INTERNATIONAL CO-OPERATION

Seychelles is a member of the African Union (see p. 183), of the Common Market for Eastern and Southern Africa (see p. 228) and of the Indian Ocean Commission (see p. 448), which aims to promote co-operation in the region. It was announced in December 1996 that Seychelles was to provide the headquarters of the Indian Ocean Tuna Commission.

Seychelles became a member of the UN in 1976 and currently has observer status at the World Trade Organization (WTO, see p. 430). Seychelles participates in the Group of 77 (G77, see p. 447) developing countries.

ECONOMIC AFFAIRS

In 2009, according to estimates by the World Bank, Seychelles' gross national income (GNI), measured at average 2007–09 prices, was US $746m., equivalent to $8,480 per head (or $16,820 per head on an international purchasing-power parity basis). During 2000–09, it was estimated, the population increased at an average annual rate of 0.9%, while gross domestic product (GDP) per head decreased, in real terms, by an average of 0.3% per year. Overall GDP increased, in real terms, at an average annual rate of 0.6% in 2000–09. However, real GDP decreased by 0.9% in 2008 and by 7.6% in 2009.

Agriculture (including forestry and fishing) contributed 2.6% of GDP in 2009, according to preliminary estimates, and accounted for 1.8% of total employment in that year. Much of Seychelles' production of coconuts has traditionally been exported in the form of copra, but exports dwindled in the late 1990s. Other cash crops include cinnamon bark, tea, patchouli, vanilla and limes. Tea, sweet potatoes, cassava, yams, sugar cane, bananas, eggs and poultry meat are produced for local consumption. However, imports of food and live animals constituted an estimated 20.4% of the value of total imports in 2009. Fishing has become increasingly important since the 1980s, and exports of canned tuna alone contributed an estimated 55.7% of the value of total exports in 2009. Licence fees from foreign fishing vessels, allowed to operate in Seychelles' waters, contribute significantly to foreign exchange. A three-year fishing protocol, worth €3.48m., was signed with the European Union (EU) in 2001; a further six-year protocol was agreed in October 2004, and in December 2005 an agreement, valid until 2011, increased the payment for fishing rights to €4.12m. a year as well as raising the value of some licences, meaning that the Government could expect payments of some €6.0m. a year. Agricultural GDP increased at an average annual rate of 1.5% during 2000–09, according to the World Bank, and by 5.0% in 2009.

Industry (including mining, manufacturing, construction and power) contributed an estimated 16.4% of GDP and accounted for 28.5% of total employment in 2009. Industrial GDP increased at an average annual rate of 2.9% during 2000–09, according to the World Bank; however, the sector declined by 2.5% in both 2008 and 2009.

The mining sector is small (it accounted for less than 0.5% of total employment in 2008) and mineral production consists mainly of quantities of construction materials, such as clay, coral, stone and sand. There are deposits of natural gas, and during the 1980s concessions were sold to several foreign companies, allowing exploration for petroleum. Exploratory drilling has so far proved unsuccessful; however, an agreement to renew exploration was made in 2005. A survey of offshore areas, initiated in 1980, revealed the presence of nodules, containing deposits of various metals, on the sea-bed. The renewed commercial exploitation of Seychelles' granite reserves is under investigation and the future development of offshore petroleum reserves is a possibility.

Manufacturing contributed an estimated 8.9% of GDP and accounted for 10.5% of total employment in 2009. Apart from a tuna-canning plant (opened in 1987), the manufacturing sector consists mainly of small-scale activities, including boat-building, printing and furniture-making. According to the World Bank, manufacturing GDP decreased at an average annual rate of 1.3% during 2000–09. However, manufacturing GDP increased by 6.8% in 2008 and by 6.3% in 2009.

Construction contributed an estimated 6.0% of GDP and, along with quarrying, accounted for 15.9% of total employment in 2009. According to official estimates, the construction sector grew at an average annual rate of 12.3% in 2004–09. The sector grew by 11.4% in 2008, but declined by 4.9% in 2009.

Energy is derived principally from oil-fired power stations. In 2008 mineral fuels and lubricants accounted for an estimated 12.4% of the total value of imports. The vast majority of fuel imports are re-exported, mainly as bunker sales to visiting ships and aircraft—exports of refined petroleum products contributed 30.0% of total export earnings in 2004, and re-exports accounted for an estimated 39.6% of the value of total exports in 2009. It is envisaged that the proceeds from re-exports will eventually fund fully fuel imports.

Services provided an estimated 81.0% of GDP and accounted for 69.8% of total employment in 2009. In 2010 tourist arrivals totalled some 174,529 and income from tourism amounted to SR $2,007m. in 2009, according to central bank estimates. The majority of visitors were from Western Europe, notably from France, Germany, Italy and the United Kingdom. The GDP of the services sector increased at an average annual rate of 1.1% during 2000–08, according to the World Bank. Services GDP declined by 7.3% in 2007, but increased by 5.7% in 2008.

In 2009 Seychelles recorded a visible trade deficit of US $326.6m., and there was a deficit of $284.2m. on the current account of the balance of payments. The principal source of imports (26.5%) in 2009 was the United Arab Emirates; other important suppliers were Singapore, South Africa, Spain, France and the United Kingdom. The principal market for domestic exports (excluding re-exports) in 2009 was the United Kingdom (38.2%); other significant purchasers were France and Italy. The principal export is canned tuna (following the expansion of the Indian Ocean Tuna Co in 1995 and increasing production thereafter); in 2009 canned tuna represented 92.3% of domestic exports. The main imports in 2009 were machinery and transport equipment, mineral fuels and lubricants, food and live animals, and basic manufactures.

In 2009 Seychelles recorded a budgetary surplus of SR 670.8m. (equivalent to 6.3% of GDP). Seychelles' general government gross debt was SR 13,659m. in 2009, equivalent to 127.3% of GDP. Seychelles' total external debt was US $1,505m. at the end of 2008, of which $654m. was public and publicly guaranteed debt. In that year the cost of debt-servicing was equivalent to 12.4% of the value of exports of goods, services and income in 2007. According to the IMF, the annual rate of inflation averaged 17.3% in 2005–09; consumer prices increased by 37.1% in 2008 and by 31.7% in 2009. Some 8.3% of the labour force were registered as unemployed in 1993.

Since the early 1970s tourism has been the mainstay of the Seychelles economy, and despite measures introduced in 1995 to develop Seychelles as an 'offshore' financial services centre (see Contemporary Political History), and to establish the islands as a centre for transshipment and air freight in the Indian Ocean area, the continuing dependence of the economy on tourism leaves the country highly vulnerable to outside economic influences, while the cost of servicing the external debt remains a major impediment to balanced growth. The new Government of President James Michel in 2004 pledged commitment to a programme of economic reform, particularly with regard to privatization. In November 2008 the rupee was allowed to float freely on foreign exchange markets, resulting in a depreciation in its value of some 48%. Inflation subsequently rose rapidly, reaching 63.3% by December, although this rate declined steadily during 2009 due to weaker international prices and slower domestic demand. A comprehensive economic reform programme, which was introduced in November with the assistance of the IMF, was adversely affected by the worsening global fiscal environment. As part of the programme, the IMF agreed a two-year stand-by arrangement valued at US $26.1m. to enable Seychelles to service its external debt (estimated to amount to some $800m., equivalent to 175% of GDP). In December 2009, following the disbursement of a further $3.4m. under the stand-by arrangement, a three-year Extended Fund Facility was approved, providing further funding amounting to $30.7m. In February 2010 it was announced that an extensive debt-cancellation agreement had been finalized between Seychelles and Libya, reducing claims from $8.1m. to some $3.4m. Meanwhile, in September 2009 an interim Economic Partnership Agreement was signed with the EU allowing Seychelles full and immediate access to European markets. In December 2010 the IMF completed its second favourable review of the country's progress under the economic reform programme, which allowed the disbursement of about $2.7m. The Government's sustained stabilization and fiscal adjustment efforts were commended, as were further planned measures to rationalize the tax system, including in preparation for the introduction of a value-added tax in mid-2012. According to the IMF, GDP growth had recovered to more than 6% in 2010 (following a contraction in 2008 and slight

SEYCHELLES

increase in 2009), and deflation of some 2% was recorded, while public external debt had been reduced to about 49% of GDP by the end of 2010. In early 2011 the Government announced the completion of a new water storage and distribution system, which was designed to mitigate the effects of drought, and, in view of the expanding tourism industry, plans for a number of construction projects.

PUBLIC HOLIDAYS

2012: 1–2 January (New Year), 6–9 April (Easter), 1 May (Labour Day), 5 June (Liberation Day, anniversary of 1977 coup), 7 June (Corpus Christi), 18 June (National Day), 29 June (Independence Day), 15 August (Assumption), 1 November (All Saints' Day), 8 December (Immaculate Conception), 25 December (Christmas Day).

Statistical Survey

Source (unless otherwise stated): Statistics and Database Administration Section, Management and Information Systems Division, POB 206, Victoria; e-mail misdstat@seychelles.net; internet www.nsb.gov.sc.

AREA AND POPULATION

Area: 455.3 sq km (175.8 sq miles), incl. Aldabra lagoon (145 sq km).

Population: 74,331 at census of 26 August 1994; 75,876 (males 37,589, females 38,287) at census of 29 August 1997. *Mid-2010* (official estimate): 86,525 (males 44,253, females 42,272).

Density (mid-2010): 190.0 per sq km.

Population by Age and Sex (official estimates at mid-2010): *0–14:* 19,691 (males 9,955, females 9,736); *15–64:* 60,023 (males 31,750, females 28,273); *65 and over:* 6,811 (males 2,548, females 4,263); *Total* 86,525 (males 44,253, females 42,272).

Principal Town: Victoria (capital), estimated population 60,000 (incl. suburbs) in 1994. *Mid-2009* (incl. suburbs, UN estimate): Victoria 26,001. (Source: UN, *World Urbanization Prospects: The 2009 Revision*).

Births, Marriages and Deaths (registrations, 2010): Live births 1,504 (birth rate 17.4 per 1,000); Marriages (of residents) 459 (marriage rate 5.3 per 1,000); Deaths 664 (death rate 7.7 per 1,000).

Life Expectancy (years at birth, official estimates): 73.2 (males 69.1; females 77.5) in 2010.

Employment (2009, averages): Agriculture, forestry and fishing 738; Manufacturing 4,419; Electricity and water 859; Construction (with quarrying) 6,646; Trade, restaurants and hotels 9,292; Transport, storage and communications 4,307; Other services 15,630; *Total* 41,891.

HEALTH AND WELFARE
Key Indicators

Total Fertility Rate (children per woman, 2009): 2.4.

Under-5 Mortality Rate (per 1,000 live births, 2008): 11.

Physicians (per 1,000 head, 2004): 1.51.

Hospital Beds (per 1,000 head, government establishments only, 2007): 4.7.

Health Expenditure (2007): US $ per head (PPP): 1,094.

Health Expenditure (2007): % of GDP: 5.1.

Health Expenditure (2007): public (% of total): 70.2.

Access to Water (% of persons, 2004): 88.

Total Carbon Dioxide Emissions ('000 metric tons, 2007): 622.9.

Carbon Dioxide Emissions Per Head (metric tons, 2007): 7.3.

Human Development Index (2007): ranking: 57.

Human Development Index (2007): value: 0.845.

For sources and definitions, see explanatory note on p. vi.

AGRICULTURE, ETC.

Principal Crops (metric tons, 2008, unless otherwise indicated): Coconuts 900*; Vegetables (incl. melons) 1,940 (2009)*; Bananas 2,000*; Other fruits (excl. melons) 2,505 (2009)*; Tea 137; Cinnamon 94.
* FAO estimate.

Livestock (head, 2008, FAO estimates): Cattle 530; Pigs 7,750; Goats 5,200. Note: No data were available for 2009.

Livestock Products (metric tons, 2009, unless otherwise indicated, FAO estimates): Pig meat 364; Chicken meat 768; Hen eggs 610 (2008).

Fishing ('000 metric tons, live weight, 2008): Capture 69.2 (Skipjack tuna 30.0; Yellowfin tuna 21.3; Bigeye tuna 9.8; Aquaculture 0.3 (Giant tiger prawn 0.3); *Total catch* 69.5.

Source: FAO.

INDUSTRY

Industrial Production (2010): Canned tuna 30,338 metric tons; Beer and stout ('000 litres) 4,781; Soft drinks ('000 litres) 5,936; Cigarettes 47m.; Electric energy 301m. kWh.

FINANCE

Currency and Exchange Rates: 100 cents = 1 Seychelles rupee (SR). *Sterling, Dollar and Euro Equivalents* (30 November 2010): £1 sterling = 19.035 rupees; US $1 = 12.259 rupees; €1 = 15.934 rupees; 100 Seychelles rupees = £5.25 = $8.16 = €6.28. *Average Exchange Rate* (Seychelles rupees per US $): 6.7011 in 2007; 9.4572 in 2008; 13.6099 in 2009. Note: In November 1979 the value of the Seychelles rupee was linked to the IMF's special drawing right (SDR). In March 1981 the mid-point exchange rate was set at SDR 1 = 7.2345 rupees. This remained in effect until February 1997, when the fixed link with the SDR was ended.

Budget (SR million, 2009, provisional figures): *Revenue:* Taxation 3,319.2 (Taxes on income, etc. 1,184.8, Domestic taxes on goods and services 1,697.3, Import duties 437.1); Other current revenue 473.6; Total 3,792.8, excl. grants received (316.8). *Expenditure:* General government services 681.7; Community and social services 102.8; Education 229.2; Health 281.2; Economic services 55.5; Agriculture, environment and fishing 122.4; Transport and communications 50.3; Other purposes 764.4; Interest payments 914.4; Capital 608.4; Total 3,810.3, excl. lending minus repayments (–371.5). Note: Figures represent the consolidated accounts of the central Government, covering the operations of the Recurrent and Capital Budgets and of the Social Security Fund.

International Reserves (US $ million at 31 December 2010): IMF special drawing rights 11.75; Reserve position in IMF 0.01; Foreign exchange 223.82; Total 235.58. Source: IMF, *International Financial Statistics*.

Money Supply (SR million at 31 December 2010): Currency outside depository corporations 580.0; Transferable deposits 4,774.6; Other deposits 1,920.5; *Broad money* 7,275.1. Source: IMF, *International Financial Statistics*.

Cost of Living (Consumer Price Index; base: 2005 = 100): All items 104.9 in 2007; 143.8 in 2008; 189.4 in 2009. Source: IMF, *International Financial Statistics*.

Expenditure on the Gross Domestic Product (SR million at current prices, 2009): Government final consumption expenditure 1,473.3; Private final consumption expenditure 7,210.1; Gross capital formation 3,630.2; *Total domestic expenditure* 12,313.6; Exports of goods and services 12,443.1; *Less* Imports of goods and services 14,030.9; *GDP in purchasers' values* 10,725.8. Source: UN National Accounts Main Aggregates Database.

Gross Domestic Product by Economic Activity (SR million at current prices, 2009, preliminary estimates): Agriculture, forestry and fishing 250.4; Manufacturing 848.9; Electricity and water 144.2; Construction 568.5; Wholesale and retail trade, and repair of motor vehicles and motorcycles 1,000.7; Trade, restaurants and hotels 1,954.7; Transport, storage and communications 1,212.8; Finance, insurance, real estate and business services 1,974.2; Education 246.0; Public administration and defence, and social security 553.0; Other services 777.6; *Sub-total* 9,530.9; Import duties, less subsidies 1,672.6; *Less* Imputed bank service charge 477.6; *GDP in purchasers' values* 10,725.8.

Balance of Payments (US $ million, 2009): Exports of goods f.o.b. 432.5; Imports of goods f.o.b. –759.1; *Trade balance* –326.6; Exports of services 404.1; Imports of services –308.2; *Balance on goods and services* –230.7; Other income received 8.5; Other income paid –119.6; *Balance on goods, services and income* –341.8; Current transfers received 67.5; Current transfers paid –9.9; *Current balance* –284.2; Capital account (net) 54.3; Direct investment abroad –5.7;

SEYCHELLES

Direct investment from abroad 248.6; Portfolio investment assets −0.1; Portfolio investment liabilities 1.0; Other investment assets −76.4; Other investment liabilities 126.8; Net errors and omissions 18.4; *Overall balance* 82.7. Source: IMF, *International Financial Statistics*.

EXTERNAL TRADE

Principal Commodities (distribution by SITC, SR million, 2009, provisional): *Imports c.i.f.:* Food and live animals 2,206.2; Mineral fuels 2,427.4; Basic manufactures 1,657.9; Machinery and transport 2,420.0; Total (incl. others) 10,792.1. *Exports f.o.b.:* Canned tuna 2,974.0; Fish (fresh/frozen) 33.5; Frozen prawns 0.0; Fish meal 96.2; Medicaments, etc. 28.0; Total (incl. others) 5,339.5 (of which domestic exports SR 3,222.6m. and re-exports SR 2,116.8m.).

Principal Trading Partners (SR million, 2009, provisional): *Imports c.i.f.:* France 671.4; Italy 412.5; Singapore 871.1; South Africa 848.3; Spain 794.0; United Arab Emirates 2,860.7; United Kingdom 601.0; Total (incl. others) 10,792.1. *Exports f.o.b.:* France 983.8; Germany 114.0; Italy 465.6; Netherlands 124.0; Sri Lanka 33.8; United Kingdom 1,232.6; Total (incl. others) 5,339.5 (of which domestic exports SR 3,222.6m. and re-exports SR 2,116.8m.).

TRANSPORT

Road Traffic (registered motor vehicles, 2009): Private 8,339; Commercial 2,886; Taxis 302; Self-drive 1,768; Motorcycles 28; Omnibuses 269; *Total* 13,592.

Shipping: *Merchant Fleet* (registered at 31 December 2009): Vessels 50; Total displacement 203,192 grt (Source: IHS Fairplay, *World Fleet Statistics*); *International Sea-borne Freight Traffic* (2009): Freight ('000 metric tons): Imports 461; Exports 5,008; Transshipment (of fish) 158.

Civil Aviation (traffic on scheduled services, 2006): Kilometres flown 16m.; Passengers carried 545,000; Passenger-km 1,359m.; Total ton-km 163m. (Source: UN, *Statistical Yearbook*). *2009:* Aircraft movements 3,751; Passengers embarked 212,000; Passengers disembarked 203,000; Freight embarked 2,054 metric tons; Freight disembarked 5,775 metric tons.

TOURISM

Foreign Tourist Arrivals ('000): 159.0 in 2008; 157.5 in 2009; 174.5 in 2010.

Arrivals by Country of Residence (2010): France 35,026; Germany 21,314; Italy 25,602; Russia 8,942; South Africa 10,425; Switzerland 6,523; United Kingdom 12,322; Total (incl. others) 174,529.

Tourism Receipts (SR million, central bank estimates): 1,194 in 2007; 1,236 in 2008; 2,007 in 2009.

COMMUNICATIONS MEDIA

Radio Receivers (1997): 42,000 in use. Source: UNESCO, *Statistical Yearbook*.

Television Receivers (2000): 16,500 in use. Source: International Telecommunication Union.

Telephones (2009): 26,100 main lines in use. Source: International Telecommunication Union.

Mobile Cellular Telephones (2009): 110,700 subscribers. Source: International Telecommunication Union.

Personal Computers: 18,000 (211.7 per 1,000 persons) in 2007. Source: International Telecommunication Union.

Internet Users (2009): 34,000 accounts. Source: International Telecommunication Union.

Broadband Subscribers (2009): 3,900. Source: International Telecommunication Union.

Book Production (1980): 33 titles (2 books, 31 pamphlets).

Daily Newspapers (2008): 2.

Non-daily Newspapers (2008): 3.

EDUCATION

Pre-primary (2010): 33 schools; 232 teachers; 2,935 pupils.

Primary (2010): 27 schools; 691 teachers (males 115, females 576); 8,671 pupils (males 4,358, females 4,313).

Secondary (2010): 13 schools; 592 teachers (males 236, females 356); 7,240 pupils (males 3,669, females 3,571).

Post-secondary (2010): 9 schools; 194 teachers; 2,280 pupils.

Vocational (2004): 7 institutions; 82 teachers; 1,099 pupils.

Special Education (2010): 2 institution; 29 teachers; 86 pupils.

Pupil-teacher Ratio (primary education): 12 in 2010.

Adult Literacy Rate (official estimate): 96% (males 96%; females 96%) in 2010.

Directory

The Government

HEAD OF STATE

President: JAMES MICHEL (took office 14 April 2004, elected 28–30 July 2006; re-elected 19–21 May 2011).

Vice-President: DANNY FAURE.

COUNCIL OF MINISTERS
(May 2011)

President, with additional responsibility for Tourism, Defence, Information and Public Relations, Legal Affairs, Risk and Disaster Management: JAMES MICHEL.

Vice-President, Minister of Finance, Trade, Information Technology and Public Administration: DANNY FAURE.

Minister of Community Development, Youth and Sports: VINCENT MERITON.

Minister of Home Affairs, the Environment and Transport: JOEL MORGAN.

Minister of Land Use and Housing: JACQUELIN DUGASSE.

Minister of Social Development and Culture: BERNARD SHAMLAYE.

Minister of Education, Employment and Human Resources Development: MACSUZY MONDON.

Minister of Foreign Affairs: JEAN-PAUL ADAM.

Minister of Investment, Natural Resources and Industry: PETER SINON.

Minister of Health: ERNA ATHANASIUS.

MINISTRIES

Office of the President: State House, POB 55, Victoria; tel. 4224155; fax 4224985; internet www.statehouse.gov.sc.

Office of the Vice-President: State House, POB 1303, Victoria; tel. 4286800; fax 4225152; e-mail jbelmont@statehouse.gov.sc.

Ministry of Community Development, Youth, Sports and Culture: Oceangate House, POB 731, Victoria; tel. 4225477; fax 4224081; e-mail oplg@seychelles.net; internet www.localgovernment.gov.sc.

Ministry of Education: POB 48, Mont Fleuri; tel. 4283283; fax 4224859; e-mail ps@eduhq.edu.sc; internet www.education.gov.sc.

Ministry of Employment and Human Resources Development: Independence House, POB 1097, Victoria; tel. 4676250; fax 4610795; e-mail ps@employment.gov.sc; internet www.employment.gov.sc.

Ministry of the Environment, Natural Resources and Transport: Independence House, POB 199, Victoria; tel. 4670504; fax 4323651; internet www.env.gov.sc.

Ministry of Finance: Liberty House, POB 113, Victoria; tel. 4382006; fax 4225265; e-mail psf@finance.gov.sc; internet www.finance.gov.sc.

Ministry of Foreign Affairs: Maison Quéau de Quinssy, POB 656, Mont Fleuri; tel. (4) 283500; fax (4) 224845; e-mail mfapesey@seychelles.net; internet www.mfa.gov.sc.

Ministry of National Development: International Conference Centre, POB 648, Victoria; tel. 4284444; fax 4225416; internet www.ict.gov.sc.

Ministry of Social Development and Health: POB 52, Mont Fleuri; tel. 4388000; fax 4226042; internet www.moh.gov.sc.

SEYCHELLES

President and Legislature

PRESIDENT
Election, 19–21 May 2011

Candidate	Votes	% of votes
James Michel (Parti Lepep)	31,966	55.46
Wavel Ramkalawan (SNP)	23,878	41.43
Philippe Boullé (Independent)	956	1.66
Ralph Volcere (NDP)	833	1.45
Total	57,633	100.00

NATIONAL ASSEMBLY
Speaker: PATRICK HERMINIE.
Election, 10–12 May 2007

Party	Votes	% of votes	Seats*
Seychelles People's Progressive Front (SPPF)	30,571	56.2	23
Seychelles National Party (SNP)-Democratic Party (DP)	23,869	43.8	11
Total	54,440	100.0	34

* Of the Assembly's 34 seats, 25 were filled by direct election and nine by allocation on a proportional basis.

Election Commission

Electoral Commission: Suite 203, Aarti Bldg, Mont Fleuri, POB 741, Victoria; tel. 4295555; fax 4225474; e-mail hendrick@seychelles.net; internet www.ecs.sc; f. 1993; Electoral Commissioner HENDRICK PAUL GAPPY.

Political Organizations

Mouvement Seychellois pour la Démocratie: Mont Fleuri; tel. 4224322; fax 4224460; f. 1992; Leader JACQUES HODOUL.

New Democratic Party (NDP): POB 169, Mont Fleuri; tel. 4224916; fax 4224302; e-mail management@dpseychelles.com; internet www.dpseychelles.com; f. 1992; successor to the Seychelles Democratic Party (governing party 1970–77); Leader RALPH VOLCERE.

Parti Lepep (People's Party): POB 1242, Victoria; tel. 4284900; fax 4225070; e-mail admin@sppf.sc; internet www.partilepep.com; fmrly the Seychelles People's United Party (f. 1964), which assumed power in 1977; renamed Seychelles People's Progressive Front in 1978; sole legal party 1978–91; assumed present name in 2009; Pres. JAMES ALIX MICHEL.

Seychelles National Party (SNP): Arpent Vert, Mont Fleuri, POB 81, Victoria; tel. 4224124; fax 4225151; e-mail secretariat@snpseychelles.sc; internet www.snpseychelles.sc; f. 1995 as the United Opposition, comprising the fmr mem. parties of a coalition formed to contest the 1993 elections; adopted present name in 1998; Leader Rev. WAVEL RAMKALAWAN; Sec.-Gen. ROGER MANCIENNE.

Diplomatic Representation

EMBASSIES AND HIGH COMMISSIONS IN SEYCHELLES

China, People's Republic: POB 680, St Louis; tel. 4671700; fax 4671730; e-mail china@seychelles.net; internet sc.china-embassy.org/eng; Ambassador WANG WEIGUO.

Cuba: Bel Eau, POB 730, Victoria; tel. 4224094; fax 4224376; e-mail cubasey@seychelles.net; internet emba.cubaminrex.cu/seychellesing; Ambassador MARIA AIDA NOGALES JIMÉNEZ.

France: La Ciotat Bldg, Mont Fleuri, POB 478, Victoria; tel. 4382500; fax 4382510; e-mail ambafrance@intelvision.net; internet www.ambafrance-sc.org; Ambassador PHILLIPE DELACROIX.

India: Le Chantier, POB 488, Francis Rachel St, Victoria; tel. 4610301; fax 4610308; e-mail hicomind@seychelles.net; internet www.seychelles.net/hicomind; High Commissioner ASIT KUMAR NAG.

Russia: Le Niol, POB 632, St Louis; tel. 4266590; fax 4266653; e-mail rfembsey@seychelles.net; Ambassador MIKHAIL I. KALININ.

United Kingdom: 3rd Floor, Oliaji Trade Centre, Francis Rachel St, POB 161, Victoria; tel. 4283666; fax 4283657; e-mail bhcvictoria@fco.gov.uk; internet ukinseychelles.fco.gov.uk/en; High Commissioner MATTHEW FORBES.

Judicial System

The legal system is derived from English Common Law and the French Code Napoléon. There are three Courts, the Court of Appeal, the Supreme Court and the Magistrates' Courts. The Court of Appeal hears appeals from the Supreme Court in both civil and criminal cases. The Supreme Court is also a Court of Appeal from the Magistrates' Courts as well as having jurisdiction at first instance. The Constitutional Court, a division of the Supreme Court, determines matters of a constitutional nature, and considers cases bearing on civil liberties. There is also an industrial court and a rent tribunal.

Supreme Court: POB 157, Victoria; tel. 4285800; fax 4224197; e-mail judiciary@seychelles.sc; Chief Justice FREDERICK EGONDE-ENTENDE.

President of the Court of Appeal: FRANCIS MACGREGOR.

Justices of Appeal: JACQUES HODOUL, SATYABHOOSUN GUPT DOMAH, ANTHONY FERNANDO, MATHILDA TWOMEY.

Puisne Judges: RANJAN PERERA, D. KARUNAKARAN, N. JUDDOO.

Attorney-General: RONNY GOVINDEN.

Religion

The majority of the inhabitants are Christians, of whom more than 85% are Roman Catholics and about 8% Anglicans. Hinduism, Islam, and the Bahá'í Faith are also practised.

CHRISTIANITY

The Anglican Communion

The Church of the Province of the Indian Ocean comprises six dioceses: four in Madagascar, one in Mauritius and one in Seychelles. The Archbishop of the Province is the Bishop of Antananarivo, Madagascar.

Bishop of Seychelles: Rt Rev. SANTOSH MARRAY, POB 44, Victoria; tel. 4321977; fax 4323879; e-mail angdio@seychelles.net.

The Roman Catholic Church

Seychelles comprises a single diocese, directly responsible to the Holy See. An estimated 85% of the total population are Roman Catholics.

Bishop of Port Victoria: Rt Rev. DENIS WIEHE, Bishop's House-Evêché, Olivier Maradan St, POB 43, Victoria; tel. 4322152; fax 4324045; e-mail rcchurch@seychelles.net.

Other Christian Churches

Pentecostal Assemblies of Seychelles: Victoria; tel. 4224598; e-mail paos@seychelles.net; Pastor HERMITTE FREMINOT.

The Press

L'Echo des Iles: POB 12, Victoria; tel. 4322262; fax 4321464; e-mail echo@seychelles.net; bi-monthly; French, Creole and English; Roman Catholic; Editor Fr EDWIN MATHIOT; circ. 2,800.

The People: Maison du Peuple, Revolution Ave, Victoria; tel. 4224455; internet www.thepeople.sc; owned by Parti Lepep; monthly; Creole, French and English; circ. 1,000.

Seychelles Nation: Information Technology and Communication Division, POB 800, Victoria; tel. 4225775; fax 4321006; e-mail seynat@seychelles.net; internet www.nation.sc; f. 1976; govt-owned; Mon.–Sat.; English, French and Creole; the country's only daily newspaper; Dir DENIS ROSE; circ. 3,500.

Seychelles Review: POB 29, Victoria; tel. 4241881; fax 4241545; e-mail surmer@seychelles.net; internet www.seychellesreview.com; f. 1994; monthly; business, politics, real estate and tourism; Editor ROLAND HOARAU.

Seychelles Weekly: POB 308, Victoria; e-mail editor@seychellesweekly.com; internet www.seychellesweekly.com; supports democracy in Seychelles; Editor (vacant).

Seychellois: POB 32, Victoria; f. 1928; publ. by Seychelles Farmers Asscn; quarterly; circ. 1,800.

Vizyon: Arpent Vert, Mont Fleuri, Victoria; tel. 4224507; fax 4224987; internet www.snpseychelles.sc/vizyon.htm; f. 2007; political fortnightly magazine of the opposition SNP; successor to weekly Regar; Creole, English and French; Editor ROGER MANCIENNE.

SEYCHELLES
Directory

Broadcasting and Communications

TELECOMMUNICATIONS

Cable and Wireless (Seychelles) Ltd: Mercury House, Francis Rachel St, POB 4, Victoria; tel. 4284000; fax 4322777; e-mail cws@seychelles.net; internet www.cwseychelles.com; f. 1990; Chief Exec. CHARLES HAMMOND.

Atlas Seychelles Ltd (XNET): POB 903, Victoria; tel. 4304060; fax 4324565; e-mail atlas@seychelles.net; internet www.seychelles.net; f. 1996 by a consortium of Space95, VCS and MBM; acquired by Cable and Wireless (Seychelles) Ltd in 2005; internet service provider; Gen. Man. ANTHONY DELORIE.

Telecom Seychelles Ltd (Airtel): POB 1358, Providence; tel. 4600609; fax 4601602; internet africa.airtel.com/seychelles; f. 1998; 100% owned by Bharti Airtel (India); provides fixed-line, mobile and satellite telephone and internet services; Chief Exec. VINOD SUD.

BROADCASTING

Radio

Seychelles Broadcasting Corpn (SBC): Hermitage, POB 321, Victoria; tel. 4289600; fax 4225641; e-mail sbcradtv@seychelles.sc; internet www.sbc.sc; f. 1983; reorg. as independent corpn in 1992; programmes in Creole, English and French; Man. Dir ANTOINE ONEZIME.

SBC Radio: Union Vale, POB 321, Victoria; tel. 4289600; fax 4289720; e-mail sbcradtv@seychelles.sc; internet www.sbc.sc; f. 1941; programmes in Creole, English and French; Man. Dir IBRAHIM AFIF.

Television

Seychelles Broadcasting Corpn (SBC): see Radio.

SBC TV: Hermitage, POB 321, Victoria; tel. 4224161; fax 4225641; e-mail sbcradtv@seychelles.sc; f. 1983; programmes in Creole, English and French; Head of TV Production JUDE LOUANGE.

Finance

(cap. = capital; res = reserves; dep. = deposits; m. = million; brs = branches; amounts in Seychelles rupees)

BANKING

In 2009 there were seven banks operating in Seychelles, of which two conducted 'offshore' business. Five of these seven banks were foreign-owned, whereas the Government of Seychelles had a majority stake in the other two banks.

Central Bank

Central Bank of Seychelles (CBS): Independence Ave, POB 701, Victoria; tel. 4282000; fax 4226104; e-mail enquiries@cbs.sc; internet www.cbs.sc; f. 1983; bank of issue; cap. 48.9m., res 20.0m., dep. 2,402.3m. (Dec. 2009); Gov. PIERRE LAPORTE.

National Banks

Development Bank of Seychelles: Independence Ave, POB 217, Victoria; tel. 4294400; fax 4224274; e-mail devbank@dbs.sc; internet www.dbs.sc; f. 1977; 55.5% state-owned; cap. 39.2m., res 43.9m., dep. 137.4m. (Dec. 2009); Chair. ANTONIO LUCAS; Man. Dir ROGER TOUSSAINT.

Seychelles International Mercantile Banking Corporation Ltd (Nouvobanq) (SIMBC): Victoria House, State House Ave, POB 241, Victoria; tel. 4293000; fax 4224670; e-mail nvb@nouvobanq.sc; internet www.nouvobanq.sc; f. 1991; 78% state-owned, 22% by Standard Chartered Bank (United Kingdom); cap. 100.0m., res 103.0m., dep. 2,774.0m. (Dec. 2009); Chair. AHMED AFIF; Pres. AHMED SAEED; 2 brs.

Seychelles Savings Bank Ltd (SSB): Kingsgate House, POB 531, Victoria; tel. 4294000; fax 4224713; e-mail ssb@savingsbank.sc; f. 1902; state-owned; term deposits, savings and current accounts; cap. and res 7.8m. (Dec. 1992), dep. 356.4m. (1999); Man. Dir MICHAEL BENSTRONG; 4 brs.

Foreign Banks

Bank of Baroda (India): Trinity House, Albert St, POB 124, Victoria; tel. 4610333; fax 4324057; e-mail ce.seychelles@bankofbaroda.com; internet www.bankofbaroda.com/seychelles.asp; f. 1978.

Barclays Bank (Seychelles) Ltd (United Kingdom): Independence Ave, POB 167, Victoria; tel. 4383838; fax 4324054; e-mail barclays@seychelles.sc; f. 1959; Seychelles Dir LOGANADEN SIDAMBARAM; 3 brs and 4 agencies.

Habib Bank Ltd (Pakistan): Frances Rachel St, POB 702, Victoria; tel. 4224371; fax 4225614; e-mail habibsez@seychelles.net; f. 1976; Vice-Pres. and Chief Man. SOHAIL ANWAR.

Mauritius Commercial Bank (Seychelles) Ltd (MCB Seychelles): POB 122, Manglier St, Victoria; tel. 4284555; fax 4322676; e-mail contact@mcbseychelles.com; internet www.mcbseychelles.com; f. 1978 as Banque Française Commerciale (BFCOI); changed name in 2003; cap. 20.0m., res 20.0m., dep. 1,232.6m. (Dec. 2009); Man. Dir JOCELYN AH-YU; 5 brs.

Offshore Bank

BMI Offshore Bank: Office 12, Marina House, Eden Island, POB 672, Victoria; tel. 4345660; e-mail enquiries@bmi.com.sc; internet www.bmi.com.sc; Dir-Gen. JAMAL ALI AL-HAZEEM.

INSURANCE

In 2010 there were four domestic and three non-domestic insurance companies in Seychelles.

H. Savy Insurance Co Ltd (HSI): Maison de la Rosière, 2nd Floor, Palm St, POB 887, Victoria; tel. 4322272; fax 4321666; e-mail insurance@mail.seychelles.net; f. 1995; all classes; majority-owned by Corvina Investments; Gen. Dir JEAN WEELING-LEE.

Seychelles Assurance Co Ltd (SACL): Pirate's Arms Bldg, POB 636, Victoria; tel. 4225000; fax 4224495; e-mail sacos@sacos.sc; internet www.sacos.sc; f. 1980; 37% owned by Opportunity Investment Company, 20% state-owned; all classes of insurance; subsidiaries include SUN Investments (Seychelles) Ltd, property-development company; fmrly State Assurance Corporation of Seychelles—SACOS; current name adopted 2006; Chair. and Man. Dir ANTONIO A. LUCAS.

Trade and Industry

GOVERNMENT AGENCIES

Seychelles Fishing Authority (SFA): POB 449, Fishing Port, Victoria; tel. 4670300; fax 4224508; e-mail management@sfa.sc; internet www.sfa.sc; f. 1984; assessment and management of fisheries resources; Chair. VÉRONIQUE HERMINIE; Man. Dir RONDOLPH PAYET.

Seychelles Trading Co Ltd (STC): Latanier Rd, POB 634, Victoria; tel. 4285000; fax 4224735; e-mail mail@stcl.sc; internet stcl.sc; f. 1984; replaced import and distribution arm of the fmr Seychelles Marketing Board (SMB) in 2008; manufacturing and marketing of products, retailing, trade; Chair. COLIN JEAN-LOUIS; CEO PATRICK VEL.

DEVELOPMENT ORGANIZATIONS

Indian Ocean Tuna Commission (IOTC) (Commission de Thons de l'Océan Indien): Le Chantier Mall, 2nd Floor, POB 1011, Victoria; tel. 4225494; fax 4224364; e-mail secretariat@iotc.org; internet www.iotc.org; f. 1996; an inter-governmental organization mandated to manage tuna and tuna-like species in the Indian Ocean and adjacent seas; to promote co-operation among its members with a view to ensuring, through appropriate management, the conservation and optimum utilization of stocks and encouraging sustainable development of fisheries based on such stocks; Exec. Sec. ALEJANDRO ANGANUZZI.

Seychelles International Business Authority (SIBA): Industrial Trade Zone, POB 991, Victoria; Bois de Rose Ave, Roche Caiman; tel. 4380800; fax 4380888; e-mail siba@seychelles.net; internet www.siba.net; f. 1995 to supervise registration of companies, transshipment and 'offshore' financial services in an international free-trade zone covering an area of 23 ha near Mahé International Airport; Chief Exec. and Man. Dir STEVE FANNY.

Seychelles Investment Bureau (SIB): POB 1167, Caravelle House, 2nd floor, Manglier St, Victoria; tel. 4295500; fax 4225125; e-mail sib@seychelles.sc; internet www.sib.gov.sc; f. 2004; CEO SHERIN RENAUD.

Small Enterprises Promotion Agency (SEnPA): Camion Hall Bldg, Victoria; tel. 4323151; fax 4324121; e-mail senpa@senpa.sc; internet www.senpa.sc; f. 2004; fmrly the Seychelles Industrial Development Corpn, f. 1988; promotes and develops small enterprises, crafts and cottage industries; CEO SYLVIANE VALMONT.

CHAMBER OF COMMERCE

Seychelles Chamber of Commerce and Industry: Ebrahim Bldg, 2nd Floor, POB 1399, Victoria; tel. 4323812; fax 4321422; e-mail scci@seychelles.int; Chair. VAITHUNASAMY RAMADOSS; Sec.-Gen. NICHOLE TIRANT-GHÉRARDI.

EMPLOYERS' ORGANIZATION

Federation of Employers' Associations of Seychelles (FEAS): POB 214, Victoria; tel. 4324969; fax 4324996; Chair. BASIL SOUNDY.

UTILITIES

Electricity

Public Utilities Corporation (Electricity Division): Electricity House, POB 174, Roche Caiman; tel. 4678000; fax 4321020; e-mail pmorin@puc.sc; Man. Dir PHILIPPE MORIN.

Seychelles Energy Commission: Room 205, Aarti Chambers, POB 1488, Victoria; tel. 4421700; e-mail mrazanajatovo@sec.sc; f. 2010; Chair. WILLS AGRICOLE.

Water

Public Utilities Corporation (Water and Sewerage Division): Unity House, POB 34, Victoria; tel. 4322444; fax 4325612; e-mail pucwater@seychelles.net; Man. Dir STEPHEN ROUSSEAU.

TRADE UNION

Seychelles Federation of Workers' Unions (SFWU): Maison du Peuple, Latanier Rd, POB 154, Victoria; tel. 4224455; fax 4225351; e-mail sfwu@seychelles.net; f. 1978 to amalgamate all existing trade unions; affiliated to Parti Lepep; 25,200 mems; Pres. OLIVIER CHARLES; Gen. Sec. ANTOINE ROBINSON.

Transport

RAILWAYS

There are no railways in Seychelles.

ROADS

In 2007 there were 508 km of roads, of which 490 km were surfaced. Most surfaced roads are on Mahé and Praslin.

SHIPPING

Privately owned ferry services connect Victoria, on Mahé, with the islands of Praslin and La Digue. At 31 December 2008 Seychelles' merchant fleet numbered 50 vessels, totalling 203,192 grt.

Seychelles Ports Authority (SPA): POB 47, Mahé Quay, Victoria; tel. 4224701; fax 4224004; e-mail enquiries@seychellesports.sc; internet www.spa.sc; Chair. Capt. GUY ADAM; CEO Lt Col ANDRÉ D. CISEAU.

Aquarius Shipping Agency Ltd: POB 865, Victoria; tel. 4225050; fax 4225043; e-mail aqua@seychelles.net; Gen. Man. ANTHONY SAVY.

Harry Savy & Co Ltd: POB 20, Victoria; tel. 4322120; fax 4321421; e-mail hsavyco@seychelles.net; shipping agents; Man. Dir GUY SAVY.

Hunt, Deltel and Co Ltd: Trinity House, Albert St, POB 14, Victoria; tel. 4380300; fax 4225367; e-mail hundel@seychelles.net; internet www.hundel.sc; f. 1937; Man. Dir E. HOUAREAU.

Mahé Shipping Co Ltd: Maritime House, POB 336, Victoria; tel. 4380500; fax 4380538; e-mail mail@maheship.sc; internet www.maheship.sc; f. 1969; shipping agents; Chair. Capt. G. C. C. ADAM.

Seychelles Shipping Line Ltd: POB 977, Providence, Victoria; tel. 4373737; fax 4373647; e-mail ssl@gondwana.sc; f. 1994; operates freight services between Seychelles and Durban, South Africa; Chair. SELWYN GENDRON; Man. Dir HASSAN OMAR.

CIVIL AVIATION

Seychelles International Airport is located at Pointe Larue, 10 km from Victoria. A new international passenger terminal and aircraft parking apron were constructed in the mid-2000s on land reclaimed in 1990; the existing terminal (which underwent SR 3m. in renovations in 2002) was to be converted into a cargo terminal. The airport also serves as a refuelling point for aircraft traversing the Indian Ocean. There are airstrips on several outlying islands.

Seychelles Civil Aviation Authority (SCAA): POB 181, Victoria; tel. 4384000; fax 4384009; e-mail secretariat@scaa.sc; internet www.scaa.sc; f. 1970; formerly Directorate of Civil Aviation; oresponsible for the Flight Information Region of 2.6m. sq km of Indian Ocean airspace; Interim Chair. CONRAD MEDERIC; CEO GILBERT FAURE.

Air Seychelles: The Creole Spirit Bldg, Quincy St, POB 386, Victoria; tel. 4381002; fax 4224305; e-mail airseymd@seychelles.net; internet www.airseychelles.net; f. 1979; operates scheduled internal flights from Mahé to Praslin; also charter services to Bird, Desroches and Denis Islands and to outlying islands of the Amirantes group; international services to Europe, Far East, East and South Africa; Acting Exec. Chair. MAURICE LOUSTAU-LALANNE.

Emirates Airlines: 5th June Ave and Manglier St, Victoria; tel. 4292700; f. 2005; Dir ABDULRAHMAN AL BALOOSHI.

Tourism

Seychelles enjoys an equable climate, and is renowned for its fine beaches and attractive scenery. There are more than 500 varieties of flora and many rare species of birds. Most tourist activity is concentrated on the islands of Mahé, Praslin and La Digue, although the potential for ecological tourism of the outlying islands received increased attention in the late 1990s. It is government policy that the development of tourism should not blight the environment, and strict laws govern the location and construction of hotels. In 1998 the Government indicated that up to 200,000 visitors (although not more than 4,000 at any one time) could be accommodated annually without detriment to environmental quality. However, several new luxury resorts were constructed in the early 2000s, and the yachting sector was also under development. Receipts from tourism totalled an estimated SR 2,007m. in 2009. In 2010 there were 174,529 tourist arrivals; most visitors are from Europe.

Compagnie Seychelloise de Promotion Hotelière Ltd: POB 683, Victoria; tel. 4224694; fax 4225291; e-mail cosproh@seychelles.net; promotes govt-owned hotels.

Seychelles Tourism Board (STB): POB 1262, Victoria; tel. 671300; fax 620620; e-mail info@seychelles.com; internet www.seychelles.travel; f. 1998 as Seychelles Tourism Marketing Authority; merged with Seychelles Tourism Office in 2005; Chair. MAURICE LOUSTAU-LALANNE.

Defence

As assessed at November 2010, the army numbered 200 men. Paramilitary forces comprised a 250-strong national guard and a 200-strong coast guard. Seychelles contributes servicemen to the East African Stand-by Brigade, a part of the African Union stand-by peace-keeping force.

Defence Expenditure: Budgeted at SR 87m. in 2010.

Commander-in-Chief of Seychelles Armed Forces: Brig. LÉOPOLD PAYET.

Education

Education is free and compulsory for children between six and 16 years of age. A programme of educational reform, based on the British comprehensive schools system, was introduced in 1980. The language of instruction in primary schools is English. The duration of primary education is six years, while that of general secondary education is five years (of which the first four years are compulsory), beginning at 12 years of age. Pre-primary and special education facilities are also available. According to UNESCO estimates, in 2008/09 enrolment at primary schools included 94% of children (males 93%; females 95%) in the relevant age-group, while the comparable ratio for secondary enrolment in that year was 97% (males 95%; females 99%). There were 2,280 students in post-secondary (non-tertiary) education in 2010. A number of students study abroad, principally in the United Kingdom. Government expenditure on education in 2009 was SR 229.2m., or about 6.0% of total expenditure.

SIERRA LEONE

Introductory Survey

LOCATION, CLIMATE, LANGUAGE, RELIGION, FLAG, CAPITAL

The Republic of Sierra Leone lies on the west coast of Africa, with Guinea to the north and east, and Liberia to the south. The climate is hot and humid, with an average annual temperature of 27°C (80°F). The rainy season lasts from May to October. The average annual rainfall is about 3,436 mm (13.5 ins). English is the official language, while Krio (Creole), Mende, Limba and Temne are also widely spoken. The majority of the population follow animist beliefs, but there are significant numbers of Islamic and Christian adherents. The national flag (proportions 2 by 3) has three equal horizontal stripes, of green, white and blue. The capital is Freetown.

CONTEMPORARY POLITICAL HISTORY

Historical Context

Sierra Leone, formerly a British colony and protectorate, achieved independence as a constitutional monarchy within the Commonwealth on 27 April 1961. The Prime Minister and leader of the Sierra Leone People's Party—SLPP, Dr (later Sir) Milton Margai, died in April 1964 and was succeeded by his half-brother, Dr (later Sir) Albert Margai, previously the Minister of Finance.

In March 1967 the army assumed control and established a ruling body, the National Reformation Council. In April 1968 a further coup was staged by army officers, and power was subsequently transferred to a civilian Government; Dr Siaka Stevens, the leader of the All-People's Congress (APC), was elected as Prime Minister. In April 1971 a republican Constitution was introduced and Stevens became executive President.

The general election in May 1973 was not contested by the SLPP, and in 1976 Stevens, the sole candidate, was unanimously re-elected to the presidency for a second five-year term of office. A new Constitution, which provided for a one-party system, was adopted by the House of Representatives in June. The APC thus became the sole legitimate political organization. Stevens was inaugurated as President for a seven-year term on 14 June 1978. He subsequently released political detainees and allocated ministerial posts to several former SLPP members (who had joined the APC).

Domestic Political Affairs

During the 1980s civil unrest, prompted by economic hardship, increased and in April 1985 Stevens announced that (contrary to earlier indications) he would not seek re-election to the presidency upon the expiry, in June, of his existing mandate. Stevens' term of office was subsequently extended for six months, to allow time for registration of voters and the nomination of a presidential candidate. At a conference of the APC in August, Maj.-Gen. Joseph Momoh, a cabinet minister and the Commander of the Army, was the sole candidate for the leadership of the party and for the presidential nomination. Momoh was elected to the national presidency in October, with 99% of the votes cast, and was inaugurated on 28 November. Although retaining his military status, Momoh appointed a civilian Cabinet, which included several members of the previous administration. Elections to the House of Representatives took place in May 1986.

Despite a campaign against financial malpractice in the public sector, Momoh's administration failed to improve the serious economic situation, and popular discontent continued. In March 1987 the Government announced that it had suppressed an attempted coup; more than 60 people were subsequently arrested, including the First Vice-President, Francis Minah. In October Minah and 15 other defendants were sentenced to death for plotting to assassinate Momoh and to overthrow the Government, and two defendants received custodial sentences on charges of treason. In October 1989 Minah and five others were executed, despite international appeals for clemency.

Following the outbreak of civil conflict in Liberia in December 1989, an estimated 125,000 Liberians took refuge in Sierra Leone. The Sierra Leonean Government contributed troops to the cease-fire monitoring group (ECOMOG) of the Economic Community of West African States (ECOWAS, see p. 257), which was dispatched to Liberia in August 1990. In November of that year Charles Taylor, the leader of the principal Liberian rebel faction, the National Patriotic Front of Liberia (NPFL), threatened to attack Freetown International Airport (alleged to be a base for ECOMOG offensives against rebel strongholds). In early April 1991, following repeated border incursions by members of the NPFL, government forces entered Liberian territory and launched a retaliatory attack against NPFL bases. By the end of that month, however, NPFL forces had advanced 150 km within Sierra Leone. The Momoh Government alleged that the rebel offensive had been instigated by Taylor, in an attempt to force Sierra Leone's withdrawal from ECOMOG, and also accused the Government of Burkina Faso of actively assisting the rebels. It was reported, however, that members of a Sierra Leonean resistance movement, the Revolutionary United Front (RUF), had joined the NPFL in attacks against government forces. In mid-1991 government troops, with the assistance of military units from Nigeria and Guinea, initiated a counter-offensive against the rebels, and succeeded in recapturing several towns in the east and south of the country.

On 29 April 1992 members of the armed forces, led by a five-member military junta, seized a radio station in Freetown and broadcast demands for improvements in conditions in the armed forces. The rebel troops later occupied the presidential offices, and the leader of the military junta, Capt. Valentine E. M. Strasser, announced that the Government had been overthrown. On the following day Momoh fled to Guinea, and Strasser announced the establishment of a governing council, to be the National Provisional Ruling Council (NPRC). Strasser affirmed the NPRC's commitment to the introduction of a multi-party system (legislation that permitted the formation of political associations had been approved in September 1991), and pledged to end the conflict in the country. On the same day the Constitution was suspended, the House of Representatives was dissolved and a state of emergency was imposed. On 1 May 1992 the NPRC (which principally comprised military officers), chaired by Strasser, was formed. Shortly afterwards a new 19-member Cabinet, which included a number of members of the NPRC, was appointed, and the Commander of the Armed Forces and the head of the security forces were replaced. On 6 May Strasser was inaugurated as Head of State.

In July 1992 Strasser replaced the three members of the NPRC in the Cabinet with civilians, and removed all civilian cabinet ministers from the NPRC. Later that month he announced extensive structural changes, which were designed to reduce the direct involvement of the NPRC in government administration: the NPRC was officially designated the Supreme Council of State, while the Cabinet was reconstituted as the Council of Secretaries (headed by the Chief Secretary of State), which was to be responsible for government administration, subject to the authority of the NPRC. In December Strasser announced a reorganization of the Council of Secretaries, in which the two remaining members of the Momoh administration were replaced. In the same month the Deputy Chairman of the NPRC, Capt. Solomon A. J. Musa, became Chief Secretary of State. Later in December, in an apparent attempt to regain public support, the Government established a 19-member National Advisory Council, comprising representatives of various non-governmental organizations, which was to draft a programme for transition to civilian rule.

At the end of December 1992 the Government announced that the security forces had suppressed a coup attempt. Shortly afterwards nine of those accused of involvement in the attempted coup were convicted by a special military tribunal, and, together with 17 prisoners who had been convicted in November on charges of treason, were summarily executed. Human rights organizations subsequently contested the Government's statement that a coup attempt had been staged, and condemned the trial by special military tribunal. In January 1993 the United Kingdom announced the suspension of economic aid to Sierra Leone in protest against the executions.

SIERRA LEONE

Transition to civilian rule

In April 1993 Strasser announced that a programme providing for a transition to civilian rule within a period of three years was to be adopted; in addition, all political prisoners were to be released, press restrictions would be relaxed, and the function of special military tribunals was to be reviewed. In July Musa was replaced as Deputy Chairman of the NPRC and Chief Secretary of State by Capt. Julius Maada Bio. Musa (who was widely believed to be responsible for the repressive measures undertaken by the Government) took refuge in the Nigerian high commission in Freetown, amid widespread speculation regarding his dismissal, and subsequently emigrated to the United Kingdom.

At the end of November 1993 Strasser announced the details of a two-year transitional programme, which provided for the installation of a civilian government by January 1996. The registration of political parties was to take place in June 1995, prior to a presidential election in November and legislative elections in December of that year. In December 1993 a five-member Interim National Electoral Commission was established to organize the registration of voters and the demarcation of constituency boundaries, in preparation for forthcoming local government elections. In the same month the National Advisory Council submitted constitutional proposals (which included a number of similar provisions to the 1991 Constitution), stipulating that: executive power was to be vested in the President, who was to be required to consult with the Cabinet, and was to be restricted to a tenure of two four-year terms of office; only Sierra Leonean nationals of more than 40 years of age were to qualify to contest a presidential election (thereby precluding Strasser and the majority of NPRC members, on grounds of age); and the legislature was to comprise a House of Representatives, which was to be elected by universal adult suffrage for a term of five years, and a 30-member upper chamber, the Senate. A draft Constitution was submitted to the NPRC in October 1994.

In January 1995 the RUF, which had been joined by disaffected members of the armed forces, gained control of the mining installations owned by the Sierra Leone Ore and Metal Company (SIEROMCO) and Sierra Rutile Ltd, and seized a number of employees of the two enterprises, including eight foreign nationals. In the same month the RUF threatened to kill the British hostages if the Sierra Leonean authorities executed an officer, who had been convicted by military tribunal of collaborating with the rebels. In February the RUF rejected appeals by the UN and the Organization of African Unity (now the African Union, see p. 183) that peace negotiations be initiated, and demanded that all troops that had been dispatched by foreign Governments to assist the Strasser administration be withdrawn as a precondition to discussions. In mid-February government forces (which had succeeded in recapturing the mining installations owned by Sierra Rutile) launched an offensive against a principal rebel base in the Kangari region, east of Freetown. Meanwhile, continued atrocities perpetrated against civilians were increasingly attributed to disaffected members of the armed forces.

In February 1995 the military administration engaged 58 Gurkha mercenaries, who had previously served in the British army, prompting further concern regarding the safety of the British hostages in Sierra Leone. In March government forces regained control of the mining installations owned by SIEROMCO and the principal town of Moyamba, 100 km south-east of Freetown (which had been captured by the RUF earlier that month). Despite the successful counter-offensives by government forces, by April the RUF had advanced towards Freetown and had initiated a series of attacks against towns in the vicinity (including Songo, which was situated only 35 km east of Freetown), apparently prior to besieging the capital. Later in April the remaining foreign nationals who had been seized by the RUF were released.

In March 1995 the Council of Secretaries was reorganized to allow principal military officials in the Government to assume active functions within the armed forces (following the advance of RUF forces towards Freetown); Lt-Col Akim Gibril became Chief Secretary of State, replacing Bio, who was appointed Chief of Defence Staff. The ban on political activity was formally ended in June; some 15 parties were subsequently granted registration (although the RUF failed to respond to government efforts to include the movement in the electoral process).

In May 1995 government forces initiated a number of counter-attacks against the RUF, and succeeded in recapturing Songo. By the end of June government forces had regained control of significant diamond-mining regions in the eastern Kono District, and part of Bo District, in a successful counter-offensive, which was generally attributed to the assistance of South African mercenaries. In September, however, the RUF launched further offensives in Bo District, while increasing reports of massacres and other violations of human rights perpetrated by the rebels against the civilian population emerged.

In December 1995 it was announced that presidential and legislative elections were to take place concurrently on 26 February 1996. In January 1996, however, Strasser was deposed by military officers, led by Bio, in a bloodless coup. Bio, who assumed the office of Head of State, announced that the coup had been instigated in response to efforts by Strasser to remain in power. (It was reported that Strasser had intended to amend restrictions on the age of prospective candidates to enable himself to contest the election.) Strasser (who had been expelled to Guinea) claimed, however, that the new military administration planned to delay the transition to civilian government. A reconstituted Supreme Council of State and Council of Secretaries were formed and it was announced that the elections were to take place as scheduled. The RUF indicated that it was prepared to enter into negotiations with the new Government, and declared a temporary cease-fire to allow voter registration to proceed throughout the country, but urged a postponement of the elections, pending a peace settlement that would allow the movement to participate in the democratic process. However, delegates at the National Consultative Conference, which was convened in early February, voted in favour of adherence to the scheduled date. The RUF subsequently abandoned the cease-fire and launched a series of attacks in various parts of the country, in an apparent attempt to undermine the electoral process.

The 1996 elections

The presidential and legislative elections duly took place on 26 February 1996. However, some 27 people were killed in attacks by armed groups, particularly in Bo and parts of Freetown, which were generally attributed to the RUF; voting was consequently extended for a further day. The reconstituted SLPP secured 36.1% of votes cast in the legislative elections, while its presidential candidate, Ahmed Tejan Kabbah, also received most support, with 35.8% of votes. A second round of the presidential election, which took place on 15 March, was contested by Kabbah and the candidate of the United National People's Party (UNPP), John Karefa-Smart (who had obtained 22.6% of votes cast in the first round): Kabbah was elected President by 59.5% of the votes. Later in March seats in the new 80-member Parliament were allocated on a basis of proportional representation, with the SLPP securing 27, the UNPP 17, the People's Democratic Party 12 and the reconstituted APC only five seats; the 12 provincial districts were represented in the legislature by Paramount Chiefs. Kabbah was inaugurated on 29 March, when the military Government officially relinquished power to the new civilian administration. In April Kabbah appointed a new Cabinet, which was subsequently approved by the new Parliament.

Following the elections, the Government announced in March 1996 that the RUF had agreed to a cease-fire; at a meeting between RUF leader Foday Sankoh and Bio in Yamoussoukro, Côte d'Ivoire, later that month, the RUF undertook to observe the cease-fire for a period of two months and to continue negotiations with the newly elected civilian Government. Following discussions between Sankoh and Kabbah in April, the Government and the RUF reaffirmed their commitment to a permanent cessation of hostilities, and announced the establishment of three joint committees, which would consider issues regarding the demobilization of rebel forces. Despite the official cease-fire, sporadic attacks by the RUF were subsequently reported and further clashes occurred later that year between government forces and the Kamajors (traditional fighters reconstituted as an auxiliary defence force).

In July 1996 the Parliament adopted legislation that formally reinstated the Constitution of 1991. In September 1996 Kabbah ordered the compulsory retirement of some 20 officers, including Strasser and Bio, from the armed forces. Shortly afterwards it was reported that a conspiracy to overthrow the Government had been thwarted by senior military officers. About 17 members of the armed forces were arrested, of whom nine were subsequently charged with involvement in the conspiracy. Following reports of a further conspiracy to overthrow the Government in January 1997, Kabbah announced that an investigative mission from Nigeria had concluded that former members of the NPRC administration had instigated the coup attempt of September 1996.

SIERRA LEONE

In November 1996 Kabbah demanded that the RUF relinquish armaments within a period of two weeks, threatening that government forces would resume military operations. At the end of that month Kabbah and Sankoh signed a peace agreement in Abidjan, Côte d'Ivoire, whereby RUF forces were to be demobilized and the movement was to be reconstituted as a political organization, while all foreign troops were to be withdrawn from the country and replaced with foreign observers. A National Commission for the Consolidation of Peace was subsequently established to monitor the peace settlement. By February 1997 all foreign mercenaries had left Sierra Leone in accordance with the agreement, while the repatriation of Sierra Leonean refugees from Liberia had commenced. However, at the end of that month (when the implementation of the peace agreement was scheduled for completion) it was reported that members of the RUF had repeatedly violated the peace agreement and had failed to report to designated centres for disarmament. In March members of the political wing of the RUF issued a declaration that Sankoh had been removed as leader of the organization, owing to his failure to implement the peace accord. Later that month, however, RUF forces loyal to Sankoh kidnapped members of the movement who had supported his replacement, together with the Sierra Leonean ambassador to Guinea; the faction issued demands for the release of Sankoh, who had been detained in Nigeria earlier that month (being reportedly in possession of armaments).

On 25 May 1997 dissident members of the armed forces, led by Maj. Johnny Paul Koroma, seized power, deposing Kabbah, who fled to Guinea. The new authorities imposed a curfew in Freetown, following widespread violent looting by armed factions, and most foreign nationals were evacuated. In early June Nigerian forces initiated a naval bombardment of Freetown in an effort to force the new military leaders to resign. However, forces loyal to the coup leaders, assisted by RUF members, succeeded in repelling Nigerian attacks. Koroma announced the establishment of a 20-member Armed Forces Revolutionary Council (AFRC), with himself as Chairman and Sankoh (who remained in detention in Nigeria) as Vice-Chairman; the AFRC (which was not internationally recognized as the legitimate Government) included a further three members of the RUF and several civilians. All political activity, the existing Constitution and government bodies were suspended, although Koroma pledged that democratic rule would be restored. Nigeria reiterated that it intended to reinstate the ousted Government with the support of ECOWAS, and a further two Nigerian warships were dispatched to the region; further clashes between Nigerian troops, who had been serving under the mandate of ECOMOG in neighbouring Liberia (q.v.), and supporters of the new military leaders occurred at the international airport at Lungi. In mid-June the AFRC announced that it had suppressed a coup attempt, following the arrest of 15 people, including several senior military officers. In the same month it was reported that troops supporting the junta had repulsed an attack by Kamajors (who remained loyal to Kabbah) at the town of Zimmi, 250 km south-east of Freetown. On 17 June Koroma was formally inaugurated as the self-proclaimed Head of State. However, despite appeals from Koroma, a campaign of civil disobedience, organized by the labour congress in protest against the coup, continued.

By early July 1997 the new military Government had been completely isolated by the international community. The Commonwealth Ministerial Action Group on the Harare Declaration (CMAG—which had been established to ensure adherence to the principles of democracy by member states) suspended Sierra Leone from meetings of the Commonwealth, pending the restoration of constitutional order and the reinstatement of a democratically elected government. The UN Security Council also condemned the coup, and expressed support for ECOWAS efforts to resolve the situation. Meanwhile, a four-member ministerial committee, comprising representatives of Nigeria, Côte d'Ivoire, Guinea and Ghana, which had been established by ECOWAS, urged the Government to relinquish power during a series of negotiations with an AFRC delegation.

In mid-July 1997 Koroma formed a cabinet, the Council of Secretaries, comprising representatives of the RUF and the army, together with a number of civilians. Later that month, following further reports of clashes between Kamajors and forces loyal to the junta in the south of the country, AFRC representatives and the ECOWAS committee, meeting in Abidjan, agreed to an immediate cease-fire; negotiations were to continue, with the aim of restoring constitutional order. At the end of July continuing discussions between the ECOWAS committee and AFRC representatives in Abidjan were abandoned, after Koroma insisted that he retain power for a tenure of four years, and refused to restore the Constitution and to end the ban on political activity. Consequently, in late August an ECOWAS conference, which was convened at Abuja, Nigeria, officially endorsed the imposition of sanctions against Sierra Leone, with the aim of obliging the AFRC to relinquish power. ECOMOG was granted a mandate to monitor the cease-fire and to enforce the economic embargo; it was also agreed that the ECOWAS monitoring committee would henceforth include Liberia (following the election of a democratic Government in that country).

The reinstatement of Kabbah

In September 1997 CMAG voted in support of the decision of the ECOWAS committee to effect the reinstatement of the Kabbah administration. In early October the UN Security Council imposed sanctions on the import of armaments and petroleum products to Sierra Leone. Following aerial bombardments of Freetown by ECOMOG troops, a mass demonstration was held in the capital to demand that the Nigerian Government withdraw its troops from Sierra Leone. Negotiations between the AFRC and the five-member committee continued, however, and later in October an agreement, which was signed in Conakry, Guinea, provided for an immediate cease-fire, and the reinstatement of Kabbah's Government by April 1998, together with immunity from prosecution for AFRC members; all troops loyal to the incumbent military administration and RUF members were to be demobilized, under the supervision of a disarmament committee, comprising representatives of the AFRC, ECOMOG and local forces loyal to Kabbah. In January 1998 ECOMOG forces again bombarded the port at Freetown (for the first time since the peace agreement in October 1997), apparently with the aim of preventing merchant vessels from contravening the sanctions.

In early February 1998 further clashes erupted near Freetown between ECOMOG troops and supporters of the military junta. Nigerian troops belonging to ECOMOG subsequently launched an intensive bombardment against Freetown and succeeded in gaining control of the capital, after senior members of the AFRC, including Koroma, fled into hiding, or surrendered to the ECOMOG forces. About 50 members of the military junta were arrested in Monrovia, Liberia, prompting protests from the Liberian Government regarding the Nigerian military intervention. It was announced that the Government that had been ousted on 25 May 1997 was to be reinstated, and that all subsequent appointments were to be considered invalid. ECOMOG forces were to remain in the country to assist in the restructuring of the armed forces. Meanwhile, following reports that troops loyal to the former military junta, with the assistance of the RUF, had taken control of Bo, ECOMOG forces were deployed in the region to support the Kamajors, and rapidly succeeded in regaining control of most of the region (prompting speculation that the Nigerian military initiative had been undertaken with the aim of gaining access to Sierra Leone's mineral resources).

On 10 March 1998 Kabbah returned from exile and was officially reinstated as President; he subsequently appointed a Cabinet (which included a number of members of his previous administration). The new Government declared a state of emergency under which members of the former military junta could be detained for a maximum of 30 days without being formally charged. It was announced that some 1,500 civilians and members of the armed forces (including Momoh) had been placed in detention and were to be charged for their alleged connections with the former military junta. Also in March the UN Security Council voted to end its embargo on imports of petroleum products to Sierra Leone (which had resulted in severe fuel shortages), although an embargo on the supply of armaments was maintained. In July the UN Security Council adopted a resolution establishing a UN Observer Mission in Sierra Leone (UNOMSIL), comprising 70 military observers, with an initial six-month mandate to monitor the security situation, supervise the disarmament of former combatants, and advise the authorities on the restructuring of the security forces. In the same month it was announced that the national army had been dissolved.

In late July 1998 the Nigerian Government returned Sankoh (who had been in detention in Nigeria since early 1997) to Sierra Leone, where he was charged with treason following his support for the military coup of May 1997. In August 1998 16 civilians, including five journalists, were sentenced to death, after being convicted of supporting the former military junta. In October 24

SIERRA LEONE

army officers were publicly executed, following their conviction for involvement with the military junta, provoking condemnation from many foreign Governments and human rights organizations, which had appealed for clemency. Death penalties imposed against a further 10 officers were commuted to terms of life imprisonment. In November a further 15 civilians, including several ministers who had served in the AFRC Government, were sentenced to death for their part in the May 1997 coup; Momoh received a custodial term of 10 years for colluding with the military junta.

Meanwhile, ECOMOG continued efforts to suppress rebel activity, particularly in the north and east of the country, and in October 1998 transferred its operational headquarters from the Liberian capital, Monrovia, to Freetown. In that month the RUF intensified hostilities, after it was announced that Sankoh had been sentenced to death by the High Court on charges of treason. In November ECOMOG forces commenced aerial bombardments of rebel bases. By late December, however, RUF forces, together with supporters of the former military junta, had advanced towards Freetown, and had seized control of the principal town of Makeni, 140 km north-east of Freetown. The Governments of Nigeria and Ghana dispatched additional troops to reinforce the ECOMOG contingent (which henceforth numbered about 15,000). At the end of December the acting Commander of the RUF, Sam Bockarie, rejected a government invitation to enter into peace negotiations, and ECOMOG forces, supported by Kamajors, attempted to repulse rebel attacks in the outskirts of Freetown.

On 6 January 1999 rebel forces attacked Freetown (where thousands of civilians from the surrounding area had taken refuge), releasing a number of supporters of the former junta from the capital's prison and seizing the Nigerian High Commission and government offices; Kabbah and a number of cabinet ministers were obliged to flee to ECOMOG headquarters. (It was subsequently discovered that two ministers had been killed by the rebels.) Bockarie announced that Freetown was under the control of the RUF, and demanded that Sankoh be released from detention. By late January ECOMOG forces claimed to have regained control of Freetown, and a cease-fire was agreed, pending peace negotiations, which were convened in Conakry, with mediation by the Governments of Guinea, Côte d'Ivoire and Togo. It was reported that Sankoh (who had been allowed by the Sierra Leonean authorities to attend the peace discussions) demanded his release and the official recognition of the RUF as a political movement as preconditions to the cessation of hostilities. Some 100 members of ECOMOG were arrested, following claims by a UN report (which were denied by ECOMOG) that suspected rebels had been summarily executed; the Kamajors were also implicated in summary killings.

Peace negotiations

Following the rebel offensive in January 1999, a number of West African Governments, particularly those of Nigeria and Ghana, reiterated claims that the Liberian Government was supporting the RUF with mercenaries and illicit exports of armaments in exchange for diamonds. ECOMOG also accused Burkina Faso and Libya of assisting rebel operations. Charles Taylor (now the Liberian President) denied any connections with the RUF, dismissing the allegations as an attempt to destabilize his administration. In April the Nigerian President-elect, Olusegun Obasanjo, agreed that the Nigerian contingent (then numbering nearly 15,000) would remain in Sierra Leone until peace was restored, apparently in response to the influence of the international community; however, a gradual withdrawal of ECOMOG troops, to be completed by early 2000, was envisaged. Formal peace negotiations between the RUF and a government delegation commenced in April 1999 in the Togolese capital, Lomé, with mediation by President Gnassingbé Eyadéma of Togo. In early May the Government and the RUF signed a cease-fire agreement, which came into effect later that month. In early July the Government and the RUF reached a power-sharing agreement, after government negotiators acceded to rebel demands that Sankoh be granted vice-presidential powers, with responsibility for the mineral resources industry, and the RUF be allocated a number of cabinet posts. The accord provided for the release of civilians who had been abducted by the rebels, and the disarmament and reintegration into the armed forces of former combatants; the RUF was to be reconstituted as a political organization. Following the completion of disarmament, legislative and presidential elections were to take place by February 2001.

In early October 1999 Sankoh (who had been conducting discussions with Taylor) and Koroma returned to Freetown from Monrovia, and pledged to co-operate with Kabbah in the implementation of the Lomé peace accord. Later that month the UN Security Council adopted Resolution 1270, establishing a 6,000-member force, the UN Mission in Sierra Leone (UNAMSIL), which was granted a six-month mandate to supervise the implementation of the peace agreement, and to assist in a programme for the disarmament and reintegration of the former rebel factions; at the same time the mandate of UNOMSIL was terminated. The withdrawal of the ECOMOG contingent was to be completed following the deployment of UNAMSIL, although, in effect, the new peace-keeping force (which was to comprise 4,000 Nigerian troops and 2,000 principally Kenyan and Indian troops) would incorporate a number of the Nigerian forces belonging to ECOMOG. On 2 November a new coalition Cabinet was officially installed; four former members of the RUF and the AFRC junta were allocated ministerial posts. Sankoh became Chairman of a commission overseeing the reconstruction of the mineral resources industry, with vice-presidential status, while Koroma was nominated Chairman of the Commission for the Consolidation of Peace. In the same month the Government announced the establishment of a Truth and Reconciliation Commission (TRC), which was to make recommendations regarding compensation for victims of human rights violations. However, reports of atrocities perpetrated against the civilian population by rebels continued, and in November division between the AFRC and RUF leadership emerged, apparently as a result of the former junta's dissatisfaction with its cabinet posts.

In early 2000 reports emerged of RUF forces in the Kailahun District of eastern Sierra Leone (where illegal diamond-mining continued) resisting disarmament and the deployment of UNAMSIL troops. In February the UN Security Council adopted a resolution in favour of expanding UNAMSIL to number 11,100, and extended its mandate for six months. In March Kabbah established a commission to supervise the elections, which, under the terms of the peace agreement, were to take place following the disarmament of the former rebel factions. By the end of that month, however, only about 17,000 of the 45,000 former combatants had been disarmed.

Peace-keeping difficulties

In April 2000 UNAMSIL troops stationed in the eastern town of Kenema repulsed attacks from rebel forces. In early May, following a further dispute over disarmament, RUF forces attacked UNAMSIL troops in Makeni and the neighbouring town of Magburaka, killing at least four Kenyan members of the contingent, and seizing a number of UN personnel as hostages. Six civilian UN observers were subsequently released, following intervention by Taylor. However, rebel forces continued to hold about 300 members of UNAMSIL (principally Zambians) hostage, while a further Zambian contingent of the peace-keeping force, numbering about 200, was reported missing. The British Government dispatched a military task force to the region (stationing troops at the airport at Lungi, and in Senegal), which evacuated most European nationals. RUF supporters guarding Sankoh's residence in Freetown fired on civilian demonstrators, who were demanding that Sankoh comply with the peace agreement; some 20 protesters were killed. (UN officials were subsequently unable to contact Sankoh, who had fled from Freetown.) Sierra Leonean government forces, led by Koroma (who continued to support the Kabbah administration), were deployed to halt rebel advances, and claimed to have recaptured territory from the RUF. In late May Sankoh was arrested in Freetown by troops loyal to Kabbah and by the end of that month the hostages held by the RUF were released. In early June, however, 21 Indian members of UNAMSIL were seized by the RUF at the eastern town of Pendembu, while a further 233 peace-keeping troops were surrounded by rebels at nearby Kailahun. By mid-June most of the British forces had withdrawn (with about 250 troops remaining in the country to train new members of the Sierra Leone armed forces, and to assist in establishing the operations of a British military advisory team).

In early July 2000 the UN Security Council adopted a resolution, proposed by the British Government, imposing an international embargo on the purchase of unauthenticated diamonds (in an effort to prevent illicit trade from RUF-held regions, thereby ending the rebels' principal source of funding for armaments); the Sierra Leonean Government was to implement a system whereby officially mined diamonds would be granted certification. In the same month government forces clashed with one of the most notorious militia groups, the West Side Boys (WSB), which had hitherto supported the former AFRC junta. In mid-July the battalion of (principally Indian) peace-keeping personnel, who had been besieged by the RUF at Kailahun, were rescued in a military operation by UNAMSIL; one member of the contingent was killed during the offensive. In early August the UN Security Council approved the establishment of an international tribunal, where Sankoh and others responsible for atrocities committed during the civil conflict would be placed on trial. The RUF leadership announced the nomination of Gen. Issa Sesay (who was reported to be a more moderate commander) to replace Sankoh. Later in August the WSB abducted 11 British military personnel and one member of the Sierra Leonean armed forces, subsequently issuing a number of demands as a precondition to releasing the hostages. Five of the British personnel were freed after negotiations, but additional British troops were dispatched to Sierra Leone, following the failure of government officials to secure an agreement on the remaining hostages. In early September about 150 British troops attacked the main WSB base, 48 km east of Freetown, and succeeded in rescuing the other seven hostages. One member of the British armed forces died during the military operation, while 25 members of the WSB were killed, and a further 18 (including the movement's leader, Foday Kallay) were captured.

In September 2000 the Indian Government announced that it was to withdraw its contingent (then numbering 3,073 troops) from UNAMSIL, despite a proposal by the UN Secretary-General that the maximum strength of the peace-keeping force be increased. In October several nations, notably Bangladesh, Ghana and Kenya, pledged to dispatch additional troops to replace those of India. The number of British troops in the country had been increased to 400, while a 500-member naval task force was deployed off Freetown to provide additional support to the UN peace-keeping operations. On 10 November, following further negotiations mediated by ECOWAS, the Government and the RUF signed a cease-fire agreement in Abuja, providing for the demobilization and disarmament of all militia forces, and the deployment of UNAMSIL throughout the country.

Meanwhile, civilians continued to flee from the country, and by August 2000 some 331,000 Sierra Leonean refugees were registered in Guinea. In September the Guinean President, Gen. Lansana Conté, claimed that Liberian and Sierra Leonean refugees were supporting the activity of rebels attempting to overthrow his Government (see the chapter on Guinea), and ordered them to leave the country. Following clashes on Guinea's border with Liberia, tripartite discussions between Guinea, Liberia and Sierra Leone commenced in October. In March 2001, however, Taylor expelled the ambassadors of Guinea and Sierra Leone from Liberia, on the stated grounds that they had been engaged in activity incompatible with their office. Kabbah retaliated by ordering the Liberian chargé d'affaires to leave the country, and announced the closure of the joint border with Liberia. As a result of the continued violence and the hostility of the Guinean authorities, large numbers of the refugees in Guinea began to return to Sierra Leone. (Diplomatic links between Liberia and Sierra Leone and Guinea were normalized in August, following a request to Taylor by ECOWAS Heads of State.)

In February 2001 the National Assembly unanimously approved a proposal by Kabbah that presidential and legislative elections, scheduled to take place in February and March, respectively, be postponed for six months, owing to the continued civil unrest in the country. At the end of March the UN Security Council adopted a resolution increasing the strength of UNAMSIL (which then numbered 9,500) to 17,500 troops. In June UNAMSIL and (British-trained) government forces regained control of part of the significant diamond-mining regions and the eastern border with Guinea and Sierra Leone (thereby forestalling renewed rebel activity originating from the neighbouring countries). The Government, the RUF and UNAMSIL subsequently agreed to a ban on diamond-mining in eastern regions still controlled by the rebels, in order to facilitate the demobilization of combatants.

In early September 2001 the Government announced that presidential and legislative elections would take place, under the aegis of the UN, on 14 May 2002 (after a further postponement, owing to the continued uncertainty of the security situation). The RUF, however, protested against the delay and threatened to withdraw from the peace process unless an interim coalition administration replaced the incumbent Government. In November 2001 representatives of the Government, the RUF and civil society agreed that parliamentary deputies in the forthcoming elections were to be elected by district (rather than under the previous system of proportional representation). In December the UN Security Council extended its ban on trade in uncertified diamonds for a further 11 months (effective from 5 January 2002).

In January 2002 the UN and the Government reached agreement on the establishment of a war crimes tribunal, to be known as the Special Court, which was to be based in Sierra Leone; the Special Court had a three-year mandate to prosecute crimes perpetrated from the end of November 1996. Meanwhile, the continuing rebel insurgency in northern Liberia, which had advanced rapidly towards Monrovia by early 2002, prompted concern that the resumption of civil conflict there would cause further instability in Sierra Leone. Despite UN pressure on the Liberian Government to end assistance for the RUF, it was reported that Bockarie, supported by 4,000 rebel forces, continued to be based in Liberia.

Following the completion of the disarmament of an estimated 45,000 former combatants in January 2002, the RUF announced its reconstitution as a political organization, the Revolutionary United Front Party (RUFP), with the aim of contesting the elections. In early March, however, Sankoh (who remained titular leader of the RUFP) was formally charged with murder, in connection with the killing of some 20 civilian protesters by his supporters in May 2000. (The trial of Sankoh, together with a further 49 former RUF members, commenced later in March 2002.) In mid-March Kabbah was elected unopposed as the presidential candidate of the SLPP. A total of 24 political parties had officially registered by this time, notably the Peace and Liberation Party (PLP), led by Koroma. However, after the collapse of an opposition alliance, which had been established in late 2001, no serious challenge to the SLPP had emerged. In early April 2002, after the authorities announced that Sankoh would not be permitted to contest the elections on behalf of the RUFP, the party's Secretary-General, Pallo Bangura, was nominated as its presidential candidate. By the end of that month an estimated 60,000 of the 150,000 Sierra Leonean refugees in Guinea and Liberia had returned voluntarily in order to participate in the elections.

Kabbah re-elected

Presidential and legislative elections took place peacefully on 14 May 2002. Kabbah was elected to a second term in office by 70.1% of the votes cast, while Ernest Bai Koroma of the APC received 22.4% of the votes. The SLPP also secured an outright majority in the expanded 124-member Parliament, with 83 seats, while the APC won 27 seats and the PLP two. Later that month Solomon Berewa (hitherto Minister of Justice) became the new Vice-President, and a reorganized Cabinet was installed.

In July 2002 the authorities announced that a seven-member TRC had been established. In August Pallo Bangura resigned his RUFP office, having secured less than 2% of votes cast in the presidential election. In September the UN Security Council adopted a resolution extending the mandate of UNAMSIL for a further six months, but also advocating that the contingent be reduced in size, while in December the UN embargo on illicit trade in diamonds was renewed for a further six months. In February 2003 a further 300 British troops were deployed in Sierra Leone, owing to concern that the intensification of hostilities between government and rebel Liberians United for Reconciliation and Democracy (LURD) forces in Liberia might destabilize the situation in Sierra Leone. (The British military presence in Sierra Leone had been reduced to number some 100 officers in July 2002.)

After the appointment of a British lawyer, Geoffrey Robertson, as President of the Special Court and a US lawyer, David Crane, as Chief Prosecutor, trial activities commenced at the end of 2002. In March 2003 the Special Court approved indictments for war crimes against seven former faction leaders, notably Sankoh, Koroma, the former RUF Commanders, Bockarie and Sesay, and the incumbent Minister of the Interior (and Kamajor leader), Sam Hinga Norman. Five of those indicted, including Hinga Norman, were taken into custody. Koroma went into hiding, following an attempt by the authorities to arrest him, while it was reported that Bockarie was supporting Liberian government forces against the LURD. In April Hinga Norman pleaded not guilty at the Special Court to charges relating to atrocities perpetrated during the civil war. Public hearings before the TRC commenced in mid-April. In early May the Liberian authorities announced that Bockarie had been killed near the border with Côte d'Ivoire, after clashing with Liberian troops attempting to arrest him, and ordered an investigation. Officials at the Special Court claimed that Bockarie and his immediate family had been captured and murdered by Liberian security forces, in an effort to prevent him from testifying against prominent regional figures.

On 4 June 2003 the Special Court officially indicted Taylor for crimes against humanity, owing to his alleged long-standing support for the RUF, and an international warrant was issued for his arrest. The indictment against Taylor immediately precipitated a major offensive against the Liberian capital by rebels demanding his resignation (see the chapter on Liberia). The renewed humanitarian crisis in Liberia during June resulted in further large numbers of Liberian refugees fleeing to southern Sierra Leone. Having accepted an offer of asylum from the Nigerian Head of State, Olusegun Obasanjo, Taylor formally resigned his office and left for exile in Nigeria on 11 August, thereby evading arrest for the charges brought against him by the Special Court. Meanwhile, progress in the case against Sankoh was hindered by the deterioration of his state of health, and, after receiving medical treatment in hospital under UN custody from March, he died at the end of July. Also in July the UN Security Council adopted a resolution recommending the gradual withdrawal of UNAMSIL by the end of 2004, in view of improved security conditions.

In early February 2004 the five-year programme for 'disarmament, demobilization and reintegration' (in which 72,490 former combatants, including 6,845 children, had been disarmed) officially ended. In March Robertson was removed from the office of President of the Special Court, after being accused of demonstrating bias against the RUF in a book he had written concerning the atrocities committed during the civil conflict. At the end of that month, owing to renewed concern that the Sierra Leonean authorities would be unable to maintain stability, particularly in view of the security situations in Guinea and Côte d'Ivoire, the UN Security Council approved a resolution in favour of maintaining a reduced UNAMSIL contingent in the country until the end of September, with further extensions possible.

On 23 September 2004 UNAMSIL officially transferred primary responsibility for security in the remaining parts of the country where it was deployed, including Freetown, to government forces. The UN Security Council approved a further resolution in the same month, authorizing the contingent's continued presence in the country until the end of June 2005.

At the end of June 2005 the UN Security Council extended the mandate of UNAMSIL for a final six months, until the end of that year. In August a further resolution provided for the creation of the United Nations Integrated Office in Sierra Leone (UNIOSIL). Following the complete withdrawal of UNAMSIL as scheduled, UNIOSIL was established on 1 January 2006, for an initial period of one year; the mission was authorized to support the consolidation of peace and assist the Government in strengthening state institutions, the rule of law, human rights, and the security sector, and the organization of presidential and legislative elections, scheduled for July 2007. In December 2006 UNIOSIL's mandate was extended until 31 December 2007. In mid-December the UN Secretary-General recommended that UNIOSIL's mandate be extended for a further nine months, to assist the Government in conducting the forthcoming elections. A new, smaller office was to replace UNIOSIL after that time, which would continue to aid the Sierra Leonean authorities in consolidating peace in the country. At the end of December the UN Security Council approved the final, nine-month extension (until September 2008) of UNIOSIL's mandate.

Meanwhile, in February 2006 the trial of Hinga Norman officially commenced at the Special Court; proceedings against him were expected to be highly controversial, owing to the popular support retained by the Kamajors. In early February 2007 Hinga Norman was taken to a hospital in Dakar, Senegal, for what was termed a routine procedure. On 22 February it was reported that he had collapsed and died in hospital. An autopsy report released the following month concluded that he died of natural causes, although Hinga Norman's family voiced their suspicions at the verdict and were believed to be considering initiating a private investigation into the circumstances surrounding his death.

In March 2006 Nigeria announced that it had received a formal request from the new Liberian Government (see chapter on Liberia) to extradite Taylor to the Special Court. Later that month Taylor fled from his residence in Nigeria in an attempt to evade custody, but was apprehended two days later, near the border with Cameroon, and dispatched to Liberia, from where he was immediately extradited by peace-keeping forces to the Special Court. In early April Taylor (who initially refused to accept the authority of the Court) pleaded not guilty to 11 charges relating to his involvement in the civil conflict in Sierra Leone. Tribunal officials subsequently requested that his trial be transferred to the International Criminal Court (see p. 340) at The Hague, Netherlands (while remaining under the jurisdiction of the Special Court), in the interests of regional stability. The Dutch authorities acceded to that request on the condition that any sentence handed down to Taylor was served in another country. The United Kingdom subsequently agreed to host Taylor should he be imprisoned and, following the unanimous approval of the UN Security Council, on 20 June Taylor was transferred to The Hague. Taylor's trial commenced in early April 2007. Taylor did not appear at the trial until July, when he spoke only to plead 'not guilty' to the charges against him. Proceedings were, however, subsequently delayed while his legal representatives prepared his case, and resumed in January 2008. (Taylor's trial concluded in March 2011 and a verdict was expected later that year.) Meanwhile, in June 2007 the Special Court imposed its first verdicts, finding three former AFRC members guilty of war crimes and crimes against humanity. The following month two of those convicted were sentenced to 50 years' imprisonment, while the third defendant received a prison term of 45 years. All three appealed against their convictions; however, in February 2008 those sentences were upheld by the Special Court. In February 2009 the last trials (of three former RUF members) to be held at the Special Court in Sierra Leone concluded with their conviction of war crimes and crimes against humanity, and in April they were sentenced to terms of imprisonment ranging from 25 to 52 years.

The presidency of Ernest Bai Koroma

Legislative and presidential elections, initially due to be held in July 2007, were postponed until August to allow more time for campaigning and logistical preparations; voting eventually took place on 11 August. Official results indicated that the opposition APC had secured the largest representation in Parliament, taking 59 of the 124 available seats. The SLPP returned 43 deputies and the People's Movement for Democratic Change (PMDC), led by Charles Margai, the son of Sir Albert Margai, took 10 seats. In the presidential election Koroma, contesting the election on behalf of the APC, secured 44.3% of votes cast, while Berewa of the SLPP received 38.3% and Margai 13.9%. As no candidate secured more than 50% of the vote, Koroma and Berewa contested a second round on 8 September, at which Koroma won 60.2% of the votes. The elections were conducted in a largely peaceful manner, despite a small number of disturbances and opposition claims of procedural irregularities. In October President Koroma, who stated the tackling of corruption as one of his priorities, named a partial cabinet list, which included Zainab Hawa Bangura as Minister of Foreign Affairs and David Carew as Minister of Finance and Development. Further appointments were announced later that month, including Abdul Serry Kamal, who assumed the position of Minister of Justice and Attorney-General, and Paolo Conteh, who was awarded the defence portfolio.

In October 2008 UNIOSIL was succeeded by the United Nations Integrated Peacebuilding Office in Sierra Leone (UNIPSIL), which was granted an initial mandate of one year. (In September 2009 the UN Security Council approved the extension of UNIPSIL's mandate until the end of September 2010.) In December 2008 a court repealed the sentences of 11 former armed rebels convicted of treason, the first time death sentences had been overturned in Sierra Leone; the decision was believed by many analysts to mark the beginning of a process to abolish the death penalty in the country. Meanwhile, in September Brig. Alfred Nelson Williams replaced Maj.-Gen. Sam Mboma as Chief of Staff of the Armed Forces.

President Koroma's pledge to address corruption resulted in a number of high-profile dismissals during 2009 and 2010. In November 2009 the Minister of State, Office of the Vice-President, Leonard Balogun Koroma, and the Minister of Health and Sanitation, Sheku Tejan Koroma, were both removed from office amid speculation of their involvement in fraud and corruption. Mohamed D. Koroma, hitherto Deputy Minister for Health and Sanitation, was named to replace Tejan Koroma, while Komba Kono replaced Balogun Koroma. The following month the Commissioner-General of the National Revenue Commission was suspended from office after allegations of financial irregularities were made against him. In late January

SIERRA LEONE

2010 the President again reiterated his intention to take action against those in public office who were found to have engaged in corrupt practices. In an official statement he accused immigration officials of selling passports to foreigners and police officers of demanding payments from civilians at checkpoints. In March Haja Afsatu Kabba, the Minister of Marine Resources and Fisheries, was charged with abuse of office and financial irregularities and was dismissed. She was replaced by Joseph Koroma, who had hitherto served as Minister of Presidential and Public Affairs.

In March 2010 health sector workers staged strike action in pursuit of increased salaries and allowances for transport and housing. Later that month, following extensive negotiations, it was reported that Koroma had agreed to a six-fold increase to rates of pay in the health service and that the strike had ended. In April the Government introduced free health care for pregnant women, breastfeeding mothers, and children under the age of five.

Recent developments: government reorganization

On 15 September 2010 the UN Security Council unanimously adopted a resolution ending the arms embargo and international travel sanctions imposed against former rebels, in view of the restoration of government control in the country. The Council approved a further resolution extending the mandate of UNIPSIL for a further year. In December Koroma effected an extensive government reorganization, in which Kamal was dismissed as Minister of Justice and Attorney-General and replaced by Frank Kargbo; other principal changes included the reassignment of Zainab Hawa Bangura as Minister of Health and Sanitation (the post having remained vacant since November 2009), while a long-standing member of the SLPP, Joseph Bandabla Dauda, was appointed as the new Minister of Foreign Affairs and International Co-operation. In addition, a Ministry of Internal Affairs and a Ministry of Youth Employment and Sports were created. Dauda subsequently resigned from the SLPP, which had suspended his membership, and that of the new Deputy Minister of Health and Sanitation, Borbor Sawyer, after they accepted ministerial posts. In early 2011 it was reported that the SLPP had continued to lose support, with many senior members leaving the party to join the APC. In April Margai publicly declared that the PMDC (which was represented in the Government) was not allied with the APC; some 50 senior members of the PMDC, including two deputy ministers, subsequently announced their resignation from the party, in protest against its leadership.

CONSTITUTION AND GOVERNMENT

Under the terms of the Constitution of 1991, executive power is vested in the President, who is directly elected by universal adult suffrage and must secure at least 25% of the votes cast in each of the four provinces. The President appoints the Cabinet (subject to approval by the legislature). The maximum duration of the President's tenure of office is limited to two five-year terms. Legislative power is vested in a unicameral Parliament, which is elected for a five-year term and comprises 112 members elected by a system of proportional representation, in 14 constituencies, and 12 Paramount Chiefs, who represent the provincial districts. Members of the Parliament are not permitted concurrently to hold office in the Cabinet.

The country is divided into four regions: the Northern, Eastern and Southern Provinces, and the Western Area, which comprise 12 districts. There are 147 chiefdoms, each controlled by a Paramount Chief and a Council of Elders, known as the Tribal Authority.

REGIONAL AND INTERNATIONAL CO-OPERATION

Sierra Leone is a member of the African Union (see p. 183) of the Economic Community of West African States (see p. 257) and of the Mano River Union (see p. 448), which aims to promote economic co-operation with Guinea and Liberia.

Sierra Leone became a member of the UN in 1961, and was admitted to the World Trade Organization (WTO, see p. 430) in 1995. Sierra Leone participates in the Group of 77 (G77, see p. 447) developing countries.

ECONOMIC AFFAIRS

In 2009, according to the World Bank, Sierra Leone's gross national income (GNI), measured at average 2007–09 prices, was US $1,938m., equivalent to $340 per head (or $790 per head on an international purchasing-power parity basis). During 2000–09, it was estimated, the population increased at an average annual rate of 3.4%, while gross domestic product (GDP) per head rose, in real terms, by an average of 6.5% per year. Overall GDP increased, in real terms, at an average annual rate of 10.1% in 2000–09; growth was 4.0% in 2009.

Agriculture (including forestry and fishing) contributed 58.8% of GDP in 2009, according to the African Development Bank (AfDB) and about 59.5% of the labour force were employed in the sector in 2011, according to FAO. The principal cash crops are cocoa beans and coffee. Staple food crops include rice, cassava, and citrus fruit. Chickens, cattle and goats are the principal livestock. In January 2010 the Sierra Leone Government issued a ban on the transport and export of logs, in an attempt to curb the largely uncontrolled logging industry that had been blamed for the depletion of the country's forests. According to the AfDB, during 2000–07 the GDP of the agricultural sector increased at an average annual rate of 5.1%; growth in agricultural GDP was 5.2% in 2009.

Industry (including mining, manufacturing, construction and power) contributed an estimated 6.1% of GDP in 2009, according to the AfDB. This sector employed 6.5% of the working population in 2004. According to the AfDB, the GDP of the industrial sector increased by an average of 11.9% per year in 2000–07; industrial GDP increased by 10.4% in 2007.

Mining and quarrying contributed 2.1% of GDP in 2009 according to the AfDB, and employed 3.6% of the working population in 2004. The principal mineral exports are diamonds (which, according to official figures, accounted for 35.7% of total export earnings in 2010), rutile (titanium dioxide), bauxite and gold. In 1995 increased rebel activity effectively suspended official mining operations (although illicit exports of diamonds by rebel forces continued). In October 2000 official exports of diamonds were resumed under a certification scheme. Following reinvestment in a major kimberlite diamond field at Koidu, production commenced at the end of 2003. The Sierra Rutile mines (the largest source of private sector employment and foreign-exchange earnings prior to 1995) resumed full mining operations in early 2006, while rehabilitation of the country's bauxite mine was completed in 2005, also allowing production to recommence in early 2006. According to the AfDB, the mining sector's GDP decreased by 21.4% in 2008.

Manufacturing contributed an estimated 2.0% of GDP in 2009, according to the AfDB, and engaged 0.5% of the employed population in 2004. The manufacturing sector consists mainly of the production of palm oil and other agro-based industries, textiles and furniture-making. During 2000–07 the GDP of the manufacturing sector increased at an average annual rate of 6.5%, according to the AfDB. Manufacturing GDP increased by 1.6% in 2009.

The construction sector contributed 1.5% of GDP in 2009, according to the AfDB, and employed 2.0% of the engaged population in 2004. According to the AfDB, the sector grew by 2.0% in 2009.

Energy is derived principally from oil-fired thermal power stations. Following long-term energy shortages, a delayed hydroelectric project at Bumbuna, in the north of the country, entered into operation in late 2009. Imports of mineral fuels comprised 22.3% of the value of total imports in 2010.

The services sector contributed 35.1% of GDP in 2009, according to the AfDB, and employed 25.0% of the engaged population in 2004. According to the AfDB, the GDP of the services sector increased by an average of 21.5% per year in 2000–07; it grew by 3.7% in 2007.

In 2009 Sierra Leone recorded an estimated trade deficit of US $241.5m., and there was a deficit of $290.1m. on the current account of the balance of payments. In 2005, according to UN estimates, the principal source of imports (17.6%) was Côte d'Ivoire; the other major supplier was the People's Republic of China. In 2003 Belgium was the principal market for exports (taking 57.0% of the total); the other significant purchaser was Germany. The principal export in 2010 was diamonds. The principal imports in that year were machinery and transport equipment, mineral fuels and lubricants, basic manufactures, food and live animals, and chemicals.

In 2009 the country recorded an overall budget deficit of Le 655,000m. Sierra Leone's general government gross debt was Le 3,879,100m. in 2009, equivalent to 61.3% of GDP. Sierra Leone's external debt totalled US $389m. at the end of 2008, of which $327m. was public and publicly guaranteed debt. The annual rate of inflation averaged 12.2% in 2003–09. Consumer prices

SIERRA LEONE

increased by 9.0% in 2009. An estimated 68,252 (3.5%) people were unemployed, according to the 2004 census.

Civil conflict, which commenced in 1991, resulted in the progressive destruction of Sierra Leone's infrastructure, and severe disruption, or complete suspension, of traditional economic activities. However, since the end of the civil war in January 2002 the country has experienced substantial real economic growth and declining inflation. Additionally, improvements in fiscal control and considerable support from international financial institutions have resulted in some progress in reconstruction. Sierra Leone's economic prospects improved further with the post-war resumption of the production and export of rutile and bauxite in early 2006, with production increasing steadily. Following the restoration of government control throughout the country, Sierra Leone became increasingly popular as a tourism destination. In May the IMF approved a three-year US $46.3m. arrangement for Sierra Leone under the existing Poverty Reduction and Growth Facility (PRGF) for low-income countries. The Fund praised the country's performance under the previous PRGF-supported programme and commended the Government's 2006–08 economic programme, which aimed, *inter alia*, to target poverty reduction and improve revenue administration. In June 2009 the IMF, after conducting its fourth review under the PRGF, agreed to the disbursement of $18.8m. to support export revenues during the global economic crisis. The completion of a delayed hydroelectric project at Bumbuna, in the north of the country, in late 2009 was expected to resolve long-term electricity shortages in the capital (although further technical difficulties were reported). In June 2010 the IMF approved a three-year Extended Credit Facility (ECF) of about $45.4m. as a successor financial arrangement to the PRGF. In December the IMF completed the first review of Sierra Leone's economic performance under the ECF-supported programme and approved a disbursement of $6.8m. GDP growth, which had slowed to 3.2% in 2009, rose to an estimated 5% in 2010, following strong output in the services and agriculture sectors, and a recovery in exports. Fiscal policy in 2011 continued to focus on increased investment in basic infrastructure, notably the expansion of the country's road network and modernization of the international airport. In January 2011 the Government announced new incentives for foreign businesses, which included exemption from an export licence requirement for the export of locally produced goods, except precious minerals.

PUBLIC HOLIDAYS

2012: 1 January (New Year's Day), 4 February* (Mouloud, Birth of the Prophet), 6–9 April (Easter), 27 April (Independence Day), 18 August* (Id al-Fitr, end of Ramadan), 26 October* (Id al-Adha, Feast of the Sacrifice), 25–26 December (Christmas and Boxing Day).

* These holidays are dependent on the Islamic lunar calendar and may vary by one or two days from the dates given.

Statistical Survey

Source (unless otherwise stated): Central Statistics Office, PMB 595, Tower Hill, Freetown; tel. (22) 223287; fax (22) 223897; internet www.sierra-leone.org/cso.html and www.statistics-sierra-leone.org.

Area and Population

AREA, POPULATION AND DENSITY

Area (sq km)	71,740*
Population (census results)†	
14 December 1985	3,515,812
4 December 2004	
Males	2,420,218
Females	2,556,653
Total	4,976,871
Population (UN estimates at mid-year)‡	
2009	5,696,471
2010	5,835,664
2011	5,977,770
Density (per sq km) at mid-2011	83.3

* 27,699 sq miles.
† Excluding adjustment for underenumeration, estimated to have been 9% in 1985.
‡ Source: UN, *World Population Prospects: The 2008 Revision*.

POPULATION BY AGE AND SEX
(UN estimates at mid-2011)

	Males	Females	Total
0–14	1,298,172	1,303,385	2,601,557
15–64	1,564,052	1,702,760	3,266,812
65 and over	52,842	56,559	109,401
Total	2,915,066	3,062,704	5,977,770

Source: UN, *World Population Prospects: The 2008 Revision*.

ADMINISTRATIVE DISTRICTS
(population at 2004 census)

	Population
Bo	463,668
Bombali	408,390
Bonthe	129,947
Kailahun	358,190
Kambia	270,462
Kenema	497,948
Koinadugu	265,758
Kono	335,401
Moyamba	260,910
Port Loko	453,746
Pujehun	228,392
Sherbo	9,740
Tonkolili	347,197
Western Area Rural District	174,2489
Western Area Urban District	772,873
Total	4,976,871

PRINCIPAL TOWNS
(population at 2004 census)

Freetown (capital)	772,873*	Makeni	82,840
Bo	149,957	Koindu	80,025
Kenema	128,402		

* Western Area Urban District.

Mid-2010 (incl. suburbs, UN estimate): Freetown 900,847 (Source: UN, *World Urbanization Prospects: The 2009 Revision*).

BIRTHS AND DEATHS
(annual averages, UN estimates)

	1995–2000	2000–05	2005–10
Birth rate (per 1,000)	42.7	41.9	40.4
Death rate (per 1,000)	23.7	18.7	16.0

Source: UN, *World Population Prospects: The 2008 Revision*.

Life expectancy (years at birth, WHO estimates): 49 (males 48; females 50) in 2008 (Source: WHO, *World Health Report*).

SIERRA LEONE

ECONOMICALLY ACTIVE POPULATION
(persons aged 10 years and over, 2004 census)

	Male	Female	Total
Agriculture, hunting and forestry	617,928	654,306	1,272,234
Fishing	33,317	17,822	51,139
Mining and quarrying	59,311	9,663	68,974
Manufacturing	7,397	2,015	9,412
Electricity, gas and water supply	7,104	1,243	8,347
Construction	28,239	10,829	39,068
Wholesale and retail trade; Repair of motor vehicles, motorcycles, and personal and household goods	102,212	167,283	269,495
Hotels and restaurants	2,619	2,312	4,931
Transport, communications and storage	14,425	1,257	15,682
Financial intermediation	3,993	2,941	6,934
Real estate, renting and business activities	5,475	5,310	10,785
Public administration and defence; compulsory social security	21,126	4,853	25,979
Education	23,254	11,326	34,580
Health and social work	9,852	9,976	19,828
Other community, social and personal service activities	44,423	39,063	83,486
Households with employed persons	3,983	4,306	8,289
Extra-territorial organizations and bodies	2,508	1,338	3,846
Total employed	**987,166**	**945,843**	**1,933,009**
Unemployed	45,936	22,316	68,252
Total labour force	**1,033,102**	**968,159**	**2,001,261**

Unemployed: 68,252 at census of 2004 (males 45,936, females 22,316).

Source: ILO.

Mid-2011 (estimates in '000): Agriculture, etc. 1,340; Total labour force 2,251 (Source: FAO).

Health and Welfare

KEY INDICATORS

Total fertility rate (children per woman, 2008)	5.2
Under-5 mortality rate (per 1,000 live births, 2008)	194
HIV/AIDS (% of persons aged 15–49, 2007)	1.7
Physicians (per 1,000 head, 2004)	0.03
Hospital beds (per 1,000 head, 2006)	0.4
Health expenditure (2007): US $ per head (PPP)	32
Health expenditure (2007): % of GDP	4.4
Health expenditure (2007): public (% of total)	31.3
Access to water (% of persons, 2008)	49
Access to sanitation (% of persons, 2008)	13
Total carbon dioxide emissions ('000 metric tons, 2007)	1,311.7
Carbon dioxide emissions per head (metric tons, 2007)	0.2
Human Development Index (2010): ranking	158
Human Development Index (2010): value	0.317

For sources and definitions, see explanatory note on p. vi.

Agriculture

PRINCIPAL CROPS
('000 metric tons)

	2006	2007*	2008*
Rice, paddy	1,062.3	1,000.0	1,000.0*
Maize	48.8	48.0	48.0*
Millet	25†	25	25*
Sorghum*	23.0	23.0	23.0
Sweet potatoes*	30.0	30.0	30.0
Cassava (Manioc)*	350.0	370.0	370.0
Sugar cane*	70	70	70
Groundnuts, with shell	115.2	115.0	115.0*
Oil palm fruit*	195.0	195.0	195.0
Tomatoes*	18.0	18.0	18.0
Plantains*	35.0	35.0	35.0
Citrus fruit*	90.0	90.0	90.0
Coffee, green*	18.0	18.0	18.0
Cocoa beans	13.9	14.0	10.5†

* FAO estimate(s).
† Unofficial figure.

2009: Cocoa beans 10.0 (unofficial figure).

Aggregate production ('000 metric tons, may include official, semi-official or estimated data): Total cereals 1,162.6 in 2006, 1,099.5 in 2007, 1,099.5 in 2008–09; Total roots and tubers 382.9 in 2006, 402.9 in 2007, 402.9 in 2008–09; Total vegetables (incl. melons) 258.0 in 2006, 268.0 in 2007, 268.0 in 2008–09; Total fruits (excl. melons) 199.8 in 2006, 200.0 in 2007, 200.0 in 2008–09.

Source: FAO.

LIVESTOCK
('000 head, year ending September)

	2006	2007*	2008*
Cattle	350.0	350.0	350.0
Pigs*	54	55	52
Sheep	470	470	470
Goats	540	540	540
Chickens*	7,600	7,700	7,700
Ducks*	80	80	75

* FAO estimates.

2009: Chickens 7,800 (FAO estimate).

Source: FAO.

LIVESTOCK PRODUCTS
('000 metric tons, FAO estimates)

	2007	2008	2009
Chicken meat	11.7	11.7	11.9
Pig meat	2.5	2.3	2.3
Game meat	3.0	3.0	n.a.
Cows' milk	18.5	18.5	18.5
Hen eggs	9.0	9.0	9.0

Source: FAO.

Forestry

ROUNDWOOD REMOVALS
('000 cubic metres, excl. bark, FAO estimates)

	2007	2008	2009
Sawlogs, veneer logs and logs for sleepers*	3.6	3.6	3.6
Other industrial wood†	120.0	120.0	120.0
Fuel wood	5,477.0	5,508.8	5,544.0
Total	**5,600.6**	**5,632.4**	**5,667.6**

* Annual output assumed to be unchanged since 1993.
† Annual output assumed to be unchanged since 1980.

Source: FAO.

SIERRA LEONE

SAWNWOOD PRODUCTION
('000 cubic metres, incl. railway sleepers)

	1991	1992	1993
Total (all broadleaved)	9.0	9.0*	5.3

* FAO estimate.

1994–2009: Annual production as in 1993 (FAO estimates).

Source: FAO.

Fishing

('000 metric tons, live weight of capture)

	2006	2007	2008
Freshwater fishes*	14.0	14.0	14.0
West African ilisha	3.3	3.9	7.8
Tonguefishes	1.0	1.2	1.3
Bobo croaker	11.1	8.7	12.2
Sardinellas	15.2	16.6	20.2
Bonga shad	60.1	52.7	86.0
Tuna-like fishes	1.4	2.3	2.7
Penaeusus shrimps	1.4	1.4	1.0
Marine molluscs	1.1	0.9	0.8
Total catch (incl. others)*	148.1	144.5	203.6

* FAO estimates.

Source: FAO.

Mining

(metric tons, unless otherwise indicated)

	2007	2008	2009
Cement (hydraulic)	235,830	254,160	236,240
Bauxite ('000 metric tons)	1,169	954	757
Diamonds ('000 carats)	604	371	401
Ilmenite	15,750	17,528	15,161
Rutile	82,527	78,908	63,864

Source: US Geological Survey.

Industry

PETROLEUM PRODUCTS
('000 metric tons, estimates)

	2005	2006	2007
Jet fuels	21	22	22
Motor spirit (petrol)	32	33	33
Kerosene	10	11	11
Distillate fuel oils	60	60	60
Residual fuel oils	35	40	40

Source: UN Industrial Commodity Statistics Database.

SELECTED OTHER PRODUCTS
('000 metric tons, unless otherwise indicated)

	2005	2006	2007
Beer and stout ('000 crates)	1,012	832	780
Soft drinks ('000 crates)	1,908	2,089	2,432
Confectionery ('000 kg)	2,074.3	2,329.9	3,141.0
Soap (metric tons)	417	n.a.	n.a.
Paint ('000 litres)	135	649	714
Cement*	172.1	234.4	235.8

* Source: US Geological Survey.

Cement: 236.2 in 2009 (Source: US Geological Survey).

Source: mainly IMF, *Sierra Leone: Selected Issues and Statistical Appendix* (January 2009).

Finance

CURRENCY AND EXCHANGE RATES

Monetary Units
100 cents = 1 leone (Le).

Sterling, Dollar and Euro Equivalents (30 November 2010)
£1 sterling = 6,508.59 leones;
US $1 = 4,191.52 leones;
€1 = 5,448.14 leones;
10,000 leones = £1.54 = $2.39 = €1.84.

Average Exchange Rate (leones per US $)
2007   2,985.19
2008   2,981.51
2009   3,385.65

CENTRAL GOVERNMENT BUDGET
(Le '000 million)

Revenue*	2008	2009	2010†
Tax	589	660	839
Personal income tax	110	122	148
Goods and services tax	62	61	76
Import duties	161	170	216
Excise duties	70	107	137
Non-tax revenue	80	89	107
Total	670	749	946

Expenditure	2008	2009	2010†
Current expenditure	1,207	1,452	1,770
Wages and salaries	334	402	506
Goods and services	285	350	339
Transfer and subsidies	109	145	170
Interest	120	103	136
Capital expenditure	359	452	619
Total	1,566	1,904	2,389

* Excluding grants received (Le '000 million): 265 in 2008; 500 in 2009; 529 in 2010 (projected).
† Projected.

Source: IMF, *Sierra Leone: Sixth Review Under the Arrangement Under the Extended Credit Facility, Request for Waiver for Nonobservance of a Performance Criterion, Request for a Three-Year Arrangement Under the Extended Credit Facility, and Financing Assurances Review—Staff Report; Press Release on the Executive Board Discussion; and Statement by the Executive Director for Sierra Leone* (June 2010).

INTERNATIONAL RESERVES
(US $ million at 31 December)

	2007	2008	2009
IMF special drawing rights	30.7	30.4	189.6
Foreign exchange	185.8	189.7	215.3
Total	216.6	220.2	405.0

2010: IMF special drawing rights 29.5.

Source: IMF, *International Financial Statistics*.

MONEY SUPPLY
(Le million at 31 December)

	2008	2009	2010
Currency outside banks	340,355	420,921	557,262
Demand deposits at commercial banks	301,741	359,688	454,007
Total money (incl. others)	666,668	807,479	1,048,055

Source: IMF, *International Financial Statistics*.

SIERRA LEONE

COST OF LIVING
(Consumer Price Index; base: 2003 = 100)

	2007	2008	2009
Food (incl. beverages)	159.3	186.4	203.2
Clothing	120.5	131.7	143.7
Rent	178.3	200.1	207.5
All items (incl. others)	160.8	182.6	199.0

Source: ILO.

NATIONAL ACCOUNTS
(million leones at current prices)

Expenditure on the Gross Domestic Product

	2007	2008	2009
Government final consumption expenditure	715,248	924,043	924,043
Private final consumption expenditure	4,336,998	4,547,239	4,547,239
Gross fixed capital formation	388,641	396,295	3,100,589
Changes in inventories	1,797,658	2,178,399	396,295
Total domestic expenditure	7,238,545	8,045,976	8,968,166
Exports of goods and services	914,841	843,671	843,671
Less Imports of goods and services	2,319,679	2,462,501	2,462,501
GDP in purchasers' values	5,833,707	6,427,146	7,349,336

Gross Domestic Product by Economic Activity

	2007	2008	2009
Agriculture, hunting, forestry and fishing	3,237,701	3,624,040	4,163,635
Mining and quarrying	246,967	171,161	146,655
Manufacturing	114,586	128,082	141,939
Electricity, gas and water	15,999	16,917	36,458
Construction	92,674	95,936	106,652
Wholesale and retail trade, restaurants and hotels	551,227	587,859	669,789
Finance, insurance, real estate and business services	291,644	317,536	358,655
Transport and communications	349,866	424,827	495,584
Public administration and defence	224,005	216,070	231,016
Other services	484,468	592,564	725,433
Sub-total	5,609,137	6,174,992	7,075,816
Less Imputed bank service charges	78,157	105,210	161,183
Indirect taxes, less subsidies	302,727	357,365	434,702
GDP in purchasers' values	5,833,707	6,427,146	7,349,336

Source: African Development Bank.

BALANCE OF PAYMENTS
(US $ million)

	2007	2008	2009
Exports of goods f.o.b.	288.9	273.5	270.3
Imports of goods f.o.b.	−395.4	−471.2	−511.9
Trade balance	−106.6	−197.7	−241.5
Exports of services	45.3	61.4	52.7
Imports of services	−98.0	−125.4	−115.9
Balance on goods and services	−159.2	−261.7	−304.8
Other income received	43.3	17.7	11.2
Other income paid	−147.6	−92.4	−46.9
Balance on goods, services and income	−263.5	−336.5	−340.5
Current transfers received	49.4	43.9	53.8
Current transfers paid	−2.8	−7.4	−3.4
Current balance	−216.9	−300.0	−290.1
Capital account (net)	239.5	61.4	68.6
Direct investment (net)	96.6	57.6	74.3
Portfolio investment (net)	—	1.6	5.6
Other investment assets	−6.1	−2.8	18.3
Other investment liabilities	0.2	39.0	236.6
Net errors and omissions	−143.2	−21.6	−212.5
Overall balance	−29.9	−164.8	−99.1

Source: IMF, *International Financial Statistics*.

External Trade

PRINCIPAL COMMODITIES
(US $ '000)

Imports c.i.f.	2008	2009	2010
Food and live animals	116,083.5	104,509.7	104,894.0
Beverages and tobacco	22,139.5	25,255.6	19,487.5
Crude materials (inedible) except fuels	14,345.3	16,142.2	13,267.3
Mineral fuels, lubricants, etc.	200,641.8	126,459.4	171,414.2
Animal and vegetable oils and fats	4,719.7	7,764.1	9,435.1
Chemicals	24,515.9	33,682.7	43,837.9
Basic manufactures	56,875.9	67,746.2	110,535.5
Machinery and transport equipment	75,586.7	95,085.7	248,698.2
Miscellaneous manufactured articles	19,231.3	43,659.2	18,217.6
Miscellaneous transactions and commodities	—	—	30,250.2
Total	534,139.6	520,304.8	770,037.5

Exports f.o.b.	2008	2009	2010
Bauxite	28,063.1	18,678.0	31,061.1
Coffee	1,487.6	13,123.6	1,698.2
Cocoa beans	14,982.0	20,544.6	37,051.2
Diamonds	98,803.7	78,374.0	113,514.7
Rutile	36,658.7	35,920.4	40,567.2
Total (incl. others)*	200,911.5	207,100.3	317,780.7

* Including re-exports: 14,755.6 in 2008; 23,561.9 in 2009; 23,445.7 in 2010.

Source: Bank of Sierra Leone.

PRINCIPAL TRADING PARTNERS

Imports c.i.f. (US $ million)	2002
Canada	23.0
China, People's Repub.	11.8
Côte d'Ivoire	129.1
Germany	9.1
India	13.2
Japan	14.9
Netherlands	19.4
United Kingdom	11.9
USA	17.4
Total (incl. others)	352.0

2005: Canada 2.0; China, People's Republic 18.8; Côte d'Ivoire 60.0; Germany 5.0; India 9.5; Japan 10.1; Netherlands 9.0; United Kingdom 15.1; USA 11.9; Total (incl. others) 341.1.

Source: UN, *International Trade Statistics Yearbook*.

Exports (Le million)	1992	1993	1994
Belgium	25,770	54	11,412
Germany	1,060	2,486	1,328
Guinea	1,315	817	1,331
Netherlands	5,307	1,201	2,815
Switzerland	7,546	486	215
United Kingdom	5,567	5,988	11,767
USA	13,832	17,564	30,431
Total (incl. others)	75,034	67,077	67,930

Source: Central Statistics Office, Freetown.

SIERRA LEONE

Transport

ROAD TRAFFIC
(motor vehicles in use at 31 December)

	2000	2001	2002
Passenger cars	2,045	2,263	11,353
Buses and coaches	2,597	3,516	4,050
Goods vehicles	2,309	2,898	3,565
Motorcycles	1,398	1,532	1,657

2007 (motor vehicles in use at 31 December): Passenger cars 16,396; Buses and coaches 390; Vans and lorries 14,054; Motorcycles and mopeds 8,198.

Source: IRF, *World Road Statistics*.

SHIPPING

Merchant Fleet
(registered at 31 December)

	2007	2008	2009
Number of vessels	302	365	330
Displacement (gross registered tons)	486,843	612,448	628,490

Source: Lloyd's Register-Fairplay, *World Fleet Statistics*.

International Sea-borne Freight Traffic
(estimates, '000 metric tons)

	1991	1992	1993
Goods loaded	1,930	2,190	2,310
Goods unloaded	562	579	589

Source: UN Economic Commission for Africa, *African Statistical Yearbook*.

CIVIL AVIATION
(traffic on scheduled services)

	2004	2005	2006
Kilometres flown (million)	1	2	2
Passengers carried ('000)	16	17	19
Passenger-km (million)	85	94	101
Total ton-km (million)	15	17	19

Source: UN, *Statistical Yearbook*.

Tourism

TOURIST ARRIVALS BY REGION OF RESIDENCE

	2006	2007	2008
Africa	10,122	10,846	11,915
Americas	6,669	6,169	6,684
Asia	4,898	2,916	3,142
Europe	10,470	11,327	12,713
Middle East	1,545	965	888
Not specified	—	—	328
Total	33,704	32,223	35,670

Tourism receipts (US $ million, excl. passenger transport): 23 in 2006; 22 in 2007; 34 in 2008.

Source: World Tourism Organization.

Communications Media

	2007	2008	2009
Telephones ('000 main lines in use)	30.3	31.5	32.8
Mobile cellular telephones ('000 subscribers)	776.0	1,008.8	1,160.0
Internet users ('000)	13.0	13.9	14.9

Radio receivers ('000 in use): 1,120 in 1997.
Daily newspapers: 1 (average circulation 20,000) in 1996.
Television receivers ('000 in use): 64 in 2006; 65 in 2007.

Sources: UNESCO, *Statistical Yearbook*; UN, *Statistical Yearbook*; and International Telecommunication Union.

Education

(2006/07, unless otherwise indicated)

	Schools*	Teachers	Males	Females	Total
Pre-primary	n.a.	1,224	11,989	12,818	24,807
Primary	2,704	30,239	693,710	628,495	1,322,205
Secondary	246	10,024	141,418	98,161	239,579
Tertiary*	n.a.	1,198	6,439	2,602	9,041

* 2001/02.

Source: mainly UNESCO Institute for Statistics.

Pupil-teacher ratio (primary education, UNESCO estimate): 43.7 in 2006/07 (Source: UNESCO Institute for Statistics).

Adult literacy rate (UNESCO estimates): 39.8% (males 51.7%; females 28.9%) in 2008 (Source: UNESCO Institute for Statistics).

Directory

The Government

HEAD OF STATE

President and Commander-in-Chief of the Armed Forces: ERNEST BAI KOROMA (elected 8 September 2007; inaugurated 15 November 2007).

Vice-President, Minister of Health and Sanitation: SAHR SAM-SUMANA.

CABINET
(May 2011)

The Government is formed by members of the All-People's Congress.

Minister of Finance and Economic Development: Dr SAMURA KAMARA.

Minister of Foreign Affairs and International Co-operation: JOSEPH BANDABLA DAUDA.

Minister of Justice and Attorney-General: FRANK KARBGO.

Minister of Information and Communications: Alhaji IBRAHIM BEN KARGBO.

Minister of Health and Sanitation: ZAINAB HAWA BANGURA.

Minister of Agriculture, Food Security and Forestry: Dr SAM SESAY.

Minister of Works, Housing and Infrastructure: ALIMAMY P. KOROMA.

Minister of Education, Science and Technology: Dr MINKAILU BAH.

Minister of Political and Public Affairs: Alhaji ALPHA SAHID BAKAR KANU.

SIERRA LEONE

Minister of Lands, Country Planning and the Environment: Capt. ALLIEU PAT SOWE.
Minister of Defence: Maj. (retd) ALFRED PALO CONTEH.
Minister of Local Government and Rural Development: DAUDA SULAIMAN KAMARA.
Minister of Internal Affairs: MUSA TARAWALLI.
Minister of Marine Resources and Fisheries: Dr SOCCOH KABIA.
Minister of Energy and Water Resources: Prof. OGUNLADE DAVIDSON.
Minister of Tourism and Cultural Affairs: VICTORIA SAIDU KAMARA.
Minister of Youth Employment and Sports: PAUL KAMARA.
Minister of Mineral Resources: Alhaji MINKAILU MANSARAY.
Minister of Labour and Social Security: HINDOLO SUMANGURU TRYE.
Minister of Trade and Industry: Dr RICHARD CONTEH.
Minister of Transport and Aviation: VANDI CHIDI MINAH.
Minister of Social Welfare, Gender and Children's Affairs: Dr DENNIS SANDY.
Minister of State, Office of the Vice-President: Dr KOMBA KONO.
Special Adviser to the President: KEMOH SESAY.
Resident Minister, Eastern Region: WILLIAM JUANA SMITH.
Resident Minister, Southern Region: MOIJUE KAIKAI.
Resident Minister, Northern Region: ALIE KAMARA.

There were also 24 Deputy Ministers and one Minister of State.

MINISTRIES

Office of the President: Freetown; tel. (22) 232101; fax (22) 231404; e-mail info@statehouse-sl.org; internet www.statehouse.gov.sl.

Ministry of Agriculture, Food Security and Forestry: Youyi Bldg, 3rd Floor, Brookfields, Freetown; tel. (22) 222242; fax (22) 241613.

Ministry of Defence: State Ave, Freetown; tel. (22) 227369; fax (22) 229380.

Ministry of Education, Science and Technology: New England, Freetown; tel. (22) 240881; fax (22) 240137.

Ministry of Energy and Water Resources: Electricity House, 4th Floor, Siaka Stevens St, Freetown; tel. (22) 226566; fax (22) 228199; e-mail info@energyandpower.gov.sl; internet www.energyandpower.gov.sl.

Ministry of Foreign Affairs and International Co-operation: Gloucester St, Freetown; tel. (22) 223260; fax (22) 225615; e-mail mfaicsl@yahoo.com.

Ministry of Health and Sanitation: Youyi Bldg, 4th Floor, Brookfields, Freetown; tel. (22) 240187; e-mail info@health.sl; internet www.health.sl.

Ministry of Information and Communications: Youyi Bldg, 8th Floor, Brookfields, Freetown; tel. (22) 240339; fax (22) 241757.

Ministry of Internal Affairs: Liverpool St, Freetown; tel. (22) 226979; fax (22) 227727.

Ministry of Justice: Guma Bldg, Lamina Sankoh St, Freetown; tel. (22) 227444; fax (22) 229366.

Ministry of Labour and Social Security: New England Ville, Freetown; tel. (22) 78341246; fax (22) 228472.

Ministry of Lands, Country Planning and the Environment: Youyi Bldg, 4th Floor, Brookfields, Freetown; tel. (22) 242013.

Ministry of Local Government and Rural Development: New England, Freetown; tel. (22) 226589; fax (22) 222409.

Ministry of Marine Resources and Fisheries: Marine House, 11 Old Railway Line, Brookfields, Freetown; tel. (22) 242117.

Ministry of Mineral Resources: Youyi Bldg, 5th Floor, Brookfields, Freetown; tel. and fax (22) 240467; e-mail contact@mmr-sl.org; internet www.mmr-sl.org.

Ministry of Political and Public Affairs: State House, State Ave, Freetown; tel. (22) 228698; fax (22) 222781.

Ministry of Social Welfare, Gender and Children's Affairs: New England, Freetown; tel. (22) 241256; fax (22) 242076.

Ministry of Tourism and Cultural Affairs: Ministerial Bldg, George St, Freetown; tel. (22) 222588.

Ministry of Trade and Industry: 6th Floor, Youyi Bldg, Brookfields, Freetown; tel. (22) 225127; e-mail info@trade.gov.sl; internet www.trade.gov.sl.

Ministry of Transport and Aviation: Ministerial Bldg, George St, Freetown; tel. (22) 221245; fax (22) 227337.

Ministry of Works, Housing and Infrastructure: New England, Freetown; tel. (22) 240937; fax (22) 240018.

Ministry of Youth Employment and Sports: New England, Freetown; tel. (22) 240881; fax (22) 240137.

President and Legislature

PRESIDENT

Presidential Election, First Round, 11 August 2007

Candidate	Votes	% of votes
Ernest Bai Koroma (APC)	815,523	44.34
Solomon Berewa (SLPP)	704,012	38.28
Charles Margai (PMDC)	255,499	13.89
Others	64,174	3.48
Total	1,839,208	100.00

Presidential Election, Second Round, 8 September 2007

Candidate	Votes	% of votes
Ernest Bai Koroma (APC)	859,144	60.22
Solomon Berewa (SLPP)	567,449	39.78
Total	1,426,593	100.00

PARLIAMENT

Speaker: Justice E. K. COWAN.

General Election, 11 August 2007

Party	Seats
All-People's Congress (APC)	59
Sierra Leone People's Party (SLPP)	43
People's Movement for Democratic Change (PMDC)	10
Total	112*

*A further 12 seats were allocated to Paramount Chiefs, who represented the 12 provincial districts.

Election Commission

National Electoral Commission (NEC): NEC Bldg, 15 Industrial Estate, Wellington, Freetown; tel. 76547299; internet www.nec-sierraleone.org; f. 2000; Chair. CHRISTIANA AYOKA MARY THORPE.

Political Organizations

A ban on political activity was rescinded in June 1995. Numerous political parties were officially granted registration, prior to elections in May 2002.

All-People's Congress (APC): 137H Fourah Bay Rd, Freetown; e-mail info@new-apc.org; internet apcparty.org; f. 1960; sole authorized political party 1978–91; merged with the Democratic People's Party in 1992; reconstituted in 1995; Leader ERNEST BAI KOROMA.

Citizens United for Peace and Progress (CUPP): e-mail info@cupp.org; internet www.cupp.org; f. 2002; Chair. ABUBAKARR YANSSANEH.

Peace and Liberation Party (PLP): Freetown; f. 2002; Leader (vacant).

People's Democratic Party (PDP): Freetown; supported Sierra Leone People's Party in May 2002 elections; Leader OSMAN KAMARA.

People's Movement for Democratic Change (PMDC): 9A Hannah Benka-Coker St, Freetown; e-mail karamohslylhorg@aol.com; internet www.pmdcsl.net; f. April 2006 by fmr mems of Sierra Leone People's Party; Leader CHARLES F. MARGAI; Sec.-Gen. ANSU B. LANSANA.

People's National Convention (PNC): Leader EDWARD JOHN KARGBO.

Sierra Leone People's Party (SLPP): 15 Wallace Johnson St, Freetown; tel. and fax (22) 2256341; e-mail info@slpp.ws; internet www.slpp.ws; f. 1951; Nat. Chair. JOHN BENJAMIN.

United National People's Party (UNPP): Leader Dr JOHN KAREFA-SMART.

Young People's Party (YPP): 19 Lewis St, Freetown; tel. (22) 232907; e-mail info@yppsl.org; internet www.yppsl.org; f. 2002; Leader SYLVIA BLYDEN; Sec.-Gen. ABDUL RAHMAN YILLA.

SIERRA LEONE

Diplomatic Representation

EMBASSIES AND HIGH COMMISSIONS IN SIERRA LEONE

China, People's Republic: 29 Wilberforce Loop, POB 778, Freetown; tel. and fax (22) 231797; e-mail chinaemb_sl@mfa.gov.cn; internet sl.china-embassy.org; Ambassador KUANG WEILIN.

Egypt: 174C Wilkinson Rd, POB 652, Freetown; tel. (22) 231245; fax (22) 234297; Ambassador GAMAL TAWFIK ABDULLAH.

The Gambia: 6 Wilberforce St, Freetown; tel. (22) 225191; fax (22) 226846; High Commissioner DEMBO BADJIE.

Ghana: 13 Walpole St, Freetown; tel. (22) 223461; fax (22) 227043; High Commissioner ELIZABETH MILLS-ROBERTSON.

Guinea: 6 Wilkinson Rd, Freetown; tel. (22) 232584; fax (22) 232496; Ambassador MOHAMED LAMIN SOMPARE.

Lebanon: 22A Spur Rd, Wilberforce, Freetown; tel. (22) 222513; fax (22) 234665; Ambassador GHASSAN ABDEL SATER.

Liberia: 10 Motor Rd, Brookfields, POB 276, Freetown; tel. (22) 230991; Chargé d'affaires a.i. THOMAS BRIMA.

Libya: 1A and 1B P. Z. Compound, Wilberforce, Freetown; tel. (22) 235231; fax (22) 234514; Ambassador Dr MOHAMED AL-HARARI ABDUL SALAAM.

Nigeria: 37 Siaka Stevens St, Freetown; tel. (22) 224224; fax (22) 2242474; High Commissioner GODSON O. ECHEGILE.

United Kingdom: 6 Spur Rd, Wilberforce, Freetown; tel. (22) 232565; fax (22) 232070; e-mail freetown.consular.enquiries@fco.gov.uk; internet ukinsierraleone.fco.gov.uk; High Commissioner IAN HUGHES.

USA: South Ridge, Hill Station, Freetown; tel. (22) 515000; fax (22) 515355; e-mail TaylorJB2@state.gov; internet freetown.usembassy.gov; Ambassador MICHAEL S. OWEN.

Judicial System

The Supreme Court

The Supreme Court is the ultimate court of appeal in both civil and criminal cases. In addition to its appellate jurisdiction, the Court has supervisory jurisdiction over all other courts and over any adjudicating authority in Sierra Leone, and also original jurisdiction in constitutional issues.

Chief Justice: UMU HAWA TEJAN JALLOH.

Supreme Court Justices: C. A. HARDING, AGNES AWUNOR-RENNER, PATRICK HAMILTON.

The Court of Appeal

The Court of Appeal has jurisdiction to hear and determine appeals from decisions of the High Court in both criminal and civil matters, and also from certain statutory tribunals. Appeals against its decisions may be made to the Supreme Court.

Justices of Appeal: S. C. E. WARNE, C. S. DAVIES, S. T. NAVO, M. S. TURAY, E. C. THOMPSON-DAVIS, M. O. TAJU-DEEN, M. O. ADOPHY, GEORGE GELAGA KING, Dr A. B. Y. TIMBO, VIRGINIA A. WRIGHT.

High Court

The High Court has unlimited original jurisdiction in all criminal and civil matters. It also has appellate jurisdiction against decisions of Magistrates' Courts.

Judges: FRANCIS C. GBOW, EBUN THOMAS, D. E. M. WILLIAMS, LAURA MARCUS-JONES, L. B. O. NYLANDER, A. M. B. TARAWALLIE, O. H. ALGHALLI, W. A. O. JOHNSON, N. D. ALHADI, R. J. BANKOLE THOMPSON, M. E. T. THOMPSON, C. J. W. ATERE-ROBERTS (acting).

Magistrates' Courts: In criminal cases the jurisdiction of the Magistrates' Courts is limited to summary cases and to preliminary investigations to determine whether a person charged with an offence should be committed for trial.

Local Courts have jurisdiction, according to native law and custom, in matters that are outside the jurisdiction of other courts.

Religion

A large proportion of the population holds animist beliefs, although there are significant numbers of Islamic and Christian adherents.

ISLAM

In 1990 Islamic adherents represented an estimated 30% of the total population.

Ahmadiyya Muslim Mission: 15 Bath St, Brookfields, POB 353, Freetown; Emir and Chief Missionary KHALIL A. MOBASHIR.

Kankaylay (Sierra Leone Muslim Men and Women's Association): 15 Blackhall Rd, Kissy, POB 1168, Freetown; tel. 33635205; fax (22) 224439; e-mail kankaylay@yahoo.com; internet www.kankaylay.com; f. 1972; 500,000 mems; Pres. Alhaji IBRAHIM ALPHA TURAY; Lady Pres. Haja MARIAM TURAY.

Sierra Leone Muslim Congress: POB 875, Freetown; f. 1928; Pres. Alhaji MUHAMMAD SANUSI MUSTAPHA.

CHRISTIANITY

Council of Churches in Sierra Leone: 4A King Harman Rd, Brookfields, POB 404, Freetown; tel. (22) 240569; fax (22) 421109; f. 1924; 17 mem. churches; Pres. Rev. MOSES B. KHANU; Gen. Sec. ALIMAMY P. KOROMA.

The Anglican Communion

Anglicans in Sierra Leone are adherents of the Church of the Province of West Africa, comprising 12 dioceses, of which two are in Sierra Leone. The Archbishop of the Province is the Bishop of Koforidua, Ghana.

Bishop of Bo: Rt Rev. SAMUEL SAO GBONDA, MacRobert St, POB 21, Bo, Southern Province; e-mail bishop@sierratel.sl.

Bishop of Freetown: Rt Rev. JULIUS O. PRINCE LYNCH, Bishopscourt, Fourah Bay Rd, POB 537, Freetown; tel. (22) 251307; fax (22) 251306; e-mail bishop@sierratel.sl.

Baptist Churches

Sierra Leone Baptist Convention: POB 64, Lunsar; 119 mem. churches; 994 mems; Pres. Rev. JOSEPH S. MANS; Sec. Rev. N. T. DIXON.

The Nigerian Baptist Convention is also active.

Methodist Churches

Methodist Church Sierra Leone: Wesley House, George St, POB 64, Freetown; tel. (22) 222216; fax (22) 227539; e-mail mcsl@ymail.com; autonomous since 1967; Pres. of Conf. Rt Rev. ARNOLD C. TEMPLE; Sec. Rev. MUSA J. JAMBAWAI; 26,421 mems.

United Methodist Church: Freetown; tel. 76444100 (mobile); e-mail sierraleoneannualconference@yahoo.com; f. 1880; Presiding Bishop JOHN K. YAMBASU; 225,000 mems.

Other active Methodist bodies include the African Methodist Episcopal Church, the Wesleyan Church of Sierra Leone, the Countess of Huntingdon's Connexion and the West African Methodist Church.

The Roman Catholic Church

Sierra Leone comprises one archdiocese and three dioceses. An estimated 5% of the total population were Roman Catholics.

Inter-territorial Catholic Bishops' Conference of The Gambia and Sierra Leone

Santanno House, POB 893, Freetown; tel. (22) 228240; fax (22) 228252.

f. 1971; Pres. Rt Rev. GEORGE BIGUZZI (Bishop of Makeni).

Archbishop of Freetown: Most Rev. EDWARD TAMBA CHARLES, Santanno House, 10 Howe St, POB 893, Freetown; tel. (22) 224590; fax (22) 224075; e-mail jhg3271@sierratel.sl.

Other Christian Churches

The following are represented: the Christ Apostolic Church, the Church of the Lord (Aladura), the Evangelical Church, the Evangelical Lutheran Church in Sierra Leone, the Missionary Church of Africa, the Sierra Leone Church and the United Brethren in Christ.

AFRICAN RELIGIONS

There is a diverse range of beliefs, rites and practices, varying between ethnic and kinship groups.

The Press

DAILIES

For di People: Freetown; independent; Editor PAUL KAMARA.

The Sierra Leone Daily Mail: 29–31 Rawdon St, POB 53, Freetown; tel. (22) 223191; internet www.sierraleonedailymail.com; f. 1931; state-owned; currently online only; Editor AIAH MARTIN MONDEH; circ. 10,000.

PERIODICALS

African Crescent: 15 Bath St, POB 353, Brookfields, Freetown; Editor MAULANA-KHALIL A. MOBASHIR.

SIERRA LEONE

The Catalyst: Christian Literature Crusade Bookshop, 92 Circular Rd, POB 1465, Freetown; tel. (22) 224382; Editor Jusu-Wai Sawi.

Concord Times: 51 Krootown Rd, Freetown; tel. (22) 229199; e-mail info@concordtimessl.com; internet www.concordtimessl.com; 3 a week; Editor Dorothy Gordon.

Leonean Sun: 49 Main Rd, Wellington, Freetown; tel. (22) 223363; f. 1974; monthly; Editor Rowland Martyn.

Liberty Voice: 139 Pademba Rd, Freetown; tel. (22) 242100; Editor A. Mahdieu Savage.

New Breed: Freetown; weekly; independent; Man. Editor (vacant).

The New Citizen: 7 Wellington St, Freetown; tel. (22) 228693; e-mail info@thenewcitizen-sl.com; internet www.thenewcitizen-sl.com; f. 1982; Man. Editor Samuel B. Conteh.

The New Globe: 49 Bathurst St, Freetown; tel. (22) 228245; weekly; Man. Editor Sam Tumoe; circ. 4,000.

The New Shaft: 60 Old Railway Line, Brookfields, Freetown; tel. (22) 241093; 2 a week; independent; Editor Franklin Bunting-Davies; circ. 10,000.

The Pool Newspaper: 1 Short St, 5th Floor, Freetown; tel. and fax (22) 220102; e-mail pool@justice.com; internet www.poolnewspaper.tripod.com; f. 1992; 3 a week; independent; Man. Dir Chernor Ojuku Sesay; circ. 3,000.

Progress: 1 Short St, Freetown; tel. (22) 223588; weekly; independent; Editor Fode Kandeh; circ. 7,000.

Sierra Leone Chamber of Commerce Journal: Sierra Leone Chamber of Commerce, Industry and Agriculture, Guma Bldg, 5th Floor, Lamina Sankoh St, POB 502, Freetown; tel. (22) 226305; fax (22) 228005; monthly.

Unity Now: 82 Pademba Rd, Freetown; tel. (22) 227466; Editor Frank Kposowa.

The Vision: 60 Old Railway Line, Brookfields; tel. (22) 241273; Editor Siaka Massaquoi.

Weekend Spark: 7 Lamina Sankoh St, Freetown; tel. (22) 223397; f. 1983; weekly; independent; Editor Rowland Martyn; circ. 20,000.

Weekly Democrat: Freetown; Editor Jon Foray.

NEWS AGENCY

Sierra Leone News Agency (SLENA): 15 Wallace Johnson St, PMB 445, Freetown; tel. (22) 224921; fax (22) 224439; f. 1980; Man. Dir Abdul Karim Jalloh (acting).

Publishers

Njala University Publishing Centre: Njala University College, PMB, Freetown; science and technology, university textbooks.

Sierra Leone University Press: Fourah Bay College, POB 87, Freetown; tel. (22) 22491; fax (22) 224439; f. 1965; biography, history, Africana, religion, social science, university textbooks; Chair. Prof. Ernest H. Wright.

United Christian Council Literature Bureau: Bunumbu Press, POB 28, Bo; tel. (32) 462; books in Mende, Temne, Susu; Man. Dir Robert Sam-Kpakra.

Broadcasting and Communications

TELECOMMUNICATIONS

Africell: 1 Pivot St, Wilberforce, Freetown; tel. 77777777 (mobile); e-mail info@africell.sl; internet www.africell.sl; f. 2005; CEO Robert el-Khoury; 742,000 subscribers (August 2009).

Airtel Sierra Leone: Zain House, 42 Main Motor Rd, Wilberforce, Freetown; tel. (22) 233222; e-mail info.africa@airtel.com; internet africa.airtel.com/sierra; f. 2000; fmrly Zain Sierra Leone, present name adopted in 2010; Man. Dir Ted Sauti-Phiri.

Comium (SL) Ltd: Comium Bldg, 30D Wilkinson Rd, Freetown; tel. 33333030 (mobile); fax 33333060 (mobile); e-mail info@comium.com.sl; internet www.comium.com.sl; f. 2005; mobile cellular telephone and broadband internet provider; Gen. Man. Paul Hyde.

Millicom SL Ltd: 117 Wilkinson Rd, Freetown; tel. 30157000 (mobile); e-mail info@tigo.sl; internet www.tigo.sl; f. 2001; subsidiary of Millicom International Cellular; operates mobile cellular telephone network under brand name Tigo; Gen. Man. Pablo Guardia.

Sierra Leone Telecommunications Co (SIERRATEL): 7 Wallace Johnson St, POB 80, Freetown; tel. (22) 222801; fax (22) 224439; internet www.sierratel.sl; state-owned telecommunications operator; Chair. Dr Tom Obaleh Kargbo; Man. Dir Alpha Sesay.

BROADCASTING

Sierra Leone Broadcasting Corpn (SBC): New England, Freetown; tel. (22) 240403; f. 1934; name changed as above in 2010 following merger of Sierra Leone Broadcasting Service and UN Radio in Sierra Leone; state-controlled; programmes mainly in English and the four main Sierra Leonean vernaculars, Mende, Limba, Temne and Krio; weekly broadcast in French; television service established 1963; Dir-Gen. Ivan Ajibola Thomas.

Finance

(cap. = capital; res = reserves; dep. = deposits; m. = million; br(s). = branch(es); amounts in leones)

BANKING

In 2010 there were 12 commercial banks and six community banks in Sierra Leone.

Central Bank

Bank of Sierra Leone: Siaka Stevens St, POB 30, Freetown; tel. (22) 226501; fax (22) 224764; e-mail info@bankofsierraleone.com; internet www.bsl.gov.sl; f. 1964; cap. 50,000.0m., res –352,030.6m., dep. 419,113.6m. (Dec. 2009); Gov. Dr Sheku S. Sesay; Dep. Gov. Andrina Rosa Coker; 1 br.

Other Banks

Access Bank Sierra Leone Ltd: 30 Siaka Stevens St, Freetown; e-mail info@accessbanksierraleone.com; f. 2007.

Ecobank Sierra Leone Ltd: 7 Lightfoot Boston St, POB 1007, Freetown; tel. (22) 221704; fax (22) 229450; e-mail info@ecobanksl.com; internet www.ecobank.com; Chair. Keili Andrew Karmoh; Man. Dir Clement Dodoo.

First International Bank (SL) Ltd: 2 Charlotte St, Freetown; tel. (22) 220038; fax (22) 221970; e-mail fib@sierratel.sl; internet fibsl.biz; f. 1998; Chair. Christian J. Smith; Man. Dir Chris Uchendu.

Guaranty Trust Bank: Sparta Bldg, 12 Wilberforce St, POB 1168, Freetown; tel. (22) 228493; fax (22) 228318; internet www.gtb.sl; f. Feb. 2002 through the acquisition of 90% of shareholding of First Merchant Bank of Sierra Leone by Guaranty Trust Bank of Nigeria; cap. 2,261.0m., total assets 17,769.0m. (Dec. 2003); Chair. Jide Ogundare; Man. Dir Ade Buraimo; 3 brs.

International Commercial Bank (Sierra Leone) Ltd: 22 Rawdon St, POB 515, Freetown; tel. (22) 222877; fax (22) 220376; e-mail enquiry@icbank-sl.com; internet www.icbank-sl.com; f. 2004; 1 br.

National Development Bank Ltd: Leone House, 6th Floor, 21–23 Siaka Stevens St, Freetown; tel. (22) 226792; fax (22) 224468; f. 1968; 99% state-owned; provides medium- and long-term finance and tech. assistance to devt-orientated enterprises; cap. 1,604.3m., total assets 2,200m. (Dec. 2003); Chair. Murray E. S. Lamin; Man. Dir Mohamed M. Turay; 3 brs.

Rokel Commercial Bank (Sierra Leone) Ltd: 25–27 Siaka Stevens St, POB 12, Freetown; tel. (22) 222501; fax (22) 222563; e-mail rokelsl@sierratel.sl; internet www.rokelsl.com; f. 1971; cap. 15,116.5m., res 29,772.8m., dep. 312,619.4m. (Dec. 2009); 51% govt-owned; Chair. Birch M. Conte; Man. Dir Henry Akintota Macauley; 11 brs.

Sierra Leone Commercial Bank Ltd: Christian Smith Bldg, 29–31 Siaka Stevens St, Freetown; tel. (22) 225264; fax (22) 225292; e-mail slcb@slcb.biz; internet www.slcb.biz; f. 1973; state-owned; cap. 12,000.0m., res 22,891.9m., dep. 274,726.8m. (Dec. 2008); Chair. Sheiki G. Bangura; Man. Dir Crispin Bishop Deigh; 8 brs.

Skye Bank Sierra Leone Ltd : 31 Siaka Stevens St, Freetown; tel. (22) 220095; fax (22) 221773; internet www.skyebanksl.com; Chair. Patrick Coker; Man. Dir Olumide Olatunji.

Standard Chartered Bank Sierra Leone Ltd: 9–11 Lightfoot-Boston St, POB 1155, Freetown; tel. (22) 225021; fax (22) 225760; e-mail scbsl@sierratel.sl; internet www.standardchartered.com/sl; f. 1894; cap. 15,255.7m., res 18,399.8m., dep. 221,661.7m. (Dec. 2009); Chair. Alex B. Kamara; CEO and Man. Dir Alberto R. Saltson; 3 brs.

Union Trust Bank Ltd: Lightfoot-Boston St, PMB 1237, Freetown; tel. (22) 226954; fax (22) 226214; e-mail info@utb.sl; internet www.utb.sl; fmrly Meridien BIAO Bank Sierra Leone Ltd; adopted present name in 1995; cap. 7,477.9m., res 8,275.1m., total assets 60,720.1m. (Dec. 2007); Chair. Alhaji Dr Sheku Tejan Kamara; Man. Dir and CEO James Sanpha Koroma; 7 brs.

United Bank For Africa Sierra Leone Ltd: 15 Charlotte St, Freetown; tel. (22) 228099; fax (22) 225395; e-mail cicsl@ubagroup.com; internet www.ubagroup.com; f. 2008; 4 brs.

SIERRA LEONE

Zenith Bank Sierra Leone Ltd: 18–20 Rawdon St, Freetown; tel. (22) 225400; fax (22) 225070; e-mail enquiry@zenithbank.com.sl; f. 2007; Chair. EDDY MARTINS EGWUENU; Man. Dir ADEWALE ADENIYI.

INSURANCE

In 2010 there were nine insurance companies in Sierra Leone.

Aureol Insurance Co Ltd: Kissy House, 54 Siaka Stevens St, POB 647, Freetown; tel. (22) 223435; fax (22) 229336; e-mail info@aureolinsurance.com; internet aureolinsurance.com; f. 1986; Chair. Dr PATRICK E. COKER; Man. Dir SOLOMON J. SAMBA.

National Insurance Co Ltd: 18–20 Walpole St, PMB 84, Freetown; tel. (22) 222535; fax (22) 226097; e-mail nic@sierratel.sl; f. 1972; state-owned; Chair. P. J. KUYEMBEH; CEO ARTHUR NATHANIEL YASKEY.

New India Assurance Co Ltd: 18 Wilberforce St, POB 340, Freetown; tel. (22) 226453; fax (22) 222494; e-mail niasl@sierratel.sl; Man. Dir A. CHOPRA.

Reliance Insurance Trust Corpn Ltd: 24 Siaka Stevens St, Freetown; tel. (22) 225115; fax (22) 228051; e-mail oonomake@yahoo.com; f. 1985; Chair. MOHAMED B. COLE; Man. Dir ALICE M. ONOMAKE.

Sierra Leone Insurance Co Ltd: 3 Howe St, POB 836, Freetown; tel. (22) 224920; fax (22) 222115; e-mail office@slico.com.sl; internet www.slico.com.sl; f. 1983; Man. Dir and CEO ALI-DAUSY MASSALLY.

Trade and Industry

GOVERNMENT AGENCY

Government Gold and Diamond Office (GGDO): c/o Bank of Sierra Leone, Siaka Stevens St, Freetown; tel. (22) 222600; fax (22) 229064; f. 1985; govt regulatory agency for diamonds and gold; combats illicit trade; Chair. Alhaji M. S. DEEN.

CHAMBER OF COMMERCE

Sierra Leone Chamber of Commerce, Industry and Agriculture: Guma Bldg, 5th Floor, Lamina Sankoh St, POB 502, Freetown; tel. (22) 226305; fax (22) 220696; e-mail info@chamberofcommerce.sl; internet www.chamberofcommerce.sl; f. 1961; 215 mems; Pres. AMADU B. NDOEKA.

TRADE AND INDUSTRIAL ASSOCIATIONS

Sierra Leone Investment and Export Promotion Agency (SLIEPA): Standard Chartered Bank Bldg, 3rd Floor, Lightfoot-Boston St, Freetown; tel. (22) 220788; e-mail info@sliepa.org; internet www.sliepa.org; f. 2007; fmrly Sierra Leone Export Development and Investment Corporation; Man. Dir CHRIS JASABE.

Small-Medium Scale Businesses Association (Sierra Leone): O.A.U. Dr., Tower Hill, PMB 575, Freetown; tel. (22) 222617; fax (22) 224439; Dir ABU CONTEH.

EMPLOYERS' ORGANIZATIONS

Sierra Leone Chamber of Mines: POB 456, Freetown; tel. (22) 226082; f. 1965; mems comprise the principal mining concerns; Pres. JOHN SISAY; Exec. Officer N. H. T. BOSTON.

Sierra Leone Employers' Federation: POB 562, Freetown; Chair. AMADU B. NDOEKA; Exec. Officer L. E. JOHNSON.

UTILITIES

Electricity

National Power Authority: Electricity House, 36 Siaka Stevens St, Freetown; tel. (22) 229868; fax (22) 227584; e-mail Sierra_Leone@iaeste.org; supplies all electricity in Sierra Leone.

Water

Guma Valley Water Co: Guma Bldg, 13/14 Lamina Sankoh St, POB 700, Freetown; tel. (22) 25887; e-mail gumasl@yahoo.co.uk; f. 1961; responsible for all existing water supplies in Freetown and surrounding villages, including the Guma dam and associated works.

TRADE UNIONS

Artisans', Ministry of Works Employees' and General Workers' Union: 4 Pultney St, Freetown; f. 1946; 14,500 mems; Pres. IBRAHIM LANGLEY; Gen. Sec. TEJAN A. KASSIM.

Sierra Leone Labour Congress: 35 Wallace Johnson St, POB 1333, Freetown; tel. (22) 226869; f. 1966; 51,000 mems in 19 affiliated unions; Pres. H. M. BARRIE; Sec.-Gen. KANDEH YILLA; 25,000 mems (2007).

Principal affiliated unions:

Clerical, Mercantile and General Workers' Union: 35 Wallace Johnson St, Freetown; f. 1945; 3,600 mems; Pres. M. D. BENJAMIN; Gen. Sec. M. B. WILLIAMS.

Sierra Leone Association of Journalists: 31 Garrisson Street, Freetown; tel. 76605811; e-mail slajalone@hotmail.com; Pres. PHILIP NEVILLE.

Sierra Leone Dockworkers' Union: 165 Fourah Bay Rd, Freetown; f. 1962; 2,650 mems; Pres. ABDUL KANISURE; Gen. Sec. A. C. CONTEH.

Sierra Leone Motor Drivers' Union: 10 Charlotte St, Freetown; f. 1960; 1,900 mems; Pres. A. W. HASSAN; Gen. Sec. ALPHA KAMARA.

Sierra Leone Teachers' Union: Regaland House, Lowcost Step—Kissy, POB 477, Freetown; f. 1951; 18,500 mems; Pres. ABDULAI KOROMA; Sec.-Gen. DAVIDSON KUYATEH.

Sierra Leone Transport, Agricultural and General Workers' Union: 4 Pultney St, Freetown; f. 1946; 1,600 mems; Pres. S. O. SAWYERR-MANLEY; Gen. Sec. S. D. KARGBO.

United Mineworkers' Union: 35 Wallace Johnson St, Freetown; f. 1944; 6,500 mems; Gen. Sec. EZEKIEL DYKE.

Also affiliated to the Sierra Leone Labour Congress: the **General Construction Workers' Union**, the **Municipal and Local Government Employees' Union** and the **Sierra Leone National Seamen's Union**.

Transport

RAILWAYS

There are no passenger railways in Sierra Leone.

Marampa Mineral Railway: Delco House, POB 735, Freetown; tel. (22) 222556; 84 km of track linking iron ore mines at Marampa (inactive since 1985) with Pepel port; Gen. Man. SYL KHANU.

ROADS

In 2002 there were an estimated 11,300 km of classified roads, including 2,138 km of main roads and 1,950 km of secondary roads; about 904 km of the total network was paved.

Sierra Leone Road Transport Corpn: Blackhall Rd, POB 1008, Freetown; tel. (22) 250442; fax (22) 250000; f. 1965; state-owned; operates transport services throughout the country; Gen. Man. DANIEL R. W. FAUX.

INLAND WATERWAYS

Established routes for launches, which include the coastal routes from Freetown northward to the Great and Little Scarcies rivers and southward to Bonthe, total almost 800 km. Although some of the upper reaches of the rivers are navigable only between July and September, there is a considerable volume of river traffic.

SHIPPING

Freetown, the principal port, has full facilities for ocean-going vessels.

Sierra Leone National Shipping Co Ltd: 45 Cline St, POB 935, Freetown; tel. (22) 229883; fax (22) 229513; f. 1972; state-owned; shipping, clearing and forwarding agency; representatives for foreign lines; Chair. Alhaji B. M. KOROMA; Man. Dir SYLVESTER B. FOMBA.

Sierra Leone Ports Authority: Queen Elizabeth II Quay, PMB 386, Cline Town, Freetown; tel. (22) 226480; fax (22) 226443; f. 1965; parastatal body, supervised by the Ministry of Transport and Aviation; operates the port of Freetown; Gen. Man. BENJAMIN O. N. DAVIES.

Sierra Leone Shipping Agencies Ltd: Deep Water Quay, Clinetown, POB 74, Freetown; tel. (22) 221709; fax (22) 293111; e-mail fna.otal@bollore.com; f. 1949; Man. Dir MICHEL MEYNARD.

CIVIL AVIATION

There is an international airport at Lungi.

Directorate of Civil Aviation: Ministry of Transport and Aviation, Ministerial Bldg, George St, Freetown; tel. (22) 222106; fax (22) 228488; Dir GEORGE GBONGBOR.

Sierra National Airlines: Leone House, 25 Pultney St, POB 285, Freetown; tel. (22) 222075; fax (22) 222026; f. 1982; state-owned; operates domestic and regional services, and a weekly flight to Paris, France; operations resumed, following civil conflict, in Nov. 2000; Chair. TAMBA MATTURI; Man. Dir ADAM CORMACK.

Tourism

The main attractions for tourists are the coastline, the mountains and the game reserves. Civil conflict throughout most of the 1990s effectively suspended tourist activity. By 2005, however, according to the World Tourism Organization, tourist arrivals had increased to 40,023, compared with 10,615 in 1999. Arrivals decreased to 35,670 in 2008. Receipts from tourism totalled an estimated US $34m. in that year.

Sierra Leone National Tourist Board: Cape Sierra Hotel, Room 100, Aberdeen, POB 1435, Freetown; tel. (22) 236620; fax (22) 236621; e-mail info@welcometosierraleone.org; internet www.welcometosierraleone.org; f. 1990; Gen. Man. CECIL J. WILLIAMS.

Defence

As assessed at November 2010, the armed forces of the Republic of Sierra Leone numbered about 10,500, with a navy of 200. In October 1999 the UN Security Council adopted a resolution establishing the UN Mission in Sierra Leone (UNAMSIL), which was to supervise the implementation of a peace agreement between the Government and rebel forces, signed in July of that year. Following the completion of disarmament in January 2002, a new army, restructured with British military assistance, was established. In September 2004 UNAMSIL transferred primary responsibility for security to the armed forces but retained its own rapid intervention capacity. Some 100 British troops remained in the country to support peace-keeping operations and to continue reorganization of the Sierra Leone armed forces. The mandate of UNAMSIL (which had been reduced from nearly its maximum authorized strength of 17,500 to about 3,400) ended at the end of 2005. Following a UN Security Council resolution in August, the United Nations Integrated Office in Sierra Leone (UNIOSIL) was established in the capital, Freetown, on 1 January 2006, for an initial period of one year, extended in December until the end of 2007. In December of that year, UNIOSIL's mandate was extended until September 2008. In October the United Nations Integrated Peacebuilding Office in Sierra Leone (UNIPSIL) officially replaced UNIOSIL with an initial mandate of one year; this was subsequently extended until September 2011. Preparations were under way in 2010 to reduce the size of the armed forces.

Defence Expenditure: Estimated at Le 57,600m. in 2009.

Commander-in-Chief of the Armed Forces: Pres. ERNEST BAI KOROMA.

Chief of Staff of the Armed Forces: Maj.-Gen. ROBERT YIRRA KOROMA.

Education

Primary education begins at five years of age and lasts for seven years. Secondary education, beginning at the age of 12, also lasts for a further seven years, comprising a first cycle of five years and a second cycle of two years. In 1987 tuition fees for government-funded primary and secondary schools were abolished. In 2000/01 primary enrolment was equivalent to 92.8% of children in the relevant age-group (males 106.0%; females 79.8%), while about 26% of children of the relevant age-group were enrolled at secondary schools (males 30%; females 20%) in 2006/07. In 2003/04 85% of the total school-age population was enrolled at primary and secondary schools. There is one university, which comprises six colleges. A total of 9,041 students were enrolled in tertiary education in 2001/02. Budgetary expenditure on education by the central Government in 2002 was Le 36,400m.

SINGAPORE

Introductory Survey

LOCATION, CLIMATE, LANGUAGE, RELIGION, FLAG, CAPITAL

The Republic of Singapore lies in South-East Asia. The country comprises one main island and some 64 offshore islands, situated approximately 137 km (85 miles) north of the Equator, off the southernmost tip of the Malay Peninsula, to which it is linked by a causeway. The climate is equatorial, with a uniformly high daily and annual temperature varying between 24°C and 27°C (75°F–80°F). Relative humidity is high (often exceeding 90%), and the average annual rainfall is 235 cm (93 ins). There are four official languages—Malay (the national language), Chinese (Mandarin), Tamil and English. The language of administration is English. Chinese dialects were spoken as a first language by 24% of the population in 2000. The principal religions are Daoism, Buddhism, Islam, Christianity and Hinduism. The national flag (proportions 2 by 3) has two equal horizontal stripes of red and white, with a white crescent moon and five white stars, arranged in a pentagram, in the upper hoist. The capital is Singapore City.

CONTEMPORARY POLITICAL HISTORY

Historical Context

In 1826 the East India Company formed the Straits Settlements by the union of Singapore and the dependencies of Penang and Malacca on the Malay Peninsula. They came under British rule in 1867 as a crown colony. Singapore was occupied by Japan for three years during the Second World War. At the end of the war in 1945, following Japan's defeat, Singapore was governed by a British military administration. When civil rule was restored in 1946, Singapore was detached from the other Straits Settlements and became a separate crown colony. A new Constitution, adopted in February 1955, introduced some measure of self-government, and in June 1959 the state achieved complete internal self-government, with Lee Kuan Yew as Prime Minister. The Federation of Malaysia came into being in September 1963, with Singapore as a constituent state. On 9 August 1965, following irreconcilable differences with the central Government in Malaysia, Singapore seceded from the federation and became an independent country. Singapore joined the UN in September and the Commonwealth in October. In December Singapore was proclaimed a republic, with a President as constitutional Head of State. In May 1973 the last major links with Malaysia, concerning currency and finance, were renounced. In September 1972 Lee Kuan Yew's ruling People's Action Party (PAP) won all 65 parliamentary seats in a general election.

Domestic Political Affairs

After independence the Government supported a strong US military presence in South-East Asia. However, with the collapse of US influence in the area during 1974–75, at the end of the war in Viet Nam, Singapore adopted a conciliatory attitude towards the People's Republic of China and its communist neighbours. The Government urged the removal of foreign bases from member states of the Association of Southeast Asian Nations (ASEAN, see p. 206), and advocated a policy of neutrality. Singapore sought to consolidate its trade links with China, although diplomatic relations were not established until 1982.

At the general election in December 1976 and again in December 1980, the PAP won all 69 seats in the enlarged Parliament. However, the PAP's monopoly ended in October 1981, when the Secretary-General of the opposition Workers' Party, J. B. Jeyaretnam, won a by-election. This posed no direct threat, but, in order to reassert its authority, the Government increased its control over trade unions and restructured the ownership of major newspapers. The PAP was again returned to power in December 1984 with a large majority in Parliament (now expanded to 79 seats), but the party lost two seats to opposition parties, and its share of the total votes was reduced to 63% from 75% in 1980. A constitutional amendment approved in July 1984 provided for up to three 'non-constituency' parliamentary seats for the opposition (with restricted voting rights) if none was won in the election. One extra seat was subsequently offered to the losing opposition candidate with the highest percentage of votes. However, this seat was refused by the Workers' Party in January 1985. In March the state President, Devan Nair, resigned. A new President, Wee Kim Wee (hitherto Chairman of the Singapore Broadcasting Corporation), was elected by Parliament in August.

In August 1986 amendments to the Parliament (Privileges, Immunities and Powers) Act were hurriedly adopted, enabling Parliament to fine, expel or imprison members who were deemed to have abused their parliamentary privileges. Parliament also approved a Newspaper and Printing Presses (Amendment) Act, which empowered the Government to restrict the distribution of foreign publications deemed to be interfering in domestic political affairs; the circulation of several foreign periodicals was subsequently restricted.

In November 1986 Jeyaretnam (one of the two opposition members of Parliament) was sentenced to one month's imprisonment and fined S $5,000 (enough, according to the Constitution, to deprive him of his parliamentary seat and prevent him from standing for election for five years), when the Supreme Court upheld a conviction for perjury in connection with bankruptcy proceedings brought against the Workers' Party four years previously. In February 1987 Jeyaretnam was also fined by a parliamentary committee for abuse of privilege, having made allegations of government interference in the judiciary; further fines were imposed on him for publishing 'distorted' accounts of an earlier hearing of the committee, and (in May) for alleged contempt of Parliament and abuse of parliamentary privilege. In October Jeyaretnam's removal from the Law Society register was ordered by a three-judge court. An appeal to the Judicial Committee of the Privy Council in the United Kingdom (then the highest court of appeal for Singapore) resulted, in October 1988, in his reinstatement as a practising lawyer. During the course of the appeal, investigations into Jeyaretnam's previous convictions found that they had been 'fatally flawed'. However, since the criminal case had been considered in the District Court, where there was no right of appeal to the Privy Council, the original convictions prevented Jeyaretnam from re-entering Parliament without a presidential pardon. This was refused by Wee Kim Wee in May 1989.

In May and June 1987 the Government detained a total of 22 people (including 10 Roman Catholic church workers and four members of the Workers' Party) without trial, under the Internal Security Act (ISA), for their alleged involvement in a 'Marxist conspiracy' to subvert state organizations. The arrests were denounced by Jeyaretnam, amid claims of intimidation. In November the Government was also criticized by international human rights groups, including Amnesty International, for its refusal to present evidence of such a conspiracy in court. By December most of the alleged conspirators had been released, but eight of them were rearrested in April 1988, after complaining that they had been tortured while in detention. Four prisoners were released by June, and in December a further four detainees were released in accordance with a ruling by the Court of Appeal, based on a fault in their detention orders. They were immediately rearrested. However, the trial had established a precedent for the judicial review of cases brought under the ISA, including the acceptability to the courts of evidence used in warrants for the arrest of suspects. In January 1989 Parliament approved legislation ensuring that the judiciary could examine such detentions only on technical grounds, and abolishing the right of appeal to the Privy Council in cases brought under the ISA. In March three detainees were released. The two remaining prisoners (of the original 22) remained in detention until June 1990.

A general election was held in September 1988. The electoral system was altered so that 39 of the existing 79 constituencies were replaced by 13 'group representation constituencies', to be contested by teams of three representatives for each party, at least one of whom was to be a member of an ethnic minority (i.e. non-Chinese). The declared aim was to ensure the presence of racial minorities in Parliament; however, in practice, opposition parties with few resources were restricted by the difficulty of presenting three candidates. The PAP won 80 of the elective seats (which now totalled 81); one was taken by the leader of the Singapore Democratic Party (SDP), Chiam See Tong. Two non-constituency seats were offered to Francis Seow (of the Workers' Party) and Lee Siew Choh (of the Socialist Front). In December, however, while Seow (who had already been detained in May under the ISA for organizing a meeting between a US diplomat and lawyers critical of the Government) was undergoing medical treatment in the USA, he was convicted *in absentia* for tax evasion and fined S $19,000: he was thus debarred from taking his seat in Parliament.

The premiership of Goh Chok Tong

In January 1989 Lee Kuan Yew began his eighth term as Prime Minister, and announced that he would retire from the premiership before the expiry of the term. This announcement was followed by a statement from the First Deputy Prime Minister, Goh Chok Tong (Lee's chosen successor), that Lee was adopting a secondary and more advisory role in the government of the country. In August Parliament unanimously re-elected Wee Kim Wee for a further four-year term as President. In early 1990 Parliament approved legislation enabling the Government to nominate as many as six unelected MPs. The politically neutral nominated MPs would be appointed for two years, and would be able to vote on all legislative proposals except those concerning financial and constitutional affairs.

On 28 November 1990 Lee Kuan Yew was duly replaced as Prime Minister by Goh Chok Tong. Lee remained in the Cabinet as Senior Minister in the Prime Minister's Office, and retained the position of Secretary-General of the PAP; Lee's son, Brig.-Gen. Lee Hsien Loong, was appointed as a Deputy Prime Minister.

In January 1991 the Constitution was amended to provide for a popularly elected presidency with extensive powers of veto on proposed financial legislation, a role as final arbiter in cases of detention for reasons of national security, and influence in civil and military appointments. The changes to the (hitherto ceremonial) functions of the President, which had been initially proposed by Lee Kuan Yew in 1984, were criticized by members of opposition parties as being intended to accommodate the former Prime Minister. Under the amendment, Wee Kim Wee was to continue in office until October 1993. Legislation empowering him with the authority of an elected president took effect from 30 November 1991. Candidates for the presidency were limited to those who had held the post of a minister, chief justice or senior civil servant or were at the head of a large company. The candidates were to be scrutinized by a new presidential election committee, which was to comprise the head of the Society of Accountants, the Chairman of the Public Service Commission and a member of the Presidential Council of Human Rights; the last two officials were appointed by the Government. The constitutional amendment also included a clause increasing the number of candidates required to contest a 'group representation constituency' in a general election to a minimum of three and a maximum of four, one of whom was to be a member of an ethnic minority.

In early 1991 the Government promoted the acceptance of five 'shared values', based on Confucian philosophy, as the basis of a national ideology. Critics alleged that the ideology would be used to reinforce support for the PAP and to obviate opposition challenges. Goh attempted, in principle, to introduce a more 'open', consultative form of government. He instituted an extensive programme of community visits to assess popular opinion, showing solicitude for the views of the minority Malay and Indian communities. Although film censorship was relaxed, the ISA and restrictions on the foreign press remained in force. In early August, seeking a popular mandate for his style of government, Goh announced that there would be a general election at the end of the month. Under a plan conceived by Chiam See Tong, the opposition parties contested only 40 of the 81 seats, thus guaranteeing an absolute majority for the incumbent PAP. Chiam issued an appeal to the electorate to take the opportunity to elect a strong opposition. Goh indicated that a failure to receive a popular endorsement would result in a return to a more authoritarian and paternalistic form of government. At the election, held on 31 August, the PAP's share of the vote was 61.0% (compared with 63.2% in 1988), and the party won 77 seats (compared with 80 in 1988). Chiam's SDP secured three seats, and the Workers' Party one seat. J. B. Jeyaretnam was unable to contest the election, as his disqualification remained in force until November. In response to Jeyaretnam's accusations that he had been deliberately excluded from the election, and also because the election schedule had prevented the PAP from presenting enough new candidates, Goh had announced, prior to the polls, that he would organize by-elections within 12–18 months of the general election.

In October 1991 Francis Seow, who had remained in exile in the USA since 1988, was convicted *in absentia* of a further 60 offences involving tax evasion, rendering him ineligible to contest any potential by-election. Later that month Jeyaretnam paid S $392,838 in legal costs to Lee Kuan Yew, thus avoiding bankruptcy, which would have prevented his candidacy. Lee had instituted a successful defamation suit against Jeyaretnam in 1990, over remarks made by Jeyaretnam at a 1988 election rally.

Following the general election, Lee Kuan Yew, who had temporarily withdrawn from public attention after Goh's accession to the premiership, resumed a prominent role in domestic politics. He attributed the decline in PAP support to neglect of the Mandarin-educated ethnic Chinese majority, and advocated a greater emphasis on Chinese culture and language. In April 1991 Goh announced that the level of electoral support among residents would be one of the criteria used to determine the order in which refurbishments would be undertaken in public housing estates (in which about 86% of Singaporeans lived). Prior to the convening of Parliament in September 1992 the Government appointed the maximum of six nominated MPs. This too was generally regarded as an attempt to discourage support for opposition candidates in the impending by-elections. In October the implementation of legislation prohibiting MPs from using the ground floors of public housing blocks as office space adversely affected all four opposition MPs, who were unable to afford commercial rents.

In November 1992 Goh announced to the Central Executive Committee of the PAP that the renewal of national leadership was the party's most urgent consideration. This statement was followed two days later by the public disclosure that both Deputy Prime Ministers, Lee Hsien Loong and Ong Teng Cheong, had been diagnosed as suffering from cancer. The revelation strengthened Goh's position as Prime Minister, since many had previously regarded his incumbency as an interim arrangement prior to Lee Hsien Loong's assumption of the premiership. In December Goh was unanimously elected to replace Lee Kuan Yew (who proposed his candidacy) as Secretary-General of the PAP.

In December 1992 Goh relinquished his parliamentary seat (which formed part of a four-member 'group representation constituency') in order to contest a by-election. Jeyaretnam was unable to contest the by-election as only three candidates from the Workers' Party registered with the authorities. The results of the by-election were regarded as an endorsement of Goh's leadership, as the four PAP candidates received 72.9% of the votes cast, while the opposition SDP secured 24.5%.

In March 1993 Chee Soon Juan, who contested the December by-election as a candidate for the SDP, was dismissed from his post as a lecturer at the National University of Singapore for 'dishonest conduct'. The Government denied that the dismissal was politically motivated, and defamation proceedings were initiated by university officials against Chee. In June, following a rejection by the SDP Central Committee of a motion of censure proposed by Chiam See Tong against Chee for bringing the party into disrepute, Chiam resigned as Secretary-General of the party. Chee replaced him as acting Secretary-General, pending party elections in early 1995. In August 1993 the SDP expelled Chiam for alleged indiscipline; however, a High Court ruling in December declared the expulsion 'illegal and invalid'. (This enabled Chiam to retain his seat in Parliament: under the Constitution a member of the legislature is obliged to relinquish his seat if he resigns or is expelled from the party he has been elected to represent.) The following month, under a judicial ruling, a 'breakaway' central executive committee, formed in 1993 by a faction of the SDP that remained loyal to Chiam, was declared void. Chee subsequently published a book entitled *Dare to Change*, which demanded greater democracy and was adopted as official party policy by the SDP in June 1994. Chee was formally elected Secretary-General of the SDP in January 1995.

Meanwhile, in August 1993 Ong Teng Cheong was elected President with 58.7% of the votes cast. However, contrary to expectation the only other candidate, Chua Kim Yeow, a former government official, who adopted an apolitical position, secured a substantial proportion (41.3%) of the vote. The candidacies of both Jeyaretnam and Tan Soo Phuan, another member of the Workers' Party, were rejected by the Presidential Election Committee on the grounds that they were unsuitable 'in regard to integrity, good character and reputation'.

In October 1996 Parliament approved amendments to the Constitution that redefined the role of the President and partially reformed the voting system. The President's powers were restricted by new provisions empowering the Government to call a referendum if the President vetoed certain constitutional amendments, and also enabling Parliament to overrule (by a two-thirds' majority) a presidential veto on senior civil service appointments. A further amendment expanded the number of 'group representation constituencies' and increased the maximum number of group candidates from four to six. The electoral reforms were opposed by the opposition parties on the grounds that the amendments favoured large, well-established parties such as the PAP, while smaller parties would have difficulty in finding and funding large numbers of candidates.

Prior to the general election, which took place on 2 January 1997, the success of the PAP was predetermined by the opposition parties' decision to contest only 36 of the 83 seats. Nevertheless, the PAP conducted a rigorous campaign in an effort to ensure that the party received two-thirds of the total votes cast, a margin regarded as sufficient endorsement of Goh and his administration. During the campaign, it was again announced that public housing improvements would be prioritized according to levels of electoral support for the PAP. The party secured a resounding victory, winning 65.0% of the votes and 81 seats (including all nine single-member constituencies). The remaining two elective seats were won by Chiam See Tong of the Singapore People's Party (SPP), for the fourth time (although previously he had been elected as a representative of the SDP), and Low Thia Khiang of the Workers' Party, for a second time. The Workers' Party, as the opposition party with the most votes but less than three seats, was also allocated a non-constituency seat; this was accepted by Jeyaretnam. The SDP lost the three seats that it had previously held.

During the election campaign, the PAP had accused Tang Liang Hong, a candidate of the Workers' Party, of being anti-Christian, of promoting Chinese interests over those of Singapore's ethnic minorities and of attempting to foment discontent among the ethnic Chinese community. Standing in the same 'group representation constituency' as Jeyaretnam, Tang failed to secure election. (Goh, unopposed in a single-member constituency, personally campaigned against Tang in the group constituency.) Tang's public rebuttal of the accusations of the PAP leaders prompted them to issue writs against him for defamation. Tang fled to Malaysia in January 1997, claiming to have received anonymous death threats. Tang was found guilty of defamation by the High Court in March, as he failed to attend the trial and provide a defence, and was ordered in May to pay a record sum of S $8m. in libel damages to Goh and 10 senior PAP leaders. Tang appealed against the judgment in September on the grounds that it contained legal errors and that the cases had been brought for political motives. The Court of Appeal ruled in November that the damages awarded against Tang were disproportionate to the injury caused, and reduced the sum to S $4.53m. In February 1998, despite this concession, Tang, against whom a warrant for arrest had been issued on 33 counts of tax evasion, was declared bankrupt.

Goh and 10 senior PAP members also sued Jeyaretnam for alleged defamation following remarks made at an election rally concerning two police reports submitted by Tang accusing the PAP leadership of criminal conspiracy and lying. In September 1997 Jeyaretnam was ordered to pay damages of S $20,000; however, the award represented only 10% of the amount sought by the PAP leadership, and the judge, who criticized Goh's lawyers for their handling of the case, ordered that Jeyaretnam pay only 60% of the legal costs. During the trial Goh admitted under cross-examination that he had authorized the unofficial disclosure of the police reports to the press, and it was put to him that the legal suits were an attempt to bankrupt Jeyaretnam and thus disqualify him from Parliament. However, the Court of Appeal dismissed an appeal by Jeyaretnam in July 1998, increasing the damages to S $100,000, and awarding full costs against him. However, it was subsequently agreed that Jeyaretnam would be permitted to pay the damages in five instalments, thereby enabling him to avoid bankruptcy proceedings and to continue as a legislator.

In November 1998 the Government revoked the remaining restrictions on the activities of the political activist Chia Thye Poh. Chia had been arrested in 1966, imprisoned for more than 22 years without trial under the ISA, confined to a fortress on an island off the coast of Singapore for a further three years, then permitted to reside in Singapore from 1992, although prohibited from taking part in any political activity. Despite this concession to Chia, government suppression of expressions of opposition continued. In January 1999 Chee Soon Juan was charged twice under the Public Entertainment Act for making unlicensed public speeches. Chee had deliberately refused to apply for licences to make the two public speeches, in which he had criticized government policy, on the grounds that freedom of expression was guaranteed under the Constitution. During the first trial Chee was represented by Jeyaretnam, who attempted to expose the alleged use of the above Act to restrict political opposition. However, Chee was found guilty at the beginning of February, and, owing to his refusal to pay a fine of S $1,400, was sentenced to seven days' imprisonment. Following his release, Chee appeared in court for a second time in February, and was sentenced, with the Assistant Secretary-General of the SDP, Wong Hong Toy, who had reportedly assisted Chee at the speech, to 12 days' imprisonment after Chee and Wong refused to pay respective fines of S $2,500 and S $2,400. The level of the fines automatically disqualified both men from seeking political office for five years; however, following an appeal, the two had their fines reduced to S $1,900 each, below the level that would have rendered them ineligible to stand for election. The Government maintained that opposition politicians had adequate opportunity to expound their views in Parliament or in the media (although in February 1998 the Government had banned political parties from producing videos and from promoting their opinions on television). In April 1999 it was reported that, subsequent to his release from prison after serving his second term of imprisonment, Chee had been fined S $600 for illegal sales of a book that he had produced on Asian opposition leaders. In March members of the PAP filed a petition to close the Workers' Party, owing to its inability to pay more than S $280,000 in damages and costs awarded against it in a defamation case. The party's closure would force the resignation of its two parliamentary representatives. It was subsequently reported that the party had lost a judicial appeal against the award.

In May 2000 Jeyaretnam was declared bankrupt by the High Court after he failed to make payments of S $30,000 in libel damages arising from a lawsuit concerning an article that appeared in the Workers' Party newspaper, *The Hammer*, in 1995. The bankruptcy ruling would have disqualified Jeyaretnam from serving in Parliament, but the orders were set aside after the outstanding debt was paid, and he was authorized to retain his non-constituency seat. In January 2001, however, Jeyaretnam was once again declared bankrupt by the High Court, with a S $235,000 debt as a result of a defamation claim against a Workers' Party newsletter. The appeal against the bankruptcy ruling was dismissed in February. In May Jeyaretnam was replaced as Secretary-General of the Workers' Party by Low Thia Khiang. In July Jeyaretnam finally lost his seat in Parliament when the Court of Appeal confirmed that it would not rescind the bankruptcy ruling against him.

Meanwhile, legislation introduced in May 1997 increased the number of nominated MPs from six to nine; the Constitution was amended accordingly in September. During the year nine Community Development Councils (CDCs) were formed. The CDCs encompassed all constituencies, including the two opposition wards, although opposition representatives would not be permitted to serve as council leaders and would have no power to disburse funds.

During 1999 Lee Hsien Loong, who had been appointed Chairman of the Monetary Authority of Singapore (MAS) in December 1997, began to assume a more prominent political role. Brig.-Gen. (retd) George Yeo, hitherto the Minister for Information and the Arts, also gained prominence following his promotion to the trade and industry portfolio in a minor cabinet reorganization in June 1999. Singapore's second presidential election was scheduled to take place in August. Ong Teng Cheong, despite his PAP affiliation, had proved an independent President, whose determination to exercise the full powers of the elected presidency had resulted in strained relations with his former government colleagues. His allegations of government obstruction of his efforts to establish the details of the Republic's financial reserves (in order to fulfil his role of guardian of those reserves as specified in the constitutional amendments of 1991) had led to a rare display of disunity among senior PAP officials, involving public disputes with both Goh and Lee Kuan Yew. Despite a medical report confirming that Ong was in complete remission from the cancer diagnosed in 1992, the PAP announced that, on the grounds of health, it would not support his candidacy should he choose to seek a second term of office. Ong, who was widely believed to command sufficient popular support to secure the presidency without a government endorsement, finally announced his decision not to contest the election in July, but unexpectedly proceeded to enumerate his political difficulties while in office. Despite Goh's expressed support for a more consultative style of governance, in mid-August a government-appointed committee declared that only one of three potential presidential candidates, S. R. Nathan (a former Singaporean ambassador to the USA whose presidential candidacy was supported by the Cabinet), had fulfilled the criteria set by the committee; Nathan was subsequently nominated as the new President of Singapore on 18 August, and was formally appointed to the position on 1 September, prompting criticism of the Government's autocratic approach.

In September 2000 the Government appeared to have relaxed its strict control over public speaking, with the opening of a 'Speakers' Corner', theoretically allowing a forum for any citizen to air issues of concern. However, in practice, speakers were obliged to register with the police beforehand, and to refrain from speaking on certain racial issues. The opportunity to speak was taken up by members of two Singaporean policy centres, after they were refused a permit to organize a marathon run to protest against the ISA in December. The gathering of around 50 people was not dispersed, but a report on the event broadcast by the Radio Corporation of Singapore was later edited at the request of the management, and the presenter who publicized the re-editing was dismissed. In April 2001 the Government permitted a rare opposition political rally. It was the first authorized protest to be openly critical of the Government since independence. The rally, intended as a pro-democracy fund-raising event for Jeyaretnam, was attended by over 1,000 people.

In July 2001 four opposition parties—the SPP, the Singapore Malay National Organization, the National Solidarity Party and the Singapore Justice Party—formed the Singapore Democratic Alliance (SDA). The new coalition was chaired by Chiam See Tong, and it was hoped that its formation would strengthen the fragmented political opposition to the PAP.

In October 2001 President Nathan unexpectedly announced that a general election was to be held in early November, significantly in advance of the August 2002 deadline. During the campaign the Government declared that the allocation of priority to public housing improvements would again be affected by levels of electoral support. Electoral boundaries were also redrawn, leading to the enlargement of 14 multi-member constituencies and to an increase in the number of parliamentary seats to 84, in order to accommodate a rise in the number of registered voters. The opposition protested that it had been disadvantaged by the rearrangements. When nominations closed in late October PAP candidates were unopposed for 55 of the 84 seats. As in previous elections, the Government thus secured victory by default before the polls opened. However, the Prime Minister urged voters to turn out on election day to decide the outcome of the contests for the remaining 29 seats, warning that Singapore confronted its 'gravest challenge since independence'. He also officially announced that he would leave office upon the conclusion of his next term.

The legislative election was held on 3 November 2001. The level of voter participation was low, owing to the large number of uncontested seats. Despite speculation that the PAP would lose ground in the election because of the deterioration in the economy, it increased its share of the votes and won 82 seats. The remaining two seats went to SDA Chairman Chiam See Tong and Low Thia Khiang of the Workers' Party. Steve Chia of the SDA was awarded a non-constituency seat.

Shortly after the election it was reported that Lee Kuan Yew and Goh were suing Chee Soon Juan of the SDP for defamation. Chee had alleged that the Government had lent more than S $17,000m. of public money to the Suharto administration in Indonesia during the 1997–98 financial crisis. He had issued a public apology for the comments soon afterwards and admitted fabricating the accusation, but had later retracted this statement, claiming that it had been made under duress. Goh claimed that, while the loan had been offered to the Suharto administration, it had never been disbursed. In February 2002 Chee was the focus of further legal action after he contravened the rule banning the discussion of racial and religious issues in 'Speakers' Corner'. He had criticized the Government's policy of banning Muslim girls from wearing headscarves in public schools and urged the promotion of cultural diversity. His comments followed the suspension of three Muslim girls from school for their wearing of headscarves.

In April 2002 Jeyaretnam made a public apology in the High Court in an attempt to bring to an end the series of defamation suits that had been brought against him by the Government; seven outstanding lawsuits were subsequently abandoned. In the same month Chee Soon Juan stated that he intended to defend the lawsuits against him. In May Chee and the Vice-Chairman of the SDP, Gandhi Ambalam, led an unauthorized rally outside the presidential palace demanding workers' rights. Following the rally, Chee and Ambalan were both sentenced to brief prison terms, having chosen not to pay the fines imposed upon them. However, Ambalan's family subsequently paid his fine, in order to enable his release from prison on the grounds of ill health. In August the High Court ordered Chee to pay damages of S $500,000 to Goh and Lee Kuan Yew, after his request for a trial was rejected; the verdict was confirmed in January 2005. Meanwhile, a constitutional amendment was approved stipulating that any member of Parliament declared bankrupt or found guilty of a crime would be banned from speaking or voting in Parliament for the duration of any appeal. In February 2003 Ambalam's appeal against his fine (which was sufficient to prohibit him from standing for political office for five years) was rejected by the Chief Justice. In October 2004 Jeyaretnam again appealed for early discharge from bankruptcy in order to secure re-entry into the political arena. However, the Court of Appeal deemed him to have been dishonest about his assets, ruling that he had failed to declare property in Johor Baru worth more than S $350,000. Consequently, the Court's original decision was upheld and Jeyaretnam's application for clemency was denied. Jeyaretnam was discharged from bankruptcy in May 2007 after paying the damages he owed.

In April 2003, meanwhile, Goh announced a cabinet reorganization, in which, *inter alia*, Deputy Prime Minister and former Minister for Defence Dr Tony Tan Keng Yam was appointed to the newly created position of Co-ordinating Minister for Security and Defence in the Prime Minister's Office (effective from August 2003). The defence portfolio was allocated to former Minister for Education Rear-Adm. (retd) Teo Chee Hean.

The premiership of Lee Hsien Loong

In August 2003 Prime Minister Goh Chok Tong announced that he intended to resign from his post at least two years prior to the country's next general election, scheduled to be held in 2007. He designated his deputy, Lee Hsien Loong, as his successor. In early 2004 Lee indicated that, following his accession to power, he would implement measures to reduce the control of the Government over Singaporean citizens and to promote a culture of political 'openness'.

On 12 August 2004 Lee Hsien Loong was formally sworn in as Prime Minister, amid claims that a dynastic succession had been contrived. Both former Prime Ministers were included within the new Cabinet: Goh was retained as Senior Minister, while Lee Kuan Yew was redesignated as Minister Mentor. Shanmugam Jayakumar became Singapore's first Deputy Minister of Indian origin. Lee retained the finance portfolio but, in an unexpected development, relinquished the chairmanship of the MAS to Goh. George Yeo was named the new Minister for Foreign Affairs and Teo Chee Hean retained the defence portfolio. Two women were appointed as Ministers of State: Lim Hwee Hua was named Minister of State for Finance and Transport, and Yu-Foo Yee Shoon became Minister of State for Community Development, Youth and Sports.

The reversal of the decline in Singapore's birth rate was immediately rendered a major government priority following Lee's inauguration. In late August 2004 Lee added responsibility for the revival of the country's population growth to the brief of Wong Kan Seng and implemented an array of measures aimed at increasing the birth rate, which since the 1960s had decreased sharply. Government bonuses were offered to parents producing a third or fourth child, maternity leave was lengthened and tax rebates were introduced for working mothers.

In 2005 the Government legalized gambling on Singapore, ending a 40-year ban and allowing for the construction of two major casino resorts, at Marina Bay and on Sentosa Island, to be built at an estimated cost of US $3,000m. The decision encountered widespread disapproval, particularly from religious groups, which accused the Government of prioritizing profit over the country's moral standing. The first hotels at the Sentosa resort opened in January 2010, and the casino commenced operations in February. A phased opening of the Marina Bay resort began in June. The resorts were expected significantly to boost the country's tourism industry and make a sizeable contribution to the Government's campaign to increase the number of tourist arrivals from 10m. in 2009 to 17m. by 2015, as well as allowing Singapore to retain the money of its nationals who had hitherto been obliged to travel abroad in order to engage in gambling activities. Furthermore, when fully completed, the two resorts were expected to employ more than 20,000 people.

Meanwhile, of the four candidates who had applied for inclusion in the presidential contest due to be held in August 2005, only the incumbent, S. R. Nathan, was granted a Certificate of Eligibility, the other three candidates being deemed to be lacking in political experience. Consequently, Nathan was returned unopposed for a second term in office; he was formally sworn in on 1 September. Also in September Minister for Home Affairs Wong Kang Seng succeeded Dr Tan, upon the latter's resignation, to become Deputy Prime Minister (while retaining the home affairs portfolio), alongside Shanmugam Jayakumar.

In April 2006, following months of speculation that Prime Minister Lee Hsien Loong was to call an early legislative election in order to take advantage of Singapore's strong economic position, it was announced that the poll (which had not been due until June 2007) would be held on 6 May 2006. At the election, opposition parties contested 47 of the 84 parliamentary seats. The PAP won 82 seats, as it had done at the 2001 election, while the SDA and the Workers' Party secured one seat each. However, the PAP's share of the votes cast decreased to 66.6%, compared with 75.3% at the 2001 election.

In February 2006, meanwhile, Chee Soon Juan was declared bankrupt by the High Court, having failed to pay the stipulated damages of S $500,000 to Lee Kuan Yew and Goh Chok Tong for the comments that he had made during the 2001 elections (see The premiership of Goh Chok Tong). Under the bankruptcy order, Chee was forbidden from contesting legislative elections for five years and was required to seek official permission to travel overseas. In the following month Chee was convicted of contempt of court for his criticism of Singapore's judiciary during the February court hearing, and was ordered to pay a fine of S$6,000. Upon his refusal to pay the fine, Chee was imprisoned for seven days, after which he again refused to pay and his imprisonment was subsequently extended for a further seven days. In April Chee and several other SDP officials were sued for defamation by Lee Kuan Yew and Lee Hsien Loong in connection with articles published in February in the party's newsletter, *The New Democrat*, which had compared the PAP Government's running of the country to the management of the National Kidney Foundation (NKF), which was embroiled in a corruption scandal. (The controversy at the NKF had emerged in July 2005; amid allegations of misuse of funds, the entire executive board of the charitable organization tendered its resignation and Goh Chok Tong's wife, hitherto the patron of NKF, also relinquished her position.) Chee Soon Juan and his sister, Chee Siok Chin, were found guilty of defamation in September 2006 in a summary judgment by the High Court, their request for a trial having been rejected, and in October 2008 the High Court ordered Chee to pay S $610,000 in defamation damages to Prime Minister Lee and his father. In November 2006 Chee was sentenced to five weeks' imprisonment for not paying a fine for speaking in public without a government permit during the 2006 election period.

Human rights issues were brought to the fore in 2006–07 as the Government sought to curb freedom of expression, attempting to restrict public gatherings, political demonstrations and views portrayed over the internet. At the annual meeting of the IMF and the World Bank in September 2006 the Government prevented five activists from attending, although it had originally yielded to international pressure by allowing access to 22 others. Despite criticism from the President of the World Bank, the Government claimed that the activists posed a security threat and could endanger the attending delegates. In February 2007 the *Far Eastern Economic Review*, a Hong Kong-based journal, failed in its second attempt to have a defamation action dismissed after the publication in July 2006 of an article entitled 'Singapore's "Martyr" Chee Soon Juan'. The *Review* vowed to defend itself vigorously against the suit filed by Lee Hsien Loong and Lee Kuan Yew, over alleged negative comments made about them and the Government by Chee. In its defence, the journal argued that, as it was published in Hong Kong and employed no Singaporean journalists, it was not bound by Singaporean law. Distribution of the journal in Singapore had been banned by the Government in September 2006 on the grounds that it had failed to comply with media regulations. In September 2008 the High Court of Singapore ruled that the *Review* had defamed the country's leaders; in October 2009 the Court of Appeal dismissed the publication's appeal against this ruling

The application of the death penalty continued to be a contentious issue following the execution of two convicted drugs-smugglers, one from Nigeria and the other from South Africa, in January 2007. The case drew international condemnation from various governments and human rights organizations, while Philip Alston, the UN Special Rapporteur on extra-judicial, summary or arbitrary executions, described it as failing to meet international legal standards for criminal prosecution.

In April 2007 it was revealed that cabinet ministers were to receive a salary increase of 60%, to be implemented by 2008. While the decision prompted large-scale public opposition, Prime Minister Lee argued that the increase was well deserved and a necessary precaution against corruption. (Lee himself was to donate his extra salary to various good causes.) Chee Soon Juan criticized the pay rises at an unauthorized forum on democracy in Asia and Europe organized by the SDP. Several members of the European Parliament, as well as two legislators from Cambodia and the Philippines, were denied permission to address the forum by the Singaporean authorities on the grounds that their contributions would constitute interference in Singaporean domestic politics and would not be in the public interest. In September the bankrupt Chee served a three-week prison sentence after failing to pay a fine for attempting to leave Singapore without permission in April 2006. Chee was arrested again in October 2007, together with three other members of the SDP, as they attempted to stage a protest outside the presidential palace in support of their demands for the full disclosure of investments by Singaporean state-controlled companies in Myanmar, following the recent violent suppression of anti-Government marches in that country. In March 2008 Chee was among 18 activists arrested and charged with unlawful assembly, after taking part in an unauthorized demonstration in protest over the rising cost of living in Singapore. His trial, one of seven that Chee awaited over the coming months, began in October. In January 2009 Chee posted a recorded plea to the new US President, Barack Obama, on the video sharing website YouTube, in which he expressed the hope that Obama would 'pay more attention to the human rights abuses of the Singapore Government' and of governments elsewhere in Asia.

In December 2007 Lee Hsien Loong relinquished responsibility for the finance portfolio to the Minister for Education, Tharman Shanmugaratnam, a former Managing Director of the MAS. In a cabinet reorganization announced in March 2008, Tharman was retained as Minister for Finance, but relinquished the education portfolio to Ng Eng Hen, hitherto Minister of Manpower. From May K. Shanmugam, a senior lawyer, was to succeed Shanmugam Jayakumar as Minister of Law, while also being appointed Second Minister for Home Affairs. Jayakumar remained as Deputy Prime Minister and Co-ordinating Minister for National Security.

Recent developments

In April 2008 veteran opposition leader J. B. Jeyaretnam established the Reform Party, urging a restructuring of the electoral system and stating his intention to bring an end to the 'enslavement' of Singapore after nearly 50 years of rule by the PAP. However, Jeyaretnam died at the end of September. The activist's son, Kenneth Jeyaretnam, was elected to replace his father as Secretary-General of the Reform Party in April 2009. In the same month Ng Teck Siong resigned as party Chairman following a vote of no confidence in his leadership; he was subsequently replaced by Edmund Ng.

In March 2009 Prime Minister Lee Hsien Loong announced a cabinet reorganization, which included the promotion, to the position of Senior Minister, of Shanmugan Jayakumar, who retained his position as Co-ordinating Minister for National Security, and the promotion, to the position of Deputy Prime Minister, of Tee Chee Hean, who retained the defence portfolio. In April Parliament approved a new Public Order Act, imposing further restrictions on the right to peaceful assembly and enhancing the powers of the police. The Government claimed that the increasing threat from international terrorist activity had necessitated the enactment of the new legislation, particularly in advance of the summit meeting of Asia-Pacific Economic Co-operation (APEC, see p. 197)—which, in the event, was convened, as planned and without incident, in Singapore in November. Amnesty International urged the Government to amend the Act in order to meet global standards of human rights and to comply with Article 14 of the Singaporean Constitution, which provided for freedom of speech and expression.

Prime Minister Lee's annual National Day Rally speech, given in August 2009, was unusually sombre and defiant in tone, reflecting the vicissitudes of Singapore's 'turbulent and challenging year'. Lee focused predominantly on the adverse effects of the global financial crisis and the need to develop and maintain a culture of social responsibility and unity across racial and religious divides. In the same month Senior Minister Goh indicated that the search for Lee's eventual replacement had already commenced, although Lee was not expected to relinquish the premiership for a number of years to come. In December Chee Soon Juan and Gandhi Ambalam were again imprisoned, for a period of one week, and fined S $1,000, after being convicted of distributing anti-PAP pamphlets without a permit during the 2006 elections. At the end of March 2010 a new political party, the United Singapore Democrats (USD), was formally established by former members of the SDP, including Narayanasamy Gogelavany, subsequently named USD President, and Jaslyn Go, USD Secretary.

In April 2010 two constitutional amendments, originally proposed by Prime Minister Lee in May 2009, were approved, whereby the maximum number of non-constituency seats was to be raised from six to nine at the next legislative election, and the system whereby the Government was able to nominate up to nine unelected, politically neutral MPs was made permanent; previously the system was subject to parliamentary approval prior to each election.

With many Singaporeans becoming increasingly vocal in their dissatisfaction with regard to the city-state's 'open-door' immigration policy for foreign workers (with about one-third of the total number of people resident in Singapore of foreign origin), Prime Minister Lee's National Day Rally speech in August 2010 focused primarily on the issue of immigration. Lee declared that Singapore should 'consolidate, slow down the pace' of immigration, stating that present rates could not be sustained indefinitely. In September the Government announced a revision to Singapore's permanent residency regulations, including an increase, from S $1.0m. to $2.5m., in the value of Singapore-based investments required to be made by foreigners aiming to become permanent residents, and the introduction of higher minimum income and residential requirements. During 2009 59,500 applications for permanent residency were approved, a significant decline on 2008, in which year some 79,200 such applications were approved.

In October 2010 former Reform Party Chairman Ng Teck Siong, together with Chia Ti Lik, a lawyer who had contested the 2006 legislative election as a candidate of the Workers' Party, formed a new political party, the Socialist Front, the stated objective of which was to establish a socialist state in Singapore, to encourage ownership and active participation of Singaporeans in the affairs and politics of the country, and to strive towards the achievement of equal opportunities for all Singaporean citizens to allow them 'to maximize their fullest potential'.

A cabinet reorganization implemented at the beginning of November 2010 was widely interpreted as part of ongoing efforts to promulgate an image of political renewal in advance of the next legislative election. Notable changes included the transfer of Deputy Prime Minister Wong from the home affairs portfolio to the position of Co-ordinating Minister for National Security, in place of Shanmugan Jayakumar. The latter remained Senior Minister in the Prime Minister's Office, but subsequently announced his intention to resign from political office. Wong was replaced as Minister of Home Affairs, a position that he had held for 17 years, by his deputy, K. Shanmugam, who concurrently retained the law portfolio, while Lui Tuck Yew, the acting Minister of Information, Communications and the Arts, was confirmed in the post on a permanent basis.

In December 2010 Edmund Ng resigned as Chairman of the Reform Party, and was replaced by Tan Tee Seng; Kenneth Jeyaretnam continued as party Secretary-General. In February 2011 at least nine members of the Reform Party, including five members of the party's central leadership, tendered their resignation from the party, citing difficulties in working with Jeyaretnam. Tan Tee Seng resigned as Chairman, also citing differences of opinion with the Secretary-General.

Meanwhile, following the conclusion of a three-year trial, in October 2010 Chee Soon Juan was convicted on four charges of speaking in public without a permit, to the consternation of the political opposition and civil liberties organizations. An appeal lodged by Chee against these convictions was rejected by the High Court in January 2011. The presiding judge ordered Chee to pay a fine of S $20,000, a punishment that would be commutable to 20 weeks' imprisonment if the fine were not paid by 10 February; however, an SDP-initiated internet appeal for donations raised the stipulated amount and Chee avoided a custodial term.

The PAP was returned to power at the general election conducted on 7 May 2011. Although the ruling party took 81 of the 87 parliamentary seats, it received only 60.1% of the votes cast (a reduction of 6.5% in comparison with the 2006 election), the outcome being regarded as the PAP's worst result since 1965. Only five PAP candidates were unopposed, compared with 37 in 2006. The Workers' Party substantially improved its representation in Parliament, winning six seats, while the SDA lost its one seat. Minister Mentor Lee Kuan Yew unexpectedly announced his retirement from the Cabinet, as did Senior Minister Goh Chok Tong and several other cabinet members. An extensive cabinet reorganization followed. Tharman Shanmugaratnam was appointed Deputy Prime Minister, retaining the finance portfolio (and also becoming Chairman of the MAS); in addition, Tharman was allocated the manpower portfolio. Teo Chee Hean remained as Deputy Prime Minister, also taking the post of Co-ordinating Minister for National Security and Minister for Home Affairs. George Yeo was replaced as Minister for Foreign Affairs by K. Shanmugam, who retained the law portfolio. Responsibility for the defence portfolio was assumed by Ng Eng Hen, hitherto the Minister of Education, who was replaced in the latter position by Heng Swee Keat.

Foreign Affairs

Regional relations

Singapore's foreign policy has been dominated by its membership of ASEAN (which comprised all 10 South-East Asian nations by mid-1999), although it has also maintained strong political and military links with more distant allies, including the USA (see Other external relations, below). In November 2000 the fourth informal summit meeting of the ASEAN + 3 group of leaders was convened in Singapore. The summit comprised the leaders of all 10 ASEAN members, as well as those of the People's Republic of China, Japan and the Republic of Korea. An outcome of the meeting was the commissioning of an East Asia Study Group to report on the feasibility of a larger East Asia political and economic grouping and free trade area. Singapore assumed the annually rotating chairmanship of the Association in 2007/08. Achievements of the 13th ASEAN summit meeting, held in Singapore in November 2007, included the adoption of a Declaration on Environmental Sustainability, which contained commitments related to environmental protection and management, climate change, and the conservation of natural resources; the approval of plans for the establishment of an Asian Economic Community by 2015; and the signature of an ASEAN Charter codifying the principles and purposes of the Association. In December 2007 Singapore became the first country to ratify the new Charter, which, having been ratified by the other nine members by October 2008, entered into force in January 2009. On 1 January 2010 a free trade agreement came into effect between the six core ASEAN members—namely Brunei, Indonesia, Malaysia, the Philippines, Singapore and Thailand—under the terms of which tariffs were to be removed on some 90% of goods traded.

Despite ASEAN's ongoing attempts to curb alleged human rights abuses by the Myanma Government, Singapore's continued support of the military regime was demonstrated in April 2007 when Minister for Foreign Affairs George Yeo visited the new Myanma administrative capital, Nay Pyi Taw. This followed the revelation that several Singaporean firms had recently signed contracts to explore for natural gas in Myanma waters, a decision seen as greatly reducing the impact of Western sanctions. Singapore's hosting of the 13th ASEAN summit and related meetings in November were overshadowed to some extent by concerns regarding the violence used to quell the anti-Government protests in Myanmar in September. Singapore had invited the UN envoy to Myanmar, Ibrahim Gambari, to address the meeting, but the Myanma Government, with the support of several other member states, succeeded in forcing the cancellation of his briefing. Bilateral relations were threatened in June 2009 when Senior Minister Goh Chok Tong, during a visit to the Myanma city of Yangon, linked the future of Singaporean investment in Myanmar to the development of democracy therein and urged the Myanma ruling junta to ensure that the forthcoming 2010 legislative elections were free, fair and genuinely inclusive, with all parties being allowed to participate. Goh's comments angered the junta, which argued that the remarks constituted a breach of ASEAN's policy of non-interference in the domestic affairs of member states. In August 2009, in what was widely perceived as an attempt to limit the damage caused by his earlier statements, Goh declared that Myanma opposition leader Aung San Suu Kyi was 'part of the problem' and should cease to dwell on the events of 1990, which he dismissed as 'history' and an obstacle to political reform; however, he maintained that Suu Kyi 'must be allowed to participate' in the 2010 elections. The extension, by a further 18 months, to Suu Kyi's house arrest in mid-August 2009 disappointed the Singaporean Ministry of Foreign Affairs, which urged the holding of 'meaningful dialogue' between the junta and the opposition. The exclusion of Suu Kyi from elections held in November 2010 (see the chapter on Myanmar) elicited expressions of concern and disappointment from the Singaporean Government, as well as others within ASEAN.

Following the resignation of Indonesian President Suharto in May 1998, Singapore's relations with Indonesia deteriorated, in part owing to Prime Minister Lee Kuan Yew's criticism of the new President, Prof. Dr Ir B. J. Habibie. In February 1999 Habibie accused Singapore of racism for allegedly discriminating against its Malay minority. However, the principal issue was Singapore's refusal to meet Indonesia's high expectations of aid in response to the regional economic crisis. Relations improved temporarily following Habibie's replacement as President by Abdurrahman Wahid in October 1999. In November 2000, however, Wahid jeopardized the relationship, as his predecessor had done, by accusing Singapore of discriminating against Malays, after Singapore rejected certain motions proposed by its neighbour at the ASEAN summit. Nevertheless, Singapore and Indonesia subsequently concluded a long-term agreement whereby Indonesia would supply the city-state with natural gas.

In February 2002 Singaporean-Indonesian relations deteriorated once more following the publication of an article in *The Straits Times* in which Lee Kuan Yew remarked that Singapore's national security was being compromised by the fact that terrorists remained at large in Indonesia. In response, the Indonesian Government summoned the Singaporean envoy to Jakarta and lodged an objection to the accusations, claiming that they were provocative and unsubstantiated. Meanwhile, Indonesian Islamic groups held protests outside Singapore's embassy in Jakarta. In March Abu Bakar Bashir, an Indonesian cleric accused of being linked to the international terrorist al-Qa'ida network, issued a writ of defamation against Lee in relation to his comments. In February 2006 the Indonesian authorities agreed to the deportation to Singapore of Mas Selamat Kastari, the alleged leader of the Singaporean branch of Jemaah Islamiah (JI), following his rearrest in Indonesia on suspicion of immigration offences. Kastari, first arrested in Indonesia in 2003, also on charges of suspected illegal immigration, had been the subject of several previous extradition requests from Singapore, which accused Kastari of a central role in an alleged plot, thwarted in late 2001, to crash a hijacked aeroplane into Changi International Airport. The Indonesian Government had rejected those requests, on the grounds that Indonesia and Singapore had no formal extradition treaty; it was unclear why Indonesia subsequently chose to reverse its decision. In February 2008 Kastari escaped from a detention centre in Singapore, where he was being held under the ISA. In May 2009 it was reported that Kastari had been reapprehended in the previous month in the Malaysian state of Johor; his arrest and renewed detention under the ISA were subsequently confirmed by the respective Governments of Singapore and Malaysia. Earlier in the year the Singaporean Government announced that it had released two suspected JI members, stating that they no longer posed a security threat. In September 2010 the Malaysian authorities confirmed the extradition to Singapore of Kastari.

Meanwhile, fires resulting from uncontrolled 'slash and burn' land-clearing practices in Indonesia caused a prolonged haze in late 2006, affecting Singapore and other countries in the region. Singapore was reported to have suffered US $50m. in economic losses. Relations between the two nations came under further pressure in February 2007 when Indonesia imposed an outright ban on all sand exports to Singapore after independent environmental experts highlighted the extensive damage caused to the environment by sand exports. (Singapore had been importing sand from Indonesia after Malaysia banned all exports in 1997.) Myanmar later offered to be Singapore's long-term supplier of sand, cement, granite and other construction materials. It was hoped that relations between Singapore and Indonesia would improve following the signature of an extradition treaty and a new agreement on defence co-operation in April 2007. However, differences emerged in May, when Indonesia sought amendments to the defence accord regarding arrangements for Singaporean troops to use Indonesian military training facilities. With Singapore refusing to consider any revisions, the ratification of both the defence and extradition agreements remained indefinitely suspended at mid-2011. Meanwhile, in March 2009 the Governments of Singapore and Indonesia signed a maritime boundary agreement that redrew the border between the Singaporean island of Sultan Shoal and Pulau Nipah in Indonesia, successfully concluding four years of negotiations. The agreement was successfully ratified by both countries in May 2010. Both Governments expressed their belief that the new, more clearly defined boundary would assist the economic development of border islands and increase Singapore's border security. It was hoped that the creation in May of six new joint working groups would further enhance bilateral economic co-operation and investment.

In September 1994 Singapore and Malaysia agreed to settle a long-standing dispute over ownership of Pedra Branca Island (Batu Puteh) by referring the case to the International Court of Justice (ICJ) in The Hague, the Netherlands. An agreement on the referral was finally signed in early 2003, and in May 2008 the ICJ ruled in favour of Singapore, by 12 votes to four. In August 1995 Singapore and Malaysia agreed on the permanent boundary of their territorial waters after 15 years of negotiations.

Relations between Singapore and Malaysia deteriorated in the latter half of 1998. In August the Malaysian Prime Minister condemned Singapore for requesting that Malaysia transfer its customs, immigration and quarantine facilities from Tanjung Pagar, a railway station in central Singapore situated on land owned by the Malaysian Government; Malaysia subsequently decided to continue using its facilities at Tanjung Pagar, while Singapore moved its customs office to a new location. In September Malaysia announced its decision to insist on prior clearance for Singaporean military aircraft wishing to enter its airspace; joint defence exercises within the context of the regional Five-Power Defence Arrangements were also terminated. In the same month the publication of the memoirs of Lee Kuan Yew, which referred to the events surrounding the secession of Singapore from the Federation of Malaysia, exacerbated bilateral tensions. An improvement in relations was perceived in November, when Goh visited Malaysia at the invitation of Malaysian Prime Minister Mahathir Mohamad. Joint defence exercises were resumed in April 1999. However, relations deteriorated again in August 2000, when Lee Kuan Yew publicly criticized Mahathir over his handling of the dismissal and detention of Anwar Ibrahim, Malaysia's former Deputy Prime Minister (see the chapter on Malaysia).

In September 2001 Lee Kuan Yew visited Malaysia and held talks with Mahathir to address the outstanding issues affecting the relationship between the two countries. A framework agreement was subsequently signed under which Malaysia agreed to relocate its facilities at Tanjung Pagar in return for Singapore's agreement to construct a railway tunnel under the strait. Lee also reported that the two countries would work together to construct a suspension bridge, which would enable the demolition of the causeway linking the two countries. However, in January 2002 the Malaysian Government denied the existence of such an agreement and proposed that Malaysia should build a suspension bridge and a railway swing bridge to replace its half of the road link, enabling the Malaysian half of the causeway to be demolished without Singapore's co-operation. Tension was also promoted by the ongoing renegotiation of the terms upon which Malaysia would continue to supply water to Singapore (based upon an agreement originally concluded in 1961 and due to expire in 2061). While an agreement had provisionally been reached in September 2001, the Malaysian Government was dissatisfied with its terms and continued to increase its demands.

In March 2002 relations were further strained when Malaysia claimed that reclamation work being carried out by Singapore in the Tebrau Straits was too close to its border and was obstructing ships sailing into ports in Johor. Malaysia later applied to the International Tribunal for the Law of the Sea (see p. 353) for a suspension of the reclamation work. The tribunal ruled in October 2003 that Singapore's reclamation work was in accordance with international law and could, therefore, proceed. The protracted dispute was ostensibly resolved in January 2005 when the respective Governments of Singapore and Malaysia issued a joint statement declaring their agreement that the

Tebrau Straits constituted a shared body of water. Meanwhile, in February 2003 Mahathir pledged that his country would continue to supply water to Singapore indefinitely. However, he stated that Malaysia would cease its provision of untreated water to the city-state upon the termination of an existing agreement in 2011 and provide filtered water instead, at what it considered to be a reasonable price. Singapore continued to insist that any proposed price was too high and that it received too little for the treated water that it supplied to Malaysia in return.

Abdullah Badawi's accession to the Malaysian premiership in October 2003 prompted expectations that Singapore's relations with Malaysia might improve, hopes that were augmented by the transfer of the Singaporean premiership to Lee Hsien Loong in August 2004. In his first National Day Rally speech, given later that month, Lee stressed his deep commitment to working in close unison with Abdullah, whom he had known for many years, in order to consolidate Singapore's links with Malaysia. In mid-2005 Abdullah announced the abandonment of his predecessor's plans for the construction of a replacement causeway linking Singapore and Malaysia, a development that it was hoped would dissipate bilateral tensions. However, in January 2006 Malaysia unexpectedly announced that it was to commence construction of its section of the new bridge, also referred to as the 'scenic bridge', in the hope that Singapore would agree in due course to the construction of its part. Construction of the Malaysian section of the bridge began in March, but was halted in the following month by Abdullah, who announced that all negotiations with Singapore pertaining to the bridge were also to be abandoned. Prime Minister Lee visited Malaysia in May 2007 for two days of informal talks with Abdullah. The main outcome of the discussions was a decision to form a joint ministerial committee to oversee collaboration on Malaysia's plan to establish a 2,217-sq-km economic development zone in its southern state of Johor, to be known as the Iskandar Development Region, with both leaders agreeing that outstanding issues of dispute, such as water sales to Singapore and the suspended construction of the bridge, should not be allowed to impede bilateral co-operation in other areas.

Singapore's relations with Malaysia appeared to be jeopardized by the appointment, in April 2009, of Najib Tun Razak as Abdullah's successor; shortly after taking office, the new Malaysian Prime Minister made several statements that seemed intent on reviving dormant bilateral disputes dating back to the premiership of Mahathir (1981–2003). However, bilateral tensions were largely defused by a week-long visit to Malaysia by Minister Mentor Lee Kuan Yew in June 2009, during which Lee held discussions with numerous senior Malaysian officials, including the Yang di-Pertuan Agong ('Supreme Head of State'), Sultan Tuanku Mizan Zainal Abidin. During a meeting between Prime Ministers Najib and Lee Hsien Loong in May 2010, the two leaders affirmed their commitment to enhancing bilateral co-operation, and agreed to the joint development of a rapid transit system between Johor Bahru and Singapore. In September the premiers finalized a land swap agreement, which provided for the exchange of six Singaporean land parcels for six pieces of Malaysian land.

Singapore and the People's Republic of China established diplomatic relations at ambassadorial level in October 1990. Nevertheless, Prime Minister Goh made his first official visit to Taiwan, with which Singapore enjoyed close military and economic links, in October 1993. In October 1996 Singapore and Australia issued a joint communiqué urging the integration of the People's Republic of China into the Asian regional security structure, and reaffirming their commitment to a co-operative dialogue with the People's Republic. However, a private visit to Singapore in January 1998 by the Taiwanese Vice-President, Lien Chan, during which he met with Goh and with Singaporean cabinet ministers, provoked the disapproval of the People's Republic, as did visits to Taiwan by Lee Kuan Yew, in September 2000 and September 2002, and by Lee Hsien Loong, in July 2004. The diplomatic furore caused by Lee's visit in 2004 served to delay the start of negotiations concerning a free trade pact between the People's Republic and Singapore, which had been due to commence in November 2004, despite Lee's insistence that his visit in no way weakened his country's commitment to the 'one China' policy that denied recognition of Taiwan. In October 2005, at a meeting in the Chinese capital, Beijing, of Singaporean and Chinese delegates, led by Lee Hsien Loong and Chinese Premier Wen Jiabao, both countries affirmed their commitment to accelerating the holding of free trade negotiations. The two countries also agreed to work together to address the regional threats of terrorism and piracy in the Straits of Melaka. China and Singapore held their first round of free trade talks in October 2006; several further sessions took place in 2007, and final negotiations in October 2008 resulted in the signing of a free trade agreement that entered into force in January 2009. Meanwhile, in early 2008 Singapore and China signed an agreement intended to increase defence and security co-operation, and in June 2009 the two countries conducted a week-long joint anti-terrorism exercise in China's Guangxi Zhuang autonomous region, China's first such exercise with foreign forces. During a visit by Prime Minister Lee to Beijing in August 2010, Chinese President Hu Jintao expressed appreciation for Singapore's continued adherence to the 'one China' policy, and both leaders pledged further to enhance bilateral relations.

Other external relations

In November 1990 representatives of the Governments of the USA and Singapore signed an agreement providing the US navy and air force with increased access to existing bases in Singapore following the planned US withdrawal from military installations in the Philippines. In January 1992 the two countries reached an agreement, in principle, on the relocation of a naval logistic command headquarters from Subic Bay, in the Philippines. However, relations with the USA were occasionally strained by attacks on the authoritarian style of government in Singapore by the liberal US media.

Following the attacks on the USA in September 2001 (see the chapter on the USA), Singapore affirmed its support for the US-led alliance against terrorism. In the aftermath of the attacks a number of suspects with alleged links to al-Qa'ida and its regional affiliates Abu Sayyaf and JI were arrested in Singapore under the ISA; among those detained were two Singaporean nationals in 2003. In March of that year the Government announced its support for the US-led military campaign to oust the regime of Saddam Hussain in Iraq. In November 2005 the Government announced that it had detained for a two-year period Mohammad Sharif Rahmat, an alleged member of JI. While JI's network seemed to have been severely damaged by the recent arrests, leading members of both JI and Abu Sayyaf remained at large in the region. In order to address the ensuing national security concerns, the Government announced the establishment of a national security secretariat, within the Ministry of Defence, intended to strengthen co-ordination between the security services of Singapore and the USA. In October 2007 Singapore's Parliament approved counter-terrorism legislation designed to give effect to the International Convention for the Suppression of Terrorist Bombings (adopted by the UN General Assembly in 1997). The new law provided for the extradition of those suspected of perpetrating terrorist bombings, even in the absence of an extradition treaty between Singapore and the other country, and gave Singapore the power to prosecute foreign nationals accused of committing terrorist offences within its territory.

Cordial relations with the USA remained largely unaffected following the inauguration of Barack Obama as the new US President in January 2009. A number of important bilateral visits were conducted during 2009–10, including that of Minister for Foreign Affairs George Yeo to Washington, DC, in April 2009, during which he met with several senior US officials, including US Secretary of State Hillary Clinton. In a joint press conference, Yeo and Clinton spoke of the 'close and constructive' relationship enjoyed between the two countries, and pledged further to increase bilateral co-operation. In October Minister Mentor Lee Kuan Yew visited New York and Washington, DC, where he met with President Obama, who himself visited Singapore in the following month to attend the APEC summit meeting, along with Secretary of State Clinton and other leading US officials. Additional discussions between Prime Minister Lee and Obama, and between Yeo and Clinton, were reported further to have enhanced the close relations between Singapore and the USA. In April 2010 Prime Minister Lee visited Washington, DC, in order to attend the Nuclear Security Summit; Lee also met with members of the Obama Administration, before travelling to Chicago, Illinois, where he met with local political and business leaders. In that year the export to Singapore of US goods totalled US $29,100m., representing an increase of 31.1% on the previous year, while the export to the USA of Singaporean goods totalled $17,500m., an increase of 11.3% on 2009.

In October 2004 officials from Bahrain, Bangladesh, Egypt, Jordan, Kuwait, Malaysia, Singapore and Thailand convened in Singapore and agreed to hold the inaugural Asia-Middle East

SINGAPORE

Dialogue (AMED) in mid-2005. This diplomatic initiative had been instigated by former Prime Minister Goh owing to concern that terrorism was being equated with Islam and also out of respect for Middle Eastern states' general suspicion of dialogues initiated by the USA or Europe. It was to focus on improving political, economic and business links between the two regions, as well as on promoting a greater level of mutual cultural understanding. The meeting was held in Singapore in June and was attended by representatives of approximately 50 Asian and Middle Eastern states. It was agreed that AMED would convene on a biennial basis, at venues alternating between Asia and the Middle East. In January 2008 Singapore concluded negotiations with the Gulf Co-operation Council (comprising Bahrain, Kuwait, Oman, Qatar, Saudi Arabia and the United Arab Emirates) on its second free trade agreement in the Middle East, the first having been signed with Jordan in May 2004. An upsurge in senior-level visits to Middle Eastern countries, including visits to Oman and Bahrain by Senior Minister Goh in January and February 2010, respectively, and to Saudi Arabia by Minister for Foreign Affairs George Yeo in May of that year, reflected Singapore's increasingly deep political and economic engagement with the region.

Relations with the United Kingdom, generally cordial, were strained in November 2010 when a British author and resident of Malaysia, Alan Shadrake, was convicted of contempt, after criticizing the use of capital punishment in Singapore and alleging a lack of impartiality within the country's judicial system in a book entitled *Once a Jolly Hangman—Singapore Justice in the Dock*; Shadrake was sentenced to six weeks' imprisonment and fined S $20,000. The verdict was received with disappointment by the British Government: Minister of State at the Foreign and Commonwealth Office Jeremy Browne expressed his 'dismay' at the author's conviction and stern sentence, appealing to Singapore to recognize 'the right to freedom of expression'. Rights groups, including the US-based Human Rights Watch, which had urged the Singaporean authorities to exonerate Shadrake, were also critical of the verdict. The author, who remained free on bail pending an appeal, lodged a formal challenge against his conviction in mid-April 2011. Human Rights Watch contended that the outcome of the appeal would have 'important implications for free expression in Singapore'.

CONSTITUTION AND GOVERNMENT

Legislative power is vested in the unicameral Parliament, with 84 members who are elected by universal adult suffrage for five years (subject to dissolution—within three months of which a general election must be held) in single-member and multi-member constituencies. As many as three additional 'non-constituency' seats may be offered to opposition parties, and up to nine non-elected, neutral MPs may be nominated: all have restricted voting rights. In May 2009 it was announced that, with effect from the next parliamentary election, opposition MPs would be afforded a maximum of nine 'non-constituency' seats; the amendment was approved in April 2010. The President is directly elected by universal adult suffrage for a six-year term as a constitutional Head of State, vested with limited powers of veto in financial matters, public appointments and detentions for reasons of national security. Effective executive authority rests with the Cabinet, led by the Prime Minister, who is appointed by the President and is responsible to Parliament.

REGIONAL AND INTERNATIONAL CO-OPERATION

Singapore is a member of the Association of Southeast Asian Nations (ASEAN, see p. 206), the Asia-Pacific Economic Co-operation (APEC, see p. 197) forum, the Asian Development Bank (ADB, see p. 202), the UN's Economic and Social Commission for Asia and the Pacific (ESCAP, see p. 37) and the Colombo Plan (see p. 446).

Singapore became a member of the UN in 1965. As a contracting party to the General Agreement on Tariffs and Trade, Singapore joined the World Trade Organization (WTO, see p. 430) on its establishment in 1995. Singapore participates in the Group of 77 (G77, see p. 447) developing nations, and is also a member of the International Labour Organization (ILO, see p. 138) and the Non-aligned Movement (see p. 461). Singapore hosts the Shangri-La Dialogue, an annual meeting of ministers responsible for defence.

ECONOMIC AFFAIRS

In 2009, according to estimates by the World Bank, Singapore's gross national income (GNI), measured at average 2007–09 prices, was US $185,655m., equivalent to $37,220 per head (or $49,850 per head on an international purchasing-power parity basis). During 2000–09, it was estimated, the population increased at an average annual rate of 2.4%, while gross domestic product (GDP) per head increased, in real terms, at an average rate of 2.5% per year. Overall GDP increased, in real terms, at an average annual rate of 5.0% in 2000–09. According to official figures, GDP contracted by 0.8% in 2009, but grew by 14.5% in 2010.

Agriculture (including fishing and quarrying—mainly of granite) contributed less than 0.1% of GDP in 2009 and, including utilities, engaged only 1.9% of the employed labour force in 2010. Vegetables, plants and orchid flowers are the principal crops. According to figures from the World Bank, agricultural GDP (again including fishing and quarrying) declined at an average annual rate of 0.7% during 2000–08. According to official figures, agricultural GDP (including fishing and quarrying) contracted by 1.7% in 2009. A further contraction, of 0.1%, occurred in 2010.

Industry (including manufacturing, construction and utilities) contributed 28.3% of GDP in 2009 and, excluding utilities, in 2010 engaged 20.1% of the employed labour force. During 2000–08, according to figures from the World Bank, industrial GDP increased at an average annual rate of 3.8%. According to official figures, the GDP of the manufacturing and construction sectors combined declined by 1.4% in 2009, but recorded a strong recovery in 2010, in which year the sector expanded by 25.0%.

Manufacturing contributed an estimated 21.4% of GDP in 2009. The sector engaged 14.8% of the employed labour force in 2010. The principal branches of manufacturing in 2008 (measured in terms of the value of output) were electronic products and components (which accounted for an estimated 26.3% of total manufacturing production), biomedical and pharmaceutical products, transport engineering (especially ship-building), chemicals and chemical products, and precision engineering. According to figures from the World Bank, manufacturing GDP increased at an average annual rate of 4.3% in 2000–08. According to official figures, manufacturing GDP contracted by 4.2% in 2009, before expanding by 29.7% in 2010.

Construction contributed 5.4% of GDP in 2009, and in 2010 the sector engaged 5.3% of the employed labour force. According to official figures, the GDP of the sector expanded by 17.1% in 2009 and by 6.1% in 2010.

Singapore relies on imports of hydrocarbons to fuel its three thermal power stations. In 2007 natural gas accounted for 78.7% of the total amount of electrical energy produced; petroleum accounted for 21.3%. In 2010 imports of mineral fuels accounted for 27.3% of total merchandise imports.

The services sector contributed 71.6% of GDP in 2009, and it engaged 77.9% of the employed labour force in 2010. Financial and business services provided 26.2% of GDP in 2009. The GDP of the financial services sector increased by 4.5% in 2008 and by 4.3% in 2009. Singapore is a major regional foreign-exchange dealing centre, and banking is an important sector. Tourism is a significant source of foreign exchange, and receipts from tourism amounted to an estimated US $10,583m. in 2008. The number of tourist arrivals rose from 9.7m. in 2009 to 11.6m. in 2010. Singapore is the world's busiest port in tonnage terms and has one of the largest merchant shipping registers in the world. According to figures from the World Bank, the GDP of the services sector increased at an average annual rate of 5.7% in 2000–08. According to official figures, the sector contracted by 0.7% in 2009 but expanded by 10.5% in 2010.

In 2009 Singapore recorded a visible trade surplus of an estimated US $30,231m., and there was a surplus of $32,628m. on the current account of the balance of payments. In 2010 the principal sources of imports were Malaysia (11.7%), the USA (11.2%), Japan, Taiwan and the Republic of Korea. Malaysia (which accounted for 11.9%), Hong Kong (11.7%), the People's Republic of China and the USA were the leading markets for exports in that year. Principal imports in 2010 included machinery and equipment (46.5% of the total imports and notably electronic components and parts), mineral fuels, miscellaneous manufactured articles and chemicals and basic manufactures. Principal exports included machinery and equipment (51.2% of the total exports and notably electronic components and parts), mineral fuels (mainly petroleum products), chemicals and miscellaneous manufactured articles. Singapore

SINGAPORE

Statistical Survey

is an important entrepôt, and re-exports accounted for 48.1% of total exports in 2010.

The 2010 budget projected revenue of S $44,581m. and expenditure of S $44,050m. The surplus was forecast to reach the equivalent of 0.1% of GDP. According to the Asian Development Bank (ADB), at the end of 2010 Singapore's external debt totalled US $498,749m. The annual rate of inflation averaged 1.6% in 2000–09; consumer prices increased by only 0.6% in 2009, before rising by 2.8% in 2010. The rate of unemployment declined to 4.1% of the labour force among Singapore citizens and permanent residents in mid-2010. The overall unemployment rate (including foreign workers) was estimated at 1.8% in March 2011, in comparison with 2.8% in June 2010.

Singapore's efforts to diversify economic activities envisaged strong growth in areas such as biomedical manufacturing and financial services. However, the country's dependency on external demand was highlighted in 2008/09, when the deterioration in global economic conditions led to a steep decline in Singapore's exports. The economy entered recession in the third quarter of 2008, and in early 2009 the Prime Minister warned that Singapore confronted its worst economic crisis since the Second World War. In comparison with the corresponding quarter of the previous year, GDP contracted by an unprecedented 11.5% in the first three months of 2009. For the year as a whole, however, GDP contracted at a slower rate than anticipated (0.8%). In early 2009 the Government announced a fiscal stimulus plan, which envisaged expenditure of about S $20,500m. The programme provided various incentives for businesses. Foreign direct investment was estimated to have increased from US $15,279m. in 2009 to $38,638m. in 2010. Although inflationary pressures eased considerably during 2009, these subsequently re-emerged, mainly owing to the increasing costs of housing, transport and food items. The pressure on prices was not expected to ease until the latter part of 2011. However, the retail sector was assisted by the 20% rise in foreign visitor arrivals in 2010. As external demand resumed and as business confidence improved, a particularly impressive recovery was recorded in the area of manufacturing. This robust growth was led by the biomedical sector, the output of which rose by 50% in 2010. The concomitant increase in exports was estimated at 31%, while the Singapore dollar appreciated by 6.8% in relation to its US counterpart. The cost of imports rose by 27.6% in 2010. Operating expenditure under the 2011/12 budget was raised in order to increase spending in areas such as health, education and housing. GDP growth in the range of 5%–7% was forecast by the Government for 2011. Meanwhile, as the Singaporean population continued to age and with foreign workers estimated to account for one-third of the labour force by 2010, the Government renewed its efforts to encourage population growth.

PUBLIC HOLIDAYS

2012: 2 January (for New Year's Day), 23–24 January (Chinese New Year), 6 April (Good Friday), 1 May (Labour Day), 17 May (Vesak Day), 9 August (National Day), 18 August* (Hari Raya Puasa, end of Ramadan), 25 October* (Hari Raya Haji, Feast of the Sacrifice), 13 November (Deepavali), 25 December (Christmas Day).

* These holidays are dependent on the Islamic lunar calendar and may vary by one or two days from the dates given.

Statistical Survey

Source (unless otherwise stated): Department of Statistics, 100 High St, 05-01 The Treasury, Singapore 179434; tel. 63327686; fax 63327689; e-mail info@singstat.gov.sg; internet www.singstat.gov.sg.

Area and Population

AREA, POPULATION AND DENSITY

Area (sq km)	710.3*
Population (census results)†	
30 June 2000	
Males	2,061,800‡
Females	1,955,900‡
Total	4,017,733
30 June 2010	5,076,700‡
Density (per sq km) at 2010 census	7,147.3

* 274.2 sq miles.
† Includes non-residents, totalling 754,524 in 2000 and 1,305,000 in 2010.
‡ Rounded figure.

POPULATION BY AGE AND SEX
('000 persons at 2010 census)*

	Males	Females	Total
0–14	334.4	320.0	654.4
15–64	1,377.0	1,401.5	2,778.9
65 and over	149.5	188.8	338.3
Total	1,861.1	1,910.6	3,771.7

Note: Totals may not be equal to the sum of components, owing to rounding.
* Resident population of Singapore only; the total population was recorded at 5,076,700.

ETHNIC GROUPS
('000 persons at 30 June 2010)*

	Males	Females	Total
Chinese	1,370.1	1,423.9	2,794.0
Malays	250.9	253.0	503.9
Indians	180.3	167.8	348.1
Others	59.8	65.9	125.8
Total	1,861.1	1,910.6	3,771.7

* Figures refer to the resident population of Singapore only.

BIRTHS, MARRIAGES AND DEATHS*

	Registered live births Number	Rate (per 1,000)	Registered marriages Number	Rate (per 1,000)	Registered deaths Number	Rate (per 1,000)
2003	37,485	10.5	21,962	5.2	16,036	4.5
2004	37,174	10.3	22,189	5.2	15,860	4.4
2005	37,492	10.2	22,992	5.3	16,215	4.4
2006	38,317	10.3	23,706	n.a.	16,393	4.4
2007	39,490	10.3	23,966	n.a.	17,140	4.5
2008	39,826	10.2	24,596	n.a.	17,127	4.4
2009	39,570	9.9	26,081	n.a.	17,101	4.3
2010	37,978	9.3	24,363	n.a.	17,525	4.3

* Data are tabulated by year of registration, rather than by year of occurrence.

Life expectancy (years at birth, WHO estimates): 81 (males 79; females 83) in 2008 (Source: WHO, *World Health Statistics*).

SINGAPORE

ECONOMICALLY ACTIVE POPULATION
('000 residents aged 15 years and over, at June of each year)*

	2008	2009	2010
Agriculture, fishing, mining and quarrying, utilities, sewage and waste management	22.7	20.9	37.6
Manufacturing	311.9	293.6	291.4
Construction	105.5	113.8	104.0
Wholesale and retail trade; repair of motor vehicles, motorcycles and personal and household goods	269.5	272.4	281.7
Hotels and restaurants	120.0	124.9	128.9
Transport and storage	182.4	179.9	191.3
Information and communications	87.0	94.3	99.9
Financial intermediation	123.6	121.9	126.0
Real estate, renting and business activities	237.5	243.4	253.4
Community, social and personal services	391.9	404.4	448.6
Total employed	**1,852.0**	**1,869.4**	**1,962.9**
Unemployed	76.2	116.3	84.4
Total labour force	**1,928.3**	**1,985.7**	**2,047.3**

*Data refer to Singapore citizens and permanent residents, but exclude foreign workers temporarily resident.

Health and Welfare

KEY INDICATORS

Total fertility rate (children per woman, 2008)	1.3
Under-5 mortality rate (per 1,000 live births, 2008)	3
HIV/AIDS (% of persons aged 15–49, 2007)	0.2
Physicians (per 1,000 head, 2004)	1.5
Hospital beds (per 1,000 head, 2006)	3.2
Health expenditure (2007): US $ per head (PPP)	1,643
Health expenditure (2007): % of GDP	3.1
Health expenditure (2007): public (% of total)	32.6
Total carbon dioxide emissions ('000 metric tons, 2007)	54,146.6
Carbon dioxide emissions per head (metric tons, 2007)	11.8
Human Development Index (2010): ranking	27
Human Development Index (2010): value	0.846

For sources and definitions, see explanatory note on p. vi.

Agriculture

PRINCIPAL CROPS
('000 metric tons)

	2007	2008	2009
Groundnut oil*	1,816	1,816	1,816
Sesame oil*	2,436	2,436	2,436
Soybean oil*	3,094	3,094	3,094
Cabbages and other brassicas	566	464	499
Spinach	2,012	1,890	2,105

* FAO estimates.

Total vegetables (incl. melons, '000 metric tons, may include official, semi-official or estimated data): 19.0 in 2007–09.

Source: FAO.

LIVESTOCK
('000 head, year ending September, FAO estimates)

	2007	2008	2009
Pigs	260	260	260
Chickens	3,000	3,000	3,200
Ducks	712	720	750

Source: FAO.

LIVESTOCK PRODUCTS
('000 metric tons)

	2007	2008	2009
Pig meat	19.2	19.3	17.5
Chicken meat*	83.1	82.6	86.2
Hen eggs	23.6	21.5	21.2

* FAO estimates.

Source: FAO.

Forestry

SAWNWOOD PRODUCTION
('000 cubic metres, incl. railway sleepers, FAO estimates)

	1990	1991	1992
Coniferous (softwood)	5	10	5
Broadleaved (hardwood)	50	20	20
Total	**55**	**30**	**25**

1993–2009: Annual production assumed to be unchanged since 1992 (FAO estimates).

Source: FAO.

Fishing

(metric tons, live weight)

	2006	2007	2008
Capture	3,103	3,522	1,623
Prawns and shrimps	460	505	132
Aquaculture	8,573	4,503	3,518
Indonesian snakehead	303	235	175
Milkfish	1,183	1,303	917
Green mussel	5,891	1,852	1,488
Total catch	**11,676**	**8,025**	**5,141**

Note: Figures exclude crocodiles, recorded by number rather than by weight. The number of estuarine crocodiles caught was: 1,712 in 2006; 1,653 in 2007; 1,877 in 2008.

Source: FAO.

Industry

PETROLEUM PRODUCTS
('000 metric tons)

	2005	2006	2007
Liquefied petroleum gas	882	669	663
Naphtha	4,783	4,606	4,483
Motor spirit (petrol)	4,879	4,699	4,574
Kerosene	619	596	581
Jet fuel	7,610	7,458	8,102
Gas-diesel (distillate fuel) oils	14,474	13,939	13,567
Residual fuel oil	8,862	8,534	8,306
Lubricating oils	2,183	2,487	2,581
Petroleum bitumen (asphalt)	1,975	1,745	1,982

Source: UN Industrial Commodity Statistics Database.

SINGAPORE

SELECTED OTHER PRODUCTS

	1988	1989	1990
Paints ('000 litres)	48,103.6	52,746.9	58,245.9
Broken granite ('000 metric tons)	6,914.0	7,007.5	6,371.7
Bricks ('000 units)	103,136	116,906	128,386
Soft drinks ('000 litres)	269,689.4	252,977.6	243,175.1
Plywood, plain and printed ('000 sq m)	31,307.0	28,871.3	26,106.9
Vegetable cooking oil (metric tons)	75,022	103,003	102,854
Animal fodder (metric tons)	110,106	115,341	104,541
Gas (million kWh)	681.1	722.4	807.1
Cassette tape recorders ('000 sets)	15,450	14,006	18,059

Source: UN, *Industrial Commodity Statistics Yearbook*.

Plywood ('000 cu m, estimates): 280 per year in 1991–2008 (Source: FAO).

Electric energy (million kWh): 41,138 in 2007; 41,717 in 2008; 41,801 in 2009 (Source: Asian Development Bank).

Finance

CURRENCY AND EXCHANGE RATES

Monetary Units
100 cents = 1 Singapore dollar (S $).

Sterling, US Dollar and Euro Equivalents (31 December 2010)
£1 sterling = S $2.0156;
US $1 = S $1.2875;
€1 = S $1.7204;
S $100 = £49.61 = US $77.67 = €58.13.

Average Exchange Rate (Singapore dollars per US $)
2008   1.4149
2009   1.4545
2010   1.3635

BUDGET
(S $ million)

Revenue*	2008	2009	2010
Tax revenue	37,519	35,272	40,662
Income tax	18,559	16,884	18,276
Corporate and personal income tax	16,403	16,861	17,206
Contributions by statutory board	2,156	23	420
Assets taxes	2,891	2,004	2,598
Taxes on motor vehicles	2,003	1,787	1,893
Customs and excise duties	2,083	2,080	2,090
Betting taxes	1,777	1,726	2,120
Stamp duty	1,838	1,989	3,097
Goods and services tax	6,632	6,633	7,699
Others	1,736	2,170	2,889
Fees and charges	3,726	2,423	3,779
Total (incl. others)	41,377	37,872	44,581

Expenditure	2008	2009	2010
Operating expenditure	28,590	29,871	32,755
Security and external relations	13,588	13,548	14,311
Social development	12,568	13,465	15,400
Education	7,298	7,419	8,517
Health	2,295	2,764	3,070
Community development and sports	1,173	1,404	1,793
Environment and water resources	560	662	661
Economic development	1,436	1,785	1,914
Trade and industry	624	652	673
Transport	374	372	420
Government administration	998	1,071	1,130
Development expenditure	8,880	10,612	11,295
Total	37,470	40,482	44,050

*Figures refer to operating revenue only; the data exclude investment income and capital revenue.

INTERNATIONAL RESERVES
(US $ million at 31 December)

	2008	2009	2010
Gold and foreign exchange	173,649	186,005	223,900
IMF special drawing rights	370	1,537	1,527
Reserve position in the IMF	174	262	297
Total	174,193	187,803	225,725

Source: IMF, *International Financial Statistics*.

MONEY SUPPLY
(S $ million at 31 December)

	2008	2009	2010
Currency outside banks	18,997	20,217	22,300
Demand deposits at commercial banks	56,706	73,255	90,166
Total money	75,703	93,472	112,466

Source: IMF, *International Financial Statistics*.

COST OF LIVING
(Consumer Price Index; base: 2009 = 100)

	2007	2008	2010
Food	90.7	97.7	101.3
Transport	99.1	103.2	110.3
Clothing and footwear	97.6	99.0	100.4
Housing	86.7	98.3	102.0
Education	96.0	99.2	102.7
Health	92.9	98.0	101.9
All items (incl. others)	93.2	99.4	102.8

NATIONAL ACCOUNTS
(S $ million at current prices)

Expenditure on the Gross Domestic Product

	2007	2008	2009
Government final consumption expenditure	25,822.2	28,847.0	28,563.6
Private final consumption expenditure	98,069.6	106,424.7	107,019.8
Change in inventories	−6,758.8	5,143.1	−6,078.5
Gross fixed capital formation	63,070.6	75,780.9	76,367.9
Statistical discrepancy	818.1	−4,340.3	−2,212.8
Total domestic expenditure	181,021.7	211,855.4	203,660.0
Exports of goods and services	584,969.9	625,462.0	533,090.6
Less Imports of goods and services	498,738.1	569,365.5	470,091.4
GDP in market prices	267,253.5	267,951.9	266,659.2
GDP at constant 2005 prices	246,845.5	250,516.1	248,587.0

Gross Domestic Product by Economic Activity

	2007	2008	2009
Agriculture, fishing and quarrying	110.4	107.6	107.3
Manufacturing	61,039.6	52,476.8	54,128.8
Electricity, gas and water	3,899.0	3,886.0	3,812.9
Construction	7,901.2	11,296.6	13,675.2
Wholesale and retail trade	47,353.3	44,447.7	41,496.7
Hotels and restaurants	5,410.5	6,010.5	5,534.6
Transport and storage	25,102.6	25,511.2	21,343.1
Information and communications	9,061.0	9,713.1	9,885.6
Financial services	30,396.9	30,568.7	31,078.8
Business services	29,944.0	34,408.2	35,089.5
Owner-occupied dwellings	8,321.1	10,641.9	11,231.6
Other services	23,194.1	24,651.6	25,368.4
Sub-total	251,733.7	253,719.9	252,752.5
Taxes on products (net)	15,519.8	14,232.0	13,906.7
GDP in market prices	267,253.5	267,951.9	266,659.2

SINGAPORE

BALANCE OF PAYMENTS
(US $ million)

	2007	2008	2009
Exports of goods f.o.b.	302,822	342,776	273,411
Imports of goods f.o.b.	−256,859	−316,161	−243,180
Trade balance	45,963	26,615	30,231
Exports of services	84,889	100,965	90,920
Imports of services	−74,747	−87,361	−82,425
Balance on goods and services	56,105	40,218	38,726
Other income received	57,333	56,126	52,676
Other income paid	−64,159	−57,522	−55,738
Balance on goods, services and income	49,279	38,822	35,665
Current transfers received	157	163	158
Current transfers paid	−2,352	−2,975	−3,196
Current balance	47,084	36,011	32,628
Capital account (net)	−259	−308	−305
Direct investment abroad	−27,645	8,478	−5,979
Direct investment from abroad	35,777	10,912	16,809
Portfolio investment assets	−37,229	−28,145	−24,444
Portfolio investment liabilities	19,349	−12,136	−5,716
Other investment assets	−78,316	−48,387	−4,105
Other investment liabilities	56,714	45,309	3,160
Net errors and omissions	4,165	1,333	−241
Overall balance	19,640	13,067	11,808

Source: IMF, *International Financial Statistics*.

External Trade

PRINCIPAL COMMODITIES
(S $ million)

Imports c.i.f.	2008	2009	2010
Mineral fuels, lubricants, etc.	128,792	89,001	115,592
Chemicals and related products	23,723	21,444	28,630
Basic manufactures	35,020	26,079	26,492
Machinery and equipment	210,232	170,767	196,902
Electronic components and parts	75,151	61,861	79,952
Miscellaneous manufactured articles	29,074	24,810	29,634
Total (incl. others)	450,893	356,299	423,221

Exports f.o.b.*	2008	2009	2010
Mineral fuels, lubricants, etc.	115,479	78,398	103,511
Petroleum products	87,339	59,192	76,886
Chemicals and related products	48,514	46,598	56,644
Basic manufactures	22,331	16,836	18,905
Machinery and equipment	242,702	203,295	244,933
Electronic components and parts	104,273	91,139	119,327
Miscellaneous manufactured articles	29,885	27,502	33,410
Total (incl. others)	476,762	391,118	478,840

* Including re-exports (S $ million): 229,144 in 2008; 191,115 in 2009; 230,231 in 2010.

PRINCIPAL TRADING PARTNERS
(S $ million)

Imports c.i.f.	2008	2009	2010
Australia	6,459	5,804	4,711
China, People's Republic	47,595	37,585	4,004
France	11,118	12,185	10,119
Germany	13,023	11,424	12,125
Hong Kong	4,909	3,894	4,004
India	11,922	8,157	12,566
Italy	4,873	3,967	3,830
Japan	36,580	27,148	33,262
Korea, Republic	25,335	20,339	24,515
Kuwait	9,222	4,006	3,607
Malaysia	53,814	41,336	49,490
Netherlands	5,819	4,608	7,280
Philippines	6,929	7,475	12,523
Saudi Arabia	20,692	11,752	15,297
Switzerland	3,643	3,585	6,181
Taiwan	23,195	18,577	25,239
Thailand	15,923	11,907	14,001
United Arab Emirates	8,908	6,206	8,693
United Kingdom	6,606	6,545	7,603
USA	52,847	41,436	47,515
Total (incl. others)	450,893	356,299	423,222

Exports f.o.b.*	2008	2009	2010
Australia	19,537	15,317	17,111
China, People's Republic	43,818	38,125	49,468
France	5,846	5,155	7,531
Germany	9,378	6,013	8,370
Hong Kong	49,526	45,274	56,081
India	16,835	13,429	18,101
Japan	23,487	17,804	22,332
Korea, Republic	17,318	18,219	19,548
Malaysia	57,639	44,809	57,114
Netherlands	10,217	7,204	8,388
Philippines	10,265	7,313	9,775
Taiwan	13,411	12,600	17,442
Thailand	18,612	14,613	17,284
United Arab Emirates	5,858	5,389	5,183
United Kingdom	9,284	7,168	8,334
USA	33,452	25,485	30,871
Viet Nam	12,280	10,114	10,061
Total (incl. others)	476,762	391,118	478,841

* Including re-exports (S $ million): 229,144 in 2008; 191,115 in 2009; 230,231 in 2010.

Transport

ROAD TRAFFIC
(registered vehicles)

	2008	2009	2010
Cars*	552,846	579,371	597,746
Motorcycles and scooters	146,120	147,215	148,160
Motor buses	15,327	16,023	16,309
Taxis	24,300	24,702	26,073
Goods and other vehicles (incl. private)	156,089	158,207	157,541
Total	894,682	925,518	945,829

* Including private, company, tuition and private hire cars.

SHIPPING

Merchant Fleet
(at 31 December)

	2007	2008	2009
Number of vessels	2,257	2,451	2,563
Displacement ('000 grt)	36,251.7	39,885.8	41,046.6

Source: IHS Fairplay, *World Fleet Statistics*.

SINGAPORE

International Sea-borne Shipping

	2008	2009	2010
Vessels entered	131,695	130,575	127,299
Total cargo ('000 metric tons)	515,415	472,300	503,342

Source: Maritime and Ports Authority of Singapore.

CIVIL AVIATION

	2008	2009	2010
Passengers:			
arrived	18,185,230	18,026,026	20,486,452
departed	18,102,820	18,062,970	20,437,264
in transit	1,406,774	1,114,982	n.a.
Mail (metric tons):			
landed	12,721	12,113	n.a.
dispatched	14,234	14,945	n.a.
Freight (metric tons):			
discharged	951,939	846,671	941,403
loaded	905,002	787,120	872,406

Source: partly Civil Aviation Authority of Singapore.

Tourism

FOREIGN VISITOR ARRIVALS
(incl. excursionists)

Country of nationality	2008	2009	2010
Australia	833,156	830,299	880,486
China, People's Republic	1,078,742	936,747	1,171,337
Germany	175,280	183,681	209,231
Hong Kong	278,115	294,420	387,552
India	778,303	725,624	828,903
Indonesia	1,765,404	n.a.	n.a.
Japan	571,040	489,987	528,817
Korea, Republic	423,018	271,987	360,673
Malaysia	647,339	n.a.	n.a.
Philippines	418,920	n.a.	n.a.
Taiwan	175,924	156,761	191,173
Thailand	333,892	n.a.	n.a.
United Kingdom	492,933	469,756	461,714
USA	396,618	370,704	416,990
Total (incl. others)	10,116,050	9,682,690	11,638,660

Tourism receipts (US $ million, excl. passenger transport): 7,545 in 2006; 9,179 in 2007; 10,583 in 2008 (Source: World Tourism Organization).

Communications Media

(at 31 December)

	2007	2008	2009
Telephones ('000 main lines in use)	1,861.8	1,876.0	1,925.6
Mobile cellular telephones ('000 subscribers)	5,924.1	6,414.8	6,879.8
Internet users ('000)	3,104.9*	3,063.5*	3,234.8
Broadband subscribers ('000)	896.2	1,023.8	1,170.7

* Estimated figure.

Personal computers: 3,410,000 (743.1 per 1,000 persons) in 2007.

Radio receivers ('000 in use): 2,550 in 1997.

Television receivers ('000 in use): 1,200 in 2000.

Daily newspapers: 11 (with average circulation of 1,542,000 copies) in 2004.

Non-daily newspapers: 9 (with average circulation of 1,134,000 copies) in 2004.

Sources: mainly International Telecommunication Union; UNESCO, *Statistical Yearbook*; UNESCO Institute for Statistics; UN, *Statistical Yearbook*.

Education

(2009)

	Institutions	Teachers	Students
Primary	172	13,493	265,104
Secondary	154	12,066	199,409
Mixed levels*	15	2,494	36,469
Pre-university	13	1,822	20,612
Institute of Technical Education	3	1,577	24,846
Polytechnics	5	4,930	80,635
National Institute of Education	1	754	4,934
Universities†	3	3,958	72,710

* Referring to schools with multiple levels, encompassing full schools (P1–S4/5), sixth-form schools (S1–JC2) and JC-plus levels (S3–JC2).

† Student and teacher numbers are not available for Singapore's fourth university (SIM University), which opened in 2005.

Pupil-teacher ratio (primary education, UNESCO estimate): 19.3 in 2007/08 (Source: UNESCO Institute for Statistics).

Adult literacy rate (official estimate): 96.3% in 2009.

Directory

The Government

HEAD OF STATE

President: SELLAPAN RAMANATHAN (S. R.) NATHAN (took office 1 September 1999).

CABINET
(May 2011)

The Cabinet comprises members of the People's Action Party.

Prime Minister: Brig.-Gen. (retd) LEE HSIEN LOONG.

Deputy Prime Minister, Co-ordinating Minister for National Security and Minister for Home Affairs: TEO CHEE HEAN.

Deputy Prime Minister and Minister for Finance and Manpower: THARMAN SHANMUGARATNAM.

Minister for Trade and Industry: LIM HNG KIANG.

Minister in the Prime Minister's Office: LIM SWEE SAY.

Minister for Information, Communications and the Arts: YAACOB IBRAHIM.

Minister for National Development: KHAW BOON WAN.

Minister for Defence: Dr NG ENG HEN.

Minister for the Environment and Water Resources: Dr VIVIAN BALAKRISHNAN.

Minister for Foreign Affairs and Law: K. SHANMUGAM.

Minister for Health: GAN KIM YONG.

Minister for Transport and Second Minister for Foreign Affairs: LUI TUCK YEW.

Minister in the Prime Minister's Office and Second Minister for Home Affairs, Trade and Industry: S. ISWARAN.

Minister for Education: HENG SWEE KEAT.

Acting Minister for Community Development, Youth and Sports and Minister of State for Ministry of Information, Communications and the Arts: CHAN CHUN SING.

MINISTRIES

Office of the President: The Istana, Orchard Rd, Singapore 238823; e-mail istana_general_office@istana.gov.sg; internet www.istana.gov.sg.

Office of the Prime Minister: The Istana, Orchard Rd, Singapore 238823; tel. 62358577; fax 68356621; e-mail pmo_hq@pmo.gov.sg; internet www.pmo.gov.sg.

SINGAPORE

Ministry of Community Development, Youth and Sports: 512 Thomson Rd, MCYS Bldg, Singapore 298136; tel. 62589595; fax 63536695; e-mail mcys_email@mcys.gov.sg; internet www.mcys.gov.sg.

Ministry of Defence: Gombak Dr., off Upper Bukit Timah Rd, Mindef Bldg, Singapore 669645; tel. 67608844; fax 67646119; internet www.mindef.gov.sg.

Ministry of Education: 1 North Buona Vista Dr., MOE Bldg, Singapore 138675; tel. 68722220; fax 67755826; e-mail contact@moe.edu.sg; internet www.moe.gov.sg.

Ministry of the Environment and Water Resources: 40 Scotts Rd, 24-00 Environment Bldg, Singapore 228231; tel. 67319000; fax 67319456; e-mail mewr_feedback@mewr.gov.sg; internet www.mewr.gov.sg.

Ministry of Finance: 100 High St, 06-03 The Treasury, Singapore 179434; tel. 62259911; fax 63327435; e-mail mof_qsm@mof.gov.sg; internet www.mof.gov.sg.

Ministry of Foreign Affairs: MFA Bldg, Tanglin, off Napier Rd, Singapore 248163; tel. 63798000; fax 64747885; e-mail mfa@mfa.gov.sg; internet www.mfa.gov.sg.

Ministry of Health: 16 College Rd, College of Medicine Bldg, Singapore 169854; tel. 63259220; fax 62241677; e-mail moh_info@moh.gov.sg; internet www.moh.gov.sg.

Ministry of Home Affairs: New Phoenix Park, 28 Irrawaddy Rd, Singapore 329560; tel. 64787010; fax 62546250; e-mail mha_feedback@mha.gov.sg; internet www.mha.gov.sg.

Ministry of Information, Communications and the Arts: 140 Hill St, 02-02 MICA Bldg, Singapore 179369; tel. 62707988; fax 68379480; e-mail mica@mica.gov.sg; internet www.mica.gov.sg.

Ministry of Law: 100 High St, 08-02 The Treasury, Singapore 179434; tel. 63328840; fax 63328842; e-mail contact@mlaw.gov.sg; internet www.mlaw.gov.sg.

Ministry of Manpower: 18 Havelock Rd, 07-01, Singapore 059764; tel. 64385122; fax 65344840; e-mail mom_hq@mom.gov.sg; internet www.mom.gov.sg.

Ministry of National Development: 5 Maxwell Rd, 21/22-00 Tower Blk, MND Complex, Singapore 069110; tel. 62221211; fax 63257254; e-mail mnd_hq@mnd.gov.sg; internet www.mnd.gov.sg.

Ministry of Trade and Industry: 100 High St, 09-01 The Treasury, Singapore 179434; tel. 62259911; fax 63327260; e-mail mti_email@mti.gov.sg; internet www.mti.gov.sg.

Ministry of Transport: 460 Alexandra Rd, 39-00 PSA Bldg, Singapore 119963; tel. 62707988; fax 63757734; e-mail mot@mot.gov.sg; internet www.mot.gov.sg.

President and Legislature

PRESIDENT

On 13 August 2005, at the end of his six-year term, the incumbent SELLAPAN RAMANATHAN (S. R.) NATHAN was again nominated as President by a state-appointed committee. S. R. Nathan was the sole candidate for the Presidency, following the rejection by the committee of three other potential candidates on the grounds of their insufficient experience. He was officially reappointed to the post on 1 September.

PARLIAMENT

Parliament House

1 Parliament Place, Singapore 178880; tel. 63326666; fax 63325526; e-mail parl@parl.gov.sg; internet www.parliament.gov.sg.

Speaker: (vacant).

General Election, 7 May 2011

Party	Seats
People's Action Party	81*
Workers' Party	6
Total	**87**

*Five seats were unopposed.

Election Commission

Elections Department of Singapore (ELD): Prime Minister's Office, 11 Prinsep Link, Singapore 187949; fax 63323428; internet www.elections.gov.sg; govt body; Chair. LEE SENG LUP.

Political Organizations

National Solidarity Party (NSP): 397 Jalan Besar, 02-01A, Singapore 209007; tel. 83823961; fax 63968645; e-mail nsp-cec@yahoogroups.com; internet www.nsp.sg; f. 1987; Pres. SEBASTIAN TEO; Sec.-Gen. KEN SUN.

People's Action Party (PAP): Blk 57B, PCF Bldg, 01-1402 New Upper Changi Rd, Singapore 463057; tel. 62444600; fax 62430114; e-mail paphq@pap.org.sg; internet www.pap.org.sg; f. 1954; governing party since 1959; 18-mem. Cen. Exec. Cttee; Chair. LIM BOON HENG; Sec.-Gen. LEE HSIEN LOONG.

Pertubuhan Kebangsaan Melayu Singapura (PKMS) (Singapore Malay National Organization): PKMS Bldg, 4th Floor, 218F Changi Rd, Singapore 1441; tel. 64470468; fax 63458724; f. 1950; est. as United Malay Nat. Org. (UMNO) of Malaysia; renamed UMNO Singapore in 1954; present name adopted 1967; seeks to advance the implementation of the special rights of Malays in Singapore, as stated in the Constitution; to safeguard and promote the advancement of Islam; and to encourage racial harmony and goodwill in Singapore; joined SDA in July 2001; Pres. OSMAN HASSAN.

Reform Party: 18A Smith St, Singapore 058932; tel. 65349641; fax 65349640; e-mail enquiries@thereformparty.net; internet www.thereformparty.net; f. 2008; Chair. TAN TEE SENG; Sec.-Gen. KENNETH JEYARETNAM.

Singapore Democratic Alliance (SDA): Singapore; f. 2001; est. to contest 2001 general election, as coalition of PKMS, SPP, NSP and SJP; NSP left coalition in 2007; Chair. CHIAM SEE TONG; Sec.-Gen. DESMOND LIM BAK CHUAN.

Singapore Democratic Party (SDP): 1357A Serangoon Rd, Singapore 328240; tel. and fax 63981675; e-mail speakup@yoursdp.org; internet www.yoursdp.org; f. 1980; 12-mem. Cen. Exec. Cttee; Chair. GANDHI AMBALAM; Sec.-Gen. CHEE SOON JUAN.

Singapore Justice Party (SJP): Singapore; f. 1972; joined SDA in July 2001; Pres. A. R. SUIB; Sec.-Gen. AMINUDDIN BIN AMI.

Singapore People's Party (SPP): 22A Upper Weld Rd, Singapore 207379; tel. 68585771; fax 62970138; e-mail feedback@spp.org.sg; internet www.spp.org.sg; f. 1993; breakaway faction of SDP, espousing more moderate policies; joined SDA in July 2001; 12-mem. Cen. Exec. Cttee; Chair. SIN KEK TONG; Sec.-Gen. CHIAM SEE TONG.

Socialist Front: 24 Peck Seah St, 05-09-11 Nehsons Bldg, Singapore 079314; e-mail contact@socialistfront.org; internet www.socialistfront.org; f. 2010; encourages participation and ownership in politics; promotes equal opportunities for citizens; Chair. NG TECK SIONG; Sec.-Gen. CHIA TI LIK.

United Singapore Democrats (USD): Singapore; f. 2010; est. by fmr mems of SDP (q. v.); Pres. NARAYANASAMY GOGELAVANY; Sec. JASLYN GO.

Workers' Party: 216G Syed Alwi Rd 02-03, Singapore 207799; tel. 62984765; fax 64544404; e-mail webmaster@wp.sg; internet www.wp.org.sg; f. 1961; active as opposition party in Singapore since 1957; merged with Barisan Sosialis (Socialist Front) in 1988; seeks to establish a democratic socialist govt with a constitution guaranteeing fundamental citizens' rights; Chair. SYLVIA LIM SWEE LIAN; Sec.-Gen. LOW THIA KHIANG.

Other parties include the Alliance Party Singapura, the Democratic People's Party, the Democratic Progressive Party, the National Party of Singapore, the Partai Rakyat, the Parti Kesatuan Ra'ayat (United Democratic Party), the People's Front, the People's Republican Party, the Persatuan Melayu Singapura, the Singapore Chinese Party, the Singapore Indian Congress, the Singapore National Front, the United National Front, the United People's Front and the United People's Party.

Diplomatic Representation

EMBASSIES AND HIGH COMMISSIONS IN SINGAPORE

Angola: 9 Temasek Blvd, 44-03 Suntec Tower Two, Singapore 038989; tel. 63419360; fax 63419367; e-mail embangola@pacific.net.sg; Ambassador FLÁVIO SARAIVA DE CARVALHO FONSECA.

Australia: 25 Napier Rd, Singapore 258507; tel. 68364100; fax 67375481; e-mail enquiries-sg@dfat.gov.au; internet www.australia.org.sg; High Commissioner DOUG CHESTER.

Bangladesh: 91 Bencoolen St, 06-01, Sunshine Plaza, Singapore 189652; tel. 62550075; fax 62551824; e-mail bdoot@singnet.com.sg; internet www.bangladesh.org.sg; High Commissioner KAMRUL AHSAN.

Belgium: 8 Shenton Way, 14-01, Singapore 068811; tel. 62207677; fax 62226976; e-mail Singapore@diplobel.fed.be; internet www.diplomatie.be/singapore; Ambassador ROLAND VAN REMOORTELE.

SINGAPORE

Brazil: 101 Thomson Rd, 10-05 United Sq., Singapore 307591; tel. 62566001; fax 62566619; e-mail cinbrem@brazil.org.sg; internet www.brazil.org.sg; Ambassador PAULO ALBERTO DE SILVEIRA SOARES.

Brunei: 325 Tanglin Rd, Singapore 247955; tel. 67339055; fax 67375275; e-mail singapore.singapore@mfa.gov.bn; High Commissioner ABDUL GHAFAR BIN ISMAIL.

Cambodia: 400 Orchard Rd, 10-03/04 Orchard Towers, Singapore 238875; tel. 63419785; fax 63419201; e-mail cambodiaembasy@pacific.net.sg; internet www.recambodia.net; Ambassador SEREY SIN.

Canada: 1 George St 11-01, Singapore 049145; tel. 68545900; fax 68545930; e-mail spore@international.gc.ca; internet www.canadainternational.gc.ca/singapore-singapour; High Commissioner DAVID SEVIGNY.

Chile: 105 Cecil St, 25-00 The Octagon Bldg, Singapore 069534; tel. 62238577; fax 62250677; e-mail contacto@chileabroad.gov.cl; internet chileabroad.gov.cl/republica-de-singapur; Ambassador GRACIELA MERCEDES FERNÁNDEZ SOBARZO.

China, People's Republic: 150 Tanglin Rd, Singapore 247969; tel. 64712117; fax 64795345; e-mail chinaemb_sg@fmprc.gov.cn; internet www.chinaembassy.org.sg; Ambassador WEI WEI.

Costa Rica: 271 Bukit Timah Rd, 04-08 Balmoral Plaza, Singapore 259708; tel. 67380566; fax 67380567; e-mail info@costaricaembassy-sg.net; internet www.costaricaembassy-sg.net; Ambassador JUAN FERNANDO CORDERO ARIAS.

Denmark: 101 Thomson Rd, 13-01/02 United Sq., Singapore 307591; tel. 63555010; fax 62533764; e-mail sinamb@um.dk; internet www.ambsingapore.um.dk; Ambassador OLE LISBORG.

Egypt: 75 Grange Rd, Singapore 249579; tel. 67371811; fax 67323422; e-mail admin@egyptemb-sin.org; internet www.mfa.gov.eg/missions/singapore/singapore/embassy/en-gb; Ambassador NASSER HAMDY.

Finland: 101 Thomson Rd, 21-03 United Sq., Singapore 307591; tel. 62544042; fax 62534101; e-mail sanomat.sin@formin.fi; internet www.finland.org.sg; Ambassador SATU MATTILA.

France: 101–103 Cluny Park Rd, Singapore 259595; tel. 68807800; fax 68807801; e-mail consulat@ambafrance-sg.org; internet www.ambafrance-sg.org; Ambassador OLIVIER CARON.

Germany: 12-00 Singapore Land Tower, 50 Raffles Place, Singapore 048623; tel. 65336002; fax 65331132; e-mail consul@sing.diplo.de; internet www.singapur.diplo.de; Ambassador JÖRG RANAU.

Hungary: 250 North Bridge Rd, 29-01 Raffles City Tower, Singapore 179101; tel. 68830882; fax 68830177; e-mail mission.sin@kum.hu; internet www.mfa.gov.hu/kulkepviselet/SG; Ambassador Dr FERENC SOMOGYI.

India: 31 Grange Rd, India House, Singapore 239702; tel. 67376777; fax 67326909; e-mail indiahc@pacific.net.sg; internet www.embassyofindia.com; High Commissioner T. C. RAGHAVAN.

Indonesia: 7 Chatsworth Rd, Singapore 249761; tel. 67377422; fax 67375037; e-mail info@kbrisingapura.com; internet www.kbrisingapura.com; Ambassador WARDANA.

Ireland: Ireland House, 541 Orchard Rd, 08-00 Liat Towers, Singapore 238881; tel. 62387616; fax 62387615; e-mail singaporeembassy@dfa.ie; internet www.embassyofireland.sg; Ambassador JOE HAYES.

Israel: 24 Stevens Close, Singapore 257964; tel. 68349200; fax 67337008; e-mail press@singapore.mfa.gov.il; internet singapore.mfa.gov.il; Ambassador AMIRA ARNON.

Italy: 101 Thomson Rd, 27-02 United Sq., Singapore 307591; tel. 62506022; fax 62533301; e-mail ambasciata.singapore@esteri.it; internet www.ambsingapore.esteri.it; Ambassador ANACLETO FELICANI.

Japan: 16 Nassim Rd, Singapore 258390; tel. 62358855; fax 67331039; e-mail eojsingfv@vsystem.com.sg; internet www.sg.emb-japan.go.jp; Ambassador YOICHI SUZUKI.

Kazakhstan: 20 Raffles Pl., 14-06 Ocean Towers, Singapore 048620; tel. 65366100; fax 64388990; e-mail office@kazakhstan.org.sg; internet www.kazakhstan.org.sg; Ambassador YERLAN BAUDARBEK-KOZHATAYEV.

Korea, Democratic People's Republic: 7500 Beach Rd, 09-320 The Plaza, Singapore 199591; tel. 64403498; fax 63482026; e-mail embdprk@singnet.com.sg; Ambassador JONG SONG IL.

Korea, Republic: 47 Scotts Rd, 08-00 Goldbell Towers, Singapore 228233; tel. 62561188; fax 62543191; e-mail info@koreaembassy.sg; internet sgp.mofat.go.kr; Ambassador OH JOON.

Kuwait: c/o The Ritz-Carlton Millenia Singapore, 7 Raffles Ave, Suite 3108, Singapore 039799; tel. 68847401; fax 64345387; e-mail embassy@kuwait.org.sg; internet www.kuwait.org.sg; Ambassador ABDULAZIZ AHMED S. AL-ADWANI.

Laos: 51 Newton Rd, 13-04/05 Goldhill Plaza, Singapore 308900; tel. 62506044; fax 62506014; e-mail laoembsg@singnet.com.sg; Ambassador THOUANE VORASARN.

Malaysia: 301 Jervois Rd, Singapore 249077; tel. 62350111; fax 67336135; e-mail mwspore@singnet.com.sg; internet www.kln.gov.my/perwakilan/singapore; High Commissioner Dato' MOHAMMED HUSSIN NAYAN.

Maldives: 101 Thomson Rd, 30-01A United Sq., Singapore 307591; tel. 67209012; fax 67209014; e-mail info@maldiveshighcommission.sg; High Commissioner AHMED KHALEEL.

Mexico: 152 Beach Rd, 06-07 Gateway East Tower, Singapore 189721; tel. 62982678; fax 62933484; e-mail embamexsing@embamexsing.org.sg; internet portal.sre.gob.mx/singapur; Ambassador JUAN JOSÉ GOMEZ CAMACHO.

Mongolia: 600 North Bridge Rd, 24-08 Parkview Sq., Singapore 188778; tel. 63480745; fax 63481753; e-mail singapore@mfat.gov.mn; internet www.realmongolia.com/singapore; Chargé d'affaires a.i. TULGA NARKHUU.

Myanmar: 15 St Martin's Dr., Singapore 257996; tel. 67350209; fax 67356236; e-mail ambassador@mesingapore.org.sg; internet www.mesingapore.org.sg; Ambassador WIN MYINT.

Netherlands: Tanglin, POB 447, Singapore 912415; tel. 67371155; fax 67371940; e-mail sin@minbuza.nl; internet www.mfa.nl/sin; Ambassador JOHANNES W. GUNIVORTUS JANSING.

New Zealand: 391A Orchard Rd, Tower A, 15-06/10 Ngee Ann City, Singapore 238873; tel. 62359966; fax 67339924; e-mail enquiries@nz-high-com.org.sg; internet www.nzembassy.com/singapore; High Commissioner PETER HAMILTON.

Nigeria: 143 Cecil St, 15-01 GB Bldg, Singapore 069542; tel. 67321743; fax 67321742; e-mail nigerhighcommission@yahoo.com.sg; internet www.nigeriahcsinga.org.sg; High Commissioner DANJUMA NANPON SHENI.

Norway: 16 Raffles Quay, 44-01 Hong Leong Bldg, Singapore 048581; tel. 62207122; fax 62202191; e-mail emb.singapore@mfa.no; internet www.norway.org.sg; Ambassador JANNE JULSRUD.

Pakistan: 1 Scotts Rd, 24-02/04 Shaw Centre, Singapore 228208; tel. 67376988; fax 67374096; e-mail secyhc@pakhicom.org.sg; internet www.parep.org.sg; High Commissioner FAUZIA M. SANA.

Panama: 16 Raffles Quay, 41-06 Hong Leong Bldg, Singapore 048581; tel. 62218677; fax 62240892; e-mail general@panamaemb.org.sg; Ambassador JOSÉ ANTONIO RUIZ BLANCO.

Peru: 390 Orchard Rd, 12-03 Palais Renaissance, Singapore 238871; tel. 67388595; fax 67388601; e-mail embperu@pacific.net.sg; internet www.embassyperu.org.sg; Ambassador J. ARTURO MONTOYA.

Philippines: 20 Nassim Rd, Singapore 258395; tel. 67373977; fax 67339544; e-mail php@pacific.net.sg; internet www.philippine-embassy.org.sg; Ambassador MINDA CRUZ.

Poland: 435 Orchard Rd, 17-02/03 Wisma Atria, Singapore 238877; tel. 62359478; fax 62359479; e-mail secretary@pacific.net.sg; internet www.singapore.polemb.net; Ambassador WALDEMAR DUBANIOWSKI.

Qatar: 8 Temasek Blvd, 41-02 Suntec Tower 3, Singapore 038988; tel. 65939900; fax 68365731; Ambassador RASHID BIN ALI HASSAN AL-KHATER.

Romania: 1 Claymore Dr., Singapore 229594; tel. 67355023; fax 67355021; e-mail comofrom@starhub.net.sg; Chargé d'affaires ALEXANDRU IRIMIA.

Russia: 51 Nassim Rd, Singapore 258439; tel. 62351834; fax 67334780; e-mail mail@russia.org.sg; internet www.russia.org.sg; Ambassador ANDREY N. ROZHKOV.

Rwanda: 6 Temasek Blvd, 27-01 Suntec Tower 4, Singapore 038986; tel. 68844621; fax 68844206; e-mail info@rwandaembassy.org.sg; internet www.rwandaembassy.org.sg; High Commissioner JEANINE KAMBANDA.

Saudi Arabia: 163 Penang Rd, 03-02/03 Winsland House 2, Singapore 238463; tel. 67345878; fax 67385291; e-mail enquiries@saudiembassy.org.sg; internet www.saudiembassy.org.sg; Ambassador Dr JAMIL MAHMOUD MERDAD.

South Africa: 331 North Bridge Rd, 15-01/06 Odeon Towers, Singapore 188720; tel. 63393319; fax 63396658; e-mail hom@southafrichc.org.sg; internet www.southafrichc.org.sg; High Commissioner Dr SIMEON SELBY RIPINGA.

Spain: 7 Temasek Blvd, 39-00 Suntec City Tower 1, Singapore 038987; tel. 67259220; fax 63333025; e-mail emb.singapur@maec.es; internet www.maec.es/Subwebs/Embajadas/singapur; Ambassador ANTONIO SÁNCHEZ JARA.

Sri Lanka: 13-07/12 Goldhill Plaza, 51 Newton Rd, Singapore 308900; tel. 62544595; fax 62507201; e-mail slhcs@lanka.com.sg; internet www.lanka.com.sg; High Commissioner JAYATHRI SAMARAKONE.

SINGAPORE

Sweden: 111 Somerset Rd, 05-01 Singapore Power Bldg, Singapore 238164; tel. 64159720; fax 64159747; e-mail ambassaden.singapore@foreign.ministry.se; internet www.swedenabroad.com/singapore; Ambassador PÄR AHLBERGER.

Switzerland: 1 Swiss Club Link, Singapore 288162; tel. 64685788; fax 64668245; e-mail sin.vertretung@eda.admin.ch; internet www.eda.admin.ch/singapore; Ambassador JÖRG ALOIS REDING.

Thailand: 370 Orchard Rd, Singapore 238870; tel. 67372158; fax 67320778; e-mail consular@thaiembassy.sg; internet www.thaiembassy.sg; Ambassador NOPADOL GUNAVIBOOL.

Turkey: Shenton Way, 10-03 SGX Centre Tower 1, Singapore 068804; tel. 65333390; fax 65333360; e-mail turksin@signet.com.sg; internet www.singapore.cg.mfa.gov.tr; Ambassador ŞAFAK GÖKTÜRK.

Ukraine: 50 Raffles Pl., 16-05 Singapore Land Tower, Singapore 048623; tel. 65356550; fax 65352116; e-mail emb_sg@mfa.gov.ua; internet www.embassy-ukraine.com; Ambassador Dr VIKTOR MASHTABEI.

United Arab Emirates: 600 North Bridge Rd, 09-01 Parkview Sq., Singapore 188778; tel. 62388206; fax 62380081; e-mail emarat@singnet.com.sg; internet www.uaeembassy-sg.com; Ambassador MOHAMMED AHMED HAMIL AL-QUBAISI.

United Kingdom: 100 Tanglin Rd, Singapore 247919; tel. 64244200; fax 64244218; e-mail consular.singapore@fco.gov.uk; internet www.ukinsingapore.fco.gov.uk; High Commissioner ANTONY PHILLIPSON.

USA: 27 Napier Rd, Singapore 258508; tel. 64769100; fax 64769340; e-mail singaporeusembassy@state.gov; internet singapore.usembassy.gov; Ambassador DAVID ADELMAN.

Uzbekistan: 20 Kramat Lane, 04-01/02 United House, Singapore 228773; tel. 67343943; fax 67345849; e-mail info@uzbekistan.org.sg; internet www.uzbekistan.org.sg; Ambassador ALISHER A. KURMANOV.

Venezuela: 3 Killiney Rd, 07-03 Winsland House 1, Singapore 239519; tel. 64911172; fax 62353167; e-mail embassy@embavenez.org.sg; Ambassador ALFREDO TORO HARDY.

Viet Nam: 10 Leedon Park, Singapore 267887; tel. 64625938; fax 64625936; e-mail vnemb@singnet.com.sg; internet www.vietnamembassy-singapore.org; Ambassador NGUYEN TRUNG THANH.

Judicial System

The judicial power of Singapore is vested in the Supreme Court and in the Subordinate Courts. The Judiciary administers the law with complete independence from the executive and legislative branches of the Government; this independence is safeguarded by the Constitution. The Supreme Court consists of the High Court and the Court of Appeal. The Chief Justice is appointed by the President if the latter, acting at his discretion, concurs with the advice of the Prime Minister. The other judges of the Supreme Court are appointed in the same way, in consultation with the Chief Justice. Under a 1979 constitutional amendment, the position of judicial commissioner of the Supreme Court was created 'to facilitate the disposal of business in the Supreme Court'. A judicial commissioner has the powers and functions of a judge, and is appointed for such period as the President thinks fit.

The Subordinate Courts consist of District Courts and Magistrates' Courts. In addition, there are also specialized courts such as the Coroner's Court, Family Court, Juvenile Court, Mentions Court, Night Court, Sentencing Courts and Filter Courts. The Primary Dispute Resolution Centre and the Small Claims Tribunals are also managed by the Subordinate Courts. The Subordinate Courts have also established the Multi-Door Courthouse, which serves as a one-stop centre for the screening and channelling of any cases to the most appropriate forum for dispute resolution.

District Courts and Magistrates' Courts have original criminal and civil jurisdiction. District Courts try offences for which the maximum penalty does not exceed 10 years of imprisonment and in civil cases where the amount claimed does not exceed S $250,000. Magistrates' Courts try offences for which the maximum term of imprisonment does not exceed three years. The jurisdiction of Magistrates' Courts in civil cases is limited to claims not exceeding S $60,000. The Coroners' Court conducts inquests. The Small Claims Tribunal has jurisdiction over claims relating to a dispute arising from any contract for the sale of goods or the provision of services and any claim in tort in respect of damage caused to any property involving an amount that does not exceed S $10,000. The Juvenile Court deals with offences committed by young persons aged under 16 years.

The High Court has unlimited original jurisdiction in criminal and civil cases. In its appellate jurisdiction it hears criminal and civil appeals from the District Courts and Magistrates' Courts. The Court of Appeal hears appeals against the decisions of the High Court in both criminal and civil matters. In criminal matters, the Court of Appeal hears appeals against decisions made by the High Court in the exercise of its original criminal jurisdiction. In civil matters, the Court of Appeal hears appeals against decisions made by the High Court in the exercise of both its original and appellate jurisdiction.

With the enactment of the Judicial Committee (Repeal) Act 1994 in April of that year, the right of appeal from the Court of Appeal to the Judicial Committee of the Privy Council in the United Kingdom was abolished. The Court of Appeal is now the final appellate court in the Singapore legal system.

Supreme Court: 1 Supreme Court Lane, Singapore 178879; tel. 63360644; fax 63379450; e-mail supcourt_qsm@supcourt.gov.sg; internet www.supcourt.gov.sg.

Attorney-General: SUNDARESH MENON.

Chief Justice: CHAN SEK KEONG.

Judges of Appeal: V. K. RAJAH, ANDREW PHANG BOON LEONG, CHAO HICK TIN.

Religion

According to the 2000 census, 64.4% of ethnic Chinese, who constituted 76.8% of the population, professed either Buddhism or Daoism (including followers of Confucius, Mencius and Lao Zi) and 16.5% of Chinese adhered to Christianity. Malays, who made up 13.9% of the population, were 99.6% Muslim. Among Indians, who constituted 7.9% of the population, 55.4% were Hindus, 25.6% Muslims, 12.1% Christians and 6.3% Sikhs, Jains or adherents of other faiths. There are small communities of Zoroastrians and Jews. Freedom of worship is guaranteed by the Constitution.

BAHÁ'Í FAITH

The Spiritual Assembly of the Bahá'ís of Singapore: 110D Wishart Rd, Singapore 098733; tel. 62226200; fax 62229166; e-mail secretariat@bahai.org.sg; internet www.bahai.org.sg.

BUDDHISM

Buddhist Union: 28 Jalan Senyum, Singapore 418152; tel. 62419419; fax 64443280; e-mail thebu@singnet.com.sg.

Singapore Buddhist Federation: 12 Ubi Ave 1, Singapore 408932; tel. 67444635; fax 67473618; e-mail buddhist@singnet.com.sg; internet www.buddhist.org.sg; f. 1948.

Singapore Buddhist Sangha Organization: 88 Bright Hill Drive, Singapore 579644.

CHRISTIANITY

National Council of Churches: 1 Coleman St, B1-27 The Adelphi, Singapore 179803; tel. 63368177; fax 63368178; e-mail admin@nccs.org.sg; internet www.nccs.org.sg; f. 1948; six mem. churches, six assoc. mems; Pres. Dr JOHN CHEW; Gen. Sec. LIM K. TAN.

Singapore Council of Christian Churches (SCCC): Singapore; f. 1956.

The Anglican Communion

The Anglican diocese of Singapore (also including Indonesia, Laos, Thailand, Viet Nam and Cambodia) is part of the Province of the Anglican Church in South-East Asia.

Bishop of Singapore: The Rt Rev. Dr JOHN HIANG CHEA CHEW, 4 Bishopsgate, Singapore 249970; tel. 64741661; fax 64791054; e-mail bpoffice@anglican.org.sg.

Orthodox Churches

The Orthodox Syrian Church and the Mar Thoma Syrian Church are both active in Singapore.

The Roman Catholic Church

Singapore comprises a single archdiocese, directly responsible to the Holy See. In December 2007 there were an estimated 177,775 adherents in the country, representing 3.9% of the total population.

Archbishop of Singapore: Most Rev. NICHOLAS CHIA, Archbishop's House, 31 Victoria St, Singapore 187997; tel. 63378818; fax 63334735; e-mail nc@veritas.org.sg.

Other Christian Churches

Brethren Assemblies: Bethesda Hall (Ang Mo Kio), 601 Ang Mo Kio Ave 4, Singapore 569898; tel. 64587474; fax 64566771; e-mail bethesdahall@gmail.com; internet www.bethesdahall.com; f. 1864; Hon. Sec. WONG TUCK KEONG.

Evangelical Fellowship of Singapore (EFOS): Singapore; f. 1980.

SINGAPORE

Methodist Church in Singapore: 70 Barker Rd, Singapore 309936; tel. 64784784; fax 64784794; e-mail mcs@methodist.org.sg; internet www.methodist.org.sg; f. 1885; 38,000 mems (Dec. 2010); Leader Bishop Dr ROBERT SOLOMON.

Presbyterian Church: 3 Orchard Rd, cnr Penang Rd, Singapore 238825; tel. 63376681; fax 63391979; e-mail orpcenglish@orpc.org.sg; internet www.orpc.org.sg; f. 1856; services in English, Chinese (Mandarin), Indonesian and German; 2,000 mems; Chair. Rev. DAVID BURKE.

Singapore Baptist Convention: 01 Goldhill Plaza, 03-19 Podium Blk, Singapore 308899; tel. 62538004; fax 62538214; e-mail info@baptistconvention.org.sg; internet www.baptistconvention.org.sg; f. 1974; Chair. Rev. EDWIN LAM HON MUN; Exec. Dir PETER TANG.

Other denominations active in Singapore include the Lutheran Church and the Evangelical Lutheran Church.

HINDUISM

Hindu Advisory Board: c/o 397 Serangoon Rd, Singapore 218123; tel. 62963469; fax 62929766; e-mail heb@pacific.net.sg; f. 1985; Chair. R. BAJAWEE; Sec. M. MADHUBALA.

Hindu Endowments Board: 397 Serangoon Rd, Singapore 218123; tel. 62963469; fax 62929766; e-mail heb@pacific.net.sg; internet www.heb.gov.sg; f. 1968; Chair. S. RAJENDRAN; Sec. P. AVADIAR.

ISLAM

Majlis Ugama Islam Singapura (MUIS) (Islamic Religious Council of Singapore): 1 Lorong 6 Toa Payoh, Singapore 319376; tel. 62568188; fax 62537572; e-mail info@muis.gov.sg; internet www.muis.gov.sg; f. 1968; Pres. Haji MOHD ALAMI MUSA; Sec. ABDUL RAZAK MARICAR.

Muslim Missionary Society Singapore (JAMIYAH): 31 Lorong, 12 Geylang Rd, Singapore 399006; tel. 62568188; fax 62537272; e-mail info@jamiyah.org.sg; internet www.jamiyah.org.sg; Pres. Haji ABU BAKAR MAIDIN; Sec.-Gen. ISMAIL ROZIZ.

SIKHISM

Central Sikh Gurdwara Board (CSGB): c/o 2 Towner Rd, 03-01, Singapore 327804; tel. 62993855; e-mail csgb@sikhs.org.sg; internet www.sikhs.org.sg; Pres. KARPAL SINGH MEHLI.

The Press

DAILIES

English Language

The Business Times: 1000 Toa Payoh North, Podium Blk, Level 3, Singapore 318994; tel. 63195318; fax 63198277; e-mail btocs@sph.com.sg; internet www.businesstimes.com.sg; f. 1976; morning; Editor ALVIN TAY; circ. 34,368.

The New Paper: 1000 Toa Payoh North, Annexe Blk, Level 6, Singapore 318994; tel. 63196319; fax 63198266; e-mail tnp@sph.com.sg; internet www.tnp.sg; f. 1988; afternoon tabloid; Editor DOMINIC NATHAN; circ. 102,616.

The Straits Times: 1000 Toa Payoh North, Singapore 318994; tel. 63195397; fax 67320131; e-mail stonline@sph.com.sg; internet www.straitstimes.com; f. 1845; morning; Editor-in-Chief PATRICK DANIEL; circ. 359,989.

Today: Caldecott Broadcast Centre, Andrew Rd, Singapore 299939; tel. 63333888; fax 65344217; e-mail news@newstoday.com.sg; internet www.todayonline.com; f. 2000; merged with *Streats*, a rival free morning tabloid, in 2004; Editor WALTER FERNANDEZ; circ. 584,000.

Chinese Language

Lianhe Wanbao: 1000 Toa Payoh North, Podium Blk, Level 4, Singapore 318994; tel. 63196319; fax 63198133; e-mail wanbao@sph.com.sg; f. 1983; evening; Editor CHUA CHIM KANG; circ. 97,082.

Lianhe Zaobao: 1000 Toa Payoh North, Podium Blk, Level 4, Singapore 318994; tel. 63196319; fax 63198228; e-mail zaobao@web1.asia1.com.sg; internet www.zaobao.com; f. 1923; Editor LIM JIM KOON; circ. 169,420.

My Paper: 1000 Toa Payoh North, News Centre, Singapore 318994; tel. 63192222; fax 63198115; e-mail mypaper@sph.com.sg; internet www.mypaper.sg; f. 2006; free tabloid aimed at bilingual working adults aged between 20 and 40 yrs; Editor APRIL PUNG KOON KING; circ. 250,000.

Shin Min Daily News (S) Ltd: 1000 Toa Payoh North, Podium Blk, Level 4, Singapore 318994; tel. 63196319; fax 63198166; e-mail shinmin@sph.com.sg; f. 1967; evening; Editor KOH LIN HOE; circ. 136,127.

Malay Language

Berita Harian: 1000 Toa Payoh North, Annexe Blk, Level 3, Singapore 318994; tel. 63195137; fax 63198255; e-mail aadeska@sph.com.sg; internet cyberita.asia1.com.sg; f. 1957; morning; Editor MOHD GUNTOR SADALI; circ. 59,193.

Tamil Language

Tamil Murasu: SPH Media Centre, 82 Genting Lane 06-07, Singapore 349567; tel. 63196319; fax 63194001; e-mail murasu4@cyberway.com.sg; internet www.tamilmurasu.com.sg; f. 1935; Editor NIRMALA MURUGAIAN; circ. 13,766.

WEEKLIES

English Language

The Edge Singapore: 150 Cecil St 13-00, Singapore 069543; tel. 62328622; fax 62328620; e-mail theedgespore@bizedge.com; internet www.theedgesingapore.com; business and investment; Editor BEN PAUL; circ. 17,870.

The New Paper on Sunday: 1000 Toa Payoh North, Annexe Blk, Level 6, Singapore 318994; tel. 63196319; fax 63198266; e-mail tnp@sph.com.sg; internet www.tnp.sg; f. 1999; tabloid; Editor DOMINIC NATHAN; circ. 125,107.

The Sunday Times: 1000 Toa Payoh North, Singapore 318994; tel. 63195397; fax 67320131; e-mail stonline@sph.com.sg; internet www.straitstimes.com; f. 1931; Editor IGNATIUS LOW; circ. 372,809(Singapore only).

Weekend Today: Caldecott Broadcast Centre, Andrew Rd, Singapore 299939; tel. 63333888; fax 65344217; e-mail today@mediacorp.com.sg; internet www.todayonline.com; f. 2002; Editor P. N. BALJI; circ. 150,000.

Chinese Language

Thumbs Up: 1000 Toa Payoh North, Annexe Blk, Level 5, Singapore 318994; tel. 63196319; fax 63198111; e-mail thumbsup@sph.com.sg; f. 2000; newspaper aimed at primary school students; Editor LIM SOON LAN; circ. 37,445.

Malay Language

Berita Minggu: 1000 Toa Payoh North, Annex Blk, Level 3, Singapore 318994; tel. 63195665; fax 63198255; e-mail aadeska@sph.com.sg; internet cyberita.asia1.com.sg; f. 1960; Sunday; Editor ISMAIL PANTEK; circ. 65,608 (Singapore only).

SELECTED PERIODICALS

English Language

8 Days: 10 Ang Mo Kio St 65, 01-06/08 Techpoint, Singapore 569059; tel. 62789822; fax 62724800; e-mail feedback@8daysonline.com; internet www.8days.sg; f. 1990; weekly; Editor-in-Chief LAU KUAN WEI; circ. 113,258.

Female: SPH Media Centre, 82 Genting Lane, Level 7, Singapore 349567; tel. 63196319; fax 63196345; e-mail magfemale@sph.com.sg; internet www.femalemag.com.sg; f. 1974; monthly; circ. 60,000.

FHM Singapore: 01-06/08, 10 Ang Mo Kio St 65, Singapore 569059; tel. 64845212; e-mail info@fhm.com.sg; internet www.fhm.com.sg; Sr Editor DAVID FURHMANN-LIM.

Her World: SPH Media Centre, 82 Genting Lane, Singapore 349567; tel. 63196319; fax 63196345; e-mail magherworld@sph.com.sg; internet www.herworld.com; f. 1960; monthly; women's; Editor NIKI BRUCE.

Her World Brides: SPH Media Centre, 82 Genting Lane, Singapore 349567; tel. 63196319; fax 63196345; e-mail maghwbrides@sph.com.sg; internet www.hwbrides.com.sg; f. 1998; quarterly; circ. 13,193.

Home and Decor: SPH Media Centre, 82 Genting Lane, 5th Floor, Singapore 349567; tel. 63196319; fax 63196345; e-mail hdecor@sph.com.sg; internet www.homeanddecor.com.sg; f. 1987; 6 a year; Editor SOPHIE KHO; circ. 27,000.

NSman: SAFRA National Service Association, 5200 Jalan Bukit Merah, Singapore 159468; tel. 63779835; fax 63779898; e-mail hq@safra.sg; internet www.safra.sg; f. 1972; est. as *Reservist*; renamed 1994; bi-monthly; publ. of SAFRA Nat. Service Asscn; Gen. Sec. TAN KOK YAM; circ. 150,000.

Pioneer: 5 Depot Rd, 05-06 Defence Technology Tower B, Singapore 109681; tel. 63731114; fax 63731111; e-mail pioneer@starnet.gov.sg; internet www.mindef.gov.sg/imindef/publications/cyberpioneer/index.html; f. 1996; monthly; publication of the Singaporean Armed Forces.

SINGAPORE

Republic of Singapore Government Gazette: Toppan Leefung Pte Ltd, 1 Kim Seng Promenade, 18-01 Great World City East Tower, Singapore 237994; tel. 68269600; fax 68203341; e-mail egazinfo@toppanleefung.com; internet www.egazette.com.sg; weekdays.

SimplyHer: SPH Media Centre, 82 Genting Lane, Level 7, Singapore 349567; tel. 63196319; fax 63196345; e-mail magsimplyher@sph.com.sg; internet www.simplyher.com.sg; f. 2004; monthly; women's; Editor PENELOPE CHAN; circ. 21,000.

Singapore Medical Journal: Singapore Medical Asscn, Level 2, Alumni Medical Centre, 2 College Rd, Singapore 169850; tel. 62231264; fax 62247827; e-mail smj@sma.org.sg; internet www.sma.org.sg/smj; f. 1959; monthly; Editor Prof. TEO ENG KIONG; circ. 5,000.

Torque: SPH Media Centre, 82 Genting Lane, Level 7, Singapore 349567; tel. 63196319; fax 63196345; e-mail seowlka@sph.com.sg; internet www.torque.com.sg; f. 1990; monthly; automobile; Editor LEE NIAN TJOE.

Young Parents: SPH Media Centre, 82 Genting Lane, Level 7, Singapore 349567; tel. 63196319; fax 63196345; e-mail magyoungparents@sph.com.sg; internet www.youngparents.com.sg; f. 1987; monthly; family; Editor STEPHANIE YEO; circ. 20,000.

Chinese Language

Characters: 1 Kallang Sector, 04-04/05 Kolam Ayer Industrial Park, Singapore 349276; tel. 67458733; fax 67458213; f. 1987; monthly; television and entertainment; Editor SAM NG; circ. 45,000.

The Citizen: People's Association, 9 Stadium Link, Singapore 397750; tel. 63405138; fax 63468657; monthly; English, Chinese, Tamil and Malay; Man. Editor OOI HUI MEI.

Icon: SPH Media Centre, 82 Genting Lane, Level 7, Singapore 349567; tel. 63196319; fax 63196345; e-mail magicon@sph.com.sg; internet www.iconsingapore.com; f. 2005; monthly; Chinese language; lifestyle; Man. Editor ELSIE YAH.

i-weekly: 10 Ang Mo Kio St 65, 01-06/08 Techpoint, Singapore 569059; tel. 64837837; fax 64837257; e-mail i-weekly@mediacorp.com.sg; f. 1981; weekly; lifestyle and entertainment; Editor-in-Chief JACKIE LIU; circ. 232,000.

NuYou: SPH Media Centre, 82 Genting Lane, Level 7, Singapore 349567; tel. 63196319; fax 63196345; internet www.nuyou.com.sg; f. 1976; monthly; Editor-in-Chief GRACE LEE.

Punters' Way: 4 Ubi View (off Ubi Rd 3), Pioneers and Leaders Centre, Singapore 408557; tel. 67458733; fax 67458321; e-mail pnlhldg@pnl-group.com; internet www.pnl-group.com; f. 1977; bi-weekly; English and Chinese; horse racing; Editor T. S. PHAN; circ. 90,000.

Racing Guide: 1 Scotts Rd, 26-03 Shaw Centre, Singapore 228208; tel. 67340111; e-mail inquiries@asiapacificpublishing.com; internet www.racingguide.com.sg; f. 1987; 2 a week; English and Chinese; sport; Editorial Consultant BENNY ORTEGA; Chinese Editor KUEK CHIEW TEONG; circ. 20,000.

Singapore Literature: Singapore Literature Society, 122B Sims Ave, Singapore 1438; quarterly; Pres. YAP KOON CHAN; Editor LUO-MING.

UW (U-Weekly): Focus Publishing Ltd,1000 Toa Payoh North, News Centre, Singapore 318994; tel. 63196319; fax 63198124; e-mail youmail@sph.com.sg; f. 2001 as You Weekly; renamed as above 2005; weekly; entertainment and lifestyle; circ. 80,000.

Young Generation: 1 New Industrial Rd, Times Centre, Singapore 536196; tel. 62139276; fax 68463440; e-mail kelenkoh@tpl.com.sg; internet www.panpaceducation.com; monthly; children's; Editor EVELYN TANG; circ. 80,000.

Malay Language

Manja: 10 Ang Mo Kio St 65, 01-06/08 Techpoint, Singapore 569059; tel. 64837118; fax 64812098; e-mail hello@manja.sg; internet www.manja.sg; f. 2000; monthly; entertainment and lifestyle; Editor RUSLINA AFFENDY.

NEWS AGENCIES

Foreign Bureaux

Various foreign bureaux operate in Singapore.

Publishers

ENGLISH LANGUAGE

Butterworths Asia: 3 Killiney Rd, 08-08 Winsland House 1, Singapore 239519; tel. 67331380; fax 67331175; e-mail help.sg@lexisnexis.com; internet www.lexisnexis.com.sg/butterworths-online; f. 1932; law texts and journals; Gen. Man. DEAN CORKERY.

Caldecott Publishing Pte Ltd: 10 Ang Mo Kio St 65, 01-06/08 Techpoint, Singapore 569059; tel. 64837118; fax 64837286; f. 1990; Editorial Dir MICHAEL CHIANG; Group Editor TAN LEE SUN.

FEP International Pte Ltd: 3A Phillips Ave, Singapore 546921; tel. 62814185; fax 67375561; f. 1960; textbooks, reference, children's and dictionaries; Gen. Man. RICHARD TOH.

Flame of the Forest Publishing Pte Ltd: Blk 5, Ang Mo Kio Industrial Park 2A, 07-22/23, AMK Tech II, Singapore 567760; tel. 64848887; fax 64842208; e-mail mail@flameoftheforest.com; internet www.flameoftheforest.com; f. 1989; Man. Dir ALEX CHACKO.

Graham Brash Pte Ltd: 45 Kian Teck Drive, Blk 1, Level 2, Singapore 628859; tel. 62624843; fax 62621519; e-mail evelyn@grahambrash.com.sg; internet www.grahambrash.com.sg; f. 1947; general, academic, educational; English, Chinese and Malay; Publr and Man. Dir CHUAN I. CAMPBELL; Gen. Man. EVELYN LEE.

Institute of Southeast Asian Studies: 30 Heng Mui Keng Terrace, Pasir Panjang Rd, Singapore 119614; tel. 67780955; fax 67756259; e-mail publish@iseas.edu.sg; internet www.iseas.edu.sg; f. 1968; scholarly works on contemporary South-East Asia and the Asia-Pacific region; Chair. Prof. WANG GUNGWU; Dir K. KESAVAPANY.

Intellectual Publishing Co: 113 Eunos Ave 3, 04-08 Gordon Industrial Bldg, Singapore 1440; tel. 67466025; fax 67489108; f. 1971; Man. POH BE LECK.

Marshall Cavendish International (Singapore) Pte Ltd: Times Centre, 1 New Industrial Rd, Singapore 536196; tel. 62139300; fax 62889254; e-mail fps@sg.marshallcavendish.com; internet www.marshallcavendish.com/education; f. 1957; fmrly Times Media Pte Ltd; academic texts; Group Publr SHANE ARMSTRONG; Publr DURIYA AZIZ.

NUS Press (Pte) Ltd: National University of Singapore, 3 Arts Link, AS3-01/02, Singapore 117569; tel. 67761148; fax 67740652; e-mail nusbooks@nus.edu.sg; internet www.nus.edu.sg/nuspress; f. 1971; scholarly; Man. Dir PAUL KRATOSKA.

Pearson Education South Asia Pte Ltd: 23–25 First Lok Yang Rd, Jurong Town, Singapore 629733; tel. 63199388; fax 62651033; e-mail info@pearsoned.com.sg; internet www.pearsonlongman.com.sg; educational; Dir, Business Support, South Asia RASMIATI HARTANTO.

Stamford Media International Pte Ltd: 209 Kallang Bahru, Singapore 339344; tel. 62947227; fax 62944396; e-mail info@stamford.com.sg; internet www.stamford.com.sg; f. 1963; est. as Stamford College Publrs; renamed Stamford Press Pte Ltd in 1983; present name adopted 2001; general, educational and journals; Man. LAWRENCE THOMAS.

Times Editions Pte Ltd: Times Centre, 1 New Industrial Rd, Singapore 536196; tel. 62139288; fax 62844733; e-mail tpl@tpl.com.sg; internet www.tpl.com.sg; f. 1978; political, social and cultural books, general works on Asia; Chair. LIM KIM SAN; Pres. and CEO LAI SECK KHUI.

World Scientific Publishing Co Pte Ltd: 5 Toh Tuck Link, Singapore 596224; tel. 64665775; fax 64677667; e-mail wspc@wspc.com.sg; internet www.worldscientific.com; f. 1981; academic and research texts and science journals; Chair. and Editor-in-Chief Prof. K. K. PHUA; Man. Dir DOREEN LIU.

MALAY LANGUAGE

Malaysia Press Sdn Bhd (Pustaka Melayu): Singapore; tel. 62933454; fax 62911858; f. 1962; textbooks and educational; Man. Dir ABU TALIB BIN ALLY.

Pustaka Nasional Pte Ltd: 548 Changi Rd, Singapore 419931; tel. 67454321; fax 67452417; e-mail enquiry@pustaka.com.sg; internet www.pustaka.com.sg; f. 1963; Arabic, English, Malay and Islamic religious books and CD-Roms; Dir SYED ALI SEMAIT.

CHINESE LANGUAGE

Shanghai Book Co (Pte) Ltd: 231 Bain St, 02-73 Bras Basah Complex, Singapore 180231; tel. 63360144; fax 63360490; e-mail shanghaibook@pacific.net.sg; f. 1925; educational and general; Man. Dir MA JI LIN.

Shing Lee Publishers Pte Ltd: 120 Hillview Ave, 05-06/07 Kewalram Hillview, Singapore 669594; tel. 67601388; fax 67623247; e-mail info@shinglee.com.sg; internet www.shinglee.com.sg; f. 1935; educational and general; Man. PEH SOH NGOH.

Union Book Co (Pte) Ltd: 231 Bain St, 03-01 Bras Basah Complex, Singapore 180231; tel. 63380696; fax 63386306; e-mail youlian@singnet.com.sg; internet www.unionbook.com.sg; f. 1952; general and reference; Gen. Man. CHOW LI-LIANG.

TAMIL LANGUAGE

EVS Enterprises: Singapore; tel. 62830002; f. 1967; children's books, religion and general; Man. E. V. SINGHAN.

SINGAPORE

GOVERNMENT PUBLISHING HOUSE

Toppan Leefung Pte Ltd: 1 Kim Seng Promenade, 18-01 Great World City East Tower, Singapore 237994; tel. 68269600; fax 68203341; e-mail enquiries@toppanleefung.com; internet www.toppanleefung.com; f. 1973; fmrly SNP Corpn Ltd; present name adopted following acquisition by Toppan Printing Co Ltd in 2008; printers and publrs; Pres. and CEO YEO CHEE TONG.

PUBLISHERS' ORGANIZATIONS

National Book Development Council of Singapore (NBDCS): 50 Geylang East Ave 1, Singapore 389777; tel. 68488290; fax 67429466; e-mail info@bookcouncil.sg; internet www.bookcouncil.sg; f. 1969; independent non-profit org.; promotes reading, writing and publishing and organizes the annual Asian Congress of Storytellers and Asian Children's Writers and Illustrators' Conference; offers professional training programmes through Centre for Literary Arts and Publishing; Chair. Prof. SERENE WEE.

Singapore Book Publishers' Association: 86 Marine Parade Central, 03-213, Singapore 440086; tel. 63447801; fax 64470897; e-mail mphua@wspc.com; internet www.publishers-sbpa.org.sg; 63 mems; Pres. TRIENA WONG.

Broadcasting and Communications

TELECOMMUNICATIONS

Infocomm Development Authority of Singapore (IDA): 8 Temasek Blvd, 14-00 Suntec Tower Three, Singapore 038988; tel. 62110888; fax 62112222; e-mail info@ida.gov.sg; internet www.ida.gov.sg; f. 1999; formed as result of merger of Nat. Computer Bd and Telecommunication Authority of Singapore; the national policy maker; regulator of telecommunications and promoter of information and communication technologies in Singapore; CEO Dr CHRISTOPHER CHIA.

MobileOne (M1): 10 International Business Park, Singapore 609928; tel. 68951111; fax 68993929; e-mail ir@m1.com.sg; internet www.m1.com.sg; f. 1997; Chair. TEO SOON HOE; CEO KAREN KOOI.

Netrust Pte Ltd: 70 Bendemeer Rd, 05-03, Luzerne, Singapore 339940; tel. 62121388; fax 62121366; e-mail infoline@netrust.net; internet www.netrust.net; f. 1997; the only licensed Certification Authority (CA) in Singapore, jtly formed by Nat. Computer Bd and Network for Electronic Transfers; verifies the identity of parties doing business or communicating in cyberspace through the issuing of electronic identification certificates, in order to enable govt orgs and private enterprises to conduct electronic transactions in a secure manner; CEO FOO JONG AI.

Singapore Technologies Telemedia: 51 Cuppage Rd, 09-01 Starhub Centre, Singapore 229469; tel. 67238777; fax 67207266; e-mail contactus@stt.st.com.sg; internet www.sttelemedia.com; Pres. and CEO LEE THENG KIAT.

Singapore Telecommunications Ltd (SingTel): 19-00 Comcentre, 31 Exeter Rd, Singapore 239732; tel. 68383388; fax 67328428; e-mail contact@singtel.com; internet info.singtel.com; f. 1992; postal and telecommunications service operator and holding co for a number of subsidiaries, serving both the corporate and consumer markets; 61.79%-owned by Temasek Holdings (Pvt) Ltd (a govt holding co), 38.21% transferred to the private sector; Chair. CHUMPOL NALAMLIENG; Group CEO CHUA SOCK KOONG.

StarHub Pte Ltd: Head Office, 51 Cuppage Rd, 01-02/03 StarHub Centre, Singapore 229469; tel. 68255000; fax 67205000; e-mail corpcomms@starhub.com; internet www.starhub.com; f. 2000; telecommunications service provider; consortium includes Singapore Technologies Telemedia Pte Ltd, Singapore Power Ltd, Nippon Telegraph and Telephone Corpn (NTT) and British Telecom (BT); CEO NEIL MONTEFIORE.

BROADCASTING

Regulatory Authority

Media Development Authority (MDA): 3 Fusionopolis Way, 16-22 Symbiosis, Singapore 138633; tel. 63773800; fax 65773888; internet www.mda.gov.sg; f. 1994; fmrly Singapore Broadcasting Authority; present name adopted 2003; licenses, regulates and promotes the devt of the media industry in Singapore; ensures the provision of an adequate range of media services to serve the interests of the general public, maintains fair and efficient market conduct and effective competition in the media industry, ensures the maintenance of a high standard of media services, regulates public service broadcasting; Chair. Dr TAN CHIN NAM; CEO Dr CHRISTOPHER CHIA.

Radio

Far East Broadcasting Associates (FEBA Ltd): 30 Lorong Ampas, 07-01 Skywaves Industrial Bldg, Singapore 328783; tel. 62508577; fax 62508422; e-mail febadmin@febaltd.com; f. 1960; Chair. GOH EWE KHENG; Exec. Dir LEE CHI KWAN (acting).

Media Corporation of Singapore: Caldecott Broadcast Centre, Andrew Rd, Singapore 299939; tel. 63333888; fax 62515628; e-mail feedback@mediacorp.com.sg; internet www.mediacorp.com.sg; f. 1994; est. as Singapore Int. Media (SIM), following corporatization of Singapore Broadcasting Corpn; holding co for 7 operating cos—Television Corpn of Singapore (TCS), Singapore Television Twelve (STV12), Radio Corpn of Singapore (RCS), MediaCorp Studios, MediaCorp News, MediaCorp Interactive and MediaCorp Publishing; Chair. HO KWON PING; CEO LUCAS CHOW.

Radio Corpn of Singapore Pte Ltd (RCS): Caldecott Broadcast Centre, Radio Bldg, Andrew Rd, Singapore 299939; tel. 63597307; fax 63597500; e-mail feedback@mediacorp.com.sg; internet www.mediacorpradio.sg; f. 1936; operates 13 domestic services—incl. in English (six), Mandarin (three), Malay (two) and Tamil (one)—and three international radio stations (manages Radio Singapore International (RSI)—services in English, Mandarin and Malay for three hours daily and service in Bahasa Indonesia for one hour daily); Man. Dir LEO GOH.

Rediffusion (Singapore) Pte Ltd: 12 New Industrial Rd, 03-03 Morningstar Centre, Singapore 536202; tel. 63832633; fax 62850421; e-mail md@rediffusion.com.sg; internet www.rediffusion.com.sg; f. 1949; commercial audio wired broadcasting service and wireless digital audio broadcasting service; broadcasts 15 regional and international channels; Man. Dir WONG BAN KUAN.

SAFRA Radio: Bukit Merah Central, POB 1315, Singapore 911599; tel. 63731924; fax 62783039; e-mail power98@pacific.net.sg; internet www.power98.com.sg; f. 1994; broadcasts in Mandarin and English.

SPH UnionWorks Pte Ltd: 1000 Toa Payoh North, News Centre, Podium Blk, Level 3, Singapore 318994; tel. 63191900; fax 63191099; e-mail webadm@sphuw.com.sg; internet www.sphuw.com.sg; f. 1991; fmrly Radio Heart and UnionWorks Pte Ltd; first private radio station; broadcasts in English and Mandarin; 2 channels covering news, music and entertainment.

Television

CNBC Asia Business News (S) Pte Ltd: 10 Anson Rd, 06-01 International Plaza, Singapore 079903; tel. 63230488; fax 62230020; e-mail contactus@cnbcasia.com; internet asia.cnbc.com; f. 1998; cable and satellite broadcaster of global business and financial news; US-controlled; broadcasts in English (24 hours daily) and Mandarin; Pres. and Man. Dir SATPAL BRAINCH.

Media Corporation of Singapore: see Radio.

Singapore Television Twelve Pte Ltd (STV12): 12 Prince Edward Rd, 05-00 Bestway Bldg, Singapore 079212; tel. 62258133; fax 62203881; internet www.stv12.com.sg; f. 1994; terrestrial TV station; 2 channels—Suria (Malay, 58 hours weekly) and Central (110.5 hours weekly); COO WOON TAI HO.

SPH MediaWorks Ltd: 1000 Toa Payoh North, News Centre, Singapore 318994; tel. 63196319; fax 63198150; e-mail sphcorp@sph.com.sg; internet www.sph.com.sg; f. 2000; subsidiary of Singapore Press Holdings Ltd (SPH); two channels—Channel U (Mandarin) and Channel i (English); also owns two radio stations; CEO ALAN CHAN HENG LOON.

Starhub CableVision Ltd: 51 Cuppage Rd, 01-02/03 Cuppage Centre, Singapore 229469; tel. 68255000; fax 67205000; internet www.starhub.com; f. 1992; fmrly Singapore CableVision Ltd; present name adopted 2002 following acquisition by Starhub Ltd; broadcasting and communications co, subscription television service; launched cable service in June 1995; offers 83 digital channels (March 2005); offers broadband access services; CEO NEIL MONTEFIORE.

Television Corpn of Singapore (TCS): Caldecott Broadcast Centre, Andrew Rd, Singapore 299939; tel. 63333888; fax 62515628; e-mail feedback@mediacorp.com.sg; internet www.mediacorp.sg; f. 1994; est. following the corporatization of Singapore Broadcasting Corpn; eight channels; broadcasts in English, Mandarin, Malay and Tamil; teletext service on one channel; also owns TVMobile, Singapore's first digital TV channel, and Digital TV; Chair. HO KWON PING; CEO LUCAS CHOW.

SINGAPORE

Finance

(cap. = capital; res = reserves; dep. = deposits; m. = million; brs = branches; amounts in Singapore dollars)

BANKING

The Singapore monetary system is regulated by the Monetary Authority of Singapore (MAS) and the Ministry of Finance. The MAS performs all the functions of a central bank and also assumed responsibility for the issuing of currency following its merger with the Board of Commissioners of Currency in October 2002. In May 2011 there were 120 commercial banks (six local, 114 foreign) and 33 representative offices in Singapore. Of the foreign banks, 26 had full licences, 50 had wholesale licences and 38 had 'offshore' banking licences.

Government Financial Institution

Monetary Authority of Singapore (MAS): 10 Shenton Way, MAS Bldg, Singapore 079117; tel. 62255577; fax 62299229; e-mail webmaster@mas.gov.sg; internet www.mas.gov.sg; merged with Board of Commissioners of Currency Oct. 2002; cap. 17,000.0m., res 18,321.3m., dep. 139,498.4m. (March 2010); Chair. GOH CHOK TONG; Man. Dir THARMAN SHANMUGARATNAM.

Domestic Full Commercial Banks

Bank of Singapore: 63 Market St, Bank of Singapore Centre, Singapore 048942; tel. 65598000; fax 65598180; internet www.bankofsingapore.com; cap. US $596.3m., dep. US $4,680.6m. (Dec. 2009); subsidiary of Oversea-Chinese Banking Corpn Ltd; fmrly ING Asia Private Bank Ltd; Chair. DAVID CONNER; CEO RENATO DE GUZMAN.

DBS Bank (Development Bank of Singapore Ltd): 6 Shenton Way, DBS Bldg, Tower One, Singapore 068809; tel. 68788888; fax 64451267; e-mail dbs@dbs.com; internet www.dbs.com/sg; f. 1968; merged with Post Office Savings Bank in 1998; 29% govt-owned; cap. 12,096m., res 7,110m., dep. 121,662m. (Dec. 2006); Chair. PETER SEAH LIM HUAT; CEO PIYUSH GUPTA; 107 local brs, 9 overseas brs.

Far Eastern Bank Ltd: 156 Cecil St, 01-00 FEB Bldg, Singapore 069544; tel. 62219055; fax 62242263; internet www.uobgroup.com; f. 1959; subsidiary of United Overseas Bank Ltd; cap. 100m., res 69.8m., dep. 645.7m. (Dec. 2006); CEO WEE EE CHEONG; 3 brs.

Oversea-Chinese Banking Corpn Ltd (OCBC): 65 Chulia St, 01-00 OCBC Centre, Singapore 049513; tel. 63187222; fax 65337955; e-mail info@ocbc.com.sg; internet www.ocbc.com.sg; f. 1932; merged with Keppel TatLee Bank Ltd in 2001; cap. 5,480.9m., res 7,923.3m., dep. 89,639.5m. (Dec. 2006); Chair. Dr CHEONG CHOONG KONG; CEO DAVID PHILBRICK CONNER; 56 local brs, 52 overseas brs.

Singapore Island Bank: POB 1900, Robinson Rd Post Office, Singapore 903750; tel. 64383883; fax 64383718; e-mail clientservice@finatiq.com; internet www.finatiq.com; f. 1954; subsidiary of Oversea-Chinese Banking Corpn Ltd; fmrly Bank of Singapore Ltd, name changed as above in Jan. 2010; Chair. DAVID PHILBRICK CONNER.

United Overseas Bank Ltd: 80 Raffles Pl., UOB Plaza, Singapore 048624; tel. 65339898; fax 65342334; internet www.uobgroup.com; f. 1935; merged with Overseas Union Bank Ltd in Jan. 2002 and with Industrial and Commercial Bank Ltd in Aug. 2002; cap. 2.013.7m., res 8,080.1m., dep. 118,501.6m. (Dec. 2007); Chair. WEE CHO YAW; CEO WEE EE CHEONG; 61 local brs, 21 overseas brs.

Foreign Banks

Full Commercial Banks

ABN AMRO Asia Merchant Bank (Singapore) Ltd (Netherlands): 63 Chulia St, Singapore 049514; tel. 62318888; fax 65323108; Chair. DAVID WONG SEE HONG; Man. Dir ROBERT R. DAVIS.

American Express Bank Ltd (USA): 16 Collyer Quay, Hitachi Tower, Singapore 049318; tel. 65384833; fax 65343022; Sr Country Exec. S. LACHLAN HOUGH.

Bangkok Bank Public Co Ltd (Thailand): 180 Cecil St, Bangkok Bank Bldg, Singapore 069546; tel. 64100400; fax 62255852; e-mail kanchana.kon@bangkokbank.com; internet www.bangkokbank.com; Sr Vice-Pres. and Gen. Man. KHUN KANCHANA KONGVANANON.

Bank of America NA (USA): 9 Raffles Place, 18-00 Republic Plaza Tower 1, Singapore 048619; tel. 62393888; fax 62393188; CEO ALAN KOH; Man. Dir GOETZ EGGELHOEFER.

Bank of China (People's Republic of China): 4 Battery Rd, Bank of China Bldg, Singapore 049908; tel. 65352411; fax 65343401; e-mail Service_SG@bank-of-china.com; internet www.bank-of-china.com; Gen. Man. ZHU HUA.

Bank of East Asia Ltd (BEA) (Hong Kong): 60 Robinson Rd, Bank of East Asia Bldg, Singapore 068892; tel. 66027702; fax 62251805; e-mail info@hkbea.com.sg; internet www.hkbea.com.sg; Gen. Man. YAP GAY-SIN.

Directory

Bank of India (India): 01-01 to 03-01, Corporate Office Bldg, 138 Robinson Rd, Singapore 068906; tel. 62220011; fax 62271275; e-mail boi.singapore@bankofindia.co.in; internet www.boi.com.sg; Chief Exec. MUNIR ALAM; Gen. Man. B. RAMASUBRAMANIAM.

PT Bank Negara Indonesia (Persero) Tbk (Indonesia): 158 Cecil St, 01-00 to 04-00 Dapenso Bldg, Singapore 069545; tel. 62257755; fax 62254757; Gen. Man. MUHAMMAD YAZEED.

Bank of Tokyo-Mitsubishi UFJ Ltd (Japan): 9 Raffles Place, 01-01 Republic Plaza, Singapore 048619; tel. 65383388; fax 65388083; internet www.bk.mufg.jp; Gen. Man. HAKOTO NAKAGAWA; Dep. Gen. Man. HIDEMITSU OTSUKA.

BNP Paribas (France): 20 Collyer Quay, Tung Centre, Singapore 049319; tel. 62101288; fax 62234459; internet www.bnpparibas.com.sg; Regional Man. JEAN-PIERRE BERNARD.

Calyon (France): 168 Robinson Rd, 23-03 Capital Tower, Singapore 068912; tel. 65354988; fax 65322422; internet www.ca-cib.com; formed through merger of Crédit Agricole Indosuez and Crédit Lyonnais.

Citibank NA (USA): Capital Square, 23 Church St, 01-01, Singapore 049481; tel. 62255225; fax 6325880; internet www.citibank.com.sg; f. 1902; Country Corporate Officer SANJIV MISRA.

HL Bank (Malaysia): 20 Collyer Quay, 01-02 Tung Centre, Singapore 049319; tel. 63498338; fax 65339340; internet www.hlb.com.my; Country Head GAN HUI TIN.

Hongkong and Shanghai Banking Corpn Ltd (Hong Kong): 01-01 HSBC Bldg, 21 Collyer Quay, Singapore 049320; tel. 65305000; fax 62214676; e-mail direct@hsbc.com.sg; internet www.hsbc.com.sg; f. 1877; CEO (Singapore) ALEX HUNGATE.

Indian Bank (India): 3 Raffles Place, Bharat Bldg, Singapore 048617; tel. 65343511; fax 65331651; e-mail indbksg@pacific.net.sg; internet indianbank-singapore.com; Gen. Man. and Chief Exec. S. K. BANDOPADHYAY.

Indian Overseas Bank (India): 64 Cecil St, IOB Bldg, Singapore 049711; tel. 62251100; fax 62244490; e-mail iobrem@iob.com.sg; internet iobsingapore.com; f. 1941; Chief Exec. V. NARAYANA MOORTHY.

JP Morgan Chase Bank (USA): 168 Robinson Rd, 15th Floor, Capital Tower, Singapore 068912; tel. 68822888; fax 68821756; internet jpmorganchase.com; Man. Dir and Sr Country Officer RAYMOND CHANG.

Maybank (Malaysia): Maybank Tower, 2 Battery Rd 01-00, Singapore 049907; tel. 65507000; fax 65333071; e-mail cs@maybank.com.sg; internet www.maybank2u.com.sg; f. 1960; CEO POLLIE SIM; 22 brs.

RHB Bank Bhd (Malaysia): 5th Floor, 90 Cecil St 05-00, Singapore 069531; tel. 63200602; fax 62255296; e-mail contactus@rhbbank.com.sg; internet rhb.com.sg; f. 1961; Country Head JASON WONG; 7 brs.

Southern Bank Bhd (Malaysia): 39 Robinson Rd, 01-02 Robinson Point, Singapore 068911; tel. 65321318; fax 65355366; Dir YEAP LAM YANG.

Standard Chartered Bank (UK): 6 Battery Rd, Singapore 049909; tel. 62258888; fax 67893756; internet www.standardchartered.com.sg; f. 1969; Group CEO PETER SANDS; Chief Exec. (Singapore) RAY FERGUSON.

Sumitomo Mitsui Banking Corpn (Japan) (SMBC): 3 Temasek Ave, 06-01 Centennial Tower, Singapore 039190; tel. 68820001; fax 68870330; internet www.smbc.co.jp; Gen. Man. MASAMI TASHIRO.

UCO Bank (India): 3 Raffles Place, Bharat Bldg, Singapore 048617; tel. 65325944; fax 65325044; e-mail general@ucobank.com.sg; internet www.ucobank.com.sg; f. 1951; Chief Exec. MAITRAYEE BANERJEE; 2 brs.

Wholesale Banks

Australia and New Zealand Banking Group Ltd (Australia): 50 Raffles Place, 01-03 Singapore Land Tower, Singapore 048623; tel. 62268899; fax 63493976; internet www.anz.com/singapore; f. 1974; CEO VISHNU SHAHANEY.

Bank of Nova Scotia (Canada): 1 Raffles Quay, 20-01 North Tower, Singapore 048583; tel. 63058388; fax 65347817; Group Head ANATOL VON HAHN.

Barclays Bank PLC (UK): 23 Church St, 13-08 Capital Sq., Singapore 049481; tel. 63953000; fax 63953139; Regional Head VIKRAM MALHOTRA; Country Man. QUEK SUAN KIAT.

Bayerische Hypo- und Vereinsbank AG (Germany): 30 Cecil St, 25-01 Prudential Tower, Singapore 049712; tel. 64133688; fax 65368591; Gen. Man. RICHARD LEE.

Bayerische Landesbank Girozentrale (Germany): 300 Beach Rd, 37-00 The Concourse, Singapore 199555; tel. 62933822; fax 62932151; e-mail sgblb@blb.de; Gen. Man. and Sr Vice-Pres. MANFRED WOLF; Exec. Vice-Pres. HEINZ HOFFMANN.

BNP Paribas Private Bank (France): 20 Collyer Quay, Tung Centre, Singapore 049319; tel. 62101288; fax 62243459; internet www.bnpparibas.com.sg; Dir and CEO BAUDOUIN PROT; Regional Head JEAN-PIERRE BERNARD.

Commerzbank AG (Germany): 8 Shenton Way, 42-01 Temasek Tower, Singapore 068811; tel. 63110000; fax 62253943; e-mail info@commerzbank.com.sg; internet www.commerzbank.com.sg; f. 1978; Man. JÜRGEN SCHMIEDING.

Crédit Lyonnais (France): 3 Temasek Ave, 11-01 Centennial Tower, Singapore 039190; tel. 63336331; fax 63336332; Gen. Man. PIERRE EYMERY.

Crédit Suisse (Switzerland): 1 Raffles Link, 05-02, Singapore 039393; tel. 62126000; fax 62126200; e-mail ask.us@credit-suisse.com; internet www.cspb.com.sg; Br. Man. SALMAN SHOAIB.

Crédit Suisse First Boston (Switzerland): 1 Raffles Link, 05-02 City Link Mall, Singapore 039393; tel. 62122000; Br. Man. ERIC M. VARVEL.

Deutsche Bank AG (Germany): 1 Raffles Quay, 17-00 South Tower, Singapore 048583; tel. 64238001; fax 62259442; internet www.db.com/singapore; f. 1971; Gen. Man. RONNY TAN CHONG TEE.

Dresdner Bank AG (Germany): 20 Collyer Quay, 22-00 Tung Centre, Singapore 049319; tel. 62228080; fax 62244008; Man. Dirs ANDREAS RUSCHKOWSKI, RAYMOND B. T. KOH, PIERS WILLIS; CEO BAUDOUIN GROONENBERGHS.

First Commercial Bank (Taiwan): 76 Shenton Way, 01-02 ONG Bldg, Singapore 079119; tel. 62215755; fax 62251905; e-mail fcbsin@singnet.com.sg; Gen. Man. LAI JEN-YU.

Habib Bank Ltd (Pakistan): 3 Phillip St, 01-03 Commerce Pt, Singapore 048693; tel. 64380055; fax 64383244; e-mail rizwan@hblsg.com; Regional Gen. Man. RIZWAN HAIDAR.

HSBC Republic Bank (Suisse) SA (Switzerland): 21 Collyer Quay, 21-01 HSBC Bldg, Singapore 049320; tel. 62248080; fax 62237146; CEO NANCIE DUPIER.

Industrial and Commercial Bank of China (People's Republic of China): 6 Raffles Quay, 12-01 John Hancock Tower, Singapore 048580; tel. 65381066; fax 65381370; e-mail icbcsg@icbc.com.sg; Chair. and Pres. JIANG JIANQING.

ING Bank NV (Netherlands): 9 Raffles Place, 19-02 Republic Plaza, Singapore 048619; tel. 65353688; fax 65338329; Country Head J. KESTEMONT.

Intesa Sanpaolo SpA (Italy): 6 Temasek Blvd, 42/04-05 Suntec Tower Four, Singapore 038986; tel. 63338270; fax 63338252; e-mail singapore.sg@intesasanpaolo.com; internet www.intesasanpaolo.com; Gen. Man. GIOVANNI FIORENDI.

KBC Bank NV (Belgium): 30 Cecil St, 12-01/08 Prudential Tower, Singapore 049712; tel. 63952828; fax 65342929; e-mail reception@kbc.com.sg; f. 1993; Gen. Man. THIERRY MEZERET.

Korea Exchange Bank (Republic of Korea): 30 Cecil St, 24-03/08 Prudential Tower, Singapore 049712; tel. 65361633; fax 65382522; e-mail kebspore@keb.co.kr; Gen. Man. JEONG OO YEOUNG.

Landesbank Baden-Württemberg (Germany): 25 International Business Park, 01-72 German Centre, Singapore 609916; tel. 65627722; fax 65627729; Man. Dr WOLFHART AUER VAN HERRENKIRCHEN.

Mega International Commercial Bank Co Ltd (Taiwan): 80 Raffles Place, 23-20 UOB Plaza II, Singapore 048624; tel. 65366311; fax 65360680; Gen. Man. HSIANG YEN-PING.

Mizuho Corporate Bank Ltd (Japan): 168 Robinson Rd, 13-00 Capital Tower, Singapore 068912; tel. 64230330; fax 64230012; Gen. Man. KOSUKE NAKAMURA.

National Australia Bank Ltd (Australia): 5 Temasek Blvd, 15-01 Suntec Tower Five, Singapore 038985; tel. 64196875; fax 63380039; f. 1981; Gen. Man. FRANK OLSSON.

National Bank of Kuwait SAK (Kuwait): 9 Raffles Place, 24-02 Republic Plaza, Singapore 048619; tel. 62225348; fax 62245438; f. 1984; Gen. Man. RICHARD MCKEGNEY.

Norddeutsche Landesbank Girozentrale (Germany): 6 Shenton Way, 16-00 DBS Bldg Tower Two, Singapore 068809; tel. 63231223; fax 63230223; e-mail nordlb.singapore@nordlb.com; internet www.nordlb.de; f. 1994; Gen. Man. and Regional Head Asia/Pacific HEINZ WERNER FRINGS.

Northern Trust Company (USA): 1 George St, 12-06, Singapore 049145; tel. 64376666; fax 64376609; e-mail LA16@ntrs.com; internet www.northerntrust.com; f. 1889; Sr Vice-Pres. LAWRENCE AU.

Rabobank International (Netherlands): 77 Robinson Rd, 09-00 SIA Bldg, Singapore 068896; tel. 65363363; fax 65363236; Regional Man. (Asia) ROB VAN ZADELHOFF.

Royal Bank of Scotland PLC (UK): 50 Raffles Place, 08-00 Singapore Land Tower, Singapore 048623; tel. 64168600; fax 62259827; Gen. Man. ALAN ROY GOODYEAR.

Société Générale (France): 80 Robinson Rd, 25-00, Singapore 068898; tel. 62227122; fax 62252609; Chief Country Officer ERIC WORMSER.

State Street Bank and Trust Co (USA): 8 Shenton Way, 33-03 Temasek Tower, Singapore 068811; tel. 63299600; fax 62259377; Br. Man. LEE YOW FEE.

UBS AG (Switzerland): 5 Temasek Blvd, 18-00 Suntec City Tower, Singapore 038985; tel. 64318000; fax 64318188; e-mail rolf-w.gerber@wdr.com; Man. Dir and Head of Br. (Singapore) BRAD ORGILL.

UniCredito Italiano SpA (Italy): 80 Raffles Pl., 51-01 UOB Plaza 1, Singapore 048624; tel. 62325728; fax 65344300; e-mail singaporebranch@gruppocredit.it; Gen. Man. MAURIZIO BRENTEGANI.

VTB Capital PLC (Russia): 9 Battery Rd, 27-01 Straits Trading Bldg, Singapore 049910; tel. 62209422; fax 62250140; internet www.vtbcapital.com; fmrly Moscow Narodny Bank Ltd; Man. Dir JOHN PETER CARDOSA.

'Offshore' Banks

ABSA Bank Ltd (South Africa): 9 Temasek Blvd, 40-01 Suntec Tower Two, Singapore 038989; tel. 63331033; fax 63331066; Gen. Man. DAVID MEADOWS.

Agricultural Bank of China (People's Republic of China): 80 Raffles Place, 27-20 UOB Plaza 2, Singapore 048624; tel. 65355255; fax 65387960; e-mail aboc@abchina.com.sg; Gen. Man. SUN MEIYU.

Arab Bank PLC (Jordan): 80 Raffles Place, 32-20 UOB Plaza 2, Singapore 048624; tel. 65330055; fax 65322150; e-mail abplc@pacific.net.com.sg; Exec. Vice-Pres. and Area Exec. Asia Pacific KIM EUN-YOUNG.

Banca Monte dei Paschi di Siena SpA (Italy): 10 Collyer Quay, 13-01 Ocean Bldg, Singapore 0104; tel. 65352533; fax 65327996; Gen. Man. GIUSEPPE DE GIOSA.

Banca di Roma (Italy): 9 Raffles Place, 20-20 Republic Plaza II, Singapore 048619; tel. 64387509; fax 65352267; e-mail bdrsi@singnet.com.sg; Gen. Man. MARIO FATTORUSSO.

Bank of Communications (People's Republic of China): 50 Raffles Place, 26-04 Singapore Land Tower, Singapore 048623; tel. 65320335; fax 65320339; Gen. Man. NIU KE RONG.

PT Bank Mandiri (Persero) (Indonesia): 16 Collyer Quay, 28-00 Hitachi Tower, Singapore 049318; tel. 65320200; fax 65320206; Gen. Man. MUHADJIR SANGIDU.

Bank of New York Mellon (USA): 1 Temasek Ave, 02-01 Millenia Tower, Singapore 039192; tel. 64320222; fax 63374302; formed through merger of Bank of New York with Mellon Financial Corpn in 2007; Sr Vice-Pres. and Man. Dir JAI ARYA.

Bank of New Zealand (New Zealand): 5 Temasek Blvd, 15-01 Suntec City Tower, Singapore 038985; tel. 63322990; fax 63322991; Gen. Man. VIVIEN KOH.

Bank of Taiwan (Taiwan): 80 Raffles Place, 28-20 UOB Plaza 2, Singapore 048624; tel. 65365536; fax 65368203; Gen. Man. CHIOU YE-CHIN.

Bumiputra Commerce Bank Bhd (Malaysia): 7 Temasek Blvd, 37-01/02/03 Suntec Tower One, Singapore 038987; tel. 63375115; fax 63371335; e-mail bpsp3700@pacific.net.sg; Gen. Man. DHANA SEGARAM.

Canadian Imperial Bank of Commerce (Canada): 16 Collyer Quay, 04-02 Hitachi Tower, Singapore 049318; tel. 65352323; fax 65357565; Br. Man. NORMAN SIM CHEE BENG.

Chang Hwa Commercial Bank Ltd (China): 1 Finlayson Green, 08-00, Singapore 049246; tel. 65320820; fax 65320374; Gen. Man. YANG JIH-CHENG.

China Construction Bank Corpn (People's Republic of China): 9 Raffles Place, 33-01/02 Republic Plaza, Singapore 048619; tel. 65358133; fax 65356533; e-mail enquiry@ccb.com.sg; internet www.ccb.com.sg; Gen. Man. JIN YU.

Commonwealth Bank of Australia (Australia): 22-04 Singapore Land Tower, 50 Raffles Place, Singapore 048623; tel. 62243877; fax 62245812; Gen. Man. ROBERT LEWIS BUCHAN.

Crédit Industriel et Commercial (France): 63 Market St, 15-01, Singapore 048942; tel. 65366008; fax 65367008; internet www.cic.com.sg; Gen. Man. JEAN-LUC ANGLADA.

Crédit Lyonnais (Suisse) SA (Switzerland): 3 Temasek Ave, 11-01 Centennial Tower, Singapore 039190; tel. 68320900; fax 63338590; e-mail singaporebranch@creditlyonnais.ch; Man. Dir ANTOINE CANDIOTTI.

Deutsche Zentral Genossenschaftsbank (DZ Bank AG) (Germany): 50 Raffles Place, 40-01 Singapore Land Tower, Singapore 048623; tel. 64380082; fax 62230082; Gen. Man. KLAUS GERHARD BORIG.

SINGAPORE

Dexia Banque Internationale à Luxembourg (Luxembourg): 9 Raffles Place, 42-01 Republic Plaza, Singapore 048619; tel. 62227622; fax 65360201; Gen. Man. ALEXANDRE JOSSET.

DnB NOR (Norway): 8 Shenton Way, 48-01/02 Temasek Tower, Singapore 068811; tel. 62206144; fax 62249743; e-mail dnbnor.singapore@dnbnor.no; internet www.dnbnor.no.

Hana Bank (Republic of Korea): 8 Cross St, 23-06 PWC Bldg, Singapore 048424; tel. 64384100; fax 64384200; Gen. Man. CHO YOUNG-SEOK.

Hang Seng Bank Ltd (Hong Kong): 21 Collyer Quay, 14-01 HSBC Bldg, Singapore 049320; tel. 65363118; fax 65363148; e-mail sgp@hangseng.com; Country Man. ANTHONY KAM PING LEUNG.

HSH Nordbank AG (Germany): 3 Temasek Ave, 32-03 Centennial Tower, Singapore 039190; tel. 65509000; fax 65509003; e-mail info@hsh-nordbank.com.sg; Gen. Man. and Regional Head KLAUS HEINER BORITZKA.

Hua Nan Commercial Bank Ltd (Taiwan): 80 Robinson Rd, 14-03, Singapore 068898; tel. 63242566; fax 63242155; e-mail accounting@hncb.com.sg; internet sg.hncb.com; Gen. Man. HUANG YUN-LUNG.

ICICI Bank Ltd (India): 9 Raffles Place, 50-01 Republic Plaza, Singapore 048619; tel. 67239288; fax 67239268; e-mail globalinvest@icicibank.com; internet www.icicibank.com.sg; Chief. Exec. SUVEK NAMBIAR.

Korea Development Bank (Republic of Korea): 8 Shenton Way, 07-01 Temasek Tower, Singapore 068811; tel. 62248188; fax 62256540; Gen. Man. KIM BYOUNG SOO.

Krung Thai Bank Public Co Ltd (Thailand): 65 Chulia St, 32-05/08 OCBC Centre, Singapore 049513; tel. 65336691; fax 65330930; e-mail br.singapore@ktb.co.th; Gen. Man. PUMIN LEELAYOOVA.

Land Bank of Taiwan: UOB Plaza 1, 34-01 Raffles Place, Singapore 048624; tel. 63494555; fax 63494545; Gen. Man. WILSON W. B. LIN.

Lloyds TSB Bank PLC (UK): 1 Temasek Ave 18-01, Millenia Tower, Singapore 039192; tel. 65341191; fax 65322493; e-mail mktg@lloydstsb.com.sg; internet www.lloydstsb.com.sg; Country Head WALLACE WONG.

Mitsubishi Trust and Banking Corpn (Japan): 50 Raffles Place, 42-01/06 Singapore Land Tower, Singapore 048623; tel. 62259155; fax 62241857; Gen. Man. MIKIO KOBAYASHI.

Natexis Banques Populaires (France): 50 Raffles Place, 41-01, Singapore Land Tower, Singapore 048623; tel. 62241455; fax 62248651; Gen. Man. PHILIPPE PETITGAS.

Nedcor Bank Ltd (South Africa): 30 Cecil St, 10-05 Prudential Tower, Singapore 049712; tel. 64169438; fax 64388350; e-mail nedsing@nedcor.com; Gen. Man. BRIAN SHEGAR.

Nordea Bank Finland Plc (Finland): 3 Anson Rd, 22-01 Springleaf Tower, Singapore 079909; tel. 63176500; fax 63275616; e-mail singapore@nordea.com; Gen. Man. THOR ERLING KYLSTAD.

Norinchukin Bank (Japan): 80 Raffles Place, 53-01 UOB Plaza 1, Singapore 048624; tel. 65351011; fax 65352883; Gen. Man. AKITA KURIHARA.

Philippine National Bank (Philippines): 96 Somerset Rd, 04-01/04 UOL Bldg, Singapore 238183; tel. 67374646; fax 67374224; e-mail singapore@pnb.com.ph; Vice-Pres. and Gen. Man. RODELO G. FRANCO.

Raiffeisen Zentralbank Österreich Aktiengesellschaft (Austria): 50 Raffles Place, 45-01 Singapore Land Tower, Singapore 048623; tel. 62259578; fax 62253973; Gen. Man. RAINER SILHAVY.

Royal Bank of Canada (Canada): 20 Raffles Place, 27-03/08 Ocean Towers, Singapore 048620; tel. 65369206; fax 65322804; Gen. Man. TREVOR DAVID WYNN.

Shinhan Bank (Republic of Korea): 50 Raffles Place, 04-02/03 Singapore Land Tower, Singapore 048623; tel. 65361144; fax 65331244; merged with Chohun Bank 2006; Gen. Man. CHOI HEUNG MIN.

Siam Commercial Bank Public Company Ltd (Thailand): 16 Collyer Quay, 25-01 Hitachi Tower, Singapore 049318; tel. 65364338; fax 65364728; Gen. Man. BANDIT ROJANAVONGSE.

Skandinaviska Enskilda Banken AB Publ (Sweden): 50 Raffles Place, 36-01 Singapore Land Tower, Singapore 048623; tel. 62235644; fax 62253047; Gen. Man. SVEN BJÖRKMAN.

State Bank of India (India): 6 Shenton Way, 22-08 DBS Bldg Tower Two, Singapore 068809; tel. 62222033; fax 62253348; e-mail sbinsgsg@pacific.net.sg; CEO PADMA RAMASUBBAN.

Sumitomo Trust & Banking Co Ltd (Japan): 8 Shenton Way, 45-01 Temasek Tower, Singapore 068811; tel. 62249055; fax 62242873; Gen. Man. MASAYUKI IMANAKA.

Svenska Handelsbanken AB (publ) (Sweden): 65 Chulia St, 21-01/04 OCBC Centre, Singapore 049513; tel. 65323800; fax 65344909; Gen. Man. JAN BIRGER DJERF.

Toronto-Dominion (South East Asia) Ltd (Canada): 15-02 Millenia Tower, 1 Temasek Ave, Singapore 039192; tel. 64346000; fax 63369500; Br. Dir AKHILESHWAR LAMBA.

Union de Banques Arabes et Françaises (UBAF) (France): 6 Temasek Blvd, 25-04/05 Suntec Tower Four, Singapore 038986; tel. 63336188; fax 63336789; e-mail ubafsg@singnet.com.sg; Gen. Man. ERIC REINHART.

Westpac Banking Corpn (Australia): 77 Robinson Rd, 19-00 SIA Bldg, Singapore 068896; tel. 65309898; fax 65326781; e-mail yhlee@westpac.wm.au; Gen. Man. CHRISTOPHER DAVID RAND.

Woori Bank (Republic of Korea): 5 Shenton Way, 17-03 UIC Bldg, Singapore 068808; tel. 62235555; fax 62259530; e-mail combksp@singnet.com.sg; Gen. Man. PARK DONG YOUNG.

Bankers' Association

The Association of Banks in Singapore: 10 Shenton Way, 12-08 MAS Bldg, Singapore 079117; tel. 62244300; fax 62241785; e-mail banks@abs.org.sg; internet www.abs.org.sg; f. 1973; Chair. DAVID P. CONNOR.

STOCK EXCHANGE

Singapore Exchange Ltd (SGX): 2 Shenton Way, 19-00 SGX Centre One, Singapore 068804; tel. 62368888; fax 65356994; e-mail query@sgx.com; internet www.sgx.com; f. 1999; demutualized and integrated securities and derivatives exchange; Chair. J. Y. PILLAY; CEO MAGNUS BÖCKER; Chief Finance Officer SECK WAI KWONG.

INSURANCE

The insurance industry is supervised by the Monetary Authority of Singapore (see Banking). In May 2011 there were 157 insurance companies, comprising 62 direct insurers (10 life insurance, 46 general insurance, six composite insurers), 28 professional reinsurers (three life reinsurers, 16 general reinsurers, nine composite reinsurers), six authorized reinsurers (two life reinsurers, three general reinsurers, one composite reinsurer) and 61 captive insurers.

Domestic Companies

Life Insurance

Aviva Ltd: 4 Shenton Way, 01-01, SGX Centre 2, Singapore 068807; tel. 68277988; fax 68277900; internet www.aviva-singapore.com.sg; f. 2002; Prin. Officer KEITH PERKINS.

Axa Life Insurance Singapore Pte Ltd: 143 Cecil St, 03-01/10 GB Bldg, Singapore 069542; tel. 68805500; fax 68805501; e-mail comsvc@axa-life.com.sg; internet www.axa-life.com.sg; Prin. Officer RICHARD MARC SHERMON.

China Life Insurance Co Ltd: 105 Cecil St, 18-00 and 19-00 The Octagon, Singapore 069534; tel. 62222366; fax 62221033; Prin. Officer SHEN NAN NING.

Friends Provident International Ltd (Singapore): 63 Market St, 06-05, Singapore 048942; tel. 63274019; fax 63274020; e-mail singapore.enquiries@fpiom.com; Prin. Officer CHRISTOPHER GAVIN GILL.

International Medical Insurers Pte Ltd: 585 North Bridge Rd, 13-00, Raffles Hospital, Singapore 188770; tel. 62982266; fax 63112396; e-mail enquiries@imi.sg; internet www.imi.sg; f. 1996; Prin. Officer VICTOR LYE.

Manulife (Singapore) Pte Ltd: 491B River Valley Rd, 07-00 Valley Pt, Singapore 248373; tel. 67371221; fax 68362374; e-mail service@manulife.com.sg; internet www.manulife.com.sg; acquired John Hancock Life Assurance Co Ltd in Dec. 2004; Pres. and CEO DARREN THOMSON.

TM Asia Life Singapore Ltd: 80 Anson Rd, 14-00 Fuji Xerox Towers, Singapore 079907; tel. 62243181; fax 62239120; e-mail asialife@asialife.com.sg; internet www.tmasialife.com; f. 1948; fmrly The Asia Life Assurance Society Ltd; Man. Dir ARTHUR LEE KING CHI.

Transamerica Life (Singapore) Ltd: 1 Finlayson Green, 13-00, Singapore 049246; tel. 62120620; fax 62120621; internet www.transamerica.com.sg; wholly owned subsidiary of Transamerica Occidental Life Insurance Co; Prin. Officer LAURENCE WONG YUEN TIN.

Transamerica Occidental Life Insurance Co: 9 Raffles Place, 53-02, Republic Plaza, Singapore 048619; tel. 62362366; fax 62362123; internet www.transamerica.com.sg; Prin. Officer LAURENCE WONG YUEN TIN.

UOB Life Assurance Ltd: 156 Cecil St, 10-01 Far Eastern Bank Bldg, Singapore 069544; tel. 62278477; fax 62243012; e-mail uoblife@uobgroup.com; internet www.uoblife.com.sg; Man. Dir TOI SEE JONG.

SINGAPORE

Zurich International Life (Singapore) Ltd: 50 Raffles Pl., 23-02 Singapore Land Tower, Singapore 048623; tel. 68766750; fax 68766751; Regional Dir CARLOS SABUGUEIRO.

General Insurance

Allianz Insurance Company of Singapore Pte Ltd: 3 Temasek Ave, 09-01 Centennial Tower, Singapore 039190; tel. 62972529; fax 62971956; e-mail askme@allianz.com.sg; internet www.allianz.com.sg; est. by merger between Allianz Insurance (Singapore) Pte Ltd and AGF Insurance (Singapore) Pte Ltd; Man. Dir ROWAN D'ARCY.

Asia Insurance Co Ltd: 2 Finlayson Green, 03-00 Asia Insurance Bldg, Singapore 049247; tel. 62243181; fax 62214355; e-mail asiains@asiainsurance.com.sg; internet www.asiainsurance.com.sg; f. 1923; Prin. Officer and Exec. Dir LARRY CHAN; Gen. Man. TAN KAH HO.

Asian Securitization and Infrastructure Assurance (Pte) Ltd: 9 Temasek Blvd, 38-01 Suntec Tower 2, Singapore 038989; tel. 63342555; fax 63342777; e-mail general@asialtd.com; Dir ELEANOR L. LIPSEY.

Aviva General Insurance Ltd: 4 Shenton Way, 21-01 SGX Centre 2, Singapore 068807; tel. 68277888; fax 68277800; e-mail service@aviva-gi.com; internet www.aviva-gi.com.sg; subsidiary of Mitsui Sumitomo Insurance Co Ltd following acquisition in 2004.

Axa Insurance Singapore Pte Ltd: 143 Cecil St, 01-01 GB Bldg, Singapore 069542; tel. 68804741; fax 68804740; e-mail customer.service@axa.com.sg; internet www.axa.com.sg; CEO BERNARD MARSEILLE.

Cosmic Insurance Corpn Ltd: 410 North Bridge Rd, 04-01 Cosmic Insurance Bldg, Singapore 188726; tel. 63387633; fax 63397805; e-mail query@cosmic.com.sg; internet www.cosmic.com.sg; f. 1971; Gen. Man. SWEE LEE CHUN.

ECICS-COFACE Guarantee Co (Singapore) Ltd: 7 Temasek Blvd, 10-03 Suntec City Tower 1, Singapore 038987; tel. 63374779; fax 63389267; e-mail ecics@ecics.com.sg; internet www.ecics.com.sg; Chair. KWAH THIAM HOCK; Asst Vice-Pres. KIM LIN MIN.

First Capital Insurance Ltd: 6 Raffles Quay 21-00, Singapore 048580; tel. 62222311; fax 62223547; e-mail enquiry@first-insurance.com.sg; internet www.first-insurance.com.sg; CEO RAMASWAMY ATHAPPAN.

India International Insurance Pte Ltd: 64 Cecil St, 04-00/05-00 IOB Bldg, Singapore 049711; tel. 63476100; fax 62244174; e-mail insure@iii.com.sg; internet www.iii.com.sg; f. 1987; all non-life insurance; CEO B. SUNDARRAMAN.

Kemper International Insurance Co (Pte) Ltd: 3 Shenton Way, 22-09 Shenton House, Singapore 068805; tel. 68369120; fax 68369121; e-mail vchia@kemper.com.sg; internet www.kemper.com.sg; Gen. Man. VIOLET CHIA.

Liberty Insurance Pte Ltd: 51 Club St, 03-00, Singapore 069428; tel. 62218611; fax 62263360; e-mail feedback@libertycitystate.com.sg; internet www.libertyinsurance.com.sg; division of Liberty Mutual Group (USA); fmrly Citystate Insurance Pte Ltd; Man. Dir A. K. CHER.

Mitsui Sumitomo Insurance (Singapore) Pte Ltd: 16 Raffles Quay, 24-01 Hong Leong Bldg, Singapore 048581; tel. 62209644; fax 62256371; internet www.ms-ins.com.sg; fmrly Mitsui Marine and Fire Insurance (Asia) Private Ltd; merged with The Sumitomo Marine and Fire Insurance Co Ltd and name changed as above in 2001; Man. Dir TAKAAKI NAKAMURA.

Royal & Sun Alliance Insurance (Singapore) Ltd: 77 Robinson Rd, 17-00 SIA Bldg, Singapore 068896; tel. 64230888; fax 64230798; e-mail customer.service@sg.royalsun.com; internet www.royalsunalliance.com.sg; Man. Dir and CEO EDMUND LIM.

SHC Capital Ltd: 302 Orchard Rd, 09-01 Tong Bldg, Singapore 238862; tel. 68299199; fax 68299249; e-mail shccapital@shcsb.com.sg; internet www.shccapital.com.sg; f. 1956; fmrly The Nanyang Insurance Co Ltd; name changed as above following takeover in June 2004; Dir and Prin. Officer QUEK SUN HUI.

Singapore Aviation and General Insurance Co (Pte) Ltd: 25 Airline Rd, 06-A Airline House, Singapore 819829; tel. 65423333; fax 65450221; f. 1976; Man. AMARJIT KAUR SIDHU.

Standard Steamship Owners' Protection and Indemnity Association (Asia) Ltd: 140 Cecil St, 15-00 PIL Bldg, Singapore 069540; tel. 65062896; fax 62211082; e-mail p&i.singapore@ctcplc.com; internet www.standard-club.com; Prin. Officer ROBERT DRUMMOND.

Tenet Insurance Co Ltd: 10 Collyer Quay, 04-01 Ocean Bldg, Singapore 049315; tel. 65326022; fax 65333871; Chair. ONG CHOO ENG.

The Tokio Marine & Fire Insurance Co (Singapore) Pte Ltd: 6 Shenton Way, 23-08 DBS Bldg Tower Two, Singapore 068809; tel. 62216111; fax 62240895; Man. Dir KYOZO HANAJIMA.

United Overseas Insurance Ltd: 156 Cecil St, 09-01 Far Eastern Bank Bldg, Singapore 069544; tel. 62227733; fax 63273870; e-mail contactus@uoi.com.sg; internet www.uoi.com.sg; f. 1971; Man. Dir DAVID CHAN MUN WAI.

Zürich Insurance (Singapore) Pte Ltd: 78 Shenton Way, 06-01, Singapore 079120; tel. 62202466; fax 62255749; Prin. Officer and Man. Dir RONALD CHENG JUE SENG.

Composite Insurance

American International Assurance Co Ltd: 1 Robinson Rd, AIA Tower, Singapore 048542; tel. 62918000; fax 65385802; internet www.aia.com.sg; Prin. Officer MARK O'DELL.

Great Eastern Life Assurance Co Ltd: 1 Pickering St, 13-01 Great Eastern Centre, Singapore 048659; tel. 62482000; fax 65322214; e-mail wecare@lifeisgreat.com.sg; internet www.lifeisgreat.com.sg; f. 1908; Dir and CEO TAN BENG LEE.

HSBC Insurance (Singapore) Pte Ltd: 3 Killiney Rd, 10-01/09, Winsland House 1, Singapore 239519; tel. 62256111; fax 62212188; internet www.insurance.hsbc.com.sg; Prin. Officer JASON DOMINIC SADLER.

NTUC Income Insurance Co-operative Ltd: 75 Bras Basah Rd, NTUC Income Centre, Singapore 189557; tel. 63363322; fax 63381500; e-mail inbox@income.wm.sg; internet www.income.com.sg; CEO TAN SUEE CHIEH; Gen. Man. ALOYSIUS TEO SENG LEE.

Overseas Assurance Corpn Ltd: 1 Pickering St, 13-01 Great Eastern Centre, Singapore 048659; tel. 62482000; fax 65322214; e-mail general@oac.com.sg; internet www.oac.com.sg; f. 1920; wholly owned subsidiary of Great Eastern Holdings; Chair. MICHAEL WONG PAKSHONG.

Prudential Assurance Co Singapore (Pte) Ltd: 30 Cecil St, 30-01 Prudential Tower, Singapore 049712; tel. 65358988; fax 65354043; e-mail customer.service@prudential.com.sg; internet www.prudential.com.sg; CEO TAN SUEE CHIEH.

Associations

General Insurance Association of Singapore: 112 Robinson Rd, 05-03 HB Robinson, Singapore 068902; tel. 62218788; fax 62272051; e-mail feedback@gia.org.sg; internet www.gia.org.sg; f. 1965; Pres. DEREK TEO; Exec. Dir MARK LIM.

Life Insurance Association, Singapore: 20 Cross St, 02-07/08 China Court, China Sq. Central, Singapore 048422; tel. 64388900; fax 64386989; e-mail lia@lia.org.sg; internet www.lia.org.sg; f. 1967; Pres. HAK LEH TAN.

Reinsurance Brokers' Association: 69 Amoy St, Singapore 069888; tel. 63723189; fax 62241091; e-mail secretariat@rbas.org.sg; internet www.rbas.org.sg; f. 1995; Chair. RICHARD AUSTEN.

Singapore Insurance Brokers' Association: 138 Cecil St, 15-00 Cecil Court, Singapore 069538; tel. 62227777; fax 62220022; e-mail siba@stcsamasmgt.com.sg; Pres. ANTHONY LIM; Vice-Pres. DAVID LUM.

Singapore Reinsurers' Association: 85 Amoy St, Singapore 069904; tel. 63247388; fax 62248910; e-mail secretariat@sraweb.org.sg; internet www.sraweb.org.sg; f. 1979; Chair. CHRISTOPHER HO SIOW SOONG.

Trade and Industry

Temasek Holdings Pte Ltd: 60B Orchard Rd, 06-18 Tower 2, The Atrium@ Orchard, Singapore 238891; tel. 68286828; fax 68211188; internet www.temasek.com.sg; f. 1974; 100% govt-owned; active shareholder and investor in banking and financial services, real estate, transport, infrastructure, telecommunications, media, bioscience and health care, education, consumer services, engineering and technology, energy and resources; revenue S $79,615m. (2008/09); Chair. S. DHANABALAN; Exec. Dir and CEO HO CHING.

GOVERNMENT AGENCIES

Housing and Development Board: 480 Lorong 6, Toa Payoh, Singapore 310480; tel. 64901111; fax 64901033; e-mail hdbmailbox@hdb.gov.sg; internet www.hdb.gov.sg; f. 1960; public housing authority; Chair. JAMES KOH CHER SIANG; CEO TAY KIM POH.

Singapore Land Authority (SLA): 55 Newton Rd, 12-01 Revenue House, Singapore 307987; tel. 63239829; fax 63239937; e-mail SLA_enquiry@sla.gov.sg; internet www.sla.gov.sg; f. 2001; est. by merger of Land Office, Singapore Land Registry, Survey Dept and Land Systems Support Unit; responsible for management and devt of state land resources; Chair. CHALY MAH; CEO VINCENT HOONG SENG LEI.

Urban Redevelopment Authority (URA): 45 Maxwell Rd, URA Centre, Singapore 069118; tel. 62216666; fax 62275069; e-mail

SINGAPORE

ura_email@ura.gov.sg; internet www.ura.gov.sg; f. 1974; est. to replace Urban Renewal Dept (f. 1967); statutory board; responsible for national planning; Chair. ALAN CHAN HENG LOON; CEO NG LANG.

DEVELOPMENT ORGANIZATIONS

Agency for Science, Technology and Research (A*STAR): 1 Fusionopolis Way, 20-10 Connexis North Tower, Singapore 138632; tel. 68266111; fax 67771711; e-mail contact@a-star.edu.sg; internet www.a-star.edu.sg; f. 1991; fmrly National Science and Technology Board; statutory board; responsible for the devt of science and technology; Chair. LIM CHUAN POH; Man. Dir LOW TECK SENG.

Applied Research Corpn (ARC): Singapore; f. 1973; independent non-profit-making research and consultancy org. aiming to facilitate and enhance the use of technology and expertise from tertiary institutions to benefit industry and businesses.

Asian Infrastructure Fund (AIF): Singapore; f. 1994; promotes and directs investment into regional projects; Chair. MOEEN QURESHI.

Economic Development Board (EDB): 250 North Bridge Rd, 28-00 Raffles City Tower, Singapore 179101; tel. 68326832; fax 68326565; e-mail clientservices@edb.gov.sg; internet www.edb.gov.sg; f. 1961; statutory body for industrial planning, devt and promotion of investments in manufacturing, services and local business; Chair. LEO YIP SENG CHEONG; Man. Dir Dr BEH SWAN GIN.

Government of Singapore Investment Corpn Pte Ltd (GIC): 168 Robinson Rd, 37-01 Capital Tower, Singapore 068912; tel. 68898888; fax 68898722; e-mail contactgic@gic.com.sg; internet www.gic.com.sg; f. 1981; Chair. LEE HSIEN LOONG; Exec. Dir Dr TONY TAN KENG YAM.

Infocomm Development Authority of Singapore (IDA): see under Telecommunications.

International Enterprise Singapore: 230 Victoria St, Level 10, Bugis Junction Office Tower, Singapore 188024; tel. 63376628; fax 63376898; e-mail enquiry@iesingapore.gov.sg; internet www.iesingapore.gov.sg; f. 1983; formed to develop and expand international trade; fmrly Trade Development Board; statutory body; Chair. SUNNY VERGHESE; CEO CHONG LIT CHEONG.

JTC Corpn: The JTC Summit, 8 Jurong Town Hall Rd, Singapore 609434; tel. 65600056; fax 65655301; e-mail askjtc@jtc.gov.sg; internet www.jtc.gov.sg; f. 1968; statutory body responsible for planning, promoting and developing industrial space; Chair. CEDRIC FOO; CEO MANOHAR KHIATANI.

Standards, Productivity and Innovation Board Singapore (SPRING): 1 Fusionopolis Way, 01-02 South Tower, Solaris, Singapore 138628; tel. 62786666; fax 62786667; e-mail enterpriseone@spring.gov.sg; internet www.spring.gov.sg; f. 1996; est. as Singapore Productivity and Standards Bd (PSB), following merger of Singapore Institute of Standards and Industrial Research and the Nat. Productivity Bd; present name adopted 2001; work-force devt, training, productivity and innovation promotion, standards devt, etc.; assistance for SMEs; Chair. PHILIP YEO; Chief Exec. PNG CHEONG BOON.

CHAMBERS OF COMMERCE

Singapore Business Federation (SBF): 10 Hoe Chiang Rd, 22-01 Keppel Towers, 089315 Singapore; tel. 68276828; fax 68276807; internet www.sbf.org.sg; f. 2002; est. following restructuring of Singapore Fed. of Chambers of Commerce and Industry; Chair. TONY CHEW LEONG CHEE; represents over 15,000 cos; constituent mems incl. the following:

Singapore Chinese Chamber of Commerce and Industry: 47 Hill St, 09-00 Singapore 179365; tel. 63378381; fax 63390605; e-mail corporate@sccci.org.sg; internet www.sccci.org.sg; f. 1906; Pres. TEO SIONG SENG; Sec.-Gen. LIM SAH SOON.

Singapore Indian Chamber of Commerce and Industry: 31 Stanley St, SICCI Bldg, Singapore 068740; tel. 62222855; fax 62231707; e-mail sicci@sicci.com; internet www.sicci.com; f. 1924; Chair. RANGARAJAN NARAYANAMOHAN; CEO HERNAIKH SINGH.

Singapore International Chamber of Commerce: 6 Raffles Quay, 10-01 John Hancock Tower, Singapore 048580; tel. 65000988; fax 62242785; e-mail general@sicc.com; internet www.sicc.com.sg; f. 1837; Chair. JENNIE CHUA.

Singapore Malay Chamber of Commerce and Industry (SMCCI): 15 Jalan Pinang, Singapore 199147; tel. 62979296; fax 63924527; e-mail inquiry@smcci.org.sg; internet www.smcci.org.sg; f. 1956; Pres. ABDUL ROHIM SARIP.

Singapore Manufacturers' Federation (SMa): 2 Bukit Merah Central, 03-00 SPRING Singapore Bldg, Singapore 159835; tel. 68263000; fax 68263008; e-mail hq@smafederation.org.sg; internet www.smafederation.org.sg; f. 1932 as Singapore Manufacturers' Asscn; renamed Singapore Confed. of Industries in 1996;

Directory

name changed as above in 2002; Pres. GEORGE HUANG; Sec.-Gen. GWEE SENG KWONG.

INDUSTRIAL AND TRADE ASSOCIATIONS

Association of Singapore Marine Industries (ASMI): 30 Tuas Ave 10, 07-01 Freight Links E-Logistics Technopark, Singapore 639150; tel. 68633038; fax 68632881; e-mail admin@asmi.com; internet www.asmi.com; f. 1968; 12 hon. mems, 70 assoc. mems, 51 ordinary mems (Oct. 2003); Pres. WONG WENG SON.

Singapore Commodity Exchange (SICOM): 2 Shenton Way, 19-00 SGX Centre 1, Singapore 068804; tel. 62368888; fax 65366648; internet www.sicom.com.sg; f. 1968; est. as Rubber Asscn of Singapore; adopted present name in 1994; regulates, promotes, develops and supervises commodity futures trading in Singapore, including the establishment and dissemination of official prices for various grades and types of rubber; provides clearing facilities; endorses certificates of origin and licences for packers, shippers and mfrs; Chair. MAGNUS BOCKER; CEO JEREMY ANG PENG LEONG.

EMPLOYERS' ORGANIZATION

Singapore National Employers Federation (SNEF): 22-00 Keppel Towers, 10 Hoe Chiang Rd, Singapore 089315; tel. 68276827; fax 68276800; e-mail webmaster@snef.org.sg; internet www.sgemployers.com; f. 1948 as Fed. of Industrialists and Traders in Singapore; name changed to Singapore Employers Fed. in 1953; present name adopted in 1980 following merger with Nat. Employers Council; Pres. STEPHEN LEE CHING YEN.

UTILITIES

Electricity and Gas

Singapore Power Ltd: 111 Somerset Rd 10-01, Singapore 238164; tel. 68238888; fax 68238188; e-mail spservices@singaporepower.com.sg; internet www.singaporepower.com.sg; incorporated in 1995 to take over the piped gas and electricity utility operations of the Public Utilities Board (see Water), which now acts as a regulatory authority for the privately owned cos; 100% owned by government holding co, Temasek Holdings Pte Ltd; f. 1995; subsidiaries incl. PowerGrid, PowerGas, SP Services, Singapore Power International, Singapore District Cooling and SP Telecommunications; Chair. NG KEE CHOE; CEO QUEK POH HUAT.

Water

Public Utilities Board: 40 Scotts Rd, 22-01 Environment Bldg, Singapore 228231; tel. 62358888; fax 62840363; e-mail pubone@singnet.com.sg; internet www.pub.gov.sg; f. 1963; statutory board responsible for water supply; manages Singapore's water system to optimize use of water resources; develops additional water sources; Chair. TAN GEE PAW; Chief Exec. KHOO TENG CHYE.

TRADE UNIONS

At the end of 2003 there were 68 employees' trade unions and associations, with 417,166 members, and three employer unions, with 2,052 members.

National Trades Union Congress (NTUC): NTUC Centre, 1 Marina Blvd 10-01, Singapore 018989; tel. 62138008; fax 63273740; e-mail membership@ntuc.org.sg; internet www.ntuc.org.sg; f. 1961; 60 affiliated unions, 6 affiliated assocs and approx. 540,000 mems (2009); Pres. JOHN DE PAYVA; Sec.-Gen. LIM SWEE SAY.

Transport

RAILWAYS

Singapore is linked to the Malaysian railway system via the Johor causeway. Branch lines provide a link to the industrial estate at Jurong.

The Mass Rapid Transit (MRT) system opened in 1990. In 2002 the extension of the East–West line to Changi Airport was completed. A 33.3-km orbital line was to link all the radial lines into the city with the last phase of construction scheduled for completion in 2012. In early 2010 the rail length of the MRT was 109.4 km.

Singapore's first Light Rapid Transit (LRT) system, the Bukit Panjang LRT, opened in 1998. Construction of the 2.1-km Sentosa Express monorail system was completed in June 2006, and operations commenced in January 2007. In 2008 the LRT covered 28.8 km of the total rail length.

Land Transport Authority: 1 Hampshire Rd, Singapore 219428; tel. 63757100; fax 63757200; internet www.lta.gov.sg; f. 1995; planning, devt and man. of the land transport system; Chair. MICHAEL LIM CHOO SAN; Chief Exec. CHEW HOCK YONG.

SMRT Corpn Ltd: 251 North Bridge Rd, Singapore 179102; tel. 63311000; fax 63340247; e-mail corpcomms@smrt.com.sg; internet

SINGAPORE

Directory

www.smrt.com.sg; f. 1987; operates the MRT and LRT rail systems, a fleet of more than 950 buses and more than 2,500 taxis (2010); Chair. KOH YONG GUAN; Pres. and CEO SAW PHAIK HWA.

ROADS

In 2007 Singapore had a total of 3,297 km of roads, of which 153 km were motorway; in that year 100% of the road network was paved. In 1990 the Government introduced a quota system to control the number of vehicles using the roads. This was replaced by a system of Electronic Road Pricing (ERP) in 1998, whereby each vehicle was charged according to road use in congested areas. The 12-km Kallang–Paya Lebar expressway, on which construction had commenced in 2001, became fully operational in September 2008; with approximately 9 km of the expressway under ground, it was the longest underground expressway in South-East Asia.

SHIPPING

Singapore is one of the world's busiest ports. The Port of Singapore Authority operates six cargo terminals: Tanjong Pagar Terminal, Keppel Terminal, Brani Terminal, Pasir Panjang Terminal, Sembawang Terminal and Jurong Port. Tanjong Pagar Terminal and Keppel Terminal have the capacity to handle 10.7m. 20-foot equivalent units (TEUs). The third container terminal, Brani, built on an offshore island connected to the mainland by a causeway, has a capacity of 5.5m. TEUs. Pasir Panjang Terminal, Singapore's main gateway for conventional cargo, has five deep-water berths, eight coastal berths and 17 lighter berths. Sembawang Terminal has three deep-water berths and one coastal berth. This terminal is the main point of entry for car carriers, and it also handles steel and timber products. Jurong Port (which handles general and dry-bulk cargo, is situated in south-western Singapore, and serves the Jurong Industrial Estate) has 20 deep-water berths and one coastal berth. A new container terminal, at Pasir Panjang, was officially opened in 2000. The second phase of building work, comprising four separate sub-phases, was completed in 2009. The final two phases of construction were scheduled for completion in 2013. In December 2009 the Singapore merchant fleet comprised 2,563 vessels, with a total displacement of 41,046,600 grt.

Maritime and Port Authority of Singapore: 460 Alexandra Rd, 18-00 PSA Bldg, Singapore 119963; tel. 63751600; fax 62759247; e-mail shipping@mpa.gov.sg; internet www.mpa.gov.sg; f. 1996; regulatory body responsible for promotion and development of the port, overseeing all port and maritime matters in Singapore; Chair. LUCIEN WONG; Chief Exec. LAM YI YOUNG.

PSA International Pte Ltd: 460 Alexandra Rd, 38th Floor, PSA Bldg, Singapore 119963; tel. 62747111; fax 62794677; e-mail gca@psa.com.sg; internet www.internationalpsa.com; f. 1964; est. as Port of Singapore Authority; made a corporate entity in 1997 in preparation for privatization; present name adopted 2003; wholly owned by Temasek Holdings Pte Ltd; responsible for the provision and maintenance of port facilities and services; participates in 28 port projects in 16 countries in Asia, Europe and the Americas; Group Chair. SIEW WAH FOCK; Group CEO EDDIE TEH.

Major Shipping Companies

American President Lines Ltd (APL): 456 Alexandra Rd, 08-00 NOL Bldg, Singapore 119962; tel. 62789000; fax 62784900; e-mail erep_asia@apl.com; internet www.apl.com; container services to North and South Asia, the USA and the Middle East; Pres. ENG AIK MENG.

Glory Ship Management Private Ltd: 24 Raffles Place, 17-01/02, Clifford Centre, Singapore 048621; tel. 65361986; fax 65361987; e-mail gene@gloryship.com.sg.

Guan Guan Shipping Pte Ltd: 2 Finlayson Green, 13-05 Asia Insurance Bldg, Singapore 049247; tel. 65343988; fax 62276776; e-mail golden@golden.com.sg; f. 1955; shipowners and agents; cargo services to East and West Malaysia, Indonesia, Pakistan, Sri Lanka, Bengal Bay ports, Persian (Arabian) Gulf ports, Hong Kong and China; Man. Dir RICHARD THIO.

IMC Shipping Co Pte Ltd: 5 Temasek Blvd, 37-01 Suntec City Tower, Singapore 038987; tel. 64119800; fax 63379715; e-mail corpcomms@imcpaa.com; internet www.imcshipping.com; Chair. FRANK TSAO WEN KING.

Maersk Singapore Pte Ltd: 200 Cantonment Rd, 10-100, South-point, Singapore 089763; tel. 63238323; fax 62247649; e-mail sinlinmng@maersk.com; f. 1929; operates under the brand name of Maersk Line; Head, Asia Pacific THOMAS KNUDSEN.

Neptune Orient Lines Ltd: 456 Alexandra Rd, 05-00 NOL Bldg, Singapore 119962; tel. 62789000; fax 62784900; e-mail nol_group_corp_comms@nol.com.sg; internet www.nol.com.sg; f. 1968; liner containerized services on the Far East/Europe, Far East/North America, Straits/Australia, South Asia/Europe and South-East Asia, Far East/Mediterranean routes; logistics services and terminals; Chair. CHENG WAI KEUNG; Group Pres. and CEO RON WIDDOWS.

Ocean Tankers (Pte) Ltd: 37 Tuas Rd, Singapore 638503; tel. 68632202; fax 68639480; e-mail corporate@oceantankers.com.sg; internet www.oceantankers.com.sg; Marine Supt V. LIM.

Osprey Maritime Ltd: 8 Cross St, 24-02/03 PWC Bldg, Singapore 048424; tel. 62129722; fax 65570450; CEO PETER GEORGE COSTALAS.

Pacific International Lines (Pte) Ltd: 140 Cecil St, 03-00 PIL Bldg, POB 3206, Singapore 069540; tel. 62218133; fax 62273933; e-mail sherry.chua@sgp.pilship.com; internet www.pilship.com; shipowners, agents and managers; liner services to South-East Asia, the Far East, India, the Red Sea, the Persian (Arabian) Gulf, West and East Africa; container services to South-East Asia; worldwide chartering, freight forwarding, container manufacturing, depot operators, container freight station operator; Exec. Chair. Y. C. CHANG; Man. Dir S. S. TEO.

Petroships Private Ltd: 460 Alexandra Rd, 25-04 PSA Bldg, Singapore 119963; tel. 62731122; fax 62732200; e-mail gen@petroships.com.sg; Man. Dir KENNETH KEE.

Syabas Tankers Pte Ltd: 10 Anson Rd, 34-10 International Plaza, Singapore 0207; tel. 62259522.

Tanker Pacific Management (Singapore) Private Ltd: 1 Temasek Ave, 38-01 Millenia Tower, Singapore; tel. 64335888; fax 63365311; internet www.tanker.com.sg; Chair. and CEO ALASTAIR MCGREGOR.

CIVIL AVIATION

Singapore's international airport at Changi was opened in 1981. Construction of a terminal solely for the use of budget carriers was completed in 2006, thereby increasing the airport's total capacity to 64m. passengers a year. Construction of a third main terminal was completed in 2008. A second airport at Seletar operates as a base for charter and training flights.

Civil Aviation Authority of Singapore: Singapore Changi Airport, POB 1, Singapore 918141; tel. 65421122; fax 65421231; e-mail thennarasee_R@caas.gov.sg; internet www.caas.gov.sg; responsible for regulatory and advisory services, air services development, airport management and development, and airspace management and organization; Chair. LEE HSIEN YANG; Dir-Gen. YAP ONG HENG.

Jetstar Asia Airways: Singapore Changi Airport T1, POB 323, Singapore 918144; tel. 93470208; internet www.jetstar.com; f. 2004; 49% owned by Qantas (Australia); service to regional destinations; merged with ValuAir in 2005; continues to operate under the Jetstar name; CEO CHONG PHIT LIAN.

SilkAir: 371 Beach Rd Unit, 17-08, Singapore 199597; tel. 62238888; fax 65426286; internet www.silkair.com; f. 1975; fmrly Tradewinds Private; wholly owned subsidiary of Singapore Airlines Ltd; began scheduled services in 1989; Chair. GOH CHOON PHONG; CEO MARVIN TAN.

Singapore Airlines Ltd (SIA): Airline House, 25 Airline Rd, Singapore 819829; tel. 65415880; fax 65456083; e-mail investor_relations@singaporeair.com.sg; internet www.singaporeair.com; f. 1972; passenger services to over 90 destinations in about 40 countries; Chair. STEPHEN LEE CHING YEN; CEO CHEW CHOON SENG.

Tiger Airways: Singapore Changi Airport, POB 82, Singapore 918143; tel. 68222300; fax 68222310; internet www.tigerairways.com; f. 2003; 49% owned by Singapore Airlines, 24% owned by US co Indigo Partners, 11% owned by Temasek Holdings Pte Ltd; services to 10 regional destinations; Chair. GERARD EE HOCK KIM; CEO TONY DAVIS.

ValuAir: Singapore Changi Airport T1, POB 323, Singapore 918144; tel. 93470208; internet www.jetstar.com/vf/en/index.aspx; f. 2003; merged with Jetstar Asia in 2005; continues to operate under the ValuAir name; provides low-cost services between Singapore and Indonesia; CEO CHONG PHIT LIAN.

Tourism

Singapore's tourist attractions include its blend of cultures and excellent shopping facilities. In 2005 the Government legalized gambling on the island, rescinding a 40-year ban and allowing for the construction of two major casino resorts, at Marina Bay and on Sentosa Island. The first hotels and the casino at the Sentosa resort opened in early 2010. A phased opening of the Marina Bay resort commenced in June 2010. The resorts were expected significantly to increase the number of visitors to Singapore. Foreign visitor arrivals rose from fewer than 9.7m. in 2009 to exceed 11.6m. in 2010. Receipts from tourism (excluding passenger transport) totalled US $10,583m. in 2008.

Singapore Tourism Board: Tourism Court, 1 Orchard Spring Lane, Singapore 247729; tel. 67366622; fax 67369423; e-mail

SINGAPORE

feedback@stb.com.sg; internet www.stb.com.sg; f. 1964; Chair. SIMON ISRAEL; Chief Exec. AW KAH PENG.

Defence

As assessed at November 2010, the total strength of the armed forces was 72,500 (including 39,000 conscripts): army 50,000 (35,000 conscripts), navy an estimated 9,000 (1,000 conscripts), air force 13,500 (3,000 conscripts). Military service lasts 24 months. Army reserves numbered an estimated 312,500. Paramilitary forces of an estimated 93,800 comprised the Singapore police force, marine and Gurkha guard battalions, and a civil defence force (numbering an estimated 81,800, including 3,200 conscripts). Singapore is a participant in the Five-Power Defence Arrangements with Malaysia, Australia, New Zealand and the United Kingdom.

Defence Expenditure: Budgeted at S $12,300m. for 2011.
Chief of the Defence Forces: Maj.-Gen. NEO KIAN HONG.
Chief of the Army: Brig.-Gen. CHAN CHUN SING.
Chief of the Air Force: Brig.-Gen. NG CHEE MENG.
Chief of the Navy: Rear-Adm. NG CHEE PENG.

Education

From 2003 education in Singapore became compulsory for the first time at primary level, the six years of which are granted free to all children. Less able pupils are afforded an additional two years in which to complete primary education, under the New Primary Education System implemented in 1979.

Despite schooling being optional at the time, in 1996 the number of children attending primary schools was equivalent to 94% of children in the relevant age-group (males 95%; females 93%) and secondary school enrolment was equivalent to 74% of children in the relevant age-group. Government expenditure on education in 2010 was estimated at S $8,517m. (19.3% of total expenditure). In 2009 there were 172 primary institutions, at which 265,104 students were enrolled; and 154 secondary institutions, at which 199,109 students were enrolled. In the same year there were 15 mixed-level schools, at which 36,469 students were enrolled, and a further 13 pre-university institutions, at which 20,612 students were enrolled.

There were 13 tertiary institutions in 2008, including the National University of Singapore, the Nanyang Technological University, the Ngee Ann Polytechnic, the Singapore Polytechnic, the Nanyang Polytechnic and the Temasek Polytechnic. In 2008 total enrolment in the universities and colleges was 172,185. The Singapore Institute of Technology, which was to provide industry-orientated qualifications in partnership with several overseas universities, opened in 2010. The Institute of Technical Education provides and regulates vocational training. It conducts institutional training for school-leavers, offers part-time continuing education and training programmes and registers apprentices. It is also responsible for setting national skills standards, the conduct of public trade testing and certification of skills.

SLOVAKIA

Introductory Survey

LOCATION, CLIMATE, LANGUAGE, RELIGION, FLAG, CAPITAL

The Slovak Republic (formerly a constituent republic of the Czech and Slovak Federative Republic, or Czechoslovakia) is a landlocked state located in central Europe, bordered to the north by Poland, to the east by Ukraine, to the south by Hungary, to the west by Austria and to the north-west by the Czech Republic. The climate is typically continental, with cold, dry winters and hot, humid summers. Average temperatures in Bratislava range from −0.7°C (30.7°F) in January to 21.1°C (70.0°F) in July. Average annual rainfall in the capital is 649 mm (26 ins). The official language is Slovak, although Hungarian, Czech and other languages are also spoken. The major religion is Christianity, the Latin-rite Catholic Church being the largest denomination, followed by the Evangelical Church of the Augsburg (Lutheran) Confession. The national flag (proportions 2 by 3) consists of three equal horizontal stripes, of white, blue and red; in the centre hoist there is a white-rimmed red shield containing a silver archiepiscopal (double-barred) cross surmounted on the central (and highest) of three blue hillocks. The capital is Bratislava.

CONTEMPORARY POLITICAL HISTORY

Historical Context

Slovaks and Czechs (who are closely related members of the western Slavic peoples) were first united in the ninth century AD, in the Great Moravian Empire, but were divided following the Empire's dissolution in 907. While the Slovaks came under Hungarian rule (which was to last, in different forms, until the early 20th century), the Czechs established a kingdom that remained an important political force until the incorporation of the Czech Lands into the Habsburg Empire in the 16th and 17th centuries.

A movement of nationalist revival, closely linked with a similar movement in the Czech Lands, evolved in Slovakia in the late 18th and 19th centuries. During the First World War (1914–18) Slovaks joined with Czechs in campaigning for an independent state, which would be composed of the Czech Lands and Slovakia. The Republic of Czechoslovakia was established on 28 October 1918, as one of the successor states to the Austro-Hungarian Empire. The country's boundaries were defined by the Treaty of Trianon of 1920, under which a large Hungarian minority was incorporated into Slovakia. Czechoslovakia's first Constitution, promulgated in 1920, made no provision for a proper federal system, and Slovak proposals for self-government were rejected by the central authorities in the capital, Prague. A further cause of Slovak disaffection was the fact that the Czech Lands were the focus of the country's economic development, while there was also an ideological divide: while the majority of Slovaks were practising Catholics, the central Government in Prague was professedly anticlerical.

In October 1938, following the Munich Agreement of 29 September (whereby the predominantly German-populated areas of Czechoslovakia were ceded to Germany), nationalists declared Slovak autonomy. On 14 March 1939, one day before Nazi armed forces occupied the Czech Lands, Germany agreed to the establishment of a separate Slovak state, under the pro-Nazi 'puppet' regime of Fr Jozef Tiso. Any opposition to the Tiso regime was ruthlessly suppressed, and the treatment of Jews was particularly severe. In August 1944 an armed resistance (the Slovak National Uprising) against Tiso's regime was begun, but it was suppressed within two months.

Following the restoration of the Czechoslovak state in 1945, at the end of the Second World War, certain concessions were made to Slovak demands for autonomy, including the establishment of a regional legislature with restricted powers (the Slovenská národná rada—Slovak National Council) and an executive, both in Bratislava, the Slovak capital. However, communists (led by Gustav Husák) seized power in Slovakia in late 1947, and in the whole of the country in 1948. In May of that year a new Constitution was approved, which declared Czechoslovakia to be a 'people's democracy'. The communists' consolidation of power was completed in June with the election of the Czech, Klement Gottwald, leader of the Communist Party of Czechoslovakia (CPCz) and Prime Minister since 1946, as President of Czechoslovakia.

In the first years of communist rule there was widespread repression. Expressions of Slovak nationalism were harshly suppressed, and in 1954 Husák and other Slovaks were imprisoned on charges of separatism. The Constitution of 1960 restricted Slovak autonomy: the executive in Bratislava was dissolved, and legislative authority was removed from the Slovenská národná rada. In January 1968 Alexander Dubček (a Slovak and hitherto leader of the Communist Party of Slovakia—CPS) was appointed First Secretary of the CPCz. The wide-ranging political and economic reforms introduced by Dubček and the new Government included plans for the creation of a federal system of two equal republics. This period of political tolerance was abruptly ended in August by the armed intervention of some 600,000 troops of the USSR and its allies. Dubček was replaced by Husák as First (subsequently General) Secretary of the CPCz, and there was a purge of party members, in particular reformists and associates of Dubček. Nevertheless, the federal system was realized in January 1969: separate Czech and Slovak Socialist Republics were established, each with its own government and legislature (Národná rada—National Council). Supreme legislative and executive power, meanwhile, were vested in the Federal Assembly and the Federal Government, respectively. However, renewed centralized rule, under Husák's leadership, left the new regional institutions largely powerless. In 1975 Husák was appointed President of Czechoslovakia. In 1987 he was replaced as General Secretary of the CPCz by Miloš Jakeš. The Government continued its repressive treatment of both the Catholic Church and the several dissident groups that had been established since the late 1970s (the most important being Charter 77). Nevertheless, the dissident movement was instrumental in organizing a series of anti-Government demonstrations, beginning in 1988, which were to culminate in the anti-communist revolution of late 1989 (see the chapter on the Czech Republic).

Elections to the Federal Assembly and to the Czech and Slovak National Councils on 8–9 June 1990 were the first to be held freely since 1946. Of the Slovak parties and movements, Public Against Violence (PAV), which, with its Czech counterpart, Civic Forum, had been the principal force in effecting the end of communist rule, emerged with the largest representation at both federal and republican levels. A coalition Slovak Government, dominated by PAV, was subsequently formed, with Vladimír Mečiar as Prime Minister.

The future of Czech-Slovak relations dominated political debate in the latter half of 1990, amid increasing support in Slovakia for greater decentralization. The Christian Democratic Movement (CDM), which formed part of the Slovak coalition Government, advocated greater Slovak autonomy within a common state; however, more radical parties—most notably the Slovak National Party (SNP), which held seats in both the federal and republican legislatures—advocated the complete secession of Slovakia. In March 1991 Mečiar was forced to resign as Slovak Prime Minister, as a consequence of his support for full autonomy for Slovakia. Mečiar left PAV and formed the Movement for a Democratic Slovakia (MDS), being replaced as Prime Minister by Ján Carnogurský, the leader of the CDM.

Domestic Political Affairs

The Government of Vladimír Mečiar

Following elections to the federal and republican legislatures on 5–6 June 1992, the MDS was the largest Slovak party both in the Federal Assembly and the National Council. In the latter body the MDS won 74 of the 150 seats available, compared with the 18 obtained by the CDM and 15 by the SNP. The Party of the Democratic Left (PDL—the successor to the CPS) secured the second largest representation (29 seats). Mečiar was reinstated as Prime Minister, heading a new, MDS-dominated Slovak Government.

On 17 July 1992 the Slovenská národná rada approved a declaration of Slovak sovereignty, and later in the month Mečiar and his Czech counterpart, Václav Klaus, reached agreement on the necessary measures to permit the separation of the two republics. On 1 September a new Slovak Constitution was adopted by the Slovenská národná rada. In November the Federal Assembly finally approved at the third attempt (and by a margin of only three votes) legislation to permit the constitutional dissolution of Czechoslovakia, which was to take effect on 1 January 1993. During late 1992 the division of federal assets and liabilities, as well as the armed forces, between the Czech and Slovak Republics accelerated. The two republics signed a co-operation agreement, and subsequently established formal diplomatic relations. Recognition was rapidly accorded to the new countries by all those states that had maintained relations with Czechoslovakia, as well as by various international bodies.

Slovakia's MDS-dominated Government and legislature remained in place. In February 1993 the Národná rada Slovenskej republiky (National Council of the Slovak Republic, as the legislature was redesignated—Národná rada) elected Michal Kováč, Deputy Chairman of the MDS and former Chairman of Czechoslovakia's Federal Assembly, as President. Internal divisions in the MDS culminated in March with the dismissal of Milan Kňažko, the strongest critic of Mečiar within the party, from his post of Deputy Prime Minister and Minister of Foreign Affairs. Also in March the SNP leader, Ludovít Černák, resigned as Minister of the Economy, leaving the Government (with the exception of two independent ministers) composed exclusively of members of the MDS. However, as a result of several defections, the party (plus affiliates) lost its majority in the legislature. A new coalition Government, in which the SNP held several principal portfolios, was formed in November. In December Mečiar ignored a demand by President Kováč for his resignation. In February 1994 six SNP deputies left the MDS to form what became the National Democratic Party—New Alternative (NDP—NA), led by Černák. In the same month the Minister of Foreign Affairs, Jozef Moravčík, and the Deputy Prime Minister, Roman Kováč, resigned from the Government, subsequently establishing the Democratic Union of Slovakia (DUS). In March the Národná rada approved a motion expressing no confidence in Mečiar's Government, prompting its resignation. A new, five-party, interim coalition was installed, led by Moravčík. Early legislative elections were scheduled for September.

The MDS was the leading party at elections to the Národná rada, held on 30 September and 1 October 1994, securing 35.0% of the votes cast and 61 seats in alliance with the Farmers' Party of Slovakia. An alliance of left-wing parties, led by the PDL, won 10.4% of the votes cast and 18 seats, followed by a coalition of Hungarian parties and the CDM (with 17 seats each). The remaining seats were taken by the DUS (15), the Association of Workers of Slovakia (AWS—13 seats) and the SNP (nine seats). Inter-party negotiations proved inconclusive, and Kováč requested that Mečiar form a Government. A coalition of the MDS, the SNP and the AWS was announced in December.

Following opposition demands for a referendum to be held on their proposals that the head of state be elected by direct popular vote, rather than chosen by the legislature, President Kováč scheduled a referendum for 23–24 May 1997. However, when the poll took place, the question on presidential elections was omitted from the ballot papers. The majority of voters consequently boycotted the referendum, and the rate of electoral participation (under 10%) rendered the vote invalid. The Minister of Foreign Affairs, Pavol Hamžík, resigned in protest at what he regarded as the Government's manipulation of the democratic process. In June several thousand people attended a rally to protest against the Government's intervention in the referendum. In February 1998, following a ruling by the Constitutional Court, Kováč announced that a new referendum would be held in April.

During January–March 1998 several attempts to elect a new President failed in the Národná rada, when candidates were unable to secure the required three-fifths' majority. The MDS had not contested the first rounds of voting, apparently confirming opposition fears that Mečiar was attempting to ensure that the presidency would remain vacant when Kováč left office, enabling him to assume a number of presidential powers. On 2 March Kováč's term expired, and certain presidential powers were transferred to the Government, in accordance with the Constitution. Mečiar immediately cancelled the referendum scheduled for April and announced the dismissal of some 28 of Slovakia's ambassadors abroad. He also granted an amnesty to various prisoners, and halted criminal proceedings relating to the May 1997 referendum. The Prime Minister's actions prompted a series of widely supported protest rallies organized by opposition parties, and were strongly criticized by the EU and the USA.

In May 1998, in preparation for legislative elections scheduled for September, the Národná rada approved amendments to the electoral law, including a stipulation that political parties obtain at least 5% of the votes cast to secure parliamentary representation. Legislation was also approved that restricted pre-election campaigning to the state-run media. In June three ethnic Hungarian parties merged to create the Party of the Hungarian Coalition (PHC), and the SDC registered officially as a single party. In July a constitutional amendment providing for the transfer of a number of presidential powers to the Chairman of the Národná rada, in the event of the presidency becoming vacant, was supported by deputies from all parties.

The Government of Mikuláš Dzurinda

The elections to the Národná rada were held on 25–26 September 1998, with the participation of 84.2% of the electorate. The MDS narrowly retained its position as the strongest party in the legislature, winning 43 seats (with 27.0% of the votes cast), but was unable to form a government, with its only possible ally, the SNP, holding 14 seats. The SDC obtained 42 seats (26.3% of the votes), the PDL 23 seats (14.7%), the PHC 15 seats and the Party of Civic Understanding (PCU—formed earlier that year) 13 seats. With a combined total of 93 seats, the SDC, the PDL, the PHC and the PCU agreed to form a new administration, and a new coalition Government, headed by Mikuláš Dzurinda, the leader of the SDC, was appointed at the end of October. Jozef Migaš, of the PDL, was elected Chairman of the Národná rada. The opposition's victory was welcomed both by Western institutions and by neighbouring countries, which anticipated improved relations with Slovakia. Dzurinda emphasized the new Government's intention to pursue early membership of the EU and NATO, pledged to combat organized crime, and outlined measures to improve Slovakia's economic situation. In December the European Parliament adopted a resolution on Slovakia's application for membership of the European Union (EU, see p. 270), recommending that the European Commission consider initiating entry talks in 1999.

In January 1999 the Národná rada approved a constitutional amendment providing for the introduction of direct presidential elections. The ruling coalition nominated Rudolf Schuster, the Chairman of the PCU, as its presidential candidate. Nine candidates contested the first round of the presidential election, which was held on 15 May. Schuster won 47.4% of the votes cast, and Mečiar obtained 37.2%. (Kováč had withdrawn his candidature in favour of Schuster.) Schuster defeated Mečiar in a second round of voting on 29 May, with 57.2% of the votes cast, and was duly inaugurated as President on 15 June, having resigned the chairmanship of the PCU.

In September 1999 a large demonstration was staged in Bratislava to protest against rising unemployment and declining living standards, resulting from austerity measures. In October Černák resigned as Minister of the Economy; the post was assumed by Lubomír Harach, the Chairman of the DUS. In January 2000, following several weeks of disputes over the future structure of the SDC, Dzurinda announced plans to form a new party, the Slovak Democratic and Christian Union (SDCU). The SDCU was officially registered in February, and was joined by several government ministers. Further SDC deputies subsequently resigned from the CDM and the DUS to join the SDCU. Following Dzurinda's election as SDCU Chairman at the party's opening congress in November, the SDC became effectively defunct.

Revisions to the Constitution, opposed by the MDS and the SNP, were adopted by a narrow majority in the legislature in February 2001. The amendments (which entered into effect on 1 July) redefined the relationship between national and international law, thereby facilitating the process of joining foreign alliances; strengthened the powers of the Constitutional Court; granted greater independence to the judiciary; and provided for public administration reform. In May Schuster replaced Pavol Hamzik, the Deputy Prime Minister for European Integration, held responsible for the misuse of EU funds, which had led to the suspension of payments in the previous month. Also in May the Minister of the Interior tendered his resignation, following increasing criticism of an investigation into mismanagement under the Mečiar administration.

In July 2001 dissension increased between the government coalition parties over new legislation providing for the establishment of a higher level of regional self-administration. Following the adoption of the reforms, which provided for the creation of eight 'higher territorial units' (VÚCs), local government elections took place on 1 and 15 December. In a reflection of increasing popular support, MDS representatives secured 146 of the 401 seats in the regional councils and six of the eight gubernatorial posts. (However, voter participation in the second round was estimated at only 22% of the registered electorate.)

In January 2002 the PDL demanded the resignation of the reformist Minister of Finance, Brigita Schmögnerová (a PDL member), after she allegedly withheld information regarding the privatization programme. Although Dzurinda initially refused to dismiss her, threats by the PDL to withdraw from the coalition finally resulted in her replacement. Schmögnerová subsequently left the PDL and formed a new political party, the Social Democratic Alternative (SDA).

In July 2002 members of the MDS who had not been selected by the party to contest the forthcoming legislative elections established a new party, the Movement for Democracy. At the elections to the Národná rada on 20–21 September, the MDS received the highest proportion of the votes cast (19.5%), obtaining 36 mandates. The SDCU received 15.1% of the votes cast and 28 seats; a centre-right party, Direction, 13.5% and 25 seats; the PHC 11.2% and 20 seats; and the CDM 8.3% and 15 seats. The New Citizens' Alliance (NCA), established in 2001, won 8.0% of the votes and 15 seats, while the Slovak Communist Party (SCP) significantly increased its share, securing 6.3% and 11 seats. However, Mečiar proved unable to form a coalition government, and in late September Schuster invited Dzurinda to establish a new administration. A coalition agreement was signed in early October by four reformist, centre-right parties (the SDCU, the PHC, the CDM and the NCA), which together held 78 of the 150 seats in the Národná rada. On 16 October Schuster formally appointed a new coalition Government. The leader of the Democratic Party (DP), which had supported the SDCU in the elections, was allocated a portfolio, although the party was not a coalition member. Mikloš was retained in the administration as the new Minister of Finance. The adoption of an austerity budget in November prompted popular protests. Local government elections took place on 6–7 December; mayoral offices were equally divided between the government coalition parties and the MDS.

In May 2003 a new party, the People's Union, was formed by disaffected members of the MDS. In the following month Mečiar was re-elected as Chairman of the MDS. At the same time, MDS members approved changing the party's name to the People's Party—Movement for a Democratic Slovakia (PP—MDS). Tensions emerged within the ruling coalition in July, after the Národná rada approved legislative amendments proposed by the NCA, easing restrictions on abortion, which were strongly opposed by the CDM. In late July Schuster vetoed the legislation, fearing the collapse of the Government. In September the Deputy Prime Minister and Minister of the Economy, Robert Nemcsics, officially resigned his post, after losing the support of the NCA, following his criticism of Pavel Rusko, the Chairman of the party. Later that month Rusko was appointed as Deputy Prime Minister and Minister of the Economy. In October Juraj Liska was appointed as Minister of Defence, replacing Ivan Simko, who had been dismissed in September. A number of deputies subsequently left the SDCU to join Simko's newly formed Free Forum, rendering the ruling coalition a minority Government, with just 68 parliamentary seats.

Ivan Gašparovič elected President

In the first round of voting in the presidential election of 3 April 2004, Mečiar won 32.7% of the votes cast, followed by the Movement for Democracy leader (and former ally of Mečiar) Ivan Gašparovič, who won 22.3% of the votes. Eduard Kukan of the SDCU, the Minister of Foreign Affairs and the preferred candidate of Dzurinda's Government, took third place, with 22.1% of the votes, while Schuster, the incumbent, obtained just 7.4% of the votes. The failure of Kukan's presidential bid prompted demands in the Národná rada for the resignation of Dzurinda, whereas Mečiar's success was regarded as a potential threat to Slovakia's planned accession to the EU (due in May). In the second round of voting, held on 17 April, Gašparovič was elected as President, receiving 59.9% of the votes cast; the rate of participation by the electorate in the second round was 43.5%. Gašparovič, who subsequently resigned from the leadership of the Movement for Democracy, was inaugurated on 15 June. Meanwhile, at Slovakia's first elections to the European Parliament in mid-June, a rate of participation by the electorate of just 17.0% was recorded, the lowest rate recorded in any EU member state. The SDCU received 17.1% of the votes, the PP—MDS 17.0%, Direction 16.9% and the CDM 16.2%; the four parties were each allocated three seats in the European Parliament. The PHC, which won 13.2% of votes, obtained two seats.

In January 2005 a new party, Direction-Social Democracy, was formed by the merger of Direction, the Social Democratic Party of Slovakia, the SDA and the PDL. In August President Gašparovič dismissed Rusko from his post as Deputy Prime Minister and Minister of the Economy, after he was implicated in a loan scandal, which revealed an apparent conflict of interest between his private business activities and his ministerial duties. (Rusko had refused to comply with an earlier request that he tender his resignation, after the CDM threatened to withdraw its 15 deputies from the Národná rada if he remained in the Government.) Deputy Prime Minister and Minister of Finance Ivan Mikloš assumed the economy portfolio, in an acting capacity. Rusko, who remained leader of the NCA, subsequently urged Dzurinda to dismiss the Minister of Health, Rudolf Zajac (who had been nominated by the NCA, but was not a party member), and the Minister of Culture, František Tóth (an NCA member), both of whom had supported Rusko's removal, threatening to withdraw the NCA from the Government should Dzurinda refuse. Members of the NCA opposed to Rusko's leadership, including two party Vice-Chairmen, Lubomír Lintner and Jirko Malchárek, and Tóth, formed a splinter faction, led by Lintner. At the beginning of September the SDCU, the CDM and the PHC agreed to expel the NCA from the ruling coalition; Zajac and Tóth were permitted to retain their posts. Lintner's group of deputies pledged its co-operation with the governing parties, and proposed Malchárek for the post of Minister of the Economy. On 11 September the NCA expelled nine members from the party, including Tóth and five Vice-Chairmen (among them Lintner and Malchárek). The following day the Government signed a co-operation agreement with Lintner's group of deputies. Opposition parties boycotted the Národná rada, but, after nine days, the Government narrowly managed to secure sufficient support to open a legislative session. In October Gašparovič appointed Malchárek as Deputy Prime Minister and Minister of the Economy.

In October 2005 DP leader Ľudovít Kaník resigned as Minister of Labour, Social Affairs and the Family. Kaník, who was replaced by Iveta Radičová, subsequently proposed a merger of the DP and the SDCU. In December a congress of the DP approved a draft agreement on the merger, which was confirmed in January 2006 at an extraordinary congress of the SDCU. The new political union was known as the SDCU-DP.

Meanwhile, on 26 November and 10 December 2005 an estimated 18% of the electorate took part in local government elections. Just 11% of the electorate participated in the second round, the lowest rate of participation in Slovakia's history. Of the parties represented in the Národná rada, the CDM secured 87 of the 412 seats in the VÚCs, Direction-Social Democracy took 70 and the SDCU won 64.

In January 2006 the Minister of Defence, Juraj Liška, tendered his resignation, after a military aircraft crashed on the Hungarian–Slovak border, killing some 42 people. Although the cause of the accident was unknown, the Government had been criticized for its decision to modernize Soviet-manufactured aircraft, rather than buying new equipment. Liška was replaced by Martin Fedor. In February the CDM announced the withdrawal of its three ministers from the Government, following Dzurinda's refusal to submit for discussion a proposal to approve a treaty with the Holy See that would enable workers to refuse to perform duties on the basis of religious objections. Dzurinda argued that any such treaty would permit the Catholic Church to interfere in civil affairs. The leader of the CDM subsequently resigned as Chairman of the Národná rada, and was replaced, in an acting capacity, by the PHC leader and Deputy Chairman of the legislature, Béla Bugár. As a result of the CDM's withdrawal, the ruling coalition controlled just 53 seats in the legislature, and three days later the Národná rada approved a proposal by Dzurinda for legislative elections, originally due to take place in September, to be held on 17 June. Gašparovič subsequently appointed Martin Pado of the SDCU-DP as Minister of the Interior, László Szigeti of the PHC as Minister of Education and Lucia Žitňanská, an independent, as Minister of Justice. In April 2006 Tóth was dismissed from his position as Minister of Culture, after being accused of misusing state funds; Rudolf Chmel, who had held the position until May 2005, was subsequently reappointed to the culture portfolio.

SLOVAKIA

The Government of Robert Fico

In legislative elections held on 17 June 2006, 50 seats were won by Fico's Direction-Social Democracy, which secured 29.1% of the votes cast. The SDCU-DP obtained 18.4% of the votes (31 seats), while the SNP and the PHC both won 11.7% (20 seats). Fifteen seats were allocated to the PP—MDS, which attracted 8.8% of the ballot, while the CDM secured 14 seats, with 8.3%. The rate of participation in the elections was 54.7%. Three days later Fico was invited by President Gašparovič to form a government. On 28 June Direction-Social Democracy voted in favour of inviting the SNP and the PP—MDS to enter into a coalition; an agreement to this end was signed on 3 July. Fico's new administration predominantly comprised members of his own party, with the SNP and the PP—MDS being allocated just three and two cabinet posts, respectively. Neither Mečiar nor SNP Chairman Ján Slota were awarded cabinet positions. None the less, the Party of European Socialists, in protest at Direction-Social Democracy's involvement with a far-right organization such as the SNP, voted to suspend temporarily the party's membership. Fico was formally appointed Prime Minister on 4 July; the new Národná rada was sworn in on the same day.

Assurances by Fico's administration that it would continue the foreign and domestic policies pursued by the previous Government, including those pertaining to Slovakia's planned accession to the euro zone, were undermined in the weeks following the general election by highly contentious statements attributed to Slota in the domestic and international press on the issues of deportation and Slovakia's ethnic Hungarian population. While the PHC appealed to prosecutors to take legal action against Slota, the SNP threatened to sue controversial PHC deputy Miklos Duray for terming it a 'fascist' party. At the end of August the Chairman of the Parliamentary Assembly of the Council of Europe (see p. 250), Rane van der Linden, denounced the manifestations of racial intolerance in Slovakia. In early September Minister of Foreign Affairs Ján Kubiš and his Hungarian counterpart, Kinga Göncz, pledged to work together to improve bilateral relations. On 7 September the Národná rada adopted a declaration against extremism and intolerance (112 deputies voted in favour of the motion, while 28 abstained). In 2006 Slovakia granted asylum to just eight individuals, from a total of 2,871 applicants.

Despite the turbulence of the first two months of his premiership, by the end of 2006 Fico appeared to have consolidated his position and introduced a period of political stability. Direction-Social Democracy performed well at the municipal elections of 2 December (in which 47.7% of the electorate participated). However, the appointment in that month of Radim Hreha, a strong supporter of Fico, as Director of Slovak Television prompted fears that the premier was applying pressure on the state media to adopt a pro-Government stance. In April an internal dispute erupted within the PHC when Duray accused outgoing Chairman Béla Bugár of co-operating with the communist-era secret police. (Bugár had been replaced as Chairman at the beginning of that month by Pál Csáky, whom many expected to adopt a more radical stance on Hungarian autonomy.)

In November 2007 the PP—MDS threatened to withdraw from the Government, in protest at Fico's dismissal of the Minister of Agriculture (a representative of that party), after evidence emerged of an illicit land sale agreement involving the Slovak State Land Fund. However, in December the Národná rada approved the budget for 2008, by 85 votes to 61, in a motion that was also regarded as expressing confidence in Fico's administration. In January 2008 the new Minister of Agriculture, Zdenka Kramplová, ordered the dismissal of the entire board of the Slovak State Land Fund. Later that month the Minister of Defence, František Kašický, resigned, following allegations that his ministry had overpriced tenders for the maintenance of military barracks; he was succeed by Jaroslav Baška, also of Direction-Social Democracy. The formation of a new political party, the Conservative Democrats of Slovakia (CDS), was announced in March by four deputies who had recently defected from the CDM; the CDS was formally registered in July. Meanwhile, in April President Gašparovič signed into law new regulations that were expected severely to restrict the activities of the print media; the new legislation, which entered into effect in June, had been drafted by the Minister of Culture, following ongoing government criticism of press statements, and had attracted objections from international organizations.

Ján Kubiš resigned as Minister of Foreign Affairs in January 2009 to become Executive Secretary of the UN Economic Commission for Europe; he was succeeded by Miroslav Lajčák, hitherto High Representative of the International Community and EU Special Representative in Bosnia and Herzegovina.

Gašparovič re-elected President

Seven candidates contested the first round of voting in a presidential election held on 21 March 2009. Gašparovič, the incumbent President, who was supported by the governing Direction-Social Democracy and SNP, secured the largest share of the valid votes cast, with 46.7%, followed by Iveta Radičová, a Vice-Chairman of the SDCU-DP and also supported by the PHC and CDM, who won 38.1%. Gašparovič defeated Radičová in a second round of voting on 4 April, receiving 55.5% of the valid votes cast. The rate of participation by the electorate was 43.6% in the first round and 51.7% in the second round.

In mid-April 2009 the Minister of Construction and Regional Development, Marian Janušek of the SNP, tendered his resignation, which had been requested by Fico after investigations by the Public Procurement Office and the Supreme Audit Office confirmed that Janušek's ministry had mishandled the tendering process for a €120m. contract that had been awarded to a consortium of two companies reported to have links to SNP Chairman Slota. In early May Ján Chrbet was dismissed as Minister of the Environment, owing to controversy concerning his involvement in the sale of carbon dioxide emissions quotas, in the previous year, at a price that was considerably lower than that received by other countries; he was replaced later in the month by Viliam Turský (also of the SNP), the hitherto Secretary of State for Agriculture. In late June the Deputy Prime Minister and Minister of Justice Stefan Harabin was elected Chairman of the Supreme Court and of the Judicial Council; he was succeeded in early July in his former position by Viera Petríková. In late August Turský was dismissed as Minister of the Environment; his dismissal followed the apparent mishandling of tendering for a contract. In response to the series of improprieties associated with activities of the ministry, the governing coalition agreed that responsibility for the Ministry of the Environment would be transferred from the SNP to Direction-Social Democracy; Jozef Medved was appointed as Minister of the Environment in late October. In March 2010 President Gašparovič dismissed Stefanov as Minister of Construction and Regional Development, following an investigation into transactions related to a contract awarded by the ministry; another member of the SNP, the Deputy Prime Minister and Minister of Education, Ján Mikolaj, also assumed responsibility for the construction portfolio, in an interim capacity, pending legislative elections, scheduled to be held on 12 June.

Recent developments: the 2010 elections and Government of Iveta Radičová

At the elections to the Národná rada, which took place on 12 June 2010, Direction-Social Democracy obtained the greatest share of the votes cast (34.8%), securing 62 of the 150 legislative seats. The SDCU-DP was placed second, with 15.4% of the votes and 28 seats, followed by a liberal party formed in 2009, Freedom and Solidarity (FAS), with 12.1% and 22 seats, the CDM (8.5% and 15 seats), Bridge, founded in 2009 to promote inter-ethnic co-operation (8.1% and 14 seats), and the SNP (5.1% and nine seats). The PHC and the PP—MDS, with less than 5% of the votes cast, both failed to secure legislative representation. Despite having obtained the highest number of seats, Direction-Social Democracy proved unable to form a coalition with a parliamentary majority, and President Gašparovič invited Radičová (who was the election leader of the SDCU-DP) to establish a coalition administration comprising the four centre-right parties in the Národná rada. On 8 July Fico and his Government resigned from office, and Radičová was appointed as Prime Minister (becoming the first woman to hold the post). On the same day Richard Sulík of Freedom and Solidarity was elected as the new parliamentary Chairman. A new Government, comprising a coalition of the SDCU-DP, the CDM, Bridge and the FAS, was subsequently installed; principal appointments included Ján Figel as First Deputy Prime Minister, Minister of Transport, Post and Telecommunications, Daniel Lipšic as Minister of the Interior and Dzurinda as Minister of Foreign Affairs. On 10 August Radičová's Government secured a vote of confidence (with 79 votes in favour) in the Národná rada. In early November President Gašparovič appointed József Nagy of Bridge to the reinstated post of Minister of the Environment (the ministry having been abolished by former Prime Minister Fico shortly before his resignation).

Following a successful public petition organized by the FAS, a referendum on political reform took place on 18 September 2010; although a large majority of votes were cast in favour of the six proposals (which included a reduction in the number of parliamentary deputies from 150 to 100, and restrictions to parliamentary immunity), only about 22.8% of the electorate participated in the poll, well below the 50% minimum required for its validation. The results of the municipal elections, which were conducted on 27 November, indicated a significant loss of support for Prime Minister Radičová's ruling coalition, following her announcement of austerity measures to reduce the budget deficit (see Economic Affairs). Fico's Direction-Social Democracy obtained majorities in 599 municipalities, with 20.6% of the votes cast, the CDM in 161, with 5.5% of the votes, and the SDCU-DP in only 159, with 5.5% of the votes. Independent candidates secured control of 979 municipalities, with 33.7% of the votes cast. Direction-Social Democracy candidates were also elected as mayors in five of the eight largest cites, including Bratislava. A rate of participation of 49.7% of the registered electorate was recorded. From late 2010 trade unions organized a series of demonstrations, in protest at the Government's proposed austerity measures. In March 2011 planned amendments to the labour code attracted particular controversy and prompted further protests; despite opposition from both trade unions and employer associations, a revised labour code was approved by the Government at the end of April.

Roma Affairs

In 1997 Mečiar appealed to the Roma population not to seek asylum abroad, after a number of Roma were repatriated from the United Kingdom. However, Slovakia's Roma continued to seek political asylum abroad (largely unsuccessfully), prompting several countries to introduce mandatory visa requirements, on a temporary basis, for Slovak citizens. Although, according to the 2001 census, there were some 89,900 Roma in Slovakia, the community was unofficially estimated to number around 200,000. In January 2004 a report by the Council of Europe concluded that Slovakia's Roma were frequently victims of racial prejudice and were disadvantaged socially. In the following month proposed reductions in social welfare prompted violent protests by the Roma minority, and some 1,000 troops were deployed to control rioting. In July new legislation was introduced prohibiting discrimination on the grounds of ethnicity. In November 2006 the European Monitoring Centre on Racism and Xenophobia, based in Vienna, Austria, criticized Slovakia, along with the Czech Republic and Hungary, for segregating its Roma populations, particularly in the education sector, but also with regard to housing and the labour market.

Foreign Affairs

Regional relations

Slovakia's relations with Hungary have been strained by the issue of the large Hungarian minority (numbering some 520,500 at the 2001 census) resident in Slovakia, who are campaigning for cultural and educational autonomy. The two countries are also involved in a dispute over the Gabčíkovo-Nagymaros hydroelectric project, a scheme initiated by the Governments of Czechoslovakia and Hungary in 1977, which involved the construction of two dams and the diversion of the River Danube. Despite Hungary's decision in 1989 to abandon the project (following pressure by environmentalist groups), the Czechoslovak Government announced that it would proceed unilaterally with its part of the construction. In early 1993 Slovakia and Hungary agreed to forward the dispute to the International Court of Justice (ICJ) in The Hague, Netherlands, and to operate a temporary water-management scheme in the mean time. In March 1995, none the less, an historic bilateral Treaty of Friendship and Co-operation was signed by the Prime Ministers of Hungary and Slovakia. The Treaty, notably, guaranteed the rights of ethnic minorities in each republic, while confirming the existing state border. However, the language law approved by the Slovak legislature in November, declaring Slovak the only official language and thereby potentially restricting the use of minority languages, was criticized both by Hungarian residents of Slovakia and by the Hungarian Government, as a violation of the Treaty. In August 1997 the Hungarian Prime Minister, Gyula Horn, and Mečiar agreed on the establishment of a joint commission to assess the implementation of the 1995 Treaty.

In September 1997 the ICJ pronounced its judgment on the Gabčíkovo-Nagymaros hydroelectric project, ruling that both countries had breached international law: Hungary was not justified in suspending work on the project, while the former Czechoslovakia should not have proceeded unilaterally. Both countries were to pay compensation for damages, and to negotiate regarding the realization of the original agreement. The participation of the PHC in the new Slovak Government, appointed in October 1998, improved prospects for the protection of minority rights. In February 1999 the first meeting of the joint minorities commission to monitor the implementation of the 1995 Treaty was held in Budapest, Hungary. In July 1999 the Národná rada approved legislation that provided for the use of an ethnic minority language in towns where the minority accounted for at least 20% of the population.

In December 1999 Hungary renounced any claim to a share of the hydroelectric energy produced by the Gabčíkovo-Nagymaros dam project, but requested an increase in the common flow of water along the Danube, for ecological reasons. In February 2001 Slovakia accepted that it had no legal means to compel Hungary to complete the project, but stated that it was to seek compensation. In December 2003 an intergovernmental commission was established to co-ordinate negotiations on the issue. Meanwhile, in January 2002 relations between Slovakia and Hungary had again become acrimonious, following Hungary's adoption of legislation that granted ethnic Hungarians resident in six neighbouring states, including Slovakia, education, employment and medical benefits. The Slovak Government protested that the new legislation violated Slovakia's sovereignty, and demanded that it be cancelled or amended. In March 2003 Hungary agreed to suspend the application of the law in Slovakia, and in December the Ministers of Foreign Affairs of Hungary and Slovakia signed an agreement on the issue. The provisions of the Hungarian 'status law' were effectively superseded by the accession of Hungary and Slovakia to the EU in May 2004 (see below). In February 2006 it was announced that Slovakia and Hungary had agreed to implement the 1997 ICJ ruling on the Gabčíkovo-Nagymaros hydroelectric project.

Tensions between Hungary and Slovakia were again apparent in August 2009, when the Slovak Ministry of Foreign Affairs prohibited the Hungarian President, László Sólyom, from entering Slovakia, despite EU regulations on freedom of movement between member states. Sólyom's visit, which was to have been in a private capacity, to unveil a statue to St István (Stephen), the first King of Hungary, in a predominantly ethnically Hungarian town in southern Slovakia, Komárno, was condemned by the Slovakian President, Prime Minister and legislative Chairman, on the grounds that it took place on 21 August, the anniversary of the 1968 invasion of Czechoslovakia by Warsaw Pact (including Hungarian) troops. The growth in support, in both Hungary and Slovakia, for extreme nationalist parties (Jobbik and the Slovak National Party, respectively) from the late 2000s was a further cause of tensions in relations. Legislation that took effect in Slovakia from 1 September placing restrictions on the use of languages other than Slovak was a further source of controversy. In early September some 10,000 people, believed to be mainly ethnic Hungarians, attended a rally in the southern town of Dunajská Streda to demand that the legislation might be amended. Concern was expressed that the legislation might criminalize the use of minority languages in private, as well as official, contexts. Slovakia and Hungary subsequently agreed that the Organization for Security and Co-operation in Europe (OSCE, see p. 385) would oversee the implementation of the law to ensure that it complied with international norms.

After elections in Hungary in April 2010 resulted in victory for centre-right party Fidesz, on 26 May the Hungarian parliament adopted legislation permitting ethnic Hungarians outside Hungary, including in Slovakia, to apply for Hungarian citizenship. This measure was described by Prime Minister Fico as a threat to security; later on 26 May the Národná rada voted in favour of amending the country's citizenship law, providing for the removal of Slovak citizenship from those who applied for citizenship of a second state. The new Government of Prime Minister Radičová (see above) stated its intention to abrogate the Fico administration's law on dual citizenship (which had entered into effect on 17 July), and also proposed to declare the Hungarian legislation as ineffective in Slovakia.

Relations with neighbouring Austria were strained by the issue of the partially constructed, Soviet-designed nuclear power station at Mochovce (north-east of Bratislava), operated by Slovenské elektrárne (Slovak Electricity), the completion of which was opposed by the Austrian Government, owing to safety concerns. An agreement on completion of the project was signed in April 1996, with Western European, Russian and Czech companies, according to which the first reactor would be commissioned by July 1998 and the second by March 1999. Tension increased in June 1998, when the first reactor was activated, despite a request from the Austrian Government that Slovakia delay the opening of the plant until an international team of inspectors, who had visited Mochovce in May, had submitted a final report on the plant's safety. In late 1999 the Slovak Government announced its decision to close two existing reactors at Jaslovské-Bohunice between 2006 and 2008, further antagonizing Austria, which had favoured closure by 2000. In May 2004, shortly after Slovakia's accession to the EU, tensions between the two countries heightened, following the Slovak Government's announcement that it intended to complete work on the Mochovce plant. Construction of Mochovce's two unfinished reactors by Slovenské elektrárne (majority owned by the Italian electricity group Enel since 2006) commenced in November 2008 and was scheduled to be completed by 2013, at an estimated cost of €2,800m.

In December 1999 Slovakia was among six countries formally invited to commence talks on accession to the EU; entry negotiations opened in February 2000. Following the return to power of a reformist coalition Government in October 2002 (see above), at an EU summit meeting held in Copenhagen, Denmark, in December, Slovakia was one of 10 nations invited to become a member in 2004. At a national referendum, which was conducted on 16–17 May 2003, 92.5% of votes were cast in favour of membership of the EU; some 52% of the electorate participated in the ballot. Slovakia's Treaty of Accession was formally ratified by the Národná rada on 1 July, and the country became a full member of the EU on 1 May 2004.

In December 2007 Slovakia, together with eight other EU member nations (including the Czech Republic, Hungary and Poland), implemented the Schengen Agreement on freedom of travel, effectively removing border controls between those states subject to the Agreement. In early 2008 the Slovak authorities announced a subsequent increase in the number of illegal immigrants detained. Following Kosovo's unilateral declaration of independence in February (see the chapter on Kosovo), Slovakia was among several EU member nations (including Spain, Romania and Cyprus) to refuse to recognize it as a sovereign state, although the Government offered it 'partnership'. The ratification of the EU's Lisbon Treaty, which was designed to reform the Union's institutions, was approved by the Národná rada in April and received presidential assent in May. The parliamentary vote had been delayed for several months, as opposition parties withheld their support for the Treaty in protest at proposed domestic legislation regulating the print media (which was also adopted in April—see above); in the event, PHC deputies finally agreed to vote in favour of ratification, while the SDCU-DP and the CDM boycotted proceedings.

In May 2008 the European Commission approved Slovakia's planned accession to the euro zone on 1 January 2009. This decision was confirmed by EU finance ministers in July 2008, and Slovakia became the 16th member of the euro zone as scheduled. In August 2010 the Národná rada voted not to pay Slovakia's share of the EU emergency assistance allocated to the severely indebted Greek economy, which had been agreed in May by the ministers responsible for finance of countries using the euro, in order to ensure regional financial stability within the euro zone. Prime Minister Radičová cited stringent domestic austerity measures planned by her Government (see Economic Affairs) as justification for the decision, which prompted criticism from the European Commission and other euro zone member states, particularly Germany.

Other external relations

In February 1994 Slovakia joined NATO's 'Partnership for Peace' programme (see p. 371). At a NATO summit meeting in Prague at the end of November 2002, Slovakia (together with six other countries) was formally invited to join the Alliance, and it became a full member on 29 March 2004. In May Slovakia hosted a plenary session of the NATO Parliamentary Assembly, and in February 2005 it hosted a summit meeting between US President George W. Bush and Russian President Vladimir Putin. President Bush praised the deployment of 100 Slovak troops to Iraq to participate in the US-led military operations there. However, in February 2007 Fico fulfilled one of his electoral promises by withdrawing his country's troops from Iraq. (This, in addition to controversial visits by the new premier to the People's Republic of China and Libya, was seen as an effort by Fico to distance himself from the pro-US stance of his predecessor.) Also in February it was agreed that some 60 Slovak troops stationed in Kabul, Afghanistan, as part of the NATO-led International Security Assistance Force (ISAF) mission, would be transferred to Kandahar, in the south of the country, by June. At early 2011 296 Slovakians were participating in ISAF. Meanwhile, in March 2007 Slovakia joined the International Energy Agency.

CONSTITUTION AND GOVERNMENT

Supreme legislative power is vested in the Národná rada Slovenskej republiky (National Council of the Slovak Republic), the 150 members of which are elected for a term of four years by universal adult suffrage. The President of the Republic (Head of State) is directly elected by universal adult suffrage for a five-year term. The President, who is restricted to two consecutive terms of office, appoints the Prime Minister and, on the latter's recommendation, the other members of the Government (the supreme body of executive power). Judicial power is exercised by the Supreme Court, regional courts and district courts. For administrative purposes, Slovakia is divided into eight 'higher territorial units' (VUCs), each with a regional council (together totalling 401 seats), and 79 electoral districts.

REGIONAL AND INTERNATIONAL CO-OPERATION

Slovakia is a member of the European Union (EU, see p. 270), the Council of Europe, the Organization for Security and Co-operation in Europe (OSCE, see p. 385), the Organisation for Economic Co-operation and Development (OECD, see p. 376) and the North Atlantic Treaty Organization (NATO, see p. 368).

Slovakia was admitted to the UN following independence in 1993 and, as a contracting party to the General Agreement on Tariffs and Trade, joined the World Trade Organization (WTO, see p. 430) on its establishment in 1995.

ECONOMIC AFFAIRS

In 2009, according to the World Bank, Slovakia's gross national income (GNI), measured at average 2007–09 prices, was US $87,402m., equivalent to $16,130 per head (or $21,600 per head on an international purchasing-power parity basis). During 2000–09, it was estimated, the population remained constant, while gross domestic product (GDP) per head increased, in real terms, by an average of 4.7% per year. Overall GDP increased, in real terms, at an average annual rate of 4.8% in 2000–10; real GDP decreased by 4.8% in 2009, but increased by 4.0% in 2010.

The agricultural sector (including hunting, forestry and fishing) contributed 3.8% of GDP in 2010, and engaged 4.0% of the employed labour force in 2008. The principal crops are sugar beet, wheat and maize. Livestock-breeding is also important. According to the World Bank, during 2000–09 the GDP of the agricultural sector increased, in real terms, at an average annual rate of 6.1%. Agricultural GDP decreased by 2.6% in 2008, but increased by 6.9% in 2009.

Industry (including mining, manufacturing, construction and power) contributed 34.8% of GDP in 2010, and engaged 39.5% of the employed labour force in 2008. The GDP of the industrial sector increased, in real terms, at an average annual rate of 9.6% during 2000–09, according to the World Bank; industrial GDP increased by 6.9% in 2009.

Mining and quarrying contributed 0.6% of GDP in 2010, and engaged 0.6% of the employed labour force in 2008. The principal minerals extracted include brown coal and lignite, copper, zinc, lead, iron ore and magnesite. There are also deposits of crude petroleum, natural gas and mercury, as well as materials used in construction (including limestone, gravel and brick loam).

The manufacturing sector contributed 20.6% of GDP in 2010, and engaged 26.6% of the employed labour force in 2008. According to the World Bank, the GDP of the manufacturing sector increased at an average annual rate of 10.8% in 2000–06; manufacturing GDP increased by 10.7% in 2006.

The construction sector contributed 9.0% of GDP in 2010, and engaged 10.5% of the employed labour force in 2008.

Energy is derived principally from nuclear power, which provided some 55% of electricity generated in 2007. In that year coal accounted for 18.7% of electricity production, and hydroelectric power for 16.0%. A nuclear power station at Jaslovské-Bohunice has been in operation since the early 1980s, although two reactors there were closed in 2006 and 2008. In mid-1998 the first block of a new nuclear power installation, at Mochovce, commenced operations; construction work on two unfinished reactors there was due to be completed by 2013. Slovakia has been heavily dependent on imported fuel and energy products. Mineral fuels and lubricants accounted for 11.8% of the value of total merchandise imports in 2009.

SLOVAKIA

The services sector contributed 61.4% of GDP in 2010, and engaged 56.5% of the employed labour force in 2008. During 2000–09, according to the World Bank, the GDP of the services sector increased, in real terms, at an average annual rate of 0.7%; services GDP increased by 7.9% in 2008, but declined by 23.6% in 2009.

In 2009 Slovakia recorded a trade surplus of US $1,715m., while there was a deficit of some $2,810m. on the current account of the balance of payments. In 2009 the principal source of imports was Germany, which accounted for 15.2% of the total; other major suppliers were the Czech Republic and Russia. Germany was also the principal market for exports in that year (accounting for 19.8%); other important purchasers were the Czech Republic, France, Hungary, Poland, Italy and Austria. The main exports in 2009 were machinery and transport equipment, basic manufactures and miscellaneous manufactured articles. The principal imports were machinery and transport equipment, basic manufactures, mineral fuels and lubricants, miscellaneous manufactured articles, and chemicals and related products.

Slovakia's overall budgetary deficit was €5,293m. in 2009, according to preliminary figures, equivalent to 8.4% of GDP. Slovakia's gross general government debt was €22.585m. in that year, equivalent to 35.7% of GDP. At the end of 2006 Slovakia's total external debt was US $27,085m., of which $4,508m. was long-term public debt. In 2003 the cost of debt-servicing was equivalent to 13.8% of the value of exports of goods and services. According to the ILO, the annual rate of inflation averaged 4.7% in 2000–09. Consumer prices increased by 1.6% in 2009, and by 0.9% in 2010. According to official figures, the average rate of unemployment was 9.6% in 2008, but increased to 12.1% in 2009.

Following independence in 1993, the economy successfully shifted from its traditional reliance on industry to services, and from state to private ownership. The country experienced more rapid economic growth than many other transition states of Central and South-Eastern Europe during the 1990s and 2000s. Particularly after the accession to power of the Government led by Mikuláš Dzurinda in 1998, which promoted extensive privatization and greater transparency, Slovakia became a favoured destination for foreign investment. This was further encouraged by the introduction of a 19% uniform rate of income tax, corporate tax and value-added tax (VAT) in 2004. Although the Government of Robert Fico, which assumed power in July 2006, adopted a more hesitant approach towards privatization than had its predecessor, the requirements of the EU's exchange rate mechanism (ERM II), which Slovakia had entered in November 2005, effectively prevented any substantial redirection of economic policy, and Slovakia adopted the euro on 1 January 2009, becoming the second country of Central and South-Eastern Europe to do so, after Slovenia. The global financial crisis from late 2008 resulted in a substantial rise in unemployment and a contraction in GDP, owing in part to the recession in Germany (a major trading partner). Despite the Government's adoption in November of a wide-ranging programme to mitigate the impact of the downturn, the state budget deficit increased from 2.3% of GDP in 2008 to some 8.4% of GDP in 2009 (remaining at about that level in 2010). Following legislative elections in June 2010, the centre-right coalition Government of Iveta Radičová pledged to reduce the budget deficit to 4.9% of GDP by 2011 and to the 3% maximum stipulated by the EU by 2013. With this objective, the Government planned to reduce sharply public sector salaries and employment, and to introduce a temporary increase in VAT, to 20%, in order to reduce state expenditure by about €970m.; the proposals prompted a series of trade union protests. In a symbolic measure, it was agreed to reduce the salaries of 2,600 senior officials, including the President, by 24% in 2010. In August the legislature voted against the payment of Slovakias's share (equivalent to about 1% of the total) of the €110,000m. emergency assistance fund that had been agreed for the severely indebted Greek economy, prompting criticism from the European Commission. However, Slovakia's participation in an EU stabilization fund, which had also been established to assist euro zone member states in avoiding insolvency, was approved; its contribution to the fund was to total some €4,300m. Following a strong recovery of GDP growth in 2010, an IMF mission issued a statement in April 2011 commending the Government's fiscal adjustment efforts and objectives.

PUBLIC HOLIDAYS

2012: 1 January (Anniversary of the Slovak Republic), 6 January (Epiphany), 13 April (Good Friday), 16 April (Easter Monday), 1 May (Labour Day), 8 May (Anniversary of Liberation), 5 July (Day of the Slav Apostles, Cyril and Methodius), 29 August (National Day, Anniversary of the Slovak National Uprising), 1 September (Constitution Day), 15 September (Our Lady of Seven Sorrows), 1 November (All Saints' Day), 17 November (Day of Freedom and Democracy), 24–26 December (Christmas).

Statistical Survey

Source: Statistical Office of the Slovak Republic, Miletičova 3, 824 67 Bratislava; tel. (2) 5023-6340; fax (2) 5556-1361; e-mail agnesa.kralikova@statistics.sk; internet www.statistics.sk.

Area and Population

AREA, POPULATION AND DENSITY

Area (sq km)	49,033*
Population (census results)	
3 March 1991	5,274,335
26 May 2001	
Males	2,612,515
Females	2,766,940
Total	5,379,455
Population (official estimates at 31 December)	
2008	5,412,254
2009	5,424,925
2010	5,435,273
Density (per sq km) at 31 December 2010	110.8

* 18,932 sq miles.

POPULATION BY AGE AND SEX
(official estimates at 31 December 2009)

	Males	Females	Total
0–14	426,381	404,939	831,320
15–64	1,962,268	1,966,203	3,928,471
65 and over	248,289	416,845	665,134
Total	**2,636,938**	**2,787,987**	**5,424,925**

POPULATION BY ETHNIC GROUP
(at 2001 census)

	Number	%
Slovak	4,614,854	85.79
Hungarian	520,528	9.68
Gypsy (Roma)	89,920	1.67
Czech	46,968	0.87
Ruthenian, Ukrainian	35,015	0.65
German	5,405	0.10
Others (incl. undeclared)	66,765	1.24
Total	**5,379,455**	**100.00**

SLOVAKIA

REGIONS
(at 31 December 2009)

	Area (sq km)	Population	Density (per sq km)
Banská Bystrica	9,455	653,186	69.1
Bratislava	2,053	622,706	303.3
Košice	6,753	778,120	115.2
Nitra	6,343	705,661	111.3
Prešov	8,993	807,011	89.7
Trenčín	4,501	599,214	133.1
Trnava	4,148	561,525	135.4
Žilina	6,788	697,502	102.8
Total	49,034	5,424,925	110.6

Note: Each region is named after its principal city.

PRINCIPAL TOWNS
(estimated population at 31 December 2002)

Bratislava (capital)	427,049	Trnava	69,868
Košice	235,509	Martin	60,017
Prešov	92,486	Trenčín	57,413
Nitra	86,958	Poprad	55,982
Žilina	85,347	Prievidza	52,658
Banská Bystrica	82,493	Zvolen	43,674

Mid-2009 ('000, incl. suburbs, UN estimate): Bratislava 428 (Source: UN, *World Urbanization Prospects: The 2009 Revision*).

BIRTHS, MARRIAGES AND DEATHS

	Registered live births		Registered marriages		Registered deaths	
	Number	Rate (per 1,000)	Number	Rate (per 1,000)	Number	Rate (per 1,000)
2002	50,841	9.5	25,062	4.7	51,532	9.6
2003	51,713	9.6	26,002	4.8	52,230	9.7
2004	53,747	10.0	27,885	5.2	51,852	9.6
2005	54,430	10.1	26,149	4.9	53,475	9.9
2006	53,904	10.0	25,939	4.8	53,301	9.9
2007	54,424	10.1	27,437	5.1	53,856	10.0
2008	57,360	10.6	28,293	5.2	53,164	9.8
2009	61,217	11.3	26,356	4.9	52,913	9.8

Life expectancy (years at birth, WHO estimates): 75 (males 71; females 79) in 2008 (Source: WHO, *World Health Statistics*).

ECONOMICALLY ACTIVE POPULATION
(labour force surveys, '000 persons)

	2006	2007	2008
Agriculture, hunting, forestry and fishing	100.8	99.3	98.0
Mining and quarrying	16.0	16.4	14.2
Manufacturing	608.6	634.2	647.6
Electricity, gas and water	41.9	40.3	42.1
Construction	226.1	237.1	256.7
Wholesale and retail trade; repair of motor vehicles, motorcycles and personal and household goods	290.6	300.0	298.9
Hotels and restaurants	101.8	102.0	107.6
Transport, storage and communications	156.2	165.3	177.7
Financial intermediation	51.8	47.6	55.2
Real estate, renting and business services	131.6	145.7	157.9
Public administration and defence; compulsory social security	161.8	159.8	167.1
Education	166.8	163.4	163.8
Health and social work	154.5	154.7	154.1

—continued	2006	2007	2008
Other community, social and personal service activities	85.3	82.1	86.4
Private households with employed persons	5.8	8.2	5.7
Extra-territorial organizations	0.2	0.8	0.7
Sub-total	2,299.5	2,356.8	2,433.5
Activities not adequately defined	1.9	0.5	0.3
Total	2,301.4	2,357.3	2,433.8
Unemployed	353.4	291.9	257.5
Total labour force	2,654.8	2,649.2	2,691.3
Males	1,470.7	1,465.1	1,488.3
Females	1,184.2	1,184.0	1,202.8

Source: ILO.

Health and Welfare

KEY INDICATORS

Total fertility rate (children per woman, 2008)	1.3
Under-5 mortality rate (per 1,000 live births, 2008)	7
HIV/AIDS (% of persons aged 15–49, 2007)	<0.1
Physicians (per 1,000 head, 2004)	3.1
Hospital beds (per 1,000 head, 2006)	6.8
Health expenditure (2007): US $ per head (PPP)	1,077
Health expenditure (2007): % of GDP	7.7
Health expenditure (2007): public (% of total)	66.8
Total carbon dioxide emissions ('000 metric tons, 2007)	36,955.1
Carbon dioxide emissions per head (metric tons, 2007)	6.8
Human Development Index (2010): ranking	31
Human Development Index (2010): value	0.818

For sources and definitions, see explanatory note on p. vi.

Agriculture

PRINCIPAL CROPS
('000 metric tons)

	2007	2008	2009
Wheat	1,379.6	1,819.5	1,537.9
Barley	659.6	891.3	675.5
Maize	623.9	1,260.6	988.1
Rye	54.4	80.3	56.9
Oats	37.4	35.0	34.6
Triticale (wheat-rye hybrid)	35.9	47.2	33.9
Potatoes	287.7	245.3	216.1
Sugar beet	846.5	678.9	898.8
Peas, dry	19.3	13.9	11.7
Sunflower seed	132.7	192.3	187.2
Rapeseed	321.1	424.4	386.7
Cabbages and other brassicas	77.2	78.6	74.1
Tomatoes	55.2	56.6	51.9
Chillies and peppers, green	26.8	24.6	26.2
Cucumbers and gherkins	27.6	27.4	12.1
Onions, dry	22.7	28.5	26.4
Carrots and turnips	31.8	37.2	35.7
Apples	17.7	41.8	50.0
Grapes	49.1	51.6	42.1
Watermelons	5.6	4.1	4.5
Tobacco, unmanufactured	0.4	—	—

Aggregate production ('000 metric tons, may include official, semi-official or estimated data): Total cereals 2,793.2 in 2007, 4,137.0 in 2008, 3,332.8 in 2009; Total roots and tubers 287.7 in 2007, 245.3 in 2008, 216.1 in 2009; Total vegetables (incl. melons) 309.0 in 2007, 334.3 in 2008, 313.4 in 2009; Total fruits (excl. melons) 127.1 in 2007, 156.0 in 2008, 150.6 in 2009.

Source: FAO.

SLOVAKIA

LIVESTOCK
('000 head, year ending 30 September)

	2007	2008	2009
Cattle	508	502	484
Pigs	1,105	749	741
Sheep	333	362	377
Goats	38	37	36
Horses	8	8	7
Chickens	12,443	10,879	13,249

Source: FAO.

LIVESTOCK PRODUCTS
('000 metric tons)

	2007	2008	2009
Cattle meat	23.0	19.9	17.7
Pig meat	113.8	102.4	88.4
Chicken meat	83.0	75.5	75.1
Cows' milk	1,074.7	1,057.3	95.7
Goats' milk*	8.2	8.2	8.2
Hen eggs	72.5	71.3	70.6
Other poultry eggs*	5.0	5.0	5.0

* FAO estimates.
Source: FAO.

Forestry

ROUNDWOOD REMOVALS
('000 cubic metres, excl. bark)

	2007	2008	2009
Sawlogs, veneer logs and logs for sleepers	4,862	5,410	4,745
Pulpwood	2,813	3,249	3,721
Other industrial wood	40	56	36
Fuel wood	417	555	586
Total	8,131	9,269	9,087

Source: FAO.

SAWNWOOD PRODUCTION
('000 cubic metres, incl. railway sleepers)

	2007	2008	2009
Coniferous (softwood)	1,872	2,063	1,605
Broadleaved (hardwood)	909	779	649
Total	2,781	2,842	2,254

Source: FAO.

Fishing
(metric tons, live weight)

	2006	2007	2008
Capture	1,718	1,994	1,655
Common carp	1,184	1,430	1,178
Goldfish	72	82	63
Northern pike	61	58	54
Pike-perch	65	68	63
Breams	95	76	69
Aquaculture	1,263	1,199	1,071
Common carp	414	273	252
Rainbow trout	784	879	761
Total catch (incl. others)	2,981	3,193	2,726

Source: FAO.

Mining
('000 metric tons, unless otherwise indicated)

	2007	2008	2009
Coal (brown and lignite)	2,111	2,423	2,572
Crude petroleum	23	21	21
Natural gas (million cu m)	134	111	110*
Limestone and other calcareous stones for cement	9,615	4,992	5,099
Sands and gravel ('000 cubic m)*	8,200	9,300	8,500*

* Estimated production.
Source: US Geological Survey.

Industry

SELECTED PRODUCTS
('000 metric tons, unless otherwise indicated)

	2005	2006	2007
Wheat flour	325	308	315
Refined sugar	88	274	151
Beer ('000 hectolitres)	3,810	3,987	3,557
Wine ('000 hectolitres)	350	319	271
Distilled alcoholic beverages ('000 hectolitres)	141	117	138
Footwear with uppers of leather ('000 pairs)	12,388	12,770	12,869
Paints and enamels dissolved in an aqueous medium	17.2	16.7	16.4
Black-coal coke	1,917	1,925	1,817
Residual fuel oils	543	654	544
Gas-diesel (distillate fuel) oil	2,455	2,587	2,819
Cement	3,282	3,389	3,504
Pig-iron*	3,681	4,145	4,145
Crude steel*	4,242	5,094	5,100
Alumina*	162.5	158.3	160.5
Passenger motor cars ('000 units)	177	263	525
Electric energy	31,455	28,056	31,418

* Source: US Geological Survey.
Source: UN Industrial Commodity Statistics Database.

2009 ('000 metric tons): Cement 3,021; Pig-iron 3,019; Crude steel 3,747; Aluminium ingot (primary) 149.6 (Source: US Geological Survey).

Finance

CURRENCY AND EXCHANGE RATES
Monetary Units
100 cent = 1 euro (€).

Sterling, Dollar and Euro Equivalents (31 December 2010)
£1 sterling = 1.172 euros;
US $1 = 0.748 euros;
€10 = £8.54 = $13.36.

Average Exchange Rate (euros per US $)
2008   0.6827
2009   0.7198
2010   0.7550

Note: Slovakia adopted the euro on 1 January 2009, replacing the former national currency at a fixed exchange rate of €1 = 30.126 koruna.

SLOVAKIA

GOVERNMENT FINANCE
(general government transactions, non-cash basis, million koruna unless otherwise indicated)

Summary of Balances

	2007	2008	2009*
Revenue	614,003	677,716	21,203
Less Expense	661,183	733,734	26,496
Net operating balance	−47,181	−56,018	−5,293
Less Net acquisition of non-financial assets	14,301	13,924	−294
Net lending/borrowing	−32,880	−42,094	−4,999

Revenue

	2007	2008	2009*
Taxes	320,669	339,518	9,959
Taxes on income, profits and capital gains	111,103	125,814	3,327
Taxes on goods and services	202,614	206,508	6,377
Social contributions	217,744	243,127	7,993
Grants	7,870	9,860	595
Other revenue	67,720	85,210	2,657
Total	614,003	677,716	21,203

Expense/Outlays

Expense by economic type	2007	2008	2009*
Compensation of employees	125,210	138,457	4,867
Use of goods and services	82,128	100,130	2,916
Compensation of fixed capital	46,191	48,450	1,715
Interest	25,257	25,551	903
Subsidies	40,744	47,667	1,057
Grants	15,622	17,574	664
Social benefits	292,536	323,634	11,949
Other expense	33,495	32,271	2,425
Total	661,183	733,734	26,496

Outlays by functions of government†	2007	2008	2009*
General public services	77,083	107,152	3,685
Defence	25,946	27,369	800
Public order and safety	35,935	39,175	1,365
Economic affairs	85,167	100,459	3,614
Environmental protection	12,738	13,177	524
Housing and community amenities	13,247	12,965	507
Health	115,035	132,225	4,698
Recreation, culture and religion	19,520	18,464	713
Education	62,419	65,731	2,701
Social protection	199,793	203,093	7,769
Statistical discrepancy	—	—	−174
Total	646,882	719,810	26,203

* Preliminary figures in € million.
† Including net acquisition of non-financial assets.

Source: IMF, *Government Finance Statistics Yearbook*.

INTERNATIONAL RESERVES
(US $ million at 31 December)

	2009	2010
Gold (Eurosystem valuation)	1,128	1,441
IMF special drawing rights	536	526
Foreign exchange	50	52
Total	1,714	2,019

Source: IMF, *International Financial Statistics*.

MONEY SUPPLY
(incl. shares, depository corporations, national residency criteria, € million at 31 December)

	2009	2010
Currency issued	7,597	7,896
Demand deposits	16,707	18,371
Other deposits	17,480	17,444
Securities other than shares	3,530	3,456
Money market fund shares	1,757	1,739
Shares and other equity	2,176	2,305
Other items (net)	−2,263	−1,896
Total	46,984	49,315

Source: IMF, *International Financial Statistics*.

COST OF LIVING
(Consumer Price Index; base December 2000 = 100)

	2008	2009	2010
Foodstuffs and non-alcoholic beverages	127.1	123.0	124.9
Alcoholic beverages and tobacco	152.1	164.2	173.6
Clothing and footwear	108.1	107.2	105.8
Housing, water, electricity, gas and other fuels	210.1	223.9	224.1
All items (incl. others)	146.5	148.9	150.3

NATIONAL ACCOUNTS
(€ million at current prices)

Expenditure on the Gross Domestic Product

	2008	2009	2010
Final consumption expenditure	50,092	51,009	51,323
Households	37,604	37,714	37,928
Non-profit institutions serving households	685	693	707
General government	11,803	12,602	12,688
Gross capital formation	18,507	12,321	14,730
Gross fixed capital formation	16,576	12,991	13,390
Changes in inventories	1,932	−670	1,340
Total domestic expenditure	68,600	63,329	66,053
Exports of goods and services	55,793	44,506	53,292
Less Imports of goods and services	57,386	44,784	53,964
Statistical discrepancy	—	—	525
GDP in purchasers' values	67,007	63,051	65,906

Gross Domestic Product by Economic Activity

	2008	2009	2010
Agriculture, hunting, forestry and fishing	2,559	2,256	2,314
Mining and quarrying	380	330	358
Manufacturing	14,033	11,216	12,410
Construction	5,897	5,440	5,416
Electricity, gas and water supply	3,197	3,169	2,750
Wholesale and retail trade; repair of motor vehicles	9,644	9,121	9,264
Hotels and restaurants	823	790	799
Transport and storage	4,485	4,061	4,523
Financial intermediation	1,999	2,331	2,251
Real estate, renting and business activities	8,710	8,642	9,269
Other services	9,076	9,982	10,854
Sub-total	60,803	57,338	60,208
Taxes, less subsidies, on products	6,204	5,714	5,697
GDP in purchasers' values	67,007	63,051	65,906

SLOVAKIA

BALANCE OF PAYMENTS
(US $ million)

	2007	2008	2009
Exports of goods f.o.b.	57,806	70,271	55,515
Imports of goods f.o.b.	−58,715	−71,170	−53,799
Trade balance	−909	−899	1,715
Exports of services	7,063	8,493	6,278
Imports of services	−6,531	−9,178	−8,007
Balance on goods and services	−376	−1,584	−13
Other income received	2,340	3,392	2,744
Other income paid	−5,628	−6,737	−4,581
Balance on goods, services and income	−3,665	−4,928	−1,851
Current transfers received	2,070	2,523	1,837
Current transfers paid	−2,508	−3,781	−2,797
Current balance	−4,103	−6,185	−2,810
Capital account	465	1,154	624
Direct investment abroad	−403	−251	−410
Direct investment from abroad	3,363	3,231	−31
Portfolio investment assets	−1,083	634	−2,686
Portfolio investment liabilities	349	1,796	1,513
Other investment assets	−1,535	−974	−3,857
Other investment liabilities	6,281	2,912	9,851
Financial derivatives assets	265	−409	585
Financial derivatives liabilities	−213	255	−231
Net errors and omissions	302	−2,312	−2,719
Overall balance	3,688	−149	−171

Source: IMF, *International Financial Statistics*.

External Trade

PRINCIPAL COMMODITIES
(distribution by SITC, US $ million)

Imports f.o.b.	2006	2007	2008
Food and live animals	1,888.2	2,539.9	3,304.5
Crude materials (inedible) except fuels	1,371.5	1,655.7	2,040.8
Mineral fuels, lubricants, etc.	5,994.9	6,396.6	9,314.9
Petroleum, petroleum products, etc.	3,453.4	4,014.0	5,472.4
Gas, natural and manufactured	1,963.2	1,600.9	2,656.6
Chemicals and related products	3,980.9	5,185.1	6,313.8
Medicinal and pharmaceutical products	1,119.4	1,573.4	1,779.8
Basic manufactures	7,586.0	10,262.3	12,338.1
Iron and steel	1,808.9	2,733.0	3,461.8
Metal manufactures	1,743.9	2,433.6	3,071.2
Machinery and transport equipment	17,394.6	25,001.3	31,210.4
General industrial machinery and equipment	2,069.1	2,534.2	3,039.0
Telecommunication and sound recording equipment	2,554.1	5,739.3	7,588.9
Electrical machinery, apparatus and appliances	3,520.0	4,441.4	5,261.5
Road vehicles	5,338.2	8,130.7	9,597.6
Miscellaneous manufactured articles	5,917.6	6,282.3	7,116.0
Professional, scientific and controlling instruments	2,485.0	1,797.6	1,779.6
Total (incl. others)	44,758.6	59,207.8	72,611.6

Exports f.o.b.	2006	2007	2008
Food and live animals	1,564.5	1,989.8	2,198.9
Mineral fuels, lubricants, etc.	2,273.0	2,591.2	3,536.9
Petroleum, petroleum products, etc.	2,124.5	2,526.9	3,364.0
Chemicals and related products	2,039.2	2,644.9	3,075.7
Basic manufactures	9,465.7	12,012.7	13,850.2
Rubber manufactures	933.6	1,135.0	1,323.1
Paper, paperboard and articles of paper pulp	970.8	1,140.2	1,451.4
Iron and steel	3,152.9	4,156.9	5,133.3
Metal manufactures	1,527.2	2,191.9	2,607.4
Machinery and transport equipment	20,017.7	30,668.3	37,873.6
General industrial machinery and equipment	1,887.6	2,544.2	3,120.7
Telecommunications and sound recording equipment	4,016.8	7,188.7	10,444.5
Electrical machinery, apparatus and appliances	2,928.8	3,761.5	4,415.4
Road vehicles	8,385.4	13,719.1	15,467.8
Miscellaneous manufactured articles	4,016.1	5,508.3	6,260.2
Total (incl. others)	41,686.2	58,036.0	70,188.7

Source: UN, *International Trade Statistics Yearbook*.

2009 (distribution by SITC, € million): *Imports*: Food and live animals 2,184; Mineral fuels, lubricants, etc. 4,586; Chemicals and related products 3,690; Basic manufactures 5,825; Machinery and transport equipment 16,443; Miscellaneous manufactured articles 4,435; Total (incl. others) 38,775. *Exports*: Food and live animals 1,526; Mineral fuels, lubricants, etc. 1,823; Chemicals and related products 1,777; Basic manufactures 7,419; Machinery and transport equipment 21,752; Miscellaneous manufactured articles 4,189; Total (incl. others) 39,721.

PRINCIPAL TRADING PARTNERS
(US $ million)

Imports f.o.b.	2006	2007	2008
Austria	1,451.3	1,755.2	2,108.1
Belgium	535.3	672.9	904.0
China, People's Republic	1,670.2	3,041.9	4,173.2
Czech Republic	5,105.6	6,453.3	8,257.4
France (incl. Monaco)	1,408.9	2,203.6	2,905.9
Germany	8,683.9	11,080.9	14,396.2
Hungary	1,952.6	3,040.8	3,599.4
Italy	1,982.4	2,253.5	2,719.6
Japan	870.1	870.0	1,051.4
Korea, Republic	1,738.8	3,031.7	4,219.5
Netherlands	578.2	753.1	886.4
Poland	1,900.3	2,346.9	2,800.2
Russia	5,074.6	5,429.9	7,744.5
Spain	664.6	861.3	888.8
Switzerland (incl. Liechtenstein)	345.4	468.6	494.7
Ukraine	564.2	601.3	751.1
United Kingdom	643.5	763.5	1,005.6
USA	559.7	605.1	897.4
Total (incl. others)	44,758.6	59,207.8	72,611.6

SLOVAKIA

Exports f.o.b.	2006	2007	2008
Austria	2,524.7	3,366.4	4,003.1
Belgium	765.0	1,238.2	1,254.5
Czech Republic	5,952.6	7,517.9	9,161.2
Denmark	352.7	571.8	612.8
France (incl. Monaco)	1,782.7	3,780.6	4,764.5
Germany	9,368.5	12,245.4	14,178.5
Hungary	2,486.5	3,684.0	4,327.4
Italy	2,689.5	3,652.1	4,132.2
Netherlands	1,749.8	2,041.6	2,129.0
Poland	2,580.5	3,596.2	4,635.5
Romania	633.8	1,040.1	1,314.1
Russia	687.3	1,308.6	2,625.9
Slovenia	358.8	455.2	544.6
Spain	1,189.5	1,783.2	1,692.2
Sweden	557.6	841.3	1,046.3
Switzerland (incl. Liechtenstein)	317.8	483.3	509.4
Turkey	408.8	657.1	932.4
Ukraine	542.7	781.1	980.1
United Kingdom	1,627.0	2,813.6	3,337.3
USA	1,342.2	1,441.7	1,200.9
Total (incl. others)	41,686.2	58,036.0	70,188.7

Source: UN, *International Trade Statistics Yearbook*.

2009 (€ million): *Imports:* Austria 1,006; China 2,165; Czech Republic 4,319; France 1,653; Germany 5,911; Hungary 1,851; Italy 1,440; Korea, Republic 2,619; Poland 1,434; Russia 3,467; United Kingdom 883; Total (incl. others) 38,775. *Exports:* Austria 2,350; Belgium 662; Czech Republic 5,277; France 3,088; Germany 7,855; Hungary 2,737; Italy 2,379; Netherlands 1,171; Poland 2,788; Russia 1,414; Spain 946; Sweden 697; Turkey 684; United Kingdom 1,822; USA 426; Total (incl. others) 39,721.

Transport

SUMMARY

	2007	2008	2009
Railway transport:			
freight ('000 metric tons)	51,813	47,910	37,603
passengers ('000)	47,070	48,744	46,667
Public road transport:			
freight ('000 metric tons)	41,169	42,639	36,920
passengers ('000)	384,637	365,519	323,142
Waterway transport: freight ('000 metric tons)	1,806	1,767	2,192

ROAD TRAFFIC
(motor vehicles in use at 31 December)

	2007	2008	2009
Passenger cars ('000)	1,434	1,545	1,589
Buses and coaches ('000)	10	11	9
Goods vehicles ('000)	196	227	247
Motorcycles ('000)	64	70	55

SHIPPING
Merchant Fleet
(registered at 31 December)

	2007	2008	2009
Number of vessels	57	51	35
Displacement ('000 gross registered tons)	233.3	189.9	146.8

Source: IHS Fairplay, *World Fleet Statistics*.

CIVIL AVIATION
(traffic on scheduled services)

	2007	2008	2009
Passengers carried ('000)	3,068	4,176	2,288
Freight carried (metric tons)	1,318	7	7

Tourism

FOREIGN TOURIST ARRIVALS
(visitors at accommodation facilities)

Country of origin	2007	2008	2009
Austria	62,661	62,052	50,065
Czech Republic	490,986	537,180	425,414
France	41,301	43,958	34,045
Germany	176,059	164,694	133,989
Hungary	93,797	90,123	56,111
Italy	58,184	54,722	50,982
Poland	243,917	308,437	164,712
United Kingdom	63,193	66,628	42,315
USA	31,977	28,739	20,815
Total (incl. others)	1,684,526	1,766,529	1,298,075

Tourism receipts (US$ million, incl. passenger transport): 1,655 in 2006; 2,352 in 2007; 3,004 in 2008 (Source: World Tourism Organization).

Communications Media

	2007	2008	2009
Telephones ('000 main lines in use)	1,150.8	1,097.8	1,021.7
Mobile cellular telephones ('000 subscribers)	6,068.1	5,520.0*	5,497.7
Internet users ('000)†	3,333.6	3,850.6	4,063.6
Broadband subscribers ('000)	472.0	604.7	777.8
Newspapers: titles	498	330	11
Newspapers: circulation ('000 copies)	234,775	147,331	n.a.
Periodicals: titles	1,047	1,805	1,289
Periodicals: circulation ('000 copies)	181,993	113,466	n.a.

*Only active mobile cellular subscribers counted from January 2008.
†Estimates.

Personal computers: 3,140,000 (580.8 per 1,000 persons) in 2008.

Radio receivers (licensed): 1,476,753 in 2005; 1,500,079 in 2006; 1,504,595 in 2007.

Television receivers (licensed): 1,381,457 in 2005; 1,400,166 in 2006; 1,404,105 in 2007.

Book production (number of titles): 2,064 in 1997; 4,386 in 1998; 3,153 in 1999.

Sources: partly International Telecommunication Union and UNESCO Institute for Statistics.

Education

(2009, unless otherwise indicated)

	Institutions	Teachers	Students
Kindergarten	2,765	13,238	133,655
Primary (basic)	2,214	29,987	437,223
Secondary: grammar	250	6,710	94,019
Secondary: specialized	493	13,473	189,265
Secondary: vocational*	181	2,589	51,882
Higher	33	10,961	144,018
Special schools	404	4,789	35,449

*2007 data.

Pupil-teacher ratio (primary education, UNESCO estimate): 16.6 in 2007/08 (Source: UNESCO Institute for Statistics).

Directory

The Government

HEAD OF STATE

President of the Republic: Ivan Gašparovič (elected 17 April 2004; inaugurated 15 June 2004; re-elected 4 April 2009, inaugurated 15 June 2009).

GOVERNMENT
(May 2011)

The Government comprises members of the Slovak Democratic and Christian Union-Democratic Party (SDCU-DP), Bridge, the Christian Democratic Movement (CDM), and Freedom and Solidarity (FAS).

Prime Minister: Iveta Radičová (SDCU-DP).
First Deputy Prime Minister, Minister of Transport, Post and Telecommunications: Ján Figeľ (CDM).
Deputy Prime Minister for Human and Minority Rights: Rudolf Chmel (Bridge).
Deputy Prime Minister, Minister of Finance: Ivan Mikloš (SDCU-DP).
Deputy Prime Minister, Minister of Labour, Social Affairs and the Family: Jozef Mihál (FAS).
Minister of the Interior: Daniel Lipšic (CDM).
Minister of Education, Science, Research and Sport: Eugen Jurzyca (SCDU-SP).
Minister of the Environment: József Nagy (Bridge).
Minister of Justice: Lucia Žitňanská (SCDU-DP).
Minister of Foreign Affairs: Mikuláš Dzurinda (SCDU-DP).
Minister of the Economy and Construction: Juraj Miškov (FAS).
Minister of Defence: Ľubomír Galko (FAS).
Minister of Culture and Tourism: Daniel Krajcer (FAS).
Minister of Health: Ivan Uhliarik (CDM).
Minister of Agriculture and Rural Development: Zsolt Simon (Bridge).

MINISTRIES

Office of the President: Hodžovo nám. 1, POB 128, 810 00 Bratislava; tel. (2) 5933-3319; fax (2) 5788-8357; e-mail informacie@prezident.sk; internet www.prezident.sk.
Office of the Government: nám. Slobody 1, 813 70 Bratislava; tel. (2) 5729-5111; fax (2) 5249-7595; e-mail urad@vlada.gov.sk; internet www.vlada.gov.sk.
Ministry of Agriculture and Rural Development: Dobrovičova 12, 812 66 Bratislava; tel. (2) 5926-6111; fax (2) 5296-3871; e-mail marcela.bodorikova@land.gov.sk; internet www.land.gov.sk.
Ministry of Culture and Tourism: nám. SNP 33, 813 31 Bratislava; tel. (2) 2048-2111; fax (2) 2048-2174; e-mail mksr@culture.gov.sk; internet www.culture.gov.sk.
Ministry of Defence and Construction: Kutuzovova 8, 832 47 Bratislava; tel. (2) 4425-8774; fax (2) 4425-3242; e-mail tlacove@mod.gov.sk; internet www.mod.gov.sk.
Ministry of the Economy: Mierová 19, 827 15 Bratislava; tel. (2) 4854-1111; fax (2) 4333-7827; e-mail palkovicova@economy.gov.sk; internet www.economy.gov.sk.
Ministry of Education, Science, Research and Sport: Stromová 1, 813 30 Bratislava; tel. (2) 5937-4111; fax (2) 5937-4335; e-mail minister@minedu.sk; internet www.minedu.sk.
Ministry of the Environment: nám. Ľ. Štúra 1, 812 35 Bratislava; tel. (2) 5956-1111; fax (2) 5956-2481; e-mail info@enviro.gov.sk; internet www.minzp.sk.
Ministry of Finance: Štefanovičova 5, POB 82, 817 82 Bratislava; tel. (2) 5958-1111; fax (2) 5958-3048; e-mail podatelna@mfsr.sk; internet www.finance.gov.sk.
Ministry of Foreign Affairs: Hlboká cesta 2, 833 36 Bratislava; tel. (2) 5978-1111; fax (2) 5978-3333; e-mail info@mzv.sk; internet www.mzv.sk.
Ministry of Health: Limbová 2, POB 52, 837 52 Bratislava; tel. (2) 5937-3111; fax (2) 5477-7983; e-mail office@health.gov.sk; internet www.health.gov.sk.
Ministry of the Interior: Pribinova 2, 812 72 Bratislava; tel. (2) 5094-1111; fax (2) 5094-4397; e-mail tokmv@minv.sk; internet www.minv.sk.
Ministry of Justice: Župné nám. 13, 813 11 Bratislava; tel. (2) 5935-3111; fax (2) 5935-3600; e-mail tlacove@justice.sk; internet www.justice.gov.sk.
Ministry of Labour, Social Affairs and the Family: Špitálska 4–6, 816 43 Bratislava; tel. (2) 2046-0000; fax (2) 5292-6136; e-mail tothova@employment.gov.sk; internet www.employment.gov.sk.
Ministry of Transport, Post and Telecommunications: nám. Slobody 6, POB 100, 810 05 Bratislava; tel. (2) 5949-4111; fax (2) 5249-4794; e-mail info@telecom.gov.sk; internet www.telecom.gov.sk.

President

Presidential Election, First Ballot, 21 March 2009

Candidates	Valid votes	%
Ivan Gašparovič	876,061	46.71
Iveta Radičová	713,735	38.05
František Mikloško	101,573	5.42
Zuzana Martináková	96,035	5.12
Milan Melník	45,985	2.45
Dagmara Bollová	21,378	1.14
Milan Sidor	20,862	1.11
Total	**1,875,629**	**100.00**

Second Ballot, 4 April 2009

Candidates	Valid votes	%
Ivan Gašparovič	1,234,787	55.53
Iveta Radičová	988,808	44.47
Total	**2,223,595**	**100.00**

Legislature

Národná rada Slovenskej republiky
(National Council of the Slovak Republic)

nám. Alexandra Dubčeka 1, 812 80 Bratislava; tel. (2) 5972-1111; fax (2) 5441-9529; e-mail info@nrsr.sk; internet www.nrsr.sk.

Chairman: Richard Sulík.

General Election, 12 June 2010

Party	Votes	% of votes	Seats
Direction-Social Democracy	880,111	34.79	62
Slovak Democratic and Christian Union-Democratic Party	390,042	15.42	28
Freedom and Solidarity	307,287	12.14	22
Christian Democratic Movement	215,755	8.52	15
Bridge	205,538	8.12	14
Slovak National Party	128,490	5.07	9
Party of the Hungarian Coalition	109,638	4.33	—
People's Party—Movement for a Democratic Slovakia	109,480	4.32	—
Party of the Democratic Left	61,137	2.41	—
Our Slovakia People's Party	33,724	1.33	—
Others	88,183	3.55	—
Total valid votes	**2,529,385**	**100.00**	**150**

Election Commission

Ústredná volebná komisia, Ministerstva vnútra (Central Elections Commission, Ministry of the Interior): Drieňova 22, 826 86 Bratislava; tel. (2) 4859-1111; fax (2) 4333-3175; e-mail ovr.svs@mvsr.vs.sk; internet www.civil.gov.sk; Chair. Edita Pfundtner.

Political Organizations

Bridge (Most/Híd): Trnavská cesta 37, 831 04 Bratislava; tel. (2) 4911-4555; fax (2) 4911-4500; e-mail office@most-hid.sk; internet www.most-hid.sk; f. 2009 by fmr mems of the Party of the Hungarian

SLOVAKIA

Coalition; promotes co-operation between all sections of society; Chair. BÉLA BUGÁR.

Christian Democratic Movement (CDM) (Kresťansko-demokratické hnutie—KDH): Bajkalská 25, 821 09 Bratislava; tel. (2) 5823-3431; fax (2) 5823-3434; e-mail tlacove@kdh.sk; internet www.kdh.sk; f. 1990; conservative; supports Christian and family values; Chair. JÁN FIGEĽ.

Communist Party of Slovakia (CPS) (Komunistická strana Slovenska—KSS): Ústredný výbor, Hattalova 12A, 831 03 Bratislava; tel. (2) 4464-4101; fax (2) 4437-2540; e-mail sekr@kss.sk; internet www.kss.sk; f. 1992 following merger of two Marxist parties, the Union of Communists of Slovakia and the Communist Party of Slovakia—91; Pres. JOZEF HRDLIČKA.

Direction-Social Democracy (Smer-Sociálna demokracia): Súmračná 25, 821 02 Bratislava; tel. and fax (2) 4342-6297; e-mail sekretariat.fico@strana-smer.sk; internet www.strana-smer.sk; f. 1999 as Direction (Smer); absorbed the Party of Civic Understanding in 2003; merged with the Social Democratic Party of Slovakia, the Social Democratic Alternative and the Party of the Democratic Left (unrelated to the party of the same name founded in 2005) in Jan. 2005, and name changed as above; absorbed the Left-wing Bloc in Dec. 2007; Chair. ROBERT FICO.

Freedom and Solidarity (FAS) (Sloboda a Solidarita—SaS): Čajakova 18, 811 05 Bratislava; fax (2) 5245-4089; e-mail sas@strana-sas.sk; internet www.strana-sas.sk; f. 2009; liberal; Chair. RICHARD SULÍK.

Green Party (Strana zelených): Sienkiewiczova 4, 811 09 Bratislava; tel. and fax (2) 5292-3231; e-mail sekretariat@stranazelenych.sk; internet www.stranazelenych.sk; f. 1989; regd 1991; supported Party of the Democratic Left in legislative elections of June 2010; Chair. PETER PILINSKÝ.

Our Slovakia People's Party (Ľudová strana Naše Slovensko—LSNS): E. F. Scherera 4801/20, 921 01 Piešťany; internet www.naseslovensko.org; f. 2000 as Party of Wine-Lovers; renamed People's Party of Social Solidarity in 2009; present name adopted in 2010; extreme nationalist; Chair MARIAN KOTLEBA.

Party of the Democratic Left (Strana demokratickej ľavice—SDL): Hurbanovo námestie 1, 811 06 Bratislava; tel. (2) 5464-2340; fax (2) 5464-2342; e-mail tlacove@mojasdl.sk; internet www.mojasdl.sk; f. 2005; social democratic; Chair. MAREK BLAHA.

Party of the Hungarian Coalition (PHC) (Strana maďarskej koalície/Magyar Koalíció Pártja): Čajakova 8, 811 05 Bratislava; tel. (2) 5249-5546; fax (2) 5249-5264; e-mail smk@smk.sk; internet www.mkp.sk; f. 1998 by merger of Coexistence (Spolužitie/Együttélés), the Hungarian Christian Democratic Movement and the Hungarian Civic Party; Chair. JÓZSEF BERÉNYI.

People's Party—Movement for a Democratic Slovakia (PP—MDS) (Ľudová strana—Hnutie za Demokratické Slovensko—LS—HZDS): POB 49, Tomášikova 32A, 830 00 Bratislava; tel. (2) 4822-0309; fax (2) 4822-0329; e-mail predseda@hzds.sk; internet www.hzds.sk; f. 1991 as Movement for a Democratic Slovakia; present name adopted in 2003; Chair. VLADIMÍR MEČIAR.

Slovak Democratic and Christian Union-Democratic Party (SDCU-DP) (Slovenská demokratická a kresťanská únia-Demokratická strana—SDKU-DS): Ružinovská 28, 827 35 Bratislava; tel. (2) 4341-4102; fax (2) 4341-4106; e-mail sdku@sdkuonline.sk; internet www.sdku-ds.sk; f. 2000 as the Slovak Democratic and Christian Union; name changed as above following merger with the Democratic Party in Jan. 2006; Chair. MIKULÁŠ DZURINDA.

Slovak National Party (SNP) (Slovenská národná strana—SNS): Šafárikovo nám. 3, 814 99 Bratislava; tel. (2) 5263-4014; fax (2) 5296-6188; e-mail sns@sns.sk; internet www.sns.sk; f. 1990; extreme nationalist; against ethnic-Hungarian representation in govt; Chair. JÁN SLOTA.

Diplomatic Representation

EMBASSIES IN SLOVAKIA

Albania: Podjavorinskej 4, 811 03 Bratislava; tel. 915678987 (mobile); Ambassador AGIM ISAKU.

Angola: Jelenia 4, 811 05 Bratislava 1; tel. (2) 5441-2164; fax (2) 5441-2182; e-mail embangola1@chello.sk; Ambassador ALBERTO CORREIA NETO.

Austria: Ventúrska 10, 811 01 Bratislava; tel. (2) 5930-1500; fax (2) 5443-2486; e-mail pressburg-ob@bmeia.gv.at; internet www.rakusko.eu; Ambassador JOSEF MARKUS WUKETICH.

Belarus: Jančova 5, 811 02 Bratislava; tel. (2) 6225-1052; fax (2) 6280-2026; e-mail slovakia@belembassy.org; internet www.belembassy.org/slovakia; Ambassador VLADIMIR SERPIKOV.

Belgium: Fraňa kráľa 5, 811 05 Bratislava; tel. (2) 5710-1211; fax (2) 5249-4296; e-mail ambabelbratis@stonline.sk; internet www.diplomatie.be/bratislava; Ambassador WALTER LION.

Brazil: Palisády 47, 811 06 Bratislava; tel. (2) 3218-1400; fax (2) 5441-8271; e-mail brasemb.bratislava@itamaraty.gov.br; Ambassador MARÍLIA SARDENBERG ZELNER GONÇALVES.

Bulgaria: Kuzmányho 1, 811 06 Bratislava 1; tel. (2) 5441-5308; fax (2) 5441-2404; e-mail bulharskoet@stonline.sk; internet www.bulgarianembassy.sk; Chargé d'affaires a.i. NACHKO GEORGIEV PEHLIVANOV.

China, People's Republic: Jančova 8B, 811 02 Bratislava; tel. and fax (2) 6280-4291; e-mail cinska.ambasada@gmail.com; internet sk.chineseembassy.org; Ambassador GU ZIPING.

Croatia: Mišikova 21, 811 06 Bratislava; tel. (2) 5720-2091; fax (2) 5443-5365; e-mail vrhbrat@mvpei.hr; internet sk.mvp.hr; Ambassador TOMISLAV CAR.

Cuba: Somolického 1A, 811 05 Bratislava; tel. (2) 5249-2777; fax (2) 5249-4200; e-mail embacuba@embacuba.sk; internet www.embacuba.sk; Ambassador DAVID PAULOVICH ESCALONA.

Cyprus: Michalská 12, 811 01 Bratislava; tel. (2) 3278-8111; fax (2) 3278-8122; e-mail office@cyembassy.sk; Ambassador MARIOS KOUNTOURIDES.

Czech Republic: POB 208, Hviezdoslavovo nám. 8, 810 00 Bratislava; tel. (2) 5920-3301; fax (2) 5920-3330; e-mail bratislava@embassy.mzv.cz; internet www.mzv.cz/bratislava; Ambassador JAKUB KARFÍK.

Denmark: Panská 27, 816 06 Bratislava; tel. (2) 5930-0200; fax (2) 5443-3656; e-mail btsamb@um.dk; internet www.ambbratislava.um.dk; Ambassador ANITA HUGAU.

Egypt: Feriencikova 14, 814 99 Bratislava 1; tel. (2) 5296-4462; fax (2) 5296-7791; e-mail egypt.embas@netax.sk; Ambassador IHAB AHMAD TALAAT NASR.

Finland: Palisády 29, 811 06 Bratislava; tel. (2) 5980-5111; fax (2) 5980-5120; e-mail sanomat.brt@formin.fi; internet www.finlandembassy.sk; Ambassador JUKKA JALMARI LEINO.

France: Hlavné nám. 7, 812 83 Bratislava; tel. (2) 5934-7111; fax (2) 5934-7199; e-mail diplo@france.sk; internet www.france.sk; Ambassador JEAN-MARIE BRUNO.

Georgia: Michalská 9, 811 01 Bratislava 1; tel. (2) 5464-6484; fax (2) 5464-6486; e-mail bratislava.emb@mfa.gov.ge; internet www.slovakia.mfa.gov.ge; Ambassador ALEKSANDR NALBANDOV.

Germany: Hviezdoslavovo nám. 10, 813 03 Bratislava; tel. (2) 5920-4400; fax (2) 5441-9634; e-mail info@germanembassy.sk; internet www.pressburg.diplo.de; Ambassador Dr AXEL HARTMANN.

Greece: Hlavné nám. 4, 811 01 Bratislava; tel. (2) 5443-4143; fax (2) 5443-4064; e-mail gremb.brt@mfa.gr; internet www.mfa.gr/bratislava; Ambassador NICOLAOS D. KANELLOS.

Holy See: Nekrasovova 17, 811 04 Bratislava; tel. (2) 5479-3528; fax (2) 5479-3529; e-mail nunziatura@nunziatura.sk; Apostolic Nuncio Most Rev. MARIO GIORDANA (Titular Archbishop of Minora).

Hungary: Sedlárska 3, 814 25 Bratislava; tel. (2) 5920-5200; fax (2) 5443-5484; e-mail mission.pzs@kum.hu; internet www.mfa.gov.hu/emb/bratislava; Ambassador ANTAL HEIZER.

India: Dunajská 4, 811 08 Bratislava; tel. (2) 5296-2915; fax (2) 5296-2921; e-mail eindia@slovanet.sk; internet www.indianembassy.sk; Ambassador RAJIV MISRA.

Indonesia: Brnianska 31, 81004 Bratislava; tel. (2) 5441-9886; fax (2) 5441-9890; e-mail indonesia@indonesia.sk; internet www.indonesia.sk; Ambassador HARSHA EDWANA JOESOEF.

Iraq: Korabinského 3, 811 02 Bratislava; tel. (2) 5413-1466; fax (2) 5413-1464; e-mail brtsemb@gmail.com; internet www.iraqembassy.sk; Ambassador MATHIL DHAJIF MAJID AL-SABTI.

Ireland: Carlton Savoy Bldg, Mostavá 2, 811 02 Bratislava 1; tel. (2) 5930-9611; fax (2) 5443-0690; e-mail bratislava@dfa.ie; internet www.embassyofireland.sk; Ambassador KATHRYN COLL.

Israel: Slávičie údolie 106, POB 6, 811 02 Bratislava; tel. (2) 5441-0557; fax (2) 5441-0850; e-mail cao-sec@bratislava.mfa.gov.il; internet bratislava.mfa.gov.il; Ambassador ALEXANDER BEN-ZVI.

Italy: Palisády 49, 811 06 Bratislava; tel. (2) 5980-0024; fax (2) 5441-3202; e-mail amb.bratislava@esteri.it; internet www.ambbratislava.esteri.it; Ambassador BRUNELLA BORZI CORNACCHIA.

Japan: Hlavné nám. 2, 813 27 Bratislava; tel. (2) 5980-0100; fax (2) 5443-2771; e-mail info@jpembassy.sk; internet www.sk.emb-japan.go.jp; Ambassador YOSHIO NOMOTO.

Korea, Republic: Dunajská 4, 811 08 Bratislava; tel. (2) 3307-0711; fax (2) 3307-0730; e-mail info@rokembassy.sk; internet svk.mofat.go.kr; f. ; Ambassador SEOK-SOONG SEO.

Kuwait: Hotel Radisson Blu Carlton, Hviezdoslavovo nám. 3, 811 02 Bratislava; tel. (2) 5939-0843; fax (2) 5939-0004; e-mail

SLOVAKIA

embassyofkuwbratislava@gmail.com; Ambassador BADER NASSER ALI AL-HOUTI.

Libya: Révova ul. 45, 811 02 Bratislava 1; tel. (2) 5441-0324; fax (2) 5441-0730; e-mail lpb@stonline.sk; Chargé d'affaires KHALIFA AHMED.

Netherlands: Fraňa Kráľa 5, 811 05 Bratislava; tel. (2) 5262-5081; fax (2) 5249-1075; e-mail btl@minbuza.nl; internet www .holandskoweb.com; Ambassador DAPHNE BERGSMA.

Norway: Palisády 29, 811 06 Bratislava; tel. (2) 5910-0100; fax (2) 5910-0115; e-mail emb.bratislava@mfa.no; internet www.norway .sk; Ambassador TRINE SKYMOEN.

Poland: Hummelova 4, 814 91 Bratislava 1; tel. (2) 5949-0211; fax (2) 5441-3184; e-mail bratyslawa.amb.sekretariat@msz.gov.pl; internet www.bratyslawa.polemb.net; Ambassador ANDRZEJ KRAWCZYK.

Portugal: Moskovská 10, 811 08 Bratislava 1; tel. (2) 5010-2211; fax (2) 5010-2222; e-mail embportbrat@stonline.sk; internet www .embport.sk; Ambassador JOAO LUÍS NIZA PINHEIRO.

Romania: Fraňa Kráľa 11, 811 05 Bratislava 1; tel. (2) 5249-1665; fax (2) 5244-4056; e-mail ro-embassy@mail.t-com.sk; internet bratislava.mae.ro; Ambassador FLORIN VODIȚĂ.

Russia: Godrova 4, 811 06 Bratislava; tel. (2) 5441-4436; fax (2) 5443-4910; e-mail info@rusemb.sk; internet www.rusemb.sk; Ambassador PAVEL M. KUZNETSOV.

Serbia: Búdková 38, 811 04 Bratislava; tel. (2) 5443-1927; fax (2) 5443-1933; e-mail embassy.serbia@internet.sk; internet www .bratislava.mfa.gov.rs; Ambassador DANKO PROKIĆ.

Slovenia: Ventúrska 5, POB 37, 813 15 Bratislava 1; tel. (2) 5726-7700; fax (2) 5245-0009; e-mail vbs@gov.si; internet www.bratislava .embassy.si; Ambassador STANISLAV VIDOVIČ.

Spain: Prepoštská 10, 811 01 Bratislava; tel. (2) 5441-5724; fax (2) 5441-5717; e-mail emb.bratislava@maec.es; internet www.maec.es/ Embajadas/bratislava; Ambassador JOSÉ ANGEL LÓPEZ JORRIN.

Switzerland: Tolstého 9, 811 06 Bratislava; tel. (2) 5930-1111; fax (2) 5930-1100; e-mail bts.vertretung@eda.admin.ch; internet www .eda.admin.ch/bratislava; Ambassador CHRISTIAN MARTIN FOTSCH.

Turkey: Holubyho 11, 811 03 Bratislava 1; tel. (2) 5441-5504; fax (2) 5441-3145; e-mail turkishembassy@nextra.sk; internet bratislava .emb.mfa.gov.tr; Ambassador FATMA DICLE KOPUZ.

Ukraine: Radvanská 35, 811 01 Bratislava; tel. (2) 5920-2810; fax (2) 5441-2651; e-mail ukremb@ukrembassy.sk; internet www.mfa.gov .ua/slovakia; Ambassador OLEH HAVAŠI.

United Kingdom: Panská 16, 811 01 Bratislava; tel. (2) 5998-2000; fax (2) 5998-2237; e-mail bebra@internet.sk; internet ukinslovakia .fco.gov.uk; Chargé d'affaires a.i. DOMINIC SCHROEDER.

USA: POB 309, 814 99 Bratislava; tel. (2) 5443-3338; fax (2) 5441-8861; e-mail consulbratislava@state.gov; internet slovakia .usembassy.gov; Ambassador THEODORE SEDGWICK.

Judicial System

The judicial system of Slovakia has three levels: district courts (45), regional courts (eight) and the Supreme Court. Regional courts serve as courts of appeal to the district courts, as well as serving as courts of first instance in some cases; the Supreme Court is the highest judicial authority in the country, operating as a court of cassation and appeal for Regional Courts. There is also a Constitutional Court to ensure compliance with the Constitution. In April 2002 an 18-member Judicial Council was elected, all of whom were lawyers, and nine of whom were judges. Three members are nominated by the President, three by the legislature, three by the Government, and eight are elected by the judges themselves. The final member is the Chairman of the Supreme Court. The Council proposes candidates for judgeships, decides on the assignment of judges, comments on the budget, and elects the Chief Justice of the Supreme Court.

Supreme Court of the Slovak Republic (Najvyšší súd Slovenskej republiky): Župné nám. 13, Bratislava 81 490; tel. (2) 5935-3111; fax (2) 5441-1535; internet www.nssr.gov.sk; Chair. STEFAN HARABIN.

Office of the Prosecutor-General: Štúrova ul. 2, 812 85 Bratislava; tel. (2) 5953-2505; fax (2) 5953-2653; e-mail generalna .prokuratura@genpro.gov.sk; internet www.genpro.gov.sk; Prosecutor-General DOBROSLAV TRNKA.

Judicial Council of the Slovak Republic (Súdna rada Slovenskej republiky): Župné nám. 13, Bratislava 81 422; tel. (2) 5935-3111; fax (2) 5935-3498; e-mail podatelna@sudnarada.gov.sk; internet www .sudnarada.gov.sk; f. 2002; Chair. STEFAN HARABIN.

Constitutional Court of the Slovak Republic (Ústavný súd Slovenskej republiky): Hlavná 110, 042 65 Košice; tel. (55) 720-7211; fax (55) 622-7639; e-mail ochodni@concourt.sk; internet www .concourt.sk; Chair. IVETTA MACEJKOVÁ.

Religion

The principal religion in Slovakia is Christianity, of which the largest denomination is Latin rite Catholicism. About 10% of the population profess no religious belief.

CHRISTIANITY

The Roman Catholic Church

Slovakia comprises four archdioceses (including one of the Slovak Byzantine rite) and five Latin rite dioceses, two Slovak Byzantine Rite eparchies, and a Military Ordinariate. At 31 December 2008 there were an estimated 4,001,754 adherents, equivalent to 73.8% of the total population. Of this number 236,894 (5.9% of the total population) were adherents of the Byzantine rite.

Bishops' Conference: Kapitulská 11, POB 13, 81 499 Bratislava; tel. (2) 5443-5234; fax (2) 5443-5913; e-mail kbs@kbs.sk; internet www.kbs.sk; Pres. Most Rev. STANISLAV ZVOLENSKÝ (Latin Rite Archbishop of Bratislava).

Latin Rite

Archbishop of Bratislava: Most Rev. STANISLAV ZVOLENSKÝ, Špitálska 7, 814 92 Bratislava; tel. (2 5720-0611; internet www .abu-bratislava.sk.

Archbishop of Košice: Most Rev. ALOJZ TKÁČ, Hlavná 28, 041 83 Košice; tel. (55) 682-8111; fax (55) 622-1034; e-mail abukosice@kbs .sk; internet www.rimkat.sk.

Archbishop of Trnava: Most Rev. RÓBERT BEZÁK, Jána Hollého 10, POB 78, 919 66 Trnava; tel. (33) 591-2111; fax (33) 591-2280; e-mail abu@abu.sk; internet www.abu.sk.

Slovak Byzantine Rite

Archbishop of Prešov: Most Rev. JÁN BABJAK, Hlavná 1, POB 135, 081 35 Prešov; tel. (51) 773-4622; fax (51) 756-2625; e-mail mons .babjak@greckokat.sk; internet www.grkatpo.sk.

The Eastern Orthodox Church

Orthodox Church in the Czech Lands and Slovakia (Pravoslávna cirkev v českých krajinách a na Slovensku): Budovateľská 1, 080 01 Prešov; tel. (51) 773-2174; fax (51) 773-4045; e-mail dzugan@ orthodox.sk; internet www.orthodox.sk; divided into two eparchies in Slovakia: Prešov and Michalovce (the first of which is an archbishopric); and two eparchies in the Czech Republic: Prague and Olomouc-Brno (q.v.); Archbishop of Prešov Rev. JÁN.

Protestant Churches

Apostolic Church in Slovakia (Apoštolská cirkev na Slovensku): Sreznevského 2, 831 03 Bratislava; tel. and fax (2) 4425-0913; e-mail rada@acs-net.sk; internet www.acs-net.sk; f. 1956; affiliated to international Assemblies of God; 4,000 mems; Pres. JÁN LACHO.

Baptist Union of Slovakia: Súľovská 2, 821 05 Bratislava; tel. and fax (2) 4342-1145; e-mail baptist@baptist.sk; internet www.baptist .sk; f. 1994; 1,973 mems (2005); Pres. Rev. TOMÁŠ KRIŠKA; Sec. Rev. TOMAS VALCHÁŘ.

Evangelical Church of the Augsburg (Lutheran) Confession in Slovakia (Evanjelická cirkev augsburského vyznania na Slovensku): Palisády 46, POB 289, 811 00 Bratislava; tel. and fax (2) 5443-2940; e-mail sekretariat@ecav.sk; internet www.ecav.sk; 321 parishes in 14 seniorates and two districts; 372,858 mems (2009); Bishop-Gen. MILOS KLÁTIK; Gen. Superintendent DELINGA PAVEL.

Reformed Christian Church of Slovakia: Synodal Office, Hlavné nám. 23, 979 01 Rimavská Sobota; tel. (47) 562-1936; fax (47) 563-3090; e-mail reformata@reformata.sk; internet www.reformata.sk; 109,735 mems and 325 parishes (2001); Bishop LÁSZLÓ FAZEKAS.

JUDAISM

Central Union of the Jewish Religious Communities in the Slovak Republic (Ústredný zväz židovských náboženských obcí v Slovenskej republike): Kozia ul. 21, 814 47 Bratislava; tel. (2) 5441-2167; fax (2) 5441-1106; e-mail uzzno@netax.sk; c. 3,000 mems; Exec. Chair. FERO ALEXANDER; Rabbi BARUCH MYERS.

The Press

The publications listed below are in Slovak, unless otherwise indicated.

PRINCIPAL DAILIES

Hospodárske noviny (Economic News): POB 35, Seberíniho 1, 820 07 Bratislava 27; tel. (24823-8330; fax (2) 4823-8369; e-mail hn@hnx

SLOVAKIA

.sk; internet www.hnonline.sk; morning; Editor-in-Chief Peter Vavro; circ. 17,232 (Oct. 2010).

Nový čas (New Time): Prievozská 14, Bratislava 821 09; tel. (2) 5822-7324; fax (2) 5822-7350; internet www.cas.sk; f. 1991; morning; Editor-in-Chief Martin Pastierovič; circ. 143,649 (Oct. 2010).

Pravda (Truth): Trnavská cesta 39A, 831 04 Bratislava; tel. (2) 4959-6111; fax (2) 4959-6281; e-mail pravda@pravda.sk; internet www.pravda.sk; f. 1920; independent; left-wing; Editor-in-Chief Pavol Minarik; circ. 52,392 (Oct. 2010).

Prešovský večerník (Prešov Evening Paper): Jarková 2, 080 01 Prešov; tel. (51) 772-4563; fax (51) 772-4163; e-mail presov@jantar.sk; internet www.vecernik.po.sk; f. 1990; Editor-in-Chief Dr Adriena Smihulová; circ. 13,000.

Sme (We Are): Lazaretská 12, 811 08 Bratislava; tel. (2) 5923-3500; fax (2) 5923-3679; e-mail redakcia@sme.sk; internet www.sme.sk; f. 1993; merged with Práca (Labour) in Oct. 2002; Editor-in-Chief Matúš Kostolný; circ. 60,226 (Oct. 2010).

Smer magazín (Direction Magazine): Horná 37, 974 01 Banská Bystrica; tel. (48) 415-1582; e-mail hospodarka.bb@petitpress.sk; internet www.regionalnenoviny.sk/?sek=rn_sdm; f. 1948; independent; Editor-in-Chief Zita Suráková.

Új szó (New Word): Lazaretská 12, 811 08 Bratislava; tel. (2) 5923-3421; fax (2) 5923-8321; e-mail redakcia@ujszo.com; internet www.ujszo.com; f. 1948; midday; in Hungarian; Editor-in-Chief Molnár Norbert; circ. 23,503 (Oct. 2010).

PRINCIPAL PERIODICALS

Avízo: Trnavská cesta 39A, 831 04 Bratislava; tel. (2) 4823-2139; e-mail obchod@avizo.sk; internet www.avizo.sk; 3 a week; advertising and information; Gen. Dir Oto Lanc; circ. 50,000 (2008).

Eurotelevízia (Eurotelevision): Einsteinova 23, 851 04 Bratislava 5; tel. (2) 3333-5701; fax (2) 3333-5733; e-mail evargova@bauermedia.sk; weekly TV and radio guide; Editor-in-Chief Eva Vargová; circ. 88,911 (Oct. 2010).

Kamarát (Friend): Lotyšská 4, 821 04 Bratislava 214; tel. and fax (2) 4525-8777; e-mail kral@kamarat.eu; internet www.kamarat.eu; f. 1950; fortnightly; magazine for teenagers; Publr Bohumil Kráľ; circ. 39,000 (Oct. 2010).

Katolícke noviny (Catholic News): Matúšova 22, POB 9, 810 01 Bratislava; tel. (2) 5930-6911; e-mail posta@katnoviny.sk; internet online.katnoviny.sk; f. 1849; weekly; Man. Editor Dr Ivan Sulík; circ. 78,161 (Oct. 2010).

Krásy Slovenska (Beauties of Slovakia): Ľubľanská 2, 831 02 Bratislava; tel. (2) 5465-2055; fax (2) 5465-2056; e-mail info@krasy-slovenska.sk; internet www.krasy-slovenska.sk; illustrated bi-monthly; Editor-in-Chief Zuzana Kollárová; circ. 10,000.

Línia: Pribišova 19A, 841 05 Bratislava; tel. (2) 6025-1123; fax (2) 6025-1130; monthly; lifestyle; Editor-in-Chief Ján Hanuška; circ. 25,000.

Romano nevo ľil/Rómsky nový list (The New Romany Journal): Jarková 4, 080 01 Prešov; tel. (51) 772-5283; fax (51) 773-3439; e-mail redakcia@rnl.sk; internet www.rnl.sk; f. 1991; in Romany, Slovak and English; publ. by the Association Jekhetane-Spolu (Together); Editor-in-Chief Roman Čonka; circ. 8,500.

Slovenka (Slovak Woman): Jaskový rad 5, 833 80 Bratislava; tel. (2) 5478-9652; fax (2) 5477-6118; e-mail slovenka@slovenka.sk; f. 1948; weekly; illustrated magazine; Editor-in-Chief Zuzana Krútka; circ. 41,697 (Oct. 2010).

Slovenské národné noviny (Slovak National News): Matica slovenská, Mudroňova 1, 036 52 Martin; tel. and fax (43) 413-4535; f. 1845; weekly; organ of Matica slovenská cultural organization; Editor-in-Chief Peter Mišák; circ. 7,000.

Trend: Tomášikova 23, 821 01 Bratislava 2; tel. (2) 2082-2222; fax (2) 2082-2223; e-mail redakcia@trend.sk; internet www.etrend.sk; f. 1991; weekly; for entrepreneurs; publ. by Trend Holding; Editor-in-Chief Pavol Suďa; circ. 13,866 (Oct. 2010).

Vasárnap (Sunday): Lazaretská 12, 811 08 Bratislava; tel. (2) 5923-3422; fax (2) 5923-3295; e-mail vasarnap@vasarnap.com; internet www.vasarnap.com; f. 1948; weekly; independent Hungarian-language magazine; Editor-in-Chief Liszka Györgyi; circ. 27,825 (Oct. 2010).

Život (Life): Prievozská 14, 821 09 Bratislava; tel. (2) 5822-7821; fax (2) 5822-7350; e-mail zivot@euroskop.ringier.sk; internet zivot.lesk.cas.sk; f. 1951; illustrated family weekly; Editor Andrej Šimončič; circ. 94,430 (Oct. 2010).

NEWS AGENCIES

Rómska tlačová agentúra (Roma Press Agency): Slovenskej jednoty 44, 040 01 Košice; tel. (55) 632-1372; e-mail rpa@mecem.sk; internet www.mecem.sk/rpa; reports on matters relating to the Roma minority, and aims to bring attention to issues affecting the community; Dir-Gen. Kristína Magdolenová.

SITA: POB 8, Mýtna 15, 810 05 Bratislava; tel. (2) 5249-2572; fax (2) 5249-3466; e-mail sita@sita.sk; internet www.sita.sk; f. 1997; independent; Chair. Ivan Sámel.

Tlačová agentúra Slovenskej republiky (TASR) (News Agency of the Slovak Republic): Pribinova 25, 811 09 Bratislava; tel. (2) 5921-0166; fax (2) 5296-3405; e-mail tasr@tasr.sk; internet www.tasr.sk; f. 1992; overseas bureaux in Belgium, Czech Republic, Hungary, Lebanon, Poland, Spain, United Kingdom and USA; Dir-Gen. Jaroslav Rezník.

PRESS ASSOCIATION

Slovenský syndikát novinárov (Slovak Syndicate of Journalists): Župné nám. 7, 815 68 Bratislava; tel. (2) 5443-5071; fax (2) 5443-2438; e-mail sekretariat@ssn.sk; internet www.ssn.sk; f. 1946; reorganized 1990; 2,500 mems; Pres. Peter Kubínyi.

Publishers

Academic Electronic Press: Bajzova 7, 821 08 Bratislava; tel. and fax (2) 5556-4495; non-fiction.

Dajama: Ľubľanská 2, 831 02 Bratislava; tel. and fax (2) 4463-1702; e-mail info@dajama.sk; internet www.dajama.sk; guide-books about Slovakia in Slovak, Hungarian, German, Polish, Russian and English.

Enigma: Javorová 4, 949 01 Nitra 1; tel. (87) 655-5551; e-mail enigma@enigma.sk; internet www.enigma.sk; f. 1991; textbooks, translations of children's books, illustrated books; Dir Vladimir Preloznik.

Epos, Ing. Miroslav Mračko: Pečnianska 27, 851 01 Bratislava 5; tel. and fax (2) 6241-2357; e-mail epos@epos.sk; internet www.epos.sk; f. 1990; economics, law, non-fiction.

Kalligram, s.r.o.: Staromestská 6D, POB 223, 810 00 Bratislava 1; tel. and fax (2) 5441-5028; e-mail kalligram@kalligram.sk; internet www.kaligram.sk; f. 1990; Slovak and Central European and world literature, literary criticism, philosophy, religion, history, social sciences, science; Dir László Szigeti.

Koloman Kertész Bagala (LCA Publishers Group): POB 99, 810 00 Bratislava 1; tel. (2) 5441-5366; fax (2) 5464-7393; e-mail lca@lca.sk; internet www.lca.sk; f. 1991; fiction; Dir Koloman Kertész Bagala.

Matica slovenská: J. C. Hronského, 036 52 Martin; tel. (43) 413-2454; fax (43) 413-3188; e-mail msba@matica.sk; internet www.matica.sk; f. 1863; literary science, bibliography, biography and librarianship; Chair. Ing. Jozef Markuš.

Poradca podnikateľa, spol. s.r.o. (Entrepreneur's Adviser): Martina Rázusa 23A, 010 01 Žilina; tel. (41) 705-3777; fax (41) 705-3214; internet www.epi.sk; books and CD-ROMs providing economic and legal information; Dir Ján Brigant.

Príroda a.s. (Nature): Koceľova 17, Bratislava 821 08; tel. (2) 5556-6176; fax (2) 5557-3052; e-mail priroda@priroda.sk; internet www.priroda.sk; f. 1949; school textbooks, encyclopedias, reference books, etc. for children and young people; Chair. Ing. Emilia Jankovitsova.

Slovenské pedagogické nakladeteľstvo—Mladé letá, s.r.o. (Slovak Educational Publishing House—Young Years): Sasinkova 5, Bratislava 811 08; tel. (2) 5022-7312; fax (2) 5542-5758; e-mail spn@spn.sk; internet www.mladeleta.sk; f. 1920; pedagogical literature, educational, school texts, dictionaries; Exec. Man. Darina Torokova.

Slovenský spisovatel a.s. (Slovak Writer): Vajnorská 128, 832 92 Bratislava 3; tel. (2) 4445-2707; fax (2) 4444-1239; e-mail slovenskyspisovatel@slovenskyspisovatel.sk; internet www.slovenskyspisovatel.sk; fiction, poetry; Dir Martin Chovanec.

Tatran: Michalská 9, 815 82 Bratislava; tel. (2) 5443-5849; fax (2) 5443-5777; f. 1949; fiction, art books, children's books, literary theory; Dir Dr Eva Mládeková.

Veda (Science): Dúbravská cesta 9, 842 34 Bratislava; tel. (2) 5477-4253; fax (2) 5477-2682; f. 1953; publishing house of the Slovak Academy of Sciences; scientific and popular scientific books and periodicals; Dir. Dr Milan Brnák.

PUBLISHERS' ASSOCIATION

Publishers' and Booksellers' Asscn of the Slovak Republic (Združenie vydavateľov a kníhkupcov Slovenskej republiky): Gregorovej 8, 821 03 Bratislava; tel. and fax (2) 4333-6700; e-mail alex.aust@post.sk; Pres. Dr Alex Aust.

Broadcasting and Communications

TELECOMMUNICATIONS

Regulatory Authority

Telecommunications Office of the Slovak Republic: Továrenská 7, POB 18, 810 06 Bratislava 16; tel. (2) 5788-1552; fax (2) 5293-2096; e-mail roman.vavro@teleoff.gov.sk; internet www.teleoff.gov.sk; Chair. Ladislav Mikuš.

Service Providers

Orange Slovensko (Orange Slovakia): Prievozská 6, 821 09 Bratislava; tel. (2) 5851-2345; e-mail info@orange.sk; internet www.orange.sk; f. 1997 as Globtel; present name adopted 2002; wholly owned by Orange (France); provides mobile cellular telecommunications services; Dir-Gen. Pavol Lančarič.

T-Com, a.s.: nám. Slobody 6, 817 62 Bratislava 15; tel. (2) 5249-2324; fax (2) 5249-2492; e-mail sekr.gr@st.sk; internet www.t-com.sk; 51% owned by Deutsche Telekom (Germany), 34% owned by Ministry of Transport, Post and Telecommunications, 15% owned by the National Property Fund of the Slovak Republic; formerly Slovenské Telekomunikácie; name changed to Slovak Telecom in Jan. 2004; name changed as above in March 2006; Pres. and Chief Exec. Miroslav Majoroš.

T-Mobile Slovensko, a.s.: Vajnorská 100A, 831 03 Bratislava; tel. (2) 4955-1111; internet www.t-mobile.sk; f. 1997; 100% owned by T-Com; provides mobile cellular telecommunications services; Gen. Dir Robert Chvátel.

Telefónica O2 Slovakia s.r.o.: Einsteinova 24, Bratislava 851 01; tel. (2) 6202-0100; fax (2) 6202-0444; internet www.sk.o2.com; f. 2007; subsidiary of Telefónica (United Kingdom); mobile cellular telecommunications services; Gen. Man. Juraj Šedivý.

BROADCASTING

Radio

Slovenský rozhlas (Slovak Radio): Mýtna 1, POB 55, 817 55 Bratislava; tel. (2) 5727-3560; fax (2) 5249-8923; e-mail interrel@slovakradio.sk; internet www.slovakradio.sk; f. 1926; Chair. Igor Gallo; Dir-Gen. Miloslava Zemková.

Television

Slovenská televízia (STV) (Slovak Television): Mlynská dolina 28, 845 45 Bratislava; tel. (2) 6542-3001; fax (2) 6542-2341; internet www.stv.sk; f. 1956; public broadcasting co; Chair. of Council Martin Kákoš; Gen. Man. Štefan Nižňanský.

TA3: Gagarinova 12, POB 31, 820 15 Bratislava; tel. (2) 4820-3511; fax (2) 4820-3549; e-mail ta3@ta3.com; internet www.ta3.com; f. 2001; privately owned; Dir-Gen. Matej Ribanský.

TV Joj: Grešákova 10, 040 01 Kosiče; tel. (55) 622-2664; fax (55) 622-1027; e-mail joj@joj.sk; internet www.joj.sk; f. 2002; privately owned subsidiary of Nova TV (Czech Republic); Dir-Gen. Vladimír Železný; Dir Milan Knažko.

TV Markíza: Bratislavská 1A, POB 7, 843 56 Bratislava 48; tel. (2) 6827-4111; fax (2) 6595-6824; e-mail markiza@markiza.sk; internet tv.markiza.sk; f. 1996; first privately owned television channel; 80% owned by Central European Media Enterprises Ltd (USA); Dir-Gen. Václav Mika.

Finance

(cap. = capital; res = reserves; dep. = deposits; m. = million; brs = branches; amounts in Slovak koruna, unless otherwise indicated)

BANKING

Central Bank

National Bank of Slovakia (Národná banka Slovenska): Imricha Karvaša 1, 813 25 Bratislava; tel. (2) 5787-1111; fax (2) 5787-1100; e-mail info@nbs.sk; internet www.nbs.sk; f. 1993; res −106,331m., dep. 490,328m., total assets 437,114m. (Dec. 2008); Gov. Jozef Makúch.

Commercial Banks

Československá obchodná banka, a.s.: Michalská 18, 815 63 Bratislava; tel. (2) 5966-8844; fax (2) 5441-4810; e-mail info@csob.sk; internet www.csob.sk; f. 1992; fmrly Istrobanka, a.s.; renamed as above after merger into Československá obchodná banka, a.s. in July 2009; 56.74% owned by Československá Obchodní banka, a.s. Prague, and 36.9% by KBC Bank NV, Brussels; cap. 5,000.0m., res 8,660.8m., dep. 183,735.0m. (Dec. 2008); Chair. Daniel Kollár; 11 brs.

Dexia banka slovensko, a.s.: Hodžova 11, 010 11 Žilina; tel. (41) 511-1111; fax (41) 562-4129; e-mail info@dexia.sk; internet www.dexia.sk; f. 1993; present name adopted 2003; 84.4% owned by Dexia Kommunalkredit Bank AG (Austria); dep. 77,251.3m., total assets 81,799.3m. (Dec. 2008); Chair. and CEO Stefaan Depaepe; 53 brs.

Komerční Banka Bratislava, a.s.: Hodžovo nám. 1A, POB 137, 810 00 Bratislava; tel. (2) 5927-7328; fax (2) 5296-1959; e-mail koba@koba.sk; internet www.koba.sk; f. 1995; cap. 500.0m., res 115.6m., dep. 9,342.2m. (Dec. 2008); Chair. and CEO Vlastimil Czabe.

OTP Banka Slovensko, a.s. (Investment and Development Bank): Stúrová 5, 813 54 Bratislava; tel. (2) 5979-1111; fax (2) 5296-3484; e-mail info@otpbanka.sk; internet www.otpbanka.sk; f. 1992; present name adopted 2002; 97.2% owned by OTP Bank (Hungary); cap. 2,064.4m., res 1,098.2m., dep. 43,610.4m. (Dec. 2008); Chair. of Bd Péter Forrai; 72 brs.

Poštová banka, a.s. (Postal Bank): Prievozska 2B, 821 09 Bratislava; tel. (2) 5960-1122; fax (2) 5960-3344; e-mail info@pabk.sk; internet www.pabk.sk; f. 1993; cap. 2,489.9m., res 1,239.3m., dep. 39,833.4m. (Dec. 2008); Chair. and CEO Marek Tarda; 24 brs.

Privatbanka, a.s.: Einsteinova 25, 851 01 Bratislava; tel. (2) 3226-6111; fax (2) 3226-6900; e-mail privatbanka@privatbanka.sk; internet www.privatbanka.sk; f. 1996; present name adopted 2005; cap. 756.9m., res 54.5m., dep. 11,740.0m. (Dec. 2008); Chair. and CEO Luboš Sevčík.

Tatra banka, a.s.: POB 42, Hodzovo nám. 3, 811 06 Bratislava; tel. (2) 5919-1000; fax (2) 5919-1110; e-mail tatrabanka@tatrabanka.sk; internet www.tatrabanka.sk; f. 1990; res 33,855.4m., dep. 250,483.0m., total assets 317,861.0m. (Dec. 2008); Chair. and Gen. Man. Igor Vida; 30 brs.

UniCredit Bank, a.s.: Sancová 1A, 813 33 Bratislava; tel. (2) 4950-2112; fax (2) 5060-2287; internet www.unicreditbank.sk; f. 1990; present name adopted 2007; 99.0% owned by Bank Austria Creditanstalt AG (Austria); cap. 7,095.5m., res 7,013.2m., dep. 124,898.6m. (Dec. 2008); Chair. of Bd and CEO Jozef Barta; 10 brs, 83 sub-brs.

Volksbank Slovensko, a.s.: Vysoká 9, POB 81, 810 00 Bratislava; tel. (2) 5965-1111; fax (2) 5441-2453; e-mail market@volksbank.sk; internet www.volksbank.sk; f. 1991 as Ludová banka; name changed as above in 2007; 91% owned by Volksbank International AG (Austria); cap. 1,000.0m., res 3,042.2m., dep. 41,741.3m. (Dec. 2008); Chair. Barbara Neiger; 47 brs.

Všeobecná úverová banka, a.s. (General Credit Bank): Mlynské Nivy 1, POB 90, 829 90 Bratislava; tel. (2) 5055-1111; fax (2) 5556-6656; e-mail kontakt@vub.sk; internet www.vub.sk; f. 1990; 96.5% owned by Intesa Holding International SA (Luxembourg); cap. 12,978m., res 2,998m., dep. 308,368m. (Dec. 2008); Chair. and CEO Ignacio Jaquotot; 240 brs.

Savings Banks

Prvá stavebná sporiteľňa, a.s.: Bajkalská 30, POB 48, 829 48 Bratislava; tel. (2) 5855-5855; fax (2) 5341-1131; internet www.pss.sk; f. 1992; cap. 1,000m.; Chair. Imrich Béreš.

Slovenská sporiteľňa, a.s. (Slovak Savings Bank): Tomášikova 48, 832 37 Bratislava; tel. (2) 5826-8111; fax (2) 5826-8670; e-mail info@slsp.sk; internet www.slsp.sk; f. 1842; 100% owned by Erste Bank (Austria); dep. 340,554m., total assets 378,282m. (Dec. 2008); Chair. and CEO Jan Rollo; 270 brs.

COMMODITY AND STOCK EXCHANGES

Bratislava Stock Exchange (Burza cenných papierov v Bratislave, a.s.): Vysoká 17, POB 151, 814 99 Bratislava 1; tel. (2) 4923-6111; fax (2) 4923-6103; e-mail info@bsse.sk; internet www.bsse.sk; f. 1991; Chair. Vladimír Kocourek; Dir-Gen. Mária Hurajová.

Commodity Exchange Bratislava (Komoditná burza Bratislava): Trnavská cesta 50A, 821 02 Bratislava; tel. (2) 5293-1010; fax (2) 5293-1007; e-mail sekretariat@kbb.sk; internet www.kbb.sk; f. 1992; Chair. Ludovít Scholtz.

INSURANCE

AEGON Životná poisťovňa, a.s.: Slávičie údolie 106, 811 02 Bratislava; tel. (2) 20668287; fax (2) 20668110; e-mail aegon@aegon.sk; internet www.aegon.sk; f. 2006; life, risk, retirement, mortgage loan; Chair. of Bd Jana Gruntová.

Allianz—Slovak Insurance Co (Allianz—Slovenská poisťovňa, a.s.): Dostojevského rad 4, 815 74 Bratislava; tel. (2) 5963-1111; fax (2) 5963-2740; e-mail allianzsp@allianzsp.sk; internet www.allianzsp.sk; 84.5% owned by Allianz AG (Germany), 15% owned by European Bank for Reconstruction and Development; majority stake divested to Allianz AG (Germany) in 2002; name changed from Slovenská poisťovňa to Allianz—Slovenská poisťovňa in 2003; Chair. Torsten Leue; 2,900 employees.

Amslico poisťovňa a.s.: Hviezdoslavovo nam. 20, 811 02 Bratislava; tel. (2) 59363225; fax (2) 59363255; e-mail amslico@amslico.sk;

SLOVAKIA

internet www.amslico.sk; f. 1995; life and accident; owned by MetLife (USA).

ERGO životná poisťovňa, a.s.: Lazaretská 12, 811 08 Bratislava; tel. (2) 32112020; fax (2) 32112099; e-mail info@ergo.sk; internet www.ergo.sk; life; Dir-Gen. Pavol Lím.

Generali Slovensko poisťovňa, a.s.: Plynárenská 7C, 824 79 Bratislava; tel. (2) 58276666; fax (2) 58276100; e-mail gsl@gsl.sk; internet www.generali.sk; f. 2008 by merger of Českej poistovne–Slovensko and Generali; life, pension and bank; Dir-Gen. Antonín Nekvinda.

ING Životná poisťovňa, a.s.: Trnavská cesta 50B, 821 02 Bratislava; tel. (2) 259313501; fax (2) 59313999; e-mail kontakt@ing.sk; internet www.ing.sk; f. 1996; subsidiary of ING Groep NV (The Netherlands); life; CEO Alexis George.

Komunálna poisťovňa, a.s.: Štefánikova 8, 811 05 Bratislava; tel. (2) 48210544; fax (2) 48210570; e-mail info@kpas.sk; internet www.kpas.sk; f. 1994; subsidiary of Vienna Insurance Group (Austria); life and non-life; CEO and Chair. Vladimir Bakeš.

Kooperativna poisťovňa, a.s.: Štefanovičova 4, 816 23 Bratislava; tel. (2) 57299198; fax (2) 52495983; e-mail info@koop.sk; internet www.koop.sk; f. 1990; subsidiary of Vienna Insurance Group (Austria); personal, car, property and liability, and travel; CEO and Chair. Juraj Lelkes.

Trade and Industry

GOVERNMENT AGENCIES

National Property Fund of the Slovak Republic (Fond Národného Majetku Slovenskej Republiky): Drieňová 27, 821 01 Bratislava; tel. (2) 4827-1111; fax (2) 4827-1289; e-mail fnm@natfund.gov.sk; internet www.natfund.gov.sk; f. 1993; supervises the privatization process; Pres. Peter Simko.

SARIO—Slovak Investment and Trade Development Agency (SARIO—Slovenská agentúra pre rozvoj investícií a obchodu): Martinčekova 17, 821 01 Bratislava; tel. (2) 5826-0100; fax (2) 5826-0109; e-mail sario@sario.sk; internet www.sario.sk; f. 1991; CEO Róbert Šimončič.

CHAMBERS OF COMMERCE

Slovak Chamber of Commerce and Industry (SOPK) (Slovenská obchodná a priemyselná komora): Gorkého 9, 816 03 Bratislava; tel. (2) 5443-3291; fax (2) 5413-1159; e-mail sopkurad@scci.sk; internet web.sopk.sk; Chair. Dr Peter Mihók.

Banská Bystrica Regional Chamber of the Slovak Chamber of Commerce and Industry (Banskobystrická Regionálna Komora SOPK): nám. S. Moysesa 4, 974 01 Banská Bystrica; tel. (48) 412-5634; fax (48) 412-5636; e-mail sopkrbb@sopk.sk; internet bb.sopk.sk; Chair. Vladimír Maňka.

Košice Regional Chamber of the Slovak Chamber of Commerce and Industry (Košická Regionálna Komora SOPK): Floriánska 19, 040 01 Košice; tel. (55) 7279-160; fax (55) 7279-156; e-mail sopkrkke@sopk.sk; internet ke.sopk.sk; Dir Ivan Pezlár.

Nitra Regional Chamber of the Slovak Chamber of Commerce and Industry (Nitrianska Regionálna Komora SOPK): Akademická 4, 949 01 Nitra; tel. (37) 653-5466; fax (37) 733-6739; e-mail sopkrknr@sopk.sk; internet nr.sopk.sk; Dir Miroslav Masarik.

Prešov Regional Chamber of the Slovak Chamber of Commerce and Industry (Prešovská Regionálna Komora SOPK): Vajanského 10, POB 246, 080 01 Prešov 1; tel. (51) 773-2818; fax (51) 773-2413; e-mail sopkrkpo@sopk.sk; internet po.sopk.sk; Dir Helena Virčíková.

Trenčín Regional Chamber of the Slovak Chamber of Commerce and Industry (Trenčíanska Regionálna Komora SOPK): ul. Jilemnického 2, 911 01 Trenčín; tel. (32) 652-3834; fax (32) 652-1023; e-mail sopkrktn@sopk.sk; internet tn.sopk.sk; Dir Štefan Bucha.

Trnava Regional Chamber of the Slovak Chamber of Commerce and Industry (Trnavská Regionálna Komora SOPK): Trhová 2, 917 01 Trnava; tel. (33) 551-2588; fax (33) 551-2603; e-mail sopkrktt@sopk.sk; internet tt.sopk.sk; Dir Eva Tománková (acting).

Žilina Regional Chamber of the Slovak Chamber of Commerce and Industry (Žilinská Regionálna Komora SOPK): ul. Halková 31, 010 01 Žilina; tel. (41) 723-5655; fax (41) 723-5653; e-mail sekrza@za.scci.sk; internet za.sopk.sk; Dir Ján Mišura.

UTILITIES

Electricity

Slovenské elektrárne, a.s. (SE) (Slovak Electricity): Hraničná 12, 827 36 Bratislava 212; tel. (2) 5866-1111; fax (2) 5341-7525; e-mail info@hq.seas.sk; internet www.seas.sk; fmr state-owned utility; 66% share acquired by Enel (Italy) in April 2006; 34% owned by the National Property Fund; Chair. and Dir-Gen. Paolo Ruzzini; Deputy Chair. Marco Arcelli.

Stredoslovenská energetika, a.s. (SSE) (Central Slovakia Energy): Republiky 5, 010 47 Žilina; tel. (41) 519-1111; fax (41) 519-2575; e-mail sse@sse.sk; internet www.sse.sk; 51% owned by the National Property Fund of the Slovak Republic, 49% by Eléctricité de France; regional electricity distributor; Chair. and Dir-Gen. Pierre Chazerain.

Východoslovenská energetika, a.s. (VSE) (East Slovakia Energy): Mlynská 31, 042 91 Košice; tel. (55) 610-2111; fax (55) 678-6516; e-mail info@vse.sk; internet www.vse.sk; 51% owned by the National Property Fund of the Slovak Republic, 49% by RWE Energie AG (Germany); regional electricity distributor; Chair. and CEO Norbert Schürmann.

Západoslovesnká energetika (ZSE) (West Slovakia Energy): Čulenova 6, 816 47 Bratislava; tel. (2) 5296-1741; fax (2) 5061-3901; e-mail kontakt@zse.sk; internet www.zse.sk; f. 1922; 51% owned by National Property Fund of the Slovak Republic, 40% by E.ON Energie AG (Germany) and 9% by the European Bank for Reconstruction and Development; regional electricity distributor; Chair. of Bd Konrad Kreuzer; Dir of Man. Bd Dr Ján Orlovský.

Gas

SPP—Slovenský Plynárenský Priemysel (Slovak Gas Co): Mlynské Nivy 44A, 825 11 Bratislava 26; tel. (2) 5869-1111; fax (2) 5869-2765; e-mail spp@spp.sk; internet www.spp.sk; 51% state-owned, 49% by consortium of cos incl. E.ON Ruhrgas (Germany) and GDF Suez (France); Chair. Jean-Jacques Ciazynski.

TRADE UNION CONFEDERATION

Confederation of Trade Unions of the Slovak Republic (Konfederácia odborových zväzov Slovenskej republiky): Odborárské nám. 3, 815 70 Bratislava; tel. (2) 5557-6065; fax (2) 5023-9102; e-mail press@kozsr.sk; internet www.kozsr.sk; Pres. Miroslav Gazdik; 347,760 mems (2007).

Transport

RAILWAYS

In 2007 the total length of railways in Slovakia was estimated at 3,629 km, of which 1,578 km were electrified.

Železnice Slovenskej republiky (Slovak State Railways): Klemensova 8, 813 61 Bratislava; tel. (2) 2029-1111; fax (2) 5296-2296; e-mail gr@zsr.sk; internet www.zsr.sk; f. 1993; became a joint-stock co with responsibility for management of rail infrastructure in 2001, when responsibility for operations was transferred to the newly established state-owned concern, Železničná spoločnosť; Chair. Juraj Mravčák; Dir-Gen. Štefan Hlinka.

Železničná spoločnosť Cargo Slovakia, a.s. (ZSSK Cargo): Drieňová 24, 820 09 Bratislava; e-mail infoservis@zscargo.sk; internet www.zscargo.sk; f. 2005, following division into two of the state railway company, Železničná spoločnosť, a.s.; operation of rail freight transport and freight-related commercial activities; state-owned; merger with ČD Cargo (Czech Republic) announced 2008; Chair. of Bd Matiej Augustín.

Železničná spoločnosť Slovensko, a.s.: Železničná 1, 041 79 Košice; tel. (2) 2029-7362; fax (2) 5341-0128; e-mail info@slovakrail.sk; internet www.slovakrail.sk; f. 2005, following division into two of the state railway company, Železničná spoločnosť, a.s.; passenger transport; state-owned; Chair. and Dir-Gen. Milan Chúpek.

Dopravný podnik Bratislava, a.s. (Bratislava Transport): Olejkárska 1, 814 52 Bratislava; tel. (2) 5950-1411; fax (2) 5950-1400; e-mail sekretariat.gr@dpb.sk; internet www.dpb.sk; tramway being upgraded to light-rail system; 11 routes with 154 stops; Dir-Gen. Robert Kadnár.

ROADS

In 2004 the total length of the road system (including motorways) was estimated at 43,000 km, of which 87.3% was paved.

Slovak Road Administration (Slovenská správa ciest): Miletičova 19, 826 19 Bratislava; tel. (2) 5025-5111; fax (2) 5556-7976; e-mail info@ssc.sk; internet www.ssc.sk; f. 1996; Dir-Gen. Ing. Roman Žembera.

INLAND WATERWAYS

The total length of navigable waterways in Slovakia (on the River Danube) is 172 km. The Danube provides a link with Germany, Austria, Hungary, Serbia, Bulgaria, Romania and the Black Sea. The main river ports are Bratislava and Komárno.

State Shipping Authority (Štátna plavebná správa): Prístavná 10, 821 09 Bratislava; tel. (2) 5556-6336; fax (2) 5556-6335; e-mail sekretariat@sps.sk; internet www.sps.sk; Dir Ing. JOZEF MORAVČÍK.

Slovak Shipping and Ports Co, a.s. (Slovenská plavba a prístavy, a.s.): Horárska 12, 815 24 Bratislava; tel. (2) 5827-1111; fax (2) 5827-1114; e-mail spap@spap.sk; internet www.spap.sk; Chair. of Bd JOZEF BLAŠKO; Gen. Man. JAROSLAV MICHALCO.

CIVIL AVIATION

There are five international airports in Slovakia: Bratislava (M. R. Štefánik Airport), Košice, Piešťany, Poprad and Sliač.

Air Slovakia: Pestovateľská ul. 2, 821 04 Bratislava; tel. (2) 4342-2744; fax (2) 4342-2742; e-mail airslovakia@airslovakia.sk; internet www.airslovakia.sk; f. 1993; scheduled passenger flights between Slovakia and Cyprus, India, Israel, Italy, Kuwait and the United Kingdom; charter and cargo services; Pres. HARJINDER SINGH SIDHU; Dir-Gen. MICHAEL HALPER.

Danube Wings (VIP Wings s. r. o.): POB 13, 820 02 Bratislava 22; tel. (2) 4363-8537; fax (2) 4363-8539; e-mail info@danubewings.eu; internet www.danubewings.eu; f. 2008; scheduled and charter passenger flights between Slovakia and various European destinations; Chair. PETER BENIK.

Tourism

Slovakia's tourist attractions include ski resorts in the High and Low Tatras and other mountain ranges, more than 20 spa resorts (with thermal and mineral springs), numerous castles and mansions, and historic towns, including Bratislava, Košice, Nitra, Bardejov, Kežmarok and Levoča. In 2009 1,298,075 foreign tourists visited Slovakia. In 2008 revenue from tourism totalled US $3,004m.

Slovak Tourist Board: nám. L. Stura 1, POB 35, 974 05 Banská Bystrica; tel. (48) 413-6146; fax (48) 413-6149; e-mail sacr@sacr.sk; internet www.sacr.sk; Dir-Gen. SVETLANA GAVOROVÁ.

Defence

As assessed at November 2010, the total active strength of Slovakia's armed forces was 16,531: army 7,322, air force 4,190, and some 5,019 centrally controlled personnel, logistical, and support staff. In December 2005 the army became fully professional. Slovakia became a full member of the North Atlantic Treaty Organization (NATO) on 29 March 2004.

Defence Expenditure: Budgeted at 760m. koruna in 2010.

Chief of the General Staff: Maj.-Gen. ALOJZ ŠTEINER.

Education

Education in Slovakia is provided free of charge at all levels in state-controlled and church-affiliated schools. Children between the ages of three and six may attend kindergarten (materská škola). Compulsory education begins at six years of age, when children enter basic school (základná škola), which takes nine years to complete (although the ninth year is optional). In 2009 437,223 pupils were enrolled at primary schools. In 2005 enrolment at primary schools included 92% of pupils in the relevant age-group, according to UNESCO estimates. There are three types of secondary school: the grammar school (gymnázium), of which there were 250 in 2009, which prepares students for higher education, the secondary specialized school (stredná odborná škola, 493) and the secondary vocational school (stredné odborné učilište, 181 in 2007), with a total enrolment of 335,166 students. In 2006 secondary enrolment was equivalent to 96% of children in the relevant age-group. In 2009 there were 33 institutions of higher education, with a total enrolment of 144,018 students. Children who have disabilities that cannot be provided for by regular schools may receive instruction at special schools. There are also private schools (basic and secondary). Of total government expenditure in 2009, €2,701m. (10.3%) was allocated to education, according to preliminary figures.

SLOVENIA

Introductory Survey

LOCATION, CLIMATE, LANGUAGE, RELIGION, FLAG, CAPITAL

The Republic of Slovenia is situated in south-central Europe. It is bounded by Austria to the north, Hungary to the north-east, Croatia to the south and east, and Italy to the west, and it has a short western coastline on the Adriatic Sea. The climate is Alpine in the mountainous areas, Mediterranean along the coast and continental in the interior. Average temperatures range from between 0°C (32°F) and 22°C (71.6°F) inland, and between 2°C (35.6°F) and 24°C (75.2°F) on the coast. Average annual rainfall ranges from 800 mm (31.5 ins) in the east to 3,000 mm (118.1 ins) in the north-west. The official language is Slovene, and, in ethnically mixed regions, also Hungarian and Italian. The majority religion in Slovenia is Roman Catholicism, although there are small communities of other Christian denominations and of Muslims and Jews. The national flag (proportions 2 by 3) consists of three horizontal stripes of white, blue and red, with a shield in the upper hoist depicting a white three-peaked mountain (Triglav), below which are two horizontal wavy blue lines and above which are three six-pointed yellow stars. The capital is Ljubljana.

CONTEMPORARY POLITICAL HISTORY

Historical Context

Following the collapse of the Austro-Hungarian Empire, the Kingdom of Serbs, Croats and Slovenes was proclaimed on 4 December 1918. (The territory of Slovenia was formally ceded by Austria by the Treaty of Saint-Germain in 1919.) In 1929 the name of the country was changed to Yugoslavia. Yugoslavia collapsed under German attack in 1941, and, during the Second World War (1939–45), Germany annexed lower Styria and Yugoslav Carinthia, while Italy annexed Istria and the territory around Ljubljana. (There was a continuing dispute with Italy over Istria; in 1954 Italy was awarded the city of Trieste, and Yugoslavia the remainder of the territory, giving Slovenia access to the sea.) Hungary occupied the plains along the Mura in north-eastern Slovenia.

The Slovene Liberation Front, formed in 1941, joined with the communist-led all-Yugoslav Partisan Army of Josip Broz (Tito), which was eventually recognized as an ally by the British and US Governments. Following the post-war proclamation of the Federal People's Republic of Yugoslavia (from 1963 the Socialist Federal Republic of Yugoslavia—SFRY), Slovenia became the most prosperous of the Yugoslav republics, but was increasingly suspicious of Serb domination. On 27 September 1989 the Slovene Assembly voted in favour of radical amendments to the Constitution of Slovenia, confirming Slovenia's sovereignty and its right to secede from the SFRY. The organization of multi-party elections was envisaged, and the establishment of opposition parties (the local League of Communists of Slovenia—LCS—having hitherto been the only legal party) was formally authorized. Slovenia was warned that the amendments contravened the Federal Constitution, and the Serbian leader, Slobodan Milošević, attempted to arrange protests in Slovenia against the Slovene leadership; however, the planned demonstrations were banned in November. Milošević subsequently instructed all Serbian enterprises to sever links with Slovenia, which retaliated by imposing reciprocal economic sanctions.

In January 1990 the Slovenian delegation withdrew from the 14th (Extraordinary) Congress of the League of Communists of Yugoslavia (LCY), following the rejection of their proposals to reform the federal party and to give greater autonomy to the respective Leagues of Communists of the republics. The LCY suffered a further reverse in February, when its Central Committee was unable to secure the quorum necessary to set a date for the reconvening of the Congress. A boycott by the entire Slovene contingent was supported by members of the Leagues of Communists of Croatia and Macedonia. The LCS suspended its links with the LCY, and changed its name to the Party of Democratic Reform (PDR). In that month Štefan Korošec of Slovenia was removed from the position of Secretary of the Presidium of the LCY Central Committee, in advance of the expiry of his mandate, and was replaced by a Serb. In March Slovenia was redesignated the Republic of Slovenia. Meanwhile, opposition parties had been formed, and in December 1989 six of the main parties formed a coalition, the Democratic Opposition of Slovenia (DEMOS). In multi-party elections, held in April 1990, DEMOS won a majority in the republican parliament, and subsequently formed a Government under Lojze Peterle, the leader of the Slovenian Christian Democrats (SCD). However, the leader of the PDR, Milan Kučan (an opponent of Milošević), was elected President of the State Presidency, and the PDR remained the largest single party in the legislature.

On 2 July 1990 the Slovenian legislature declared the sovereignty of the republic. An amendment to the republican Constitution, resolving that republican laws should take precedence over federal laws, was approved by the legislature on 27 September. Slovenia also assumed control over the local territorial defence force, thereby bringing the republic into direct confrontation with the Serb-dominated federal army, which attempted to reassert its authority by confiscating weapons and seizing the headquarters of the republican force. Slovenian and Croatian proposals to reform the Yugoslav Federation were rejected, and Serbia imposed economic sanctions on imports from the secessionist states. None the less, in a referendum held in Slovenia on 23 December, some 89% of those who voted (about 94% of the electorate) endorsed Slovenian independence.

Relations between Slovenia and the SFRY deteriorated further in January 1991, when the Slovenian authorities refused to implement an order by the SFRY Presidency to disarm all paramilitary groups. In the same month Slovenia and Croatia signed friendship and military co-operation agreements. Although the Slovenian Government approved a programme for Slovenian dissociation from the SFRY in February, both Slovenia and Croatia remained willing to consider a federation of sovereign states. However, following the Serbian-led crisis in the Federal State Presidency in March (see the chapter on Serbia), the Slovenian Government became more resolved to withdraw from the federation. In May Slovenia declared its intention to secede before the end of June, and legislation was adopted that would enable eventual independence, including the establishment of a Slovenian army. Tensions with the federal authorities were exacerbated when Slovenia attempted to take control of the collection of customs duties.

Domestic Political Affairs

Slovenia and Croatia declared their independence from the SFRY on 25 June 1991. In response, Serb-dominated federal troops were mobilized on 27 June, and tanks were dispatched from Belgrade, the Serbian and Yugoslav capital. Sporadic fighting ensued, and, despite attempts by the European Community (EC—now European Union—EU, see p. 270) to arrange a cease-fire, there was an aerial bombardment of Brnik (Ljubljana) airport. On 7–8 July an EC-mediated cease-fire agreement between Slovenia and the SFRY ended all hostilities in Slovenia. According to official figures, 79 people were killed in the fighting in Slovenia. On 8 October (following the expiry of a three-month moratorium on dissociation, agreed as part of the EC cease-fire accord) Slovenia proclaimed its full independence, introduced its own currency, the tolar, and recalled all of its citizens serving in federal institutions. All federal army units had withdrawn from Slovenia by 26 October. A new Slovenian Constitution, providing for a bicameral legislature, was promulgated on 23 December. Slovenia was recognized by the EC in January 1992. The USA recognized the country in April, and withdrew sanctions against Slovenia (imposed on all states in the territory of the former SFRY in the previous year) in August. Slovenia was admitted to the UN in May.

Peterle's administration experienced increasing difficulties, as the struggle for independence became less of a unifying factor. In October 1991 the Slovenian Democratic Union, one of the larger and most influential DEMOS parties, split into two factions, both of which remained in the coalition. A liberal wing formed the Democratic Party (DP) under the Minister of Foreign Affairs, Dr Dmitrij Rupel, while the majority of the party's parliamentary delegates supported a more conservative programme and formed the National Democratic Party, led by the Minister of Justice and Administration, Dr Rajko Pirnat. DEMOS was dissolved in December, although it was envisaged that the Peterle administration would remain in power pending the organization of elections (to take place under the terms of the new Constitution). However, the Government lost a parliamentary motion of no confidence in April 1992, and Peterle resigned. He was replaced by Dr Janez Drnovšek, the leader of the Liberal Democratic Party (LDP) and a former President of the SFRY Presidency.

The 1992 parliamentary and presidential elections

Parliamentary and presidential elections took place on 6 December 1992. About 85% of the registered electorate participated in elections to the Državni zbor (National Assembly). Although the LDP returned the greatest number of deputies (22) to the 90-member body, it failed to secure a majority of seats in the legislature. Among the groupings that obtained representation were the SCD, with a total of 15 seats, the United List (a four-party electoral alliance), with 14 seats, and the extreme nationalist Slovenian National Party (SNP), which won 12 seats. In the presidential election, Kučan (standing as an independent candidate) was re-elected to what had become, under the terms of the 1991 Constitution, a largely ceremonial post, obtaining 63.9% of the votes cast. His nearest rival, Ivan Bizjak of the SCD, secured 21.1% of the votes. Voting was held concurrently for the 22 directly elected members of the advisory Državni svet (National Council); its remaining 18 members were chosen by an electoral college shortly afterwards.

In January 1993 Drnovšek formed a coalition Government, comprising members of the LDP, the SCD, the United List (later renamed the United List of Social Democrats—ULSD), the Greens of Slovenia and the Social Democratic Party of Slovenia (SDPS). Peterle was appointed Minister of Foreign Affairs, and Bizjak Minister of Internal Affairs. In July the Minister of Defence, Janez Janša, was among several senior politicians implicated in a scandal involving the sale of armaments to Bosnian Muslims (Bosniaks), in contravention of the UN embargo on the transfer of military equipment between the former Yugoslav republics. Earlier in the year Janša (the President of the SDPS) had accused Kučan of protecting former officials of the communist regime. Janša was dismissed from the Government in March 1994, after a ministerial commission found that security forces under the command of the Ministry of Defence had ill-treated a former ministry employee. The SDPS withdrew from the Government, protesting that the coalition agreement had been breached. In addition, the party cited as its reasons for leaving the Government continuing high-level corruption and the change in the coalition's structure, following the merger in March of the LDP with three other organizations to form a new party, Liberal Democracy of Slovenia (LDS). The LDS, led by Drnovšek, also included the DP and the Greens of Slovenia—Eco-Social Party (comprising the parliamentary members of the Greens of Slovenia), and numbered 30 deputies in the Državni zbor. Drnovšek subsequently formed a new coalition Government with the SCD and the ULSD. However, Bizjak resigned as Minister of Internal Affairs in May, following allegations that security forces controlled by his ministry had been involved in criminal activities in Austria.

In September 1994 the appointment of an LDS member, Jožef Školjč, to the presidency of the Državni zbor prompted Peterle's resignation from the Government, in protest at what he regarded as the excessive concentration of authority among members of the LDS. Although the SCD remained within the government coalition, Drnovšek refused to accede to the party's demand that Peterle's successor should also be a member of the SCD. In January 1995 an agreement was finally reached whereby Zoran Thaler of the LDS was appointed Minister of Foreign Affairs, and Janko Deželak of the SCD assumed the post of Minister of Economic Relations and Development (a portfolio hitherto held by the LDS).

The 1996 legislative elections

In January 1996 the ULSD withdrew from the governing coalition, following the Prime Minister's proposal to replace the ULSD Minister of Economic Affairs, Dr Maks Tajnikar. Tajnikar was subsequently replaced by an independent deputy, Metod Dragonja, and the three other positions left vacant by the ULSD withdrawal were allocated to one member of the LDS and two of the SCD. In May Thaler was defeated in a motion of no confidence, prompted by his acceptance of a compromise solution to a dispute with Italy (which had prevented Slovenia's accession to associate membership of the EU—see Regional Affairs) opposed by the SCD.

At the elections to the Državni zbor, which took place on 10 November 1996, the LDS returned 25 deputies to the chamber, and subsequently increased its overall strength to 45 seats, having secured the support of the ULSD, the Democratic Party of Pensioners of Slovenia (DeSUS), the SNP and the representatives of the Hungarian and Italian minorities. A newly formed opposition alliance, Slovenian Spring, comprising the Slovenian People's Party (SPP), the SCD and the SDPS, also held 45 seats in the Državni zbor. Consequently, Kučan's nomination of Drnovšek to the office of Prime Minister failed to obtain the requisite majority of more than one-half of the deputies. Eventually, an SCD deputy withdrew from the party to become an independent deputy, and agreed to support Drnovšek's candidacy, and in January 1997 Drnovšek was re-elected as Prime Minister. However, the continued absence of a majority in the Državni zbor impeded the formation of a new government, with the parties belonging to Slovenian Spring refusing to accept an administration headed by Drnovšek. Drnovšek consequently failed to secure sufficient support for his proposed coalition administration, which was to include representatives of all the parties in the legislature. In late February the SPP (which held 19 seats) finally agreed to join a coalition Government with the LDS and DeSUS, which was approved by 52 votes in the Državni zbor. In July Thaler resigned as Minister of Foreign Affairs. Boris Frlec was appointed to the post in September.

A presidential election took place on 23 November 1997. Kučan won a second term of office, with 55.6% of the votes cast. His nearest rival, the President of the Državni zbor, Janez Podobnik, secured 18.4% of the votes. Indirect elections to the Državni svet followed on 26 November.

The 2000 legislative elections

In January 2000 Frlec resigned as Minister of Foreign Affairs, following criticism of his failure to resolve long-standing disputes between the Governments of Slovenia and Croatia. He was replaced in February by Dr Dmitrij Rupel. In March it was announced that the SPP and the SCD would merge in the following month, and that the nine ministers belonging to the SPP would resign from the Government. Drnovšek was obliged to resign in April, after his proposed new government was rejected by the Državni zbor. The SPP and SCD merged as planned, and subsequently formed a new alliance, Coalition Slovenia, with the SDPS. Coalition Slovenia nominated Andrej Bajuk as a candidate for the premiership, and in early May, having twice been narrowly rejected by the Državni zbor, Bajuk was endorsed as Prime Minister. The Government, which was approved by the Državni zbor in June, notably included Peterle as Minister of Foreign Affairs and Janša as Minister of Defence.

In July 2000 the approval by 70 of the 90 deputies in the Državni zbor of constitutional amendments, providing for the introduction of a system of proportional representation in the forthcoming elections, resulted in division within the SPP. Bajuk (who had opposed the new legislation) announced his resignation from the reconstituted SPP and his intention of establishing a new breakaway party. Kučan subsequently declared that the legislative elections would take place in October. In August Bajuk was elected Chairman of the newly formed New Slovenia—Christian People's Party (NSi), which was also joined by Peterle. The elections to the Državni zbor on 15 October were conducted under the new system, with 88 deputies elected on the basis of proportional representation, and the remaining two deputies elected as representatives of the Italian and Hungarian minority communities. The LDS secured 34 seats (an increase of nine seats compared with 1996), while the SDPS won 14 seats, the ULSD 11 seats, the SPP nine seats and the NSi eight seats. Drnovšek was re-elected to the premiership by the Državni zbor in early November, and a coalition agreement was reached by the LDS, the ULSD, the SPP and DeSUS. A new Government, which included several prominent members of Drnovšek's previous administrations, was endorsed by the legislature at the end of November. Drnovšek announced that administrative reforms essential to EU requirements were to be expedited.

The presidential election on 10 November 2002 was contested by nine candidates. (Kučan was prohibited, under the terms of the Constitution, from seeking election for a third term.) Drnovšek won the highest proportion of votes, with 44.4%, but failed to secure an outright majority; a second round between him and Barbara Brezigar, a state prosecutor, who was supported by the SDPS and the NSi (and had received 30.8% of the votes), was

SLOVENIA

scheduled for 1 December. At this second ballot, Drnovšek was elected to the presidency, with 56.5% of the votes cast. Anton Rop, also a member of the LDS and hitherto Minister of Finance, was nominated to replace Drnovšek as Prime Minister, and on 19 December a new Government was approved by the Državni zbor. Drnovšek was inaugurated as President on 22 December. In September 2003 the SDPS was reconstituted as the Slovenian Democratic Party (SDP).

In early 2004 the Državni zbor approved legislation providing for the restoration of citizenship to 18,000 nationals of former Yugoslav republics, who (resident in Slovenia at the time of its independence) had been removed from population records and lost their residency rights. However, at a referendum, which was conducted in April, following pressure from the SNP and three right-wing parties, some 94% of the votes cast by 31% of the electorate rejected adoption of the new legislation. Following the referendum, the SPP, the only party in the governing coalition to have supported the referendum, withdrew from the Government (which was subsequently reorganized). Following the accession of Slovenia to full membership of the EU on 1 May (see Regional Affairs), the first elections to the European Parliament took place on 13 June, in which about 28% of the electorate participated. The NSi, the SDP and the LDS each obtained two mandates, while the ULSD received one seat. In July Rop dismissed Rupel as Minister of Foreign Affairs; Rupel had announced that he was transferring his support to the opposition SDP prior to forthcoming legislative elections. Ivo Vajgl, hitherto ambassador to Germany, was appointed to the post.

The 2004 legislative elections

At the legislative elections on 3 October 2004, the centre-right SDP secured 29.1% of the votes cast and 29 seats in the 90-member Državni zbor, defeating the ruling LDS (with 22.8% of the votes and 23 seats). Janša was appointed Prime Minister on 9 November. Following lengthy inter-party negotiations, the SDP reached a coalition agreement with the SPP, the NSi and DeSUS, and a new Government was approved by 51 votes in the Državni zbor on 3 December. In April 2005 the ULSD was reconstituted as the Social Democrats (SD), under the continued leadership of Borut Pahor. In November trade unions organized a mass demonstration in Ljubljana (the largest to be staged since 1991), in protest at government plans for extensive economic reforms.

At a first round of voting in the presidential election of 21 October 2007, of the six candidates, Peterle, who contested the election as an independent with the support of the SDP, the SPP and the NSi, won 28.7% of the votes cast, while Danilo Türk, a former UN diplomat and an independent candidate supported by DeSUS and the SD, won 24.5% of the votes and Gaspari obtained 24.1%. At the second round of voting, contested by Peterle and Türk on 11 November, Türk was elected President, with 68.0% of the votes cast. In mid-November the Government won a motion of confidence proposed by Janša, who had complained that opposition criticism was impeding preparations to adopt the rotational presidency of the EU. Türk was inaugurated on 22 December, upon the expiry of the mandate of Drnovšek (who died in early 2008).

Recent developments: Borut Pahor's Government

Prior to the elections to the Državni zbor conducted on 21 September 2008, a Finnish television broadcast had implicated government members, including Prime Minister Janša, in a scandal involving the alleged receipt of unauthorized payments from a Finnish state-owned company, Patria, in association with a tender to supply military vehicles. In the event, the SD secured 29 seats in the chamber, with 30.5% of the votes cast, narrowly defeating Janša's SDP, which won 28 seats (29.3% of the votes); For Real—New Politics (Zares—a party established in 2007 by breakaway members of the LDS) received nine seats (9.4%), DeSUS seven seats (7.5%), the SNP five seats (5.4%), the SPP (allied with the Youth Party of Slovenia) five seats (5.2%) and the LDS five seats (5.2%), while the NSi failed to achieve the minimum percentage required for representation. The rate of voter participation was 63.1%. In October Janša initiated criminal proceedings against the journalist responsible for the Finnish broadcast.

On 3 November 2008 Türk officially nominated the President of the SD, Borut Pahor, as Prime Minister; a coalition agreement was subsequently reached between the SD, Zares, DeSUS and the LDS, which together held 50 of the 90 seats in the legislature. Pahor's new Government was approved by the Državni zbor on 21 November; it contained seven independent members, including Samuel Žbogar (hitherto Slovenia's ambassador to the USA) as Minister of Foreign Affairs. A new post of Minister without Portfolio, responsible for Slovenes Abroad, was also created. Pahor pledged that the introduction of measures to combat the effects of the international financial crisis would be a priority for the Government.

In elections to the European Parliament, held on 7 June 2009, the SDP and the SD each obtained two seats, while the NSi, the LDS and Zares each secured one. The rate of participation by the electorate was 28.3%. In late January 2010 the President of DeSUS, Karl Erjavec, lost a motion of confidence in the Državni svet, proposed by Pahor, and consequently resigned from the position of Minister of the Environment and Physical Planning that he had occupied since November 2008. The motion had been prompted by a ruling of the Court of Audit, accusing the Ministry of the Environment and Physical Planning of financial mismanagement, and criticizing its failure to establish an efficient, separate waste-management system. However, Erjavec's supporters claimed that the Court's ruling constituted a breach of the principle of separating judicial and executive powers. In early July 2010 the Minister of the Economy, Matej Lahovnik, resigned from his post, three days after leaving Zares, apparently owing to disagreement with the Zares leader and Minister of Higher Education, Science and Technology, Gregor Golobič. In December Dusa Busan of DeSUS was appointed as Minister without Portfolio, responsible for Local Self-Government and Regional Policy, following the resignation of Henrik Gjerkës. However, she resigned in mid-April, citing lack of trust. The remaining members of DeSUS subsequently announced their intention to leave the coalition, although ministers were to remain in their posts until a planned referendum on pensions reform had taken place.

Regional Affairs

Areas of disputed border territory with Croatia, most notably the maritime boundary in the Bay of Piran in Istria, undermined otherwise harmonious relations between the two countries following independence. In November 1993 Slovenian proposals to decommission the country's nuclear power plant, at Krško (constructed by the former federal authorities to supply energy to both Slovenia and Croatia), prompted protests by Croatia, which was reliant on the installation for one-quarter of its energy requirements. In October 1994 the Croatian Government submitted a formal protest to Slovenia, following the approval of legislation providing for a reorganization of local government boundaries in Slovenia, as part of which four villages in the disputed area were to be included within the Slovenian municipality of Piran (Pirano). In February 1995 a meeting of the Slovenian-Croatian joint border commission agreed that, since the process of delineating the border would be lengthy, this should be pursued separately from other bilateral concerns. In March Slovenia and Croatia agreed to divide ownership of the Krško nuclear station equally between the two countries.

In July 1998 Slovenia ceased distributing electricity generated at the Krško nuclear power plant to Croatia, claiming that it had failed to pay for power, valued at some US $14m., already supplied. In the same month Slovenia privatized its share of the Krško power plant. Croatia was reported to have resumed payments to Slovenia in August, and subsequently the transfer of electricity was restored. In November it was announced that the dispute over the Krško nuclear power plant would be resolved on the basis of co-ownership. Following the election of a new Government in Croatia in early 2000, bilateral relations improved significantly. After lengthy negotiations between Drnovšek and the Croatian Prime Minister, Ivica Račan, an agreement resolving the outstanding issues of contention between Slovenia and Croatia was signed in July 2001. The accord (which required endorsement by the legislatures of the two countries) granted Slovenia access to the Adriatic Sea through the Bay of Piran, and provided for continued joint management of the Krško nuclear installation; the four disputed border villages were to remain under Croatian sovereignty. In 2003 a further dispute erupted between Slovenia and Croatia, after the Croatian Government announced plans to establish an economic zone in the Adriatic Sea, which would remove Slovenia's direct access to international waters. The Slovenian Government temporarily withdrew its ambassador in Croatia.

In August 2005 it was announced that Croatia had withdrawn its ambassador to Slovenia, following the Slovenian Government's decision to declare a fishing zone in the border region. (The ambassador was returned by early September.) After the Državni zbor approved the Government's decision, Croatia declared the fishing zone to be illegitimate and demanded that the issue be referred to international arbitration. The Slovenian Government demonstrated reluctance to enter into international arbitration and, following the official opening of Croatia's accession negotiations with the EU earlier that month, threatened to obstruct Croatian membership. The Slovenian Government also continued to reject claims by Croatia that it was liable for outstanding debts owed to Croatian citizens by the former Ljubljanska Banka of Slovenia. At the end of 2005 the Croatian national power utility submitted to an international centre for investment disputes a demand for compensation for undelivered electricity from the Krško installation. In January 2007 the dispute between Croatia and Slovenia over the joint maritime boundary was revived with a diplomatic protest by Slovenia that the Croatian Government had pre-empted a border demarcation by extending concessions for petroleum exploration in the disputed region. At the beginning of 2008 Croatia implemented legislation enforcing its environmental fishing zone in the Adriatic Sea, which it had declared in 2003 with the objective of protecting fishing stocks; Slovenia, together with Italy, opposed the measure, which would result in significant financial damage for their fleets. Slovenia (which had assumed the EU's rotational presidency) indicated that the issue would impede Croatia's ongoing EU integration process. In March 2008, following continued pressure from the EU, Croatia agreed that implementation of the environmental fishing zone would be postponed until its anticipated accession to the Union.

In October 2008 the Slovenian Government demanded that Croatia withdraw documentation submitted as part of its EU accession negotiations, which was considered to predetermine the common maritime border that remained under dispute. At an intergovernmental conference in December, Croatia was prevented by a Slovenian veto from making progress in 11 negotiating chapters. The Croatian Government issued a statement denying that the documentation predetermined the maritime border. The European Commission expressed concern at Slovenia's decision to impede the accession negotiations and urged both countries to resolve the issue through bilateral discussions; however, Croatian Prime Minister Ivo Sanader demanded that the dispute be referred to international arbitration.

In early February 2009 the Državni zbor ratified the protocols for Croatia's accession to the North Atlantic Treaty Organization (NATO), which had been supported by Slovenia's governing coalition on the grounds that it would improve regional stability. Later in February, however, following an initiative by the SPP that a referendum be conducted on Croatia's prospective NATO membership, the Državni zbor adopted a declaration that Slovenia's national interests be protected during Croatia's NATO accession process and stating its territorial claim. A meeting between Sanader and his Slovenian counterpart, Borut Pahor, in Mokrice, Slovenia, in late February, failed to produce any agreement; Sanader continued to insist that the border issue be referred to the International Court of Justice, while the Slovenian Government announced its acceptance of a proposal by the European Commissioner responsible for Enlargement, Olli Rehn, that the European Commission mediate a resolution to the dispute. Nevertheless, Türk ratified Croatia's NATO accession protocol in late March; Croatia was admitted as a member of the Alliance in early April. Later in April the EU cancelled a round of entry negotiations with Croatia, owing to the continued dispute with Slovenia. Following discussions between new Croatian Prime Minister Jadranka Kosor and Pahor, it was finally agreed in early September that the border dispute should not present an obstacle to the resumption of Croatia's EU accession negotiations, and that the dispute would be resolved through international arbitration. On 29 September a Slovenian parliamentary committee on EU affairs voted in favour of ending its veto on Croatia's accession in the Council of the EU. On 4 November the Governments of Croatia and Slovenia signed an agreement allowing international arbitrators to delineate the joint border, and the agreement was ratified by Croatia in late November. In late March the Slovenian Supreme Court ruled the agreement to be constitutional, and it was ratified by the legislature on 19 April. A legally binding referendum on the agreement took place in June, at which some 51.5% of the participating electorate voted in support of the initiative.

Slovenia and Croatia are united in their opposition to movements for Istrian autonomy and to any revision to their detriment of the 1975 Treaty of Osimo, which had defined the borders between the SFRY and Italy, and had provided for the payment by the SFRY of compensation for Italian property transferred to Yugoslav sovereignty after 1947. In 1993 some 35,000 Italians were reported to be demanding compensation for, or the restitution of, property in Slovenia. Consequently, in July 1994 the Italian Government of Silvio Berlusconi stated that until the Slovenian authorities agreed to compensate Italian nationals who had fled after 1947 from territory now held by Slovenia, and whose property had been confiscated under communist rule, Italy would block efforts by Slovenia to achieve further integration with Western Europe. Italy thus prevented scheduled negotiations on an association agreement between Slovenia and the EU until March 1995, when the new Italian Government of Lamberto Dini withdrew the veto. However, it was not until May 1996 that Slovenia and Italy agreed to a compromise solution proposed by Spain, whereby Slovenia was to allow EU nationals to purchase property in Slovenia, on a reciprocal basis, within four years of the association agreement's ratification, and EU citizens who had previously permanently resided in Slovenia for a period of three years (thus including Italian nationals who had fled after the Second World War) would be permitted to buy immediately. In June Slovenia finally signed an association agreement with the EU, and simultaneously applied for full membership of the organization. In July 1997 the Državni zbor voted in favour of amending the Constitution in accordance with the agreement.

Formal accession negotiations with the EU commenced in November 1998. In December 2002, at a summit meeting in Copenhagen, Denmark, Slovenia was one of 10 nations officially invited to become members of the EU with effect from 2004. Meanwhile, at a summit meeting in Prague, Czech Republic, in November 2002, Slovenia was formally invited to join NATO in 2004. A national referendum on the issue of joining both organizations was conducted on 23 March 2003; some 89.6% of voters endorsed membership of the EU, and 66.1% membership of NATO. On 29 March 2004 Slovenia was officially admitted to NATO, together with Bulgaria, Estonia, Latvia, Lithuania, Romania and Slovakia, at a ceremony in Washington, DC, USA. Slovenia's accession to the EU followed on 1 May. In June 2006 EU leaders, meeting in Brussels, Belgium, approved Slovenia's application to adopt the European common currency, the euro, with effect from 1 January 2007. The decision was confirmed by EU Ministers of Finance on 11 July 2006, and Slovenia joined the euro zone as scheduled. In December 2007 Slovenia implemented the EU's Schengen Agreement on freedom of travel, effectively removing border controls between those states subject to the Agreement. Ratification of the EU's Lisbon Treaty, which was designed to reform the Union's institutions, was approved by the Državni zbor in January 2008 and received presidential assent in the following month.

CONSTITUTION AND GOVERNMENT

The Constitution of the Republic of Slovenia was enacted on 23 December 1991. Under the terms of the Constitution, as subsequently modified, legislative power is vested in the 90-member Državni zbor (National Assembly). Of the 90 deputies, who serve a term of four years, 88 are elected on the basis of proportional representation; two members are representatives of the Hungarian and Italian minorities. The Državni svet (National Council), which is elected for five years, comprises 22 directly elected members and 18 members chosen by an electoral college to represent various social, economic, trading, political and local interest groups; the Council's role is mainly advisory, but it is empowered to veto decisions of the Državni zbor. The Prime Minister, who is elected by the Državni zbor, nominates the Government (subject to the approval of the legislature). The President of the Republic has largely ceremonial powers, and is directly elected for a maximum of two five-year terms. The judicial branch of government is independent. The Supreme Court is the highest court for civil and criminal cases in the republic. For administrative purposes, Slovenia is divided into 193 municipalities, 11 of which are designated as city municipalities.

REGIONAL AND INTERNATIONAL CO-OPERATION

Slovenia is a member of the European Bank for Reconstruction and Development (see p. 265) and the Council of Europe (see p. 250). The country acceded to full membership of the European Union (EU, see p. 270) and the North Atlantic Treaty Organization (NATO, see p. 368) in 2004. Slovenia was invited to join the Organisation for Economic Co-operation and Development (see p. 376) in 2010.

SLOVENIA

Slovenia became a member of the UN in 1992, and joined the World Trade Organization (see p. 430) in 1995.

ECONOMIC AFFAIRS

In 2009, according to the World Bank, Slovenia's gross national income (GNI), measured at average 2007–09 prices, was US $48,063m., equivalent to $23,520 per head (or $26,340 per head on an international purchasing-power parity basis). During 2000–09, it was estimated, the population increased at an average annual rate of 0.3%, while gross domestic product (GDP) per head increased, in real terms, by an average of 2.6% per year. Overall GDP increased, in real terms, at an average annual rate of 2.7% in 2000–10, according to official figures. Real GDP decreased by 8.1% in 2009, but increased by 1.2% in 2010.

Agriculture (including hunting, forestry and fishing) contributed 2.4% of GDP in 2009 and engaged 4.0% of the employed labour force in 2010. The principal crops are cereals (particularly maize and wheat), potatoes, sugar beet and fruits (especially grapes and apples). Slovenia's forests, which cover about one-half of the country, are an important natural resource. Agricultural GDP declined at an average rate of 0.6% per year during 2000–09. The GDP of the sector increased by 5.5% in 2008, but decreased by 8.5% in 2009.

Industry (including mining, manufacturing, construction and power) contributed 31.1% of GDP in 2009 and engaged 33.7% of the employed labour force in 2009. Industrial GDP increased at an average rate of 2.5% per year in 2000–09. Sectoral GDP increased by 1.5% in 2008, but decreased by 15.7% in 2009.

Mining and quarrying contributed 0.4% of GDP in 2009 and engaged 0.4% of the employed labour force in 2010. The principal activity is coal-mining; lead and zinc are also extracted, together with relatively small amounts of natural gas, petroleum and salt. Slovenia also has small deposits of uranium. The GDP of the mining sector increased at an average rate of 1.9% per year in 2000–098. Mining GDP increased by 1.2% in 2008, but declined by 3.4% in 2009.

Manufacturing contributed 19.6% of GDP in 2009 and engaged 22.5% of the employed labour force in 2010. Manufacturing GDP increased at an average rate of 2.2% per year in 2000–09. GDP in the manufacturing sector increased by just 0.1% in 2008, and decreased by 16.7% in 2009.

Construction contributed 7.9% of GDP in 2009 and engaged 8.8% of the employed labour force in 2010. The GDP of the sector increased at an average rate of 3.4% per year in 2000–09. Growth in the construction sector was 5.5% in 2008, but the sector contracted by 15.5% in 2009.

A nuclear power station was constructed in Slovenia by the former Yugoslav authorities to provide energy for both Slovenia and Croatia (see Contemporary Political History). In 2007 nuclear power stations provided 37.9% of energy requirements, coal-fired electricity-generating stations provided 36.5%, and hydroelectric power stations provided 21.7%. Imports of fuel products comprised 11.3% of the value of merchandise imports in 2009.

The services sector contributed 66.5% of GDP in 2009 and engaged 62.3% of the employed labour force in 2010. Tourism is a significant source of revenue; tourist activity was adversely affected by the political instability of 1991, but the number of arrivals recovered, reaching 1,823,900 in 2009. The GDP of the services sector increased at an average rate of 3.5% per year in 2000–09. Growth in the services sector was 4.5% in 2008, but the sector contracted by 3.9% in 2009.

In 2009 Slovenia recorded a visible trade deficit of US $991m., and there was a deficit of $720m. on the current account of the balance of payments. In that year Slovenia's principal source of imports was Germany (accounting for 18.3% of the total); other major suppliers were Italy, Austria and France. Germany was also the principal market for exports (taking 19.8% of the total in that year); Italy, Croatia, Austria and France were also significant purchasers. The major imports in 2009 were machinery and transport equipment (particularly road vehicles and parts, and electrical machinery), basic manufactures (particularly iron and steel), chemical products, mineral fuels, miscellaneous manufactured articles, food and live animals, and crude materials. The principal exports in that year were machinery and transport equipment (particularly road vehicles and parts, and electrical machinery), basic manufactures (notably metal manufactures), chemicals (particularly pharmaceuticals) and miscellaneous manufactured articles.

Slovenia's overall budgetary deficit for 2010 was €18.9m., equivalent to 0.05% of GDP. Slovenia's general government gross debt was €10.253m. in 2009, equivalent to 29.4% of GDP. At the end of 2009 total central government debt amounted to US $15,891.2m. The annual rate of inflation averaged 4.4% in 2000–09. Consumer prices increased by 0.8% in 2009. The rate of unemployment was 11.8% in 2010.

By April 2003 Slovenia had achieved sustained convergence in per-head income to about 70% of the average for the countries of the European Union (EU, see p. 270). Slovenia formally acceded to the EU on 1 May 2004 and, following the successful adoption of measures to reduce inflation, achieved entry into the exchange rate mechanism (ERM II) in June. The continued reduction of inflation in order to meet EU levels was central to government policy, and Slovenia adopted the euro on 1 January 2007. Slovenia was severely affected by the global economic crisis from late 2008, and real GDP declined by 8.1% in 2009. Although there was a slight increase in GDP in 2010, of 1.2%, in January 2010 the Government reached agreement with employers and trade unions to increase the minimum wage by 22.9% during 2010–12, attracting fears among some observers of an increase in the rate of unemployment, which had already risen to 10.3% in 2009, compared with 7.0% in 2008; the rate of unemployment recorded in 2010 was 11.8%. In March 2010 the Government announced a 'crisis exit' strategy, which aimed to promote competitiveness and increase economic growth. The Government planned to reduce public expenditure, and reform the pensions and health care systems, as well as to reduce its stake in principal industrial sectors and reorientate the economy towards the services sector. In December the legislature approved a bill on pensions reform, which was to be submitted for approval by referendum in mid-2011. The IMF and the Organisation for Economic Co-operation and Development (OECD) welcomed the Government's efforts to reform the pensions system, but urged that further reforms be implemented in order to ensure its long-term sustainability. In April 2011 proposed legislation that would have placed restrictions on the amount of short-term work available to students and pensioners was rejected by some 80% of voters in a referendum.

PUBLIC HOLIDAYS

2012: 1–2 January (New Year), 8 February (Prešeren Day, National Day of Culture), 6–9 April (Easter), 27 April (Resistance Day), 1–2 May (Labour Day), 25 June (National Statehood Day), 15 August (Assumption), 31 October (Reformation Day), 1 November (All Saints' Day), 25 December (Christmas Day), 26 December (Independence Day).

SLOVENIA

Statistical Survey

Source (unless otherwise indicated): Statistical Office of the Republic of Slovenia, 1000 Ljubljana, Vožarski pot 12; tel. (1) 2415104; fax (1) 2415344; e-mail info.stat@gov.si; internet www.stat.si.

Area and Population

AREA, POPULATION AND DENSITY

Area (sq km)	20,273*
Population (census results)	
31 March 1991	1,913,355
31 March 2002	
Males	958,576
Females	1,005,460
Total	1,964,036
Population (official estimates at 1 January)†	
2008	2,025,866
2009	2,032,362
2010	2,046,976
Density (per sq km) at 1 January 2010	101.0

* 7,827 sq miles.
† Estimates are calculated on a *de jure* basis.

POPULATION BY AGE AND SEX
(official estimates at 1 January 2010)

	Males	Females	Total
0–14	147,808	139,467	287,275
15–64	732,992	688,444	1,421,436
65 and over	133,307	204,958	338,265
Total	1,014,107	1,032,869	2,046,976

POPULATION BY ETHNIC GROUP
(2002 census)

Ethnic group	Number	%
Slovenes	1,631,363	83.06
Serbs	38,964	1.98
Croats	35,642	1.81
Bosniaks	21,542	1.10
Muslims*	10,467	0.53
Others†	226,058	11.51
Total (incl. others)	1,964,036	100.00

* Including persons claiming Muslim ethnicity rather than religious adherence.
† Including unknown and not declared.

REGIONS
(official estimates at 1 January 2010)

	Area (sq km)	Population	Density (per sq km)
Pomurska	1,337	119,548	89.4
Podravska	2,170	323,343	149.0
Koroška	1,041	72,812	69.9
Savinjska	2,384	260,025	109.1
Zasavska	264	44,706	169.3
Spodnjeposavska	885	70,192	79.3
Jugovzhodna Slovenija	2,675	142,092	53.1
Osrednjeslovenska	2,555	529,646	207.3
Gorenjska	2,137	202,903	94.9
Notranjsko-kraška	1,456	52,217	35.9
Goriška	2,325	119,080	51.2
Obalno-kraška	1,044	110,412	105.8
Total	20,273	2,046,976	101.0

PRINCIPAL TOWNS
(population at 1 January 2010, official estimates)

Ljubljana (capital)	279,653	Celje	48,783
Maribor	112,364	Novo mesto	35,966
Kranj	54,781	Nova Gorica	32,089
Koper (Capodistria)	52,212		

BIRTHS, MARRIAGES AND DEATHS

	Registered live births		Registered marriages		Registered deaths	
	Number	Rate (per 1,000)	Number	Rate (per 1,000)	Number	Rate (per 1,000)
2002	17,501	8.8	7,064	3.5	18,701	9.4
2003	17,321	8.7	6,756	3.4	19,451	9.7
2004	17,961	9.0	6,558	3.3	18,523	9.3
2005	18,157	9.1	5,769	2.9	18,825	9.4
2006	18,932	9.4	6,368	3.2	18,180	9.1
2007	19,823	9.8	6,373	3.2	18,584	9.2
2008	21,817	10.8	6,703	3.3	18,308	9.1
2009	21,856	10.7	6,542	3.2	18,750	9.2

Life expectancy (years at birth, WHO estimates): 79 (males 75; females 82) in 2008 (Source: WHO, *World Health Statistics*).

IMMIGRATION AND EMIGRATION

	2007	2008	2009
Long-term immigrants	29,193	30,693	30,296
Long-term emigrants	14,943	12,109	18,788

ECONOMICALLY ACTIVE POPULATION
('000 persons aged 15 years and over, December)

	2008	2009	2010
Agriculture, hunting, forestry and fishing	38.8	37.7	33.1
Mining and quarrying	3.4	3.1	2.9
Manufacturing	216.3	190.6	184.1
Electricity, gas and water supply	16.7	17.0	16.9
Construction	89.5	83.3	72.1
Wholesale and retail trade; repair of motor vehicles, motorcycles, and personal and household goods	116.9	113.5	109.4
Hotels and restaurants	34.3	33.8	32.5
Transport, storage and communications	51.4	48.8	46.9
Information and communication	22.4	22.5	22.6
Financial intermediation	24.6	24.2	24.2
Real estate, renting and business activities	74.8	75.9	77.3
Public administration and defence; compulsory social security	50.8	51.6	51.5
Education	61.0	62.6	64.3
Health and social work	51.6	52.1	53.3
Other social and personal services	27.2	27.6	27.4
Private households with employed persons	0.5	0.5	0.5
Total employed	880.3	844.7	819.0
Unemployed	66.2	96.7	110.0
Total labour force	946.5	941.4	929.0

SLOVENIA

Health and Welfare

KEY INDICATORS

Total fertility rate (children per woman, 2008)	1.4
Under-5 mortality rate (per 1,000 live births, 2008)	3.0
HIV/AIDS (% of persons aged 15–49, 2007)	<0.1
Physicians (per 1,000 head, 2005)	2.4
Hospital beds (per 1,000 head, 2006)	4.8
Health expenditure (2007): US $ per head (PPP)	2,099
Health expenditure (2007): % of GDP	7.8
Health expenditure (2007): public (% of total)	71.5
Access to water (% of total population, 2008)	99
Total carbon dioxide emissions ('000 metric tons, 2007)	15,095.7
Carbon dioxide emissions per head (metric tons, 2007)	7.5
Human Development Index (2010): ranking	29
Human Development Index (2010): value	0.828

For sources and definitions, see explanatory note on p. vi.

Agriculture

PRINCIPAL CROPS
('000 metric tons)

	2007	2008	2009
Wheat	133.3	160.3	136.3
Barley	67.9	76.8	70.8
Maize	308.3	319.9	302.6
Oats	5.5	5.0	4.3
Triticale (wheat-rye hybrid)	12.0	13.3	13.5
Potatoes	131.1	100.3	103.4
Cabbages and other brassicas	22.2	28.9	30.4
Lettuce and chicory	12.5	13.2	15.3
Tomatoes	4.4	4.7	4.3
Chillies and peppers, green	3.7	4.3	4.6
Onions, dry	4.5	5.3	6.0
Apples	114.5	102.9	95.7
Pears	11.8	9.3	9.9
Peaches and nectarines	9.3	6.8	10.0
Plums	6.3	4.1	4.1
Grapes	122.5	105.7	112.9

* FAO estimate.

Aggregate production ('000 metric tons, may include official, semi-official or estimated data): Total cereals 535.4 in 2007, 583.2 in 2008, 536.3 in 2009; Total roots and tubers 131.1 in 2007, 100.3 in 2008, 103.4 in 2009; Total vegetables (incl. melons) 66.4 in 2007, 80.3 in 2008, 85.1 in 2009; Total fruits (excl. melons) 271.5 in 2007, 234.7 in 2008; 240.5 in 2009.

Source: FAO.

LIVESTOCK
('000 head)

	2007	2008	2009
Cattle	454	480	470
Pigs	575	543	432
Sheep	132	131	139
Goats	28	28	24
Horses	19*	20	20*
Chickens	2,919	4,354	4,387
Turkeys	110	158	145

* FAO estimate.
Source: FAO.

LIVESTOCK PRODUCTS
('000 metric tons)

	2007	2008	2009
Cattle meat	38.4	36.9	35.3
Pig meat	57.3	54.6	44.1
Sheep meat	1.7	1.6	1.7
Chicken meat	42.7	52.2	55.1
Turkey meat	6.7	6.7	6.3
Cows' milk	642.3	666.5	653.7
Hen eggs	15.8	19.4	21.5

Source: FAO.

Forestry

ROUNDWOOD REMOVALS
('000 cubic metres, excl. bark)

	2007	2008	2009
Sawlogs, veneer logs and logs for sleepers	1,699	1,686	1,514
Pulpwood	353	316	370
Other industrial wood	41	60	63
Fuel wood	788	928	983
Total	**2,881**	**2,990**	**2,930**

Source: FAO.

SAWNWOOD PRODUCTION
('000 cubic metres, incl. railway sleepers)

	2007	2008	2009
Coniferous (softwood)	464	367	321
Broadleaved (hardwood)	146	108	76
Total	**610**	**475**	**397**

Source: FAO.

Fishing

(metric tons, live weight)

	2006	2007	2008
Capture	1,131	1,111	869
Common carp	80	74	89
European pilchard (sardine)	298	249	306
European anchovy	410	407	184
Aquaculture	1,369	1,352	1,315
Common carp	204	195	166
Rainbow trout	894	799	775
European seabass	30	15	50
Mediterranean mussel	163	301	224
Total catch	**2,500**	**2,463**	**2,184**

Source: FAO.

SLOVENIA

Statistical Survey

Mining

(metric tons, unless otherwise indicated)

	2007	2008	2009
Brown coal ('000 metric tons)	483	489	511
Lignite ('000 metric tons)	4,079	4,032	3,918
Natural gas ('000 cu m)	3,418	2,610	2,575
Crude petroleum (42-gallon barrels)	2,060	1,170	994
Bentonite*	130	130	130
Silica sand	350,000*	353,983	326,636
Sand and gravel (excl. glass sand)	21,548,000	19,171,000	19,000,000*
Pumice*	40,000	40,000	40,000
Salt*	2,000	2,000	2,000

* Estimate(s).

Source: US Geological Survey.

Industry

SELECTED PRODUCTS

('000 metric tons, unless otherwise indicated)

	2007	2008	2009
Wine ('000 hectolitres)	312	260	258
Footwear (excl. rubber) ('000 pairs)	3,683	3,483	3,269
Veneer sheets ('000 cubic metres)	453	454	338
Plywood ('000 cubic metres)*	171	70	75
Mechanical wood pulp*†	50	175	164
Newsprint*‡	120	137	119
Household and sanitary paper*‡	61	60	41
Wrapping and packaging paper and paperboard	320	304	296
Cement†§	1,300	1,300	1,000
Crude steel ingots (incl. crude steel for casting)‖	638	642	430
Refined lead†§	15.0	15.0	14.0
Electric energy (million kWh)	15,043	16,398	16,401

* Source: FAO.
† Estimated production.
‡ Unofficial figure.
§ Source: US Geological Survey.
‖ Source: International Iron and Steel Institute (Brussels, Belgium).

Finance

CURRENCY AND EXCHANGE RATES

Monetary Units
100 cent = 1 euro (€).

Sterling, Dollar and Euro Equivalents (31 December 2010)
£1 sterling = 1.172 euros;
US $1 = 0.748 euros;
€10 = £8.54 = $13.36.

Average Exchange Rate (euros per US $)
2008 0.6827
2009 0.7198
2010 0.7550

The tolar was introduced in October 1991, replacing (initially at par) the Yugoslav dinar. Slovenia participated in the common European currency, the euro, with effect from 1 January 2007; a fixed exchange rate of €1 = 239.640 tolars was in operation. The euro and the tolar circulated alongside each other until 14 January, after which time the euro (comprising 100 cent) became the sole legal tender.

BUDGET
(€ '000)*

Revenue	2008	2009	2010†
Tax revenue	13,937,365	12,955,413	12,848,340
Taxes on income and profits	3,442,172	2,805,088	2,490,703
Taxes on payroll, property, etc.	258,037	28,490	28,076
Social security contributions	5,095,009	5,161,254	5,234,485
Domestic taxes on goods and services	4,805,321	4,660,212	4,780,628
Taxes on international trade and transactions	120,092	90,533	90,699
Other current revenue	854,903	684,060	920,423
Capital revenue and grants	127,653	117,688	186,654
Transferred revenues	53,916	54,303	109,427
Receipts from EU budget	365,374	596,534	724,676
Total	**15,339,211**	**14,407,999**	**14,789,520**

Expenditure‡	2008	2009	2010†
Current expenditure (excl. transfers)	6,557,500	6,800,822	6,958,887
Interest payments	335,166	336,091	488,097
Current transfers	6,742,228	7,339,430	7,625,384
Capital expenditure (excl. transfers)	1,255,495	1,294,057	1,305,791
Capital transfers	458,605	494,618	389,059
Payments to EU budget	427,915	439,301	396,785
Total	**15,441,743**	**16,368,229**	**16,675,906**

* Figures represent a consolidation of the accounts of the central Government (State Budget, Pension Fund and Health Insurance Fund) and local administrative authorities.
† Preliminary.
‡ Excluding net lending (€ '000): −86,109 in 2008; −263,494 in 2009; −164,475 in 2010 (preliminary).

Source: Ministry of Finance, Ljubljana.

INTERNATIONAL RESERVES
(US $ million at 31 December)

	2008	2009	2010
Gold (Eurosystem valuation)	88.46	113.71	145.26
IMF special drawing rights	11.80	310.61	305.20
Reserve position in IMF	46.35	65.99	114.41
Foreign exchange	809.91	589.55	543.18
Total	**956.52**	**1,079.86**	**1,108.05**

Source: IMF, *International Financial Statistics*.

MONEY SUPPLY
(incl. shares, depository corporations, national residency criteria, € million at 31 December)

	2008	2009	2010†
Currency issued	3,255	3,536	3,686
Demand deposits	6,842	7,375	8,375
Other deposits	12,121	12,416	12,155
Securities other than shares	1,762	3,829	5,056
Money market fund shares	17	14	12
Shares and other equity	5,016	5,410	5,384
Other items (net)	−298	−216	−48
Total	**28,715**	**32,364**	**34,620**

Source: IMF, *International Financial Statistics*.

COST OF LIVING
(Consumer Price Index for urban areas; base: 2000 = 100)

	2007	2008	2009
Food (incl. beverages)	137.0	150.8	151.6
Fuel and light	155.2	171.6	172.9
Clothing (incl. footwear)	115.0	120.0	119.3
Rent	199.5	210.7	209.6
All items (incl. others)	138.6	146.5	147.7

Source: ILO.

SLOVENIA

NATIONAL ACCOUNTS
(€ million at current prices)

Expenditure on the Gross Domestic Product

	2007	2008	2009
Final consumption expenditure	24,207.7	26,519.1	26,775.4
Households	17,944.2	19,477.5	19,355.9
Non-profit institutions serving households	274.0	283.3	251.3
General government	5,989.6	6,758.3	7,168.3
Gross capital formation	10,955.7	11,918.8	8,149.2
Gross fixed capital formation	9,571.3	10,743.4	8,471.6
Changes in inventories / Acquisitions, less disposals, of valuables	1,384.4	1,175.4	−322.4
Total domestic expenditure	35,163.4	38,437.9	34,924.6
Exports of goods and services	24,040.7	25,132.4	20,571.6
Less Imports of goods and services	24,635.9	26,265.6	20,111.8
GDP in purchasers' values	34,568.2	37,304.7	35,384.4

Gross Domestic Product by Economic Activity

	2007	2008	2009
Agriculture, hunting and forestry	757.3	819.9	751.9
Fishing	3.3	3.1	4.0
Mining and quarrying	135.6	137.5	137.8
Manufacturing	7,112.0	7,230.8	6,046.0
Electricity, gas and water supply	853.9	980.6	985.5
Construction	2,393.5	2,727.2	2,428.7
Wholesale and retail trade; repair of motor vehicles, motorcycles and personal and household goods	3,713.4	4,139.9	3,856.5
Hotels and restaurants	703.6	753.8	722.0
Transport, storage and communications	2,339.5	2,492.2	2,215.9
Financial intermediation	1,404.4	1,486.8	1,557.5
Real estate, renting and business activities	5,269.9	5,799.4	5,626.2
Public administration and defence; compulsory social security	1,682.6	1,870.5	1,961.1
Education	1,567.9	1,664.5	1,746.7
Health and social work	1,383.5	1,546.2	1,750.0
Other community, social and personal services	1,000.0	1,065.7	1,054.1
Private households with employed persons	21.0	23.0	24.3
Gross value added at basic prices	30,341.5	32,741.2	30,868.3
Taxes on products	4,420.4	4,769.2	4,727.8
Less Subsidies	193.7	205.7	211.7
GDP in market prices	34,568.2	37,304.7	35,384.4

BALANCE OF PAYMENTS
(US $ million)

	2007	2008	2009
Exports of goods f.o.b.	27,151	29,583	22,532
Imports of goods f.o.b.	−29,466	−33,467	−23,524
Trade balance	−2,314	−3,884	−991
Exports of services	5,691	7,426	6,010
Imports of services	−4,264	−5,212	−4,456
Balance on goods and services	−887	−1,670	563
Other income received	1,609	1,850	933
Other income paid	−2,693	−3,372	−2,013
Balance on goods, services and income	−1,971	−3,191	−518
Current transfers received	1,295	1,276	1,350
Current transfers paid	−1,622	−1,716	−1,551
Current balance	−2,298	−3,632	−720
Capital account (net)	−72	−33	−18

—continued	2007	2008	2009
Direct investment abroad	−1,800	−1,427	−167
Direct investment from abroad	1,531	1,937	−579
Portfolio investment assets	−4,468	−371	27
Portfolio investment liabilities	1,379	932	6,408
Financial derivatives assets	−46	54	45
Financial derivatives liabilities	26	14	−46
Other investment assets	−6,396	−704	−467
Other investment liabilities	12,337	3,304	−4,799
Net errors and omissions	−393	−109	390
Overall balance	−199	−34	76

Source: IMF, *International Financial Statistics*.

External Trade

PRINCIPAL COMMODITIES
(distribution by SITC, € million)

Imports c.i.f.	2007	2008	2009
Food and live animals	1,197.5	1,338.0	1,303.7
Crude materials (inedible) except fuels	1,218.2	1,196.4	818.7
Mineral fuels, lubricants, etc.	2,020.3	2,943.7	1,933.7
Petroleum, petroleum products, etc.	1,348.3	2,231.1	1,373.2
Chemicals and related products	2,590.6	2,717.3	2,312.9
Basic manufactures	4,850.1	4,686.2	3,139.3
Textile yarn, fabrics, etc.	444.6	405.7	302.3
Iron and steel	1,348.3	1,357.0	713.4
Non-ferrous metals	842.6	735.8	448.7
Other metal manufactures	843.9	872.1	634.5
Machinery and transport equipment	7,383.2	7,716.3	5,479.8
Machinery specialized for particular industries	616.8	717.7	405.6
General industrial machinery, equipment and parts	1,002.0	1,040.1	777.7
Electrical machinery, apparatus, etc.	1,206.4	1,263.6	1,025.5
Road vehicles (incl. air-cushion vehicles) and parts (excl. tyres, engines and electrical parts)	2,838.1	2,741.4	1,750.5
Miscellaneous manufactured articles	2,037.0	2,173.4	1,890.5
Clothing and accessories (excl. footwear)	409.8	460.1	424.9
Total (incl. others)	21,507.6	23,045.7	17,115.3

SLOVENIA

Statistical Survey

Exports f.o.b.	2007	2008	2009
Chemicals and related products	2,672.8	2,859.6	2,629.2
Medicinal and pharmaceutical products	1,395.8	1,560.6	1,510.5
Basic manufactures	4,855.1	4,705.7	3,335.9
Paper, paperboard and articles thereof	519.3	519.8	477.0
Textile yarn, fabrics, etc.	449.4	411.8	346.5
Iron and steel	833.8	886.9	439.5
Non-ferrous metals	785.4	637.8	394.6
Other metal manufactures	1,027.3	1,070.6	749.2
Machinery and transport equipment	7,848.7	7,887.2	6,449.7
General industrial machinery, equipment and parts	1,211.6	1,228.2	935.2
Electrical machinery, apparatus, etc.	1,865.1	1,890.7	1,605.3
Road vehicles (incl. air-cushion vehicles) and parts (excl. tyres, engines and electrical parts)	3,111.4	2,855.8	2,840.6
Miscellaneous manufactured articles	2,423.2	2,423.4	1,910.0
Furniture and parts; bedding mattresses, etc.	825.9	733.2	517.4
Clothing and accessories (excl. footwear)	281.2	276.4	218.8
Total (incl. others)	19,405.9	19,808.2	16,017.7

PRINCIPAL TRADING PARTNERS
(€ million)

Imports c.i.f.	2007	2008	2009
Austria	2,691.5	2,830.5	2,243.0
Belgium	494.9	483.0	388.0
China, People's Republic	346.0	441.1	346.1
Croatia	849.4	835.0	629.9
Czech Republic	506.2	564.0	440.8
France	1,151.6	1,176.9	946.9
Germany	4,177.9	4,318.2	3,136.1
Hungary	758.3	896.1	646.5
Italy	3,927.6	4,159.6	3,027.9
Japan	90.8	100.7	58.9
Netherlands	762.1	751.3	567.0
Poland	355.3	410.8	359.1
Russia	490.0	355.9	208.0
Slovakia	283.4	309.3	238.3
Spain	529.4	602.9	464.0
Sweden	165.2	181.8	109.6
Switzerland	210.5	198.2	249.5
Turkey	180.0	167.6	144.7
United Kingdom	347.2	333.2	219.9
USA	280.3	421.0	330.6
Total (incl. others)	21,507.6	23,045.7	17,115.3

Exports f.o.b.	2007	2008	2009
Austria	1,512.8	1,555.1	1,251.1
Belgium	185.0	202.0	178.8
Bosnia and Herzegovina	535.6	626.3	500.8
Croatia	1,569.7	1,693.9	1,240.9
Czech Republic	489.4	486.5	388.4
France	1,278.4	1,292.9	1,360.8
Germany	3,652.2	3,744.5	3,166.1
Hungary	647.1	616.0	458.8
Italy	2,565.4	2,394.6	1,862.5
Macedonia, former Yugoslav republic	144.2	181.3	160.4
Netherlands	316.1	343.2	254.2
Poland	616.5	694.7	468.4
Russia	691.6	799.9	519.4
Serbia	669.9	708.5	532.4
Slovakia	310.9	360.7	275.4
Spain	356.3	270.0	189.8
Switzerland	189.8	168.9	159.6
United Kingdom	526.2	471.4	378.1
USA	329.3	276.5	209.4
Total (incl. others)	19,405.9	19,808.2	16,017.7

Transport

RAILWAYS
(traffic)

	2007	2008	2009
Passenger journeys ('000)	16,124	16,661	16,355
Passenger-km (million)	812	834	840
Freight carried ('000 metric tons)	17,575	17,270	13,098
Freight ton-km (million)	3,603	3,520	2,668

ROAD TRAFFIC
(registered motor vehicles at 31 December)

	2007	2008	2009
Motorcycles	34,162	41,612	46,185
Mopeds	37,331	40,384	42,243
Passenger cars	1,014,122	1,045,183	1,058,858
Buses	2,330	2,378	2,394
Lorries	62,635	67,585	68,122
Agricultural tractors	80,193	84,316	87,108
Total (incl. others)	1,286,903	1,343,252	1,366,561

SHIPPING

Merchant Fleet
(at 31 December)

	2007	2008	2009
Number of vessels	6	7	7
Displacement (grt)	1,628	2,126	2,126

Source: IHS Fairplay, *World Fleet Statistics*.

International Sea-borne Freight Traffic
('000 metric tons)

	2006	2007	2008
Goods loaded	188	202	235
Goods unloaded	3,206	2,956	3,827

CIVIL AVIATION
(traffic)

	2007	2008	2009
Kilometres flown ('000)	22,087	24,146	23,646
Passengers carried ('000)	1,136	1,302	1,144
Passenger-km (million)	1,186	1,349	1,193
Freight carried (metric tons)	4,481	2,321	1,854
Freight ton-km ('000)	3,724	1,953	1,682

Tourism

FOREIGN TOURIST ARRIVALS
('000)*

Country of origin	2007	2008	2009
Austria	207.2	210.2	207.4
Croatia	106.4	123.1	104.0
France	60.5	66.2	60.5
Germany	211.1	222.2	195.2
Italy	368.7	406.7	417.8
Netherlands	56.8	66.6	63.8
United Kingdom	87.1	86.9	69.4
Total (incl. others)	1,751.3	1,957.7	1,823.9

*Figures refer to arrivals at accommodation establishments.

Receipts from tourism (US $ million, incl. passenger transport): 1,911 in 2006; 2,465 in 2007; 3,115 in 2008 (Source: World Tourism Organization).

SLOVENIA

Communications Media

	2006	2007	2008
Telephones ('000 main lines in use)*	837.5	857.1	1,009.8
Mobile cellular telephones ('000 subscribers)*	1,819.6	1,928.4	2,054.9
Television subscriptions ('000)	624	609	614
Internet users ('000)*†	1,083.1	1,140.5	1,162.3
Broadband subscribers ('000)*	279.8	344.7	426.6
Daily newspapers	9	14	15
Non-daily newspapers	226	180	193
Other periodicals	1,425	1,429	1,346
Book production (titles published, including pamphlets)	4,684	5,129	6,358

* Source: International Telecommunication Union.
† Estimated figures.

2009: Telephones ('000 main lines in use) 1,034.2; Mobile cellular telephones ('000 subscribers) 2,100.4; Internet users ('000, estimate) 1,298.5; Broadband subscribers ('000) 465.7 (Source: International Telecommunication Union).

Personal computers: 858,000 (425.1 per 1,000 persons) in 2007 (Source: International Telecommunication Union).

Education

(2008/09, unless otherwise indicated)

	Institutions	Teachers	Males	Females	Total
Pre-primary*	863	8,906	34,158	36,966	71,124
Elementary†	483	18,206	84,084	79,138	163,222
Upper secondary†	244	11,297	49,465	48,154	97,619
Higher education‡	49	5,673	37,066§	54,163§	91,229§

* 2009/10 figures.
† Including education of adults.
‡ 2006/07.
§ Excluding post-graduate students.

Pupil-teacher ratio (primary education, UNESCO estimate): 17.4 in 2007/08 (Source: UNESCO Institute for Statistics).

Adult literacy rate (UNESCO estimates): 99.7% (males 99.7%; females 99.7%) in 2008 (Source: UNESCO Institute for Statistics).

Directory

The Government

HEAD OF STATE

President: Dr Danilo Türk (elected 11 November 2007; inaugurated 22 December 2007).

GOVERNMENT
(May 2011)

A coalition comprising representatives of the Social Democrats (SD), For Real—New Politics (Zares), Liberal Democracy of Slovenia (LDS) and the Democratic Party of Pensioners of Slovenia (DeSUS), and Independents.

Prime Minister: Borut Pahor (SD).
Minister of Agriculture, Forestry and Food: Dejan Židan (Independent).
Minister of Labour, Family and Social Affairs: Dr Ivan Svetlik (Independent).
Minister of Finance: Dr Franc Križanič (SD).
Minister of the Economy: Darja Radić (Zares).
Minister of Public Administration: Irma Pavlinič-Krebs (Zares).
Minister of Culture: Majda Širca (Zares).
Minister of Internal Affairs: Katarina Kresal (LDS).
Minister of Defence: Dr Ljubica Jelušič (SD).
Minister of the Environment and Physical Planning: Roko Žarnić (DeSUS).
Minister of Justice: Aleš Zalar (LDS).
Minister of Transport: Dr Patrick Vlačič (SD).
Minister of Education and Sport: Dr Igor Lukšič (SD).
Minister of Higher Education, Science and Technology: Gregor Golobič (Zares).
Minister of Health: Dorijan Marušič (Independent).
Minister of Foreign Affairs: Samuel Žbogar (Independent).
Minister without Portfolio, responsible for Development and European Affairs: Mitja Gaspari (Independent).
Minister without Portfolio, responsible for Slovenes Abroad, and acting Minister for Local Self-Government and Regional Policy: Dr Boštjan Žekš (Independent).

MINISTRIES

Office of the President: 1000 Ljubljana, Erjavčeva 17; tel. (1) 4781222; fax (1) 4781357; e-mail gp.uprs@up-rs.si; internet www.up-rs.si.

Office of the Prime Minister: 1000 Ljubljana, Gregorčičeva 20; tel. (1) 4781000; fax (1) 4781721; e-mail gp.kpv@gov.si; internet www.kpv.gov.si.

Government Office for Development and European Affairs: 1000 Ljubljana, Gregorčičeva 25–25a; tel. (1) 4782451; fax (1) 4782500; e-mail gp.svrez@gov.si; internet www.svrez.gov.si.

Government Office for Local Self-Government and Regional Policy: 1000 Ljubljana, Kotnikova 28; tel. (1) 3083178; fax (1) 4783619; e-mail gp.svlr@gov.si; internet www.svlr.gov.si.

Government Office for Slovenes Abroad: 1000 Ljubljana, Komenskega 11; tel. (1) 2308000; fax (1) 2308017; e-mail urad.slovenci@gov.si; internet www.uszs.gov.si.

Ministry of Agriculture, Forestry and Food: 1000 Ljubljana, Dunajska 22; tel. (1) 4789000; fax (1) 4789021; e-mail gp.mkgp@gov.si; internet www.mkgp.gov.si.

Ministry of Culture: 1000 Ljubljana, Maistrova 10; tel. (1) 3695900; fax (1) 3695901; e-mail gp.mk@gov.si; internet www.mk.gov.si.

Ministry of Defence: 1000 Ljubljana, Vojkova cesta 55; tel. (1) 4712211; fax (1) 4712978; e-mail glavna.pisarna@mors.si; internet www.mors.si.

Ministry of the Economy: 1000 Ljubljana, Kotnikova 5; tel. (1) 4003311; fax (1) 4001031; e-mail gp.mg@gov.si; internet www.mg.gov.si.

Ministry of Education and Sport: 1000 Ljubljana, Masarykova 16; tel. (1) 4005200; fax (1) 4005321; e-mail gp.mss@gov.si; internet www.mss.gov.si.

Ministry of the Environment and Physical Planning: 1000 Ljubljana, Dunajska cesta 48; tel. (1) 4787400; fax (1) 4787422; e-mail gp.mop@gov.si; internet www.mop.gov.si.

Ministry of Finance: 1502 Ljubljana, Župančičeva 3; tel. (1) 3695200; fax (1) 3696659; e-mail gp.mf@gov.si; internet www.mf.gov.si.

Ministry of Foreign Affairs: 1001 Ljubljana, Prešernova 25; tel. (1) 4782000; fax (1) 4782340; e-mail info.mzz@gov.si; internet www.mzz.gov.si.

Ministry of Health: 1000 Ljubljana, Štefanova 5; tel. (1) 4786001; fax (1) 4786058; e-mail gp.mz@gov.si; internet www.mz.gov.si.

Ministry of Higher Education, Science and Technology: 1000 Ljubljana, Kotnikova 38; tel. (1) 4784600; fax (1) 4784719; e-mail gp.mvzt@gov.si; internet www.mvzt.gov.si.

Ministry of Internal Affairs: 1000 Ljubljana, Štefanova 2; tel. (1) 4284000; fax (1) 2514330; e-mail gp.mnz@gov.si; internet www.mnz.gov.si.

Ministry of Justice: 1000 Ljubljana, Župančičeva 3; tel. (1) 3695200; fax (1) 3695783; e-mail gp.mp@gov.si; internet www.mp.gov.si.

Ministry of Labour, Family and Social Affairs: 1000 Ljubljana, Kotnikova 5; tel. (1) 3697700; fax (1) 3697832; e-mail gp.mddsz@gov.si; internet www.mddsz.gov.si.

SLOVENIA

Ministry of Public Administration: 1000 Ljubljana, Tržaška cesta 21; tel. (1) 4788330; fax (1) 4788331; e-mail gp.mju@gov.si; internet www.mju.gov.si.

Ministry of Transport: 1535 Ljubljana, Langusova 4; tel. (1) 4788000; fax (1) 4788139; e-mail gp.mpz@gov.si; internet www.mzp.gov.si.

President

Presidential Election, First Ballot, 21 October 2007

Candidate	Votes	% of votes
Lojze Peterle (Independent)	283,412	28.73
Danilo Türk (Independent)	241,349	24.47
Mitja Gaspari (Independent)	237,632	24.09
Zmago Jelinčič Plemeniti (Slovenian National Party)	188,951	19.16
Darko Krajnc (Youth Party of Slovenia)	21,526	2.18
Others	13,559	1.37
Total	**986,429**	**100.00**

Second Ballot, 11 November 2007

Candidate	Votes	% of votes
Danilo Türk (Independent)	677,333	68.03
Lojze Peterle (Independent)	318,288	31.97
Total	**995,621**	**100.00**

Legislature

The Slovenian legislature is bicameral, comprising the Državni zbor (National Assembly), the directly elected lower chamber, and the Državni svet (National Council), the indirectly elected upper chamber.

Državni zbor (National Assembly)

1102 Ljubljana, Šubičeva 4; tel. (1) 4789400; fax (1) 4789845; e-mail gp@dz-rs.si; internet www.dz-rs.si.

President: Dr PAVEL GANTAR.

General Election, 21 September 2008

Party	Votes	%	Seats
Social Democrats	320,248	30.45	29
Slovenian Democratic Party	307,735	29.26	28
For Real—New Politics	98,526	9.37	9
Democratic Party of Pensioners of Slovenia	78,353	7.45	7
Slovenian National Party	56,832	5.40	5
Slovenian People's Party–Youth Party of Slovenia	54,809	5.21	5
Liberal Democracy of Slovenia	54,771	5.21	5
Others*	80,553	7.65	2
Total	**1,051,827**	**100.00**	**90**

*Two of the 90 seats in the Državni zbor are reserved for representatives of the Italian and Hungarian minorities.

Državni svet (National Council)

1000 Ljubljana, Šubičeva 4; tel. (1) 4789798; fax (1) 4789851; e-mail janez.susnik@ds-rs.si; internet www.ds-rs.si.

There are 40 councillors in the Državni svet, who are indirectly elected for a five-year term by an electoral college.

President: BLAŽ KAVČIČ.

Election Commission

Republic Electoral Commission: 1000 Ljubljana, Slovenska 54; tel. (1) 4322002; fax (1) 4331269; e-mail rvk@gov.si; internet www.dvk.gov.si; Chair. ANTON GAŠPER FRANTAR.

Political Organizations

Democratic Party of Pensioners of Slovenia (DeSUS) (Demokratična stranka upokojencev Slovenije): 1000 Ljubljana, Kersnikova 6/VI; tel. (1) 4397350; fax (1) 4314113; e-mail desus@siol.net; internet www.desus.si; Pres. KARL VIKTOR ERJAVEC.

For Real—New Politics (Zares—Nova Politika—Zares): 1000 Ljubljana, Župančičeva 8; tel. (1) 2428750; fax (1) 2428753; e-mail info@zares.si; internet www.zares.si; f. 2007 by fmr mems of Liberal Democracy of Slovenia; Pres. GREGOR GOLOBIČ.

Greens of Slovenia (Zeleni Slovenije): 10000 Ljubljana, Komenskega 11; tel. (2) 7781071; fax (2) 7878543; e-mail zeleni@zeleni.si; internet www.zeleni.si; f. 1989; in 1993 the party split into two factions, one retaining the original name, the other, more radical, wing adopting the title Greens of Slovenia—Eco-Social Party; Chair. Prof. VLADO ČUŠ.

Liberal Democracy of Slovenia (LDS) (Liberalna demokracija Slovenije): 1000 Ljubljana, Slovenski cesta 29; tel. (1) 2000310; fax (1) 2000311; e-mail lds@lds.si; internet www.lds.si; f. 1994 by a merger of the Liberal Democratic Party, the Greens of Slovenia—Eco-Social Party, the Democratic Party and the Socialist Party of Slovenia; Chair. KATARINA KRESAL; 18,000 mems.

New Slovenia—Christian People's Party (NSi) (Nova Slovenija—Krščanska ljudska stranka): 1000 Ljubljana, Cankarjeva 11; tel. (1) 2416650; fax (1) 2416670; e-mail tajnistvo@nsi.si; internet www.nsi.si; f. 2000 by mems of the Slovenian People's Party; Pres. LJUDMILA NOVAK.

Party of the Slovene People (Stranka Slovenskega Naroda—SSN): 2000 Maribor, Efenkova 10; tel. and fax (2) 6205025; e-mail ssn@ssn.si; internet www.ssn.si; nationalist; Pres. MIHA MAJC.

Slovenian Democratic Party (SDP) (Slovenska Demokratska Stranka—SDS): 1000 Ljubljana, Trstenjakova 8; tel. (1) 4345450; fax (1) 4345452; e-mail tajnistvo@sds.si; internet www.sds.si; f. 1989 as Social Democratic Party of Slovenia; name changed in 2003; centre-right; Pres. JANEZ JANŠA; Sec.-Gen. ANJA BAH ŽIBERT; 26,000 mems.

Slovenian National Party (SNP) (Slovenska nacionalna stranka—SNS): 1000 Ljubljana, Tivolska 13; tel. (1) 2529020; fax (1) 2529022; e-mail info@sns.si; internet www.sns.si; f. 1991; nationalist; Pres. ZMAGO JELINČIČ PLEMENITI; Exec. Sec. MIŠA GLAŽAR; 8,000 mems (2008).

Slovenian People's Party (SPP) (Slovenska ljudska stranka—SLS): 1000 Ljubljana, Beethovnova 4; tel. (1) 2418820; fax (1) 2511741; e-mail sls@sls.si; internet www.sls.si; f. 1989 as the Slovenian Farmers' Asscn; merged with the Slovenian Christian Democrats in April 2000; Pres. RADOVAN ŽERJAV.

Social Democrats (SD) (Socialni demokrati): 1000 Ljubljana, Levstikova 15; tel. (1) 2444100; fax (1) 2444111; e-mail info@socialnidemokrati.si; internet www.socialnidemokrati.si; f. 1993 as United List of Social Democrats; renamed 2005; Pres. BORUT PAHOR; Gen. Sec. UROŠ JAUŠEVEC; 23,000 mems.

Diplomatic Representation

EMBASSIES IN SLOVENIA

Albania: 1000 Ljubljana, Zaloška cesta 69; tel. (1) 5473650; fax (1) 5473652; e-mail embassy.ljubljana@mfa.gov.al; Ambassador SANDËR KOVAÇI.

Austria: 1000 Ljubljana, Prešernova cesta 23; tel. (1) 4790700; fax (1) 2521717; e-mail laibach-ob@bmaa.gv.at; internet www.bmeia.gv.at/laibach; Ambassador ERWIN KUBESCH.

Belgium: 1000 Ljubljana, trg Republike 3/IX; tel. (1) 2006010; fax (1) 4266395; e-mail ljubljana@diplobel.org; internet www.diplomatie.be/ljubljanafr; Ambassador LOUIS ENGELEN.

Bosnia and Herzegovina: 1000 Ljubljana, Kolarjeva 26; tel. (1) 2343250; fax (1) 2343261; e-mail ambihlju@siol.net; Ambassador ZDRAVKO BEGOVIĆ.

Brazil: 1000 Ljubljana, Kongresni trg 3; tel. (1) 2442400; fax (1) 2442420; e-mail mail@brazil.si; Ambassador DÉBORA VAINER BARENBOIM.

Bulgaria: 1000 Ljubljana, Opekarska cesta 35; tel. (1) 2832899; fax (1) 2832901; e-mail bgembassysl@siol.net; internet www.mfa.bg/ljubljana; Ambassador FILIP BOKOV.

China, People's Republic: 1000 Ljubljana, Koblarjeva 3; tel. (1) 4202855; fax (1) 2822199; e-mail kitajsko.veleposlanistvo@siol.net; internet si.china-embassy.org; Ambassador SUN RONGMIN.

Croatia: 1000 Ljubljana, Gruberjevo nabrežje 6; tel. (1) 4256220; fax (1) 4258106; e-mail croemb.slovenia@mvp.hr; internet si.mvp.hr; Ambassador Dr SVJETLAN BERKOVIĆ.

SLOVENIA

Cyprus: 1000 Ljubljana, Komenskega 12; tel. (1) 2321542; fax (1) 2302002; e-mail embassy.cyprus@siol.net; Ambassador CHARALAMBOS PANAYIDES.

Czech Republic: 1000 Ljubljana, Riharjeva 1; tel. (1) 4202450; fax (1) 2839259; e-mail ljubljana@embassy.mzv.cz; internet www.mzv.cz/ljubljana; Ambassador PETR VOZNICA.

Denmark: 1000 Ljubljana, Tivolska 48, Eurocenter; tel. (1) 4380800; fax (1) 4317417; e-mail ljuamb@um.dk; internet www.ambljubljana.um.dk; Ambassador KARSTEN VAGN NIELSEN.

Egypt: 1000 Ljubljana, Opekarska cesta 18A; tel. (1) 4295420; fax (1) 2839122; e-mail embassy.ljubljana@mfa.gov.eg; Ambassador AHMED FAROUK.

Finland: 1000 Ljubljana, Ajdovščina 4/8; tel. (1) 3002120; fax (1) 3002139; e-mail sanomat.lju@formin.fi; internet www.finland.si; Chargé d'affaires a.i. LARS VILHELM CANTELL.

France: 1000 Ljubljana, Barjanska cesta 1; tel. (1) 4790400; fax (1) 4790410; e-mail ambafrance_si@siol.net; internet www.ambafrance-si.org; Ambassador NICOLE MICHELANGELI.

Germany: 1000 Ljubljana, Prešernova cesta 27; tel. (1) 4790300; fax (1) 4250899; e-mail germanembassy-slovenia@siol.net; internet www.ljubljana.diplo.de; Ambassador WERNER BURKART.

Greece: 1000 Ljubljana, Trnovski pristan 14; tel. (1) 4201400; fax (1) 2811114; e-mail grcon.lub@mfa.gr; internet www.mfa.gr/ljubljana; Ambassador DIONYSSIOS COUNDOUREAS.

Holy See: 1000 Ljubljana, Krekov trg 1; tel. (1) 4339204; fax (1) 4315130; e-mail apostolska.nunciatura@rkc.si; Apostolic Nuncio (vacant).

Hungary: 1210 Ljubljana, ul. Konrada Babnika 5; tel. (1) 5121882; fax (1) 5121878; e-mail huemblju@siol.net; internet www.mfa.gov.hu/kulkepviselet/SLO/hu; Ambassador ISTVÁN SZENT-IVÁNYI.

India: 1000 Ljubljana, Maurerjeva 29; tel. (1) 5133110; fax (1) 5133116; e-mail info@indianembassy.si; internet www.indianembassy.si; Ambassador JAYAKAR JEROME.

Iran: 1000 Ljubljana, Dunajska cesta 154; tel. (1) 5882500; e-mail sayyed.alenabi@telemach.net; Ambassador MOHAMMAD RAHIM AGHAEIPOUR.

Ireland: 1000 Ljubljana, Palača kapitelj, Poljanski nasip 6; tel. (1) 3008970; fax (1) 2821096; e-mail ljubljanaembassy@dfa.ie; internet www.irishembassy.si; Ambassador THOMAS BRADEY.

Italy: 1000 Ljubljana, Snežniška 8; tel. (1) 4262194; fax (1) 4253302; e-mail archivio.lubiana@esteri.it; internet www.amblubiana.esteri.it; Ambassador ALESSANDRO PIETROMARCHI.

Japan: 1000 Ljubljana, trg Republike 3/XI; tel. (1) 2008281; fax (1) 2511822; e-mail info@embjp.si; internet www.si.emb-japan.go.jp; Ambassador TOSHIMITSU ISHIGURE.

Kosovo: 1000 Ljubljana, Dvorec Sela, Zaloška cesta 69; tel. (1) 5415410; fax (1) 5415411; e-mail embassy.slovenia@ks-gov.net; Ambassador ANTON BERISHA.

Latvia: 1000 Ljubljana, Ajdovščina 4; tel. (1) 4341620; fax (1) 4341622; e-mail juris.poikans@mfa.gov.lv; Ambassador BAHTIJORS HASANS.

Lithuania: 1000 Ljubljana, Emonska cesta 8; tel. (1) 2445600; fax (1) 2445603; e-mail amb.si@urm.lt; internet si.mfa.lt; Ambassador RIMUTIS KLEVEČKA.

Macedonia, former Yugoslav republic: 1000 Ljubljana, Prešernova 2; tel. (1) 4210021; fax (1) 4210023; e-mail makamb@siol.net; Ambassador IGOR POPOV.

Montenegro: 1000 Ljubljana, Njegoševa cesta 14; tel. (1) 4395364; fax (1) 4395360; e-mail eslovenia@mfa.gov.me; Ambassador RANKO MILOVIĆ.

Netherlands: 1000 Ljubljana, Palača Kapitelj, Polijanski nasip 6; tel. (1) 4201460; fax (1) 4201470; e-mail lju@minbuza.nl; internet www.netherlands-embassy.si; Ambassador JOHANNES DOUMA.

Norway: 1000 Ljubljana, Ajdovščina 4/8; tel. (1) 3002140; fax (1) 3002150; e-mail emb.ljubljana@mfa.no; internet www.norway.si; Ambassador GURO KATHARINA HELWIG VIKØR.

Poland: 1000 Ljubljana, Bežigrad 10; tel. (1) 4364712; fax (1) 4362521; e-mail ambpol.si@siol.net; internet www.lublana.polemb.net; Ambassador CEZARY KRÓL.

Portugal: 1000 Ljubljana, trg Republika 3/10; tel. (1) 4790540; fax (1) 4790550; e-mail embportlju@siol.net; Ambassador MARIA DO CARMO ALLEGRO DE MAGALHÃES.

Romania: 1000 Ljubljana, Smrekarjeva 33A; tel. (1) 5058294; fax (1) 5055432; e-mail embassy.of.romania@siol.net; internet ljubljana.mae.ro; Ambassador DANA MANUELA CONSTANTINESCU.

Russia: 1000 Ljubljana, Tomšičeva 9; tel. (1) 4256875; fax (1) 4256878; e-mail ambrus.slo@siol.net; internet www.rus-slo.mid.ru; Ambassador DOKU ZAVGAYEV.

Serbia: 1000 Ljubljana, Slomškova 1; tel. (1) 4380110; fax (1) 4342688; e-mail ambasada@ambasadasrbije.si; internet www.ambasadasrbije.si; Ambassador PREDRAG FILIPOV.

Slovakia: 1000 Ljubljana, Tivolska cesta 4; tel. (1) 4255425; fax (1) 4210524; e-mail emb.ljubljana@mzv.sk; internet www.mzv.sk/lublana; Ambassador Dr MARIANNA ORAVCOVÁ.

Spain: 1000 Ljubljana, Trnovski pristan 24; tel. (1) 4202330; fax (1) 4202333; e-mail emba.espa.eslovenia@siol.net; Ambassador ANUNCIADA FERNÁNDEZ DE CÓRDOVA ALONSO-VIGUERA.

Switzerland: 1000 Ljubljana, trg Republike 3/VI; tel. (1) 2008640; fax (1) 2008669; e-mail lju.vertretung@eda.admin.ch; internet www.eda.admin.ch/ljubljana; Ambassador ROBERT REICH.

Turkey: 1000 Ljubljana, Livarska 4; tel. (1) 2364150; fax (1) 4365240; e-mail vrtucije@siol.net; internet www.ljubljana.emb.mfa.gov.tr; Ambassador DERYA KANBAY.

Ukraine: 1000 Ljubljana, Teslova 23; tel. (1) 4210604; fax (1) 4210603; e-mail emb_si@mfa.gov.ua; internet www.mfa.gov.ua/slovenia; Ambassador VADYM V. PRYMACHENKO.

United Kingdom: 1000 Ljubljana, trg Republike 3/IV; tel. (1) 2003910; fax (1) 4250174; e-mail info@british-embassy.si; internet ukinslovenia.fco.gov.uk; Ambassador ANDREW PAGE.

USA: 1000 Ljubljana, Prešernova cesta 31; tel. (1) 2005500; fax (1) 2005555; e-mail usembassyljubljana@state.gov; internet slovenia.usembassy.gov; Ambassador JOSEPH A. MUSSOMELI.

Judicial System

The Slovenian Constitution guarantees the independence of the judiciary.

The 44 district courts decide minor cases. The 11 regional courts act as courts of the first instance in all cases other than those for which the district courts have jurisdiction. Four regional courts act as courts of the second instance. There are, in addition, labour courts and social courts, which adjudicate in disputes over pensions, welfare allocations and other social benefits. A Higher Labour and Social Court has jurisdiction in the second instance. The Supreme Court is the highest authority for civil and criminal law. There is also a Constitutional Court, composed of nine judges, each elected for a single term of nine years.

Constitutional Court of the Republic of Slovenia (Ustavno sodišča Republike Slovenije): 1000 Ljubljana, Beethovnova 10; tel. (1) 4776400; fax (1) 2510451; e-mail info@us-rs.si; internet www.us-rs.si; Pres. Dr ERNEST PETRIČ.

Supreme Court of the Republic of Slovenia (Vrhovno Sodišče Republike Slovenije): 1000 Ljubljana, Tavčarjeva 9; tel. (1) 3664200; fax (1) 3664301; e-mail urad.vsrs@sodisce.si; internet www.sodisce.si; Pres. BRANKO MASLEŠA.

Office of the State Prosecutor-General: 1000 Ljubljana, trg OF 13; tel. (1) 4341935; fax (1) 4341945; e-mail dtrs@dt-rs.si; internet www.dt-rs.si; State Prosecutor-General ZVONKO FIŠER.

Religion

Most of the population are Christian, predominantly adherents of the Roman Catholic Church. There are few Protestant Christians, despite the importance of a Calvinist sect (the Church of Carniola) to the development of Slovene literature in the 16th century. At the census of 2002 some 57.8% of the population described themselves as Roman Catholics, 10.1% as atheists, 2.4% as Muslims, 2.3% as Orthodox Christians and 0.8% as Protestants; 22.8% of all respondents did not answer the question requesting their religious allegiance.

CHRISTIANITY

The Roman Catholic Church

The Roman Catholic Church in Slovenia comprises two archdioceses and four dioceses. There are an estimated 1,592,644 adherents (equivalent to 78.8% of the total population).

Bishops' Conference: 1000 Ljubljana, p.p. 121/III, Ciril Metodov trg 4; tel. (1) 2342600; fax (1) 2314169; e-mail ssk@rkc.si; f. 1993; Pres. Most Rev. ALOJZIJ URAN (Archbishop of Ljubljana).

Archbishop of Ljubljana: Most Rev. ALOJZIJ URAN, 1001 Ljubljana, p.p. 1990, Ciril Metodov trg 4; tel. (1) 2342600; fax (1) 2314169; e-mail nadskofija.lubljana@rkc.si.

Archbishop of Maribor: Most Rev. MARJAN TURNŠEK, 2000 Maribor, Slomškov trg 19; tel. (2) 2290401; fax (2) 2523092; e-mail ordinariat@slomsek.net.

SLOVENIA   Directory

Protestant Church

Evangelical Lutheran Church of Slovenia: 9226 Moravske Toplice, 11 Levstikova; tel. (2) 5381323; fax (2) 5381324; e-mail evang.cerkev.si@siol.net; f. 1561; 20,000 mems; Chair. GEZA ERNIŠA.

ISLAM

Islamic Association in the Republic of Slovenia (Islamska Skupnost V Republiki Sloveniji): 1000 Ljubljana, Grabiovičeva 14; tel. (1) 2313625; fax (1) 2313626; internet www.islamska-skupnost.si; Dir NEVZET PORIĆ.

The Press

The publications listed below are in Slovene, unless otherwise indicated.

PRINCIPAL DAILIES

Delo (Event): 1509 Ljubljana, Dunajska 5; tel. (1) 4737417; fax (1) 4737406; e-mail urednistvo@delo.si; internet www.delo.si; f. 1959; morning; Editor-in-Chief ROMANA DOBNIKAR-ŠERUGA; circ. 93,781.

Dnevnik (Daily): 1000 Ljubljana, Kopitarjeva 2; tel. (1) 3082300; fax (1) 3082329; e-mail info@dnevnik.si; internet www.dnevnik.si; f. 1951; evening; independent; Man. Dir BRANKO PAVLIN; Editor-in-Chief ZLATKO SETINC; circ. 63,000.

Slovenske novice (Slovene News): 1509 Ljubljana, Dunajska 5; tel. (1) 4737700; fax (1) 1737352; e-mail info@slovenskenovice.si; internet www.slovenskenovice.si; f. 1991; Editor-in-Chief BOJAN BUDJA; circ. 80,000.

Večer (Evening): 2504 Maribor, Svetozarevska 14; tel. (2) 2353500; fax (2) 2353368; internet www.vecer.si; f. 1945; evening; Dir UROŠ SKUHALA; Editor-in-Chief TOMAŽ RANC; circ. 70,000.

PERIODICALS

Avto magazin: 1000 Ljubljana, Vošnjakova 3; tel. (1) 3000700; fax (1) 3000713; e-mail avtomagazin@adriamedia.si; internet www.avto-magazin.si; f. 1967; fortnightly; cars, motorcycles and sports; Editor DUŠAN LUKIČ; circ. 16,000.

Delavska enotnost (Workers' Unity): 1000 Ljubljana, Dalmatinova 4; tel. (1) 4341200; fax (1) 2317298; e-mail delavska.enotnost@union-zsss.si; f. 1942; weekly, Thursdays except in Aug.; trade union issues; Editor-in-Chief MOJCA MATOZ; circ. 16,000.

Dolenjski list: 8000 Novo mesto, ul. Germova 4/212; tel. (7) 3930500; fax (7) 3930540; e-mail info@dolenjskilist.si; internet www.dolenjskilist.si; f. 1950; weekly; general and local information; Editor-in-Chief JOŽICA DORNIŽ; circ. 24,000.

Družina: 1001 Ljubljana, trg Krekov 1; tel. (1) 1316202; fax (1) 3602800; e-mail druzina@druzina.si; internet www.druzina.si; f. 1952; Christian; Editor-in-Chief FRANCI PETRIČ; circ. 70,000.

Finance: 1538 Ljubljana, Dalmatinova 2; tel. (1) 3091540; fax (1) 3091545; e-mail finance@finance.si; internet www.finance.si; f. 1992; 2 a week; Editor-in-Chief PETER FRANKL; circ. 8,500.

Gea: 1536 Ljubljana, Slovenska 29; tel. (1) 2413230; fax (1) 1252836; e-mail gea@mkz-lj.si; f. 1990; monthly; popular science; Editor-in-Chief ANJA LESKOVAR; circ. 16,000.

Gorenjski glas (Voice of Gorenjska): 4000 Kranj, Bleiweisova cesta 4; tel. (4) 2014200; fax (4) 2014213; e-mail info@g-glas.si; internet www.gorenjskiglas.si; f. 1947; 2 a week; general and regional information; Editor-in-Chief MARIJA VOLČJAK; circ. 18,000 (2010).

Jana: 1509 Ljubljana, Dunajska 5; tel. (1) 4738201; fax (1) 4738220; e-mail jana@delo-revije.si; internet www.jana.si; f. 1972; weekly; women's interest; Editor-in-Chief MELITA BERZELAK; circ. 62,000.

Kaj: 62000 Maribor, Svetozarevska 14; tel. (2) 26951; fax (2) 227736; f. 1984; weekly; popular; Editor-in-Chief MILAN PREDAN; circ. 16,500.

Kmečki glas: 1000 Ljubljana, p.p. 47, Železna cesta 14; tel. (1) 4735350; fax (1) 4735377; e-mail info@czd-kmeckiglas.si; internet www.kmeckiglas.com; weekly; general and agricultural news; Dir PETER ZADEL; circ. 38,000.

Lipov list: 1000 Ljubljana, Miklosičeva 38/6; tel. (1) 4341670; fax (1) 4341680; e-mail info@turisticna-zveza.si; monthly; Editor-in-Chief RENATA PICEJ.

Mag: 1000 Ljubljana, Njegoševa 14; tel. (1) 319480; fax (1) 1329158; f. 1995; weekly; news and politics; Editor-in-Chief JANEZ MARKES.

Mladina: 1000 Ljubljana, Dunajska 51; tel. (1) 2306500; fax (1) 2306510; e-mail desk@mladina.si; internet www.mladina.si; f. 1942; weekly; news magazine; Editor-in-Chief GREGA REPOVŽ; circ. 30,000.

Moj mikro: 1509 Ljubljana, Dunajska 5; tel. (1) 4738111; fax (1) 4738111; e-mail mojmikro@mojmikro.si; internet www.mojmikro.si; monthly; personal computers; Editor-in-Chief MARJAN KODELJA.

Nova Muska: 1000 Ljubljana, Cesta 27, Aprila 31; tel. (1) 1317039; e-mail revijamuska@gmail.com; internet www.novamuska.org; f. 2010; monthly; music; successor to the fmr music magazine *Muska*; Editor-in-Chief Dr JOŽE VOGRINC.

Naš Čas (Our Time): 63320 Velenje, Foltova 10; tel. (3) 855450; fax (3) 851990; f. 1956; weekly; general and regional information; Editor-in-Chief STANE VOVK; circ. 6,250.

Nedeljski dnevnik (Weekly Record): 1000 Ljubljana, Kopitarieva 2; tel. (1) 3082100; fax (1) 3082329; e-mail zlatko.setinc@dnevnik.si; internet www.dnevnik.si/nedeljski_dnevnik; f. 1961; weekly; popular; Editor-in-Chief ZLATKO SETINC; circ. 145,000 (2006).

Novi tednik (New Weekly): 3000 Celje, Prešernova 19; tel. (3) 4225100; fax (3) 5441032; e-mail tednik@nt-rc.si; internet www.novitednik.com; f. 1945; weekly; general and local information; Editor-in-Chief TATJANA CVIRN; circ. 16,980.

Obrtnik: 1000 Ljubljana, Celovška 71; tel. (1) 5830507; fax (1) 5054373; e-mail miran.jarec@ozs.si; internet www.ozs.si/obrtnik; f. 1971; monthly; small businesses; Editor-in-Chief MIRAN JAREC; circ. 60,000.

PIL: 1000 Ljubljana, Slovenska 29; tel. (1) 2413220; fax (1) 4252836; e-mail pil@mkz.si; internet www.pil-on.net; monthly; for children aged 9 to 12 years; Editor JANA ZIRKELBACH; circ. 21,000.

Podjetnik: 1000 Ljubljana, Celovška 71; tel. (1) 5830500; fax (1) 5054373; e-mail info@podjetnik.si; internet www.podjetnik.si; f. 1992; monthly; business and management; Editor-in-Chief PRIMOŽ KAUČIČ; circ. 8,500.

Primorske novice (News from the Primorska region): 6000 Koper, ul. Of. 12; tel. (5) 6648100; fax (5) 6648122; e-mail editors@primorske.si; internet www.primorske.si; f. 1947; daily; general and regional information; Editor-in-Chief SILVA KRIŽMAN; circ. 23,000.

Profit: 1000 Ljubljana, Dunajska 7; tel. (1) 4304310; fax (1) 2318940; e-mail profit.uredmistvo@sid.net; 2 a month; business; Editor-in-Chief JOŽE SIMČIČ.

Rodna gruda (Native Breast): 1000 Ljubljana, Cankarjeva 1/II, Združenje Slovenska izseljenska matica; tel. (1) 2410280; fax (1) 4251673; e-mail rodna.gruda@zdruzenje-sim.si; internet www.zdruzenje-sim.si; f. 1951; monthly; national issues and news; Editor-in-Chief VIDA POSINKOVIČ; circ. 2,100.

Slovenian Business Report: 1000 Ljubljana, Sarhova 8; tel. and fax (1) 4305309; e-mail info@sbr.si; internet www.sbr.si; f. 1991; quarterly; in English; economic affairs; Editor-in-Chief ROBERT MULEJ; circ. 4,000 (2009).

Slovenija: 1000 Ljubljana, Cankarjeva 1/II; tel. (1) 2410280; fax (1) 4251673; e-mail sim@siol.net; f. 1987; quarterly; in English; news about Slovenia and Slovenes; Man. Editor (vacant); circ. 3,500.

Štajerski Tednik: 2250 Ptuj, Raičeva 6; tel. (2) 7493410; fax (2) 7493435; e-mail nabiralnik@radio-tednik.si; internet www.radio-tednik.si; f. 1948; weekly; politics, local information; Dir JOŽE BRAČIČ; circ. 12,000.

Stop: 1000 Ljubljana, Dunajska 5; tel. (1) 4738151; fax (1) 4738169; e-mail info@revijastop.si; internet www.revijastop.si; f. 1967; weekly; leisure, film, theatre, pop music, radio and television programmes; Editor-in-Chief MARTIN SENICA; circ. 44,600.

Tretji dan (Third Day): 1000 Ljubljana, Jurčičev trg 2; tel. (1) 4268477; fax (1) 4268478; e-mail info@drustvo-skam.si; internet www.drustvo-skam.si/td; weekly; Editor-in-Chief LENART RIHAR.

Tribuna: 1000 Ljubljana, Kersnikova 4; tel. (1) 4380263; fax (1) 4380264; e-mail urednistvo@tribuna.si; internet www.tribuna.si; 3 a week; student newspaper; Dir ROMAN DIDOVIČ.

Vestnik Murska Sobota (Murska Sobota Herald): 9000 Murska Sobota, ul. Arhitekta Novaka 13; tel. (2) 5381710; fax (2) 5381711; e-mail vestnik@vestnik.si; internet www.p-inf.si; f. 1949; weekly; popular; Editor-in-Chief JANEZ VOTEK; circ. 20,000.

Zdravje (Health): 1509 Ljubljana, Dunajska 5; tel. (1) 4738136; fax (1) 4738253; e-mail zdravje@zdravje.si; internet www.zdravje.si; monthly; Editor-in-Chief MARTA KRPIČ.

PRESS AGENCIES

Morel: 1000 Ljubljana, Reboljeva 13, statti Parmova 41–45; tel. (1) 2321723; fax (1) 4361223; e-mail morel@siol.net; internet www.morel.si; f. 1993; Dir and Chief Editor EMIL LUKANČIČ-MORI.

Slovenska Tiskovna Agencija (STA): 1000 Ljubljana, Cankarjeva 5, p.p. 145; tel. (1) 2410100; fax (1) 4342970; e-mail desk@sta.si; internet www.sta.si; f. 1991; Gen. Man. BOJAN VESELINOVIČ; Editor-in-Chief BARBARA STRUKELJ.

Publishers

Cankarjeva Založba: 1000 Ljubljana, Kopitarjeva 2; tel. (1) 3603720; fax (1) 3603787; e-mail import.books@cankarjeva-z.si;

SLOVENIA

Directory

internet www.cankarjeva-z.si; f. 1945; philosophy, science and popular science, dictionaries and reference books, Slovenian and translated literature, international co-productions; Dir-Gen. JOŽE KORINŠEK.

DZS d.d.: 1538 Ljubljana, Dalmatinova 2; tel. (1) 3069700; fax (1) 3069877; e-mail info@dzs.si; internet www.dzs.si; f. 1945; textbooks, manuals, world classics, natural sciences, art books, encyclopedias, dictionaries, educational CD-ROMs; Exec. Dir ADA DE COSTA PETAN.

Mladinska Knjiga Založba: 1000 Ljubljana, Slovenska 29; tel. (1) 2413288; fax (1) 4252294; e-mail intsales@mkz-lj.si; f. 1945; books for youth and children, incl. general, fiction, science, travel and school books, language courses, magazines and videos; Dir MILAN MATOS.

Slovenska Matica: 1000 Ljubljana, Kongresni trg 8; tel. and fax (1) 4224340; e-mail drago.jancar@siol.net; f. 1864; poetry, science, philosophy; Pres. Prof. Dr MILČEK KOMELJ.

Založba Lipa Koper: Koper; tel. (5) 6274883; fiction; Dir Prof. JOŽE A. HOČEVAR.

Založba Obzorja d.d. Maribor: 2000 Maribor, Partizanska 3–5; tel. (2) 2348100; fax (2) 2348135; e-mail info@zalozba-obzorja.si; internet www.zalozba-obzorja.si; f. 1950; popular science, general literature, periodicals, etc.; Man. Dir GORAZD ZEMLJARIČ.

Broadcasting and Communications

TELECOMMUNICATIONS

Telecommunications Agency (Agencija za telekomunikacije, radiodifuzijo in pošto Republike Slovenije—ATRP): 1000 Ljubljana, Kotnikova 19A; tel. (1) 4734900; fax (1) 4328036; e-mail urst.box@gov .si; internet www.atrp.si; Dir JOŽE KLEŠNIK (acting).

Si.mobil—Vodafone: 1000 Ljubljana, Šmartinska cesta 134B; tel. (1) 5440000; fax (1) 5440099; e-mail info@simobil.si; internet www .simobil.com; f. 1999; subsidiary of Mobilkom Austria; Chair. of Bd DEJAN TURK; 370,000 subscribers (March 2006).

T-2: 2000 Maribor, Streliška cesta 150; e-mail pr@t-2.net; internet www.t-2.net; f. 2004; mobile cellular telecommunications services.

Telekom Slovenije: 1000 Ljubljana, Cigaletova 15; tel. (1) 2341000; fax (1) 2314736; e-mail info@telekom.si; internet www.telekom.si; f. 1949; 62.5% state-owned; Pres. BOJAN DREMELJ.

  Mobitel: 1537 Ljubljana, Vilharjeva 23; tel. (1) 4722200; fax (1) 4722990; e-mail info@mobitel.si; internet www.mobitel.si; f. 1991; 100% owned by Telekom Slovenije; mobile cellular telecommunications services; Chief Exec. KLAVDIJ GODNIČ.

Tušmobil: 3000 Celje, Resljeva ul. 16; tel. (1) 6000999; fax (1) 6002021; internet www.tusmobil.si; f. 2007; mobile cellular telecommunications services.

BROADCASTING

Regulatory Authority

Slovenian Broadcasting Council (Svet za Radiodifuzijo—SRDF): 1000 Ljubljana, Stegne 7; tel. (1) 5836300; fax (1) 5111101; e-mail srdf .box@apek.si; internet www.srdf.si; f. 1994; nine mems; protects independence of radio and television programmes; supervises the activities of broadcasting and cable operators; Chair. Dr DEJAN JELOVAC.

Radio

Radiotelevizija Slovenija (RTV Slo): 1550 Ljubljana, Kolodvorska 2; tel. (1) 4752154; fax (1) 4752150; e-mail webmaster@ rtvslo.si; internet www.rtvslo.si; f. 1928; three radio programmes nationally; broadcasts in Slovene, Hungarian and Italian; Gen. Man. MARKO FILLI.

Radio Koper Capodistria: 6000 Koper, ul. Of 15; tel. (5) 6485483; fax (5) 6485488; e-mail radio.koper@rtvslo.si; internet www.rtvslo .si; Dir DRAGOMIR MIKELIĆ.

Radio Slovenia International: 2000 Maribor, Ilichova 33; tel. (2) 4299132; fax (2) 4299215; e-mail srecko.trglec@rtvslo.si; internet www.rtvslo.si; f. 2001; state-owned; broadcasts in Slovene, English and German 24 hours a day; Editor-in-Chief SREČKO TRGLEC.

Television

Radiotelevizija Slovenija (RTV Slo): 1550 Ljubljana, Kolodvorska 2; tel. (1) 4752154; fax (1) 4752150; e-mail webmaster@ rtvslo.si; internet www.rtvslo.si/html/radio-slo/; f. 1928; three television programmes (TV1, TV2 and TV3) nationally; broadcasts in Slovene, Hungarian and Italian; Gen. Man. ANTON GUZEJ.

Kanal A: 1000 Ljubljana, Tivolska 50; tel. (1) 1334133; fax (1) 1334222; Pres. DOUGLAS FULTON.

Pop TV: 1000 Ljubljana, Kranjčeva 26; tel. (1) 1893200; fax (1) 1612222; Editor TOMAŽ PEROVIČ.

TV 3: PRVA TV d.o.o, 1000 Ljubljana, Vojkova 58; tel. (1) 2807800; fax (1) 2807840; internet www.mtg.se/en/Contact; Editor-in-Chief MLADEN SICHROVSKY.

Finance

BANKS

(cap. = capital; res = reserves; dep. = deposits; m. = million; amounts in euros, unless otherwise indicated; brs = branches)

In January 1999 new banking legislation allowed foreign banks to establish branches in Slovenia for the first time.

National Bank

Banka Slovenije (Bank of Slovenia): 1505 Ljubljana, Slovenska 35; tel. (1) 4719000; fax (1) 2515516; e-mail bsl@bsi.si; internet www.bsi .si; fmrly National Bank of Slovenia, as part of the Yugoslav banking system; assumed central bank functions in 1991; cap. and res 751.8m., dep. 1,408.3m. (Dec. 2008); Gov. Dr MARKO KRANJEC.

Selected Banks

Abanka Vipa d.d.: 1517 Ljubljana, Slovenska 58, POB 368; tel. (1) 4718100; fax (1) 4325165; e-mail info@abanka.si; internet www .abanka.si; f. 1955 as Ljubljana Branch of Yugoslav Bank for Foreign Trade; present name adopted 1989; cap. 30.0m., res 291.2m., dep. 3,516.5m. (Dec. 2008); Pres. ALES ZAJDELA; 32 brs.

Banka Celje d.d.: 3001 Celje, Vodnikova 2, POB 431; tel. (3) 4221000; fax (3) 4221100; e-mail info@banka-celje.si; internet www.banka-celje.si; cap. 16.9m., res 164.2m., dep. 1,549.8m. (Dec. 2008); Chair. of Bd DUŠAN DROFENIK.

Banka Koper d.d.: 6502 Koper, Pristaniška 14; tel. (5) 6661000; fax (5) 6662006; e-mail info@banka-koper.si; internet www.banka-koper .si; f. 1955; cap. 22.1m., res 212.5m., dep. 1,639.5m. (Dec. 2008); Pres. of Management Bd VOJKO ČOK; 14 brs.

Deželna banka Slovenije d.d.: 1000 Ljubljana, Kolodvorska 9; tel. (1) 4727100; fax (1) 4727405; e-mail info@dbs.si; internet www.dbs .si; f. 1990; present name adopted 2004; cap. 15.8m., res 59.9m., dep. 751.7m. (Dec. 2008); Pres. of Bd PETER VRISK; 10 brs.

Gorenjska Banka d.d. Kranj: 4000 Kranj, Bleiweisova cesta 1, POB 147; tel. (4) 2084000; fax (4) 2084491; e-mail info@gbkr.si; internet www.gbkr.si; f. 1955; cap. 13.8m., res 323.4m., dep. 1,455.2m. (Dec. 2008); CEO GORAZDA TRČEK; 5 brs.

Hypo Alpe-Adria-Bank d.d.: 1000 Ljubljana, Dunajska cesta 117; tel. (1) 5804000; fax (1) 5804001; e-mail hypo-bank@hypo.si; internet www.hypo-alpe-adria.si; f. 1999; cap. 174.0m., res 19.9m., dep. 2,044.9m. (Dec. 2008); Pres. ANTON ROMIH.

Nova Kreditna banka Maribor d.d. (Nova KBM): 2505 Maribor, Vita Kraigherja 4; tel. (2) 2292290; fax (2) 2524333; e-mail info@ nkbm.si; internet www.nkbm.si; f. 1955; present name adopted 1994; 51.1% state-owned; cap. 27.4m., res 301.4m., dep. 4,182.0m. (Dec. 2008); Pres. and CEO MATJAŽ KOVAČIČ; 90 brs and sub-brs.

Nova Ljubljanska banka d.d. (NLB): 1520 Ljubljana, trg Republike 2; tel. (1) 4763900; fax (1) 2522500; e-mail info@nlb.si; internet www.nlb.si; f. 1994; commercial, investment and savings bank; 33% state-owned, 31% owned by KBC Bank NV (Belgium); cap. 74.3m., res 1,045.9m., dep. 10,802.1m. (Dec. 2008); CEO BOŽO JAŠOVIČ; 198 brs.

Probanka d.d.: 2000 Maribor, trg Leona Štuklja 12; tel. (2) 2520500; fax (2) 2526029; e-mail info@probanka.si; internet www.probanka.si; f. 1991; cap. 15.8m., res 93.4m., dep. 1,121.1m. (Dec. 2008); Pres. and Chair. ROMANA PAJENK.

Raiffeisen banka d.d: 2000 Maribor, Zagrebška cesta 76; tel. (2) 2293100; fax (2) 2223502; e-mail info@raiffeisen.si; internet www .raiffeisen.si; f. 1992; present name adopted 2007; cap. 14.1m., res 44.4m., dep. 1,005.1m. (Dec. 2008); Chair. KLEMENS NOWOTNY; 14 brs.

SKB Banka d.d.: 1000 Ljubljana, Ajdovščina 4; tel. (1) 4715555; fax (1) 2314549; e-mail info@skb.si; internet www.skb.si; f. 1978; 99.6% owned by Société Générale (France); cap. 52.8m., res 165.1m., dep. 2,504.4m. (Dec. 2008); Pres. and Chief Exec. CVETKA SELŠEK; 58 brs.

UniCredit Banka Slovenija d.d.: 1000 Ljubljana, Smartinska 140; tel. (1) 5876600; fax (1) 5876684; e-mail info@unicreditgroup .si; internet www.unicreditgroup.si; f. 1991; fmrly Bank Austria Creditanstalt d.d. Ljubljana; name changed as above Sept. 2007; cap. 16.2m., res 153.6m., dep. 2,687.2m. (Dec. 2008); Chair. FRANCE ARHAR.

STOCK EXCHANGE

Ljubljana Stock Exchange (Ljubljanska Borza d.d.): 1000 Ljubljana, Slovenska 56; tel. (1) 4710211; fax (1) 4710213; e-mail info@ljse .si; internet www.ljse.si; f. 1989; operative 1990; 81.0% owned by

SLOVENIA

Wiener Börse (Vienna Stock Exchange), Austria; Pres. Andrej Šketa.

INSURANCE

Adriatic Insurance Co: 6503 Koper, Ljubljanska cesta 3 A; tel. (5) 6643100; fax (5) 6643109; e-mail info@adriatic-slovenica.si; internet www.adriatic.si; f. 1990; CEO Gabrijel Škof.

Grawe Insurance Co d.d.: 2000 Maribor, Gregorčičeva 39; tel. (2) 2285500; fax (2) 2285526; e-mail grawe@grawe.si; internet www.grawe.si; Pres. Božo Emeršič.

Maribor Insurance Co: 2507 Maribor, Cankarjeva 3; tel. (2) 2332100; fax (2) 2332530; e-mail info@zav-mb.si; internet www.zav-mb.si; Chair. Drago Cotar.

Merkur Insurance Co: 1000 Ljubljana, Dunajska 58; tel. (1) 3005450; fax (1) 4361092; e-mail info@merkur-zav.si; internet www.merkur-zav.si; f. 1992; CEO Denis Stroligo.

Sava Insurance Co (Sava Re) (Pozavarovalnica Sava dd Ljubljana): 1000 Ljubljana, Dunajska 56; tel. (1) 4750200; fax (1) 4750264; e-mail info@sava-re.si; internet www.sava-re.si; f. 1973; Chair. of Bd Zvonko Ivanušič.

Triglav Insurance Co (Zavarovalnica Triglav d.d.): 1000 Ljubljana, Miklošičeva 19; tel. (1) 4747200; fax (1) 4326302; e-mail info-triglav@triglav.si; internet www.triglav.si; CEO Matjaž Rakovec; Chair. of Supervisory Bd Borut Jamnik.

Trade and Industry

GOVERNMENT AGENCY

Agency of the Republic of Slovenia for Restructuring and Privatization (Agencija Republike Slovenije za Prestrukturiranje in Privatizacijo—ARSPIP): 1000 Ljubljana, Kotnikova 28; tel. (1) 1316030; fax (1) 1316011; e-mail webmaster@arspip.si; Dir Mira Puc.

CHAMBERS OF COMMERCE

Chamber of Commerce and Industry of Slovenia (Gospodarska Zbornica Slovenije): 1504 Ljubljana, Dimičeva 13; tel. (1) 5898313; fax (1) 5898317; e-mail infolink@gzs.si; internet www.gzs.si; Pres. Josko Cuk.

Chamber of Small Businesses of Slovenia: 1000 Ljubljana, Celovška 71; tel. (1) 4593241; fax (1) 4559270; Pres. Miha Grah; Sec. Anton Filipič; 50,000 mems.

UTILITIES

Electricity

Elektro-Slovenija d.o.o. (ELES): 1000 Ljubljana, Hajdrihova 2; tel. (1) 1301440; fax (1) 1250333; e-mail info@eles.si; internet www.eles.si; national electricity distributor; Dir-Gen. Vitoslav Türk.

Nuklearna Elektrarna p.o. (NEK): 8270 Krško, Vrbina 12; tel. (7) 4802000; fax (7) 4921006; e-mail nek@nek.si; internet www.nek.si; f. 1974; 50% owned by GEN energija Ljubljana, 50% owned by Hrvatska Elektropriveda Zagreb (Croatia); production and distribution of electricity from nuclear power plant at Krško.

Gas

Geoplin d.o.o.: 1000 Ljubljana, Ljubljanska brigade 11; tel. (1) 5820600; fax (1) 5820601; e-mail info@geoplin.si; internet www.geoplin.si; f. 1975; national gas co; Gen. Man. Alojz Stana.

TRADE UNIONS

The Association of Independent Trade Unions of Slovenia: 1000 Ljubljana, Dalmatinova 4; tel. (1) 4317983; fax (1) 4318294; Pres. Dušan Semolič.

Independence—Confederation of New Trade Unions of Slovenia (Sindikat Ljubljanske regije KNSS—Neodvisnost): 1000 Ljubljana, Linhartova cesta 13; tel. (1) 3063951; fax (1) 4391815; e-mail neodvisnost.knss@siol.net; internet www.knss-neodvisnost.eu; f. 1990; Pres. Drago Lombar.

Transport

RAILWAYS

Slovenske Železnice (SŽ) (Slovenian Railways): 1506 Ljubljana, Kolodvorska 11; tel. (1) 2914001; fax (1) 2914800; e-mail boris.zivec@slo-zeleznice.si; internet www.slo-zeleznice.si; Dir-Gen. Boris Živec.

ROADS

In 2007 the country had 38,709 km of roads, of which 579 km were motorways and expressways and 975 km were highways, main or national roads. An 84-km motorway links Ljubljana with the coastal region in the south-west.

Directorate for Roads: Ministry of Transport, 1535 Ljubljana, Langusova 4; tel. (1) 1788000; fax (1) 1788139; e-mail drsc-info@gov.si.

SHIPPING

Slovenia's principal international trading port, at Koper, handles some 3m. tons of freight annually.

Luka Koper d.d.: 6501 Koper, Vojkovo nabrežje 38; tel. (5) 6656100; fax (5) 6395020; e-mail portkoper@luka-kp.si; internet www.luka-kp.si; f. 1957; Pres. of Management Bd Robert Casar.

Principal Shipping Company

Splošna Plovba: 6320 Portorož, Obala 55, POB 60; tel. (5) 6766000; fax (5) 6766130; e-mail plovba@5-plovba.si; transport of all types of cargo; regular liner service; Man. Dir Aldo Krejačič.

CIVIL AVIATION

There are three international airports in Slovenia, at Brnik (Ljubljana), Maribor and Portorož.

Adria Airways: 1000 Ljubljana, Kuzmičeva 7; tel. (1) 3691000; fax (1) 4369233; e-mail info@adria.si; internet www.adria.si; f. 1961; operates international scheduled services to destinations in Europe and the Middle East; Pres. Tadej Tufek.

Tourism

Slovenia offers a variety of tourist attractions, including Mediterranean resorts to the west, the Julian Alps and the lakes of Bled and Bohinj to the north, and, in the south, the karst limestone regions, with more than 6,000 caves. The number of foreign tourist arrivals increased steadily from the mid-1990s, reaching 1,823,900 in 2009. Tourism receipts totalled US $3,115m. in 2008.

Slovenian Tourist Board: 1000 Ljubljana, Dunajska 156; tel. (1) 5891840; fax (1) 5891841; e-mail info@slovenia.info; internet www.slovenia.info; f. 1996; Gen. Man. Dimitrij Piciga.

Defence

As assessed at November 2010, the active Slovenian armed forces numbered 7,600 (with 1,700 reserves). There was a paramilitary police force of 4,500 (plus 5,000 reserves). In September 2003 the Government announced the abolition of compulsory military service, prior to the country's official accession to the North Atlantic Treaty Organization (NATO) on 29 March 2004.

Defence Expenditure: Budgeted at 483m. tolars for 2011.

Chief of Staff of the Slovenian Army Supreme Headquarters: Maj.-Gen. Alojz Steiner.

Education

Primary education is free and compulsory for all children between the ages of six and 15 years. In ethnically mixed regions, two methods of schooling have been developed: bilingual or with instruction in the minority languages. Various types of secondary education, beginning at 15 and lasting between two and five years, are also available. In 2005/06 95% of children in the relevant age-group (males 96%; females 95%) were enrolled at primary schools, while enrolment in secondary education included 90% of children in the appropriate age-group (males 90%; females 91%). Slovenia's four universities are situated in Ljubljana, Maribor, Koper (the University of Primorska) and Nova Gorica, with 60,284, 23,363, 6,490 and 725 students, respectively, in 2008/09; a further 7,266 students were enrolled in other higher education institutions in that year. In 2008 expenditure on education by all levels of government was equivalent to 6.2% of GDP.

Ministry of Education and Sport: see The Government (Ministries).

Ministry of Higher Education, Science and Technology: see The Government (Ministries).

SOLOMON ISLANDS

Introductory Survey

LOCATION, CLIMATE, LANGUAGE, RELIGION, FLAG, CAPITAL

Solomon Islands is a scattered Melanesian archipelago in the south-western Pacific Ocean, east of Papua New Guinea. The country includes most of the Solomon Islands (those to the north-west being part of Papua New Guinea), Ontong Java Islands (Lord Howe Atoll), Rennell Island and the Santa Cruz Islands, about 500 km (300 miles) to the east. The climate is equatorial, with small seasonal variations, governed by the trade winds. In Honiara the average temperature is about 27°C (81°F) and the average annual rainfall about 2,160 mm (85 ins). The official language is standard English, although pidgin English is more widely used and understood. More than 80 different local languages exist, and no vernacular is common to the whole country. More than 95% of the inhabitants profess Christianity, and most of the remainder follow traditional beliefs. The national flag (proportions 1 by 2) comprises two triangles, one of blue (with its base at the hoist and its apex in the upper fly) and one of dark green (with its base in the fly and its apex in the lower hoist), separated by a narrow yellow diagonal stripe (from lower hoist to upper fly), with five white five-pointed stars (arranged to form a diagonal cross) in the upper hoist. The capital is Honiara, on the island of Guadalcanal.

CONTEMPORARY POLITICAL HISTORY

Historical Context

The northern Solomon Islands became a German protectorate in 1885 and the southern Solomons a British protectorate in 1893. Rennell Island and the Santa Cruz Islands were added to the British protectorate in 1898 and 1899. Germany ceded most of the northern Solomons and Ontong Java Islands to the United Kingdom between 1898 and 1900. The whole territory, known as the British Solomon Islands Protectorate, was placed under the jurisdiction of the Western Pacific High Commission (WPHC), with its headquarters in Fiji.

The Solomon Islands were invaded by Japan in 1942, but, after a fierce battle on Guadalcanal, most of the islands were recaptured by US forces in 1943. After the Second World War the protectorate's capital was transferred from Tulagi Island to Honiara. In January 1953 the headquarters of the WPHC also moved to Honiara. Meanwhile, elected local councils were established on most of the islands, and by 1966 almost the whole territory was covered by such councils.

Domestic Political Affairs

Under a new Constitution, introduced in October 1960, a Legislative Council and an Executive Council were established for the protectorate's central administration. Initially, all members of both bodies were appointed, but from 1964 the Legislative Council included elected members, and the elective element was gradually increased. Another Constitution, introduced in March 1970, established a single Governing Council of 17 elected members, three ex officio members and (until the end of 1971) up to six public service members. A new Governing Council of 24 directly elected members was formed in 1973, when a ministerial system was introduced.

A further new Constitution, adopted in April 1974, instituted a single Legislative Assembly, containing 24 members who chose a Chief Minister with the right to appoint his own Council of Ministers. A new office of Governor of the Protectorate was also created, to assume almost all of the functions previously exercised in the territory by the High Commissioner for the Western Pacific. Solomon Mamaloni, leader of the newly founded People's Progressive Party (PPP), was appointed the first Chief Minister in August 1974. The territory was officially renamed the Solomon Islands in June 1975, although it retained protectorate status.

In January 1976 the Solomon Islands received internal self-government, with the Chief Minister presiding over the Council of Ministers in place of the Governor. In June elections were held for an enlarged Legislative Assembly, and in July the Assembly elected one of its new members, Peter Kenilorea, to the position of Chief Minister. Solomon Islands (as it was restyled, without the definite article) became an independent state, within the Commonwealth, on 7 July 1978. The Legislative Assembly became the National Parliament and designated Kenilorea the first Prime Minister. The main political issue confronting the new nation was the proposed decentralization of authority to the regions, support for which was particularly strong in the Western District, the most commercially developed part of the country.

The first general election since independence took place in August 1980. Independent candidates won more seats than any of the three parties. Parliament again elected Kenilorea Prime Minister by an overwhelming majority. In August 1981, however, Parliament approved a motion expressing no confidence in Kenilorea, and chose Mamaloni, who now led the People's Alliance Party (PAP) following the merger of the PPP with the Rural Alliance Party in 1979, to succeed him as Prime Minister.

After legislative elections in October 1984, Sir Peter Kenilorea (as he had become) was again elected as Prime Minister. The new Government consisted of a coalition of nine members of Kenilorea's Solomon Islands United Party (SIUPA), three members of the newly formed Solomone Ano Sagufenua (SAS) party and three independents. The five provincial ministries, established by Mamaloni, were abolished, in accordance with Kenilorea's declared policy of restoring to central government control some of the powers held by the provincial governments.

In October 1985 a new political party, which sought a resolution of ongoing land disputes, the Nationalist Front for Progress (NFP), was formed, under the leadership of Andrew Nori. The SAS subsequently withdrew from the coalition, and Kenilorea formed a new Cabinet, comprising nine members of the SIUPA, three of the NFP and three independents. Kenilorea resigned following the approval of a motion of no confidence (two others having previously been defeated); in December Ezekiel Alebua, the former Deputy Prime Minister, assumed the premiership.

A report by a specially commissioned constitutional review committee, chaired by Mamaloni, was published in March 1988, and proposed that Solomon Islands become a federal republic within the Commonwealth, and that the President of the Republic be a native of the territory. In January 1989 the PAP announced that Solomon Islands would be declared a republic if the party won the next general election, scheduled to take place in February. At the election the PAP won 11 of the 38 seats, the largest representation obtained by any party, while Alebua's party, the United Party, secured only four seats. In March Mamaloni was elected Prime Minister. His Cabinet included the former Governor-General of Solomon Islands, Sir Baddeley Devesi, and was the first since independence to comprise the members of a single party.

In October 1990 Mamaloni resigned as leader of the PAP, one week before Parliament was due to vote on another motion of no confidence in his premiership, declaring that he would remain as an independent Prime Minister. He dismissed five members of the Cabinet, replacing them with four members of the opposition and a PAP backbencher. The Prime Minister defied persistent demands for his resignation by a majority of the members of Parliament. The remaining 10 ministers of the PAP were expelled from the party in February 1991, following their refusal to resign from their posts in the interests of party unity. Later in that year, as a result of continuing economic decline, the Solomon Islands Council of Trade Unions issued an ultimatum demanding Mamaloni's resignation.

At elections to the recently enlarged National Parliament in May 1993 the Group for National Unity and Reconciliation (GNUR), led by Mamaloni, won 21 of the 47 seats. However, a newly formed coalition of opposition parties and independents, the National Coalition Partners (NCP), was successful in electing an independent member, Francis Billy Hilly, to the premiership in June. Hilly defeated Mamaloni by a single vote.

In October 1994 a constitutional crisis arose, following attempts by the Governor-General, Moses (later Sir Moses) Pitakaka, to dismiss Hilly on the grounds that he no longer held a parliamentary majority. However, Hilly remained in office, with the support of a High Court ruling, and confusion intensified when Pitakaka appointed the opposition leader, Mamaloni, to the position of Prime Minister. Hilly finally resigned at the end of October, and the post was declared vacant. In a parliamentary election to the premiership in November, Mamaloni defeated the former Governor-General, Devesi, by 29 votes to 18.

In late 1995 and early 1996 Mamaloni's Government incurred a series of allegations of corruption and misconduct, particularly in relation to claims that seven ministers had received payments from foreign logging companies between 1993 and 1995; in February 1996, however, all seven were acquitted.

Controversy arose in mid-1996 over constituency payments by parliament members, and the reinstatement of the Constituency Development Fund, which entitled each member to US $66,000, and which had been widely used by members at the previous general election to secure re-election by purchasing gifts for voters. In September the regional trades union organization, the South Pacific and Oceanic Council of Trade Unions (SPOCTU), cited the prevalence of corruption as the greatest obstacle to the islands' development, and stated that, in consequence, investors and aid donors would remain reluctant to make financial commitments to Solomon Islands. In February 1997 legislation to reform the provincial government system, which had been approved by Parliament but vehemently opposed by the larger provinces, was declared invalid by the High Court.

In May 1997 Mamaloni announced his intention to hold an early general election, following which he would resign as leader of the GNUR. Meanwhile, Alebua resigned from the leadership of the NCP, following accusations of misconduct, and was replaced by Edward Hunuehu. A general election took place on 6 August to a legislature that had recently been enlarged to 50 seats. The GNUR won 24 seats and a new grouping, the Solomon Islands Alliance for Change Coalition (SIACC), secured the remainder. In late August Bartholomew Ulufa'alu was elected Prime Minister, defeating the newly elected leader of the GNUR, Danny Philip, by 26 votes to 22. The new Government announced a programme of extensive structural reforms, including a rationalization of the public sector, a reduction in the number of ministerial portfolios (from 16 to 10), and measures to expand the private sector and to encourage greater participation of non-governmental organizations in the country's socio-economic development. The measures aimed to restore a degree of economic stability to Solomon Islands and to attract increased foreign investment. Legislation proposing that a politician seeking to change party allegiance would automatically lose his or her seat and be subject to a by-election was similarly intended to increase political stability.

In April 1998 Job Dudley Tausinga, whose Coalition for National Advancement (CNA) constituted the largest group outside the Government, was appointed Leader of the Opposition. Numerous defections between the Government and opposition in 1998 created ongoing political instability, which prompted the Government to reiterate its proposal for legislation to restrict the rights of elected members of Parliament to change party allegiance. In September Solomon Mamaloni was elected Leader of the Opposition. Mamaloni died in January 2000 and was succeeded by Manasseh Sogavare, under whose leadership the CNA subsequently reverted to its original name of the PPP.

Unrest and insecurity

From April 1998 violent unrest in Honiara was attributed to ethnic tensions, mainly between the inhabitants of Guadalcanal and Malaita provinces. One underlying cause of the disturbances was the alienation of land by the Government since independence. Title to some land thus expropriated had been returned to Guadalcanal, but this had not allayed a widespread feeling of resentment in the province at the financial burden imposed by hosting the country's capital. It was reported that a group styling itself the 'Guadalcanal Revolutionary Army' (GRA) had begun a campaign of militancy to force the Government to relocate the capital. The unrest intensified in early 1999, prompting the Government to establish a peace committee for the province. In mid-1999 talks between the Premier of Guadalcanal Province, Ezekiel Alebua, and the Solomon Islands Prime Minister failed to alleviate inter-ethnic tensions in the province. Riots broke out in Honiara, and some 80 Malaitan immigrants were evacuated following threats by armed GRA militants. Following Ulufa'alu's demands that peace be restored to the province before the implementation of any further measures, the GRA ordered an immediate halt to its activities. The Guadalcanal Provincial Assembly subsequently declared that it had accepted an initial payment of SI $500,000 in compensation for accommodating the national capital. A reconciliation ceremony was held between the two parties, during which Alebua appealed to the GRA to lay down its arms. However, the Malaitans subsequently demanded that they too be given compensation, amounting to US $600,000, for damage to their property by the GRA militants.

Throughout 1999 violent clashes led to many deaths and forced thousands to abandon their villages, prompting the Government to announce a state of emergency in Guadalcanal. A Commonwealth Special Envoy and a UN peace-keeping force arrived to assist in the negotiation of a peace agreement with the Isatabu Freedom Movement (IFM, formerly the GRA, and also known in 1999 as the Isatabu Freedom Fighters—IFF), led by Andrew Te'e. A number of peace agreements reached throughout 1999 quickly broke down, and a peace-monitoring group from Fiji and Vanuatu, jointly funded by Australia and New Zealand, arrived in Guadalcanal in October. In January 2000 a new guerrilla group emerged, the Malaita Eagle Force (MEF), and demanded US $40m. in compensation payments for loss of property incurred by Malaitans as a result of the conflict. Among their spokesmen was the former Minister for Finance, Andrew Nori.

Following further outbreaks of violence in the province that led to the death of four people, including two police officers, in February 2000, the Governor-General issued a decree outlawing membership of both the IFM and the MEF. Further clashes between the two rebel groups were reported in early March, and later in that month riots took place in Honiara during which Malaitan immigrants stoned the headquarters of the Guadalcanal Provincial Government. In May the order that outlawed the groups was suspended. In early June members of the MEF, armed with weapons obtained in raids on police armouries, seized control of Honiara, placing Ulufa'alu under house arrest. The rebels demanded the immediate resignation of the Prime Minister, claiming that he, himself an ethnic Malaitan, had failed to compensate displaced Malaitans within the established deadline (allegedly set for that day) and also demanded the appointment of a new Commissioner of Police, the de facto head of national security. In renewed outbreaks of violence, up to 100 people were reportedly killed. The MEF, meanwhile, claimed to have gained control of the police force, 98% of the military-style weapons in the territory, broadcasting services and the telecommunications infrastructure. Ulufa'alu was released after four days, following an agreement between the MEF and government negotiators that a special parliamentary sitting would be convened during which Ulufa'alu would be subject to a motion of no confidence. A 14-day cease-fire was called to guarantee the safe passage of a Commonwealth monitoring team. In mid-June Ulufa'alu resigned, one day before the scheduled no-confidence vote, but remained as interim Prime Minister for a 14-day transitional period during which negotiations between the MEF, the IFM and a Commonwealth Special Envoy, Professor Ade Adefuye of Nigeria, were to take place. However, negotiations foundered following the MEF's refusal to hand over its weapons, pending the appointment of a new prime minister, which was to take place in an extraordinary parliamentary session in late June. As this session failed to raise the necessary quorum, the election of a new prime minister was delayed until the end of June, when Sogavare, the Leader of the Opposition, defeated Rev. Leslie Boseto, incumbent Minister for Lands and Housing, by 23 votes to 21. Sogavare declared that he would seek to establish peace without making significant changes to the policy of the previous Government. None the less, the new Prime Minister announced a comprehensive reallocation of ministerial posts and restructuring of ministries. A new Ministry for National Unity, Reconciliation and Peace was established, and plans to create a Solomon Islands Defence Force and Ministry of Defence were announced. (Previously defence issues had fallen within the remit of the police service, which had become compromised because of reported MEF infiltration, and by allegations that about 75% of officers were ethnic Malaitans.)

New negotiations in August 2000 resulted in the declaration of a 90-day cease-fire between the IFM and the MEF, although intermittent violent disorder continued in Guadalcanal. In late August IFM dissidents kidnapped the brother of Deputy Prime Minister Allan Kemakeza, demanding that SI $6.5m. in compensation be paid to the displaced persons of Guadalcanal. Kemakeza was released unharmed after 10 days without the payment of a ransom. In September a breakaway group from the IFM, which had reverted to the former name of the GRA under the leadership of Harold Keke, held an airline pilot hostage with a demand for SI $2m.; he was released unharmed without the demands being acceded to, although Keke later claimed that the Government had paid him US $200,000.

The Townsville Peace Agreement and 2001 election

A further session of talks in Australia, led to the signing on 15 October 2000, of a treaty known as the Townsville Peace Agreement, by the MEF, the IFM, the Solomon Islands Government and the Provincial Governments of Malaita and Guadalcanal. An amnesty for all those involved in crimes associated with the ethnic conflict was to be granted, subject to the surrender of all weaponry within 30 days. The agreement also envisaged the creation of an international peace-monitoring team (which was to work alongside a locally appointed Peace Monitoring Council), and the repatriation to their home villages of all MEF and IFM soldiers at the expense of the Solomon Islands Government. Infrastructure and services in the two provinces would be restored and developed. The two provinces would also be granted a greater degree of administrative autonomy. Malaita Province was to receive additional funding to reflect the demands placed on the region by the influx of 20,000 displaced persons from Guadalcanal.

The implementation of the peace process, overseen by monitors from Australia and New Zealand, was threatened in mid-November 2000, when four people were killed in a shooting in Gizo, Western Province. Among the dead were two members of Papua New Guinea's secessionist Bougainville Revolutionary Army (BRA). Moreover, delays in the disarmament process involving the MEF and the IFM caused the deadline for the surrender of arms to be extended until 15 December. In mid-November, following an announcement that the Guadalcanal Provincial Government headquarters (which had been occupied by members of the MEF since June) was to be rehabilitated as a symbol of national unity, arsonists, believed to be linked with the MEF, attacked the building. Despite a series of ceremonies in late November and early December, in which members of the IFM and MEF surrendered weapons, it was believed that at least 400 illegally held weapons remained in circulation at the end of December. The legislation granting immunity to those who had committed crimes during the conflict was approved by Parliament in mid-December, and was criticized by the prominent human rights organization Amnesty International. Also in December, new legislation provided for the appointment of two further ministers, a Minister for Rehabilitation, Reconstruction and Redirection, and a Minister for Economic Reform and Structural Adjustment. In late December one man was injured in an attack on a motel, in Honiara, in which disarmed former IFM rebels recruited to join the police were resident. Responsibility for the attack was attributed to a group calling itself the Marau Eagle Force, from the eastern Marau region of Guadalcanal, which was subject to separate peace negotiations. The Guadalcanal Liberation Force (GLF), as the GRA had been restyled, led by Harold Keke, also announced that it had not accepted the cease-fire.

In January 2001 it was reported that the Government was contemplating an extension of the amnesty. Further violence broke out between Guadalcanal militants and members of the Marau Eagle Force. A peace agreement between the group and the IFM was signed in February, although the Peace Monitoring Council observed that the infrastructure of the Marau region had been almost entirely destroyed since 1998 and that there was little immediate prospect of recovery. Violent incidents between the Marau Eagle Force, the GLF and government patrols throughout March–April 2001 led the International Peace Monitoring Team from Australia to state that the cease-fire arrangement reached under the Townsville Peace Agreement had been breached. In June the Premier of Guadalcanal, Ezekiel Alebua, was shot and seriously injured in an assassination attempt, apparently carried out on the orders of former leaders of the IFM. Harold Keke met the Deputy Prime Minister and the secretary of the Peace Monitoring Council in June and, in October, he voiced his support for the imminent general elections. However, the failure of former militia groups to surrender their guns was the main obstacle to a lasting peace throughout 2001, and officials estimated that there remained some 500 high-powered weapons in the community, in addition to handmade weapons. The Government declared an 'arms amnesty' in April 2002. Militants surrendered some 2,000 guns with impunity. Weapons disposal began in June, coinciding with the International Peace Monitoring Team's departure from the country.

Meanwhile, in the second half of 2000 Western, Choiseul, and Temutu provinces all declared themselves to be semi-autonomous states within Solomon Islands. On 1 September the legislature of the latter, representing 20,000 inhabitants, approved a bill allowing for a referendum on the province's proposed independence; the worsening economic situation caused by the conflict in Guadalcanal was believed to be a determining factor. Additionally, movements in Guadalcanal and Makira provinces demanding greater autonomy were reported to have gained strength at this time. In November the Minister for Provincial Government and Rural Development, Nathaniel Waena, announced that legislation to amend the Constitution would be submitted in 2001, in order to institute a federal system of government. In March 2001 the Government announced that it would introduce legislation to extend the life of Parliament for a further year, to expire in August 2002, stating that the social and economic problems of the islands would not facilitate the holding of elections as scheduled in August 2001. This proposal attracted widespread opposition, including that of churches, trade unions, all provincial premiers, and the principal overseas aid donors to Solomon Islands. When it became apparent that he would not possess a parliamentary majority to support the legislation, Sogavare withdrew the bill from Parliament in early May; later in that month it was announced that the elections would be held in December, funded wholly from overseas. In October the High Court began hearing a case brought by former Prime Minister Ulufa'alu; he had challenged the legality of the Government, seeking a ruling that the coup and subsequent election that had ousted him in June 2000 were unconstitutional (he lost the case in November 2001).

In October 2001 public services deteriorated as nation-wide power cuts resulted from the inability of the Solomon Islands Electricity Authority (SIEA) to pay for its supplies of diesel fuel. The Government announced the introduction of health charges in order to maintain medical services, and was forced to appeal to Australia and New Zealand for assistance in policing, as violent crime was becoming endemic. A storage container holding weapons relinquished under the Townsville Peace Agreement was broken into and, in November, the revelation that compensation totalling SI $17.4m. had been paid to former members of the MEF for alleged property damage precipitated a violent demonstration by protesters demanding similar recompense. The Prime Minister was prevented from leaving his office (to attend a session of the UN General Assembly in New York), and the house of the Deputy Prime Minister was vandalized.

Accusations and rumours of bribery and intimidation were rife during the campaigning that preceded the general election, held on 5 December 2001. The electoral grouping of the SIACC won 12 seats, the PAP secured nine and the PPP six, while 22 seats were won by independent candidates. In the absence of a clear SIACC leader, 11 elected members of the coalition convened with 11 elected independents to decide upon an acceptable premier. Following various shifts in allegiances, Sir Allan Kemakeza (as he had become), leader of the PAP and former Deputy Prime Minister, was declared Prime Minister. Despite having previously been accused of misappropriating state funds, the former Minister for Finance, Snyder Rini, was appointed Deputy Prime Minister and Minister for National Planning.

However, the new Government was unable to improve the increasingly desperate political and economic situation on the islands. A peace summit, organized by the Peace Monitoring Council, scheduled to be held in March 2002, was postponed until June, and, as the security situation in the country deteriorated further, numerous international peace monitors began withdrawing from the islands. In March Kemakeza dismissed Michael Maina, the Minister for Finance, after the latter failed to consult the Cabinet prior to announcing a number of drastic budgetary measures, the most significant of which was his decision to devalue the national currency by 25%. Maina was replaced by Laurie Chan, who revalued the currency in April.

There were reports of further disturbances on the western coast of Guadalcanal in June 2002 during which it was claimed that 11 Malaitans, who were part of a force attempting to capture the GLF leader, Harold Keke, had been killed. In July water and electricity supplies to the capital were interrupted after the SIEA was once again unable to purchase fuel to power its generators, and the Solomon Islands Water Authority (SIWA) had failed to pay rental arrears to the landowners of the Kongulai water source. The country was further adversely affected by a series of strikes in mid-August by public-sector workers in protest at the non-payment of their salaries. Later in that month the Minister for Youth and Sports and Women's Affairs, Rev. Augustin Geve, was assassinated. It was subsequently reported that Keke had claimed responsibility for the murder. Following further violence attributed to the GLF, in September Kemakeza made a formal request to the UN for a peace-keeping force to address the increasing state of lawlessness in the country, and in the following month a delegation of four UN officials visited the islands to assess the situation.

The National Peace Council

In mid-October 2002 the Cabinet approved the establishment of the National Peace Council, an interim body, to replace the Peace Monitoring Council, the mandate of which expired on 15 October under the terms of the Townsville Peace Agreement. A permanent body was to be established after 16 January 2003. However, it was confirmed in the same month that more weapons were in circulation in the country than when the peace agreement was signed in October 2000. The National Peace Council expressed a belief that many of the weapons surrendered under the arms amnesty of April 2002 had been removed for use by police officers in their campaign to capture Keke.

In mid-December 2002 the Minister for Finance, Laurie Chan, resigned. The Government claimed that this action was in response to criticism of his budget, which had recently been approved by the Cabinet. However, Radio New Zealand reported that his resignation was in protest at the Government's decision to pay unscheduled allowances to the 'special constables' (former militants from the ethnic conflict who were allowed to join the police force as part of the peace agreement) who had demanded the payments with threats and violence. The latter had included an incident in which gunshots were fired at the Prime Minister's residence by a group of 'special constables'. The Government confronted a serious challenge in mid-December when six independent members of Parliament resigned because of what they described as a 'leadership problem' within the coalition. However, the Government defeated an opposition motion of no confidence by 28 votes to 17.

The country's precarious peace process suffered a major reversal in February 2003 when a leading member of the National Peace Council, Sir Frederick Soaki, was assassinated. There was speculation that the killing might have been connected to his involvement in a 'demobilization' programme for 'special constables'. A report by Amnesty International in March claimed that the country's 'special constables' had tortured and killed numerous people in the operation against Harold Keke along the southern coast of Guadalcanal. In April three of Keke's close associates deserted him and reported that in recent weeks they had witnessed him committing nine murders, mostly, it was believed, of his own supporters whom he had suspected of collaborating with the police. In May it was reported that Keke had taken six missionaries hostage in southern Guadalcanal. In a separate incident on Malaita, in the same month, an Australian missionary was beheaded.

In early June 2003 Kemakeza travelled to the Australian capital of Canberra for a meeting with Prime Minister John Howard, at which he reiterated the Solomon Islands' request for direct foreign intervention in order to address the country's worsening law and order crisis. (Former Prime Minister Sogavare had made a similar appeal for Australia to send troops to the country at the time of the signing of the Townsville Peace Agreement in October 2000, but the request had been rejected.) In mid-June 2003 senior officials from Australia and New Zealand arrived in Solomon Islands to assess the possibility of mounting a regional intervention in the country. At a meeting of the Pacific Islands Forum in Sydney, Australia, later that month, delegates from the 16 member nations agreed unanimously to send a multinational intervention force to Solomon Islands; eight island members stated their intention to commit personnel to the force. The proposed action was to constitute the largest armed intervention in the South Pacific region since the Second World War.

Meanwhile, reports of violence and intimidation by Keke and his rebel forces continued during June 2003. At least 23 people (including 11 members of a religious order) were taken hostage and several more were killed. An estimated 1,000 villagers fled their homes after Keke took control of a police post, thereby expanding the area under his control. The rebel leader also burned two villages where he believed that local people had informed the authorities of his activities. Furthermore, in the same month his militia forced some 1,200 people at gunpoint to stand along several stretches of beach in order to serve as a human shield and thereby prevent a planned police landing in the area. Atrocities continued in the following month when another settlement (of some 500 inhabitants) was burned on Keke's orders and a number of people (including several children) were beaten to death or beheaded.

Following further discussions in July 2003 the Australian Government stated its requirements for the intervention to proceed, which included unhindered access to the country's financial records and the appointment of up to 100 foreign nationals to senior positions in the islands' public service and government sectors. The economic component of the proposed intervention would also provide for the payment of Solomon Islands' domestic and foreign debts through increased aid from Australia and New Zealand. Displaced villagers (estimated to total 20,000 since ethnic violence intensified in 2000) were to receive a specific allocation of $A100,000 in aid from Australia. The Solomon Islands Government unanimously approved legislation to allow the Australian-led force, the Regional Assistance Mission to Solomon Islands (RAMSI) as it became known, into the country, and the Australian warship *HMAS Manoora* subsequently arrived in Honiara with 400 personnel, followed by a total of 2,225 troops and police from various other countries, including New Zealand, Papua New Guinea, Fiji, Tonga, Vanuatu and Samoa.

In early August 2003 the UN Secretary-General, Kofi Annan, commended the Pacific island countries for their efforts to support Solomon Islands and stated that the UN was prepared to contribute actively to any future peace process in the country. On 13 August Harold Keke surrendered and was arrested, along with 10 of his close associates; Keke handed over a large number of firearms and was taken away on *HMAS Manoora* for his own safety. Later in that month a 17-member 'economic assistance team' arrived in Solomon Islands, some of whom were to assume strategic roles in government and the public service in order to implement major reforms. The Australian Prime Minister also made a one-day visit to the islands. By early September the regional forces announced that they had collected a total of 3,850 weapons since the start of a firearms amnesty a month earlier. Australia began to withdraw its troops in late October and by early December more than one-half of its personnel had left the islands. In November 2004, however, the murder of an Australian soldier prompted Australia to increase the number of its defence personnel in Solomon Islands by 100.

The capture and arrest of members of various militia groups, including two individuals who had been signatories to the Townsville Peace Agreement, continued during late 2003. Police Superintendent Mannaseh Maelanga, who had served as the MEF's Supreme Commander, was arrested in November and sentenced to one year's imprisonment in March 2004. Andrew Te'e, former Supreme Commander of the IFM, was arrested and charged with the murder of three people. In February 2004 Keke and two of his associates were found guilty of the murder in 2002 of Augustine Geve (see The Townsville Peace Agreement and 2001 election). He was expected to stand trial for other alleged offences, including the murder of seven missionaries, in the following months.

The Government was subject to considerable embarrassment in December 2003 when the Minister for Communications, Aviation and Meteorology, Daniel Fa'afunua, was arrested and charged with the assault of his wife and of a female police officer, with being drunk and disorderly and with demanding money with menaces. The former minister was found guilty in February 2004 and received a lengthy prison sentence. In September of that year the Minister for Agriculture and Livestock, Alex Bartlett, was arrested on charges relating to violent offences that had occurred during 2000, when he was involved in the leadership of the MEF.

In June 2004 Nathaniel Waena, the former Minister for National Unity, Reconciliation and Peace, was elected Governor-General, with 27 parliamentary votes.

In early 2005 the Minister for Provincial Government, Clement Rojumana, was arrested on 25 corruption charges and the Minister for Police, Michael Maina, was charged with theft. Both ministers were replaced in March. In April the former Minister for Finance, Francis Zama, was charged with official corruption over the alleged granting to himself of an exemption from the payment of goods tax during his period in office. Moreover, a police investigation in mid-2005 claimed that the Minister for Health, Benjamin Una, had been involved in two shooting incidents in 2004 that had targeted personnel from the regional intervention force, including the killing of an Australian officer. Una denied the allegations. In October 2005 the Minister for Fisheries and Marine Resources, Paul Maenu'u, was forced to resign following his vote at a meeting of the International

Whaling Commission in favour of a reintroduction of commercial whaling, in defiance of the Government's stated position. Mathias Taro was appointed to replace Maenu'u. In November Una submitted his resignation as Minister for Health, having been arrested and charged with stealing aid funds that had been donated for a development project in his parliamentary constituency. Johnson Koli was named as the new Minister for Health. Alfred Sasako was appointed as Minister for Infrastructure and Development in the same month (but was dismissed in March 2006 following allegations of misconduct). In November 2005 the Prime Minister became involved in controversy with regard to the allocation of loans from a Taiwanese bank. It was claimed that during his tenure of the post of Minister for National Unity and Reconciliation in 2001, Sir Allan Kemakeza had received compensation of US $121,000 for personal losses incurred during ethnic unrest. Following an audit, it was revealed that millions of dollars could not be accounted for and that the Cabinet had remained unaware of the situation.

The 2006 legislative election and subsequent events

In the legislative election held on 5 April 2006 around one-half of the incumbent members of Parliament lost their seats. It was believed that only 16 of the 50 incoming members had formally declared their party affiliation prior to the election, confirming that electors tended to vote for individuals rather than for representatives of specific political parties. It was subsequently reported that independents occupied 29 seats and that the recently formed Solomon Islands Party for Rural Advancement (SIPRA), led by Job Dudley Tausinga, held four seats, the National Party four seats, the PAP four seats and the Solomon Islands Democratic Party three seats, with the remainder being distributed among various other parties. On 18 April three candidates participated in the contest for the post of Prime Minister, but none secured the requisite majority in the first session of voting in Parliament. Manasseh Sogavare was thus eliminated and a second ballot took place, at which Snyder Rini, leader of the Independent Democratic Party (IDP—as the Association of Independent Members of Parliament had been renamed in 2004 on its registration as a political party) and former Deputy Prime Minister, received 27 parliamentary votes, while Job Dudley Tausinga won 23.

Rini's appointment as Prime Minister led to widespread protests. A group calling itself People's Power delivered a petition to the Governor-General demanding Rini's immediate resignation, claiming that he had been involved in corruption and bribery. It was variously alleged that Rini had accepted funding from the local Chinese business community and from both mainland Chinese and Taiwanese supporters who hoped to influence the electoral process. Snyder Rini was nevertheless sworn in on 20 April 2006. Public dissatisfaction culminated in two days of the most serious rioting witnessed in the country for many years. Much of the capital was left in ruins, and in particular many local Chinese businesses and homes were destroyed in arson attacks. It was reported that more than 300 citizens of the People's Republic of China had been evacuated from Honiara to their homeland. A curfew was imposed, and in an attempt to restore law and order in the capital Australia dispatched reinforcements of 110 soldiers and 70 police officers. Several opposition politicians were among those arrested in connection with the rioting. However, shortly before a parliamentary vote of no confidence was scheduled to take place, and after only eight days in the post of Prime Minister, Rini announced his decision to resign. He remained in office in an acting capacity, pending a fresh parliamentary ballot to choose the next prime minister. On 4 May Manasseh Sogavare was elected, securing 28 votes; Fred Fono, who had briefly served as Deputy Prime Minister in the interim Government, received 22 votes. The majority of Solomon Islanders appeared to welcome the appointment of Sogavare, who on the following day announced the composition of his Cabinet. Job Dudley Tausinga was appointed as Deputy Prime Minister, also assuming responsibility for the portfolio of forestry, environment and conservation. Bartholomew Ulufa'alu was named Minister for Finance and Treasury; Patterson Oti became Minister for Foreign Affairs; and Bernard Ghiro was appointed Minister for Home Affairs.

Following his assumption of office, Prime Minister Sogavare announced that the country's economic strategies were to be reorientated and that a new policy regarding the management of Taiwanese financial aid to Solomon Islands was to be formulated, to permit greater transparency in the use of such funds. Francis Billy Hilly was dismissed from the post of Minister for Commerce, Industries and Employment in August 2006 following his alleged refusal to denounce a memorandum of understanding signed by his National Party with China. In October a parliamentary no-confidence motion submitted by Fred Fono, the Leader of the Opposition, against Sogavare, failed to gain sufficient votes to succeed. Sogavare subsequently effected a minor reorganization of the Cabinet, in which Ulufa'alu, the Minister for Finance and Treasury, was replaced by Gordon Darcy Lilo, hitherto Minister for National Reform and Aid Co-ordination, while Steve Abana became Minister for Planning and Aid Co-ordination. In December Tausinga resigned as Deputy Prime Minister, apparently over a dispute related to logging, and was replaced by Toswell Kaua, who retained the agriculture and livestock portfolio.

In early April 2007 a large earthquake in the South Pacific caused a tsunami that resulted in more than 50 fatalities in Solomon Islands and destroyed the homes of thousands in the Western and Choiseul provinces. Aftershocks continued to hamper international and local relief efforts. Australia and Taiwan both supported emergency operations in the area. (In April 2011 a special report commissioned by the Office of the Auditor General revealed serious mismanagement of aid and relief supplies on the part of the local authorities.)

In May 2007 the Minister for Public Service, Joses Sanga, died. Sanga's portfolio was allocated to Deputy Prime Minister Kaua, while the agriculture and livestock portfolio, hitherto the responsibility of Kaua, was transferred to a new cabinet member, Severino Nuaiasi. In the same month Francis Zama was convicted of official corruption (see The National Peace Council), receiving a 20-month prison sentence. Zama's sentence was subsequently suspended, and in October he was appointed Minister for Justice and Legal Affairs, before being transferred to the finance and treasury portfolio, and later to education and human resources. In November Sir Allan Kemakeza, the former Prime Minister, was convicted of larceny, intimidation and demanding money with menaces, relating to a raid by members of the MEF on the local office of an Australian law firm in 2002.

In November 2007 13 members of Sogavare's Government resigned, including the Deputy Prime Minister, Toswell Kaua, and the Minister for Education and Human Resources Development, Derek Sikua. Together with the opposition, the dissident group urged Sogavare himself to resign owing to the lack of confidence in his leadership. Sogavare's failure to attend an earlier meeting of the Pacific Islands Forum, along with his handling of the Moti affair (see Relations with Australia and the Pacific Islands), were widely criticized. Both sides claimed to have the support of a parliamentary majority, and several members of the opposition reportedly joined the Government after being appointed to cabinet posts. However, in mid-December a no-confidence motion submitted against Sogavare succeeded by a narrow margin; Derek Sikua was elected to replace him as Prime Minister.

The premiership of Derek Sikua

Sikua's Cabinet included several ministers who had been members of the Sogavare Government prior to the defections, including Toswell Kaua, who was appointed Minister for Law and Justice, and Gordon Darcy Lilo, who assumed responsibility for environment, conservation and meteorology. Other notable appointments included Fred Fono as Deputy Prime Minister and William Haomae as Minister for Foreign Affairs. The Government announced its intention to reduce the number of political appointments in an attempt to curb government spending.

In January 2008 the opposition was further weakened by the withdrawal of support of four of its members. It was reported in June that the Government was promoting the federalization of Solomon Islands and was soon to introduce legislation to that effect. In July the opposition filed a motion of no confidence against the Government, citing public dissatisfaction with increasing food prices, among other factors. However, the motion, which was presented to Parliament in August, was defeated by a considerable margin. Meanwhile, the dismissal of an appeal against the conviction of Sir Allan Kemakeza, Minister for Forestry and former Prime Minister, resulted in his departure from the Cabinet as well as from Parliament, which in turn precipitated a minor ministerial reorganization in September: Matthew Wale was appointed as Minister for Education and Human Resources Development, to replace Job Dudley Tausinga, who assumed responsibility for the forestry portfolio. In October the Prime Minister was acquitted of drink-driving charges brought against him in January. In April 2009, furthermore, Sikua and the Secretary to the Cabinet, Jeremiah Manele, filed a joint defamation suit in the High Court against the *Island Sun* newspaper, for an article which alleged that the two men had become intoxicated and behaved inappropriately at the UN General Assembly in New York in October 2008.

In early 2009 heavy rainfall resulted in severe flooding in areas including Malaita and Central provinces. The Government proclaimed a national disaster as the number of fatalities rose to 13.

In May 2009 Sikua effected a major cabinet reorganization, including the appointment of Peter Tom as the Minister for Home Affairs, while Laurie Chan replaced Toswell Kaua as Minister for Justice and Legal Affairs, the latter reportedly being removed for health reasons. Sikua also dismissed six Permanent Secretaries who had been appointed under the Sogavare Government. The dismissed officials successfully sued the Government for compensation, claiming breach of contract. In June Frank Kabui, a former Attorney-General, was elected Governor-General, receiving 30 parliamentary votes; he took office in July.

In April 2009 an official report into the 2006 riots found the Royal Solomon Islands Police responsible for the violence, owing to incompetence and a failure properly to fulfil its duty, while unsatisfactory urban living conditions were also cited as a contributory factor. However, the report concluded that there was no conspiracy connected to the violence. Following its release, the Government was accused of editing the report to remove information regarding specific individuals and groups found to be responsible for the riots; the Government denied this charge.

Also in April 2009 the Government officially established the Solomon Islands Truth and Reconciliation Commission. The panel was charged with investigating the causes of the violent conflict in Guadalcanal that occurred between 1997 and 2003. The Commission was composed of five members: its chairman, Rev. Sam Ata, and two other Solomon Islands citizens, a former Vice-President of Fiji, Ratu Joni Madraiwiwi, and a Peruvian human rights activist. However, Amnesty International expressed concern that the establishment of the Commission might be detrimental to future court cases against alleged perpetrators of the violence, as any evidence brought before the Commission would thus become inadmissible in trials. Public hearings by the Commission commenced in Honiara in March 2010 (further hearings, in Malaita, took place in May), when victims of the ethnic conflict presented their testimonies. Also in March discussions between the political leaders of Guadalcanal and Malaita provinces began in Honiara, with the aim of achieving reconciliation and peaceful co-existence. In the same month the Australian-owned Gold Ridge gold mine, on Guadalcanal, which had been forced to close 10 years previously at the height of the period of ethnic violence, was formally reopened following a ceremony of reconciliation among local landowning communities; the mine was expected to make a large contribution to the country's economy. During 2010 a resettlement programme was launched which was to involve the construction of around 300 new homes for the displaced landowners. In March 2011 the first gold bar from the mine was poured.

Meanwhile, in January 2010 a new political party, the Ownership, Unity and Responsibility (OUR) Party, was inaugurated, with Manasseh Sogavare, the Leader of the Opposition and former Prime Minister, as its president and Patterson Oti, the former Minister for Foreign Affairs, as its general secretary. By March it was reported that 11 new parties had been formed to contest the forthcoming general election. Among these new groups was the Twelve Pillars to Peace and Prosperity (TP4), led by Delmah Nori, which was to represent the views of the country's women and to encourage the greater involvement of women in government. In April the six parties forming the incumbent governing coalition (known as the Coalition for National Unity and Rural Advancement—CNURA) announced that they would contest the election jointly. Also in April, however, proposed legislation on the reform of the political party system, in order to increase stability (in particular by limiting the ability of members of the legislature to change their party allegiance), was defeated in Parliament; on the following day Sikua dismissed five ministers whom he accused of failing to support the proposed legislation, and also removed several members of the legislature from their posts as chairmen of state-owned enterprises, including the national investment corporation, the postal service and the ports authority. The dismissed ministers included the Minister for Finance and Treasury, Snyder Rini, who was replaced by Francis Billy Hilly (the former Prime Minister and hitherto Minister for Commerce, Industry and Employment), the Minister for Justice and Legal Affairs, Laurie Chan, whose post was assumed by Augustine Taneko, and the Minister for Environment and Conservation, Gordon Darcy Lilo, who was replaced by Clement Kengava. In March, meanwhile, it was announced that the European Union (EU) and the UN would provide experts to monitor the poll. Parliament was dissolved on 24 April, pending the holding of the general election in August. Concern was expressed in some quarters over the donation of US $1.2m. to the Rural Constituency Development Fund presented to the outgoing members of Parliament by the Taiwanese Government and over the significant pay rise that the legislators awarded themselves prior to their leaving office.

Recent developments: the 2010 election and premiership of Danny Philip

At least 19 parties contested the legislative election held on 4 August 2010. Although there were a number of complaints of minor voting irregularities, the poll was reported to have been conducted in a relatively orderly and peaceful manner. Of the 50 parliamentary seats, 28 were taken by independents, while the Solomon Islands Democratic Party secured 12 seats and Sogavare's OUR Party and SIPRA each took 3 seats. The IDP, led by former Prime Minister Rini, itself officially obtained only one seat in Parliament, but was believed to have the support of more than 20 independent legislators. Despite the recent formation of the TP4 party and the participation of 22 female candidates in the election, no women succeeded in securing a seat in the legislature. A number of prominent politicians, including Deputy Prime Minister Fred Fono, the Minister for Finance and Treasury, Francis Billy Hilly, and the General Secretary of the OUR party, Patterson Oti, lost their seats at the election. Several weeks of difficult negotiations ensued as the various parties attempted to garner sufficient support to form a viable coalition government. On 25 August Danny Philip, the leader of the Reformed Democratic Party, was elected as the new Prime Minister in a parliamentary ballot, defeating his only rival, Steve Abana of the Solomon Islands Democratic Party, by 26 votes to 23 (there was one spoiled ballot). Philip appointed a new Government, entitled the National Coalition for Reform and Advancement (NCRA), which was composed of the IDP, SIPRA, the Reformed Democratic Party, the Rural and Urban Political Party, the Direct Development Party and independents. Among the members of the new Cabinet were two somewhat controversial appointees: Manasseh Maelanga, who became Deputy Prime Minister and Minister for Home Affairs, and Jimmy Lusibaea, who was appointed as Minister for Fisheries and Marine Resources. Both were former leaders of the now-defunct MEF and had served prison sentences for offences relating to the ethnic violence.

Following reports of disagreements over the allocation of the remaining unfilled portfolios, Gordon Darcy Lilo became Minister for Finance and Treasury and Snyder Rini as Minister for Development Planning and Aid Co-ordination (a newly created ministry). Steve Abana was appointed as Leader of the Opposition by the National Parliamentary Opposition Group, and Clay Forau was identified as the Leader of the Independent Group in Parliament. In early September Sir Allan Kemakeza was elected as the new Speaker of the National Parliament; Francis Billy Hilly and Fred Fono were the two other, unsuccessful, candidates. In the following month Prime Minister Philip announced in an official policy statement that his Government intended to implement two wide-ranging reform programmes over the following four years: one covering constitutional reform (including proposed amendments to the electoral laws and the utilization of the country's valuable natural resources) and the other sector development reform (in an attempt to lessen the over-reliance of the economy on the logging industry). In November skirmishes were reported in the capital when the High Court sentenced cabinet minister Jimmy Lusibaea to 33 months in prison for his involvement in incidents relating to the ethnic violence a decade previously. Lusibaea's sentence (for unlawful wounding and for assaulting a police officer) resulted in the automatic loss of his parliamentary seat and of his cabinet position. In early December the Prime Minister dismissed the Minister for Forestry, Bodo Dettke, over the latter's decision to seize a logging ship; however, Dettke was reinstated in the Cabinet a few days later as the new Minister for Fisheries and Marine Resources (a portfolio left vacant as a result of Lusibaea's recent conviction).

In mid-January 2011 the opposition expressed outrage at Lusibaea's early release from prison, but the Government insisted that the former minister, who, because of the brevity of his time spent in prison, was now entitled to resume his parliamentary seat, had received no special treatment and that his release (less than two months after he had been sentenced) had been officially approved by the Correctional Services Parole Board. The opposition pledged to launch a legal challenge to Lusibaea's pardon. A few days later the opposition demanded the resignation of Prime Minister Philip following the defection of at least five cabinet ministers, including Bodo Dettke, who claimed no longer to have confidence in Philip's leadership or in the Minister for Finance and Treasury, Gordon Darcy Lilo. In early February Dettke and another opposition MP escaped unharmed from a shooting incident in Honiara; the police were unable to determine whether the attack had been politically motivated. In the same week the chairman of the Correctional Services Parole Board, Philip Tegevota, resigned from his post, claiming to have been informed that his life was under threat. As lobbying among the members of Parliament intensified during February and a number of defectors revoked their decision to leave the Cabinet, the Prime Minister refused to consider the opposition's demand for the recall of Parliament and the holding of a no-confidence motion, claiming that the Government had the support of a parliamentary majority. In mid-February, having overseen a conciliatory meeting between the Prime Minister and Leader of the Opposition Steve Abana, the Speaker of the National Parliament, Sir Allan Kemakeza, announced that Parliament would be convened in late March to debate the annual budget. Later in February the trial of the Minister for Energy, Mines and Rural Electrification, Mark Kemakeza (brother of the Speaker), opened in Honiara; the minister was accused of having illegally used public funds that had been allocated for a fishing project in his constituency. The Government's position was considerably strengthened in the latter half of February by a number of reported defections by members of the opposition to the NCRA ranks. The opposition was further destabilized at the end of March following the resignation of Steve Abana as Leader of the Opposition in response to an internecine power struggle; Abana was replaced by Derek Sikua.

Within days of assuming his new post, Sikua submitted a parliamentary motion of no confidence in Philip's administration; however, the motion was subsequently rejected by the Speaker, who asserted that the parliamentary schedule and lack of time did not permit its consideration. Despite opposition disapproval, Jimmy Lusibaea was officially readmitted as a member of Parliament. In early April 2011 the Government's power was further consolidated by the defection to its ranks of six more opposition MPs, including Abana and the Leader of the Independent Group in Parliament, Clay Forau, and by the smooth passage of the budget. Later that month Prime Minister Philip carried out a cabinet reorganization, dismissing six ministers, four of whom (among them being Mark Kemakeza) had changed their party allegiance several times in recent months. The seven new appointees to the Cabinet included five MPs (among them being Forau) who had recently crossed over from the opposition. The Prime Minister pledged to restore stability to the government system and to make his Cabinet more effective. At the end of April Governor-General Kabui refused officially to approve the appointment of Jimmy Lusibaea as Minister for Fisheries and Marine Resources, asserting that the MP was disqualified from holding a cabinet post according to the Constitution (Kabui claimed that, despite his early release from prison, the term of Lusibaea's original sentence remained the same—i.e. more than the maximum of six months' imprisonment allowed by the Constitution for individuals to be eligible to hold a government post).

Environmental Concerns

The exploitation of Solomon Islands' timber resources provides a major source of foreign exchange, but has proved difficult to regulate. From 2004 the huge increase in the production of round logs in Solomon Islands led to considerable disquiet among community representatives, landowners and environmentalists. The total harvest of round logs in that year was estimated at more than 900,000 cu m, which was equivalent to five times the sustainable limit for timber production in the country. In November a petition of more than 1,000 signatures was delivered to the Government, demanding a reduction in the current rate of logging, increased regulation of logging activity by foreign companies and a greater role for local communities in decisions made about their forestry resources. The petition, which contained endorsements from every province in Solomon Islands, urged the Government to approve legislation providing for the sustainable management of the forestry industry. However, the Government postponed consideration of the proposed legislation, and it was reported that logging rates had increased yet further in anticipation of its introduction. In April 2008 the incoming Government of Derek Sikua announced that more stringent environmental controls were to be imposed on the country's logging operations (see Economic Affairs). Although demand for timber exports declined in 2009, owing to the global recession, exploitation continued at an unsustainable rate, and in December a senior forestry official estimated that sources of timber for commercial logging would be exhausted within two or three years. A report issued in April 2010 described numerous illegal practices perpetrated with impunity by logging companies, together with corruption, social problems and conflict among traditional landowning communities as a result of the companies' activities. In March 2011 the Government stated that it would further promote the replacement of the natural forest with the establishment of plantations (by both smallholders as well as by the large-scale logging companies) in an effort to counterbalance the excessive deforestation activities. With the aim of educating the Pacific nations about the importance of conserving their forests, the Secretariat of the Pacific Community had earlier designated 2011 as the International Year of the Forests.

The country's practice of capturing and exporting large numbers of live dolphins drew international criticism in mid-2003, when police mounted a large-scale security operation around Honiara Airport to prevent journalists from filming some 200 dolphins being loaded into a cargo aeroplane bound for Mexico. Several reports of harassment and violence against foreign journalists were received. It was believed that, owing to the high price commanded by the sale of the animals, senior Solomon Islands officials were likely to be involved. The trade in wild dolphins had been prohibited by most developed countries under the Convention on International Trade in Endangered Species of Wild Flora and Fauna. In December 2004 a consignment of dolphins was prevented from being exported after representatives from the fishing industry complained that the trade was harming the reputation of the islands' important tuna industry (widely perceived by Western countries to be 'dolphin-friendly'). The export of dolphins was subsequently banned upon the entry into force in November 2005 of a new law. In June 2007, however, the ban was removed, and in October of that year a consignment of 28 dolphins was sent to the United Arab Emirates, provoking criticism from environmentalists. In January 2010 it was reported that the Solomon Islands Government had approved the export of up to 100 dolphins per year, and in February 2011 Robert Satu, the director of the Solomon Islands Marine Mammal Educational Centre and Exporters Ltd, claimed to have orders from a number of European and Middle Eastern countries for the export of live dolphins.

In May 2009 Solomon Islands concluded an agreement with five other nations (Timor-Leste, Indonesia, Malaysia, Papua New Guinea and the Philippines) to protect the 'Coral Triangle', a huge area of biologically diverse coral reefs, which also contains spawning grounds vital for tuna fisheries. In March 2010 the National Parliament adopted legislation on establishing protected areas and conserving biodiversity in Solomon Islands' remaining areas of forest and elsewhere.

Regional Affairs

As a small Pacific island nation Solomon Islands is vulnerable to economic and environmental pressures, and depends on investment and aid from other countries, chiefly Australia, Japan and Taiwan, and from international sources.

Relations with Australia and the Pacific Islands

Australia is Solomon Islands' most influential neighbour and a major source of economic assistance, as well as providing administrative, police and military personnel under RAMSI (see The National Peace Council). Relations between Solomon Islands and Australia became strained in 2006 over the extradition of Julian Moti, an Australian citizen who in September had been appointed as the Attorney-General of Solomon Islands. Moti, who was wanted by the Australian authorities on a charge of statutory rape (allegedly committed in Vanuatu several years previously), had been arrested in Papua New Guinea but contravened the conditions of his bail and gained refuge in the Solomon Islands' High Commission in Port Moresby in October. Shortly thereafter he was flown, reportedly on an aircraft of the Papua New Guinea Defence Force, to Solomon Islands, where he was arrested by police officers serving under RAMSI and charged with illegal immigration. In mid-October Prime Minister Sogavare declared his unwillingness to give assent to any Australian extradition requests and claimed that Moti's detention was unlawful. Sogavare's threat to suspend the mandate for RAMSI and reappraise Australia's role in the mission attracted criticism from the parliamentary opposition, and fears were raised about the repercussions of the dispute on the security and stability of Solomon Islands, and on Australian aid. The rift deepened when RAMSI officers carried out a forcible search of Sogavare's office to obtain evidence relating to the Moti case, while Sogavare was abroad attending a meeting of the Pacific Islands Forum. At the meeting Australia was accused by both Sogavare and the Papua New Guinean Prime Minister, Sir Michael Somare, of violating the sovereignty of their respective countries; one of the conclusions of the summit meeting was the establishment of a commission to review RAMSI and its operations. Peter Shanel, the Minister for Commerce, Employment and Trade, was arrested for allegedly having given misleading information with regard to Moti's entry into Solomon Islands; it was reported that the dismissal of Police Commissioner Shane Castles, an Australian citizen, in December, was related in part to Shanel's arrest and to the raid on Sogavare's office. In mid-December immigration charges against Moti were dismissed. The Solomon Islands Government then proposed a dialogue between Moti and the Australian authorities. In January 2007 Australia appointed a new High Commissioner to succeed Patrick Cole, who had been expelled from Solomon Islands in September 2006 because of his alleged interference in domestic politics. However, RAMSI remained a point of contention: in February 2007 the Australian Minister for Foreign Affairs, in an open letter published in a Solomon Islands newspaper, appealed to the islanders to support the mission; in the same month the Solomon Islands Minister for Foreign Affairs, Patterson Oti, urged the formulation of an exit strategy for RAMSI. In July, having been suspended for several months, Moti was sworn in as Attorney-General, an act that was described by Australian Prime Minister John Howard as 'provocative and insensitive'. Sogavare, for his part, threatened to take Australia to the International Court of Justice, claiming that its pursuit of Moti was related to political interests. Australia applied for Moti's extradition, but was refused in September.

Relations between the two countries improved following the replacement of Sogavare by Derek Sikua as Prime Minister, and the subsequent extradition of Moti to Australia in December 2007 (the case against him was dismissed by an Australian court in September 2009; this decision was, however, overturned by an Australian court of appeal in July 2010). Sikua visited Australia in January 2008, reportedly assuring the new Australian Prime Minister, Kevin Rudd, of his approval of RAMSI; Rudd paid a reciprocal visit to Solomon Islands in March, and in April 2009 Australia's Minister for Trade, Simon Crean, visited the Solomons to discuss trade and economic development issues, including a prospective free trade agreement, PACER Plus, between Australia and Pacific Island Forum members. In May Rudd was reported to have expressed displeasure at the slow progress of projects in Solomon Islands financed by Australian aid. In mid-August 2010 RAMSI admitted responsibility for the death of a local man in Honiara when it fired shots to disperse a crowd of rioters; the Solomon Islands police force subsequently launched an investigation into the death. On assuming the premiership at the end of the month, Danny Philip stated that he hoped that the situation would be such that RAMSI could withdraw from the Solomon Islands within five to six years. In February 2011 a team of independent experts arrived in Honiara to review the partnership framework between RAMSI and the Solomon Islands Government. In the same month allegations were made in an unauthorized 'intelligence report' (by an unknown source) published in the *Island Sun* claiming that RAMSI and the Australian Government was implicated in ongoing attempts by the opposition to bring about the collapse of the Government of Danny Philip and that it exerted undue influence over the islands' judiciary. The Australian authorities strenuously denied these accusations and Prime Minister Philip, who also asserted that the allegations were baseless, stressed that his Government was committed to working closely with RAMSI.

In 1990 relations between Papua New Guinea and Solomon Islands deteriorated, following allegations by the latter that patrol boats from Papua New Guinea were interfering with the traditional crossing between Bougainville Island (Papua New Guinea) and the Shortland Islands. The Papua New Guinea Government accused Solomon Islands of harbouring members of the rebel BRA and of providing them with supplies. Despite the signing in that year of an agreement on joint border surveillance and arrangements to host peace negotiations between the BRA and the Papua New Guinea Government, relations worsened considerably in 1992 when Papua New Guinea forces carried out several unauthorized incursions into the Shortland Islands, in which a fuel depot was destroyed and two Solomon Islanders were killed. Alleging Australian involvement in the incursions, Prime Minister Mamaloni suspended surveillance flights by the Australian air force over the country's territory. Despite the initiation of discussions between Solomon Islands and Papua New Guinea in January 1993, further incursions were reported in April. Following the election of a new Government in May in Solomon Islands, negotiations between the two countries resulted in an agreement to close the BRA office in Honiara. However, in 1996, as violence on Bougainville intensified, numerous incursions by Papua New Guinea defence forces into Solomon Islands' waters were reported, while the Papua New Guinea Government repeated accusations that Solomon Islands was harbouring BRA activists. Nevertheless, in June 1997 Papua New Guinea and Solomon Islands concluded a maritime border agreement, following several years of negotiations. The purpose of the agreement was not only to delineate the sea boundary between the two countries but also to provide a framework for co-operation in matters of security, natural disaster, customs, quarantine, immigration and conservation. In December 1997 the Prime Ministers of the two countries paid an extended visit to Bougainville to express support for the recently established truce agreement. Furthermore, the Governor of Bougainville was sympathetic to the problem of increasing numbers of Solomon Islanders from the Western Province crossing to Bougainville in late 2001. Many were trading goods in Bougainville in exchange for food and services. Discussions regarding the border of Papua New Guinea were held in April 2002; both Governments were concerned about the increase of weapons-trafficking from Bougainville to the Western Province. Renewed border discussions took place between the two countries in June 2003. A development agreement that included joint infrastructural development, technical assistance and information sharing was signed by the two Governments in March 2005. In January 2008 the new Solomon Islands Prime Minister, Derek Sikua, visited Papua New Guinea to improve relations between the two countries, which, he maintained, had been damaged by the Moti affair and its consequences. During a return visit in October 2009 by the Papua New Guinea Prime Minister, Sir Michael Somare, the two heads of government discussed investment promotion and protection, and the possibility of a double taxation treaty.

In March 1988 Solomon Islands signed an agreement with Vanuatu and Papua New Guinea to form the Melanesian Spearhead Group. The new group regarded as its principal aims the preservation of Melanesian cultural traditions and the attainment of independence by the French Overseas Territory of New Caledonia. In March 1990 the Melanesian Spearhead Group admitted the Front de Libération Nationale Kanak Socialiste (FLNKS—the main Kanak, or Melanesian, political group in New Caledonia). In mid-1994 the group concluded an agreement regarded as the first stage in the establishment of a free trade area by the three countries. Fiji was admitted to the group in mid-1996. Solomon Islands announced its commitment to further economic integration with the countries of the Melanesian Spearhead Group in late 1997. The members of the Melanesian Spearhead Group signed a constitution in March 2007. In July 2010 Prime Minister Sikua officially opened the chancery housing Solomon Islands diplomatic mission in the Fijian capital of Suva. In February 2011 Prime Minister Philip announced proposals to develop a Pan Melanesian Economic Union to promote large-scale investment in the region.

In October 1995 Solomon Islands became a signatory to the Federated States of Micronesia Agreement on Regional Fisheries Access. In early 1997 Solomon Islands and Vanuatu agreed to undertake negotiations on the maritime boundaries between the two countries in an attempt to clarify uncertainty regarding fishing rights.

Other regional relations

Diplomatic relations with Taiwan were established in 1983: Solomon Islands thus became one of the relatively few nations to accord diplomatic recognition to Taiwan, rather than to the People's Republic of China. A seven-member parliamentary delegation, including five cabinet ministers, travelled to Taiwan in September 2004 to discuss mutual co-operation and aid. In January 2005, during a visit to Solomon Islands as part of a tour of the Pacific islands, the Taiwanese President denied that his

SOLOMON ISLANDS

country was practising 'dollar diplomacy' (providing aid in exchange for diplomatic recognition). In May 2006 it was announced that Taiwan's first payment to the Rural Constituency Development Fund (RCDF) had been released. The payments proved controversial because they were made directly to members of the legislature for use in their respective constituencies, and were perceived as potentially open to abuse. In December 2007 the new Prime Minister of Solomon Islands, Derek Sikua, pledged to continue his country's pro-Taiwan policy. During 2009 negotiations were undertaken on a free trade agreement between the two countries. In March 2010 the Taiwanese President, Ma Ying-jeou, paid an official visit to Solomon Islands, during which Sikua reiterated that his country supported Taiwan in its 'struggle for recognition'. Ma reportedly commented that misuse of Taiwanese aid was unacceptable, and Sikua subsequently stated that greater transparency would be required in accounting for RCDF expenditure.

Japan is a major provider of aid for Solomon Islands. The two countries' relations attracted international attention in mid-2005, when, following receipt of US $6.7m. from the Japanese Government for a major project to improve Honiara Airport, Solomon Islands voted with Japan in favour of the removal of a 20-year moratorium on commercial whaling at a meeting of the International Whaling Commission (thereby reneging on a recent commitment to abstain from the vote). In May 2009 Sikua expressed gratitude for Japanese assistance, especially in energy, infrastructure and fisheries, and reiterated his Government's support for Japan's application to become a permanent member of the UN Security Council.

CONSTITUTION AND GOVERNMENT

Under the 1978 Constitution, executive authority is vested in the British monarch, as Head of State, and is exercisable by the monarch's representative, the Governor-General, who is appointed on the advice of Parliament and acts on the advice of the Cabinet. Legislative power is vested in the unicameral National Parliament, with 50 members elected by universal adult suffrage for four years (subject to dissolution) in single-member constituencies. The Cabinet is composed of the Prime Minister, elected by Parliament, and other ministers appointed by the Governor-General on the Prime Minister's recommendation. The Cabinet is responsible to Parliament. Judicial power is exercised by the High Court, magistrates' courts and local courts. Appeals from the High Court are heard by the Court of Appeal, the members of which are senior judges from Australia, New Zealand and Papua New Guinea. The country comprises four Districts, within which there are nine local government councils, elected by universal adult suffrage. The Constitution provides for further devolution of power to provincial authorities.

REGIONAL AND INTERNATIONAL CO-OPERATION

Solomon Islands is a member of the Pacific Community (see p. 410), the Pacific Islands Forum (see p. 413), the Asian Development Bank (see p. 202) and the UN's Economic and Social Commission for Asia and the Pacific (ESCAP, see p. 37), and is a signatory to the Lomé Conventions and the successor Cotonou Agreement (see p. 327) with the European Union (EU). The country is also a member (with Fiji, Papua New Guinea and Vanuatu) of the Melanesian Spearhead Group, which provides for free trade among member countries

Solomon Islands joined the UN in 1978 and acceded to membership of the World Trade Organization (WTO, see p. 430) in 1996. The country is a member of the Commonwealth, and in early 2010 the Commonwealth Pacific Governance Facility was established in Honiara.

ECONOMIC AFFAIRS

In 2009, according to estimates by the World Bank, Solomon Islands' gross national income (GNI), measured at average 2007–09 prices, was US $478m., equivalent to $910 per head (or $1,860 on an international purchasing-power parity basis). During 2000–09, it was estimated, the population increased at an average annual rate of 2.6%, while gross domestic product (GDP) per head increased, in real terms, at an average annual rate of 0.4%. According to figures from the Asian Development Bank (ADB), overall GDP increased, in real terms, at an average annual rate of 3.2% in 2000–09. Having increased by 7.3% in 2008, GDP declined by 1.2% in 2009.

Agriculture (including hunting, forestry and fishing) contributed 35.6% of GDP in 2009, according to UN estimates. In 2004 an estimated 28.7% of those working in the formal sector of the economy were involved in agriculture. In 2011, according to FAO, 67.5% of the labour force, including the informal sector, were projected to be engaged in agricultural activities. The principal cash crops have traditionally included coconuts, cocoa, rice and oil palm. Earnings from copra (which was for many years the country's main export) decreased from SI $45.6m. in 2006 to $36.8m. in 2007. The value of cocoa exports increased from SI $30.3m. in 2006 to $70.8m. in 2007. Meanwhile, the rehabilitation of the palm oil industry involved plans to replant thousands of hectares of the former plantations and to clear other areas for new plantations. Spices are cultivated for export on a small scale. The production of tuna is important, and fish accounted for 11.8% of export earnings in 2007. The forestry sector is the leading source of revenue, timber exports accounting for 65.2% of total export receipts in 2007. However, the dramatic increase in the production of timber from the early 1990s prompted several international organizations to express alarm at the rate of logging in the country (see Contemporary Political History). Output of timber reached 1,148,000 cu m in 2007, in comparison with 536,000 cu m in 2000. The value of timber exports rose from SI $190.5m. in 2000 to $838.7 in 2007. According to ADB data, agricultural GDP expanded by an annual average of 5.7% during 2000–09, increasing by 6.7% in 2008, but declining by 7.3% in 2009.

Industry (including mining, manufacturing, construction and power) contributed 7.5% of GDP in 2009, according to UN estimates. The sector employed 6.4% of wage-earners in 2004. The mining sector's contribution to GDP is negligible. Gold has been the sole mineral export of significance. The other (mainly undeveloped) mineral resources include deposits of copper, lead, zinc, silver, cobalt, asbestos, phosphates, nickel and high-grade bauxite. In 2008 a Japanese company was reported to have identified significant deposits of nickel on the island of Choiseul. According to figures from the ADB, the industrial GDP decreased at an average annual rate of 1.8% during 2000–09; the sector's GDP expanded by 2.0% in 2009.

According to UN estimates, manufacturing contributed 5.3% of GDP in 2009. The sector employed 15.6% of wage-earners in 1995. The most important branches are food-processing (notably fish-canning), coconut-based products, brewing, saw-milling, logging and handicrafts. According to ADB data, the GDP of the manufacturing sector contracted by an annual average of 3.2% during 2000–09, expanding by 2.0% in 2008, but declining by 1.0% in 2009.

Construction contributed 0.7% of GDP in 2009, according to UN estimates. The sector employed 2.7% of wage-earners in 2004. Construction activity was reported to have increased in 2010.

Energy is derived principally from hydroelectric power, with solar energy being increasingly utilized. Mineral fuels accounted for 23.7% of the total import costs in 2007. Several potential petroleum-producing areas in the islands have been identified. Coconut bio-fuel has been introduced in some areas. Electricity output totalled 75m. kWh in 2009.

Service industries contributed 56.9% of GDP in 2009, according to UN estimates, and engaged 64.9% of wage-earners in 2004. Earnings from the tourism sector reached only US $10.3m. in 2006, compared with $13m. in 1998. Tourist arrivals were estimated to have increased from 13,748 in 2007 to 16,264 in 2008. According to figures from the ADB, during 2000–09 services GDP increased by an annual average of 1.8%, rising by 4.6% in 2009.

In 2009 there was a visible trade deficit of US $75.78m. and a deficit of $207.90m. on the current account of the balance of payments. In 2009 the principal sources of imports were Singapore (which accounted for 24.4%), Australia (22.7%), New Zealand, Fiji and Papua New Guinea, while the principal markets for exports were the People's Republic of China (50.3%), the Republic of Korea, the Philippines, Spain, Italy and Thailand. The principal exports in 2007 were timber, fish, palm oil, cocoa and copra. The principal imports were mineral fuels, foodstuffs, machinery and transport equipment, basic manufactures, beverages and tobacco.

The 2009 budget projected total expenditure of SI $1,701.6m., with revenue (including grants) expected to total SI $1,704.8m. According to the ADB, there was a fiscal surplus equivalent to 2.4% of GDP in 2010. Aid from Australia was projected at $A225.7m. in 2010/11. Financial assistance from New Zealand was budgeted at $NZ38.0m. in 2010/11. Assistance from the European Union (EU) was expected to amount to US $20m. in 2010. In 2009, according to the ADB, the country's external debt totalled US $134m. The cost of debt-servicing was equivalent to

SOLOMON ISLANDS

Statistical Survey

6.8% of the value of exports of goods and services in 2008. The average annual rate of inflation in Honiara in 2000–09 was 8.8%. The rate of inflation was estimated by the ADB to have declined from 7.1% in 2009 to 3.0% in 2010. The extent of the islands' informal sector impedes an accurate assessment of the rate of unemployment; however, youth unemployment, particularly in urban areas, has remained at a high level.

The economy of Solomon Islands remains one of the least developed in the Pacific region. Progress has been impeded by inadequate infrastructure and a very high rate of population growth. The country's major commodity exports are vulnerable to adverse weather conditions and to variations in prices on international markets. The regional intervention of 2003 (see Contemporary Political History) included an economic recovery programme involving increased assistance from Australia (totalling some $A1,000m. over 10 years). The destruction of numerous businesses in the rioting of early 2006 was a deterrent to potential investors. Furthermore, the islands' heavy dependence upon forestry, with logging being the prime constituent of both taxation and export revenues, has become a major economic, as well as environmental, concern. With the industry having continued to operate at an unsustainable rate, in April 2008 the new Government announced various measures to counter the detrimental impact of logging activities on the nation's forests. Henceforth all companies, including those engaged in the mining and agricultural sectors, were to be required to obtain a public environment report prior to commencing operations. With the onset of the global financial crisis in 2008 there were substantial rises in prices for essential commodities such as rice and petroleum; in August of that year the rate of inflation was reported to have reached a peak of 25%. Mainly owing to a substantial increase in log exports, in 2010 the economy recovered well from the decline of the previous year, with GDP growth reaching an estimated 4.0%. A significant decrease in the cost of rice imports helped to curtail inflationary pressures in 2010, but consumer prices were expected to increase once again in 2011 as the costs of fuel and other commodities rose. The Government's budget for 2011 accorded priority to the improvement of public services (notably education) through more efficient modes of expenditure; clarification of the complex land tenure system, in an attempt to attract greater investment, was also emphasized. The ADB anticipated that the commencement of commercial operations at the Australian-owned Gold Ridge gold mine on Guadalcanal in 2011 would contribute to an acceleration in the rate of GDP growth to 7.5% in that year.

PUBLIC HOLIDAYS

2012 (provisional): 2 January (for New Year's Day), 6–9 April (Easter), 4 June (Queen's Official Birthday), 11 June (Whit Monday), 7 July (Independence Day), 25–26 December (Christmas).

Statistical Survey

Source (unless otherwise indicated): National Statistics Office, Ministry of Finance, P.O. Box G6, Honiara; tel. (677) 27835; fax (677) 23951; e-mail Stats_management@mof.gov.sb; internet www.spc.int/prism/country/sb/stats.

AREA AND POPULATION

Area: 27,556 sq km (10,639 sq miles).

Population: 409,042 (males 211,381, females 197,661) at census of 21–22 November 1999; 515,870 at census of 21–22 November 2009 (provisional result). *Mid-2011* (Secretariat of the Pacific Community estimate): 564,303 (males 290,219, females 274,084) (Source: Pacific Regional Information System).

Density (mid-2011): 20.5 per sq km.

Population by Age and Sex (Secretariat of the Pacific Community estimates at mid-2011): *0–14:* 228,864 (males 118,091, females 110,773); *15–64:* 317,772 (males 163,115, females 154,657); *65 and over:* 17,667 (males 9,013, females 8,654); *Total* 564,303 (males 290,219, females 274,084) (Source: Pacific Regional Information System).

Ethnic Groups (census of November 1986): Melanesians 268,536; Polynesians 10,661; Micronesians 3,929; Europeans 1,107; Chinese 379; Others 564.

Principal Towns (population at 1999 census): Honiara (capital) 49,107; Noro 3,482; Gizo 2,960 (Source: Thomas Brinkhoff, *City Population*—internet www.citypopulation.de). *Mid-2009* (incl. suburbs, UN estimate) Honiara 71,921 (Source: UN, *World Urbanization Prospects: The 2009 Revision*).

Births and Deaths (annual averages, 2005–10, UN estimates): Birth rate 30.8 per 1,000; Death rate 6.2 per 1,000 (Source: UN, *World Population Prospects: The 2008 Revision*).

Life Expectancy (years at birth, WHO estimates): 70 (males 68; females 71) in 2008. Source: WHO, *World Health Statistics*.

Employment (excluding informal sector, 2004, estimates): Agriculture 6,342; Forestry 3,482; Fishing 5,114; Manufacturing (incl. mining and quarrying) 1,476; Electricity and water 469; Construction 1,397; Trade, restaurants and hotels 3,274; Transport, storage and communications 1,246; Finance, insurance, real estate and business services 806; Administration 6,758; Other community, social and personal service activities 21,757; Total 52,121. *2006* (excluding informal sector, estimate): Total employed 59,161. Source: IMF, *Solomon Islands: Tax summary and Statistical Appendix* (November 2008).

HEALTH AND WELFARE

Key Indicators

Total Fertility Rate (children per woman, 2008): 3.9.

Under-5 Mortality Rate (per 1,000 live births, 2008): 36.

Physicians (per 1,000 head, 2003): 0.1.

Hospital Beds (per 1,000 head, 2005): 1.5.

Health Expenditure (2007): US $ per head (PPP): 123.

Health Expenditure (2007): % of GDP: 4.6.

Health Expenditure (2007): public (% of total): 92.4.

Access to Water (% of persons, 2006): 70.

Access to Sanitation (% of persons, 2006): 32.

Total Carbon Dioxide Emissions ('000 metric tons, 2007): 197.9.

Carbon Dioxide Emissions Per Head (metric tons, 2007): 0.4.

Human Development Index (2010): ranking: 123.

Human Development Index (2010): value: 0.494.

For sources and definitions, see explanatory note on p. vi.

AGRICULTURE, ETC.

Principal Crops ('000 metric tons, 2008, FAO estimates, unless otherwise indicated): Coconuts 276; Oil palm fruit 188; Rice, paddy 2.8; Cocoa beans 4.7 (2009); Sweet potatoes 86; Yams 32; Taro 44; Vegetables (incl. melons) 8.2 (2009); Fruits (excl. melons) 21.3 (2009).

Livestock ('000 head, year ending September 2008, FAO estimates): Cattle 14.5; Pigs 55; Chickens 235. Note: No data were available for 2009.

Livestock Products (metric tons, 2009, FAO estimates): Cattle meat 740; Pig meat 2,320; Chicken meat 280; Hen eggs 488; Cows' milk 1,430.

Forestry ('000 cu m, 2009): *Roundwood Removals* (excl. bark): Sawlogs and veneer logs 1,233 (FAO estimate); Fuel wood 127 (FAO estimate); Total 1,360. *Sawnwood Production:* 27 (FAO estimate, all broadleaved, incl. railway sleepers).

Fishing (metric tons, live weight, 2008): Skipjack tuna 7,564; Yellowfin tuna 8,530; Bigeye tuna 88; Total catch (incl. others): 26,235 (FAO estimate). Note: Figures exclude FAO estimates of capture data for trochus shells (18 metric tons) and of aquaculture data for aquatic plants (144 metric tons).

Source: FAO.

MINING

Production (kilograms, 2006): Gold 10. Source: US Geological Survey.

SOLOMON ISLANDS

INDUSTRY

Production (metric tons, 2007, unless otherwise indicated): Copra 28,000; Coconut oil 741,000; Palm oil 22,000; Electric energy 75 million kWh (2009). Source: Asian Development Bank.

FINANCE

Currency and Exchange Rates: 100 cents = 1 Solomon Islands dollar (SI $). *Sterling, US Dollar and Euro Equivalents* (31 December 2010): £1 sterling = SI $12.625; US $1 = SI $8.065; €1 = SI $10.776; SI $100 = £7.92 = US $12.40 = €9.28. *Average Exchange Rate* (SI $ per US $): 7.7479 in 2008; 8.0550 in 2009; 8.0645 in 2010.

Budget (SI $ million, 2009): *Revenue:* Taxes 1,307.4; Non-tax revenue 181.3; Grants 216.0; Statistical discrepancy 3.6; Total 1,704.8. *Expenditure:* Total 1,701.6 (Current expenditure 1,427.2, Capital expenditure 274.4). Source: Asian Development Bank.

Official Development Assistance (US $ million, 2000): Bilateral 22.1; Multilateral 46.3; Total 68.4 (Grants 69.7, Loans –1.3). *2007:* Total 246.1. Source: UN, *Statistical Yearbook for Asia and the Pacific*.

International Reserves (excl. gold, US $ million at 31 December 2010): IMF special drawing rights 14.26; Reserve position in IMF 0.85; Foreign exchange 250.73; *Total* 265.84. Source: IMF, *International Financial Statistics*.

Money Supply (SI $ million at 31 December 2009): Currency outside depository corporations 305.22; Transferable deposits 822.33; Other deposits 703.20; *Broad money* 1,830.75. Source: IMF, *International Financial Statistics*.

Cost of Living (Consumer Price Index for Honiara, average of quarterly figures; base: October–December 1992 = 100): 342.8 in 2006; 369.0 in 2007; 433.0 in 2008; 443.7 in 2009. Source: Asian Development Bank.

Gross Domestic Product (SI $ million at constant 2005 prices): 372.5 in 2007; 399.8 in 2008; 391.1 in 2009. Source: UN Statistics Division, National Accounts Main Aggregates Database.

Expenditure on the Gross Domestic Product (SI $ million at current prices, 2009): Government final consumption expenditure 2,117.4; Private final consumption expenditure 4,254.9; Changes in inventories 72.3; Gross fixed capital formation 727.9; *Total domestic expenditure* 7,172.5; Exports of goods and services 2,004.1; *Less* Imports of goods and services 3,127.2; Statistical discrepancy –295.7; *GDP in purchasers' values* 5,753.7. Source: UN Statistics Division, National Accounts Main Aggregates Database.

Gross Domestic Product by Economic Activity (SI $ million at current prices, 2009): Agriculture, hunting, forestry and fishing 2,012.4; Mining, manufacturing and utilities 384.7 (Manufacturing 298.7); Construction 38.9; Trade, restaurants and hotels 780.5; Transport, storage and communications 536.8; Other services 1,893.5; *Gross value added* 5,646.8; Net taxes on products 106.9 (obtained as residual); *GDP in market prices* 5,753.7. Source: UN Statistics Division, National Accounts Main Aggregates Database.

Balance of Payments (US $ million, 2009): Exports of goods f.o.b. 163.42; Imports of goods f.o.b. –239.19; *Trade balance* –75.78; Exports of services 72.48; Imports of services –98.92; *Balance on goods and services* –102.22; Other income received 12.91; Other income paid –138.12; *Balance on goods, services and income* –227.42; Current transfers received 31.80; Current transfers paid –12.28; *Current balance* –207.90; Capital account (net) 27.09; Direct investment abroad –2.98; Direct investment from abroad 117.65; Other investments assets 13.88; Other investment liabilities 14.90; Net errors and omissions 6.52; *Overall balance* –30.85. Source: IMF, *International Finance Statistics*.

EXTERNAL TRADE

Principal Commodities (SI $ '000, 2007): *Imports c.i.f.:* Food and live animals 231,381; Mineral fuels, etc. 434,324; Basic manufactures 95,429; Machinery and transport equipment 206,847; Total (incl. others) 1,836,334. *Exports f.o.b.:* Fish 151,392; Copra 36,768; Palm oil 105,281; Timber 838,693; Cocoa 70,838; Total (incl. others) 1,285,651.

Principal Trading Partners (US $ million, 2009): *Imports:* Australia 69.5; China, People's Republic 11.9; Fiji 13.6; India 7.4; Japan 9.7; Malaysia 12.1; New Zealand 15.0; Papua New Guinea 13.2; Singapore 74.4; Thailand 6.5; Total (incl. others) 305.5. *Exports:* Australia 4.0; China, People's Republic 162.0; Italy 11.2; Japan 6.1; Korea, Republic 18.6; Malaysia 6.1; Papua New Guinea 4.1; Philippines 18.1; Spain 14.5; Thailand 10.8; Total (incl. others) 322.1. Note: Data reflect the IMF's direction of trade methodology and, as a result, the totals may not be equal to those presented for trade in commodities.

Source: Asian Development Bank.

TRANSPORT

Road Traffic (motor vehicles in use at 30 June 1986): Passenger cars 1,350; Commercial vehicles 2,026.

Shipping: *Traffic* (international traffic, '000 metric tons, 1990): Goods loaded 278; Goods unloaded 349 (Source: UN, *Monthly Bulletin of Statistics*). *Merchant Fleet* (registered at 31 December 2009): Vessels 38; Total displacement ('000 grt) 12.9 (Source: IHS Fairplay, *World Fleet Statistics*).

Civil Aviation (traffic on scheduled services, 2006): Kilometres flown 3 million; Passengers carried 101,000; Passenger-km 85 million; Total ton-km 8. Source: UN, *Statistical Yearbook*.

TOURISM

Visitor Arrivals by Country (2008): Australia 7,413; Japan 589; New Zealand 1,097; Papua New Guinea 906; United Kingdom 457; USA 1,105; Vanuatu 518; Total (incl. others) 16,264.

Tourism Receipts (US $ million, excl. passenger transport, unless otherwise indicated): 8.1 in 2005 (incl. passenger transport); 10.3 in 2006 (incl. passenger transport); 3.5 in 2007; 3.5 in 2008.

Source: World Tourism Organization.

COMMUNICATIONS MEDIA

Non-daily Newspapers (1996): 3; estimated circulation 9,000.

Radio Receivers (1997): 57,000 in use.

Television Receivers (2001): 12,000 in use.

Telephones (2009): 8,200 main lines in use.

Mobile Cellular Telephones (2009): 30,000 subscribers.

Personal Computers: 22,000 (46.4 per 1,000 persons) in 2005.

Internet Users (2009): 10,000.

Broadband Subscribers (2009): 2,000.

Sources: UNESCO, *Statistical Yearbook*; International Telecommunication Union.

EDUCATION

Pre-primary (2002/03): 16,469 pupils.

Primary: 523 schools (1993); 3,014 teachers (1999); 83,232 pupils (2006/07).

Secondary: 23 schools (1993); 1,337 teachers (2000); 27,332 pupils (2006/07).

Overseas Centres (1988): 405 students.

Source: UNESCO, *Statistical Yearbook*; UNESCO Institute for Statistics.

Adult Literacy Rate (estimate based on census data): 76.6% in 2003. Source: UN Development Programme, *Human Development Report*.

SOLOMON ISLANDS

Directory

The Government

HEAD OF STATE

Queen: HM Queen ELIZABETH II.
Governor-General: FRANK OFAGIORO KABUI (sworn in 7 July 2009).

CABINET
(May 2011)

The Government is formed by the National Coalition for Reform and Advancement, which includes the Reformed Democratic Party, the Independent Democratic Party, the Solomon Islands Democratic Party, OUR Party, independents and others.

Prime Minister: DANNY PHILIP.
Deputy Prime Minister and Minister for Home Affairs: MANASSEH MAELANGA.
Minister for Foreign Affairs and Trade Relations: PETER SHANEL AGOVAKA.
Minister for Finance and Treasury: GORDON DARCY LILO.
Minister for Commerce, Industry and Employment: ELIJAH DORO MUALA.
Minister for Development Planning and Aid Co-ordination: SNYDER RINI.
Minister for Agriculture and Livestock: CONNELLY SANDAKABATU.
Minister for Fisheries and Marine Resources: (vacant).
Minister for Forestry: BRADLEY TOVOSIA.
Minister for Communication and Aviation: ANDREW HANARIA KENIASINA.
Minister for Culture and Tourism: SAMUEL MANETOALI.
Minister for Education and Human Resources Development: DICKSON HA'AMORI.
Minister for Energy, Mines and Rural Electrification: MOSES GARU.
Minister for Environment, Conservation and Meteorology: JOHN MOFFAT FUGUI.
Minister for Health and Medical Services: CHARLES SIGOTO.
Minister for Infrastructure Development: JACKSON FIULAUA.
Minister for Justice and Legal Affairs: COMMINS ASTON MEWA.
Minister for Lands, Housing and Survey: JOSEPH ONIKA.
Minister for National Unity, Peace and Reconciliation: HYPOLITE TAREMAE.
Minister for Police, National Security and Correctional Services: CLAY FORAU SOALAOI.
Minister for Provincial Government and Institutional Strengthening: WALTER FOLOTALU.
Minister for Public Service: RICKY HOUENIOPWELA.
Minister for Women, Youth and Children's Affairs: DICKSON MUA.
Minister of Rural Development and Indigenous Affairs: LIONEL ALEX.

MINISTRIES

Office of the Prime Minister: POB G1, Honiara; tel. 21867; fax 26088; internet www.pmc.gov.sb.
Ministry of Agriculture and Livestock Development: POB G13, Honiara; tel. 27987; fax 28365; e-mail psagriculture@pmc.gov.sb.
Ministry of Commerce, Industries, Labour and Immigration: Honiara; tel. 28614; fax 25084; e-mail commerce@commerce.gov.sb; internet www.commerce.gov.sb.
Ministry of Communication and Aviation: Honiara; tel. 28049; fax 28054.
Ministry of Culture and Tourism: POB G26, Honiara; tel. 26848; fax 26875.
Ministry of Development Planning and Aid Co-ordination: Honiara; tel. 28608; fax 30163.
Ministry of Education and Human Resources: POB G28, Honiara; tel. 28643; fax 22042; e-mail pseducation@pmc.gov.sb.
Ministry of Energy, Mines and Rural Electrification: POB G37, Honiara; tel. 28609; fax 25811; e-mail psmines@pmc.gov.sb.
Ministry of Environment, Conservation and Meteorology: Honiara; tel. 28611; fax 28735; e-mail psforestry@pmc.gov.sb.
Ministry of Finance and Treasury: POB 26, Honiara; tel. 24102; fax 28619; e-mail psfinance@pmc.gov.sb.
Ministry of Fisheries and Marine Resources: POB G13, Honiara; tel. 39143; e-mail psfisheries@pmc.gov.sb.
Ministry of Foreign Affairs and External Trade: POB G10, Honiara; tel. 28612; fax 20351; e-mail psforeign@pmc.gov.sb.
Ministry of Forestry: POB G13, Honiara; tel. 28611; fax 28735.
Ministry of Health and Medical Services: POB 349, Honiara; tel. 20830; fax 20085; e-mail pshealth@pmc.gov.sb.
Ministry of Home Affairs: POB G11, Honiara; tel. 28602; fax 25591; e-mail psaffairs@pmc.gov.sb.
Ministry of Infrastructure Development: POB G30, Honiara; tel. 28605; fax 28705; e-mail kudu@mnpd.gov.sb.
Ministry of Justice and Legal Affairs: Honiara; tel. 21632; fax 22702; e-mail hclibrary@courts.gov.sb.
Ministry of Lands, Housing and Survey: POB G38, Honiara; tel. 22750; fax 27298; e-mail pslands@pmc.gov.sb.
Ministry of National Unity, Reconciliation and Peace: POB 1548, Honiara; tel. 28616.
Ministry of Police, National Security and Correctional Services: POB G1723, Honiara; tel. 28607; fax 28423; e-mail pspolice@pmc.gov.sb.
Ministry of Provincial Government and Institutional Strengthening: POB G35, Honiara; tel. 28606; fax 28708; e-mail psprovincial@pmc.gov.sb.
Ministry of Public Service: POB G1, Honiara; tel. 28617; fax 25559; e-mail pspublic@pmc.gov.sb.
Ministry of Rural Development and Indigenous Affairs: Honiara; tel. 25238; fax 22170.
Ministry of Women, Youth and Children's Affairs: Honiara; tel. 28602; fax 23547.

Legislature

National Parliament

POB G19, Honiara; tel. 21751; fax 23866; internet www.parliament.gov.sb.

Speaker: Sir ALLAN KEMAKEZA.

General Election, 4 August 2010 (provisional results)

Party	Seats
Solomon Islands Democratic Party	12
Ownership, Unity and Responsibility (OUR) Party	3
Solomon Islands Party for Rural Advancement	3
Independent Democratic Party	1
National Party	1
Rural and Urban Political Party	1
Solomon Islands Liberal Party	1
Independents and others	28
Total	**50**

Note: in many cases party affiliations were subject to review in the immediate aftermath of the election.

Election Commission

Electoral Commission: Ministry of Home Affairs, POB 1500, Honiara; tel. 21198; fax 26161; Chair. Sir PETER KENILOREA; Chief Electoral Officer POLYCARP HAUNUNU.

Political Organizations

Parties in the National Parliament can have a fluctuating membership and an influence disproportionate to their representation. There is a significant number of independents who are loosely associated in the amorphous, but often decisive, 'Independent Group'. The following parties represent the main groupings:

Autonomous Solomon Islanders Party: Honiara; f. 2010; advocates return of Solomon Islands' ownership to the people; Pres. ELIJAH OWA.

SOLOMON ISLANDS

Independent Democratic Party: c/o National Parliament, POB G19, Honiara; f. 2004; fmrly the Assen of Independent Members of Parliament; Sec.-Gen. SNYDER RINI; Pres. Sir THOMAS CHAN.

National Party: c/o National Parliament, POB G19, Honiara; f. 1996; Leader FRANCIS BILLY HILLY.

Ownership, Unity and Responsibility (OUR) Party: c/o National Parliament, POB G19, Honiara; f. 2010; est. by opponents of Govt of Derek Sikua; Pres. MANASSEH SOGAVARE; Interim Gen. Sec. PATTERSON OTI.

People's Alliance Party (PAP): Honiara; f. 1979; est. by merger of People's Progressive Party (f. 1973) and Rural Alliance Party (f. 1977); advocates establishment of a federal republic; Pres. JAMES MEKAB; Sec. EDWARD KINGMELE.

People's Congress Party: Honiara; f. 2010; advocates reform of the Rural Constituency Development Fund; Leader FRED FONO.

People's Federation Party: Honiara; f. 2010; aims to improve national infrastructure, education, health and medical services, and the stability of the political culture; Sec.-Gen. RUDDOLF DORAH.

Reformed Democratic Party: c/o National Parliament, POB G19, Honiara; f. 2010; Pres. DANNY PHILIP.

Rural and Urban Political Party (RUPP): Honiara; f. 2010; Pres. SAMUEL MANETOALI.

Solomon Islands Democratic Party: c/o National Parliament, POB G19, Honiara; campaigns for self-reliance and for ending of country's dependence on external aid; Leader STEVE WILLIAM ABANA; Gen. Sec. JOHN KENIAPISIA.

Solomon Islands Liberal Party (SILP): c/o National Parliament, POB G19, Honiara; f. 1976; est. as National Democratic Party (NADEPA); present name adopted in 1986; Leader RICHARD ULU-FA'ALU.

Solomon Islands Party for Rural Advancement (SIPRA): Honiara; f. 2006; advocates the decentralization of powers and the recognition of community governance structures and traditional values; Pres. and Leader JOB DUDLEY TAUSINGA; Deputy Pres. GORDON DARCY LILO.

Other parties that contested the 2010 election included the Direct Development Party (f. 2010 by Dick Ha'amori), New Nations Solomon Islands Party (f. 2010 by Belani Tekulu), People's Power Action Party (f. 2010 by Robert Wales Feratelia), Rural Congress People's Party (f. 2010 by Rev. Milton Talasasa), United Party (interim Pres. Joel Konofilia), Twelve Pillars to Peace and Prosperity Party (TP4, f. 2010 by Delmah Nori to represent the views of women).

Diplomatic Representation

EMBASSIES AND HIGH COMMISSIONS IN SOLOMON ISLANDS

Australia: Hibiscus Ave, POB 589, Honiara; tel. 21561; fax 23691; e-mail austhoniara.enquiries@dfat.gov.au; internet www.solomonislands.embassy.gov.au; High Commissioner MATTHEW ANDERSON.

Japan: Mendana Ave, POB 560, Honiara; tel. 22953; fax 21006; Chargé d'affaires AKIRA IWANADE.

New Zealand: Mendana Ave, POB 697, Honiara; tel. 21502; fax 22377; e-mail nzhicom@solomon.com.sb; High Commissioner MARK RAMSDEN.

Papua New Guinea: POB 1109, Honiara; tel. 20561; fax 20562; High Commissioner AIWA OLMI.

Taiwan (Republic of China): Bairiki, Tarawa; tel. 22557; fax 22535; e-mail Kir@mofa.gov.tw; Ambassador BENJAMIN HO.

United Kingdom: Telekom House, Mendana Ave, POB 676, Honiara; tel. 21705; fax 21549; e-mail bhc@solomon.com.sb; internet ukinsolomonislands.fco.gov.uk; High Commissioner TIMOTHY SMART.

Judicial System

The High Court is a Superior Court of Record with unlimited original jurisdiction and powers (except over customary land) as prescribed by the Solomon Islands Constitution or by any law for the time being in force in Solomon Islands. The Judges of the High Court are the Chief Justice, resident in Solomon Islands and employed by its Government, and the Puisne Judges (of whom there are usually three). Appeals from this Court go to the Court of Appeal, the members of which are senior judges from Australia, New Zealand and Papua New Guinea. The Chief Justice and judges of the High Court are ex officio members of the Court of Appeal.

In addition there are Magistrates' Courts staffed by qualified and lay magistrates exercising limited jurisdiction in both civil and criminal matters. There are also Local Courts staffed by elders of the local communities, which have jurisdiction in the areas of established native custom, petty crime and local government by-laws. In 1975 Customary Land Appeal Courts were established to hear land appeal cases from Local Courts, which have exclusive original jurisdiction over customary land cases.

Office of the Registrar: High Court and Court of Appeal, POB G21, Honiara; tel. 21632; fax 22702; Registrar of the High Court GAVIN WITHERS.

President of the Court of Appeal: Sir ROBIN AULD.

Chief Justice of the High Court: Sir ALBERT ROCKY PALMER.

Attorney-General: BILLY TITIULU.

Religion

More than 95% of the population profess Christianity, and the remainder follow traditional beliefs. According to the census of 1976, about 34% of the population adhered to the Church of Melanesia (Anglican), 19% were Roman Catholics, 17% belonged to the South Seas Evangelical Church, 11% to the United Church (Methodist) and 10% were Seventh-day Adventists. Most denominations are affiliated to the Solomon Islands Christian Association. In many areas Christianity is practised alongside traditional beliefs, especially ancestor worship.

CHRISTIANITY

Solomon Islands Christian Association: POB 1335, Honiara; tel. 23350; fax 26150; e-mail essica@solomon.com.sb; f. 1967; five full mems, seven assoc. mem. orgs; Chair. Most Rev. ADRIAN SMITH; Gen. Sec. EMMANUEL IYABORA.

The Anglican Communion

Anglicans in Solomon Islands are adherents of the Church of the Province of Melanesia, comprising eight dioceses: six in Solomon Islands (Central Melanesia, Malaita, Temotu, Ysabel, Hanuato'o and Central Solomons, which was established in May 1997) and two in Vanuatu (one of which also includes New Caledonia). The Archbishop is also Bishop of Central Melanesia and is based in Honiara. The Church had an estimated 180,000 members in 1988.

Archbishop of the Province of Melanesia: Rt Rev. DAVID VUNAGI, Archbishop's House, POB 19, Honiara; tel. 21892; fax 21098; e-mail epogo@comphq.org.sb.

General Secretary: GEORGE KIRIAU, Provincial Headquarters, POB 19, Honiara; tel. 21892; fax 21098; e-mail gkiriau@comphq.oeg.sb.

The Roman Catholic Church

For ecclesiastical purposes, Solomon Islands comprises one archdiocese and two dioceses. At 31 December 2007 there were an estimated 101,564 adherents in the country. The Bishops participate in the Bishops' Conference of Papua New Guinea and Solomon Islands (based in Papua New Guinea).

Archbishop of Honiara: Most Rev. ADRIAN THOMAS SMITH, Holy Cross, GPOB 237, Honiara; tel. 21943; fax 26426; e-mail chancery@solomon.com.sb.

Other Christian Churches

Assembly of God: POB 928, Honiara; tel. and fax 25512; f. 1971; Gen. Supt Rev. JERIEL OTASUI.

Christian Fellowship Church: Church, Paradise, Munda, Western Province; f. 1960; over 5,000 mems in 24 villages; runs 12 primary schools in Western Province.

Seventh-day Adventist Mission: POB 63, Honiara; tel. 21191; over 9,000 mems on Guadalcanal and over 6,800 on Malaita (Oct. 2000); Pres. of Western Pacific Region NEIL WATTS; Sec. Pastor J. PIUKI TASA.

South Seas Evangelical Church: POB 16, Honiara; tel. 22388; fax 20302; Pres. ERIC TAKILA; Gen. Sec. CHARLES J. RAFEASI.

United Church in Solomon Islands: POB 82, Munda, Western Province; tel. 61125; fax 61143; e-mail ucsihq@solomon.com.sb; a Methodist church; Bishop of Solomon Islands Region Rev. PHILEMON RITI; Gen. Sec. GINA TEBULU.

BAHÁ'Í FAITH

National Spiritual Assembly: POB 245, Honiara; tel. 22475; fax 25368; e-mail bahainsa@welkam.solomon.com.sb.

ISLAM

Solomon Islands Muslim League: POB 219, Honiara; tel. 21773; fax 24243; Gen. Sec. Dr MUSTAPHA RAMO; 66 mems.

SOLOMON ISLANDS

The Press

Agrikalsa Nius (Agriculture News): POB G13, Honiara; tel. 21211; fax 21955; f. 1986; monthly; Editor ALFRED MAESULIA; circ. 1,000.

Citizens' Press: Honiara; monthly.

Link: Solomon Islands Development Trust, POB 147, Honiara; tel. 21130; fax 21131; pidgin and English; 3 or 4 a year.

Solomon Nius: POB 718, Honiara; tel. 22031; fax 26401; monthly; Dept of Information publication; Editor-in-Chief THOMAS KIVO; monthly; circ. 2,000.

Solomon Star: POB 255, Honiara; tel. 22062; fax 25290; e-mail solstar@solomon.com.sb; internet www.solomonstarnews.com; f. 1982; daily; English; Dir JOHN W. LAMANI; Editor EDNAL PALMER; circ. 7,000.

Solomon Times: POB 707, Honiara; tel. 23272; fax 39197; internet www.solomontimes.com; daily; online newspaper; Chief Editor and Man. Dir EDWARD KINGMELE.

Solomon Voice: POB 1235, Honiara; tel. 20116; fax 20090; f. 1992; weekly; circ. 10,000; Editor CAROL COLVILLE.

Broadcasting and Communications

TELECOMMUNICATIONS

The Telecommunications Bill 2009, approved by Parliament in August of that year, ended the long-standing monopoly of the Solomon Telekom Company. In December 2010 the Telecommunications Commission announced plans to invite bids for a third telecommunications licence.

Regulatory Authority

Telecommunications Commission of the Solomon Islands (TCSI): POB 2180, Honiara; tel. 23855; fax 23860; internet www.tcsi.org.sb; f. 2010; Commr NICHOLAS WILLIAMS.

Service Providers

Bemobile: 50% owned by Telikom PNG Pty Ltd; provides mobile telephone services; commenced operations in August 2010; CEO MICHAEL AH KOY.

Telekom (Solomon Telekom Company Ltd): Mendana Ave, POB 148, Honiara; tel. 21576; fax 23110; e-mail info@ourtelekom.com.sb; internet www.solomon.com.sb; 64.74% owned by Solomon Islands National Provident Fund, 32.58% by Cable and Wireless plc, 2.68% by Investment Corpn of Solomon Islands; operates national and international telecommunications links; Chair. JOHN BEVERLEY; Chief Exec. LOYLEY NGIRA.

BROADCASTING

Radio

Solomon Islands Broadcasting Corporation: POB 654, Honiara; tel. 20051; fax 23159; e-mail sibcnews@solomon.com.sb; internet www.sibconline.com.sb; f. 1976; daily transmissions in English and pidgin; broadcasts total 112 hours per week; Chair. AUGUSTINE TANEKO; Gen. Man. CORNELIUS RATHAMANA; Editor WALTER NALANGU.

Finance

BANKING

(cap. = capital; res = reserves; dep. = deposits; brs = branches; amounts in Solomon Islands dollars)

Central Bank

Central Bank of Solomon Islands: POB 634, Honiara; tel. 21791; fax 23513; e-mail info@cbsi.com.sb; internet www.cbsi.com.sb; f. 1983; sole bank of issue; cap. 20m., res 248.1m., dep.359.5m. (Dec. 2008); Gov. DENTON RARAWA; Deputy Gov. GANE SIMBE.

Development Bank

Development Bank of Solomon Islands: POB 911, Honiara; tel. 21595; fax 23715; e-mail dbsi@welkam.solomon.com.sb; f. 1978; declared insolvent in Sept. 2004 and placed under the administration of the Central Bank of Solomon Islands; Chair. JOHN MICHAEL ASIPARA; Man. Dir LUKE LAYMAN ETA; 4 brs; 5 sub-brs.

Commercial Banks

Australia and New Zealand Banking Group Ltd (Australia): Mud Alley, POB 10, Honiara; tel. 21111; fax 26937; e-mail solomons@anz.com; internet www.anz.com/SolomonIslands; Gen. Man. BARRY SOWMAN.

Bank South Pacific Ltd (Papua New Guinea): tel. 21874; fax 24674; e-mail bsp@solomon.com.sb; internet www.bsp.com.sb; fmrly National Bank of Solomon Islands Ltd; became br. of Bank of South Pacific Ltd following acquisition in 2007; Gen. Man. MARK CORCORAN.

Westpac Banking Corporation (Australia): National Provident Fund Bldg, 721 Mendana Ave, POB 466, Honiara; tel. 21222; fax 23419; e-mail westpacsolomons@westpac.com.au; internet www.westpac.com.sb; Man. GIAN TAVIANI.

INSURANCE

A number of British and Australian insurance companies maintain agencies in Solomon Islands.

Trade and Industry

GOVERNMENT AGENCY

Investment Corporation of Solomon Islands: POB 570, Honiara; tel. 22511; fax 21263; holding company through which the Government retains equity stakes in a number of corporations; Chair. (vacant).

DEVELOPMENT ORGANIZATION

Solomon Islands Development Trust (SIDT): POB 147, Honiara; tel. 23409; fax 21131; e-mail sidt@welkam.solomon.com.sb; f. 1982; development org.; Exec. Dir ABRAHAM BAENESIA.

CHAMBER OF COMMERCE

Solomon Islands Chamber of Commerce and Industry (SICCI): NPF Bldg, 2nd Floor, POB 650, Honiara; tel. 39542; fax 39544; e-mail sicci@solomon.com.sb; internet www.solomonchamber.com.sb; 69 member cos (July 2004); Chair. JAMES KIM; CEO CALVIN ZIRU.

INDUSTRIAL AND TRADE ASSOCIATIONS

Association of Mining and Exploration Companies: c/o POB G24, Honiara; f. 1988; Pres. NELSON GREG YOUNG.

Commodities Export Marketing Authority: POB 54, Honiara; tel. 22528; fax 21262; e-mail cema@solomon.com.sb; regulator of agricultural commodities such as coconut, cocoa, coffee, palm oil, spices and ngali nut products; agencies at Honiara, Noro and Yandina; Chair. (vacant); Gen. Man. PITAKIA MOSES PELOMO.

Livestock Development Authority: POB 525, Honiara; tel. 29649; fax 22214; f. 1977; privatized 1996; Man. Dir WARREN TUCKER.

Solomon Islands Small Business Enterprise Centre: POB 972, Honiara; tel. 26650; fax 26653; e-mail manager.sbec@solomon.com.sb; Man. RILEY MESEPITU.

Solomon Islands Forest Industries Association: POB 1617, Honiara; tel. 26026; fax 20267; Chair. and Sec. KAIPUA TOHI.

EMPLOYERS' ORGANIZATIONS

Chinese Association: POB 1209, Honiara; tel. 22351; fax 23480; asscn of business people from the ethnic Chinese community.

Federation of Solomon Islands Business: POB 320, Honiara; tel. 22902; fax 21477.

UTILITIES

Electricity

Solomon Islands Electricity Authority (SIEA): POB 6, Honiara; tel. 39422; fax 39472; e-mail mike@siea.com.sb; internet www.siea.com.sb; f. 1961; autonomous, govt-owned entity responsible for generation, transmission, distribution and sale of electrical energy; Chair. Hon. FRANCIS ZAMA; CEO MICHAEL NATION.

Water

Solomon Islands Water Authority (SIWA): POB 1407, Honiara; tel. 23985; fax 20723; f. 1994; Chair. (vacant); Gen. Man. DONALD MAKINI.

CO-OPERATIVE SOCIETIES

Central Co-operative Association (CCA): Honiara.

Salu Fishing Co-operative Association: POB 1041, Honiara; tel. 26550.

Solomon Islands Consumers Co-operative Society Ltd: Honiara; tel. 21798; fax 23640.

Western General Co-operative Association (WGCA): Gizo, Western Province.

SOLOMON ISLANDS

TRADE UNIONS

There are 14 registered trade unions in Solomon Islands.

Solomon Islands Council of Trade Unions (SICTU): National Centre for Trade Unions, POB 271, Honiara; tel. 22566; fax 23171; f. 1986; Pres. DAVID P. TUHANUKU; Sec. TONY KAGOVAI; the principal affiliated unions are:

Media Association of Solomon Islands (MASI): POB 654, Honiara; tel. 20051; fax 23300; e-mail sibcnews@welkam.solomon.com.sb; Pres. GEORGE HERMING.

Solomon Islands Medical Association: Honiara.

Solomon Islands National Teachers' Association (SINTA): POB 967, Honiara; f. 1985; Pres. K. SANGA; Gen. Sec. JOHN HOUAINIMA.

Solomon Islands Post and Telecommunications Union: Honiara; tel. 21821; fax 20440; Gen. Man. SAMUEL SIVE.

Solomon Islands Public Employees' Union (SIPEU): POB 360, Honiara; tel. 21967; fax 23110; Pres. MARTIN KARANI; Sec.-Gen. PAUL BELANDE.

Solomon Islands Seamen's Association: POB G32, Honiara; tel. 24942; fax 23798.

Transport

ROADS

There are about 1,391 km of roads maintained by the central and provincial governments. In addition, there are 800 km of privately maintained roads mainly for plantation use. Honiara has a main road running about 65 km each side of it along the north coast of Guadalcanal, and Malaita has a road 157 km long running north of Auki and around the northern end of the island to the Lau Lagoon, where canoe transport takes over; and one running south for 35 km to Masa. On Makira a road links Kira Kira and Kakoranga, a distance of 35 km.

SHIPPING

Regular shipping services (mainly cargo) exist between Solomon Islands and Australia, New Zealand, Hong Kong, Japan, Singapore, Taiwan and European ports. The four main ports are at Honiara, Yandina, Noro and Gizo.

Solomon Islands Ports Authority: POB 307, Honiara; tel. 22646; fax 23994; e-mail ports@solomon.com.sb; f. 1956; responsible for the ports of Honiara and Noro; Chair. (vacant); Gen. Man. WILLIAM BARILE.

Sullivans (SI) Ltd: POB 3, Honiara; tel. 21643; fax 23889; e-mail shipping@sullivans.com.sb; shipping agents, importers, wholesalers; CEO KEVIN CHANT.

Tradco Shipping Ltd: POB 114, Honiara; tel. 22588; fax 23887; e-mail tradco@solomon.com.sb; f. 1984; shipping agents; Man. Dir GERALD STENZEL.

CIVIL AVIATION

Two airports are open to international traffic and a further 25 serve internal flights. Air Niugini (Papua New Guinea) and Qantas (Australia) fly to Honiara International Airport (located 13 km from the capital).

Director of Civil Aviation: DEMETRIUS T. PIZIKI.

Solomon Airlines Limited: POB 23, Honiara; tel. 20031; fax 20232; e-mail it.man@flysolomons.com; internet www.flysolomons.com; f. 1968; govt-owned; international and domestic operator; scheduled services between Honiara and Port Moresby (Papua New Guinea), Nadi (Fiji), Brisbane (Australia) and Port Vila (Vanuatu); Chair. BILL TYSON; CEO RON SUMSUM.

Tourism

The development of the tourism sector is hindered by the relative inaccessibility of the islands and the inadequacy of tourist facilities. In 2008 tourism receipts (excluding passenger transport) amounted to an estimated US $3.5m. Tourist arrivals were reported to have risen from 13,748 in 2007 to 16,264 in 2008.

Solomon Islands Tourism Industry Association (SITIA): Honiara; tel. 26848; fax 26875; f. 2008; Pres. WILSON MAELAUA.

Solomon Islands Visitors Bureau: POB 321, Honiara; tel. 22442; fax 23986; e-mail info@sivb.com.sb; internet www.visitsolomons.com.sb; f. 1980; Gen. Man. MICHAEL TOKURU; Marketing Man. FREDA UNUSI.

Defence

In July 2003, as the security situation on Guadalcanal deteriorated, the Regional Assistance Mission to Solomon Islands (RAMSI), an Australian-led force comprising more than 2,500 troops and police from various countries in the region, arrived in Solomon Islands to restore law and order. Assisting the local security forces, RAMSI personnel remained in the country at mid-2010.

Commissioner of Police: WALTER KOLA (acting).

Education

About two-thirds of school-age children receive formal education, mainly in state schools. About 30% of the children who complete a primary school education receive secondary schooling, either in one of eight national secondary schools (at least one of which is run by the Government and the remainder by various churches) or in one of 12 provincial secondary schools, which are run by provincial assemblies. The provincial secondary schools provide curricula of a practical nature, with a bias towards agriculture, while the national secondary schools offer more academic courses.

In 1993 there were 523 primary schools and 23 secondary schools. In 2002/03 pre-primary pupils numbered 16,469. In 2006/07 primary pupils totalled 83,232 and secondary students numbered 27,332. In 2003 the Church of Melanesia announced plans to establish a new secondary school in each of the country's six dioceses. There are two teacher-training schools and a technical institute. According to the 1999 census, 57% of children aged between five and 14 attended school. In 2006/07 the total enrolment at primary schools was equivalent to 67% of children in the relevant age group, while enrolment in secondary schools included only 30% of children in the relevant age-group. Scholarships are available for higher education at various universities overseas. In 1977 the Solomon Islands Centre of the University of the South Pacific (based in Fiji) opened in Honiara. Central government expenditure on education in 1991 was SI $24m., or 7.9% of total spending.

SOMALIA

Introductory Survey

LOCATION, CLIMATE, LANGUAGE, RELIGION, FLAG, CAPITAL

The Somali Republic lies on the east coast of Africa, with Ethiopia to the north-west and Kenya to the west. There is a short frontier with Djibouti to the north-west. Somalia has a long coastline on the Indian Ocean and the Gulf of Aden, forming the 'Horn of Africa'. The climate is generally hot and dry, with an average annual temperature of 27°C (80°F). It is hotter in the interior and on the Gulf of Aden, but cooler on the Indian Ocean coast. Average annual rainfall is less than 430 mm (17 ins). The national language is Somali, but Arabic is also in official use. English and Italian are widely spoken. The state religion is Islam, and the majority of Somalis are Sunni Muslims. There is a small Christian community, mostly Roman Catholics. The national flag (proportions 2 by 3) is pale blue, with a large five-pointed white star in the centre. The capital is Mogadishu.

CONTEMPORARY POLITICAL HISTORY

Historical Context

Somalia was formed by a merger of two former colonial territories: British Somaliland, in the north, and its larger and more populous neighbour, Italian Somaliland. The United Kingdom established a protectorate in British Somaliland in 1886. Italian Somaliland originated in 1889, when Italy concluded agreements with two local rulers, who placed their territories under Italian protection. Italy's occupation of the region was subsequently extended along the coast and inland, and Italian control was completed in 1927. During the Second World War British Somaliland was conquered temporarily by Italian troops, but in 1941 it was recaptured by a British counter-offensive, which also forced the Italians to withdraw from Eritrea, Italian Somaliland and Ethiopia. A British military administration was then established in British and Italian Somaliland.

Under the provisions of the post-war peace treaty of February 1947, Italy renounced all rights to Italian Somaliland. In December 1950, however, the pre-war colony became the UN Trust Territory of Somalia, with Italy returning as the administering power for a 10-year transitional period, prior to independence. The territory's first general election on the basis of universal adult suffrage was held in March 1959, when 83 of the 90 seats in the Legislative Assembly were won by the Somali Youth League (SYL), a pro-Western party led by the Prime Minister, Seyyid Abdullah Issa.

British Somaliland reverted to civilian rule in 1948. The British colonial authorities prepared the territory for self-government, and the first general election took place in March 1959. Fresh elections, for a new legislative council, were held in February 1960, with all parties in favour of early independence and the unification of all Somali territories. Representatives of British Somaliland and the Trust Territory of Somalia met in April and agreed on a merger of the two territories in an independent republic. British Somaliland was granted independence on 26 June, and the merger received unanimous approval by the legislature on the following day.

Accordingly, the union of former British and Italian Somaliland took effect on 1 July 1960, when the independent Somali Republic was proclaimed. Dr Aden Abdullah Osman, hitherto President of the legislature of the southern territory, was elected to be the first President of the new Republic, and the legislatures of the two Somali regions merged to create a single National Assembly. The two dominant parties in former British Somaliland joined with the SYL to form a tripartite coalition Government. Dr Abd ar-Rashid Ali Shermarke of the SYL became Prime Minister. In June 1964 Shermarke resigned as Prime Minister and was replaced by Abd ar-Razak Hussein, who formed a Cabinet exclusively from members of the SYL. In June 1967, however, Shermarke was elected by the National Assembly to replace President Osman. He appointed a new Cabinet, led by Mohamed Ibrahim Egal, the former Prime Minister of British Somaliland.

On 15 October 1969 President Shermarke was assassinated. Six days later the army seized control in a coup on the eve of a planned presidential election. Power was assumed by the armed forces' Commander-in-Chief, Maj.-Gen. Mohamed Siad Barre, who proclaimed the Somali Democratic Republic. The 1960 Constitution was suspended, political parties were abolished and the National Assembly was dissolved. In October 1970 Siad Barre declared Somalia a socialist state and began a revolutionary programme of national unification and social and economic reform. In July 1976 power was transferred to the newly formed Somali Revolutionary Socialist Party (SRSP), with Siad Barre as Secretary-General.

A new Constitution came into force in September 1979. Elections were held in December for a new legislature, the People's Assembly, which, in January 1980, elected Siad Barre as President of the Republic. Constitutional amendments, approved by the Assembly in November 1984, effectively transferred all powers of government to the President. Despite continuing internal unrest, at elections to the Assembly, in December, a single list of SRSP candidates was reportedly endorsed by 99.9% of voters.

A presidential election, at which Siad Barre was the sole candidate, took place in December 1986, confirming his presidency for a further seven-year term by 99.9% of a reported 4.9m. votes cast. Although Lt-Gen. Mohamed Ali Samater was appointed to the newly created post of Prime Minister in February 1987, the President continued to dominate Somalia's political life.

Domestic Political Affairs

Anti-Government demonstrations in Mogadishu in July 1989, in protest against the arrest of several leading Muslim clerics, were violently suppressed by the armed forces, resulting in the deaths of more than 400 demonstrators. Two recently created opposition groups, the United Somali Congress (USC—composed of Hawiye clan intellectuals) and the National United Front of Somalia (allegedly dominated by disaffected army officers), were thought to have orchestrated the demonstrations. In August there were reports of fighting between government troops and members of the Ogadeni clan in southern Somalia, and Western sources claimed that the only areas of the country that remained under government control were Mogadishu, parts of Hargeysa and Berbera.

As Siad Barre's authority declined, in July 1990 the Council of Ministers endorsed earlier proposals for the democratization of Somalia's political system. It was decided that, following a review by the People's Assembly, a new constitution would be submitted to a national referendum in October, and that multi-party legislative and local government elections would be held in February 1991. In August 1990 the USC, the Somali National Movement (SNM) and the Somali Patriotic Movement (SPM) agreed to co-ordinate their separate military campaigns to overthrow Siad Barre. In October the Government announced the immediate introduction of the new Constitution and a new electoral code. Siad Barre relinquished the post of Secretary-General of the SRSP, in accordance with the Constitution, which stipulated that the President should hold no responsibilities other than those of the presidency. Despite the apparent readiness of the new Government to hasten the process of political reform, the principal insurgent groups showed no signs of relaxing their military campaigns, and on 1 January 1991 the USC announced that it had captured most areas of Mogadishu and that it had besieged the home of Siad Barre. On 27 January Siad Barre was reported to have fled the capital with those forces remaining loyal to him, and the USC took power. It immediately invited all former opposition groups to participate in a national conference to discuss the democratization of Somalia. On 29 January the USC appointed Ali Mahdi Mohamed (a government minister in the 1960s) as President, in a temporary capacity, and he, in turn, invited Umar Arteh Ghalib (a former foreign affairs minister) to form a government that would prepare the country for democracy. The provisional Government was approved by the President on 2 February.

By mid-March 1991, however, Somalia was close to anarchy. Opposition movements rejected the USC's invitation to take part in a national conference, and the SNM was reported to have formed an 11-member administration and a legislature to govern the former territory of British Somaliland. In May the SNM announced its official support for the secession of that territory, and later that month the SNM Central Committee elected Abd ar-Rahman Ahmed Ali 'Tur' as President of the self-proclaimed 'Republic of Somaliland'. In June the Committee approved a 17-member government to administer the territory for a period of two years, after which free elections were to be held.

The SNM declined an invitation issued by the USC to participate in a conference of national reconciliation in June 1991, stating that it did not concern 'Somaliland'. The conference, convened in Djibouti, was attended by representatives of the USC, the Somali Democratic Movement (SDM), the SPM and the Democratic Front for the Salvation of Somalia, and mandated delegates from the four organizations to travel to 'Somaliland' to persuade the SNM to abandon its declaration of independence. The SNM insisted, however, that the secession of 'Somaliland' from Somalia was irreversible. At a second reconciliation conference in July the four groups that had met in June were joined by the United Somali Front (USF) and the Somali Democratic Alliance. The leaders of the six groups signed a manifesto, which, *inter alia*, committed them to defeat the forces of Siad Barre (which had regrouped as the Somali National Front—SNF), to readopt the 1960 Constitution, which Siad Barre had suspended in 1969, and to implement a general cease-fire. The manifesto also confirmed Ali Mahdi in his position as Somalia's President for a period of two years pending free elections. Ali Mahdi was sworn in as President on 18 August 1991, and in September he reappointed Ghalib as Prime Minister; in October the latter announced the formation of a newly expanded Government, comprising 72 ministers and deputy ministers, in order to ensure equal representation for the six participating groups.

Meanwhile, in June 1991 a major rift had developed within the USC, and supporters of President Ali Mahdi clashed with those of the USC's military commander, Gen. Mohamed Farah Aidid, in Mogadishu. Aidid objected to Ali Mahdi's assumption of the presidency, since he had commanded the military campaign to overthrow Siad Barre. In October Aidid rejected the legitimacy of the Government appointed earlier that month, and in November his faction launched a major offensive on the President's positions in the capital. The fighting intensified, and in December Ali Mahdi appealed to the UN to send a peace-keeping force to intervene in the conflict. The UN responded by sending a special envoy to Mogadishu in January 1992. However, the envoy's attempts met with failure, and the mission was followed by an escalation in violence. In mid-January Aidid appointed his own 21-member administration. By the end of March it was estimated that 14,000 people (mostly civilians) had been killed and 27,000 wounded in the hostilities in Mogadishu.

International intervention

In January 1992 the UN imposed an embargo on the sale of armaments to Somalia. In the following month the UN, the Organization of African Unity (OAU, now the African Union—AU, see p. 183), the League of Arab States (the Arab League, see p. 361) and the Organization of the Islamic Conference (OIC, see p. 400) issued a joint appeal for a cease-fire, stating that it was a prerequisite for the granting of humanitarian aid to Somalia. Representatives from the rival factions in Mogadishu subsequently agreed to the terms of a cease-fire accord devised by the international organizations. In March, in discussions with a joint mission of the UN, the OAU, the OIC and the Arab League in Mogadishu, Aidid agreed to the monitoring of the cease-fire by a foreign observer mission. In April the UN Security Council approved the establishment of a 'UN Operation in Somalia' (UNOSOM), comprising a 50-strong observer mission to monitor the cease-fire, while it also agreed, in principle, to dispatch forces to protect UN personnel and supplies at Mogadishu's port, and to escort food supplies to distribution points. However, the Security Council needed to obtain consent for the peace-keeping force from both parties involved in the conflict, and Aidid was opposed to the deployment of foreign military personnel in Somalia.

In April 1992 the SNF advanced to within 40 km of Mogadishu, but Gen. Aidid's militias decisively repelled them, pursuing them to the south of the country. Siad Barre fled, with some 200 supporters, to Kenya. (Siad Barre was refused political asylum in Kenya, and in May he moved to Nigeria, where he died in January 1995.) In May Aidid's forces and those of the SPM, the SDM and the Southern Somali National Movement (SSNM), with which he had formed a military alliance known as the Somali Liberation Army (SLA), captured Kismayu, which had been held by the SNF. By June the SLA was in control of most of central and southern Somalia. In late June the UN secured agreement from the principal factions in Mogadishu for the deployment of the observer mission envisaged in the March cease-fire accord. In August Aidid agreed to the deployment of 500 UN troops mandated with escorting food aid from Mogadishu's port and airport to distribution points.

Also in August 1992 the coalition of Gen. Aidid's faction of the USC with the SPM, the SDM and the SSNM was consolidated with the formation of the Somali National Alliance (SNA), of which Aidid was the leader. Meanwhile, Ali Mahdi strengthened ties with other armed groups hostile to Aidid, and forged links with Gen. Mohamed Siad Hersi 'Morgan' (who had led the SNF since the departure of his father-in-law, Siad Barre).

By November 1992 the 500 UN troops had still been prevented from implementing their mandate to secure delivery of food aid. The USA subsequently offered to lead a military operation in the country, which was sanctioned by the Security Council in early December. Shortly afterwards an advance contingent of 1,800 US marines landed on the beaches of Mogadishu and took control of the port and airport. The US members of the Unified Task Force (UNITAF) were reinforced subsequently by troops from 21 other countries.

In January 1993 14 of Somalia's political organizations attended peace negotiations in Addis Ababa, Ethiopia, under the auspices of the UN, which resulted in agreements on an immediate cease-fire, disarmament under UN supervision and the holding of a conference of national reconciliation in March, at which an accord providing for the establishment of a Transitional National Council as the supreme authority in Somalia, with a mandate to hold elections within two years, was reached. The Council was to comprise 74 members: one from each of the 15 organizations represented at the conference, three from each of the 18 proposed administrative regions (inclusive of 'Somaliland') and five from Mogadishu.

Agreement on the future government of Somalia was reached hours after the UN Security Council approved the establishment of UNOSOM II, which was to take over responsibility for maintaining security from UNITAF by 1 May 1993. UNOSOM II was to be the UN's largest ever peace-keeping operation, comprising 28,000 military personnel and 2,800 civilian staff, and its first where peace-enforcement without consent from parties within the country was authorized. UNOSOM II was, in addition, to be responsible for overseeing the rehabilitation of the country and the repatriation of Somali refugees. In May the USA transferred responsibility for international efforts in Somalia to UNOSOM II, the forces of which embarked on a series of armed initiatives, including air-strikes, against suspected strategic positions of the SNA. Despite the increased scale of UNOSOM operations, Aidid avoided injury or capture during June, prompting the Security Council to issue a formal warrant for his arrest. The violent deaths of three Italian UNOSOM soldiers in July provoked Italian media claims that the military emphasis of the mission, promoted by the USA in pursuit of Aidid, was threatening the security of UN personnel and jeopardizing diplomatic initiatives undertaken by the Italian Government. The situation was exacerbated by a US helicopter attack on a suspected pro-Aidid command centre, which resulted in the deaths of 50–100 Somalis, and the murder, in retaliation, of four foreign journalists by enraged Somali crowds.

Uncompromising media coverage of the deaths of three US soldiers in September 1993, and a violent exchange in the capital in October (which resulted in the deaths of some 300 Somalis, 18 US servicemen and the capture, by local militia, of a US helicopter pilot and a Nigerian soldier), prompted widespread public outrage in the USA. The US President, Bill Clinton, subsequently announced that all US troops were to be withdrawn by the end of March 1994, regardless of the outcome of attempts to negotiate a political settlement to the conflict by that date. Clinton's decision later in October 1993 to withdraw immediately the US special forces (which had been deployed to apprehend Aidid) prompted speculation that the release of the US pilot and the Nigerian soldier, secured in mid-October following discussions between representatives of the US Government and Aidid, had been achieved as part of an undisclosed bilateral agreement. Despite Aidid's declaration of a unilateral cease-fire prior to the talks, and subsequent indications of his willingness to enter into negotiations with the USA (in preference to the UN), fighting between pro-Aidid and pro-Mahdi factions escalated.

UN and US withdrawal

In February 1994, in the context of the imminent withdrawal of UNOSOM contingents from the USA and several other Western nations, the UN Security Council revised UNOSOM's mandate, reducing the troop strength of the mission to a maximum of 22,000. In November 1994 the UN Security Council extended UNOSOM's mandate by four months, to a final date of 31 March 1995. As the deadline for UNOSOM's departure approached, the competition for control of installations currently held by the UN, in particular the port and airport, became the focus of factional hostility. In November 1994 UN forces began to withdraw from positions outside Mogadishu in the first stages of UNOSOM's departure. 'Operation United Shield', to ensure the safe evacuation of the UN troops and civilian personnel, as well as most of the equipment brought in under UNOSOM, was organized and led by the USA. The USA stationed several thousand marines in warships off the Somali coast in December, and in early 1995 they were joined by a multinational force of naval and air force units in order to protect departing UN employees (some 136 members of UNOSOM had been killed since the beginning of the operation).

In late February 1995 1,800 US and 400 Italian marines landed on Mogadishu's beaches, and command of the remaining 2,400 UN troops and of the whole operation was passed from the UN to the US commander. The marines secured the port and airport, and evacuated the remaining UN soldiers. The departure of the last UN personnel on 2 March (almost one month ahead of schedule) was closely followed by that of the US and Italian marines themselves. Somali looters overran the airport, but armoured cars from Aidid's faction, reportedly accompanied by UN-trained police officers, took control of the area. Ali Mahdi's Abgal clansmen gained control of the eastern section of the airport, and skirmishes were reported between the two sides. Aidid and Ali Mahdi subsequently agreed terms for the reopening of the port; however, fighting for control of the crucial sites rapidly resumed.

Significant divisions within the SNA became more apparent in June 1995, following an attempt by disaffected members to replace Aidid with his former aide, Osman Hassan Ali 'Ato', as Chairman of the party. SNA members loyal to Aidid immediately rejected the legitimacy of the actions of the Ali 'Ato' faction and announced the expulsion of the faction from the SNA. In mid-June a conference of reconciliation, convened in southern Mogadishu by representatives of 15 pro-Aidid factions, elected Aidid President of the Republic of Somalia for a three-year term. However, Aidid's presidency and mandate to govern were immediately rejected in a joint statement issued by Ali Mahdi and Ali 'Ato'. In September Aidid's forces seized Baidoa.

Fighting between Gen. Aidid's supporters and those loyal to Ali 'Ato' intensified in early 1996. In July pro-Aidid factions clashed with supporters of Ali Mahdi in Mogadishu, resulting in some 90 fatalities. Aidid was wounded during the skirmishes, and on 1 August he died as a result of his injuries. Despite initial hopes that Aidid's death might result in a cessation of hostilities and the resumption of peace negotiations, on 4 August one of his sons, Hussein Mohamed Aidid (a former US marine and hitherto Aidid's chief of security), was appointed interim President by the SNA leadership council. Hussein Aidid (who was subsequently elected Chairman of the SNA) vowed to continue his father's struggle, and factional fighting quickly resumed.

In December 1996 representatives of some 26 Somali factions (notably excluding the SNA) held protracted talks in Sodere, Ethiopia, under the auspices of the Ethiopian Government and the Intergovernmental Authority on Development (IGAD). The conference culminated in January 1997 in the formation of a 41-member National Salvation Council (NSC), with an 11-member executive committee and a five-member joint chairmanship committee, to act as an interim government charged with drafting a transitional charter and holding a national reconciliation conference. Aidid condemned the establishment of the NSC and accused the Ethiopian authorities of interfering in Somali affairs.

In September 1999 the UN Secretary-General, Kofi Annan, announced that the UN Security Council was to consider a solution to the Somalia problem, following a proposal made by the Somali Peace Alliance (under the chairmanship of 'Puntland' Leader Abdullahi Yussuf) that central authority in Somalia be gradually rebuilt, beginning with regionally based administrations. This proposal was, however, immediately rejected by the Mogadishu faction leaders and President Egal of 'Somaliland'. In October IGAD delegates met in Addis Ababa to discuss President Ismaïl Omar Guelleh of Djibouti's proposed peace plan for Somalia. In February 2000 IGAD member states endorsed Guelleh's plan, which envisaged the staging of a Somali national reconciliation conference in Djibouti in early May, to be attended by representatives of various sections of Somali society. Under the plan, they would elect a new national legislature, which would, in turn, elect a President. The President would choose a Prime Minister, subject to the approval of the legislature, who would head a transitional government for a period of no longer than two years, during which time a national constitution would be drafted and elections would be scheduled. However, although the peace plan was unanimously approved by OAU foreign ministers in March, and also won the approval of the UN and the USA, Egal announced that 'Somaliland' would refuse any attempts to unite it with Somalia.

Formation of the Transitional National Assembly

The Somali national reconciliation conference opened in Arta, Djibouti, on 2 May 2000, with some 400 delegates, representing various Somali clans and political and armed groups, in attendance. By mid-June the number of delegates had risen to around 900, although notably only one of the principal Somali faction leaders, Ali Mahdi, was present. In early July the conference produced a draft national charter, which envisaged the Somali Republic adopting a federal system of government, after a three-year interim period, comprising 18 regional administrations. Furthermore, it provided for the creation of the Somali Transitional National Assembly (TNA), to comprise 225 members, of whom 25 would be women. Each of the four major Somali clans (Dir, Hawiye, Darod and Rahanwin) was allocated 44 parliamentary seats, and an alliance of small clans was to receive 24 seats; the remaining 25 seats were reserved for women from the four major clans and the alliance of small clans, each of which would receive five seats. However, disagreements between clans and sub-clans over the distribution of seats ensued, and in early August President Guelleh intervened, suggesting the appointment of a further 20 members to the Assembly, thus increasing the total number to 245. Guelleh's proposal was accepted, and on 13 August the TNA held its inaugural session in Arta. On 26 August it was announced that Abdulkasim Salad Hasan, a member of the Hawiye clan, who had held several ministerial positions in the Siad Barre administration, had been elected President of Somalia by the TNA. Hasan was sworn in as President on the following day at a ceremony in Arta. On 30 August 2000 President Hasan returned to Mogadishu, where he was greeted by tens of thousands of Somalis. On 8 October President Hasan appointed Ali Khalif Galaydh, a former Minister of Industry in the Siad Barre regime, to the post of Prime Minister; later that month Galaydh announced a 32-member Cabinet

Relations between Somalia and Ethiopia deteriorated in January 2001, after Galaydh accused Ethiopia of providing arms to factions opposed to the Transitional National Government (TNG). Relations between the two countries were further strained in March, when the Ethiopian authorities allowed several Somali faction leaders to convene in Addis Ababa for a series of meetings, which resulted in the creation of the Somali Reconciliation and Restoration Council (SRRC), headed by Hussein Aidid.

In mid-October 2001 a group of dissatisfied TNA members proposed a motion of no confidence in the TNG, citing the administration's failure to promote the reconciliation process and its lack of progress regarding the constitution of regional administrations. Later that month 141 of the 174 TNA members participating in the vote approved the motion to dismiss the Galaydh administration.

In mid-November 2001 President Hasan appointed Col Hassan Abshir Farah, hitherto Minister of Water and Mineral Resources, as Prime Minister. Farah announced that his first priority was to implement a programme of national reconciliation, and thus the appointment of a new cabinet was delayed until after the conclusion of further peace talks between the SRRC and members of the TNA, which were scheduled to take place in Nairobi later that month. Although the talks were further postponed until mid-December, they were attended by senior members of the SNA (again with the notable exception of Hussein Aidid) and representatives of several other Mogadishu faction leaders. On 24 December, in the Kenyan town of Nakura, Farah, on behalf of the TNA, and Mowlid Ma'aneh Mohamed, the Secretary-General of the SRRC, signed a peace agreement, which provided for the formation of an 'all-inclusive government' to ensure equitable power-sharing among all Somali clans and the establishment of a Nairobi-based secretariat to oversee the implementation of the Somali peace process and to solicit funds for it.

SOMALIA

In mid-February 2002 Farah formed a new 31-member Cabinet, which notably included Dr Hussein Mohamed Usman Jimbir, a former senior member of the SRRC, as Minister of Education. However, several members of factions that had signed the Nakura peace agreement in December 2001 were reported to have requested to be excluded from the new Government until a parliamentary committee, established to investigate a proposed increase in the number of parliamentary seats, had released its recommendations. The reconciliation process in Somalia was further endangered in early April 2002, when the Rahanwin Resistance Army (RRA) announced that it had established a new autonomous region in south-western Somalia, based in Baidoa, to be known as the 'State of South-western Somalia'. The Chairman of the RRA, Mohamed Hasan Nur Shatigadud, was elected as 'President' of the new region for a four-year period.

Renewed reconciliation efforts

An IGAD-sponsored reconciliation conference opened in the Kenyan town of Eldoret in mid-October 2002 in the presence of representatives of the Governments of Ethiopia, Kenya, Uganda, Sudan, Djibouti and Eritrea. Following the conclusion of the first phase of the conference, the TNG and a number of Somali factions signed a temporary cease-fire and agreed to abide by the final outcome of the conference; to establish an all-inclusive federal system of government; to combat terrorism; and to enhance the safety of aid workers in the country. Further progress was slowed by continuing deadlock over the allocation of seats to the plenary session of the conference. However, by early December the TNG and Mogadishu-based faction leaders Hussein Aidid, Mohammed Qanyare Afrah, Muse Sudi Yalahow and Ali 'Ato' signed a declaration committing themselves to ending violence in the Somali capital. In January 2003, however, Yalahow announced that he would no longer participate in the conference. Yalahow's departure followed the earlier withdrawal of Qanyare Afrah from the proceedings. In February the conference was moved to Nairobi, and in the following month the TNG and the remaining faction leaders provisionally agreed on the formation of an administration for Mogadishu and further measures to bring peace to the capital.

In early July 2003 delegates at the Nairobi conference reached a provisional agreement, providing for the establishment of a transitional unicameral parliament, which would comprise 351 members selected by political leaders, and would remain in operation for four years. However, President Hasan rejected the agreement, which had been signed by Farah, stating that it would divide the country, and in August divisions between Hasan and Farah intensified. Later that month, just days before the expiry of the three-year mandate of the TNG, Hasan dismissed Farah and the Speaker of the TNA. Hasan insisted that the existing governing institutions would remain in place, despite the expiry of their mandate, until a new President, government and parliament had been installed. Dr Abdi Guled Mohamed, the Minister of Air and Land Transport, was appointed premier, in an acting capacity.

Despite the expiry of his mandate in August 2003, President Hasan appointed Mohamed Abdi Yusuf, hitherto Deputy Speaker of the TNA, as Prime Minister in early December. In January 2004 the TNA approved the appointment of a new 37-member TNG, which included three Deputy Prime Ministers. In the same month talks reconvened in Nairobi, with the aim of restoring the faltering peace process. Following a period of intense negotiations, during which Yalahow and the leaders of the Juba Valley Alliance (JVA), the RRA and the SNF rejoined the discussions, later that month representatives from more than 20 factions in attendance agreed to establish a new transitional parliament, comprising 275 members (rather than the 351 previously agreed), who would serve five-year terms. The parliament would appoint a President, who, in turn, would nominate a Prime Minister to form a government. It was envisaged that each of the four major Somali clans would select 61 members of the new legislature, while a coalition of smaller clans would be responsible for choosing the remaining 31 members. Agreement on a new Transitional Federal Charter (replacing the transitional national charter) was reached in Nairobi; it was approved by the TNA on 8 February and subsequently endorsed by a presidential decree.

In June 2004 an arbitration committee was formed in Nairobi to oversee the nomination of members to the new parliament, and by mid-August the majority of the new members of the Transitional Federal Parliament (TFP) had been nominated and inauguration ceremonies commenced in Nairobi. On 15 September Sharif Hassan Sheikh Adan, a Mogadishu-based business executive, was elected Speaker of the TFP and later that month nominations were invited for the position of President. Following two rounds of voting in the TFP on 10 October, two presidential candidates remained: Col Abdullahi Yussuf Ahmed, the President of the autonomous region of 'Puntland' (see below), and Abdallah Ahmed Addow, a former Somali ambassador to the USA. At a third round of voting held later that day, Yussuf secured 189 of the 268 votes cast and was sworn in as President of Somalia at a ceremony in Nairobi on 14 October. In early November Yussuf appointed Ali Mohammed Ghedi, a member of the Hawiye clan and a former AU official, as Prime Minister.

The presidency of Abdullahi Yussuf Ahmed

Shortly after he had taken office, President Yussuf had appealed to the AU and the UN to approve the deployment of a peace-keeping force of up to 20,000 troops to assist with the relocation of the TFP and the Transitional Federal Government (TFG) to Mogadishu and to disarm militias in the Somali capital. However, ongoing violence in the city caused plans to be stalled. In early January 2005 the AU stated its readiness 'in principle' to deploy a contingent of peace-keepers to Somalia. Despite further concerns over the security situation in the capital, plans for the relocation proceeded, and in early February a delegation of 30 members of the TFP arrived in Mogadishu, followed by a further 50 parliamentarians, led by Sheikh Adan, a few days later. As an AU mission arrived in Mogadishu in mid-February to assess the security situation, thousands of people staged protests against the proposed peace-keeping force and a bomb exploded in the capital, killing two people. In late February Yussuf and Ghedi arrived in Somalia to head a delegation to investigate possible locations for the TFG. The delegation returned to Kenya in early March, and Ghedi's special adviser announced that other towns were being considered as a temporary base for the new administration until violence in the capital subsided.

In mid-March 2005 IGAD defence ministers agreed to deploy a 10,000-strong peace-keeping force, the IGAD Peace Support Mission to Somalia (IGASOM), in the country from 30 April, to be replaced at an unspecified later date by an AU force. Demonstrations were held days later in Mogadishu opposing the deployment of peace-keeping troops from neighbouring countries, and members of the TFP were involved in a violent confrontation, following a vote to reject the planned deployment. In an attempt to allay fears in Somalia, the IGAD Council of Ministers proposed a compromise solution, in which a reduced IGASOM force of 6,800 would initially be deployed, comprised solely of Sudanese and Ugandan troops. In late March the Somali Government announced that it would temporarily relocate to Baidoa and Jowhar, 90 km north of Mogadishu. However, heavy fighting in Baidoa later in March between supporters of Yussuf and militia opposed to the relocation of the TFG outside of Mogadishu resulted in at least 14 fatalities, and in late April the 80 parliamentarians situated in Mogadishu rejected appeals from the President and the UN-led Joint Co-ordination and Monitoring Committee to return to Nairobi, stating that a return to exile would jeopardize ongoing efforts to 'pacify' the capital.

At the end of April 2005 a bomb exploded in Mogadishu, killing 15 people and injuring at least 50 others, at a rally attended by Ghedi. In early May 100 members of the TFP opposed to Yussuf's relocation plans, including Sheikh Adan, boycotted a parliamentary vote in Nairobi, where supporters of the President approved the planned relocation to Baidoa and Jowhar and the deployment of the proposed peace-keeping force. Days later Qanyare Afrah, Yalahow and Ali 'Ato' undertook to combine their militias and withdraw them from Mogadishu, and a partial disarmament of their forces took place at a ceremony in the capital. Also in April, the AU approved plans to send 1,700 peace-keeping troops to Somalia but stated that the force would only arrive when its security could be guaranteed. In mid-May 30 members of the TFP accompanied Sheikh Adan upon his return to Mogadishu, while a spokesman for the President announced that Jama had been removed from office. In June Ghedi and the remaining ministers and members of parliament left Nairobi and arrived in Jowhar, despite the opposition of local militia. Fears of renewed conflict between the opposing factions were raised in early July as Yussuf announced plans to gather a group of militiamen in Jowhar, and in August tensions escalated, when the Mogadishu-based members of the TFP accused Yussuf of planning a civil war with military assistance from Ethiopia. In September, speaking before the UN General Assembly, Yussuf urged the UN Security Council to lift the arms embargo, which he claimed had hindered the establishment of a national security force and had prevented the deployment of peace-keepers in Somalia. A convoy carrying Ghedi on a visit to Mogadishu was attacked with grenades and a land mine in early November. Three people were killed in the apparent assassination attempt, although Ghedi was uninjured in the attack. Later that month 11 people were killed during fighting in Mogadishu, after the Union of Islamic Courts (UIC) of Mogadishu, which had established a court system in the capital based on *Shari'a* (Islamic) law, attempted to seize control of cinemas it had accused of encouraging immoral and criminal behaviour.

The rise of the Somali Supreme Islamic Courts Council

In early January 2006 Yussuf and Sheikh Adan signed an agreement for the TFP to meet in Somalia within 30 days, following further talks held in San'a, and in late January members of the group led by Sheikh Adan signalled their willingness to support a process of reconciliation. Despite the absence of Ali 'Ato', Yalahow and several other prominent ministers opposed to Yussuf, 205 parliamentarians assembled in Baidoa on 26 February as the TFP met for the first time since returning from Kenya. In late February a number of formerly opposed faction leaders, including Qanyare Afrah and Yalahow, formed a new political alliance—the Alliance for the Restoration of Peace and Counter-Terrorism (ARPCT)—which aimed to combat Islamist extremism in Somalia. Militia supported by the ARPCT were in conflict with forces loyal to the UIC in the south of Mogadishu, and at least 33 people were killed before a cease-fire was negotiated by Somali elders. However, some 140 people were killed and thousands fled the capital in late March as fighting resumed, and attempts by elders to renegotiate a cease-fire between the two factions continued. Unrest continued in the capital during early May with more than 80 people reported to have been killed in clashes between the two sides.

In early June 2006 the UIC claimed to have seized control of Mogadishu. Later that month, at a meeting convened by the Arab League in Khartoum, Sudan, the Government signed an agreement of mutual recognition with the UIC, in an attempt to avert a potential attack on Baidoa. Shortly after the agreement was signed, the UIC underwent a reorganization and was renamed the Somali Supreme Islamic Courts Council (SSICC). The US-led Contact Group on Somalia urged the Somali Government to enter further discussions with the SSICC to avoid more widespread conflict. Talks were initially scheduled for mid-July, but the Government requested their postponement, accusing the SSICC of breaching cease-fire agreements. President Yussuf subsequently agreed to meet with SSICC leaders; however, they, in turn, refused to negotiate. In late July and early August some 40 ministers and assistant ministers resigned, citing their dissatisfaction with Prime Minister Ghedi's apparent unwillingness to negotiate with the SSICC. On 28 July the Minister of Constitutional and Federal Affairs, Abdallah Derow Isaq, was shot dead outside a mosque in Baidoa, and two days later Prime Minister Ghedi narrowly defeated a vote of no confidence in the TFP. However, President Yussuf dissolved the Cabinet on 7 August and instructed Ghedi to form a new administration. In late August Ghedi nominated 31 ministers, 31 assistant ministers and five state ministers to form a new TFG.

Tensions continued between the Government and the SSICC, and during late August 2006 SSICC forces took control of several towns to the north of Mogadishu, and continued to demand the withdrawal of all Ethiopian troops from Somalia, the presence of whom had repeatedly been denied by both the Somali and the Ethiopian Governments. Further peace talks took place in Khartoum on 4 September under the auspices of the Arab League, and the following day IGAD convened a meeting in Nairobi at which regional leaders agreed to deploy an international peace force to Somalia, despite continued opposition to the proposal from the SSICC. IGAD also increased pressure on the UN to remove the arms embargo, which would allow President Yussuf to form a national security force; many observers feared that lifting the embargo would lead to a resurgence of fighting. In late September the remaining port outside SSICC control, at Kismayu, was seized by that organization.

Meanwhile, in mid-September 2006 President Yussuf narrowly escaped an assassination attempt outside the Parliament buildings. In exchanges of fire that followed the explosion 11 people were killed, including Yussuf's brother, which served further to increase tensions between the weakened Government and the SSICC, although the latter denied any involvement in the incident.

Attempts to establish peace-keeping missions

Further peace talks were scheduled to take place in Khartoum in October 2006, but the SSICC refused to enter into discussions while the Ethiopian military remained in Somalia, and in early November negotiations were postponed. The SSICC issued a peace initiative to the Somali Government on 11 November; however, the Government rejected this and the following day violent conflict erupted, igniting fears that the situation could escalate into a regional war. Ethiopian reinforcements arrived in Baidoa, while SSICC troops were deployed to positions close to the Ethiopian border. In early December the Ethiopian Government reported attacks by insurgents who had crossed the border. At the same time, violence escalated in the area surrounding Baidoa as opposing troops sought to exert control over the seat of government. The UN Security Council hurriedly adopted a resolution (No. 1725) providing for peace-keeping missions from other African nations to enter Somalia in support of government forces. Meanwhile, the SSICC, although lacking military strength, was securing wider popular support. The SSICC claimed that the majority of the country, under Islamist control, remained peaceful and that international intervention was the cause of much of the conflict. Nevertheless, in mid-December the SSICC issued an ultimatum to the Ethiopian forces to leave Somalia within seven days or face a full-scale war. The Ethiopian Government (which only officially admitted to military involvement in Somalia in late December) rejected these demands, and civilians fled Baidoa and the surrounding areas as fighting broke out once more. During a meeting with the European Union (EU, see p. 270) Commissioner for Development and Humanitarian Aid on 20 December the SSICC declared that it would honour its commitment to attending peace talks in Sudan, and there followed reports that fighting had begun to subside. However, Ethiopian troops advanced towards Mogadishu, forcing the SSICC to retreat. Pro-Government forces began to regain control over the capital and popular support for the SSICC reportedly waned.

On 1 January 2007, with the SSICC forces driven out of the capital, Prime Minister Ghedi announced a three-day amnesty during which civilians were to surrender their weapons. The UN warned that the continued presence of Eritrean forces in Somalia remained a threat to the fragile peace, and as Ethiopia began to withdraw troops from Somalia there was increased pressure on the AU to establish a peace-keeping force in the region. Remaining pro-Government troops were subjected to guerrilla attacks in the weeks that followed, although these were reported to be small in scale, and the success of the peace process remained uncertain. The USA launched a series of air-strikes against Islamists who continued to pose a threat in southern areas of Somalia.

In January 2007 Sheikh Adan was dismissed as Speaker of the TFP, amid allegations that he supported the Islamist extremists and had failed to attend parliamentary meetings. Shaykh Adan Madobe was elected to replace Sheikh Adan on 31 January. Meanwhile, in mid-January 154 members of the TFP voted in favour of declaring martial law, to be imposed for a period of three months from 31 January.

At the end of January 2007 an AU summit convened in Addis Ababa, Ethiopia, concluded, having secured less than 4,000 troops of the 8,000 pledged to constitute a peace-keeping force. However, President Yussuf agreed to stage a national reconciliation conference with the aim of bringing an end to the conflict in the country and it was subsequently agreed that the reconciliation conference would be held in April. In February the UN Security Council adopted a resolution (No. 1744) authorizing the establishment of the AU Mission in Somalia (AMISOM), with an initial mandate of six months. It was envisaged that this force would replace the withdrawing Ethiopian troops and provide support to the TFG, although in early March insurgents attacked the first AMISOM contingent to arrive in Somalia.

A tentative cease-fire was agreed on 22 March 2007 between elders of the Hawiye clan and Ethiopian military officials. However, it broke down almost immediately when government forces attacked Islamist militia in the southern region of the capital in an attempt to consolidate their control and the fighting escalated into what many observers claimed was the most violent conflict in 15 years. Fighting continued into early April and by that time, according to the office of the UN High Commissioner for Refugees (UNHCR), some 47,000 people had fled Mogadishu and it was reported that some 1,500 people had been killed, while several thousand more had been injured. The reconciliation talks were postponed until June.

SOMALIA

Meanwhile, in February 2007 Prime Minister Ghedi effected a cabinet reshuffle; four ministers were redesignated, including the Deputy Prime Minister and Minister of Interior and Security, Hussein Aidid, who was demoted to the position of Minister of Public Works and Housing. Further governmental changes were implemented in April, including the appointment of Husayn Elabe Fahiye as Minister of Foreign Affairs.

Government institutions return to Mogadishu

On 12 March 2007 the TFP voted to relocate the TFG and the following day the office of the President moved from Baidoa to Mogadishu. Cabinet ministers began preparations to transfer their offices to the capital, but progress was hindered by continuing violence in the city. The TFG announced in mid-March that additional security measures were to be implemented to quell the unrest, including deploying trained Ethiopian and AU troops to the worst affected areas. A UN agency reported that by late April more than 300,000 people—almost one-third of the city's population—had left Mogadishu, and in May Hawiye clan elders conceded defeat in the capital and the TFG urged the group to enter into negotiations over disarmament.

The reconciliation conference finally began in mid-July 2007; among the most pressing issues for discussion were the holding of future elections and the resolution of clan divisions, and the international community encouraged the TFG to include moderate Islamists in the conference. However, Islamists and Hawiye clan elders refused to attend the meeting, on the grounds that while Ethiopian troops remained in the country the conference would not provide a neutral base for discussions. The outcome of the seven-week conference, largely considered successful by Somali organizers, was undermined by the absence of key parties, according to international observers. In late August AMISOM's mandate was extended for a further six months.

The opposition conference began in early September 2007, attended by Sheikh Hassan Dahir Aweys, Chairman of the SSICC, who had been in hiding since being driven from Mogadishu by Ethiopian forces earlier that year. At the meeting, also attended by UN and EU observers, SSICC and opposition leaders formed a coalition, the Alliance for the Re-liberation of Somalia (ARS). The ARS aimed to remove the Ethiopian-backed Government and would be guided by a 191-member committee, headed by the former Speaker of the TFP, Sheikh Adan. A 10-member executive committee was elected, with Sheikh Sharif Sheikh Ahmed named as Chairman.

Relations between President Yussuf, a member of the Darod clan, and Prime Minister Ghedi of the Hawiye clan had become increasingly strained in 2007. Ghedi had opposed suggestions by Yussuf that cabinet ministers no longer needed to be members of the TFP, while the two had also clashed over the control of petroleum concessions in 'Puntland' and funding pledged by Saudi Arabia. In late October Prime Minister Ghedi tendered his resignation following further outbreaks of violence involving insurgents and Ethiopian troops. Nur Hassan Hussein, the Secretary-General of the Somali Red Crescent humanitarian organization and a Hawiye, was named as the new Prime Minister and sworn into office on 24 November. Earlier in that month fighting in Mogadishu escalated, forcing thousands of residents to flee the capital.

Prime Minister Hussein announced his new Cabinet in December 2007, but his nominations were criticized by the Ethiopian Government, particularly that of Minister of Foreign Affairs and International Co-operation Mohamed Ali Hamud, who was believed to have close ties to Arab governments. Shortly after their appointment, five ministers submitted their resignation, claiming that the composition of the new administration did not fully represent their clans. Having failed to gain approval for his first Cabinet, Hussein formed a new TFG in mid-January 2008, which included Salim Aliow Ibrow as Minister of Justice and Religious Affairs and Acting Minister of Labour and Social Affairs, Aydid Abdullahi Ilka Hanaf as Minister of Education and Culture and Acting Minister of Health, and Muhammad Abdisalan Adan as Minister of Information, Youth Affairs and Sports; all three were also awarded the status of Deputy Prime Minister.

In late January 2008 AU security officials submitted a proposal for measures to establish lasting peace and security. The plan included increased efforts towards achieving reconciliation; ensuring a safe environment for humanitarian aid workers; and fostering greater co-operation from the international community in peace-keeping operations. In February Prime Minister Hussein conceded that the TFG was willing to meet opposition leaders in an attempt to revive the faltering reconciliation process. The UN was considering the deployment of a UN peace-keeping force to replace AMISOM, which by mid-April comprised only 2,450 troops and had largely been restricted to protecting transport facilities in Mogadishu and providing security for government officials. In February the UN Security Council had authorized the extension of AMISOM's mandate until late August. In late March it was reported that at least 19 civilians were killed in Mogadishu when fighting broke out between government troops and Islamist insurgents. Meanwhile, rebel forces launched a raid on Jowhar and in the same month the USA formally designated the militant Islamist group, al-Shabaab ('The Youth'), which had been established in 2007 by former members of the UIC, as a terrorist organization, claiming that it was linked to the al-Qa'ida network (see below). In March 2008 the Somali representative of UNHCR announced that, owing to the continuing violence, about 20,000 civilians were fleeing Mogadishu each month, and around 1m. Somalis were internally displaced.

Islamist insurgents seized the town of Adado, in the central region of Galgudud, in April 2008, reportedly killing 15 people. In the same month Sudan Ali Ahmed, the Chairman of the Elman Human Rights Organization, claimed that fighting in Mogadishu had killed 81 people, as a result of Ethiopian troops using heavy artillery in residential areas. Meanwhile, a report by Amnesty International accused Ethiopian forces of committing extrajudicial killings during a raid on a mosque in Mogadishu. In early May a leader of al-Shabaab, Aden Hashi Ayro, was killed in an air-strike launched by US forces on the town of Dhuusa Mareeb, which resulted in the deaths of at least seven other people. Later that month UN-sponsored peace talks between the TFG and the ARS commenced in Djibouti; however, Islamist leaders in Somalia, including hard-line elements of the ARS led by Aweys, reiterated their refusal to enter into negotiations until Ethiopian forces had been withdrawn from Somalia. Also in mid-May the UN Security Council approved the establishment of a joint planning unit and recommended the relocation of the UN Political Office for Somalia (UNPOS) from Nairobi to Mogadishu. UNPOS was to support the TFG in the development of a constitution and organization of a referendum and democratic elections in 2009. Meanwhile, tens of thousands of people staged violent protests in Mogadishu against the sharp increase in food prices; the rioting lasted for two days and there were reports that five people were killed when security forces fired on the crowds.

Withdrawal of Ethiopian troops

In June 2008 an agreement was concluded by members of the TFG and a moderate faction of the ARS present in Djibouti, which included provisions for the withdrawal of Ethiopian troops from Somalia and the deployment of a UN peace-keeping force to replace them; it was also agreed that a cease-fire would be implemented within 30 days. (The agreement was officially signed in August.) Hard-line Islamists in Somalia, who had boycotted the talks, dismissed the agreement and in July the group split into two separate factions (the moderate 'Djibouti wing' and the more hard-line 'Asmara wing'). Despite the agreement, intense fighting continued between insurgents and government forces, with reports of clashes in Mogadishu that resulted in the deaths of at least 28 people. Furthermore, two policemen were killed when their vehicle was destroyed in a bomb attack in which three other people died, and in late June the SSICC claimed to have captured the cities of Hawdar, Wajid and Balad Weyn in central and south-west Somalia. In the following month the head of the UN Development Programme office in Mogadishu, Usman Ali Ahmad, was shot dead near his residence in the city, although it was not clear who was responsible for the killing. The attack was part of a wider campaign by insurgents, in particular those affiliated to al-Shabaab, to target aid workers in the country, at least 20 of whom were believed to have been murdered, and a further 17 kidnapped, between January and July.

The UN Security Council extended the mandate of AMISOM for a further six months in August 2008, while Ethiopian Prime Minister Meles Zenawi announced plans to begin the withdrawal of Ethiopian troops from Somalia. Nevertheless, violence continued in Mogadishu, while two Western journalists were kidnapped near the capital, and Islamists captured the southern port of Kismayu, after three days of intense fighting in which some 100 people were killed and thousands more were displaced. (The journalists were released in November 2009.) Meanwhile, on 2 August 2008 it was reported that nine ministers and one deputy minister had resigned from the TFG, apparently in response to Hussein's dismissal of the Governor of the Banaadir region, Mohammed Umar Habeeb; Hussein subsequently appointed six new ministers to the TFG. In October the security situation in Mogadishu deteriorated further and there were also bombings in the capital of 'Somaliland' as well as co-ordinated suicide attacks against government buildings in 'Puntland'. None the less, a new peace treaty was signed between the TFG and the 'Djibouti wing' of the ARS, in which they agreed to implement an official cease-fire the following month. It was also revealed that Ethiopian troops would begin withdrawing from Somalia on 21 November; the Ethiopian Government subsequently announced that it would remove all of its forces by the end of the year. Meanwhile, al-Shabaab had taken control of large areas of central and southern Somalia, and with the imminent withdrawal of Ethiopian forces there were concerns that it would succeed in capturing Mogadishu.

In mid-December 2008 Yussuf announced that he had dismissed Prime Minister Hussein, following his attempts to establish a power-sharing administration with moderate Islamists. Hussein rejected this decision, insisting that only the TFP had the power to remove him, but, despite the TFP voting in favour of reinstating Hussein, the President later named Mohamed Mohamud Guled as the new Prime Minister. On 24 December Guled announced his resignation, stating that his appointment was causing dissension within the Government. President Yussuf, in turn, resigned on 29 December; he was replaced in an acting capacity by the Speaker of the TFP, Adan Madobe.

Sheikh Sharif Sheikh Ahmed becomes President

Amid the uncertainty that followed Yussuf's resignation in December 2008, the violence continued as insurgents shelled government forces and AMISOM positions in Mogadishu, while a number of Islamist groups began to fight among themselves. New groups, seeking to take advantage of the potential power vacuum created by the departure of Ethiopian troops, had formed in late December, including the Ahlu-Sunna Wal-Jama, which declared a *jihad* (holy war) against hard-line Islamist factions. On 16 January 2009 the UN Security Council adopted a resolution (No. 1863) expressing its intention to establish a peace-keeping force in Somalia to replace AMISOM and extending the mission's mandate for a further six months.

In late January 2009 Ethiopia completed the withdrawal of its forces. Shortly afterwards, al-Shabaab insurgents seized control of Baidoa, where the TFP had formerly been based. The TFP, which had been convened in Djibouti, agreed to increase its composition by 275 members to 550 deputies; 149 new members from the 'Djibouti wing' of the ARS were appointed to the TFP. On 30 January the TFP elected Sheikh Sharif Sheikh Ahmed, the leader of the 'Djibouti wing' of the ARS, as President. Sheikh Ahmed defeated Gen. Maslah Mohamed Siyad (the son of Siad Barre) in a second round of voting by 293 votes to 126.

In February 2009 President Sheikh Ahmed appointed a new Prime Minister, Omar Abdirashid Ali Sharmarke (hitherto Somalia's ambassador-designate to the USA), and on 21 February Ali Sharmarke formed a new Cabinet. Former TFP Speaker Sheikh Adan was appointed Deputy Prime Minister and Minister of Finance, while Shaykh Abdulqadir Ali Umar, a senior member of the SSICC, became Minister of Internal Affairs. Nevertheless, fighting continued in Mogadishu, where at least 11 Burundian troops serving with the AMISOM peace-keeping force were reported to have been killed. On 10 March the TFG voted in favour of introducing *Shari'a* law, in an attempt to pacify al-Shabaab insurgents; however, the heavy fighting persisted, and later that month Osama bin Laden, the leader of the al-Qa'ida (Base) organization (see Other external relations), released an audio recording urging al-Shabaab to oust the administration of Sheikh Ahmed. In April at least eight people were killed following a mortar attack on the TFP building. (The legislative body had relocated to Mogadishu in March.)

Islamist insurgents advance to capital

By May 2009 al-Shabaab forces (reportedly supported by volunteer foreign combatants) had seized control of Jowhar and advanced to Mogadishu, prompting large numbers of civilians to flee from the capital. In late May the UN Security Council extended the mandate of AMISOM until the end of January 2010. Some 26 people, including the city's police commander, were killed in clashes between insurgents and government forces in Mogadishu in June 2009; al-Shabaab was also responsible for a suicide bomb attack in the town of Beledweyne, near the border with Ethiopia, which killed at least 30 people, including the Minister of National Security. On 22 June Sheikh Ahmed declared a state of emergency; nevertheless, heavy fighting, also involving AMISOM troops, continued in Mogadishu. In August Ali Sharmarke extensively reorganized the TFG; Abdallah Boss Ahmed, who originated from 'Somaliland', was appointed Minister of Defence, while Ali Jama Ahmed Jengeli became Minister of Foreign Affairs (having held the post under President Yussuf).

In September 2009 it was reported that al-Shabaab had threatened intensive attacks against Western targets, in reprisal for the killing of a prominent al-Qa'ida commander, Saleh Ali Saleh Nabhan, in a military operation by US special forces near the southern town of Baraawe. Two days later, some 15 AMISOM personnel were killed in a suicide bomb attack against AMISOM headquarters. Fighting in the capital Mogadishu continued sporadically throughout October, including a fierce exchange of fire between al-Shabaab insurgents and government forces and AMISOM near the international airport, in which some 30 people were killed. Also in October al-Shabaab secured control of the southern town of Kismayu, following the collapse of its power-sharing agreement with Hizbul Islam (a major insurgent group which had emerged at the beginning of 2009). In early December some 22 people, including three ministers, were killed and 60 others injured in a suicide bomb attack at a graduation ceremony at a hotel in Mogadishu. Public indignation prompted the first ever demonstration against al-Shabaab in Mogadishu, which was organized by Ahlu-Sunna Wal-Jama. The TFG was subsequently reorganized.

Heavy fighting in Mogadishu continued in early 2010 and further protests against al-Shabaab were staged; UNHCR reported that some 17,000 civilians in the capital had become displaced by January. Renewed clashes between Ahlu-Sunna Wal-Jama and al-Shabaab, in the central region of Galgaduud, were also reported in that month. On 28 January the UN Security Council issued a resolution extending the mandate of AMISOM for a further year and requesting that the number of troops in the mission (then about 3,700) be increased to its total authorized strength of 8,000. Following negotiations, the TFG reached an agreement with Ahlu-Sunna Wal-Jama in February, whereby the milita group pledged to support efforts to suppress the al-Shabaab insurgency and was to be offered a number of government posts. (The power-sharing agreement was officially signed in Addis Ababa in mid-March.) Also in February al-Shabaab (which was reported to have divided into two factions) announced its alignment with al-Qa'ida. In March, amid the intensification of the conflict, the mayor of Mogadishu urged its remaining residents to flee the capital.

In mid-May 2010 the TFP convened for the first time since December 2009, although during the session the parliament building came under attack from al-Shabaab and it was reported that at least 24 people had been killed. Nevertheless, proceedings continued and Adan Madobe claimed that a vote of no confidence in Prime Minister Ali Sharmarke had been approved by 280 of the deputies present. However, it was later stated that the motion had actually been taken on Adan Madobe's position and the following day he announced his resignation as Speaker. Ali Sharmarke maintained that he would remain in his post and that President Sheikh Ahmed, who had indicated that he had dissolved the Government, did not have the power to effect his dismissal. Sheikh Ahmed subsequently confirmed that Ali Sharmarke and his Government would remain in office. On 28 May Sheikh Adan was again elected Speaker of the TFP.

Al-Shabaab staged its first attack outside Somalia in July 2010, when bombs were detonated at two locations in Kampala, Uganda, killing 74 people and injuring a further 70. Al-Shabaab claimed responsibility for the bombings and stated that they were in retaliation for military action by AMISOM Ugandan troops in Mogadishu. On 24 August al-Shabaab, which had threatened to mount a large-scale offensive if the AU proceeded with plans to increase the military strength of AMISOM, attacked the Muna hotel in Mogadishu, killing at least 33 people, including six parliamentary deputies and several government officials; the perpetrators subsequently committed suicide after security forces surrounded the hotel. Later that month al-Shabaab forces fired mortars at the presidential palace, killing four Ugandan soldiers serving with AMISOM. In September numerous attacks by al-Shabaab in Mogadishu included a suicide bomb attack at the airport, in which at least 14 people were killed; Hizbul Islam claimed responsibility for a thwarted suicide attack attempt against the presidential palace.

SOMALIA

Recent developments: new government military offensive

In early September 2010 Sheikh Ahmed dismissed the Chief of Staff, Gen. Mohamed Gelle Kahiye, following allegations that he had sold weapons illegally. On 21 September, with a vote of confidence in him pending, Sharmarke announced his resignation, citing continuing differences with the President. (The Deputy Prime Minister and Minister of Energy and Fuel, Abdiwahid Ilmi Gonjeh, became premier on an acting basis.) On 14 October Sheikh Ahmed appointed a former diplomat, Mohamed Abdullahi Mohamed, as the new Prime Minister of the TFG. A new, 18-member Cabinet formed by Mohamed, in which only Minister of Finance and the Treasury Hussein Abdi Halane retained his post, was approved by the TFP on 27 November. On 22 December, amid continued fighting in Mogadishu, the UN Security Council adopted a resolution authorizing an extension of the existing AMISOM mandate until 30 September 2011 and an increase in the strength of the mission from 8,000 troops to a maximum of 12,000; it was reported that al-Shabaab forces occupied about one-half of the capital at that time. On 3 February 2011 the TFP voted to extend its legislative mandate (which had been due to expire in August) for a further three years; the UN, the EU, the USA, and other donor states and international organizations expressed concern at the extension of the transitional period. In mid-February a demonstration at the presidential palace in Mogadishu, which had been organized by local authorities in support of peace, was violently dispersed by government troops, resulting in an exchange of fire in which three people were killed. (It was estimated that some 22,000 people had been killed in the capital since the concentration of hostilities there.) Sheikh Ahmed replaced all senior security officials in early March. On 28 March the TFG announced that it would extend its own mandate for an additional year, until August 2012. Meanwhile, in February 2011 government forces supported by AMISOM and ethnic militia began a concerted offensive, succeeding in regaining control of strategic locations in the capital; in March it was reported that hostilities had also surrounded al-Shabaab bases near the borders with Ethiopia and Kenya, and that (despite denials by the Somalian and Ethiopian authorities) Ethiopian troops were again assisting military action against al-Shabaab.

The 'Republic of Somaliland'

In May 1993 Egal, who had been Somalia's Prime Minister in 1967–69, was elected as the new President of 'Somaliland'. In June Egal announced the composition of a 14-member council of ministers for 'Somaliland'. By late September a two-year transitional programme for reconstruction had been approved by a 47-member bicameral parliament (comprising a council of elders and a council of representatives). The administration's hopes that the prevailing atmosphere of peace in the north-western region would inspire the international community's prompt recognition of 'Somaliland' were largely frustrated, in October, by the OAU Secretary-General's rejection of the territory's independent status. Relations between the Egal administration and UNOSOM officials improved in late 1993, following the assurances of the UN Secretary-General that the mission would not interfere in the region's affairs but would provide funding for reconstruction and the rehabilitation of the police force. Nevertheless, in August 1994 Egal expelled UN representatives from 'Somaliland', accusing them of interfering in internal affairs. This was apparently precipitated by talks between the new UN Special Representative to Somalia, James Victor Gbeho (appointed in July), and Ahmed Ali 'Tur', who was courted by both the UN and Gen. Aidid following his disavowal of secession for 'Somaliland'. In October the rift between Egal and Ahmed Ali 'Tur' culminated in violent confrontations in Hargeysa between military units remaining loyal to Egal and those defecting to support Ahmed Ali 'Tur'. By mid-December it was estimated that three-quarters of the population of Hargeysa had fled, many thousands of them seeking refuge in Ethiopia (see below). Fighting spread to other parts of 'Somaliland', and in April 1995 government forces were in conflict with fighters from the Garhadji clan who had recently formed an alliance with Issa militiamen belonging to the anti-secessionist USF. Despite Egal's weakened position, he persevered with the introduction of a new currency for the territory, the 'Somaliland shilling'.

In August 1995 four sub-committees were established to draft a new constitution for 'Somaliland'. A provisional document was published in March 1996. Peace talks between the territory's warring factions were conducted in December 1995, and in May 1996 it was reported that rebel armed forces had surrendered their weapons at an official disarmament ceremony in Hargeysa. In February 1997, shortly after it was announced that the constitution had become effective for a three-year interim period, Egal was re-elected (by an electoral college) President of 'Somaliland' for a five-year term.

At a referendum held in late May 2001, according to official results, 91.7% of the voters in 'Somaliland' approved a new constitution for the territory, which contained a clause confirming the self-declared state's independence. However, the outcome appeared unlikely to persuade the international community to grant recognition to 'Somaliland'. In mid-January 2002 Egal's term of office, which had been due to expire at the end of February, prior to scheduled presidential and parliamentary elections, was extended for one year by the council of elders. In early May, however, Egal died from complications following surgery in South Africa; the Vice-President, Dahir Riyale Kahin, was inaugurated as President of 'Somaliland'. Kahin appointed Ahmed Yusuf Yassin as Vice-President later that month, and in July Kahin announced that a presidential election would be held in January 2003. The election was delayed on a number of occasions, but finally proceeded on 14 April. According to results published by the 'Somaliland' Election Commission, Kahin defeated his nearest rival, Ahmad Muhammad Silanyo, by just 80 votes, securing 205,595 (42.1%) of the total 498,639 votes cast. A third candidate, Faysal Ali Warabe, received 77,433 votes (15.5%). Silanyo immediately contested the result of the election and announced his intention to appeal against the outcome. However, in the following month the 'Somaliland' constitutional court confirmed the legitimacy of Kahin's victory, and he was sworn in as President on 16 May.

On 29 September 2005 candidates from three political parties contested the 82 seats in the House of Representatives. Kahin's Unity, Democracy and Independence Party (UDUB) emerged as the largest of the three parties with 33 seats, the Peace, Unity and Development Party (KULMIYE) won 28 seats and the Justice and Development Party (UCID) 21. At the official opening of parliament in November a disagreement over the election of a speaker developed into a physical confrontation between members of the Council. The role was eventually allocated to Abdirahman Mohamed Abdullahi of the UCID, and in mid-December the 'Somaliland' parliament held its first full session. In March 2009 it was announced that a presidential election, originally scheduled for August 2008 but postponed due to instability in the region, would instead be held in September 2009. In September opposition deputies in the House of Representatives introduced a motion accusing Kahin and members of his administration of 'corruption and constitutional violations' and demanding his impeachment. The election commission announced a further postponement of the presidential election, owing to the continuing unstable conditions and to allow the resolution of the technical issues related to voter registration. UDUB, KULMIYE and UCID agreed to a series of proposals drafted by the international sponsors of Somaliland's election process, whereby changes would be made to the electoral commission, the election would be conducted on the basis of voter registration, and the election date would be established by the commission, after consultation between all three political parties. In October the parliament approved the establishment of a new electoral commission. In May 2010 it was announced that the election was to take place on 26 June. On that day Silanyo was decisively elected with 49.6% of votes cast, defeating Kahin, who received 33.2% of the votes. The new President was sworn in on 27 July. The elections were conducted without incident and were endorsed by international observers. Three countries were represented when he assumed office: Kenya, Djibouti and Ethiopia. In September the 'Somaliland' parliament voted to extend the mandates of both the upper chamber, the House of Elders, and the House of Representatives, and of appointed municipal and regional representatives, on the grounds that existing conditions did not permit the organization of further elections in the region. Meanwhile, the increase in violent incidents was attributed to the emergence of a rebel movement, with connections to the Islamist insurgents in southern and central Somalia, that opposed 'Somaliland's secession from Somalia.

'Puntland'

In July 1998 Col Abdullahi Yussuf Ahmed announced the formation of 'Puntland', a new autonomous administration in north-eastern Somalia. In August Abdullahi Yussuf, as President of the new administration, appointed a Cabinet, which was subsequently approved by the recently inaugurated 69-

member parliament (empowered to act as the legislature for a three-year transitional period, prior to the holding of regional elections). A charter for 'Puntland', released shortly afterwards, precluded 'Puntland' from seceding from Somalia, while it envisaged the adoption of a federal system of national government, with similar regional governments emerging around the country. Hussein Aidid declared his opposition to the administration, accusing the Ethiopian authorities of encouraging 'Puntland' to secede. In late June 2001 Yussuf's mandate was controversially extended for a further three years by the 'Puntland' parliament, at the behest of clan elders. The legality of the decision was challenged by several opposition figures, and the 'Puntland' High Court issued a decree, effective from 1 July, placing all security services and other government institutions under its supervision. The Chief Justice of 'Puntland', Yussuf Haji Nur, subsequently proclaimed himself President of the territory; senior clan elders confirmed Haji Nur as acting President until 31 August. However, Yussuf rejected this decision, and heavy fighting ensued between followers of Yussuf and Haji Nur. In late August a general congress, attended by representatives of all major 'Puntland' clans, opened in Garowe, the region's capital, to elect a new President and Vice-President, as well as members to a new 'Puntland' assembly, and in mid-November Jama Ali Jama and Ahmad Mahmud Gunle were sworn in as President and Vice-President, respectively. In April 2002 Yussuf and Ali Jama met for talks in Ethiopia, but no agreement was reached. Fighting continued in 'Puntland' during 2002 and early 2003, with numerous casualties reported on both sides. In May 2003 Yussuf sought to stabilize 'Puntland' by concluding a power-sharing agreement with opposition forces, under the terms of which opposition members were granted a number of ministerial portfolios. In July 2004, following a presidential decree which reduced the Government's term in office from two years to six months, Yussuf formed a new 15-member Government. In October Yussuf was elected President of Somalia (see above) and Mohamed Abdi Hashi succeeded him as President of 'Puntland' in an acting capacity. In early January 2005 Gen. Mohamud Muse Hersi 'Adde', a former Somali diplomat, secured the support of 35 members of the 'Puntland' parliament, thus defeating Hashi, who won 30 votes, and was elected President of 'Puntland'. Hassan Dahir Afqurac was elected Vice-President.

In late February 2006 an armed confrontation between security forces and a group loyal to the Minister for Planning, Abdirahman Farole, which had occupied the parliamentary building, resulted in at least three deaths. In early March parliament approved a new Cabinet, in which incumbent ministers retained their portfolios, with the exception of Farole, whom Hersi had dismissed following the siege. Meanwhile, in October 2005 it emerged that 'Puntland' had issued mineral and petroleum exploration rights to Range Resources of Australia in an agreement that included the regions of Sanaag and Sool, disputed by 'Puntland' and the neighbouring region of 'Somaliland', prompting vociferous criticism from the 'Somaliland' administration. From September 2004 troops from both regions had reportedly been engaged in heavy fighting near the border between the two self-declared states. In December 2007 Hersi effected a cabinet reorganization, which included the establishment of a new Ministry of Oil and Minerals. In January 2009 the parliament elected Farole as the new President of 'Puntland', with 49 of the 66 members voting for him. Farole named a new Cabinet in which only three members of the previous administration were retained. Following a process of constitutional review, which had begun under the previous administration, in June parliament officially approved a new constitution, which provided for the adoption of a multi-party system. In November Farole issued a decree appointing his son, Muhammad Abdirahman Farole, as presidential advisor for media services; it was reported that the Government intended to introduce legislation to govern the media. In December the 'Puntland' parliament adopted a new state flag.

In July 2010 a conference, organized by the Hawadle clan, to establish a local administration in Hiiraan, a central region with secessionist aspirations, took place in the Kenyan capital, Nairobi. In August it was reported that Mohamed Abdi Gab had been appointed in Nairobi as the first 'President' of Hiiraan.

Refugees

The escalation of hostilities between the Siad Barre Government and the rebel forces increased the flow of refugees from Somalia to Ethiopia and Kenya. Following the SNM's assumption of control in northern Somalia in early 1991, thousands of refugees returned from Ethiopia. Many more returned to their home territory in 'Somaliland' in late 1991 and early 1992, as a result of the ethnic conflict in south-western Ethiopia. The intensification of hostilities in the south of Somalia from April 1992 precipitated a huge movement of refugees. In early 1993 the International Committee of the Red Cross estimated that three-quarters of Somalia's population had been internally displaced by the civil conflict, although by late 1994 many thousands had returned to their villages. According to UNHCR, at the beginning of 2010 there were an estimated 560,000 Somali refugees world-wide, including 309,000 in Kenya, 163,000 in Yemen, and 59,000 in Ethiopia; at that time the number of internally displaced persons in Somalia totalled 1,550,000. Despite the presence of AMISOM peace-keeping forces (see above), violence in southern and central Somalia continued during 2010, and intensive fighting in the capital prompted the further flight of many thousands of people. By early 2011 the number of Somali refugees in neighbouring countries had risen to an estimated 680,000.

Foreign Affairs

Regional relations

In April 1988 a decade of hostile relations between Somalia and Ethiopia, following the war in 1977–78 over the Ogaden area of Ethiopia (which is inhabited by ethnic Somalis), ended with a peace accord. It was agreed to re-establish diplomatic relations, to withdraw troops from border areas and to exchange prisoners of war. Following the overthrow of the Mengistu regime in May 1991, the new Government in Ethiopia declared itself neutral with regard to the factions fighting for control of Somalia. Ethiopia hosted peace conferences for the warring Somali factions in 1993, 1996 and 1997. The Egyptian, Kenyan and Libyan authorities also fostered peace initiatives for Somalia from the late 1990s.

Following the outbreak of the Eritrean–Ethiopian border conflict in mid-1998, rival Somali factions were the recipients of increasingly large consignments of weapons from the two warring countries, which sought to secure Somali allegiance to their causes. Growing concern about the activities of Eritrean-supported Somali militias prompted Ethiopia to launch cross-border raids into Somalia against warlords, and in June 1999 the RRA, assisted by Ethiopian troops, captured the town of Baidoa from Hussein Aidid's SNA. Aidid's continuing support of the Eritrean Government and Ethiopian insurgent groups led neutral observers to believe that the conflict was in danger of spreading elsewhere in the Horn of Africa. The Ethiopian Government claimed, however, that its actions were merely attempts to protect the border from attacks initiated by Somali-based rebel opposition groups. In September Ali 'Ato' and Aidid attended a meeting with the Ethiopian Minister of Foreign Affairs, Seyoum Mesfin, in Libya where an agreement was reached whereby Aidid would withdraw support for Ethiopian Oromo rebels in return for Ethiopian disengagement from Somalia. In November the SNA announced that it had disarmed several hundred Oromo Liberation Front (OLF) rebels living in Somalia, had closed down their offices and had asked the OLF leaders to leave the country. It was, however, reported that Ethiopian incursions into Somalia continued in the early 2000s.

In December 2004 a long-term ally of the Ethiopian authorities, Abdullahi Yussuf Ahmed, became President of Somalia (see Domestic Political Affairs). In mid-2006 the forces of the SSICC gained control of much of Somalia, including the capital; in July the SSICC declared a *jihad* on Ethiopia, which it accused of launching a military offensive against Islamist troops. The Ethiopian Government had repeatedly denied any military presence in Somalia, but in October the Ethiopian Prime Minister, Meles Zenawi, announced that his country was 'technically' at war with the Islamist forces. (The Ethiopian Government officially admitted to military involvement in Somalia for the first time in late December.) Ethiopian forces increasingly engaged in conflict in Somalia and by the end of that year had assisted government troops in regaining control of much of the country; violence continued, with militant Islamists refusing to participate in peace discussions unless Ethiopian troops withdrew. In November 2008 the Ethiopian Government announced the withdrawal of its troops from Somalia under a peace agreement, and the process was completed by mid-January 2009.

Amid international concern at the intensifying anti-Government insurgency in 2009, it was widely believed that the Eritrean Government provided support to al-Shabaab and Hizbul Islam, and that senior officers of the Islamist groups had trained in Eritrean camps. In May the AU joined the regional Intergovernmental Authority on Development in urging the

SOMALIA

Introductory Survey

imposition of UN sanctions against Eritrea, in reprisal for its assistance of the Somali insurgents and undermining of the Somali peace process. (The Eritrean Government dismissed the accusations and suspended membership of the AU.) In December the UN Security Council adopted a resolution expressing concern at Eritrea's rejection of the 2008 peace accord in Somalia and imposing an armaments embargo against Eritrea, together with travel sanctions against its senior political and military officials.

Other external relations

Following the suicide attacks on New York and Washington, DC, on 11 September 2001, for which the USA held the al-Qa'ida (Base) organization of Osama bin Laden responsible, the USA 'froze' the foreign assets of Somalia's al-Barakat bank, as it suspected that much of the estimated US $500m. remitted from Somalis abroad to the bank was being funnelled to terrorist organizations. Furthermore, al-Ittihad al-Islam was among 27 groups designated as foreign terrorist organizations in September by the US Government, which believed that al-Ittihad al-Islam had links to al-Qa'ida. In November the new Somali Prime Minister, Hassan Abshir Farah, denied that his Government had any links to al-Ittihad al-Islam or to al-Qa'ida and stated that he would not object to the deployment of US troops inside Somalia to monitor and detect alleged terrorist activities. In the following month US officials were reported to have held talks with several Somali faction leaders regarding the possible existence of al-Qa'ida camps in areas under their control. US special forces raided a Mogadishu hospital in March 2003 and seized a suspected al-Qa'ida operative, who was believed to have been involved in the bombing of an Israeli-owned hotel in Mombasa, Kenya, in November 2002, which resulted in the deaths of 18 people. A report published by the UN in November 2003 stated that the al-Qa'ida cell that had launched the attack on the hotel had used Somalia as a base, and warned of the possibility of further acts of terrorism being plotted, after it discovered evidence of attempts by extremist groups to procure weapons in Mogadishu. US naval forces stationed in Djibouti and Bahrain conducted patrols along the coast of Somalia throughout 2005 following a reported increase in piracy, and in late January 2006 13 suspected pirates were captured following an armed pursuit near the coast involving a US guided missile destroyer. In early March US naval forces launched a missile attack on the southern town of Dobley, targeting a Kenyan national suspected of involvement with the bombings of the US embassies in Tanzania and Kenya in August 1998, and the November 2002 Mombasa attack.

According to a report published in October 2007 by the International Maritime Bureau (IMB), the number of maritime pirate attacks off the coast of Somalia increased significantly during the first nine months of 2007, with 26 reported incidents compared with eight during the same period of 2006. By early 2008, in response to increasingly frequent attacks, particularly in the busy shipping lanes in the Gulf of Aden, there were demands for an international response to the problem. The US and French Governments proposed amendments to international law that would allow naval forces to pursue pirates into Somalia's territorial waters, and arrest and prosecute them. In April pirates seized a French tourist yacht off the coast of Somalia with 30 crew members on board; all those taken hostage were freed after a ransom was paid. The Somali Government then granted France permission to pursue the pirates on to Somali territory, where they were caught and detained by a French navy helicopter. On 2 June the UN Security Council adopted a resolution allowing any state or regional organization, in co-operation with the Somali Government, to enter Somalia's territorial waters in order to combat piracy. (The initial period of authorization was subsequently renewed.) In October the IMB announced that there had been 63 reported cases of pirate attacks off the coast of Somalia between January and September 2008, and that the attacks were increasingly ambitious in scale: in November pirates captured a Saudi-owned oil tanker, and demanded a US $25m. ransom for its return. (The vessel was released in January 2009 following the reported payment of $3m.) In January some 24 countries formed the Contact Group on Piracy off the Coast of Somalia under the aegis of the UN (which was subsequently expanded to 47 states and 10 international organizations). Nevertheless, an IMB report indicated a further increase in piracy activity off the east coast of Somalia and in the Gulf of Aden, where a total of 32 vessels had been hijacked by Somali pirates in the first nine months of 2009, with 533 crew members taken hostage. In November pirates seized a Greek-owned oil supertanker, one of the largest ships that had been captured; it was released in January 2010, following the reported payment of $7m. In June 2010 five Somali nationals were sentenced in the Netherlands to five years' imprisonment each, after they were convicted of attempting to seize a Dutch Antilles-owned vessel in January 2009 (in an attack that was suppressed by Danish marines). In November 2010 the trial of 10 Somalis, who were accused of taking control of a German container ship in April, began in Germany. In the same month two British hostages, who had been kidnapped by Somali pirates in October 2009, were released following ransom payments by their relatives. In January 2011 the IMB announced that incidents of piracy had again increased significantly, with a total of 49 ships seized and 1,016 crew members taken hostage off the coast of Somalia during 2010; at the end of that year 28 vessels and 638 hostages continued to be held for ransom by Somali pirates. (However, the number of incidents in the Gulf of Aden had been reduced considerably, which was attributed principally to the presence of international naval units patrolling the region.)

CONSTITUTION AND GOVERNMENT

In July 2000 a Somali national reconciliation conference, sponsored by President Guelleh of Djibouti, approved a Transitional National Charter, which envisaged the Somali Republic adopting a federal system of government, comprising 18 regional administrations, after a three-year interim period. The Charter provided for the creation of a Transitional National Assembly (TNA), which was to exercise legislative power in Somalia during the interim period. The 245-member TNA was inaugurated in August and elected a President of Somalia. Despite the expiry of its mandate in August 2003, the TNA remained in place, pending the election of a new legislative body. In February 2004, following protracted negotiations in Kenya, a new Transitional Federal Charter (replacing the previous Charter) was approved by the TNA; it provided for the establishment of a new 275-member Transitional Federal Parliament (TFP), to comprise 61 representatives from each of the four major clans and 31 from an alliance of smaller clans. Once established, the TFP elected a national President in October, who, in turn, nominated a Prime Minister. In January 2009 the composition of the TFP (which remained based in Baidoa, owing to the adverse security situation in Mogadishu) was increased by a further 275 members.

REGIONAL AND INTERNATIONAL CO-OPERATION

Somalia is a member of the African Union (see p. 183) and the Islamic Development Bank (see p. 357).

Somalia became a member of the UN in 1960 and participates in the Group of 77 (G77) developing countries.

ECONOMIC AFFAIRS

In 2009, according to estimates by the UN, Somalia's gross national income (GNI) was US $1,931m., equivalent to $211 per head. In 2009 gross domestic product (GDP) was an estimated $2,012m., equivalent to $298 per head. During 2000–09, it was estimated, the population increased at an average annual rate of 2.4%. GDP increased, in real terms, at an average annual rate of 2.9% in 2000–09; growth of 2.6% was recorded in 2009.

According to UN estimates, agriculture (including forestry and fishing) contributed 60.2% of GDP in 2009. According to FAO estimates, 65.6% of the working population were employed in agriculture in mid-2010. Agriculture is based on the breeding of livestock, which accounted for 49% of GDP in 1989 and 38.4% of the total value of exports in 1988. Bananas have traditionally been the principal cash crop, accounting for 40.3% of export earnings in 1988. The GDP of the agricultural sector increased by an average of 2.9% per year in 2000–09; agricultural GDP increased by 2.9% in 2009. Total cereals production was 207,800 metric tons in 1999, the lowest annual yield since 1993, but recovered to an estimated 359,000 metric tons in 2005, before declining to 196,000 metric tons in 2007.

According to UN estimates, industry (including mining, manufacturing, construction and power) contributed 7.4% of GDP in 2009, and employed an estimated 12.0% of the working population in 2002. The combined GDP of the mining, manufacturing, construction and power sectors increased by an average of 3.2% per year in 2000–09; growth in 2009 was 2.3%.

Mining (including utilities) contributed 0.7% of GDP in 2009, according to the UN. Somalia's mineral resources include salt, limestone, gypsum, gold, silver, nickel, copper, zinc, lead, manganese, uranium and iron ore. Deposits of petroleum and natural gas have been discovered, but remain unexploited: US petroleum companies were granted exploration rights covering two-thirds of the country by Siad Barre, and were expected to start investigations once there was a durable peace. In February 2001 it was reported that the French petroleum company TotalFinaElf had signed an agreement with the transitional Somali Government to carry out oil exploration in the south of the country. Discussions commenced in January 2003 between the 'Somaliland' administration and a British-based company regarding the possible granting of contracts for petroleum exploration. An Australian mining company, Range Resources, began mineral and petroleum exploration in 'Puntland' and in October 2005 it signed a contract with the 'Puntland' Government, granting it 50.1% of exploration rights for the entire region, including territory disputed by neighbouring 'Somaliland'. However, the TFG later declared the contract void. The combined GDP of the mining and utilities sector increased by an average of 3.4% per year in 2000–09; growth in 2009 was 1.9%.

According to UN estimates, manufacturing contributed 2.5% of GDP in 2009. The most important sectors are food-processing, especially sugar-refining, the processing of hides and skins, and the refining of petroleum. Manufacturing GDP increased by an average of 3.3% per year in 2000–09; growth in 2009 was 2.1%.

According to UN estimates, construction contributed 4.2% of GDP in 2009. The GDP of the sector increased at an average annual rate of 2.7% in 2000–09; growth of 2.4% was recorded in 2009.

Energy is derived principally from oil-fired generators. Imports of fuel products comprised 14% of the value of merchandise imports in 1990.

The services sector contributed 32.5% of GDP in 2009, and engaged an estimated 21.1% of the employed labour force in 2002. Tourism accounted for some 9.3% of GDP in 1988, although since the outbreak of civil unrest there has been little tourist activity in Somalia. The GDP of the services sector increased at an average annual rate of 3.0% in 2000–09; growth of 2.5% was recorded in 2009.

In 1989 Somalia recorded a visible trade deficit of US $278.6m., and there was a deficit of $156.7m. on the current account of the balance of payments. In 1982 the principal source of imports (34.4%) was Italy, while Saudi Arabia was the principal market for exports (86.5%). Other major trading partners in that year were the United Kingdom, the Federal Republic of Germany and Kenya. The principal exports in 1988 were livestock and bananas. The principal imports were petroleum, fertilizers, foodstuffs and machinery. Livestock and bananas remained the principal exports in the late 1990s, while the United Arab Emirates emerged as Somalia's main trading partner.

In 1988 Somalia recorded a budget deficit of 10,009.4m. Somali shillings. A provisional budget for 1991 was projected to balance at 268,283.2m. Somali shillings. Somalia's total external debt was US $2,944m. at the end of 2007, of which $1,979m. was long-term public debt. In 2000–03 the average annual rate of inflation was 10.2%. Consumer prices remained static in 2003. The rate of unemployment was estimated at 47.4% in 2002.

Somalia's long history of civil unrest, together with unreliable climatic conditions, have undermined the traditional agricultural base of the economy. In December 2001 the UN announced that Somalia was on the verge of economic collapse. This was attributed largely to the US Administration's decision to enforce the closure of the al-Barakat banking and telecommunications organization, owing to its suspected links to terrorist organizations, thus severing the remittance process on which so much of the country is heavily dependent. The formation of a new Government in late 2004 raised hopes that central authority would be restored to the country, thus providing a degree of stability; in that year Coca-Cola opened a soft drinks plant in Mogadishu, representing the largest single investment in the country. In 2007 the China National Offshore Oil Corporation signed an agreement with the Somali Government, which allowed the former the opportunity to explore any land with potential reserves of natural resources. However, despite pledges of significant humanitarian aid by the international community, ongoing conflict continued to prevent the development of an economic infrastructure. Meanwhile, a significant increase in piracy off the coast of Somalia from 2008 adversely affected trade, while interrupting humanitarian supplies. Conditions deteriorated further in 2009, when the effects of severe drought were compounded by the escalation of hostilities between government troops and Islamist forces, which had reached the capital. Potential donors failed to pledge funding, deterred by the lack of functioning central government and concerns that Islamist insurgents would seize aid. In January 2010 the TFG announced that it had reopened the central bank (which had not functioned since 1991). The humanitarian crisis continued during 2010, with hostilities concentrated in the capital (see Domestic Political Affairs), prompting the further displacement of many thousands of people. In October it was reported that the main Islamist insurgent group, al-Shabaab, had prohibited the transfer of foreign remittances to Somalia (which then contributed about 23% of household income), on religious grounds. In early 2011 the International Crisis Group issued a report condemning the continuing incompetence and corruption of the TFG. In March, following further drought and sharp rises in the price of grain in many areas, FAO estimated that some 2.4m. of the population required humanitarian assistance, of whom nearly 1.5m. had been displaced by conflict. Meanwhile, it was reported that the Government had succeeded in regaining control of strategic parts of the capital from al-Shabaab, after launching a concerted military offensive.

PUBLIC HOLIDAYS

2012: 1 January (New Year's Day), 4 February* (Mouloud, birth of the Prophet), 1 May (Labour Day), 26 June (Independence Day), 1 July (Foundation of the Republic), 18 August* (Id al-Fitr, end of Ramadan), 26 October* (Id al-Adha, Feast of the Sacrifice), 5 December* (Ashoura).

* These holidays are dependent on the Islamic lunar calendar and may vary by one or two days from the dates given.

SOMALIA

Statistical Survey

Sources (unless otherwise stated): Economic Research and Statistics Dept, Central Bank of Somalia, Mogadishu, and Central Statistical Dept, State Planning Commission, POB 1742, Mogadishu; tel. (1) 80385.

Area and Population

AREA, POPULATION AND DENSITY

Area (sq km)	637,657*
Population (census results)†	
7 February 1975	3,253,024
February 1986 (provisional)	
Males	3,741,664
Females	3,372,767
Total	7,114,431
Population (UN estimates at mid-year)‡	
2009	9,133,124
2010	9,358,602
2011	9,605,189
Density (per sq km) at mid-2011	15.1

* 246,201 sq miles.
† Excluding adjustment for underenumeration.
‡ Source: UN, *World Population Prospects: The 2008 Revision*.

POPULATION BY AGE AND SEX
(UN estimates at mid-2011)

	Males	Females	Total
0–14	2,163,166	2,144,385	4,307,551
15–64	2,484,702	2,552,804	5,037,506
65 and over	117,596	142,536	260,132
Total	4,765,464	4,839,725	9,605,189

Source: UN, *World Population Prospects: The 2008 Revision*.

PRINCIPAL TOWNS
(estimated population in 1981)

Mogadishu (capital)	500,000	Berbera	65,000
Hargeysa	70,000	Merca	60,000
Kismayu	70,000		

Mid-2010 ('000, including suburbs, UN estimate): Mogadishu 1,500 (Source: UN, *World Urbanization Prospects: The 2009 Revision*).

BIRTHS AND DEATHS
(annual averages, UN estimates)

	1995–2000	2000–05	2005–10
Birth rate (per 1,000)	45.9	45.7	44.2
Death rate (per 1,000)	17.9	16.2	15.9

Source: UN, *World Population Prospects: The 2008 Revision*.

Life expectancy (years at birth, WHO estimates): 48 (males 47; females 49) in 2008 (Source: WHO, *World Health Statistics*).

ECONOMICALLY ACTIVE POPULATION
(estimates, '000 persons, 1991)

	Males	Females	Total
Agriculture, etc.	1,157	1,118	2,275
Industry	290	46	336
Services	466	138	604
Total labour force	1,913	1,302	3,215

Source: UN Economic Commission for Africa, *African Statistical Yearbook*.

2002 (percentage distribution): Agriculture 66.9; Industry 12.0; Services 21.1 (Source: The World Bank and United Nations Development Programme, *Socio-Economic Survey 2002 Somalia*).

Mid-2011 (estimates in '000): Agriculture, etc. 2,502; Total labour force 3,843 (Source: FAO).

Health and Welfare

KEY INDICATORS

Total fertility rate (children per woman, 2008)	6.4
Under-5 mortality rate (per 1,000 live births, 2008)	200
HIV/AIDS (% of persons aged 15–49, 2007)	0.5
Physicians (per 1,000 head, 1997)	0.04
Hospital beds (per 1,000 head, 1997)	0.42
Health expenditure (2001): US $ per head (PPP)	18
Health expenditure (2001): % of GDP	2.6
Health expenditure (2001): public (% of total)	44.6
Total carbon dioxide emissions ('000 metric tons, 2007)	600.9
Carbon dioxide emissions per head (metric tons, 2007)	0.1
Access to water (% of persons, 2008)	30
Access to sanitation (% of persons, 2008)	23

For sources and definitions, see explanatory note on p. vi.

Agriculture

PRINCIPAL CROPS
('000 metric tons, FAO estimates unless otherwise indicated)

	2005	2006	2007
Rice, paddy	18	18	16
Maize	200	97	99
Sorghum	140	145*	80
Sweet potatoes	8	7	7
Cassava (Manioc)	85	82	82
Sugar cane	210	220	215
Groundnuts, with shell	9	5	6
Sesame seed	30	30	30
Watermelons	8	7	8
Grapefruit and pomelos	6	6	6
Bananas	38	38	38
Oranges	9	9	9
Lemons and limes	8	8	8
Dates	11	12	12

* Unofficial figure.

2008: Figures assumed to be unchanged from 2007 (FAO estimates).

Note: No data were available for individual crops in 2009.

Aggregate production ('000 metric tons, may include official, semi-official or estimated data): Total cereals 359 in 2005, 261 in 2006, 196 in 2007–09; Total roots and tubers 93 in 2005, 89 in 2006, 89 in 2007–09; Total vegetables (incl. melons) 92 in 2005, 83 in 2006, 84 in 2007–09; Total fruits (excl. melons) 208 in 2005, 209 in 2006, 209 in 2007–09.

Source: FAO.

LIVESTOCK
('000 head, year ending September, FAO estimates)

	2004	2005	2006
Cattle	5,400	5,500	5,350
Sheep	14,500	14,700	13,100
Goats	13,800	14,600	12,700
Pigs	5	5	4
Asses and mules	44	44	n.a.
Camels	7,210	7,230	7,000
Chickens	3	3	3

2007–08: Production assumed to be unchanged from 2006 (FAO estimates).

Note: No data were available for 2009.

Source: FAO.

SOMALIA

LIVESTOCK PRODUCTS
('000 metric tons, FAO estimates)

	2005	2006	2007
Cows' milk	450	437	435
Goats' milk	413	394	393
Sheep's milk	475	468	468
Cattle meat	68	66	66
Sheep meat	53	48	48
Goat meat	39	42	42
Hen eggs	3	3	3

2008–09: Production assumed to be unchanged from 2007 (FAO estimates).
Source: FAO.

Forestry

ROUNDWOOD REMOVALS
('000 cubic metres, excl. bark, FAO estimates)

	2007	2008	2009
Sawlogs, veneer logs and logs for sleepers*	28	28	28
Other industrial wood	82	82	82
Fuel wood	11,461	11,806	12,163
Total	11,571	11,916	12,273

* Annual output assumed to be unchanged since 1975.
Source: FAO.

SAWNWOOD PRODUCTION
('000 cubic metres, incl. railway sleepers)

	1973	1974	1975
Total (all broadleaved)	15*	10	14

* FAO estimate.

1976–2009: Production assumed to be unchanged from 1975 (FAO estimates).
Source: FAO.

Fishing

('000 metric tons, live weight, FAO estimates)

	1999	2000	2001
Marine fishes	23.5	19.8	26.3
Total catch (incl. others)	24.8	20.8	27.5

2002–08: Figures assumed to be unchanged from 2001 (FAO estimates).
Source: FAO.

Mining

('000 metric tons, estimates)

	2002	2003	2004
Salt	1	1	1
Gypsum	2	2	2

Source: US Geological Survey.

Industry

SELECTED PRODUCTS
('000 metric tons, unless otherwise indicated)

	1986	1987	1988
Sugar*	30.0	43.3	41.2
Canned meat (million tins)	1.0	—	—
Canned fish	0.1	—	—
Pasta and flour	15.6	4.3	—
Textiles (million yards)	5.5	3.0	6.3
Boxes and bags	15.0	12.0	5.0
Cigarettes and matches	0.3	0.2	0.1
Petroleum products	128	44	30

* Data from FAO.

Raw sugar ('000 metric tons): 20 in 2004; 15 in 2005; 20 in 2006 (Source: UN Industrial Commodity Statistics Database).

Electric energy (million kWh): 301 in 2005; 307 in 2006; 326 in 2007 (Source: UN Industrial Commodity Statistics Database).

Finance

CURRENCY AND EXCHANGE RATES

Monetary Units
100 cents = 1 Somali shilling (So. sh.).

Sterling, Dollar and Euro Equivalents (31 December 2010)
£1 sterling = 49,939.42 Somali shillings;
US $1 = 31,900.00 Somali shillings;
€1 = 42,624.78 Somali shillings;
100,000 Somali shillings = £2.00 = $3.13 = €2.35.

Average Exchange Rate (Somali shillings per US $)
1987   105.18
1988   170.45
1989   490.68

Note: A separate currency, the 'Somaliland shilling', was introduced in the 'Republic of Somaliland' in January 1995. The exchange rate was reported to be US $1 = 2,750 'Somaliland shillings' in March 2000.

CURRENT BUDGET
(million Somali shillings)

Revenue	1986	1987	1988
Total tax revenue	8,516.4	8,622.4	12,528.1
Taxes on income and profits	1,014.8	889.7	1,431.0
Income tax	380.5	538.8	914.8
Profit tax	634.3	350.9	516.2
Taxes on production, consumption and domestic transactions	1,410.4	1,274.2	2,336.4
Taxes on international transactions	6,091.2	6,458.5	8,760.6
Import duties	4,633.2	4,835.2	6,712.1
Total non-tax revenue	6,375.2	8,220.4	7,623.4
Fees and service charges	274.1	576.1	828.8
Income from government property	633.4	656.4	2,418.9
Other revenue	5,467.2	6,987.9	4,375.7
Total	14,891.6	16,842.8	20,151.5

Expenditure	1986	1987	1988
Total general services	11,997.7	19,636.7	24,213.6
Defence	2,615.9	3,145.0	8,093.9
Interior and police	605.0	560.7	715.4
Finance and central services	7,588.3	14,017.8	12,515.6
Foreign affairs	633.0	1,413.9	2,153.1
Justice and religious affairs	248.5	290.2	447.0
Presidency and general administration	93.0	148.0	217.4
Planning	189.0	24.9	24.3
National Assembly	25.0	36.2	46.9

SOMALIA

Expenditure—continued	1986	1987	1988
Total economic services	1,927.6	554.1	600.3
Transportation	122.2	95.2	94.5
Posts and telecommunications	94.3	76.7	75.6
Public works	153.9	57.5	69.8
Agriculture	547.2	59.4	55.3
Livestock and forestry	459.0	89.5	109.9
Mineral and water resources	318.8	85.2	93.1
Industry and commerce	131.0	45.1	43.9
Fisheries	101.2	45.5	58.2
Total social services	1,050.5	900.1	930.8
Education	501.6	403.0	478.1
Health	213.8	203.5	255.2
Information	111.5	135.0	145.8
Labour, sports and tourism	139.6	49.3	51.7
Other	84.0	109.3	—
Total	**14,975.8**	**21,091.0**	**25,744.7**

1989 (estimates): Budget to balance at 32,429.0m. Somali shillings.
1990 (estimates): Budget to balance at 86,012.0m. Somali shillings.
1991 (estimates): Budget to balance at 268,283.2m. Somali shillings.

CENTRAL BANK RESERVES
(US $ million at 31 December)

	1987	1988	1989
Gold*	8.3	7.0	6.9
Foreign exchange	7.3	15.3	15.4
Total	**15.6**	**22.3**	**22.3**

*Valued at market-related prices.
Source: IMF, *International Financial Statistics*.

MONEY SUPPLY
(million Somali shillings at 31 December)

	1987	1988	1989
Currency outside banks	12,327	21,033	70,789
Private sector deposits at central bank	1,771	1,555	5,067
Demand deposits at commercial banks	15,948	22,848	63,971
Total money	**30,046**	**45,436**	**139,827**

Source: IMF, *International Financial Statistics*.

COST OF LIVING
(Consumer Price Index; base: 2000 = 100)

	2001	2002	2003
All items	111.5	133.8	133.8

2004–06: Consumer prices assumed to be unchanged from 2003.
Source: African Development Bank.

NATIONAL ACCOUNTS
('000 million Somali shillings at current prices)
Expenditure on the Gross Domestic Product

	2006	2007	2008
Government final consumption expenditure	3,092.8	3,352.0	3,321.3
Private final consumption expenditure	25,828.3	27,991.4	27,740.0
Gross fixed capital formation	7,230.9	7,836.1	7,767.1
Changes in inventories	23.1	25.1	24.9
Total domestic expenditure	**36,175.1**	**39,204.6**	**38,853.3**
Exports of goods and services	112.1	121.4	120.4
Less Imports of goods and services	604.3	654.9	649.1
GDP at purchasers' values	**35,682.9**	**38,671.0**	**38,324.5**

Gross Domestic Product by Economic Activity

	2006	2007	2008
Agriculture, hunting, forestry and fishing	22,222.1	24,083.0	23,867.2
Mining and quarrying	1,164.3	1,261.8	1,250.5
Manufacturing	916.3	993.0	984.1
Construction	1,553.6	1,683.7	1,668.6
Trade, restaurants and hotels	3,927.4	4,256.2	4,218.1
Transport and communications	3,571.7	3,870.8	3,836.1
Other services	4,542.5	4,922.9	4,878.8
Sub-total	**37,897.9**	**41,071.4**	**40,703.4**
Indirect taxes (net)	−1,298.6	−1,407.4	−1,394.8
Less Imputed bank service charges	916.3	993.0	984.1
GDP at purchasers' values	**35,682.9**	**38,671.0**	**38,324.5**

Source: African Development Bank.

BALANCE OF PAYMENTS
(US $ million)

	1987	1988	1989
Exports of goods f.o.b.	94.0	58.4	67.7
Imports of goods f.o.b.	−358.5	−216.0	−346.3
Trade balance	**−264.5**	**−157.6**	**−278.6**
Imports of services	−127.7	−104.0	−122.0
Balance on goods and services	**−392.2**	**−261.6**	**−400.6**
Other income paid	−52.0	−60.6	−84.4
Balance on goods, services and income	**−444.2**	**−322.2**	**−485.0**
Current transfers received	343.3	223.7	331.2
Current transfers paid	−13.1	—	−2.9
Current balance	**−114.0**	**−98.5**	**−156.7**
Investment liabilities	−22.8	−105.5	−32.6
Net errors and omissions	39.0	22.4	−0.8
Overall balance	**−97.9**	**−181.7**	**−190.0**

Source: IMF, *International Financial Statistics*.

External Trade

PRINCIPAL COMMODITIES
(million Somali shillings)

Imports*	1986	1987	1988
Foodstuffs	1,783.3	3,703.6	1,216.1
Beverages and tobacco	298.1	183.6	6.2
Manufacturing raw materials	230.0	626.9	661.4
Fertilizers	1.8	238.0	2,411.4
Petroleum	2,051.0	3,604.2	3,815.9
Construction materials	981.4	2,001.9	307.8
Machinery and parts	1,098.3	1,203.6	957.1
Transport equipment	1,133.8	1,027.6	195.2
Total (incl. others)	**8,443.4**	**13,913.7**	**11,545.5**

*Figures cover only imports made against payments of foreign currencies. The total value of imports in 1986 was 20,474 m. Somali shillings.

Exports	1986	1987	1988
Livestock	4,420.3	7,300.0	3,806.5
Bananas	1,207.2	2,468.8	3,992.3
Hides and skins	294.0	705.2	492.0
Total (incl. others)	**6,372.5**	**10,899.9**	**9,914.1**

1992 (estimates, US $ million): Imports 150; Exports 80.

2000 (US $ million): Imports 160; Exports 69 (Source: African Development Bank).

2008 (selected commodities, US $ million): *Imports:* Refined sugar 59; Vegetables 49; Wheat or meslin flour 48; Vegetable products 46. *Exports:* Live goats 28; Waste and scrap of gold 27; Cattle 16; Wood charcoal 13; Live sheep 11 (Source: African Development Bank).

SOMALIA

PRINCIPAL TRADING PARTNERS
('000 Somali shillings)

Imports	1980	1981	1982
China, People's Repub.	46,959	40,962	89,772
Ethiopia	43,743	146,853	155,775
Germany, Fed. Repub.	104,117	430,548	214,873
Hong Kong	5,351	13,862	3,972
India	41,467	19,638	4,801
Iraq	2,812	67,746	402
Italy	756,800	662,839	1,221,146
Japan	28,900	54,789	48,371
Kenya	86,515	105,627	198,064
Saudi Arabia	120,208	160,583	82,879
Singapore	18,569	15,592	73,652
Thailand	19,296	40,527	106,474
United Kingdom	172,613	935,900	238,371
USA	201,662	141,823	154,082
Total (incl. others)	2,190,627	3,221,715	3,548,805

Exports	1980	1981	1982
Djibouti	6,640	3,209	2,458
Germany, Fed. Repub.	11,376	1,956	20,086
Italy	107,661	58,975	77,870
Kenya	2,425	6,929	4,211
Saudi Arabia	583,768	803,631	1,852,936
United Kingdom	1,233	—	3,169
USA	1,301	—	6,970
Yemen, People's Dem. Repub.	3,182	—	—
Total (incl. others)	844,012	960,050	2,142,585

Source: the former Ministry of Planning, Mogadishu.

1986: *Imports* (estimates, million Somali shillings) China, People's Repub. 553; France 341; Germany, Fed. Repub. 1,481; Japan 836; United Kingdom 773; USA 1,816; Total (incl. others) 8,443; *Exports* (estimates, million Somali shillings) China, People's Repub. 4; France 27; Germany, Fed. Repub. 11; United Kingdom 31; USA 5; Total (incl. others) 6,373 (Source: UN Economic Commission for Africa, *African Statistical Yearbook*).

2000 (US $ million): Imports 160; Exports 69 (Source: African Development Bank).

2008 (selected trading partners, US $ million): *Imports:* Brazil 9; Ethiopia 77; India 99; Kenya 187; United Arab Emirates 194. *Exports:* India 9; Nigeria 7; Oman 14; United Arab Emirates 29; Yemen 48 (Source: African Development Bank).

Transport

ROAD TRAFFIC
(estimates, '000 motor vehicles in use)

	1994	1995	1996
Passenger cars	2.8	2.0	1.0
Commercial vehicles	7.4	7.3	6.4

Source: International Road Federation, *World Road Statistics*.

SHIPPING
Merchant Fleet
(registered at 31 December)

	2007	2008	2009
Number of vessels	18	16	15
Total displacement ('000 grt)	9.9	6.0	5.2

Source: IHS Fairplay, *World Fleet Statistics*.

International Sea-borne Freight Traffic
('000 metric tons)

	1989	1990	1991
Goods loaded	325	324	n.a.
Goods unloaded	1,252*	1,118	1,007*

* Estimate.

Source: UN Economic Commission for Africa, *African Statistical Yearbook*.

CIVIL AVIATION
(traffic on scheduled services)

	1989	1990	1991
Kilometres flown (million)	3	3	1
Passengers carried ('000)	89	88	46
Passenger-km (million)	248	255	131
Freight ton-km (million)	8	9	5

Source: UN, *Statistical Yearbook*.

Tourism

	1996	1997	1998
Tourist arrivals ('000)	10	10	10

Source: World Bank.

Communications Media

	1995	1996	1997
Radio receivers ('000 in use)	400	450	470
Television receivers ('000 in use)	124	129	135
Telephones ('000 main lines in use)*	15	15	15
Daily newspapers	1	2	n.a.

*Estimates.

2003: Mobile cellular telephones (subscribers) 200,000; Telephones (main lines in use, estimate) 100,000; Internet users 30,000.

2004: Mobile cellular telephones (subscribers) 500,000; Telephones (main lines in use, estimate) 100,000; Internet users 86,000.

2005: Mobile cellular telephones (subscribers) 500,000; Telephones (main lines in use, estimate) 100,000; Internet users 90,000.

2006: Mobile cellular telephones (subscribers) 550,000; Internet users 94,000.

2007: Mobile cellular telephones (subscribers) 600,000; Internet users 98,000.

2008: Mobile cellular telephones (subscribers) 627,000; Telephones (main lines in use, estimate) 100,000; Internet users 102,000.

2009: Mobile cellular telephones (subscribers) 641,000; Telephones (main lines in use, estimate) 100,000; Internet users 106,000.

Sources: UNESCO, *Statistical Yearbook*; International Telecommunication Union.

Education

(1985, unless otherwise indicated)

	Institutions	Teachers	Pupils
Pre-primary	16	133	1,558
Primary	1,224	10,338	196,496
Secondary:			
general	n.a.	2,149	39,753
teacher training	n.a.	30*	613*
vocational	n.a.	637	5,933
Higher	n.a.	817†	15,672†

* Figure refers to 1984.
† Figure refers to 1986.

Source: UNESCO, *Statistical Yearbook*.

1990 (UN estimates): 377,000 primary-level pupils; 44,000 secondary-level pupils; 10,400 higher-level pupils.

1991: University teachers 549; University students 4,640.

Adult literacy rate (UNESCO estimates): 24.0% in 2002 (Source: UN Development Programme, *Human Development Report*).

SOMALIA

Directory

The Government

HEAD OF STATE

President: SHEIKH SHARIF SHEIKH AHMED (took office 31 January 2009).

CABINET
(May 2011)

Prime Minister: MOHAMED ABDULLAHI MOHAMED.
Deputy Prime Minister and Minister of Foreign Affairs: MOHAMED ABDULLAHI OMAAR.
Deputy Prime Minister and Minister of Defence: ABDIHAKIM MOHAMOUD HAJI-FAQI.
Deputy Prime Minister and Minister of Planning and International Co-operation: DR ABDIWELI ALI.
Minister of Justice, Religious Affairs and Endowment: ABDULLAHI ABYAN NUR.
Minister of the Interior and National Security: ABDISHAKUR SHEIKH HASSAN FARAH.
Minister of Finance and the Treasury: HUSSEIN ABDI HALANE.
Minister of Women's Development and Family Welfare: DR MARYAN QASIM AHMED.
Minister of Commerce and Industry: MOHAMUD ABDI IBRAHIM.
Minister of Education, Higher Education and Culture: Dr ABDINUR SHEIKH MOHAMED.
Minister of Information, Posts and Telecommunications: Prof. ABDULKAREEM HASSAN JAMA.
Minister of Ports and Marine, Air and Land Transport: Prof. AHMED ABDIRAHMAN ABADE.
Minister of Public Works and Reconstruction: ABDIRASHID HASHI.
Minister of Mineral Resources, Water, Energy and Petroleum: ABDIRISAK SHEIKH MUHYADIN.
Minister of Constitutional and Federal Affairs: MOHAMUD MOHAMED BOONOW.
Minister of Health and Human Services: Dr ADEN HAJI IBRAHIM DAUD.
Minister of Agriculture and Livestock: YUSUF MOALLIM AMIN.
Minister of Youth, Sports, Labour and Workforce Development: ABDINUR MOALLIM MOHAMUD.
Minister of Fisheries, Marine Resources and Environment: Dr MOHAMED MOALLIM HASSAN MOHAMED.

MINISTRIES

Office of the President: 1 Villa Baidao, 2525 Baydhabo; e-mail president@president.somaligov.net; internet www.president.somaligov.net.
Office of the Prime Minister: 1 Villa Somalia, 2525 Mogadishu; tel. (5) 543050; fax (5) 974242; e-mail primeminister@opm.somaligov.net; internet www.opm.somaligov.net.
Ministry of Agriculture and Livestock: 1 Villa Somalia, 2525 Mogadishu; internet www.moa.somaligov.net.
Ministry of Commerce and Industry: 1 Villa Somalia, 2525 Mogadishu; internet www.moin.somaligov.net.
Ministry of Constitutional and Federal Affairs: Mogadishu.
Ministry of Defence: Mogadishu; internet www.mod.somaligov.net.
Ministry of Education, Higher Education and Culture: Mogadishu.
Ministry of Finance and the Treasury: 1 Villa Somalia, 2525 Mogadishu; tel. (5) 404240; internet www.mof.somaligov.net.
Ministry of Fisheries, Marine Resources and Environment: 1 Villa Somalia, 2525 Mogadishu; internet www.mofmr.somaligov.net.
Ministry of Foreign Affairs: 1 Villa Somalia, 2525 Mogadishu; tel. and fax (5) 424640; internet www.mfa.somaligov.net.
Ministry of Health and Human Services: 1 Villa Somalia, 2525 Mogadishu; tel. and fax (5) 424640; internet www.moh.somaligov.net.
Ministry of Information, Posts and Telecommunications: 1 Villa Somalia, 2525 Mogadishu; tel. and fax (5) 424640; internet www.moi.somaligov.net.
Ministry of the Interior and National Security: 1 Villa Somalia, 2525 Mogadishu; internet www.mois.somaligov.net.
Ministry of Justice, Religious Affairs and Endowment: Mogadishu.
Ministry of Minerals Resources, Water, Energy and Petroleum: Mogadishu.
Ministry of Planning and International Co-operation: 2525 Mogadishu.
Ministry of Ports and Marine, Air and Land Transport: Mogadishu.
Ministry of Public Works and Reconstruction: 1 Villa Somalia, 2525 Mogadishu; internet www.mopwh.somaligov.net.
Ministry of Women's Development and Family Welfare: 1 Villa Somalia, 2525 Mogadishu; internet www.mowfa.somaligov.net.
Ministry of Youth, Sports, Labour and Workforce Development: 1 Villa Somalia, 2525 Mogadishu; internet www.moys.somaligov.net.

Legislature

TRANSITIONAL FEDERAL PARLIAMENT

Speaker: SHARIF HASAN SHEIKH ADAN.

In January 2004, following protracted negotiations in Kenya, an agreement was signed that provided for the establishment of a new 275-member transitional national parliament, to comprise 61 representatives from each of the four major clans and 31 from an alliance of smaller clans. Members were sworn in to the Transitional Federal Parliament (TFP) in August. In January 2009 it was agreed that the composition of the TFP would be increased by a further 275 members.

Political Organizations

Alliance for the Re-liberation of Somalia (ARS): f. 2007; split into two factions in 2008; 'Djibouti wing' led by SHEIKH SHARIF SHEIKH AHMED signed a peace agreement with the TNG, while the 'Asmara wing' led by SHEIKH HASSAN DAHIR AWEYS remained in conflict with the Government.
Islamic Party (Hizb al-Islam): radical Islamist party; Chair. SHEIKH AHMAD QASIM.
Islamic Union Party (al-Ittihad al-Islam): aims to unite ethnic Somalis from Somalia, Ethiopia, Kenya and Djibouti in an Islamic state.
Juba Valley Alliance (JVA): f. 1999; alliance of militia and businessmen from the Habr Gedir and Marehan clans; Pres. BARE ADAN SHIRE.
National Democratic League: Beled Weyne; f. 2003; Chair. Dr ABDIRAHMAN ABDULLE ALI; Sec.-Gen. ABDIKARIM HUSAYN IDOW.
Peace and Development Party: Mogadishu; f. 2002; Chair. ABDULLAHI HASAN AFRAH.
Rahanwin Resistance Army (RRA): guerrilla force active around Baidoa; Chair. HASAN MUHAMMAD NUR SHATIGADUD.
Al-Shabaab (The Youth): f. 2007 by former members of the Union of Islamic Courts; Leader IBRAHIM HAJI JAMA.
Somali Democratic Alliance (SDA): f. 1989; represents the Gadabursi ethnic grouping in the north-west; opposes the Isaaq-dominated SNM and its declaration of an independent 'Republic of Somaliland'; Leader MOHAMED FARAH ABDULLAH.
Somali Democratic Movement (SDM): represents the Rahanwin clan; movement split in early 1992, with this faction in alliance with ALI MAHDI MOHAMED; Leader ABDULKADIR MOHAMED ADAN.
Somali Eastern and Central Front (SECF): f. 1991; opposes the SNM's declaration of the independent 'Republic of Somaliland'; Chair. HIRSI ISMAIL MOHAMED.
Somali National Alliance (SNA): f. 1992 as alliance between the Southern Somali National Movement (which withdrew in 1993) and the factions of the United Somali Congress, Somali Democratic Movement and Somali Patriotic Movement given below; Chair. HUSSEIN MOHAMED AIDID.

    Somali Democratic Movement (SDM): represents the Rahanwin clan; Chair. ADAM UTHMAN ABDI; Sec.-Gen. Dr YASIN MA'ALIM ABDULLAHI.
    Somali Patriotic Movement (SPM): f. 1989; represents Ogadenis (of the southern Darod clan); Chair. GEDI UGAS MADHAR.

Somali National Front (SNF): f. 1991; guerrilla force active in southern Somalia, promoting Darod clan interests and seeking restoration of SRSP Govt; a rival faction (led by OMAR HAJI MASALEH)

SOMALIA

is active in southern Somalia; Leader Gen. MOHAMED SIAD HERSI 'MORGAN'.

Somali National Salvation Council: f. 2003; Chair. MUSE SUDI YALAHOW.

Somali Patriotic Movement (SPM): f. 1989 in southern Somalia; represents Ogadenis (of the Darod clan) in southern Somalia; this faction of the SPM has allied with the SNF in opposing the SNA; Chair. Gen. ADEN ABDULLAHI NOOR ('Gabio').

Somali People's Democratic Union (SPDU): f. 1997; breakaway group from the SSDF; Chair. Gen. MOHAMED JIBRIL MUSEH.

Somali Reconciliation and Restoration Council (SRRC): f. 2001 by faction leaders opposed to the establishment of the Hasan administration; aims to establish a rival national govt; Co-Chair. HUSSEIN MOHAMED AIDID, HILOWLE IMAN UMAR, ADEN ABDULLAHI NOOR, HASAN MOHAMED NUR, ABDULLAHI SHAYKH ISMA'IL; Sec.-Gen. MOWLID MA'ANEH MOHAMED.

Somali Revolutionary Socialist Party (SRSP): f. 1976 as the sole legal party; overthrown in Jan. 1991; conducts guerrilla operations in Gedo region, near border with Kenya; Sec.-Gen. (vacant); Asst Sec.-Gen. AHMED SULEIMAN ABDULLAH.

Somali Salvation Democratic Front (SSDF): f. 1981 as the Democratic Front for the Salvation of Somalia (DFSS), as a coalition of the Somali Salvation Front, the Somali Workers' Party and the Democratic Front for the Liberation of Somalia; operates in cen. Somalia, although a smaller group has opposed the SNA around Kismayu in alliance with the SNF; Chair. MOHAMED ABSHIR MONSA.

Somali Solidarity Party: Mogadishu; f. 1999; Chair. ABD AL-RAHMAN MUSA MOHAMED; Sec.-Gen. SA'ID ISA MOHAMED.

Southern Somali National Movement (SSNM): based on coast in southern Somalia; Chair. ABDI WARSEMEH ISAR.

Supreme Somali Islamic Courts Council: formerly the Union of Islamic Courts; seeks to create a Somali state under the guiding principles of *Shari'a* (Islamic) law; Chair. Sheikh HASSAN DAHIR AWEYS.

United Somali Congress (USC): f. 1989 in cen. Somalia; overthrew Siad Barre in Jan. 1991; party split in 1991, with this faction dominated by the Abgal sub-clan of the Hawiye clan, Somalia's largest ethnic group; Leader ABDULLAHI MA'ALIN; Sec.-Gen. MUSA NUR AMIN.

United Somali Congress—Somali National Alliance (USC—SNA): f. 1995 by dissident mems of the SNA's USC faction; represents the Habr Gedir sub-clan of the Hawiye; Leader OSMAN HASSAN ALI 'ATO'.

United Somali Congress—Somali Salvation Alliance (USC—SSA): Leader MUSE SUDI YALAHOW.

United Somali Party (USP): opposes the SNM's declaration of the independent 'Republic of Somaliland'; Leader MOHAMED ABDI HASHI.

Unity for the Somali Republic Party (USRP): f. 1999; the first independent party to be established in Somalia since 1969; Leader ABDI NUR DARMAN.

Diplomatic Representation

EMBASSIES IN SOMALIA

Note: Following the overthrow of Siad Barre in January 1991, all foreign embassies in Somalia were closed and all diplomatic personnel left the country. Some embassies were reopened, including those of France, Sudan and the USA, following the arrival of the US-led Unified Task Force (UNITAF) in December 1992; however, nearly all foreign diplomats left Somalia in anticipation of the withdrawal of the UN peace-keeping force, UNOSOM, in early 1995.

Cuba: Mogadishu.

Djibouti: Mogadishu; Ambassador DAYIB DOUBAD ROBLEH.

Korea, Democratic People's Republic: Via Km 5, Mogadishu; Ambassador KIM RYONG SU.

Ethiopia: POB 368, Mogadishu; Ambassador ABDULAZIZ AHMED ADAM.

Libya: Via Medina, POB 125, Mogadishu; Ambassador SAID RABIC.

Pakistan: Via Afgoi, Km 5, POB 339, Mogadishu; tel. (1) 80856.

Sudan: Via al-Mukarah, POB 552, Mogadishu; Chargé d'affaires a.i. FADIL AL-JASULI MUSTAFA.

Turkey: Via Km 6, POB 2833, Mogadishu; tel. (1) 81975.

United Arab Emirates: Via Afgoi, Km 5, Mogadishu; tel. (1) 23178.

Yemen: K4, Mogadishu; Ambassador AHMED HAMID ALI UMAR.

Judicial System

Constitutional arrangements in operation until 1991 provided for the judiciary to be independent of the executive and legislative powers. Laws and acts having the force of law were required to conform to the provisions of the Constitution and to the general principles of Islam.

Attorney-General: ABDULLAH DAHIR BARRE.

Supreme Court: Mogadishu; the court of final instance in civil, criminal, administrative and auditing matters; Chair. Sheikh AHMAD HASAN.

Military Supreme Court: Mogadishu; f. 1970; tried mems of the armed forces.

National Security Court: Mogadishu; heard cases of treason.

Courts of Appeal: Mogadishu; sat at Mogadishu and Hargeysa, with two sections, General and Assize.

Regional Courts: There were eight Regional Courts, with two sections, General and Assize.

District Courts: There were 84 District Courts, with Civil and Criminal Divisions. The Civil Division had jurisdiction over all controversies where the cause of action had arisen under *Shari'a* (Islamic) Law or Customary Law and any other Civil controversies where the matter in dispute did not involve more than 3,000 shillings. The Criminal Division had jurisdiction with respect to offences punishable with imprisonment not exceeding three years, or fines not exceeding 3,000 shillings, or both.

Qadis: District Courts of civil jurisdiction under Islamic Law.

Following the withdrawal of the UN peace-keeping force, UNOSOM, in early 1995, most regions outside Mogadishu reverted to clan-based fiefdoms where Islamic (*Shari'a*) law (comprising an Islamic Supreme Council and local Islamic high courts) prevailed. In October 1996 Ali Mahdi Mohamed endorsed a new Islamic judicial system under which appeals could be lodged on all sentences passed by Islamic courts, and no sentence imposed by the courts could be implemented prior to an appeal court ruling. In April 2009 the Transitional Parliament voted in favour of the introduction of *Shari'a* throughout Somalia.

Religion

ISLAM

Islam is the state religion. Most Somalis are Sunni Muslims.

Imam: Gen. MOHAMED ABSHIR.

CHRISTIANITY

The Roman Catholic Church

Somalia comprises a single diocese, directly responsible to the Holy See. The total number of Roman Catholics in Somalia was estimated at just 100.

Bishop of Mogadishu: (vacant), POB 273, Ahmed bin Idris, Mogadishu; tel. (1) 20184; e-mail evechcat@intnet.dj.

The Anglican Communion

Within the Episcopal Church in Jerusalem and the Middle East, the Bishop in Egypt has jurisdiction over Somalia.

The Press

The Country: POB 1178, Mogadishu; tel. (1) 21206; f. 1991; daily.

Dalka: POB 388, Mogadishu; tel. (1) 500533; e-mail dalka@somaliinternet.com; internet www.dalka-online.com; f. 1967; current affairs; weekly.

Heegan (Vigilance): POB 1178, Mogadishu; tel. (1) 21206; f. 1978; weekly; English; Editor MOHAMOUD M. AFRAH.

Horseed: POB 1178, Mogadishu; tel. (1) 21206; e-mail horseednet@gmail.com; internet www.horseednet.com; weekly; in Somali and English.

Huuriya (Liberty): Hargeysa; daily.

Jamhuuriya (The Republic): Hargeysa; e-mail webmaster@jamhuuriya.info; internet www.jamhuuriya.info; independent; daily; Editor-in-Chief HASSAN SAID FAISAL ALI; circ. 2,500.

Al-Mujeehid: Hargeysa; weekly.

New Era: POB 1178, Mogadishu; tel. (1) 21206; quarterly; in English, Somali and Arabic.

Qaran Press (Maalinle Madaxbannaan): Mogadishu; tel. (1) 215305; internet www.qaranpress.com; financial information; daily; in Somali; Editor ABDULAHI AHMED ALI; circ. 2,000.

Riyaaq (Happiness): Bossasso.

SOMALIA

Sahan (Pioneer): Bossasso; Editor MUHAMMAD DEEQ.
Somalia in Figures: Ministry of National Planning, POB 1742, Mogadishu; tel. (1) 80384; govt statistical publ; 3 a year; in English.
Somalia Times: POB 555, Mogadishu BN 03040; e-mail info@somalpost.com; internet www.somaliatimes.com; Somali; weekly; circ. 50,000.

NEWS AGENCIES

Horn of Africa News Agency: Mogadishu; e-mail info@hananews.org; internet www.hananews.org; f. 1990.
Somali National News Agency (SONNA): POB 1748, Mogadishu; tel. (1) 24058; Dir MUHAMMAD HASAN KAHIN.

Publishers

Government Printer: POB 1743, Mogadishu.
Somalia d'Oggi: Piazzale della Garesa, POB 315, Mogadishu; law, economics and reference.

Broadcasting and Communications

TELECOMMUNICATIONS

Ministry of Information: POB 1748, Mogadishu; tel. (1) 999621; Dir-Gen. A. ALI ASKAR.
Somali Telecom (Olympic Telecommunications): Mogadishu.
Somaliland Telecommunications Corpn: Hargeysa; Dir MOHAMED ARWO.
Telcom Somaliland: Telcom Somaliland Bldg, Togdheer St, Hargeysa; tel. (2) 300161; fax (2) 300162; e-mail info@telcomsomaliland.com; internet www.telcomsomaliland.com; f. 2003; provides local, national long distance and int. telecommunications, mobile communications and data services.

BROADCASTING

Radio

Holy Koran Radio: Mogadishu; f. 1996; religious broadcasts in Somali.
Radio Awdal: Boorama, 'Somaliland'; operated by the Gadabursi clan.
Radio Banaadir: Tahlil Warsame Bldg, 4 Maka al-Mukarama Rd, Mogadishu; tel. (5) 2960268; e-mail rbb@radiobanadir.com; internet www.radiobanadir.com; f. 2000; serves Mogadishu and its environs.
Radio Free Somalia: tel. (5) 630838; e-mail admin@radiofreesomalia.com; internet www.radiofreesomalia.com; f. 1993; operates from Galacaio in north-eastern Somalia; relays humanitarian and educational programmes.
Radio Gaalkayco: operates from 'Puntland'.
Radio Hargeysa, the Voice of the 'Republic of Somaliland': POB 14, Hargeysa; tel. 155; e-mail radiohargeysa@yahoo.com; internet www.radiosomaliland.com/radiohargeisa.html; serves the northern region ('Somaliland'); broadcasts in Somali, and relays Somali and Amharic transmission from Radio Mogadishu; Dir of Radio IDRIS EGAL NUR.
Radio HornAfrique: Mogadishu; f. 1999; commercial independent station broadcasting music and programmes on social issues; Dir (vacant).
Radio Mogadishu, Voice of the Masses of the Somali Republic: southern Mogadishu; f. 1993 by supporters of Gen. Aidid after the facilities of the fmr state-controlled radio station, Radio Mogadishu (of which Gen. Aidid's faction took control in 1991), were destroyed by UNOSOM; broadcasts in Somali, Amharic, Arabic, English and Swahili; Chair. FARAH HASAN AYOBOQORE.
Radio Mogadishu, Voice of Somali Pacification: Mogadishu; f. 1995 by supporters of Osman Hassan Ali 'Ato'; broadcasts in Somali, English and Arabic; Dir-Gen. MUHAMMAD DIRIYEH ILMI.
Radio Mogadishu, Voice of the Somali Republic: northern Mogadishu; f. 1992 by supporters of Ali Mahdi Mohamed; Chair. FARAH HASSAN AYOBOQORE.
Radio Shabelle: Mogadishu; e-mail ali.dahir@shabelle.net; internet www.shabelle.net; Chair. and CEO ABDIMAALIK YUSUF.
Radio Somaliland: internet www.radiosomaliland.com
Voice of Peace: Galkayo; tel. 90795026 (mobile); e-mail codkanabadda@gmail.com; internet www.codkanabadda.com; f. 1993; aims to promote peace and reconstruction in Somalia; receives support from UNICEF and the AU.

Some radio receivers are used for public address purposes in small towns and villages.

Note: In January 2007 the Transitional National Government was granted emergency powers to proscribe four media companies in an attempt to restore order in Mogadishu. HornAfrique Media and Shabelle Media were believed to have ceased operations although others condemned the ban and refused to close.

Television

A television service, financed by Kuwait and the United Arab Emirates, was inaugurated in 1983. Programmes in Somali and Arabic are broadcast for three hours daily, extended to four hours on Fridays and public holidays. Reception is limited to a 30-km radius of Mogadishu.

Somali Television Network (STN): Mogadishu; f. 1999; broadcasts 22 channels in Somali, English, French, Hindi, Gujarati, Bengali, Punjabi, Italian and Arabic; Man. Dir ABURAHMAN ROBLEY ULAYEREH.
Television HornAfrique: Mogadishu; f. 1999; broadcasts 6 channels in Somali and Arabic; CEO ALI IMAN SHARMARKEH.

Finance

(cap. = capital; res = reserves; m. = million; brs = branches; amounts in Somali shillings unless otherwise stated)

BANKING

Central Bank

Central Bank of Somalia: 1 Villa Somalia, Mogadishu; tel. (1) 657733; fax (1) 215026; internet www.somalbanca.org; Chair. ABDULLAHI JAMA ALI.
A central bank (with 10 branches) is also in operation in Hargeysa (in the self-proclaimed 'Republic of Somaliland').

Commercial Banks

Commercial Bank of Somalia: Via Primo Luglio, POB 203, Mogadishu; tel. (1) 22861; f. 1990 to succeed the Commercial and Savings Bank of Somalia; state-owned; cap. 1,000m. (May 1990); 33 brs.
Universal Bank of Somalia: Mogadishu; f. 2002; cap. US $10m.; Gen. Man. MAHAD ADAN BARKHADLE (acting).

Private Bank

Somali-Malaysian Commercial Bank: Mogadishu; f. 1997; cap. US $4m.

Development Bank

Somali Development Bank: Via Primo Luglio, POB 1079, Mogadishu; tel. (1) 21800; f. 1968; state-owned; cap. and res 2,612.7m. (Dec. 1988); Pres. MOHAMED MOHAMED NUR; 4 brs.

INSURANCE

Cassa per le Assicurazioni Sociali della Somalia: POB 123, Mogadishu; f. 1950; workers' compensation; Dir-Gen. HASSAN MOHAMED JAMA; 9 brs.
State Insurance Co of Somalia: POB 992, Mogadishu; f. 1974; Gen. Man. ABDULLAHI GA'AL; brs throughout Somalia.

Trade and Industry

DEVELOPMENT ORGANIZATIONS

Agricultural Development Corpn: POB 930, Mogadishu; f. 1971 by merger of fmr agricultural and machinery agencies and grain marketing board; supplies farmers with equipment and materials and purchases growers' cereal and oil seed crops; Dir-Gen. MOHAMED FARAH ANSHUR.
Livestock Development Agency: POB 1759, Mogadishu; f. 1966; Dir-Gen. HASSAN WELI SHEIKH HUSSEN; brs throughout Somalia.
Somali Co-operative Movement: Mogadishu; Chair. HASSAN HAWADLE MADAR.
Somali Oil Refinery: POB 1241, Mogadishu; Chair. NUR AHMED DARAWISH.
Water Development Agency: POB 525, Mogadishu; Dir-Gen. KHALIF HAJI FARAH.

CHAMBER OF COMMERCE

Somali Chamber of Commerce and Industry (SCCI): Somali Chamber Bldg, nr Banadir Hotel, Shibis District, Mogadishu; tel. (1)

643081; fax (1) 221560; e-mail info@somalicci.com; internet www.somalicci.com; f. 1970; Pres. IMAN ALI.

TRADE ASSOCIATION

National Agency of Foreign Trade: POB 602, Mogadishu; tel. (1) 120485; major foreign trade agency; state-owned; brs in Berbera and over 150 centres throughout Somalia; Dir-Gen. JAMA AW MUSE.

UTILITIES

Water Development Agency: POB 525, Mogadishu; Dir-Gen. KHALIF HAJI FARAH.

TRADE UNION

National Union of Somali Journalists (NUSOJ): Tree Biano Bldg, Via al-Mukarah Km 4, Mogadishu; fax (1) 859944; e-mail nusoj@nusoj.org; internet www.nusoj.org; f. 2002 as Somali Journalists' Network (SOJON); name changed as above in 2005; Chair. BURHAN AHMED DAHIR; Sec.-Gen. MOHAMED IBRAHIM (acting); 6 brs across Somalia.

Transport

RAILWAYS

There are no railways in Somalia.

ROADS

In 2000 there were an estimated 22,100 km of roads, of which some 11.8% were paved.

SHIPPING

Merca, Berbera, Mogadishu and Kismayu are the chief ports. An EU-sponsored development project for the port of Berbera (in 'Somaliland') was announced in February 1996. It was reported that the port of Mogadishu, which had been largely closed since 1995, was reopened to commercial traffic in August 2006. There was a large increase in piracy off the coast of Somalia during the late 2000s.

Berbera Port Authority: Berbera; tel. (2) 740198; fax (2) 770224; e-mail bportadm@telesom.net; Gen. Man. ALI OMER MOHAMED.

Somali Ports Authority: POB 935, Mogadishu; tel. (1) 30081; Port Dir AHMED HAGI ALI ADANI.

Juba Enterprises Beder & Sons Ltd: POB 549, Mogadishu; privately owned.

National Shipping Line: POB 588, Mogadishu; tel. (1) 23021; state-owned; Gen. Man. Dr ABDULLAHI MOHAMED SALAD.

Puntland Shipping Service: Bossasso.

Shosman Commercial Co Ltd: North-Eastern Pasaso; privately owned.

Somali Shipping Corpn: POB 2775, Mogadishu; state-owned.

CIVIL AVIATION

Mogadishu has an international airport. There are airports at Hargeysa and Baidoa and six other airfields. It was reported that a daily service had been inaugurated in April 1994 between Hargeysa (in the self-declared 'Republic of Somaliland') and Nairobi, Kenya. Mogadishu international airport (closed since 1995) was officially re-opened in mid-1998, but continuing civil unrest hampered services. In August 2006 the airport reopened to commercial flights.

Air Somalia: Mogadishu; f. 2001; operates internal passenger services and international services to destinations in Africa and the Middle East; Chair. ALI FARAH ABDULLEH.

Jubba Airways: POB 6200, 30th St, Mogadishu; tel. (1) 217000; fax (1) 227711; e-mail jubbaair@emirates.net.ae; internet www.jubba-airways.com; f. 1998; operates domestic flights and flights to destinations in Djibouti, Saudi Arabia, the United Arab Emirates and Yemen; Man. Dir ABDULLAHI WARSAME.

Defence

Of total armed forces of 64,500 in June 1990, the army numbered 60,000, the navy 2,000 and the air force 2,500. In addition, there were 29,500 members of paramilitary forces, including 20,000 members of the People's Militia. Following the overthrow of the Siad Barre regime in January 1991, there were no national armed forces. Somalia was divided into areas controlled by different armed groups, which were based on clan, or sub-clan, membership. Following his election to the presidency in August 2000, Abdulkasim Salad Hasan announced his intention to recruit former militiamen into a new national force: by December some 5,000 Somalis had begun training under the supervision of Mogadishu's Islamic courts. However, efforts to establish a new national armed force have made little progress since the Government's return to Somalia from exile in 2005. In November 2008 it was estimated that the armed forces of the Transitional Federal Government (TFG) numbered around 2,000. The total armed forces of the self-proclaimed 'Republic of Somaliland' were estimated to number 15,000, while the armed forces of 'Puntland' were believed to number around 5,000–10,000. The AU Mission in Somalia had an estimated 7,250 troops present in the country (mostly from Burundi and Uganda) in late 2010.

Chief of General Staff: Col ABDI AHMAD GULED.

Air Force Commander: NUR ILMI ADAWE.

Navy Commander: Col MUSE SA'ID MOHAMED.

Army Commander: Gen. MUHAMMAD GHELLE KAHIYE.

Commander of Rapid Reaction Forces: Gen. ABDI'AZIZ ALI BARRE.

Education

Following the overthrow of Mohamed Siad Barre's Government in January 1991 and the ensuing internal disorder, Somalia's education system collapsed. In January 1993 a primary school was opened in the building of Somalia's only university, the Somali National University in Mogadishu (which had been closed in early 1991). A number of schools operating in the country were under the control of fundamentalist Islamic groups.

SOUTH AFRICA

Introductory Survey

LOCATION, CLIMATE, LANGUAGE, RELIGION, FLAG, CAPITAL

The Republic of South Africa occupies the southern extremity of the African mainland. It is bordered by Namibia to the north-west, by Botswana and Zimbabwe to the north, by Mozambique to the north-east, and by Swaziland to the east. Lesotho is completely surrounded by South African territory. The climate is generally sub-tropical, but with considerable regional variations. Temperatures in Cape Town, on the south-west coast, vary from 7°C (45°F) to 26°C (79°F), with an annual average of about 17°C (63°F). Annual rainfall averages 510 mm (20 ins) at Cape Town, and 1,101 mm (43 ins) at Durban, on the east coast. The official languages are Sepedi, Sesotho, Setswana, siSwati, Tshivenda, Xitsonga, Afrikaans, English, isiNdebele, isiXhosa and isiZulu. About 79.4% of the population are black, 9.2% are white, 8.8% are Coloured (of mixed race), and 2.6% are Asian (mainly of Indian origin). Most of the inhabitants profess Christianity, although traditional African religions are still adhered to. There are also small minorities of Hindus (nearly all Asians) and Muslims (mainly Coloureds and Asians). The national flag (proportions 2 by 3) has a green 'Y' shape extending from the upper and lower hoist corners to the centre of the fly end, bordered in white on its outer edges, and in light orange on its inner edges near the hoist; the areas above and below the horizontal band of the 'Y' are red and blue respectively, with a black triangle at the hoist. The administrative capital is Pretoria, the legislative capital is Cape Town, and the judicial capital is Bloemfontein.

CONTEMPORARY POLITICAL HISTORY

Historical Context

On 31 May 1910 four British dependencies were merged to form the Union of South Africa, a dominion under the British Crown. In 1931 the British Parliament recognized the Union as an independent country within the Commonwealth. From the establishment of South Africa until 1984, national administration was the exclusive preserve of the white population.

The National Party (NP), which acceded to power in 1948, introduced the doctrine of apartheid (in theory the separate, but equal, development of all racial groups, in practice leading to white, particularly Afrikaner, supremacy). The principal opposition to government policy during the 1950s took the form of a campaign of civil disobedience, led by the multiracial African National Congress of South Africa (ANC). In 1959 some members of the ANC formed the exclusively black Pan-Africanist Congress (PAC). In 1960 the ANC and the PAC protested against the 'pass laws' (which required blacks to be in possession of special documentation in designated white urban areas); at one demonstration, in Sharpeville, 67 blacks were killed by security forces, prompting international outrage, and further demonstrations within South Africa, as a result of which the ANC and the PAC were declared illegal. Both movements subsequently formed military wings, based outside South Africa, to conduct campaigns of sabotage. An influential leader of the ANC, Nelson Mandela, was detained in 1962 and sentenced to life imprisonment on a charge of sabotage in 1964, but remained a focus for opposition to apartheid.

On 31 May 1961, following a referendum among white voters in October 1960, South Africa became a republic, and left the Commonwealth. Dr Hendrik Verwoerd was Prime Minister from 1958 until his assassination in September 1966. He was succeeded by the former Minister of Justice, Balthazar Johannes (B. J.) Vorster.

As an integral part of the policy of apartheid, the territorial segregation of African ethnic groups was enforced, on the grounds that the Native Reserves (comprising only 13% of national territory) constituted the historic 'homelands' (Bantustans) of different African nations. In 1963 Transkei was accorded 'self-governing' status, with an Executive Council, headed by a Chief Minister, to be elected by a Legislative Assembly. Bophuthatswana (June 1972), Ciskei (August 1972), Lebowa (October 1972), Gazankulu (February 1973), KwaZulu (April 1973), Qwaqwa (November 1974), KwaNdebele (October 1977), and KaNgwane (August 1984) were subsequently granted 'self-government'. Transkei was declared 'independent' in October 1976, Bophuthatswana in December 1977, Venda in September 1979 and Ciskei in December 1981. The population of the 'independent homelands' was not entitled to South African citizenship. The 'independent homelands' were not recognized by any government other than that of South Africa.

Domestic Political Affairs

The numerous discriminatory laws regulating the lives of the country's black, 'Coloured' (a term used to denote people of mixed race) and 'Indian' (Asian) populations, combined with stringent security legislation, led to the detention without trial of many of the Government's opponents, the banning of black political organizations outside the 'homelands', and the forced removal of hundreds of thousands of blacks in accordance with the provisions of the Group Areas Act of 1966 (which imposed residential segregation of the races) and the 'homelands' policy. In June 1976 violent riots occurred in Soweto (South-Western Townships), near Johannesburg, and rapidly spread to other black urban areas. Vorster used the executive's virtually limitless powers, conferred by the newly adopted Internal Security Act, to suppress riots and strikes. Several hundred people died in confrontations with the security forces, and many more were detained without trial. Allegations of human rights violations by security forces culminated in international indignation at the death in detention of a black community leader, Steve Biko, in September 1977. In 1978 black, Coloured and Indian activists founded the Azanian People's Organization (AZAPO).

In September 1978 Vorster resigned as Prime Minister, and was succeeded by Pieter Willem (P. W.) Botha, hitherto the Minister of Defence. In February 1981 a new, 60-member advisory body, the President's Council, comprising representatives of the white, Coloured and Indian population, was formed to consider constitutional reform. Its recommendations to include Coloureds and Indians (but not blacks) in a three-chamber Parliament, with a multiracial government (led by an executive President), exacerbated inter-party differences: the 'verligte' (liberal) wing of the NP, led by Botha, advocated the establishment of a confederation of South Africa and the 'homelands', with separate citizenships but a common South African nationality, and was strongly opposed by the 'verkrampte' (uncompromising) wing of the party.

Constitutional reforms were approved by the House of Assembly in September 1983, and by about 66% of voters in an all-white referendum in November. In the same month the Progressive Federal Party (PFP) decided to take part in the reformed system. However, six 'homeland' leaders, including Chief Mangosuthu Gatsha Buthelezi, the Chief Minister of KwaZulu (who had consistently opposed the 'homelands' policy), rejected the constitutional reforms on the grounds that blacks remained excluded from participation in the central Government. Despite a previous pledge by the Prime Minister to assess Coloured and Indian opinion on the reforms, elections to the Coloured and Indian chambers of the new Parliament, known as the House of Representatives and the House of Delegates, respectively, took place in August 1984, without prior referendums. As a result, the boycott that had been organized by the principal legal opposition movement, the United Democratic Front (UDF), was widely observed: about 18% of the eligible Coloured population voted in the elections to the House of Representatives, with the Coloured Labour Party (LP) winning 76 of the 80 directly elected seats, while only 16.6% of eligible Indian voters participated in the elections to the House of Delegates, with the National People's Party (NPP) winning 18 and the Solidarity Party 17 of the 40 directly elected seats. (The House of Assembly, as elected in 1981, remained in office.)

The new Constitution came into effect in September 1984. Under its terms, legislative power was vested in the State President and the tricameral Parliament, comprising the 178-member House of Assembly (for the representation of whites), the 85-member House of Representatives (for Coloureds) and the 45-member House of Delegates (for Indians). The post of Prime Minister was abolished and Botha was unanimously elected to the new office of State President (which combined the powers of Head of State and Prime Minister) by an electoral college, comprising members of all three parliamentary chambers. A President's Council, a new Cabinet and three Ministers' Councils (one for each population group) were subsequently established. The Cabinet comprised only two non-white members, the Chairmen of the Indian and Coloured Ministers' Councils, neither of whom was given a portfolio.

During 1985–86 a number of the laws on which apartheid was based were modified or repealed, prompting strong right-wing opposition. The Immorality Act (1927) and the Prohibition of Mixed Marriages Act (1949), which banned sexual relations and marriage between members of different races, were repealed in April 1985, and in the following month it was announced that the Prohibition of Political Interference Act (1967), prohibiting members of different racial groups from belonging to the same political party, was to be abrogated. In April 1986 the Government promulgated legislation that provided for the removal of a number of restrictions on the movement, residence and employment of blacks in white urban areas. On 1 July the 'pass laws' were officially repealed, with the introduction of uniform identity documents for all South African citizens. On the same day reforms concerning the structure of local and provincial government were implemented, and legislation granting blacks limited rights to own property in black urban areas entered into force. In the same month it was announced that citizens of the four 'independent homelands' who were residing and working permanently in South Africa were to regain South African citizenship; in effect, however, only a small proportion of the population of the 'homelands' was eligible. Following discussions, initiated by Buthelezi in April 1986, regarding the establishment of a joint authority for his 'homeland', KwaZulu, and the province of Natal, the Government agreed to the formation of an administrative body, the Joint Executive Authority (which was installed in November 1987).

The introduction of the new Constitution in September 1984 prompted severe rioting in the black townships. Factional clashes within the black community also occurred, notably between supporters of the ANC and of the Inkatha Movement, a Zulu organization led by Buthelezi. In July 1985 the Government declared a state of emergency in 36 districts; by March 1986 it was estimated that 757 people had been killed, and almost 8,000 arrested. In June of that year Botha declared a nation-wide state of emergency, on the grounds that national security was endangered by subversive elements. Press censorship subsequently became progressively stricter, and the powers of the security forces were extended. Opposition to the Government emerged from the influential Congress of South African Trade Unions (COSATU).

In January 1989 Botha withdrew from his official duties, owing to ill health; in February he resigned as leader of the NP, and was succeeded by Frederik Willem (F. W.) de Klerk, hitherto Minister of National Education. Despite almost unanimous demands from the party that he should share power with de Klerk before retiring at the next general election, Botha refused to allow his power as State President to be eroded, and in March he resumed his official duties. In April the PFP, the Independent Party (which had been formed by one of a number of 'verligte' defectors from the NP in 1988) and the National Democratic Movement (established by dissident PFP members in late 1987) merged to form the Democratic Party (DP).

The state of emergency was extended for a further 12 months in June 1989. In August Botha claimed that members of his Cabinet had omitted to inform him of a prospective visit by de Klerk to Zambia to meet with President Kenneth Kaunda (which he opposed, owing to Kaunda's support for the ANC). Following a confrontation with the Cabinet, Botha resigned as State President. Shortly afterwards de Klerk was appointed acting President.

Elections to the three Houses of Parliament took place in September 1989. The NP won 93 of the 166 elective seats in the House of Assembly, while the Conservative Party (CP) secured 39 seats, and the DP 33 seats. Less than 12% of the Coloured electorate voted in the general election to the House of Representatives, at which the LP won 69 of the 80 directly-elective seats. Some 20% of the Indian electorate voted in the general election to the House of Delegates: the Solidarity Party secured 16 of the 40 directly-elective seats, while the NPP won nine. In mid-September, following his inauguration as State President, de Klerk stated that the implementation of constitutional reforms was his highest priority.

The release of Nelson Mandela

On 2 February 1990 de Klerk announced several radical reforms, including the legalization of the ANC, the PAC, the South African Communist Party (SACP), the UDF and more than 30 other banned political organizations. Mandela and a further 120 political prisoners were to be released unconditionally. In addition, most emergency regulations restricting the media were to be removed, as were repressive measures imposed on former political detainees; detention without trial was to be limited to a maximum of six months. De Klerk confirmed that the Government intended to initiate negotiations with the black opposition, with the aim of drafting a new democratic constitution. Leaders of the extreme right-wing parties reacted to de Klerk's reforms with threats of violence.

Mandela's release from prison, on 11 February 1990, received much international attention. In March he was elected Deputy President of the ANC. In spite of appeals by Mandela for reconciliation between rival factions within the black community, the continuing violence in Natal between supporters of the Inkatha Movement and mainly Xhosa-speaking supporters of the ANC intensified in March and April, and unrest erupted in several black townships. In May legislation was introduced that granted temporary immunity from prosecution to political exiles who had committed crimes, including leaders of the ANC. In July Buthelezi reconstituted the Inkatha Movement as the Inkatha Freedom Party (IFP), in order to participate in future constitutional negotiations. The following month the ANC and the Government reached an agreement whereby, in preparation for constitutional negotiations, the ANC was to suspend its guerrilla activities, and the Government was to release more than 3,000 political prisoners and to facilitate the return to South Africa of an estimated 40,000 exiles. However, the ANC subsequently continued to train recruits for its military wing (Umkhonto we Sizwe—MK) and to stockpile ammunition, thereby contravening the terms of its cease-fire and causing the Government to delay the release of political prisoners and the repatriation of exiles.

During August 1990 factional fighting between supporters of the IFP and of the ANC escalated in the black townships surrounding Johannesburg; more than 500 people were reported to have been killed by the end of that month. Nevertheless, in October the state of emergency was revoked in Natal. (It had been revoked in all other provinces in June.) Also that month the Separate Amenities Act of 1953 (which had imposed racial segregation with regard to public amenities) was repealed, prompting right-wing protests, particularly from the Afrikaanse Weerstandsbeweging (AWB), a paramilitary organization that had been formed in 1973 under the leadership of Eugene Terre'Blanche. During October the NP opened its membership to all races.

In February 1991 de Klerk announced that he was to introduce draft legislation to repeal the principal remaining apartheid laws: the Land Acts of 1913 and 1936 (which stipulated that the black population was entitled to own only 13.6% of the land), the Group Areas Act, the Black Communities Act of 1984 (which enforced the separate status of black townships) and the Population Registration Act of 1950 (which decreed that all South Africans should be registered at birth according to race) were subsequently abolished. In the same month the Government agreed to assume joint administrative powers in Ciskei, following increasing pressure within the 'independent homeland' for its reincorporation into South Africa and for the resignation of its military ruler. In mid-February the Government and the ANC reached agreement on the release of political prisoners, the return of exiles and the curtailment of activities by the MK. However, increasing township violence continued to impede constitutional negotiations.

In July 1991, at a national congress of the ANC, Nelson Mandela was elected as its President and Cyril Ramaphosa, hitherto leader of the National Union of Mineworkers, was elected Secretary-General of the organization. A multi-party conference on South Africa's future, the Convention for a Democratic South Africa (CODESA), was convened in December. CODESA was attended by the Government and 18 political organizations, including the ANC, the NP, the DP, the LP, the NPP, New Solidarity (formerly the Solidarity Party) and representatives of the 'homelands' (including the IFP, which represented KwaZulu); the conference was boycotted by the PAC, AZAPO and the CP. The negotiating body's stated aim to create an undivided South Africa was rejected by the IFP, which favoured the concept of a South African federation of independent states, and by the Bophuthatswana administration, which demanded total independence from South Africa.

In mid-1992 the ANC announced that it was to organize a series of demonstrations in protest against 'homeland' leaders who wished their territories (Bophuthatswana, Ciskei, KwaZulu and Qwaqwa) to retain a strong measure of autonomy in the future South Africa. In September Ciskei security forces killed 28 ANC demonstrators, and injured about 200, prompting international outrage. The ANC accused the South African security forces (some of whose members had been seconded to Ciskei) of complicity in the incident. In mid-September de Klerk announced that measures to reduce the 'independence' of the 'homelands' would be implemented. In late 1992 the leaders of Bophuthatswana, Ciskei and KwaZulu formed a pressure group (the Concerned South Africans Group—COSAG) to campaign for a maximum degree of regional autonomy.

In March 1993 it was decided that CODESA was to be reconstituted, with the PAC, the IFP and the CP granted equal status with the other representatives, and in June 1993 legislation providing for the abolition of the President's Council was approved by Parliament. The IFP, CP and KwaZulu delegations subsequently withdrew from the negotiating forum, while the remaining representatives continued discussions on the precepts of a multiracial interim constitution. The interim Constitution, promulgated in July, entrenched equal rights for citizens regardless of race, and vested executive power in a President and a Cabinet, which was to comprise representatives of the political parties that held a stipulated number of seats in the legislature. Legislative authority was vested in a bicameral Parliament, comprising a 400-member National Assembly (to be elected by proportional representation) and a Senate (with 10 members elected by each regional legislature). The National Assembly and Senate formed the Constitutional Assembly, which was to draft a new constitution, with adherence to the principles stipulated by the negotiating forum. Although the interim Constitution included provisions for the establishment of regional legislatures, it was rejected by COSAG (while the IFP, KwaZulu and CP delegations continued to boycott negotiations).

In early September 1993 the negotiating forum approved legislation providing for the establishment of a multiracial Transitional Executive Council (TEC), which was to rule in conjunction with the existing Government pending the elections, thereby allowing blacks to participate in central government for the first time. The TEC was to comprise representatives of the groups involved in the negotiating process; however, the IFP, the CP, the governments of Bophuthatswana, Ciskei and KwaZulu, and the PAC refused to participate. Later in September Parliament adopted legislation providing for the installation of the TEC, and the establishment of an Independent Electoral Commission (IEC), and an independent media commission and broadcasting authority.

In October 1993 the constituent members of COSAG, together with the Afrikaner Volksfront (AVF—an informal alliance of right-wing organizations), formed the Freedom Alliance (FA), with the stated objective of negotiating concessions regarding regional autonomy. The Bophuthatswana and Ciskei delegations subsequently withdrew from the negotiating forum. In November the negotiating forum repealed legislation providing for detention without trial. Later that month agreement was reached regarding the establishment of a new security force, which was to be under the control of both central and provincial government, and a reconstituted national defence force, which was to comprise members of the existing armed forces of South Africa and the 'independent homelands', and the military wings of political organizations.

Approval of the new Constitution

On 18 November 1993, following intensive discussions, 19 of the 21 delegations remaining in the negotiating forum approved the interim Constitution, which incorporated several amendments to the draft promulgated in July. A number of significant compromises between the Government and the ANC had been achieved: the Government abandoned its demand that cabinet decisions require a two-thirds' majority (thereby accepting that power-sharing would not be constitutionally entrenched), while the ANC agreed to a fixed five-year period for transition to majority rule. The President was to be elected by the National Assembly, and was to exercise executive power in consultation with at least two Deputy Presidents, who were to be nominated by parties with a minimum of 80 seats in the National Assembly (equivalent to 20% of the national vote). A Constitutional Court was to be appointed by the President from a list of candidates nominated by an independent judicial commission. As a concession to the FA, the interim Constitution included a provision that entitled the legislatures of the nine redesignated provinces to draft their own constitutions, subject to the principles governing the national Constitution. Nevertheless, the FA, together with the PAC, rejected the interim Constitution.

In early December 1993 the negotiating forum reached agreement on the reincorporation of the four 'independent homelands' into South Africa on 27 April 1994, when the interim Constitution was to enter into force. On 1 January South African citizenship was to be restored to the population of the 'homelands', who would be entitled to vote in the elections. However, the governments of Bophuthatswana and Ciskei refused to recognize the decision. On 7 December 1993 the TEC commenced sessions, but was, as expected, boycotted by a number of delegations. In mid-December the IEC was established. On 22 December Parliament ratified the interim Constitution, thereby effecting its own dissolution as an organ of the apartheid regime.

In February 1994, in accordance with a decision by the TEC, de Klerk announced that the elections, which were to be monitored by international observers, would take place between 26 and 28 April. The IFP confirmed that it intended to boycott the elections, after the Zulu tribal monarch, King Goodwill Zwelithini (who was Buthelezi's nephew), rejected the interim Constitution and declared sovereignty over the territory traditionally owned by the Zulus. In mid-February Nelson Mandela announced a number of proposed amendments to the interim Constitution. The FA, however, rejected the concessions, on the grounds that the powers of regional government remained inadequate, and refused to attend discussions on the proposed amendments, which were, nevertheless, adopted by the negotiating forum. In early March, after the ANC and IFP agreed to accept international mediation regarding the issue of regional autonomy, Buthelezi announced that he was to register the IFP provisionally to contest the elections. The IFP, however, failed to present a list of candidates by the stipulated date, while Zwelithini continued to urge his followers to boycott the elections.

In March 1994 the President of Bophuthatswana, Lucas Mangope (a member of the FA), announced that the population of the 'homeland' would not participate in the elections. Following widespread protests in Bophuthatswana, Mangope fled from the capital, Mmabatho, after disaffected members of the security forces demanded that he allow participation in the elections and refused to take action against the demonstrators. At the apparent instigation of the AVF, some 5,000 armed right-wing extremists, principally members of the AWB, entered Bophuthatswana and occupied Mmabatho, with the aim of reinstating Mangope. Shortly afterwards the Government dispatched some 2,000 members of the armed forces to Bophuthatswana, which, together with disaffected local troops, regained control of the 'homeland'. The Government and the TEC formally deposed Mangope, whose removal signified the effective dissolution of the FA. Later in March members of the armed forces were deployed in Ciskei to maintain civil order, following the resignation of the 'homeland's' military ruler in response to a strike by reformist members of the security forces. (The TEC and the Government assumed joint responsibility for administration in Bophuthatswana and Ciskei pending the elections.)

In April 1994 an agreement was reached whereby the IFP was to participate in the elections, in exchange for guarantees that the institutions of the Zulu monarch and kingdom were to be recognized in the interim Constitution. Under the terms of a proposed draft constitution for KwaZulu/Natal (as Natal had been redesignated in February), the Zulu monarch was to be granted additional territorial powers and sovereignty with regard to traditional law and custom. However, the AVF announced that it would continue to boycott the elections. In April Terre'Blanche threatened that a campaign of recent bomb attacks would continue unless the Government acceded to demands for Afrikaner self-determination. Under the terms of an accord between the Government, the ANC and the Freedom Front (FF)—led by Gen. (retd) Constand Viljoen—earlier in April, the level of support for the FF in the elections was to be used to determine whether a separate Afrikaner state might be established in any region with the approval of the majority of the resident population.

On 27 April 1994 the interim Constitution came into force, with voting commencing on the previous day, as scheduled.

SOUTH AFRICA

Although a number of reports of electoral malpractice emerged, the IEC declared that the elections had been free and fair. The promulgation of the official results was delayed, owing, in part, to disputed ballots in KwaZulu/Natal; following negotiations between the IFP and the ANC, it was agreed that the IFP would be allocated 50.3% of the vote in the province, thereby allowing it a majority of one seat in the regional legislature. On 2 May, after partial results indicated a substantial majority in favour of the ANC, de Klerk conceded defeat, prompting widespread jubilation. Shortly afterwards it was announced that the ANC had secured 62.7% of votes cast, while the NP had won 20.4%, the IFP 10.5% and the FF 2.2%. Consequently, the ANC narrowly failed to obtain a parliamentary majority of two-thirds, which, under the terms of the interim Constitution, would have allowed its members to draft and adopt the new constitution without consulting other parties. The NP, which secured a majority in the province of Northern Cape, received the stipulated percentage of the national vote entitling it to nominate a Deputy President. Mandela subsequently appointed a senior official of the ANC, Thabo Mbeki, as First Deputy President, while de Klerk was nominated as Second Deputy President.

The Mandela presidency

Mandela was officially elected as President by the National Assembly on 9 May 1994, and was inaugurated on the following day at a ceremony that was attended by a large number of international heads of state. A Cabinet of National Unity, comprising 18 representatives of the ANC, six of the NP and three of the IFP, was subsequently formed, with Buthelezi allocated the portfolio of home affairs. Later in May the provincial legislatures elected a 90-member Senate, comprising 60 representatives of the ANC, 17 of the NP, five of the IFP and FF, respectively, and three of the DP. The ANC thus held a slightly higher majority in the Constitutional Assembly than in the National Assembly, but failed, nevertheless, to obtain a two-thirds' majority. The Secretary-General of the ANC, Cyril Ramaphosa, was subsequently elected Chairman of the Constitutional Assembly.

The new Government adopted a Reconstruction and Development Programme (RDP), which comprised extensive measures for social and economic development, including the reform of the education and health services. The Government also announced plans to establish a 'Truth and Reconciliation Commission' (TRC), composed of eminent citizens, which would investigate violations of human rights perpetrated under the apartheid regime; the TRC was to be empowered to grant indemnity to individuals who confessed to politically motivated crimes committed before 5 December 1993 (when the TEC was effectively installed). Although the FF had failed to obtain the level of support in the elections stipulated as a precondition to the consideration of its demands, the Government subsequently agreed to the establishment of a 'volkstaat council', in which Viljoen and other right-wing Afrikaners were to debate the issue of self-determination. Meanwhile, it was disclosed that de Klerk had authorized the transfer of state-owned land (comprising one-third of the territory of KwaZulu/Natal) to Zwelithini shortly before the elections. The ANC denied knowledge of the agreement.

In June 1994 it was announced that the new South African National Defence Force (SANDF) was to be constituted over a period of three years. In mid-June a cabinet committee decided that Zwelithini was to remain the statutory trustee of the territory in KwaZulu/Natal that had been transferred to his control prior to the elections. In September the Government officially ended the state of emergency in KwaZulu/Natal that had been imposed in March. In October the IFP majority in the provincial legislature of KwaZulu/Natal adopted legislation that provided for the establishment of an advisory council of Zulu chiefs, the House of Traditional Leaders, in which Zwelithini would be equal in status to other chiefs (including Buthelezi).

In November 1994 the Government adopted legislation that formally restored the rights of land ownership to members of the black population who had been dispossessed following the introduction of discriminatory legislation beginning in 1913; the Restitution of Land Rights Act provided for the establishment of a special commission and court to investigate and arbitrate claims.

In January 1995 the National Intelligence Service (NIS) was replaced with two new bodies, incorporating elements of the ANC's security department and agencies of the former 'homelands': the South African Secret Service, under the command of the former head of the NIS, was to control international intelligence, while the National Intelligence Agency (NIA), headed by a former ANC security official, was to be responsible for internal intelligence. In the same month, amid reports of increasing political violence between ANC and IFP supporters in KwaZulu/Natal, Buthelezi was elected Chairman of the House of Traditional Leaders.

An 11-member Constitutional Court was installed in February 1995; the Court was to ensure that the executive, legislative and judicial organs of government adhered to the principles entrenched in the interim Constitution, and was to endorse a final constitutional text with respect to these principles. In the same month Mandela confirmed that he would not contest the elections in 1999.

At a party conference on constitutional policy in April 1995, the ANC rejected NP proposals that the principle of power-sharing be entrenched in the final constitution, thereby extending the tenure of the coalition Government. The conference also failed to accept IFP demands for international mediation on regional autonomy, and adopted constitutional proposals that provided for a Senate comprising members of provincial legislatures, which would be empowered to veto provincial legislation. Buthelezi subsequently suspended IFP participation in the Constitutional Assembly, and indicated that the IFP would not accept a constitution that had been drafted by the remaining parties in the Assembly. In late May Mandela consented to foreign mediation on constitutional discussions. In the same month the National Assembly approved draft legislation providing for the establishment of the TRC; only the FF deputies opposed the enactment of the legislation.

At the local elections, which took place in most parts of the country on 1 November 1995, the ANC secured 66.4% of the votes cast and the majority of the seats on the local councils, while the NP won 16.2% and the FF 4.0%. Elections in KwaZulu/Natal were postponed until March 1996, owing to continuing violence in the region. Voting took place in some parts of Western Cape, but not in the metropolitan area of Cape Town, nor in some rural areas of the province, as a result of delays in the demarcation of electoral boundaries. After further delays, the local elections in KwaZulu/Natal took place on 26 June, amid relative calm. The IFP won the largest share (44.5%) of the votes cast.

Meanwhile, in November 1995 Gen. Magnus Malan, the Minister of Defence in 1980–91, and a further 10 prominent officials in the former armed forces were arrested on charges relating to the killing of 13 people in KwaMakutha (south of Durban) in 1987; they were accused of involvement in the establishment in 1985 of a military camp in Namibia where IFP commandos were trained to perpetrate attacks on prominent ANC supporters. The arrest and subsequent indictment of Gen. Malan and the other former officers provoked great controversy; Mandela was accused by members of the NP and FF of political bias in his refusal to grant temporary indemnity to the accused until their cases could be heard by the TRC, which was to commence sessions in April 1996. (In late November 1995 Archbishop Desmond Tutu was appointed as Chairman of the Commission.) Buthelezi was cited in the indictment as having in 1985 requested the assistance of the security forces in creating paramilitary units to combat the ANC.

The Truth and Reconciliation Commission

The trial of Gen. Malan and his 19 co-defendants began in Durban in early March 1996. (In May charges were abandoned against three of the former security force commanders, owing to insufficient evidence.) In mid-March the Government withdrew indemnity from prosecution that had been granted by de Klerk's Government to 73 ANC members, including Mbeki and Joe Modise. In April the TRC, comprising Archbishop Tutu (who retired from the archbishopric in June) and 16 other members drawn from all racial groups and a variety of professions, commenced hearings, which were to continue for up to two years. The Commission was empowered to grant judicial amnesties to perpetrators of human rights violations committed during the apartheid era, if it was satisfied that a full disclosure had been made and that the crime in question had been politically motivated (depending on the gravity of the crime). The TRC was also to advise on appropriate reparations to the victims (or to their families) of crimes committed.

On 8 May 1996 Parliament approved the final version of the Constitution, with the NP voting in favour, in spite of its reservations over some provisions. The IFP maintained its boycott of the Constitutional Assembly, while the 10 FF deputies abstained; only the two deputies of the African Christian Democratic Party (ACDP) voted against the adoption of the Constitution. The new Constitution incorporated an extensive Bill of

Rights, and provided for the establishment of a commission to guarantee the rights of the white minority. A National Council of Provinces was to replace the existing Senate, and was designed to increase the influence of the provinces on the policy of the central Government (although falling short of the provincial powers demanded by the IFP). De Klerk subsequently announced that the NP was to withdraw from the Government of National Unity, attributing the decision to the diminishing influence of his party on government policy, the refusal of the ANC to include power-sharing arrangements in the new Constitution, and the necessity, in the interests of democracy, for an effective opposition. The NP later withdrew from all the Provincial Governments except for that of Western Cape (where it was in the majority). Mandela appointed members of his own party to the ministerial portfolios vacated by NP members and abolished the position of Second Deputy President.

In late August 1996 Mbeki made a statement to the TRC regarding violations of human rights perpetrated during the apartheid era, including the execution of 34 people at the ANC's camps in Angola, asserting that these were justified in the context of the struggle against apartheid. De Klerk apologized before the TRC for the suffering that the apartheid policies of the NP had caused, but denied that any violations of human rights had been authorized during his time in government. Also in late August Eugene de Kock, a former commander of the notorious counter-insurgency 'hit squad', the Vlakplaas, was convicted of 89 charges relating to the activities of the unit, including six charges of murder. In September de Kock detailed to the Supreme Court his involvement in the apartheid regime's campaign against its opponents, claiming that de Klerk and Botha had both had full knowledge of these operations, which included assassinations.

In early September 1996 the Constitutional Court ruled that the new Constitution failed to adhere to the principles enshrined in the interim Constitution in a number of respects, notably with regard to the powers of the provinces, which the Court deemed insufficient. The Constitutional Assembly was to amend the document accordingly within a period of 90 days. The amended Constitution was approved by both chambers of Parliament on 11 October, with the ANC and the NP having negotiated a slight increase in the powers of the provinces. The new Constitution was returned to the Constitutional Court for final endorsement, and was promulgated by the President at a ceremony in Sharpeville on 10 December. The new Constitution entered into force on 4 February 1997. On 6 February the inaugural session of the new National Council of Provinces, which replaced the Senate as the second chamber of Parliament, was held.

Meanwhile, in October 1996 Gen. Malan and his co-defendants were acquitted of all charges in connection with the massacre in Kwa-Makutha. Although it was accepted that the killings had been committed by IFP supporters who had been trained by the former armed forces, the prosecution failed to prove that the attack had been authorized by military or political leaders. The judgment was regarded as a set-back for the TRC, with Gen. Malan urging former members of the armed forces not to seek amnesties from the TRC, but to submit to trial in the courts if charged (thus discouraging potential confessions to the Commission). Later in October the TRC proposed that the final date for indemnity be extended from 6 December 1993 to 10 May 1994 (the date of Mandela's inauguration as President). Shortly afterwards a former police commissioner submitted evidence to the TRC implicating Botha in an attack against the headquarters of the South African Council of Churches in 1988. Botha declared that he would not submit evidence to the Commission and denied involvement in any crimes for which he needed to apply for amnesty. Following discussions with Tutu, however, he agreed to co-operate with the TRC by means of correspondence. In late October Tutu criticized the ANC for failing to submit amnesty applications from its members, and subsequently threatened to resign from the TRC if such applications were not made. The ANC responded by assuring the TRC that applications by its members would be made where necessary.

On 13 December 1996 (the eve of the deadline for applications for amnesty from the TRC) Mandela announced that the final dates for the period in which crimes had been committed and the deadline for the receipt of amnesty applications were to be extended, to 10 May 1994 and 10 May 1997, respectively. The ANC confirmed that some 360 of its members, including three cabinet ministers, had applied for amnesty.

By the 10 May 1997 deadline nearly 8,000 amnesty applications had been received. Also in May 1997 de Klerk made a second appearance before the TRC; his continued insistence that he had been unaware of the violations of human rights perpetrated during the period of apartheid prompted an angry response from Tutu, who accused de Klerk of being responsible for abuses. The NP subsequently suspended co-operation with the TRC, and initiated legal action against the TRC on the grounds of political bias. At the end of August de Klerk resigned from the leadership of the NP and retired from active politics; he was replaced by Marthinus van Schalkwyk. In December 1997 Mandela resigned from the presidency of the ANC, as anticipated, and was succeeded by Mbeki, who was elected unopposed. Jacob Zuma was elected Deputy President of the party.

In October 1998 the TRC commenced reparation payments to victims of human rights violations under the apartheid system and at the end of that month Tutu presented to Mandela the TRC's interim report detailing human rights violations committed in 1960–64, based on statements from some 21,000 victims of abuses and about 7,000 amnesty applicants. The report concluded that the apartheid system constituted a crime against humanity; it was alleged that, while the State was primarily accountable for violations of human rights, the ANC had also committed abuses in its legitimate struggle against apartheid (notably in the MK's torture and execution of suspected dissidents in detention camps outside South Africa). Botha, as President of the State Security Council in 1978–89, was considered to be responsible for an increase in killings of government opponents and to have ordered the bomb attacks by state agents in the 1980s. Buthelezi was deemed accountable for human rights violations perpetrated by the IFP (which was responsible for the highest proportion of killings in 1990–94). The report also cited Viljoen and Terre'Blanche as being responsible for serious violations of human rights. It was stated that the South African business community had benefited from the apartheid system, and the introduction of a 'wealth tax' to assist in social reconstruction was proposed. The prosecution of those responsible for human rights violations who had not applied for amnesty, or who had been denied amnesty, was recommended. Buthelezi and Viljoen dismissed the findings of the report as reflecting pro-ANC bias in the TRC, and Buthelezi subsequently threatened to prosecute the Commission, particularly with regard to the report's allegation that the IFP had colluded with the apartheid regime. In December 1998 Mandela confirmed that perpetrators of crimes committed under the apartheid regime would not be granted a general amnesty, which had been urged by the NP, IFP and some members of the ANC. Under TRC regulations, applicants would only be granted amnesty after submitting a full confession and evidence that the crime was politically motivated.

Mbeki replaces Mandela

More than 16m. voters participated in legislative elections, which took place peacefully, at national and provincial level, on 2 June 1999. The ANC secured 266 of the 400 seats in the National Assembly, with 66.4% of votes cast; the DP increased its representation in the Assembly from seven to 38 seats, while the IFP won 34, and the New National Party (NNP, as the NP had been reconstituted), which had lost much support to the DP, only 28 seats. The ANC subsequently formed a coalition with an Indian party, the Minority Front, thereby securing a two-thirds' majority in the National Assembly. The IFP reached a coalition agreement with the ANC in KwaZulu/Natal, where the IFP Premier retained his post. In Western Cape no party won a majority of seats in the provincial legislature, and, after intensive negotiations, the NPP and DP established a coalition Government to prevent the ANC, which had obtained the highest number of votes, from gaining power. On 16 June Mbeki was inaugurated as President, in a ceremony also marking the formal retirement of Mandela. The IFP joined the ANC in a further coalition Government, in which Buthelezi remained Minister of Home Affairs. Zuma became Deputy President.

In July 1999 the TRC released a report containing evidence from former members of the security forces that implicated Botha in the killing of eight anti-apartheid activists in 1988. (Botha died in October 2006.) In August the TRC granted amnesty to former NP Minister of Law and Order, Adriaan Vlok, the former Commissioner of Police, Gen. Johan van der Merwe, de Kock, and a further 14 members of the former security forces, in respect of ordering the bombing of the offices of the South African Council of Churches in 1988. In September the Minister of Justice announced that further cases were to be submitted to judges specially nominated by Mbeki. In October the trial of Wouter Basson, the head of the apartheid regime's chemical and biological armaments programme in 1982–92, on

64 charges (including responsibility for the killing of 200 members of the South West Africa People's Organisation of Namibia—SWAPO), commenced at the High Court in Pretoria. He was acquitted of 15 charges in June 2001, and the remaining charges in April 2002. Later in October 1999 the TRC granted amnesty to nine former members of the security forces, including de Kock, who had provided evidence regarding the bombing of the ANC offices in London in 1982. In December 1999 10 members of the AWB were granted amnesty for the bombing campaign in 1994.

In January 2000 the National Assembly adopted extensive legislation prohibiting discrimination on any grounds and the use of racist terms in language. In June it was announced that the NNP and DP were to form a new coalition, the Democratic Alliance (DA), to contest the local government elections.

In September 2001 the South African Medical Research Council reported that HIV/AIDS was the largest single cause of death in South Africa, responsible for approximately 40% of adult deaths, and estimated that, without effective treatment, up to 7m. people could die from the disease by 2010. Mbeki had attracted criticism in August 2001 after urging the Minister of Health to reduce the budget for HIV/AIDS treatment, citing mortality figures from 1995 (when the disease accounted for only 2.2% of deaths). In December the Ministry of Health lost a case brought by the Treatment Action Campaign (TAC), a group of AIDS activists, when the High Court in Pretoria ordered it to provide antiretroviral drugs to all pregnant women infected with HIV to reduce the chance of transmission to their children; the Government had argued that the drugs were toxic and excessively expensive to administer. (The Government lost its appeal against the ruling in April 2002.) In February 2002 Buthelezi, as Minister of Home Affairs, ordered the distribution of antiretroviral drugs in KwaZulu/Natal, in contravention of official government policy, and in March the High Court upheld the ruling that ordered state provision of antiretroviral drugs. The Government sought leave to appeal the ruling, but it was overturned by the Constitutional Court in July; in October the Government announced that it would investigate means of providing antiretroviral drugs through the public health system. In November 2003 the Government also announced that it would spend R 12,100m. on combating HIV/AIDS over the next four years; R 1,900m. was to be allocated for the provision of antiretroviral drugs. At that time the Government committed to providing free antiretroviral treatment to some 53,000 people by March 2004; however, by November of that year the number of people receiving treatment was estimated at only 18,500.

Meanwhile, in July 2001 the PAC drew attention to what it considered the Government's inadequate housing and land redistribution policies, by seizing land belonging to farmers and the Provincial Government in east Johannesburg and inviting thousands of homeless people to settle there. Within two weeks the Government had removed the estimated 7,000 squatters from the land, using armed police officers. COSATU and affiliated unions organized a two-day general strike in August in protest at the proposed privatization of public assets, which, it claimed, would result in large-scale redundancies. COSATU estimated that 4m. workers had participated in the strike, a figure that the Government described as exaggerated. In August Agri South Africa, an organization representing commercial farmers (mainly white) and 'emerging' black farmers, reported that there had been more than 6,000 attacks on South African farms since 1991, resulting in the deaths of more than 1,000 people; it was widely feared that the motivation for the attacks was land redistribution, as had been the case in Zimbabwe since the late 1990s. The South African Government declared land seizures illegal in August.

The leader of the NNP, van Schalkwyk, announced in October 2001 that the party was suspending its participation in the DA, following differences with the DP; the DP had dismissed the mayor of Cape Town, a prominent figure in the NNP, while the DP suspected the NNP of attempting to increase membership in an attempt to take overall control of the DA. Van Schalkwyk announced that the NNP would seek an accommodation with the ANC, as the IFP had done, retaining its independence, but holding positions in the Cabinet. In late November the ANC and NNP announced a power-sharing agreement in Western Cape (the only province not previously under ANC control), and the NNP also took seats in seven of the eight other Provincial Governments (all except KwaZulu/Natal, where the ANC had an agreement with the IFP). Discord within the NNP emerged when Gerald Morkel resigned as Premier of Western Cape in November, after publicly refusing to support closer co-operation with the ANC; he was replaced by Peter Marais. However, Marais resigned in May 2002 over allegations of sexual harassment and was replaced by van Schalkwyk.

A ruling by the Constitutional Court in late 2002, allowing national and provincial deputies to change parties without losing their seats, led to significant changes in the political landscape: in April 2003 the ANC secured a two-thirds' parliamentary majority when members of the United Democratic Movement and the NNP defected to the ruling party, while the FA and the Afrikaner Eenheidsbeweging lost all their seats. At provincial level, members of the IFP defected to the ANC in KwaZulu/Natal and assumed further positions in the Cabinet, although the premiership of the province remained under IFP control.

The TRC's final report was presented to Mbeki in March 2003. The Commission had granted amnesty to 1,200 people, but had rejected more than 5,000 applications. Tutu recommended that some US $240m. ($12,000 each) be paid to the 20,000 people identified as victims of apartheid, and urged companies that had benefited through their involvement with the apartheid regime to contribute to the reparations process. Publication of the final report had been delayed by a legal challenge brought by the IFP, which was heavily implicated in the perpetration of human rights violations. In April, having rejected the suggestion that a special tax be imposed on companies that had gained from apartheid, Mbeki announced that those designated victims by the TRC would receive single payments of just over $3,800 each.

In 2003 ambitious empowerment charters were created for the financial and mining sectors, which envisaged large increases in the number of non-white company executives and mine owners, respectively. In 1994 the Government had promised to transfer 30% of white-owned farms to non-whites over the next five years, but by 2004 only 2% had been transferred.

The 2004 elections

Meanwhile, elections to the National Assembly and the provincial legislatures took place concurrently on 14 April 2004. The ANC won 279 of the National Assembly's 400 seats, with 69.7% of the valid votes cast. The DA took 50 seats, with 12.4% of votes cast, and the IFP 28, with 7.0%. The ANC secured overall control of seven of the nine provincial assemblies; although it failed to win outright majorities in KwaZulu/Natal and Western Cape, the ANC subsequently nominated premiers to head all nine provincial governments. The IEC declared the elections to have been free and fair. On 23 April members of the National Assembly voted unanimously to re-elect Mbeki to the presidency. President Mbeki announced the composition of a new Cabinet, which included most senior members of the previous administration: Zuma was reappointed Deputy President, while Mantombanza (Manto) Tshabalala-Msimang retained the health portfolio despite the slow progress regarding the provision of antiretroviral drugs to combat HIV/AIDS. The two IFP representatives who had been allocated ministerial portfolios did not take up their posts when the new Government was sworn in on 29 April.

In August 2004 van Schalkwyk announced that the NNP was to merge with ANC and that the NNP would be disbanded in September 2005. The NNP leader also stated his intention to join the ANC and urged all NNP members to do the same. Former President de Klerk subsequently announced his resignation from the NNP in protest at the decision. (The NNP officially ceased to exist at the end of February 2006.)

Meanwhile, in August 2003, the National Director of Public Prosecutions, Bulelani Ngcuka, had announced that Deputy President Zuma would not be prosecuted for alleged corruption in connection with an arms-procurement deal, despite an apparent recommendation from investigators that he be charged. This prompted accusations of government interference in the legal process and opposition demands for Zuma's resignation. Zuma repeatedly rejected the allegations against him; however, in early June 2005 his financial adviser, Schabir Shaik, was found guilty of corruption and fraud and sentenced to 15 years' imprisonment by the Durban High Court. The Court found evidence of a corrupt relationship between Shaik and Zuma, and that a series of payments made by Shaik on behalf of Zuma were intended to influence Zuma to benefit Shaik's business. Although Zuma did not give evidence, the trial revealed that Zuma had been party to a bid to solicit a bribe from a French defence company involved in the arms-procurement deal.

President Mbeki came under increasing pressure to dismiss Zuma and on 14 June 2005 he announced that the Deputy President would be 'released' from his duties. Zuma was replaced by Phumzile Mlambo-Ngcuka, hitherto the Minister of Energy and Mineral Affairs. In early August it was reported that the new Deputy President advocated the forced expropriation of white farms to accelerate the process of land distribution. At an education conference later that month Mlambo-Ngcuka was also reported to have called for South Africa to model its land redistribution programme on that of Zimbabwe. Zuma's trial commenced in the High Court in late July 2006. In mid-September the High Court judge dismissed the case, stating that Zuma had suffered social prejudice as a result of the publicity the case had received. The judge also cited failures of the State to hear legal challenges to raids carried out on the property of Zuma and his advisers, adding that further investigations into the case should have been conducted. Zuma's supporters believed that the result would increase the likelihood of him being elected to the presidency in 2009, and urged President Mbeki, who was constitutionally prohibited from serving a third term, to reinstate him as Deputy President. Nevertheless, tensions remained between Mbeki and Zuma and differences continued to divide the ANC.

In November 2005 it was also reported that Zuma was under investigation for the alleged rape of a female family friend; he was charged with the offence in early December but strenuously denied the allegation and was acquitted in early May 2006. In a separate investigation into missing funds 16 current and former ministers were found guilty of theft and fraud in October 2006. As much as R 17m. had been stolen and parliamentary travel privileges had been abused.

In May 2007 Helen Zille, the Mayor of Cape Town, was elected leader of the DA, replacing Tony Leon who had led the party since its formation in 2000. In June 2007 the ANC held a national policy conference following which it was announced that both Mbeki and Zuma could contest the leadership of the party at its national conference in December. Internal tensions had continued to divide the ruling tripartite coalition, although Mbeki warned in June that he would not be dictated to regarding government policies by the SACP. Zuma had secured the support of senior members of the SACP, and in September he received the endorsement of COSATU for his leadership campaign.

As the leadership contest gained momentum, senior members of the ANC exerted pressure on both Mbeki and Zuma to withdraw their candidatures, claiming that their rivalry was causing a major rift within the party. Neither candidate was prepared to concede, and in December 2007 ANC members elected Zuma to the party presidency after he secured 2,329 votes to Mbeki's 1,505; Kgalema Motlanthe was appointed ANC Deputy President. However, later that month the National Prosecuting Authority (NPA) indicted Zuma on charges of corruption and fraud. The Supreme Court of Appeal had ruled in November that Zuma could again be tried in connection with the arms-procurement deal. Zuma once more denied the allegations. In early 2008 differences between Mbeki and Zuma continued, deepening divides within both the ANC and the Government. In February the DA and the Independent Democrats (ID) announced their intention to seek a vote of no confidence in Mbeki and force an early general election. Zuma's impending trial threatened to damage his chances of success in the election and the ANC demanded that Motlanthe, considered a potential alternative candidate, be given a cabinet post. Reflecting the declining influence of Mbeki's power, in April he agreed to include Motlanthe in the National Assembly.

Public frustration escalated in May 2008 amid worsening economic conditions; rising food and fuel prices placed greater strain on resources and in mid-May clashes broke out in several townships between local residents and foreigners. It was in these areas that Mbeki was perceived to be failing in his responsibilities as President, and dissatisfaction with Mbeki's Government continued to increase. Some 20 people were killed in the fighting and several hundred more were injured, while aid workers in the area reported that as many as 30,000 people had been displaced by the violence. Mbeki received further criticism later that month from the DA, which claimed that the country now lacked strong leadership, evidenced by Mbeki's delayed decision to deploy the armed forces to suppress the recent fighting and his continued stance of 'quiet diplomacy' in relation to the volatile situation in Zimbabwe (see below).

Mbeki's power continued to decline and in July 2008 the ANC National Executive Committee (NEC) appointed Motlanthe to the newly created post of Minister in the Presidency, responsible for Government Business. As such, Motlanthe assumed de facto control over the Government. At the same time the NEC dismissed three of Mbeki's allies, including Nosimo Balindlela, Premier of Eastern Cape, and Ebrahim Rasool, Premier of Western Cape, highlighting divisions within the ANC.

In September 2008 the High Court dismissed the charges brought against Zuma, and ruled that there was evidence of political interference from high-ranking officials in the investigation. This caused the rift within the ANC to widen and it was subsequently announced that Mbeki had relinquished the presidency at the party's request, effective from 25 September. His resignation was followed by that of 11 cabinet ministers, including Mlambo-Ngcuka and Trevor A. Manuel, the long-serving Minister of Finance. A parliamentary vote elected Motlanthe as the new President with a clear majority and he was to remain in the post until the legislative elections in April 2009. It was rumoured that Zuma had not been elected for fear that it would appear he had assumed the role clandestinely. Widely thought to be the leading candidate for the presidency, the ANC preferred to have Zuma's legitimacy confirmed with a democratic election. Baleka Mbete, hitherto the Speaker of the National Assembly, was subsequently named Deputy President and Charles Nqakula was appointed Minister of Defence, while Manuel was reappointed Minister of Finance; Gwen Mahlangu-Nkabinde replaced Mbete as Speaker.

Divisions within the ANC deepened and in November 2008 a group of former ANC members and allies of Mbeki, led by Mosiuoa Lekota, formed a new political party, the Congress of the People (COPE). The ANC launched a formal complaint against the name of the new party, claiming that the ANC was regularly referred to in political spheres by the same name. Nevertheless, COPE was officially launched in December with members claiming that the party would provide a serious challenge to the ANC; COPE members won 12 seats in local by-elections that month.

As preparations for the general election began in early 2009, Zuma faced a further reverse when an appeal court overturned the earlier ruling that dismissed the corruption charges brought against him. However, in June the trial date was postponed indefinitely. In March Zuma approached the prosecutor's office with a deal offering to refrain from appointing only close ANC allies to high-profile positions, should he be elected in April, in return for all charges against him being dismissed. Meanwhile, Mlambo-Ngcuka announced that he had left the ANC to join COPE.

Recent developments: the Zuma administration

On 22 April 2009 elections duly took place to the National Assembly and to South Africa's nine provincial legislatures. Final results confirmed the overwhelming victory of the ANC, which, with 65.9% of total votes cast, won 264 of the National Assembly's 400 seats. The DA took 67 seats, with 16.7% of votes cast, and COPE secured 30 seats with 7.4%. The ANC also secured overall control of eight provincial assemblies. More than 77% of the registered electorate participated. As expected, Zuma was elected President by the National Assembly with 277 votes and was inaugurated on 9 May. The following day Zuma announced his new Government and the reorganization of a number of ministries: a National Planning Commission and a performance monitoring and evaluation competency were created within the presidency, to be led by Manuel and Collins Chabane, respectively; the Ministry of Minerals and Energy was divided into two separate ministries; and the Ministry for Education was separated into the Ministry of Basic Education and the Ministry of Higher Education. Appointments made to the enlarged administration included Motlanthe as Deputy President, Pravin Gordhan (the Commissioner of the South African Revenue Service) as Minister of Finance and Jeff Radebe as Minister of Justice and Constitutional Development; the hitherto Minister of Foreign Affairs, Nkosazana Dlamini-Zuma, was moved to the Ministry of Home Affairs. Also of note was the appointment of the leader of the Afrikaner nationalist Vryheidsfront Plus party, Dr Pieter Mulder, as Deputy Minister of Agriculture, Forestry and Fisheries.

Although the ANC had been unable to secure the two-thirds' majority of seats in the National Assembly that would have allowed it to amend the Constitution, it remained the dominant political organization. Furthermore, many opposition parties subsequently experienced significant difficulties. In June 2009 the ACDP announced that it would no longer participate with the DA in the Western Cape provincial administration (the only non-ANC controlled province), following the DA's decision the previous month to remove an ACDP member from his position of Deputy Mayor of Cape Town. Meanwhile, COPE, which had failed to perform as strongly as expected in the national elections, was confronted with a number of organizational problems and growing dissatisfaction with Lekota's leadership. In July two senior party officials resigned, and in early May 2010 the party's Deputy President, Mbhazima Shilowa, formally stated his intention to challenge Lekota for the party presidency at COPE's national conference, which was scheduled to be held later that month. In April Lekota had held a press conference at which he claimed to have evidence of possible fraud with relation to monies allocated to COPE through Parliament. As the party's chief whip, Shilowa was the officer responsible for accounting for parliamentary party funds. Lekota lost a vote of confidence in his leadership at the COPE conference in late May, leaving Shilowa as acting President of the party. In response, Lekota initiated a successful legal challenge against the vote and was reinstated as COPE President in June, although the deep divisions within the party, which had been highlighted in a very public manner, remained.

Meanwhile, in August 2009 members of the South African military commenced industrial action and demanded pay increases and improved employment conditions. A demonstration, attended by some 1,300 soldiers in Pretoria, degenerated into violent clashes between police officers and protesters, during which at least 18 people were injured. Concerns were raised regarding the potential threat to national security posed by the industrial action, and senior military officials expressed their objection to the absence of legislation preventing members of the military from joining a trade union. The previous month as many as 50,000 construction workers went on strike, bringing work on a number of projects related to the hosting of the 2010 Fédération Internationale de Football Association World Cup to a halt, while later in July 2009 violent disturbances in protest against a lack of basic services were reported in townships in Johannesburg, Western Cape, and the north-eastern region of Mpumalanga. The construction sector strike was brought to an end after seven days, following the award of a 12% pay increase. In December President Zuma announced that a pay increase of up to 65% (as well as one-off bonuses) were to be offered to low-ranking soldiers, although funding to finance the increased expenditure had not been allocated in the 2009/10 budget.

President Zuma came under increasing pressure during early 2010, following a number of controversial incidents. In January Zuma married for the fifth time, taking a third concurrent spouse (he was also engaged to be married to a fourth), and while traditionalists supported his choice to uphold Zulu practices, his polygamy was denounced by many members of society as inconsistent with modern customs. In February the DA accused the President of contradicting the Government's message on HIV/AIDS prevention after it was revealed that he had fathered a child outside of wedlock with the daughter of a family friend. The following month the DA leader, Helen Zille, demanded an official investigation into Zuma's failure to declare his financial interests within 60 days of taking office, and in mid-March COPE and the DA unsuccessfully brought a motion of no confidence against Zuma.

In April 2010 Eugene Terre'Blanche, the AWB leader who was released from prison in 2004 after serving three years of a five-year sentence for attempted murder, was killed after a dispute over unpaid wages with two farm workers, both of whom were subsequently charged with his murder. The AWB and President Zuma appealed for calm, although a spokesman for the former had initially blamed the killing on the recent public recital of an apartheid-era song by the President of the ANC Youth League, Julius Malema. The High Court had issued a ruling in March 2010 banning Malema from performing the song, but the ANC had contested that decision. It was reported that more than 3,000 white South African farmers were believed to have been murdered since 1994.

New government proposals that had the potential to limit freedom of expression caused considerable controversy in mid-2010. Zuma argued that the Protection of Information Act, which would impose harsh penalties for revealing (or attempting to reveal) classified information and would allow the authorities to restrict a greater range of such information, was necessary to protect national security. He also claimed that the Media Appeals Tribunal, which could potentially have the authority to censor the media, would protect citizens from libellous allegations. However, critics condemned the proposals as damaging to press freedom and government transparency, designed solely to protect the political and business élites, and possibly unconstitutional. Meanwhile, in July former National Commissioner of Police Jacob 'Jackie' Sello Selebi was convicted of accepting payments from a high-profile drugs trafficker, ostensibly in exchange for ignoring his criminal activities. Selebi initiated an appeal against his 15-year gaol sentence in September.

Aware of the weakness of the DA, and the opposition in general, Zille announced in August 2010 that her party would merge with the ID by 2014 in order to present the ANC with a stronger challenge in the legislative elections scheduled to be held in that year. Zille also declared that the DA would seek meetings with other parties to discuss the formation of a possible opposition coalition.

From mid-August 2010 public sector workers staged nationwide strikes, reportedly involving over 1m. people, to demand increased salaries. Clashes occurred between strikers and the police, and soldiers were mobilized in some cases to deter further violence. The industrial action caused widespread disruption within the education system, and the Government was forced to deploy military medics to hospitals to ensure that the provision of essential medical services was maintained. The strikes were ended in early September, after the Government offered a 7.5% pay raise and an R 800 housing allowance, which was accepted by the public sector unions in the following month. It was expected that the Government would have to arrange loans to pay for the wage increases, placing extra pressure on the country's already strained fiscal position.

In late October 2010 Zuma effected a cabinet reorganization. Seven ministers were removed from their posts, including those responsible for communications, labour, public enterprises and public works, although the major portfolios were unaltered. A number of new deputy ministerial positions were also created. The cabinet changes were generally welcomed by opposition parties and the public since several unpopular ministers were dismissed, such as Minister of Communications Siphiwe Nyanda, who had frequently been accused of corrupt practices.

Foreign Affairs
Regional relations

South Africa became increasingly isolated politically in southern Africa after Zimbabwe (formerly Rhodesia) underwent the transition to independence in April 1980. During the 1980s South Africa's continued occupation of Namibia resulted in frequent clashes between SWAPO guerrillas and South African troops (see the chapter on Namibia). In 1971 the International Court of Justice had declared South Africa's presence in Namibia to be illegal and the UN had, in 1973, recognized SWAPO as the 'authentic representative of the Namibian people'. Following the collapse of the semi-autonomous internal administration, South Africa resumed direct rule of Namibia in January 1983. In February 1984 South Africa and Angola agreed on a cease-fire along the Angola–Namibia border, and established a joint commission to monitor the withdrawal of South African troops from Angola. On 22 December 1988 Angola, Cuba and South Africa signed a formal treaty designating 1 April 1989 as the commencement date for the process leading to Namibian independence, as well as a treaty requiring all 50,000 Cuban troops to be withdrawn from Angola by July 1991. Elections were held in Namibia in November 1989, and independence for the former South African territory was achieved on 21 March 1990, under a SWAPO-controlled Government. The strategic port of Walvis Bay and 12 offshore islands, to which Namibia laid claim, remained under South African jurisdiction until September 1991, when the two countries agreed to administer the disputed territories jointly. In August 1993 South Africa relinquished sovereignty over Walvis Bay and the 12 islands, which were officially transferred to Namibia in March 1994. In August 2001 the South African and Namibian foreign ministers met to discuss the issue of their joint border on the Orange river; Namibia claimed the border extended to the middle of the river, while South Africa claimed it lay on the northern bank, provoking differences over mineral and fishing rights.

In 1984 South Africa signed a mutual non-aggression pact with Mozambique (the Nkomati accord), which implied that South Africa would withdraw its covert support for the Resistência Nacional Moçambicana (Renamo), while Mozambique would prevent the ANC from using its territory as a base for attacks on South Africa. In September 1985 the South African Government conceded that there had been 'technical' violations of the accord. In May 1988 Mozambican and South African officials agreed to reactivate the Nkomati accord, and in September President Botha visited President Joaquim Chissano of Mozambique, his first state visit to a black African nation. Following his election as President, Mandela made an official visit to Mozambique in July 1994. In August of that year South Africa, Mozambique and Swaziland signed a security co-operation accord, in an effort to combat the continuing illicit transport of armaments. In February 1997 South Africa appealed to the Government of Swaziland to release Swazi trade union leaders from detention. The Swazi Government protested at action mounted by COSATU in support of its Swazi counterparts, stating that it represented interference in the internal affairs of Swaziland. In April 2006 protests were staged by COSATU, the SACP and its Youth League, and the Swaziland Solidarity Network in support of Swaziland's campaign for democracy and human rights. Demonstrators attempted to blockade several crossing points on the Swaziland border and more than 20 people were arrested.

In 1979 the Southern African Development Co-ordination Conference (SADCC) was established by southern African countries, to work towards a reduction of their economic dependence on South Africa. SADCC reformed in August 1992 as the Southern African Development Community (SADC, see p. 420), which aimed to achieve closer economic integration between its member states. South Africa was admitted to SADC in August 1994. In April 1997 members of the South African armed forces participated in military training exercises in Zimbabwe, as part of a nascent SADC regional peace-keeping force. In September 1998 about 600 South African and 200 Botswanan troops were dispatched to restore order in the Lesotho capital, Maseru, under the aegis of SADC, following a coup attempt by junior military officers. About 750 South African troops, together with some 350 Botswanan troops, remained in Lesotho to maintain civil order, before their withdrawal in May 2000.

In April 2000 Mbeki, together with the Presidents of Namibia and Mozambique, visited Zimbabwe to increase pressure on President Robert Mugabe to prevent the illegal occupation of white-owned farmland (see the chapter on Zimbabwe). Despite international condemnation of Mugabe and requests by a number of countries, most notably the United Kingdom, for more unequivocal criticism of President Mugabe's actions from South Africa, President Mbeki attempted to maintain 'constructive engagement' towards Zimbabwe. Following Mugabe's re-election as President in March 2002, the ANC issued a statement endorsing the ballot, despite allegations that Mugabe's party, the Zimbabwe African National Union—Patriotic Front, had intimidated voters and engaged in electoral fraud. The South African Government's position strained relations with the United Kingdom and the USA, and the latter threatened to withdraw support for the New Partnership for Africa's Development (NEPAD, see below) if the Government did not condemn Mugabe. However, later in March Mbeki was part of a Commonwealth troika (also comprising the President of Nigeria and the Prime Minister of Australia) that decided to suspend Zimbabwe from meetings of that organization for a period of one year. Mbeki had previously ignored pleas from Morgan Tsvangirai, the leader of the main opposition party in Zimbabwe, the Movement for Democratic Change, to impose sanctions on Zimbabwe prior to the election. In March 2003 Donald (Don) McKinnon, the Secretary-General of the Commonwealth, stated that the troika had concluded that Zimbabwe's suspension from the organization's meetings should remain in force for a further nine months. However, South Africa subsequently denied that it had agreed to the extension of the suspension. Zimbabwe withdrew from the Commonwealth in December 2003, shortly before the conclusion of the organization's Heads of Government meeting, at which the country's suspension had been extended indefinitely. Mbeki had criticized the decision to maintain the suspension, claiming that some Commonwealth members had failed to understand the question of land ownership in Zimbabwe. The Commonwealth appointed South Africa to a six-member advisory panel charged with monitoring the situation in Zimbabwe. Mbeki met separately with Mugabe and Tsvangirai in that month in an unsuccessful attempt to persuade them to form a coalition government. Mbeki continued to mediate between Mugabe and Tsvangirai prior to the Zimbabwean presidential and legislative elections held in March 2008, and brokered the introduction of new election legislation requiring electoral officials to post the number of votes cast at individual polling stations. However, following the decision of the Zimbabwe Electoral Commission not to release the results of the presidential election, in April Mugabe boycotted an emergency SADC summit in Zambia called to discuss the situation in Zimbabwe. Mbeki travelled to Harare for talks with Mugabe, but the former's policy of 'quiet diplomacy' attracted criticism from a number of international observers, while Tsvangirai appealed for Mbeki to relinquish his role as mediator to Zambian President Levy Mwanawasa. Despite his resignation from the South African presidency, Mbeki continued to chair negotiations between Tsvangirai and Mugabe and in September the two sides concluded the Interparty Political Agreement (see chapter on Zimbabwe), which provided for a power-sharing arrangement. Further discussions, again with mediation by Mbeki, resulted in the installation of a new Council of Ministers in February 2009 and the appointment of Tsvangirai to the Zimbabwean premiership. Following his election in May 2009, South African President Jacob Zuma succeeded Mbeki as the Chairman of SADC and principal mediator in negotiations between the government parties in Zimbabwe. Zuma's approach to Zimbabwe during 2010 suggested that his predecessor's strategy of 'quiet diplomacy' would be maintained. Meanwhile, in September the Government announced that deportations of illegal Zimbabwean migrants, suspended since April 2009, would recommence from the end of 2010 (subsequently postponed until the end of March 2011) due to the improving situation in Zimbabwe. Human rights organizations and diaspora groups criticized the Government's decision, arguing that conditions in Zimbabwe were still too unstable to justify the resumption of large-scale repatriations. By the end of 2010 some 275,000 undocumented Zimbabweans had applied to normalize their status, although this was believed to represent only a fraction of the illegal Zimbabwean population in South Africa.

In November 1996 South Africa was criticized for its approval of a substantial sale of weapons to Rwanda, which was believed to be providing military support to rebels in eastern Zaire who were engaged in conflict with the Zairean army. In response to international pressure, the South African Government subsequently decided to suspend the sale of armaments to Rwanda. During 1996 South Africa supported efforts to achieve reconciliation in Angola and in early 1997 was involved in intensive diplomatic activity, along with other African countries, with the aim of negotiating an end to the civil war in Zaire. Following the assumption of power by Alliance des forces démocratiques pour la libération du Congo-Zaïre, led by Laurent-Désiré Kabila, in May, South Africa became the first foreign government to recognize the new regime and pledged to assist in reconstruction efforts and in the holding of elections in the renamed Democratic Republic of the Congo (DRC). In October 2001 South African soldiers were dispatched to Burundi (q.v.) as part of a proposed 700-member peace-keeping mission, in an effort to enforce national security and to support the formation of a multi-ethnic transitional government. Mandela had been instrumental in negotiating a peace accord (signed in August 2000), whereby the Hutu and Tutsi ethnic groups, which had been engaged in civil conflict since 1993, were each to hold the presidency for 18 months during a three-year transitional period. Meanwhile, in March 2005 South Africa dispatched some 300 troops to Darfur, Sudan (q.v.), to join an African Union (AU, see p. 183) mission to investigate and monitor events in the region. By early 2010 South Africa had 950 security personnel (including 781 soldiers) stationed in Darfur as part of the joint AU-UN hybrid peace-keeping operation in Darfur (UNAMID), which had been established in mid-2007.

In February 2007 South Africa signed a defence agreement with the Central African Republic committing to the provision of military training and the donation of surplus military supplies. In April 2008 South Africa signed a memorandum of understanding with the Republic of the Congo to develop co-operation between the two countries' military services, indicating that South Africa may be preparing to work more closely with other central African countries within the framework of the military organization established under the Communauté économique des états de l'Afrique centrale (see p. 446).

In June 2010 former head of the Rwandan armed forces Lt-Gen. Faustin Kayumba Nyamwasa, who had sought asylum in South Africa after being accused by the Rwandan authorities of orchestrating a series of deadly grenade attacks in the country earlier in the year (a charge he rejected), was shot outside his home in Johannesburg in an apparent assassination attempt. After fleeing to South Africa, Nyamwasa had become a prominent critic of Rwandan President Paul Kagame. Rwandans were reportedly among the suspects subsequently arrested by South African police, and the Ministry of International Relations and Co-operation later revealed that members of a foreign security service had been involved in the shooting. The Rwandan Government strenuously denied any complicity in the attack and expressed its discontent at the 'insinuations emanating from

SOUTH AFRICA

official circles in South Africa'. The incident strained bilateral relations, culminating in August in the South African Government's withdrawal of its ambassador to Rwanda 'for consultations'.

In October 2001 the New Partnership for Africa's Development (NEPAD) was launched, as part of a long-term strategy for socio-economic recovery in Africa, in accordance with a decision taken at the Organization of African Unity (OAU—now the AU) summit held in Lusaka, Zambia, in July. Mbeki formulated NEPAD's founding documents, in conjunction with the heads of state of Algeria, Egypt, Nigeria and Senegal, and South Africa was to host the Secretariat. In mid-2004 the AU agreed that the Pan-African Parliament (PAP) would be based in South Africa; the Government subsequently announced that the PAP would be housed in Midrand (between Johannesburg and Pretoria). The second session of the PAP—its first in South Africa—took place at temporary headquarters in Midrand in mid-September that year.

Other external relations

Following the implementation of political reforms in South Africa from February 1990, international sanctions imposed during the 1980s were reviewed. During 1991 South Africa was readmitted to international sporting competition, after many years of exclusion. In July the USA officially withdrew economic sanctions (which were, however, retained by a number of US states and cities). In October Commonwealth Heads of Government endorsed the withdrawal of cultural sanctions against South Africa; however, sanctions on finance, arms and trade and investment remained. Japan ended all its sanctions during that month. In 1992 the European Community (EC, now the European Union—EU, see p. 270) withdrew a number of sanctions against South Africa. In September 1993, following the adoption of legislation providing for the installation of a multiracial transitional administration (see above), the international community ended the remaining economic sanctions against South Africa. The UN Security Council ended its mandatory embargo on armaments, following the establishment of an interim Government of National Unity in May 1994; South Africa subsequently established diplomatic relations with more than 165 countries. South Africa became a member of the Commonwealth on 1 June, and joined the OAU later that month. The People's Republic of China refused to establish formal diplomatic links while South Africa maintained relations with Taiwan. In November 1996 President Mandela announced that South Africa's diplomatic relations with Taiwan were to be severed in favour of the People's Republic of China, with effect from the end of 1997. In response, Taiwan withdrew its ambassador indefinitely and announced that the majority of its aid projects in South Africa would be suspended.

In December 1995 a joint US-South African commission was established, chaired by Mbeki and the US Vice-President, Al Gore. In February 1998 it was announced that South Africa and the USA were to normalize their defence trade agreement, thereby allowing South African armaments companies to trade with their US counterparts for the first time. In August 1998 two people were killed, and about 27 injured, in a bomb attack on a US restaurant in Cape Town. A supporter of an organization styled Muslims Against Global Oppression (MAGO) claimed to have perpetrated the bombing, apparently in retaliation for US air attacks on Sudan and Afghanistan (although MAGO officially denied responsibility for the incident).

In March 1998, following four years of negotiations, the EU approved the terms for a comprehensive free-trade agreement with South Africa. The agreement provisionally came into force on 1 January 2000; a continuing dispute with the Governments of Italy, Spain, Portugal and Greece, which had refused to sign the accord on wines and spirits, was resolved after South Africa agreed to discontinue the use of traditional European names for alcoholic drinks within five years. In December 2000 a framework agreement was reached on a free-trade accord with the Southern Common Market (known as Mercosur—Mercado Común del Sur, comprising Argentina, Brazil, Paraguay and Uruguay). The Southern African Customs Union (SACU), consisting of South Africa and the smaller states of Botswana, Lesotho, Namibia and Swaziland, concluded a preferential trade agreement with Mercosur in December 2004. A revised version of this agreement was signed by representatives of Mercosur and SACU in December 2008 and April 2009, respectively.

CONSTITUTION AND GOVERNMENT

Under the terms of the Constitution, which was adopted on 8 May 1996 and entered into force on 4 February 1997, legislative power is vested in a bicameral Parliament, comprising a National Assembly and a National Council of Provinces (formerly the Senate). The National Assembly is elected by universal adult suffrage under a system of proportional representation and has between 350 and 400 members. The 90-member National Council of Provinces comprises six permanent delegates and four special delegates from each of the provincial legislatures (see below). The President, who is elected by the National Assembly from among its members, exercises executive power in consultation with the other members of the Cabinet. Any party that holds a minimum of 80 seats in the National Assembly (equivalent to 20% of the national vote) is entitled to nominate an Executive Deputy President. A Constitutional Court ensures that the executive, legislative and judicial organs of government adhere to the provisions of the Constitution.

Each of the nine provinces has a legislature, which is elected under a system of proportional representation. Each legislature is entitled to draft a constitution for the province, subject to the principles governing the national Constitution, and to elect a Premier, who heads an Executive Council. Parties that hold a minimum of 10% of seats in the provincial legislature are entitled to a proportional number of portfolios in the Executive Council.

REGIONAL AND INTERNATIONAL CO-OPERATION

South Africa is a member of the Southern African Customs Union (with Botswana, Lesotho, Namibia and Swaziland), of the Southern African Development Community (SADC, see p. 420) and of the African Union (see p. 183). The Secretariat of the New Partnership for Africa's Development (see p. 184) is located in South Africa.

South Africa was a founder member of the UN on its establishment in 1945. As a contracting party to the General Agreement on Tariffs and Trade, South Africa joined the World Trade Organization (WTO, see p. 430) on its establishment in 1995. South Africa participates in the G20 and in the Group of 77 (G77, see p. 447) developing countries. In recognition of South Africa's rising international prominence, in December 2010 the country joined the informal grouping of major developing nations known as BRIC (consisting of Brazil, Russia, India and China, and subsequently redesignated BRICS). South Africa began a two-year term as a non-permanent member of the UN Security Council on 1 January 2011.

ECONOMIC AFFAIRS

In 2009, according to estimates by the World Bank, South Africa's gross national income (GNI), measured at average 2007–09 prices, was US $284,499m., equivalent to $5,770 per head (or $10,060 per head on an international purchasing-power parity basis). During 2000–09, it was estimated, the population increased at an average annual rate of 1.3%, while gross domestic product (GDP) per head, in real terms, increased by 2.2%. Overall GDP increased, in real terms, at an average annual rate of 3.6% in 2003–10, according to figures from the South African Reserve Bank; overall GDP declined by 1.7% in 2009, but grew by 2.8% in 2010.

Agriculture (including forestry and fishing) contributed 2.5% of GDP in 2010. Some 5.1% of the employed labour force were engaged in the sector in 2009. Maize (also the principal subsistence crop), fruit and sugar are exported, and livestock-rearing is also important; wool is another significant export. The GDP of the agricultural sector increased by an average of 1.9% per year in 2003–10. Agricultural GDP declined by 3.0% in 2009, but increased by 0.9% in 2010.

Industry (including mining, manufacturing, construction and power) contributed 30.8% of GDP in 2010, and engaged 25.0% of the employed labour force in 2009. Industrial GDP increased at an average annual rate of 2.6% in 2003–10. Industrial GDP declined by 6.5% in 2009, but grew by 4.5% in 2010.

Mining contributed 9.6% of GDP in 2010, and engaged 2.4% of the employed labour force in 2009. South Africa was the world's second largest producer of gold in 2007, with the major mineral export accounting for about 10.9% of total world production. China overtook South Africa as the world's leading producer of gold in 2007. Coal, platinum, iron ore, diamonds, chromium, manganese, vanadium, vermiculite, antimony, limestone, asbestos, fluorspar, uranium, copper, lead and zinc are also important mineral exports. There are reserves of petroleum, natural gas, sillimanite, titanium and zirconium. The GDP of the mining sector decreased by an average of 0.4% per year in 2003–10. Mining GDP contracted by 4.2% in 2009, but increased by 5.8% in 2010.

Manufacturing contributed 14.6% of GDP in 2010, and engaged 13.7% of the employed labour force in 2009. The GDP of the manufacturing sector increased at an average annual rate of 2.7% in 2003–10. Manufacturing GDP declined by 10.4% in 2009, but increased by 5.0% in 2010.

The construction sector contributed 3.8% of GDP in 2010, and engaged 8.3% of the employed labour force in 2009. The real GDP of the construction sector increased by an average of 9.2% per year in 2003–10; the sector's GDP increased by 7.4% in 2009 and by only 1.5% in 2010.

Energy is derived principally from coal-based electricity (94.7% in 2007); this is supplemented by nuclear power and by hydroelectric power (4.3% and 0.4%, respectively). The construction of a plant to convert natural gas into liquid fuel was completed in 1992. Exploitation of petroleum reserves in oilfields located 140 km south-west of the Southern Cape commenced in 1997. In 2001 substantial reserves of natural gas were discovered off the Western Cape. Imports of mineral fuels and lubricants comprised 21.5% of the value of total imports in 2009.

The services sector contributed 66.7% of GDP in 2010, and engaged 69.8% of the employed labour force in 2009. The real GDP of the services sector increased by an average of 4.3% per year in 2003–10. Services GDP increased by 2.2% in 2010.

In 2009 South Africa recorded a visible trade surplus of US $534m., while there was a deficit of $11,327m. on the current account of the balance of payments. In 2009 the principal source of imports for South Africa was the People's Republic of China (which provided 13.1% of the total); other major suppliers of imports were Germany, the USA and Saudi Arabia. The principal market for exports in that year was also China (10.5%); other important purchasers were the USA, Japan, Germany and the United Kingdom. The principal exports in 2009 were basic manufactures (particularly platinum, iron and steel and diamonds), machinery and transport equipment, mineral fuels, metalliferous ores and metal scrap, chemical products and food and live animals. The principal imports were machinery and transport equipment (especially road vehicles), mineral fuels (particularly petroleum) and chemical products.

In the financial year 2010/11 South Africa's estimated budget deficit was R 143,360.6m. South Africa's general government gross debt was R 747,393m. in 2009, equivalent to 30.1% of GDP. At the end of 2008 South Africa's total foreign debt was US $41,943.2m., of which $13,173.2m. was public and publicly guaranteed debt. The cost of debt-servicing in that year was equivalent to 4.4% of the value of exports of goods, services and income. The annual rate of inflation averaged 6.0% in 2000–10; consumer prices increased by 4.3% in 2010. According to official figures, 24.0% of the labour force were unemployed in 2009.

Following the removal of economic sanctions (imposed by the international community in protest against apartheid) in late 1993, and democratic elections in April 1994, foreign governments pledged considerable financial assistance to South Africa, and by 1999 financial market conditions had improved considerably, resulting in lower inflation, increased real GDP and greater investor confidence. Economic progress continued in the 2000s, but many problems remained, including widespread poverty, a high level of unemployment and the devastating social and economic impact of the HIV/AIDS epidemic. Several initiatives aimed at reducing social disparities had been introduced, such as the Broad-Based Black Empowerment Act (instituted in 2004) to redistribute the nation's wealth among the black population, while the Government's land reform programme aimed to transfer 30% of commercial agricultural land to previously disadvantaged groups by 2014. The country was negatively affected by the global economic slowdown from late 2008, with declining exports, dwindling production levels in the manufacturing and mining sectors, rising unemployment, and a resultant GDP contraction of 1.8% in 2009, although the construction industry was buoyed by the increase in resources allocated to infrastructure projects in advance of South Africa's hosting of the 2010 Fédération Internationale de Football Association World Cup. The Government's countercyclical strategy, combined with rising demand for the country's key exports, led to an economic recovery from the second half of 2009, and the IMF projected renewed GDP growth of 3.2% in 2010. With the recovery underway, the 2010 budget reduced public spending in order to lower the fiscal deficit, although key expenditure on social and infrastructure programmes remained unaltered. The World Cup was held successfully in June, resulting in tourist numbers for the year increasing by over 15%. The tournament cost some R 40,000m. to stage, of which an estimated R 38,000m. would be recovered through the concomitant economic growth, and the Government was hopeful that the legacy of new infrastructure and the country's improved international standing would enhance investment and tourism in the future. However, there were concerns regarding the agricultural sector following torrential rains during December 2010 and January 2011, which caused extensive flooding of farmland. The IMF forecast real GDP expansion of 3.6% in 2011, although the Fund noted that annual growth of around 6% would be needed to lower the persistently high unemployment rate (which stood at around 25% during 2010). The 2011 budget focused on addressing unemployment, with measures including: an increase in government spending on labour-intensive construction projects; a R 9,000m. job creation fund; a wage subsidy scheme to encourage companies to hire young unemployed people; and tax reductions for the important manufacturing industry.

PUBLIC HOLIDAYS

2012: 1 January (New Year's Day), 21 March (Human Rights Day), 6 April (Good Friday), 9 April (Family Day), 27 April (Freedom Day), 1 May (Workers' Day), 16 June (Youth Day), 9 August (National Women's Day), 24 September (Heritage Day), 16 December (Day of Reconciliation), 25 December (Christmas Day), 26 December (Day of Goodwill).

Statistical Survey

Source (unless otherwise indicated): Statistics South Africa, Private Bag X44, Pretoria 0001; tel. (12) 3108911; fax (12) 3108500; e-mail info@statssa.pwv.gov.za; internet www.statssa.gov.za.

Area and Population

(Note: Population estimates exclude adjustment for the effect of deaths related to HIV/AIDS)

AREA, POPULATION AND DENSITY

Area (sq km)	1,220,813*
Population (census results)	
9 October 1996	40,583,573
9 October 2001	
Males	21,434,041
Females	23,385,737
Total	44,819,778
Population (official estimates at mid-year)	
2008	48,687,300
2009	49,320,500
2010	49,991,300
Density (per sq km) at mid-2010	40.9

* 471,358 sq miles.

POPULATION BY AGE AND SEX
(official estimates at mid-2010)

	Males	Females	Total
0–14	7,807,300	7,696,900	15,504,200
15–64	15,501,600	16,510,100	32,011,700
65 and over	1,020,100	1,455,300	2,475,400
Total	24,329,000	25,662,300	49,991,300

ETHNIC GROUPS
(at mid-2010, estimates)

	Number	% of total
Africans (Blacks)	39,682,600	79.4
Europeans (Whites)	4,584,700	9.2
Coloureds	4,424,100	8.8
Asians	1,299,900	2.6
Total	49,991,300	100.00

PROVINCES
(official estimates of population at mid-2010)

	Area (sq km)	Population	Density (per sq km)	Capital
Eastern Cape	168,966	6,743,800	39.9	Bisho
Free State*	129,825	2,824,500	21.8	Bloemfontein
Gauteng†	18,178	11,191,700	615.7	Johannesburg
KwaZulu/Natal	94,361	10,645,400	112.8	Pietermaritzburg
Limpopo‡	125,754	5,439,600	43.3	Pietersburg
Mpumalanga§	76,495	3,617,600	47.3	Nelspruit
Northern Cape	372,889	1,103,900	3.0	Kimberley
North-West	104,882	3,200,900	30.5	Mmabatho
Western Cape	129,462	5,223,900	40.4	Cape Town
Total	1,220,813	49,991,300	40.9	

* Formerly the Orange Free State.
† Formerly Pretoria-Witwatersrand-Vereeniging.
‡ Known as Northern Province (formerly Northern Transvaal) until February 2002.
§ Formerly Eastern Transvaal.

Note: Figures for population are rounded estimates based on the cohort-component compilation method.

PRINCIPAL TOWNS
(metropolitan areas, population at 2001 census)

Johannesburg	3,225,812	Springs	80,776
Durban	3,090,122	Vanderbijlpark	80,201
Cape Town*	2,893,247	Vereeniging	73,288
Pretoria*	1,985,983	Uitenhage	71,668
Port Elizabeth	1,005,779	Rustenburg	67,201
Soweto	858,649	Kimberley	62,526
Tembisa	348,687	Brakpan	62,115
Pietermaritzburg	223,518	Witbank	61,092
Botshabelo	175,820	Somerset West	60,609
Mdantsane	175,783	Klerksdorp	59,511
Boksburg	158,650	Midrand	44,566
East London	135,560	Newcastle	44,119
Bloemfontein*	111,698	Welkom	34,158
Benoni	94,341	Potchefstroom	26,725
Alberton	89,394	Carletonville	18,362
Krugersdorp	86,618	Westonaria	8,440

* Pretoria is the administrative capital, Cape Town the legislative capital and Bloemfontein the judicial capital.

Mid-2010 (incl. suburbs, UN estimates): Johannesburg 3,669,725; Cape Town 3,404,807; East Rand (Ekurhuleni) 3,201,805; Durban 2,879,233; Pretoria 1,428,987; Vereeniging 1,142,544; Port Elizabeth 1,067,679 (Source: UN, *World Urbanization Prospects: The 2009 Revision*).

BIRTHS AND DEATHS
(annual averages, UN estimates)

	1995–2000	2000–05	2005–10
Birth rate (per 1,000)	25.2	24.2	22.1
Death rate (per 1,000)	9.9	13.4	15.1

Source: UN, *World Population Prospects: The 2008 Revision*.

Registered live births ('000): 1,200 in 2007; 1,278 in 2008; 1,255 in 2009.

Registered deaths: 612,778 in 2006; 603,094 in 2007; 592,073 in 2008.

Registered marriages: 183,030 in 2007; 186,522 in 2008; 171,989 in 2009.

Life expectancy (years at birth, UN estimates): 53 (males 52; females 55) in 2008 (Source: WHO, *World Health Statistics*).

IMMIGRATION AND EMIGRATION

	2001	2002	2003
Immigrants:			
Africa	1,419	2,472	4,961
Europe	1,714	1,847	2,567
Asia	1,289	1,738	2,328
Americas	213	244	354
Oceania	51	65	99
Total (incl. others and unspecified)	4,832	6,545	10,578
Emigrants:			
Africa	1,584	1,461	2,611
Europe	5,316	4,637	6,827
Asia	226	218	445
Americas	1,713	1,473	2,090
Oceania	2,912	2,523	3,248
Total (incl. others and unspecified)	12,260	10,890	16,165

Immigrants (2004): Africa 5,235; Europe 2,638; Asia 2,225; Americas 343; Total (incl. others) 10,714.

SOUTH AFRICA

ECONOMICALLY ACTIVE POPULATION
('000 persons aged 15 to 65 years, annual labour force survey)*

	2007	2008	2009
Agriculture, hunting, forestry and fishing	737	780	679
Mining and quarrying	367	329	312
Manufacturing	1,960	1,954	1,805
Electricity, gas and water	86	94	93
Construction	1,051	1,136	1,096
Trade, restaurants and hotels	3,342	3,150	2,927
Transport, storage and communications	717	766	740
Financing, insurance, real estate and business services	1,459	1,656	1,719
Community, social and personal services	2,490	2,616	2,642
Private households	1,258	1,230	1,199
Total employed	13,467	13,713	13,216
Unemployed	3,871	4,075	4,167
Total labour force	17,338	17,788	17,383

* Figures have been assessed independently, so totals are not always equal to the sum of the component parts.

Health and Welfare

KEY INDICATORS

Total fertility rate (children per woman, 2008)	2.5
Under-5 mortality rate (per 1,000 live births, 2008)	67
HIV/AIDS (% of persons aged 15–49, 2007)	18.1
Physicians (per 1,000 head, 2004)	0.8
Hospital beds (per 1,000 head, 2005)	2.8
Health expenditure (2007): US $ per head (PPP)	819
Health expenditure (2007): % of GDP	8.6
Health expenditure (2007): public (% of total)	41.4
Access to water (% of persons, 2008)	91
Access to sanitation (% of persons, 2008)	77
Total carbon dioxide emissions ('000 metric tons, 2007)	433,172.7
Carbon dioxide emissions per head (metric tons, 2007)	9.0
Human Development Index (2010): ranking	110
Human Development Index (2010): value	0.597

For sources and definitions, see explanatory note on p. vi.

Agriculture

PRINCIPAL CROPS
('000 metric tons)

	2007	2008	2009
Wheat	1,905	2,130	1,958
Barley	222.5	192.0	216.0
Maize	7,125	12,700	12,050
Oats	45.0*	45.0*	n.a.
Sorghum	176.0	255.0	276.5
Potatoes	1,972.4	2,098.6	1,819.3
Sweet potatoes	50.6	48.5	62.7
Sugar cane	20,300.0*	20,500.0*	n.a.
Beans, dry	39.5	59.0	67.0
Soybeans (Soya beans)	205.0	282.0	516.0
Groundnuts, with shell	58.0	88.8	99.5
Sunflower seed	300.0	872.0	801.0
Seed cotton	29.3	26.3	23.0*
Cabbages and other brassicas	143.7	152.9	136.6
Tomatoes	491.2	540.5	532.7
Pumpkins, squash and gourds	81.2	72.9	n.a.
Onions, dry	432.9	496.4	461.9
Carrots and turnips	148.3	170.5	147.9
Maize, green*	310	310	n.a.
Watermelons	64.7	5.6	73.4
Bananas	345.7	393.1	373.6
Oranges	1,410.3	1,524.7	1,445.3
Tangerines, mandarins, clementines and satsumas	135.0*	135.0*	n.a.
Lemons and limes	194.7	229.9	214.4
Grapefruit and pomelos	388.7	340.9	370.4

—continued	2007	2008	2009
Apples	708.1	770.7	702.3
Pears	336.4	337.1	340.2
Apricots	55.4	43.6	46.3
Peaches and nectarines	170.0	162.7	157.8
Plums and sloes	52.8	62.6	60.7
Grapes	1,813.0	1,791.6	n.a.
Mangoes, mangosteens and guavas	82.9	78.4	41.5
Avocados	65.2	83.5	75.9
Pineapples	146.2	124.6	123.1
Tobacco, unmanufactured	20.0*	20.0*	n.a.

* FAO estimate(s).

Aggregate production ('000 metric tons, may include official, semi-official or estimated data): Total cereals 9,514 in 2007, 15,363 in 2008, 14,586 in 2009; Total roots and tubers 2,023 in 2007, 2,147 in 2008, 1,882 in 2009; Total vegetables (incl. melons) 2,115 in 2007, 2,245 in 2008, 2,196 in 2009; Total fruits (excl. melons) 5,994 in 2007, 6,172 in 2008, 5,967 in 2009.

Source: FAO.

LIVESTOCK
('000 head, year ending September)

	2006	2007	2008
Cattle	13,532	13,911	13,865
Pigs	1,662	1,651	1,615
Sheep	24,983	25,082	25,094
Goats	6,400	6,265	6,529
Horses*	270	290	295
Asses*	150	150	150
Chickens	125,840	126,000*	126,160*
Ducks*	360	365	365
Geese and guinea fowls*	130	135	135
Turkeys*	500	500	510

* FAO estimate(s).

2009: Cattle 13,761; Pigs 1,613; Sheep 24,989; Goats 6,358.

Source: FAO.

LIVESTOCK PRODUCTS
('000 metric tons)

	2007	2008	2009
Cattle meat*	805	777	n.a.
Sheep meat*	98.9	94.1	94.9
Goat meat*	35.8	37.2	36.3
Pig meat	224.6	296.3	313.0
Chicken meat	974*	974*	n.a.
Cows' milk	3,066	3,200	3,091
Hen eggs	438	473	450
Wool, greasy*	45	45	n.a.

* FAO estimate(s).

Source: FAO.

Forestry
(including Namibia)

ROUNDWOOD REMOVALS
('000 cubic metres, excl. bark, FAO estimates)

	2007	2008	2009
Sawlogs, veneer logs and logs for sleepers	4,367.4	5,093.4	4,374.8
Pulpwood	13,875.6	13,661.7	12,940.7
Other industrial wood	1,268.8	1,112.2	1,572.1
Fuel wood	12,000.0	12,000.0	12,000.0
Total	31,511.8	31,867.3	30,887.6

Source: FAO.

SOUTH AFRICA

SAWNWOOD PRODUCTION
('000 cubic metres, incl. railway sleepers)

	2007	2008	2009
Coniferous (softwood)	1,845.3	1,878.3	1,753.3
Broadleaved (hardwood)	149.6	177.5	122.3
Total	1,995.0	2,055.8	1,875.6

Source: FAO.

Fishing

('000 metric tons, live weight)

	2006	2007	2008
Capture*	618.6	678.8	643.7
Cape hakes (Stokvisse)	132.9	141.4	131.7
Southern African pilchard	217.3	139.5	91.0
Whitehead's round herring	42.7	48.1	64.7
Southern African anchovy	134.4	252.8	265.8
Cape horse mackerel	27.0	31.7	30.5
Aquaculture*	3.0	2.7	3.2
Total catch*†	621.7	681.4	646.9

* FAO estimates.

† Excluding aquatic plants ('000 metric tons, FAO estimates): 12.8 in 2006; 15.5 in 2007; 13.6 in 2008.

Note: Figures exclude aquatic animals, recorded by number rather than weight. The number of Nile crocodiles captured was: 24,089 in 2006; 34,837 in 2007; 40,197 in 2008.

Source: FAO.

Mining

('000 metric tons unless otherwise indicated)

	2006	2007	2008
Hard coal	244,782	247,666	252,213
Crude petroleum ('000 barrels)	4,441	2,559	1,976
Natural gas	1,795	1,800*	1,800*
Iron ore†	26,000	26,500	30,800
Copper ore (metric tons)†	89,700	97,000	109,000
Nickel ore (metric tons)†	41,800	37,917	31,675
Lead concentrates (metric tons)†	48,273	41,857	46,440
Zinc ore (metric tons)†	34,444	30,859	29,002
Manganese ore and concentrates (metallurgical and chemical)‡	5,213	5,995	6,806
Chromium ore‡	7,418	9,665	9,682
Vanadium ore (metric tons)‡	23,780	23,486	20,295
Zirconium concentrates (metric tons)*	398,000	398,000	398,000
Antimony concentrates (metric tons)†	4,362	3,354	3,370
Cobalt ore (metric tons)*†	400	400	400
Silver (kg)	86,951	68,919	75,199
Uranium oxide (metric tons)	639	619	654
Gold (kg)	272,128	252,598	212,744
Platinum-group metals (kg)	307,528	304,032	275,677
Kaolin	51.6	50.8	39.5
Magnesite—crude	73.3	80.7	83.9
Phosphate rock‡	2,629	2,556	2,287
Fluorspar	256	285	299
Salt	464.9	411.5	416.0
Diamonds ('000 carats)	15,153	15,250	12,901
Gypsum—crude	554.0	627.4	571.3
Mica (metric tons)	828	437	393
Talc (metric tons)	10,966	14,281	5,145
Pyrophyllite (metric tons)	74,886	123,573	80,704

* Estimated figure(s).

† Figures refer to metal content of ores and concentrates.

‡ Gross weight.

Source: US Geological Survey.

Industry

SELECTED PRODUCTS
('000 metric tons, unless otherwise indicated)

	2005	2006	2007
Wheat flour*	2,153	2,217	2,242
Chemical wood pulp	1,118	1,306	1,394
Newsprint	336	343	349
Motor spirit (petrol)	7,858	7,938	7,876
Kerosene	618	624	610
Jet fuel	1,840	1,908	1,688
Distillate fuel oils	9,201	9,873	6,219
Petroleum bitumen—asphalt	802	778	490
Cement (sales)†	12,975	14,257	15,316
Pig-iron†	6,130	6,159	5,358
Crude steel†	9,494	9,718	9,098
Refined copper—unwrought†	99.4	104.1	113.6
Electric energy (million kWh)	244,920	253,798	263,479

* Twelve months ending September.

† Source: US Geological Survey.

Sugar—refined: 1,141 in 2002; 1,232 in 2003.

Footwear ('000 pairs): 19,699 in 2002; 17,317 in 2003.

Rubber tyres ('000): 12,038 in 2002; 12,804 in 2003.

Lubricating oils: 412 in 2002; 446 in 2003; 376 in 2004.

Colour television receivers ('000): 271 in 2002; 359 in 2003.

Passenger motor cars—assembled ('000): 300 in 2002; 306 in 2003.

Lorries—assembled ('000): 129 in 2002; 125 in 2003.

Source: mostly UN Industrial Commodity Statistics Database.

2008 ('000 metric tons): Cement (sales) 14,719; Pig-iron 5,350; Crude steel 8,550; Refined copper—unwrought 93.0 (Source: US Geological Survey).

Finance

CURRENCY AND EXCHANGE RATES

Monetary Units
100 cents = 1 rand (R).

Sterling, Dollar and Euro Equivalents (31 December 2010)
£1 sterling = 10.38 rand;
US $1 = 6.63 rand;
€1 = 8.86 rand;
100 rand = £9.63 = $15.08 = €11.29.

Average Exchange Rate (rand per US $)
2008   8.2612
2009   8.4737
2010   7.3212

BUDGET
(million rand, year ending 31 March)

Revenue	2008/09	2009/10	2010/11*
Tax revenue (gross)	625,100.2	598,705.4	672,200.0
Taxes on incomes and profits	383,482.7	359,044.8	380,080.0
Individuals	195,115.0	205,145.0	228,000.0
Companies (including secondary tax)	185,395.9	150,351.2	149,000.0
Retirement funds	143.3	42.7	—
Other	2,828.6	3,505.9	3,080.0
Taxes on payroll and workforce	7,327.5	7,804.8	8,420.0
Taxes on property	9,477.1	8,826.4	9,365.0
Domestic taxes on goods and services	201,416.1	203,666.8	247,540.0
Value-added tax	154,343.1	147,941.3	181,335.0
Excise duties	21,354.0	22,565.2	24,800.0
Levies on fuel	24,883.8	28,832.5	34,300.0

SOUTH AFRICA

Revenue—continued	2008/09	2009/10	2010/11*
Air departure tax	549.4	580.3	705.0
Other	285.7	405.7	1,200.0
Stamp duties and fees	571.8	49.5	5.0
State Miscellaneous Revenue	−27.4	−5.7	—
Taxes on international trade and transactions	22,852.4	19,318.9	26,790.0
Departmental revenue	12,616.2	8,888.5	12,254.0
Sub-total	637,716.4	607,593.3	684,454.0
Less SACU payments†	28,920.6	27,915.4	14,991.3
Other adjustments	—	—	−2,900.0
Total	608,795.7	579,678.6	666,562.7

Expenditure	2008/09	2009/10	2010/11*
Central government administration	49,167.6	51,564.2	61,552.7
The Presidency	308.8	659.1	766.9
Parliament	1,071.5	1,009.0	1,201.6
Cooperative governance and traditional affairs	33,386.0	33,661.6	41,748.5
Foreign affairs	5,472.3	5,417.4	4,715.8
Home affairs	4,666.6	5,195.4	5,834.4
Public works	4,197.0	5,533.6	7,138.7
Women, children and people with disabilities	61.9	77.5	106.2
Financial and administrative services	29,409.2	59,945.9	41,879.6
Government communication and information system	427.5	495.4	550.2
National treasury	23,762.8	53,240.6	38,375.4
Public Enterprises	3,265.1	3,983.3	555.5
Public services and administration	630.6	670.8	656.7
Statistics South Africa	1,323.1	1,555.8	1,741.7
Social services	126,166.0	139,815.5	155,292.6
Arts and culture	2,114.5	2,224.9	2,339.7
Education	25,151.8	28,538.7	32,850.2
Health	16,424.5	19,168.6	22,218.7
Labour	1,507.2	1,698.7	1,793.2
Social development	76,096.7	85,318.2	94,841.0
Sport and Recreation South Africa	4,871.4	2,866.4	1,249.6
Justice and protection services	90,602.9	102,433.8	110,078.5
Correctional services	12,822.6	13,687.3	15,232.5
Defence	27,801.3	31,324.2	30,442.6
Independent complaints directorate	99.3	106.2	131.4
Justice and constitutional development	8,244.4	9,653.5	10,742.3
Safety and security	41,635.2	47,662.5	53,529.7
Economic services and infrastructure	75,274.9	82,624.1	91,116.3
Agriculture and forestry	3,464.9	3,961.8	4,003.9
Communications	2,328.6	2,301.9	2,138.0
Economic development	220.4	314.6	384.5
Energy	2,961.7	3,690.9	5,648.7
Environmental affairs	1,789.9	2,124.3	2,359.8
Human settlements	13,269.5	16,407.4	19,305.9
Mineral resources	768.3	853.8	995.8
Rural development and land reform	6,669.8	5,863.8	7,293.4
Tourism	1,202.2	1,145.6	1,183.8
Science and technology	3,703.5	4,183.9	4,128.0
Trade and industry	4,836.7	5,923.3	6,075.5
Transport	28,161.7	28,664.0	29,989.4
Water affairs	5,797.8	7,188.6	7,609.7
Sub-total	370,620.6	436,383.5	459,919.7
State debt costs	54,393.7	57,129.2	66,570.4
Provincial equitable share	201,795.6	236,890.8	265,139.4
Skills levy and seats	7,234.1	7,815.6	8,424.2
Members' remuneration	304.2	398.8	392.7
Judges' salaries	1,601.1	1,774.9	1,929.9
President and deputy-president salary	4.0	3.8	4.6
General fuel levy sharing with metros	—	6,800.1	7,542.4
Total	635,953.3	747,196.8	809,923.3

* Estimates.
† Payments to Botswana, Lesotho, Namibia and Swaziland, in accordance with Southern African Customs Union agreements.

Source: National Treasury, Pretoria.

INTERNATIONAL RESERVES
(US $ million at 31 December)

	2008	2009	2010
Gold (national valuation)	3,485	4,438	5,654
IMF special drawing rights	344	2,803	2,754
Reserve position in IMF	2	2	2
Foreign exchange	30,238	32,432	35,419
Total	34,069	39,675	43,829

Source: IMF, *International Financial Statistics*.

MONEY SUPPLY
(million rand at 31 December)

	2008	2009	2010
Currency outside depository corporations	57,362	61,784	65,079
Transferable deposits	363,384	361,281	408,363
Other deposits	1,150,864	1,154,169	1,217,424
Securities other than shares	342,591	370,544	392,113
Broad money	1,914,200	1,947,777	2,082,979

Source: IMF, *International Financial Statistics*.

COST OF LIVING
(Consumer Price Index; base: 2000 = 100)

	2006	2007	2008
Food	147.8	163.1	190.0
Clothing	84.6	76.8	87.7
Housing	118.2	129.7	142.2
Electricity, gas and other fuels	141.9	153.3	182.8
All items (incl. others)	134.0	143.5	160.0

2009: All items 171.4.
2010: All items 178.7.
Source: ILO.

NATIONAL ACCOUNTS
(million rand at current prices, preliminary)

National Income and Product

	2008	2009	2010
Compensation of employees	999,629	1,083,733	1,198,951
Net operating surplus	716,559	727,641	820,901
Consumption of fixed capital	301,840	333,377	352,159
Gross domestic product (GDP) at factor cost	2,018,028	2,144,751	2,372,011
Taxes on production	279,781	274,769	314,196
Less Subsidies	23,670	23,551	23,450
GDP at market prices	2,274,139	2,395,969	2,662,757
Primary incomes received from abroad	48,254	34,075	34,099
Less Primary incomes paid abroad	122,129	87,593	87,022
Gross national income at market prices	2,200,264	2,342,451	2,609,834
Current transfers received from abroad	11,483	10,334	9,089
Less Current transfers paid abroad	30,389	32,762	25,851
Gross national disposable income at market prices	2,181,358	2,320,023	2,593,072

SOUTH AFRICA

Expenditure on the Gross Domestic Product

	2008	2009	2010
Government final consumption expenditure	428,852	505,469	573,540
Private final consumption expenditure	1,398,236	1,456,089	1,575,642
Increase in stocks	−11,958	−62,069	−8,561
Gross fixed capital formation	524,678	531,957	521,613
Residual item	3,424	−14,361	4,896
Total domestic expenditure	2,343,232	2,417,085	2,667,130
Exports of goods and services	809,644	657,192	728,621
Less Imports of goods and services	878,737	678,308	732,994
GDP at market prices	2,274,139	2,395,969	2,662,757
GDP at constant 2005 prices	1,814,134	1,783,617	1,834,292

Gross Domestic Product by Economic Activity

	2008	2009	2010
Agriculture, forestry and fishing	63,384	63,888	59,543
Mining and quarrying	201,381	198,180	230,402
Manufacturing	340,623	330,310	352,176
Electricity, gas and water	45,803	60,280	66,812
Construction (contractors)	72,894	87,116	91,973
Wholesale and retail trade, catering and accommodation	271,237	294,260	335,562
Transport, storage and communication	188,231	199,065	220,039
Finance, insurance, real estate and business services	442,121	467,126	511,332
Government services	299,373	340,837	386,352
Other community, social and personal services	119,220	135,537	152,747
Gross value added at basic prices	2,044,267	2,176,597	2,406,938
Taxes, less subsidies, on products	229,872	219,370	255,819
GDP at market prices	2,274,139	2,395,967	2,662,757

BALANCE OF PAYMENTS
(US $ million)

	2007	2008	2009
Exports of goods f.o.b.	76,435	86,118	66,542
Imports of goods f.o.b.	−81,596	−90,566	−66,009
Trade balance	−5,160	−4,448	534
Exports of services	13,818	12,805	12,020
Imports of services	−16,481	−16,976	−14,808
Balance on goods and services	−7,824	−8,619	−2,254
Other income received	6,882	5,944	3,988
Other income paid	−16,725	−15,076	−10,377
Balance on goods, services and income	−17,667	−17,751	−8,643
Current transfers received	1,099	1,377	1,242
Current transfers paid	−3,450	−3,709	−3,926
Current balance	−20,018	−20,083	−11,327
Capital account (net)	28	25	26
Direct investment abroad	−2,982	2,120	−1,311
Direct investment from abroad	5,737	9,645	5,354
Portfolio investment assets	−3,439	−6,720	−1,746
Portfolio investment liabilities	13,681	−7,583	13,368
Other investment assets	517	8,921	3,101
Other investment liabilities	7,196	5,372	−2,489
Net errors and omissions	5,017	10,528	−804
Overall balance	5,737	2,225	4,171

Source: IMF, *International Financial Statistics*.

External Trade

PRINCIPAL COMMODITIES
(distribution by SITC, US $ million)

Imports c.i.f.	2007	2008	2009
Food and live animals	2,839.6	3,184.8	2,873.1
Crude materials (inedible) except fuels	2,516.2	2,891.0	1,261.8
Mineral fuels, lubricants, etc.	14,847.3	19,555.0	13,663.3
Petroleum, petroleum products, etc.	14,317.6	18,512.8	12,949.0
Crude petroleum oils, etc.	10,917.9	14,957.2	10,294.4
Chemicals and related products	7,163.9	8,549.9	6,673.8
Basic manufactures	9,241.4	9,048.1	6,611.5
Non-metallic mineral manufactures	2,200.0	1,936.1	1,234.7
Machinery and transport equipment	29,795.2	30,670.0	22,201.3
Power generating machinery and equipment	1,696.5	2,627.8	1,762.0
Machinery specialized for particular industries	4,158.7	4,417.2	2,605.1
General industrial machinery, equipment and parts	3,881.9	4,271.9	3,341.7
Office machines and automatic data-processing equipment	3,108.2	3,020.8	2,452.4
Telecommunications and sound equipment	3,818.2	3,913.3	3,172.3
Other electrical machinery, apparatus, etc.	3,259.2	3,627.7	2,987.7
Road vehicles	7,746.2	6,161.2	4,339.8
Passenger motor vehicles (excl. buses)	4,410.3	2,749.7	2,335.8
Other transport equipment	1,599.7	2,038.2	1,107.8
Miscellaneous manufactured articles	6,412.4	6,468.1	5,729.1
Total (incl. others)	79,872.6	87,593.1	63,766.1

Exports f.o.b.	2007	2008	2009
Food and live animals	3,196.8	4,124.1	4,132.8
Vegetables and fruit	1,883.6	2,050.9	2,076.8
Beverages and tobacco	967.8	1,078.1	1,132.9
Crude materials (inedible) except fuels	7,139.8	10,624.6	8,448.0
Metalliferous ores and metal scrap	5,305.1	8,252.7	6,806.7
Mineral fuels, lubricants, etc.	6,759.0	7,120.3	6,022.7
Coal, lignite and peat	3,386.4	4,785.5	4,215.1
Petroleum, petroleum products, etc.	3,226.0	2,198.7	1,675.5
Chemicals and related products	4,340.2	5,723.7	4,100.2
Basic manufactures	26,106.9	26,946.0	17,535.4
Non-metallic mineral manufactures	2,901.8	2,647.1	1,588.8
Pearl, precious and semi-precious stones, unworked or worked	2,533.8	2,339.0	1,307.1
Diamonds (non-industrial), not mounted or set	2,487.8	2,282.5	1,300.8
Iron and steel	7,460.1	8,859.7	5,116.2
Pig-iron, etc.	3,889.1	5,954.6	2,912.7
Non-ferrous metals	13,018.7	12,578.3	8,614.0
Silver, platinum and other platinum group metals	9,842.1	9,817.6	6,769.7
Platinum group metals, unwrought, unworked or semi-manufactured	9,823.1	9,801.0	6,766.6
Aluminium	2,201.4	2,071.0	1,464.3
Aluminium and aluminium alloys, unwrought	1,608.8	1,348.4	1,004.2

SOUTH AFRICA

Statistical Survey

Exports f.o.b.—continued	2007	2008	2009
Machinery and transport equipment	13,411.6	16,229.1	10,786.6
General industrial machinery, equipment and parts	4,051.3	4,078.9	2,489.2
Road vehicles	5,164.9	7,522.3	5,096.1
Passenger motor vehicles (excl. buses)	2,635.5	4,535.6	3,062.5
Miscellaneous manufactured articles	1,628.9	1,777.4	1,408.1
Total (incl. others)	64,026.6	73,965.5	53,863.9

Source: UN, *International Trade Statistics Yearbook*.

PRINCIPAL TRADING PARTNERS
(US $ million)*

Imports f.o.b.	2007	2008	2009
Angola	1,645.8	2,686.5	1,370.6
Argentina	1,018.7	1,003.2	858.2
Australia	1,458.5	1,630.4	1,083.0
Belgium	988.0	1,128.2	927.2
Brazil	1,658.6	1,661.1	1,242.2
China, People's Repub.	8,562.7	9,909.3	8,325.3
France (incl. Monaco)	2,680.3	2,502.6	1,993.2
Germany	9,316.9	9,914.0	7,438.3
India	1,777.5	2,261.9	1,811.6
Iran	2,955.5	3,290.4	2,599.1
Ireland	809.1	857.5	n.a.
Italy	2,218.1	2,133.8	1,608.2
Japan	5,249.4	4,882.6	3,093.7
Korea, Repub.	1,791.5	1,437.1	1,135.3
Malaysia	1,064.6	1,084.6	865.8
Netherlands	1,276.3	1,213.2	1,157.9
Nigeria	1,771.8	1,892.4	1,839.0
Saudi Arabia	3,606.3	5,523.0	3,204.1
Singapore	654.7	887.9	575.8
Spain	1,112.7	1,063.7	756.9
Sweden	1,152.3	1,614.7	1,104.3
Thailand	1,466.6	1,756.1	1,352.5
United Kingdom	3,863.5	3,556.2	2,526.1
USA	6,166.1	7,038.0	4,949.4
Total (incl. others)	79,872.6	87,593.1	63,766.1

Exports f.o.b.	2007	2008	2009
Angola	772.2	897.8	682.0
Australia	1,278.4	1,494.4	725.8
Belgium	1,748.8	2,046.6	1,282.2
China, People's Repub.	4,169.6	4,309.8	5,670.1
Congo, Democratic Repub.	621.8	1,125.2	573.8
France (incl. Monaco)	1,382.9	1,447.2	841.3
Germany	5,106.0	5,748.9	3,512.7
Hong Kong	655.5	645.1	963.4
India	1,349.5	2,279.5	2,067.7
Israel	785.3	841.4	575.5
Italy	1,429.8	1,595.2	1,080.6
Japan	7,039.3	8,119.6	4,096.1
Kenya	643.3	709.9	872.4
Korea, Repub.	1,161.6	1,506.7	900.8
Mozambique	1,267.2	1,609.0	1,606.6
Netherlands	2,880.7	3,463.6	2,036.6
Nigeria	683.8	955.0	678.1
Spain	1,757.7	1,876.6	1,088.5
Switzerland-Liechtenstein	1,370.5	1,556.4	2,273.3
United Arab Emirates	708.6	769.9	610.4
United Kingdom	4,907.3	4,905.9	3,002.1
USA	7,528.7	7,987.4	4,859.7
Zambia	1,421.2	1,965.4	1,416.0
Zimbabwe	1,194.8	1,689.0	1,608.0
Total (incl. others)	64,026.6	73,965.5	53,863.9

* Imports by country of origin; exports by country of destination.

Source: UN, *International Trade Statistics Yearbook*.

Transport

RAILWAYS
(traffic, year ending 31 March)*

	1997/98	1998/99	1999/2000
Passenger-km (million)	1,775	1,794	3,930
Net ton-km (million)	103,866	102,777	106,786

* Including Namibia.

Source: UN, *Statistical Yearbook*.

2008 (estimates): Passengers ('000) 613,435; Total freight carried ('000 metric tons) 183,106.

2009 (estimates): Passengers ('000) 643,893; Total freight carried ('000 metric tons) 183,483.

2010 (preliminary): Passengers ('000) 519,801; Total freight carried ('000 metric tons) 185,986.

ROAD TRAFFIC
(registered motor vehicles at 31 December)

	2005	2006	2007
Passenger cars	4,890,206	4,574,972	5,160,844
Buses and coaches	302,947	288,513	316,540
Lorries and vans	1,968,198	1,824,088	2,125,784
Motorcycles and mopeds	280,693	237,556	312,046

Source: IRF, *World Road Statistics*.

SHIPPING

Merchant Fleet
(vessels registered at 31 December)

	2007	2008	2009
Number of vessels	250	261	273
Displacement ('000 grt)	192.6	195.1	202.9

Source: IHS Fairplay, *World Fleet Statistics*.

International Sea-borne Freight Traffic

	2003	2004	2005
Goods loaded (metric tons)	128,477,183	124,370,762	127,408,557
Goods unloaded (metric tons)	42,845,843	43,820,161	43,847,748
Containers loaded (TEU)	1,194,400	1,290,883	1,484,009
Containers unloaded (TEU)	1,220,167	1,341,888	1,530,227

Source: National Ports Authority of South Africa.

CIVIL AVIATION
(traffic on scheduled services)

	2004	2005	2006
Kilometres flown (million)	194	218	217
Passengers carried ('000)	9,879	11,845	12,921
Passenger-km (million)	26,048	29,191	30,797
Total ton-km (million)	3,270	3,580	3,845

Source: UN, *Statistical Yearbook*.

2007: Passengers carried ('000) 12,870.3 (Source: World Bank, World Development Indicators database).

2008: Passengers carried ('000) 13,135.4 (Source: World Bank, World Development Indicators database).

Tourism

FOREIGN VISITOR ARRIVALS*

Country of origin	2006	2007	2008
Botswana	765,705	821,070	807,292
France	108,713	118,175	131,512
Germany	263,225	259,856	243,578
Lesotho	1,919,889	2,171,954	2,165,505
Mozambique	926,496	1,085,556	1,228,979
Namibia	225,020	221,360	222,817
Netherlands	126,327	130,878	130,083
Swaziland	993,030	1,041,235	1,090,056
United Kingdom	494,955	506,481	493,415
USA	259,674	282,062	292,884
Zambia	160,984	184,358	193,677
Zimbabwe	989,614	977,101	1,248,043
Total (incl. others and unspecified)	8,508,806	9,207,697	9,728,860

* Figures include same-day visitors (excursionists), but exclude arrivals of South African nationals resident abroad. Border crossings by contract workers are also excluded.

Tourism receipts (US $ million, excl. passenger transport): 8,967 in 2006; 9,890 in 2007; 8,861 in 2008.

Source: World Tourism Organization.

Communications Media

	2007	2008	2009
Telephones ('000 main lines in use)	4,532	4,425	4,320
Mobile cellular telephones ('000 subscribers)	42,300*	45,000	46,436
Internet users ('000)	3,966	4,187	4,420
Broadband subscribers ('000)	378	426	481

* Estimate.

2001: Radio receivers ('000 in use): 11,696; Television receivers ('000 in use): 7,708.

Daily newspapers: 18 (total average circulation 1,408,000) in 2004.

Non-daily newspapers: 314 (total average circulation 7,630,000) in 2004.

Book production: 5,418 titles in 1995.

Personal computers: 3,966,000 (84.6 per 1,000 persons) in 2005.

Sources: partly UNESCO, *Statistical Yearbook*; UN, *Statistical Yearbook*; International Telecommunication Union.

Education

(2009)*

	Institutions	Teachers	Students
Primary	14,380	181,805	5,851,605
Secondary	6,304	141,841	3,856,946
Combined	4,611	71,035	2,158,052
Intermediate and middle	611	18,386	361,360
ABET centres†‡	2,395	15,657	297,900
ELSEN centres§	418	8,618	100,717
Further education and training‡	49	6,255	420,475
ECD‖	3,312	10,046	237,471
Higher education‡	23	16,320	837,779

* Figures for public and independent institutions, unless otherwise indicated.
† Adult basic education and training.
‡ Figures refer to public institutions only.
§ Education for learners with special needs.
‖ Early childhood development.

Source: Department of Education.

Pupil-teacher ratio (primary education, UNESCO estimate): 31.0 in 2006/07 (Source: UNESCO Institute for Statistics).

Adult literacy rate (UNESCO estimates): 89.0% (males 89.9%; females 88.1%) in 2008 (Source: UNESCO Institute for Statistics).

Directory

The Government

HEAD OF STATE

President: JACOB ZUMA (inaugurated 9 May 2009).
Deputy President: KGALEMA MOTLANTHE.

THE CABINET
(May 2011)

Minister of Agriculture, Forestry and Fisheries: TINA JOEMAT-PETTERSSON.
Minister of Arts and Culture: PAUL MASHATILE.
Minister of Basic Education: ANGIE MOTSHEKGA.
Minister of Communications: RADHAKRISHNA 'ROY' PADAYACHIE.
Minister of Co-operative Governance and Traditional Affairs: SICELO SHICEKA.
Minister of Correctional Services: NOSIVIWE MAPISA-NQAKULA.
Minister of Defence and Military Veterans: LINDIWE NONCEBA SISULU.
Minister of Economic Development: EBRAHIM PATEL.
Minister of Energy: DIPUO PETERS.
Minister of Finance: PRAVIN JAMNADAS GORDHAN.
Minister of Health: Dr AARON MOTSOALEDI.
Minister of Higher Education and Training: Dr BLADE NZIMANDE.
Minister of Home Affairs: Dr NKOSAZANA DLAMINI-ZUMA.
Minister of Human Settlements: TOKYO SEXWALE.
Minister of International Relations and Co-operation: MAITE NKOANA-MASHABANE.
Minister of Justice and Constitutional Development: JEFF RADEBE.
Minister of Labour: MILDRED OLIPHANT.
Minister of Mining: SUSAN SHABANGU.
Minister of Police: NATHI MTHETHWA.
Minister of Public Enterprises: MALUSI GIGABA.
Minister for the Public Service and Administration: RICHARD BALOYI.
Minister of Public Works: GWEN MAHLANGU-NKABINDE.
Minister of Rural Development and Land Reform: GUGILE NKWINTI.
Minister of Science and Technology: NALEDI PANDOR.
Minister of Social Development: BATHABILE DLAMINI.
Minister of Sport and Recreation: FIKILE MBALULA.

SOUTH AFRICA

Minister of State Security: SIYABONGA CWELE.
Ministers in the Presidency: TREVOR MANUEL (National Planning Commission), COLLINS CHABANE (Performance Monitoring, Evaluation and Administration).
Minister of Tourism: MARTHINUS VAN SCHALKWYK.
Minister of Trade and Industry: Dr ROB DAVIES.
Minister of Transport: SBUSISO JOEL NDEBELE.
Minister of Water and Environmental Affairs: EDNA MOLEWA.
Minister of Women, Youth, Children and People with Disabilities: LULU XINGWANA.

In addition, there were 32 Deputy Ministers.

MINISTRIES

The Presidency: Union Bldgs, West Wing, Government Ave, Pretoria 0001; Private Bag X1000, Pretoria 0001; tel. (12) 3005200; fax (12) 3238246; e-mail president@po.gov.za; internet www.thepresidency.gov.za.

Ministry in The Presidency: National Planning Commission: Union Bldgs, 2nd Floor, Government Ave, Pretoria 0001; Private Bag X1000, Pretoria 0001; tel. (12) 3005277; fax (12) 3238246; e-mail minister@po.gov.za; internet www.thepresidency.gov.za.

Ministry in The Presidency: Performance Monitoring, Evaluation and Administration in The Presidency: Union Bldgs, 2nd Floor, Government Ave, Pretoria 0001; Private Bag X1000, Pretoria 0001; tel. (12) 3005331; fax (12) 3218870; e-mail samson@po.gov.za; internet www.thepresidency.gov.za.

Ministry of Agriculture, Forestry and Fisheries: Agriculture Bldg, 20 Beatrix St, Arcadia, Pretoria 0002; Private Bag X250, Pretoria 0001; tel. (12) 3197317; fax (12) 3197856; e-mail cco@nda.agric.za; internet www.doa.agric.za.

Ministry of Arts and Culture: 481 Church St, 10th Floor, cnr Church and Beatrix Sts, Kingsley Centre, Arcadia, Pretoria; Private Bag X899, Pretoria 0001; tel. (12) 4413709; fax (12) 4404485; e-mail sandile.memela@dac.gov.za; internet www.dac.gov.za.

Ministry of Basic Education: Sol Plaatje House, 123 Schoeman St, Pretoria 0002; Private Bag X603, Pretoria 0001; tel. (12) 3125501; fax (12) 3235989; internet www.education.gov.za.

Ministry of Communications: Nkululeko House, iParioli Office Park, 399 Duncan St, cnr Park St, Hatfield, Pretoria 0083; Private Bag X860, Pretoria 0001; tel. (12) 4278177; fax (12) 3626915; e-mail joe@doc.gov.za; internet www.doc.gov.za.

Ministry of Co-operative Governance and Traditional Affairs: 87 Hamilton St, Arcadia, Pretoria 0001; Private Bag X802, Pretoria 0001; tel. (12) 3340705; fax (12) 3264478; internet www.cogta.gov.za.

Ministry of Correctional Services: Poyntons Bldg, West Block, cnr Church and Schubart Sts, Pretoria 0002; Private Bag X853, Pretoria 0001; tel. (12) 3072000; fax (12) 3286149; e-mail communications@dcs.gov.za; internet www.dcs.gov.za.

Ministry of Defence and Military Veterans: Armscor Bldg, Block 5, Nossob St, Erasmusrand 0181; Private Bag X427, Pretoria 0001; tel. (12) 3556101; fax (12) 3470118; e-mail mil@mil.za; internet www.dod.mil.za.

Ministry of Economic Development: DTI Campus, 3rd Floor, Block A, 77 cnr Meintjies and Esselen Sts, Sunnyside, Pretoria; Private Bag X149, Pretoria 0001; tel. (012) 3941006; fax (86) 3940255.

Ministry of Energy: Mineralia Centre, 234 Visagie St, Pretoria 0002; Private Bag X59, Pretoria 0001; tel. (12) 3178000; fax (12) 3223416; internet www.dme.gov.za.

Ministry of Health: 226 Prinsloo St, Pretoria 0001; Private Bag X399, Pretoria 0001; tel. (12) 3120546; fax (12) 3255526; e-mail bhengu@health.gov.za; internet www.doh.gov.za.

Ministry of Higher Education and Training: Sol Plaatje House, 123 Schoeman St, Pretoria 0002; Private Bag X893, Pretoria 0001; tel. (12) 3125555; fax (12) 3235618; internet www.education.gov.za.

Ministry of Home Affairs: cnr Maggs and Petroleum Sts, Watloo, Pretoria; Private Bag X114, Pretoria 0001; tel. (12) 8108039; fax (12) 8107312; e-mail csc@dha.gov.za; internet www.home-affairs.gov.za.

Ministry of Human Settlements: Govan Mbeki House, 240 Walker St, Sunnyside, Pretoria 0002; Private Bag X644, Pretoria 0001; tel. (12) 4211310; fax (12) 3418513; e-mail mareldia@housing.gov.za; internet www.housing.gov.za.

Ministry of International Relations and Co-operation: Union Bldgs, East Wing, 1 Government Ave, Arcadia, Pretoria 0002; Private Bag X152, Pretoria 0001; tel. (12) 3511000; fax (12) 3291000; e-mail minister@foreign.gov.za; internet www.dfa.gov.za.

Ministry of Justice and Constitutional Development: Momentum Centre, 329 Pretorius St, cnr Pretorius and Prinsloo Sts, Pretoria 0001; Private Bag X276, Pretoria 0001; tel. (12) 313578217; fax (12) 3151749; e-mail znqayi@justice.gov.za; internet www.doj.gov.za.

Ministry of Labour: Laboria House, 215 Schoeman St, Pretoria 0002; Private Bag X117, Pretoria 0001; tel. (12) 3094000; fax (12) 3094030; e-mail page.boikanyo@labour.gov.za; internet www.labour.gov.za.

Ministry of Mining: Mineralia Centre, 391 Andries St, Pretoria 0002; Private Bag X59, Pretoria 0001; tel. (12) 3178000; fax (12) 3223416; internet www.dme.gov.za.

Ministry of Police: Wachthuis, 7th Floor, 231 Pretorius St, Pretoria; Private Bag X463, Pretoria 0001; tel. (12) 3932810; fax (12) 3932812; e-mail bloemb@saps.org.za.

Ministry of Public Enterprises: Infotech Bldg, Suite 401, 1090 Arcadia St, Hatfield, Pretoria 0083; Private Bag X15, Hatfield 0028; tel. (12) 4311000; fax (86) 5012624; e-mail info@dpe.gov.za; internet www.dpe.gov.za.

Ministry of Public Service and Administration: Batho Pele House, 116 Proes St, Pretoria 0001; Private Bag X916, Pretoria 0001; tel. (12) 3361701; fax (12) 3267802; e-mail natasha@dpsa.gov.za; internet www.dpsa.gov.za.

Ministry of Public Works: AVN Bldg, 6th Floor, cnr Skinner and Andries Sts, Pretoria 0002; Private Bag X65, Pretoria 0001; tel. (12) 3105951; fax (12) 3105184; internet www.publicworks.gov.za.

Ministry of Rural Development and Land Reform: Old Bldg, 184 cnr Jacob Mare and Paul Kruger Sts, Pretoria; Private Bag X833, Pretoria 0001; tel. (12) 3128911; fax (12) 3236072; internet www.ruraldevelopment.gov.za.

Ministry of Science and Technology: DST Bldg (No. 53), Meiring Naude Rd, Brummeria 0001; Private Bag X894, Pretoria 0001; tel. (12) 8436300; fax (12) 3242687; e-mail nelvis.qekema@dst.gov.za; internet www.dst.gov.za.

Ministry of Social Development: HSRC Bldg, North Wing, 134 Pretorius St, Pretoria 0002; Private Bag X901, Pretoria 0001; tel. (12) 3127500; fax (12) 3122502; e-mail lakelak@dsd.gov.za; internet www.dsd.gov.za.

Ministry of Sport and Recreation: cnr Vermeulen and Queen Sts, 66 Queen St, Pretoria; Private Bag X896, Pretoria 0001; tel. (12) 3045000; fax (12) 3230795; e-mail stofile@srsa.gov.za; internet www.srsa.gov.za.

Ministry of State Security: Bogare Bldg, 2 Atterbury Rd, Menlyn, Pretoria; POB 1037, Menlyn 0077; tel. (12) 3670700; fax (12) 3670749; e-mail lornad@mweb.co.za; internet www.intelligence.gov.za.

Ministry of Tourism: Fedsure Forum Bldg, North Tower, 1st and 2nd Floors, 315 Pretorius St, cnr Pretorius and van der Walt Sts, Pretoria 0001; Private Bag X424, Pretoria 0001; tel. (12) 3103611; fax (12) 3220082; internet www.tourism.gov.za.

Ministry of Trade and Industry: 77 Meintjies St, Sunnyside, Pretoria 0002; Private Bag X84, Pretoria 0001; tel. (12) 3949500; fax (12) 3949501; e-mail contactus@thedti.gov.za; internet www.thedti.gov.za.

Ministry of Transport: Forum Bldg, 159 Struben St, Pretoria 0002; Private Bag X193, Pretoria 0001; tel. (12) 3093000; fax (12) 3283194; e-mail khozac@dot.gov.za; internet www.transport.gov.za.

Ministry of Water and Environmental Affairs: Sedibeng Bldg, 10th Floor, 185 Schoeman St, Pretoria 0002; Private Bag X313, Pretoria 0001; tel. (12) 3368733; fax (12) 3367817; e-mail pagel@dwaf.gov.za; internet www.dwaf.gov.za.

Ministry of Women, Youth, Children and People with Disabilities: Union Buildings, Room 290A, Government Ave., Pretoria; Private Bag X1000, Pretoria 0001; tel. (12) 3005575; e-mail tseleng@po.gov.za.

National Treasury: 40 Church Sq., Pretoria 0002; Private Bag X115, Pretoria 0001; tel. (12) 3155372; fax (12) 3233262; e-mail dumisa.jele@treasury.gov.za; internet www.treasury.gov.za.

Legislature

PARLIAMENT

National Council of Provinces

Chairman: MNINWA JOHANNES MAHLANGU.

The National Council of Provinces (NCOP), which replaced the Senate under the new Constitution, was inaugurated on 6 February 1997. The NCOP comprises 90 members, with six permanent delegates and four special delegates from each of the nine provinces.

National Assembly

Speaker: MAX VUYISILE SISULU.

SOUTH AFRICA

General Election, 22 April 2009

Party	Votes	% of votes	Seats
African National Congress	11,650,748	65.90	264
Democratic Alliance	2,945,829	16.66	67
Congress of the People	1,311,027	7.42	30
Inkatha Freedom Party	804,260	4.55	18
Independent Democrats	162,915	0.92	4
United Democratic Movement	149,680	0.85	4
Vryheidsfront Plus	146,796	0.83	4
African Christian Democratic Party	142,658	0.81	3
United Christian Democratic Party	66,086	0.37	2
Pan-Africanist Congress of Azania	48,530	0.27	1
Minority Front	43,474	0.25	1
Azanian People's Organization	38,245	0.22	1
African People's Convention	35,867	0.20	1
Others	134,614	0.76	—
Total	**17,680,729**	**100.00**	**400**

Provincial Governments
(May 2011)

EASTERN CAPE
Premier: Noxolo Kiviet (ANC).
Speaker of the Legislature: Fikile Xasa (ANC).

FREE STATE
Premier: Ace Magashule (ANC).
Speaker of the Legislature: Moeketsi Sesele (ANC).

GAUTENG
Premier: Nomvula Paula Mokonyane (ANC).
Speaker of the Legislature: Lindiwe Maseko (ANC).

KWAZULU/NATAL
Premier: Dr Zweli Lawrence Mkhize (ANC).
Speaker of the Legislature: Neliswa Peggy Nkonyeni (ANC).

LIMPOPO
Premier: Cassel Mathale (ANC).
Speaker of the Legislature: Rudoph Phala (ANC).

MPUMALANGA
Premier: David D. Mabuza (ANC).
Speaker of the Legislature: Jackson Mthembu (ANC).

NORTHERN CAPE
Premier: Hazel Jenkins (ANC).
Speaker of the Legislature: Ghoolam Acharwaray (ANC).

NORTH-WEST
Premier: Thandi Modise (ANC).
Speaker of the Legislature: Nono Dumile Maloy (ANC).

WESTERN CAPE
Premier: Helen Zille (DA).
Speaker of the Legislature: Shahid Esau (DA).

Election Commission

Independent Electoral Commission: Election House, 260 Walker St, Sunnyside, Pretoria; tel. (12) 4285700; fax (12) 4285863; e-mail iec@elections.org.za; internet www.elections.org.za; f. 1996; Chair. Dr Brigalia Bam.

Political Organizations

A total of 26 parties contested the elections to the National Assembly in April 2009, while 38 parties presented candidates in the concurrent provincial elections.

African Christian Democratic Party (ACDP): Stats Building, 1st Floor, 2 Fore St, POB 1677, Alberton; tel. (11) 8693941; fax (86) 6564411; e-mail office@acdp.org.za; internet www.acdp.org.za; f. 1993; Leader Rev. Kenneth Meshoe.

African National Congress of South Africa (ANC): 54 Sauer St, Johannesburg 2001; POB 61884, Marshalltown 2107; tel. (11) 3761000; fax (11) 3761100; e-mail nmtyelwa@anc.org.za; internet www.anc.org.za; f. 1912; in alliance with the South African Communist Party (SACP) and the Congress of South African Trade Unions (COSATU); governing party since April 1994; Pres. Jacob Zuma; Deputy Pres. Kgalema Motlanthe; Sec.-Gen. Gwede Mantashe; Pres. of the Youth League Julius Malema.

African People's Convention (APC): Dr Neil Aggett House, 4th Floor, 90 President St, between Kruis and Small Sts, Johannesburg 2001; tel. (11) 4985535; fax (11) 4985938; e-mail mmazibuko@gpl.gov.za; internet www.theapc.org.za; f. 2008; Pres. Themba Godi; Sec.-Gen. Hlabirwa R. D. Mathume.

Afrikaner Weerstandsbeweging (AWB) (Afrikaner Resistance Movement): POB 274, Ventersdorp 2710, Johannesburg; tel. and fax (18) 2642516; e-mail awb@awb.co.za; internet www.awb.co.za; f. 1973; Afrikaner (Boer) nationalist group seeking self-determination for the Afrikaner people in South Africa; Leader Steyn van Ronge.

Al Jama-ah: The Business Hub, 1A Forest Pl., Pinelands, Cape Town 7405; tel. (21) 5314273; internet www.aljama.co.za; Muslim party; Leader Mogamad Ganief Ebrahim Hendricks.

Azanian People's Organization (AZAPO): 141 Commissioner St, Kine Centre, 19th Floor, Johannesburg 2001; POB 4230, Johannesburg 2000; tel. (11) 3316430; fax (11) 3316433; e-mail azapo@mail.ngo.za; internet www.azapo.org.za; f. 1978; to seek the establishment of a unitary, democratic, socialist republic; excludes white mems; Pres. Jacob Dikobo; Nat. Chair. Zithulele Nyangana Absalom Cindi.

Boerestaat Party (Boer State Party): POB 4995, Luipaardsvlei 1743; tel. (11) 7623841; fax (11) 7623842; e-mail info@boerestaatparty.co.za; internet www.boerestaatparty.co.za; f. 1988; seeks the reinstatement of the Boer Republics in a consolidated Boerestaat; Leader Coen Vermaak.

Christian Democratic Alliance (CDA): Cape Town; tel. (21) 4033518; fax (21) 4033518; e-mail national.office@cda.org.za; internet www.cda.org.za; f. 2008; Leader Louis Michael Green; Sec.-Gen. Kevin Southgate.

Congress of the People (COPE): Braampark, 1st Floor, Forum II, 33 Hoofd St, Braamfontein, Johannesburg 2000; tel. (11) 3396060; fax (11) 3396064; e-mail info@congressofthepeople.org.za; internet www.congressofthepeople.org.za; f. 2008 following split in the ANC; Pres. Mosiuoa Lekota.

Democratic Alliance (DA): POB 1475, Cape Town 8000; 2nd Floor, Theba Hosken House, cnr Breda and Mill Sts, Gardens, Cape Town; tel. (21) 4651431; fax (21) 4615559; e-mail info@da.org.za; internet www.da.org.za; f. 2000 by opposition parties, incl. the Democratic Party, the Federal Alliance and the New National Party (NNP), to contest that year's municipal elections; NNP withdrew in late 2001; Leader Helen Zille; Chair. Joe Seremane.

Herstigte Nasionale Party (HNP): 199 Neethling St, Eloffsdal, POB 1888, Pretoria 0001; tel. (12) 3358523; fax (12) 3358518; e-mail info@hnp.org.za; internet www.hnp.org.za; f. 1969 by fmr mems of the National Party; advocates 'Christian Nationalism'; Leader Andries Breytenbach; Gen. Sec. Louis J. van der Schyff.

Independent Democrats (ID): Rm 28, Marks Bldg, Parliament Plein St, POB 751, Cape Town 8000; tel. (21) 4038696; fax (21) 4032350; e-mail id@id.org.za; internet www.id.org.za; f. 2003; announced intention in 2010 to merge with the Democratic Alliance by the 2014 legislative elections; Pres. Patricia de Lille; Chair. Mervyn Cirota.

Inkatha Freedom Party (IFP): 2 Durban Club Pl., Durban, 4000; POB 4432, Durban 4000; tel. (31) 3651300; fax (31) 3074964; e-mail ifpinfo@iafrica.com; internet www.ifp.org.za; f. 1975 as Inkatha National Cultural Liberation Movement with mainly Zulu support; reorg. in 1990 as a multiracial political party; Pres. Chief Mangosuthu Gatsha Buthelezi.

Minority Front: 347 Florence Nightingale Dr., Westcliff, Chatsworth; tel. (31) 4033360; fax (31) 4033354; e-mail mf@mf.org.za; internet www.mf.org.za; f. 1993; Indian support; Leader Amichand Rajbansi.

National Democratic Convention (NADECO): 1615 Commercial City, 40 Commercial Rd, Durban 4001; tel. (31) 3042098; fax (31) 3042944; e-mail mbathah@nadeco.org; internet www.nadeco.org; f. 2005; Pres. Rev. Hawu Mbatha; Chair. Themba Mbutho.

Pan-Africanist Congress of Azania (PAC): 10th Floor, Renaissance House, 16–22 New St, Ghandi Sq., Johannesburg; POB 6010, Johannesburg 2000; tel. (11) 8389380; fax (11) 8389384; e-mail pacazania@telkomsa.net; internet www.panafricanperspective.com/pac/index.html; f. 1959; Pres. Dr Motsoko Pheko; Nat. Exec. Sec. Mfanelo Skwatsha.

SOUTH AFRICA

Progressive Independent Party (PIP): Indian support; Leader FAIZ KHAN.

South African Communist Party (SACP): Cosatu House, 3rd Floor, 1 Leyds St, Braamfontein; POB 1027, Johannesburg 2000; tel. (11) 3393633; fax (11) 3396880; e-mail info@sacp.org.za; internet www.sacp.org.za; f. 1921; reorg. 1953; supports the ANC; Chair. GWEDE MANTASHE; Gen. Sec. BLADE NZIMANDE.

United Christian Democratic Party (UCDP): POB 3010, Mmabatho; tel. (18) 3815691; fax (18) 3817346; e-mail ucdpheadoff@ucdp.org.za; internet www.ucdp.org.za; f. 1972 as the Bophuthatswana Nat. Party; name changed to Bophuthatswana Dem. Party in 1974; present name adopted in 1991; multiracial; Leader KGOSI L. M. MANGOPE; Sec.-Gen. M. N. MATLADI; Nat. Chair. I. SIPHO MFUNDISI.

United Democratic Movement (UDM): Tomkor Bldg, 2nd Floor, cnr Vermeulen and Du Toit Sts, Pretoria; POB 26290, Arcadia 0007; tel. (12) 3210010; fax (12) 3210014; e-mail info@udm.org.za; internet www.udm.org.za; f. 1997; multiracial support; demands effective measures for enforcement of law and order; Pres. BANTU HOLOMISA; Sec.-Gen. BONGANI MSOMI.

Vryheidsfront Plus (Freedom Front Plus—VF Plus/FF Plus): Blok 8, Highveld Office Park, Highveld, Centurion Pretoria; POB 67391, Highveld, 0169; tel. (12) 6650564; fax (12) 6652420; e-mail info@vf.co.za; internet www.vryheidsfront.co.za; f. 1994 as Freedom Front; name changed after incorporating the Conservative Party and Afrikaner Eenheidsbeweging in Sept. 2003; right-wing electoral alliance; Leader Dr PIETER W. A. MULDER; Chair. ABRIE OOSTHUIZEN.

Diplomatic Representation

EMBASSIES AND HIGH COMMISSIONS IN SOUTH AFRICA

Algeria: 950 Arcadia St, Hatfield, Pretoria 0083; POB 57480, Arcadia 0007; tel. (12) 3425074; fax (12) 3426479; Ambassador MOHAMED LAMINE LAABAS.

Angola: 1030 Schoeman St, Hatfield, Pretoria 0083; POB 8685, Pretoria 0001; tel. (12) 3420049; fax (12) 3427039; Ambassador MIGUEL GASPAR FERNANDES NETO.

Argentina: 200 Standard Plaza, 440 Hilda St, Hatfield, Pretoria 0083; POB 11125, Pretoria 0028; tel. (12) 4303524; fax (12) 4303521; e-mail argembas@global.co.za; Ambassador CARLOS SERSALE DI CERISANO.

Australia: 292 Orient St, Arcadia, Pretoria 0083; Private Bag X150, Pretoria 0001; tel. (12) 4236000; fax (12) 3428442; e-mail pretoria.info@dfat.gov.au; internet www.australia.co.za; High Commissioner ANN JACQUELINE HARRAP.

Austria: Momentum Office Park, 1109 Duncan St, Brooklyn, Pretoria 0181; POB 95572, Waterkloof 0145; tel. (12) 4529155; fax (12) 4601151; e-mail pretoria-ob@bmeia.gv.at; internet www.bmeia.gv.at/pretoria; Ambassador Dr OTTO DITZ.

Bangladesh: 410 Farenden St, Sunnyside, Pretoria 0002; tel. (12) 3432105; fax (12) 3435222; e-mail bangladeshpta@iburst.co.za; High Commissioner M. D. SHAHIDUL ISLAM.

Belarus: 327 Hill St, Arcadia, Pretoria 0083; POB 4107, Pretoria 0001; tel. (12) 4307664; fax (12) 3426280; e-mail sa@belembassy.org; internet www.rsa.belembassy.org; Chargé d'affaires a.i. ALEKSEI LESNOY.

Belgium: 625 Leyds St, Muckleneuk, Pretoria 0002; tel. (12) 4403201; fax (12) 4403216; e-mail pretoria@diplobel.fed.be; internet www.diplomatie.be/pretoria; Chargé d'affaires a.i ROLAND PROVOT.

Benin: 900 Park St, cnr Orient and Park Sts, Arcadia, Pretoria 0083; POB 26484, Arcadia 0007; tel. (12) 3426978; fax (12) 3421823; e-mail embbenin@yebo.co.za; internet www.maebenin.bj/Pretoria.htm; Ambassador CLAUDE RUBEN FASSINOU.

Botswana: 24 Amos St, Colbyn, Pretoria 0083; POB 57035, Arcadia 0007; tel. (12) 4309640; fax (12) 3421845; High Commissioner MOTLHAGODI MOLOMO.

Brazil: Hillcrest Office Park, Woodpecker Pl., 1st Floor, 177 Dyer Rd, Hillcrest, Pretoria 0083; POB 3269, Pretoria 0001; tel. (12) 3665200; fax (12) 3665299; e-mail pretoria@brazilianembassy.org.za; internet www.brazilianembassy.org.za; Ambassador JOSÉ VICENTE DE SÁ PIMENTEL.

Bulgaria: 1071 Church St, Hatfield, Pretoria 0083; POB 29296, Arcadia 0007; tel. (12) 3423720; fax (12) 3423721; e-mail embulgsa@iafrica.com; internet www.bulgarianembassy.co.za; Ambassador VOLODYA CHANEV NEYKOV.

Burundi: 20 Glyn St, Colbyn, Pretoria 0083; POB 12914, Hatfield 0028; tel. (12) 3424881; fax (12) 3424885; Ambassador REGINE RWAMIBANGO.

Directory

Cameroon: 800 Duncan St, Brooklyn, Pretoria 0075; POB 13790, Hatfield 0028; tel. (12) 3624731; fax (12) 3624732; e-mail hicocam@cameroon.co.za; High Commissioner ADRIEN KOUAMBO JOMAGUE.

Canada: 1103 Arcadia St, cnr Hilda St, Hatfield, Pretoria 0083; Private Bag X13, Hatfield 0028; tel. (12) 4223000; fax (12) 4223052; e-mail pret@international.gc.ca; internet www.dfait-maeci.gc.ca/southafrica/menu-en.asp; High Commissioner ADÈLE DION.

Chile: Delmondo Office Park, 169 Garsfontein Rd, Ashlea Gardens, Pretoria 0081; POB 2449, Brooklyn Sq. 0075; tel. (12) 4608090; fax (12) 4608093; e-mail chile@iafrica.com; internet www.embchile.co.za; Ambassador FRANCISCO JAVIER MARAMBIO.

China, People's Republic: 965 Church St, Arcadia, Pretoria 0083; POB 95764, Waterkloof 0145; tel. (12) 4316500; fax (12) 3424244; e-mail reception@chinese-embassy.org.za; internet www.chinese-embassy.org.za; Ambassador ZHONG JIANHUA.

Colombia: Park Corner Bldg, 3rd Floor, 1105 Park St, Hatfield, Pretoria 0083; POB 12791, Hatfield 0028; tel. (12) 3420211; fax (12) 3420216; e-mail info@embassyofcolombia.co.za; Ambassador EDGAR JOSÉ PEREA-ARIAS.

Comoros: 817 Thomas St, cnr Church and Eastwood Sts, Arcadia, Pretoria 0083; tel. (12) 3439483; fax (12) 3420138; Ambassador AHMED MOHAMED THABIT.

Congo, Democratic Republic: 791 Schoeman St, Arcadia, Pretoria 0083; POB 28795, Sunnyside 0132; tel. (12) 3446475; fax (12) 3444054; e-mail rdcongo@lantic.net; Ambassador BENE M'POKO.

Congo, Republic: 960 Arcadia St, Arcadia, Pretoria 0083; POB 40427, Arcadia 0007; tel. (12) 3425508; fax (12) 3425510; Ambassador ROGER ISSOMBO.

Côte d'Ivoire: 795 Government Ave, Arcadia, Pretoria 0083; POB 13510, Hatfield 0028; tel. (12) 3426913; fax (12) 3426713; Ambassador ZOGOÉ HERVÉ-BRICE ABIE.

Croatia: 1160 Church St, Colbyn, Pretoria 0083; POB 11335, Hatfield 0028; tel. (12) 3421206; fax (12) 3421819; internet za.mfa.hr; Ambassador IVAN PICUKARIĆ.

Cuba: 45 Mackenzie St, Brooklyn, Pretoria 0181; POB 11605, Hatfield 0028; tel. (12) 3462215; fax (12) 3462216; e-mail sudafri@iafrica.com; internet emba.cubaminrex.cu/sudafricaing; Ambassador ANGEL VILLA HERNÁNDEZ.

Cyprus: cnr Church St and Hill St, Arcadia, Pretoria 0083; POB 14554, Hatfield 0028; tel. (12) 3425258; fax (12) 3425596; e-mail cyprusjb@mweb.co.za; High Commissioner ARGYROS ANTONIOU.

Czech Republic: 936 Pretorius St, Arcadia, Pretoria 0083; POB 13671, Hatfield 0028; tel. (12) 4312380; fax (12) 4302033; e-mail pretoria@embassymzv.cz; internet www.mzv.cz/pretoria; Ambassador MARTIN POHL.

Denmark: iParioli Office Park, Block B2, Ground Floor, 1166 Park St, Hatfield, Pretoria; POB 11439, Hatfield 0028; tel. (12) 4309340; fax (12) 3427620; e-mail pryamb@um.dk; internet www.ambpretoria.um.dk; Ambassador DAN E. FREDERIKSEN.

Dominican Republic: 276 Anderson St., Brooklyn, Pretoria 0181; tel. (12) 3602463; fax (12) 5679613; e-mail dominican.embassy@gmail.com; Ambassador RAÚL FERNANDO BARRIENTOS-LARA.

Ecuador: Suite 3, 36 Selati St, Selati Park, Alphen Park, Pretoria; tel. (12) 3461662; fax (12) 3467082; e-mail eecusudafrica@mmrree.gov.ec; Ambassador Dr JOSÉ VALENCIA.

Egypt: 270 Bourke St, Muckleneuk, Pretoria 0002; POB 30025, Sunnyside 0132; tel. (12) 3431590; fax (12) 3431082; e-mail egyptemb@global.co.za; Ambassador MOHAMED BADR ELDIN MOSTAFA ZAYED.

Equatorial Guinea: 48 Florence St, Colbyn, Pretoria; POB 12720, Hatfield 0028; tel. (12) 3429945; fax (12) 3427250; Ambassador F. EDU NGUA.

Eritrea: 1281 Cobham Rd, Queenswood, Pretoria 0186; POB 11371, Queenswood 0121; tel. (12) 3331302; fax (12) 3332330; Ambassador SALIH OMAR ABDU.

Ethiopia: 47 Charles St, Bailey's Muckleneuk, Brooklyn 0181; POB 11469, Hatfield 0028; tel. (12) 3463542; fax (12) 3463867; e-mail ethiopia@sentechsa.com; Ambassador MELESE MARIMO MARASSO.

Finland: 628 Leyds St, Muckleneuk, Pretoria 0002; POB 443, Pretoria 0001; tel. (12) 3430275; fax (12) 3433095; e-mail sanomat.pre@formin.fi; internet www.finland.org.za; Ambassador TIINA MYLLYNTAUSTA.

France: 250 Melk St, cnr Melk and Middle Sts, New Muckleneuk, Pretoria 0181; tel. (12) 4251600; fax (12) 4251689; e-mail france@ambafrance-rsa.org; internet www.ambafrance-rsa.org; Ambassador JACQUES LAPOUGE.

Gabon: 921 Schoeman St, Arcadia, Pretoria 0083; POB 9222, Pretoria 0001; tel. (12) 3424376; fax (12) 3424375; Ambassador MARCEL-JULES ODONGUI-BONNARD.

Germany: 180 Blackwood St, Arcadia, Pretoria 0083; POB 2023, Pretoria 0001; tel. (12) 4278900; fax (12) 3433606; e-mail

GermanEmbassyPretoria@gonet.co.za; internet www.pretoria.diplo.de; Ambassador DIETER WALTER HALLER.

Ghana: 1038 Arcadia St, Hatfield, Pretoria 0083; POB 12537, Hatfield 0028; tel. (12) 3425847; fax (12) 3425863; High Commissioner LEE OCRAN.

Greece: Hadefields Office Park, 1st Floor, 1267 Church St, Block G, Hatfield, Pretoria 0001; tel. (12) 4307351; fax (12) 4304313; e-mail embgrsaf@global.co.za; Ambassador SPYRIDON THEOCHAROPOULOS.

Guinea: 336 Orient St, Arcadia, Pretoria 0083; POB 13523, Hatfield 0028; tel. and fax (12) 3427348; e-mail embaguinea@iafrica.com; Ambassador GAOUSSOU TOURÉ.

Haiti: 808 George St, Arcadia, Pretoria 0007; POB 14362, Hatfield 0028; tel. (12) 4307560; fax (12) 3427042; Ambassador YOLETTE AZOR-CHARLES.

Holy See: Argo St, Waterkloof Ridge, Pretoria 0181; POB 95200, Waterkloof 0145; tel. (12) 3464235; fax (12) 3461494; e-mail nunziosa@iafrica.com; Apostolic Nuncio Most Rev. JAMES PATRICK GREEN (Titular Archbishop of Altino).

Hungary: 959 Arcadia St, Hatfield, Pretoria 0083; POB 13843, Hatfield 0028; tel. (12) 4303030; fax (12) 4303029; e-mail mission.prt@kum.hu; Ambassador ISTVÁN EMRI.

India: 852 Schoeman St, Arcadia, Pretoria 0083; POB 40216, Arcadia 0007; tel. (12) 3425392; fax (12) 3425310; e-mail polinf@hicomind.co.za; internet www.indiainsouthafrica.com; High Commissioner VIRENDRA GUPTA.

Indonesia: 949 Schoeman St, Arcadia, Pretoria 0082; POB 13155, Hatfield, Pretoria 0028; tel. (12) 3423350; fax (12) 3423369; e-mail fpanggabean@indonesia-pretoria.org.za; internet www.indonesia-pretoria.org.za; f. 1995; Ambassador SJAHRIL SABARUDDIN.

Iran: 1002 Schoeman St, Hatfield, Pretoria 0083; POB 12546, Hatfield 0083; tel. (12) 3425880; fax (12) 3421878; e-mail office@iranembassy.org.za; internet www.iranembassy.org.za; Ambassador ASGHAR EBRAHIMI ASL.

Iraq: 803 Duncan St, Brooklyn, Pretoria 0181; POB 11089, Hatfield 0028; tel. (12) 3622048; fax (12) 3622027; Chargé d'affaires a.i. RAFID BAHIDH DAWOOD AR-RIKABI.

Ireland: Southern Life Plaza, 1st Floor, 1059 Schoeman St, cnr Festival and Schoeman Sts, Arcadia, Pretoria 0083; POB 4174, Arcadia 0001; tel. (12) 3425062; fax (12) 3424752; e-mail pretoria@dfa.ie; internet www.embassyireland.org.za; Ambassador BRENDAN MCMAHON.

Israel: 428 King's Hwy, Elizabeth Grove St, Lynnwood, Pretoria; Private Bag X50, Menlo Park 0102; tel. (12) 4703500; fax (12) 4703555; e-mail publicaffairs@pretoria.mfa.gov.il; internet pretoria.mfa.gov.il; Ambassador DOV SEGEV-STEINBERG.

Italy: 796 George Ave, Arcadia, Pretoria 0083; tel. (12) 4230001; fax (12) 4305547; e-mail segreteria.pretoria@esteri.it; internet www.ambpretoria.esteri.it; Ambassador ELIO MENZIONE.

Jamaica: 1119 Burnett St, Hatfield, Pretoria 0083; tel. (12) 3626667; fax (12) 3668510; e-mail jhcpretoria@telkomsa.net; High Commissioner TAYLOR ROBERTS.

Japan: 259 Baines St, cnr Frans Oerder St, Groenkloof, Pretoria 0181; Private Bag X999, Pretoria 0001; tel. (12) 4521500; fax (12) 4603800; e-mail info@embjapan.org.za; internet www.japan.org.za; Ambassador TOSHIRO OZAWA.

Jordan: 252 Olivier St, Brooklyn, Pretoria 0075; POB 14730, Hatfield 0028; tel. (12) 3468615; fax (12) 3468611; e-mail embjordpta@telkomsa.net; Ambassador O. J. NADIF.

Kenya: 302 Brooks St, Menlo Park, Pretoria 0081; POB 35954, Menlo Park 0012; tel. (12) 3622249; fax (12) 3622252; e-mail info@kenya.org.za; internet www.kenya.org.za; High Commissioner THOMAS AMOLO.

Korea, Democratic People's Republic: 958 Waterpoort St, Faerie Glen, Pretoria; POB 1238, Garsfontein 0042; tel. (12) 9918661; fax (12) 9918662; e-mail dprkembassy@lantic.net; Ambassador AN HUI JONG.

Korea, Republic: Greenpark Estates, Bldg 3, 27 George Storrar Dr., Groenkloof, Pretoria 0081; POB 939, Groenkloof 0027; tel. (12) 4602508; fax (12) 4601158; e-mail korrsa@mweb.co.za; internet zaf.mofat.go.kr; Ambassador KIM HAN-SOO.

Kuwait: 890 Arcadia St, Arcadia, Pretoria 0083; Private Bag X920, Pretoria 0001; tel. (12) 3420877; fax (12) 3420876; e-mail safarku@global.co.za; Ambassador HASSAN BADER KAREEM AL-OQAB.

Lebanon: 788 Government St, Pretoria; POB 941, Groenkloof 0027; tel. (12) 4302130; fax (12) 4302238; e-mail embassyoflebanon@telkomsa.net; Ambassador MICHEL THOMAS KATRA.

Lesotho: 391 Anderson St, Menlo Park, Pretoria 0081; POB 55817, Arcadia 0007; tel. (12) 4607648; fax (12) 4607469; High Commissioner LINEO LYDIA KHECHANE-NTOANE.

Liberia: Suite 9 Section 7, Schoeman St Forum, 1157 Schoeman St, Hatfield, Pretoria; POB 14082, Hatfield, Pretoria; tel. (12) 3422734; fax (12) 3422737; e-mail libempta@pta.lia.net; Ambassador LOIS LEWIS BRUTHUS.

Libya: 900 Church St, Arcadia, Pretoria 0083; POB 40388, Arcadia 0007; tel. (12) 3423902; fax (12) 3423904; e-mail libyasa@telkomsa.net; Ambassador Dr ABDULLAH ABDUSSALAM AZ-ZUBEDI.

Madagascar: 90B Tait St, Colbyn, Pretoria; POB 11722, Queenswood 0120; tel. (12) 3420983; fax (12) 3420995; e-mail consul@infodoor.co.za; Ambassador DENIS ANDRIAMANDROSO.

Malawi: 770 Government Ave, Arcadia, Pretoria 0083; POB 11172, Hatfield 0028; tel. and fax (12) 3421759; fax (12) 3420147; e-mail highcommalai@telkomsa.net; High Commissioner (vacant).

Malaysia: 1007 Schoeman St, Arcadia, Pretoria 0083; POB 11673, Hatfield 0028; tel. (12) 3425990; fax (12) 4307773; internet www.kln.gov.my/web/zaf_pretoria; High Commissioner M. KENNEDY JAWAN.

Mali: 876 Pretorius St, Arcadia 0083; POB 12978, Hatfield, Pretoria 0028; tel. (12) 3427464; fax (12) 3420670; Ambassador BALLADJI DIAKITE.

Mauritania: 146 Anderson St, Brooklyn, Pretoria; tel. (12) 3623578; fax (12) 3623304; e-mail rimambapretoria@webmail.co.za; Ambassador MOHAMED OULD HANNANI.

Mauritius: 1163 Pretorius St, Hatfield, Pretoria 0083; tel. (12) 3421283; fax (12) 3421286; e-mail mhcpta@mweb.co.za; High Commissioner MOHAMED ISMAEL DOSSA.

Mexico: 570 Ferhsen St, Parkdev Bldg, Ground Floor, Brooklyn Bridge, Pretoria 0181; POB 9077, Pretoria 0001; tel. (12) 4601004; fax (12) 4600973; e-mail embamexza@mweb.co.za; Ambassador LUIS CABRERA CUARON.

Morocco: 799 Schoeman St, cnr Farenden St, Arcadia, Pretoria 0083; POB 12382, Hatfield 0028; tel. (12) 3430230; fax (12) 3430613; e-mail sifmapre@mwebbiz.co.za; Chargé d'affaires HABIB DEFOUAD.

Mozambique: 529 Edmund St, Arcadia, Pretoria 0083; POB 40750, Arcadia 0007; tel. (12) 4010300; fax (12) 3266388; e-mail highcomm@embamoc.co.za; High Commissioner FERNANDO ANDRADE FAZENDA.

Myanmar: 201 Leyds St, Arcadia, Pretoria 0083; POB 12121, Queenswood 0121; tel. (12) 3412557; fax (12) 3412553; e-mail euompta@global.co.za; Chargé d'affaires a.i HLAIMGN PHONE MYINT.

Namibia: 197 Blackwood St, Arcadia, Pretoria 0083; POB 29806, Sunnyside 0132; tel. (12) 4819100; fax (12) 3445998; e-mail secretary@namibia.org.za; High Commissioner MARTEN NENKETE KAPEWASHA.

Nepal: 453 Fehersen St, Baileys Muckleneuk, Pretoria; tel. (12) 346 2399; fax (12) 3460521; Ambassador ARUN PRASAD DHITAL.

Netherlands: 210 Queen Wilhelmina Ave, New Muckleneuk 0181, Pretoria; tel. (12) 4254500; fax (12) 4254511; e-mail pre@minbuza.nl; internet www.dutchembassy.co.za; Ambassador ROBERT GERARD DE VOS.

New Zealand: 125 Middel St, Muckleneuk, Pretoria 0181; Private Bag X25, Brooklyn Sq. 0075; tel. (12) 4359000; fax (12) 4359002; e-mail enquiries@nzhc.co.za; internet www.nzembassy.com/south-africa; High Commissioner Dr GEOFFREY JOHN RANDAL.

Nigeria: 971 Schoeman St, Arcadia, Pretoria 0083; POB 27332, Sunnyside 0132; tel. (12) 3420805; fax (12) 3421668; High Commissioner Brig.-Gen. (retd) MOHAMMED BUBA MARWA.

Norway: iParioli Bldg, A2, 1166 Park St, Hatfield, Pretoria 0083; POB 11612, Hatfield 0028; tel. (12) 3426100; fax (12) 3426099; e-mail emb.pretoria@mfa.no; internet www.norway.org.za; Ambassador TOR CHRISTIAN HILDAN.

Oman: 42 Nicholson St, Muckleneuk, Pretoria 0081; POB 2650, Brooklyn 0075; tel. (12) 3460808; fax (12) 3461660; e-mail sult-oman@telkom.net; Ambassador KHALID BIN SULAIMAN BIN ABDUL RAHMAN BA'OMAR.

Pakistan: 312 Brooks St, Menlo Park, Pretoria 0181; POB 11803, Hatfield 0028; tel. (12) 3624072; fax (12) 3623967; e-mail pareppretoria@worldonline.co.za; High Commissioner ZAIGHAMUDDIN AZAM.

Panama: 229 Olivier St, Brooklyn, Pretoria; tel. (12) 4606677; fax (12) 3465474; e-mail panamaembassy@bodamail.co.za; Ambassador RODRIGO GUILLERMO CHIARI.

Paraguay: 189 Strelitzia Rd, Waterkloof Heights, Pretoria 0181; POB 95774, Waterkloof 0145; tel. (12) 3471047; fax (12) 3470403; e-mail embaparsudafrica@mre.gov.py; Ambassador JOSÉ MARTÍNEZ LEZCANO.

Peru: 200 Saint Patrick St, Muckleneuk Hill, Pretoria 0083; POB 907, Groenkloof 0027; tel. (12) 4401030; fax (12) 4401054; e-mail embaperu2@telkomsa.net; Ambassador DAÚL MATUTE-MEJÍA.

Philippines: 54 Nicholson St, Muckleneuk, Pretoria 0181; POB 2562, Brooklyn Sq. 0075; tel. (12) 3460451; fax (12) 3460454; e-mail pretoriape@mweb.co.za; internet mzone.mweb.co.za/residents/pretoriape; Chargé d'affaires a.i ERIC R AQUINO, Jr.

SOUTH AFRICA

Poland: 14 Amos St, Colbyn, Pretoria 0083; POB 12277, Queenswood 0121; tel. (12) 4302631; fax (12) 4302608; e-mail amb.pol@pixie.co.za; internet www.pretoria.polemb.net; Ambassador MARCIN KUBIAK.

Portugal: 599 Leyds St, Muckleneuk, Pretoria 0002; POB 27102, Sunnyside 0132; tel. (12) 3412340; fax (12) 3413975; e-mail portemb@global.co.za; Ambassador JOÃO NUGENT RAMOS PINTO.

Qatar: 355 Charles St, Waterkloof, Pretoria 0181; Private Bag X13, Brooklyn Sq. 0075; tel. (12) 4521700; fax (12) 3466732; e-mail qatar-emb@lantic.net; Ambassador Dr BASHIR ISSA AL-SHIRAWI.

Romania: 117 Charles St, Brooklyn, Pretoria 0181; POB 11295, Hatfield 0028; tel. (12) 4606940; fax (12) 4606947; e-mail romembsa@global.co.za; Ambassador RADU GABRIEL SAFTA.

Russia: 316 Brooks St, Menlo Park, Pretoria 0081; POB 6743, Pretoria 0001; tel. (12) 3621337; fax (12) 3620116; e-mail ruspospr@mweb.co.za; internet www.russianembassy.org.za; Ambassador ANATOLY A. MAKAROV.

Rwanda: 983 Schoeman St, Arcadia, Pretoria; POB 55224, Arcadia 0007; tel. (12) 3426536; fax (12) 3427106; e-mail ambapretoria@minaffet.gov.rw; internet www.southafrica.embassy.gov.rw; Ambassador VINCENT KAREGA (designate).

Saudi Arabia: 711 Duncan St, cnr Lunnon St, Hatfield, Pretoria 0083; POB 13930, Hatfield 0028; tel. (12) 3624230; fax (12) 3624239; Ambassador MOHAMMED MAHMOUD BIN ALI AL-ALI.

Senegal: Charles Manor, 57 Charles St, Baileys Muckleneuk, Pretoria 0181; POB 2948, Brooklyn Sq. 0075; tel. (12) 4605263; fax (12) 3465550; e-mail ambassenepta@telkomsa.za; Ambassador CHEIKH NIANG.

Serbia: 163 Marais St, Brooklyn, Pretoria; POB 13026, Hatfield 0028; tel. (12) 4605626; fax (12) 4606003; e-mail info@scgembassy.org.za; internet www.scgembassy.org.za; Ambassador GORAN VUJIČIĆ.

Singapore: 980 Schoeman St, Arcadia, Pretoria 0083; POB 11809, Hatfield 0028; tel. (12) 4306035; fax (12) 3424425; e-mail sporehc@mweb.co.za; High Commissioner BERNARD WILLIAM BAKER.

Slovakia: 930 Arcadia St, Pretoria 0083; POB 12736, Hatfield 0028; tel. (12) 3422051; fax (12) 3423688; e-mail slovakemb@telkomsa.net; internet www.mfa.sk/zu; Ambassador LADISLAV STRAKA.

Spain: Lord Charles Bldg, 337 Brooklyn Rd, Menlo Park, Pretoria 0181; POB 1633, Pretoria 0001; tel. (12) 4600123; fax (12) 4602290; e-mail emb.pretoria@mae.es; Ambassador PABLO BENAVIDES ORGAZ.

Sri Lanka: 410 Alexander St, Brooklyn, Pretoria 0181; tel. (12) 4607690; fax (12) 4607702; e-mail srilanka@global.co.za; internet www.srilanka.co.za; High Commissioner DHARMASENA WIJESINGHE.

Sudan: 1203 Pretorius St, Hatfield, Pretoria 0083; POB 25513, Monument Park 0105; tel. (12) 3424538; fax (12) 3424539; internet www.sudani.co.za; Ambassador ALI YOUSIF AHMED.

Suriname: Suite No. 4, Groenkloof Forum Office Park, 57 George Storrar Drive, Groenkloof, 0181 Pretoria; POB 149, Pretoria; tel. (12) 3467627; fax (12) 3460802; e-mail embsur@lantic.net; Ambassador EDWARD RUDOLF BRAAFHEID.

Swaziland: 715 Government Ave, Arcadia, Pretoria 0007; POB 14294, Hatfield 0028; tel. (12) 3441910; fax (12) 3430455; Ambassador SOLOMON MNUKWA DLAMINI.

Sweden: iParioli Bldg, 1166 Park St, Hatfield 0083; POB 13477, Hatfield 0028; tel. (12) 4266400; fax (12) 4266464; e-mail sweden@iafrica.com; internet www.swedenabroad.com/pretoria; Ambassador PETER TEJLER.

Switzerland: 225 Veale St, Parc Nouveau, New Muckleneuk, Pretoria 0181; POB 2508, Brooklyn Sq. 0075; tel. (12) 4520660; fax (12) 3466605; e-mail pre.vertretung@eda.admin.ch; internet www.eda.admin.ch/pretoria; Ambassador RUDOLF BÄRFUSS.

Syria: 963 Schoeman St, Arcadia, Pretoria 0083; POB 12830, Hatfield 0028; tel. (12) 3424701; fax (12) 3424702; e-mail syriaemb@telkomsa.net; Chargé d'affaires a.i. BASSAM DARWISH.

Tanzania: 822 George Ave, Arcadia, Pretoria 0007; POB 56572, Arcadia 0007; tel. (12) 3424393; fax (12) 4304383; e-mail thc@tanzania.org.za; internet www.tanzania.org.za; High Commissioner RADHIA NAIMA MTENGETI MSUYA.

Thailand: 428 cnr Hill and Pretorius Sts, Arcadia, Pretoria 0028; POB 12080, Hatfield 0083; tel. (12) 3424600; fax (12) 3424805; e-mail info@thaiembassy.co.za; internet www.thaiembassy.co.za; Chargé d'affaires a.i. THARIT CHARUNGVAT.

Trinidad and Tobago: 258 Lawley St, Waterkloof, 0181 Pretoria; POB 95872, Waterkloof, Pretoria 0145; tel. (12) 4609688; fax (12) 3467302; e-mail tthepretoria@telkomsa.net; High Commissioner HARRY PARTAP.

Tunisia: 850 Church St, Arcadia, Pretoria 0083; POB 56535, Arcadia 0007; tel. (12) 3426282; fax (12) 3426284; Ambassador Prof. Dr AHMED MAHJOUB.

Turkey: 1067 Church St, Hatfield, Pretoria 0083; POB 56014, Arcadia 0007; tel. (12) 3426055; fax (12) 3426052; e-mail pretbe@global.co.za; internet www.turkishembassy.co.za; Ambassador AHMET VAKUR GÖKDERNIZLER.

Uganda: 882 Church St, Pretoria 0083; POB 12442, Hatfield 0083; tel. (12) 3426031; fax (12) 3426206; e-mail ugacomer@mweb.co.za; High Commissioner KWERONDA RUHEMBA.

Ukraine: 398 Marais St, Brooklyn, Pretoria 0181; POB 57291, Menlo Park 0102; tel. (12) 4601943; fax (12) 4601944; e-mail emb_za@mfa.gov.ua; Ambassador VALERY HREBENIUK.

United Arab Emirates: 992 Arcadia St, Arcadia, Pretoria 0083; POB 57090, Arcadia 0007; tel. (12) 3427736; fax (12) 3427738; e-mail uae@mweb.co.za; Ambassador ISMAEL OBAID YUSUF AL-ALI.

United Kingdom: 255 Hill St, Arcadia, Pretoria 0002; tel. (12) 4217600; fax (12) 4217555; e-mail media.pretoria@fco.gov.uk; internet ukinsouthafrica.fco.gov.uk; High Commissioner Dr NICOLA BREWER.

USA: 877 Pretorius St, Arcadia, Pretoria 0083; POB 9536, Pretoria 0001; tel. (12) 4314000; fax (12) 3422299; e-mail embassypretoria@state.gov; internet southafrica.usembassy.gov; Ambassador DONALD HENRY GIPS.

Uruguay: 301 MIB House, 3rd Floor, Hatfield Sq., 1119 Burnett St, Hatfield, Pretoria 0083; POB 14818, Pretoria 0028; tel. (12) 3626521; fax (12) 3626523; Ambassador LUIS BERMUDEZ ALVAREZ.

Venezuela: Hatfield Gables South Bldg, 1st Floor, Suite 4, 474 Hilda St, Pretoria 0083; POB 11821, Hatfield 0028; tel. (12) 3626593; fax (12) 3626591; e-mail embasudaf@icon.co.za; Ambassador ANTONIO MONTILLA-SALDIVIA.

Viet Nam: 87 Brooks St, Brooklyn, Pretoria 0181; POB 13692, Hatfield 0028; tel. (12) 3628119; fax (12) 3628115; e-mail embassy@vietnam.co.za; Ambassador MANH HUNG NGUYEN.

Yemen: 329 Main St, Waterkloof 0181; POB 13343, Hatfield 0028; tel. (12) 4250760; fax (12) 4250762; e-mail info@yemenembassy.org.za; internet www.yemenembassy.org.za; Chargé d'affaires Dr ALI ABDUL-QAWI AL-GHAFFARI.

Zambia: 570 Ziervogel St, Arcadia, Pretoria 0083; POB 12234, Hatfield 0028; tel. (12) 3261854; fax (12) 3262140; High Commissioner BIZWAYO NEWTON NKUNIKA.

Zimbabwe: Zimbabwe House, 798 Merton St, Arcadia, Pretoria 0083; POB 55140, Arcadia 0007; tel. (12) 3425125; fax (12) 3425126; e-mail zimpret@lantic.net; Ambassador PHELEKEZELA MPHOKO.

Judicial System

The common law of the Republic of South Africa is the Roman-Dutch law, the uncodified law of Holland as it was at the time of the secession of the Cape of Good Hope in 1806. The law of England is not recognized as authoritative, although the principles of English law have been introduced in relation to civil and criminal procedure, evidence and mercantile matters.

The Constitutional Court, situated in Johannesburg, consists of a Chief Justice, a Deputy Chief Justice and nine other justices. Its task is to ensure that the executive, legislative and judicial organs of government adhere to the provisions of the Constitution. It has the power to reverse legislation that has been adopted by Parliament. The Supreme Court of Appeal, situated in Bloemfontein, comprises a President, a Deputy President and a number of judges of appeal, and is the highest court in all but constitutional matters. There are also High Courts and Magistrates' Courts. A National Director of Public Prosecutions is the head of the prosecuting authority and is appointed by the President of the Republic. A Judicial Service Commission makes recommendations regarding the appointment of judges and advises central and provincial government on all matters relating to the judiciary.

Constitutional Court: cnr Queen and Sam Hancock/Hospital Sts, Constitution Hill, Braamfontein 2017; tel. (11) 3597400; fax (11) 4036524; e-mail cases@concourt.org.za; internet www.constitutionalcourt.org.za; f. 1995; Chief Justice SANDILE NGCOBO.

Supreme Court of Appeal: cnr Elizabeth and President Brand Sts, Bloemfontein 9301; POB 258, Bloemfontein 9300; tel. (51) 4127437; fax (86) 6445991; e-mail astreet@justice.gov.za; internet www.supremecourtofappeal.gov.za; f. 1910; Pres. LEX MPATI.

Religion

Some 80% of the population profess the Christian faith. Other religions that are represented are Hinduism, Islam, Judaism and traditional African religions.

SOUTH AFRICA

CHRISTIANITY

At mid-2000 there were an estimated 12.4m. Protestants and 18.7m. adherents of other forms of Christianity.

South African Council of Churches: POB 62098, Marshalltown 2107; tel. (11) 2417800; fax (11) 4921448; internet www.sacc.org.za; f. 1968; 26 mem. churches; Pres. Prof. RUSSEL BOTMAN; Gen. Sec. EDDIE MAKUE.

The Anglican Communion

Most Anglicans in South Africa are adherents of the Anglican Church of Southern Africa (formerly the Church of the Province of Southern Africa), comprising 25 dioceses (including Angola, Lesotho, Namibia, St Helena, Swaziland and two dioceses in Mozambique). The Church had an estimated 4.5m. communicant members at mid-2006.

Archbishop of Cape Town and Metropolitan of the Province of Southern Africa: Most Rev. THABO CECIL MAKGOBA, 20 Bishopscourt Dr., Bishopscourt, Claremont, Cape Town 7700; tel. (21) 7612531; fax (21) 7614193; e-mail archbish@bishopscourt-cpsa.org.za; internet www.anglicanchurchsa.org.

The Dutch Reformed Church (Nederduitse Gereformeerde Kerk—NGK)

In 2005/06, including confirmed and baptized members, the Dutch Reformed Churches in South Africa consisted of: the Dutch Reformed Church, with 1,155,001 (mainly white) members; the Uniting Reformed Church, with 1,039,606 (mainly Coloured and black) members; the Reformed Church in Africa, with 1,708 Indian members; and the Dutch Reformed Church in Africa, with an estimated 150,000 (mainly black) members. All congregations were desegregated in 1986.

General Synod: POB 13528, Hatfield, Pretoria 0028; tel. (12) 3420092; fax (12) 3420380; e-mail algemenesinode@ngkerk.org.za; internet www.ngkerk.org.za; Moderator Prof. PIET STRAUSS; Gen. Sec. Dr KOBUS GERBER.

The Lutheran Churches

Lutheran Communion in Southern Africa (LUCSA): POB 7170, Bonaero Park 1622; tel. (11) 9731873; fax (11) 3951615; e-mail info@lucsa.org; internet www.lucsa.org; f. 1991; co-ordinating org. for the Lutheran churches in southern Africa, incl. Angola, Botswana, Malawi, Mozambique, Namibia, South Africa, Swaziland, Zambia and Zimbabwe; 1,618,720 mems (1999); Pres. Bishop C. K. MOENGA; Exec. Dir Bishop Dr A. MOYO.

Evangelical Lutheran Church in Southern Africa (ELCSA): POB 7231, 1622 Bonaero Park; tel. (11) 9731853; fax (11) 3951888; e-mail elcsaadmin@mweb.co.za; f. 1975 by merger of four non-white churches; Presiding Bishop Dr N. P. PHASWANA (acting); 580,377 mems (2009).

Evangelical Lutheran Church in Southern Africa (Cape Church): POB 3466, 7602 Matieland; tel. (21) 8869747; fax (21) 8869748; e-mail rohwernj@afrihost.co.za; Pres. Bishop NILS ROHWER; 4,347 mems (2010).

Evangelical Lutheran Church in Southern Africa (N-T): Church Council, 24 Geldenhuys Rd, Bonaero Park, Johannesburg; POB 7095, Bonaero Park 1622; tel. (11) 9731851; fax (11) 3951862; e-mail bishop@elcsant.org.za; internet www.elcsant.org.za; f. 1981; Pres. Bishop HORST MUELLER; 10,016 mems (2010).

Moravian Church in Southern Africa: 63 Albert Rd, POB 24111, Lansdowne 7779; tel. (21) 7614030; fax (21) 7614046; e-mail mcsa@iafrica.com; f. 1737; Pres. LENNOX MCBUSI; 50,000 mems (2010).

The Roman Catholic Church

An estimated 6.3% of the total population were Roman Catholics.

Southern African Catholic Bishops' Conference (SACBC) Khanya House, 140 Visagie St, Pretoria 0001; POB 941, Pretoria 0001; tel. (12) 3236458; fax (12) 3266218; e-mail sacbclib@wn.apc.org; internet www.sacbc.org.za.

f. 1947 mems representing South Africa, Botswana and Swaziland; Pres. JOSEPH BUTI TLHAGALE (Archbishop of Johannesburg); Sec.-Gen. Fr RICHARD MENATSI.

Archbishop of Bloemfontein: JABULANI ADATUS NXUMALO, Archbishop's House, 7A Whites Rd, Bloemfontein 9301; POB 362, Bloemfontein 9300; tel. (51) 4481658; fax (51) 4472420; e-mail bfnarch@mweb.co.za.

Archbishop of Cape Town: Most Rev. STEPHEN BRISLIN, Cathedral Place, 12 Bouquet St, Cape Town 8001; POB 2910, Cape Town 8000; tel. (21) 4622417; fax (21) 4619330; e-mail info@catholic-ct.org.za; internet www.catholic-ct.co.za.

Archbishop of Durban: Cardinal WILFRID NAPIER, Archbishop's House, 154 Gordon Rd, Durban 4001; POB 47489, Greyville 4023; tel. (31) 3031417; fax (31) 3121848; e-mail vg@catholic-dbn.org.za.

Archbishop of Johannesburg:: Most Rev. BUTI JOSEPH TLHAGALE, Archbishop's House, PMB X10, Doornfontein 2028; tel. (11) 4026400; fax (11) 4026406; e-mail catholic@icon.co.za.

Archbishop of Pretoria: Most Rev. WILLLIAM SLATTERY, Jolivet House, 140 Visagie St, Pretoria 0002; POB 8149, Pretoria 0001; tel. (12) 3265311; fax (12) 3253994; e-mail ptadiocese@absamail.co.za.

Other Christian Churches

In addition to the following Churches, there are a large number of Pentecostalist groups, and more than 4,000 independent African Churches.

African Gospel Church: POB 32312, 4060 Mobeni; tel. (31) 9074377; Moderator Rev. F. D. MKHIZE; Gen. Sec. O. MTOLO; 100,000 mems.

Afrikaanse Protestantse Kerk (Afrikaans Protestant Church): POB 11488, Hatfield 0028; tel. (12) 3621390; fax (12) 3622023; internet www.apkerk.co.za; f. 1987 by fmr mems of the Dutch Reformed Church (Nederduitse Gereformeerde Kerk) in protest at the desegregation of church congregations; c. 33,623 mems.

Apostolic Faith Mission of South Africa: Bldg no. 14, Central Office Park, 257 Jean Ave, POB 9450, Centurion; tel. (12) 6440490; fax (12) 6440732; e-mail admin@afm-ags.org; internet www.afm-ags.org; f. 1908; Pres. Dr ISAK BURGER; Gen. Sec. Pastor M. G. MAHLABO; 136,000 mems.

Assemblies of God: POB 51065, Musgrave 4062; tel. (21) 9144386; fax (21) 9144387; e-mail brian@assemblies.org.za; internet www.assemblies.org.za; f. 1915; Chair. Rev. ISAAC HLETA; Gen. Sec. Rev. C. P. WATT; 300,000 mems.

Baptist Union of Southern Africa: Private Bag X45, Wilropark 1731; tel. (11) 7685980; fax (11) 7685983; e-mail secretary@baptistunion.org.za; internet www.baptistunion.org.za; f. 1877; Pres. Rev. TSHILILO PANEAH EDSON MAGOLOI; Gen. Sec. Rev. ANGELO SCHEEPERS; 52,000 mems (2009).

Black Dutch Reformed Church: POB 137, Bergvlei 2012; Leader Rev. SAM BUTI; c. 1m. mems.

Church of England in South Africa: POB 2180, Clareinch 7740; tel. (21) 6717070; fax (21) 6712553; e-mail cameronb@cesa.org.za; internet www.cesa.org.za; Bishop Rt Rev. FRANK RETIEF (presiding), Bishop Rt Rev. MARTIN MORRISON, Bishop Rt Rev. Dr WARWICK COLE-EDWARDES, Bishop Rt Rev. DESMOND INGLESBY; 207 churches.

Evangelical Presbyterian Church in South Africa: POB 31961, Braamfontein 2017; tel. (11) 3391044; fax (11) 4034144; e-mail secretary@epcsa.org.za; internet www.epcsa.org.za; f. 1875; Gen. Sec. Rev. J. S. NGOBE; Treas. Rev. H. D. MASANGU; 60,000 mems.

The Methodist Church of Southern Africa: Methodist Connexional Office, POB 50216, Musgrave 4062; tel. (31) 2024214; fax (31) 2017674; e-mail general@mco.org.za; internet www.mco.org.za; f. 1883; Pres. Bishop I. M. ABRAHAMS; Sec. Rev. VUYANI G. NYOBOLE; 800,000 mems.

Nederduitsch Hervormde Kerk van Afrika: POB 2368, Pretoria 0001; tel. (12) 3228885; fax (12) 3203279; e-mail fanie@nhk.co.za; internet www.nhk.co.za; f. 1652; Gen. Sec. Dr S. P. PRETORIUS; 193,561 mems.

Nederduitse Gereformeerde Kerk in Afrika: Portland Pl., 37 Jorissen St, 2017 Johannesburg; tel. (11) 4031027; 6 synods (incl. 1 in Swaziland); Moderator Rev. S. P. E. BUTI; Gen. Sec. W. RAATH; 350,370 mems.

Presbyterian Church of Africa: POB 72, Nyanga, Cape Town 7755; tel. (21) 3850687; e-mail faleni@absamail.co.za; internet www.presbyterianchurchofafrica.co.za; f. 1898; 8 presbyteries (incl. 1 in Malawi and 1 in Zimbabwe); Moderator Rt Rev. MZUKISI WELCOME FALENI; 1,231,000 mems.

Reformed Church in South Africa (Die Gereformeerde Kerke): POB 20004, Noordbrug 2522, Potchefstroom; tel. (18) 2973986; fax (18) 2931042; e-mail direkteur@gksa.org.za; internet www.gksa.org.za; f. 1859; Prin. Officer Dr C. J. SMIT; 158,973 mems.

Seventh-day Adventist Church: POB 468, Bloemfontein 9300; tel. (51) 4478271; fax (51) 4488059; e-mail sau.president@adventist.org.za; internet www.adventist.org.za; Pres. Dr T. LETSELI; Sec. Pastor T. KUNENE; 126,175 mems.

United Congregational Church of Southern Africa: POB 96014, Brixton; tel. and fax (21) 6839665; e-mail dave@uccsa.co.za; internet www.uccsa.org.za; f. 1799; Pres. Rev. IAN BOOTH; Gen. Sec. Rev. DES VAN DER WATER; 400,000 mems in 350 churches.

Uniting Presbyterian Church in Southern Africa: POB 96188, Brixton 2019; tel. (11) 3392471; fax (11) 3396938; e-mail gensec@presbyterian.org.za; internet www.upcsa.org.za; f. 1999; Moderator Rt Rev. W. D. POOL; Gen. Sec. Rev. V. S. VELLEM; Clerk of the Assembly T. W. COULTER; 130,000 mems.

Zion Christian Church: Zion City, Moria; f. 1910; South Africa's largest black religious group; Leader Bishop BARNABAS LEKGANYANE; c. 4m. mems.

SOUTH AFRICA

ISLAM

In 2003 there were some 455 Mosques and 408 Muslim colleges in South Africa.

United Ulama Council of South Africa (UUCSA): POB 4118, Cape Town 8000; tel. (21) 6965150; fax (21) 6968502; f. 1994; Pres. SHEIKH EBRAHIM GABRIELS; Sec.-Gen. MOULANA YUSUF PATEL.

JUDAISM

According to the South African Jewish Board of Deputies, in 2006 there were about 80,000 Jews in South Africa, and about 200 organized Jewish communities.

African Jewish Congress: POB 51663, Raedene 2124; tel. (82) 4402621; fax (86) 6146724; e-mail moshe@beyachad.co.za; internet www.africanjewishcongress.com; f. 1994; co-ordinating body representing Jewish communities in sub-Saharan Africa; Pres. MERVYN SMITH; Spiritual Leader Rabbi MOSHE SILBERHAFT.

South African Jewish Board of Deputies: POB 87557, Houghton 2041; tel. (11) 6452523; fax (11) 6452559; e-mail sajbod@iafrica.com; internet www.jewish.org.za; f. 1903; the representative institution of South African Jewry; Pres. RUSSELL GADDIN; Chair. MICHAEL BAGRAIM; Nat. Dir WENDY KAHN.

BAHÁ'Í FAITH

National Spiritual Assembly: 209 Bellairs Dr., North Riding 2169, POB 932, Banbury Cross 2164; tel. (11) 4620100; fax (11) 4620129; e-mail nsa.sec@bahai.org.za; internet www.bahai.org.za; f. 1956; Gen. Sec. SHOHREH RAWHANI; 11,000 mems resident in 320 localities.

The Press

Government Communication and Information System (GCIS): Midtown Bldg, cnr Vermeulen and Prinsloo Sts, Pretoria; Private Bag X745, Pretoria 0001; tel. (12) 3142911; fax (12) 3252030; e-mail information@gcis.gov.za; internet www.gcis.gov.za; govt agency; CEO MZWANELE JIMMY MANYI.

South African Press Ombudsman: POB 47221, Parklands 2121, Johannesburg; tel. (11) 7884837; fax (11) 7884990; e-mail pressombudsman@ombudsman.org.za; internet www.presscouncil .org.za; Ombudsman JOE THLOLOE.

DAILIES

Eastern Cape

Die Burger (Oos-Kaap): 52 Cawood St, POB 525, Port Elizabeth 6001; tel. (41) 5036111; fax (41) 5036138; e-mail kontak@dieburger .com; internet www.dieburger.com; f. 1937; morning; Afrikaans; Publr ANDRE OLIVIER; circ. 23,849.

Daily Dispatch: 35 Caxton St, POB 131, East London 5200; tel. (43) 7022000; fax (43) 7022968; e-mail letters@dispatch.co.za; internet www.dispatch.co.za; f. 1872; publ. by Dispatch Media (Pty) Ltd; afternoon; also publ. *Weekend Dispatch* (Sat.); English; Editor MPUMELELO MKHABELA; circ. 33,338 (Mon.–Fri.), 27,927 (Sat.).

The Herald: Newspaper House, 19 Baakens St; POB 1117, Port Elizabeth 6000; tel. (41) 5047911; fax (41) 5853947; e-mail heraldletters@avusa.co.za; internet www.theherald.co.za; f. 1845; fmrly *Eastern Province Herald*; publ. by Johnnic Publishing Ltd; morning; English; Editor RIC WILSON; circ. 29,719 (Mon.–Fri.), 25,000 (Sat.).

Free State

Die Volksblad: 79 Voortrekker St, POB 267, Bloemfontein 9300; tel. (51) 4047600; fax (51) 4306949; e-mail nuus@volksblad.com; internet www.volksblad.com; f. 1904; publ. by Media 24; morning; Afrikaans; Editor JONATHAN CROWTHER; circ. 29,018 (Mon.–Fri.), 23,000 (Sat.).

Gauteng

Beeld: Media Park, Kingsway 69, Auckland Park, Johannesburg; POB 333, Auckland Park 2006; tel. (11) 7139000; fax (11) 7139960; e-mail nuus@beeld.com; internet www.beeld.com; f. 1974; publ. by Media 24; morning; weekly: *Kampus-Beeld*, student news and information, and *JIP* youth supplement; Afrikaans; Editor-in-Chief PEET KRUGER; Editor TIM DU PLESSIS; circ. 105,618 (Mon.–Fri.), 88,402 (Sat.).

Business Day: POB 1745, Saxonwold 2132; tel. (11) 2803000; fax (11) 2805505; internet www.bday.co.za; f. 1985; publ. by BDFM Publrs (Pty) Ltd; afternoon; English; financial; incl. *Wanted* arts and leisure magazine; Editor JIM JONES; circ. 40,451 (Mon.–Fri.).

The Citizen: POB 43069, Industria 2042; tel. (11) 2486000; fax (11) 2486213; e-mail news@citizen.co.za; internet www.citizen.co.za; f. 1976; publ. by Caxton Publrs & Printers Ltd; Mon.–Sat., morning; English; Editor M. WILLIAMS; circ. 76,183 (Mon.–Fri.), 57,935 (Sat.).

The Daily Sun: POB 121, Auckland Park 2006; tel. (11) 8776000; fax (11) 8776020; e-mail news@dailysun.co.za; internet www.dailysun .co.za; Editor THEMBA KHUMALO.

The New Age: 52 Lechwe St, Corporate Park, Old Pretoria Rd, Midrand 1685; tel. (11) 5421222; fax (86) 7337000; e-mail info@ thenewage.co.za; internet www.thenewage.co.za; f. 2010; Editor HENRY JEFFREYS.

The Pretoria News: 216 Vermeulen St, Pretoria 0002; POB 439, Pretoria 0001; tel. (12) 3002000; fax (12) 3257300; e-mail pta .newsdesk@inl.co.za; internet www.ptanews.co.za; f. 1898; publ. by Independent Newspapers Gauteng Ltd; afternoon; English; Editor ZINGISA MKHUMA; circ. 28,690 (Mon.–Fri.), 17,406 (Sat.).

Sowetan: 61 Commando Rd, Industria West, Johannesburg 2000; POB 6663, Johannesburg 2000; tel. (11) 4714000; fax (11) 4748834; e-mail editor@sowetan.co.za; internet www.sowetan.co.za; f. 1981; publ. by New Africa Publs (NAP) Ltd; morning; English; Acting Editor THABO LESHILO; circ. 4,122,825 (Mon.–Fri.).

The Star: 47 Sauer St, POB 1014, Johannesburg 2000; tel. (11) 6339111; fax (11) 8343918; e-mail starnews@star.co.za; internet www.star.co.za; f. 1887; publ. by Independent Newspapers Gauteng Ltd; morning; English; also publ. *The Saturday Star*; Editor MOEGSIEN WILLIAMS; circ. 166,461 (Mon.–Fri.), 137, 385 (Sat.).

KwaZulu/Natal

The Daily News: 18 Osborne St, Greyville 4001; POB 47549, Greyville 4023; tel. (31) 3082106; fax (31) 3082185; internet www .iol.co.za; f. 1878; Mon.–Fri., afternoon; English; Editor ALAN DUNN; circ. 50,000.

The Mercury: 18 Osborne St, Greyville 4001; POB 47397, Greyville 4023; tel. (31) 3082472; fax (31) 3082662; e-mail mercnews@inl.co.za; internet themercury.co.za; f. 1852; publ. by Independent Newspapers KZN; morning; English; Editor ANGELA QUINTAL; circ. 34,541 (Mon.–Fri.).

Witness: 45 Willowton Rd, POB 362, Pietermaritzburg 3200; tel. (33) 3551111; fax (33) 3551122; e-mail johnc@witness.co.za; internet www.witness.co.za; f. 1846; publ. by Natal Witness Printing and Publishing Co Ltd; morning; English; also publ. *Weekend Witness*; Editor J. CONYNGHAM; circ. 23,700 (Mon.–Fri.), 29,000 (Sat.).

Northern Cape

Diamond Fields Advertiser: POB 610, cnr Bean and Villiers Sts, Kimberley 8300; tel. (53) 8326261; fax (53) 8328902; e-mail pbe@ independent.co.za; internet www.iol.co.za; publ. by Independent Newspapers Gauteng Ltd; morning; English; Editor KEVIN RITCHIE; circ. 8,948 (Mon.–Fri.).

North-West

Rustenburg Herald: 13 Coetzer St, POB 2043, Rustenburg 0300; tel. (14) 5928329; fax (14) 5921869; e-mail mailbag@ rustenburgherald.co.za; internet www.rustenburg.co.za; f. 1924; English and Afrikaans; Man. Editor WALDIE WOLSCHENK; circ. 20,368.

Western Cape

Die Burger: 40 Heerengracht, POB 692, Cape Town 8000; tel. (21) 4062222; fax (21) 4062913; e-mail kontak@dieburger.com; internet www.dieburger.com; f. 1915; publ. by Media 24; morning; Afrikaans; Editor BUN BOOYENS; circ. 104,102 (Mon.–Fri.), 117,092 (Sat.).

Cape Argus: 122 St George's St, POB 56, Cape Town 8000; tel. (21) 4884911; fax (21) 4884075; e-mail argusnews@ctn.independent.co .za; internet www.capeargus.co.za; f. 1857; publ. by Independent Newspapers Cape Ltd; afternoon; English; also publ. *Weekend Argus*; Editor CHRIS WHITFIELD; circ. 73,230 (Mon.–Fri.), 103,953 (Sat. and Sun.).

Cape Times: Newspaper House, 122 St George's Mall, Cape Town 8001; POB 11, Cape Town 8000; tel. (21) 4884776; fax (21) 4884744; e-mail alide.dasnois@inl.co.za; internet www.capetimes.co.za; f. 1876; publ. by Independent Newspapers Cape Ltd; morning; English; Dep. Editor ALIDE DASNOIS; circ. 49,526 (Mon.–Fri.).

WEEKLIES AND FORTNIGHTLIES

Eastern Cape

Weekend Post: 19 Baakens St, Private Bag X6071, Port Elizabeth 6000; tel. (41) 5047251; fax (41) 5854966; e-mail weekend@johnnicec .co.za; internet www.weekendpost.co.za; publ. by Johnnic Publishing Co Ltd; English; Editor JEREMY MCCABE; circ. 33,372 (Sat.).

SOUTH AFRICA

Free State

Vista: POB 1027, Welkom 9460; tel. (57) 3571304; fax (57) 3532427; e-mail mwill@volksblad.com; internet www.media24.com/eng/newspapers/vista.html; f. 1971; weekly; English and Afrikaans; Editor Marti Will; circ. 38,000 (2005).

Gauteng

City Press: POB 3413, Johannesburg 2000; tel. (11) 7139002; fax (11) 7139977; e-mail news@citypress.co.za; internet www.citypress.co.za; f. 1983; publ. by RCP Media Bpk; weekly; English; Editor-in-Chief Ferial Haffejee; circ. 173,922 (Sun.).

Engineering News/Mining Weekly: POB 75316, Garden View 2047; tel. and fax (11) 6223744; fax (11) 6229350; e-mail newsdesk@engineeringnews.co.za; internet www.miningweekly.com; f. 1981; publ. by Creamer Media; weekly; Editor Terence Creamer; circ. 20,000.

Financial Mail: Johncom Bldg, 4 Biermann Ave, Rosebank 2196; POB 1744, Saxenwold 2132; tel. (11) 2803016; fax (11) 2805800; e-mail fmmail@fm.co.za; internet www.financialmail.co.za; weekly; English; Editor Barney Mthombothi; circ. 33,000.

Mail and Guardian: POB 91667, Auckland Park 2006; tel. (11) 2507300; fax (11) 2507303; e-mail newsdesk@mg.co.za; internet www.mg.co.za; publ. by M&G Media (Pty) Ltd; weekly; English; CEO Govin Reddy; Editor Nic Dawes; circ. 40,162 (Fri.).

Noordwes Gazette: POB 515, Potchefstroom 2520; tel. (18) 2930750; e-mail potchherald@media24.com; weekly; English and Afrikaans; Editor H. Stander; circ. 35,000.

Northern Review: 16 Grobler St, POB 45, Pietersburg 0700; tel. (152) 2959167; fax (152) 2915148; weekly; English and Afrikaans; Editor R. S. de Jager; circ. 10,300.

Potchefstroom and Ventersdorp Herald: POB 515, Potchefstroom 2520; tel. (18) 2930750; fax (18) 2930759; e-mail potchherald@media24.com; internet www.potchefstroomherald.co.za; f. 1908; Friday; English and Afrikaans; Editor H. Stander; Man. Dir Rassie van Zyl; circ. 8,000.

Rapport: POB 333, Auckland Park 2006; tel. (11) 7139002; fax (11) 7139977; e-mail rapport@rapport.co.za; internet www.naspers.co.za/rapport; publ. by RCP Media; weekly; Afrikaans; Sr Gen. Man. and Publr Sarel du Plessis; Editor Liza Albrecht; circ. 322,731 (Sun.).

South African Jewish Report: Suite 175, Postnet X10039, Randburg 2125; tel. (11) 8860162; fax (11) 8864202; e-mail geoffs@icon.co.za; internet www.sajewishreport.co.za; weekly; publ. by SA Jewish Report (Pty) Ltd; Editor Geoff Sifrin.

Springs and Brakpan Advertiser: 48, 5th Ave, POB 761, Springs 1560; tel. (11) 8124800; fax (11) 8124823; e-mail springseditorial@caxton.co.za; f. 1916; English and Afrikaans; Editor Cathy Grosvenor; circ. 13,000.

Sunday Times: POB 1742, Saxonwold 2132; tel. (11) 2805155; fax (11) 2805111; e-mail makhanyam@sundaytimes.co.za; internet www.sundaytimes.co.za; f. 1906; weekly; English; also published in Zulu; Editor-in-Chief Mondli Makhanya; circ. 505,402 (Sun.).

Vaalweekblad: 27 Ekspa Bldg, D. F. Malan St, POB 351, Vanderbijlpark 1900; tel. (16) 817010; fax (16) 810604; internet www.vaalweekblad.com; weekly; Afrikaans and English; Editor W. J. Buys; circ. 16,000.

Die Vrye Afrikaan: PO Box 675, Durbanville 7551; tel. (12) 3268646; e-mail redakteur@vryeafrikaan.co.za; internet www.vryeafrikaan.co.za; f. 2004; weekly; Afrikaans; Editor Johann Roussouw; circ. 13,000.

KwaZulu/Natal

Farmers' Weekly: 368 Jan Smuts Ave, Craighall, Johannesburg 2196; tel. (11) 8890836; fax (11) 8890862; e-mail farmersweekly@caxton.co.za; internet www.farmersweekly.co.za; f. 1911; weekly; agriculture and horticulture; Editor Chris Burgess; circ. 17,000.

Ilanga: 19 Timeball Blvd, The Point, Durban 4001; POB 2159 Durban 4000; tel. (31) 3374000; fax (31) 3379785; e-mail peterc@ilanganews.co.za; internet www.ilanganews.co.za; f. 1903; publ. by Mandla Matla Publishing Co (Pty) Ltd; 2 a week; also publ. *Ilanga Lange Sonto* (Sun. circ. 87,000); Zulu; Editor Sipho Ngobese; circ. 107,000; circ. 100,000 (Mon. and Thur.).

Independent On Saturday: 18 Osborne St, Greyville 4001; POB 47397, Greyville 4023; tel. (31) 3082900; fax (31) 3082185; e-mail satmail@inl.co.za; internet www.nn.independent.co.za; f. 1878; publ. by Independent Newspapers KZN; English; Editor Clyde Bawden; circ. 56,216.

Kwana in the City: POB 35559, Northway 4065; tel. (31) 5641230; fax (31) 5649807; e-mail vrydag@eastcoast.co.za; internet www.kwana.co.za; f. 1995; publ. by Kwana Group; English; free community newspaper with focus on consumer and human rights issues; also publ. *Kwana on Track* (f. 2004, English and Zulu, circ. 50,000) aimed at rail commuters; Publr Shelley Seid; Editor Dr Hilda Grobler; circ. 20,000.

Ladysmith Gazette: POB 10019, Ladysmith 3370; tel. (36) 6376801; fax (36) 6372283; f. 1902; weekly; English, Afrikaans and Zulu; Editor Diana Procter; circ. 7,000.

Post: 18 Osborne St, Greyville, Durban 4000; POB 47397, Greyville 4023; tel. (31) 3082400; fax (31) 3082427; e-mail post@inl.co.za; internet www.thepost.co.za; f. 1955 as *Golden City Post*; publ. by Independent Newspapers KZN; weekly; English; focus on the Indian community; Editor Brijlall Ramguthee; circ. 45,500 (Wed.).

Sunday Tribune: 18 Osborne St, POB 47549, Greyville 4023; tel. (31) 3082911; fax (31) 3082662; e-mail tribunenews@inl.co.za; internet www.sundaytribune.co.za; f. 1937; publ. by Independent Newspapers KZN; weekly; English; Editor Alan Dunn; circ. 109,774 (Sun.).

Umafrika: 35A Intersite Ave, Umgeni Business Park, Durban; tel. (31) 2684500; fax (31) 2684545; e-mail editor@umafrika.co.za; f. 1911; owned by Izimpoondo Communications; Friday; Zulu and English; Editor and Publisher Cyril Madlala; circ. 32,000.

Northern Cape

Die Gemsbok: POB 60, Upington 8800; tel. 27017; fax 24055; English and Afrikaans; Editor D. Jones; circ. 8,000.

Western Cape

Drum: Naspers Bldg, 7th Floor, 5 Protea Place, Sandown 2096; POB 653284, Benmore 2010; tel. (11) 3220888; fax (11) 3220891; e-mail pmdluli@media24.com; f. 1951; English and Zulu; Editor Esmare Weideman; Publr John Relihan; circ. 79,895 (2006).

Eikestadnuus: 44 Alexander St, POB 28, Stellenbosch 7600; tel. (2231) 72874; fax (2231) 99538; internet www.news24.com/Eikestad; weekly; English and Afrikaans; Editor R. Gerber; circ. 7,000.

Fair Lady: POB 785266, Cape Town 2146; tel. (11) 3220858; fax (11) 8836617; e-mail flmag@fairlady.com; internet www.fairlady.com; fortnightly; English; Editor Suzy Brokensha; circ. 103,642.

Huisgenoot: 40 Heerengracht, POB 1802, Cape Town 8000; tel. (21) 4062115; fax (21) 4063316; e-mail hgnbrief@huisgenoot.com; internet www.huisgenoot.com; f. 1916; weekly; Afrikaans; Editor Esmaré Weideman; circ. 355,487.

Move! Magazine: Media City, 10th Floor, 1 Heerengracht St, Foreshore, Cape Town 8001; tel. (21) 4461232; fax (21) 4461206; e-mail move@media24.com; f. 2005; weekly; English; Editor Sbu Mpungose.

The Southern Cross: POB 2372, Cape Town 8000; tel. (21) 4655007; fax (21) 4653850; e-mail editor@scross.co.za; internet www.scross.co.za; f. 1920; publ. by Catholic Newspapers and Publishing Co Ltd; weekly; English; Roman Catholic interest; Editor Günther Simmermacher; circ. 11,000 (Wed.).

tvplus: Media City, 10th Floor, 1 Heerengracht St, Cape Town 8001; POB 7197, Roggebaai 8012; tel. (21) 4461222; fax (21) 4461206; e-mail tvplus@media24.com; internet www.tvplus.co.za; f. 2000; weekly; English and Afrikaans; Editor Wicus Pretorius.

Tyger-Burger: 40 Heerengracht, POB 2271, Cape Town 8000; tel. (21) 4062121; fax (21) 4062913; weekly; Afrikaans and English; Editor Abie von Zyl.

Weekend Argus: 122 St George's Mall, POB 56, Cape Town 8000; tel. (21) 4884911; fax (21) 4884762; internet www.iol.co.za; f. 1857; Sat. and Sun.; English; Editor Chris Whitfield; circ. 108,294.

You Magazine: Naspers Bldg, 7th Floor, 40 Heerengracht St, Cape Town 8001; POB 7167, Roggebaai 8012; tel. (21) 4062166; fax (21) 4062937; e-mail you@you.co.za; internet www.you.co.za; f. 1987; weekly; English; Editor Esmaré Weideman; circ. 222,845 (2004).

MONTHLIES

Free State

Wamba: POB 1097, Bloemfontein; publ. in seven vernacular languages; educational; Editor C. P. Senyatsi.

Gauteng

Boxing World: 5A Dover St, Randburg, Gauteng; tel. (11) 8868558; e-mail info@boxingworld.co.za; f. 1976; Editor Peter Leopeng; circ. 10,000.

Nursing News: POB 1280, Pretoria 0001; tel. (12) 3432315; fax (12) 3440750; f. 1978; English and Afrikaans; magazine of the Dem. Nursing Org; circ. 76,000.

SOUTH AFRICA

KwaZulu/Natal

Bona: POB 32083, Mobeni 4060; tel. (31) 422041; fax (31) 426068; f. 1956; English, Sotho, Xhosa and Zulu; Editor (vacant); circ. 256,631.

Living and Loving: POB 218, Parklands, Johannesburg 2121; tel. (11) 8890621; fax (11) 8890668; e-mail livingandloving@caxton.co.za; internet www.livingandloving.co.za; publ. by Caxton Magazines; English; parenting magazine; Editor CARLIEN WESSELS; circ. 55,000.

Rooi Rose: POB 412982, Craighall 2024; tel. (11) 8890665; fax (11) 8890975; e-mail rooirose@caxton.co.za; internet www.rooirose.co.za; f. 1942; Afrikaans; women's interest; Editor MARTIE PANSEGROUW; circ. 122,296.

World Airnews: POB 35082, Northway 4065; tel. (31) 5641319; fax (31) 5637115; e-mail tom@airnews.co.za; internet www.airnews.co.za; f. 1973; owned by TCE Publications; monthly; aviation news; Man. Editor TOM CHALMERS; circ. 13,312 (2011).

Your Family: POB 473016, Parklands 2121; tel. (11) 8890749; fax (11) 8890642; e-mail yourfamily@caxton.co.za; internet www.yourfamily.co.za; f. 1973; English; cooking, crafts, DIY; Editor ANGELA WALLER-PATON; circ. 164,115.

Western Cape

Car: Ramsay, Son & Parker (Pty) Ltd, Digital Publishing, 3 Howard Dr., Pinelands, Cape Town; POB 180, Howard Place 7450; tel. (21) 5303100; fax (21) 5322698; e-mail car@rsp.co.za; internet www.cartoday.com; English; Editor J. BENTLEY; circ. 99,411 (2008).

Femina: 21 St John's St, POB 3647, Cape Town 8000; tel. (21) 4646248; fax (21) 4612501; Editor ROBYNNE KAHN; circ. 68,591.

Reader's Digest (South African Edition): 5 Protea Pl., Protea Park, Sandown, Johannesburg 2146; POB 785266, Sandton 2146; tel. (11) 3220700; fax (11) 8839495; e-mail magazine.sa@readersdigest.com; internet www.readersdigest.co.za; f. 1948; English; Editor ANTHONY JOHNSON; circ. 62,399.

Sarie: POB 785266, Sandton 2146; tel. and fax (21) 4062366; e-mail mvanbre@sarie.com; internet www.natmags.com; monthly; Afrikaans; women's interest; Editor MICHELLE VAN BREDA; circ. 137,970 (2004).

South African Medical Journal: MASA House, Central House, Private Bag X1, Pinelands 7430; tel. (21) 5306520; fax (21) 5314126; e-mail danjn@telkomsa.net; internet www.samj.org.za; f. 1884; publ. by the South African Medical Asscn; Editor-in-Chief DANIEL J. NCAYIYANA; circ. 20,000.

Die Voorligter: Private Bag, Tyger Valley 7536; tel. (21) 9177000; fax (21) 9141333; e-mail lig@cnw-inter.net; internet www.christene.co.za; f. 1937; journal of the Dutch Reformed Church of South Africa; Editor Dr F. M. GAUM; circ. 50,000.

Wineland Magazine: VinPro, POB 1411, Suider-Paarl 7624; tel. (21) 8634524; fax (21) 8634851; e-mail cas@wineland.co.za; internet www.wineland.co.za; f. 1931; publ. by VinPro wine producers' org.; viticulture and the wine and spirit industry; incorporates *Wynboer* technical guide for wine producers; Editor CASSIE DU PLESSIS; circ. 7,000.

The Wisden Cricketer: POB 16368, Vlaeberg 8018; tel. (21) 4083813; e-mail aevlambi@touchline.co.za; internet www.wisdencricketer.co.za; f. 2005; Publr NIC WIDES; Editor ROB HOUWING.

Woman's Value: POB 1802, Cape Town 8000; tel. (21) 4062629; fax (21) 4062929; e-mail wvdited@womansvalue.com; internet www.women24.com; English; Editor and Publr TERENA LE ROUX; circ. 134,749.

PERIODICALS

Eastern Cape

African Journal of AIDS Research (AJAR): Centre for AIDS Development, Research and Evaluation, Institute of Social and Economic Research, Rhodes University, POB 94, Grahamstown 6140; tel. (46) 6038553; fax (46) 6038769; e-mail ajar@ru.ac.za; internet www.cadre.org.za; f. 2002; quarterly; Man. Editor KEVIN KELLY.

Gauteng

Africa Insight: Africa Institute of South Africa, POB 630, Pretoria 0001; tel. (12) 3049700; fax (12) 3261778; e-mail ngobenis@ai.org.za; internet www.ai.org.za; f. 1960; quarterly; journal of the Africa Institute of South Africa; Editor SOLANI NGOBENI; circ. 1,200.

Africanus: Unisa Press, POB 392, UNISA, 0003 Pretoria; tel. (12) 4292953; fax (12) 4293449; e-mail delpoa@unisa.ac.za; 2 a year; journal of the Centre for Development Studies, Unisa; African and Third World developmental issues; Editor LINDA CORNWELL.

Codicillus: Unisa Press, POB 392, UNISA, 0003 Pretoria; tel. (12) 4292953; fax (12) 4293449; e-mail delpoa@unisa.ac.za; 2 a year; journal of the School of Law at the Univ. of South Africa; South African and international law; Editor Prof. H. C. ROODT.

The ScienceScope: POB 395, Pretoria 0001; tel. (12) 8414625; fax (12) 8413789; e-mail edaconceicao@csir.co.za; internet www.csir.co.za; f. 1991 as *Technobrief*; quarterly; publ. by the South African Council for Scientific and Industrial Research; Editor EUNICE DA CONCEIÇÃO; circ. 6,000.

South African Journal of Economics: 4.45 EBW Bldg, University of Pretoria, Pretoria 0002; POB 73354, Lynnwood Ridge 0040; tel. (12) 4203525; fax (12) 3625266; e-mail saje@up.ac.za; internet www.essa.org.za; f. 1933; quarterly; English and Afrikaans; journal of the Economic Soc. of South Africa; publ. by Blackwells; Man. Editor P. A. BLACK.

KwaZulu/Natal

South African Journal of Chemistry: School of Chemistry, University of KwaZulu-Natal, Durban 4000; tel. (31) 2601096; fax (31) 2603091; e-mail taford@vodamail.co.za; internet search.sabinet.co.za/sajchem; f. 1921; publ. by the South African Chemical Institute; digital; Co-ordinating Editor TONY FORD.

North-West

Historia: c/o Dept of Historical and Heritage Studies, Faculty of Humanities, Humanities Bldg (Main Campus), University of Pretoria, Pretoria 0002; tel. (12) 4202323; fax (12) 4202656; e-mail moutofa@unisa.ac.za; f. 1956; 2 a year; journal of the Historical Asscn of South Africa; South African and African history; Co-ordinating Editor ALEX MOULTON.

Western Cape

Economic Prospects: Bureau for Economic Research, Economics and Management Sciences Bldg, 7th Floor, Bosman St, Stellenbosch 7600; Private Bag 5050, Stellenbosch 7599; tel. (21) 8872810; fax (21) 8839225; e-mail hhman@sun.ac.za; quarterly; forecast of the South African economy for the coming 18–24 months; Man. Editor P. LAUBSCHER.

Ecquid Novi: c/o South African Journal for Journalism Research, POB 106, Stellenbosch 7599; tel. (21) 8082625; fax (21) 8083488; e-mail novi@sun.ac.za; internet www.sun.ac.za/ecquidnovi; f. 1980; 2 a year; focus on role of the media in southern Africa and Africa; Editor ARNOLD S. DE BEER.

The Motorist: Highbury Monarch Pty, 8th Floor, Metlife Centre, 7 Coen Steytler Ave, Foreshore, 8001 Cape Town; tel. (21) 4160141; fax (21) 4187312; e-mail themotorist@monarchc.co.za; f. 1966; journal of the Automobile Asscn of SA; Editor FIONA ZERBST; circ. 131,584 (2000).

NEWS AGENCIES

East Cape News (ECN) Pty Ltd: POB 897, Grahamstown 6140; tel. (46) 6361050; e-mail editor@ecn.co.za; internet www.ecn.co.za; f. 1997; fmrly East Cape News Agencies; Dir MIKE LOEWE.

South African Press Association (SAPA): Cotswold House, Greenacres Office Park, cnr Victory and Rustenburg Rds, Victory Park; POB 7766, Johannesburg 2000; tel. (11) 7821600; fax (11) 7821587; e-mail comms@sapa.org.za; internet www.sapa.org.za; f. 1938; Man. WIM J. H. VAN GILS; Editor MARK A. VAN DER VELDEN; 40 mems.

PRESS ASSOCIATIONS

Foreign Correspondents' Association of South Africa: POB 1136, Auckland Park 2006; tel. and fax (11) 4860490; e-mail fca@onwe.co.za; internet www.fcasa.co.za; represents 175 int. journalists; Chair. JOHN CHIAHEMEN; Sec. MARTINA SCHWIKOWSKI.

Newspaper Association of South Africa: Nedbank Gardens, 5th Floor, 33 Bath Ave, Rosebank 2196, Johannesburg; POB 47180, Parklands 2121; tel. (11) 7213200; fax (11) 7213254; e-mail na@printmedia.org.za; internet www.printmedia.org.za; f. 1882; represents 42 national daily and weekly newspapers, and 178 community newspapers; Pres. PRAKASH DESAI.

Print Media SA: 2nd Floor, 7 St David's, St David's Office Park, St David's Place, Parktown 2193; POB 47180, Parklands 2121; tel. (11) 5519600; fax (11) 5519650; e-mail mamosat@printmedia.org.za; internet www.printmedia.org.za; f. 1995 following the restructuring of the Newspaper Press Union of Southern Africa; represents all aspects of the print media (newspapers and magazines); over 700 mems; CEO INGRID LOUW.

SOUTH AFRICA   *Directory*

Publishers

Acorn Books: POB 4845, Randburg 2125; tel. (11) 8805768; fax (11) 8805768; e-mail acornbook@iafrica.com; f. 1985; Africana, general, natural history; Propr and Publr ELEANOR-MARY CADELL.

Jonathan Ball Publishers: 10–14 Watkins St, Denver Ext. 4, Johannesburg 2094; POB 33977, Jeppestown 2043; tel. (11) 6222900; fax (11) 6018183; e-mail orders@jonathanball.co.za; internet www.jonathanball.co.za; acquired by Via Afrika (Naspers Group) in 1992; fiction, reference, bibles, textbooks, general; imprints incl. AD Donker (literature), Delta (general fiction and non-fiction) and Sunbird; Man. Dir JONATHAN BALL.

Bible Society of South Africa: Bible House, 134 Edward St, POB 5500, Tyger Valley 7536; tel. (21) 9108777; fax (21) 9108799; e-mail biblia@biblesociety.co.za; internet www.biblesociety.co.za; f. 1820; bibles and religious material in 11 official languages; CEO Rev. G. S. KRITZINGER.

Brenthurst Press (Pty) Ltd: Federation Rd, POB 87184, Houghton 2041; tel. (11) 5445400; fax (11) 4861651; e-mail orders@brenthurst.co.za; internet www.brenthurst.org.za; f. 1974; Southern African history; Dir MARCELLE GRAHAM.

Christelike Uitgewersmaatskappy (CUM): POB 1599, Vereeniging 1930; tel. (16) 4407000; fax (16) 4211748; e-mail orders@cabooks.co.za; internet www.cum.co.za; religious fiction and non-fiction.

Clever Books: POB 13816, Hatfield 0028; tel. (12) 3423263; fax (12) 4302376; e-mail info@cleverbooks.co.za; internet www.cleverbooks.co.za; f. 1981; subsidiary of MacMillan Publrs; Gen. Man. ELNA HARMSE.

Fisichem Publishers: 19 Hofmeyer St, Private Bag X3, Matieland 7602; tel. (21) 8870900; fax (21) 8839635; e-mail info@fisichem.co.za; internet fisichem.co.za; f. 1985; owned by FRJ Trust; science, maths and accounting study guides; Man. RETHA JORDAAN.

Flesch Publications: 11 Peninsula Rd, Zeekoevlei, Cape Town 7941; POB 31353, Grassy Park 7888; tel. (21) 7054317; fax (21) 7060766; e-mail sflesch@iafrica.com; f. 1954; biography, cookery, aviation; CEO STEPHEN FLESCH.

Fortress Books: POB 2475, Knysna 6570; tel. (44) 3826805; fax (44) 3826848; e-mail fortress@iafrica.com; internet www.uys.com/fortress; f. 1973; military history, biographies, financial; Man. Dir I. UYS.

Heinemann Publishers (Pty) Ltd: Heinemann House, Grayston Office Park, Bldg 3, 128 Peter Rd, Atholl Ext. 12, Sandton 2196; POB 781940, Sandown, Sandton 2146; tel. (11) 3228600; fax (11) 3228715; e-mail customerliaison@heinemann.co.za; internet www.heinemann.co.za; educational; incl. imprints Lexicon, Isando and Centaur; Man. Dir ORENNA KRUT.

Home Economics Publishers (Huishoudkunde Uitgewers): POB 7091, Stellenbosch 7599; tel. and fax (21) 8864722; e-mail mcv1@sun.ac.za; Man. M. C. VOSLOO.

HSRC Press: Human Sciences Research Council Private, Bag X9182, Cape Town 8000; tel. (21) 4668000; fax (21) 4610836; e-mail publishing@hsrc.ac.za; internet www.hsrcpress.ac.za; Chair. Prof. DAN NCAYIYANA.

Juta and Co Ltd: POB 14373, Lansdowne 7780, Cape Town; tel. (11) (21) 7633500; fax (21) 7633560; e-mail cserv@juta.co.za; internet www.juta.co.za; f. 1853; academic, educational, law, electronic; imprints incl. Double Storey (general contemporary), and University of Cape Town Press (scholarly and academic); CEO R. J. WILSON.

LAPA Publishers (Lees Afrikaans Praat Afrikaans): 380 Bosman St, POB 123, Pretoria 0001; tel. (12) 4010700; fax (12) 3244460; f. 1996 as the publishing arm of the Afrikaans Language and Culture Asscn; present name adopted in 2000; Afrikaans; general fiction and non-fiction; CEO WIM DE WET.

Learning Matters Africa: 341 West St, Durban 4001; POB 466, Durban 4000; tel. (31) 3053791; fax (31) 3077356; e-mail padams@adamsbooks.co.za; f. 2002; educational; CEO BRYAN PHILLIPS.

Lemur Books (Pty) Ltd (The Galago Publishing (1999) (Pty) Ltd): POB 1645, Alberton 1450; tel. (11) 9072029; fax (11) 8690890; e-mail lemur@mweb.co.za; internet www.galago.co.za; f. 1980; military, political, history, hunting, general; Man. Dir F. STIFF.

LexisNexis Butterworths SA: 215 North Ridge Rd, Morningside, Durban 4001; POB 792, Durban 4000; tel. (31) 2683111; fax (31) 2683108; e-mail customercare@lexisnexis.co.za; internet www.lexisnexis.co.za; f. 1948 as Butterworths; adopted LexisNexis name in 2001; jtly owned by Reed Elsevier, USA, and Kagiso Media; law, tax, accountancy; Chair. W. ROGER JARDINE; CEO WILLIAM J. LAST.

Lux Verbi-BM: POB 5, Wellington 7654; tel. (21) 8648210; fax (21) 8648295; e-mail jmc@luxverbi-bm.co.za; internet www.luxverbi-bm.com; f. 1818 as the Dutch Reformed Church Publishing Co; merged with Bible Media in 1999; subsidiary of the Naspers Group; imprints incl. Hugenote, NG Kerk Uitgewers, Protea, and Waterkant; Christian media; Man. Dir H. S. SPIES; Editor-in-Chief W. BOTHA.

Maskew Miller Longman (Pty) Ltd: cnr Forest Dr. and Logan Way, Pinelands 7405; POB 396, Cape Town 8000; tel. (21) 5326000; fax (21) 5310716; e-mail customerservices@mml.co.za; internet www.mml.co.za; f. 1893 as Miller Maskew; merged with Longman in 1983; jtly owned by Pearson Education and Caxton Publrs and Printers Ltd; imprints incl. Kagiso Publishing (f. 1994; fmrly De Jager-HAUM) and Phumelela Books; educational and general; CEO JAPIE PIENAAR.

Methodist Publishing House: POB 13128, Woodstock, Cape Town 7915; tel. (21) 4483640; fax (21) 4483716; e-mail george@methbooks.co.za; f. 1894; Christian books and church supplies; Gen. Man. GEORGE VINE.

Nasou—Via Afrika: 40 Heerengracht, Cape Town 8001; POB 5197, Cape Town 8000; tel. (21) 4063005; fax (21) 4063086; e-mail CGilittt@nasou.com; internet www.nasou-viaafrika.com; f. 1963; subsidiary of Via Afrika (Naspers Group); educational; imprints incl. Acacia, Action Publrs, Afritech, Afro, Atlas, Era, Juta, KZN Books, Gariep, Idem, Phoenix Education, Shortland and Y-Press Grade R-3; Man. Dir CLIVE GILLITT.

NB Publishers: Naspers Bldg, 12th Floor, 40 Heerengracht, Roggebai 8012; POB 879, Cape Town 8000; tel. (21) 4063033; fax (21) 4063812; e-mail nb@nb.co.za; internet www.nb.co.za; English, Afrikaans, Xhosa and Zulu; Human & Rousseau (f. 1959; general, children's and youth literature, cookery and self-help), Kwela (f. 1994; fiction), Pharos (dictionaries), Tafelberg (f. 1950; fiction and non-fiction, politics, children's and youth literature) and Best Books (educational texts); Head of Publishing C. T. BREYTENBACH.

Oxford University Press: POB 12119, N1 City, Cape Town 7463; tel. (21) 5962300; fax (21) 5961234; e-mail oxford.za@oup.com; internet www.oxford.co.za; f. 1914; Man. Dir LIEZE KOTZE.

Protea Book House: 1067 Burnett St, Hatfield, Pretoria; POB 35110, Menlo Park, 0102 Pretoria; tel. (12) 3623444; fax (12) 3625688; e-mail protea@intekom.co.za; internet www.proteaboekhuis.co.za; f. 1997; art and photography, Afrikaans fiction, South African history, spiritual, academic and general; Dir NICOL STASSEN.

Random House Struik (Pty) Ltd South Africa: POB 2002, Houghton 2041; tel. (11) 4843538; fax (11) 4846180; e-mail lindad@randomstruik.co.za; f. 1966; general fiction; Man. Dir S. E. JOHNSON.

Shuter & Shooter Publishers (Pty) Ltd: 110CB Downes Rd, Pietermaritzburg; POB 13016, Cascades, Pietermaritzburg 3202; tel. (33) 8468700; fax (33) 8468701; e-mail sales@shuters.com; internet www.shuters.com; f. 1921; educational, general and African languages and trade books; Man. Dir PRIMI CHETTY.

University of KwaZulu-Natal Press (UKZN Press): Private Bag X01, Scottsville 3209; tel. (33) 2605226; fax (33) 2605801; e-mail books@ukzn.ac.za; internet www.uknzpress.co.za; academic and scholarly; Publr GLENN COWLEY; Editor SALLY HINES.

Van Schaik Publishers: 1064 Arcadia St, POB 12681, Hatfield 0028; tel. (12) 3422765; fax (12) 4303563; e-mail vanschaik@vanschaiknet.com; internet www.vanschaiknet.com; f. 1915; acquired by Nasionale Pers, latterly Via Afrika-Naspers Group in 1986; English and Afrikaans; academic and scholarly; CEO LEANNE MARTINI.

Wits University Press: PO Wits, Johannesburg 2050; tel. (11) 4845910; fax (11) 4845971; e-mail Veronica.Klipp@wits.ac.za; internet witspress.wits.ac.za; f. 1922; general trade, non-fiction and scholarly; Publr VERONICA KLIPP.

PUBLISHERS' ASSOCIATION

Publishers' Association of South Africa (PASA): Suite 305, 2nd Floor, The Foundry, Prestwich St, Green Point, Cape Town 8005; tel. (21) 4252721; fax (21) 4213270; e-mail pasa@publishsa.co.za; internet www.publishsa.co.za; f. 1992; promotes and protects the rights and responsibilities of the independent publishing sector in South Africa; Exec Dir. DUDLEY H. SCHROEDER.

Broadcasting and Communications

REGULATORY AUTHORITY

Independent Communications Authority of South Africa (ICASA): Pinmill Farm, Blocks A, B, C and D, 164 Katherine St, Sandton 2146; Private Bag X10002, Marlboro 2063; tel. (11) 5663000; fax (11) 4441919; e-mail info@icasa.org.za; internet www.icasa.org.za; f. 2000 as successor to the Independent Broadcasting Authority (f. 1993) and South African Telecommunications Regulatory Authority (f. 1996); regulates telecommunications and broadcasting; Chair. Dr STEPHEN SIPHO MNCUBE.

SOUTH AFRICA   *Directory*

TELECOMMUNICATIONS

Cell C (Pty) Ltd: 150 Rivonia Rd, Sandown 2196; Private Bag X36, Benmore 2010, Johannesburg; tel. (11) 3244000; fax (11) 3244009; e-mail customerservice@cellc.co.za; internet www.cellc.co.za; f. 2000; subsidiary of 3C Telecommunications (60% owned by Oger Telecom South Africa, 40% by CellSAf); mobile cellular telecommunications provider; Chair. TALAAT LAHAM; CEO LARS P. REICHELT.

Mobile Telephone Networks (Pty) Ltd (MTN): 3 Alice Lane, Ext. 38, PMB 9955, Sandton 2146; tel. (11) 3016000; fax (11) 3018448; internet www.mtn.co.za; f. 1994; mobile cellular telecommunications provider; operations in 21 countries in Africa and the Middle East; 11m. subscribers in South Africa (2006); Chair. MATAMELA CYRIL RAMAPHOSA; CEO SIFISO DABENGWA.

Neotel: 44 Old Pretoria Main Rd, Midrand, Johannesburg; PostNet Suite 612, Private Bag X29, Gallo Manor, Johannesburg, 2052; tel. (11) 585 1000; fax (11) 585 0001; e-mail info@neotel.co.za; internet www.neotel.co.za; Man. Dir and CEO AJAY PANDEY.

Telkom SA Ltd: Telkom Towers North, 152 Proes St, Pretoria 0002; POB 925, Pretoria 0001; tel. (12) 3111007; fax (12) 3114031; e-mail letlapll@telkom.co.za; internet www.telkom.co.za; f. 1991; 38% govt-owned; ICT solutions service provider; Chair. LAZARUS ZIM; CEO NOMBULELO MOHOL.

Virgin Mobile South Africa (Pty) Ltd (VMSA): CitiGroup Bldg, 2nd Floor, 145 West St, Sandton, Johannesburg; POB 78331, Sandton 2146; tel. (11) 3244000; fax (11) 3244113; e-mail CustomerCare@virginmobile.co.za; internet www.virginmobile.co.za; f. 2006; jt venture btwn Cell C and Virgin Mobile Telecoms Ltd, United Kingdom; mobile cellular telecommunications provider; CEO STEVE BAILEY.

Vodacom Group (Pty) Ltd: Vodacom Corporate Park, 082 Vodacom Blvd, Vodavalley, Midrand 1685; tel. (11) 6535000; e-mail corporate.affairs@vodacom.co.za; internet www.vodacom.co.za; f. 1993; 50% owned by Telkom SA Ltd, 50% by Vodafone Group PLC, United Kingdom; subsidiaries in the DRC (f. 2002), Lesotho (f. 1996), Mozambique (f. 2003) and Tanzania (f. 1999); Chair. MTHANDAZO PETER MOYO; CEO PIETER UYS.

BROADCASTING

Radio

South African Broadcasting Corpn (SABC)—Radio: Private Bag X1, Auckland Park 2006, Johannesburg; tel. (11) 7149111; fax (11) 7149744; e-mail rpsales@sabc.co.za; internet www.sabc.co.za; f. 1936; comprises 15 public radio stations and three commercial radio stations broadcasting in 11 languages; Chair. Dr BEN NGUBANE; CEO SOLLY MOKOETLE.

Domestic Services

SAfm; Afrikaans Stereo; 5 FM; Radio 2000; Good Hope Stereo; Radio Kontrei; RPN Stereo; Jacaranda Stereo; Radio Algoa (www.algoafm.co.za; regional services); Radio Lotus (Indian service in English); Radio Metro (African service in English); Thobela FM; Ikwekwezi FM; Radio Sesotho; Setswana Stereo; Radio Swazi; Radio Tsonga; Radio Xhosa; Radio Zulu; Lesedi FM; Ligwalagwala FM; Motsweding FM; Phaphala FM; Radio Sonder Grense (Afrikaans); Tru FM; Ukhozi FM; Umhlobo Wenene FM; X-K FM.

External Service

567 CapeTalk: Suite 7D, Somerset Sq., Highfield Rd, Cape Town; Private Bag 567, Vlaeberg 8018; tel. (21) 4464700; fax (21) 4464800; e-mail 567webmaster@capetalk.co.za; internet www.capetalk.co.za; Man. COLLEEN LOUW.

Channel Africa Network: POB 91313, Auckland Park 2006; tel. (11) 7142255; fax (11) 7142072; e-mail molotod@sabc.co.za; internet www.channelafrica.org; f. 1966; external service of SABC; broadcasts 217 hours per week in English, French, Portuguese, Kiswahili, Chinyanja and Silozi; Gen. Man. DAVID MOLOTO.

Classic FM: Jorissen Place, 6th Floor, 66 Jorissen St, Braamfontein; POB 782, Auckland Park 2006; tel. (11) 4031027; fax (11) 4035451; e-mail info@classicfm.co.za; internet www.classicfm.co.za.

East Coast Radio: Durban; tel. (31) 5709495; fax (86) 6794951; e-mail news@ecr.co.za; internet www.ecr.co.za.

94.7 Highveld Stereo: Primedia Place, 5 Gwen Lane, cnr Gwen Lane and Fredman Dr., Sandown, Gauteng; POB 3438, Rivonia 2128; tel. (11) 5063947; fax (11) 5063393; e-mail comments@highveld.co.za; internet www.highveld.co.za.

Jacaranda 94.2: 1 Samrand Ave, Kosmosdal, POB 11961, Centurion 0046; tel. 800609942; e-mail enquiries@jacarandafm.com; internet www.jacarandafm.com.

Kaya FM 95.9: 1 Central Pl., 30 Jeppe St, Newtown, Johannesburg; POB 434, Newtown 2113; tel. (11) 6349500; fax (11) 6349574; e-mail pr@kayafm.co.za; internet www.kayafm.co.za; f. 1997.

Talk Radio 702: Primedia House, 2nd Floor, 5 Gwen Lane, Sandown, Sandton; POB 5572, Rivonia 2128; tel. (11) 5063702; e-mail 702webmaster@702.co.za; internet www.702.co.za.

YFM 99.2: Albury Rd, Dunkeld Cres., South West Blocks, Dunkeld West, Ext 8, Sandton 2196; tel. (11) 2807070; fax (11) 2807556; e-mail webmaster@yfm.co.za; internet www.yworld.co.za; f. 1997; Man. Dir and CEO KANTHAN PILLAY.

Television

In February 2007 the Government announced that the country would begin digital terrestrial broadcasting in November 2008 and that the country's analogue signal would be switched off by December 2013.

e.tv: 5 Summit Rd, Hyde Park, Johannesburg 2196; Private Bag, X9944, Sandton 2146; tel. (11) 5379300; e-mail info@etv.co.za; internet www.etv.co.za; f. 1998; CEO MARCEL GOLDING.

Naspers: 40 Heerengracht, Cape Town 8001; tel. (21) 4062121; e-mail GKGreen@multichoice.co.za; internet www.naspers.co.za; provides subscription television through Multichoice, M-Net and SuperSport packages; Chief Executive KOOS BEKKER.

South African Broadcasting Corpn (SABC)—Television: Private Bag X41, Auckland Park 2006; tel. (11) 7149111; fax (11) 7145055; e-mail enterpri@sabc.co.za; internet www.sabc.co.za; transmissions began in 1976; broadcasts television services in 11 languages over three channels; SABC1 broadcasts in English, isiZulu, isiXhosa, isiNdebele and siSwati; SABC2 broadcasts in English, Afrikaans, Sesotho, Setswana, Sepedi, Xitsonga and Tshivendi; SABC3 broadcasts documentaries, educational programmes and sport in English; Chair. Dr BEN NGUBANE; CEO SOLLY MOKOETLE.

Finance

(cap. = capital; auth. = authorized; res = reserves; dep. = deposits; m. = million; brs = branches; amounts in rand)

BANKING

In early 2011 the South African banking sector comprised 19 registered banks, two mutual banks, 13 local branches of foreign banks and 41 foreign banks with approved local representative offices. The five largest banks—Standard Bank, Nedbank, ABSA, FirstRand and Investec—controlled some 90% of total banking assets.

Central Bank

South African Reserve Bank: 370 Church St, POB 427, Pretoria 0002; tel. (12) 3133911; fax (12) 3133197; e-mail info@resbank.co.za; internet www.reservebank.co.za; f. 1921; cap. 2.0m., res 9,875.2m., dep. 181,196.5m. (March 2010); Gov. GILL MARCUS; Sen. Dep. Gov. X. P. GUMA; 7 brs.

Commercial Banks

ABSA Bank Ltd: ABSA Towers East, 3rd Floor, 170 Main St, Johannesburg 2001; POB 7735, Johannesburg 2000; tel. (11) 3504000; fax (11) 3504009; e-mail absa@absa.co.za; internet www.absa.co.za; subsidiary of Barclays Bank PLC; cap. 303m., res 17,675m., dep. 597,772m. (Dec. 2009); Chair. GARTH GRIFFIN; Group Chief Exec. MARIA RAMOS; 726 brs.

African Bank Ltd: 59 16th Rd, Private Bag X170, Midrand 1685; tel. (11) 2569000; fax (11) 2569217; e-mail ymistry@africanbank.co.za; internet www.africanbank.co.za; f. 1975; owned by African Bank Investments Ltd; cap. 121m., res 3,096m., dep. 16,794m. (Sept. 2009); CEO LEONIDAS KIRKINIS; 268 brs.

Albaraka Bank Ltd: 2 Kingsmead Blvd, Kingsmead Office Park, Stalwart Simelane St, Durban 4001; POB 4395, Durban 4000; tel. (31) 3649000; fax (31) 3649001; e-mail marketing@albaraka.co.za; internet www.albaraka.co.za; f. 1989; operates according to Islamic principles; cap. 150.0m., dep. 1,624.2m., total assets 1,870.7m. (Dec. 2008); Chair. ADNAN AHMED YOUSIF; CEO SHABIR CHOHAN.

Capitec Bank: 1 Quantum St, Techno Park, Stellenbosch 7600; tel. (21) 8095900; e-mail clientcare@capitecbank.co.za; internet www.capitecbank.co.za; f. 2001; Chair. MICHIEL SCHOLTZ DU PRÉ LE ROUX; CEO RIAAN STASSEN.

Bidvest Bank Ltd: Rennie House, 11th Floor, 19 Ameshoff St, Braamfontein 2001, Johannesburg; POB 185, Johannesburg 2000; tel. (11) 4073000; fax (11) 4073322; e-mail letstalk@bidvestbank.co.za; internet www.bidvestbank.co.za; f. 1850 as Rennies Bank Ltd; renamed as above in 2007; subsidiary of Bidvest Group Ltd; foreign exchange, trade finance and related activities; cap. 1.8m., res 603.1m., dep. 873.8m. (June 2009); Chair. J. L. PAMENSKY; Man. Dir A. C. SALOMON; over 60 brs.

FirstRand Bank Ltd: 4th Floor, 4 First Place, cnr Fredman Dr. and Rivonia Rd, Bank City, Sandton 2196; POB 786273, Sandton 2146;

SOUTH AFRICA

tel. (11) 2821808; fax (11) 2828088; e-mail information@firstrand.co.za; internet www.firstrand.co.za; f. 1971 as First National Bank of Southern Africa; merged with Rand Bank in 1998; cap. 4m., res 13,965m., dep. 496,512m. (June 2010); CEO SIZWE NXASANA; 600 brs.

GBS Mutual Bank: 18–20 Hill St, Grahamstown 6139; POB 114, Grahamstown 6140; tel. (46) 6227109; fax (46) 6228855; e-mail gbs@gbsbank.co.za; internet www.gbsbank.co.za; f. 1877; total assets 659.0m. (Mar. 2003); Chair. T. C. S. TAGG; CEO A. M. VORSTER; 4 brs.

Habib Overseas Bank Ltd: N77 Oriental Plaza, Fordsburg, Johannesburg 2092; POB 62369, Marshalltown, Johannesburg 2107; tel. (11) 8347441; fax (11) 8347446; e-mail habib@global.co.za; internet www.habiboverseas.co.za; f. 1992; cap. 20m., dep. 691m., total assets US $102m. (Dec. 2009); Chair. HABIB MOHAMED D. HABIB; 5 brs.

HBZ Bank Ltd: 135 Jan Hofmeyr Rd, Westville, Durban 3631; POB 1536, Wandsbeck 3631; tel. (31) 2674400; fax (31) 2671193; e-mail sazone@hbzbank.co.za; internet www.hbzbank.co.za; f. 1995; subsidiary of Habib Bank Ltd; cap. 10.0m., res 141.9m., dep. 1,746.1m. (Dec. 2009); Chair. MUHAMMAD HABIB; CEO ZAFAR ALAM KHAN; 6 brs.

Mercantile Bank Ltd: Mercantile Lisbon House, 142 West St, Sandown 2196; POB 782699, Sandton 2146; tel. (11) 3020300; fax (11) 3020700; internet www.mercantile.co.za; f. 1965; subsidiary of Mercantile Lisbon Bank Holdings; cap. 1,483.3m., res 74.2m., dep. 4,265.0m. (Dec. 2009); Chair. Dr JOAQUIM A. S. DE ANDRADE CAMPOS; CEO D. J. BROWN; 14 brs.

Nedbank Ltd: 135 Rivonia Rd, Sandown 2196, Johannesburg 2001; tel. (11) 2944444; fax (11) 2950999; e-mail Gawien@nedbank.co.za; internet www.nedbankgroup.co.za; f. 1988; name changed from Nedcor Bank Ltd Nov. 2002; subsidiary of Nedbank Group Ltd; cap. 5,397m., res 32,596m., dep. 476,698m. (Dec. 2009); Chair. REUEL J. KHOZA; CEO MIKE BROWN; 472 brs.

South African Bank of Athens Ltd: Bank of Athens Bldg, 116 Marshall St, Johannesburg 2001; POB 7781, Johannesburg 2000; tel. (11) 6344300; fax (11) 8381001; e-mail info@bankofathens.co.za; internet www.bankofathens.co.za; f. 1947; 99.51% owned by National Bank of Greece; cap. 13.9m., res 166.5m., dep. 1,058.1m. (Dec. 2009); Chair. A. LEOPOULOS; CEO HECTOR ZARCA; 11 brs.

The Standard Bank of South Africa Ltd: Standard Bank Centre, 5 Simmonds St, Johannesburg 2001; POB 7725, Johannesburg 2000; tel. (11) 2994701; fax (11) 6364207; e-mail information@standardbank.co.za; internet www.standardbank.co.za; f. 1862; cap. 60m., res 43,147m., dep. 696,805m. (Dec. 2009); Chair. DEREK E. COOPER; CEO J. H. MAREE; 1,000 brs.

Ubank Ltd: Sanhill Park, 1 Eglin Rd, Sunninghill; Private Bag X101, Sunninghill 2157; tel. (11) 5185000; fax (86) 5457966; e-mail corpcomm@tebabank.com; internet www.tebabank.co.za; f. 2000; fmrly Teba Bank Ltd, name changed as above in 2010; specializes in microfinance and providing financial services to mining communities; total assets 2,639m. (Feb. 2008); Chair. AYANDA MJEKULA; CEO MARK WILLIAMS; 90 brs, 29 agencies.

Merchant Bank

Grindrod Bank Ltd: 1st Floor North, 20 Kingsmead Blvd, Kingsmead Office Park, Durban 4001; POB 3211, Durban 4001; tel. (31) 3336600; fax (31) 5710505; internet www.grindrodbank.co.za; f. 1994; present name adopted 2006; Man. Dir DAVID POLKINGHORNE.

Investment Banks

Cadiz Holdings: Fernwood House, 1st Floor, The Oval, 1 Oakdale Rd, Newlands 7700; POB 44547, Claremont 7735; tel. 6578300; fax 6578301; e-mail reception@cadiz.co.za; internet www.cadiz.co.za; f. 1993; 15% owned by Investec, 11% by Makana Financial Services; total assets 298.1m. (Dec. 2003); Chair. RAY CADIZ; CEO RAM BARKAI.

Investec Bank Ltd: 100 Grayston Dr., Sandown, Sandton 2196; POB 785700, Sandton 2146; tel. (11) 2867000; fax (11) 2867777; e-mail investorrelations@investec.com; internet www.investec.com; f. 1974; cap. 25m., res 16,400m., dep. 143,000m. (Mar. 2010); CEO S. KOSEFF; 6 brs.

Sasfin Bank Ltd: 29 Scott St, Waverley 2090; POB 95104, Grant Park 2051; tel. (11) 8097500; fax (11) 8872489; e-mail info@sasfin.com; internet www.sasfin.com; f. 1951; subsidiary of Sasfin Holdings Ltd; cap. 1.7m., res 383.5m., dep. 925.1m. (June 2009); Chair. MARTIN GLATT; CEO ROLAND SASSOON.

Development Bank

Development Bank of Southern Africa (DBSA): 1258 Lever Rd, Headway Hill; POB 1234, Halfway House, Midrand 1685; tel. (11) 3133911; fax (11) 3133086; e-mail info@dbsa.org; internet www.dbsa.org; total assets 23,684.5m. (March 2004); f. 1983; Chair. JABU MOLEKETI; CEO PAUL BALOYI.

Bankers' Association

Banking Association South Africa: Sunnyside Office Park, Bldg D, 3rd Floor, 32 Princess of Wales Terrace, Parktown 2193; tel. (11) 6456700; fax (11) 6456800; e-mail webmaster@banking.org.za; internet www.banking.org.za; f. 1993; fmrly Banking Council of South Africa; name changed as above in 2005; 15,000 mems; Chair. STEPHEN KOSEFF; Man. Dir CASSIM COOVADIA.

STOCK EXCHANGE

JSE Ltd: One Exchange Sq., 2 Gwen Lane, Sandown, Sandton; Private Bag X991174, Sandton 2146; tel. (11) 5207000; fax (11) 5208584; e-mail info@jse.co.za; internet www.jse.co.za; f. 1887 as Johannesburg Stock Exchange; present name adopted in 2005; in late 1995 legislation was enacted providing for the deregulation of the Stock Exchange; automated trading commenced in June 1996; demutualized in July 2005 and became a listed co in June 2006; CEO R. M. LOUBSER.

INSURANCE

In 2010 South Africa was served by 100 short-term and 81 long-term insurers, and 13 reinsurance firms.

Allianz Insurance Ltd: 40 Ashford Rd, Parkwood, Johannesburg 2001; POB 62228, Marshalltown 2107; tel. (11) 4421111; fax (11) 4421125; e-mail baini@allianz.co.za; internet www.allianz.co.za; Chair. D. DU PREEZ; Man. Dir IAN BAIN.

Clientèle Life Assurance Co: Clientèle House, Morning View Office Park, cnr Rivonia and Alon Rds, Morningside, Johannesburg; POB 1316, Rivonia 2128; tel. (11) 3203333; e-mail services@clientelelife.com; internet www.clientelelife.com; f. 1997; subsidiary of Hollard Insurance Group; Chair. GAVIN ROUTLEDGE; Man. Dir BASIL WILLIAM REEKIE.

Credit Guarantee Insurance Corpn of Africa Ltd: 31 Dover St, POB 125, Randburg 2125; tel. (11) 8897000; fax (11) 8861027; e-mail info@cgic.co.za; internet www.creditguarantee.co.za; f. 1956; Chair. PETER TODD; Man. Dir MIKE C. TRUTER.

Discovery: 16 Fredman Dr., Sandton 2146; POB 784262, Sandton 2146; tel. (11) 5292888; fax (11) 5293590; e-mail worldinfo@discovery.co.za; internet www.discoveryworld.co.za; f. 1992; 64% owned by FirstRand; health and life assurance; Chair. MONTY HILKOWITZ; CEO ADRIAN GORE.

Liberty Life: Liberty Life Centre, 1 Ameshoff St, Braamfontein, Johannesburg 2001; POB 10499, Johannesburg 2000; tel. (11) 4083911; fax (11) 4082109; e-mail info@liberty.co.za; internet www.liberty.co.za; f. 1958; Chair. SAKI MACOZOMA; CEO BRUCE HEMPHILL.

Old Mutual (South African Mutual Life Assurance Society): Mutualpark, Jan Smuts Dr., POB 66, Cape Town 8001; tel. (21) 5099111; fax (21) 5094444; e-mail contact@oldmutual.com; internet www.oldmutual.com; f. 1845; Chair. MICHAEL J. LEVETT; CEO JAMES SUTCLIFFE.

Regent Insurance Co Ltd: 146 Boeing Rd East, Elma Park, POB 674, Edenvale 1609; tel. (11) 8795000; fax (11) 4539533; e-mail email@bob.co.za; internet www.regent.co.za; f. 1989; 100% owned by Imperial Holdings; Gen. Man. JONO SOAMES.

Santam Ltd: Santam Head Office, 1 Sportica Cres., Bellville 7530; POB 3881, Tyger Valley 7536; tel. (21) 9157000; fax (21) 9140700; e-mail info@santam.co.za; internet www.santam.co.za; f. 1918; Chair. D. K. SMITH; CEO IAN KIRK.

South African National Life Assurance Co Ltd (SANLAM): 2 Strand Rd, Bellville; POB 1, Sanlamhof 7532; tel. (21) 9479111; fax (21) 9479440; e-mail life@sanlam.co.za; internet www.sanlam.co.za; f. 1918; Chair. Dr J. VAN ZYL.

Zurich Insurance Co South Africa Ltd: 70 Fox St, Johannesburg 2001; tel. (11) 3709111; fax (11) 8368018; e-mail info@insurance.za.org; internet www.saeagle.co.za; fmrly South African Eagle Insurance Co Ltd; rebranded as above in 2007; Chair. M. C. SOUTH; CEO N. V. BEYERS.

Association

South African Insurance Association (SAIA): JCC House, 3rd Floor, 27 Owl St, Milpark; POB 30619, Braamfontein 2017; tel. (11) 7265200; fax (11) 7265351; e-mail adele@saia.co.za; internet www.saia.co.za; f. 1973; represents short-term insurers; Chair. RONNIE NAPIER; CEO BARRY SCOTT.

Trade and Industry

GOVERNMENT AGENCIES

National Empowerment Fund: West Block, 187 Rivonia Rd, Morningside 2057; POB 31, Melrose Arch, Melrose North 2076;

SOUTH AFRICA

tel. (11) 3058000; fax (11) 3058001; e-mail info@nefcorp.co.za; internet www.nefcorp.co.za; f. 1998; CEO Philisiwe Buthelezi.

Small Enterprise Development Agency (SEDA): DTI Campus, Block G, 77 Meintjies St, Sunnyside, POB 56714, Pretoria; tel. (12) 4411000; e-mail info@seda.org.za; internet www.seda.org.za; f. 2004; CEO Hlonela Nelisa Lupuwana.

DEVELOPMENT ORGANIZATIONS

Business Partners Ltd: 37 West St, Houghton Estate, Johannesburg 2198; POB 7780, Johannesburg 2000; tel. (11) 7136600; fax (11) 7136650; e-mail enquiries@businesspartners.co.za; internet www.businesspartners.co.za; f. 1981 as Small Business Devt Corpn; invests in, and provides services to, small and medium-sized enterprises; Chair. Johann Rupert; Man. Dir Nazeem Martin.

Independent Development Trust: Glenwood Office Park, cnr Oberon and Sprite Sts, Faerie Glen, Pretoria; POB 73000, Lynnwood Ridge 0043; tel. (12) 8452000; fax (12) 3480894; e-mail info@idt.org.za; internet www.idt.org.za; f. 1990; advances the national devt programme working with govt and communities in fields incl. poverty relief, infrastructure, empowerment, employment and capacity building; CEO Thembi Nwedamustwu.

Industrial Development Corpn of South Africa Ltd (IDC): 19 Fredman Dr., Sandown 2196; POB 784055, Sandton 2146; tel. (11) 2693000; fax (11) 2693116; e-mail callcentre@idc.co.za; internet www.idc.co.za; f. 1940; promotes entrepreneurship and competitiveness; total assets 90,421m. (March 2008); Chair. Dr Wendy Y. N. Luhabe; CEO G. M. Qhena.

Productivity SA: Private Bag 235, Midrand 1685; tel. (11) 8485300; fax (11) 8485555; e-mail info@productivitysa.co.za; internet www.productivitysa.co.za; f. 1968; Chair. Dr J. M. Laubscher (acting); Exec. Dir Dr Bongani Coka (acting).

CHAMBERS OF COMMERCE

Bloemfontein Chamber of Commerce and Industry: 1st Floor, Tourism Centre, 30 Park Rd, Bloemfontein; POB 87, Bloemfontein 9301; tel. (51) 4473369; fax (51) 4475064; internet www.bcci.co.za; f. 2004; Pres. Nancy de Sousa; c. 550 mems (2010).

Cape Town Regional Chamber of Commerce and Industry: Cape Chamber House, 19 Louis Gradner St, Foreshore, Cape Town 8001; tel. (21) 4024300; fax (21) 4024302; e-mail info@capechamber.co.za; internet www.capechamber.co.za; f. 1804; Pres. Jeremy Wiley; 4,632 mems.

Chamber of Commerce and Industry–Johannesburg: JCC House, 6th Floor, 27 Owl St, cnr Empire Rd, Milpark; Private Bag 34, Auckland Park 2006; tel. (11) 7265300; fax (11) 4822000; e-mail info@jcci.co.za; internet www.jcci.co.za; f. 1890; CEO Keith Brebnor; 3,800 mems.

Durban Chamber of Commerce and Industry: Chamber House, 190 Stanger St, POB 1506, Durban 4000; tel. (31) 3351000; fax (31) 3321288; e-mail chamber@durbanchamber.co.za; internet www.durbanchamber.co.za; CEO Gugu Mazibuko; 3,500 mems.

Gauteng North Chamber of Commerce and Industry (GNCCI): Tshwane Events Centre, Soutter St, Pretoria; POB 2164, Pretoria 0001; tel. (12) 3271487; fax (12) 3271490; internet www.gncci.co.za; f. 1929; fmrly Pretoria Business and Agricultural Centre; merged with Pretoria Sakekamer in 2004; Chair. Bert Badenhorst; CEO Wim du Plessis; over 900 mems.

Pietermaritzburg Chamber of Business (PCB): POB 11734, Dorpspruit, Pietermaritzburg 3206; tel. (33) 3452747; fax (33) 3944151; e-mail pcb@pcb.org.za; internet www.pcb.org.za; f. 2002 as successor to the Pietermaritzburg Chamber of Commerce and Industries (f. 1910); CEO Andrew Layman; 880 mems.

Port Elizabeth Regional Chamber of Commerce and Industry (PERCCI): 200 Norvic Dr., Greenacres, Port Elizabeth 6045; KPMG House, POB 63866, Greenacres 6057; tel. (41) 3731122; fax (41) 3731142; e-mail info@pechamber.org.za; internet www.percci.co.za; f. 1994; Pres. Siya Mhlaluka; 814 mems.

South African Chamber of Commerce and Industry (SACCI): 24 Sturdee Ave, Rosebank, Johannesburg 2196; POB 213, Saxonwold 2132; tel. (11) 4463800; fax (11) 4463850; e-mail info@sacci.org.za; internet www.sacci.org.za; f. 1990 by merger of Asscn of Chambers of Commerce and Industry and South African Federated Chamber of Industries; fmrly known as South African Chamber of Business; Pres. Prof. Alwyn Louw; CEO Neren Rau.

Wesvaal Chamber of Business (WESCOB): POB 7167, Flamwood 2572; tel. (18) 4627109; fax (86) 6936365; e-mail chamber@gds.co.za; internet www.wesvaalchamber.co.za; f. 1898; Pres. Johan Smit; c. 100 mems.

INDUSTRIAL AND TRADE ORGANIZATIONS

Association of Cementitious Material Producers (ACMP): POB 168, Halfway House 1685; tel. (11) 2073037; fax (12) (11) 3150315; e-mail naudek.acmp@mweb.co.za; internet www.acmp.co.za; f. 2002; Exec. Dir Dhiraj B. K. Rama.

Cape Wools: Wool House, 18 Grahamstown Rd, North End, Port Elizabeth 6001; POB 2191, Port Elizabeth 6056; tel. (41) 544301; fax (41) 546760; e-mail capewool@capewools.co.za; internet www.capewools.co.za; f. 1997; Section 21 service company; seven mems: three appointed by wool producer orgs, two by the Wool Textile Council, one by Wool Brokers and Traders and one by Labour; Chair. Geoff Kingwill; Gen. Man. André Strydom.

Chamber of Mines of South Africa: Chamber of Mines Bldg, 5 Hollard St, POB 61809, Marshalltown 2107; tel. (11) 4987100; fax (11) 8341884; e-mail webmaster@bullion.org.za; internet www.bullion.org.za; f. 1889; Pres. Dr Xolani Humphrey Mkhwanazi; CEO Bheki Sibiya.

Clothing Trade Council (CloTrade): 35 Siemers Rd, 6th Floor, Doornfontein; POB 2303, Johannesburg 2000; tel. (11) 4020664; fax (11) 4020667; f. 2002; successor to the Clothing Fed. of South Africa; Pres. Jack Kipling.

Grain Milling Federation: Embankment Park, 194 Kwikkie Cres., Centurion 0046; POB 7262, Centurion 0046; tel. (12) 6631660; fax (12) 6633109; e-mail gmf@grainmilling.org.za; internet www.grainmilling.org.za; f. 1944; Exec. Dir Jannie de Villiers.

Master Builders South Africa (MBSA): POB 1619, Halfway House, Midrand 1685; tel. (11) 2059000; fax (11) 3151644; e-mail info@mbsa.org.za; internet www.mbsa.org.za; f. 1904; fmrly known as Building Industries Fed. South Africa; President Jean-Marie Talbot; CEO Pierre Fourie; 4,000 mems.

Master Diamond Cutters' Association of South Africa: Private Bag X1, Suite 105, Excom 2023; tel. (11) 3341930; fax (11) 3341933; e-mail info@masingita.co.za; f. 1928; Pres. MacDonald Temane; 76 mems.

National Association of Automobile Manufacturers of South Africa: Nedbank Plaza, 1st Floor, cnr Church and Beatrix Sts, Pretoria 0002; POB 40611, Arcadia 0007; tel. (12) 3232980; fax (12) 3263232; e-mail naamsa@iafrica.com; internet www.naamsa.co.za; f. 1935; Dir N. M. W. Vermeulen; 19 full mems and 21 assoc. mems.

National Chamber of Milling, Inc: POB 7262, Centurion 0046; tel. (12) 6631660; fax (12) 6633109; e-mail info@grainmilling.org.za; internet www.grainmilling.org.za; f. 1936; Exec. Dir Jannie de Villiers.

National Textile Manufacturers' Association: POB 81, New Germany 3620; tel. (31) 7104410; fax (31) 7056257; f. 1947; Sec. Peter McGregor; 9 mems.

Plastics Federation of South Africa: 18 Gazelle Rd, Corporate Park South, Old Pretoria Rd, Midrand; Private Bag X68, Halfway House, Midrand 1685; tel. (11) 3144021; fax (11) 3143764; internet www.plasticsinfo.co.za; f. 1979; Exec. Dir David Hughes; 10 mems.

Printing Industries Federation of South Africa (PIFSA): Block D, The Braids, 113 Bowling Ave, Gallo Manor 2191; POB 1396, Gallo Manor 2052; tel. (11) 2871160; fax (11) 2871179; e-mail pifsa@pifsa.org; internet www.pifsa.org; f. 1916; CEO Patrick Lacy; c. 820 mems (representing 65% of printers in South Africa); six additional regional brs.

Retail Motor Industry Organization (RMI): POB 2940, Randburg 2125; tel. (11) 8866300; fax (11) 7894525; e-mail rmi@rmi.org.za; internet www.rmi.org.za; f. 1908; affiliates throughout southern Africa; CEO Jeff Osborne; 7,400 mems.

South African Dairy Foundation: POB 72300, Lynnwood Ridge, Pretoria 0040; tel. (12) 3485345; fax (12) 3486284; e-mail dairy-foundation@pixie.co.za; f. 1980; Sec. S. L. van Coller; 59 mems.

South African Federation of Civil Engineering Contractors (SAFCEC): 12 Skeen Blvd, POB 644, Bedfordview 2008; tel. (11) 4090900; fax (11) 4501715; e-mail admin@safcec.org.za; internet www.safcec.org.za; f. 1939; Exec. Dir H. P. Langenhoven; 300 mems.

South African Fruit and Vegetable Canners' Association (Pty) Ltd (SAFVCA): Hoofstraat 258 Main St, POB 6175, Paarl 7620; tel. (21) 8711308; fax (21) 8725930; e-mail info@safvca.co.za; internet www.safvca.co.za; f. 1953; Gen. Man. Jill Atwood-Palm; 9 mems.

South African Inshore Fishing Industry Association (Pty) Ltd: POB 2066, Cape Town 8000; tel. (21) 4252727; e-mail safish@new.co.za; f. 1953; Chair. W. A. Lewis; Man. S. J. Malherbe; 4 mems.

South African Oil Expressers' Association: Cereal Centre, 6th Floor, 11 Leyds St, Braamfontein 2017; tel. (11) 7251280; f. 1937; Sec. Dr R. du Toit; 14 mems.

South African Paint Manufacturers' Association: POB 751605, Gardenview, Johannesburg 2047; tel. (11) 4552503; e-mail sapma@sapma.org.za; internet www.sapma.org.za; Chair. Terry Ashmore; 100 mems.

South African Petroleum Industry Association (SAPIA): ABSA Centre, 14th Floor, Adderley St, Cape Town 8001; POB

7082, Roggebai 8012; tel. (21) 4198054; fax (21) 4198058; internet www.sapia.co.za; f. 1994; represents South Africa's six principal petroleum cos; Chair. JAMES SEUTLOADI; Dir AVHAPFANI TSHIFULARO.

South African Sugar Association (SASA): 170 Flanders Dr., POB 700, Mount Edgecombe 4300; tel. (31) 5087000; fax (31) 5087199; internet www.sugar.org.za; Exec. Dir M. K. TRIKAM.

Includes:

South African Sugar Millers' Association Ltd (SASMAL): POB 1000, Mt Edgecombe 4300; tel. (31) 5087300; fax (31) 5087310; e-mail sasmal@sasa.org.za; represents interests of sugar millers and refiners within the operations of SASA; Exec. Dir D. W. HARDY; 6 mem. cos.

Sugar Manufacturing and Refining Employers' Association (SMREA): POB 1000, Mount Edgecombe 4300; tel. (31) 5087300; fax (31) 5087310; e-mail sasmal@sasa.org.za; f. 1947; regulates relations between mems and their employees; participates in the Bargaining Council for the sugar manufacturing and refining industry; Chair. B. V. LANE; 6 mem. cos.

South African Wool Textile Council: POB 2201, North End, Port Elizabeth 6056; tel. (41) 4845252; fax (41) 4845629; Sec. BEATTY-ANNE STARKEY.

Steel and Engineering Industries Federation of South Africa (SEIFSA): 42 Anderson St, POB 1338, Johannesburg 2000; tel. (11) 2989400; fax (11) 2989500; e-mail info@seifsa.co.za; internet www.seifsa.co.za; f. 1943; Exec. Dir BRIAN ANGUS; 38 affiliated trade asscns representing 2,350 mems.

VinPro (SA): POB 1411, Suider-Paarl 7624; tel. (21) 8073322; fax (21) 8632079; e-mail info@vinpro.co.za; internet www.vinpro.co.za; f. 1979; represents wine producers; Chair. ABRIE BOTHA; Exec. Dir JOS LE ROUX.

UTILITIES
Electricity

Electricity Supply Commission (ESKOM): POB 1091, Johannesburg 2000; tel. (11) 8008111; fax (11) 8004390; e-mail PAIA@eskom.co.za; internet www.eskom.co.za; f. 1923; state-controlled; Chair. and CEO MPHO MAKWANA (acting).

Gas

SASOL Gas: POB 4211, Randburg 2125; tel. (11) 8897600; fax (11) 8897955; e-mail gascustomercare@sasol.com; internet www.sasol.com; f. 1964; Man. Dir HANS NAUDÉ.

Water

Umgeni Water: 310 Burger St, Pietermaritzburg 3201; POB 9, Pietermaritzburg 3200; tel. (331) 3411111; fax (331) 3411167; e-mail info@umgeni.co.za; internet www.umgeni.co.za; f. 1974; CEO MZIMKULU MSIWA.

Water Research Commission: Private Bag X03, Gezina 0031; tel. (12) 3300340; fax (12) 3312565; e-mail orders@wrc.org.za; internet www.wrc.org.za; Chair. Prof. J. B. ADAMS; CEO Dr RIVKA KFIR.

TRADE UNIONS

According to COSATU, some 40% of workers were unionized at March 2005. Under amendments to the Labour Relations Act (LRA), 1995, introduced in 2002, the Government sought to eliminate illegitimate trade unions and employers' organizations. The provisions of the LRA also stipulated that organizations that failed to provide annual audited financial accounts would be deregistered.

Trade Union Federations

Confederation of South African Workers' Unions (CONSAWU): 21 Adriana Cres., Gateway Industrial Park, Rooishuiskraal X25, Centurion; tel. (12) 6614265; fax (12) 6611793; e-mail consawu@mweb.co.za; internet www.consawu.co.za; f. 2003; Pres. JOEL MFINGWANA; Gen. Sec. KHULILE NKUSHUBANA; 290,000 mems (2007).

Affiliates with 20,000 or more mems include:

National Union of Public Service and Allied Workers (NUPSAW): NUPSAW House, 814 Church St, Eastwood, Pretoria; POB 11459, Tramshed 0126; tel. (12) 3421674; fax (86) 6724354; e-mail generalsecretary@nupsaw.co.za; internet www.nupsaw.co.za; f. 1998; Pres. EZRA MFINGWANA; Gen. Sec. SUCCESS MATAITSANE; c. 42,000 (2005).

Other organizations affiliated to CONSAWU include: the Asscn of Metal, Iron and General Workers' Union; the Asscn Trade Union of South African Workers; the Brick and General Workers' Union; Building, Wood and Allied Workers' Union of South Africa; the Building Workers' Union; the Food and Gen. Workers' Union; the Commercial Workers' Union of South Africa; the Food, Cleaning and Security Workers' Union; the Fed. Council of Retail and Allied Workers; the Hotel and Allied Restaurant Workers' Union; the Movement for Social Justice; the Nat. Certified Fishing and Allied Workers' Union; the Nat. Construction, Building and Allied Workers' Union; the Nat. Union of Tertiary Education of South Africa; the Professional Educators' Union; the Professional Employees' Trade Union of South Africa; the Progressive Gen. Employees' Asscn of South Africa; the Progressive Trade Union of South Africa; Solidarity; the South African Building and Allied Workers' Org.; the South African Domestic and Gen. Workers' Union; the South African Food, Retail and Agricultural Workers' Union; the Transport Action, Retail and Gen. Workers' Union; the Trawler and Line Fishermen's Union; the Westcoast Workers' Union; and the Workers' Labour Council–South Africa.

Congress of South African Trade Unions (COSATU): COSATU House, 4th Floor, 1–5 Leyds St, Braamfontein; POB 1019, Johannesburg 2000; tel. (11) 3394911; fax (11) 3396940; e-mail patrick@cosatu.org.za; internet www.cosatu.org.za; f. 1985; 21 trade union affiliates representing c. 1.8m. paid-up mems; Pres. SDUMO DLAMINI; Gen. Sec. ZWELINZIMA VAVI.

Affiliates with 20,000 or more mems include:

Chemical, Energy, Paper, Printing, Wood and Allied Workers' Union (CEPPWAWU): Umoya House, 3rd Floor, 2–6 New St, South Ghandi Sq., Johannesburg 2001; POB 3219, Johannesburg 2000; tel. (11) 8332870; fax (11) 8332883; e-mail secretariat@ceppwawu.org.za; internet www.ceppwawu.org; f. 1999 by merger of the Chemical Workers' Industrial Union and Paper, Printing, Wood and the Allied Workers' Union; represents workers in the petrochemical, consumer chemical, rubber, plastics, glass and ceramics, printing, pulp and paper, furniture and woodworking industries; Pres. JACOB MABENA; Gen. Sec. SIMON MOFOKENG; Nat. Treas. LEMMY MOKOENA; 61,768 mems (2006).

Communication Workers' Union (CWU): 29 Rissik St, 3rd Floor, Johannesburg 2001; POB 10248, Johannesburg 2000; tel. (11) 8384848; fax (11) 8385962; e-mail membership@cwu.org.za; internet www.cwu.org.za; f. 1996 by merger of the Post Office Employees' Asscn, the Post and Telecommunication Workers' Asscn and the South African Post Telecommunication Employees' Asscn; Pres. JOE CHAUKE; Gen. Sec. GALLANT ROBERTS; 44,000 mems (2006).

Democratic Nursing Organisation of South Africa (DENOSA): 605 Church St, Pretoria 0001; POB 1280, Pretoria 0001; tel. (12) 3432315; fax (12) 3440750; e-mail info@denosa.org.za; internet www.denosa.org.za; f. 1996; Pres. DOROTHY MATEBENI; Gen. Sec. THEMBEKA T. GWAGWA; 64,165 mems (2006).

Food and Allied Workers' Union (FAWU): Vuyisile Mini Centre, cnr NY1 and NY110, Guguletu, Cape Town; POB 1234, Woodstock 7915; tel. (21) 6379040; fax (21) 6379190; e-mail admin@fawu.org.za; internet www.fawu.org.za; Pres. ATWELL NAZO; Gen. Sec. KATISHI MASEMOLA; 111,029 mems (2006).

National Education, Health and Allied Workers' Union (NEHAWU): 56 Marshall St, Marshalltown, Johannesburg; POB 10812, Johannesburg 2001; tel. (11) 8332902; fax (11) 8330757; e-mail bongi@nehawu.org.za; internet www.nehawu.org.za; f. 1987; Pres. MZWANDILE MICHAEL MAKWAYIBA; Gen. Sec. FIKILE MAJOLA; 192,739 mems (2006).

National Union of Metalworkers of South Africa (NUMSA): NUMSA Bldg, 153 Bree St, cnr Becker St, Newtown, Johannesburg 2001; POB 260483, Excom 2023; tel. (11) 6891700; fax (11) 8336408; e-mail mziwakheh@numsa.org.za; internet www.numsa.org.za; represents workers in the engineering, motor, tyre, rubber and automobile assembly industries; Pres. CEDRIC SABELO GINATOM; Gen. Sec. IRVIN JIM; 216,808 mems (2006).

National Union of Mineworkers (NUM): 7 Rissik St, cnr Frederick St, Johannesburg 2000; POB 2424, Johannesburg 2000; tel. (11) 3772000; fax (11) 8360367; e-mail Tmlabatheki@num.org.za; internet www.num.org.za; f. 1982; represents workers in the mining, energy, construction, building material manufacturing, civil engineering and building industries; Pres. SENZENI ZOKWANA; Gen. Sec. FRANS BALENI; 262,042 mems (2006).

Police and Prisons Civil Rights Union (POPCRU): 1 Marie Rd, Auckland Park 0183; tel. 861403040; fax (11) 7268834; e-mail gs@popcru.org.za; internet www.popcru.org.za; Pres. ZIZAMELE CEBEKHULU; Gen. Sec. NKOSINATHI THELEDI; 95,864 mems (2006).

SASBO: The Finance Union: SASBO House, Fourmall Office Park West, Roos St, Fourways, Johannesburg; Private Bag X84, Bryanston 2021; tel. (11) 4670192; fax (11) 4670188; e-mail michelek@sasbo.org.za; internet www.sasbo.org.za; f. 1916 as the South African Soc. of Bank Officials; Gen. Sec. SHAUN OELSCHIG; 67,500 mems (2010).

Southern African Clothing and Textile Workers' Union (SACTWU): Industria House, 350 Victoria Rd, Salt River, Cape Town; POB 1194, Woodstock 7915; tel. (21) 4474570; fax (21) 4474593; e-mail headoffice@sactwu.org.za; internet www.sactwu.org.za; Pres. THEMBA KHUMALO; Gen. Sec. ANDRE KRIEL; 110,216 mems (2006).

SOUTH AFRICA

South African Commercial, Catering and Allied Workers' Union (SACCAWU): SACCAWU House, 11 Leyds St, Braamfontein; POB 10730, Johannesburg 2000; tel. (11) 4038333; fax (11) 4030309; e-mail secretariatadmin@saccawu.org.za; internet www.saccawu.org.za; f. 1975; represents workers in the service industry, commercial, catering, tourism, hospitality and finance sectors; Pres. AMOS MOTHAPO; Gen. Sec. BONES SKULU; 107,553 mems (2006).

South African Democratic Teachers' Union (SADTU): Matthew Goniwe House, cnr Goud and Marshall Sts, Johannesburg 2000; POB 6401, Johannesburg 2000; tel. (11) 3344830; fax (11) 3344836; e-mail dmbetse@sadtu.org.za; internet www.sadtu.org.za; f. 1990; Pres. THOBILE NTOLA; Gen. Sec. THULAS NXESI; 224,387 mems (2006).

South African Municipal Workers' Union (SAMWU): Trade Union House, 8 Beverly St, Athlone, Cape Town; Private Bag X9, Athlone 7760; tel. (21) 6971151; fax (21) 6969175; e-mail soraya.solomon@samwu.org.za; internet www.samwu.org.za; f. 1987; Pres. SAM MOLOPE; Gen. Sec. MTHANDEKI NHLAPO; 118,973 (2006).

South African Transport and Allied Workers' Union (SATAWU): Marble Towers, 6th Floor, cnr Jeppe and Von Wielligh Sts, Johannesburg 2000; POB 9451, Johannesburg 2001; tel. (11) 3336127; fax (11) 3338918; e-mail cecilia@satawu.org.za; internet www.satawu.org.za; f. 2000; Pres. EZROM MABYANA; Gen. Sec. ZENZO MAHLANGU; 134,000 mems (2006).

Other organizations affiliated to COSATU include: the Musicians' Union of South Africa; the Performing Arts Workers' Equity; the Public and Allied Workers' Union of South Africa; the South African Democratic Nurses' Union; the South African Football Players' Union; the South African Medical Association; and the South African State and Allied Workers' Union.

Federation of Unions of South Africa (FEDUSA): Fedusa House, 10 Kingfisher St, Horizon Park, Roodepoort 1725; POB 7779, Westgate 1734; tel. (11) 2791800; fax (11) 2791821; e-mail dennis@fedusa.org.za; internet www.fedusa.org.za; f. 1997 by merger of the Fed. of South African Labour Unions and Fed. of Civil Servants; 22 mem. unions; politically non-aligned; proposed 'super fed.' with the Nat. Council of Trade Unions and Confed. of South African Workers' Unions delayed in 2006; Pres. DANIE CARSTENS; Gen. Sec. DENNIS GEORGE; 360,000 mems (2007).

Affiliated unions with 10,000 or more mems include:

Health and Other Service Personnel Trade Union of South Africa (HOSPERSA): POB 231, Kloof 3640, Durban, Pretoria 0121; tel. (12) 7654625; fax (12) 7658455; e-mail officegs@hospersa.co.za; internet www.hospersa.co.za; f. 1958; represents workers in the public and private health, welfare and services sectors, and the public safety and security and education sectors; Pres. GODFREY SELEMATSELA; Gen. Sec. NOEL DESFONTAINES; 72,000 mems (2009).

National Security and Unqualified Workers' Union (NASAWU): United Bldg, 10th Floor, 58 Field St, Durban; POB 63015, Bishopsgate, Durban 4008; tel. (31) 3059320; fax (31) 3059621; Gen. Sec. HAROLD MDINEKA; 13,000 mems (2006).

National Union of Leather and Allied Workers (NULAW): Mercury House, 6th Floor, Rm 67, 320 Smith St, Durban; POB 839, Durban 4000; tel. (31) 3076420; fax (31) 3043077; e-mail nulaw@mweb.co.za; internet www.nulaw.org.za; Gen. Sec. MARTIN PAULSEN; 13,180 mems (2005).

Professional Transport Workers' Union (PTWU): Sable Centre, 3rd Floor, 41 De Korte St, Braamfontein, Johannesburg; POB 31415, Braamfontein 2017; tel. (11) 3394249; fax (11) 6820444; e-mail ptwu@wol.co.za; represents workers in the road freight, private security and cleaning sectors; Gen. Sec. PAUL WA MALEMA; c. 10,000 mems (2002).

South African Typographical Union (SATU): SATU House, 166 Visagie St, Pretoria 0001; POB 1993, Pretoria 0001; tel. (12) 3236097; fax (12) 3231284; e-mail martind@satu.co.za; internet www.satu.co.za; f. 1982; represents workers in the printing, newspaper and packaging industries; Gen. Sec. MARTIN DEYSEL; 17,796 mems (2001).

Suid-Afrikaanse Onderwysersunie (SAOU) (South African Teachers' Union): SAOU Bldg, 278 Serene St, Garsfontein, Pretoria; POB 90120, Garsfontein 0042; tel. (12) 3489641; fax (12) 3489658; e-mail saou@saou.co.za; internet www.saou.co.za; Pres. JOHANNES S. ROUX; CEO EDWARD H. DAVIES; 24,247 (2006).

UASA—The Union: UASA Office Park, 42 Goldman St, Florida 1709; POB 565, Florida 1710; tel. (11) 4723600; fax (11) 6744057; e-mail andre.venter@uasa.org.za; internet www.uasa.org.za; f. 1998 by merger of the Administrative, Technical and Electronic Asscn of South Africa and Officials' Asscn of South Africa; fed. of 31 unions incl. the fmr Nat. Employees' Trade Union; represents workers in the mining, motor, transport, manufacturing and engineering industries; fmrly United Association of South Africa; CEO J. P. L. 'KOOS' BEZUIDENHOUT; 86,000 mems (2008).

Other organizations affiliated to FEDUSA include: the Airline Pilots' Association of South Africa; the Care, Catering and Retail Allied Workers' Union of South Africa; the Construction and Engineering Industrial Workers' Union; the Insurance and Banking Staff Association; the Internal Staff Association; the Jewellers and Goldsmiths' Union; the Millennium Workers' Union; the Mouth Peace Workers' Union; the National Democratic Change and Allied Workers' Union; the National Teachers' Union; the National Union of Hotel, Restaurant, Catering, Commercial, Health and Allied Workers; the South African Communications Union; the South African Parastatal and Tertiary Institutions Union; the United National Public Servants' Association of South Africa and Allied Workers' Union; and the United Transport and Allied Trade Union.

National Council of Trade Unions (NACTU): Metropolitan Life Centre, 4th Floor, 108 Fox St, Johannesburg; POB 10928, Johannesburg 2000; tel. (11) 8331040; fax (11) 8331032; e-mail info@nactu.org.za; internet www.nactu.org.za; f. 1986 by merger of the Council of Unions of South Africa and Azanian Confed. of Trade Unions; fed. of 22 African trade unions; aligned to the Pan-Africanist Congress of Azania party; Pres. JOSEPH MAQHEKENI; Gen. Sec. MANENE SAMELA; 310,000 mems (2007).

Affiliates with 10,000 or more mems include:

Building, Construction and Allied Workers' Union (BCAWU): Glencairn Bldg, 8th Floor, 73 Market St, Johannesburg; POB 96, Johannesburg 2000; tel. (11) 3339180; fax (11) 3339944; e-mail bcawu@netactive.co.za; f. 1974; Gen. Sec. NARIUS MOLOTO; c. 25,000 mems (2003).

Media Workers' Association of South Africa (MWASA): 208-212 cnr Jeppe and von Wielligh Sts, POB 11136, Johannesburg; tel. (11) 3371019; fax (11) 3371806; internet www.mwasa.org.za; f. 1978 as the Writers' Asscn of South Africa, successor to the Union of Black Journalists; present name adopted in 1986; applied to become a political party in 2005; Pres. TUWANI GUMANI; Sec.-Gen. ALBERT MAKGOBA; c. 27,000 mems (1998).

Metal and Electrical Workers' Union of South Africa (MEWUSA): Elephant House, 5th Floor, 107 Market St, Johannesburg; POB 3669, Johannesburg 2000; tel. and fax (11) 3369425; e-mail mewusa@lantic.net; internet www.mewusa.org.za; f. 1989; Pres. DANIEL LENGOABALA; Gen. Sec. NKRUMAH RAYMOND KGAGUDI; c. 10,000 paid-up mems (2005).

National Union of Food, Beverages, Wine, Spirit and Allied Workers (NUFBWSAW): 8 Stannic Bldg, 4th Floor, New St, South Ghandi Sq., Johannesburg; POB 5718, Johannesburg 2000; tel. (11) 8331140; fax (11) 8331503; Pres. ARMSTRONG NTOYAKHE; Nat. Organizer ANTHONY HENDRICKS; c. 10,000 mems (2005).

South African Chemical Workers' Union (SACWU): 29 Klerk St, btwn Harrison and Dirk Sts, 11th Floor, Johannesburg; POB 236, Johannesburg 2000; tel. (11) 8386581; fax (11) 8386622; e-mail samela@sacwu.co.za; Pres. JOSEPH MAQHEKENI; c. 40,000 mems (2003).

Other organizations affiliated to NACTU include: the Banking, Insurance and Finance Workers' Union; the Hospitality Industry and Allied Workers' Union; the Hotel, Liquor, Catering, Commercial and Allied Workers' Union of South Africa; the Municipality, Education, State, Health and Allied Workers' Union; the National Clothing and Textile Workers' Union of South Africa; the National Services and Allied Workers' Union; the National Union of Farm Workers; the National Union of Furniture and Allied Workers; the Parliamentary Staff Union; the Transport and Allied Workers Union; and the Transport and Omnibus Workers' Union.

Non-affiliated Union

Public Servants' Association of South Africa (PSA): PSA Head Office Bldg, 563 Belvedere St, Arcadia, Pretoria; POB 40404, Arcadia 0007; tel. (12) 3036500; fax (12) 3036652; e-mail ask@psa.co.za; internet www.psa.co.za; withdrew affiliation from FEDUSA in 2006; Chair. PAUL SELLO; Pres. KOOT MYBURGH; Gen. Man. DANNY ADONIS; 185,500 mems (2006).

Transport

Most of South Africa's railway network and the harbours and airways are administered by the state-owned Transnet Ltd. There are no navigable rivers. Private bus services are regulated to complement the railways.

Transnet Ltd: Carlton Centre, 150 Commissioner St, Johannesburg 2001; POB 72501, Parkview 2122; tel. (11) 3083000; fax (11) 3082638; e-mail unathi.mgobozi@transnet.net; internet www.transnet.net; CEO BRIAN MOLEFE.

SOUTH AFRICA — Directory

RAILWAYS

With the exception of commuter services, the South African railways system is operated by Transnet Freight Rail Ltd (formerly Spoornet), the rail division of Transnet. The network comprised some 34,000 track-km in 2010, of which 16,946 km was electrified. Extensive rail links connect Transnet Freight Rail with the rail networks of neighbouring countries. In 2010 construction of the 80-km rapid rail network Gautrain was under way in the province of Gauteng. The first phase of the system linking O. R. Tambo International Airport and Sandton was opened for commercial service in June 2010. The second phase linking Pretoria and Johannesburg was expected to be completed in mid-2011.

Transnet Freight Rail: Inyanda House, 21 Wellington Rd, Parktown 2193; Private Bag X47, Johannesburg 2000; tel. (11) 5449368; fax (11) 5449515; e-mail dan.motaung@transnet.net; internet www.spoornet.co.za; fmrly Spoornet; renamed as above in 2007; Acting CEO Tau Morwe.

ROADS

In 2001 there were an estimated 364,131 km of classified roads, including 239 km of motorways.

South African National Roads Agency Ltd (SANRAL): Ditsela Pl., 1204 Park St, cnr Duncan St, Hatfield, Pretoria; POB 415, Pretoria 0001; tel. (12) 4266000; fax (12) 3622116; e-mail info@nra.co.za; internet www.nra.co.za; f. 1998; responsible for design, construction, management and maintenance of 16,150 km of the national road network (2008); Chair. Maduke Lot Ndlovu; CEO Nazir Alli.

SHIPPING

The principal harbours are at Richards Bay, Durban, Saldanha, Cape Town, Port Elizabeth, East London, Ngqura (Coega), and Mossel Bay. The deep-water port at Richards Bay has been extended and its facilities upgraded. Both Richards Bay and Saldanha Bay are major bulk-handling ports, while Saldanha Bay also has an important fishing fleet. More than 30 shipping lines serve South African ports.

South African Maritime Safety Authority (SAMSA): 161 Lynnwood Rd, cnr Duncan St, Brooklyn, Pretoria; POB 13186, Hatfield 0028; tel. (12) 3662600; fax (12) 3662601; e-mail info@samsa.org.za; internet www.samsa.org.za; advises the Govt on matters connected with sea transport to, from or between South Africa's ports, incl. safety at sea, and prevention of pollution by petroleum; CEO Tsietsi Mokhele.

Transnet National Ports Authority: POB 32696, Braamfontein 2017; tel. (11) 2429003; fax (11) 2424027; internet www.transnetnationalportsauthority.net; f. 2000; fmrly part of Portnet; subsidiary of Transnet; controls and manages the country's eight major seaports; CEO Khomotso Phihlela.

Transnet Port Terminals: Kingsmead Office Park, cnr Stalwart and Stanger Sts, Durban 4001; tel. (86) 1204485; fax (31) 3088352; e-mail tptwebmaster@transnet.net; internet www.transnetportterminals.net; f. 2000 as South African Port Terminals, renamed as above in 2008; fmrly part of Portnet; subsidiary of Transnet; operates 13 container, bulk, breakbulk and car terminals at six of the country's major ports; CEO Tau Morwe.

CIVIL AVIATION

Civil aviation is controlled by the Minister of Transport. The Chief Directorate: Civil Aviation Authority at the Department of Transport is responsible for licensing and control of domestic and international air services.

Airports Company South Africa (ACSA): 24 Johnson Rd, Riverwoods, Bedfordview 2008; POB 75480, Gardenview 2047; tel. (11) 7231400; fax (11) 4539353; internet www.airports.co.za; f. 1993; owns and operates South Africa's 10 principal airports, of which four (at Johannesburg, Cape Town, Durban and Pilanesburg) are classified as international airports; Chair. Sindi Zilwa; Man. Dir Monhla Hlahla.

Civil Aviation Authority (CAA): Ikhaya Lokundiza, Bldg 16, Treur Close, Waterfall Park, Bekker St, Midrand; Private Bag X73, Halfway House 1685; tel. (11) 5451000; fax (12) 5451465; e-mail mail@caa.co.za; internet www.caa.co.za; CEO Colin Jordaan.

Airlink Airline: No.3, Greenstone Hill Office Park, Emerald Blvd, Greenstone Hill, Modderfontein; POB 7529, Bonaero Park 1622; tel. (11) 9611700; fax (11) 3951076; e-mail info@flyairlink.com; internet www.saairlink.co.za; f. 1992; internal and external scheduled services and charters in Southern Africa; Man. Dirs Rodger Foster, Barrie Webb.

COMAIR Ltd: cnr Atlas Rd and Marignane Dr., Bonaero Park 1619; POB 7015, Bonaero Park 1622; tel. (11) 9210111; fax (11) 9733913; e-mail cr@comair.co.za; internet www.comair.co.za; f. 1946; scheduled domestic, regional and international services; Chair. D. Novick; Jt CEOs Erik Venter, Gidon Novick.

Interair South Africa: Ground Floor, Finance House, Ernest Oppenheimer Rd, Bruma Lake Office, Bruma, Johannesburg; Private Bag 8, OR Tambo Int. Airport, Johannesburg 1627; tel. (11) 6160636; fax (11) 6160930; e-mail info@interair.co.za; internet www.interair.co.za; Exec. Chair. David P. Tokoph.

Safair (Pty) Ltd: Northern Perimeter Rd, Bonaero Park 1619; POB 938, Kempton Park 1620; tel. 9280000; fax 3951314; e-mail marketing@safair.co.za; internet www.safair.co.za; f. 1965; part of the Aergo Group; aircraft leasing, engineering and maintenance services; CEO Christo Kok.

South African Airways (SAA): Airways Park, Jones Rd, Private Bag X13, Johannesburg 1627; tel. (11) 9782888; fax (11) 9789567; e-mail voyager@flysaa.com; internet www.flysaa.com; f. 1934; state-owned; internal passenger services linking all the principal towns; international services to Africa, Europe, North and South America and Asia; Chair. Jakes Gerwel; CEO Siza Mzimela.

South African Express Airways (SA Express): Tambo International Airport, Johannesburg; tel. (11) 9789905; fax (11) 9785578; e-mail reservations@flyexpress.aero; internet www.flyexpress.aero; f. 1994; CEO Inati Ntshanga.

Tourism

Tourism is an important part of South Africa's economy. The chief attractions for visitors are the climate, scenery and wildlife reserves. In 2008 some 9.7m. tourists visited South Africa. In that year receipts from tourism amounted to US $8,861m.

South African Tourism: Bojanala House, 90 Protea Rd, Chislehurston, Johannesburg 2196; Private Bag X10012, Sandton 2146; tel. (11) 8953000; fax (11) 8953001; internet www.southafrica.net; f. 1947; 11 overseas brs; CEO Moeketsi Mosola.

Defence

As assessed at November 2010, the South African National Defence Force (SANDF) totalled about 62,082: army 37,141, navy 6,244, air force 10,653 and a medical corps numbering 8,044. The SANDF comprised members of the former South African armed forces, together with personnel from the former military wings of the ANC and the Pan-Africanist Congress, and the former 'homelands' militias. In 2010 a total of 1,980 South African troops were stationed abroad; of these, 29 were observers.

Defence Expenditure: Budgeted at R33,900m. in 2011.

Chief of the South African National Defence Force: Lt-Gen. Godfrey Nhlanhla Ngwenya.

Chief of the South African Air Force: Lt-Gen. Carlo Gagiano.

Chief of the South African Army: Maj.-Gen. Solly Zacharia Shoke.

Chief of the South African Navy: Vice-Adm. Johannes Refiloe Mudimu.

Education

School attendance is compulsory for children of all population groups between the ages of seven and 16 years. From 1991 state schools were permitted to admit pupils of all races, and in 1995 the right to free state education for all was introduced. According to UNESCO estimates, in 2006/07 enrolment at primary schools included 87% of pupils in the relevant age-group (males 87%; females 88%), while enrolment in secondary schools included 72% of pupils in the relevant age-group (males 70%; females 74%). In 2009 there were 23 higher education institutions, with a total of 837,779 students. Initial budget estimates for 20010/11 indicated the allocation of R32,850.2m. (4.1% of total expenditure) to education.

SPAIN

Introductory Survey

LOCATION, CLIMATE, LANGUAGE, RELIGION, FLAG, CAPITAL

The Kingdom of Spain, in south-western Europe, forms more than four-fifths of the Iberian peninsula. The country also includes the Balearic Islands in the Mediterranean Sea, the Canary Islands in the Atlantic Ocean and a few small enclaves in North Africa. Mainland Spain is bounded to the north by Andorra and France and to the west by Portugal. To the east is the Mediterranean Sea, and Morocco lies 30 km to the south. The climate is less temperate than in most of Western Europe, with hot summers and, in the hilly interior, cold winters. The official national language is Spanish. Catalan, and its close relative Valencian, are widely spoken in the north-east, Basque in the north and Galician in the north-west; all have co-official status in their respective regions. The majority of the population are Roman Catholics, but the Constitution states that Spain has no official state religion. The national flag (proportions 2 by 3) carries three horizontal stripes, of red, yellow (one-half of the depth) and red. The state flag carries, in addition, the national coat of arms. The capital is Madrid.

CONTEMPORARY POLITICAL HISTORY

Historical Context

After winning the civil war of 1936–39, the Nationalist forces, led by Gen. Francisco Franco, established an authoritarian rule which restricted individual liberties and severely repressed challenges to its power. In 1942 Gen. Franco revived the traditional legislative assembly, the Cortes (Courts), with limited powers. After keeping Spain neutral in the Second World War, Franco announced in 1947 that the monarchy (abolished in 1931) would be restored after his death or retirement. In 1967, in the first elections since the civil war, a portion of the Cortes was directly elected under a limited franchise. In July 1969 Franco nominated Prince Juan Carlos de Borbón (grandson of the last reigning monarch, King Alfonso XIII) as his successor, and in June 1973 relinquished the post of President of the Government (Prime Minister) to Adm. Luis Carrero Blanco, who was killed in December. Responsibility for the assassination was claimed by Euskadi ta Askatasuna (ETA—Basque Homeland and Liberty), the Basque separatist organization. Carlos Arias Navarro became Prime Minister in January 1974.

Franco died in November 1975. He was succeeded as Head of State by King Juan Carlos, and in December a more liberal Council of Ministers was formed. In 1976 restrictions on political activity were lifted. In July Arias Navarro resigned at the King's request, and was replaced by Adolfo Suárez. The introduction of democratic government then proceeded rapidly, and an elected bicameral legislature was established. Most of the numerous de facto political parties were able to take part in the general elections for the Cortes, held in June 1977. An overall majority was won by the Unión de Centro Democrático (UCD), a coalition party headed by the Prime Minister. In December 1978 a new Constitution was endorsed by referendum and ratified by the King. It confirmed Spain as a parliamentary monarchy, with freedom for political parties, and guaranteed the right of Spain's 'nationalities and regions' to autonomy.

Domestic Political Affairs

A general election was held in March 1979, resulting in little change in the distribution of seats in the Cortes. The new Government was again headed by Suárez. Basque and Catalan autonomous parliaments were established in March 1980 and, in elections to both parliaments, the UCD was heavily defeated by the moderate regionalist parties. Confidence in Suárez diminished and in January 1981 he resigned. Leopoldo Calvo-Sotelo Bustelo, hitherto the Deputy Prime Minister, was named as his successor.

On 23 February 1981 a group of armed civil guards, led by Lt-Col Antonio Tejero Molina, stormed into the Cortes, taking hostage all 350 deputies. The military commander of Valencia, Lt-Gen. Jaime Milans del Bosch, declared a state of emergency in that region and sent tanks on to the streets of the city of Valencia. King Juan Carlos acted swiftly to secure the loyalty of other military commanders, and by the following morning, having declared his support for the Constitution in a televised address, had been able to persuade Milans del Bosch himself to stand down. Tejero surrendered, and the deputies were released unharmed. More than 30 military officers were subsequently brought to trial, and both Tejero and Milans del Bosch received lengthy prison sentences. (Milans del Bosch was released in 1990 and Tejero in 1996.)

Immediately after the attempted coup, Calvo-Sotelo was formally installed as Prime Minister and formed a new Council of Ministers, resisting pressure to establish a coalition government. The Prime Minister addressed various contentious issues during his term of office, including his decision to take Spain into the North Atlantic Treaty Organization (NATO, see p. 368). Following Calvo-Sotelo's replacement as UCD leader in July, Suárez defected to found a rival party, the Centro Democrático y Social (CDS). Desertion from the UCD continued and in August, with the party no longer commanding a workable majority, an early general election was called. In October, shortly before the election, a right-wing plot to stage a pre-emptive military coup was uncovered. Four colonels were arrested (three of whom were subsequently sentenced to prison terms), and Milans was also implicated. The election resulted in a decisive victory for the Partido Socialista Obrero Español (PSOE—Spanish Socialist Workers' Party), led by Felipe González, who formed a new Council of Ministers in December 1982.

Following large-scale demonstrations against Spain's membership of NATO, in March 1986 a long-awaited referendum on the question of Spain's continued membership of the alliance was held. Contrary to expectations, the Spanish people voted to remain within NATO, following Prime Minister González's reversal on the issue and an extensive campaign by the Government. In an early general election held in June 1986 the PSOE was returned to power, defeating the Coalición Popular (CP), which incorporated the conservative Alianza Popular (AP), the Partido Demócrata Popular (subsequently Democracia Cristiana) and the Partido Liberal. A new Council of Ministers was appointed in July, again led by González. Following its defeat, the CP fell into disarray, and in December Manuel Fraga, the leader of the AP, resigned.

In January 1989 Fraga returned to the leadership of the AP, which was relaunched as the Partido Popular (PP) and which was subsequently joined by Democracia Cristiana and the Partido Liberal. The unity of the PSOE was undermined by the establishment of a dissident faction and by the defection to Izquierda Unida (IU—United Left, an alliance comprising the Partido Comunista de España and other left-wing parties) of 100 PSOE members. Nevertheless, at the general election, held eight months early, in October, the PSOE was returned to power on a provisional basis, pending investigations into allegations of polling irregularities. After several months of controversy, the PSOE's representation in the Congreso de los Diputados (Congress of Deputies) was reduced to 175 of the 350 seats, the PP holding 107 seats. The PSOE, however, was able to retain a majority by subsequently entering into a tactical alliance with the CDS, the Catalan nationalist Convergència i Unió (CiU) and the Euzko Alderdi Jeltzalea-Partido Nacionalista Vasco (EAJ-PNV—the Basque Nationalist Party).

At the general election in June 1993 the PSOE failed to obtain an absolute majority in the Congreso de los Diputados. The PSOE's negotiations with CiU and the EAJ-PNV failed to result in the conclusion of a formal coalition agreement. In July, therefore, González commenced his fourth term as Prime Minister, at the head of a minority administration. With the Spanish economy in recession the Prime Minister appealed for support for drastic measures to address the economic crisis. In November, however, thousands of protesters demonstrated against the Government's economic policies. Controversial labour legislation was approved by the Congreso in March 1994.

In 1994–95 the Government came under increasing pressure over suggestions that it had been involved in the establishment of the Grupos Antiterroristas de Liberación (GAL), a counter-terrorist grouping which had been formed in 1983 with the aim of combating ETA. It was alleged that members of the Ertzaintza (Basque Country police force) had given support to the organization, which was suspected of responsibility for the murders of 27 ETA members exiled in France. Investigations into the affair had begun in 1988, and in 1991 a senior police officer and an accomplice were convicted of organizing the groups of mercenaries. In December 1994, following further questioning of the pair and the reopening of the case, Julián Sancristóbal, a former director-general of state security in the Ministry of the Interior, was arrested on suspicion of financing and assisting GAL. The Prime Minister denied that the Government had been connected in any way with the so-called 'dirty war' of the 1980s against ETA. However, in February 1995 Baltasar Garzón, an investigating judge at the National Court, ordered the arrest of Rafael Vera, the former Secretary of State for Security, on suspicion of involvement in the kidnapping in 1983 of Segundo Marey, a French business executive mistaken for an ETA member, and of misuse of public funds. In April 1995, concluding that GAL had been established and financed by the Ministry of the Interior, Garzón indicted a total of 14 former officials, including Vera and Sancristóbal. Garzón's final report into the origins and financing of GAL implicated González along with the former Deputy Prime Minister and Minister of Defence, Narcís Serra, the Minister of the Interior during 1982–88, José Barrionuevo, and other PSOE officials.

In September 1995 Judge Eduardo Móner was appointed by the Supreme Court to examine the allegations against the Prime Minister and the other senior politicians; Sancristóbal, Vera and Barrionuevo were subsequently charged with misuse of public funds, while Barrionuevo was also charged with illegal detention and association with an armed group. However, Móner reported that he had found no evidence linking González to the activities of the death squads, while Serra was also exonerated. Móner concluded his inquiry into the abduction of Marey in April 1997, and in September the Supreme Court confirmed that 12 defendants were to stand trial. At the conclusion of the trial in July 1998, Barrionuevo, Vera and Sancristóbal were found guilty of kidnapping and misappropriation of public funds; each received a prison sentence of 10 years. The sentences of the other nine defendants ranged from two to nine years. A further trial began in September 2001, with González among some 100 witnesses called upon to testify. In January 2002 Barrionuevo was absolved of the charge of misappropriation of funds; however, Vera was sentenced to seven years' imprisonment and barred from holding public office for 18 years.

The Partido Popular in power

At an early general election in March 1996, the PP took 156 of the 350 seats in the Congreso de los Diputados, thus falling short of an outright majority. The PSOE, its reputation severely damaged by the ongoing investigation into the GAL affair, won 141 seats, while IU took 21 and CiU 16. The King invited José María Aznar, the President of the PP, to form a government. Having secured the support of CiU, the five EAJ-PNV deputies and of the four representatives of Coalición Canaria (CC), the new Prime Minister's investiture finally took place in early May. (However, the EAJ-PNV abandoned its pact with the Government in September 1997, before withdrawing its support entirely in December 1999.)

One of the new administration's main priorities was the reduction of the budget deficit. Several aspects of the Government's policies, however, aroused intense opposition. In December 1996 civil servants took part in a 24-hour strike to protest against the Government's imposition of a pay freeze, while in February 1997 a two-week strike by truck drivers, in support of improved working conditions, caused severe disruption and led to the closure of the country's road borders. In early 1998 one miner died during violent protests in northern Spain, where the coal-miners of Asturias were demonstrating against proposed job losses (the Government having been obliged to plan decreases in coal output in order to comply with European Union (EU, see p. 270) directives regarding reductions in subsidies to state-owned industries). At the end of January, after a month-long strike that attracted much public sympathy, agreement was reached when the Government granted concessions on the terms of early retirement for miners.

The ruling party's strong performance at the legislative election held on 12 March 2000 was largely attributed to the Government's record of economic success (in particular its reduction of the unemployment rate). In the lower house the PP won 183 of the 350 seats, thus unexpectedly securing an absolute majority.

The PSOE's representation was reduced to 125 seats, while IU, which had conducted a joint campaign with the PSOE, suffered a sharp decline in support, losing 13 of its 21 seats in the Congreso de los Diputados. The moderate regional parties, CiU and the EAJ-PNV, took 15 and seven seats, respectively. Aznar was sworn in for a second term of office in April, having secured the support of CiU and CC. Joaquín Almunia resigned as leader of the PSOE immediately after the election. At the party congress in July José Luis Rodríguez Zapatero, a lawyer, was elected to the leadership. Zapatero, who excluded left-wingers from the new national executive committee, declared his intention to modernize the party in order to form an effective opposition.

In January 2002 the PP re-elected Aznar as its President, but he made clear his intention not to seek a third term as Prime Minister in 2004. In May 2002, as a result of the failure of negotiations between the Government, trade unions and employers' representatives over proposed reforms to employment law, the leading trade unions announced plans to hold the first general strike since 1988. The day after the unions' announcement, the Government approved the imposition of reforms to unemployment subsidies by decree. The general strike proceeded in June 2002. Revised legislation on labour reform, which annulled the main provisions of the controversial decree, was approved by the Congreso de los Diputados in October.

In November 2002 the Aznar Government was faced with a serious crisis following the sinking of the Liberian-registered, Greek-owned oil tanker *Prestige* 240 km off the coast of Galicia. The vessel, which had reported to the authorities that its hull had ruptured and that it was leaking oil, had been refused landfall and had been towed out to sea, where it split in two and sank six days later. An estimated 12,000 metric tons of the vessel's 77,000-ton capacity was believed to have been released into the sea in the first slick, around one-half of which soon reached the Galician coast, requiring the imposition of a prohibition of fishing in that area. It was subsequently revealed that the oil remaining in the wreck was still leaking (in early January 2003 the total amount of spillage was revised to 25,000 tons). Massive clean-up operations were launched, mostly by environmental groups and by the local population; a significant lack of aid from the Spanish military aroused widespread public discontent. Demonstrations were attended by some 150,000 people in Santiago de Compostela in December and by around 100,000 people in Vigo in January 2003, at which participants protested at the perceived mishandling of the disaster by both the regional and national PP authorities and demanded the resignation of Aznar. A local commission launched by the regional Government of Galicia met with obstruction from the central Government, which also delayed the setting up of a national investigation. Meanwhile, the oil slicks spread to the Basque region, and also reached the coastlines of France and Portugal.

Amid the increasing likelihood of US-led military action in Iraq in early 2003, Aznar was one of eight European leaders to sign a declaration at the end of January in support of US moves towards an ultimatum. Public opinion, however, already swayed against the PP by the Government's handling of the *Prestige* disaster, was, in general, strongly against military action, with 3m. people participating in anti-war demonstrations in February, and opinion polls suggesting that at least 80% of the population was against the launching of an armed conflict. None the less, in late February Aznar expressed his support for US-led military action with a UN mandate. As the US intention to commence armed intervention with or without UN approval became clear, Aznar assured the Spanish people that Spain would not contribute to any military coalition. A summit meeting hosted in the Azores, Portugal, in March led to a joint declaration by Aznar, the British Prime Minister, Tony Blair, and the US President, George W. Bush, condemning the regime of Saddam Hussain and expressing support for necessary military actions. The subsequent announcement by the USA of its intention to act, if need be, without international ratification received the PP Government's concerted support. In July, despite the level of popular feeling against the war (which had commenced on 20 March) and the dissent of all the opposition parties, the Government committed 1,300 troops to the peace-keeping force. In November seven Spanish intelligence officers were killed in Iraq, bringing the total number of Spaniards to have died as a direct result of the conflict to 10. Opinion polls reported that an estimated 90% of the Spanish population believed that the instigation of armed conflict in Iraq by the US-led coalition had been a mistake, and Zapatero, the leader of the PSOE, stated that if his party won the general election in March 2004, Spanish troops would be withdrawn from Iraq.

The Madrid bombings; the first Zapatero Government

On 11 March 2004, three days before the general election, 10 bombs exploded in four commuter trains in Madrid, killing 191 people and injuring more than 1,500. The Government immediately indicated that ETA was the principal suspect; however, Batasuna, ETA's political wing, was swift to condemn the attacks. Campaigning for the election was suspended, and three days of national mourning were declared. Despite the Government's initial supposition that the bombings had been carried out by ETA, suspicion increasingly came to rest on Islamist militants; in the days following the attacks three Moroccans were arrested, who were suspected of having links to the al-Qa'ida organization of the Saudi-born militant Islamist Osama bin Laden (who was killed by US forces in May 2011) and to the May 2003 suicide bombings in Casablanca, Morocco.

Opinion polls conducted before the attacks had widely predicted that the PP would win the general election with a reduced majority. However, the bombings became the central issue in the election, which took place as scheduled on 14 March 2004. Following the emergence of evidence suggesting that Islamists had perpetrated the attacks, the Government was criticized for its premature response in blaming ETA and its unwillingness to consider other possibilities. In the event, the PSOE secured an unexpected victory in the elections to the Congreso de los Diputados, winning 164 seats, while the PP, led by the Deputy Prime Minister, Mariano Rajoy, obtained 148 seats. The PP retained its majority in the Senado (Senate), however, emerging with a total of 126 seats compared to the PSOE's 111. The election turn-out, at 77.2%, was nine percentage points higher than in 2000. Immediately after his party's victory Zapatero reiterated his pledge to withdraw Spanish troops from Iraq if control in that country were not handed over by the US-led coalition authorities to the UN by 30 June. However, on assuming office he announced that the troops would be withdrawn as quickly as possible, and the Spanish withdrawal was completed by the end of May. Zapatero announced that he did not intend to form a coalition government; rather, the PSOE made pacts with smaller parties in the two legislative chambers, effectively isolating the PP. Having won a congressional vote of confidence, Zapatero and his new Council of Ministers were inaugurated in April.

On 2 April 2004, meanwhile, a bomb of the same type discovered on the trains involved in the earlier Madrid attacks was defused on the railway line between Madrid and Seville (Sevilla). The following day seven men who were suspected of involvement in the bombings apparently blew themselves up, killing one police officer, during a police raid on an apartment in Leganés, a suburb of Madrid; Abdelmajid Farkhet, the man suspected of organizing the 11 March attacks, was among the dead. In May a parliamentary commission of inquiry into the train bombings was established. Specifically, the commission was to investigate information on the attacks provided by the PP Government, that Government's anti-terrorist policy, and the trafficking of illegal arms in Spain. In late November the former Prime Minister, Aznar, was questioned by the commission. Aznar maintained that ETA was linked to the Islamist militants suspected of carrying out the bomb attacks. Zapatero, who subsequently appeared before the commission, alleged that the PP administration had deleted all government computer records relating to the train bombings before leaving office. In March 2005 the preliminary findings of the commission, supported by all the parliamentary groups except the PP, were published. Recommendations included an increase in the implementation of security measures; however, the commission was criticized by some observers for being overly political in its handling of the inquiry.

Despite opposition from leaders of the Roman Catholic church, legislation permitting marriage between couples of the same sex was adopted by the Senado in June 2005, following its approval by the Congreso de los Diputados in April. In November 2005 new defence legislation was passed that required any deployment of Spanish troops abroad to be approved by the Cortes, and limited the circumstances in which such a deployment might occur. In February 2006 Spain's highest consultative body, the Council of State, voted to support the Government's proposed amendments to the Constitution. Among the changes anticipated were the alteration of the law of royal succession, removing the preference for a male heir, a restructuring of the Senado and an increase in the power of the Autonomous Communities in the upper house; also to be addressed was the contentious issue of whether the Autonomous Communities should be regarded as 'nations'. However, in May 2007 Zapatero announced that the Government was abandoning constitutional reform for the duration of the current legislature owing to lack of support from the PP.

During 2007 a principal topic of political debate concerned proposals, presented personally by Zapatero as Prime Minister, to introduce a 'law on historic memory' that was intended to provide formal recognition to those who had lost their lives during and immediately before the civil war, and to those who had been the victims of political repression under the Franco regime. The draft legislation was subject to criticism from both the PP, which regarded the proposals contained within the law as potentially socially divisive and unwarranted, and from human rights groups and the Catalan nationalist allies of the Government, the ERC, which considered the measures to be insufficiently rigorous. None the less, the Congreso de los Diputados approved the legislation at the end of October. Public funds were to be provided to organizations involved in locating mass graves, and to identifying, exhuming and re-burying the dead. Trials on political charges conducted during the period of Franco's rule were to be declared illegitimate (sentences passed were not, however, to be repealed outright), while political rallies at Franco's place of burial were to be prohibited and public monuments to Franco and his regime were to be removed. Meanwhile, also in late October, tens of thousands of Spanish pilgrims paraded in the Vatican City to commemorate the beatification by the Roman Catholic Church of some 498 priests and members of religious orders killed during the Civil War, principally by Republican forces. In November 2008, following a request by surviving relatives and representatives of the victims, the investigating judge Baltasar Garzón launched a criminal investigation into the disappearance of tens of thousands of Spaniards during the civil war and Franco's dictatorship, and ordered the exhumation of several mass graves. Garzón claimed jurisdiction on the grounds that the crimes committed during this period constituted 'crimes against humanity' rather than political crimes, and were consequently not covered by an amnesty law of 1977 nor by any statute of limitations. Later that month, however, the National Court ruled that Garzón did not have the authority to launch such an investigation and that inquiries into such crimes must be carried out by courts in the regions where the crimes were committed. Also in November it was announced that some 500,000 descendants of those Spaniards who fled the country during the civil war and Franco's rule would be permitted to apply for Spanish citizenship.

Meanwhile, in February 2007 the trial began at the National Court in Madrid of 29 men suspected of involvement of the Madrid train bombings in March 2004—mostly Moroccan nationals, but including three Spanish citizens who had supplied the explosives. In October 21 of the defendants were convicted of the attacks, while seven were acquitted, including an Egyptian citizen, Rabei Osman el-Sayed Ahmed, who had been accused of organizing the attacks. (Charges had been dropped against the remaining suspect, on grounds of lack of evidence.) Three defendants were sentenced to the equivalent of the maximum permissible prison term of 40 years, having been found guilty of murdering 191 people, procuring two involuntary abortions (as two of those killed in the attacks were pregnant women) and conspiring to cause the deaths of the 1,856 people injured in the attacks. In July 2008 four of the 21 convicts had their sentences overturned by the Supreme Court, which also upheld the acquittal of el-Sayed Ahmed. A further principal suspect in the attacks, Hicham Ahmidan, was arrested in January 2008 in Morocco; in December he was sentenced to 10 years' imprisonment by a court in that country, having been convicted of providing logistical support to the bombers.

The second Zapatero Government

At the general election held on 9 March 2008, both the PSOE and PP increased their share of the votes cast, and their representation in the Congreso de los Diputados, compared with the results of the 2004 election, to 43.6% and 169 seats, and 40.1% and 154 seats, respectively. The representation of IU and of the ERC decreased, to two and three seats, respectively, while CiU won 10 seats and the EAJ-PNV six. Four other parties, mostly representing regional interests, obtained representation in the chamber. As in the outgoing lower chamber, no party controlled an overall majority of seats. In concurrent elections to the Senado, the PP remained the largest faction, with 98 of the directly elected seats, and (following the appointment, in the following month, of senators to represent the Autonomous Community of Andalusia, in which an election to the regional legislature had been held concurrently with the general election) a further 24 appointed seats. The PSOE obtained 79 directly elected seats, and held 14 appointees. Zapatero was confirmed as Prime Minister in April by a simple majority vote in the Congreso de los Diputados, and the appointment of a new Government, including the formation of two new ministries—of Equality and of Science and Innovation—was announced later in the month. Several principal positions remained unchanged from the outgoing administration: Miguel Ángel Moratinos retained his post as Minister of Foreign Affairs and Co-operation; Alfredo Pérez Rubalcaba remained as Minister of the Interior; María Teresa Fernández de la Vega as First Deputy Prime Minister, Minister of the Presidency and Government Spokesperson; and Pedro Solbes as Second Deputy Prime Minister and Minister of the Economy and Finance. New appointments included Carme Chacón as Minister of Defence—the first woman to assume that post in Spain. Indeed, excluding the premiership, women accounted for exactly one-half of the ministerial appointments.

Zapatero's new Government was faced with growing problems precipitated by the world economic slowdown. In the year to March 2009 unemployment in the country nearly doubled as some 2m. people lost their jobs and the construction industry collapsed. In response to the economic downturn, the Government introduced stimulus plans in April, August and November. Faced with growing levels of unemployment, in January 2009 the Government announced an incentive aimed at unemployed immigrants in Spain, under the terms of which they could cash in their unemployment benefits for a lump sum of some €10,000, on condition that they returned to their home countries and agreed not to return to Spain to seek work for at least three years.

In April 2009 Zapatero effected a cabinet reorganization in order to boost the PSOE's flagging popularity amid the economic crisis and prior to the forthcoming European Parliament elections. Among the most notable appointments was the replacement of the Second Deputy Prime Minister and Minister of the Economy and Finance, Pedro Solbes, by Elena Salgado Méndez. Solbes had openly disagreed with Zapatero over future fiscal stimulus plans, opposing a further widening of the country's budget deficit. None the less, the PSOE suffered losses at the election to the European Parliament in June, taking 21 of the 50 available seats compared with the 23 won by the PP. The result was interpreted as an expression of public discontent with the Government's handling of the economic crisis and as a vindication of the PP leader, Rajoy, whose leadership had been subject to sustained criticism from sections of his party in the preceding months.

The Government came into renewed conflict with the Roman Catholic Church and the conservative opposition in 2009 over its plans, approved by the Council of Ministers in May, to reform the law on abortion. In October a demonstration, attended by more than 1m. people according to some reports, took place in Madrid in protest at the proposed measures, which would, *inter alia*, allow abortion on demand until the 14th week of pregnancy and allow girls over the age of 16 years to obtain an abortion without parental consent. (Existing legislation provided for abortion only in cases of rape, foetal malformation or potential danger to a woman's physical or mental health, although the latter provision was reported to be interpreted liberally in practice.) The draft legislation was approved by the Congreso de los Diputados in December and by the Senado in February 2010.

In April 2010 an investigating judge at the Supreme Court, Luciano Varela, ordered Garzón to stand trial on a charge of knowingly exceeding his judicial authority by investigating, in 2008, the disappearances that had occurred under Franco, despite being prohibited by the 1977 amnesty law. Varela's indictment was based on allegations brought by a right-wing anti-corruption organization, Manos Limpias (Clean Hands), supported by Falange Española de las JONS, a successor grouping to the official political movement of the Franco regime. Later in April 2010 an estimated 60,000 people demonstrated in Madrid in support of Garzón (who denied all the allegations against him), while similar marches were held in other Spanish cities. The affair prompted accusations of political motivation against both Garzón and his opponents. In March Zapatero had publicly praised the investigative judge's actions in the fight against Basque terrorism, leading the opposition to criticize the Prime Minister for attempting to influence the Supreme Court's decision. In May the General Council of the Judiciary suspended Garzón from his post at the National Court for the duration of the proceedings against him. Later in May Garzón was granted leave to work as an adviser at the International Criminal Court in The Hague, Netherlands. In March 2011 Garzón filed a case at the European Court of Human Rights challenging his prosecution on the grounds that it violated Spain's obligations under the European Convention on Human Rights, in particular the obligation to protect judicial independence. In April another investigating judge at the Supreme Court, Alberto Jorge Barreiro, announced that Garzón would be tried on charges of perversion of the course of justice for ordering recordings of conversations between imprisoned suspects and their lawyers while investigating a corruption scandal involving members of the opposition PP in 2009.

Recent developments: austerity measures

The Government was subjected to renewed political pressure arising from the economic crisis in the first half of 2010, suffering a further decline in public approval as it attempted to address the country's acutely high public deficit. In May, amid fears that Spain would require financial assistance from the EU and the IMF to avoid defaulting on its sovereign debt (following a similar package of loans to Greece agreed earlier in the month), Zapatero announced the introduction of emergency legislation intended to reduce the deficit from 11.2% of gross domestic product (GDP) in 2009 to 6% in 2011. The proposed measures, which included a 5% reduction in public sector salaries, were approved in the Congreso de los Diputados by a margin of just one vote, indicating the fragility of parliamentary support for the PSOE administration. In June 2010 the Government declared its intention to bring to a conclusion a long-running debate over the liberalization of labour market laws, indicating that it would unilaterally approve a reform if negotiations with trade unions and employers' organizations failed to reach agreement. The talks broke down later in the month and the Government duly announced its proposals, which included a reduction in severance pay for workers on permanent contracts, the relaxation of conditions for dismissal, and measures intended to discourage the use of temporary contracts. These measures entered into force immediately on a provisional basis pending parliamentary approval, and a definitive version of the reform was finally approved by the Cortes in September. The PP joined other centre-right parties in abstaining from the vote, claiming that the reform was insufficient, while the measures were opposed by the trade unions and the far-left parties. Later in September the trade unions organized a one-day general strike, the first since 2002 and the first against Zapatero's Government. Fears that the Government might be unable to complete its parliamentary term (which was due to expire in March 2012) were allayed in October 2011 when it concluded agreements with the EAJ-PNV and CC, under which the smaller parties promised to support the 2011 budget and other key economic policies; the Government was thus ensured of a small majority in the Congreso de los Diputados. As part of the deal with the EAJ-PNV, the further devolution of powers from the central Government to the Basque regional administration (under the terms of the region's Statute of Autonomy) was agreed.

In October 2010 Zapatero announced a reorganization of the Council of Ministers. Two of the longest-serving ministers in the PSOE Government, Fernández de la Vega and Moratinos, were among the six ministers dismissed; Trinidad Jiménez replaced Moratinos as Minister of Foreign Affairs and Co-operation, while Rubalcaba added Fernández de la Vega's former titles of First Deputy Prime Minister and Government Spokesman to his existing responsibilities as Minister of the Interior. Ramón Jáuregui was appointed to the cabinet as Minister of the Presidency, while Valeriano Gómez became Minister of Labour and Immigration in place of Celestino Corbacho, who had previously indicated his intention to step down. In early April 2011 Zapatero sought to end speculation about his future leadership by announcing that he did not intend to seek a third term as Prime Minister at the general election due in March 2012. The PSOE suffered significant losses at the regional and local elections held on 22 May 2011. A primary election to choose the PSOE's prime ministerial candidate was expected to be held in June. However, opinion polls indicated that, even under a new leader, the PSOE was likely to suffer a heavy defeat by Rajoy's PP at the forthcoming general election.

The Autonomous Communities

Following the promulgation of the 1978 Constitution, Spain's historic regions were swift to take advantage of the new provisions for self-government. Autonomous regional parliaments were established in the Basque Country (País Vasco/Euskadi) and in Catalonia (Cataluña/Catalunya) in 1980. The parliaments of Galicia and Andalucía were established in October 1981 and May 1982, respectively, and the remaining 13 legislative assemblies of the Autonomous Communities (Comunidades Autónomas) were elected in May 1983.

In September 2005 the Catalan Parliament overwhelmingly approved the draft of a revised Statute of Autonomy, to replace the existing document which had been in force since 1979. The proposed statute provoked considerable controversy elsewhere in the country over its definition of Catalonia as a 'nation' and its provision for greater fiscal and judicial independence. In March 2006 the Congreso de los Diputados approved a revised version of the statute that significantly reduced the extent of financial independence that would be granted to Catalonia, despite the opposition of ERC, which favoured full independence, and the PP, which claimed that the statute violated the Constitution. The new Statute of Autonomy was approved by 73.2% of voters in a referendum held in Catalonia in June, and came into force in August. Meanwhile, in July the PP submitted an appeal to the Constitutional Court against the new statute. The party alleged that a number of the document's articles were unconstitutional, including the definition of Catalonia as a 'nation', the privileged status afforded to the Catalan language and the provisions for judicial independence. The Constitutional Court finally delivered its judgment in July 2010 after repeated delays. Although it upheld the majority of the statute, it declared unconstitutional or ordered the reinterpretation of some 41 articles; notably, it allowed the use of the term 'nation' to refer to the region's historical and cultural identity but ruled that it could have no constitutional meaning. On the following day more than 1m. people attended a demonstration in Barcelona in favour of Catalan autonomy and against the court's decision. At the election to the Catalan Parliament held in November 2010, the outgoing coalition Government led by the Partit dels Socialistes de Catalunya (PSC–Socialist Party of Catalonia, allied to the PSOE) suffered a heavy defeat; the PSC took 28 of the 135 seats, compared to 37 in the previous Parliament. CiU increased its standing as the largest party in the legislature, taking 62 seats. Artur Mas, the leader of CiU, was subsequently inaugurated as President of the Generalitat (the regional administration) at the head of a minority CiU Government.

Several other autonomous communities, including Aragón, the Balearic Islands (Illes Balears), the Canary Islands (Canarias), Castilla-La Mancha and Galicia, began proceedings to reform their statutes of autonomy in 2005 and 2006. In April 2006 a new statute for the Valencia region entered into force, which, *inter alia*, defined Valencia as an 'historic nationality' (a term traditionally applied to Catalonia, the Basque Country and Galicia), made Valencian an official language and increased judicial and tax-raising independence. A new statute for Andalucía, which also defined the region as an 'historic nationality', took effect in March 2007, after being approved by 87% of the participating electorate in a referendum in February.

The conflict in the Basque region

The violent Basque separatist organization, ETA, founded in 1959 as a radical offshoot of the EAJ-PNV, came to increased prominence during the late 1960s. Having claimed its first victim, a civil guard, in 1968, the group achieved its most high-profile success in 1973 with the assassination of Adm. Carrero Blanco. Despite the establishment of the Basque Country Autonomous Community in 1979, ETA continued to demand a sovereign state comprising the three provinces of the Basque Country together with Navarra (Navarra—which was established as a separate Autonomous Community in 1982) and the historic Basque provinces of south-west France. In 1980 alone a total of 92 murders was attributed to the group. Despite bomb attacks in Bilbao in February 1983 and Madrid in July 1986, the central Government maintained its offer of social reintegration, instigated in mid-1984, to former ETA members.

The explosion in June 1987 of a bomb beneath a crowded Barcelona supermarket, which killed 21 and injured 45, was the most devastating attack committed by the organization, prompting Herri Batasuna (HB), ETA's political wing, to issue an unprecedented statement criticizing the attack. Co-operation with the authorities of France and Algeria (where numerous ETA members were discovered to be living) was strengthened, and in October the French police arrested 67 Basque suspects. In December five children were among the 12 killed in a bomb attack on the married quarters of a Civil Guard barracks in Zaragoza, which provoked a further public outcry and prompted the Government to break off negotiations with ETA early in the following year. In January 1988, after protracted negotiations, six parties (all of those represented in the Basque Parliament except HB) signed the Ajuria Enea Pact, rejecting terrorism as a means of determining the region's future. In January 1989 ETA declared a unilateral truce in an effort to reopen negotiations with the Government. Subsequent discussions between representatives of the Government and of ETA collapsed in April. A resolution declaring the right of the Basque people to self-determination was approved by the Basque Parliament in February 1990.

During the early and mid-1990s the authorities achieved considerable success in their counter-terrorist activities against ETA, particularly with increased co-operation from France. In July 1992 ETA's offer of a truce (to coincide with the forthcoming Olympic Games in Barcelona), in return for the reopening of dialogue, was rebuffed by the Government, which continued to insist upon the group's permanent renunciation of violence. Moreover, between then and February 1993 (when a major arsenal was discovered in France and ETA's operational head was captured) more than 500 ETA suspects were arrested. However, hopes of thereby forcibly and judicially terminating ETA's campaign of violence were ended in June by two car bomb explosions (one of which killed seven people) in Madrid.

Several senior ETA leaders were captured in late 1994 and in mid-1995, but attacks on police officers continued. In January 1995 Gregorio Ordóñez, a member of the Basque Parliament and the PP candidate for the mayoralty of San Sebastián at the forthcoming municipal elections, was shot dead, the first politician since 1992 to be murdered by ETA. In April 1995 Aznar, leader of the opposition PP, narrowly survived a car-bomb attempt on his life in Madrid, which injured 19 others. In August the authorities announced that a plot to assassinate King Juan Carlos had been foiled. Successive murders of politicians in early 1996 provoked a public outcry.

In July 1996, following a brief truce and the new PP Government's conditional offer of dialogue in the previous month, ETA renewed its bombing campaign, this time targeting the tourism industry. However, the authorities continued to arrest and convict ETA activists. A resurgence of violence in 1997 culminated in the abduction in July of Miguel Angel Blanco, a PP councillor in the Basque town of Ermua. ETA issued an ultimatum that prisoners belonging to the separatist organization be transferred to gaols in the Basque Country. Despite numerous appeals, including a message from the Pope, Blanco was duly shot upon the expiry of ETA's 48-hour deadline. His death provoked an unprecedented display of public outrage. In the largest demonstration since the attempted military coup of 1981, millions of Spaniards took to the streets, including Prime Minister Aznar, who led a protest march in Madrid. The Prime Minister vowed to intensify the Government's campaign against ETA, while urging (along with the moderate Basque parties) the isolation of HB.

In December 1997 the 23 members of the collective leadership of HB were each sentenced to seven years' imprisonment for collaborating with an armed group. In a significant development, for the first time the direct relationship between ETA and HB, which continued to claim to be independent of the terrorist organization, was recognized by the judiciary. The members of the collective leadership were released in July 1999, when their imprisonment was ruled unconstitutional. Meanwhile, in early 1998 a new HB leadership was elected, pledging to continue with the policies of its predecessors.

ETA declares a cease-fire

In September 1998, apparently attempting to pre-empt any ban on its activities and while still declining to renounce the use of violence, HB announced that it was to contest the forthcoming elections as Euskal Herritarrok (EH). In the same month both the PP and the opposition PSOE expressed reservations at the conclusion of an agreement (the Lizarra Pact) by the EAJ-PNV, Eusko Alkartasuna (EA), HB and IU on proposals for unconditional discussions with ETA. Nevertheless, following several months of secret talks between representatives of the EAJ-PNV and HB, on 16 September ETA declared an indefinite truce. In a conciliatory gesture, the Prime Minister indicated his willingness to transfer a number of ETA convicts to prisons in the Basque Country.

At the Basque elections held in October 1998, the EAJ-PNV again received the greatest support, while the PP supplanted the Partido Socialista de Euskadi-Euskadiko Ezkerra (PSE-EE, affiliated to the PSOE) as the party with the second largest representation in the regional parliament. In December, with the support of EH, an entirely nationalist coalition Government was established, with Juan José Ibarretxe of the EAJ-PNV as Lehendakari (President). Meanwhile, in November the central Government announced the inauguration of direct contact with representatives of ETA, which reaffirmed its commitment to the cease-fire.

In July 1999, for the first time, EH joined other Basque parties in signing a declaration rejecting the use of violence. In early September, as the first anniversary of the truce approached, it was revealed that a total of 180 ETA prisoners had been released within the last year. However, official monitoring of ETA activity continued and at the end of September three ETA suspects were arrested in France. On 28 November, on the eve of the opening in Paris of the trial of 13 ETA defendants, the terrorist organization announced the end of the 14-month cease-fire. Hours before the expiry of the truce on 3 December, the EAJ-PNV, along with other signatories of the Lizarra Pact, invited EH to sign a document demanding full sovereignty for the Basque Country and criticizing the policies of both the Spanish and French Governments. Despite successful official action against ETA activities, in January 2000 the organization successfully exploded two car bombs in Madrid, one of which killed an army officer. In February a Basque socialist politician and his bodyguard were killed in a bomb attack in Vitoria, prompting Ibarretxe to sever all links with EH, which subsequently announced that it was withdrawing from the Basque Parliament.

During 2000 some 100 members or collaborators of ETA were detained following covert Civil Guard operations; six command units were dismantled; and 12 members of ETA were successfully extradited. However, street disturbances in Basque cities continued to escalate, and there were 23 fatalities resultant from ETA attacks. Violence and assassinations by ETA continued during 2001, as did arrests of ETA suspects by the Spanish and French authorities.

At early elections to the Basque Parliament held in May 2001 the electoral coalition of the EAJ-PNV and EA, led by Ibarretxe, retained power. Following the election, HB, which had lost support, elected new members to its leadership and declared that henceforth it was to be known as Batasuna (Unity).

In October Ibarretxe warned that he was determined to hold a referendum on self-determination for the Basque Country, should the Government in Madrid continue to reject dialogue and ETA continue its campaign of violence. However, Prime Minister Aznar condemned the proposal as unconstitutional.

Batasuna is outlawed

In May 2002 the trial of Arnaldo Otegi, the spokesman for Batasuna, for vocal support of ETA was dismissed by the Supreme Court, to the consternation of the Government, which attempted to intervene. After a number of ETA actions during the EU summit in Seville in June, however, the Senado approved measures to outlaw political parties deemed to support terrorist organizations. The legislation was widely seen as targeting Batasuna, and, indeed, in August a parliamentary vote outlawed the party, while a separate Supreme Court order enforced the closure of party offices and a three-year suspension of party activities. Subsequently, in March 2003, the Supreme Court officially outlawed Batasuna. (The party was banned for a further two years in early 2006.) In December 2003 an attempt to circumvent the banning of Batasuna led the party to establish another organization, Sozialista Abertzaleak (Patriotic Socialists), in the hope of contesting regional elections later that year. In June 2009 the European Court of Human Rights rejected an appeal by Batasuna against the decision to ban it, ruling that the Spanish authorities' actions were justified.

In January 2003 the Cortes approved anti-terrorist legislation, extending the maximum sentence for terrorist activities from 30 to 40 years, and in February the Basque-language newspaper *Euskaldunon Egunkaria* was shut down on the grounds of its alleged links with ETA. Prior to regional and municipal elections in May, the central Government banned some 1,500 candidates from standing on the grounds of their alleged links with ETA. In response, ETA urged the lodging of protest votes in support of the banned politicians.

Immediately following the PSOE's victory in the general election in March 2004, ETA expressed a desire to begin a dialogue with the new Government; this was rejected, however, by the incoming administration of premier Zapatero. In late 2004, following the establishment of a Franco-Spanish anti-terrorism police force in September, a series of arrests of suspected members of ETA took place in France and Spain, including the capture in October of the alleged leader of the organization, Mikel 'Antza' Albizu Iriarte, in France. Subsequently Batasuna announced that it was prepared to negotiate. However, in December and January 2005 a series of bombs were detonated around Spain, and in early February ETA exploded a car bomb, injuring over 40 people, at a conference centre in Madrid, which was due to be visited by the King and President Vicente Fox of Mexico.

Meanwhile, in September 2003 Ibarretxe presented to the regional legislature his plan for shared sovereignty over the Basque Country, which proposed the 'free association' of the Basque Country with Spain, the creation of a separate judiciary and education system and the right of the Basque Country to conduct international relations. The proposals—known as the 'Ibarretxe plan'—were not widely supported in the region, and were strongly criticized by Madrid-based politicians and media on the grounds that it would be in breach of the Spanish Constitution. In December 2004 the Basque Parliament voted in favour of the Ibarretxe plan, with the last-minute support of Sozialista Abertzaleak, the perceived successor to Batasuna in the Parliament. In February 2005 the plan was debated by the Congreso de los Diputados and rejected by an overwhelming majority, although Zapatero declared that he was prepared to enter into negotiations on the status of the Basque Country within Spain. Ibarretxe responded by bringing the date of the Basque regional elections forward to 17 April. The election was seen as a gauge of the popularity of the 'Ibarretxe plan'. Prior to the poll, Aukera Guztiak, a radical nationalist party, was banned on the grounds of being close to ETA. However, a legal but hitherto inactive party, Euskal Herrialdeetako Alderdi Komunista (EHAK, also known as the Partido Comunista de las Tierras Vascas—PCTV), subsequently declared that it would contest the election with the same electoral programme proposed by Aukera Guztiak and Batasuna. In the event, Ibarretxe's EAJ-PNV and EA coalition won a reduced majority of 29 seats, while EHAK won nine seats.

Further cease-fire and negotiations

In May 2005 the Congreso de los Diputados approved government plans to open negotiations with ETA, should the group consent to disarm. ETA continued its bombing campaign around Spain during 2005 and early 2006, although no fatalities were caused. However, in March 2006 the group declared a 'permanent cease-fire', the first time in its history that it had taken such a step. It was speculated that the cease-fire had been prompted by the arrest of many of the organization's leaders. Zapatero responded to ETA's unilateral declaration by stating in May that the Government intended to enter into peace talks with the group. Despite these advances, during late 2006 ETA issued a number of statements indicating that it was not prepared to abandon violence or relinquish its weapons until the Basque Country became independent of Spain. In December, less than two weeks after the Government held its first formal meeting with ETA officials, a car bomb exploded at Barajas airport in Madrid, killing two people. Although ETA claimed responsibility for the attack, it claimed that its permanent cease-fire remained intact; none the less, Zapatero suspended talks in response to the bombing. (In May 2010 the National Court convicted three members of ETA of perpetrating the attack and sentenced them to lengthy prison terms.)

In June 2007 ETA announced an immediate end to its cease-fire, issuing a statement accusing the Government of 'pursuing detentions, torture and persecution' of its members. Several days later Otegi, who had been convicted of glorifying terrorism in April 2006, began serving a 15-month prison sentence after his appeal was rejected by the Supreme Court. In August an explosion in Durango, in which two police officers were injured, constituted the first attack by ETA since the formal expiry of its cease-fire.

In September 2007, in response to a request by Judge Baltasar Garzón, some 23 senior members of Batasuna were arrested during a clandestine meeting of the organization in Segura. Batasuna described the arrests as constituting a 'declaration of war' by the Spanish authorities; the EAJ-PNV was also critical of the arrests. In December two Spanish civil guards were shot by suspected members of ETA in Southern France; one of the officers was killed and the other left in a coma. The killing was believed to constitute the first killing perpetrated by ETA in France for some 30 years. In February 2008, in response to a further request by Garzón, the National Court suspended the operations, for a period of three years, of EHAK and another radical nationalist party, Acción Nacionalista Vasca (ANV), which had come to prominence at the municipal elections in May 2007. Garzón declared that the both parties were linked to Batasuna. In September the two parties were definitively outlawed by the Supreme Court.

In September 2007 Ibarretxe announced plans to hold a referendum on the Basque Country's future political status in the following year. The proposals were immediately rejected by the Spanish Government, which maintained that, constitutionally, only it could authorize referendums. Nevertheless, in June 2008 the Basque Parliament voted in favour of the referendum, which was scheduled for 25 October (the anniversary of the signing of the region's statute of autonomy in 1979) and which would gauge support for a negotiated settlement with ETA and for negotiations on 'the Basque people's right to decide'. However, in September the Constitutional Court ruled that the planned referendum was unconstitutional since it did not have central government approval. On 25 October an estimated 20,000 protesters marched in six towns in the Basque Country demanding that a referendum on Basque self-determination take place.

Violence by ETA continued throughout 2008, including fatal attacks against a civil guard barracks in Legutiano in May and a military academy in Santoña in September, and the assassination of the owner of a construction company in December. Also in May Francisco Javier López Peña, the suspected political leader of ETA, was arrested in Bordeaux, France, after some 20 years in hiding. In July it was announced by the Spanish authorities that the most active ETA cell, the 'Vizcaya commando', had been dismantled. Nine people were arrested, including Arkaitz Goikoetxea, the suspected cell leader. In November Miguel de Garikoitz Aspiazu Rubina (alias 'Txeroki'), the suspected military leader of ETA, was arrested in the French Pyrenees. In December 2008 the French authorities arrested Aspiazu Rubina's apparent successor as military leader, Aitzol Iriondo, and only four months later, in April 2009, Iriondo's successor, Jurdan Martitegi, was also arrested in France.

Non-nationalist Basque government elected

At elections to the Basque Parliament held in March 2009 the EAJ-PNV won 30 of the 75 seats. The PSE-EE performed well, winning 25 seats, while the PP took 13; the nationalist parties Aralar and EA won four seats and one seat, respectively, while Ezker Batua-Berdeak (affiliated to IU) and the non-nationalist Unión Progreso y Democracia (UPyD) each took one seat. No party with links to ETA managed to circumvent the legal prohibitions and contest the election, with the result that the new legislature was free of any connection with the violent separatist movement for the first time since 1980. In May, with the EAJ-PNV unable to achieve the required absolute majority of 38 seats, the PSE-EE's Patxi López was elected Lehendakari with the support of the PP and UPyD, becoming the Basque Government's first non-nationalist leader. The new Government set out as its priority the fight against ETA.

Attacks by ETA continued in 2009, despite the recent arrests among its leadership. In June a police inspector involved in anti-terrorism operations was killed in a suburb of Bilbao by a bomb attached to his car. In late July, coinciding with the 50th anniversary of ETA's foundation, two bomb attacks occurred within 48 hours against the Civil Guard in Burgos and on Mallorca; the first, outside a barracks, left more than 50 people injured, while the second caused the deaths of two officers. A co-ordinated series of bomb explosions in Palma de Mallorca in August, apparently targeted at tourists, caused no injuries. None the less, the high rate of police action against ETA continued. Later in August three suspected militants were arrested in Le Corbier in the French Alps, and in the following week the French authorities seized a significant quantity of weapons and explosives believed to have been used by the group in southern France. In October Otegi (who had been released from gaol in August 2008) and a number of other senior members of Batasuna were arrested in San Sebastián on suspicion of attempting to resurrect the illegal party. In March 2010 Otegi was sentenced to two months' imprisonment by the National Court on a charge of glorifying terrorism. Meanwhile, later in October 2009 Aitor Elizarán Aguilar, believed to be López Peña's successor as political leader of ETA, was arrested in a joint operation between Spanish and French police in Carnac, north-west France. Evidence of ETA's increasing use of Portugal as a base for its operations emerged in February 2010 when, for the first time, Portuguese police discovered a cache of explosives in a house in Obidos. At the end of February the suspected military leader of ETA, Ibon Gogeaskoetxea, was arrested along with two other militants in Normandy, France; he was the fourth successive head of the organization to be detained in 15 months. In the following month a French police officer died after a gun battle with suspected ETA militants near Paris. Gogeaskoetxea's suspected successor as military leader of ETA, Mikel Kabikoitz Carrera Sarobe (alias 'Ata'), was arrested in May along with his deputy in Bayonne, France. On 5 September ETA declared a cease-fire, stating in a communiqué that it had decided some months ago not to carry out armed attacks and that it was committed to achieving an independent Basque Country by democratic means. The Basque and Spanish Governments immediately declared the group's announcement insufficient, since it did not amount to a permanent or verifiable renunciation of violence. It was widely believed that ETA's truce was in response not only to the recent weakening of its military capability as a result of police action, but also to political pressure from within the Basque separatist movement; indeed, earlier in September Batasuna had endorsed a statement (the 'Brussels Declaration'), published in March by an international group of former peace negotiators and statesmen, that demanded a permanent and internationally verifiable cease-fire as a precondition for a negotiated end to the conflict. Following a number of further declarations by Batasuna and other Basque nationalist parties in support of a permanent end to the violence, on 10 January 2011 ETA declared a 'permanent and general' cease-fire that would be 'verifiable by the international community'. However, the Government maintained that the declaration still did not go far enough, demanding that the group renounce violence unconditionally and that it take steps towards disarmament and dissolution. In February 2011 the foundation was announced of a new radical nationalist party, to be called Sortu, that explicitly rejected violence (including that of ETA), and which intended to contest the municipal elections scheduled for 22 May. The Government cautiously welcomed the new party's foundation, describing the rejection of violence by the radical nationalist movement as an important step, but stressed that the courts would decide if the new party could legally be registered. The case was subsequently referred to the Supreme Court, which in March ruled that Sortu was a successor to the illegal Batasuna and, as such, could not be registered as a legal political party. Seven of the court's 16 judges issued a dissenting opinion, stating that there was insufficient evidence that the new party was directly linked to Batasuna and that it appeared to comply with the 2002 law on political parties. In April 2011 former members of Sortu formed a coalition called Bildu. Initially this was also banned by the Supreme Court, but the ban was lifted in the Constitutional Court, permitting Bildu to contest the May 2011 regional and local elections, at which it won seven of the 50 seats in the Navarre legislative assembly.

Foreign Affairs
Regional relations

Spanish ratification of the Treaty on European Union (the Maastricht Treaty) was completed in November 1992. A national referendum on the EU Treaty establishing a Constitution for Europe took place in Spain on 20 February 2005, with 76.2% of the votes cast being in favour of ratifying the treaty. The turnout, however, was equivalent to only 42.3% of the electorate. Following the rejection of this treaty by voters in France and the Netherlands later that year, in December 2007 a new, amended treaty was signed in Lisbon, Portugal, and Spain ratified the resultant Treaty of Lisbon by parliamentary approval in July 2008.

Spain continues to claim sovereignty over the neighbouring British dependency of Gibraltar (q.v.). In 1997 the United Kingdom rejected Spanish initiatives entailing joint sovereignty for up to 100 years prior to an eventual transfer of power to Spain. In December Spanish proposals that, following a period of joint sovereignty, Gibraltar became an Autonomous Community were similarly rebuffed by the British Government. In April 2000 Spain and the United Kingdom signed an agreement relating to the administrative status of Gibraltar. The territory's identity cards would henceforth be accepted by Spain as valid for travel within the EU. Furthermore, the agreement permitted the implementation of numerous EU directives, long obstructed by Spain, which had refused to recognize the Government of Gibraltar as a 'competent authority' in EU affairs. It was also agreed that Spain and Gibraltar would communicate indirectly through a facility, based in London, provided by the British authorities. Following a meeting between Spanish and British officials in Brussels, Belgium, in mid-2001, the Minister of Foreign Affairs, Josep Piqué, and his British counterpart, Jack Straw, held discussions in October, during which they agreed to work towards solving the dispute by December 2002. The issue of the right of Gibraltarians to vote on any agreement reached by the two Governments continued to impede the progress of the discussions, with Piqué warning the British Government that Spain would not accept the results of such a referendum. In January 2002 it was reported that the Spanish Government had agreed to modify its demand for outright sovereignty over the territory and reconsider the option of sharing sovereignty over the territory with the United Kingdom for an indefinite period. In May, however, Aznar announced that Spain would never withdraw its territorial claim to Gibraltar. Negotiations progressed in mid-2002, although a stalemate emerged when Spain disagreed with the British conditions for joint sovereignty—that it be permanent, that the military base would remain under British control, and that all changes be approved by a referendum put to the people of Gibraltar. In a referendum organized by the local administration of Gibraltar in November, which was not, however, recognized by the Spanish or British Governments, the electorate voted overwhelmingly against joint sovereignty with Spain.

In December 2004 the first of what was to be an annual tripartite meeting between the United Kingdom, Spain and Gibraltar was held in the United Kingdom, and it was subsequently announced that henceforth decisions on the territory's future must be agreed by all three parties. In early 2006 Spain opposed the inclusion of references to the right to self-determination of Gibraltarians in a proposed new constitution for Gibraltar. However, in March Straw assured the Spanish Government that the draft constitution would not change the current international status or sovereignty of the territory, nor affect Spanish rights over Gibraltar under the Treaty of Utrecht, which would constrain the right to self-determination, in the view of the British Government, and that independence would therefore only be a future option for Gibraltar with Spain's consent. The Constitution was subsequently approved in a referendum in the territory in December. Meanwhile, in September 2006 a meeting was held in Córdoba between the Spanish Minister of Foreign Affairs and Co-operation, Miguel Angel Moratinos, the British Minister of State for Europe, Geoff Hoon, and the Gibraltarian Chief Minister, Peter Caruana, the first ever meeting between members of all three Governments. An agreement was signed which, *inter alia*, envisaged the expansion of Gibraltar airport, with a new terminal building straddling the border, and allowed Spain to open a branch of the Spanish cultural organization, the Instituto Cervantes, in Gibraltar. While relations between Spain and the United Kingdom improved from 2006, tensions still remained. In January 2009 several Spanish opposition parliamentarians accused a Gibraltarian development company of 'illegal incursion' into Spanish waters, after it proposed to erect platforms on the seabed. In March the Spanish Government made a formal complaint to the British authorities over a proposed visit to the territory by a member of the British royal family, describing it as 'an affront' to Spain. None the less, in July 2009 Moratinos became the first Spanish minister to visit Gibraltar when he attended the annual ministerial meeting of the tripartite Forum of Dialogue.

Relations with Morocco have been dominated by the issues of sovereignty of the Spanish exclaves of Ceuta and Melilla, illegal immigration and drugs-trafficking, and by disputes over fishing rights. By 2000 the problems of illegal immigration (not only via Spanish North Africa but increasingly via the Canary Islands) had become a major political issue. In May, during a visit to Morocco, the Spanish Prime Minister confirmed that the recently implemented immigration law, one of the most liberal within the EU, was to be reformed. Since its entry into force earlier in the year, the new legislation had encouraged more than 82,000 illegal migrants to apply for Spanish residency permits. Protests against the reforms were staged in Spanish North Africa as well as in mainland Spain. Negotiations on the renewal of the fishing agreement between Morocco and the EU, permitting Spanish vessels access to Moroccan waters, commenced in September 1999. The agreement expired in November and Morocco indicated that it would not be renewed. Relations were severely strained in July 2002 following the occupation of a small uninhabited islet near Ceuta, the Isla de Perejil (Laila), by 12 Moroccan soldiers. Spain lodged a formal protest against this action on 12 July, but Morocco refused to withdraw its men, claiming that Perejil had been a part of Morocco since independence in 1956. Spanish soldiers reoccupied the island on 17 July, and a subsequent US-mediated agreement between Spain and Morocco left the island unoccupied. Issues over the sovereignty of Ceuta and Melilla continued to be problematic, however, and in September Morocco accused Spain of repeated violations of its airspace and territorial waters and reasserted its claims over the exclaves before the UN. Meetings in December 2002 and January 2003 contributed to the re-establishment of diplomatic relations between the two countries in February. However, a visit to the disputed territories by King Juan Carlos in November 2007 provoked protests by the Moroccan Government.

Other external relations

In 1988 Spain and the USA renewed their bilateral defence agreement, permitting the USA's continued use of bases in Spain. An amendment to the accord was agreed in 2002. In mid-2003, despite widespread public opposition, Spain sent 1,300 peace-keeping troops to Iraq to join the US-led coalition forces, and in October of that year pledged €250m. to the reconstruction process in Iraq. Following the election of the PSOE Government in March 2004, however, the withdrawal of the Spanish troops was completed by the end of May. The hasty withdrawal of troops, together with Zapatero's expressed hostility towards the US Administration of George W. Bush, contributed to a sharp deterioration of relations with the USA. By 2007 tensions had eased, and in June US Secretary of State Condoleezza Rice visited Madrid, becoming the first senior US official to visit Spain since the PSOE Government took office.

In November 1992 Spain dispatched a substantial contingent of troops to Bosnia and Herzegovina, the first Spanish soldiers to serve in a UN peace-keeping operation. Continuing to assume a greater international role, Spain contributed troops to the multinational force deployed in Albania in April 1997, and again in April 1999 during the NATO offensive against Yugoslavia. Spain committed 1,200 ground troops to the international peace-keeping force deployed in Kosovo in June 1999. Spain was one of five EU countries that refused to recognize Kosovo's unilateral declaration of independence from Serbia in 2008, and in March 2009 it was announced that the remaining 600 Spanish troops in Kosovo would be withdrawn later that year. The withdrawal of Spanish troops was completed in September. In mid-2011 Spain was contributing to a number of international peace-keeping missions, including the United Nations Interim Force in Lebanon, in which some 1,100 Spanish troops were serving, and the International Security Assistance Force in Afghanistan, in which some 1,000 Spanish troops were serving. Spain also contributed five aircraft to the international mission to impose a no-fly zone over Libya that commenced in March 2011.

From 1998, under Spanish law, persons accused of crimes against humanity, no matter where they had taken place, could be tried in a Spanish court. In the late 1990s criminal proceedings continued in Spain against former Argentine and Chilean officials of the military dictatorships of Argentina (1976–83) and of Chile (1979–90), during which numerous Spanish citizens had been killed. In November 1998, following the arrest in the United Kingdom of Gen. Augusto Pinochet and the instigation by Judge Garzón of extradition proceedings against the former Chilean President, Chile's ambassador to Madrid was recalled for consultations. In October 1999 a British judge ruled that the former Chilean President could be extradited to Spain to answer 35 charges of torture and conspiracy. In March 2000, however, Pinochet was permitted to return to Chile from the United Kingdom, where he had remained under house arrest, extradition proceedings having been abandoned on medical grounds. In April 2005, following an indictment by Garzón, Adolfo Scilingo, an Argentine former army officer, was given a prison sentence of 640 years (although, under Spanish law, he would serve a maximum of 30 years) for crimes against humanity under the military rule in Argentina during 1976–83; Scilingo was the first person to be convicted in Spain according to the principle of universal jurisdiction. In November 2009 legislation took effect which limited the power of the courts to prosecute crimes against humanity to those cases in which there was a clear link to Spain, or in which the alleged perpetrator was present on Spanish territory.

CONSTITUTION AND GOVERNMENT

Under the Constitution approved in 1978, Spain is an hereditary monarchy, with the King as Head of State. He appoints the President of the Government (Prime Minister) and, on the latter's recommendation, other members of the Council of Ministers. Legislation is initiated for discussion in the Cortes (national assembly) in Madrid, in the Parliaments of the Autonomous Communities, or by popular petition. The King's actions in state affairs must receive the prior approval of the

Cortes, to which the Government is responsible. The Council of State is the supreme consultative organ of the Government.

Legislative power is vested in the Cortes Generales, comprising two chambers, elected by direct universal adult suffrage for four years (subject to dissolution). The Congreso de los Diputados (Congress of Deputies) has 350 members, elected by proportional representation, and the Senado (Senate) has 208 directly elected members, plus 51 regional representatives, elected by the autonomous parliaments. A party can gain representation only if it obtains at least 3% of the votes.

Regional self-government was established in the 1978 Constitution. In October 1979 the statutes of the first of 17 Autonomous Communities were approved by referendum. The first Legislative Assemblies (Basque and Catalan) were elected in March 1980. The Galician Legislative Assembly was elected in October 1981 and that of Andalucía in May 1982. The remaining 13 were constituted in May 1983, thus completing the process of devolution. The regions possess varying degrees of autonomy. Each Legislative Assembly is elected for four years.

Spain comprises 50 provinces, each with its own Council (Diputación Provincial). The system of Civil Governors was replaced (by royal decree) in April 1997: a government subdelegate is appointed by each Autonomous Community's government delegate.

REGIONAL AND INTERNATIONAL CO-OPERATION

Spain is a member of the European Union (EU, see p. 270), the Council of Europe (see p. 250) and the Organization for Security and Co-operation in Europe (OSCE, see p. 385).

Spain was admitted to the UN in 1955; the headquarters of the World Tourism Organization (see p. 177) is in Madrid. As a contracting party to the General Agreement on Tariffs and Trade, Spain joined the World Trade Organization (WTO, see p. 430) on its establishment in 1995. Spain is also a member of the North Atlantic Treaty Organization (NATO, see p. 368) and the Organisation for Economic Co-operation and Development (OECD, see p. 376).

ECONOMIC AFFAIRS

In 2009, according to estimates by the World Bank, Spain's gross national income (GNI), measured at average 2007–09 prices, was US $1,464,739m., equivalent to $31,870 per head (or $31,630 per head on an international purchasing-power parity basis). During 2000–09, it was estimated, the population increased at an average annual rate of 1.5%, while gross domestic product (GDP) per head increased, in real terms, by an average of 0.8% per year. Overall GDP increased, in real terms, at an average annual rate of 2.3% in 2000–09; real GDP growth was 0.9% in 2008, but GDP contracted by 3.6% in 2009.

Agriculture (including forestry and fishing) contributed 2.7% of GDP in 2010 and engaged 4.3% of the employed labour force in the same year. The principal crops are barley, wheat, sugar beet, vegetables, citrus fruits, grapes and olives; wine and olive oil are important products. The fishing industry is significant. The Spanish fishing fleet is one of the largest in the world. Agricultural GDP shrank at an average annual rate of 1.0% in 2000–08, according to the World Bank; it declined by 10.0% in 2005, mainly owing to severe drought, but increased by 2.4% in 2006 and by 3.8% in 2007, followed by a decline of 0.6% in 2008.

Industry (including mining, manufacturing, power and construction) contributed 25.7% of GDP in 2010, and engaged 23.1% of the employed labour force in the same year. According to the World Bank, industrial GDP increased at an average annual rate of 2.1% in 2000–08; it increased by 3.1% in 2007, but declined by 2.4% in 2009.

The mining and quarrying industry provided less than 1.0% of GDP in 2004 and engaged 0.2% of the employed labour force in that year. The principal minerals produced include cement, industrial sand and gravel, aluminium, copper, gold, silver and zinc. Although coal is plentiful in Spain, the production costs are relatively high.

Manufacturing contributed an estimated 12.6% of GDP in 2010 and engaged 12.8% of the employed labour force in the same year. Important industries include passenger cars, shipbuilding, chemicals, steel, textiles and footwear. Investment is being made in new manufacturing industries, such as information technology and telecommunications equipment. Manufacturing GDP increased at an average annual rate of 1.4% in 2000–07, according to the World Bank; the rate of growth was 2.8% in 2006 and 2.7% in 2007.

The construction sector contributed 10.1% of GDP in 2010, and engaged 8.9% of the employed labour force in the same year.

Energy (comprising mining and power) contributed an estimated 3.1% of GDP in 2010, and employed 1.3% of the labour force in the same year. Energy is derived principally from petroleum, most of which is imported. In 2008 imports of mineral fuels and lubricants accounted for 19.4% of total import costs (petroleum and petroleum products accounted for 14.5%). Natural gas became an increasingly important fuel source in the late 1990s. Some natural gas requirements are obtained from the Bay of Biscay, the remainder is imported by pipeline from Algeria. Nuclear energy provided 53.9% of total electricity production in 2007, while coal provided 22.0% and hydroelectric power 8.8%. Wind and solar power together accounted for 9.1% of the electricity supply in the same year. According to official estimates, energy GDP increased by 2.0% annually in 2000–07; energy GDP grew by 0.8% in 2007.

In 2010 the services sector accounted for an estimated 71.7% of GDP, while it engaged 72.6% of the employed labour force in the same year. The tourism industry makes an important contribution to the Spanish economy. In 2009 the number of tourist arrivals was estimated at 52.2m. (25.5% from the United Kingdom), and receipts from tourism totalled €56,352m in 2008. Remittances from emigrants are also significant; in 2007 remittances amounted to €5.3m. According to the World Bank, the GDP of the services sector increased at an average annual rate of 3.7% in 2000–08; services GDP increased by 2.4% in 2008.

In 2009 Spain recorded a visible trade deficit of US $62,833m. and there was a deficit of $80,375m. on the current account of the balance of payments. In 2008 the principal sources of imports were Germany (13.9%) and France, Italy and China. France was the main export market in that year (18.2%), followed by Germany, Portugal, Italy, and the United Kingdom. Other members of the European Union (EU, see p. 270) are also important trading partners. The principal imports in 2008 were machinery and transport equipment, mineral fuels and lubricants, basic manufactures, chemical products, miscellaneous manufactured articles, and food and live animals. The main exports were machinery and transport equipment, basic manufactures, chemicals and related products, and food and live animals (particularly fruit and vegetables).

In 2009 the budget deficit was €117,306.0m., equivalent to 11.1% of GDP. Spain's general government gross debt was €560,587.0m. in 2009, equivalent to 53.2% of GDP. The annual rate of inflation averaged 2.9% in 2000–09; consumer prices decreased by an average of 0.4% in 2009, but rose by 1.9% in 2010. The unemployment rate was 18.0% in 2009.

Spain underwent an extended period of rapid expansion in the late 1990s and 2000s, driven by consumer demand based on the availability of inexpensive credit, a rapid rise in property prices and the expansion of the construction sector. The contraction of credit on the global financial markets from 2007 caused a collapse of the housing market, which was already saturated with new properties, and the subsequent global downturn had a severe effect on the Spanish economy as a whole. According to official estimates, GDP declined by 3.6% in 2009 and 0.1% in 2010 and by the first quarter of 2010 unemployment had surpassed 20%. During 2008–09 the Government of José Luis Rodríguez Zapatero implemented stimulus measures to support the economy, including tax rebates and increased investment in public infrastructure projects. However, increased government spending caused a rapid deterioration of the fiscal balance, which went from a surplus of 2.3% in 2007 to a deficit of 11.1% of GDP in 2009, significantly above the EU's deficit limit of 3% of GDP. Harsh austerity measures, including a 5% reduction in public sector pay, were announced in January and May 2010, partly in response to concern among international investors that Spain was at risk of defaulting on its sovereign debt. Concern remained over the potential cost to the economy and public finances of any further loss of confidence in Spain's indebted regional savings banks (*cajas de ahorros*), which were heavily exposed to the fall in property values; the Banco de España had been forced to intervene in Caja Castilla La Mancha in March 2009 and CajaSur in May 2010 in order to prevent their collapse. In January 2011, having urged the savings banks to continue their process of merger and consolidation, the Government announced its intention to nationalize any savings bank that failed to secure sufficient capital investment by September. Meanwhile, the Government hoped that reforms to the labour market laws approved definitively in September 2010 would help to reduce the country's

SPAIN

Statistical Survey

high level of structural unemployment by facilitating the hiring and dismissal of workers on permanent contracts. In February 2011 the Government concluded an agreement with the principal trade unions and employers' organizations to raise the legal retirement age from 65 to 67 years by 2027; further agreement on reform of the collective bargaining system remained pending. None the less, in the first quarter of 2011 unemployment reached its highest level for 14 years, at 21.3%. Official figures published in April 2011 forecast GDP growth of 1.3% for that year; however, the IMF in October 2010 predicted growth of just 0.7% in 2011.

PUBLIC HOLIDAYS

2012: 1 January (New Year's Day), 6 January (Epiphany)*, 5 April (Maundy Thursday)*, 6 April (Good Friday), 1 May (Labour Day), 15 August (Assumption), 12 October (National Day), 1 November (All Saints' Day), 6 November (Constitution Day), 8 December (Immaculate Conception), 25 December (Christmas Day).

In addition, various holidays are established by the Autonomous Communities and municipal authorities, giving an annual total of 14 public holidays.

* May not be observed in all Autonomous Communities.

Statistical Survey

Source (unless otherwise stated): Instituto Nacional de Estadística, Paseo de la Castellana 183, 28071 Madrid; tel. (91) 5839100; fax (91) 5839158; internet www.ine.es.

Area and Population

AREA, POPULATION AND DENSITY*

Area (sq km)	505,988†
Population (census results)	
1 March 1991	38,872,268
1 November 2001	
Males	20,012,882
Females	20,834,489
Total	40,847,371
Population (official estimates at 1 January)	
2009	45,828,172
2010	45,989,016
2011	46,152,925
Density (per sq km) at 1 January 2011	91.2

* Including the Spanish External Territories (Spanish North Africa—area 33 sq km), an integral part of Spain. Ceuta had a population of 75,763 on 1 January 2011, while Melilla's population was 74,078.
† 195,363 sq miles.

POPULATION BY AGE AND SEX
(official estimates at 1 January 2011)

	Males	Females	Total
0–14	3,582,254	3,382,832	6,965,085
15–64	15,787,086	15,522,957	31,310,043
65 and over	3,355,525	4,522,270	7,877,798
Total	22,724,866	23,428,060	46,152,925

Note: Totals may not be equal to the sum of components, owing to extrapolation methodologies.

AUTONOMOUS COMMUNITIES AND CITIES
(population at 1 January 2011)*

	Area (sq km)	Population	Density (per sq km)	Capital
Autonomous Communities				
Andalucía (Andalusia)	87,598	8,256,297	94.3	Sevilla (Seville)
Aragón	47,720	1,314,906	27.6	Zaragoza
Principado de Asturias	10,604	1,055,557	99.5	Oviedo
Illes Balears (Balearic Is)	4,992	1,088,514	218.1	Palma de Mallorca
Canarias (Canary Is)	7,447	2,100,235	282.0	Las Palmas de Gran Canaria/ Santa Cruz de Tenerife†
Cantabria	5,321	578,632	108.7	Santander
Castilla-La Mancha	79,462	2,046,717	25.8	Toledo
Castilla y León	94,225	2,491,420	26.4	Valladolid
Cataluña/Catalunya (Catalonia)	32,113	7,333,530	228.4	Barcelona
Comunidad Valenciana/ Comunitat Valenciana	23,255	5,004,475	215.2	Valencia
Extremadura	41,635	1,083,259	26.0	Mérida
Galicia	29,574	2,736,636	92.5	Santiago de Compostela
Comunidad de Madrid	8,028	6,369,167	793.4	Madrid
Región de Murcia	11,313	1,468,127	129.8	Murcia
Comunidad Foral de Navarra (Navarre)	10,390	622,125	59.9	Pamplona
País Vasco/Euskadi (Basque Country)	7,235	2,140,339	295.8	Vitoria-Gasteiz
La Rioja	5,045	313,149	62.1	Logroño
Autonomous Cities				
Ceuta	19	75,763	3,987.5	—
Melilla	13	74,078	5,698.3	—
Total	505,988	46,152,925	91.2	

* Including residents temporarily abroad.
† Joint capitals.

PRINCIPAL TOWNS*
(population at 1 January 2010)

Madrid (capital)	3,273,049	Vitoria-Gasteiz	238,247
Barcelona	1,619,337	Elche	230,822
Valencia	809,267	Oviedo	225,155
Sevilla (Seville)	704,198	Santa Cruz de Tenerife	222,643
Zaragoza	675,121	Badalona	218,886
Málaga	568,507	Cartagena	214,165
Murcia	441,345	Terrassa	212,724
Palma de Mallorca	404,681	Jerez de la Frontera	208,896
Las Palmas de Gran Canaria	383,308	Sabadell	207,338
Bilbao	353,187	Móstoles	206,015
Alacant (Alicante)	334,418	Alcalá de Henares	204,120
Córdoba	328,547	Fuenlabrada	198,973
Valladolid	315,522	Pamplona	197,488
Vigo	297,124	Almería	190,013
Gijón	277,198	Leganés	187,227
Hospitalet de Llobregat	258,642	Donostia-San Sebastián	185,506
A Coruña (La Coruña)	246,047	Santander	181,589
Granada	239,154	Castelló (Castellón) de la Plana	180,690

* Population figures refer to *municipios*, each of which may contain some rural area as well as the urban centre.

SPAIN

BIRTHS, MARRIAGES AND DEATHS

	Registered live births Number	Rate (per 1,000)	Registered marriages Number	Rate (per 1,000)	Registered deaths Number	Rate (per 1,000)
2002	418,846	10.1	211,522	5.1	368,618	8.9
2003	441,881	10.5	212,300	5.0	384,828	9.2
2004	454,591	10.7	216,149	5.1	371,934	8.7
2005	466,371	10.8	208,146	4.7	387,355	8.9
2006	482,957	11.0	203,453	4.6	371,478	8.4
2007	492,527	10.9	201,579	4.5	385,361	8.6
2008	519,779	11.2	194,022	4.3	386,324	8.4
2009	492,931	10.7	172,540	3.8	383,486	8.4

Life expectancy (years at birth, WHO estimates): 81 (males 78; females 84) in 2008 (Source: WHO, *World Health Statistics*).

ECONOMICALLY ACTIVE POPULATION
('000 persons aged 16 years and over)

	2008	2009	2010
Agriculture, hunting, forestry and fishing	818.9	786.1	793.0
Mining and quarrying	52.9	45.9	44.8
Manufacturing	2,951.8	2,519.5	2,370.1
Electricity, gas and water supply	194.2	209.6	195.6
Construction	2,453.4	1,888.3	1,650.8
Wholesale and retail trade; repair of motor vehicles, motorcycles and personal and household goods	3,203.3	2,974.7	2,909.4
Hotels and restaurants	1,452.5	1,421.2	1,370.3
Transport, storage and communications	1,525.1	1,426.7	1,415.6
Financial intermediation	507.7	474.1	463.5
Real estate, renting and business activities	1,921.3	1,841.8	1,829.7
Public administration and defence; compulsory social security	1,276.5	1,367.3	1,406.3
Education	1,149.1	1,160.1	1,181.6
Health and social work	1,261.7	1,323.4	1,364.6
Other community, social and personal service activities	734.3	722.0	711.7
Private households with employed persons	752.6	725.3	747.0
Extra-territorial organizations and bodies	2.3	2.1	2.7
Total employed	20,257.6	18,888.0	18,456.5
Total unemployed	2,590.6	4,149.5	4,632.4
Total labour force	22,848.2	23,037.5	23,088.9
Males	13,031.7	12,938.5	12,819.2
Females	9,816.5	10,099.0	10,269.7

Health and Welfare

KEY INDICATORS

Total fertility rate (children per woman, 2008)	1.4
Under-5 mortality rate (per 1,000 live births, 2008)	4
HIV/AIDS (% of persons aged 15–49, 2007)	0.5
Physicians (per 1,000 head, 2004)	3.3
Hospital beds (per 1,000 head, 2005)	3.4
Health expenditure (2007): US $ per head (PPP)	2,671
Health expenditure (2007): % of GDP	8.5
Health expenditure (2007): public (% of total)	71.8
Total carbon dioxide emissions ('000 metric tons, 2007)	358,965.7
Carbon dioxide emissions per head (metric tons, 2007)	8.0
Human Development Index (2010): ranking	20
Human Development Index (2010): value	0.863

For sources and definitions, see explanatory note on p. vi.

Agriculture

PRINCIPAL CROPS
('000 metric tons)

	2007	2008	2009
Wheat	6,436	6,714	4,797
Rice, paddy	723	665	899
Barley	11,945	11,261	7,400
Maize	3,611	3,629	3,479
Oats	1,309	1,149	906
Potatoes	2,480	2,366	2,481
Sugar beet	4,910	3,988	4,154
Olives	6,140	5,475	6,205
Sunflower seed	733	822	876
Lettuce	948	1,003	1,000*
Tomatoes	4,081	3,923	4,749
Chillies and peppers, green	1,058	992	1,012
Onions, dry	1,184	1,098	1,195
Oranges	2,740	3,367	2,780
Tangerines, mandarins, clementines and satsumas	1,987	2,213	2,026
Lemons and limes	507	689	620
Apples	721	688	553
Pears	552	558	404
Peaches and nectarines	1,221	1,299	1,226
Grapes	5,963	6,020	5,286
Watermelons	791	722	827
Cantaloupes and other melons	1,183	1,022	1,006

* FAO estimate.

Aggregate production ('000 metric tons, may include official, semi-official or estimated data): Total cereals 24,484 in 2007, 23,904 in 2008, 17,872 in 2009; Total roots and tubers 2,512 in 2007, 2,398 in 2008, 2,513 in 2009; Total vegetables (incl. melons) 13,060 in 2007, 12,622 in 2008, 13,626 in 2009; Total fruits (excl. melons) 15,114 in 2007, 16,278 in 2008, 14,373 in 2009.

Source: FAO.

LIVESTOCK
('000 head, year ending September)

	2007	2008	2009
Horses*	250	248	n.a.
Asses and mules*	252	252	n.a.
Cattle	6,585	6,585	6,020
Pigs	26,061	26,026	26,290
Sheep	22,194	19,952	19,718
Goats	2,892	2,959	2,265
Chickens*	137,000	138,000	138,000

* FAO estimates.

Source: FAO.

LIVESTOCK PRODUCTS
('000 metric tons)

	2007	2008	2009
Cattle meat	620	658	598
Sheep meat	203	157	124
Goat meat	10	9	8
Pig meat	3,439	3,484	3,291
Horse meat	5	6	n.a.
Rabbit meat	75	69	n.a.
Chicken meat	1,131	1,082	1,179
Cows' milk	6,143	6,340	n.a.
Sheep's milk	414	441	439*
Goats' milk	489	593	473
Hen eggs	825†	800	n.a.
Honey	32	30	n.a.
Wool, greasy	29	29†	n.a.

* Unofficial figure.
† FAO estimate.

Source: FAO.

Forestry

ROUNDWOOD REMOVALS
('000 cubic metres, excl. bark)

	2007	2008	2009
Sawlogs, veneer logs and logs for sleepers	4,532	5,273	3,193
Pulpwood	7,531	8,566	8,119
Other industrial wood	483	589	589
Fuel wood	1,982	2,600	2,600
Total	14,528	17,027	14,502

Source: FAO.

SAWNWOOD PRODUCTION
('000 cubic metres, incl. railway sleepers)

	2007	2008	2009
Coniferous (softwood)	2,180	2,295	2,295*
Broadleaved (hardwood)	1,152	846	846*
Total	3,332	3,142	3,142

* FAO estimate.
Source: FAO.

Fishing

('000 metric tons, live weight)

	2006	2007	2008
Capture	961.2*	820.1*	917.2
Blue whiting (Poutassou)	56.7	37.5	25.2
European pilchard (sardine)	70.1	60.3	56.5
Skipjack tuna	169.2	106.0	131.1
Yellowfin tuna	88.9	56.6	76.3
Jack and horse mackerels	44.4	43.0	44.7
Aquaculture	292.9	281.2	249.1
Blue mussel	228.8	209.6	180.3
Total catch*	1,254.2	1,101.4	1,166.3

* FAO estimate(s).
Note: Figures exclude Sardinia coral (metric tons): 6 in 2006; 5 in 2007–08.
Source: FAO.

Mining

('000 metric tons unless otherwise indicated)

	2007	2008	2009
Anthracite	7,872	7,238	6,952
Lignite	6,180	—	—
Crude petroleum ('000 barrels)	334	298	250
Natural gas (million cu m)	330	330*	330*
Copper*†	10	10	10
Kaolin	489	356	300*
Potash salts (crude)*	435	435	435
Sepiolite	718	708	770
Dolomite*	15,000	15,000	15,000
Fluorspar‡	152	149	122
Salt (unrefined)	4,182	4,141	4,058
Gypsum (crude)*	15,000	15,000	15,000

* Estimated production.
† Figures refer to the metal content of ores.
‡ Figures refer to total CaF_2 content (acid and metallurgical grades).
Source: US Geological Survey.

Industry

SELECTED PRODUCTS
('000 metric tons unless otherwise indicated)

	2005	2006	2007
Fish (tinned)	384.1	389.0	n.a.
Wheat flour	3,073	3,036	3,144
Vinegar	1,002	1,034	1,037
Distilled alcohol ('000 hl)	4,815	4,341	4,474
Wine ('000 hl)	40,302	36,118	35,756
Beer ('000 hl)	31,156	34,032	33,502
Soft drinks ('000 hl)	59,889	58,672	58,880
Cigarettes (million units)	47,506	39,798	41,906
Washing powders and detergents	2,225.0	2,228.1	2,180.1
Aluminium (primary)*	394.2	349.0	408.0†
Refined copper (primary)*	302.3	290.0†	290.0†
Pig-iron*	4,200	4,200†	4,200†
Cement (Portland)*	50,347	54,033	54,000†
Motorcycles ('000)	197	193	154
Passenger cars ('000)	2,375.4	2,220.1	2,385.2
Electricity (million kWh)	294,077	299,454	303,292

* Data from the US Geological Survey.
† Estimated figure.
Source: mainly UN Industrial Commodity Statistics Database.

2008 ('000 metric tons unless otherwise indicated, estimates): Aluminium (primary) 408.0; Refined copper (primary) 255.0; Pig-iron 4,200; Cement (Hydraulic) 42,088 (Source: US Geological Survey).

2009 ('000 metric tons unless otherwise indicated, estimates): Aluminium (primary) 408.0; Refined copper (primary) 255.0; Pig-iron 4,200; Cement (Hydraulic) 29,505 (Source: US Geological Survey).

Finance

CURRENCY AND EXCHANGE RATES

Monetary Units
100 cent = 1 euro (€).

Sterling and Dollar Equivalents (31 December 2010)
£1 sterling = 1.172 euros;
US $1 = 0.7484 euros;
€10 = £8.54 = $13.36.

Average Exchange Rate (euros per US $)
2008   0.6827
2009   0.7198
2010   0.7550

Note: The national currency was formerly the peseta. From the introduction of the euro, with Spanish participation, on 1 January 1999, a fixed exchange rate of €1 = 166.386 pesetas was in operation. Euro notes and coins were introduced on 1 January 2002. The euro and local currency circulated alongside each other until 28 February, after which the euro became the sole legal tender.

BUDGET
(€ million)

Revenue	2009	2010	2011
Current operations	139,962	119,213	105,544
Direct taxation	77,041	66,393	55,239
Indirect taxation	50,202	40,736	36,142
Rates and other revenue	3,732	3,147	3,384
Current transfers	5,807	5,491	4,715
Estate taxes	3,181	3,445	6,063
Capital operations	1,148	1,993	476
Transfer of real investments	120	107	104
Capital transfers	1,028	1,886	372
Financial assets	2,340	3,192	13,370
Total	143,450	124,398	119,390

SPAIN

Statistical Survey

Expenditure*	2009	2010	2011
Current	133,528	157,448	132,406
Social security	7,386	8,291	8,092
Autonomous communities	38,644	43,192	16,098
Autonomous organs	4,315	18,706	17,810
Local corporations	14,848	13,147	13,544
Private companies	225	214	174
Foreign contributions	12,742	12,744	12,275
Families	3,096	2,967	2,970
Personnel	26,848	27,572	26,982
Purchase of goods and services	3,502	3,515	3,385
Interest	17,424	23,224	27,421
Contingency fund	3,251	3,745	2,472
Capital	21,125	23,842	15,178
Investment	10,408	9,390	5,817
Capital transfers	10,717	14,452	9,362
Financial assets	34,292	15,998	12,960
Financial liabilities	33,973	35,409	46,595
Total	226,169	236,443	209,612

*Calculated according to recognized obligations rather than payments made.

Source: Ministerio de Economía y Hacienda, Madrid.

INTERNATIONAL RESERVES
(US $ million at 31 December)

	2008	2009	2010
Gold (market prices)	7,832	9,996	12,768
IMF special drawing rights	223	4,639	4,517
Reserve position in IMF	650	780	1,323
Foreign exchange	11,540	12,787	13,306
Total	20,245	28,202	31,914

Source: IMF, *International Financial Statistics*.

MONEY SUPPLY
(incl. shares, depository corporations, national residency criteria, € '000 million at 31 December)

	2008	2009	2010
Currency issued	79.44	91.74	95.50
Banco de España	86.56	84.07	80.14
Demand deposits	473.98	523.15	510.13
Other deposits	1,160.09	1,144.59	1,178.45
Securities other than shares	398.63	439.88	432.74
Money market fund shares	28.06	13.44	8.13
Shares and other equity	256.23	285.11	297.65
Other items (net)	−98.08	−130.62	−152.76
Total	2,298.35	2,367.28	2,369.84

Source: IMF, *International Financial Statistics*.

COST OF LIVING
(Consumer Price Index; base: 2006 = 100)

	2008	2009	2010
Food (excl. alcoholic beverages and tobacco)	109.8	108.6	107.7
Alcohol and tobacco	111.2	121.1	134.3
Household expenses	105.2	106.8	107.4
Clothing (incl. footwear)	101.7	100.1	99.7
Rent	110.6	112.0	116.0
Transport	108.0	101.7	108.7
All items (incl. others)	107.0	106.7	108.6

NATIONAL ACCOUNTS
(€ million at current prices)

National Income and Product

	2007	2008	2009
Compensation of employees	502,182	531,293	516,799
Gross operating surplus and mixed income	441,918	463,250	460,711
Gross domestic product (GDP) at factor cost	944,100	994,543	977,510
Taxes, less subsidies, on production and imports	109,437	93,581	76,404
GDP in market prices	1,053,537	1,088,124	1,053,914
Primary incomes (net)	−24,695	−30,355	−24,373
Gross national income	1,028,842	1,057,769	1,029,541
Less Consumption of fixed capital	165,482	176,671	183,866
Net national income	863,360	881,098	845,675
Current transfers (net)	−9,835	−11,959	−10,972
Gross national disposable income	853,525	869,139	834,703

Expenditure on the Gross Domestic Product

	2008	2009	2010
Final consumption expenditure	834,229	819,206	841,291
Households	612,165	586,554	610,459
Non-profit institutions serving households	9,785	9,870	10,057
General government	212,279	222,782	220,775
Gross capital formation	316,514	257,370	244,294
Gross fixed capital formation	311,830	252,961	238,667
Changes in inventories	4,684	4,409	5,627
Total domestic expenditure	1,150,743	1,076,576	1,085,585
Exports of goods and services	288,016	246,364	279,001
Less Imports of goods and services	350,635	269,026	301,995
GDP in market prices	1,088,124	1,053,914	1,062,591

Gross Domestic Product by Economic Activity

	2008	2009	2010
Agriculture, hunting, forestry and fishing	26,494	25,955	26,062
Mining and quarrying; electricity, gas and water supply*	28,360	28,208	29,684
Manufacturing	141,310	121,917	122,132
Construction	113,511	105,522	97,791
Private sector service industries	535,523	540,133	538,609
Public sector service industries	150,813	157,964	158,125
Gross value added in basic prices	996,011	979,699	972,403
Import duties, value-added tax and other taxes, less subsidies on products	92,113	74,215	90,188
GDP in market prices	1,088,124	1,053,914	1,062,591

*Including refinery products.

BALANCE OF PAYMENTS
(US $ million)

	2007	2008	2009
Exports of goods f.o.b.	264,053	284,346	223,981
Imports of goods f.o.b.	−389,291	−412,631	−286,813
Trade balance	−125,238	−128,285	−62,833
Exports of services	128,148	143,497	122,912
Imports of services	−96,492	−104,763	−87,446
Balance on goods and services	−93,582	−89,550	−27,366
Other income received	79,614	79,397	56,735
Other income paid	−120,986	−132,271	−98,855
Balance on goods, services and income	−134,953	−142,424	−69,486
Current transfers received	25,637	25,008	25,552
Current transfers paid	−35,223	−39,016	−36,441
Current balance	−144,540	−156,432	−80,375

SPAIN

Statistical Survey

—continued	2007	2008	2009
Capital account (net)	6,374	8,184	5,647
Direct investment abroad	−139,545	−74,326	−7,685
Direct investment from abroad	66,682	74,226	6,451
Portfolio investment assets	−5,888	31,401	1,316
Portfolio investment liabilities	124,060	−26,313	71,739
Financial derivatives liabilities	−5,915	−11,801	−7,716
Other investment assets	−47,980	−26,678	−3,611
Other investment liabilities	147,199	185,683	25,278
Net errors and omissions	−233	−3,256	−5,074
Overall balance	215	687	5,970

Source: IMF, *International Financial Statistics*.

External Trade

PRINCIPAL COMMODITIES
(distribution by SITC, US $ million)

Imports c.i.f.	2006	2007	2008
Food and live animals	22,053.4	27,298.0	29,973.5
Fish, crustaceans and molluscs, and products thereof	6,426.2	7,075.6	7,149.5
Vegetables and fruit	3,647.8	4,677.9	4,938.3
Beverages and tobacco	3,618.4	4,316.8	4,705.0
Alcoholic beverages	1,830.7	2,074.1	2,180.6
Tobacco and tobacco manufactures	1,546.1	1,870.6	2,151.4
Mineral fuels and lubricants	51,803.1	58,399.6	81,328.4
Petroleum, petroleum products etc.	39,728.8	45,230.7	60,547.9
Gas, natural and manufactured	9,942.8	10,643.0	16,947.1
Chemicals and related products	36,445.5	43,233.0	49,129.5
Organic chemicals	8,622.7	9,529.8	10,150.2
Medicinal and pharmaceutical products	9,628.9	12,171.3	15,273.9
Basic manufactures	43,194.3	53,649.3	51,213.3
Paper, paperboard and related products	4,674.9	5,480.0	5,421.4
Textile yarn, fabrics and articles thereof	4,771.1	5,356.8	5,203.5
Iron and steel	12,127.2	15,623.6	15,321.6
Non-ferrous metals	5,841.9	7,528.9	6,328.4
Manufactures of metal	7,108.2	8,955.5	9,175.4
Machinery and transport equipment	120,981.2	142,727.0	135,663.4
Telecommunications, sound recording and reproducing equipment	13,284.7	15,090.5	14,280.8
Electrical machinery, apparatus and appliances	14,190.6	19,304.6	25,082.3
Road vehicles	48,034.8	58,170.6	47,321.7
Passenger cars	24,175.4	29,105.9	22,187.4
Miscellaneous manufactured articles	35,353.4	42,124.6	45,787.7
Total (incl. others)	329,975.8	391,236.9	418,728.3

Exports f.o.b.	2006	2007	2008
Food and live animals	23,332.6	27,363.7	31,438.0
Vegetables and fruit	12,411.3	14,152.9	15,749.0
Tomatoes	1,009.9	1,179.1	1,252.5
Oranges, mandarins, clementines etc.	2,388.2	2,929.7	3,102.8
Beverages and tobacco	2,972.2	3,614.6	4,127.0
Wine	2,059.8	2,568.7	2,963.6
Mineral fuels and lubricants	9,852.5	11,976.8	18,259.4
Animals and vegetable oils, fats and waxes	2,665.7	3,168.5	3,997.4
Olive oil	2,271.2	2,605.3	2,845.4
Chemicals and related products	25,563.0	31,655.4	34,918.4
Medicinal and pharmaceutical products	7,595.7	9,819.5	11,358.0
Basic manufactures	37,910.4	45,782.1	50,668.6
Ceramic products	2,949.3	3,357.4	3,528.0
Iron and steel	8,380.0	11,444.7	14,283.5
Machinery and transport equipment	84,784.6	97,800.1	99,616.9
Electrical machinery, apparatus and appliances	9,191.5	10,082.1	10,767.6
Road vehicles	44,245.5	53,178.3	53,665.1
Miscellaneous manufactured articles	18,558.2	21,571.4	24,020.3
Total (incl. others)	214,061.2	253,753.9	279,231.5

Source: UN, *International Trade Statistics Yearbook*.

PRINCIPAL TRADING PARTNERS
(US $ million)

Imports c.i.f.	2006	2007	2008
Algeria	5,766.6	6,145.3	9,503.1
Austria	2,804.4	3,916.7	3,637.8
Belgium	9,638.8	10,955.6	10,524.4
Brazil	2,718.7	4,196.5	4,623.5
China, People's Republic	18,050.4	25,382.7	30,279.4
France (incl. Monaco)	42,106.0	48,041.7	46,502.5
Germany	46,830.4	59,906.2	58,377.6
Ireland	4,994.7	5,677.2	6,210.2
Italy	27,296.5	34,108.8	32,189.1
Japan	7,433.4	8,348.6	7,566.6
Korea, Republic	4,872.2	4,946.6	3,974.5
Libya	3,756.8	3,559.1	4,640.8
Mexico	3,416.6	4,134.3	4,730.5
Morocco	3,087.1	4,100.5	4,171.3
Netherlands	13,200.4	15,578.8	15,908.0
Nigeria	4,757.6	5,025.7	6,934.2
Poland	2,697.5	3,704.8	3,949.3
Portugal	10,718.5	12,720.5	13,746.8
Russia	9,325.3	10,830.4	11,071.6
Saudi Arabia	3,845.2	4,461.7	6,209.8
Sweden	4,286.7	4,871.0	4,441.0
Switzerland-Liechtenstein	4,405.9	4,238.8	4,262.6
United Kingdom	16,688.4	19,416.3	19,245.9
USA	10,790.0	13,802.8	16,709.3
Total (incl. others)	329,975.8	391,236.9	418,728.3

Exports f.o.b.	2006	2007	2008
Algeria	1,351.5	1,851.2	3,191.8
Austria	1,767.5	1,919.6	2,151.3
Belgium	6,253.0	7,155.6	8,353.1
China, People's Rep.	2,163.0	2,916.7	3,176.7
France (incl. Monaco)	40,058.2	47,708.9	50,896.9
Germany	23,350.4	27,282.1	29,361.4
Greece	2,396.1	3,032.1	3,812.3
Italy	18,265.6	22,595.3	22,396.5
Mexico	3,791.4	4,364.5	4,141.4
Morocco	3,269.1	4,203.3	5,406.3

SPAIN

Exports f.o.b.—continued	2006	2007	2008
Netherlands	7,079.7	8,287.7	8,760.5
Poland	2,315.3	3,354.9	4,008.4
Portugal	19,056.5	21,947.5	24,672.3
Russia	1,901.0	2,870.6	4,186.3
Sweden	2,057.9	2,326.6	2,418.5
Switzerland-Liechtenstein	3,313.5	3,335.9	3,693.5
Turkey	3,498.3	4,041.6	4,436.4
United Kingdom	17,054.7	19,582.6	19,746.3
USA	9,453.8	10,208.0	11,134.3
Total (incl. others)	214,061.2	253,753.9	279,231.5

Source: UN, *International Trade Statistics Yearbook*.

Transport

RAILWAYS
(RENFE only)

	2006	2007	2008
Number of passengers ('000)	516,369	506,620	499,700
Passenger-km (million)	20,259	19,965	22,074
Freight ('000 metric tons)	14,818	24,737	22,012
Freight ton-km (million)	11,011	10,547	9,737

ROAD TRAFFIC
('000 motor vehicles in use at 31 December)

	2006	2007	2008
Passenger cars	21,052.6	21,760.2	22,145.4
Buses	60.4	61.0	62.2
Lorries	4,910.3	5,140.6	5,192.2
Motorcycles	2,058.0	2,311.3	2,500.8
Tractors	204.1	212.7	213.4
Other vehicles	768.7	832.6	855.3

SHIPPING

Merchant Fleet
(registered at 31 December)

	2007	2008	2009
Number of vessels	1,648	1,728	1,790
Displacement (grt)	3,061,813	3,054,871	2,880,418

Source: IHS Fairplay, *World Fleet Statistics*.

International Sea-borne Freight Traffic

	2003	2004	2005
Goods loaded ('000 metric tons)	68,227	74,576	81,066
Goods unloaded ('000 metric tons)	221,455	236,200	259,214

Source: partly Puertos del Estado, Ministerio de Fomento, Madrid.

CIVIL AVIATION
(domestic and international traffic on scheduled services)

	2005	2006	2007
Passengers carried ('000)	181,200	193,500	210,500
Goods carried ('000 metric tons)	610,145	582,876	607,129

Passengers carried ('000): 203,800 in 2008.

Source: Dirección General de Aviación Civil, Ministerio de Fomento, Madrid.

Tourism

FOREIGN TOURIST ARRIVALS
(incl. Spaniards resident abroad)

Country of residence	2007	2008	2009
Belgium	1,724,409	1,636,636	1,596,898
France	9,004,008	8,149,265	7,916,164
Germany	10,080,606	10,062,629	8,925,908
Ireland	1,630,335	1,658,899	1,458,151
Italy	3,623,091	3,354,251	3,181,559
Netherlands	2,503,495	2,479,928	2,094,633
Portugal	2,414,562	2,224,304	2,051,988
Switzerland	1,376,470	1,286,725	1,141,226
United Kingdom	16,296,132	15,775,243	13,324,626
USA	1,046,698	1,124,493	1,137,654
Total (incl. others)	58,665,504	57,192,013	52,231,098

Receipts from tourism (incl. excursionists, € million): 52,255 in 2006; 56,220 in 2007; 56,352 in 2008.

Source: Instituto de Estudios Turísticos, Madrid.

Communications Media

	2007	2008	2009
Telephones ('000 main lines in use)	20,192.5	20,576.1	20,333.8
Mobile cellular telephones ('000 subscribers)	48,422.5	49,623.3	51,083.9
Internet users ('000)*	24,276.7	26,509.4	28,117.7
Broadband subscribers ('000)	7,990.4	9,054.2	9,706.7

*Estimates.

Personal computers: 17,640,000 (393.1 per 1,000 persons) in 2007.

Radio receivers ('000 in use, 1997): 13,100.

Book production (2003): titles ('000) 72.0; copies (million) 238.7.

Daily newspapers (2004): 151 (with combined average circulation of 6,183,000 copies per issue).

Non-daily newspapers (1999): 11 (with combined average circulation of 5,371,000).

Sources: partly UN, *Statistical Yearbook*; UNESCO Institute for Statistics; UNESCO, *Statistical Yearbook*; and International Telecommunication Union.

Education

(2009/10 unless otherwise indicated)

	Institutions	Teachers	Students
Pre-primary	20,619	346,661	1,822,142
Primary	14,005		2,702,415
Special education	1,514*	8,843†	30,616
Secondary: general	7,389	305,897	1,793,205
Secondary: vocational and university entrance	11,707		1,183,853
Universities, etc.	72‡	107,905§	1,404,115

*Referring to special schools and special education units which are mainstream alternatives to special education.
† Referring to special school teachers in special education classrooms and mainstream alternatives to special education.
‡ 2005/06 figure.
§ 2007/08 figure.

Source: Ministerio de Educación y Ciencia, Madrid.

Pupil-teacher ratio (primary education, UNESCO estimate): 12.4 in 2007/08 (Source: UNESCO Institute for Statistics).

Adult literacy rate (UNESCO estimates): 97.6% (males 98.4%; females 96.9%) in 2008 (Source: UNESCO Institute for Statistics).

Directory

The Government

HEAD OF STATE

King of Spain: HM King JUAN CARLOS I (acceded to the throne 22 November 1975).

COUNCIL OF MINISTERS
(May 2011)

A minority Government of the Partido Socialista Obrero Español (PSOE—Spanish Socialist Workers' Party).

President of the Government (Prime Minister): JOSÉ LUIS RODRÍGUEZ ZAPATERO.

First Deputy Prime Minister, Minister of the Interior and Government Spokesman: ALFREDO PÉREZ RUBALCABA.

Second Deputy Prime Minister and Minister of the Economy and Finance: ELENA SALGADO MÉNDEZ.

Third Deputy Prime Minister and Minister of Regional Policy and Public Administration: MANUEL CHAVES GONZÁLEZ.

Minister of Foreign Affairs and Co-operation: TRINIDAD JIMÉNEZ GARCÍA-HERRERA.

Minister of Justice: FRANCISCO CAAMAÑO DOMÍNGUEZ.

Minister of Defence: CARME CHACÓN PIQUERAS.

Minister of Development: JOSÉ BLANCO LÓPEZ.

Minister of Education: ÁNGEL GABILONDO PUJOL.

Minister of Labour and Immigration: VALERIANO GÓMEZ SÁNCHEZ.

Minister of Industry, Tourism and Trade: MIGUEL SEBASTIÁN GASCÓN.

Minister of the Environment, Rural and Marine Affairs: ROSA AGUILAR RIVERO.

Minister of the Presidency: RAMÓN JÁUREGUI ATONDO.

Minister of Culture: ÁNGELES GONZÁLEZ-SINDE REIG.

Minister of Health, Social Policy and Equality: LEIRE PAJÍN IRAOLA.

Minister of Science and Innovation: CRISTINA GARMENDIA MÉNDIZABAL.

MINISTRIES

Office of the President of the Government: Complejo de la Moncloa, Avda de Puerta de Hierro s/n, 28071 Madrid; fax (91) 3900217; e-mail jlrzapatero@presidencia.gob.es; internet www.la-moncloa.es.

Ministry of Culture: Plaza del Rey 1, 28004 Madrid; tel. (91) 7017000; fax (91) 7017352; e-mail contacte@mcu.es; internet www.mcu.es.

Ministry of Defence: Paseo de la Castellana 109, 28071 Madrid; tel. (91) 3955000; e-mail infodefensa@mde.es; internet www.mde.es.

Ministry of Development: Paseo de la Castellana 67, 28071 Madrid; tel. (91) 5977000; fax (91) 5978573; e-mail fomento@fomento.es; internet www.fomento.es.

Ministry of the Economy and Finance: Alcalá 9, Paseo de la Castellana 162, 28014 Madrid; tel. (91) 5958000; fax (91) 5958486; e-mail informacion.alcala@meh.es; internet www.meh.es.

Ministry of Education: Alcalá 36, 28071 Madrid; tel. (91) 7018098; fax (91) 7018648; e-mail prensa@educacion.es; internet www.educacion.es.

Ministry of the Environment, Rural and Marine Affairs: Paseo Infanta Isabel 1, 28071 Madrid; tel. (91) 3475368; fax (91) 3475412; e-mail informac@mapa.es; internet www.marm.es.

Ministry of Foreign Affairs and Co-operation: Plaza de la Provincia 1, 28012 Madrid; tel. (91) 3799700; e-mail informaec@maec.es; internet www.maec.es.

Ministry of Health, Social Policy and Equality: Paseo del Prado 18–20, 28014 Madrid; tel. 901 400100; fax (91) 5964480; e-mail oiac@msps.es; internet www.msps.es.

Ministry of Industry, Tourism and Trade: Paseo de la Castellana 160–162, 28046 Madrid; tel. (902) 446006; fax (91) 4578066; e-mail info@mityc.es; internet www.mityc.es.

Ministry of the Interior: Paseo de la Castellana 5, 28046 Madrid; tel. (91) 5371111; fax (91) 5371003; e-mail estafeta@mir.es; internet www.mir.es.

Ministry of Justice: San Bernardo 45, 28015 Madrid; tel. (91) 3904500; fax (91) 3902244; e-mail prensa@mjusticia.es; internet www.mjusticia.es.

Ministry of Labour and Immigration: Nuevos Ministerios, Agustín de Bethencourt 4, 28003 Madrid; tel. (91) 3630111; e-mail informacionmtin@mtin.es; internet www.mtin.es.

Ministry of the Presidency: Complejo de la Moncloa, Avda de Puerta de Hierro s/n, 28071 Madrid; tel. (91) 3214000; e-mail sec@mpr.es; internet www.mpr.es.

Ministry of Regional Policy and Public Administration: Paseo de la Castellana 3, 28071 Madrid; tel. (91) 2731029; fax (91) 2731012; e-mail prensa@mpt.es; internet www.map.es.

Ministry of Science and Innovation: Albacete 5, 28027 Madrid; tel. (90) 2218600; e-mail informa@micinn.es; internet web.micinn.es.

COUNCIL OF STATE

The Council of State is the supreme consultative organ of the Government. It comprises eight permanent members, 11 ex officio members (including, *inter alia*, the Director of the Real Academia Española, the General Prosecutor, the General Chief of Staff of Defence and the Governor of the Banco de España) and up to 10 elective members appointed by the Government, as well as a President and a Secretary-General. In addition, former Prime Ministers may sit as ex officio members if they so choose.

Consejo de Estado: Mayor 79, 28013 Madrid; tel. (91) 5166262; fax (91) 5166244; e-mail tramitaciones@consejo-estado.es; internet www.consejo-estado.es.

President: FRANCISCO RUBIO LLORENTE.

Legislature

LAS CORTES GENERALES

Congreso de los Diputados
(Congress of Deputies)

Carrera de Floridablanca s/n, 28071 Madrid; tel. (91) 3906000; fax (91) 4298707; e-mail informacion@congreso.es; internet www.congreso.es.

President: JOSÉ BONO MARTÍNEZ (PSOE).

First Vice-President: TERESA CUNILLERA I MESTRES (PSOE).

General Election, 9 March 2008

	%	Seats
Partido Socialista Obrero Español (PSOE)*	43.87	169
Partido Popular (PP)†	39.93	154
Convergència i Unió (CiU)	3.03	10
Euzko Alderdi Jeltzalea/Partido Nacionalista Vasco (EAJ/PNV)	1.19	6
Esquerra Republicana de Catalunya (ERC)	1.13	3
Izquierda Unida (IU)	3.77	2
Bloque Nacionalista Galego (BNG)	0.83	2
Coalición Canaria—Partido Nacionalista Canario (CC-PNC)	0.69	2
Union Progreso y Democracia (UPyD)	1.19	1
Nafarroa Bai (Na Bai)	0.24	1
Total (incl. others)	100.00	350

* Including Partit dels Socialistes de Catalunya.
† Including the two deputies of the Unión del Pueblo Navarro, which severed its alliance with the PP in October 2008.

Senado
(Senate)

Plaza de la Marina Española 8, 28071 Madrid; tel. (91) 5381000; fax (91) 5381003; e-mail informacion@senado.es; internet www.senado.es.

President: FRANCISCO JAVIER ROJO GARCÍA (PSE-EE).

First Vice-President: ISIDRE MOLAS I BATLLORI (PSC-PSOE).

The Senate comprises 264 members, 208 of whom are directly elected for a term of four years. The remaining 56 regional representatives are chosen by the assemblies of the autonomous regions and are renewed following legislative elections in those regions. At early May

SPAIN

2011 the composition of the Senate by legislative grouping was as follows (excluding one elected seat, which remained vacant):

Grouping	Directly elected	Appointed	Total
Partido Popular (PP)	99	24	123
Partido Socialista Obrero Español (PSOE)	86	19	105
Entesa Catalana de Progrés*	12	3	15
Convergència i Unió (CiU)	4	4	8
Senadores Nacionalistas†	2	2	4
Others	4	4	8
Total	207	56	263

*An alliance of the Esquerra Republicana de Catalunya, the Esquerra Unida i Alternativa, the Iniciativa per Catalunya Verds and the Partit dels Socialistes de Catalunya.
† Comprising the Euzko Alderdi Jeltzalea/Partido Nacionalista Vasco (EAJ/PNV) and the Bloque Nacionalista Galego (BNG).

Legislative Assemblies of the Autonomous Communities

(For full names of political parties, see Political Organizations)

Note: At the time of going to press, in late May 2011, the new Presidents of the Governments and Parliaments of those Autonomous Communities that held elections on 22 May had not yet been elected.

ANDALUCÍA (ANDALUSIA)

President of the Government (Junta): José Antonio Griñán Martínez (PSOE).
President of the Parliament: Fuensanta Coves (PSOE).
Election, 9 March 2008

	Seats
PSOE	56
PP	47
IU-LV-CA*	6
Total	109

*Convocatoria por Andalucía.

ARAGÓN

President of the Government: Marcelino Iglesias Ricou (PSOE).
President of the Parliament (Cortes): Francisco Pina Cuenca (PSOE).
Election, 22 May 2011

	Seats
PP	30
PSOE	22
PAR	7
CHA	4
IU	4
Total	67

PRINCIPADO DE ASTURIAS

President: Vicente Alberto Álvarez Areces (PSOE).
President of the Parliament (Junta General del Principado): María Jesús Álvarez González (PSOE).
Election, 22 May 2011

	Seats
FA	16
PSOE	15
PP	10
IU-LV	4
Total	45

BALEARIC ISLANDS (SEE ILLES BALEARS)
BASQUE COUNTRY (SEE PAÍS VASCO)
CANARIAS (CANARY ISLANDS)

President of the Government: Paulino Rivero Baute (CC).
President of the Parliament: Antonio A. Castro Cordobez (CC).
Election, 22 May 2011

	Seats
PP	21
CC	21
PSOE	15
NC	3
Total	60

CANTABRIA

President: Miguel Ángel Revilla Roiz (PRC).
President of the Parliament: Miguel Ángel Palacio García (PSOE).
Election, 22 May 2011

	Seats
PP	20
PRC	12
PSOE	7
Total	39

CASTILLA Y LEÓN (CASTILE AND LEON)

President of the Government (Junta): Juan Vicente Herrera Campo (PP).
President of the Parliament (Cortes): José Manuel Fernández Santiago (PP).
Election, 22 May 2011

	Seats
PP	53
PSOE	29
UPL	1
IUCYL*	1
Total	84

*Izquierda Unida Castilla y León.

CASTILLA-LA MANCHA (CASTILE-LA MANCHA)

President of the Government (Junta de Comunidades): José María Barreda Fontes (PSOE).
President of the Parliament (Cortes): Francisco José Pardo Piqueras (PSOE).
Election, 22 May 2011

	Seats
PP	25
PSOE	24
Total	49

CATALUÑA/CATALUNYA (CATALONIA)

President of the Government (Generalitat): Artur Mas i Gavarró (CiU).
President of the Parliament: Núria de Gispert i Català (CiU).
Election, 28 November 2010

	Seats
CiU	62
PSC-PSOE	28
PP	18
ICV-EUiA*	10
ERC	10
SI	4
C's	3
Total	135

*Coalition of Iniciativa per Catalunya Verds (ICV) and Esquerra Unida i Alternativa (EUiA).

SPAIN   *Directory*

COMUNIDAD VALENCIANA/COMUNITAT VALENCIANA (VALENCIA)

President of the Government (Generalitat): Francisco Enrique Camps Ortiz (PP).
President of the Parliament (Corts): María Milagrosa Martínez Navarro (PP).
Election, 22 May 2011

	Seats
PP	55
PSOE	33
Compromís*	6
EUPV	5
Total	99

* A coalition of Bloc Nacionalista Valenciana, Iniciativa del Poble Valencià (IdPV) and Els Verds Esquerra Ecologista del País Valencià (EV-EE).

EXTREMADURA

President of the Government (Junta): Guillermo Fernández Vara (PSOE).
President of the Parliament (Asamblea): Juan Ramón Ferreira Díaz (PSOE).
Election, 22 May 2011

	Seats
PSOE	32
PP	30
IU-SIEX	3
Total	65

GALICIA

President of the Government (Xunta): Alberto Núñez Feijóo (PP).
President of the Parliament: Pilar Rojo Noguera (PP).
Election, 1 March 2009

	Seats
PP	39
PS de G-PSOE	24
BNG	12
Total	75

ILLES BALEARS (BALEARIC ISLANDS)

President of the Government: Francesc Antich i Oliver (PSOE).
President of the Parliament: Aino Rado Ferrando (PSOE).
Election, 22 May 2011

	Seats
PP	35
PSOE	14
PSM-IV-ExM	4
PSOE-PACTE*	4
PSM-EN	1
GxF-PSOE	1
Total	59

* Pacte Progressista d'Eivissa.

MADRID

President: Esperanza Aguirre Gil de Biedma (PP).
President of the Parliament (Asamblea): Elvira Rodríguez Herrer (PP).
Election, 22 May 2011

	Seats
PP	72
PSOE	36
IU-LV	13
UPyD	8
Total	129

REGIÓN DE MURCIA

President of the Government: Ramón Luis Valcárcel Siso (PP).
President of the Parliament (Asamblea Regional): Francisco Celdrán Vidal (PP).
Election, 22 May 2011

	Seats
PP	33
PSOE	11
IU-VRM*	1
Total	45

* Izquierda Unida-Verdes de la Región de Murcia.

COMUNIDAD FORAL DE NAVARRA (NAVARRE)

President of the Government: Miguel Sanz Sesma (UPN).
President of the Parliament: María Elena Torres Miranda (PSN-PSOE).
Election, 22 May 2011

	Seats
UPN	19
PSN-PSOE	9
Na-Bai	8
Bildu*	7
PP	4
IZQ-EZK	3
Total	50

* Coalition of Eusko Alkartasuna (EA) and Alternatiba.

PAÍS VASCO/EUSKADI (BASQUE COUNTRY)

Lehendakari (President): Patxi López Álvarez (PSE-EE/PSOE).
President of the Parliament: Arantza Quiroga Cia (PP).
Election, 1 March 2009

	Seats
EAJ-PNV	30
PSE-EE/PSOE	24
PP	13
Aralar	4
EA	2
EB-B	1
UPyD	1
Total	75

LA RIOJA

President of the Government: Pedro María Sanz Alonso (PP).
President of the Parliament: José Ignacio Ceniceros González (PP).
Election, 22 May 2011

	Seats
PP	20
PSOE	11
PR	2
Total	33

VALENCIA (SEE COMUNIDAD VALENCIANA)

Political Organizations

PRINCIPAL NATIONAL PARTIES

Izquierda Unida (IU) (United Left): Olimpo 35, 28043 Madrid; tel. (91) 7227500; fax (91) 3880405; e-mail secretaria.organizacion@izquierda-unida.es; internet www.izquierda-unida.es; f. 1986 as coalition of Partido Comunista de España and other left-wing parties; Co-ordinator-Gen. Cayo Lara.

   Partido Comunista de España (PCE) (Communist Party of Spain): Olimpo 35, 28043 Madrid; tel. (91) 3004969; fax (91) 3004744; e-mail comitefederal@pce.es; internet www.pce.es; f. 1922; Euro-communist; absorbed Partido Comunista Obrero Español (PCOE) in 1986, and most of Partido Comunista de los Pueblos de España (PCPE) in Jan. 1989; Sec.-Gen. José Luis Centella.

SPAIN

Partido Popular (PP) (People's Party): Génova 13, 28004 Madrid; tel. (91) 5577300; fax (91) 3122322; e-mail partidopopular@pp.es; internet www.pp.es; f. 1976 as Alianza Popular; adopted current name 1989; absorbed Democracia Cristiana (fmrly Partido Demócrata Popular) and Partido Liberal in early 1989; centre-right; Christian Democrat; 750,000 mems (2008); Pres. MARIANO RAJOY BREY; Sec.-Gen. MARÍA DOLORES DE COSPEDAL GARCÍA.

Partido Socialista Obrero Español (PSOE) (Spanish Socialist Workers' Party): Ferraz 70, 28008 Madrid; tel. (91) 5820444; fax (91) 5820422; e-mail infopsoe@psoe.es; internet www.psoe.es; f. 1879; affiliated to the Socialist International; merged with the Partido Socialista Popular in 1978; joined by Partido de los Trabajadores de España-Unidad Comunista (PTE-UC) in 1991 and Partido de Nueva Izquierda (PDNI) in 2001; 551,469 mems (2006); Pres. MANUEL CHAVES GONZÁLEZ; Sec.-Gen. JOSÉ LUIS RODRÍGUEZ ZAPATERO.

Unión Progreso y Democracia (UPyD): Orense 25, 6°, 628080 Madrid; tel. (91) 5982286; fax (91) 7700078; e-mail informacion@upyd.es; internet www.upyd.es; f. 2007; centrist; advocates constitutional and democratic reform; Spokesperson ROSA DÍEZ GONZÁLEZ.

Los Verdes (LV) (The Greens): C/ Imagen nº 6, 4° B1, 41003 Sevilla; tel. (95) 4214756; fax (95) 4226888; e-mail losverdes@verdes.es; internet www.verdes.es; f. 1984; confederation of various regional environmentalist parties.

REGIONAL PARTIES

There are branches of the main national parties in most autonomous communities, some of which bear alternative or additional names. There are also numerous regional parties, including the following:

Andalucía
(Andalusia)

Partido Andalucista (PA): Rastro N 8, 41004 Sevilla; tel. (95) 4502167; fax (95) 4212887; e-mail ejecutivanacional@partidoandalucista.org; internet www.partidoandalucista.org; f. 1971; Sec.-Gen. PILAR GONZÁLEZ MODINO.

Aragón

Chunta Aragonesista (CHA): Conde de Aranda 14–16, 1°, 50003 Zaragoza; tel. (976) 284242; fax (976) 281311; e-mail sedenacional@chunta.com; internet www.chunta.com; f. 1986; left-wing; Pres. NIEVES IBEAS VUELTA.

Partido Aragonés (PAR): Coso 87, 50001 Zaragoza; tel. (976) 200616; e-mail sugerencias@partidoaragones.es; internet www.partidoaragones.es; f. 1977; fmrly Partido Aragonés Regionalista; centre-right; Pres. JOSÉ ANGEL BIEL; Sec.-Gen. ARTURO ALIAGA LÓPEZ.

Asturias

Foro Asturias (FA) (Asturias Forum): General Elorza 75A, 1° A, 33002 Oviedo; tel. (98) 5202745; fax (98) 5223554; e-mail asturias@foroasturias.es; internet www.foroasturias.es; Pres. FRANCISCO ÁLVAREZ-CASCOS.

Unión Renovadora Asturiana (URAS): Menéndez Valdés 2, 1°, 33201 Gijón; tel. (98) 5353245; e-mail correo@uras.org; internet www.uras.org; f. 1999 following split in PP of Asturias; in 2004 formed coalition, Unión Asturianista, with Partíu Asturianista (PAS); Pres. JAVIER LÓPEZ ALONSO; Sec.-Gen. FERNANDO EXPÓSITO VENAYAS.

Canarias
(Canary Islands)

Agrupación Herreña Independiente (AHI): La Constitución 4, 38900 Valverde, El Hierro, Santa Cruz de Tenerife; tel. (922) 551134; fax (922) 551224; party of El Hierro island; Pres. TOMÁS PADRÓN HERNÁNDEZ.

Coalición Canaria (CC): Buenos Aires 24, 35001 Las Palmas, Gran Canaria; tel. (928) 363142; e-mail lagomera@coalicioncanaria.org; internet www.coalicioncanaria.org; f. 1993 as coalition of Canary Islands parties incl. Agrupaciones Independientes de Canarias, Centro Canario Nacionalista, Iniciativa Canaria and Asamblea Majorera; united as a single party in 2005; Pres. CLAUDINA MORALES.

Nueva Canarias (NC): C/Venegas 1, Of. 2 y 4; tel. (928) 234234; fax (928) 230275; e-mail nc@nuevacanarias.org; internet nuevacanarias.org; f. 2005; Pres. ROMÁN RODRÍGUEZ RODRÍGUEZ.

Partido Nacionalista Canario (PNC): Méndez Núñez 27, 35008 38001, Santa Cruz de Tenerife; tel. and fax (922) 292475; e-mail partidonacionalistacanario@hotmail.com; internet www.pnc-canarias.eu; f. 1924; National Pres. JUAN MANUEL GARCÍA RAMOS; National Sec.-Gen. GUSTAVO DAVILA DE LEÓN.

Cantabria

Partido Regionalista de Cantabria (PRC): Amós de Escalante 2, 2°D, 39002 Santander; tel. (942) 229177; fax (942) 362337; e-mail prc@prc.es; internet www.prc.es; f. 1978; centre-right; Sec.-Gen. MIGUEL ANGEL REVILLA ROIZ.

Castilla y León
(Castile and Leon)

Unión del Pueblo Leonés (UPL): Avda República Argentina 13, 1°, 24004 León; tel. (987) 263309; fax (987) 204499; e-mail sede@upl.es; internet www.upl.es; f. 1986 as Unión Leonesista; advocates autonomy for León region; 4,000 mems; Pres. PEDRO ANGEL GALLEGO; Sec.-Gen. JAVIER CHAMORRO RODRÍGUEZ.

Cataluña/Catalunya
(Catalonia)

Ciutadans—Partit de la Ciutadania/Ciudadanos—Partido de la Ciudadanía (C's) (Citizens—Citizenship Party): Passeig de Gràcia 55, 7°, 3A, 08008 Barcelona; tel. (90) 2140306; e-mail info@ciudadanos-cs.org; internet www.ciudadanos-cs.org; f. 2006; opposes Catalan nationalism; Pres. ALBERT RIVERA DÍAZ; Sec.-Gen. MATÍAS ALONSO RUIZ.

Convergència i Unió (CiU): Còrsega 331–333, 08037 Barcelona; tel. (93) 2363100; fax (93) 2363105; e-mail ciu@ciu.info; internet www.ciu.info; f. 1978 as an electoral alliance; became confederation of parties in March 2001; Catalan nationalist, conservative; Pres. ARTUR MAS I GAVARRÓ; Sec.-Gen. JOSEP ANTONI DURAN I LLEIDA; an alliance of the following two parties:

  Convergència Democràtica de Catalunya (CDC): Còrsega 331–333, 08037 Barcelona; tel. (93) 2363100; fax (93) 2363105; e-mail cdc@convergencia.org; internet www.convergencia.org; f. 1974; Catalan nationalist, centrist; Pres. JORDI PUJOL I SOLEY; Sec.-Gen. ARTUR MAS I GAVARRÓ.

  Unió Democràtica de Catalunya (UDC): Napols 35–39, 08018, Barcelona; tel. (93) 2402200; fax (93) 2402201; e-mail info@unio.org; internet www.unio.org; f. 1931; Christian democrat; Pres. RAMON ESPADALER I PARCERISAS; Sec.-Gen. JOSEP MARIA PELEGRÍ I AIXUT.

Esquerra Republicana de Catalunya (ERC) (Republican Left of Catalonia): Calàbria 166, 08015 Barcelona; tel. (93) 4536005; fax (93) 3237122; e-mail info@esquerra.org; internet www.esquerra.cat; f. 1931; advocates independence for Catalonia within European context, a just society and national solidarity of Catalan people; Pres. JOAN PUIGCERDÓS; Sec.-Gen. JOAN RIDAO.

Esquerra Unida i Alternativa (EUiA): Doctor Aiguader 10-12, 08003 Barcelona; tel. (93) 3170034; fax (93) 3179251; e-mail euia@euia.cat; internet www.euia.cat; federation of 5 communist and left-wing parties in Catalonia; republican; affiliated to Izquierda Unida; Co-ordinator-Gen. JORDI MIRALLES I CONTE.

Iniciativa per Catalunya Verds (ICV): Passatge del Rellotge 3, 08002 Barcelona; tel. (93) 3010612; e-mail srieger@iniciativa.cat; internet www.iniciativa.cat; f. 1987 as Iniciativa per Catalunya, a federation of left-wing parties; adopted current name in 1998 following alliance with Els Verds (Confederació Ecologista de Catalunya); Pres. JOAN SAURA LAPORTA; Sec.-Gen. JOAN HERRERA TORRES.

Partit dels Socialistes de Catalunya (PSC-PSOE): Nicaragua 75-77, 08029 Barcelona; tel. (93) 4955400; fax (93) 4955435; e-mail info@socialistes.org; internet www.socialistes.cat; f. 1978 by merger of various Catalan parties of socialist ideology; allied to PSOE; Pres. ISIDRE MOLAS I BATLLORI; First Sec. JOSÉ MONTILLA AGUILERA.

Solidaritat Catalana per la Independència (SI): Passeig Domènec Sert 16, 3r 1a, 08552 Taradell (Barcelona); e-mail info@solidaritatcatalana.cat; internet www.solidaritatcatalana.cat; f. 2010; advocates independence for Catalonia; Pres. TONI STRUBELL; Sec.-Gen. URIEL BERTRAN I ARRUÉ.

Comunidad Valenciana/Comunitat Valenciana
(Valencia)
(see also Cataluña)

Bloc Nacionalista Valencià: Sant Jacint 28, entresòl, 46008 Valencia; tel. (96) 3826606; fax (96) 3826276; e-mail bloc@bloc.ws; internet www.bloc.ws; f. 1998 as federation of Unitat del Poble Valencià (f. 1982), Partit Valencià Nacionalista (f. 1990) and Nacionalistes d'Alcoi (f. 1994); progressive Valencian nationalist party; Pres. JOSEP MARIA PAÑELLA ALCACER; Sec.-Gen. ENRIC XAVIER MORERA CATALÀ.

Esquerra Unida del País Valencià (EUPV): Gran Via Ramón i Cajál 55, 2°, 46007 Valencia; tel. (963) 841888; fax (963) 847678; e-mail eupv@eupv.org; internet www.eupv.org; left-wing; affiliated to Izquierda Unida; Co-ordinator MARGA SANZ.

Partido Socialista del País Valenciano (PSPV-PSOE) (Valencian Socialist Party): Palau de les Corts Valencianes, Plaza San Lorenzo 4, 46003 Valencia; e-mail info@socialistesvalencians.org; internet www.socialistesvalencians.org; affiliated to PSOE; Pres. ÓSCAR TENA; Sec.-Gen. JORGE ALARTE GORBE.

Extremadura

Socialistas Independientes de Extremadura (SIEX): Mérida; Leader José Antonio Jiménez García.

Galicia

Bloque Nacionalista Galego (BNG): Avda Rodríguez de Viguri 16, baixo, 15703 Santiago de Compostela; tel. (981) 555850; fax (981) 555851; e-mail sedenacional@bng-galiza.org; internet www.bng-galiza.org; f. 1982; Galician nationalist; Leader Guillerme Vázquez.

Partido dos Socialistas de Galicia (PS de G-PSOE) (Galician Socialist Party): Rua do Pino 1–9, 15704 Santiago de Compostela; tel. (981) 552030; fax (981) 588708; e-mail ceng@psdeg-psoe.org; internet www.psdeg-psoe.org; Galician branch of the PSOE; Sec.-Gen. Manuel (Pachi) Vázquez Fernandez.

Illes Balears
(Balearic Islands)
(see also Cataluña)

Alternativa Esquerra Unida-Els Verds: Sindicat 74, 1r 2a, 07001 Palma de Mallorca; tel. (971) 724488; fax (971) 971711836; alliance of Esquerra Unida de les Illes Baleares (affiliated to Izquierda Unida) and Els Verds de Mallorca; Spokespersons Eberhard Grosske, Miquel Àngel Llauger.

Eivissa pel Canvi (ExC) (Ibiza for Change): Apdo Correos 40, Santa Gertrudis, Santa Eulària des Riu, Eivissa; e-mail info@eivissapelcanvi.cat; internet www.eivissapelcanvi.org; f. 2006; opposes municipal corruption.

Entesa per Mallorca (ExM): C/d'en Morey 11, Palma de Mallorca; tel. (971) 713127; e-mail mallorca@entesapermallorca.org; internet www.entesapermallorca.org; f. 2006; created following a split from Partit Socialista de Mallorca; Pres. Biel Huguet; Sec.-Gen. Jaume Sansó.

Gent per Formentera (GxF): Palma de Mallorca; e-mail gentxformentera@gmail.com; internet www.gentxformentera.org; f. 2007; contested the 2011 regional election in alliance with the Partido Socialista Obrero Español (PSOE).

IniciativaVerds (IV): Carrer Costa i Llobera 28, 07005 Palma de Mallorca; tel. (971) 728241; fax (971) 728241; e-mail info@iniciativaverds.org; internet www.iniciativaverds.org; f. 2010; Co-ordinator-Gen. David Abril.

PSM-Entesa Nacionalista (PSM-EN): Isidoro Antillón 9, baixos, 07006 Palma de Mallorca; tel. (971) 775252; fax (971) 774848; e-mail federacio@psm-entesa.cat; internet www.psm-entesa.org; f. 1989 as Federació de l'Esquerra Nacionalista de les Illes Baleares (FENIB); federation of PSM-Entesa Nacionalista de Mallorca (f. 1976 as Partit Socialista de les Illes, renamed Partit Socialista de Mallorca—PSM in 1977), PSM-Entesa Nacionalista de Menorca (f. 1977 as Partit Socialista de Menorca), Entesa Nacionalista i Ecologista d'Eivissa (f. 1989) and other groups; Socialist, Catalan nationalist, environmentalist; Sec.-Gen. Gabriel Barceló.

Navarra
(Navarre)
(see also País Vasco)

Aralar: Aduanaren txokoa 16–18, 31001 Pamplona; tel. (948) 206362; fax (948) 206003; e-mail nafarroa@aralar.net; internet www.aralar.net; f. 2002 by fmr dissident mems of Euskal Herritarrok (subsequently Batasuna) opposed to that party's links with ETA; Basque separatist, left-wing; rejects violence; active throughout the Basque region; Co-ordinator-Gen. Patxi Zabaleta.

Bildu (Gather): Pamplona; e-mail nafarroa@bildu.info; internet www.bildu.info; f. 2011; coalition of Eusko Alkartasuna (EA) and Alternatiba; separatist; Leaders Pello Urizar, Oskar Matute, Bakartxo Ruiz.

Convergencia de Demócratas de Navarra (CDN): Avda Carlos III 7, 1°, 2A, 31002 Pamplona; tel. (948) 228185; fax (948) 227336; e-mail cdn@cdn.es; internet www.cdn.es; f. 1995; progressive centrist party; promotes Navarrese identity and opposes integration with Basque Country; Pres. José Andrés Burguete Torres; Sec. Angel Luis Fortún Moral.

Izquierda-Ezkerra (IZQ-EZK): Pamplona; internet www.izquierda-ezkerra.org; f. 2011; a coalition of Izquierda Unida de Navarra (IUN-NEB) and Batzarre.

    Batzarre (Assembly): Navarrería 15, 1°C, 31001 Pamplona; tel. (948) 224757; fax (948) 210063; e-mail info@batzarre.org; internet www.batzarre.org; f. 1987; left-wing Basque nationalist party of Navarre.

    Izquierda Unida de Navarra—Nafarroako Ezker Batua (IUN-NEB): Calle Mayor 20, 31001 Pamplona; tel. (948) 220405; fax (948) 212941; e-mail info@iun-neb.org; internet www.iun-neb.org; f. 1986; pursues social changes based on the principles of liberty, equality and solidarity; Co-ordinator-Gen. José Miguel Nuin Moreno.

Nafarroa Bai (Na Bai) (Navarre Yes): Plaza del Castillo 32, 1° izqda, 31001 Pamplona; tel. (948) 203033; fax (948) 203034; e-mail nafarroabai@nafarroabai.net; internet www.nafarroabai.org; coalition of Basque nationalist parties in Navarre: Aralar, Batzarre, Eusko Alkartasuna and EAJ-PNV; Leader Patxi Zabaleta.

Partido Socialista de Navarra (PSN): Paseo de Sarasate 15, 2°, 31002 Pamplona; tel. (948) 225003; fax (948) 221534; e-mail info@psn-psoe.org; internet www.psn-psoe.org; Navarrese branch of PSOE; Sec.-Gen. Roberto Jiménez Alli.

Unión del Pueblo Navarro (UPN): Plaza Príncipe de Viana 1, 4° dcha, 31002 Pamplona; tel. (948) 223402; fax (948) 210810; e-mail administrador@upn.org; internet www.upn.org; f. 1979; centre-right; opposes closer ties between Navarre and Basque Country; Pres. Yolanda Barcina; Sec.-Gen. Carlos García Adanero.

País Vasco/Euskadi
(Basque Country)

Aralar: see Navarra above.

Eusko Alkartasuna (EA) (Basque Solidarity): Camino de Portuetxe 23, 1°, 20018 San Sebastián; tel. (943) 020130; fax (943) 020131; e-mail gipuzkoa@euskoalkartasuna.org; internet www.euskoalkartasuna.org; f. 1985 (as Eusko Abertzaleak—Basque Nationalists) by dissident group of progressive EAJ-PNV mems; Sec.-Gen. Pello Urizar Karetxe.

Euzko Alderdi Jeltzalea-Partido Nacionalista Vasco (EAJ-PNV): Sabin Etxea, Ibáñez de Bilbao 16, 48001 Bilbao; tel. (94) 4039400; fax (94) 4039415; e-mail idazkaria.ebb@eaj-pnv.com; internet www.eaj-pnv.com; f. 1895; Basque nationalist; seeks to achieve autonomy through peaceful means; 32,000 mems; Pres. Iñigo Urkullu Renteria; Sec. Belén Greaves Badillo.

Ezker Batua-Berdeak (EB-B): Fernández del Campo 24, 48010 Bilbao; tel. (94) 4702100; fax (94) 4701012; internet www.ezkerbatua-berdeak.org; f. 1986 as a coalition of left-wing, social democratic and environmentalist parties; Pres. Javier Madrazo.

Partido Socialista de Euskadi-Euskadiko Ezkerra (PSE-EE) (Basque Socialist Party-Basque Left): Alameda de Recalde 27, 4°, 48009 Bilbao; tel. (94) 4242142; fax (94) 4238904; e-mail info@socialistasvascos.com; internet www.socialistasvascos.com; f. 1993 by merger of PSE-PSOE (Basque branch of PSOE) and Euskadiko Ezkerra; affiliated to PSOE; Pres. Jesús Eguiguren; Sec.-Gen. Patxi López Álvarez.

La Rioja

Partido Riojano (PR): Portales 17, 1°, 26001 Logroño; tel. (941) 238199; fax (941) 254396; e-mail partidoriojano@partidoriojano.es; internet www.partidoriojano.es; f. 1982; Pres. Miguel González de Legarra; Sec.-Gen. Javier Sáenz Torre Merino.

ILLEGAL ORGANIZATIONS

The principal illegal armed organization is the Basque separatist Euskadi ta Askatasuna (ETA—Basque Homeland and Liberty, f. 1959). The Political Parties law of June 2002 facilitated the banning of parties deemed to support violence or terrorism. The legislation was employed against a number of parties in the Basque Country, most notably Batasuna (f. 1978 as Herri Batasuna), a radical separatist party led by Arnaldo Otegi Mondragón, which was banned by the Supreme Court in March 2003 on account of its links to ETA. Other parties deemed to be alternatives to Batasuna that have been outlawed include Eusko Abertzale Ekintza/Acción Nacionalista Vasca (EAE/ANV) and Euskal Herrialdeetako Alderdi Komunista/Partido Comunista de las Tierras Vascas (EHAK/PCTV), both of which were banned in September 2008. Sortu, which was founded in February 2011 and publicly rejected violence, was nevertheless banned in March 2011 as a successor party to Batasuna. Its members subsequently joined in the formation of Bildu (see above), which was initially banned but later permitted to contest the regional and local elections in May 2011.

Election Commission

Junta Electoral Central: Congreso de los Diputados, Carretera de San Jerónimo 36, 28071 Madrid; tel. (91) 3906367; fax (91) 4297778; internet www.juntaelectoralcentral.es; independent; Pres. Antonio Martín Valverde.

SPAIN

Diplomatic Representation

EMBASSIES IN SPAIN

Afghanistan: Umbría 8, 28043 Madrid; tel. (91) 7218581; fax (91) 7216832; e-mail embajadadeafganistanenmadrid@gmail.com; Ambassador Massod Khalili.

Albania: María de Molina 64, 5°b, 28006 Madrid; tel. (91) 5612118; fax (91) 5613775; e-mail cancilleria@albania.e.telefonica.net; Ambassador Kastriot Robo.

Algeria: General Oraá 12, 28006 Madrid; tel. (91) 5629705; fax (91) 5629877; e-mail embargel@tsai.es; Ambassador Mohammed Haneche.

Andorra: Alcalá 73, 28009 Madrid; tel. (91) 4317453; fax (91) 5776341; e-mail embajada@embajadaandorra.es; Ambassador Manuel M. Pujadas Domingo.

Angola: Serrano 64, 3°, 28001 Madrid; tel. (91) 4356430; fax (91) 5779010; e-mail gabinete@embajadadeangola.com; internet www.embajadadeangola.com; Ambassador Víctor Manuel Rita da Fonseca Lima.

Argentina: Serrano 90, 6° y 7°, 28001 Madrid; tel. (91) 7710500; fax (91) 7710526; e-mail embajada@portalargentino.net; internet www.portalargentino.net; Ambassador Carlos Antonio Bettini.

Armenia: Avda de Lisboa 22, 28928 Madrid; tel. and fax (91) 6425356; e-mail embarmit@tin.it; Chargé d'affaires a.i. Khoren Terteryan.

Australia: Paseo de la Castellana 259d, Planta 24, Torre Espacio, 28046 Madrid; tel. (91) 3536600; fax (91) 3536692; e-mail madrid.embassy@dfat.gov.au; internet www.spain.embassy.gov.au; Ambassador Zorica McCarty.

Austria: Paseo de la Castellana 91, 9°, 28046 Madrid; tel. (91) 5565315; fax (91) 5973579; e-mail madrid-ob@bmeia.gv.at; internet www.bmeia.gv.at/madrid; Ambassador Rudolf Lennkh.

Azerbaijan: Ronda de la Avutarda 38, 28043 Madrid; tel. (91) 7596010; fax (91) 7597056; e-mail info@azembajada.es; internet www.azembassy.es; Ambassador Altai Vasifoglu Efendiev.

Bangladesh: Diego de León 69, 2°d, 28006 Madrid; tel. (91) 4019932; fax (91) 4029564; e-mail chancery@bdoot-mad.e.telefonica.net; Ambassador Ikhtiar Momin Chowdhury.

Belgium: Paseo de la Castellana 18, 6°, 28046 Madrid; tel. (91) 5776300; fax (91) 4318166; e-mail madrid@diplobel.fed.be; internet www.diplomatie.be/madrid; Ambassador Johan Swinnen.

Bolivia: Velázquez 26, 3°a, 28001 Madrid; tel. (91) 5780835; fax (91) 5773946; e-mail embajada@embajadadebolivia.es; internet www.embajadadebolivia.es; Ambassador María Del Carmen Almendras Camargo.

Bosnia and Herzegovina: Lagasca 24, 2°, 28001 Madrid; tel. (91) 5750870; fax (91) 4355056; e-mail ambasada@ctv.es; Ambassador Zeljana Zovko.

Brazil: Fernando el Santo 6, 28010 Madrid; tel. (91) 7004650; fax (91) 7004660; e-mail gabinete@embajadadebrasil.es; internet www.brasil.es; Ambassador Paulo Cesar de Oliveira Campos.

Bulgaria: Santa María Magdalena 15, 28016 Madrid; tel. (91) 3455761; fax (91) 3591201; e-mail embulmad@yahoo.es; internet www.mfa.bg/madrid; Ambassador Ivan Yankov Hristov.

Cameroon: Rosario Pino 3, 28020 Madrid; tel. (91) 5711160; fax (91) 5712500; e-mail ambcammadrid@telefonica.net; internet ambacam-madrid.com; Ambassador (vacant).

Canada: Torre Espacio, Paseo de la Castellana 259d, 28046 Madrid; tel. (91) 3828400; fax (91) 3828490; e-mail mdrid@international.gc.ca; internet www.canadainternational.gc.ca/spain-espagne; Ambassador Graham S. Shantz.

Chile: Lagasca 88, 6°, 28001 Madrid; tel. (91) 4319160; fax (91) 5775560; e-mail echilees@tsai.es; internet chileabroad.gov.cl/espana; Ambassador Sergio Romero Pizarro.

China, People's Republic: Arturo Soria 113, 28043 Madrid; tel. (91) 5194242; fax (91) 5192035; e-mail embajadachina@embajadachina.es; internet www.embajadachina.es; Ambassador Zhu Bangzao.

Colombia: General Martínez Campos 48, 28010 Madrid; tel. (91) 7004770; fax (91) 3102869; e-mail emadrid@cancilleria.gov.co; internet www.embacol.com; Ambassador Orlando Sardi de Lima.

Congo, Democratic Republic: Paseo de la Castellana 255, 1°c, 28046 Madrid; tel. (91) 7332647; fax (91) 3231575; e-mail ambardc47@yahoo.es; Ambassador (vacant).

Costa Rica: Paseo de la Castellana 164, 17°, 28046 Madrid; tel. (91) 3459622; fax (91) 3533709; e-mail embajada@embcr.org; internet www.embajadadecostarica.es; Ambassador Ekhart Peters Seevers.

Côte d'Ivoire: Serrano 154, 28006 Madrid; tel. (91) 5626916; fax (91) 5622193; internet www.ambaci.es; Ambassador Paul Ambohalé Ayoman.

Croatia: Claudio Coello 78, 2°, 28001 Madrid; tel. (91) 5776881; fax (91) 5776905; e-mail madrid@mvpei.hr; internet es.mvp.hr; Ambassador Neven Pelicarić.

Cuba: Paseo de la Habana 194, 28036 Madrid; tel. (91) 3592500; fax (91) 3596145; e-mail secreembajada@ecubamad.com; internet emba.cubaminrex.cu/espana; Ambassador Alejandro González Galiano.

Cyprus: Paseo de la Castellana 45, 4–5° izqda, 28046 Madrid; tel. (91) 5783114; fax (91) 5782189; e-mail embajadachipre@telefonica.net; internet www.mfa.gov.cy/embassymadrid; Ambassador Nearchos Palas.

Czech Republic: Avda Pío XII 22–24, 28016 Madrid; tel. (91) 3531880; fax (91) 3531885; e-mail madrid@embassy.mzv.cz; internet www.mfa.cz/madrid; Ambassador Karel Beran.

Denmark: Serrano 26, 7°, 28001 Madrid; tel. (91) 4318445; fax (91) 4319168; e-mail madamb@um.dk; internet www.ambmadrid.um.dk; Ambassador Lars Thuesen.

Dominican Republic: Paseo de la Castellana 30, 1°, 28046 Madrid; tel. (91) 4315395; fax (91) 4358139; e-mail embajada@embajadadominicana.es; internet www.embajadadominicana.es; Ambassador César Augusto Medina Abreu.

Ecuador: Velázquez 114, 2°, 28006 Madrid; tel. (91) 5627215; fax (91) 7450244; e-mail embajada@mecuador.es; Ambassador Galo Alfredo Chiriboga Zambrano.

Egypt: Velázquez 69, 28006 Madrid; tel. (91) 5776308; fax (91) 5781732; Ambassador Ayman Abdulsamie Omar Zaineldine.

El Salvador: General Oraá 9–5°, 28006 Madrid; tel. (91) 5628002; fax (91) 5630584; e-mail madrid@embasalva.com; Ambassador Dr Edgardo Suárez Mallagray.

Equatorial Guinea: Avda Pío XII 14, 28016 Madrid; tel. (91) 3532169; fax (91) 3532165; e-mail rge@embarege-madrid.com; Ambassador Narciso Ntugu.

Estonia: Claudio Coello 91, 1°, 28006 Madrid; tel. (91) 4261671; fax (91) 4261672; e-mail embassy.madrid@mfa.ee; internet www.estemb.es; Ambassador Toomus Kahur.

Finland: Paseo de la Castellana 15, 28046 Madrid; tel. (91) 3196172; fax (91) 3083901; e-mail sanomat.mad@formin.fi; internet www.finlandia.es; Ambassador Markku Keinänen.

France: Salustiano Olózaga 9, 28001 Madrid; tel. (91) 4238900; fax (91) 4238908; e-mail chancellerie@ctv.es; internet www.ambafrance-org; Ambassador Bruno Delaye.

Gabon: Francisco Alcántara 3, 28002 Madrid; tel. (91) 4138211; fax (91) 4131153; e-mail emb-gabon-es@nemo.es; Ambassador Simón Wilfrid Ntoutoume Emane.

Georgia: Felipe IV 10, 28014 Madrid; tel. (91) 4293329; fax (91) 4296883; e-mail embassymadrid@mfa.gov.ge; internet www.spain.mfa.gov.ge; Ambassador Nikoloze Natlibadz.

Germany: Fortuny 8, 28010 Madrid; tel. (91) 5579000; fax (91) 3197508; e-mail info@madrid.diplo.de; internet www.madrid.diplo.de; Ambassador Reinhard Silberberg.

Ghana: Capitán Haya 38, 10°a, 28020 Madrid; tel. (91) 5670390; fax (91) 5670393; e-mail mission@ghanaembassyspain.com; Ambassador Fidelis Woenenyo Yao Ekar.

Greece: Avda Dr Arce 24, 28002 Madrid; tel. (91) 5644653; fax (91) 5644668; e-mail gremb.mad@mfa.gr; Ambassador Nicholas Zafiropoulos.

Guatemala: Rafael Salgado 3, 10°, 28036 Madrid; tel. (91) 3440347; fax (91) 4587894; e-mail informacion@embajadaguatemala.es; internet www.embajadaguatemala.es; Ambassador Anamaría Diéguez Arévalo.

Haiti: Marques del Duero 3, 1°, 28001 Madrid; tel. (91) 5752624; fax (91) 4314600; Ambassador Yolette Azor-Charles.

Holy See: Avda Pío XII 46, 28016 Madrid; tel. (91) 7668311; fax (91) 7667085; e-mail nunap@planalfa.es; Apostolic Nuncio Most Rev. Renzo Fratini (Titular Archbishop of Botriana).

Honduras: Paseo de la Castellana 164, 2°b, 28046 Madrid; tel. (91) 3531806; fax (91) 3458193; e-mail info@embahonduras.es; internet www.embahonduras.es; Ambassador Norman García Paz.

Hungary: Fortuny 6, 4°, 28010 Madrid; tel. (91) 4137011; fax (91) 4134138; e-mail mission.mad@kum.hu; internet www.mfa.gov.hu/emb/madrid; Ambassador Edit Bucsi-Szabó.

India: Avda Pío XII 30–32, 28016 Madrid; tel. (91) 3098870; fax (91) 3451112; e-mail amb@embassyindia.es; internet www.embajadaindia.com; Ambassador Sujata Mehta.

Indonesia: Agastia 65, 28043 Madrid; tel. (91) 4130294; fax (91) 4138994; e-mail kbri@embajadadeindonesia.es; internet www.embajadadeindonesia.es; Ambassador Adiyatwidi Adiwoso Asmady.

Iran: Jerez 5, Villa El Altozano, Chamartín, 28016 Madrid; tel. (91) 3450112; fax (91) 3451190; e-mail embiran@hotmail.com; Ambassador Morteza Saffari Natanzi.

Iraq: Sotilla, 1°, Parque Conde de Orgaz, 28043 Madrid; tel. (91) 7591282; fax (91) 7593180; e-mail embajadairak@yahoo.es; Ambassador Dr ZIAD KHALED A. ALI.

Ireland: Paseo de la Castellana 46, 4°, 28046 Madrid; tel. (91) 4364093; fax (91) 4351677; e-mail madridembassy@dfa.ie; internet www.embassyofireland.es; Ambassador JUSTIN HARMAN.

Israel: Velázquez 150, 7°, 28002 Madrid; tel. (91) 7829500; fax (91) 7829555; e-mail embajada@embajada-israel.es; internet www.embajada-israel.es; Ambassador RAPHAEL SCHUTZ.

Italy: Lagasca 98, 28006 Madrid; tel. (91) 4233300; fax (91) 5757776; e-mail archivio.ambmadrid@esteri.it; internet www.ambmadrid.esteri.it; Ambassador LEONARDO VISCONTI DI MODRONE.

Japan: Serrano 109, 28006 Madrid; tel. (91) 5907600; fax (91) 5901321; internet www.es.emb-japan.go.jp; Ambassador FUMIAKI TAKAHASHI.

Jordan: General Martínez Campos 41, 5°, 28010 Madrid; tel. (91) 3191100; fax (91) 3082536; e-mail jordania@telefonica.net; internet www.embjordaniaes.org; Ambassador ZAID M. AL-LOZI.

Kazakhstan: Sotillo 10, 28043 Madrid; tel. (91) 7216290; fax (91) 7219374; e-mail embajada@kazesp.org; internet www.kazesp.org; Ambassador YERGALI BULEGENOV.

Kenya: Jorge Juan 9, 3A, 28001, Madrid; tel. (91) 5710925; fax (91) 5705611; e-mail info@kenyaembassyspain.es; internet www.kenyaembassyspain.es; Ambassador BRAMWEL KISUYA (designate).

Korea, Republic: González Amigó 15, 28033 Madrid; tel. (91) 3532000; fax (91) 3532001; e-mail embspain.adm@mofat.go.kr; internet esp.mofat.go.kr; Ambassador OH DAE-SUNG.

Kuwait: Avda de Miraflores 61, 28035 Madrid; tel. (91) 5792467; fax (91) 5702109; Ambassador ADIL HAMAD M. AL-AYYAR.

Latvia: Alfonso XII 52, 1°, 28014 Madrid; tel. (91) 3691362; fax (91) 3690020; e-mail lespan@telefonica.net; Ambassador ROLANDS LAPPUĶE.

Lebanon: Paseo de la Castellana 178, 3° izqda, 28046 Madrid; tel. (91) 3451368; fax (91) 3455631; e-mail leem-e@teleline.es; Ambassador (vacant).

Libya: Pisuerga 12, 28002 Madrid; tel. (91) 5635753; fax (91) 5643986; e-mail oficinapopularlibia-madrid@hotmail.com; internet www.embajadalibia.es; Ambassador AJELI ABDUSSALAM ALI BRENI.

Lithuania: Pisuerga 5, 28002 Madrid; tel. (91) 7022116; fax (91) 3104018; e-mail amb.es@urm.lt; internet es.mfa.lt; Ambassador AUDRA PLEPYTĖ-JARA.

Luxembourg: Claudio Coello 78, 1°, 28001 Madrid; tel. (91) 4359164; fax (91) 5774826; e-mail madrid.amb@mae.etat.lu; internet www.madrid.mae.lu/es; Ambassador JEAN A. WELTER.

Macedonia, former Yugoslav republic: Don Ramón de la Cruz 107, 2°B, 28006 Madrid; tel. (91) 5717298; fax (91) 5713481; e-mail emb.mkd.madrid@gmail.com; Ambassador METODIJA BELEVSKI.

Malaysia: Paseo de la Castellana 91, Edif. Centro 23, 10°, 28046 Madrid; tel. (91) 5550684; fax (91) 5555208; e-mail malmadrid@kin.gov.my; Ambassador NAIMUN ASHAKLI MOHAMMAD.

Mali: Velazquez 114, 3°D, 28006 Madrid; tel. (91) 3105230; fax (91) 3105256; e-mail consuladodemali@hotmail.com; Ambassador SEKOU DIT GAOUSSOU CISSE.

Malta: Paseo de la Castellana 45, 6° dcha, 28046 Madrid; tel. (91) 3913061; fax (91) 3913066; e-mail maltaembassy.madrid@gov.mt; Ambassador TANYA VELLA.

Mauritania: Velázquez 90, 3°, 28006 Madrid; tel. (91) 5757006; fax (91) 4359531; e-mail ambarim@embajadamauritania.es; internet www.embajadamauritania.es; Ambassador MOHAMED M. OULD ABDELLAHI OULD BOYE.

Mexico: Carrera de San Jerónimo 46, 28014 Madrid; tel. (91) 3692814; fax (91) 4202292; e-mail embamex@embamex.es; internet www.embamex.es; Ambassador JORGE ZERMEÑO INFANTE.

Monaco: Villanueva 12, 28001 Madrid; tel. (91) 5782048; fax (91) 4357132; e-mail espagne@ambassade-monaco.org; Ambassador PATRICK VAN KLAVEREN.

Morocco: Serrano 179, 28002 Madrid; tel. (91) 5631090; fax (91) 5617887; e-mail correo@embajada-marruecos.es; internet www.embajada-marruecos.es; Ambassador AHMED OULD SOUILEM.

Mozambique: Velázquez 109, 4°B, 28006 Madrid; tel. (91) 5776382; fax (91) 5776705; e-mail embamoc.madrid@hotmail.com; Ambassador FERNANDA E. MOISES LICHALE.

Netherlands: Paseo de la Castellana 259D, 328046 Madrid; tel. (91) 3537500; fax (91) 3537565; e-mail mad@minbuza.nl; internet www.mfa.nl/mad; Ambassador PETER VAN WULFFTEN PALTHE.

New Zealand: Pinar 7, 3°, 28006 Madrid; tel. (91) 5230226; fax (91) 5230171; e-mail embnuevazelanda@telefonica.net; internet www.nzembassy.com/spain; Ambassador ROBERT MOORE-JONES.

Nicaragua: Paseo de la Castellana 127, 1°B, 28046 Madrid; tel. (91) 5555513; fax (91) 4555737; Ambassador AUGUSTO C. ZAMORA RODRÍGUEZ.

Nigeria: Segre 23, 28002 Madrid; tel. (91) 5630911; fax (91) 5636320; e-mail info@nigeriainspain.org; internet www.nigeriainspain.org; Ambassador OBED WADZANI.

Norway: Serrano 26, 5°, 28001 Madrid; tel. (91) 4363840; fax (91) 3190969; e-mail emb.madrid@mfa.no; internet www.noruega.es; Ambassador TORGEIR LARSEN.

Oman: Cardenal Herrera Oria 138, 28034 Madrid; tel. (91) 7364445; fax (91) 7354536; e-mail oman.emb.madrid@gmail.com; Ambassador HILAL BIN MARHOON BIN SALIM AL-MAAMARY.

Pakistan: Avda Pío XII 11, 28016 Madrid; tel. (91) 3458995; fax (91) 3458158; e-mail cancilleria@embajada-pakistan.org; internet www.embajada-pakistan.org; Ambassador HUMAIRA HASAN.

Panama: Claudio Coello 86, 1° dcha, 28006 Madrid; tel. (91) 5765001; fax (91) 5767161; Ambassador ALVARO E. TOMAS.

Paraguay: Doctor Fleming 3, 1°, 28036 Madrid; tel. (91) 45709234; fax (91) 3084905; e-mail embapar@arrakis.es; Ambassador OSCAR J. CABELLO SARUBBI.

Peru: Príncipe de Vergara 36, 5° dcha, 28001 Madrid; tel. (91) 4314242; fax (91) 5776861; e-mail lepru@embajadaperu.es; internet www.embajadaperu.es; Ambassador JAIME CÁCERES SAYÁN.

Philippines: Eresma 2, 28002 Madrid; tel. (91) 7823830; fax (91) 4116606; e-mail madridpe@terra.es; internet www.philmadrid.com; Ambassador CARLOS C. SALINAS.

Poland: Guisando 23 bis, 28035 Madrid; tel. (91) 3736605; fax (91) 3736624; e-mail madryt.amb.sekretariat@msz.gov.pl; internet www.madrid.polemb.net; Ambassador RYSZARD SCHNEPF.

Portugal: Pinar 1, 28006 Madrid; tel. (91) 7824960; fax (91) 7824972; e-mail embmadrid@emb-portugal.es; internet www.embajadaportugal-madrid.org; Ambassador ALVARO JOSÉ DE MENDONÇA E MOURA.

Qatar: Paseo de la Castellana 15, 5°, 28046 Madrid; tel. (91) 3106926; fax (91) 3104851; Ambassador HAMAD BIN HAMAD AL-IBRAHIM AL-ATTIYYA.

Romania: Avda Alfonso XIII 157, 28016 Madrid; tel. (91) 3501881; fax (91) 3452917; e-mail secretariat@embajadaderumania.es; internet madrid.mae.ro; Ambassador MARIA LIGOR.

Russia: Velázquez 155, 28002 Madrid; tel. (91) 4110807; fax (91) 5629712; e-mail embrues@infonegocio.com; internet www.spain.mid.ru; Ambassador ALEKSANDR KUZNETSOV.

San Marino: Padre de Jesús Ordóñez 18, 3°, 28002 Madrid; tel. (91) 5639000; fax (91) 5631931; e-mail embamadrid@sanmarino1.net; Ambassador ENRICO MARIA PASQUINI (resident in Rome, Italy).

Saudi Arabia: Dr Alvarez Sierra 3, 28033 Madrid; tel. (91) 3834300; fax (91) 3021145; e-mail info@arabiasaudi.org; internet www.arabiasaudi.org; Ambassador Prince SA'UD BIN NAIF BIN ABD AL-AZIZ AL-SA'UD.

Senegal: Príncipe de Vergara 90, 1° A y B, 28001 Madrid; tel. (91) 7451003; fax (91) 7451148; Ambassador ABAS NDIOUR.

Serbia: Velázquez 162, 28002 Madrid; tel. (91) 5635045; fax (91) 5630440; e-mail office@embajada-serbia.es; internet www.embajada-serbia.es; Ambassador JELA BAĆOVIĆ.

Slovakia: Pinar 20, 28006 Madrid; tel. (91) 5903861; fax (91) 5903868; e-mail mail@embajadaeslovaquia.es; Ambassador JÁN ŠKODA.

Slovenia: Hermanos Bécquer 7, 2°, 28006 Madrid; tel. (91) 4116893; fax (91) 5646057; e-mail vma@gov.si; Ambassador (vacant).

South Africa: Claudio Coello 91, 28006 Madrid; tel. (91) 4363780; fax (91) 5777414; e-mail embassy@sudafrica.com; Ambassador FIKILE SYLVIA MAGUBANE.

Sudan: Paseo de la Castellana 115, 2° izqda, 28046 Madrid; tel. (91) 4174903; fax (91) 5972516; e-mail sudani49@hotmail.com; Ambassador (vacant).

Sweden: Caracas 25, 28010 Madrid; tel. (91) 7022000; fax (91) 7022040; e-mail ambassaden.madrid@foreign.ministry.se; internet www.swedenabroad.com/madrid; Chargé d'affaires a.i. JÖRGEN PERSSON.

Switzerland: Núñez de Balboa 35A, 7°, 28001 Madrid; tel. (91) 4363960; fax (91) 4363980; e-mail vertretung@mad.rep.admin.ch; internet www.eda.admin.ch/madrid; Ambassador URS JOHANN ZISWILER.

Syria: Plaza de Platerías Martínez 1, 1°, 28014 Madrid; tel. (91) 4203946; fax (91) 4202681; Ambassador HUSSAM EDDIN ALA.

Thailand: Joaquín Costa 29, 28002 Madrid; tel. (91) 5632903; fax (91) 5640033; e-mail madthai@temb.e.telefonica.net; Ambassador KULKUMUT SINGHARA NA AYUDHAYA.

SPAIN

Tunisia: Avda Alfonso XIII 64–68, 28016 Madrid; tel. (91) 4473508; fax (91) 5938416; e-mail ambtnmad@terra.es; Ambassador MUHAMMAD RIDHA KECHRID.

Turkey: Rafael Calvo 18, 2°A y B, 28010 Madrid; tel. (91) 3198064; fax (91) 3086602; e-mail info@tcmadridbe.org; internet www.tcmadridbe.org; Ambassador ENDER ARAT.

Ukraine: Ronda de la Abubilla 52, 28043 Madrid; tel. (91) 7489360; fax (91) 3887178; e-mail ucremb@ya.com; internet www.mfa.gov.ua/spain; Ambassador ANATOLIY A. SHCHERBA.

United Arab Emirates: Capitán Haya 40, 28020 Madrid; tel. (91) 5701003; fax (91) 5715176; Ambassador Dr HASSA ABDULLAH AL-OTAIBA.

United Kingdom: Paseo de la Castellana 259D, Torre Espacio, 28046 Madrid; tel. (91) 7146300; fax (91) 7146301; e-mail enquiries.madrid@fco.gov.uk; internet ukinspain.fco.gov.uk; Ambassador GILES PAXMAN, LVO.

USA: Serrano 75, 28006 Madrid; tel. (91) 5872200; fax (91) 5872303; e-mail amemb@embusa.es; internet madrid.usembassy.gov; Ambassador ALAN D. SOLOMONT.

Uruguay: Paseo del Pintor Rosales 32, 1° D, 28008 Madrid; tel. (91) 7580475; fax (91) 5428177; e-mail urumatri@urumatri.com; Ambassador CARLOS PITA.

Uzbekistan: Paseo de la Castellana 45, 4° dcha, 28046 Madrid; tel. (91) 3101639; fax (91) 3103123; Ambassador GULNARA KARIMOVA.

Venezuela: Capitán Haya 1, 13°, Edif. Eurocentro, 28020 Madrid; tel. (91) 5981200; fax (91) 5971583; e-mail embajada@espana.gob.ve; Ambassador (vacant).

Viet Nam: Arturo Soria 201, 1°A, 28043 Madrid; tel. (91) 5102867; fax (91) 4157067; e-mail claudiomes@yahoo.com; internet www.embavietnam-madrid.org; Ambassador TRUONG TRIEU DUONG.

Yemen: Paseo de la Castellana 117, 8°D, 28046 Madrid; tel. (91) 4119950; fax (91) 5623865; e-mail secretaria@embajadayemen.es; internet www.embajadayemen.es; Ambassador MUSTAPHA AHMAD NOMAN.

Judicial System

Consejo General del Poder Judicial (CGPJ)
(General Council of the Judiciary)
Marqués de la Ensenada 8, 28071 Madrid; tel. (91) 7006100; fax (91) 7006358; e-mail webmaster@cgpj.es; internet www.poderjudicial.es.

The highest governing body of the judiciary; comprises a President, 20 members elected by the Cortes and appointed by the King for a five-year term (10 by the Congreso de los Diputados and 10 by the Senado); supervises the judicial system; independent of the Ministry of Justice; Pres. CARLOS JOSÉ DÍVAR BLANCO

General Prosecutor: CÁNDIDO CONDE-PUMPIDO.

CONSTITUTIONAL COURT

Tribunal Constitucional: Domenico Scarlatti 6, 28003 Madrid; tel. (91) 5508000; fax (91) 5449268; e-mail buzon@tribunalconstitucional.es; internet www.tribunalconstitucional.es; Pres. PASCUAL SALA SÁNCHEZ.

SUPREME COURT

Tribunal Supremo: Palacio de Justicia, Plaza de la Villa de París s/n, 28071 Madrid; tel. (91) 3971200; e-mail webmaster@cgpj.es; internet www.poderjudicial.es; Composed of 5 courts: civil; criminal; litigation; company; and military, each with its president and its respective judges; Pres. CARLOS JOSÉ DÍVAR BLANCO.

HIGH COURTS

Audiencia Nacional (National Court): García Gutiérrez 1, 28004 Madrid; tel. (91) 3973381; fax (91) 3973306; internet www.audiencianacional.es; f. 1977; consists of 3 divisions: Penal, Social and Contencioso-Administrativo, each with its president and respective judges; attached to Second Court of Supreme Court; deals primarily with crimes associated with a modern industrial society, such as corruption, forgery, drugs-trafficking, as well as terrorism; Pres. ANGEL JUANES.

OTHER COURTS

The Higher Courts of Justice in the Autonomous Communities comprise civil, criminal, administrative and labour divisions, while Provincial Courts hear proceedings for prosecutions of offences by lengthy prison terms, and appeals against the rulings of lower courts. The lower courts are the Criminal, Administrative, Labour, Juvenile and Prison Supervisory Courts of First Instance and Trial Courts. In municipalities where there are no Courts of First Instance and Trial, there is a Magistrates' Court.

Religion

CHRISTIANITY

About 92% of Spain's inhabitants profess adherence to Roman Catholicism, and the country contains some 61,000 churches, with about 500 persons in each parish. The Roman Catholic organization Opus Dei, which seeks to integrate religious faith and professional work, plays an important role in Spanish society. There are some 30,000 Protestants in Spain.

The Roman Catholic Church

For ecclesiastical purposes, Spain (including Spanish North Africa) comprises 14 metropolitan archdioceses and 55 dioceses. At 31 December 2006 there were an estimated 40.8m. adherents, equivalent to 92.0% of the population.

Bishops' Conference

Conferencia Episcopal Española, Añastro 1, 28033 Madrid; tel. (91) 3439600; fax (91) 3439602; e-mail conferenciaepiscopal@planalfa.es; internet www.conferenciaepiscopal.es.
f. 1977; Pres. Cardinal ANTONIO MARÍA ROUCO VARELA (Archbishop of Madrid); Sec.-Gen. JUAN ANTONIO MARTÍNEZ CAMINO.

Archbishop of Barcelona: Cardinal LLUÍS MARTÍNEZ SISTACH.
Archbishop of Burgos: Most Rev. FRANCISCO GIL HELLÍN.
Archbishop of Granada: Most Rev. FRANCISCO JAVIER MARTÍNEZ FERNÁNDEZ.
Archbishop of Madrid: Cardinal ANTONIO MARÍA ROUCO VARELA.
Archbishop of Mérida-Badajoz: Most Rev. SANTIAGO GARCÍA ARACIL.
Archbishop of Oviedo: Most Rev. JESÚS SANZ MONTES.
Archbishop of Pamplona and Tudela: Most Rev. FRANCISCO PÉREZ GONZÁLEZ.
Archbishop of Santiago de Compostela: Most Rev. JULIÁN BARRIO BARRIO.
Archbishop of Sevilla: Most Rev. JUAN JOSÉ ASENJO PELEGRINA.
Archbishop of Tarragona: Most Rev. JAUME PUJOL BALCELLS.
Archbishop of Toledo: Most Rev. BRAULIO RODRÍGUEZ PLAZA.
Archbishop of Valencia: Most Rev. CARLOS OSORO SIERRA.
Archbishop of Valladolid: Most Rev. RICARDO BLÁZQUEZ PÉREZ.
Archbishop of Zaragoza: Most Rev. MANUEL UREÑA PASTOR.

Other Christian Churches

Iglesia Española Reformada Episcopal (IERE) (Spanish Reformed Episcopal Church): Beneficencia 18, 28004 Madrid; tel. (91) 4452560; fax (91) 5944572; e-mail eclesiae@arrakis.es; internet www.anglicanos.org; f. 1860; mem. of the Anglican Communion; 17 congregations (2004); Bishop Rt Rev. CARLOS LÓPEZ LOZANO.

Unión Evangélica Bautista Española (UEBE) (Baptist Evangelical Union of Spain): San Jacinto 26, 3°, 46008 Valencia; tel. (963) 591633; fax (963) 134581; e-mail secretaria@uebe.org; internet www.uebe.org; f. 1922; Pres. Rev. JUAN MARCOS VÁZQUEZ VARELA; Gen. Sec. Rev. MANUEL SARRIAS.

ISLAM

It is estimated that there are some 1m. Muslims in Spain, many of whom are Moroccan migrant workers.

Comisión Islámica de España: Anastasio Herrero 5, 28020 Madrid; tel. (91) 5714040; fax (91) 5708889; e-mail cie@teleline.es; umbrella org.; negotiates with Govt on Islamic affairs; Sec.-Gen. MANSUL ESCUDERO.

Federación Española de Entidades Religiosas Islámicas (FEERI): La Unión 47, 29006 Málaga; f. 1989; 57 mem. groups; Pres. FÉLIX ANGEL HERRERO.

Unión de Comunidades Islámicas de España (UCIDE): Anastasio Herrero 5, Madrid 28020; tel. (91) 5714040; e-mail secretariogeneralcie@hotmail.com; Pres. RIAY TATARY BAKRY.

Comunidad Ahmadía del Islam en España: La Mezquita Basharat, 14630 Pedro Abad (Córdoba); tel. (957) 186203; fax (957) 186300; e-mail info@alislam.org; internet www.alislam.org; Pres. MUBARIK AHMAD KHAN.

JUDAISM

There are an estimated 48,000 Jews in Spain.

Federación de Comunidades Judías de España (Federation of Jewish Communities of Spain): Miguel Ángel 7, 1° C, 28010 Madrid; tel. (91) 7001208; fax (91) 3915717; e-mail fcje@fcje.org; internet www.fcje.org; 30 communities; Pres. ISAAC QUERUB CARO.

SPAIN *Directory*

The Press

The most widely read newspapers are *ABC*, *El Mundo*, *El País* and *La Razón*, published in Madrid, and *La Vanguardia*, published in Barcelona. Important regional newspapers include *El Periódico de Catalunya* (Barcelona), *El Correo* (Bilbao) and *La Voz de Galicia* (A Coruña). Sporting dailies, notably *Marca* and *As*, enjoy very high circulation figures. Much of the Spanish media is owned by large corporations, of which the most prominent are Grupo PRISA (*El País*) and Vocento (*ABC* and various regional titles).

PRINCIPAL DAILIES
(arranged by province)

Albacete

La Tribuna de Albacete: Paseo de la Cuba 14, 02005 Albacete; tel. (967) 191000; fax (967) 240386; e-mail redaccion@latribunadealbacete.es; internet www.latribunadealbacete.es; Propr Promecal; Dir Francisco Javier Martínez García.

Alicante

Información: Avda Dr Rico 17, Apdo 214, 03005 Alicante; tel. (96) 5989100; fax (96) 5989165; e-mail redaccion@epi.es; internet www.diarioinformacion.com; f. 1940; Propr Editorial Prensa Ibérica; Dir Juan R. Gil; circ. 32,303.

Almería

La Voz de Almería: Avda Mediterráneo 159, 1°, Edif. Cadena Ser, 04007 Almería; tel. (950) 280036; fax (950) 256458; e-mail lavoz@lavozdealmeria.com; internet www.lavozdealmeria.com; morning; Dir Pedro Manuel de la Cruz Alonso; circ. 10,575.

Asturias

El Comercio: Diario El Comercio 1, 33207 Gijón; tel. (98) 5179800; fax (98) 5340955; e-mail elcomercio@elcomerciodigital.es; internet www.elcomerciodigital.com; f. 1878; Propr Vocento; Dir Íñigo Noriega Gómez; circ. 26,102.

La Nueva España: Calvo Sotelo 7, Edif. Sedes, 33007 Oviedo; tel. (98) 5279700; fax (98) 5279711; e-mail pam@lne.es; internet www.lne.es; f. 1937; Propr Editorial Prensa Ibérica; Dir Isidoro Nicieza; circ. 60,469.

El Periódico—La Voz de Asturias: La Lila 6, bajo, 33002 Oviedo; tel. (98) 5101500; fax (98) 5101505; e-mail vozredaccion@elperiodico.com; internet www.lavozdeasturias.es; f. 1923; Propr Grupo Zeta; Dir Luis Mugueta San Martín; circ. 10,077.

Badajoz

Hoy—Diario de Extremadura: Carretera Madrid–Lisboa 22, 06008 Badajoz; tel. (924) 252511; fax (924) 205297; e-mail hoyredaccion@hoy.es; internet www.hoy.es; f. 1933; Catholic; Badajoz and Cáceres editions; Propr Vocento; Dir Julián Quirós; circ. 23,365.

Barcelona

Ara: Diputació 119, 08015 Barcelona; tel. (93) 2029595; fax (93) 4519264; e-mail web@ara.cat; internet www.ara.cat; f. 2010; Catalan; Dir Carles Capdevila.

Avui: Enric Granados 84, entresòl, 08008 Barcelona; tel. (93) 3163900; fax (93) 3163936; e-mail info@avui.cat; internet www.avui.cat; f. 1976; Catalan; Exec. Pres. Antoni Cambredó; Dir Xavier Bosch; circ. 28,591.

Mundo Deportivo: Avda Diagonal 577, 5°, 08036 Barcelona; tel. (93) 3444100; fax (93) 3444250; e-mail contacto@elmundodeportivo.es; internet www.elmundodeportivo.es; f. 1906; sport; Propr Grupo Godó; Dir Santi Nolla Zayas; circ. 96,561.

El Periódico de Catalunya: Consell de Cent 425–427, 08009 Barcelona; tel. (93) 2655353; fax (93) 4846512; e-mail atencion.lector@elperiodico.com; internet www.elperiodico.com; daily; f. 1978; parallel edns in Spanish and Catalan; Propr Grupo Zeta; Dir Rafael Nadal; circ. 177,830.

Sport: Consell de Cent 425–427, 6°, 08009 Barcelona; tel. (93) 2279400; fax (93) 2279410; e-mail redaccion@diariosport.com; internet www.sport.es; Propr Grupo Zeta; Dir Joan Vehils; circ. 104,987.

La Vanguardia: Avda Diagonal 477, 08036 Barcelona; tel. (93) 4812200; fax (93) 3185587; e-mail lavanguardia@lavanguardia.es; internet www.lavanguardia.es; f. 1881; Propr Grupo Godó; Dir José Antich; circ. 209,735.

Burgos

Diario de Burgos: Avda Castilla y León 62–64, 09006 Burgos; tel. (947) 268375; fax (947) 268003; e-mail redaccion@diariodeburgos.es; internet www.diariodeburgos.es; f. 1891; Catholic; Propr Promecal; Dir Antonio José Mencía Gullón; circ. 14,266.

Cádiz

Diario de Cádiz: Edif. Fénix, Avda de El Puerto 2, 11007 Cádiz; tel. (956) 297900; fax (956) 261460; e-mail redaccion@diariodecadiz.es; internet www.diariodecadiz.es; f. 1867; Propr Grupo Joly; Dir José Joaquín León; circ. 26,073.

Diario de Jerez: Patricio Garvey s/n, Apdo 316, 11402 Jerez de la Frontera; tel. (956) 321411; fax (956) 349904; e-mail redaccion@diariojerez.es; internet www.diariodejerez.com; f. 1984; Propr Grupo Joly; Dir Rafael Navas Renedo; circ. 8,695.

Cantabria

Alerta—el Diario de Cantabria: 1 de Mayo s/n, Barrio San Martín, 39011 Peñacastillo; tel. (942) 320033; fax (942) 322046; e-mail administracion@eldiarioalerta.com; internet www.eldiarioalerta.com; f. 1937; independent; Dir Ciriaco Díaz Porras; circ. 30,619.

El Diario Montañés: La Prensa s/n, La Albericia, 39012 Santander; tel. (942) 354000; fax (942) 341806; e-mail redaccion.dm@eldiariomontanes.es; internet www.eldiariomontanes.es; f. 1902; Propr Vocento; Dir Manuel Angel Castañeda Pérez; circ. 39,901.

Castellón

El Periódico Mediterráneo: Carretera de Almassora s/n, 12005 Castellón de la Plana; tel. (964) 349500; fax (964) 349505; e-mail mediterraneo@elperiodico.com; internet www.elperiodicomediterraneo.com; f. 1938; Propr Grupo Zeta; Dir José Luis Valencia; circ. 10,810.

Ciudad Real

El Día de Ciudad Real: Plaza Cervantes 6, 13001 Ciudad Real; tel. (926) 223033; fax (926) 227185; e-mail redaccion@eldiadeciudadreal.com; internet www.eldiadeciudadreal.com; f. 2002; independent; Dir Santiago Mateo Sahuquillo; circ. 4,500.

La Tribuna de Ciudad Real: Pedro Muñoz 3, 13005 Ciudad Real; tel. (926) 215301; fax (926) 215306; e-mail ciudadreal@diariolatribuna.com; internet www.diariolatribuna.com; Propr Promecal; Dir Oscar Gálvez Maté; circ. 3,976.

Córdoba

Córdoba: Ing. Juan de la Cierva 18 (Polígono Torrecilla), Apdo 2, 14013 Córdoba; tel. (957) 420302; fax (957) 204648; e-mail cordoba2@elperiodico.com; internet www.diariocordoba.com; f. 1941; Propr Grupo Zeta; Dir Francisco Luis Córdoba Berjillos; circ. 15,503.

A Coruña

El Correo Gallego: Preguntoiro 29, 15704 Santiago de Compostela; tel. (981) 543700; fax (981) 543701; e-mail grupocorreogallego@elcorreogallego.es; internet www.elcorreogallego.es; f. 1878; Propr Grupo Correo Gallego; Dir José Manuel Rey Nóvoa; circ. 18,238.

Galicia Hoxe: Preguntoiro 29, 15704 Santiago de Compostela; tel. (981) 543700; fax (981) 543701; e-mail info@galicia-hoxe.com; internet www.galicia-hoxe.com; f. 1994 as *O Correo Galego*; refounded under current name 2003; Galician; Propr Grupo Correo Gallego; Dir José Manuel Rey Nóvoa.

El Ideal Gallego: Polígono de Pocomaco, C12, 15190 Mesoiro; tel. (981) 173040; fax (981) 299327; e-mail elidealgallego@elidealgallego.com; internet www.elidealgallego.com; f. 1917; independent; Dir Juan Ramón Díaz García; circ. 15,500 (Sun. 20,000).

La Voz de Galicia: Avda de la Prensa 84–85, Polígono de Sabón, 15142 Arteixo; tel. (981) 180180; fax (981) 180410; e-mail redac@lavoz.com; internet www.lavozdegalicia.com; f. 1882; Propr Grupo Voz; Dir Xosé Luis Vilela Conde; circ. 103,702.

Girona

El Punt: Santa Eugènia 42, 17005 Girona; tel. (972) 186400; fax (972) 186420; e-mail girona@elpunt.cat; internet www.elpunt.cat; f. 1979; Catalan; various regional edns; also publishes weekly edns covering Valencia and Perpignan (France); Dir Emili Gispert; circ. 24,134 July 2008–June 2009.

Granada

Ideal: Huelva 2, Polígono de Asegra, 18210 Peligros; tel. (958) 809809; fax (958) 402480; e-mail cartasdirector@ideal.es; internet www.ideal.es; f. 1932; Propr Vocento; Dir Eduardo Peralta de Ana; circ. 32,887; edns in Granada, Jaén and Almería.

Guipúzcoa

El Diario Vasco: Camino de Portuetxe 2, Barrio de Ibaeta, Apdo 201, 20018 San Sebastián; tel. (943) 410700; fax (943) 410814; e-mail

SPAIN

contactanos@diariovasco.com; internet www.diariovasco.com; f. 1934; Propr Vocento; Dir José Gabriel Mujika; circ. 98,700 (Sat.–Sun. 121,000).

Gara: Camino Portuetxe 23, 2°, 20018 San Sebastián; tel. (943) 316999; fax (943) 316998; internet www.gara.net; f. 1999; Basque and Spanish; left-wing Basque nationalist; independent; Dir Josu Juaristi.

Illes Balears

Diari de Balears: Paseo Mallorca, 9°A, 07011 Palma de Mallorca; tel. (971) 788300; fax (971) 455740; e-mail redaccio@ddbalears.cat; internet dbalears.cat; f. 1939 as *Baleares*; refounded as Catalan daily in 1996; Propr Grupo Serra; Dir Miquel Serra Magraner.

Diario de Ibiza: Avda de la Paz, 07800 Ibiza; tel. (971) 190000; fax (971) 190322; e-mail diariodeibiza@epi.es; internet www.diariodeibiza.es; Propr Editorial Prensa Ibérica; Dir Joan Serra Tur; circ. 7,615.

Diario de Mallorca: Puerto Rico 15, Polígono de Levante, 07006 Palma de Mallorca; tel. (971) 170300; fax (971) 170301; e-mail secretaria.diariodemallorca@epi.es; internet www.diariodemallorca.es; f. 1953; Propr Editorial Prensa Ibérica; Dir José Eduardo Iglesias Barca; circ. 22,350.

Menorca, Diario Insular: Cap de Cavalleria 5, 07714 Mahón, Menorca; tel. (971) 351600; fax (971) 351983; e-mail redaccion@menorca.info; internet www.menorca.info; f. 1941; Dir Joan Bosco Marquès Bosch; circ. 6,609.

Última Hora: Paseo Mallorca 9A, 07011 Palma de Mallorca; tel. (971) 788333; fax (971) 454190; e-mail master@ultimahora.es; internet www.ultimahora.es; f. 1893; Propr Grupo Serra; Dir Pedro Comas Barceló; circ. 36,487.

León

Diario de León: Carretera León–Astorga, Km 4,5, 24010 León; tel. (987) 840300; fax (987) 840340; e-mail web@diariodeleon.com; internet www.diariodeleon.es; Dir Fernando Aller González; circ. 16,100.

Lleida (Lérida)

Segre: Riu 6, Apdo 543, 25007 Lérida; tel. (973) 248000; fax (973) 246031; e-mail redaccio@diarisegre.com; internet www.diarisegre.com; f. 1982; Catalan and Spanish edns; independent; Dir Juan Cal Sánchez; circ. 13,184.

Lugo

El Progreso: Ribadeo s/n, 27002 Lugo; tel. (982) 298100; fax (982) 298102; e-mail correo@elprogreso.es; internet www.elprogreso.es; f. 1908; Dir Luis Rodríguez García; Editor-in-Chief Blanca García Montenegro; circ. 15,509.

Madrid

ABC: Juan Ignacio Luca de Tena 7, 28027 Madrid; tel. (91) 3399000; fax (91) 3203680; e-mail cartas@abc.es; internet www.abc.es; f. 1905; conservative, monarchist; various regional edns; Propr Vocento; Dir José Antonio Zarzalejos; circ. 230,422.

As: Albasanz 14, 4°, 28037 Madrid; tel. (91) 3752500; fax (91) 3752558; e-mail diarioas@diarioas.es; internet www.as.com; f. 1967; sport; Propr Grupo PRISA; Dir Alfredo Relaño Estapé; circ. 225,670.

Cinco Días: Gran Vía 32, 2°, 28013 Madrid; tel. (91) 3537900; fax (91) 3537991; e-mail redaccion@cinodias.com; internet www.cincodias.com; f. 1978; economic; Propr Grupo PRISA; Dir Jorge Rivera; circ. 37,945.

El Economista: Condesa de Venadito 1, 3°, 28027 Madrid; tel. (91) 3246700; fax (91) 3246727; e-mail comunicacion@eleconomista.es; internet www.eleconomista.es; f. 2006; originally f. 1886 as weekly; daily; Pres. Alfonso de Salas; Dir Amador G. Ayora; circ. 22,516.

Expansión: Paseo de la Castellana 66, 28046 Madrid; tel. (91) 3373220; fax (91) 3373266; e-mail expansion@recoletos.es; internet www.expansion.com; economic; Propr Unidad Editorial, SA; Dir Jesús Martínez de Rioja Vázquez; circ. 50,394.

La Gaceta de los Negocios: Pantoja 14, 28002 Madrid; tel. (91) 4327600; fax (91) 4327733; e-mail jpv@negocios.com; internet www.negocios.com; f. 1989; daily; business and finance; Dir José María García Hoz; circ. 37,902.

Marca: Paseo de la Castellana 66, 2°, 28046 Madrid; tel. (91) 3373220; fax (91) 3373276; e-mail marca.com@unidadeditorial.es; internet www.marca.com; f. 1938 as weekly in San Sebastián, 1942 as daily in Madrid; sport; Propr Unidad Editorial, SA; Dir Rafael Alique; circ. 310,793.

El Mundo (del Siglo Veintiuno): Pradillo 42, 28002 Madrid; tel. (91) 5864800; fax (91) 5864848; internet www.elmundo.es; f. 1989; centre-right; various regional edns; Propr Unidad Editorial, SA; Pres. Carmen Iglesias; Dir Pedro J. Ramírez Codina; circ. 337,172.

El País: Miguel Yuste 40, 28037 Madrid; tel. (91) 3378200; fax (91) 3377758; e-mail redaccion@elpais.com; internet www.elpais.com; f. 1976; centre-left; regional edns in Andalusia, Basque Country, Catalonia, Galicia and Valencia; Propr Grupo PRISA; Pres. Ignacio Polanco Moreno; Dir Javier Moreno Barber; circ. 425,927.

El Mundo (del Siglo Veintiuno): Pradillo 42, 28002 Madrid; tel. (91) 5864800; fax (91) 5864848; internet www.elmundo.es; f. 1989; centre-right; various regional edns; Propr Unidad Editorial, SA; Pres. Carmen Iglesias; Dir Pedro J. Ramírez Codina; circ. 337,172.

Qué!: Orense 81, 3°, 28020 Madrid; tel. (91) 5726200; fax (91) 5710085; e-mail redaccion@quediario.com; internet www.quediario.com; f. 2005; free; 15 local edns; Propr Vocento; Dir Ana I. Pereda; circ. 959,283.

La Razón: Josefa Valcárcel 42, 28027 Madrid; tel. (91) 3247000; fax (91) 7423604; e-mail sugerencias@larazon.es; internet www.larazon.es; f. 1998; conservative; Pres. Mauricio Casals; Dir José Alejandro Vara; circ. 149,559.

20 Minutos: Condesa de Venadito 1, 1°, 28027 Madrid; tel. (91) 7015600; fax (91) 7015660; e-mail grupo20minutos@20minutos.es; internet www.20minutos.es; f. 2000; free; 15 regional edns; Dir Arsenio Escolar; circ. 850,000.

Málaga

La Opinión de Málaga: Granada 42, 29015 Málaga; tel. (95) 2126200; fax (95) 2126255; e-mail secretaria@epi.es; internet www.laopiniondemalaga.es; f. 1999; Propr Editorial Prensa Ibérica; Dir Joaquín Marín Alarcón; circ. 7,589.

Sur: Avda Dr Marañón 48, 29009 Málaga; tel. (95) 2649600; fax (95) 2279508; e-mail redaccion.su@diariosur.es; internet www.diariosur.es; f. 1937; Propr Vocento; Dir José Antonio Frías Ruiz; circ. 60,000 (also publishes free English weekly, circ. 32,293).

Murcia

La Verdad: Camino Viejo de Monteagudo s/n, 30160 Murcia; tel. (968) 369100; fax (968) 369147; e-mail lectores@laverdad.es; internet www.laverdad.es; f. 1903; local edns published in Albacete and Alicante; propr Vocento; Dir José María Esteban Ibáñez; circ. 29,794.

Navarra

Diario de Navarra: Carretera Zaragoza s/n, 31191 Cordovilla (Navarra); tel. (948) 236050; fax (948) 150320; e-mail cartas@diariodenavarra.es; internet www.diariodenavarra.es; f. 1903; conservative; independent; Dir Inés Artajo Ayesa; circ. 57,893.

Diario de Noticias: Altzutzate 8, Polígono Areta, 31620 Huarte; tel. (948) 332533; fax (948) 332518; e-mail cad@noticiasdenavarra.com; internet www.noticiasdenavarra.com; f. 1994; independent; Dir Joseba Santamaría; circ. 18,135.

Ourense

La Región: Polígono Industrial de San Cibrao das Viñas C4, 32091 Ourense; tel. (988) 600102; e-mail info@laregion.es; internet www.laregion.es; f. 1910; independent; Pres. José Luis Outeiriño Rodríguez; Dir Alfonso Sánchez Izquierdo; circ. 11,405.

Las Palmas de Gran Canaria

Canarias 7: Profesor Lozano 7, Urbanización El Sebadal, 35008 Las Palmas; tel. (928) 301300; fax (928) 301434; e-mail infocan@canarias7.es; internet www.canarias7.es; f. 1982; Dir Francisco Suárez Álamo; circ. 30,544.

La Provincia—Diario de las Palmas: Alcalde Ramírez Bethencourt 8, 35003 Las Palmas; tel. (928) 479410; fax (928) 479401; e-mail laprovincia@epi.es; internet www.laprovincia.es; *La Provincia* f. 1911, *Diario de las Palmas* f. 1895; Propr Editorial Prensa Ibérica; Dir Ángel Tristán Pimienta; circ. 30,990.

Pontevedra

Faro de Vigo: Factoría de Chapela, 36320 Redondela; tel. (986) 814600; fax (986) 814615; e-mail redaccion@farodevigo.es; internet www.farodevigo.es; f. 1853; Propr Editorial Prensa Ibérica; Dir Juan Carlos Da Silva; circ. 40,263.

La Rioja

La Rioja: Vara del Rey 74, Apdo 28, 26002 Logroño; tel. (941) 279107; fax (941) 279106; e-mail redaccion@larioja.com; internet www.diariolarioja.com; f. 1889; Propr Vocento; Dir Ramón Alonso; circ. 16,780.

SPAIN

Salamanca

La Gaceta Regional de Salamanca: Avda de los Cipreses 81, 37004 Salamanca; tel. (923) 252020; fax (923) 256155; e-mail admon@lagacetadesalamanca.com; internet www.lagacetadesalamanca.es; f. 1920; independent; Dir IÑIGO DOMÍNGUEZ DE CALATAYUD; circ. 14,985.

Santa Cruz de Tenerife

El Día: Avda de Buenos Aires 71, Apdo 97, 38005 Santa Cruz; tel. (922) 238300; fax (922) 214247; e-mail redaccioneldia@eldia.es; internet www.eldia.es; f. 1910; Dir JOSÉ E. RODRÍGUEZ RAMÍREZ; circ. 24,352.

Diario de Avisos: Salamanca 5, 38006 Santa Cruz; tel. (922) 272350; fax (922) 241039; e-mail redaccion@diariodeavisos.com; internet www.diariodeavisos.com; f. 1890; refounded 1976; Dir LEOPOLDO FERNÁNDEZ CABEZA DE VACA; circ. 12,293.

La Opinión de Tenerife: Plaza Santa Cruz de la Sierra 2, 38003 Santa Cruz; tel. (922) 471800; fax (922) 471801; e-mail tenerife@laopinion.es; internet www.laopinion.es; Propr Editorial Prensa Ibérica; Dir CARMEN RUANO; circ. 6,317.

Sevilla (Seville)

El Correo de Andalucía: Américo Vespucio 39, Isla de la Cartuja. 41092 Sevilla; tel. (95) 4999251; fax (95) 4517635; e-mail redaccion@correoandalucia.es; internet www.correoandalucia.es; f. 1899; independent; Pres. JOSÉ RODRÍGUEZ DE LA BORBOLLA CAMOYÁN; Dir ANTONIO HERNÁNDEZ-RODICIO; circ. 15,470.

Diario de Sevilla: Rioja 14, 41001 Sevilla; tel. (95) 4506200; fax (95) 4506222; e-mail secretaria@diariodesevilla.es; internet www.diariodesevilla.es; f. 1999; Propr Grupo Joly; Dir JOSÉ ANTONIO CARRIZOSA; circ. 22,378.

Tarragona

Diari de Tarragona: Domènech Guansé 2, 43005 Tarragona; tel. (977) 299700; fax (977) 223013; e-mail diari@diaridetarragona.com; internet www.diaridetarragona.com; f. 1808; Spanish and Catalan; Dir RAMON PEDRÓS; circ. 14,082.

Valencia

Levante—El Mercantil Valenciano (EMV): Traginers 7, 46014 Valencia; tel. (96) 3992200; fax (96) 3992276; e-mail levante.rdc@epi.es; internet www.levante-emv.es; f. 1872; Propr Editorial Prensa Ibérica; Dir FERRAN BELDA; circ. 44,345.

Mini Diario: Jesús 40, 1°, 46007 Valencia; tel. (96) 3462624; fax (96) 3462620; e-mail redaccion@minidiario.com; internet www.minidiario.com; f. 1992; free; edns in Valencia and Alicante; Dir JUAN PÉREZ; circ. 56,360.

Las Provincias: Polígono Industrial Vara de Quart, Gremis 1, 46014 Valencia; tel. (96) 3502211; fax (96) 3590188; e-mail lasprovincias@lasprovincias.es; internet www.lasprovincias.es; f. 1866; rightist; Propr Vocento; Dir PEDRO ORTIZ SIMARRO; circ. 41,487.

Valladolid

El Día de Valladolid: Edif. Promecal, Los Astros s/n, 47009 Valladolid; tel. (983) 325045; fax (983) 325047; e-mail redaccion@diavalladolid.es; internet www.eldiadevalladolid.com; f. 2000; Propr Promecal; Pres. ANTONIO MÉNDEZ POZO.

El Norte de Castilla: Vázquez de Menchaca 10 (Polígono de Argales), 47008 Valladolid; tel. (983) 412100; fax (983) 412111; e-mail redaccion.nc@nortecastilla.es; internet www.nortecastilla.es; f. 1854; Propr Vocento; Dir CARLOS ROLDÁN SAN JUAN; circ. 36,422.

Vizcaya (Bizkaia)

El Correo: Pintor Losada 7, Apdo 205, 48004 Bilbao; tel. (94) 4870100; fax (94) 4870111; e-mail info@diario-elcorreo.es; internet www.elcorreodigital.com; f. 1910; edns in Vizcaya and Álava; Propr Vocento; Dir ÁNGEL ARNEDO GIL; circ. 119,601.

Deia: Carretera Bilbao Galdácano 8 (Bolueta), 48004 Bilbao; tel. (94) 4599100; fax (94) 4599120; e-mail cartas@deia.com; internet www.deia.com; f. 1997; Basque nationalist, associated with the EAJ-PNV; publishes weekly satirical supplement, *Caduca Hoy*; circ. 21,179.

Zaragoza

Heraldo de Aragón: Paseo de la Independencia 29, Apdo 175, 50001 Zaragoza; tel. (976) 765000; fax (976) 765001; e-mail redaccion@heraldo.es; internet www.heraldo.es; f. 1895; independent; also publishes edn in Huesca; Dir GUILLERMO FATÁS CABEZA; circ. 53,865.

El Periódico de Aragón: Hernán Cortés 37, bajo, 50005 Zaragoza; tel. (976) 700400; fax (976) 700458; e-mail eparagon@elperiodico.com; internet www.elperiodicodearagon.com; f. 1990; Propr Grupo Zeta; Dir JAIME ARMENGOL; circ. 12,481.

SELECTED PERIODICALS

The Arts

Arquitectura y Diseño: RBA Revistas, SA, Pérez Galdós 36 bis, 08012 Barcelona; internet www.rba.es; monthly; architecture and design; Dir-Gen. ARIADNA HERNÁNDEZ; circ. 47,741 (June 2007).

Claves de Razón Práctica: Julián Camarillo 29B, 1°, 28004 Madrid; tel. (91) 5386104; fax (91) 5222291; e-mail claves@progresa.es; internet claves.progresa.es; f. 1990; monthly; books and culture; Dirs JAVIER PRADERA, FERNANDO SAVATER; circ. 4,500.

El Croquis: Avda de los Reyes Católicos 9, El Escorial, 28280 Madrid; tel. (91) 8969414; fax (91) 8969415; e-mail elcroquis@elcroquis.es; internet www.elcroquis.es; 6 a year; architecture, in Spanish and English; Dirs FERNANDO MÁRQUEZ CECILIA, RICHARD LEVENE; circ. 15,078 (2010).

Experimenta: Churruca 27, 4° ext. dcha, 28004 Madrid; tel. (91) 5214049; fax (91) 5213212; e-mail info@experimenta.es; internet www.experimenta.es; f. 1989; architecture and design; Dir PIERLUIGI CATTERMOLE FIORAVANTI.

Insula: P° de Recoletos 4, 2°, 28001; tel. and fax (91) 4233743; internet www.insula.es; f. 1946; monthly; literature and social sciences; Editor ARANTXA GÓMEZ SANCHO; circ. 6,000.

Letra Internacional: Monte Esquinza 30, 3° dcha, 28010 Madrid; tel. (91) 3104313; fax (91) 3194585; e-mail editorial@fpabloiglesias.es; internet www.fpabloiglesias.es; f. 1986; quarterly; culture; Dir SALVADOR CLOTAS I CIERCO.

El Magisterio Español: Jose Abascal 46, 4° dcha, 28003 Madrid; tel. (91) 5199131; fax (91) 4151124; e-mail jollero@magisnet.com; internet www.magisnet.com; f. 1866; Wed.; education; Dir JOSÉ MARÍA DE MOYA ANEGÓN; circ. 10,320 (2009).

Ritmo: Isabel Colbrand 10, Oficina 87, 28050 Madrid; tel. (91) 3588774; fax (91) 3588944; e-mail correo@ritmo.com; internet www.ritmo.com; monthly; classical music; Dir (vacant).

Qué Leer: Passeig de Sant Gervasi 16–20, 08022 Barcelona; tel. (93) 2541250; fax (93) 2541263; e-mail queleer@hachette.es; internet www.que-leer.com; f. 1996; monthly; book news, etc.; Dir ANTONIO G. ITURBE; circ. 26,608.

Current Affairs, History, Religion, etc.

A Nosa Terra: Rúa Príncipe 22, 36202 Vigo; tel. (986) 222405; fax (986) 223101; e-mail info@anosaterra.com; internet www.anosaterra.com; f. 1907; weekly; Galician; Dir AFONSO EÍRÉ LÓPEZ.

Aceprensa: Núñez de Balboa 125, 6°, 28006 Madrid; tel. (91) 5158975; fax (91) 5631243; e-mail redaccion@aceprensa.com; internet www.aceprensa.com; f. 1973; weekly; news and features; Editorial Dir IGNACIO ARÉCHAGA DUQUE; circ. 4,000.

Boletín Oficial del Estado (BOE): Avda de Manoteras 54, 28050 Madrid; tel. (902) 365303; fax (91) 3841555; internet www.boe.es; f. 1936; successor of *Gaceta de Madrid*, f. 1661; daily except Sun.; laws, decrees, orders, etc.; Dir-Gen. JULIO SEAGE MARIÑO; circ. 60,000.

Cambio 16: Arroyo de Fontarrón 51, 28030 Madrid; tel. (91) 4201199; fax (91) 3601302; e-mail cambio16@cambio16.info; internet www.cambio16.info; f. 1972; weekly, Wed.; general; Dir MANUEL DOMÍNGUEZ MORENO.

El Ciervo: Calvet 56, 08021 Barcelona; tel. (93) 2005145; fax (93) 2011015; e-mail redaccion@elciervo.es; internet www.elciervo.es; f. 1951; monthly; politics and culture; Dir ROSARIO BOFILL; circ. 5,000.

Ciudad Nueva: José Picón 28, 28028 Madrid; tel. (91) 7259530; fax (91) 7130452; e-mail revista@ciudadnueva.com; internet www.ciudadnueva.com; f. 1964; monthly; Dir JAVIER RUBIO; circ. 7,000.

La Clave: Avda de Argón 336, 28022 Madrid; tel. (91) 8373131; fax (91) 8373136; e-mail redaccion@laclave.com; internet www.laclave.com; f. 2001; weekly; news magazine; Dir JOSÉ LUIS BALBIN; circ. 60,000.

Clío: Passeig San Gervasi 16–20, 08022 Barcelona; tel. (93) 2232136; fax (93) 4322907; e-mail clio@hachette.es; internet www.cliorevista.com; f. 2001; monthly; history; Dir JOSEP A. BORRELL; circ. 36,401.

Ecclesia: Alfonso XI 4, 28014 Madrid; tel. (91) 5315400; fax (91) 5225561; e-mail ecclesia@planalfa.es; f. 1941; weekly; religious information; Dir JESÚS DE LAS HERAS MUELA; Editor-in-Chief MIGUEL DE SANTIAGO; Propr Conferencia Episcopal Española; circ. 24,000.

Época: Paseo de la Castellana 36–38, 28046 Madrid; tel. (91) 5109100; fax (91) 5109149; weekly; Dir CARLOS DAVILA.

Historia 16: Rufino González 13,1°, 28037 Madrid; tel. (91) 3271171; fax (91) 3271220; e-mail h16redaccion@telefonica.net; f. 1976; monthly; history; Dir MARÍA ALDAVE; circ. 25,000.

SPAIN

El Jueves: Avda Diagonal 468, 5°, 08006 Barcelona; tel. (93) 2922217; fax (93) 2375824; e-mail redaccion@eljueves.es; internet www.eljueves.es; f. 1977; weekly, Wed.; satirical; Dir Manel Fontdevila; circ. 105,029 (2010).

Mundo Cristiano: Paseo de la Castellana 210, 2°B, 28046 Madrid; tel. (91) 3507862; fax (91) 3590230; e-mail mundoc@edicionespalabra.es; f. 1963; monthly; Dir Dario Chimeno Cano; Editor-in-Chief José M. Navalpotro; circ. 12,747 (June 2007).

Nueva Revista: Javier Ferrero 2, 28002 Madrid; tel. (91) 5199756; fax (91) 4151254; e-mail nuevarevista@tst.es; internet www.nuevarevista.net; f. 1990; 6 a year; politics, culture, art; Pres. Antonio Fontán Pérez.

Política—Revista Republicana: Ríos Rosas 10, 1° B, 28003 Madrid; tel. (902) 158935; fax (91) 4411165; e-mail ir@bitmailer.net; internet www.izquierdarepublicana.com; f. 1934; bi-monthly; organ of Izquierda Republicana; Dir Isabelo Herreros.

Revista de Estudios Políticos: Plaza de la Marina Española 9, 28071 Madrid; tel. (91) 5401950; fax (91) 5419574; e-mail editer@cepc.es; internet www.cepc.es; f. 1941; quarterly; publishes research papers, original and unpublished, on the Theory of the Constitution, State Theory, Political Science, History and History of Political Thought; publ. by Centro de Estudios Políticos y Constitucionales; Dirs Pedro de Vega, Juan J. Solozábal Echavarría; circ. 1,000.

El Socialista: Gobelas 31, 28023 Madrid; tel. (91) 5820044; fax (91) 5820045; e-mail elsocialista@elsocialista.es; internet www.elsocialista.es; f. 1866; monthly; general information; Dir Joaquín Tagar; circ. 185,000.

El Temps: Octubre Centre de Cultura Contemporània, Sant Ferran 12, 46001 Valencia; tel. (96) 3535100; fax (96) 3534569; e-mail eltemps@eltemps.net; internet www.eltemps.net; f. 1984; weekly; general information; in Catalan; Dir Jordi Fortuny i Batalla; circ. 25,000.

Tiempo: O'Donnell 12, 3°, 28009 Madrid; tel. (91) 5863300; fax (91) 5863346; e-mail contacta.tiempo@zetadigital.es; internet www.tiempodehoy.com; weekly; Dir Jesús Rivasés; circ. 43,408 (June 2007).

Treball: Passatge del Rellotge 3, 08002 Barcelona; tel. (93) 3010612; fax (93) 4124252; e-mail treball@iniciativa.cat; internet www.iniciativa.cat; f. 1991; 6 a year; organ of Iniciativa per Catalunya Verds; Dir Marc Rius; circ. 6,000.

Vida Nueva: Impresores 2, Urbanización Prado del Espino, 28660 Boadilla del Monte, Madrid; tel. (91) 4226255; fax (91) 4226118; e-mail director.vidanueva@ppc-editorial.com; internet www.vidanueva.es; f. 1958; weekly; society and religion; Dir Juan Rubio; circ. 20,000.

Finance

Actualidad Económica: Paseo de la Castellana 66, 4°, 28046 Madrid; tel. (91) 3370346; fax (91) 5628415; e-mail aeconomica@recoletos.es; internet www.actualidad-economica.com; f. 1958; weekly, Mon.; Dir Miguel Ángel Belloso; circ. 32,866 (June 2010).

Capital: Castellana 192, 11°, 28046 Madrid; tel. (91) 3832476; fax (91) 3832571; e-mail mmoreno@gyj.es; internet www.capital.es; f. 2000; monthly; business and economics; publ. by Grupo G+J; Dir José Luis Gómez; circ. 35,088 (June 2010).

Dinero: Sepúlveda 7B, 28108 Madrid; tel. (91) 4327672; fax (91) 4327765; e-mail cgarcia@negocios.com; monthly; business and finance; Dir Miguel Ormaetxea Arroyo; circ. 11,586 (June 2007).

El Empresario: Diego de León 50, 3°, 28006 Madrid; tel. (91) 4116161; fax (91) 5645269; e-mail cepyme@@cepyme.es; internet www.cepyme.es; monthly; economics and business; circ. 15,000.

Información Comercial Española—Revista de Economía: Paseo de la Castellana 162, 5°, 28046 Madrid; tel. (91) 3493627; fax (91) 3493634; 8 a year; published by Ministry of the Economy and Finance; Dir Antonio Hernández García.

Mi Cartera de Inversión: José Abascal 56, 7°, 28003 Madrid; tel. (91) 4563320; fax (91) 4563328; e-mail sugerenciashoyinversion@vocento.com; internet www.hoyinversion.com; Dir Rafael Rubio Gómez-Caminero; circ. 16,788 (Dec. 2006).

El Mundo Financiero: Peña Sacra 1, 28260 Madrid; tel. and fax (91) 8583547; e-mail jlbarcelo@elmundofinanciero.com; internet www.elmundofinanciero.com; f. 1946; monthly; Dir José Luis Barceló Mezquita; circ. 15,000.

El Nuevo Lunes de la Economía y la Sociedad: Ferrocarril 37 duplicado, entreplanta, 28045 Madrid; tel. (91) 5160801; fax (91) 5160819; e-mail nuevolunes@elnuevolunes.com; internet www.elnuevolunes.es; weekly; Pres. José García Abad.

Home, Fashion and General

Casa Diez: Avda Cardenal Herrera Oria 3, 28034 Madrid; tel. (91) 7287000; fax (91) 7289144; e-mail malvarez@hachette.es; internet www.casadiez.orange.es; monthly; home decoration; Dir Milagros Alvarez Gortari; circ. 207,517 (June 2010).

Clara: Avda Diagonal 189, 08018 Barcelona; tel. (93) 4157374; fax (93) 2177378; f. 1992; monthly; Dir Hortensia Galí Pérez; circ. 196,948 (June 2010).

Cosmopolitan: Albasanz 15, Edif. A, 28037 Madrid; tel. (91) 4369820; fax (91) 4358701; e-mail cosmopolitanweb@cosmohispano.com; internet www.cosmohispano.com; f. 1990; monthly; Dir Lala Herrero; circ. 222,419 (June 2010).

Diez Minutos: Santa Engracia 23, 28010 Madrid; tel. (91) 7287000; fax (91) 7289132; e-mail diezminutos@hachette.es; internet www.diezminutos.es; f. 1951; weekly; celebrity gossip; Dir Cristina Acebal; circ. 481,672 (June 2010).

Elle: Santa Engracia 23, 28010 Madrid; tel. (91) 7287000; fax (91) 7289306; e-mail elle@hachette.es; internet www.elle.es; f. 1986; monthly; Dir Susana Martínez Vidal; circ. 264,671 (June 2010).

Elle Deco: Santa Engracia 23, 28010 Madrid; tel. (91) 7287000; fax (91) 7289144; e-mail elledeco@hachette.es; internet www.elledeco.es; f. 1989; 5 a year; Dir Milagros Alvarez Gortari.

GEO: Albasanz 15, Edif. A, 28037 Madrid; tel. (91) 5752617; fax (91) 4369977; e-mail vtraba@gps.grupogyj.es; internet www.georevista.es; f. 1987; monthly; geography, nature, people, photo-journalism, travel; Dir David Corral; circ. 55,925 (June 2010).

GQ: Paseo de la Castellana 9–11, 2°, 28046 Madrid; tel. (91) 7004170; fax (91) 7004199; e-mail gq@condenast.es; internet www.revistagq.com; monthly; men's magazine; Dir Javier Fernández de Angulo; circ. 77,160 (July 2010).

¡Hola!: Miguel Angel 1, 3°, 28010 Madrid; tel. (91) 7021820; fax (91) 3197298; e-mail publinet@hola.com; internet www.hola.com; f. 1944; weekly; general illustrated; Dir Eduardo Sánchez Pérez; circ. 540,902 (June 2007).

Interviú: O'Donnell 12, 5°, 28009 Madrid; tel. (91) 5863300; fax (91) 5863498; e-mail interviu@grupozeta.es; internet www.interviu.es; f. 1976; weekly; Dir Teresa Viejo; circ. 115,487 (Sept. 2010).

Labores del Hogar: Avda Diagonal 189, 08018 Barcelona; tel. (93) 4157374; fax (93) 2177378; e-mail labores@hymsa.com; f. 1926; monthly; home textile crafts; Dir Eulàlia Ubach; circ. 66,313 (June 2010).

Lecturas: Avda Diagonal 189, 08018 Barcelona; tel. (93) 4157374; fax (93) 2177378; e-mail lecturas@hymsa.com; internet www.lecturas.es; f. 1921; weekly, Fri.; Dir Javier de Montini; circ. 342,129 (June 2010).

Mía: Albasanz 15, Edif. A, 28037 Madrid; tel. (91) 4369800; fax (91) 5752617; e-mail mia@gyj.es; internet www.miarevista.es; f. 1986; weekly; Dir Ketty Rico Oliver; circ. 214,512 (June 2010).

Nuevo Estilo: Avda Cardenal Herrera Oria 3, 28034 Madrid; tel. (91) 7287000; fax (91) 7289135; e-mail nuevoestilo@hachette.es; internet www.nuevo-estilo.es; f. 1977; monthly; home decoration; Dir Marta Riopérez; circ. 131,800 (June 2010).

Nuevo Vale: Gran Vía de Carlos III 124, 5°, 08034 Barcelona; tel. (93) 2061540; fax (93) 2805555; e-mail buzon@publicacionesheres.com; weekly; Dir Esther Giralt; circ. 87,019 (June 2010).

Pronto: Gran Vía de Carlos III 124, 5°, 08034 Barcelona; tel. (93) 2061540; fax (93) 2805555; e-mail pronto@publicacionesheres.com; f. 1972; weekly; general information; Dir Antonio Gómez Abad; circ. 1,093,138 (June 2010).

Semana: Cuesta de San Vicente 28, 28008 Madrid; tel. (91) 5472300; fax (91) 5413642; e-mail redaccion@semana.es; internet www.semana.es; f. 1942; weekly; general, illustrated; Dir Charo Carracedo Armada; circ. 281,814 (June 2010).

Ser Padres Hoy: Albasanz 15, Edif. A, 28037 Madrid; tel. (91) 4369800; fax (91) 5767881; e-mail publicidad@gyj.es; internet www.serpadres.es; f. 1974; monthly; for parents; Dir Javier J. García González; circ. 37,462 (June 2008).

Súper Pop: Gran Vía Carlos III 124, 1°, 08034 Barcelona; tel. (93) 2521452; fax (93) 2521450; e-mail info@superpop.es; f. 1976; fortnightly; teenage magazine; Dir Silvia Alemán; circ. 113,614 (June 2007).

Telva: Avda de San Luis 25, 28033 Madrid; tel. (91) 4435000; fax (91) 3373143; e-mail telva@telva.com; internet www.telva.com; f. 1963; beauty, fashion, weddings, interviews, cookery and fitness; monthly; Dir Nieves Fontana Líbano; circ. 253,136 (June 2010).

Vogue España: Paseo de la Castellana 9–11, 28046 Madrid; tel. (91) 7004170; fax (91) 7004199; e-mail vogue@condenast.es; internet www.vogue.es; f. 1988; monthly; Dir Yolanda Sacristán; circ. 188,445 (June 2010).

Woman: Bailén 84, 2°, 08009 Barcelona; tel. (93) 5863300; fax (93) 2324630; e-mail woman@grupozeta.es; internet www.woman.es; f. 1992; monthly; Dir Empar Prieto; circ. 1211,778 (June 2010).

SPAIN — *Directory*

Leisure Interests and Sport

Automóvil: Ancora 40, 28045 Madrid; tel. (91) 3470100; fax (91) 3470152; e-mail automovil@mpib.es; internet www.motorpress-iberica.es; monthly; motoring; Dir FERNANDO GÓMEZ BLANCO; circ. 114,286 (June 2010).

Autopista: Ancora 40, 28045 Madrid; tel. (91) 3470100; fax (91) 3470135; e-mail autopista@mpib.es; internet www.motorpress-iberica.es; weekly; motoring; Editor ARANCHA PATO; circ. 43,000 (June 2010).

Cinemanía: Progresa (Grupo Prisa), Julián Camarillo 29B, 1°, 28037 Madrid; tel. (91) 5386104; fax (91) 5222291; e-mail cinemania@progresa.es; internet www.progresa.es; f. 1995; monthly; films; Dir CARLOS MARAÑÓN; circ. 55,220 (June 2010).

Coche Actual: Ancora 40, 28045 Madrid; tel. (91) 3470154; fax (91) 3470152; e-mail cocheactual@mpib.es; internet www.motorpress-iberica.es; weekly; cars; Dir ANTONIO RONCERO FERNÁNDEZ; circ. 46,837 (June 2010).

Don Balón: Avda Diagonal 435, 1–2°, 08036 Barcelona; tel. (93) 2092000; fax (93) 2412358; e-mail info@donbalon.org; internet www.donbalon.com; f. 1975; weekly; sport; Editor-in-Chief ANTONIO CASALS; circ. 22,880 (June 2010).

Fotogramas: Santa Engracia 23, 28010 Madrid; tel. (91) 7287000; fax (91) 7289306; e-mail fotogramas@hachette.es; internet www.fotogramas.es; f. 1946; monthly; cinema; Dir TONI ULLED NADAL; circ. 151,654 (June 2010).

Guía del Ocio—La Semana de Barcelona: Muntaner 492, bajos, 08022 Barcelona; tel. (93) 4185005; fax (93) 4173363; e-mail redaccion@guiadelociobcn.com; internet www.guiadelociobcn.com; f. 1977; weekly, Fri.; listings and reviews of events; Dir XAVIER MUNIESA CALDERÓ; circ. 50,000.

Guía del Ocio—La Semana de Madrid: Alcalá 106, 2°, 28009 Madrid; tel. (91) 4367500; fax (91) 4367501; e-mail guiadelocio@guiadelociomad.com; internet www.guiadelocio.com; weekly, Fri.; listings and reviews of events; Dir-Gen. MARCOS DE MINONDO RUIZ-MORALES.

Motociclismo: Ancora 40, 28045 Madrid; tel. (91) 3470100; fax (91) 3470152; e-mail motociclismo@mpib.es; internet www.motociclismo.es; f. 1951; weekly; motorcycling; Dir and Editor AUGUSTO MORENO DE CARLOS; circ. 46,522 (June 2010).

Sport Life: Ancora 40, 28045 Madrid; tel. (91) 3470100; fax (91) 3470236; e-mail sportlife@mpib.es; internet www.motorpress-iberica.es; monthly; Editor FRANCISCO JESÚS CHICO; circ. 83,284 (June 2010).

Supertele: Santa Engracia 23, 28010 Madrid; tel. (91) 7287000; fax (91) 7289306; e-mail supertele@hachette.es; internet www.supertele.es; f. 1992; weekly; TV magazine; Dir PURIFICACIÓN BLANCO PAÍNO; circ. 99,005 (June 2010).

Tele Digital: C/ Juan Bravo, 3A, 28006 Madrid; tel. (91) 4451950; fax (91) 4450621; internet www.sateliteinfos.com; Dir JOSÉ DA CUNHA.

Tele Indiscreta: Avda Cardenal Herrera Oria 3, 28034 Madrid; tel. (91) 7287000; fax (91) 3581348; e-mail teleindiscreta@hachette.es; weekly; popular illustrated; TV programme; Dir PURIFICACIÓN BLANCO PAÍNO; circ. 31,852 (June 2007).

Telenovela: Santa Engracia 23, 28010 Madrid; tel. (91) 7287000; fax (91) 7289306; e-mail telenovela@hachette.es; internet www.tele-novela.orange.es; f. 1993; TV series; Dir AGUSTÍN DE TENA; circ. 74,579 (June 2010).

TP Teleprograma: Santa Engracia 23, 28010 Madrid; tel. (91) 7287000; fax (91) 7289129; e-mail tp@hachette.es; internet www.teleprograma.tv; f. 1966; weekly; TV, cinema and video; Dir PURIFICACIÓN BLANCO PAÍNO; circ. 113,285 (June 2010).

Viajar: O'Donnell 12, 3°, 28009 Madrid; tel. (91) 5863300; fax (91) 5863411; e-mail mlopez.viajar@grupozeta.es; internet www.revistaviajar.es; f. 1978; monthly; travel; Dir MARIANO LÓPEZ; circ. 75,000.

Medicine, Science and Technology

Arbor: Vitruvio 8, 28006 Madrid; tel. (91) 5616651; fax (91) 5855326; e-mail director.arbor@csic.es; internet arbor.revistas.csic.es; f. 1944; monthly; science, thought and culture; publ. by Consejo Superior de Investigaciones Científicas (CSIC); Dir ALBERTO SÁNCHEZ ÁLVAREZ-INSUA.

Avión Revue: Pais Valenciano 55, 46900 Torrent; tel. (91) 3470154; fax (91) 3470152; e-mail avionrevue@mpib.es; f. 1982; monthly; aeroplanes; Dir (vacant); circ. 21,307 (June 2010).

Computerworld: Fortuny 18, 5°, 28010 Madrid; tel. (91) 3496600; fax (91) 3196104; e-mail computerworld@idg.es; internet www.idg.es/computerworld; f. 1981; weekly; also available: *CIO, Comunicaciones World, Dealer World, iWorld, MacWorld, PC World Digital, PC World PRO*; Editor-in-Chief ESTHER MACÍAS; circ. 9,182 (March 2010).

El Ecologista: Marqués de Laganés 12, 28004 Madrid; tel. (91) 5312389; fax (91) 5312611; e-mail comunicacion@ecologistasenaccion.org; internet www.ecologistasenaccion.org; f. 1979; quarterly; ecological issues; Dir JOSÉ LUIS GARCÍA CANO; circ. 13,000.

Gaceta Médica de Bilbao: Lersundi 9, Apdo 5073, 48009 Bilbao; tel. (94) 4233768; fax (94) 4232161; e-mail gacetamedica@telefonica.net; f. 1894; quarterly; official publication of the Academia de Ciencias Médicas de Bilbao/Bilboko Sendalarintz Jakindia; Dir Dr JUAN IGNACIO GOIRIA ORMAZABAL; circ. 5,000.

Investigación y Ciencia: Muntaner 339, Pral 1°, 08021 Barcelona; tel. (93) 4143344; fax (93) 4145413; e-mail precisa@investigacionyciencia.es; internet www.investigacionyciencia.es; f. 1976; quarterly; Dir JOSÉ MARÍA VADERAS GALLARDO; circ. 30,055 (Dec. 2009).

Mundo Científico: Pérez Galdós 36, 08012 Barcelona; tel. (93) 4157374; fax (93) 2177378; monthly; Dir JORGE ALCALDE.

Muy Interesante: Albasanz 15, 28037 Madrid; tel. (91) 4369800; fax (91) 5752617; e-mail publicidad@gyj.es; internet www.muyinteresante.es; f. 1981; monthly; history, medicine, nature, science; Dir JOSÉ PARDINA CANCER; circ. 295,342 (June 2010).

PC Actual: López de Hoyos 141, 1°, 28002 Madrid; tel. (91) 5106600; fax (91) 5194813; e-mail javier-perez@rba.es; internet www.pc-actual.com; monthly; Dir SUSANA HERRERO.

Tiempos Médicos: Editores Médicos, SA, Alsasua 16, 28023 Madrid; tel. (91) 3768140; fax (91) 3739907; e-mail edimsa@edimsa.es; internet www.edimsa.es; 10 a year; Dir Dr A. CHICHARRO PAPIRI; circ. 10,549 (Dec. 2009).

NEWS AGENCIES

Agencia EFE, SA: Espronceda 32, 28003 Madrid; tel. (91) 3467100; fax (91) 3467134; e-mail efe@efe.es; internet www.efe.es; f. 1939; national and international news; 140 bureaux and correspondents abroad; sports, features, radio and television, and photographic branches; Pres. ÁLEX GRIJELMO; Gen. Man. LOLA ÁLVAREZ.

Colpisa: José Abascal 56, 1°, 28003 Madrid; tel. (91) 4564600; fax (91) 4564701; f. 1972; Pres. JOSÉ MARÍA BERGARECHE; Dir ROGELIO RODRÍGUEZ.

Europa Press Noticias: Paseo de la Castellana 210, 3°, 28046 Madrid; tel. (91) 3592600; fax (91) 3503251; e-mail noticias@europapress.es; internet www.europapress.es; Dir ANGEL EXPÓSITO MORA.

Iberia Press: Velázquez 46, 1°, 28001 Madrid; tel. and fax (91) 8155319; e-mail press-bulletin@jet.es; f. 1977; Dir JOSÉ RAMÓN ALONSO.

PRESS ASSOCIATIONS
National Organizations

Asociación de Corresponsales de Prensa Extranjera (ACPE): Monte Esquinza 41, 1°, 28010 Madrid; tel. (91) 3101433; fax (91) 3080950; e-mail acpe.corresponsales@wanadoo.es; internet www.acpe-corresponsales.com; f. 1923; foreign correspondents' asscn; Pres. SAID IDA HASSAN; Sec.-Gen. CARLOS MEZA; 150 mems.

Asociación de Editores de Diarios Españoles (AEDE): Orense 69, 2°, 28020 Madrid; tel. (91) 4251085; fax (91) 5796020; e-mail maribel@aede.es; internet www.aede.es; f. 1978; 33 mems, representing 95 daily newspapers (2008); Pres. PILAR DE YARZA.

Asociación de Revistas Culturales en España (ARCE): Hortaleza 75, 28004 Madrid; tel. (91) 3086066; fax (91) 3199267; e-mail info@arce.es; internet www.arce.es; f. 1983.

Federación de Asociaciones de Periodistas de España (FAPE): Juan Bravo 6, 28006 Madrid; tel. (91) 5850038; fax (91) 5850035; e-mail fape@fape.es; internet www.fape.es; f. 1922; Pres. FERNANDO GONZÁLEZ URBANEJA; Sec.-Gen. LUIS SERRANO ALTIMIRAS; 48 mem. asscns.

Unión de Escritores y Periodistas Españoles: Madrid; f. 1978; journalists' asscn; Pres. ANTONIO ARIAS PIQUERAS; Sec.-Gen. ELOY S. CASTAÑARES; 4,000 mems.

Provincial Organizations
Barcelona

Centre Internacional de Premsa de Barcelona: Rambla de Catalunya 10, 1°, 08007 Barcelona; tel. (93) 4121111; fax (93) 3178386; e-mail cipb@periodistes.org; internet www.periodistes.org; f. 1988; facilities and services for journalists; Pres. XAVIER BATALLA GARCÍA; Dir MÓNICA VIÑAS.

Bilbao

Asociación de Periodistas de Bizkaia (Bizkaiko Kazetarien Elkartea): Dr Achucarro 10, 1°, 48011 Bilbao; tel. and fax (94)

SPAIN

4168748; e-mail asociacion@periodistasvascos.com; internet www.periodistasvascos.com; Pres. JOSÉ MANUEL ALONSO; Sec. BLANCA GARCÍA-EGOCHEAGA.

Madrid

Asociación de la Prensa de Madrid: Juan Bravo 6, 28006 Madrid; tel. (91) 5850010; fax (91) 5850050; e-mail apm@apmadrid.es; internet www.apmadrid.es; f. 1895; Pres. FERNANDO GONZÁLEZ URBANEJA; Sec.-Gen. LUIS SERRANO ALTIMIRAS; 7,000 mems.

Centro de Prensa de Madrid: Claudio Coello 98, 28006 Madrid; tel. (91) 5850010; fax (91) 5850050; Sec.-Gen. JOSÉ MARÍA LORENTE TORIBIO.

Sevilla

Asociación de la Prensa de Sevilla: Plaza de San Francisco 9, 1°, 41004 Sevilla; tel. (95) 4500468; fax (95) 4225299; e-mail aps@asociacionprensa.org; internet www.asociacionprensa.org; f. 1909; Pres. ANA MARÍA CARVAJAL LLORENS; Sec.-Gen. PILAR SURIÑACH MUÑOZ.

Zaragoza

Centro de Prensa de Zaragoza: Cinco de Marzo 9, 50004 Zaragoza; tel. (976) 223210; fax (976) 222963; e-mail aparagon@aparagon.es; internet www.aparagon.es/centrop.asp; Pres. RAMÓN J. BUETAS CORONAS; Sec. ROBERTO GARCÍA BERMEJO.

Publishers

Agencia Española de Cooperación Internacional para el Desarrollo: Avda Reyes Católicos 4, 28040 Madrid; tel. (91) 5838379; fax (91) 5838311; internet www.aecid.es; f. 1943; arts, law, history, economics for circulation in Latin America; Literary and Artistic Dir ANTONIO PAPELL.

Alianza Editorial: Juan Ignacio Luca de Tena 15, 28027 Madrid; tel. (91) 3938888; fax (91) 3207480; e-mail alianzaeditorial@alianzaeditorial.es; internet www.alianzaeditorial.es; f. 1959; advanced textbooks, fiction, general non-fiction, reference, paperbacks; imprint of Grupo Anaya; Gen. Man. VALERIA CIOMPI.

Barcino Editorial: Carrer Acàcies 15, 08027 Barcelona; tel. and fax (93) 3495935; e-mail barcino@editorialbarcino.cat; internet www.editorialbarcino.com; f. 1924; Catalan classics, general; Dir CARLES DUARTE MONTSERRAT.

Carroggio, SA de Ediciones: Rambla Catalunya 38, 08001 Barcelona; tel. (93) 4949922; fax (93) 4949923; e-mail carroggio@carroggio.com; internet www.carroggio.es; f. 1911; art, literature, reference books, multimedia; Man. Dir SANTIAGO CARROGGIO GUERIM.

Columna Edicions: Peu de la Creu 4, 08001 Barcelona; tel. (93) 4437100; fax (93) 4417130; e-mail info@columnaedicions.cat; internet www.columnaedicions.cat; f. 1985; imprint of Grup 62; fiction and non-fiction in Catalan.

Durvan, SA de ediciones: Avda Manoteras 50, 28050 Madrid; tel. (91) 3842022; e-mail editorial@durvan.com; internet www.durvan.com; f. 1960; Sociedad Anónima de Promoción y Ediciones; Dir JAVIER PEREDA PRADO.

EDHASA (Editora y Distribuidora Hispano-Americana, SA): Avda Diagonal 519–521, 2°, 08029 Barcelona; tel. (93) 4949720; fax (93) 4194584; e-mail info@edhasa.es; internet www.edhasa.com; f. 1946; contemporary fiction, non-fiction, pocket books, historical fiction and non-fiction, crime, philosophy; Editorial Dir and Man. DANIEL FERNÁNDEZ.

Ediciones Cátedra: Juan Ignacio Luca de Tena 15, 28027 Madrid; tel. (91) 3938787; fax (91) 7412118; e-mail catedra@catedra.com; internet www.catedra.com; f. 1973; imprint of Grupo Anaya; literature, literary criticism, history, humanities, linguistics, arts, cinema, music, feminism; Pres. JOSÉ MANUEL GÓMEZ.

Ediciones Destino: Avda Diagonal 662–664, 08034 Barcelona; tel. (93) 4967001; fax (93) 4967002; e-mail edicionesedestino@edestino.es; internet www.edestino.es; f. 1942; imprint of Grupo Planeta; general fiction, history, art, children's books.

Ediciones Deusto: Avda Diagonal 662–664, 08034 Barcelona; tel. (94) 4356161; fax (94) 4356166; e-mail deustomail@ediciones-deusto.es; internet www.ediciones-deusto.es; f. 1960; imprint of Grupo Planeta; management and law.

Ediciones Encuentro: Ramírez de Arellano 17, 10°, 28043 Madrid; tel. (91) 5322607; fax (91) 5322346; e-mail encuentro@ediciones-encuentro.es; internet www.ediciones-encuentro.es; f. 1978; theology, philosophy, art, history, biography, society, politics, literature.

Ediciones Mensajero, SAU: Sancho de Azpeitia 2, 48014 Bilbao; tel. (94) 4470358; fax (94) 4472630; e-mail mensajero@mensajero.com; internet www.mensajero.com; f. 1915; arts, biography, theology, psychology, pedagogy, social sciences and paperbacks; Editorial Dir JOSU LEGUINA ECHEBERRÍA.

Ediciones Morata, SL: Mejía Lequerica 12, 28004 Madrid; tel. (91) 4480926; fax (91) 4480925; e-mail morata@edmorata.es; internet www.edmorata.es; f. 1920; psychology, psychiatry, pedagogics, sociology; Dir FLORA MORATA.

Ediciones Obelisco: Pedro IV 78, 3 y 5°, 08005 Barcelona; tel. (93) 3098525; fax (93) 3098523; e-mail info@edicionesobelisco.com; internet www.edicionesobelisco.com; f. 1981; general fiction and non-fiction; Dir JULI PERADEJORDI.

Ediciones Omega: Plató 26, 08006 Barcelona; tel. (93) 2010599; fax (93) 2097362; e-mail omega@ediciones-omega.es; internet www.ediciones-omega.es; f. 1948; biology, field guides, geography, geology, agriculture, photography; Chair. ANTONIO PARICIO.

Ediciones Pirámide: Juan Ignacio Luca de Tena 15, 28027 Madrid; tel. (91) 3938989; fax (91) 7423661; e-mail piramide@anaya.es; internet www.edicionespiramide.es; f. 1973; scientific and technical books, business, economics, psychology; imprint of Grupo Anaya; Man. Dir MARIANO JOSÉ NORTE.

Ediciones Polígrafa: Balmes 54, 2°, 08007 Barcelona; tel. (93) 3968846; fax (93) 4672172; e-mail info@edicionespoligrafa.com; internet www.edicionespoligrafa.com; f. 1960; arts, leisure; Man. Dir JUAN DE MUGA DÒRIA; Editor-in-Chief FRANCISCO REI.

Ediciones Siruela: Almagro 25, 28010 Madrid; tel. (91) 3555720; fax (91) 3552201; e-mail atencionlector@siruela.com; internet www.siruela.com; f. 1982; history, literature, art, children's books, translations; Dir JACOBO FITZ-JAMES STUART.

Ediciones Universidad de Navarra, SA (EUNSA): Plaza de los Sauces 1 y 2, 31010 Barañain–Pamplona (Navarra); tel. (948) 256850; fax (948) 256854; e-mail info@eunsa.es; internet www.eunsa.es; f. 1967; architecture, natural sciences, law, history, social sciences, theology, philosophy, medical, engineering, journalism, education, economics and business administration, biology, literature, library science, paperbacks, etc.; Chair. GUIDO STEIN.

Ediciòns Xerais de Galicia: Doutor Marañón 12, 36211 Vigo; tel. (986) 214888; fax (986) 201366; e-mail xerais@xerais.es; internet www.xerais.es; f. 1979; imprint of Grupo Anaya; literature, education, history and reference books in Galician; Dir MANUEL BRAGADO RODRÍGUEZ.

Editorial Anagrama: Pedró de la Creu 58, 08034 Barcelona; tel. (93) 2037652; fax (93) 2037738; e-mail anagrama@anagrama-ed.es; internet www.anagrama-ed.es; f. 1969; fiction, essays, foreign literature in translation; Editor and Dir JORGE HERRALDE.

Editorial Bosch: Comte d'Urgell 51 bis, Apdo 928, 08011 Barcelona; tel. (93) 4521050; fax (93) 4521057; e-mail bosch@bosch.es; internet www.bosch.es; f. 1934; law, social sciences, classics; Man. ALBERT FERRÉ.

Editorial Castalia: Castelló 24, 1°, 28001 Madrid; tel. (91) 3195857; fax (91) 3102442; e-mail castalia@castalia.es; internet www.castalia.es; f. 1945; classics, literature; Pres. AMPARO SOLER GIMENO.

Editorial CEAC: Avda Diagonal 662–664, 08034 Barcelona; tel. (93) 4926956; e-mail info@ceacedit.com; internet www.editorialceac.com; f. 1947; imprint of Grupo Planeta; textbooks, education, leisure; Man. JAIME PINTANEL.

Editorial Desclée de Brouwer: Henao 6, 3° dcha, 48009 Bilbao; tel. (94) 4246843; fax (94) 4237594; e-mail info@edesclee.com; internet www.edesclee.com; f. 1945; general non-fiction in Spanish and Basque; Pres. JAVIER GOGEASCOECHEA.

Editorial Edaf: Jorge Juan 68, 1°, 28009 Madrid; tel. (91) 4358260; fax (91) 4315281; e-mail edaf@edaf.net; internet www.edaf.net; f. 1967; literature, dictionaries, occult, natural health, paperbacks; Dir-Gen. JOSÉ ANTONIO FOSSATI SEDDON.

Editorial Everest: Carretera León–Coruña, Km 5, Apdo 339, 24080 León; tel. (987) 844200; fax (987) 844202; e-mail info@everest.es; internet www.everest.es; f. 1957; general; Dir-Gen. JOSÉ ANTONIO LÓPEZ MARTÍNEZ.

Editorial Galaxia: Avda de Madrid 44, 36204 Vigo (Pontevedra); tel. (986) 432100; fax (986) 223205; e-mail galaxia@editorialgalaxia.es; internet www.editorialgalaxia.es; f. 1950; literary works, reviews, popular, children's, Galician literature; Dir VÍCTOR F. FREIXANES.

Editorial Gredos: Sánchez Pacheco 85, 28002 Madrid; tel. (91) 7444920; fax (91) 5192033; e-mail comercial@editorialgredos.com; internet www.editorialgredos.com; f. 1944; linguistics, philology, humanities, art, literature, dictionaries; Dir JOSÉ MANUEL MARTOS CARRASCO.

Editorial Gustavo Gili: Rosselló 87–89, 08029 Barcelona; tel. (93) 3228161; fax (93) 3229205; e-mail info@ggili.com; internet www.ggili.com; f. 1902; photography, art, architecture, design, fashion; Dirs GABRIEL GILI, MÓNICA GILI.

SPAIN

Editorial Hispano-Europea: Primer de Maig, 21, Pol. Ind. Gran Via Sud, 08908 L'Hospitalet de Llobregat (Barcelona); tel. (93) 2018500; fax (93) 4142635; e-mail hispanoeuropea@hispanoeuropea.com; internet www.hispanoeuropea.com; f. 1954; technical, scientific, sport, pets and reference; Propr and Man. Dir JORGE J. PRAT ROSAL.

Editorial Juventud: Provença 101, 08029 Barcelona; tel. (93) 4441800; fax (93) 4398383; e-mail info@editorialjuventud.es; internet www.editorialjuventud.es; f. 1923; general fiction, biography, history, art, music, reference, dictionaries, travel books, children's books, paperbacks, in Catalan and Spanish; Dir LUIS ZENDRERA.

Editorial Marfil: San Eloy 17, 03804 Alcoy; tel. (96) 5523311; fax (96) 5523496; e-mail editorialmarfil@editorialmarfil.com; internet www.editorialmarfil.com; f. 1947; textbooks, psychology, pedagogy, university texts, literature; Man. RAFAEL LLORÉNS FIGUEROLA.

Editorial Nerea: Aldamar, 36 bajo, 20003 San Sebastián; tel. (943) 432227; fax (943) 433379; e-mail nerea@nerea.net; internet www.nerea.net; f. 1987; architecture, art, history. photography; Chair. MARTA CASARES.

Editorial Reus, SA: Preciados 23, 2°, 28013 Madrid; tel. (91) 5213619; fax (91) 5312408; e-mail reus@editorialreus.es; internet www.editorialreus.es; f. 1852; law; Pres. JESÚS M. PINTO VARELA.

Editorial Reverté: Loreto 13–15, Local B, 08029 Barcelona; tel. (93) 4193336; fax (93) 4195189; e-mail reverte@reverte.com; internet www.reverte.com; f. 1947; scientific and technical; Dir JAVIER REVERTÉ MASCÓ.

Editorial Seix Barral: Avda Diagonal 662–664, 7°, 08034 Barcelona; tel. (93) 4967003; fax (93) 4967004; e-mail editorial@seix-barral.es; internet www.seix-barral.es; f. 1911; literary fiction.

Editorial Tecnos: Juan Ignacio Luca de Tena 15, 28027 Madrid; tel. (91) 3938686; fax (91) 7426631; e-mail foro_tecnos@anaya.es; internet www.tecnos.es; f. 1947; law, social and political science, philosophy and economics; imprint of Grupo Anaya; Man. MANUEL GONZÁLEZ MORENO.

Editorial Teide: Viladomat 291, 08029 Barcelona; tel. (902) 233030; fax (93) 3212646; e-mail info@editorialteide.com; internet www.editorialteide.es; f. 1942; educational, scientific, technical and art; Man. Dir FEDERICO RAHOLA.

La Esfera de los Libros: Avda de Alfonso XIII 1, bajos, 28002 Madrid; tel. (91) 2960200; fax (91) 2960206; e-mail laesfera@esferalibros.com; internet www.esferalibros.com; history, journalism, biography; Dir-Gen. JOSÉ MARÍA CALVÍN.

Espasa Libros: Avda Diagonal 662–664, 08034 Barcelona; tel. (91) 4230370; fax (91) 4233743; e-mail sugerencias@espasa.es; internet www.espasa.es; f. 1860; encyclopaedias, history, dictionaries, literature, biographies, paperbacks, etc.; CEO JESÚS BADENES.

Fondo de Cultura Económica de España, SL (FCE España): Librería Juan Rulfo México, Fernando el Católico 86, 28015 Madrid; tel. (91) 7632800; e-mail directora.general@fondodeculturaeconomica.com; internet www.fondodeculturaeconomica.com; f. 1974; sciences, literature, children's books, history, academic; Dir JUAN GUILLERMO LÓPEZ.

Galaxia Gutenberg: Travessera de Gràcia 47–49, 08021 Barcelona; tel. (93) 3660100; fax (93) 3660104; e-mail galaxiagutenberg@circulo.es; f. 1995; literary fiction, poetry, economics.

Grup 62: Peu de la Creu 4, 08001 Barcelona; tel. (93) 4437100; fax (93) 4437130; e-mail correu@grup62.com; internet www.grup62.com; f. 1962; 18 imprints publishing titles in Catalan and Spanish, including Art 62, Edicions 62, Editorial Empúries, Editorial Selecta, Ediciones Península, El Aleph Editores, Enciclopèdia Catalana, Luciérnaga, Nous Negocis, Planeta, Pòrtic i Mina, Proa, Salsa Books; Pres. J. M. MARTOS.

Grupo Anaya: Juan Ignacio Luca de Tena 15, 28027 Madrid; tel. (91) 3938800; fax (91) 7426631; e-mail administrador@anaya.es; internet www.anaya.es; f. 1959; imprints include Algaida, Alianza Editorial, Anaya, Barçanova, Clé Internacional, Del Prado, Ediciones Cátedra, Ediciones Pirámide, Edicións Xerais de Galicia, Editorial Tecnos, Eudema, Larousse and Oberon; reference, sciences, arts, literature, education; Pres. JOSÉ MANUEL GÓMEZ.

Grupo Edebé: Paseo San Juan Bosco 62, 08017 Barcelona; tel. (93) 2037408; fax (93) 2054670; e-mail informacion@edebe.net; internet www.edebe.com; f. 1888; imprints include Giltza, Rodeira, Marjal and Guadiel; children's and educational publications; Man. JOSÉ ALDUNATE JURÍO.

Grupo Editorial Bruño: Juan Ignacio Luca de Tena 15, 28027 Madrid; tel. (91) 7244800; fax (91) 3613133; e-mail informacion@editorial-bruno.es; internet www.editorial-bruno.es; f. 1898; education, children's books.

Grupo Editorial Luis Vives: Xaudaró 25, 28034 Madrid; tel. (91) 3344883; fax (91) 3344882; e-mail dediciones@edelvives.es; internet www.grupoeditorialluisvives.com; f. 1890; imprints include Edelvives, Baula (Catalan), Alhucema, Ibaizabal (Basque) and Tambre (Galician); children's books, textbooks, reference under the imprints.

Grupo Editorial Santillana: Torrelaguna 60, 28043 Madrid; tel. (91) 7449060; fax (91) 7449019; e-mail grupo@santillana.es; internet www.gruposantillana.com; f. 1960; part of Grupo PRISA; imprints include Aguilar, Alfarguara, Altea, Richmond Publishing and Taurus; Pres. EMILIANO MARTÍNEZ.

Grupo Océano: Milanesado 21–23, 08017 Barcelona; tel. (93) 2802020; fax (93) 2041073; e-mail info@oceano.com; internet www.oceano.com; f. 1950; imprints include Circe, Instituto Gallach de Librería y Ediciones and Oceano; general; Chair. JOSÉ LLUIS MONREAL.

Grupo Planeta: Avda Diagonal 662–664, 08034 Barcelona; tel. (93) 4928000; fax (93) 4928565; e-mail info@planeta.es; internet www.planeta.es; f. 1949; imprints include Ediciones Destino, Ediciones Deusto, Ediciones Minotauro, Ediciones Temas de Hoy, Editorial CEAC, Editorial Crítica, Editorial Planeta, Emcé Editores, GeoPlaneta, MR Ediciones, Timun Mas; Pres. JOSÉ MANUEL LARA BOSCH.

Herder Editorial, SA: Provença 388, 08025 Barcelona; tel. (93) 4762626; fax (93) 2073448; e-mail herder@herdereditorial.com; internet www.herdereditorial.com; f. 1944; literature, language, theology, sociology, psychology; Dir RAIMUND HERDER.

Iberoamericana de Libros y Ediciones, SL: Amor de Dios 1, 28014 Madrid; tel. (91) 4293522; fax (91) 4295397; e-mail info@iberoamericanalibros.com; internet www.ibero-americana.net; f. 1996; owned by Verveut Verlagsgesellschaft (Germany); academic books.

Larousse Editorial: Mallorca, 45, 3°, 08029 Barcelona; tel. (93) 2413505; fax (93) 2413511; e-mail larousse@larousse.es; internet www.larousse.es; f. 1912; encyclopaedias, dictionaries, atlases, linguistics.

Marcombo, SA de Boixareu Editores: Gran Vía de les Corts Catalanes 594, 08007 Barcelona; tel. (93) 3180079; fax (93) 3189339; e-mail info@marcombo.com; internet www.marcombo.com; f. 1945; reference, sciences, textbooks; Pres. and Man. Dir JOSEP M. BOIXAREU VILAPLANA.

Montagud Editores: Ausiàs March 25, 1°, 08010 Barcelona; tel. (93) 3182082; fax (93) 3025083; e-mail montagud@montagud.com; internet www.montagud.com; f. 1906; business; Chair. FRANCISCO ANTOJA GIRALT.

MR Ediciones, SA: Recoletos 4, 3°, 28001 Madrid; tel. (91) 4230314; fax (91) 4230306; e-mail info@mrediciones.es; internet www.edicionesmartinezroca.com; f. 1965; fmrly Ediciones Martínez Roca; fiction, New Age, spirituality, sport, 'how-to' books, psychology, psychiatry; Dir LAURA FALCÓ.

Narcea, SA de Ediciones: Avda Dr Federico Rubio y Galí 9, 28039 Madrid; tel. (91) 5546484; fax (91) 5546487; e-mail narcea@narceaediciones.es; internet www.narceaediciones.es; f. 1968; humanities, pedagogy, psychology, spirituality, textbooks; Man. Dir MONICA B. GONZÁLEZ NAVARRO.

Nivola Libros y Ediciones, SL: Apartado de Correos 113, 28760 Tres Cantos (Madrid); tel. (902) 105185; fax (91) 8041482; e-mail contacto@nivola.com; internet www.nivola.com; science.

Plaza y Janés: Travessera de Gràcia 47–49, 08021 Barcelona; tel. (93) 3660300; fax (93) 2002219; internet www.plaza.es; f. 1959; fiction and non-fiction, reference; imprint of Random House Mondadori.

Random House Mondadori: Travessera de Gràcia 47–49, 08021 Barcelona; tel. (93) 3660300; fax (93) 3660449; e-mail gestionweb@rhm.es; internet www.randomhousemondadori.es; f. 2001 as a joint venture between Random House (Germany and USA) and Mondadori (Italy); imprints include Areté, Beascoa, Debate, Electa, Grijalbo, Lumen, Montena, Plaza y Janés, Rosa dels Vents and Sudamericana; Gen. Man. NURIA CABUTÍ.

Siglo XXI de España, Editores: Sector Foresta 1, 28760 Tres Cantos (Madrid); tel. (91) 8061996; fax (91) 8044028; e-mail atencion.cliente@akal.com; internet www.sigloxxieditores.com; f. 1967; pocket collections, reference, history, social sciences; Pres. PABLO GARCÍA-ARENAL.

SM Grupo: Impresores 2, Urbanización Prado del Espino, 28660 Boadilla del Monte, (Madrid); tel. (91) 4228800; fax (91) 5089927; e-mail clientes@grupo-sm.com; internet www.grupo-sm.com; f. 1940; textbooks, children's, reference, travel, literature; Pres. JUAN DE ISASA GONZÁLEZ UBIETA; Man. Dir JAVIER CORTÉS SORIANO.

Thomson Reuters Aranzadi: Camino de Galar 15, 31190 Cizur Menor (Navarra); tel. (902) 444144; fax (948) 297200; e-mail clientes@aranzadi.es; internet www.aranzadi.es; f. 1929; fmrly Editorial Aranzadi; law; Dir JUAN CARLOS FRANQUET CASAS.

Tusquets Editores: Cesare Cantú 8, 08023 Barcelona; tel. (93) 2530400; fax (93) 4176703; internet www.tusquets-editores.es; art, general fiction and non-fiction.

SPAIN

Vicens Vives: Polígono Industrial Pratense, 111, parcela 16, El Prat de Llobregat, 08820 Barcelona; tel. (93) 4782755; fax (93) 4783659; e-mail e@vicensvives.es; internet www.vicensvives.es; f. 1961; school and university, educational; Dir ROSARIO RAHOLA DE ESPONA.

PUBLISHERS' ASSOCIATIONS

Asociación de Editores de Madrid: Santiago Rusiñol 8, 28040 Madrid; tel. (91) 5544745; fax (91) 5532553; e-mail editoresmadrid@editoresmadrid.org; internet www.editoresmadrid.org; f. 1977; Pres. JAVIER CORTÉS SORIANO; Sec.-Gen. AMALIA MARTÍN PEREDA.

Asociación de Editoriales Universitarias Españolas (AEUE): Plaza de las Cortes 2, 7°, 28014 Madrid; tel. (91) 3600698; fax (91) 3601201; e-mail secretariatecnica@une.es; Pres. MAGDA POLO PUJADAS; Sec. ISABEL TERROBA PASCUAL.

Associació d'Editors en Llengua Catalana (Association of Publishers in Catalan Language): València 279, 1°, 08009 Barcelona; tel. (93) 2155091; fax (93) 2155273; e-mail info@editorsencatala.org; internet www.catalanpublishers.org; f. 1978; Pres. MANUEL SANGLAS MUCHART; Sec.-Gen. SEGIMON BORRÀS.

Federación de Gremios de Editores de España (Federation of Publishers' Associations of Spain): Cea Bermúdez 44, 2° dcha, 28003 Madrid; tel. (91) 5345195; fax (91) 5352625; e-mail fgee@fge.es; internet www.federacioneditores.org; f. 1978; Pres. ANTONI COMAS; Exec. Dir ANTONIO MARÍA AVILA.

Gremi d'Editors de Catalunya: València 279, 1°, 08009 Barcelona; tel. (93) 2155091; fax (93) 2155273; e-mail info@gremieditorscat.es; internet www.gremieditorscat.es; Pres. JOSEP M. PUIG DE LA BELLACASA; Sec.-Gen. SEGIMON BORRÀS.

Gremio de Editores de Euskadi/Euskadiko Editoreen Elkartea: Lehendakari Aguirre 11, 3°, 48014 Bilbao; tel. (94) 4764313; fax (94) 4761980; internet www.editores-euskadi.com; Pres. JAVIER GOGEASCOECHEA ARRIEN; Man. Dir ANDRÉS FERNÁNDEZ SECO.

Broadcasting and Communications

TELECOMMUNICATIONS

The telecommunications market was fully deregulated in December 1998.

BT España: Edif. Herre, Salvador de Madariaga 1, 28027 Madrid; tel. (91) 2708000; fax (91) 2708888; internet www.btglobalservices.com/business/es/es/index.html; Dir-Gen. JACINTO CAVESTANY VALLEJO.

Euphony: Plaza de la Independencia 10, 28001 Madrid; tel. (91) 5239577; e-mail serviciocliente.es@euphony.com; internet www.euphony.es; fixed-line and mobile cellular telecommunications services, internet service provider; Chief Exec. GILES REDPATH.

Euskaltel: Parque Tecnológico Edificio 809, 48160 Derio (Vizcaya); tel. (94) 4011000; fax (94) 4011020; internet www.euskaltel.com; f. 1995; offers fixed-line and mobile cellular telecommunications, digital cable television, and broadband internet services in the Basque Country; Chair. JOSÉ ANTONIO ARDANZA GARRO; CEO ALBERTO GARCÍA ERAUZKIN.

Jazztel: Anabel Segura 11, Edif. C, 28108 Alcobendas, Madrid; tel. (91) 1839000; fax (91) 1839943; e-mail contact@jazztel.com; internet www.jazztel.com; Pres. LEOPOLDO FERNÁNDEZ PUJALS.

ONO: Basauri 7 y 9, 28023 Madrid; tel. (91) 1809300; internet www.ono.es; f. 1998; broadband internet, telephone and television; owns Grupo Auna; Pres. JOSÉ MARÍA CASTELLANO; CEO ROSALÍA PORTELA.

Orange: Parque Empresarial La Finca, Paseo del Club Deportivo 1, Edif. 8, 28223 Pozuelo de Alarcón (Madrid); internet www.orange.es; f. 2006; owned by France Telecom España; fmrly Uni2 and Amena; CEO JEAN MARC VIGNOLLES.

Telefónica: Gran Vía 28, 28013 Madrid; tel. (91) 7406918; e-mail prensa@telefonica.es; internet www.telefonica.es; f. 1924; privatized in 1997; monopoly on telephone services removed in 1998; incl. mobile network Telefónica Móviles; provides services in 41 countries (2007); Pres. CÉSAR ALIERTA; CEO JULIO LINARES.

Vodafone España: Avda Europa 1 (Central), Parque Empresarial La Moraleja, 28108 Alcobendas, Madrid; tel. (607) 133333; internet www.vodafone.es; f. 1998; fmrly Airtel; mobile services; Pres. and CEO FRANCISCO ROMÁN.

Xfera Moviles: Avda de la Vega 15, Alcobendas, 28100 Madrid; tel. (91) 1315200; fax (91) 1315202; e-mail prensa@yoigo.com; internet www.yoigo.com; f. 2006; 76.6% owned by TeliaSonera (Sweden); provides mobile cellular communications services under the brand name Yoigo; Dir-Gen. JOHAN ANDSJÖ.

Regulatory Authorities

Comisión del Mercado de las Telecomunicaciones (Telecommunications Market Commission—CMT): Marina 16–18, Edif. Torre Mapfre, 08005 Barcelona; tel. (93) 6036200; e-mail cmt@cmt.es; internet www.cmt.es; f. 1996; Pres. REINALDO RODRÍGUEZ ILLERA; Sec. IGNACIO REDONDO ANDREU.

Secretaría de Estado de Telecommunicaciones y para la Sociedad de la Información: Ministerio de Industria, Turismo y Comercio, Capitán Haya 41, 2°, 28071 Madrid; tel. (91) 3461583; fax (91) 3461520; e-mail planavanza@mityc.es; internet www.planavanza.es.

BROADCASTING

Corporación Radio Televisión Española (RTVE): Edif. Prado del Rey, 28223 Pozuelo de Alarcón, Madrid; tel. (91) 5815461; fax (91) 5815454; e-mail direccion.comunicacion@rtve.es; internet www.rtve.es; state-owned company; controls and co-ordinates radio and television; incorporates Televisión Española, Televisión Española Internacional, Televisión Española Temática, Radio Nacional de España, Instituto Oficial de Radio y Televisión and the Orquesta Sinfónica y Coro; formerly Ente Público Radio Televisión Española; renamed and reformed in 2007 to become independent of govt influence; Pres. ALBERTO OLIART.

Independent Companies

Compañía de Radio y Televisión de Galicia (CRTVG): Bando-San Marcos, 15820 Santiago de Compostela (A Coruña); tel. (981) 540640; fax (981) 540829; e-mail info@crtvg.es; internet www.crtvg.es; f. 1985; Galician language station; Dir-Gen. ALFONSO SÁNCHEZ IZQUIERDO.

Corporació Catalana de Mitjans Audiovisuals (CCMA): Ganduxer 117, 08022 Barcelona; tel. (93) 4444800; fax (93) 4444824; e-mail comunicacio@ccma.cat; internet www.ccma.cat; f. 1983; Catalan language station; 7 television channels and 4 radio stations; Pres. ENRIC MARÍN I OTTO; Dir-Gen. RAMON MATEU I LLEVADOT.

Euskal Irrati Telebista (EITB)/Radiotelevisión Vasca: 48215 Iurreta (Vizcaya); tel. (94) 6031000; fax (94) 6034937; e-mail bisitak@eitb.com; internet www.eitb.com; f. 1982; Basque station; 2 television channels, 2 international television channels and 5 radio stations; Dir-Gen. ALBERTO SURIO.

Onda Regional de Murcia: Avda Libertad 6, bajo, 30009 Murcia; tel. (968) 200000; fax (968) 230850; e-mail felipe.nicolas@orm.es; internet www.orm.es; f. 1990; Dir-Gen. JOAQUIN AZPARREN IRIGOYEN.

Ràdiotelevisió Valenciana (RTVV): Polígono Accés Ademús s/n, 46100 Burjassot (Valencia); tel. (96) 3183000; fax (96) 3183001; e-mail dgen@rtvv.es; internet www.rtvv.es; f. 1984; Dir-Gen. JOSÉ LÓPEZ JARABA.

Radio Televisión de Andalucía (RTVA): Sede Central RTVA, Pabellón de Canal Sur (Antigua Pabellón de Andalucía), José de Gálvez s/n, 41090 San Juan de Aznalfarache (Sevilla); tel. (95) 5054600; fax (95) 5054937; e-mail comunicacion@rtva.es; internet www.rtva.es; f. 1988; Dir-Gen. JOSÉ MARÍA GILLÉN MARISCAL.

Radio Televisión Madrid (RTVM): Paseo del Príncipe 3, Ciudad de la Imagen, 28223 Pozuelo de Alarcón (Madrid); tel. (91) 5128200; fax (91) 5128300; e-mail prensa@telemadrid.es; internet www.telemadrid.es; Dir-Gen. ISABEL LINARES LIÉBANA.

Radiotelevisión Canaria (RTVC): Avda Bravo Murillo 5, Edif. Mapfre, 1°, 38003 Santa Cruz de Tenerife; tel. (922) 470600; fax (922) 273173; e-mail tvcanaria@tvcanaria.tv; internet www.tvcanaria.tv; f. 1997; broadcasts in the Canaries; Dir-Gen. GUILLERMO (WILLY) GARCÍA-MACHIÑENA GARCÍA-CHECA.

Radiotelevisión Castilla-La Mancha (RTVCM): Río Alberche s/n, Edif. RTVCM, Polígono Santa María de Benquerencia, 45007 Toledo; tel. (925) 288600; fax (925) 287883; e-mail comunicacion@rtvcm.es; internet www.rtvcm.es; Dir-Gen. JORDI GARCÍA CANDAU.

Federation

Federación de Asociaciones de Radio y Televisión de España: Evaristo San Miguel 8, 28008 Madrid; tel. (91) 5481222; fax (91) 5593630; e-mail rtvmadrid@telefonica.net; Pres. FEDERICO SÁNCHEZ AGUILAR.

RADIO

Radio Nacional de España (RNE): Avda de la Radio y la Televisión 4, 28223 Pozuelo de Alarcón (Madrid); tel. (91) 5817000; fax (91) 5183240; e-mail secretario_general.rne@rtve.es; internet www.rne.es; broadcasts Radio 1, Radio Clásica, Radio 3, Radio 4, Radio 5 Todo Noticias; 17 regional stations; Dir-Gen. SANTIAGO GONZÁLEZ.

Radio Exterior de España (REE): Avda de la Radio y la Televisión 4, 28223 Pozuelo de Alarcón (Madrid); tel. (91) 3461034; fax (91) 3461815; e-mail ree@rtve.es; internet www.rtve.es/radio/radio-exterior; overseas service of RNE; broadcasts in 10 languages; includes a world service in Spanish; Dir JOSEFINA BENÉITEZ.

SPAIN	*Directory*

Independent Stations

Ambiente Musical: Paseo de la Castellana 210, 10°, 28046 Madrid; tel. (91) 3454000; fax (91) 3591321; e-mail estudio@musicam.net; Dir-Gen. Manel Sallés Carceller.

Cadena 100: Alfonso XI 4, 28014 Madrid; tel. (91) 5951244; fax (91) 5225454; e-mail contacto@cadena100.es; internet www.cadena100.es; Dir Javier Llano Abril.

Cadena M80: Gran Vía 32, 8°, 28013 Madrid; tel. (91) 3477740; fax (91) 5324769; e-mail consultas@m80radio.com; internet www.m80radio.com; Dir Manuel Dávila Moreno.

Cadena Dial: Gran Vía 32, 8°, 28013 Madrid; tel. (91) 3477740; fax (91) 5324769; e-mail direccion@cadenadial.com; internet www.cadenadial.com; Dir Juan Carlos Chaves.

Cadena Ona Catalana: Aragón 390–394, 2°, 08013 Barcelona; tel. (93) 2449990; fax (93) 2459459; e-mail onacatalana@onacatalana.com; internet www.onacatalana.com; Dir-Gen. Josep Puigbó.

Cadena Ondacero RadioVoz Galicia: Ronda de Outeiro 1, bajo, 15006 A Coruña; tel. (981) 180600; fax (981) 180477; e-mail manuel.mantilla@radiovoz.es; internet www.radiovoz.es; Dir Manuel Mantilla Fernández.

Cadena de Ondas Populares Españolas/Radio Popular, SA (COPE): Alfonso XI 4, 3°, 28014 Madrid; tel. (91) 5951200; fax (91) 5322008; e-mail internet.usuarios@cope.es; internet www.cope.es; f. 1959; controlled by Roman Catholic Church; numerous medium-wave and FM stations; Pres. and CEO Alfonso Coronel de Palma.

Cadena Radio España/Radio España Madrid: Manuel Silvela 9, 28010 Madrid; tel. (91) 4475300; fax (91) 5938413; Pres. and Dir-Gen. José Antonio Sánchez.

Cadena Radiolé: Gran Vía 32, 7°, 28013 Madrid; tel. (91) 3477740; fax (91) 5324769; e-mail direccion@radiole.com; internet www.radiole.com; Dir Juan Carlos Chaves.

Cadena TOP Radio España: Manuel Silvela 9, 28010 Madrid; tel. (91) 4475300; fax (91) 4477026; internet www.topradio.es; Pres. José Antonio Sánchez.

Catalunya Ràdio, SRG, SA: Avda Diagonal 614–616, 08021 Barcelona; tel. (93) 3069200; fax (93) 3069201; e-mail informatius@catradio.cat; internet www.catradio.cat; f. 1983; run by Catalan autonomous govt; four channels: Catalunya Ràdio, Catalunya Música, Catalunya Informació, iCat; 6 internet channels; Dir Ramon Mateu.

COMRàdio: Travessera de les Corts 131–159, 08028 Barcelona; tel. (93) 5080600; fax (93) 5080810; e-mail comradio@comradio.com; internet www.comradio.com; Dir-Gen. Francesc Triola.

EITB Radio: Miramón Pasealekua 172, 20014 San Sebastián; tel. (943) 012300; fax (943) 012295; e-mail info@eitb.com; internet www.eitb.com; run by Basque autonomous govt; broadcasts on FM and MW as Euskadi Irratia, Radio Euskadi (Bilbao), Radio Vitoria (Vitoria-Gasteiz) and EITB Irratia; Dir Alberto Surio.

Europa FM: Bueso Pineda 7, 28043 Madrid; tel. (91) 4134361; fax (91) 4137175; e-mail europafm@europafm.com; internet europafm.com; Dir Patricio Sánchez.

Grupo Pevesa Comunicación, SL—Radio Ondas Riojanas: Santo Domingo 5, 26580 Arnedo; tel. (941) 383350; fax (941) 383383; e-mail ondarioja@ondarioja.com; internet www.ondarioja.com; Pres. Pedro Vega Hernández.

Los 40 Principales: Gran Vía 32, 8°, 28013 Madrid; tel. (91) 3470705; fax (91) 5317370; internet www.los40.com; Dir Carlos Montoya.

Muinmo, SL: Castelló 36, 28001 Madrid; tel. (91) 3598079; fax (91) 3500704; Dir-Gen. Miguel Angel Montero Quevedo.

Onda Cero Radio (OCR): José Ortega y Gasset 22–24, 28006 Madrid; tel. (91) 436400; fax (91) 436101; e-mail ondacero@ondacero.es; internet www.ondacero.es; owned by Telefónica; Dir-Gen. Francisco Espinar.

Radio Autonomía Madrid, SA: Paseo del Príncipe 3, Ciudad de la Imagen, 28223 Pozuelo de Alarcón, Madrid; tel. (91) 5128649; fax (91) 5123752; e-mail ondamadrid@ondamadrid.com; internet www.ondamadrid.es; f. 1985; Dir Miguel Pérez-Pla de Viu.

Ràdio Autonomia Valenciana, SA/Ràdio Nou: Avda Blasco Ibáñez 136, 46022 Valencia; tel. (96) 3183600; fax (96) 3183601; internet www.radionou.com; Dir Javier Gomar Albert.

Radio ECCA: Avda Escaleritas 64, 1°, 35011 Las Palmas de Gran Canaria; tel. (928) 257400; fax (928) 207395; e-mail info@radioecca.org; internet www.radioecca.org; adult education; Dir-Gen. María del Carmen Palmés Pérez.

Radio Galega (RG): San Marcos, 15820 Santiago de Compostela; tel. (981) 540940; fax (981) 540919; e-mail radiogalega@crtvg.es; internet www.crtvg.es; f. 1985; run by Galician autonomous Govt; Man. Dir Rosa Martínez.

Radio Surco-Castilla La Mancha: Concordia 14, Bajo C, 13700 Tomelloso (Ciudad Real); tel. (926) 505959; fax (926) 505961; e-mail r.surco@retemail.es; internet www.radiosurco.es; Dir Francisco Castellanos Cuellar.

Punto Radio: Juan Ignacio Luca de Tena 7, 28027 Madrid; tel. (91) 3399535; fax (91) 7417589; e-mail info@puntoradio.com; internet www.puntoradio.com; f. 2005; Dir-Gen. Héctor Casado.

Sociedad Española de Radiodifusión (Cadena SER): Gran Vía 32, 28013 Madrid; tel. (91) 3477700; fax (91) 3470709; e-mail gprensa@unionradio.es; internet www.cadenaser.com; f. 1924; 235 regional stations; owned by Grupo PRISA; Dir-Gen. Raúl Rodríguez.

Digital Radio

In March 1999 two digital radio licences were awarded for the frequencies MF-1 and MF-2. MF-1 was controlled by Cope, Intereconomía, Recoletos and *El Mundo*, while MF-2 was controlled by SER, Onda Rambla-Planeta, Onda Cero, Radio España, Onda Digital and Prensa Española. MF-1 began broadcasting in Madrid and Barcelona in July 2000.

Radio Association

Asociación Española de Radiodifusión Comercial (AERC): Plaza Independencia 2, 4° dcha, 28001 Madrid; tel. (91) 4357072; fax (91) 4356196; e-mail aerc@aerc.es; groups nearly all commercial radio stations; Dir-Gen. Alfonso Ruiz de Assin.

TELEVISION

Analogue broadcasts ceased in April 2010.

Televisión Española (TVE): Edif. Prado del Rey, 28223 Pozuelo de Alarcón, Madrid; tel. (91) 3464968; fax (91) 3463055; e-mail consultas@rtve.es; internet www.tve.es; broadcasts on TVE-1 and La 2; production centres in Barcelona and Las Palmas de Gran Canaria and 15 regional centres; broadcasts to Europe and the Americas on Canal Internacional; Dir Santiago González.

Independent Stations

Antena 3 Televisión: Avda de Isla Graciosa s/n, 28703 San Sebastián de los Reyes, Madrid; tel. (91) 6230657; fax (91) 6230994; e-mail antena3tv@antena3tv.com; internet www.antena3tv.com; f. 1989; owned by Grupo Planeta; Pres. José Manuel Lara Bosch.

Canal 9—Televisió Autonómica Valenciana (TVV): Polígon Accés Ademús, 46100 Burjassot (Valencia); tel. (96) 3183000; fax (96) 3183001; e-mail wmaster@rtvv.es; internet www.rtvv.es; f. 1989; second channel commenced operations in 1997; Dir José López Jaraba.

Canal Sur Televisión: Carretera San Juan de Aznalfarache, Apdo 132, 41920 San Juan de Aznalfarache, Sevilla; tel. (95) 5054600; fax (95) 5054925; e-mail comunicacion@rtva.es; internet www.canalsur.es; f. 1989; regional station for Andalusia; Dir-Gen. Jesús Vigorra.

Euskal Telebista—ETB (TV Vasca): Capuchinos de Basurtu 2, 48013 Bilbao; tel. (94) 6563000; fax (94) 6563095; e-mail info@eitb.com; internet www.eitb.com; f. 1982; 2 channels broadcasting to Basque Country, 1 in Basque, 1 in Spanish; Dir Bingen Zupiria Gorostidi.

Popular TV: Alfonso XI 4, 28014 Madrid; tel. (91) 3096669; e-mail populartv@populartv.net; internet www.populartv.net; broadcasts on a local and national level; Pres. and Dir-Gen. Fernando Giménez Barriocanal.

La Sexta: Virgilio 2, Edif. 4, Ciudad de la Imagen, 28223 Pozuelo de Alarcón (Madrid); tel. (91) 8382966; fax (91) 8382958; e-mail info@lasexta.com; internet www.lasexta.com; f. 2006; national terrestrial channel; Pres. Emilio Aragón; CEO José Miguel Contreras.

Sogecable: Avda de los Artesanos 6, 28760 Tres Cantos (Madrid); tel. (91) 7367000; fax (91) 7368695; e-mail prensa@sogecable.com; internet www.sogecable.es; f. 1989; satellite and digital television, internet services; operates Cuatro (national terrestrial channel), Digital+ (digital provider), Canal Satélite Digital, CNN+, Compañía Independiente de Televisión, Gestsport, Sogecine; owned by Grupo PRISA; Pres. Rodolfo Martín Villa; CEO Pedro García Guillén.

Grupo Telecinco: Federico Monpou 5B, 28049 Madrid; tel. (91) 3966300; fax (91) 3966478; e-mail telecinco@telecinco.es; internet www.telecinco.es; f. 1990; private commercial national network; jtly owned by Grupo Mediaset (Italy), Grupo Correo de Comunicación, Ice Finance (The Netherlands); Pres. Alejandro Echevarría.

Televisió de Catalunya (TV3): Carrer de la TV3, s/n, 08970 Sant Joan Despi, Barcelona; tel. (93) 4999333; fax (93) 4730671; internet www.tv3.cat; f. 1983; broadcasts in Catalan; Dir Mònica Terribas i Sala.

Televisión de Galicia (TVG): San Marcos, Apdo 707, 15820 Santiago de Compostela; tel. (981) 540640; fax (981) 540719; e-mail crtvg@crtvg.es; internet www.crtvg.es; f. 1985; broadcasts in Galician; Dir-Gen. Alfonso Sánchez Izquierdo.

SPAIN

Televisión Autonomía Madrid, SA (Telemadrid): Paseo del Príncipe 3, 28223 Pozuelo de Alarcón (Madrid); tel. (91) 5128200; fax (91) 5128300; e-mail correo@telemadrid.com; internet www.telemadrid.es; commenced transmissions in 1989; controlled by RTVM; cultural channel, laOtra, commenced transmission in March 2001; Dir-Gen. ISABEL LINARES LIÉBANA.

Other Satellite, Cable and Digital Television

Chello Multicanal: Saturno 1, Pozuelo de Alarcón, 28224 Madrid; tel. (91) 7141080; fax (91) 3516873; e-mail lineadirecta@chellomulticanal.com; internet www.chellomulticanal.com/es; f. 1996; cable; operates 9 channels; Dir-Gen. EDUARDO ZULUETA.

Grupo Auna: Basauri 7 y 9, 28023 Madrid; internet www.auna.es; part of ONO; telecommunications, internet and cable TV; operates the cable telecommunications providers Aragón de Cable, Cabletelca, Cable i Televisió de Catalunya, Madritel, Supercable de Andalucía, Supercable Sevilla and Supercable Almería.

Hispasat: Gobelas 41, 2°, 28023 Madrid; tel. (91) 7102540; fax (91) 3729000; e-mail comunicacion@hispasat.es; internet www.hispasat.com; satellite; Pres. PETRA MATEOS.

Telecable de Asturias: Parque Científico y Tecnológico de Gijón, Carretera de Cabueñes, 33203 Gijón; tel. (984) 191000; fax (984) 191001; e-mail info@telecable.es; internet www.telecable.es; cable; f. 1995; operator for Asturias; Pres. JUAN GARCIA CONDE; Dir-Gen. ALEJANDRO MARTÍNEZ PEÓN.

Telefónica Cable: Calle Virgilio 2, Edif. 2, 2°, 28223 Pozuelo de Alarcón (Madrid); tel. (91) 5129510; e-mail cac@tcable.es; f. 1997; cable.

Veo TV: Plaza de la Castellana 40, 28046 Madrid; internet www.veo.es; f. 2001; digital; Dir EDUARDO SÁNCHEZ ILLANA.

Associations

Agrupación de Operadores de Cable (AOC): Obenque 4, 28042 Madrid; f. 1998; by CYC Madrid, Retecal, Telecable and Grupo Cable; group of cable telecommunications operators; Dir JESÚS PELEGRÍN.

Promoción e Identificación de Servicios Emergentes de Telecomunicaciones Avanzadas (PISTA): Secretaría de Estado de Telecomunicaciones y para la Sociedad de la Información, Capitán Haya 41, 28071 Madrid; tel. (91) 3461500; fax (91) 3461567; e-mail jmontalban@mityc.es; part of Ministry of Industry, Tourism and Trade; initiative for the promotion and identification of emerging advanced telecommunications.

Unión de Televisiones Comerciales Asociadas (UTECA): Miguel Ángel 7, 1°B, 28010 Madrid; tel. (91) 3086746; fax (91) 3910049; e-mail uteca@uteca.com; internet www.uteca.com; f. 1998; represents commercial television interests; Pres. ALEJANDRO ECHEVARRÍA; Sec.-Gen. JORGE DEL CORRAL Y DÍEZ DEL CORRAL.

Finance

(cap. = capital, res = reserves, dep. = deposits, brs = branches, m. = million, amounts in euros)

BANKING

Central Bank

Banco de España: Alcalá 48, 28014 Madrid; tel. (91) 3386063; fax (91) 3385884; e-mail bde@bde.es; internet www.bde.es; f. 1782; granted exclusive right of issue in 1874; nationalized 1962; granted a degree of autonomy in 1994; cap. 1,000.0m., res 1,000.0m., dep. 75,105.1m. (Dec. 2008); Gov. MIGUEL ÁNGEL FERNÁNDEZ ORDÓÑEZ; 22 brs.

Principal Commercial and Development Banks

Banca March SA: Avda Alejandro Rosselló 8, 07002 Palma de Mallorca; tel. (971) 779100; fax (971) 779187; e-mail divinter@bancamarch.es; internet www.bancamarch.es; f. 1926; 100% owned by the March family; cap. 29.2m., res 1,188.6m., dep. 9,083.7m. (Dec. 2008); Pres. JOSÉ CARLOS MARCH DELGADO; Man. Dir FRANCISCO VERDÚ PONS; 270 brs.

Banco de Andalucía: Fernández y González 4, 41001 Sevilla; tel. (95) 4594700; fax (95) 4594802; internet www.bancoandalucia.es; f. 1844; 80.1% owned by Grupo Banco Popular; cap. 16.3m., res 938.0m., dep. 11,153.2m. (Dec. 2007); Pres. MIGUEL DE SOLÍS Y MARTÍNEZ CAMPOS; Gen. Man. FRANCISCO PARDO MARTÍNEZ; 298 brs.

Banco Bilbao Vizcaya Argentaria (BBVA): Paseo de la Castellana 81, 28046 Madrid; tel. (91) 4876000; fax (91) 4876417; internet www.bbva.es; f. 2000 by merger; cap. 1,837.0m., res 20,619.0m., dep. 495,873.0m. (Dec. 2008); Pres. JOSÉ IGNACIO GOIRIGOLZARRI TELLAECHE; Chair. and Chief Exec. FRANCISCO GONZÁLEZ RODRÍGUEZ; 3,375 brs.

Banco Caixa Geral: Juan Ignacio Luca de Tena 1, 28027 Madrid; tel. (91) 3099000; fax (91) 3209275; e-mail extranjero@bancaixageral.es; internet www.bancocaixageral.es; f. 1969; present name adopted 2006; 99.6% owned by Caixa Geral de Depósitos (Portugal); cap. 442.8m., res −34.1m., dep. 5,854.0m. (Dec. 2008); Pres. ANTÓNIO MALDONADO GONELHA; Chief Exec. FERNANDO FARIA DE OLIVEIRA.

Banco de Castilla: Plaza de los Bandos 10, 37002 Salamanca; tel. (923) 290000; fax (923) 211902; internet www.bancocastilla.es; f. 1915; 95.2% owned by Grupo Banco Popular; cap. 26.0m., res 404.2m., dep. 4,272.8m. (Dec. 2006); Pres. GABRIEL GANCEDO DE SERAS; Gen. Man. JOSÉ BRAVO JIMÉNEZ; 199 brs.

Banco Cooperativo Español: Virgen de los Peligros 6, 28013 Madrid; tel. (91) 5956700; fax (91) 5956800; internet www.cajarural.com; f. 1990; cap. 73.0m., res 137.1m., dep. 8,202.7m. (Dec. 2008); Chair. JOSÉ LUIS GARCÍA PALACIOS; Gen. Man. JAVIER PETIT ASUMENDI; 4,100 brs.

Banco Español de Crédito S.A. (Banesto): Gran Vía de Hortaleza 3, 28043 Madrid; tel. (91) 3383100; fax (91) 3381883; e-mail uninternac@banesto.es; internet www.banesto.es; f. 1902; cap. 543.0m., res 4,551.9m., dep. 112,781.6m. (Dec. 2009); Chair. ANA PATRICIA BOTÍN-SANZ DE SAUTUOLA Y O'SHEA; CEO JOSÉ A. GARCÍA CANTERA; 1,703 brs.

Banco de Galicia: Policarpo Sanz 23, Pontevedra, 36202 Vigo; tel. (986) 822100; fax (986) 822101; internet www.bancogalicia.es; f. 1918; part of Grupo Banco Popular Español; cap. 9.1m., res 337.7m., dep. 3,624.3m. (Dec. 2006); Pres. JESÚS PLATERO; Gen. Man. JUAN J. RUBIO; 141 brs.

Banco Gallego S.A.: Avda Linares Rivas 30, 15005 A Coruña; tel. (981) 127950; fax (981) 126582; e-mail intervenciongeneral@bancogallego.com; internet www.bancogallego.es; f. 1847; cap. 119.0m., res 78.7m., dep. 4,043.9m. (Dec. 2008); Pres. JUAN MANUEL URGOITI LÓPEZ-OCAÑA; Gen. Man. JOSÉ LUIS LOSADA RODRÍGUEZ; 163 brs.

Banco Guipuzcoano, SA: Avda de la Libertad 21, 20004 San Sebastián; tel. (943) 418100; fax (943) 418337; e-mail bgintnal@bancogui.com; internet www.bancogui.es; f. 1899; cap. 37.4m., res 581.0m., dep. 9,542.4m. (Dec. 2009); Pres. JOSÉ MARÍA AGUIRRE GONZÁLEZ; Gen. Man. JUAN LUIS ARRIETA; 265 brs.

Banco Pastor: Cantón Pequeño 1, Edif. Pastor, 15003 La Coruña; tel. (981) 127600; fax (981) 210301; internet www.bancopastor.es; f. 1776; cap. 86.4m., res 1,259.8m., dep. 25,166.6m. (Dec. 2008); Chair. JOSÉ MARÍA ARIAS MOSQUERA; Chief Exec. JORGE GOST GIJÓN; 568 brs.

Banco Popular Español: Velázquez 34, 28001 Madrid; tel. (91) 5207000; fax (91) 5783274; internet www.bancopopular.es; f. 1926; cap. 133.3m., res 7,700.6m., dep. 118,346.1m. (Dec. 2009); Pres. and CEO ANGEL CARLOS RON GÜIMIL; 2,224 brs.

Banco de Sabadell: POB 1, Plaza Sant Roc 20, Sabadell, 08201 Barcelona; tel. (93) 7289289; fax (93) 7270606; e-mail info@bancsabadell.com; internet www.bancsabadell.com; f. 1881; cap. 150.0m., res 3,804.1m., dep. 75,041.4m. (Dec. 2008); Chair. JOSEP OLIU; 1,186 brs.

Banco Santander: Plaza de Canalejas 1, 28014 Madrid; tel. (91) 5581111; internet www.santander.com; f. 1857; cap. 3,127.1m., res 44,550.3m., dep. 812,543.0m. (Dec. 2007); Chair. EMILIO BOTÍN-SANZ DE SAUTUOLA Y GARCÍA DE LOS RÍOS; Man. Dir JUAN BOTÍN; 8,848 brs.

Banco Urquijo, SA: Príncipe de Vergara 131, 28002 Madrid; tel. (91) 3372000; fax (91) 3372096; internet www.bancourquijo.es; f. 1870; part of Grupo Banco de Sabadell; cap. 92.7m., res 148.7m., dep. 3,675.0m. (Dec. 2004); Pres. FERDINAND VERDONCK; CEO ALFONSO TOLCHEFF; 60 brs.

Banco de Valencia: Pintor Sorolla 2–4, 46002 Valencia; tel. (96) 3984500; fax (96) 3984570; e-mail division.internacional@bancodevalencia.es; internet www.bancodevalencia.es; f. 1900; cap. 118.4m., res 1,055.7m., dep. 21,334.4m. (Dec. 2009); Pres. JOSÉ LUIS OLIVAS MARTÍNEZ; Gen. Man. DOMINGO PARRA SORIA; 428 brs.

Banco de Vasconia: Plaza del Castillo 39, 31001 Pamplona; tel. (948) 179600; fax (948) 179665; e-mail serviciocentrales@bancovasconia.es; internet www.bancovasconia.es; f. 1901; 96.9% owned by Banco Popular Español; cap. 9.6m., res 173.5m., dep. 3,351.4m. (Dec. 2006); Pres. JOSÉ R. RODRÍGUEZ GARCÍA; Gen. Man. MIGUEL MOZO LOBATO; 121 brs.

Bankinter: Paseo de la Castellana 29, 28046 Madrid; tel. (91) 3397500; fax (91) 3397556; e-mail international@bankinter.es; internet www.bankinter.com; f. 1965; finances industrial and business dealings with medium- and long-term loans and investments; cap. 142.0m., res 2,290.9m., dep. 50,820.4m. (Dec. 2009); Chair. PEDRO GUERRERO; CEO MARÍA DOLORES DANCAUSA; 253 brs.

Barclays Bank SA: Plaza de Colón 1, 28046 Madrid; tel. (91) 3361000; fax (91) 3361134; internet www.barclays.es; f. 1974; cap. 157.8m., res 814.7m., dep. 30,096.0m. (Dec. 2008); 99.7% owned by Barclays Bank PLC (United Kingdom); Chair. C. MARTÍNEZ DE CAMPOS; 163 brs.

SPAIN

Deutsche Bank SAE: Avda Diagonal 446, 08006 Barcelona; tel. (93) 3673788; fax (93) 3673311; internet www.deutsche-bank.es; f. 1950; present name adopted 1994; 99.7% owned by Deutsche Bank AG (Germany); cap. 67.4m., res 668.2m., dep. 17,361.2m. (Dec. 2008); Chair. HERMANN-JOSEF LAMBERTI.

Savings Banks

Bilbao Bizkaia Kutxa (BBK): Gran Vía 30–32, 48009 Bilbao; tel. (94) 4017000; fax (94) 4017800; e-mail bbktelefono@bbk.es; internet www.bbk.es; f. 1907 as Caja de Ahorros Municipal de Bilbao; merged with Caja de Ahorros Vizcaina and adopted current name 1990; cap. 0.0m., res 3,804.5m., dep. 24,864.6m. (Dec. 2009); Chair. and Chief Exec. MARIO FERNÁNDEZ PELAZ; 330 brs.

CAIXANOVA (Caixa de Aforros de Vigo, Ourense e Pontevedra): Avda García Barbon 1–3, 36201 Vigo; tel. (986) 828200; fax (986) 828238; e-mail internacionalcx@caixanova.com; internet www.caixanova.com; f. 1929; present name adopted 2000; res 1,027.4m., dep. 28,431.6m. (Dec. 2008); Pres. and Chair. JULIO FERNÁNDEZ GAYOSO; Gen. Man. JOSÉ LUIS PEGO ALONSO; 526 brs.

Caixa d'Estalvis de Catalunya (Caixa Catalunya): Plaza Antonio Maura 6, 08003 Barcelona; tel. (93) 4845000; fax (93) 4845141; e-mail international.services@caixacatalunya.es; internet www.caixacatalunya.es; f. 1926; res 2,664.8m., dep. 60,631.4m., total assets 67,551.4m. (Dec. 2006); Pres. NARCÍS SERRA; Gen. Man. JOSEP ADOLF TODÓ; 936 brs.

Caixa d'Estalvis de Tarragona (Caixa Tarragona): Plaza Imperial Tàrraco 6, 43005 Tarragona; tel. (977) 299200; fax (977) 299250; e-mail liniapreferent@caixatarragona.es; internet www.caixatarragona.es; f. 1952; res 450.9m., dep. 10,790.4m., total assets 11,371.0m. (Dec. 2008); Pres. GABRIEL FERRATÉ PASCUAL; Gen. Man. RAFAEL JENÉ VILLAGRASA; 289 brs.

Caja de Ahorros de Asturias (CAJASTUR): Plaza de la Escandalera 2, 33003 Oviedo; tel. (98) 5102222; fax (98) 5215649; e-mail extranjero@cajastur.es; internet www.cajastur.es; f. 1945; res 1,508.8m., dep. 13,477.5m., total assets 15,450.7m. (Dec. 2008); Pres. and CEO MANUEL MENÉNDEZ MENÉNDEZ; 343 brs.

Caja de Ahorros de Castilla la Mancha (CCM): Parque San Julián 20, 16002 Cuenca; tel. (969) 177314; fax (969) 177606; e-mail webmaster@ccm.es; internet www.ccm.es; f. 1992; management assumed by Banco de España in March 2009; merger into Caja de Ahorros de Asturias agreed Nov. 2009; cap. 0.0m., res 1,029.7m., dep. 26,052.5m. (Dec. 2008); Pres. (vacant); 390 brs.

Caja de Ahorros de Galicia (Caixa Galicia): Rúa Nueva 30, 15003 A Coruña; tel. (981) 188000; fax (981) 188001; internet www.caixagalicia.es; f. 1978; cap. 0.0m., res 2,032.2m., dep. 43,536.7m. (Dec. 2008); Pres. MAURO VARELA PÉREZ; Gen. Man. JOSÉ LUIS MÉNDEZ LÓPEZ; 866 brs.

Caja de Ahorros de la Inmaculada de Aragón (CAI): Paseo Independencia 10, 50004 Zaragoza; tel. (976) 718100; fax (976) 718377; e-mail info.corporativa@cai.es; internet www.cai.es; f. 1905; res 786.2m., dep. 9,370.7m., total assets 10,403.7m. (Dec 2008); Pres. ANTONIO AZNAR GRASA; 247 brs.

Caja de Ahorros del Mediterráneo (CAM): San Fernando 40, 03001 Alicante; tel. (96) 5905000; fax (96) 5905044; e-mail cam@cam.es; internet www.cam.es; f. 1875; cap. 3.0m., res 3,059.4m., dep. 68,365.7m. (Dec. 2009); Chair. VICENTE SALA BELLÓ; Gen. Man. ROBERTO LÓPEZ ABAD; 1,067 brs.

Caja de Ahorros y Monte de Piedad de las Baleares 'Sa Nostra': Ramón Llull 2, 07001 Palma de Mallorca; tel. (971) 171717; fax (971) 171797; e-mail sanostra@sanostra.es; internet www.sanostra.es; res 632.7m., dep. 13,475.1m., total assets 14,343.8m. (Dec. 2008); Chair. FERNANDO ALZAMORA CARBONELL; Gen. Man. PEDRO BATLE MAYO; 229 brs.

Caja de Ahorros y Monte de Piedad del Círculo Católico de Obreros de Burgos (CajaCírculo): Avda de los Reyes Católicos 1, 09005 Burgos; tel. (947) 288200; fax (947) 288210; internet www.cajacirculo.es; f. 1909; res 505.8m., dep. 4,323.3m., total assets 4,974.1m. (Dec. 2008); Chair. JOSÉ IGNACIO MIJANGOS LINAZA; Gen. Man. SANTIAGO RUIZ DIEZ; 176 brs.

Caja de Ahorros y Monte de Piedad de Guipúzcoa y San Sebastián (Kutxa) (Gipuzkoa eta Donstiako Aurrezki Kutxa): Garibai 15, Apdo 1389, 20004 San Sebastián; tel. (943) 001000; fax (943) 001045; e-mail infokutxa@kutxa.es; internet www.kutxa.es; f. 1896; cap. 180.3m., res 2,078.5m., dep. 18,469.1m. (Dec. 2009); Pres. and Chair. XABIO ITURBE OTAEGI; 330 brs.

Caja de Ahorros y Monte de Piedad de Madrid (Caja Madrid): Plaza de Celenque 2, 28013 Madrid; tel. (91) 3792000; fax (91) 5216980; e-mail bvegasga@cajamadrid.es; internet www.cajamadrid.es; f. 1869; res 9,154.2m., dep. 168,802.9m., total assets 180,970.9m. (Dec. 2008); Pres. MIGUEL BLESA DE LA PARRA; 1,914 brs.

Caja de Ahorros y Monte de Piedad de Navarra (Caja Navarra): Avda de Carlos III 8, 31002 Pamplona; tel. (948) 222333; fax (948) 208269; e-mail sac@can.es; internet www.can.es; f. 1921; cap. 0.0m., res 937.2m., dep. 17,490.8m. (Dec. 2008); Pres. MIGUEL SANZ SESMA; Gen. Man. ENRIQUE GOÑI BELTRÁN DE GARIZURIETA; 323 brs.

Caja de Ahorros y Monte de Piedad de Zaragoza, Aragón y Rioja (IBERCAJA): Plaza del Paraíso 2, 50008 Zaragoza; tel. (976) 767676; fax (976) 214417; internet www.ibercaja.es; f. 1876; res 1,995.5m., dep. 32,420.1m., total assets 35,237.2m. (Dec. 2006); Chair. AMADO FRANCO LAHOZ; Gen. Man. JOSÉ LUIS AGUIRRE LOASO; 1,008 brs.

Caja de Ahorros de Murcia (Cajamurcia): Gran Vía Escultor Salzillo 23, 30005 Murcia; tel. (968) 361600; fax (968) 306160; internet www.cajamurcia.es; f. 1965; cap. 0.0m., res 1,248.7m., dep. 14,649.8m., total assets 16,719.6m. (Dec. 2006); Pres. JUAN ROCA GUILLAMÓN; Gen. Man. CARLOS EGEA KRAUEL; 415 brs.

Caja de Ahorros y Pensiones de Barcelona (La Caixa): Avda Diagonal 621–629, 08028 Barcelona; tel. (93) 4046000; fax (93) 3395703; e-mail estudis@lacaixa.es; internet www.lacaixa.es; f. 1990; res 14,462.7m., dep. 217,391.5m., total assets 260,827.4m. (Dec. 2008); Chair. ISIDRO FAINÉ; Pres. and Chief Exec. JUAN MARÍA NIN; 5,053 brs.

Caixa d'Estalvis Unió de Caixes de Manlleu, Sabadell i Terrassa (Unnim): Plaça Catalunya 9, 08002 Barcelona; tel. (902) 480808; e-mail info@unnim.cat; internet www.unnim.cat; f. 2010 by merger of 3 savings banks (Manlleu, Sabadell and Terrassa); Pres. SALVADOR SOLEY I JUNOY; Dir-Gen. ENRIC MATA TARRAGÓ.

Caja de Ahorros de Valencia, Castellón y Alicante (BANCAJA) (Caixa d'Estalvis de València, Castelló i Alacant): Pintor Sorolla, 8, 46002 Valencia; tel. (96) 3875500; fax (96) 3527550; internet www.bancaja.es; f. 1878; res 3,410.7m., dep. 103,729.3m., total assets 111,459.2m. (Dec. 2009); Chair. JOSÉ LUIS OLIVAS MARTÍNEZ; Gen. Man. JOSÉ FERNANDO GARCÍA CHECA; 1,055 brs.

Caja Duero (Caja de Ahorros de Salamanca y Soria): Plaza de los Bandos 15–17, 37002 Salamanca; tel. (923) 279300; fax (923) 270680; internet www.cajaduero.es; f. 1881; res 1,080.6m., dep. 19,271.9m., total assets 20,743.6m. (Dec. 2008); Pres. and Chair. JULIO FERMOSO; Gen. Man. LUCAS HERNÁNDEZ; 563 brs.

Caja España (Caja España de Inversiones, Caja de Ahorros y Monte de Piedad): Ordoño II 17, 24001 León; tel. (987) 218683; fax (987) 218067; e-mail buzon@cajaespana.es; internet www.cajaespana.es; f. 1900; res 862.9m., dep. 23,557.3m., total assets 24,804.3m. (Dec. 2008); Chair. SANTOS LLAMAS LLAMAS; Gen. Man. JOSÉ IGNACIO LAGARTOS RODRÍGUEZ; 538 brs.

Caja Insular de Ahorros de Canarias (La Caja de Canarias): Triana 20, 35002 Las Palmas; tel. (928) 442254; fax (928) 442599; e-mail ciac@lacajadecanarias.es; internet www.lacajadecanarias.es; f. 1939; res 365.5m., dep. 8,862.7m., total assets 9,354.4m. (Dec. 2008); Pres. ANTONIO MARRERO HERNÁNDEZ.

Caja Laboral Popular Coop. de Crédito (Caja Laboral): Paseo José María Arizmendiarrieta s/n, 20500 Mondragón, Guipúzcoa; tel. (943) 719500; fax (943) 719778; e-mail cajalaboral.net@cajalaboral.es; internet www.cajalaboral.es; f. 1959; cap. 458.4m., res 797.6m., dep. 19,448.2m. (Dec. 2008); Pres. JUAN M. OTAEGUI MURUA; Gen. Man. ELIAS ATUCHA ARESTI; 389 brs.

Confederación Española de Cajas de Ahorros (CECA): Alcalá 27, 28014 Madrid; tel. (91) 5965000; fax (91) 5965742; e-mail admin@ceca.es; internet www.ceca.es; f. 1928; national asscn of savings banks; cap. 30.1m., res 575.8m., dep. 17,226.9m. (Dec. 2008); Pres. ISIDRO FAINÉ; 22,445 brs.

Montes de Piedad y Caja de Ahorros de Ronda, Cádiz, Almería, Málaga y Antequera (Unicaja): Avda Andalucía 10–12, 29007 Málaga; tel. (952) 138000; fax (952) 138130; e-mail info@personal.unicaja.es; internet www.unicaja.es; f. 1991; cap. 0.0m., res 2,196.3m., dep. 28,805.2m. (Dec. 2008); Pres. BRAULIO MEDEL CAMARÁ; Gen. Man. MIGUEL ANGEL CABELLO JURADO; 870 brs.

Banking Associations

Asociación Española de Banca (AEB): Velázquez 64–66, 28001 Madrid; tel. (91) 7891311; fax (91) 7891310; f. 1977; Pres. MIGUEL MARTÍN; Sec.-Gen. PEDRO PABLO VILLASANTE.

Fondo de Garantía de Depósitos (FGD): José Ortega y Gasset 22, 28006 Madrid; tel. (91) 4316645; fax (91) 5755728; e-mail fogade@fgd.es; internet www.fgd.es; f. 1977; deposit guarantee fund; Pres. JOSÉ MARÍA VIÑALS IÑIGUEZ.

STOCK EXCHANGES

Bolsas y Mercados Españoles (BME): Palacio de la Bolsa, Plaza de la Lealtad 1, 28014 Madrid; tel. (91) 7095000; fax (91) 5326816; e-mail accionista@bolsasymercados.es; internet www.bolsasymercados.es; integrates cos that manage securities market and financial system; Pres. ANTONIO J. ZOIDO MARTÍNEZ.

SPAIN

Bolsa de Barcelona: Paseo de Gracia 19, 08007 Barcelona; tel. (93) 4013555; fax (93) 4013650; e-mail informacion@borsabcn.es; internet www.borsabcn.es; f. 1915; Pres. JOAN HORTALÀ I ARAU.

Bolsa de Bilbao: José M. Olabarri 1, 48001 Bilbao; tel. (94) 4034400; fax (94) 4034430; e-mail bolsabilbao@bolsabilbao.es; internet www.bolsabilbao.es; f. 1890; CEO JOSÉ LUIS DAMBORENEA.

Bolsa de Madrid: Plaza de la Lealtad 1, 28014 Madrid; tel. (91) 5891161; fax (91) 5312290; e-mail internacional@bolsamadrid.es; internet www.bolsamadrid.es; f. 1831; 49 mems; Chair. and CEO ANTONIO ZOIDO MARTÍNEZ.

Bolsa de Valores de Valencia: Libreros 2 y 4, 46002 Valencia; tel. (96) 3870100; fax (96) 3870133; e-mail webmaster@bolsavalencia.es; internet www.bolsavalencia.es; f. 1980; Vice-Pres. and CEO MANUEL ESCÁMEZ SÁNCHEZ.

Regulatory Authority

Comisión Nacional del Mercado de Valores (CNMV): Miguel Ángel 11, 28010 Madrid; tel. (91) 5851500; fax (91) 3193373; internet www.cnmv.es; f. 1988; national securities and exchange commission; Pres. JULIO SEGURA SÁNCHEZ.

INSURANCE

Aegon Unión Aseguradora: Príncipe de Vergara 156, 28002 Madrid; tel. (91) 5636222; fax (91) 5639715; internet www.aegon.es; f. 1944; owned by Aegon NV (The Netherlands); life, property, health and personal insurance and reinsurance; Chair. ALEJANDRO ROYO-VILLANOVA PAYÁ; CEO JESÚS QUINTANAL SAN EMETERIO.

Allianz, Compañía de Seguros y Reaseguros: Paseo de la Castellana 39, 28046 Madrid; tel. (91) 5960400; fax (91) 5578702; internet www.allianz.es; f. 1999; total premiums 2,292m. (2004); Pres. DETLEV BREMKAMP; CEO VICENTE TARDÍO.

Ascat Vida: Provença 398–404, 08025 Barcelona; tel. (93) 484600; tel. (93) 4846002; e-mail info_ascat@ascat.es; internet www.ascat.es; f. 1986; subsidiary of Caixa Catalunya.

Asistencia Sanitaria Interprovincial de Seguros (ASISA): Caracas 12, 28010 Madrid; tel. (91) 3190191; fax (91) 4103836; e-mail asisa.informacion@asisa.es; internet www.asisa.es; Pres. FRANCISCO CARREÑO CASTILLA.

Axa: Paseo de la Castellana 79, 28046 Madrid; tel. (91) 5388200; fax (91) 5553197; internet www.axa.es; Pres. EDUARDO DE AGUIRRE ALONSO-ALLENDE.

Banco Vitalicio de España, Compañía Anónima de Seguros: Paseo de Gracia 11, 08007 Barcelona; tel. (93) 4840100; fax (93) 4840239; internet www.vitalicio.es; f. 1880; total premiums 1,221.2m. (2004); Pres. JOSÉ MARÍA AMUSÁTEGUI DE LA CIERVA.

BBVA Seguros: Alcalá 17, 28014 Madrid; tel. (91) 5379231; fax (91) 3747266; e-mail seguros@grupobbva.com; internet www.bbvaseguros.com.

Bilbao, Cía Anónima de Seguros y Reaseguros (Seguros Bilbao): Paseo del Puerto 20, 48990 Neguri-Getxo (Vizcaya); tel. (94) 4898100; fax (94) 4898263; internet www.segurosbilbao.com; f. 1918; gen. insurance, represented throughout Spain; part of Grupo Catalana Occidente; Pres. FRANCISCO JOSÉ ARREGUI; Man. Dir IÑAKI ALVARES.

Caja de Seguros Reunidos, Cía de Seguros y Reaseguros (Caser Seguros): Plaza de la Lealtad 4, 28014 Madrid; tel. (91) 5955000; fax (91) 5955018; e-mail informacion@caser.es; internet www.caser.es; f. 1942; represented throughout Spain; total premiums 1,587.9m. (2005); Dir-Gen. IGNACIO EYRIES GARCÍA DE VINUESA.

Crédito y Caución (Compañía Española de Seguros y Reaseguros): Paseo de la Castellana 4, 28046 Madrid; tel. (91) 4326300; fax (91) 4326506; e-mail sac@creditoycaucion.es; internet www.creditoycaucion.com; f. 1929; total premiums 361m. (2005); Pres. JESÚS SERRA FARRÉ; CEO ISIDRO UNDA URZAIZ.

Estrella Seguros: Orense 2, 28020 Madrid; tel. (91) 5905656; fax (91) 5907674; e-mail clientes@laestrella.es; internet www.laestrella.es; f. 1901; all classes of insurance and reinsurance; total premiums 1,007.3m. (2005); Pres. Duque CARLOS ZURITA DELGADO; CEO MÓNICA MONDARDINI.

Grupo Catalana Occidente: Avda Alcalde Barnils 63, 08174 Sant Cugat del Vallés (Barcelona); tel. (93) 5820500; fax (93) 5820560; e-mail calidad@catalanaoccidente.com; internet www.catalanaoccidente.com; insurance and reinsurance; Pres. JOSÉ MARÍA SERRA FARRÉ.

Mapfre Mutualidad (Mapfre Mutualidad de Seguros y Reaseguros): Carretera de Pozuelo a Majadahonda, Km 3800, 28820 Majadahonda, Madrid; tel. (91) 6262100; fax (91) 6262308; internet www.mapfre.com; f. 1933; car insurance; Pres. JOSÉ A. REBUELTA GARCÍA.

Mapfre Seguros Generales: Paseo de Recoletos 23, 28004 Madrid; tel. (91) 5816300; fax (91) 5815252; internet www.mapfre.com; Pres. RAFAEL GALARRAGA SOLORES.

Mapfre Vida: Avda General Perón 40, 28020 Madrid; tel. (91) 5811400; fax (91) 5811592; internet www.mapfre.com; life; Man. Dir SEBASTIÁN HOMET DUPRA.

Mutua General de Seguros (MGS): Avda Diagonal 543, 08029 Barcelona; tel. (93) 3221212; fax (93) 3220971; e-mail sac@mgs.es; internet www.mgs.es; f. 1907; Pres. JORGE LUQUE VICO.

Mutua Madrileña: Paseo de la Castellana 33, 28046 Madrid; tel. (902) 555555, (91) 5578200; fax (91) 3105223; internet www.mutua-mad.es; f. 1930; Pres. IGNACIO GARRALDA RUÍZ DE VELASCO.

Ocaso, SA, Compañía de Seguros y Reaseguros: Princesa 23, 28008 Madrid; tel. (91) 5380100; fax (91) 5418509; e-mail ocaso@ocaso.es; internet www.ocaso.es; f. 1920; total premiums 513m., cap. 100m. (2002); 370 brs in Spain, 1 in London, 1 in Puerto Rico; Pres. ISABEL CASTELO D'ORTEGA; Dir-Gen. D. ANTONIO DOMÍNGUEZ CUERDO.

Sanitas de Seguros: Ribera del Loira 52, 28042 Madrid; tel. 902 230220; fax (91) 5852516; e-mail iferrando@sanitas.es; internet www.sanitas.es; health; Pres. JUAN JOSÉ LÓPEZ-IBOR.

SantaLucía Seguros: Plaza de España 15, 28008 Madrid; tel. (91) 5419387; fax (91) 5410133; e-mail atencion@santalucia.es; internet www.santalucia.es; f. 1922; Pres. CARLOS J. ALVAREZ NAVARRO.

Vidacaixa: General Almirante 6, 08014 Barcelona; tel. (93) 2278700; fax (93) 3324441; internet www.vidacaixa.es; subsidiary of Grupo CaiFor; Pres. TOMÁS MUNIESA ARANTEGUI.

Zurich: Vía Augusta 192–200, 08021 Barcelona; tel. (93) 2099111; fax (93) 2014849; e-mail zurich.seleccion-es@zurich.com; internet www.zurichspain.com.

Regulatory Authority

Dirección General de Seguros y Fondos de Pensiones: Paseo de la Castellana 44, 28046 Madrid; tel. (91) 3397000; fax (91) 3397113; e-mail dirseguros@meh.es; internet www.dgsfp.meh.es; supervisory body; part of Ministry of the Economy and Finance; Dir-Gen. RICARDO LOZANO ARAGÜÉS.

Insurance Association

Unión Española de Entidades Aseguradoras y Reaseguradoras (UNESPA): Núñez de Balboa 101, 28006 Madrid; tel. (91) 7451530; fax (91) 7451531; internet www.unespa.es; f. 1977; Pres. PILAR GONZÁLEZ DE FRUTOS; Sec.-Gen. MIRENCHU DEL VALLE; c. 300 mem. cos.

Trade and Industry

GOVERNMENT AGENCIES

Comisión Nacional de la Competencia (CNC): Barquillo 5, 28004 Madrid; tel. (91) 5680510; fax (91) 5680590; e-mail informacion@cncompetencia.es; internet www.cncompetencia.es; f. 2007 by merger of the Servicio de Defensa de la Competencia and the Tribunal de Defensa de la Competencia; investigates anti-competitive practices and enforces competition law; Pres. LUIS BERENGUER FUSTER.

Instituto Español de Comercio Exterior (ICEX): Paseo de la Castellana 14-16, 28046 Madrid; tel. (91) 3496100; fax (91) 4316128; internet www.icex.es; f. 1982; institute for foreign trade; Pres. SILVIA IRANZO GUTIÉRREZ.

Secretaría General de Comercio Exterior: Secretaría de Estado de Comercio y Turismo, Paseo de la Castellana 160, 28046 Madrid; tel. (902) 446006; fax (91) 4578066; part of Ministry of Industry, Tourism and Trade; Sec.-Gen. ALFREDO BONET BAIGET.

DEVELOPMENT ORGANIZATIONS

Ade Gestión Sodical, SGECR: Jacinto Benavente 2, 3°, 47195 Valladolid; tel. (983) 343811; fax (983) 330702; e-mail sodical@sodical.es; internet www.sodical.es; f. 1982 as Sociedad para el Desarrollo Industrial de Castilla y León (SODICAL); promotes devt in Castile and Leon; Dir-Gen. MANUEL FERNÁNDEZ DÍEZ.

Instituto Andaluz de la Reforma Agraria (IARA): Tabladilla s/n, 41071 Sevilla; tel. (95) 5032000; fax (95) 5032149; empowered to expropriate land under the agricultural reform programme; Pres. MARÍA ISABEL SALINAS GARCÍA.

Instituto Galego de Promoción Económica (IGAPE): Complejo Administrativo Barrio de San Lázaro s/n, 15703 Santiago de Compostela (A Coruña); tel. (981) 541147; fax (981) 558844; e-mail igape@igape.es; internet www.igape.es; promotes devt in Galicia; overseas brs in People's Republic of China, Germany, Japan, Poland and USA; Dir-Gen. ÁLVARO ÁLVAREZ-BLÁZQUEZ FERNÁNDEZ; Sec.-Gen. JOSÉ MARÍA PENELAS FIGUEIRA.

Instituto Madrileño de Desarrollo (IMADE): José Abascal 57, 28003 Madrid; tel. (91) 3997400; e-mail informacion@imade.es; internet www.imade.es; f. 1984; public devt institution for Madrid region; Dir AURELIO GARCÍA DE SOLA Y ARRIAGA.

Sociedad de Desarrollo de Navarra (SODENA): Avda Carlos III el Noble 36, 1° dcha, 31003 Pamplona; tel. (848) 421942; fax (848) 421943; e-mail info@sodena.com; internet www.sodena.com; promotes devt in Navarra; Pres. JOSÉ ROIG ALDASORO.

Sociedad para el Desarrollo Económico de Canarias (Sodecan): Villalba Hervás 4, 6°, 38002 Santa Cruz de Tenerife; tel. (922) 298020; fax (922) 298131; e-mail sodecantf@sodecan.es; internet www.sodecan.es; promotes devt in the Canary Islands; Pres. JOSÉ MANUEL SORIA LÓPEZ.

Sociedad para el Desarrollo Industrial de Extremadura (Sodiex): Avda Ruta de la Plata 13, 10001 Cáceres; tel. (927) 224878; fax (927) 243304; e-mail sodiex@sodiex.es; internet www.sodiex.es; f. 1977; promotes industrial devt in Extremadura.

CHAMBERS OF COMMERCE

Cámara de Comercio Internacional (International Chamber of Commerce): Avda Diagonal 452-454, 08006 Barcelona; tel. (93) 4169300; fax (93) 4169301; e-mail iccspain@cambrabcn.es; internet www.iccspain.org; f. 1922; Pres. MIQUEL VALLS MASEDA; Sec.-Gen. LUIS SOLÁ VILARDELL.

Confederación Española de Comercio (CEC): Orense 25, 2°C, 28020 Madrid; tel. (91) 5981050; fax (91) 5520967; e-mail cec@confespacomercio.com; internet www.confespacomercio.com; f. 1984; Pres. PERE LLORENS LORENTE; Sec.-Gen. MIQUEL ÁNGEL FRAILE VILLAGRASA; 450,000 mems.

Consejo Superior de Cámaras Oficiales de Comercio, Industria y Navegación de España (High Council of Official Chambers of Commerce, Industry, and Navigation of Spain): Ribera del Loira 12, 28042 Madrid; tel. (91) 5906900; fax (91) 5906913; e-mail info@cscamaras.es; internet www.camaras.org; f. 1922; Pres. JOSÉ ANTONIO QUIROGA Y PIÑEYRO; Dir-Gen. GONZALO ORTIZ AMOR; comprises 85 Chambers throughout Spain, incl. the following:

Cámara de Comercio de Bilbao/Bilboko Merkataritza Ganbera: Gran Vía 13, 48001 Bilbao; tel. (94) 4706500; fax (94) 4436171; e-mail atencionalcliente@çamarabilbao.com; internet www.camarabilbao.com; Pres. JOSÉ ÁNGEL CORRES ABÁSOLO; Dir-Gen. JUAN LUIS LASKURAIN ARGARATE.

Cámara Oficial de Comercio e Industria de Madrid: Ribera del Loira 56-58, 28042 Madrid; tel. (91) 5383500; fax (91) 5383677; e-mail camara@camaramadrid.es; internet www.camaramadrid.es; f. 1887; Pres. SALVADOR SANTOS CAMPANO; Dir-Gen. MIGUEL GARRIDO; 511,804 mems.

Cámara Oficial de Comercio, Industria y Navegación de Sevilla: Plaza de la Contratación 8, 41004 Sevilla; tel. (902) 932320; fax (954) 225619; e-mail ccinsevilla@camaradesvilla.com; internet www.camaradesevilla.com; Pres. FRANCISCO LEÓN HERRERO; f. 1886.

Cámara Oficial de Comercio, Industria y Navegación de Valencia: Jesús, 19, 46007 Valencia; tel. (96) 3103900; fax (96) 3531742; e-mail info@camaravalencia.com; internet www.camaravalencia.com; f. 1886; Pres. ARTURO VIROSQUE RUÍZ; Dir FERNANDO ZÁRRAGA QUINTANA.

Cambra de Comerç de Barcelona: Avda Diagonal 452–454, 08006 Barcelona; tel. (90) 2448448; fax (93) 4169301; e-mail cambra@cambrabcn.org; internet www.cambrabcn.es; f. 1886; Dir XAVIER CARBONELL I ROURA.

INDUSTRIAL AND TRADE ASSOCIATIONS

Agrupación de Fabricantes de Cemento de España (OFICEMEN): José Abascal 53, 28003 Madrid; tel. (91) 4411688; fax (91) 4423817; e-mail info@oficemen.com; internet www.oficemen.com; cement manufacturers; Pres. JOAQUIN ESTRADA; Dir-Gen. ANICETO ZARAGOZA; 13 mem. cos.

Asociación de Comercio de Cereales y Oleaginosas de España (ACCOE): Doctor Fleming 56, 3°D, 28036 Madrid; tel. (91) 3504305; fax (91) 3455009; e-mail info@accoe.org; internet www.accoe.org; f. 1977; cereal traders; Pres. FRANCISCO ÁLVAREZ DE LA LAMA.

Asociación de Criadores Exportadores de Sherry (ACES): Avda Alcalde Alvaro Domecq 6, 2°D, 11405 Jerez de la Frontera; tel. (956) 341046; fax (956) 346081; sherry exporters; Pres. FRANCISCO VALENCIA JAÉN.

Asociación de Empresas de Electrónica, Tecnologías de la Información y Telecomunicaciones de España (AETIC): Príncipe de Vergara 74, 4°, 28006 Madrid; tel. (91) 5902300; e-mail aetic@aetic.es; internet www.aetic.es; f. 1984; electronic, information and telecommunication industries; Pres. JESÚS BANEGAS NÚÑEZ; Dir-Gen. GONZALO CARO SANTA CRUZ; c. 3,000 mem. cos.

Asociación Española de Exportadores de Electrónica e Informática (SECARTYS): Gran Vía de les Corts Catalanes 774, 4°, 08013 Barcelona; tel. (93) 1828800; fax (93) 2478561; e-mail secartys@secartys.org; internet www.secartys.org; f. 1968; electronics exporters; Pres. JOSEP ROF; Dir-Gen. CARLOS VIVAS; 1,200 mem. cos.

Asociación Española de Fabricantes de Automóviles y Camiones (ANFAC): Fray Bernardino Sahagún 24, 28036 Madrid; tel. (91) 3431343; fax (91) 3450377; e-mail prensa@anfac.com; internet www.anfac.es; car and lorry manufacturers; Pres. FRANCISCO JAVIER GARCÍA SANZ.

Asociación Española de Fabricantes de Equipos y Componentes para Automoción (SERNAUTO): Castelló 120, 28006 Madrid; tel. (91) 5621041; e-mail sernauto@sernauto.es; internet www.sernauto.es; f. 1967; asscn of manufacturers of equipment and components for automobile industry; Pres. JOSÉ MARÍA PUJOL ARTIGAS; Dir-Gen. JOSÉ ANTONIO JIMÉNEZ SACEDA.

Asociación Española de la Industria y Comercio Exportador de Aceite de Oliva (ASOLIVA): José Abascal 40, 2°, 28003 Madrid; tel. (91) 4468812; fax (91) 5931918; e-mail asoliva@asoliva.es; internet www.asoliva.es; f. 1928; olive oil exporters; Pres. JOSÉ PONT AMENOS.

Asociación Española de Productoras de Fibras Químicas (PROFIBRA): Via Laietana 46, 2°, 08003 Barcelona; tel. (93) 2682644; fax (93) 2682630; e-mail profibra@profibra.com; f. 1977; chemical fibre producers; Pres. RAFAEL ESPAÑOL NAVARRO; Sec.-Gen. GUILLERMO GRAELL DENIEL.

Asociación de Exportadores de Pescado y Cefalopodos Congelados (AEPYCC): Diego de León 44, 28006 Madrid; tel. (91) 4113156; fax (91) 5618178; fish exporters; Pres. RAMÓN MASO; Sec. IGNACIO MONTENEGRO GONZÁLEZ.

Asociación Industrial Textil de Proceso Algodonero (AITPA): Gran Vía de les Corts Catalanes 670, 08010 Barcelona; tel. (93) 3189200; fax (93) 3026235; e-mail aitpa@aitpa.es; internet www.aitpa.es; cotton textile industry; Pres. MANUEL DÍAZ.

Asociación Nacional Española de Fabricantes de Hormigón Preparado (ANEFHOP): Bretón de los Herreros 43, bajo, 28003 Madrid; tel. (91) 4416634; fax (91) 3993497; e-mail tecnico.anefhop@nauta.es; internet www.anefhop.com; f. 1968; concrete manufacturers; Pres. MANUEL A. SOBRAL CRUZ; Dir-Gen. FRANCISCO JAVIER MARTÍNEZ DE EULATE.

Asociación Nacional de Fabricantes de Pastas Papeleras, Papel y Cartón (ASPAPEL): Avda de Baviera 15, 28028 Madrid; tel. (91) 5763003; fax (91) 5774710; e-mail aspapel@aspapel.es; internet www.aspapel.es; f. 1977; paper and cardboard manufacturers; Pres. FLORENTINO NESPEREIRA; Dir-Gen. CARLOS REINOSO TORRES.

Comité de Gestión de Cítricos (CGC): Monjas de Santa Catalina 8, 4°, 46002 Valencia; tel. (96) 3521102; fax (96) 3510718; e-mail comite@citricos.org; internet www.citricos.org; citrus fruit exporters; Pres. VICENTE BORDILS RAMÓN; Dir JOSÉ MARTÍNEZ SERRANO.

Confederación de Cooperativas Agrarias de España (CCAE) (Confederation of Spanish Agrarian Co-operatives): Agustín de Bethencourt 17, 4°, 28003 Madrid; tel. (91) 5351035; fax (91) 5540047; e-mail ccae@ccae.es; internet www.ccae.es; Pres. FERNANDO MARCÉN; Dir-Gen. EDUARDO BAAMONDE NOCHE.

Confederación Española de Organizaciones Empresariales del Metal (CONFEMETAL): Príncipe de Vergara 74, 5°, 28006 Madrid; tel. (91) 5625590; fax (91) 5635758; e-mail informacion@confemetal.es; internet www.confemetal.es; metal asscns; Pres. CARLOS PÉREZ DE BRICIO OLARIAGA; Sec.-Gen. ANDRÉS SÁNCHEZ DE APELLÁNIZ.

Confederación Nacional de la Construcción (CNC): Diego de León 50, 2°, 28006 Madrid; tel. (91) 5624585; fax (91) 5615269; e-mail cnc@cnc.es; internet www.cnc.es; f. 1977; construction industry; Pres. JUAN FRANCISCO LAZCANO ACEDO.

Consejo Intertextil Español (CIE): Alvarez de Baena 7, 28006 Madrid; tel. (91) 5158180; fax (91) 5635085; e-mail cie@fedecon.es; internet www.consejointertextil.com; textile industry; Pres. JOSEP CASAS; Sec.-Gen. JORDI FONT; 7 mem. asscns.

Federación Empresarial de la Industria Química Española (FEIQUE): Hermosilla 31, 1°, 28001 Madrid; tel. (91) 4317964; fax (91) 5763381; e-mail info@feique.org; internet www.feique.org; chemical industry; Pres. FERNANDO ITURRIETA; Dir-Gen. FERNANDO GALBIS.

Federación Española de Asociaciones de Productores y Exportadores de Frutas, Hortalizas, Flores y Plantas Vivas (FEPEX): Miguel Angel 13, 4°A, 28010 Madrid; tel. (91) 3191050; fax (91) 3103812; e-mail fepex@fepex.es; internet www.fepex.es; f. 1987; fruit and vegetable producers and exporters; Pres. JORGE BROTONS; Dir JOSÉ MARÍA POZANCOS; 26 mem. asscns.

Federación Española de Industrias de la Alimentación y Bebidas (FIAB): Diego de León 44, 1° izqda, 28006 Madrid; tel.

SPAIN

(91) 4117211; fax (91) 4117344; e-mail fiab@fiab.es; internet www.fiab.es; f. 1977; food and drink industries; Pres. Jesús Serafín Pérez; Dep. Sec.-Gen. Horacio Gonzalez Aleman; 48 mem. asscns.

Federación de Industrias del Calzado Español (FICE): Núñez de Balboa 116, 3°, 28006 Madrid; tel. (91) 5627003; fax (91) 5620094; e-mail info@fice.es; internet www.fice.es; f. 1977; footwear; Pres. Rafael Calvo Rodríguez; Dir-Gen. Patricia Piñeiro Orellano.

Fundación Cotec: Marqués de Salamanca 11, 2° izqda, 28006 Madrid; tel. (91) 4364774; fax (91) 4311239; internet www.cotec.es; f. 1990; promotes technological innovation and understanding; Pres. José Ángel Sánchez Asiaín; Dir Juan Mulet.

Sociedad Estatal de Participaciones Industriales (SEPI): Velázquez 134, 28006 Madrid; tel. (91) 3961000; fax (91) 5628789; e-mail informacion@sepi.es; internet www.sepi.es; f. 1996; asscn of state-owned cos; Pres. Enrique Martínez Robles; Sec.-Gen. Fernando Sequeira Fuentes; 36 mems.

Unión de Empresas Siderúrgicas (UNESID): Castelló 128, 3°, 28006 Madrid; tel. (91) 5624010; fax (91) 5626584; e-mail unesid@unesid.org; internet www.unesid.org; f. 1968; asscn of Spanish producers of steel; Chair. Gonzalo Urquijo; Dir-Gen. Andrés Barceló.

EMPLOYERS' ORGANIZATIONS

Círculo de Empresarios: Paseo de la Castellana 15, 6°, 28046 Madrid; tel. (91) 5781472; fax (91) 5774871; e-mail asociacion@circulodeempresarios.org; internet www.circulodeempresarios.org; f. 1977; comprises CEOs of more than 180 major cos; Pres. Claudio Boada Pallerés; Sec.-Gen. Pedro Morenés Eulate.

Confederación Española de Organizaciones Empresariales (CEOE) (Spanish Confederation of Employers' Organizations): Diego de León 50, 28006 Madrid; tel. (91) 5663400; fax (91) 5622562; e-mail ceoe@ceoe.es; internet www.ceoe.es; f. 1977; covers industry, agriculture, commerce and service sectors; comprises 210 orgs; Pres. Gerardo Díaz Ferrán; Sec.-Gen. José María Lacasa Aso.

Confederación Empresarial de Madrid (CEIM) (Madrid Confederation of Employers and Industries): Diego de León 50, 1°, 28006 Madrid; tel. (91) 4115317; fax (91) 5627537; internet info@ceim.es; internet www.ceim.es; f. 1978; small, medium and large businesses; Pres. Arturo Fernández Alvarez; Sec. Alejandro Couceiro.

Confederación Empresarial Valenciana (CEV): Plaza Conde de Carlet 3, 46003 Valencia; tel. (96) 3155720; fax (96) 3923199; e-mail cev@cev.es; internet www.cev.es; f. 1977; Pres. José Vicente González Pérez; Sec.-Gen. Enrique Soto Ripoll.

Confederación Empresarial Vasca/Euskal Entrepresarien Konfederakuntza (CONFEBASK): Gran Vía 45, 2°, 48011 Bilbao; tel. (94) 4021331; fax (94) 4021333; e-mail confebask@confebask.es; internet www.confebask.es; f. 1983; Pres. Miguel Lazpiur; Sec.-Gen. José Guillermo Zubía Guinea.

Confederación Española de la Pequeña y Mediana Empresa (CEPYME): Diego de León 50, 3°, 28006 Madrid; tel. (91) 4116161; fax (91) 5645269; e-mail cepyme@cepyme.es; internet www.cepyme.es; small and medium businesses; Pres. Antonio Masa Godoy; Sec.-Gen. José Manuel Vilar Martínez.

Fomento del Trabajo Nacional/Foment del Treball Nacional—Confederación Empresarial de Catalunya: Vía Laietana 32, 08003 Barcelona; tel. (93) 4841200; fax (93) 4841230; e-mail foment@foment.com; internet www.foment.com; f. 1771 as Real Compañía de Hilados de Algodón del Principado de Catalunya; devt of national labour; Pres. Joan Rosell Lastortras; Sec.-Gen. Juan Pujol Segarra.

UTILITIES

Comisión Nacional de Energía (CNE): Alcalá 47, 28014 Madrid; tel. (91) 4329600; fax (91) 5776218; e-mail dre@cne.es; internet www.cne.es; f. 1999; part of Ministry of Industry, Tourism and Trade; regulates energy systems; Pres. María Teresa Costa Campi.

Instituto para la Diversificación y Ahorro de la Energía (IDAE): Madera 8, 28004 Madrid; tel. (91) 4564900; fax (91) 5230414; e-mail comunicacion@idae.es; internet www.idae.es; f. 1974 as Centro de Estudios de la Energía; under control of General Secretariat of Energy (Ministry of Industry, Tourism and Trade); Dir-Gen. Enrique Jiménez Larrea.

Secretaría General de Energía: Paseo de la Castellana 160, 28046 Madrid; tel. (902) 446006; fax (91) 4587704; e-mail secgenenergia@mityc.es; internet www.mityc.es/energia; part of Ministry of Industry, Tourism and Trade; Sec.-Gen. Pedro Marín Uribe.

Electricity

Asociación Española de la Industria Eléctrica (UNESA): Francisco Gervás 3, 28020 Madrid; tel. (91) 5674800; fax (91) 5674987; e-mail info@unesa.es; internet www.unesa.es; f. 1944; groups principal electricity cos; Pres. Eduardo Montes; Sec.-Gen. Pascual Sala.

Operador del Mercado Ibérico de Energía—Polo Español (OMEL): Alfonso XI 6, 4° y 5°, 28014 Madrid; tel. (91) 6598900; fax (91) 5240396; e-mail info@omel.es; internet www.omel.es; f. 1997; Spanish branch of the Iberian Energy Market; Pres. and CEO Pedro Mejía Gómez.

Red Eléctrica de España (REE): Paseo del Conde de los Gaitanes 177, 28109 Madrid; tel. (91) 6508500; fax (91) 6504542; e-mail redelectrica@ree.es; internet www.ree.es; manages and operates the national grid; Chair. Luis Atienza Serna.

Principal Electricity Companies

Endesa: Ribera del Loira 60, Campo de las Naciones, 28042 Madrid; tel. (91) 2131000; fax (91) 5638181; internet www.endesa.es; f. 1983; generator, distributor and vendor of electricity; also provides gas; 92% owned by Enel (Italy); Pres. Borja Prado Eulate; CEO Andrea Brentan.

E.ON España: Medio 12, 39003 Santander; tel. (942) 246000; fax (942) 246034; e-mail informacion@eon.com; internet www.eon-espana.com; f. 2008 following the acquisition of Enel Viesgo; subsidiary of E.ON AG (Germany); generation, distribution and supply; also provides gas; CEO Miguel Antoñanzas.

Gas Natural Fenosa: see Gas.

HC Energía: Plaza de la Gesta 2, 33007 Oviedo (Asturias); tel. (98) 5230300; e-mail hcenergia@hcenergia.com; internet www.hcenergia.com; f. 1919; fmrly Hidroeléctrica del Cantábrico; generation, distribution and supply; also provides gas; owned by Electricidade de Portugal; Pres. Manuel Menéndez Menéndez.

Iberdrola: Cardenal Gardoqui 8, 48008 Bilbao; tel. (944) 151411; fax (944) 154579; e-mail informacion@iberdrola.com; internet www.iberdrola.com; generation, distribution and supply; supplies mainly hydroelectric power; also provides gas; Pres. and CEO José Ignacio Sánchez Galán.

Gas

Enagás: Paseo de los Olmos 19, 28005 Madrid; tel. (902) 443700; e-mail contacta@enagas.es; internet www.enagas.es; operates gas transportation network; f. 1972; Pres. Antoni Llardén Carratlá.

Endesa: see Electricity.

Gas Natural Fenosa: Plaça del Gas 1, 08003 Barcelona; tel. (902) 199199; fax (93) 4029317; internet www.gasnatural.com; f. 1991 as Gas Natural; acquired Unión Fenosa (f. 1982) and adopted current name 2009; distributor of gas; generator, distributor and supplier of electricity; comprises regional distribution cos; Pres. Salvador Gabarró Serra; CEO Rafael Villaseca Marco.

Naturgas Energía: Plaza Pío Baroja 3, 2°, 48001 Bilbao; tel. (94) 4035700; fax (94) 4249733; e-mail webnaturgas@naturgasenergia.com; internet www.naturgasenergia.com; f. 1982; 65.6% owned by HC Energía; distributor of gas and electricity; Pres. Manuel Menéndez.

Water

Dirección General del Agua: Plaza de San Juan de la Cruz s/n, 28071 Madrid; tel. (91) 5976660; part of Ministry of the Environment, Agriculture and the Marine; co-ordinates water policy and supervises water management; Dir-Gen. Jaime Palop Piqueras.

Grupo Agbar: Torre Agbar, Avda Diagonal 211, 08009 Barcelona; tel. (93) 3422000; fax (93) 3422662; e-mail comunicacion@agbar.es; internet www.agbar.es; treatment of water and waste liquid; provision of sanitation and certification services; Pres. Jorge Mercader Miró; Dir-Gen. Angel Simón Grimaldos.

Grupo Aguas de Valencia: Gran Vía Marqués del Turia 19, 46005 Valencia; tel. (96) 3860600; e-mail aquas.valencia@aquasvalencia.es; internet www.aguasdevalencia.es; water and sewerage services; Pres. Eugenio Calabuig Gimeno.

TRADE UNIONS

Central Sindical Independiente y de Funcionarios (CSI-CSIF): Maudes 15, 1°, 28003 Madrid; tel. (91) 3100662; fax (91) 3102376; e-mail justicia@csi-csif.es; internet www.csi-csif.es; Pres. Domingo Fernández Veiguela; Sec.-Gen. Lourdes Blanco Amillategui.

Confederación General de Trabajo (CGT) (General Confederation of Labour): Sagunto 15, 1°, 28010 Madrid; tel. (91) 4475769; fax (91) 4453132; e-mail sp-comunicacion@cgt.es; internet www.cgt.es; Sec.-Gen. Jacinto Ceacero Cubillo.

Confederación Intersindical Galega (CIG): Rua Miguel Ferro Caaveiro 10, 3°, 15073 Santiago de Compostela; tel. (981) 564300; fax (981) 571082; e-mail secretarioxeral@galizacig.net; internet www

.galizacig.com; Galician confederation; Sec.-Gen. Xésus E. Seixo Fernández.

Confederación Nacional del Trabajo (CNT) (National Confederation of Labour): Secretariado Permanente del Comité Nacional, Julián Ceballos 23, 39300 Torrelavega, Cantabria; tel. (647) 892023; fax (942) 940983; e-mail sp_cn@cnt.es; internet www.cnt.es; f. 1910; Sec.-Gen. Fidel Manrique.

Confederación Sindical de Comisiones Obreras (CCOO) (Workers' Commissions): Fernández de la Hoz 12, 28010 Madrid; tel. (91) 7028000; fax (91) 3104804; e-mail ccoo@ccoo.es; internet www.ccoo.es; f. 1956; independent left-wing; Sec.-Gen. Ignacio Fernández Toxo; 1,050,000 mems (2005).

Eusko Langilleen Alkartasuna/Solidaridad de Trabajadores Vascos (ELA—Euskal Sindikatua) (Basque Workers' Solidarity): Barrainkua 13, 48009 Bilbao; tel. (94) 4037700; fax (94) 4037777; e-mail naziorte@elasind.org; internet www.ela-sindikatua.org; f. 1911; legally recognized 1977; independent; Sec.-Gen. Adolfo Muñoz Sanz; 109,318 mems.

Unión General de Trabajadores (UGT) (General Union of Workers): Hortaleza 88, 28004 Madrid; tel. (91) 5897601; fax (91) 5897603; e-mail info@cec.ugt.org; internet www.ugt.es; f. 1888; 8 affiliated federations; Sec.-Gen. Cándido Méndez Rodríguez.

Unión Sindical Obrera (USO) (Workers' Trade Union): Príncipe de Vergara 13, 7°, 28001 Madrid; tel. (91) 5774113; fax (91) 5772959; e-mail uso@uso.es; internet www.uso.es; f. 1960; independent; mem of European Trade Union Confederation and the International Trade Union Confederation; Sec.-Gen. Julio Salazar Moreno; 105,000 mems.

Transport

RAILWAYS

In 2008 the total rail network was 15,288 km. Spain's high-speed rail network includes a route from Madrid to Barcelona, which was completed in 2008, and was scheduled to be extended as far as the French border by 2012, and a link from Madrid to Valencia, which was completed in late 2010. Construction of a high-speed line linking Madrid with the Portuguese capital, Lisbon, was expected to be completed by 2013. From January 2005 the state railway company, RENFE, was divided into an operating and a management division, and the goods transport sector was open to competition. RENFE's monopoly on cross-border passenger transport ended in 2010.

Administrador de Infraestructuras Ferroviarias (Adif): Paseo del Rey 30, 28008 Madrid; tel. (91) 3008080; e-mail vialia@adif.es; internet www.adif.es; f. 2005; state-owned; fmrly part of state-owned railway co, Red Nacional de los Ferrocarriles Españoles (RENFE); manages railway infrastructure; Pres. Antonio González Marín; Sec.-Gen. María Rosa Sanz Cerezo.

RENFE Operadora: Avda Pío XII 110, 28036 Madrid; tel. (91) 3006600; e-mail comunicacion@renfe.es; internet www.renfe.es; f. 2005 following liberalization of railway sector; fmrly Red Nacional de los Ferrocarriles Españoles (RENFE); state-owned; Pres. José Salgueiro Carmona; Sec.-Gen. José L. Marroquín Mochales.

Eusko Trenbideak—Ferrocarriles Vascos (ET/FV) (Eusko-Tren): Atxuri 6, 48006 Bilbao; tel. (94) 4019900; fax (94) 4019901; e-mail attcliente@euskotren.es; internet www.euskotren.es; f. 1982; controlled by the Basque Govt; 188 km of 1,000 mm gauge; Dir-Gen. José Miguel Múgica Peral.

Ferrocarriles de Vía Estrecha (Feve) (Narrow Gauge Railways): Plaza de los Ferroviarios, 33012 Oviedo; tel. (98) 5297656; fax (98) 5281708; e-mail info@feve.es; internet www.feve.es; f. 1965 by integration of private cos; state-owned co. attached to the Ministry of Development; operates an extensive suburban and inter-urban network in northern Spain and the Murcia region; 1,194 km (2006) of 1,000 mm gauge track (of which 317 km were electrified); Pres. Angel Villalba Álvarez; Dir-Gen. Amador Robles Tascón.

Ferrocarrils de la Generalitat de Catalunya (FGC): Pau Casals 24, 8°, 08021 Barcelona; tel. (93) 3663000; fax (93) 3663350; e-mail nalba@fgc.net; internet www.fgc.net; f. 1979; 290 km, of which 161 km are electrified; Pres. Joan Torres i Carol.

Ferrocarrils de la Generalitat de València (FGV): Partida de Xirivelleta, 46014 Valencia; tel. (96) 3976565; fax (96) 3976580; e-mail webmaster_fgv@gva.es; internet www.fgv.es; f. 1986; 237 km of track; also operates Valencia Metro, with 4 lines and 143 km of track, and Tram Alicante (93 km); Pres. Mario Flores Lanuza; Dir-Gen. Marisa Gracia Giménez.

Metro de Bilbao: Navarra 2, 48001 Bilbao; tel. (94) 4254000; e-mail info@metrobilbao.net; internet www.metrobilbao.com; f. 1995; 38.9 km; 2 lines and 36 stations; Dir-Gen. Rafael Sarria Ansoleaga.

Metro de Madrid: Cavanilles 58, 28007 Madrid; tel. 902 444403; fax (91) 7212957; e-mail prensa@metromadrid.es; internet www.metromadrid.es; 283 km, 13 lines, 231 stations, also light railway network (Metro Ligero) of 28 km, 3 lines, 38 stations; Pres. Manuel Melis Maynar; Dir Ildefonso de Matías Jiménez.

Transports Metropolitans de Barcelona (TMB): Carrer 60, 21–31, Sector A. Polígono industrial Zona Franca, 08040 Barcelona; tel. (93) 2987000; e-mail tmb@tmb.net; internet www.tmb.net; 85.8 km, 6 lines, 104 stations (2008); Chair. Assumpta Escarp Gilbert Tintoré.

ROADS

The total road network in 2007 was 667,064 km, including 13,014 km of motorway, 12,832 km of main roads and 140,165 of secondary roads.

Dirección General de Carreteras: Paseo de la Castellana 67, 28071 Madrid; tel. (91) 5977000; fax (91) 5978535; part of Ministry of Development; Dir-Gen. Juan Francisco Lazcano Acedo.

SHIPPING

Spain has many ports. Among the most important are Algeciras, Barcelona, Valencia, Tarragona, Bilbao, Cartagena, Gijón, Huelva and Santa Cruz de Tenerife. The 1,790 ships of the merchant fleet totalled 2.9m. grt at December 2009.

Asociación de Navieros Españoles (ANAVE): Dr Fleming 11, 1° dcha, 28036 Madrid; tel. (91) 4580040; fax (91) 4579780; e-mail anave@anave.es; internet www.anave.es; shipowners' asscn; Pres. Juan Riva Francos; Dir Manuel Carlier de Lavalle.

Dirección General de la Marina Mercante: Ruíz de Alarcón 1, 28014 Madrid; tel. (91) 5979118; fax (91) 5979120; part of Ministry of Development; Dir-Gen. Felipe Martínez Martínez.

Puertos del Estado: Avda del Partenón 10, 28042 Madrid; tel. (91) 5245500; fax (91) 5245501; e-mail webmaster@puertos.es; internet www.puertos.es; Pres. Mariano Navas Gutiérrez.

Principal Shipping Companies

Acciona Trasmediterránea: Avda de Europa 10, Parque Empresarial La Moraleja, 28018 Alcobendas (Madrid); tel. (91) 4238500; fax (91) 4238555; e-mail info@trasmediterranea.es; internet www.trasmediterranea.es; f. 1917; Spanish ports, Balearic and Canary Is and Spanish North African, Algerian and Moroccan ports; Pres. Miguel Angel Fernández Villamandos; Dir-Gen. José Manuel Fernández Villamandos.

Agencia Marítima Española Evge: Avda Francesc Cambó 17, 08003 Barcelona; tel. (93) 3905800; fax (93) 2681750; e-mail evge@evgebcn.com; internet www.evgebcn.com; f. 1959; international shipping agents; Man. Dir Ramón Oliete Cossio.

Auximar, SL (Marítima del Norte): Miño 4, 28002 Madrid; tel. (91) 7454300; fax (91) 7454303; e-mail central@auximar.es; internet www.auximar.es; f. 1957; ship management, refrigerated cargo vessels, liquefied gas tankers; Dirs Iñigo de Sendagorta, Javier de Sendagorta.

Compañía Remolcadores Ibaizabal: Muelle de Tomás Olabarri 4, 5°, 48930 Las Arenas (Vizcaya); tel. (94) 4645133; fax (94) 4645565; e-mail ibaizabal@ibaizabal.org; internet www.remolcadoresibaizabal.com; f. 1906; ocean-going, coastal, harbour, salvage; Pres. Alejandro Aznar Sainz.

Compañía Trasatlántica Española: José Abascal 58, 3°, 28003 Madrid; tel. (91) 4514244; fax (91) 3993736; internet www.trasatlantica.com; f. 1850; freight services to Europe, North Africa, Caribbean, South America; Man. Dir Javier Villasante.

Empresa Naviera Elcano S.A.: José Abascal, 4°, 28003 Madrid; tel. (91) 5369800; fax (91) 4451324; e-mail elcanox@elcano.sa.es; internet www.navieraelcano.com; Pres. José Silvera.

Ership: Lagasca 88, 28001 Madrid; tel. (91) 4263400; fax (91) 5750883; e-mail chart@ership.com; internet www.ership.com; fmrly TAC; CEO Gonzalo Alvargonzález.

Naviera Pinillos: Capitán Haya 21, 28020 Madrid; tel. (91) 5556711; fax (91) 5569777; e-mail pinillos@pinillos.com; internet www.pinillos.com; f. 1840; part of Grupo Boluda; services between Canary Is and other Spanish ports; Pres. Vicente Boluda; Dir Angel Mato.

Nenufar Shipping: Manuel Ferreo 13, 28036 Madrid; tel. (91) 3158393; fax (91) 3158384; e-mail nenufar@nenufar.com; internet www.nenufar.com; f. 1983; part of Grupo Boluda; services to Spanish ports, Canary Is, Italy, Portugal, the United Kingdom, Morocco and Mauritania.

Repsol Naviera Vizcaina: Juan de Aguriaguerra 35, 2°, 48009 Bilbao; tel. (94) 4251100; fax (94) 4251143; f. 1956; world-wide, but particularly Mediterranean, Near East and Persian (Arabian) Gulf to Spain and transatlantic trade; Man. Dir Javier González Juliá.

CIVIL AVIATION

In 2011 there were more than 50 airports, almost all of which were equipped to receive international flights.

Dirección General de Aviación Civil: Paseo de la Castellana 67, 28071 Madrid; tel. (91) 5975356; fax (91) 5975357; internet www.fomento.es/aviacioncivil; Dir-Gen. MANUEL AMEIJEIRAS VALES.

Aeropuertos Españoles y Navegación Aérea (AENA): Arturo Soria 109, 28043 Madrid; tel. (91) 3211000; fax (91) 3212571; e-mail servicios-aeroportuarios@aena.es; internet www.aena.es; f. 1990; network of airports in Spain; Pres. MANUEL AZUAGA MORENO.

Principal Airlines

Air Europa Líneas Aéreas: Centro Empresarial Globalia, Apdo. Correos-132, 07620 Llucmajor; tel. (971) 178190; fax (971) 178353; internet www.air-europa.com; f. 1986; charter and scheduled services to Canary and Balearic Is, North Africa, Central, Southern and Eastern Europe; also Mexico, Cuba and Dominican Republic; Pres. JUAN JOSÉ HIDALGO ACERA; Dir-Gen. MANUEL PANADERO.

Binter Canarias: Aeropuerto de Gran Canaria, Parcela 9, del ZIMA Apdo 50, Gran Canaria; tel. (928) 579601; fax (928) 579603; e-mail info@bintercanarias.es; internet www.bintercanarias.com; f. 1988; scheduled services within Canary Islands and to Madeira, Morocco, Western Sahara and Mauritania; subsidiary of Grupo Iberia; Pres. PEDRO AGUSTÍN DEL CASTILLO; CEO RODOLFO NÚÑEZ RUANO.

Clickair: Solsones 2, Esc. B., 3° 1, Parc de Negocis Mas Blau, Prat de Llobregat, 08820 Barcelona; tel. (93) 3784400; e-mail info@clickair.com; internet www.clickair.com; f. 2006; low-cost airline; flights from Barcelona to other Spanish destinations (incl. Canary Islands), and to destinations in Europe, Israel, Russia and North Africa; Dir-Gen. ALEX CRUZ DE LLANO.

Iberia: Velázquez 130, 28006 Madrid; tel. (91) 5878787; internet www.iberia.com; f. 1927; domestic and international passenger and freight services to 106 destinations in 43 countries; provides maintenance, handling in airport, IT system solutions; merged with British Airways PLC (United Kingdom) to form International Airlines Group in Jan. 2011; Chair. and CEO ANTONIO VÁZQUEZ ROMERO.

Iberworld Airlines: Gran Vía Asima 23, Polígono Son Castelló, 07009 Palma de Mallorca; tel. (91) 229144; fax (91) 713184; e-mail iberworld@iberworld.com; internet www.iberworld.com; domestic, international and intercontinental charter flights.

Spanair: Edif. Spanair, Plaça Europa 54–56, 08902 L'Hospitalet de Llobregat; tel. (930) 002121; e-mail comunicacion@spanair.com; internet www.spanair.com; f. 1986; passenger scheduled and charter services within Spain, incl. Canary and Balearic Islands and within Europe, and to Algeria and The Gambia; 84.69% stake acquired by Iniciatives Empresarials Aeronàutiques in Jan. 2009; 11.6% owned by SAS Group (Denmark/Norway/Sweden); Pres. FERRAN SORIANO; CEO MIKE SZUCS.

Vueling Airlines: Edif. Muntadas, Berguedà 1, Parque de Negocios Mas Blau, El Prat de Llobregat, 08820 Barcelona; tel. (93) 3787878; fax (93) 3787879; e-mail clients@vueling.com; internet www.vueling.com; f. 2004; low-cost airline; domestic and international flights; Pres. JOSEP PIQUÉ; CEO LARS NYGAARD.

Tourism

Spain's tourist attractions include its climate, beaches and historic cities. Tourism makes an important contribution to the country's economy. In 2009 52.2m. foreign tourists visited Spain (57.2m. in 2008). Receipts from tourism totalled €56,352m. in 2008.

Instituto de Turismo de España (Turespaña): José Lázaro Galdiano 6, 28036 Madrid; tel. (91) 3433500; e-mail infosmile@tourspain.es; internet www.tourspain.es; promotes tourism; offices in Spain and abroad; Pres. JOAN MESQUIDE FERRANDO; Dir-Gen. ANTONIO BERNABÉ GARCÍA.

Secretaría de Estado de Comercio y Turismo: Paseo de la Castellana 160, 28071 Madrid; fax (91) 4578066; internet www.comercio.es; Sec. PEDRO MEJÍA GÓMEZ.

Defence

Military service was compulsory in Spain until December 2002. Conscription was abolished in 2000, while the final stages of professionalization were completed in 2003. Legislation to permit the entry of women to all sections of the armed forces took effect in early 1989. As assessed at November 2010, the total strength of the armed forces was 142,212, comprising: army 78,121; navy 21,606 (including 5,300 marines); air force 21,172; and 21,313 in joint service. The paramilitary Guardia Civil (Civil Guard) numbered 79,950. Spain became a member of the North Atlantic Treaty Organization (NATO, see p. 368) in May 1982. In December 1997 Spain's full integration into the military structure of NATO (with effect from January 1999) was approved by the alliance. Spain joined Western European Union (WEU, see p. 463) in November 1988. The US military presence in Spain totalled 1,256 at November 2010. In November of the same year the European Union (EU) ministers responsible for defence agreed to create a number of 'battlegroups' (each comprising about 1,500 men), which could be deployed at short notice to crisis areas around the world. The EU battlegroups, two of which were to be ready for deployment at any one time, following a rotational schedule, reached full operational capacity from 1 January 2007. Spain was the sole contributor to one battlegroup and led another with the participation of Germany, France and Portugal. Spain also participated in the Spanish-Italian Amphibious battlegroup, which was led by Italy.

Defence Budget: €7,150m. in 2011.

General Chief of Staff of Defence: Gen. JOSÉ JULIO RODRÍGUEZ FERNANDEZ.

Chief of Staff of the Army: Gen. FULGENCIO COLL BUCHER.

Chief of Staff of the Navy: Adm. Gen. MANUEL REBOLLO GARCÍA.

Chief of Staff of the Air Force: Gen. JOSÉ JIMÉNEZ RUIZ.

Education

Responsibility for education is divided between the central Government and the Autonomous Communities. Education is compulsory, and available free of charge, from the ages of six to 16 years. Pre-primary education caters for children up to six years of age and comprises two three-year stages. Primary education begins at six years of age and also comprises two three-year cycles. Lower secondary education (*Educación Secundaria Obligatoria—ESO*), which lasts for four years, is followed between the ages of 12 and 16 and culminates in the awarding of the *Graduado en ESO* certificate. Thereafter, students may take a vocational training course, lasting one or two years, or the two-year *Bachillerato* course, in preparation for university entrance; alternatively, they may follow a two-year specialist artistic or sports course. Private schools (which may be publicly funded), many of which are administered by the Roman Catholic Church, are responsible for the education of approximately one-third of Spanish children. In those Autonomous Communities in which a language other than Spanish is co-official (the Basque Country, the Balearic Islands, Catalonia, Galicia and Valencia), the teaching of the language of the Autonomous Community is compulsory at all levels, but the language of instruction varies according to location. In 2008/09 98.7% of children aged from three to five years were attending pre-primary institutions. In 2007/08 enrolment at primary schools included 100% of children in the relevant age-group, while enrolment at secondary schools in that year included 95% of children in the appropriate age-group.

Higher education includes university education, advanced vocational training, and advanced studies in the arts, plastic arts and design, and sport. In 2007 reforms to the university system were enacted with the aim of conforming to the Bologna Process, which sought to harmonize university systems within the European Higher Education Area. Under the reformed system, which was to be implemented during the 2010/11 academic year, there are three cycles within university education: Bachelor's (*Grado*), Master's (*Máster*) and Doctorate (*Doctor*). This replaced the previous three-cycle structure, which comprised the degrees of *Diplomatura*, *Licenciatura* and *Doctor*, complemented by degrees in engineering and architecture. Some 1.4m. students were attending university in 2009/10. There were 72 universities in that year, including the open university (Universidad Nacional de Educación a Distancia—UNED).

In 2008 total public expenditure on education was estimated at €49,887.2m.

SPANISH EXTERNAL TERRITORIES

The Spanish External Territories comprise mainly Ceuta and Melilla, two enclaves within Moroccan territory on the north African coast. Attached to Melilla, for administrative purposes, are Peñón de Vélez de la Gomera, a small fort on the Mediterranean coast, and two groups of islands, Peñón de Alhucemas and the Chafarinas. Ceuta and Melilla are seen as integral parts of Spain by the Spanish Government and have the status of autonomous cities, although Morocco has put forward a claim to both. Sovereignty over the uninhabited island of Perejil (known as Laila to the Moroccans) is disputed between Spain and Morocco.

CEUTA

Introductory Survey

LOCATION, CLIMATE, LANGUAGE, RELIGION

Ceuta, one of the two main enclaves of Spanish North Africa, is situated on the north African coast opposite Gibraltar, the Strait here being about 25 km wide. The average temperature is 17°C. Spanish and Arabic are spoken. The majority of Europeans are Roman Catholic, most North Africans being Muslim. There are small Hindu and Jewish communities.

CONTEMPORARY POLITICAL HISTORY

The population of the enclave is mostly Spanish. The proportion of Arab residents, however, has increased, owing to the large number of immigrants from Morocco. Those born in the territory are Spanish citizens and subjects. An ancient port and walled city, Ceuta was retained by Spain upon Moroccan independence from France in 1956. Having developed as a military and administrative centre for the former Spanish Protectorate in Morocco, Ceuta now functions as a bunkering and fishing port. In 1974 the town became the seat of the Capitanía General de Africa. Two-thirds of Ceuta's land area are used exclusively for military purposes.

In November 1978 King Hassan of Morocco stated his country's claim to Ceuta and the other main Spanish enclave in North Africa, Melilla, a claim that was reiterated following the opening of the Spanish frontier with Gibraltar in early 1985. In October 1981 Spain declared before the UN that Ceuta and Melilla were integral parts of Spanish territory. Spain rejects any comparison between the two enclaves and Gibraltar. From 1984 there was increasing unease over Spanish North Africa's future, following rioting in Morocco in January and the signing of the treaty of union between Libya and Morocco in August. In July 1985 the joint Libyan-Moroccan assembly passed a resolution calling for the 'liberation' of Ceuta and Melilla.

Details of Ceuta and Melilla's new draft statutes, envisaging the establishment of two local assemblies, with jurisdiction over such matters as public works, agriculture, tourism, culture and internal trade, were approved by the central Government in December 1985. Unlike Spain's other regional assemblies, however, those of Ceuta and Melilla were not to be vested with legislative powers. After negotiations with representatives of the Muslim community, in May 1986 the central Government agreed to grant Spanish nationality to more than 2,400 Muslims resident in the enclaves. At the general election held in June, the ruling Partido Socialista Obrero Español (PSOE) was successful in Ceuta.

In February 1988 it was announced that, in accordance with regulations of the European Community (EC, now European Union—EU, see p. 270), to which Spain had acceded in 1986, Moroccan citizens would in due course require visas to enter Spain. Entry to Spanish North Africa, however, was to be exempt from the new ruling.

In March 1988, after several months of negotiations, the central Government and principal opposition parties in Madrid reached a broad consensus on draft autonomy statutes for Spanish North Africa. Although it was envisaged that Spain would retain the territories, the possibility of a negotiated settlement with Morocco was not discounted. In July, seven years after the enclaves' first official request for autonomy, the central Government announced that the implementation of the territories' autonomy statutes was to be accelerated. Meanwhile, in October Morocco's Minister of Foreign Affairs formally presented his country's claim to Ceuta and Melilla to the UN General Assembly. In 1989 Spain and Morocco agreed to hold annual summit meetings in an effort to improve relations. At the general election held in October 1989, the ruling PSOE retained its Ceuta seats, despite allegations by the opposition Partido Popular (PP) that many names on the electoral register were duplicated.

In April 1990 the Spanish Government presented the autonomy statutes for discussion in the territories. It was confirmed that the enclaves were to remain an integral part of Spain, and that they were to be granted self-government at municipal, rather than regional, level. Moroccan political parties were united in their denunciation of what they considered an attempt to legalize Spanish possession of the territories. The draft autonomy statutes of Ceuta and Melilla were submitted to the Congreso de los Diputados (Congress of Deputies) in Madrid for discussion in October 1991. In November thousands of demonstrators, many of whom had travelled from the enclaves, attended a protest march in Madrid (organized by the Governments of Ceuta and Melilla), in support of demands for full autonomy for the territories. In early 1992, however, the central Government confirmed that the assemblies of Ceuta and Melilla were not to be granted full legislative powers. At the general election of June 1993 the PSOE of Ceuta lost its one seat in the Congreso and its two seats in the Senado (Senate) to the PP.

The final statutes of autonomy were approved by the Spanish Government in September 1994, in preparation for their presentation to the Cortes (parliament). The statutes provided for 25-member local assemblies, with powers similar to those of the municipal councils of mainland Spain. Each assembly would elect from among its members a city president. The proposals for limited self-government were not well received in Ceuta where, in October, a general strike received widespread support, while demonstrations subsequently took place in both Ceuta and Madrid. Following their approval by the Congreso de los Diputados in December, the autonomy statutes were ratified by the Senado in February 1995. Approval of the statutes by the Spanish Cortes was denounced by Morocco, which declared that the recovery of Ceuta and Melilla was to be one of its major objectives.

Elections for the new local assemblies were held in May 1995. In Ceuta the PP won nine of the 25 seats, Progreso y Futuro de Ceuta (PFC) six, the nationalist Ceuta Unida (CEU) four and the PSOE three. Basilio Fernández López of the PFC was re-elected Mayor/President, heading a coalition with CEU and the PSOE. Mustafa Mizziam Ammar, leader of the Partido Democrático y Social de Ceuta (PDSC), became the first Muslim candidate ever to be elected in the territory.

In February 1996 the Spanish and Moroccan Prime Ministers met in Rabat, Morocco, for their first summit meeting since December 1993. At the general election held in March 1996, the three PP delegates to the Cortes in Madrid were re-elected. In July Mayor/President Fernández López resigned after seven months at the head of a minority administration, and was replaced by Jesús Fortes Ramos of the PP, who urged that the enclave be considered a fully autonomous region.

In mid-1996 attention focused once again on the issue of illegal immigration from Africa. Both Ceuta and Melilla appealed to the EU for financial assistance to counter the problems arising from the enclaves' attractive location as an entry point to Europe and from the recent implementation of the EU's Schengen Agreement permitting the free movement of persons among the accord's signatory countries. Negotiations in Madrid in October between the Spanish Minister of the Interior and his Moroccan counterpart resulted in an agreement on the establishment of two joint commissions to address the specific problems of illegal immigration and drugs-trafficking. At further discussions in December, for the first time since the signing of a joint accord in 1992, Morocco agreed to the readmission of illegal immigrants held in the Spanish enclaves. In September the Secretary-General of the North Atlantic Treaty Organization (NATO) confirmed that Ceuta and Melilla would remain outside the Alliance's sphere of protection if Spain were to be fully integrated into NATO's military structure.

At the elections of June 1999 the most successful party was the Grupo Independiente Liberal (GIL), which secured 12 of the 25 seats in the Assembly. Antonio Sampietro Casarramona of the GIL replaced Jesús Fortes Ramos of the PP as Mayor/President in August, following the latter's removal from office by a motion of censure supported by a rebel PSOE deputy, Susana Bermúdez. The defection to the GIL of the socialist deputy was ostensibly due to the PSOE's apparent refusal to allocate her the education and culture portfolio, as desired. The authorities subsequently announced that a judicial inquiry into the defection of Bermúdez was to be conducted.

Both the PSOE and the PP accused the GIL of having bribed the deputy to transfer her allegiance. In March 2000 Sampietro and Bermúdez were charged with bribery. At the general election held on 12 March, Ceuta's three PP representatives in Madrid, one deputy and two senators, all secured re-election.

In early 1999 it was conceded that the security barrier along Ceuta's border with Morocco was proving inadequate. The EU-funded project had been initiated five years previously but remained unfinished. Between January and July alone a total of 21,411 illegal immigrants were apprehended on Ceuta's frontier and returned to Morocco. In November border security was reinforced by the army. Further improvements to the barrier were completed in February 2000. The implementation in that month of new legislation relating to immigrants' rights obliged the border post at Ceuta to provide legal assistance to those being denied entry to Spain by the police. In May it was revealed that during 1999 a total of 700,000 illegal immigrants had been refused admission to Spanish North Africa.

In Morocco, meanwhile, King Hassan died in July 1999. In January 2000 Prime Minister José María Aznar visited Ceuta and Melilla (although in his capacity as President of the PP, rather than President of the Government), describing the enclaves as constant parts of Spain's future. Morocco subsequently cancelled a scheduled official visit of the Spanish Minister of Foreign Affairs (although the official reason given by the Moroccan authorities for the cancellation was that King Muhammad VI was on holiday). In May Aznar declared that the controversial immigration law, which had taken effect in February, would need to be reviewed, as, since its entry into force, more than 82,000 immigrants had applied for Spanish residency permits. Large numbers of immigrants continued to enter the two enclaves illegally throughout 2000, and further clashes between migrants and the security forces were reported. The immigration law reforms, which entered into force in January 2001, intended to assist those seeking asylum but offered severe penalties to illegal immigrants and to traffickers in and employers of illegal immigrants. Protests against the reforms were staged in Spanish North Africa, as in Spain.

In September 2000, following a ruling in the Spanish courts that Ceuta and Melilla could not be considered to be autonomous communities, the ruling GIL proposed in the Ceuta Assembly that the Spanish Government grant Ceuta greater autonomy. Discussions on the proposal, which proved highly emotive, led to disturbances within the Assembly. However, the motion was subsequently carried by a majority vote.

In January 2001 five Ceuta councillors resigned their posts and announced their departure from the GIL, thus depriving the party of its majority in the Assembly. Former PSOE deputy Bermúdez subsequently withdrew her support for the GIL, which had previously enabled the party to assume office. A motion of censure against Sampietro, proposed by the PP, the PSOE, the PDSC and one of the former GIL councillors, was carried in February, with the support of 17 of the 25 deputies, and Juan Jesús Vivas Lara of the PP was appointed Mayor/President. A new Council was subsequently announced, including the five 'rebel' councillors (now members of the Grupo Mixto). The Vice-President of the Council, Jesús Simarro Marín, resigned in July; Cristina Bernal Durán was appointed to replace him.

The Government announced in September 2001 that the identification papers of Moroccans wishing to enter Ceuta and Melilla would be examined more closely and increased the police presence at the frontiers. In August the human rights organization Amnesty International had accused the Spanish Government of the systematic abuse of the rights of homeless children from Morocco and Algeria, citing Melilla and Ceuta as regions where the worst offences occurred.

Relations with Morocco remained tense in late 2001, especially following that country's abrupt withdrawal of its ambassador from Madrid in October. Relations were threatened again in July 2002, after the occupation of Perejil, a small islet near Ceuta, by 12 Moroccan soldiers. Spain made a formal protest to the Moroccan Government on 12 July, but Morocco refused to withdraw its men, claiming that Perejil (known as Laila to the Moroccans) had been a part of Morocco since independence in 1956. Four Spanish gunboats were dispatched to patrol the locality and Spanish soldiers reoccupied the island on 17 July. A subsequent US-mediated arrangement resulted in agreement by both countries to leave the islet unoccupied. However, in September Morocco reasserted its claims to Ceuta and Melilla at the UN. Later in the month Morocco additionally accused Spain of violating its airspace and territorial waters more than 90 times since July, and cancelled a scheduled meeting with Spain in protest against the alleged landing of a Spanish military helicopter on Perejil; Spain denied the claim. In response to several border incidents and in an attempt to halt illegal immigration, Spain ordered the permanent closure of the border with Morocco at Benzu in October.

A bilateral immigration accord signed by Spain and Morocco in February 2003 proposed the repatriation to Morocco of 200 illegal immigrant minors from Ceuta and Melilla in March. In early 2003 measures to strengthen border security were increased. Moreover, a series of suicide bombings launched against Western targets in Casablanca in May, killing up to 45 people, resulted in a further tightening of border security. It was believed that one of the leaders of the militant Islamist group thought to be responsible for the attacks was a resident of Ceuta, and that others involved in the bombings had subsequently fled to mainland Spain via Ceuta. In June the Spanish Government's delegate in Ceuta initiated a request to the Ministry of Foreign Affairs in Madrid to withdraw citizenship from any dual-nationals in the enclave who were proven criminals, members of fundamentalist groups or pro-Moroccan. At the regional elections held in May 2003, the PP achieved an absolute majority in Ceuta for the first time, winning 19 of 25 seats, while the Unión Demócrata Ceutí (UDCE), which represented the Muslim population, secured three. Juan Jesús Vivas Lara remained as Mayor/President.

In September 2003 Aznar visited Morocco for bilateral discussions, although the issue of sovereignty over Spain's North African possessions was reportedly avoided. In 2003 it was estimated that around 3,000 immigrants passed through Ceuta, and the enclave received more than 1,400 asylum requests, compared with 372 in 2002 and 82 in 2001. Official figures stated that 18% of the requests processed in 2003 were successful. In December 2003 Morocco and Spain made progress towards reaching an accord on the repatriation of illegal immigrant minors; however, a final agreement was not signed. Human rights groups criticized the two centres provided by the Spanish Government for immigrants as inadequate.

At the general election held on 14 March 2004, the PP retained the deputy and senators elected by Ceuta. In September the Mayor/President, Vivas Lara, met with the newly elected Spanish Prime Minister, José Luis Rodríguez Zapatero, to discuss the possible change in status of Ceuta from Ciudad Autónoma (Autonomous City) to Comunidad Autónoma (Autonomous Community), in line with other areas of Spain. In that year the height of the barrier separating Ceuta and Morocco reached 6 m. In November the central Government unveiled plans to build reception centres for immigrants on the mainland, to which illegal immigrants arrested in Ceuta and Melilla would be transported.

In 2005 potential immigrants continued to attempt to gain access to Europe through Ceuta and Melilla, with a succession of groups of would-be immigrants attempting to scale the walls separating the enclaves from Morocco. In September five would-be immigrants were killed by security forces during an attempt by some 600 people to climb the wall into Ceuta. It was announced at a Spanish-Moroccan summit held in late September in Seville, Spain, that security on both sides of the border would be increased following the attempts; however, the waves of immigration continued in early October, and more deaths resulted. Concern arose that immigrants captured by Moroccan security forces were being abandoned in Morocco's south-western desert. In October the Spanish Government authorized €3m. to improve facilities for immigrants in the enclaves. Heightened security reduced the number of attempts being made to climb the walls, but it appeared that immigrants were looking for new (and potentially more dangerous) routes to Europe via the Canary Islands.

In October 2005 the Congreso de los Diputados in Madrid reaffirmed the integral Spanish nature of the enclaves. In early 2006 Zapatero made the first official visit by a Prime Minister to the enclaves in over 25 years. His visit was condemned by the Moroccan authorities as a provocation, despite the fact that relations between Spain and Morocco had been favourable during the first two years of Zapatero's administration, with increasing co-operation on immigration issues. In the same month the Government Delegate in Ceuta, Jerónimo Nieto, was replaced by José Jenaro García-Arreciado Batanero.

In February 2007 the Spanish Government reached an agreement with the Governments of Ceuta and Melilla to abandon plans to change the cities' status to that of Autonomous Communities. In return, more powers would be devolved to the cities in the areas of employment and social services, and their budgets would be increased. At elections held on 27 May, the PP retained its absolute majority in the Assembly, again winning 19 of the 25 seats; the UDCE, in alliance with the left-wing Izquierda Unida, secured four seats, while the PSOE won two. Vivas Lara resumed office as Mayor/President. The entire regional executive of the PSOE, headed by Secretary-General Antonia Palomo, resigned as a result of the party's poor performance in the elections. In October ongoing divisions within the local branch of the PSOE led to its dissolution, and the party's national leadership delegated a commission to assume temporary responsibility for PSOE activities in Ceuta. (The local branch of the PSOE resumed activities under a newly elected Secretary-General, José Antonio Carracao Meléndez, in December 2008.)

In early November 2007 a two-day visit to Ceuta and Melilla by King Juan Carlos, his first since acceding to the throne in 1975, was warmly welcomed by residents, but provoked considerable anger in Morocco. The Moroccan Government recalled its ambassador from Madrid for consultations ahead of the visit, which it deemed regret-

SPANISH EXTERNAL TERRITORIES

Ceuta

table and provocative. The Spanish Prime Minister sought to defuse tensions, insisting that relations with Morocco, which had improved in recent years, remained strong. However, Morocco's King Muhammad VI noted that Spain risked jeopardizing bilateral relations, and urged Spain to engage in dialogue with Morocco over the disputed enclaves. Later in November the Moroccan Government postponed a planned visit to Rabat by the Spanish Minister of Development. The Moroccan ambassador to Spain returned to Madrid in January 2008, following a visit to Rabat by the Spanish Minister of Foreign Affairs and Co-operation, Miguel Angel Moratinos, who delivered a conciliatory letter from Prime Minister Zapatero to King Muhammad.

At the general election held on 9 March 2008, the PP retained Ceuta's one seat in the Congreso de los Diputados and its two seats in the Senado. In April the Government of Ceuta opposed plans to reorganize the Spanish armed forces, amid fears that they would result in a substantial reduction in the number of troops stationed in the city. However, the central Government rejected this suggestion, insisting that the composition of the forces deployed in its North African territories would change, but that it did not intend to reduce overall numbers. In the following month José Fernández Chacón was appointed to replace José Jenaro García-Arreciado Batanero as Government Delegate in Ceuta.

Efforts to strengthen border security were increased in late 2008, after the militant Islamist al-Qa'ida Organization in the Land of the Islamic Maghreb (AQIM) announced that it intended to intensify its campaign of violence against the governments of North Africa. (Previously confined largely to Algeria, the group had latterly staged several bomb attacks in neighbouring countries, and its leader, Abu Musab Abd al-Wadud, had reportedly stated his intention to expand its activities into Europe.) In April 2011 a group thought to be affiliated to AQIM issued a threat to carry out bomb attacks in Ceuta and Melilla during Easter celebrations later that month.

In October 2009 the Vice-President and Councillor of the Presidency, Pedro Gordillo Durán, was forced to resign from office, following allegations that he had demanded favours of a sexual nature from a female job-seeker in return for granting her employment in the civil service.

In late April 2011 it was estimated that a total of seven political organizations were to contest elections to the Assembly, which were due to be held on 22 May.

CONSTITUTION AND GOVERNMENT

Following the adoption of statutes of autonomy and the establishment of local assemblies in 1995, Ceuta and Melilla remain integral parts of Spain, but have greater jurisdiction over matters such as public works, internal trade and tourism. Each enclave has its own Mayor/President. Ceuta, Melilla and the island dependencies are known as *plazas de soberania*, fortified enclaves over which Spain has full sovereign rights. In both Ceuta and Melilla civil authority is vested in a Government Delegate (Delegado del Gobierno) directly responsible to the Ministry of the Interior in Madrid. This official is usually assisted by a government sub-delegate. There is also one delegate from each of the Ministries in Madrid.

ECONOMIC AFFAIRS

In 2008, according to official estimates, the gross domestic product (GDP) of Ceuta was equivalent to €22,320 per head, ranking 11th (in terms of GDP per head) in a list of the 19 Spanish autonomous regions. According to preliminary official estimates, total GDP was €1,611.1m. in 2009. The population of Ceuta increased by an annual average of 0.2% in 2002–09. Real GDP growth for 2008 was estimated at 1.8%.

Agricultural activity in Ceuta is negligible, as is employment in the sector; according to preliminary estimates, the sector contributed just 0.2% of GDP in 2009.

Industry is on a limited scale (although there is a local brewery), but the sector contributed 13.7% of GDP in 2009, and 10.8% of the employed population were engaged in the sector, on average, during the final quarter of that year. Construction contributed 7.4% of GDP in 2009, and 5.0% of the employed population were engaged in the sub-sector, on average, in the final quarter of the same year.

Services contributed an estimated 86.1% of GDP in 2009, and some 88.4% of the employed population were engaged in the sector, on average, in the final quarter of that year.

Most of the population's food is imported, with the exception of fish, which is obtained locally (sardines and anchovies are among the most significant catches). A large proportion of the tinned fish is sold outside Spain. More important to the economies of Ceuta and Melilla is the port activity; most of their exports take the form of fuel supplied—at very competitive rates—to ships. Most of the fuel comes from the Spanish refinery in Tenerife. Ceuta's port received a total of 12,545 ships in 2010. Most trade is conducted with other parts of Spain. In 2010 Ceuta's trade deficit was around €270m. In that year the principal source of imports (accounting for some 24.1% of the total value) was the Netherlands; other major suppliers were the People's Republic of China and Portugal. Switzerland was the principal market for exports. The principal imports in 2010 were mineral fuels and oils (accounting for more than 61% of the total value), and textiles and clothing. The principal exports in the same year were plastics. Tourism makes a significant contribution to the territory's economy. In 2009 there were 77,659 visitors to Ceuta, attracted by duty-free goods. In 2004 there was an estimated budget surplus of €750,000, equivalent to 0.1% of GDP. The annual rate of inflation averaged 2.6% in 2002–10; the rate was 1.5% in 2010. According to provisional estimates, on average, some 24.8% of the labour force were unemployed during the final quarter of 2010.

Upon the accession in January 1986 of Spain to the European Community (EC, now European Union—EU, see p. 270), Ceuta was considered a Spanish city and therefore as European territory, and joined the organization as part of Spain. It retained its status as a free port. The statute of autonomy, adopted in early 1995, envisaged the continuation of the territory's fiscal benefits. Euro notes and coins became the sole legal tender on 28 February 2002.

Sustained Spanish economic growth in the 2000s and successive enlargements of the EU that took place during that decade limited Spain's access to EU aid, with the result that, although income in the enclave had not improved significantly, subsidies for Ceuta would be progressively reduced during the period 2007–13, with a view to their eventual withdrawal. The city's consolidated budget for 2010 included current and capital transfers from the Spanish state of €66.6m and €12.3m., respectively. Ceuta's economy relies heavily on a transient Moroccan work-force; unofficial estimates of unemployment among Ceuta's permanent residents suggest a rate of some 35%, the highest in Spain.

Statistical Survey

Sources (unless otherwise stated): Administración General del Estado, Beatriz de Silva 4, 51001 Ceuta; tel. (956) 512616; fax (956) 511893; Instituto Nacional de Estadística, Paseo de la Castellana 183, 28071 Madrid; tel. (91) 5839100; fax (91) 5839158; internet www.ine.es; *Memoria Socioeconómico y Laboral de 2004:* Consejo Económico y Social, Edif. La Tahoma, Esquina Salud Tejero y Dueñas, Ceuta; tel. (956) 519131; fax (956) 519146; e-mail ces-ceuta@ceuta.es.

AREA AND POPULATION

Area: 19.7 sq km (7.6 sq miles).

Population (census results): 67,615 at 1 March 1991; 71,505 at 1 November 2001 (males 35,991, females 35,514). *2010* (official estimate at 1 July): 75,417 (males 37,967, females 37,450).

Density (1 July 2010): 3,828 per sq km.

Population by Age and Sex (official estimates at 1 July 2010): *0–14:* 14,865 (males 7,602, females 7,264); *15–64:* 51,310 (males 24,763, females 24,956); *65 and over:* 9,242 (males 4,009, females 5,231); *Total* 75,417 (males 37,967, females 37,450).

Births, Marriages and Deaths (2009, provisional): Live births 1,516 (birth rate 20.1 per 1,000); Marriages 393 (marriage rate 5.4 per 1,000); Deaths 526 (death rate 7.3 per 1,000).

Life Expectancy (years at birth, 2008): 79.6 (males 77.0; females 82.1).

Immigration and Emigration (excl. Spanish territory, 2009): Immigrants 423; Emigrants 117.

Economically Active Population ('000 persons aged 16 years and over, October–December 2010, estimates): *Total employed* 24.2; Unemployed 8.0; *Total labour force* 32.2 (males 20.1, females 12.1).

AGRICULTURE, ETC.

Livestock (animals slaughtered, 2004): Sheep 1,025; Goats 108.

Fishing (metric tons, live weight of catch): 304.1 in 2002; 310.8 in 2003; 236.8 in 2004.

FINANCE

Currency and Exchange Rates: 100 cent = 1 euro (€). *Sterling and Dollar Equivalents* (31 December 2010): £1 sterling = 1.172 euros; US $1 = 0.748 euros; 10 euros = £8.54 = $13.36. *Average Exchange Rate* (euros per US $): 0.6827 in 2008; 0.7198 in 2009; 0.7550 in 2010. Note: The local currency was formerly the Spanish peseta. From the introduction of the euro, with Spanish participation, on 1 January 1999, a fixed exchange rate of €1 = 166.386 pesetas was in effect. Euro notes and coins were introduced on 1 January 2002. The euro and local currency circulated alongside each other until 28 February, after which the euro became the sole legal tender.

SPANISH EXTERNAL TERRITORIES

Ceuta

Budget (€ '000, 2004): *Revenue:* Current operations 170,621.8 (Direct taxation 6,397.6, Indirect taxation 90,247.4, Rates and other revenue 14,342.8, Current transfers 54,106.2, Estate taxes 5,527.7); Capital operations 49,002.7 (Capital transfers 31,715.2, Transfers of real investments 3,073.4, Assets 704.3, Liabilities 13,509.7); Total 219,624.5. *Expenditure:* Current operations 153,214.7 (Wages and salaries 74,948.9, Goods and services 55,016.6, Financial 3,561.4, Current transfers 19,687.8); Capital operations 65,659.8 (Real investments 53,365.5, Capital transfers 0.0, Assets 1,705.0, Liabilities 10,589.2); Total 218,874.5.

Cost of Living (Consumer Price Index; base: 2006 = 100): All items 105.8 in 2008; 106.4 in 2009; 108.0 in 2010.

Gross Domestic Product (€ million at current prices, provisional): 1,558.4 in 2007; 1,611.8 in 2008; 1,611.1 in 2009.

Gross Domestic Product by Economic Activity (€ million at current prices, 2009, provisional): Agriculture and fishing 3.4; Energy 61.9; Construction 110.8; Other industry 32.4; Services 1,287.6; *Sub-total* 1,496.1; Net taxes on products 115.0; *GDP at market prices* 1,611.1.

EXTERNAL TRADE

Principal Commodities (€ million, 2010): *Imports:* Milk and dairy products, eggs, honey, etc. 15.4; Mineral fuels and oils, and products thereof 166.1; Textile and clothing 29.4; Footwear 10.0; Machinery and equipment (incl. electrical), and parts thereof 6.3; Vehicles (excl. rail or tram), and parts thereof 8.0; Total (incl. others) 271.0. *Exports:* Total 0.1.

Principal Trading Partners (€ million, 2010): *Imports:* China, People's Republic 31.5; Netherlands 65.2; Portugal 14.1; Total (incl. others) 271.4. *Exports:* Switzerland 0.1; Total (incl. others) 0.1.

Source: Foreign Trade Database, Agencia Tributaria (Madrid).

TRANSPORT

Road Traffic (Ceuta and Melilla, 2009): Vehicles registered 5,085 (Passenger cars 3,435, Buses, etc. 7, Lorries and vans 737, Motorcycles 894, Tractors 2, Other 10).

Shipping (domestic and international, 2010): Vessels entered 12,545; Goods handled ('000 metric tons) 1,952; Passenger movements ('000) 1,894.

Civil Aviation (2008, preliminary): Flights 2,754; Passengers carried ('000) 25; Goods transported 3 metric tons.

TOURISM

Visitor Arrivals (by country of residence, 2002): France 2,653; Germany 700; Italy 1,076; Portugal 1,062; Spain 41,593; United Kingdom 1,430; USA 2,939; Total (incl. others) 61,356. *2009:* Total 77,659 (Spain 60,275).

COMMUNICATIONS MEDIA

Telephones (main lines in use, 2004): 24,849.

EDUCATION

(2005/06)

Pre-primary: 24 schools; 149 teachers; 2,961 students.

Primary: 22 schools; 411 teachers (excl. 42 engaged in both pre-primary and primary teaching); 5,948 students.

Secondary: First Cycle: 16 schools (of which 6 schools also provided second-cycle education and 5 provided vocational education, see below); 209 teachers (excl. 34 engaged in both secondary and primary teaching and 234 engaged in more than one cycle of secondary); 3,874 students.

Secondary: Second Cycle: 34 teachers; 1,298 students.

Secondary: Vocational: 83 teachers; 970 students.

Source: Ministry of Education and Science, Madrid.

Directory

Government

HEAD OF STATE

King of Spain: HM King JUAN CARLOS I (succeeded to the throne 22 November 1975).

Government Delegate in Ceuta: JOSÉ FERNÁNDEZ CHACÓN.

MEMBERS OF THE SPANISH PARLIAMENT

Deputy elected to the Congress in Madrid: FRANCISCO ANTONIO GONZÁLEZ PÉREZ (PP).

Representatives to the Senate in Madrid: NICOLÁS FERNÁNDEZ CUCURULL (PP), LUZ ELENA SANÍN NARANJO (PP).

COUNCIL OF GOVERNMENT
(May 2011)

The executive was formed by members of the Partido Popular (PP).

Mayor/President: JUAN JESÚS VIVAS LARA.
Councillor of Development: JUAN MANUEL DONCEL DONCEL.
Councillor of the Economy and Employment: GUILLERMO MARTÍNEZ ARCAS.
Councillor of Education, Culture and Women: MARÍA ISABEL DEU DEL OLMO.
Councillor of the Environment and Urban Services: YOLANDA BEL BLANCA.
Councillor of Health and Consumer Affairs: ADELA MARÍA NIETO SÁNCHEZ.
Councillor of the Interior: JOSÉ ANTONIO RODRÍGUEZ GÓMEZ.
Councillor of Finance: FRANCISCO MÁRQUEZ DE LA RUBIA.
Councillor of Social Affairs: CAROLINA PÉREZ GÓMEZ.
Councillor of Youth, Sports and New Technology: KISSY CHANDIRAMANI RAMESH.

GOVERNMENT OFFICES

Delegación del Gobierno: Beatriz de Silva 4, 51001 Ceuta; tel. (956) 984400; fax (956) 513671; e-mail roberto@ceuta.map.es.
Office of the Mayor/President: Plaza de Africa s/n, Asamblea, 1°, 51001 Ceuta; tel. and fax (956) 528309; e-mail presidencia@ceuta.es; internet www.ceuta.es.
Council of Development: Plaza de Africa s/n, Asamblea, 3°, 51001 Ceuta; tel. and fax (956) 528240; e-mail fomento@ceuta.es.
Council of the Economy and Employment: Edif. Ceuta Center, 1°, 51001 Ceuta; tel. and fax (956) 528386; e-mail economia@ceuta.es.
Council of Education, Culture and Women: Plaza de Africa s/n, Asamblea, 2°, 51001 Ceuta; tel. and fax (956) 528153; e-mail educacion@ceuta.es.
Council of the Environment and Urban Services: Plaza de Africa s/n, Asamblea, 3°, 51001 Ceuta; tel. and fax (956) 528164; e-mail medioambiente@ceuta.es; internet www.ceuta.es/medioambiente.
Council of Finance: Edif. Ceuta Center, 51001 Ceuta; e-mail hacienda@ceuta.es.
Council of Health and Consumer Affairs: Carretera San Amaro 12, Ceuta; tel. and fax (856) 200680; fax (856) 200723; e-mail sanidad@ceuta.es; internet www.ceuta.es/sanidad.
Council of the Interior: Edif. Polifuncional, Avda España, 51001 Ceuta; tel. (956) 528076.
Council of Social Affairs: Carretera San Amaro 12, Ceuta; tel. and fax (856) 200684; e-mail bsocial@ceuta.es.
Council of Youth, Sports and New Technologies: Avda de Africa s/n, Ceuta; tel. (956) 518844; fax (956) 510295.

Assembly

Election, 22 May 2011

	Seats
Partido Popular (PP)	18
Caballas*	4
Partido Socialista Obrero Español (PSOE)	3
Total	**25**

* Coalition of Unión Demócrata Ceutí (UDCE) and Parti Socialista del Pueblo del Ceuta (PSPC).

Election Commission

Junta Electoral de Zona y Provincial de Ceuta: Ceuta; Sec. FRANCISCO JAVIER IZQUIERDO CARBONERO.

Political Organizations

Izquierda Unida (IU): General Yagüe, 4-1°, 51001 Ceuta; tel. (956) 811941; e-mail izquierdaunidaceuta@hotmail.com; internet www.izquierda-unida.es; alliance of left-wing parties; Leader ROSA RODRÍGUEZ.

SPANISH EXTERNAL TERRITORIES

Ceuta

Partido Democrático y Social de Ceuta (PDSC): Bolivia 35, 51001 Ceuta; Muslim party; Leader MUSTAFA MIZZIAM AMMAR.

Partido Popular (PP): Teniente Arrabal 4, Edif. Ainara, Bajo, 51001 Ceuta; tel. (956) 518191; fax (956) 513218; e-mail ceuta@pp.es; internet www.ppceuta.es; fmrly Alianza Popular; national-level, centre-right party; Pres. JUAN JESUS VIVAS LARA; Sec.-Gen. JUAN MANUEL DONCEL DONCEL.

Partido Socialista Obrero Español (PSOE): Daóiz 1, 51001 Ceuta; tel. (956) 515553; e-mail infopsoe@psoe.es; internet www.ceuta.psoe.es; national-level, left-wing party; Sec.-Gen. JOSÉ ANTONIO CARRACAO MELÉNDEZ.

Partido Socialista del Pueblo de Ceuta (PSPC): Echegarray 1, Local 1D, 51001 Ceuta; tel. and fax (956) 518869; e-mail pspc@pspc.info; internet www.pspc.es; f. 1986 by dissident members of PSOE and others; contested May 2011 elections as part of 'Caballas' coalition with Unión Demócrata Ceutí; Sec.-Gen. IVÁN CHAVES.

Unión Demócrata Ceutí (UDCE): Avda Teniente-Coronel Gautier 22, 2° dcha, Ceuta; Muslim party; contested May 2011 elections as part of 'Caballas' coalition with Partido Socialista del Pueblo de Ceuta; Leader MUHAMMAD ALÍ.

There are also various civic associations.

Judicial System

Tribunal Superior de Justicia de Andalucía, Ceuta y Melilla: Plaza Nueva, 10, Palacio de la Real Chancillería, 18071 Granada, Spain; tel. (958) 002600; fax (958) 002720; e-mail webmaster.ius@juntadeandalucia.es; internet www.juntadeandalucia.es; Pres. LORENZO DEL RÍO.

Religion

CHRISTIANITY

The Roman Catholic Church

Bishop of Cádiz and Ceuta: ANTONIO CEBALLOS ATIENZA (resident in Cádiz), Vicar-Gen. FRANCISCO CORRERO TOCÓN, Obispado de Ceuta, Plaza de Nuestra Señora de Africa, 51001 Ceuta; tel. (956) 517732; fax (956) 513208; e-mail obispadoceuta@planalfa.es; internet www.obispadodecadizyceuta.org.

OTHER RELIGIONS

Ceuta has a large Muslim population (estimated at around 30,000), as well as Jewish and Hindu communities.

The Press

El Faro de Ceuta: Sargento Mena 8, 51001 Ceuta; tel. (956) 524035; fax (956) 524147; e-mail ceuta@grupofaro.es; internet www.elfaroceutamelilla.es; f. 1934; morning; Pres. RAFAEL MONTERO PALACIOS; Editors-in-Chief JOSÉ M. GALLARDO, TAMARA CRESPO; circ. 5,000.

El Pueblo de Ceuta: Independencia 11, 1°, 51001 Ceuta; tel. (956) 514367; fax (956) 517650; e-mail elpuebloredaccion@telefonica.net; internet www.elpueblodeceuta.es; f. 1995; daily; Dir and Editor-in-Chief SALVADOR VIVANCOS CANALES.

NEWS AGENCY

Agencia EFE: Milán Astray 1, 1°, Of. 8, 51001 Ceuta; tel. (956) 517550; fax (956) 516639; e-mail ceuta@agenciaefe.net; Correspondent RAFAEL PEÑA SOLER.

PRESS ASSOCIATION

Asociación de la Prensa: Beatriz de Silva 14, 1° E, 51001 Ceuta; tel. (956) 403713; fax (956) 528205; Pres. RAFAEL PEÑA SOLER.

Broadcasting

RADIO

Onda Cero Radio Ceuta: Delgado Serrano 1, 1° dcha, 51001 Ceuta; tel. (956) 200068; fax (956) 200179; internet www.ondacero.es; Dir RAFAEL ROMAGUERA MENA.

Radio Nacional de España: Real 90, 51001 Ceuta; tel. (956) 524688; fax (956) 519067; e-mail prensa@rtve.es; internet www.rtve.es; Dir EDUARDO SÁNCHEZ DORADO.

Radio Popular de Ceuta/COPE: Sargento Mena 8, 1°, 11701 Ceuta; tel. (956) 524200; fax (956) 524202; internet www.cope.es; Dir DANIEL OLIVA.

Radio Televisión Ceuta: Avda Alcalde Sánchez, Prado 3–5, Ceuta; tel. and fax (956) 524420; e-mail televidente@rtvce.es; internet www.rtvce.es; f. 2000; owned by Sociedad Española de Radiodifusión; commercial; Dir DANIEL OLIVA MARTÍN.

TELEVISION

Radio Televisión Ceuta: Real 90, Portón 4, 1° dcha, 51001 Ceuta; tel. (956) 511820; fax (956) 516820; internet www.rtvce.es; Dir MANUEL GONZÁLEZ BOLORINO.

Finance

BANKING

In 2007 there were nine banks operating in Ceuta, all of which were based in mainland Spain.

Banco Bilbao Vizcaya Argentaria (BBVA): Gonzalez de la Vega 8, 51001 Ceuta; tel. (956) 201238; fax (956) 510585; internet www.bbva.es; 4 brs.

Banco de España: Plaza de España 2, 51001 Ceuta; tel. (956) 513253; fax (956) 513108; internet www.bde.es.

Banco Español de Crédito (Banesto): Camoens 5, 51001 Ceuta; tel. (956) 524028; internet www.banesto.es.

Banco Popular Español: Paseo del Revellín 1, 51001 Ceuta; tel. (956) 515340; fax (956) 512970; internet www.bancopopular.es.

Banco Santander Central Hispano (BSCH): Paseo del Revellín 17–19, 51001 Ceuta; tel. (956) 511371; internet www.gruposantander.es; 2 brs.

Caja de Ahorros y Pensiones de Barcelona (La Caixa): Gran Vía s/n, 51001 Ceuta; tel. (956) 515886; fax (956) 513972; internet www.lacaixa.es; 4 brs.

Caja Duero: Sargento Coriat 5, 51001 Ceuta; tel. (956) 518040; fax (956) 517019; tel. www.cajaduero.es; 1 br.

Caja Madrid: Plaza de los Reyes s/n, 51001 Ceuta; tel. (956) 524016; fax (956) 524017; internet www.cajamadrid.es; 6 brs.

Montes de Piedad y Caja de Ahorros de Ronda, Cádiz, Almería, Málaga y Antequera (Unicaja): Paseo Revellín 21, 51001 Ceuta; tel. (956) 518340; fax (956) 519561; internet www.unicaja.es; 2 brs.

INSURANCE

MAPFRE: Paseo Marina Española 92, Edif. Patio Paramo, 51001 Ceuta; tel. (956) 519638; fax (956) 513916; e-mail balfaro@mapfre.com; internet www.mapfre.com; Commercial Man. BORJA ALFARO INFANTE; 3 offices.

Trade and Industry

Cámara Oficial de Comercio, Industria y Navegación: Dueñas 2, 51001 Ceuta; tel. (956) 509590; fax (956) 509589; e-mail camerceuta@camaras.org; internet www.camaraceuta.org; chamber of commerce; Pres. LUIS MORENO NARANJO; Sec.-Gen. MARÍA DEL ROSARIO ESPINOSA SUÁREZ.

Confederación de Empresarios de Ceuta: Paseo de las Palmeras, Edif. Corona 26–28, 51001 Ceuta; tel. (856) 200038; fax (956) 512010; e-mail info@confeceuta.es; internet www.confeceuta.es; employers' confed; Pres. RAFAEL MONTERO AVALOS; Sec.-Gen. JOSEFA GUERRERO RÍOS.

UTILITIES

Aguas de Ceuta Empresa Municipal, SA (ACEMSA): Solis 1, Edif. San Luis, Ceuta; tel. (956) 524619; e-mail aguasdeceuta@acemsa.es; internet www.acemsa.es; Pres. YOLANDA BEL BLANCO; Dir-Gen. MANUEL GÓMEZ HOYOS.

Empresa de Alumbrado Eléctrico de Ceuta SA: Beatriz de Silva 2, Ceuta; tel. (956) 511901; e-mail info@electricadeceuta.com; internet www.electricadeceuta.com; generates and transmits electricity; Rep. ALBERTO RAMÓN GAITÁN RODRÍGUEZ.

TRADE UNION

Confederación Sindical de Comisiones Obreras (CCOO): Alcalde Fructuoso Miaja 1, 51001 Ceuta; tel. (956) 516243; fax (956) 517991; e-mail ccoo.ce@ceuta.ccoo.es; internet www.ccoo.es; 3,214 mems (2004); Sec.-Gen. JOSÉ LUIS ARÓSTEGUI RUIZ.

Transport

Much of the traffic between Spain and Morocco passes through Ceuta; there are ferry services to Algeciras, Melilla, Málaga and Almería. Plans for an airport are under consideration. Helicopter services to Málaga are provided by Helisureste. There were 37 km of paved roads in Ceuta in 2009. Construction of a highway between the Port of Ceuta and the Moroccan border was due to be completed in

SPANISH EXTERNAL TERRITORIES

2011. The Port of Ceuta is one of the most important in the Mediterranean. In 2010 2.0m. metric tons of goods, 1.9m. passengers and 12,545 ships passed through the port.

Port of Ceuta: Autoridad Portuaria de Ceuta, Muelle de España s/n, 51001 Ceuta; tel. (956) 527000; fax (956) 527001; e-mail apceuta@puertodeceuta.com; internet www.puertodeceuta.com; Pres. JOSÉ FRANCISCO TORRADO LÓPEZ.

Acciona Trasmediterránea: Muelle Cañorero Dato 6, 51001 Ceuta; tel. (956) 505390; fax (956) 504714; e-mail info@trasmediterranea.es; internet www.trasmediterranea.es; f. 1917; services between Algeciras and Ceuta.

Euroferrys: Muelle Cañorero Dato, 51001 Ceuta; tel. (956) 507070; fax (956) 505588; e-mail clientes@euroferrys.com; internet www.euroferrys.com; f. 1998; owned by Acciona Trasmediterránea; passenger and cargo services between Algeciras and Ceuta; Pres. JOAQUÍN GONZÁLEZ SANJUÁN.

Tourism

Visitors are attracted by the historical monuments, the Parque Marítimo and the museums, as well as by the Shrine of Our Lady of Africa. There were 77,659 visitors to Ceuta in 2009, of whom 60,275 were from mainland Spain.

Servicios Turísticos de Ceuta: Baluarte de los Mallorquines, Edrissis s/n, 51001 Ceuta; tel. (856) 200560; fax (856) 200565; e-mail turismo@ceuta.es; internet www.ceuta.es/turismo.

Defence

Military authority is vested in a commandant-general. The enclaves are attached to the military region of Sevilla. In August 2003 Spain had 8,100 troops deployed in Spanish North Africa, compared with 21,000 in mid-1987. Two-thirds of Ceuta's land area are used exclusively for military purposes.

Commandant-General: ENRIQUE VIDAL DE LOÑO.

Education

The conventional Spanish facilities are available; however, there are also teachers of the Islamic religion in the city. The 22 primary schools in Ceuta had a total enrolment of 5,948 students in 2005/06, while 16 first cycle (from the ages of 12 to 16) secondary schools had an enrolment of 3,874 students; six secondary schools enrolled some 1,298 students for the *bachillerato*, and five schools also had 970 students enrolled on vocational courses. In higher education, links with the University of Granada are maintained and there is a branch of the Spanish open university (Universidad Nacional de Educación a Distancia—UNED).

MELILLA

Introductory Survey

LOCATION, CLIMATE, LANGUAGE, RELIGION

Melilla is situated on a small peninsula jutting into the Mediterranean Sea. The average temperature is 17°C. Spanish and Arabic are spoken. The majority of Europeans are Roman Catholic, most North Africans being Muslim.

CONTEMPORARY POLITICAL HISTORY

The population of Melilla is mostly Spanish. The proportion of Arab residents, however, has greatly increased, owing to the large number of immigrants from Morocco. Those born in the territory are Spanish citizens and subjects. Melilla was the first Spanish town to rise against the Government of the Popular Front in July 1936, at the beginning of the Spanish Civil War. Like Ceuta, Melilla was retained by Spain when Morocco became independent in 1956. In addition to its function as a port, Melilla now serves as a military base, more than one-half of the enclave's land area being used solely for military purposes. In October 1978 King Hassan of Morocco attempted to link the question of the sovereignty of Melilla to that of the return of the British dependent territory of Gibraltar to Spain. (See the chapter on Ceuta for details on Morocco's relationship with Spain and the North African enclaves.)

After negotiations with representatives of the Muslim community, in May 1986 the central Government in Madrid agreed to grant Spanish nationality to more than 2,400 Muslims resident in Melilla and Ceuta, under the terms of legislation introduced in July 1985 requiring all foreigners resident in Spain to register with the authorities. At that time only some 7,000 of the estimated 27,000-strong Muslim community in Melilla held Spanish nationality. In response to protests, particularly in Melilla, the central Government had given assurances that it would assist the full integration into Spanish society of Muslims in the enclaves. By mid-1986, however, the number of Muslims applying for Spanish nationality in Melilla had reached several thousand. As a result of delays in the processing of the applications, Aomar Muhammadi Dudú, the leader of the newly founded Muslim Partido de los Demócratas de Melilla (PDM), accused the Government of failing to fulfil its pledge to the Muslim residents.

At the general election of June 1986, the ruling Partido Socialista Obrero Español (PSOE) was defeated by the centre-right Coalición Popular (CP) in Melilla, the result indicating the strong opposition of the Spanish community to the Government's plan to integrate the Muslim population. Tight security surrounded the elections, and 'parallel elections', resulting in a vote of confidence in the PDM leader, were held by the Muslim community. Polling was accompanied by several days of unrest. Talks in Madrid between representatives of the main political parties in Melilla and the Ministry of the Interior resulted in concessions to the enclave. In September Dudú agreed to accept a senior post in the Ministry, with responsibility for relations with the Muslim communities of Spain. In November, however, Muslim leaders in Melilla announced that they wished to establish their own administration in the enclave, in view of the Madrid Government's failure to fulfil its promise of Spanish citizenship for Muslim residents. The Spanish Minister of the Interior reiterated assurances of the Government's commitment to integrating the Muslim community. Later in the month thousands of Muslims took part in a peaceful demonstration in support of Dudú, who had resigned his Madrid post after only two months in office. (He subsequently went into exile in Morocco and lost the support of Melilla's Muslim community.)

In February 1987 police reinforcements were dispatched from Spain, in response to a serious escalation of inter-racial tensions in Melilla. Numerous demonstrators were detained, and several prominent Muslims were charged with sedition and briefly held in custody. King Hassan reaffirmed his support for the Muslims of the Spanish enclaves.

In March 1988, after several months of negotiations, the central Government and main opposition parties in Madrid reached a broad consensus on draft autonomy statutes for the Spanish External Territories. (See the chapter on Ceuta for details of the statutes.)

At the general election held in October 1989 the election results were declared invalid, following the discovery of serious irregularities. At the repeated ballot, in March 1990, both seats in the Senado (Senate) and the one seat in the Congreso de los Diputados (Congress of Deputies) were won by the Partido Popular (PP), the latter result depriving the PSOE of its overall majority in the Madrid lower chamber. By 1990 almost all residents were in possession of an identity card.

At elections to the municipal council held in May 1991, the PP secured 12 of the 25 seats, and Ignacio Velázquez Rivera of the right-wing Partido Nacionalista de Melilla (PNM) was elected Mayor of the enclave, replacing the previous PSOE mayor. At the general election of June 1993 the PSOE candidate defeated the incumbent PP member in the Congreso de los Diputados; the PP also lost one of its two seats in the Senado.

The final statutes of autonomy for Ceuta and Melilla were approved by the Spanish Government in September 1994, in preparation for their presentation to the Cortes (parliament—see the chapter on Ceuta). At elections for the new local assembly, held in May 1995, the level of participation was less than 62%. The PP won 14 of the 25 seats, the PSOE five seats, the Coalición por Melilla (CpM), a new Muslim grouping, four seats and the right-wing Unión del Pueblo Melillense (UPM) two seats. Ignacio Velázquez (PP/PNM) was returned to the position of Mayor/President.

At the general election held in March 1996, the PSOE lost its seat in the lower house to the PP, which also took both seats in the Senado. In the same month thousands of Muslims took part in a demonstration, organized by the CpM, to protest against their position on the margins of society.

In March 1997 a motion of censure against Ignacio Velázquez resulted in the Mayor/President's defeat, owing to the defection to the opposition of two PP councillors, Enrique Palacios and Abdelmalik Tahar. The opposition then declared Palacios to be Mayor/President, although the central Government continued to recognize Velázquez as the rightful incumbent. In May, for the first time, the Mayor/Presidents of both Ceuta and Melilla attended a conference of the autonomous regions' presidents, held in Madrid. Despite the attempted 'coup' in Melilla, the territory was represented by Ignacio Velázquez. In November, from Tenerife, Abdelmalik Tahar accused Velázquez and five associates of having subjected him to blackmail and threats, as a result of which he had relinquished his seat on the Council, thereby permitting the PP to replace him and to regain its majority. In December Tahar, who was now under police protection, declared to the investigating judge that he had been offered 50m. pesetas (of which he had received 3m.) and a monthly sum of 200,000 pesetas. Following a judicial ruling leading to the successful revival of the motion of censure against Velázquez in February 1998, Palacios took office as Mayor/President of Melilla, accusing his predecessor of serious financial mismanagement. A new motion of censure, presented by the PP urging that (despite the bribery charges against him) Velázquez be restored to office, was deemed to be illegal and therefore rejected in a decree issued by Palacios, who also ordered the temporary closure of the local assembly. In July Palacios accused the PP of having employed public funds, amounting to more than 200m. pesetas, to secure the votes of some 2,500 Muslims at the 1995 local elections. The allegations were denied by the PP.

During 1997 there was increased concern regarding the numbers of illegal immigrants. In June police reinforcements were drafted into Melilla, following renewed disturbances in which one immigrant died. More than 100 illegal immigrants were immediately returned to Morocco as part of a special security operation, and on the same day a total of 873 Moroccans were denied entry to Melilla. (More than 10,000 Moroccans continued to cross the border legally each day, in order to work in the enclave.) In August the Spanish General Prosecutor demanded emergency measures to address the immigration crisis, having urged the Ministry of the Interior in June to find an immediate solution. In the same month various non-governmental organizations condemned the rudimentary conditions in which more than 900 illegal immigrants, mainly from sub-Saharan Africa and Algeria, were being held in Melilla. In December the Spanish Government announced that 1,206 sub-Saharan Africans were to be transferred from Ceuta and Melilla to the mainland.

In January 1999, after 12 years' exile in Morocco, Aomar Muhammadi Dudú returned to Melilla, in preparation for the local elections to be held in June. At the elections the Grupo Independiente Liberal (GIL), recently founded by Jesús Gil, the controversial Mayor of Marbella, Spain, secured seven of the 25 seats in the assembly of Melilla. In July the two newly elected PSOE councillors defied a central directive to vote with the five PP delegates (in order to obstruct the accession of the GIL to the city presidency), and instead gave their support to Mustafa Aberchán Hamed of the CpM, which had won five seats. Aberchán was thus elected to replace Enrique Palacios as Mayor/President of Melilla. In mid-July Aberchán and the GIL agreed to form a minority Government. The two rebel PSOE councillors subsequently relinquished their seats. In October, following a disagreement between the CpM and the GIL, Aberchán was able to reach a broad agreement with members of the PP and UPM, enabling him to remain in office. In November the Melilla branch of the GIL announced that henceforth it was to operate independently of the mainland party. In the same month, a new agreement between Aberchán and the GIL having been concluded, the latter grouping declared its intention to renew its participation in the Government of Melilla. As a result, the socialist councillors withdrew from the administration.

In December 1999 the Mayor/President announced the composition of a new coalition Government, the post of First Vice-President being allocated to Crispin Lozano, the local leader of the GIL, while Enrique Palacios of the newly founded Partido Independiente de Melilla (PIM) became Second Vice-President. In the same month Ignacio Velázquez, the former PP Mayor/President, was barred from public office for six years, having been found guilty of neglecting his duty during his tenure of office. The conviction was in respect of an incident in 1992 when Velázquez had convened a session of the Council, which was scheduled to vote on a motion of censure against him, in full knowledge of the fact that at least one member was due to be in Madrid that day, thus rendering any vote invalid. However, he was acquitted of charges of misappropriation of public funds. In May 2000, following the defection to the opposition of two GIL deputies and one UPM representative, Aberchán declared that, despite the Government's loss of its majority, he would not resign. The opposition subsequently announced that they would request a vote of no confidence in Aberchán's Government at the earliest opportunity. Later in the month the national leadership of the PP and the PSOE met in Madrid in an attempt to negotiate a solution to the political crisis in Melilla. The two parties agreed that, if Aberchán's Government was removed from office, they would form a coalition government in partnership with the UPM, whose leader, Juan José Imbroda Ortiz, would be nominated Mayor/President. In July the remaining five GIL members left the Government and joined the opposition. The opposition subsequently introduced a motion of censure against Aberchán, whom they accused of nepotism, of a lack of transparency, and of harassment of the opposition. Aberchán, who described the accusations as being racially motivated, announced that the CpM was to withdraw from the legislature. In mid-July some 2,000 Muslim citizens of Melilla demonstrated in support of Aberchán. At the same time Palacios suspended the motion of censure by decree, reportedly without having consulted Aberchán. (Palacios was subsequently barred from public office for seven years, having been found guilty of perversion of the course of justice.) The opposition later successfully overturned the decree in the courts, and the vote on the motion of censure against Aberchán was therefore able to proceed. The motion was adopted in September, with the support of 16 of the 25 deputies, and Imbroda was elected as Mayor/President. In late 2000 four members of the GIL announced their departure from the party. In January 2002 Velázquez resigned as Councillor of the Presidency, after the Supreme Court upheld his 1999 conviction.

At the regional elections held in May 2003, a coalition of the PP and the UPM won 15 seats, with the CpM taking seven. The incumbent Mayor/President, Juan José Imbroda Ortiz, remained in power. At the general election held on 14 March 2004, meanwhile, the PP retained Melilla. In September Imbroda met the recently elected Spanish Prime Minister, José Luis Rodríguez Zapatero, to discuss the possibility that Melilla would become a Comunidad Autónoma (Autonomous Community), a move that would give legislative powers to the government of the territory. The plan was, however, abandoned in February 2007, owing to disagreement over the content of the proposed statute of autonomy; instead, the Spanish Government agreed to devolve more powers to Ceuta and Melilla in the areas of education and social services.

In May 2004, meanwhile, the Government of Melilla announced plans to improve security along the border with Morocco. In August, however, in the first mass entry for three years, some 450 people attempted to enter Melilla illegally by climbing the security fence; as many as 40 people were believed to have succeeded in entering the territory. During August–October 2005 increasing numbers of would-be migrants attempted to scale the security barriers separating Melilla from Morocco. A number of deaths were said to have resulted from these attempts, and in October it was reported that six people had been shot during violent clashes with Moroccan security forces. It was subsequently announced that one barrier would be doubled in height (to 6 m), and that border security would be increased. Meanwhile, the Spanish Government announced funding of €17m. for security in Melilla.

At the local election held on 27 May 2007, the PP (which had absorbed its coalition partner, the UPM) obtained 15 seats in the Assembly, the same number as previously, thereby retaining its overall majority; the CpM and the PSOE each won five seats. The constitution of the Assembly was delayed until early July owing to an appeal against the election result levied by the CpM, which alleged that the PP had engaged in acts of electoral fraud, including the falsification of postal ballots. The appeal was rejected by the Supreme Court of Justice of Andalusia, which ruled that the evidence presented by the CpM was not sufficient to indicate irregularity. Imbroda was subsequently re-elected as Mayor/President.

A two-day visit to Melilla and Ceuta by King Juan Carlos and Queen Sofía in early November 2007 was strongly condemned by the Moroccan authorities (see the chapter on Ceuta). Several thousand Moroccans, including politicians and trade union representatives, took part in a demonstration at the border with Melilla to protest against the presence of the Spanish King. The Government of Melilla issued a statement accusing the Moroccan Government of interfering in Spanish domestic affairs by criticizing the visit.

At the general election held on 9 March 2008, the PP retained Melilla's one seat in the Congreso de los Diputados, although only by a narrow margin, as well as its two seats in the Senado. Later that month Esther Donoso García-Sacristán was appointed as Councillor of Contracting and Heritage to replace María del Carmen Dueñas Martínez, who had been elected to the Senado. In April Gergorio Escobar was appointed to replace José Fernández Chacón as Government Delegate in Ceuta. At the regional PP congress held in late October 2008, Juan José Imbroda Ortiz was appointed to succeed Arturo Esteban Albert as local President of the PP.

In April 2008 the Government of Melilla urged the Spanish Ministry of Defence to suspend plans to restructure the armed forces, claiming that these would entail a reduction in the number of troops stationed in the city. For its part, the central Government maintained that although there would be changes in the composition of the forces deployed in Melilla, overall numbers would not be reduced.

Two suspected Islamist militants were detained in Melilla at the beginning of April 2008, in accordance with international arrest warrants issued by the Moroccan Government in connection with their alleged involvement in terrorist activities, including a series of suicide bombings against Western targets in Casablanca in May 2003, in which 45 people died.

Attempts by illegal migrants to cross the border between Melilla and Morocco increased in late October 2008, after heavy flooding damaged the recently fortified fence separating the two territories. Although additional security forces were deployed to patrol the

SPANISH EXTERNAL TERRITORIES

Melilla

damaged areas, it was reported that in one incident almost one-half of a group of some 60 sub-Saharan Africans succeeded in entering Melilla; 17 others were reportedly arrested. In the weeks that followed further attempts were made to breach the fence: more than 150 people were reported to have tried to enter Melilla during November; and a number of people were injured in clashes with Moroccan and Spanish security forces (including several members of the security forces).

In April 2011 a group thought to be affiliated to the militant Islamist al-Qa'ida Organization in the Land of the Islamic Maghreb issued a statement, warning of bomb attacks in the enclave during Easter celebrations later that month. Meanwhile, also in April, a deputy Councillor was forced to resign from the Council of Government and as a PP candidate for the forthcoming Assembly election—scheduled to take place on 22 May—after it was revealed that he had received a conviction for domestic violence in 2006.

CONSTITUTION AND GOVERNMENT

See the chapter on Ceuta.

ECONOMIC AFFAIRS

In 2008, according to official estimates, the gross domestic product (GDP) of Melilla was equivalent to €21,493 per head, ranking 12th (in terms of GDP per head) in a list of the 19 Spanish autonomous regions. In 2009, according to preliminary figures, GDP totalled €1,495.9m. The population of Melilla increased by an annual average of 0.8% in 2002–09. Real GDP growth was estimated at 1.2% for 2008.

Agricultural activity in Melilla is negligible, as is employment in that sector; according to preliminary estimates, the sector contributed just 0.6% of GDP in 2009.

Although industry is on a limited scale, the sector contributed 12.8% of GDP in 2009, and 12.3% of the employed population were engaged in the sector, on average, during the final quarter of the same year. Construction contributed 9.0% of GDP in 2009, and the sub-sector engaged 10.5% of the employed population, on average, in the final quarter of that year.

Services contributed an estimated 86.6% of GDP in 2009, and some 87.7% of the employed population were engaged in the sector, on average, in the final quarter of the same year.

Most of the population's food is imported, with the exception of fish, which is obtained locally (sardines and anchovies are among the most significant catches). A large proportion of the tinned fish is sold outside Spain. More important to the economies of Melilla and Ceuta is the port activity; most of their exports take the form of fuel supplied—at very competitive rates—to ships. Most of the fuel comes from the Spanish refinery in Tenerife. Apart from the ferries from Málaga and Almería in mainland Spain, Melilla's port is not busy—a total of 1,235 vessels entered in 2010—and its exports are correspondingly low. Most trade is conducted with other parts of Spain. In 2010 Melilla recorded a trade deficit of €121.0m. In 2010 the principal source of imports (accounting for more than 26.5% of the total value) was the People's Republic of China; other major suppliers were the USA and Thailand. Morocco was the principal market for exports, taking more than 90% of the total value. The principal imports in 2009 were fruits and vegetables (some 24.5% of the total value), textiles, and clothing and cereals. The principal exports in the same year were man-made filaments (almost 60% of the total value). Tourism makes a significant contribution to the territory's economy. In 2009 visitor arrivals numbered 45,152. The annual rate of inflation averaged 2.9% in 2002–10; the rate was 2.2% in 2010. On average, some 26.1% of the labour force were unemployed during the final quarter of 2010.

Upon the accession in January 1986 of Spain to the European Community (EC, now European Union—EU, see p. 270), Melilla was considered a Spanish city and European territory, and joined the organization as part of Spain. It retained its status as a free port. The statute of autonomy, adopted in early 1995, envisaged the continuation of the territory's fiscal benefits. Euro notes and coins became the sole legal tender on 28 February 2002.

In June 1994 the EU announced substantial regional aid: between 1995 and 1999 Melilla was to receive a total of ECU 45m., of which ECU 18m. was to be in the form of direct aid. However, successive enlargements of the EU and sustained Spanish economic growth during the 2000s limited Spain's access to EU aid, with the result that, although income in the enclave had not improved significantly, subsidies for Melilla would be progressively reduced during the period 2007–13, with a view to their eventual withdrawal. The city's consolidated budget for 2010 included current and capital transfers from the Spanish state of €105.9m. and €10.3m., respectively. In May 2009 it was reported that the Spanish Government was considering increasing existing tax concessions to the aviation industry in some non-peninsular regions of Spain, including Melilla, as part of a new initiative to stimulate economic growth.

THE PEÑÓN DE VÉLEZ DE LA GOMERA, PEÑÓN DE ALHUCEMAS AND CHAFARINAS ISLANDS

These rocky islets, situated, respectively, just west and east of al-Hocima (Alhucemas) and east of Melilla off the north coast of Morocco, are administered with Melilla. The three Chafarinas Islands lie about 3.5 km off Ras el-Ma (Cabo de Agua). The Peñón de Alhucemas is situated about 300 m from the coast. The Peñón de Vélez de la Gomera is situated about 80 km further west, lying 85 m from the Moroccan shore, to which it is joined by a narrow strip of sand. A small military base is maintained on the Peñón de Vélez, while a military garrison of fewer than 100 men is stationed on the Peñón de Alhucemas, and a garrison of about 100 Spanish soldiers is maintained on the Isla del Congreso, the most westerly of the Chafarinas Islands. A supply ship calls at the various islands every two weeks. Prospective visitors must obtain the necessary military permit in Ceuta or Melilla.

Statistical Survey

Source (unless otherwise stated): Instituto Nacional de Estadística, Paseo de la Castellana 183, 28071 Madrid; tel. (91) 5839100; fax (91) 5839158; internet www.ine.es.

AREA AND POPULATION

Area: 12.5 sq km (4.8 sq miles).

Population (census results): 56,600 at 1 March 1991; 66,411 at 1 November 2001 (males 33,224, females 33,187). *2010* (official estimate at 1 July): 73,822 (males 37,039, females 36,782).

Density (1 July 2010): 5,906 per sq km.

Population by Age and Sex (official estimates at 1 July 2010): *0–14:* 16,079 (males 8,212, females 7,866); *15–64:* 49,436 (males 25,380, females 24,057); *65 and over:* 8,308 (males 3,447, females 4,859); *Total* 73,822 (males 37,039, females 36,782).

Births, Marriages and Deaths (2009, provisional): Live births 1,509 (birth rate 20.4 per 1,000); Marriages 395 (marriage rate 5.6 per 1,000); Deaths 421 (death rate 6.0 per 1,000).

Life Expectancy (years at birth, 2008): 79.6 (males 75.4; females 84.1).

Immigration and Emigration (excl. Spanish territory, 2009): Immigrants 687; Emigrants 165.

Economically Active Population ('000 persons aged 16 years and over, October–December 2010, estimates): *Total employed* 21.8; Unemployed 7.7; *Total labour force* 29.5 (males 16.9, females 12.6).

FINANCE

Currency and Exchange Rates: 100 cent = 1 euro (€). *Sterling and Dollar Equivalents* (31 December 2010): £1 sterling = 1.172 euros; US $1 = 0.748 euros; 10 euros = £8.54 = $13.36. *Average Exchange Rate* (euros per US $): 0.6827 in 2008; 0.7198 in 2009; 0.7550 in 2010. Note: The local currency was formerly the Spanish peseta. From the introduction of the euro, with Spanish participation, on 1 January 1999, a fixed exchange rate of €1 = 166.386 pesetas was in effect. Euro notes and coins were introduced on 1 January 2002. The euro and local currency circulated alongside each other until 28 February, after which the euro became the sole legal tender.

Cost of Living (Consumer Price Index, annual averages; base: 2006 = 100): All items 106.7 in 2008; 106.8 in 2009; 109.1 in 2010.

Gross Domestic Product (€ million at current prices, provisional): 1,442.0 in 2007; 1,494.8 in 2008; 1,495.9 in 2009.

Gross Domestic Product by Economic Activity (€ million at current prices, 2009, provisional): Agriculture and fishing 8.8; Energy 28.7; Construction 124.7; Other industry 24.4; Services 1,202.5; *Sub-total* 1,389.2; Net taxes on products 106.7; *GDP at market prices* 1,495.9.

EXTERNAL TRADE

Principal Commodities (€ million, 2010): *Imports:* Fruits and vegetables 30.5; Coffee, tea, maté and spices 12.0; Cereals 11.8; Textile and clothing 17.9; Footwear 4.0; Vehicles (excl. rail or tram), and parts thereof 7.6; Total (incl. others) 124.6. *Exports:* Man-made filaments 2.1; Clothing and made-up textile articles 0.7; Total (incl. others) 3.6.

Principal Trading Partners (€ million, 2010): *Imports:* Canada 9.0; China, People's Republic 33.0; Germany 8.4; Netherlands 6.7;

SPANISH EXTERNAL TERRITORIES

Melilla

Thailand 12.2; USA 17.2; Total (incl. others) 124.7. *Exports:* Morocco 3.3; Total (incl. others) 3.6.

Source: Foreign Trade Database, Agencia Tributaria (Madrid).

TRANSPORT

Road Traffic (Ceuta and Melilla, 2009): Vehicles registered 5,085 (Passenger cars 3,435, Buses, etc. 7, Lorries and vans 737, Motorcycles 894, Tractors 2, Other 10).

Shipping (domestic and international, 2010): Vessels entered 1,235; Goods handled ('000 metric tons) 818; Passenger movements ('000) 633.

Civil Aviation (2008, preliminary): Flights 10,539; Passengers transported ('000) 307; Goods transported 386 metric tons.

TOURISM

Visitor Arrivals (by country of residence, 2002): France 476; Germany 432; Italy 331; Netherlands 425; Spain 23,648; Total (incl. others) 31,812. *2009:* Total 45,152 (Spain 35,951).

EDUCATION

(2005/06)

Pre-primary: 20 schools; 159 teachers, 3,237 students.

Primary: 15 schools; 422 teachers (excl. 20 engaged in both pre-primary and primary teaching); 5,996 students.

Secondary: First Cycle: 9 schools (of which 4 schools also provided second-cycle education and 5 provided vocational education); 255 teachers (excl. 10 engaged in both primary and secondary teaching, and 198 engaged in more than one secondary cycle, and excl. 33 specialists); 3,923 students.

Secondary: Second Cycle: 53 teachers; 1,339 students.

Secondary: Vocational: 703 students; 65 teachers.

Source: Ministry of Education and Science, Madrid.

Directory

Government

HEAD OF STATE

King of Spain: HM King JUAN CARLOS I (succeeded to the throne 22 November 1975).

Government Delegate in Melilla: GREGORIO ESCOBAR.

MEMBERS OF THE SPANISH PARLIAMENT

Deputy elected to the Congress in Madrid: ANTONIO GUTIÉRREZ MOLINA (PP).

Representatives to the Senate in Madrid: MARÍA DEL CARMEN DUEÑAS MARTÍNEZ (PP), JUAN JOSÉ IMBRODA ORTIZ (PP).

COUNCIL OF GOVERNMENT

(May 2011)

The executive was formed by members of the Partido Popular (PP).

Mayor/President of Melilla: JUAN JOSÉ IMBRODA ORTIZ.

First Vice-President and Councillor of Public Administration: MIGUEL MARÍN COBOS.

Second Vice-President and Councillor of the Presidency and Civic Participation: ABDELMALIK EL-BARKANI ABDELKADER.

Councillor of Finance and Budgeting: GUILLERMO FRÍAS BARRERA.

Councillor of the Economy, Employment and Tourism: DANIEL CONESA MÍNGUEZ.

Councillor of Development: RAFAEL RICARDO MARÍN FERNÁNDEZ.

Councillor of Social Welfare and Health: MARÍA ANTONIA GARBÍN ESPIGARES.

Councillor of the Environment: RAMÓN GAVILÁN ARAGÓN.

Councillor of Culture: SIMI CHOCRÓN CHOCRÓN.

Councillor of Civic Security: RAMÓN ANTÓN MOTA.

Councillor of Education and Voluntary Organizations: ANTONIO MIRANDA MONTILLA.

Councillor of Contracting and Heritage: ESTHER DONOSO GARCÍA-SACRISTÁN.

Councillor of Youth and Sport: FRANCISCO ROBLES FERRÓN.

GOVERNMENT OFFICES

Delegación del Gobierno: Avda de la Marina Española 3, 52001 Melilla; tel. (95) 2675840; fax (95) 2672657; e-mail puri@melilla.map.es.

Office of the Mayor/President: Palacio de la Asamblea, Plaza de España, 52001 Melilla; tel. (95) 2699100; fax (95) 2679230; e-mail presidencia@melilla.es; internet www.melilla.es.

Council of Civic Security: Jefatura Policía Local, General Astilleros 25, Melilla; tel. (95) 2698111; fax (95) 2698121; e-mail policialocal@melilla.es.

Council of Contracting and Heritage: Palacio de la Asamblea, Plaza de España, 52001 Melilla; tel. (95) 2699151; fax (95) 2699158; e-mail consejeriacontratacion@melilla.es.

Council of Culture: Palacio de la Asamblea, Plaza de España, 52001 Melilla; tel. (95) 2699193; fax (95) 2699158; e-mail consejeriacultura@melilla.es.

Council of Development: Antiguo Edif. Mantelete, Duque de Ahumada s/n, 52071 Melilla; tel. (95) 2699223; fax (95) 2699224; e-mail consejeriafomento@melilla.es.

Council of the Economy, Employment and Tourism: Justo Sancho Miñano 2, 52801 Melilla; tel. (95) 2676241; fax (95) 2676242; e-mail consejeriaeconomia@melilla.es.

Council of Education and Voluntary Organizations: Querol 7, 52001 Melilla; tel. (95) 2699214; fax (95) 2699279; e-mail educacion@melilla.es.

Council of the Environment: Palacio de la Asamblea, Plaza de España, 52001 Melilla; tel. (95) 2699134; fax (95) 2699161; e-mail consejeriamedioambiente@melilla.es.

Council of Finance and Budgeting: Palacio de la Asamblea, Plaza de España, 52001 Melilla; tel. (95) 2699157; fax (95) 2699160; e-mail conserjeriahacienda@melilla.es.

Council of the Presidency and Civic Participation: Palacio de la Asamblea, Plaza de España, 52001 Melilla; tel. (95) 2699207; fax (95) 2699137; e-mail consejeriapresidencia@melilla.es.

Council of Public Administration: Palacio de la Asamblea, Plaza de España, 52001 Melilla; tel. (95) 2699102; fax (95) 2699103; e-mail cap@melilla.es.

Council of Social Welfare and Health: Carlos Ramírez de Arellano 10, Melilla; tel. (95) 2699301; fax (95) 2699302; e-mail consejeriabienstarsocial@melilla.es.

Council of Youth and Sport: Palacio de la Asamblea, Plaza de España, 52001 Melilla; tel. (95) 2699225; fax (95) 2699208; e-mail semananautica@melilla.es.

Assembly

Election, 22 May 2011

	Seats
Partido Popular (PP)	15
Coalición por Melilla (CpM)	6
Partido Socialista Obrero Español (PSOE)	2
Partido Populares en Libertad (PPL)	2
Total	25

Election Commission

Junta Electoral de Zona y Provincial de Melilla: Melilla; Sec. RUPERTO MANUEL GARCÍA HERNÁNDEZ.

Political Organizations

Coalición por Melilla (CpM): Ejército Español 21, 1° dcha, 52001 Melilla; tel. (95) 2969188; fax (95) 2699247; f. 1995 by merger of Partido del Trabajo y Progreso de Melilla and Partido Hispano Bereber; majority of members are from the Muslim community; mem. of left-wing Izquierda Unida coalition; Pres. MUSTAFA HAMED MO ABERCHÁN; Sec.-Gen. HASSAN MOHATAR.

Partido Popular (PP): Roberto Cano 2, 1° izqda, POB 384, 52001 Melilla; tel. (95) 2681095; fax (95) 2684477; e-mail melilla@pp.es; internet www.ppmelilla.es; national-level, centre-right party; absorbed the Unión del Pueblo Melillense in 2007; Pres. JUAN JOSÉ IMBRODA ORTIZ; Sec.-Gen. MARÍA DEL CARMEN DUEÑAS MARTÍNEZ.

Partido Populares en Libertad (PPL): Calle Carlos V, n° 21, Local 1, 52006 Melilla; tel. (95) 2694007; fax (95) 2694627; e-mail popularesenlibertad@gmail.com; internet www.popularesenlibertad.es; f. March 2011; centrist, liberal party formed

SPANISH EXTERNAL TERRITORIES

to contest elections of May 2011; Pres. Ignacio Velázquez Rivera; Sec.-Gen. Alberto Weil González.

Partido Socialista de Melilla-Partido Socialista Obrero Español (PSME-PSOE): Doctor García Martínez 3, 52006 Melilla; tel. (95) 2677807; fax (95) 2679857; e-mail infopsoe@psoe.es; internet www.psoe.es; national-level, left-wing party; Pres. Andrés Visiedo Segura; Sec.-Gen. Dionisio Muñoz Pérez.

There are also various civic associations in Melilla.

Religion

As in Ceuta, most Europeans are Roman Catholics. The registered Muslim community numbered 20,800 in 1990. The Jewish community numbered 1,300. There is also a Hindu community.

ISLAM

Comisión Islámica de Melilla (CIM): García Cabrelles 13, Melilla; Sec.-Gen. Abderramán Benyahya.

CHRISTIANITY

The Roman Catholic Church

Melilla is part of the Spanish diocese of Málaga.

The Press

El Faro de Melilla: Castelar 5, 1°, Melilla; tel. (95) 2690029; fax (95) 2683992; e-mail melilla@grupofaro.es; internet www.elfaroceutamelilla.es; Pres. Rafael Montero Palacios; Editor-in-Chief Angela M. Perazzi.

Melilla Hoy: Polígono Industrial SEPES, La Espiga, Naves A-1/A-2, 52006 Melilla; tel. (95) 2690000; fax (95) 2675725; e-mail redaccion@melillahoy.es; internet www.melillahoy.es; f. 1985; Pres. Enrique Bohórquez López-Dóriga; Editor-in-Chief Mustafa Hamed; circ. 2,000.

Sur: Músico Granados 2, 52001 Melilla; tel. (95) 2691283; fax (95) 2673674; e-mail surmelilla@rusadirmedia.com; internet www.diariosur.es; local edn of Málaga daily; Perm. Rep. Avelino Gutiérrez Pérez.

El Telegrama de Melilla: Polígono La Espiga, Nave A-8, 52006 Melilla; tel. (95) 2691443; fax (95) 2691469; e-mail telegramademelilla@yahoo.es; internet www.eltelegrama.com; Dir Juan Carlos Heredia.

NEWS AGENCY

Agencia EFE: Cándido Lobera 4, 1° izqda, 52001 Melilla; tel. (95) 2685235; fax (95) 2680043; e-mail melilla@efe.es; Correspondent (vacant).

PRESS ASSOCIATION

Asociación de la Prensa: Apartado de Correos 574, 29880 Melilla; tel. (95) 2681854; fax (95) 2675725; Pres. Miguel Gómez Bernardi.

Broadcasting

RADIO

Cadena Dial Melilla: Muelle Ribera 18B, 52005 Melilla; tel. (95) 2682328; fax (95) 2681573; e-mail radiomelilla@unionradio.es; internet www.cadenadial.com; Rep. Rocío González Justo.

Onda Cero Radio Melilla: Músico Granados 2, 52004 Melilla; tel. (95) 2691283; e-mail ondaceromelilla@ondaceromelilla.net; internet www.ondaceromelilla.net; Dir José Jesús Navajas Trobat.

Radio Melilla: Muelle Ribera s/n, 52005 Melilla; tel. (95) 2681708; fax (95) 2681573; e-mail radiomelilla@unionradio.es; internet www.cadenaser.com; owned by Sociedad Española de Radiodifusión; commercial; Dir Antonia Ramos Peláez.

Radio Nacional de España (RNE): Duque de Ahumada 5, 52001 Melilla; tel. (95) 2681907; fax (95) 2683108; internet www.rtve.es; state-controlled; Rep. Montserrat Cobos Ruano.

TELEVISION

A fibre optic cable linking Melilla with Almería was laid in 1990. From March 1991 Melilla residents were able to receive three private TV channels from mainland Spain: Antena 3, Canal+ and Tele 5.

Antena 3: Edif. Melilla, Urbanización Rusadir, 29805 Melilla; tel. (95) 2688840; internet www.antena3.com.

Finance

BANKING

There were seven banks operating in Melilla in 2007, all of which were based in mainland Spain.

Banco Bilbao Vizcaya Argentaria (BBVA): Teniente Aguilar De Mera 3 52001 Melilla; tel. (952) 686076; fax (952) 685249; internet www.bbva.es; 5 brs.

Banco de España: Plaza de España 3, 52001 Melilla; tel. (95) 2683940; fax (95) 2683942; internet www.bde.es.

Banco Español de Crédito (Banesto): Avda Juan Carlos I 12, 52001 Melilla; tel. (95) 2684348; fax (95) 2683645; internet www.banesto.es; 2 brs.

Banco Popular Español: Avda Juan Carlos I 14, 52001 Melilla; tel. (95) 2684847; fax (95) 2676844; internet www.bancopopular.es.

Banco Santander Central Hispano (BSCH): Ejército Español 1, 52001 Melilla; tel. (95) 2681422; internet www.gruposantander.es; 3 brs.

Caja de Ahorros y Pensiones de Barcelona (La Caixa): Avda Juan Carlos I 28, 52001 Melilla; tel. (95) 2685760; fax (95) 2960276; internet www.lacaixa.es; 2 brs.

Montes de Piedad y Caja de Ahorros de Ronda, Cádiz, Almería, Málaga y Antequera (Unicaja): Ejército Español 9, 52001 Melilla; tel. (952) 682595; fax (952) 683684; internet www.unicaja.es; 4 brs.

INSURANCE

MAPFRE: Avda Democracia 9, 52004 Melilla; tel. (95) 2673189; fax (95) 2674977; e-mail maberna@mapfre.com; internet www.mapfre.com; Commercial Man. Bernabe Escoz; 2 offices.

Trade and Industry

Cámara Oficial de Comercio, Industria y Navegación: Cervantes 7, 52001 Melilla; tel. (95) 2684840; fax (95) 2683119; e-mail info@camaramelilla.es; internet www.camaramelilla.es; f. 1906; chamber of commerce; Pres. Margarita López Almendáriz; Vice-Pres. Hamed Maanan Benaisa Bouji.

Confederación de Empresarios de Melilla (CEME-CEOE): Plaza 1 de Mayo, Bajo Dcha, 52003 Melilla; tel. (95) 2673696; fax (95) 2676175; e-mail ceme@cemelilla.org; internet www.cemelilla.org; f. 1979; employers' confed; Pres. Margarita López Almendáriz; Sec.-Gen. Jerónimo Pérez Hernández.

UTILITIES

The Spanish electricity company Endesa operates an oil-fired power station in Melilla. In 2007 a new 12.6-MW generator was installed, increasing capacity by 22%.

TRADE UNION

Confederación Sindical de Comisiones Obreras (CCOO): Plaza 1° de Mayo s/n, 2°, 52004 Melilla; tel. (95) 2676535; fax (95) 2672571; e-mail orga.melilla@melilla.ccoo.es; internet www.ccoo.es; Sec.-Gen. Angel Gutiérrez Gómez.

Transport

There is a daily ferry service to Málaga and a service to Almería. Melilla airport, situated 4 km from the town, is served by daily flights to various destinations on the Spanish mainland, operated by Iberia Regional/Air Nostrum. There were 26 km of paved roads in Melilla in 2009. The Port of Melilla handled 818,099 metric tons of goods and 633,044 passengers in 2009; 1,235 ships passed through the port in that year.

Port of Melilla: Autoridad Portuaria de Melilla, Avda de la Marina Española 4, 52001 Melilla; tel. (95) 2673600; fax (95) 2674838; e-mail puertodemelilla@puertodemelilla.es; internet www.puertomelilla.es; Pres. Arturo Esteban; Dir José Luis Almazán.

Acciona Trasmediterránea: Avda General Marina 1, 52001 Melilla; tel. (95) 2681635; fax (95) 2682685; e-mail correom@trasmediterranea.es; internet www.trasmediterranea.es; operates ferry service between Melilla and Almería and Málaga, in mainland Spain.

Tourism

There is much of historic interest to the visitor, while Melilla is also celebrated for its modernist architecture. Several new hotels, including a luxury development, were constructed in the 1990s. In 2009 tourist arrivals numbered 45,152 (including 35,591 visitors from mainland Spain).

Oficina Provincial de Turismo: Pintor Fortuny 21, 52004 Melilla; tel. (95) 2976151; fax (95) 2976153; e-mail info@melillaturismo.com; internet www.melillaturismo.com.

Defence

(See Ceuta.) More than one-half of Melilla's land area is used solely for military purposes.

Commandant-General: Gen. CÉSAR MURO BENAYAS.

Education

In addition to the conventional Spanish facilities, the Moroccan Government finances a school for Muslim children in Melilla, the languages of instruction being Arabic and Spanish. The 15 primary schools in Melilla had a total enrolment of 5,996 students in 2005/06, while nine secondary schools had an enrolment of 3,923 for the first cycle of secondary education (between the ages of 12 and 16); four of these schools offered second cycle and five offered vocational education, with 1,339 students enrolled for the *bachillerato* and 703 students enrolled on vocational courses. The Spanish open university (Universidad Nacional de Educación a Distancia—UNED) maintains a branch in Melilla.

SRI LANKA

Introductory Survey

LOCATION, CLIMATE, LANGUAGE, RELIGION, FLAG, CAPITAL

The Democratic Socialist Republic of Sri Lanka lies in southern Asia. It comprises one large island and several much smaller ones, situated in the Indian Ocean, about 80 km (50 miles) east of the southern tip of India. The climate is tropical, with an annual average temperature of about 27°C (81°F) in Colombo. There is very little seasonal variation in temperature: the monthly average in Colombo ranges from 25°C (77°F) to 28°C (82°F). The south-western part of the island receives rain from both the south-west and the north-east monsoons: average annual rainfall in Colombo is 2,365 mm (93 ins). Sinhala and Tamil are the two official languages, the former being spoken by more than 70% of the population. Tamil was made a recognized national language in 1978 and became the country's second official language in 1988. According to the 2001 census, in 18 out of 25 districts 76.7% of the population were Buddhist, 8.5% were Muslim, 7.9% were Hindu and 6.1% were Roman Catholic. The census results did not cover the Tamil-dominated (and therefore mainly Hindu) northern and eastern districts. The national flag (proportions 1 by 2) consists mainly of a dark crimson rectangular panel, with a yellow border, in the fly. In the centre of the panel is a gold lion, carrying a sword, while in each corner (also in gold) there is a leaf of the bo (bodhi) tree, which is sacred to Buddhists. At the hoist are two vertical stripes, also edged in yellow, to represent Sri Lanka's minorities: one of green (for Muslims) and one of orange (for Tamils). The commercial capital is Colombo. In 1982 the ancient capital of Sri Jayawardenepura (Kotte) became the administrative capital.

CONTEMPORARY POLITICAL HISTORY

Historical Context

Sri Lanka, known as Ceylon until 1972, gained its independence from the United Kingdom in February 1948. From then until 1956, for a brief period in 1960 and from 1965 to 1970 the country was ruled, latterly in coalition, by the United National Party (UNP), which was concerned to protect the rights of the Tamils, Hindu members of an ethnic minority (closely linked with the inhabitants of the southern Indian state of Tamil Nadu), who are concentrated in the north (and, to a lesser extent, in the east) of the main island. The socialist Sri Lanka Freedom Party (SLFP), formed in 1951 by Solomon Bandaranaike, emphasized the national heritage, winning the support of groups that advocated the recognition of Sinhala as the official language and the establishment of Buddhism as the predominant religion. The SLFP won the 1956 elections decisively and remained in power, except for a three-month interruption in 1960, until 1965, having formed a coalition Government with the Lanka Sama Samaj Party (LSSP), a Trotskyist group, in 1964. Following the assassination of Solomon Bandaranaike in 1959, his widow, Sirimavo Bandaranaike, assumed the leadership of the SLFP. At the 1970 elections the SLFP became the leading partner of a United Front coalition Government with the LSSP and the Communist Party of Sri Lanka (CPSL). In 1971 the United Front Government suppressed an uprising led by the left-wing Janatha Vimukthi Peramuna (JVP—People's Liberation Front). A state of emergency was declared, and the party was banned.

Domestic Political Affairs

In 1976 the main Tamil party, the Federal Party, and other Tamil groups formed the Tamil United Liberation Front (TULF), demanding a separate Tamil state ('Eelam') in the northern and eastern parts of the country. In December of that year the communists supported strikes in the transport sector, which were initiated by the UNP and the LSSP (the latter had been expelled from the governing coalition in 1975). The strikes ended in January 1977, and in February Sirimavo Bandaranaike prorogued the National State Assembly until May. Several members of the SLFP resigned, and seven members of the CPSL left the coalition Government, forming an independent group within the opposition. In February the state of emergency, which had been imposed in 1971, was lifted and the JVP was legalized again.

Sri Lanka under Junius Richard Jayewardene (1977–88)

A general election was held in July 1977, accompanied by widespread violence. The UNP won the election, with an overwhelming majority, and the party's leader, Junius Richard Jayewardene, became Prime Minister. In August riots broke out between the Sinhalese majority and the Tamil minority. The TULF, which had become the main opposition party, increased its demands for an independent Tamil state. In October a constitutional amendment was passed to establish a presidential system of government, and in February 1978 Jayewardene became the country's first executive President.

Continued violence and pressure from the Tamils during 1978 led the Government to make some concessions, such as the recognition of the Tamil language (not as an official language, but under the new status of 'national language'), in the new Constitution of the Democratic Socialist Republic of Sri Lanka, which came into force in September. In view of this, the Ceylon Workers' Congress (CWC) joined the Government, but the TULF remained undecided, mainly for fear of reprisals by Tamil extremists. Further violence prompted the declaration of a state of emergency in July 1979 in the northern district of Jaffna, where the Tamils were in a majority. At the same time, stringent anti-terrorist legislation was passed in Parliament (as the National State Assembly had been renamed in 1978), and a presidential commission was established to study the Tamil issue.

In June 1980 a general strike, called by left-wing trade unions seeking higher wages, led to the declaration of a state of emergency between July and August, and more than 40,000 government workers lost their jobs. In August the TULF agreed to the establishment of district development councils, providing for a wide measure of regional autonomy. Elections to these, held in June 1981, were boycotted by the SLFP, the LSSP and the CPSL, and the UNP won control of 18 of the 24 councils. Subsequent communal disturbances between Sinhalese and Tamils led to the imposition of a state of emergency in the north for five days in June, and throughout the country from August 1981 to January 1982. Tamil MPs proposed a motion of no confidence in the Government and subsequently boycotted Parliament until November 1981, when a peace initiative to ease ethnic tension was proposed by the Government.

Meanwhile, in October 1980 former Prime Minister Sirimavo Bandaranaike was found guilty of having abused her position by a special presidential commission, which deprived her of all civic rights and effectively prevented her from standing in the next elections.

In August 1982 Parliament approved an amendment to the 1978 Constitution that enabled President Jayewardene to call a presidential election before his term of office expired, i.e. after four years instead of six. Sri Lanka's first presidential election was held in October 1982, and Jayewardene was returned to office with 53% of the votes cast. The SLFP candidate, Hector Kobbekaduwa, polled 39%, despite his party's disarray and Sirimavo Bandaranaike's loss of civic rights.

Following this success, the President announced, with the approval of Parliament and the Supreme Court, that, instead of a general election, a referendum would be held to decide whether to prolong the life of Parliament for a further six years after the session ended in July 1983. A state of emergency was in force between October 1982 and January 1983, and all opposition newspapers were closed by the Government. Sirimavo Bandaranaike was allowed to campaign in the referendum, which took place in December 1982 and resulted in approval of the proposal to prolong Parliament until 1989. On a 71% turn-out, some 55% (3.1m.) voted in favour, with the dissenting minority of 2.6m. being concentrated mainly in and around Jaffna.

A state of emergency was declared in May 1983 to combat mounting terrorism, and in June Tamil militant activity led to army reprisals and the worst outbreak of violence for many years, with more than 400 deaths and particularly severe rioting in Jaffna and Colombo. A curfew and press censorship were imposed, and three left-wing parties (including the JVP) were banned. In July the 16 TULF MPs resigned in protest at the extension of Parliament, as approved by the referendum. In August Parliament passed a 'no-separation' amendment to the Constitution, depriving those espousing Tamil separatism of their civic rights. In October the TULF MPs were found to have forfeited their seats because of their parliamentary boycott. After much discussion and with the informal mediation of India, an All-Party Conference (APC) began in January 1984. The APC comprised representatives of the Buddhist, Christian and Muslim faiths as well as political leaders from the Sinhalese and Tamil communities. The Government proposed to establish provincial councils, with some regional autonomy, throughout the country. The TULF, however, demanded regional devolution that would enable the northern province, with its Tamil majority, to amalgamate with the eastern province where the Tamils were in a minority and thus create a Tamil state within the framework of a united Sri Lanka. The Sinhalese and the Muslims were implacably opposed to this proposal. The APC was finally abandoned in December, without agreement on the crucial question of the extent of regional autonomy.

An escalation in violence in the northern part of the island in November and December 1984 led to the proclamation of another state of emergency. There were widespread accusations of gross military indiscipline, along with condemnation of government-sponsored settlement of Sinhalese in Tamil areas in the eastern province. A restricted zone was established between Mannar and Mullaitivu, to prevent contact with the Indian state of Tamil Nadu, where many of the Tamil militants were reportedly based.

In February 1986 there was a resurgence of violence in the northern and eastern provinces. In May a series of explosions in Colombo was widely believed to have been carried out by Tamil extremists. The Government intensified its campaign against the insurgents by increasing defence expenditure and by launching an offensive against the militant Tamils in the Jaffna peninsula. This offensive made little headway, but the government cause was helped by internecine fighting between two of the principal Tamil militant groups, the Tamil Eelam Liberation Organization (TELO) and the Liberation Tigers of Tamil Eelam (LTTE—also known as the Tamil Tigers), the latter of which, over the year, emerged as the dominant Tamil separatist group under the leadership of Velupillai Prabhakaran. In May Tamil militants renewed their attacks on Sinhalese villagers who had been settled by the Government in Tamil-dominated areas in the eastern province.

In January 1987, in response to an announcement by the LTTE that they intended to seize control of the civil administration of Jaffna, the Government suspended, indefinitely, the distribution of all petroleum products to the peninsula. In the same month all the powers previously vested in the Prime Minister, Ranasinghe Premadasa, as Minister of Emergency Civil Administration were transferred to a new Ministry of National Security, directly supervised by the President. In February the Government launched an offensive against the insurgents in the Batticaloa district of the eastern province. The situation worsened in April, when the LTTE, having rejected an offer of a cease-fire by the Sri Lankan Government, carried out a series of outrages against the civilian population, including a bomb explosion in Colombo's main bus station, which killed more than 100 people. In response, the Government attempted to regain control of the Jaffna peninsula, the stronghold of the LTTE. During the resultant struggle between the LTTE and government forces, India demonstrated its support for the Tamils by violating Sri Lankan airspace to drop food and medical supplies in Jaffna. On 29 July, however, an important breakthrough was made when President Jayewardene and the Indian Prime Minister, Rajiv Gandhi, signed an accord which attempted to settle the country's ethnic crisis. The main points were: the provision of an Indian Peace-Keeping Force (IPKF) to oversee its proper implementation; a complete cessation of hostilities, and the surrender of all weapons held by the Tamil militants; the amalgamation of the northern and eastern provinces into one administrative unit, with an elected provincial council (together with the creation of provincial councils in the seven other provinces); the holding of a referendum in the eastern province at a date to be decided by the Sri Lankan President, to determine whether the mixed population of Tamils, Sinhalese and Muslims supported an official merger with the northern province into a single Tamil-dominated north-east province; a general amnesty for all Tamil militants; the repatriation of some 130,000 Tamil refugees from India to Sri Lanka (by early 1991 the number of Tamil refugees in India had risen to an estimated 210,000, and in early 1992 the Indian Government began to repatriate them, allegedly on a voluntary basis); the prevention of the use of Indian territory by Tamil militants for military or propaganda purposes; the prevention of the military use of Sri Lankan ports by any country in a manner prejudicial to Indian interests; and the provision that Tamil and English should have equal status with Sinhala as official languages. The accord encountered widespread disapproval among the Sinhalese population and from the SLFP, which claimed that it granted too much power to the Tamil minority.

In July and August 1987 more than 7,000 Indian troops were dispatched to Sri Lanka. After a promising start, the surrender of arms by the Tamil militant groups became more sporadic, and the implementation of the peace accord was impeded by further bitter internecine fighting among the Tamil militias (involving the LTTE in particular), which necessitated direct intervention by the IPKF. By early October the surrender of arms by the LTTE had virtually ceased; the group resumed its terrorist attacks on Sinhalese citizens, and declared itself to be firmly opposed to the peace accord. In response to the resurgence in violence, the IPKF launched an offensive against the LTTE stronghold in the Jaffna peninsula. The Indian troops encountered fierce and prolonged resistance from the Tamil militants, which resulted in the deployment of thousands of reinforcements. By the end of October, however, the IPKF had gained control of Jaffna city, while most of the LTTE militants had escaped to establish a new base for guerrilla operations, in the Batticaloa district of the eastern province. Both sides had suffered heavy casualties.

Owing to the continuing violence, the Sri Lankan Government abandoned its plan to create an interim administrative council for the northern and eastern provinces. However, in November 1987, despite strong opposition from the SLFP (which vehemently opposed the proposed merger of the northern and eastern provinces), Parliament adopted the legislation establishing provincial councils.

Another major threat to the successful implementation of the peace accord was the re-emergence in 1987 of the outlawed Sinhalese group, the JVP, which had been officially banned in 1983 and which was based mainly in the south of the island. This group claimed that the accord conceded too much power to the Tamils. As part of its anti-accord campaign, the JVP was widely believed to have been responsible for an assassination attempt on President Jayewardene in August, in which one MP was killed and several cabinet ministers were seriously wounded, and to have murdered more than 200 UNP supporters by February 1988, including the Chairman of the UNP, Harsha Abeywardene, and the leader of the left-wing Sri Lanka Mahajana (People's) Party (SLMP), Vijaya Kumaratunga, who supported the accord.

In February 1988 a new opposition force emerged when an alliance, named the United Socialist Alliance (USA), was formed between the SLMP, the LSSP, the CPSL, the Nava Sama Samaja Party, and (most notably) the Tamil rights group entitled the Eelam People's Revolutionary Liberation Front (EPRLF). Although the USA group, led by Chandrika Bandaranaike Kumaratunga (the widow of the SLMP leader and the daughter of Sirimavo Bandaranaike), comprised opposition parties, it expressed support for the peace accord.

Elections to seven of the new provincial councils were held in April and June 1988 (in defiance of the JVP's threats and violence); elections in the northern and eastern provinces were postponed indefinitely. The UNP won a majority and effective control in all seven, while the USA emerged as the main opposition group. The SLFP boycotted the elections, in protest at the continuing presence of the IPKF (which now numbered about 50,000) in Sri Lanka. In September President Jayewardene officially authorized the merger of the northern and eastern provinces into a single north-eastern province, prior to provincial council elections there. The JVP reacted violently to this development, and was widely believed to have been responsible for the murder of the Minister of Rehabilitation and Reconstruction at the end of the month. In protest against the proposed elections in the new north-eastern province and the presidential election (due to be held in December), the JVP organized a series of strikes and violent demonstrations in the central, western and southern provinces in October. In an effort to curb the increasing violence, the Government applied extensive emergency regulations, imposed curfews in areas of unrest, and deployed armed riot police. Despite boycotts and threats by both the JVP and the LTTE, elections to the new north-eastern provincial council took place in November. The moderate and pro-accord Tamil groups, the EPRLF and the Eelam National Democratic Liberation Front (ENDLF), together with the Sri Lanka Muslim Congress (SLMC), were successful in the elections, while the UNP won only one seat. In early December Parliament unanimously approved a constitution amendment bill to make Tamil one of the country's two official languages (with Sinhala), thus fulfilling one of the major commitments envisaged in the peace accord. On 19 December the presidential election took place, in circumstances of unprecedented disruption, and was boycotted by the LTTE and the JVP. None the less, about 55% of the total electorate was estimated to have voted. Prime Minister Ranasinghe Premadasa (the UNP's candidate) won by a narrow margin, with 50.4% of the total votes, while Sirimavo Bandaranaike, the President of the SLFP (whose civil rights had been restored in January 1986), received 44.9%. On the following day Parliament was dissolved in preparation for a general election.

The United National Party (UNP) retains power under President Ranasinghe Premadasa (1989–93)

In January 1989 Premadasa was sworn in as Sri Lanka's new President, and an interim Cabinet was appointed. In the same month the Government repealed the state of emergency, which had been in force since May 1983, and abolished the Ministry of National Security. Concurrently, however, special security measures were invoked in an attempt to curb the escalating violence. Shortly after his inauguration, Premadasa offered to confer with the extremists and invited all groups to take part in the electoral process. The JVP and the LTTE, however, intensified their campaigns of violence in protest at the forthcoming general election. In early February 1989 the moderate, pro-accord Tamil groups, the EPRLF, the ENDLF and the TELO, formed a loose alliance, under the leadership of the TULF, to contest the general election. In the election, which was held on 15 February and which was, again, marred by widespread violence, the UNP won 125 of the 225 contested seats. The new system of proportional representation, which was introduced at this election, was especially advantageous to the SLFP, which became the major opposition force in Parliament, with 67 seats. The comparatively low electoral participation of 64% confirmed that the intimidatory tactics employed by the LTTE and the JVP had once more an effect on the voters. A few days later President Premadasa installed a new Cabinet, and in March he appointed the Minister of Finance, Dingiri Banda Wijetunga, as the country's new Prime Minister.

Between January and April 1989 five battalions of the IPKF left Sri Lanka, and in May the Sri Lankan Government announced that it wanted all Indian troops to have left Sri Lanka by the end of July. In response, Rajiv Gandhi stressed that the timetable for a complete withdrawal would have to be decided mutually, and that, before the Indian forces left, he wanted to ensure the security of the Tamils and the devolution of real power to the elected local government in the north-eastern province. In protest against the continued presence of the IPKF in Sri Lanka, the JVP organized a series of demonstrations and strikes. As a result of the escalating unrest, the Government reimposed a state of emergency on 20 June. In the same month, shortly after the murders of several prominent Tamil leaders, peace negotiations between the Sri Lankan Government and the LTTE that had been instigated in May were temporarily discontinued. In September the Governments of Sri Lanka and India signed an agreement in Colombo, under which India promised to make 'all efforts' to withdraw its remaining 45,000 troops from Sri Lanka by the end of the year, and the IPKF was to declare an immediate unilateral cease-fire. In turn, the Sri Lankan Government pledged immediately to establish a peace committee for the north-eastern province in an attempt to reconcile the various Tamil groups and to incorporate members of the LTTE into the peaceful administration of the province.

The JVP suffered a very serious set-back in November 1989 when its leader, Rohana Wijeweera, and his principal deputy were shot dead by the security forces. In the following month the head of the military wing of the JVP, Saman Piyasiri Fernando, was killed in a gunfight in Colombo. Between September 1989 and the end of January 1990 the Sri Lankan security forces effectively destroyed the JVP as a political force, thus substantially transforming the country's political scene. All but one member of the JVP's political bureau and most leaders at district level had been killed. It was estimated, however, that the number of civilians killed in the lengthy struggle between the JVP and the Government might have been as high as 25,000–50,000.

As the Indian troops increased the speed of their withdrawal from Sri Lanka in the latter half of 1989, the LTTE initiated a campaign of violence against its arch-rivals, the more moderate Indian-supported EPRLF, which was mustering a so-called Tamil National Army, with Indian help, in the north-eastern province, to resist the LTTE. The LTTE accused the EPRLF and its allies of forcibly conscripting thousands of Tamil youths into this army. Following months of peace talks with the Government, however, the political wing of the LTTE was recognized as a political party by the commissioner of elections in December. The LTTE leaders then proclaimed that the newly recognized party would take part in the democratic process (it demanded immediate fresh elections in the north-eastern province) under the name of the People's Front of the Liberation Tigers (PFLT). By the end of 1989 the inexperienced and undisciplined Tamil National Army had been virtually destroyed by the LTTE, which now appeared to have the tacit support of the central Government and had taken control of much of the territory in the north-eastern province.

Following further talks between the Governments of Sri Lanka and India, the completion date for the withdrawal of the IPKF was postponed until the end of March 1990. In early March the EPRLF-dominated north-eastern provincial council, under the leadership of Annamalai Varadharajah Perumal, renamed itself the 'National Assembly of the Free and Sovereign Democratic Republic of Eelam' and gave the central Government a one-year ultimatum to fulfil a charter of demands. Two weeks later, however, Perumal was reported to have fled to southern India. The last remaining IPKF troops left Sri Lanka on 24 March, a week ahead of schedule. In the following month the Government eased emergency regulations (including the ban on political rallies) in an effort to restore a degree of normality to the country after years of violence. At the same time, Sri Lanka's security forces, encouraged by the relative lull in violence, halted all military operations against the now much-weakened JVP and the Tamil militant groups. A fragile peace was maintained until June, when the LTTE abandoned their negotiations with the Government and renewed hostilities with surprise attacks on military and police installations in the north and north-east. Consequently, the Sri Lankan security forces were compelled to launch a counter-offensive. In mid-June the Government dissolved the north-eastern provincial council (despite protests by the EPRLF), and the holding of fresh elections in the province was postponed indefinitely pending the LTTE's agreement to participate in them (as earlier promised). In August the LTTE intensified their campaign of violence in the eastern province against the Muslim population, which retaliated with counter-attacks. At the end of August the Government launched a major offensive against the Tamil strongholds in the Jaffna peninsula. It was widely suspected that the LTTE were responsible for the assassination in March 1991 of the Minister of Plantation Industries and Minister of State for Defence, Ranjan Wijeratne (who had been in charge of both the government forces' successful campaign against the JVP, several years earlier, and the ongoing offensive against the LTTE), and for the bomb attack on an armed-forces building in Colombo in June. More significantly, for its regional implications, the LTTE were believed to have been responsible for the assassination of the former Indian Prime Minister, Rajiv Gandhi, near Madras (now known as Chennai), the state capital of Tamil Nadu, in May. In early 1992 the Indian Government proscribed the LTTE and banned their activities on Indian territory.

In August 1991 the opposition, with the support of a number of UNP parliamentary members, began proceedings for the impeachment of the President. The impeachment motion, which listed 24 instances of alleged abuse of power, was rejected in October by the Speaker of Parliament on the grounds that some of the signatures on the resolution were invalid. Eight erstwhile UNP parliamentary members, including two former cabinet members, Lalith Athulathmudali and Gamini Dissanayake, who were expelled from the party (thus losing their parliamentary seats as well) by Premadasa for supporting the impeachment motion, formed a new party in December, called the Democratic United National Front (DUNF), to which they hoped to attract dissident members of the UNP.

The security forces suffered a serious reversal in August 1992, when 10 senior officers, including the northern military commander and the Jaffna peninsula commander, were killed in a land-mine explosion near Jaffna. Tension between the Muslim and Tamil populations in the north-eastern district of Polonnaruwa drastically increased following the massacre of more than 170 Muslim villagers by suspected LTTE guerrillas in October. In the next month the LTTE were also widely believed to have been responsible for the murder of the naval commander Vice-Admiral Clancy Fernando in Colombo.

The assassination of Premadasa and the assumption of power by Dingiri Banda Wijetunga (1993–94)

In April 1993 the opposition DUNF accused Premadasa's Government of having been responsible for the assassination of the party's leader, Lalith Athulathmudali. In response, Premadasa alleged that the perpetrators of the murder had been LTTE terrorists; the LTTE, however, denied any responsibility for the killing. The country was thrown into greater political turmoil on 1 May, when President Premadasa was assassinated in a bomb explosion in Colombo. The LTTE were officially blamed for the murder, although, again, they strenuously denied any involvement. A few days later Parliament unanimously elected the incumbent Prime Minister, Dingiri Banda Wijetunga, to serve the remaining presidential term (expiring in December 1994), and the erstwhile Minister of Industries, Science and Technology, Ranil Wickremasinghe, was appointed to replace him in the premiership. In provincial elections held in mid-May 1993 the UNP won control of four of the seven councils; no polling was carried out in the area covered by the now defunct north-eastern province (the province was officially declared invalid by the Supreme Court in October 2006). Although the ruling party received 47% of the votes, it was the first time since 1977 that its percentage of total votes had fallen below 50%, an indication of an erosion of its support base.

The Sri Lankan forces achieved considerable success in their fight against ethnic violence in the eastern province in 1993, but were forced to abandon a massive military offensive in the Jaffna peninsula in October owing to the ferocity of the LTTE resistance. In the following month both sides suffered heavy casualties in the course of the battle over the military base at Pooneryn on the Jaffna lagoon. Despite the continuing violence, provincial elections were held in the eastern province and in the northern town of Vavuniya in early March 1994; the UNP secured the greatest number of seats, while independent Tamil groups also performed well. The LTTE and the TULF boycotted the poll. The ruling party suffered its first major electoral reverse for 17 years at the end of the month, however, when an opposition grouping known as the People's Alliance (PA, of which the main constituents were the SLFP and the traditional Marxist left and which was headed by the former leader of the USA group, Chandrika Kumaratunga) won a clear majority in elections to the southern provincial council.

The Sri Lanka Freedom Party (SLFP) returns to power under Chandrika Kumaratunga (1994–2001)

In June 1994, in an apparent attempt to catch the opposition by surprise, the President dissolved Parliament and announced that early legislative elections were to be held on 16 August, ahead of the presidential election. Wijetunga's ploy failed, however: the PA obtained 48.9% of the votes, thus securing a narrow victory over the UNP, which received 44% of the poll. Under the prevailing system of proportional representation, this translated into 105 seats for the PA and 94 for the UNP in the 225-seat Parliament. The 17-year parliamentary rule of the UNP had thus come to an end. On 18 August Chandrika Kumaratunga was appointed Prime Minister, the PA having secured the support of the SLMC, the TULF, the Democratic People's Liberation Front and a small, regional independent group. A new Cabinet was appointed on the following day, almost all members of which belonged to the SLFP. In line with her electoral pledge to abolish the executive presidency and to establish a parliamentary system in its place, the Prime Minister removed the finance portfolio from the President and assumed responsibility for it herself. Although Wijetunga retained the title of Minister of Defence, actual control of the ministry was expected to be exercised by the Deputy Minister of Defence. The Prime Minister's mother, Sirimavo Bandaranaike, was appointed as Minister without Portfolio. With regard to the Tamil question, overtures were made between the new Government and the LTTE concerning unconditional peace talks (these commenced in October) and at the end of August, as a gesture of goodwill, the Government partially lifted the economic blockade on LTTE-occupied territory. In addition, the Prime Minister created a new Ministry of Ethnic Affairs and National Integration and assumed the portfolio herself, thus illustrating her determination to seek an early solution to the civil strife.

In September 1994 Kumaratunga was unanimously elected by the PA as its candidate for the forthcoming presidential poll, while Gamini Dissanayake, the leader of the opposition (who had left the DUNF and returned to the UNP in 1993), was chosen as the UNP's candidate. The election campaign was thrown into confusion, however, on 24 October 1994, when Dissanayake was assassinated by a suspected LTTE suicide bomber in a suburb of Colombo; more than 50 other people, including the General Secretary of the UNP, Gamini Wijesekara, and the leader of the SLMP, Ossie Abeyagoonasekera, were also killed in the explosion. The Government declared a state of emergency and suspended the ongoing peace talks with the LTTE. Dissanayake had been an outspoken critic of these talks and had been one of the architects of the 1987 Indo-Sri Lankan accord. His widow, Srima Dissanayake, was chosen by the UNP to replace him as the party's presidential candidate. The state of emergency was revoked on 7 November (with the exception of the troubled areas in the north and east) to facilitate the fair and proper conduct of the presidential election, which was held on 9 November. Kumaratunga won the election, with 62.3% of the votes, while Srima Dissanayake obtained 35.9%. The Government viewed the victory as a clear mandate for the peace process initiated earlier that year. Sirimavo Bandaranaike was subsequently appointed Prime Minister for the third time. The new President pledged to abolish the executive presidency before mid-July 1995, on the grounds that she believed that the post vested too much power in one individual, and promised to initiate a programme of social, economic and constitutional change.

Following the failure of peace talks with the LTTE in the early months of 1995, in July the Government launched another major offensive in the Jaffna peninsula. As the offensive was intensified in October, tens of thousands of civilians were compelled by the LTTE to flee the area. Rather than actively confronting the troops, the LTTE detonated explosives on the country's two largest oil storage facilities near Colombo, which received virtually all of Sri Lanka's imported petroleum. As a result, about 20% of the island's petroleum supply was destroyed. In December the Sri Lankan army achieved a major victory in capturing the city of Jaffna and subsequently much of the Jaffna peninsula. The Government's short-term strategy with regard to the Jaffna peninsula was to attempt to persuade the tens of thousands of civilians now living in refugee camps to return there and to establish a fully functional civil administration in the region. Although the LTTE's military strength and morale had been undermined, the rebels, as expected, reverted to guerrilla warfare and further terrorist activity following the recapture of Jaffna; at the end of January 1996 more than 100 people were killed and about 1,400 were injured in a suicide bomb attack on the Central Bank in Colombo. Against a background of continuing conflict between the Tamil militants and the government forces in the north and east of the country, the President extended the state of emergency to cover the whole country in April (since coming to power in November 1994, the PA administration had restricted the emergency provisions to the troubled northern and eastern regions and Colombo). In May 1996 the army announced that it now controlled the whole of the Jaffna peninsula and claimed that, of the 300,000 Tamil civilians who had been displaced by the ethnic violence, about 250,000 had returned to the government-held areas. Despite the army's controlling presence in the peninsula, the LTTE were by no means a spent force. In July the Tamil militants attacked and overran the isolated military base at Mullaitivu on the north-eastern coast of Sri Lanka, inflicting heavy casualties on the army. About one week later the LTTE were suspected of planting a bomb on a crowded suburban train near Colombo, which killed more than 70 people. In September the army seized control of the northern town of Kilinochchi, which had served as the LTTE's new headquarters since April. In the following month Prabhakaran and nine other militants were charged with more than 700 criminal acts of terrorism, including the bombing of the Central Bank in January. This constituted the first occasion that the Government had taken legal action against the LTTE leader. Fierce fighting between the Tamil militants and government troops continued into 1997, both in the north and in the east of the country.

The Government was given a considerable boost in March 1997, following its overwhelming success in local elections, in which it won more than 80% of the contested bodies (voting did not take place in the troubled northern and eastern provinces).

In May government forces launched a fresh military offensive against the LTTE, with the aim of gaining control of the strategically important 75-km stretch of the A9 highway between Vavuniya and Elephant Pass, which is the point of entry to the Jaffna peninsula. In October 18 people were killed and more than 100 injured (including about 35 foreigners) when a bomb exploded in the car park of a Colombo hotel. It was widely believed that the LTTE deliberately targeted foreigners in this attack following the US Administration's decision a few days earlier to place the organization on its official list of international terrorist groups. In late January 1998 16 people were killed in a suspected LTTE suicide bombing in Kandy at Sri Lanka's most sacred Buddhist temple, the Dalada Maligawa ('Temple of the Tooth'). The following day the Government formally outlawed the LTTE, thus apparently ruling out the prospect of further peace negotiations in the near future and focusing instead on a military solution. Also in late January the UNP rejected the Government's proposed constitutional amendments regarding devolution. The UNP disagreed with the Government's proposal to devolve wide-ranging powers to regional councils—including a Tamil-administered area—and favoured the concept of power-sharing at the centre. Also at the end of January, polls were conducted in Jaffna for the first time in 15 years. The local authority elections, which were monitored by tens of thousands of troops, were contested by a number of moderate Tamil political parties but were, not surprisingly, boycotted by the LTTE. The largest number of seats was won by the Eelam People's Democratic Party (EPDP), but the turn-out was a mere 28%, owing to LTTE threats to disrupt the voting.

In May 1998 the recently elected mayor of Jaffna (the first person to hold that position in 14 years), Sarojini Yogeswaran, who was a member of the moderate TULF, was assassinated by two suspected LTTE gunmen after refusing demands by Tamil militants to resign. In September Yogeswaran's replacement, Ponnuthurai Sivapalan, who was also a leading member of the TULF, was killed, along with 19 others, in a suspected LTTE bomb explosion in Jaffna city hall.

By the end of 1998, despite fierce fighting and large numbers of casualties on both sides, the army had still failed to capture completely the northern A9 highway, which, if opened, would provide the military with a vital land route to the Jaffna peninsula. In December the Government announced its decision to cancel the operation to capture the highway, which, since it was launched in May 1997, had cost the lives of more than 3,000 government troops.

In January 1999 the ruling PA won the elections to the north-western provincial council by a significant margin, although the result was marred by allegations of widespread electoral fraud and violence against opposition activists. In elections to five other provincial elections that were held in April, the PA won control in four provinces and retained power in the fifth—the polls were very keenly contested, however, with the PA achieving about 43% of the total votes and the UNP obtaining around 41%. Elections to the southern province, which were held in May, also resulted in a PA-led administration. One noteworthy feature of this series of provincial polls was the resurgence of the JVP as a credible political force.

Meanwhile, in March 1999 the army launched another offensive against the LTTE in the northern province, the objective of which was to reduce the area under the effective control of the Tamil guerrillas. In July the TULF Vice-President, Neelan Tiruchelvam, who was a leading peace campaigner and human rights activist, was assassinated by a suspected LTTE suicide bomber in Colombo. In November the Government suffered a debilitating set-back following a rapid series of LTTE victories in the north-eastern Wanni region, thus reversing more than two years of territorial gains by the military. As a result of these demoralizing defeats and amid reports of large-scale desertions and mutiny in the army ranks, the Government announced a tightening of existing military censorship on domestic news coverage in an attempt to stem adverse publicity and reorganized the northern military command.

A few days before an early presidential election, which was held on 21 December 1999 (almost one year ahead of schedule), Kumaratunga survived an assassination attempt by a suspected LTTE suicide bomber in Colombo; the explosion killed more than 20 people, while the President sustained wounds to her right eye. The election, which was contested by 13 candidates and attracted a 73% turn-out of the electorate, was marred by widespread allegations of vote-rigging, intimidation and violence. Kumaratunga was returned to power by a narrow majority (possibly having garnered a considerable sympathy vote), winning 51% of the total votes, while her main rival, Ranil Wickremasinghe of the UNP, secured 43%.

In early 2000 the Government confirmed that, at Kumaratunga's request, the Norwegian Government had agreed to play an intermediary role in any peace negotiations with the LTTE. The Norwegian Minister of Foreign Affairs, Knut Vollebæk, arrived in Colombo in February to discuss with Kumaratunga and Wickremasinghe the modalities for commencing direct peace talks between the Sri Lankan Government and the LTTE. Earlier that month Vollebæk had met a senior LTTE official in London, United Kingdom, to assess the separatists' opinions regarding peace negotiations. According to commentators, the preconditions of both sides (respectively, the abandonment by the LTTE of their demand for an independent state and the withdrawal of all government troops from Tamil areas) were the most serious obstacles to the commencement of talks.

Despite the steps being taken towards the instigation of peace talks, heavy fighting continued between the army and the LTTE in the north. In April 2000 the LTTE announced that they had captured the large military base at Elephant Pass at the strategic entrance point to the peninsula. In response to the escalating military crisis, the Government imposed draconian security measures, banning all activities perceived as a threat to national security and giving extensive powers to the armed forces and police, and renewed press censorship. By mid-May the LTTE claimed to be only 1 km from the administrative centre of Jaffna, and thousands of terrified civilians were reported to be fleeing from the embattled city. In late May, as the army and the LTTE continued to struggle for control of the peninsula, the Government appealed for new army recruits, and Norway launched a fresh diplomatic initiative to find a peaceful solution to the crisis. In early June the Minister of Industrial Development, Clement V. Gunaratna, and more than 20 others were killed by a suspected LTTE suicide bomber in Colombo. At the end of the month President Kumaratunga and Wickremasinghe began discussions on the draft of a new constitution designed to resolve the ethnic conflict. The Government and UNP agreed on a draft document, which recommended converting the country into a de facto federal state through the establishment of eight semi-autonomous regional councils. However, the Tamil parliamentary parties rejected the proposals as providing inadequate autonomy to the Tamil regions of the country. Senior Buddhist monks also opposed the reforms, owing to fears that devolution would threaten the Sinhalese-dominated population and prominence of Buddhism in Sri Lanka. In July the UNP withdrew its support for the reforms; the President subsequently postponed indefinitely a parliamentary vote on the issue as it became clear that the Government would not obtain the two-thirds' majority required to secure the passage of the legislation. On 10 August Sirimavo Bandaranaike announced her resignation as Prime Minister, owing to ill health (she died later that year). She was replaced by Ratnisiri Wickremanayake, the erstwhile Minister of Public Administration, Home Affairs and Plantation Industries. Parliament was dissolved in preparation for a general election.

In September 2000 the Minister of Shipping and Shipping Development, Mohammad H. M. Ashraff, and the President of the SLMC, along with 14 others, were killed in a helicopter crash in Kegalle district. A high-level investigation into the incident was ordered; there was widespread speculation that the aircraft had been shot down by LTTE guerrillas.

The parliamentary elections of 10 October 2000 were marred by allegations of electoral malpractice and by systematic violence and intimidation. Nevertheless, the elections attracted a turn-out of 75% of the electorate. Neither the PA nor the UNP won an absolute majority (taking 107 and 89 of the 225 parliamentary seats, respectively), but, having gained the support of the EPDP and National Unity Alliance (NUA—primarily a constituent of the SLMC), the PA was able to form a new, expanded coalition under the premiership of Wickremanayake.

In June 2001, following the dismissal of the leader of the SLMC, Abdul Rauf Hakeem, from his position as Minister of Internal and International Trade, Commerce, Muslim Religious Affairs and Shipping Development, several members of the SLMC withdrew their support for the ruling PA, thereby reducing the coalition Government to a minority in Parliament. Immediately afterwards, opposition parties challenged the Government with a no-confidence motion. In order to prevent the motion from being debated in Parliament, on 10 July the President suspended the legislature until 7 September, and announced that a referendum on a new constitution would take place on 21 August. The UNP-led opposition organized a series of demonstrations against the President's decision to prorogue Parliament. The President also faced opposition within the Cabinet itself, particularly with regard to the referendum. As a result, Kumaratunga announced in August that the referendum would be postponed until mid-October.

Meanwhile, efforts by Norwegian emissaries to bolster the peace process from late 2000 met with little progress. In July 2001 President Kumaratunga circumvented Parliament and reimposed a state of emergency under anti-terrorist regulations. The ban on the LTTE was also extended. In late July the LTTE launched attacks on the capital's international airport and an adjacent airbase. Several hours of shooting between Tamil militants and the army ended with all 13 guerrillas and seven soldiers killed; several military and civilian aircraft were also destroyed. The assault on the country's only international airport, hitherto renowned for its impenetrable security, adversely affected the tourist industry (and thus the economy), and raised questions about the air force and airport's defence system.

In an attempt to resolve the political crisis, the Prime Minister and senior cabinet members conducted negotiations on the possible establishment of a coalition government. The Government's overtures to the UNP were rebuffed, but in early September 2001 the JVP formally agreed to support the minority Government for one year (but not to join the administration), in return for a set of conditions. The President had already granted the JVP two of its demands by cancelling the referendum and reconvening Parliament. In addition, the President agreed to suspend negotiations with the LTTE for one year and to postpone the privatization programme. In accordance with further JVP's demands, in mid-September the size of the Cabinet was halved to 22 members. However, three senior cabinet members resigned, refusing to participate in an administration supported by the left-wing party. Several members of the PA criticized the pact and doubted its longevity. At the end of September a motion of no confidence in the Government was resubmitted to Parliament. On 10 October 13 members of the PA, including several ministers, defected to the opposition, thereby reducing the coalition once again to a minority. In order to forestall defeat in the vote of no confidence due to take place the following day, President Kumaratunga dissolved Parliament. The opposition condemned the decision, although the dissolution was constitutional (one year had passed since the previous legislative elections).

The UNP holds parliamentary power under an SLFP President (2001–04)

The general election on 5 December 2001, one of the most violent in Sri Lanka's history, was also marred by incidents of vote-rigging and other electoral malpractices. Some tens of thousands of Tamil voters were barred from voting after the army prevented them from leaving LTTE-controlled areas to cast their vote. Nevertheless, 72% of the electorate voted. The UNP won 109 of the 225 seats (with 45.6% of the vote) and the PA received 77 seats (37.2%). The JVP secured 16 seats (9.1%) and the Tamil Nationalist Alliance (TNA—a Tamil opposition alliance, comprising the TULF, TELO, EPRLF and All Ceylon Tamil Congress, formed prior to the election) won 15 seats (3.9%). The UNP leader, Ranil Wickremasinghe, formed the United National Front (UNF) with the SLMC to ensure a majority of 114 seats in Parliament, and on 9 December he was sworn in as Prime Minister. For the first time since 1984, the Prime Minister and the President were from two opposing parties. The President was at first reluctant to relinquish her defence and finance portfolios, which she eventually gave up in return for full control over the élite Presidential Security Division that was deployed for her personal protection. After lengthy negotiations, a new coalition Government, including representatives of the TNA and 12 members of the former PA administration, was sworn in on 12 December. In 2002 the right of the President to dissolve Parliament after one year from the date of the last election loomed over the new Government. In an attempt to curb the President's powers and to ensure stability for the peace process, the Government recommended that parliamentary resolutions determine future elections; however, the President refused to support this suggestion.

The UNP's victory in December 2001 was largely attributed to the party's eagerness to resume negotiations with the LTTE. Significantly, the TNA was a member of the coalition Government. On 19 December the LTTE announced a unilateral one-month cease-fire from 25 December, and on 21 December the Government responded with the declaration of a reciprocal cease-fire as a 'gesture of goodwill'. The Prime Minister also announced that the free movement of food, medicine and other non-military supplies into the Tamil-controlled areas would be allowed (a concession refused, hitherto, by the President). In early January 2002 the Government announced the reduction of economic sanctions on the northern areas controlled by the LTTE. One week later a delegation of Norwegian diplomats, led by Norway's Deputy Minister of Foreign Affairs, Vidar Helgesen, arrived in Colombo to conduct negotiations with the Prime Minister and President, and eventually to facilitate peace talks between the Government and the LTTE. At the end of January both sides extended the cease-fire by one month. On 22 February 2002 the Government and LTTE signed an agreement on an internationally monitored indefinite cease-fire to take effect the following day. Norway was requested to monitor the cease-fire.

In March 2002 Prime Minister Wickremasinghe visited Jaffna, the first premier to do so since 1982. In early April the Government lifted a six-year ban on domestic flights and allowed commercial airlines to resume flights to Jaffna. A week later an important road linking the Jaffna peninsula with the rest of the country was opened for the first time in 12 years. On 10 April Prabhakaran addressed an international press conference for the first time in more than 10 years. He demanded the lifting of the ban on the LTTE as a prerequisite to negotiations and declared his commitment to peace and full support of the cease-fire. A few days later he signed a pact with the SLMC, allowing the largest Muslim party in Sri Lanka to participate in proposed negotiations with the Government. It was also agreed that nearly 100,000 Muslims expelled from the north by the LTTE about 10 years ago would be permitted to return to their homes. In May a Tamil-owned trawler, reported to have been illegally importing weapons, was destroyed by the Sri Lankan navy in an exchange of gunfire off the coast of the eastern Batticaloa district—the first major violation of the cease-fire to have occurred. The LTTE refuted allegations that they had been smuggling arms and accused the army of attacking a civilian fishing boat in an effort to undermine the cease-fire. Later in the month the Norwegian-led Sri Lanka Monitoring Mission (SLMM) issued a statement conveying concern over the increasing number of cases of civilians being harassed by the LTTE.

Meanwhile, the first direct talks for seven years between the Government and the LTTE took place in May 2002 on the Jaffna peninsula. Although the August deadline for the commencement of formal peace negotiations was not achieved, the cease-fire was upheld. According to the Office of the UN High Commissioner for Refugees (UNHCR, see p. 71), by mid-August 103,000 displaced families had returned to their homes since the beginning of the cease-fire in February. In early September the Government lifted the official ban on the LTTE, and the first round of official peace talks took place in mid-September in Thailand. The Minister of Constitutional Affairs, Prof. G. L. Peiris, acted as chief negotiator for the Government, while Anton Balasingham led negotiations on behalf of the LTTE. The talks proved successful: both sides agreed to establish a joint committee to deal with security issues, and a joint task force to concentrate on the reconstruction of areas destroyed by war, the clearing of landmines and the resettling of 800,000 internally displaced people to high-security zones. On the final day of negotiations Balasingham unexpectedly renounced the LTTE's long-standing demand for independence, instead agreeing to consider regional autonomy and self-government.

In early October 2002 four people were killed and 15 injured in clashes between government and LTTE forces in Ampara district, in one of the most serious violations of the cease-fire to date. At the end of the month a Sri Lankan court convicted Prabhakaran, *in absentia*, for his role in a 1996 truck bombing in Colombo and sentenced him to 200 years' imprisonment. Despite these events, the second round of peace negotiations commenced on 31 October in Thailand. The talks concentrated mainly on humanitarian issues, but concluded in a breakthrough, with both sides agreeing to create a subcommittee to examine a political solution to the conflict. Balasingham announced that the LTTE were willing to participate in the democratic process, would allow other political parties to operate in the areas under their control and would cease the recruitment of child soldiers. The LTTE also abandoned their demand for an interim government in the north-east. Both sides agreed to establish subcommittees to deal with rehabilitation and military de-escalation. Meanwhile, Sinhalese nationalists opposed to the peace process questioned the sincerity of the LTTE, dismissing the progress at the negotiations as an attempt to win publicity and international favour. Nevertheless, the peace process gained momentum in late November when Balasingham arrived in Norway to enter negotiations with the Norwegian Prime Minister on the eve of a one-day international donor conference in support of Sri Lanka's quest for a lasting peace. A few days later Prabhakaran confirmed in his annual address that the LTTE were prepared to accept regional autonomy rather than an independent state, but warned that violence would resume if negotiations collapsed.

In December 2002, at the third round of peace talks, held in Oslo, Norway, the two sides agreed on 'internal self-determination' based on a federal system of government within a united Sri Lanka. Peiris and Balasingham described the developments as unprecedented and historic. However, in order to achieve the two-thirds' majority required in Parliament to pass a constitutional amendment, the Government needed to secure the support of the President. Although Kumaratunga welcomed the peace agreement, she had repeatedly criticized the Government for making too many concessions during the peace process. In mid-December a close adviser of the President stated that the PA would not support a political solution unless the LTTE disarmed. However, at the fourth round of negotiations, held in Thailand in January 2003, Balasingham refused to yield to pressure to disarm the Tamil forces prior to a political settlement. The talks concluded with an agreement to accelerate the rate of return and resettlement of up to 250,000 displaced people. Meanwhile, despite Tamil promises to halt the forced recruitment of children, the SLMM reported that the LTTE had enlisted hundreds of child soldiers since the instigation of the cease-fire. The fifth round of negotiations, held in Germany in February, focused on human rights issues; it was agreed that UNICEF would monitor a joint programme to rehabilitate child soldiers.

In February 2003 President Kumaratunga censured the Prime Minister for granting a licence to the LTTE radio station, Voice of Tigers, amid rising tension in the 'cohabitation Government'. Prabhakaran failed to attend a meeting with Norwegian peace mediators in mid-March, reportedly owing to the sinking of a civilian Tamil ship by the Sri Lankan navy several days earlier. Furthermore, the sixth round of negotiations, held in Japan on 18–21 March, ended without agreement, amid reports of renewed violence in Sri Lanka. An international donor meeting in Washington, DC, USA, to consider aid for Sri Lanka's reconstruction in preparation for a major donor conference to be held in Japan in June, took place in mid-April. The LTTE, however, were not invited: the USA had not yet lifted its ban on the Tamil organization; neither had India, one of the attendees at the meeting. On 21 April the LTTE announced that they were temporarily withdrawing from the peace negotiations and that they would not attend the donor conference in Japan in June since they had been excluded from the aid conference in the USA. They also expressed their dissatisfaction with the manner in which the cease-fire had been implemented (government troops remained stationed in many parts of the Tamil-controlled areas in a clear violation of the cease-fire) and the way in which the Government was carrying out rehabilitation and relief measures. Although the LTTE expressed their intention to uphold the cease-fire, the President placed the security forces on high alert.

Efforts to revive the peace process suffered a set-back in May 2003 when the Government refused the LTTE's request to establish an interim administration for the north-east of the country. Informal talks, however, continued to take place. In June a senior leader of the EPRLF, Subathran, was shot dead. Subathran was the most senior of 30 politicians from rival Tamil parties and suspected army informants to have been assassinated since the beginning of the cease-fire; the LTTE were believed to have been responsible for the shooting, creating serious doubts over the Tamil organization's commitment to multi-party politics. Also in June, an LTTE oil tanker exploded and sank during a confrontation with a Sri Lankan navy patrol. The LTTE and Government offered conflicting versions of the incident: military officials reported that the ship was smuggling weapons and that Tamil militants aboard the vessel refused to stop despite several warnings and caused the explosion to avoid being caught; the LTTE denied the charges, claiming that the Sri Lankan navy fired at the ship after capturing the crew. At the end of the month the LTTE organized a demonstration to demand the return of thousands of homes on the Jaffna peninsula occupied by the Sri Lankan army as high-security zones since the 1980s; some 150,000 people attended the rally. Although the Government was committed to vacating these zones, the army believed that a sudden withdrawal would give the LTTE the opportunity to seize complete control of the Jaffna peninsula. In August the SLMM reported that the Tamil militants had failed to comply with the terms of the cease-fire agreement by refusing to dismantle a camp in the north-eastern district of Trincomalee. Controversy over the issue intensified with allegations by the military and opposition that the LTTE had established 13 new camps since the beginning of the cease-fire; the Tamil militants denied the charges.

On 4 November 2003 the country was plunged into a constitutional crisis when President Kumaratunga took advantage of the Prime Minister's absence abroad and suspended the legislature for a period of two weeks, dismissed the Minister of Interior and Christian Affairs, the Minister of Defence and of Transport, Highways and Aviation, and the Minister of Mass Communication, assuming these portfolios herself, and deployed troops to key positions in the capital in the stated interest of preserving national security. The President claimed that Wickremasinghe, who returned from the USA on 7 November, had made too many concessions to the LTTE during peace negotiations. Kumaratunga and Wickremasinghe held two meetings in an attempt to resolve the crisis, with little success: the Prime Minister rejected the offer to form a government of national unity and suggested that, since the President had assumed the defence portfolio, Kumaratunga should lead the peace negotiations. However, the two leaders agreed to appoint a committee to establish new power-sharing arrangements by mid-December. In the mean time, the Norwegian peace negotiators announced that they would withdraw from the peace process until it was clarified who held power and authority in Sri Lanka.

In January 2004 the crisis worsened when President Kumaratunga declared that she had held an undisclosed inauguration ceremony in 2000 to give herself another year in office, thereby extending her term to December 2006. Analysts debated whether the action was constitutional. Later in January 2004 the SLFP and the JVP formed the United People's Freedom Alliance (UPFA). The UPFA was joined by four other left-wing parties (including the JVP), which had been members of the erstwhile PA, in early February. On 7 February Kumaratunga dissolved Parliament and called a general election for 2 April, almost four years ahead of schedule. Both the Cabinet and the LTTE condemned the decision, amid fears that the election would further undermine the peace process.

In March 2004 a rift within the LTTE appeared after a senior Tamil eastern regional commander declared his independence from the rest of the group. V. Muralitharan (commonly known as Col Karuna) withdrew his 6,000 fighters from the 15,000-strong LTTE in a dispute with the northern-based LTTE leader, Prabhakaran. Karuna, who accused northern Tamil groups of ignoring and discriminating against eastern groups, stated that he would not recognize the cease-fire agreement between the Government and Prabhakaran, and instead demanded a separate truce agreement with the Sri Lankan administration. In late March the LTTE vowed to remove Karuna from Sri Lanka and in early April fighting between the two Tamil factions broke out around the eastern town of Batticaloa. Four days later it was reported that Karuna had fled from his base and gone into hiding, that his forces had dispersed and that the LTTE had assumed full control of the eastern areas.

The United People's Freedom Alliance gains control of Parliament

At the general election, which took place on 2 April 2004, the UPFA won 105 of the 225 seats, having taken 45.6% of the votes cast; Wickremasinghe's UNP retained 82 seats (with 37.8% of the votes), while the TNA won 22 seats (with 7.0%). In an unexpected development, the Buddhist Jathika Hela Urumaya (JHU—National Heritage Party) secured nine seats. The LTTE, which had openly supported the TNA during the election campaign, described the large number of seats won by the Tamil alliance as an endorsement and recognition of the LTTE as 'the sole representative' of the Tamil population. Participation at the election was reported to have reached 75% of eligible voters and the poll concluded peacefully. However, there were claims of voter intimidation and electoral malpractice, particularly in the north and east of the country. Mahinda Rajapakse, a senior member of the SLFP, was sworn in as Prime Minister on 6 April and a few days later a new Cabinet was inaugurated. In September the UPFA Government achieved a legislative majority when the CWC, which had eight seats in Parliament, announced that it would join the ruling coalition. In the following month three members of the opposition SLMC defected to the UPFA, further strengthening the Government.

Meanwhile, the cease-fire between the LTTE and the Government came under increasing pressure from June 2004 onwards. During discussions with the SLMM, the LTTE accused the Sri Lankan armed forces of sheltering Col Karuna and of assisting him in waging a campaign against them. Despite initially denying it, the armed forces eventually admitted that they had helped Karuna to escape, while insisting that the plan had been carried out without the Government's knowledge. Fears that the cease-fire was close to collapse were heightened when a suicide bomber blew herself up during questioning at a police station in Colombo in early July, having first attempted to meet the Secretary-General of the EPDP, Douglas Devananda, who was a long-standing opponent of the LTTE. Although the LTTE denied any involvement in the attack, they were widely believed to have been responsible both for the bombing, and for the assassination of another EPDP politician in Ampara district later that month. In the mean time, clashes continued to occur between the LTTE and members of the breakaway Karuna faction. In December the LTTE formally rejected a new proposal by the Government that the two sides restart peace negotiations. The LTTE attributed their decision to the fact that the JVP, one of the members of the coalition Government, opposed their condition that any negotiations should be based upon their concept of an Interim Self-Governing Authority (ISGA, a body that had been proposed by the LTTE in October 2003 to administer the north-east of the country).

Political events were overshadowed by a natural disaster that struck the country at the end of 2004. Sri Lanka was one of the countries most seriously affected by the devastating tsunami caused by a massive earthquake in the Indian Ocean on 26 December. More than 31,000 Sri Lankans were killed in the disaster, which also left thousands homeless and without livelihoods. The tourism industry was badly affected by the catastrophe, with many hotels and resorts being damaged or destroyed. It was initially hoped that the scale of the disaster would serve to ease tensions between the Government and the LTTE, particularly as the Tamil areas of the island were among those worst hit. However, conflicts soon surfaced over the distribution of aid; the LTTE claimed that the Government was restricting the flow of international aid into Tamil-controlled areas and demanded that it be delivered directly to them. In June 2005 the Government finally signed an agreement—entitled the Post-Tsunami Operational Management Structure (P-TOMS)—that would allow the LTTE to participate in the distribution of aid for the reconstruction effort. The agreement had only been reached following the withdrawal from the ruling coalition of the JVP, which had remained staunchly opposed to any deal with the LTTE. The JVP's exit left the Government with a minority in the legislature, although the opposition UNP had assured the Government of its support for the aid-sharing mechanism. In the following month, however, in response to a petition from the JVP and the JHU, the Supreme Court suspended the implementation of the P-TOMS, ruling that several of its clauses were illegal. Meanwhile, increasing tensions between the LTTE and government forces, complicated by the former's ongoing clashes with the rebel Karuna faction, led to an upsurge in violence that prompted international donors to warn the two sides that the cease-fire was under threat. At the end of May the chief of military intelligence in Colombo, Maj. Nizam Muthalif, had become the most senior official to have been assassinated by the LTTE since the signing of the cease-fire in February 2002.

In August 2005 the peace process between the Government and the LTTE was further jeopardized when the Minister of Foreign Affairs, Lakshman Kadirgamar, was assassinated by unidentified gunmen at his home in Colombo. Although they denied involvement, the LTTE were held responsible for the attack. In the aftermath of the murder, President Kumaratunga declared a state of emergency, granting the security forces broad powers of detention. Amid widespread fears that the cease-fire would collapse, both sides announced their commitment to its maintenance, and the LTTE promised to meet with the Government to review the truce agreement. In September the LTTE declined a Norwegian proposal that the talks should be held at the international airport near Colombo, while the Government rejected the LTTE's suggestion that they be held in Kilinochchi, the political centre of LTTE-controlled northern Sri Lanka. Later in the same month the European Union (EU) issued a statement banning LTTE delegations from visiting any of its member states. Sporadic violence continued throughout the following months.

Meanwhile, there was controversy over the schedule for the next presidential election. While, under the terms of the Constitution, the next election was due to be held in December 2005, President Kumaratunga claimed that the holding of an undisclosed inauguration ceremony in 2000 had actually extended her second term until December 2006. In July 2005 the SLFP announced that its presidential candidate would be Prime Minister Rajapakse. In August the Supreme Court brought an end to the controversy, ruling that the election should be held by 22 November 2005. Former Prime Minister Ranil Wickremasinghe subsequently declared that he would stand as the candidate of the UNP.

Mahinda Rajapakse assumes the presidency; the four-year cease-fire collapses

On 17 November 2005 14 candidates contested the presidential election. Rajapakse secured a narrow victory over his closest rival, Wickremasinghe, winning 50.3% of the vote, compared with 48.4% for Wickremasinghe. The election was notable for the low turn-out amongst the country's Tamil population, particularly in the LTTE-controlled northern and eastern areas. While the LTTE had stated that they would not prevent people from voting, there was widespread evidence that they had done so. Rajapakse subsequently nominated the incumbent Minister of Agriculture, Public Security, Law and Order and of Buddha Sasana, Ratnasiri Wickremanayake, as Prime Minister. In the new Cabinet, announced shortly afterwards, neither the JVP nor the JHU were awarded any portfolios.

There was an escalation in violence in December 2005. At least 60 people died over the course of the month as a result of various attacks believed to have been co-ordinated by the LTTE. In early January 2006 a suicide bomb attack on a naval patrol vessel resulted in the deaths of 13 sailors, constituting the largest loss of military life since the cease-fire began. A further nine sailors were killed in a land-mine explosion later in that month. In February negotiators representing the LTTE and the Government convened in Geneva, Switzerland, to hold talks on the recent upsurge in violence. A joint statement issued following the conclusion of the talks committed both sides to upholding the cease-fire, which appeared in imminent danger of collapse. The LTTE agreed to attempt to prevent further attacks on the security forces, while the Government pledged to try to disarm the Karuna faction of the LTTE, which was believed to have been acting on behalf of the armed forces against its erstwhile comrades. However, in April the LTTE stated that it would not attend the second round of talks scheduled to be held in Geneva that month, alleging that government forces had carried out attacks on Tamil civilians and that the Sri Lankan navy had prevented the LTTE commanders in the east of the country from meeting the LTTE political leaders in the north. In late April a suicide bombing believed to have been perpetrated by the LTTE at the army headquarters in Colombo killed at least 11 people and seriously injured the Chief of Staff of the Army, Lt-Gen. (later Gen.) Sarath Fonseka. The Government subsequently ordered a number of air strikes on alleged LTTE bases near Trincomalee, which, according to the LTTE, caused the displacement of approximately 15,000 people. The violence continued, further jeopardizing the ongoing cease-fire: in May the SLMM acknowledged that a 'low intensity war' was taking place. At the end of the month the EU classified the LTTE as a terrorist organization, which entailed a suspension of LTTE fund-raising in EU member states, a freeze on the organization's assets and a ban on travel to the EU. The LTTE responded by demanding the withdrawal of EU members of the SLMM, resulting in the departure of Danish, Finnish and Swedish monitors in July and August. Amid escalating violence the LTTE withdrew from peace talks planned for June. In mid-June fears about the intensification of the conflict were realized when landmine explosions killed some 64 civilians on a crowded bus in Kebithigollewa. Despite the LTTE's condemnation of the attack, the Government retaliated by launching air strikes on Kilinochchi. A new front in the conflict opened up over access to the Maavil-Aru waterway, which became the scene of a number of air and ground offensives in July. The violence spread to the town of Muttur, north of the waterway, forcing thousands of inhabitants, many of them Muslims, to flee in August. Clashes between LTTE fighters and army troops continued in the north and east of the country, with rising death tolls of civilians, rebels and government forces. At the end of September the SLMM estimated that the resumption of hostilities had resulted in the displacement of some 200,000 people. In October, following a suicide bombing near Habarana that killed approximately 100 naval officers, it was feared that relatively unaffected areas of the country would be drawn into the conflict when the LTTE attacked a naval base in the southern town of Galle. Little progress was made at peace talks held in Geneva at the end of October, although both sides agreed to uphold the terms of the cease-fire agreement. In November it was reported that an army attack on a Tamil refugee camp in LTTE-held territory had resulted in at least 65 civilian fatalities. Shortly afterwards a TNA member of Parliament was assassinated in Colombo, with no group claiming responsibility. At the end of November Prabhakaran declared the cease-fire to be 'defunct' and blamed the Government for failing to find a solution. In early December the Government amended existing laws to extend the powers of security officials and support anti-terrorist operations. Anton Balasingham, the chief LTTE negotiator, died in mid-December.

The violence continued into 2007, with government forces reportedly securing the eastern town of Vakarai in January after a series of battles and the displacement of an estimated 30,000 people. In February the ambassadors of Italy and the USA were injured in mortar fire during a visit to Batticaloa; the attack was blamed on the LTTE. In March there was a renewal of hostilities in eastern areas, reportedly as part of a larger government drive to secure the east of the country, as concerns mounted for the estimated 155,000 civilians left homeless by the fighting. Later that month the strengthened capability of LTTE forces was demonstrated by an air attack on the government airbase at Katunayake, which was followed in late April by air bombings of fuel depots in the Colombo area.

Meanwhile, at the end of June 2006 Rajapakse was elected unopposed to replace Kumaratunga as President of the SLFP. In January 2007 more than 20 dissident politicians from the opposition parties (including the UNP and the SLMC) joined the Government, thus giving it a parliamentary majority. In June two former SLFP ministers founded a new political party, the Sri Lanka Freedom Party—Mahajana Wing (SLFP—M), in reaction to the 'path of extremism' that they believed the SLFP to be taking. In December the SLMC withdrew its support for the governing coalition, and the party's leader, Abdul Rauf Hakeem, resigned from his position as Minister of Posts and Telecommunication.

As fighting continued in the north and east of the country, in mid-2007 it was estimated that the resumption of hostilities had resulted in approximately 5,000 fatalities since 2005. There were frequent reports of human rights violations on both sides. In February 2007 the Government approved the establishment of a special committee, the International Independent Group of Eminent Persons (IIGEP), which was to examine alleged instances of human rights violations in Sri Lanka alongside a presidential commission of inquiry. (However, in March 2008 the IIGEP announced that it was unilaterally suspending its operations in Sri Lanka owing to its reservations over the effectiveness and credibility of the government inquiry process.) In June 2007 hundreds of Tamils were apparently forced to leave Colombo by the police, and accounts of abductions and disappearances were commonplace. The LTTE, in turn, was criticized for its alleged recruitment of children, forced recruitment and abduction of adults, and political killings. The UN High Commissioner for Human Rights also expressed concern over human rights violations reportedly committed by Col Karuna's troops. However, the Government declined the Commissioner's offer to establish an office in the country. In July the army claimed that its operations in the eastern province had resulted in a decisive victory over the LTTE and had led to its recapture of the region. The front line shifted as fighting intensified in the north of the country. Both sides suffered set-backs in late 2007 and early 2008. In October 2007 the LTTE conducted an aerial and land attack on the Anuradhapura airbase, reportedly killing tens of military officers and destroying eight aircraft. S. P. Thamilselvan, the head of the LTTE's political wing and a leading member of its negotiating team, was killed in an aerial bombardment by the military in the following month. In early January 2008 a senior LTTE intelligence official was reportedly killed in a landmine explosion; his death was followed within days by that of D. M. Dassanayake, the Minister of Nation Building, in a bomb attack. The Government, having given notice of its intention to withdraw from the cease-fire agreement, formally did so on 16 January; this appeared to confirm the Government's preference thenceforth for a military solution to the conflict (attested by the considerable enlargement of the armed forces over the preceding two years). As a result, the SLMM announced the end of its activities in Sri Lanka. Also in January, Col Karuna, who had been apprehended while attempting to enter the United Kingdom using a counterfeit passport in late 2007, was sentenced to nine months' imprisonment by a British court on charges of identity fraud. Speculation had arisen over the links between Karuna's faction and the Sri Lankan Government, and the role that this alleged alliance had played in the Government wresting control of the eastern province from the LTTE. In July 2008 the British authorities deported Karuna from the United Kingdom. In March 2009, having left his faction's political front, the Tamileela Makkal Viduthalai Pulikal (TMVP), and joined the SLFP, Karuna (using his civilian name, Vinayagamoorthy Muralidharan) was appointed as Minister of National Integration and Reconciliation (a non-cabinet post). Meanwhile, in April 2008 the Minister of Highways and Road Development, Jeyaraj Fernandopulle, (together with at least 14 other people) was killed in a suspected LTTE suicide bombing carried out near Colombo, while a suicide attack in the centre of the capital itself in May left around 10 people dead.

Defeat of the LTTE and the end of the 26-year civil war

In the latter half of 2008 the Sri Lankan army made considerable advances against the LTTE, which, nevertheless, put up fierce resistance and increasingly resorted to terrorist attacks across the country. Both sides suffered heavy casualties, although, owing to stringent restrictions placed on the media by the Government, exact numbers were impossible to confirm. There was also growing international concern over the mounting casualties among (mainly) Tamil civilians as a result of the army's offensive against the LTTE. In response, the Government claimed that the retreating LTTE was using the civilian population as a human shield. In early January 2009 the rebels lost control of their de facto capital, Kilinochchi, and later that month their last remaining stronghold, Mullaitivu, fell to the advancing government troops. By April the LTTE were cornered in a small stretch of coastal territory in the north-east of the country. Despite the Government having established a designated 5 sq km no-fire zone for the thousands of civilians fleeing from the violence, hundreds of civilians were reported to have been killed by both sides in the conflict. The LTTE and the army both denied any responsibility for civilian deaths, and the latter claimed to have stopped using heavy artillery (although the evidence of intensive shelling suggested otherwise). The humanitarian crisis facing the Government was severe, with more than 200,000 refugees living in makeshift accommodation, and medical and food provisions in short supply. There were growing demands from the international community (including the US Administration and the UN) for an immediate cease-fire to allow the safe evacuation of the 50,000 civilians trapped in the conflict zone. However, the government forces, in their determination to rout the LTTE, refused to halt their bombardment, while the rebels, for their part, continued to attempt to prevent the refugees from leaving the conflict zone. On 17 May the Government reported that all the civilians remaining in the war zone had been freed and claimed to have defeated the last remnants of the rebel forces (who were holding out in a small area on the coast), thus bringing the 26-year civil conflict that had claimed at least 70,000 lives to its conclusion. The LTTE were reported to have finally laid down their arms and released a statement declaring that their struggle had 'reached its bitter end'. On the following day there were unconfirmed reports that Prabhakaran, together with several other senior LTTE officials, had been killed while attempting to escape the advancing army. Amid scenes of jubilation on the streets of Colombo, President Rajapakse formally announced the army's victory over the LTTE on 19 May and declared the following day as a public holiday. In an attempt to allay the concerns of the Tamil population, Rajapakse pledged immediately to address the political issues arising from the conflict's conclusion by negotiating some form of power-sharing agreement with the Tamils in the north and east of the island.

However, the army's victory created a further humanitarian problem. Around 290,000 non-combatant Tamils were herded into refugee camps around Mullaitivu and in other locations in the northern province. The fate of these displaced Tamils became the focus of a campaign by the Tamil diaspora groups (mainly in Canada and Europe). In addition, a number of European countries, including the United Kingdom, France and Germany, demanded an international investigation into alleged war crimes committed by both the Sri Lankan forces and the LTTE in the civil war's final phases. On 25 May 2009 the UN Human Rights Council convened a special emergency session on Sri Lanka at the request of 17, mostly European, countries. The proposed resolution sought to condemn the Sri Lankan Government for its alleged disregard for civilian life during the last stage of the fight against the LTTE, but was rejected. Instead, a resolution tabled by the Sri Lankan Government itself, commending its handling of the war and, in particular, its commitment to human rights, was passed by a vote of 29 to 12. Among those who voted in support of the Sri Lankan Government were the two main Asian regional powers, China and India, as well as Cuba, Russia, Pakistan and Egypt. During the year many aid and human rights agencies expressed concern over the poor conditions suffered by the 'internally displaced persons' (IDPs) in the overcrowded internment camps ('welfare villages'), and there were also complaints regarding the Government's slow rate of release of the IDPs. The Government claimed that the process of resettlement had been delayed by the need for the authorities to identify any disguised LTTE fighters or cadres among the IDPs. In October, however, the Government accelerated the pace of resettlement of the IDPs under the reported threat of the imposition of EU trading sanctions. In December the Government finally gave permission for the remaining 130,000 IDPs to leave the camps if they so wished (although it was expected that many of them would remain in the camps indefinitely since either their villages had been destroyed or the journey would be too perilous given the number of unexploded landmines and ordnance).

Recent Developments: Rajapakse consolidates his power following the defeat of the LTTE

In October 2009 the UPFA won its eighth successive victory in provincial elections when it took control of the provincial council in the southern province. A few days later it was announced that legislative and presidential elections would be held by April 2010. Although elections to Parliament were due by that date, Rajapakse's presidential term was not scheduled to expire until November 2011; the President's decision to call an early election appeared to reflect the Government's confidence in its popularity and strength in the aftermath of the defeat of the LTTE.

In the mean time, following the victory of the army in May 2009, there were reports of growing friction between the Government and the army commander who had masterminded and led the defeat of the LTTE, Gen. Sarath Fonseka. In July these rumours appeared to be confirmed when Fonseka was moved to the largely ceremonial post of Chief of Defence Staff. In November Fonseka resigned from this position and announced his intention to contest the forthcoming presidential election as the candidate of the recently formed New Democratic Front and with the support of the revived opposition alliance of the UNF. He claimed that President Rajapakse had become increasingly corrupt and dictatorial and that he had done little to promote national reconciliation since the demise of the LTTE. Such was the level of antipathy felt by the Tamil population towards Rajapakse, that the TNA (the long-standing spokesbody of the LTTE) pledged its support for Fonseka in the presidential poll. In the election, which was held on 26 January 2010 with a turn-out of 74.5%, President Rajapakse was returned to power for a second term, securing 57.9% of the votes cast, while Fonseka obtained 40.2%. In early February the Supreme Court ruled that Rajapakse could begin his new term in November rather than immediately, thus effectively giving him almost an extra year in power. In the following week Fonseka, who had vowed to contest the presidential election results, was arrested on charges of conspiring to overthrow the Government while he was in command of the army. Fonseka and the opposition immediately condemned his detention as a violation of human rights and politically motivated, and denounced the accusations of a conspiracy as completely baseless. Violent clashes between thousands of government supporters and opposition activists ensued in Colombo. Fonseka further angered the Government when he quoted allegations that high-ranking military officials, including Defence Secretary Gotabhaya Rajapakse, had ordered army officers to shoot and kill surrendering LTTE troops in the closing days of the conflict. In March Fonseka appeared before a court martial in Colombo on charges of engaging in politics while serving in the armed forces and of violating military procurement procedures; the court martial was subsequently adjourned.

The ruling UPFA secured an overwhelming victory in the general election held on 8 April 2010, winning 144 of the 225 parliamentary seats; the UNP (which contested the election on its own and not at the head of the UNF) won 60 seats, the Ilankai Tamil Arasu Katchi (a constituent party of the TNA) 14 seats and the newly formed Democratic National Alliance (DNA, led by Fonseka) seven seats (one of which was secured by Fonseka himself). President Rajapakse appointed the veteran statesman and incumbent Minister of Plantation Industries, D. M. Jayaratne, as Prime Minister on 21 April and a new, substantially reduced Cabinet was sworn in two days later. The President was accused of nepotism by some observers following the appointment of his older brother, Chamal Rajapakse, as Speaker of Parliament (two other brothers also held government posts) and the procurement of a parliamentary seat by his son, Namal Rajapakse. In early May the Government announced the partial relaxation of emergency regulations that had been in place since 2006.

In mid-May 2010 the Government announced plans for the establishment of a Lessons Learnt and Reconciliation Commission (LLRC), which was to investigate the reasons behind the collapse of the cease-fire in 2008, promote national unity and determine compensation for the numerous victims of the civil conflict. However, the LLRC's mandate would not cover investigations into allegations of the violation of humanitarian law by government forces and the LTTE during the final stages of the war (although it would reportedly look into cases concerning individual responsibility). In the same month a study undertaken by the International Crisis Group (ICG—an independent non-governmental organization based in Brussels, Belgium) was published, which claimed that the Sri Lankan army and the LTTE were responsible for the deaths of thousands more civilians than previously estimated and that there was strong evidence that the government forces had deliberately targeted hospitals and humanitarian operations during their final onslaught against the Tamil militants. The ICG estimated that as many as 75,000 civilians, who were known to have been alive in the no-fire zone in February 2009, remained unaccounted for. The Government denied having committed any war crimes and described the UN's reported proposals officially to investigate its conduct of the war against the LTTE as unjustifiable. The new Sri Lankan Minister of External Affairs, Prof. G. L. Peiris, stressed that any foreign intervention in Sri Lanka's internal affairs would not only be highly unwelcome but would also be detrimental to the work of the LLRC. None the less, in late June 2010 the UN Secretary-General, Ban Ki-Moon, appointed a special three-member panel of experts to advise him on appropriate courses of action regarding alleged war crimes perpetrated by both sides in the final months of the civil war. The UN estimated that around 7,000 civilians were killed in the last five months of the conflict (and a total of approximately 100,000 during the course of the entire 26-year-long conflict). The Sri Lankan Government announced that the establishment of the UN human rights advisory panel, which was headed by a former Attorney-General of Indonesia, Marzuki Darusman, was unnecessary and that it would not be allowed to enter the country. In early July the Minister of Construction and Engineering Services, and of Housing and Common Amenities, Wimal Weerawansa, led a demonstration of hundreds of protesters who laid siege to the UN's office compound in Colombo in protest at the controversial advisory panel. The Government had earlier refused to grant visas to the panel's three members on the grounds that their investigation violated Sri Lankan sovereignty. The UN responded to the protests (which were reported to have the tacit support of the Sri Lankan Government) by temporarily recalling its envoy to Sri Lanka and by closing its compound in Colombo.

In August 2010 Fonseka was found guilty by a court martial of having engaged in politics while on active military service and was sentenced to a dishonourable discharge and divested of all military ranks and privileges; this verdict was subsequently approved by President Rajapakse in his capacity as Commander-in-Chief of the Sri Lankan armed forces. In the same month, amid much international scepticism regarding its credibility, the LLRC, headed by former Attorney-General C. R. de Silva, held its first public session. A number of high-profile human rights organizations, including Amnesty International, refused to give evidence to the commission on the grounds that it exercised no real mandate to investigate the truth and that it was flawed by its non-neutral status.

In early September 2010 Rajapakse's hold on power was considerably strengthened by the Supreme Court's approval of a constitutional reforms bill that had been proposed by the Government. The legislation included provisions allowing an individual to hold the presidency for an unlimited number of terms (previously limited to two terms). Claiming that the President was acting in an increasingly dictatorial manner, members of the opposition staged a parliamentary walkout and thousands of demonstrators took to the streets of the capital to protest against the proposed constitutional amendments (which, among other things, would allow Rajapakse to stand for the presidency again in 2016 on the expiry of his second term). However, the Eighteenth Amendment Bill was passed on 8 September by a clear two-third's majority in Parliament, despite the voting being boycotted by the UNP. The main provisions of the bill (aside from the lifting of the limit on the tenure of the presidency) were: the replacement of a 10-member constitutional council that had been created as a check on the President by a five-member parliamentary council that would have no power of veto over presidential constitutional initiatives; and the bestowal on the President of final authority over appointments to the judiciary, police, electoral commission and the civil service. This latter measure effectively rescinded the Seventeenth Amendment Bill that had been introduced in 2001 in an attempt to curb presidential power by depoliticizing important state appointments. At the end of the month President Rajapakse endorsed the 30-month prison term imposed on Fonseka by a second court martial for the violation of military tender procedures. Fonseka, who still faced a number of other charges (including conspiracy to overthrow the Government) in different civil courts, was immediately transferred to a high-security prison in Colombo. (In January 2011 Fonseka lost his appeal against his conviction to the Supreme Court which would have enabled him to retain his parliamentary seat; the Court ruled that the utilization of the courts martial system had been legal.)

On 19 November 2010 President Rajapakse was formally sworn in for his second term in office in a ceremony that was boycotted by the main opposition parties. A few days later the President appointed a new, considerably enlarged, Cabinet; the majority of senior ministers, including Prime Minister Jayaratne, retained their portfolios. Abdul Rauf Hakeem, the leader of the SLMC, which had recently left the ranks of the opposition to join the UPFA, was appointed as Minister of Justice. Despite its stated wish to seek reconciliation for all parties in the aftermath of the civil war, the Government risked heightening ethnic tension in December when it abandoned the Tamil language version of the national anthem. Earlier in the year Tamil anger had also been provoked by the Government's destruction of several graveyards holding the remains of former Tamil militants.

Political events in Sri Lanka were temporarily overshadowed in December 2010–January 2011 by the devastating monsoon floods that affected more than 1.2m. people and destroyed vast areas of agricultural crops (mostly in the eastern province).

The ruling UPFA won an overwhelming mandate in local elections that were held throughout the country in March 2011, securing power in 205 of the 234 bodies where polling took place. In the following month the UN panel of experts submitted its report on alleged human rights violations (thenceforth widely referred to as the Darusman Report) to the UN Secretary-General and to the Sri Lankan Government. The latter immediately rejected the findings of the report, describing them as 'fundamentally flawed' and 'patently biased', while continuing to maintain that government forces had not wittingly been responsible for any civilian deaths during the final phase of the battle against the LTTE in 2009. To express their outrage at the panel's accusations of war crimes (made against both the Sri Lankan army and the Tamil militants), the UPFA staged a mass rally (headed by Rajapakse) in Colombo on 1 May 2011.

Foreign Affairs

While officially adhering to a policy of non-alignment, Sri Lanka has long fostered close diplomatic and economic relations with its large neighbour India. Following its direct intervention in 1987–90 in the Sri Lankan civil conflict, when an Indian peace-keeping force was dispatched to the island to oversee the implementation of a peace accord between the Sri Lankan Government and the Tamil militants, India subsequently resisted further demands that it become directly involved again. Since the defeat of the LTTE in 2009 India has played a major role in the resettlement and rehabilitation of thousands of displaced Tamil civilians and in the reconstruction of the war-ravaged north-east of Sri Lanka (including the reopening, after nearly 30 years, of a ferry service across the Palk Strait). In 2010 India opened two new consulates in Sri Lanka, one in the southern city of Hambantota and the other in Jaffna, and announced further investment in Sri Lanka (notably in the energy sector). During an official visit to India by President Rajapakse in June 2010 an agreement was signed regarding the possibility of Sri Lanka supplying India with electricity (following the commissioning of new coal and thermal power plants). Feasibility studies were to be conducted on connecting the electricity grids of the two countries through an undersea power line. In January 2011 relations between Sri Lanka and India came under pressure as a result of the alleged shooting of two Indian fishermen in two separate incidents by the Sri Lankan navy.

As relations between Sri Lanka and the West came under pressure as a result of growing concerns over the former's human rights record (in August 2010 the EU temporarily suspended Sri Lanka's preferential access to EU markets under the Generalised System of Preferences known as GSP Plus), Sri Lanka looked increasingly towards its Asian neighbours to foster closer ties. In recent years relations between Sri Lanka and the People's Republic of China have strengthened considerably. China has invested heavily in Sri Lanka, especially in the areas of energy and infrastructure development; the large international port at Hambantota (the first phase of which was completed in August 2010) and the nearby Mattala International Airport, which are both currently being built with Chinese funding, are of particular note. In June 2010 Chinese Vice-Premier Zhang Dejiang visited Colombo for talks with President Rajapakse, during which the two leaders signed six agreements on co-operation in industry and technology. Pakistan, which provided the Sri Lankan Government with large amounts of advanced military equipment during the civil war, has also promoted the development of closer ties with Sri Lanka, particularly with regard to the expansion of bilateral trade (which totalled an estimated US $500m. in 2010). In April 2011 President Rajapakse paid a three-day official visit to Bangladesh, in the course of which the two countries signed five memorandums of understanding on a number of subjects, including export promotion, education and agricultural research.

CONSTITUTION AND GOVERNMENT

The Constitution of Sri Lanka was approved by the National State Assembly (renamed Parliament) on 17 August 1978, and promulgated on 7 September 1978.

A presidential form of government was adopted in October 1977 and confirmed in the Constitution of September 1978. The Constitution provides for a unicameral Parliament as the supreme legislative body, its members being elected by a system of modified proportional representation. Executive powers are vested in the President, who is Head of State. The President is directly elected for a term of six years and is not accountable to Parliament. The President has the power to appoint or dismiss the Prime Minister and members of the Cabinet; may assume any portfolio; and is empowered to dismiss Parliament. In 1982 the Constitution was amended, allowing the President to call a presidential election before his/her first term of office was completed. In 1983 the Constitution was further amended to include a 'no-separation' clause, making any division of Sri Lanka illegal, and any advocates of separatism liable to lose their civic rights. In 2010 a constitutional amendment abolished the stipulation restricting the President to two terms of office.

Sri Lanka comprises nine provinces and 25 administrative districts, each with an appointed Governor and elected Development Council. A network of 68 Pradeshiya Sabhas (district councils) was inaugurated throughout the country in 1988.

REGIONAL AND INTERNATIONAL CO-OPERATION

Sri Lanka is a member of the Asian Development Bank (ADB, see p. 202) and a founder member of both the South Asian Association for Regional Co-operation (SAARC, see p. 417) and the Colombo Plan (see p. 446), which seek to improve regional co-operation, particularly in economic and social development.

Having joined the UN in 1955, Sri Lanka is a member of the Economic and Social Commission for Asia and the Pacific (ESCAP, see p. 37). As a contracting party to the General Agreement on Tariffs and Trade (GATT), Sri Lanka joined the World Trade Organization (WTO, see p. 430) on its establishment in 1995.

ECONOMIC AFFAIRS

In 2009, according to estimates by the World Bank, Sri Lanka's gross national income (GNI), measured at average 2007–09 prices, was US $40,390m., equivalent to $1,990 per head (or $4,720 per head on an international purchasing-power parity basis). During 2000–09, it was estimated, the population increased at an average annual rate of 0.9%, while gross domestic product (GDP) per head grew, in real terms, by an average of 3.9% per year. Overall GDP increased, in real terms, at an average annual rate of 4.9% in 2000–09. According to the Asian Development Bank (ADB), real GDP rose by 6.0% in 2008, by 3.5% in 2009 and by 7.6% in 2010.

In 2010 agriculture (including hunting, forestry and fishing) contributed an estimated 12.8% of GDP, while 33.4% of the employed labour force (excluding inhabitants of the northern and eastern provinces) were engaged in the sector in 2009. The principal cash crops are tea (which accounted for an estimated 22.3% of total export earnings in 2009), rubber and coconuts. In 2004 Sri Lanka was the world's second largest tea exporter, having been overtaken by Kenya in that year. Rice production is also important. Cattle, buffaloes, goats and poultry are the principal livestock. According to the World Bank, during 2000–09 agricultural GDP increased at an average annual rate of 2.5%. According to the ADB, agricultural GDP expanded by 2.8% in 2007, by 4.6% in 2008 and by 3.2% in 2009.

Industry (including mining and quarrying, manufacturing, construction and power) contributed an estimated 29.4% of GDP in 2010 and engaged 26.2% of the employed labour force (excluding inhabitants of the northern and eastern provinces) in 2009. According to the World Bank, during 2000–09 industrial GDP increased at an average annual rate of 4.1%. According to the ADB, industrial GDP rose by 8.9% in 2007, by 9.4% in 2008 and by 4.2% in 2009.

Mining and quarrying contributed an estimated 1.6% of GDP in 2010, and, according to the ADB, engaged 1.8% of the employed labour force in 2001. Diamonds are the major mineral export (accounting for an estimated 6.0% of total export earnings in 2009). Another commercially important mineral in Sri Lanka is graphite, and there are also deposits of iron ore, monazite, uranium, ilmenite sands, limestone and clay.

Manufacturing contributed an estimated 18.0% of GDP in 2010 and engaged 18.7% of the employed labour force (excluding inhabitants of the northern and eastern provinces) in 2009. The principal branches of manufacturing include wearing apparel (excluding footwear), textiles, food products, and also petroleum and coal products. The garment industry is Sri Lanka's largest earner of foreign exchange, with sales of garments and textiles providing an estimated 56.3% of total export earnings in 2008. During 2000–09 manufacturing GDP increased by an average of 3.2% per year, according to the World Bank. The GDP of the manufacturing sector rose by 10.4% in 2008 and by 3.3% in 2009, according to the ADB.

Construction contributed an estimated 7.6% of GDP in 2010. According to the ADB, during 2000–09 construction GDP increased at an average annual rate of 9.0%; the sector grew by 10.5% in 2008 and by 5.6% in 2009.

Energy is derived principally from petroleum, which accounted for 59.9% of electricity production in 2007. In the same year hydroelectric power accounted for 39.9% of electricity produced. In 2007 construction of a coal-fired electricity plant at Norochcholai in the north-west of the country commenced; once fully operational (by 2013 according to the schedule), the plant was expected to alter significantly the structure of the energy sector. Imports of petroleum comprised 21.2% of the value of total imports in 2009.

The services sector, which is dominated by tourism, contributed an estimated 57.8% of GDP in 2010 and engaged 40.4% of the employed labour force (excluding inhabitants of the northern and eastern provinces) in 2009. According to the World Bank, during 2000–09 services GDP increased at an average annual rate of 6.2%. According to the ADB, the sector's GDP grew by 9.2% in 2007, by 24.9% in 2008 and by 3.3% in 2009.

In 2009 Sri Lanka recorded a visible trade deficit of US $2,101m. and there was a deficit of $292m. on the current account of the balance of payments. In 2009 the principal source of imports (21.2%) was India, while the USA was the principal market for exports (20.4%). Other major trading partners were the People's Republic of China, Singapore and the United Kingdom. The principal exports in 2009 were textiles and garments, and agricultural products (principally tea). The principal imports were petroleum, textiles and machinery and transport equipment.

The estimated budgetary deficit for 2010 totalled Rs 933,982m. Sri Lanka's total external debt was US $15,154m. at the end of 2008, of which $12,624 was public and publicly guaranteed debt. In that year the cost of debt-servicing was equivalent to 9.3% of earnings from the exports of goods, services and income. During 1997–2009 the average annual rate of inflation was 10.5%; according to the ADB, the rate was 20.4% in 2007, 29.8% in 2008 and 2.5% in 2009. According to the ADB, 5.9% of the labour force were unemployed in 2009.

Despite a strong recovery from the devastating effects of the tsunami in late 2004, the persistent fiscal deficit remained a considerable obstacle to Sri Lanka's development in the latter half of the 2000s. The Government increasingly relied on external creditors to finance this deficit, thus contributing to escalating levels of public debt and higher rates of inflation. Moreover, escalating security problems and the official lifting of a four-year cease-fire between the Government and the Tamil militants in early 2008 (see Contemporary Political History) engendered additional expenditure on defence and deterred foreign investment. Following the resolution of the civil conflict in May 2009, the subsequent rehabilitation and reconstruction programmes (many of which were funded by China) provided a significant boost to the economy, and helped to attract greater levels of domestic and foreign investment. In December 2009 the main highway to the Jaffna peninsula was reopened for the first time in 25 years, thus facilitating the economic integration and recovery of the northern and eastern areas of the island that were previously controlled by the insurgents. Despite the slow global recovery from the economic crisis of the late 2000s, the Sri Lankan economy showed robust growth in 2010, with GDP increasing by 7.6%, compared with 3.5% in 2009. In 2010 it was reported that Sri Lanka was the highest ranked country among the South Asian nations in the World Prosperity Index. The tourism sector performed particularly well in 2010, with tourist arrivals rising by 46% to reach a record high. However, following a massive decrease in the rate of inflation in 2009 (to a 25-year low of 3.4%), consumer prices rose again in 2010, mainly as a result of escalating global commodity costs (notably food). Nevertheless, by expanding the revenue base and by reducing public expenditure, the Government succeeded in narrowing the budget deficit from 9.9% of GDP in 2009 to 8.0% in 2010. As a result of Sri Lanka's fiscal prudence, during 2010 the IMF released three more tranches of the standby loan of US $2,600m. that had been approved in July 2009. In spite of the EU's temporary withdrawal of Sri Lanka's preferential trade access to European markets in August 2010 (owing to concerns over human rights issues) and the serious flooding that affected the eastern provinces in early 2011, the economy was forecast to remain in vigorous health, with the services and industry sectors fuelling projected GDP growth of 8.0% in 2011. Among the main economic challenges still facing the Government were the reform of the tax system and an increase in the level of private sector investment.

PUBLIC HOLIDAYS

2012: 15 January (Tamil Thai Pongal Day), 4 February (Independence Commemoration Day, and Milad un-Nabi, Birth of the Prophet), 20 February (Maha Shivaratri), 6 April (Good Friday), 13 April (Sinhala and Tamil New Year's Eve), 14 April (Sinhala and Tamil New Year's Day), 1 May (May Day), 18 August (Id al-Fitr, Ramazan Festival Day), 25 October (Id al-Adha, Hadji Festival Day), 13 November (Diwali—Festival of Lights), 25 December (Christmas Day).

Note: A number of Hindu, Muslim and Buddhist holidays depend on lunar sightings. There is a holiday every lunar month on the day of the full moon.

SRI LANKA

Statistical Survey

Source (unless otherwise stated): Department of Census and Statistics, 15/12 Maitland Crescent, POB 563, Colombo 7; tel. (11) 2682176; fax (11) 2697594; e-mail dcensus@lanka.com.lk; internet www.statistics.gov.lk.

Area and Population

AREA, POPULATION AND DENSITY

Area (sq km)	65,525*
Population (census results)	
17 March 1981	14,846,750
17 July 2001 (provisional)†	
Males	8,343,964
Females	8,520,580
Total	16,864,544
Population (official estimates at mid-year)‡	
2008	20,217,000
2009	20,450,000
2010	20,653,000
Density (per sq km) at mid-2010	315.2

* 25,299 sq miles. This figure includes inland water (3,189 sq km).
† Figures refer to 18 out of 25 districts where enumeration was carried out completely. Enumeration was only partially conducted in Mannar, Vavuniya, Batticaloa and Trincomalee districts, owing to security concerns; data from these districts brought the total enumerated population to approximately 17,560,000. The census was not conducted in the districts of Jaffna, Mullaitivu and Kilinochchi, also owing to security concerns. The total estimated population for the entire country at July 2001 was 18,732,255.
‡ Provisional.

POPULATION BY AGE AND SEX
('000, official estimates at mid-2010)

	Males	Females	Total
0–14	2,757	2,674	5,431
15–64	6,888	7,033	13,921
65 and over	604	697	1,301
Total	10,249	10,404	20,653

ETHNIC GROUPS
(census results)

	1981	2001*†
Sinhalese	10,979,561	13,810,664
Sri Lankan Tamil	1,886,872	736,484
Indian Tamil	818,656	855,888
Sri Lankan Moors	1,046,926	1,349,845
Others	114,735	111,663
Total	14,846,750	16,864,544

* Provisional.
† Figures refer to 18 out of 25 districts.

DISTRICTS
(population estimates at mid-2010)

	Area (sq km, excl. inland water)*	Population ('000)	Density (persons per sq km)
Colombo	676	2,553	3,777
Gampaha	1,341	2,177	1,623
Kalutara	1,576	1,135	720
Kandy	1,917	1,431	746
Matale	1,952	497	255
Nuwara Eliya	1,706	761	446
Galle	1,617	1,084	670
Matara	1,270	839	661
Hambantota	2,496	571	229
Jaffna	929	611	658
Mannar	1,880	104	55
Vavuniya	1,861	174	93
Mullaitivu	2,415	148	61
Kilinochchi	1,205	156	129
Batticaloa	2,610	543	208
Ampara	4,222	644	153
Trincomalee	2,529	374	148
Kurunegala	4,624	1,563	338
Puttalam	2,882	779	270
Anuradhapura	6,664	830	125
Polonnaruwa	3,077	410	133
Badulla	2,827	886	313
Moneragala	5,508	440	80
Ratnapura	3,236	1,125	348
Kegalle	1,685	818	485
Total	62,705	20,653	329

* As at 1988; revised total land area is 62,336 sq km.

PRINCIPAL TOWNS
(provisional, population at 2001 census)

Colombo (Kolamba)*	642,020	Sri Jayawardenepura (Kotte)†	115,826
Dehiwala-Mount Lavinia	209,787	Kandy (Maha Nuwara)	110,049
Moratuwa	177,190	Kalmunai (Galmune)	94,457
Jaffna (Yapanaya)	145,600‡	Galle (Galla)	90,934
Negombo (Migamuwa)	121,933		

* Commercial capital.
† Administrative capital.
‡ Estimated population at mid-1997 (Source: Provincial Councils, Department of Elections).

Source: Thomas Brinkhoff, *City Population* (internet www.citypopulation.de).

Mid-2009 (incl. suburbs, UN estimates): Colombo (Kolamba) 681,484; Sri Jayawardenepura (Kotte) 123,090 (Source: UN, *World Urbanization Prospects: The 2009 Revision*).

BIRTHS, MARRIAGES AND DEATHS
(year of registration, provisional)

	Registered live births Number	Rate (per 1,000)	Registered marriages Number	Registered deaths Number	Rate (per 1,000)
2002	363,549	19.1	190,832	110,637	5.8
2003	363,343	18.9	193,387	114,310	5.9
2004	360,220	18.5	191,985	112,568	5.8
2005	370,424	18.8	194,352	129,822	6.6
2006	371,264	18.7	197,458	115,424	5.8
2007	380,069	19.0	195,193	116,883	5.8
2008*	379,912	18.8	198,578	118,279	5.9
2009*	376,843	18.4	194,970	120,085	5.9

* Provisional.

Life expectancy (years at birth, WHO estimates): 69 (males 63; females 76) in 2008 (Source: WHO, *World Health Statistics*).

SRI LANKA

ECONOMICALLY ACTIVE POPULATION
('000 persons aged 10 years and over, excluding northern and eastern provinces)

	2007	2008	2009
Agriculture, hunting, forestry and fishing	2,202.1	2,344.4	2,318.6
Manufacturing	1,331.4	1,354.9	1,301.3
Mining and quarrying			
Electricity, gas and water	542.5	533.1	521.4
Construction			
Wholesale and retail trade, repair of motor vehicles, motorcycles and personal household goods	932.1	924.5	913.4
Restaurants and hotels	118.5	103.8	133.2
Transport, storage and communications	456.8	426.0	419.6
Financing, insurance, real estate and business services	215.2	236.0	221.0
Public administration and defence	433.0	462.6	487.4
Education	259.5	298.8	300.1
Health and social work	115.9	110.9	128.5
Other community, social and personal services	104.6	128.8	104.6
Private households with employed persons	87.4	84.1	96.1
Sub-total	6,799.0	7,008.0	6,945.2
Activities not adequately defined	242.9	166.7	194.3
Total employed	7,041.9	7,174.7	7,139.5
Unemployed	447.0	394.0	432.9
Total labour force	7,488.9	7,568.7	7,527.4

Health and Welfare

KEY INDICATORS

Total fertility rate (children per woman, 2008)	2.3
Under-5 mortality rate (per 1,000 live births, 2008)	17
HIV/AIDS (% of persons aged 15–49, 2007)	<0.1
Physicians (per 1,000 head, 2006)	0.6
Hospital beds (per 1,000 head, 2000)	2.9
Health expenditure (2007): US $ per head (PPP)	179
Health expenditure (2007): % of GDP	4.2
Health expenditure (2007): public (% of total)	47.5
Access to water (% of persons, 2008)	90
Access to sanitation (% of persons, 2008)	91
Total carbon dioxide emissions ('000 metric tons, 2007)	12,303.7
Carbon dioxide emissions per head (metric tons, 2007)	0.6
Human Development Index (2010): ranking	91
Human Development Index (2010): value	0.658

For sources and definitions, see explanatory note on p. vi.

Agriculture

PRINCIPAL CROPS
('000 metric tons)

	2007	2008	2009
Rice, paddy	3,131	3,875	3,652
Maize	56	113	130
Potatoes	77	75	62
Sweet potatoes	49	52	47
Cassava (Manioc)	220	241	278
Sugar cane	783	799	920
Beans, dry	9	9	9*
Cow peas, dry	11	12	13
Coconuts	2,131	2,211	n.a.
Cabbages	69	77	63
Tomatoes	65	85	74
Pumpkins, squash and gourds	97	97	117
Cucumbers and gherkins	28	31	32
Aubergines (Eggplants)	93	104	106
Chillies and peppers, green	49	51	46
Onions, dry	149	107	128
Beans, green	41	43	41
Carrots and turnips	38	40	36
Plantains	519	530	512
Lemons and limes	5	5	5
Guavas, mangoes and mangosteens	85	79	82
Pineapples	53	52	50
Coffee, green	6	5	5
Tea	305	318	290
Pepper	19	23	25
Cinnamon	13	13	15
Natural rubber	118	129	136

* FAO estimate.

Aggregate production ('000 metric tons, may include official, semi-official or estimated data): Total cereals 3,193 in 2007, 3,994 in 2008, 3,788 in 2009; Total roots and tubers 346 in 2007, 368 in 2008, 389 in 2009; Total vegetables (incl. melons) 720 in 2007, 722 in 2008, 730 in 2009; Total fruits (excl. melons) 728 in 2007, 732 in 2008, 715 in 2009.

Source: FAO.

LIVESTOCK
('000 head, year ending September)

	2007	2008	2009
Buffaloes	318	319	372
Cattle	1,206	1,196	1,137
Sheep	16	10	8
Goats	389	377	377
Pigs	94	89	81
Chickens	13,779	14,331	13,615

Source: FAO.

LIVESTOCK PRODUCTS
('000 metric tons)

	2007	2008	2009
Cattle meat	23.5	22.3	22.9
Buffalo meat*	3.7	3.7	4.4
Goat meat	1.3	1.2	1.3
Pig meat	2.3	1.6	1.6
Chicken meat	100.1	102.5	99.3
Cows' milk	143.4	145.6	155.5
Buffaloes' milk	27.3	30.1	41.6
Goats' milk*	5.0	5.0	5.0
Hen eggs	51.9	59.0	64.8

* FAO estimates.

Source: FAO.

SRI LANKA

Forestry

ROUNDWOOD REMOVALS
('000 cubic metres, excl. bark, FAO estimates)

	2007	2008	2009
Sawlogs, veneer logs and logs for sleepers	117	35	34
Other industrial wood	577	577	577
Fuel wood	5,431	5,357	5,283
Total	6,125	5,969	5,894

Source: FAO.

SAWNWOOD PRODUCTION
('000 cubic metres, incl. railway sleepers)

	1999*	2000	2001
Coniferous (softwood)	—	—	30
Broadleaved (hardwood)	5	29	31
Total	5	29	61

*FAO estimates.

2002–09: Production assumed to be unchanged from 2001 (FAO estimates).
Source: FAO.

Fishing

('000 metric tons, live weight)

	2006	2007	2008
Capture	274.0	307.3	327.6
Tilapias	19.3	22.5	25.2
Demersal percomorphs	11.2	13.9	12.7
Clupeoids	56.2	63.5	66.9
Skipjack tuna	54.3	73.2	78.9
Carangids	9.6	11.4	11.2
Mackerels	15.6	16.3	18.3
Sharks, rays, skates etc.	5.7	3.3	3.9
Aquaculture	5.7	8.2	7.5
Total catch	279.7	315.5	335.0

Source: FAO.

Mining

('000 metric tons, unless otherwise indicated)

	2007	2008*	2009
Natural graphite (metric tons)	9,593	6,615	7,000
Salt—unrefined	70	111	112
Kaolin	11	10	10
Phosphate rock (gross weight)	40	42	42

*Estimates.
Sources: US Geological Survey.

Industry

SELECTED PRODUCTS
('000 metric tons, unless otherwise indicated)

	2005	2006	2007
Raw sugar	60	70	75
Cigarettes (million units)	4,832	4,832	4,719
Jet fuel	114	131	171
Motor gasoline—petrol	161	194	163
Kerosene	139	144	97
Distillate fuel oil	591	628	445
Residual fuel oil	762	809	810
Cement*	1,500	1,600	1,700
Plywood ('000 cu m)†	14	14	14
Electric energy (million kWh)	8,769	9,389	9,814

*Estimates.
† FAO estimates.

Naphtha ('000 metric tons): 99 in 2003; 103 in 2004; 118 in 2005.

2008: Cement ('000 metric tons) 1,800 (estimate); Plywood ('000 cu m) 6 (unofficial figure); Electric energy (million kWh) 9,901.

2009: Cement ('000 metric tons) 1,900; Plywood ('000 cu m) 6 (unofficial figure); Electric energy (million kWh) 9,882.

Sources: US Geological Survey; Asian Development Bank, *Key Indicators of Developing Asian and Pacific Countries*; FAO; UN, *Industrial Commodity Statistics Yearbook* and Database.

Finance

CURRENCY AND EXCHANGE RATES

Monetary Units
100 cents = 1 Sri Lanka rupee (R).

Sterling, Dollar and Euro Equivalents (31 December 2010)
£1 sterling = Rs 173.661;
US $1 = Rs 110.930;
€1 = Rs 148.225;
1,000 Sri Lanka rupees = £5.76 = $9.01 = €6.75.

Average Exchange Rate (rupees per US $)
2008   108.334
2009   114.945
2010   113.066

BUDGET
(Rs million)

Revenue	2008	2009	2010*
Taxation	585,770	619,182	726,014
Taxes on income and profits	126,541	139,558	160,344
Taxes on domestic goods and services	320,480	311,908	376,014
Value-added tax	202,984	171,118	206,730
Excise duty (ordinance)	27,404	28,516	32,080
Excise duty (special provisions)	73,534	69,067	83,663
Stamp duty	3,751	3,328	4,390
Taxes on international trade	136,958	164,448	186,076
Import duties	63,994	79,810	84,257
Licence taxes and other	1,791	3,269	3,580
Non-tax revenue	91,474	101,255	109,359
Capital revenue	13,646	12,056	15,997
Other	77,828	89,199	93,362
Foreign grants	22,143	25,922	19,000
Total	699,388	746,359	854,373

SRI LANKA

Statistical Survey

Expenditure by category	2008	2009	2010*
Recurrent expenditure	736,594	881,984	952,179
Personal emoluments	175,790	130,499	130,859
Salaries and wages	116,278	130,499	130,859
General public services	22,745	30,387	39,671
Transfers	246,602	266,355	279,816
Retirement benefits	76,091	86,305	92,254
Provincial councils	76,807	77,783	85,047
Interest payments	212,094	303,177	337,227
Other purposes	79,363	69,645	74,239
Capital expenditure	296,927	348,788	379,396
Public debt repayments	379,204	516,131	456,780
Domestic	285,516	387,003	393,567
Foreign	93,689	129,128	63,213
Total expenditure	1,412,725	1,746,902	1,788,355

Expenditure by institution	2008	2009	2010*
Special spending units	10,138	11,780	15,539
Ministries	1,402,587	1,735,122	1,772,816
Finance and planning	605,297	831,712	850,908
Defence	206,867	214,637	202,217
Health	46,898	48,976	53,097
Public administration and home affairs	94,800	106,380	114,169
Local government and provincial councils	97,777	102,211	113,263
Total expenditure	1,412,725	1,746,902	1,788,355

* Forecasts.

Source: Ministry of Finance and Planning, Colombo.

INTERNATIONAL RESERVES
(excluding gold, US $ million at 31 December)

	2007	2008	2009
IMF special drawing rights	7	2	20
Reserve position in IMF	76	74	75
Foreign exchange	3,297	2,393	4,521
Total	3,380	2,469	4,616

2010: IMF special drawing rights 2; Reserve position in IMF 74.

Source: IMF, *International Financial Statistics*.

MONEY SUPPLY
(Rs million at 31 December)

	2007	2008	2009
Currency outside banks	147,183	155,023	181,840
Demand deposits at commercial banks	119,407	122,285	154,849
Total money (incl. others)	268,005	278,553	339,036

Source: IMF, *International Financial Statistics*.

COST OF LIVING
(Consumer Price Index for Colombo; base: 2002 = 100)

	2008	2009	2010
Food (incl. beverages)	213.3	219.2	234.2
Clothing (excl. footwear)	154.8	165.3	n.a.
Rent	226.8	227.5	n.a.
All items (incl. others)	199.9	206.8	219.1

Source: ILO.

NATIONAL ACCOUNTS
(Rs million at current prices)

Expenditure on the Gross Domestic Product

	2008	2009	2010*
Government final consumption expenditure	713,788	851,549	872,610
Private final consumption expenditure	3,085,296	3,116,221	3,684,738
Gross capital formation	1,215,247	1,181,449	1,556,769
Total domestic expenditure	5,014,331	5,149,219	6,114,117
Exports of goods and services	1,095,679	1,031,289	1,215,007
Less Imports of goods and services	1,699,328	1,345,216	1,726,803
GDP at market prices	4,410,682	4,835,293	5,602,321
GDP at factor cost, at constant 2002 prices	2,365,501	2,449,214	2,645,432

* Provisional.

Gross Domestic Product by Economic Activity

	2008	2009	2010*
Agriculture, hunting, forestry and fishing	590,114	613,694	716,892
Mining and quarrying	71,768	79,204	89,100
Manufacturing	791,898	875,562	1,009,003
Construction	327,138	366,248	423,414
Electricity, gas and water	104,666	113,687	127,625
Transport, storage and communications	530,980	599,934	709,400
Wholesale and retail trade	949,372	948,425	1,096,323
Hotels and restaurants	20,611	24,988	33,213
Finance and real estate	413,322	499,304	597,540
Ownership of dwellings	141,794	161,485	171,871
Public administration	380,765	445,543	500,547
Private services	88,255	107,219	127,393
GDP at market prices	4,410,682	4,835,293	5,602,321

* Provisional.

Source: Central Bank of Sri Lanka, Colombo.

BALANCE OF PAYMENTS
(US $ million)

	2007	2008	2009
Exports of goods f.o.b.	7,640	8,111	7,085
Imports of goods f.o.b.	−10,167	−12,682	−9,186
Trade balance	−2,527	−4,571	−2,101
Exports of services	1,775	2,002	1,892
Imports of services	−2,602	−3,010	−2,522
Balance on goods and services	−3,354	−5,579	−2,732
Other income received	449	225	122
Other income paid	−807	−1,197	−609
Balance on goods, services and income	−3,711	−6,551	−3,219
Current transfers received	2,502	2,918	3,330
Current transfers paid	−288	−353	−403
Current balance	−1,498	−3,986	−292
Capital account (net)	269	291	233
Direct investment abroad	−55	−62	−20
Direct investment from abroad	603	752	404
Portfolio investment assets	326	−174	−47
Portfolio investment liabilities	−322	−488	−382
Other investment assets	−281	210	−435
Other investment liabilities	−257	−234	−625
Net errors and omissions	−159	724	−140
Overall balance	−1,374	−2,968	−1,304

Source: IMF, *International Financial Statistics*.

External Trade

PRINCIPAL COMMODITIES
(Rs million)

Imports c.i.f.	2007	2008	2009*
Consumer goods	221,371	277,135	226,487
Wheat	25,891	40,563	29,769
Durables	103,627	113,369	83,388
Intermediate goods	721,473	903,187	651,492
Petroleum	276,899	364,284	248,959
Textiles	180,689	184,404	165,717
Investment goods	297,266	330,272	281,441
Machinery and transport equipment	178,325	191,846	166,411
Total (incl. others)	1,250,386	1,525,705	1,172,618

Exports f.o.b.	2007	2008	2009*
Agricultural products	166,945	200,739	194,206
Tea	113,565	137,600	136,171
Petroleum products	18,693	27,551	15,484
Rubber based products	53,318	58,671	44,163
Diamonds	38,588	45,328	36,383
Textiles and garments	369,696	376,025	376,146
Total (incl. others)	660,389	667,187	609,513

* Provisional.

Source: Central Bank of Sri Lanka, Colombo.

PRINCIPAL TRADING PARTNERS
(US $ million)

Imports c.i.f.	2007	2008	2009
China, People's Republic	923.8	1,786.9	1,559.5
Hong Kong	724.8	458.2	343.5
India	2,610.1	2,731.9	2,413.0
Iran	844.2	1,109.7	721.7
Japan	413.2	408.5	224.6
Malaysia	283.5	467.6	375.0
Singapore	1,118.5	1087.6	836.6
United Arab Emirates	333.2	438.0	284.9
United Kingdom	229.8	246.9	n.a.
USA	412.1	311.6	252.5
Total (incl. others)	11,301.0	14,421.2	11,408.6

Exports f.o.b.	2007	2008	2009
France	175.9	175.2	150.7
Germany	437.9	446.0	389.3
India	515.3	382.0	337.4
Italy	394.9	406.6	405.7
Japan	159.6	187.4	166.7
Russia	202.6	273.3	232.9
United Arab Emirates	209.2	264.2	265.1
United Kingdom	1,018.0	1,035.4	948.0
USA	1,970.0	1,882.3	1515.9
Total (incl. others)	7,740.0	8,523.9	7,448.8

Note: Data reflect the IMF's direction of trade methodology and, as a result, the totals may not be equal to those presented for trade in commodities.

Source: Asian Development Bank.

Transport

RAILWAYS

	2007	2008	2009
Passengers (million)	110.5	104.6	101.8
Freight carried ('000 metric tons)*	1,707	1,694	1,647

* Excluding livestock.

ROAD TRAFFIC
(motor vehicles in use at 31 December)

	2000	2001	2002
Passenger cars	233,018	241,444	253,447
Buses and coaches	64,963	66,273	67,702
Lorries and vans	300,712	312,495	328,913
Road tractors	133,092	138,879	146,043
Motorcycles and mopeds	834,586	868,705	923,467
Total	1,566,371	1,627,796	1,719,572

2007: Passenger cars 361,211; Buses and coaches 79,870; Lorries and vans 718,338; Motorcycles and mopeds 1,966,375.

2008: Passenger cars 381,448; Buses and coaches 81,050; Lorries and vans 761,364; Motorcycles and mopeds 2,167,131.

Source: International Road Federation, *World Road Statistics*.

SHIPPING

Merchant Fleet
(registered at 31 December)

	2007	2008	2009
Number of vessels	85	88	84
Displacement ('000 grt)	163.3	174.3	167.6

Source: IHS Fairplay, *World Fleet Statistics*.

International Sea-borne Shipping
(freight traffic, '000 metric tons, Colombo, Trincomalee and Galle only)

	2007	2008	2009
Goods loaded	17,724	20,131	19,494
Goods unloaded	28,621	30,451	29,283

CIVIL AVIATION
(traffic on scheduled services)

	2004	2005	2006
Kilometres flown (million)	43	42	45
Passengers carried ('000)	2,413	2,818	3,101
Passenger-km (million)	8,310	8,599	9,271
Total ton-km (million)	1,068	1,089	1,164

Source: UN, *Statistical Yearbook*.

Tourism

FOREIGN TOURIST ARRIVALS*

Country of residence	2006	2007	2008
Australia	21,665	20,241	19,145
Belgium	6,373	4,653	2,394
Canada	14,863	11,862	9,745
France	22,703	9,540	10,703
Germany	47,296	35,016	30,154
India	128,52	105,906	88,628
Italy	12,353	11,451	9,137
Japan	16,217	14,274	10,578
Maldives	24,505	29,550	31,458
Netherlands	19,460	17,532	13,180
Pakistan	11,165	10,173	7,702
Switzerland	7,729	4,911	5,261
United Kingdom	88,531	94,089	80,214
USA	20,825	16,476	13,458
Total (incl. others)	559,603	494,008	438,475

* Excluding Sri Lanka nationals residing abroad.

Tourism receipts (US $ million, incl. passenger transport): 733 in 2006; 750 in 2007; 803 in 2008.

Sources: World Tourism Organization.

Communications Media

	2007	2008	2009
Telephones ('000 main lines in use)	2,742.1	3,446.4	3,436.0
Mobile cellular telephones ('000 subscribers)	7,983.5	11,082.5	14,095.3
Internet users ('000)	771.7	1,163.5	1,776.2
Broadband subscribers ('000)	63.3	101.9	169.6

Radio receivers ('000 in use): 3,850 in 1997.

Television receivers ('000 in use): 2,200 in 2001.

Newspapers (titles): 189 in 2001.

Books published: 1,818 titles in 2000; 7.4m. copies in 2001.

Personal computers: 734,000 (37.3 per 1,000 persons) in 2005.

Sources: UN, *Statistical Yearbook*; UNESCO, *Statistical Yearbook*; Telecommunications Regulatory Commission of Sri Lanka and International Telecommunication Union.

Education

(1995)

	Institutions	Teachers	Students
Primary	9,657	70,537	1,962,498
Secondary	5,771*	103,572	2,314,054
Universities and equivalent	n.a.	2,344	40,035
Distance learning	n.a.	206	20,601

* 1992 figure.

1996: Primary: 9,554 institutions, 66,339 teachers, 1,843,848 students.

1997: Primary: 60,832 teachers, 1,807,751 students; Secondary: 2,313,511 students.

1998: Primary: 1,798,162 students.

2009 (all levels, provisional): *Schools:* Total 10,205 (state 9,410, private 98, Pirivenas (monastic colleges) 697). *Teachers:* Total 225,338 (state 213,694, private 5,701, Pirivenas (monastic colleges) 5,943). *Pupils:* Total 4,033,248 (state 3,860,176, private 114,974, Pirivenas (monastic colleges) 58,098).

Higher education (2008, provisional): 14 institutions, 4,043 teachers (including temporary staff), 66,675 students.

Source: Ministry of Education, Colombo.

Pupil-teacher ratio (primary education, UNESCO estimate): 23.5 in 2007/08 (Source: UNESCO Institute for Statistics).

Adult literacy rate (UNESCO estimates): 90.6% (males 92.2%; females 89.1%) in 2008 (Source: UNESCO Institute for Statistics).

Directory

The Government

HEAD OF STATE

President: MAHINDA RAJAPAKSE (sworn in 19 November 2005; re-elected 26 January 2010; sworn in for a second term 19 November 2010).

THE CABINET
(May 2011)

The Cabinet is formed by the United People's Freedom Alliance.

Prime Minister and Minister of Buddha Sasana and Religious Affairs: D. M. JAYARATNE.

Minister of Defence, of Highways, of Finance and Planning, and of Ports and Aviation: MAHINDA RAJAPAKSE.

Senior Minister and Minister of Good Governance and Infrastructure Facilities: RATHNASIRI WICKRAMANAYAKA.

Senior Minister and Minister of Human Resources: D. E. W. GUNASEKERA.

Senior Minister and Minister of Rural Affairs: ATHAUDA SENEVIRATNE.

Senior Minister and Minister of Food Security: P. DAYARATNE.

Senior Minister and Minister of Urban Affairs: A. H. M. FOWZIE.

Senior Minister and Minister of Social Services: MILROY FERNANDO.

Senior Minister and Minister of Consumer Welfare: S. B. NAVINNE.

Senior Minister and Minister of National Assets: PIYASENA GAMAGE.

Senior Minister and Minister of Scientific Affairs: Prof. TISSA VITHARANA.

Senior Minister and Minister of International Monetary Co-operation: SARATH AMUNUGAMA.

Minister of Irrigation and Water Resources Management: NIMAL SIRIPALA DE SILVA.

Minister of Health: MAITHRIPALA SIRISENA.

Minister of Petroleum Industries: SUSIL PREMAJAYANTHA.

Minister of Livestock and Rural Community Development: ARUMUGAM THONDAMAN.

Minister of Water Supply and Drainage: DINESH C. R. GUNAWARDENA.

Minister of Traditional Industries and Small Enterprise Development: DOUGLAS DEVANANDA.

Minister of Local Government and Provincial Councils: A. L. M. ATHAULLAH.

Minister of Industry and Commerce: RISHAD BATHIYUTHEEN.

Minister of Power and Energy: CHAMPIKA RANAWAKA.

Minister of Construction, Engineering Services, Housing and Common Amenities: WIMAL WEERAWANSA.

Minister of Justice: RAUFF HAKEEM.

Minister of Economic Development: BASIL RAJAPAKSE.

Minister of National Languages and Social Integration: VASUDEVA NANAYAKKARA.

Minister of Higher Education: S. B. DISSANAYAKE.

Minister of External Affairs: Prof. G. L. PEIRIS.

Minister of Public Administration and Home Affairs: W. D. J. SENEVIRATNE.

Minister of Parliamentary Affairs: SUMEDHA JAYASENA.

Minister of Postal Services: JEEWAN KUMARANATUNGA.

Minister of Technology and Research: PAVITHRA WANNIARACHCHI.

Minister of Environment: ANURA PRIYADARSHANA YAPA.

Minister of Child Development and Women's Affairs: TISSA KARALIYADDE.

Minister of Labour and Labour Relations: GAMINI LOKUGE.

Minister of Education: BANDULA GUNAWARDENA.

Minister of Plantation Industries: MAHINDA SAMARASINGHE.

Minister of Fisheries and Aquatic Resources: RAJITHA SENARATNE.

Minister of Land and Land Development: JANAKA BANDARA TENNEKOON.

Minister of Social Services: FELIX PERERA.

Minister of Private Transport Services: C. B. RATHNAYAKE.

Minister of Agriculture: MAHINDA YAPA ABEYWARDENA.

Minister of Mass Media and Information: KEHELIYA RAMBUKWELLA.

Minister of Transport: KUMARA WELGAMA.

Minister of Youth Affairs: DULLAS ALAHAPERUMA.

Minister of Co-operatives and Internal Trade: JOHNSTON FERNANDO.

SRI LANKA

Minister of Rehabilitation and Prison Reforms: CHANDRASIRI GAJADEERA.
Minister of Indigenous Medicine: SALINDA DISSANAYAKE.
Minister of Minor Export Crops Promotion: REGINALD COORAY.
Minister of Foreign Employment Promotion and Welfare: DILAN PERERA.
Minister of Coconut Development and State Plantations Development: JAGATH PUSHPAKUMARA.
Minister of Culture and the Arts: T. B. EKANAYAKE.
Minister of Disaster Management: MAHINDA AMARAWEERA.
Minister of Agrarian Services and Wildlife: S. M. CHANDRASENA.
Minister of Resettlement: GUNARATNE WEERAKOON.
Minister of Public Coordination and Public Affairs: MERVIN SILVA.
Minister of Sports: MAHINDANANDA ALUTHGAMAGE.
Minister of State Assets and Enterprise Development: DAYASRITHA TISSERA.
Minister of Telecommunications and Information Technology: RANJITH SIYAMBALAPITIYA.
Minister of National Heritage: JAGATH BALASURIYA.
Minister of Productivity Promotion: LAKSHMAN SENEVIRATNE.
Minister of State Management Reforms: NAVIN DISSANAYAKE.
Minister of Civil Aviation: PRIYANKARA JAYARATNA.

MINISTRIES

President's Secretariat: Republic Sq., Colombo 1; tel. (11) 2324801; fax (11) 2331246; e-mail priu@presidentsoffice.lk; internet www.president.gov.lk.

Prime Minister's Office: 58 Sir Ernest de Silva Mawatha, Colombo 7; tel. (11) 2575317; fax (11) 2575454; e-mail slpm@pmoffice.gov.lk; internet www.pmoffice.gov.lk.

Ministry of Agrarian Services and Wildlife: 80/5 Govijana Mandiraya, Rajamalwatta Ave, Battaramulla, Colombo; tel. (11) 2887421; fax (11) 2887481; e-mail bkva@yahoo.com.

Ministry of Agriculture: 'Govijana Mandiraya', 80/5 Rajamalwatta Rd, Battaramulla, Colombo; tel. (11) 2869553; fax (11) 2868910; e-mail ituagrimin@gmail.com; internet www.mimrd.gov.lk.

Ministry of Buddha Sasana and Religious Affairs: 115 Wijerama Mawatha, Colombo 7; tel. (11) 2690896; fax (11) 2690897; e-mail herathmudi@yahoo.com.

Ministry of Child Development and Women's Affairs: 177 Nawala Rd, Narahenpita, Colombo 5; tel. (11) 2368096; fax (11) 2369294; e-mail directorwb_womens@mymail.lk; internet www.childwomenmin.gov.lk.

Ministry of Civil Aviation: 19 Chaithya Rd, Colombo 1; tel. (11) 2439350; fax (11) 2433387; e-mail civimyad@sltnet.lk; internet www.ports-aviation.gov.lk.

Ministry of Coconut Development and Janatha Estate Development: 493/1, T. B. Jayah Mawatha, Colombo 10; tel. (11) 2693620; fax (11) 2693620; e-mail pjpushpakumara@yahoo.com.

Ministry of Construction, Engineering Services, Housing and Common Amenities: 'Sethsiripaya', 2nd Floor, Battaramulla, Colombo; tel. (11) 2888151; fax (11) 2867952; e-mail minister@enghousing.net; internet www.constructionmin.gov.lk.

Ministry of Co-operatives and Internal Trade: 'Rakshana Mandiraya', 7th Floor, 21 Vauxhall St, Colombo 2; tel. (11) 2435602; fax (11) 2447669; e-mail sltradeweb@yahoo.com.

Ministry of Culture and the Arts: 'Sethsiripaya', 8th Floor, Battaramulla, Colombo; tel. (11) 2872001; fax (11) 2872024; e-mail itasst@cultural.gov.lk; internet www.cultural.gov.lk.

Ministry of Defence: 15/5 Baladaksha Mawatha, POB 572, Colombo 3; tel. (11) 2430860; fax (11) 2446300; e-mail webinfo@defence.lk; internet www.defence.lk.

Ministry of Disaster Management: 2 Wijerama Mawatha, Colombo 7; tel. (11) 2695013; fax (11) 2681980; e-mail info@dmhr.gov.lk; internet www.disastermin.gov.lk.

Ministry of Economic Development: 177 Galle Rd, Colombo 3; tel. (11) 2394764; fax (11) 2394763; e-mail secedip@sltnet.lk; internet www.med.gov.lk.

Ministry of Education: 'Isurupaya', Battaramulla, Colombo; tel. (11) 2785141; fax (11) 2785162; e-mail isurupaya@moe.gov.lk; internet www.moe.gov.lk.

Ministry of Environment: 82 Sampath Paya, Rajamalwatte Rd, Battaramulla, Colombo; tel. (11) 2882112; fax (11) 2863652; e-mail promotion@menr.lk; internet www.environmentmin.gov.lk.

Ministry of External Affairs: Republic Bldg, Colombo 1; tel. (11) 2325371; fax (11) 2446091; e-mail publicity@formin.gov.lk; internet www.slmfa.gov.lk.

Ministry of Finance and Planning: Galle Face Secretariat, Colombo 1; tel. (11) 2484500; fax (11) 2449823; e-mail info@mo.treasury.gov.lk; internet www.treasury.gov.lk.

Ministry of Fisheries and Aquatic Resources: New Secretariat, Maligawatta, Colombo 10; tel. (11) 2446183; fax (11) 2541184; e-mail secretary@fisheries.gov.lk; internet www.fisheries.gov.lk.

Ministry of Foreign Employment Promotion and Welfare: 12th Floor, Central Bank Bldg, Janadhipathi Mawatha, Colombo 1; tel. (11) 2477971; fax (11) 2477955.

Ministry of Health: 'Suwasiripaya', 385 Wimalawansha Himi Mawatha, Colombo 10; tel. (11) 2694033; fax (11) 2692694; e-mail dhi@health.gov.lk; internet www.health.gov.lk.

Ministry of Higher Education: 18 Ward Place, Colombo 7; tel. (11) 2694486; fax (11) 2697239; e-mail mioh.hied@sltnet.lk; internet www.mohe.gov.lk.

Ministry of Indigenous Medicine: Old Kottawa Rd, Nawinna, Maharagama, Colombo; tel. (11) 2850093; fax (11) 5651966; e-mail ita@ayurveda.gov.lk; internet www.indigenousmedimini.gov.lk.

Ministry of Industry and Commerce: 73/1 Galle Rd, Colombo 3; tel. (11) 2392149; fax (11) 2449402; e-mail misec@sltnet.lk; internet www.industry.gov.lk.

Ministry of Irrigation and Water Resources Management: 11 Jawatta Rd, Colombo 5; tel. (11) 2554001; fax (11) 2554015; e-mail dgiirrig@.sltnet.lk; internet www.irrigation.gov.lk.

Ministry of Justice: Superior Courts Complex Bldg, Colombo 12; tel. (11) 2323022; fax (11) 2320785; e-mail justiceminist@sltnet.lk; internet www.justiceministry.gov.lk.

Ministry of Labour and Labour Relations: Labour Secretariat, 2nd Floor, Narahenpita, Colombo 5; tel. (11) 2583164; fax (11) 2588950; e-mail slmol@slt.lk; internet www.labourdept.gov.lk.

Ministry of Land and Land Development: 'Govijana Mandiraya', 80/5 Rajamalwatta Rd, Battaramulla, Colombo; tel. (11) 2868908; fax (11) 2887442; e-mail pmltd@sltnet.lk; internet www.landmin.gov.lk.

Ministry of Livestock and Rural Community Development: 45 St Michael's Rd, POB 562, Colombo 3; tel. (11) 2541369; fax (11) 2430365; e-mail geethacb@hotmail.com; internet www.livestock.gov.lk.

Ministry of Local Government and Provincial Councils: 330 Union Place, Colombo 2; tel. (11) 2305326; fax (11) 2347529; e-mail secpl@minhaprolo.gov.lk.

Ministry of Mass Media and Information: 163 Kirulappona Mawatha, Polhengoda, Colombo 5; tel. (11) 2513459; fax (11) 2513462; e-mail dammika.yapa@media.gov.lk; internet www.media.gov.lk.

Ministry of Minor Export Crop Promotion: 'Govijana Mandiraya', 80/5 Rajamalwatta Ave, Battaramulla, Colombo; tel. (11) 22878678; fax 2863548.

Ministry of National Heritage: 'Sethsiripaya', 8th Floor, Battaramulla, Colombo 3; tel. (11) 2879082; fax (11) 2885970.

Ministry of National Languages and Social Integration: 40 Buthgamuwa Rd, Rajagiriya; tel. (11) 2883926; fax (11) 2883929; e-mail info@lanintegrationmin.gov.lk.

Ministry of Parliamentary Affairs: 464B Pannipitiya Rd, Pelewatta, Battaramulla, Colombo; tel. (11) 2786966; fax (11) 2786968; e-mail webmaster@parliament.lk; internet www.minparliament.gov.lk.

Ministry of Petroleum Industries: 80 Sir Ernest De Silva Mawatha, Colombo 7; tel. (11) 2564355; fax (11) 2375163; internet www.petroleummin.gov.lk.

Ministry of Plantation Industries: 55/75 Vauxhall Lane, Colombo 2; tel. (11) 2445397; fax (11) 2438031; e-mail secypi@sltnet.lk; internet www.plantationindustries.gov.lk.

Ministry of Ports and Highways: 45 Leyden Bastian Rd, Colombo 1; tel. (11) 2432249; fax (11) 2435142; e-mail sec@slpa.lk (ports); e-mail sec@mohsl.gov.lk (highways); internet www.mohsl.gov.lk.

Ministry of Postal Services: 310 D. R. Wijewardene Mawatha, Colombo 10; tel. (11) 2422591; fax (11) 2323465; e-mail info@telepost.gov.lk; internet www.telepost.gov.lk.

Ministry of Power and Energy: 493/1 T. B. Jaya Mawatha, Colombo 10; tel. (11) 2687013; fax (11) 2687014; e-mail pepeland@eureka.lk; internet www.power.lk.

Ministry of Private Transport Services: 241 Park Rd, Colombo 5; tel. (11) 2587372; fax (11) 2503680; e-mail cbr@cbratnayake.org.

Ministry of Productivity Promotion: 318 High Level Rd, Colombo 6; tel. (11) 2812161; fax (11) 2812162.

SRI LANKA

Ministry of Public Administration and Home Affairs: Independence Sq., Colombo 7; tel. (11) 2662340; fax (11) 2693304; e-mail minister@pubad.gov.lk; internet www.pubad.gov.lk.

Ministry of Public Management Reforms: 29/2 D. P. Wijesinghe Mawatha, Pellawatte, Battaramulla; tel. (11) 2786658; fax (11) 2784199; e-mail secmpmr@sltnet.lk; internet www.reformsmin.gov.lk.

Ministry of Public Relations and Public Affairs: 115 Anagarika Dharmapala Mawatha, Colombo 7; tel. (11) 2334249; fax (11) 2334182; e-mail wijesekaraw@yahoo.com.

Ministry of Rehabilitation and Prison Reforms: 35A Dr N. M. Perera Mawatha, Colombo 8; tel. (11) 2697912; fax (11) 2697910; e-mail prisons@sltnet.lk; internet www.prisons.gov.lk/About%20us/ministry.htm.

Ministry of Resettlement: 146 Galle Rd, Colombo 3; tel. (11) 2395109; fax (11) 2395521; e-mail resettlementmin@yahoo.com; internet www.resettlementmin.gov.lk.

Ministry of Social Services: 'Sethsiripaya', 5th Floor, Battaramulla, Colombo; tel. (11) 2584320; fax (11) 2877381; e-mail msssec@sltnet.lk; internet www.socialwelfare.gov.lk.

Ministry of Sports: 7A Reid Ave, Colombo 7; tel. (11) 2685079; fax (11) 2689161; e-mail sportssec@yahoo.com; internet www.sportsmin.gov.lk.

Ministry of State Resources and Enterprise Development: 561/3 Elvitigala Mawatha, Colombo 5; tel. (11) 2368358; fax (11) 2369180.

Ministry of Technology and Research: 408 Galle Rd, POB 1571, Colombo 3; tel. (11) 2374700; e-mail mstsasad@sltnet.lk; internet www.most.gov.lk.

Ministry of Telecommunications and Information Technology: 79/1, 5th Lane, Colombo 3; tel. (11) 2577777; fax (11) 2301712; e-mail info@ictmin.gov.lk; internet www.ictmin.gov.lk.

Ministry of Traditional Industries and Small Enterprise Development: 780 Maradana Rd, Colombo 10; tel. (11) 2669269; fax (11) 2669281; e-mail mintised@sltnet.lk; internet www.risepmin.gov.lk.

Ministry of Transport: 1 D. R. Wijewardene Mawatha, POB 588, Colombo 10; tel. (11) 2687105; fax (11) 2684930; e-mail mintrans@sltnet.lk; internet www.transport.gov.lk.

Ministry of Water Supply and Drainage: 34 Thakahashi Bldg, Narahenpita Rd, Nawala, Colombo; tel. (11) 2808135; fax (11) 2808137; internet www.mwsd.gov.lk.

Ministry of Youth Affairs and Skills Development: 420 Bouddhaloka Mawatha, Colombo 7; tel. (11) 2669237; fax (11) 2683569; e-mail youthmin@sltnet.lk; internet www.youthmin.gov.lk.

President and Legislature

PRESIDENT

Presidential Election, 26 January 2010

Candidate	Valid votes	% of votes
Mahinda Rajapakse (SLFP)	6,015,934	57.88
Gen. Sarath Fonseka (New Democratic Front)	4,173,185	40.15
Total (incl. others)*	10,393,613	100.00

*In addition to the two main candidates, there were 20 other candidates, none of whom won more than 0.4% of valid votes.

PARLIAMENT

Speaker: CHAMAL RAJAPAKSE.
Deputy Speaker: PRIYANKARA JAYARATNE.

General Election, 8 April 2010

Party/Alliance	Votes	% of votes	Seats
United People's Freedom Alliance	4,846,388	60.33	144
United National Party	2,357,057	29.34	60
Democratic National Alliance	441,251	5.49	7
Ilankai Tamil Arasu Katchi	233,190	2.90	14
Others	155,831	1.94	—
Total	8,033,717	100.00	225

Election Commission

Department of Elections: Elections Secretariat, Sarana Mawatha, Rajagiriya, Jayawardenapura; tel. (11) 2868441; fax (11) 2868445; e-mail comelesl@sltnet.lk; internet www.slelections.gov.lk; f. 1947; govt dept; Commr of Elections MAHINDA DESHAPRIYA.

Political Organizations

Akhila Ilankai Tamil United Front (AITUK): e-mail secretary@tamilunitedfront.com; internet www.tamilunitedfront.com; f. 2006; Tamil; advocates federal solution to ethnic conflict; Gen. Sec. Dr K. VIGNESWARAN.

Democratic National Alliance (DNA): Royal Ave, Colombo; f. 2010; Leader Gen. SARATH FONSEKA; Sec.-Gen. VIJITHE HERATH.

Janatha Vimukthi Peramuna (JVP) (People's Liberation Front): 464/20 Pannipitiya Rd, Pelawatte, Battaramulla, Colombo; tel. (11) 2785612; fax (11) 2786050; e-mail jvplanka@sltnet.lk; internet www.jvpsrilanka.com; f. 1965; banned following a coup attempt in 1971, regained legal status in 1977, banned again in 1983, but regained legal status in 1994; Marxist; Sinhalese support; Leader SOMAWANSA AMARASINGHE; Gen. Sec. TILVIN SILVA.

Democratic Workers' Congress (DWC) (Political Wing): 70 Bankshall St, POB 1009, Colombo 11; tel. (11) 2439199; fax (11) 2435961; f. 1978 as political wing of DWC trade union (f. 1939); aims to eliminate discrimination against the Tamil-speaking Sri Lankans of recent Indian origin; 201,382 mems (1994); Pres. ASHRAF AZIZ.

Deshapriya Janatha Viyaparaya (DJV) (Patriotic People's Movement): militant, Sinhalese group; associated with the JVP.

Eelam National Democratic Liberation Front (ENDLF): 315 Kandy Rd, Kilinochchi; internet www.endlf.com; Tamil; supports 1987 Indo-Sri Lankan peace accord; has operated as a national political party since Sept. 1988; Pres. G. GNANASEKARAN; Dep. Gen. Sec. P. RAJARATNAM.

Eksath Lanka Podujana Pakshaya: 100/16 Via Kurunduwatte Rd, Nawala Rd, Rajagiriya; tel. (11) 2867069; Sec. SUNIL W. JINASENA.

Liberal Party: 88/1 Rosmead Place, Colombo 7; tel. (11) 2691589; fax (11) 2699772; e-mail libparty@sri.lanka.net; internet www.liberalparty-srilanka.org; f. 1987; Sec.-Gen. KAMAL NISSANKA; Pres. SWARNA AMARATUNGA.

Muslim National Unity Alliance (MNUA): Dharussalam, 53 Vauxhall Lane, Colombo 2; tel. (11) 2424187; affiliate party of the Sri Lanka Muslim Congress; has operated as a national political party since 1986; Leader FARIEL ASHRAFF.

Muslim United Liberation Front: 134 Hulftsdorp St, Colombo 12; tel. (11) 2501198; has operated as a national political party since Sept. 1988.

Nava Sama Samaja Party (NSSP) (New Equal Society Party): Left Front, 17 Barracks Lane, Colombo 2; tel. (11) 2430621; fax (11) 2305963; e-mail nssp.lk@gmail.com; internet www.nssp.info; f. 1977; Trotskyist; Gen. Sec. LINUS JAYATILAKE; Presidium Member Dr VICKRAMABAHU KARUNARATHNE.

New Democratic Front: Colombo; f. 2009 as breakaway faction of Democratic United National Front; Leader ARIYAWANSA DISSANAYAKE; Sec. SHAMILA PERERA.

New Democratic Party (NDP): S47, 3rd Floor, C. C. S. M. Complex, Colombo 11; tel. (71) 4302909; fax (11) 2473757; e-mail info@ndpsl.org; internet www.ndpsl.org; f. 1978 as the Sri Lanka Communist Party; adopted current name in 1991; upholds Marxist-Leninist-Mao Zedong philosophy in anti-imperialist campaigning for social justice; publs monthly party newsletter Puthiya Poomi; Gen. Sec. S. K. SENTHIVEL.

Singhalaye Nithahas Peramuna (Sinhalese Freedom Front): Sri Panchananda Charity Bldg, Kelani Railway Station Rd, Colombo; f. 1994; nationalist, Buddhist; Pres. ARYA SENA TERA; Sec. Prof. NALIN DE SILVA.

Sri Lanka Progressive Front: 7 7th Lane, Pagoda Rd, Nugegoda; tel. (11) 2826564; f. 1996 following split from Janatha Vimukthi Peramuna; leftist nationalist party; Sec. ROHAN JAYATUNGA.

Tamil Makkal Viduthalai Pulikal (TMVP) (Tamil Peoples Liberation Tigers—Karuna Group): 2 Anderawatta Rd, Polhengoda, Colombo 5; f. 2004; political and paramilitary group, fmrly of LTTE; joint asscn with the Eelam National Democratic Liberation Front (India); Leader SIVANESATHURAI CHANDRAKANTHAN ('PILLAYAN'); Gen. Sec. A. KAILESVARARAJAH.

Tamil National Alliance (TNA): 3rd Floor, Parliamentary Complex, Sri Jeyawardanapura Kotte, Colombo; tel. (11) 2778470; fax (11) 2778470; e-mail enquiries@tamilalliance.net; internet www.tamilalliance.net; f. 2001; alliance of Tamil parties; Leader RAJAVAROTHIAM SAMPANTHAN.

SRI LANKA

All Ceylon Tamil Congress: Colombo; f. 1944; aims to secure Tamil self-determination; joined TNA in 2001; Leader GAJENDRAKUMAR PONNAMBALAM.

Eelam People's Revolutionary Liberation Front (EPRLF): 85/9 Pokuna Rd, Hendala, Wattala; tel. (11) 2685826; internet www.eprlf.net; Tamil rights group; the party split into two factions, one led by ANNAMALAI VARADHARAJAH PERUMAL, known as the Varadharajah faction, and the other by SURESH K. PREMACHANDRAN, known as the Premachandran faction; c. 1,000 mems.

Ilankai Tamil Arasu Katchi (ITAK): 3rd Floor, Parliamentary Complex, Sri Jeyawardanapura Kotte, Colombo; Tamil; Leader RAJAVAROTHIAM SAMPANTHAN; Gen. Sec. MAVAI SENATHIRAJAH.

Tamil Eelam Liberation Organization (TELO): 34 Ammankovil Rd, Pandarikulam, Vavuniya; tel. (24) 2222977; fax (24) 2224457; e-mail teloheadoffice@yahoo.com; internet www.telo.org; supports 1987 Indo-Sri Lankan peace accord; has operated as a national political party since Sept. 1988; pro-LTTE; Pres. SELVAM ADAIKALANTHAN.

Tamil United Liberation Front (TULF): 30/1B Alwis Place, Colombo 3; tel. and fax (11) 2347721; f. 1972 by several Tamil parties, incl. All Ceylon Tamil Congress; subsumed Federal Party (f. 1949) in 1976; Pres. VEERASINGHAM ANANDASANGAREE.

United National Front (UNF): Colombo; f. 2001; revived 2009 to contest 2010 legislative election; Leader RANIL WICKREMASINGHE.

Democratic People's Front: 72 Bankshall St, Colombo 11; tel. (11) 2473511; fax (11) 2435961; has operated as a national political party since Sept. 1988; Leader MANO GANESHAN; Dep. Leader and Gen. Sec. NALLIAH KUMARAGURUPARAN.

Sri Lanka Freedom Party—Mahajana Wing (SLFP—M): Colombo; f. 2007 as breakaway faction of the Sri Lanka Freedom Party, under the leadership of fmr Minister of Foreign Affairs and fmr Minister of Port Development; advocates constitutional reform, incl. revisions to the Executive President's authority; memorandum of understanding signed with United National Party in July 2007 whereby the two parties pledged to contest future elections as a broad coalition (the 'National Congress'); Founder and Leader MANGALA SAMARAWEERA.

Sri Lanka Muslim Congress (SLMC): Dharussalam, 53 Vauxhall Lane, Colombo 2; tel. (74) 717720; fax (74) 717722; e-mail info@slmc.org.uk; internet www.slmc.org; Leader RAUFF HAKEEM; Sec.-Gen. M. T. HASSEN ALI.

United National Party (UNP): 30 Sir Marcus Fernando Mawatha, Colombo 7; tel. (11) 5636551; fax (11) 2682905; e-mail info@unp.lk; internet www.unp.lk; f. 1946; democratic socialist; aims at a non-aligned foreign policy, supports Sinhala and Tamil as the official languages and state aid to denominational schools; Leader RANIL WICKREMASINGHE; Chair. RUKMAN SENANAYAKE; Gen. Sec. TISSA ATTANAYAKE.

United People's Freedom Alliance (UPFA): 301, T. B. Jaya Mawatha, Colombo 10; tel. (60) 2700259; fax (11) 2674363; e-mail slfpmedia@gmail.com; internet www.sandanaya.lk; f. 2004; left wing coalition incl. communists and Trotskyists; Leader MAHINDA RAJAPAKSE; Gen. Sec. SUSIL PREMAJAYANTHA.

Ceylon Workers' Congress (CWC): 'Savumia Bhavan', 72 Ananda Coomarasamy Mawatha, POB 1294, Colombo 7; tel. (11) 2301359; fax (11) 2301355; e-mail cwconline@sltnet.lk; f. 1939 as Ceylon Indian Congress; name changed as above in 1950; represents the interests of workers in the mercantile and local government sectors and of workers on tea, rubber and coconut plantations; 250,000 mems; Pres. and Gen. Sec. S. R. ARUMUGAN THONDAMAN.

Communist Party of Sri Lanka (CPSL): 91 Dr N. M. Perera Mawatha, Colombo 8; tel. (11) 2688942; fax (11) 2691610; f. 1943; advocates establishment of socialist society; seeks broadening of democratic rights and processes, political solution to ethnic problem, defence of social welfare and presses for social justice; supports national sovereignty, territorial integrity and national unity of the country; Gen. Sec. D. E. W. GUNASEKERA.

Democratic United National Front (DUNF): 60 1st Lane, Rawathawatte, Moratuwa; tel. and fax (11) 2645566; f. 1991 by dissident group of UNP politicians; 500,000 mems; Pres. D. M. G. EKANAYAKE; Gen. Sec. M. C. MOHAMED ISMAIL.

Desha Vimukthi Janatha Pakshaya (National Liberation People's Party): 152/1, 1/2 Baddagana HS, Duwa Rd, Baddagana; tel. (11) 2338812; has operated as a national political party since Sept. 1988; Sec. P. M. PODIAPPUHAMY.

Eelam People's Democratic Party (EPDP): 121 Park Rd, Colombo 5; tel. (11) 2551015; fax (11) 2585255; e-mail epdp@sltnet.lk; internet www.epdpnews.com; Tamil; Sec.-Gen. DOUGLAS DEVANANDA.

Jathika Hela Urumaya (JHU) (National Heritage Party): 1047/3A Denzil Kobbekaduwa Mawatha, Pannipitiya Rd, Pelawatte, Battaramulla, Colombo; tel. (11) 2882585; fax (11) 2866125; e-mail jhu2004@gmail.com; f. 2004; Buddhist; Sinhalese nationalist; Sec. Dr OMALPE SOBHITHA THERO.

Jathika Nidahas Peramuna (JNP) (National Freedom Front): 21/1 Asoka Mawatha, Battaramulla, Colombo; tel. (11) 3071340; fax (11) 2882176; e-mail info@nffsrilanka.com; internet www.jnpsrilanka.com; f. 2008 as a breakaway faction of the JVP; Chair. WIMAL WEERAWANSA; Gen. Sec. PRIYANJITH WITHARANA.

Lanka Sama Samaja Party (LSSP) (Lanka Equal Society Party): 457 Dr Colvin R. de Silva Mawatha, Colombo 2; tel. (11) 2676770; f. 1935; Trotskyist; Gen. Sec. WIMALASIRI DE MEL.

Mahajana Eksath Peramuna (MEP) (People's United Front): 10/4 Lake Rd, Maharagama, Colombo; tel. and fax (11) 2872318; f. 1956; Sinhalese and Buddhist support; left-wing; advocates economic self-reliance; Pres. DINESH C. R. GUNAWARDENA; Sec. D. M. KARUNATHILAKA DISSANAYAKE.

Sri Lanka Freedom Party (SLFP): 301 T. B. Jayah Mawatha, Colombo 10; tel. (11) 2696289; fax (11) 2685563; e-mail slfp@srilankafreedomparty.org; f. 1951; democratic socialist; advocates a non-aligned foreign policy, industrial development in both the state sector and the private sector, rapid modernization in education and in the economy, and safeguards for minorities; Chair. MAHINDA RAJAPAKSE; Gen. Sec. MAITHRIPALA SIRISENA.

Sri Lanka Mahajana Pakshaya (SLMP) (Sri Lanka People's Party): 196 Kolonnawa Rd, Wellampitiya; f. 1984 by fmr mems of the SLFP; social democrats; Leader SARATH KONGAHAGE; Gen. Sec. PREMASIRI PERERA.

Upcountry People's Front: 56, Rosita Housing Scheme, Kotagala; tel. (52) 2258227; represents interests of workers (mainly of Indian Tamil origin) on tea plantations; Chair. P. CHANDRASEKARAN.

Tamil separatist groups also include the Liberation Tigers of Tamil Eelam (LTTE; Leader SELVARASA PATHMANATHAN), the Tamil Eelam Liberation Front (TELF; Gen. Sec. M. K. EELAVENTHAN), the People's Liberation Organization of Tamil Eelam (PLOTE; Leader DHARMALINGAM SIDDHARTHAN; Vice-Pres. KARUVAI A. SRIKANTHASAMI), the People's Revolutionary Action Group, the Ellalan Force and the Tamil People's Protection Party.

Diplomatic Representation

EMBASSIES AND HIGH COMMISSIONS IN SRI LANKA

Australia: 21 Gregory's Rd, Colombo 7; tel. (11) 2463200; fax (11) 2686453; e-mail austcom@sltnet.lk; internet www.srilanka.embassy.gov.au; High Commissioner KATHY KLUGMAN.

Bangladesh: 5 Ward Pl., Colombo 7; tel. (11) 2303943; fax (11) 2695556; e-mail bdootlanka@sltnet.lk; High Commissioner MAHBUB UZ ZAMAN.

Canada: 33A 5th Lane, Colpetty, Colombo 3; tel. (11) 5226232; fax (11) 5226296; e-mail clmbo@international.gc.ca; internet www.canadainternational.gc.ca/sri_lanka; High Commissioner BRUCE LEVY.

China, People's Republic: 381/A Bauddhaloka Mawatha, Colombo 7; tel. (11) 2694491; fax (11) 2693799; e-mail chinaemb_lk@mfa.gov.cn; internet lk.china-embassy.org; Ambassador YANG XIUPING.

Cuba: 15/9 Maitland Cres., Colombo 7; tel. (11) 2677170; fax (11) 2669380; e-mail cubaembalk@sltnet.lk; internet embacuba.cubaminrex.cu/srilankaing; Ambassador NIRSIA CASTRO GUEVARA.

Egypt: 39 Dr Lester James Peries Mawatha, Colombo 5; tel. (11) 2508752; fax (11) 2585292; e-mail egyptemb@sltnet.lk; Ambassador FAWZI MUHAMMAD EL-SAID GOHAR.

France: 89 Rosmead Pl., POB 880, Colombo 7; tel. (11) 2639400; fax (11) 2639402; e-mail ambfrclb@sltnet.lk; internet www.ambafrance-lk.org; Ambassador CHRISTINE ROBICHON.

Germany: 40 Alfred House Ave, POB 658, Colombo 3; tel. (11) 2580431; fax (11) 2580440; e-mail info@colombo.diplo.de; internet www.colombo.diplo.de; Ambassador JENS UWE PLOETNER.

Holy See: 220 Bauddhaloka Mawatha, Colombo 7 (Apostolic Nunciature); tel. (11) 2582554; fax (11) 2580906; e-mail nuntius@sltnet.lk; Apostolic Nuncio Most Rev. Dr JOSEPH SPITERI (Titular Archbishop of Serta).

India: 36–38 Galle Rd, Colombo 3; tel. (11) 2421605; fax (11) 2446403; e-mail cpic@sltnet.lk; internet www.hcicolombo.org; High Commissioner ASHOK K. KANTHA.

Indonesia: 400/50 Sarana Rd, off Bauddhaloka Mawatha, Colombo 7; tel. (11) 2674337; fax (11) 2678668; e-mail indocol@indonesia-colombo.lk; internet indonesia-colombo.lk; Ambassador DJAFAR HUSEIN.

Iran: 5 Independence Ave, Colombo 7; tel. (11) 2681018; fax (11) 2681017; e-mail emb_colombo@mfa.gov.ir; Ambassador MAHMOUD RAHIMI GORGI.

SRI LANKA

Directory

Iraq: 19 Barnes Place, POB 79, Colombo 7; tel. (1) 698733; fax (1) 697676; e-mail iraqiya@sol.lk; Ambassador KAHTAAN TAHA KHALAF.

Italy: 55 Jawatta Rd, Colombo 5; tel. (11) 2588388; fax (11) 2596344; e-mail ambasciata.colombo@esteri.it; internet www.ambcolombo.esteri.it; Ambassador PIO MARIANI.

Japan: 20 Gregory's Rd, Colombo 7; tel. (11) 2693831; fax (11) 2698629; e-mail cultujpn@sltnet.lk; internet www.lk.emb-japan.go.jp; Ambassador KUNIO TAKAHASHI.

Korea, Democratic People's Republic: Colombo; Ambassador HAN CHANG ON.

Korea, Republic: 98 Dharmapala Mawatha, Colombo 7; tel. (11) 2699036; fax (11) 2696699; e-mail korembsl@mofat.go.kr; internet lka.mofat.go.kr; Ambassador CHOI KI-CHUL.

Kuwait: 292 Bauddhaloka Mawatha, Colombo 7; tel. (11) 2597958; fax (11) 2597954; e-mail cmb@kuwaitembassysl.org; Ambassador YAQOUB AL-ATEEQI.

Libya: 120 Horton Pl., POB 155, Colombo 7; tel. (11) 2693700; fax (11) 5338881; Ambassador HAFIM M. A. MAHFOM.

Malaysia: 33 Bagatalle Rd, Colombo 3; tel. (11) 2554681; fax (11) 2554684; e-mail mwcolombo@dialogsl.net; internet www.kln.gov.my/perwakilan/colombo; High Commissioner ROSLI ISMAIL.

Maldives: 25 Melbourne Ave, Colombo 4; tel. (11) 2587827; fax (11) 2581200; e-mail info@maldiveshighcom.lk; internet www.maldiveshighcom.lk; High Commissioner HUSSAIN SHIHAB.

Myanmar: 4A Rosmead Ave, Rosmead Pl., Colombo 7; tel. (11) 2696440; fax (11) 2682052; e-mail mmembcmb@eureka.lk; Ambassador OHN THWIN.

Nepal: 153 Kynsey Rd, Colombo 8; tel. (11) 2689657; fax (11) 2689655; e-mail nepalembassy@eureka.lk; Ambassador SUSHIL CHANDRA AMATYA.

Netherlands: 25 Torrington Ave, Colombo 7; tel. (11) 2510200; fax (11) 2502855; e-mail col@minbuza.nl; internet www.hollandinsrilanka.org; Ambassador LEUNI CUELENAERE.

Norway: 49 Bullers Lane, Colombo 7; tel. (11) 2352500; fax (11) 2352599; e-mail emb.colombo@mfa.no; internet www.norway.lk; Ambassador HILDE HARALDSTAD.

Pakistan: 53/6 Gregory's Rd, Colombo 7; tel. (11) 2696301; fax (11) 2695780; e-mail parepcolombo@sltnet.lk; internet www.pakistanhc.lk; High Commissioner SEEMA ILLAHI BALOCH.

Qatar: 11 Rajakeeya Mawatha, Old Race Course Ave, Colombo 7; tel. (11) 2690440; fax (11) 2690443; Ambassador SAEED BIN ABDULLAH AL-MANSOORI.

Romania: 9 Queens Terrace, Colombo 3; tel. (11) 2505005; fax (11) 2505006; e-mail romania@sltnet.lk; internet www.colombo.mae.ro; Chargé d'affaires a.i. VICTOR CHIUJDEA.

Russia: 62 Sir Ernest de Silva Mawatha, Colombo 7; tel. (11) 2573555; fax (11) 2574957; e-mail rusemb@itmin.net; internet www.sri-lanka.mid.ru; Ambassador VLADIMIR P. MIKHAYLOV.

Saudi Arabia: 39 Sir Ernest de Silva Mawatha, Colombo 7; tel. (11) 2682087; fax (11) 2682088; e-mail lkemb@mofa.gov.sa; Ambassador ABDUL ASIA BIN AL-JEMAZ.

South Africa: 114 Rosmead Pl., Colombo 7; tel. (11) 2689926; fax (11) 2688670; e-mail sahc_general@sltnet.lk; High Commissioner BUYISIWE MAUREEN PHETO.

Switzerland: 63 Gregory's Rd, POB 342, Colombo 7; tel. (11) 2695117; fax (11) 2695176; e-mail col.vertretung@eda.admin.ch; internet www.eda.admin.ch/colombo; Ambassador THOMAS LITSCHER.

Thailand: Greenlanka Towers, 9th Floor, 46/46 Nawam Mawatha, Colombo 2; tel. (11) 2302500; fax (11) 2304511; e-mail thaicmb@sltnet.lk; internet www.thaiembassy.org/colombo; Ambassador THINAKORN KANASUTA.

United Arab Emirates: 44 Sir Ernest de Silva Mawatha, Colombo 7; tel. (11) 2565052; fax (11) 2564104; Ambassador MAHMOUD MUHAMMAD AL-MAHMOUD.

United Kingdom: 389 Bauddhaloka Mawatha, Colombo 7; tel. (11) 5390639; fax (11) 5390694; e-mail colombo.general@fco.gov.uk; internet ukinsrilanka.fco.gov.uk; High Commissioner JOHN JAMES RANKIN.

USA: 210 Galle Rd, Colombo 3; tel. (11) 2498500; fax (11) 2429070; e-mail commercialcolombo@state.gov; internet srilanka.usembassy.gov; Ambassador PATRICIA A. BUTENIS.

Judicial System

The judicial system consists of the Supreme Court, the Court of Appeal, the High Court, District Courts, Magistrates' Courts and Primary Courts. The last four are Courts of the First Instance and appeals lie from them to the Court of Appeal and from there, on questions of law or by special leave, to the Supreme Court. The High Court deals with all criminal cases and the District Courts with civil cases. There are Labour Tribunals to decide labour disputes.

The Judicial Service Commission comprises the Chief Justice and two judges of the Supreme Court, nominated by the President. All judges of the Courts of First Instance (except High Court Judges) and the staff of all courts are appointed and controlled by the Judicial Service Commission. The Supreme Court consists of the Chief Justice and not fewer than six and not more than 10 other judges. The Court of Appeal consists of the President and not fewer than six and not more than 11 other judges.

Chief Justice of the Supreme Court: SHIRANEE BANDARANAYAKE (acting).

Attorney-General: MOHAN PEIRIS.

Religion

According to the 2001 census, the distribution of the population by religion in 18 out of 25 districts was: Buddhist 76.7%, Muslim 8.5%, Hindu 7.9%, Roman Catholics 6.1% and other Christians 0.8%. The census results did not cover the Tamil-dominated northern and eastern districts, where a higher proportion of Hindus could be expected.

BUDDHISM

Theravada Buddhism is the predominant sect. There are an estimated 53,000 Buddhist *bhikkhus* (monks), living in about 6,000 temples.

All Ceylon Buddhist Congress: 380 Bauddhaloka Mawatha, Colombo 7; tel. (11) 2688517; fax (11) 2691695; e-mail acbc@isplanka.lk; internet www.acbc.lk; f. 1919; Pres. JAGATH SUMATHIPALA; Jt Secs Maj.-Gen. (retd) JALIYA NAMMUNI, RANJITH EKANAYAKE.

Sri Lanka Regional Centre of the World Fellowship of Buddhists: 380 Bauddhaloka Mawatha, Colombo 7; tel. (11) 2681886; fax (11) 2833362; e-mail nationlanka@sltnet.lk; Pres. D. M. JAYATILAKA DISSANAYAKE; Sec. Prof. JAYANTHA WEERAKOON.

HINDUISM

The majority of the Tamil population are Hindus. According to the 2001 census the Hindu population in 18 out of 25 districts was 1,329,020.

CHRISTIANITY

National Christian Council of Sri Lanka: 368/6 Bauddhaloka Mawatha, Colombo 7; tel. (11) 2671723; fax (11) 2671721; e-mail sec@nccsl.org; internet www.nccsl.org; f. 1945; 13 mem. bodies; Gen. Sec. Rev. Dr JAYASIRI PEIRIS.

The Anglican Communion

The Church of Ceylon (Sri Lanka) comprises two Anglican dioceses. In 1985 there were about 78,000 adherents.

Bishop of Colombo: Rt Rev. DULEEP KAMIL DE CHICKERA, Bishop's House, 358/2 Bauddhaloka Mawatha, Colombo 7; tel. (11) 2684810; fax (11) 2684811; e-mail bishop@eureka.lk; diocese f. 1845.

Bishop of Kurunegala: Rt Rev. KUMARA BANDARA SAMUEL ILLANGASINGHE, Bishop's House, Kandy Rd, Kurunegala; tel. (37) 22191; fax (37) 26806; e-mail bishopkg@sltnet.lk; diocese f. 1950.

The Roman Catholic Church

For ecclesiastical purposes, Sri Lanka comprises one archdiocese and 10 dioceses. At 31 December 2009 there were an estimated 1,359,788 adherents in the country.

Catholic Bishops' Conference in Sri Lanka: 19 Balcombe Place, Cotta Rd, Borella, Colombo 8; tel. (11) 2697062; fax (11) 2699619; e-mail conferencesl@sltnet.lk; internet www.cbcsl.com; f. 1975; Pres. Most Rev. JOSEPH VIANNEY FERNANDO (Bishop of Kandy); Sec.-Gen. Rt Rev. Dr NORBERT M. ANDRADI.

Archbishop of Colombo: Cardinal ALBERT MALCOLM RANJITH, Archbishop's House, Borella, Colombo 8; tel. (11) 2695471; fax (11) 2692009; e-mail sunilde@sltnet.lk; internet www.archdioceseofcolombo.com.

The Church of South India

The Church comprises 21 dioceses, including one, Jaffna, in Sri Lanka. The diocese of Jaffna, with an estimated 18,500 adherents in 1997, was formerly part of the South India United Church (a union of churches of the Congregational and Presbyterian/Reformed traditions), which merged with the Methodist Church in South India and the four southern dioceses of the (Anglican) Church of India to form the Church of South India in 1947.

SRI LANKA

Bishop in Jaffna: Rt Rev. Dr DANIEL S. THIAGARAJAH, 36 5/2, Sinsapa Rd, Colombo 6; tel. (11) 2150795; fax (11) 2505805; e-mail bishop@csijaffnadiocese.com; internet csijaffnadiocese.com.

Other Christian Churches

Christian Reformed Church: General Consistory Office, 363 Galle Rd, Colombo 6; tel. (11) 2360861; fax (11) 2582469; e-mail crcsl1642@gmail.com; f. 1642; Pres. of Gen. Consistory Rev. CHARLES N. JANSZ.

Methodist Church: Methodist Headquarters, 252 Galle Rd, Colombo 3; tel. (11) 2575630; fax (11) 2436090; e-mail methhq@sltnet.lk; internet www.gbgm-umc.org/methchsrilan; 30,139 mems (2000); Pres. of Conference Rev. W. P. EBENEZER JOSEPH; Sec. of Conference Rev. J. C. S. ROHITHA DE SILVA.

Other denominations active in the country include the Sri Lanka Baptist Sangamaya.

BAHÁ'Í FAITH

Spiritual Assembly: Bahá'í National Centre, 65 Havelock Rd, Colombo 5; tel. and fax (11) 2587360; e-mail nsasrilanka@sltnet.lk.

The Press

NEWSPAPERS

Newspapers are published in Sinhala, Tamil and English. There are five main newspaper publishing groups:

Associated Newspapers of Ceylon Ltd: Lake House, 35 D. R. Wijewardene Mawatha, POB 248, Colombo 10; tel. (11) 2429429; fax (11) 2429329; e-mail webmanager@lakehouse.lk; internet www.lakehouse.lk; f. 1926; nationalized 1973; publr of *Daily News*, *Evening Observer*, *Thinakaran*, *Lak Janatha* and *Dinamina* (dailies); three Sunday papers: *Sunday Observer*, *Silumina* and *Thinakaran Vaara Manjari*; and 11 periodicals; Chair. BANDULA PADMAKUMARA; CEO TIKIRI KOBBEKADUWA.

Express Newspapers (Ceylon) Ltd: 185 Grandpass Rd, POB 160, Colombo 14; tel. (11) 5322735; fax (11) 2327827; e-mail md@expressnewspapers.lk; internet www.virakesari.lk; f. 1930; publr of *Virakesari Daily*, *Mithran Varamalar*, *Metro News* and *Virakesari Weekly* (Sunday); Chair. HARI SELVANATHAN; Man. Dir KUMAR NADESAN.

Leader Publications (Pvt) Ltd: 24 Katukurunduwatte Rd, Ratmalana; tel. (11) 4977220; fax (11) 4641942; e-mail editor@thesundayleader.lk; internet www.thesundayleader.lk; f. 1994; publr of *The Sunday Leader* and *Irida Peramuna*; Chair. LAL WICKREMATUNGE.

Upali Newspapers Ltd: 223 Bloemendhal Rd, POB 133, Colombo 13; tel. (11) 2497500; fax (11) 2497543; e-mail prabath@unl.upali.lk; f. 1981; publr of *The Island*, *Divaina* (dailies), two Sunday papers, *Sunday Island* and *Sunday Divaina*, four weeklies, *Vidusara*, *Navaliya*, *Bindu* and *The Island International* (for sale abroad only), and one bi-weekly, *Vathmana–News Magazine*; English and Sinhala; Editor-in-Chief PRABATH SAHABANDU; Chair. LAKMENI WIJAYWARDANA WELGAMA.

Wijeya Newspapers Ltd: 8 Hunupitiya Cross Rd, Colombo 2; tel. (11) 2314714; fax (11) 2449504; e-mail pradeep@admin.wnl.lk; internet www.wijeya.lk; f. 1979; publr of *Daily Mirror*, *The Sunday Times*, *Lankadeepa*, *Irida Lankadeepa* and *Sirikatha*; Sinhala and English; Chair. RANJIT SUJIVA WIJEWARDENE.

Dailies

Budusarana: Lake House, 35 D. R. Wijewardene Mawatha, POB 248, Colombo 10; tel. (11) 2429598; fax (11) 2449069; e-mail budusarana@lakehouse.lk; internet www.lakehouse.lk/budusarana; Editor N. S. PERERA.

Daily Mirror: 8 Hunupitiya Cross Rd, Colombo 2; tel. (11) 2479479; fax (11) 5530811; e-mail dmnews@dailymirror.wnl.lk; internet www.dailymirror.lk; f. 1996; English and Sinhala; Editor CHAMPIKA LIYANAARACHCHI; circ. 30,000.

Daily News: Lake House, 35 D. R. Wijewardene Mawatha, POB 248, Colombo 10; tel. (11) 2429224; fax (11) 2343694; e-mail editor@dailynews.lk; internet www.dailynews.lk; f. 1918; morning; English; Editor JAYATHILLEKE DE SILVA; circ. 65,000.

Dinakara: 95 Maligakanda Rd, Colombo 10; tel. (11) 2595754; f. 1978; morning; Sinhala; publ. by Rekana Publrs; official organ of the Sri Lanka Freedom Party; Editor MULEN PERERA; circ. 12,000.

Dinamina: Lake House, 35 D. R. Wijewardene Mawatha, POB 248, Colombo 10; tel. (11) 2429241; fax 2429250; e-mail editor@dinamina.lk; internet www.dinamina.lk; f. 1909; morning; Sinhala; Editor MAHINDA ABEYSUNDARA; circ. 140,000.

Divaina: 223 Bloemendhal Rd, POB 133, Colombo 13; tel. (11) 4609000; fax (11) 2344253; e-mail divaina@unl.upali.lk; internet www.divaina.com; f. 1982; morning and Sunday; Chief Editor MERRILL PERERA.

Eelanadu: Jaffna; tel. (21) 22389; f. 1959; morning; Tamil; Chair. S. RAVEENTHIRANATHAN; Editor M. SIVANANTHAM; circ. 15,000.

The Island: 223 Bloemendhal Rd, POB 133, Colombo 13; tel. (11) 4609174; fax (11) 2448185; e-mail prabath@unl.upali.lk; internet www.island.lk; f. 1981; English; Editor PRABATH SAHABANDU; circ. 80,000.

Lak Janatha: Lake House, 35 D. R. Wijewardene Mawatha, POB 248, Colombo 10; tel. (11) 2421181; f. 2005; evening; Sinhala; Editor SUJEEWA DISSANAYAKE.

Lakbima: 445/1 Sirimavo Bandaranayake Mawatha, Colombo 14; tel. (11) 2330673; fax (11) 2449593; e-mail lakbima@isplanka.lk; internet www.lakbima.lk; publ. by Sumathi Newspapers Pvt Ltd; Chief Editor JATILA WELLABODA.

Lankadeepa: 8 Hunupitiya Cross Rd, Colombo 2; tel. (11) 2479214; fax (11) 2448323; e-mail siri@wijeya.lk; internet www.lankadeepa.lk; f. 1986; Sinhala and English; Editor SIRI RANASINGHE; circ. 160,000.

Namathu Eelanadu: Jaffna; f. 2002; Tamil; Editor SIVASUBRAMANIAM RAGURAM.

New Uthayan Publications Pvt Ltd: 361 Kasthuriyar Rd, Jaffna; tel. (21) 2229933; fax (21) 2223837; e-mail uthayandaily@gmail.com; internet www.uthayan.com; f. 1985; Tamil; Man. Dir E. SARAVANAPAVAN; Chief Editor M. V. KAANAMYLNATHAN; circ. 22,000.

Peraliya: Borella Supermarket Complex, 2nd Floor, Colombo 8; Editor SUJEEWA GAMAGE.

Thinakaran: Lake House, 35 D. R. Wijewardene Mawatha, POB 248, Colombo 10; tel. (11) 2429271; fax (11) 2429270; e-mail editor.tkn@lakehouse.lk; internet www.thinakaran.lk; f. 1932; morning; Tamil; Editor K. V. SIVASUPRAMANIAM; circ. daily 14,000.

Thinakkural: 68 Ellie House Rd, Colombo 15; tel. (11) 2522555; fax (11) 2540691; e-mail thinakkural@yahoo.com; internet www.thinakkural.com; Tamil; also publ. from Jaffna; Chief Editor V. THANABALASINGHAM.

Valampurii: 3, 2nd Lane, Brown Rd, Jaffna; tel. (21) 2227829; fax (21) 2223378; e-mail valampurii@yahoo.com; internet www.valampurii.com; f. 1999; Tamil; Chief Editor N. VIJAYASUNTHARAM; circ. 10,000.

Virakesari Daily: 185 Grandpass Rd, POB 160, Colombo 14; tel. (11) 5322750; fax (11) 2448205; e-mail kesari25@virakesari.lk; internet www.virakesari.lk; f. 1931; morning; Tamil; Man. Dir KUMAR NADESAN; Chief Editor R. PRABAGAN; circ. 60,000.

Sunday Newspapers

Irida Lankadeepa: 8 Hunupitiya Cross Rd, Colombo 2; tel. (11) 2347248; fax (11) 2314886; e-mail ariyad@wijeya.lk; internet www.lankadeepa.lk; Sinhala; Chief Editor ARIYANANDA DOBAGAHAWATTA.

Janasathiya: 47 Jayantha Weerasekara Mawatha, Colombo 10; f. 1965; Sinhala; publ. by Suriya Publishers Ltd; Editor SARATH NAWANA; circ. 50,000.

Mithran Varamalar: 185 Grandpass Rd, POB 160, Colombo 14; tel. (11) 2323841; fax (11) 4614374; e-mail kesari22@virasekari.lk; internet www.virakesari.lk; f. 1969; Tamil; Man. Dir KUMAR NADESAN; Chief Editor V. THEVARAJ; circ. 29,000.

The Nation: 742 Maradana Rd, Colombo 10; tel. (11) 4708888; fax (11) 4708800; e-mail editor@nation.lk; internet www.nation.lk; publ. by Rivira Media Corpn Ltd; Chief Editor GAMINI ABEYWARDANE; circ. 132,376 (2010).

Silumina: Lake House, 35 D. R. Wijewardene Mawatha, POB 248, Colombo 10; tel. (11) 2429261; fax (11) 2429260; e-mail editor@silumina.lk; internet www.silumina.lk; f. 1930; Sinhala; Editor KARUNADASA SOORIYARACHCHI; circ. 264,000.

Sunday Island: 223 Bloemendhal Rd, POB 133, Colombo 13; tel. (11) 2421599; fax (11) 2448185; e-mail manik@unl.upali.lk; f. 1981; English; Editor MANIK DE SILVA; circ. 40,000.

Sunday Lakbima: 445/1 Sirimavo Bandaranayake Mawatha, Colombo 14; tel. (11) 4619312; fax (11) 4617902; e-mail news@lakbima.lk; internet www.lakbimanews.lk; Chief Editor SUNDARA NIHATHAMANI DE MEL.

The Sunday Leader: 24 Katukurunduwatte Rd, Ratmalana; tel. (75) 2365892; fax (75) 2365891; e-mail editor@thesundayleader.lk; internet www.thesundayleader.lk; English; Editor FREDERICA JANSZ.

Sunday Observer: Lake House, 35 D. R. Wijewardene Mawatha, POB 248, Colombo 10; tel. (11) 2429231; fax (11) 2429230; e-mail editor@sundayobserver.lk; internet www.sundayobserver.lk; f. 1923; English; Editor DINESH WEERAWANSA; circ. 125,000.

SRI LANKA

Directory

Sunday Thinakkural: 68 Ellie House Rd, Colombo 15; internet www.thinakkural.com/sundaythinakkural; Tamil; also publ. from Jaffna; Editor A. SIYANESACHELVAN.

The Sunday Times: 8 Hunupitiya Cross Rd, Colombo 2; tel. (11) 2326247; fax (11) 2423922; e-mail editor@sundaytimes.wnl.lk; internet www.sundaytimes.lk; f. 1986; English and Sinhala; Editor SINGHA RATNATUNGA; circ. 116,000.

Thinakaran Vaara Manjari: Lake House, 35 D. R. Wijewardene Mawatha, POB 248, Colombo 10; tel. (11) 2221181; internet www.thinakaran.lk/vaaramanjari; f. 1948; Tamil; Editor R. SRIKANTHAN; circ. 35,000.

Virakesari Weekly: 185 Grandpass Rd, POB 160, Colombo 14; tel. (11) 5322760; fax (11) 4614374; e-mail kesari22@virakesari.lk; internet www.virakesari.lk; f. 1931; Tamil and English; Man. Dir KUMAR NADESAN; Chief Editor V. THEVARAJ; circ. 110,000.

PERIODICALS
(weekly unless otherwise stated)

Aththa: 91 Dr N. M. Perera Mawatha, Colombo 8; tel. (11) 2691450; fax (11) 2691610; e-mail dew128@dialogsl.net; f. 1964; Sinhala; publ. by the Communist Party of Sri Lanka; Editor GUNASENA VITHANA; circ. 28,000.

Business Lanka: Trade Information Service, Sri Lanka Export Development Board, Level 7, 42 Navam Mawatha, POB 1872, Colombo 2; tel. (11) 2300705; fax (11) 2305211; e-mail edb@tradenetsl.lk; f. 1981; quarterly; information for visiting business executives, etc.; Editor (vacant).

Ceylon Medical Journal: 6 Wijerama Mawatha, Colombo 7; tel. (11) 2693324; fax (11) 2698802; e-mail office@cmj.slma.lk; internet www.sljol.info/index.php/CMJ; f. 1887; quarterly; Editors Prof. H. JANAKA DE SILVA, Dr A. ABEYGUNASEKERA.

The Economic Times: 130/C/8 Jothikarama Mawatha, Kalalgoda, Pannipitiya; tel. (11) 2796134; fax (11) 4305787; f. 1970; Editor THIMSY FAHIM.

The Financial Times: 323 Union Place, POB 330, Colombo 2; quarterly; commercial and economic affairs; Man. Editor CYRIL GARDINER.

Gnanarthapradeepaya: Colombo Catholic Press, 2 Gnanarthapradeepaya Mawatha, Borella, Colombo 8; tel. (11) 2695984; fax (11) 2692586; e-mail pradeepaya@sltnet.lk; internet www.colombocatholicpress.lk; f. 1866; Sinhala; Roman Catholic; Chief Editor Rev. Fr CYRIL GAMINI FERNANDO; Exec. Dir Rev. Fr ROHAN DE ALWIS; circ. 45,000.

Irudina: Lithira Publications (Pvt) Ltd, 24 Katukurunduwatta Rd, Ratmalana, Colombo; tel. (60) 2178456; fax (11) 5515937; e-mail editor@irudina.lk; internet www.irudina.lk; f. 2004; Sinhala; Editor MOHAN LAL PIYADASA.

Janakavi: 47 Jayantha Weerasekera Mawatha, Colombo 10; fortnightly; Sinhala; Assoc. Editor KARUNARATNE AMERASINGHE.

Manasa: 150 Dutugemunu St, Dehiwala, Colombo; tel. (11) 2553994; f. 1978; Sinhala; monthly; science of the mind; Editor SUMANADASA SAMARASINGHE; circ. 6,000.

Mihira: Lake House, 35 D. R. Wijewardene Mawatha, POB 248, Colombo 10; tel. (11) 2429583; fax (11) 2429329; f. 1964; Sinhala children's magazine; Editor AJITH DHARMASIRI; circ. 145,000.

Morning Star: 36-5/2, Sinsapa Rd, Colombo 6; tel. (60) 2150795; fax (11) 2505805; e-mail editor@csijaffnadiocese.com; internet csijaffnadiocese.com; f. 1841; English and Tamil; monthly newsletter; publ. by the Jaffna diocese of the Church of South India.

Nava Yugaya: Lake House, 35 D. R. Wijewardene Mawatha, POB 248, Colombo 10; tel. (11) 2429521; fax (11) 2429329; e-mail dissbhanu@yahoo.com; f. 1956; literary; fortnightly; Sinhala; Editor SUJEEWA DISSANAYAKE; circ. 57,000.

Navaliya: 223 Bloemendhal Rd, Colombo 13; tel. (11) 2331688; fax (11) 2344252; e-mail navaliya@unl.upali.lk; internet www.navaliya.com; Sinhala; women's interest; Editor WASANTHA SRIYAKANYHI; circ. 86,000.

Navamani: 156 Hospital Rd, Kalubowila, Dehiwala, Colombo; tel. (11) 4204766; fax (11) 4204765; e-mail navamani@wow.lk; f. 1996; Man. Dir M. D. M. RIZVI; Chief Editor M. P. M. AZHAR.

Pathukavalan: POB 2, Jaffna; f. 1876; Tamil; publ. by St Joseph's Catholic Press; Editor Rev. Fr RUBAN MARIAMPILLAI; circ. 7,000.

Puthiya Ulaham: 115 4th Cross St, Jaffna; f. 1976; Tamil; six a year; publ. by Centre for Better Society; Editor Rev. Dr S. J. EMMANUEL; circ. 1,500.

Ravaya: 83 Piliyandala Rd, Maharagama, Colombo; tel. (11) 2851672; e-mail mkvictorivan@gmail.com; Sinhala; Editor VICTOR IVAN.

Sarasaviya: Lake House, 35 D. R. Wijewardene Mawatha, POB 248, Colombo 10; tel. (11) 2429586; e-mail sarasaviya@lakehouse.lk; internet www.sarasaviya.lk; f. 1963; Sinhala; films; Editor-in-Chief GAMINI SAMARASINGHE; circ. 56,000.

Sinhala Bauddhaya: Maha Bodhi Mandira, 130 Rev. Hikkaduwe Sri Sumangala Nahimi Mawatha, Colombo 10; e-mail mahabodhi@asia.com; f. 1906; publ. by The Maha Bodhi Society of Ceylon; Hon. Sec. KIRTHI KALAHE; circ. 25,000.

Sirikatha: 8 Hunupitiya Cross Rd, Colombo 2; tel. (11) 2423920; fax (11) 2314651; e-mail siri@wijeya.lk; Sinhala women's magazine; Chief Editor SIRI RANASINGHE.

Sri Lanka Government Gazette: Government Press, POB 507, Colombo; tel. (11) 2691460; fax (11) 2698653; f. 1802; Sinhala and Tamil; official govt bulletin; circ. 54,000.

Subasetha: Lake House, 35 D. R. Wijewardene Mawatha, POB 248, Colombo 10; tel. (11) 2429429; internet www.subasetha.lk; f. 1967; Sinhala; astrology, the occult and indigenous medicine; Editor Capt. K. CHANDRA SRI KULARATNE; circ. 100,000.

Tharunee: Lake House, 35 D. R. Wijewardene Mawatha, POB 248, Colombo 10; tel. (11) 2429591; fax (11) 2449069; f. 1969; Sinhala; women's journal; Editor GAMINI SAMARASINGHE; circ. 95,000.

Vidusara: 223 Bloemendhal Rd, Colombo 13; tel. (11) 2331687; fax (11) 2344252; e-mail rajendra@unl.upali.lk; internet www.vidusara.com; Sinhala; Chief Editor RAJENDRA KULASINGHE; circ. 103,992.

NEWS AGENCIES

Lankapuvath (National News Agency of Sri Lanka): 30/75A, Longdon Pl., Colombo 07; tel. (11) 2585927; fax (11) 2585930; e-mail office@lankapuvath.net; internet www.lankapuvath.lk; f. 1978; Chair. (vacant); Editor (vacant).

TamilNet: e-mail tamilnet@tamilnet.com; internet www.tamilnet.com; f. 1997; reports on Tamil affairs.

PRESS ASSOCIATIONS

Foreign Correspondents' Association of Sri Lanka: 27th Floor, East Tower, World Trade Centre, Colombo 1; tel. (11) 2346166; fax (11) 2357909; e-mail simon.gardner@reuters.com; Pres. SIMON GARDNER.

Sri Lanka Press Association: Media House, 17A, 2/1, Stanley Tillakaratne Mawatha, Nugegoda, Colombo; tel. (11) 2775606; fax (11) 2816516; Pres. B. H. S. JAYAWARDHANA; Sec.-Gen. MUDITHA KARIYAKARAWANA.

Publishers

W. E. Bastian and Co (Pvt) Ltd: 23 Canal Row, Fort, Colombo 1; tel. (11) 2432752; f. 1904; art, literature, technical; Dirs H. A. MUNIDEVA, K. HEWAGE, N. MUNIDEVA, G. C. BASTIAN.

Buddhist Publication Society: 54 Sangaraja Mawatha, POB 61, Kandy; tel. (81) 2237283; fax (81) 2238901; e-mail bps@sltnet.lk; internet www.bps.lk; f. 1958; philosophy, religion and theology; Pres. Bhikkhu BODHI; Editor BHIKKU NYANATUSITA.

Colombo Catholic Press: 2 Gnanarthapradeepaya Mawatha, Borella, Colombo 8; tel. (11) 2678106; fax (11) 2692586; e-mail colombocp@sltnet.lk; f. 1865; religious; publrs of *The Messenger*, *Gnanarthapradeepaya*, *The Weekly*; Exec. Dir Rev. Fr ROHAN DE ALWIS.

M. D. Gunasena and Co Ltd: 217 Olcott Mawatha, POB 246, Colombo 11; tel. (11) 2323981; fax (11) 2323336; e-mail publishingmgr@mdgunasena.com; internet www.mdgunasena.com; f. 1913; educational and general; Chair M. D. PERCY GUNASENA; Man. Dir M. D. ANANDA GUNASENA.

Lake House Printers and Publishers Ltd: 41 W. A. D. Ramanayake Mawatha, POB 1458, Colombo 2; tel. (11) 2433271; fax (11) 2449504; e-mail wnl@wijeya.lk; f. 1965; Chair. R. S. WIJEWARDENE; Sec. D. P. ANURA NISHANTHA KUMARA.

Pradeepa Publishers: 34/34 Lawyers' Office Complex, Colombo 12; tel. and fax (11) 2435074; academic and fictional; Propr K. JAYATILAKE.

Saman Publishers Ltd: 49/16 Iceland Bldg, Colombo 3; tel. (11) 2223058; fax (11) 2447972.

Sarexpo International Ltd: Caves Bookshop, 81 Sir Baron Jayatilleke Mawatha, POB 25, Colombo 1; tel. (11) 2422676; fax (11) 2447854; e-mail sarexpo@eureka.lk; f. 1876; history, arts, law, medicine, technical, educational; Man. Dir C. J. S. FERNANDO.

K. V. G. de Silva and Sons (Colombo) Ltd: Shop No. 5, Liberty Plaza, Colombo 3; tel. (11) 7455646; fax (11) 7555543; f. 1898; art, philosophy, scientific, technical, academic, 'Ceyloniana', fiction; Man. FREDERICK JAYARATNAM.

SRI LANKA

PUBLISHERS' ASSOCIATION

Sri Lanka Association of Publishers: 112 S. Mahinda Himi Mawatha, Maradana, Colombo 10; tel. (11) 2695773; fax (11) 2696653; e-mail dayawansa@dayawansajayakody.com; f. 1972; Pres. DAYAWANSA JAYAKODY; Sec.-Gen. DHARMADASA PANDITHARATNA.

Broadcasting and Communications

TELECOMMUNICATIONS

Telecommunications Regulatory Commission of Sri Lanka: 276 Elvitigala Mawatha, Manning Town, Colombo 8; tel. (11) 2689345; fax (11) 2689341; e-mail dgtsl@trc.gov.lk; internet www.trc.gov.lk; f. 1996; Chair. LALITH WEERATHUNGA; Dir-Gen. PRIYANTHA KARIYAPPERUMA.

Bharti Airtel Lanka: 598 Elvitigala Mawatha, Colombo 5; tel. and fax 755755755 (mobile); e-mail 555@airtel.lk; internet www.airtel.lk; f. 2009; subsidiary of Bharti Airtel (India); digital mobile services; CEO AMALI NANAYAKKARA; 1m. subscribers.

Dialog Telekom PLC: 475 Union Pl., Colombo 2; tel. (11) 7678678; fax (11) 2678692; e-mail dialog@dialog.lk; internet www.dialog.lk; operates Dialog GSM, Sri Lanka's largest mobile telephone network; Chair. DATUK AZZAT KAMALUDIN; Chief Exec. Dr SHRIDHIR SARIPUTTA HANSA WIJAYASURIYA.

Etisalat Sri Lanka: 78 Mukthar Plaza Bldg, 3rd Floor, Grandpass Rd, Colombo 14; tel. 722123123 (mobile); fax 722541100 (mobile); e-mail customercare@int.tigo.lk; internet www.etisalat.lk; f. 2010; following takeover of Tigo Sri Lanka by Etisalat (UAE); CEO DUMINDRA RATNAYAKA.

Hutchison Telecommunications Lanka (Pvt) Ltd: 234 Galle Rd, Bambalapitiya, Colombo 4; tel. 785785785 (mobile); e-mail cs@hutchison.lk; internet www.hutch.lk; f. 2004; subsidiary of Hutchison Telecommunications Int. Ltd; CEO SHANKAR BALI.

Lanka Communication Services (Pvt) Ltd: 65C Dharmapala Mawatha, Colombo 7; tel. (11) 2437545; fax (11) 2537547; e-mail webmaster@lankacom.net; internet www.lankacom.net; f. 1991; subsidiary of Singapore Telecom International; Man. Dir ROHITH UDALAGAMA.

Sri Lanka Telecom Ltd: Telecom Headquarters, 7th Floor, Lotus Rd, POB 503, Colombo 1; tel. (11) 2329711; fax (11) 2440000; e-mail pr@slt.lk; internet www.slt.lk; 35% owned by Nippon Telegraph and Telephone Corpn (Japan), 49.5% by Govt of Sri Lanka and 3.5% by employees; Chair. LEISHA DE SILVA CHANDRASENA; Chief Exec. GREG YOUNG.

Mobitel (Pvt) Ltd: 108 W. A. D. Ramanayake Mawatha, Colombo 2; tel. 712755777 (mobile); fax (11) 2330396; e-mail info@mobitel.lk; internet www.mobitel.lk; acquired by Sri Lanka Telecom Ltd in 2002; mobile telecommunications services; CEO SUREN AMERASEKERA.

RADIO

Sri Lanka Broadcasting Corpn: Independence Sq., POB 574, Colombo 7; tel. (11) 2697491; fax (11) 2691568; e-mail dg@slbc.lk; internet www.slbc.lk; f. 1967; under Ministry of Mass Media and Information; controls all broadcasting in Sri Lanka; regional stations at Anuradhapura, Kandy and Matara; transmitting stations at Ambewela, Ampara, Anuradhapura, Diyagama, Ekala, Galle, Kanthalai, Mahiyangana, Maho, Matara, Puttalam, Ratnapura, Seeduwa, Senkadagala, Weeraketiya; home service in Sinhala, Tamil and English; foreign service also in Tamil, English, Sinhala, Hindi, Kannada, Malayalam, Nepali and Telugu; 893 broadcasting hours per week: 686 on domestic services, 182 on external services and 126 on education; Chair. HUDSON SAMARASINGHE; Dir-Gen. SAMANTHA WELIWERIYA.

Asura FM: 52, 5th Lane, Colombo 3; tel. (11) 2575000; fax (11) 2301082; e-mail asura@tnlradio.com; broadcasts 24 hrs daily in Sinhala; Gen. Man. CHANDANA THILAKARATNA.

Colombo Communications (Pvt) Ltd: 686 Galle Rd, Colombo 3; tel. (11) 5577777; fax (11) 2505796; e-mail info@efm.lk; internet www.efm.lk; commercial station; three channels broadcast 24 hrs daily in English, Sinhala and Tamil.

Lite FM: 52, 5th Lane, Colombo 3; tel. (11) 7777555; fax (11) 2301082; e-mail litefm@tnlradio.com; internet www.litefm.me; f. 1999; commercial station; broadcasts 24 hrs daily in English; Chair. NIRAJ WICKREMESINGHE.

MBC Networks (Pvt) Ltd: 7 Braybrooke Pl., Colombo 2; tel. (11) 5340111; fax (11) 5340116; e-mail info@maharaja.lk; internet www.capitalmaharaja.com; commercial station comprising four channels; broadcasts 24 hrs daily in English, Sinhala and Tamil; Dir NEDRA WEERASINGHE.

TNL Radio Network Pvt Ltd: 52, 5th Lane, Colombo 3; tel. (11) 7777555; fax (11) 2301082; e-mail info@tnlradio.com; internet www.rhythmfm.me; f. 1993; commercial station; broadcasts 24 hrs daily in English; CEO and Chair. NIRAJ WICKREMESINGHE.

Trans World Radio: Orchid Pl., off Swarnadisi Pl., Koswatte, Nawala, Colombo; tel. (5) 559321; fax (11) 2877750; e-mail rkoch@twr.org; internet www.twr.org; f. 1978; religious station; broadcasts 2–3 hrs every morning and 6.5 hrs each evening to Indian subcontinent; Dir (Finance/Admin) ROGER KOCH; Eng. P. VELMURUGAN.

TELEVISION

Sri Lanka Rupavahini Corpn (SLRC): Independence Sq., POB 2204, Colombo 7; tel. (11) 2501050; fax (11) 2580929; e-mail dg@rupavahini.lk; internet www.rupavahini.lk; f. 1982; studio at Colombo; transmitting stations at nine locations; broadcasts 18 hrs daily on Channel I, 15 hrs daily on Channel II; Chair. SARATH KONGAHAGE.

Independent Television Network (ITN): Wickremasinghepura, Battaramulla; tel. (11) 2774424; fax (11) 2774591; e-mail itnch@slt.lk; internet www.itn.lk; broadcasts about 18 hrs daily; operates Lakhanda Radio (24 hrs; daily); Chair. ROSMAND SENARATHNA; Gen. Man. W. P. A. M. WIJESINGHE.

EAP Network (Pvt) Ltd: 676 Galle Rd, Colombo 3; tel. (11) 2503819; fax (11) 2503788; e-mail eapnet@slt.lk; Chair. SOMA EDIRISINGHE; Man. Dir JEEVAKA EDIRISINGHE.

MTV Channel (Pvt) Ltd: 36 Araliya Uyana, Depanama, Pannipitiya; tel. (11) 2851371; fax (11) 2851373; e-mail info@media.maharaja.lk; internet www.capitalmaharaja.com/mtvchannels.html; f. 1992; broadcasts on three channels in English, Sinhala and Tamil; Group Dir MANO WICKRAMANAYAKE.

National Television of Tamil Eelam (NTT): e-mail ntt_news@yahoo.com; f. 2005; broadcasts for two hrs daily.

Telshan Network (Pvt) Ltd (TNL): 9D Tower Bldg, 25 Station Rd, Colombo 4; tel. (11) 2596241; fax (11) 2706125; e-mail tnltvr@slt.lk; Chair. and Man. Dir SHANTILAL NILKANT WICKREMESINGHE.

Finance

(cap. = capital; res = reserves; dep. = deposits; m. = million; brs = branches; amounts in Sri Lanka rupees)

BANKING

Central Bank

Central Bank of Sri Lanka: 30 Janadhipathi Mawatha, POB 590, Colombo 1; tel. (11) 2477000; fax (11) 2477712; e-mail cbslgen@cbsl.lk; internet www.cbsl.gov.lk; f. 1950; sole bank of issue; cap. 25,000m., dep. 220,361m. (Dec. 2009), res 125,978.2m. (Dec 2008); Gov. and Chair. of the Monetary Board AJITH NIVARD CABRAAL; Dep. Govs K. G. D. D. DHEERASINGHE, P. D. J. FERNANDO; 4 brs.

Commercial Banks

Bank of Ceylon: 4 Bank of Ceylon Mawatha, POB 241, Colombo 1; tel. (11) 2446811; fax (11) 2320864; e-mail boc@boc.lk; internet www.boc.lk; f. 1939; 100% state-owned; cap. 5,000m., res 4,078m., dep. 442,811m. (Dec. 2009); Chair. Dr GAMINI WICKRAMASINGHE; Gen. Man. B. A. C. FERNANDO; 307 brs in Sri Lanka, 3 brs abroad.

Commercial Bank of Ceylon PLC: Commercial House, 21 Bristol St, POB 856, Colombo 1; tel. (11) 2430416; fax (11) 2449889; e-mail e-mail@combank.net; internet www.combank.net; f. 1969; 29.77% owned by DFCC Bank, 29.91% by govt corpns and 40.32% by public; cap. 10,607m., res 17,891m., dep. 264,649m. (Dec. 2009); Chair. M. J. C. AMARASURIYA; Man. Dir A. L. GOONERATNE; 168 brs.

Hatton National Bank Plc: 479 T. B. Jayah Mawatha, POB 837, Colombo 10; tel. (11) 2664664; fax (11) 2446523; e-mail moreinfo@hnb.net; internet www.hnb.net; f. 1970; as Hatton National Bank Ltd; name changed to above in 2007; 11% owned by individuals, 89% by institutions; cap. 5,084m., res 14,967m., dep. 220,352m. (Dec. 2009); Chair. Dr RANEE JAYAMAHA; Man. Dir and CEO RAJENDRA THEAGARAJAH; 187 brs.

Nations Trust Bank Plc: 242 Union Pl., Colombo 2; tel. (11) 4313131; fax (11) 2307854; e-mail info@nationstrust.com; internet www.nationstrust.com; f. 1999 as Nations Trust Bank Ltd; privately owned; acquired Mercantile Leasing Ltd by merger to form Nations Leasing business; name changed as above in 2008; cap. 3,109m., res 1,076m., dep. 46,612m. (Dec. 2009); Chair. AJIT GUNEWARDENE; CEO SALIYA RAJAKARUNA.

Pan Asia Banking Corpn PLC: 450 Galle Rd, Colombo 3; tel. (11) 2565556; fax (11) 2565558; e-mail pabc@pabcbank.com; internet www.pabcbank.com; f. 1995; 100% privately owned (87.6% owned by local shareholders, 12.4% by foreign shareholders); cap. 1,106m., res

349m., dep. 16,328m. (Dec. 2009); Chair. A. G. Weerasinghe; CEO Claude Peiris; 41 brs.

People's Bank: 75 Sir Chittampalam A. Gardiner Mawatha, POB 728, Colombo 2; tel. (11) 2327841; fax (11) 2433127; e-mail info@peoplesbank.lk; internet www.peoplesbank.lk; f. 1961; 92% owned by Govt, 8% by co-operatives; cap. 7,201m., res 10,578m., dep. 401,157m. (Dec. 2009); Chair. W. Karunajeewa; Gen. Man. N. Vasantha Kumar; 325 brs.

Sampath Bank Plc: Sampath Centre Bldg, 110 Sir James Peiris Mawatha, POB 997, Colombo 2; tel. (11) 2303050; fax (11) 2303085; e-mail info@sampath.lk; internet www.sampath.lk; f. 1987 as Investment and Credit Bank Limited; name changed as above in 2008; cap. 1,581m., res 10,264m., dep. 128,577m. (Dec. 2009); Chair. I. W. Senanayake; Man. Dir Harris Premaratne; 131 brs.

Seylan Bank PLC: Ceylinco Seylan Towers, 90 Galle Rd, POB 400, Colombo 3; tel. (11) 2456789; fax (11) 2456456; e-mail info@seylan.lk; internet www.eseylan.com; f. 1988 as Seylan Bank Ltd; cap. 5,567m., res 5,014m., dep. 106,694m. (Dec. 2009); Chair. Eastman Narangoda; Exec. Dir R. Nadarajah; 116 brs.

Union Bank of Colombo Ltd: 15a Alfred Pl., Colombo 3; tel. (11) 2370870; fax (11) 4525576; e-mail info@unionb.com; internet www.unionb.com; f. 1995; cap. 1,813m., res 14m., dep. 11,963m. (Dec. 2009); Chair. Ajita de Zoysa; CEO and Dir Anil Amarasuriya; 25 brs.

Development Banks

DFCC Bank: 73/5 Galle Rd, POB 1397, Colombo 3; tel. (11) 2442442; fax (11) 2440376; e-mail info@dfccbank.com; internet www.dfccbank.com; f. 1956 as Development Finance Corpn of Ceylon; name changed as above 1997; provides long- and medium-term credit, investment banking and consultancy services; cap. 4,695m., res 10,034m., dep. 7,823m. (March 2010); Chair. J. M. S. Brito; CEO A. N. Fonseka; 19 brs.

National Development Bank Plc: DHPL Bldg, 42 Nawam Mawatha, POB 1825, Colombo 2; tel. (11) 2448448; fax (11) 2314642; e-mail contact@ndbbank.com; internet www.ndbbank.com; f. 1979 by an Act of Parliament as National Development Bank of Sri Lanka; subsequently privatized and name changed as above in June 2008; provides long-term finance for projects, equity financing and merchant banking services; cap. 1,032m., res 10,061m., dep. 60,748m. (Dec. 2009); Chair. Manik Nagahawatte; CEO Russell de Mel; 48 brs.

State Mortgage and Investment Bank: 269 Galle Rd, Colombo 3; tel. (11) 2573561; fax (11) 2573346; e-mail agmit@smib.lk; internet www.smib.lk; f. 1979; following the merger of the Ceylon State Mortgage Bank and the Agricultural and Industrial Credit Corporation of Ceylon; Chair. W. M. Dayasinghe; 14 brs.

Merchant Banks

Merchant Bank of Sri Lanka Plc: Bank of Ceylon Merchant Tower, 28 St Michael's Rd, POB 1987, Colombo 3; tel. (11) 4711711; fax (11) 4711743; e-mail mbslbank@mbslbank.com; internet www.mbslbank.com; f. 1982; 53.8% owned by Bank of Ceylon; public ltd liability co; cap. p.u. 2,500m., total assets 2,128m. (2003); Chair. M. R. Shah; CEO Gamini Karunathileka; 11 brs.

People's Merchant Plc: 21 Navam Mawatha, Colombo 2; tel. (11) 2300191; fax (11) 2300190; e-mail pmbank@sltnet.lk; internet www.peoplesmerchantbank.lk; f. 1984 as a subsidiary of People's Bank; Chair. P. A. Ajith Panditharatne; Man. Dir and CEO Anura Wickremasinghe; 10 brs.

Financial Association

The Finance Houses' Association of Sri Lanka: 181/1a Dharmapala Mawatha, Colombo 7; tel. (11) 2362669; fax (11) 2362668; e-mail finass@sltnet.lk; internet www.fhalanka.lk; f. 1958; represents the finance cos registered and licensed by the Central Bank of Sri Lanka; Chair. Hafeez Rajudin.

STOCK EXCHANGES

Securities and Exchange Commission of Sri Lanka: East Tower, 28th and 29th Floors, World Trade Centre, Echelon Sq., Colombo 1; tel. (11) 2439144; fax (11) 2439149; e-mail mail@sec.gov.lk; internet www.sec.gov.lk; f. 1987; Dir-Gen. Malik Cader; Chair. Indrani Sugathadasa.

Colombo Stock Exchange: 04-01, West Block, World Trade Centre, Echelon Sq., Colombo 1; tel. (11) 2446581; fax (11) 2445279; e-mail cse@cse.lk; internet www.cse.lk; f. 1896; stock market; 21 mem. firms and 234 listed cos; Chair. Nihal Fonseka; CEO Surekha Sellahewa.

INSURANCE

Aviva NDB Insurance: Eagle House, 75 Kumaran Ratnam Rd, Colombo 2; tel. (11) 2310310; fax (11) 2447620; e-mail info@avivandb.com; internet www.avivandb.com; f. 1988 as CTC Eagle Insurance Co Ltd; renamed as above in 2010; general and life insurance; mem. of Aviva International Holdings Ltd; Chair. T. R. Ramachandran; Man. Dir Shah Rouf.

Ceylinco Insurance Plc: Ceylinco House, 4th Floor, 69 Janadhipathi Mawatha, Colombo 1; tel. (11) 2485757; fax (11) 2485769; e-mail jagath@lanka.com.lk; internet www.ceylinco-insurance.com; f. 1987; general and life insurance; Chair. J. G. Perera; Man. Dir and CEO A. R. Gunawardena.

Hayleys PLC: Hayley Bldg, 400 Deans Rd, Colombo 10; tel. (11) 2696331; fax (11) 2699299; e-mail info@cauhayleys.com; internet www.hayleys.com; f. 1952; Chair. A. M. Pandithage.

National Insurance Corpn Ltd: 47 Muttiah Rd, POB 2202, Colombo 2; tel. (11) 2445738; fax (11) 2445733; e-mail nicopl@slt.lk; general; Chair. T. M. S. Nanayakkara; Sec. A. C. J. de Alwis.

Sri Lanka Insurance Corporation Ltd: 'Rakshana Mandiraya', 21 Vauxhall St, POB 1337, Colombo 2; tel. (11) 2357457; fax (11) 2447742; e-mail slic@srilankainsurance.com; internet www.srilankainsurance.com; f. 1961; privatized in 2003; all classes of insurance; CEO and Man. Dir Mohan de Alwis.

Union Assurance Ltd: Union Assurance Centre, 20 St Michael's Rd, Colombo 3; tel. (11) 2428428; fax (11) 2343065; e-mail unionassurance@ualink.lk; internet www.ualink.lk; f. 1987; general and life insurance; CEO Dirk Pereira.

Trade and Industry

GOVERNMENT AGENCIES

Board of Investment of Sri Lanka: World Trade Centre, West Tower, 26th Floor, Echelon Sq., Colombo 1; tel. (11) 2434403; fax (11) 2447995; e-mail infoboi@boi.lk; internet www.investsrilanka.com; f. 1978 as the Greater Colombo Economic Commission; promotes foreign direct investment and administers the eight Export Processing Zones at Katunayake, Biyagama, Koggala, Mirigama, Malwatta, Horana, Mawathagama and Polgahawela; also administers industrial township at Watupitiwala and industrial parks at Seetawaka and Kandy; Chair. and Dir-Gen. Jayampathi Bandaranayake.

Sri Lanka Gem and Jewellery Exchange: World Trade Centre, East Low Blk, Levels 4 and 5, Echelon Sq., Colombo 1; tel. 777536674 (mobile); e-mail gemautho@sltnet.lk; internet www.srilankagemautho.com; f. 1990; testing and certification of gems, trading booths; Dir-Gen. Ravi Samaranayake.

National Gem and Jewellery Authority: 25 Galle Face Terrace, Colombo 3; tel. (11) 2390645; fax (11) 2320758; e-mail gemautho@slnet.lk; internet www.srilankagemautho.com; f. 1971 as State Gem Corpn; Chair. Gen. Rohan De S. Daluwatte; Dir-Gen. Ajith Perera (acting).

Trade Information Service: Sri Lanka Export Development Board, Level 7, 42 Navam Mawatha, POB 1872, Colombo 2; tel. (11) 2300677; fax (11) 2300676; e-mail tisinfo@edb.tradenetsl.lk; internet www.srilankabusiness.com; f. 1981 to collect and disseminate commercial information and to provide advisory services to trade circles; Chair. and Chief Exec. Janaka Ratnayake; Dir-Gen. Sujatha Weerakoon.

DEVELOPMENT ORGANIZATIONS

Coconut Development Authority: 54 Nawala Rd, Narahenpita, POB 1572, Colombo 5; tel. (11) 2502502; fax (11) 2508729; e-mail dgcda@sltnet.lk; internet www.cda.lk; f. 1972; state body; promotes the coconut industry through financial assistance for mfrs of coconut products, market information, consultancy services and quality assurance; Chair. Sugath Handunge.

Industrial Development Board of Ceylon (IDB): 615 Galle Rd, Katubedda, POB 09, Moratuwa; tel. (11) 2605326; fax (11) 2607002; e-mail idb@sltnet.lk; internet www.idb.lk; f. 1969; under Ministry of Traditional Industries and Small Enterprise Development; promotes industrial development through provincial network; Chair. Udayasri Kariyawasam.

Centre for Industrial and Technology Information Services (CITIS): 615 Galle Rd, Katubedda, POB 09, Moratuwa 10400; tel. (11) 2605372; fax (11) 2607002; e-mail idbitd@sltnet.lk; internet www.idb.lk; f. 1989; disseminates information to small and medium-sized enterprises; Dir U. Wimalasooriya (acting).

Information and Communication Technology Association of Sri Lanka (ICTA): 160/24 Kirimandala Mawatha, Colombo 5; tel. (11) 2369100; fax (11) 2369091; e-mail dilanp@icta.lk; internet www.icta.lk; f. 2003; responsible for development of information communication technology in Sri Lanka; govt-owned; Chair. Prof. P. W. Epasinghe (acting).

Janatha Estates Development Board: 55/75 Vauxhall St, Colombo 2; fax (11) 2446577; f. 1975; manages tea and spice plantations; 10,164 employees; 1 regional office.

Sri Lanka Export Development Board: Trade Information Service, Level 7, 42 Navam Mawatha, Colombo 2; tel. (11) 2300705; fax (11) 2305211; e-mail edb@tradenetsl.lk; internet www.srilankabusiness.com; f. 1979; Chair. and Chief Exec. JANAKA RATNAYAKE; Dir-Gen. SUJATHA WEERAKOON.

CHAMBERS OF COMMERCE

Federation of Chambers of Commerce and Industry of Sri Lanka: 53 Vauxhall Lane, 3rd Floor, Colombo 2; tel. (11) 2304253; fax (11) 2304255; e-mail sg@fccisl.lk; internet www.fccisl.lk; f. 1973; a central org. of 53 chambers of commerce and industry and trade asscns representing 12,500 cos throughout Sri Lanka; Pres. TISSA JAYAWEERA; Sec.-Gen. THUSITHA TENNAKOON.

Ceylon Chamber of Commerce: 50 Navam Mawatha, POB 274, Colombo 2; tel. (11) 2421745; fax (11) 2449352; e-mail info@chamber.lk; internet www.chamber.lk; f. 1839; 517 mems; Chair. ANURA EKANAYAKE; Sec.-Gen. and CEO HARIN MALWATTE.

Ceylon National Chamber of Industries (CNCI): Galle Face Court 2, Apt No. 20, 1st Floor, POB 1775, Colombo 3; tel. (11) 2452181; fax (11) 2331443; e-mail info@cnci.biz; internet www.cnci.biz; f. 1960; 325 mems; Chair. SUNIL LIYANAGE; Sec.-Gen. and CEO KUMARA KANDALAMA.

International Chamber of Commerce Sri Lanka: Ground Floor, 53 Vauxhall St, POB 1733, Colombo 2; tel. (11) 2307825; fax (11) 2307841; e-mail iccsl@sltnet.lk; internet www.iccsrilanka.com; f. 1955; Chair. TISSA JAYAWEERA; CEO GAMINI PEIRIS.

National Chamber of Commerce of Sri Lanka (NCCSL): NCCSL Bldg, 450 D. R. Wijewardene Mawatha, POB 1375, Colombo 10; tel. (11) 2689600; fax (11) 2689596; e-mail sg@nccsl.lk; internet www.nccsl.lk; f. 1948; Pres. ASOKA HETTIGODA; Sec.-Gen. E. M. WIJETILLEKE.

INDUSTRIAL AND TRADE ASSOCIATIONS

Association of Computer Training Organizations: 51 Sir Marcus Fernando Mawatha, Colombo 7; tel. (11) 2665261; fax (11) 4713821; e-mail actos@infotel.lk; internet www.actos.lk; f. 1991; 29 mems; Pres. KAPILA GIRAGAMA.

Ceylon Coir Fibre Exporters' Association: c/o Volanka Ltd, 193 Minuwangoda Rd, Kotugoda; tel. (11) 2232476; fax (11) 2232477; e-mail com@volanka.com; internet www.volanka.com; Chair. INDRAJITH PIYASENA.

Ceylon Hardware Merchants' Association: 159 1/5 Mahavidyalaya Mawatha, Colombo 13; fax (11) 2423342; 191 mems; Pres. S. T. S. ARULANANTHAN.

Ceylon Planters' Society: 40/1 Sri Dhammadara Mawatha, Ratmalana; tel. (11) 2715656; fax (11) 2716758; e-mail planterssociety@yahoo.com; f. 1936; 500 mems (plantation mans); Pres. SANJAYA DISSANAYAKE; Sec. D. N. R. WIJEWARDENA.

Coconut Products Association: c/o Ceylon Chamber of Commerce, 50 Navam Mawatha, POB 274, Colombo 2; tel. (11) 2421745; fax (11) 2449352; e-mail info@chamber.lk; internet www.chamber.lk; f. 1925; Chair. THARAKA DADAGAMUWA; Sec. E. P. A. COORAY.

Colombo Rubber Traders' Association (CRTA): c/o Ceylon Chamber of Commerce, 50 Navam Mawatha, POB 274, Colombo 2; tel. (11) 5588881; fax (11) 2449352; e-mail info@chamber.lk; internet www.chamber.lk; f. 1918; Chair. M. RAHEEM; Gen. Sec. DAVID JANSZE.

Colombo Tea Traders' Association: c/o Ceylon Chamber of Commerce, 50 Navam Mawatha, POB 274, Colombo 2; tel. (11) 5588801; fax (11) 2449352; e-mail info@chamber.lk; internet www.chamber.lk; f. 1894; 203 mems; Chair. AVINDRA DE SILVA.

Exporters Association of Sri Lanka (EASL): 50 Nawam Mawatha, Colombo 2; tel. (11) 2421745; fax (11) 2449352; e-mail irangika@chamber.lk; internet www.exporterssrilanka.org; f. 1997; Chair. NIRMALI SAMARATUNGA.

Fabric Apparel Accessory Manufacturers' Association (FAAMA): c/o JAAF Secretariat, 16 De Fonseka Rd, Colombo 5; e-mail info@faama.lk; internet www.faama.lk; f. 2003; Chair. BEAUNO FERNANDO; 59 mems.

Free Trade Zone Manufacturers' Association: Plaza Complex, Unit 6 (Upper Floor), IPZ, Katunayake; tel. (11) 2259875; fax (11) 2252813; e-mail ftzma@sltnet.lk; f. 1979; Chair. DHAMMIKA FERNANDO.

Joint Apparel Association Forum (JAAF): 16 De Fonseka Rd, Colombo 5; tel. (11) 4528494; fax (11) 2501753; e-mail info@jaafsl.com; internet www.jaafsl.com; f. 2002; co-ordinates and develops apparel industry; Chair. A. SUKUMARIN; Sec.-Gen. ROHAN MASAKORALE.

Sea Food Exporters' Association: c/o Tropic Frozen Foods Ltd, 16/1 Thammita Rd, Negombo; tel. (31) 2222959; fax (31) 2233348.

Software Exporters' Association: 65 Walukarama Rd, Colombo 3; tel. (11) 4721194; fax (11) 4721198; e-mail mano@eurocenter.lk; f. 1999; 52 mems; Chair. MANO SEKARAM.

Sri Lanka Apparel Exporters' Association: 45 Rosmead Pl., Colombo 7; tel. (11) 2675050; fax (11) 2683118; e-mail sl-apparel@sltnet.lk; internet www.srilanka-apparel.com; f. 1982; Chair. ROHAN ABAYAKOON; Sec. HEMAMALI SIRISENA.

Sri Lanka Association of Manufacturers and Exporters of Rubber Products (SLAMERP): Associated Motorways Ltd, Nagoda, Kalutara; tel. (34) 2227066; fax (34) 2226476; e-mail slamerp@panlanka.net; f. 1984; Chair. ANANDA CALDERA; Pres. ANANDA CALDERA.

Sri Lanka Association of Printers (SLAP): 290 D. R. Wijewardene Mawatha, Colombo 10; tel. (11) 2472315; fax (11) 2386716; e-mail slap@srilankaprint.com; internet www.srilankaprint.com; f. 1956; 390 mems; publs quarterly magazine *Printceylon*; Pres. DHARANI KARUNARATNE; Sec. V. KUMARAN.

Sri Lanka Chamber of Garment Exporters (SLCGE): 108A-1 Maya Ave, Colombo 6; tel. (11) 2504379; fax (11) 4517585; e-mail info@srilankagarments.com; internet www.srilankagarments.com; f. 1992; Pres. JAYASIRI SILVA; Gen. Sec. J. J. SOURJAH; 78 mems.

Sri Lanka Chamber of the Pharmaceutical Industry: 15 Tichbourne Passage, Colombo 10; tel. (11) 2231560; fax (11) 2671877; e-mail aperera@sol.lk; internet www.slcpi.org; f. 1999; 31 mems; Pres. ANANDA SAMARASINGHE; Sec. SUDARSHANA JAYATILLEKE.

Sri Lanka Fruit and Vegetables Producers, Processors and Exporters' Association: c/o Consolidated Business Systems, 27A Papiliya Rd, Nugegoda, Colombo; tel. (11) 2821013; fax (11) 2856476; e-mail sarathds@sri.lanka.net; internet www.srilankafruit.com; f. 1981; 50 mems; Pres. SARATH DE SILVA.

Sri Lanka Gem and Jewellery Association (SLGJA): Subud Home, 2nd Floor, 38 Frankfort Pl., Colombo 4; tel. (11) 2597226; fax (11) 2597250; e-mail info@slgja.org; internet www.slgja.org; f. 2003, following merger of Sri Lanka Gem Traders' Asscn, Sri Lanka Jewellery Manufacturing Exporters' Asscn, Sri Lanka Lapidarists' and Exporters' Asscn and Sri Lanka Jewellers' and Gem Merchants' Fed.; 297 mems; Chair. DESHABANDU M. MACKY HASIM; Sec. ZIQUFI ISMAIL.

Sri Lanka Shippers' Council (SLSC): c/o Ceylon Chamber of Commerce, 50 Nawam Mawatha, POB 274, Colombo 2; tel. (11) 2421745; fax (11) 2449352; e-mail slsc@chamber.lk; f. 1966; Pres. RANDOLPH PERERA; Sec.-Gen. PREMA COORAY.

Sri Lanka Tea Board: 574 Galle Rd, POB 1750, Colombo 3; tel. (11) 2587814; fax (11) 2589132; e-mail teaboard@pureceylontea.com; internet www.pureceylontea.com; f. 1976 for development of tea industry through quality control and promotion in Sri Lanka and in world markets; Chair. SUSANTHA RATNAYAKE; Dir-Gen. H. D. HEMARATNE.

EMPLOYERS' ORGANIZATION

Employers' Federation of Ceylon: 385 J3 Old Kotte Rd, Rajagiriya, Colombo; tel. (11) 2867966; fax (11) 2867942; e-mail efc@empfed.lk; internet www.employers.lk; f. 1929; mem. of International Organization of Employers and Confederation of Asia Pacific Employers; 510 mems; Chair. C. L. K. P. JAYASURIA; Dir-Gen. R. L. P. PEIRIS.

UTILITIES

Electricity

Ceylon Electricity Board: 50 Sir Chittampalam A. Gardiner Mawatha, POB 540, Colombo 2; tel. (11) 2324471; fax (11) 2323935; e-mail admin@ceb.lk; internet www.ceb.lk; f. 1969; Chair. V. D. AMARAPALA.

Water

National Water Supply and Drainage Board (NWSDB): Galle Rd, Ratmalana, Colombo; tel. (11) 2638999; fax (11) 2636449; e-mail gm@waterboard.lk; internet www.waterboard.lk; f. 1975; govt corpn; Chair. KARUNASENA HETTIARACHCHI; Gen. Man. K. L. L. PREMANATH.

CO-OPERATIVES

In 2000 there were an estimated 11,793 co-operative societies in Sri Lanka, with membership totalling 17,235,000.

National Co-operative Council of Sri Lanka (NCC): 455 Galle Rd, POB 1469, Colombo 03; tel. (11) 2585496; fax (11) 2587062; e-mail nccsec@sltnet.lk.

In January 2008 the top five co-operatives in Sri Lanka were:

Mahiyangana Multi-Purpose Co-operative: Mahiyangana; f. 1971; food and agriculture; Chair. P. M. C. BANDARA.

SRI LANKA   *Directory*

Matara District Tea Producers' Co-operative: f. 1998; food and agriculture; c. 3,000 mems (2003); Chair. B. RANWAKA.

Morawakkorale Tea Producers' Co-operative Society: Deniyaya Rd, Kotapola; tel. (41) 2271259; e-mail info@mkteacoop.com; internet mkteacoop.com; f. 1953; 3,800 mems (2008); Chair. MAHINDA VIDANAPATHIRANA; Gen. Man. W. W. LEENAS PRIYASHANTHA.

Negombo Multi-Purpose Co-operative: 358 Main St, Negombo; tel. (31) 2238846; f. 1971; diversified financials.

Polonnaruwa District Milk Producers' Co-operative: Polonnaruwa; f. 1979; food and agriculture.

TRADE UNIONS

In 2009 there were more than 1,650 trade unions registered in Sri Lanka, many of which had fewer than 50 members, and 19 trade union federations. Many of the trade unions have political affiliations.

All Ceylon Federation of Free Trade Unions (ACFFTU): 94-1/6 York Bldg, York St, Colombo 1; tel. (11) 2431847; fax (11) 2470874; e-mail nwc@itmin.com; 10 affiliated unions; 84,000 mems; Pres. MARCELL C. RAJAHMONEY; Sec.-Gen. ANTON LODWICK.

All Ceylon Trade Union Federation (ACTUF): 198/19 Panchikawatte Rd, Colombo 10; tel. (11) 2595566; fax (11) 5358783; e-mail editor@unions.lk; internet www.unions.lk; f. 1941; Pres. K. D. LAL KANTHA.

Ceylon Federation of Labour (CFL): 457 Union Pl., Colombo 2; tel. (11) 2694273; fax (11) 2686188; f. 1957; 16 affiliated unions; 155,969 mems; Pres. PERCY WICKRAMASEKARA; Gen. Sec. H. A. PIYADASA.

Ceylon Mercantile, Industrial and General Workers' Union (CMU): 3, 22nd Lane, Colombo 3; tel. (11) 2328158; fax (11) 2434025; e-mail gscmu@sltnet.lk; Gen. Sec. BALA TAMPOE.

Ceylon Workers' Congress (CWC): 'Savumia Bhavan', 72 Ananda Coomarasamy Mawatha, POB 1294, Colombo 7; tel. (11) 2301359; fax (11) 2301355; e-mail cwconline@sltnet.lk; f. 1939; political entity; represents mainly plantation workers of recent Indian origin; 50 district offices and seven regional offices; 250,000 mems; Pres. S. ARUMUGAN THONDAMAN.

Democratic Workers' Congress (DWC): 70 Bankshall St, POB 1009, Colombo 11; tel. (11) 2423746; fax (11) 2435961; f. 1939; 201,382 mems (1994); Pres. MANO GANESHAN; Gen. Sec. R. KITNAN.

Government Workers' Trade Union Federation (GWTUF): 457 Union Pl., Colombo 2; 52 affiliated unions; 100,000 mems; Leader P. D. SARANAPALA.

Inter Company Employees Union: 158/18 E. D. Dabare Mawatha, Colombo 5; tel. (11) 5358782; fax (11) 5358783; union of private-sector workers; Gen. Sec. VASANTHA SAMARASINGHE.

Jathika Sevaka Sangamaya (JSS) (National Employees' Union): 416 Kotte Rd, Pitakotte, Colombo; tel. (11) 2865436; fax (11) 2865438; e-mail jathika.ss@gmail.com; f. 1959; 357,000 mems; represents over 70% of unionized manual and clerical workers of Sri Lanka; Gen. Sec. SIRINAL DE MEL.

Lanka Jathika Estate Workers' Union (LJEWU): 60 Bandaranayakepura, Sri Jayawardenepura Mawatha, Welikada, POB 1918, Rajagiriya; tel. (11) 2865138; fax (11) 2862262; e-mail ljewusl@gmail.com; f. 1958; 13 affiliated unions; Pres. RAVINDRA SAMARAWEERA; Gen. Sec. K. VELAYUDAM.

National Trade Union Federation: 60 Bandaranayakepura Mawatha, Welikada, Rajagiriya; tel. (11) 2885599; fax (11) 2862262; e-mail ntufsl@gmail.com.

National Workers' Congress: 1/6 York Bldg, 94 York St, Colombo 1; tel. (11) 2431847; fax (11) 2470874; e-mail nwc@itmin.net; internet www.slnwc.org; f. 1947; Pres. M. C. RAJAHMONEY; Sec.-Gen. and Treas. A. LODWICK.

Public Services National Trade Union Federation (PSNTUF): Colombo; internet www.psntuf.lk; f. 1973; 48 affiliated unions; 25,000 mems; Pres. JOSEPH M. PERERA; Gen. Sec. J. M. L. R. JAYASUNDARA.

Sri Lanka Nidahas Sewaka Sangamaya (Sri Lanka Free Workers' Union): 301 T. B. Jayah Mawatha, POB 1241, Colombo 10; tel. and fax (11) 2694074; f. 1960; 834 br. unions; 88,000 mems; Pres. ALAVI MOWLANA; Gen. Sec. LESLIE DEVENDRA.

Trade Union Confederation: Colombo; f. 2008; 40 affiliated unions; Pres. K. S. WEERASEKERA; Sec. H. M. NAWARATNE BANDARA.

United Federation of Labour: 17 Barrack Lane, Colombo 2; tel. (11) 2324053; Pres. LINUS JAYATILLAKE.

Transport

RAILWAYS

In 2009 the total length of the Sri Lankan railways network was 1,447 km. In that year the network transported 102m. passengers and 1.8m. tons of freight. In early 2010 a 10-year railway development strategy was introduced by the Government. Plans for a project to reconstruct the Northern Railway Line from Medawachchiya to Thalaimannar, with funding from Indian sources, were finalized in mid-2010. An electrified line connecting Veyangoda and Kalutara South was scheduled to be completed by 2013.

Sri Lanka Railways Authority (SLRA): Colombo; f. 2003; responsible for running of nat. railway network; Gen. Man. T. LALITHASIRI GUNARUWAH.

Sri Lanka Railways (SLR): Olcott Mawatha, POB 335, Colombo 10; tel. (11) 2431177; fax (11) 2446490; e-mail gmr-slr@sltnet.lk; internet www.railway.gov.lk; f. 1864; under Ministry of Transport; operates 1,447 track-km; 10 railway lines across the country and 164 stations, with 134 sub-stations (2008); Gen. Man. T. L. GUNARUWAN.

ROADS

In 2011 there were an estimated 116,113 km of roads in Sri Lanka, of which 2,900 km were highways, 1,706 km provincial roads and 35,755 km rural roads. Delayed construction of a four-lane Southern Expressway, extending from Colombo to Mattara and jointly funded by the Asian Development Bank and the Japanese Bank for International Co-operation, was scheduled to be completed by 2011. The Colombo–Katunayake Expressway, Outer Circular Highway and Colombo–Matara Expressway were scheduled to be completed by 2013. There were also plans to extend the Southern Expressway from Mattara to Hambantota to improve the connectivity between the western and southern parts of the country.

Department of Motor Traffic: 341 Elvitigala Mawatha, POB 533, Colombo 5; tel. (11) 2694331; fax (11) 2694338; e-mail comm@dmt.gov.lk; internet www.dmt.gov.lk; Commr BADULLAGE WIJAYARATNE.

Sri Lanka Transport Board: 200 Kirula Rd, Narahenpita, POB 1435, Colombo 5; tel. (11) 2581120; fax (11) 2368921; e-mail chairmanctb@sltnet.lk; f. 1958; nationalized organization responsible for road passenger transport services consisting of a central transport board, 11 Cluster Bus Cos and one regional transport board; fleet of 4,077 buses (2006); Chair. TUDER CAYARATNE; Sec. D. P. W. DE LIVERA.

SHIPPING

Colombo is one of the most important ports in Asia and is situated at the junction of the main trade routes. The other main ports of Sri Lanka are Trincomalee, Galle and Jaffna. Trincomalee is the main port for handling tea exports.

Ceylon Association of Ships' Agents (CASA): 56 Ward Pl., Colombo 7; tel. (11) 2696227; fax (11) 2698648; e-mail casa@sltnet.lk; internet www.casa.lk; f. 1944; primarily a consultative organization; represents mems in dealings with govt authorities; 110 mems; Chair. NIMAL RANCHIGODA; Sec.-Gen. DHAMMIKA WALGAMPAYA.

Sri Lanka Ports Authority: 19 Chaithya Rd, POB 595, Colombo 1; tel. (11) 2421201; fax (11) 2440651; e-mail info@slpa.lk; internet www.slpa.lk; f. 1979; responsible for all cargo handling operations and harbour development and maintenance in the ports of Colombo, Galle, Kankasanthurai, Trincomalee, Oluvil, Point Pedro and Hambantota; Chair. PRIYATH BANDU WICKRAMA; Man. Dir Capt. NIHAL KEPPETIPOLA.

Shipping Companies

Ceylon Ocean Lines Ltd: 'Sayuru Sevana', 46/12 Nawam Mawatha, Colombo 2; tel. (11) 2434928; fax (11) 2439245; e-mail oceanlines@col.lk; f. 1956; shipping agents, freight forwarders, charterers, container freight station operators and bunkers; Dirs Capt. L. P. WEINMAN, Capt. A. V. RAJENDRA.

Ceylon Shipping Corpn Ltd: MICH Bldg, 27 Bristol St, Colombo 1; tel. (11) 2328772; fax (11) 2449486; e-mail cscl@cscl.lk; internet www.cscl.lk; f. 1971 as a govt corpn; became govt-owned limited liability co in 1992; operates fully containerized service to Europe, the Far East, the Mediterranean, USA and Canada (East Coast); Chair. PRASAD GALHENA.

Ceylon Shipping Lines Ltd: 450 D. R. Wijewardene Mawatha, POB 891, Colombo 10; tel. (11) 2689500; fax (11) 2689510; e-mail cslmgmt@sltnet.lk; internet www.ceylonshippinglines.com; f. 1954; shipping agents, travel agents, off dock terminal operators; Chair. ARMYNE WIRASINHA; Man. Dir D. P. C. LAWRENCE.

Colombo Dockyard Ltd: Port of Colombo, Graving Docks, POB 906, Colombo 15; tel. (11) 2429000; fax (11) 2446441; e-mail coldock@cdl.lk; internet www.cdl.lk; f. 1974; 51% owned by Onomichi Dockyard Co Ltd, Japan, and 49% by Sri Lankan public and

SRI LANKA

government institutions; four dry-docks, seven repair berths (1,200 m), repair of ships up to 125,000 dwt, and builders of steel/aluminium vessels of up to 3,000 dwt; Chair. AKIHIKO NAKAUCHI; Man. Dir and CEO M. P. B. YAPA.

Mercantile Shipping Co Ltd: Bohen House, 108 Aluthmawatha Rd, Colombo 15; tel. (11) 2331792; fax (11) 2331799; e-mail info@mscl.lk; internet www.mscl.lk; f. 1981; Gen. Man. STEPHAN KUEHL.

Sri Lanka Shipping Co Ltd: 46/5 Robert Sennayake Bldg, Navam Mawatha, POB 1125, Colombo 2; tel. (11) 2336853; fax (11) 2437479; e-mail lankaship@slsc.lk; internet www.srilankashipping.com; f. 1956; Chair. Capt. LESTER POEL WEINMAN.

INLAND WATERWAYS

There are more than 160 km of canals open for traffic.

CIVIL AVIATION

There are airports at Batticaloa, Colombo (Bandaranaike for external flights and Ratmalana for internal), Gal Oya, Palali, Jaffna and Trincomalee. Construction work on a second international airport, located about 180 km south of Colombo at Mattara, near Hambantota, commenced in late 2009 and was scheduled to be completed by the end of 2012.

Civil Aviation Authority of Sri Lanka: Supreme Bldg, 64 Galle Rd, Colombo 3; tel. (11) 2433213; fax (11) 2440231; e-mail info@caa.lk; internet www.caa.lk; f. 2002; under the supervision of the Ministry of Ports and Aviation; Chair. W. D. R. M. J. GOONETILEKE; CEO and Dir-Gen. Civil Aviation H. M. C. NIMALSIRI.

Deccan Aviation (Lanka) Pvt Ltd: 385, Galle Rd, Colombo 03; f. 2004; only co. authorized to operate both helicopters and fixed wing aircraft in the country.

Expo Aviation Pvt Ltd: tel. (11) 2576941; fax (11) 2576943; e-mail expoair@expoavi.com; internet www.expoavi.com; f. 1997; private carrier of int. cargo in Sri Lanka; Man. Dir SHAFIK KASSIM.

Helitours: Air Headquarters, POB 594, Colombo 2; tel. (11) 2342577; fax (11) 2343969; e-mail ops1@slaf.gov.lk; commercial wing of Sri Lankan Air Force; charter services to domestic destinations; Dir Wing-Commdr DAYAL WIJERATNE.

Mihin Lanka: No. 61, W. A. D. Ramanayake Mawatha, Colombo 2; tel. (11) 7800310; fax (11) 7800307; e-mail info@mihinlanka.com; internet www.mihinlanka.com; f. 2007; govt-owned; int. services to India, the Maldives, United Arab Emirates, Thailand and Singapore; Chair. SAJIN VAS GUNAWARDENA.

SriLankan Airlines Ltd: Airline Centre, Bandaranaike International Airport, Katunayake, Colombo; tel. (11) 97335555; fax (11) 97335122; e-mail ulweb@srilankan.aero; internet www.srilankan.aero; f. 1979 as Air Lanka Ltd, name changed as above in 1999; int. services to Europe, the Middle East, South Asia and the Far East; Chair. NISHANTA WICKREMASINGHE; CEO MANOJ GUNAWARDENA.

Tourism

As a stopping place for luxury cruises and by virtue of the spectacle of its Buddhist festivals, ancient monuments and natural scenery, Sri Lanka is one of Asia's most important tourist centres.

Sri Lanka's tourism industry was adversely affected by the intercommunal violence in 1983–2009. However, following the end of the civil war in May 2009, the tourism sector began to recover strongly; according to figures from the Sri Lanka Tourism Development Authority, tourist arrivals increased by 2.1% in 2009, compared with the previous year, to 447,890, before expanding by an impressive 46.1% in 2010, to 654,476. Receipts from tourism (not including passenger transport) increased from US $319.5m. in 2008 to an estimated $326.3m. in 2009.

Sri Lanka Convention Bureau (SLCB): Hotel School Bldg, 4th Floor, 78 Galle Rd, Colombo 03; tel. (11) 4865050; fax (11) 2472985; e-mail slcb@sltnet.lk; internet www.visitsrilanka.net; f. 2005 as one of several entities replacing the Sri Lanka Tourism Board; aims to promote Sri Lanka as a prime destination for meetings, incentives, conferences and exhibitions (MICE) tourism; Chair. Dr NALAKA GODAHEWA; Gen. Man. VIPULA WANIGASEKARA.

Sri Lanka Tourism Development Authority (SLTDA): 80 Galle Rd, Colombo 3; tel. (11) 2437059; fax (11) 2440001; e-mail info@sltda.gov.lk; internet www.sltda.gov.lk; f. 2005 as one of several entities replacing the Sri Lanka Tourism Board; Chair. NALAKA GODAHEWA; Dir-Gen. S. KALAISELVAM.

Sri Lanka Tourism Promotion Bureau (SLTPB): 80 Galle Rd, Colombo 3; tel. (11) 2426900; fax (11) 2440001; e-mail info@srilanka.travel; internet www.srilanka.travel; f. 2005 as one of several entities replacing the Sri Lanka Tourism Board; Chair. BERNARD GOONETILLEKE; Man. Dir DILEEP MUDADENIYA.

Defence

As assessed at November 2010, the total strength of the active armed forces was some 160,900 (including recalled reservists): army 117,900, navy 15,000, air force 28,000; the reserve forces numbered 5,500. There were also paramilitary forces of an estimated 62,200 (including an estimated 15,000 National Guard, 13,000 Home Guard and a 3,000-strong anti-guerrilla Special Task Force). Military service is voluntary.

Defence Budget: Estimated at Rs 215,220m. for 2011 (equivalent to 11.0% of total expenditure).

Chief of Defence Staff: Air Chief Marshal W. D. R. M. J. GOONETILEKE.

Commander of the Army: Lt.-Gen. JAGATH JAYASURIYA.

Commander of the Air Force: Air Vice Marshal HARSHA ABEYWICKREMA.

Commander of the Navy: Vice-Adm. D. W. A. S. DISSANAYAKE.

Education

The formulation of educational policy is the responsibility of the Ministry of Education and the Ministry of Higher Education. The administration and management of the school system is divided into 15 regions. The 2010 budget allocated Rs 23,453m. to the Ministry of Education and Rs 11,993m. to the Ministry of Higher Education, together representing 3.7% of total recurrent expenditure.

Since 1945 education has been available free of charge. In 2009 about 4.0m. pupils attended schools, and teachers numbered an estimated 225,338. The total number of schools (including denominational schools and Pirivenas, which are attended by Buddhist clergy and lay students) was estimated at 10,205 in that year.

School attendance is officially compulsory for 11 years between five and 15 years of age, and each year about 350,000 new pupils start school. Schools are streamed according to the language medium used, either Sinhala or Tamil. Improving the standard of English, which is a compulsory second language, is one of the policy priorities of the Government. In 1960 almost all denominational schools were brought under state control.

SUDAN

Introductory Survey

LOCATION, CLIMATE, LANGUAGE, RELIGION, FLAG, CAPITAL

The Republic of Sudan lies in north-eastern Africa. It is bordered by Egypt to the north, by the Red Sea, Eritrea and Ethiopia to the east, by the Central African Republic, Chad and Libya to the west, and by Kenya, Uganda and the Democratic Republic of the Congo (formerly Zaire) to the south. The climate shows a marked transition from the desert of the north to the rainy equatorial south. Temperatures vary with altitude and latitude. The annual average for the whole country is about 21°C (70°F). Arabic is the official language, although other languages are spoken and English is widely understood. Most northern Sudanese are Muslims, while in the south most of the inhabitants are animists or Christians. The national flag (proportions 1 by 2) has three equal horizontal stripes, of red, white and black, with a green triangle at the hoist. The capital is Khartoum.

CONTEMPORARY POLITICAL HISTORY

Historical Context

The Sudan (as the country was known before 1975) achieved independence as a parliamentary republic on 1 January 1956. In May 1969 power was seized by a group of officers, led by Col Gaafar Muhammad Nimeri. All existing political institutions and organizations were abolished, and the 'Democratic Republic of the Sudan' was proclaimed, with supreme authority in the hands of the Revolutionary Command Council (RCC). In October 1971 a referendum confirmed Nimeri's nomination as President. A new Government was formed, the RCC was dissolved, and the Sudanese Socialist Union (SSU) was recognized as the only political party.

An early problem facing the Nimeri Government concerned the disputed status of the three southern provinces (Bahr al-Ghazal, Equatoria and Upper Nile), whose inhabitants are racially and culturally distinct from most of the country's population. Rebellion against rule from the north had first broken out in 1955, and fighting continued until March 1972, when an agreement to give the three provinces a degree of autonomy was concluded between members of the Government and representatives of the South Sudan Liberation Movement. A High Executive Council (HEC) for the Southern Region was established in April 1972, and Sudan's permanent Constitution was endorsed in April 1973. Elections to the Regional People's Assembly for southern Sudan took place in November 1973, followed by elections to the National People's Assembly in April 1974.

In April 1983 President Nimeri was re-elected for a third six-year term. During that year Sudan's north–south conflict escalated, and in June Nimeri finally decided to redivide the south into three smaller regions, each with its own assembly, in an effort to quell the unrest. In September Nimeri suddenly announced the imposition of strict Islamic law (the *Shari'a*), provoking anger in the largely non-Muslim south, and in April 1984 Nimeri proclaimed a state of emergency. The stringent application of *Shari'a* law aggravated tensions within the country and strained relations between Sudan and its allies, Egypt and the USA.

In May 1984 Nimeri replaced his Council of Ministers with a 64-member Presidential Council, in accordance with the '*Shoura*' (consultation) principle of *Shari'a* law. In July, however, the National People's Assembly rejected his proposed constitutional amendments to make Sudan a formal Islamic state. In October Nimeri ended the state of emergency and offered to revoke the redivision of the south, if a majority of southerners desired it. The situation in the south continued to deteriorate, with the emergence of the Sudan People's Liberation Movement (SPLM), whose armed forces, the Sudan People's Liberation Army (SPLA), rapidly gained military control over large areas of the provinces of Bahr al-Ghazal and Upper Nile.

Domestic Political Affairs

On 6 April 1985, while Nimeri was visiting the USA, he was deposed in a bloodless military coup. The country's new leader, Gen. Abdel-Rahman Swar al-Dahab (who had recently been made Minister of Defence and Commander-in-Chief of the army by Nimeri), appointed a Transitional Military Council (TMC) to govern the country, but he pledged a return to civilian rule after a one-year transitional period. The SSU and the National People's Assembly were dissolved, and hundreds of Nimeri's officials were arrested; Nimeri went into exile in Cairo, Egypt. A transitional Constitution was introduced in October that allowed new political groupings to emerge in preparation for a general election, and in December the name of the country was officially changed to 'the Republic of Sudan'.

In a general election in April 1986 the Umma Party (UP), led by Sadiq al-Mahdi, won 99 of the 264 seats in the new National Assembly, followed by the Democratic Unionist Party (DUP), with 63 seats. A coalition Government was formed by the UP and DUP, with four portfolios in the Council of Ministers allocated to southern parties. Al-Mahdi became Prime Minister and Minister of Defence, and a six-member Supreme Council assumed the functions of Head of State. With these appointments, the TMC was dissolved, signifying a return to civilian rule.

In response to the April 1985 coup, the SPLM initially declared a cease-fire, but presented the new regime with a series of demands concerning the southern region. Despite Swar al-Dahab's offer of various concessions to the south, the SPLM refused to negotiate with the TMC, and fighting resumed. In June al-Mahdi announced that the coalition parties had agreed that laws based on a 'Sudanese legal heritage' would replace those unacceptable to non-Muslims, who would be exempted from Islamic taxation and special penalties. However, the SPLM continued to demand a total abrogation of Islamic law, while the National Islamic Front (NIF) demanded that the Islamic code be imposed on the whole country.

In February 1989 Dr Hassan al-Turabi, the leader of the NIF, was appointed Deputy Prime Minister. Although a peace agreement concluded by the DUP and the SPLM in November had been widely endorsed, the NIF opposed its provision for the suspension of Islamic laws as a prelude to the negotiation of a peace settlement. The NIF was consequently excluded from a new Government formed in March. Peace negotiations between a government delegation and the SPLM commenced in Ethiopia in April, and at the beginning of May the SPLM leader, Col John Garang, proclaimed a one-month cease-fire (subsequently extended to 30 June), renewing hopes for peace. The negotiations culminated in an agreement to suspend Islamic laws, pending the proposed convening, in September, of a constitutional conference.

Al-Bashir seizes power

On 30 June 1989 a bloodless coup, led by Brig. (later Lt-Gen.) Omar Hassan Ahmad al-Bashir, removed al-Mahdi's Government. Al-Bashir formed a 15-member Revolutionary Command Council for National Salvation (RCC), which declared its primary aim to be the resolution of the southern conflict. Al-Bashir, who became Head of State, Chairman of the RCC, Prime Minister and Minister of Defence, and Commander-in-Chief of the armed forces, abolished the Constitution, the National Assembly and all political parties and trade unions, and declared a state of emergency.

The SPLM's response to the coup was cautious. In July 1989 Lt-Gen. al-Bashir declared a one-month unilateral cease-fire and offered amnesty to those opposing the Government 'for political reasons'. By August the SPLM's terms for a negotiated settlement to the conflict included the immediate resignation of the RCC, prior to the establishment of an interim government, in which the SPLM, the banned political parties and other groupings would be represented. However, the new regime's proximity to the NIF had become apparent, and the negotiations collapsed immediately over the issue of Islamic law. Hostilities, which had been in abeyance since the beginning of May, resumed at the end of October.

In February 1991 the RCC enacted a decree instituting a new, federal system of government. Sudan was divided into nine states, each of which had its own governor, deputy governor and cabinet of ministers, and assumed responsibility for local administration and the collection of some taxes. The central Government retained control over foreign policy, military affairs, the economy and the other principal areas of administration. At the beginning of February it had been announced that a new penal code, based on *Shari'a* law, would take effect in March, but would not apply in the three southern states, pending the establishment there of elected assemblies to resolve the issue. The SPLM nevertheless regarded the application of Islamic law in the northern states as unacceptable, citing the large numbers of non-Muslims resident there.

The overthrow, in May 1991, of the Ethiopian Government, led by Mengistu Haile Mariam, had implications for the SPLA forces, who had previously enjoyed Ethiopian support. In late May armed clashes were reported within Ethiopia between SPLA forces and those of the new Ethiopian Government, and the Sudanese Government declared its recognition of, and support for, the new Ethiopian regime. In October Sudan and Ethiopia signed a treaty of friendship and co-operation.

In February 1992 al-Bashir appointed all 300 members of a new transitional National Assembly, which included the entire RCC, all government ministers and the governors of Sudan's nine states. The Assembly was accorded legislative authority, with the power to examine all decrees issued by the RCC, and responsibility for preparing the country for parliamentary elections. In October 1993 al-Bashir announced political reforms in preparation for presidential and legislative elections in 1994 and 1995, respectively. The RCC was dissolved after it had appointed al-Bashir as President and as head of a new civilian Government.

In January 1994 the two principal rival factions of the SPLA were reported to have agreed on a cease-fire. In February Sudan was redivided into 26 states instead of the nine that had formed the basis of administration since 1991. The executive and legislative powers of each state government were to be expanded, and southern states were to be exempted from *Shari'a* law. In March delegations representing the Government and two factions of the SPLA participated in peace talks held in Nairobi, Kenya, under the auspices of the Intergovernmental Authority on Drought and Development (IGADD—superseded in 1996 by the Intergovernmental Authority on Development—IGAD, see p. 336), which in September 1993 had formed a committee on the Sudanese conflict comprising the Heads of State of Kenya, Ethiopia, Uganda and Eritrea. All parties to the talks agreed to allow the free passage of relief supplies to southern Sudan. A further round of IGADD-sponsored peace negotiations was held in Nairobi in July, but divergent positions on the issues of the governance of the south and the role of religion in government quickly led to deadlock.

In March 1995 Garang announced that his faction of the SPLA was to mount a new northern offensive in collaboration with other northern rebels. The New Sudan Brigade aimed to unite other insurgent groups against the Government, but did not appear to gain the support of rival SPLA factions. In late March, following mediation by former US President Jimmy Carter, the Government declared a unilateral cease-fire for a period of two months, and offered rebel groups an amnesty if they surrendered their weapons. The SPLA and the South Sudan Independence Movement (SSIM) responded by also declaring cease-fires. In late May the Government extended its cease-fire for two months. However, it soon became apparent that the army was continuing to conduct military operations.

The 1996 elections

Legislative and presidential elections took place in March 1996. Some 5.5m. of Sudan's 10m. eligible voters were reported to have participated in the election of 275 deputies to a new, 400-seat National Assembly. The remaining 125 deputies had been appointed at a national conference in January. Representatives of opposition groups and parties alleged that electoral malpractice had been widespread. In the presidential election al-Bashir obtained 75.7% of the total votes cast, and formally commenced a five-year term of office on 1 April. On the same day al-Turabi was unanimously elected President of the National Assembly.

Rumours of an attempted *coup d'état* in late March 1996 prejudiced the newly constituted regime's claim that the elections signified the beginning of a new period of stability and reconciliation, as did reports of serious unrest in Khartoum in early April. On 10 April a 'political charter for peace' was signed by the Government, the SSIM and the splinter group SPLA-United, pledging to preserve Sudan's national unity and to take joint action to develop those areas of the country that had been affected by the civil war. The charter also provided for the holding of a referendum as 'a means of realizing the aspirations of southern citizens' and affirmed that Islamic law would be the basis of future legislation. On 17 April Sudan's First Vice-President was reported to have invited Garang to sign the charter on behalf of his faction of the SPLA, prompting speculation that this was part of an ongoing attempt to form a new government of national unity. However, the new Cabinet, announced on 21 April, retained the military, Islamist cast of its predecessor.

In April 1997 a peace accord, covering major issues such as power-sharing and *Shari'a* law, and promising a referendum on southern secession after a four-year transition period, was signed by six rebel groups. Both the Eritrea-based National Democratic Alliance (NDA) and the SPLA, however, rejected the agreement. In August, in accordance with the terms of the agreement, the Southern States Co-ordination Council (SSCC) was established; Dr Riek Mashar Teny-Dhurgon, the leader of the Southern Sudan Defence Force (SSDF), was sworn in as its Chairman. At the beginning of September the SPLA-United declared a cease-fire, and its commander, Dr Lam Akol, returned to Khartoum in the following month.

In March 1998 al-Bashir announced a government reorganization in which a number of former rebel leaders were appointed to the Cabinet, including Akol as Minister of Transport. In April a new Constitution was approved by the National Assembly and endorsed by 96.7% of voters in a referendum held between 1 and 20 May. New legislation approved in November provided for the establishment of an independent election commission and of a Constitutional Court, and for the legalization of political associations. Registration of political parties began in January 1999.

In May 1999 former President Nimeri returned to Sudan after 14 years in exile in Egypt. His return was welcomed by the Government, although opposition parties demanded his prosecution for crimes he had allegedly committed while President. In the same month al-Turabi held talks in Switzerland with Sadiq al-Mahdi, with the aim of initiating a process of reconciliation. At the end of May a meeting took place in Kampala, Uganda, between al-Mahdi, Garang and Mubarak al-Mahdi (of the NDA), to discuss several issues regarding their conflict with the Sudanese Government.

In August 1999 the Government accepted a Libyan peace initiative, which envisaged a cease-fire, an end to media propaganda, direct talks through a conference of national dialogue and the establishment of a preparatory committee. The peace effort was to be co-ordinated jointly by Egypt and Libya. In September the SPLA stated that it supported the Egyptian-Libyan peace initiative 'in principle', although after a meeting with the US Secretary of State in October (see below) Garang discounted the Egyptian-Libyan initiative in favour of the IGAD-sponsored peace process.

At a conference, held in Cairo in October 1999, the leaders of the NDA decided to examine ways of combining the peace initiative sponsored by IGAD and the Egyptian-Libyan initiative, in order to unite the parties of the NDA, a number of whom opposed the pursuit of two parallel initiatives. At the end of November Djibouti hosted a regional IGAD summit meeting, attended by Kenya, Ethiopia and Sudan, to discuss issues related to development and stability in the region. While in Djibouti, President al-Bashir met the UP leader, al-Mahdi, following which the Sudanese Government and the UP signed a declaration of principles, envisaging a federal system of government and the holding of a referendum within four years to allow southerners to choose between the division of the country or unity with decentralized powers. The agreement was welcomed by many parties; however, it was criticized by the NDA, and later rejected by Garang.

During 1999 there were increasing reports of rivalry between al-Bashir and al-Turabi, particularly following the introduction of a bill in the National Assembly that sought to remove the President's power to appoint and dismiss state governors. Consideration of the draft legislation was repeatedly delayed, but a vote was scheduled to be held in mid-December in which the National Assembly was widely expected to approve it. However, on 12 December al-Bashir dissolved the National Assembly and imposed a three-month state of emergency, claiming that he had taken these measures in order to end the 'duality' in the administration. An emergency order suspended some articles of the Constitution, although provincial councils and governors were to continue working. Al-Turabi accused al-Bashir of having carried out a *coup d'état*, although a legal challenge, mounted against the measures, was later rejected by the Constitutional Court.

In March 2000 the Government extended the state of emergency until the end of the year, and approved a law allowing the formation of political parties (superseding the 1998 law), although this was rejected by the opposition, as it still incorporated provisions to suspend the activities of any party. In the same month the UP announced its decision to suspend its membership of the NDA during a meeting in Asmara. In April 2000 it was reported that a presidential election was planned for October; the ruling National Congress Party (NCP) had nominated al-Bashir as its candidate in October 1999. However, most opposition parties, including the UP, indicated that they would not participate in any elections prior to the convening of a national conference to discuss the problems in Sudan.

IGAD-sponsored peace talks, held in April 2000, ended inconclusively, and in May the SPLM suspended its participation in protest against the Government's alleged continued bombing of civilian targets. It reaffirmed its commitment to the unification of the IGAD process and the Egyptian-Libyan initiative, but did not indicate on what conditions it would resume talks. The next round of IGAD-sponsored talks had been scheduled to begin on 17 May. In June the SPLM announced it would rejoin the peace talks, and in that month al-Bashir declared a general amnesty for all opponents of the Government; however, it was rejected by a number of opposition groups, including the SPLM. Later that month al-Turabi announced the formation of a new political party, the Popular National Congress (PNC), whose registration was formally approved in August.

Al-Bashir re-elected

Presidential and legislative elections were held concurrently over a 10-day period in mid-December 2000, although they were boycotted by the main opposition parties. As expected, al-Bashir was re-elected President, with 86.5% of the votes cast, comfortably defeating his nearest rival, former President Nimeri, who obtained 9.6% of the vote. Voting did not take place in the three southern states. The NCP secured 355 seats in the new 360-member National Assembly; the remaining five seats were won by small opposition parties. On 3 January 2001 al-Bashir extended the state of emergency for a further year.

On 21 February 2001 al-Turabi was arrested at his home in Khartoum after it was announced that the PNC and the SPLM had signed a memorandum of understanding in Switzerland urging the Sudanese people to participate in 'peaceful popular resistance' against the al-Bashir regime. In early March al-Turabi and several other members of the PNC's leadership council were reported to have been charged with criminal conspiracy, undermining the constitutional order, waging war on the state and calling for violent opposition to public authority. (In late May al-Turabi was released from prison and placed under house arrest.) Meanwhile, the day after al-Turabi's arrest, al-Bashir implemented a major reorganization of the Cabinet and replaced many of the country's state governors. Several new ministries were created, and, although the new, 32-member Cabinet was dominated by NCP members, al-Bashir incorporated four members of two minor opposition parties into the Government.

In early July 2001 it was reported that the Sudanese Government and the NDA had both provisionally accepted a renewed Libyan-Egyptian peace initiative, which provided for an immediate cease-fire, the establishment of a transitional government and a number of constitutional reforms. Later that month the leadership council of the NCP approved the Libyan-Egyptian plan. However, al-Bashir maintained that he would not support any proposals that involved the separation of state and religion or the partition of the country, thus endangering the success of the initiative, as the NDA concurrently reiterated its demand for the right of the southern states to be granted self-determination. In mid-December the state of emergency was again extended for a further 12 months.

In January 2002 talks sponsored jointly by the USA and Switzerland commenced in Buergenstock, Switzerland. Following six days of intensive discussions, the Sudanese Government and the SPLA agreed to observe a six-month cease-fire, to be supervised by a joint military commission, in the central Nuba region in order to facilitate the delivery of vital aid supplies to the area. However, the following month the USA announced that it had suspended discussions with the Sudanese Government, after two separate incidents earlier that month in which Sudanese air force planes had bombed civilians collecting food supplies in the Bahr al-Ghazal province. The Sudanese Minister of External Relations subsequently issued an apology for the attack and in mid-March the USA brokered an agreement between the SPLA and the Sudanese Government, which aimed to guarantee the protection of civilians from military attacks; the agreement was to be monitored by two teams of international observers. The cease-fire was extended for a further six months in July, and again, in late December. In August al-Bashir renewed the detention order that had been placed on al-Turabi the previous year for a further 12 months, and in September al-Turabi was transferred to prison. In December the state of emergency was once again extended for a further 12 months.

Towards the Comprehensive Peace Agreement

Meanwhile, in June 2002 a new round of IGAD-sponsored peace talks between the Government and the SPLM opened in Machakos, Kenya. A major breakthrough in the conflict was achieved on 20 July, when delegations from the SPLM and the Government signed an accord, known as the Machakos Protocol, which provided for a six-year period of autonomy for the south, to be followed by an internationally monitored referendum on self-determination. The Protocol also stated that Sudan's Constitution would be rewritten to ensure that *Shari'a* law would not be applied to non-Muslim southerners. Nevertheless, negotiations between the Government and the SPLM were halted in November, after no agreement could be reached on the number of government and civil service posts to be allocated to southerners and the distribution of petroleum revenues. Disputes also remained over control of the Abyei, Blue Nile and Nuba Mountains provinces in central Sudan and the religious status of Khartoum. The two sides did, however, agree to extend the cease-fire until the end of March 2003.

Talks resumed in Nairobi in January 2003, and the following month a memorandum of understanding was signed under which the Government and the SPLM agreed to allow international observers to monitor the cease-fire. In April al-Bashir and Garang met for only the second time in 20 years and reaffirmed their commitment to the Machakos Protocol and pledged to facilitate unrestricted delivery of humanitarian assistance to those in the south of the country. However, negotiations continued to progress at a very slow pace, and in August the discussions were extended until mid-September in order to give both sides additional time to resolve their outstanding differences.

In mid-September 2003 the SPLA and the Sudanese Government agreed to extend their cease-fire for a further two months, and days later the two sides signed a landmark security agreement. Under the terms of the arrangement, two separate armed forces were to be created, as well as a number of integrated units, comprising both government and SPLA troops. Both sides agreed to contribute 12,000 soldiers to a joint force, the Sudan Armed Forces (SAF), to be deployed in southern Sudan, and a further 6,000 soldiers from each side were to be dispatched to the disputed Nuba Mountains and Blue Nile provinces. Furthermore, 80% of the government forces in southern Sudan would be withdrawn to the north no later than two-and-a-half years after the signing of a Comprehensive Peace Agreement (CPA). It was also agreed that both sides' forces would be reduced at a later, unspecified date and that they would be placed under the command of a joint defence board composed of SPLM and government officials. In October the US Secretary of State, Colin Powell, secured assurances from the Sudanese Government and the SPLM that a comprehensive settlement would be reached by the end of the year. Nevertheless, later in October US sanctions on Sudan (see below) were extended for a further 12 months. Also in October al-Turabi was released from detention, and all restrictions on the PNC's activities were lifted.

In early December 2003 SPLM delegates visited Khartoum for the first time since the escalation of the north–south conflict in 1983, prior to convening for further talks with the Government in Naivasha, Kenya. On 7 January 2004 the two sides signed an accord on wealth- and revenue-sharing, which also provided for the establishment of two separate banking systems for the north and the south, as well as a new national currency on the signing of a final peace settlement. Although talks resumed in Kenya in mid-February, progress on other matters remained slow. Furthermore, in April the UN announced that it had been forced to suspend aid operations in southern Sudan, owing to renewed violence, and that some 50,000 people had fled their homes in the region during the previous month.

The Government and the SPLM signed three protocols on 26 May 2004, which removed the remaining obstacles to the conclusion of a comprehensive peace accord. Specifically, the protocols stated that the SPLM and other southern groups would hold 30% of government seats in the north, while holding 70% of seats in the south; that the contested regions of the Blue Nile and the Nuba Mountains would be governed by an administration in which 55% of the seats would be taken by government officials and 45% by the SPLM, while the petroleum-rich region of Abyei would be granted special status and be governed by the presidential office; and that Khartoum would remain under Islamic law with certain protections for non-Muslims.

The final round of the IGAD-sponsored talks began in Naivasha in late June 2004, although progress was delayed by the Sudanese authorities' attempts to involve other pro-Government southern militias in the talks. Talks eventually resumed in October and on 31 December a permanent cease-fire was agreed by the Sudanese Government and the SPLM. On 9 January 2005 Garang and Vice-President Ali Osman Muhammad Taha signed the CPA in Nairobi in the presence of Powell and representatives from the UN, the European Union (EU, see p. 270), the African Union (AU, see p. 183) and IGAD, thus formally bringing an end to more than 20 years of civil conflict between the SPLA and successive governments. Under the agreement, Garang was to assume the position of Sudanese Vice-President and would act as President of Southern Sudan during the six-year period of autonomy, after which a referendum on secession would be held. Meanwhile, in mid-January the Government signed a peace accord with the NDA in Cairo, which allowed for the return of NDA leaders to Sudan and granted them the right to conduct their political activities in the country.

The UN appealed for the international community to assist with the reconstruction of southern Sudan's infrastructure, which had been extensively damaged during the civil conflict. On 25 January 2005 the UN announced that it had restored diplomatic ties with Sudan and would contribute some €50m. in aid, to be divided equally between the north and the south, and in late March the UN Security Council unanimously approved Resolution 1590, which provided for the establishment of the UN Mission in Sudan (UNMIS), comprising up to 10,000 peace-keeping troops and 715 civilian personnel, to be deployed in southern Sudan for an initial period of six months (which was subsequently repeatedly renewed); a contingent of Nepalese soldiers duly commenced duties at the end of the month.

In June 2005 al-Bashir announced the release of 'all political detainees', among them al-Turabi. Earlier that month the President had lifted the ban prohibiting all political activity by the PNC. On 6 July the National Assembly ratified the new interim Constitution (see below) and on 9 July Garang was appointed First Vice-President of the new presidential council, replacing Taha who took the role of Vice-President, and as President of Southern Sudan. In mid-July government troops withdrew from Juba (in southern Sudan) and the surrounding area in accordance with the CPA, which stipulated that 17% of government troops be redeployed within six months of signing the agreement, and Garang named the SPLM deputy leader, Commdr (later Lt-Gen.) Salva Kiir Mayardit, as Vice-President of the new southern administration. Interim governors were also appointed to each of the 10 states in southern Sudan. On 1 August it was announced that Garang had been killed in a helicopter crash. Salva Kiir succeeded Garang as leader of the SPLA/SPLM, and was later appointed as First Vice-President of Sudan and President of Southern Sudan. During August differences regarding wealth-sharing and the allocation of the energy portfolio continued to obstruct the formation of a government of national unity. However, in late September an agreement was reached and the list of government ministers was announced, in which 16 portfolios (including those of defence, interior, finance and energy and mining) were awarded to members of the NCP, nine to the SPLM and four to members of smaller opposition parties. In January 2006 the National Assembly adopted controversial legislation prohibiting any member of the armed forces (excluding al-Bashir and Salva Kiir), the police, the security forces or the SPLA, judges, diplomats and high-ranking civil servants from joining a political party; it also made provisions for any party to be dissolved, or prevented from participating in elections, if it was believed to be undertaking activities that breached the CPA. Claiming that this contravened the Constitution, the NDA withdrew from the National Assembly.

The Darfur conflict

Meanwhile, in February 2003 a new area of conflict emerged in the Darfur region of western Sudan. The Sudan Liberation Movement (SLM) announced the commencement of an armed campaign to end Darfur's political and economic marginalization and to combat the Government's 'ethnic cleansing' activities in the region. The SLM, which was reported to have some 1,500 troops and received support from Eritrea, subsequently attacked the provincial capital, al-Fasher. In an attempt to suppress the revolt the Sudanese authorities armed pro-Government ethnic Arab militias, known as the *Janjaweed*, who systematically razed entire villages to the ground and carried out indiscriminate killings. In April the Sudanese authorities refused offers of talks with the rebels, dismissed senior security officials in the region, and deployed additional forces to Darfur to retake most of the territory that had been lost to the SLM. In December aid agencies maintained that the Sudanese Government was preventing food and medical supplies from reaching the Darfur region, and in January 2004 Sudanese planes reportedly bombed a number of villages in the border area, just weeks after the rebels claimed to have killed some 700 government troops. By March it was estimated that more than 130,000 Sudanese had entered Chad and as many as 900,000 people had been displaced as a result of the ongoing conflict and the rapidly deteriorating humanitarian situation. At the end of that month indirect peace talks between the Government, the SLM and the Justice and Equality Movement (JEM), attended by international observers, commenced in Chad, and on 8 April a 45-day humanitarian cease-fire was signed by representatives of the three parties. By early June it was estimated that as a result of continued violence in Darfur more than 30,000 people had been killed and a further 1m. people had been displaced, with 350,000 of those at risk from starvation and disease.

Following visits from Powell and the UN Secretary-General, Kofi Annan, to refugee camps in Darfur in late June 2004 and the threat of the imposition of UN sanctions on the *Janjaweed*, in early July the Sudanese authorities committed to a series of actions, including the more aggressive use of the security forces to deal with the militia, the easing of travel restrictions for aid workers and the deployment of AU troops in Darfur. There followed a marginal improvement in access granted to humanitarian aid agencies but the security situation remained precarious as militias continued to attack civilian populations. In mid-July AU-sponsored peace talks between the Sudanese Government and the rebels opened in Addis Ababa, Ethiopia. The talks swiftly collapsed after the Government rejected the preconditions set out by the SLM and the JEM for further negotiations, which included the disarmament of the *Janjaweed* and the removal of those *Janjaweed* fighters absorbed by the police and army; the observation of the April cease-fire agreement; the prosecution of the perpetrators of crimes and an inquiry into allegations of genocide; unimpeded humanitarian access for aid agencies; the release of prisoners of war; and a 'neutral' venue for future talks. In late July the US House of Representatives approved a resolution declaring the human rights abuses in Darfur a 'genocide' and on 30 July the UN Security Council adopted a resolution urging the Sudanese Government to end the conflict in Darfur, to facilitate the delivery of humanitarian aid, and to grant AU peace monitors access to the region. The resolution was rejected by the Sudanese Government and the armed forces spokesman, Gen. Muhammad Bashir Suleiman, described it as a 'declaration of war'.

In mid-September 2004 the UN Security Council approved a second resolution, stating that it would consider imposing sanctions affecting Sudan's petroleum industry should it fail to take steps to disarm the *Janjaweed* and protect civilians from further attacks. The UN was also to establish a commission to investigate claims that the human rights abuses in Darfur amounted to genocide, while the AU planned to increase the size of its monitoring force in the region (the African Union Mission in Sudan—AMIS) from 350 to some 3,500. Further peace talks held days earlier between the Government, the SPLA and the JEM in Abuja, Nigeria, ended without agreement. In early October the British Prime Minister, Tony Blair, arrived in Sudan for talks with President al-Bashir in an attempt to resolve the Darfur issue. A five-point peace plan, proposed by Blair, was accepted by the President. In agreeing to the plan, the Sudanese Government pledged to allow an increase in the number of AU troops in the country; to identify its forces in Darfur to enable the effective monitoring of the cease-fire; to commit to a cessation of hostilities in Darfur within three months and to negotiate a comprehensive agreement to the ongoing conflict in southern Sudan (see above) by the end of 2004; and to assist with the distribution of humanitarian aid.

In mid-November 2004, following talks in Abuja, the Government agreed to establish a 'no-fly' zone over the Darfur region (the rebels had accused government forces of using aircraft to support *Janjaweed* attacks). In December AU cease-fire monitors reported that they had witnessed large quantities of arms and ammunition being delivered to government forces in Darfur. Continued *Janjaweed* attacks were reported and in early February 2005 a UN commission of inquiry revealed that although serious crimes against humanity had taken place, these did not amount to genocide. It did, however, identify 51 suspected war criminals and recommended that they be tried by the International Criminal Court (ICC, see p. 340), which was to undertake preparatory analysis of the situation prior to deciding whether to commence a full investigation into allegations of war crimes committed in Darfur. Al-Bashir pledged not to send any Sudanese nationals abroad for trial, but the Minister of External Relations, Dr Mustafa Osman Ismail, subsequently offered to hold any future ICC trial in Sudan. In late April the AU confirmed that additional peace-keeping troops would arrive in Darfur by the end of September, increasing the number of AMIS troops to 7,731.

In mid-May 2005 the SLM and the JEM agreed to maintain a cease-fire and to engage in further talks with the Government. However, according to the UN there was an increase in the number of reported instances of rape and kidnapping in the region during the month of April and attacks on civilians by *Janjaweed* fighters continued. In May a conference for international donor countries was held in Addis Ababa and US $200m. was pledged to fund the enlarged AU peace-keeping operation in Darfur. NATO had previously announced that it would provide training, logistics and technical support to the mission. In June the ICC commenced an investigation into allegations that the Sudanese Government and the *Janjaweed* had committed crimes against humanity in the Darfur region. Also in that month the Government established a court at which 162 people accused of committing crimes against humanity in the Darfur region were to be tried, and referred to the institution as 'an alternative' to the ICC. In October four AU peace-keepers were killed in southern Darfur and concerns over escalating violence prompted the UN to withdraw all non-essential staff from Darfur. The human rights organization Human Rights Watch (HRW) released a report in December, which accused al-Bashir, Taha and several other senior government officials of involvement in crimes against humanity committed in Darfur. The report also appealed for them to be investigated by the ICC and added to a UN list of suspects eligible for sanctions. ICC investigators were subsequently refused permission by the Government to visit Darfur to gather evidence of alleged crimes against humanity.

Proposed UN intervention in Darfur

In January 2006 Annan urged the USA and European countries to contribute logistical support and troops for a planned UN peace-keeping mission in Darfur. Sudan declared its vehement opposition to the proposal and al-Bashir reportedly stated that Darfur would become a 'graveyard' for any foreign troops deployed in the region. In late January the SLM and the JEM announced the formation of the Alliance of Revolutionary Forces in West Sudan, in a move intended to strengthen the rebels' position in negotiations which had resumed in Abuja. In early March the AU voted to extend the mandate of AMIS until September, when a UN force was expected to assume peace-keeping duties. However, Arab League heads of state, meeting in Khartoum in late March, agreed to provide funds for the AU force to remain and voted to support Sudanese opposition to the deployment of non-African peace-keeping troops. In late April the UN Security Council approved a resolution, imposing sanctions on four individuals suspected of involvement in crimes committed in the Darfur region: Maj.-Gen. Gaafar Muhammad el-Hassan, Commander of the Western Military Region for the Sudanese Air Force; the Commander of the SLA, Adam Yacub Shant; the Field Commander of the rebel National Movement for Reform and Development, Gabril Abdulkareem Badri; and Sheikh Musa Hilal of the *Janjaweed* militia were banned from travelling outside of Sudan and any assets they held abroad were to be 'frozen'. Also in late April the Government agreed to accept an AU peace agreement. However, the 30 April deadline was twice extended by two days, and officials from the USA and United Kingdom arrived in Abuja to aid the negotiations.

On 4 May 2006 the JEM and the SLM faction led by Abd al-Wahid Muhammad al-Nur rejected the agreement. Nevertheless, the faction led by Minni Minawi announced that it had accepted the proposals, despite reservations regarding certain conditions, and the Darfur Peace Agreement (DPA) was signed on 5 May. The measures stipulated in the document included, *inter alia*, a Government undertaking to disarm completely the *Janjaweed* by mid-October; the establishment of buffer zones around refugee camps and access routes for humanitarian aid organizations; the integration of rebel forces into the Sudanese armed forces and police; the allocation of eight seats in the National Assembly to Minawi's group; and the transfer of US $300m. to a reconstruction and development fund for Darfur, and further annual transfers of $200m. for two years thereafter. The agreement also proposed that a referendum be held to decide upon the issue of Darfur being recognized as a region rather than as three separate states. However, the JEM and the al-Nur-led SLM faction maintained their opposition to the DPA.

In June 2006 a joint AU-UN delegation arrived in Darfur to assess the needs of AMIS and the feasibility of its replacement by a UN force. In July, at an AU Summit in Banjul, The Gambia, the UN Secretary-General announced that President al-Bashir had refused to allow UN troops to take over from AMIS. It was also announced that the AU would withdraw its peace-keeping force from the region at the end of September. A conference convened in mid-July under the auspices of the UN also failed to convince the Sudanese Government to accept a UN peace-keeping force, although participating countries pledged some US $200m. in funds, the majority of which would be used to assist the increasingly overwhelmed AU troops. Minawi repeatedly appealed for UN forces to be sent to the troubled region and in mid-June he threatened to withdraw from the peace agreement, claiming that the deal would collapse without the immediate support of the international community. In July the two signatories of the DPA, the Government and Minawi's faction of the SLM, launched violent attacks on the rebel groups who had rejected the peace agreement. New factions had begun to emerge to challenge Minawi's increasing power in the north of Darfur, joining forces to form the National Redemption Front (NRF). Fighting subsequently spread from northern Darfur towards the west of the region.

On 31 August 2006 the UN Security Council adopted a resolution, which provided for some 17,300 additional military personnel and 3,300 civilian police to be dispatched to Sudan to support UNMIS, and for its mandate to be extended to assume the responsibilities of AMIS in Darfur. Violence in the region had escalated during that month and the UN, the AU and humanitarian agencies alleged that Minawi's troops had joined Government forces and the *Janjaweed* militia in fighting the rebel groups. The Sudanese Government continued to refuse to allow UN forces into Darfur and reinforcements were deployed to the region; AU forces remaining in the area reported that Government troops had bombed rebel-held villages, threatening the delivery of aid supplies. In response the AU increased the number of peace-keeping personnel and stated that AMIS would remain in Darfur until the end of the year.

On 27 September 2006 President al-Bashir issued a decree establishing an interim authority in Darfur, in accordance with the terms of the DPA. The authority was to be headed by Minawi, in his capacity as senior assistant to the President, a position to which he was appointed following the signing of the CPA. He was to be supported by a group of advisers, including the Governors of the three states in Darfur.

In October 2006 the Government issued a statement that a plan had been devised to fulfil the commitments of the DPA, including the disarmament of the Arab militia group. The plan was submitted to the AU and was to be implemented over a two-month period, extending the original deadline for disarming the militia group by two months. The following month Minawi alleged that the Government was rearming and mobilizing the *Janjaweed* and appealed for the international community to act swiftly to find a resolution to the conflict.

In November 2006 discussions took place in Addis Ababa on measures to reinforce the AMIS forces, which had thus far failed to halt the violence in Darfur. Proposals were made for a joint AU-UN force, with a greater role to be assumed by the UN troops. Sudan again reiterated its opposition to the presence of UN troops; however, later that month Sudan announced that it accepted, in principle, the proposal of a hybrid force, but requested further discussions on key issues before any changes could be implemented. Meanwhile, the AU agreed to extend the mandate of AMIS until mid-2007 as the UN temporarily withdrew non-essential staff from the capital of Northern Darfur state, amid fears of escalating violence between rebel fighters and the *Janjaweed*.

The UN Security Council continued with efforts to persuade Sudan to accept a joint AU-UN mission in Darfur, and in late December 2006 al-Bashir accepted the proposals, stating that

UN plans required immediate implementation. However, it was stipulated that the AU was to remain in command of the hybrid force. A three-part UN plan was initiated: the first phase included reinforcing the much-weakened AU force with UN troops and supplies, to be followed by further support packages. The third phase required the overhaul of the size and command of the force, in favour of a greater UN role, to which Sudan remained resolutely opposed. Nevertheless, by 31 December the AU had secured a tentative cease-fire agreement from rebel groups in northern Darfur.

Breakdown of the Darfur cease-fire

Peace efforts were undermined on 1 January 2007, when insurgent-held positions were bombed in violation of the cease-fire. Al-Bashir subsequently admitted that government troops had bombed rebel forces, but claimed that this did not breach the cease-fire agreement since they were defending themselves from rebel attacks. The Government subsequently agreed to measures to restore peace, including a 60-day cease-fire and an AU-UN-sponsored peace summit, to be held in Ethiopia later that month. In January the ICC dispatched a team of officials to Khartoum to investigate crimes committed during the conflict in Darfur and in February the ICC indicted the former Minister of State for the Interior, Ahmad Muhammad Harun, and the leader of the *Janjaweed* militia, Ali Muhammad Ali Abd al-Rahman, on multiple charges of war crimes and crimes against humanity. The following month the Sudanese authorities announced that they had suspended all co-operation with the ICC. In May that body issued arrest warrants for Harun and al-Rahman. Meanwhile, a further shift in the stance of the Sudanese Government was reported in early February when al-Bashir appointed two members of rebel factions to executive positions in the Council of Ministers and in the Darfur administration.

With increasingly widespread acceptance that the DPA signed in May 2006 had broken down, rebel factions agreed upon a need to collaborate in order to challenge the power of the ruling NCP. By the end of December an alliance had formed, uniting many of the rebel groups that had refused to sign the DPA, styled the Non-Signatory Factions (NSF). A conference of NSF and remaining NRF commanders, due to be held in early 2007 to renegotiate the terms of the failed peace agreement, was delayed as government forces carried out a series of bomb attacks in the area where the conference was to take place. Al-Nur's faction of the SLM, fearful of being overpowered by the NSF, joined with remaining non-signatories to threaten the credibility of the impending conference. Despite further clashes, the conference eventually commenced in February 2007.

As the conflict in western Sudan continued, the people of eastern Sudan, including the Rashaida and the Beja communities, expressed their increasing resentment towards the Government. The eastern regions had been severely affected by drought and famine and, encouraged by the success of the SPLA in forcing negotiations with the Government, some of the Beja launched an armed struggle, supported by NDA and SPLA forces. The Beja Congress, which emerged during the 1960s, was joined during the 1990s by the Rashaida Free Lions group, and in 2005 the two groups merged to form the Eastern Front (EF). Although their forces were much smaller than those rebel groups fighting in Darfur, they occupied strategic points, launching attacks on the road and rail routes that provided access to the only port on the coast of Sudan, and threatened to destabilize the country's economy. Military offensives by government forces failed to prevent the EF from launching more attacks on eastern Sudan's transport and economic infrastructure and in 2006 the Government agreed to negotiate with the group. In June 2006 talks were held in Asmara, presided over by the Eritrean authorities, and on 19 June the Government and the EF signed an agreement on a set of principles for developing a peace agreement; a cease-fire was also implemented, to be monitored by Eritrean military officials. Peace talks resumed in July and, after lengthy negotiations, a power-sharing agreement was signed on 9 October. The following day the positions of presidential assistant and presidential adviser were assigned to members of the rebel group, along with other positions in the Government at both national and regional level. The peace deal was ratified by the Sudanese authorities on 18 October, ending several years of conflict between the Government and the EF.

Concerns were raised in late 2005 that the ongoing conflict in Darfur could spread into neighbouring Chad. In late November Sudan accused the Chadian air force of violating Sudanese airspace by flying over the Darfur region and claimed that Chadian armed forces had crossed the border into Darfur to steal cattle. Chad responded with accusations that Sudan had provided weapons to a group of soldiers who had deserted the Chadian army and were planning to overthrow the President of Chad, Gen. Idriss Deby Itno. In mid-December Chadian rebels based in Darfur attacked the border town of Adre and the Chadian Government declared 'a state of belligerence' with Sudan, which it held ultimately responsible for the assault. In February 2006 the two countries held talks in Libya aimed at preventing further escalation in the dispute and agreement was reached to restore diplomatic relations and to prevent rebels from using territory to launch cross-border raids. However, in March Deby publicly questioned Sudan's commitment to the accord following a series of attacks on villages in Chad by the *Janjaweed*, allegedly with Sudanese assistance. In April Deby expelled the Sudanese ambassador to Chad and ordered the closure of the land border between the two countries following an attack on the Chadian capital, N'Djamena, by rebel forces. However, a threat to forcibly return Sudanese refugees was subsequently withdrawn. In August, at a meeting convened in N'Djamena the two countries agreed to restore diplomatic relations and reopen border crossings and embassies. By November it had become apparent that the conflict in Darfur had spread into the Central African Republic (CAR). In the north of that country, groups of rebel fighters had begun to join together, forming allegiances with Chadian factions and providing a route through to Chad for the Sudanese rebels. In February 2007 a summit was held under the auspices of French President Jacques Chirac, during which the CAR, Chad and Sudan agreed that they would cease support for rebel fighters in either of the three countries. In early May, following mediation by Saudi Arabia's King Abdallah, Presidents al-Bashir and Deby agreed to co-operate with the AU and the UN in their attempts to stabilize the Chad–Sudan border. Both countries approved the formation of a joint border force, and pledged to cease training and funding rebel groups and to stop all cross-border attacks.

In June 2007, following further discussions in Addis Ababa, the Government of Sudan agreed to accept a joint AU-UN peace-keeping force, comprising up to 20,000 troops. However, shortly after issuing a statement accepting the deployment of peace-keeping personnel, the Government began to delay the process, questioning the command structure of the operation. Nevertheless, the following month the UN Security Council adopted Resolution 1769 establishing UNAMID, the UN-AU hybrid operation in Darfur, with an initial mandate of 12 months. Further disagreements threatened to disrupt the process when, in August, the AU announced that UNAMID peace-keeping forces would comprise only African personnel, safeguarding the AU's lead role in Sudan. UNAMID assumed peace-keeping operations on 31 December but was severely under-resourced with less than one-half of the pledged 20,000 troops deployed. In February 2008 a legal framework was agreed, which would allow UNAMID peace-keepers to move freely within the country without fear of attacks by government forces. In July the UN Security Council extended UNAMID's mandate until July 2009. Meanwhile, further peace negotiations were initiated by President Abdoulaye Wade of Senegal and in March 2008, at a meeting in Dakar, Senegal, attended by regional leaders and EU and UN representatives, Chad and Sudan signed a non-aggression agreement renewing their commitment to restoring peace. Nevertheless, violence in the region continued and thousands more civilians were reported to have crossed the border into Chad to escape the conflict. In May Sudan accused Chadian rebels of involvement in an attack on Sudan's largest city, Omdurman, and severed diplomatic relations with Chad. Chad subsequently accused Sudan of attacking a town on the common border, although Sudan denied the allegations. In June military leaders from Chad and Sudan met in Senegal to discuss mechanisms for ensuring security in the border region, including the deployment of troops at strategic positions along the border, and diplomatic ties were later restored. However, in August hundreds of people implicated in the Omdurman attack remained in detention without charge.

Renewed hostilities in Darfur

In September 2007 the UN Secretary-General, Ban Ki-Moon, announced that a further round of peace talks on Darfur had been scheduled for the following month, to take place in Tripoli, Libya. The Government later agreed to comply with the terms of a cease-fire agreement, to be enforced during the peace negotiations. Talks commenced in Tripoli on 27 October; however, in response to continued attacks by government forces, many rebel groups declined to attend the meeting and instead held separate talks in Juba, convened by the Government of Southern Sudan (GOSS). The Tripoli talks had been further hindered by the collapse of the coalition Government in Khartoum earlier that month. In mid-October the SPLM withdrew from the Government in protest against delays in implementing the CPA. Al-Bashir subsequently reorganized the Council of Ministers, naming SPLM members Deng Alor Kol as Minister of Foreign Affairs and Mansur Khaled as Minister of Foreign Trade among the new appointments. Salva Kiir also effected changes to the GOSS in which two ministers were dismissed and two new presidential advisers were appointed. Additional governmental changes were implemented in December when seven SPLM members were appointed to the central Government. Akol, who had been demoted from the position of Minister of Foreign Affairs to Minister of Cabinet Affairs in the October reshuffle, was dismissed from the cabinet and replaced by Pagan Amum of the SPLM. Akol had been accused by fellow SPLM members of developing close ties with the NCP. Al-Bashir carried out a further minor reorganization of the Government in mid-February 2008. Lt-Gen. Nhial Deng Nhial was named GOSS Minister of SPLA Affairs following the death of his predecessor, Dominic Dim Deng, in a plane crash in May.

Reports emerged in September 2008 that government forces had launched a renewed campaign of violence in eastern Darfur, attacking rebel strongholds in an attempt to secure access to oil reserves and transport routes to Chad. Rebels in the nearby province of Kordofan were mobilized to support the offensive, evoking concerns that the crisis in Darfur could spread eastwards. As fighting continued in Darfur, al-Bashir announced a unilateral cease-fire in November, including the disarmament of pro-Government militia, on the condition that sufficient measures for monitoring the situation were implemented. However, rebel leaders demanded that the *Janjaweed* be disarmed before they would consider relinquishing their own weapons. Reinforcements from Pakistan and Ethiopia were deployed to Darfur in December to assist the peace-keeping operation, increasing the number of UNAMID troops to some 12,737. (Additional African troops were pledged in early 2009, and, following the renewal of its mandate in August, UNAMID's personnel had been increased to 16,852 by February 2010.)

Meanwhile, renewed violence in the ethnically divided Abyei region broke out in early 2008 after a period of relative calm. Clashes between the SPLA and members of the Misseriya ethnic group (supported by the NCP) threatened to exacerbate the situation in Darfur and undermine progress towards holding presidential and legislative elections planned for July 2009. Nevertheless, a national census commenced in April 2008 in an attempt to ensure the general election could take place, although rebel groups opposed the census. It was also agreed that the dispute over Abyei's status should be referred to the Permanent Court of Arbitration (PCA) in The Hague, Netherlands. An interim administration was established in the Abyei region in August; Arop Moyak of the SPLM was named Chief Administrator, while the NCP's Rahama Abuldrahman al-Nur was appointed Deputy Chief Administrator.

In July 2009, following a ruling by the PCA, a compromise agreement was reached regarding the boundary lines of the Abyei region. The border to the north, as established in 2005, would remain while new lines were drawn to the east and west that would return the Heglig oilfields and the oil pipeline infrastructure to government control. However, large portions of fertile land and other oilfields would remain outside of these lines, in provinces that retained the possibility of joining the semi-autonomous south. While both parties appeared to accept the ruling, tensions nevertheless remained as discussions on the composition of the Abyei electorate continued to be disputed and violent clashes between the north and the south intensified, exacerbated by internal division within the GOSS. The security policy of the GOSS was based on the belief that conflict with the north was likely and measures to strengthen the border between the north and the south were implemented. In September 2009 it was reported that the Sudanese Government was withholding oil revenue from the GOSS, placing further strain on relations between the two sides. (The CPA stated that some 50% of revenue from the oilfields in southern Sudan was to be allocated to the GOSS, and this accounted for almost 98% of budgetary funding in the south.) With the terms of the CPA scheduled to come to an end in 2011, and a referendum on independence for the south to be held upon its expiry, the discontent over oil revenues and a dispute over the required proportion of votes required in order to approve secession again placed significant strain on relations between the NCP and the SPLM at national government level. The NCP demanded that 75% of the vote in favour of independence would be required at the referendum, while the SPLM insisted that a simple majority would suffice. However, in December 2009 the National Assembly approved legislation that required 60% of the electorate in southern Sudan to vote for the ballot to be deemed legitimate, but also stated that a simple majority of 51% would suffice in order to secure independence.

Having been suspended in June 2009, peace talks on Darfur resumed in August in an attempt to reconcile the rebel factions. However, the negotiations were not attended by the SPLM. A UN report published in November claimed that armed factions in Darfur continued to use excessive force in breach of the UN arms embargo, infringe human rights and impede the peace process. An earlier report issued by the AU recommended the continued use of inclusive dialogue in an effort to resolve the conflict. Following months of faltering negotiations, some progress was achieved in February 2010 when, with mediation from Chadian authorities, the Sudanese Government signed a framework agreement with the JEM, providing for a cease-fire and the possibility of further peace negotiations. Al-Bashir, who approved the release from prison of 57 members of the JEM involved in an attack on Khartoum in mid-2008, claimed that the agreement had resolved the conflict in Darfur.

Multi-party elections

In March 2009 an international arrest warrant for al-Bashir was formally issued, following evidence presented in July 2008 by the Chief Prosecutor of the ICC, Luis Moreno Ocampo, in respect of war crimes committed in Darfur from March 2003. A demonstration was subsequently staged in Khartoum in his support. The indictment, the first to be brought by the ICC against an incumbent Head of State, was rejected by Sudan (which had refused to extradite al-Rahman and Harun), and prompted a mixed response from regional leaders and the international community; although the decision was welcomed by the US Administration and international human rights groups, it was notably opposed by the AU and the Arab League. In February 2010 judges at the ICC ruled that an appeal could be heard that, if successful, would result in charges of genocide being added to the seven counts of crimes against humanity and war crimes, with which al-Bashir had already been charged and for which the arrest warrant had been issued.

Having initially been scheduled to take place in July 2009, and then in February 2010, it was announced that, following a further postponement (after a number of political parties threatened to boycott the ballot amid demands for changes to legislation on civil liberties and freedom of speech), the first democratic, multi-party elections to take place in Sudan for 24 years would be held in April 2010. In addition to national presidential and legislative polls, the President of Southern Sudan and provincial governors were also to be elected. Prior to the commencement of voter registration in November 2009, Salva Kiir had issued a strong statement in favour of two separate northern and southern states. In January 2010 Salva Kiir confirmed that he would not seek the national presidency and that Yasir Saeed Arman would contest that office on behalf of the SPLM. Later that month al-Bashir announced that the NCP would not present a candidate in the poll to elect the President of Southern Sudan, and in the period immediately preceding the elections a number of opposition parties announced their withdrawal from the various electoral contests.

Voting in the elections commenced on 11 April 2010; however, the initial three-day voting period was extended by two days, after technical issues and delays in delivering ballot papers in a number of regions. On 26 April the National Elections Commission (NEC) announced the results of the presidential election, according to which al-Bashir secured 68.2% of the votes cast; Arman took 21.7%, despite having withdrawn from the poll at the end of March, citing concerns over potential irregularities in the conduct of the ballot. The Umma National Party (UNP, as the UP had been restyled) had also withdrawn from the presidential election (although al-Mahdi's name remained on the ballot paper and he received about 1.0% of the votes cast). Salva Kiir was overwhelmingly re-elected as President of Southern Sudan, with about 93.0% of votes cast. On 21 May Salva Kiir was sworn in for a further presidential term. Al-Bashir, who had pledged that the referendum on the secession of southern Sudan would take place in January 2011 as scheduled, was inaugurated for a further five-year term on 27 May 2010 (at a ceremony that was boycotted by many Arab and African Heads of State). According to the final results of the legislative elections, the NCP secured a total of 323 of the 450 seats in the National Assembly, while the SPLM won 99 seats (with the UNP boycotting the elections). Several opposition parties denounced the election results as fraudulent, and alleged that widespread malpractice had been perpetrated. Observer missions dispatched by the EU and the US Carter Center declared that the elections had failed to meet international standards; the Carter Center subsequently issued a report criticizing the conduct of the voting, and urging the NEC to review the results. On 24 May the new National Assembly held its first session and re-elected Ahmad Ibrahim al-Tahir of the NCP as its Speaker. Gen. George Athor, formerly a general in the Southern Sudanese army, and a small contingent of troops under his command began to stage rebel attacks in protest against the outcome of legislative elections. Following a declaration of dissatisfaction with the conduct of the elections, the JEM suspended its participation in peace negotiations and escalated military operations. Fighting consequently intensified in Darfur, and almost 600 people were killed in May.

In mid-June 2010 al-Bashir announced a new 35-member coalition Government, which included nine members of the SPLM (two more than required under the terms of the CPA); Salva Kiir retained the office of First Vice-President and Taha of Second Vice-President. Lual Achwel Deng of the SPLM, who had served as Minister of Foreign Affairs in the previous Government, was appointed as Minister of Petroleum (a decision that was designed to placate southern suspicions following the alleged siphoning of oil revenues under the previous Government, and to ensure high-level SPLM involvement in discussions on a post-secession oil-sharing agreement). Meanwhile, President Salva Kiir formed a new GOSS administration; notably, Deng Alor, a former Sudan Minister of Foreign Affairs and a senior member of the SPLM, was appointed as the Southern Sudan Minister of Regional Co-operation, while the Secretary-General of the SPLM, Pagan Amum, became the Minister of Peace and CPA Implementation.

On 12 July 2010 the ICC issued a second arrest warrant for President al-Bashir, on three counts of genocide committed in the Darfur region. (However, the AU instructed member states not to arrest al-Bashir and he continued to make official regional visits.) At the end of July the UN Security Council extended the mandate of UNAMID for a further year. In September it was announced that the Government had delayed until mid-November the registration of voters for the referendum on secession for southern Sudan, in order to allow further preparations, prompting concerns that it would be postponed. However, in early October the Government announced a timetable for the referendum on secession, confirming that it was scheduled for 9 January 2011. Later in October 2010 NCP officials declared that a postponement of a parallel referendum in Abyei (which had also been stipulated under the CPA) was likely, after negotiations between the North and South Sudan authorities in Addis Ababa failed to result in agreement over the composition of the region's electoral commission, the eligibility of voters and the demarcation of borders. The Government also rejected a UN proposal to deploy peace-keeping forces at the north–south border. On 14 October the UN Security Council adopted a resolution extending until October 2011 the mandate of a four-member panel of experts (originally established in March 2005), to monitor the arms embargo in the Darfur region. The voter registration process commenced on 15 November as scheduled and was extended for an additional week, until 8 December. The NCP accused the SPLM of intimidating potential voters in Khartoum.

Recent developments: referendum on the secession of southern Sudan

The referendum on the secession of southern Sudan was conducted on 9–15 January 2011; preliminary results indicated that more than 98% of the population had voted in favour of secession, with only about 1% voting for unity with the north. Ethnic clashes continued in Abyei in early January, including fighting, in which some 37 people were killed, between the northern loyalist Misseriya and the Dinka Ngok, who were allied with the SPLM. The parallel referendum on secession for Abyei had been postponed as expected. According to the final results of the referendum, which were announced on 7 February, about 98.8% of the population of southern Sudan had voted to secede from the north and officially form their own country. Some 97.6% of the electorate had participated in the poll (far higher than the 60% required to validate the results). On 16 February the Southern Sudan Government approved the banner of the SPLM as the official flag for the new nation, and the SPLA as its official army. On the following day Southern Sudanese political parties endorsed 'South Sudan' as the name of the new state, which was to be inaugurated on 9 July. In early February some 50 people were killed in southern Sudan in a mutiny over the redeployment of the northern and southern armies, which began in the southern town of Malakal. Meanwhile, despite a cease-fire signed with the Government in January, attacks by the rebel group led by Athor continued in the region of the towns of Fangak and Dor, in Jonglei state.

In early February 2011 Jimmy Lemi Milla, the Southern Sudan Minister of Co-operatives and Rural Development, was shot and killed inside the ministry building in Juba, apparently as a result of a family dispute. Later in February it was announced that al-Bashir would not seek re-election in 2015. In March 2011 the SPLM suspended negotiations with the NCP over a number of post-secession arrangements, including citizenship rights, accusing the northern Government of training and arming insurgent groups to destabilize southern Sudan. (At that time about 250,000 southerners had returned from northern Sudan, and the displacement of many more was expected after the Republic of South Sudan officially came into existence.) Meanwhile, tensions increased in Abyei, and reports emerged that both SAF and SPLA troops were deployed there. The SPLA also clashed with rebel militia in Unity and Upper Nile states, of which the two most prominent groups were led by Athor and Col Gatluak Gai, a former SPLM officer who had resigned from his post after accusing the SPLM of fraud in the national elections in southern Sudan. On 24 April the NEC announced that a referendum would be conducted in Darfur on 1–2 July, in accordance with the DPA, to determine the permanent administrative status of the region; however, the JEM and other rebel groups rejected the legitimacy of a referendum, insisting that the issue be resolved through further negotiations. Later in April disputes within the NCP resulted in al-Bashir's dismissal of a senior presidential security adviser.

Refugees

In addition to civil war and economic crisis, Sudan has experienced drought and famine, and the problem has been compounded by a very large number of refugees in the southern provinces, mainly from Ethiopia and Chad. At the end of 2008, according to estimates from the office of the UN High Commissioner for Refugees (UNHCR), there were some 419,248 Sudanese refugees abroad, of whom 267,966 were in Chad, 56,883 in Uganda, 28,496 in Kenya, and 25,913 in Ethiopia. Sudan was also host to some 181,605 refugees at that time, of whom 124,785 were originally from Eritrea. By late 2004, as a result of the Darfur conflict, it was estimated by UNHCR that some 1.6m. people were displaced within Darfur and that some 200,000 people had fled to neighbouring Chad. In early 2010 it was believed that almost 2.7m. people were classified as internally displaced in the Darfur region alone, while the total number of internally displaced persons in Sudan had reached 4.9m. Following a referendum overwhelmingly in favour of the secession of southern Sudan in January 2011 (see above), UNHCR appealed for donor assistance to support the displacement of southerners moving back from Khartoum and other parts of northern Sudan; it was envisaged that a further 800,000 southerners would return from northern Sudan during that year.

Foreign Affairs
Regional relations

In January 2006, at the sixth AU summit, which took place in Khartoum, the emergence of al-Bashir as the leading candidate for the chairmanship of the organization provoked widespread criticism from the international community and proved unacceptable to representatives from a number of AU member states. Following two days of negotiations, it was agreed that the President of the Republic of the Congo, Gen. Denis Sassou-Nguesso, would assume the chairmanship in 2006, to be succeeded by al-Bashir in 2007. Faced with unanimous opposition, in January 2007 al-Bashir withdrew his candidacy and the President of Ghana, John Kufuor, assumed the role of Chairman.

Following an unsuccessful coup attempt in 1976, Sudan severed diplomatic relations with Libya and established a mutual defence pact with Egypt. Diplomatic links between Sudan and Libya were restored in 1978, but relations became strained in 1981, during Libya's occupation of Chad, and President Nimeri frequently accused Libya of supporting plots against him. After the 1985 coup, Libya was the first country to recognize the new regime, and relations between the two countries improved significantly. Although Libya's military involvement in Chad declined, some Libyan forces remained in north-western Sudan, despite repeated Sudanese demands for their withdrawal. The regime that took power in Sudan in 1985 adopted a foreign policy of non-alignment, in contrast to Nimeri's strongly pro-Western attitude, and sought improved relations with Ethiopia and the USSR, to the concern of Sudan's former allies, Egypt and the USA. In 1990, after Lt-Gen. al-Bashir had visited Col Qaddafi, the Libyan leader, in Tripoli, Sudan and Libya signed a 'declaration of integration' that envisaged the complete union of the two countries within four years. In 1995 Sudan, Libya and Chad were reported to be discussing integration after eventual legislative elections in Chad. Tension subsequently arose between Libya and Sudan as a result of Libya's expulsion of Sudanese expatriate workers, but did not, apparently, detract from the two countries' commitment to integration, reiterated in 1996. Talks between delegates from Libya, Sudan and Eritrea were held in Tripoli in March 2010 to discuss means of increasing security in the region. However, in June the Sudanese Government announced the closure of its border with Libya in order to protect travellers from rebel attack. Meanwhile, in January Chadian and Sudanese authorities signed an agreement on the normalization of relations between the two countries, including a pledge to establish a joint force to be deployed later that year along the common border in an attempt to foster greater security and to assist in efforts to resolve the Darfur situation. In February President al-Bashir announced that an official visit to Khartoum by Chad's President Idriss Deby Itno had put a 'definitive end' to the troubled relations between Sudan and Chad. The decision of the Chadian authorities to repel JEM leader Khalil Ibrahim from the country in May, when the rebel commander and his entourage were denied entry at N'Djamena international airport, and had their Chadian passports destroyed, demonstrated Deby's commitment to the new agreement.

In September 1995 Ethiopia accused Sudan of harbouring terrorists implicated in the attempted assassination of Egyptian President Hosni Mubarak in June and, in response, announced the closure of some Sudanese diplomatic facilities in the country and of non-governmental organizations connected with Sudan. In April 1996 Sudan claimed that Ethiopian government forces had collaborated with the SPLA in attacks on two towns in south-eastern Sudan, while in June Ethiopia accused Sudan of attempting to destabilize the region. In January 1997 relations deteriorated further when, following alleged attacks on Sudan, President al-Bashir declared a *jihad* (holy war) against Ethiopian aggression and ordered a general mobilization. Ethiopia, however, denied any involvement in the attacks. An improvement in relations was reported during 1998, although in December the Ethiopian Minister of Foreign Affairs stated that relations between the two countries would not improve until Sudan handed over those responsible for the attempted assassination of the Egyptian President. One of the suspects was extradited in 1999 (see below), and in November, on his return from a visit to Ethiopia, al-Bashir stated that relations with that country were fully normalized. The common border was reopened in early 2000, and in March the Sudanese and Ethiopian Governments signed a number of agreements, which provided for increased co-operation in political, cultural, commercial and transport sectors. Further agreements regarding border security were signed in the following month. Relations between the two countries were temporarily strained in late April 2001 after an internal Ethiopian flight was hijacked and diverted to Khartoum. Although the incident was brought to a swift conclusion, and all passengers on board the aircraft were released unharmed, the Sudanese authorities refused Ethiopia's request for the hijackers to be extradited to Ethiopia for trial. A seven-year dispute over border demarcation appeared to have been resolved in June 2008 when an accord was concluded, under which Ethiopia returned small pockets of land to the al-Qadaref region. However, Ethiopians complained that the Ethiopian Government had failed to consult its citizens on the matter and that the agreement granted Sudanese nationals the right to occupy certain areas of holy or historic importance. The chair of the joint border committee declared he would repeal the decision, although the Sudanese Government insisted that progress on the issue had been made. In November 2009 Ethiopia deployed a 200-strong air force unit to Darfur, in support of the 1,600 ground troops already stationed in the region.

Sudan's relations with Eritrea deteriorated after 1991, and in December 1994 Eritrea severed diplomatic relations with Sudan. Eritrea has sponsored meetings of the principal groups opposed to the Sudanese regime, which it accused of lending support to the insurgent Eritrean Islamic Jihad. In December 1994 Eritrea sponsored a meeting between various Sudanese opposition groups, which resulted in a 'Declaration of Political Agreement'. The signatories included the SPLA, the UP and the DUP. A further deterioration in relations occurred after a conference of the Sudanese opposition, organized by the NDA, was held in the Eritrean capital, Asmara, in June. In July 1996 Sudanese government forces claimed that attacks had been launched against them from within Eritrea. In April 1997 Sudan protested to the UN over Eritrean aggression on its territory. In June Sudan denied Eritrean accusations that the Sudanese Government had masterminded a plot to assassinate the Eritrean President. The border was closed in June 1997, and again in February 1998, as a result of the violence; further attacks were reported in the border area by both Eritrea and Sudan throughout 1998. Following talks held in November 1998, in Qatar, the two sides signed an agreement for the open discussion of bilateral issues. A further meeting, held in May 1999, resulted in an accord, signed by the Presidents of Sudan and Eritrea, in which they agreed to restore diplomatic relations, to refrain from hostile propaganda and to establish joint committees, both to implement the terms of the accord and to study any further issues that might arise between the two countries, although tensions between the two countries remained. In June the two countries established joint committees in accordance with the terms of the 1999 Doha agreement. A further agreement was signed in Asmara in January 2000, providing for the immediate reopening of the two countries' borders and the resumption of flights between their airports. In February the Presidents of Eritrea and Sudan held talks in Khartoum, and it was agreed to issue passports to residents in the border area. Furthermore, they declared that they would not allow opposition groups located in their respective countries to launch cross-border raids. However, relations between the two countries deteriorated in July, when the Sudanese Government accused Eritrea of assisting the NDA with a planned offensive in eastern Sudan. In October Eritrean President Issaias Afewerki visited Khartoum, where he held talks with al-Bashir, during which both sides expressed their desire for a fresh beginning to their bilateral relations and agreed to take measures to settle differences between the two countries in a peaceful manner. In July 2001 Eritrea and Sudan signed an agreement on border security, which aimed to eradicate smuggling and illegal infiltration, as well as ensure the safe passage of people and goods. Relations between the two countries deteriorated again in mid-2002, and in October the Sudanese authorities closed the common border, claiming that Eritrea had been involved in an NDA offensive in eastern Sudan. Following a meeting with the Yemeni President, Ali Abdullah Saleh, and the Ethiopian Prime Minister, Meles Zenawi, in December 2003, President al-Bashir accused Eritrea of arming and training rebels in the Darfur region of Sudan and maintained that Eritrea was a destabilizing force in the region. Eritrea refuted the allegations. In October 2004 Eritrea accused Sudan of complicity in an attempt to assassinate President Afewerki, while Sudan maintained that Eritrea had provided rebels with arms in an attempt to destabilize the Sudanese Government. Relations between the two countries were again strained in June 2005, when Sudan accused Eritrea of providing assistance to rebel forces who had attacked Sudanese government troops in eastern Sudan earlier that month. However, at a meeting in Khartoum in October Akol, who had earlier been appointed Minister of Foreign Affairs, signed an agreement with his Eritrean acting counterpart to work towards the normalization of relations between Sudan and Eritrea. In June 2006 President Afewerki met al-Bashir in Khartoum, and later that month the two countries agreed to restore diplomatic relations to ambassadorial level. Following Eritrean mediation, the Sudanese Government and the rebel Eastern Front signed a peace agreement in Asmara in October (see above). In June 2008 the Sudanese authorities banned all activity of Eritrean opposition groups that had been operating from Sudan, demonstrating a marked improvement in relations between the two countries. Al-Bashir visited Asmara in March 2009, when he reiterated his commitment to the June 2008 agreement.

Sudan and Uganda have accused each other of supporting groups opposed to their respective regimes, and in 1995 Uganda broke off diplomatic relations with Sudan. A further deterioration in relations in December brought the two countries to the brink of open war. In 1996 Sudan and Uganda agreed to restore diplomatic relations, provided that each side undertook to cease its support for rebel factions operating from the other's territory, and to participate in an international committee to monitor the agreement. In August 1997 President Nelson Mandela of South Africa hosted talks between the two countries, following mutual accusations of troops incursions. Relations between Sudan and Uganda improved during 1999, and in December, following a meeting in Nairobi, mediated by former US President Jimmy Carter, the two countries signed an accord in which they agreed to restore diplomatic relations and to end support to each other's rebel groups; shortly afterwards it was announced that eight leaders of the Lord's Resistance Army (LRA) were to be relocated from Sudan to a country of their choice in accordance with the agreement. In February 2000, however, Uganda expressed its dissatisfaction with Sudan's implementation of the accord and appealed for Sudan to disarm the LRA and to disband all LRA camps within Sudan. Sudan reaffirmed its commitment to the agreement and in June 2001 the two countries exchanged diplomats. In August the Ugandan embassy in Khartoum reopened and a chargé d'affaires was appointed. In March 2002 the two countries signed an agreement whereby Sudan temporarily authorized Ugandan troops to pursue LRA rebels within Sudan, and later that month the Ugandan Government announced that its troops had captured all four main bases in Sudan belonging to the LRA. In late November the Sudanese authorities agreed to extend permission for Ugandan troops to remain on its territory for as long as Uganda deemed necessary. Meanwhile, the two countries upgraded relations to ambassadorial level. In August 2006 peace talks between the LRA and the Ugandan Government, which had commenced in Juba, southern Sudan, in July, resulted in a cease-fire agreement. However, continuing negotiations regarding the demobilization of the LRA collapsed in April 2008. In July the Southern Sudanese Government demanded that Ugandan troops withdraw from the region, claiming that they were responsible for attacks on civilians during anti-LRA operations. In late 2010 the Governments of Uganda, Sudan, the Central Africa Republic and the Democratic Republic of the Congo were engaged in negotiations to establish a joint cross-border force, with AU support, in order to co-ordinate military action against the LRA.

President Nimeri was one of very few Arab leaders to support President Sadat of Egypt's initiative for peace with Israel in 1978. Sudan's close relations with Egypt were consolidated in 1982, when a 'charter of integration' was signed. The first session of the joint 'Nile Valley Parliament', created by the charter, was convened in 1983 with 60 Sudanese and 60 Egyptian members. Relations with Egypt deteriorated in 1991, as a result of the Sudanese Government's support for Iraq during the Gulf crisis. Egypt also expressed concern at the perceived growth of Islamic 'fundamentalism' in Sudan. The two countries are involved in a dispute over the Halaib border area, and in early 1992 relations deteriorated sharply following the announcement that Sudan had awarded a Canadian company a concession to explore for petroleum there. Relations deteriorated further, as Egypt repeatedly accused Sudan of supporting illegal Islamic fundamentalist groups in Egypt, while Sudan alleged that Egypt was supporting the SPLA. In August the Sudanese Government sought international arbitration on the Halaib issue, claiming that Egypt had been settling families in the area in an effort to bring it under Egyptian control. In January 1993 Sudan complained to the UN Security Council that Egyptian troops had infringed Sudan's territorial integrity. In March Egypt announced the construction of a new road link to Halaib. Sudan retaliated by appropriating the Khartoum campus of the University of Cairo. In June Sudan announced that it was closing two Egyptian consulates in Sudan and two of its own consulates in Egypt. In January 1995 Egypt rejected a request by Sudan to refer the dispute over the Halaib border area to a meeting of the OAU's council of Ministers of Foreign Affairs in Addis Ababa. In June relations suffered a further serious setback after the attempted assassination of President Mubarak of Egypt on his arrival in Addis Ababa to attend the annual conference of the OAU. The Egyptian Government immediately accused Sudan of complicity in the attack, and the OAU made the same allegation in September. In January 1996 the UN Security Council condemned Sudan's role in the attempted assassination and adopted Resolution 1044 seeking the extradition of three individuals implicated in the attack. Relations between Sudan and Egypt appeared to improve in 1997; in December talks were held between President al-Bashir and senior Egyptian officials, and in January 1998 it was agreed that a joint chamber of commerce would be established. In May a joint Sudanese-Egyptian technical committee met in Khartoum to finalize details for the return of several institutions in Sudan to Egyptian control. Both sides agreed that the institutions should be returned, although differences remained over the time period for this operation. In October Sudan and Egypt agreed on a plan to hasten the normalization of relations. In July 1999 it was announced that Sudan had extradited one of the three suspects implicated in the attempted assassination of Mubarak. In December the two countries agreed to normalize their relations and to resolve their dispute over the Halaib issue amicably. In March 2000 it was announced that the University of Cairo in Khartoum was to be reopened, and later that month Egypt appointed an ambassador to Sudan for the first time since the assassination attempt on Mubarak. In September the Sudanese and Egyptian ministers responsible for foreign affairs held the first session of the Egyptian-Sudanese Commission for 10 years, at which the two countries expressed their commitment to further bilateral economic development. In May 2003 Mubarak visited Khartoum for the first time since the attempted assassination. In March 2011 al-Bashir became the first Arab leader to visit Egypt after the resignation of Mubarak in February (see the chapter on Egypt); the new Egyptian authorities, which planned that the country join the ICC, issued assurances that they would support Sudan's case with regard to the arrest warrant issued by the Court against al-Bashir.

Other external relations

The USA has been one of the severest critics of the present Sudanese Government, frequently expressing concern about Sudan's links with Iran. Allegations of Sudanese involvement in terrorism resulted in the detention in the USA, in 1993, of five Sudanese residents suspected of plotting to blow up buildings and road tunnels in New York, USA and to assassinate President Mubarak of Egypt on a visit to the USA; the USA subsequently added Sudan to its list of countries accused of sponsoring terrorism. In August 1997 the USA imposed economic sanctions against Sudan, owing to its alleged continued support for terrorism. In late August 1998 the USA launched a missile attack on what it claimed was a chemical weapons factory in Khartoum. Immediately after the attack, however, the Sudanese Government denied these claims and stated that it was, in fact, a private pharmaceuticals plant. Sudan recalled its ambassador to the USA and refused permission for US aircraft to use its airspace; its requests for a UN inquiry into the attack were unanimously refused by the Security Council, despite backing from the League of Arab States (see p. 361) and the Organization of the Islamic Conference (see p. 400). By February 1999 it had become evident that the US intelligence on which the attack had been based was fundamentally flawed. In May Sudan requested compensation for the damage caused by the bomb attack, and in July 2000 the proprietor of the factory announced his intention to sue the US Government for damages. Meanwhile, in April 1999 the USA had announced its decision to ease sanctions on the export of food and medicine to Sudan, and at the end of May Sudan fulfilled one of the conditions set by the USA for a review of the sanctions regime by signing a treaty banning chemical weapons. In November, however, the USA enacted controversial legislation allowing food aid to be delivered direct to the Sudanese rebels. An improvement in relations was evident in March 2000 following a visit to Sudan by a US diplomat to discuss the possibility of reopening the US embassy in Khartoum; in mid-April the embassy was duly reopened. However, relations once again deteriorated in December, when Sudan lodged an official complaint with the UN after the US Assistant Secretary of State, Susan Rice, visited rebel-held areas of southern Sudan in November, without the permission of the Sudanese Government. Following the election of a new US Administration, under the leadership of President George W. Bush, in January 2001, there was some uncertainty regarding the USA's policy towards Sudan. In July the Bush Administration outlined its three main policy objectives for Sudan: to deal with the humanitarian crisis, to end Sudan's role as a sanctuary for terrorism, and to promote a just peace by bringing the warring parties together. In September Bush appointed a former senator, John Danforth, as his special envoy to Sudan.

Following the September 2001 suicide attacks on New York and Washington, DC, Sudan agreed to assist the USA with its search for terrorist suspects, and by late September the Sudanese authorities had arrested some 30 individuals resident in

SUDAN

Sudan who were suspected of having links to Osama bin Laden, a Saudi-born Islamist activist, and the al-Qa'ida (Base) organization, which the USA held responsible for the attacks. Nevertheless, US sanctions remained in place, and Sudan continued to be listed by the US Department of State as a sponsor of terrorism. Furthermore, two Sudanese banks were among numerous institutions under US investigation as possible sources of financial support for bin Laden. Sudan expressed criticism of the US-led military strikes on Afghanistan, which commenced in November, and later that month the USA extended sanctions until November 2002. In October 2002 Bush approved legislation that allowed the USA to impose further sanctions, including the suspension of multilateral loans, on the Sudanese Government, should it fail to negotiate in good faith with the southern rebels or interfere with humanitarian efforts in the south of the country. The USA also froze the financial assets of 12 Sudanese companies, including the National Broadcasting Corporation. Under the Sudan Peace Act, conditions in Sudan would be evaluated every six months, although the law also made provision for the expenditure of US $100m. a year by the USA until 2005 in areas of Sudan not under the Sudanese Government's control. In October 2003 the US Agency for International Development pledged a further $40m. to finance initiatives to assist Sudan to recover from the civil war. However, the additional aid was conditional on the implementation of a CPA. In mid-November the US embassy in Khartoum was temporarily closed in response to a 'specific threat' to US interests in Sudan. The conflict in Darfur (see above) resulted in the deterioration of relations between Sudan and the USA and in September 2004 the US Administration accused the Sudanese Government of committing genocide. The USA subsequently proposed a draft UN resolution, which threatened to impose sanctions on Sudan's petroleum industry if the Sudanese authorities did not act to end the violence in the region. In late July 2005 the US Secretary of State, Condoleezza Rice, who met al-Bashir in Khartoum and also visited the Abu Shouk refugee camp in the Darfur region, urged action from the Sudanese administration to resolve the conflict in Darfur. During the visit, Rice also indicated that the USA was to send an ambassador to Khartoum for the first time since 1997. In October 2006 President Bush approved the Darfur Peace and Accountability Act of 2006, which provided for the imposition of sanctions against those responsible for genocide, war crimes, and crimes against humanity, and supported humanitarian efforts and measures to secure peace in the region of Darfur. He also issued an executive order freezing the assets and property of the Sudanese Government and prohibiting financial transactions with that body. The USA threatened to impose economic sanctions on state-controlled companies in Sudan in April 2007 unless the Government agreed to co-operate in restoring peace to the Darfur region. The following month President Bush implemented measures to exclude Sudanese companies from the US financial system. Following his election to the US presidency in November 2008, Barack Obama announced a new US strategy on Sudan, moving away from Bush's exclusionary stance. President Obama pledged to engage the Sudanese authorities in meaningful dialogue, with a focus on ending the conflict in Darfur, ensuring the implementation of the CPA with a view to securing peace in the region and continuing to address the threat of terrorism. After the organization of a referendum on secession for southern Sudan in January 2011 (see above), the US Administration announced that it would begin to normalize relations with Sudan.

Sudan's relations with the United Kingdom deteriorated in May 1998, following a statement made by the British Secretary of State for International Development in which she accused Sudan of using food aid as a weapon in Bahr al-Ghazal. The Sudanese Government vehemently denied this and accused the United Kingdom of having a negative attitude towards forthcoming peace negotiations. The British Government played an active role in attempting to end the violence in Darfur—the British Secretary of State for Foreign and Commonwealth Affairs, Jack Straw, visited the region in August 2004, and Prime Minister Blair visited Khartoum in October to increase diplomatic pressure on the Sudanese Government. After the ICC formally issued an international arrest warrant for President al-Bashir in March 2009 (see above), the United Kingdom urged the Sudanese Government to co-operate with the Court. Sudan retaliated against the warrant by expelling a number of international aid agencies, including Oxfam, that had been operating in the country.

CONSTITUTION AND GOVERNMENT

In early July 2005 the National Assembly approved an interim Constitution as part of the CPA, which had been signed in January between the Sudanese Government and the Sudan People's Liberation Movement (SPLM). The interim Constitution provided for the establishment of a Government of National Unity, representation in which was to be divided between northerners and southerners, with the former holding 70% of the posts and the latter 30%. Following a transitional period, presidential and legislative elections took place in April 2010, in accordance with the CPA. The President is directly elected for a five-year term, and appoints the Government. The National Assembly comprises 450 members, of whom 270 are directly elected in single seat constituencies, 68 are elected on the basis of proportional representation from party lists, and a further 112 women representatives are elected on the basis of proportional representation.

The President of the Government of Southern Sudan is elected directly by the people of southern Sudan for a five-year mandate, renewable only once. Following legislative elections in April 2010, the Southern Sudan Legislative Assembly comprised 170 members, of whom 102 are directly elected in single seat constituencies, 25 are elected on the basis of proportional representation from party lists, and a further 43 women representatives are elected on the basis of proportional representation from party lists. In accordance with the terms of the CPA, a referendum on the secession of southern Sudan was conducted in January 2011; 98.8% of the population (with a participation rate of 97.6% of the electorate) voted to secede from the north and officially form their own country, which was to be named 'South Sudan' and be inaugurated on 6 July.

Sudan is divided into 26 states. A governor is responsible for each state, assisted by five (in the case of the southern states six) state ministers.

REGIONAL AND INTERNATIONAL CO-OPERATION

Sudan is a member of the African Union (see p. 183) and the Council of Arab Economic Unity (see p. 247). In 1997 Sudan's membership of both the Arab Fund for Economic and Social Development (AFESD, see p. 194) and the Arab Monetary Fund (see p. 195) was suspended. Membership of the AFESD was restored in April 2000.

Sudan became a member of the UN in 1956, and participates in the Group of 77 (G77, see p. 447) developing countries.

ECONOMIC AFFAIRS

In 2009, according to estimates by the World Bank, Sudan's gross national income (GNI), measured at average 2007–09 prices, was US $51,629m., equivalent to $1,220 per head (or $2,000 on an international purchasing-power parity basis). During 2000–09, it was estimated, the population increased at an average annual rate of 2.2%, while gross domestic product (GDP) per head increased, in real terms, by an average of 4.7% per year. Overall GDP increased, in real terms, at an average annual rate of 6.9% in 2000–09; growth in 2009 was 4.0%.

Agriculture (including forestry and fishing) contributed an estimated 30.7% of GDP in 2009, according to the African Development Bank (AfDB). According to FAO, the sector employed about 50.6% of the labour force in mid-2011. The principal cash crop is sesame seed (including oil cake), which accounted for 1.6% of total export earnings in 2009. The principal subsistence crops are sorghum, millet and wheat. The GDP of the agricultural sector increased by an average of 2.8% per year in 2000–09, according to the World Bank. Agricultural GDP increased by 4.3% in 2009.

Industry (including mining, manufacturing, construction and power) contributed an estimated 29.1% of GDP in 2009, according to the AfDB, and employed 7.9% of the labour force in 1983. In 2000–09 industrial GDP increased at an average annual rate of 10.9%, according to the World Bank. Industrial GDP increased by 7.5% in 2008 and by 14.7% in 2009.

Mining accounted for an estimated 15.3% of GDP in 2009, according to the AfDB. Only 0.1% of the labour force was employed in the mining sector in 1983; however, this figure had risen considerably by the late 2000s. Sudan has reserves of petroleum, chromite, gypsum, gold, iron ore and wollastonite. Sudan began to develop its petroleum reserves in the mid-1990s; proven reserves totalled 6,700m. barrels at the end of 2009, sufficient to sustain production at current levels for more than 37 years. In 2007 Sudan was the sixth largest producer of petroleum in Africa. In 2009 petroleum and petroleum products accounted for 78.8% of total export earnings. According to the AfDB, the GDP of the mining sector increased by 10.5% in 2009.

Manufacturing contributed an estimated 7.9% of GDP in 2009, according to the AfDB. The most important branch of the sector is food-processing, especially sugar-refining, while the textile industry, cement production and petroleum-refining are also significant. Some 4.6% of the labour force were employed in manufacturing in 1983. According to the World Bank, in 2000–09 manufacturing GDP increased at an average annual rate of 4.1%. Manufacturing GDP increased by 8.0% in 2009.

The construction sector contributed an estimated 4.2% of GDP in 2009, according to the AfDB; it engaged some 2.3% of the employed labour force in 1983. According to the AfDB, the GDP of the sector increased by 8.5% in 2009.

Energy is derived from petroleum (which contributed 68.0% of total output in 2007) and hydroelectric power (32.0%). In May 2004 the Government announced plans to provide 90% of the country with electricity over the following five years by harnessing more of the hydroelectric potential of the Nile. Sudan is a net exporter of fuels, with imports of refined petroleum products comprising an estimated 4.0% of the total value of imports in 2009, compared to 5.0% in 2006.

Services contributed an estimated 40.2% of GDP in 2009, according to the AfDB, and employed 18.8% of the labour force in 1983. During 2000–09, according to the World Bank, the GDP of the services sector increased at an average annual rate of 8.2%. In 2008 the GDP of the services sector rose by 8.3%, but it declined by 3.0% in 2009.

In 2009 Sudan recorded a visible trade deficit of US $694.3m., and there was a deficit of $3,908.2m. on the current account of the balance of payments. In 2009 the principal sources of imports were the People's Republic of China (accounting for 16.6% of the total), Japan, Saudi Arabia, the United Arab Emirates (UAE) and India. In 2009 the principal market for Sudanese exports was also the People's Republic of China (taking 65.3%); the UAE and Canada were the other major purchasers. The principal exports in 2009 were mineral products (especially petroleum and petroleum products and gold). The principal imports in 2009 were machinery and transport equipment, iron and steel, food and live animals, and chemicals and related products.

In 2009, according to preliminary figures from the IMF, Sudan recorded an overall budget deficit of 5,865m. new Sudanese pounds, equivalent to 4.6% of GDP in that year. Sudan's general government gross debt was 101,363m. new Sudanese pounds in 2009, equivalent to 80.6% of GDP. At the end of 2008 Sudan's total external debt was US $19,633m., of which $12,599m. was public and publicly guaranteed debt. In that year the cost of debt-servicing was equivalent to 2.5% of the total value of exports of goods, services and income. In 2003–09 the average annual rate of inflation was 9.6%. Consumer prices increased by an average of 14.3% in 2008 and by 11.3% in 2009.

Sudan's formidable economic problems, originating in the 1970s, when the country's agricultural potential was neglected, have been compounded by civil conflict. Sudan began exporting petroleum in late 1999 and further discoveries of petroleum in 2001 led to a vast increase in export revenues; however, much of these earnings were used by the Government to fund the war against the rebels in the south of the country. Following the CPA signed by the Government and the SPLM in January 2005, levels of foreign investment increased, thus providing capital for reconstruction programmes in the regions affected by the civil war. However, the donor community remained deeply concerned by the ongoing conflict and humanitarian crisis in the Darfur region. In November 2008 the UN requested some US $2,000m. of humanitarian aid to fund projects in 2009, one-half of which would target the Darfur region. Significantly, while many companies from Europe and North America have been reluctant to invest in Sudan, companies from the People's Republic of China, India and Malaysia have acquired major stakes in a number of Sudanese oil concessions. Uganda and Sudan, meanwhile, opened a new trading centre in Juba, which was expected to facilitate a large increase in commerce between southern Sudan and Uganda. Juba has emerged as a major distribution centre for the south of the country since the signing of the CPA. In a staff-monitored programme covering June 2009–December 2010, the IMF set objectives for the Government of Sudan, including maintaining macro-economic stability in the recovery period following the global economic crisis and safeguarding and rebuilding foreign exchange reserves. The IMF also recommended a number of fiscal policy reforms, including reducing the rate of value-added tax, in response to the decline in world oil prices in 2009. GDP growth of 4.0% was estimated in 2009, although the IMF forecast that this rate would recover slightly to 5.5% in 2010 as the impact of the global economic downturn became less severe. In February 2011, after the secession of southern Sudan was overwhelmingly approved in a referendum (see Domestic Political Affairs), it was announced that agreement had been reached on the allocation of the proceeds of Sudan's oil reserves, principally located in southern Sudan. On independence (which was scheduled for 6 July), the newly established 'South Sudan' would assume control of about three-quarters of the country's current production, amounting to some 490,000 barrels a day, and pay the northern Government a transit fee for the use of a pipeline for oil exports. The IMF envisaged that the new state would receive technical assistance from the Fund in establishing a monetary system, including a new currency. The organization of the referendum, following multi-party elections in April 2010, was expected to improve Sudan's relations with the international community. However, uncertainties remained over the settlement of other outstanding issues between northern and southern Sudan (including debt-sharing, nationality and borders), and continuing insurgent activity in Darfur and other regions. The further mass displacement of southerners returning from northern Sudan after the secession referendum, which was expected to continue during 2011, exacerbated the humanitarian situation, compounding the effects of crop failure in many areas; in early 2011 it was estimated that 2.7m. people were dependent on food aid.

PUBLIC HOLIDAYS

2012: 1 January (Independence Day), 4 February* (Mouloud, Birth of the Prophet), 6 April (Uprising Day, anniversary of 1985 coup), 16 April (Sham al-Nassim, Coptic Easter Monday), 30 June (Revolution Day), 18 August* (Id al-Fitr, end of Ramadan), 26 October* (Id al-Adha, Feast of the Sacrifice), 15 November* (Muharram, Islamic New Year), 25 December (Christmas).

* The dates of Islamic holidays are determined by sightings of the moon, and may be slightly different from those given above.

SUDAN

Statistical Survey

Source (unless otherwise stated): Department of Statistics, Ministry of Finance and National Economy, POB 735, Khartoum; tel. (183) 777563; fax (183) 775630; e-mail info@mof-sudan.net; internet www.mof-sudan.net; Central Bureau of Statistics, POB 700, Khartoum; tel. (183) 777255; fax (183) 771860; e-mail info@cbs.gov.sd; internet www.cbs.gov.sd.

Area and Population

AREA, POPULATION AND DENSITY

Area (sq km)	2,505,813*
Population (census results)†	
1 February 1993	24,940,683
22 April 2008	
Males	20,073,977
Females	19,080,513
Total	39,154,490
Population (official estimate at mid-year)	
2009	40,299,000
Density (per sq km) at mid-2009	16.1

* 967,500 sq miles.
† Excluding adjustments for underenumeration, estimated to have been 6.7% in 1993.

POPULATION BY AGE AND SEX
(population at 2008 census)

	Males	Females	Total
0–14	8,718,975	7,964,829	16,683,804
15–64	10,606,796	10,538,986	21,145,782
65 and over	748,206	576,698	1,324,904
Total	20,073,977	19,080,513	39,154,490

PROVINCES
(1983 census, provisional)*

	Area (sq miles)	Population	Density (per sq mile)
Northern	134,736	433,391	3.2
Nile	49,205	649,633	13.2
Kassala	44,109	1,512,335	34.3
Red Sea	84,977	695,874	8.2
Blue Nile	24,009	1,056,313	44.0
Gezira	13,546	2,023,094	149.3
White Nile	16,161	933,136	57.7
Northern Kordofan	85,744	1,805,769	21.1
Southern Kordofan	61,188	1,287,525	21.0
Northern Darfur	133,754	1,327,947	9.9
Southern Darfur	62,801	1,765,752	28.1
Khartoum	10,883	1,802,299	165.6
Eastern Equatoria	46,073	1,047,125	22.7
Western Equatoria	30,422	359,056	11.8
Bahr al-Ghazal	52,000	1,492,597	28.7
Al-Buhayrat	25,625	772,913	30.2
Sobat	45,266	802,354	17.7
Jonglei	47,003	797,251	17.0
Total	967,500	20,564,364	21.3

* In 1991 a federal system of government was inaugurated, whereby Sudan was divided into nine states, which were sub-divided into 66 provinces and 281 local government areas. A constitutional decree, issued in February 1994, redivided the country into 26 states.

PRINCIPAL TOWNS
(population at 1993 census)

Omdurman	1,271,403	Nyala	227,183
Khartoum (capital)	947,483	El-Gezira	211,362
Khartoum North	700,887	Gedaref	191,164
Port Sudan	308,195	Kosti	173,599
Kassala	234,622	El-Fasher	141,884
El-Obeid	229,425	Juba	114,980

Source: UN, *Demographic Yearbook*.

Mid-2010 ('000, including suburbs, UN estimate): Khartoum 5,172 (Source: UN, *World Urbanization Prospects: The 2009 Revision*).

BIRTHS AND DEATHS
(annual averages, UN estimates)

	1995–2000	2000–05	2005–10
Birth rate (per 1,000)	38.1	34.5	31.6
Death rate (per 1,000)	12.0	11.0	10.3

Source: UN, *World Population Prospects: The 2008 Revision*.

Life expectancy (years at birth, WHO estimates): 57 (males 57; females 58) in 2008 (Source: WHO, *World Health Statistics*).

ECONOMICALLY ACTIVE POPULATION*
(persons aged 10 years and over, 1983 census, provisional)

	Males	Females	Total
Agriculture, hunting, forestry and fishing	2,638,294	1,390,411	4,028,705
Mining and quarrying	5,861	673	6,534
Manufacturing	205,247	61,446	266,693
Electricity, gas and water	42,110	1,618	43,728
Construction	130,977	8,305	139,282
Trade, restaurants and hotels	268,382	25,720	294,102
Transport, storage and communications	209,776	5,698	215,474
Financing, insurance, real estate and business services	17,414	3,160	20,574
Community, social and personal services	451,193	99,216	550,409
Activities not adequately defined	142,691	42,030	184,721
Unemployed persons not previously employed	387,615	205,144	592,759
Total	4,499,560	1,843,421	6,342,981

* Excluding nomads, homeless persons and members of institutional households.

Mid-2011 (estimates in '000): Agriculture, etc. 7,145; Total 14,133 (Source: FAO).

Health and Welfare

KEY INDICATORS

Total fertility rate (children per woman, 2008)	4.2
Under-5 mortality rate (per 1,000 live births, 2008)	109
HIV/AIDS (% of persons aged 15–49, 2007)	1.4
Physicians (per 1,000 head, 2005)	0.3
Hospital beds (per 1,000 head, 2005)	0.7
Health expenditure (2007): US $ per head (PPP)	71
Health expenditure (2007): % of GDP	3.5
Health expenditure (2007): public (% of total)	36.8
Access to water (% of persons, 2008)	57
Access to sanitation (% of persons, 2008)	34
Total carbon dioxide emissions ('000 metric tons, 2007)	11,512.3
Carbon dioxide emissions per head (metric tons, 2007)	0.3
Human Development Index (2010): ranking	154
Human Development Index (2010): value	0.379

For sources and definitions, see explanatory note on p. vi.

SUDAN

Agriculture

PRINCIPAL CROPS
('000 metric tons)

	2007	2008	2009
Wheat	803	587	642
Rice, paddy	23	30	23
Maize	70	62	66
Millet	796	721	630
Sorghum	4,999	3,869	4,192
Potatoes	264	273	284
Cassava (Manioc)	10*	10*	n.a.
Yams	137*	137*	n.a.
Sugar cane	7,467	7,453	7,527
Beans, dry	16	17	12
Broad beans, horse beans, dry	162	140	113
Groundnuts, with shell	564	716	942
Sunflower seed	73	100	247
Sesame seed	242	350	318
Melonseed	46*	46*	n.a.
Seed cotton	244	107	169
Tomatoes	642	432	453
Pumpkins, squash and gourds	68*	68*	n.a.
Aubergines (Eggplants)	70	235	756
Onions, dry	59*	59*	n.a.
Garlic	36	38	25
Canteloupes (incl. other melons)	28*	28*	n.a.
Watermelons	145*	145*	n.a.
Dates	332	336	339
Oranges	18*	18*	n.a.
Lemons and limes	63*	63*	n.a.
Grapefruits and pomelos	68*	68*	n.a.
Guavas, mangoes and mangosteens	195*	195*	n.a.
Bananas	74*	74*	n.a.

* FAO estimate.

Aggregate production ('000 metric tons, may include official, semi-official or estimated data): Total cereals 6,691 in 2007, 5,269 in 2008, 5,552 in 2009; Total roots and tubers 420 in 2007, 429 in 2008, 440 in 2009; Total vegetables (incl. melons) 2,058 in 2007, 2,021 in 2008, 1,898 in 2009; Total fruits (excl. melons) 1,167 in 2007, 1,171 in 2008, 1,174 in 2009.

Source: FAO.

LIVESTOCK
('000 head, year ending September)

	2007	2008	2009
Horses*	26	26	26
Asses*	750	751	751
Cattle	41,000	41,400	41,563
Camels	4,250	4,400	4,521
Sheep	50,944	51,100	51,555
Goats	42,987	43,100	43,270
Chickens	40,624	41,502	42,400*

* FAO estimate(s).
Source: FAO.

LIVESTOCK PRODUCTS
('000 metric tons)

	2007	2008	2009
Cattle meat*	340	340	340
Sheep meat*	148	152	153
Goat meat*	186	189	190
Chicken meat	26	27	30*
Cows' milk	5,292	5,309	5,328*
Sheep's milk	498	504	n.a.
Goats' milk	1,456	1,475	n.a.
Hen eggs*	47	47	n.a.
Wool, greasy*	46	46	n.a.

* FAO estimate(s).
Source: FAO.

Forestry

ROUNDWOOD REMOVALS
('000 cubic metres, FAO estimates)

	2007	2008	2009
Sawlogs, veneer logs and logs for sleepers	123	123	123
Other industrial wood	2,050	2,050	2,050
Fuel wood	18,110	18,326	18,547
Total	20,283	20,499	20,720

Source: FAO.

Gum arabic ('000 metric tons, year ending 30 June): 24 in 1993/94; 27 in 1994/95; 25 in 1995/96 (Source: IMF, *Sudan—Recent Economic Developments*, March 1997).

Fishing

('000 metric tons, live weight)

	2005*	2006*	2007
Capture	59.0	57.0	65.5
Nile tilapia	20.3	19.8	22.9
Other freshwater fishes	33.5	32.2	36.9
Marine fishes	5.2	5.0	5.7
Aquaculture	1.6	1.6	2.0*
Total catch	60.6	58.6	67.5*

* FAO estimate(s).
2008: Catch assumed to be unchanged from 2007 (FAO estimates).
Source: FAO.

Mining

('000 metric tons, unless otherwise stated)

	2007	2008	2009
Crude petroleum ('000 barrels)	176,574	168,898	173,453
Salt (unrefined)	22.9	10.6	35.8
Chromite	15.5	27.1	14.1
Gold ore (kilograms)*	2,703	2,276	1,922

* Figures refer to the metal content of ores.
Source: US Geological Survey.

Industry

PETROLEUM PRODUCTS
(metric tons)

	2007	2008	2009*
Motor spirit (petrol)	10,279	9,244	9,200
Naphtha	170	219	200
Jet fuels	929	836	800
Kerosene	239	251	200
Gas-diesel (distillate fuel) oils	15,410	13,903	13,800
Residual fuel oils	4,175	4,534	4,500

* Estimates.
Source: US Geological Survey.

SUDAN

Statistical Survey

SELECTED OTHER PRODUCTS
('000 metric tons)

	2005	2006	2007
Wheat flour	1,300	1,200	n.a.
Raw sugar	728	767	743
Cement	244	227	327

2002 ('000 metric tons): Refined sugar 674; Vegetable oils 63.

Source: UN Industrial Commodity Statistics Database.

Electric energy (million kWh): 5,021.0 in 2007; 5,506.0 in 2008; 6,372 in 2009.

Finance

CURRENCY AND EXCHANGE RATES

Monetary Units
100 piastres = 1 new Sudanese pound (SDG).

Sterling, Dollar and Euro Equivalents (30 September 2010)
£1 sterling = 3.776 new Sudanese pounds;
US $1 = 2.373 new Sudanese pounds;
€1 = 3.238 new Sudanese pounds;
10 new Sudanese pounds = £2.65 = $4.21 = €3.09.

Average Exchange Rate (new Sudanese pounds per US $)
2007   2.0161
2008   2.0902
2009   2.3015

Note: On 1 March 1999 the Sudanese pound (£S) was replaced by the Sudanese dinar (SDD), equivalent to £S10. The pound was withdrawn from circulation on 31 July 1999. A new Sudanese pound (SDG), equivalent to 100 dinars (and 1,000 old pounds) was introduced on 10 January 2007. The new currency was to circulate along with previous currencies (the old pound had continued to circulate in some regions) for a transitional period, but became the sole legal tender on 1 July 2007.

CENTRAL GOVERNMENT BUDGET
(million new Sudanese pounds)

Revenue*	2008	2009†	2010‡
Tax revenue	7,680	8,619	10,067
Petroleum revenue	17,338	9,519	13,156
Sales to refineries	3,513	2,840	2,792
Export revenues	13,825	6,679	10,364
Other non-petroleum non-tax revenue	833	923	1,258
Total	25,852	19,061	24,481

Expenditure	2008	2009†	2010‡
Current expenditure	24,331	22,073	26,060
Wages	5,951	6,836	7,649
Goods and services	2,919	2,375	2,403
Interest	1,088	1,254	1,364
Subsidies	2,519	712	1,380
Fuel	2,195	447	1,272
Transfers	11,575	9,799	11,874
To South	6,159	4,485	5,464
To North	5,396	5,288	6,353
Other current expenditure	279	1,097	1,390
Capital expenditure	3,838	3,572	3,748
Total	28,169	25,645	29,808

* Excluding grants totalling (million new Sudanese pounds): 572 in 2008; 719 in 2009 (preliminary); 1,061 in 2010 (projection).
† Preliminary.
‡ Projections.

Source: IMF, *Sudan: Second Review Under the 2009–10 Staff-Monitored Program —Staff Report; Staff Supplement; and Statement by the Executive Director for Sudan* (April 2011).

INTERNATIONAL RESERVES
(US $ million at 31 December)

	2007	2008	2009
IMF special drawing rights	—	—	197.2
Foreign exchange	1,377.9	1,399.0	897.0
Total	1,377.9	1,399.0	1,094.2

2010: IMF special drawing rights 193.5.

Source: IMF, *International Financial Statistics*.

MONEY SUPPLY
(million Sudanese dinars at 31 December)

	2007	2008	2009
Currency outside depository corporations	5,640	6,775	8,066
Transferable deposits	6,777	8,045	9,595
Other deposits	7,271	8,049	10,624
Broad money	19,688	22,869	28,285

Source: IMF, *International Financial Statistics*.

COST OF LIVING
(Consumer Price Index for middle income group; base: 2007 = 100)

	2008	2009
Food and beverages	118.6	133.1
Clothing and footwear	107.5	118.3
Housing	118.0	128.1
Household operations	106.7	116.4
Health care	107.8	118.1
Transport	103.2	107.7
Entertainment	103.8	109.5
Education	100.4	119.2
All items (incl. others)	114.3	127.2

NATIONAL ACCOUNTS
(million new Sudanese pounds at current prices)

Expenditure on the Gross Domestic Product

	2007	2008	2009
Government final consumption expenditure	9,635	10,811	13,130
Private final consumption expenditure	85,780	92,073	107,349
Changes in inventories	7,373	5,852	6,919
Gross fixed capital formation	16,170	18,645	19,462
Total domestic expenditure	118,958	127,381	146,860
Exports of goods and services	18,665	25,401	31,635
Less Imports of goods and services	23,607	25,035	27,067
GDP in purchasers' values	114,018	127,747	151,428

Gross Domestic Product by Economic Activity

	2007	2008	2009
Agriculture, hunting, forestry and fishing	32,985	37,481	44,970
Mining and quarrying	17,824	20,064	22,409
Manufacturing	8,782	9,726	11,508
Electricity, gas and water	1,981	2,242	2,513
Construction	4,651	5,239	6,171
Wholesale and retail trade, restaurants and hotels	16,728	18,376	21,108
Transport and communications	13,781	15,046	17,076
Finance, insurance, real estate and business services	7,809	8,961	10,399
Government services	5,944	6,681	7,482
Other services	2,255	2,503	2,729
Sub-total	112,740	126,319	146,365
Less Imputed bank service charge	1,095	1,126	1,244
Indirect taxes (net)	2,373	2,553	6,307
GDP in purchasers' values	114,018	127,747	151,428

Source: African Development Bank.

SUDAN

BALANCE OF PAYMENTS
(US $ million)

	2007	2008	2009
Exports of goods f.o.b.	8,879.2	11,670.5	7,833.7
Imports of goods f.o.b.	−7,722.4	−8,229.4	−8,528.0
Trade balance	1,156.8	3,441.1	−694.3
Exports of services	384.3	492.8	392.0
Imports of services	−2,938.7	−2,619.5	−2,684.0
Balance on goods and services	−1,397.6	1,314.4	−2,986.3
Other income received	183.7	43.4	36.1
Other income paid	−2,436.8	−3,056.5	−2,438.4
Balance on goods, services and income	−3,650.7	−1,698.6	−5,388.6
Current transfers received	2,321.5	4,023.6	3,441.9
Current transfers paid	−2,117.9	−3,638.6	−1,961.5
Current balance	−3,447.1	−1,313.6	−3,908.2
Direct investment abroad	—	−89.2	—
Direct investment from abroad	2,425.6	2,600.5	2,682.2
Portfolio investment assets	62.1	−33.4	−22.4
Portfolio investment liabilities	−16.6	−0.1	−0.5
Other investment assets	−535.3	−866.5	532.4
Other investment liabilities	1,060.6	−101.6	2,259.7
Net errors and omissions	26.9	−125.4	−1,835.1
Overall balance	−423.8	70.8	−291.9

Source: IMF, *International Financial Statistics*.

External Trade

PRINCIPAL COMMODITIES
(US $ million)

Imports c.i.f.	2007	2008	2009
Food and live animals	465.4	1,152.5	1,191.7
Cereals and cereal preparations	205.2	569.5	537.4
Unmilled durum wheat	161.2	493.1	386.9
Mineral fuels, lubricants, etc.	32.3	14.3	346.9
Refined petroleum products	32.2	13.8	346.7
Chemicals and related products	1,027.8	395.5	920.6
Medicinal and pharmaceutical products	814.7	216.6	284.6
Basic manufactures	1,017.1	1,352.1	1,807.3
Textiles and textile products (excl. clothing)	152.9	125.3	243.8
Cement	91.5	129.1	109.7
Iron and steel	211.5	768.0	620.3
Machinery and transport equipment	6,264.3	8,774.5	3,254.6
Power generating machinery and equipment	649.7	252.8	317.0
Machinery specialized for particular industries	1,110.5	393.3	520.1
Miscellaneous industrial machinery	260.5	249.6	298.7
Telecommunication and recording equipment	1,310.8	221.1	205.2
Road vehicles	1,043.9	953.9	1,223.2
Passenger vehicles (excl. buses)	301.3	401.9	405.0
Lorries and special purpose vehicles	495.6	327.0	567.9
Miscellaneous manufactured articles	898.1	652.1	817.5
Total (incl. others)	9,853.6	16,416.7	8,589.9

Exports f.o.b.	2006	2008*	2009
Food and live animals	150.8	126.1	298.4
Live animals	109.9	71.5	249.7
Sheep and goats	106.5	50.0	224.2
Sheep	103.2	49.4	220.4
Crude materials (inedible) except fuels	291.2	370.8	281.1
Oil seeds and oleaginous fruit	147.5	173.6	153.8
Sesame seeds	143.7	167.9	147.5
Cotton	71.1	58.3	40.2
Mineral fuels, lubricants, etc.	4,796.1	8,935.4	7,151.8
Petroleum and petroleum products	4,791.7	8,934.0	7,151.8
Machinery and transport equipment	58.3	33.0	46.3
Other commodities and transactions	174.2	3.2	1,279.5
Non-monetary gold, unwrought	148.2	—	1,278.5
Total (incl. others)	5,478.7	9,500.9	9,079.5

* Data for 2007 were not available.

Source: UN, *International Trade Statistics Yearbook*.

PRINCIPAL TRADING PARTNERS
(US $ million)

Imports c.i.f.	2007	2008	2009
Australia	116.0	287.9	278.3
Canada	136.7	257.0	92.7
China, People's Repub.	1,614.0	1,295.6	1,426.7
Egypt	357.2	422.8	410.3
France (incl. Monaco)	258.3	147.4	113.3
Germany	481.9	119.7	328.4
India	276.6	579.4	548.5
Indonesia	196.0	17.0	46.6
Italy	192.7	124.7	248.5
Japan	744.7	632.1	817.1
Jordan	268.3	126.2	86.2
Kenya	36.8	254.5	63.7
Korea, Repub.	265.3	174.2	205.4
Malaysia	22.1	43.6	52.9
Netherlands	218.9	63.7	90.6
Russia	30.5	738.8	97.3
Saudi Arabia	1,429.6	4,096.6	650.4
Sweden	476.7	64.6	99.1
Switzerland (incl. Liechtenstein)	57.3	16.3	n.a.
Turkey	65.2	80.9	381.0
Ukraine	31.2	621.9	83.3
United Arab Emirates	714.2	499.3	634.0
United Kingdom	564.0	1,075.4	192.0
USA	59.1	43.0	288.3
Total (incl. others)	9,853.6	16,416.7	8,589.9

Exports f.o.b.	2006	2008*	2009
Canada	66.8	0.1	802.1
China, People's Repub.	4,324.3	7,553.5	5,932.2
Egypt	68.6	130.8	93.5
France	15.2	22.8	35.1
Germany	21.3	17.6	9.7
India	22.2	72.6	164.6
Indonesia	5.1	119.1	143.3
Japan	299.0	690.9	213.1
Korea, Repub.	6.5	55.6	7.9
Malaysia	—	107.8	40.6
Saudi Arabia	154.7	114.7	254.4
Singapore	12.2	70.9	94.5
United Arab Emirates	280.5	221.4	951.1
United Kingdom	50.8	7.5	24.0
Yemen	1.2	170.1	24.4
Total (incl. others)	5,478.7	9,500.9	9,079.5

* Data for 2007 were not available.

Source: UN, *International Trade Statistics Yearbook*.

Transport

RAILWAY TRAFFIC

	2007	2008	2009
Passengers carried ('000)	51	91	87
Passenger-km (million)	50	67	62
Freight carried ('000 metric tons)	1,091	1,033	907
Freight ton-km (million)	781	919	800

ROAD TRAFFIC
(motor vehicles in use)

	2000	2001	2002
Passenger cars	46,000	46,400	47,300
Commercial vehicles	60,500	61,800	62,500

Source: UN, *Statistical Yearbook*.

SHIPPING
Merchant Fleet
(registered at 31 December)

	2007	2008	2009
Number of vessels	19	19	18
Displacement (grt)	25,904	25,904	25,072

Source: IHS Fairplay, *World Fleet Statistics*.

International Sea-borne Freight Traffic
(estimates, '000 metric tons)

	1991	1992	1993
Goods loaded	1,290	1,387	1,543
Goods unloaded	3,800	4,200	4,300

Source: UN Economic Commission for Africa, *African Statistical Yearbook*.

CIVIL AVIATION
(traffic on scheduled services)

	2004	2005	2006
Kilometres flown (million)	8	8	9
Passengers carried ('000)	473	511	563
Passenger-km (million)	898	992	1,072
Total ton-km (million)	116	128	142

Source: UN, *Statistical Yearbook*.

2007: Passengers carried ('000) 598.2 (Source: World Bank, World Development Indicators database).

2008: Passengers carried ('000) 617.8 (Source: World Bank, World Development Indicators database).

Tourism

	2006	2007	2008
Foreign visitor arrivals	328,148	436,295	439,661
Tourism receipts (US $ million, excl. passenger transport)	167	262	331

Source: World Tourism Organization.

Communications Media

	2007	2008	2009
Telephones ('000 main lines in use)	345.2	366.2	370.4
Mobile cellular telephones ('000 subscribers)	8,218	11,992	15,340
Internet users ('000)	3,501.4	4,200.9	n.a.
Broadband subscribers ('000)	42.5	44.6	162.7

1996: Daily newspapers 5 (average circulation 737,000 copies).
1997: Radio receivers ('000 in use) 7,550.
1998: Non-daily newspapers 11 (average circulation 5,644,000); Periodicals 54 (average circulation 68,000 copies).
2000: Television receivers ('000 in use) 8,500.
2004: Daily newspapers 22; Non-daily newspapers 3.
2006: Personal computers 4,237,096 (107.1 per 1,000 persons).

Sources: UNESCO, *Statistical Yearbook*; UN, *Statistical Yearbook*; International Telecommunication Union.

Education

(2008/09 unless otherwise stated)

	Institutions*	Teachers	Males	Females	Total
Pre-primary	5,984	20,738	316,792	315,443	632,235
Primary	11,982	123,633	2,539,712	2,204,756	4,744,468
Secondary	3,512	82,665	992,446	845,010	1,837,456
Universities, etc.	n.a.	4,486†	n.a.	n.a.	200,538†

* Figures refer to 1998.
† Estimates for 2000.

Source: UNESCO Institute for Statistics.

Pupil-teacher ratio (primary education, UNESCO estimate): 38.4 in 2008/09 (Source: UNESCO Institute for Statistics).

Adult literacy rate (UNESCO estimates): 69.3% (males 79.0%; females 59.6%) in 2008 (Source: UNESCO Institute for Statistics).

Directory

The Government

HEAD OF STATE

President: Lt-Gen. OMAR HASSAN AHMAD AL-BASHIR (took power as Chairman of the Revolutionary Command Council for National Salvation (RCC) on 30 June 1989; appointed President by the RCC on 16 October 1993; elected President in March 1996; re-elected in December 2000 and in April 2010).
First Vice-President: Lt-Gen. SALVA KIIR MAYARDIT.
Second Vice-President: ALI OSMAN MUHAMMAD TAHA.

COUNCIL OF MINISTERS
(May 2011)

The Government is formed by members of the National Congress Party (NCP), the Sudan People's Liberation Movement (SPLM), the Democratic Unionist Party—Original (DUPO) and the United Democratic Salvation Front (UDSF).

Prime Minister: Lt-Gen. OMAR HASSAN AHMAD AL-BASHIR (NCP).
Minister of the Presidency: Maj.-Gen. BAKRI HASSAN SALIH (NCP).
Minister of Cabinet Affairs: (vacant).
Minister of Defence: Maj.-Gen. Eng. ABD AL-RAHIM MOHAMED HUSSEIN (NCP).
Minister of the Interior: IBRAHIM MAHMOOD HAMID (NCP).
Minister of Foreign Affairs: ALI AHMED KARTI (NCP).
Minister of Justice: MOHAMED BUSHARA DOUSA.
Minister of Finance and National Economy: ALI MAHMOOD ABD AL-RASOOL (NCP).
Minister of Human Resources Development: KAMAL ABD AL-LATIF (NCP).
Minister of Agriculture: ABD AL-HALIM ISMAIL AL-MUTAAFI.
Minister of Industry: AWAD AHMED AL-JAZ (NCP).
Minister of Guidance and Endowments: AZHARI AL-TIGANI AWAD AL-SAYID (NCP).

SUDAN

Minister of Information: Kamal Mohamed Obeid (NCP).
Minister of International Co-operation: Jalal Yousif al-Degair (DUPO).
Minister of Petroleum: Lual Achwel Deng (SPLM).
Minister of Higher Education and Scientific Research: Peter Adok Neyaba (SPLM).
Minister of General Education: Dr Farah Mustafa Abdalla (SPLM).
Minister of Irrigation and Water Resources: Eng. Kamal Ali Mohamed (NCP).
Minister of Electricity and Dams: Osama Abdalla Mohamed al-Hassan.
Minister of Science and Technology: Eissa Bushra Mohamed (NCP).
Minister of Culture: Al-Samawa'al Khalafalla al-Quraish.
Minister of Health: Abdalla Tiya Guma'a.
Minister of Welfare and Social Security: Amira al-Fadil Mohamed al-Fadil.
Minister of Youth and Sports: Haj Magid Siwar (NCP).
Minister of Transportation: Chol Ram Pang.
Minister of Investment: Prof. George Poreng Neombe (SPLM).
Minister of Foreign Trade: Elias Neyama Lel.
Minister of Minerals: Abd al-Bagi al-Gailani.
Minister of Antiquities, Tourism and Wildlife: Ahmed Babiker Nihar (NCP).
Minister of the Environment, Forestry and Urban Development: Joseph Malwal Dong (UDSF).
Minister of Roads and Bridges: Abd al-Wahab Mohamed Osaman.
Minister of Parliamentary Affairs: Halima Hassaballa al-Naeem.
Minister of Labour: Dak Dop Pishop.
Minister of Animal Resources and Fisheries: Faisal Hassan Ibrahim.
Minister of Humanitarian Affairs: Joseph Lual Achwel (SPLM).
Minister of Communications and Information Technology: Yahiya Abdalla Mohamed Hamad.

In addition, there is one presidential adviser and 42 Ministers of State.

GOVERNMENT OF SOUTHERN SUDAN
(May 2011)

President: Lt-Gen. Salva Kiir Mayardit.
Vice-President: Dr Riek Machar.
Minister of Cabinet Affairs: Kosti Manibe Ngai.
Minister of Peace and CPA Implementation: Pagan Amum.
Minister of SPLA and Veteran Affairs: Lt-Gen. Nhial Deng Nhial.
Minister of Regional Co-operation: Deng Alor.
Minister in the Office of the President: Dr Cirino Hitend Ofuho.
Minister of Legal Affairs and Constitutional Development: John Luyk Jok.
Minister of Internal Affairs: Maj.-Gen. Gier Cuang Aluong.
Minister of Parliamentary Affairs: Michael Makuei Lueth.
Minister of Finance and Economic Planning: David Deng Athorbei.
Minister of Investment: Gen. Oyay Deng Ajak.
Minister of Labour and Public Services: Awut Deng Acuil.
Minister of Information: Dr Barnaba Marial Benjamin.
Minister of Health: Dr Luka Tombekana Manoja.
Minister of Agriculture and Forestry: Dr Anne Itto Leonardo.
Minister of Roads and Transport: Anthony Lino Makana.
Minister of Education: Dr Michael Milli.
Minister of Commerce and Industry: Stephen Dhieu.
Minister of the Environment: Isaac Awan Maper.
Minister of Housing and Physical Planning: Jema Nunu Kumba.
Minister of Communications and Postal Services: Madut Biar Yel.
Minister of Energy and Mining: Garang Diing Akuong.
Minister of Gender, Child and Social Welfare: Agnes Kwaje Lauba.
Minister of Co-operatives and Rural Development: (vacant).
Minister of Humanitarian Affairs and Disaster Management: James Kok Ruea.
Minister of Irrigation and Water Resources: Paul Mayom Akec.
Minister of Higher Education, Research, Science and Technology: Joseph Ukel.
Minister of Wildlife Conservation and Tourism: (vacant).
Minister of Animal Resources and Fisheries: Nyalok Tiong Gatluak.
Minister of Human Resources Development: Mary Jervas Yak.
Minister of Youth, Sport and Recreation: Makuac Teny Yoh.
Minister of Culture and Heritage: Gabriel Changson Cheng.
Minister without Portfolio: Dr Priscilla Nyanyang.

MINISTRIES

Ministry of Agriculture: POB 285, al-Gamaa Ave, Khartoum; tel. (183) 780951; e-mail moafcc@sudanmail.net.
Ministry of Animal Resources and Fisheries: Khartoum.
Ministry of Antiquities, Tourism and Wildlife: POB 2424, Khartoum; tel. (183) 471329; fax (183) 471437; e-mail admin@sudan-tourism.com.
Ministry of Cabinet Affairs: POB 931, Khartoum; tel. (183) 784205; fax (183) 771331; e-mail info@sudan.gov.sd; internet www.sudan.gov.sd/en.
Ministry of Communications and Information Technology: Khartoum.
Ministry of Culture: Khartoum.
Ministry of Defence: POB 371, Khartoum; tel. (183) 774910.
Ministry of Electricity and Dams: Khartoum.
Ministry of the Environment and Urban Development: POB 300, Khartoum; tel. (183) 462604.
Ministry of Finance and National Economy: POB 735, Khartoum; tel. (183) 777563; fax (183) 775630; e-mail info@mof-sudan.net; internet mof-sudan.com.
Ministry of Foreign Affairs: POB 873, Khartoum; tel. (183) 773101; fax (183) 772941; e-mail ministry@mfa.gov.sd; internet www.sudanmfa.com.
Ministry of Foreign Trade: Khartoum; tel. (183) 772793; fax (183) 773950.
Ministry of General Education: Khartoum; tel. (183) 772808; e-mail moe-sd@moe-sd.com; internet www.moe-sd.com.
Ministry of Guidance and Endowments: Khartoum.
Ministry of Health: POB 303, Khartoum; tel. (183) 773000; e-mail inhsd@sudanet.net; internet www.fmoh.gov.sd.
Ministry of Higher Education and Scientific Research: POB 2081, Khartoum; tel. (183) 779312; fax (183) 783394; e-mail srp@mohe.gov.sd; internet mohe.gov.sd.
Minister of Human Resources Development: Khartoum.
Ministry of Humanitarian Affairs: POB 1976, Khartoum; tel. (183) 780675; e-mail human@mha.gov.sd; internet www.mha.gov.sd.
Ministry of Industry: POB 2184, Khartoum; tel. (183) 777830.
Ministry of Information: Khartoum.
Ministry of the Interior: POB 2793, Khartoum; tel. (183) 776554.
Ministry of International Co-operation: POB 2092, Khartoum; tel. (183) 772169; fax (183) 780115; e-mail info@micsudan.com; internet www.micsudan.com.
Ministry of Investment: POB 6286, Khartoum; tel. (183) 787194; fax (183) 787199; internet www.sudaninvest.gov.sd.
Ministry of Irrigation and Water Resources: POB 878, Khartoum; tel. (183) 783221; fax (183) 773388; e-mail oehamad@hotmail.com.
Ministry of Justice: POB 302, al-Nil Ave, Khartoum; tel. (183) 774842; fax (183) 771479.
Ministry of Labour: Khartoum.
Ministry of Minerals: POB 2087, Khartoum; tel. (183) 775595; fax (183) 775428.
Ministry of Parliamentary Affairs: Khartoum.
Ministry of Petroleum: Khartoum.
Ministry of Presidential Affairs: Khartoum.
Ministry of Roads and Bridges: POB 300, Khartoum; tel. (183) 781629; fax (183) 780507.
Ministry of Science and Technology: Khartoum.
Ministry of Transportation: Khartoum.
Ministry of Welfare and Social Security: Khartoum.
Ministry of Youth and Sports: Khartoum.

STATE GOVERNORS
(May 2011)

Al-Buhayrat: Lt-Gen. Chol Tong Maya (SPLM).

SUDAN

Bahr al-Jabal: Maj.-Gen.(retd) CLEMENT WANI KONGA (SPLM).
Blue Nile: MALIK AGAR EYARE (SPLM).
Eastern Equatoria: LOUIS LOBONG LOJORE (SPLM).
Gadarif: KARAM ALLAH ABBAS (NCP).
Gezira: Dr AL-ZUBEIR BASHIR TAHA (NCP).
Jonglei: KUOL MANYANG JUUK (SPLM).
Kassala: MOHAMMED YUSUF ADAM BESHIR (NCP).
Khartoum: Dr ABD AL-RAHMAN AL-KHIDIR (NCP).
Northern: FETHI KHALIL MOHAMMED (NCP).
Northern Bahr al-Ghazal: PAUL MALONG AWAN ANEI (SPLM).
Northern Darfur: OSMAN MUHAMMAD YUSUF KIBIR (NCP).
Northern Kordofan: MOATASIM MIRGHANI ZAKI EL-DIN (NCP).
Red Sea: MOHMED TAHEIR AILA (NCP).
River Nile: ABDULLAH MOHAMMED (NCP).
Sennar: AHMED ABBAS (NCP).
Southern Darfur: ABD AL-HAMID KASHA (NCP).
Southern Kordofan: AHMED HAROUN (NCP).
Upper Nile: SIMON KON FUJ (SPLM).
Wahdah: Brig. TABAN DENG GAI (SPLM).
Warab: NYANDENG MALEK DELIECH (SPLM).
Western Bahr al-Ghazal: RIZIK HASSAN ZACHARIAH (SPLM).
Western Darfur: JAAFER ABD AL-HAKAM (NCP).
Western Equatoria: Col BANGASI JOSEPH BAKOSORO (Ind.).
White Nile: YUSUF AHMED EL-SHANBALY.

President and Legislature

PRESIDENT
Election, 11–15 April 2010

Candidate	Votes	% of votes
Omar Hassan Ahmad al-Bashir (National Congress Party)	6,901,694	68.24
Yasir Saeed Arman (Sudan People's Liberation Movement)	2,193,826	21.69
Abdullah Deng Nhial Ayom (Popular Congress Party)	396,139	3.92
Hatim as-Sir Ali Sikunji (Democratic Unionist Party)	195,668	1.93
Others	426,983	4.22
Total	10,114,310	100.00

MAJLIS WATANI
(National Assembly)

Speaker: AHMAD IBRAHIM AL-TAHIR.
Deputy Speakers: ANGELO BEDA, ABDALLAH AL-HARDELLO.
Election, 11–15 April 2010, provisional results

Party	A	B	C	Total
National Congress Party	180	50	82	312
Sudan People's Liberation Movement	56	17	26	99
Popular Congress Party	—	1	3	4
United Democratic Party	4	—	—	4
Independents	3	—	—	3
Umma Federal Party	2	—	1	3
Sudan People's Liberation Movement—Democratic Change	2	—	—	2
Umma Reform and Renewal Party	2	—	—	2
Democratic Unionist Party—Original	1	—	—	1
Muslim Brotherhood	1	—	—	1
Umma National Party	1	—	—	1
Total	252†	68	112	432†

* There are 450 members of the Majlis Watani of which 270 (A) are directly elected in single seat constituencies; 68 'party members' (B) are elected on the basis of proportional representation at the state level from separate and closed party lists; and a further 112 women members (C) are elected on the basis of proportional representation at the state level from separate and closed party lists.
† Voting in 16 constituencies was postponed, the result in one seat was not released and one seat was declared vacant.

President and Legislature of Southern Sudan

PRESIDENT
Election, 11–15 April 2010

Candidate	Votes	% of votes
Lt-Gen. Salva Kiir Mayardit (Sudan People's Liberation Movement)	2,616,613	92.99
Dr Lam Akol Ajawin (Sudan People's Liberation Movement—Democratic Change)	197,217	7.01
Total	2,813,830	100.00

LEGISLATIVE ASSEMBLY

Speaker: JAMES WANI IQQA.
Election 11–15 April 2010

Party	A	B	C	Total
Sudan People's Liberation Movement	93	25	42	160
Independents	6	—	—	6
Sudan People's Liberation Movement—Democratic Change	2	—	1	3
National Congress Party	1	—	—	1
Total	102	25	43	170

* There are 170 members of the Legislative Assembly of which 102 (A) are directly elected in single seat constituencies; 25 'party members' (B) are elected on the basis of proportional representation at the state level from separate and closed party lists; and a further 43 women members (C) are elected on the basis of proportional representation at the state level from separate and closed party lists.

Election Commission

National Elections Commission (NEC): Khartoum; tel. (183) 520282; e-mail info@nec.org.sd; internet www.nec.org.sd; Chairman MAULANA ABEL ALIER.

Political Organizations

The right to political association, subject to compliance with the law, was guaranteed in the Constitution approved by referendum in June 1998. (All political organizations had been banned following the military coup of 30 June 1989.) The registration of parties began in January 1999. The following parties are among the most active:

Communist Party of Sudan (CPS): Khartoum; e-mail cpsudan@gmail.com; internet www.midan.net; f. 1946; Gen. Sec. MOHAMED IBRAHIM NUGUD MUNAWAR.

Democratic Unionist Party—Original (DUPO): Khartoum; Leader MUHAMMAD OSMAN AL-MIRGHANI; participates in National Democratic Alliance (see below).

Free Sudanese National Party (FSNP): Khartoum; Chair. Fr PHILIP ABBAS GHABBUSH.

Independent Democrats: Khartoum; Leader AS-SAMAWITT HUSAYN OSMAN MANSUR.

Islamic-Christian Solidarity: Khartoum; Founder HATIM ABDULLAH AL-ZAKI HUSAYN.

Islamic Revival Movement: Khartoum; Founder SIDDIQ AL-HAJ AL-SIDDIQ.

Islamic Socialist Party: Khartoum; Leader SALAH AL-MUSBAH.

Islamic Ummah Party: Khartoum; Chair. WALI AL-DIN AL-HADI AL-MAHDI.

Justice Party: Khartoum; f. 2002 by fmr members of the NCP.

Moderate Trend Party: Khartoum; Leader MAHMUD JIHA.

Muslim Brotherhood: Khartoum; Islamist fundamentalist; Leader Dr HABIR NUR AL-DIN.

National Congress Party (NCP): Khartoum; successor to National Islamic Front; Pres. Lt-Gen. OMAR HASSAN AHMAD AL-BASHIR; Sec.-Gen. Prof. IBRAHIM AHMAD UMAR.

SUDAN

National Democratic Party: Khartoum; f. 2002 following merger of the Union of Nationalistic Forces, the Communist Party and the National Solidarity Party.

New National Democratic: Leader MUNEER SHEIKH EL-DIN JALAB.

Nile Valley Conference: Khartoum; Founder Lt-Gen. (retd) UMAR ZARUQ.

Popular Congress Party (PCP): Khartoum; f. 2000; Founder HASSAN AT-TURABI.

Popular Masses' Alliance: Khartoum; Founder FAYSAL MUHMAD HUSAYN.

Socialist Popular Party: Khartoum; Founder SAYYID KHALIFAH IDRIS HABBANI.

Sudan Green Party: Khartoum; Founder Prof. ZAKARAIA BASHIR IMAM.

Sudan National Alliance (SNA): f. 1994; Leader ABDEL AZIZ KHALID.

Sudan People's Liberation Movement (SPLM): Khartoum; e-mail info@splmtoday.com; internet www.splmtoday.com; Leader Lt-Gen. SALVA KIIR MAYARDIT; Sec.-Gen. PAGAN AMUM.

Sudan People's Liberation Movement—Democratic Change (SPLM—DC): Juba; f. 2009; Leader Dr LAM AKOL AJAWIN.

Sudanese Central Movement: Khartoum; Founder Dr MUHAMMAD ABU AL-QASIM HAJ HAMAD.

Sudanese Initiative Party: Khartoum; Leader J'AFAR KARAR.

Sudanese National Party (SNP): Khartoum; Leader HASAN AL-MAHI; participates in the National Democratic Alliance (see below).

Sudanese Socialist Democratic Union (SSDU): Leader FATIMA AHMED ABDEL MAHMOUD MOHAMED.

Umma National Party (UNP): internet www.umma.org; f. 1945; Mahdist party based on the Koran and Islamic traditions; Chair. Dr UMAR NUR AL-DA'IM; Leader SADIQ AL-MAHDI; withdrew from the National Democratic Alliance (see below) in March 2000.

Umma Reform and Renewal Party: Khartoum; f. 2002; Leader MUBARAK AL-FADIL.

Union of Sudan African Parties (USAP): f. 1987; Chair. JOSEPH OKELLO; Sec.-Gen. Prof. AJANG BIOR.

United Democratic Party.

United Democratic Salvation Front (UDSF): Khartoum; political wing of the Sudan People's Defence Force; Chair. Dr GABRIEL CHANGSON CHANG.

A number of opposition movements are grouped together in the Asmara-based **National Democratic Alliance (NDA)** (Chair. OSMAN AL-MIRGHANI; Sec.-Gen. JOSEPH OKELU). These include the **Beja Congress** (Sec.-Gen. Amna Dirar), the **Legitimate Command (LC)**, the **Sudan Alliance Forces (SAF)** (f. 1994; Commdr-in-Chief Brig. ABD AL-AZIZ KHALID OSMAN), and the **Sudan Federal Democratic Alliance (SFDA)** (f. 1994; advocates a decentralized, federal structure for Sudan; Chair. AHMAD DREIGE).

In 2003 two rebel groups, the **Sudan Liberation Movement (SLM)** (Leader MINNI ARKUA MINAWI) and the **Justice and Equality Movement (JEM)** (Chair. Dr KHALIL IBRAHIM MOHAMED), began an armed rebellion in the Darfur region of western Sudan.

At a meeting convened in Asmara, Eritrea, in 2006 the **National Redemption Front (NRF)** was formed by the leader of the JEM, Dr KHALIL IBRAHIM MOHAMED, his counterpart, AHMAD DREIGE of the SFDA, and KHAMIS ABDALLA ABAKAR, the former Deputy Chairman of Abd al-Wahid Muhammad al-Nur's faction of the SLM, and leader of the **Group of 19 (G-19)**. The G-19 emerged as the principal faction of the NRF, originally formed as a group of commanders who defected from al-Nur's faction during the Abuja, Nigeria, negotiations. In December 2006 a group of Arab rebels, opposed to the Sudanese army and the *Janjaweed*, formed an alliance called the **Popular Forces Troops (PFT)**.

Diplomatic Representation

EMBASSIES IN SUDAN

Afghanistan: Madinatol Riyadh, Shareol Moshtal Sq. 10, House No. 81, Khartoum; tel. (183) 221852; fax (183) 222059; e-mail afembsudan@hotmail.com; Chargé d'affaires a.i. KHALILURRAHMAN HANANI.

Algeria: Blvd El-Mechtel Eriad, POB 80, Khartoum; tel. (183) 234773; fax (183) 224190; Ambassador MUHAMMAD YARKI.

Brazil: Kamel Magzob St, House No. 110, Block 21, al-Amarat, POB 8255, Riyadh, 12217 Khartoum; tel. (183) 217079; fax (183) 217049; e-mail ambassador@brasilemb-sd.org; Ambassador ANTONIO CARLOS DO NASCIMENTO PEDRO.

Bulgaria: St 31, House No. 9, Block 10, al-Amarat, POB 1690, 11111 Khartoum; tel. (183) 560106; fax (183) 560107; e-mail bgembsdn@yahoo.co.uk; Chargé d'affaires a.i. SVILEN BOZHANOV.

Chad: St 57, al-Amarat, Khartoum; tel. (183) 471612; Ambassador MAHAMAT ABDERAHIM ACYL.

China, People's Republic: POB 1425, Khartoum; tel. (183) 272730; fax (183) 271138; e-mail ssddssgg@yahoo.com.cn; Ambassador LI CHENGWEN.

Congo, Democratic Republic: St 13, Block 12 CE, New Extension, 23, POB 4195, Khartoum; tel. (183) 471125; Chargé d'affaires a.i. BAWAN MUZURI.

Egypt: University St, POB 1126, Khartoum; tel. (183) 777646; fax (183) 778741; e-mail sphinx-egysud@yahoo.com; Ambassador ABDUL-GHAFFAR AL-DEEB.

Eritrea: St 39, House No. 26, POB 1618, Khartoum 2; tel. (183) 483834; fax (183) 483835; e-mail erena@sudanet.net; Ambassador Gen. ISSA AHMED ISSA.

Ethiopia: Plot No. 4, Block 384BC, POB 844, Khartoum; tel. (183) 471379; fax (183) 471141; e-mail eekrt@hotmail.com; Ambassador ATO ALI ABDO.

France: al-Amarat, St 13, Plot No. 11, Block 12, POB 377, 11111 Khartoum; tel. (183) 471082; fax (183) 465928; e-mail cad.khartoum-amba@diplomatie.gouv.fr; internet www.ambafrance-sd.org; Ambassador PATRICK NICOLOSO.

Germany: 53 Baladia St, Block No. 8D, Plot 2, POB 970, Khartoum; tel. (183) 777990; fax (183) 777622; e-mail reg1@khar.auswaertiges-amt.de; internet www.khartum.diplo.de; Ambassador RAINER EBERLE.

Holy See: Kafouri Belgravia, POB 623, Khartoum (Apostolic Nunciature); tel. (183) 330037; fax (183) 330692; e-mail kanuap@yahoo.it; Apostolic Nuncio Most Rev. LEO BOCCARDI (Titular Archbishop of Bitetto).

India: 61 Africa Rd, POB 707, Khartoum II; tel. (183) 574001; fax (183) 574050; e-mail ambassador@indembsdn.com; internet www.indembsdn.com; Ambassador AVANINDRA KUMAR PANDEY.

Indonesia: St 60, 84, Block 12, ar-Riyadh, POB 13374, Khartoum; tel. (183) 225106; fax (183) 225528; e-mail kbri_khartoum@sudanmail.com; Ambassador Dr M. A. SUJATMIKO.

Iran: Sq. 15, House No. 4, Mogran, POB 10229, Khartoum; tel. (183) 781490; fax (183) 778668; e-mail iransud@yahoo.com; Ambassador REZA AMERI.

Iraq: Sharia ash-Shareef al-Hindi, POB 1969, Khartoum; tel. (183) 271867; fax (183) 271855; e-mail krtemb@iraqmofamail.net; Ambassador Dr SALEH HUSSEIN ALI.

Italy: St 39, Block 61, POB 793, Khartoum; tel. (183) 471615; fax (183) 471217; e-mail ambasciata.khartoum@esteri.it; internet www.ambkhartoum.esteri.it; Ambassador ROBERTO CANTONE.

Japan: St 43, House No. 67, POB 1649, Khartoum; tel. (183) 471601; fax (183) 471600; internet www.sdn.emb-japan.go.jp; Ambassador AKINORI WADA.

Jordan: St 33, House No. 13, POB 1379, Khartoum; tel. (183) 483125; fax (183) 471038; Ambassador MUNTHER QUBAAH.

Kenya: Plot No. 516, Block 1 West Giraif, POB 8242, Khartoum; tel. (155) 772800; fax (155) 772802; e-mail kenemb@yahoo.com; Ambassador ROBERT MUTUA NGESU.

Korea, Republic: House No. 2, St 1, New Extension, POB 2414, Khartoum; tel. (183) 451136; fax (183) 452822; e-mail ssudan@mofat.go.kr; Ambassador DONG EOK KIM.

Kuwait: Africa Ave, near the Tennis Club, POB 1457, Khartoum; tel. (183) 781525; Ambassador MUNTHIR BADR SALMAN.

Lebanon: St 5, Al-Amarat, Khartoum; tel. (183) 461320; fax (113) 461246; e-mail amliban@hotmail.com; Ambassador SHARBEL STEPHAN.

Libya: 50 Africa Rd, POB 2091, Khartoum; Secretary of People's Bureau (vacant).

Malaysia: St 3, Block 2, al-Amarat, POB 11668, Khartoum; tel. (183) 482763; fax (183) 482762; e-mail malkhtoum@kln.gov.my; internet www.kln.gov.my/web/sdn_khartoum/home; Chargé d'affaires a.i. DEDDY FAISAL BIN AHMAD SALLEH.

Morocco: St 19, 32, New Extension, POB 2042, Khartoum; tel. (183) 473068; fax (183) 471053; e-mail sifmasoud@sudan.mail.net; Ambassador MUHAMMAD MAA EL-AININE.

Netherlands: St 47, House No. 76, POB 391, Khartoum; tel. (183) 471200; fax (183) 480304; e-mail kha@minbuza.nl; internet www.mfa.nl/afrika/sudan/ambassade_khartoem; Ambassador N. W. M. BRAAKHUIS.

Nigeria: St 17, Sharia al-Mek Nimr, POB 1538, Khartoum; tel. (183) 779120; fax (183) 771491; Ambassador SALIHU AHMED-SAMBO.

SUDAN

Norway: St 49, House No. 63, POB 13096, Khartoum; tel. (183) 578336; fax (183) 577180; e-mail emb.khartoum@mfa.no; internet www.norway-sudan.org; Ambassador SVEIN SEVJE.

Oman: St 1, New Extension, POB 2839, Khartoum; tel. (183) 471606; fax (183) 471017; Ambassador ABDULLAH BIN-RASHID BIN-ALI AL-MEDELWI.

Pakistan: Dr Mehmood Sharif St, House No. 78, Block 25, POB 1178, Khartoum; tel. (183) 265599; fax (183) 273777; e-mail embkhartoum@yahoo.com; Ambassador MUHAMMAD ALAM BROHI.

Qatar: Elmanshia Block 92H, POB 223, Khartoum; tel. (183) 261113; fax (183) 261116; e-mail qatarembkht@yahoo.com; Ambassador ALI HASSAN ABDULLAH AL-HAMADI.

Romania: Kassala Rd, Plot No. 172–173, Kafouri Area, POB 1494, Khartoum North; tel. (185) 338114; fax (185) 341497; e-mail ambro_khartoum@hotmail.com; Ambassador Dr EMIL GHITULESCU.

Russia: A10 St, B1, New Extension, POB 1161, Khartoum; tel. (183) 471042; fax (183) 471239; e-mail rfsudan@hotmail.com; Ambassador ENVARBIK M. FAZELIYANOV.

Rwanda: Al-Amarat, St 57, House No. 4, Block 10. POB 243, Khartoum; tel. (183) 595848; fax (183) 595847; e-mail rwaembassy@gmail.com; internet www.sudan.embassy.gov.rw; Chargé d'affaires a.i. JOSEPH RUTABANA.

Saudi Arabia: St 11, New Extension, Khartoum; tel. (183) 741938; Ambassador MOHAMMED IBN ABAS AL-KALABI.

Somalia: St 23–25, New Extension, POB 1857, Khartoum; tel. (183) 744800; Ambassador Prof. MAHDI ABUKAR.

South Africa: St 11, House No. 16, Block B9, al-Amarat, POB 12137, Khartoum; tel. (183) 585301; fax (183) 585082; e-mail khartoum@foreign.gov.za; Ambassador Dr MANELISI GENGE.

Switzerland: St 15, House No. 7, Amarat, POB 1707, Khartoum; tel. (183) 471010; fax (183) 472804; e-mail kha.vertretung@eda.admin.ch; internet www.eda.admin.ch/khartoum; Ambassador ANDREJ MOTYL.

Syria: St 3, New Extension, POB 1139, Khartoum; tel. (183) 471152; fax (183) 471066; Ambassador HABIB ALI ABBAS.

Tunisia: St 15, 35, al-Amarat, Khartoum; tel. (183) 487947; fax (183) 487950; e-mail at_khartoum@yahoo.fr; Ambassador SAÏD NACEUR BENROMDHANE.

Turkey: Baladia St, House No. 21, Block 8H, POB 771, Khartoum; tel. (183) 794215; fax (183) 794218; e-mail hartumbe@gmail.com; Ambassador (vacant).

Uganda: POB 2676, Khartoum; tel. (183) 158571; fax (183) 797868; e-mail ugembkht@hotmail.com; Ambassador BETTY AKECH.

United Arab Emirates: St 3, New Extension, POB 1225, Khartoum; tel. (183) 744476; e-mail uaembassy@sudanmail.net; Ambassador HASSAN AHMED SULIEMAN AL-SHIHI.

United Kingdom: St 10, off Baladia St, POB 801, Khartoum; tel. (183) 777105; fax (183) 776457; e-mail media.khartoum@fco.gov.uk; internet www.britishembassy.gov.uk/sudan; Ambassador Dame Dr ROSALIND MARY MARSDEN.

USA: Kilo 10, Soba, off Wad Medani Highway, POB 699, Khartoum; tel. 1-870-2-2000; internet sudan.usembassy.gov; Chargé d'affaires ROBERT E. WHITEHEAD.

Yemen: St 11, New Extension, POB 1010, Khartoum; tel. (183) 743918; Ambassador SALAH AL-ANSI.

Judicial System

In September 1983 President Nimeri replaced all existing laws with Islamic (*Shari'a*) law. However, following the coup in April 1985, the *Shari'a* courts were abolished, and it was announced that the previous system of criminal courts was to be revived. In 1987 a new legal code, based on a 'Sudanese legal heritage', was introduced. Islamic law was reintroduced in March 1991, but was not applied in the southern states of Equatoria, Bahr al-Ghazal and Upper Nile.

Chief Justice: GALAL EL-DIN MUHAMMAD OSMAN.

Religion

The majority of the northern Sudanese population are Muslims, while in the south the population are principally Christians or animists.

ISLAM

Islam is the state religion. Sudanese Islam has a strong Sufi element, and is estimated to have more than 15m. adherents.

CHRISTIANITY

Sudan Council of Churches: Inter-Church House, St 35, New Extension, POB 469, Khartoum; tel. (183) 742859; f. 1967; 12 mem. churches; Chair. Most Rev. PAOLINO LUKUDU LORO (Roman Catholic Archbishop of Juba); Gen. Sec. Rev. CLEMENT H. JANDA.

Roman Catholic Church

Latin Rite

Sudan comprises two archdioceses and seven dioceses. Roman Catholics represented about 12% of the total population.

Sudan Catholic Bishops' Conference
General Secretariat, POB 6011, Khartoum; tel. (183) 225075. f. 1971; Pres. Mgr RUDOLF DENG MAJAK (Bishop of Wau); Sec.-Gen. JOHN DINGI MARTIN.

Archbishop of Juba: Most Rev. PAOLINO LUKUDU LORO, Catholic Church, POB 32, Juba, Equatoria State; tel. 820303; fax 820755; e-mail archbishopofjuba@hotmail.com.

Archbishop of Khartoum: Cardinal GABRIEL ZUBEIR WAKO, Catholic Church, POB 49, Khartoum; tel. (183) 782174; fax (183) 783518; e-mail taban_roko@yahoo.com.uk.

Maronite Rite

Maronite Church in Sudan: POB 244, Khartoum; Rev. Fr YOUSEPH NEAMA.

Melkite Rite

Patriarchal Vicariate of Egypt and Sudan: Greek Melkite Catholic Patriarchate, 16 Sharia Daher, 11271 Cairo, Egypt; tel. (2) 5905790; fax (2) 5935398; e-mail grecmelkitecath_egy@hotmail.com; General Patriarchal Vicar in Egypt and Sudan Mgr (JOSEPH) JULES ZEREY (Titular Archbishop of Damietta); Patriarchal Vicar in Sudan Mgr Exarkhos GEORGE BANNA; POB 766, Khartoum; tel. (183) 777910.

Syrian Rite

Syrian Church in Sudan: Under the jurisdiction of the Patriarch of Antioch; Protosyncellus Rt Rev. JOSEPH-CLÉMENT HANNOUCHE (Bishop of Cairo).

Orthodox Churches

Coptic Orthodox Church

Metropolitan of Khartoum, Southern Sudan and Uganda: Rt Rev. ANBA DANIAL, POB 4, Khartoum; tel. (183) 770646; fax (183) 785646; e-mail metaous@email-sudan.net.

Bishop of Atbara, Omdurman and Northern Sudan: Rt Rev. ANBA SARABAMON, POB 628, Omdurman; tel. (183) 550423; fax (183) 556973.

Greek Orthodox Church

Metropolitan of Nubia: POB 47, Khartoum; tel. (183) 772973; Archbishop DIONYSSIOS HADZIVASSILIOU.

The Ethiopian Orthodox Church is also active.

The Anglican Communion

Anglicans are adherents of the (Episcopal) Church of the Province of the Sudan. The Province, with 24 dioceses and about 1m. adherents, was established in 1976.

Archbishop in Sudan and Bishop of Juba: Most Rev. DANIEL DENG BUL YAK, ECS Liaison Office, POB 604, Khartoum; tel. (11) 485720; fax (11) 485717; e-mail ecsprovince@hotmail.com.

Other Christian Churches

Evangelical Church: POB 57, Khartoum; c. 1,500 mems; administers schools, literature centre and training centre; Chair. Rev. RADI ELIAS.

Presbyterian Church: POB 40, Malakal; autonomous since 1956; 67,000 mems (1985); Gen. Sec. Rev. THOMAS MALUIT.

The Africa Inland Church, the Sudan Interior Church and the Sudanese Church of Christ are also active.

The Press

DAILIES

Abbar al-Youm: Khartoum; tel. (183) 779396; daily; Editor AHMED AL-BALAL AL-TAYEB.

SUDAN

Al-Anbaa: Khartoum; tel. (183) 466523; f. 1998; Editor-in-Chief NAJIB ADAM QAMAR AL-DIN.

Al-Isteqlal: Juba; f. 2011; second Arabic language daily in South Sudan; Man. Editor GAMAL DALMAN.

Al-Mussir: Juba; f. 2011; first Arabic language daily in South Sudan.

Al-Nasr: Khartoum; tel. (183) 772494; Editor Col YOUNIS MAHMOUD.

Al-Rai al-Akhar: Khartoum; tel. (183) 777934; daily; Editor MOHI AL-DIN TITTAWI.

Al-Rai al-Amm: Khartoum; tel. (183) 778182; fax (183) 772176; e-mail info@rayaam.net; internet www.rayaam.net; daily; Editor SALAH MUHAMMAD IBRAHIM.

Al-Wan: Khartoum; tel. (183) 775036; e-mail alwaan@cybergates.net; daily; independent; pro-Govt; Editor HOUSSEN KHOGALI.

The Citizen: Hai Amarat, Airport Road, Juba; tel. 908760789 (mobile); e-mail thecitizen2006@yahoo.com; f. 2005; Editor-in-Chief NHIAL BOL.

Khartoum Monitor: St 61, New Extension, Khartoum; e-mail khartoummonitor@hotmail.com; Chair. and Editor ALFRED TABAN; Man. Editor WILLIAM EZEKIEL.

Sudan Mirror: POB 59163, 00200 Nairobi, Kenya; tel. and fax (20) 3876439; e-mail daneiffe@gmail.com; internet www.sudanmirror.co.ke; f. 2003; Dir DANIEL EIFFE.

Sudan Standard: Ministry of Information and Communication, Khartoum; daily; English.

PERIODICALS

Al-Guwwat al-Musallaha (The Armed Forces): Khartoum; f. 1969; publs a weekly newspaper and monthly magazine for the armed forces; Editor-in-Chief Maj. MAHMOUD GALANDER; circ. 7,500.

New Horizon: POB 2651, Khartoum; tel. (183) 777913; f. 1976; publ. by the Sudan House for Printing and Publishing; weekly; English; political and economic affairs, devt, home and international news; Editor AL-SIR HASSAN FADL; circ. 7,000.

Sudanow: POB 2651, Khartoum; tel. (183) 777913; f. 1976; publ. by the Sudan House for Printing and Publishing; monthly; English; political and economic affairs, arts, social affairs and diversions; Editor-in-Chief AHMED KAMAL ED-DIN; circ. 10,000.

NEWS AGENCIES

Sudan News Agency (SUNA): Sharia al-Gamhouria, POB 1506, Khartoum; tel. (183) 775770; e-mail suna@sudanet.net; internet www.suna-sd.net; Dir-Gen. ALI ABD AL-RAHMAN AL-NUMAYRI.

Sudanese Press Agency: Khartoum; f. 1985; owned by journalists.

Publishers

Ahmad Abd ar-Rahman al-Tikeine: POB 299, Port Sudan.

Al-Ayyam Press Co Ltd: Aboulela Bldg, POB 363, United Nations Sq., Khartoum; f. 1953; general fiction and non-fiction, arts, poetry, reference, newspapers, magazines; Man. Dir BESHIR MUHAMMAD SAID.

Al-Sahafa Publishing and Printing House: POB 1228, Khartoum; f. 1961; newspapers, pamphlets, fiction and govt publs.

Al-Salam Co Ltd: POB 944, Khartoum.

Claudios S. Fellas: POB 641, Khartoum.

Khartoum University Press: POB 321, Khartoum; tel. (183) 776653; f. 1964; academic, general and educational in Arabic and English; Man. Dir ALI EL-MAK.

GOVERNMENT PUBLISHING HOUSE

El-Asma Printing Press: POB 38, Khartoum.

Broadcasting and Communications

TELECOMMUNICATIONS

Canar Telecommunication (Canartel): Al-Qibla Centre, Block 37, cnr Al-Sahafa and Madani Rds, POB 8182, Khartoum; tel. (15) 5550000; fax (15) 5550055; e-mail support@canar.sd; internet www.canar.sd; f. 2005; operates fixed-line telephone and internet services; CEO ALI BIN-JARSH.

Ministry of Information and Communication: Khartoum; regulatory body; Sec.-Gen. Eng. AWAD E. WIDAA.

MTN-Sudan: 264 Garden City, POB 34611111, Khartoum; tel. (92) 1111111; internet www.mtn.sd; f. 2005; mobile cellular telephone provider; CEO HASSAN JABER; 1.4m. subscribers (2007).

Posts and Telegraphs Public Corpn: Khartoum; tel. (183) 770000; fax (183) 772888; e-mail sudanpost@maktoob.com; regulatory body; Dir-Gen. AHMAD AL-TIJANI ALALLIM.

Sudan Telecom Co (SUDATEL): Sudatel Tower, POB 11155, Khartoum; tel. (183) 797400; fax (183) 782322; e-mail info@sudatel.net; internet www.sudatel.sd; f. 1993; service provider for Sudan; Chair. TAREK HASSAN SHALAB; CEO IMAD ADDIN HUSSIEN AHMED.

Zain: Khartoum; tel. 91230000; e-mail info@sd.zain.com; internet www.sd.zain.com; f. 1997 as MobiTel; name changed as above in 2007; provides mobile cellular telephone services; Man. Dir ELFATIH M. ERWA.

BROADCASTING

Radio

South Sudan Radio: Juba; Dir-Gen. AROP BAGAT TINGLOTH.

Sudan Radio: POB 572, Omdurman; tel. (187) 559315; fax (187) 560566; e-mail info@sudanradio.info; internet www.sudanradio.info; f. 1940; state-controlled service broadcasting daily in Arabic, English, French and Swahili; Dir-Gen. MUTASIM FADUL USUD.

Sudan Radio Service (SRS): Umeme Plaza, Old Naivasha Rd, off Ngong Rd, Dagoretti, POB 4392, 00100 Nairobi, Kenya; tel. (20) 3870906; fax (20) 3876520; e-mail srs@sudanradio.org; internet www.sudanradio.org; f. 2003; by the Education Development Center with support from the United States Agency for International Development; broadcasts in 10 languages including Dinka, Bari, Nuer, Zande, Shilluk, Arabic, Juba-Arabic and English; Chief of Party JON NEWSTROM.

Voice of Sudan: e-mail informationsec@ndasudan.org; active since 1995; run by the National Democratic Alliance; Arabic and English.

Television

An earth satellite station operated on 36 channels at Umm Haraz has much improved Sudan's telecommunications links. A nation-wide satellite network is being established with 14 earth stations in the provinces. There are regional stations at Gezira (Central Region) and Atbara (Northern Region).

South Sudan TV: Juba; Dir-Gen. AROP BAGAT TINGLOTH.

Sudan Television: POB 1094, Omdurman; tel. (15) 550022; internet www.sudantv.net; f. 1962; state-controlled; 60 hours of programmes per week; Head of Directorate HADID AL-SIRA.

Finance

(cap. = capital; res = reserves; dep. = deposits; m. = million; brs = branches; amounts in new Sudanese pounds, unless otherwise indicated)

BANKING

All domestic banks are controlled by the Bank of Sudan. Foreign banks were permitted to resume operations in 1976. In December 1985 the Government banned the establishment of any further banks. It was announced in December 1990 that Sudan's banking system was to be reorganized to accord with Islamic principles. In May 2000 the Bank of Sudan issued new policy guidelines under which Sudan's banks were to merge into six banking groups to improve their financial strength and international competitiveness; plans for implementing this merger were ongoing in 2010. In 2009 there were a total of 38 banks in Sudan.

Central Bank

Bank of Sudan: Gamhoria St, POB 313, Khartoum; tel. (183) 782246; fax (183) 787226; e-mail sudanbank@sudanmail.net; internet www.bankofsudan.org; f. 1960; bank of issue; cap. and res 274.2m., dep. 8,695.2m. (Dec. 2009); Gov. MOHAMMAD KHAIR AL-ZUBAIR; 13 brs.

Commercial Banks

Al-Baraka Bank: Baraka Tower, Zubeir Pasha St, POB 3583, Khartoum; tel. (183) 785810; fax (183) 778948; e-mail khairy@albarakasudan.com; internet www.albaraka.com.sd; f. 1984; 87.8% owned by Al-Baraka Banking Group (Bahrain); investment and export promotion; cap. SDD 3,353.6m., res SDD 4,042.7m., dep. SDD 37,220.2m. (Dec. 2006); Chair. OSMAN AHMED SULIMAN; Gen. Man. ABDALLAH KHAIRY HAMID; 24 brs.

Al-Shamal Islamic Bank: Al-Shamal Islamic Tower, al-Sayid Abd al-Rahman St, POB 10036, 11111 Khartoum; tel. (183) 779078; fax (183) 772661; e-mail info@alshamalbank.com; internet www.alshamalbank.com; f. 1990; total assets SDD 18,258.0m. (Dec. 2003); Pres. GAFAAR OSMAN FAGIR; Gen. Man. ABDELMONEIM HASSAN SAYED (acting); 17 brs.

SUDAN
Directory

Bank of Khartoum: Intersection Gamhouria St and El-Gaser St, POB 1008, Khartoum; tel. 156660000; fax (183) 781120; e-mail info@bok.sd; internet www.bok-sd.com; f. 1913; 60% owned by Dubai Islamic Bank PJSC (United Arab Emirates); absorbed National Export/Import Bank and Unity Bank in 1993; cap. 381m., res 92.9m., dep. 2,818.2m. (Dec. 2009); Chair. Dr KHALID M. ALI AL KAMDA; Gen. Man. FADI SALIM AL-FAQIH; 118 brs.

Blue Nile Mashreg Bank: Barlaman St, POB 984, Khartoum; tel. (183) 776092; fax (183) 782562; e-mail info@bluemashreg.com; internet www.bluemashreg.com; cap. 74.8m., res 21.2m., dep. 357.1m. (Dec. 2009); Chair. MUHAMMAD ISMAIL MUHAMMAD; Gen. Man. ISAAM USMAN MAHGOUB.

Buffalo Commercial Bank: BCB Junction, Juba; e-mail info@buffalocommercialbank.com; internet www.buffalocommercialbank.com; f. 2008; Chair. Dr LUAL ACUEK LUAL DENG; CEO BISWASH GAUCHAN.

Farmers Commercial Bank: POB 11984, Al-Qasr Ave, Khartoum; tel. (183) 774960; fax (183) 773687; e-mail mozarea@alnlilin.com; internet www.fcbsudan.com; f. 1960 as Sudan Commercial Bank; name changed as above in 1999 following merger with Farmers Bank for Investment and Rural Development; cap. 69.7m., res 13.5m., dep. 377.1m. (Dec. 2009); Chair. AL-TAYB ELOBEID BADR; Pres. SULIMAN HASHIM MOHAMED TOUM; 28 brs.

National Bank of Sudan: Kronfli Bldg, Zubeir Pasha St, POB 1183, Khartoum; tel. (183) 778153; fax (183) 779545; e-mail contactus@nbs.com.sd; internet www.nbs.com.sd; f. 1982; 70% owned by Bank Audi SAL, Lebanon; cap. 150.0m., res 39.3m., dep. 164.9m. (Dec. 2009); Chair. Dr IMAD ITANI; 13 brs in Sudan, 2 abroad.

Omdurman National Bank: Al-Qaser Ave, POB 11522, Khartoum; tel. (183) 770400; fax (183) 770263; e-mail info@omd-bank.com; internet www.omd-bank.com; f. 1993; cap. 523.3m., res 116.9m., dep. 5,597.0m. (Dec. 2009); Gen. Man. ABDEL RAHMAN HASSAN ABDEL RAHMAN; 17 brs; 852 employees.

Sudanese French Bank: Plot No. 6, Block A, Al-Qasr St, POB 2775, Khartoum; tel. (183) 771730; fax (183) 790391; e-mail info@sfbank.net; internet www.sfbank.net; f. 1978 as Sudanese Investment Bank; name changed as above in 1993; cap. 100.1m., res 34.0m., dep. 896.2m. (Dec. 2009); Chair. OSMAN SALMAN MOHAMED NOUR; Gen. Man. MASSAD MOHAMMED AHMED ABDUL KARIM; 20 brs.

Tadamon Islamic Bank: Baladia St, POB 3154, Khartoum; tel. (183) 771505; fax (183) 773840; e-mail info@tadamonbank-sd.com; internet www.tadamonbank-sd.com; f. 1981; cap. 81.5m., res 141.0m., dep. 1,115.9m. (Dec. 2009); Chair. Dr HASSAN OSMAN SAKOTA; Gen. Man. ABBAS ABDALLA ABBAS; 18 brs.

Foreign Banks

Byblos Bank Africa Ltd: 21 al-Amarat St, POB 8121, Khartoum; tel. (183) 566444; fax (183) 566454; e-mail Byblosbankafrica@byblosbank.com; internet www.byblosbank.com.lb; 65% owned by Byblos Bank SAL (Lebanon); f. 2003; cap. 93.3m., res 43.8m., dep. 394.2m. (Dec. 2009); Chair. Dr FRANÇOIS S. BASSIL; Gen. Man. NADIM GHANTOUS.

Faisal Islamic Bank (Sudan) (Saudi Arabia): Faih'a Bldg, Ali al-Latif St, POB 2415, Khartoum; tel. (183) 777920; fax (183) 780193; e-mail fibsudan@fibsudan.com; internet www.fibsudan.com; f. 1977; cap. 110.0m., res 10.4m., dep. 1,800.0m. (Dec. 2009); Chair. Prince MUHAMMAD AL-FAISAL AL-SA'UD; Gen. Man. ALI OMAR IBRAHIM FARAH; 30 brs.

Saudi Sudanese Bank: Baladia St, POB 1773, Khartoum; tel. (183) 780307; fax (183) 781836; e-mail saudi-sud@saudisb.sd; internet www.saudisb.sd; f. 1986; cap. 60.0m., res −49.8m., dep. 372.8m. (Dec. 2009); Chair. ABDEL GALIL EL-WASIA; Gen. Man. MUDATHIR ALI AL-BASHIR (acting); 13 brs.

Sudanese Egyptian Bank (SEB): Ingaz Rd, Elsafia, Khartoum; tel. (183) 745583; fax (183) 745580; e-mail msiralkhatim@sebank.sd; internet www.sebank.sd; f. 2005; total assets 422,671,880 (Dec. 2008); Man. Dir AMR BAHAA; 5 brs.

Development Banks

Agricultural Bank of Sudan: Ghoumhoria Ave, POB 1263, Khartoum; tel. (183) 777432; fax (183) 778296; e-mail agribank@yahoo.com; f. 1957; cap. SDD 5,200.0m., res SDD 3,609.4m., dep. SDD 18,864.9m. (Dec. 2003); provides finance for agricultural projects; Pres. AL-SAYID GAFFAR MUHAMMAD AL-HASSAN; Gen. Man. AL-SAYID AL-KINDI MUHAMMAD OSMAN; 40 brs.

Islamic Co-operative Development Bank (ISCOB): Et-Tanmha Tower, Kolyat Eltib St, POB 62, Khartoum; tel. (183) 777789; fax (183) 777715; e-mail info@iscob.com; internet www.iscob.com; f. 1983; cap. and res SDD 3,821.0m., total assets SDD 28,250.4m. (Dec. 2003); Chair. El-Haj ATTA EL-MANAN IDRIS; 6 brs.

El-Nilein Bank: United Nations Sq., POB 1722, Khartoum; tel. (183) 771984; fax (183) 785811; e-mail info@nidbg.com; internet www.nidbg.com; f. 1993 by merger of En-Nilein Bank and Industrial Bank of Sudan; name changed as above in 2007; 99% owned by Bank of Sudan; provides tech. and financial assistance for private sector industrial projects and acquires shares in industrial enterprises; cap. SDD 3,282.6m., res SDD −861.4m., dep. SDD 54,046.9m. (Dec. 2005); Man. Dir MOHAMED ABBAS AGAB; 37 brs.

NIMA Development and Investment Bank: Hashim Hago Bldg, As-Suk al-Arabi, POB 665, Khartoum; tel. (183) 779496; fax (183) 781854; f. 1982 as National Devt Bank; name changed as above 1998; 90% owned by NIMA Groupe, 10% private shareholders; finances or co-finances economic and social devt projects; cap. £S 4,000m., res £S 106m. (Dec. 1998); Dir-Gen. SALIM AS-SAFI HUGIR; 6 brs.

Real Estates Commercial Bank: Baladia St, POB 309, Khartoum; tel. (183) 777917; fax (183) 779465; f. 1967; mortgage bank financing private sector urban housing devt; cap. and res £S 1,700m., total assets £S 9,500m. (Dec. 1994); Chair. Eng. MUHAMMAD ALI EL-AMIN; 6 brs.

STOCK EXCHANGE

Sudanese Stock Exchange: Al-Baraka Tower, 5th Floor, POB 10835, Khartoum; tel. (183) 776235; fax (183) 776134; f. 1995; Chair. HAMZA MUHAMMAD JENAWI; 27 mems.

INSURANCE

African Insurance Co (Sudan) Ltd: New Abu Ella Bldg, Parliament Ave, Khartoum; tel. (183) 173402; fax (183) 177988; f. 1977; fire, accident, marine and motor; Gen. Man. AL-NOMAN AL-SANUSI.

Blue Nile Insurance Co (Sudan) Ltd: Al-Qasr Ave, Blue Nile Insurance Bldg, POB 2215, Khartoum; tel. (183) 170580; fax (183) 172405; internet www.blue-nile-insurance.com; f. 1965; Gen. Man. MUHAMMAD al-AMIN MIRGHANI.

Foja International Insurance Co Ltd: POB 879, Khartoum; tel. (183) 784470; fax (183) 783248; fire, accident, marine, motor and animal; Gen. Man. MAMOON IBRAHIM ABD ALLA.

General Insurance Co (Sudan) Ltd: El-Mek Nimr St, POB 1555, Khartoum; tel. (183) 780616; fax (183) 772122; f. 1961; Gen. Man. AL-SAMAWL AL-SAYED HAFIZ.

Islamic Insurance Co Ltd: Al-Faiha Commercial Bldg, Ali Abdullatif St, POB 2776, Khartoum; tel. (183) 772656; fax (183) 778959; e-mail islamicins@sudanmail.net; internet www.islamicinsur.com; f. 1979; all classes; CEO Dr KAMAL JADKAREEM.

Khartoum Insurance Co Ltd: Al-Taminat Bldg, Al-Jamhouriya St, POB 737, Khartoum; tel. (183) 778647; f. 1953; Chair. MUDAWI M. AHMAD; Gen. Dir YOUSIF KHAIRY.

Juba Insurance Co Ltd: Al-Baladiya St, Sayen Osnam Al-Amin Bldg, 2nd Floor, POB 10043, Khartoum; tel. (183) 783245; fax (183) 781617; Gen. Man. ABDUL AAL AL-DAWI.

Middle East Insurance Co Ltd: Al-Qasr St, Kuronfuli Bldg, 1st Floor, POB 3070, Khartoum; tel. (183) 772202; fax (183) 779266; f. 1981; fire, marine, motor and general liability; Chair. AHMAD I. MALIK; Gen. Dir ALI MUHAMMAD AHMED EL-FADL.

Sudanese Insurance and Reinsurance Co Ltd: Al-Gamhouria Ave, Nasr Sq., Abd Al-Rahman Makawi Bldg, 3rd Floor, POB 2332, Khartoum; tel. (183) 770812; fax (183) 771820; e-mail info@sudinreco.com; internet www.sudinreco.com; f. 1967; Gen. Man. HASSAN EL-SAYED MUHAMMAD ALI.

United Insurance Co (Sudan) Ltd: Makkawi Bldg, Al-Gamhouria St, POB 318, Khartoum; tel. (183) 776630; fax (183) 770783; e-mail abdin@unitedinsurance.ws; internet www.unitedinsurance.ws; f. 1968; Chair. HASHIM EL-BERIER; Dir-Gen. MUHAMMAD ABDEEN BABIKER.

Trade and Industry

GOVERNMENT AGENCIES

Agricultural Research Corpn (ARC): POB 126, Wadi Medani; tel. (51) 1842226; fax (51) 1843213; e-mail arcdg@sudanmail.net; internet www.arcsudan.sd; f. 1967; Dir-Gen. Prof. ELSADIG SULIMAN MOHAMED.

Animal Production Public Corpn: POB 624, Khartoum; tel. (183) 778555; Gen. Man. Dr FOUAD RAMADAN HAMID.

General Petroleum Corpn: POB 2649, Khartoum; tel. (183) 777554; fax (183) 773663; e-mail secretarygeneral@spc.sd; f. 1976; Chair. Dr AWAD AHMED AL-JAZZ; Sec.-Gen. Dr OMER MOHAMED KHEIR.

Gum Arabic Co Ltd: POB 857, Khartoum; tel. (183) 462111; fax (183) 467923; e-mail info@gac-arabicgum.com; internet www.gac-arabicgum.com; f. 1969; Chair. ABD EL-HAMID MUSA KASHA; Gen. Man. HASSAN SAAD AHMED.

Industrial Production Corpn: POB 1034, Khartoum; tel. (183) 771278; f. 1976; Dir-Gen. OSMAN TAMMAM.

SUDAN

Cement and Building Materials Sector Co-ordination Office: POB 2241, Khartoum; tel. (183) 774269; Dir T. M. KHOGALI.
Food Industries Corpn: POB 2341, Khartoum; tel. (183) 775463; Dir MUHAMMAD AL-GHALI SULIMAN.
Leather Industries Corpn: POB 1639, Khartoum; tel. (183) 778187; f. 1986; Man. Dir IBRAHIM SALIH ALI.
Oil Corpn: POB 64, Khartoum North; tel. (183) 332044; Gen. Man. BUKHARI MAHMOUD BUKHARI.
Spinning and Weaving General Co Ltd: POB 765, Khartoum; tel. (183) 774306; f. 1975; Dir MUHAMMAD SALIH MUHAMMAD ABDALLAH.
Sudan Tea Co Ltd: POB 1219, Khartoum; tel. (183) 781261.
Sudanese Mining Corpn: POB 1034, Khartoum; tel. (183) 770840; f. 1975; Dir IBRAHIM MUDAWI BABIKER.
Sugar and Distilling Industry Corpn: POB 511, Khartoum; tel. (183) 778417; Man. MIRGHANI AHMAD BABIKER.
Mechanized Farming Corpn: POB 2482, Khartoum; Man. Dir AWAD AL-KARIM AL-YASS.
National Cotton and Trade Co Ltd: POB 1552, Khartoum; tel. (183) 80040; f. 1970; Chair. ABD EL-ATI A. MEKKI; Man. Dir ABD AL-RAHMAN A. MONIEM; Gen. Man. ZUBAIR MUHAMMAD AL-BASHIR.
Port Sudan Cotton Trade Co Ltd: POB 590, Port Sudan; POB 590, Khartoum; Gen. Man. SAID MUHAMMAD ADAM.
Public Agricultural Production Corpn: POB 538, Khartoum; Chair. and Man. Dir ABDALLAH BAYOUMO; Sec. SAAD AL-DIN MUHAMMAD ALI.
Public Corpn for Building and Construction: POB 2110, Khartoum; tel. (183) 774544; Dir NAIM AL-DIN.
Public Corpn for Irrigation and Excavation: POB 619, Khartoum; tel. (183) 780167; Gen. Sec. OSMAN AL-NUR.
Public Corpn for Oil Products and Pipelines: POB 1704, Khartoum; tel. (183) 778290; Gen. Man. ABD AL-RAHMAN SULIMAN.
Rahad Corpn: POB 2523, Khartoum; tel. (183) 775175; financed by the World Bank, Kuwait and the USA; Man. Dir HASSAN SAAD ABDALLA.
State Trading Corpn: POB 211, Khartoum; tel. (183) 778555; Chair. E. R. M. TOM.
  Automobile Corpn: POB 221, Khartoum; tel. (183) 778555; importer of vehicles and spare parts; Gen. Man. DAFALLA AHMAD SIDDIQ.
  Captrade Engineering and Automobile Services Co Ltd: POB 97, Khartoum; tel. (183) 789265; fax (183) 775544; e-mail cap1@sudanmail.net; f. 1925; importers and distributors of engineering and automobile equipment; Gen. Man. ESSAM MOHD EL-HASSAN KAMBAL.
  Gezira Trade and Services Co: POB 17, Port Sudan; tel. (311) 825109; fax (311) 822029; e-mail gtsportsudan@hotmail.com; f. 1980; importer of agricultural machinery, spare parts, electrical and office equipment, foodstuffs, clothes and footwear; exporter of oilseeds, grains, hides and skins and livestock; provides shipping insurance and warehousing services; agents for Lloyds and P & I Club; Chair. NASR EL-DIN M. OMER.
  Khartoum Commercial and Shipping Co: POB 221, Khartoum; tel. (183) 778555; f. 1982; import, export and shipping services, insurance and manufacturing; Gen. Man. IDRIS M. SALIH.
  Silos and Storage Corpn: POB 1183, Khartoum; stores and handles agricultural products; Gen. Man. AHMAD AL-TAIEB HARHOOF.
Sudan Cotton Co Ltd: POB 1672, Khartoum; tel. (183) 775755; fax (183) 770703; e-mail sccl@sudanmail.net; internet www.sudan-cotton.com; f. 1970; exports and markets cotton; Chair. ABBAS ABD AL-BAGI HAMMAD; Dir-Gen. Dr ABDIN MUHAMMAD ALI.
Sudan Gezira Board: POB 884, HQ Barakat Wadi Medani, Gezira Province; tel. 2412; Sales Office, POB 884, Khartoum; tel. (183) 740145; f. 1950; responsible for Sudan's main cotton-producing area; the Gezira scheme is a partnership between the Govt, the tenants and the Board. The Govt provides the land and is responsible for irrigation. Tenants pay a land and water charge and receive the work proceeds. The Board provides agricultural services at cost, technical supervision and execution of govt agricultural policies relating to the scheme. Tenants pay a percentage of their proceeds to the Social Development Fund. The total potential cultivable area of the Gezira scheme is c. 850,000 ha and the total area under systematic irrigation is c. 730,000 ha. In addition to cotton, groundnuts, sorghum, wheat, rice, pulses and vegetables are grown for the benefit of tenant farmers; Man. Dir Prof. FATHI MUHAMMAD KHALIFA.
Sudan Oilseeds Co Ltd: Parliament Ave, POB 167, Khartoum; tel. (183) 780120; f. 1974; 58% state-owned; exporter of oilseeds (groundnuts, sesame seeds and castor beans); importer of foodstuffs and other goods; Chair. SADIQ KARAR AL-TAYEB; Gen. Man. KAMAL ABD AL-HALIM.

DEVELOPMENT CORPORATIONS

Sudan Development Corpn (SDC): 21 al-Amarat, POB 710, Khartoum; tel. (183) 472151; fax (183) 472148; f. 1974 to promote and co-finance devt projects with special emphasis on projects in the agricultural, agri-business and industrial sectors; cap. p.u. US $200m.; Man. Dir ABDEL WAHAB AHMED HAMZA.
  Sudan Rural Development Co Ltd (SRDC): POB 2190, Khartoum; tel. (183) 773855; fax (183) 773235; e-mail srdfc@hotmail.com; f. 1980; SDC has 27% shareholding; cap. p.u. US $20m.; Gen. Man. EL-AWAD ABDALLA H. HIJAZI.
  Sudan Rural Development Finance Co (SRDFC): POB 2190, Khartoum; tel. (183) 773855; fax (183) 773235; f. 1980; Gen. Man. OMRAN MUHAMMAD ALI.

CHAMBERS OF COMMERCE

Southern Sudan Chamber of Commerce, Industry and Agriculture (SSCC): Juba; Chair. BENJAMIN BOL; Sec.-Gen. SIMON AKUEI DENG.
Union of Sudanese Chambers of Commerce: POB 81, Khartoum; tel. (183) 772346; fax (183) 780748; e-mail chamber@sudanchamber.org; f. 1908; Pres. AL-TAYEB AHMED OSMAN; Sec.-Gen. IBRAHIM MUHAMMAD OSMAN.

INDUSTRIAL ASSOCIATION

Sudanese Chambers of Industries Association: Africa St, POB 2565, Khartoum; tel. (183) 471716; fax (183) 471720; e-mail info@sudanindustries.org; internet www.sudanindustry.org; f. 1974; Chair. NOUR ELDIN SAEED AL-SAID; Sec.-Gen. Dr EL FATIH ABBAS.

UTILITIES

Public Electricity and Water Corpn: POB 1380, Khartoum; tel. (183) 81021; Dir Dr YASIN AL-HAJ ABDIN.

CO-OPERATIVE SOCIETIES

There are about 600 co-operative societies, of which 570 are officially registered.
Central Co-operative Union: POB 2492, Khartoum; tel. (183) 780624; largest co-operative union operating in 15 provinces.

TRADE UNIONS

All trade union activity was banned following the 1989 coup. The following organizations were active prior to that date.

Federations

Sudan Workers Trade Unions Federation (SWTUF): POB 2258, Khartoum; tel. (183) 777463; includes 42 trade unions representing c. 1.75m. public service and private sector workers; affiliated to the Int. Confed. of Arab Trade Unions and the Org. of African Trade Union Unity; Pres. IBRAHIM GHANOUR; Gen. Sec. YOUSUF ABU SHAMA HAMED.
Sudanese Federation of Employees and Professionals Trade Unions: POB 2398, Khartoum; tel. (183) 773818; f. 1975; includes 54 trade unions representing 250,000 mems; Pres. IBRAHIM AWADALLAH; Sec.-Gen. KAMAL AL-DIN MUHAMMAD ABDALLAH.

Transport

RAILWAYS

The total length of railway in operation in 2002 was 5,978 route-km. The main line runs from Wadi Halfa, on the Egyptian border, to al-Obeid, via Khartoum. Lines from Atbara and Sinnar connect with Port Sudan. There are lines from Sinnar to Damazin on the Blue Nile (227 km) and from Aradeiba to Nyala in the south-western province of Darfur (689 km), with a 446-km branch line from Babanousa to Wau in Bahr al-Ghazal province. The latter was reopened in 2010, having ceased operations during the civil war. In 2009 plans were announced for the construction of a 10,000-km transcontinental railway project linking Port Sudan with Dakar, Senegal. In December 2010 plans were under way for a 750-km railway linking Juba, South Sudan, with Tororo, Uganda.
Sudan Railways Corpn (SRC): Sudan Railways Corpn Bldg, al-Tabia St, POB 1812, Khartoum; tel. (183) 774009; fax (183) 770652; internet www.sudanrailways.gov.sd; f. 1875; Chair. MOHAMMED AHMED; Gen. Man. HAMZA MOHAMED OSMAN.

ROADS

Roads in northern Sudan, other than town roads, are only cleared tracks and often impassable immediately after rain. Motor traffic on roads in the former Upper Nile province is limited to the drier months of January–May. There are several good gravelled roads in the

Equatoria and Bahr al-Ghazal provinces which are passable all the year, but in these districts some of the minor roads become impassable after rain.

Over 48,000 km of tracks are classed as 'motorable'; there were 3,160 km of main roads and 739 km of secondary roads in 1985. A 484-km highway links Khartoum, Haiya and Port Sudan. In September 2010 the Government of Southern Sudan announced its intention to construct 30,000 km of all-weather roads.

National Transport Corpn: POB 723, Khartoum; Gen. Man. MOHI AL-DIN HASSAN MUHAMMAD NUR.

Public Corpn for Roads and Bridges: POB 756, Khartoum; tel. (183) 770794; f. 1976; Chair. ABD AL-RAHMAN HABOUD; Dir-Gen. ABDOU MUHAMMAD ABDOU.

INLAND WATERWAYS

The total length of navigable waterways served by passenger and freight services is 4,068 km, of which approximately 1,723 km is open all year. From the Egyptian border to Wadi Halfa and Khartoum navigation is limited by cataracts to short stretches, but the White Nile from Khartoum to Juba is almost always navigable.

River Navigation Corpn: Khartoum; f. 1970; jtly owned by Govts of Egypt and Sudan; operates services between Aswan and Wadi Halfa.

River Transport Corpn (RTC): POB 284, Khartoum North; operates 2,500 route-km of steamers on the Nile; Chair. ALI AMIR TAHA.

SHIPPING

Port Sudan, on the Red Sea, 784 km from Khartoum, and Suakin are the only commercial seaports.

Axis Trading Co Ltd: POB 1574, Khartoum; tel. (183) 775875; f. 1967; Chair. HASSAN A. M. SULIMAN.

Red Sea Shipping and Services Co: POB 308, Khartoum; tel. (183) 580885; fax (183) 5119090; e-mail redseaco@redsea-sd.com; internet www.redsea-sd.com; Gen. Man. AWAD HAG ALI HAMED.

Sea Ports Corpn: Port Sudan; tel. (311) 822061; fax (311) 822258; e-mail info@sudanports.gov.sd; internet sudanports.gov.sd; f. 1906; Gen. Man. IBRAHIM EL-AMEEN.

Sudan Shipping Line Ltd: POB 426, Port Sudan; tel. 2655; POB 1731, Khartoum; tel. (183) 780017; f. 1960; 10 vessels totalling 54,277 dwt operating between the Red Sea and western Mediterranean, northern Europe and United Kingdom; Chair. ISMAIL BAKHEIT; Gen. Man. SALAH AL-DIN OMER AL-AZIZ.

United African Shipping Co: POB 339, Khartoum; tel. (183) 780967; Gen. Man. MUHAMMAD TAHA AL-GINDI.

CIVIL AVIATION

In June 2005 the Government announced that preliminary construction work had been completed for a new international airport at a site 40 km south-west of Khartoum. Work to build runways and two passenger terminals was scheduled to be completed by the late 2000s. The airport was expected to open in 2012.

Civil Aviation Authority: Sharia Sayed Abd al-Rahman, POB 430, Khartoum; tel. (183) 787757; fax (183) 779715; e-mail info@caa.gov.sd; internet www.caa-sudan.net; f. 1936; Dir-Gen. ABOU BAKR GAAFAR AHMAD.

Azza Transport: Mak Nimir St, POB 11586, Khartoum; tel. (183) 783761; fax (183) 770408; e-mail info@azzatransport.com; internet www.azzatransport.com; f. 1993; charter and dedicated freight services to Africa and the Middle East; Man. Dir Dr GIBRIL I. MOHAMED.

Badr Airlines: Arkaweet Block 65, Bldg No. 393, POB 6899, Khartoum; tel. 249912327000 (mobile); fax 249155144662; e-mail badr@badrairlines.com; internet www.badrairlines.com; operates cargo and passenger air services for humanitarian aid.

Sudan Airways Co Ltd: Sudan Airways Complex, 161 Obeid Khatim St, Riadh Nlock No. 10, POB 253, Khartoum; tel. (183) 243738; fax (183) 115951; e-mail gm@sudanair.com; internet www.sudanair.com; f. 1947; internal flights and international services to Africa, the Middle East and Europe; Man. Dir ALOBIED FADLULMULA ALI.

Sudanese Aeronautical Services (SASCO): POB 8260, al-Amarat, Khartoum; tel. (183) 7463362; fax (183) 4433362; fmrly Sasco Air Charter; chartered services; Chair. M. M. NUR.

Trans Arabian Air Transport (TAAT): POB 1461, Africa St, Khartoum; tel. (183) 451568; fax (183) 451544; e-mail ftaats@sudanmail.net; f. 1983; dedicated freight services to Africa, Europe and Middle East; Man. Dir EL-FATI ABDIN.

United Arabian Airlines: POB 3687, Office No. 3, Elekhwa Bldg, Atbara St, Khartoum; tel. (183) 773025; fax (183) 784402; e-mail krthq@uaa.com; f. 1995; charter and dedicated freight services to Africa and the Middle East; Man. Dir M. KORDOFANI.

Tourism

Although tourism in Sudan remains relatively undeveloped, the eastern Red Sea coast and Nile tributaries offer opportunities for water sports. Other attractions include ancient Egyptian remains and the Ad-Dinder National Tourist Park, a game reserve established in 1935. In 1991 Sudan's first Marine National Park opened on Sanganeb atoll. A total of 439,661 tourists visited Sudan in 2008. Receipts from tourism in that year were US $331m.

Public Corpn of Tourism and Hotels: POB 7104, Khartoum; tel. (183) 781764; f. 1977; Dir-Gen. Maj.-Gen. EL-KHATIM MUHAMMAD FADL.

Defence

As assessed at November 2010, the armed forces comprised: army an estimated 105,000; navy an estimated 1,300; air force 3,000. A paramilitary Popular Defence Force included 17,500 active members and 85,000 reserves. Military service is compulsory for males aged 18–30 years and lasts for two years.

Defence Expenditure: Budgeted at US $696m. for 2009.

Chief of Staff of the Air Forces and the Air Defence Forces: Gen. MOHYDEEN AHMED ABDALLA.

Chief of Staff of the Ground Forces: Gen. MUSTAFA OSMAN OBEID.

Chief of Staff of the Marine Forces: Gen. MOHAMED FADL.

Education

The Government provides free primary education from the ages of six to 13 years. Secondary education begins at 14 years of age and lasts for up to three years. In 2000/01 enrolment at primary schools included 49% of children in the relevant age-group (boys 54%; girls 45%), according to UNESCO estimates, while in 1998/99 enrolment at secondary schools was equivalent to 30% of children in the relevant age-group (boys 31%; girls 29%). There are 26 public universities in Sudan.

SURINAME

Introductory Survey

LOCATION, CLIMATE, LANGUAGE, RELIGION, FLAG, CAPITAL

The Republic of Suriname lies on the north-east coast of South America. It is bordered by Guyana to the west, by French Guiana to the east, and by Brazil to the south. The climate is sub-tropical, with fairly heavy rainfall and average temperatures of between 21°C (70°F) and 30°C (86°F). Average annual rainfall varies from 3,720 mm (146 ins) in the north to 804 mm (32 ins) in the south. The official language is Dutch. The other main languages are Hindustani and Javanese. The majority of the people can speak the native language Sranang Tongo, a Creole language known as Negro English or taki-taki, while Chinese, English, French and Spanish are also used. The principal religions are Christianity (professed by about 48% of the population), Hinduism (24%) and Islam (16%). The national flag (proportions 2 by 3) has five horizontal stripes: a broad central band of red (with a five-pointed yellow star in the centre), edged with white, between bands of green. The capital is Paramaribo.

CONTEMPORARY POLITICAL HISTORY

Historical Context

Settlers from England landed in Suriname in the 1630s, and the territory was alternately a British and a Dutch colony until it was eventually awarded to the Netherlands by the Treaty of Vienna in 1815. The colony's economy depended on large sugar plantations, for which labour was provided by slaves of African origin. Following the abolition of slavery in 1863, immigration of labourers from India and the then Dutch East Indies was encouraged, and many of them settled permanently in Suriname. This history explains the country's current ethnic diversity: there are small communities of the original Amerindian population (mainly in the interior) and of ethnic Chinese and Europeans; a Creole population, largely of African descent, constitutes about one-third of the population, as do the Asian-descended 'East' Indians (known locally as Hindustanis); the Indonesian-descended 'Javanese' form about 15% of the population, and another Creole group, the 'boschnegers' or Bush Negroes, forms a further 10% (the Bush Negroes are the Dutch-speaking descendants of escaped slaves, long-established in the rainforest as a tribalized society of four clans). Under a Charter signed in December 1954, Suriname (also known as Dutch Guiana) became an equal partner in the Kingdom of the Netherlands, with the Netherlands Antilles and the Netherlands itself, and gained full autonomy in domestic affairs.

Domestic Political Affairs

The Hindustani-dominated Government, in power since 1969 and led by Dr Jules Sedney, resigned in February 1973. General elections in November were won by an alliance of parties, the Nationale Partij Kambinatie (NPK), which favoured complete independence from the Netherlands, and in December Henck Arron, leader of the Nationale Partij Suriname (NPS—a predominantly Creole party), became Prime Minister. Suriname became independent on 25 November 1975. Dr Johan Ferrier, hitherto the Governor of Suriname, became the new republic's first President. Some 40,000 Surinamese emigrated to the Netherlands after independence, leaving Suriname with a severely underskilled work-force. Border disputes with French Guiana and Guyana also ensued. The general election of October 1977 resulted in a clear majority for the NPK, and Arron continued as Prime Minister.

Military rule

The Arron administration was overthrown in February 1980 by a group of soldiers, who formed a military council, the Nationale Militaire Raad (NMR). President Ferrier refused to agree to the retention of supreme power by the NMR, and in March he appointed a civilian administration led by Dr Henk Chin-A-Sen, a former leader of the Partij Nationalistische Republiek. In August the Army Chief of Staff, NMR member Sgt-Maj. (later Lt-Col) Désiré (Desi) Bouterse (subsequently Commander-in-Chief of the armed forces), led a coup. Ferrier was replaced by Chin-A-Sen; the legislature was dissolved, and a state of emergency declared. A Hindustani-inspired counter-coup, led by Sgt-Maj. Wilfred Hawker, failed in March 1981. In September the President announced details of a draft Constitution, which sought to limit the army to a supervisory role in government. The army responded with the formation of the Revolutionary People's Front, a comprehensive political alliance headed by Bouterse and two other members of the NMR, Maj. Roy Horb and Lt (later Commdr) Iwan Graanoogst, together with three leaders of workers' and students' organizations. In February 1982 the NMR, led by Bouterse, seized power from Chin-A-Sen and his civilian Government. The Vice-President of the Supreme Court, L. Fred Ramdat Misier, was appointed interim President. Hawker was executed after attempting a further coup in March.

A state of siege was declared, and martial law was imposed, as a result of the attempted coup of March 1982. In order to prevent the Netherlands from suspending its aid, a 12-member Cabinet of Ministers with a civilian majority was appointed, and a moderate economist, Henry Neyhorst, became Prime Minister, although Bouterse remained effectively in control. Failure to effect promised social and economic changes lost Bouterse the support of left-wing groups and trade unions, which supported the business community in demanding a return to constitutional rule. In October the arrest of Cyriel Daal, the leader of Suriname's principal trade union (De Moederbond), prompted strikes and demonstrations. In order to avert a general strike, Bouterse agreed to arrange for the election of a constituent assembly to draft a new constitution by March 1983 (to be followed by the establishment of an elected government), but he later reneged on this commitment. In December 1982 members of the armed forces burned down several buildings used by the opposition. During the ensuing disturbances, 15 prominent citizens, including Daal, were killed, in what became known as the 'December Murders'. The Government resigned, the Netherlands and the USA halted all aid, and the country was placed under rule by decree; an interim, military-dominated Government was appointed. An attempted coup in January 1983, the sixth since February 1980, resulted in the dismissal of two-thirds of the officers of the armed forces and the death of Maj. Horb. In February 1983 Dr Errol Alibux, a former Minister of Social Affairs, was appointed Prime Minister. He formed a new Cabinet of Ministers, composed of members of two left-wing parties, the Progressieve Arbeiders en Landbouwers Unie (PALU) and the Revolutionaire Volkspartij. The new Government immediately ended the restrictions imposed in December 1982.

The restoration of civilian rule

In January 1984, after a series of widely observed strikes in support of demands for the restoration of civilian rule and the organization of free elections, Bouterse dismissed the Cabinet of Ministers. Agreement was reached with the strike organizers, following the withdrawal of proposals to increase taxation rates. An interim Government, with Wim Udenhout, a former adviser to Bouterse, as Prime Minister, was created in February to formulate a timetable for the gradual restoration of constitutional rule. Nominees of the trade unions and business sector were also included in the new Government. Bouterse hoped to consolidate his position by securing a political base through Standvaste (the 25 February Movement), which he had founded in November 1983. In December 1984 plans for a nominated National Assembly (comprising representatives of Standvaste, the trade unions and the business community) were announced. The Netherlands Government, however, refused to consider the changes as a significant move towards democratic rule, deeming them insufficient to merit the resumption of aid. None the less, the National Assembly was inaugurated in January 1985. A new Cabinet of Ministers, based on the previous administration, was formed by Udenhout.

The tripartite administration collapsed in April 1985, after the withdrawal of three of the four trade union nominees. A reconstituted Cabinet, formed in June, contained new members with links to traditional political parties. In November the ban on political parties was revoked, and in the same month, former NPS Prime Minister Henck Arron, together with Jaggernath

Lachmon of the Hindustani-based Vooruitstrevende Hervormings Partij (VHP) and Willy Soemita of the Kaum Tani Persatuan Indonesia (KTPI), accepted an invitation to join the NMR, renamed the Topberaad (Supreme Council). By July 1986 only two military officers remained on the Topberaad. In that month Bouterse appointed a new Cabinet of Ministers, including representatives from industry, business, political parties, trade unions and Standvaste. Pretaap Radhakishun, a business executive and member of the VHP, was appointed Prime Minister. The Cabinet drafted a new Constitution, which was approved by a national referendum in September 1987.

From July 1986 anti-Government guerrillas began a series of attacks on military posts on the eastern border of the country. The guerrillas were led by Ronnie Brunswijk (a former presidential bodyguard). Mainly Bush Negroes, they claimed that government resettlement policies threatened the autonomy of their tribal society, as guaranteed by treaties, signed in 1760, with the former Dutch authorities. It was reported that financial support for the guerrillas (known as the Jungle Commando, or Surinamese Liberation Army—SLA) was being provided by Surinamese exiles in the Netherlands. By November most of the eastern district of Marowijne was under guerrilla control, and the rebels had also occupied the area near Zanderij (later renamed Johan Adolf Pengel) International Airport, south of Paramaribo. Rebel attacks on the mining town of Moengo forced the closure of the country's principal bauxite mines. The town was recaptured by the armed forces in December, but the mines remained closed. At the beginning of December a state of emergency was declared in eastern and southern Suriname, and a curfew was imposed. Reports that some 200 civilians had been massacred by government troops in the search for guerrillas led to protests by the Netherlands and US Governments.

In February 1987 five members of the Cabinet of Ministers, including Radhakishun, resigned. Jules Wijdenbosch, hitherto the Minister of Internal Affairs and a member of Standvaste, was appointed Prime Minister. The entire Cabinet resigned at the end of March, and a new Cabinet, led by Wijdenbosch, was appointed by Bouterse in April.

In 1987, in preparation for the general election that was to be held in November, several political parties resumed their activities. Standvaste was reconstituted, under Wijdenbosch, as the Nationale Democratische Partij (NDP—National Democratic Party). Three major opposition parties, the NPS, the VHP and the KTPI, announced an electoral alliance, the Front voor Demokratie en Ontwikkeling (FDO—Front for Democracy and Development). Brunswijk's SLA observed a cease-fire for the duration of the voting.

The FDO won a decisive victory in elections to the 51-seat National Assembly held in November 1987. In January 1988 the National Assembly unanimously elected Ramsewak Shankar (a former Minister of Agriculture) as President of the Republic, and Henck Arron was elected Vice-President and thus (in accordance with the new Constitution) Prime Minister. In December 1987 Bouterse was appointed leader of a five-member Military Council, established under the new Constitution to 'guarantee a peaceful transition' to democracy. In July 1988 the Netherlands agreed to resume aid to Suriname, but under more restrictive conditions until the Suriname Government implemented the IMF's structural adjustment programme. However, relations remained tense, largely owing to the Dutch administration's mistrust of the intentions of the Surinamese army.

In July 1989 representatives of the Government and the SLA, meeting in French Guiana, signed an agreement at Kourou, which was ratified by the National Assembly in August. The main provisions of the Kourou Accord were: a general amnesty for those involved in the recent conflicts; the ending of the state of emergency; the incorporation of many members of the SLA into a special police unit for the interior of the country; and significant investment in the interior. The armed forces declared their opposition to the Accord, but took no direct action against continuing negotiations. However, at the end of August there was a further outbreak of guerrilla activity, in the west of the country, by an Amerindian group critical of some of the provisions of the Accord. The group, known as the Tucayana Amazonica, principally opposed the involvement of the SLA in the proposed police force for the interior; it also requested the restoration of the Bureau for Amerindian Affairs. Several of the group's demands were similar to those of the army command, and there were allegations that Tucayana were being armed and encouraged by the military, exploiting the traditional antipathy between the Amerindians and many of the Bush Negroes. In October, however, the Tucayana spokesmen were augmented by elected representatives of the Amerindian communities (the Commission of Eight) and the two groups met representatives of the National Assembly, who stated that the Government was prepared to supplement, but not rescind, the Kourou Accord.

Also in October 1989 Tucayana received the support of another new insurgent group, the Mandela Bush Negro Liberation Movement (BBM), which declared itself to be dissatisfied with the Kourou Accord. The BBM was formed by members of the most westerly (and, hitherto, least involved in the civil war) of the Bush Negro clans, the Matauriërs. In the same month, however, Brunswijk's SLA secured the support of another new insurgent group, the Union for Liberation and Democracy (UBD), which occupied the mining town of Moengo. The UBD declared its support for the Accord.

On 22 December 1990 Bouterse resigned as Commander-in-Chief of the armed forces, after President Shankar failed to issue an official protest at the Netherlands' treatment of Bouterse, who was denied access to the country at Amsterdam's airport. Suspicions that Bouterse's resignation might portend a military coup were realized two days later, when the acting Commander-in-Chief of the armed forces, Graanoogst, seized power. The coup was immediately condemned by the Dutch Government, which suspended development aid to Suriname. Johan Kraag (honorary chairman of the NPS and a former Minister of Labour) was appointed provisional President on 29 December, and promptly invited Bouterse to resume command of the armed forces, thus substantiating speculation that Kraag was merely acting on behalf of Bouterse. A transitional Government (led by Jules Wijdenbosch) was sworn in in early January 1991, and it was announced that a general election would take place within 100 days, later extended to 150 days. In March Brunswijk and Bouterse (who had continued negotiations intermittently since 1989) signed a peace accord in the rebel stronghold of Drietabbetje. In April four rebel groups, the SLA, Tucayana, the BBM and Angula (or 'Defiance', led by Carlos Maassi), signed a further agreement with the Government, promising to respect the law and not to obstruct the conduct of free elections.

The election of Venetiaan

The elections, which were monitored by a delegation from the Organization of American States (OAS, see p. 391), were held in May 1991. The Nieuw Front (NF), an electoral alliance comprising the members of the former FDO and the Surinaamse Partij van de Arbeid, secured 30 seats in the National Assembly, while the NDP won 12. The remaining nine seats were won by a new coalition, Democratisch Alternatief 1991 (DA '91), mainly comprising former members of the FDO critical of the Government's failure to curb the political influence of the military. Despite the fact that it had not secured the two-thirds' majority in the Assembly necessary to elect its presidential candidate, Runaldo R. Venetiaan, automatically, the NF refused to consider the possibility of any agreement involving the formation of a coalition government or the cession of ministerial posts or policy commitments to either the NDP or DA '91. When a series of meetings of the National Assembly in July failed to result in any one presidential candidate securing a majority, the Chairman of the Assembly, Jaggernath Lachman, in accordance with the Constitution, convened the Vereinigde Volksvergadering (United People's Assembly), a body comprising the members of the National Assembly and representatives of the municipal and district councils, in order to elect a President. Venetiaan was elected with an overwhelming 79% of the votes. One of Venetiaan's first acts as President was to announce, in October, the reduction of the armed forces by two-thirds and a reduction in the defence budget of 50%. These measures were introduced as part of a government programme of 'socialization' of the armed forces. In addition, amendments to the Constitution, approved in March 1992, included measures to curb the political influence of the military. In April the Military Council, established under the 1987 Constitution, was abolished.

In August 1992 a peace agreement was signed by the Government and the SLA and the Tucayana; the BBM also committed itself to the agreement. Under the terms of the agreement, the amnesty law envisaged under the Kourou Accord of 1989, covering all civil conflicts since 1985 and amended to include insurgent groups formed since the ratification of the Kourou Accord, was to be implemented. All weapons were to be surrendered to the Government, under OAS supervision. Following disarmament, members of all the groups would be eligible for recruitment into a special police force for the interior of the country. In addition, the Government gave assurances that the interior would receive priority in its programmes for economic development and social welfare.

In November 1992 Bouterse resigned as Commander-in-Chief of the armed forces, prompting public concern that the move might once again signal a coup. Venetiaan's appointment of Col (retd) Arthy Gorré as Bouterse's successor resulted in a confrontation between the Government and senior military officers in April 1993. (Gorré had supported the 1980 coup staged by Bouterse, but had resigned from the armed forces in 1987, following a disagreement with the latter.) Graanoogst, who had occupied the position of Commander-in-Chief on an interim basis since Bouterse's resignation, refused to concede the post to Gorré. He was supported by his fellow members of the military high command and by Bouterse, who, despite his resignation, remained effectively in control of the armed forces. Venetiaan subsequently deferred Gorré's appointment until May, when it was endorsed by a majority in the National Assembly, despite veiled threats of a military coup and an attack on the national television station, which had allegedly been instigated by Bouterse. All four members of the military high command subsequently acceded to a request by the National Assembly for their resignations. Three of them, including Graanoogst, later accepted posts as advisers to the Government, thus assuaging fears of an escalation of the conflict. Indications that the Netherlands might intervene to assist the Government were also considered influential in averting further military defiance of civilian rule.

The election of Wijdenbosch

At a general election conducted in May 1996 no single party secured a legislative majority. Venetiaan, having rejected an offer from Bouterse to form a coalition government, unsuccessfully negotiated with the three other parties with representation in the legislature. Neither Venetiaan nor the candidate of the NDP, former Prime Minister Jules Wijdenbosch, were able to command the two-thirds' majority in the National Assembly necessary to secure the presidency, and responsibility for choosing the president consequently passed to the Vereinigde Volksvergadering, which elected Wijdenbosch. The KTPI and a dissident faction of the VHP, the Basispartij voor Vernieuwing en Democratie (BVD), subsequently left the NF alliance, joining an NDP-led coalition. The new coalition Government, appointed in September, comprised members of the NDP, KTPI, BVD and the Hernieuwde Progressieve Partij (HPP).

In August 1997 the Government recalled its ambassador to the Netherlands for consultations, following the decision by the Dutch Government to seek an international arrest warrant for Bouterse on charges of illegal drugs-trafficking. Bouterse was reportedly in hiding following the issue of the warrant. Talks aimed at improving relations between the Governments of Suriname and the Netherlands were conducted, at ministerial level, in New York, USA, in April 1998. However, the fact that Bouterse was continuing to serve on the Council of State remained a serious source of dissatisfaction for the Netherlands' delegation. In March 1999 the Dutch authorities began legal proceedings against Bouterse *in absentia*, on charges of corruption and drugs-trafficking. Similar *in absentia* court proceedings were initiated in the Netherlands against the guerrilla leader Ronnie Brunswijk (who was found guilty on charges of drugs-trafficking in April, and sentenced to eight years' imprisonment) and the President of the Central Bank of Suriname, Henk Goedschalk, who was accused of deliberate financial mismanagement. Despite the Suriname Government's refusal to accede to Dutch demands for the extradition of Bouterse, in April President Wijdenbosch dismissed Bouterse from the Council of State, claiming that he represented a divisive force in Surinamese politics. In July Bouterse was convicted and sentenced, *in absentia*, to 16 years in prison (later reduced to 11 years) and fined US $2.3m. The Attorney-General of the Netherlands filed further charges (this time for torture resulting in death) against Bouterse in January 2000. The new charges concerned the 1982 December Murders and arose because of a complaint filed by relatives of the victims.

Dissatisfaction with the Government's management of the economy increased in 1998 and 1999. In June 1998 widespread industrial action brought chaos to the country for several days. There was further labour unrest in the agriculture and mining sectors later in the year. Following another national strike, which brought the country to a virtual standstill, the entire Cabinet resigned in May 1999. In June the National Assembly passed a vote of no confidence in the President. However, the result fell short of the two-thirds' majority needed to force him from office and Wijdenbosch refused to tender his own resignation. Instead he called for early elections to be held by 25 May 2000. Prior to the election, in an apparent attempt to distance himself from Bouterse, Wijdenbosch left the NDP and formed a new electoral coalition, Democratisch Nationaal Platform 2000 (DNP 2000).

The re-election of Venetiaan

Voting proceeded on 25 May 2000, when Venetiaan's NF (an electoral alliance comprising the NPS, the Pertajah Luhur, the Surinaamse Partij van de Arbeid, and the VHP) secured a majority of seats. Having narrowly failed to secure the two-thirds' majority to appoint a new President directly, the NF entered into coalition negotiations with the smaller parties. On 4 August Venetiaan was elected to the presidency for the second time. On assuming office the new President pledged to fight corruption, accelerate economic development and reduce debt. In October the Dutch Government agreed to resume aid to Suriname, which had been suspended since 1998.

On 1 November 2000 the Suriname Court of Justice ruled that Bouterse must stand trial in Suriname in connection with the December Murders. In September 2001 the Dutch High Court ruled that Bouterse could not be prosecuted in the Netherlands under the UN's Convention on Torture, as the legislation had not been ratified in that country until 1989, seven years after the atrocities took place. However, in the following month it upheld Bouterse's 1999 conviction for drugs-trafficking and demanded that he be extradited to serve his 11-year prison sentence—a measure that could not be enacted, as the Surinamese Constitution prohibited extradition of its citizens.

In June 2002 the Dutch Government dispatched forensic specialists to assist Surinamese police officers investigating the December Murders. In December a judge presiding over the case ordered the exhumation of the remains of the 15 murder victims. As a result of a four-year investigation, a military court indicted Bouterse and 25 other suspects for the 1982 December Murders in December 2004. In March 2007 Bouterse publicly apologized to the families of the 15 victims, although he denied direct involvement in their deaths, and advocated an amnesty for the suspects. In February 2009 proceedings began against Bouterse and 23 other suspects formally accused of the December Murders. Bouterse's election as President in July 2010 meant that in theory he would be able to pardon himself if he were found guilty of involvement in the murders. The trial was ongoing in early 2011. In August 2005 the OAS's Inter-American Court of Human Rights instructed the Government to investigate a massacre that occurred in the village of Moiwana in 1986, during Bouterse's presidency, and to pay US $13,000 compensation to the 130 survivors. President Venetiaan formally apologized for the massacre at a ceremony in Moengo in July 2006.

In March 2005 the NDP formally nominated Bouterse as its candidate in the indirect presidential election that was to follow the legislative ballot in May. The USA reacted to the NDP's nomination by threatening to sever diplomatic links with Suriname in the event of Bouterse being re-elected President. The NDP accused the USA of political interference and lodged a formal complaint with the Caribbean Community and Common Market (CARICOM, see p. 219) and the OAS. At the election the NF retained its position as the largest party in the National Assembly, although it lost its majority. The NDP increased its legislative representation. Bouterse and former guerrilla leader Ronnie Brunswijk were both elected to the legislature.

Following the election the NF entered into negotiations with smaller parties in order to garner the two-thirds' parliamentary majority needed to re-elect Venetiaan to the presidency. As a result, on 13 July 2005 Venetiaan was nominated by a coalition of the NF, the DA '91 and the A-Combinatie (a coalition that included the Algemene Bevrijdings- en Ontwikkeling Partij— General Liberation and Development Party—led by Brunswijk). In an unexpected move, two days later the NDP presidential candidate Bouterse withdrew from the contest, nominating his former running mate Rabin Parmessar in his stead. The NDP and the Volksalliantie Voor Vooruitgang (People's Alliance for Progress), formed a coalition, nominating Wilfried Roseval, formerly Wijenbosch's running mate, for the vice-presidency. However, neither Venetiaan nor Parmessar secured the requisite two-thirds' majority during the two rounds of voting. Responsibility for electing the new head of state once again passed to the 891-member Vereinigde Volksvergadering, which opted for Venetiaan. At his inauguration President Venetiaan pledged to combat criminal activity and to continue to pursue established financial policies and budgetary discipline to achieve economic stability.

In an attempt to reduce the cost of imported petroleum, in July 2005 the Government signed the PetroCaribe energy accord with Venezuela, thereby gaining access to favourable energy concessions and the option of preferential terms should the price of petroleum exceed US $40 per barrel. However, the steep increases in the retail cost of petroleum products, and consequently of transportation, led to civil unrest in the latter half of 2005 and early 2006. Unrest continued in 2007 and 2008, when workers from four different sectors staged strikes to draw attention to their poor working conditions. In November 2007 over 1,000 teachers left their positions, seeking higher wages and a fair system of benefits. The strike continued until early 2008, when the Government agreed to increase wages by 10%. In early 2008 the workers in the bauxite industry as well as employees at the Jarikaba banana plant went on strike in support of demands for more substantial salary increases.

Recent developments: the election of Bouterse

A total of 20 parties, mostly grouped into coalitions, contested the general election on 25 May 2010. With 40.2% of the votes cast, the Megacombinatie (an alliance headed by former President Desi Bouterse that included the NDP, Nieuw Suriname, PALU and the KTPI) became the largest grouping within the National Assembly after gaining control of 23 of the 51 legislative seats. The NF secured 14 seats, while Brunswijk's A-Combinatie and the Volksalliantie (a coalition of four Javanese parties) won seven and six seats, respectively. The rate of participation by the electorate was high, at 73.2%. OAS and CARICOM observation missions declared the election fair and peaceful. After securing the support of the A-Combinatie and the Volksalliantie, on 19 July Bouterse was elected as President by the National Assembly, winning the votes of 36 of the 51 deputies (and thus exceeding the necessary two-thirds' parliamentary majority). Bouterse was inaugurated on 12 August, but the ceremony was not attended by any foreign leaders, an indication of the international community's reluctance to engage with a President with a dictatorial past, a drugs-trafficking conviction and connections to the December Murders.

Six A-Combinatie members received positions in Bouterse's Cabinet of Ministers, including Martin Misiedjan, who was appointed Minister of Justice and the Police. The Volksalliantie was allocated three government posts, with Soewarto Moestadja becoming the new Minister of Home Affairs. The remaining eight ministries were assigned to members of the Megacombinatie; most notably, Winnie Boedhoe became Minister of Finance, Winston Lackin received the foreign affairs portfolio and Lamuré Latour was given responsibility for defence. Robert Ameerali, an independent, was awarded the position of Vice-President. Controversially, Bouterse also appointed Alice Amafo as the new Minister of Social Affairs and Housing; Amafo had resigned the transport portfolio in 2007 due to allegations that she had misused public funds. Bouterse declared that economic development and attracting foreign investment were the main priorities of his Government.

In commemoration of the 25 February 1980 coup, in early 2011 Bouterse controversially reintroduced the 25 February national holiday, which had been abrogated by Venetiaan in 1991. Bouterse described the 'revolution' that resulted in the overthrow of Arron's administration as 'legitimate'.

Foreign Affairs

Suriname has a territorial dispute with Guyana over an estimated 15,000 sq km (6,000 sq miles) of land in the Corentije region, and another with French Guiana over land to the east of the Litani river. In 1990, with the mediation of the UN High Commissioner for Refugees, France and Suriname agreed terms providing for the repatriation of an estimated 10,000 Surinamese refugees from French Guiana. In 2002 the Suriname Government delivered an official protest to the French authorities concerning the alleged compulsory repatriation of refugees. Relations with France deteriorated in 2007 when the French Government designated a 2m.-ha region along the disputed border with French Guiana as a national park. Under its new protected status, the traditional hunting and fishing practices of the indigenous Surinamese communities were strictly prohibited in the park. The Organization of Indigenous People in Suriname protested against the restrictions to the French Government.

In 1995 Guyana and Suriname reached agreement on the establishment of a joint commission in order to seek a resolution of the countries' territorial dispute. In 1998 Guyana granted the Canadian-based company CGX Energy Inc a concession to explore for petroleum and gas along the continental margin off Guyana, part of which lay within the disputed maritime area. In May 2000 Suriname formally claimed that Guyana had violated its territorial integrity, and invited Guyana to begin negotiations regarding the maritime boundary. In June the Surinamese Navy forced CGX to remove the drilling platform. In 2001 the two countries issued a declaration of their Governments' commitment to peace and co-operation and in the following year revived the Guyana–Suriname Bilateral Co-operation Council. The two Governments agreed to investigate the possibility of a joint exploration for petroleum in the disputed territory and to improve co-operation in trade, investments and joint ventures. However, relations again became strained in 2003 when the Surinamese Government decreed that maps of the country circulated by diplomatic missions in Paramaribo must include the disputed territory. Guyana lodged a formal protest and sent a naval detachment to patrol the Corentijn River. Both countries subsequently strengthened their military presence in the area and in February 2004 two Surinamese gunboats expelled a Canadian company, exploring for oil with Guyana's permission, from the area. At the end of that month Guyana referred the maritime boundary dispute to arbitration at the UN's International Tribunal for the Law of the Sea, in Hamburg, Germany. In 2007 the Tribunal ruled in favour of Guyana, granting sovereignty over 33,152 sq km (12,800 sq miles) of coastal waters; Suriname was awarded 17,891 sq km (6,900 sq miles). Guyana's subsequent claims for compensation of US $34m. for damage arising from the expulsion of the oil rig were dismissed by the UN Permanent Court of Arbitration, which ruled that Suriname had not used armed force.

In September 2010 President Bouterse travelled to Guyana for talks with his Guyanese counterpart, Bharrat Jagdeo. The two leaders agreed to put aside any unresolved border issues and concentrate instead upon enhancing bilateral co-operation in areas of mutual interest such as trade and security. Relations continued to improve in late 2010 following further amicable discussions, during which plans to build a bridge across the Corentyne river were revived. Construction work was expected to begin in 2011.

Violent clashes between local residents and Brazilian mineworkers in the Surinamese town of Albina in December 2009 highlighted the issue of ethnic tensions connected with the presence of large numbers of migrant workers in Suriname. An initial incident, which resulted in the murder of a Surinamese national, led to violence in which many people were injured and buildings and local businesses were set alight, leaving some 100 people homeless (most of whom were Brazilian, Chinese or Javanese). Following negotiations with Brazil, in December 2010 a bilateral immigration accord was concluded to monitor the flow of peoples across their shared border.

In March 2002 the Surinamese and Dutch Ministers of Foreign Affairs approved the establishment of a Returned Emigration Committee to oversee the voluntary repatriation of Surinamese with Dutch nationality without the loss of social benefits. In October 2004 customs officials in Suriname and the Netherlands reached an agreement to share information in an attempt to reduce tax evasion on imports from the Netherlands. The Dutch authorities, while acknowledging the choice made by the Surinamese electorate, expressed dissatisfaction at Bouterse's election as President in July 2010 and declared that he would only be permitted entry into the Netherlands if he were arriving to commence his prison sentence for drugs-trafficking (Bouterse, *in absentia*, had been found guilty of this crime by a Dutch court in 1999). The Netherlands also announced that engagement with the new Surinamese administration would not progress beyond the 'functional necessities', while the provision of Dutch finance and training for the Surinamese police force was cancelled.

CONSTITUTION AND GOVERNMENT

Under the 1987 Constitution, legislative power is held by the National Assembly, with 51 members, elected by universal adult suffrage for a five-year term. The Assembly elects the President and the Vice-President of the Republic. Executive power is vested in the President, who appoints the Cabinet of Ministers, led by the Vice-President, who is also the Prime Minister. The Cabinet is responsible to the National Assembly. A Council of State, comprising civilians and members of the armed forces, advises the President and the Cabinet of Ministers on policy, and

SURINAME

has power of veto over legislation approved by the Assembly. Suriname comprises 10 administrative districts.

REGIONAL AND INTERNATIONAL CO-OPERATION

In February 1995 Suriname was granted full membership of the Caribbean Community and Common Market (CARICOM, see p. 219). It was also one of the six founder members of CARICOM's Caribbean Single Market and Economy (CSME), established on 1 January 2006. The CSME was intended to enshrine the free movement of goods, services and labour throughout the CARICOM region, although persistent delays in implementation meant that the CSME was not expected to be fully operational until 2015. Suriname is a member of the Organization of American States (see p. 391), the Association of Caribbean States (see p. 445) and the Inter-American Development Bank (see p. 333). The country joined the UN in December 1975. As a contracting party to the General Agreement on Tariffs and Trade, Suriname joined the World Trade Organization (see p. 430) on its establishment in 1995. The country is also a member of the Group of 77 (see p. 447) organization of developing states.

ECONOMIC AFFAIRS

In 2008, according to estimates by the World Bank, Suriname's gross national income (GNI), measured at average 2006–08 prices, was US $2,455m., equivalent to $4,760 per head (or $6,690 per head on an international purchasing-power parity basis). During 2000–09, it was estimated, the population increased at an average annual rate of 1.2%, while gross domestic product (GDP) per head increased, in real terms, by an average of 4.0 per year over 2000–08. According to World Bank figures, overall GDP increased, in real terms, at an average annual rate of 5.3 in 2000–08; growth totalled 2.5% in 2009.

Agriculture (including hunting, forestry and fishing) contributed 5.8% of GDP (excluding the informal sector) in 2009, according to the UN, and the sector engaged 8.0% of the employed population at the 2004 census. The principal crop is rice, which supplies domestic demand and provided 1.9% of export earnings in 2008. Bananas are cultivated for export, together with plantains, sugar cane and citrus fruits, while Suriname also produces coconuts, maize and vegetables. In 2005 some US $23m. was granted by the Dutch Government to assist the diversification of the agricultural sector and to improve rural roads and irrigation systems. Livestock is being developed, as are the extensive timber reserves (more than 80% of Suriname's total land area is covered by forest). Commercial fishing is important (exports of shrimp and fish providing an estimated 7.3% of total export revenue in 2007). According to the World Bank, agricultural GDP increased by 1.4% per year in 2000–08; the sector fell by 5.0% in 2008.

Industry (including mining, manufacturing, public utilities and construction) contributed 44.3% of GDP (excluding the informal sector) in 2009, according to the UN, and the sector engaged some 22.9% of the employed labour force at the 2004 census. The principal activity is the bauxite industry, which dominates both the mining and manufacturing sectors. According to the World Bank, industrial GDP increased by an annual average of 8.6% in 2000–08; the sector increased by 2.3% in 2008.

Mining, quarrying and utilities contributed 17.4% of GDP in 2009, according to the UN, and the sector engaged 5.9% of the employed labour force at the 2004 census. The principal product is bauxite (used in the manufacture of aluminium), of which Suriname is one of the world's leading producers (providing an estimated 4.0m. metric tons in 2009). Two new bauxite mines, operated by US-based aluminium company Alcoa and Australian company BHP Billiton, began operations in 2006. In 2008 the Government stated that it aimed to establish a state-owned aluminium company in order to increase revenue from the sector. Gold was also a significant contributor to the economy. In 2002 the Canadian gold-mining corporation Cambior began construction of new facilities at Gross Rosebel. Extraction began in 2004, and in that year gold production reportedly reached a record 8,513 kg, rising to 12,192 kg by 2009. In 2007 gold contributed some 35.9% of total export revenue and in 2008 earnings from the industry were estimated at US $53.5m. Reserves of petroleum in Suriname are exploited at a rate of around 12,500 barrels per day. Some 40% of production is for export, but much is used domestically in the bauxite industry. Unproven reserves are also thought to exist in the Saramacca district. Petroleum production earned some US $187.7m. in 2008. Suriname also has extensive deposits of iron ore and reserves of manganese, copper, nickel, platinum and kaolin. According to government estimates, the GDP of the mining sector increased by an average of 10.6% per year in 2000–04.

Manufacturing contributed 22.4% of GDP (excluding the informal sector) in 2009, according to the UN, and the sector engaged an estimated 7.0% of the employed labour force at the 2004 census. Bauxite refining and smelting is the principal industry (alumina accounted for an estimated 47.5% of export revenue in 2007), but there are also important food-processing industries and manufacturers of cigarettes, beverages and chemical products. According to the World Bank, manufacturing GDP increased by an estimated average of 8.5% per year in 2000–08; the sector contracted by 2.6% in 2008.

The construction sector contributed 4.5% of GDP (excluding the informal sector) in 2009, according to the UN, and the sector engaged an estimated 9.0% of the employed labour force at the 2004 census.

Energy is derived principally from hydroelectricity and hydrocarbon fuels, which are mainly imported; in 2008 mineral fuels and lubricants accounted for 15.6% of total merchandise imports. The country has considerable potential for the further development of hydroelectric power. In 2007 Suriname produced 1,618m. kWh of electricity, derived mostly from hydroelectric power.

The services sector contributed 49.9% of GDP (excluding the informal sector) in 2009, according to the UN, and the sector engaged an estimated 64.3% of the employed labour force at the 2004 census. According to the World Bank, the GDP of the services sector increased by an average of 5.5% per year in 2000–08; sectoral growth was 7.1% in 2008.

In 2009 Suriname recorded a visible trade surplus of US $108.8m., and there was a surplus of $209.5m. on the current account of the balance of payments. The principal source of imports in 2005 was the USA (providing 24.4% of total imports); other significant suppliers in that year were the Netherlands, Trinidad and Tobago and Japan. The principal markets for exports in 2005 were Norway (some 23.9% of the value of total exports), the USA and France. The principal imports in 2008 were machinery and transport equipment, basic manufactures, mineral fuels and lubricants, food and live animals and chemicals. The principal exports (excluding re-exports) in that year were crude petroleum and mineral fuels and lubricants.

In 2007 there was an estimated budgetary surplus of 195.5m. Surinamese dollars (equivalent to around 3.0% of GDP, excluding the contributions of the informal sector). Suriname's general government gross debt was 1,651m. Surinamese dollars in 2009, equivalent to 20.4% of GDP. At the end of 2002 the total external public debt stood at an estimated US $319.8m., of which $161.9m. was public and publicly guaranteed debt. By the end of December 2007 total external public debt had declined marginally, to US $161.1m. In December 2009 public debt was equivalent to some 19% of GDP. According to official figures, the annual rate of inflation averaged 6.8% in 2006–10. Consumer prices remained virtually constant in 2009, but increased by 6.9% in 2010. According to official sources, the rate of unemployment was 9.5% in 2004. The informal sector contributed around 14.3% of GDP in 2006.

Economic activity is relatively diversified in range, with the dominant sector being the bauxite/alumina industry. Agriculture is also important, particularly the production of rice and bananas, but the sector remains relatively undeveloped. GDP growth slowed to 2.5% in 2009 in response to the global economic crisis. The IMF noted that Suriname had fared better than many of its neighbours during the downturn because of growth in the gold-mining and construction industries. A recovery in demand and prices for the country's key mineral commodities in 2010 led to an increase in export revenues and contributed to estimated GDP growth of 4.5% in that year. However, rising food prices and public sector salaries resulted in inflation increasing to 10% by the end of the year (compared with around 1% in late 2009). Further inflationary pressures were generated in January 2011, when the Government effected a 16% devaluation of the Surinamese dollar and introduced a series of tax increases, including a rise in fuel duty. Nevertheless, it was anticipated that these measures would also stabilize the fiscal deficit (which had risen steadily during the previous year). In the same month the Government announced a new scheme to regulate the illegal gold-mining sector, in order to bring the industry into the formal income tax system, and it was hoped that the resultant boost in tax receipts would further reduce the fiscal deficit. The IMF forecast economic expansion of about 5% in 2011, driven by continued high demand for alumina and gold, while the planned construction of a new bauxite mine and the country's second

SURINAME

industrial-scale gold mine was expected to contribute to robust growth in the medium term.

PUBLIC HOLIDAYS

2012: 1 January (New Year's Day), 23 January (Chinese New Year), 25 February (Day of the Revolution), 8 March* (Phagwa), 6–9 April (Easter), 1 May (Labour Day), 1 July (Emancipation Day), 18 August (Id al-Fitr, end of Ramadan), 26 October (Id al-Adha, Feast of the Sacrifice), 13 November (Diwali), 25 November (Republic Day), 25–26 December (Christmas).

* Exact date dependent upon sightings of the moon.

Statistical Survey

Sources (unless otherwise stated): Algemeen Bureau voor de Statistiek, Kromme Elleboogstraat 10, POB 244, Paramaribo; tel. 473927; fax 425004; e-mail info@statistics-suriname.org; internet www.statistics-suriname.org; Ministry of Trade and Industry, Havenlaan 3, POB 9354, Paramaribo; tel. 402080; fax 402602.

AREA AND POPULATION

Area: 163,820 sq km (63,251 sq miles).

Population: 355,240 (males 175,814, females 179,426) at census of 1 July 1980; 492,829 (males 247,846, females 244,618, not known 365) at census of 2 August 2004. *Mid-2011* (estimate): 528,971. Source: UN, *World Population Prospects: The 2008 Revision*.

Density (at mid-2011): 3.2 per sq km.

Population by Age and Sex (UN estimates at mid-2011): *0–14:* 149,157 (males 76,136, females 73,021); *15–64:* 345,251 (males 174,058, females 171,193); *65 and over:* 34,563 (males 14,767, females 19,796); *Total* 528,971 (males 264,961, females 264,010) (Source: UN, *World Population Prospects: The 2008 Revision*).

Ethnic Groups (1980 census, percentage): Creole 34.70; Hindustani 33.49; Javanese 16.33; Bush Negro 9.55; Amerindian 3.10; Chinese 1.55; European 0.44; Others 0.84.

Administrative Districts (population at census of 2 August 2004): Paramaribo 242,946; Wanica 85,986; Nickerie 36,639; Coronie 2,887; Saramacca 15,980; Commewijne 24,649; Marowijne 16,642; Para 18,749; Brokopondo 14,215; Sipaliwini 34,136; *Total* 492,829.

Principal Towns (census of 2 August 2004): Paramaribo (capital) 205,000; Lelydorp 15,600; Nieuw Nickerie 11,100. Source: Thomas Brinkoff, *City Population* (internet www.citypopulation.de).

Births, Marriages and Deaths (2004): Registered live births 9,062 (birth rate 18.6 per 1,000); Marriages 1,951 (4.0 per 1,000); Registered deaths 3,319 (death rate 6.8 per 1,000). *2007:* Birth rate 19.3 per 1,000; Death rate 7.6 per 1,000. *2008:* Birth rate 19.0 per 1,000; Death rate 7.6 per 1,000. *2009:* Birth rate 18.7 per 1,000; Death rate 7.6 per 1,000. *2010:* Birth rate 18.5; Death rate 7.6. Sources: UN, *Demographic Yearbook*; Pan American Health Organization.

Life Expectancy (years at birth): 69.4 (males 65.9; females 73.1) in 2010. Source: Pan American Health Organization.

Economically Active Population ('000 persons aged 15–64 years, census of 2004): Agriculture, hunting, forestry and fishing 12,593; Mining and quarrying 9,308; Manufacturing 10,971; Utilities 1,659; Construction 14,031; Trade 25,012; Hotels, restaurants and bars 4,833; Transport, storage and communication 8,711; Financial intermediation 2,723; Real estate, renting and business activities 6,350; Public administration and defence 27,995; Education 8,355; Health and social work 6,797; Other community, social and personal service activities 9,911; *Sub-total* 149,249; Unknown 7,456; *Total employed* 156,705 (males 101,919, females 54,768, unknown 18); Unemployed 16,425; *Total labour force* 173,130.

HEALTH AND WELFARE

Key Indicators

Total Fertility Rate (children per woman, 2010): 2.3.

Under-5 Mortality Rate (per 1,000 live births, 2010): 29.7.

HIV/AIDS (% of persons aged 15–49, 2007): 2.4.

Physicians (per 1,000 head, 2008): 0.9.

Hospital Beds (per 1,000 head, 2007): 3.1.

Health Expenditure (2007): US $ per head (PPP): 527.

Health Expenditure (2007): % of GDP: 7.6.

Health Expenditure (2007): public (% of total): 47.4.

Access to Water (% of persons, 2008): 93.

Access to Sanitation (% of persons, 2008): 84.

Total Carbon Dioxide Emissions ('000 metric tons, 2007): 2,436.6.

Carbon Dioxide Emissions Per Head (metric tons, 2007): 4.8.

Human Development Index (2010): ranking: 94.

Human Development Index (2010): value: 0.646.

Source: partly Pan American Health Organization; for other sources and definitions, see explanatory note on p. vi.

AGRICULTURE, ETC.

Principal Crops ('000 metric tons, 2008, FAO estimates): Rice, paddy 183; Roots and tubers 4; Sugar cane 120; Coconuts 9; Vegetables 14; Bananas 89; Plantains 9; Oranges 13; Other citrus fruit 2. Note: No data were available for 2009.

Livestock ('000 head, 2008, FAO estimates): Cattle 50; Sheep 6; Goats 4; Pigs 27; Chickens 5,010. Note: No data were available for 2009.

Livestock Products ('000 metric tons, 2008, unless otherwise indicated, FAO estimates): Cattle meat 2; Pig meat 2 (2009); Chicken meat 8; Cows' milk 6; Hen eggs 1.

Forestry ('000 cu metres, 2009, FAO estimates): *Roundwood Removals:* Sawlogs, veneer logs and logs for sleepers 200; Other industrial wood 8; Fuel wood 47; Total 255. *Sawnwood Production:* Total (incl. railway sleepers) 74.

Fishing ('000 metric tons, 2008): Capture 23.8 (FAO estimate—Marine fishes 17.2; Penaeus shrimps 0.2; Atlantic seabob 6.0); Aquaculture 0.0; *Total catch* 23.8 (FAO estimate).

Source: FAO.

MINING

Selected Products (2009, estimates): Crude petroleum ('000 barrels) 5,650; Bauxite 4,000; Gold (Au content, kg) 12,193. Sources: US Geological Survey.

INDUSTRY

Selected Products ('000 metric tons, 2007 unless otherwise indicated): Gold-bearing ores 300 (kg, 2004); Gravel and crushed stone 85 (2002); Distillate fuel oil 41; Residual fuel oils 360; Cement 65 (2004); Alumina 1,929 (2005); Beer of barley 21 (2008); Coconut oil 0.87 (2009); Palm oil 0.17 (2009); Cigarettes 483 (million, 1996); Plywood 1 ('000 cubic metres, 2008); Electricity 1,618 (million kWh). Sources: mainly UN Industrial Commodity Statistics Database and FAO.

FINANCE

Currency and Exchange Rates: 100 cents = 1 Surinamese dollar. *Sterling, Dollar and Euro Equivalents* (31 December 2010): £1 sterling = 4.297 Surinamese dollars; US $1 = 2.745 Surinamese dollars; €1 = 3.668 Surinamese dollars; 100 Surinamese dollars = £23.27 = US $36.43 = €27.26. *Average Exchange Rate* (Surinamese dollars per US $): 2.745 in 2008; 2.745 in 2009; 2.745 in 2010. *Note:* Between 1971 and 1993 the official market rate was US $1 = 1.785 guilders. A new free market rate was introduced in June 1993, and a unified, market-determined rate took effect in July 1994. A mid-point rate of US $1 = 401.0 guilders was in effect between September 1996 and January 1999. A new currency, the Surinamese dollar, was introduced on 1 January 2004, and was equivalent to 1,000 old guilders. Some data in this survey are still presented in terms of the former currency.

Budget (million Surinamese dollars, 2007, estimates): *Revenue:* Direct taxation 778.8; Indirect taxation 804.0 (Domestic taxes on goods and services 368.8, Taxes on international trade 430.9, Other taxes (incl. bauxite levy) 4.3); Non-tax revenue 319.7; Total 1,902.5 (excl. grants 99.5). *Expenditure:* Wages and salaries 678.4; Subsidies and transfers 217.0; Goods and services 590.1; Interest payments 94.5; Capital 225.4; Total 1,805.4 (excl. net lending 1.1). Source: IMF, *Suriname: Statistical Appendix* (August 2008).

SURINAME

International Reserves (US $ million at 31 December 2010): Gold (national valuation) 87.95; IMF special drawing rights 124.20; Reserve position in IMF 9.43; Foreign exchange 505.25; Total 726.83. Source: IMF, *International Financial Statistics*.

Money Supply ('000 Surinamese dollars at 31 December 2010): Currency outside depository corporations 669,197; Transferable deposits 2,315,720; Other deposits 2,441,332; Securities other than shares 80,034; *Broad money* 5,506,283. Source: IMF, *International Financial Statistics*.

Cost of Living (Consumer Price Index for Paramaribo area; base: April–June 2009 = 100): 101.4 in 2008; 101.3 in 2009; 108.3 in 2010.

Gross Domestic Product ('000 Surinamese dollars at constant 2005 prices): 5,370 in 2007; 5,692 in 2008; 5,834 in 2009. Source: UN National Accounts Main Aggregates Database.

Expenditure on the Gross Domestic Product ('000 Surinamese dollars at current prices, 2009): Government final consumption expenditure 366,995; Private final consumption expenditure 1,279,348; Gross capital formation 6,247,334; *Total domestic expenditure* 7,893,677; Exports of goods and non-factor services 5,252,160; *Less* Imports of goods and non-factor services 4,859,925; Statistical discrepancy −144,456; *GDP in purchasers' values* 8,141,456. Source: UN National Accounts Main Aggregates Database.

Gross Domestic Product by Economic Activity ('000 Surinamese dollars at current prices, 2009): Agriculture, hunting, forestry and fishing 373,519; Mining, quarrying and utilities 1,130,358; Manufacturing 1,452,545; Construction 289,001; Wholesale, retail trade, hotels and restaurants 848,683; Transport, storage and communications 493,599; Other services 1,895,094; *Sub-total* 6,482,798; Net of indirect taxes 1,658,658 (obtained as residual); *GDP in purchasers' values* 8,141,456. Source: UN National Accounts Main Aggregates Database.

Balance of Payments (US $ million, 2009): Exports of goods f.o.b. 1,404.3; Imports of goods f.o.b. −1,295.5; *Trade balance* 108.8; Exports of services 286.7; Imports of services −285.3; *Balance on goods and services* 110.2; Other income received 29.8; Other income paid −24.5; *Balance on goods, services and income* 115.5; Current transfers received 147.2; Current transfers paid −53.2; *Current balance* 209.5; Capital account (net) 87.4; Direct investment from abroad −93.4; Portfolio investment assets −9.9; Portfolio investment liabilities −0.9; Other investment assets 3.7; Other investment liabilities 37.9; Net errors and omissions −41.2; *Overall balance* 193.1. Source: IMF, *International Financial Statistics*.

EXTERNAL TRADE

Principal Commodities (US $ million, 2008): *Imports c.i.f.*: Food and live animals 144.8; Mineral fuels, lubricants, etc. 190.4; Chemicals 124.2; Basic manufactures 249.4; Machinery and transport equipment 399.6; Total (incl. others) 1,304.4. *Exports (excl. re-exports) f.o.b.*: Crude materials (inedible) except fuels 714.8; Mineral fuels, lubricants, etc. 185.4; Total (incl. others) 1,689.0. *Re-exports*: Beverages and tobacco 14.5; Total (incl. others) 54.4. *2007*: Total exports 1,360.8 (Alumina 645.7; Gold 488.8; Shrimp and fish 99.2; Crude oil 107.5; Rice 18.1) (Source: IMF, *Suriname: Statistical Appendix*—August 2008).

Principal Trading Partners (US $ million, 2005): *Imports c.i.f.*: Belgium 23.6; Brazil 39.3; Canada 10.1; China, People's Repub. 59.5; Germany 23.9; Japan 47.5; Netherlands 160.0; Trinidad and Tobago 116.0; United Kingdom 18.3; USA 267.9; Total (incl. others) 1,099.9. *Exports f.o.b.*: Barbados 6.6; France 74.8; Iceland 26.9; Japan 10.7; Netherlands 24.2; Norway 222.4; Trinidad and Tobago 20.7; USA 155.6; Total (incl. others) 929.1. Source: IMF, *Suriname: Statistical Appendix* (May 2007).

TRANSPORT

Road Traffic (registered motor vehicles, 2006): Passenger cars 81,778; Buses and coaches 3,029; Lorries and vans 25,745; Motor-cycles and mopeds 40,889 (Source: IRF, *World Road Statistics*).

Shipping: *International Sea-borne Freight Traffic* (estimates, '000 metric tons, 2001): Goods loaded 2,306; Goods unloaded 1,212. *Merchant Fleet* (registered at 31 December 2009): Number of vessels 15; Total displacement 4,687 grt. Source: IHS Fairplay, *World Fleet Statistics*.

Civil Aviation (traffic on scheduled services, 2006): Kilometres flown (million) 6; Passengers carried ('000) 307; Passenger-km (million) 1,676; Total ton-km (million) 205. Source: UN, *Statistical Yearbook*.

TOURISM

Tourist Arrivals (number of non-resident arrivals at national borders, '000): 160.0 in 2005; 152.9 in 2006; 162.5 in 2007.

Tourism Receipts (US $ million, incl. passenger transport): 109 in 2006; 73 in 2007; 83 in 2008.

Source: World Tourism Organization.

COMMUNICATIONS MEDIA

Radio Receivers (1997): 300,000 in use.
Television Receivers (2000): 110,000 in use.
Telephones (2009): 83,700 main lines in use.
Mobile Cellular Telephones (2009): 763,900 subscribers.
Personal Computers: 20,000 (40.0 per 1,000 persons) in 2005.
Internet Users (2009): 163,000.
Broadband Subscribers (2009): 8,600.
Daily Newspapers (2005): 4.
Non-daily Newspapers (2005): 4.

Sources: mainly UNESCO, *Statistical Yearbook*; UN, *Statistical Yearbook*; International Telecommunication Union.

EDUCATION

Pre-primary (2007/08): 813 teachers; 17,467 pupils.
Primary (2007/08 unless otherwise stated, incl. special education): 308 schools (2001/02); 4,354 teachers; 69,604 pupils.
Secondary (2007/08 unless otherwise stated, incl. teacher-training): 141 schools (2001/02); 3,373 teachers (2006/07); 48,134 pupils.
University (2001/02): 1 institution; 350 teachers; 3,250 students.
Other Higher (2001/02): 3 institutions; 200 teachers; 1,936 students.
Pupil-teacher Ratio (primary education, UNESCO estimate): 16.0 in 2007/08.
Adult Literacy Rate (UNESCO estimates): 90.7% (males 93.0%; females 88.4%) in 2008.

Source: mainly UNESCO Institute for Statistics.

Directory

The Government

HEAD OF STATE

President: DESIRÉ (DESI) DELANO BOUTERSE (took office 12 August 2010).

Council of State: Chair. DESIRÉ (DESI) DELANO BOUTERSE (President of the Republic); 14 mems; 10 to represent the political parties in the National Assembly, one for the Armed Forces, two for the trade unions and one for employers.

CABINET OF MINISTERS
(May 2011)

The current Government is formed by members of the Megacombinatie (MC), A-Combinatie (AC) and Volksalliantie (VA) alliances.

Vice-President: ROBERT AMEERALI (Ind.).
Minister of Finance: WINNIE BOEDHOE (MC).
Minister of Foreign Affairs: WINSTON LACKIN (MC).
Minister of Defence: LAMURÉ LATOUR (MC).
Minister of Home Affairs: SOEWARTO MOESTADJA (VA).
Minister of Justice and the Police: LAMURÉ LATOUR (acting).
Minister of Sport and Youth Affairs: PAUL ABENA (AC).
Minister of Agriculture, Animal Husbandry and Fisheries: HENDRIK SETROWIDJOJO (VA).
Minister of Transport, Communications and Tourism: VALISI PINAS (AC).

SURINAME

Minister of Public Works: RAMON ABRAHAMS (MC).
Minister of Social Affairs and Housing: ALICE AMAFO (AC).
Minister of Trade and Industry: MICHAEL MISKIN (MC).
Minister of Regional Development: LINUS DIKO (AC).
Minister of Education and Community Development: RAYMOND SAPOEN (VA).
Minister of Health: CELCIUS WALDO WATERBERG (AC).
Minister of Labour, Technological Development and the Environment: GINMARDO KROMOSOETO (MC).
Minister of Natural Resources: JIM HOK (MC).
Minister of Physical Planning, Land and Forestry Management: MARTINUS SASTROREDJO (MC).

MINISTRIES

Office of the President: Kleine Combéweg 2–4, Centrum, Paramaribo; tel. 472841; fax 475266; e-mail secretariaat@president.gov.sr; internet www.kabinet.sr.org.

Office of the Vice-President: Dr Sophie Redmondstraat 118, Paramaribo; tel. 474805; fax 472917; e-mail office_vicepres@sr.net.

Ministry of Agriculture, Animal Husbandry and Fisheries: Letitia Vriesdelaan 7, Paramaribo; tel. 477698; fax 470301; e-mail minlvv@sr.net.

Ministry of Defence: Kwattaweg 29, Paramaribo; tel. 474244; fax 420055; e-mail defensie@sr.net.

Ministry of Education and Community Development: Dr Samuel Kafiluddistraat 117–123, Paramaribo; tel. 498383; fax 495083; e-mail minond@sr.net.

Ministry of Finance: Tamarindelaan 3, Paramaribo; tel. 472610; fax 476314; e-mail financien@sr.net; internet www.minfin.sr.

Ministry of Foreign Affairs: Lim A. Postraat 25, POB 25, Paramaribo; tel. 471209; fax 410411; e-mail buza@sr.net.

Ministry of Health: Henck Arronstraat 64, POB 201, Paramaribo; tel. 477601; fax 473923; e-mail info@volksgezondheid.gov.sr; internet www.volksgezondheid.gov.sr.

Ministry of Home Affairs: Wilhelminastraat 3, Paramaribo; tel. 476461; fax 421170; e-mail minbiza@sr.net.

Ministry of Justice and the Police: Henck Arronstraat 1, Paramaribo; tel. 473033; fax 412109; e-mail min.jus-pol@sr.net; internet www.juspolsuriname.org.

Ministry of Labour, Technological Development and the Environment: Wageswegstraat 22, POB 911, Paramaribo; tel. 475241; fax 410465; e-mail voorlichting@atm.sr.org; internet www.atm.sr.org.

Ministry of Natural Resources: Dr J. C. de Mirandastraat 11–13, Paramaribo; tel. 410160; fax 472911; e-mail minnh@sr.net.

Ministry of Physical Planning, Land and Forestry Management: Cornelis Jongbawstraat 10–12, Paramaribo; tel. 470728; fax 473316; e-mail mpjong@datsunsuriname.com.

Ministry of Public Works: Verlengde Jagernath Lachmonstraat 167, Paramaribo; tel. 462500; fax 464901; e-mail minow@sr.net.

Ministry of Regional Development: Van Rooseveltkade 2, Paramaribo; tel. 471574; fax 424517; e-mail regon@sr.net.

Ministry of Social Affairs and Housing: Waterkant 30, Paramaribo; tel. 472340; fax 470516; e-mail soza@sr.net.

Ministry of Sport and Youth Affairs: Paramaribo.

Ministry of Trade and Industry: Havenlaan 3, POB 9354, Paramaribo; tel. 402080; fax 402602; e-mail hi.voorlichting@minhi.gov.sr; internet www.minhi.gov.sr.

Ministry of Transport, Communications and Tourism: Prins Hendrikstraat 24–26, Paramaribo; tel. 411951; fax 420425; e-mail odc@mintct.sr; internet www.mintct.sr.

Legislature

NATIONAL ASSEMBLY

Chairman: JENNIFER GEERLINGS-SIMONS.

General Election, 25 May 2010

Party	% of votes cast	Seats
Megacombinatie*	40.22	23
Nieuw Front†	31.65	14
A-Combinatie‡	4.70	7
Volksalliantie§	12.98	6
Partij voor Demokratie en Ontwikkeling in Eenheid	5.09	1
Basispartij voor Vernieuwing en Democratie/ Politieke Vleugel van de FAL	5.07	—
Other parties	0.29	—
Total	**100.00**	**51**

* An alliance of the Kerukunan Tulodo Pranatan Inggil (KTPI), the Nationale Democratische Partij (NDP), the Nieuw Suriname (NS) and the Progressieve Arbeiders en Landbouwers Unie (PALU).
† An alliance of the Nationale Partij Suriname (NPS), the Surinaamse Partij van de Arbeid (SPA) and the Vooruitstrevende Hervormings Partij (VHP).
‡ Including candidates of the Algemene Bevrijdings- en Ontwikkelingspartij (ABOP) and the Broederschap en Eenheid in Politiek (BEP).
§ An alliance of the Democraten van de 21, Pertijajah Luhur (PL), the Progressieve Surinaamse Volkspartij (PSV) and the Unie van Progressieve Surinamers (UPS).

Election Commission

Centraal Hoofdstembureau (CHS) (Central Polling Authority): Wilhelminastraat 3, Paramaribo; tel. 410362; independent; Chair. LOTHAR BOKSTEEN.

Political Organizations

A-Combinatie (AC): Paramaribo; electoral alliance including:

Algemene Bevrijdings- en Ontwikkelingspartij (ABOP) (General Liberation and Development Party): Jaguarstraat 15, Paramaribo; e-mail webmaster@abop-suriname.net; internet www.abop-suriname.net; f. 1990; Pres. RONNIE BRUNSWIJK; Sec. C. ADA.

Broederschap en Eenheid in Politiek (BEP): Theodorusstraat 55, Land van Dijk, Paramaribo; tel. 402509; fax 422996; e-mail info@bep.sr; internet beppartij.org; f. 1957 as Maroon Party Suriname (MPS); name changed as above in 1987; Chair. CAPRINO ALLENDY; Sec. WENSLEY MISIEDJAN.

Seeka: Paramaribo; Chair. PAUL ABENA.

Basispartij voor Vernieuwing en Democratie (BVD) (Base Party for Renewal and Democracy): Hoogestraat 28–30, Paramaribo; tel. 422231; e-mail info@bvdsuriname.org; internet www.bvdsuriname.org; contested the 2010 election in coalition with the Politiek Vleugel van de FAL (PVF—q.v.); Chair. DILIPKOEMAR SARDJOE; Sec. JERREL CASTLE ROCK.

Democratisch Alternatief 1991 (DA '91) (Democratic Alternative 1991): Gladiolenstraat 17, POB 91, Paramaribo; tel. 432342; fax 493121; e-mail info@da91.sr; internet da91.org; f. 1991 as the Alternatief Forum (AF); social democratic; Chair. WINSTON JESSERUN; Sec. WILFRIED MEYER.

Hernieuwde Progressieve Partij (HPP) (Renewed Progressive Party): Tourtonnelaan 51, Paramaribo; tel. 426965; e-mail hpp@cq-link.sr; f. 1986; Chair. PRIM RAMTAHALSING.

Megacombinatie (MC) (Mega Combination): Paramaribo; Leader DESIRÉ (DESI) DELANO BOUTERSE; alliance formed to contest the 2010 election, comprising:

Kerukunan Tulodo Pranatan Inggil (KTPI) (Party for National Unity and Solidarity): Bonistraat 64, Geyersvlijt, Paramaribo; tel. 456116; f. 1949 as the Kaum Tani Persatuan Indonesia; largely Indonesian; Leader WILLY SOEMITA; Sec. ROBBY DRAGMAN.

Nationale Democratische Partij (NDP) (National Democratic Party): Dr H. D. Benjaminstraat 38, Paramaribo; tel. 499183; fax 432174; e-mail ndpsur@sr.net; internet www.ndp.sr; f. 1987 by Standvaste (the 25 February Movt); army-supported; Chair. DESIRÉ (DESI) DELANO BOUTERSE; Sec. DENNIS MENZO.

Nieuw Suriname (NS) (New Suriname): Paramaribo; f. 2003; Pres. JOHN NASIBDAR; Sec. SAFIEK JAHANGIER.

Progressieve Arbeiders en Landbouwers Unie (PALU) (Progressive Workers' and Farm Labourers' Union): Dr S. Kafiluddis-

SURINAME

traat 27, Paramaribo; tel. 400115; e-mail palu@sr.net; internet palu-suriname.org; f. 1977; socialist party; Chair. JIM K. HOK; Vice-Chair. HENK RAMNANDANLAL.

Nationale Unie (NU): Postbus 5193, Paramaribo; tel. 499675; fax 499678; e-mail info@nationaleunie.net; internet www.nationaleunie.net; f. 1991; Leader MAHIN JANKIE; Sec.-Gen. SOENIEL DEWKALI.

Naya Kadam (New Step): Naarstraat 5, Paramaribo; tel. 482014; fax 481012; e-mail itsvof@sr.net; Chair. INDRA DJWALAPERSAD; Sec. WALDO RAMDIHAL.

Nieuw Front (NF) (New Front): Paramaribo; f. 1987 as Front voor Demokratie en Ontwikkeling (FDO—Front for Democracy and Devt); name changed as above in 1991; Pres. RUNALDO R. VENETIAAN; an alliance comprising:

Nationale Partij Suriname (NPS) (Suriname National Party): Grun Dyari, Johan Adolf Pengelstraat 77, Paramaribo; tel. 477302; fax 475796; e-mail nps@sr.net; internet www.nps.sr; f. 1946; predominantly Creole; Pres. RUNALDO VENETIAAN; Sec. S. OEMRAWSINGH.

Surinaamse Partij van de Arbeid (SPA) (Suriname Labour Party): Rust en Vredestraat 64, Paramaribo; tel. 425912; fax 420394; f. 1987; affiliated with C-47 trade union; social democratic party; joined NF in 1991; Chair. GUNO CASTELEN; Sec.-Gen. ROY ADEMA.

Vooruitstrevende Hervormings Partij (VHP) (Progressive Reformation Party): Jagernath Lachmonstraat 130, Paramaribo; tel. 425912; fax 420394; internet www.parbo.com/vhp; f. 1949 as Verenigde Hindostaanse Partij (United Indian Party); name changed as above in 1973; leading left-wing party; predominantly Indian; Leader RAMDIN SARDJOE; Sec. MAHINDER RATHIPAL.

Partij voor Demokratie en Ontwikkeling in Eenheid (DOE) (Party for Democracy and Development in Unity): Prinsenstraat 47, Hoek Waaldijkstraat, Paramaribo; tel. 491701; e-mail info@doepartij.org; internet www.doepartij.org; f. 1999; Chair. CARL BREEVELD; Sec. PAUL BRANDON.

Pendawa Lima: Bonistraat 115, Geyersvlij, Paramaribo; tel. 551802; f. 1977; predominantly Indonesian; Chair. RAYMOND SAPOEN; Sec. RANDY KROMODIHARDJO.

Permanente Voorspoed Republiek Suriname (PVRS) (Lasting Prosperity Party of Suriname): Engelslootstraat 8, Projectsloot, Paramaribo; tel. 493928; e-mail info@nieuwpvrs.com; internet www.nieuwpvrs.com; Chair. CHAS MIJNALS.

Politieke Vleugel van de FAL (PVF): Keizerstraat 150, Paramaribo; f. 1995; political wing of farmers' org. Federatie van Agrariërs en Landarbeiders; contested the 2010 election in coalition with the Basispartij voor Vernieuwing en Democratie (BVD—q.v.); Chair. SOEDESCHAND JAIRAM; Sec. RADJOE BIKHARIE.

Progressieve Bosneger Partij (PBP): f. 1968; resumed political activities 1987; represents members of the Bush Negro (Boschneger) ethnic group; associated with the Pendawa Lima (see above); Chair. ARMAND KANAPE.

Volksalliantie (People's Alliance): Paramaribo; alliance formed to contest the 2010 election; Leader PAUL SALAM SOMOHARDJO.

Democraten van de 21 (D21) (Democrats of the 21st Century): Goudstraat 22, Paramaribo; f. 1996; Chair. SOEWARTO MOESTADJA; Sec. KANIMAN PASIRAN.

Pertijajah Luhur (PL) (Full Confidence Party): Hoek Gemenlandsweg-Daniel Coutinhostraat, Paramaribo; tel. 401087; fax 420394; internet www.pertjajahluhur.org; f. 1998; left Nieuw Front alliance in 2010; Pres. PAUL SALAM SOMOHARDJO.

Progressieve Surinaamse Volkspartij (PSV) (Suriname Progressive People's Party): Keizerstraat 122, Paramaribo; tel. 472979; internet www.middenblok.com; f. 1947; resumed political activities 1987; contested the 2010 election in coalition with the Unie van Progressieve Surinamers (UPS—q.v.); Christian democratic party; Chair. RONALD GRUNBERG.

Unie van Progressieve Surinamers (UPS): Keizerstraat 122, Paramaribo; tel. 472979; internet www.middenblok.com; f. 2004; contested the 2010 election in coalition with the Progressieve Surinaamse Volkspartij (PSV—q.v.); Chair. HENRI ORI.

Diplomatic Representation

EMBASSIES IN SURINAME

Brazil: Maratakkastraat 2, Zorg en Hoop, POB 925, Paramaribo; tel. 400200; fax 400205; e-mail brasemb@sr.net; internet www2.mre.gov.br/suriname/index.asp; Ambassador JOSÉ LUIZ MACHADO E COSTA.

China, People's Republic: Anton Dragtenweg 131, POB 3042 Paramaribo; tel. 451570; fax 452540; e-mail chinaemb_sr@mfa.gov.cn; internet sr.chineseembassy.org; Ambassador YUAN NANSHENG.

Cuba: Brokopondolaan 4, Paramaribo; tel. 434917; fax 432626; e-mail embacubasuriname@parbo.net; internet embacu.cubaminrex.cu/surinaming; Ambassador ANDRÉS MARCELO GONZÁLEZ GARRIDO.

France: Henck Arronstraat 5–7, POB 2648, Paramaribo; tel. 476455; fax 471208; e-mail ambafrance.paramaribo@diplomatie.gouv.fr; internet www.ambafrance-sr.org; Ambassador RICHARD BARBEYRON.

Guyana: Gravenstraat 82, POB 785, Paramaribo; tel. 477895; fax 472679; e-mail guyembassy@sr.net; Ambassador MERLIN UDHO.

India: Dr Sophie Redmondstraat 221, POB 1329, Paramaribo; tel. 498344; fax 491106; e-mail india@sr.net; internet www.indembassysuriname.com; Ambassador KANWAL JIT SINGH SODDHI.

Indonesia: Van Brussellaan 3, Uitvlugt, POB 157, Paramaribo; tel. 431230; fax 498234; e-mail indonemb@sr.net; internet www.paramaribo.deplu.go.id; Ambassador NUR SYAHRIR RAHARDJO.

Japan: Henck Arronstraat 23–25, POB 2921, Paramaribo; tel. 474860; fax 412208; e-mail eojparbo@sr.net; Ambassador TASUAKI IWATA (resident in Venezuela).

Netherlands: Van Roseveltkade 5, POB 1877, Paramaribo; tel. 477211; fax 477792; e-mail prm@minbuza.nl; internet www.nederlandseambassade.sr; Ambassador AART JACOBI.

Russia: Anton Dragtenweg 7, POB 8127, Paramaribo; tel. and fax 472387; Ambassador PAVEL SERGIEV.

USA: Dr Sophie Redmondstraat 129, POB 1821, Paramaribo; tel. 472900; fax 425690; e-mail embuscen@sr.net; internet suriname.usembassy.gov; Ambassador JOHN R. NAY.

Venezuela: Henck Arronstraat 23–25, POB 3001, Paramaribo; tel. 475401; fax 475602; e-mail embajador@suriname.gob.ve; internet www.embavenezsuriname.com; Ambassador FRANCISCO DE JESÚS SIMANCAS.

Judicial System

The administration of justice is entrusted to a Court of Justice, the six members of which are nominated for life, and three Cantonal Courts. Suriname recognized the Caribbean Court of Justice (CCJ) on matters of original jurisdiction pertaining to international trade. The CCJ was inaugurated in Port of Spain, Trinidad and Tobago, on 16 April 2005.

President of the Court of Justice: EWALD OMBRE.
Attorney-General: SUBHAAS PUNWASI.

Religion

CHRISTIANITY

According to the 2004 census, Christians represent approximately 48% of the population.

Committee of Christian Churches: Paramaribo; tel. 476306; Chair. Rev. WILHELMUS DE BEKKER (Bishop of Paramaribo).

The Roman Catholic Church

For ecclesiastical purposes, Suriname comprises the single diocese of Paramaribo, suffragan to the archdiocese of Port of Spain (Trinidad and Tobago). The Bishop participates in the Antilles Episcopal Conference (currently based in Port of Spain, Trinidad and Tobago). Some 25% of the population are Roman Catholics.

Bishop of Paramaribo: WILHELMUS ADRIANUS JOSEPHUS MARIA DE BEKKER, Bisschopshuis, Henck Arronstraat 12, POB 1230, Paramaribo; tel. 425918; fax 471602; e-mail cabisdom@sr.net.

The Anglican Communion

Within the Church in the Province of the West Indies, Suriname forms part of the diocese of Guyana. The Episcopal Church is also represented.

Anglican Church: St Bridget's, Hoogestraat 44, Paramaribo.

Protestant Churches

Evangelisch Lutherse Kerk in Suriname: Waterkant 102, POB 585, Paramaribo; tel. 425503; fax 425503; e-mail elks@sr.net; f. 1741; Pres. MARY-AN MOLGO; 3,500 mems.

Moravian Church in Suriname (Evangelische Broeder Gemeente): Maagdenstraat 50, POB 1811, Paramaribo; tel. 473073; fax 475794; e-mail ebgs@sr.net; f. 1735; Praeses MAARTEN MINGOEN; 40,000 mems (2004).

Adherents to the Moravian Church constitute some 15% of the population. Also represented are the Christian Reformed Church, the Dutch Reformed Church, the Baptist Church, the Evangelical

Methodist Church, Pentecostal Missions, the Seventh-day Adventists and the Wesleyan Methodist Congregation.

HINDUISM

According to the 2004 census, 24% of the population are Hindus.

Arya Dewaker: Johan Adolf Pengelstraat 210, Paramaribo; tel. 400706; e-mail aryadewaker@sr.net; members preach the Vedic Dharma; disciples of Maha Rishi Swami Dayanand Sarswati, the founder of the Arya Samaj in India; f. 1929; Chair. INDERDATH TILAKDHARIE.

Sanatan Dharm: Koningstraat 31–33, POB 760, Paramaribo; tel. 404190; f. 1930; Pres. Dr R. M. NANNAN PANDAY; over 150,000 mems.

ISLAM

Some 16% of the population are Muslims, according to the 2004 census.

Federatie Islamitische Gemeenten in Suriname: Paramaribo; Indonesian Islamic org.; Chair. K. KAAIMAN.

Stichting der Islamitische Gemeenten Suriname: Verlengde Mahonielaan 39, Paramaribo; Indonesian Islamic org.

Surinaamse Islamitische Organisatie (SIO): Watermolenstraat 10, POB 278, Paramaribo; tel. 475220; fax 472075; e-mail ijamaludin@hotmail.com; f. 1978; Pres. Dr I. JAMALUDIN; Sec. Dr K. M. MOENNE; 6 brs.

Surinaamse Moeslim Associatie: Kankantriestraat 55–57, Paramaribo; Javanese Islamic org.

JUDAISM

The Dutch Jewish Congregation and the Dutch Portuguese-Jewish Congregation are represented in Suriname.

Jewish Community: The Synagogue Neve Shalom, Keizerstraat, POB 1834, Paramaribo; tel. 400236; fax 402380; e-mail rene-fernandes@cq-link.sr; internet www.ujcl.org; f. 1854; mem. of Union of Jewish Congregations of Latin America and the Caribbean (UJCL); Officiant JACQUES VAN NIEL; 300 mems (2005).

The Press

DAILIES

Dagblad Suriname: Zwartenhovenbrugstraat 154, POB 975, Paramaribo; tel. 426336; fax 471718; e-mail general@dbsuriname.com; internet www.dbsuriname.com; f. 2002; Dir FARIED PIERKHAN; Editor LAL MAHOMED JAMES.

De Ware Tijd: Malebatrumstraat 9, POB 1200, Paramaribo; tel. 472833; fax 411169; e-mail infodwt@dwt.net; internet www.dwtonline.com; f. 1957; morning; Dutch; independent/liberal; Dir STEVE JONG TJIEN FA; Editor-in-Chief RICARDO CARROT.

De West: Dr J. C. de Mirandastraat 2–6, POB 176, Paramaribo; tel. 473327; fax 470322; e-mail dewest@cq-link.sr; internet www.dewestonline.cq-link.sr; f. 1909; midday; Dutch; liberal; Editor GEORGE D. C. FINDLAY; circ. 15,000–18,000.

PERIODICALS

Advertentieblad van de Republiek Suriname: Henck Arronstraat 120, POB 56, Paramaribo; tel. 473501; fax 454782; f. 1871; 2 a week; Dutch; govt and official information bulletin; Editor E. D. FINDLAY; circ. 1,000.

CLO Bulletin: Gemenelandsweg 95, Paramaribo; f. 1973; irreg.; Dutch; labour information publ. by civil servants' union.

Kerkbode: Burenstraat 17–19, POB 219, Paramaribo; tel. 473079; fax 475635; e-mail stadje@sr.net; f. 1906; weekly; religious; CEO CONSTAN LANDVREUGD; circ. 1,200.

Omhoog: Henck Arronstraat 21, POB 1802, Paramaribo; tel. 425992; fax 426782; e-mail rkomhoog@sr.net; f. 1952; Dutch; weekly; Catholic bulletin; Editor S. MULDER; circ. 5,000.

Xtreme Magazine: Uranusstraat 49, Paramaribo; tel. 456969.

Publishers

Afaka International NV: Residastraat 23, Paramaribo; tel. and fax 530640; e-mail info@afaka.biz; internet www.afaka.net; f. 1996; Dir GERRIT BARRON.

Educatieve Uitgeverij Sorava NV: Latourweg 10, POB 8382, Paramaribo; tel. and fax 480808.

IMWO, Universiteit van Suriname: Universiteitscomplex, Leysweg 1, POB 9212, Paramaribo; tel. 465558; fax 462291; e-mail bmhango@yahoo.com.

Ministerie van Onderwijs en Volksontwikkeling (Ministry of Education and Community Development): Dr Samuel Kafilludistraat 117–123, Paramaribo; tel. 498850; fax 495083.

Okopipi Publ. (Publishing Services Suriname): Van Idsingastraat 133, Paramaribo; tel. 472746; e-mail pssmoniz@sr.net; fmrly I. Krishnadath.

Papaya Media Counseling: Plutostraat 30, POB 8304, Paramaribo; tel. and fax 454530; e-mail roy_bhikharie@sr.net; f. 2002; Man. Dir ROY BHIKHARIE.

Stichting Wetenschappelijke Informatie (Foundation for Information and Development): Prins Hendrikstraat 38, Paramaribo; tel. 475232; fax 422195; e-mail swin@sr.net; internet www.swi77.org; f. 1977; Chair. JACK MENKE.

Tabiki Productions: Weidestraat 34, Paramaribo; tel. 478525; fax 478526; e-mail insightsuriname@yahoo.com.

VACO, NV: Domineestraat 26, POB 1841, Paramaribo; tel. 472545; fax 410563; f. 1952; Dir EDUARD HOGENBOOM.

PUBLISHERS' ASSOCIATION

Publishers' Association Suriname: Domineestraat 32, POB 1841, Paramaribo; tel. 472545; fax 410563.

Broadcasting and Communications

TELECOMMUNICATIONS

Regulatory Authority

Telecommunications Authority Suriname (TAS): Dr J. F. Nassylaan 23, Paramaribo; tel. 421464; fax 421465; e-mail tasur@sr.net; f. 2007; Dir JETTIE OLFF.

Major Service Providers

Digicel Suriname: Henck Arronstraat 27–29, POB 1848, Paramaribo; tel. 462626; fax 475502; internet www.digicelsuriname.com; mobile operating licence granted in Aug. 2006; operations commenced Dec. 2007; Dir of the Bd COLM DELVES; CEO HANS LUTE.

International Telecommunication Suriname NV (IntelSur NV): Paramaribo; mobile operating licence granted in August 2006 formalized in April 2007; CEO ERIC LELIENHOF.

Telecommunication Corporation Suriname (Telesur): Heiligenweg 14, POB 1839, Paramaribo; tel. 473944; fax 421919; internet www.telesur.sr; liberalization of the telecommunications sector ended Telesur's monopoly in April 2007; supervisory function of Telesur assumed by new regulatory body, Telecommunication Authority Suriname (q.v.); Man. Dir DIRK M. R. CURRIE.

BROADCASTING

Radio

ABC Radio (Ampie's Broadcasting Corporation): Maystraat 57, Paramaribo; tel. 464555; fax 464680; e-mail info@abcsuriname.com; internet www.abcsuriname.com; f. 1975; re-opened in 1993; commercial; Dutch and some local languages.

Radika Radio & TV: Indira Gandhiweg 165, Paramaribo; tel. 482800; fax 482910; e-mail radika@sr.net; internet www.radikartv.com; f. 1962; re-opened in 1989; Dutch and Hindi; Dir ROSHNI RADHAKISHUN.

Radio Apintie: Verlengde Gemenelandsweg 37, POB 595, Paramaribo; tel. 400500; fax 400684; e-mail apintie@sr.net; internet www.apintie.sr; f. 1958; commercial; Dutch and some local languages; Dir CHARLES VERVUURT.

Radio Bersama: Bonnistraat 115, Paramaribo; tel. 551802; fax 551803; internet www.radio-bersama.com; f. 1997; Gen. Man. AJOEB MOENTARI.

Radio Boskopu: Roseveltkade 1, Paramaribo; tel. 410300; govt-owned; Sranang Tongo and Dutch; Head LEO VAN VARSSEVELD.

Radio Nickerie (RANI): Waterloostraat 3, Nieuw Nickerie; tel. 231462; commercial; Hindi and Dutch.

Radio Paramaribo (Rapar): Verlengde Jagernath Lachmonstraat 34, POB 975, Paramaribo; tel. 499995; fax 493121; e-mail rapar@sr.net; f. 1957; commercial; Dutch and some local languages; Dir FARIED PIERKHAN.

Radio Sangeet Mala: Indira Gandhiweg 40, Paramaribo; tel. 485893; e-mail info@sgmsuriname.com; internet www.sgmsuriname.com; f. 1998; Dutch and Hindi; Dirs RADJEN SOEKHRADJ, SOEDESH RAMSARAN.

Radio SRS (Stichting Radio Omroep Suriname): Jacques van Eerstraat 20, POB 271, Paramaribo; tel. 498115; fax 498116; e-mail adm@radiosrs.com; internet www.radiosrs.com; f. 1965; com-

SURINAME

mercial; govt-owned; Dutch and some local languages; Dir Roseline A. Daan.

Radio & Televisie Garuda: Goudstraat 14–16, Paramaribo; tel. 456869; f. 2001; Dir Tommy Radji.

Radio Ten: Stadionlaan 3, POB 110, Paramaribo; tel. 410881; fax 422294; e-mail info@radio10.sr; internet www.radio10.sr; Dir Werner Duttenhofer.

Other stations include: Radio KBC, Radio Koyeba, Radio Pertjaya, Radio Shalom, Radio Zon, Ramasha Radio, Rasonic Radio and Trishul Radio.

Television

ABC Televisie (Ampie's Broadcasting Corporation): Maystraat 57, Paramaribo; tel. 464555; fax 464680; e-mail info@abcsuriname.com; internet www.abcsuriname.com; Channel 4.

Algemene Televisie Verzorging (ATV): van het Hogerhuysstraat 58-60; tel. 404611; fax 402660; e-mail info@atv.sr; internet www.atv.sr; f. 1985; govt-owned; commercial; Dutch, English, Portuguese, Spanish and some local languages; Channel 12; Man. Guno Cooman.

Radio & Televisie Garuda: see Radio & Televisie Garuda in Radio section.

Radika Radio & TV: see Radika Radio & TV in Radio section; Hindi entertainment TV channel.

STVS (Surinaamse Televisie Stichting): Letitia Vriesdelaan 5, POB 535, Paramaribo; tel. 473032; fax 477216; e-mail info@stvs.sr; internet www.stvs.sr; f. 1965; govt-owned; commercial; local languages, Dutch and English; Channels 6, 8, 11 and 13; Dir Kenneth Oostburg.

Finance

(cap. = capital; res = reserves; dep. = deposits; m. = million; brs = branches; amounts in Surinamese dollars)

BANKING

Central Bank

Centrale Bank van Suriname: 18–20 Waterkant, POB 1801, Paramaribo; tel. 473741; fax 476444; e-mail info@cbvs.sr; internet www.cbvs.sr; f. 1957; cap.and res. 210.7m., dep. 858.2m. (Dec. 2009); Gov. Gilmore Hoefdraad; Exec. Dir O. Ezechiëls.

Commercial Banks

Finabank NV: Dr Sophie Redmondstraat 59–61, Paramaribo; tel. 472266; fax 422672; e-mail finabank@sr.net; internet www.finabanknv.com; f. 1991; cap. 1.0m., res. 5.1m., dep. 157.0m. (Dec. 2009); Chair. Jules A. Tjin Wong Joe; Gen. Man. Merleen Atmodikromo.

Handels-Krediet- en Industriebank (Hakrinbank NV): Dr Sophie Redmondstraat 11–13, POB 1813, Paramaribo; tel. 477722; fax 472066; e-mail hakrindp@sr.net; internet www.hakrinbank.com; f. 1936; cap. 0.1m., res 75.3m., dep. 1,004.9m. (Dec. 2009); Pres. and Chair. A. K. R. Shyamnarain; CEO J. D. Bousaid; 6 brs.

Landbouwbank NV: FHR Lim A Postraat 34, POB 929, Paramaribo; tel. 475945; fax 411965; e-mail lbbank@sr.net; f. 1972; govt-owned; agricultural bank; Chair. D. Ferrier; Pres. D. Hindori; 5 brs.

RBTT Bank (Suriname) NV: Kerkplein 1, Paramaribo; tel. 471555; fax 411325; internet www.rbtt.com/sr/personal; f. 1856.

Stichting Surinaamse Volkscredietbank (VCB): Waterkant 104, POB 1804, Paramaribo; tel. 472616; fax 473257; e-mail info@vcbbank.sr; internet www.vcbbank.sr; f. 1949; Man. Dir Thakoerdien Ramlakhan; 3 brs.

Surichange Bank NV: Dr Sophie Redmondstraat 71, Paramaribo; tel. 471151; fax 474554; e-mail info@surichange.sr; internet www.scbbank.sr; cap. 4.5m., res. 3.5m., dep. 87.4m. (Dec. 2009); Exec. Dirs Stanley Mathura, Rajindrekoemar Merhai.

De Surinaamsche Bank NV: Henck Arronstraat 26–30, POB 1806, Paramaribo; tel. 471100; fax 411750; e-mail info@dsbbank.sr; internet www.dsbbank.sr; f. 1865; cap. 0.8m., res 124.5m., dep. 1,751.4m. (Dec. 2009); Chair. S. Smit; CEO Sigmund L. J. Proeve; 8 brs.

Surinaamse Postspaarbank: Knuffelsgracht 10–14, POB 1879, Paramaribo; tel. 472256; fax 472952; e-mail spsbdir@sr.net; f. 1904; savings and commercial bank; Man. Alwin R. Baarh (acting); 2 brs.

INSURANCE

Assuria NV: Grote Combeweg 37, POB 1501, Paramaribo; tel. 477955; fax 472390; e-mail assurialeven@assuria.sr; internet www.assuria.sr; f. 1961; life and indemnity insurance; Man. Dir Dr S. Smit.

Directory

Assuria Schadeverzekering NV: Henck Arronstraat 5–7, POB 1030, Paramaribo; tel. 473400; fax 476669; e-mail customer.service@assuria.sr; internet www.assuria.sr; Chair. J. J. Healy; Man. Dir Dr S. Smit.

Fatum Levensverzekering NV: Noorderkerkstraat 5–7, Paramaribo; tel. 471541; fax 410067; e-mail fatum@sr.net; internet www.fatum-suriname.com; Chair. C. A. Calor; Exec. Dir N. W. Lalbiharie.

Hennep Verzorgende Verzekering NV: Dr Sophie Redmondstraat 246, Paramaribo; tel. 425205; fax 425209; e-mail hennep@sr.net; internet www.uitvaarthennep.com; f. 1896; Man. Dir H. J. Hennep.

Parsasco NV: Henck Arronstraat 119, Paramaribo; tel. 421212; fax 421325; e-mail parsasco@sr.net; internet www.parsasco.com; f. 1995; Man. Dir Amar Randjitsing.

Self Reliance: Heerenstraat 48–50 en Henck Arronstraat 69–71, Paramaribo; tel. 472582; fax 472475; e-mail self-reliance@sr.net; internet www.self-reliance.sr; f. 1980; general and life insurance; Pres. Maurice L. Roemer.

Trade and Industry

DEVELOPMENT ORGANIZATIONS

Centre for Industry and Export Development: Rust en Vredestraat 79–81, POB 1275, Paramaribo; tel. 474830; fax 476311; f. 1981; Man. R. A. Leter.

Stichting Planbureau Suriname (National Planning Office of Suriname): Dr Sophie Redmondstraat 118, POB 172, Paramaribo; tel. 447408; fax 475001; e-mail dirsps@sr.net; internet www.planbureau.net; f. 1951; responsible for regional and socio-economic long- and short-term planning; Man. Dir Lilian J. M. Monsels-Thompson.

CHAMBERS OF COMMERCE

Kamer van Koophandel en Fabrieken (Chamber of Commerce and Industry): Dr J. C. de Mirandastraat 10, POB 149, Paramaribo; tel. 474536; fax 474779; e-mail chamber@sr.net; f. 1910; Pres. Robert Ameerali; 16,109 mems.

Surinaams–Nederlandse Kamer voor Handel en Industrie (Suriname–Netherlands Chamber of Commerce and Industry): Jagernath Lachmonstraat 158, Paramaribo; tel. and fax 476909.

INDUSTRIAL AND TRADE ASSOCIATIONS

Associatie van Surinaamse Fabrikanten (ASFA) (Suriname Manufacturers' Assen): Jaggernath Lachmonstraat 187, POB 3046, Paramaribo; tel. 434014; fax 439798; e-mail info@asfasuriname.com; internet www.asfasuriname.com; f. 1980; Chair. Rahid Doekhie; 317 mems.

Vereniging Surinaams Bedrijfsleven (Suriname Trade and Industry Association): Prins Hendrikstraat 18, POB 111, Paramaribo; tel. 475286; fax 475287; e-mail info@vsbstia.org; internet www.vsbstia.org; Pres. Marcel A. Meyer; 290 mems.

UTILITIES

Electricity

NV Energie Bedrijven Suriname (EBS): Noorderkerkstraat 2–14, POB 1825, Paramaribo; tel. 471045; fax 474866; e-mail g.lau@nvebs.com; internet www.nvebs.com; f. 1932 as Nederlands-Indische Gas Maatschappij; present name adopted in 1968; electricity and gas distribution; owns and operates Electricity Co of Paramaribo (EPAR) and Ogane Paramaribo (OPAR); Dir Gerard Lau.

Staatsolie Maatschappij Suriname NV: Dr Ir H. S. Adhinstraat 21, POB 4069, Paramaribo; tel. 499649; fax 491105; e-mail mailstaatsolie@staatsolie.com; internet www.staatsolie.com; f. 1980; state petroleum exploration and exploitation co; electricity and steam generation and supplies; produces 16,000 barrels per day of Saramacca Crude oil; Man. Dir Marc C. H. Waaldijk; 750 employees.

Paradise Oil Company: Dr Ir H. S. Adhinstraat 21, POB 4069, Paramaribo; tel. 439781; fax 530093; e-mail madaal@staatsolie.com; f. 2003; 100% owned by Staatsolie Maatschappij Suriname NV; oil exploration co; Operations Man. Patrick Brunings.

Water

NV Surinaamsche Waterleiding Maatschappij (SWM): Henck Arronstraat 9–11, POB 1818, Paramaribo; tel. 471414; fax 476343; e-mail swmsecretariaat@swm.sr; internet www.swm.sr; f. 1932; govt-owned; Dir Scen Sjauw Koen Sa; 465 employees (2008).

TRADE UNIONS

Council of the Surinamese Federation of Trade Unions (RAVAKSUR) (Raad van Vakcentrales Suriname): f. 1987; Sec. MICHAEL MISKIN; comprises:

Algemeen Verbond van Vakverenigingen in Suriname 'De Moederbond' (AVVS) (General Confederation of Trade Unions): Verlengde Jagernath Lachmonstraat 134, POB 2951, Paramaribo; tel. 465118; fax 463116; e-mail avvsmoederbond51@hotmail.com; right-wing; Pres. ERROLL G. SNIJDERS; Gen. Sec. ALESSANDRO SPRONG; 15,000 mems.

Centrale Landsdienaren Organisatie (CLO) (Central Organization for Civil Service Employees): Gemenelandsweg 743, Paramaribo; tel. 499839; Pres. RONALD HOOGHART; 13,000 mems.

Organisatie van Samenwerkende Autonome Vakbonden (OSAV): Noorderkerkstraat 2–10, Paramaribo; fax 478548; Pres. SONNY CHOTKAN.

Progressieve Werknemers Organisatie (PWO) (Progressive Workers' Organization): Limesgracht 80, POB 406, Paramaribo; tel. 475840; fax 477814; f. 1948; covers the commercial, hotel and banking sectors; Pres. ANDRE KOORNAAR; Sec. EDWARD MENT; 4,000 mems.

Progressive Trade Union Federation (C-47): Wanicastraat 230, Paramaribo; tel. 401120; fax 401149; e-mail c47@sr.net; Pres. ROBBY BERENSTEIN; Gen. Sec. CLAUDETTE ETNEL.

Federation of Farmers and Agrarians (FAL): Keizerstraat 150, Paramaribo; tel. 420833; fax 474517; Pres. JIWAN SITAL; Gen. Sec. ANAND DWARKA.

Nickerie Banana Workers' Union (BABN): Paramaribo; f. 2008; Pres. DAYANAND DWARKA.

Transport

RAILWAYS

There are no public railways operating in Suriname.

ROADS

In 2003 Suriname had an estimated 4,304 km (2,674 miles) of roads, of which 26.3% were paved. The principal east–west road, 390 km in length, links Albina, on the eastern border, with Nieuw Nickerie, in the west.

SHIPPING

Suriname is served by many shipping companies and has about 1,500 km (930 miles) of navigable rivers and canals. There are two ferry services linking Suriname with Guyana, across the Corantijn river, and with French Guiana, across the Marowijne river. In late 2010 a feasibility study into construction of a bridge across the Corantijn river was begun by Suriname and Guyana.

Maritieme Autoriteit Suriname (Suriname Maritime Authority): Cornelis Jongbawstraat 2, POB 888, Paramaribo; tel. 476733; fax 472940; e-mail info@mas.sr; internet www.mas.sr; fmrly Dienst voor de Scheepvaart; govt authority supervising and controlling shipping in Surinamese waters; Man. of Maritime Operations A. T. EDENBURG.

Scheepvaart Maatschappij Suriname NV (SMS) (Suriname Shipping Line Ltd): Waterkant 44, POB 1824, Paramaribo; tel. 472447; fax 474814; e-mail surinam_line@sr.net; f. 1936; state-owned; passenger services in the interior; Chair. A. T. EDENBURG.

Suriname Coast Traders NV: Flocislaan 4, Industrieterrein Flora, POB 9216, Paramaribo; tel. 463040; fax 463831; internet www.pasonsgroup.com; f. 1981; subsidiary of Pasons Group.

NV VSH United Suriname Shipping Company: van 't Hogerhuysstraat 9–11, POB 1860, Paramaribo; tel. 402558; fax 403515; e-mail sales@vshunited.com; internet www.vshunited.com/shipping.html; shipping agents and freight carriers; Man. RICHARD STEENLAND.

CIVIL AVIATION

The main airport is Johan Adolf Pengel International Airport, 45 km from Paramaribo. Domestic flights operate from Zorg-en-Hoop Airport, located in a suburb of Paramaribo. There are 35 airstrips throughout the country.

Surinaamse Luchtvaart Maatschappij NV (SLM) (Suriname Airways): Mr Jagernath Lachmonstraat 136, POB 2029, Paramaribo; tel. 465700; fax 491213; e-mail publicrelations@slm.firm.sr; internet www.slm.nl; f. 1962; services to Amsterdam (Netherlands) and to destinations in North America, South America and the Caribbean; Vice-Pres. CLYDE CAIRO.

Gonini Air Service Ltd: Doekhiweg 1, Zorg-en-Hoop Airport, POB 1614, Paramaribo; tel. 499098; fax 498363; f. 1976; privately owned; licensed for scheduled and unscheduled national and international services (charters, lease, etc.); Man. Dir GERARD BRUNINGS.

Gum Air NV: Doekhieweg 3, Zorg-en-Hoop Airfield, Paramaribo; tel. 498760; fax 491740; e-mail info@gumair.com; internet www.gumair.com; f. 1974; privately owned; unscheduled domestic and regional flights; Man. DEAN GUMMELS.

Tourism

Efforts were made to promote the previously undeveloped tourism sector in the 1990s. Attractions include the varied cultural activities, a number of historical sites and an unspoiled interior with many varieties of plants, birds and animals. There are 13 nature reserves and one nature park. There were an estimated 162,500 stop-over arrivals in 2007, of which a majority came from the Netherlands. In 2008 tourism receipts totalled US $83m.

Suriname Tourism Foundation: Dr J. F. Nassylaan 2, Paramaribo; tel. 424878; fax 477786; e-mail info@suriname-tourism.org; internet www.suriname-tourism.org; f. 1996; Exec. Dir ARMAND LI-A-YOUNG.

Defence

The National Army numbered an estimated 1,840 men and women, as assessed at November 2010. There is an army of 1,400, a navy of 240 and an air force of some 200.

Defence Budget: an estimated 134,000m. Surinamese dollars in 2010.

Commander-in-Chief: Col HEDWICH GILAARD.

Education

Education is compulsory for children between the ages of seven and 12. Primary education lasts for six years, and is followed by a further seven years of secondary education, comprising a junior secondary cycle of four years followed by a senior cycle of three years. All education in government and denominational schools is provided free of charge. In 2007/08 enrolment in primary education included 90% of children in the relevant age-group, while in 2004/05, according to UNESCO estimates, enrolment in secondary education included 65% of children in the relevant age-group. Higher education was provided by four technical and vocational schools and by the University of Suriname at Paramaribo. In 2003 the Inter-American Development Bank approved a US $12.5m. loan to fund the reform of the basic education system into a single 10-year cycle. It was hoped that the funds would result in a 10% increase in the number of pupils who finished sixth grade and a 20% reduction in drop-out and repetition rates. A further $13m. grant for the sector was approved by the Dutch Government in 2005.

SWAZILAND

Introductory Survey

LOCATION, CLIMATE, LANGUAGE, RELIGION, FLAG, CAPITAL

The Kingdom of Swaziland is a land-locked country in southern Africa, bordered by South Africa to the north, west, south and south-east, and by Mozambique to the east. The average annual temperature is about 16°C (61°F) on the Highveld, and about 22°C (72°F) in the sub-humid Lowveld, while annual rainfall ranges from 1,000 mm (40 ins) to 2,280 mm (90 ins) on the Highveld, and from 500 mm (20 ins) to 890 mm (35 ins) in the Lowveld. English and siSwati are the official languages. About 60% of the population profess Christianity, while most of the remainder adhere to traditional beliefs. The national flag (proportions 2 by 3) is blue, with a yellow-edged horizontal crimson stripe (one-half of the depth) in the centre. On this stripe is a black and white Swazi shield, superimposed on two spears and a staff, all lying horizontally. The capital is Mbabane.

CONTEMPORARY POLITICAL HISTORY

Historical Context

Swaziland, which was previously under the joint rule of the United Kingdom and the South African (Transvaal) Republic, became a British protectorate in 1903, and one of the High Commission Territories in 1907, the others being the colony of Basutoland (now the Kingdom of Lesotho) and the protectorate of Bechuanaland (now the Republic of Botswana). The British Act of Parliament that established the Union of South Africa in 1910 also provided for the inclusion in South Africa of the three High Commission Territories, subject to consultation with the local inhabitants.

Swaziland's first Constitution, which was introduced by the British Government, entered into force in January 1964. The Paramount Chief (iNgwenyama—the Lion), King Sobhuza II, subsequently established a traditionalist political party, the Imbokodvo National Movement (INM), which secured all of the seats in the new Legislative Council at elections in June of that year. In 1965, in response to continued pressure from the INM, the British Government established a committee to draft proposed constitutional amendments. A new Constitution, which was promulgated in 1966 and came into effect in April 1967, provided for the introduction of internal self-government pending the attainment of full independence by the end of 1969. Executive power was vested in King Sobhuza as the hereditary monarch and constitutional Head of State. The Legislative Council was dissolved in March 1967, and elections to the new bicameral Parliament took place in April. The INM secured all 24 elective seats in the House of Assembly, although the Ngwane National Liberatory Congress (NNLC) received 20% of the votes cast. In May King Sobhuza formed Swaziland's first Cabinet, appointing the leader of the INM, Prince Makhosini Dlamini, as Prime Minister. On 6 September 1968 Swaziland was granted full independence within the Commonwealth, and a new Constitution (based on the existing Constitution) was adopted.

In April 1973, in accordance with a parliamentary resolution, King Sobhuza repealed the Constitution, imposed a state of emergency under which all political activity was suspended, introduced legislation providing for detention without trial for a period of 60 days, and announced the formation of a national army. A new Constitution, promulgated on 13 October 1978, confirmed the King's control of executive and legislative decisions. The functions of the bicameral parliament, comprising a House of Assembly and a Senate, were confined to debating government proposals and advising the King. The existing 40 traditional local councils (Tinkhundla—singular: Inkhundla) were each to nominate two members to an 80-member electoral college, which was, in turn, to elect 40 deputies to the House of Assembly. Members of the House of Assembly were to select 10 members of the Senate, while the King was to nominate a further 10 members to each chamber. All political parties (including the INM) were prohibited. Legislative elections took place later that year, and the parliament was inaugurated in January 1979. In June 1982 the Swaziland National Council, an advisory body on matters of Swazi tradition, comprising members of the royal family, was redesignated as the Supreme Council of State (Liqoqo).

Domestic Political Affairs

King Sobhuza died in August 1982. In accordance with Swazi tradition, the powers of Head of State devolved upon the Queen Mother (Ndlovukazi—Great She Elephant) Dzeliwe, who was authorized to act as Regent until King Sobhuza's designated successor, Prince Makhosetive (born in 1968), attained the age of 21. Shortly afterwards Queen Regent Dzeliwe appointed the Liqoqo, which was to advise her in all affairs of State. Competition to secure supreme executive power subsequently emerged between the Prime Minister, Prince Mabandla N. F. Dlamini, and several prominent members, led by Prince Mfanasibili Dlamini, of the Liqoqo. In March 1983 Prince Mabandla was replaced as Prime Minister by a traditionalist, Prince Bhekimpi Dlamini. In August, under the powers of the 'Authorized Person' (an important hereditary post, held by Prince Sozisa Dlamini, the Chairman of the Liqoqo), Queen Regent Dzeliwe was deposed, apparently as a result of her reluctance to dismiss Prince Mabandla. Following an attempt by Queen Regent Dzeliwe to appeal against her deposition, Prince Mfanasibili and his followers obtained an official declaration that the High Court had no jurisdiction in matters concerning Swazi custom and tradition. Widespread opposition to the deposition of Queen Regent Dzeliwe was suppressed, and in September Queen Ntombi, the mother of Prince Makhosetive, was officially invested as Regent. In November elections to the Libandla took place, and a new Cabinet was appointed, in which only Prince Bhekimpi and the Minister of Foreign Affairs, Richard Dlamini, were retained.

In October 1985, following protests by prominent members of the royal family at the Liqoqo's monopoly of power, Queen Regent Ntombi dismissed Prince Mfanasibili. It was subsequently announced that the Liqoqo was to be reconstituted in its former capacity as an advisory body on matters pertaining to traditional law and custom. In December all those convicted of conspiracy in late 1984 were pardoned and released. In January 1986 it was announced that Prince Makhosetive was to be crowned in April, three years earlier than expected, in order to end the competition for power among vying royal factions.

Prince Makhosetive was crowned on 25 April 1986, and assumed the title of King Mswati III. In May King Mswati dissolved the Liqoqo, thereby consolidating his power. In July the King reorganized the Cabinet, and in October he appointed a former senior member of the security forces, Sotsha Dlamini, as Prime Minister. In May 1987 12 prominent officials, including Prince Bhekimpi and Prince Mfanasibili, were charged with sedition and treason, in connection with the removal from power of Queen Regent Dzeliwe in 1983. In November King Mswati established a special tribunal to preside over all cases involving alleged offences against the King or the Queen Regent; defendants appearing before the tribunal were not to be granted the right to legal representation or appeal. In March 1988 10 of those accused of involvement in the deposition of Queen Regent Dzeliwe were convicted of treason by the special tribunal, and received custodial sentences; two defendants were acquitted. In July, however, it was reported that the 10 convicted in March had been released.

In November 1987 elections to the legislature took place, one year earlier than scheduled. In July 1989 King Mswati dismissed Sotsha Dlamini for alleged disobedience, replacing him with Obed Dlamini, a former leader of the Swaziland Federation of Trade Unions (SFTU).

In early 1990 the People's United Democratic Movement (PUDEMO), which had been established in 1983, distributed tracts questioning the legitimacy of the monarchy in its existing form and demanding constitutional reform. Security forces subsequently arrested a number of suspected members of PUDEMO, who were variously charged with treason, sedition or conspiring to form a political party. All the defendants were acquitted of the principal charges, although five were convicted of illegally attending a political gathering (the sentences of two of the five were annulled on appeal in October 1991). In November King Mswati dismissed the reformist Minister of Justice, Reginald Dhladhla, reportedly on the advice of the Swaziland National Council (which had been reconstituted from the former Liqoqo), prompting public concern that it continued to exert undue influence on government policies. Later in November five members of PUDEMO (who had previously been acquitted of all charges) were arrested under legislation enabling the detention of suspects without trial. In March 1991 the prisoners were released, as a result of international pressure. In an attempt to advance its objectives through legal bodies, PUDEMO subsequently established a number of affiliated organizations, including the Human Rights Association of Swaziland (HUMARAS) and the Swaziland Youth Congress (SWAYOCO), but these were not accorded official recognition.

In September and October 1991 a committee, termed Vusela (Greetings), conducted a series of public forums throughout the country to elicit popular opinion on political reforms. Widespread demands for the abolition of the existing electoral system were reported, while there was substantial criticism of the composition of the Vusela committee itself. In October King Mswati announced an extensive reorganization of the Cabinet. In February 1992 PUDEMO declared itself a legal opposition party (in contravention of the prohibition on political associations), rejected King Mswati's efforts to institute political reform, and demanded a constitutional referendum. Two further opposition movements, the Swaziland United Front (SUF) and the Swaziland National Front (SWANAFRO), subsequently re-emerged. In February King Mswati appointed a second committee (Vusela 2), which was to present recommendations for consideration by the King, based on the conclusions of the first committee.

In October 1992 King Mswati approved several proposals submitted by Vusela 2. The House of Assembly (redesignated the National Assembly) was to be expanded to 65 deputies (of whom 55 were to be directly elected by secret ballot from candidates nominated by the Tinkhundla, and 10 appointed by the King), and the Senate to 30 members (10 selected by the National Assembly and 20 appointed by the King); in addition, the legislation providing for detention without trial was to be abrogated, and a new constitution, incorporating the amendments, enshrining an hereditary monarchy and confirming the fundamental rights of the individual and the independence of the judiciary, was to be drafted. However, opposition groups protested at the committee's failure to recommend the immediate restoration of a multi-party political system: the issue was to be postponed until the forthcoming elections, in order to determine the extent of public support. PUDEMO announced its opposition to the electoral reforms, and demanded that the Government organize a national convention to determine the country's constitutional future. King Mswati subsequently dissolved parliament, and announced that he was to rule by decree, with the assistance of the Council of Ministers (as the Cabinet had been restyled), pending the adoption of a new constitution and the holding of parliamentary elections. Later in October King Mswati announced that elections to the National Assembly would take place in the first half of 1993. At a series of public meetings doubts were expressed as to the viability of the reformed electoral system; in early 1993, in response to public concern, it was announced that legislation preventing the heads of the Tinkhundla from exerting undue influence in the nomination of candidates had been introduced.

The 1993 elections

The first round of elections to the expanded National Assembly took place on 25 September 1993. The second round of parliamentary elections, on 11 October, was contested by the three candidates in each Inkhundla who had obtained the highest number of votes in the first poll; the majority of members of the former Council of Ministers (which had been dissolved in late September), including Obed Dlamini, failed to secure seats in the Assembly. Later in October King Mswati nominated a further 10 deputies to the National Assembly, which elected 10 of its members to the Senate; King Mswati subsequently appointed the remaining 20 senators, among them Obed Dlamini and Prince Bhekimpi. In November the former Minister of Works and Construction, Prince Jameson Mbilini Dlamini, considered a traditionalist, was appointed Prime Minister, and a new Council of Ministers was formed.

In February 1994 it was announced that King Mswati was to appoint a 15-member commission, comprising representatives of organs of State and non-governmental organizations, to draft a new constitution, and a national policy council, which was to prepare a manifesto of the Swazi people. Elections to the Tinkhundla (which had been postponed from March) finally took place, although a high rate of abstention by voters was reported. (The heads of the Tinkhundla had previously been appointed by the King.)

In January 1996 PUDEMO announced a campaign of protests and civil disobedience, owing to the Government's failure to respond to demands for the installation of a multi-party system and for the adoption of a constitution restricting the monarch to a largely ceremonial role. Security forces intervened to suppress demonstrations by SFTU members, and violent clashes ensued, in which three people were reported to have been killed. The SFTU refused to enter into negotiations with the Government, stipulating that the 1973 decree and restrictions on trade unions be revoked prior to discussions. Meanwhile, it was reported that some members of the Government, including Obed Dlamini, also favoured political reform. King Mswati accused the trade unions of attempting to overthrow the monarchy, and threatened to order his traditional warriors to suppress the strike. The SFTU subsequently suspended strike action to allow negotiations to proceed with the Government (which continued to reject the unions' preconditions for discussions). In May 1996 King Mswati indicated that a 'People's Parliament', comprising a series of consultative meetings between citizens and government leaders, had been initiated to solicit public opinion regarding constitutional reform. At the same time King Mswati dismissed Prince Mbilini as Prime Minister, and announced that he would appoint his successor in consultation with the Swaziland National Council.

In late July 1996, following an emergency meeting (attended by the Heads of State of Mozambique, Botswana, Zimbabwe and South Africa) to discuss Swaziland's political situation, King Mswati appointed a Constitutional Review Commission, comprising chiefs, political activists and trade unionists, to collate submissions from the Swazi people and subsequently draft proposals for a new constitution. (The Commission received substantial funds from international donors.) At the same time, Dr Barnabas Sibusiso Dlamini, an IMF Executive Director and former Minister of Finance, was appointed Prime Minister.

In December 1996 the Prime Minister announced that a 'task force', composed of workers, employers and government representatives, had discussed the SFTU's demands made in March 1995, and that the implementation of the recommendations outlined in the resulting report was to be overseen by the Labour Advisory Board. In January 1997, however, the SFTU claimed that there had been no response to its demands for democratic reform, and resolved to begin indefinite strike action from February. Meanwhile, the PUDEMO President, Mario Masuku, declared that Swaziland's leaders were not committed to change, and withdrew from the Constitutional Review Commission. At the end of January the four main leaders of the SFTU were arrested and subsequently charged with intimidating bus owners into joining the forthcoming strike. The strike, pronounced illegal by the Government, proceeded, and was apparently observed by approximately one-half of the labour force. On the ninth day of industrial action six strikers were seriously injured in violent clashes with the security forces. The SFTU leaders declined the Government's offer to release them on condition that they end the strike; their trial was dismissed in February, owing to lack of evidence. At the beginning of March the Congress of South African Trade Unions (COSATU), which had asserted its support for the SFTU throughout the strike, initiated a one-day blockade of the Swazi border. The SFTU decided to suspend the strike shortly afterwards, as the Government had agreed to commence negotiations, but resolved to continue industrial action on the first two days of each month until its 27 demands had been met. In April 1997 the SFTU postponed a further blockade indefinitely, in order to allow the Government adequate time to review the situation.

In August 1998 King Mswati dissolved the National Assembly, in preparation for elections scheduled for October. Opposition groups urged voters to boycott the polls, in the absence of the immediate legalization of political parties. Some 350 candidates were nominated by the Tinkhundla to contest the 55 elective seats in the Assembly. Voting took place on 16 and 24 October; turn-out was reportedly low. A new Cabinet, with Sibusiso Dlamini as Prime Minister, was appointed in mid-November, and a new Senate and Swaziland National Council were formed.

In April 1999 the NNLC, PUDEMO and the SFTU united to form the Swaziland Democratic Alliance (SDA). The NNLC leader, Obed Dlamini, was elected Chairman. However, following warnings from the police that the proposed inauguration of the party, scheduled for 19 April, was illegal and would not be permitted to take place, the executive of the SDA met and cancelled the event.

A judicial crisis developed in late 2002 when, with reference to decrees issued by the King in connection with the evictions of some 200 people from their homes in October 2000, the six South African judges of the Swaziland Court of Appeal resigned in protest at the Government's refusal to accept two rulings that the King had no power to overrule the National Assembly. The judges of the High Court subsequently announced that they would refuse to sit or set dates for hearings, and a strike by members of the legal profession ensued. In April 2003 a report by the International Bar Association attributed the judicial crisis to the lack of clearly defined roles for the executive, legislature and judiciary. In May the Government withdrew a statement in which it had accused the judges of being under external influence. In mid-September 2004 the Government reversed its position on the rulings which had provoked the crisis. Hearings were scheduled to resume at the Court of Appeal in November on condition that those evicted were allowed to return to their villages.

Meanwhile, in June 2001 King Mswati provoked international criticism by promulgating a decree that, it was claimed, effectively amounted to the declaration of a state of emergency; the legislation ensured that no person or body, including the courts, had the authority to challenge the King, prevented newspapers from challenging publishing bans, allowed the King to appoint judges and traditional chiefs personally, and made ridiculing or impersonating the King a criminal offence. Opposition groups in Swaziland condemned the decree as reinforcing tyrannical rule, and criticized the international community's lack of interest in the country's political situation. The King revoked the decree in July, in response to international diplomatic pressure, notably a threat by the USA to impose economic sanctions. However, at the same time the King issued a new decree that retained certain sections of the original decree, including a provision allowing the detention of Swazi citizens without the option of bail for some offences.

Constitutional review

In August 2001 the Constitutional Review Commission submitted its report, which recommended that the King's powers be extended and political parties remain outlawed, but stated that the introduction of a bill of rights that was not in conflict with Swazi laws and customs was a possibility. In February 2002 a 15-member committee, appointed by the King, began drafting a new constitution; PUDEMO criticized the Government for allegedly manipulating the Commission's report and selecting members of the drafting committee who were sympathetic to government policy. In May Prince David, the King's brother, and Chairman of the constitution-drafting committee, announced a new draft constitution, which, *inter alia*, envisaged the retention of the Tinkhundla system for forthcoming elections to the National Assembly.

King Mswati introduced the Internal Security Bill in June 2002, intended to suppress political dissent. It provided variously for fines and prison sentences for those found guilty of carrying or wearing banners or flags of banned political formations, or of participating in mass strikes or boycotts. Training abroad to commit acts of insurgency in Swaziland would be punishable by up to 20 years' imprisonment. The bill was severely criticized by the SFTU, PUDEMO and various foreign governments, which considered it to be inconsistent with the bill of rights and the proposed constitutional reform.

In May 2003 King Mswati announced the dissolution of the National Assembly. Pending elections to a new Assembly, scheduled for October, a council, styled the King's Order-in-Council, was charged with debating and enacting legislation in collaboration with the King. The elections to the National Assembly, duly held in October, were reportedly marked by a very low turn-out, many voters having apparently heeded an appeal by pro-democracy groups for a boycott of the polls. Although several members of proscribed political organizations stood as independent candidates, a Commonwealth monitoring team subsequently declared that the elections had been largely meaningless, in view of the lack of basic democratic freedoms that prevailed in Swaziland. In November the King appointed Themba Dlamini, a former incumbent on various parastatal bodies and a close associate of the royal family, as the new Prime Minister. At the same time, the King accepted a new draft constitution that, observers noted, safeguarded many of the monarchy's existing prerogatives. Among the provisions of the proposed new basic law was that the King should remain the head of the executive and retain responsibility for appointing the Prime Minister. He would, furthermore, retain a power of veto over any bill that received parliamentary approval. However, the draft Constitution did propose the removal of the King's power to rule by decree and provided for the replacement of the Court of Appeal by a new Supreme Court as Swaziland's highest judicial body.

Meanwhile, in March 2004 Marwick Khumalo resigned as Speaker of the National Assembly and was replaced, in May, by Charles S'gayoyo Magongo. Khumalo claimed that he had been forced to resign, owing to his opposition to government attempts to purchase a private aircraft for the King. In May the National Assembly voted to suspend itself in protest at the Government's stated intention to review the Industrial Court's ruling that the Clerk of Parliament had been illegally dismissed by the previous Prime Minister and should be reinstated. Also in May the National Constituent Assembly (NCA—a pressure group composed of churches, political parties, and labour and human rights organizations) announced a legal challenge to what it claimed was the King's intention of promulgating the proposed new Constitution by decree. In mid-June the NCA petitioned the High Court, demanding that the constitution-drafting committee should be required to hold public hearings and receive submissions from interested parties. The High Court agreed that it would hear the petition in August, although no date was fixed.

In January 2005 the SFTU commenced a two-day general strike in protest at the proposed constitutional reform, which it maintained entrenched the power of the monarchy. The new Constitution was finally approved by a joint sitting of the Senate and the National Assembly in early June. It was ratified by King Mswati on 26 July and came into effect on 7 February 2006. The Constitution was viewed as being socially progressive, according greater rights to women—legally recognized as adults for the first time—and guaranteeing the right to primary education, but politically conservative: executive power was concentrated in the King and the Tinkhundla remained as the basis of the parliamentary system; the King would also continue to appoint the Prime Minister and the Cabinet, Chiefs and High Court judges and could dissolve the legislature. A bill of rights guaranteed freedom of assembly and speech; however, these rights could be suspended by the King if he considered it to be in the public interest. Furthermore, while there existed provision for the judiciary to interpret the Constitution, ultimate authority was vested with the King. There also remained considerable ambiguity regarding the legality of political parties, although the Constitution stated that the 'people of Swaziland have a right to be heard through and represented by their own freely chosen representatives in the government of the country'.

In late February 2006 the King effected a reorganization of the Cabinet. Moses Mathendele Dlamini was appointed Minister of Foreign Affairs and Trade, replacing Mabili Dlamini, who assumed the housing and urban development portfolio vacated by Dumsile Sukati. Sukati was appointed Minister of Natural Resources and Energy, replacing Mfofmfo Nkambule, who took over the health and social welfare portfolio from Chief Sipho Shongwe. A minor government reshuffle was carried out in May in which Nkambule was replaced by Njabulo Mabuza. In September the Deputy Prime Minister, Albert Shabangu, collapsed and died at his home. He was replaced by Constance Simelane, hitherto the Minister of Education, in October. Themba Msibi assumed responsibility for the education portfolio, while Magongo replaced him as Minister of Public Service and Information.

Recent developments: the 2008 elections

In February 2008 six opposition parties announced that they would boycott forthcoming legislative elections, which were scheduled for later that year, and demanded the introduction of a system of multi-party democracy. A spokesman for PUDEMO stated that it was important to 'deny the state legitimacy' by refusing to take part. In April the Deputy President of that party, Gabriel Mkhumane, was shot dead in South Africa, where he had lived in exile for 24 years. The following month the Elections and Boundaries Commission announced that voter registration had begun for the elections, which were scheduled for September, although political parties were still effectively proscribed. In June the King dissolved the House of Assembly (as the lower legislative body had been redesignated in the 2006 Constitution), and on 19 September the elections proceeded as scheduled, despite demonstrations by pro-democracy activists who denounced it as a farce. The SFTU organized a march in Mbabane, and a further demonstration was planned on the border with South Africa; however, this was suppressed by the security forces and a number of activists were arrested. In the same month an extravagant ceremony was held to celebrate the King's 40th birthday and the 40th anniversary of Swaziland's independence.

Following the announcement of the election results there were reports that two men had been killed, and a third injured, when a bomb exploded on a road close to the King's Lozitha palace, east of Mbabane: it was believed that the men were planning to detonate the bomb near the royal palace but that it exploded prematurely. The injured man, a South African national, was taken into custody and charged with treason, while a fourth man who was involved managed to escape; one of those who died in the attempted bombing, Jack Govender, was a founding member of the anti-royalist Swaziland Solidarity Network (SSN). In October 2008 the King reappointed Sibusiso Dlamini as Prime Minister, and a new Council of Ministers was subsequently formed with a number of new appointments, including Themba Masuku as Deputy Prime Minister. Lutfo Dlamini succeeded Moses Mathendele Dlamini as Minister of Foreign Affairs, and Benedict Xaba replaced Mabuza as Minister of Health, while Princess Tsandzile (one of five female appointments to the Cabinet) was named as Minister of Natural Resources and Energy, in place of Sukati.

In November 2008 the President of PUDEMO, Mario Masuku, was arrested and charged under new anti-terrorism laws in connection with the attempted bomb attack on the royal palace. In the same month Prime Minister Dlamini formally listed four opposition organizations (PUDEMO, the Swaziland Liberation Army, the SSN and SWAYOCO) as terrorist groups. The Attorney-General, Majahenkhaba Dlamini, also warned journalists that reports in which they criticized the Government could lead to their arrest under the Suppression of Terrorism Act 2008. In February 2009 SWAYOCO Secretary-General Thabile Zwane was arrested for alleged terrorist activities, while in September Masuku was eventually acquitted and released from prison following a court ruling. In March 2010 he appealed for the imposition of political and economic sanctions on members of the Swazi ruling élite.

In April 2010 Prime Minister Dlamini urged the Swazi people to resist the increasing demands made by prominent members of Swazi society for the holding of a referendum on multi-party democracy prior to the 2013 legislative elections, and instead to rely upon the ongoing dialogue processes to decide on the preferred system of governance for the Kingdom.

In early May 2010 a PUDEMO supporter, Sipho Jele, was arrested at a trade union rally, reportedly for wearing a t-shirt displaying that party's emblem; he was later found hanged in his gaol cell. The police declared his death a suicide, but this explanation was dismissed by his family and by Masuku (although the results of a subsequent investigation corroborated the suicide theory). Jele's funeral was raided by several hundred police officers, who confiscated PUDEMO and SWAYOCO banners, while Masuku was detained temporarily under anti-terrorism legislation after he made a speech at the rescheduled funeral in late May in which he briefly mentioned PUDEMO. Properties belonging to Masuku and other opposition leaders were searched by police in June, and up to 16 SWAYOCO members were arrested in the same month for their alleged involvement in a series of recent bomb attacks against police, judicial and political targets.

The Minister of Justice and Constitutional Affairs, Ndumiso Mamba, resigned in August 2010. The SSN claimed that Mamba had been forced to step down after it was discovered that he had been having an affair with King Mswati's 12th wife. Prime Minister Dlamini appointed the Minister of Home Affairs, Chief Mgwagwa Gamedze, as acting justice minister.

In early September 2010 the major trade unions staged demonstrations in Manzini, attended by several hundred people, to demand democracy and greater rights for workers. Violent clashes between demonstrators and the security forces were reported, and SWAYOCO leader Wandile Dludlu was detained and allegedly assaulted by police officers after joining the march. Masuku and approximately 50 other opposition activists were arrested the day before the protest action commenced; Masuku, along with most of the other detainees, was swiftly released, but he was prevented by the police from participating in the demonstrations, while several COSATU members who had intended to join the protests were deported to South Africa. Human rights organization Amnesty International strongly criticized the 'police harassment and intimidation'. Further protests took place in March and April 2011 against proposed reductions to the size of the civil service and wage freezes.

Meanwhile, the Senate in February 2011 ruled that the discounted sale of state-owned land to six cabinet members (the Prime Minister, the Deputy Prime Minister, and the ministers responsible for home affairs, economic planning, natural resources, and agriculture), which had been authorized by Minister of Housing and Urban Development Lindiwe Dlamini in 2009, was unconstitutional and demanded that the land be returned to the state. The Constitution stipulated that only Land Management Boards had the authority to sell crown land, which was to be subject to public auction, a process that Lindiwe Dlamini had dismissed as 'time consuming'. A House of Assembly select committee was also conducting an inquiry into the corruption scandal in March 2011.

HIV/AIDS

Swaziland has been severely affected by the HIV/AIDS pandemic. The Government has been criticized for its reluctance to confront the problem directly; proposed measures have included sterilizing or branding those infected with HIV. In an attempt to prevent the spread of the disease, in September 2001 the Government ordered women aged 18 years or younger to remain celibate and avoid shaking hands with men for a period of five years. In February 2004 the Prime Minister declared a national disaster, brought about by Swaziland's high incidence of HIV infection in combination with drought, land degradation and rising poverty. Following a visit to the country, in mid-March 2006 the UN Secretary-General's special envoy reported that 42.6% of the adult population (aged between 15 and 49 years) was infected with HIV; a recent survey of pregnant women between the ages of 25 and 29 had indicated a prevalence rate of 56.3%. It was anticipated that by 2010 orphaned children would represent between 10% and 15% of the population. In August 2007 a new national health policy was launched, aimed at addressing the decline in the quality of health care services by 2015 and limiting the spread of HIV/AIDS. In September it was announced that a new, decentralized strategy for combating HIV/AIDS was to be implemented, affording communities the responsibility of determining the action required in that area. Prompted by research that indicated that circumcision dramatically reduced HIV transmission rates, the Government initiated a US $15m. circumcision programme in early 2011, with funding provided by the USA.

Foreign Affairs

During the apartheid era Swaziland pursued a policy of dialogue and co-operation with South Africa. In 1982 the two countries signed a secret non-aggression pact; several members of the African National Congress of South Africa (ANC), which had increasingly used Swaziland as a base for guerrilla attacks into South Africa, were subsequently arrested and expelled from Swaziland. The signing, in March 1984, of the Nkomati accord between South Africa and Mozambique (which banned both countries from harbouring dissidents) led many ANC members to flee from Mozambique to neighbouring Swaziland. Following the murder, in 1984, of the deputy chief of the Swazi security police, the Government initiated a campaign to arrest all ANC fugitives remaining in the country (the ANC denied involvement in the killing). In 1986 leading Swazi politicians expressed opposition to the imposition of economic sanctions against South Africa, owing to the dependence of Swaziland's own economy on that country. Detentions and deportations of ANC members by the Swazi Government continued, while several suspected ANC members were abducted by South African security forces or killed in Swaziland by gunmen who were widely assumed to be South African. Following the legalization of the ANC in 1990, the Swazi Prime Minister, Obed Dlamini, pledged to conduct an inquiry (which, however, he failed to initiate) into state operations against ANC members. Formal diplomatic relations were established in 1993. From the late 1990s prominent South African organizations, including the ANC and COSATU, expressed support for the SFTU's demands for political reform, prompting the Swazi Government to protest of interference in its domestic affairs. In April 1995 the South African Government announced that it had rejected a long-standing claim by Swaziland to a region in the Mpumalanga province (formerly Eastern Transvaal). However, King Mswati declared in a letter to South African President Thabo Mbeki in early 2001 that he had not

SWAZILAND

abandoned his intention to reincorporate parts of Mpumalanga and KwaZulu/Natal provinces into Swaziland. In 2003 the Chairperson of the Swaziland Border Adjustment Committee, Prince Khuzulwandle, criticized Mbeki for declining to discuss realignments of the border. In February 2010 the Swaziland Democracy Campaign was launched by domestic and South African organizations with a view to creating global momentum for democracy in Swaziland.

Following the ratification of the October 1992 peace accord in Mozambique (q.v.), an agreement signed by the Governments of Swaziland and Mozambique and the office of the UN High Commissioner for Refugees in August 1993 provided for the repatriation of some 24,000 Mozambican nationals from Swaziland. In December the number of Swazi troops deployed at the border with Mozambique was increased, following clashes between Swazi and Mozambican forces in the region. Mozambique subsequently protested at alleged border incursions by members of the Swazi armed forces. In early 1994 discussions took place between Swazi and Mozambican officials to seek mutually satisfactory arrangements for the joint patrol of the border, and in 1995 it was announced that the Mhlumeni border post, closed since the 1970s, would reopen as the second official transit point between the two countries. In September 1997, during the first visit to Swaziland made by a Mozambican Prime Minister, a bilateral extradition agreement was signed, with the aim of reducing cross-border crime. In December 1999 the Swazi authorities expelled some 500 Mozambican citizens who had been declared illegal immigrants.

CONSTITUTION AND GOVERNMENT

The Constitution of 7 February 2006 vests supreme executive power in the hereditary King, who is the Head of State, and provides for a bicameral legislature, comprising a House of Assembly and a Senate. The functions of the legislature are confined to debating government proposals and advising the King. Executive power is exercised through the Cabinet, which is appointed by the King.

The Parliament of Swaziland consists of the Senate, comprising not more than 31 members (of whom 20 are appointed by the King—at least eight of these are women—and 10 elected by the House of Assembly, one-half of these being women) and the House of Assembly, which comprises not more than 76 members. Of these, 60 are directly elected from candidates nominated by traditional local councils, known as Tinkhundla, and 10 are appointed by the King, one-half of whom are women. Additionally one woman is selected from each of the four regions of Swaziland and the Attorney-General is also an ex officio member.

The King appoints the Prime Minister and the Cabinet and has the power to dissolve the bicameral legislature. The Swazi National Council (Sibaya) constitutes the highest policy and advisory council of the nation and functions as the annual general meeting of the nation. A Council of Chiefs, composed of 12 chiefs drawn from the four regions of Swaziland advises the King on customary issues and any matter relating to chieftancy.

REGIONAL AND INTERNATIONAL CO-OPERATION

Swaziland is a member of the Common Market for Eastern and Southern Africa (see p. 228), of the Southern African Development Community (SADC, see p. 420) and of the Southern African Customs Union (SACU), which also includes Botswana, Lesotho, Namibia and South Africa.

Swaziland became a member of the UN in 1968. As a contracting party to the General Agreement on Tariffs and Trade, Swaziland joined the World Trade Organization (WTO, see p. 430) on its establishment in 1995. Swaziland participates in the Group of 77 (G77, see p. 447) developing countries.

ECONOMIC AFFAIRS

In 2009, according to estimates by the World Bank, Swaziland's gross national income (GNI), measured at average 2007–09 prices, was US $2,787m., equivalent to $2,350 per head (or $4,580 per head on an international purchasing-power parity basis). During 2000–09, it was estimated, the population increased at an average annual rate of 1.0%, while gross domestic product (GDP) per head increased, in real terms, by an average of 1.2% per year. Overall GDP increased, in real terms, at an average annual rate of 2.3% in 2000–09; growth in 2009 was 0.4%.

Agriculture (including forestry) contributed 7.3% of GDP in 2009, according to World Bank estimates. About 28.1% of the labour force was employed in the agricultural sector in mid-2011 (including subsistence farming), according to FAO. However, according to IMF estimates, at June 2005 only 20.8% of those in paid employment were engaged in agriculture. The principal cash crops are sugar cane (sugar accounted for 14.1% of domestic export earnings in 2007), cotton, citrus fruits, pineapples and maize. Tobacco and rice are also cultivated. Livestock-rearing is traditionally important. Commercial forestry (which employs a significant proportion of the population) provides wood for the manufacture of pulp. During 2000–09, according to the World Bank, agricultural GDP increased by an average of 0.7% per year. Agricultural GDP increased by 0.4% in 2009.

According to the World Bank, industry (including mining, manufacturing, construction and power) contributed 49.4% of GDP in 2009, and engaged 28.8% of those in paid employment in June 2005. During 2000–09, according to the World Bank, industrial GDP increased at an average annual rate of 1.7%. Industrial GDP increased by 0.4% in 2009.

Mining contributed 0.3% of GDP in 2008, according to African Development Bank (AfDB), and engaged 1.3% of those in paid employment in June 2005. Swaziland has extensive reserves of coal, much of which is exported. Asbestos is also an important mineral export. In addition, Swaziland has reserves of tin, kaolin, talc, iron ore, pyrophyllite and silica. During 2000–04, according to the IMF, mining GDP declined by an average of 5.0% per year; mining GDP declined by 20.2% in 2003 but increased by 9.0% in 2004.

Construction contributed 2.9% of GDP in 2008, according to AfDB estimates, and in June 2005 engaged 21.2% of those in paid employment.

Manufacturing contributed 44.4% of GDP in 2009, according to the World Bank, and in June 2005 engaged 5.4% of those in paid employment. During 2000–09 manufacturing GDP increased at an annual average rate of 1.7%. Manufacturing GDP increased by 0.4% in 2009.

Swaziland imports most of its energy requirements from South Africa. The Swazi Government aimed to increase domestic energy output to cover approximately 50% of the country's needs, following the construction of a hydroelectric power station on the Maguga Dam, which began operations in 2002. However, in 2005 80.7% of total electrical energy generated and imported was obtained from South Africa and Mozambique, compared with 77.1% in 2002. Mineral fuels and lubricants accounted for an estimated 14.1% of imports in 2007. In the mid-2000s plans were being discussed for the construction of a 100-MW thermal power station in the Lowveld using bagasse, the waste left from processing sugar cane.

The services sector contributed 43.3% of GDP in 2009 and engaged 50.3% of those in paid employment in June 2005. According to the World Bank, the GDP of the services sector increased by an average of 3.4% per year in 2000–09. Services GDP increased by 0.4% in 2008.

In 2009, according to the IMF, Swaziland recorded a visible trade deficit of US $121.3m., while there was a deficit of $415.1m. on the current account of the balance of payments. In 2007 the principal source of imports was South Africa (81.3%), which was also the principal market for exports (79.8%); Italy was also an important export market. The principal imports in 2007 were machinery and transport equipment, food and live animals, and mineral fuels and lubricants; the principal exports in 2007 were chemicals and chemical products, and food and live animals.

In the financial year ending 31 March 2011 there was an estimated overall budgetary surplus of E3,855m. Swaziland's general government gross debt was E3,669m. in 2009, equivalent to 14.5% of GDP. Swaziland's external debt totalled US $362m. at the end of 2008, of which $348m. was public and publicly gunranteed debt. In 2007 the cost of debt-servicing was equivalent to 1.9% of the value of exports of goods and services. In 2000–09 annual inflation averaged 7.6%; consumer prices increased by an average of 7.5% in 2009. It was estimated that 40% of the labour force were unemployed in 1995.

Swaziland's economy is vulnerable to fluctuations in international prices for some major exports, including sugar, as well as to the effects of unfavourable weather conditions. In addition, prevailing economic conditions in neighbouring South Africa have a pronounced impact on the Swazi economy: although Swaziland may determine the exchange rate of its currency, the lilangeni, this has remained at par with the South African rand. The removal in January 2005 of World Trade Organization quotas for textile exports to the USA brought Swaziland into direct competition with exporters based in Asia, while the

SWAZILAND

European Union's (EU) sugar tariff modifications lowered the price paid for Swazi sugar from 2007. The EU did, however, allocate €100m. to assist Swazi farmers in diversifying into alternative crops, such as cotton, and in early 2008 the European Commission granted Swazi sugar producers €15m. to protect them from the lowering in prices. Food security remained a concern, however, with the country heavily dependent on maize imports. In early 2010 the Government announced it was to implement a plan of subsidies to help stabilize the situation of poor nutrition. (In 2009 around 20% of the population were malnourished.) Meanwhile, the securing of much-needed foreign investment in Swaziland remained dependent on a satisfactory political settlement. The US had imposed economic sanctions on Swaziland, restricting financial assistance, but in September 2009 these were lifted and assistance resumed after the Swaziland Government approved new legislation prohibiting the smuggling and trafficking of people in the country. The global financial crisis had a severe impact upon Swaziland's economy during 2009, with the resulting decline in trade leading to a reduction in activity in the manufacturing sector and a drastic contraction in vital revenues from the Southern African Customs Union (SACU). According to the IMF, GDP grew by just 1.2% in that year. SACU receipts continued to decline in 2010, prompting a liquidity crisis in the country, which was exacerbated by the spiralling public sector wage bill. In order to stabilize the fiscal position, in October the Government revealed plans to raise taxes, decrease non-essential spending, reduce the size of the civil service and freeze public sector salaries. Despite the fiscal crisis, the IMF estimated that GDP expanded by 2.0% in 2010, due in part to the improvement in the international economic climate and the resurgence in demand for Swaziland's mineral exports. However, the IMF projected negligible GDP growth of 0.5% in 2011, while the proposed restructuring of SACU tariffs (which would further lower Swaziland's customs revenues), combined with the long-standing problems of poverty, unemployment and HIV/AIDS, presented an enormous challenge to the authorities.

PUBLIC HOLIDAYS

2012: 1 January (New Year's Day), 6–9 April (Easter), 19 April (Birthday of King Mswati), 25 April (National Flag Day), 1 May (Workers' Day), 17 May (Ascension Day), 22 July (Birthday of the late King Sobhuza), 6 September (Somhlolo—Independence—Day), 24 October (UN Day), 25–26 December (Christmas and Boxing Day).

The Incwala and Umhlanga Ceremonies are held in December or January, and August or September (respectively), but the exact dates are variable each year.

Statistical Survey

Source (unless otherwise stated): Central Statistical Office, POB 456, Mbabane; internet www.gov.sz/home.asp?pid=75.

Area and Population

AREA, POPULATION AND DENSITY

Area (sq km)	17,363*
Population (census results)†	
11–12 May 1997	929,718
11 May 2007 (provisional)‡§	
Males	460,498
Females	493,026
Total	953,524
Population (UN estimate at mid-year)‖	
2009	1,185,000
2010	1,202,000
2011	1,218,602
Density (per sq km) at mid-2011	70.2

* 6,704 sq miles.
† Excluding absentee workers.
‡ Source: UN, *Population and Vital Statistics Report*.
§ Population data are *de jure*, although the totals were the subject of some dispute on publication; in early 2009 the Ministry of Economic Planning and Development published the State of Swaziland Population Report, which contained a revised population estimate of 1,018,449 for 2007.
‖ Source: UN, *World Population Prospects: The 2008 Revision*.

POPULATION BY AGE AND SEX
(UN estimates at mid-2011)

	Males	Females	Total
0–14	234,623	232,577	467,200
15–64	345,237	364,112	709,349
65 and over	17,701	24,352	42,053
Total	597,561	621,041	1,218,602

Source: UN, *World Population Prospects: The 2008 Revision*.

ETHNIC GROUPS
(census of August 1986)

Swazi	661,646
Other Africans	14,468
European	1,825
Asiatic	228
Other non-Africans	412
Mixed	2,403
Unknown	77
Total	681,059

REGIONS
(population at census of May 2007, provisional figures)

	Area (sq km)	Population	Density (per sq km)
Hhohho	3,569	263,761	73.9
Manzini	5,945	293,260	49.3
Shiselweni	4,070	202,686	49.8
Lebombo	3,779	193,817	51.3
Total	17,363	953,524	54.9

Source: UN, *2010 World Population and Housing Census Programme*.

PRINCIPAL TOWNS
(population at census of May 1997)

Mbabane (capital)	57,992		Manzini	25,571

Mid-2009 (incl. suburbs, UN estimate): Mbabane 73,815 (Source: UN, *World Urbanization Prospects: The 2009 Revision*).

BIRTHS AND DEATHS
(annual averages, UN estimates)

	1995–2000	2000–05	2005–10
Birth rate (per 1,000)	34.3	31.9	30.0
Death rate (per 1,000)	10.4	15.4	15.7

Source: UN, *World Population Prospects: The 2008 Revision*.

Life expectancy (years at birth, WHO estimates): 48 (males 48; females 48) in 2008 (Source: WHO, *World Health Statistics*).

SWAZILAND

EMPLOYMENT
(persons in paid employment at June)

	2003	2004	2005
Agriculture, hunting, forestry and fishing	21,491	20,804	19,955
Mining and quarrying	1,153	1,407	1,283
Manufacturing	19,485	19,874	20,272
Electricity, gas and water	1,418	1,389	859
Construction	4,824	5,293	5,115
Distribution	9,021	9,988	11,454
Transportation	2,491	2,265	3,007
Finance	6,422	5,202	6,430
Social services	26,758	27,247	27,228
Total employed	**93,063**	**93,469**	**95,603**

Source: IMF, *Kingdom of Swaziland: Selected Issues and Statistical Appendix* (March 2008).

Mid-2011 (estimates in '000): Agriculture, etc. 139; Total labour force 494 (Source: FAO).

Health and Welfare

KEY INDICATORS

Total fertility rate (children per woman, 2008)	3.5
Under-5 mortality rate (per 1,000 live births, 2008)	83
HIV/AIDS (% of persons aged 15–49, 2007)	26.1
Physicians (per 1,000 head, 2004)	0.16
Hospital beds (per 1,000 head, 2006)	2.1
Health expenditure (2007): US $ per head (PPP)	287
Health expenditure (2007): % of GDP	6.0
Health expenditure (2007): public (% of total)	62.5
Access to water (% of persons, 2008)	69
Access to sanitation (% of persons, 2008)	55
Total carbon dioxide emissions ('000 metric tons, 2007)	1,062.6
Carbon dioxide emissions per head (metric tons, 2007)	0.9
Human Development Index (2010): ranking	121
Human Development Index (2010): value	0.498

For sources and definitions, see explanatory note on p. vi.

Agriculture

PRINCIPAL CROPS
('000 metric tons)

	2005	2006	2007
Maize	74.5	67.1	26.2
Potatoes*	6.7	6.0	6.0
Sweet potatoes*	2.6	2.3	2.3
Sugar cane	5,200	5,000	5,000*
Groundnuts, with shell*	4.3	4.1	4.1
Tomatoes*	3.6	3.4	3.4
Oranges*	40	36	36
Grapefruit and pomelos*	40	37	37
Pineapples*	32	31	31

* FAO estimate(s).

2008: Production assumed to be unchanged from 2007 (FAO estimates). Note: No data were available for individual crops in 2009.

Aggregate production ('000 metric tons, may include official, semi-official or estimated data): Total cereals 76 in 2005, 68 in 2006, 27 in 2007–09; Total roots and tubers 56 in 2005, 54 in 2006–09; Total vegetables (incl. melons) 11 in 2005, 11 in 2006–09; Total fruits (excl. melons) 119 in 2005, 105 in 2006–09.

Source: FAO.

LIVESTOCK
('000 head, year ending September, FAO estimates)

	2005	2006	2007
Horses	1.4	1.4	1.5
Asses	14.8	14.8	14.8
Cattle	615	580	585
Pigs	37	30	30
Sheep	27	27	28
Goats	274	275	276
Chickens	3,600	3,200	3,200

2008: Figures assumed to be unchanged from 2007 (FAO estimates). Note: No data were available for 2009.

Source: FAO.

LIVESTOCK PRODUCTS
('000 metric tons, FAO estimates)

	2005	2006	2007
Cattle meat	14.3	17.5	17.5
Goat meat	1.9	1.9	1.9
Pig meat	1.4	1.2	1.2
Chicken meat	7.4	4.9	4.9
Cows' milk	38.7	37.5	39.0

2008–09: Production assumed to be unchanged from 2007 (FAO estimates).

Source: FAO.

Forestry

ROUNDWOOD REMOVALS
('000 cubic metres, excl. bark, FAO estimates)

	2007	2008	2009
Sawlogs, veneer logs and logs for sleepers	260	260	260
Other industrial wood	70	70	70
Fuel wood	1,012	1,028	1,045
Total	**1,342**	**1,358**	**1,375**

Source: FAO.

SAWNWOOD PRODUCTION
('000 cubic metres, incl. railway sleepers, FAO estimates)

	1995	1996	1997
Total (all coniferous)	90	100	102

1998–2009: Production assumed to be unchanged from 1997 (FAO estimates).

Source: FAO.

Fishing

(metric tons, live weight)

	1999	2000*	2001*
Capture	70*	70	70
Aquaculture	61	69	72
Common carp	18	20	20
Mozambique tilapia	20	25	25
Redbreast tilapia	12	13	15
North African catfish	5	6	6
Red claw crayfish	6	5	6
Total catch	**131***	**139**	**142**

* FAO estimate(s).

2002–08 (metric tons, live weight, FAO estimate): Capture 70.

Source: FAO.

SWAZILAND

Mining

(metric tons unless otherwise indicated)

	2007	2008	2009
Coal	241,283	174,807	170,000
Ferrovanadium	500	500	500*
Quarrystone ('000 cu m)	208	241	240*

* Estimated production.

Source: US Geological Survey.

Industry

SELECTED PRODUCTS

	2005	2006	2007
Raw sugar ('000 metric tons)	653	623	631
Electrical energy (million kWh)	408	436	454

Source: UN Industrial Commodity Statistics Database.

Wood pulp ('000 metric tons, FAO estimates): 160.7 in 2006; 170.4 in 2007; 142.2 in 2008–09 (Source: FAO).

Finance

CURRENCY AND EXCHANGE RATES

Monetary Units
100 cents = 1 lilangeni (plural: emalangeni).

Sterling, Dollar and Euro Equivalents (31 December 2010)
£1 sterling = 10.382 emalangeni;
US $1 = 6.6316 emalangeni;
€1 = 8.8611 emalangeni;
100 emalangeni = £9.63 = $15.08 = €11.29.

Average Exchange Rate (emalangeni per US $)
2008   8.261
2009   8.474
2010   7.321

Note: The lilangeni is at par with the South African rand.

BUDGET
(million emalangeni, year ending 31 March)

Revenue*	2005/06	2006/07	2007/08
Tax revenue	5,189.5	7,682.8	7,564.9
Taxes on net income and profits	1,267.4	1,534.3	1,644.4
Companies	472.5	560.9	522.1
Individuals	761.7	892.4	1,058.4
Non-resident dividends and interest	33.3	81.0	63.9
Taxes on property	13.3	10.3	18.1
Taxes on goods, services, and international trade	3,894.4	6,102.2	5,886.0
Receipts from Southern African Customs Union	3,101.1	5,321.8	4,989.9
Levies on sugar exports	21.1	33.1	32.1
Hotel and gaming taxes	7.8	9.6	13.5
Sales tax	734.9	620.1	725.0
Licences and other taxes	29.4	27.2	30.3
Other taxes	14.4	36.0	16.4
Other current revenue	137.3	172.0	713.5
Property income	53.4	89.6	596.6
Fees, fines, and non-industrial sales	83.9	82.3	116.9
Total	5,326.8	7,854.8	8,278.4

Expenditure†	2005/06	2006/07	2007/08
Current expenditure	4,416.3	4,681.3	5,217.3
Wages and salaries	2,443.0	2,588.7	2,750.2
Other purchases of goods and services	995.8	1,202.8	1,343.0
Interest payments	194.4	163.4	211.3
Domestic	31.6	35.3	84.9
Foreign	162.9	128.1	126.4
Subsidies and other current transfers	783.1	726.4	912.8
Capital expenditure	1,409.7	1,436.6	1,732.7
Health	47.8	48.5	69.8
Education	18.9	42.6	82.2
Agriculture	171.6	321.4	587.7
Transport and communications	387.0	632.3	745.6
Other	784.4	391.9	247.4
Total	5,826.0	6,117.9	6,950.0

* Excluding grants received (million emalangeni): 172.2 in 2005/06; 165.6 in 2006/07; 62.8 in 2007/08.
† Excluding net lending (million emalangeni): –68.3 in 2005/06; –55.2 in 2006/07; 43.0 in 2007/08.

Source: IMF, *Kingdom of Swaziland: Selected Issues and Statistical Appendix* (October 2008).

2008/09 (million emalangeni, year ending 31 March): Total revenue (incl grants) 9,627; Total expenditure (incl. net lending) 9,669 (Source: IMF, *Kingdom of Swaziland: 2010 Article IV Consultation—Staff Report; Staff Supplement; Public Information Notice on the Executive Board Discussion; and Statement by the Executive Director for Swaziland*—January 2011).

2009/10 (million emalangeni, year ending 31 March): Total revenue (incl grants) 9,222; Total expenditure (incl. net lending) 11,038 (Source: IMF, *Kingdom of Swaziland: 2010 Article IV Consultation—Staff Report; Staff Supplement; Public Information Notice on the Executive Board Discussion; and Statement by the Executive Director for Swaziland*—January 2011).

2010/11 (million emalangeni, year ending 31 March, estimates): Total revenue (incl grants) 6,944; Total expenditure (incl. net lending) 10,799 (Source: IMF, *Kingdom of Swaziland: 2010 Article IV Consultation—Staff Report; Staff Supplement; Public Information Notice on the Executive Board Discussion; and Statement by the Executive Director for Swaziland*—January 2011).

INTERNATIONAL RESERVES
(excl. gold, US $ million at 31 December)

	2008	2009	2010
IMF special drawing rights	3.93	69.62	68.39
Reserve position in IMF	10.11	10.29	10.11
Foreign exchange	737.90	878.96	677.85
Total	751.94	958.87	756.35

Source: IMF, *International Financial Statistics*.

MONEY SUPPLY
(million emalangeni at 31 December)

	2008	2009	2010
Currency outside depository corporations	279.82	327.63	349.35
Transferable deposits	1,692.33	2,009.35	2,189.70
Other deposits	4,110.81	5,376.24	5,783.69
Broad money	6,082.96	7,713.23	8,322.74

COST OF LIVING
(Consumer Price Index; base: 2000 = 100, unless otherwise indicated)

	2006	2007	2008
Food	194.1	228.3	271.5
Clothing	114.6	113.9	116.0
Housing*	101.3	102.5	113.0
All items (incl. others)	147.3	159.2	179.8

* Base 2005 = 100.

2009 (Consumer Price Index; base: 2000 = 100): All items 193.2.

Source: ILO.

SWAZILAND

NATIONAL ACCOUNTS
(million emalangeni at current prices)

Expenditure on the Gross Domestic Product

	2006	2007	2008
Government final consumption expenditure	2,771	3,041	3,338
Private final consumption expenditure	15,111	16,107	22,242
Gross capital formation	2,558	2,644	2,756
Total domestic expenditure	20,440	21,792	28,336
Exports of goods and services	15,294	16,281	14,741
Less Imports of goods and services	15,772	16,558	18,129
GDP at purchasers' values	19,962	21,515	24,947

Gross Domestic Product by Economic Activity

	2006	2007	2008
Agriculture, forestry and fishing	1,152	1,277	1,460
Mining	57	54	52
Manufacturing	6,078	6,686	7,816
Electricity, gas and water	139	149	175
Construction	588	568	551
Wholesale and retail trade; restaurants and hotels	1,678	1,774	2,007
Finance, insurance and real estate	1,403	1,558	1,850
Transport and communications	972	1,199	1,363
Public administration and defence	2,712	2,859	3,358
Other services	251	272	306
Sub-total	15,030	16,396	18,938
Indirect taxes	5,264	5,491	6,441
Less Imputed bank service charge	332	372	432
GDP at purchasers' values	19,962	21,515	24,947

Source: African Development Bank.

BALANCE OF PAYMENTS
(US $ million)

	2007	2008	2009
Exports of goods f.o.b.	1,744.8	1,568.6	1,660.1
Imports of goods f.o.b.	−2,015.9	−1,578.5	−1,781.3
Trade balance	−271.1	−9.9	−121.3
Exports of services	454.7	224.6	200.0
Imports of services	−506.8	−650.7	−562.3
Balance on goods and services	−323.3	−435.9	−483.5
Other income received	280.8	298.0	290.8
Other income paid	−217.0	−303.2	−413.4
Balance on goods, services and income	−259.5	−441.1	−606.2
Current transfers received	403.5	417.7	404.9
Current transfers paid	−209.5	−208.0	−213.8
Current balance	−65.5	−231.4	−415.1
Capital account (net)	−30.2	−8.8	−4.0
Direct investment abroad	−23.2	7.9	−7.0
Direct investment from abroad	37.5	105.7	65.7
Portfolio investment assets	4.2	−75.5	122.8
Portfolio investment liabilities	1.0	43.9	−6.6
Other investment assets	357.8	190.1	249.7
Other investment liabilities	53.7	176.0	48.4
Net errors and omissions	−700.8	12.0	−55.0
Overall balance	−365.5	219.9	−1.1

Source: IMF, *International Financial Statistics*.

External Trade

PRINCIPAL COMMODITIES
(US $ million)

Imports c.i.f.	2005	2006	2007
Food and live animals	230.1	158.8	222.2
Beverages and tobacco	29.9	20.6	26.1
Crude materials (inedible)	26.9	21.2	25.8
Minerals, fuels and lubricants	194.0	180.4	178.5
Chemicals and chemical products	324.4	158.5	166.8
Basic manufactures	323.7	250.5	243.4
Machinery and transport equipment	308.8	279.9	240.6
Miscellaneous manufactures	180.1	134.3	146.8
Total (incl. others)	1,656.1	1,242.4	1,270.1

Exports f.o.b. (incl. re-exports)	2005	2006	2007
Food and live animals	230.5	366.0	230.2
Beverages and tobacco	10.0	16.4	4.8
Crude materials (inedible)	114.3	134.6	85.2
Minerals, fuels and lubricants	8.4	15.1	14.0
Chemicals and chemical products	598.1	638.8	600.9
Basic manufactures	31.1	36.3	31.8
Machinery and transport equipment	57.6	52.7	44.8
Miscellaneous manufactures	222.6	199.0	99.2
Total (incl. others)	1,277.8	1,462.8	1,113.3

Source: UN, *International Trade Statistics Yearbook*.

PRINCIPAL TRADING PARTNERS
(US $ million)

Imports c.i.f.	2005	2006	2007
China, People's Repub.	65.9	24.6	50.8
Germany	1.2	25.4	0.9
Hong Kong	11.8	19.8	2.2
India	0.4	10.7	16.2
Japan	5.8	26.1	30.1
Mozambique	57.3	11.3	17.0
South Africa	1,339.3	995.2	1,033.2
United Kingdom	32.6	8.5	8.5
USA	11.5	10.1	17.4
Zimbabwe	15.8	13.2	4.9
Total (incl. others)	1,656.1	1,242.4	1,270.1

Exports f.o.b.	2005	2006	2007
Australia	441.5	2.3	2.2
Botswana	6.6	13.1	3.3
Italy	0.1	0.4	153.5
Lesotho	8.0	25.6	1.3
Mozambique	96.6	247.4	20.2
Namibia	8.3	11.5	31.1
New Zealand	0.4	22.9	0.9
South Africa	478.8	446.1	888.5
Uganda	0.0	246.7	0.0
United Kingdom	128.4	4.6	1.3
USA	56.2	48.9	1.1
Zimbabwe	0.6	369.0	0.0
Total (incl. others)	1,277.8	1,462.8	1,113.3

Source: UN, *International Trade Statistics Yearbook*.

Transport

RAILWAYS
(traffic)

	2002	2003	2004
Net total ton-km (million)	728	726	710

Source: UN, *Statistical Yearbook*.

SWAZILAND

ROAD TRAFFIC
(motor vehicles in use at 31 December 2007)

Passenger cars	52,223
Buses and coaches	8,124
Lorries and vans	41,778
Motorcycles and mopeds	3,482

Source: IRF, *World Road Statistics*.

CIVIL AVIATION
(traffic on scheduled services)

	1998	1999	2000
Kilometres flown (million)	1	1	2
Passengers carried ('000)	41	12	90
Passenger-km (million)	43	13	68
Total ton-km (million)	4	1	6

Source: UN, *Statistical Yearbook*.

Tourism

TOURIST ARRIVALS
(at hotels)

Country of residence	2005	2006	2007
Australia	1,527	4,192	2,120
Mozambique	15,597	11,702	8,413
Portugal	733	8,188	10,674
South Africa	99,176	130,783	146,605
United Kingdom	15,737	11,948	11,684
Total (incl. others)	311,656	316,082	299,226

Tourism receipts (US $ million, incl. passenger transport): 77 in 2005; 75 in 2006; 32 in 2007.

Source: World Tourism Organization.

Communications Media

	2007	2008	2009
Telephones ('000 main lines in use)	44.0	44.0	44.0
Mobile cellular telephones ('000 subscribers)	380.0	531.6	656.0
Internet users ('000)	47.2	80.0	90.1
Broadband subscribers ('000)	n.a.	0.8	1.5

Source: International Telecommunication Union.

Personal computers: 42,000 (36.9 per 1,000 persons) in 2006 (Source: International Telecommunication Union).

Radio receivers (year ending 31 March 1998): 155,000 in use (Source: UN, *Statistical Yearbook*).

Television receivers (2002): 32,000 in use (Source: International Telecommunication Union).

Daily newspapers (2004): 2 (estimated circulation 27,000) (Source: UNESCO Institute for Statistics).

Education

(2006/07, unless otherwise indicated)

	Institutions	Teachers	Students
Pre-primary*	n.a.	451	14,554
Primary	541†	7,169	232,572
Secondary	182†	4,358	83,049
University‡	1§	462||	5,692||

* 2004/05.
† Figure for 2001/02.
‡ Figures exclude vocational, technical and teacher-training colleges. In 2000 there were 1,822 students enrolled at these institutions, which numbered 10 in 2003.
§ Figure for 2000.
\|\| Figure for 2005/06.

Source: UNESCO Institute for Statistics.

Pupil-teacher ratio (primary education, UNESCO estimate): 32.4 in 2006/07 (Source: UNESCO Institute for Statistics).

Adult literacy rate (UNESCO estimates): 86.5% (males 87.4%; females 85.6%) in 2008 (Source: UNESCO Institute for Statistics).

Directory

The Government

HEAD OF STATE

King: HM King MSWATI III (succeeded to the throne 25 April 1986).

COUNCIL OF MINISTERS
(May 2011)

Prime Minister: BARNABAS SIBUSISO DLAMINI.
Deputy Prime Minister: THEMBA MASUKU.
Minister of Economic Planning and Development: Prince HLANGUSEMPHI.
Minister of Finance: MAJOZI SITHOLE.
Minister of Foreign Affairs: LUTFO DLAMINI.
Minister of Public Works and Transport: NTUTHUKO DLAMINI.
Minister of Health: BENEDICT XABA.
Minister of Commerce, Industry and Trade: JABULILE MASHWAMA.
Minister of Housing and Urban Development: Pastor LINDIWE GWEBU.
Minister of Education and Training: WILSON NTJANGASE.
Minister of Agriculture: CLEMENT DLAMINI.
Minister of Tourism and Environmental Affairs: MACFORD SIBANDZE.
Minister of Labour and Social Security: PATRICK MAGWEBETANE MAMBA.
Minister of Natural Resources and Energy: Princess TSANDZILE.
Minister of Sports, Culture and Youth Affairs: HLOBSILE NDLOVU.
Minister of Information, Communication and Technology: NEL'SIWE SHONGWE.
Minister of Home Affairs: Chief MGWAGWA GAMEDZE.
Minister of Public Service: MTITI FAKUDZE.
Minister of Justice and Constitutional Affairs: DAVID MATSE.

MINISTRIES

Office of the Prime Minister: POB 433, Swazi Plaza, Mbabane; tel. 24042251; fax 24043943; internet www.gov.sz.

Office of the Deputy Prime Minister: POB 433, Swazi Plaza, Mbabane; tel. 24042723; fax 24044085.

Ministry of Agriculture: POB 162, Mbabane; tel. 24042731; fax 24044700.

Ministry of Commerce, Industry and Trade: Eastern Wing, Interministerial Complex, POB 451, Mbabane; tel. 24043201; fax 24044711; e-mail mee@realnet.co.sz.

Ministry of Economic Planning and Development: POB 602, Mbabane; tel. 24043765; fax 24042157.

Ministry of Education and Training: Hospital Rd, POB 39, Mbabane; tel. 24042491; fax 24043880.

SWAZILAND

Ministry of Finance: POB 443, Mbabane; tel. 24048148; fax 24043187.
Ministry of Foreign Affairs: POB 518, Mbabane; tel. 24042661; fax 24042669; e-mail ps_foreignaffairs@gov.sz.
Ministry of Health: POB 5, Mbabane; tel. 24042431; fax 4042092.
Ministry of Home Affairs: Justice Bldg, 1st Floor, Mhlambanyatsi Rd, POB 432, Mbabane; tel. 24042941; fax 25514060.
Ministry of Housing and Urban Development: Income Tax Bldg, 3rd and 5th Floors, Mhlambanyatsi Rd, POB 1832, Mbabane; tel. 24046035; fax 24044085.
Ministry of Information, Communication and Technology: Interministerial Complex, Block 8, 3rd Floor, Mbabane; tel. 24083123; fax 24040651; e-mail dlaminimart@gov.sz.
Ministry of Justice and Constitutional Affairs: POB 924, Mbabane; tel. 24046010; fax 24043533; e-mail ps@justice.gov.sz.
Ministry of Labour and Social Security: Mbabane.
Ministry of Natural Resources and Energy: Income Tax Bldg, 4th Floor, Mhlambanyatsi Rd, POB 57, Mbabane; tel. 24046244; fax 24042436; e-mail mnre@realnet.co.sz.
Ministry of Public Service: POB 338, Mbabane; tel. 24042761; fax 24042774.
Ministry of Public Works and Transport: Mhlambanyatsi Rd, POB 58, Mbabane; tel. 24099000; e-mail nkanmbulep@gov.sz.
Ministry of Sports, Culture and Youth Affairs: Phutfumani Bldg, Warner St, Mbabane.
Ministry of Tourism and Environmental Affairs: Income Tax Bldg, 2nd Floor, Mhlambanyatsi Rd, POB 2652, Mbabane; tel. 24044556; fax 24045415; e-mail mdlulim@gov.sz.

Legislature

SENATE

The Senate comprises not more than 31 members, of whom 20 are appointed by the King—at least eight of these are women—and 10 elected by the House of Assembly, one-half of whom are women.
President: GELANE ZWANE.

HOUSE OF ASSEMBLY

The House of Assembly comprises not more than 76 members. Of these, not more than 60 are directly elected from candidates nominated by traditional local councils, known as Tinkhundla, and not more than 10 are appointed by the King, one-half of whom are women. Additionally, one woman is selected from each of the four regions of Swaziland and the Attorney-General is also an ex officio member. The latest elections to the House of Assembly took place on 19 September 2008.
Speaker: PRINCE GUDUZA.

Election Commission

Elections and Boundaries Commission: POB 4842, Mbabane; tel. 24162813; fax 24161970; five mems; Chair. Chief GIJA DLAMINI.

Political Organizations

Party political activity was banned by royal proclamation in April 1973, and formally prohibited under the 1978 Constitution. Since 1991, following indications that the Constitution was to be revised, a number of political associations have re-emerged. Following the introduction of the new Constitution in February 2006, the legal status of party political activity remained unclear.
African United Democratic Party (AUDP): f. 2006; advocates full democratization of Swaziland; Pres. STANLEY MAUNDZISA; Sec.-Gen. SIBUSISO DLAMINI.
Imbokodvo National Movement (INM): f. 1964 by King Sobhuza II; traditionalist movement, which also advocates policies of devt and the elimination of illiteracy; Leader (vacant).
Ngwane National Liberatory Congress (NNLC): Ilanga Centre, Martin St, Manzini; tel. 25053935; f. 1962 by fmr mems of the SPP; advocates democratic freedoms and universal suffrage, and seeks abolition of the Tinkhundla electoral system; Pres. OBED DLAMINI; Sec.-Gen. DUMISA DLAMINI.
People's United Democratic Movement (PUDEMO): POB 4588, Manzini; tel. and fax 25054181; internet pudemo.org; f. 1983; seeks constitutional limitation of the powers of the monarchy; affiliated orgs include the Human Rights Asscn of Swaziland and the Swaziland Youth Congress (SWAYOCO—Pres. ALEX LANGWENYA; Sec.-Gen. KENNETH KUNENE); Pres. MARIO BONGANI MASUKU; Sec. SIKHUMBUZO PHAKATHI.
Swaziland National Front (SWANAFRO): Mbabane; Pres. ELMOND SHONGWE; Sec.-Gen. GLENROSE DLAMINI.
Swaziland Progressive Party (SPP): POB 6, Mbabane; tel. 22022648; f. 1959; Pres. J. J. NQUKU.
Swaziland United Front (SUF): POB 14, Kwaluseni; f. 1962 by fmr mems of the SPP; Leader MATSAPA SHONGWE.

Diplomatic Representation

EMBASSIES IN SWAZILAND

Mozambique: Princess Dr., POB 1212, Mbabane; tel. 24041296; fax 24048482; e-mail moz.high@swazi.net; Ambassador TIAGO CATIGO RECIBO.
South Africa: The New Mall, 2nd Floor, Dr Sishayi Rd, POB 2507, Mbabane; tel. 24044651; fax 24044335; e-mail sahc@africaonline.co.sz; High Commissioner Dr R. J. M. MAMPANE.
Taiwan (Republic of China): Makhosikhosi St, Mbabane; tel. 24044739; fax 24046688; e-mail rocembassy@africaonline.co.sz; Ambassador TSAI MING-YAW.
USA: Central Bank Bldg, 7th Floor, Mahlokohla St, Mbabane Pl., POB 199, Mbabane; tel. 24046441; fax 24045959; internet swaziland.usembassy.gov; Ambassador EARL MICHAEL IRVING.

Judicial System

Following the introduction of the new Constitution, the Swaziland Superior Court of Judicature comprised the Supreme Court and the High Court, which replaced the existing Court of Appeal and the High Court. The Supreme Court is headed by the Chief Justice and consists of not fewer than four other Justices of the Supreme Court, and is the final Court of Appeal. The High Court consists of the Chief Justice and not fewer than four Justices of the High Court, and has unlimited original jurisdiction in civil and criminal matters.

Religion

About 60% of the adult Swazi population profess Christianity. Under the new Constitution, which came into effect on 7 February 2006, Christianity ceased to be recognized as the country's official religion. There was a growing Muslim population, reported to number some 10,000 adherents. Most of the remainder of the population hold traditional beliefs.

CHRISTIANITY

At mid-2000 there were an estimated 153,000 Protestants and 466,000 adherents professing other forms of Christianity.
Council of Swaziland Churches: Mandlenkosi Ecumenical House, 142 Esser St, Manzini; POB 1095, Manzini; tel. 25053697; fax 25055841; e-mail c.o.c@africaonline.co.sz; f. 1976; Chair. Bishop MESHACK MABUZA; Gen. Sec. KHANGEZILE I. DLAMINI; 10 mem. churches incl. Roman Catholic, Anglican, Kukhany'okusha Zion Church and Lutheran.
League of African Churches: POB 230, Lobamba; asscn of 48 independent churches; Chair. SAMSON HLATJWAKO.
Swaziland Conference of Churches: 175 Ngwane St, POB 1157, Manzini; tel. and fax 25055253; e-mail scc@africaonline.co.sz; internet www.swazilandcc.org; f. 1929; Pres. Rev. JOHANNES V. MAZIBUKO; Gen. Sec. Rev. S. F. DLAMINI.

The Anglican Communion

Swaziland comprises a single diocese within the Church of the Province of Southern Africa. The Metropolitan of the Province is the Archbishop of Cape Town, South Africa. The Church had some 40,000 members at mid-2000.
Bishop of Swaziland: Rt Rev. MESHACK BOY MABUZA, Bishop's House, Muir St, POB 118, Mbabane; tel. 24043624; fax 24046759; e-mail anglicanchurch@africaonline.co.sz.

The Roman Catholic Church

The Roman Catholic Church was established in Swaziland in 1913. For ecclesiastical purposes, Swaziland comprises the single diocese of Manzini, suffragan to the archdiocese of Pretoria, South Africa. Some 6% of the total population are adherents of the Roman Catholic Church. The Bishop participates in the Southern African Catholic Bishops' Conference (based in Pretoria, South Africa).

SWAZILAND

Bishop of Manzini: Rt Rev. LOUIS NCAMISO NDLOVU, Bishop's House, Sandlane St, POB 19, Manzini; tel. 25056900; fax 25056762; e-mail bishop@africaonline.co.sz.

Other Christian Churches

Church of the Nazarene: POB 832, Manzini; tel. 25054732; f. 1910; 7,649 adherents (1994).

The Evangelical Lutheran Church in Southern Africa: POB 117, Mbabane; tel. 24043411; fax 24041847; f. 1902; Bishop JEREMIAH BHEKI MAGAGULA; 2,800 adherents in Swaziland (1994).

Mennonite Central Committee: POB 329, Mbabane; tel. 24042805; fax 24044732; f. 1971; Co-ordinator HLOB'SILE NXUMALO.

The Methodist Church in Southern Africa: POB 42, Mbabane; tel. 26321975; e-mail brianj@bcmc.co.za; internet www.methodist.org.za; f. 1880; Bishop BRIAN C. JENNINGS; 2,578 adherents (1992).

United Christian Church of Africa: POB 1345, Nhlangano; tel. 22022648; f. 1944; Pres. Rev. WELLINGTON B. MKHALIPHI; Founder and Gen. Sec. Dr J. J. NQUKU.

The National Baptist Church, the Christian Apostolic Holy Spirit Church in Zion and the Religious Society of Friends (Quakers) are also active.

BAHÁ'Í FAITH

National Spiritual Assembly: POB 298, Mbabane; tel. 25052689; f. 1960; mems resident in 153 localities.

ISLAM

Ezulwini Islamic Institute: Al Islam Dawah Movement of Swaziland, POB 133, Ezulwini; c. 3,000 adherents (1994).

The Press

PRINCIPAL NEWSPAPERS

The Guardian of Swaziland: POB 4747, Mbabane; tel. 2404838; f. 2001; daily newspaper; Editor THULANI MTHETHWA.

The Swazi News: Sheffield Rd, POB 156, Mbabane; tel. 24042520; fax 24042438; e-mail swazinews@times.co.sz; internet www.times.co.sz; f. 1983; weekly; English; owned by *The Times of Swaziland*; Editor THULANI THWALA; circ. 24,000.

Swazi Observer: Observer House, 3 West St, POB A385, Swazi Plaza, Mbabane; tel. 24049600; fax 24045503; e-mail info@observer.org.sz; internet www.observer.org.sz; f. 1981; owned by Tibiyo Taka Ngwane; Mon.–Sat.; *Weekend Observer* (Sun.); publ. suspended Feb. 2000, resumed March 2001; CEO S. MYZO MAGAGULA; Editor-in-Chief MUSA NDLANGAMANDLA.

Swaziland Today: POB 395, Mbabane; tel. 24041432; fax 24043493; weekly; govt newsletter.

The Times of Swaziland: Sheffield Rd, POB 156, Mbabane; tel. 24042211; fax 24042438; e-mail editor@times.co.sz; internet www.times.co.sz; f. 1897; Mon.–Fri., Sun.; also monthly edn; English; other publs incl. *What's Happening* (tourist interest); Man. Editor MBOGANI MBINGO; circ. 18,000.

PRINCIPAL PERIODICALS

The Nation: Mbabane House, 3rd Floor, Mahlokohla St, POB 4547, Mbabane; tel. and fax 24046611; e-mail thenation@realnet.co.sz; f. 1997; monthly; independent news magazine; publ. suspended briefly May 2001; Editor BHEKI MAKHUBU.

Swaziview: Mbabane; tel. 24042716; monthly magazine; general interest; circ. 3,500.

UNISWA Research Journal of Agriculture, Science and Technology: Private Bag 4, Kwaluseni; tel. 25274418; fax 25274428; e-mail research@uniswa.sz; internet www.uniswa.sz; 2 a year; publ. of the Faculties of Agriculture, Health Sciences and Science of the Univ. of Swaziland; Chair. Prof. E. M. OSSOM.

Publishers

Apollo Services (Pty) Ltd: POB 35, Mbabane; tel. 24042711.

GBS Printing and Publishing (Pty) Ltd: POB 1384, Mbabane; tel. 25052779.

Jubilee Printers: POB 1619, Matsaka; tel. 25184557; fax 25184558.

Longman Swaziland (Pty) Ltd: POB 2207, Manzini; tel. 25053891.

Macmillan Boleswa Publishers (Pty) Ltd: POB 1235, Manzini; tel. 25184533; fax 25185247; e-mail macmillan@africaonline.co.sz; f. 1978; textbooks and general; CEO DUSANKA STOJAKOVIC.

Swaziland Printing & Publishing Co Ltd: POB 28, Mbabane; tel. 24042716; fax 24042710.

Whydah Media Publishers Ltd: Mbabane; tel. 24042716; f. 1978.

Broadcasting and Communications

TELECOMMUNICATIONS

MTN Swaziland: Karl Grant St, POB 5050, H100 Mbabane; tel. 24060000; fax 24046217; e-mail yellohelp@mtn.co.sz; internet www.mtn.co.sz; f. 1998; jt venture between MTN Group, South Africa, and Swaziland Posts and Telecommunications Corpn; operates mobile cellular telephone network; 213,000 subscribers (2005); Chair. DAVID DLAMINI; CEO AMBROSE DLAMINI.

Swaziland Posts and Telecommunications Corpn (SPTC): Phutfumani Bldg, Mahlokohla St, POB 125, H100 Mbabane; tel. 24052000; fax 24052001; e-mail info@sptc.co.sz; internet www.sptc.co.sz; f. 1983; Chair. AMON DLAMINI; Man. Dir ZWANE ELIJAH.

BROADCASTING

Radio

Swaziland Broadcasting and Information Service: POB 338, Mbabane; tel. 24042763; fax 24046953; e-mail sbisnews@africaonline.co.sz; f. 1966; broadcasts in English and siSwati; Dir PERCY SIMELANE.

Swaziland Commercial Radio (Pty) Ltd: POB 1586, Alberton 1450, South Africa; tel. (11) 24344333; fax (11) 24344777; privately owned commercial service; broadcasts to Southern Africa in English and Portuguese; music and religious programmes; Man. Dir A. DE ANDRADE.

Trans World Radio: POB 64, Manzini; tel. 25052781; fax 25055333; internet www.twr.org; f. 1974; religious broadcasts from five transmitters in 30 languages to Southern, Central and Eastern Africa and to the Far East.

Television

Swaziland Television Authority (Swazi TV): POB A146, Swazi Plaza, Mbabane; tel. 24043036; fax 24042093; e-mail swazitv.eng@africaonline.co.sz; f. 1978; state-owned; broadcasts seven hours daily in English; Acting CEO MBUSI DLAMINI.

Finance

(cap. = capital; res = reserves; dep. = deposits; m. = million; brs = branches; amounts in emalangeni)

BANKING

In 2010 there were four commercial banks in Swaziland.

Central Bank

Central Bank of Swaziland: POB 546, Mahlokohla St, Mbabane; tel. 24082000; fax 24040013; e-mail info@centralbank.org.sz; internet www.centralbank.org.sz; f. 1974; bank of issue; cap. 21.8m., res 31.4m., dep. 1,388.7m. (March 2006); Gov. MARTIN G. DLAMINI; Dep. Gov. S. G. MDLULI.

Commercial Banks

First National Bank of Swaziland Ltd: Sales House Bldg, 2nd Floor, Swazi Plaza, POB 261, Mbabane; tel. 25184637; fax 24044735; e-mail hnsibande@fnb.co.za; internet www.fnbswaziland.co.sz; f. 1988; fmrly Meridien Bank Swaziland Ltd; wholly owned by FirstRand Bank Holdings Ltd, Johannesburg; cap. and res 61.5m., dep. 484.5m. (June 2002); Chair. Dr D. M. J. VON WISSEL; Man. Dir DAVE WRIGHT; 7 brs.

Nedbank (Swaziland) Ltd: cnr Plaza-Dr Sishayi St and Bypass Rd, POB 68, Mbabane; tel. 24081000; fax 24044060; e-mail info@nedbank.co.sz; internet www.nedbank.co.sz; f. 1974; fmrly Standard Chartered Bank Swaziland Ltd; 23.1% state-owned; cap. 11.9m., res 134.6m., dep. 1,006.2m. (Dec. 2007); Chair. MABILI DLAMINI; Man. Dir FIKILE NKOSI; 6 brs and 1 agency.

Development Banks

Standard Bank Swaziland Ltd: Standard House, 1st Floor, Swazi Plaza, POB A294, Mbabane; tel. 24046587; fax 24045899; e-mail standardbankswaziland@iafricaonline.co.sz; internet www.standardbank.co.sz; f. 1988; fmrly Stanbic Bank Swaziland, present name adopted 1997; merged with Barclays Bank of Swaziland in Jan.

SWAZILAND

1998; 25% state-owned; cap. 14.6m., res 89.3m., dep. 1,454.3m. (Dec. 2005); Chair. R. J. Rossouw (acting); Man. Dir Tineyi Mawocha; 10 brs, 1 agency.

Swaziland Development and Savings Bank (SwaziBank—Libhange LeSive): Engungwini Bldg, Gwamile St, POB 336, Mbabane; tel. 24042551; fax 24041214; e-mail swazibank@swazibank.sz; internet www.swazibank.co.sz; f. 1965; state-owned; taken over by central bank in 1995; under independent management since 2000; cap. and res 143.0m., total assets 557.9m. (March 2002); Acting Chair. Noah M. Nkambule; Man. Dir Stanley M. N. Matsebula; 8 brs.

Financial Institution

Swaziland National Provident Fund: POB 1857, Manzini; tel. 25082000; fax 25082001; internet www.snpf.co.sz; f. 1974; provides benefits for employed persons on retirement from regular employment or in the event of becoming incapacitated; employers are required by law to pay a contribution for every eligible staff member; total assets 290m. (June 1996); Chair. Mduduzi Gina; CEO Prince Lonkhokhela Dlamini.

STOCK EXCHANGE

Swaziland Stock Exchange: Capital Markets Development Unit, Infumbe Bldg, 1st Floor, Warner St, POB 546, Mbabane; tel. 24082164; fax 24049493; e-mail info@ssx.org.sz; internet www.ssx.org.sz; f. 1990 as Swaziland Stock Market (SSM); state-owned; Chair. Martin G. Dlamini.

INSURANCE

Between 1974 and 1999 the state-controlled Swaziland Royal Insurance Corpn (SRIC) operated as the country's sole authorized insurance company, although cover in a number of areas not served by SRIC was available from several specialized insurers. In 1999 it was proposed that legislation would be enacted to end SRIC's monopoly and provide for the company's transfer to private sector ownership. The legislation was adopted as the Insurance Act in 2005.

Insurance Companies

Swaziland Royal Insurance Corpn (SRIC): SRIC House, Somhlolo Rd, Gilfillan St, POB 917, H100 Mbabane; tel. 24043231; fax 24046415; e-mail sric@sric.sz; internet www.sric.sz; f. 1974; 41% state-owned, 59% owned by Munich-Reinsurance Co of Africa Ltd, Mutual and Fed. Insurance Co of South Africa Ltd, Swiss Re Southern Africa Ltd, S.A. Eagle Insurance Co Ltd, Old Mutual, and Mutual and Federal; Chair. Kenneth Mbuli; Gen. Man. Zombodze R. Magagula.

Metropolitan Life Swaziland: Mbabane; tel. 24090282; e-mail info@metropolitan.co.sz; internet www.metropolitan.co.sz; f. 2008; Chair. Stanley Matsebula; Man. Dir Muzi Dlamini.

Insurance Association

Insurance Brokers' Association of Swaziland (IBAS): POB 222, Mbabane H100; tel. 24043226; fax 24046412; e-mail mzamo_dlamini@aon.co.sz; f. 1983; Chair. Mzamo Elliot Dlamini; 4 mems.

Trade and Industry

GOVERNMENT AGENCIES

Small Enterprise Development Co (SEDCO): POB A186, Swazi Plaza, Mbabane; tel. 24042811; fax 24040723; e-mail business@sedco.co.sz; internet www.sedco.biz; f. 1970; devt agency; supplies workshop space, training and expertise for 165 local entrepreneurs at eight sites throughout the country; Chair. Pholile Dlamini; CEO Dorrington Matiwane.

Swaziland Investment Promotion Authority (SIPA): Mbandzeni House, 7th Floor, Church St, POB 4194, Mbabane; tel. 24040472; fax 24043374; e-mail info@sipa.org.sz; internet www.sipa.org.sz; f. 1998; Chair. Nick Jackson; CEO Phiwayinkosi Ginindza.

DEVELOPMENT ORGANIZATIONS

National Industrial Development Corpn of Swaziland (NIDCS): POB 866, Mbabane; tel. 24043391; fax 24045619; f. 1971; state-owned; administered by Swaziland Industrial Devt Co; Admin. Dir P. K. Thamm.

Swaziland Coalition of Concerned Civic Organisations (SCCCO): Smithco Industrial Centre, Mswati III Ave, 11th St, Matsapha; POB 4173, Mbabane; tel. and fax 25187688; e-mail webmaster@swazicoalition.org.sz; internet www.swazicoalition.org.sz; f. 2003; promotes constitutional democracy, poverty alleviation, fiscal discipline, economic stability, competitive regional and international trade, social justice, and the rule of law; Sec.-Gen. Musa Hlope; 9 mems incl.:

Coordinating Assembly of Non-Governmental Organisations (CANGO): POB A67, Swazi Plaza, Mbabane; tel. 24044721; fax 24045532; e-mail director@cango.org.sz; internet www.cango.org.sz; f. 1983; Exec. Dir Emmanuel Ndlangamandla; over 70 mem. orgs.

Federation of Swaziland Employers and Chamber of Commerce (FSECC): Emafini Business Center, Malagwane Hill, POB 72, Mbabane; tel. 24040768; fax 24090051; e-mail fsecc@business-swaziland.com; internet www.business-swaziland.com; f. 2003 by merger of Fed. of Swaziland Employers (f. 1964) and Swaziland Chamber of Commerce (f. 1916); CEO Zodwa Mabuza; c. 500 mems (2005).

Swaziland Industrial Development Co (SIDC): Dhlan'Ubeka House, 5th Floor, cnr Mdada and Lalufadlana Sts, POB 866, Mbabane; tel. 24044010; fax 24045619; e-mail info@sidc.co.sz; internet www.sidc.co.sz; f. 1986; 35% state-owned; finances private sector projects and promotes local and foreign investment; cap. E24.1m., total assets E577m. (June 2010); Chair. Tim Zwane; Man. Dir Tambo Gina.

Swaki (Pty) Ltd: Liqhaga Bldg, 4th Floor, Nkoseluhlaza St, POB 1839, Manzini; tel. 25052693; fax 25052001; e-mail info@swaki.co.sz; jtly owned by SIDC and Kirsh Holdings; comprises a number of cos involved in manufacturing, services and the production and distribution of food.

Swaziland Solidarity Network (SSN): c/o COSATU House, 3rd Floor, 1–5 Leyds St, Braamfontein, South Africa; POB 1027, Johannesburg 2000, South Africa; tel. (11) 23393621; fax (11) 23394244; e-mail ssnnetwork@gmail.org.za; internet www.swazisolidarity.org; f. 1997; umbrella org. promoting democracy; incorporates mems from Swaziland and abroad incl. PUDEMO, SWAYOCO, and the Swaziland Democratic Alliance (f. 1999); also incl. the African National Congress of South Africa, South African Communist Party and Congress of South African Trade Unions.

Tibiyo Taka Ngwane (Bowels of the Swazi Nation): POB 181, Kwaluseni, Manzini; tel. 25184306; fax 25184399; internet www.tibiyo.com; f. 1968; national devt agency, with investment interests in all sectors of the economy; participates in domestic and foreign jt investment ventures; total assets: E604m. (1999); Chair. Prince Logcogco Mangaliso; Man. Dir Absalom Themba Dlamini.

CHAMBERS OF COMMERCE

Sibakho Chamber of Commerce: POB 2016, Manzini; tel. and fax 25057347.

Swaziland Chamber of Commerce and Industry: see Fed. of Swaziland Employers and Chamber of Commerce.

INDUSTRIAL AND TRADE ASSOCIATIONS

National Agricultural Marketing Board: POB 4261, Manzini; tel. 25055314; fax 25054072; internet www.namboard.co.sz; Chair. Dr Micah B. Masuku; CEO Obed N. Hlongwane.

National Maize Corpn (NMC): 11th St Matsapha Indstrial Sites; tel. 25187432; fax 25184461; e-mail info@nmc.co.sz; internet www.nmc.co.sz; f. 1985; Chair. Nathi Gumedze; Acting CEO Sifiso Nxumalo.

Swaziland Citrus Board: Sokhamila Bldg, cnr Dzeliwe and Mdada Sts, POB 343, Mbabane H100; tel. 24044266; fax 24043548; e-mail citrus@realnet.co.sz; f. 1969; Chair. H. C. Noddeboe.

Swaziland Commercial Board: POB 509, Mbabane; tel. 24042930; Man. Dir J. M. D. Fakudze.

Swaziland Cotton Board: POB 220, Manzini; tel. and fax 25052775; e-mail dlaminiaa@gov.sz; f. 1967; CEO Tom Jele.

Swaziland Dairy Board: Enguleni Bldg, 3rd Floor, 287 Mahleka St, POB 2975, Manzini; tel. 25058262; fax 25058260; e-mail ceo-swazidairy@africaonline.co.sz; internet swazidairy.org; f. 1971; Gen. Man. N. T. Gumede.

Swaziland Sugar Association: 4th Floor, cnr Dzeliwe and Msakato Sts, POB 445, Mbabane; tel. 24042646; fax 24045005; e-mail info@ssa.co.sz; internet www.ssa.co.sz; CEO Dr Michael Matsebula.

EMPLOYERS' ORGANIZATIONS

Building Contractors' Association of Swaziland: POB 518, Mbabane; tel. 24040071; fax 24044258; e-mail soconswad@realnet.co.sz.

Swaziland Association of Architects, Engineers and Surveyors: Swazi Plaza, POB A387, Mbabane; tel. 24042227.

Swaziland Institute of Personnel and Training Managers: c/o UNISWA, Private Bag, Kwaluseni; tel. 25184011; fax 25185276.

UTILITIES

Electricity

Swaziland Electricity Company: POB 258, Mbabane; tel. 24094000; fax 24042335; e-mail sifiso.dhlamini@sec.co.sz; internet www.sec.co.sz; statutory body; f. 1963; Chair. S'THOFENI GININDZA; Man. Dir PIUS GUMBI.

Water

Swaziland Water Services Corpn: Emtfonjeni Bldg, Below Gables Shopping Complex, Ezulwini, MR103, POB 20, Mbabane H100; tel. 24163621; fax 24163617; e-mail headoffice@swsc.co.sz; internet www.swsc.co.sz; state authority; Chair. ESAU N. ZWANE; CEO PETER N. BHEMBE.

CO-OPERATIVE ASSOCIATIONS

Swaziland Central Co-operatives Union: POB 551, Manzini; tel. 25052787; fax 25052964.

There are more than 123 co-operative associations, of which the most important is:

Swaziland Co-operative Rice Co Ltd: handles rice grown in Mbabane and Manzini areas.

TRADE UNIONS

At mid-2005 there were 55 organizations recognized by the Department of Labour. Only non-managerial workers may belong to a union.

Trade Union Federations

Swaziland Amalgamated Trade Unions (SATU): POB 7138, Manzini; tel. 25059544; fax 25052684; f. 2003 by merger of five industrial unions; Sec.-Gen. FRANK NKULULEKO MNCINA; 3,500 mems (2005).

Swaziland Federation of Labour (SFL): Swazi Plaza, POB 1173, Mbabane; tel. 24045216; fax 24044261; e-mail sufiaw@realnet.co.sz; Sec.-Gen. VINCENT V. NCONGWANE; 10,900 mems (2007).

Swaziland Federation of Trade Unions (SFTU): POB 1158, Manzini; tel. and fax 25056575; internet www.cosatu.org.za/sftu; f. 1973; prin. trade union org. since mid-1980s; represents workers in the agricultural, private and public sectors; Pres. BARNES DLAMINI; Sec.-Gen. JAN SITHOLE; 83,000 mems (2007).

21 affiliated mem. unions incl.:

Swaziland Agriculture and Plantation Workers' Union (SAPWU): POB 2010, Manzini; tel. 24526010; fax 24526106; Sec.-Gen. ARCHIE SAYED.

Swaziland Communications Workers' Union (SCWU): c/o Swaziland Post and Telecommunications Corpn, POB 125, Mbabane; fax 24042093; fmrly Swaziland Post and Telecommunications Workers' Union; present name adopted in 2006; Pres. INNOCENT NGWENYA; Sec.-Gen. MDUDUZI ZWANE.

Swaziland Manufacturing and Allied Workers' Union (SMAWU): Agora Shopping Complex, King Mswati III Ave, Matsapha, POB 2379, Manzini; tel. 25186503; fax 25187028; e-mail smawu@realnet.co.sz; Gen. Sec. SIPHO PETERSON MAMBA; 7,000 mems (2004).

Swaziland National Association of Civil Service (SNACS): POB 2811, Manzini M200; tel. 2557882; fax 2557887; e-mail snacs@swazi.net; f. 1980; reportedly suspended from the SFTU in 2006; Pres. CHARLES KHUMALO; Gen. Sec. ABSOLOM DLAMINI; 3,855 mems (2002).

Swaziland Nurses' Association (Swaziland National Association of Nurses): POB 6191, Manzini; tel. and fax 25058070; f. 1965; Pres. BHEKI MAMBA; Gen. Sec. JULIA JABULILE ZIYANÉ.

Swaziland Transport and Allied Workers' Union (STAWU): POB 3362, Manzini; Sec.-Gen. SIMANGA SHONGWE.

Other unions affiliated to the SFTU include the Building and Construction Workers' Union of Swaziland; the Swaziland Commercial and Allied Workers' Union; the Swaziland Conservation Workers' Union; the Swaziland Electricity Supply, Maintenance and Allied Workers' Union; the Swaziland Hotel, Catering and Allied Workers' Union; the Swaziland Manufacturing and Allied Workers' Union; the Swaziland Media and Publications Workers' Union; the Swaziland Mining, Quarrying and Allied Workers' Union; the Swaziland Motor Engineering Allied Workers' Union; the Swaziland Union of High Learning Institutions; the Workers' Union of Swaziland Security Guards; the Workers' Union of Town Councils; and the Swaziland Water and Co-operation Workers' Union.

Swaziland National Association of Teachers (SNAT): POB 1575, M200 Manzini; tel. 25052603; fax 25060386; e-mail snatcentre@africaonline.co.sz; internet www.snat.org.sz; Pres. SIMON BRIAN MAKHANYA; Sec.-Gen. MUZI GLADWELL MHLANGA; 9,000 mems.

Swaziland Union of Financial Institutions and Allied Workers (SUFIAW): 100 Johnson St, Mbabane; tel. 24044261; fax 24045216; e-mail sufiaw@realnet.co.sz; Pres. BRIAN MABUZA; Sec.-Gen. VINCENT V. NCONGWANE.

Other registered unions include the Association of Lecturers and Academic Personnel of the University of Swaziland, and the University of Swaziland Workers' Union.

Staff Associations

Three staff associations exist for employees whose status lies between that of worker and that of management: the Nyoni Yami Irrigation Scheme Staff Association, the Swazican Staff Association and the Swaziland Electricity Board Staff Association.

Transport

Buses are the principal means of transport for many Swazis. Bus services are provided by private operators; these are required to obtain annual permits for each route from the Road Transportation Board, which also regulates fares.

RAILWAYS

The rail network, which totalled 297 km in 1998–99, provides a major transport link for imports and exports. Railway lines connect with the dry port at Matsapha, the South African ports of Richards Bay and Durban in the south, the South African town of Komatipoort in the north and the Mozambican port of Maputo in the east. Goods traffic is mainly in wood pulp, sugar, molasses, coal, citrus fruit and canned fruit. In June 1998 the Trans Lebombo rail service was launched to carry passengers from Durban to Maputo via Swaziland. The service was terminated in May 2000, owing to insufficient demand. In August 2004 the Government announced plans to privatize Swaziland Railways.

Swaziland Railways: Swaziland Railway Bldg, cnr Johnston and Walker Sts, POB 475, Mbabane; tel. 24047211; fax 24047210; internet www.swazirail.co.sz; f. 1962; Chair. B. A. G. FITZPATRICK; CEO GIDEON J. MAHLALELA.

ROADS

In 2002 there were an estimated 3,594 km of roads, including 1,465 km of main roads and 2,129 km of secondary roads. About 30% of the road network was paved in that year. The rehabilitation of about 700 km of main roads and 600 km of district gravel-surfaced roads began in 1985, financed by World Bank and US loans totalling some E18m. In 1991 work commenced on the reconstruction of Swaziland's main road artery, connecting Mbabane to Manzini, via Matsapha, and in 2001 the Government announced the construction of two main roads in the north of the country, financed by Japanese loans.

Roads Department: Ministry of Public Works and Transport, POB 58, Mbabane; tel. 24042321; fax 24045825; e-mail tshabalalatr@gov.sz; Chief Roads Engineer T. M. TSHABALALA.

SHIPPING

Royal Swazi National Shipping Corpn Ltd: POB 1915, Manzini; tel. 25053788; fax 25053820; f. 1980 to succeed Royal Swaziland Maritime Co; 76% owned by Tibiyo Taka Ngwane; owns no ships, acting only as a freight agent; Gen. Man. M. S. DLAMINI.

CIVIL AVIATION

Swaziland's only airport is at Matsapha, near Manzini, about 40 km from Mbabane. In mid-1997 the Government initiated a three-year programme to upgrade the airport. In early 2003 construction began of an international airport at Sikhupe, in eastern Swaziland. In March 2006 Swaziland Airlink was one of 92 airlines banned from landing at European Union airports owing to safety concerns.

Swaziland Airlink: POB 939, Matsapha Airport, Manzini; tel. 25186155; fax 25186148; f. 1999; fmrly Royal Swazi Nat. Airways Corpn; jt venture between SA Airlink, South Africa (40%) and the Govt of Swaziland; scheduled passenger services from Manzini to Johannesburg, South Africa; Chair. LINDIWE KHUMALO-MATSE.

Tourism

Swaziland's attractions for tourists include game reserves (at Malolotja, Hawane, Mlawula and Mantenga) and magnificent mountain scenery. In 2007 tourist arrivals at hotels totalled 299,226; receipts from tourism amounted to US $32m. in that year.

Hotel and Tourism Association of Swaziland: Oribi Court, 1st Floor, Gwamile St, POB 462, Mbabane; tel. 24042218; fax 24044516;

SWAZILAND

e-mail aliand@realnet.co.sz; internet www.visitswazi.com/tourismassoc; f. 1979.

Swaziland National Trust Commission (SNTC): POB 100, Lobamba; tel. 24161516; fax 24161875; e-mail director@sntc.org.sz (parks and wildlife); e-mail curator@sntc.org.sz (museums and monuments); internet www.sntc.org.sz; f. 1972; parastatal org. responsible for conservation of nature and cultural heritage (national parks, museums and monuments); CEO T. DLAMINI.

Swaziland Tourism Authority (STA): POB A1030, Swazi Plaza, Mbabane H101; tel. 24049693; fax 24049683; e-mail secretary@tourismauthority.org.sz; internet www.welcometoswaziland.com; f. 2001; CEO ERIC SIPHO MASEKO.

Defence

The Umbutfo Swaziland Defence Force was created in 1973. Compulsory military service of two years was introduced in 1983.

Defence Expenditure: Budgeted at E168m. for 2001/02.

Commander of the Umbutfo Swaziland Defence Force: Maj.-Gen. STANLEY S. DLAMINI.

Deputy Commander of the Umbutfo Swaziland Defence Force: Brig.-Gen. PATRICK V. MOTSA.

Education

Education is not compulsory in Swaziland. Primary education begins at six years of age and lasts for seven years. Secondary education begins at 13 years of age and lasts for up to five years, comprising a first cycle of three years and a second of two years. According to UNESCO estimates, in 2006/07 83% of children in the relevant age-group (males 82%; females 84%) were enrolled at primary schools, while in that year secondary enrolment included 29% of children in the appropriate age-group (males 31%; females 26%). In 2005/06 5,692 students were enrolled at the University of Swaziland, which has campuses at Luyengo and Kwaluseni. There are also a number of other institutions of higher education: in 2000 there were 1,822 students enrolled at 10 vocational, technical and teacher-training colleges. In 2008 21.6% of total government expenditure was allocated to education.

SWEDEN

Introductory Survey

LOCATION, CLIMATE, LANGUAGE, RELIGION, FLAG, CAPITAL

The Kingdom of Sweden lies in north-western Europe, occupying about two-thirds of the Scandinavian peninsula. It is bordered by Finland to the north-east, and by Norway to the north-west and west. About 15% of Sweden's area lies north of the Arctic Circle. The Baltic Sea and the Gulf of Bothnia are to the east, the Skagerrak and Kattegat channels to the south-west. The country is relatively flat and is characterized by thousands of inland lakes and small coastal islands. There is a mountain range, the Kjolen mountains, in the north-west. Winters are cold and summers mild. In Stockholm the mean summer temperature is 18°C (64°F) and the mean winter temperature −3°C (27°F). The national language is Swedish, but there are Finnish and Lapp (Sámi) minorities (the latter numbering between 17,000 and 20,000), retaining their own languages. A majority of the inhabitants profess Christianity, and about 78% are adherents of the Evangelical Lutheran Church of Sweden. The national flag (proportions 5 by 8) is light blue with a yellow cross, the upright of the cross being to the left of centre. The capital is Stockholm.

CONTEMPORARY POLITICAL HISTORY

Historical Context

Sweden has been a constitutional monarchy, traditionally neutral, since the early 19th century. During this time the country has not participated in any war or entered any military alliance. Norway, formerly united with Sweden, became independent in 1905. Sweden adopted parliamentary government in 1917, and universal adult suffrage was introduced in 1921. From 1932 until 1976, except for a short break in 1936, Sweden was governed by the Socialdemokratiska Arbetareparti (SAP—Social Democratic Labour Party), either alone or as the senior partner in coalitions (1936–45 and 1951–57). During those 44 years the country had only three Prime Ministers, all Social Democrats. Since the Second World War Sweden has become an active member of many international organizations, including the UN (to which it has given military support), the Council of Europe (see p. 250) and, from 1995, the European Community (EC, now European Union—EU, see p. 270).

Domestic Political Affairs

Olof Palme succeeded Dr Tage Erlander as Prime Minister and leader of the SAP in October 1969. After a general election in September 1970, Palme formed a minority Government. Under a constitutional reform, the Riksdag (Parliament) was reconstituted from January 1971, its two chambers being replaced by a unicameral assembly. King Gustaf VI Adolf, who had reigned since 1950, died in September 1973 and was succeeded by his grandson, Carl XVI Gustaf. A revised Constitution, effective from January 1975, ended the monarch's prerogative to appoint the Prime Minister: the Speaker of the Riksdag was to have this responsibility in future.

At the September 1976 election, dissatisfaction with high rates of taxation, necessary to maintain the advanced social welfare system that Sweden had developed, brought about the defeat of the SAP. Thorbjörn Fälldin, leader of the Centerpartiet (CP—Centre Party), formed a centre-right coalition in October. The wish of the CP to abandon Sweden's nuclear power programme caused serious controversy in June 1978, when an independent commission recommended its continuation. This view was endorsed by the Folkpartiet (FP—Liberals) and Moderata Samlingspartiet (MS—Moderates), whose rejection of a proposal by Fälldin to submit the nuclear issue to a national referendum precipitated the Government's resignation in October 1978. The FP formed a minority Government, led by Ola Ullsten. Following a general election in September 1979, Fälldin returned as Prime Minister of a coalition comprising members of the CP, the MS and the FP, with an overall parliamentary majority of only one seat. A referendum on the future of nuclear power was held in March 1980, at which a narrow majority of the electorate approved a limited programme of nuclear reactor development, to be progressively eliminated by 2010 and replaced by alternative energy resources.

During 1980 the Government's economic policies came under attack, mainly because of the rising rate of inflation, and there was severe industrial unrest. The MS, who disagreed with proposed tax reforms, left the coalition in May 1981. At the next general election, held in September 1982, the SAP was returned to power, securing 166 of the 349 seats in the Riksdag, but gaining an overall majority over the three non-socialist parties. In October Palme formed a minority Government, following an undertaking by the Vänsterpartiet—Kommunisterna (VpK—Left Party—Communists), which held 20 seats, to support the SAP. Palme's Government was returned to power in September 1985, with the support of the VpK. The SAP and the VpK together won 178 seats, while the three main non-socialist parties took 171 seats. The FP increased its share of seats in the legislature from 21 to 51.

In February 1986 Palme was murdered by an unknown assailant in Stockholm. In March the Deputy Prime Minister, Ingvar Carlsson, took office as Prime Minister. Carlsson retained Palme's Cabinet and declared that he would continue the policies of his predecessor. In mid-1989 Christer Pettersson, a man with a history of mental illness and violent crime, was convicted of Palme's murder amid some controversy, only to be acquitted on appeal in October. In May 1998, in response to a petition by the public prosecutor's office, the Supreme Court ruled that there was insufficient new evidence to conduct a retrial.

Meanwhile, ecological concerns were heightened in 1988 by two disasters affecting the marine environment along Sweden's coast, both of which were attributed to the effects of pollutants. At the general election in September the environmentalist Miljöpartiet de Gröna (MP—Green Party) gained parliamentary representation for the first time, but the SAP remained in power with the continued support of the VpK. The MS remained the second largest party in the Riksdag. In February 1990 the VpK (subsequently restyled the Vänsterpartiet—VP—Left Party) and the MP refused to support the Government's proposed austerity measures. Carlsson resigned, but, having secured support for a more moderate set of proposals, he formed another minority Government.

During 1990 the Swedish economy entered into recession, and in December the Riksdag approved a new programme of austerity measures. The Government was forced to abandon the long-held belief that the commitment to full employment and the defence of the welfare state (supported by high levels of taxation and of public expenditure) should be overriding priorities.

The MS-led Government of Carl Bildt

The popularity of the SAP continued to decline, and in the general election of September 1991 the party did not win enough seats to form a government, although, with 138 seats, it remained the largest party in the Riksdag. The MS increased their representation to 80 seats, while the Kristdemokratiska Samhällspartiet (KdS—Christian Democrats) and a recently formed right-wing party, Ny demokrati (ND—New Democracy), won 26 and 25 seats respectively, at the expense of the FP and the CP; the MP failed to secure 4% of the total votes cast, and thereby lost its seats. Carlsson resigned as Prime Minister for the second time, and in early October Carl Bildt, the leader of the MS (the largest non-socialist party in the legislature), formed a minority Government comprising members of four non-socialist parties—the MS, the CP, the FP and the KdS. The coalition was obliged to rely on the ND for support in securing approval for legislation. Without delay, the new Government began to accelerate the deregulation of the economy already undertaken by its predecessor.

Although the Government's austerity measures succeeded in reducing inflation, the high level of the budgetary deficit was a cause of concern in 1992. In September speculation on the international currency markets caused a rapid outflow of capital, and in November a fresh outflow of capital, following the SAP's refusal to approve reductions in public expenditure, forced the Government to allow the krona to 'float' in relation to other currencies, thereby effectively devaluing it by some 10%. In March 1993 the Government was defeated in the Riksdag when the ND refused to support budgetary proposals, but later in the same month the Government won a parliamentary vote of confidence (the ND abstained from voting). In June 1994 the leader of the CP, Olof Johansson, resigned from his post as Minister of the Environment in protest at the Government's approval of plans to construct a link with Denmark across the Öresund strait (see Foreign Affairs).

SAP-led minority Governments: 1994–2002

At the general election in September 1994 the SAP increased its representation to 161 seats. The VP won 22 seats and the MP 18. Although the MS maintained the level of support they had gained at the previous election, the other parties in the incumbent coalition Government fared badly. Bildt resigned as Prime Minister, and in October 1994 Carlsson formed a minority SAP Government. The results appeared to indicate a trend of increased support for parties opposed to Sweden's joining the EU (as the EC had become). Despite opposition to EU membership within the SAP, Carlsson declared that a major objective of his Government would be to secure a mandate for Sweden to join the EU in a national referendum. He also emphasized the need for stringent economic measures to reduce unemployment, stabilize the budgetary deficit and safeguard welfare provisions. Following approval by referendum in November, Sweden became a member of the EU on 1 January 1995 (see Foreign Affairs).

In March 1996 Carlsson relinquished his dual posts as Prime Minister and leader of the SAP, in order to retire from political life. Göran Persson, hitherto Minister of Finance, was elected unopposed as Prime Minister and leader of the SAP. In November an independent study group, which had been commissioned by the Government to consider Sweden's proposed participation in Economic and Monetary Union (EMU, see p. 311), recommended that Sweden should not join EMU until the unemployment rate had been significantly reduced. In February 1997, however, the central bank advocated membership of EMU from its inception in 1999. Nevertheless, in June 1997 the Government announced that Sweden would not be participating in the first stage of EMU, citing a lack of public support for the project. In October it was also announced that Sweden had no intention of participating in the European Exchange Rate Mechanism (ERM).

In August 1997 details of a national programme of enforced sterilization conducted during 1935–75 against some 60,000 individuals assessed to be of inferior intellectual or physical capabilities, reported in the Swedish press, provoked national outrage and prompted the Government to announce the creation of a public inquiry into the country's post-First World War eugenics programme. It was subsequently revealed that minimal compensation had been paid to only 16 victims of the programme during the previous 10 years. In March 1999 the Ministry of Health and Social Affairs announced that compensation amounting to a maximum of 175,000 kronor would be paid to each surviving victim of the programme. In August 2001 the State Sterilization Compensation Board stated that of some 2,000 applicants, about 1,500 had received compensation, the total amount paid out being approximately 256m. kronor.

At the general election held in September 1998 the SAP maintained its position as the largest party in the Riksdag (winning 131 seats), despite a substantial reduction in its representation. This was the SAP's worst electoral performance for some 70 years, and the party required the support of the VP and the MP to remain in government. The MS retained the position of second largest party in the Riksdag, obtaining 82 seats. At about 81%, the participation rate at the election was the lowest for some 50 years. Post-electoral analysis identified the SAP's pursuit of financial regularity at the perceived expense of socialist policies as the probable cause of its poor performance. It was reported that, in return for its support, the VP would seek to persuade the Government to increase expenditure on social welfare and employment, and would encourage the slower repayment of Sweden's national debt, higher taxes, the complete decommissioning of Sweden's nuclear power stations, and a less stringent programme of privatization. Both the VP and the MP remained strongly opposed to any future participation by Sweden in EMU. In early October the new Government presented its statement of policy, which envisaged a more active role in Europe for Sweden, and measures intended to achieve sustainable economic growth and a reduction in unemployment. Following the announcement of former premier Bildt's retirement from party politics, in August 1999 Bo Lundgren was elected to succeed him as leader of the MS.

In late 1999 it was reported that public spending on defence equipment was to be reduced drastically. Additionally, proposed reform of the national defence system was likely to result in the loss of some 10,000 military and civilian jobs. Earlier in the year the military high command had indicated that the Government's programme of defence rationalization would lead to an eventual halving of the strength of the armed forces, in terms of both personnel and equipment, prompting speculation that Sweden might be about to reconsider its neutral status with regard to regional security. In November 2000 Persson announced proposals to that effect. He asserted that neutrality was no longer relevant after the end of the Cold War, and that it did not cover all aspects of Sweden's security policy, such as disarmament, the non-proliferation of nuclear weapons and stability in Europe. However, Persson did not propose to join the North Atlantic Treaty Organization (NATO, see p. 368), asserting that it was essential for the stability of northern Europe that Sweden remain non-aligned.

SAP-led minority Government: 2002–06

At the general election held on 15 September 2002 the SAP maintained its position as the largest party in the Riksdag, winning 144 of the 349 seats. Persson formed a minority SAP Government with the parliamentary support of the MP and the VP. In return for their support, the MP and the VP required the Government to espouse some of their policies, including a reduction of 6,000m. kronor in defence expenditure over five years and a moratorium on cod-fishing in the Baltic Sea from 1 January 2003, with compensation for the fishing industry.

In March 2000 a national congress of the SAP had endorsed the adoption of future EMU entry as official party policy, despite a significant degree of opposition. Following the 2002 general election, Persson announced that a referendum would be held on the adoption of the euro in September 2003. The SAP remained divided on the issue; the MS and other centre-right parties supported entry into EMU. The campaign for the adoption of the euro was supported by the national media and the business community, whereas opposition to the new currency was focused in the trade unions, the MP and the VP. Opponents of EMU feared that membership would force Sweden to reduce public spending so as not to breach the 3% budget deficit limit imposed by the EU's Stability and Growth Pact. In September, four days prior to the referendum on entry into EMU, the Minister for Foreign Affairs, Anna Lindh, one of the Government's most effective campaigners for the adoption of the euro, was stabbed in central Stockholm; she died of her injuries the following day. Sympathy for Lindh did not prevent voters from rejecting the adoption of the euro. The result of the referendum was 42.0% in favour of entry to EMU, 55.9% against and 2.1% blank votes. Only in Stockholm did the proposal to adopt the euro receive a majority of the votes cast. A Swede of Serbian origin, who had a history of mental illness and claimed there was no political motive for the attack, was convicted of Lindh's murder and sentenced to life imprisonment in March 2004.

With the prospect of the enlargement of the EU from 15 to 25 countries on 1 May 2004, concerns arose that the Swedish welfare system would be unduly burdened by an influx of workers from the new member states. In April, however, the Riksdag rejected government-proposed legislation providing for welfare and labour restrictions on migrant workers from the 10 accession countries for at least two years, meaning that Sweden was one of the few EU countries without any such restrictions.

The perceived failure of the main political parties adequately to address the strong current of scepticism concerning the EU, as expressed in Sweden's rejection of the euro, led to the formation, in February 2004, of a new political grouping, the Junilistan (June List), which opposed further integration with the EU, but did not advocate withdrawal. The grouping stressed that it was not itself a political party, and went as far as appending its candidates' usual party affiliation to their names on the ballots for the forthcoming elections to the European Parliament. This strategy proved successful, allowing the June List to draw support from across the political spectrum. At the elections, held on 13 June, the June List won three of Sweden's 19 seats in the European Parliament. The SAP, by contrast, obtained five seats, while the MS won four. The VP and FP each won two seats, and the CP, MP and the Kristdemokraterna (Kd, as the KdS had been renamed) one apiece. Despite expectations that the June List's success in the European elections might increase pressure on the Government to hold a national referendum on the ratification of the EU constitutional treaty, which had been approved by the Council of the EU in June 2004, the Government chose to present the treaty for approval (or otherwise) in the Riksdag. However, following the rejection of the treaty at national referendums in France and the Netherlands in mid-2005, Sweden was one of several member states to delay the ratification process indefinitely. The Treaty of Lisbon, which replaced the constitutional treaty, was ratified by the Riksdag in November 2008, finally entering into force in December 2009.

In March 2006 Laila Freivalds resigned as Minister for Foreign Affairs, following criticism of her ministry's involvement in forcing the temporary closure, in February, of the website of *SD-Kuriren*—the newspaper of the far-right Sverigedemokraterna (SD, Swedish Democrats)—which had asked readers to submit cartoons of the Prophet Muhammad. (The publication of caricatures depicting the Prophet in a Danish newspaper in late 2005, and in a number of other European newspapers in early 2006, as a gesture in support of press freedom, had led to world-wide protests by Muslims—see the chapter on Denmark.) Freivalds had already come under pressure to resign in December 2005 after an independent commission held her partly responsible for the Government's slow response to the tsunamis in South-East Asia on 26 December 2004 (which killed more than 500 Swedes). Jan Eliasson, the President of the UN General Assembly, was appointed as the new Minister for Foreign Affairs; he was to hold both positions until the expiry of his UN term in September 2006.

Reinfeldt's MS-led Government

At the general election, held on 17 September 2006, the centre-right Alliance for Sweden, comprising the MS, the FP, the CP and the Kd, emerged as the largest group in the Riksdag, the four parties together winning 178 seats. Of those, the MS, led by Fredrik Reinfeldt, won 97 seats (compared with 55 seats in the 2002 elections), the CP 29, the FP 28 and the Kd 24. The four main non-socialist parties had presented a joint programme for government, which included plans to reduce welfare dependency and increase the labour supply by means of tax cuts for the lower paid and reductions in the levels of unemployment benefit, to reduce the role of the state in the economy through the privatization of state-owned companies and to introduce private sector competition in health care and education. In contrast to its partners in the Alliance, the FP suffered a significant decline in support, recording a loss of 20 seats, compared with the 2002 elections. The revelation of a scandal regarding a group of FP activists, who, during the election campaign, had gained illegal access to the computer network of the SAP and distributed information they had obtained to fellow activists in the FP, was considered to have been a decisive factor in the party's poor electoral performance. The SAP, despite remaining the largest party in the Riksdag (with 130 seats), recorded its worst electoral result since 1914. Persson immediately resigned as Prime Minister and announced that he would relinquish the leadership of the SAP in March 2007. As the leader of the largest party in the Alliance, Reinfeldt assumed the role of Prime Minister.

Reinfeldt's appointments to the new coalition Government in October 2006 included Maud Olofsson, of the CP, as Deputy Prime Minister and Minister for Enterprise and Energy, and the former Prime Minister, Bildt, as Minister for Foreign Affairs. The appointment of Nyamko Sabuni, a former refugee from Zaire (now the Democratic Republic of the Congo), as Minister for Integration and Gender Equality in the new Cabinet was controversial, with Muslim groups organizing a petition calling for her resignation, in response to her outspoken views on integration. Shortly after assuming office the Minister for Culture, Cecilia Stegö Chilò, and the Minister for Foreign Trade, Maria Borelius, both of the MS, were forced to resign, following allegations of irregularities in their personal finances. Lena Adelsohn Liljeroth and Sten Tolgfors, also both of the MS, assumed the culture and foreign trade portfolios, respectively.

Mona Sahlin was elected to succeed Persson as party leader at an SAP party conference in March 2007. In April, at the trial of six people on charges relating to the illegal accessing of SAP computer data by FP activists, three of the defendants were convicted and received substantial fines, while three members of the FP, including a former party secretary, were acquitted. In that month Lars Leijonborg, the Minister for Education and Research, whose leadership of the FP had been the subject of criticism for several months, announced that he would resign as party leader following the party conference, scheduled for September. He was replaced as leader of the FP by Jan Björklund.

A Swedish artist, Lars Vilks, provoked anger among Muslim communities in August 2007, when he depicted the head of the Prophet Muhammad on a dog's body. The decision by the Swedish newspaper *Nerikes Allehanda* to print the caricature resulted in formal protests by Egypt, Iran and Pakistan. In September Reinfeldt met with diplomats from a number of Muslim countries in an effort to defuse the tension. He apologized for any offence the image might have caused, but defended the right of Swedish citizens to freedom of expression. Vilks was subsequently placed under police protection, following reports that Islamist militants had offered a reward for his murder. In March 2010 seven people were arrested in Ireland and charged with plotting to murder Vilks; several Swedish newspapers then reprinted the caricature, in solidarity with the artist, provoking further protests. In July a Swedish court sentenced two men who had attacked the artist's home in May to two and three years' imprisonment, respectively, having convicted them of attempted arson.

A minor government reorganization took place in September 2007. Sten Tolgfors, the Minister for Foreign Trade, was appointed Minister for Defence, following Mikael Odenberg's decision to resign from the post over government proposals to reduce the defence budget by up to 4,000m. kronor by 2010. Ewa Björling succeeded Tolgfors as the Minister for Foreign Trade.

Six people were arrested in Sweden and Norway in February 2008, on suspicion of financing militant organizations and planning terrorist acts. Three of the suspects, who were reported to be Swedish citizens, were apprehended in Stockholm. In June the Riksdag narrowly approved a controversial bill allowing for all cross-border e-mails and telephone calls to be monitored for reasons of national security. The law took effect from 1 January 2009 and was strongly criticized by many commentators as an attack on civil liberties.

The country's opposition parties in December 2008 announced plans to form a coalition government if they were to win sufficient votes in the general election, scheduled for September 2010. The SAP, MP and VP stated that they would campaign as separate parties but would present a joint economic policy prior to the election. This followed previous attempts to form a coalition, which had been frustrated by the VP's reluctance to accept certain areas of the SAP-MP agreement, particularly in relation to economic policy.

In February 2009, despite divisions between the four governing parties on the issue, Reinfeldt announced the reversal of the decision to phase out the country's remaining nuclear power stations, as part of a new programme to combat global warming and increase energy security. Although the phased decommissioning of nuclear plants had been ratified in a referendum in 1980, by 2009 only two of the country's 12 nuclear reactors had been closed. Reinfeldt claimed that as the referendum result had not specified the means by which nuclear power would be replaced, the Government should not be bound by it. The new programme, which envisaged the replacement of the 10 ageing reactors with new models, also aimed to ensure that the country would use 50% renewable energy by 2020, reduce greenhouse gas emissions by 40% and become carbon neutral by 2050. The Government's proposals, which specified that the replacement reactors could only be constructed at existing sites and would not be permitted to exceed 10 in number, were narrowly approved by the Riksdag in June 2010.

At elections to the European Parliament, held in early June 2009, the SAP won five of the 18 allocated seats, the MS four, the FP three and the MP two, while the VP, the CP and the Kd won one seat apiece, as did the Pirate Party, which had been formed in 2006 to campaign against laws that make the sharing of internet files a criminal offence. Birgitta Ohlsson, of the FP, took office as Minister for EU Affairs in February 2010, succeeding Cecilia Malmström, who had been appointed to the European Commission.

Recent developments: 2010 election

At a general election held on 19 September 2010, the four parties of the governing centre-right Alliance won a total of 173 of the 349 seats in the Riksdag, just two seats short of a majority, with the MS securing 107 seats, the FP 24, the CP 23 and the Kd 19. The MS was the only party in the coalition to increase its representation (from 97 seats in the 2006 elections). The Red-Green alliance, comprising the SAP, the MP and the VP, together took 156 seats, 15 fewer than in 2006. Although the SAP narrowly retained its position as the largest single party, it suffered a further loss of support, its strength declining from 130 seats to 112, while the MP, hitherto the smallest parliamentary party, became the third largest as a result of the election, increasing its representation to 25 seats. The far-right SD, which advocated a drastic reduction in immigration, entered the Riksdag for the first time, winning 20 seats and effectively depriving the MS-led Alliance of its majority. A turn-out of 84.6% was recorded.

In early October 2010 Prime Minister Reinfeldt announced the formation of a minority Government, in which many of the ministerial posts remained unchanged. With the FP having supplanted the CP as the second largest party in the coalition, Jan Björklund, the FP's leader and Minister for Education, became Deputy Prime Minister, replacing Olofsson, who remained Minister for Enterprise and Energy. New appointees included Erik Ullenhag, of the FP, as Minister for Integration and Deputy Minister for Employment and Peter Norman, of the MS, as Minister for Financial Markets. Reinfeldt had ruled out any co-operation with the SD, the electoral success of which had prompted the organization of several rallies in protest against the party's policies, hoping instead to gain the support of the MP and the SAP in securing approval for legislation. In November Mona Sahlin announced her intention to resign as leader of the SAP; Håkan Juholt was elected as her replacement at a party congress held in March 2011.

A number of constitutional amendments were adopted by the Riksdag in November 2010, receiving the support of all parliamentary parties except the SD, and took effect in January 2011. The reforms notably enshrined Sweden's membership of the EU in the Constitution, reduced the threshold for independent candidates to be elected to the Riksdag from 8% of the votes cast to 5%, and required the conduct of a parliamentary confidence vote in the Prime Minister within two weeks of an election.

Sweden experienced its first suicide bombing in December 2010, when an Iraqi-born Swede detonated a car bomb in central Stockholm before killing himself when a second device exploded; two other people were injured in the second explosion. Shortly before the incident the Swedish security service and a news agency had received messages threatening attacks on Swedes in retribution for the deployment of Swedish forces in Afghanistan and also referring to the caricature of the Prophet Muhammad by Lars Vilks.

The minority Government suffered a reverse in March 2011 in its plans to proceed with the privatization of a range of state-owned companies, when the opposition parties united in the Riksdag to approve legislation aimed at preventing the planned divestment of government stakes in four companies: the power utility Vattenfall; the telecommunications company TeliaSonera; the postal service Posten; and SBAB Bank.

Foreign Affairs

Sweden's tradition of neutrality has prevented it from joining NATO, but it is an active member of many international organizations, both in Europe and world-wide, and is a significant donor of development assistance.

Regional relations

Sweden attaches considerable importance to co-operation with its Nordic and Baltic neighbours. It was a founder member of the Nordic Council (in 1952), the Nordic Council of Ministers (in 1962), and of the Council of the Baltic Sea States (established in 1992 and including the former Soviet Baltic republics).

In March 1991 the Swedish and Danish Governments agreed to construct a 16-km combined bridge and tunnel for road and rail traffic, across the Öresund strait, between Malmö and Copenhagen (to be known as the Öresund Link). The plan aroused opposition in Sweden, on the grounds that the link might hinder the flow of water into the Baltic Sea, as well as increasing pollution by emissions from vehicles. In May 1994 a Swedish marine commission concluded that plans for the link did not provide sufficient guarantees to protect the flow of water into the Baltic. In the following month, however, the Swedish Government approved construction plans, and the link was opened in July 2000.

In November 2009 the Swedish Government gave its approval for the construction within its territorial waters of Nord Stream, a double pipeline beneath the Baltic Sea, to carry natural gas from Russia to Germany. The Government declared itself satisfied with commitments by the construction consortium to safeguard fisheries, shipping and the environment. The pipeline was expected to begin operating in late 2011.

Within the wider European context, Sweden was a founder member of the Council of Europe in 1949, and of the European Free Trade Association (EFTA, see p. 447) in 1960. It also belongs to the Organization for Security and Co-operation in Europe (see p. 385) (founded in 1995 as a permanent organ of the Conference on Security and Co-operation in Europe, first held in 1973). Prior to Sweden's membership of the EU, trade with EU countries was conducted by means of a free trade area, the European Economic Area (EEA), created in 1994 under the aegis of EFTA. Negotiations on admission to the EU began in February 1993, when the Bildt Government declared that the country's tradition of neutrality would not prevent Sweden from participating fully in the common foreign and security policy of the EU. The negotiations were concluded in March 1994. Sweden obtained safeguards for its traditional policy of freedom of official information, and for its strict environmental standards, and won concessions on the maintenance of subsidies for agriculture in remote areas. A national referendum on membership was held on 13 November, producing a 52.2% majority in favour of joining the EU. The Riksdag formally ratified membership in December, and Sweden's accession to the EU took effect from 1 January 1995 (whereupon Sweden withdrew from EFTA). It was widely held that concern about the possible effects on the domestic economy of remaining outside the EU, together with fears regarding Sweden's ability to influence international affairs, such as the maintenance of effective environmental controls, had been major factors in the outcome of the referendum. Following the vote, the Carlsson Government reiterated that Sweden would retain its non-aligned policy within the EU, although it successfully applied for observer status within Western European Union (WEU) with effect from 1995. Sweden remained outside European Monetary Union (EMU) following the electorate's rejection in 2003 of proposals to join EMU (see Domestic Political Affairs, above). From the beginning of 2008 Swedish forces formed part of the Nordic Battlegroup, under the EU's rotating schedule of forces on standby for deployment to areas of crisis.

Other external relations

Although not a member of NATO, Sweden co-operated with NATO in the latter's Partnership for Peace programme from 1994 onwards, and in the Euro-Atlantic Partnership Council (established in 1997), and has participated in NATO-led peacekeeping operations in the Balkan region and Afghanistan.

The Swedish Government expressed its opposition to the US-led military operation against the regime of Saddam Hussain in Iraq from early 2003. However, Sweden contributed funds towards the reconstruction of Iraq, in addition to humanitarian aid.

In 2010 Sweden was the world's third largest donor of development assistance in proportion to its gross national income (GNI), after Norway and Luxembourg, providing 0.97% of its GNI, or 32,602m. kronor.

Sweden's relations with Turkey were strained in March 2010, following the adoption by the Riksdag of a resolution recognizing as 'genocide' the killing of some 1.5m. Armenians under the Ottoman Empire during 1915–23. The Turkish ambassador was withdrawn from Sweden in response, but returned to the country at the end of the month, after Swedish Prime Minister Reinfeldt distanced his Government from the legislature's decision.

Attempts by the Swedish authorities to prosecute Julian Assange, the Australian founder of the website Wikileaks, an organization publishing leaked private and classified content, for sexual offences allegedly committed during a visit to Sweden in August 2010, attracted considerable international media attention. In February 2011 a British court ruled that Assange should be extradited from the United Kingdom to Sweden, but Assange appealed against the decision, denying the allegations against him, which he claimed were politically motivated.

CONSTITUTION AND GOVERNMENT

The Swedish Constitution is based on four fundamental laws and the Riksdag Act of 1974. The four fundamental laws are the Instrument of Government (originally dating from 6 June 1809), the Act of Succession (1810), the Freedom of the Press Act (1949) and the Fundamental Law on Freedom of Expression (1992). A new Instrument of Government came into force in 1975. Further constitutional amendments took effect in 2011. Sweden is a constitutional monarchy. The hereditary monarch is head of state, but has very limited formal prerogatives. Executive power rests with the Cabinet (Regeringen), which is responsible to the legislature (Riksdag). The unicameral Riksdag was introduced in January 1971. It has 349 members, elected by universal adult suffrage for four years, on the basis of proportional representation. The Prime Minister is nominated by the Speaker of the Riksdag and later confirmed in office by the whole House. The country is divided into 21 counties (Län) and 288 municipal districts (Kommun). Both counties and municipalities have popularly elected councils.

SWEDEN

Introductory Survey

REGIONAL AND INTERNATIONAL CO-OPERATION

Sweden is a founding member of the Nordic Council (see p. 461) and the Nordic Council of Ministers (see p. 461). Sweden is a member of the European Union (EU, see p. 270), although it does not use the single currency, the euro. It is a founding member of both the Council of Europe (see p. 250) and the Council of the Baltic Sea States (see p. 248), which is based in Stockholm. It participates in the Organization for Security and Co-operation in Europe (OSCE, see p. 385) and the Arctic Council (see p. 445).

Sweden joined the UN in 1946. As a contracting party to the General Agreement on Tariffs and Trade, Norway joined the World Trade Organization (WTO, see p. 430) on its establishment in 1995. Although not a member of NATO, Sweden has participated in NATO's Partnership for Peace programme since 1994. It is a member of the Organisation for Economic Co-operation and Development (OECD, see p. 376).

ECONOMIC AFFAIRS

In 2009, according to estimates by the World Bank, Sweden's gross national income (GNI), measured at average 2007–09 prices, was US $455,198m., equivalent to $48,930 per head (or $38,560 on an international purchasing-power parity basis). During 2000–09, it was estimated, the population grew at an average annual rate of 0.5%, while gross domestic product (GDP) per head increased, in real terms, by an average of 1.0% per year. Sweden's overall GDP increased, in real terms, by an average of 1.6% per year in 2000–09. According to official figures, GDP contracted by 5.3% in 2009, but grew by 5.5% in 2010.

Agriculture (including hunting, forestry and fishing) contributed 1.9% of GDP in 2010 and employed 2.2% of the working population in 2008. The main agricultural products are dairy produce, meat, cereals and potatoes, primarily for domestic consumption. In 2009 forestry products (wood, pulp and paper) accounted for 11.8% of total merchandise exports. Agricultural GDP increased by an average of 3.8% per year during 2000–08; it grew by an estimated 0.6% in 2009 and 1.0% in 2010.

Industry (including mining, manufacturing, construction and power) provided 26.6% of GDP in 2010 and employed 21.7% of the working population in 2008. Industrial GDP increased by an average of 3.0% per year in 2000–08. Industrial GDP contracted by 16.3% in 2009, but grew by 14.9% in 2010.

Mining contributed 1.4% of GDP in 2010 and employed 0.2% of the working population in 2008. The principal product is iron ore, but there are also large reserves of uranium (some 15% of the world's total known reserves), copper, lead and zinc. The GDP of the mining and quarrying sector declined, in real terms, by an average of 2.8% per year in 2003–07, according to Statistics Sweden; it decreased by 10.2% in 2008, 17.2% in 2009, but increased by 37.6% in 2010.

Manufacturing contributed 21.0% of GDP in 2010 and employed 14.3% of the working population in 2008. Sweden's principal manufactures were paper and paper products, motor vehicles, chemicals, basic iron and steel, television and radio transmitters and other communications apparatus and general purpose machinery. Manufacturing GDP increased, in real terms, by an average of 4.7% per year in 2003–07, according to Statistics Sweden; it declined by 5.2% in 2008 and by 18.0% in 2009, but growth resumed in the following year and the sector grew by 15.4% in 2010.

Construction contributed 6.9% of GDP in 2010 and employed 6.7% of the working population in 2008. Construction GDP increased by an average of 5.7% a year in 2005–07, but declined by 5.8% in 2008 and 5.5% in 2009.

Energy is derived principally from hydroelectric power and nuclear power, which provided 46.9% and 42.0% of electricity generated in 2008, respectively. Fossil fuels contributed 9.7% of electricity and wind power 1.4%. In February 2009, despite a resolution to phase out nuclear power that was approved in a referendum in 1980, the Swedish Government announced proposals to replace the 10 remaining nuclear reactors in Sweden as they became obsolete. The decision reflected ambitious targets for climate change and the desire for energy security. The legislation phasing out nuclear power was repealed in June 2010. Imports of petroleum and petroleum products accounted for 9.9% of total imports in 2009.

The services sector contributed 71.6% of GDP in 2010 and engaged 76.1% of the employed population in 2008. The GDP of the services sector increased, in real terms, at an average annual rate of 2.1% during 2000–08; it contracted by 4.4% in 2009, but grew by 4.7% in 2010.

In 2009 Sweden recorded a visible trade surplus of US $14,015m., and there was a surplus of $31,460m. on the current account of the balance of payments. The European Union (EU, see p. 270) dominates Swedish trade: in 2007 it provided 71.6% of imports and took 61.3% of exports. The European Free Trade Association (EFTA, see p. 447) is also an important trading partner. In 2009 the principal single source of imports was Germany (contributing 17.9% of total imports); other major suppliers were Norway and Denmark (9.0%), the Netherlands (6.9%), the United Kingdom (5.7%) and Finland (5.2%). Norway was the principal market for exports in that year (accounting for 10.6% of total exports); other major purchasers were Germany (10.2%), Switzerland (9.8%), the United Kingdom (7.4%), Denmark (7.3%) and Finland (6.4%). The principal exports in 2009 were machinery and transport equipment, chemicals and basic manufactured goods. The principal imports in 2009 were machinery and transport equipment, and basic and other manufactures.

In 2009 there was a budget deficit of €2,694.1m., equivalent to 0.9% of GDP. In the same year Sweden's general government gross debt was equivalent to 41.9% of GDP. The annual rate of inflation averaged 1.6% in 2000–09; consumer prices decreased by an average of 0.3% in 2009, but increased by 1.2% in 2010. The unemployment rate averaged 8.4% in 2010.

Sweden is a small open economy, which is more diversified than is usual for a country of its size, with important sectors such as engineering, high technology, domestic aviation, nuclear power, automotive manufacturing, armaments and telecommunications. High levels of taxation in the country traditionally financed a generous social welfare system. However, this also proved an obstacle to entrepreneurship and to the attraction and retention of skilled labour from abroad. From 2006 the centre-right coalition Government attempted to reduce welfare dependency and increase the labour supply, by lowering income taxes for low- and medium-income groups and curtailing unemployment benefits, while there were plans to sell stakes in many state-owned companies and lower the level of public debt. However, the economic programme encountered significant difficulties as the global financial and economic crisis adversely affected the economy, with GDP contracting by 0.6% in 2008. In October 2008 the Riksdag approved the establishment of a stability fund to guarantee banks' medium-term loans and provide emergency support to financial institutions. In April 2009 the Government announced that it had provided a total of 45,000m. kronor to stimulate the economy during 2009, and would allocate a further 60,000m. kronor for this purpose in 2010. The central bank, meanwhile, reduced its key interest rate, the repo rate, to a record low point of 0.25% in July 2009, in an attempt to mitigate the effects of the financial crisis. Despite these expansionary policies, GDP contracted by 5.3% in 2009, while the rate of unemployment rose as major companies reduced their workforces. However, the economy recovered strongly in 2010: GDP expanded by 5.5%, exceeding forecasts and comfortably outperforming other Western European economies, with faster growth recorded in each successive quarter, reaching 7.7% on a year-on-year basis in the final quarter. In response to this rapid growth, from July 2010 the central bank gradually increased the repo rate, to a level of 1.75% by April 2011, in an effort to restrain inflation. Although on a downward trend, the unemployment rate remained high, at 8.1% in March 2011 (compared with 9.0% a year earlier). The Government forecast more moderate GDP growth of 4.6% for 2011 and estimated that the budgetary deficit that had resulted from its efforts to revive the economy would be eliminated by 2012.

PUBLIC HOLIDAYS*

2012: 1 January (New Year's Day), 6 January (Epiphany), 6 April (Good Friday), 8 April (Easter), 9 April (Easter Monday), 1 May (May Day), 17 May (Ascension Day), 28 May (Whit Sunday), 6 June (National Day), 23 June (Midsummer Holiday), 3 November (All Saints' Day), 25 December (Christmas), 26 December (Boxing Day).

* The eve of a holiday is as important or more so than the holiday itself. Most Swedes have the day off work, including those working in the civil service, banks, public transport, hospitals, shops and the media. Others have at least a half-day. This applies especially to Midsummer's Eve, All Saints' Day Eve and Christmas Eve. The eve of May Day is sometimes called Valborg Eve or St Walpurgis. When a holiday falls on a Thursday many Swedes have the following Friday off in addition. When a holiday falls on a Saturday or Sunday it is not taken on the following Monday.

SWEDEN

Statistical Survey

Sources (unless otherwise stated): Statistics Sweden, Klostergatan 23, 701 89 Örebro; tel. (19) 17-60-00; fax (19) 17-70-80; e-mail information@scb.se; internet www.scb.se.

Area and Population

AREA, POPULATION AND DENSITY

Area (sq km)	
Land	410,335
Inland waters	39,960
Total	450,295*
Population (census results)†	
1 November 1985	8,360,178
1 November 1990	
Males	4,242,351
Females	4,345,002
Total	8,587,353
Population (official estimates at 31 December)†	
2008	9,256,347
2009	9,340,682
2010	9,415,570
Density (per sq km) at 31 December 2010	22.9‡

* 173,859 sq miles.
† Population is de jure.
‡ Density refers to land area only.

POPULATION BY AGE AND SEX
(official estimates at 31 December 2010)

	Males	Females	Total
0–14	803,712	761,247	1,564,959
15–64	3,106,754	3,006,611	6,113,365
65 and over	779,778	957,468	1,737,246
Total	4,725,326	4,690,244	9,415,570

COUNTIES
(31 December 2010)

	Land area (sq km)*	Population	Density (per sq km)
Stockholms län	6,519.3	2,054,343	315.1
Uppsala län	7,036.7	335,882	47.7
Södermanlands län	6,103.1	270,738	44.4
Östergötlands län	10,604.6	429,642	40.5
Jönköpings län	10,495.4	336,866	32.1
Kronobergs län	8,467.3	183,940	21.7
Kalmar län	11,219.1	233,536	20.8
Gotlands län	3,151.4	57,269	18.2
Blekinge län	2,946.7	153,227	52.0
Skåne län	11,035.4	1,243,329	112.7
Hallands län	5,461.6	299,484	54.8
Västra Götalands län	23,956.1	1,580,297	66.0
Värmlands län	17,591.3	273,265	15.5
Örebro län	8,546.3	280,230	32.8
Västmanlands län	6,317.9	252,756	40.0
Dalarnus län	28,195.6	277,047	9.8
Gävleborgs län	18,200.1	276,508	15.2
Västernorrlands län	21,684.5	242,625	11.2
Jämtlands län	49,343.1	126,691	2.6
Västerbottens län	55,189.7	259,286	4.7
Norrbottens län	98,249.0	248,609	2.5
Total†	410,335.4	9,415,570	22.9

* According to new estimates for land area.
† Including area of 21.2 sq km outside of existing county boundaries.

PRINCIPAL TOWNS
(estimated population of municipalities at 31 December 2010)*

Stockholm (capital)	847,073	Örebro	135,460
Göteborg (Gothenburg)	513,751	Norrköping	130,050
Malmö	298,963	Helsingborg	129,177
Uppsala	197,787	Jönköping	127,382
Linköping	146,416	Umeå	115,473
Västerås	137,207	Lund	110,488

* According to the administrative subdivisions of 1 January 2006.

BIRTHS, MARRIAGES AND DEATHS

	Registered live births		Registered marriages		Registered deaths	
	Number	Rate (per 1,000)	Number	Rate (per 1,000)	Number	Rate (per 1,000)
2003	99,157	11.0	39,041	4.3	92,961	10.4
2004	100,928	11.2	43,088	4.8	90,532	10.0
2005	101,346	11.2	44,381	4.9	91,710	10.1
2006	105,913	11.6	45,551	5.0	91,177	10.0
2007	107,421	11.7	47,898	5.2	91,729	10.0
2008	109,301	11.8	50,332	5.4	91,449	9.9
2009	111,801	12.0	48,033	5.1	90,080	9.6
2010	115,641	12.3	50,730	5.4	90,487	9.6

Life expectancy (years at birth, WHO estimates): 81 (males 79; females 83) in 2008 (Source: WHO, *World Health Statistics*).

IMMIGRATION AND EMIGRATION

	2008	2009	2010
Immigrants	101,171	102,280	98,801
Emigrants	45,294	39,240	48,853

ECONOMICALLY ACTIVE POPULATION
(sample surveys, '000 persons aged 16 to 64 years)

	2006	2007	2008
Agriculture, hunting and forestry	84	99	99
Fishing	2	3	2
Mining and quarrying	8	9	9
Manufacturing	653	658	655
Electricity, gas and water supply	25	25	24
Construction	270	290	306
Wholesale and retail trade, repair of motor vehicles, motorcycles and personal and household goods	536	557	563
Hotels and restaurants	128	143	148
Transport, storage and communications	274	281	275
Financial intermediation	84	89	93
Real estate, renting and business activities	603	664	698
Public administration and defence, compulsory social security, extra-territorial organizations and bodies	249	260	261

SWEDEN

—continued

	2006	2007	2008
Education	480	491	485
Health and social work	701	724	721
Other community, social and personal service activities, private households with employed persons	233	240	249
Sub-total	4,332	4,533	4,589
Activities not adequately defined	9	8	4
Total employed	4,341	4,541	4,593
Unemployed	246	298	305
Total labour force	4,587	4,839	4,898
Males	2,404	2,539	2,574
Females	2,181	2,298	2,323

Source: ILO.

Health and Welfare

KEY INDICATORS

Total fertility rate (children per woman, 2008)	1.9
Under-5 mortality rate (per 1,000 live births, 2008)	3
HIV/AIDS (% of persons aged 15–49, 2007)	0.1
Physicians (per 1,000 head, 2004)	3.3
Hospital beds (per 1,000 head, 1997)	5.2
Health expenditure (2007): US $ per head (PPP)	3,323
Health expenditure (2007): % of GDP	9.1
Health expenditure (2007): public (% of total)	81.7
Total carbon dioxide emissions ('000 metric tons, 2007)	49,207.5
Carbon dioxide emissions per head (metric tons, 2007)	5.4
Human Development Index (2010): ranking	9
Human Development Index (2010): value	0.885

For sources and definitions, see explanatory note on p. vi.

Agriculture

PRINCIPAL CROPS
('000 metric tons; holdings of more than 2 ha of arable land)

	2007	2008	2009
Wheat	2,255.7	2,202.2	2,284.0
Rye	137.6	168.8	218.9
Barley	1,439.0	1,671.6	1,676.6
Oats	889.8	820.0	750.0
Triticale (wheat-rye hybrid)	276.1	274.1	255.4
Potatoes	789.0	853.2	854.3
Rapeseed	216.1	254.5	298.4
Sugar beet	2,137.7	1,974.9	2,405.8

Aggregate production ('000 metric tons, may include official, semi-official or estimated data): Total cereals 5,057.6 in 2007, 5,195.0 in 2008, 5,249.2 in 2009; Total roots and tubers 789.0 in 2007, 853.2 in 2008, 854.3 in 2009; Total vegetables (incl. melons) 301.5 in 2007, 297.7 in 2008, 317.2 in 2009; Total fruits (excl. melons) 39.2 in 2007, 40.3 in 2008, 40.1 in 2009.

Source: FAO.

LIVESTOCK
('000 head, year ending September; holdings of more than 2 ha of arable land, or with large numbers of livestock)

	2007	2008	2009
Cattle	1,559.7	1,558.4	1,538.3
Sheep	508.9	524.8	540.5
Pigs	1,676.3	1,609.3	1,528.7
Horses*	95.0	95.0	95.0
Chickens	7,080	7,195	7,159
Turkeys	101	101*	n.a.

* FAO estimate(s).
Source: FAO.

LIVESTOCK PRODUCTS
('000 metric tons)

	2007	2008	2009
Cattle meat	133.5	128.8	150.5
Horse meat	0.9	1.0	0.9*
Sheep meat	4.6	4.6	5.1
Pig meat	264.9	270.8	260.7
Chicken meat	105.4	107.2	105.2
Game meat	16.2	16.0*	16.0*
Cows' milk	3,025.0	3,029.0	2,974.0
Hen eggs	95.0	95.0†	95.0†

* FAO estimate.
† Unofficial figure.
Source: FAO.

Forestry

ROUNDWOOD REMOVALS
('000 cubic metres; rounded figures)

	2007	2008	2009
Sawlogs, veneer logs and logs for sleepers	39,800	32,000	30,100
Pulpwood	32,000	32,400	28,600
Fuel wood	5,900	5,900	5,900
Other industrial wood	500	500	500
Total	78,200	70,800	65,100

Source: FAO.

SAWNWOOD PRODUCTION
('000 cubic metres, incl. railway sleepers; rounded figures)

	2007	2008	2009
Coniferous (softwood)	18,637	17,500	16,100
Broadleaved (hardwood)	101	101	100
Total	18,738	17,601	16,200

Source: FAO.

Fishing

('000 metric tons, live weight)

	2006	2007	2008
Capture	269.3	238.3	231.3
Atlantic cod	13.2	13.6	12.6
Blue whiting (Poutassou)	0.3	0.5	—
Sandeels (Sandlances)	32.8	8.1	12.5
Atlantic herring	103.4	99.5	94.7
European sprat	102.7	100.4	95.6
Aquaculture	7.5	5.4	7.6
Total catch	276.8	243.6	238.9

Note: Figures exclude aquatic mammals, recorded by number rather than by weight. The number of harbour porpoises caught was: 2 in 2006; 3 in 2007; 1 in 2008.

Source: FAO.

SWEDEN

Mining

('000 metric tons, unless otherwise indicated)

	2006	2007	2008*
Iron ore*	13,980	14,820	14,280
Copper ore	86.7	62.9	57.7
Gold (kilograms)	6,848	5,159	5,530
Silver (metric tons)	292.3	323.2	293.1
Zinc ore	210.0	214.6	174.8
Lead ore	55.6	63.2	65.1

* Estimates.

Note: Figures relate to the metal content of ores.

Source: US Geological Survey.

Industry

SELECTED PRODUCTS
('000 metric tons unless otherwise indicated)

	2006	2007	2008
Pig-iron and sponge-iron*	3,577	3,816	3,583
Crude steel*	5,435	5,673	5,198
Aluminium*†‡	133.2	130.0	113.5
Copper (refined)*†‡	254	239	253
Lead (refined)*†‡	114.0	77.9	99.4
Mechanical wood pulp§	3,489	3,672	3,570
Chemical wood pulp§	8,466	8,464	8,227
Newsprint§	2,541	2,547	2,560
Printing and writing paper§	3,413	3,835	4,158
Other paper and paperboard§	6,112	5,979	5,839
Cement (hydraulic)*	2,600	2,500†	2,500
Dwellings completed (number)	29,832	30,527	32,021
Electricity (million kWh)‖	143,299	148,849	n.a.

* Source: US Geological Survey.
† Estimate(s).
‡ Primary and secondary metals.
§ Source: FAO.
‖ Source: UN Industrial Commodity Statistics Database.

Finance

CURRENCY AND EXCHANGE RATES

Monetary Units
100 öre = 1 Swedish krona (plural: kronor).

Sterling, Dollar and Euro Equivalents (31 December 2010)
£1 sterling = 10.504 kronor;
US $1 = 6.710 kronor;
€1 = 8.966 kronor;
100 Swedish kronor = £9.52 = $14.90 = €11.15.

Average Exchange Rate (kronor per US $)
2008   6.5911
2009   7.6538
2010   7.2075

STATE BUDGET
(million kronor)

Revenue	2008	2009	2010*
Tax revenue	750,174	638,989	701,045
Other current revenue	52,964	48,115	40,856
Capital revenue	76,519	102	29
Loan repayment	1,881	1,736	1,615
Computed revenue	8,700	8,912	9,104
Contributions from the European Union	11,036	11,682	13,713
Total	**901,274**	**709,536**	**766,362**

Expenditure	2008	2009	2010*
Justice	32,693	33,645	35,583
Defence	43,030	42,106	43,319
Health	49,131	53,065	56,493
Social insurance for the sick and disabled	115,862	109,969	99,629
Social insurance for the elderly	42,591	42,304	41,405
Social insurance for families and children	66,393	68,080	70,270
Social insurance for the unemployed	51,781	5,332	5,319
Employment	1,031	60,620	69,454
Education and university research	44,524	49,263	52,907
Community planning and housing	2,075	1,906	1,539
Communications	61,484	40,573	40,842
Agriculture, forestry and fisheries	16,508	16,369	18,212
General grants to municipalities	64,770	81,589	75,690
Interest on central government debt	48,206	36,463	20,112
Contributions to the European Union	31,526	19,192	27,727
Total (incl. others)	**766,076**	**885,673**	**787,317**

* Forecasts.

INTERNATIONAL RESERVES
(US $ million at 31 December)

	2008	2009	2010
Gold	3,821	4,431	5,735
IMF special drawing rights	306	3,591	3,522
Reserve position in IMF	463	725	1,123
Foreign exchange	25,127	38,543	37,919
Total	**29,717**	**47,290**	**48,299**

Source: IMF, *International Financial Statistics*.

MONEY SUPPLY
(million kronor at 31 December)*

	2008	2009	2010
Currency outside depository corporations	99,410	100,070	96,390
Transferable deposits	1,235,500	1,357,790	1,460,960
Other deposits	504,760	435,600	447,080
Securities other than shares	1,103,050	1,122,060	827,540
Broad money	**2,942,710**	**3,015,510**	**2,831,970**

* Figures are rounded to the nearest 10m. kronor.

Source: IMF, *International Financial Statistics*.

COST OF LIVING
(Consumer Price Index; base: 1980 = 100)

	2007	2008	2009
Food and non-alcoholic beverages	244.8	261.7	269.3
Alcoholic beverages and tobacco	382.6	412.2	423.8
Clothing and footwear	168.7	166.9	169.4
Housing, water, electricity and fuels	352.4	376.4	359.1
Furniture and household goods	221.3	221.9	225.8
Health	772.7	763.1	769.4
Transport	372.1	386.5	389.0
Communication	181.9	173.5	168.0
Recreation and culture	187.8	182.3	183.3
Restaurants and hotels	420.2	442.8	456.3
Miscellaneous goods and services	327.1	332.9	340.6
All items	**290.5**	**300.5**	**299.7**

SWEDEN

NATIONAL ACCOUNTS
(million kronor at current prices)

National Income and Product

	2008	2009	2010
Compensation of employees	1,724,586	1,709,497	1,773,594
Net operating surplus }	539,358	413,069	541,890
Net mixed income }			
Domestic factor incomes	2,263,944	2,122,566	2,315,484
Consumption of fixed capital	416,568	439,651	443,725
Gross domestic product (GDP) at factor cost	2,680,512	2,562,217	2,759,209
Taxes on production and imports	581,575	585,953	601,838
Less Subsidies	57,767	58,989	59,975
GDP in market prices	3,204,320	3,089,181	3,301,072
Primary incomes received from abroad (net)	113,249	55,680	60,752
Gross national income	3,317,569	3,144,861	3,361,824
Less Consumption of fixed capital	416,568	439,651	443,725
Net national income	2,901,001	2,705,210	2,918,099
Other current transfers from abroad (net)	−45,300	−48,309	−49,703
Net national disposable income	2,855,701	2,656,901	2,868,396

Expenditure on the Gross Domestic Product

	2008	2009	2010
Final consumption expenditure	2,339,941	2,384,613	2,499,618
Households	1,456,872	1,476,911	1,549,320
Non-profit institutions serving households	47,905	49,767	51,516
General government	835,164	857,935	898,782
Gross capital formation	648,038	503,124	607,709
Gross fixed capital formation	641,807	549,869	586,825
Changes in inventories	6,231	−46,745	20,884
Total domestic expenditure	2,987,979	2,887,737	3,107,327
Exports of goods and services	1,715,236	1,495,225	1,648,816
Less Imports of goods and services	1,498,895	1,293,781	1,455,071
GDP in market prices	3,204,320	3,089,181	3,301,072
GDP at constant 2009 prices	3,263,209	3,089,181	3,260,201

Gross Domestic Product by Economic Activity

	2008	2009	2010
Agriculture, forestry and fishing	49,831	47,645	53,999
Mining and quarrying	20,662	16,106	31,080
Manufacturing	496,786	417,701	473,000
Electricity, gas and water	89,127	89,327	104,262
Construction	146,350	140,698	155,700
Wholesale and retail trade	322,942	309,319	334,506
Hotels and restaurants	40,967	40,196	43,183
Transport, storage and communications	186,203	175,109	185,952
Financial intermediation	109,684	120,669	119,952
Real estate and business services*	597,582	571,825	586,312
Government services	561,874	566,353	580,680
Education, health and social services	84,649	90,779	98,685
Other community, social and personal services	64,042	64,653	66,422
Non-profit institutes serving households	39,151	41,008	42,356
Sub-total	2,809,850	2,691,388	2,876,089
Taxes on products	411,265	415,174	442,018
Less Subsidies on products	16,795	17,381	17,035
GDP in market prices	3,204,320	3,089,181	3,301,072

* Including imputed rents of owner-occupied dwellings.

Note: Financial intermediation services indirectly measured data are distributed to production sectors.

BALANCE OF PAYMENTS
(US $ million)

	2007	2008	2009
Exports of goods f.o.b.	172,155	185,494	134,918
Imports of goods f.o.b.	−154,381	−170,082	−120,902
Trade balance	17,774	15,412	14,015
Exports of services	62,511	70,594	59,598
Imports of services	−45,884	−52,289	−44,373
Balance on goods and services	34,401	33,716	29,241
Other income received	66,200	73,344	45,613
Other income paid	−55,323	−55,874	−38,310
Balance on goods, services and income	45,277	51,185	36,543
Current transfers received	5,602	6,784	4,854
Current transfers paid	−10,669	−12,910	−9,936
Current balance	40,210	45,059	31,460
Capital account (net)	579	159	423
Direct investment abroad	−36,725	−31,937	−31,913
Direct investment from abroad	27,361	38,815	11,538
Portfolio investment assets	−49,428	−19,191	−18,497
Portfolio investment liabilities	64,689	−7,572	81,009
Financial derivatives assets	39,427	79,006	116,006
Financial derivatives liabilities	−40,377	−77,468	−118,230
Other investment assets	−48,342	847	18,018
Other investment liabilities	34,255	40,665	−50,720
Net errors and omissions	−31,665	−66,633	−23,936
Overall balance	−14	1,750	15,159

Source: IMF, *International Financial Statistics*.

OFFICIAL ASSISTANCE TO DEVELOPING COUNTRIES
(million kronor)

	2007	2008	2009
Bilateral assistance	19,814	21,009	22,997
Multilateral assistance	9,506	10,617	11,747
Total	29,320	31,625	34,744

External Trade

PRINCIPAL COMMODITIES
(distribution by SITC, million kronor)

Imports c.i.f.	2007	2008	2009
Food and live animals	64,766	73,200	77,687
Fresh fruit and vegetables	15,699	16,708	16,806
Crude materials (inedible) except fuels	38,362	35,562	27,744
Mineral fuels, lubricants, etc.	114,703	158,860	105,455
Petroleum, petroleum products, etc.	99,094	136,678	90,197
Chemicals and related products	110,866	122,106	115,107
Organic chemicals	19,179	23,023	22,813
Medical and pharmaceutical preparations	24,780	27,590	31,282
Unprocessed plastics	19,799	19,883	15,810
Basic manufactures	174,808	169,233	124,237
Iron and steel	58,599	53,673	30,504

SWEDEN

Statistical Survey

Imports c.i.f.—*continued*	2007	2008	2009
Machinery and transport equipment	400,173	399,612	327,555
Power-generating machinery and equipment	27,428	29,486	23,481
Telecommunications and sound equipment	54,641	52,754	49,272
Other electrical machinery, apparatus, etc.	65,748	67,937	64,677
Road vehicles and parts*	112,543	104,013	76,119
Miscellaneous manufactured articles	118,171	124,098	118,014
Clothing and accessories (excl. footwear)	24,808	26,151	26,301
Other miscellaneous manufactured articles	37,698	41,116	41,650
Total (incl. others)	1,034,450	1,097,903	911,236

Exports f.o.b.	2007	2008	2009
Crude materials (inedible) except fuels	70,613	71,280	60,785
Wood, lumber and cork	30,238	25,740	25,284
Pulp and waste paper	17,139	18,131	15,225
Mineral fuels, lubricants, etc.	62,750	94,304	65,785
Petroleum, petroleum products, etc.	57,252	85,762	60,154
Chemicals and related products	125,873	130,565	134,247
Medical and pharmaceutical preparations	59,152	59,734	68,184
Basic manufactures	237,856	241,460	191,174
Paper, paperboard and manufactures	73,180	77,773	77,067
Iron and steel	76,819	75,450	41,701
Manufactures of metals	33,797	35,327	27,872
Machinery and transport equipment	501,667	501,536	387,335
Power-generating machinery and equipment	45,257	43,387	36,980
Machinery specialized for particular industries	52,431	56,376	39,557
General industrial machinery, equipment and parts	81,408	85,510	71,177
Telecommunications and sound equipment	77,259	79,157	67,304
Other electrical machinery, apparatus, etc.	53,420	56,973	57,120
Road vehicles and parts*	154,269	142,923	82,665
Miscellaneous manufactured articles	96,925	104,351	104,666
Total (incl. others)	1,139,674	1,194,411	998,603

* Data on parts exclude tyres, engines and electrical parts.

2009 (revised totals, '000 million kronor): Imports 912.9; Exports 996.7.

2010 ('000 million kronor, preliminary): Imports 1,066.2; Exports 1,136.2.

PRINCIPAL TRADING PARTNERS
(million kronor)

Imports c.i.f.	2007	2008	2009
Austria	11,208	12,041	10,414
Belgium	42,984	42,622	35,341
China, People's Repub.	35,735	36,935	34,607
Denmark	94,224	103,027	81,695
Estonia	8,040	8,241	7,066
Finland	64,781	63,527	47,006
France	50,835	55,379	46,121
Germany	189,412	194,064	163,150
Hong Kong	8,571	8,484	7,952
Ireland	12,422	11,402	11,560
Italy	36,211	37,534	28,256

Imports c.i.f.—*continued*	2007	2008	2009
Japan	17,750	16,998	14,075
Netherlands	63,009	65,154	59,511
Norway	88,277	97,437	82,458
Poland	29,737	35,949	27,734
Russia	29,199	44,422	31,240
Spain	14,567	14,735	11,723
Switzerland	8,958	9,324	8,918
United Kingdom	76,885	70,378	51,934
USA	32,267	33,860	34,568
Total (incl. others)	1,034,450	1,097,903	911,236

Exports f.o.b.	2007	2008	2009
Australia	13,033	13,593	12,782
Austria	11,677	12,069	9,302
Belgium	52,327	51,945	36,568
Canada	11,001	11,101	8,638
China, People's Repub.	22,190	25,916	31,302
Denmark	83,729	88,254	73,323
Finland	70,977	75,645	64,211
France	57,244	58,558	50,717
Germany	118,901	123,950	101,791
Italy	36,065	37,154	30,563
Japan	13,951	13,175	12,541
Netherlands	57,639	61,025	46,576
Norway	107,274	113,482	105,667
Poland	27,911	30,077	25,205
Russia	22,702	28,883	14,042
Spain	32,721	27,602	23,947
Switzerland	10,246	11,020	9,797
United Kingdom	81,665	87,584	74,114
USA	86,511	78,651	63,767
Total (incl. others)	1,139,674	1,194,411	998,603

2009 (revised totals, '000 million kronor): Imports 912.9; Exports 996.7.

2010 ('000 million kronor, preliminary): Imports 1,066.2; Exports 1,136.2.

Transport

RAILWAYS
(traffic)

	2004	2005	2006
Passengers (million)	147	150	159
Passenger-km (million)	8,658	8,936	9,642
Freight (million metric tons)	60	63	65
Freight ton-km (million)	20,856	21,675	22,271

Freight ton-km (million): 20,856 in 2004.

ROAD TRAFFIC
('000 motor vehicles in use at 31 December)

	2005	2006	2007
Passenger cars	4,154	4,202	4,258
Buses and coaches	13	14	13
Lorries and vans	461	480	504
Motorcycles	250	269	287

SHIPPING

Merchant Fleet
(registered at 31 December)

	2007	2008	2009
Number of vessels	572	566	538
Total displacement ('000 grt)	4,044.9	4,389.3	4,044.9

Source: Lloyd's Register-Fairplay, *World Fleet Statistics*.

SWEDEN

International Sea-borne Freight Traffic

	2004	2005	2006
Vessels entered ('000 grt)	106,690	115,715	119,917
Vessels cleared ('000 grt)	102,311	110,059	115,788
Goods loaded ('000 metric tons)	65,547	69,275	74,494
Goods unloaded ('000 metric tons)	79,088	82,641	83,267

CIVIL AVIATION
(traffic on scheduled services)*

	2004	2005	2006
Kilometres flown (million)	133	119	110
Passengers carried ('000)	11,624	10,808	10,561
Passenger-km (million)	11,976	11,389	10,237
Total ton-km (million)	1,452	1,410	1,224

* Including an apportionment (3/7) of the international services of Scandinavian Airlines System (SAS), operated jointly with Denmark and Norway.

Source: UN, *Statistical Yearbook*.

Tourism

VISITORS BY ORIGIN
(nights in all types of tourist accommodation)

	2006	2007	2008
Denmark	1,038,498	953,890	1,348,399
Finland	428,219	418,957	475,634
France	238,919	258,632	270,828
Germany	2,123,566	2,108,213	2,690,148
Italy	244,413	264,361	262,240
Japan	112,313	103,719	100,991
Netherlands	716,702	698,625	750,975
Norway	2,709,794	2,817,122	3,084,018
Russia	167,128	187,239	206,394
United Kingdom	642,792	636,464	648,227
USA	421,230	437,944	393,153
Total (incl. others)	10,951,666	11,200,371	12,495,002

Tourism receipts (US $ million, excl. passenger transport): 10,485 in 2006; 13,697 in 2007; 14,399 in 2008.

Source: World Tourism Organization.

Communications Media

	2007	2008	2009
Telephones ('000 main lines in use)	5,505.8	5,345.7	5,151.3
Mobile cellular telephones ('000 subscribers)	10,117	10,892	11,642
Internet users ('000)*	7,511.4	8,203.1	8,398.3
Broadband subscribers ('000)	2,776	2,899	2,942
Daily newspapers: titles	169	168	171
average net circulation ('000 copies)	3,833	3,725	3,605
Weekly newspapers and periodicals: titles	443	436	427
average net circulation ('000 copies)	22,121	22,738	22,328

* Estimates.

Book production: 19,829 titles in 2009.

Personal computers: 8,000,000 (881.0 per 1,000 persons) in 2005 (Source: International Telecommunication Union).

Television receivers ('000 in use, 2001): 8,600.

Radio receivers ('000 in use, 1997): 8,250.

Sources: mainly International Telecommunication Union, UN, *Statistical Yearbook*, and UNESCO, *Statistical Yearbook*.

Education

(2007/08 unless otherwise indicated)

	Institutions	Teachers[1]	Students
Primary: grades 1–6	4,755	108,233[2]	1,023,724
Secondary: grades 7–9			
Integrated upper secondary schools	641[3]	37,640[2]	347,713[4]
Higher education	64	20,000[5]	397,679[6]
People's colleges	147[3]	n.a.	98,855
Municipal adult education	400	6,593[2]	170,318

[1] Full-time and part-time teachers and teachers on leave.
[2] 2004/05.
[3] 1996/97.
[4] At 15 October 2004.
[5] 1994/95.
[6] 2003/04.

Pupil-teacher ratio (primary education, UNESCO estimate): 9.6 in 2007/08 (Source: UNESCO Institute for Statistics).

Directory

The Government

HEAD OF STATE

Monarch: HM King CARL XVI GUSTAF (succeeded to the throne 15 September 1973).

THE CABINET
(May 2011)

A coalition of the parties comprising Alliansen (The Alliance): the Moderata Samlingspartiet (MS), the Centerpartiet (CP), the Folkpartiet Liberalerna (FP) and the Kristdemokraterna (Kd).

Prime Minister: FREDRIK REINFELDT (MS).
Deputy Prime Minister and Minister for Education: JAN BJÖRKLUND (FP).
Minister for EU Affairs: BIRGITTA OHLSSON (FP).
Minister for Justice: BEATRICE ASK (MS).
Minister for Migration and Asylum Policy: TOBIAS BILLSTRÖM (MS).
Minister for Foreign Affairs: CARL BILDT (MS).
Minister for International Development Co-operation: GUNILLA CARLSSON (MS).
Minister for Trade: EWA BJÖRLING (MS).
Minister for Defence: STEN TOLGFORS (MS).
Minister for Health and Social Affairs: GÖRAN HÄGGLUND (Kd).
Minister for Children and the Elderly: MARIA LARSSON (Kd).
Minister for Public Administration and Housing: STEFAN ATTEFALL (Kd).
Minister for Social Security: ULF KRISTERSSON (MS).
Minister for Finance: ANDERS BORG (MS).
Minister for Financial Markets: PETER NORMAN (MS).
Minister for Gender Equality and Deputy Minister for Education: NYAMKO SABUNI (FP).
Minister for Rural Affairs: ESKIL ERLANDSSON (CP).
Minister for the Environment: ANDREAS CARLGREN (CP).
Minister for Enterprise and Energy: MAUD OLOFSSON (CP).
Minister for Information Technology and Regional Affairs: ANNA-KARIN HATT (CP).
Minister for Infrastructure: CATHARINA ELMSÄTER-SVÄRD (MS).

SWEDEN

Minister for Culture and Sport: LENA ADELSOHN LILJEROTH (MS).
Minister for Employment: HILLEVI ENGSTRÖM (MS).
Minister for Integration and Deputy Minister for Employment: ERIK ULLENHAG (FP).

MINISTRIES

Prime Minister's Office: Rosenbad 4, 103 33 Stockholm; tel. (8) 405-10-00; fax (8) 723-11-71; e-mail registrator@primeminister.ministry.se; internet www.regeringen.se; incl. EU Affairs.

Ministry of Rural Affairs: Fredsgt. 8, 103 33 Stockholm; tel. (8) 405-10-00; fax (8) 20-64-96; e-mail registrator@agriculture.ministry.se; internet www.regeringen.se/sb/d/1473.

Ministry of Culture: Drottningt. 16, 103 33 Stockholm; tel. (8) 405-10-00; fax (8) 21-68-13; e-mail registrator@culture.ministry.se; internet www.regeringen.se/sb/d/8339.

Ministry of Defence: Jakobsgt. 9, 103 33 Stockholm; tel. (8) 405-10-00; fax (8) 723-11-89; e-mail registrator@defence.ministry.se; internet www.regeringen.se/sb/d/495.

Ministry of Education and Research: Drottninggt. 16, 103 33 Stockholm; tel. (8) 405-10-00; fax (8) 723-11-92; e-mail registrator@education.ministry.se; internet www.regeringen.se/sb/d/1454.

Ministry of Employment: Mäster Samuelsgt. 70, 103 33 Stockholm; tel. (8) 405-10-00; fax (8) 411-36-16; e-mail registrator@employment.ministry.se; internet www.regeringen.se/sb/d/8270.

Ministry of Enterprise, Energy and Communications: Mäster Samuelsgt. 70, 103 33 Stockholm; tel. (8) 405-10-00; fax (8) 411-36-16; e-mail registrator@enterprise.ministry.se; internet www.regeringen.se/sb/d/1470.

Ministry of the Environment: Tegelbacken 2, 103 33 Stockholm; tel. (8) 405-10-00; fax (8) 24-16-29; e-mail registrator@environment.ministry.se; internet www.regeringen.se/sb/d/1471.

Ministry of Finance: Drottninggt. 21, 103 33 Stockholm; tel. (8) 405-10-00; fax (8) 21-73-86; e-mail registrator@finance.ministry.se; internet www.regeringen.se/sb/d/1468.

Ministry for Foreign Affairs: Gustav Adolfs torg 1, 103 39 Stockholm; tel. (8) 405-10-00; fax (8) 723-11-76; e-mail registrator@foreign.ministry.se; internet www.regeringen.se/sb/d/1475.

Ministry of Health and Social Affairs: Fredsgt. 8, 103 33 Stockholm; tel. (8) 405-10-00; fax (8) 723-11-91; e-mail registrator@social.ministry.se; internet www.regeringen.se/sb/d/1474.

Ministry of Justice: Rosenbad 4, 103 33 Stockholm; tel. (8) 405-10-00; fax (8) 20-27-34; e-mail registrator@justice.ministry.se; internet www.regeringen.se/sb/d/584.

Ministry of Rural Affairs: Fredsgt. 8, 103 33 Stockholm; tel. (8) 405-10-00; fax (8) 20-64-96; e-mail registrator@agriculture.ministry.se; internet www.regeringen.se/sb/d/1473.

Legislature

SVERIGES RIKSDAG

100 12 Stockholm; tel. (8) 786-40-00; e-mail riksdagsinformation@riksdagen.se; internet www.riksdagen.se.

Speaker: PER WESTERBERG.

General Election, 19 September 2010

Party	Votes	% of votes	Seats
Sveriges Socialdemokratiska Arbetareparti (SAP)*	1,827,497	30.66	112
Moderata Samlingspartiet (MS)†	1,791,766	30.06	107
Miljöpartiet de Gröna (MP)*	437,435	7.34	25
Folkpartiet Liberalerna (FP)†	420,524	7.06	24
Centerpartiet (CP)†	390,804	6.56	23
Sverigedemokraterna (SD)	339,610	5.70	20
Vänsterpartiet (VP)*	334,053	5.60	19
Kristdemokraterna (Kd)†	333,696	5.60	19
Others	85,023	1.43	—
Total	5,960,408	100.00	349

* Contested the election as part of De rödgröna (The Red-Greens).
† Contested the election as part of Alliansen (The Alliance).

Election Commission

Valmyndigheten (Election Authority): Solna Strandväg 78, POB 4210, 171 04 Solna; tel. (8) 635-69-00; fax (8) 635-69-20; e-mail valet@val.se; internet www.val.se; independent; Chair. MARIANNE ELIASON.

Political Organizations

Centerpartiet (CP) (Centre Party): Stora Nygt. 4, POB 2200, 103 15 Stockholm; tel. (8) 617-38-00; fax (8) 617-38-10; e-mail info@centerpartiet.se; internet www.centerpartiet.se; f. 1910 as an agrarian party; aims at social, environmental and progressive development and decentralization; Leader MAUD OLOFSSON; 68,000 mems.

Feministiskt initiativ (Fi) (Feminist Initiative): POB 498, 101 29 Stockholm; tel. (0) 706-100-190; e-mail info@feministisktinitiativ.se; internet www.feministisktinitiativ.se; f. 2005; Principal Speakers CARL EMANUELSSON, STINA SVENSSON, SISSELA NORDLING BLANCO.

Folkpartiet Liberalerna (FP) (Liberal Party): POB 2253, Stora Nygt. 2A, 103 16 Stockholm; tel. (8) 410-242-00; fax (8) 509-116-60; e-mail info@liberal.se; internet www.folkpartiet.se; f. 1902; advocates market-orientated economy and social welfare system; Chair. JAN BJÖRKLUND.

Junilistan (June List): Vasagt. 40, 111 20 Stockholm; tel. and fax (8) 23-01-11; fax (8) 23-02-11; e-mail kg.svenson@junilistan.se; internet www.junilistan.se; f. 2004 to contest elections to the European Parliament; opposes further powers for EU; Pres (vacant).

Kristdemokraterna (Kd) (Christian Democratic Party): POB 2373, Munkbron 1, 103 18 Stockholm; tel. (8) 723-25-00; fax (8) 723-25-10; e-mail info@kristdemokraterna.se; internet www.kristdemokraterna.se; f. 1964 as Kristdemokratiska Samhällspartiet (KdS); promotes emphasis on Christian values in political life; Chair. GÖRAN HÄGGLUND; 24,000 mems.

Miljöpartiet de Gröna (MP) (Green Party): International Secretary, Swedish Parliament, 100 12 Stockholm; tel. (8) 786-57-86; fax (8) 786-53-75; e-mail international@mp.se; internet www.mp.se; f. 1981; Principal Speakers MARIA WETTERSTRAND, PETER ERIKSSON; c. 9,400 mems.

Moderata Samlingspartiet (MS) (Moderate Party): POB 2080, Stora Nygt. 30, 103 12 Stockholm; tel. (8) 676-80-00; fax (8) 21-61-23; e-mail info@moderat.se; internet www.moderat.se; f. 1904; advocates liberal-conservative policies and market-orientated economy; Chair. FREDRIK REINFELDT; Sec.-Gen. SOFIA ARKELSTEN; 100,000 mems.

Piratpartiet (Pirate Party): POB 307, 101 26 Stockholm; tel. (8) 720-04-00; e-mail info@piratpartiet.se; internet www.piratpartiet.se; f. 2006; advocates the citizen's right to complete and exclusive control of information pertaining to his or her private life and the abolition of copyright on all material for non-commercial use; Chair. ANNA TROBERG.

Sverigedemokraterna (SD) (Sweden Democrats): POB 200 85, 104 60 Stockholm; tel. (8) 50-00-00-50; fax (8) 643-92-60; e-mail info@sverigedemokraterna.se; internet www.sverigedemokraterna.se; f. 1988; nationalist, anti-immigration; Leader JIMMIE ÅKESSON.

Sveriges Socialdemokratiska Arbetareparti (SAP) (Swedish Social Democratic Party): Sveavägen 68, 105 60 Stockholm; tel. (8) 700-26-00; fax (8) 20-42-57; e-mail info@socialdemokraterna.se; internet www.socialdemokraterna.se; f. 1889; egalitarian; Chair. HÅKAN JUHOLT; Sec.-Gen. CARIN JÄMTIN; 100,000 mems.

Vänsterpartiet (VP) (Left Party): Kungsgt. 84, POB 12 660, 112 93 Stockholm; tel. (8) 654-08-20; fax (8) 653-23-85; e-mail vansterpartiet@riksdagen.se; internet www.vansterpartiet.se; f. 1917 as Left Social Democratic Party of Sweden; renamed the Communist Party 1921; renamed Left Party—Communists 1967; renamed Left Party 1990; policies based on the principles of Marxism, feminism and other theories; Chair. LARS OHLY.

Diplomatic Representation

EMBASSIES IN SWEDEN

Albania: Capellavägen 7, 181 32 Lidingö; tel. (8) 731-09-20; fax (8) 767-65-57; e-mail embassy.stockholm@mfa.gov.al; Ambassador RUHI HADO.

Algeria: Danderydsgt. 3–5, POB 26027, 100 41 Stockholm; tel. (8) 679-91-30; fax (8) 611-49-57; e-mail embassy.algeria@telia.com; internet www.embalgeria.se; Ambassador FATAH MAHRAZ.

Angola: Skeppsbron 8, POB 3199, 103 64 Stockholm; tel. (8) 24-28-90; fax (8) 34-31-27; e-mail info@angolaemb.se; internet www.angolaemb.se; Ambassador DOMINGOS CULOLO.

Argentina: POB 14039, 104 40 Stockholm; Narvavägen 32, 3rd Floor, Apartment 3, 115 22 Stockholm; tel. (8) 663-19-65; fax (8) 661-00-09; e-mail cancilleria@argemb.se; Ambassador HERNÁN MASSINI EZCURRA.

Australia: Sergels Torg 12, 11th Floor, POB 7003, 103 86 Stockholm; tel. (8) 613-29-00; fax (8) 613-29-82; e-mail reception@austemb.se; internet www.sweden.embassy.gov.au; Ambassador PAUL STEPHENS.

Austria: Kommendörsgt. 35, 5th Floor, 114 58 Stockholm; tel. (8) 665-17-70; fax (8) 662-69-28; e-mail stockholm-ob@bmeia.gv.at; internet www.aussenministerium.at/stockholm; Ambassador Dr ULRIKE TILLY.

Azerbaijan: Karlavägen 60, 114 49 Stockholm; tel. (8) 661-58-50; fax (8) 411-24-58; e-mail azerembassy@gmail.com; internet www.azembassy.se; Ambassador RAFAEL IBRAHIMOV.

Bangladesh: Anderstorpsvägen 12, 1st Floor, 171 54 Solna; tel. (8) 730-58-50-52; fax (8) 730-58-70; e-mail banijya@bangladeshembassy.se; Ambassador A. F. M. GOUSAL AZAM SARKER.

Belarus: Herserudsvägen 5, 4th Floor, 181 34 Lidingö; tel. (8) 731-57-41; fax (8) 767-07-46; e-mail belarusambassador@telia.com; internet www.sweden.belembassy.org; Ambassador ANDREI M. GRINKEVICH.

Belgium: POB 1040, 101 38 Stockholm; Kungsbroplan 2, 2nd Floor, 112 27 Stockholm; tel. (8) 534-802-00; fax (8) 534-802-07; e-mail stockholm@diplobel.fed.be; internet www.diplomatie.be/stockholm; Ambassador MARC BAPTIST.

Bolivia: Södra Kungsvägen 60, 181 32 Lidingö; tel. (8) 731-58-30; fax (8) 767-63-11; e-mail embolivia-estocolmo@telia.com; Ambassador MILTON RENÉ SOTO SANTIESTEBAN.

Bosnia and Herzegovina: Birger Jarlsgt. 55, POB 7102, 103 87 Stockholm; tel. (8) 440-05-40; fax (8) 24-98-30; e-mail amb.bih.sto@telia.com; Ambassador DARKO ZELENIKA.

Botswana: Tyrgt. 11, POB 26024, 100 41 Stockholm; tel. (8) 545-258-00; fax (8) 723-00-87; e-mail botstock@gov.bw; Ambassador BERNADETTE SEBAGE RATHEDI.

Brazil: Odengt. 3, 114 24 Stockholm; tel. (8) 545-163-00; fax (8) 545-163-14; e-mail stockholm@brazilianembassy.se; internet www.brazilianembassy.se; Ambassador LEDA LÚCIA MARTINS CAMARGO.

Bulgaria: Karlavägen 29, 114 31 Stockholm; tel. (8) 723-09-38; fax (8) 21-45-03; e-mail bg.embassy@telia.com; internet www.bulgarien.se; Ambassador IVAN TZVETKOV.

Canada: Tegelbacken 4, 7th Floor, POB 16129, 103 23 Stockholm; tel. (8) 453-30-00; fax (8) 453-30-16; e-mail stkhm@international.gc.ca; internet www.canadainternational.gc.ca/sweden-suede; Ambassador ALEXANDRA VOLKOFF.

Chile: Sturegt. 8, 3rd Floor, 114 35 Stockholm; tel. (8) 679-82-80; fax (8) 679-85-40; e-mail echilese@embassyofchile.se; internet www.embassyofchile.se; Ambassador JOSÉ MIGUEL CRUZ SÁNCHEZ.

China, People's Republic: Lidovägen 8, 115 25 Stockholm; tel. (8) 579-364-37; fax (8) 579-364-54; e-mail protocol@chinaembassy.se; internet www.chinaembassy.se; Ambassador LAN LIJUN.

Colombia: Östermalmsgt. 46, 3rd Floor, POB 5627, 114 86 Stockholm; tel. (8) 21-43-20; fax (8) 21-84-90; e-mail embcol@telia.com; Ambassador RAFAEL NIETO NAVIA.

Congo, Democratic Republic: Stockholmsvägen 33, 4th Floor, POB 1171, 181 23 Lidingö; tel. (8) 765-83-80; fax (8) 765-85-91; e-mail rdcongo6@hotmail.com; Chargé d'affaires a.i. HENRI MBAYAHE NDUNGO.

Congo, Republic: Dalagt. 32, 1st Floor, 113 24 Stockholm; tel. (8) 300-59-0; e-mail ambassade@private.as; Ambassador ANDRÉ HOMBESSA.

Croatia: Engelbrektsplan 2, 3rd Floor, 144 34 Stockholm; tel. (8) 440-52-80; fax (8) 678-83-20; e-mail croemb.stockholm@mvpei.hr; Ambassador VLADIMIR MATEK.

Cuba: Sturevägen 9, 182 73 Stocksund; tel. (8) 545-83-277; fax (8) 545-83-270; e-mail primero.enero59@swipnet.se; internet emba.cubaminrex.cu/suecia; Ambassador FRANCISCO ROBERTO FLORENTINO GRAUPERA.

Cyprus: Birger Jarlsgt. 37, 4th Floor, POB 7649, 103 94 Stockholm; tel. (8) 24-45-18; fax (8) 24-45-18; e-mail info@cyprusemb.se; internet www.cyprusemb.se; Ambassador GEORGE CHACALLI.

Czech Republic: POB 26156, 100 41 Stockholm; Villagt. 21, 114 32 Stockholm; tel. (8) 440-42-10; fax (8) 440-42-11; e-mail stockholm@embassy.mzv.cz; internet www.mzv.cz/stockholm; Ambassador JAN KÁRA.

Denmark: Jakobs Torg 1, POB 16119, 103 23 Stockholm; tel. (8) 406-75-00; fax (8) 791-72-20; e-mail stoamb@um.dk; internet www.ambstockholm.um.dk; Ambassador KIRSTEN MALLING BIERING.

Dominican Republic: Kungsholmsgt. 10, 5th Floor, POB 5584, 112 27 Stockholm; tel. (8) 667-46-11; fax (8) 667-51-05; e-mail stockholm@domemb.se; Ambassador MARINA ISABEL CÁCERES DE ESTÉVEZ.

Ecuador: Engelbrektsgt. 13, 114 32 Stockholm; tel. (8) 679-60-43; fax (8) 611-55-93; e-mail mecuador.suecia@embecu.se; internet www.embecu.se; Ambassador MARIO ANÍBAL GUERRERO.

Egypt: Strandvägen 35, POB 14230, 104 40 Stockholm; tel. (8) 459-98-60; fax (8) 661-26-64; e-mail embassyofegypt@telia.com; Ambassador MUHAMMAD OSAMA TAHA EL-MAGDOUB.

El Salvador: Herserudsvägen 5A, 5th Floor, 181 34 Lidingö; tel. (8) 765-86-21; fax (8) 731-72-42; e-mail embassy@elsalvador.se; Ambassador MARTIN ALBERTO RIVERA GÓMEZ.

Eritrea: Stjärnvägen 2B, 4th Floor, POB 1164, 181 23 Lidingö; tel. (8) 441-71-70; fax (8) 446-73-40; e-mail info@eritrean-embassy.se; internet www.eritrean-embassy.se; Chargé d'affaires a.i. YONAS MANNA BAIRU.

Estonia: POB 26076, 100 41 Stockholm; Tyrgt. 3/3A, 114 27 Stockholm; tel. (8) 545-122-80; fax (8) 545-122-99; e-mail info@estemb.se; internet www.estemb.se; Ambassador JAAK JÕERÜÜT.

Finland: Gärdesgt. 11, POB 24285, 104 51 Stockholm; tel. (8) 676-67-00; fax (8) 20-74-97; e-mail info@finland.se; internet www.finland.se; Ambassador HARRY GUSTAF HELENIUS.

France: Kommendörsgt. 13, POB 5135, 102 43 Stockholm; tel. (8) 459-53-00; fax (8) 459-53-41; e-mail presse@ambafrance-se.org; internet www.ambafrance-se.org; Ambassador JOËL DE ZORZI.

Georgia: Humlegårdsgt. 19, 1st Floor, 114 46 Stockholm; tel. (8) 678-02-60; fax (8) 678-02-64; e-mail geoemb.sweden@telia.com; internet www.sweden.mfa.gov.ge; Ambassador AMIRAN KAVTARADZE.

Germany: POB 27832, 115 93 Stockholm; Skarpögt. 9, 115 27 Stockholm; tel. (8) 670-15-00; fax (8) 670-15-72; e-mail info@stockholm.diplo.de; internet www.stockholm.diplo.de; Ambassador Dr JOACHIM RÜCKER.

Greece: Kommendörsgt. 16, POB 55565, 102 04 Stockholm; tel. (8) 545-660-10; fax (8) 660-54-70; e-mail grembstockholm@greekembassy.se; internet www.greekembassy.se; Ambassador ALIKI HADJI.

Guatemala: Munkbron 3, 111 28 Stockholm; tel. (8) 660-52-29; fax (8) 660-42-29; e-mail embassy@guatemala.se; internet www.guatemala.se; Ambassador FERNANDO MOLINA GIRÓN.

Holy See: Svalnäsvägen 10, 182 63 Djursholm; tel. (8) 446-51-10; fax (8) 622-51-10; e-mail nunciature@telia.com; Apostolic Nuncio Most Rev. EMIL PAUL TSCHERRIG (Titular Archbishop of Voli).

Honduras: Stjärnvägen 2, 7th Floor, 181 34 Lidingö; tel. (8) 731-50-84; fax (8) 636-99-83; e-mail hondurasembassy@telia.com; internet www.hondurasembassy.se; Ambassador HERNÁN ANTONIO BERMÚDEZ AGUILAR.

Hungary: Dag Hammarskjölds Väg 10, POB 24125, 104 51 Stockholm; tel. (8) 661-67-62; fax (8) 660-29-59; e-mail embassy.stockholm@kum.hu; internet www.mfa.gov.hu/emb/stockholm; Ambassador GÁBOR SZENTIVÁNYI.

Iceland: Kommendörsgt. 35, 114 58 Stockholm; tel. (8) 442-83-00; fax (8) 660-74-23; e-mail icemb.stock@utn.strj.is; internet www.iceland.org/se; Ambassador GUÐMUNDUR ÁRNI STEFÁNSSON.

India: Adolf Fredriks Kyrkogt. 12, POB 1340, 111 83 Stockholm; tel. (8) 10-70-08; fax (8) 24-85-05; e-mail information@indianembassy.se; internet www.indianembassy.se; Ambassador ASHOK SAJJANHAR.

Indonesia: Sysslomansgt. 18/I, POB 12520, 102 29 Stockholm; tel. (8) 545-55-880; fax (8) 650-87-50; e-mail kbri@indonesiskaambassaden.se; internet www.indonesiskaambassaden.se; Chargé d'affaires a.i. ELMAR I. LUBIS.

Iran: Västra Yttringe Gård, Elfviksvägen, POB 6031, 181 06 Lidingö; tel. (8) 636-36-77; fax (8) 636-36-13; internet www.iran.se; Ambassador RASOUL ESLAMI.

Iraq: Baldersgt. 6A, POB 26031, 100 41 Stockholm; tel. (8) 411-44-43; fax (8) 796-83-66; e-mail stkemb@iraqmofamail.net; internet www.iraqembassy.se; Ambassador Dr HUSSAIN MAHDI ABID AL-AMERI.

Ireland: Hovslagargt. 5, POB 10326, 100 55 Stockholm; tel. (8) 545-040-40; fax (8) 660-13-53; e-mail stockholmembassy@dfa.ie; internet www.embassyofireland.se; Ambassador DONAL HAMILL.

Israel: Storgt. 31, POB 14006, 104 40 Stockholm; tel. (8) 528-065-00; fax (8) 528-065-55; e-mail info@stockholm.mfa.gov.il; internet stockholm.mfa.gov.il; Ambassador BENNY DAGAN.

Italy: Oakhill, Djurgården, 115 21 Stockholm; tel. (8) 545-671-00; fax (8) 660-05-05; e-mail info.stockholm@esteri.it; internet www.ambstoccolma.esteri.it; Ambassador ANGELO PERSIANI.

Japan: Gärdesgt. 10, 115 27 Stockholm; tel. (8) 579-353-00; fax (8) 661-88-20; e-mail protocol@japansamb.se; internet www.se.emb-japan.go.jp; Ambassador YOSHIKI WATANABE.

Kenya: Birger Jarlsgt. 37, 2nd Floor, POB 7694, 103 95 Stockholm; tel. (8) 21-83-04; fax (8) 20-92-61; e-mail kenya.embassy@telia.com; Ambassador PURITY W. MUHINDI.

Korea, Democratic People's Republic: Norra Kungsvägen 39, 181 31 Lidingö; tel. (8) 767-38-36; fax (8) 767-38-35; e-mail koryo@telia.com; Ambassador RI HUI CHOL.

Korea, Republic: Laboratoriegt. 10, POB 27237, 102 53 Stockholm; tel. (8) 545-894-00; fax (8) 660-28-18; e-mail koremb.sweden@mofat.go.kr; internet swe.mofat.go.kr; Ambassador EOM SEOCK-JEONG.

Kosovo: Birger Jarlsgt. 33, 1st Floor, 111 45 Stockholm; tel. (8) 0722-25-56-51; fax (8) 588-18-51-0; e-mail embassy.sweden@ks-gov.net; Ambassador LULZIM PECI.

SWEDEN

Kuwait: Banérgt. 37, POB 10030, 100 55 Stockholm; tel. (8) 450-99-80; fax (8) 450-99-55; e-mail kuwaitambassad@telia.com; Ambassador ALI I. AL-NIKHAILAN.

Laos: Badstrandsvägen 11, POB 34050, 112 65 Stockholm; tel. (8) 618-20-10; fax (8) 618-20-01; e-mail info@laoembassy.se; internet www.laoembassy.se; Ambassador SOUTHAM SAKONHNINHOM.

Latvia: Odengt. 5, POB 19167, 104 32 Stockholm; tel. (8) 700-63-00; fax (8) 14-01-51; e-mail embassy.sweden@mfa.gov.lv; internet www.stockholm.mfa.gov.lv; Ambassador MAIJA MANIKA.

Lebanon: Kommendörsgt. 35, POB 5360, 102 49 Stockholm; tel. (8) 665-19-65; fax (8) 662-68-24; internet www.lebanonembassy.se; Ambassador NASRAT AL-ASSAD.

Libya (People's Bureau): Valhallavägen 74, POB 10133, 100 55 Stockholm; tel. (8) 14-34-35; fax (8) 10-43-80; e-mail libyanembassy06@hotmail.com; Ambassador (vacant).

Lithuania: Grevgt. 5, 114 53 Stockholm; tel. (8) 667-54-55; fax (8) 667-54-56; e-mail info@litemb.se; internet www.litemb.se; Ambassador REMIGIJUS MOTUZAS.

Macedonia, former Yugoslav republic: Riddargt. 35, POB 10128, 100 55 Stockholm; tel. (8) 661-18-30; fax (8) 661-03-25; e-mail stockholm@mfa.gov.mk; Ambassador KIRE ILIOSKI.

Malaysia: Karlavägen 37, POB 26053, 100 41 Stockholm; tel. (8) 440-84-00; fax (8) 791-87-60; e-mail mwstholm@algohotellet.se; Ambassador Dato' KAMARUDIN MUSTAFA.

Mexico: Grevgt. 3, 114 53 Stockholm; tel. (8) 663-51-70; fax (8) 663-24-20; e-mail suecia.embamex@telia.com; internet www.sre.gob.mx/suecia; Ambassador NORMA BERTHA PENSADO MORENO.

Moldova: Engelbrektsgt. 10, 114 32 Stockholm; tel. (8) 411-40-64; fax (8) 411-40-74; e-mail stockholm@moldovaembassy.se; internet www.suedia.mfa.md; Ambassador EMIL DRUC.

Mongolia: Svärdvägen 25B, 182 33 Danderyd; tel. (8) 753-11-35; fax (8) 753-11-38; e-mail stockholm@mfat.gov.mn; Ambassador ENKHMANDAKH BALDAN.

Morocco: Kungsholmstorg 16, 112 21 Stockholm; tel. (8) 545-511-30; fax (8) 545-511-39; e-mail morocco@telia.com; Ambassador ZOHOUR ALAOUI.

Mozambique: Sturegt. 46, 4th Floor, POB 5801, 102 48 Stockholm; tel. (8) 666-03-50; fax (8) 663-67-29; e-mail info@embassymozambique.se; internet www.embassymozambique.se; Ambassador PEDRO COMISSÁRIO AFONSO.

Namibia: Luntmakargt. 86–88, POB 19151, 104 32 Stockholm; tel. (8) 442-98-00; fax (8) 612-66-55; e-mail info@embassyofnamibia.se; internet www.embassyofnamibia.se; Ambassador DANIEL RUDOLPH SMITH.

Netherlands: Götgt. 16A, POB 15048, 104 65 Stockholm; tel. (8) 556-933-00; fax (8) 556-933-11; e-mail sto@minbuza.nl; internet www.nlemb.se; Ambassador JAN EDWARD CRAANEN.

New Zealand: Nybrogt. 11, 114 39 Stockholm; tel. (8) 459-69-40; fax (8) 459-69-59; e-mail nzemb.skm@mft.net.nz; internet www.nzembassy.com/sweden; Ambassador BARBARA BRIDGE.

Nicaragua: Sandhamnsgt. 40, 6th Floor, 115 28 Stockholm; tel. (8) 667-18-57; fax (8) 662-41-60; e-mail embajada.nicaragua@telia.se; Chargé d'affaires a.i. FRANCISCO RAMÓN CHAVARRIA.

Nigeria: Tyrgt. 8, POB 628, 101 32 Stockholm; tel. (8) 24-63-90; fax (8) 24-63-98; e-mail nigerian.embassy@swipnet.se; internet nigerianembassy.se; Chargé d'affaires a.i. NAOMI CHUKWUMAEZE.

Norway: Skarpögt. 4, POB 27829, 115 93 Stockholm; tel. (8) 665-63-40; fax (8) 782-98-99; e-mail emb.stockholm@mfa.no; internet www.norge.se; Ambassador ANNE K. LUND.

Pakistan: POB 5872, 102 40 Stockholm; Karlavägen 65, 1st Floor, 114 49 Stockholm; tel. (8) 20-33-00; fax (8) 24-92-33; e-mail info@pakistanembassy.se; internet www.pakistanembassy.se; Ambassador NADEEM RIYAZ.

Panama: Östermalmsgt. 59, POB 55547, 102 04 Stockholm; tel. (8) 662-65-35; fax (8) 662-89-91; e-mail panaembasuecia@tele2.se; Ambassador RICARDO QUINTERO NASSAR.

Paraguay: Stureplan 4C, 114 35 Stockholm; tel. (8) 463-32-07; fax (8) 463-10-10; e-mail jose_gorostiagap@hotmail.com; Chargé d'affaires JOSÉ EMILIO GOROSTIAGA PEÑA.

Philippines: POB 2219, 103 15 Stockholm; Skeppsbron 20, 1st Floor, 111 30 Stockholm; tel. (8) 23-56-65; fax (8) 14-07-14; e-mail stockholm@philembassy.se; internet www.philembassy.se; Ambassador MARIA ZENEIDA ANGARA COLLINSON.

Poland: Karlavägen 35, 114 31 Stockholm; tel. (8) 505-750-00; fax (8) 505-750-86; e-mail info.polen@polemb.se; internet www.sztokholm.polemb.net; Ambassador ADAM HALACINSKI.

Portugal: Narvavägen 32, 2nd Floor, POB 10194, 100 55 Stockholm; tel. (8) 545-670-60; fax (8) 662-53-29; e-mail portugal@embassyportugal.se; internet www.embassyportugal.se; Ambassador FRANCISCO PIMENTEL DE MELO RIBEIRO DE MENEZES.

Romania: Östermalmsgt. 36, POB 26043, 100 41 Stockholm; tel. (8) 10-86-03; fax (8) 10-28-52; e-mail info@romanianembassy.se; internet www.stockholm.mae.ro; Ambassador RADUTA DANA MATACHE.

Russia: Gjörwellsgt. 31, 112 60 Stockholm; tel. (8) 13-04-41; fax (8) 618-27-03; e-mail rusembassy@telia.com; internet www.ryssland.se; Ambassador IGOR NEVEROV.

Rwanda: Dalvägen 2, 3rd Floor, 169 27 Solna; tel. (8) 500-019-70; fax (8) 500-019-73; e-mail ambastockholm@minaffet.gov.rw; internet sweden.embassy.gov.rw; Ambassador VENETIA SEBUDANDI.

Saudi Arabia: Sköldungagt. 5, POB 26073, 100 41 Stockholm; tel. (8) 23-88-00; fax (8) 796-99-56; Ambassador Dr ABD AL-RAHMAN GDAIA.

Senegal: Birger Jarlsgt. 37, 3rd Floor, POB 7384, 103 91 Stockholm; tel. (8) 411-71-60; fax (8) 411-71-68; e-mail senegalembassy@telia.com; Ambassador HENRI-ANTOINE TURPIN.

Serbia: Valhallavägen 70, POB 26209, 100 41 Stockholm; tel. (8) 21-84-36; fax (8) 21-84-95; e-mail serbiaemb@telia.com; Ambassador Prof. Dr DUŠAN CRNOGORČEVIĆ.

Slovakia: Arsenalsgt. 2, 3rd Floor, POB 7183, 103 88 Stockholm; tel. (8) 545-039-60; fax (8) 545-039-69; e-mail emb.stockholm@mzv.sk; internet www.mzv.sk/stockholm; Ambassador PETER KMEC.

Slovenia: Styrmansgt. 4, 1st Floor, 114 54 Stockholm; tel. (8) 545-65-885; fax (8) 662-92-74; e-mail vst@gov.si; Chargé d'affaires a.i. METODA MIKUZ.

South Africa: Fleminggt. 20, 4th Floor, 112 26 Stockholm; tel. (8) 24-39-50; fax (8) 660-71-36; e-mail saemb.swe@telia.com; internet www.southafricanemb.se; Ambassador MANDISA DONA MARASHA.

Spain: Djurgårdsvägen 21, Djurgården, POB 10295, 100 55 Stockholm; tel. (8) 52-28-08-00; fax (8) 663-30-34; e-mail emb.estocolmo@maec.es; internet www.maec.es/embajadas/estocolmo; Ambassador ANTONIO NÚÑEZ GARCIA-SAÚCO.

Sri Lanka: Strandvägen 39, 1st Floor, POB 24055, 104 50 Stockholm; tel. (8) 663-65-23; fax (8) 660-00-89; e-mail slembassy@comhem.se; internet www.slembassy.se; Ambassador RANJITH PEMSIRI JAYASOORIYA.

Sudan: Stockholmsvägen 33, POB 26142, 181 33 Lidingö; tel. (8) 611-77-80; fax (8) 611-77-82; e-mail sudanembassy@telia.com; Chargé d'affaires a.i. BADRELDIN ALI MOHAMED ELGUAIFRI.

Switzerland: Valhallavägen 64, POB 26143, 100 41 Stockholm; tel. (8) 676-79-00; fax (8) 21-15-04; e-mail sto.vertretung@eda.admin.ch; internet www.eda.admin.ch/stockholm; Ambassador KURT M. HOECHNER.

Syria: Vendevägen 90, 5th Floor, POB 4, 182 11 Danderyd; tel. (8) 622-18-70; fax (8) 660-88-05; e-mail info@syrianembassy.se; internet www.syrianembassy.se; Ambassador MILAD ATIEH.

Tanzania: Näsby Allé 6, 183 55 Täby; tel. (8) 732-24-30; fax (8) 732-24-32; e-mail mailbox@tanemb.se; internet www.tanemb.se; Ambassador MUHAMMED MWINYI MZALE.

Thailand: Floragt. 3, POB 26220, 100 40 Stockholm; tel. (8) 791-73-40; fax (8) 791-73-51; e-mail info@thaiembassy.se; internet www.thaiembassy.se; Ambassador THANARAT THANAPUTTI.

Tunisia: Narvavägen 32, 1st Floor, POB 24030, 104 50 Stockholm; tel. (8) 545-855-20; fax (8) 662-19-75; e-mail at.stockholm@swipnet.se; Chargé d'affaires EMNA ABBES.

Turkey: Dag Hammarskjölds Väg 20, POB 24105, 104 51 Stockholm; tel. (8) 23-08-40; fax (8) 663-55-14; e-mail turkbe@turkemb.se; internet www.turkemb.se; Ambassador ZERGÜN KORUTÜRK.

Ukraine: Stjärnvägen 2A, 181 34 Lidingö; tel. (8) 522-28-400; fax (8) 522-28-411; e-mail emb_se@mfa.gov.ua; internet www.mfa.gov.ua/sweden; Ambassador YEVGEN PEREBYINIS.

United Arab Emirates: Torsgt. 2, 5th Floor, 101 23 Stockholm; tel. (8) 411-12-44; fax (8) 411-12-45; e-mail uae@uaeembassy.se; internet www.uaeembassy.se; Ambassador Sheikha NAJLA MOHAMED SALEM AL-QASSIMI.

United Kingdom: Skarpögt. 6–8, POB 27819, 115 93 Stockholm; tel. (8) 671-30-00; fax (8) 671-31-04; e-mail info@britishembassy.se; internet ukinsweden.fco.gov.uk/en; Ambassador PAUL JOHNSTON.

USA: Dag Hammarskjölds Väg 31, 115 89 Stockholm; tel. (8) 783-53-00; fax (8) 661-19-64; e-mail stockholmweb@state.gov; internet stockholm.usembassy.gov; Ambassador (vacant).

Uruguay: Kommendörsgt. 35, 114 58 Stockholm; tel. (8) 660-31-96; fax (8) 665-31-66; e-mail urustoc@uruemb.se; Chargé d'affaires a.i. ALEJANDRO GARÓFALI ACOSTA.

Venezuela: Engelbrektsgt. 35B, POB 26012, 100 41 Stockholm; tel. (8) 411-09-96; fax (8) 21-31-00; e-mail venezuela.embassy@comhem.se; Chargé d'affaires a.i. ZULIMA ROJAS MAVARES.

Viet Nam: Örby Slottsvägen 26, 125 71 Älvsjö; tel. (8) 556-210-70; fax (8) 556-210-80; e-mail info@vietnamemb.se; internet www.vietnamemb.se; Ambassador NGUYEN DUC HOA.

Zambia: Gårdsvägen 18, 3rd Floor, POB 3056, 169 03 Solna; tel. (8) 679-90-40; fax (8) 679-68-50; e-mail info@zambiaembassy.se; internet www.zambiaembassy.se; Ambassador ANNE LUZONGO MTAMBOH.

Zimbabwe: POB 3253, 103 65 Stockholm; Herserudsvägen 5A, 7th Floor, 181 34 Lidingö; tel. (8) 765-53-80; fax (8) 21-91-32; e-mail mbuya@stockholm.mail.telia.com; Ambassador STEPHEN CLETUS CHIKETA.

Judicial System

The judiciary and the executive are separate, although judges are appointed by the Government. A judge can be removed by an authority other than a court, but may, in such an event, request a judicial trial of the decision.

To supervise the courts in administrative matters, there is a central authority, Domstolsverket, in Jönköping. This authority has no control over the judicial process, in which the court is independent even of the legislature and Government.

There are state officers who exercise control over the judiciary as well as the administrative authorities. The Justitiekansler (Chancellor of Justice or Attorney-General) and the four Justitieombudsmän supervise the courts and the general administration including the armed forces. The Justitiekansler performs his functions on behalf of the Government. The Justitieombudsmän are appointed by and act on behalf of the legislature.

Attorney-General (Justitiekansler): GÖRAN LAMBERTZ.

SUPREME COURT

Högsta domstolen (Supreme Court in Stockholm): POB 2066, 103 12 Stockholm; Riddarhustorget 8, 111 28 Stockholm; tel. (8) 561-666-00; fax (8) 561-666-86; e-mail hogsta.domstolen@dom.se; internet www.hogstadomstolen.se; the Supreme Court in Stockholm, consisting of a minimum of 14 members, is the Court of Highest Instance. The Court works in three chambers, each of which is duly constituted of five members. Certain cases are decided by full session of the Court. There are also special divisions with three members (or, in simple cases, one member) which decide whether the Court is to consider a case.

Chairman of the Supreme Court: MARIANNE LUNDIUS.

Justices: LEIF THORSSON, DAG VICTOR, SEVERIN BLOMSTRAND, TORGNY HÅSTAD, AGNETA BÄCKLUND, JOHNNY HERRE, ANN-CHRISTINE LINDEBLAD, ELLA NYSTRÖM, KERSTIN CALISSENDORFF, PER VIRDESTEN, GÖRAN LAMBERTZ, GUDMUND TOIJER, STEFAN LINDSKOG, LENA MOORE.

APPELLATE COURTS

The Court of Appeal, the Court of Second Instance, consists of a president, judges of appeal and associate judges of appeal. The work is apportioned between various divisions, each of which has five or six members. In criminal cases the bench consists of three professional judges and two lay assessors; in petty and civil cases there are three professional judges only. There are six Courts of Appeal (*hovrätter*).

President of the Court of Appeal (Stockholm): FREDRIK WERSÄLL.

President of the Court of Appeal (Jönköping): KATHRIN FLOSSING.

President of the Court of Appeal (Malmö): LENNART SVENSÄTER.

President of the Court of Appeal (Göteborg): GUNNEL WENNBERG.

President of the Court of Appeal (Sundsvall): STEN ANDERSSON.

President of the Court of Appeal (Umeå): ANDERS IACOBÆUS.

DISTRICT COURTS

The District Court acts as a Court of First Instance in both civil and criminal cases. In 2010 there were 48 District Courts (*tingsrätter*). In criminal cases the court is composed of a presiding professional judge and three or, in serious cases, five lay assessors; in petty cases the court consists of the professional judge only. In civil cases the court is ordinarily composed of three professional judges; however, preparatory sessions are conducted by one professional judge. In family law cases, the court is composed of a professional judge and three lay assessors. The lay assessors are elected for a period of four years (during which they are on duty for about 10 days a year). They act as members of the bench and should consequently be distinguished from the jurors of other countries. In certain types of case technical experts may sit alongside the judges.

ADMINISTRATIVE COURTS

In each of the 23 administrative districts of the country there is a County Administrative Court (*länsrätt*). This court handles appeal cases concerning the assessment of social security and welfare. The bench ordinarily consists of a professional judge and three lay assessors, although in simple cases a professional judge may preside alone.

Appeals against decisions by the County Administrative Courts may be made to Administrative Courts of Appeal (*kammarrätter*) consisting of a president, judges of appeal and associate judges of appeal. The courts work in divisions, each of which normally has six members. The bench consists of at least three and not more than four judges. In certain cases there are, however, three professional judges and two lay assessors. There are four Administrative Courts of Appeal.

The Supreme Administrative Court of Sweden (*Regeringsrätten*) in Stockholm, consisting of 19 members, is the Court of Highest Instance in Administrative cases. The composition of the court is governed by rules very similar to those that apply to the Supreme Court.

Chairman of the Supreme Administrative Court: STEN HECKSCHER.

President of the Administrative Court of Appeal (Stockholm): THOMAS ROLÉN.

President of the Administrative Court of Appeal (Göteborg): CARL GUSTAV FERNLUND.

President of the Administrative Court of Appeal (Sundsvall): BERTIL EKHOLM.

President of the Administrative Court of Appeal (Jönköping): PETER ROSÉN.

SPECIAL COURTS

Special courts exist for certain categories of cases, such as real estate courts (*fastighetsdomstolar*).

OMBUDSMEN

The post of Justitieombudsman was created in 1800 to supervise the manner in which judges, government officials and other civil servants observe the laws, and to prosecute those who act illegally, misuse their position or neglect their duties. The Ombudsman is allowed access to all documents and information and has the right to be present at the considerations of the courts and other authorities. Government ministers in Sweden are not subject to supervision by the Ombudsman. The term of office is four years.

Ombudsmen: MATS MELIN, KERSTIN ANDRÉ, CECILIA NORDENFELT, HANS-GUNNAR AXBERGER.

Religion

CHRISTIANITY

About 78% of the population were members of the Svenska Kyrkan (Church of Sweden) in 2004. Since the constitutional link between the Church and the state was severed in 2000 a significant number of people have left the Church each year.

Sveriges Kristna Råd (Christian Council of Sweden): Ekumeniska Centret, Starrbäcksgt. 11, 172 99 Sundbyberg; tel. (8) 453-68-00; fax (8) 453-68-29; e-mail info@skr.org; internet www.skr.org; f. 1993; 27 mem. churches; Chair. Rev. KARIN WIBORN; Gen. Sec. SVEN-BERNHARD FAST.

Church of Sweden

Svenska kyrkan

Kyrkokansliet, Sysslomansgt. 4, 751 70 Uppsala; tel. (18) 16-95-00; fax (18) 16-95-38; e-mail info@svenskakyrkan.se; internet www.svenskakyrkan.se.

Evangelical Lutheran; 13 dioceses, 2,225 parishes, 3,500 active clergy (including missionaries in the mission fields); the Archbishop of Uppsala is head of the Church.

Archbishop of Uppsala: Most Rev. ANDERS WEJRYD, 751 70 Uppsala; tel. (18) 16-95-00; fax (18) 16-96-25.

Evangeliska Fosterlands-Stiftelsen (Swedish Evangelical Mission): Sysslomansgt. 4, 751 70 Uppsala; tel. (18) 16-98-00; fax (18) 16-98-01; e-mail efs@efs.svenskakyrkan.se; internet www.efs.nu; f. 1856; an independent mission org. within the Church of Sweden; 17,994 mems; Chair. RAY RAWALL; Mission Dir ANDERS SJÖBERG.

Other Protestant Churches

Eesti Evangeeliumi Luteri Usu Kirik (Estonian Evangelical Lutheran Church): POB 450 74, 104 30 Stockholm 45; tel. (8) 20-69-78; e-mail ingo.jaagu@bredband.net; 12,000 mems; Dean INGO TIIT JAAGU; Gen. Sec. IVAR NIPPAK.

Metodistkyrkan i Sverige (United Methodist Church): Danska vägen 20, 412 66 Göteborg; tel. (31) 733-78-40; fax (31) 733-87-49; e-mail info@metodistkyrkan.se; internet www.metodistkyrkan.se;

SWEDEN

f. 1868; 3,565 mems; Bishop ØYSTEIN OLSEN; Pres. of Conference Board ANDERS SVENSSON.

Sjundedags Adventistsamfundet (Seventh-day Adventists): Olof Palmes Gt. 25, POB 536, 101 30 Stockholm; tel. (8) 545-297-70; fax (8) 20-48-68; e-mail info@adventist.se; internet www.adventist.se; f. 1880; 2,800 mems; Pres. BOBBY SJÖLANDER; Sec. AUDREY ANDERSSON.

Svenska Baptistsamfundet (Baptist Union of Sweden): Starrbäcksgt. 11, 172 99 Sundbyberg; tel. (8) 564-827-00; fax (8) 564-827-27; e-mail info@baptist.se; internet www.baptist.se; f. 1848; 215 churches, 17,748 mems (2008); mem. European Baptist Fed., Baptist World Alliance and Christian Council of Sweden (Sveriges Kristna Råd); Pres. Rev. KARIN WIBORN; Gen. Sec. LARS DALESJÖ.

Svenska Missionskyrkan (Mission Covenant Church of Sweden): Tegnérgt. 8, POB 6302, 113 81 Stockholm; tel. (8) 674-07-00; fax (8) 674-07-93; e-mail info@missionskyrkan.se; internet www.missionskyrkan.se; f. 1878; 61,769 mems; Pres. GÖRAN ZETTERGREN; Chair. of Board ULF HÅLLMARKER.

The Roman Catholic Church

For ecclesiastical purposes, Sweden comprises the single diocese of Stockholm, directly responsible to the Holy See. At 31 December 2006 there were 140,000 adherents in the country, representing 1.5% of the total population.

Scandinavian Bishops' Conference

POB 135, 421 22 Västra Frölunda; tel. (31) 709-57-15; fax (31) 49-21-70; e-mail nbk@bishopsoffice.org.

f. 1960 new statutes approved 2000; covers Sweden, Norway, Denmark, Finland and Iceland; Pres. Rt Rev. ANDERS ARBORELIUS; Sec.-Gen. Rt Rev. GEORG MÜLLER.

Bishop of Stockholm: Rt Rev. ANDERS ARBORELIUS, Götgt. 68, POB 4114, 102 62 Stockholm; tel. (8) 462-66-00; fax (8) 702-05-55; e-mail info@katolskakyrkan.se; internet www.katolskakyrkan.se.

Other Denominations

Other Christian Churches include the Pentecostal Movement (with an estimated 90,000 mems in 2004), the Orthodox Churches of the Greeks, Romanians, Russians, Serbians and Finnish (together numbering about 100,000 mems in 2004), the Church of Jesus Christ of Latter-day Saints (Mormons—9,000 mems in 2004), the Swedish Alliance Missionary Society (12,895 mems in 1997), the Jehovah's Witnesses (23,000 mems in 2004) and the Salvation Army (25,531 mems in 1997).

ISLAM

In 2004 there were approximately 300,000 to 350,000 Muslims in Sweden, of whom around 100,000 were believed to be religiously active.

Islamiska Radet i Sverige (Islamic Council of Sweden—IRIS): POB 3053, 14503 Norsborg; tel. (8) 531-707-95; fax (8) 531-706-65; f. 1986.

Islamiska Kulturcenterunionen i Sverige (Union of the Islamic Cultural Centres in Sweden—IKUS): POB 3053, 145 03 Norsborg; tel. (8) 531-707-95; fax (8) 531-706-65; f. 1984.

Sveriges Muslimska Förbund (SMUF): Stockholms Moske, Kapellgränd 10, 116 25 Stockholm; tel. (8) 509-109-00; f. 1981; Chair. MAHMOUD ALDEBE; 70,000 mems.

Sveriges Muslimska Råd (Muslim Council of Sweden—SMR): Stockholms Moske, Kapellgränd 10, 116 25 Stockholm; tel. and fax (8) 509-109-00; e-mail info@sverigesmuslimskarad.se; internet www.sverigesmuslimskarad.se; f. 1990; members include the Sveriges Muslimska Förbund; Chair. HELENA BENAOUDA.

JUDAISM

In 2004 the total number of Jews living in Sweden was estimated to be approximately 18,500–20,000; however, the Jewish community estimated 10,000 active, or practising, members. There are Orthodox, Conservative and Reform Jewish synagogues. The largest Jewish community is in Stockholm.

Judiska Församlingen i Stockholm (Jewish Community in Stockholm): Wahrendorffsgt. 3B, POB 7427, 103 91 Stockholm; tel. (8) 587-858-00; fax (8) 587-858-58; e-mail info@jfst.se; internet www.jfst.se; f. 1776; c. 4,500 mems; Exec. Dir THOMAS BAB.

OTHER RELIGIONS

In 2004 there were approximately 3,000–4,000 Buddhists and a similar number of Hindus in Sweden.

The Press

Press freedom in Sweden dates from a law of 1766. The 1949 Freedom of the Press Act, a fundamental law embodying the whole of the press legislation in the Constitution, guarantees the press's right to print and disseminate ideas; protects those supplying information by forbidding editors to disclose sources under any circumstances; authorizes all public documents to be publicly available, official secrets being the only exception; and contains provision for defamation. Press offences are to be referred to common law, and all cases against the press must be heard by jury.

In 1916 the Press Council was founded by press organizations to monitor ethical matters within the press. Lacking judicial status, it has powers to rehabilitate persons wronged by the press who refuse to apply to courts of law. Its judgments are widely published and highly respected.

In 1969 the office of Press Ombudsman was established to supervise adherence to ethical standards. Public complaints shall be directed to the Press Ombudsman, who is also entitled to act on his own initiative. He may dismiss a complaint if unfounded, or if the newspaper agrees to publish a retraction or rectification acceptable to the complainant. When he finds that the grievance is of a more serious nature, he will file a complaint with the Press Council, which will then publish a statement acquitting or criticizing the newspaper. The findings of the Council are published in the newspaper concerned.

The dominating influence of the few major dailies is largely confined to Stockholm, the provinces having a strong press of their own. The major dailies are: *Aftonbladet, Dagens Nyheter, Expressen, Svenska Dagbladet, Dagens Industri* (all Stockholm), *Göteborgs-Posten* (Gothenburg), *Sydsvenskan* (Malmö). In 2009 there were 171 daily newspapers with a combined circulation of 3.6m.

The two principal magazine publishers in Sweden are the Bonnier group (also a large book publisher and the majority shareholder in the newspapers *Dagens Nyheter, Expressen* and *Sydsvenskan*) and the Aller company. Four other companies produce most of the remainder of Sweden's magazine circulation. The most popular weekly periodicals include the family magazines *Aret Runt, Hemmets Veckotidning, Allers* and *Hemmets Journal*, and the home and household magazine *ICA Kuriren. Vi* caters for serious cultural and political discussion, and *Bonniers Litterära Magasin* specializes in literary topics.

PRINCIPAL NEWSPAPERS

Newspapers with a circulation exceeding 15,000 are listed below.

Ängelholm

Nordvästra Skånes Tidningar: 262 83 Ängelholm; tel. (431) 84-000; fax (431) 26-177; f. 1847; daily; Conservative; Editor-in-Chief BENNIE OHLSSON.

Borås

Borås Tidning: 501 85 Borås; tel. (33) 700-07-00; fax (33) 10-14-36; f. 1826; morning; Conservative; Editor JAN ÖJMERTZ; circ. 53,000 (2001).

Eksjö

Smålands-Tidningen: POB 261, 575 23 Eksjö; tel. (381) 13-200; fax (381) 17-145; f. 1899; morning; independent; Editor BENGT WENDLE.

Eskilstuna

Eskilstuna-Kuriren Strengnäs Tidning: POB 120, 631 02 Eskilstuna; tel. (16) 15-60-00; fax (16) 51-63-04; e-mail redaktion@ekuriren.se; internet www.ekuriren.se; f. 1890; morning; Liberal; Editor PEO WÄRRING; circ. 33,000 (2006).

Falkenberg

Hallands Nyheter: 311 81 Falkenberg; tel. (346) 29-000; fax (346) 29-115; e-mail redaktionen@hn.se; internet www.hn.se; f. 1905; morning; Centre; Editor ANNA KARIN LITH; circ. 31,000 (2001).

Falun

Dala-Demokraten: POB 825, Stigaregat. 17, 791 29 Falun; tel. (23) 47-500; fax (23) 20-668; e-mail redaktionen@deladem.se; internet www.dalademokraten.se; f. 1917; morning; Social Democrat; Editor GÖRAN GREIDER.

Falu-Kuriren: POB 265, 791 26 Falun; tel. (23) 93-500; fax (23) 12-073; e-mail red@falukuriren.se; internet www.falukuriren.se; f. 1894; morning; Liberal; Editor CHRISTER GRUHS.

Gävle

Arbetarbladet: POB 287, 801 04 Gävle; tel. (26) 15-93-00; fax (26) 12-14-06; f. 1902; morning; Social Democrat; Editor KENNET LUTTI.

SWEDEN

Gefle Dagblad: POB 367, 801 05 Gävle; tel. (26) 15-95-00; fax (26) 15-97-00; f. 1895; morning; Liberal; Editor Robert Rosén.

Göteborg
(Gothenburg)

Göteborgs-Posten: Polhemsplatsen 5, 405 02 Göteborg; tel. (31) 62-40-00; fax (31) 62-45-85; e-mail redaktion@gp.se; internet www.gp.se; f. 1858; morning; Liberal; Editor-in-Chief Peter Hjorne; circ. 245,600 (2006).

Halmstad

Hallandsposten: 301 81 Halmstad; tel. (35) 14-75-00; fax (35) 14-76-88; e-mail redaktionen@hallandsposten.se; internet www.hallandsposten.se; f. 1850; morning; Liberal; Editor Viveka Hedbjörk.

Hässleholm

Norra Skåne: 281 81 Hässleholm; tel. (451) 74-50-00; fax (451) 74-50-32; e-mail chefred@nsk.se; internet www.nsk.se; f. 1899; morning; Centre; Editor Billy Bengtsson; circ. 21,800 (2001).

Helsingborg

Helsingborgs Dagblad: Vasatorpsvägen 1, 251 83 Helsingborg; tel. (242) 489-90-00; e-mail redaktionen@hd.se; internet hd.se; f. 1867; morning; independent; Editor-in-Chief Lars Johansson.

SD-Kuriren: POB 130 45, 250 13 Helsingborg; tel. (73) 62-60-661; fax (455) 151-33; e-mail redaktion@sdkuriren.se; internet www.sdkuriren.se; f. 1988; organ of the Sverigedemokraterna; Editor-in-Chief Richard Jomshof; circ. 30,000.

Hudiksvall

Hudiksvalls Tidning: POB 1201, 824 15 Hudiksvall; tel. (650) 355-00; fax (650) 355-60; e-mail redaktion@ht.se; internet www.ht.se; f. 1909; includes Hälsinglands Tidning; morning; Centre; Man. Dir Ruben Jacobsson; Editor Jörgen Bengtson.

Jönköping

Jönköpings-Posten/Smålands Allehanda: 551 80 Jönköping; tel. (36) 30-40-50; fax (36) 12-61-11; f. 1865; morning; independent; Editor Stig Fredriksson.

Kalmar

Barometern med Oskarshamns-Tidningen: 391 88 Kalmar; tel. (480) 59-100; fax (480) 59-131; f. 1841; morning; Conservative; Editor Gunilla Andreasson.

Karlskrona

Blekinge Läns Tidning: 371 89 Karlskrona; tel. (455) 77-000; fax (455) 82-170; e-mail kudcenter@blt.se; internet www.blt.se; f. 1869; morning; Liberal; Editor-in-Chief Kerstin Johansson; circ. 36,800 (2003).

Sydöstra Sveriges Dagblad: Landbrogt. 17, 371 88 Karlskrona; tel. (455) 19-000; fax (455) 82-237; f. 1903; morning; Social Democrat; Editor Anders Hagquist.

Karlstad

Nya Wermlands-Tidningen: POB 28, 651 02 Karlstad; tel. (54) 19-90-00; fax (54) 19-96-00; e-mail redaktion@nwt.se; internet www.nwt.se; f. 1836; morning; Conservative; Editor Staffan Ander.

Värmlands Folkblad: POB 67, 651 03 Karlstad; tel. (54) 17-55-06; fax (54) 15-16-59; e-mail kundtjanst@vf.se; internet www.vf.se; f. 1918; morning; Social Democrat; Editor Peter Franke.

Kristianstad

Kristianstadsbladet: 291 84 Kristianstad; tel. (44) 18-55-00; fax (44) 21-17-01; e-mail kb@kristianstadsbladet.se; internet www.kristianstadsbladet.se; f. 1856; morning; Liberal; Man. Dir Bo Wigernäs; Editor Håkan Bengtsson; circ. 31,900 (2004).

Lidköping

Nya Läns-Tidningen: 531 81 Lidköping; tel. (510) 89-700; fax (510) 89-796; e-mail post@nlt.se; f. 1903; morning; 3 a week; Liberal; Editor Lennart Hörling.

Linköping

Östgöta Correspondenten: 581 89 Linköping; tel. (13) 28-00-00; fax (13) 28-03-24; e-mail nyhet@corren.se; internet www.corren.se; f. 1838; morning; Liberal; Editor Ola Sigvardsson; circ. 59,300 (2006).

Luleå

Norrbottens-Kuriren: 971 81 Luleå; tel. (920) 37-500; fax (920) 67-107; f. 1861; morning; Conservative.

Norrländska Socialdemokraten: 971 83 Luleå; tel. (920) 36-000; fax (920) 36-279; f. 1919; morning; Social Democrat; Editor Lennart Håkansson.

Malmö

Kvällsposten: 205 26 Malmö; tel. (40) 28-16-00; fax (40) 93-92-24; f. 1990; evening; Liberal; Editor Lars Klint.

Skånska Dagbladet: Östergt. 11, POB 165, 201 21 Malmö; tel. (40) 660-55-00; fax (40) 97-47-70; f. 1888; morning; Centre; Editor Jan A. Johansson.

Sydsvenskan: 205 05 Malmö; tel. (40) 28-12-00; fax (40) 93-54-75; e-mail sydsvenskan@sydsvenskan.se; internet sydsvenskan.se; f. 1848; morning; Liberal independent; Editors Jonas Gruvö, Heidi Avellan; circ. 136,400 (2003).

Norrköping

Norrköpings Tidningar: 601 83 Norrköping; tel. (11) 20-00-00; fax (11) 20-02-40; e-mail redaktionen@nt.se; internet www.nt.se; f. 1758; morning; Conservative; Editor Charli Nilsson; circ. 49,900 (2000).

Nyköping

Södermanlands Nyheter: 611 79 Nyköping; tel. (155) 76-700; fax (155) 26-88-01; e-mail redaktionen@sn.se; internet www.sn.se; f. 1893; morning; Editor Göran Carlstorp; circ. 25,300 (2006).

Örebro

Nerikes Allehanda: 701 92 Örebro; tel. (19) 15-50-00; fax (19) 12-03-83; e-mail redaktionen@na.se; internet www.na.se; f. 1843; morning; Liberal; Editor Krister Linner.

Örnsköldsvik

Örnsköldsviks Allehanda: POB 110, 891 23 Örnsköldsvik; tel. (660) 29-50-00; fax (660) 15-064; e-mail jimmie.naslund@allehanda.se; internet allehanda.se; f. 1843; morning; Liberal; Editor Jimmie Näslund; circ. 20,800 (2001).

Östersund

Länstidningen: 831 89 Östersund; tel. (63) 15-55-00; fax (63) 15-55-95; f. 1924; morning; Social Democrat; Editors Peter Swedenmark, Christer Sjöström; circ. 17,000 (2003).

Östersunds-Posten: POB 720, 831 28 Östersund; tel. (63) 16-16-00; fax (63) 10-58-02; f. 1877; morning; Centre; Editors Bosse Svensson, Håkan Larsson.

Piteå

Piteå-Tidningen: POB 193, 941 24 Piteå; tel. (911) 64-500; fax (911) 64-650; f. 1915; morning; Social Democrat; Editor Olov Carlsson.

Skara

Skaraborgs Läns Tidning: POB 214, 532 23 Skara; tel. (511) 13-010; fax (511) 18-815; f. 1884; morning; Liberal; Editor Hans Olofsson.

Skellefteå

Norra Västerbotten: POB 58, 931 21 Skellefteå; tel. (910) 57-700; fax (910) 57-875; e-mail redaktionsavderlning@norran.se; internet www.norran.se; f. 1910; morning; 6 days a week; Liberal; Editor Ola Theander; circ. 30,500 (2000).

Skövde

Skaraborgs Allehanda: POB 407, 541 28 Skövde; tel. (500) 46-75-00; fax (500) 48-05-82; e-mail redaktion@sla.se; internet www.sla.se; f. 1884; morning; Conservative; Editor Måns Johnson.

Södertälje

Länstidningen: 151 82 Södertälje; tel. (8) 550-921-00; fax (8) 550-877-72; e-mail redaktion@lt.se; f. 1861; morning; 6 a week; Centre; Editor Torsten Carlsson; circ. 17,600 (2002).

Stockholm

Aftonbladet: 105 18 Stockholm; tel. (8) 725-20-00; fax (8) 600-01-70; e-mail redaktion@aftonbladet.se; internet www.aftonbladet.se; f. 1830; evening; Social Democrat independent; Editor-in-Chief Kalle Jungkvist.

SWEDEN

Dagen: 105 36 Stockholm; tel. (8) 619-24-00; fax (8) 619-60-51; e-mail info@dagen.se; f. 1945; morning; 4 a week; Christian independent; Editor DANIEL GRAHN; circ. 20,200 (2003).

Dagens Industri: 113 90 Stockholm; tel. (8) 736-50-00; fax (8) 31-19-06; internet di.se; f. 1976; 6 a week; business news; Editor LINUS PAULSSON.

Dagens Nyheter: 105 15 Stockholm; tel. (8) 738-10-00; fax (8) 738-21-80; e-mail info@dn.se; internet www.dn.se; f. 1864; morning; independent; Editor-in-Chief THORBJÖRN LARSSON; CEO LENA HERRMANN; circ. 344,000 (2007).

Expressen: Gjörwellsgt. 30, 105 16 Stockholm; tel. (8) 738-30-00; fax (8) 738-33-40; e-mail redaktionen@expressen.se; internet www.expressen.se; f. 1945; evening; Liberal; Editor OTTO SJÖBERG; circ. 353,000 (2003).

Svenska Dagbladet: 105 17 Stockholm; tel. (8) 13-50-00; fax (8) 13-56-80; e-mail svd@svd.se; internet www.svd.se; f. 1884; morning; Conservative; Editor-in-Chief LENA K. SAMUELSSON; circ. 170,000 (2000).

Sundsvall

Sundsvalls Tidning: 851 72 Sundsvall; tel. (60) 19-70-00; fax (60) 15-44-33; e-mail redaktion@st.nu; internet www.st.nu; f. 1841; morning; Liberal; Editor KJELL CARNBRO; circ. 35,700 (2005).

Trollhättan

Trollhättans Tidning: POB 54, 461 22 Trollhättan; tel. (520) 49-42-00; fax (520) 49-43-19; f. 1906; morning; 5 a week; independent; Editor TORBJÖRN HÅKANSSON.

Uddevalla

Bohusläningen med Dals Dagblad: 451 83 Uddevalla; tel. (522) 99-000; fax (522) 51-18-88; f. 1878; morning; Liberal; Editor ULF JOHANSSON.

Umeå

Västerbottens-Kuriren: 901 70 Umeå; tel. (90) 15-10-00; fax (90) 77-00-53; e-mail info@vk.se; internet www.vk.se; f. 1900; morning; Liberal.

Uppsala

Upsala Nya Tidning: Danmarksgt. 28, POB 36, 751 03 Uppsala; tel. (18) 478-00-00; fax (18) 12-95-07; e-mail hakan.holmberg@unt.se; internet www.unt.se; f. 1890; morning; Liberal; Editor-in-Chief HÅKAN HOLMBERG; circ. 52,800 (2009).

Värnamo

Värnamo Nyheter: 331 84 Värnamo; tel. (370) 30-19-56; fax (370) 493-95; e-mail redaktion@varnamonyheter.se; internet www.varnamonyheter.se; f. 1917; morning; independent; Editor STIG-ERIC EINARSSON; circ. 23,000 (2000).

Västerås

Vestmanlands Läns Tidning: POB 3, 721 03 Västerås; tel. (21) 19-90-00; fax (21) 19-90-60; e-mail nyheter@vlt.se; internet www.vlt.se; f. 1831; morning; Liberal; Editor ELISABETH BÄCK; circ. 48,000 (2003).

Växjö

Smålandsposten: 351 70 Växjö; tel. (470) 77-05-00; fax (470) 209-49; f. 1866; morning; Conservative; Editor CLAES-GÖRAN HEGNELL.

Ystad

Ystads Allehanda: 271 81 Ystad; tel. (411) 55-78-00; fax (411) 13-955; e-mail nyheter@ystadsallehanda.se; internet www.ystadsallehanda.se; f. 1873; morning; Liberal; Editor MARGARETHA ENGSTRÖM; circ. 26,100 (2004).

POPULAR PERIODICALS

Allas Veckotidning: Allers Förlag, 205 35 Malmö; tel. (40) 38-59-00; fax (40) 38-59-64; e-mail allas@aller.se; internet www.allas.se; f. 1931; owned by Aller Media; weekly; family; Editor-in-Chief GUNILLA HÅKANSSON; circ. 117,700.

Allers: Aller Media AB, Landskronavägen 23, 251 85 Helsingborg; tel. (42) 17-35-00; fax (42) 17-35-68; e-mail redaktionen@allers.se; f. 1877; weekly; family; Editor-in-Chief LOTTA HYLANDER; circ. 213,800.

Allt om Mat: Sveavägen 53, 105 44 Stockholm; tel. (8) 736-53-00; fax (8) 34-00-88; e-mail red@aom.bonnier.se; internet www.alltommat.se; f. 1970; 18 a year; food specialities; Editor-in-Chief KATRIN ALSTRÖM; circ. 125,800.

Antik och Auktion: Landskronåvagen 23, 251 85 Helsingborg; tel. (42) 12-35-00; fax (42) 17-37-40; e-mail carin.stentorp@aller.se; internet www.antikochauktion.se; f. 1978; monthly; antiques; Editor CARIN STENTORP; circ. 57,900.

Året Runt: 105 44 Stockholm; tel. (8) 736-52-00; fax (8) 30-49-00; f. 1946; weekly; family; Editor LILLIAN EHRENHOLM-DAUN; circ. 243,500.

Bilsport: POB 529, 371 23 Karlskrona; tel. (455) 33-53-25; fax (455) 186-60; e-mail bilsport@fabas.se; internet www.bilsport.se; f. 1962; fortnightly; motor-sport, cars; Editor-in-Chief FREDRIK SJÖQVIST; circ. 67,300.

Damernas Värld: Sveavägen 53, 105 44 Stockholm; tel. (8) 736-53-00; fax (8) 24-46-46; e-mail martina.bonnier@dv.bonnier.se; internet www.damernasvarld.se; f. 1940; monthly; women's interest; Editor MARTINA BONNIER; circ. 118,800.

Elle: POB 27700, 115 91 Stockholm; Humlegårdsgatan 6, 114 46 Stockholm; tel. (8) 457-80-00; fax (8) 457-80-80; e-mail ellered@hachette.se; internet www.elle.se; f. 1988; monthly; women's interest; Editor HERMINE COYET OHLÉN; circ. 81,900.

Femina Månadens Magasin: Landskronavägen 23, 251 85 Helsingborg; tel. (42) 17-35-00; fax (42) 17-36-82; e-mail femina@aller.se; e-mail femina.se; f. 1981; monthly; women's interest; Editor ULRIKA NORBERG; circ. 118,000.

Frida: Hammarby Kaj 18, 120 30 Stockholm; tel. (8) 587-481-00; fax (8) 587-481-07; e-mail frida@frida.forlag.se; internet www.frida.se; f. 1981; fortnightly; for teenage girls; Editor-in-Chief CAMILLA LORD; circ. 67,000.

Hänt Extra: POB 27704, 115 91 Stockholm; tel. (8) 679-46-00; fax (8) 679-46-77; f. 1986; weekly; family; Editor-in-Chief BENGT GUSTAVSSON; circ. 129,500 (2010).

Hänt i Veckan: POB 27704, 115 91 Stockholm; tel. (8) 679-46-00; fax (8) 679-46-33; f. 1964; weekly; family; Editor-in-Chief STEN HEDMAN; circ. 132,300.

Hemmets Journal: Egmont Tidskrifter AB, 205 07 Malmö; tel. (40) 38-52-00; fax (40) 38-53-98; e-mail red.hj@egmont.se; internet www.hemmetsjournal.se; f. 1920; weekly; family; Editor-in-Chief HÅKAN STRÖM; circ. 202,100 (2010).

Hemmets Veckotidning: Allers Förlag AB, 205 35 Malmö; tel. (40) 38-59-00; fax (40) 38-59-14; f. 1929; weekly; family; Editor ULLA COCKE; circ. 215,300.

Hus & Hem: ICA Förlaget AB, POB 6630, 113 84 Stockholm; tel. (8) 728-23-00; fax (8) 34-56-37; e-mail kundtjanst.husohem@formapg.se; internet www.husohem.se; 12 a year; for house-owners; Editor ANNA LILJEBERG; circ. 86,500 (2010).

ICA Kuriren: Hälsingegt. 49, POB 6630, 113 84 Stockholm; tel. (8) 728-23-00; fax (8) 728-23-50; e-mail red.kuriren@forlaget.ica.se; internet www.icakuriren.se; f. 1942; weekly; home and household; Editor ANN DAHL; circ. 158,100 (2010).

Kalle Anka & Co: 205 08 Malmö; tel. (40) 693-94-00; fax (40) 693-94-95; e-mail webeditor@egmont.se; internet www.kalleanka.se; f. 1948; weekly; comics; Editor TORD JÖNSSON; circ. 65,300 (2010).

Kvällsstunden: Tidningshuset Kvällsstunden AB, Klockartorpsgt. 14, POB 1080, 721 27 Västerås; tel. (21) 19-04-00; fax (21) 13-62-62; e-mail info@tidningshuset.com; internet www.tidningshuset.com; weekly; family magazine; Editor ÅKE LINDBERG; circ. 45,800 (2010).

Må Bra: Tysta Gt. 12, POB 27780, 115 93 Stockholm; tel. (8) 679-46-00; fax (8) 667-34-39; e-mail liselotte.stalberg@mabra.aller.se; internet mabra.com; f. 1978; monthly; health and nutrition; Editor-in-Chief LISELOTTE STÅLBERG; circ. 85,700 (2010).

Privata Affärer: Sveavägen 53, 105 44 Stockholm; tel. (8) 736-53-00; fax (8) 31-25-60; e-mail pren@privataaffarer.se; internet www.privataaffarer.se; f. 1978; monthly; personal money management; Editor-in-Chief PER HAMMARLUND; circ. 59,500 (2010).

Röster i Radio/TV: POB 27704, 115 91 Stockholm; tel. (8) 679-46-00; fax (8) 679-46-33; f. 1934; weekly; family magazine and programme guide to radio and television; Editor-in-Chief EDGAR ANTONSSON; circ. 140,000.

Sköna hem: Sveavägen 53, 105 44 Stockholm; tel. (8) 736-53-00; fax (8) 33-74-11; e-mail skonahem@skh.bonnier.se; internet www.skonahem.com; f. 1979 (*Sköna hem*), 1956 (*Allt i Hemmet*), merged 1992; monthly; interior decoration; Editor-in-Chief CLAES BLOM; circ. 93,400 (2010).

Svensk Damtidning: Humlegårdsgt. 6, POB 27710, 115 91 Stockholm; tel. (8) 679-46-00; fax (8) 679-47-50; e-mail svenskdam@aller.se; internet www.svenskdam.se; f. 1980; weekly; women's interest; Editor-in-Chief KARIN LENMOR; circ. 149,600 (2010).

Tara: Kungsgt. 34, 105 44 Stockholm; tel. (8) 736-52-00; e-mail red@tara.bonnier.se; internet www.tara.se; for middle-aged women; fitness, nutrition, fashion, relationships; Editor-in-Chief ANN FREDLUND.

SWEDEN

Teknikens Värld: Rådmansgt. 49, 105 44 Stockholm; tel. (8) 736-53-00; fax (8) 736-00-11; e-mail ventilen@tv.bonnier.se; internet www.teknikensvarld.se; f. 1948; fortnightly; motoring; Editor-in-Chief DANIEL FRODIN; circ. 43,400 (2010).

Vecko-Revyn: Kungsgt. 34, 105 44 Stockholm; tel. (8) 736-52-00; fax (8) 24-16-02; e-mail ebba@veckorevyn.com; internet veckorevyn.net; f. 1935; weekly; young women's interest; Editor EBBA VON SYDOW; circ. 43,200 (2010).

Vi Bilägare: Ynglingagt. 12, POB 23800, 104 35 Stockholm; tel. (8) 736-12-00; fax (8) 736-12-49; e-mail redaktionen@vibilagare.se; internet www.vibilagare.se; f. 1930; fortnightly; auto and travel; Editor NILS-ERIC FRENDIN; circ. 118,400 (2010).

Vi Föräldrar: Sveavägen 53, 105 44 Stockholm; tel. (8) 736-53-00; fax (8) 34-00-43; e-mail red@vf.bonnier.se; internet www.viforaldrar.se; f. 1968; 14 a year; parents' magazine; Editor-in-Chief ASA RYDGREN (acting); circ. 45,000 (2010).

SPECIALIST PERIODICALS

Aktuellt i Politiken: Sveavägen 68, 105 60 Stockholm; tel. (8) 700-26-00; fax (8) 11-65-42; weekly; social, political and cultural affairs; organ of Social Democratic Labour Party; Editor FREDRIK KORNEBÄCK; circ. 55,000.

Allt om Jakt & Vapen: POB 3263, 103 65 Stockholm; tel. (8) 30-16-30; fax (8) 28-59-74; e-mail jaktochvapen@pressdata.se; internet www.jaktovapen.com; 11 a year; hunting; Editor ERIK WALLIN; circ. 41,500.

Arbetsledaren: POB 12069, 102 22 Stockholm; tel. (8) 652-01-20; fax (8) 653-99-68; f. 1908; 10 a year; journal for foremen and supervisors; Editor INGRID ASKEBERG; circ. 87,400.

Barn: 107 88 Stockholm; tel. (8) 698-90-00; fax (8) 698-90-14; e-mail barn@rb.se; internet www.rb.se/barn; owned by Rädda Barnen (Save the Children Sweden); 6 a year; children's rights; Editor-in-Chief SOFIE ARNÖ; circ. 115,700 (2011).

Båtliv: POB 8097, 371 38 Karlskrona; tel. (445) 297-80; fax (455) 36-97-99; e-mail info@batliv.se; internet www.batliv.se; 5 a year; for boat-owners and boat-club members; Editor LARS-ÅKE REDÉEN; circ. 147,100 (2010).

Byggnadsarbetaren: Hagagt. 2, 106 32 Stockholm; tel. (8) 728-48-00; fax (8) 728-49-80; e-mail redaktionen@byggnadsarbetaren.se; internet www.byggnadsarbetaren.se; f. 1949; 15 a year; construction; Editor KENNETH PETTERSON; circ. 114 900 (2010).

Dina Pengar: Konsument Göteborg, POB 11364, 404 28 Göteborg; tel. (8) 573-650-60; fax (8) 573-651-00; e-mail redaktionen@dinarpengar.se; internet www.di.se; 9 a year; finance; Editor LINUS PAULSSON; circ. 83,000.

Du&jobbet: Långholmsgt. 34, POB 17550, 118 91 Stockholm; tel. (8) 442-46-00; fax (8) 442-46-08; e-mail redaktionen@duochjobbet.se; internet www.duochjobbet.se; f. 1912; monthly; working environment, health, management; Editor-in-Chief EVA BERLIN; circ. 15,400 (2010).

Handelsnytt: POB 1146, 111 81 Stockholm; tel. (8) 412-68-00; fax (8) 21-43-33; e-mail handelsnytt@handels.se; internet www.handelsnytt.se; f. 1906; 11 a year; organ of the Union of Commercial Employees; Editor ANNA FILIPSSON; circ. 147,900 (2010).

Hundsport: POB 20136, 161 02 Bromma; tel. (8) 80-85-65; fax (8) 80-85-95; monthly; for dog-owners; Editor TORSTEN WIDHOLM; circ. 99,700 (2010).

Jaktmarker och Fiskevatten: Västra Torggt. 18, 652 24 Karlstad; tel. (54) 10-03-70; fax (54) 10-09-83; 11 a year; hunting and fishing; circ. 48,100.

Kommunalarbetaren: Hagagt. 2, POB 19034, 104 32 Stockholm; tel. (8) 728-28-00; fax (8) 30-61-42; e-mail kommunalarbetaren@kommunal.se; internet www.ka.se; 22 a year; organ of the Union of Municipal Workers; Editor LIV BECKSTRÖM; circ. 535,500 (2010).

Kyrkans Tidning: Kungsholmstorg 5, POB 22543, 104 22 Stockholm; tel. (8) 462-28-00; fax (8) 644-76-86; e-mail redaktionen@kyrkanstidning.se; internet www.kyrkanstidning.se; f. 1982; weekly; organ of the Church of Sweden; Man. Dir THOMAS GRAHL; Editor ANDERS AHLBERG; circ. 35,700 (2010).

LAND-Familjetidningen: Gävlegt. 22, 113 92 Stockholm; tel. (8) 588-550-10; fax (8) 588-369-59; e-mail land@lrfmedia.lrf.se; internet www.tidningenland.com; f. 1971; weekly; organ of the farmers' asscn; circ. 234,000 (2006).

LAND Lantbruk: Gävlegt. 22, 113 92 Stockholm; tel. (8) 787-51-00; fax (8) 787-55-02; e-mail internetredaktionen@lantbruk.com; internet www.lantbruk.com; f. 1971; weekly; organ of the farmers' asscn; agriculture, forestry; Editor OLLE ERIKSSON; circ. 118,700.

Lärarförbundet: Segelbåtsvägen 15, POB 12229, 102 26 Stockholm; tel. (8) 737-65-00; fax (8) 656-94-15; e-mail sten.svensson@lararforbundet.se; internet www.lararforbundet.se; 22 a year; for teachers; Editor-in-Chief STEN SVENSSON; circ. 225,000.

Directory

Metallarbetaren: Olof Palmesgt. 11, 105 52 Stockholm; tel. (8) 10-68-30; fax (8) 11-13-02; f. 1888; weekly; organ of Swedish Metal Workers' Union; Editor PER AHLSTRÖM; circ. 415,400.

Motor: POB 23142, 104 35 Stockholm; tel. (8) 690-38-00; fax (8) 690-38-22; monthly; cars and motoring; circ. 117,300 (2010).

Motorföraren: Heliosgt. 11, 120 30 Stockholm; tel. (8) 555-765-55; fax (8) 555-765-95; e-mail info@mhf.se; internet www.mhf.se; f. 1927; 8 a year; motoring and tourism; Editor ARNE WINERDAL; circ. 31,400 (2010).

Ny Teknik: Mäster Samuelsgt. 56, 106 12 Stockholm; tel. (8) 796-66-00; fax (8) 613-30-28; e-mail redaktion@nyteknik.se; internet www.nyteknik.se; f. 1967; weekly; technical publication owned by the two largest engineering societies of Sweden; Editor-in-Chief JAN HUSS (acting); circ. 155,50 (2010).

PRO-Pensionären: POB 3274, 103 65 Stockholm; tel. (8) 701-67-00; fax (8) 20-33-58; e-mail info@pro.se; internet www.pro.se; f. 1942; 10 a year; magazine for pensioners; Editor BETTAN ANDERSSON; circ. 303,200 (2010).

SEKO-magasinet: Barnhusgt. 10, POB 1102, 111 81 Stockholm; tel. (8) 791-41-00; fax (8) 21-16-94; f. 1955; 11 a year; organ of the National Union of Services and Communications Employees; Editor-in-Chief JESPER BENGTSSON; circ. 154,700.

SIA-Skogsindustriarbetaren: Olof Palmesgt. 31, POB 1138, 111 81 Stockholm; tel. (8) 470-83-00; fax (8) 20-79-04; e-mail sia@skogstrafacket.org; monthly; forestry; circ. 69,100.

SIF-Tidningen: SIF-huset, Olof Palmesgt. 17, 105 32 Stockholm; tel. (8) 508-970-00; fax (8) 508-970-12; e-mail bjorn.oijer@sif.se; 19 a year; organ of the Union of Clerical and Technical Employees; Editor-in-Chief BJORN OIJER; circ. 331,800.

Skog & Såg: Sag i Syd, POB 37, 551 12 Jönköping; tel. (36) 34-30-00; fax (36) 12-86-10; f. 1966; 4 a year; sawmills and forestry; Editor SVEN MAGNUSSON; circ. 73,800 (2010).

SKTF-Tidningen: POB 7825, 103 97 Stockholm; tel. (8) 789-63-00; fax (8) 789-64-79; e-mail sktftidningen@sktf.se; internet www.sktftidningen.se; 20 a year; organ of the Union of Municipal Employees; Editor KENT KÄLLQVIST; circ. 159,200 (2010).

Sunt Förnuft: 114 95 Stockholm; tel. (8) 613-17-00; fax (8) 21-38-58; 8 a year; taxpayers' magazine; circ. 65,200 (2010).

Svensk Bokhandel (Journal of the Swedish Book Trade): Birkagt. 16C, POB 6888, 113 86 Stockholm; tel. (8) 545-417-70; fax (8) 545-417-75; e-mail redaktion@svb.se; internet www.svb.se; co-publ. by Swedish Publrs' Asscn and Swedish Booksellers' Asscn, for booksellers, publishers, antiquarians and librarians; Editor LASSE WINKLER; circ. 3,300 (2010).

Svensk Golf: POB 84, 182 11 Danderyd; tel. (8) 622-15-00; fax (8) 755-84-39; e-mail info@golf.se; internet www.golf.se; f. 1946; 10 a year; golf; Editor TOBIAS BERGMAN; circ. 315,000 (2010).

Svensk Jakt: Öster Malma, 611 91 Nyköping; tel. (155) 24-62-90; fax (155) 24-62-95; e-mail redaktionen@svenskjakt.se; internet www.jagareforbundet.se/svenskjakt; f. 1862; 11 a year; for hunters and dog breeders; circ. 141,900 (2010).

Sveriges Natur: Åsögt. 115, POB 4625, 116 91 Stockholm; tel. (8) 702-65-00; fax (8) 702-27-02; e-mail sveriges.natur@snf.se; f. 1909; 5 a year; organ of Swedish Society for Nature Conservation; Editor CARL-AXEL FALL; circ. 112,000 (2010).

Tidningen C: POB 2200, 103 15 Stockholm; tel. (8) 617-38-30; fax (8) 617-38-10; e-mail c.redaktionen@centrepartiet.se; f. 1929; 4 a year; organ of the Centre Party; Editor SUSANNE SIGNAHL; circ. 68,000.

Transportarbetaren: POB 714, 101 33 Stockholm; tel. (8) 723-77-00; fax (8) 723-00-76; 11 a year; organ of the Swedish Transport Workers' Union; Editor JAN LINDKVIST; circ. 63,400 (2010).

Turist: 101 20 Stockholm; tel. (8) 463-21-00; 6 a year; tourism and travel; Editor MONIKA TROZELL; circ. 160,700 (2010).

NEWS AGENCIES

Svenska Nyhetsbyrån (Swedish Conservative Press Agency): POB 3553, 103 69 Stockholm; tel. (8) 14-07-50; fax (8) 10-10-48; e-mail red@snb.se; internet www.snb.se; Pres. FREDRIK HAAGE; Editor-in-Chief and Dir PER SELSTAM.

Svensk-Internationella Pressbyrån AB (SIP) (Swedish-International Press Bureau): Stymansgt. 4, 114 54 Stockholm; tel. (8) 528-088-10; fax (8) 528-088-30; e-mail ld@publicitet.com; internet www.publicitet.se; f. 1927; Editor-in-Chief CHRISTER LIEDHOLM.

Tidningarnas Telegrambyrå (TT) (Swedish News Agency): Katarinavägen 15, 105 12 Stockholm; tel. (8) 692-26-00; fax (8) 692-28-55; e-mail redaktionen@tt.se; internet www.tt.se; f. 1921; co-operative news agency, working in conjunction with Reuters, AFP and other agencies; Chair. RAOUL GRÜNTHAL; Gen. Man. and Editor-in-Chief THOMAS PETERSSOHN.

SWEDEN   *Directory*

PRESS ASSOCIATIONS

Pre Cent (Centre Party's Press Agency): POB 2033, 103 11 Stockholm; tel. (8) 786-48-84; fax (8) 24-30-04; e-mail red@precent.se; f. 1987; Editor-in-Chief JIMMY DOMINIUS; 33 mems.

Svenska Journalistförbundet (Swedish Union of Journalists): POB 1116, 111 81 Stockholm; tel. (8) 613-75-00; fax (8) 21-26-80; e-mail kansliet@sjf.se; internet www.sjf.se; f. 1901; Pres. AGNETA LINDBLOM HULTHÉN; 19,000 mems.

Svenska Tidningsutgivareföreningen (Swedish Newspaper Publishers' Asscn): Kungsholmstorg 5, POB 22500, 104 22 Stockholm; tel. (8) 692-46-00; fax (8) 692-46-38; e-mail info@tu.se; internet www.tu.se; f. 1898; Man. DIR PÄR FAGERSTRÖM; 200 mems.

Sveriges Tidskrifter (Swedish Magazine Publishers' Asscn): Vasagt. 50, 111 20 Stockholm; tel. (8) 545-298-90; fax (8) 14-98-65; e-mail info@sverigestidskrifter.se; internet www.sverigestidskrifter.se; f. 1943; Man. DIR LARS STRANDBERG.

Sveriges Vänsterpressförening (Liberal Press Asscn): 901 70 Umeå; tel. (90) 15-10-00; fax (90) 77-46-47; f. 1905; Pres. OLOF KLEBERG; Sec. MATS OLOFSSON; c. 130 mems.

Publishers

Alfabeta Bokförlag AB: Bondegt. 21, POB 4284, 102 66 Stockholm; tel. (8) 714-36-30; fax (8) 643-24-31; e-mail info@alfamedia.se; internet www.alfamedia.se; fiction, psychology, biography, cinema, art, music, travel guides, children's books; Man. DIR DAG HERNRIED.

Bokförlaget Arena: Fersens väg 9, 211 42 Malmö; tel. (40) 10-92-55; fax (40) 10-92-51; e-mail info@arenabok.se; internet www.arenabok.se; f. 1920; non-fiction; Publr JOHANNA EKBERG.

Bokförlaget Atlantis AB: Sturegt. 24, 114 36 Stockholm; tel. (8) 545-660-70; fax (8) 545-660-71; e-mail info@atlantisbok.se; internet www.atlantisbok.se; f. 1977; fiction, non-fiction, art; imprint: Signum; Man. DIR PETER LUTHERSSON.

Berghs Förlag AB: Observatoriegt. 10, POB 45084, 104 30 Stockholm; tel. (8) 31-65-59; fax (8) 32-77-45; e-mail info@berghsforlag.se; internet www.berghsforlag.se; f. 1954; non-fiction for adults and children, picture books and fiction for children, craft books, popular science, New Age literature; Publr LENA ANDERSSON.

Bonnier Carlsen Bokförlag AB: Sveavägen 56, POB 3159, 103 63 Stockholm; tel. (8) 696-89-30; fax (8) 696-89-31; e-mail info@carlsen.bonnier.se; internet www.bonniercarlsen.se; picture books, juvenile books, non-fiction, board books, comics; Man. DIR ANNA BORNÉ MINBERGER.

Bonnierförlagen AB: Sveavägen 56, POB 3159, 103 63 Stockholm; tel. (8) 696-80-00; fax (8) 696-80-46; e-mail info@bok.bonnier.se; internet www.bok.bonnier.se; f. 1837; fiction, non-fiction, encyclopaedias, reference books, quality paperbacks; includes Albert Bonniers Förlag AB, Bonnier Utbildning AB, Bokförlaget Forum AB, Wahlström & Widstrand, Autumn Publishing, Bonnier Audio, Bonnier Carlsen, Bokförlaget Rebus, Bokförlaget Max Ström, Reseförlaget; Chair. JACOB DALBORG.

Bokförlaget Bra Böcker: Ångbåtsbron 1, POB 892, 201 80 Malmö; tel. (40) 665-46-00; internet www.bbb.se; f. 1965; fiction, biography, books in translation; Man. DIR ERIK JOHANSSON.

Brombergs Bokförlag AB: Hantverkargt. 26, POB 12886, 112 98 Stockholm; tel. (8) 562-620-80; fax (8) 562-620-85; e-mail info@brombergs.se; internet www.brombergs.se; literary fiction, non-fiction; Man. DIR DOROTEA BROMBERG.

Brutus Östlings Bokförlag Symposion: Rönneholm 604, 240 36 Stehag; tel. (413) 606-90; fax (413) 109-48; e-mail order@symposion.se; internet www.symposion.se; poetry, drama, non-fiction.

Carlsson Bokförlag AB: Stora Nygt. 31, 111 27 Stockholm; tel. (8) 657-95-00; fax (8) 796-84-57; e-mail info@carlssonbokforlag.se; internet www.carlssonbokforlag.se; art, photography, ethnology, history, politics; Man. DIR TRYGVE CARLSSON.

Bokförlaget DN: POB 703 21, 107 23 Stockholm; tel. (8) 696-87-90; fax (8) 696-83-67; e-mail marknad@forum.se; internet www.bokforlagetdn.se; publishing division of Dagens Nyheter newspaper; Publr and Pres. ALBERT BONNDER.

Bokförlaget T. Fischer & Co: Svartmangt. 18, POB 2036, 103 11 Stockholm; tel. (8) 643-38-46; fax (8) 643-38-98; e-mail bokforlaget@fischer-co.se; internet www.fischer-co.se; non-fiction; owned by Lind & Co.

Forma Publishing Group: Port-Anders-Gt., T3, 721 85 Västerås; tel. (21) 19-40-00; fax (21) 19-41-36; e-mail patrik.widlund@formapg.se; internet www.formapg.se; f. 1945 as ICA Förlaget AB; present name adopted 2004; non-fiction, cookery, handicrafts, gardening, natural history, popular psychology, health, domestic animals, sports; magazine publisher; Chair. CLAES-GÖRAN SYLVÉN; Man. DIR PATRIK WIDLUND.

Forum Publishers: Sveavägen 56, POB 3159, 103 63 Stockholm; tel. (8) 696-84-40; fax (8) 696-83-47; e-mail brittinger.nordstrand@forum.se; internet www.forum.se; f. 1944; general fiction, non-fiction; Man. DIR MAGNUS NYTELL.

Gehrmans Musikförlag AB: POB 42026, 126 12 Stockholm; Västberga allé 5, 126 30 Hägersten; tel. (8) 610-06-00; fax (8) 610-06-27; e-mail info@gehrmans.se; internet www.gehrmans.se; f. 1893; orchestral and choral music; general music publishing; Pres. JOE LINDSTRÖM; CEO GUNNAR HELGESSON.

Hermods AB: Warfvinges väg 33, 112 51 Stockholm; tel. (8) 410-251-00; e-mail keith.fransson@hermods.se; internet www.liberhermods.se; f. 1993; further and higher education; Man. DIR KEITH FRANSSON.

Informationsförlaget: Sveavägen 61, POB 6884, 113 86 Stockholm; tel. (8) 545-560-50; fax (8) 31-39-03; e-mail red@informationsforlaget.se; internet www.informationsforlaget.se; f. 1979; publishers of books for cos and orgs on demand; reference, encyclopaedias, gastronomy, illustrated books; Man. DIR ULF HEIMDAHL.

Liber AB: 113 98 Stockholm; tel. (8) 690-90-00; fax (8) 690-93-36; e-mail export@liber.se; internet www.liber.se; general and educational publishing; owned by Wolters Kluwer NV (Netherlands); Man. DIR JERKER NILSSON.

J. A. Lindblads Bokförlags AB: Warfvingesväg 30, POB 30195, 104 25 Stockholm; tel. (8) 618-78-98; e-mail bertil.wahlstrom@lindblads.se; fiction, non-fiction, juvenile, paperbacks; Man. DIR BERTIL WAHLSTRÖM.

Abraham Lundquist AB Musikförlag: POB 93, 182 11 Danderyd; tel. (8) 732-92-35; fax (8) 732-92-38; e-mail info@abrahamlundquist.se; internet www.abrahamlundquist.se; f. 1838; music; Man. DIR (vacant).

Bokförlaget Natur och Kultur: Karlavägen 31, POB 27323, 102 54 Stockholm; tel. (8) 453-86-00; fax (8) 453-87-90; e-mail info@nok.se; internet www.nok.se; f. 1922; textbooks, general literature, fiction; Man. DIR GUNN JOHANSSON.

Norstedts Förlagsgrupp: Tryckerigt. 4, POB 2052, 103 12 Stockholm; tel. (8) 769-87-00; fax (8) 769-88-64; e-mail www.norstedts.se; internet www.norstedts.se; subsidiaries: Norstedts Förlag, Norstedts Akademiska Förlag, Rabénförlagen; Man. DIR PETER WILCKE.

  Norstedts Förlag AB: Tryckerigt. 4, POB 2052, 103 12 Stockholm; tel. (8) 769-88-50; fax (8) 769-88-64; e-mail info@norstedts.se; internet www.norstedts.se; f. 1823; fiction, non-fiction; imprints: Norstedts, Prisma, Nautiska, Norstedts Pocket and Norstedts Audio; part of Norstedts Förlagsgrupp; Man. DIR PETER WILCKE.

Norstedts Juridik AB: 106 47 Stockholm; tel. (8) 598-191-00; fax (8) 598-191-91; e-mail kundservice@nj.se; internet www.nj.se; f. 1837; owned by Wolters Kluwer NV (Netherlands); fmrly C. E. Fritzes AB; CEO OLOV SUNDSTRÖM.

Bokförlaget Opal AB: Tegelbergsvägen 31, POB 20113, 161 02 Bromma; tel. (8) 28-21-79; fax (8) 29-66-23; e-mail opal@opal.se; internet www.opal.se; f. 1973; Man. DIR BENGT CHRISTELL.

Ordfront Förlag AB: Bellmansgt. 30, POB 17506, 118 91 Stockholm; tel. (8) 462-44-00; fax (8) 462-44-90; e-mail info@ordfront.se; internet www.ordfront.se; fiction, history, politics; Man. DIR JAN-ERIK PETTERSSON.

Prisma Bokförlaget: Tryckerigt. 4, POB 2052, 103 12 Stockholm; tel. (8) 769-87-00; fax (8) 769-89-13; e-mail info@prismabok.se; internet www.prismabok.se; f. 1963; imprint of Nordstedts Bokförlag AB; Dir VIVECA EKELUND.

Rabén & Sjögren: Tryckerigt. 4, POB 2052, 102 12 Stockholm; tel. (8) 769-88-50; fax (8) 769-88-13; e-mail info@eriksson-lindgren.se; internet www.eriksson-lindgren.se; children's; Man. DIR ANN SKÖLD NILSSON.

Rabénförlagen: Tryckerigt. 4, POB 2052, 103 12 Stockholm; tel. (8) 769-88-00; fax (8) 769-88-13; e-mail info@raben.se; internet www.raben.se; f. 1942; general, juvenile; imprints: Rabén & Sjögren, Gammafon, Tiden, Eriksson & Lindgren; part of Norstedts Förlagsgrupp; Dir ERIK LIEDBERG.

Bokförlaget Semic: Esplanaden 3B, POB 1243, 172 25 Sundbyberg; tel. (8) 799-30-50; fax (8) 799-30-64; e-mail info@semic.se; internet www.semic.se; handbooks, calendars, comic magazines, juvenile; Pres. RICKARD EKSTRÖM.

Stenströms Bokförlag AB: Linnégt. 98, POB 24086, 104 50 Stockholm; tel. (8) 663-76-01; fax (8) 663-22-01; f. 1983; Man. DIR BENGT STENSTRÖM.

Reseförlaget: Sveavägen 56, POB 3159, 103 63 Stockholm; tel. (8) 696-80-00; fax (8) 696-80-46; e-mail info@reseforlaget.se; internet www.reseforlaget.se; f. 1990 as Streiffert Förlag AB; acquired by Bonnierförlagen AB and adopted current name 2006; travel guides.

Timbro Förlag/SFN: Kungsgt. 60, POB 3037, 103 61 Stockholm; tel. (8) 587-898-00; fax (8) 667-00-37; e-mail info@timbro.se; internet www.timbro.se; economics, political science; Man. Dir Markus Uvell.

Verbum Förlag AB: St Paulsgt. 2, POB 15169, 104 65 Stockholm; tel. (8) 743-65-00; fax (8) 641-45-85; e-mail info.forlag@verbum.se; internet www.verbum.se; f. 1911; theology, fiction, juvenile, music; imprints: Verbum and Nordia; Man. Dir Claes-Göran Gunnarsson.

Wahlström & Widstrand: Sveavägen 58, POB 3159, 103 63 Stockholm; tel. (8) 696-84-80; fax (8) 696-83-80; e-mail info@wwd.se; internet www.wwd.se; f. 1884; fiction, non-fiction, biography, history, science, paperbacks; owned by Bonnierförlagen AB; Man. Dir Kerstin Angelin.

PUBLISHERS' ASSOCIATIONS

Föreningen Svenska Läromedel (Swedish Asscn of Educational Publishers): Vegagt. 14, 113 29 Stockholm; tel. (8) 588-314-00; fax (8) 736-19-44; e-mail info@svenskalaromedel.se; internet svenskalaromedel.se; f. 1973; Chair. Jerker Nilsson; Dir Rickard Vinde; 11 mems.

Svenska Förläggareföreningen (Swedish Publishers' Asscn): Drottninggt. 97, 113 60 Stockholm; tel. (8) 736-19-40; fax (8) 736-19-44; e-mail info@forlaggare.se; internet www.forlaggare.se; f. 1843; Chair. Eva Bonnier; Man. Dir Kristina Ahlinder; 60 mems.

Broadcasting and Communications

TELECOMMUNICATIONS

Regulatory Authority

Post- och Telestyrelsen (PTS) (Post and Telecom Agency): Valhallavägen 117, POB 5398, 102 49 Stockholm; tel. (8) 678-55-00; fax (8) 678-55-05; e-mail pts@pts.se; internet www.pts.se; Dir-Gen. Göran Marby.

Major Service Providers

Hi3G Access AB: Lindhagensgt. 98, POB 30213, 104 25 Stockholm; tel. (7) 633-333-33; fax (7) 633-372-00; e-mail info@tre.se; internet www.tre.se; f. 2003; mobile communications; 60% shares owned by Hutchison Whampoa Ltd (Hong Kong), 40% owned by Investor AB (Sweden); CEO Peder Ramel.

Tele 2 AB: Skeppsbron 18, POB 2094, 103 13 Stockholm; tel. (85) 562-000-60; fax (85) 562-000-40; e-mail press.relations@tele2.com; internet www.tele2.com; f. 1993; Pres. and CEO Mats Granryd.

Telefonaktiebolaget LM Ericsson: Torshamngt. 23, 164 83 Stockholm; tel. (8) 719-00-00; fax (8) 719-19-76; e-mail investor.relations.se@ericsson.com; internet www.ericsson.com; parent co of the Ericsson group; mobile and fixed network provider; represented in 140 countries; Chair. Michael Treschow; CEO Carl-Hans Vestberg.

Telenor Sverige AB: Campus Gräsvik 12, 371 80 Karlskrona; tel. (4) 553-310-00; fax (4) 553-312-22; internet www.telenor.se; fmrly Vodafone Sverige AB; provides mobile cellular communications under brand name Djuice, as well as broadband internet access and digital television services; acquired by Telenor AS (Norway) in 2005; Man. Dir Lars-Åke Norling.

TeliaSonera AB: Stureplan 8, 106 63 Stockholm; tel. (8) 504-550-00; fax (8) 504-550-01; e-mail teliasonera@teliasonera.se; internet www.teliasonera.se; f. by merger of Telia AB (Sweden) with Sonera Ltd (Finland); 37.3% owned by Govt of Sweden, 13.7% by Govt of Finland; Chair. Anders Narvinger; Pres. and CEO Lars Nyberg.

Teracom AB: Esplanaden 3c, POB 1366, 172 27 Sundbyberg; tel. (8) 555-420-00; fax (8) 555-420-01; e-mail webmaster@teracom.se; internet www.teracom.se; provides digital television and radio services, fixed-line telephony and broadband internet access; Pres. Stephan Guiance; Dir Crister Fritzson.

BROADCASTING

Until the end of 1992 public service radio and television were organized within the state broadcasting corporation, Sveriges Radio AB, a public service organization financed by licence fees; this operated two national television channels and three national radio channels, together with 24 local radio stations. On 1 January 1993 the state corporation was replaced by three companies, Sveriges Radio AB, Sveriges Television AB, and Sveriges Utbildningsradio AB, responsible for radio, television, and educational radio and television, respectively. The operations of these companies are regulated by law and by agreements with the Government. From 1 January 1994 the three companies came into the ownership of three foundations.

Radio

There are four public service radio channels, as well as neighbourhood radio stations and private local radio stations (financed by advertising).

IBRA Radio AB: Regulatorvägen 11, 141 99 Stockholm; tel. (8) 608-96-00; fax (8) 608-96-50; e-mail info@ibra.se; internet www.ibra.se; non-commercial private Christian co broadcasting to all continents; Pres. Jack-Tommy Ardenfors; Dir Lars Anderås.

Sveriges Radio AB (SR): Oxenstiernsgt. 20, 105 10 Stockholm; tel. (8) 784-50-00; fax (8) 784-15-00; e-mail lyssnarservice@sr.se; internet sverigesradio.se; f. 1993; independent co responsible for national radio broadcasting; Man. Dir Mats Svegfors.

Sveriges Utbildningsradio AB: Tulegt. 7, 113 95 Stockholm; tel. (8) 784-40-00; fax (8) 784-43-91; e-mail kundtjanst@ur.se; internet www.ur.se; f. 1978; public service co responsible for educational broadcasting on radio and television; CEO Erik Fichteliu.

Television

There are two public service television channels (SVT 1 and SVT 2). The broadcasts are financed by licence fees. In 1991 the Government awarded the licence for a third terrestrial nation-wide television channel to TV 4 (which is financed by advertising). Television channels transmitted by satellite and cable, and directed at the Swedish audience, include: TV 3, Kanal 5, TV 6, Kanal 9, Z-TV, and the film channels TV 1000, FilmMax, Filmnet Plus and Filmnet Movie.

Kanal 5: Rådmansgt. 42, 114 99 Stockholm; tel. (8) 520-555-55; fax (8) 612-05-95; e-mail info@kanal5.se; internet kanal5.se; commercial satellite channel; owned by ProSiebenSat1 (Germany); Dir-Gen. Jonas Sjögren.

Sveriges Television AB (SVT): Oxenstiernsgt. 26-34, 105 10 Stockholm; tel. (8) 784-00-00; fax (8) 784-15-00; e-mail eva.hamilton@svt.se; internet www.svt.se; f. 1956; independent; operates 7 channels: SVT1, SVT2, SVT24, SVT Barnkanalen, Kunskapskanalen, SVT Europa and SVT HD; CEO Eva Hamilton.

Sveriges Utbildningsradio AB: see Radio.

TV 3: Stockholm; tel. (8) 562-023-00; fax (8) 562-023-30; e-mail info@tv3.se; internet www.tv3.se; commercial satellite channel.

TV 4: Tegeluddsvägen 3, 115 79 Stockholm; tel. (8) 459-40-00; fax (8) 459-44-44; internet www.tv4.se; commercial terrestrial channel; Man. Dir Jan Scherman.

Finance

(cap. = capital; res = reserves; dep. = deposits; m. = million; brs = branches; amounts in kronor unless otherwise stated)

SUPERVISORY BODY

Finansinspektionen (Financial Supervisory Authority): Brunnsgt. 3, POB 7821, 103 97 Stockholm; tel. (8) 787-80-00; fax (8) 24-13-35; e-mail finansinspektionen@fi.se; internet www.fi.se; f. 1991 by merger of Bankinspektionen (Bank Inspection Board, f. 1907) and Försäkringsinspektionen (Private Insurance Supervisory Service, f. 1904), for the supervision of commercial and savings banks, financial companies, insurance companies, insurance brokers, friendly societies, mortgage institutions, securities firms and unit trusts, the stock exchange and clearing functions, the securities registry centre and the information registry centre; Chair. Bengt Westerberg; Dir-Gen. Martin Andersson.

BANKING

At the end of 2007 there were 126 banks in Sweden, comprising 28 commercial banks, 31 foreign banks, 65 savings banks and two co-operative banks.

Central Bank

Sveriges Riksbank: Brunkebergstorg 11, 103 37 Stockholm; tel. (8) 787-00-00; fax (8) 21-05-31; e-mail registratorn@riksbank.se; internet www.riksbank.se; f. 1668; bank of issue; led by an executive board of 6 members (including a Governor), appointed by a General Council of 11 members, all of whom are, in turn, appointed by the Riksdag; cap. 1,000m., res 63,025m., dep. 455,999m. (Dec. 2009); Chair., Gen. Council Johan Gernandt; Gov. Stefan Ingves; 2 brs.

Commercial Banks

Danske Bank i Sverige: Norrmalmstorg 1, POB 7523, 103 92 Stockholm; tel. (8) 524-800-00; e-mail danskebank@danskebank.com; internet www.danskebank.se; f. 1837 as Östgöta Enskilda Bank; subsidiary of Den Danske Bank (Denmark); Chair. Peter Straarup; Pres. and CEO Ulf Lundahl; 30 brs.

SWEDEN

Nordea Bank AB: Smålandsgt. 17, 105 71 Stockholm; tel. (8) 614-70-00; fax (8) 20-08-46; internet www.nordea.com; f. 1974 as Post- och Kreditbanken; present name adopted 2001; part of Nordea Group; 19.9% owned by Swedish Govt; cap. €5,102m., res –€518m., dep. €444,034m. (Dec. 2009); Chair. Hans Dalborg; Pres. and CEO Christian Clausen; 252 brs in Sweden.

Skandinaviska Enskilda Banken AB (SEB): Kungsträdgårdsgt. 8, 106 40 Stockholm; tel. (8) 771-62-10-00; fax (8) 763-83-89; internet www.seb.se; f. 1972; cap. 21,942m., res 33,811m., dep. 1,903,573m. (Dec. 2009); Chair. Marcus Wallenberg; Pres. and Group CEO Annika Falkengren; 260 brs.

Svenska Handelsbanken AB: Kungsträdgårdsgt. 2, 106 70 Stockholm; tel. (8) 701-10-00; fax (8) 701-24-37; e-mail info@handelsbanken.se; internet www.handelsbanken.se; f. 1871 as A. B. Stockholms Handelsbank; present name adopted 1956; cap. 2,899m., res m., dep. 1,929,464m. (Dec. 2009); Chair. Hans Larsson; Pres. and CEO Pär Boman; 459 brs in Sweden.

Swedbank AB: Brunkebergstorg 8, 105 34 Stockholm; tel. (8) 585-900-00; fax (8) 796-80-92; internet www.swedbank.se; f. 1997 by merger of Föreningsbanken and Sparbanken Sverige; present name adopted 2006; cap. 14,918m., res 6,489m., dep. 1,096,414m. (Dec. 2008); Chair. Lars Idermark; Pres. and CEO Michael Wolf; 470 brs in Sweden.

Banking Organization

Svenska Bankföreningen (Swedish Bankers' Asscn): Regeringsgt. 38, POB 7603, 103 94 Stockholm; tel. (8) 453-44-00; fax (8) 796-93-95; e-mail info@bankforeningen.se; internet www.bankforeningen.se; f. 1880; Pres. Jan Lidén; Man. Dir Pär Boman; 29 mems.

STOCK EXCHANGE

NASDAQ OMX Nordic Exchange Stockholm: Tullvaktsvägen 15, 105 78 Stockholm; tel. (8) 405-60-00; fax (8) 405-60-01; internet www.nasdaqomx.com; f. 1863 under govt charter; automated trading system introduced by 1990; Stockholmsbörsen merged with OMX AB in 1998; acquired by NASDAQ Stock Market, Inc (USA) in 2008; part of OMX Nordic Exchange with the Copenhagen (Denmark), Helsinki (Finland) and Reykjavík (Iceland) exchanges; Group CEO Robert Greifeld.

INSURANCE

The assets of Swedish insurance companies at the end of 2010 totalled 2,950,000m. kronor.

Principal Insurance Companies

Folksam: Bohusgt. 14, 106 60 Stockholm; tel. (8) 772-60-00; fax (8) 702-99-22; e-mail info@floksam.se; internet www.folksam.se; f. 1908; all branches of life and non-life insurance; Pres. and CEO Anders Sundström.

Skandia Insurance Co Ltd: Sveavägen 44, 103 50 Stockholm; tel. (8) 788-10-00; fax (8) 788-30-80; e-mail contact@oldmutual.com; internet www.skandia.com; f. 1855; owned by Old Mutual PLC (United Kingdom); all branches of life insurance; Chair. Lars Otterbeck; Pres. and CEO Julian Roberts.

Trygg-Hansa: Flemminggt. 18, 106 26 Stockholm; tel. (8) 243-10-00; fax (8) 650-93-67; internet www.trygghansa.se; f. 1828; all branches of non-life insurance; owned by Codan Forsikring A/S (Denmark); CEO Rickard Gustafson.

Insurance Associations

Konsumernternas försäkringsbyrå (Swedish Consumers' Insurance Bureau): Karlavägen 108, POB 24215, 104 51 Stockholm; tel. (8) 22-58-00; fax (8) 24-88-91; e-mail angela.olsson@konsumernternas.se; internet www.konsumernternasforsakringsbyra.se; f. 1979; provides free advice to consumers on various insurance matters; principles are the Konsumentverket (Swedish Consumer Agency), the Finansinpektionen (Financial Supervisory Authority) and the Sveriges Försäkringsförbund (Swedish Insurance Fed.); Chair. Gunnar Olsson.

Svenska Försäkringsföreningen (Swedish Insurance Society): Karlavägen 108, 6th Floor, POB 24213, 104 51 Stockholm; tel. (8) 522-789-00; fax (8) 522-789-95; e-mail info@forsakringsforeningen.se; internet www.forsakringsforeningen.se; f. 1875; promotes sound development of the Swedish insurance business; Chair. Lars Rosén; Sec. Sara Råsmar.

Sveriges Försäkringsförbund (Swedish Insurance Federation): Karlavägen 108, POB 24043, 104 50 Stockholm; tel. (8) 522-785-00; fax (8) 522-785-15; e-mail info@forsakringsforbundet.com; internet www.forsakringsforbundet.com; Chair. Torbjörn Magnusson; Man. Dir Christina Lindenius.

Directory

Trade and Industry

GOVERNMENT AGENCIES

Arbetsförmedlingen (Public Employment Service): Hälsingegt. 38, 113 99, Stockholm; tel. (8) 508-801-00; fax (8) 586-064-99; e-mail registrator@arbetsformedlingen.se; internet www.arbetsformedlingen.se; f. 2008 to replace Arbetsmarknadsverket and Arbetsmarknadsstyrelsen; central agency, responsible for administration of Sweden's labour market; main aims: to match those seeking employment to suitable vacancies, to encourage those outside the labour market to seek employment, and to maintain a high level of employment within the labour market; managed by a board appointed by Govt; Chair. Thomas Franzén; Dir-Gen. Angeles Bermudez-Svankvist.

Exportrådet (Swedish Trade Council): World Trade Center, Klarabergsviadukten 70, POB 240, 101 24 Stockholm; tel. (8) 588-660-00; fax (8) 588-661-90; e-mail info@swedishtrade.se; internet www.swedishtrade.se; f. 1972; Chair. Bo Dankis; Man. Dir Ulf Berg.

Tillväxtverket (Swedish Agency for Economic and Regional Growth): Götgt. 74, 106 21 Stockholm; tel. (8) 681-91-00; fax (8) 19-68-26; e-mail tillvaxtverket@tillvaxtverket.se; internet www.tillvaxtverket.se; Dir-Gen. Christina Lugnet.

CHAMBERS OF COMMERCE

Handelskammaren Jönköpings Län: Elmiavägen 11, 554 54 Jönköping; tel. (36) 30-14-30; fax (36) 12-95-79; e-mail info@jonkoping.cci.se; internet www.jonkoping.cci.se; f. 1975; Pres. Johan Svedberg; Man. Dir Göran Kinnander; 400 mems.

Handelskammaren Mälardalen: Drottninggt. 26, POB 8044, 700 08 Örebro; tel. (19) 16-61-60; fax (19) 11-77-50; e-mail info@handelskammarenmalardalen.se; internet www.handelskammaren malardalen.se; f. 1907; Pres. Christer Henebäck; Man. Dir Merit Israelsson.

Handelskammaren Mittsverige (Mid-Sweden Chamber of Commerce): Kyrkogt. 26, 852 32 Sundsvall; tel. (60) 17-18-80; fax (60) 61-86-40; e-mail info@midchamber.se; internet www.midchamber.se; f. 1913; Chair. Rolf Johannesson; Man. Dir Dick Jansson; 350 mems.

Handelskammaren Värmland: Södra Kyrkogt. 6, 652 24 Karlstad; tel. (54) 22-14-80; fax (54) 22-14-90; e-mail info@handelskammarenvarmland.se; internet www.handelskammarenvarmland.se; f. 1912; Pres. Helene Rinstad; Sec. Ulf Ljungdahl; 1,200 mems.

Mellansvenska Handelskammaren: POB 296, 801 04 Gävle; tel. (26) 66-20-80; fax (26) 66-20-99; e-mail chamber@mhk.cci.se; internet www.mhk.cci.se; f. 1907; Pres. Ove Anonsen; Man. Dir Anders Franck; 465 mems.

Norrbottens Handelskammare: Kyrkogt. 13, 972 38 Luleå; tel. (920) 45-56-60; fax (920) 45-56-66; internet www.north.cci.se; f. 1904; Chair. Hans Eriksson; Man. Dir Andreas Lind.

Östsvenska Handelskammaren: Nya Rådstugugt. 3, 602 24 Norrköping; tel. (11) 28-50-30; fax (11) 13-77-19; e-mail info@east.cci.se; internet www.east.cci.se; f. 1913; covers Östergötland, Södermanland and Gotland; c. 600 mem. cos; Chair. Ann Krumlinde; Man. Dir Jonas Sjöbom.

Stockholms Handelskammare: Västra Trädgårdsgt. 9, POB 16050, 103 21 Stockholm; tel. (8) 555-100-00; fax (8) 566-316-20; e-mail info@chamber.se; internet www.chamber.se; f. 1902; Pres. Jens Spendrup; Vice-Pres. Peter Wallenberg, Jr.

Sydsvenska Industri- och Handelskammaren: Skeppsbron 2, 211 20 Malmö; tel. (40) 690-24-00; fax (40) 690-24-90; e-mail info@handelskammaren.com; internet www.handelskammaren.com; f. 1905; Pres. Lars Frithiof; Man. Dir Stephan Müchler; 2,500 mems.

Västsvenska Industri- och Handelskammaren: Mässans Gt. 18, POB 5253, 402 25 Göteborg; tel. (31) 83-59-00; fax (31) 83-59-36; e-mail info@handelskammaren.net; internet www.handelskammaren.net; f. 1661; Chair. Finn Johnsson; Man. Dir Anders Källström; c. 2,600 mems.

INDUSTRIAL AND TRADE ASSOCIATIONS

Svenskt Näringsliv (Confederation of Swedish Enterprise): Storgt. 19, 114 82 Stockholm; tel. (8) 553-430-00; fax (8) 553-430-99; e-mail info@svensktnaringsliv.se; internet www.svensktnaringsliv.se; f. 2001 by merger of Sveriges Industriförbund (f. 1910) and Svenska Arbetsgivareföreningen (f. 1902); central org. representing Swedish business and industry; Pres. Signhild Arnegård Hansen; Dir-Gen. Urban Bäckström; consists of 50 mem. asscns, representing c. 60,000 cos.

Företagarna (Federation of Private Enterprises): Regeringsgt. 52, 106 67 Stockholm; tel. (8) 406-17-00; fax (8) 24-55-26; e-mail info@

SWEDEN

Directory

foretagarna.se; internet www.foretagarna.se; f. 1990; Chair. JAN CARLZON; Man. Dir ANNA-STINA NORDMARK NILSSON; 55,000 mems.

Grafiska Företagens Förbund (Graphic Companies' Federation): Karlavägen 108, POB 24184, 104 51 Stockholm; tel. (8) 762-68-00; fax (8) 611-08-28; e-mail info@grafiska.se; internet www.grafiska.se; Chair. GÖRAN GUSTAFSSON; Man. Dir LARS JOSEFSSON.

Jernkontoret (Steel Producers' Assen): Kungsträdgårdsgt. 10, POB 1721, 111 87 Stockholm; tel. (8) 679-17-00; fax (8) 611-20-89; e-mail office@jernkontoret.se; internet www.jernkontoret.se; f. 1747; Chair. OLOF FAXANDER; Man. Dir ELISABETH NILSSON.

Lantbrukarnas Riksförbund (LRF) (Federation of Swedish Farmers): Franzéngt. 6, 105 33 Stockholm; tel. (0) 771-573-573; e-mail info@lrf.se; internet www.lrf.se; Chair. LARS-GÖRAN PETTERSSON; Man. Dir ANDERS KÄLLSTRÖM; 167,743 mems.

Plast- & Kemiföretagen (Swedish Plastics and Chemicals Assen): Storgt. 19, POB 5501, 114 85 Stockholm; tel. (8) 783-86-00; fax (8) 663-63-23; e-mail info@plastkemiforetagen.se; internet www.plastkemiforetagen.se; f. 2003 by merger of the Assen of Swedish Chemical Industries and the Plastics and Chemicals Fed.; Pres. JAN SVÄRD; Man. Dir MAGNUS HUSS; c. 230 mems.

Skogsindustrierna (Swedish Forest Industries' Federation): POB 55525, 102 04 Stockholm; tel. (8) 762-72-60; fax (8) 611-71-22; e-mail terese.sundberg@skogsindustrierna.org; internet www.forestindustries.se; Chair. MAGNUS HALL; Dir-Gen. MARIE S. ARWIDSON.

SveMin (Föreningen för gruvor, mineral- och metallproducenter i Sverige) (Swedish Assen of Mines, Mineral and Metal Producers): Kungsträdgårdsgt. 10, POB 1721, 111 87 Stockholm; tel. (8) 762-67-55; fax (8) 678-02-10; e-mail info@svemin.se; internet www.svemin.se; f. 2004; Pres. LENNART EVRELL; Man. Dir BENGT HULDT; 40 mem. cos.

Svensk Handel (Swedish Federation of Trade): Regeringsgt. 60, 103 29 Stockholm; tel. (10) 471-85-00; fax (10) 471-86-65; e-mail info@svenskhandel.se; internet www.svenskhandel.se; Chair. CHRISTIAN W. JANSSON; Man. Dir DAG KLACKENBERG; 13,000 mems.

Svensk Industriförening (Swedish Industry Assen): Klara Norra Kyrkogt. 31, POB 22307, 104 22 Stockholm; tel. (8) 440-11-70; fax (8) 440-11-71; e-mail info@sinf.se; internet www.sinf.se; f. 1941; Man. Dir ANDERS EKDAHL; 1,500 mems.

TEKO (Textile and Clothing Industries' Assen): Storgt. 5, POB 5510, 114 85 Stockholm; tel. (8) 762-68-80; fax (8) 762-68-87; e-mail teko@teko.se; internet www.teko.se; f. 1907; Chair. SVEN GATENHEIM; Man. Dirs OLA TOFTEGAARD; 263 mems.

EMPLOYERS' ORGANIZATIONS

Almega: Sturegat. 11, POB 55545, 102 04 Stockholm; tel. (8) 762-69-00; fax (8) 762-69-48; e-mail almega.epost@almega.se; internet www.almega.se; f. 1921; 7 mem. asscns: Swedish IT and Telecom Industries, Almega Samhall Employers' Assen, Almega Service Asscns, Almega Service Employers' Assen, Media and Information Employers' Assen, Assen of Private Care Providers, Swedish Assen of Staff Agencies; Chair. HÅKAN BRYNGELSON; Dir-Gen. JONAS MILTON; 10,000 mems.

Byggnadsämnesförbundet (Building Material Manufacturers Employers): Kungsträdgårdsgt. 10, POB 1721, 111 87 Stockholm; tel. (8) 762-65-35; fax (8) 762-65-12; e-mail info@baf.se; internet www.baf.se; Chair. JOHAN SKOGLUND; Man. Dir LARS DICANDER; c. 200 mem. cos.

Elektriska Installatörsorganisationen EIO (The Swedish Electrical Contractors' Association): Rosenlundsgt. 40, POB 17537, 118 91 Stockholm; tel. (8) 762-75-00; fax (8) 668-86-17; e-mail info@eio.se; internet www.eio.se; Chair. THOMAS CARLSSON; Man. Dir JAN SIEZING; 2,600 mem. cos.

Försäkringsbranschens Arbetsgivareorganisation (Insurance Employers): Karlavägen 108, 6th Floor, POB 24168, 104 51 Stockholm; tel. (8) 522-786-00; fax (8) 522-786-70; e-mail info@fao.se; internet www.fao.se; Chair. TORBJÖRN MAGNUSSON; Man. Dir CHRISTINA LINDENIUS; 145 mem. cos.

Livsmedelsföretagen (Li) (Food Industry): Storgt. 19, POB 55680, 102 15 Stockholm; tel. (8) 762-65-00; fax (8) 762-65-12; e-mail info@li.se; internet www.li.se; f. 2001 by merger of Livsmedelsbranschens Arbetsgivareförbund and Livsmedelsindustriena; Chair. PER STENSTRÖM; Man. Dir AGNETA DREBER; c. 900 mems.

Maskinentreprenörerna (Earth-moving Contractors): Storgt. 19, POB 1609, 111 86 Stockholm; tel. (8) 762-70-65; fax (8) 611-85-41; e-mail kaisa.makiranta@me.se; internet www.maskinentreprenorerna.se; Man. Dir HAMPE MOBÄRG; c. 3,600 mem. cos.

Plåtslageriernas Riksförbund (Platers): Årstaängsvägen 19C, POB 17536, 118 91 Stockholm; tel. (8) 762-75-85; fax (8) 616-00-72; e-mail info@plr.se; internet www.plr.se; Chair. PER ANDERSSON; Man. Dir THOMAS DAHLBERG; 900 mem. cos.

Stål och Metall Arbetsgivareförbundet (Steel and Metal Industry Employers): Kungsträdgårdsgt. 10, POB 1721, 111 87 Stockholm; tel. (8) 762-67-35; fax (8) 611-62-64; e-mail info@metallgruppen.se; internet www.stalometall.se; f. 1906; Pres. PETER GOSSAS; Man. Dir BENGT HULDT; 200 mems with 44,000 employees.

SVEMEK (Welding Engineering): POB 1721, 111 87 Stockholm; tel. (8) 762-67-35; fax (8) 611-62-64; e-mail info@metallgruppen.se; internet www.svemek.se; fmrly Svets Mekaniska Arbetsgivareförbundet; Pres. PER LINDE; Man. Dir BENGT HULDT; 414 mems with 4,629 employees.

Sveriges Bageriförbund (Bakery and Confectionery Employers): Storgt. 19, POB 55680, 102 15 Stockholm; tel. (8) 762-60-00; fax (8) 678-66-64; e-mail martin@bageri.se; internet www.bageri.se; f. 1900; Chair. STEFAN FRITZDORF; Man. Dir MARTIN LUNDELL; 530 mems.

Sveriges Byggindustrier (Swedish Construction Federation): Storgt. 19, POB 5054, 102 42 Stockholm; tel. (8) 698-58-00; fax (8) 698-59-00; e-mail info@bygg.org; internet www.bygg.org; Chair. LEIF STRIDH; Man. Dir BO ANTONI; c. 3,000 mem. cos.

Teknikföretagen (Assen of Swedish Engineering Industries): Storgt. 5, POB 5510, 114 85 Stockholm; tel. (8) 782-08-00; fax (8) 782-09-00; e-mail info@teknikforetagen.se; internet www.teknikforetagen.se; f. 1896 as VI Sveriges Verkstadsindustrier; Pres. LEIF ÖSTLING; Man. Dir ANDERS NARVINGER; 3,400 mem. cos.

TransportGruppen (Transport Industry): Storgt. 19, POB 5384, 102 49 Stockholm; tel. (8) 762-71-00; fax (8) 611-46-99; e-mail info@transportgruppen.se; internet www.transportgruppen.se; 8 mem. asscns: Swedish Road Transport Employers' Assen, Swedish Bus and Coach Employers' Assen, Swedish Air Transport Industry Employers' Assen, Swedish Motor Trade Employers' Assen, Employers' Assen of the Swedish Petroleum Industry, Swedish Shipowners Employers' Assen, Assen Ports of Sweden, Swedish International Freight Assen; Chair. PER OLOF JANSSON; Dir PETER JEPPSSON.

Trä- och Möbelindustriförbundet (Swedish Wood Products Industry Employers' Assen): Storgt. 19, POB 55525, 103 21 Stockholm; tel. (8) 762-72-50; fax (8) 762-72-24; e-mail info@tmf.se; internet www.tmf.se; Chair. ULF ADOLFSSON; Man. Dir LEIF G. GUSTAFSSON; 800 mem. cos.

VVS Företagen (Heating, Plumbing, Refrigeration and Insulation Employers): Årstaängsvägen 19C, POB 47160, 100 74 Stockholm; tel. (8) 762-73-00; fax (8) 669-41-19; e-mail info@vvsforetagen.se; internet www.vvsforetagen.se; f. 1918; Chair. ÖSTEN LINDGREN; Man. Dir ROINE KRISTIANSON; c. 1,400 mems.

UTILITIES

Regulatory Authority

Energimyndigheten (Swedish Energy Agency): Kungsgt. 43, POB 310, 631 04 Eskilstuna; tel. (16) 544-20-00; fax (16) 544-20-99; e-mail registrator@energimyndigheten.se; internet www.energimyndigheten.se; f. 1998; monitors and advises electricity and natural gas cos, also undertakes research into renewable energy; Dir-Gen. TOMAS KÅBERGER.

Electricity and Gas

E.ON Sverige AB: Carl Gustafs väg 1, 205 09 Malmö; tel. (40) 25-50-00; e-mail info@eon.se; internet www.eon.se; f. 2001; frmly Sydkraft AB; part of E.ON Group (Germany); generation, distribution and supply of electricity and natural gas; Pres. and CEO HÅKAN BUSKHE.

Fortum AB: Hangövägen 19, 115 77 Stockholm; tel. (8) 671-70-00; fax (8) 671-77-77; e-mail res.koncernkommunikationsverige@fortum.com; internet www.fortum.se; f. 1998 by merger of Imatran Voima and Neste Oyj (both Finland); mem. of Fortum Corpn (Finland), international energy co with core businesses in gas, power and heat; electricity production, distribution and supply; Chair. MATTI LEHTI; Dir-Gen. MIKAEL LILIUS.

Göteborg Energi AB: POB 53, 401 20 Gothenberg; tel. (31) 62-60-00; fax (31) 15-25-01; internet www.goteborgenergi.se; distribution of electricity and natural gas; co-owns electricity supplier Plusenergi with Vattenfall; Man. Dir ANDERS HEDENSTEDT.

Lunds Energi AB: Råbyvägen 37, POB 25, 221 00 Lund; tel. (46) 35-60-00; fax (46) 18-92-62; e-mail kundservice@lundsenergi.se; internet www.lundsenergi.se; f. 1907; distribution, supply of electricity and natural gas; subsidiaries incl.: Billinge Energi AB, Kraftringen Service AB, KREAB Energi AB, Nynäshamn Energi; Man. Dir JAN SAMUELSSON.

Öresundskraft AB: Västra Sandgt. 4, POB 642, 251 06 Helsingborg; tel. (42) 490-30-00; fax (42) 490-30-60; e-mail info@oresundskraft.se; internet www.oresundskraft.se; f. 1859; distribution and supply of electricity and natural gas; Man. Dir ANDERS ÖSTLUND.

Umeå Energi AB: Storgt. 34, POB 224, 901 05 Umeå; tel. (90) 16-00-00; fax (90) 16-00-10; e-mail umea.energi@umeaenergi.se; internet

SWEDEN

Directory

www.umeaenergi.se; production, distribution and supply of electricity; Man. Dir KURT ÅSTRÖM.

Vattenfall AB: 162 87 Stockholm; tel. (8) 739-50-00; fax (8) 739-51-29; e-mail info@vattenfall.se; internet www.vattenfall.se; f. 1909; became limited liability co in 1992; state-owned; power generation and distribution; co-owns electricity supplier Plusenergi with Göteborg Energi AB; some 90 directly or indirectly owned operational subsidiaries; interests in Denmark, Finland, Germany and Poland; Pres. and CEO ØYSTEIN LØSETH.

Water

Responsibility for water supply lies with the municipalities. Since the 1990s many municipalities have formed limited companies under public ownership to manage water supply, such as the supplier for the capital (Stockholm Vatten AB). Several municipalities have contracted private companies to manage water supply.

TRADE UNIONS
Principal Federations

Landsorganisationen i Sverige (LO) (Swedish Trade Union Confederation): Barnhusgt. 18, 105 53 Stockholm; tel. (8) 796-25-00; fax (8) 796-28-00; e-mail mailbox@lo.se; internet www.lo.se; f. 1898; affiliated to ITUC; Pres. WANJA LUNDBY-WEDIN; 14 affiliated unions, with a total membership of 1.7m. (October 2009).

Sveriges Akademikers Centralorganisation (SACO) (Swedish Confederation of Professional Asscns): Lilla Nygt. 14, POB 2206, 103 15 Stockholm; tel. (8) 613-48-00; fax (8) 24-77-01; e-mail kansli@saco.se; internet www.saco.se; f. 1947; affiliated to ITUC and ETUC; Chair. ANNA EKSTRÖM; 24 affiliated unions and professional orgs, 604,000 mems (Dec. 2009).

Tjänstemännens Centralorganisation (TCO) (Confederation of Professional Employees): Linnégt. 14, 114 94 Stockholm; tel. (8) 782-91-00; fax (8) 663-75-20; e-mail info@tco.se; internet www.tco.se; f. 1944; affiliated to ITUC, European Trade Union Confed. and Council of Nordic Trade Unions; Pres. STURE NORDH; 15 affiliated unions with total membership of 1.2m.

Principal Unions

Fackförbundet ST (Civil Servants): Sturegt. 15, POB 5308, 102 47 Stockholm; tel. (8) 790-51-00; fax (8) 24-29-24; e-mail st@st.org; internet www.st.org; f. 1904; fmrly Statstjänstemannaförbundet; affiliated to TCO; Pres. ANNETTE CARNHEDE; 93,000 mems.

Fastighetsanställdas Förbund (Building Maintenance Workers): Upplandsgt. 4, 2nd Floor, POB 70446, 107 25 Stockholm; tel. (8) 696-11-50; fax (8) 24-46-90; e-mail info.fk@fastighets.se; internet www.fastighets.se; f. 1936; affiliated to LO; Pres. HANS ÖHLUND; 39,243 mems (Dec. 2005).

Finansförbundet (Bank Employees): Olof Palmesgt. 17, POB 720, 101 34 Stockholm; tel. (8) 614-03-00; fax (8) 611-38-98; e-mail info@finansforbundet.se; internet www.finansforbundet.se; affiliated to TCO; Pres. LILLEMOR SMEDENVALL; 375 mem. cos.

GS, Facket för Skogs-, Trä- och Grafisk bransch (Forestry, Woodworking and Graphic Workers): Olof Palmesgt 31, 5th Floor POB 1152, 111 81 Stockholm; tel. (10) 470-83-00; fax (8) 20-79-04; e-mail kontakt@gsfacket.se; internet www.gsfacket.se; f. 2009 by merger of Grafiska Fackförbundet—Mediafacket and Skogs- och Träfacket; affiliated to LO; Pres. PER-OLOF SJÖÖ; 65,000 mems (June 2009).

Handelsanställdas Förbund (Commercial Employees): Upplandsgt. 5, POB 1146, 111 81 Stockholm; tel. (8) 412-68-00; fax (8) 10-00-62; e-mail handels@handels.se; internet www.handels.se; f. 1906; affiliated to LO; Pres. LARS-ANDERS HÄGGSTRÖM; 150,000 mems.

Hotell- och Restaurang Facket (Hotel and Restaurant Workers): Olof Palmesgt. 31, 3rd Floor, POB 1143, 111 81 Stockholm; tel. (0) 771-57-58-59; fax (8) 411-71-18; e-mail medlem@hrf.net; internet www.hrf.net; f. 1918; affiliated to LO; Pres. ELLA NIIA; 60,000 mems (Dec. 2005).

IF Metall: Olof Palmesgt. 11, 105 52 Stockholm; tel. (8) 786-80-00; fax (8) 240-86-74; e-mail postbox.fk@ifmetall.se; internet www.ifmetall.se; f. 2006 by merger of Industrifacket and Svenska Metallindustriarbetareförbundet; affiliated to LO; Pres. STEFAN LÖFVEN; c. 370,000 mems.

Jusek: Nybrogt. 30, POB 5167, 102 44 Stockholm; tel. (8) 665-29-00; fax (8) 662-79-23; e-mail vaxel@jusek.se; internet www.jusek.se; affiliated to SACO; asscn of graduates in law, business administration and economics, computer and systems science, personnel management and social science; Pres. GÖRAN ARRIUS; 65,000 mems.

Kommunal—Svenska Kommunalarbetareförbundet (Swedish Municipal Workers' Union): Liljeholmsvägen 32, POB 19039, 104 32 Stockholm; tel. (10) 442-70-00; fax (8) 31-87-45; e-mail kommunal.forbundet@kommunal.se; internet www.kommunal.se; affiliated to LO; Pres. YLVA THÖRN; 573,600 mems.

Lärarförbundet (Teachers): Segelbåtsvägen 15, POB 12229, 102 26 Stockholm; tel. (8) 737-65-00; fax (8) 656-94-15; e-mail kansli@lararforbundet.se; internet www.lararforbundet.se; affiliated to TCO; Pres. EVA-LIS SIRÉN; 225,000 mems.

Lärarnas riksförbund (National Union of Teachers in Sweden): Sveavägen 50, POB 3529, 103 69 Stockholm; tel. (8) 613-27-00; fax (8) 21-91-36; e-mail lr@lr.se; internet www.lr.se; f. 1884; affiliated to SACO; Pres. METTA FJELKNER; 80,000 mems.

Ledarna—Sveriges chefsorganisation (Professional and Managerial Staff): St Eriksgt. 26, POB 12069, 102 22 Stockholm; tel. (8) 598-990-00; fax (8) 598-990-10; e-mail ledarna@ledarna.se; internet www.ledarna.se; f. 1905; affiliated to TCO; Pres. ANNIKA ELIAS; 70,000 mems.

SEKO—Facket för Service och Kommunikation (Services and Communications Employees): Barnhusgt. 6, POB 1105, 111 81 Stockholm; tel. (8) 791-41-00; fax (8) 21-89-53; e-mail seko@seko.se; internet www.seko.se; f. 1970; present name since 1995; affiliated to LO; Pres. JANNE RUDÉN; c. 131,986 mems.

SKTF (Local Government Officers): Kungsgt. 28A, POB 7825, 103 97 Stockholm; tel. (771) 44-00-00; fax (8) 789-64-81; e-mail sktfdirekt@sktf.se; internet www.sktf.se; fmrly Sveriges Kommunaltjänstemannaförbund; affiliated to TCO; Pres. EVA NORDMARK; 160,000 mems.

Svenska Byggnadsarbetareförbundet (Byggnads) (Building Workers): Liljeholmsvägen 32, 106 32 Stockholm; tel. (8) 728-48-00; fax (8) 34-50-51; e-mail forbundet@byggnads.se; internet www.byggnads.se; affiliated to LO; Pres. HANS TILLY; 118,000 mems.

Svenska Elektrikerförbundet (Electricians): Upplandsgt. 14, 1st Floor, POB 1123, 111 81 Stockholm; tel. (8) 412-82-82; fax (8) 412-82-01; e-mail postbox.fk@sef.com; internet www.sef.com; f. 1906; affiliated to LO; Pres. JONAS WALLIN; 26,000 mems.

Svenska Livsmedelsarbetareförbundet (Food Workers): Upplandsgt. 3, POB 1156, 111 81 Stockholm; tel. (8) 769-29-00; fax (8) 796-29-03; e-mail info@livs.se; internet www.livs.se; f. 1896; affiliated to LO; Pres. HANS-OLOF NILSSON; 48,285 mems (Dec. 2005).

Svenska Målareförbundet (Painters): Olof Palmesgt. 31, POB 1113, 111 81 Stockholm; tel. (8) 587-274-00; fax (8) 587-274-99; e-mail post@malareforbundet.se; internet www.malareforbundet.se; f. 1887; affiliated to LO; Chair. LARS-ÅKE LUNDIN; 15,900 mems.

Svenska Musikerförbundet (Musicians): Alströmergt. 25B, POB 49144, 101 29 Stockholm; tel. (8) 587-060-00; fax (8) 16-80-20; e-mail info@musikerforbundet.se; internet www.musikerforbundet.se; f. 1907; affiliated to LO; Pres. JAN GRANVIK.

Svenska Pappersindustriarbetareförbundet (Swedish Paperworkers' Union): Olof Palmesgt. 11, 5th Floor, POB 1127, 111 81 Stockholm; tel. (8) 796-61-00; fax (8) 411-41-79; e-mail info@pappers.se; internet www.pappers.se; f. 1920; affiliated to LO; Pres. JAN-HENRIK SANDBERG; 22,665 mems (2006).

Svenska Transportarbetareförbundet (Transport Workers): Olof Palmesgt. 29, 6th Floor, POB 714, 101 33 Stockholm; tel. (10) 480-30-00; fax (8) 24-03-91; e-mail transport.fk@transport.se; internet www.transport.se; f. 1897; affiliated to LO; Chair. LARS LINDGREN; c. 73,000 mems.

Sveriges Ingenjörer (Swedish Asscn of Graduate Engineers): Malmskillnadsgt. 48, POB 1419, 111 84 Stockholm; tel. (8) 613-80-00; fax (8) 796-71-02; e-mail info@sverigesingenjorer.se; internet www.sverigesingenjorer.se; affiliated to SACO; Pres. ULF BENGTSSON; 120,000 mems.

Unionen (Clerical and Technical Employees): Olof Palmesgt. 17, 105 32 Stockholm; tel. (8) 508-970-00; fax (8) 508-970-01; e-mail kontakt@unionen.se; internet www.unionen.se; f. 2008 by merger of HTF and Sif; affiliated to TCO; Pres. CECILIA FAHLBERG; 500,000 mems.

Vårdförbundet (Swedish Asscn of Health Professionals): Adolf Fredriks Kyrkgt. 11, POB 3260, 103 65 Stockholm; tel. (8) 14-77-00; fax (8) 411-42-29; e-mail info@vardforbundet.se; internet www.vardforbundet.se; fmrly Svenska Hälso- och Sjukvårdens Tjänstemannaförbund; affiliated to TCO; Pres. ANNA-KARIN EKLUND; 110,000 mems.

Transport

RAILWAYS

In mid-2007 there were 11,904 km of standard- and narrow-gauge railways, of which 9,683 km of track was electrified. A new railway line extending 190 km, connecting Nyland and Umeå on the northeastern coast of Sweden, entered into service in August 2010.

SJ AB (Statens Järnvägar): 105 50 Stockholm; tel. (10) 751-50-00; fax (10) 751-54-24; e-mail sjinfo@sj.se; internet www.sj.se; f. 1856;

state-owned; runs passenger traffic on all state-owned railway track; Chair. ULF ADELSOHN; CEO JAN FORSBERG.

Banverket: Jussi Björlings väg 2, 781 85 Borlänge; tel. (243) 44-50-00; e-mail banverket@banverket.se; internet www.banverket.se; primarily govt funded; manages Sweden's state-owned railway infrastructure; Dir-Gen. MINOO AKHTARZAND.

Malmö-Limhamns Järnvägs AB: POB 30022, 200 61 Limhamn; tel. (40) 36-15-04; fax (40) 15-86-24; 5 km of 1,435-mm gauge; Dir UWE JÖHNSON; Traffic Man. K. HOLMBERG.

TGOJ Trafik AB: Gredbyvägen 3–5, 632 21 Eskilstuna; tel. (16) 17-26-61; fax (16) 17-26-66; e-mail info@tgojtrafik.se; internet www.tgojtrafik.se; f. 1877; 300 km of 1,435-mm gauge electrified railways; Chair. JAN SUNDLING; Pres. BENGT FORS.

ROADS

At 31 December 2008 there were an estimated 574,741 km of roads, of which 1,806 km were motorways, 15,325 km were main or national roads and 83,131 km of secondary or regional roads. In 2000 a road-rail link between Malmö and Copenhagen (Denmark), across the 16-km Öresund strait, was opened.

SHIPPING

The principal ports in terms of cargo handled are Göteborg (Gothenberg), Brofjorden, Trelleborg, Luleå and Malmö. Stockholm is also an important port. At 31 December 2009 the Swedish merchant fleet numbered 538 vessels, with a combined displacement of 4.0m. grt.

Principal Shipping Companies

Broström Ship Management AB: POB 39, 471 21 Skärhamn; tel. (304) 67-67-00; fax (304) 67-11-10; e-mail info@brostrom.se; internet www.brostrom.se; 97.3% owned by Maersk Product Tankers AB; management co, operating specialized tanker services; Man. Dir LENART SIMONSSON.

Broström Tankers AB: 403 30 Göteborg; tel. (31) 61-60-00; fax (31) 61-60-12; e-mail brotank@brostrom.se; internet www.brostrom.se; f. 1990; specializes in transporting petroleum products, in north-west Europe and world-wide; Man. Dir TORE ANGERVALL.

Rederi AB Transatlantic: Södra Hamnen 27, POB 32, 471 21 Skärhamn; tel. (304) 67-47-00; fax (304) 67-47-70; e-mail info@rebt.se; internet www.rabt.se; f. 2005 by merger of B&N Nordsjöfrakt AB (f. 1972) and Gorthon Lines AB (f. 1915); freight shipping, forwarding, storage, agency, ice-breaking; Man. Dir CARL-JOHAN HAGMAN.

Stena AB: Masthuggskajen, 405 19 Göteborg; tel. (31) 85-50-00; fax (31) 12-06-51; e-mail info@stenaline.com; internet www.stena.com; f. 1939; parent co of Stena Line, Stena Bulk, Stena RoRo, Stena Teknik, Concordia Maritime and Northern Marine Management; CEO DAN STEN OLSSON.

Wallenius Lines AB: Swedenborgsgt. 19, POB 17086, 104 62 Stockholm; tel. (8) 772-05-00; fax (8) 640-68-54; e-mail info@walleniuslines.com; internet www.walleniuslines.com; f. 1934; car and truck carriers; Pres. LONE FØNSS SCHRØDER.

Associations

Föreningen Sveriges Sjöfart och Sjöförsvar (Swedish Maritime League): Kastellet, Kastellholmen, 111 49 Stockholm; tel. (8) 611-74-81; fax (8) 611-74-76; e-mail fsss@algonet.se; f. 1983 by merger of Swedish General Shipping Asscn and Swedish Navy League; Pres. CLAES TORNBERG; Gen. Sec. STEN GÖTHBERG; 2,000 mems.

Sveriges Redareförening (Swedish Shipowners' Asscn): Södra Hamntg. 53, POB 330, 401 25 Göteborg; tel. (31) 62-95-25; fax (31) 15-23-13; e-mail srf@sweship.se; internet www.sweship.se; f. 1906; Pres. LARS HØGLAND; Man. Dir HÅKAN FRIDBERG.

CIVIL AVIATION

The main international airport is at Arlanda, 42 km from Stockholm. Gothenburg (Göteborg) and Malmö are also served by international airports. There are regular flights between the main cities in Sweden. Many domestic flights operate from Bromma (Stockholm's city airport).

Luftfartsstyrelsen (Swedish Civil Aviation Authority): Vikboplan 7, 601 73 Norrköping; tel. (11) 415-20-00; e-mail luftfartsstyrelsen@luftfartsstyrelsen.se; internet www.luftfartsstyrelsen.se; f. 1923 as Luftfartsverket; present name adopted 2005; state body; central govt authority for matters concerning civil aviation; Dir-Gen. NILS GUNNAR BILLINGER.

Scandinavian Airlines System (SAS): Frösundavik Allé 1, Solna, 195 87 Stockholm; tel. (8) 797-00-00; fax (8) 797-15-15; internet www.sas.se; f. 1946; the national carrier of Denmark, Norway and Sweden. It is a consortium owned two-sevenths by SAS Danmark A/S, two-sevenths by SAS Norge ASA and three-sevenths by SAS Sverige AB. Each parent org. is a limited co owned 50% by Govt and 50% by private shareholders. The SAS group includes the consortium and the subsidiaries in which the consortium has a majority or otherwise controlling interest; the Board consists of two members from each of the parent cos and the chairmanship rotates among the three national chairmen on an annual basis. SAS absorbed Linjeflyg AB (domestic passenger, newspaper and postal services in Sweden) in 1993; strategic alliance with Lufthansa (Germany) formed in 1995; Chair. FRITZ H. SCHUR; Pres. and CEO RICKARD GUSTAFSON.

Transwede Airways AB: POB 2011, 438 11 Landvetter; tel. (31) 94-79-80; fax (31) 94-79-90; e-mail trygve.gjertsen@transwede.com; internet www.transwede.se; f. 1985 as Aerocenter Trafikflyg AB; current name adopted 1986; relaunched 2005; operates charter passenger services within Scandinavia; CEO TRYGVE GJERTSEN.

West Air Sweden: Prästgårdsgt. 1, POB 5433, 402 29 Göteborg; tel. (31) 703-04-50; fax (31) 703-04-55; e-mail info@westair.se; internet www.westair.se; f. 1963; present name adopted 1993; Pres. GUSTAF THUREBORN.

Tourism

Sweden offers a variety of landscape, from the mountains of the 'Midnight Sun', north of the Arctic Circle, to the white sandy beaches of the south. There are many lakes, waterfalls and forests, and Stockholm is famed for its beautiful situation and modern architecture. Most tourists come from the other Scandinavian countries, Germany and the United Kingdom. In 2008 tourism arrivals totalled 12.5m. and receipts an estimated US $14,399m.

Svenska Turistföreningen (Swedish Touring Club): Ameralitetsbacken 1, POB 25, 101 20 Stockholm; tel. (8) 463-21-00; fax (8) 678-19-58; e-mail info@stfturist.se; internet www.stfturist.se; f. 1885; 300,000 mems; owns and operates mountain hotels and youth hostels; co-ordinates nature and cultural activities in local clubs; Pres. TORGNY HÅSTAD; Sec.-Gen. YVONNE ARENTOFT.

Turistdelegationen: POB 4044, 102 61 Stockholm; tel. (8) 681-90-00; e-mail nutek@nutek.se; internet www.nutek.se/turistnaringen; f. 1995; Swedish Tourist Authority became part of Nutek, the Swedish Agency for Economic and Regional Growth, in January 2006; state-owned; promotes enterprise and entrepreneurship in the tourist industry in Sweden and produces and disseminates tourism information; Dir DENNIS BEDEROFF.

Defence

As assessed at November 2010, Sweden maintained total armed forces of 14,525, compared with 53,100 in 1999. The army consisted of 7,332 men, of whom 2,167 were conscripts; the navy 3,423 men, including 1,083 conscripts; and the air force 3,770 men, including 711 conscripts. There were also 6,454 staff. In addition, there were voluntary defence reservists totalling 200,000, compared with 570,000 in 1999. Compulsory military service was abolished from July 2010. In November 2004 the European Union (EU) ministers responsible for defence agreed to create a number of 'battlegroups' (each comprising about 1,500 men), which could be deployed at short notice to crisis areas around the world. The EU battlegroups, two of which were to be ready for deployment at any one time, following a rotational schedule, reached full operational capacity from 1 January 2007. Sweden contributed 2,300 troops to the Nordic battlegroup of 2,800 troops, with smaller contingents from Finland, Norway, Ireland and Estonia, and was also committed to being the sole contributor to a Swedish battlegroup.

Defence Expenditure: forecast at 43,319m. kronor in 2010.

Supreme Commander of the Swedish Armed Forces: Gen. SVERKER GÖRANSON.

Education

The Swedish National Agency for Education *Skolverket* is one of main central authorities responsible for education at pre-school, comprehensive, upper secondary and municipal adult levels. Non-compulsory pre-primary education is provided by the municipalities to children between one and five years of age. Basic education, which is compulsory, extends for nine years, starting at the age of six or seven years, and is received at the comprehensive school (*grundskola*). At the end of this period a pupil may enter the integrated upper secondary school (*gymnasieskola*). Courses at upper secondary schools last three years, and are organized into 17 nationally defined study programmes of which 14 are vocational. All publicly funded schools follow a national curriculum. However, most schools are operated by municipal authorities, which have some autonomy over the profile of each school. In addition, parents have the right to send their children to independent schools, which are publicly funded and must share the same objectives as municipally run schools, but may differ in character and methods. Enrolment at pre-primary level included 94.8% of children in the relevant age-group in 2005/06. Enrolment at primary schools in 2007/08 included 95.0% of children in the relevant age-group, while the comparable ratio for secondary enrolment in that year was 99%.

Higher education is administered by the Swedish National Agency for Higher Education *Högskoleverket*. There were 64 higher education institutions in Sweden in 2007/08, consisting of universities and university colleges as well as independent colleges. Slightly more than 30% of young people in Sweden proceed to higher education within five years of completing their upper secondary schooling.

The budget for 2009 allocated 48,756. kronor (5.6% of total expenditure) to education and university research.

SWITZERLAND

Introductory Survey

LOCATION, CLIMATE, LANGUAGE, RELIGION, FLAG, CAPITAL

The Swiss Confederation lies in central Europe, bounded to the north by Germany, to the east by Austria and Liechtenstein, to the south by Italy and to the west by France. The climate is generally temperate, but varies considerably with altitude and aspect. In Zürich the average temperature ranges from −1°C (30°F) in winter to 16°C (61°F) in summer. There are four national languages: German, French, Italian and Romansh (Rumantsch), spoken by 72.5%, 21.0%, 4.3% and 0.6% of resident Swiss nationals, respectively, in 2000. Other languages are spoken by the remaining 1.6% of the population. Including resident aliens, the linguistic proportions in 2000 were: German 63.7%, French 20.4%, Italian 6.5%, Romansh 0.5% and other languages 9.0%. Most Swiss citizens profess Christianity: in 2000 42.7% were Protestants and 41.2% Roman Catholics. Of the total resident population in 2000, 35.3% were Protestants and 41.8% Roman Catholics. The Federal flag, which is square, consists of a white upright cross in the centre of a red ground. The capital is Bern (Berne).

CONTEMPORARY POLITICAL HISTORY

Historical Context

Switzerland, whose foundation is traditionally dated to 1291, has occupied its present area since its borders were fixed by treaty in 1815. At the same time, it was internationally recognized as a neutral country. Despite the strategic importance of Switzerland, its 'permanent neutrality' has never since been violated. The country has not entered any military alliances, and it avoided participation in both World Wars. The federal system of government dates back to 1848. Executive authority is exercised on a collegial basis by the Federal Council (cabinet), with a President who serves, for only one year at a time, as 'the first among equals'. Owing to the restricted powers of the Federal Council, initiatives and referendums form the core of the political process. Switzerland is a confederation of 26 cantons. In 1979 the mainly French-speaking region of Jura seceded from the predominantly German-speaking canton of Bern, becoming the first new canton to be established since 1815.

Despite the fact that Switzerland has long been the headquarters of many international organizations, the country did not join the UN until 2002, owing to concerns that it would conflict with the country's traditional neutrality. Switzerland was a founder member of the European Free Trade Association (EFTA, see p. 447) in 1960 and joined the Council of Europe (see p. 250) in 1963.

Domestic Political Affairs

The enfranchisement of women in federal elections was approved at a referendum in February 1971. However, the cantons of Appenzell Ausserrhoden and Appenzell Innerrhoden introduced female suffrage only in 1989 and 1990, respectively. In October 1984 the Federal Assembly elected Switzerland's first female cabinet minister, Dr Elisabeth Kopp of the Radical Democratic Party, who became Head of the Federal Department of Justice and Police. In December 1988 the Assembly elected Kopp to be Vice-President of the Swiss Confederation for 1989, concurrently with her other duties in the Federal Council. In the same month, however, she announced her resignation from her post as Head of the Federal Department of Justice and Police, following allegations that she had violated regulations concerning official secrecy. In February 1989, following an investigation of the case, Kopp was replaced as Vice-President; in February 1990, however, she was acquitted by the Federal Supreme Court.

The commission that had investigated the allegations against Kopp during 1989 subsequently revealed that the office of the Federal Public Prosecutor held about 900,000 secret files on some 200,000 Swiss citizens and foreigners. In March 1990 riots ensued when around 30,000 people demonstrated in Bern in protest at the existence of such files. The Government subsequently announced that it would commission a report on the activities of the security services and introduce new laws regulating state security; it also opened most of the files to public scrutiny. Published in June 1993, the report found that security service observation had been largely restricted to left-wing groups since 1945 and that security service personnel had at times behaved in an unprofessional manner.

In November 1989 64.4% of voters in a referendum rejected a proposal to abolish the armed forces by 2000. Following the referendum, which had been instigated by the Group for Switzerland Without an Army (an alliance of socialist, pacifist, youth and ecological organizations), the Federal Military (Defence) Department established a working party to examine proposals for reforms in the armed forces; consequently, the strength of the armed forces was considerably reduced during the early 1990s.

Meanwhile, in 1986 the Government introduced legislation that aimed to restrict the number of refugees who were to be granted political asylum in Switzerland. However, the new legislation was criticized by socialist, religious and humanitarian groups, and in April 1987 a national referendum on the issue was held. Of the 41.8% of the electorate who voted at the referendum, a substantial majority was in favour of the new restrictions. In March 1994, in an attempt to control increasing drugs-related crime (following allegations that immigrants trading in illicit drugs were exploiting the asylum laws to avoid extradition), the Government approved legislation restricting the rights of asylum seekers and immigrants, which included provisions for their arrest and detention without trial for failure to possess the requisite identification documents; further stringent measures against foreigners suspected of trafficking in illegal drugs were approved by national referendum in December. Civil rights groups accused the Government of yielding to popular xenophobic sentiment in an effort to divert attention from its failure to overcome the drugs problem.

The rise of the Swiss People's Party

The elections to the National Council and the Council of States held in October 1999 were characterized by the strong performance of the Swiss People's Party, which, in terms of votes gained, became the country's largest party. In the National Council the Swiss People's Party overtook both the Radical Democratic Party and the Christian Democratic People's Party to become the second largest party after the Social Democratic Party. Seats in the National Council are allotted in proportion to votes gained. However, the complex, 'cantonal' nature of the electoral system ensured ultimate victory for the Social Democratic Party. In the Council of States, the Swiss People's Party obtained seven seats, thereby becoming the third largest party (after the Radical Democrats and the Christian Democrats).

In the early years of the 21st century the stability of the 'grand coalition' that had governed Switzerland since 1959 was increasingly threatened by the growing influence of the Swiss People's Party. Under the so-called 'magic formula' traditionally used to determine the distribution of government seats among the coalition partners, the Social Democratic Party, the Radical Democratic Party and the Christian Democratic People's Party each received two seats and the Swiss People's Party received only one. However, at the general election in October 2003 the Swiss People's Party received the largest share of the votes cast and thus for the first time became the largest party in the National Council, with 55 seats. The party demanded a second seat on the Federal Council to reflect this (to be taken by Christoph Blocher), and threatened to withdraw from the coalition, effectively ending the era of consensus politics, if its demand was not met. Traditionally, Swiss ministers were reappointed at each election, and kept their seats until such time as they resigned. However, when the Federal Assembly elected the Federal Council in December, Blocher contested the seat held by Ruth Metzler of the Christian Democratic People's Party, and, after three ballots, won with a majority of just five votes. This was the first ministerial deselection for 130 years, and the first time the composition of the governing coalition had been changed in 44 years. When the new Federal Council took office on 1 January 2004, Blocher became Head of the Federal Department of Justice and Police, which carried with it responsibility not only for policy

SWITZERLAND

on immigration and asylum but also for negotiating with the European Union (EU, see p. 270) on Swiss membership of the Schengen Agreement (which binds signatories to the abolition of border controls) and the Dublin Convention on Asylum (relating to common formal arrangements on asylum).

In June 2004 the National Council approved a two-tier immigration policy whereby priority was to be given to EU and EFTA nationals, with immigration otherwise restricted to only highly skilled workers in the agricultural, construction, health and tourism sectors. At a national referendum held in September, a government plan to ease citizenship procedures for Swiss-born second-generation immigrants was opposed by 56.8% of those who participated, while a plan to grant automatic citizenship to third-generation immigrants was rejected by 51.6%. At a national referendum in September 2006, 67.8% of the valid votes cast were in favour of a proposal, supported by the Swiss People's Party, further to curtail the rights of asylum seekers and foreign migrants to Switzerland. Under the proposals, refugees would be required to present valid identification documents to the authorities within two days of their arrival in Switzerland and the issuance of work permits to non-skilled individuals from non-EU and -EFTA countries would effectively be ended.

Recent developments: events following the 2007 general election

Campaigning for the general election in October 2007 was characterized by the increased polarization of the electorate. In September controversy arose following accusations of racism against the Swiss People's Party by a UN official in Switzerland, which followed that party's use of images deemed to be xenophobic in its campaign posters. In early October the campaign was marred by violent clashes in the capital, Bern, between police and left-wing activists who had attempted to disrupt a rally held by the Swiss People's Party. At the election, which was held on 21 October, the Swiss People's Party strengthened its position as the largest party, winning 62 seats in the National Council. The Social Democratic Party performed poorly, taking just 43 seats, while the Radical Democratic Party and the Christian Democratic People's Party won 31 seats apiece. The Green Party increased its representation, winning 20 seats.

Opposition to the Swiss People's Party centred increasingly on Blocher. Many Federal Assembly members opposed Blocher's re-election to the Federal Council, in particular the Green Party, which announced its intention to propose its own candidate. However, prior to the vote, which took place in December 2007, the Green Party withdrew its candidate in favour of a moderate member of the Swiss People's Party, Eveline Widmer-Schlumpf, who eventually defeated Blocher. In defiance of the party leadership, Widmer-Schlumpf announced that she would accept a role in the Federal Council. The Swiss People's Party subsequently withdrew its support for the Government.

Following Blocher's deselection, both Widmer-Schlumpf and the Head of the Federal Department of Defence, Civil Protection and Sports, Samuel Schmid, were excluded from the party's parliamentary group, on the grounds that their moderate views conflicted with those of the majority of the party's supporters. In March 2008 the party leadership initiated measures to expel Widmer-Schlumpf. When the executive of the Graubünden cantonal organization—of which Widmer-Schlumpf was a leading figure—refused to revoke her membership of the party, it was replaced by a committee of more right-wing members. The attempt by the Swiss People's Party to impose discipline upon its regional organizations prompted the secession, in June, of executives in other traditionally moderate cantonal sections, notably Bern, where dissident members formed a new party, the Conservative Democratic Party. The former Swiss People's Party executives in Glarus and Graubünden subsequently formed parties under the same name in their respective cantons. The new parties immediately gained representation in the Federal Council, as Widmer-Schlumpf and Schmid were among the leading members. The Conservative Democratic Party was formally inaugurated as a national party at a special conference held in Glarus in November 2008; Hans Grunder was elected as party President.

In November 2008 Schmid announced his intention to resign from the Federal Council. (He had been subject to media criticism since mid-2008, following an incident at a military training camp in which six soldiers died, and the resignation of the head of the armed forces in July, following allegations of personal misconduct.) At the election for Schmid's successor in December, the list of candidates included three members of the Swiss People's Party, notably Blocher and the head of the Zürich cantonal organization, Ueli Maurer; Maurer was elected to the role. Following his election, Maurer confirmed his commitment to bipartisan government, although the President of the Swiss People's Party, Toni Brunner, called for the party to receive a second cabinet seat. The Radical Democratic Party and the Liberal Party of Switzerland merged as FDP.The Liberals in January 2009; Fulvio Pelli, previously the leader of the Radical Democratic Party, became President of the new formation. In June Pascal Couchepin, Head of the Federal Department of Home Affairs, announced his retirement from the Federal Council. In September Didier Burkhalter (who, like Couchepin, was a French-speaking member of FDP.The Liberals) was elected to succeed him.

In early 2009 the Swiss Government was subject to intense pressure from several countries, including France, Germany and the USA, over its continued reluctance to implement changes to the country's laws on banking secrecy. In February the Federal Council appointed a committee of financial and legal experts to recommend measures designed to uphold banking secrecy. In March, however, the cabinet approved proposals to relax the legislation to permit the sharing of information on accounts held in Swiss banks with investigators in certain individual cases where allegations of tax evasion could be proven. Nevertheless, the Government insisted that it continued to endorse the principle of banking secrecy and that the reform would affect a very small number of cases. In April the Organisation for Economic Co-operation Development (OECD, see p. 376) notably included Switzerland in a so-called 'grey' list of states that had adopted OECD standards on exchanging tax information but had not yet substantially implemented them. Switzerland secured its removal from this list in September, however, after signing a 12th bilateral agreement on the exchange of tax information. Meanwhile, in August, in the most significant case of its kind to date, an agreement was reached whereby Switzerland's largest bank, UBS, was to accede within 12 months to a US request for information concerning 4,450 accounts held by US citizens who were suspected of tax evasion. After the Federal Administrative Court ruled in January 2010 that the release of confidential banking data to US investigators was illegal, the Swiss Government was forced to seek parliamentary approval of the agreement, which was narrowly secured in June.

In a referendum held in November 2009, 57.5% of voters approved an initiative proposed by the Swiss People's Party to ban the construction of minarets in Switzerland. The party had once again been subject to accusations of racism in its campaign in favour of the initiative, which it maintained was intended to halt what it claimed was the increasing Islamization of the country and to uphold Swiss democratic values. (It was reported, however, that of the approximately 200 mosques in Switzerland just four had a minaret, and that, in practice, planning consent for new minarets was rarely granted.) The Government—which, together with the other principal political parties, had opposed the initiative—announced that it would abide by the decision of the electorate, but declared that freedom of religion in Switzerland was not compromised by the new legislation and that it would seek to ease tensions with Muslim countries and organizations engendered by the referendum.

Moritz Leuenberger, the Head of the Federal Department of the Environment, Transport, Communications and Energy, announced his resignation from the Federal Council in July 2010, as did Hans-Rudolf Merz, the Head of the Federal Department of Finance, in August. Critics of Merz had accused him of weakening banking secrecy and of being slow to respond to the dispute with the US authorities over allegations of tax evasion by US clients of UBS. Simonetta Sommaruga, of the Social Democratic Party, and Johann Schneider-Ammann, of FDP.The Liberals, were elected to the Federal Council in September, replacing party colleagues Leuenberger and Merz, respectively. The second-placed candidate in both votes was Jean-François Rime of the Swiss People's Party. Sommaruga's election produced a female majority in the cabinet for the first time. A reorganization of the Federal Council was announced a few days later and took effect at the beginning of November. Schneider-Ammann became Head of the Federal Department of Economic Affairs and Sommaruga Head of the Federal Department of Justice and Police, while their predecessors in these posts, Doris Leuthard and Widmer-Schlumpf, assumed responsibility for the Federal Department of the Environment, Transport, Communications and Energy and the Federal Department of Finance, respectively. In December Micheline Calmy-Rey, the Head of the

Federal Department of Foreign Affairs, was elected President of the Confederation for 2011.

An initiative proposed by the Swiss People's Party on the mandatory deportation of foreigners convicted of serious crimes (ranging from murder to social security fraud) was approved by 52.3% of voters in a referendum in November 2010. A less extreme counter-proposal submitted by the Federal Assembly, amid concerns that automatic expulsion would violate Switzerland's commitments under international law, was rejected by 52.6% of voters.

'Nazi Gold'

In September 1995 the Swiss Bankers' Association (SBA) announced the introduction of measures that would enable relatives to trace and recover the assets deposited in Swiss bank accounts by victims of the Nazi massacre of Jews in the Second World War. To assist in this process an accord was signed in May 1996 by the SBA and the World Jewish Congress establishing an Independent Committee of Eminent Persons (ICEP), which was to be responsible for auditing all dormant Swiss bank accounts. In September documents were released from British and US archives, claiming that gold valued at several thousand million dollars, at current prices, had been deposited in Swiss banks during the Second World War. Much of it was suspected to have belonged to Jews killed in the Holocaust. The Swiss Federal Assembly subsequently approved legislation establishing an independent panel to investigate the ownership of these assets, and legislation ordering banks to release all records that might pertain to dealings with the Nazi regime in Germany or its victims. In December the Federal Government appointed an international commission to conduct a broad historical investigation of Switzerland's role as a financial centre during the Second World War.

Meanwhile, the issue of 'Nazi gold' had received much coverage in the international press. Jewish organizations threatened to boycott Swiss financial institutions, claiming that insufficient efforts were being made to recover their assets. In March 1997 three of Switzerland's most prominent banks, Crédit Suisse, Swiss Bank Corporation and Union Bank of Switzerland, established a special humanitarian fund for impoverished survivors of the Holocaust, under the administration of the Federal Government; the first payments from the fund were made in November. In December Swiss banks issued the first payments to claimants of funds from dormant accounts that had been opened prior to and during the Second World War.

In March 1998 senior US public finance officials, threatening an imminent boycott of Swiss banks and industrial interests, placed the former under increasing pressure to agree to a swift 'global settlement' of the issue of Holocaust victims' accounts, involving the establishment of a victims' fund and a timetable for payment; soon afterwards (against the wishes of the Swiss Government, which believed the ICEP to be making adequate progress in assessing claims) Swiss Bank Corporation and Union Bank of Switzerland, which subsequently merged to form UBS, and Crédit Suisse announced their intention to negotiate such a settlement. In August UBS and Crédit Suisse agreed to pay US $1,250m. to the World Jewish Congress as compensation for the role of Swiss financial institutions in retaining dormant Jewish assets, handling gold deposited by the Nazis and lending money during the Second World War to German companies that had utilized Jewish slave labour. In return, all threats of boycotts and legal action against Swiss concerns were withdrawn.

In December 1999 the ICEP reported that its audit of all dormant Swiss bank accounts had shown that some 54,000 of these might have belonged to Jews murdered in the Holocaust (although the figure was subsequently reduced to 36,000). The Committee recommended that details of 25,000 of the 54,000 accounts should be publicized in order to alert survivors of the Holocaust or their heirs to their existence. The Committee did not attempt to value the funds held in the accounts, but stated that the total would probably not exceed the US $1,250m. already committed by UBS and Crédit Suisse to the World Jewish Congress. The publication of the ICEP report was followed, almost immediately, by that of the international historical commission appointed in December 1996. The commission concluded that, by closing its border to an estimated 24,500 fugitive Jews from 1942, Switzerland bore partial responsibility for their deaths at the hands of the Nazis. Following the release of the historical commission's report, the Government formally apologized for Switzerland's role in the Second World War. Further details emerged in August 2001, which indicated that several of Switzerland's largest companies, including Nestlé, had ignored reports of Nazi atrocities and had continued to trade with Germany during the Second World War. In December a further report indicated that Switzerland had harboured substantial amounts of Nazi funds and assets, and even concealed entire German companies, during the Second World War and had provided a refuge for several prominent Nazi war criminals following the end of hostilities.

The proposed settlement of US $1,250m. to end the threat of litigation by Holocaust survivors against Swiss banks was approved by a judge in the USA in July 2000. The two banks formally agreed the settlement in August; four Swiss insurers added a further $50m. in response to claims that the insurance policies of Holocaust survivors had not been honoured. Swiss companies that had used forced labour during the Second World War were also required to contribute. In February 2001 Swiss banks published lists of dormant bank accounts, thought to be linked to the Holocaust, to be claimed by the account-holders or their heirs.

Foreign Affairs

Regional relations

Switzerland began to emerge from its traditional isolation in the early 1990s. This was largely due to economic pressures resulting from the world recession and the further integration of the European Community (EC). In May 1992 the Federal Council announced that it was to apply for membership of the EC. In a referendum in December, however, the Swiss electorate voted against ratification of an agreement, signed in May, to create a free trade zone encompassing both EC and EFTA member states. (The European Economic Area was established, without Switzerland, in January 1994.) Despite this setback, the Government declared its intention to continue to pursue its application for membership of the EC. During 1993 Switzerland confined itself to seeking bilateral negotiations with the EC (which became the EU in that year) on issues of particular national interest. Agreement was reached in December 1996 to phase out Swiss work permits for citizens of EU member states over a period of six years. By February 2000 the Government had negotiated seven bilateral free trade agreements with the EU. The accords, which were approved in a referendum in May, included the gradual elimination of immigration controls between Switzerland and the EU over a period of 12 years. In a referendum in March 2001 77% of voters rejected a motion to begin 'fast-track' accession negotiations with the EU. The result was believed to have been influenced in part by a letter from the European Commission in February, widely perceived as coercive, which urged the acceleration of negotiations with the EU regarding co-operation against customs fraud and tax evasion. The Government insisted that the vote did not represent a rejection of the EU, but rather reflected the desire to move towards accession at a slower pace, and that its plans for eventual membership of the EU remained unchanged.

In December 2004 the Federal Assembly approved a second set of bilateral agreements with the EU, which had been signed in October. Under the agreements Switzerland was to introduce (incrementally between 1 July 2005 and 2011) a withholding tax of 35% on the income of EU citizens' savings held in Switzerland, with banking secrecy to be retained. The agreements also provided for co-operation against customs fraud and for Switzerland's associate membership of the Schengen Agreement and Dublin Convention, as well as for the extension of the first set of bilateral agreements to the 10 states that had acceded to full membership of the EU earlier in the year. At a referendum in June 2005 54.6% of participating voters supported Switzerland's adherence to the Schengen/Dublin accords. (The Schengen/Dublin accords were duly implemented on 12 December 2008.) The extension of existing bilateral agreements to the new EU member states was approved by 56.0% of voters at a referendum held in September 2005. During 2010 the Swiss Government came under increasing pressure from the EU to reform its relations with the Union. However, although the President of the Confederation, Doris Leuthard, acknowledged in August that changes might be desirable, establishing a working group to consider the issue, she insisted that the Government would not agree to the automatic adoption of EU rules, as advocated by the Union, and would instead seek the negotiation of a third set of bilateral agreements. Leuthard's successor, Micheline Calmy-Rey, reiterated this position during talks with senior EU officials in February 2011.

SWITZERLAND

Other external relations

In June 1993 the Federal Assembly approved legislation that sought permission for Swiss forces to be included in future UN peace-keeping operations. However, at a referendum on the issue, which took place in June 1994, 57.3% of voters rejected the proposal. Switzerland did subsequently join the Partnership for Peace programme of the North Atlantic Treaty Organization (NATO, see p. 368) in 1996. Swiss peace-keepers have participated in operations in Bosnia and Herzegovina, while Swiss truce-verifiers have worked in Kosovo under the Organization for Security and Co-operation in Europe (OSCE, see p. 385). In November 2000 a referendum was held on proposals to reduce the military budget by one-third; the motion was rejected by 62.4% of voters. A further proposal to abolish the armed forces was rejected by 78.1% of voters in a referendum held in December 2001; 76.8% of voters also rejected a replacement civilian force.

Until 2002, although Switzerland maintained a permanent observer at the UN and had joined the organization's non-political specialized agencies, it was not a full member of the UN. At a referendum in 1986 some 75.7% of voters had rejected full membership of the UN. In September 2001 the Federal Assembly approved proposals for Switzerland to join the UN. At a referendum in March 2002 the proposals were narrowly adopted. Switzerland was formally admitted as a member of the UN in September.

In the late 1990s a series of high-profile money-laundering cases threatened to damage Switzerland's reputation as a stable financial centre. Most notably, these included the freezing of assets and accounts linked to Gen. Sani Abacha and Slobodan Milošević, the former leaders of Nigeria and Yugoslavia, respectively, and the former head of the Peruvian secret service, Vladimiro Montesinos. Suspect funds found in Swiss bank accounts were linked to missing IMF aid paid to Russia and also to the former leader of the Philippines, Ferdinand Marcos. The total value of suspect funds under investigation in Switzerland increased from 333m. Swiss francs in 1999 (representing 160 cases) to 1,543m. Swiss francs (representing 370 cases) in 2000. In August 2003 Switzerland declared itself willing to co-operate with Nigeria's efforts to recover funds stolen by Abacha. The Nigerian Government estimated that Abacha had embezzled some US $2,000m., of which about $700m. was believed to have been deposited in Switzerland. The Swiss Government announced in April 2006 that it had returned all of the funds to the Nigerian Government. Appeals from the Abacha family for ownership of the money had been rejected. According to an agreement reached between Switzerland and Nigeria, the World Bank was to ensure the returned funds were used for development projects in health, education and basic infrastructure. In 2006 the Federal Supreme Court ruled that indefinite freezes imposed by the Government on privately held assets in Swiss banks were unconstitutional. Non-governmental organizations expressed fears that the ruling could lead to the release of further assets whose provenance was suspected to be illegal, including an estimated 7.7m. Swiss francs believed to have been deposited by former President Mobutu Sese Seko of Zaire (now the Democratic Republic of the Congo). In April 2009 the Swiss federal prosecutor ruled that, owing to the statute of limitations, assets believed to have been deposited by former President Mobutu should be returned to his family upon the expiry of the order freezing those funds at the end of April. An appeal to the Federal Criminal Court by a private individual against the decision to release the funds was rejected in July, and Mobutu's assets were duly released. In early 2011 the Government froze assets held in Switzerland by several current or former heads of state: the President of Côte d'Ivoire, Laurent Gbagbo, who was refusing to concede defeat following a presidential election in that country; the former Presidents of Tunisia and Egypt, Zine al-Abidine Ben Ali and Hosni Mubarak, who had both left office following popular uprisings; and Col Muammar al-Qaddafi, the leader of Libya, where opposition protests had been violently suppressed. New legislation, designed to facilitate the freezing, confiscation and restitution of suspect funds deposited in Swiss banks by heads of state, came into effect in February. The law, which was aimed particularly at resolving cases in which the country of origin of the assets was unable to conduct a criminal procedure that met the requirements of Swiss legislation on international mutual assistance, allowed the authorities to act without having received a formal request from the state in question and removed the statute of limitations on the return of illegally acquired assets. It also stipulated that restored funds should be used for the good of the people of the country of origin. The Swiss Government subsequently initiated legal proceedings to return assets of the former Haitian President Jean-Claude Duvalier, which had been frozen since 1986, to the Haitian Government.

Relations with Libya deteriorated markedly from July 2008 after Hannibal al-Qaddafi, the son of Col Muammar al-Qaddafi, was arrested along with his wife in Geneva on charges of assault. The couple were swiftly released on bail and left Switzerland; however, the Libyan authorities responded with a number of retaliatory measures, including the closure of Swiss companies in Libya, the withdrawal of some US $5,000m. from Swiss banks and the restriction of air travel between the two countries. Moreover, in the same month two Swiss business executives in Libya, Rachid Hamdani and Max Göldi, were temporarily detained on charges of violating the terms of their visas, and were subsequently denied permission to leave the country. The Swiss Government initially refused to accede to Libyan demands for an apology over the treatment of Hannibal al-Qaddafi and his wife (the charges against whom were withdrawn in September), arguing that the matter fell within the jurisdiction of the cantonal authorities in Geneva and that the police there had acted within the law. However, in August 2009 the President of the Confederation, Hans-Rudolf Merz, travelled to Libya and issued a public apology for the incident. Following talks with the Libyan Government, Merz announced that the two countries had agreed to 'normalize' their relationship and that Hamdani and Göldi would be allowed to leave Libya. Nevertheless, the pair were arrested once again in September and were subsequently removed to an unknown location. In November Switzerland suspended the agreement signed in August, citing Libya's refusal to co-operate in the case of the two businessmen, and declared a ban on the issuing of entry visas to 188 prominent Libyans. (The ban applied to visas issued by all signatories of the Schengen Agreement, and led to strained relations between Switzerland and the EU, especially after Libya imposed its own entry ban on nationals of Schengen-area countries in February 2010.) In December 2009 Hamdani and Göldi, who had both taken refuge in the Swiss embassy in Libya, were each sentenced, *in absentia*, to 16 months' imprisonment by a Libyan court for visa irregularities and tax evasion. Hamdani was acquitted on appeal in the following month and left Libya in February 2010, but Switzerland continued to demand the release of Göldi, whose sentence had been reduced to four months after he surrendered to the Libyan authorities. Meanwhile, the approval in a referendum in November 2009 of legislation outlawing the construction of minarets in Switzerland contributed to a further deterioration in relations between the two countries, and in February 2010 Col Qaddafi urged all Muslims to wage *jihad* (holy war) against Switzerland in response to the ban. None the less, both countries lifted their respective visa restrictions in March, and Göldi was permitted to return to Switzerland in June, a day after the Head of the Federal Department of Foreign Affairs, Micheline Calmy-Rey, had signed an agreement on the normalization of bilateral relations with her Libyan counterpart.

CONSTITUTION AND GOVERNMENT

The Swiss Confederation, composed of 26 cantons, has a republican federal Constitution. Originally promulgated in 1848, it was wholly revised in 1874 and again in 2000. Legislative power is held by the bicameral Federal Assembly: the Council of States, with 46 members, elected for three to four years, representing the cantons (of which 20 send two members each and six, known as 'half-cantons', are represented by one member each); and the National Council, with 200 members directly elected by universal adult suffrage for four years, on the basis of proportional representation. Executive power is held by the Federal Council, which has seven members elected for four years by a joint session of the Federal Assembly. The Assembly also elects one of the Federal Councillors to be President of the Confederation (head of state) for one year at a time.

National policy is the prerogative of the Federal Government, but considerable power is vested in the cantons. Under the Constitution, the autonomous cantons hold all powers not specifically delegated to the federal authorities. The Swiss citizen shares three distinct allegiances—communal, cantonal and national. Direct participation is very important in communal government, and all adult Swiss residents may take part in the communal assemblies or referendums, which decide upon local affairs. Each canton has its own written constitution, government and legislative assembly. The referendum, which can be on a communal, cantonal or national scale, further ensures the possibility of direct public participation in decision-making.

REGIONAL AND INTERNATIONAL CO-OPERATION

Switzerland was a founder member of the European Free Trade Association (EFTA, see p. 447), and is a member of the Council of Europe (see p. 250). Switzerland has signed a number of bilateral free trade agreements with the European Union (EU, see p. 270), and is a signatory to the EU's Schengen Agreement on border controls and the Dublin Convention on Asylum. It is also a member of the Organization for Security and Co-operation in Europe (OSCE, see p. 385).

Switzerland joined the UN in 2002 following a referendum, although many of the UN's institutions had been located in Geneva since 1946. It joined the World Trade Organization (WTO, see p. 430) in 1995, and was a founder member of the Organisation for Economic Co-operation and Development (OECD, see p. 376). Switzerland participates in the Partnership for Peace programme of the North Atlantic Treaty Organization (NATO, see p. 368).

ECONOMIC AFFAIRS

In 2008, according to estimates by the World Bank, Switzerland's gross national income (GNI), measured at average 2006–08 prices, was US $431,136m., equivalent to $56,370 per head (or $41,830 per head on an international purchasing-power parity basis). During 2000–09, it was estimated, the population grew by an average of 0.8% per year, while during 2000–08 gross domestic product (GDP) per head increased, in real terms, at an average annual rate of 1.1%. Overall GDP increased, in real terms, by an average of 1.9% per year in 2000–08; real GDP increased by 1.8% in 2008, but contracted by 1.9% in 2009.

Agriculture (including forestry and fishing) contributed an estimated 1.2% of GDP in 2009, according to provisional figures. The sector engaged 3.4% of the employed labour force in 2010. The principal cash crops are sugar beet, potatoes and wheat. Dairy products, notably cheese, are also important. At a national referendum held in November 2005, 55.7% of voters approved a five-year ban on the use of genetically modified crops. In March 2010 the moratorium was extended until November 2013. According to the World Bank, agricultural GDP declined at an average annual rate of 1.1% in 2000–07; it contracted by 4.3% in 2006, but grew by 5.2% in 2007.

Industry (including mining and quarrying, manufacturing, power and construction) contributed an estimated 26.8% of GDP in 2009, according to provisional figures. The sector engaged 22.5% of the employed labour force in 2010. In 2000–07 industrial GDP increased by an average of 2.4% per year. It rose by 3.9% in 2007.

Switzerland is not richly endowed with mineral deposits, and only rock salt and building materials are mined or quarried in significant quantities. In 2010 only 0.1% of the working population were employed in mining and quarrying. The sector contributed an estimated 0.2% of GDP in 2006.

The manufacturing sector, which contributed an estimated 19.9% of GDP in 2006, engaged 14.6% of the employed labour force in 2010. The most important branches are precision engineering (in particular clocks and watches, which provided 7.4% of export revenue in 2010), heavy engineering, machine-building, textiles, chocolate, chemicals and pharmaceuticals.

The construction sector contributed an estimated 5.6% of GDP in 2009, according to provisional figures. The sector engaged 7.0% of the employed labour force in 2010.

Of total electricity output in 2007, 53.0% was provided by hydroelectric power and 42.0% by nuclear power (from five reactors with a total generating capacity of 3,077 MW). Imports of mineral fuels comprised 7.2% of the value of total imports in 2009 (including imports to Liechtenstein). Switzerland is a net exporter of electricity. Following damage to a nuclear power station in Japan after a severe earthquake, in March 2011 the Government announced that it was suspending the approvals process for three new reactors, pending safety assessments.

The services sector contributed an estimated 72.0% of GDP in 2009, according to provisional figures. The sector engaged 74.1% of the employed labour force in 2010. Switzerland plays an important role as a centre of international finance, and Swiss markets account for a significant share of international financial transactions. The insurance sector is also highly developed, and Swiss companies are represented throughout the world. Switzerland draws considerable revenue from tourism; receipts from tourism provisionally totalled 15,005m. Swiss francs in 2009. In 2000–07 services GDP increased by an average of 1.8% per year. It rose by 3.6% in 2007.

In 2009 Switzerland recorded a visible trade surplus of US $1,391m., and there was a surplus of $38,972m. on the current account of the balance of payments. The European Union (EU, see p. 270) accounted for the majority of Switzerland's trade, providing 81.2% of the country's imports and taking 62.0% of exports in 2008. In 2010 the principal source of imports was Germany (providing 32.9% of total imports), followed by Italy and France. Germany was also the principal market for exports (accounting for 19.4% of total exports), followed by the USA, Italy and France. The principal exports in 2010 were chemicals, machinery, clocks and watches, precision instruments and metals. The main imports in that year were chemicals, machinery, precision instruments, motor vehicles, and textiles, clothing and footwear.

According to official estimates, Switzerland recorded a consolidated budgetary surplus of 8,928m. Swiss francs (equivalent to 1.7% of GDP) in 2009. Switzerland's general government gross debt was 208,886m. Swiss francs in 2009, equivalent to 39.0% of GDP. The annual rate of inflation averaged 0.9% in 2000–09; consumer prices decreased by 0.5% in 2009, but increased by 0.7% in 2010. The rate of unemployment averaged 4.0% in 2010. Of all the major European countries, Switzerland has the highest percentage of foreign workers (23% of the working population in 2010).

Switzerland is a prosperous country, despite its small size, with a high level of income per head. Its economic success, built around financial services and a modern industrial sector, is in large part due to a highly educated labour force and a flexible labour market. Although Switzerland is not a member of the EU, it is nevertheless largely dependent on the euro area for economic growth and enjoys privileged access to the EU's internal market through numerous bilateral agreements. From 2004–08 Switzerland enjoyed continued growth in real GDP, partly owing to the success of the private banking and insurance sectors. However, the prominence of the financial services sector left the Swiss economy vulnerable to the effects of the global financial crisis from 2008. In October the Swiss National Bank (SNB) provided some 6,000m. Swiss francs of additional capital to the country's largest bank, UBS, which subsequently revealed losses of some 20,000m. Swiss francs for the year. The Government introduced three sets of stimulus measures in November 2008, March and June 2009, with a total value of nearly 3,000m. Swiss francs. A fall in demand, concomitant with a strong currency, precipitated a steep decline in the value of exports from late 2008, while a decline in consumer spending prompted the SNB to reduce interest rates, in an attempt to offset the risk of deflation. Real GDP contracted by 1.9% in 2009, but increased by an estimated 2.6% in 2010. The recovery in 2010 was broadly based, with both domestic and external demand rising, and the performance of the financial sector also improved. Interest rates remained extremely low throughout 2010, while the SNB intervened in the foreign exchange market in the first half of the year in an attempt to curb the appreciation of the Swiss franc against the euro, as a surge in inflows of capital reflected concerns regarding sovereign debt in the euro area. However, the Swiss currency strengthened further (not just against the euro), adversely affecting exports towards the end of the year. A continued slowdown in exports was expected to result in more moderate growth in 2011.

PUBLIC HOLIDAYS

2012: 1 January (New Year's Day), 6 April (Good Friday)*, 9 April (Easter Monday)*, 17 May (Ascension Day), 28 May (Whit Monday)*, 1 August (National Day), 25 December (Christmas Day), 26 December (St Stephen's Day)*.

In addition, various cantonal and local holidays are observed.

* Observation varies by canton.

SWITZERLAND

Statistical Survey

Source (unless otherwise stated): Federal Statistical Office, Information Service, 10 Espace de l'Europe, 2010 Neuchâtel; tel. 327136011; fax 327136012; e-mail info@bfs.admin.ch; internet www.bfs.admin.ch.

Area and Population

AREA, POPULATION AND DENSITY

Area (sq km)	41,284*
Population (census results)	
4 December 1990	6,873,687
5 December 2000	
Males	3,567,567
Females	3,720,443
Total	7,288,010
Population (official estimates at 31 December)†	
2007	7,593,494
2008	7,701,856
2009	7,785,806
Density (per sq km) at 31 December 2009	188.6

* 15,940 sq miles.
† Figures refer to permanent resident population.

POPULATION BY AGE AND SEX
(official estimates at 31 December 2009)

	Males	Females	Total
0–14	608,065	573,156	1,181,221
15–64	2,663,676	2,632,218	5,295,894
64 and over	558,825	749,866	1,308,691
Total	3,830,566	3,955,240	7,785,806

LANGUAGES
(Swiss nationals, %)

	1980	1990	2000
German	73.5	73.4	72.5
French	20.1	20.5	21.0
Italian	4.5	4.1	4.3
Romansh	0.9	0.7	0.6
Others	1.0	1.3	1.6

REGIONS AND CANTONS

Region/Canton	Area (sq km)*	Population (2009)† Total ('000)	Per sq km	Capital (with population, 2000‡)
Région lémanique	8,718.7	1,462.2	167.7	—
Genève	282.4	453.3	1,605.2	Genève (177,964)
Valais	5,224.4	307.4	58.8	Sion (27,171)
Vaud	3,211.9	701.5	218.4	Lausanne (124,914)
Espace Mittelland	10,062.0	1,741.8	173.1	—
Bern	5,959.3	974.2	163.5	Bern (128,634)
Fribourg	1,670.6	273.2	163.5	Fribourg (35,547)
Jura	838.5	70.1	83.6	Delémont (11,353)
Neuchâtel	802.5	171.6	213.7	Neuchâtel (32,914)
Solothurn	790.7	252.7	319.6	Solothurn (15,489)
Nordwestschweiz	1,958.2	1,060.7	541.7	—
Aargau	1,403.6	600.0	427.5	Aarau (15,470)
Basel-Stadt	37.0	187.9	5,078.4	Basel (166,558)
Basel-Landschaft	517.6	272.8	527.0	Liestal (12,930)
Zürich	1,728.9	1,351.3	781.6	Zürich (363,273)
Ostschweiz	11,521.1	1,094.3	95.0	—
Appenzell Ausserrhoden	242.8	53.0	218.3	Herisau (15,882)
Appenzell Innerrhoden	172.5	15.7	91.0	Appenzell (5,447)
Glarus	685.1	38.5	56.2	Glarus (5,556)
Graubünden	7,105.5	191.9	27.0	Chur (32,989)
St Gallen	2,025.7	474.7	234.3	St Gallen (72,626)
Schaffhausen	298.5	75.7	253.6	Schaffhausen (33,628)
Thurgau	991.0	244.8	247.0	Frauenfeld (21,954)

Region/Canton—continued	Area (sq km)*	Population (2009)† Total ('000)	Per sq km	Capital (with population, 2000‡)
Zentralschweiz	4,483.6	739.7	165.0	—
Luzern	1,493.5	373.0	249.7	Luzern (59,496)
Nidwalden	275.9	40.8	147.9	Stans (6,983)
Obwalden	490.6	35.0	71.3	Sarnen (9,145)
Schwyz	908.2	144.7	159.3	Schwyz (13,802)
Uri	1,076.7	35.3	32.8	Altdorf (8,541)
Zug	238.7	110.9	464.6	Zug (22,973)
Ticino	2,812.2	335.7	119.4	Bellinzona (16,463)
Total	41,284.2	7,785.8	188.6	—

* Figures exclude lakes larger than 5 sq km (total area 1,289.5 sq km). Also excluded are special territories (total area 7.2 sq km).
† Estimated permanent resident population at 31 December.
‡ Census figures.

PRINCIPAL TOWNS
(estimated population at 1 January 2009)

Zürich (Zurich)	365,132	Biel (Bienne)	50,013
Genève (Genf or Geneva)	183,287	Thun (Thoune)	42,129
Basel (Bâle)	164,937	Köniz	37,974
Bern (Berne, capital)	122,925	La Chaux-de-Fonds	37,240
Lausanne	122,284	Schaffhausen (Schaffhouse)	34,630
Winterthur (Winterthour)	98,238	Fribourg (Freiburg)	34,084
St Gallen (Saint-Gall)	72,040	Chur (Coire)	32,957
Luzern (Lucerne)	59,241	Neuchâtel (Neuenburg)	32,592

BIRTHS, MARRIAGES AND DEATHS

	Registered live births Number	Rate (per 1,000)	Registered marriages Number	Rate (per 1,000)	Registered deaths Number	Rate (per 1,000)
2002	72,372	9.9	40,213	5.5	61,768	8.5
2003	71,848	9.8	40,056	5.4	63,070	8.6
2004	73,082	9.9	39,460	5.3	60,180	8.1
2005	72,903	9.8	40,139	5.4	61,124	8.2
2006	73,371	9.8	39,817	5.3	60,283	8.1
2007	74,494	9.8	40,330	5.3	61,089	8.0
2008	76,691	10.0	41,534	5.4	61,233	8.0
2009	78,286	10.1	41,918	5.4	62,476	8.0

Life expectancy (years at birth, WHO estimates): 82 (males 80; females 84) in 2008 (Source: WHO, *World Health Statistics*).

ECONOMICALLY ACTIVE POPULATION*
(quarterly averages, April–June, '000 persons aged 15 years and over)

	2008	2009	2010
Agriculture, hunting, forestry and fishing	161	152	154
Mining and quarrying	5	5	5
Manufacturing	699	690	668
Electricity, gas and water supply	39	39	40
Construction	316	314	319
Wholesale and retail trade; repair of motor vehicles, motorcycles and personal and household goods	677	678	674

SWITZERLAND

—continued	2008	2009	2010
Hotels and restaurants	256	252	254
Transport, storage and communications	373	373	371
Financial intermediation	243	250	248
Real estate, renting and business activities	540	559	566
Public administration and defence; compulsory social security	175	175	184
Education	297	303	302
Health and social work	521	539	549
Other community, social and personal service activities	170	170	171
Private households with employed persons	61	72	82
Total employed	4,533	4,571	4,588
Unemployed	148	183	190
Total labour force	4,681	4,754	4,778
Males	2,557	2,589	2,619
Females	2,122	2,165	2,159

* Refers to workers who are employed for at least one hour per week, and includes foreign workers ('000): 1,198 in 2008; 1,242 in 2009; 1,255 in 2010.

Note: Totals may not be equal to the sum of components, owing to rounding.

Health and Welfare

KEY INDICATORS

Total fertility rate (children per woman, 2008)	1.5
Under-5 mortality rate (per 1,000 live births, 2008)	5
HIV/AIDS (% of persons aged 15–49, 2007)	0.6
Physicians (per 1,000 head, 2006)	4.0
Hospital beds (per 1,000 head, 2005)	5.7
Health expenditure (2007): US $ per head (PPP)	4,417
Health expenditure (2007): % of GDP	10.8
Health expenditure (2007): public (% of total)	59.3
Total carbon dioxide emissions ('000 metric tons, 2007)	37,962.7
Carbon dioxide emissions per head (metric tons, 2007)	5.0
Human Development Index (2010): ranking	13
Human Development Index (2010): value	0.874

For sources and definitions, see explanatory note on p. vi.

Agriculture

PRINCIPAL CROPS
('000 metric tons)

	2007	2008	2009
Wheat	543.0	548.1	549.4
Barley	210.5	200.3	198.1
Maize	177.6	170.7	174.0
Rye	10.1	12.1	15.9
Oats	10.1	9.5	10.5
Triticale (wheat-rye hybrid)	58.7	58.9	56.3
Potatoes	491.0	473.0	517.0
Sugar beet	1,572.9	1,625.2	1,719.7
Rapeseed	61.0	62.1	67.0
Cabbages and other brassicas	29.7	31.8	34.3
Lettuce and chicory	63.5	63.2	70.5
Tomatoes	30.6	33.5	34.5
Onions and shallots, green	27.2	27.0	33.6
Carrots and turnips	53.8	58.7	69.9
Apples	276.9	258.5	252.1
Pears	83.6	83.2*	73.9
Grapes	131.8	136.1	141.0

* Unofficial figure.

Aggregate production ('000 metric tons, may include official, semi-official or estimated data): Total cereals 1,012 in 2007, 1,002 in 2008, 1,006 in 2009; Total roots and tubers 491 in 2007, 473 in 2008, 517 in 2009; Total vegetables (incl. melons) 313.5 in 2007, 325.8 in 2008, 366.1 in 2009; Total fruits (excl. melons) 533 in 2007, 508 in 2008, 507 in 2009.

Source: FAO.

LIVESTOCK
('000 head, year ending September)

	2007	2008	2009
Cattle	1,566.9	1,604.3	1,597.5
Horses	57.7	59.3	60.2
Asses	5.9	6.2	6.0*
Pigs	1,573.1	1,540.1	1,557.2
Sheep	443.6	446.2	431.9
Goats	79.1	81.4	85.1
Chickens	8,101	8,474	8,741

* FAO estimate.

Source: FAO.

LIVESTOCK PRODUCTS
('000 metric tons)

	2007	2008	2009
Cattle meat	132.9	135.4	141.6
Sheep meat	5.4	5.4	5.4
Pig meat	242.0	231.0	237.8
Chicken meat	58.4	62.4	63.8
Cows' milk	3,911.5	4,071.3	4,073.1
Goats' milk	21.3	21.4	21.3
Hen eggs	38.8	39.3	41.3

Source: FAO.

Forestry

ROUNDWOOD REMOVALS
('000 cubic metres, excluding bark)

	2007	2008	2009
Sawlogs, veneer logs and logs for sleepers	3,648	3,203	2,822
Pulpwood	628	535	415
Other industrial wood	21	18	15
Fuel wood	1,222	1,195	1,325
Total	5,519	4,951	4,577

Source: FAO.

SAWNWOOD PRODUCTION
('000 cubic metres, including railway sleepers)

	2007	2008	2009
Coniferous (softwood)	1,463	1,448	1,413
Broadleaved (hardwood)	78	93	68
Total	1,541	1,541	1,481

Source: FAO.

Fishing

(metric tons, live weight)

	2006	2007	2008
Capture	1,422	1,377	1,582
Roach	166	168	176
European perch	267	242	292
Whitefishes	822	801	956
Aquaculture	1,214	1,214	1,214
Rainbow trout	1,107	1,110	1,110
Total catch	2,636	2,591	2,796

Source: FAO.

SWITZERLAND

Industry

SELECTED PRODUCTS
('000 metric tons unless otherwise indicated)

	2005	2006	2007
Cement*	4,022	4,000	4,000
Cigarettes (million)	42,190	48,937	54,348
Aluminium (unwrought, primary)*	44,458	40,000	25,000
Flour (wheat)	367	370	368
Chocolate and chocolate products	160.3	168.3	181.3
Motor spirit (petrol, '000 barrels)*	10,000	10,000	10,000
Distillate fuel oils ('000 barrels)*	20,000	20,000	20,000
Residual fuel oil ('000 barrels)*	30,000	30,000	30,000
Electric energy (million kWh)†	59,612	64,038	67,950

* Source: US Geological Survey.
† Including Liechtenstein.

Source (unless otherwise indicated): UN Industrial Commodity Statistics Database.

Watches ('000 exported): 17,840 in 1984; 25,137 in 1985; 28,075 in 1986.

New dwellings (units completed): 35,961 in 1997; 33,734 in 1998; 33,108 in 1999.

2009 ('000 barrels, unless otherwise indicated): Cement ('000 metric tons) 4,000; Motor spirit (petrol) 10,000; Distillate fuel oils 16,000; Residual fuel oil 4,000 (Source: US Geological Survey).

Finance

CURRENCY AND EXCHANGE RATES

Monetary Units
100 Rappen (centimes) = 1 Schweizer Franken (franc suisse) or Swiss franc.

Sterling, Dollar and Euro Equivalents (31 December 2010)
£1 sterling = 1.4709 francs;
US $1 = 0.9396 francs;
€1 = 1.2555 francs;
100 Swiss francs = £67.98 = $106.43 = €79.65.

Average Exchange Rates (Swiss francs per US $)
2008   1.0831
2009   1.0881
2010   1.0429

BUDGET
(million Swiss francs)*

Revenue†	2002	2003	2004
Taxes	95,697	94,568	97,643
Taxes on income and wealth	64,935	63,418	65,412
Income and wealth tax	45,591	45,986	46,590
Corporation and capital gains tax	12,615	12,118	12,218
Pre-paid tax	2,628	1,641	2,628
Other taxes on income and wealth	4,101	3,673	3,976
Stamp duty	2,819	2,624	2,755
Taxes on property and goods	1,895	1,937	1,960
Taxes on motor vehicles	1,774	1,820	1,851
Taxes on consumption	23,735	24,204	25,052
Value-added tax	16,857	17,156	17,666
Taxes on traffic	1,067	999	993
Customs duty	1,091	1,090	1,054
Agricultural duty	3	3	4
Duty from drivers	86	105	124
Duty from casinos	65	189	291
Other revenue	38,913	35,246	36,581
Total	**134,610**	**129,814**	**134,224**

Expenditure	2002	2003	2004
General administration	8,818	9,204	8,855
Public order and safety	7,514	7,872	7,970
Defence	5,162	5,066	4,979
Foreign relations	2,373	2,365	2,427
Education	25,786	26,560	27,684
Culture and leisure activities	4,187	4,212	4,249
Health	18,047	18,839	19,326
Social welfare	25,411	26,481	27,742
Transport and administration	14,671	14,024	14,411
Environment	4,909	4,897	4,907
National economy	7,058	6,466	6,344
Finances and taxes	10,317	9,825	9,486
Total	**134,253**	**135,811**	**138,379**

* Incorporates federal, cantonal and communal budgets, but excludes social security obligations. The consolidated accounts (including social security obligations) were (million Swiss francs): *Revenue:* 162,213 in 2002; 161,932 in 2003; 165,097 in 2004. *Expenditure:* 163,687 in 2002; 167,981 in 2003; 170,738 in 2004.
† Not including parish taxes.

2005 (million Swiss francs): Total revenue 174,543; Total expenditure 174,356 (Source: Swiss National Bank).

2006 (million Swiss francs): Total revenue 183,777; Total expenditure 175,527 (Source: Swiss National Bank).

2007 (million Swiss francs): Total revenue 190,777; Total expenditure 179,869 (Source: Swiss National Bank).

2008 (million Swiss francs): Total revenue 190,162; Total expenditure 187,023 (Source: Swiss National Bank).

2009 (million Swiss francs, estimates): Total revenue 197,854; Total expenditure 188,926 (Source: Swiss National Bank).

2010 (million Swiss francs, estimates): Total revenue 187,043; Total expenditure 194,232 (Source: Swiss National Bank).

2011 (million Swiss francs, budget forecasts): Total revenue 195,330; Total expenditure 201,339 (Source: Swiss National Bank).

INTERNATIONAL RESERVES
(US $ million at 31 December)

	2007	2008	2009
Gold (national valuation)	30,898	29,013	37,055
IMF special drawing rights	248	229	5,391
Reserve position in IMF	359	681	1,194
Foreign exchange	43,867	44,151	91,614
Total	**75,372**	**74,074**	**135,254**

2010: IMF special drawing rights 4,993; Reserve position in IMF 1,141; Foreign exchange 217,203.

Source: IMF, *International Financial Statistics*.

MONEY SUPPLY
('000 million Swiss francs at 31 December)

	2007	2008	2009
Currency outside banks	44.26	49.16	49.97
Demand deposits at deposit money banks	194.85	239.04	311.77
Total money (incl. others)	**247.78**	**325.39**	**406.72**

Source: IMF, *International Financial Statistics*.

COST OF LIVING
(Consumer Price Index; annual averages; base: December 2010 = 100)

	2008	2009	2010
Foodstuffs	103.0	102.8	101.6
Alcoholic beverages and tobacco	95.6	98.2	99.4
Clothing and footwear	90.0	92.1	93.2
Housing and energy	98.0	96.9	99.3
Household equipment, etc.	99.7	100.5	100.1
Health	100.3	100.7	100.4
Transport	100.4	97.1	99.4
Communication	106.7	101.5	100.0
Education	96.3	97.8	98.9
Recreation and culture	103.3	102.7	100.5
Restaurants and hotels	97.6	99.2	100.1
Other goods and services	98.4	98.9	100.2
All items	**99.5**	**99.0**	**99.7**

SWITZERLAND

Statistical Survey

NATIONAL ACCOUNTS
(million Swiss francs at current prices)

National Income and Product

	2007	2008*	2009*
Compensation of employees	315,543	332,850	342,885
Operating surplus	99,097	99,735	81,482
Domestic factor incomes	414,640	432,585	424,367
Consumption of fixed capital	89,933	94,443	95,724
Gross domestic product (GDP) at factor cost	504,573	527,028	520,091
Indirect taxes	35,625	36,890	35,733
Less Subsidies	19,098	19,723	20,541
GDP in purchasers' values	521,101	544,196	535,282
Factor income received from abroad	147,181	92,509	99,666
Less Factor income paid abroad	142,056	130,706	77,454
Gross national product	526,226	505,998	557,495
Less Consumption of fixed capital	89,933	94,443	95,724
National income in market prices	436,293	411,555	461,771

* Provisional figures.

Expenditure on the Gross Domestic Product

	2007	2008*	2009*
Final consumption expenditure	353,169	367,276	371,108
Households and non-profit institutions serving households	296,789	308,629	310,459
General government	56,379	58,647	60,649
Gross capital formation	114,393	114,946	105,601
Gross fixed capital formation	112,221	115,200	108,176
Changes in inventories	1,253	−1,238	−4,472
Acquisitions, less disposals, of valuables	920	983	1,898
Total domestic expenditure	467,562	482,222	476,709
Exports of goods and services	293,067	307,454	276,637
Less Imports of goods and services	239,528	245,480	218,064
GDP in market prices	521,101	544,196	535,282

* Provisional figures.

Gross Domestic Product by Economic Activity

	2007	2008*	2009*
Agriculture, hunting, forestry and fishing	5,939	6,506	5,964
Construction	26,516	27,810	28,407
Other industry	108,996	114,310	107,132
Wholesale and retail trade; hotels and restaurants; transport, storage and communications	106,241	113,704	111,218
Financial intermediation; insurance and real estate; research and development and other business activities	119,319	121,140	118,718
General government, education, health, community and personal services	124,129	129,863	134,025
Sub-total	491,140	513,333	505,465
Taxes on products	32,865	33,807	32,809
Less Subsidies on products	2,904	2,945	2,992
GDP in market prices	521,101	544,196	535,282

* Provisional figures.

BALANCE OF PAYMENTS
(US $ million)

	2007	2008	2009
Exports of goods f.o.b.	200,491	241,163	206,119
Imports of goods f.o.b.	−187,257	−227,680	−204,728
Trade balance	13,234	13,482	1,391
Exports of services	65,865	77,939	70,043
Imports of services	−31,747	−36,592	−39,072
Balance on goods and services	47,352	54,829	36,362
Other income received	122,418	85,894	96,244
Other income paid	−119,874	−121,580	−81,322
Balance on goods, services and income	49,896	19,143	51,284
Current transfers received	22,706	27,153	25,384
Current transfers paid	−32,223	−39,828	−37,696
Current balance	40,379	6,468	38,972
Capital account (net)	−4,171	−3,480	−3,325
Direct investment abroad	−52,001	−53,561	−33,609
Direct investment from abroad	33,410	15,999	27,588
Portfolio investment assets	−20,344	−65,608	−35,411
Portfolio investment liabilities	1,626	30,024	7,019
Financial derivatives assets	−3,794	65,928	17,642
Financial derivatives liabilities	−6,605	−59,493	−15,658
Other investment assets	−293,439	303,974	119,464
Other investment liabilities	295,320	−248,458	−49,352
Net errors and omissions	13,082	12,061	−25,193
Overall balance	3,463	3,853	48,137

Source: IMF, *International Financial Statistics*.

External Trade

Note: Swiss customs territory includes the Principality of Liechtenstein, the German enclave of Büssingen and the Italian commune of Campione, but excludes the free zone of the Samnaun Valley.

PRINCIPAL COMMODITIES
(million Swiss francs)

Imports c.i.f.	2003	2004	2005
Agricultural and forestry products	10,368.7	10,505.2	10,997.4
Mineral fuels	6,905.7	7,767.7	11,194.4
Textiles and items of clothing	8,611.5	8,699.3	8,846.2
Clothing (excl. footwear)	5,384.9	5,435.2	5,655.5
Paper, paperboard and graphics	4,478.2	4,901.0	5,049.5
Leather, rubber and plastic products	4,453.1	4,835.9	5,198.8
Chemical products	27,489.4	29,606.7	32,796.5
Chemical elements and unmoulded plastics	6,603.4	7,499.4	8,933.6
Pharmaceutical products	16,104.3	17,411.5	19,166.4
Metal products	9,789.9	11,571.9	12,367.2
Machinery (incl. electrical)	26,009.6	27,659.7	29,972.3
Industrial machinery	9,105.2	9,631.8	10,548.6
Office machines	5,929.2	5,796.3	6,019.7
Electronics	7,439.9	8,375.8	9,311.0
Passenger cars	7,639.0	7,761.6	7,790.3
Precision instruments	4,463.3	4,882.4	5,373.6
Precious metals and gemstones	5,202.9	5,698.2	6,499.6
Total (incl. others)	134,986.7	143,996.2	157,544.5

SWITZERLAND

Statistical Survey

Exports f.o.b.	2003	2004	2005
Agricultural and forestry products	4,427.0	4,863.4	5,192.2
Chemical products	45,193.6	49,601.9	54,838.0
Chemical elements and unmoulded plastics	5,815.7	6,331.8	6,425.0
Pharmaceutical products	30,947.8	34,819.8	39,792.5
Metals and metal products	9,976.0	11,112.5	11,663.7
Machinery (incl. electrical)	31,183.3	33,839.3	35,172.0
Industrial machinery	20,047.7	21,650.8	21,803.8
Electronics	8,488.6	9,513.1	10,715.1
Precision instruments	9,757.6	10,204.6	11,500.2
Clocks and watches	10,216.9	11,157.9	12,390.3
Precious metals and gemstones	4,521.9	5,085.2	4,791.1
Total (incl. others)	141,157.5	152,756.5	162,991.1

2006 (million Swiss francs): *Imports:* Machinery, equipment and electronics 32,018; Precision instruments, watches and jewellery 12,171; Chemicals 35,785; Textiles, clothing and footwear 9,392; Motor vehicles 15,495; Total (incl. others) 165,410. *Exports:* Machinery, equipment and electronics 38,630; Precision instruments 12,925; Watches 13,743; Chemicals 62,975; Textiles, clothing and footwear 4,405; Metals 13,424; Total (incl. others) 177,475 (Source: Swiss National Bank).

2007 (million Swiss francs): *Imports:* Machinery, equipment and electronics 35,118; Precision instruments, watches and jewellery 13,678; Chemicals 41,260; Textiles, clothing and footwear 10,040; Motor vehicles 17,098; Total (incl. others) 183,578. *Exports:* Machinery, equipment and electronics 43,065; Precision instruments 13,977; Watches 15,956; Chemicals 68,811; Textiles, clothing and footwear 4,637; Metals 15,498; Total (incl. others) 197,533 (Source: Swiss National Bank).

2008 (million Swiss francs): *Imports:* Machinery, equipment and electronics 35,118; Precision instruments, watches and jewellery 15,139; Chemicals 38,272; Textiles, clothing and footwear 10,040; Motor vehicles 16,750; Total (incl. others) 186,884. *Exports:* Machinery, equipment and electronics 43,806; Precision instruments 14,909; Watches 17,034; Chemicals 71,918; Textiles, clothing and footwear 4,468; Metals 15,276; Total (incl. others) 206,330 (Source: Swiss National Bank).

2009 (million Swiss francs): *Imports:* Machinery, equipment and electronics 29,250; Precision instruments, watches and jewellery 15,378; Chemicals 34,964; Textiles, clothing and footwear 9,042; Motor vehicles 14,961; Total (incl. others) 160,187. *Exports:* Machinery, equipment and electronics 33,741; Precision instruments 13,835; Watches 13,229; Chemicals 71,771; Textiles, clothing and footwear 3,687; Metals 10,489; Total (incl. others) 180,534 (Source: Swiss National Bank).

2010 (million Swiss francs): *Imports:* Machinery, equipment and electronics 31,422; Precision instruments, watches and jewellery 18,396; Chemicals 37,767; Textiles, clothing and footwear 8,953; Motor vehicles 16,600; Total (incl. others) 173,685. *Exports:* Machinery, equipment and electronics 36,439; Precision instruments 14,388; Watches 16,139; Chemicals 75,879; Textiles, clothing and footwear 3,386; Metals 12,736; Total (incl. others) 193,253 (Source: Swiss National Bank).

PRINCIPAL TRADING PARTNERS
(million Swiss francs)*

Imports c.i.f.	2003	2004	2005
Austria	5,662.6	6,085.7	7,219.9
Belgium	4,031.0	4,249.5	4,793.7
China, People's Republic	2,423.0	2,840.9	3,378.4
France	15,297.8	15,107.2	15,804.4
Germany	42,738.3	46,341.9	49,732.2
Ireland	4,796.1	4,692.5	5,652.4
Italy	14,076.4	15,848.3	16,530.1
Japan	2,845.8	3,046.6	2,918.1
Netherlands	6,555.6	6,989.6	7,551.5
Russia	1,202.8	1,042.0	1,023.1
Spain	3,193.5	3,440.1	3,980.4
Sweden	1,675.3	1,676.1	1,484.5
United Kingdom	5,609.3	5,842.1	6,951.0
USA	7,356.6	7,253.6	8,328.0
Total (incl. others)	134,986.7	143,996.2	157,544.5

Exports f.o.b.	2003	2004	2005
Austria	4,660.6	4,901.2	5,169.1
Belgium	2,757.8	2,855.9	2,932.5
Canada	1,437.6	1,994.2	2,268.6
China, People's Republic	2,485.1	3,107.0	3,466.8
France	12,416.9	13,511.7	14,136.3
Germany	29,224.1	30,922.2	31,691.8
Hong Kong	4,144.4	4,237.0	4,011.8
Israel	710.1	746.5	776.6
Italy	12,782.6	13,712.0	14,816.2
Japan	5,408.9	5,722.3	5,892.1
Netherlands	4,484.6	4,462.8	5,548.2
Singapore	1,365.3	1,500.7	1,633.1
Spain	4,903.8	5,975.9	6,595.2
Sweden	1,628.6	1,651.0	1,605.8
Turkey	1,692.7	1,997.1	2,054.4
United Kingdom	6,768.2	7,676.8	8,803.2
USA	15,442.4	15,780.0	17,513.2
Total (incl. others)	141,157.5	152,756.5	162,991.1

*Imports by country of production; exports by country of consumption.

2006 (million Swiss francs): *Imports:* Austria 7,496.6; Belgium 5,093.3; China, People's Republic 3,918.6; France 17,096.7; Germany 55,099.8; Ireland 4,613.1; Italy 18,426.0; Netherlands 8,267.0; Spain 4,038.4; United Kingdom 6,006.6; USA 8,308.4; Total (incl others) 165,410.3. *Exports:* Austria 5,829.1; China, People's Republic 3,753.0; France 15,224.8; Germany 35,827.6; Hong Kong 3,562.0; Italy 15,913.8; Japan 6,361.0; Netherlands 6,034.1; Spain 6,880.7; United Kingdom 8,343.1; USA 18,255.0; Total (incl others) 177,474.8 (Source: Swiss National Bank).

2007 (million Swiss francs): *Imports:* Austria 8,047.8; Belgium 5,332.2; China, People's Republic 4,765.7; France 17,857.7; Germany 62,170.8; Ireland 6,023.8; Italy 20,588.6; Netherlands 8,748.3; Spain 4,123.5; United Kingdom 7,076.3; USA 9,426.2; Total (incl others) 183,577.8. *Exports:* Austria 6,254.7; China, People's Republic 4,786.1; France 16,662.2; Germany 41,149.2; Hong Kong 4,196.8; Italy 17,524.2; Japan 6,165.7; Netherlands 6,126.1; Spain 7,524.1; United Kingdom 9,413.1; USA 18,406.8; Total (incl others) 197,532.7 (Source: Swiss National Bank).

2008 (million Swiss francs): *Imports:* Austria 7,885.2; Belgium 5,685.0; China, People's Republic 4,980.4; France 18,044.2; Germany 64,775.0; Ireland 4,915.1; Italy 21,351.0; Netherlands 8,999.6; Spain 3,901.8; United Kingdom 5,990.6; USA 9,445.6; Total (incl others) 186,883.6. *Exports:* Austria 5,966.1; China, People's Republic 5,528.5; France 17,728.0; Germany 41,805.6; Hong Kong 4,559.5; Italy 18,232.7; Japan 6,288.2; Netherlands 6,258.7; Spain 7,331.7; United Kingdom 9,695.0; USA 19,467.4; Total (incl others) 206,330.4 (Source: Swiss National Bank).

2009 (million Swiss francs): *Imports:* Austria 7,156.7; Belgium 4,439.1; China, People's Republic 5,139.2; France 15,264.3; Germany 53,839.7; Ireland 4,239.12; Italy 17,922.1; Netherlands 7,633.8; Spain 3,713.6; United Kingdom 5,562.9; USA 8,029.1; Total (incl others) 160,187.0. *Exports:* Austria 5,438.6; China, People's Republic 5,399.5; France 15,225.2; Germany 35,283.4; Hong Kong 3,759.7; Italy 15,454.7; Japan 6,823.7; Netherlands 5,322.3; Spain 6,505.6; United Kingdom 8,521.3; USA 17,654.0; Total (incl others) 180,533.9 (Source: Swiss National Bank).

2010 (million Swiss francs): *Imports:* Austria 7,853.2; Belgium 4,682.9; China, People's Republic 6,064.4; France 15,235.5; Germany 57,169.9; Ireland 5,853.6; Italy 18,401.5; Netherlands 8,265.4; Spain 4,133.0; United Kingdom 6,224.2; USA 8,147.7; Total (incl others) 173,684.6. *Exports:* Austria 6,133.7; China, People's Republic 7,075.5; France 15,132.7; Germany 37,574.0; Hong Kong 5,297.3; Italy 15,540.9; Japan 6,416.7; Netherlands 5,763.7; Spain 6,344.2; United Kingdom 9,082.8; USA 19,472.0; Total (incl others) 193,252.8 (Source: Swiss National Bank).

SWITZERLAND

Transport

RAILWAY TRAFFIC

	2006	2007	2008
Passengers carried (million)*	379	403	n.a.
Passenger-km (million)	16,578	17,434	18,028
Freight carried (million metric tons)	70.2	71.1	n.a.
Freight ton-km (million)	12,466	11,952	12,265

* Excluding multiple journeys.

ROAD TRAFFIC
(motor vehicles in use at 30 September)

	2004	2005	2006
Passenger cars	3,811,351	3,863,807	3,899,917
Buses and coaches	44,784	45,785	46,445
Lorries and vans	298,193	307,264	314,020
Agricultural vehicles	180,898	182,093	185,450
Other industrial vehicles	50,957	51,860	53,437
Motorcycles	583,010	592,194	608,648

INLAND WATERWAYS
(freight traffic at port of Basel, '000 metric tons)

	1996	1997	1998
Goods loaded	876.9	837.5	688.4
Goods unloaded	6,283.4	7,002.4	7,420.3

Source: Federal Department of Transport.

SHIPPING
Merchant Fleet
(at 31 December)

	2007	2008	2009
Number of vessels	32	35	35
Displacement ('000 grt)	588.6	640.4	640.6

Source: IHS Fairplay, *World Fleet Statistics*.

CIVIL AVIATION
(traffic on scheduled services)

	2004	2005	2006
Kilometres flown (million)	172	166	165
Passengers carried ('000)	9,287	9,663	10,849
Passenger-km (million)	20,602	20,476	22,140
Total ton-km (million)	2,986	2,994	3,282

Source: UN, *Statistical Yearbook*.

2007: Passengers carried ('000) 12,298.5 (Source: World Bank, World Development Indicators database).

2008: Passengers carried ('000) 14,352.8 (Source: World Bank, World Development Indicators database).

Tourism

FOREIGN TOURIST ARRIVALS
(at hotels and similar establishments)

Country of residence	2006	2007	2008
Austria	160,031	175,683	189,159
Belgium	218,743	227,719	246,741
France	585,472	634,305	670,663
Germany	2,106,860	2,249,431	2,344,337
Italy	498,702	542,201	552,953
Japan	347,299	324,554	277,657
Netherlands	329,022	362,993	412,559
Spain	189,121	211,692	215,365
United Kingdom	784,963	834,783	825,719
USA	725,497	727,387	651,876
Total (incl. others)	7,862,957	8,447,718	8,608,337

Tourism receipts (million Swiss francs): 13,544 in 2006; 14,621 in 2007; 15,598 in 2008; 15,005 in 2009 (provisional).

Source: mainly World Tourism Organization.

Communications Media

	2007	2008	2009
Telephones ('000 main lines in use)	4,927.2	4,827.9	4,673.2*
Mobile cellular telephones ('000 subscribers)	8,208.9	8,896.7	9,255.0†
Internet users ('000)	5,679.3	5,823.4	6,152.5
Broadband subscribers ('000)	2,380.5	2,556.2	2,685.6†
Books published (titles)	11,410	11,126	11,105
Newspapers:			
number	208	203	n.a.
circulation ('000)	2,202.7	2,158.2	n.a.

* Estimate.
† Provisional figure.

Personal computers: 7,360,000 (962.4 per 1,000 persons) in 2008.
Source: mainly International Telecommunication Union.

Television receivers ('000 in use): 4,000 in 2001.

Radio licences ('000, 1996): 2,805.

Education

(2008/09 unless otherwise indicated)

	Institutions*	Teachers†	Students
Pre-primary	5,006	13,592‡	152,919
Compulsory primary§	6,141	42,168‡	777,394
Compulsory secondary§		35,688‡	
Upper secondary	893	13,900‡	
General	n.a.	13,900‡	337,145
Vocational	n.a.	n.a.	
Higher	382	87,238	234,799
Vocational	n.a.	n.a.	50,043
Universities of applied sciences	n.a.	37,236‖	63,747
Universities	n.a.	50,002‖	121,009

* 2004.
† 2007/08.
‡ May include double-counted data.
§ Excluding schools with special curriculums.
‖ Including teaching assistants and administrative and technical personnel.

Pupil-teacher ratio (primary education, UNESCO estimate): 12.6 in 2007/08 (Source: UNESCO Institute for Statistics).

Directory

The Government

FEDERAL COUNCIL
(May 2011)

President of the Swiss Confederation for 2011 and Head of the Federal Department of Foreign Affairs: MICHELINE CALMY-REY (Social Democratic Party).

Vice-President of the Swiss Confederation for 2011 and Head of the Federal Department of Finance: EVELINE WIDMER-SCHLUMPF (Conservative Democratic Party).

Head of the Federal Department of Defence, Civil Protection and Sports: UELI MAURER (Swiss People's Party).

Head of the Federal Department of Economic Affairs: JOHANN N. SCHNEIDER-AMMANN (FDP.The Liberals).

Head of the Federal Department of the Environment, Transport, Communications and Energy: DORIS LEUTHARD (Conservative Democratic People's Party).

Head of the Federal Department of Home Affairs: DIDIER BURKHALTER (FDP.The Liberals).

Head of the Federal Department of Justice and Police: SIMONETTA SOMMARUGA (Social Democratic Party).

Chancellor of the Swiss Confederation: CORINA CASANOVA (Christian Democratic People's Party).

FEDERAL DEPARTMENTS

Federal Chancellery: Bundeshaus West, 3003 Bern; tel. 313223791; fax 313223706; e-mail webmaster@admin.ch; internet www.bk.admin.ch.

Federal Department of Defence, Civil Protection and Sports: Bundeshaus Ost, 3003 Bern; tel. 313222111; fax 313245104; e-mail postmaster.vbs@gs-vbs.admin.ch; internet www.vbs.admin.ch.

Federal Department of Economic Affairs: Bundeshaus Ost, 3003 Bern; tel. 313222007; fax 313222194; e-mail info@gs-evd.admin.ch; internet www.evd.admin.ch.

Federal Department of the Environment, Transport, Energy and Communications: Bundeshaus Nord, Kochergasse 10, 3003 Bern; tel. 313222111; fax 313222692; e-mail info@gs-uvek.admin.ch; internet www.uvek.admin.ch.

Federal Department of Finance: Bernerhof, Bundesgasse 3, 3003 Bern; tel. 313226033; fax 313233852; e-mail info@gs-efd.admin.ch; internet www.efd.admin.ch.

Federal Department of Foreign Affairs: Bundeshaus West, 3003 Bern; tel. 313222111; fax 313234001; e-mail info@eda.admin.ch; internet www.eda.admin.ch.

Federal Department of Home Affairs: Schwanengasse 2, 3003 Bern; tel. 313228041; fax 313227901; e-mail info@gs-edi.admin.ch; internet www.edi.admin.ch.

Federal Department of Justice and Police: Bundeshaus West, 3003 Bern; tel. 313222111; fax 313227832; e-mail info@gs-ejpd.admin.ch; internet www.ejpd.admin.ch.

Legislature

BUNDESVERSAMMLUNG/ASSEMBLÉE FÉDÉRALE
(Federal Assembly)

Nationalrat/Conseil National
(National Council)

Parlamentsgebäude, 3003 Bern; tel. 313228790; e-mail information@pd.admin.ch.

President: JEAN-RENÉ GERMANIER (2010/11).

General Election, 21 October 2007

	Seats
Swiss People's Party	62*
Social Democratic Party	43
Radical Democratic Party	31†
Christian Democratic People's Party	31
Green Party	20
Liberal Party	4†
Green Liberal Party	3
Evangelical People's Party	2

—continued	Seats
Workers' Party	1
Union of Federal Democrats	1
Ticino League	1
Christian Socialist Party	1
Total	200

* In September 2008 four representatives of the Swiss People's Party left that party and joined the Conservative Democratic Party.
† The Radical Democratic Party and the Liberal Party merged, as FDP.The Liberals, on 1 January 2009.

Ständerat/Conseil des Etats
(Council of States)

Parlamentsgebäude, 3003 Bern; tel. 313228790; e-mail information@pd.admin.ch.

President: HANSHEIRI INDERKUM (2010/11).

Elections, 2007

	Seats
Christian Democratic People's Party	15
Radical Democratic Party	12*
Social Democratic Party	9
Swiss People's Party	7†
Green Party	2
Green Liberal Party	1
Total	46

Note: Members are elected by canton; method and period of election differs from canton to canton
* The Radical Democratic Party and the Liberal Party merged to form FDP.The Liberals on 1 January 2009.
† In September 2008 a representative of the Swiss People's Party left that party and joined the Conservative Democratic Party.

Political Organizations

Bürgerlich-Demokratische Partei (BDP) (Conservative Democratic Party): Postfach 119, 3000 Bern 6; tel. 313521482; fax 313521471; e-mail mail@bdp.info; internet www.bdp.info; f. Nov. 2008 by fmr mems of Swiss People's Party (q.v.); cantonal orgs in Aargau, Basel-Landschaft, Bern, Fribourg, Glarus, Graubünden, Luzern, St Gallen, Schwyz, Solothurn, Thurgau, Valais and Zürich; Pres. HANS GRUNDER.

Christlichdemokratische Volkspartei der Schweiz/Parti démocrate-chrétien suisse (CVP) (Christian Democratic People's Party): Klaraweg 6, Postfach 5835, 3001 Bern; tel. 313573333; fax 313522430; e-mail info@cvp.ch; internet www.cvp.ch; f. 1912; advocates a Christian outlook on world affairs, federalism and Christian social reform by means of professional asscns; non-sectarian; Pres. CHRISTOPHE DARBELLAY; Gen. Sec. TIM FREY; Leader of Parliamentary Group URS SCHWALLER.

Christlichsoziale Partei/Parti chrétien-social (CSP) (Christian Social Party): Eichenstr. 79, 3184 Wünnewil; tel. 264963074; e-mail info@csp-pcs.ch; internet www.csp-pcs.ch; f. 1997; Pres. MARIUS ACHERMANN; Sec. MARLIES SCHAFER-JUNGO.

Eidgenössisch-Demokratische Union/Union Démocratique Fédérale (EDU) (Federal Democratic Union): Frutigenstr. 8, Postfach 2144, 3601 Thun; tel. 332223637; fax 332223744; e-mail info@edu-schweiz.ch; internet www.edu-schweiz.ch; conservative Christian principles; Pres. HANS MOSER.

Evangelische Volkspartei der Schweiz/Parti évangélique suisse (EVP) (Evangelical People's Party): Nägeligasse 9, Postfach 294, 3000 Bern 7; tel. 313517171; fax 313517102; e-mail info@evppev.ch; internet www.evppev.ch; f. 1919; Pres. HEINER STUDER; Gen. Sec. JOEL BLUNIER.

FDP.Die Liberalen/PLR.Les Libéraux-Radicaux (FDP.The Liberals): Neuengasse 20, Postfach 6136, 3001 Bern; tel. 313203535; fax 313203500; e-mail info@fdp.ch; internet www.fdp.ch; f. 2009 by merger of the Radical Democratic Party (Freisinnig-Demokratische Partei der Schweiz/Parti radical-démocratique suisse—FDP) and the Liberal Party of Switzerland (Liberale Partei der Schweiz/Parti liberal suisse); predecessor org. led the movement that gave rise to the Federative State and the Constitution of 1848; promotes a strong Fed. Govt, while respecting the legitimate rights of the cantons and all the minorities; liberal democratic principles;

SWITZERLAND

Pres. Dr FULVIO PELLI; Leader of Parliamentary Group GABI HUBER; Gen. Sec. STEFAN BRUPBACHER.

Freiheits-Partei der Schweiz/Die Auto-Partei (Freedom Party of Switzerland/The Automobile Party): Eigasse 13, Postfach 332, 4622 Egerkingen; tel. 623983838; fax 623984848; e-mail zs@freiheits-partei.ch; internet www.freiheits-partei.ch; f. 1985 to support motorists' rights; subsequently campaigned for restricted immigration; Pres. PETER COMMARMOT; Sec. WALTER MÜLLER.

Grüne Partei der Schweiz/Les Verts—Parti écologiste suisse (GPS) (Green Party of Switzerland): Waisenhauspl. 21, 3011 Bern; tel. 313126660; fax 313126662; e-mail gruene@gruene.ch; internet www.gruene.ch; f. 1983; Pres. UELI LEUENBERGER; Leader of Parliamentary Group THERESE FRÖSCH; Gen. Sec. MIRIAM BEHRENS.

Grünliberale Partei Schweiz (GLP) (Green Liberal Party of Switzerland): Postfach 367, 3000 Bern 7; tel. 313230530; e-mail schweiz@grunliberale.ch; internet www.grunliberale.ch; f. 2004; Pres. MARTIN BÄUMLE; Gen. Sec. SANDRA GURTNER-OESCH.

Lega dei Ticinesi (Ticino League): via Monte Boglia 3, CP 2311, 6904 Lugano; tel. 919731048; fax 919731040; internet www.legaticinesi.ch; f. 1991; 1,500 mems; Pres. GIULIANO BIGNASCA; Sec. MAURO MALANDRA.

Liberal-Demokratische Partei Basel-Stadt (Die Liberalen) (Liberal-Democratic Party Basel-City): 4010 Basel; tel. 612721236; fax 612721743; e-mail info@ldp.ch; internet www.ldp.ch; Pres. CHRISTOPH BÜRGENMEIER.

Mouvement Citoyens Genevois (MCG) (Geneva Citizens' Movement): CP 340, 1211 Geneva 17; tel. 228497333; fax 223214507; e-mail info@mcge.ch; internet www.mcge.ch; f. 2005; Pres. ERIC STAUFFER.

Partei der Arbeit der Schweiz/Parti suisse du travail (Parti ouvrier et populaire) (Workers' Party): Postfach 533, 3000 Bern 22; tel. 442417722; e-mail secret-pst-pda@gouvernement.ch; internet www.pst.ch; f. 1944; Pres. NELLY BUNTSCHU.

Schweizer Demokraten/Démocrates suisses (SD) (Swiss Democrats): Postfach 8116, 3001 Bern; tel. 319742010; fax 319742011; e-mail schweizer-demokraten@bluewin.ch; internet www.schweizer-demokraten.ch; f. 1961 as Nationale Aktion gegen die Überfremdung von Volk und Heimat/Action nationale; present name adopted 1990; 6,000 mems; main objectives are preservation of the country's political independence and of individual freedom, protection of the environment, and restriction of immigration; Pres. MARKUS BORNER; Gen. Sec. ROLAND SCHÖNI.

Schweizerische Volkspartei/Union démocratique du centre (SVP) (Swiss People's Party): Brückfeldstr. 18, Postfach 8252, 3001 Bern 26; tel. 313005858; fax 313005859; e-mail gs@svp.ch; internet www.svp.ch; f. 1971; Pres. TONI BRUNNER; Leader of Parliamentary Group CASPAR BAADER; Gen. Sec. MARTIN BALTISSER.

Sozialdemokratische Partei der Schweiz/Parti socialiste suisse (SP) (Social Democratic Party): Spitalgasse 34, 3001 Bern; tel. 313296969; fax 313296970; e-mail sekretariat@sp-ps.ch; internet www.sp-ps.ch; f. 1888; bases its policy on democratic socialism; mem. of Socialist International and assoc. mem. of Party of European Socialists; c. 33,000 mems; Pres. CHRISTIAN LEVRAT; Leader of Parliamentary Group URSULA WYSS; Sec.-Gen. THOMAS CHRISTEN.

Partito Socialista, sezione ticinese del PSS (Socialist Party): piazza Governo 4, 6500 Bellinzona; tel. 918259462; fax 918259601; e-mail segreteria@ps-ticino.ch; internet www.ps-ticino.ch; f. 1992; fmrly the Partito Socialista Unitario; Pres. MANUELE BERTOLI.

Diplomatic Representation

EMBASSIES IN SWITZERLAND

Afghanistan: 63 rue de Lausanne, 1202 Geneva; tel. 227311616; fax 227314510; e-mail mission.afghanistan@bluewin.ch; internet www.mission-afghanistan.ch; Chargé d'affaires a.i. OBAID KHAN NOORI.

Albania: Pourtalèsstr. 45A, 3074 Muri bei Bern; tel. 319526010; fax 319526012; e-mail emalb@bluewin.ch; Ambassador MEHMET ELEZAJ.

Algeria: Willadingweg 74, 3000 Bern 15; tel. 313501050; fax 313501059; e-mail info@ambassade-algerie.ch; internet www.ambassade-algerie.ch; Ambassador EL-HAOUÉS RIACHE.

Angola: Laubegstr. 18, 3006 Bern; tel. 313518585; fax 313518586; e-mail berna@ambassadeangola.ch; internet www.ambassadeangola.ch; Ambassador APOLINARIO JORGE CORREIA.

Argentina: Jungfraustr. 1, 3005 Bern; tel. 313564343; fax 313564340; e-mail esuiz@mrecic.gov.ar; internet www.suiza.embajada-argentina.gov.ar; Chargé d'affaires a.i. FERNANDO RAUL LERENA.

Armenia: 28 ave du Mail, 1205 Geneva; tel. 223201100; fax 223206148; e-mail arm.mission@deckpoint.ch; Ambassador CHARLES AZNAVOUR.

Austria: Kirchenfeldstr. 77–79, 3005 Bern; tel. 313565252; fax 313515664; e-mail bern-ob@bmeia.gv.at; internet www.aussenministerium.at/bern; Ambassador Dr HANS PETER MANZ.

Azerbaijan: Dalmaziquai 27, 3005 Bern; tel. 313505040; fax 313505041; e-mail bern@mission.mfa.gov.az; internet www.azembassy.ch; Ambassador MURAD NAJAFBAYLI.

Bangladesh: 65 Rue de Lausanne, 1202 Geneva; tel. 229068020; fax 227384616; e-mail mission.bangladesh@ties.itu.int; Ambassador ABDUL HANNAN.

Belarus: Quartierweg 6, CP 438, 3074 Muri bei Bern; tel. 319527914; fax 319527616; e-mail swiss@belembassy.org; internet www.swiss.belembassy.org; Chargé d'affaires a.i. ANDREI KULAZHANKA.

Belgium: Jubiläumsstr. 41, Postfach 150, 3000 Bern; tel. 313500150; fax 313500165; e-mail bern@diplobel.fed.be; internet www.diplomatie.be/bern; Ambassador MARC VAN CRAEN.

Benin: 28 chemin du Petit-Saconnex, 1209 Geneva; tel. 229068460; fax 229068461; e-mail info@missionbenin.ch; Ambassador SÉRAPHIN LISSASSI.

Bhutan: 17–19 chemin du Champ-d'Anier, 1209 Geneva; tel. 227990890; fax 227990899; e-mail mission.bhutan@ties.itu.int; Ambassador YESHEY DORJI.

Bosnia and Herzegovina: Thorackerstr. 3, 3074 Muri bei Bern; tel. 313511052; fax 313511079; e-mail emb-ch-brn@vtxmail.ch; Ambassador JAKOB FINCI.

Brazil: Monbijoustr. 68, 3007 Bern; tel. 313718515; fax 313710525; e-mail info@brasbern.ch; internet www.brasbern.ch; Ambassador MARIA STELA POMPEU BRASIL FROTA.

Bulgaria: Bernastr. 2–4, 3005 Bern; tel. 313511455; fax 313510064; e-mail bulembassy@bluewin.ch; internet www.bulembassy.ch; Chargé d'affaires a.i. EMIL GENDOV.

Burkina Faso: 51 ave Blanc, 1202 Geneva; tel. 227346330; fax 227346331; e-mail info@ambaburkinafaso-ch.org; internet www.ambaburkinafaso-ch.org; Ambassador PROSPER VOKOUMA.

Burundi: 44 rue de Lausanne, 1201 Geneva; tel. 227327705; fax 227327734; e-mail mission.burundi@bluewin.ch; Ambassador PIERRE CLAVER NDAYIRAGIJE.

Cambodia: Chemin Taverney 3, CP 213, 1218 Le Grand-Saconnex; tel. 227887773; fax 227887774; e-mail cambodge@bluewin.ch; Ambassador SUN SUON.

Cameroon: Brunnadernrain 29, 3006 Bern; tel. 313524737; fax 313524736; e-mail ambacam.berne@yahoo.fr; internet www.ambacamberne.ch; Ambassador LÉONARD HENRI BINDZI.

Canada: Kirchenfeldstr. 88, 3005 Bern; tel. 313573200; fax 313573210; e-mail bern@international.gc.ca; internet www.canadainternational.gc.ca/switzerland-suisse; Ambassador ROBERTA SANTI.

Cape Verde: 47 ave Blanc, 1202 Geneva; tel. (22) 7313336; fax 227313540; e-mail cap.vert@bluewin.ch; Ambassador JOSÉ LUIS MONTEIRO.

Central African Republic: 9 chemin de Taverney, 1218 Le Grand-Saconnex; tel. 227888883; fax 227888885; Ambassador LÉOPOLD SAMBA.

Chile: Eigerpl. 5, 12th Floor, 3007 Bern; tel. 313700058; fax 313720025; e-mail embajada@embachile.ch; Ambassador ENRIQUE MIGUEL MELKONIAN STUERMER.

China, People's Republic: Kalcheggweg 10, 3006 Bern; tel. 313527333; fax 313514573; e-mail chinaemb_ch@mfa.gov.cn; internet www.china-embassy.ch; Ambassador WU KEN.

Colombia: Dufourstr. 47, 3005 Bern; tel. 313511700; fax 313501409; e-mail eberna@cancilleria.gov.co; internet www.emcol.ch; Ambassador CLAUDIA TURBAY QUINTERO.

Congo, Democratic Republic: Sulgenheimweg 21, CP 5261, 3001 Bern; tel. 313713538; fax 313727466; e-mail rdcambassy@bluewin.ch; Chargé d'affaires a.i. SÉBASTIEN MUTOMB MUJING.

Congo, Republic: 8 rue Chabray, 1201 Geneva; tel. 227318821; fax 227318817; e-mail missioncongo@bluewin.ch; Ambassador LUC-JOSEPH OKIO.

Costa Rica: Schwarztorstr. 11, 3007 Bern; tel. 313727887; fax 313727834; e-mail costa.rica@bluewin.ch; Chargé d'affaires a.i. ROBERTO AVENDANO SANCHO.

Côte d'Ivoire: Thormannstr. 51, CP 170, 3005 Bern; tel. 313508080; fax 313508081; e-mail acibe-1@acibe.org; internet www.acibe.org; Ambassador MAMADOU DIARRASSOUBA.

Croatia: Thunstr. 45, 3005 Bern; tel. 313520275; fax 313520373; e-mail croemb.bern@mvpei.hr; Ambassador JAKŠA MULJAČIĆ.

Cuba: Gesellschaftsstr. 8, CP 5275, 3012 Bern; tel. 313022111; fax 313029830; e-mail embacuba.berna@bluewin.ch; internet emba.cubaminrex.cu/suiza; Ambassador ISAAC ROBERTO TORRES BARRIOS.

SWITZERLAND

Czech Republic: Muristr. 53, CP 537, 3000 Bern 31; tel. 313504070; fax 313504098; e-mail bern@embassy.mzv.cz; internet www.mfa.cz/bern; Ambassador Dr Boris Lazar.

Denmark: Thunstr. 95, 3006 Bern 31; tel. 313505454; fax 313505464; e-mail brnamb@um.dk; internet www.ambbern.um.dk; Ambassador Hans Klingenberg.

Dominican Republic: Weltpoststr. 4, CP 22, 3000 Bern 15; tel. 313511585; fax 313511587; e-mail embaj.rep-dom@sunrise.ch; Ambassador Teresita Migdalia Torres García.

Ecuador: Kramgasse 54, 3011 Bern; tel. 313516254; fax 313512771; e-mail embecusuiza@bluewin.ch; Ambassador Rafael Alfonso Paredes Proano.

Egypt: Elfenauweg 61, 3006 Bern; tel. 313528012; fax 313520625; Ambassador Magdy Galal Sharawy.

Ethiopia: 56 rue de Moillebeau, CP 338, 1211 Geneva 19; tel. 229197010; fax 229197029; e-mail mission.ethiopia@ties.itu.int; internet www.ethiopianmission.ch; Chargé d'affaires a.i. Petros Tetemke.

Finland: Weltpoststr. 4, Postfach 11, 3015 Bern 15; tel. 313504100; fax 313504107; e-mail sanomat.brn@formin.fi; internet www.finlandia.ch; Ambassador Alpo Rusi.

France: Schosshaldenstr. 46, 3006 Bern; tel. 313592111; fax 313592191; e-mail scac@ambafrance-ch.org; Ambassador Alain Pierre Catta.

Georgia: 1 rue Richard Wagner, 1202 Geneva; tel. 229191010; fax 227339033; e-mail geomission.geneva@bluewin.com; internet www.switzerland.mfa.gov.ge; Ambassador Zurab Tchiaberashvili.

Germany: Willadingweg 83, Postfach 250, 3000 Bern 15; tel. 313594111; fax 313594444; e-mail info@bern.diplo.de; internet www.bern.diplo.de; Ambassador Dr Axel Berg.

Ghana: Belpstr. 11, Postfach, 3001 Bern; tel. 313817852; fax 313814941; e-mail ghanaemb@tcnet.ch; internet www.ghanaembassy.ch; Ambassador Ellen Serwaa Nee-Whang.

Greece: Weltpostr. 4, 3015 Bern; tel. 313561414; fax 313681272; e-mail gremb.brn@mfa.gr; Ambassador John Mourikis.

Holy See: Thunstr. 60, CP 259, 3006 Bern (Apostolic Nunciature); tel. 313526040; fax 313525064; e-mail nunziaturach@yahoo.com; Apostolic Nuncio Most Rev. Francesco Canalini (Titular Archbishop of Valeria).

Hungary: Muristr. 31, CP 216, 3000 Bern 15; tel. 313528572; fax 313512001; e-mail mission.brn@kum.hu; internet www.mfa.gov.hu/emb/bern; Ambassador Erzebet Nagy.

India: Kirchenfeldstr. 28, 3005 Bern; tel. 313501130; fax 313511557; e-mail india@indembassybern.ch; internet www.indembassybern.ch; Ambassador Chitra Narayanan.

Indonesia: Elfenauweg 51, 3006 Bern; tel. 313520983; fax 313516765; e-mail kbribern@bgb.ch; internet www.indonesia-bern.org; Ambassador Djoko Susilo.

Iran: Thunstr. 68, CP 227, 3006 Bern 6; tel. 313510801; fax 313515652; e-mail secretariat@iranembassy.ch; internet www.iranembassy.ch; Ambassador Alireza Salari Sharifabadi.

Iraq: Elfenstr. 6, 3006 Bern; tel. 313514043; fax 313518312; e-mail bernemb@iraqmofamail.net; internet www.irakembassy.ch; Ambassador Pirot Ahmed Ibrahim Ibrahim.

Ireland: Kirchenfeldstr. 68, Postfach 262, 3005 Bern; tel. 313521442; fax 313521455; e-mail berne@dfa.ie; internet www.embassyofireland.ch; Ambassador Martin Burke.

Israel: Alpenstr. 32, 3006 Bern 6; tel. 313563500; fax 313563556; e-mail info@bern.mfa.gov.il; internet bern.mfa.gov.il; Ambassador Ilan Elgar.

Italy: Elfenstr. 14, 3000 Bern 16; tel. 313500777; fax 313500711; e-mail ambasciata.berna@esteri.it; internet www.ambberna.esteri.it; Ambassador Giuseppe Deodato.

Japan: Engestr. 53, 3000 Bern 9; tel. 313002222; fax 313002255; e-mail eojs@bluewin.ch; internet www.ch.emb-japan.go.jp; Ambassador Ichiro Komatsu.

Jordan: Thorackerstr. 3, 3074 Muri bei Bern; tel. 313840404; fax 313840405; e-mail info@jordanembassy.ch; Ambassador Nabil Saleem Masarweh.

Kazakhstan: Alleeweg 15, 3006 Bern; tel. 313517972; fax 313517975; e-mail kasachische.botschaft@freesurf.ch; internet www.kazakhstan-bern.ch; Ambassador Mukhtar Tileuberdi.

Korea, Democratic People's Republic: Pourtalèsstr. 43, 3074 Muri bei Bern; tel. 319516621; fax 319515704; e-mail dprk.embassy@bluewin.ch; Ambassador So Se-Phyong.

Korea, Republic: Kalcheggweg 38, 3006 Bern 15; tel. 313562444; fax 313562450; e-mail swiss@mofat.go.kr; internet che-berne.mofat.go.kr; Ambassador Kim Jong-Il.

Kosovo: Amthausgasse 3, 3011 Bern; tel. 313100690; fax 313100691; e-mail embassy.switzerland@ks-gov.net; Ambassador Naim Malaj.

Kuwait: Brunadernrain 19, Postfach 458, 3006 Bern; tel. 313567000; fax 313567001; e-mail info@kuwaitembassy.ch; internet www.kuwaitembassy.ch; Ambassador Dr Suhail Khalil Yousef Shuhaiber.

Kyrgyzstan: 4–6 rue du Lac, 1ère étage, 1207 Geneva; tel. 227079220; fax 227079221; e-mail kyrgyzmission@bluewin.ch; internet www.kyrgyzmission.net; Ambassador Gulnora T. Iskakova.

Laos: 14 bis route de Colovrex, 1218 Le Grand-Saconnex; tel. 227982441; fax 227982440; e-mail laomission_geneva@bluewin.ch; Ambassador Yong Chanthalangsy.

Lebanon: Thunstr. 10, 3074 Muri bei Bern; tel. 319506565; fax 319506566; e-mail ambalibch@hotmail.com; internet ambassadeliban.ch; Ambassador Hussein Rammal.

Lesotho: 45–47 rue de Lausanne, 2ème étage, 1201 Geneva; tel. 229061050; fax 229000525; e-mail mission.lesotho@ties.itu.int; Ambassador Anthony Mothae Maruping.

Libya: Tavelweg 2, 3006 Bern 31; tel. 313513076; fax 313511325; Ambassador (vacant).

Liechtenstein: Willadingweg 65, Postfach, 3000 Bern 15; tel. 313576411; fax 313576415; e-mail info@bbrn.llv.li; internet www.bern.liechtenstein.li; Ambassador Dr Hubert Ferdinand Büchel.

Lithuania: Kramgasse 12, 3011 Bern; tel. 313525291; fax 313525292; e-mail amb.ch@urm.lt; internet ch.mfa.lt; Chargé d'affaires a.i. Virginija Umbrasiené.

Luxembourg: Kramgasse 45, Postfach 619, 3000 Bern 8; tel. 313114732; fax 313110019; e-mail berne.am@mae.etat.lu; internet berne.mae.lu/ge; Ambassador Gérard Philipps.

Macedonia, former Yugoslav republic: Kirchenfeldstr. 30, 3005 Bern; tel. 313520002; fax 313520037; e-mail makedamb@bluewin.ch; Ambassador Ramadan Nazifi.

Madagascar: 32 ave de Riant-Parc, 1209 Geneva; tel. 227401650; fax 227401616; e-mail ambamadsuisse@bluewin.ch; internet www.madagascar-diplomatie.ch; Ambassador Rajemison Rakotomaharo.

Malaysia: Jungfraustr. 1, 3005 Bern; tel. 313504700; fax 313504702; e-mail malberne@kln.gov.my; Ambassador Ho May Yong.

Mali: 20 route de Pré-Bois, 1215 Geneva 15 Aéroport; tel. 227100960; fax 227100696; e-mail malisuisse@yahoo.fr; Ambassador Sidiki Lamine Sow.

Mexico: Weltpoststr. 20, 3015 Bern; tel. 313574747; fax 313574748; e-mail embamex1@swissonline.ch; internet www.sre.gob.mx/suiza; Ambassador Luciano Joublanc Montano.

Monaco: Hallwylstr. 34, 3006 Bern; tel. 313562858; fax 313562855; e-mail ambassademonaco@bluewin.ch; Ambassador Robert Fillon.

Montenegro: 147 rue de Lausanne, 1202 Geneva; tel. 227326680; fax 227326682; e-mail missionofmontenegro@bluewin.ch; Ambassador Ljubisa Perovic.

Morocco: Helvetiastr. 42, 3005 Bern; tel. 313510362; fax 313510364; e-mail sifamaberne2@bluewin.ch; internet www.amb-maroc.ch; Ambassador Muhammad Saïd Benryane.

Netherlands: Seftigenstr. 7, 3007 Bern; tel. 313508700; fax 313508710; e-mail ben@minbuza.nl; internet www.nlembassy.ch; Ambassador Dr Peter Schönherr.

Nigeria: Zieglerstr. 45, Postfach 574, 3007 Bern; tel. 313842600; fax 313842626; e-mail info@nigerianbern.org; internet www.nigerianbern.org; Chargé d'affaires a.i. Ifeanyi Eugene Nwosu.

Norway: Bubenbergpl. 10, Postfach 5264, 3011 Bern; tel. 313105555; fax 313105550; e-mail emb.bern@mfa.no; internet www.amb-norwegen.ch; Ambassador Rolf Trolle Andersen.

Pakistan: Bernastr. 47, 3005 Bern; tel. 313501790; fax 313501799; e-mail parepberne@bluewin.ch; Chargé d'affaires a.i. Hasnain Yousaf.

Paraguay: Kramgasse 58, Postfach 523, 3000 Bern 8; tel. 313123222; fax 313123432; e-mail embapar@embapar.ch; Ambassador Rodolfo Luis González Garabelli.

Peru: Thunstr. 36, 3005 Bern; tel. 313518555; fax 313518570; e-mail info@embaperu.ch; Ambassador Juan Carlos Gamarra.

Philippines: Kirchenfeldstr. 73–75, 3005 Bern; tel. 313501717; fax 313522602; e-mail info@philembassyberne.ch; internet www.philembassyberne.ch; Ambassador (vacant).

Poland: Elfenstr. 20A, 3000 Bern 15; tel. 313580202; fax 313580216; e-mail berno.amb.sekretariat@msz.gov.pl; internet www.berno.polemb.net; Ambassador Jarosław Starzyk.

Portugal: Weltpoststr. 20, 3015 Bern; tel. 313528668; fax 313514432; e-mail mail@scber.dgaccp.pt; Ambassador José Manuel de Carvalho.

SWITZERLAND

Romania: Kirchenfeldstr. 78, 3005 Bern; tel. 313523522; fax 313526455; e-mail ambasada@roamb.ch; internet berna.mae.ro; Ambassador Dr IONEL NICU SAVA.

Russia: Brunnadernrain 37, 3006 Bern; tel. 313520566; fax 313525595; e-mail rusbotschaft@bluewin.ch; internet www.switzerland.mid.ru; Ambassador IGOR B. BRATCHIKOV.

Rwanda: 37–39 rue de Vermont, 4ème étage, 1202 Geneva; tel. 229191000; fax 229191001; e-mail ambageneve@minaffet.gov.rw; internet switzerland.embassy.gov.rw; Ambassador SOLINA NYIRAHABIMANA.

Saudi Arabia: Kramburgstr. 12, 3006 Bern; tel. 313521555; fax 313514581; e-mail chemb@mofa.gov.sa; Ambassador HAZEM M. S. KARAKOTLY.

Serbia: Seminarstr. 5, 3006 Bern; tel. 313524996; fax 313514474; e-mail info@ambasadasrbije.ch; internet www.ambasadasrbije.ch; Ambassador MILAN PROTIĆ.

Slovakia: Thunstr. 63, 3074 Muri bei Bern; tel. 313563930; fax 313563933; e-mail slovak@spectraweb.ch; Ambassador JAN FOLTIN.

Slovenia: Schwanengasse 9, 3011 Bern; tel. 313109000; fax 313124414; e-mail vbe@gov.si; internet bern.embassy.si; Ambassador BOJAN GROBOVŠEK.

South Africa: Alpenstr. 29, Postfach, 3000 Bern 6; tel. 313501313; fax 313513944; e-mail bern.admin@foreign.gov.za; internet www.southafrica.ch; Ambassador GEORGE HENRY JOHANNES.

Spain: Kalcheggweg 24, Postfach 99, 3000 Bern 15; tel. 313505252; fax 313505255; e-mail emb.berna@maec.es; internet www.maec.es/embajadas/berna; Ambassador MIGUEL ANGEL DE FRUTOS GÓMEZ.

Sudan: 51–53 ave Blanc, 3ème étage, 1202 Geneva; tel. 227312663; fax 227161970; e-mail mission.sudan@bluewin.ch; internet www.sudanembassy-mission.ch; Chargé d'affaires a.i. JOHN OMER HASSAN AHMED.

Sweden: Bundesgasse 26, Postfach, 3011 Bern; tel. 313287000; fax 313287001; e-mail ambassaden.bern@foreign.ministry.se; internet www.swedenabroad.com/bern; Ambassador PER THÖRESSON.

Thailand: Kirchstr. 56, 3097 Liebefeld-Bern; tel. 319703030; fax 319703035; e-mail thai.bern@bluewin.ch; Ambassador ARBHORN MANASVANICH.

Timor-Leste: 16 route de Colovrex, 2ème étage, 1218 Le Grand-Saconnex; tel. 227883562; fax 227883564; e-mail info@timor-lestemission.ch; Ambassador JOAQUIM ANTÓNIO MARIA LOPES DA FONSECA.

Tunisia: Kirchenfeldstr. 63, 3005 Bern; tel. 313528226; fax 313510445; e-mail at.berne@bluewin.ch; Chargé d'affaires a.i. SAMI SAIDI.

Turkey: Lombachweg 33, 3006 Bern; tel. 313597070; fax 313528819; e-mail tcbern@tr-botschaft.ch; internet www.tr-botschaft.ch; Ambassador TANJU SÜMER.

Turkmenistan: 29 route de Pré-Bois, 1215 Geneva 15 Aéroport; tel. 229295775; fax 227910885; e-mail tm_ch@live.com; Ambassador ESEN AYDOGDYEV (Resident in Vienna, Austria).

Uganda: 6 bis rue Antoine Carteret, 1202 Geneva; tel. 223398810; fax 223407030; e-mail mission.uganda@ties.itu.ch; internet www.ugandamission.ch; Ambassador MAURICE KIWANUKA KAGIMU.

Ukraine: Feldeggweg 5, 3005 Bern; tel. 313522316; fax 313516416; e-mail emb_ch@mfa.gov.ua; internet www.mfa.gov.ua/switzerland; Ambassador IHOR DIR.

United Kingdom: Thunstr. 50, 3000 Bern 15; tel. 313597700; fax 313597701; e-mail info@britishembassy.ch; internet ukinswitzerland.fco.gov.uk; Ambassador SARAH GILLETT.

USA: Sulgeneckstr. 19, 3007 Bern; tel. 313577011; fax 313577344; internet bern.usembassy.gov; Ambassador DONALD STERNOFF BEYER, Jr.

Uruguay: Kramgasse 63, 3011 Bern; tel. 313122226; fax 313112747; e-mail uruhelve@bluewin.ch; Ambassador LUIS RICARDO NARIO FAGÚNDEZ.

Venezuela: Schosshaldenstr. 1, Postfach 1005, 3000 Bern 15; tel. 313505757; fax 313505758; e-mail embajada@embavenez-suiza.ch; internet www.embavenez-suiza.ch; Ambassador CÉSAR OSVELIO MÉNDEZ GONZÁLEZ.

Viet Nam: Schlösslistr. 26, 3008 Bern; tel. 313887872; fax 313887879; e-mail info@vietnam-embassy.ch; internet www.vietnam-embassy.ch; Ambassador HOANG VAN NHA.

Judicial System

Switzerland has had a common Civil Code since 1912, but the Penal Code was only unified in 1942. Under the Code, capital punishment was abolished by the few cantons that still retained it. The individual cantons continue to elect and maintain their own magistracy, and retain certain variations in procedure. The canton of Zürich, for example, has justices of the peace (Friedensrichter—normally one for each commune), District Courts (Bezirksgerichte), Labour Courts (Arbeitsgerichte), Courts for Tenancy Matters, an Appeal Court (Obergericht) with various specialized benches, a Cassation Court (Kassationsgericht), and, for the more important cases under penal law, a Jury Court (Geschworenengericht).

At the federal level, the Federal Supreme Court has, in principle, jurisdiction over judicial matters. However, federal appeals commissions adjudicate appeals against rulings by the federal authority. From 1997 a revision of the federal judicial system was undertaken that saw the establishment of two new judicial bodies of first instance, in order to alleviate the burden on the Federal Supreme Court. These were the Federal Criminal Court (from April 2004) and the Federal Administrative Court (from January 2007). In January 2007 the competences of the Federal Insurance Court were assumed by the Federal Supreme Court. There are also military courts at the federal level.

Most disputes relating to the application of federal administrative law are first judged by the Federal Administrative Court. In January 2007 the Federal Administrative Court replaced some 30 federal appeals commissions as well as the current departmental appeals services.

FEDERAL SUPREME COURT

Schweizerisches Bundesgericht—Tribunal fédéral
Schweizerhofquai 6, 6004 Luzern; 29 ave du Tribunal fédéral, 1000 Lausanne 14; tel. 213189111; fax 213233700; e-mail direktion@bger.admin.ch; internet www.bger.ch.

Composed of 38 judges elected for a six-year term by the Federal Assembly. According to the Constitution any citizen eligible for election to the National Council can theoretically be elected Justice to the Court, but in practice only lawyers are considered for this office. All of the official Swiss languages must be represented in the Court. The President of the Federal Supreme Court is elected by the Federal Assembly for a two-year term, with no possibility of re-election, from among the senior judges of the Court. The Court is divided into six permanent branches or chambers, each of which has jurisdiction over cases pertaining to a specific subject, namely: (a) two 'Public', i.e. Constitutional and Administrative Law Divisions, being composed of seven and six judges, respectively; (b) two Civil or Private Law Divisions of six judges each, which serve mainly as Courts of Appeal in civil matters; (c) the Debt Execution and Bankruptcy Law Chamber of three judges (members of the Second Civil Law Division); (d) the Criminal Law Division, the so-called Court of Cassation, which is composed of five judges and which hears mainly appeals in criminal law matters. There are also four non-permanent divisions hearing exclusively cases that involve certain crimes against the Confederation, certain forms of terrorism, and other offences related to treason.

President: LORENZ MEYER.

Vice-President: SUZANNE LEUZINGER.

FEDERAL CRIMINAL COURT

Bundesstrafgericht—Tribunal pénal fédéral
CP 2720, 6501 Bellinzona; Viale Stefano Franscini 3, 6500 Bellinzona; tel. 918226262; fax 918226242; e-mail info@bstger.admin.ch; internet www.bstger.ch.

f. 2004; composed of 17 judges elected by the Federal Assembly; court of first instance for criminal cases assigned to federal jurisdiction; in particular, may adjudicate offences such as crimes and misdemeanours against the Confederation's interests, offences committed using explosives, economic crime, organized crime or money-laundering beyond the internal or external borders of Switzerland.

President: ANDREAS J. KELLER.

Vice-President: DANIEL KIPFER FASCIATI.

FEDERAL ADMINISTRATIVE COURT

Bundesverwaltungsgericht—Tribunal administratif fédéral
Postfach, 3000 Bern 14; tel. 587052626; fax 587052980; e-mail info@bvger.admin.ch; internet www.bvger.ch.

Composed of 72 judges elected by the Federal Assembly for a renewable period of six years; court of first instance for cases arising from administrative decisions at the federal level; appeals in some cases relating to civil and public law matters may be heard in the Federal Supreme Court.

President: CHRISTOPH BANDLI.

Vice-President: MARKUS METZ.

SWITZERLAND

Religion

According to the 2000 census, the religious adherence of the total resident population was as follows: Roman Catholic 41.8%, Protestant 35.3%, Orthodox Church 1.8%, Old Catholic 0.2%, Muslim 4.3%, Jewish 0.2%, other religions (including Buddhist and Hindu) 0.8% and those without religion 11.1%.

CHRISTIANITY

The Roman Catholic Church

For ecclesiastical purposes, Switzerland comprises six dioceses and two territorial abbacies. All of the dioceses and abbacies are directly responsible to the Holy See. At 31 December 2006 there were an estimated 3,183,081 adherents (some 44.4% of the total population).

Bishops' Conference

Secrétariat de la Conférence des Evêques Suisses, CP 278, 1701 Fribourg; tel. 265101515; fax 265101516; e-mail secretariat@conferencedeseveques.ch; internet www.kath.ch/sbk-ces-cvs.

f. 1863; Pres. Rt Rev. NORBERT BRUNNER (Bishop of Sion); Sec.-Gen. Abbé FELIX GMÜR.

Bishop of Basel: Rt Rev. KURT KOCH, Bischöfliches Ordinariat, Baselstr. 58, Postfach 216, 4501 Solothurn; tel. 326255825; fax 326255845; e-mail generalvikariat@bistum-basel.ch; internet www.bistum-basel.ch.

Bishop of Chur: Rt Rev. VITUS HUONDER, Bischöfliches Ordinariat, Hof 19, Postfach 133, 7002 Chur; tel. 812586000; fax 812586001; e-mail ordinariat@bistum-chur.ch; internet www.bistum-chur.ch.

Bishop of Lausanne, Geneva and Fribourg: Rt Rev. BERNARD GENOUD, 86 rue de Lausanne, CP 512, 1701 Fribourg; tel. 263474850; fax 263474851; e-mail chancellerie@diocese-lgf.ch; internet www.diocese-lgf.ch.

Bishop of Lugano: Rt Rev. PIER GIACOMO GRAMPA, Via Borghetto 6, CP 5382, 6901 Lugano; tel. 919138989; fax 919138990; e-mail segretaria.vescovo@catt.ch; internet www.catt.ch.

Bishop of Sankt Gallen: Rt Rev. MARKUS BÜCHEL, Bischöfliches Ordinariat, Klosterhof 6B, Postfach 263, 9001 Sankt Gallen; tel. 712273340; fax 712273341; e-mail kanzlei@bistum-stgallen.ch; internet www.bistum-stgallen.ch.

Bishop of Sion: Rt Rev. NORBERT BRUNNER, 12 rue de la Tour, CP 2124, 1950 Sion 2; tel. 273291818; fax 273291836; e-mail diocese.sion@cath-vs.ch; internet www.cath-vs.ch.

Protestant Churches

Federation of Swiss Protestant Churches (Schweizerischer Evangelischer Kirchenbund—Fédération des Eglises protestantes de Suisse): Sulgenauweg 26, Postfach, 3000 Bern 23; tel. 313702525; fax 313702580; e-mail info@sek-feps.ch; internet www.sek-feps.ch; f. 1920; comprises the reformed cantonal churches of Aargau, Appenzell (incl. Appenzell Ausserrhoden and Appenzell Innerrhoden), Basel-Landschaft, Basel-Stadt, Bern-Jura-Solothurn, Fribourg, Geneva, Glarus, Graubünden, Luzern, Neuchâtel, Nidwalden, Obwalden, St Gallen, Schaffhausen, Schwyz, Solothurn, Thurgau, Ticino, Uri, Valais, Vaud, Zug, Zürich, the Free Evangelical Church of Geneva and the United Methodist Church; the exec. organ is the Council of the Federation (Rat des Schweizerischen Evangelischen Kirchenbundes—Conseil de la Fédération); Pres. Rev. THOMAS WIPF.

The Old Catholic Church

Christkatholische Kirche der Schweiz (Old Catholic Church of Switzerland): Willadingweg 39, 3006 Bern; tel. 313513530; fax 313529560; e-mail bischof@christkath.ch; internet www.christkath.ch; f. 1874; c. 13,500 mems; Pres., Synodical Council URS STOLZ; Bishop Dr HARALD REIN.

ISLAM

According to the 2000 census there were 310,807 Muslims recorded in Switzerland, making Islam the second largest religion in the country. There are two major mosques, one in Zürich and one in Geneva, and approximately 200 Islamic centres located throughout the country.

Federation of Islamic Organizations in Switzerland (Föderation Islamischer Dachorganisationen in der Schweiz—Fédération d'Organisations Islamiques de Suisse): Bahnstr. 80, 8105 Regensdorf; tel. 714551383; fax 714551387; e-mail info@fids.ch; internet www.fids.ch; f. 2006; 12 mem. orgs; Pres. Dr HISHAM ABU MAIZAR.

Föderation Islamischer Gemeinschaften in der Schweiz: Hohlstrasse 615A, 8050 Zürich; tel. 443013151; f. 1978.

JUDAISM

According to the 2000 census there were 17,900 Jews in Switzerland.

Schweizerischer Israelitischer Gemeindebund—Fédération suisse des communautés israélites: Gotthardstr. 65, Postfach 2105, 8027 Zürich; tel. 433050777; fax 433050766; e-mail info@swissjews.ch; internet www.swissjews.ch; f. 1904; Pres. Dr HERBERT WINTER; Gen. Sec. JONATHAN KREUTNER.

The Press

Freedom of the press in Switzerland is guaranteed by Article 17 of the amended 1999 Constitution, and the only formal restrictions on the press are the legal restraints concerned with abuses of this freedom.

Switzerland's federal constitutional structure and the coexistence of diverse languages and religions have tended to produce a decentralized press, fragmented into numerous local papers, often with very low circulations. The majority of newspapers are regional, even such high circulation ones as *Berner Zeitung*, *Tages-Anzeiger* and national dailies such as *Neue Zürcher Zeitung*. About 67% of newspapers are printed in German, 27% in French, 4% in Italian and less than 1% in Romansh. Some 100,000 copies of French, German, Italian and Spanish newspapers are imported daily.

PRINCIPAL DAILIES

Baden

Aargauer Zeitung: Stadtturmstr. 19, 5400 Baden; tel. 582005858; fax 582005859; e-mail azredaktion@azag.ch; internet www.aargauerzeitung.ch; f. 1996 by merger of *Aargauer Tagblatt* and *Badener Tagblatt*; Editor-in-Chief PETER BURI; circ. 129,321 (2007).

Basel/Bâle

Basler Zeitung: Aeschenpl. 7, 4002 Basel; tel. 616391111; fax 616311582; e-mail redaktion@baz.ch; internet www.baz.ch; f. 1976; liberal; Editor-in-Chief MATTHIAS GEERING; circ. 94,084 (2007).

Bellinzona

La Regione Ticino: Via Ghiringhelli 9, 6500 Bellinzona; tel. 918211121; fax 918211122; e-mail info@laregione.ch; internet www.laregione.ch; f. 1992; Editor GIACOMO SALVIONI; circ. 32,555 (2009).

Bern/Berne

Berner Zeitung: Nordring/Dammweg 9, 3001 Bern; tel. 3133003111; fax 313327724; e-mail redaktion@bernerzeitung.ch; internet www.bzonline.ch; f. 1844; independent; Editors-in-Chief MARKUS EISENHUT, MICHAEL HUG; circ. 213,544 (2007).

Der Bund: Bubenbergpl. 8, 3001 Bern; tel. 313851111; fax 313851112; e-mail redaktion@derbund.ch; internet www.ebund.ch; f. 1850; liberal; Editor-in-Chief ARTUR K. VOGEL; circ. 60,500 (2005).

Biel/Bienne

Bieler Tagblatt: Robert-Walser-Pl. 7, 2502 Biel; tel. 323219111; fax 323219119; e-mail btredaktion@bielertagblatt.ch; internet www.bielertagblatt.ch; independent; Editor-in-Chief CATHERINE DUTTWEILER; circ. 27,576 (2007).

Brig

Walliser Bote: Furkastr. 21, 3900 Brig; tel. 279229988; fax 279229989; e-mail info@walliserbote.ch; internet www.walliserbote.ch; Catholic; Editor-in-Chief PIUS RIEDER; circ. 26,727 (2007).

La Chaux-de-Fonds

L'impartial: 14 rue Neuve, 2300 La Chaux-de-Fonds; tel. 329102000; fax 329102009; e-mail redaction@limpartial.ch; internet www.limpartial.ch; f. 1880; independent; Editor-in-Chief NICOLAS WILLEMIN; circ. 15,182 (2007).

Chur/Coire

Bündner Tagblatt: Comercialstr. 22, 7007 Chur; tel. 812555000; fax 812555123; e-mail redaktion-bt@suedostschweiz.ch; internet www.suedostschweiz.ch/medien/bt; f. 1852; independent; Editor-in-Chief CHRISTIAN BUXHOFER.

La Quotidiana: Via Centrala 4, 7130 Glion; tel. 819200710; fax 819200715; e-mail redaktion-lq@suedostschweiz.ch; f. 1997; in Romansh; Publr Südostschweiz Presse AG; Editor-in-Chief MARTIN CABALZAR.

Die Südostschweiz: Comercialstr. 22, 7007 Chur; tel. 812255050; fax 812255102; e-mail zentralredaktion@suedostschweiz.ch; internet www.suedostschweiz.ch; publ. regional editions for Gaster und See and Glarus; independent; Publr Südostschweiz Presse AG; Editor-in-Chief ANDREA MASÜGER; circ. 126,697 (2007).

Delémont

Le Quotidien Jurassien: 6 route de Courroux, 2800 Delémont; tel. 324211818; fax 324211890; e-mail lqj@lqj.ch; internet www.lqj.ch; f. 1993; independent; Editor-in-Chief PIERRE-ANDRÉ CHAPATTE; circ. 21,246 (2007).

Dielsdorf

Zürcher Unterländer: Schulstr. 12, 8157 Dielsdorf; tel. 18548282; fax 18530690; e-mail redaktion@zuonline.ch; internet www.zuonline.ch; Editor-in-Chief CHRISTINE FIVIAN; circ. 22,544 (2007).

Frauenfeld

Thurgauer Zeitung: Promenadenstr. 16, 8501 Frauenfeld; tel. 527235757; fax 527235707; e-mail redaktion@thurgauerzeitung.ch; internet www.thurgauerzeitung.ch; f. 1798; independent; Publrs Huber & Co AG; Editor-in-Chief URSULA FRAEFEL; circ. 39,406 (2007).

Freiburg/Fribourg

La Liberté: 42 blvd de Pérolles, 1705 Fribourg; tel. 264264411; fax 264264444; e-mail redaction@laliberte.ch; internet www.laliberte.ch; Editor-in-Chief LOUIS RUFFIEUX; circ. 38,735 (2007).

Genève
(Geneva)

Le Temps: 3 pl. de Cornavin, CP 2570, 1211 Geneva 2; tel. 227995858; fax 227995859; e-mail info@letemps.ch; internet www.letemps.ch; f. 1998; Dir and Editor-in-Chief JEAN-JACQUES ROTH; circ. 45,103 (2007).

Tribune de Genève: CP 5115, 11 rue des Rois, 1211 Geneva 11; tel. 223224000; fax 227810107; e-mail alain.giroud@edipresse.ch; internet www.tdg.ch; f. 1879; independent; morning; Editor-in-Chief PIERRE RUETSCHI; circ. 62,003 (2007).

Herisau

Appenzeller Zeitung: Kasernenstr. 64, 9100 Herisau; tel. 713546474; fax 713546475; e-mail redaktion@appon.ch; internet www.appenzellerzeitung.ch; radical democratic; f. 1828; Publrs Appenzeller Medienhaus Schläpfer AG; Editor-in-Chief MONIKA EGLI.

Lausanne

Le Matin: 33 ave de la Gare, 1001 Lausanne; tel. 213494949; fax 21494929; internet www.lematin.ch; f. 1862; independent; Editor-in-Chief PETER ROTHENBÜHLER; circ. 70,012 (2007).

24 heures: 33 ave de la Gare, 1001 Lausanne; tel. 213494444; fax 213494419; internet www.24heures.ch; f. 1762; independent; Editor-in-Chief THIERRY MAYER; circ. 89,102 (2007).

Lugano

Corriere del Ticino: Via Industria, 6933 Muzzano; tel. 919603131; fax 919682779; e-mail cdt@cdt.ch; internet www.cdt.ch; f. 1891; independent; Dir GIANCARLO DILLENA; circ. 38,108 (2007).

Giornale del Popolo: Via San Gottardo 50, 6900 Lugano; tel. 919223800; fax 919223805; e-mail redazione@gdp.ch; internet www.gdp.ch; f. 1926; independent; Pres. PIER GIACOMO GRAMPA; circ. 18,057 (2007).

Luzern/Lucerne

Neue Luzerner Zeitung: Maihofstr. 76, 6006 Lucerne; tel. 414295252; fax 414295181; e-mail redaktion@neue-lz.ch; internet www.zisch.ch; f. 1996; Editor-in-Chief THOMAS BORNHAUSER; circ. 130,213 (2007).

Neuchâtel/Neuenburg

L'Express: 39 rue de la Pierre-à-Mazel, 2000 Neuchâtel; tel. 327235300; fax 327235209; e-mail redaction@lexpress.ch; internet www.lexpress.ch; f. 1738; independent; Editor-in-Chief NICOLAS WILLEMIN; circ. 23,344 (2007).

Sankt Gallen/Saint-Gall

St Galler Tagblatt: Fürstenlandstr. 122, 9001 St Gallen; tel. 712727711; fax 712727476; e-mail zentralredaktion@tagblatt.ch; internet www.tagblatt.ch; f. 1839; liberal; Editor-in-Chief GOTTLIEB F. HÖPLI; circ. 101,732 (2007).

Schaffhausen/Schaffhouse

Schaffhauser Nachrichten: Vordergasse 58, 8201 Schaffhausen; tel. 526333111; fax 526333401; e-mail redaktion@shn.ch; internet www.shn.ch; f. 1861; liberal; Editor-in-Chief NORBERT NEININGER; circ. 24,657 (2007).

Sion

Le Nouvelliste: 13 rue de l'Industrie, 1950 Sion; tel. 273297511; fax 273297578; e-mail redaction@nouvelliste.ch; internet www.lenouvelliste.ch; Catholic; Editor-in-Chief JEAN-FRANÇOIS FOURNIER; circ. 42,671 (2007).

Stäfa

Zürichsee-Zeitung: Seestr. 86, 8712 Stäfa; tel. 19285555; fax 19285550; e-mail redstaefa@zsz.ch; internet www.zsz.ch; f. 1845; radical democratic; Editor-in-Chief BENJAMIN GEIGER; circ. 45,519 (2007).

Thun/Thoune

Berner Oberländer: Rampenstr. 1, 3602 Thun; tel. 332251515; fax 332251505; e-mail redaktion-bo@bom.ch; internet www.berneroberlaender.ch; f. 1898; independent; Publrs Berner Oberland Medien AG; Editor-in-Chief RENÉ E. GYGAX; circ. 23,500 (2005).

Thuner Tagblatt: Rampenstr. 1, 3602 Thun; tel. 332251515; fax 332251505; e-mail redaktion-tt@bom.ch; internet www.thunertagblatt.ch; independent; publ. by Berner Oberland Medien AG; Editor-in-Chief RENÉ E. GYGAX; circ. 24,000 (2005).

Wetzikon

Zürcher Oberländer: Rapperswilerstr. 1, 8620 Wetzikon; tel. 19333333; fax 19323232; e-mail redaktion@zol.ch; internet www.zo-medien.ch; f. 1852; liberal; Editor-in-Chief CHRISTOPH VOLLENWEIDER; circ. 38,663 (2007).

Winterthur/Winterthour

Der Landbote: Garnmarkt 1–10, Postfach, 8401 Winterthur; tel. 522669901; fax 522669911; e-mail redaktion@landbote.ch; internet www.landbote.ch; f. 1836; independent; morning; Editor-in-Chief COLETTE GRADWOHL; circ. 35,898 (2007).

Zofingen

Zofinger Tagblatt: Vordere Henzmannstr. 20, 4800 Zofingen; tel. 627459393; fax 627459419; e-mail ztredaktion@ztonline.ch; internet www.zofingertagblatt.ch; f. 1873; liberal; Editor BEAT KIRCHHOFER.

Zürich

Blick: Dufourstr. 23, 8008 Zürich; tel. 442596262; fax 442596665; e-mail redaktion@blick.ch; internet www.blick.ch; independent; Editor-in-Chief BERNHARD WEISSBERG; circ. 240,066 (2007).

Neue Zürcher Zeitung: Falkenstr. 11, Postfach, 8021 Zürich; tel. 442581111; fax 442521329; e-mail redaktion@nzz.ch; internet www.nzz.ch; f. 1780; independent liberal; Editor-in-Chief MARKUS SPILLMANN; circ. 143,875 (2007).

Tages-Anzeiger: Werdstr. 21, 8021 Zürich; tel. 442484411; fax 442484471; e-mail redaktion@tages-anzeiger.ch; internet www.tagesanzeiger.ch; f. 1893; independent; Editors-in-Chief MARKUS EISENHUT, RES STREHLE; circ. 216,411 (2007).

20 Minuten: Werdstr. 21, Postfach, 8021 Zürich; tel. 442486820; fax 442486821; e-mail redaktion@20minuten.ch; internet www.20min.ch; f. 1999; distributed free of charge; six regional editions: Bern/Basel, Geneva, Luzern, Région, St Gallen and Zürich; Editor-in-Chief MARCO BOSELLI; circ. 435,460 (2007).

PERIODICALS AND JOURNALS

Allgemeine Schweizerische Militärzeitschrift: Brunnenstr. 7, 8604 Volketswil; tel. 449084560; fax 449084540; e-mail redaktion@asmz.ch; internet www.asmz.ch; f. 1834; 11 a year; Editor-in-Chief ROLAND BECK; circ. 21,000.

Die Alpen: Monbijoustr. 61, Postfach, 3000 Bern 23; tel. 313701885; fax 313701890; e-mail alpen@sac-cas.ch; internet www.sac-cas.ch; monthly; publ. by Schweizer Alpen-Club; circ. 98,891.

Auto & Lifestyle (ACS Clubmagazin): Wasserwerkgasse 39, 3000 Bern 13; tel. 313283111; fax 313110310; e-mail acszv@acs.ch; internet www.acs.ch; publ. by the Automobile Club of Switzerland; 10 a year; circ. 63,200.

Automobil Revue: Dammweg 9, 3001 Bern; tel. 313303034; fax 313303032; e-mail office@automobilrevue.ch; internet www.automobilrevue.ch; f. 1906; weekly publ. in German and French (*Revue automobile*); Editor PIERRE-ANDRÉ SCHMIDT; circ. 67,412.

SWITZERLAND

Beobachter: Förrlibuckstr. 70, 8021 Zürich; tel. 434445252; fax 434445353; e-mail redaktion@beobachter.ch; internet www.beobachter.ch; f. 1927; 2 a month; circ. 306,531.

Bilanz: Förrlibuckstr. 70, 8021 Zürich; tel. 434445520; fax 434445521; e-mail redaktion@bilanz.ch; internet www.bilanz.ch; f. 1977; review of business in Switzerland; circ. 57,548.

Courrier neuchâtelois: 2013 Colombier; tel. 328417250; fax 328411521; weekly; Editor René Gessler; circ. 88,087.

Du—Zeitschrift für Kultur: Du Verlags AG, Holbeinstr. 8, 8008 Zürich; tel. 432434600; fax 432434611; f. 1941; monthly art review; Editor Andreas Kläui; circ. 31,915.

Echo Magazine: 12 rue de Meyrin, CP 80, 1211 Geneva 7; tel. 225930303; fax 225930319; e-mail abo.echo.magazine@saripress.ch; internet www.echomagazine.ch; f. 1929; weekly; Editor-in-Chief Patrice Favre; circ. 22,000.

L'Eco dello Sport: via San Gottardo 25, 6500 Bellinzona; tel. 918262710; fax 91575750; circ. 44,000.

Finanz und Wirtschaft: Verlag Finanz und Wirtschaft AG, Hallwylstr. 71, Postfach, 8021 Zürich; tel. 442983535; fax 442983500; e-mail verlag@fuw.ch; internet www.fuw.ch; f. 1928; 2 a week; finance and economics; circ. 34,604 (2007).

Freisinn: Postfach 6136, 3001 Bern; tel. 313203535; fax 313203500; e-mail zila@fdp.ch; internet www.fdp.ch; f. 1979; monthly; politics; Editor-in-Chief Nico Zila; circ. 71,160.

GlücksPost: Dufourstr. 49, 8008 Zürich; tel. 442596912; fax 442596930; e-mail glueckspost@ringier.ch; internet www.glueckspost.ch; women's interest; f. 1977; weekly; Editor-in-Chief Béatrice Zollinger; circ. 148,737.

Handelszeitung: Seestr. 37, 8027 Zürich; tel. 442883555; fax 442883575; e-mail redaktion@handelszeitung.ch; internet www.handelszeitung.ch; f. 1862; financial, commercial and industrial weekly; Publr Jörg Tobuschat; Editor-in-Chief Beat Balzli; circ. 33,044.

L'Hebdo: Pont Bessières 3, POB 6682, 1002 Lausanne; tel. 213317600; fax 213317601; e-mail courrier.hebdo@ringier.ch; internet www.hebdo.ch; f. 1981; weekly; news magazine; Editor-in-Chief Alain Jeannet; circ. 48,451 (2007).

L'Illustré: Pont Bessières 3, POB 6505, 1002 Lausanne; tel. 213317500; fax 213317501; e-mail illustre@ringier.ch; internet www.illustre.ch; f. 1921; weekly; Chief Editor Michel Jeanneret; circ. 97,974.

Museum Helveticum: Steinentorstr. 13, 4010 Basel; tel. 612789565; fax 612789566; e-mail verlag@schwabe.ch; internet www.schwabe.ch; f. 1944; publ. by Schwabe AG; 2 a year; Swiss journal for classical philology, ancient history and classical archaeology; Editors Prof. M. Guggisberg, Prof. S. Rebenich, Prof. Thomas Schmidt, Prof. H. Harich-Schwarzbauer.

Music Scene: Neuenhoferstr. 101, 5401 Baden; tel. 562032272; fax 562032299; e-mail info@music-scene.ch; internet www.music-scene.ch; f. 1924; young people's fortnightly; circ. 50,000.

Nebelspalter: Bahnhofstr. 17, 9326 Horn; tel. 718468876; fax 718468879; e-mail verlag@nebelspalter.ch; internet www.nebelspalter.ch; f. 1875; publ. by Engeli & Partner Verlag; 10 a year; satirical; Editor-in-Chief Marco Ratschiller; circ. 12,600.

Revue militaire suisse: 3 ave de Florimont, 1006 Lausanne; tel. 213114817; fax 213119709; e-mail info@jcrc.ch; internet www.revuemilitairesuisse.ch; f. 1856; 8 a year; Editor-in-Chief Lt Col Alexandre Vautravers.

Revue suisse de zoologie: Muséum d'Histoire Naturelle, CP 6434, 1211 Geneva 6; tel. 224186300; fax 224186301; e-mail danielle.decrouez@mhn.ville-ge.ch; f. 1893; quarterly; Dir Danielle Decrouez.

Schweizer Archiv für Neurologie und Psychiatrie (Archives Suisses de Neurologie et de Psychiatrie): EMH Schweizerischer Ärzteverlag AG, Farnsburgerstr. 8, 4132 Muttenz; tel. 614678555; fax 614678556; e-mail sanp@emh.ch; internet www.sanp.ch; f. 1917; 8 a year; Publr Dr Natalie Marty.

Schweizer Familie: Werdstr. 21, Postfach, 8021 Zürich; tel. 442486106; fax 444248096; e-mail redaktion@schweizerfamilie.ch; internet www.schweizerfamilie.ch; f. 1893; weekly; Editor-in-Chief Daniel Dunkel; Man. Dir Josef Burch; circ. 205,529.

Schweizer Illustrierte: Dufourstr. 23, 8008 Zürich; tel. 442596363; fax 442620442; e-mail info@schweizer-illustrierte.ch; internet www.schweizer-illustrierte.ch; f. 1911; illustrated weekly; Chief Editor Nik Niethammer; circ. 232,519.

Schweizer Monat: Vogelsangstr. 52, 8006 Zürich; tel. 443612606; fax 443637005; e-mail info@schweizermonatshefte.ch; internet www.schweizermonatshefte.ch; f. 1921; political, economic and cultural monthly; Editor-in-Chief René Scheu; circ. 2,500.

Schweizerisches Handelsamtsblatt (Feuille officielle suisse du commerce): POB 1025, 3000 Bern; tel. 313240992; fax 313240961; e-mail info@sogc.ch; internet www.shab.ch; f. 1883; commercial daily; publ. by State Secretariat for Economic Affairs (SECO); Editor-in-Chief Markus Tanner; circ. 10,000.

Snowactive: Strike Media Schweiz AG, Gösgerstr. 15, POB 170, 5012 Schönenwerd; tel. 628582820; fax 628582829; e-mail j.weibel@snowactive.ch; internet www.snowactive.ch; f. 1968; 7 a year; German and French/Italian editions; Editor Joseph Weibel; circ. 85,000.

Swiss Engineering (STZ): Les Cerisiers, 1585 Bellerive; tel. 266773270; fax 266773269; e-mail mediakom@bluewin.ch; internet www.swissengineering-stz.ch; 10 a year; technical journal in German; Editor-in-Chief Christa Rosatzin-Strobel; circ. 20,000.

Swiss Journal of Psychology/ Schweizerische Zeitschrift für Psychologie/ Revue suisse de psychologie: Länggassstr. 76, Postfach, 3000 Bern 9; tel. 313004500; fax 313004593; e-mail verlag@hanshuber.com; internet www.verlag-hanshuber.com; f. 1942; quarterly; in German, French and English; Editor-in-Chief Prof. Dr Friedrich Wilkening.

Swiss Medical Weekly: EMH Swiss Medical Publrs Ltd, Steinentorstr. 13, 4010 Basel; tel. 614678555; fax 614678556; e-mail red@smw.ch; internet www.smw.ch; f. 1871; fortnightly; Man. Editor Dr Natalie Marty.

TCS-Zürich: Geissbüelstr. 24–26, 8604 Volketswil; tel. 442868636; fax 442868607; official organ of the Zürich Touring Club; monthly; Chief Editor Reto Cavegn; circ. 200,000.

Tele: Förrlibuckstrasse 70, Postfach, 8021 Zürich; tel. 434445950; fax 434445999; e-mail telesekr@ringier.ch; internet www.tele.ch; f. 1967; television, cinema and multimedia; weekly; Editor Gion Stecher; circ. 214,214.

Touring: Maulbeerstr. 10, 3001 Bern; tel. 313805000; fax 313805006; f. 1935; fortnightly; German, French and Italian editions; Chief Editor Stefan Senn; circ. 1,306,000.

TV 8: 3 Pont Bessières, 1005 Lausanne; tel. 213317000; fax 213317001; e-mail tv8@ringier.ch; weekly; circ. 83,119 (2007).

Vox Romanica: Centre de dialectologie, Université de Neuchâtel, 6 ave DuPeyrou, 2000 Neuchâtel; tel. 327181720; fax 327181721; e-mail andres.kristol@unine.ch; internet www.unine.ch/dialectologie/vox/vox.html; f. 1936; annual review of Romance linguistics and medieval literature; publ. by Collegium Romanicum (Swiss Association of Romanists); Editors Prof. Dr Rita Franceschini, Prof. Andres Kristol.

Weltwoche: Förrlibuckstr. 70, 8021 Zürich; tel. 434445700; fax 434445669; e-mail redaktion@weltwoche.ch; internet www.weltwoche.ch; f. 1933; weekly; independent; Editor-in-Chief Roger Köppel; circ. 92,337.

Werk, Bauen + Wohnen: Talstr. 39, 8001 Zürich; tel. 442181430; fax 442181434; e-mail wbw.zh@bluewin.ch; internet www.werkbauenundwohnen.ch; f. 1913; monthly; architecture; circ. 8,000.

NEWS AGENCY

Schweizerische Depeschenagentur AG/Agence Télégraphique Suisse SA (SDA/ATS) (Swiss News Agency): Länggassstr. 7, 3001 Bern; tel. 313093333; fax 313093030; e-mail sekretariat.reda@sda.ch; internet www.sda.ch; f. 1894; agency for political and general news; Chair., Management Bd Markus Schwab; Chief Editor Bernard Maissen.

PRESS ASSOCIATIONS

Impressum—Die Schweizer Journalistinnen/Les journalistes suisses/I giornalisti svizzeri: Grand'Places 14A, 1701 Fribourg; tel. 263471500; fax 263471509; e-mail info@impressum.ch; internet www.impressum.ch; Pres Antoine Gessler, Stefan Rohrbach.

Presse Suisse: 1 ave de Florimont, 1006 Lausanne; tel. 213434090; fax 213434099; e-mail admin@pressesuisse.ch; internet www.pressesuisse.ch; f. 1921 as Union Romande des éditeurs de journaux et de périodiques; present name adopted 2006; 54 mems and 6 assoc. mems; Pres. Valérie Boagno.

Verband Schweizer Presse: Konradstr. 14, Postfach 1202, 8021 Zürich; tel. 3186464; fax 3186462; e-mail contact@schweizerpresse.ch; internet www.schweizerpresse.ch; f. 1899; Pres. Hanspeter Lebrument; c. 150 mems.

Publishers

FRENCH-LANGUAGE PUBLISHING HOUSES

Academic Press Fribourg: 42 blvd de Pérolles, CP 176, 1705 Fribourg; tel. 264264311; fax 264264300; e-mail info@paulusedition.ch; internet www.paulusedition.ch; Dir Maurice Greder.

SWITZERLAND

Editions l'Age d'Homme SA: 10 rue de Genève, Postfach 5076, 1002 Lausanne 9; tel. 213120095; fax 213208440; e-mail info@agedhomme.com; internet www.lagedhomme.com; f. 1966; fiction, biography, music, art, social sciences, science fiction, literary criticism; Man. Dir VLADIMIR DIMITRIJEVIC.

Editions de l'Aire SA: 15 rue de l'Union, CP 57, 1800 Vevey; tel. 219236836; fax 219236823; e-mail editionaire@bluewin.ch; internet www.editions-aire.ch; f. 1978; literature, history, philosophy, religion; Man. MICHEL MORET.

La Bibliothèque des Arts: 55 ave de Rumine, 1005 Lausanne; tel. 213123667; fax 213123615; e-mail webmaster@bibliotheque-des-arts.com; internet www.bibliotheque-des-arts.com; f. 1954; art, culture; Dir OLIVIER DAULTE.

Librairie Droz SA: 11 rue Firmin-Massot, POB 389, 1211 Geneva 12; tel. 223466666; fax 223472391; e-mail droz@droz.org; internet www.droz.org; f. 1924; history, medieval literature, French literature, linguistics, social sciences, economics, archaeology; Dir MAX ENGAMMARE.

Edipresse Publications SA: 33 ave de la Gare, 1001 Lausanne; tel. 213494545; fax 213494540; e-mail epsa.info@edipresse.ch; internet www.edipresse.com; f. 1988; newspapers, magazines; Pres. PIERRE LAMUNIÈRE.

Editions Eiselé SA: 42 Confrérie, CP 128, 1008 Prilly; tel. 21623650; fax 216236359; e-mail info@eisele.ch; internet www.eisele.ch; arts, education, popular science, textbooks.

Editions d'En Bas: 30 rue des Côtes-de-Montbenon, 1003 Lausanne; tel. 213233918; fax 213212240; e-mail enbas@bluewin.ch; internet www.enbas.ch; f. 1976; literature, politics, history, sociology, memoirs, travel, poetry, photography; Dir JEAN RICHARD.

Françoise Gonin Editions d'Art: 1Ch. Du Grand-Praz 1, 1012 Lausanne-Chailly; tel. and fax 217285948; e-mail ogonin@freesurf.ch; internet www.gonin.org/editions; f. 1926; art books.

Editions du Grand-Pont: 2 place Bel-Air, 1003 Lausanne; tel. 213124466; fax 213113222; f. 1971; general, art books and literature; Dir JEAN-PIERRE LAUBSCHER.

Editions du Griffon: 17 Faubourg du Lac, 2000 Neuchâtel; tel. 327252204; f. 1944; science, arts.

Editions Ides et Calendes: Évole 19, 2000 Neuchâtel; tel. 327253861; fax 327255880; e-mail info@idesetcalendes.com; internet www.idesetcalendes.com; f. 1941; art, photography, literature; Dir ALAIN BOURET.

Institut de Hautes Etudes Internationales et du Développement: 20 rue Rothschild, CP 136, 1211 Geneva 21; tel. 229085700; fax 229065947; e-mail webmaster@graduateinstitute.ch; internet graduateinstitute.ch; f. 1927; educational, development; Dir PHILIPPE BURRIN.

La Joie de Lire SA: 5 chemin Neuf, 1207 Geneva; tel. 228073399; fax 228073392; e-mail info@lajoiedelire.ch; internet www.lajoiedelire.ch; f. 1987; juvenile; Dir FRANCINE BOUCHET.

Editions Labor & Fides SA: 1 rue Beauregard, 1204 Geneva; tel. 223113290; fax 227813051; e-mail g.montmollin@laboretfides.com; internet www.laboretfides.com; f. 1924; theological and religious publs; Dir GABRIEL DE MONTMOLLIN.

Loisirs et Pédagogie SA (LEP): en Budron B4A, 1052 Le Mont-sur-Lausanne; tel. 216512570; fax 216535751; e-mail contact@editionslep.ch; internet www.editionslep.ch; f. 1980; Dir PHILIPPE BURDEL.

Médecine et Hygiène: 46 chemin de la mousse, 1225 Chêne-Bourg; tel. 227029311; fax 227029355; e-mail admin@medhyg.ch; internet www.medhyg.ch; f. 1943; medicine, psychology, general science, university textbooks; Man. Dir BERTRAND KIEFER.

Editions Mondo SA: 12 Entre Deux Villes, CP 720, 1800 Vevey; tel. 219241450; fax 219245048; e-mail info@mondo.ch; internet www.mondo.ch; Dir ARSLAN ALAMIR.

Olizane: 11 rue des Vieux-Grenadiers, 1205 Geneva; tel. 223285252; fax 223285796; e-mail guides@olizane.ch; internet www.olizane.ch; f. 1981; travel, tourism, orientalism, photography; Dir MATTHIAS HUBER.

Editions Payot Lausanne: Nadir SA, 18 ave de la Gare, CP 529, 1001 Lausanne; tel. 213290264; fax 213290266; f. 1875; technical, textbooks, medicine, law, popular science, art books, tourism, history, music, general non-fiction, academic publs; Dir JACQUES SCHERRER.

Presses Polytechniques et Universitaires Romandes: EPFL, Centre-Midi, CP 119, 1015 Lausanne-Ecublens; tel. 216932130; fax 216934027; e-mail ppur@epfl.ch; internet www.ppur.org; f. 1980; technical and scientific; also publishes in English as EPFL Press; Man. Dir OLIVIER BABEL.

Slatkine Reprints: 5 rue des Chaudronniers, CP 3625, 1211 Geneva 3; tel. 227762551; fax 227763527; e-mail slatkine@slatkine.com; internet www.slatkine.com; Dir M. E. SLATKINE.

Editions du Tricorne: 14 rue Lissignol, 1201 Geneva; tel. 227388366; fax 227319749; e-mail tricorne@tricorne.org; internet www.tricorne.org; f. 1976; philosophy, human sciences, art, religion, psychology, mathematics; Dir SERGE KAPLUN.

Editions Zoé: 11 rue des Moraines, 1227 Carouge-Geneva; tel. 223093606; fax 223093603; e-mail info@editionszoe.ch; internet www.editionszoe.ch; literature, criticism, fiction, essays, theatre, art, music, cookery; Dir CAROLINE COUTAU.

GERMAN-LANGUAGE PUBLISHING HOUSES

Arche Literatur Verlag AG: Heinrichstr. 249, 8005 Zürich; tel. 447605171; fax 447602068; internet www.arche-verlag.com; f. 1944; literature; Dir NIKOLAUS HANSEN.

Benteli Verlags AG: Steinackerstr. 8, 8583 Sulgen; tel. 716449131; fax 716449139; e-mail info@benteli.ch; internet www.benteli.ch; f. 1898; fine arts, photography, non-fiction, philology; Dir TILL SCHAAP.

Birkhäuser Verlag AG: Viaduktstr. 42, Postfach 133, 4010 Basel; tel. 615689800; fax 612050799; e-mail info@birkhauser.ch; internet www.birkhauser.ch; books and journals; mathematics, biology, architecture, design; Man. Dir SVEN FUND.

Carl-Huter-Verlag GmbH: Ohm-Str. 14, 8050 Zürich; tel. 443117471; fax 443117485; e-mail verlag@carl-huter.ch; internet www.carl-huter.ch; physiognomy and nature; Dirs FRITZ AERNI, ELISABETH AERNI.

Cosmos Verlag AG: Kräyigenweg 2, 3074 Muri bei Bern; tel. 319506464; fax 319506460; e-mail info@cosmosverlag.ch; internet www.cosmosverlag.ch; f. 1923; fiction, literature, local history, reference, children's, tax management; Dir RETO M. AEBERLI.

Diogenes Verlag AG: Sprecherstr. 8, 8032 Zürich; tel. 442548511; fax 442528407; e-mail info@diogenes.ch; internet www.diogenes.ch; f. 1952; belles-lettres, fiction, graphic arts, children's; Publrs DANIEL KEEL, RUDOLF C. BETTSCHART.

Europa Verlag AG: Scheuchzerstrasse 50, 8006 Zürich; tel. 443622023; fax 443622025; e-mail mail@europaverlag.ch; internet www.europa-verlag.ch; f. 1933; politics, philosophy, history, biography, sociology, fiction; Dir LARS SCHULTZE-KOSSACK.

Hallwag Kümmerly+Frey AG: Grubenstr. 109, 3322 Schönbühl; tel. 318503131; fax 318503100; e-mail info@swisstravelcenter.ch; internet www.swisstravelcenter.ch; f. 1912; maps and guides, road maps, atlases, travel guides; CEO PETER NIEDERHAUSER.

H. E. P. Verlag AG: Brunngasse 36, Postfach, 3000 Bern 7; tel. 313102929; fax 313183135; e-mail info@hep-verlag.ch; internet www.hep-verlag.ch; imprints Baufachverlag and Ott Verlag; educational and training material; Dir PETER EGGER.

S. Karger AG: Allschwilerstr. 10, Postfach, 4009 Basel; tel. 613061111; fax 613061234; e-mail karger@karger.ch; internet www.karger.com; f. 1890 in Berlin, 1937 in Basel; international medical journals, books on medicine, chemistry, psychology; Pres. Dr THOMAS KARGER; CEO GABRIELLA KARGER, RALPH WEIL.

Peter Lang AG: Moosstr. 1, Postfach 350, 2542 Pieterlen; tel. 323761717; fax 323761727; e-mail info@peterlang.com; internet www.peterlang.com; f. 1977; humanities, social sciences, German language and literature, Romance literatures and languages, linguistics, music, art, theatre, ethnology; CEO TONY ALBALÁ.

Müller Rüschlikon Verlags AG: Gewerbestr. 10, 6330 Cham; tel. 417417755; fax 417417115; e-mail info@bucheli-verlag.ch; f. 1936; non-fiction; Dir HEINZ JANSEN.

Nagel & Kimche AG, Verlag: Neptunstr. 20, 8032 Zürich; tel. 443666680; fax 443666688; e-mail info@nagel-kimche.ch; internet www.nagel-kimche.ch; f. 1983; belles-lettres, juvenile; Dir Dr DIRK VAIHINGER.

Neptun Verlag AG: Erlenstr. 2, 8280 Kreuzlingen; tel. 716779655; fax 716779650; e-mail neptun@bluewin.ch; internet www.neptunart.ch; f. 1946; travel books, children's, contemporary history; Dir H. BERCHTOLD-MÜHLEMANN.

Neue Zürcher Zeitung, Buchverlag: Postfach, 8021 Zürich; tel. 442581505; fax 442581399; e-mail buch.verlag@nzz.ch; internet www.nzz-libro.ch; Man. HANS-PETER THÜR.

Verlag Niggli AG: Steinackerstr. 8, Postfach 135, 8583 Sulgen; tel. 716449111; fax 716449190; e-mail info@niggli.ch; internet www.niggli.ch; f. 1950; art, architecture, design, typography; Gen. Man. Dr J. CHRISTOPH BÜRKLE.

Orell Füssli Verlag: Dietzingerstr. 3, Postfach, 8036 Zürich; tel. 444667711; fax 444667412; e-mail info@ofv.ch; internet www.ofv.ch; f. 1519; management, history, law, schoolbooks, trade directories.

Verlag Pro Juventute/Atlantis Kinderbücher: Thurgauerstr. 39, 8050 Zürich; tel. 442567777; fax 442567778; e-mail info@projuventute.ch; internet www.projuventute.ch; social sciences, children's, families; Man. URS GYSLING.

SWITZERLAND

Friedrich Reinhardt Verlag: Missionsstr. 36, Postfach 393, 4012 Basel; tel. 612646450; fax 612646488; e-mail verlag@reinhardt.ch; internet www.reinhardt.ch; f. 1900; belles-lettres, theology, periodicals; Dir ALFRED RÜDISÜHLI.

Rex-Verlag: Arsenalstr. 24, 6011 Kreins; tel. 414194719; fax 414194711; e-mail info@rex-verlag.ch; internet www.rex-verlag.ch; f. 1931; theology, pedagogics, fiction, juvenile; Dir MARKUS KAPPELER.

Ringier AG: Dufourstr. 23, 8008 Zürich; tel. 442596111; fax 442598635; e-mail info@ringier.ch; internet www.ringier.ch; f. 1831; newspapers, magazines, online services, television, print; CEO MARC WALDER.

Sauerländer Verlage AG: Industriestr. 1, 5000 Aarau; tel. 628368686; fax 628368695; e-mail verlag@sauerlaender.ch; internet www.sauerlaender.ch; f. 1807; juvenile, school books, textbooks, history, chemistry, periodicals (professional, trade, science); Man. Dir FRANK THALHOFER.

Schulthess Juristische Medien AG: Zwinglipl. 2, Postfach, 8022 Zürich; tel. 442002929; fax 442002998; e-mail buch@schulthess.com; internet www.schulthess.com; f. 1791; legal, social sciences, university textbooks; Man. Dir ANDREAS HOHNHEISER.

Schwabe AG: Steinentorstr. 13, 4010 Basel; tel. 612789565; fax 612789566; e-mail verlag@schwabe.ch; internet www.schwabe.ch; f. 1488; medicine, art, history, philosophy; Dir DAVID MARC HOFFMANN.

Stämpfli Verlag AG: Wölflistr. 1, Postfach 8326, 3001 Bern; tel. 313006311; fax 313006688; e-mail verlag@staempfli.com; internet www.staempfliverlag.com; f. 1799; law, economics, history, art; Man. Dir Dr RUDOLF STÄMPFLI.

Tobler Verlag AG: Quellenstr. 4E, 9402 Mörschwil; tel. 718452010; fax 718452091; e-mail info@klv.ch; internet www.tobler-verlag.ch; f. 1995; part of Kaufmännischer Lehrmittelverlag AG since 2011; Dir SASCHA GLOOR.

TVZ Theologischer Verlag Zürich AG: Badenerstr. 73, Postfach, 8026 Zürich; tel. 442993355; fax 442993358; e-mail tvz@ref.ch; internet www.tvz-verlag.ch; f. 1934; religion, theology; Dir MARIANNE STAUFFACHER.

Ch. Walter Verlag AG: Dorfstr. 81/87, Postfach 121, 8706 Meilen; tel. 449233177; e-mail info@walter-verlag.ch; internet www.walter-verlag.ch; f. 1992; children's books, history, literature; Pres. Dr CHLAUS WALTER.

Wepf & Co AG Verlag: Eisengasse 5, 4001 Basel; tel. 612698515; fax 612630244; e-mail wepf@dial.eunet.ch; internet www.wepf.ch; f. 1755; architecture, engineering, ethnology, geography, geology, mineralogy; Dir H. HERRMANN.

PUBLISHERS' ASSOCIATIONS

Association Suisse des Editeurs de Langue Française: 2 ave Agassiz, CP 1215, 1001 Lausanne; tel. 213197111; fax 213197910; e-mail aself@centrepatronal.ch; f. 1975; asscn of French-speaking publrs; Pres. FRANCINE BOUCHET; Vice-Pres. OLIVIER BABEL; Sec.-Gen. FRANÇOIS PERRET; 75 mems.

Schweizer Buchhändler- und Verleger-Verband (SBVV): Alderstr. 40, Postfach, 8034 Zürich; tel. 444213600; fax 444213618; e-mail sbvv@swissbooks.ch; internet www.swissbooks.ch; f. 1849; asscn of German-speaking Swiss booksellers and publrs; Central Pres. MARIANNE SAX; Dir DANI LANDOLF; 516 mem. and affiliated firms.

Broadcasting and Communications

TELECOMMUNICATIONS

Cablecom GmbH: Zollstr. 42, 8021 Zürich; tel. 2779111; internet www.cablecom.ch; f. 1994; offers cable television, broadband internet access and fixed-line and mobile cellular telecommunications; owned by Liberty Global, Inc. (USA); Man. Dir. ERIC TVETER.

In & Phone SA: Rue de Lausanne 33, 1800 Vevey; tel. 219221941; fax 219221940; e-mail info@inphone.ch; internet www.inphone.ch; f. 2003; mobile communications; owned by Unify Group Holding; Gen. Man. OLIVIER LEUENBERGER.

Orange Communications SA: Hardturmstr. 161, 8005 Zürich; tel. 212161010; fax 212161515; internet www.orange.ch; f. 1999; mobile cellular communications and broadband internet access; owned by Orange SA (France); CEO THOMAS SIEBER; 1.6m. subscribers (Dec. 2010).

Sunrise Communications AG: Binzmühlestr. 130, Postfach, 8050 Zürich; tel. 587777777; fax 587777778; internet www.sunrise.ch; f. 1997; mobile cellular and fixed-line telecommunications and internet access; owned by TDC A/S (Denmark); CEO OLIVER STEIL; 2.9m. subscribers (Dec. 2009).

Swisscom AG: Alte Tiefenaustr. 6, 3048 Worblaufen; tel. 313421111; fax 313422549; e-mail swisscom@swisscom.com; internet www.swisscom.com; fmrly Swiss Telecom PTT; 56.9% owned by Federal Govt; Chair. ANTON SCHERRER; CEO CARSTEN SCHLOTER.

Tele2 Schweiz: Postfach 171, 8833 Samstagern; tel. 842242420; fax 842242422; internet www.tele2.ch; f. 1998; broadband internet access, fixed-line and mobile cellular telecommunications; CEO MATS TILLY.

BROADCASTING

The Swiss Broadcasting Corporation (SBC) is a private non-profit-making company, which fulfils a public duty on the basis of a licence granted to it by the Federal Government. The SBC uses the electrical and radio-electrical installations of Swisscom AG for public broadcasting of radio and television programmes. Swisscom is responsible for all technical aspects of transmission. Some 75.1% of the receiver licence fee is allocated to the SBC, while Swisscom takes 24.2% and the remainder is distributed among local radio and television stations.

SRG SSR idée suisse (Swiss Broadcasting Co—SBC; Schweizerische Radio- und Fernsehgesellschaft; Société suisse de radiodiffusion et télévision): Giacomettistr. 1, 3000 Bern 31; tel. 313509111; fax 313509256; e-mail info@srgssrideesuisse.ch; internet www.srgssrideesuisse.ch; f. 1931; Pres. JEAN-BERNARD MÜNCH; Dir-Gen. ROGER DE WECK; Deputy Dir-Gen. DANIEL ECKMANN; SRG SSR idée suisse is composed of the following regional companies:

Radio e Televisiun Rumantscha (RTR): Via da Masans 2, 7002 Chur; tel. 812557575; fax 812557500; internet www.rtr.ch; Pres. DURI BEZZOLA.

Radio-Télévision suisse romande (RTSR): 40 ave du Temple, CP 78, 1010 Lausanne; tel. 213186975; fax 213181976; e-mail info@rtsr.ch; internet www.rtsr.ch; Pres. JEAN CAVADINI.

Società cooperativa per la radiotelevisione Svizzera di lingua italiana (CORSI): Segreteria CORSI, via Canevascini 5, 6903 Lugano; tel. 918036325; fax 918036337; e-mail info@corsi-rsi.ch; internet www.corsi-rsi.ch; Pres. CLAUDIO GENERALI.

SRG Idée suisse DEUTSCHSCHWEIZ (Radio- und Fernsehgesellschaft DRS): Fernsehstr. 1–4, Postfach, 8052 Zürich; tel. 443056611; fax 443056710; e-mail info@srgdeutschschweiz.ch; internet www.srgdeutschschweiz.ch; formerly Radio- und Fernsehgesellschaft der Deutschen und der Rätoromanischen Schweiz (RDRS); Pres. VIKTOR BAUMELER.

Radio

Digital audio broadcasting (DAB) began in 1999 in Bern, Biel, Interlaken and Solothurn and had expanded to cover most of the German-speaking cantons, the Italian-speaking canton of Ticino, Geneva and Lausanne by 2007. DAB programmes were received by approximately 90% of the population in 2009.

Radio Rumantsch (RR): Via da Masans 2, 7002 Chur; tel. 812557575; fax 812557500; e-mail contact@rtr.ch; internet www.rtr.ch; operated by Radio e Televisiun Rumantscha (RTR); 24-hour programming in Romansh; Dir ERWIN ARDÜSER.

Radio svizzera di lingua italiana (RSI): CP, 6903 Lugano; tel. 918035111; fax 918035355; e-mail info@rsi.ch; internet www.rsi.ch; operated by Radiotelevisione svizzera di lingua italiana (RTSI); operates three Italian-language stations: **Rete Uno** current affairs and reportage, also general entertainment programmes and public service broadcasts, **Rete Due** educational and general interest programmes, music and news, **Rete Tre** rock and pop music; Dir of Radio DINO BALESTRA.

Radio Télévision Suisse (RTS): 40 ave du Temple, CP 78, 1010 Lausanne; tel. 213181111; fax 216523719; internet www.rts.ch; offers four stations: **La Première** news and background reports, stories, entertainment and music; **Espace 2** classical and contemporary music, jazz and folk, with features on the arts, history and society, radio plays and concert broadcasts; **Couleur 3** youth station playing rock and pop, with current affairs features; **Option Musique** music station with news bulletins, traffic reports and weather forecasts; Dir GILLES MARCHAND; Dir of Programmes GILLES PACHE; Dir of Information JEAN-JACQUES ROTH.

Schweizer Radio DRS (SR DRS): Brunnenhofstr. 22, 8042 Zürich; tel. 443661111; e-mail kommunikation@srdrs.ch; internet www.drs.ch; SR DRS is the Swiss national radio programme for the German part of Switzerland with three main studios in Zürich, Basel and Bern from which it operates six radio stations: **DRS 1** current affairs, traffic and weather reports and entertainment, six regional news magazines report regularly from around Switzerland; **DRS 2** classical music, jazz, culture, science, economics, politics and philosophy; **DRS 3** pop music and information, specializes in live concert broadcasts; **DRS 4 News** non-stop news; **DRS Musikwelle** traditional music of all genres, with news and **DRS 1** programmes; **DRS Virus** youth and multimedia; Dir Iso RECHSTEINER.

SWITZERLAND

Directory

Swiss Satellite Radio (SsatR): Novarastr. 2, Postfach, 4002 Basel; tel. 613653831; fax 613653839; three Swiss Satellite Radio music channels, broadcast via the internet, cable and satellite; **Radio Swiss Pop** music-only service; **Radio Swiss Classic** classical music service with minimal presentation; **Radio Swiss Jazz** music service playing jazz, blues and soul; Dir LARISSA ERISMANN.

There are also 48 local and regional radio stations active in Switzerland.

Television

A complete television programme service for each linguistic region and regular broadcasts in Romansh are provided on the 1st (VHF) channel. The 2nd and 3rd (UHF) channels are used in each linguistic region for transmitting programmes of the other two linguistic regions. Limited direct advertising is allowed.

Digital Video Broadcasting (DVB) began in 2005, with analogue broadcasting due to be discontinued in 2015.

Radio Télévision Suisse (RTS): see above; offers two channels: **TSR1** news on society, culture and entertainment; **TSR2** sports, documentaries, cultural programmes.

Schweizer Fernsehen (SF): Fernsehstr. 1–4, Postfach, 8052 Zürich; tel. 443056611; fax 443055660; e-mail sf@sf.tv; internet www.sf.tv; operates **SF1**, **SF zwei** and a third channel, **SF info**, which repeats current affairs programmes from **SF1**, **SF zwei** and **Presse TV** in hourly and half-hourly blocks; Dir UELI HALDIMANN.

Televisione svizzera di lingua italiana (TSI): CP, 6903 Lugano; tel. 918035111; fax 918035355; e-mail info@rtsi.ch; internet www.rtsi.ch; operated by Radiotelevisione svizzera di lingua italiana (RTSI); two Italian-language channels: **TSI1** full-service channel aimed at a broad audience, **TSI2** complementary channel with sport, children's programmes and repeats of news programmes from **TSI1**; Dir of TV DINO BALESTRA.

Televisiun Rumantscha (TvR): Via da Masans 2, 7002 Chur; tel. 812557575; fax 812557500; e-mail contact@rtr.ch; internet www.rtr.ch; operated by Radio e Televisiun Rumantscha (RTR); provides programming in Romansh (*Telesguard* and *Cuntrasts*) which is broadcast on SF1; Dir MARIANO TSCHUOR.

There are also 83 local and regional television stations, 18 of which have high transmission activity.

Finance

(cap. = capital; res = reserves; dep. = deposits; m. = million; brs = branches; all values are in Swiss francs)

REGULATORY AUTHORITY

Eidgenössische Finanzmarktaufsicht (FINMA) (Swiss Financial Market Supervisory Authority): Schwanengasse 2, 3003 Bern; tel. 313279100; fax 313279101; e-mail info@finma.ch; internet www.finma.ch; f. 2009 by merger of the Federal Office of Private Insurance, the Swiss Federal Banking Commission and the Anti-Money Laundering Control Authority; supervises banks, insurance cos, stock exchanges, securities dealers and other financial intermediaries; Chair. Dr EUGEN HALTINER; CEO Dr PATRICK RAAFLAUB.

BANKING

Switzerland's banks have a long-standing reputation as a secure repository for foreign capital. The Swiss Banking Law of 1934 declared it a penal offence for a bank to provide information about its clients without their explicit authorization, unless a court had ordered otherwise. When foreign authorities wish to investigate Swiss accounts, criminal charges must have been made in a foreign court and accepted as valid by Switzerland. The system of numbered accounts has also shielded depositors' shares from investigation. However, the abuse of bank secrecy by organized crime led Switzerland and the USA to sign a treaty in May 1973, whereby banking secrecy rules may be waived in the case of common-law crime (although not for non-criminal tax evasion and anti-trust law infringements). Further amendments to banking secrecy legislation were introduced in 1990 and 1998.

In June 1977 the Swiss banks agreed a code of practice which required the introduction of stricter controls over the handling of foreign funds. The opening of numbered accounts was subjected to closer scrutiny and the practice of actively encouraging the flow of foreign money into the country was checked. The agreement was modified in 1982. In 1987, following the withdrawal from the agreement of the Swiss National Bank, the code was adapted by the Swiss Bankers' Association into rules of professional conduct; further modifications to the code were introduced in 1992. In 1978, in view of the steady increase in Swiss banks' international business, the Federal Banking Commission was given greater supervisory powers. Banks were required for the first time to submit consolidated balance sheets to the Commission and new consolidation requirements forced banks to raise capital to between 6% and 8% of total liabilities. The capital requirement is now one of the highest in the world.

On 1 January 2009 the Federal Banking Commission merged with two other federal bodies to form the Swiss Financial Market Supervisory Authority (FINMA), which assumed responsibility for regulating the entire financial services sector.

At the end of 2009 there were 326 banks operating in Switzerland. The 24 cantonal banks are mostly financed and controlled by the cantons, and their activities are co-ordinated by the Association of Swiss Cantonal Banks. In 2009 they had 745 branches and controlled more than one-third of Switzerland's savings deposits.

Central Bank

Schweizerische Nationalbank/Banque nationale suisse (Swiss National Bank): Börsenstr. 15, Postfach 2800, 8022 Zürich; tel. 446313111; fax 446313911; e-mail snb@snb.ch; internet www.snb.ch; f. 1907; conducts the country's monetary policy as an independent central bank; obliged by the Constitution and statute to act in accordance with the interests of the country as a whole; primary goal is to ensure price stability, while taking due account of economic developments; Dept I handles international affairs, economic affairs, legal and administrative affairs, human resources and communications; Dept II handles cash, finance and controlling, financial stability and oversight, and security; Dept III handles financial markets, asset management, risk management, banking operations and information technology; cap. 25m., res 22,872m., dep. 76,019m. (Dec. 2007); Chair., Governing Bd PHILIPP HILDEBRAND.

Canton Banks

There are 24 cantonal banks, of which the following are the largest:

Aargauische Kantonalbank: Bahnhofstr. 58, 5001 Aarau; tel. 628357777; fax 628357778; e-mail akb@akb.ch; internet www.akb.ch; f. 1913; cap. 200m., res 387m., dep. and bonds 16,253m. (Dec. 2009); Pres. ARTHUR ZELLER; CEO RUDOLF DELLENBACH; 30 brs.

Banca dello Stato del Cantone Ticino: Viale H. Guisan 5, 6501 Bellinzona; tel. 918037111; fax 918037170; internet www.bancastato.ch; f. 1915; cap. 100m., res 152m., dep. and bonds 7,089m. (Dec. 2009); Chair. FULVIO PELLI; Pres., Exec. Bd DONATO BARBUSCIA; 4 brs.

Banque Cantonale de Fribourg: 1 blvd de Pérolles, 1701 Fribourg; tel. 848223223; fax 263507709; e-mail info@bcf.ch; internet www.bcf.ch; f. 1892 as Banque de l'Etat de Fribourg; present name adopted 1996; cap. 70m., res 466m., dep. and bonds 9,732m. (Dec. 2008); Chair. GILBERT MONNERON; CEO ALBERT MICHEL; 26 brs.

Banque Cantonale de Genève: 17 quai de l'Ile, CP 2251, 1211 Geneva; tel. 582112100; fax 582112199; e-mail info@bcge.ch; internet www.bcge.ch; f. 1994; cap. 360m., res 409m., dep. and bonds 12,586m. (Dec. 2008); Chair. MICHEL MATTACCHINI; CEO BLAISE GOETSCHIN; 23 brs.

Banque Cantonale du Jura: 10 rue de la Chaumont, CP 278, 2900 Porrentruy; tel. 324651301; fax 324651495; e-mail bcj@bcj.ch; internet www.bcj.ch; f. 1979; cap. 42m., res 67m., dep. and bonds 1,706m. (Dec. 2009); Chair. Dr PAUL-ANDRÉ SANGLARD; Gen. Man. BERTRAND VALLEY; 12 brs.

Banque Cantonale du Valais: 8 pl. des Cèdres, CP 133, 1951 Sion; tel. 848765765; fax 273246666; e-mail info@bcvs.ch; internet www.bcvs.ch; f. 1917; cap. 150m., res 301m., dep. and bonds 8,298m. (Dec. 2008); Chair. BERNARD STALDER; CEO JEAN-DANIEL PAPILLOUD; 20 brs.

Banque Cantonale Neuchâteloise: 4 pl. Pury, 2001 Neuchâtel; tel. 327236111; fax 327236236; e-mail info@bcn.ch; internet www.bcn.ch; f. 1883; cap. 125m., res 166m., dep. 5,651m. (Dec. 2008); Pres. JEAN-PIERRE GHELFI; Gen. Man. JEAN-NOËL DUC; 1 br.

Banque Cantonale Vaudoise: 14 pl. St François, CP 300, 1003 Lausanne; tel. 212121000; fax 212121596; e-mail info@bcv.ch; internet www.bcv.ch; f. 1845; cap. 258m., res 2,561m., dep. 30,470m. (Dec. 2008); Chair. OLIVIER STEIMER; CEO PASCAL KIENER; 66 brs.

Basellandschaftliche Kantonalbank: Rheinstr. 7, 4410 Liestal; tel. 619259494; fax 619259674; e-mail info@blkb.ch; internet www.blkb.ch; f. 1864; cap. 217m., res 393m., dep. and bonds 14,893m. (Dec. 2008); Pres. WILHELM HANSEN; CEO Dr BEAT OBERLIN; 8 brs.

Basler Kantonalbank: Spiegelgasse 2, 4002 Basel; tel. 612662555; fax 612662915; e-mail bkb@bkb.ch; internet www.bkb.ch; f. 1899; cap. 254m., res 451m., dep. and bonds 14,923m. (Dec. 2008); Chair. Dr ANDREAS C. ALBRECHT; CEO HANS-RUDOLF MATTER; 19 brs.

BEKB/BCBE (Berner Kantonalbank/Banque Cantonale Bernoise): Bundespl. 8, 3001 Bern; tel. 316661111; fax 316666040; e-mail bekb@bekb.ch; internet www.bekb.ch; f. 1834 as Banque Cantonale de Berne; present name adopted 1991; cap. 186m., res 1,537m., dep. and bonds 20,968m. (Dec. 2009); Pres. Dr JÜRG RIEBEN; CEO JEAN-CLAUDE NOBILI; 78 brs.

Graubündner Kantonalbank: Postfach, 7002 Chur; tel. 812569111; fax 812599588; e-mail info@gkb.ch; internet www.gkb

SWITZERLAND

.ch; f. 1870; cap. 250m., res 1,448m., dep. and bonds 13,649m. (Dec. 2009); Pres. Dr Hans Hatz; CEO Alois Vinzens; 74 brs.

Luzerner Kantonalbank: Pilatusstr. 12, 6002 Lucerne; tel. 844822811; fax 412062090; e-mail info@lukb.ch; internet www.lukb.ch; f. 1850; cap. 357m., res 805m., dep. and bonds 20,767m. (Dec. 2009); Chair. Fritz Studer; CEO Bernard Kobler; 26 brs.

Schwyzer Kantonalbank (SKZB): Bahnhofstr. 3, 6431 Schwyz; tel. 588002020; fax 588002021; e-mail kundenzentrum@szkb.ch; internet www.szkb.ch; f. 1889 as Kantonalbank Schwyz, present name adopted 1997; cap. 50m., res 323m., dep. and bonds 10,256m. (Dec. 2009); Pres. Alois Camenzind; CEO Gottfried Weber; 27 brs.

St Galler Kantonalbank: St Leonhardstr. 25, Postfach 2063, 9001 St Gallen; tel. 712313131; fax 712313232; e-mail info@sgkb.ch; internet www.sgkb.ch; f. 1871; cap. 390m., res 1,180m., dep. and bonds 20,201m. (Dec. 2008); Chair. Dr Franz-Peter Oesch; Pres., Exec. Bd Roland Ledergerber; 37 brs.

Thurgauer Kantonalbank: Bankpl. 1, Postfach 160, 8570 Weinfelden; tel. 848111444; fax 848111445; e-mail info@tkb.ch; internet www.tkb.ch; f. 1871; cap. 400m., res 1,052m., dep. and bonds 13,750m. (Dec. 2009); Chair. René Bock; CEO Peter Hinder; 30 brs.

Urner Kantonalbank: Bahnhofstr. 1, 6460 Altdorf; tel. 418756000; fax 418756313; e-mail info@urkb.ch; internet www.urkb.ch; f. 1915; cap. 30m., res 188m., dep. and bonds 1,776m. (Dec. 2009); Pres. Dr Hansruedi Stadler; CEO Peter Zgraggen; 9 brs.

Zuger Kantonalbank: Baarerstr. 37, 6301 Zug; tel. 417091111; fax 417091555; e-mail service@zugerkb.ch; internet www.zugerkb.ch; f. 1892; cap. 144m., res 263m., dep. and bonds 6,917m. (Dec. 2008); Chair. and Pres. Beat Bernet; Gen. Man. Toni Luginbühl; 10 brs.

Zürcher Kantonalbank: Bahnhofstr. 9, 8010 Zürich; tel. 442939393; fax 442923802; e-mail info@zkb.ch; internet www.zkb.ch; f. 1870; cap. 1,925m., res 5,008m., dep. and bonds 90,624m. (Dec. 2008); Chair. Dr Urs Oberholzer; CEO Martin Scholl; 103 brs.

Commercial Banks (Selected List)

Baloise Bank SoBa: Amthauspl. 4, Postfach 262, 4502 Solothurn; tel. 326260375; fax 326233692; e-mail bank@baloise.ch; internet www.baloise.ch; f. 1994; subsidiary of Bâloise-Gruppe; Group Chair. Dr Rolf Schäuble; Group CEO Martin Strobel.

Bank Julius Baer & Co Ltd: Bahnhofstr. 36, 8010 Zürich; tel. 588881111; fax 588881122; internet www.juliusbaer.com; f. 1890; cap. 575m., res 2,602m., dep. and bonds 31,403m. (Dec. 2008); Chair. Raymond J. Baer; CEO Boris Collardi; 13 brs.

Banque Thaler SA: 3 rue Pierre-Fatio, Postfach 3335, 1211 Geneva 3; tel. 227070909; fax 227070910; e-mail info@banquethaler.ch; internet www.banquethaler.ch; f. 1982 as KBC Bank (Suisse) SA; present name adopted 2000; cap. 20m., res 8m., dep. 68m. (Dec. 2008); Pres. Robert Cuypers; Gen. Man. Dirk Eelbode.

BNP Paribas (Suisse) SA: 2 pl. de Hollande, 1211 Geneva; tel. 582122111; fax 582122222; internet www.bnpparibas.ch; f. 1961 as United Overseas Bank SA; present name adopted 2001; cap. 320m., res 2,079m., dep. and bonds 42,520m. (Dec. 2008); Chair. George Chodron de Courcel; CEO Pascal Boris; 5 brs.

BSI SA: Via Franscini 8, 6900 Lugano; tel. 588093111; fax 588093678; e-mail info@bsibank.com; internet www.bsibank.com; f. 1873 as Banca della Svizzera italiana; present name adopted 1998; absorbed Banca del Gottardo in 2008; cap. 1,840m., res 408m., dep. and bonds 17,433m. (Dec. 2008); Chair. Dr Giorgio Ghiringhelli; CEO Dr Alfredo Gysi; 7 brs.

Clariden Leu AG: Bahnhofstr. 32, 8001 Zürich; tel. 582052111; fax 582052191; e-mail info@claridenleu.com; internet www.claridenleu.com; f. 2007 by merger of Bank Hofmann, Bank Leu, BGP Banca di Gestione Patrimoniale, Clariden Bank and Crédit Suisse Fides; Chair. Peter Eckert; CEO Hans Nützi; 8 brs.

Crédit Suisse Group: Paradepl. 8, Postfach 100, 8070 Zürich; tel. 442121616; fax 443332587; internet www.credit-suisse.ch; f. 1856; cap. 47m., res 49,108m., dep. and bonds 852,602m. (Dec. 2009); Group CEO Brady W. Dougan; CEO, Switzerland Hans-Ulrich Meister; 290 brs.

Migros Bank AG: Seidengasse 12, 8021 Zürich; tel. 442298111; fax 442298715; e-mail info@migros.ch; internet www.migrosbank.ch; f. 1958; cap. 700m., res 435m., dep. and bonds 27,971m. (Dec. 2008); Chair. Herbert Bolliger; Pres., Exec. Bd Dr Harald Nedwed; 54 brs.

Neue Aargauer Bank: Bahnhofstr. 49, 5001 Aarau; tel. 564627100; fax 564627542; e-mail webmaster@nab.ch; internet www.nab.ch; f. 1989; 98.6% owned by Crédit Suisse Group; cap. 134m., res 818m., dep. and bonds 17,966m. (Dec. 2008); Pres. Josef Meier; CEO Peter Bühlmann; 33 brs.

Raiffeisen Schweiz Genossenschaft/Raiffeisen Switzerland Cooperative: Raffeisenpl., 9001 St Gallen; tel. 712258888; fax 712258887; e-mail info@raiffeisen.ch; internet www.raiffeisen.ch; f. 1902; cap. 536m., res 7,447m., dep. and bonds 127,979m. (Dec. 2009); Chair., Bd of Dirs Franz Marty; Chair., Exec. Bd Dr Pierin Vincenz; 367 associated banks.

RBS Coutts Bank Ltd: Stauffacherstr. 1, 8022 Zürich; tel. 432455111; fax 432455396; internet www.rbscoutts.com; f. 1930; fmrly Coutts Bank von Ernst; current name adopted 2008; cap. 110m., res 1,029m., dep. 15,914m. (Dec. 2008); Chair. David Douglas-Home, Earl of Home; 5 brs.

Swissquote Bank: 33 chemin de la Créteaux, CP 391, 1196 Gland; tel. 229999898; fax 229999412; e-mail info@swissquote.ch; internet www.swissquote.ch; f. 2000; Chair. Mario Fontana; CEO Marc Bürki.

UBS AG: Bahnhofstr. 45, 8021 Zürich; tel. 442341111; fax 442399111; e-mail info@ubs.com; internet www.ubs.com; f. 1998 by merger of Union Bank of Switzerland (f. 1912) and Swiss Bank Corpn (f. 1872); cap. 293m., res 17,751m., dep. 1,732,867m. (Dec. 2008); Chair. Kaspar Villiger; Group CEO Oswald Grübel; 357 brs.

Union Bancaire Privée: 96–98 rue du Rhône, CP 1320, 1211 Geneva 1; tel. 588192111; fax 588192200; e-mail ubp@ubp.ch; internet www.ubpbank.com; f. 1990 by merger of TDB American Express Bank (f. 1956) and Compagnie de Banque et d'Investissements (f. 1969); cap. 300m., res 1,214m., dep. and bonds 17,415m. (Dec. 2009); Chair. Edgar de Picciotto; CEO Guy de Picciotto; 6 brs.

Valiant Bank: Bundespl. 4, 3001 Bern; tel. 313209111; fax 313209112; internet www.valiant.ch; f. 2001 by merger of Spar- und Leihkasse in Bern, Gewerbekasse in Bern, bank in Langnau, BB Bank Belp and Ersparniskasse Murten; cap. 110m., res 1,044m., dep. and bonds 16,925m. (Dec. 2008); Chair. Prof. Dr Roland von Büren; CEO Michael Hobmeier; 88 brs.

Private Banks

Switzerland's private banking sector is the largest, in terms of assets, in the world. In 2009 there were 14 privately owned banks in Switzerland, of which the following are among the most important:

Banque Privée Edmond de Rothschild SA: 18 rue de Hesse, 1204 Geneva; tel. 588189111; fax 588189121; e-mail contact@bper.ch; internet www.lcf-rothschild.ch; f. 1924; cap. 45m., res 441m., dep. and bonds 2,599m. (Dec. 2008); Chair. Baron Benjamin de Rothschild; CEO Claude Messulam; 2 brs.

EFG Bank: Bahnhofstr. 16, Postfach 2255, 8022 Zürich; tel. 442261717; fax 442261729; e-mail enquiries_ch@efgbank.com; internet www.efgbank.com; f. 1997 as EFG Private Bank SA; present name adopted 2005; cap. 162m., res 439m., dep. 11,463m. (Dec. 2008); Chair. Jean-Pierre Cuoni; CEO Lukas Ruflin.

HSBC Private Bank (Suisse) SA: 2 quai Général Guisan, CP 3580, 1211 Geneva 3; tel. 587055555; fax 587055151; internet www.hsbcprivatebank.com; f. 1988 as Republic National Bank New York (Suisse) SA; present name adopted 2004; cap. 708m., res 2,303m., dep. 66,423m. (Dec. 2008); Chair. Peter Widmer; CEO Alexandre Zeller; 3 brs.

Hyposwiss Private Bank AG: Schützengasse 4, 8021 Zürich; tel. 442143111; fax 442115223; e-mail info@hyposwiss.ch; internet www.hyposwiss.ch; f. 1889 as Schweizerische Hypothekenbank; present name adopted 2002; cap. 26m., res 76m., dep. and bonds 1,037m. (Dec. 2008); Chair. Roland Ledergerber; CEO Siegfried R. Peyer.

Lombard Odier Darier Hentsch & Cie: 11 rue de la Corraterie, 1211 Geneva 11; tel. 227092111; fax 227092911; e-mail geneva@lombardodier.com; internet www.lombardodier.com; f. 2002 by merger of Lombard Odier & Cie (f. 1796) and Darier Hentsch & Cie (f. 1991); Snr Partners Pierre Darier, Thierry Lombard; Man. Partners Patrick Odier, Jean Pastré, Bernard Droux, Anne-Marie de Weck, Christophe Hentsch, Hubert Keller.

Pictet & Cie Banquiers: 60 route des Acacias, 1211 Geneva 73; tel. 583232323; fax 583232324; e-mail info@pictet.com; internet www.pictet.com; f. 1805; Snr Partner Ivan Pictet; Partners Claude Demole, Jacques de Saussure, Nicolas Pictet, Philippe Bertherat, Jean-François Demole, Renaud de Planta, Rémy Best.

Central Co-operative Credit Institution

Bank Coop AG: Aeschenpl. 3, 4002 Basel; tel. 612862121; fax 612714595; e-mail info@bankcoop.ch; internet www.bankcoop.ch; f. 1927 as Co-operative Central Bank; present name adopted 2001; 56.3% stake owned by Basler Kantonalbank; cap. 338m., res 468m., dep. and bonds 11,947m. (Dec. 2008); Chair. Dr Ralph Lewin; Pres., Exec. Bd Andreas Waspi; 33 brs.

Bankers' Organizations

Association of Foreign Banks in Switzerland: Löwenstr. 51, Postfach 1211, 8021 Zürich; tel. 442244070; fax 442210029; e-mail info@foreignbanks.ch; internet www.foreignbanks.ch; f. 1972; 144 mems (Dec. 2007); Chair. Dr Alfredo Gysi; Sec. Gen. Dr Martin Maurer.

SWITZERLAND

Schweizerische Bankiervereinigung/Association Suisse des Banquiers (Swiss Bankers' Asscn): Aeschenpl. 7, Postfach 4182, 4002 Basel; tel. 612959393; fax 612725382; e-mail office@sba.ch; internet www.swissbanking.org; f. 1912; 363 institutional mems and 16,000 individual mems; Chair. PATRICK ODIER; CEO Dr URS P. ROTH.

Verband Schweizerischer Kantonalbanken/Union des Banques Cantonales Suisses (Asscn of Swiss Cantonal Banks): Wallstr. 8, 4002 Basel; tel. 612066666; fax 612066667; e-mail vskb@vskb.ch; internet www.kantonalbank.ch; f. 1907; perm. office est. 1971; Chair. PAUL NYFFELER.

STOCK EXCHANGES

BX Berne eXchange (Berner Börsenverein): Aarbergergasse 36, 3011 Bern; tel. 313294040; fax 313115309; e-mail office@berne-x.com; internet www.bernerboerse.ch; f. 1884; 9 mems, 6 assoc. mems; Dir ANDREAS OBERLI BALLI.

SIX Swiss Exchange: Selnaustr. 30, 8021 Zürich; tel. 588542091; fax 588543091; e-mail six@six.com; internet www.six-swiss-exchange.com; f. 1873; 51 mems; Pres. Prof. Dr PETER GOMEZ; Group CEO Dr URS RÜEGSEGGER.

INSURANCE

In December 2008 there were 218 insurance companies in Switzerland.

Allianz Suisse: Bleicherweg 19, Postfach, 8022 Zürich; tel. 583587111; fax 583584042; e-mail contact@allianz-suisse.ch; internet www.allianz-suisse.ch; subsidiaries: Allianz Suisse Versicherungen, Allianz Suisse Leben, Allianz Suisse Personal Financial Services; Chair. ULRICH ZIMMERLI; CEO Dr MANFRED KNOF.

AXA Winterthur: Gen. Guisan-Str. 40, Postfach 357, 8401 Winterthur; tel. 522611111; fax 522136620; e-mail info.ch@axa-winterthur.ch; internet www.axa-winterthur.ch; f. 1875; fmrly Winterthur Schweizerische Versicherungs-Gesellschaft; owned by AXA Group (France); Pres. ALFRED BOUCKAERT; CEO PHILIPPE EGGER.

Basler Versicherungen: Aeschengraben 21, Postfach 2275, 4002 Basel; tel. 612858585; fax 612857070; e-mail insurance@baloise.ch; internet www.baloise.ch; f. 1864; all classes; part of Bâloise-Gruppe; CEO OLAV NOACK.

Generali (Schweiz) Holding AG: Soodmattenstr. 10, 8134 Adliswil 1; tel. 584724040; fax 584724425; e-mail info@generali.ch; internet www.generali.ch; life and non-life; part of Generali Group (Italy); CEO ALFRED LEU.

Helvetia Versicherungen: St Alban-Anlage 26, 4002 Basel; tel. 582801000; fax 582801001; internet www.helvetia.ch; f. 1861; owned by Helvetia Holding; life, fire, burglary, accident liability, motor; Chair. Dr ERICH WALSER; CEO, Switzerland PHILIPP GMÜR.

Schweizerische Mobiliar Versicherungsgesellschaft (Die Mobiliar): Bundesgasse 35, 3001 Bern; tel. 313896111; fax 313896852; e-mail info@mobi.ch; internet www.mobi.ch; f. 1826; accident, sickness, fire and damage by the elements, theft, valuables, damage by water, glass breakage, machines, construction work, interruption of business, epidemics, warranty, guarantee, third-party liability, motor vehicles, travel, transport; CEO URS BERGER.

Schweizerische National-Versicherungs-Gesellschaft (Nationale Suisse): Steinengraben 41, 4003 Basel; tel. 612752111; fax 612752656; e-mail info@nationalesuisse.ch; internet www.nationalesuisse.ch; CEO HANS KÜNZLE.

SCOR Holding (Switzerland) Ltd: General Guisan-Quai 26, Postfach, 8022 Zürich; tel. 446399393; fax 446399390; e-mail scor@scor.com; internet www.scor.com; fmrly Converium; acquired by SCOR Group (France) in 2007; Group Chair. DENIS KESSLER; CEO BENJAMIN GENTSCH.

Swiss Life: General Guisan-Quai 40, POB 2831, 8022 Zürich; tel. 432843311; fax 432846311; e-mail info.com@swisslife.ch; internet www.swisslife.com; f. 1857; specializes in international employee benefit and pension plans; brs in France, Germany, Liechtenstein, Luxembourg and Singapore; Group CEO BRUNO PFISTER.

Swiss Re (Schweizerische Rückversicherungs-Gesellschaft) (Swiss Reinsurance Co): Mythenquai 50/60, 8022 Zürich; tel. 442852121; fax 442852999; e-mail contact@swissre.com; internet www.swissre.com; f. 1863; world-wide reinsurance; Chair. WALTER KIELHOLZ; CEO STEFAN LIPPE.

Vaudoise Assurances: Pl. de Milan, 1001 Lausanne; tel. 216188080; fax 216188181; internet www.vaudoise.ch; f. 1895; subsidiaries: Vaudoise Générale (non-life), Vaudoise Vie (life); Pres. ROLF MEHR.

Zürich Versicherungs-Gesellschaft: Thurgauerstrasse 80, 8085 Zürich; tel. 446282828; fax 446288444; e-mail kontakt@zurich.ch; internet www.zurich.ch; f. 1922; part of Zurich Financial Services group; life; Group CEO JAMES J. SCHIRO.

Insurance Organization

Schweizerischer Versicherungsverband—Association suisse d'assurances (SVV—ASA) (Swiss Insurance Asscn): C. F. Meyer-Str. 14, Postfach 4288, 8022 Zürich; tel. 442082828; fax 442082800; e-mail info@svv.ch; internet www.svv.ch; f. 1901; Pres. ERICH WALSER; Dir LUCIUS DÜRR; 72 mems.

Trade and Industry

GOVERNMENT AGENCY

Osec Business Network Switzerland: Stampfenbachstr. 85, Postfach 2407, 8021 Zürich; tel. 443655151; fax 443655221; e-mail info@osec.ch; internet www.osec.ch; offices in Lausanne and Lugano; promotes trade; CEO DANIEL KÜNG.

PRINCIPAL CHAMBERS OF COMMERCE

Aargauische Industrie- und Handelskammer: Entfelderstr. 11, 5001 Aarau; tel. 628371818; fax 628371819; e-mail info@aihk.ch; internet www.aihk.ch; Pres. DANIEL KNECHT.

Berner Handelskammer: Gutenbergstr. 1, Postfach 5464, 3001 Bern; tel. 313888787; fax 313888788; e-mail info@bern-cci.ch; internet www.bern-cci.ch; Pres. NIKLAUS J. LÜTHI.

Camera di commercio, dell'industria, dell'artigianato e dei servizi del Cantone Ticino (Cc-Ti): Corso Elvezia 16, 6901 Lugano; tel. 919151111; fax 919151112; e-mail info@cc-ti.ch; internet www.cciati.ch; f. 1917; Dir LUCA ALBERTONI; 760 mems.

Chambre de commerce Fribourg (CCF): 37 route du Jura, CP 304, 1701 Fribourg; tel. 263471220; fax 263471239; e-mail info@ccfribourg.ch; internet www.ccfribourg.ch; f. 1917; Pres. CHARLES PHILLOT.

Chambre de commerce, d'industrie et des services de Genève (CCIG): 4 blvd du Théâtre, 1211 Geneva 11; tel. 228199111; fax 228199100; e-mail ccig@cci.ch; internet www.ccig.ch; f. 1865; Pres. FRANÇOIS NAEF; Dir JACQUES JEANNERAT; 1,700 mems.

Chambre de commerce et d'industrie du Jura: 23 rue de l'Avenir, CP 274, 2800 Delémont 1; tel. 324214545; fax 324214540; e-mail ccjura@cci.ch; internet www.ccij.ch; Pres. JEAN-PAUL RENGGLI; Dir JEAN-FRÉDÉRIC GERBER; 400 mems.

Chambre neuchâteloise du commerce et de l'industrie: 4 rue de la Serre, 2001 Neuchâtel; tel. 327221515; fax 327221520; e-mail cnci@cnci.ch; internet www.cnci.ch; Pres. FRÉDÉRIC GEISSBUHLER; Dir PIERRE HILTPOLD; 800 mem. cos.

Chambre valaisanne de commerce et d'industrie: 6 rue Pré-Fleuri, CP 288, 1951 Sion; tel. 273273535; fax 273273536; e-mail info@cci-valais.ch; internet www.cci-valais.ch; Pres. BERNARD BRUTTIN; Dir VINCENT RIESEN; 356 mem. cos.

Chambre vaudoise du commerce et de l'industrie (CVCI): 47 ave d'Ouchy, CP 315, 1001 Lausanne; tel. 216133535; fax 216133505; e-mail cvci@cvci.ch; internet www.cvci.ch; Pres. BERNARD RÜEGER; Dir CLAUDINE AMSTEIN; 2,700 mems.

Glarner Handelskammer: Spielhof 14A, 8750 Glarus; tel. 556401173; fax 556403639; e-mail glhk@landolt-althaus.ch; internet www.glhk.ch; Pres. ANDERS HOLTE; Sec. Dr KARLJÖRG LANDOLT.

Handelskammer beider Basel: Aeschenvorstadt 67, Postfach, 4010 Basel; tel. 612706060; fax 612706005; e-mail hkbb@hkbb.ch; internet www.hkbb.ch; f. 1997 by merger of Basler Handelskammer (f. 1876) and Verband der Industriellen Baselland (f. 1919); Pres. THOMAS STAEHELIN; 800 mem. cos.

Handelskammer und Arbeitgeberverband Graubünden: Hinterm Bach 40, 7000 Chur; tel. 812543800; fax 812543809; e-mail info@hkgr.ch; internet www.hkgr.ch; Pres. LUDWIG LOCHER.

Handelskammer und Arbeitgebervereinigung Winterthur (HAW): Neumarkt 15, 8401 Winterthur; tel. 522130763; fax 522089934; e-mail info@haw.ch; internet www.haw.ch; f. 1992; Pres. THOMAS ANWANDER; Dir CHRISTIAN MODL.

Industrie- und Handelskammer St Gallen-Appenzell: Gallusstr. 16, Postfach, 9001 St Gallen; tel. 712241010; fax 712241060; e-mail sekretariat@ihk.ch; internet www.ihk.ch; f. 1466; Pres. Dr KONRAD HUMMLER; Dir Dr KURT WEIGELT; 1,300 mems.

Industrie- und Handelskammer Thurgau: Schmidstr. 9, Postfach 396, 8570 Weinfelden; tel. 716221919; fax 716226257; e-mail info@ihk-thurgau.ch; internet www.ihk-thurgau.ch; Pres. PETER A. SCHIFFERLE; Dir PETER MAAG; 600 mems.

Solothurner Handelskammer: Grabackerstr. 6, Postfach 1554, 4502 Solothurn; tel. 326262424; fax 326262426; e-mail info@sohk.ch; internet www.sohk.ch; f. 1874; Pres. KURT LOOSLI; Dir ROLAND FÜRST.

SWITZERLAND

Zentralschweizerische Handelskammer: Kapellpl. 2, Postfach 2941, 6002 Lucerne; tel. 414106865; fax 414105288; e-mail info@hkz.ch; internet www.hkz.ch; f. 1889; Pres. Hans Wicki; Dir Felix Howald; 500 mems.

Zürcher Handelskammer: Bleicherweg 5, Postfach 3058, 8022 Zürich; tel. 442174050; fax 442174051; e-mail direktion@zurichcci.ch; internet www.zurichcci.ch; f. 1873; represents businesses in Zürich, Schaffhausen and Zug cantons; Pres. Peter Quadri; CEO Dr Lukas Briner; 1,800 mems.

INDUSTRIAL AND TRADE ASSOCIATIONS

Associazione Industrie Ticinesi: Corso Elvezia 16, CP 5130, 6901 Lugano; tel. 919118484; fax 919234636; e-mail info@aiti.ch; internet www.aiti.ch; f. 1962; Pres. Daniele Lotti; Dir Stefano Modenini.

Chocosuisse—Verband Schweizerischer Schokoladefabrikanten: Münzgraben 6, 3000 Bern 7; tel. 313100990; fax 313100999; e-mail info@chocosuisse.ch; internet www.chocosuisse.ch; f. 1901; asscn of chocolate mfrs; Pres. Walter Anderau; Dir Dr Franz Schmid; 18 mems, 2 assoc. mems.

Economiesuisse (Swiss Business Federation): Hegibachstr. 47, Postfach 1072, 8032 Zürich; tel. 444213535; fax 444213434; e-mail info@economiesuisse.ch; internet www.economiesuisse.ch; f. 1870; as Schweizerischer Handels- und Industrie-Verein; present name adopted 2000; Pres. Gerold Bührer; Exec. Dir Dr Pascal Gentinetta; 163 mems.

Electrosuisse: Luppmenstr. 1, 8320 Fehraltorf; tel. 449561111; fax 449561122; e-mail info@electrosuisse.ch; internet www.electrosuisse.ch; f. 1889 as Swiss Electrotechnical Association; electronics; Chair. Willy R. Gehrer; Man. Dir Dr Ueli Betschart; 1,750 mem. cos.

Fédération de l'Industrie Horlogère Suisse (FH): 6 rue d'Argent, 2501 Bienne; tel. 323280828; fax 323280880; e-mail info@fhs.ch; internet www.fhs.ch; f. 1982 by merger of Swiss Chamber of Watchmaking and Swiss Watchmaking Fed.; watch industry; Pres. Jean-Daniel Pasche; 542 mems.

Föderation der Schweizerischen Nahrungsmittel-Industrien: Thunstr. 82, Postfach 1009, 3000 Bern 6; Münzgraben 6, 3000 Bern 7; tel. 313562121; fax 313510065; e-mail info@thunstrasse82.ch; internet www.fial.ch; foodstuffs; Pres. Rolf Schweiger; 199 mems.

Schweizerischer Baumeisterverband (SBV): Weinbergstr. 49, Postfach, 8035 Zürich; tel. 442588111; fax 442588335; e-mail verband@baumeister.ch; internet www.baumeister.ch; f. 1897; building contractors; Pres. Werner Messmer; Dir Daniel Lehmann; 3,000 mems.

Schweizerischer Gewerbeverband (SGV) (Swiss Union of Small and Medium Enterprises): Schwarztorstr. 26, 3007 Bern; tel. 313801414; fax 313801415; e-mail info@sgv-usam.ch; internet www.sgv-usam.ch; f. 1879; Pres. Edi Engelberger; Dir Dr Pierre Triponez; 257 mems and 25 cantonal sections.

Schweizerischer Verband für visuelle Kommunikation (Viscom): Speichergasse 35, Postfach 678, 3000 Bern 7; tel. 582255500; fax 582255510; e-mail info@viscom.ch; internet www.viscom.ch; f. 1869; printing industry; Pres. Peter Edelmann; Dir Thomas Gsponer; 750 mem. cos.

Schweizerischer Versicherungsverband: (see under Insurance).

SGCI Chemie Pharma Schweiz (Swiss Society of Chemical Industries): Nordstr. 15, Postfach, 8021 Zürich; tel. 443681711; fax 443681770; e-mail mailbox@sgci.ch; internet www.sgci.ch; f. 1882; branch asscn of the chemical and pharmaceutical industry; Pres. C. Mäder; Dir-Gen. Dr B. Moser; c. 250 mems.

Swiss Cigarette: Monbijoustr. 14, CP 5236, 3001 Bern; tel. 313909918; fax 313909903; e-mail office@swiss-cigarette.ch; internet www.swiss-cigarette.ch; f. 1933; formerly Communauté de l'industrie suisse de la cigarette; cigarette mfrs; Dir Chantal Aeby Pürro; three mem. cos.

Swiss Retail Federation: Marktgasse 50, 3000 Bern 7; tel. 313124040; fax 313124041; e-mail info@swiss-retail.ch; internet www.swiss-retail.ch; formerly Verband der Schweizerischen Waren- und Kaufhäuser; Pres. Bruno Frick; 31 mem. cos.

Textilverband Schweiz: Beethovenstr. 20, Postfach 2900, 8022 Zürich; tel. 442897979; fax 442897980; e-mail zuerich@swisstextiles.ch; internet www.swisstextiles.ch; f. 1874; textiles and fashion; Pres. Max R. Hungerbühler; Dir Dr Thomas Schweizer; 220 mems.

Verband Schweizerischer Kreditbanken und Finanzierungsinstitute (VSKF): Toblerstr. 97/Neuhausstr. 4, 8044 Zürich; tel. 442504340; fax 442504349; e-mail office@gigersimmen.ch; internet www.vskf.org; f. 1945; asscn of credit banks and finance institutes; Pres. Heinz Hofer; Sec. Dr Robert Simmen; 13 mems.

Verband Schweizerische Ziegelindustrie: Elfenstr. 19, 3006 Bern; tel. 313521188; fax 313521185; e-mail mail@domoterra.ch; internet www.domoterra.ch; f. 1874; heavy clay; Sec.-Gen. Dr Peter R. Burkhalter; 11 mem. cos.

EMPLOYERS' ORGANIZATIONS

Central Organizations

Schweizerischer Arbeitgeberverband (Confed. of Swiss Employers): Hegibachstr. 47, Postfach, 8032 Zürich; tel. 444211717; fax 444211718; e-mail verband@arbeitgeber.ch; internet www.arbeitgeber.ch; f. 1908; Pres. Dr Rudolf Stämpfli; Dir Thomas Daum; 80 mems.

Schweizerischer Bauernverband (Union Suisse des Paysans, Lega svizzera dei contadini, Swiss Farmers' Union): Laurstr. 10, 5201 Brugg; tel. 564625111; fax 564415348; e-mail info@sbv-usp.ch; internet www.sbv-usp.ch; f. 1897; Pres. Hansjörg Walter; Dir Jacques Bourgeois.

Principal Regional Organizations

Arbeitgeberverband Basel: Aeschenvorstadt 71, Postfach 4010 Basel; tel. 612059600; fax 612059609; e-mail info@arbeitgeberbasel.ch; internet www.arbeitgeberbasel.ch; f. 2007 by merger of Basler Volkswirtschaftsbund and Arbeitgeber-Verband Basel; Pres. Marc R. Jaquet; Dir Barbara Gutzwiller-Holliger; 2,500 mems.

Fédération des entreprises romandes: 98 rue de Saint-Jean, CP 5278, 1211 Geneva 11; tel. 227153111; fax 227153122; e-mail info@fer-sr.ch; internet www.fer-sr.ch; f. 1947; Pres. Nicolas Brunschwig; Sec.-Gen. Blaise Matthey.

Luzerner Industrie-Vereinigung: c/o Zentralschweizerische Handelskammer, Kapellpl. 2, Postfach 2941, 6002 Lucerne; tel. 414106889; fax 414105288; e-mail info@hkz.ch; internet www.liv-luzern.ch; f. 1918; Pres. Mark Bachmann; Dir Felix Howald; 120 mems.

Union des associations patronales genevoises: 98 rue de Saint-Jean, 1211 Geneva 11; tel. 227153241; fax 227380434; e-mail uapg@uapg.ch; internet www.uapg.ch; union of employers' asscns in Geneva; Pres. André Galiotto.

Union des industriels valaisans: 6 rue de Lausanne, 1950 Sion; tel. 273232992; fax 273232288; e-mail info@uiv.ch; internet www.uiv.ch; f. 1955; Pres. Grégoire Iten.

Verband der Arbeitgeber Region Bern (VAB): Kapellenstr. 14, Postfach 6916, 3001 Bern; tel. 313902581; fax 313902582; e-mail info@berner-arbeitgeber.ch; internet www.berner-arbeitgeber.ch; f. 1919; employers' asscn for the Bern region; Pres. Enrico Casanovas; Dir Dr Claude Thomann.

Vereinigung Zürcherischer Arbeitgeberorganisationen: Selnaustr. 30, 8021 Zürich; tel. 442012875; fax 442012877; e-mail dieter.sigrist@swx.com; f. 1947; asscn of Zürich employers' orgs; Pres. Thomas Isler; Sec. Dieter Sigrist.

Sectional Organizations

Arbeitgeberverband Schweizerischer Papier-Industrieller: Bergstr. 110, 8032 Zürich; tel. 442669920; fax 442669949; e-mail zpk@zpk.ch; internet www.zpk.ch; paper mfrs; Pres. Frank R. Ruepp; Dir Max Fritz; 11 mems.

Convention Patronale de l'Industrie Horlogère Suisse: 65 ave Léopold-Robert, 2301 La Chaux-de-Fonds; tel. 329100383; fax 329100384; e-mail info@cpih.ch; internet www.cpih.ch; f. 1937; watch mfrs; Pres. Elisabeth Zölch; Gen. Sec. François Matile; seven mems.

Swissmem (Swiss Mechanical and Electrical Engineering Industries): Kirchenweg 4, Postfach, 8032 Zürich; tel. 443844111; fax 443844242; internet www.swissmem.ch; f. 1905; Pres. Hans Hess; Dir Peter Dietrich; c. 1000 mems.

UTILITIES

Electricity

Verband Schweizerischer Elektrizitätsunternehmen: Hintere Bahnhofstr. 10, Postfach, 5001 Aarau; tel. 628252525; fax 628252526; e-mail info@strom.ch; internet www.strom.ch; electricity producers' asscn; f. 1895; Pres. Kurt Rohrbach; Dir Josef Dürr.

Gas

Verband der Schweizerischen Gasindustrie: Grütlistr. 44, Postfach, 8027 Zürich; tel. 412883131; fax 412021834; e-mail vsg@erdgas.ch; internet www.erdgas.ch; f. 1920; Pres. Dr Hajo Leutenegger; Dir Jean-Marc Hentsch.

Water

The cantons are responsible for the supply of water, but delegate to the municipalities and communes. As a result Switzerland has some 3,000 water companies. Water is usually supplied by a public company or co-operative, such as the municipal water suppliers for Basel,

SWITZERLAND

Winterthur and Zürich (Industrielle Werke Basel, Stadtwerk Winterthur, Wasserversorgung Zürich).

TRADE UNIONS
National Federations

Schweizerischer Gewerkschaftsbund (SGB) (Swiss Fed. of Trade Unions): Monbijoustr. 61, 3007 Bern; tel. 313770101; fax 313770102; e-mail info@sgb.ch; internet www.sgb.ch; f. 1880; main trade union org.; 16 affiliated unions; affiliated to ITUC; Pres. PAUL RECHSTEINER; c. 390,000 mems.

Travail.Suisse: Hopfenweg 21, Postfach 5775, 3001 Bern; tel. 313702111; fax 313702109; e-mail info@travailsuisse.ch; internet www.travailsuisse.ch; f. 2002 by merger of Confédération des Syndicats Chrétiens de Suisse and Fédération des Sociétés Suisses d'Employés; 12 affiliated unions; Pres. MARTIN FLÜGEL; 168,352 mems (Jan. 2008).

Principal Unions

Angestellte Schweiz (Employees Switzerland): Rigipl. 1, Postfach, 8033 Zürich; tel. 443601111; fax 443601112; e-mail info@angestellte.ch; internet www.angestellte.ch; fed. of 80 unions representing workers in engineering, electrical, metal, chemical and pharmaceutical industries; mem. union of Travail.Suisse; Pres. BENNO VOGLER; 24,237 mems (Jan. 2008).

Comedia (Media): Monbijoustr. 33, Postfach 6336, 3001 Bern; tel. 313906611; fax 313906691; e-mail info@comedia.ch; internet www.comedia.ch; f. 1858; mem. union of SGB; Pres DANIÈLE LENZIN, ROLAND KREUZER; c. 15,000 mems.

Gewerkschaft Kommunikation (Communications): Looslistr. 15, Postfach 370, 3027 Bern; tel. 319395211; fax 319395262; e-mail zentralsekretariat@syndicom.ch; internet www.gewerkschaftkom.ch; f. 1999; represents workers in postal service, telecommunications, ICT and air-traffic control sectors; mem. union of SGB; Pres. ALAIN CARRUPT; c. 37,000 mems.

Hotel & Gastro Union (Hotel and Restaurant Workers): Adligenswilerstr. 22, 6006 Luzern; tel. 414182222; fax 414120372; internet www.hotelgastrounion.ch; f. 1886 as Union Helvetia; present name adopted 2000; mem. union of Travail.Suisse; Pres. BRUNO POMA; 17,721 mems (Jan. 2008).

Organizzazione Christiano-Sociale Ticinese (OCST): Via Balestra 19, 6900 Lugano; tel. 919211551; fax 919235365; e-mail segretariato.cantonale@ocst.com; internet www.ocst.com; f. 1919; Pres. ROMANO ROSSI; 37,086 mems (Jan. 2008).

Schweizerischer Eisenbahn- und Verkehrspersonal-Verband (SEV) (Railway and Transport Workers): Steinerstr. 35, Postfach, 3000 Bern 6; tel. 313575757; fax 313575858; internet www.sev-online.ch; f. 1919; mem. union of SGB; Pres. JÜRG HURNI; c. 48,000 mems.

Schweizerischer Verband des Personals öffentlicher Dienste (Public Services): Birmensdorferstr. 67, Postfach 8279, 8036 Zürich; tel. 442665252; fax 442665253; e-mail vpod@vpod-ssp.ch; internet www.vpod-ssp.ch; f. 1905; mem. union of SGB; Pres. CHRISTINE GOLL; Gen. Sec. STEFAN GIGER; c. 35,000 mems.

Syna (Syndicat Interprofessionnel/Sindicato Interprofessionale): Josefstr. 59, 8031 Zürich; tel. 442797171; fax 442797172; e-mail zuer@syna.ch; internet www.syna.ch; f. 1998 to replace Landesverband freier Schweizer Arbeitnehmer (f. 1919); represents workers in all sectors; mem. union of Travail.Suisse; Pres. KURT REGOTZ; 65,924 mems (Jan. 2008).

Unia: Weltpoststr. 20, Postfach 272, 3000 Bern 15; tel. 313502111; fax 313502211; e-mail info@unia.ch; internet www.unia.ch; f. 2004 by merger of Gewerkschaft Bau und Industrie (GBI), Gewerkschaft Industrie, Gewerbe, Dienstleistungen (SMUV), Gewerkschaft Verkauf, Handel, Transport, Lebensmittel (VHTL) and Gewerkschaft unia; represents construction and engineering industries as well as employees in the retail and catering sectors; mem. union of SGB; Pres RENZO AMBROSETTI, ANDREAS RIEGER; c. 200,000 mems (2009).

Transport

RAILWAYS

Construction of the 35-km Lötschberg base tunnel was completed in June 2007, shortening travel time between Germany and the Italian city of Milan by about one hour. Excavation of a further 57-km rail tunnel, the Gotthard Base Tunnel, was completed in 2010; the tunnel was scheduled to become operational in 2017 and was expected to reduce journey times between Zürich and Milan by one-and-a-half hours.

Schweizerische Bundesbahnen (SBB) (Chemins de fer fédéraux suisses): Hochschulstr. 6, 3000 Bern 65; tel. 512201111; fax 512204265; e-mail railinfo@sbb.ch; internet www.sbb.ch; f. 1902; 3,034 km in 2007 (of which 1,707 km were multiple track); Chair. THIERRY LALIVE D'EPINAY; CEO ANDREAS MEYER.

Small private companies control private railways in Switzerland, chiefly along short mountain routes, with a total length of around 2,032 km. The following are among the principal private railways:

BLS AG: Genfergasse 11, Postfach, 3001 Bern; tel. 313272727; fax 313272910; e-mail info@bls.ch; internet www.bls.ch; f. 1906 as Berner Alpenbahn-Gesellschaft Bern–Lötschberg–Simplon (BLS); present co f. 2006 by merger; 520 km; network includes the 35-km Lötschberg base tunnel; regional passenger services; cargo services on Lötschberg–Simplon route; direct car-train connection from Bern to the Valais and Italy; boat services on Lakes Thun and Brienz; commuter rail services in Bern area; CEO BERNARD GUILLELMON.

Centovalli Railway: Via Franzoni 1, CP 146, 6601 Locarno; tel. 917560400; fax 917560499; e-mail fart@centovalli.ch; internet www.centovalli.ch; f. 1923; 19 km of track in Switzerland; Locarno–Camedo-Domodossola (Italy); Dir MAURO CARONNO.

Matterhorn Gotthard Bahn AG: Nordstr. 20, 3900 Brig; tel. 279277777; fax 279277779; e-mail info@mgbahn.ch; internet www.mgbahn.ch; f. 2003 by merger of BVZ Zermatt-Bahn AG and Furka Oberalp Bahn AG; 25% state-owned, 75% owned by BVZ Holding AG; Zermatt–Brig–Disentis and Andermatt–Göschenen; 144 km; Chair. DANIEL LAUBER; Dir HANS-RUDOLF MOOSER.

Matterhorn Gotthard Bahn Infrastruktur AG: Nordstr. 20, 3900 Brig; tel. 279277777; fax 279277779; e-mail info@mgbahn.ch; internet www.mgbahn.ch; 100% state-owned; responsible for track, overhead catenary equipment, operating control centres, station bldgs and workshops; Pres. ROLF ESCHER.

Matterhorn Gotthard Bahn Verkehrs AG: Nordstr. 20, 3900 Brig; tel. 279277777; fax 279277779; e-mail info@mgbahn.ch; internet www.mgbahn.ch; 75% owned by BVZ Holding AG, 25% state-owned; controls all railway operations, incl. rolling stock, depots and related maintenance; Pres. DANIEL LAUBER.

Montreux-Oberland Bernois: CP 1426, 1820 Montreux; tel. 219898181; fax 219898100; e-mail mob@mob.ch; internet www.mob.ch; f. 1899; 75 km; Montreux–Château d'Oex–Gstaad–Zweisimmen–Lenk im Simmental; operates tour services incl. GoldenPass Panoramic, GoldenPass Classic, Belle Epoque, Rochers-de-Naye, Les Pléiades and the Chocolate Train; operates funicular railways on Vevey–Chardonne–Mont-Pèlerin and Les Avants–Sonloup routes; Dir R. KUMMROW.

Rhätische Bahn AG (Rhaetian Railway): Bahnhofstr. 25, 7002 Chur; tel. 812549100; fax 812549118; internet www.rhb.ch; f. 1889; 375 km; the most extensive of the privately run railways; Chair., Management Bd ERWIN RUTISHAUSER.

Südostbahn AG: Bahnhofpl. 1A, 9001 St Gallen; tel. 712282323; fax 712282333; e-mail info@sob.ch; internet www.sob.ch; f. 1889; f. 2001 by merger of Schweizerische Südostbahn and Bodensee–Toggenburg-Bahn; 35.8% owned by Federal Govt; 120 km; Pres. GEORG HESS.

ROADS

In 2008 Switzerland had 71,355 km of roads, including 1,766 km of motorways and expressways and 18,143 km of highways or main roads. The 17-km road tunnel through the Saint Gotthard Pass, a European road link of paramount importance, was opened in 1980.

Swiss Federal Roads Office (Bundesamt für Strassen/Office fédéral des routes): Mühlestr. 2, Ittigen, 3003 Bern; tel. 313229411; fax 313232303; e-mail info@astra.admin.ch; internet www.astra.admin.ch; Dir RUDOLF DIETERLE.

INLAND WATERWAYS

Inland navigation legislation is the responsibility of the Confederation, but sovereignty over the waterways rests with the cantons. This means, in practice, that the Confederation limits its activities to the supervision of the licensed shipping companies (passenger ships and the related infrastructure, such as landing stages) and pilots; the cantons supervise pleasure-boat navigation (sports boats, i.e. sail and motor boats, etc.) and the non-licensed passenger vessels and goods shipping on the lakes and rivers.

SHIPPING

Although Switzerland is landlocked, the Rhine river is navigable by sea-going vessels as far as Basel; in addition, Swiss-registered merchant ships operate on the world's oceans. In 2009 Switzerland's registered merchant fleet comprised 35 vessels, with an aggregate displacement of some 640,600 grt. The principal shipping companies in Switzerland are:

ABCmaritime: 1 rue Perdtemps, 1260 Nyon; tel. 223657100; fax 223657111; e-mail info@abcmaritime.ch; internet www.abcmaritime.ch; f. 1982; ship management; Man. Dir PETER ZÜRCHER.

Agility Logistics AG: Sankt Jakobs-Str. 220, 4002 Basel; tel. 613165151; fax 613135557; e-mail switzerland@agilitylogistics

SWITZERLAND

.com; internet www.agilitylogistics.com; fmrly Natural AG; shipping management and freight forwarder; COO, Europe MARIO CAVALLUCCI.

Keller Shipping Ltd: Holbeinstr. 68, Postfach 3479, 4002 Basel; tel. 612818686; fax 612818679; e-mail info@lloydsagency.ch; internet www.lloydagency.ch; agency of Lloyds of London (United Kingdom) in Switzerland and Liechtenstein; Pres. A. R. KELLER.

Mediterranean Shipping Co SA: 40 ave Eugène-Pittard, 1206 Geneva; tel. 227038888; fax 227038787; e-mail info@mscgva.ch; internet www.mscgva.ch; f. 1970; operates 376 container vessels (March 2008); Dir G. APONTE.

Reederei Zürich AG: Bergstr. 109, 8030 Zürich; tel. 4112571040; fax 616393466; e-mail webmaster@reedereizurich.com; internet www.reedereizurich.com; ship management.

Suisse-Atlantique, Société de Navigation Maritime SA: 7 ave des Baumettes, CP 48, 1020 Renens 1; tel. 216372201; fax 216372202; e-mail activity@suisat.com; world-wide tramping services; Pres. E. ANDRE; Dir C. DIDAY.

CIVIL AVIATION

Switzerland's principal airports are situated at Zürich and Geneva. A major airport at Basel-Mulhouse-Freiburg (EuroAirport) serves northern Switzerland, but is situated across the border in France.

Baboo: 46 rue de Frontenex, 1207 Geneva; tel. 848445445; internet www.flybaboo.com; f. 2003; scheduled services to destinations in Europe; CEO MARK DARBY.

Darwin Airline: Lugano Airport, 6982 Agno; tel. 916124500; fax 916124520; e-mail info@darwinairline.com; internet www.darwinairline.com; f. 2003; low-cost airline; flights from four Swiss airports to destinations in Italy and Spain; Pres. SERGIO ERMOTTI; CEO FABIO PARINI.

Edelweiss Air: Operations Center, Postfach, 8058 Zürich-Flughafen; tel. 438165060; fax 438165061; e-mail office@edelweissair.ch; internet www.edelweissair.ch; f. 1995; operates charter flights to destinations world-wide; acquired by Swiss in 2008; CEO KARL KISTLER.

Helvetic Airways AG: Postfach 250, 8058 Zürich-Flughafen; tel. 442708500; e-mail info@helvetic.com; internet www.helvetic.com; f. 2003; charter flights and scheduled services to destinations in Italy and Germany; Chair. LEONARDO DE LUCA; CEO BRUNO JANS.

Swiss (Swiss International Air Lines): Postfach, 4002 Basel; tel. 615820000; fax 615823333; e-mail communications@swiss.com; internet www.swiss.com; f. 1979 as Crossair, took over operations from Swissair and adopted current name in 2002; national carrier operating routes to 76 destinations in 42 countries; subsidiary of Deutsche Lufthansa AG (Germany); CEO HARRY HOHMEISTER.

Tourism

Switzerland's principal attractions are the lakes and lake resorts and the mountains. Walking, mountaineering and winter sports are among the chief pastimes. Foreign tourist arrivals at hotels and similar establishments totalled 8.6m. in 2008. Receipts from tourism totalled 15,598m. Swiss francs in 2008 and a provisional 15,005m. Swiss francs in 2009.

Switzerland Tourism: Tödistr. 7, 8027 Zürich; tel. 442881111; fax 442881205; e-mail info@myswitzerland.com; internet www.myswitzerland.com; f. 1917; Dir JÜRG SCHMID.

Defence

National defence is based on compulsory military service for all able-bodied male citizens; women may serve voluntarily. Switzerland maintains no standing army except for a small permanent personnel of commissioned and non-commissioned officers primarily concerned with training. Military service consists of 18 weeks' compulsory recruit training at the age of 19–20 years, followed by seven three-week 'refresher' training courses between the ages of 20 and 30 years. Each soldier keeps his equipment in his own home, and receives compulsory marksmanship training between periods of service. As assessed at November 2010, the total strength of the armed forces, when mobilized, was 197,511, comprising an active force of 25,620 and reserves of 171,891 (army 121,998; air force 26,436; command support organization 14,136; and logistics organization 9,321). In addition, there was a civil defence force numbering 80,000 reservists. The Confederation belongs to no international defence organizations, and the strategy of the army and air force is defensive. In December 1996 Switzerland signed the Partnership for Peace framework document of the North Atlantic Treaty Organization (NATO). It was emphasized, however, that this in no way compromised the country's 'permanent neutrality', and that Switzerland had no intention of joining NATO itself.

Defence Expenditure: Budgeted at 4,090m. Swiss francs for 2011.

Chief of the General Staff: Maj.-Gen. ANDRÉ BLATTMANN.

Education

Pre-primary education in Switzerland is largely financed by the 26 cantons. Depending on the canton, pupils may undertake one or two years of kindergarten education, before commencing compulsory education. Primary and secondary education are controlled by the cantons as well, with the result that there are 26 different systems in operation. Responsibility for higher education is shared between the cantons and the Federal Government. Education is compulsory for children between the ages of seven and 16 years. The duration of primary education, which commences at the age of six or seven, is nine years. The duration and system of secondary education depends on individual cantonal policy. Some 20% of 17-year-olds continue their studies at a higher secondary school (*Gymnasium/collège*), and a leaving certificate (*Matura/maturité*) from one of these is a prerequisite for entry to academic higher education. About 70% proceed to vocational training (trade and technical) for a period of three to four years. There are 10 cantonal universities, two Federal Institutes of Technology (of university standing) and one Academic Institute (a teacher-training college of university standing), as well as nine universities of applied sciences. Numerous private schools exist, as well as one private university of applied sciences, and many foreign children receive part of their education in Switzerland. In 2007/08 enrolment at pre-primary level included 75.0% of children in the relevant age-group; enrolment at primary and secondary levels included 84.0% and 85.0% of children in the relevant age-group, respectively. In 2008/09 the number of students enrolled at Swiss universities stood at 184,756. In 2007 federal, cantonal and communal expenditure on education amounted to 28,440m. Swiss francs (19.5% of total public expenditure).

SYRIA

Introductory Survey

LOCATION, CLIMATE, LANGUAGE, RELIGION, FLAG, CAPITAL

The Syrian Arab Republic lies in western Asia, with Turkey to the north, Iraq to the east and Jordan to the south. Lebanon and Israel are to the south-west. Syria has a coastline on the eastern shore of the Mediterranean Sea. Much of the country is mountainous and semi-desert. The coastal climate is one of hot summers and mild winters. The inland plateau and plains are dry but cold in winter. Average temperatures in Dimashq (Damascus) range from 2°C to 12°C (36°F to 54°F) in January and from 18°C to 37°C (64°F to 99°F) in August. The national language is Arabic, with Kurdish a minority language. According to the UN Relief and Works Agency for Palestine Refugees in the Near East (UNRWA), at June 2010 there were 477,700 Palestinian refugees registered in Syria. More than 80% of the population are Muslims (mostly Sunnis), but there is a substantial Christian minority of various sects. The national flag (proportions 2 by 3) has three equal horizontal stripes, of red, white and black, with two five-pointed, green stars in the centre of the white stripe. The capital is Damascus.

CONTEMPORARY POLITICAL HISTORY

Historical Context

Syria was formerly part of Turkey's Ottoman Empire. Turkish forces were defeated in the First World War (1914–18), and Syria was occupied in 1920 by France, in accordance with a League of Nations mandate. Syrian nationalists proclaimed an independent republic in September 1941. French powers were transferred in January 1944, and full independence was achieved on 17 April 1946. In December 1949 Syria came under a military dictatorship, led by Brig. Adib Shishekly. He was elected President in July 1953, but was overthrown by another army coup in February 1954.

In February 1958 Syria merged with Egypt to form the United Arab Republic (UAR). In September 1961, following a military coup in Damascus, Syria seceded and formed the independent Syrian Arab Republic. In 1963 Maj.-Gen. Amin al-Hafiz formed a Government in which members of the Arab Socialist Renaissance (Baath) Party were predominant. In February 1966 the army deposed the Government of President al-Hafiz, replacing him with Dr Nur el-Din al-Atasi. However, in November 1970, after a bloodless coup, the military (moderate) wing of the Baath Party seized power, led by Lt-Gen. Hafiz al-Assad, who was elected President in March 1971. In March 1972 the National Progressive Front (NPF), a grouping of the five main political parties (including the Baath Party), was formed under the leadership of President Assad.

Domestic Political Affairs

Syria's regional influence under President Hafiz al-Assad

Increasing border tension between Syria and Israel was a major influence leading to the Six-Day War of June 1967, when Israel attacked its Arab neighbours in reprisal for the closure of the Strait of Tiran by the UAR (Egypt). Israeli forces made swift territorial gains, including the Golan Heights region of Syria, which remains under Israeli occupation. An uneasy truce lasted until October 1973, when Egyptian and Syrian forces launched simultaneous attacks on Israeli-held territory. On the Syrian front, there was fierce fighting in the Golan Heights until a cease-fire was agreed after 18 days. In May 1974 the US Secretary of State, Henry Kissinger, secured an agreement for the disengagement of forces. Israel's formal annexation of the Golan Heights in December 1981 effectively impeded the prospect of a negotiated Middle East settlement at this time.

Syria disapproved of the second interim Egyptian-Israeli Disengagement Agreement, signed in September 1975, but agreed to acknowledge it as a *fait accompli* in return for Egypt's acceptance of Syria's role in Lebanon. Syria had progressively intervened in the Lebanese civil war during 1976, finally providing the bulk of the 30,000-strong Arab Deterrent Force (ADF). Syria condemned the Egyptian President, Anwar Sadat, for Egypt's peace initiative with Israel in November and December 1977, the Camp David agreements signed by Egypt and Israel in September 1978, and the subsequent peace treaty concluded between them.

From 1977 frequent assassinations of Alawites (the minority Islamic sect to which Assad belonged) indicated sectarian tension within Syrian society. Assad attributed much of the opposition to the Muslim Brotherhood, a conservative Islamist group, and he ordered the brutal suppression of an uprising in Hamah (Hama), led by the outlawed Brotherhood, in February 1982. From November 1983, after Assad suffered a heart attack, rivals to the succession—including Col Rifaat al-Assad, the President's brother—vied for pre-eminence. In March 1984, following Assad's recovery, the appointment of three Vice-Presidents had the effect of equally distributing power among the President's potential successors and giving none the ascendancy. Assad was also able to rely on a cadre of loyal officers who ensured the army's continued support for the President.

The ADF, based in northern Lebanon, was unable to act when Israel invaded southern Lebanon in June 1982 and surrounded Beirut, trapping Syrian troops and fighters of the Palestine Liberation Organization (PLO). The Syrian and Palestinian forces in Beirut were evacuated in August, under the supervision of a multinational peace-keeping force, and some 50,000 Syrian troops, deployed in the Beqa'a valley and northern Lebanon, opposed 25,000 Israelis in the south of the country, even though the ADF's mandate had expired. Syria rejected the May 1983 Israel-Lebanon peace agreement, formulated by US Secretary of State George Shultz, refusing to withdraw its forces from Lebanon and continuing to supply the militias of the Lebanese Druze and Shi'ite factions in their fight against the Lebanese Government and the Christian Phalangists. From May 1983 Syria supported a revolt against Yasser Arafat and the leadership of Fatah (the Palestine National Liberation Movement), and by November Syrian and rebel PLO forces had cornered Arafat, the PLO Chairman, in the Lebanese port of Tarabulus (Tripoli). Arafat and some 4,000 of his supporters were eventually evacuated, under UN protection, in December.

In March 1984 President Amin Gemayel of Lebanon capitulated to Syria's influence over Lebanese affairs, and abrogated the May 1983 agreement with Israel. In April President Assad approved Gemayel's plans for a Lebanese government of national unity, giving equal representation to Muslims and Christians. In September 1984 Syria arranged a truce to end fighting in Tripoli between the pro-Syrian Arab Democratic Party and the Sunni Tawhid Islami (Islamic Unification Movement). The Lebanese army entered the city in late 1984, under the terms of a Syrian-backed extended security plan, to assert the authority of the Lebanese Government. Syria also authorized Lebanon's participation in talks with Israel to co-ordinate the departure of the Israeli Defence Force from southern Lebanon (with that of other security forces), in order to prevent an outbreak of civil violence. After the final stage of the Israeli withdrawal in June 1985, several hundred Israeli troops and advisers remained in Lebanon to assist the Israeli-backed 'South Lebanon Army' in policing a narrow buffer zone along the Lebanese side of the international border. Syria removed 10,000–12,000 troops from the Beqa'a valley in July, leaving some 25,000 in position.

President Assad was re-elected for a third seven-year term of office in February 1985, and his administration involved itself in seeking to resolve Lebanon's sectarian unrest. Through its proxy, Amal, Syria sought to prevent Yasser Arafat from re-establishing a power base in Beirut, and around 650 people died in the fighting before a cease-fire was agreed in Damascus in June. In December the three main Lebanese militias—the Druze, Amal and Lebanese Forces (LF) Christian militia—met in Damascus to sign a Syrian-brokered accord outlining a politico-military settlement of the civil war. However, the Shi'ite Hezbollah and Sunni Murabitoun militias were not party to the accord and President Gemayel, who had not been consulted during the drafting of the agreement, refused to endorse it. Opposition to the accord was further manifested following Samir

Geagea's promotion to the leadership of the LF in January 1986. Syria brokered another cease-fire in June, this time in the Palestinian refugee camps around Beirut (where fighting between Palestinian guerrillas and Shi'ite Amal militiamen had recently escalated); this proved to be the first stage in a Syrian-sponsored peace plan for Muslim west Beirut. The co-operation of the Amal, Druze and Sunni militias was dependent upon the deployment of uniformed Syrian troops in Beirut for the first time since 1982. Though the activities of the militias in west Beirut were temporarily curbed, the plan was strongly opposed in Christian east Beirut and was not extended to the predominantly Shi'ite southern suburbs, where most of the city's Palestinian refugees lived. By early 1987 heavy fighting had resumed in west Beirut, between Amal forces and an alliance of Druze, Murabitoun and Communist Party militias. Syrian troops (soon numbering some 7,500) succeeded in enforcing a cease-fire in the central and northern areas of west Beirut, but were not deployed in the southern suburbs.

At a general election held in February 1986 the Baath Party and other members of the NPF (excluding the Communist Party, which contested the poll independently) obtained 151 of the 195 seats in the People's Assembly. The communists won nine seats, and independents 35. In November 1987, following the resignation of Abd al-Rauf al-Kassem as Prime Minister, Mahmoud al-Zoubi, the Speaker of the Assembly, was appointed premier. In May 1988 Syria's interest in the Lebanese presidential election, scheduled to be held in August of that year, prompted an intense period of fighting between Amal and Hezbollah in Beirut's southern suburbs. Overt Syrian support for the candidacy of Sulayman Franjiya (President of Lebanon during 1970–76), and later for Mikhail al-Daher (after the first postponement of the election), aroused the opposition of Lebanese Christian leaders, who objected to candidates imposed by foreign powers. Consequently, Syria refused to recognize the interim military administration appointed by President Gemayel shortly before his term of office expired. From March 1989 Christian forces, commanded by Gen. Michel Aoun (the head of the interim Lebanese Government), attempted to expel Syrian forces from Lebanon, thereby provoking one of the most violent confrontations of the entire civil war.

In October 1989, under the auspices of the League of Arab States (the Arab League, see p. 361), the Lebanese National Assembly endorsed a charter of national reconciliation (the Ta'if agreement). The Lebanese authorities envisaged a continuing role for the Syrian army in Lebanon by stipulating that it should assist in the implementation of two security plans incorporated in the accord, which also included the constitutional amendments that Syria had long sought to effect in Lebanon. (For further details concerning the Ta'if agreement, see the chapter on Lebanon.) In May 1991 Syria and Lebanon signed a treaty of 'fraternity, co-operation and co-ordination', which was immediately denounced by Israel as a further step towards the formal transformation of Lebanon into a Syrian protectorate. Israel responded by deploying armed forces inside the buffer zone in southern Lebanon, and any likelihood of Israel's compliance with UN Security Council Resolution 425 (adopted in March 1978), which demanded the withdrawal of Israeli armed forces from southern Lebanon, diminished. Syria was the only Arab state which refused to recognize the independent Palestinian state (proclaimed by the Palestine National Council in November 1988), in accordance with its long-standing policy of preventing any other force in Lebanon from acquiring sufficient power to challenge Syrian interests. Meanwhile, Syria persistently denied claims, principally by the USA, that it was sponsoring international terrorism, and refused to restrict the activities of Palestinian groups on its territory. Following a series of bomb attacks in Europe in 1985–86, in November 1986 members of the European Community (EC, now European Union—EU, see p. 270), excluding Greece, imposed limited diplomatic and economic sanctions against Syria, as did the USA and Canada. However, the EC (with the exception of the United Kingdom) ended its ban on ministerial contacts with Syria in July 1987; financial aid was resumed in September, although a ban on the sale of weapons to Syria remained in force.

Domestic affairs following the end of Lebanon's civil war

At elections to the People's Assembly (now expanded to 250 seats) in May 1990, the Baath Party won 134 seats and other parties 32, while 84 seats were reserved for independent candidates. In December 1991 it was announced that 2,864 political prisoners were to be released; this was regarded as the first indication of President Assad's intention to liberalize Syria's political system. In March 1992 Assad indicated that new political parties might in future be established, but he rejected the implementation of foreign democratic frameworks as unsuited to the country's level of economic development. In January 1994 Basel al-Assad, President Assad's eldest son and presumed successor, was killed in a road accident; the President's second son, Bashar, was reportedly instructed to assume the role of his late brother in order to avoid a power struggle. In August senior government officials, including the Commander of the Special Forces, were removed from office in an apparent attempt by Assad to consolidate his position and improve Syria's international standing.

The ruling Baath Party and its NPF allies reinforced their dominance of Syrian affairs at elections to the People's Assembly in August 1994, winning 167 of the 250 seats. In November 1995—the 25th anniversary of President Assad's seizure of power—some 1,200 political prisoners, including members of the banned Muslim Brotherhood, were released under an amnesty, while a number of the Brotherhood's leaders were allowed to return from exile. During 1996 there were reports of several explosions in Damascus, in addition to a number of attacks on Syrian targets in Lebanon. In January 1997 the Syrian-based Islamic Movement for Change claimed responsibility for a bomb attack in central Damascus the previous month, in which 11 people died.

In February 1998 President Assad unexpectedly dismissed his brother, Col Rifaat al-Assad, as Vice-President (a post he had held since 1984, although he had spent much of the intervening period overseas). In July President Assad appointed new chiefs of both the Syrian army and the intelligence service, prompting speculation that he was seeking to extend the political influence of his second son, Bashar.

Elections to the People's Assembly were held on 30 November and 1 December 1998, at which the NPF, led by the ruling Baath Party, again won 167 of the 250 seats. On 11 February 1999 a national referendum ratified the incoming Assembly's decision to nominate President Assad for a fifth term of office. It was widely speculated that Bashar would be promoted to the vice-presidency in a new administration, having already been promoted to the rank of army colonel in January and reportedly granted new powers over important domestic matters. In June the Syrian authorities were said to be undertaking an 'unprecedented' campaign, led by Bashar al-Assad, to counter corruption in public office. Details emerged in September of large-scale arrests (involving 1,000 people, according to some reports) by security forces in Damascus and Latakia against supporters and relatives of Rifaat al-Assad. Subsequent closures of Rifaat's interests (including port facilities in Latakia) provoked several days of violent clashes between his supporters and the security forces, in which, according to reports rejected by the Government, hundreds of people were killed or injured.

Having accepted the resignation of Mahmoud al-Zoubi and his administration in March 2000, President Assad named Muhammad Mustafa Mero, formerly governor of Halab (Aleppo), as Prime Minister. A new cabinet was subsequently inaugurated, with a programme to accelerate social and economic reforms, to strengthen anti-corruption measures and to resume peace negotiations with Israel. In all, 22 new ministers were appointed (including a number of younger technocrats and supporters of Bashar al-Assad), although the foreign affairs, defence and interior portfolios remained unchanged. In May al-Zoubi was expelled from the Baath Party for alleged 'irregularities and abuses' during his period in office. His assets were subsequently seized, and he was expected to stand trial on corruption charges. However, in late May official sources reported that al-Zoubi had committed suicide.

Bashar al-Assad's succession to the presidency

President Assad died on 10 June 2000. Shortly after his death the People's Assembly amended the Constitution, lowering the minimum age required of a president from 40 to 34 years, thus enabling Bashar al-Assad to assume the presidency. Bashar was also nominated as Commander-in-Chief of the Armed Forces, and his military rank was upgraded to that of Lieutenant-General. Following approval of Bashar's nomination for the presidency by the People's Assembly in late June (the Baath Party having already endorsed his candidacy), a nation-wide referendum on the succession was scheduled for July; the First Vice-President, Abd al-Halim Khaddam, assumed the role of acting President. In mid-June Bashar al-Assad was elected Secretary-General of the Baath Party. Rifaat al-Assad claimed that the assumed succession by Bashar was unconstitutional, and declared that he would challenge his nephew for the presidency. (The Syrian authorities reportedly issued a warrant for Rifaat's arrest should he attempt to enter the country from exile.) At the national referendum held on 10 July, Bashar al-Assad (the sole presidential candidate) received the endorsement of a reported 97.29% of voters. In his inaugural address to the People's Assembly on 17 July, President Assad emphasized as priorities for his administration economic reform, the elimination of official corruption and the conclusion of a peace treaty with Israel.

In July 2000 the new President released a significant number of political prisoners, the majority of whom were communists and members of the Muslim Brotherhood. Nevertheless, in September a statement by 99 Syrian intellectuals, published in the Lebanese press, demanded increased democracy and freedom of expression, an end to the state of emergency (in force since 1963) and the release of political detainees. In November the army was sent into the southern region of al-Suweida to quell three days of violent clashes between members of the Sunni bedouin and Druze communities, in which 20 people died.

In January 2001 a group of at least 1,000 intellectuals, among them a prominent businessman and deputy, Riad Seif, urged the Syrian regime to approve political reforms. They demanded the suspension of martial law, the holding of free elections, a free press, the release of political prisoners and an end to discrimination against women. Meanwhile, following a decision by the Baath Party in November 2000 to permit the other political parties in the NPF to issue their own newspapers, it was announced in early 2001 that the first non-state-controlled newspaper for several decades was to be published by the Communist Party. Syria's first privately owned newspaper for almost 40 years was also issued from February.

An independent deputy, Mamoun al-Homsi, was detained in August 2001 after starting a hunger strike in protest at official corruption and the Government's failure to end martial law. In September the leader of the Communist Party, Riad al-Turk, was taken into custody on charges of defaming the presidency (he had reportedly criticized the system of 'hereditary succession'). A few days later Riad Seif, who had held an 'illegal' discussion forum on political reform (the authorities had recently required that such forums be approved in advance), was arrested. Trial proceedings began in October against al-Homsi and Seif, and in March 2002 al-Homsi was convicted of 'attempting to change the Constitution by illegal means' and sentenced to a five-year custodial term. Seif also received a five-year gaol sentence in April, having been convicted on similar charges. In June 2002 al-Turk was sentenced to two-and-a-half years' imprisonment, although he was freed by President Assad in November, reportedly on 'humanitarian grounds'. Meanwhile, in November 2001 some 120 political prisoners were released under a general amnesty. In January 2002 legislation relating to private broadcasting was relaxed.

President Assad effected an extensive reorganization of the Government in December 2001. Prime Minister Mero retained his post, as did the Ministers of Defence and Foreign Affairs (the long-serving Minister of Foreign Affairs, Farouk al-Shara', additionally became the fourth Deputy Prime Minister), although a new Minister of the Interior, Maj.-Gen. Ali Hammoud (former head of the intelligence service), was named. However, several 'pro-reform' ministers were appointed to strategic portfolios relating to the economy, among them Muhammad al-Atrash as Minister of Finance.

Meanwhile, there was increasing agitation in Lebanon for a cessation of Syrian influence on Lebanese political affairs after the inauguration of a new Syrian President and the Israeli withdrawal from southern Lebanon. In July 2000 Maronite Christian leaders in Lebanon requested that President Assad release all Lebanese political prisoners held in Syria, and in the following month a coalition of Christian political parties in Lebanon urged voters then to boycott the forthcoming parliamentary elections, on the grounds that Syria would predetermine the outcome of the poll. The results of the elections, at which former premier Rafiq Hariri resoundingly defeated the Syrian-sponsored Government of Selim al-Hoss, served to intensify speculation about Syria's future role in Lebanese affairs. Syrian officials reacted angrily when the Lebanese Druze leader and traditional ally of Syria, Walid Joumblatt, demanded a 're-evaluation' of Syria's role in Lebanon. In December 46 Lebanese prisoners (many of whom were Christians detained by Syrian troops during the civil war) were released from Syrian detention; hitherto, Syria had never confirmed that it was holding Lebanese political prisoners.

In June 2001 Syria withdrew some 6,000–10,000 of its armed forces from predominantly Christian districts of east and south Beirut, and from Mount Lebanon; some of the troops were redeployed in the Beqa'a valley. However, Syria retained a number of military bases in strategic areas of the Lebanese capital. Redeployments of Syrian troops from central Lebanon took place in April 2002, and from northern Lebanon in February 2003. The new Lebanese Government formed under Hariri in April was widely considered to be the most pro-Syrian administration in Lebanon for more than a decade. In June unidentified assailants fired rockets at the studios of Hariri's Future Television in central Beirut. Syria was blamed for having organized the attack, chiefly as a warning to the Lebanese Prime Minister following remarks he made on a state visit to Brazil in which Hariri appeared to call for an improvement in Arab–Israeli relations. Moreover, the attack coincided with a further redeployment of Syrian troops from Lebanon.

Developments following the 2003 legislative elections

Elections to the People's Assembly were held on 2 and 3 March 2003, at which the NPF, led by the ruling Baath Party, again won 167 of the 250 seats, with the remaining 83 going to independents. Opposition parties, under an umbrella grouping called the National Democratic Rally, boycotted the election on the grounds that it was undemocratic. On 9 March the newly reconvened legislature elected the Deputy Prime Minister in charge of Public Services, Muhammad Naji al-Otari, as the new Speaker of the People's Assembly. Al-Otari was replaced as Deputy Prime Minister by Muhammad Safi Abu Wdan in late March.

In July 2003 it was reported that President Bashar al-Assad had adopted a decree effectively ending the Baath Party's monopoly on government, military and public sector positions. In September Prime Minister Mero resigned, along with his cabinet, apparently as a result of his failure to accelerate the process of political reform. Al-Otari was appointed as the new Prime Minister, and his first cabinet was announced at the end of the month. Soon afterwards at least 16 government officials were dismissed as part of a new anti-corruption campaign. In May 2004 Maj.-Gen. Mustafa Tlass retired from the posts of Minister of Defence and Deputy Commander-in-Chief of the Armed Forces; he was succeeded in both posts by armed forces Chief of Staff Hassan al-Turkmani, who was in turn replaced by Gen. Ali Habib Mahmoud (hitherto Special Forces Commander).

Issues of civil rights came to the fore in early 2004. In February a prominent lawyer and human rights activist, Haitham al-Maleh, was prevented from travelling to the United Arab Emirates (UAE); the Syrian Human Rights Association claimed that al-Maleh was being punished for having criticized the ongoing state of emergency in a speech he made to the German Bundestag (Federal Assembly) two months earlier. At the same time the Lebanese newspaper *An-Nahar* published a petition signed by 1,500 Syrian intellectuals, democratic activists and lawyers urging the Government to instigate radical reforms, including the lifting of the state of emergency and the release of political prisoners. At the end of the month foreigners were banned from studying at the 20 Islamic schools licensed by the Ministry of Labour and Social Affairs; they would henceforth only be allowed to study Islamic law at Damascus University. Although the official reason given was that the degrees awarded by the schools were not yet officially recognized, the decision was widely regarded as a crackdown by the secular regime on foreign Islamists who were using their studies as a cover for militant, fund-raising or recruitment activities.

There was a widespread outbreak of violent, predominantly Kurdish, protest in March 2004. The unrest started in the north-eastern town of Al-Qamishli, close to the border with Turkey, when fighting at a football match escalated into large-scale anti-Government protests and fighting between the Arab majority and Kurdish minority; a number of deaths were reported. Minister of the Interior Hammoud travelled to the region to oversee the quelling of the violence, and the Government accused Kurdish political groups of deliberately inciting the riots. However, the unrest quickly spread to the town of Al-Hasakah, and Kurdish émigrés in many European countries staged demonstrations of solidarity with the Kurds outside Syrian embassies. By April it appeared that hundreds of Kurds were still being detained by the authorities in connection with the clashes, and Amnesty International called for an independent inquiry into the unrest and for any remaining detainees to be either charged or released. In the same month a car bomb exploded outside the former offices of the UN Disengagement Observer Force in Damascus; an exchange of fire between police and four people fleeing the scene resulted in the deaths of two assailants, a police officer and a bystander; the other two attackers were arrested by the authorities.

In July and August 2004, as part of an amnesty declared by President Assad, 251 political prisoners were freed, including members of the Muslim Brotherhood and Imad Shiash, who had been serving a prison sentence since 1975 for his membership of the proscribed Arab Communist Organization. In October 2004 Assad announced a significant reorganization of the Council of Ministers, dismissing eight ministers from their posts. Prominent appointees included Maj.-Gen. Ghazi Kanaan, a former head of Syrian military intelligence in Lebanon, who assumed the interior portfolio from Hammoud, and Mahdi Dakhlallah, a well-known journalist, who was appointed Minister of Information.

Demonstrating Syria's continued influence on Lebanese political affairs, Prime Minister Hariri, following meetings with Syrian officials, withdrew his objection to the extension, in August 2004, of Lebanese President Emile Lahoud's mandate by three years. However, international pressure on Syria increased following the adoption in early September of UN Security Council Resolution 1559, which, without referring to Syria explicitly, demanded that Lebanon's sovereignty be respected and that all foreign forces leave the country. (See the chapter on Lebanon for further details of Lebanese domestic affairs and of the UN resolution.) The Syrian army subsequently redeployed about 3,000 special forces from positions south of Beirut, and further troops were withdrawn in December from the northern town of Batrun and from Beirut's southern suburbs and airport to the Beqa'a valley. However, the new Lebanese Government approved by the legislature in November (in which Rafiq Hariri had been replaced as Prime Minister by Omar Karami) was regarded as being even more favourable than its predecessor to continued Syrian influence in Lebanese affairs. In December a number of Lebanese political parties issued a joint statement demanding the cessation of foreign interference in the country.

Former Lebanese Prime Minister Rafiq Hariri was killed in a car bombing in Beirut on 14 February 2005. Although President Assad condemned the attack, the USA, without accusing Syria of any involvement, withdrew its ambassador to Damascus for consultations, and later demanded the complete withdrawal of Syrian troops from Lebanon and a thorough and transparent investigation into the incident. Meanwhile, Syria and Iran agreed to form a 'united front' against foreign threats to their states. Syria declared later in the month that it would redeploy all of its troops in Lebanon to the Beqa'a valley. Mass protests against Syria's influence on Lebanese affairs, and against the Syrian military presence in Lebanon, followed, and in late February US President George W. Bush demanded that Syria: withdraw all troops and security service personnel from Lebanon; stop using its territory to support militant groups; support free and fair elections in Lebanon; and adhere to UN Security Council Resolution 1559 (see above). The UN Secretary-General, Kofi Annan, called on Syria to withdraw its troops from Lebanon by April.

In early March 2005 Presidents Assad and Lahoud agreed at a summit meeting to the withdrawal of Syrian troops to the Beqa'a valley by the end of March; Syria later promised to withdraw all troops before Lebanon's general election in May, and to provide the UN with a timetable for the withdrawal. Syria reportedly withdrew 4,000–6,000 of its troops from Lebanon to Syria in mid-March, removing Syrian soldiers and intelligence agents from their barracks and offices around Tripoli and Beirut; 8,000–10,000 troops reportedly remained in the Beqa'a valley. A UN report released in late March blamed Syria for allowing political tension in Lebanon to mount before the murder of Hariri; it also criticized Lebanon's initial attempts to investigate the incident. In early April the UN Security Council approved Resolution 1595, which established an International Independent Investigation Commission (UNIIIC) to investigate Hariri's murder. The German prosecutor Detlev Mehlis was appointed to head the commission. The formation of a new Lebanese administration, headed by newly appointed Prime Minister Najib Miqati, was announced in mid-April. Later in the month Syria declared that it had withdrawn all of its troops and security forces from Lebanon, and in early May a UN team dispatched to Lebanon to confirm the withdrawal announced that thus far it had not found a single Syrian soldier in areas that it had inspected.

President Assad and Prime Minister Otari met the new Lebanese premier Fouad Siniora in Syria in August 2005. The two states reportedly agreed to improve relations based on mutual respect, and Siniora emphasized Lebanon's support of Syria and its commitment to bilateral agreements. Various prominent Lebanese figures opposed to Syrian influence in Lebanon were killed or injured in bomb attacks during mid- to late 2005, including George Hawi, the former Secretary-General of the Parti communiste libanais (Lebanese Communist Party), who was killed in a car bombing in Beirut in June.

At the 10th national congress of the Baath Party in June 2005, President Assad was re-elected as Secretary-General. Vice-President and member of the party leadership Abd al-Halim Khaddam reportedly asked to be relieved of all of his duties, citing a wish to allow more young people to be represented in the party and state leadership. Although there was no confirmation that Khaddam's resignation as Vice-President had been accepted, it was announced that he had not been re-elected to the party leadership. The political committee of the Baath Party endorsed proposals to relax laws relating to the state of emergency, and to produce legislation allowing the formation of independent parties and increased freedom of the press; however, by early 2011 the proposed reforms had yet to be introduced.

In December 2005 Khaddam, who had been living in exile in Paris, France, since his resignation, held an interview with the Dubai (UAE)-based satellite television station Al-Arabia in which he accused Assad of having personally threatened Rafiq Hariri a few months prior to his assassination. Khaddam subsequently declared that, in his view, Assad had ordered Hariri's killing, although he awaited the final decision of the investigating commission. He declared that the current Syrian regime could not be reformed, and appealed to opposition groups in Syria to co-operate to defeat it. In early January 2006 the Baath Party announced that it had formally expelled Khaddam, accusing him of treachery against the party, his country and the Arab nation for his accusations against the Syrian President. Meanwhile, in December 2005 the People's Assembly unanimously approved a motion demanding that Khaddam be brought to trial on charges of treason and corruption. In January 2006 the Syrian Government froze Khaddam's assets, and in April a military court formally charged the former Vice-President with a series of offences, including inciting a foreign attack on Syrian soil and plotting to seize political and civil power.

The UN investigation into the assassination of Rafiq Hariri

In response to reports that Syrian intelligence agents might not have completely withdrawn from Lebanon, the UN announced in June 2005 that it was considering sending a commission to the country to investigate the claims. (Syria continued to assert that it had removed all of its security personnel.) UNIIIC began its inquiry into Rafiq Hariri's assassination in mid-June, with a three-month mandate. In August UNIIIC arrested three former Lebanese security officials with close ties to Syria, who had tendered their resignations in April, for questioning regarding the assassination. A fourth security chief, who had retained his post after Hariri's murder, subsequently handed himself in to the organization. A former, pro-Syrian parliamentary deputy was also detained. In mid-October, shortly before UNIIIC issued its first report on the investigation, the official Syrian Arab News Agency announced the death, by suicide, of the Minister of the Interior, Maj.-Gen. Ghazi Kanaan; a formal investigation subsequently confirmed the cause of death. Shortly before his apparent suicide, Kanaan had issued a statement to a Lebanese radio station defending Syria's role in Lebanon and announcing that he had been questioned by UNIIIC, but had not given any evidence against Syria. Some analysts noted that Kanaan, a potential alternative to the Syrian President who had opposed the decision to extend Lebanese President Lahoud's tenure by three years in 2004 (see above), had been seen as a threat to Assad.

According to its first report, issued in October 2005, UNIIIC had found evidence that Lebanese and Syrian intelligence and security services were directly involved in the assassination of Rafiq Hariri. Moreover, the report reasoned, the act was too complex and too well planned to have taken place without the approval of senior Syrian security officials and their Lebanese counterparts. UNIIIC expressed its extreme concern at the lack of co-operation of the Syrian authorities. Lebanon and Syria both rejected the report, criticizing the investigation's findings as politically motivated, and Syria announced that it had established a special judicial commission to deal with all matters relating to UNIIIC's mission. The UN commission was granted an extension to its mandate to mid-December. The UN Security Council reacted to the report by adopting Resolution 1636 at the end of October, establishing measures against suspects in the assassination, including prohibitions on travel and the freezing of assets, and urging Syria to co-operate fully with the investigation commission and to detain persons identified by the inquiry as suspects in Hariri's assassination, threatening unspecified 'further action' should Syria not fulfil the resolution's demands. The Security Council gave Syria until 15 December to comply with the resolution, which was sponsored by the USA, France and the United Kingdom. Syria reported in November that it had arrested six government officials for questioning. Meanwhile, in late October, the UN Special Envoy, Terje Rød-Larsen, published his report on compliance with UN Security Council Resolution 1559, in which he commended Syria's withdrawal of its troops from Lebanon, but criticized Lebanon for not complying with the resolution's demands.

In his second report to the UN Security Council, issued in December 2005, Mehlis noted that Syria had presented five officials suspected of involvement in the murder of Hariri to UNIIIC for interrogation in Vienna, Austria. However, the report again accused Syria of reluctance to co-operate with the investigating body. UNIIIC had found further evidence of the involvement of the Lebanese and Syrian intelligence and security services in the assassination, and Mehlis identified 19 suspects, six of whom were Syrian (of which five were those currently under interrogation in Vienna). Mehlis resigned as head of UNIIIC shortly after he presented the report, citing personal and professional reasons; he was replaced by Serge Brammertz. UNIIIC's mandate was extended to 15 June 2006.

In January 2006, after Abd al-Halim Khaddam accused President Assad of having personally threatened Hariri (see above), UNIIIC investigators declared that they wished to question President Assad and Syria's Minister of Foreign Affairs al-Shara'. However, the Minister of Information, Mahdi Dakhlallah, declared that Syria would not permit UNIIIC to interview the President. Brammertz met al-Shara' and other unspecified Syrian officials in late February. Al-Shara' announced in March that he had reached an agreement with UNIIIC providing for full Syrian co-operation with the investigation, while maintaining the country's 'sovereignty and dignity'. Meanwhile, Khaddam reiterated his claims that Assad was ultimately responsible for Hariri's assassination, and called for a popular revolt to effect the President's removal from office.

President Assad effected a comprehensive reorganization of the Council of Ministers in February 2006. Al-Shara' was appointed as Vice-President to replace Khaddam, and given additional responsibility for Foreign Affairs and Information; he was replaced as Minister of Foreign Affairs by Walid Mouallem. Brig.-Gen. Bassam Abd al-Majid was accorded the interior portfolio, which had been vacant since the death of Ghazi Kanaan in October 2005. In March 2006 Dr Najah al-Attar was also named as a Vice-President.

In May 2006 274 Lebanese and Syrian intellectuals and activists signed the Beirut-Damascus Declaration, a petition urging the Syrian Government to reassess its policy on Lebanon, to respect the sovereign independence of that country and to establish normal diplomatic relations. Many of those who signed the Declaration were subsequently arrested, and in early 2007 five prominent activists were convicted on charges of disseminating false information and damaging national morale; they were sentenced to terms of imprisonment of between three and 10 years.

Meanwhile, the third and fourth UNIIIC reports on the assassination of Hariri were published in March and June 2006, respectively. Recent Syrian co-operation was described as 'generally satisfactory', and the investigators claimed to have made considerable progress with regard to their understanding both of the circumstances surrounding the murder and of the links between the planners and the perpetrators of the killing. However, the report acknowledged that more thorough investigation was required into alleged links between Hariri's assassination and 14 other attacks against anti-Syrian figures in Lebanon since October 2004. In mid-June 2006 UNIIIC's mandate was extended for another year. The fifth UNIIIC report was released by Brammertz in September, and again described Syrian co-operation with the investigation as 'generally satisfactory'.

Syria was forced to deny accusations that it had orchestrated the assassination of Pierre Gemayel, the Lebanese Minister of Industry, a well-known opponent of Syrian influence in Lebanon, who was shot dead in his car on the outskirts of Beirut in November 2006 (see the chapter on Lebanon). Among those quick to apportion the blame firmly on Syria was Rafiq Hariri's son, Saad. During 2007 the Syrian leadership continued to oppose demands by the international community, including the US Administration, that an international tribunal be established in order to try suspects in Hariri's murder. In response to the adoption by the UN Security Council, in May, of Resolution 1757, establishing a special tribunal for this purpose, Syria emphasized its position that the tribunal represented a violation of Lebanese sovereignty, and that it would refuse to hand over any Syrian suspects to the new body.

Domestic unrest following the 2007 legislative elections

In January 2007, in preparation for legislative elections scheduled to take place in April, President Assad approved amendments to electoral legislation, including the introduction of stricter regulations on the financing of campaigns. No changes were made to the quota system by which 167 of the 250 seats were reserved for the NPF, despite widespread demands for its abolition from reformists. Ten days before the polls the Government announced that the number of seats reserved for the NPF would actually be increased to 170, thus reducing the number of seats set aside for independent candidates to just 80. At the elections to the People's Assembly on 22–23 April, voter turn-out was officially reported at 56.1% of the registered electorate; however, opponents of the Government claimed that the true rate of participation was, at most, 10%–20%. Speaking at an official press conference on 26 April, the Minister of the Interior announced that the NPF had in fact secured 172 seats; the number of independents thus fell to 78. The opposition, which had boycotted the polls, called upon the international community to condemn the elections and to acknowledge the illegitimacy of the newly installed legislature. Moreover, both domestic and external human rights groups and even government-controlled newspapers denounced the elections as undemocratic. In the following month the legislature unanimously approved the Baath Party's nomination of Bashar al-Assad for a second term as President, a national referendum on which was duly held on 27 May. Assad was endorsed for another seven-year term of office by a reported 97.6% of votes; turn-out was officially declared to have been more than 95.8%.

In October 2005 a coalition of political activists and members of banned political organizations had issued a document entitled the Damascus Declaration for Democratic National Change, which urged the establishment, through peaceful means, of a democratic state, built on moderate Islamic principles, with a new constitution to guarantee liberty and human rights for all. The Declaration also appealed for a democratic solution to the issue of Kurdish nationalism. In December 2007 168 signatories convened to reaffirm the Declaration's message and to elect a National Council; Fida' al-Hourani, daughter of Akram al-Hourani, one of the founders of the Baath Party, was elected President. In the weeks following the meeting up to 40 members of the movement were detained, and legal proceedings against 12 dissidents were initiated in July on charges including spreading false information and weakening national morale. The accused, who had pleaded not guilty to all charges, were convicted in October and accorded sentences of between two and two-and-a-half years' imprisonment. In a report published in February 2009, the US-based organization Human Rights Watch appealed for the abolition of the Supreme State Security Court, an extra-judicial organ of state which, the group stated, was used primarily to try suspected dissidents without granting them proper legal representation or the right of appeal.

In February 2008 Imad Mughniyeh, a senior member of Hezbollah, was killed in a car bombing in Damascus. Hezbollah claimed that the attack had been carried out by Israeli secret service operatives, an allegation that was denied by Israel. The Syrian authorities immediately launched an investigation into the incident. However, the fact that no findings were released prompted widespread speculation concerning the possible involvement of Syrian or other Arab nationals in the bombing. Brig.-Gen. Muhammad Suleiman, an adviser and close ally of President Assad, was shot dead near the port city of Tartous in August. After an initial refusal to comment on Suleiman's death, the Government confirmed the assassination some days later.

Suleiman had allegedly acted as a liaison with Hezbollah, as well as with the International Atomic Energy Agency (IAEA—which was investigating Syria's alleged nuclear facility, see The Israeli-Syrian track of the Middle East peace process). In September 2008 a car bomb, detonated close to both a security forces' base and an important Shi'a shrine, on the outskirts of Damascus, killed 17 people. In November Syrian state television broadcast what it claimed were the confessions of 11 militants responsible for the bombing, which was the deadliest attack on Syrian territory for more than 20 years. The 10 men and one woman, as well as a 12th operative who had carried out the suicide attack, were described as members of Fatah al-Islam, a militant Sunni Islamist group active in the Palestinian refugee camps in Lebanon. The confessions also contained the allegation that the group had been funded by Saad Hariri's Future Movement. the Future Movement strongly denied this allegation, and countered with the claim that Fatah al-Islam was in fact, funded by the Syrian intelligence authorities. Unsubstantiated reports in December suggested that the leader of Fatah al-Islam, Shakir al-Abssi, had been either captured or killed by security forces in Syria. In October, meanwhile, there were violent clashes between Syrian security forces and suspected militants at the Yarmuk Palestinian refugee camp, close to Damascus, in which two Iraqi men and a police officer were reportedly killed.

A protracted political crisis in Lebanon, during which pro-Syrian factions, including Hezbollah, obstructed a new presidential election (the tenure of President Lahoud having ended in November 2007), threatened to escalate into civil war in that country during 2008. Syria was swift to deny claims by many Western governments that it was preventing the presidential vote from taking place, and that it was seeking to bring about the collapse of Lebanon's Western-backed Government by providing military assistance to Hezbollah and its allies. However, following the signing of the Qatari-brokered Doha Agreement in May 2008, which led to the formation of a national unity administration and the election of Michel Suleiman as President, renewed rapprochement between Syria and Lebanon became possible. In fact, Syria's support for the agreement was regarded as providing the catalyst for a marked improvement in its international standing generally. A landmark agreement was reached between Lebanon and Syria in July, when the two countries announced that they were to enter into diplomatic relations and open embassies in one another's capitals for the first time. Syria's Minister of Foreign Affairs, Walid Mouallem, visited Beirut in that month for further talks on bilateral relations, and President Suleiman made a two-day state visit to Syria in August. During Suleiman's visit it was announced that the work of a committee to demarcate the Lebanese–Syrian border would be resumed. The countries also agreed jointly to investigate the issue of persons missing since Lebanon's civil war and to review existing bilateral agreements. President Assad issued a decree formally establishing diplomatic relations with Lebanon in October. Ziad Baroud, Lebanon's Minister of the Interior, visited his Syrian counterpart in Damascus for talks on security co-operation in November, and, in an unexpected development, Gen. Michel Aoun, leader of the Christian opposition in Lebanon and a former adversary of Syria (see above), was a guest of President Assad in December. By late March 2009 both countries had opened their respective embassies and approved their ambassadors' nominations. The Special Tribunal for Lebanon (STL), established to try those suspected of involvement in the assassination of Rafiq Hariri, had begun operating earlier that month in Leidschendam, Netherlands. One of the main suspects in the case, Zuhair al-Siddiq, a former officer in the Syrian intelligence service, was reportedly arrested in Dubai in April.

Continuing criticism of Syria's human rights record

President Assad announced a significant reorganization of the Council of Ministers in April 2009, appointing six new ministers. Notable changes included the appointment of Gen. Saeed Muhammad Sammour, a senior military intelligence officer, as Minister of the Interior, in place of Brig.-Gen. Bassam Abd al-Majid, and the appointment of Ahmad Hammoud Younis, a judge and former deputy in the People's Assembly, as the new Minister of Justice. The Ministry of Local Administration and Environment was divided into two separate ministries: Kawkab al-Sabagh Muhammad Jamil al-Dayeh was appointed to the new post of Minister of State for Environmental Affairs, while Tamer Fouad al-Hijeh became Minister of Local Administration. In a further reorganization in June, Lt-Gen. Hassan al-Turkmani, hitherto Minister of Defence, was appointed Assistant Vice-President with the rank of Minister. Turkmani's former post was accorded to Lt-Gen. Ali Habib Mahmoud, who was replaced as Chief of Staff of the Armed Forces by Gen. Dawood Rajiha.

In October 2009 Syria attracted international criticism following the arrest of the prominent human rights campaigner Haitham al-Maleh, on charges of spreading false information that would undermine national morale. In an interview with a British-based Arabic television channel shortly before his arrest, al-Maleh, a former judge, had condemned the arbitrary and undemocratic exercise of power by the Government and the security forces. Trial proceedings against al-Maleh commenced in a military court in Damascus in April 2010, and in early July he was given a three-year prison term; the sentence led a number of international human rights groups and foreign governments to demand al-Maleh's immediate release. In late June 2010 another lawyer and leading human rights activist, Muhammad al-Hassani, had been found guilty of a similar offence and sentenced to a prison term of the same duration; al-Hassani was detained in July 2009 after having accused the Syrian authorities of conducting 'unfair trials' of political prisoners. In early March 2010 a petition seeking early release for 12 signatories to the Damascus Declaration, imprisoned in October 2008 (see above), was rejected in the Court of Appeals. In April the authorities released 36 political prisoners, who were either elderly or suffering from ill health.

The new Lebanese Prime Minister, Saad Hariri, made a landmark visit to Damascus to meet President Assad in December 2009. Hariri's March 14 Alliance had secured victory in the Lebanese national elections in June and, after protracted negotiations, had formed a new, national unity Government in November. The Lebanese Prime Minister, who had blamed Syria for the assassination of his father in 2005, stated that his visit represented the beginning of a 'new phase' in relations between the two countries. Furthermore, in what was regarded by observers as an indication of waning anti-Syrian sentiment among the supporters of the March 14 Alliance, in late March 2010 Walid Joumblatt, leader of the Parti socialiste progressiste, also travelled to Damascus for talks with President Assad. During a second visit by Hariri to Damascus in mid-May the Lebanese and Syrian leaderships held discussions on bilateral and regional issues prior to a scheduled trip by the Lebanese Prime Minister to the USA at the end of the month. In early September Hariri stated in an interview with a United Kingdom-based newspaper, *Asharq al-Awsat*, that he had been mistaken in accusing Syria of involvement in his father's murder.

In mid-July 2010, in response to evidence that increasing numbers of Syrian women were choosing to wear the *niqab* (veil), the Government ordered all universities and colleges to ban female students from wearing the veil on their campuses. The new policy apparently demonstrated the secular regime's determination to prevent the rise in Islamist fundamentalism seen in other countries of the region from taking hold in Syria. It was also reported that about 1,000 primary school teachers who continued to wear the *niqab* had been transferred to administrative posts. A report published by Human Rights Watch at this time, entitled *A Wasted Decade: Human Rights in Syria during Bashar al-Asad's First Ten Years in Power*, asserted that Syria's poor record on individual freedoms and human rights had essentially remained unchanged since President Assad assumed the role from his father in July 2000. The organization castigated the Syrian authorities for practices such as the: repression of any form of dissent by members of the opposition and Kurdish minority journalists and human rights activists; continued use of emergency legislation; mistreatment and torture of prisoners; heavy censorship of the media; and lack of accountability in state institutions.

Recent developments: anti-Government unrest

Syria was initially little affected by the mass popular protests that took place in many Arab countries from early 2011, although it was reported in February that individuals demonstrating in support of the uprising in Egypt (see chapter on Egypt) had been detained by the security forces. However, in mid-March people in Dar'a began protesting, initially against the arrest of a group of children who had been writing anti-regime slogans (as popularized during the uprisings in Egypt and Tunisia) on walls in the town. Demonstrations, with demands including the release of political prisoners and an end to corruption, continued in Dar'a and nearby towns over the following days, and were repressed by security forces; a number of protesters were reported to have been shot dead, including 15 during the funeral of some earlier victims. On 25 March protests erupted in towns across Syria and continued in Dar'a; army troops were subsequently deployed to that town and to Latakia, where some 12 people were killed after the offices of the Baath Party were set on fire by protesters. The Government attributed the deaths in Latakia to sectarian strife (the town and its surroundings are divided between Sunni and Alawite communities), and declared that it intended to meet one of the demonstrators' principal demands, the lifting of the long-standing state of emergency. On 29 March President Assad accepted the resignation of the Council of Ministers led by al-Otari, apparently in an effort to appease the protesters, and on the following day he made his first public intervention since the start of the crisis in a speech to the People's Assembly. However, although he declared the need for reform he did not announce an immediate end to the state of emergency, and denounced 'foreign conspirators' as the cause of the ongoing unrest.

Protests, by this time increasingly demanding the fall of Assad's regime and the introduction of democracy, continued in early April 2011, notably in Dar'a, Homs and the town of Douma, north-east of Damascus, and were again violently repressed. On 3 April Assad appointed Dr Adel Safar, hitherto Minister of Agriculture and Agrarian Reform, to form a new Council of Ministers. In further efforts to appease forces hostile to the Government, in the following days the ban on the wearing of the *niqab* by teachers was rescinded, while some 200,000 stateless Kurds were granted Syrian citizenship. However, the protests continued to spread across the country, taking hold in Banias, where troops were deployed. On 14 April the composition of Safar's new Council of Ministers was announced: this notably included the appointment of Muhammad Ibrahim al-Shaar as Minister of the Interior and Muhammad al-Jleilati as Minister of Finance, although the ministers responsible for defence and foreign affairs retained their posts. (The new Council was sworn in by President Assad two days later.) On 15 April large-scale protests took place in Damascus for the first time. The lifting of the state of emergency was officially announced on 19 April; however, legislation restricting the right to demonstrate was simultaneously introduced, provoking an angry response from protesters. Moreover, on the same day a prominent left-wing activist, Mahmoud Issa, was arrested at his home in Homs, shortly after he had given an interview to the Qatar-based satellite television channel Al Jazeera. Anti-Government protests and violent repression by the army and security forces continued to escalate across the country into May. It was widely reported that prominent human rights campaigners and political activists were among those arrested by security forces; in mid-May domestic human rights organizations estimated that up to 850 people had been killed and more than 7,000 arrested since the unrest began.

The Israeli-Syrian track of the Middle East peace process

In July 1991, following a meeting with the US Secretary of State, James Baker, President Assad agreed for the first time to participate in direct negotiations with Israel at a regional peace conference, for which the terms of reference would be a comprehensive settlement based on UN Security Council Resolutions 242 (of 1967) and 338 (1973). In August 1991 the Israeli Cabinet formally agreed to attend a peace conference on terms proposed by the USA and the USSR. An initial, 'symbolic' session of the conference was held in Madrid, Spain, in October, and attended by Israeli, Syrian, Egyptian, Lebanese and Palestinian-Jordanian delegations. Syria's principal aim was to recover the Golan Heights, occupied by Israel since 1967. However, it emphasized that it was not prepared to achieve national goals at the expense of a comprehensive Middle East peace settlement. Syria regarded the Declaration of Principles on Palestinian Self-Rule in the Occupied Territories—the basis of a peace settlement signed by Israel and the PLO in September 1993—as deeply flawed. Furthermore, President Assad viewed the secret negotiations between Israel and the PLO prior to the Declaration of Principles as having undermined the united Arab position in the peace process, and Syria gave no indication that it would cease to support those Palestinian factions, such as the Damascus-based Popular Front for the Liberation of Palestine—General Command (PFLP—GC), which actively opposed the accord.

President Assad met US President Bill Clinton in Geneva, Switzerland, in January 1994—his first such meeting with a US leader since 1977—in an attempt to give fresh impetus to the Syrian track of the peace process. In June 1994 Syria reacted warily to the signing by Jordan and Israel of 'sub-agendas' for future bilateral discussions, and continued to adhere to the principle of a united Arab approach to negotiation with Israel.

In September Israel published details of a plan for the partial withdrawal of its armed forces from the Golan Heights; Syria rejected the proposals, although President Assad continued to affirm his willingness to achieve peace with Israel. Clinton visited Damascus in October for talks with Assad (the first visit by a US President to Syria for some 20 years), in a further attempt to facilitate the resumption of dialogue between Syria and Israel. However, it was not until March 1995 that bilateral negotiations finally resumed.

In May 1995 Israel and Syria concluded a 'framework understanding on security arrangements', in order to facilitate the participation in the discussions of the two countries' military Chiefs of Staff. Israel stated publicly that it had proposed a four-year timetable for the withdrawal of its armed forces from the Golan Heights, but that Syria had insisted on one of 18 months. In June the Israeli and Syrian Chiefs of Staff held talks in Washington, DC. Negotiations became deadlocked once again, however, and the situation was aggravated by political turmoil in Israel following the assassination of the Prime Minister, Itzhak Rabin, in November. The acting Israeli Prime Minister, Shimon Peres, indicated that no further discussions would take place until after the Israeli general election in May 1996, owing to Syria's refusal to condemn the violence in Israel and to take firmer action against terrorism generally. Following the election to the Israeli premiership of Likud leader Binyamin Netanyahu, an emergency Arab League summit meeting, held in Cairo, Egypt, in June, urged the new right-wing Government in Israel not to abandon the principle of negotiating 'land-for-peace', and demanded the removal of all Israeli settlements in the Golan Heights and their return to Syria. Netanyahu rejected the 'land-for-peace' policies of his Labour predecessor and also insisted that continued Israeli sovereignty over the Golan Heights must be the basis of any peace settlement with Syria. The redeployment, in September, of Syrian armed forces in Lebanon to positions in the Beqa'a valley gave rise to speculation in Israel that Syria, frustrated at the lack of progress in the peace process, might be preparing an attack on Israeli forces.

In early 1997 prospects of a resumption in negotiations were further frustrated after the Israeli Knesset (parliament) approved a preliminary reading of proposed legislation stipulating that the return of land to Syria would require the approval of at least two-thirds of deputies. In March 1998 Syria accused Israel of attempting to sabotage its relationship with Lebanon after the Israeli Prime Minister offered to withdraw from southern Lebanon in exchange for a security arrangement before reaching a formal agreement with Syria regarding the Golan Heights. Both Syria and Lebanon reiterated that any withdrawal must be unconditional, in compliance with UN Security Council Resolution 425. Syria was sceptical regarding the likely success of the US-brokered Wye Memorandum, signed in October by Israel and the Palestinian (National) Authority (PA), towards achieving a lasting peace in the Middle East, and President Assad again demanded a resumption of 'land-for-peace' negotiations.

Syria welcomed the success of Ehud Barak and his Labour-led One Israel coalition in the Israeli elections of May 1999. Barak reportedly proposed a five-phase plan to negotiate peace with Syria and to effect an Israeli withdrawal from southern Lebanon. Syria responded with the demand that Barak uphold his pre-election pledge to withdraw from Lebanon within one year of his election, and to resume peace talks from their point of deadlock in 1996. At the inauguration of the new Israeli Cabinet in early July 1999, Barak promised to negotiate a bilateral peace with Syria, based on UN Security Council Resolutions 242 and 338, thus apparently signalling to the Assad regime his intention to return most of the occupied Golan Heights to Syria in exchange for peace and normalized relations. In mid-July, prior to a meeting in Washington, DC, between Barak and President Clinton, Syria was reported to have warned dissidents of Damascus-based Palestinian organizations to cease their military operations against Israel, and to have interrupted the supply of Iranian weapons to Hezbollah guerrillas in southern Lebanon. Moreover, in late July Syria reported a 'cease-fire' with Israel, although mutual disagreements remained, most notably over the point at which previous negotiations had been suspended. In September, as Israel and the PA signed the Sharm el-Sheikh Memorandum (or Wye Two—see the chapter on Israel) in Egypt, US Secretary of State Madeleine Albright held talks with President Assad in Damascus.

In early December 1999, following mediation by Clinton, Israel and Syria agreed to resume negotiations from the point at which they had stalled in 1996. The first round of discussions between the Syrian Minister of Foreign Affairs, Farouk al-Shara', and the Israeli premier, Ehud Barak, was opened by the US President in mid-December 1999 in Washington, DC. Both sides agreed to resume discussions in the following month, and in late December Syria and Israel were reported to have agreed an informal 'cease-fire' in order to limit the conflict in Lebanon. A second round of talks between al-Shara' and Barak proceeded in early January 2000 in Shepherdstown, West Virginia, again with Clinton's involvement. Syria and Israel had agreed meanwhile on the establishment of committees to discuss simultaneously the issues of borders, security, normalization of relations, and water-sharing. However, in mid-January the peace talks were postponed indefinitely. Syria declared that it required a 'written' commitment from Israel to withdraw from the Golan Heights prior to a resumption of talks, while Israel demanded the personal involvement of President Assad in the negotiating process, and that Syria take action to restrain Hezbollah in southern Lebanon. In March the Israeli Cabinet voted unanimously to withdraw its forces from Lebanon by July, even in the absence of a peace settlement with Syria, while the Knesset voted to change the majority required in the event of an Israeli withdrawal from the Golan from 50% of participating voters to 50% of the registered electorate.

In May 2000 al-Shara' hosted discussions in Palmyra with his Egyptian and Saudi Arabian counterparts in an effort to co-ordinate a united Arab position towards the USA and Israel prior to the planned Israeli withdrawal from southern Lebanon. Reports following the talks suggested that Saudi Arabia and Egypt had pledged military support to Syria in the event of Israeli aggression. The accelerated withdrawal of Israeli armed forces from southern Lebanon was completed on 24 May, several weeks ahead of the original Israeli deadline. Following the death, in June, of President Assad, and the succession of his second son, Bashar al-Assad, in July (see Domestic Political Affairs), the Israeli-Syrian track of the Middle East peace process remained stalled. Nevertheless, Bashar indicated a desire to resume negotiations in the near future, although he emphasized that Syrian policy on the Golan Heights remained unchanged. The escalation of the Palestinian al-Aqsa *intifada* from September strained Syria's relations with Israel and, as tensions increased throughout the Middle East, Israel accused Syria of involvement in the abduction of Israeli military personnel by Hezbollah in the disputed Shebaa Farms area of southern Lebanon. (Shebaa Farms was designated by the UN as being part of Syria, and thus subject to the Syrian track of the peace process.)

Following the election of Likud leader Ariel Sharon to the Israeli premiership in February 2001, President Assad again reiterated Syria's position: namely, that negotiations would only be resumed upon a full Israeli withdrawal from the Golan Heights. Tensions between the two sides increased in April following an attack by Israeli forces on a Syrian radar station in eastern Lebanon, in which at least one Syrian soldier died. In December, following talks in Damascus between Egypt's President Hosni Mubarak and President Assad, Egypt and Syria issued a joint statement condemning Israeli military actions in the West Bank and Gaza, and appealed to the international community to exert pressure on Israel to halt its 'aggression'. In January 2003 a Syrian soldier was killed during a rare exchange of gunfire between Israeli and Syrian forces in the Golan Heights. In November 2004 Assad announced that he was willing to resume peace talks with Israel unconditionally (although it was unclear whether the Syrian President intended for negotiations to resume from where they had collapsed in 2000—see above); however, Israel demanded that Syria first close the headquarters of the Islamic Resistance Movement (Hamas) and Islamic Jihad, and Assad rejected Israel's setting of conditions as unacceptable.

In April 2003 US President George W. Bush handed to the Israeli and Palestinian leaderships the so-called 'roadmap' peace plan, which had been drawn up by the Quartet group (comprising the USA, the UN, Russia and the EU). The plan envisaged an end to the Arab–Israeli conflict and the creation of a sovereign Palestinian state by 2005–06 (for full details of the roadmap, see the chapter on Israel). A fully negotiated peace settlement between Israel and Syria was one of the objectives of the roadmap, but Syria was keen to emphasize that the new plan must run in tandem with the Syrian track of negotiations on the Golan Heights issue; however, in May 2003 President Assad reportedly assured Javier Solana, the EU's High Representative for the Common Foreign and Security Policy, that Syria would unconditionally accept the roadmap. An offer from Syria to resume peace talks with Israel in July was firmly rejected by Israeli Prime Minister Ariel Sharon as 'insincere'. In the following month Israel accused Syria of masterminding an attack by Hezbollah in Shebaa Farms. In October Israeli forces launched an air attack against an alleged Palestinian militant training camp inside Syria. Israel claimed that the camp at Ain Saheb near Damascus was being used by Hamas and Islamic Jihad, which the latter group denied, while another Palestinian militant group, the Popular Front for the Liberation of Palestine (PFLP), stated that the facility at Ain Saheb was in fact not in use. Israel insisted that the attack was not directed against Syria, but was in retaliation for a suicide bomb attack in Haifa, Israel, in which 19 Israelis were killed. In January 2004 President Assad rejected Israeli offers to resume peace negotiations, describing them as a 'media manoeuvre'. Following an Israeli warning of military action against Syria for its presumed involvement in suicide attacks in Israel that killed 16 people in August, a senior Hamas official was assassinated in Damascus in September.

In December 2006 Israeli Prime Minister Ehud Olmert rejected an appeal from President Assad for a resumption of formal peace negotiations with Syria. Olmert accused Assad of merely trying to solicit international approval at a time when Syria was under intense scrutiny for its alleged complicity in the assassinations in Lebanon of Rafiq Hariri and Pierre Gemayel (see Domestic Political Affairs). In January 2007 a former Israeli diplomat claimed that Israel and Syria had in fact conducted secret negotiations concerning a possible peace deal between September 2004 and July 2006, in which month the outbreak of the conflict between Israel and Hezbollah (see the chapters on Israel and Lebanon) had abruptly brought the proceedings to a close. (According to reports in the Israeli media, prior to the collapse of talks, mutual understandings had been reached with regard to an Israeli withdrawal from the Golan Heights and other issues of contention.) The diplomat's claims were strongly denied by the Syrian Government; however, Israeli officials acknowledged that meetings might have been held between non-governmental representatives from the two countries. In March 2007 President Assad was reported to have confirmed that in fact secret talks had taken place between 'non-official' channels.

In June 2007, amid reports that Olmert had established a ministerial committee with the task of examining Israel's military preparedness for a potential conflict with Syria, the Israeli premier was said to have declared that he was ready to engage in direct negotiations with the Syrian regime, without preconditions. The Israeli media commented that Olmert had relayed to Syria, through Turkish and German officials, the proposal that Israel withdraw from the Golan Heights in exchange for Syria's undertaking to 'gradually dissolve' its links with Iran and militant organizations in Lebanon and the Palestinian territories. Tensions between Israel and Syria worsened in September, after Israel carried out an air-strike on a military installation at al-Kibar, 'deep within' Syrian territory. In October President Assad stated that the Israeli strike had hit a military building that was under construction and denied media reports speculating that it might have been a concealed nuclear reactor. In April 2008 US intelligence officials reportedly presented evidence that the target of the Israeli air-strike was in fact a nuclear facility that was being constructed with assistance from the Democratic People's Republic of Korea (North Korea); the Syrian authorities again strongly rejected the claims. An investigation of the site was carried out by the IAEA in June; however, the remains of the original building had been razed and buried under the concrete foundations of a new construction. The IAEA investigators stated in November that traces of uranium had been discovered, although the source of the material remained uncertain. While the IAEA insisted that its findings warranted further investigation, the Syrian authorities refused to grant the agency additional access to al-Kibar, or to a number of other sites, stating that the source of the uranium was Israeli missiles used in the bombing of the installation. In a report issued in February 2009, the IAEA contended there was a 'low probability' that Israeli munitions were the source of the radioactive material, and described Syria's co-operation with their investigation as unsatisfactory. Two further IAEA reports published at the end of May and in late November 2010 again criticized the Syrian authorities for failing to co-operate with the Agency's investigations into the exact purpose of the al-Kibar facility and three other apparently related military sites.

Meanwhile, in May 2008 Turkey's Minister of Foreign Affairs, Ali Babacan, confirmed that indirect talks aimed at achieving a comprehensive peace agreement between Israel and Syria, through Turkish mediation, were to begin in Istanbul. Four rounds of talks were held between May and August. However, a fifth round of talks, scheduled for September, was postponed due to the political uncertainty in Israel following the resignation of Prime Minister Olmert (see the chapter on Israel). Following Israel's military offensive against Hamas targets in the Gaza Strip, launched in December 2008 (see the chapters on Israel and the Palestinian Autonomous Areas), President Assad formally suspended the talks with Israel. During the campaign for Israel's general election, which took place in February 2009, the Likud leader, Binyamin Netanyahu, declared his outright opposition to the surrender of the Golan Heights as part of any peace agreement with Syria. After a new Israeli coalition Government was sworn in, under Netanyahu's premiership, in April, his Minister of Foreign Affairs, Avigdor Lieberman (leader of the right-wing Israel Beytenu), ruled out any Israeli withdrawal from the Golan Heights.

It was reported in November 2009 that Israeli forces in the Mediterranean Sea had intercepted en route to Syria a cargo ship, the *Francop*, which Israel claimed was carrying a large consignment of Iranian-made weapons destined for Hezbollah militants in Lebanon. Syria's Minister of Foreign Affairs, Walid Mouallem, denied the allegations, stating that the vessel had been carrying commercial goods. In early February 2010 Lieberman issued a controversial statement, in which he demanded that Syria relinquish all territorial claims over the Golan Heights and asserted that any act of aggression by Syria towards Israel would result in the removal of President Assad from power. The outburst was prompted by an earlier comment by Assad that Israel was pushing the region towards war. Israel held a series of military exercises in that month that reportedly simulated a major assault on Syrian territory. In mid-April Israeli President Shimon Peres publicly accused Syria of delivering long-range Scud missiles and providing relevant training to Hezbollah militants; the allegations were denied by Syria, Hezbollah and the Lebanese Prime Minister, Saad el-Din Hariri. In early May Israeli defence officials also issued claims that Syria was transferring advanced missiles, capable of inflicting damage on cities across Israel, to militants in Lebanon. Although Assad expressed his willingness to resume Turkish-mediated peace talks with Israel, the Syrian leadership was strongly critical of Israel's military raid on a Turkish ship attempting to break the Israeli blockade of Gaza at the end of May, which resulted in the deaths of nine pro-Palestinian Turkish activists. The Syrian President warned on several occasions during 2010 that the prospects of war in the Middle East were increasing. Moreover, the likelihood of reaching an Israeli-Syrian peace settlement appeared more remote when, in late November, the Knesset approved legislation stating that any withdrawal from the Golan Heights would require the prior endorsement of Israeli voters in a national referendum.

Foreign Affairs
Relations with the USA
The Syrian Government condemned the suicide attacks carried out in New York and Washington, DC, on 11 September 2001. However, Syria was openly critical of the decision of the US Administration of George W. Bush—as part of its world-wide 'war on terror'—to launch a military campaign against targets in Afghanistan linked to the Taliban regime and to the militant Islamist organization held principally responsible for the attacks, the al-Qa'ida network of Osama bin Laden. In October the British Prime Minister, Tony Blair, undertook an official visit to Syria, to garner Arab support for the US-led campaign in Afghanistan, and asked the Syrian leadership to end its support for militant groups such as Hezbollah and the PFLP. However, President Bashar al-Assad condemned the West's bombing of Afghan civilians and stated that organizations engaged in fighting the Israeli occupation were 'legitimate'. The Syrian leadership refused US demands, in November 2002, that it close the Damascus office of Islamic Jihad, following a renewed campaign by the Palestinian organization against targets in Israel. In December President Assad became the first Syrian leader to visit the United Kingdom, where he expressed his opposition to a likely US-led military campaign to bring about 'regime change' in Iraq, and rejected Blair's demand to curb militant Palestinian groups operating in Syria.

As the US-led coalition forces launched their campaign to oust the regime of Saddam Hussain in Iraq in March 2003, the USA also increasingly hinted that Syria might be the next target for a US-imposed 'regime change'. Damascus referred to the campaign in Iraq as an 'illegal invasion'. Moreover, Syrians were angered in late March when a bus close to the border with Iraq was hit by a stray US missile, killing five Syrian civilians. Damascus strongly denied claims by the Bush Administration that it was providing military equipment to Iraq during the conflict. The USA alleged that Syria had assisted leading members of the Iraqi Baath Party to flee the country after the collapse of Saddam Hussain's regime and that Iraqi weapons of mass destruction might have been transported to cross the border into Syria. However, in April President Bush declared that Syria was co-operating with the US-led coalition, having recently sealed its border with Iraq. Nevertheless, US officials from the Department of the Treasury estimated that US $3,000m. of Iraqi money was being held by Syrian-controlled banks in Damascus and Lebanon, in contravention of a UN resolution calling on all Iraqi funds held abroad to be handed over to the US-controlled Iraqi Fund for Development.

In December 2003 US President Bush signed the Syria Accountability Act, which allowed the USA to impose a range of sanctions on Syria unless the country met a series of conditions (including ending its support for terrorist groups). The sanctions were eventually put in place on 11 May 2004; they included a ban on all US exports to Syria other than food or medicine, and a halt to flights between the two countries. Syria rejected the sanctions, asserting that they would not affect the country or its economy, and in October Syria signed a bilateral agreement with the EU for greater economic co-operation, with Syria agreeing to renounce proliferation of nuclear weapons. In December it was reported that evidence had been found that Syria was permitting the training on its territory of militants to be used as insurgent fighters in Iraq, as well as allowing insurgents across the border between the two countries; Syria denied the claims.

In March 2007 Syria called for a 'serious dialogue' with the USA on a wide range of concerns pertaining to the Middle East. In the following month Nancy Pelosi, Speaker of the US House of Representatives (the third highest ranking elected official in the USA after the President and Vice-President), visited Damascus as part of a wider tour of the region, thus becoming the most senior US official to visit Syria since 2003. Pelosi's unauthorized visit drew strong criticism from President Bush, who, angered by the challenge to his Administration's policy of isolation towards the Syrian Government, accused her of usurping executive powers and of sending 'mixed signals' to a 'state sponsor of terrorism'. Pelosi, of the Democratic Party, dismissed such censure, pointing out that three Republican congressmen had also visited Syria very recently without attracting any disapproval from the Bush Administration. The Syrian ambassador to the USA, Imad Moustapha, described Pelosi's overture as a 'positive step', but one that offered little likelihood of a change in US policy. However, in May 2007 US Secretary of State Condoleezza Rice held talks with Syrian Minister of Foreign Affairs Mouallem on the sidelines of a major summit meeting held in Egypt, intended to address the situation in Iraq. The sideline negotiations represented the first official high-level talks between the two countries since the murder of Rafiq Hariri in Lebanon (see Domestic Political Affairs). During the talks Rice urged the Syrian leadership to take further action to prevent foreign fighters from crossing into Iraq from Syria in order to participate in the anti-US insurgency.

It was hoped that Syrian–US tensions would be eased when, in November 2007, Syria agreed to send a low-level delegation to the international peace meeting held under US auspices in Annapolis, Maryland, USA, with the aim of relaunching the Middle East peace process. However, such optimism proved to be shortlived. In February 2008 President Bush approved an expanded range of sanctions against the Syrian regime, which he accused of destabilizing both Iraq and Lebanon. The new sanctions included a freeze on the assets of prominent Syrian officials or businessmen deemed to have benefited from corrupt practices. In March the US Administration also announced that maritime vessels docking in US ports that had previously visited Syrian ports would henceforth be placed on a Port Security Advisory List, amid US concerns regarding Syrian links with international terrorist networks. The Bush Administration extended sanctions further against Syria in May, imposing a further embargo on certain exports to the country. This tighter sanctions regime was imposed following allegations by US intelligence agencies that there existed a covert nuclear co-operation between Syria and North Korea (see The Israeli-Syrian track of the Middle East peace process).

Notwithstanding President Bush's reassertion, in a speech to the UN in September 2008, that Syria was a state sponsor of terrorism, Secretary of State Rice held further talks on regional affairs with Walid Mouallem in New York. However, in an incident that threatened to curtail the potential progress in US-Syrian relations, four US military helicopters, flying from Iraq, carried out a covert raid some 10 km inside Syrian territory in late October, targeting a building under construction in the Abu Kamal district. Official Syrian sources claimed that eight civilians, among them children, had been killed. This account was disputed by an unnamed US intelligence source, which asserted that the operation had successfully targeted a prominent associate of al-Qa'ida, Abu Ghadiya, who was allegedly responsible for smuggling foreign militants and weapons across the Syrian border into Iraq, and that all those killed were militants. Mouallem, who was in the United Kingdom at the time of the raid for talks on improving Syria's ties with Europe, described the operation as a 'criminal and terrorist act'. At the end of October thousands of protesters took part in a demonstration close to the US embassy in Damascus, which was protected by a cordon of Syrian riot police.

Following the inauguration of Barack Obama as the new US President in January 2009, there was renewed optimism concerning US-Syrian relations. In the opening weeks of his presidency Obama announced his intention to pursue a pragmatic and reconciliatory foreign policy approach in the Middle East. During late January and February three separate US congressional delegations visited Damascus for talks with President Assad on improving bilateral relations. Imad Moustapha, Syria's ambassador to the USA, held talks in Washington, DC, with Jeffrey Feltman, Acting Assistant Secretary of the Bureau of Near Eastern Affairs at the US Department of State, in late February; Moustapha described the meeting as constructive. The process of dialogue continued to grow in significance when Feltman, along with Daniel Shapiro, a senior White House official who had been involved in drafting the Syria Accountability Act in 2003, held talks in Damascus with Minister of Foreign Affairs Mouallem. While both sides emphasized the positive aspects of the dialogue, neither denied that there remained significant obstacles to a full normalization of relations—notably Syria's support for Hamas and Hezbollah, and its relationship with Iran, and the USA's continued policy of diplomatic and economic sanctions against Syria, and support for Israel.

Although in May 2009 the US Administration renewed its programme of sanctions against Syria, in June diplomatic relations advanced to a higher level, following the visit to Damascus of George Mitchell, the US special envoy to the Middle East, for discussions with President Assad on US efforts to relaunch the stalled Middle East peace process. Mitchell asserted that Syria could play a crucial role in efforts to secure a comprehensive peace settlement. In February 2010 Robert Ford, a former envoy in Algeria, was formally nominated as US ambassador to Syria, the post having been vacant since the withdrawal of the former envoy in 2005, in protest at Syria's alleged involvement in the assassination of Rafiq Hariri. Immediately following the nomination, US Under Secretary of State for Political Affairs William Burns visited Damascus for talks with Assad on strengthening bilateral relations. Despite reports that the new ambassadorial appointment might be postponed owing to Syria's alleged transfer of missiles to Hezbollah in Lebanon, Ford's appointment was approved by the US Senate Foreign Relations Committee in April 2010. However, the Senate subsequently failed to ratify it (owing to the concerns of many US senators regarding the return of an ambassador to Syria), leading President Obama to appoint Ford directly during a congressional recess at the end of December.

The US sanctions programme was extended for a further year on 3 May 2010, since the Obama Administration assessed that Syria remained an 'extraordinary threat' to US national security and foreign policy with its 'continuing support for terrorist organisations and pursuit of weapons of mass destruction and missile programmes'. The US President did acknowledge, however, that the Syrian Government had achieved some success in efforts to prevent foreign insurgents from crossing its border into Iraq. Furthermore, the USA removed its objections to Syria acceding to the World Trade Organization (WTO), and the country was granted observer status at the WTO on 4 May as a preliminary step to being granted full membership. However, prospects of an improvement in relations receded following the Syrian authorities' response to anti-Government protests in the country from March 2011 (see Recent Developments): in April President Obama denounced the violent repression of demonstrators by Syrian security forces and urged Assaf to 'change course now and heed the calls of his own people'. On 18 May Obama signed an Executive Order implementing targeted sanctions against President Assad and six prominent Syrian officials, including al-Shara', Prime Minister Safar, and the Ministers of the Interior and Defence.

Regional relations

In August 1999 a diplomatic crisis developed between Syria and the Palestinian authorities after the Syrian Deputy Prime Minister and Minister of Defence, Maj.-Gen. Mustafa Tlass, publicly accused Yasser Arafat of having 'sold Jerusalem and the Arab nation' in peace agreements concluded with Israel since 1993, and made other personal insults against the Palestinian leader. The PA demanded that Tlass resign (and Fatah reportedly issued a death warrant against Tlass), while President Assad was apparently angered by the minister's remarks. Arafat attended the funeral of President Hafiz al-Assad, and in mid-2000 the PA renewed its demand that Syria free all remaining Palestinian prisoners from its gaols; seven Palestinians were released into Lebanese custody in December. Amid Syrian efforts to support the Palestinians in their escalating conflict with the Israelis, and following talks between Bashar al-Assad and Arafat during the summit meeting of Arab League states in Jordan in March 2001, the two leaders declared that they had achieved a reconciliation. In December 2004 PLO leader Mahmud Abbas made the first official Palestinian visit to Damascus since 1996. Abbas, the Palestinian Prime Minister, Ahmad Quray, the Minister of Foreign Affairs, Dr Nasser al-Kidwa, and President Assad discussed the current situation in the Palestinian territories and preparations for the presidential election scheduled to be held there in January 2005. Assad emphasized Syria's support for the Palestinian people and their struggle for national unity, while Abbas stressed the importance of co-operation between Syria and the PA. By June 2010 there were 477,700 Palestinian refugees registered in Syria.

In October 1998 the Jordanian Government demanded 'immediate answers' from Syria concerning a list of 239 Jordanians allegedly missing in Syria, and a further 190 who it claimed were being held in Syrian prisons. The Syrian authorities agreed to investigate the matter, but stated that most of those listed were in fact members of Palestinian organizations linked with Jordan and had violated Syrian laws. In February 1999 President Assad unexpectedly attended the funeral of King Hussein of Jordan, and reportedly held a private meeting with the new monarch. Syria had welcomed the succession of King Abdullah, and the new Jordanian King made his first official visit to Syria in April. The two leaders urged a resumption of the peace process and increased bilateral co-operation; Syria agreed to supply Jordan with water during 1999, as the latter was undergoing a drought, and both sides agreed to hold future discussions regarding the Jordanian prisoners in Syria. King Abdullah made an unscheduled visit to Syria in July, at a time when Jordan was concerned that any separate peace settlement between Syria and Israel might undermine the Palestinian position in future negotiations. The joint Syrian-Jordanian Higher Committee met in August in Amman under the chairmanship of both countries' premiers—the first time in almost a decade that a senior Syrian delegation had visited Jordan's capital. Meanwhile, the Syrian Government stated that many of the Jordanian prisoners held in Syria had been released under a general amnesty granted in July 2000 (see Domestic Political Affairs) and that the 'very few' who remained in Syrian gaols were non-political detainees. Following the death of President Assad in June of that year, King Abdullah visited Damascus in July for talks with Syria's new President, Bashar al-Assad; Syria again agreed to supply Jordan with water during that summer. It was reported in November that Syria had upgraded its diplomatic representation in Jordan to ambassadorial level. In February 2004 Syria and Jordan launched the Wahdah Dam project on Jordan's River Yarmuk. The project, which was completed in September 2006, aimed to provide Jordan with water and Syria with electricity.

Relations between Syria and Iraq had been strained since the early 1970s due to a rivalry between the respective factions of the Baath Party in Damascus and Baghdad. Notably, Syria supported Iran in its war with Iraq in 1980–88. Although an extraordinary summit meeting of the Arab League in November 1987 produced a unanimous statement expressing solidarity with Iraq and condemning Iran for prolonging the war and for its occupation of Arab territory, Syria announced subsequently that a reconciliation with Iraq had not taken place, and that Syrian relations with Iran remained fundamentally unchanged. Syria also used its veto to prevent the adoption of an Iraqi proposal to readmit Egypt to the Arab League, but it could not prevent the inclusion in the final communiqué of a clause permitting individual member nations to re-establish diplomatic relations with Egypt. However, Egypt's recognition of the newly proclaimed Palestinian state in November 1988 gave fresh impetus to attempts to achieve a reconciliation between Egypt and Syria. These culminated in the restoration of bilateral relations in December 1989, and in the visit of Egypt's President Hosni Mubarak to Damascus.

Syria appeared keen to take advantage of the diplomatic opportunities arising from Iraq's invasion of Kuwait in August 1990, and in particular to improve its relations with the USA. Syria endorsed Egypt's efforts to co-ordinate an Arab response to the invasion, and agreed to send troops to Saudi Arabia as part of a pan-Arab deterrent force, supporting the US-led effort to deter an Iraqi invasion of Saudi Arabia; Syria also committed itself to the demand for an unconditional Iraqi withdrawal from Kuwait. Indications that Syria's participation in the multinational force was transforming its relations with the West were confirmed in November when diplomatic ties were restored with the United Kingdom. Iraq's overwhelming military defeat by the US-led multinational force in February 1991 strengthened Syria's position with regard to virtually all its major regional concerns. In March the Ministers of Foreign Affairs of the members of the Co-operation Council for the Arab States of the Gulf (Gulf Co-operation Council, see p. 243) met their Egyptian and Syrian counterparts in Damascus to discuss regional security. The formation of an Arab peace-keeping force, comprising mainly Egyptian and Syrian troops, was subsequently announced, although in May Egypt declared its intention to withdraw its forces from the Gulf region within three months. Syria's decision to ally itself, in opposition to Iraq, with the Western powers and the 'moderate' Arab states led the USA to realize that it could no longer seek to exclude Syria from any role in the resolution of the Arab–Israeli conflict. A shift in Syria's relations with the USSR, a major source of military assistance but whose programmes of political liberalization President Assad had recently criticized, provided another reason for its realignment with the West.

After Iraq's defeat by the multinational force in February 1991, Syria became a centre for elements of the Iraqi opposition. However, it remained committed to the territorial integrity of Iraq, fearing that disintegration might encourage minorities within Syria (particularly the Kurds) to pursue their own autonomy. Three crossing points on the Syria–Iraq border were reopened in June 1997 to facilitate bilateral trade (Syria closed its border with Iraq in 1980), and in September 1998 Iraq, Iran and Syria agreed to establish a joint forum for foreign policy co-ordination (particularly with regard to the USA). In the same month Syria and Iraq reopened commercial centres in one another's capitals, and in April 1999 a series of mutual agreements were signed, as part of the process of normalizing relations. Throughout 1998–2002 the Syrian Government criticized US and British air-strikes against Iraqi air defence targets, as well as the maintenance of UN sanctions against Iraq.

In August 2000 a rail link between Aleppo and the Iraqi capital was reopened after an interval of some 20 years, and in December the Syrian authorities reportedly removed all restrictions on Iraqi citizens travelling to Syria. In November, furthermore, Iraq was reported to have begun transporting crude petroleum to Syria via a pipeline not used since the early 1980s. When the US Secretary of State, Colin Powell, visited Damascus in February 2001, his discussions with the Syrian President apparently centred on Syria's alleged violation of UN sanctions regarding the supply of petroleum from Iraq. In August the Syrian Prime Minister, leading a ministerial and commercial delegation, became the most senior Syrian official to visit Iraq for two decades. Syria was particularly concerned (as was Turkey) by the potential ascendance of Iraqi Kurdish groups should the incumbent regime in Baghdad be overthrown, although, visiting these countries in March 2002, the Patriotic Union of Kurdistan leader, Jalal Talabani, gave assurances that Iraq's Kurdish groups had no intention of establishing their own state. There were reports in mid-2002 that Syria (having been elected as a non-permanent member of the UN Security Council for 2002–03) was involved in mediation efforts between Iraq and Kuwait.

Despite its unexpected support for UN Security Council Resolution 1441, approved in November, which imposed strict terms according to which Iraq must disarm or else face probable military action, Syria expressed its firm opposition to the US-led military campaign against the Iraqi regime, which began in March 2003 (see the chapter on Iraq).

In February 2006 Syria and Iraq announced that they were to restore full diplomatic relations and exchange ambassadors as soon as a new government was installed in Iraq. Relations were formally restored in November, ending a hiatus of more than 20 years, and the two sides also agreed to co-operate on security issues. It was hoped that the renewal of diplomatic ties would facilitate the policing of the shared border, across which a large number of militants were still reported to be entering Iraq. In February 2007 a spokesman for the Iraqi Government claimed that 50% of those who had committed suicide bomb attacks in Iraq had entered the country from Syria, although this was staunchly denied by the Syrian Government. The office of the UN High Commissioner for Refugees estimated the number of displaced Iraqis in Syria at some 1m. people in January 2011. New regulations requiring Iraqi citizens to obtain a visa before entering Syria were introduced in October 2007; access to Syria from Iraq had been unrestricted since 2000. Following a visit to Baghdad by Minister of Foreign Affairs Mouallem in March 2009, Prime Minister al-Otari led a ministerial delegation on a two-day visit to Iraq in April, during which talks were held on border security, economic co-operation and regional affairs.

Iraqi Prime Minister Nuri al-Maliki paid an official visit to Damascus on 18 August 2009, during which he held talks with President Assad and senior Syrian officials on security issues, including US and Iraqi allegations that Syria was failing to take adequate measures to stem the flow of foreign militants across its border into Iraq. However, a series of bomb attacks targeting government buildings in Baghdad on 19 August led to a diplomatic crisis between the two countries. The Iraqi authorities claimed to have evidence that the attacks had been directed and financed by two former Iraqi Baath Party officials living in exile in Syria, and responded by withdrawing their ambassador from Syria and demanding the extradition of the alleged conspirators. The Syrian authorities rejected Iraq's allegations and recalled their own ambassador from Baghdad. None the less, in September the Iraqi and Syrian ministers responsible for foreign affairs entered into talks, mediated by Turkey, aimed at resolving the dispute. In March 2010 Iraqi Vice-President Tariq al-Hashimi travelled to Syria to examine arrangements for the participation of displaced Iraqis in the forthcoming national elections in Iraq. During his visit al-Hashimi also held talks on bilateral relations with Assad and Mouallem, which were described as 'successful and constructive'. As was the case with Iraq's other neighbours, Syria played a role in the protracted negotiations towards forming a new Iraqi coalition government following the elections to the Council of Representatives; a 'partial' Government under Prime Minister al-Maliki was finally approved in late December. President Assad had stated during a visit by al-Maliki to Damascus in mid-October that a new Iraqi administration, provided that it represented national unity, would lead to improved relations between their countries. It was agreed in that month to return ambassadors to Baghdad and Damascus, marking an end to the diplomatic crisis that had begun in August 2009.

Allegations about Syria's involvement in the assassination of Rafiq Hariri, in February 2005, and its role in Lebanon generally, led to increasing international and regional isolation, which, in turn, increased the strategic importance of Syria's ties with Iran. In August President Assad visited the recently elected Iranian President, Mahmoud Ahmadinejad, in Tehran, and the two leaders announced their solidarity in the face of common foreign threats. Several presidential summits were subsequently held in both Tehran and Damascus between early 2006 and mid-2009. Despite the widely held opinion that Syria's growing rapprochement with the USA, from early 2009, would necessitate a weakening of relations with Iran, President Assad continued to promote close ties with the Iranian Government during 2010. In late February, following the nomination of a new US ambassador to Syria, Ahmadinejad travelled to Damascus for consultations on regional affairs with Assad. The summit was seen as a symbolic response to a statement by US Secretary of State Hillary Clinton a few days earlier that the USA was urging Syria to distance itself from Iran and cancel its support for militant groups in Lebanon, the Palestinian Autonomous Areas and Iraq. In a further gesture of defiance, President Assad also hosted an official banquet attended by Ahmadinejad and the Secretary-General of Hezbollah, Sheikh Hasan Nasrallah. In early January 2011 Iran's acting Minister of Foreign Affairs, Ali Akbar Salehi, welcomed the Speaker of the People's Assembly, Mahmoud al-Abrash, to Tehran, reiterating the desire of the Iranian Government to strengthen its bilateral relationship with Syria in all areas.

A summit meeting of Arab League member states, held in Damascus in March 2008, was boycotted by several leading officials; notable absentees were Egypt's President Mubarak and Saudi Arabia's King Abdullah, both of whom blamed Syria and Iran for contributing to the crisis in Lebanon through their support for the Hezbollah-led opposition. When Saudi Arabia had transferred its ambassador in Damascus to Qatar in February, it declined to appoint a new ambassador to Syria. Relations with Saudi Arabia remained strained throughout 2008, and the two countries' conflicting interests in the region were highlighted again by their divergent responses to Israel's military offensive in Gaza, launched in December (see The Israeli-Syrian track of the Middle East peace process). President Assad attended an emergency Arab League meeting in Doha in January 2009, convened by Qatar with the stated aim of formulating a unified Arab response to the crisis in Gaza. However, the Doha summit was boycotted by several nations, notably Egypt and Saudi Arabia, and did not achieve the quorum of 15 participating states required to grant the meeting official status. Shortly afterwards, however, during the Arab Economic, Social and Development Summit in Kuwait, Assad attended a private meeting hosted by the Saudi King and also attended by the leaders of Qatar, Egypt and Kuwait, which was heralded as achieving significant progress towards greater Arab unity. In early March the Saudi Minister of Foreign Affairs, Prince Sa'ud al-Faisal, met with President Assad in Damascus for talks on Arab reconciliation and other regional issues. Al-Faisal extended an invitation to Assad to visit Saudi Arabia, and both sides described the talks as positive and constructive. On 11 March King Abdullah hosted a one-day summit on regional affairs attended by President Assad (in his first visit to Saudi Arabia for four years), President Mubarak of Egypt and the Kuwaiti Amir, Sheikh al-Sabah. Foremost among the objectives of the summit were the promotion of Arab unity and support for the Egyptian-brokered reconciliation talks between the rival Palestinian factions, Fatah and Hamas.

The appointment, in July 2009, of a new Saudi ambassador to Syria confirmed the positive trend in bilateral relations. In September, following his attendance at the inauguration of a new university in Jeddah, Saudi Arabia, President Assad held discussions on bilateral relations and regional affairs with King Abdullah. In October the Saudi monarch, accompanied by a senior-level ministerial delegation, completed his first official visit to Syria since acceding to the throne in 2005; discussions included plans to promote Saudi investment in Syrian infrastructure projects. At the summit's conclusion King Abdullah and President Assad issued a statement confirming their joint support for: the establishment of a government of national unity in Lebanon; joint Arab measures in support of the Palestinian cause; and the safeguarding of stability and national unity in Yemen. President Assad made a reciprocal visit to Riyadh, the Saudi capital, in mid-January 2010, during which talks continued on a range of key regional issues. The Saudi and Syrian leaders held a tripartite summit meeting with the Lebanese President, Michel Suleiman, in Beirut at the end of July, in an effort to persuade Lebanon's competing Sunni and Shi'ite political factions from once again resorting to violence. The meeting was convened amid growing tensions in Lebanon over reports that an indictment by the STL (the UN-sponsored tribunal investigating the murder of former premier Rafiq Hariri—see Domestic Political Affairs) was imminent, and that members of the (Shi'ite) Hezbollah were likely to be named. However, in mid-January 2011, with the first indictments expected to be issued later that month, the Lebanese 'national unity' Government collapsed, following the resignations of 11 cabinet ministers led by Hezbollah and its allies. The previous day the Saudi and Syrian Governments were reported to have failed to achieve a compromise agreement for Lebanon, with some sources claiming that the USA had intervened to prevent a political deal from enabling Hezbollah to avoid censure by the STL.

Relations between Syria and Turkey became increasingly strained in the 1990s, owing to disagreements over the sharing of water from the Euphrates river. No permanent agreement on this resource has been concluded, and both Syria and Iraq are concerned that new dams in Turkey will reduce their share of water from the Euphrates. Syria's relations with Turkey deteriorated sharply in April 1996 after it was revealed that Turkey and Israel had concluded a military co-operation agreement earlier in the year. In October 1998 Turkey threatened to invade Syria if its demands for an end to alleged Syrian support for the separatist Kurdistan Workers' Party (Partiya Karkeren Kurdistan—PKK) were not met. The Turkish authorities also demanded the extradition of the PKK leader, Abdullah Öcalan (who, they claimed, was directing PKK operations from Damascus), and insisted that Syria renounce its historic claim on the Turkish province of Hatay. Turkey's aggressive stance was viewed by Syria as evidence of a Turkish-Israeli military and political alliance, and as a result both Syria and Turkey ordered troops to be deployed along their joint border. Diplomatic efforts to defuse the crisis by Egypt, Iran and the UN, and Syrian assurances that Öcalan was not residing in Syria, allowed a degree of normalization in bilateral relations. In late October, following two days of negotiations in southern Turkey, representatives of the two countries signed an agreement whereby the PKK was to be banned from entering Syrian territory, while the organization's active bases in Syria and Lebanon's Beqa'a valley were to be closed.

Despite persistent Syrian concerns regarding the close nature of Turkish-Israeli relations, it was reported in March 2000 that Syrian and Turkish officials were holding discussions in Damascus on a memorandum of principles, intended to establish a new framework for future bilateral relations. In September Syria and Turkey signed a co-operation agreement relating to countering terrorism and organized crime, and in June 2002 they signed two military co-operation accords. Moreover, reports in February that the Turkish army was to begin the clearance of land-mines along its border with Syria were seen as evidence of a steady improvement in bilateral relations. In December 2003 relations were strengthened by Syria's decision to hand over 22 suspects sought by the Turkish authorities in connection with four suicide bomb attacks in Istanbul in November, in which at least 60 people were killed. In January 2004 President Assad made the first ever visit by a Syrian head of state to Turkey. Turkey's membership of the North Atlantic Treaty Organization, and hence its relatively close relationship with the USA, as well as shared concerns about a possible 'ripple-effect' of increased Kurdish autonomy in northern Iraq following the removal of the regime of Saddam Hussain in early 2003, were believed to be among the principal reasons for Syria's initiative to improve its relations with Turkey. In January 2007 an agreement between the Syrian and Turkish Governments to create a bilateral free trade zone took effect. A Joint Technical Committee on water resources, involving Syria, Turkey and Iraq, was reconvened in May, after some 15 years of inactivity, and by early 2010 various joint initatives aimed at resolving disagreements over water resources were under discussion; these included a proposed joint Turkish-Syrian dam on the Orontes river at the border between Syria and Turkey. The so-called 'friendship dam' construction project commenced in February 2011. Meanwhile, political and economic relations with Turkey continued to progress in 2008, with Turkey adopting the role of mediator for indirect Syrian-Israeli peace talks (see The Israeli-Syrian track of the Middle East peace process) and several new agreements on trade and investment co-operation being signed in December.

A bilateral summit convened in Istanbul in September 2009 reflected the growing strength of Syrian-Turkish relations. President Assad and Turkish Prime Minister Recep Tayyip Erdoğan discussed the development of a joint response to the stalled Middle East peace process and other regional issues. An accord establishing a High-Level Strategic Co-operation Council and an agreement on the removal of reciprocal visa requirements were also signed by the respective Ministers of Foreign Affairs. Following the inaugural meeting of the Strategic Co-operation Council in Damascus in December, attended by the respective premiers and the ministers responsible for portfolios including foreign affairs, the interior, justice and agriculture, more than 50 agreements were signed on co-operation in various areas, including security, economy and trade, water, energy, health, education, culture, environment and transport. Assad completed another official visit to Turkey in May 2010, during which he participated in a tripartite summit with the Turkish and Qatari leaders, and pledged his support for Turkey's efforts to mediate in the international dispute concerning Iran's nuclear programme (see the chapter on Iran). A second meeting of the Strategic Co-operation Council was held in the Turkish capital,

Ankara, in December, at which a further 11 co-operation accords were signed. The Syrian and Turkish delegations also pledged to increase the volume of bilateral trade and tourism, and discussed the possibility of establishing a joint oil exploration company, as well as a Syrian-Turkish bank. Having initially taken a cautious stance over Syria's response to the anti-Government protests which had erupted in March 2011, in a television interview in May Erdoğan urged Assad to heed the protesters' 'indispensable requests for peace and democracy', although he did not call for Assad himself to stand down.

Other external relations

In January 2005 President Assad visited Russia for official talks with President Vladimir Putin. Earlier in the month reports that Russia was to sell missiles to Syria that could be used against targets in Israel provoked anger in that country. In February Russia confirmed its intention to sell missiles to Syria, asserting that the weapons would only be used for defensive purposes. Assad again visited Russia in August 2008, where discussions were held with President Dmitrii Medvedev on defence co-operation. Work subsequently commenced on the development of an extensive Russian naval facility at the Syrian port of Tartous, which would be protected by Russian cruise missiles. A reciprocal visit by Medvedev to Syria in early May 2010—the first by a Russian head of state since 1917—was seen as demonstrating the growing importance of Russia in the Middle East region, particularly as the US Administration, having just renewed sanctions against the Syrian regime (see above) was still widely perceived among Arab states as being pro-Israeli. The talks reportedly focused on how to achieve a comprehensive regional peace settlement, and on increased co-operation between Syria and Russia in the fields of defence and energy, including a possible collaboration on the construction of a Syrian nuclear power plant. A formal agreement finalizing Syria's purchase of Russian fighter planes, anti-tank missiles and air defence systems was signed a few days after Medvedev's visit.

Syria's relations with France became increasingly strained following the killing of Rafiq Hariri in February 2005. French President Jacques Chirac, a friend and supporter of Hariri, accused Syria of involvement in the assassination, and Chirac's successor, Nicolas Sarkozy, announced in December 2007 that his Government would cease all diplomatic contacts with Syria until the regime demonstrated that it was committed to enabling the Lebanese National Assembly to elect a successor to President Lahoud (see the chapter on Lebanon). However, after the signing of the Doha Agreement in May 2008 (see Domestic Political Affairs) there was a rapid rapprochement of Syria and France. In July President Assad was invited to Paris by Sarkozy to attend a summit on the French President's new Union for the Mediterranean initiative. In August Syria appointed a new ambassador to France—the post having been vacant since the retirement of the previous envoy some 18 months previously. In the same week the French Minister of Foreign Affairs, Bernard Kouchner, launched what he termed a 'new era of relations' when he held talks with his Syrian counterpart and Assad in Damascus. Sarkozy began a two-day official visit to Syria in September, the first visit by a French President since 2002. During the visit a quadripartite summit was held by the leaders of France, Syria, Turkey and Qatar; foremost on the agenda were the ongoing Turkish-mediated indirect talks between Syria and Israel. In early August 2010 President Sarkozy announced that Jean-Claude Cousseran, formerly France's ambassador in both Syria and Egypt, was to act as a mediator between Syria and Israel in order to facilitate the resumption of discussions regarding the Israeli-Syrian track of the Middle East peace process.

The EU had resumed a formal dialogue with Syria in March 2007, when Javier Solana, the Secretary-General of the Council of the EU and High Representative for the Common Foreign and Security Policy, met with Walid Mouallem and President Assad in Damascus. In October 2008 Solana made a further visit to the Syrian capital, signalling the resumption of negotiations on an EU association agreement, which had stalled after the assassination of Rafiq Hariri in 2005. Abdullah al-Dardari, the Deputy Prime Minister, responsible for Economic Affairs, held two days of negotiations in Brussels, Belgium, with Benita Ferrero-Waldner, the EU Commissioner responsible for External Relations and European Neighbourhood Policy, in November. These negotiations led to the signing, in December, of a draft co-operation agreement, with ratification of an association agreement anticipated by mid-2009. However, following a decision by the Government of the Netherlands to attach a clause allowing for a suspension of the association agreement should Syria commit human rights violations, ratification was postponed until late October. In mid-October the Syrian Government indicated that it was not yet ready to conclude the agreement and postponed indefinitely a decision on ratification. In addition to the human rights issue, Syria was believed to have concerns about exposing the beleaguered agricultural sector, weakened by several years of severe drought, to increased international competition. Also in October Mouallem made an official visit to the United Kingdom, and in November the British Secretary of State for Foreign and Commonwealth Affairs, David Miliband, visited Damascus for talks with President Assad: their discussions encompassed bilateral relations, intelligence co-operation and regional affairs. The visit was the first by a senior member of the British Government since 2001. In early September 2010 the European Parliament expressed concern regarding the apparent deterioration in Syria's human rights situation, citing in particular the recent imprisonment of lawyers who had openly criticized the authorities (see Domestic Political Affairs), and urged the Syrian leadership to address such issues as part of the ongoing dialogue regarding the country's association agreement with the EU.

CONSTITUTION AND GOVERNMENT

A new and permanent Constitution was endorsed in a national referendum held on 12 March 1973. Under the 1973 Constitution (as subsequently amended), legislative power is vested in the unicameral People's Assembly, with 250 members elected by universal adult suffrage to serve a four-year term. Executive power is vested in the President, elected by direct popular vote for a seven-year term. (Following the death of President Hafiz al-Assad on 10 June 2000, the Constitution was amended to allow his son, Lt-Gen. Bashar al-Assad, to accede to the presidency.) He governs with the assistance of an appointed Council of Ministers, led by the Prime Minister. Syria has 14 administrative districts (*mohafazat*).

REGIONAL AND INTERNATIONAL CO-OPERATION

Syria is a member of the League of Arab States (Arab League, see p. 361) and the Organization of Arab Petroleum Exporting Countries (OAPEC, see p. 397). Syria joined the UN on its establishment in October 1945. In May 2010 the World Trade Organization (WTO, see p. 430) agreed to commence accession negotiations with Syria. The country also participates in the Organization of the Islamic Conference (OIC, see p. 400).

ECONOMIC AFFAIRS

In 2009, according to estimates by the World Bank, Syria's gross national income (GNI), measured at average 2007–09 prices, was US $50,869m., equivalent to $2,410 per head (or $4,620 per head on an international purchasing-power parity basis). During 2000–09, it was estimated, the population increased at an average annual rate of 2.8%, while gross domestic product (GDP) per head increased, in real terms, by an average of 1.6% per year. Overall GDP increased, in real terms, at an average annual rate of 4.4% in 2000–09; growth was 6.0% in 2009, according to provisional official figures.

Agriculture (including forestry and fishing) contributed an estimated 22.3% of GDP in 2009, and engaged 15.2% of the employed labour force (excluding foreign workers) in that year. The principal cash crops are cotton (which accounted for about 2.4% of export earnings in 2003), and fruit and vegetables. According to official estimates, agricultural GDP increased at an average annual rate of 1.9% in 2000–09; the sector's GDP declined by an estimated 7.1% in 2008, but increased by 12.8% in 2009.

Industry (comprising mining, manufacturing, construction and utilities) provided an estimated 27.9% of GDP in 2009, and engaged 32.5% of the employed labour force (excluding foreign workers) in the same year. The GDP of the industrial sector increased at an average annual rate of 2.4% during 2000–09, according to official preliminary figures; industrial GDP increased by 3.7% in 2009.

Mining contributed an estimated 19.7% of GDP in 2003, and employed 0.3% of the working population (excluding foreign workers) in 1999. Crude petroleum is the major mineral export, accounting for 58.5% of total export earnings in 2003, and phosphates are also exported. Syria also has reserves of natural gas and iron ore. At the end of 2008 Syria had proven oil reserves of 2,500m. barrels, and estimated average oil production was 398,000 barrels per day (b/d), having declined from 596,000 b/d in 1995. However, the Government hoped to reverse this trend with the award of contracts (anticipated in 2011) to international companies seeking to explore, develop and produce oil and gas in eight onshore blocks in the north and east of the country. Syria was estimated to have 280,000m. cu m of proven natural gas reserves at the end of 2008, and in that year production of natural gas reached an estimated daily average of 5,500m. cu m. In 2001 Syria and Lebanon signed an agreement under which Syria was to supply gas to northern Lebanon. However, although the pipeline intended to supply the natural gas was completed in 2005, the two countries did not implement the agreement owing to political differences.

Manufacturing contributed an estimated 7.3% of GDP in 2004, and employed 12.7% of the working population in 1999. Along with mining, the sector contributed an estimated 24.8% of GDP in 2009. The principal branches of manufacturing, measured by gross value of output, are: food products, beverages and tobacco; chemicals, petroleum, coal, rubber and plastic products; textiles, clothing, leather products and footwear; metal products, machinery, transport equipment and appliances; and non-metallic mineral products. According to the World Bank, the GDP of the manufacturing sector increased by an average of 13.4% per year during 2000–09; manufacturing GDP increased by 5.0% in 2009.

Building and construction contributed an estimated 3.1% of GDP in 2009, and employed 16.2% of the working population in that year. According to official estimates, the GDP of the sector increased by an average of 6.6% per year during 2000–09; construction GDP declined by 8.1% in 2008, before increasing by 5.3% in 2009.

Energy is derived principally from petroleum (providing 59.7% of total electricity production in 2007), and also natural gas (31.2%) and hydroelectric power (9.1%). Imports of mineral fuels and lubricants comprised 12.8% of the value of total imports in 2009.

Services accounted for an estimated 49.8% of GDP in 2009, and engaged 52.3% of the employed labour force (excluding foreign workers) in that year. According to official estimates, the GDP of the services sector increased at an average rate of 8.4% per year in 2000–09; growth of the sector was 5.0% in 2009.

In 2008 Syria recorded a visible trade deficit of US $773m., and there was a surplus of $66m. on the current account of the balance of payments. In 2009 the principal source of imports (8.5%) was the People's Republic of China; other important suppliers were Turkey, Russia and Egypt. Germany was the primary market for exports in that year (9.1%); other major purchasers were France, Italy and Saudi Arabia. The principal exports in 2009 were mineral fuels and lubricants, food and live animals basic manufactures, and chemicals and related products while the principal imports were basic manufactures, food and live animals, machinery and transport equipment, mineral fuels and lubricants, and chemicals.

According to preliminary figures from the IMF, a budget deficit of £S70,100m. was recorded in 2008 and an increased deficit of £S133,400m. was projected for 2009. Syria's general government gross debt was £S667,143m. in 2009, equivalent to 27.3% of GDP. At the end of 2006 Syria's total external debt was US $6,508m., of which $5,640m. was long-term public debt. The cost of debt-servicing in that year was equivalent to 1.9% of the total value of exports of goods and services. Annual inflation averaged 5.6% in 2000–10. Consumer prices increased by 4.4% in 2010, compared with an increase of 2.8% in 2009. According to official figures, 8.1% of the labour force were unemployed in 2009.

During 2010, a decade since President Bashar al-Assad assumed office, the Syrian regime continued its programme of gradual economic liberalization. The reduction of the economy's dependence on revenue from petroleum was a priority since Syria had become a net importer of petroleum, and oil industry sources estimated in 2010 that its reserves would be exhausted by 2030. The authorities' Development Plan for 2011–15 focused on improving living standards, creating job opportunities, encouraging investment and stimulating GDP growth. Other planned reforms included the introduction, with IMF assistance, of a value-added tax in 2011 (deferred from 2008), and the phasing out of petroleum price subsidies; the Government raised petrol prices by 10% in September 2010. Liberalization of the financial sector had commenced in 2003, and a stock exchange was opened in 2009. In January 2010 the authorities announced plans to increase the maximum permitted level of foreign ownership in the banking sector from 49% to 60%. In July 2010 new legislation was introduced permitting the establishment of investment banks, although the £S20,000m. minimum capital requirement was expected to deter many banks from applying for a licence. Meanwhile, in May the People's Assembly approved a bill to restructure the telecommunications sector and establish an independent regulator; however, the Syrian Telecommunications Establishment (Syrian Telecom) was to remain under state control. In August the Government invited bids for companies to operate Syria's third mobile telecommunications licence. In May 2010 the US Administration of President Barack Obama renewed the economic sanctions regime imposed by the Administration of George W. Bush in 2004 and tightened in 2008 (see Contemporary Political History). However, the USA removed its objection to Syria joining the World Trade Organization. In recent years Syria's economic performance has been influenced by the presence of large numbers of refugees from Iraq (estimated at around 1m. in early 2011), with the consequent increased levels of demand and rise in inflation. According to official figures, GDP growth in 2009 was 6.0% (the IMF had forecast 4.0%), with modest increases in agricultural and hydrocarbons output, and income from tourism remaining strong; indeed, the global financial crisis of 2008–09 had a relatively moderate impact on the Syrian economy. Assessing the economy in September 2010, the Deputy Prime Minister, responsible for Economic Affairs, Abdallah Dardari, projected growth of about 5.8% for that year and of an average of 5.5%–6% over the next five years; Dardari announced that the Government planned to attract $55,000m. in foreign direct investment during this period. However, the widespread civil unrest that began in March 2011 was considered likely to represent a major deterrent to foreign investment and tourism, as well as disrupting the wider economy.

PUBLIC HOLIDAYS

2012: 1 January (New Year's Day), 4 February* (Mouloud/Yum al-Nabi, Birth of Muhammad), 8 March (Revolution Day), 21 March (Mother's Day), 13–16 April (Greek Orthodox Easter), 17 April (Independence Day), 1 May (Labour Day), 6 May (Martyrs' Day), 16 June* (Leilat al-Meiraj, Ascension of Muhammad), 18 August* (Id al-Fitr, end of Ramadan), 6 October (Anniversary of October War), 25 October* (Id al-Adha, Feast of the Sacrifice), 14 November* (Muharram, Islamic New Year), 25 December (Christmas Day),

* These holidays are dependent on the Islamic lunar calendar and may vary by one or two days from the dates given.

SYRIA

Statistical Survey

Sources (unless otherwise stated): Central Bureau of Statistics, rue Abd al-Malek bin Marwah, Malki Quarter, Damascus; tel. (11) 3335830; fax (11) 3322292; e-mail infocbs@cbssyr.org; internet www.cbssyr.org; Central Bank of Syria, place du 17 avril, Damascus; tel. (11) 2216802; fax (11) 2248329; e-mail info@bcs.gov.sy; internet www.banquecentrale.gov.sy.

Area and Population

AREA, POPULATION AND DENSITY

Area (sq km)	
Land	184,050
Inland water	1,130
Total	185,180*
Population (census results)	
3 September 1994	13,782,315
22 September 2004	
Males	9,196,878
Females	8,723,966
Total	17,920,844
Population (official estimate at 1 January)	
2008	22,331,000
2009	23,027,000
2010	23,695,000
Density (per sq km) at 1 January 2010	128.0

* 71,498 sq miles; including the Israeli-occupied Golan region (1,154 sq km).

Note: According to the United Nations Relief and Works Agency for Palestine Refugees in the Near East (UNRWA), there were 472,109 Palestinian refugees in Syria at 31 December 2009.

POPULATION BY AGE AND SEX
('000 persons at 2004 census)

	Males	Females	Total
0–14	3,637	3,434	7,071
15–64	5,213	5,046	10,259
65 and over	311	280	591
Total	9,161	8,760	17,921

GOVERNORATES
(official estimates at 1 January 2010)

	Area (sq km)	Population ('000)	Density (per sq km)
Dar'a	3,730	1,085	290.9
Deir el-Zor	33,060	1,623	49.1
Dimashq (Damascus, capital)	—	1,749	—
Halab (Aleppo)	18,500	5,680	307.0
Hamah (Hama)	10,160	2,052	202.0
Al-Hasakah	23,330	1,540	66.0
Hims (Homs)	40,940	2,087	51.0
Idleb	6,100	1,997	327.4
Al-Ladhiqiyah (Latakia)	2,300	1,207	524.8
Quneitra	1,860	475	255.4
Al-Raqqah (Rakka)	19,620	966	49.2
Rif Dimashq (Rural Damascus)	18,140*	1,820	100.3
Al-Suweida	5,550	476	85.8
Tartous	1,890	938	496.3
Total	185,180	23,695	128.0

* Includes area for Dimashq (Damascus, capital).

BIRTHS, MARRIAGES AND DEATHS
(excl. nomad population and Palestinian refugees, estimates)

	Registered live births		Registered marriages	Registered deaths
	Number	Rate (per 1,000)		
1997	496,140	32.9	128,146	53,366
1998	505,008	32.4	130,835	57,893
1999	503,473	31.3	136,157	56,564
2000	505,484	31.0	139,843	57,759
2001	524,212	31.4	153,842	60,814
2002	471,970	27.6	174,449	53,252
2003	492,639	28.1	n.a.	53,778
2004	491,476	n.a.	178,166	57,855

2007: Live births 727,439; Deaths 76,064.
2009: Live births 670,793; Deaths 76,650.
Source: UN, *Demographic Yearbook*.

Life expectancy (years at birth, WHO estimates): 72 (males 70; females 75) in 2008 (Source: WHO, *World Health Statistics*).

ECONOMICALLY ACTIVE POPULATION
(labour force sample survey, persons aged 15 years and over, 2009)*

	Males	Females	Total
Agriculture, hunting, forestry and fishing	636,095	122,191	758,286
Mining and quarrying; manufacturing; and electricity, gas and water	764,870	53,338	818,208
Construction	801,496	7,172	808,668
Trade, restaurants and hotels	780,818	38,188	819,006
Transport, storage and communications	366,051	14,136	380,187
Financing, insurance, real estate and business services	93,073	19,226	112,299
Community, social and personal services	931,480	370,926	1,302,406
Sub-total	4,373,883	625,177	4,999,060
Activities not adequately defined	169	—	169
Total employed	4,374,052	625,177	4,999,229
Unemployed	263,676	179,277	442,953
Total labour force	4,637,728	804,454	5,442,182

* Figures refer to Syrians only, excluding armed forces.

Health and Welfare

KEY INDICATORS

Total fertility rate (children per woman, 2008)	3.2
Under-5 mortality rate (per 1,000 live births, 2008)	16
HIV/AIDS (% of persons aged 15–49, 2003)	<0.1
Physicians (per 1,000 head, 2006)	0.5
Hospital beds (per 1,000 head, 2006)	1.4
Health expenditure (2007): US $ per head (PPP)	154
Health expenditure (2007): % of GDP	3.6
Health expenditure (2007): public (% of total)	45.9
Access to water (% of persons, 2008)	89
Access to sanitation (% of persons, 2008)	96
Total carbon dioxide emissions ('000 metric tons, 2007)	69,835.8
Carbon dioxide emissions per head (metric tons, 2007)	3.5
Human Development Index (2010): ranking	111
Human Development Index (2010): value	0.589

For sources and definitions, see explanatory note on p. vi.

SYRIA

Agriculture

PRINCIPAL CROPS
('000 metric tons)

	2007	2008	2009
Wheat	4,041.1	2,139.3	3,701.8
Barley	784.5	261.1	845.7
Maize	177.0	281.3	183.3
Potatoes	570.1	720.5	709.6
Sugar beet	1,366.5	1,104.9	732.7
Chick-peas	50.0	27.1	57.4
Lentils	109.0	34.1	102.5
Almonds	76.1	82.6	97.0
Olives	495.3	827.0	885.9
Cabbages and other brassicas	34.0	39.0	44.8
Lettuce and chicory	62.2	52.4	53.1
Tomatoes	1,232.5	1,163.3	1,165.6
Cauliflowers	37.3	29.6	35.9
Pumpkins, squash and gourds	121.1	135.3	121.8
Cucumbers and gherkins	146.5	139.9	132.9
Aubergines (Eggplants)	153.1	165.2	147.0
Chillies and peppers, green	78.8	67.2	48.4
Onions and shallots, green	46.4	47.3	74.9
Onions, dry	99.8	94.2	79.4
Oranges	602.9	657.7	689.8
Lemons and limes	130.6	137.3	140.6
Apples	280.2	360.7	361.0
Apricots	112.7	100.9	98.9
Sweet cherries	75.0	48.3	76.1*
Peaches and nectarines	57.4	56.4	62.6
Grapes	273.0	280.9	358.0
Watermelons	606.7	366.7	749.7
Cantaloupes and other melons	158.8	61.0	106.5
Figs	41.1	40.3	53.7
Cotton lint*	365	244	228
Cotton seed	463	454	424

* FAO estimate(s).
Aggregate production ('000 metric tons, may include official, semi-official or estimated data): Total cereals 5,011 in 2007, 2,685 in 2008, 4,736 in 2009; Total roots and tubers 570 in 2007, 720 in 2008, 710 in 2009; Total oilcrops 201 in 2007, 266 in 2008, 276 in 2009; Total vegetables (incl. melons) 3,102 in 2007, 2,700 in 2008, 3,078 in 2009; Total fruits (excl. melons) 1,970 in 2007, 2,090 in 2008, 2,261 in 2009.
Source: FAO.

LIVESTOCK
('000 head, year ending September)

	2007	2008	2009
Horses	14.0	15.3	n.a.
Asses	107.0	100.8	92.7
Cattle	1,168.3	1,109.0	1,084.5
Camels	27.4	27.5	32.5
Sheep	22,865.4	22,865.4	n.a.
Goats	1,561.3	1,579.0	1,508.0
Chickens	26,096	23,143	24,490

Source: FAO.

LIVESTOCK PRODUCTS
('000 metric tons)

	2007	2008	2009
Cattle meat	65.5	63.8	63.0
Sheep meat	204.6	184.5	189.5
Chicken meat	173.4	178.9	182.2
Cows' milk	1,705.9	1,609.0	1,600.3
Sheep's milk	873.7	712.9	706.0
Goats' milk	97.0	99.2	97.0
Hen eggs	171.4	151.4	162.4
Wool, greasy*	50.0	50.0	n.a.

* FAO estimates.
Source: FAO.

Forestry

ROUNDWOOD REMOVALS
('000 cubic metres, excl. bark, FAO estimates)

	2007	2008	2009
Sawlogs, veneer logs and logs for sleepers	16	16	16
Other industrial wood	24	24	24
Fuel wood	25	26	27
Total	65	66	67

Sawnwood production ('000 cubic metres): *1980*: Coniferous (softwood) 6.6; Broadleaved (hardwood) 2.4; Total 9.0. *1981–2009*: Production as in 1980 (FAO estimates).
Source: FAO.

Fishing

(metric tons, live weight)

	2006	2007	2008
Capture	8,264	9,456	6,996
Freshwater fishes	4,869	6,075	3,784
Aquaculture	8,902	8,425	8,595
Common carp	4,387	3,967	3,696
Tilapias	3,460	2,921	3,874
Total catch	17,166	17,881	15,591

Source: FAO.

Mining

('000 metric tons, unless otherwise indicated)

	2007	2008	2009
Phosphate rock	3,678	3,221	2,466
Salt (unrefined)	81	89	78
Gypsum	448	573	403
Natural gas (million cu m)	5,581	5,488	5,814
Crude petroleum	20,632	19,841	18,699

Sources: US Geological Survey; BP, *Statistical Review of World Energy*.

Industry

SELECTED PRODUCTS
('000 metric tons, unless otherwise indicated)

	2007	2008	2009
Plywood (cu m)*	7.8	7.8	7.8
Paper and paperboard	75	75*	75
Cement (hydraulic)	5,104	5,336	5,497
Olive oil (virgin)	98.3	156.3	168.2
Soybean oil†	61.9	64.5	93.6
Cottonseed oil	30.4	31.6	33.4
Motor spirit (petrol, '000 barrels)	12,921	12,958	12,958
Distillate fuel oils ('000 barrels)	29,346	29,346	29,346
Residual fuel oils ('000 barrels)	32,887	32,887	32,887

* FAO estimate(s).
† Unofficial figures.
Sources: FAO; US Geological Survey.

Electric energy (million kWh): 38,784 in 2007; 41,170 in 2008; 43,406 in 2009.

Finance

CURRENCY AND EXCHANGE RATES

Monetary Units
100 piastres = 1 Syrian pound (£S).

Sterling, Dollar and Euro Equivalents (31 December 2010)
£1 sterling = £S17.573;
US $1 = £S11.225;
€1 = £S14.999;
£S1,000 = £56.91 sterling = $89.09 = €66.67.

Exchange Rate: Between April 1976 and December 1987 the official mid-point rate was fixed at US $1 = £S3.925. On 1 January 1988 a new rate of $1 = £S11.225 was introduced. In addition to the official exchange rate, there is a promotion rate (applicable to most travel and tourism transactions) and a flexible rate.

BUDGET
(£S '000 million)

Revenue	2005	2006	2007
Oil-related proceeds	106.2	127.0	99.6
Non-oil tax revenue	160.3	196.3	221.4
Income and profits	59.3	65.0	74.2
International Trade	30.7	32.9	33.4
Excises	4.5	6.6	9.1
Other	65.8	91.9	104.7
Non-oil non-tax revenue	89.9	111.5	137.5
Total	356.3	434.9	458.6

Expenditure	2005	2006	2007
Current expenditure	277.0	317.2	325.7
Wages and salaries	157.0	207.0	223.2
Goods and services	21.5	22.5	24.3
Interest payments	29.0	29.5	30.0
Subsidies and transfers	69.5	51.2	41.6
Development expenditure	154.4	176.5	194.8
Social	60.3	65.7	68.8
Agriculture	15.5	17.9	22.5
Extractive industries	8.1	11.6	16.7
Manufacturing industries	8.4	9.4	7.7
Utilities	34.6	39.9	39.3
Construction	0.4	0.9	0.7
Trade	1.8	3.9	2.6
Transport and communications	21.3	24.8	31.2
Finance	2.4	3.3	4.4
Other	1.5	0.2	1.0
Total	431.4	493.7	520.5

2008 (£S '000 million, estimates): Total revenue 600.0; Total expenditure 600.0.

2009 (£S '000 million, estimates): Total revenue 685.0; Total expenditure 685.0.

2010 (£S '000 million, estimates): Total revenue 754.0; Total expenditure 754.0.

Source: Ministry of Finance, Damascus.

2008 (£S '000 million, preliminary): *Revenue:* Oil-related proceeds 131.4; Non-oil tax revenue 258.0; Non-oil non-tax revenue 101.5; Total 491.2. *Expenditure:* Current expenditure 388.3; Development expenditure 173.1; Total 561.3 (Source: IMF, *Syrian Arab Republic: 2009 Article IV Consultation—Staff Report; and Public Information Notice—*March 2010).

2009 (£S '000 million, projections): *Revenue:* Oil-related proceeds 111.2; Non-oil tax revenue 296.2; Non-oil non-tax revenue 125.3; Total 533.0. *Expenditure:* Current expenditure 415.8; Development expenditure 250.6; Total 666.4 (Source: IMF, *Syrian Arab Republic: 2009 Article IV Consultation—Staff Report; and Public Information Notice—*March 2010).

INTERNATIONAL RESERVES
(excluding foreign exchange, US $ million at 31 December)

	2007	2008	2009
Gold (national valuation)	39	38	38
IMF special drawing rights	58	56	438
Total	97	94	476

2010: IMF special drawing rights 430.

Source: IMF, *International Financial Statistics*.

MONEY SUPPLY
(£S million at 31 December)

	2007	2008	2009
Currency outside depository corporations	422,357	468,820	480,952
Transferable deposits	351,707	469,456	507,088
Other deposits	548,881	717,811	810,695
Broad money	1,322,946	1,656,087	1,798,734

Source: IMF, *International Financial Statistics*.

COST OF LIVING
(Consumer Price Index; base: 2000 = 100)

	2008	2009	2010
Food and beverages	181.8	182.2	190.8
Electricity, gas and other fuels (incl. water)	173.4	228.6	249.4
Clothing and footwear	139.0	134.9	141.9
Rent	182.7	177.2	176.8
All items (incl. others)	161.4	165.9	173.2

Source: ILO.

NATIONAL ACCOUNTS
(£S million at current prices)

Expenditure on the Gross Domestic Product

	2007	2008	2009*
Government final consumption expenditure	248,300	274,879	301,787
Private final consumption expenditure	1,192,230	1,390,933	1,508,579
Gross fixed capital formation	412,136	408,725	451,766
Changes in stocks	148,802	367,501	309,175
Total domestic expenditure	2,001,468	2,442,038	2,571,307
Exports of goods and services	779,930	902,067	732,502
Less Imports of goods and services	763,573	899,045	784,658
GDP in market prices	2,017,825	2,445,060	2,519,151
GDP at constant 2000 prices	1,284,035	1,341,516	1,422,178

* Provisional.

Gross Domestic Product by Economic Activity

	2007	2008	2009*
Agriculture, hunting, forestry and fishing	389,828	453,746	566,360
Mining and quarrying			
Manufacturing	628,143	787,430	628,661
Electricity, gas and water			
Construction	72,585	78,174	78,646
Wholesale and retail trade	372,894	513,092	577,777
Transport and communications	201,156	225,157	249,859
Finance and insurance	113,289	128,380	127,362
Government services	200,662	224,304	243,724
Other community, social and personal services	48,307	53,621	61,664
Non-profit private services	954	1,002	1,152
Sub-total	2,027,818	2,464,906	2,535,205
Import duties	33,405	33,112	32,821
Less Imputed bank service charges	43,398	52,958	48,875
GDP in market prices	2,017,825	2,445,060	2,519,151

* Estimates.

SYRIA

BALANCE OF PAYMENTS
(US $ million)

	2006	2007	2008
Exports of goods f.o.b.	10,245	11,756	15,334
Imports of goods f.o.b.	−9,359	−12,277	−16,107
Trade balance	886	−521	−773
Exports of services	2,924	3,862	4,040
Imports of services	−2,520	−3,013	−3,202
Balance on goods and services	1,290	328	65
Other income received	428	594	540
Other income paid	−1,363	−1,283	−1,689
Balance on goods, services and income	355	−361	−1,084
Current transfers received	770	1,040	1,335
Current transfers paid	−235	−220	−185
Current balance	890	459	66
Capital account (net)	18	118	73
Direct investment from abroad	659	1,242	1,467
Portfolio investment assets	—	—	−55
Other investment assets	−710	−746	−646
Other investment liabilities	−281	216	83
Net errors and omissions	−1,488	−746	−937
Overall balance	−912	544	50

Source: IMF, *International Financial Statistics*.

External Trade

PRINCIPAL COMMODITIES
(distribution by SITC major group, £S million)

Imports	2007	2008	2009
Food and live animals	68,802	96,531	122,366
Beverages and tobacco	5,651	3,829	10,697
Crude materials, inedible, except fuels	25,696	36,603	44,173
Mineral fuels and lubricants	225,666	265,332	91,544
Animal and vegetable oils and fats	5,370	7,034	10,097
Chemicals and related products	78,368	102,839	98,915
Basic manufactures	147,949	217,264	204,515
Machinery and transport equipment	117,840	98,469	119,882
Total (incl. others)	684,557	839,419	714,216

Exports	2007	2008	2009
Food and live animals	93,079	87,576	107,950
Beverages and tobacco	5,040	53,583	9,996
Crude materials, inedible, except fuels	9,296	26,462	13,500
Mineral fuels and lubricants	219,541	261,275	169,577
Animal and vegetable oils and fats	13,595	7,629	4,465
Chemicals and related products	28,755	35,198	31,796
Basic manufactures	70,321	118,927	54,888
Machinery and transport equipment	26,936	31,575	18,216
Total (incl. others)	579,034	707,798	488,330

PRINCIPAL TRADING PARTNERS
(£S million)

Imports c.i.f.	2007	2008	2009
China, People's Republic	54,363	91,500	60,621
Egypt	29,723	28,701	40,522
France	14,435	9,351	10,475
Germany	17,116	17,414	21,055
India	17,352	17,223	15,317
Italy	45,658	39,164	25,786
Japan	12,505	9,545	8,815
Lebanon	7,839	7,885	7,221
Netherlands	12,685	11,253	6,356
Romania	3,548	5,641	9,537
Russia	66,726	108,790	42,879
Saudi Arabia	37,989	31,030	28,908
Spain	5,403	11,724	8,724
Turkey	28,127	23,064	54,269
United Arab Emirates	15,492	15,043	9,559
USA	14,867	16,390	21,740
Total (incl. others)	684,557	839,419	714,216

Exports f.o.b.	2007	2008	2009
Egypt	20,507	34,011	16,927
France	61,279	47,434	31,474
Germany	7,513	75,984	44,409
Italy	126,396	55,147	27,537
Jordan	24,626	21,006	16,182
Lebanon	17,169	62,179	16,292
Netherlands	9,190	9,593	11,205
Russia	1,912	667	586
Saudi Arabia	56,596	48,019	27,418
Spain	12,958	19,860	15,907
Turkey	27,966	29,593	14,707
United Arab Emirates	12,301	8,799	8,101
USA	13,019	16,373	10,459
Total (incl. others)	579,034	707,798	488,330

Transport

RAILWAYS
(traffic)

	2007	2008	2009
Passengers carried ('000)	2,492	3,365	3,657
Passenger-km ('000)	744,110	1,120,021	1,223,432
Freight ('000 metric tons)	9,450	9,307	8,842
Freight ton-km (million)	2,551	2,370	2,263

ROAD TRAFFIC
(motor vehicles in use)

	2007	2008	2009
Passenger cars	446,132	551,858	637,604
Buses	5,154	6,201	6,611
Lorries, trucks, etc.	516,167	552,841	623,359
Motorcycles	186,945	205,518	242,090

SHIPPING
Merchant Fleet
(registered at 31 December)

	2007	2008	2009
Number of vessels	139	117	67
Total displacement ('000 grt)	361.0	317.2	247.2

Source: IHS Fairplay, *World Fleet Statistics*.

SYRIA

International Sea-borne Traffic

	1996	1997	1998
Vessels entered ('000 net regd tons)	2,901*	2,640	2,622
Cargo unloaded ('000 metric tons)	4,560	4,788	5,112
Cargo loaded ('000 metric tons)	1,788	2,412	2,136

* Excluding Banias.

Vessels entered ('000 net registered tons): 2,928 in 1999; 2,798 in 2000; 2,827 in 2001.

Source: mainly UN, *Monthly Bulletin of Statistics* and *Statistical Yearbook*.

CIVIL AVIATION
(traffic on scheduled services)

	2004	2005	2006
Kilometres flown (million)	11	12	24
Passengers carried ('000)	1,170	1,240	1,252
Passenger-km (million)	2,212	2,520	2,340
Total ton-km (million)	219	249	228

Source: UN, *Statistical Yearbook*.

2006: Passengers carried ('000) 1,252.1 (Source: World Bank, World Development Indicators database).

2007: Passengers carried ('000) 1,371.5 (Source: World Bank, World Development Indicators database).

2008: Passengers carried ('000) 1,358.5 (Source: World Bank, World Development Indicators database).

Tourism

FOREIGN VISITOR ARRIVALS
(incl. excursionists)*

Country of nationality	2006	2007	2008
Iran	270,915	330,369	361,605
Iraq	1,289,250	1,530,458	889,463
Jordan	882,501	914,822	1,044,564
Kuwait	98,892	110,388	126,977
Lebanon	1,786,943	1,448,809	1,587,115
Saudi Arabia	408,186	353,103	403,140
Turkey	480,553	485,953	562,832
Total (incl. others)	5,681,751	5,434,253	6,950,852

* Figures exclude Syrian nationals resident abroad.

Tourism receipts (US $ million, incl. passenger transport): 2,035 in 2005; 2,113 in 2006; 2,972 in 2007.

Source: World Tourism Organization.

Communications Media

	2007	2008	2009
Telephones ('000 main lines in use)	3,452	3,633	3,871
Mobile cellular telephones ('000 in use)	6,235	7,056	9,982*
Internet users ('000)	3,470	3,565	4,469
Broadband subscribers ('000)	7.0	11.1	34.7

* Data until 30 November.

1992: Book production 598 titles.
1996: Daily newspapers 8 (average circulation 287,000 copies).
1997 ('000 in use): Radio receivers 4,150.
2000 ('000 in use): Television receivers 1,080.
2004: Daily newspapers 4.
Personal computers: 1,800,000 (89.6 per 1,000 persons) in 2007.

Sources: UNESCO, *Statistical Yearbook*; UN, *Statistical Yearbook*; International Telecommunication Union.

Education

(2008/09, unless otherwise indicated)

	Institutions*	Teachers	Males	Females	Total
Pre-primary	1,431	8,465	76,083	69,333	145,416
Primary	n.a.	132,099†	1,240,904	1,142,319	2,383,223
Secondary: general	1,140	162,758†	1,306,251	1,256,317	2,562,568
Secondary: vocational	595	18,439	60,990	40,777	101,767
Higher*	5	8,084	141,310	138,304	279,614

* Excluding private universities; data for 2006/07.
† 2007/08.

Source: mainly UNESCO Institute for Statistics.

Pupil-teacher ratio (primary education, UNESCO estimate): 17.8 in 2007/08 (Source: UNESCO Institute for Statistics).

Adult literacy rate (UNESCO estimates): 83.6% (males 90.0%; females 77.2%) in 2008 (Source: UNESCO Institute for Statistics).

Directory

The Government

HEAD OF STATE

President: Lt-Gen. BASHAR AL-ASSAD (assumed office 17 July 2000).
Vice-President, responsible for Foreign Affairs and Information: FAROUK AL-SHARA'.
Vice-President: Dr NAJAH AL-ATTAR.
Assistant Vice-President with rank of Minister: Lt-Gen. HASSAN AL-TURKMANI.

COUNCIL OF MINISTERS
(May 2011)

Prime Minister: Dr ADEL SAFAR.
Minister of Defence: Lt-Gen. ALI MUHAMMAD HABIB MAHMOUD.
Minister of Foreign Affairs and Expatriates: WALID MOUALLEM.
Minister of Information: Dr ADNAN HASSAN MAHMOUD.
Minister of the Interior: Maj.-Gen. MUHAMMAD IBRAHIM AL-SHAAR.
Minister of Local Administration: OMAR IBRAHIM GHALAWANJI.
Minister of Education: SALEH AL-RASHED.
Minister of Higher Education: ABD AL-RAZZAQ SHEIKH ISSA.
Minister of Electricity: IMAD MUHAMMAD DEEB KHAMIS.
Minister of Culture: MUHAMMAD RIYAD HUSSEIN ISMAT.
Minister of Transport: Dr FAISAL ABBAS.
Minister of Petroleum and Mineral Resources: SUFIAN ALLAW.
Minister of Industry: ADNAN SALKHO.
Minister of Finance: MUHAMMAD AL-JLEILATI.
Minister of Economy and Trade: MUHAMMAD NIDAL AL-SHAAR.
Minister of Housing and Construction: HALA MUHAMMAD AL-NASSER.
Minister of Justice: TAYSIR QALA AWWAD.
Minister of Agriculture and Agrarian Reform: RIYAD FARID HIJAB.
Minister of Irrigation: GEORGE MALKI SOUMI.
Minister of Communications and Technology: IMAD ABD AL-GHANI SABOUNI.
Minister of Health: Dr WAEL NADER AL-HALQI.

SYRIA

Minister of Awqaf (Religious Endowments): MUHAMMAD ABD AL-SATTAR AL-SAYYID.
Minister of Labour and Social Affairs: RADWAN AL-HABIB.
Minister of Tourism: LAMIA MEREI AASI.
Minister of Presidential Affairs: MANSOUR AZZAM.
Minister of State for Environmental Affairs: KAWKAB AL-SABAGH MUHAMMAD JAMIL AL-DAYEH.
Ministers of State: YOUSUF SULEIMAN AL-AHMAD, HUSSEIN MAHMOUD FARZAT, HASSAN AL-SARRI, GHIATH JARAATLI, JOSEPH SUWAID.

MINISTRIES

Office of the President: Damascus.
Office of the Prime Minister: rue Chahbandar, Damascus; tel. (11) 2226000; fax (11) 2237842.
Ministry of Agriculture and Agrarian Reform: rue Jabri, place Hedjaz, Damascus; tel. (11) 2213613; fax (11) 2244078; e-mail agre-min@syriatel.net; internet www.syrian-agriculture.org.
Ministry of Awqaf (Religious Endowments): place al-Misat, Damascus; tel. (11) 4470005; fax (11) 4470006; e-mail admin@syrianawkkaf.org; internet www.syrianawkkaf.org.
Ministry of Communications and Technology: rue Abed, Damascus; tel. (11) 3320807; fax (11) 2246403; e-mail admin@moct.gov.sy; internet www.moct.gov.sy.
Ministry of Culture: rue George Haddad, Rawda, Damascus; tel. (11) 3331556; fax (11) 3342606; e-mail info@moc.gov.sy; internet www.moc.gov.sy.
Ministry of Defence: place Omayad, Damascus; tel. (11) 7770700; fax (11) 2237842.
Ministry of Economy and Trade: rue Maysaloun, Damascus; tel. (11) 2324680; fax (11) 2225695; e-mail econ-min@net.sy; internet www.syrecon.org.
Ministry of Education: rue Shahbander, al-Masraa, Damascus; tel. (11) 4444800; fax (11) 4420435; e-mail info@syrianeducation.org.sy; internet www.syrianeducation.org.sy.
Ministry of Electricity: BP 4900, rue al-Kouatly, Damascus; tel. (11) 2119934; fax (11) 2227736; e-mail peegt@net.sy.
Ministry of Expatriates: Island 20, Dummar, Damascus; tel. (11) 3193999; fax (11) 3134301; e-mail azari36@gmail.com; internet www.moex.gov.sy.
Ministry of Finance: BP 13136, rue Jule Jammal, Damascus; tel. (11) 2211300; fax (11) 2224701; e-mail mof@net.sy; internet www.syrianfinance.org.
Ministry of Foreign Affairs: rue al-Rashid, Damascus; tel. (11) 3331200; fax (11) 3327620; e-mail syr-mofa@scs-net.org.
Ministry of Health: rue Majlis al-Sha'ab, Damascus; tel. (11) 3311020; fax (11) 3311114; e-mail health-min@net.sy; internet www.moh.gov.sy.
Ministry of Higher Education: BP 9251, place Mezzeh Gamarik, Damascus; tel. (11) 2119865; fax (11) 2128919; e-mail mhe@shern.net; internet www.mhe.gov.sy.
Ministry of Housing and Construction: place Yousuf al-Azmeh, al-Salheyeh, Damascus; tel. (11) 2217571; fax (11) 2459400; e-mail diwan@mhc.gov.sy; internet www.mhc.gov.sy.
Ministry of Industry: BP 12835, rue Maysaloun, Damascus; tel. (11) 3720959; fax (11) 2231096; e-mail industry-min@mail.sy; internet www.syrianindustry.org.
Ministry of Information: Immeuble Dar al-Baath, Autostrade Mezzeh, Damascus; tel. and fax (11) 6664681; fax (11) 6664681; e-mail info@moi.gov.sy; internet www.moi.gov.sy.
Ministry of the Interior: rue al-Bahsah, al-Marjeh, Damascus; tel. (11) 2313471; fax (11) 2324835; e-mail admin@civilaffair-moi.gov.sy; internet www.civilaffair-moi.gov.sy.
Ministry of Irrigation: BP 4451, Harasta nr the Panorama, Damascus; tel. (11) 5318268; fax (11) 5312948; e-mail ministry@irrigation.gov.sy; internet www.irrigation.gov.sy.
Ministry of Justice: rue al-Nasr, Damascus; tel. (11) 2214105; fax (11) 2246250.
Ministry of Labour and Social Affairs: place Yousuf al-Azmeh, al-Salheyeh, Damascus; tel. (11) 2455089; fax (11) 2247499; internet www.molsa.gov.sy.
Ministry of Local Administration: BP 3311, Damascus; tel. (11) 2317911; fax (11) 2316921; e-mail info@mlae-sy.org; internet www.mlae-sy.org.
Ministry of Petroleum and Mineral Resources: BP 40, al-Adawi, Insha'at, Damascus; tel. (11) 4451624; fax (11) 4463942; e-mail mopmr-central@mail.sy; internet www.petroleum.gov.sy.
Ministry of State for Environmental Affairs: BP 3773, Damascus; tel. (11) 2138682; fax (11) 2320885.
Ministry of Tourism: BP 6642, rue Barada, Damascus; tel. (11) 2210122; fax (11) 2242636; e-mail min-tourism@mail.sy; internet www.syriatourism.org.
Ministry of Transport: BP 33999, rue al-Jala'a, Damascus; tel. (11) 3316840; fax (11) 3323317; e-mail min-trans@net.sy; internet www.mot.gov.sy.

Legislature

Majlis al-Sha'ab
(People's Assembly)

People's Council, Damascus; tel. (11) 2226127; fax (11) 3712532; e-mail raedbk@parliament.gov.sy; internet www.parliament.gov.sy.
Speaker: MAHMOUD AREF AL-ABRASH.

Election, 22 and 23 April 2007

Party	Seats
National Progressive Front*	172
Independents	78
Total	250

*The National Progressive Front reportedly comprised 10 political parties, headed by the Baath Arab Socialist Party.

Political Organizations

The **National Progressive Front (NPF—Al-Jabha al-Wataniyah al-Taqadumiyah)**, headed by the late President Hafiz al-Assad, was formed in March 1972 as a coalition of five political parties. The Syrian Constitution defines the Baath Arab Socialist Party as 'the leading party in the society and the state'. At the time of the legislative elections in April 2007, the NPF consisted of 10 parties:

Arab Democratic Unionist Party (Hizb al-Ittihad al-'Arabi al-Dimuqrati): f. 1981, following split from the Arab Socialist Union; considers the concerns of the Arab world in general as secondary to those of Syria itself in the pursuit of pan-Arab goals; Chair. GHASSAN AHMAD OSMAN.

Arab Socialist Movement (Harakat al-Ishtiraki al-'Arabi): Damascus; f. 1963, following split from Arab Socialist Union; contested the 2007 election to the People's Assembly as two factions (see also National Vow Movement); Leader AHMAD AL-AHMAD.

Arab Socialist Union (al-Ittihad al-Ishtiraki al-'Arabi): Damascus; f. 1973, following the separation of the Syrian branch from the international Arab Socialist Union; Nasserite; supportive of the policies of the Baath Arab Socialist Party; Leader SAFWAN AL-QUDSI.

Baath Arab Socialist Party (al-Hizb al-Ba'th al-'Arabi al-Ishtiraki): National Command, BP 9389, Autostrade Mezzeh, Damascus; tel. (11) 6622142; fax (11) 6622099; e-mail baath@baath-party.org; internet www.baath-party.org; Arab nationalist socialist party; f. 1947, as a result of merger between the Arab Revival (Baath) Movement (f. 1940) and the Arab Socialist Party (f. 1940); in power since 1963; supports creation of a unified Arab socialist society; approx. 1m. mems in Syria; brs in most Arab countries; Pres. Lt-Gen. BASHAR AL-ASSAD.

Democratic Socialist Unionist Party (al-Hizb al-Wahdawi al-Ishtiraki al-Dimuqrati): f. 1974, following split from the Arab Socialist Union; Chair. FADLALLAH NASR AL-DIN.

National Vow Movement (Harakat al-'ahd al-Watani): a breakaway party from the Arab Socialist Union; a faction of the Arab Socialist Movement; awarded three seats in 2007 election to the People's Assembly; Leader GHASSAN ABD AL-AZIZ OSMAN.

Socialist Unionists (Al-Wahdawiyyun al-Ishtirakiyyun): e-mail alwahdawinet@hotmail.com; internet www.alwahdawi.net; f. 1961, through split from the Baath Arab Socialist Party following that organization's acceptance of Syria's decision to secede from the United Arab Republic; Nasserite; aims for Arab unity, particularly a new union with Egypt; produces weekly periodical *Al-Wehdawi*; Chair. FAYEZ ISMAIL.

Syrian Arab Socialist Union Party: Damascus; tel. (11) 239305; Nasserite; Sec.-Gen. SAFWAN KOUDSI.

Syrian Communist Party (Bakdash) (al-Hizb al-Shuyu'i al-Suri): BP 7837, Damascus; tel. (11) 4455048; fax (11) 4446390; e-mail info@syriancp.org; internet www.syriancp.org; f. 1924 by Fouad Shamal in Lebanon and Khalid Bakdash (died 1995); until 1943 part of joint Communist Party of Syria and Lebanon; party split into two factions under separate leaders, Bakdash and Faisal (q.v.), in 1986; Marxist-Leninist; publishes fortnightly periodical *Sawt al-Shaab*; Sec.-Gen. AMMAR BAKDASH.

SYRIA

Syrian Communist Party (Faisal) (al-Hizb al-Shuyu'i al-Suri): Damascus; f. 1986, following split of Syrian Communist Party into two factions under separate leaders, Faisal and Bakdash (q.v.); aims to end domination of Baath Arab Socialist Party and the advantages given to mems of that party at all levels; advocates the lifting of the state of emergency and the release of all political prisoners; publishes weekly periodical *An-Nour*; Sec.-Gen. YOUSUF RASHID FAISAL.

Syrian Social Nationalist Party (Centralist Wing) (al-Hizb al-Suri al-Qawmi al-Ijtima'i): e-mail webmaster@ssnp.info; internet www.ssnp.com; f. 1932 in Beirut, Lebanon; joined the NPF in 2005; also known as Parti populaire syrien; seeks creation of a 'Greater Syrian' state, incl. Syria, Lebanon, Jordan, the Palestinian territories, Iraq, Kuwait, Cyprus and parts of Egypt, Iran and Turkey; advocates separation of church and state, the redistribution of wealth, and a strong military; supports Syrian involvement in Lebanese affairs; has brs world-wide, and approx. 90,000 mems in Syria; Chair. ISSAM MAHAYIRI.

There are numerous opposition parties, within Syria or in exile, which are forced to operate on a clandestine basis. Formed in 1980, the **National Democratic Rally** (NDR—Tajammu' al-Watani al-Dimuqrati) is an alliance of banned, secularist opposition parties, several of which are opposition wings of parties that joined the ruling NPF.

A current member of the NDR, the **Syrian Democratic People's Party** (al-Hizb al-Sha'ab al-Suri al-Dimuqrati—leader ABULLAH HOSHA) was founded in 1973 as the Syrian Communist Party (Political Bureau), following the decision by founder Riad at-Turk to split from that party after its leader, Khalid Bakdash, decided to allow the organization to join the NPF. The party adopted its current name in 2005. The party publishes an online newsletter (www.arraee.com).

There is also a **Marxist-Leninist Communist Action Party**, which regards itself as independent of all Arab regimes.

An illegal Syrian-based organization, the **Islamic Movement for Change (IMC)**, claimed responsibility for a bomb attack in Damascus in December 1996.

Diplomatic Representation

EMBASSIES IN SYRIA

Algeria: Immeuble Noss, Raouda, Damascus; tel. (11) 3331446; fax (11) 3334698; Ambassador SALEH BOUSHEH.

Argentina: BP 116, Damascus; tel. (11) 3334167; fax (11) 3327326; e-mail easir@net.sy; Ambassador ROBERTO AHUAD.

Armenia: BP 33241, Ibrahim Hanono St, Malki, Damascus; tel. (11) 6133560; fax (11) 6130952; e-mail am309@net.sy; Ambassador ARSHAK POLADIAN.

Austria: BP 5634, Immeuble Mohamed Naim al-Deker, 1 rue Farabi, Mezzeh Est, Damascus; tel. (11) 61380100; fax (11) 6116734; e-mail damaskus-ob@bmeia.gv.at; Ambassador MARIA KUNZ.

Bahrain: BP 36225, Damascus; tel. (11) 6132314; fax (11) 6130502; e-mail damascus.mission@mofa.gov.bh; Ambassador ABD AL-RAHMAN MUBARAK AL-SULEITTI.

Belarus: BP 16239, 27 rue Qurtaja, Mezzeh Est, Damascus; tel. (11) 6118097; fax (11) 6132802; e-mail syria@belembassy.org; Ambassador OLEG YERMALOVICH.

Belgium: 10 rue al-Salaam, 2e–3e étage, Mezzeh Est, Damascus; tel. (11) 61399931; fax (11) 61399977; e-mail damascus@diplobel.fed.be; internet www.diplomatie.be/damascus; Ambassador FRANÇOISE GUSTIN.

Brazil: BP 2219, 39 rue al-Farabi, Mezzeh Est, Damascus; tel. (11) 6124551; fax (11) 6124553; e-mail braemsyr@net.sy; Ambassador EDGAR ANTONIO CASIANO.

Bulgaria: BP 2732, 8 rue Pakistan, place Arnous, Damascus; tel. (11) 3318445; fax (11) 4419854; e-mail bul_emb@abv.bg; internet www.mfa.bg/bg/62/; Chargé d'affaires DIMITAR MIHAILOV.

Canada: BP 3394, Damascus; tel. (11) 6116692; fax (11) 6114000; e-mail dmcus@international.gc.ca; internet www.canadainternational.gc.ca/syria-syrie; Ambassador GLENN DAVIDSON.

Chile: BP 3561, 6 rue Ziad bin Abi Soufian, Rawda, Damascus; tel. (11) 3338443; fax (11) 3331563; e-mail embachile.siria@gmail.com; internet chileabroad.gov.cl/siria; Ambassador RICARDO FIEGELIST SCHMIDT.

China, People's Republic: BP 2455, 83 rue Ata Ayoubi, Damascus; tel. (11) 3339594; fax (11) 3338067; e-mail chinaemb_sy@mfa.gov.cn; internet sy.chineseembassy.org; Ambassador LI HUAXIN.

Cuba: Immeuble Istouani and Charbati, 40 rue al-Rachid, Damascus; tel. (11) 3339624; fax (11) 3333802; e-mail embacubasy@net.sy; Ambassador LUIS ERINEL MARISY FIGUEREDO.

Cyprus: BP 9269, 278G rue Malek bin Rabia, Mezzeh Ouest, Damascus; tel. (11) 6130812; fax (11) 6130814; e-mail cyembdam@scs-net.org; Ambassador ANTONIS GRIVAS.

Czech Republic: BP 2249, place Abou al-Ala'a al-Maari, Damascus; tel. (11) 3331383; fax (11) 3338268; e-mail damascus@embassy.mzv.cz; internet www.mzv.cz/damascus; Ambassador EVA FILIPI.

Denmark: BP 2244, Fatmeh Idriss 6, rue al-Ghazzawi, Mezzeh Ouest, Damascus; tel. (11) 61909000; fax (11) 61909033; e-mail damamb@um.dk; internet www.ambdamaskus.um.dk; Ambassador CHRISTINA MARKUS LASSEN.

Egypt: BP 12443, rue al-Gala'a, Abou Roumaneh, Damascus; tel. (11) 3330756; fax (11) 33500911; e-mail egypt@tvcabo.co.mz; Ambassador SHAWKI ISMAIL ALI SOLIMAN.

Eritrea: BP 12846, Autostrade al-Mazen West, 82 rue Akram Mosque, Damascus; tel. (11) 6112357; fax (11) 6112358; Chargé d'affaires a.i. HUMMED MOHAMED SAEED KULU.

Finland: BP 3893, Immeuble 164A, rue Doha, Area 3, Mezzeh Est, Damascus; tel. (11) 6127570; fax (11) 6119777; e-mail sanomat.dam@formin.fi; internet www.finland.sy; Ambassador HARRI MÄKI-REINIKKA.

France: BP 769, rue Ata al-Ayoubi, al-Afif, Damascus; tel. (11) 3390200; fax (11) 3390221; e-mail ambafr@net.sy; internet www.ambafrance-sy.org/spip.php?rubrique=1; Ambassador ERIC CHEVALLIER.

Germany: BP 2237, 16 rue Abd al-Mun'im Riyad, al-Malki, Damascus; tel. (11) 37900000; fax (11) 3718768; e-mail info@damaskus.diplo.de; internet www.damaskus.diplo.de; Ambassador ANDREAS REINICKE.

Greece: BP 30319, Immeuble Pharaon, 11 rue Farabi, Mezzeh Est, Damascus; tel. (11) 6113035; fax (11) 6114920; e-mail gremb.dam@mfa.gr; internet www.mfa.gr/damascus; Ambassador ATHANASSIOU TASSIA.

Holy See: BP 2271, 1 place Ma'raket Ajnadin, al-Malki, Damascus (Apostolic Nunciature); tel. (11) 3332601; fax (11) 3327550; e-mail noncesy@mail.sy; Apostolic Nuncio Most Rev. MARIO ZENARI (Titular Archbishop of Iulium Carnicum).

Hungary: BP 2607, 12 rue al-Salam, Mezzeh Est, Damascus; tel. (11) 6117966; fax (11) 6117917; e-mail mission.dam@kum.hu; internet www.mfa.gov.hu/kulkepviselet/sy; Ambassador JÁNOS BUDAI.

India: BP 685, 3455 rue ibn al-Haitham, Abou Roumaneh, Damascus; tel. (11) 3347351; fax (11) 3347912; e-mail damascus@mea.gov.in; Ambassador V. PRANATHARTHI HARAN.

Indonesia: BP 3530, Immeuble 26, Bloc 270A, 132 rue al-Madina al-Munawar, Mezzeh Est, Damascus; tel. (11) 6119630; fax (11) 6119632; e-mail kbridams@net.sy; Ambassador ASSAYID WAHIB.

Iran: BP 2691, Autostrade Mezzeh, nr al-Razi Hospital, Damascus; tel. (11) 6117675; fax (11) 6110997; e-mail iran-dam@net.sy; Ambassador SAYED AHMAD MOUSSAVI.

Iraq: Damascus; tel. (11) 3341290; fax (11) 3341291; e-mail dmkemb@iraqmofamail.net; Ambassador Dr ALA'A HUSSAIN AL-JAWADI.

Italy: BP 2216, rue al-Ayoubi, Damascus; tel. (11) 3338338; fax (11) 3320325; e-mail ambasciata.damasco@esteri.it; internet www.ambdamasco.esteri.it; Ambassador ACHILLE FRANCO LUIGI AMERIO.

Japan: BP 3366, 3537 Sharkasiya, rue al-Jala'a, Abou Roumaneh, Damascus; tel. (11) 3338273; fax (11) 3339920; Ambassador TOSHIRO SUZUKI.

Jordan: rue Abou Roumaneh, Damascus; tel. (11) 3334642; fax (11) 3336741; internet www.jordanembassydemascus.gov.jo; Ambassador OMAR AL-AMED.

Korea, Democratic People's Republic: rue Fares al-Khouri-Jisr Tora, Damascus; Ambassador CHOE SU HON.

Kuwait: rue Ibrahim Hanano, Damascus; tel. (11) 6118851; fax (11) 6117640; e-mail damascus@mofa.gov.kw; Ambassador AZIZ RAHIM AL-DIHANI.

Lebanon: Abou Roumaneh, Damascus; Ambassador MICHEL EL-KHOURY.

Libya: Abou Roumaneh, Damascus; Head of People's Bureau AHMAD ABD AL-SALAM BIN KHAYAL.

Malaysia: Immeuble 117, Mezzeh Est Villas, Damascus; tel. (11) 6122811; fax (11) 6122814; e-mail malsyria@kln.gov.my; Ambassador MAT DRIS BIN Haji YAACOB.

Mauritania: ave al-Jala'a, rue Karameh, Damascus; tel. (11) 3339317; fax (11) 3330552; Ambassador AAL OULD AHMADO.

Morocco: 35 rue Abu Bakr al-Karkhi Villas, Mezzeh Est, Damascus; tel. (11) 6110451; fax (11) 6117885; e-mail sifmar@scs-net.org; Ambassador MUHAMMAD LAKHSASSI.

Netherlands: BP 702, Immeuble Tello, rue al-Jala'a, Abou Roumaneh, Damascus; tel. (11) 3336871; fax (11) 3339369; e-mail dmc@

SYRIA

minbuza.nl; internet syrie.nlambassade.org; Ambassador DOLF HOGEWONING.

Norway: BP 7703, 2 rue Shafei, Mezzeh Est, Damascus; tel. (11) 6122941; fax (11) 6112798; e-mail emb.damascus@mfa.no; internet www.norway.org.sy; Ambassador ROLF WILLY HANSEN.

Oman: BP 9635, rue Ghazzawi, Mezzeh Ouest, Damascus; tel. (11) 6115176; fax (11) 6114589; e-mail oman-em@scs-net.org; Ambassador MUHAMMAD BIN SALEM BIN SAID AL-SHANFARI.

Pakistan: BP 9284, rue al-Farabi, Mezzeh Est, Damascus; tel. (11) 6132694; fax (11) 6132662; e-mail parepdam@scs-net.org; Ambassador NAWABZADA AMINALLAH KHAN RAISANI.

Panama: Bldg 10, Office 4, rue al-Bizm, Malki St, Damascus; tel. (11) 3739001; fax (11) 3738801; e-mail consuladodepanamadamasco@gmail.com; Chargé d'affaires CARLOS A. DE GRACIA.

Philippines: BP 36849, 56 rue Hamzeh bin al-Mutaleb, Mezzeh, Damascus; tel. (11) 6132626; fax (11) 6132626; e-mail info@ambaphilsyria.com; Ambassador WILFREDO R. CUYUGAN.

Poland: BP 501, rue Baha Eddin Aita, Abou Roumaneh, Damascus; tel. (11) 3333010; fax (11) 3315318; e-mail damaszek.amb.sekretariat@msz.gov.pl; internet www.damaszek.polemb.net; Ambassador MICHAŁ MURKOCIŃSKI.

Qatar: BP 4188, rue Ahmed Shouki, Abou Roumaneh, Damascus; e-mail damascus@mofa.gov.qa; tel. (11) 3336717; fax (11) 3342455; Ambassador ZAYED BIN SAEED AL-KHAYAREEN.

Romania: BP 4454, 8 rue Ibrahim Hanano, Damascus; tel. (11) 3327570; fax (11) 3327571; e-mail damascamb@gmail.com; Ambassador DANUT FLORIN SANDOVICI.

Russia: BP 3153, rue Umar bin al-Khattab, al-Dawi, Damascus; tel. (11) 4423155; fax (11) 4423182; e-mail rusemb@scs-net.org; Ambassador SERGEI KIRPICHENKO.

Saudi Arabia: rue al-Jala'a, Abou Roumaneh, Damascus; tel. (11) 3334914; fax (11) 3337383; e-mail syemb@mofa.gov.sa; Chargé d'affaires a.i. FALEH AL-REHAILI.

Serbia: BP 739, 18 rue al-Jala'a, Abou Roumaneh, Damascus; tel. (11) 3336222; fax (11) 3333690; e-mail ambasada@srbija-damask.org; internet www.srbija-damask.org; Ambassador JOVAN VUJASINOVIĆ.

Slovakia: BP 33115, 158 rue al-Shafi, Mezzeh Est, Damascus; tel. (11) 6132114; fax (11) 6132598; e-mail emb.damascus@mzv.sk; internet www.damascus.mfa.sk; Ambassador MILAN HUPCEJ.

Somalia: ave Ata Ayoubi, al-Afif, Damascus; Ambassador BASHIR HAJI OSMAN.

South Africa: BP 9141, rue al-Ghazaoui, 7 Jadet Kouraish, Mezzeh Ouest, Damascus; tel. (11) 61351520; fax (11) 6111714; e-mail admin.damascus@foreign.gov.za; Ambassador SHAUN EDWARD BYNEVELDT.

Spain: BP 392, rue al-Shafi, Mezzeh Est, Damascus; tel. (11) 6132900; fax (11) 6132941; e-mail emb.damascus@maec.es; Ambassador JULIO ALBI DE LA CUESTA.

Sudan: BP 3940, Immeuble al-Kassar Assadi, Damascus; tel. (11) 6112901; fax (11) 6112904; e-mail sud-emb@net.sy; Ambassador ABD AL-RAHMAN DIRAR.

Sweden: BP 4266, Immeuble du Patriarcat Catholique, rue Chakib Arslan, Abou Roumaneh, Damascus; tel. (11) 33400700; fax (11) 3327749; e-mail ambassaden.damaskus@foreign.ministry.se; internet www.swedenabroad.com/damascus; Ambassador NIKLAS KEBBON.

Switzerland: BP 234, 2 rue al-Shafi, Mezzeh Est, Damascus; tel. (11) 6111972; fax (11) 6111976; e-mail dam.vertretung@eda.admin.ch; internet www.eda.admin.ch/damascus; Ambassador MARTIN AESCHBACHER.

Tunisia: BP 4114, 6 rue al-Shafi, blvd Fahim, Mezzeh, Damascus; tel. (11) 6132700; fax (11) 6132704; e-mail at.damas@net.sy; Ambassador MUHAMMAD AOUITI.

Turkey: BP 3738, 56–58 ave Ziad bin Abou Soufian, Damascus; tel. (11) 33501930; fax (11) 3339243; e-mail turkemb.damascus@mfa.gov.tr; internet damascus.emb.mfa.gov.tr; Ambassador ÖMER ONHUN.

Turkmenistan: Miset, 4097 Ruki el-Din, 2e étage, Damascus; tel. (11) 2241834; fax (11) 3320905.

Ukraine: BP 33944, 14 rue al-Salam, Mezzeh Est, Damascus; tel. (11) 6113016; fax (11) 6121355; e-mail emb_sy@mfa.gov.ua; internet www.mfa.gov.ua/syria; Ambassador OLEH SEMENETS.

United Arab Emirates: Immeuble Housami, 62 rue Raouda, Damascus; tel. (11) 3330308; fax (11) 3327961; e-mail emirate-damas@net.sy; Ambassador SALEM AL-QATAM AL-ZA'ABI.

United Kingdom: BP 37, Immeuble Kotob, 11 rue Muhammad Kurd Ali, Malki, Damascus; tel. (11) 3391513; fax (11) 3921873; e-mail british.embassy.damascus@fco.gov.uk; internet ukinsyria.fco.gov.uk; Ambassador SIMON COLLIS.

USA: BP 29, 2 rue al-Mansour, Abou Roumaneh, Damascus; tel. (11) 33914444; fax (11) 33913999; e-mail damasweb-query@state.gov; internet syria.usembassy.gov; Ambassador ROBERT S. FORD.

Venezuela: BP 2403, Immeuble al-Tabbah, 5 rue Lisaneddin bin al-Khateb, place Rauda, Damascus; tel. (11) 6124835; fax (11) 6124833; e-mail embavenez@tarassul.sy; internet www.embavensiria.com; Ambassador IMAD SAAB SAAB.

Yemen: Abou Roumaneh, Charkassieh, Damascus; Ambassador (vacant).

Judicial System

The Courts of Law in Syria are principally divided into two juridical court systems: Courts of General Jurisdiction and Administrative Courts. Since 1973 the Supreme Constitutional Court has been established as the paramount body of the Syrian judicial structure.

THE SUPREME CONSTITUTIONAL COURT

This is the highest court in Syria. It has specific jurisdiction over: (i) judicial review of the constitutionality of laws and legislative decrees; (ii) investigation of charges relating to the legality of the election of members of the Majlis al-Sha'ab (People's Assembly); (iii) trial of infractions committed by the President of the Republic in the exercise of his functions; (iv) resolution of positive and negative jurisdictional conflicts and determination of the competent court between the different juridical court systems, as well as other bodies exercising judicial competence. The Supreme Constitutional Court is composed of a Chief Justice and four Justices. They are appointed by decree of the President of the Republic for a renewable period of four years.

Chief Justice of the Supreme Court: ADNAN ZUREIQ, Damascus; tel. (11) 3331902.

COURTS OF GENERAL JURISDICTION

The Courts of General Jurisdiction in Syria are divided into six categories: (i) The Court of Cassation; (ii) The Courts of Appeal; (iii) The Tribunals of First Instance; (iv) The Tribunals of Peace; (v) The Personal Status Courts; (vi) The Courts for Minors. Each of the above categories (except the Personal Status Courts) is divided into Civil, Penal and Criminal Chambers.

(i) The Court of Cassation: This is the highest court of general jurisdiction. Final judgments rendered by Courts of Appeal in penal and civil litigations may be petitioned to the Court of Cassation by the Defendant or the Public Prosecutor in penal and criminal litigations, and by any of the parties in interest in civil litigations, on grounds of defective application or interpretation of the law as stated in the challenged judgment, on grounds of irregularity of form or procedure, or violation of due process, and on grounds of defective reasoning of judgment rendered. The Court of Cassation is composed of a President, seven Vice-Presidents and 31 other Justices (Councillors).

(ii) The Courts of Appeal: Each court has geographical jurisdiction over one governorate (*mohafazat*). Each court is divided into Penal and Civil Chambers. There are Criminal Chambers which try felonies only. The Civil Chambers hear appeals filed against judgments rendered by the Tribunals of First Instance and the Tribunals of Peace. Each Court of Appeal is composed of a President and sufficient numbers of Vice-Presidents (Presidents of Chambers) and Superior Judges (Councillors). There are 54 Courts of Appeal.

(iii) The Tribunals of First Instance: In each governorate there are one or more Tribunals of First Instance, each of which is divided into several Chambers for penal and civil litigations. Each Chamber is composed of one judge. There are 72 Tribunals of First Instance.

(iv) The Tribunals of Peace: In the administrative centre of each governorate, and in each district, there are one or more Tribunals of Peace, which have jurisdiction over minor civil and penal litigations. There are 227 Tribunals of Peace.

(v) Personal Status Courts: These courts deal with marriage, divorce, etc. For Muslims, each court consists of one judge, the 'Qadi Shari'i'. For Druzes, there is one court consisting of one judge, the 'Qadi Mazhabi'. For non-Muslim communities, there are courts for Roman Catholics, Orthodox believers, Protestants and Jews.

(vi) Courts for Minors: The constitution, officers, sessions, jurisdiction and competence of these courts are determined by a special law.

PUBLIC PROSECUTION

Public prosecution is headed by the Attorney-General, assisted by a number of Senior Deputy and Deputy Attorneys-General, and a sufficient number of chief prosecutors, prosecutors and assistant prosecutors. Public prosecution is represented at all levels of the Courts of General Jurisdiction in all criminal and penal litigations and also in certain civil litigations as required by the law. Public prosecution controls and supervises enforcement of penal judgments.

SYRIA

ADMINISTRATIVE COURTS SYSTEM

The Administrative Courts have jurisdiction over litigations involving the state or any of its governmental agencies. The Administrative Courts system is divided into two courts: the Administrative Courts and the Judicial Administrative Courts, of which the paramount body is the High Administrative Court.

MILITARY COURTS

The Military Courts deal with criminal litigations against military personnel of all ranks and penal litigations against officers only. There are two military courts: one in Damascus, the other in Aleppo. Each court is composed of three military judges. There are other military courts, consisting of one judge, in every governorate, which deal with penal litigations against military personnel below the rank of officer. The different military judgments can be petitioned to the Court of Cassation.

Religion

The majority of Syrians follow a form of Islamic Sunni orthodoxy. There are also a considerable number of religious minorities: Shi'a Muslims; Isma'ili Muslims; the Isma'ili of the Salamiya district, whose spiritual head is the Aga Khan; a large number of Druzes, the Nusairis or Alawites of the Jebel Ansariyeh (a schism of the Shi'ite branch of Islam, to which about 11% of the population, including President Assad, belong) and the Yezidis of the Jebel Sinjar; and a minority of Christians.

The Constitution states only that 'Islam shall be the religion of the head of the state'. The original draft of the 1973 Constitution made no reference to Islam at all, and this clause was inserted only as a compromise after public protest. The Syrian Constitution is thus unique among the constitutions of Arab states (excluding Lebanon) with a clear Muslim majority in not enshrining Islam as the religion of the state itself.

ISLAM

Grand Mufti: Sheikh AHMAD BADER EL-DIN HASSOUN, BP 7410, Damascus; tel. (11) 2688601; fax (11) 2637650; e-mail info@drhassoun.com; internet www.drhassoun.com.

CHRISTIANITY

Orthodox Churches

Greek Orthodox Patriarchate of Antioch and all the East: BP 9, Damascus; tel. (11) 5424400; fax (11) 5424404; e-mail info@antiochpat.org; internet www.antiochpat.org; Patriarch of Antioch and all the East His Beatitude IGNATIUS HAZIM; has jurisdiction over Syria, Lebanon, Iran and Iraq.

Syrian Orthodox Patriarchate of Antioch and all the East: BP 22260, Bab Touma, Damascus; tel. (11) 54498989; e-mail patriarch-z-iwas@scs-net.org; Patriarch of Antioch and all the East His Holiness IGNATIUS ZAKKA I IWAS; the Syrian Orthodox Church includes one Catholicose (of India), 37 Metropolitans and one Bishop, and has an estimated 4m. adherents throughout the world.

The Armenian Apostolic Church is also represented in Syria.

The Roman Catholic Church

Armenian Rite

Patriarchal Exarchate of Syria: Exarchat Patriarcal Arménien Catholique, BP 22281, Bab Touma, Damascus; tel. (11) 5413820; fax (11) 5419431; e-mail damazmcath@hotmail.com; f. 1985; represents the Patriarch of Cilicia (resident in Beirut, Lebanon); 4,500 adherents (31 Dec. 2010); Exarch Patriarchal Bishop JOSEPH ARNAOUTIAN.

Archdiocese of Aleppo: Archevêché Arménien Catholique, BP 97, 33 al-Tilal, Aleppo; tel. (21) 2123946; fax (21) 2116637; e-mail armen.cath@mail.sy; 17,500 adherents (31 Dec. 2007); Archbishop BOUTROS MARAYATI.

Diocese of Kamichlié: Evêché Arménien Catholique, BP 17, al-Qamishli; tel. (53) 424211; fax (53) 426211; e-mail armen.cath@mail.sy; 4,000 adherents (31 Dec. 2007); Bishop JOSEPH ARNAOUTI.

Chaldean Rite

Diocese of Aleppo: Evêché Chaldéen Catholique, BP 4643, 1 rue Patriarche Elias IV Mouawwad, Soulémaniyé, Aleppo; tel. (21) 4441660; fax (21) 4600800; e-mail audoa@scs-net.org; 15,000 adherents (31 Dec. 2007); Bishop ANTOINE AUDO.

Latin Rite

Apostolic Vicariate of Aleppo: BP 327, 19 rue al-Fourat, Aleppo; tel. (21) 2682399; fax (21) 2689413; e-mail vicariatlatin@mail.sy; f. 1762; 12,000 adherents (31 Dec. 2008); Vicar Apostolic GIUSEPPE NAZZARO (Titular Bishop of Forma).

Maronite Rite

Archdiocese of Aleppo: Archevêché Maronite, BP 203, 57 rue Fares el-Khoury, Aleppo; tel. and fax (21) 2118048; e-mail maronite@scs-net.org; 4,000 adherents (31 Dec. 2007); Archbishop YOUSUF ANIS ABI-AAD.

Archdiocese of Damascus: Archevêché Maronite, BP 2179, 6 rue al-Deir, Bab Touma, Damascus; tel. (11) 5412888; fax (11) 5436002; e-mail mgrsamirnassar@gmail.com; f. 1527; 14,000 adherents (31 Dec. 2007); Archbishop SAMIR NASSAR.

Diocese of Latakia: Evêché Maronite, BP 161, rue Hamrat, Tartous; tel. (43) 223433; fax (43) 322939; 33,000 adherents (31 Dec. 2007); Bishop YOUSUF MASSOUD MASSOUD.

Melkite Rite

Melkite Greek Catholic Patriarchate of Antioch: Patriarcat Grec-Melkite Catholique, BP 22249, 12 ave al-Zeitoun, Bab Charki, Damascus; tel. (11) 5441030; fax (11) 5417900; e-mail pat.melk@scs-net.org; internet www.pgc-lb.org; or BP 70071, Antélias, Lebanon; tel. (4) 413111; fax (4) 418113; f. 1724; jurisdiction over 1.5m. Melkites throughout the world (incl. 234,000 in Syria); Patriarch of Antioch and all the East, of Alexandria and of Jerusalem His Beatitude GREGORIOS III LAHAM; the Melkite Church includes the patriarchal sees of Damascus, Cairo and Jerusalem and four other archdioceses in Syria; seven archdioceses in Lebanon; one in Jordan; one in Israel; and six eparchies (in the USA, Brazil, Canada, Australia, Venezuela, Argentina and Mexico).

Archdiocese of Aleppo: Archevêché Grec-Catholique, BP 146, 9 place Farhat, Aleppo; tel. (21) 2119307; fax (21) 2119308; e-mail gr.melkcath@mail.sy; 17,000 adherents (31 Dec. 2007); Archbishop JEAN-CLÉMENT JEANBART.

Archdiocese of Busra and Hauran: Archevêché Grec-Catholique, Khabab, Hauran; tel. (15) 855012; e-mail derbosra@hotmail.com; 27,000 adherents (31 Dec. 2007); Archbishop BOULOS NASSIF BORKHOCHE.

Archdiocese of Homs: Archevêché Grec-Catholique, BP 1525, rue el-Mo'tazila, Boustan al-Diwan, Homs; tel. (31) 2482587; fax (31) 2464587; e-mail isidore_battikha@yahoo.fr; 30,000 adherents (31 Dec. 2007); Archbishop (vacant).

Archdiocese of Latakia: Archevêché Grec-Catholique, BP 151, rue al-Moutannabi, Latakia; tel. (41) 460777; fax (41) 476002; e-mail saouafnicolas@yahoo.fr; 10,000 adherents (31 Dec. 2007); Archbishop NICOLAS SAWAF.

Syrian Rite

Archdiocese of Aleppo: Archevêché Syrien Catholique, place Mère Teresa de Calcutta, Azizié, Aleppo; tel. (21) 2126750; fax (21) 2126752; e-mail a_chahda@hotmail.com; 8,000 adherents (31 Dec. 2007); Archbishop DENYS ANTOINE CHAHDA.

Archdiocese of Damascus: Archevêché Syrien Catholique, BP 2129, 157 rue Al-Mustaqeem, Bab Charki, Damascus; tel. and fax (11) 5445343; e-mail psamirm@cyberia.met.lb; 14,000 adherents (31 Dec. 2007); Archbishop GRÉGOIRE ELIAS TABÉ.

Archdiocese of Hassaké-Nisibi: Archevêché Syrien Catholique, BP 6, Hassaké; tel. (52) 320812; e-mail b.hindo@hotmail.com; 35,000 adherents (31 Dec. 2007); Archbishop JACQUES BEHNAN HINDO.

Archdiocese of Homs: Archevêché Syrien Catholique, BP 303, rue Hamidieh, Homs; tel. (31) 221575; fax (21) 224350; 10,000 adherents (31 Dec. 2007); Archbishop THÉOPHILE GEORGES KASSAB.

The Anglican Communion

Within the Episcopal Church in Jerusalem and the Middle East, Syria forms part of the diocese of Jerusalem (see the chapter on Israel).

Other Christian Groups

Protestants in Syria are largely adherents of either the National Evangelical Synod of Syria and Lebanon or the Union of Armenian Evangelical Churches in the Near East (for details of both organizations, see the chapter on Lebanon).

The Press

Since the Baath Arab Socialist Party came to power, the structure of the press has been modified according to socialist patterns. Most publications are issued by political, religious or professional associations (such as trade unions), and several are published by govern-

SYRIA

ment ministries. However, two privately owned daily newspapers have been launched in recent years. Anyone wishing to establish a new paper or periodical must apply for a licence.

The major dailies are *Al-Baath* (the organ of the party), *Tishreen*, *Al-Thawra* and the *Syria Times*, all published in Damascus.

PRINCIPAL DAILIES

Al-Baath (Renaissance): BP 9389, Autostrade Mezzeh, Damascus; tel. (11) 6622142; fax (11) 6622099; e-mail baath@baath-party.org; internet www.albaath.news.sy; f. 1946; morning; Arabic; organ of the Baath Arab Socialist Party; Editor ILYAS MURAD; circ. 45,000.

Baladna: BP 2000, al-Huda Bldg, al-Eskandaria St, Damascus; tel. (11) 6122515; fax (11) 6122514; e-mail info@ug.com.sy; internet www.baladnaonline.net; Arabic; privately owned; publ. by United Group for Publishing, Advertising and Marketing; Chief Editor SAMIR AL-SHIBANI.

Champress: Immeuble Arnos, place Arnos, Damascus; tel. (11) 44681199; fax (11) 44681190; e-mail mail@champress.com; internet www.champress.com; privately owned; political; online only; Arabic; Dir ALI JAMALO.

Al-Fida' (Redemption): Hama; Al-Wahda Foundation for Press, Printing and Publishing, BP 2448, Dawar Kafr Soussat, Damascus; tel. (11) 225219; fax (11) 2216851; e-mail fedaa@thawra.com; internet fedaa.alwehda.gov.sy; morning; Arabic; political; Editor A. AULWANI; circ. 4,000.

Al-Furat: Al-Wahda Foundation for Press, Printing and Publishing, BP 2448, Dawar Kafr Soussat, Damascus; tel. (51) 224494; fax (51) 218418; e-mail furat@thawra.com; internet furat.alwehda.gov.sy; Editor ADNAN OWAID.

Al-Horubat: Homs; Al-Wahda Foundation for Press, Printing and Publishing, BP 2448, Dawar Kafr Soussat, Damascus; tel. (11) 225219; fax (11) 2216851; e-mail ouroba@thawra.com; internet ouruba.alwehda.gov.sy; morning; Arabic; political; circ. 5,000.

Al-Jamahir (The People): Aleppo; Al-Wahda Foundation for Press, Printing and Publishing, BP 2448, Dawar Kafr Soussat, Damascus; tel. (21) 214309; fax (21) 214308; e-mail jamahir@thawra.com; internet jamahir.alwehda.gov.sy; Arabic; political; Chief Editor MORTADA BAKACH; circ. 10,000.

Syria Times: BP 5452, Medan, Damascus; tel. (11) 2247359; fax (11) 2231374; e-mail syriatimes@teshreen.com; internet syriatimes.tishreen.info; English; publ. by Tishreen Foundation for Press and Publishing; Editor FOUAD MARDOUD; circ. 15,000.

Al-Thawra (Revolution): Al-Wahda Foundation for Press, Printing and Publishing, BP 2448, Dawar Kafr Soussat, Damascus; tel. (11) 2210850; fax (11) 2216851; e-mail admin@thawra.com; internet thawra.alwehda.gov.sy; f. 1963; morning; Arabic; political; Editor ASAAD ABBOUD; circ. 40,000.

Tishreen (October): BP 5452, Medan, Damascus; tel. (11) 2131100; fax (11) 2246860; e-mail tnp@mail.sy; internet www.tishreen.info; Arabic; publ. by Tishreen Foundation for Press and Publishing; Chief Editor KHALAF AL-JARAAD; circ. 50,000.

Al-Wahda (Unity): Latakia; Al-Wahda Foundation for Press, Printing and Publishing, BP 2448, Dawar Kafr Soussat, Damascus; tel. (11) 225219; fax (11) 2216851; e-mail wehda@thawra.com; internet wehda.alwehda.gov.sy; Arabic; political.

Al-Watan: Duty Free Zone, Damascus; tel. (11) 2137400; fax (11) 2139928; internet www.alwatan.sy; f. 2006; Arabic; political; privately owned; Chief Editor WADDAH ABED RABBO.

WEEKLIES AND FORTNIGHTLIES

Abyad wa Aswad (White and Black): 8 rue Hekmat Alasale, Almastaba 4, Muhajirin; tel. (11) 3739968; fax (11) 3739949; e-mail a-and-a@scs-net.org; internet www.awaonline.net; f. 2002; weekly; Arabic; political; privately owned; Editor AYMAN AL-DAQUQ.

Al-Iqtisadiya: rue Abd al-Munim Riyad 13, Damascus; tel. (11) 3737344; fax (11) 3737348; e-mail info@iqtissadiya.com; internet www.iqtissadiya.com; f. 2001; weekly; Arabic; economic; privately owned; Editor WADDAH ABD AL-RABBO.

Kantsasar: BP 133, Aleppo; tel. and fax (21) 2246753; e-mail kantsasar@excite.com; internet www.periotem.com; weekly; publ. by Armenian Prelacy of Aleppo; Editor MARY MERDKHANIAN.

Kassioun: BP 35033, Damascus; tel. (11) 3346681; fax (11) 3346681; e-mail general@kassioun.org; internet www.kassioun.org; weekly; publ. by the Syrian Communist Party (Bakdash).

Kifah al-Oummal al-Ishtiraki (The Socialist Workers' Struggle): Fédération Générale des Syndicats des Ouvriers, rue Qanawat, Damascus; weekly; Arabic; labour; publ. by Gen. Fed. of Labour Unions; Editor SAEED AL-HAMAMI.

Al-Maukef al-Riadi (Sport Stance): Al-Wahda Foundation for Press, Printing and Publishing, BP 2448, Dawar Kafr Soussat, Damascus; tel. (11) 225219; e-mail riadi@thawra.com; internet riadi.alwehda.gov.sy; weekly; Arabic; sports; circ. 50,000.

Directory

An-Nour (Light): BP 7394 Damascus; tel. (11) 3324914; fax (11) 3342571; e-mail annour@mail.sy; internet www.an-nour.com; f. 2001; weekly; Arabic; political and cultural; organ of the Syrian Communist Party (Faisal); Editor-in-Chief YAQUB GARRO.

Sawt al-Shaab (Voice of the People): Damascus; f. 1937, but publ. suspended in 1939, 1941, 1947 and 1958; relaunched in 2001; fortnightly; Arabic; organ of the Syrian Communist Party (Bakdash).

OTHER PERIODICALS

Al-Arabieh (The Arab Lady): Syrian Women's Association, BP 3207, Damascus; tel. (11) 3313275; fax (11) 3311078; monthly; Editor MAJEDA KUTEIT.

Al-Fikr al-Askari (The Military Idea): BP 4259, blvd Palestine, Damascus; fax (11) 2125280; f. 1950; 6 a year; Arabic; official military review publ. by the Political Administration Press.

Al-Ghad (Tomorrow): Association of Red Cross and Crescent, BP 6095, rue Maysat, Damascus, tel. (11) 2242552; fax (11) 7777040; monthly; environmental health; Editor K. ABED-RABOU.

Al-Irshad al-Zirai (Agricultural Information): Ministry of Agriculture and Agrarian Reform, rue Jabri, Damascus; tel. (11) 2213613; fax (11) 2216627; 6 a year; Arabic; agriculture.

Jaysh al-Sha'ab (The People's Army): Ministry of Defence, BP 3320, blvd Palestine, Damascus; fax (11) 2125280; f. 1946; monthly; Arabic; army magazine; publ. by the Political Dept of the Syrian Army.

Al-Kalima (The Word): Al-Kalima Association, Aleppo; monthly; Arabic; religious; Publr and Editor FATHALLA SAKAL.

Al-Kanoun (The Law): Ministry of Justice, rue an-Nasr, Damascus; tel. (11) 2214105; fax (11) 2246250; monthly; Arabic; juridical.

Layalina: Damascus; tel. (11) 6122515; fax (11) 6122514; e-mail info@layalinamag.com; internet layalina.sy.pressera.com; monthly; Arabic; social and lifestyle; publ. by United Group for Publishing, Advertising and Marketing; Chair. MAJD SULEIMAN.

Al-Maaloumatieh (Information): National Information Centre, BP 11323, Damascus; tel. (11) 2127551; fax (11) 2127648; e-mail nice@net.sy; f. 1994; quarterly; computer magazine; Editor ABD AL-MAJID AL-RIFAI; circ. 10,000.

Al-Ma'arifa (Knowledge): Ministry of Culture, rue al-Rouda, Damascus; tel. (11) 3336963; f. 1962; monthly; Arabic; literary; Editor ABD AL-KARIM NASIF; circ. 7,500.

Al-Majalla al-Batriarquia (The Magazine of the Patriarchate): Syrian Orthodox Patriarchate, BP 914, Damascus; tel. (11) 4447036; f. 1962; monthly; Arabic; religious; Editor SAMIR ABDOH; circ. 15,000.

Al-Majalla al-Tibbiya al-Arabiyya (Arab Medical Magazine): rue al-Jala'a, Damascus; tel. (11) 3331890; e-mail kfkallas@net.sy; internet www.arabmedmag.com; monthly; Arabic and English; publ. by Arab Medical Comm; Dir KHALID KALLAS; Editor Dr AL-LOUJAMI MAZEN.

Majallat Majma' al-Lughat al-Arabiyya bi-Dimashq (Magazine of the Arab Language Academy of Damascus): Arab Academy of Damascus, BP 327, Damascus; tel. (11) 3713145; fax (11) 3733363; e-mail mla@net.sy; f. 1921; quarterly; Arabic; Islamic culture and Arabic literature, Arabic scientific and cultural terminology; Chief Editor Dr SHAKER FAHAM; circ. 1,600.

Al-Mouallem al-Arabi (The Arab Teacher): National Union of Teachers, BP 2842-3034, Damascus; tel. (11) 225219; f. 1948; monthly; Arabic; educational and cultural.

Al-Mouhandis al-Arabi (The Arab Engineer): Order of Syrian Engineers and Architects, BP 2336, Immeuble Dar al-Mouhandisen, place Azme, Damascus; tel. (11) 2214916; fax (11) 2216948; e-mail lbosea@net.sy; f. 1961; 4 a year; Arabic; scientific and cultural; Dir Eng. M. FAYEZ MAHFOUZ; Chief Editor Dr Eng. AHMAD AL-GHAFARI; circ. 50,000.

Al-Munadel (The Militant): c/o BP 11512, Damascus; fax (11) 2126935; f. 1965; monthly; Arabic; magazine of Baath Arab Socialist Party; Dir Dr FAWWAZ SAYYAGH; circ. 100,000.

Al-Nashra al-Iktissad (Economic Bulletin): Damascus Chamber of Commerce; tel. (11) 2218339; fax (11) 2225874; e-mail dcc@dcc-sy.com; f. 1922; quarterly; finance and investment; Editor GHASSAN KALLA; circ. 3,000.

Al-Sinaa (Industry): Damascus Chamber of Commerce, BP 1305, rue Mou'awiah, Harika, Damacus; tel. (11) 2222205; fax (11) 2245981; e-mail dcc@dcc-sy.com; monthly; commerce, industry and management; Editor Y. HINDI.

Souriya al-Arabiyya (Arab Syria): Ministry of Information, Immeuble Dar al-Baath, Autostrade Mezzeh, Damascus; tel. (11) 6622141; fax (11) 6617665; monthly; publicity; in four languages.

Syria Today: Baramkeh, Free Zone, Damascus; tel. (11) 88270310; fax (11) 2137343; e-mail mail@syria-today.com; internet www.syria-today.com; monthly; English; economic and social development; Chair. LOUMA TARABINE; Man. Editor FRANCESCA DE CHÂTEL.

SYRIA

Al-Tamaddon al-Islami (Islamic Civilization Society): Darwichiyah, Damascus; tel. (11) 2240562; fax (11) 3733563; e-mail isltmddn@hotmail.com; f. 1932; monthly; Arabic; religious; published by Al-Tamaddon al-Islami Assen; Pres. of Assen AHMAD MOUAZ AL-KHATIB.

Al-Yakza (The Awakening): Al-Yakza Association, BP 6677, rue Sisi, Aleppo; f. 1935; monthly; Arabic; literary social review of charitable institution; Dir HUSNI ABD AL-MASSIH; circ. 12,000.

Al-Zira'a (Agriculture): Ministry of Agriculture and Agrarian Reform, rue Jabri, Damascus; tel. (11) 2213613; fax (11) 2244023; f. 1985; monthly; Arabic; agriculture; circ. 12,000.

NEWS AGENCY

Syrian Arab News Agency (SANA): BP 2661, Baramka, Damascus; tel. (11) 2129702; fax (11) 2228265; e-mail public-relation@sana.sy; internet www.sana.sy; f. 1966; supplies bulletins on Syrian news to foreign news agencies; 16 offices abroad; 16 foreign correspondents; Dir-Gen. (vacant).

Publishers

Arab Advertising Organization: BP 2842-3034, 28 rue Moutanabbi, Damascus; tel. (11) 2225219; fax (11) 2220754; e-mail sy-adv@net.sy; f. 1963; exclusive govt establishment responsible for advertising; publishes Directory of Commerce and Industry, Damascus International Fair Guide, Daily Bulletin of Official Tenders; Dir-Gen. MONA F. FABAH.

Damascus University Press: Baramkeh, Damascus; tel. (11) 2119890; fax (11) 2235779; e-mail noubough@gmail.com; internet www.damascusuniversity.edu.sy; f. 1923; medicine, engineering, social sciences, law, agriculture, arts, etc.; Dir NOUBOUGH YASSIN.

Dar al-Awael: BP 10181, Damascus; tel. (11) 44676270; fax (11) 44676273; e-mail alawael@daralawael.com; internet www.daralawael.com; f. 1999; academic publr; Dir-Gen. ISMAIL ABDULLAH.

Dar al-Fikr: BP 962, Damascus; tel. (11) 2211166; fax (11) 2239716; e-mail fikr@fikr.com; internet www.fikr.com; f. 1957; Islamic studies, academic and gen. non-fiction; Dir-Gen. MUHAMMAD ADNAN SALIM.

Institut Français du Proche-Orient: BP 344, Damascus; tel. (11) 3330214; fax (11) 3327887; e-mail secretariat@ifporient.org; internet www.ifporient.org; f. 1922; sociology, anthropology, Islamic studies, archaeology, history, language and literature, arts, philosophy, geography, religion; publs include *Syria* (bi-annual journal), *Bulletin d'Etudes Orientales* (annual journal), *Bibliotheque Archeologique et Historique* (series), *Publications de l'Instituit Français de Damas* (series); Dir FRANÇOIS BURGAT.

OFA-Business Consulting Center—Documents Service: BP 3550, 3 place Chahbandar, Damascus; tel. (11) 3318237; fax (11) 4426021; e-mail ofa1@net.sy; internet www.ofa-bcc.com; f. 1964; numerous periodicals, monographs and surveys on political and economic affairs; Dir-Gen. SAMIR A. DARWICH; has one affiliated br., OFA-Business Consulting Centre (foreign co representation and services).

The Political Administration Press: BP 3320, blvd Palestine, Damascus; fax (11) 2125280; publishes *Al-Fikr al-Askari* (six a year) and *Jaysh al-Sha'ab* (monthly).

Syrian Documentation Papers: BP 2712, Damascus; f. 1968; publishers of *Bibliography of the Middle East* (annual), *General Directory of the Press and Periodicals in the Arab World* (annual), and numerous publications on political, economic, literary and social affairs, as well as legislative texts concerning Syria and the Arab world; Dir-Gen. LOUIS FARÈS.

Tishreen Foundation for Press and Publishing: BP 5452, Medan, Damascus; tel. (11) 2131100; fax (11) 2246860; publishes *Syria Times* and *Tishreen* (dailies).

United Group for Publishing, Advertising and Marketing: Immeuble al-Huda, rue al-Eskandaria, Mazzeh, Damascus; tel. (11) 6122515; fax (11) 6122514; e-mail info@ug.com.sy; internet www.ug.com.sy; publs *Baladna* newspaper, *Layalina* magazine, *What's On* magazine; Chair. MAJD SULEIMAN.

Al-Wahda Foundation for Press, Printing and Publishing (Institut al-Ouedha pour l'impression, édition et distribution): BP 2448, Dawar Kafr Soussat, Damascus; tel. (11) 225219; internet www.alwehda.gov.sy; publs *Al-Fida'*, *Al-Horubat*, *Al-Jamahir*, *Al-Thawra* and *Al-Wahda* (dailies), *Al-Maukef al-Riadi* (weekly) and other commercial publs; Dir-Gen. FAHD DIYAB.

Broadcasting and Communications

TELECOMMUNICATIONS

Syrian Telecommunications Establishment (STE—Syrian Telecom): BP 11774, Autostrade Mezzeh, Damascus; tel. (11) 2240000; fax (11) 6110000; e-mail ste-gm@net.sy; internet www.ste.gov.sy; f. 1975; Gen. Dir Dr NAZEM BAHSAS.

MTN Syria: BP 34474, Immeuble al-Mohandis al-Arabi, Autostrade Mezzeh, Damascus; fax (11) 6666094; e-mail customercare@mtn.com.sy; internet www.mtnsyria.com; f. 2001 as Spacetel Syria; name changed to Areeba Syria in 2004; present name adopted in 2007 following the acquisition of a 75% stake by MTN Group (South Africa); provider of mobile telephone services; Chair. JAMAL RAMADAN; CEO ISMAIL JAROUDI; 129.2m. subscribers (June 2010).

Syriatel: Immeuble STE, 6e étage, rue Thawra, Damascus; tel. (11) 932190000 (mobile); fax (11) 3341917; e-mail info@syriatel.com.sy; internet syriatel.sy; f. 2000; provider of mobile telephone services; Chair. RAMI MAKHLOUF; CEO NADER KALAI; 3.5m. subscribers (Oct. 2007).

BROADCASTING

Radio

General Organization of Radio and Television (ORTAS—Organisme de la Radio-Télévision Arabe Syrienne): place Omayyad, Damascus; tel. (11) 720700; fax (11) 2234930; e-mail contact@rtv.gov.sy; internet www.rtv.gov.sy; radio broadcasts started in 1945, television broadcasts in 1960; radio directorate consists of four departments: Radi, Shaab, Shabab FM, and a multilingual news service; television directorate operates one satellite and two terrestrial channels, broadcasting in Arabic, English and French; Dir-Gen. FAYEZ AL-SAYEGH; Dirs NAIF HAMMOUD (Radio), Dr FOUAD SHERBAJI (Television).

Television

General Organization of Radio and Television: see Radio.

Addounia TV: Damascus; tel. (11) 4472630; fax (11) 4472632; e-mail info@addounia.tv; internet www.addounia.tv; privately owned news channel; awarded broadcasting licence mid-2007; began broadcasting Oct. 2008; Gen. Man. FOUAD AL-SHARBAJI.

Finance

(cap. = capital; res = reserves; dep. = deposits; m.= million; brs = branches; amounts in £S unless otherwise indicated)

BANKING

Central Bank

Central Bank of Syria (Banque Centrale de Syrie): place du 17 avril, Damascus; tel. (11) 2212642; fax (11) 2248329; e-mail info@bcs.gov.sy; internet www.banquecentrale.gov.sy; f. 1956; cap. and res 5,027m., dep. 620,946m. (Dec. 2008); Gov. Dr ADIB MAYALEH; 12 brs.

Other Banks

Agricultural Co-operative Bank: BP 4325, rue al-Tajehiz, Damascus; tel. and fax (11) 2213462; fax (11) 2241261; e-mail syrianagrobank@gmail.com; internet www.agrobank.org; f. 1888; cap. 10,000m., res 671m., dep. 12,000m. (Dec. 2001); Chair. Dr ABD AL-RAZZAQ KASSEM; 106 brs.

Arab Bank Syria SA (ABS): BP 38, rue al-Mahdi bin Barakeh, Abou Roumaneh, Damascus; tel. (11) 3348125; fax (11) 3349844; e-mail ali.zatar@arabbank-syria.com; internet www.arabbank-syria.com; f. 2005; jt venture between Syrian investors (51%) and Arab Bank (Jordan—49%); private commercial bank; cap. 3,000m., res 180m., dep. 30,533m. (Dec. 2009); Chair. Dr KHALID WASSIF AL-WAZANI; Gen. Man. MUHAMMAD AL-HASSAN; 9 brs.

Bank Audi Syria SA: BP 6228, Damascus; e-mail contactus.syria@banqueaudi.com; internet www.banqueaudi.com/basy/syria.html; f. 2005; 47% owned by Audi Saradar Group (Lebanon), 26% by Syrian investors, 2% by a Saudi investor; remaining 25% oversubscribed in an initial public offering in Aug. 2005; private commercial bank; cap. 5,000m., res 171m., dep. 68,114m. (Dec. 2009); Chair. GEORGES ACHI; CEO BASSEL S. HAMWI; 19 brs.

Bank of Syria and Overseas: BP 3103, Harika-Bab Barid, Lawyers' Syndicate Bldg, nr Chamber of Commerce, Damascus; tel. (11) 2460560; fax (11) 2460555; e-mail bsomail@bso.com.sy; internet www.bso.com.sy; f. 2004; jt venture between Banque du Liban et d'Outre Mer (BLOM, Lebanon—39%), the World Bank's Int. Finance Corpn (10%) and Syrian investors (51%); private commercial bank; cap. 3,000m., res 571m., dep. 66,153m. (Dec. 2009); Chair. Dr RATEB AL-SHALLAH; CEO AMR AZHARI; 11 brs.

Banque BEMO Saudi Fransi SA (BBSF): 39 rue Ayyar, Salhiah, Damascus; tel. (11) 2317778; fax (11) 2318778; e-mail bbsf@mail.sy; internet www.bbsfbank.com; f. 2004; jt venture between Syrian investors (51%), Banque Saudi Fransi (Saudi Arabia—27%) and Banque Européenne pour le Moyen-Orient (Lebanon—22%); private commercial bank; cap. 3,250m., res 483m., dep. 92,462m. (Dec. 2009); Chair. RIAD OBEGI; Gen. Man. and CEO ROBIN DE MOUXY; 22 brs.

Byblos Bank Syria: BP 5424, al-Chaalan, rue Amine Loutfi Hafez, Damascus; tel. (11) 3348240; fax (11) 3348205; e-mail byblosbanksyria@byblosbank.com; internet www.byblosbank.com.lb/aboutbbkgroup/bbk_sa/board/index.shtml; f. 2005; 41.5% owned by Byblos Bank SAL (Lebanon), 51% by Syrian investors and 7.5% by the Org. of Petroleum Exporting Countries' Fund for Int. Devt; private commercial bank; cap. 2,000m., res −36m., dep. 29,877m. (Dec. 2009); Chair. SEMAAN BASSIL; 9 brs.

CHAM Bank: BP 33979, place al-Najmeh, Damascus; tel. (11) 3348720; fax (11) 3348731; e-mail info@chambank.com; internet www.chambank.com; f. 2006; jt venture between Dar Investment Co (Kuwait—12.5%), Commercial Bank of Kuwait (10%), Islamic Devt Bank (Kuwait—9%) and several Syrian and other Gulf investors; cap. 2,501m., dep. 8,793m., total assets 11,073m. (Dec. 2009); private commercial bank run on Islamic principles; Chair. JAMAL ABD AL-HAMID AL-MUTAW'A; Man. Dir ALI IBRAHIM ABDULLA.

Commercial Bank of Syria (Banque Commerciale de Syrie): BP 933, place Yousuf al-Azmeh, Damascus; tel. (11) 2218890; fax (11) 2216975; e-mail cbos@mail.sy; internet www.cbs-bank.com; f. 1967; govt-owned bank; cap. US $1,616m., res $699m., dep. $13,237m. (Dec. 2009); Chair. MUHAMMAD YASSER MURTADA; Gen. Man. Dr DOURAID DERGHAM; 84 brs.

Industrial Bank: BP 7578, Immeuble Dar al-Mohandessin, rue Maysaloon, Damascus; tel. and fax (11) 2222222; e-mail info@industrialbank.gov.sy; internet www.industrialbank.gov.sy; f. 1959; nationalized bank providing finance for industry; cap. 257m., total assets 8,131m. (Dec. 2001); Gen. Man. ANIS AL-MARAWI; 17 brs.

The International Bank for Trade and Finance: place Hejazz, Damascus; tel. (11) 2460500; fax (11) 2460505; e-mail info@ibtf.com; internet www.ibtf.com.sy; f. 2004; 49% owned by Housing Bank for Trade and Finance (Jordan), 51% by Syrian investors; cap. 3,000m., res 488m., dep. 57,402m. (Dec. 2009); private commercial bank; Chair. Dr MICHAEL MARTO; CEO SULTAN AL-ZU'BI; 30 brs.

Popular Credit Bank: BP 2841, 6e étage, Immeuble Dar al-Mohandessin, rue Maysaloon, Damascus; tel. (11) 2227604; fax (11) 2211291; f. 1967; govt-owned bank; provides loans to the services sector and is sole authorized issuer of savings certificates; Pres. and Gen. Man. MUHAMMAD HASSAN AL-HOUJJEIRI; 50 brs.

Real Estate Bank: BP 2337, place Yousuf al-Azmeh, Damascus; tel. (11) 2218602; fax (11) 2233107; e-mail realestate@realestate-sy.com; internet www.reb.sy; f. 1966; govt-owned bank; provides loans and grants for housing, schools, hospitals and hotel construction; cap. 10,000m., res 6,051m., dep 167,003m. (Dec. 2009); Chair. MUHAMMAD SALEH KENG; Gen. Man. Dr MULHAM DIBO; 21 brs.

Syria International Islamic Bank: BP 35494, Damascus; tel. (11) 2241135; fax (11) 2241132; e-mail info@siib.sy; internet www.siib.sy; f. 2007; 49% Qatari-owned (incl. Qatar Int. Islamic Bank—30%); private commercial bank run on Islamic principles; cap. 5,000m., res −132m., dep. 52,230m. (Dec. 2009); Chair. YOUSUF AHMAD AL-NAAMA; CEO ABD AL-QADER AL-DUWAIK; 14 brs.

Syrian Lebanese Commercial Bank SAL (SLCB): c/o Commercial Bank of Syria, BP 933, Immeuble G.M., 6e étage, place Yousuf Azmeh, Damascus; tel. (11) 2225206; fax (11) 2243224; e-mail hamra@slcbk.com; internet www.slcb.com.lb; f. 1974; 84.2% owned by Commercial Bank of Syria, 10% by Banque du Crédit Populaire SAL, 5% by Syrian Insurance Co; head office in Beirut, Lebanon; brs in Damascus and Aleppo; cap. 125,000m., res 26,331m., dep. 516,142m. (Dec. 2009); Chair. and Gen. Man. Dr DOURAID AHMAD DERGHAM; 2 brs.

STOCK EXCHANGE

Six companies were listed on the Damascus Securities Exchange when it opened for trading in March 2009.

Damascus Securities Exchange: BP 6564, Damascus; tel. (11) 5190000; fax (11) 5190099; e-mail info@dse.sy; internet www.dse.sy; f. 2009; 18 listed cos (Sept. 2010); Chair. Dr RATEB AL-SHALLAH.

Supervisory Body

Syrian Commission on Financial Markets and Securities: BP 31845, Damascus; tel. (11) 3310487; fax (11) 3310722; e-mail info@scfms.sy; internet www.scfms.sy; f. 2005; Chair. MUHAMMAD AL-IMADY.

INSURANCE

A legislative decree, issued in 2005, allowed for the establishment of privately owned insurance companies.

Arabia Insurance Co—Syria (AICS): rue al-Alam, Damascus; tel. (11) 6627745; fax (11) 6627750; e-mail arabia-insurance@arabiasyria.com; f. 2006; Asst Gen. Man. ROGER COTON.

General Social Security Organization: BP 2684, rue Port Said, Damascus; tel. (11) 2316932; fax (11) 2323115; e-mail taminat@gov.sy; internet www.taminat.gov.sy; Dir-Gen. KHALAF AL-ABDULLAH.

Syria International Insurance (Arobe Syria): BP 33015, Immeuble Malki 18, rue Zuheir Ben Abi Sulma, Rawda, Damascus; fax (11) 3348144; e-mail info@aropesyria.com; internet www.aropesyria.com; f. 2006; owned by Arope Insurance (Lebanon); all classes of insurance; Chair. AMR AZHARI.

Syrian General Organization for Insurance (Syrian Insurance Co): BP 2279, 29 rue Ayyar, Damascus; tel. (11) 2218430; fax (11) 2220494; e-mail syrinsur@syrian-insurance.com; internet www.syrian-insurance.com; f. 1953; auth. cap. 1,000m.; nationalized co; operates throughout Syria; Chair. ADEL AL-KADAMANI; Dir-Gen. SULAYMAN AL-HASSAN.

Syrian Kuwaiti Insurance Co: BP 5778, Immeuble 4, King Abd al-Aziz Al Sa'ud St, Abou Roumaneh, Damascus; tel. (11) 3328060; fax (11) 3328061; e-mail info@skicins.com; internet www.skicins.com; f. 2006; owned by Gulf Insurance Co of Kuwait; cap. 850m.; all classes of insurance; Chair. KHALID SAUD AL-HASSAN.

Trust Syria Insurance Co: BP 30578, Immeuble Trust, rue Murshid Khatir, Damascus; tel. (11) 4472650; fax (11) 4472652; e-mail mail@trustsyria.com; internet www.trustsyria.com; f. 2006; all classes of insurance; CEO TAHER BIN TALEB KAMAL AL-HERAKI.

United Insurance Co: BP 4419, Damascus; tel. (11) 3341933; fax (11) 3341934; e-mail info@uic.com.sy; internet www.uic.com.sy; awarded Syria's first-ever private insurance co licence in 2006; Gen. Man. MUHAMMAD AL-SABI.

Supervisory Body

Syrian Insurance Supervisory Commission (SISC): BP 5648, 5e étage, Immeuble Insurance, rue 29 mai, Damascus; fax (11) 2226224; e-mail sisc.sy@mail.sy; internet www.sisc.sy; f. 2004; Gen. Man. EYAD ZAHRA.

Trade and Industry

STATE ENTERPRISES

Syrian industry is almost entirely under state control. There are national organizations responsible to the appropriate ministry for the operation of all sectors of industry, of which the following are examples:

Cotton Marketing Organization: BP 729, rue Bab al-Faraj, Aleppo; tel. (21) 2238486; fax (21) 2218617; e-mail cmo-aleppo@mail.sy; internet www.cmo.gov.sy; f. 1965; governmental authority for purchase of seed cotton, ginning and sales of cotton lint; Pres. and Dir-Gen. Dr AHMAD SOUHAD GEBBARA.

General Company for Phosphate and Mines (GECOPHAM): BP 288, Homs; tel. (31) 2751122; fax (31) 2751123; e-mail gecopham@net.sy; internet www.gecopham.com; f. 1970; production and export of phosphate rock; Gen. Dir Eng. FARHAN AL-MOHSEN.

General Organization for Engineering Industries: BP 3120, Damascus; tel. (11) 2121834; fax (11) 2116201; e-mail g.o.eng.ind@net.sy; internet www.handasieh.org; 13 subsidiary cos.

General Organization for the Exploitation and Development of the Euphrates Basin (GOEDEB): Rakka; Dir-Gen. Dr Eng. AHMAD SOUHAD GEBBARA.

General Organization for Food Industry (GOFI): BP 105, rue al-Fardous, Damascus; tel. (11) 2457008; fax (11) 2457021; e-mail foodindustry@mail.sy; internet www.syriafoods.net; f. 1975; food-processing and marketing; Chair. and Gen. Dir KHALIL JAWAD.

General Organization for the Textile Industries: BP 620, rue al-Fardoss, Bawabet al-Salhieh, Damascus; tel. (11) 2216200; fax (11) 2216201; e-mail syr-textile@mail.syr; internet textile.org.sy; f. 1975; control and planning of the textile industry and supervision of textile manufacture; 27 subsidiary cos; Dir-Gen. Dr JAMAL AL-OMAR.

Syrian Petroleum Company (SPC): BP 2849, Damascus; tel. (11) 3137935; fax (11) 3137979; e-mail spccom1@scs-net.org; internet www.spc-sy.com; f. 1958; state agency; holds the oil and gas concession for all Syria; exploits the Suweidiya, Karatchouk, Rumelan and Jbeisseh oilfields; also organizes exploration, production and marketing of oil and gas nationally; Chair. and Man. Dir Dr Eng. OMAR AL-HAMAD.

Al-Furat Petroleum Company: BP 7660, Damascus; tel. (11) 6183333; fax (11) 6184444; e-mail afpc@afpc.net.sy; internet www.afpc-sy.com; f. 1985; 50% owned by SPC and 50% by a foreign consortium of Syria Shell Petroleum Devt B.V. and Deminex Syria

SYRIA

GmbH; exploits oilfields in the Euphrates river area; Chair. SAID HUNEDI; Gen. Man. OLE MYKLESTAD.

DEVELOPMENT ORGANIZATIONS

State Planning Commission: Rukeneddin, Damascus; tel. (11) 5161015; fax (11) 5161010; e-mail info@planning.gov.sy; internet www.planning.gov.sy; Head AMER HOSNI LUTFI.

Syrian Consulting Bureau for Development and Investment: BP 12574, Bldg 1, 2nd Floor, cnr Zuheir Ben Abi Sulma St and ibn al-Khateeb St, Rawda, Damascus; tel. (11) 3345757; fax (11) 3340711; e-mail scb@scbdi.com; internet www.scbdi.com; f. 1991; independent; Man. Dir NABIL SUKKAR.

CHAMBERS OF COMMERCE AND INDUSTRY

Federation of Syrian Chambers of Commerce: BP 5909, rue Mousa Ben Nousair, Damascus; tel. (11) 3337344; fax (11) 3331127; e-mail syr-trade@mail.sy; internet www.fedcommsyr.org; f. 1975; Pres. GHASSAN AL-QALLA'A; Sec.-Gen. BASSAM GHRAWI.

Aleppo Chamber of Commerce: BP 1261, Aleppo; tel. (21) 2238236; fax (21) 2213493; e-mail alepchmb@mail.sy; internet www.aleppochamber.org; f. 1885; Pres. Dr HASSAN ZEIDO; Gen. Sec. MUHAMMAD MANSOUR.

Aleppo Chamber of Industry: BP 1859, rue al-Moutanabbi, Aleppo; tel. (21) 3620601; fax (21) 3620040; e-mail info@aleppo-coi.org; internet www.aleppo-coi.org; f. 1935; Pres. SALEH AL-MALLAH; Gen. Man. MUHAMMAD GHREWATI; 7,705 mems.

Damascus Chamber of Commerce: BP 1040, rue Mou'awiah, Damascus; tel. (11) 2245475; fax (11) 2225874; e-mail dcc@net.sy; internet www.dcc-sy.com; f. 1890; Pres. MUHAMMAD GHASSAN AL-QALLAA; Gen. Sec. BASSAM GHRAOUI; 11,500 mems.

Damascus Chamber of Industry: BP 1305, rue Harika Mou'awiah, Damascus; tel. (11) 2215042; fax (11) 2245981; e-mail dci@mail.sy; internet www.dci-syria.org; Pres. Eng. IMAD GHRIWATI; Sec. Eng. AYIMEN MAOULAWI.

Hama Chamber of Commerce and Industry: BP 147, rue al-Kouatly, Hama; tel. (33) 525203; fax (33) 517701; e-mail hamacham@scs-net.org; internet hama-chamber.org; f. 1934; Pres. MU'TAZ GHANDOUR; Man. Dir ABD AL-RAZZAK AL-HAIT.

Homs Chamber of Commerce: BP 440, rue Abou al-Of, Homs; tel. (31) 2471000; fax (31) 2464247; e-mail hcc@homschamber.org.sy; internet www.homschamber.org.sy; f. 1928; Pres. Eng. M. ADEL TAYYARA; Gen. Man. M. FARES AL-HUSSAMY.

Latakia Chamber of Commerce and Industry: 8 rue Attar, Latakia; tel. (41) 479531; fax (41) 478526; e-mail lattakia@chamberlattakia.com; internet www.chamberlattakia.com; Pres. KAMAL ISMAIL AL-ASSAD.

Tartous Chamber of Commerce and Industry: POB 403, Tartous; tel. (43) 329852; fax (43) 329728; e-mail info@tcci-sy.com; internet tcci-sy.net; Pres. WAHIB KAMEL MERI; Gen. Man. MANAH ASSAF.

EMPLOYERS' ORGANIZATIONS

Fédération de Damas: Damascus; f. 1949.

Fédération Générale à Damas: Damascus; f. 1951; Dir TALAT TAGLUBI.

Fédération des Patrons et Industriels à Lattaquié: Latakia; f. 1953.

UTILITIES

Electricity

Public Establishment for Electricity Generation and Transmission (PEEGT): BP 3386, 17 rue Nessan, Damascus; tel. (11) 2229654; fax (11) 2229062; e-mail peegt@net.sy; f. 1965; present name adopted 1994; state-owned; operates 11 power stations through subsidiary cos; Dir-Gen. Dr AHMAD AL-ALI; Gen. Man. HISHAM MASIAJ.

Gas

Syrian Gas Company: BP 4499, Homs; tel. (31) 2451925; fax (31) 2451933; e-mail info@sgc.gov.sy; internet www.sgc.gov.sy; f. 2003; state-owned; responsible for production, processing and distribution of gas supplies; Dir-Gen. ALI ABBAS.

Water

The Ministry of Housing and Construction is responsible for planning and regulation in the Syrian water sector; it oversees the operations of 14 regional water establishments that manage the provision of drinking water and sewerage facilities. The Ministry of Irrigation is responsible for the management of water resources and the provision of irrigation water. An Integrated Water Resource Management Project, co-ordinated by the State Planning Commission, was initiated in 2006 with the aim of modernizing and integrating the various authorities responsible for the sector (see www.water.co.sy).

TRADE UNIONS

General Federation of Labour Unions (Ittihad Naqabat al-'Ummal al-'Am fi Suriya): BP 2351, rue Qanawat, Damascus; f. 1948; Chair. MUHAMMAD SHAABAN AZZOUZ; Sec. MAHMOUD FAHURI.

Order of Syrian Engineers and Architects: BP 2336, Immeuble al-Mohandessin, place Azmeh, Damascus; tel. (11) 2214916; fax (11) 2216948; e-mail osea@net.sy; internet www.syrianengineers.com; Pres. M. FAYEZ MAHFOUZ.

Transport

RAILWAYS

In 2009 the main railway system totalled 2,495 km of track. A new railway line linking Aleppo with Mersin in southern Turkey began operating in March 2009. Another new line connecting Aleppo with Gaziantep, also in southern Turkey, was inaugurated in December; services commenced in late 2010. Meanwhile, plans for a mixed underground/elevated metro system in Damascus were at the planning stages in early 2011. Construction work on the Green Line, consisting of a 16.5-km line and 17 stations, was scheduled to commence in 2012, with completion anticipated by 2016.

General Establishment of Syrian Railways: Ministry of Transport, BP 182, Aleppo; tel. (21) 2294602; fax (21) 2283162; e-mail cfs-syria@net.sy; internet www.cfssyria.org; f. 1897; Dir-Gen. GEORGE MAKABARI.

General Organization of the Hedjaz-Syrian Railway: BP 2978, rue Hedjaz, Damascus; tel. (11) 3331625; e-mail generaldirector@hijazerail.com; internet hijazerail.com; f. 1908; the Hedjaz Railway has 347 km of track (gauge 1,050 mm) in Syria; services operate between Damascus and Amman, Jordan, on a branch line of about 24 km from Damascus to Katana, and there is a further line of 64 km from Damascus to Serghaya; Dir-Gen. MAHMOUD SAQBANI.

ROADS

Arterial roads run across the country linking the north to the south and the Mediterranean to the eastern frontier. In 2009 Syria's total road network was 68,157 km, of which 43,753 km were asphalted. Plans to construct a Damascus Ring Highway, at an estimated cost of US $380m., were under discussion in early 2011. In mid-2009 the Government announced plans for the construction of two major new motorways: a north–south highway linking Bab al-Hawha, near the Turkish border, with Nasib, on the border with Jordan; and an east–west highway linking the Mediterranean port of Tartous with the Iraqi border.

Public Establishment for Road Communications: BP 34203, Damascus; tel. (11) 2458411; fax (11) 2452682; e-mail director-g@perc.gov.sy; internet www.perc.gov.sy; f. 2003; Dir-Gen. HUSSAIN AL-ARNOUS.

PIPELINES

The Syrian Company for Oil Transport operates a network of domestic oil and gas pipelines, including a 560-km crude oil pipeline linking fields in Al-Hasakah province with Tartous, as well as some 2,000 km of gas pipelines. A 1,200-km Arab Gas Pipeline, to distribute Egyptian gas in the region, was announced by Egypt, Syria, Lebanon and Jordan in 2004. The first stage of the Syrian section was completed in 2008.

Syrian Co for Oil Transport (SCOT): BP 13, Banias; tel. (43) 711300; fax (43) 710418; e-mail scot50@scs-net.org; internet www.scot-syria.com; f. 1972; Gen. Man. NUMIR HABIB MAKHLOUF.

SHIPPING

Latakia is Syria's principal port; it has a 972-m quay with draughts ranging from 11.8 m–13.3 m. A concession to manage and operate the container terminal at Latakia was awarded to a consortium led by the French CMA CGM Group in March 2009. The concessionaire announced plans to increase capacity to 1m. 20-ft equivalent units (TEU) by 2012. Latakia handled 6.1m. tons of cargo in 2009. The other major ports are at Banias and Tartous. Tartous handled 14.1m. tons of cargo in 2009.

Regulatory and Port Authorities

General Directorate of Syrian Ports: BP 505, Latakia; tel. (41) 473333; fax (41) 475805; e-mail gdp-itm@syrianport.com; internet www.syrianports.com; Dir-Gen. Rear-Adm. MOHSEN HASSAN.

SYRIA

Latakia Port Authority: BP 220, rue Baghdad, Latakia; tel. (41) 476452; fax (41) 475760; e-mail info@lattakiaport.gov.sy; internet www.lattakiaport.gov.sy; Gen. Man. SULEIMAN A. BALOUCH.

Syrian General Authorities for Maritime Transport (SYRIA-MAR): BP 314, place Zat al-Sawary, Latakia; tel. (41) 370681; fax (41) 371013; internet syriamar.net.

Tartous Port Authority: BP 86, Tartous; tel. (43) 225150; fax (43) 315602; e-mail ta-pco@mail.sy; internet www.tartousport.com; Gen. Man. ZAKI E. NAJIB.

Principal Shipping Companies

Ismail, A. M., Shipping Agency Ltd: BP 74, rue al-Mina, Tartous; tel. (43) 221987; fax (43) 318949; operates 8 general cargo vessels; Man. Dir MAHMOUD ISMAIL.

Muhieddine Shipping Co: BP 1099, rue al-Chourinish, Tartous; tel. (43) 323090; fax (43) 317139; e-mail info@muhieddineshipping.net; internet www.muhieddineshipping.net; operates 7 general cargo ships.

Riamar Shipping Co Ltd: BP 284, Immeuble Tarwin, rue du Port, Tartous; tel. (43) 314999; fax (43) 212616; e-mail aksabra@riamar.org; operates 6 general cargo vessels; Chair. and Man. Dir ABD AL-KADER SABRA.

Al-Sham Shipping Co: BP 33436, Damascus; tel. (11) 3311960; fax (11) 3311961; e-mail al-sham@al-sham.com; internet www.al-sham.com; f. 1994; operates two general cargo vessels; Chair. MUHAMMAD A. HAYKAL.

Syro-Jordanian Shipping Co: BP 148, rue Port Said, Latakia; tel. (41) 471635; fax (41) 470250; e-mail syjomar@net.sy; f. 1976; operates 2 general cargo ships; Chair. OSMAN LEBBADY; Tech. Man. M. CHOUMAN.

Tartous International Container Terminal JSC: BP 870, Tartous; tel. (43) 328882; fax (43) 328831; e-mail info@ictsi.sy; internet www.ictsi-sy.com; f. 2006; owned by Int. Container Terminal Services, Inc; awarded 10-year concession to operate a container terminal at Tartous; CEO and Gen. Man. ROMEO A. SALVADOR.

CIVIL AVIATION

There are international airports at Damascus and Aleppo. Plans to expand the capacity of Damascus airport were under discussion in early 2011. Syrianair also operates domestic flights from airports in al-Qamishli and Deir el-Zor. Extensive renovation work at Deir el-Zor was completed in 2008. Damascus International Airport handled 3.7m. passengers in 2009, while Aleppo handled 0.5m. passengers in the same year.

Syrian Civil Aviation Authority (SCAA): BP 6257, place Nejmeh, Damascus; tel. (11) 3331306; fax (11) 2232201; internet www.scaasy.com; Dir-Gen. Dr WAFIK HASAN.

Cham Wings Airlines: rue al-Fardous, Damascus; tel. (11) 2244086; fax (11) 2454506; e-mail info@chamwings.com; internet www.chamwings.com; f. 2007; first private int. airline in Syria; flights from Damascus serving seven destinations in the Middle East and Europe; Chair. ISSAM SHAMMOUT.

Syrian Arab Airlines (Syrianair): BP 417, Social Insurance Bldg, 5th Floor, Youssef al-Azmeh Sq., Damascus; tel. (11) 2220700; fax (11) 224923; e-mail syr-air@syriatel.net; internet www.syriaair.com; f. 1946; refounded 1961 to succeed Syrian Airways, after revocation of merger with Misrair (Egypt); domestic passenger and cargo services (from Damascus, Aleppo, Latakia and Deir el-Zor) and routes to Europe, the Middle East, North Africa and the Far East; Chair. and Man. Dir NACHAAT NUMIR; Dir-Gen. GHAYDA ABD AL-LATIF.

Syrian Pearl Airlines: BP 31219, Damascus; tel. (11) 5010; fax (11) 3349557; e-mail info@flysyrianpearl.com; internet www.flysyrianpearl.com; f. 2008; commenced operations May 2009; 69% owned by CHAM Holding, 25% by Syrian Arab Airlines and 6% by Kuwaiti investors; domestic flights, and services to Sharm el-Sheikh (Egypt), Jeddah (Saudi Arabia) and İstanbul (Turkey); flights suspended in June 2009; Chair. Dr ABD AL-RAHMAN AL-ATTAR; CEO FINN THAULOW.

Tourism

Syria's tourist attractions include a pleasant Mediterranean coastline, the mountains, town bazaars, and the antiquities of Damascus, Aleppo and Palmyra, as well as hundreds of deserted ancient villages in the north-west of the country. In 2008 some 7.0m. tourists visited Syria; tourism receipts totalled US $2,972m. in 2007.

Ministry of Tourism: BP 6642, rue Barada, Damascus; tel. (11) 2210122; fax (11) 2242636; e-mail min-tourism@mail.sy; internet www.syriatourism.org; f. 1972; Counsellor to the Minister SAWSAN JOUZY; Dir of Tourism Promotion and Marketing NIDAL MACHFEJ.

Middle East Tourism: BP 201, Malki St, Shawki ave, Damascus; tel. (11) 3325655; fax (11) 3326266; e-mail daadouche@net.sy; internet www.daadouche.com; f. 1952; Pres. MAHER DAADOUCHE; 7 brs.

Syrian Arab Co for Hotels and Tourism (SACHA): BP 5549, Mezzeh, Damascus; tel. (11) 2223286; fax (11) 2219415; f. 1977; Chair. DIRAR JUMA'A; Gen. Man. ELIAS ABOUTARA.

Defence

Commander-in-Chief of the Armed Forces: Lt-Gen. BASHAR AL-ASSAD.

Minister of Defence and Deputy Commander-in-Chief of the Armed Forces: Lt-Gen. ALI MUHAMMAD HABIB MAHMOUD.

Chief of Staff of the Armed Forces: Gen. DAWOOD BIN ABDULLAH RAJIHA.

Air Force Commander: Gen. MUHAMMAD AL-KHOULI.

Republican Guard Commander: Maj.-Gen. ALI HASSAN.

Defence Budget (2010): £S89,500m.

Military Service: 30 months (Jewish population exempted).

Total Armed Forces (as assessed at November 2010): 295,000 (army 220,000—including conscripts; air defence command—an army command—40,000; navy 5,000; air force 30,000); reserves 314,000 (army 280,000; air force 10,000; air defence 20,000; navy 4,000).

Paramilitary Forces (as assessed at November 2010): an estimated 108,000 (Gendarmerie—under control of Ministry of the Interior—8,000; Baath Party Workers' Militia an estimated 100,000).

Education

Primary education, which begins at six years of age and lasts for six years, is officially compulsory. In 2002/03 primary enrolment included 95% of children in the relevant age-group. In 2008/09 an estimated 2,383,223 pupils were enrolled in primary education (males 1,240,904; females 1,142,319). Secondary education, beginning at 12 years of age, lasts for a further six years, comprising two cycles of three years each. In 2008/09 enrolment at secondary schools included 69% of children in the appropriate age-group. An estimated 2,562,568 pupils (males 1,306,251; females 1,256,317) were enrolled in secondary education (excluding vocational courses) in 2008/09.

There are agricultural and technical schools for vocational training, and by 2006/07 there were eight private universities and numerous private schools. In that year there were 250,000 students at state universities, 6,000 at private institutions and a further 2,500 at the Syrian Virtual University (established in 2002 and which offers degree courses via the internet). The main language of instruction in schools is Arabic, but English and French are widely taught as second languages. The combined budgetary expenditure of the Ministries of Education and of Higher Education in 2008 was an estimated S£63,286m. (equivalent to some 10.5% of total spending).

The UN Relief and Works Agency for Palestine Refugees in the Near East (UNRWA) provides education for Palestinian refugees in Syria. During the academic year 2010/11 UNWRA operated 118 elementary and preparatory schools in Syria, with a total enrolment of 66,014 pupils.

TAIWAN

Introductory Survey

LOCATION, CLIMATE, LANGUAGE, RELIGION, FLAG, CAPITAL

The Republic of China has, since 1949, been confined mainly to the province of Taiwan (comprising one large island and several much smaller ones), which lies off the south-east coast of the Chinese mainland. The territory under the Republic's effective jurisdiction consists of the island of Taiwan (also known as Formosa) and nearby islands, including the P'enghu (Pescadores) group, together with a few other islands which lie just off the mainland and form part of the province of Fujian (Fukien), west of Taiwan. The largest of these is Kinmen (Jinmen), also known as Quemoy, which, with three smaller islands, is about 10 km from the port of Xiamen (Amoy), while five other islands under Taiwan's control, chiefly Matsu (Mazu), lie further north, near Fuzhou. Taiwan itself is separated from the mainland by the Taiwan (Formosa) Strait, which is about 130 km (80 miles) wide at its narrowest point. The island's climate is one of rainy summers and mild winters. Average temperatures are about 15°C (59°F) in the winter and 26°C (79°F) in the summer. The average annual rainfall is 2,580 mm (102 in). The official language is Northern Chinese (Mandarin), but Taiwanese, a dialect based on the language of Fujian Province, is widely spoken. The predominant religions are Buddhism and Daoism (Taoism), but there are also adherents of I-kuan Tao, Christianity and Islam. The philosophy of Confucianism has a large following. The national flag (proportions 2 by 3) is red, with a dark blue rectangular canton, containing a white sun, in the upper hoist. The capital is Taipei.

CONTEMPORARY POLITICAL HISTORY

Historical Context

China ceded Taiwan to Japan in 1895. The island remained under Japanese rule until the end of the Second World War in 1945, when it was returned to Chinese control, becoming a province of the Republic of China, then ruled by the Kuomintang (KMT, Nationalist Party). The leader of the KMT was Gen. Chiang Kai-shek, President of the Republic since 1928. The KMT Government's forces were defeated in 1949 by the Communist revolution in China. President Chiang and many of his supporters withdrew from the Chinese mainland to Taiwan, where they established a KMT regime in succession to their previous all-China administration. This regime continued to assert that it was the rightful Chinese Government, in opposition to the People's Republic of China, proclaimed by the victorious Communists in 1949. The Nationalists successfully resisted attacks by their Communist rivals, and declared that they intended to recover control of mainland China.

Although its effective control was limited to Taiwan, the KMT regime continued to be dominated by politicians who had formerly been in power on the mainland. Unable to replenish their mainland representation, the National Assembly (last elected fully in 1947) and other legislative organs extended their terms of office indefinitely, although fewer than one-half of the original members were alive on Taiwan by the 1980s. The political domination of the island by immigrants from the mainland caused some resentment among native Taiwanese, and led to demands for increased democratization and for the recognition of Taiwan as a state independent of China. The KMT consistently rejected demands for independence, restating the party's long-standing policy of seeking political reunification, although under KMT terms, with the mainland.

The KMT regime continued to represent China at the UN (and as a permanent member of the UN Security Council) until October 1971, when it was replaced by the People's Republic. After 1971 a number of countries broke off diplomatic relations with Taiwan and recognized the People's Republic. Nationalist China was subsequently expelled from several other international organizations. In November 1991, however, as 'Chinese Taipei', Taiwan joined the Asia-Pacific Economic Co-operation (APEC, see p. 197) forum. In September 1992, under the name of the 'Separate Customs Territory of Taiwan, P'enghu, Kinmen and Matsu', Taiwan was granted observer status at the General Agreement on Tariffs and Trade (GATT) and was finally approved for membership of the successor body in September 2001: on 1 January 2002 Taiwan formally became a member of the World Trade Organization (WTO, see p. 430). In June 1995 Taiwan offered to make a donation of US $1,000m., to be used for the establishment of an international development fund, if the island were permitted to rejoin the UN. In February 2004 it was announced that Taiwan would become a member of the Commission for the Conservation and Management of Highly Migratory Fish Stocks in the Western and Central Pacific Ocean (responsible for implementing the 1995 UN Fish Stocks Agreement). Following its admission to the WTO, therefore, this represented the second recognition of Taiwan by an international organization.

In September 2006, for the 14th consecutive year, the General Committee of the UN General Assembly rejected a proposal urging Taiwan's participation in the UN. The Taiwanese leadership pledged to continue the island's campaign to gain re-entry, stating that henceforth it would make its application under the name of Taiwan, rather than the 'Republic of China'. In September 2007, however, the island's membership application, as Taiwan, was again rejected. In September 2008 a further proposal urging Taiwan's entry to the UN was rejected. The issue was submitted to Taiwanese voters in two referendums held in March 2008, but the results were declared invalid owing to the low level of voter participation (see Domestic Political Affairs). As Taiwan began to consider the adoption of a different approach to the issue of UN representation, the island was expected to focus henceforth on securing representation in selected UN specialized agencies. In September 2009 the Ministry of Foreign Affairs confirmed that it was renouncing its immediated quest for a seat at the UN. This change of strategy was confirmed in August 2010. In May 2003, meanwhile, the People's Republic of China strongly opposed a US proposal that Taiwan be permitted to participate in the World Health Organization (WHO). The People's Republic reiterated its view in May 2008, when for the 12th time the World Health Assembly (the WHO governing body) rejected a proposal, supported by The Gambia and by the Pacific nation of Palau, that Taiwan be granted observer status in WHO. In April 2009 China abandoned its objections to Taiwan's attendance as an observer, under the name of Chinese Taipei, at the World Health Assembly. In May 2011, however, the Taiwanese President claimed that China had exerted pressure on WHO to refer to Taiwan as a Chinese province in its documentation.

Domestic Political Affairs

In December 1972 legislative elections were held, for the first time in 24 years, to fill 53 seats in the National Assembly. The new members, elected for a fixed term of six years, joined 1,376 surviving 'life-term' members of the Assembly. President Chiang Kai-shek remained in office until his death in April 1975. He was succeeded as leader of the ruling KMT by his son, Gen. Chiang Ching-kuo, who had hitherto been Premier. Dr Yen Chia-kan, Vice-President since 1966, became the new President. In 1978 President Yen retired and was succeeded by Gen. Chiang. At elections for 71 seats in the Legislative Yuan in December 1983, the KMT won an overwhelming victory, confirming its dominance over the independent 'Tangwai' (non-party) candidates. In March 1984 President Chiang was re-elected for a second six-year term, and Lee Teng-hui, a former mayor of Taipei and a native Taiwanese, became Vice-President. President Chiang died in January 1988 and was succeeded by Lee Teng-hui.

In September 1986 135 leading opposition politicians formed the Democratic Progressive Party (DPP), in defiance of the KMT's ban on the formation of new political parties. Partial elections to the National Assembly and the Legislative Yuan were held in December. The KMT achieved a decisive victory, but the DPP received about one-quarter of the total votes, and more than doubled the non-KMT representation. In February 1987 the KMT began to implement a programme of political reform. Martial law (which had remained in force since 1949) was replaced by the National Security Law in July 1987: political parties other than the KMT were permitted, and civilians were removed from the jurisdiction of military courts. In April, in a reorganization of the Executive Yuan (cabinet), seven major posts were allocated to reformist members of the KMT. In November the second annual Congress of the DPP approved a resolution declaring that Taiwanese citizens had the right to advocate independence. In January 1988, however, two opposition activists were imprisoned on charges of sedition.

In February 1988 a plan to restructure the legislative bodies was approved by the Central Standing Committee of the KMT. Voluntary resignations were to be sought from 'life-term' members of the Legislative Yuan and National Assembly, and seats were no longer to be reserved for representatives of mainland constituencies. Following a decision to hold free elections for two-thirds of the members of the KMT's Central Committee, numerous new members were elected at the party congress in July, and the proportion of native Taiwanese increased sharply. In January 1989 three legislative measures were enacted: a revision of regulations concerning the registration of political parties; a retirement plan for those members of the three legislative assemblies who had been elected by mainland constituencies in 1947; and a new law to give greater autonomy to the Taiwan Provincial Government (which retained responsibility for the general administration of the island, with the exception of the cities of Taipei and Kaohsiung) and the Provincial Assembly. In the following month the KMT became the first political party to register under the new legislation. Despite its objections to the size of the retirement pensions being offered and the terms of the Civic Organizations Law (under which political parties were obliged to reject communism and any notion of official political independence for Taiwan), the DPP applied for official registration in April.

Partial elections to the Legislative Yuan and the Taiwan Provincial Assembly were held in December 1989. A total of 101 seats in the Legislative Yuan were contested, with the KMT obtaining 72 seats and the DPP winning 21, thus securing the prerogative to propose legislation in the Legislative Yuan. In February 1990 the opening of the National Assembly's 35-day plenary session, convened every six years to elect the country's President, was disrupted by DPP members' violent action in a protest against the continuing domination of the Assembly by elderly KMT politicians, who had been elected on the Chinese mainland prior to 1949 and who had never been obliged to seek re-election. Many injuries resulted from clashes between riot police and demonstrators. In March 1990 DPP members were barred from the National Assembly for refusing to swear allegiance to the 'Republic of China', attempting instead to substitute 'Taiwan' upon taking the oath. Various amendments to the Temporary Provisions, which for more than 40 years had permitted the effective suspension of the Constitution, were approved by the National Assembly in mid-March. Revisions included measures to strengthen the position of the mainland-elected KMT members, who were granted new powers to initiate and veto legislation, and also an amendment to permit the National Assembly to meet annually. The revisions were opposed not only by the DPP but also by more moderate members of the KMT, and led to a large protest rally in Taipei, demanding the abolition of the National Assembly and the holding of direct presidential elections. Nevertheless, President Lee was duly re-elected, unopposed, by the National Assembly for a six-year term, two rival KMT candidates having withdrawn.

The National Affairs Conference (NAC) convened in June 1990 to discuss proposals for reform. A Constitutional Reform Planning Group was subsequently established. The NAC reached consensus on the issue of direct presidential elections, which would permit the citizens of Taiwan, rather than the members of the National Assembly, to select the head of state. Meanwhile, the Council of Grand Justices had ruled that elderly members of the National Assembly and of the Legislative Yuan should step down by the end of 1991. The National Unification Council (NUC), chaired by President Lee, was formed in October. In the same month the Mainland Affairs Council, comprising heads of government departments and led by the Vice-Premier of the Executive Yuan, was founded. In December President Lee announced that Taiwan would formally end the state of war with the mainland; the declaration of emergency was to be rescinded by May 1991. Plans were announced for gradual constitutional reform. Meanwhile, in early December 1990 Huang Hwa, the leader of a faction of the DPP and independence activist, had received a 10-year prison sentence upon being found guilty of 'preparing to commit sedition'.

In April 1991 the National Assembly was convened, the session again being marred by violent clashes between KMT and DPP members. The DPP subsequently boycotted the session, arguing that a completely new constitution should be introduced and that elderly KMT delegates, who did not represent Taiwan constituencies, should not have the right to make amendments to the existing Constitution. Some 20,000 demonstrators attended a DPP-organized protest march. Nevertheless, the National Assembly duly approved the constitutional amendments, and at midnight on 30 April the 'period of mobilization for the suppression of the Communist rebellion' and the Temporary Provisions were formally terminated. The existence, but not the legitimacy, of the Government of the People's Republic was officially acknowledged by President Lee. Furthermore, Taiwan remained committed to its 'one China' policy. In May 1991 widespread protests following the arrest of four advocates of independence for Taiwan led to the abolition of the Statute of Punishment for Sedition. The law had been adopted in 1949 and had been frequently employed by the KMT to suppress political dissent.

A senior UN official visited the island in August 1991, the first trip by such a representative since Taiwan's withdrawal from the organization in 1971. Large-scale rallies to demand the holding of a referendum on the issue of Taiwan's readmission to the UN as an independent state took place in September and October 1991, resulting in clashes between demonstrators and the security forces.

In August 1991 the opposition DPP officially announced its alternative draft constitution for 'Taiwan', rather than for the 'Republic of China', thus acknowledging the de facto position regarding sovereignty. In September, after being reinstated in the Legislative Yuan, Huang Hsin-chieh, the Chairman of the DPP, relinquished his seat in the legislature and urged other senior deputies to do likewise. Huang had been deprived of his seat and imprisoned in 1980, following his conviction on charges of sedition. At the party congress in October 1991, Huang was replaced as DPP Chairman by Hsu Hsin-liang. The DPP congress adopted a resolution henceforth to advocate the establishment of 'the Republic of Taiwan'.

Elections to the new 405-member National Assembly, which was to be responsible for amending the Constitution, took place in December 1991. The 225 seats open to direct election were widely contested. The campaign was dominated by the issue of independence. However, the DPP suffered a humiliating defeat. The KMT secured a total of 318 seats (179 of which were won by direct election), while the DPP won 75 seats (41 by direct election). All elderly mainland-elected delegates were obliged to relinquish their seats. In February 1992 20,000 demonstrators protested against the sedition laws and demanded a referendum on the issue of independence.

In March 1992, at a plenary session of the KMT Central Committee, it was agreed to reduce the President's term of office from six to four years. However, the important question of arrangements for future presidential elections remained unresolved. In April street demonstrations were organized by the DPP to support demands for direct presidential elections. In May the National Assembly adopted eight amendments to the Constitution, one of which empowered the President to appoint members of the Control Yuan.

Taiwan's first full elections since the establishment of Nationalist rule in 1949 were held in December 1992. The KMT retained 102 of the 161 seats in the Legislative Yuan. However, the DPP garnered 31% of the votes and more than doubled its representation in the legislature, winning 50 seats. Following this setback, the Premier and the KMT Secretary-General resigned. In February 1993 Lien Chan, hitherto Governor of Taiwan Province, became the island's first Premier of Taiwanese descent.

In May 1993 about 30 conservative rebels resigned from the KMT, and formed the New Alliance Nationalist Party. Furthermore, in June the Government was defeated in the Legislative Yuan, when a group of KMT deputies voted with the opposition to approve legislation on financial disclosure requirements for elected and appointed public officials. The unity of the KMT was further undermined in August, when six dissident legislators belonging to the New Kuomintang Alliance, which had registered as a political group in March, announced their decision to leave the ruling party in order to establish the New Party (NP). Nevertheless, at the KMT congress in August Lee Teng-hui was re-elected Chairman of the party. A new 31-member Central Standing Committee and 210-member Central Committee, comprising mainly Lee's supporters, were selected. In a conciliatory gesture by the KMT Chairman, four vice-chairmanships were created, the new positions being filled by representatives of different factions of the party.

In September 1993, following a series of bribery scandals, the Executive Yuan approved measures to combat corruption. In the same month a KMT member of the Legislative Yuan was sentenced to 14 years' imprisonment for bribery of voters during the 1992 election campaign; similar convictions followed. At local government elections held in November 1993, although its share of the votes declined, the KMT secured 15 of the 23 posts at stake. The DPP, which accused the KMT of malpractice, won only six posts, despite receiving a substantial proportion of the votes; it retained control of Taipei County. Following allegations of extensive bribery at further local polls in early 1994 (at which the DPP and independent candidates made strong gains), the Ministry of Justice intensified its campaign against corruption. Proposals for constitutional amendments to permit the direct election in 1996 of the Taiwanese President by popular vote (rather than by electoral college) and to limit the powers of the Premier were approved by the National Assembly in July 1994.

At gubernatorial and mayoral elections in December 1994 the DPP took control of the Taipei mayoralty, in the first such direct polls for 30 years, while the KMT succeeded in retaining the provincial governorship of Taiwan, in the first ever popular election for the post, and the mayoralty of Kaohsiung. The NP established itself as a major political force, its candidate for the mayoralty of Taipei having received more votes than the KMT incumbent.

Elections to the Legislative Yuan were held in December 1995. A major campaign issue was that of corruption. The KMT's strength declined to 84 of the 164 seats, the party faring particularly badly in Taipei. The DPP increased its representation to 53 seats. The NP, which favoured reconciliation with the mainland, secured 21 seats. In mid-March 1996 a DPP demonstration on the streets of Taipei, in support of demands for Taiwan's independence, was attended by 50,000 protesters. At Taiwan's first direct presidential election, held on 23 March, the incumbent President Lee received 54.0% of the votes cast, thus securing his re-election for a four-year term. At the concurrent elections for the National Assembly, the KMT took 183 of the 334 seats. The DPP won 99 seats and the NP 46 seats. The Chairman of the DPP, Shih Ming-teh, resigned and Hsu Hsin-liang, who had resigned in November 1993, returned to the post.

In June 1996 the President's announcement of the composition of the new Executive Yuan aroused much controversy. Although several members retained their previous portfolios, the President (apparently under pressure from within the KMT) demoted the popular Ministers of Justice and of Transportation and Communications, both of whom had exposed malpractice and initiated campaigns against corruption. Other changes included the replacement of the Minister of Foreign Affairs by John Chang, the grandson of Chiang Kai-shek. However, the most controversial nomination was the reappointment as Premier of Lien Chan, despite his recent election as the island's Vice-President. Opposition members of the Legislative Yuan, along with a number of KMT deputies, demanded that the President submit the membership of the Executive Yuan to the legislature for approval.

In December 1996 the multi-party National Development Conference (NDC), established to review the island's political system, held its inaugural meeting. The convention approved KMT proposals to abolish the Legislative Yuan's right to confirm the President's choice of Premier, to permit the legislature to introduce motions of no confidence in the Premier and to empower the President to dissolve the legislature. The Provincial Governor, (James) Soong Chu-yu, subsequently tendered his resignation in protest at the NDC's recommendations that elections for the provincial governorship and assembly be abolished, as the first stage of the dissolution of the system of provincial administration. An historical legacy duplicating many of the functions of central and local government, the Provincial Government had remained responsible for the entire island, with the exception of the cities of Taipei and Kaohsiung. In January 1997 President Lee refused to accept the Governor's resignation, but the affair drew attention to the uneasy relationship between the island's President and its Governor. In July the National Assembly approved a series of constitutional reforms, implementing the NDC's recommendations.

In May 1997 more than 50,000 demonstrators, protesting against the increase in violent crime, demanded the resignation of President Lee. Three members of the Executive Yuan subsequently resigned. The appointment of Yeh Chin-feng as Minister of the Interior (the first woman to oversee Taiwan's police force) did little to appease the public, which remained highly suspicious of the alleged connections between senior politicians and the perpetrators of organized crime. Thousands of protesters again took to the streets of Taipei, renewing their challenge to President Lee's leadership and demanding the immediate resignation of Premier Lien Chan. In June a 'Say No to China' rally attracted as many as 70,000 supporters.

In July 1997 the National Assembly approved various constitutional reforms, including the freezing of the Provincial Government. (The Provincial Government was abolished in December 1998.) Other revisions that received approval were to empower the President of Taiwan to appoint the Premier without the Legislative Yuan's confirmation; the legislature was to be permitted to hold a binding vote of no confidence in the Executive Yuan, while the President gained the right to dissolve the Legislative Yuan.

In August 1997 Vincent Siew, former Chairman of the Council for Economic Planning and Development and also of the Mainland Affairs Council, replaced Lien Chan as Premier (the latter retained the post of Vice-President), and John Chang was appointed Vice-Premier. In the same month President Lee was re-elected unopposed as Chairman of the ruling KMT. The KMT experienced a serious set-back in elections at mayoral and magistrate levels, held in November. The DPP, which had campaigned on a platform of more open government, secured 12 of the 23 constituency posts contested, while the KMT won only eight posts. More than 70% of Taiwan's population was thus to come under DPP administration. The Secretary-General of the KMT resigned and was replaced by John Chang. A major reorganization of the party followed.

At local elections held in January 1998, the KMT won an overwhelming majority of the seats contested, while the DPP, in a reversal of fortune, performed badly. In April the Minister of Justice tendered, and then subsequently withdrew, his resignation, claiming that lawmakers with connections to organized crime were exerting pressure on the Government to dismiss him. However, in July he was forced to resign, following his mishandling of an alleged scandal concerning the acting head of the Investigation Bureau.

In June 1998 the first-ever direct election for the leadership of the DPP was held. Lin Yi-hsiung won a convincing victory, assuming the chairmanship of the party in August. Meanwhile, at local elections in June, the KMT suffered a set-back, winning fewer than 50% of the seats contested. Independent candidates performed well. In August 17 new members were elected to the KMT Central Standing Committee, the 16 others being appointed by President Lee.

Elections to the newly expanded 225-member Legislative Yuan took place in December 1998. The KMT won 46.4% of the votes cast, securing 125 seats, the DPP received 29.6% of the votes and won 72 seats, while the pro-unification NP obtained only 7.1% of the votes and took 11 seats. The New Nation Alliance, a breakaway group from the DPP (formed in September), won only one seat (with 1.6% of the votes cast). In the simultaneous election to select the mayor of Taipei, the KMT candidate, Ma Ying-jeou, a popular former Minister of Justice, defeated the DPP incumbent, Chen Shui-bian. However, Frank Hsieh, the DPP candidate, won the office of mayor of Kaohsiung. The KMT retained control of both city councils.

Chiou I-jen resigned as Secretary-General of the DPP in December 1998 and was replaced by Yu Shyi-kun. Later in that month Chao Shu-po, a Minister without Portfolio, was appointed Governor of Taiwan Province, replacing the elected incumbent, James Soong, as part of the plans to dismantle the provincial government, agreed in 1997. In March 1999 an unprecedented vote of no confidence in the leadership of Premier Vincent Siew was defeated in the Legislative Yuan. The motion was presented by the opposition following Siew's decision to reduce the tax on share transactions, apparently as a result of pressure from President Lee. In September the National Assembly approved a controversial constitutional amendment, which, *inter alia*, extended the terms of the deputies from May 2000 to June 2002. Election to the Assembly was henceforth to be on the basis of party proportional representation. Shortly afterwards, the KMT leadership expelled the Speaker of the National Assembly, Su Nan-cheng, from the party on the grounds that he had violated its policy on the tenure extension, thereby also removing him from his parliamentary seat and the post of Speaker. In March 2000, however, the Council of Grand Justices of the

TAIWAN

Judicial Yuan ruled the National Assembly's action to be unconstitutional. The DPP and the KMT then reached an agreement on the abolition of the National Assembly and the cancellation of elections scheduled for early May. In April the National Assembly convened, and approved a series of constitutional amendments, which effectively deprived the body of most of its powers, and reduced it to an ad hoc institution. The powers to initiate constitutional amendments, to impeach the President or Vice-President and to approve the appointment of senior officials were transferred to the Legislative Yuan. The National Assembly was to retain the functions of ratifying constitutional amendments and impeachment proceedings, in which case 300 delegates, appointed by political parties according to a system of proportional representation, would convene for a session of a maximum duration of one month.

In November 1999 it was announced that a presidential election was to be held in March 2000. Five candidates registered: Lien Chan (with Vincent Siew as candidate for Vice-President) was the KMT nominee, while Chen Shui-bian, a former mayor of Taipei, was to stand for the DPP (with the feminist Annette Lu as vice-presidential candidate), and Li Ao was to represent the NP; the former DPP Chairman, Hsu Hsin-liang, qualified as an independent candidate, as did James Soong who, along with a number of his supporters, was consequently expelled from the KMT, his prospects being jeopardized by charges of embezzlement. In January 2000 Lien Chan proposed that the KMT's extensive business holdings be placed in trust and that the party terminate its direct role in the management of the numerous companies in which it owned shares. The KMT adopted the proposal shortly afterwards. In a reflection of the tense political situation between Taiwan and China, Chen Shui-bian of the DPP modified the party's stance and pledged not to declare formal independence for the island unless Chinese forces attacked.

The administration of President Chen

The presidential election of 18 March 2000 was won by Chen Shui-bian, who obtained 39.3% of the votes cast. James Soong, his closest rival, received 36.8% of the votes. Lien Chan of the KMT secured only 23.1% of the votes. The remaining candidates obtained less than 1%. (Upon his inauguration in May, Chen thus became Taiwan's first non-KMT President since 1945.) Violence erupted as disappointed KMT supporters besieged the party's headquarters, attributing the KMT's defeat to the leadership's expulsion of James Soong and the resultant division of the party. Lee Teng-hui subsequently resigned from the chairmanship of the party, and Lien Chan assumed the leadership. However, as the KMT continued to dominate the Legislative Yuan, the party did not entirely relinquish its influence, and in April 2000 it gave permission for Tang Fei, a KMT member and hitherto Minister of National Defense, to serve as Premier, although he was to be suspended from party activities while in the post. Following protracted negotiations, the membership of the new Executive Yuan, which incorporated 11 DPP members and 13 KMT members, was approved in early May. The incoming Government largely lacked ministerial experience. Furthermore, the DPP's lack of a legislative majority impeded the passage of legislation. In July Frank Hsieh replaced Lin Yi-hsiung as Chairman of the DPP.

In October 2000 Tang Fei resigned as Premier, ostensibly owing to ill health. It was suggested that his departure from the post was due to the Government's failure to agree upon the fate of Taiwan's fourth nuclear power plant, the DPP being opposed to the project. Vice-Premier Chang Chun-hsiung was appointed Premier, and a minor reorganization of the Executive Yuan was effected. Changes included the appointment of Yen Ching-chang as Minister of Finance. In the same month the Minister of Economic Affairs, Lin Hsin-yi, was expelled from the KMT for 'seriously opposing KMT policies and impairing the people's interests' after he had demonstrated his support for the cancellation of the nuclear power project. Chang Chun-hsiung announced that the Executive Yuan had decided to halt construction of the plant for financial reasons. The outraged KMT rejected the Government's right to cancel a project previously approved by the legislature. Together with the NP and the People First Party (PFP—founded by James Soong immediately after the election), the KMT began collecting legislators' signatures for the recall (censure) of Chen Shui-bian. Despite Chen's subsequent apology, the Legislative Yuan approved revised legislation on the process for presidential impeachment. KMT member Vincent Siew refused to act as the President's representative to the annual APEC forum in Brunei in November. The business community, furthermore, issued an unprecedented public message that economic recovery should take priority over political differences, but in December some 10,000 protesters in Taipei demanded that Chen resign. In November the Government requested a constitutional interpretation of the issue from the Council of Grand Justices, which in January 2001 ruled that the Government should have sought the legislature's approval before terminating the project. The Government therefore decided to resume construction of the nuclear plant. In March a minor government reorganization was effected. The most notable change was the appointment of Hu Ching-piao, hitherto a Minister without Portfolio, as Chairman of the Atomic Energy Council, replacing Hsia Der-yu.

In July 2001 the KMT issued a radical policy document arguing that Taiwan's best option in terms of its relations with China was to form a 'confederation' with the mainland. However, the KMT's Central Standing Committee refrained from adopting the proposal, reflecting the party's uncertainty over mainland policy. In August the Taiwan Solidarity Union (TSU) was formally established with the support of former President Lee Teng-hui. Led by the former Minister of the Interior, Huang Chu-wen, and consisting of breakaway members of the KMT and DPP, the party hoped to secure for President Chen a majority in the forthcoming legislative elections. Lee was expelled from the KMT in September.

At the elections held on 1 December 2001 the DPP emerged as the biggest single party in the new legislature, having won 36.6% of the votes cast and 87 of the 225 seats. The KMT won 31.3% of votes and 68 seats, thereby losing its dominance of the Legislative Yuan for the first time in its history. The PFP came third, winning 20.3% of the votes and 46 seats, while the newly formed TSU came fourth, with 8.5% of the votes and 13 seats. The NP won only 2.9% of the votes and one seat. Independents took nine seats. The level of voter participation was registered as 66.2%.

In January 2002 President Chen reorganized the Executive Yuan, appointing his Secretary-General, Yu Shyi-kun, as Premier. Other notable appointments included Chen Shih-meng, hitherto Deputy Governor of the Central Bank, as the Secretary-General to the President, replacing Yu. Lin Hsin-i, hitherto Minister of Economic Affairs, was appointed Vice-Premier and Chairman of the Council for Economic Planning and Development. Eugene Chien was appointed as Minister of Foreign Affairs, and Lee Yung-san became Minister of Finance. The new administration incorporated several members of the KMT, including Gen. Tang Yao-ming, hitherto Chief of the General Staff, who was appointed as Minister of National Defense; Tang was the first native-born Taiwanese to hold the newly augmented defence post in a military dominated by mainlanders. The ministers in charge of mainland and Overseas Chinese affairs were retained.

At elections for provincial city and town councils, held in January 2002, the KMT won the largest number of seats. In February an alliance of the KMT and PFP ('pan-blue' camp) successfully blocked the candidate of the DPP-TSU ('pan-green' camp) for the post of Vice-President of the Legislative Yuan, electing Chiang Ping-kun of the KMT to that position. At the same time, the incumbent President of the legislature, Wang Jin-pyng of the KMT, was re-elected to his post. The KMT-PFP alliance immediately challenged the new Government by attempting to force it to accept revisions to local budget allocations, which had been hastily approved by the outgoing Legislative Yuan, but the alliance failed to secure the majority necessary in the new legislature. However, an early set-back for the DPP administration occurred in March 2002 when the Minister of Economic Affairs, Christine Tsung, resigned, citing a hostile political environment. She was replaced by her deputy, Lin Yi-fu.

A major scandal emerged in March 2002 when it was reported that the Government of former President Lee Teng-hui had, in co-operation with the island's intelligence service (National Security Bureau—NSB), clandestinely established an unauthorized fund of US $100m. in order to finance covert operations on the mainland and to further Taiwanese interests among influential lobby groups abroad. It was widely believed that the source of the 'leaks' was a former NSB colonel who had embezzled US $5.5m. and then fled the island.

In April 2002 the Executive Yuan approved plans to abolish the posts of Speaker and Deputy Speaker of the National Assembly, and replace them with that of a chairman of the session. In May the Government revealed proposals to reform the electoral system, which would reduce the number of seats in the Legislative Yuan from 225 to 150 and extend the term of legislators from three to four years. Some 90 seats would be filled from single-seat constituencies (thereby eliminating the need for candidates from the same party to compete against each other, as in the existing multi-seat constituencies), with the remaining seats divided proportionally among parties that received more than 5% of the total vote. Also in May, KMT Chairman Lien Chan announced that his party would form an official alliance with the PFP in order to strengthen opposition to the ruling DPP. In the same month thousands of people demonstrated in favour of changing Taiwan's official name from the 'Republic of China' to 'Taiwan'.

In June 2002 Premier Yu Shyi-kun appointed Liu Shyh-fang as the first female Secretary-General of the Executive Yuan, replacing Lee Ying-yuan, who was standing as the DPP's candidate in elections for the mayoralty of Taipei, in December. In July President Chen Shui-bian formally assumed the chairmanship of the DPP. In September the Executive Yuan approved drafts of the new Political Party Law, which would ban political parties from operating or investing in profit-making enterprises, and allow the Government to investigate and confiscate assets unlawfully obtained by political parties. Although ostensibly aimed at creating greater political fairness and financial openness, the draft legislation was viewed as being directed at the KMT; during the its decades of rule, the KMT had amassed a vast commercial fortune, estimated at NT $53,750m. by 2001. As a result, the party would be obliged to sell many of its assets.

A new political dispute emerged in late September 2002 over planned reforms of the debt-ridden agricultural and fishermen's credit co-operatives. The Government sought to reduce the activities of these local financial bodies, which had traditionally been used as a source of funds and influence for local KMT politicians. However, opposition to the reforms was so intense that by late November President Chen was forced to suspend the plans. At the same time, more than 120,000 farmers and fishermen marched through Taipei to protest against the reforms, in what was the largest demonstration on the island since Chen took office. Premier Yu Shyi-kun offered to resign, but was retained by Chen, who instead accepted the resignations of the Minister of Finance, Lee Yung-san, and the Chairman of the Council of Agriculture, Fan Chen-tsung. They were replaced by Lin Chuan and Lee Chin-lung, respectively. The departure of the respected Lee Yung-san, and the appointment of the third finance minister in as many years, raised concerns about political stability.

Meanwhile, attention began to focus on elections for the mayoralties of Taipei and Kaohsiung, which took place in early December 2002. In Taipei the incumbent mayor, Ma Ying-jeou of the KMT, defeated his DPP rival, Lee Ying-yuan, winning 64.1% of the votes cast. Thus, he immediately emerged as a potential presidential candidate. His popularity complicated efforts by the KMT and PFP to select one of their respective party chairmen, Lien Chan or James Soong, as the joint presidential candidate of the 'pan-blue' camp. In Kaohsiung the incumbent mayor, Frank Hsieh of the DPP, narrowly defeated his KMT rival, Huang Chun-ying, by 50.0% to 46.8% of the votes cast.

In February 2003 President Chen appointed Chiou I-jen, hitherto Secretary-General of the National Security Council, as Secretary-General to the President, while Kang Ning-hsiang, hitherto Vice-Minister of National Defense, succeeded Chiou in his former position. Following criticism of his handling of the outbreak of Severe Acute Respiratory Syndrome (SARS), the Minister of Health, Twu Shiing-jer, resigned in May 2003. By June the virus had killed more than 80 people on the island.

The issue of Taiwan's very identity came to the fore once again in September 2003, when as many as 150,000 independence activists, led by former President Lee Teng-hui, rallied in Taipei to demand that the island's name be formally changed from the 'Republic of China' to 'Taiwan'. The continued use of the former had remained the source of much international confusion, and it was believed that the adoption of 'Taiwan' would facilitate wider diplomatic recognition. A rival rally, attended mainly by veterans of the civil war and their descendants (who continued to favour eventual reunification with the mainland), attracted several thousand supporters. Also in September, President Chen proposed the drafting of a new constitution for Taiwan.

In November 2003 Taiwan's legislature approved a new law to allow referendums to be held on the island, prompting strong criticism from China (see Cross-straits Relations). The approval of the legislation followed President Chen's formal declaration of his intention to stand for re-election in the 2004 presidential election. In December 2003 President Chen announced plans to hold a referendum on the issue of China's deployment of missiles against Taiwan, to coincide with the forthcoming presidential poll. Also in December, President Chen confirmed that Vice-President Annette Lu, a vocal supporter of Taiwanese independence, would also stand for re-election. Opposition presidential candidate Lien Chan and vice-presidential candidate James Soong, of the KMT and of the allied PFP, respectively, as well as the popular mayor of Taipei, Ma Ying-jeou of the KMT, expressed strong opposition to the proposed referendum. In February 2004 demonstrations involving more than 70,000 people took place in southern Taiwan in support of the referendum. At the end of February, in Taiwan's largest ever demonstration, an estimated 1.5m. people formed a 500-km 'human chain', linking hands across the island to protest against China's deployment of missiles. Meanwhile, the wording of the referendum question had been modified to ask voters whether, in the event of China's refusal to withdraw its missiles, they would favour a strengthening of Taiwan's defence system.

President Chen's re-election and subsequent events

In a dramatic development on the day prior to the presidential election, while campaigning in Tainan both President Chen and Vice-President Lu were injured in a shooting incident. (The alleged assailant, Chen Yi-hsiung, was an unemployed man who was reported to have committed suicide shortly afterwards; however, further doubts with regard to these events were subsequently raised—see below). Neither Chen nor Lu were seriously hurt in the apparent assassination attempt, and the poll proceeded as planned on 20 March 2004. President Chen was re-elected by a narrow margin of 29,518 votes, equivalent to only 0.2% of valid votes, with 337,297 ballot papers being declared invalid. A turn-out of 80.28% of the electorate was recorded. However, in the concurrent referendum on the issue of Taiwan's response to the deployment of mainland missiles, the majority of citizens declined to vote on President Chen's proposals, thus indicating widespread division within Taiwan on the issue of the island's relationship with China. President Chen's re-election was immediately challenged by opposition candidate Lien Chan, who claimed that there had been irregularities in the electoral process and demanded a recount of the votes. Supporters of Lien rioted in Taipei and other cities.

In April 2004 the Minister of the Interior, Yu Cheng-hsien, resigned, citing the failure to prevent the shooting of President Chen as the reason for his departure. In the same month the Minister of Foreign Affairs, Eugene Chien, resigned in connection with the departure of the head of the American Institute in Taiwan (see Foreign Affairs). A recount of votes cast in the presidential election was completed on 19 May. It was estimated that 38,000 ballots were controversial, and that of these 23,000 were votes for Chen. Nevertheless, President Chen was inaugurated for a second term on 20 May, and on the same day he announced appointments to the new Executive Yuan. Yu Shyi-kun was retained as Premier. In July remarks by Vice-President Annette Lu suggesting a resettlement of Taiwan's aboriginal communities to South America caused widespread offence among the island's indigenous population. In the same month a new political party, the pro-independence Formosa Party, was inaugurated. In August the Legislative Yuan approved a bill on constitutional changes, which included plans for a reduction in the number of legislators and for reform of the electoral system. Also in August, there was controversy surrounding the establishment of an independent committee to investigate the shooting of President Chen, with the President of the Judicial Yuan claiming that the investigatory powers being given to this body were unconstitutional. In September protests took place in Taipei against the special budget of NT $610,800m. for the purchase of US weapons, which had been approved by the Executive Yuan in June.

In the election for the Legislative Yuan in December 2004 the 'pan-green' alliance of the DPP and the TSU secured 101 seats, whereas the 'pan-blue' alliance, comprising the KMT, the PFP and the NP, won 114 seats. The resulting opposition majority in the legislature was expected to hinder President Chen's plans for constitutional changes. Chen resigned as DPP Chairman after the election, taking responsibility for the party's failure to secure a larger number of seats. Meanwhile, disputes over the legitimacy of President Chen's victory in March continued, with a High Court rejecting two opposition attempts, in November and December respectively, to nullify the presidential election result.

In January 2005 the Executive Yuan approved a draft amendment to the referendum law (see above), requiring any changes to Taiwan's boundaries to be approved by the population. Later in

TAIWAN

January Premier Yu Shyi-kun and all members of the Executive Yuan resigned prior to the first meeting of the new Legislative Yuan. President Chen subsequently appointed Frank Hsieh, mayor of Kaohsiung and a leading member of the DPP, as Premier. Most outgoing ministers were reappointed to their former posts. Also in January, Secretary-General Su Tseng-chang was appointed Chairman of the DPP, replacing Chen; former Premier Yu Shyi-kun was subsequently appointed Secretary-General in his place. In February Premier Hsieh appointed Wu Rong-i as Vice-Premier and Minister of the Consumer Protection Commission.

In March 2005 a large rally, attended by President Chen, took place in Taipei in protest at the approval of anti-secession legislation by China's National People's Congress (NPC). On 14 May elections were held for an ad hoc National Assembly, which was to convene in order to ratify or reject the range of constitutional amendments approved by the Legislative Yuan in August 2004. The DPP secured 127 of the Assembly's 300 seats, having received 42.5% of votes cast, while the KMT won 117 seats. When the Assembly came to vote in June 2005, 248 members were in favour of the amendments, 23 more than the two-thirds' majority required for ratification. The amendments to the Constitution were thus passed into law. They included a reduction in the number of seats in the Legislative Yuan (from 225 to 113), reforms to the electoral system, the transfer of the power to impeach the President and Vice-President from the National Assembly to the Judicial Yuan, and the ratification of all future constitutional amendment proposals by popular referendum (requiring the approval of 50% of eligible voters, following approval by 75% of the Legislative Yuan). These reforms were due to come into effect before the next legislative elections, scheduled for 2007. Meanwhile, in June and again in September 2005 the Supreme Court rejected the appeals of the 'pan-blue' alliance to have the results of the presidential election declared invalid. In July Ma Ying-jeou, the mayor of Taipei, was chosen as Chairman of the KMT, in the party's first leadership election. Ma received 72.4% of votes cast by party members to defeat Wang Jin-pyng, President of the Legislative Yuan. In August the Supreme Prosecutor's Office announced that it was closing its investigation into the shooting of President Chen and Vice-President Lu in the previous year.

The mid-term elections for city mayors and county magistrates held in December 2005 resulted in significant gains for the KMT, which took 14 of the 23 contested constituencies, leading to considerable embarrassment for the DPP, which won in only six. The KMT also outperformed the DPP in elections for county councillors, township governors and magistrates. Su Tseng-chang resigned from the post of Chairman of the DPP, and Yu Shyi-kun, the former Premier and latterly Secretary-General to the President, was subsequently elected as his replacement.

In January 2006 Frank Hsieh resigned as Premier, citing the failure of the legislature to approve his proposed budget for 2006 as the main reason for his departure, while also hinting at policy disagreements with President Chen; in his farewell speech Hsieh warned Chen that the policy of a separate sovereign identity for Taiwan was not supported by the majority of the population. The DPP's poor electoral performance was also regarded by some as a contributory factor in his resignation, as was a scandal over allegations of corruption and exploitation surrounding the construction of the metro system in the city of Kaohsiung, where hundreds of Thai construction workers had reportedly rioted in August 2005 in protest at their poor living and working conditions. President Chen appointed Su Tseng-chang to replace Hsieh; the new appointee thereby became Chen's fifth Premier since the President's accession to power in 2000. The new Executive Yuan was sworn in on 25 January 2006. Tsai Ing-wen became Vice-Premier and Minister of the Consumer Protection Commission, Lee Yi-yang was appointed Minister of the Interior, Huang Chih-fang was the new Minister of Foreign Affairs, and Joseph J. C. Lyu took the post of Minister of Finance. In all, 14 new appointments were made, while the remaining 29 members of the Executive Yuan were retained from the previous administration. Meanwhile, President Chen appointed the former Minister of Foreign Affairs, Dr Tan Sun Chen, to the position of Secretary-General to the President, after the post was reportedly refused by Hsieh, who stated his intention to withdraw from politics.

President Chen's reiteration in January 2006 of his commitment to the ratification by referendum of a new constitution by 2008, his proposed abolition of the NUC and his declaration that he intended to reapply for membership of the UN under the name of 'Taiwan' (see above) drew strong criticism from the opposition. Joseph Wu, Minister of the Mainland Affairs Council, noted that the NUC had not in fact convened since 1999 and was so poorly funded as to be effectively useless. In February 2006 the DPP administration announced its intention to change Taiwan's official name, its flag, its national anthem and the definition of its territory. In April Chen participated in an unprecedented televised meeting with Ma Ying-jeou. On the following day the special defence budget proposed in June 2004 was opposed for the 50th time by the 'pan-blue' alliance in the Legislative Yuan.

In May 2006 President Chen's authority was greatly undermined by the detention of his son-in-law, Chao Chien-ming, on charges of insider dealing. It was alleged that in 2005 Chao had purchased in his mother's name 20m. shares in the Taiwan Development Corporation, a state-owned property company, having learned that the value of the company's stock was about to increase. Chao relinquished his membership of the DPP in an attempt to protect the party's image. (Subsequently indicted, along with his father and three others, Chao was sentenced to six years' imprisonment in December.) Although Chen had apologized to the nation for his family's involvement in the affair, the PFP instigated a campaign to remove the President from office.

Also in May 2006, former DPP legislator Shen Fu-hsiung confirmed an allegation that in the 1990s, during his campaign for the mayoralty of Taipei, President Chen had received no fewer than six political donations from the fugitive tycoon Chen You-hao. (Chen You-hao, the former head of the Tuntex group, had fled Taiwan in 2002 when the conglomerate was in financial difficulties; he was subsequently accused of embezzling funds from the group.) Shen also claimed that he had accompanied Chen You-hao on a visit to the President's wife, Wu Shu-jen (also a former legislator), to whom the tycoon had given nearly US $200,000, an accusation that Wu had previously denied. Two days later the 'pan-blue' alliance submitted a recall motion to the legislature, in the hope of removing President Chen.

On 1 June 2006, under intense political pressure, President Chen ceded much of his authority to Premier Su Tseng-chang. Henceforth the President would no longer have the power to dictate policy or to appoint members of the Executive Yuan, but would remain in charge of foreign and defence policy and would oversee relations with the People's Republic. The President also announced that he would play no further active role within the DPP. However, opposition politicians continued to demand Chen's resignation; protest rallies were held in the days that followed in an effort to increase pressure on the President to stand down. In a live televised speech Chen defended his administration and denied the allegations that had been made against his family. The motion of recall was voted upon in late June: despite gaining some support from the KMT (90 votes, including that of Wang Jin-pyng, the President of the Legislative Yuan, who was supposed to remain neutral), the 'pan-blue' alliance received just 119 votes, thus falling short of the number of votes (two-thirds of the seats currently occupied) required to submit the motion to a national referendum.

At the end of June 2006 it was announced that Ho Chih-chin, an academic, would succeed Joseph J. C. Lyu as Minister of Finance. Lyu, who had come under criticism for his handling of negotiations over the management of Mega Financial Holding (a major provider of financial services), retained a position within the Executive Yuan, as Minister without Portfolio. In early July party factions within the DPP unanimously approved the candidacy of former Premier Frank Hsieh in the forthcoming Taipei mayoral election.

The increasing unpopularity of President Chen

Controversy surrounding President Chen continued. In July 2006 prosecutors questioned Wu Shu-jen in relation to allegations that the President's wife and her doctor, Huang Fang-yen, had acted on behalf of businessmen who wished to acquire the Sogo department store, and that in return Wu had accepted gift vouchers worth about US $185,000. A newspaper report claimed that forged receipts to the value of around US $600,000 had been submitted for reimbursement under the special allowances budget of the Office of the President. This was confirmed by a KMT legislator, Chiu Yi, who accused the President of having embezzled the money, although Chiu failed to provide any evidence to support his allegation. The Office of the President also came under scrutiny for the alleged improper use of taxpayers' money from May 2000 to pay the wages of the housekeeper at an apartment occupied by the President before his move to his official residence in January 2001, and which subsequently became the home of his daughter. DPP legislators in turn accused KMT Chairman Ma Ying-jeou of remitting a proportion of his official allowance as mayor of Taipei into his personal account for private use, and reported their suspicions to the National Audit Office. Meanwhile, Premier Su Tseng-chang appeared to be consolidating his position within the DPP after the Conference on Sustaining Taiwan's Economic Development, held in late July 2006, during which he gained the support of local business groups and trade unions. At the DPP convention, also held in July, the party voted by a small majority to dissolve its factions in an attempt to promote unity.

In August 2006 the Executive Yuan underwent a further reorganization when the Minister of Economic Affairs, Hwang In-san, who had resigned on the grounds of ill health, was replaced by his deputy, Chen Ruey-long. Also in August, the Minister of Transportation and Communications, Kuo Yao-chi, offered to resign, in order to take responsibility for a scandal that had arisen from the controversial awarding of a contract for an electronic motorway toll collection system. She was replaced by Tsai Duei. Prosecutors began to question President Chen over the alleged misuse of public funds. Meanwhile, the President continued to antagonize the KMT (and mainland China) by reiterating that he intended to draft a new constitution and that Taiwan should apply to join the UN as an observer under the name of 'Taiwan'. In early August the PFP announced that it would begin an attempt to impeach Chen. Shih Ming-teh, a former DPP chairman, subsequently announced the formation of a 'one million people' mass movement to remove the President from office. Within days Shih's campaign had attracted more than 1m. supporters, each of whom donated NT $100 to show their commitment to the cause. Shih vowed that he and his supporters would stage a round-the-clock protest outside the presidential office in the following month and that they would not disperse until the President resigned. Neither the KMT nor the PFP was prepared officially to participate in the campaign, instead encouraging party members to attend the rallies.

In September 2006 at least 100,000 demonstrators took to the streets of Taipei, wearing red to signify their anger at Chen's alleged corruption. Despite inclement weather conditions, around 4,000 spent the night in front of the presidential office, and many stayed for several days until a march later in the month; the DPP organized a rival rally the next day. The PFP again attempted to initiate a recall motion against the President, and in late September the Legislative Yuan voted by 106 to 82 to refer the motion for review by a parliamentary committee prior to a full debate in the Legislative Yuan in October. By mid-October the momentum against the President had increased, with violent skirmishes (including a scuffle between two rival legislators from the DPP and KMT) marring the official National Day celebrations. Demonstrators caused serious disruption of the events, obstructing Chen's motorcade, blocking roads and effectively besieging the presidential office. None the less, the next recall motion against Chen again failed when the opposition secured only 116 votes, still short of the requisite two-thirds' majority. Later in October the opposition once more blocked a controversial arms bill involving multi-million dollar weapons purchases from the USA (see above).

In early October 2006 President Chen's wife, Wu Shu-jen, had been cleared by prosecutors of wrongdoing during the takeover of the Sogo department store on the basis of lack of evidence. In early November, however, prosecutors declared that they had sufficient evidence to charge Chen with misuse of public funds and that they were prevented from doing so only by his presidential immunity. However, no such immunity protected Wu Shu-jen, who was indicted along with three former presidential aides on charges of forgery and corruption. According to the prosecutors, Wu and the three senior aides had misappropriated NT $14.8m. from the 'state affairs fund'. While the prosecutors accepted Chen's explanation that in two of the six cases being investigated the funds had been used for secret diplomatic missions, they concluded that the use of such assets in four other cases could not be verified. Opposition members immediately demanded Chen's resignation and urged the DPP to join them in approving a motion of recall against the President, who attributed the apparent irregularities in the use of the state affairs fund to poorly defined regulations. Meanwhile, thousands of protesters once more took to the streets of Taipei, again demanding the President's resignation. The demonstration was spurned by the PFP and the KMT; however, the latter warned that the President could be impeached only by formal legal proceedings. The opposition then initiated a third recall motion against the President. Furthermore, disagreements began to emerge within the ranks of the DPP, when two members resigned from the Legislative Yuan in order to demonstrate dissatisfaction with their party's handling of the scandal. DPP legislators filed a lawsuit against Ma Ying-jeou, accusing him of embezzling public funds.

When the crucial recall vote was held in late November 2006, the DPP again rallied to support its leader, boycotting the vote and thus preventing the motion from obtaining the requisite two-thirds' majority. Moreover, at mayoral elections held in Taipei and Kaohsiung in December the DPP performed better than anticipated. Although the DPP candidate in Taipei, Frank Hsieh, lost to his KMT rival, Hau Long-bin, Hsieh nevertheless garnered 40.9% of the votes, an increase of 5.0% in comparison with the mayoral election of 2002. In Kaohsiung the DPP candidate, Chen Chu, won by a narrow margin to become the island's first female mayor.

Party differences were temporarily, and somewhat unexpectedly, put aside in late December 2006 when the KMT voted with the Government to place the long-delayed arms procurement bill (see above) on the legislative agenda. The proposed legislation, which the KMT had previously boycotted along with the PFP, would provide for the purchase of US weapons from the annual budget of the Ministry of National Defense, rather than from a special budget. However, the passage of the legislation remained uncertain, as the KMT voted against a motion providing for the bill to be referred directly for a second reading. In June 2007 budget legislation, which encompassed funding for military procurement that had been debated and altered by the Legislative Yuan, was finally approved.

In January 2007 the KMT and PFP formalized a party alliance, undertaking to present a single candidate in each district in the legislative election scheduled for the end of the year. In March Lee Jye, the Minister of National Defense, was expelled from the KMT as a result of a dispute regarding a government order to remove statues of Chiang Kai-shek from military premises, a decision with which Lee had complied. Ma Ying-jeou had resigned from the chairmanship of the KMT in February following accusations of forgery and of the embezzlement of NT $11.2m. during his tenure of the mayoralty of Taipei. Ma denied the allegations and reiterated his intention to stand as a presidential candidate in 2008. Although he was replaced as KMT Chairman in April by Wu Poh-hsiung, in May the party confirmed Ma's candidacy for the presidency of Taiwan, and in August 2007 he was acquitted of all charges. Meanwhile, in May 2007, following his defeat by former Premier Frank Hsieh in the contest for the nomination of the DPP presidential candidate, Su Tseng-chang resigned as Premier. President Chen appointed Chang Chun-hsiung, who had served as Premier in 2000–02, to replace Su. Premier Chang Chun-hsiung subsequently effected a government reorganization, although many of the incumbent members of the Executive Yuan were retained; notable exceptions included Tsai Ing-wen, who was succeeded by Chiou I-jen as Vice-Premier and Minister of the Consumer Protection Commission, and Lee Jye, who was replaced by Lee Tien-yu in the position of Minister of National Defense.

In September 2007 several prominent members of the DPP, including Chairman Yu Shyi-kun, Vice-President Annette Lu and former Minister of Foreign Affairs (Mark) Chen Tan-sun, were indicted on charges of corruption and forgery. Yu Shyi-kun, who resigned from the DPP chairmanship with immediate effect, was charged with the misuse of funds, which he claimed had been spent on public, rather than private, affairs. Meanwhile, similar charges against the DPP's presidential candidate, Frank Hsieh, and his vice-presidential candidate, Su Tseng-Chang, were abandoned. President Chen returned to the position of DPP Chairman in October. In September the DPP had adopted a resolution affirming Taiwan's separate identity and appealing for a new constitution and a referendum on the issue of sovereignty; the name of Taiwan, it was stated, should enter into common usage without necessarily abolishing the official designation of the 'Republic of China'. The DPP continued its campaign against the commemoration of Chiang Kai-shek, cancelling two public holidays honouring the former President in August, and removing Chiang's name from a memorial hall in Taipei in December.

The return to power of the KMT

Legislative elections held on 12 January 2008 resulted in a resounding victory for the KMT, which secured 81 seats (out of a reduced total of 113 seats in accordance with the constitutional amendments of 2005); the DPP, with only 27 seats, was thus defeated by a considerable margin. The Non-Partisan Solidarity

Union (NPSU) won three seats and the KMT's alliance partner, the PFP, only one. Turn-out was extremely low in comparison with previous elections, at approximately 58%. Wang Jin-pyng was subsequently re-elected President of the Legislative Yuan. Voters were also presented with two proposals at referendums, both of which were rejected: the first proposed measure was the seizure of state assets allegedly appropriated by the KMT during and after its assumption of power in 1945; the second, submitted by the KMT, entailed additional anti-corruption measures. The results were widely regarded as an indication of public opposition to the DPP's forceful stance on sovereignty and Taiwan's status, as well as of the fear of jeopardizing relations with the mainland and of alienating the island's strategic allies. Following the DPP's defeat, Chen resigned as the party's Chairman and was replaced by Frank Hsieh. Premier Chang Chun-hsiung and the other members of the Executive Yuan submitted their resignations, but President Chen refused to accept these, citing a need for stability. In February, however, the Premier accepted the resignation of Lee Tien-yu from the post of Minister of National Defense, owing to criticism of his role in the establishment of a weapons company, the majority of which was privately owned. In mid-March the Minister of Finance, Ho Chih-chin, resigned, following his involvement in a scuffle at the offices of the DPP's presidential candidate, Frank Hsieh. Meanwhile, the election pledges of presidential candidate Ma Ying-jeou included an undertaking to pursue neither unification nor independence.

On 22 March 2008 Ma Ying-jeou of the KMT was elected the island's President, having received almost 58.5% of the votes cast, thus defeating Frank Hsieh, who subsequently announced that he would resign as Chairman of the DPP. At 76.3%, the level of participation by voters in the presidential election was high. However, the results of two concurrent referendums on the issue of the island's application for membership of the UN were declared invalid: although the number of votes in favour of each proposal exceeded 50% of the ballots cast, the total number of votes exercised failed to reach the requisite threshold of 50% of the registered electorate. The first proposal, which sought approval for the island's application under the name of Taiwan, was supported by the DPP; the KMT urged that this referendum be boycotted. The second referendum, initiated by the KMT, asked voters if they supported an application to return to the UN as 'the Republic of China' or alternatively as Taiwan or under any other suitable designation. Liu Chao-shiuan, a former Vice-Premier and hitherto President of Soochow University, was subsequently nominated as the island's Premier by the President-elect. In early May, just weeks before the swearing-in of the new Government, Vice-Premier Chiou I-jen and Minister of Foreign Affairs Huang Chih-fang submitted their resignations as a result of a funding controversy: it was alleged that an attempt in 2006 to persuade Papua New Guinea to transfer diplomatic recognition from China to Taiwan, using almost US $30m. in aid, had failed, and that one of the intermediaries had absconded with the money. As the scandal widened, President Chen also denied his involvement in the affair; however, he and several others were subsequently prosecuted and brought to trial (see below). It was feared that the scandal had damaged Taiwan's reputation by drawing international attention to the practice of so-called 'chequebook diplomacy'.

Ma Ying-jeou was sworn in as President on 20 May 2008. Important appointments to the Executive Yuan, led by incoming Premier Liu Chao-shiuan and incorporating many who had served as ministers in the previous KMT administration, included that of Li Sush-der as Minister of Finance and that of Francisco H. L. Ou as Minister of Foreign Affairs. The new cabinet also included a record 11 women, notably Wang Ching-feng as Minister of Justice. Almost immediately, his presidential immunity having been removed upon his departure from office, it emerged that a corruption inquiry involving former President Chen had been instigated; in August, amid further allegations of financial impropriety, Chen left the DPP. Meanwhile, in May Tsai Ing-wen, a former Vice-Premier, was elected Chairwoman of the DPP, replacing Frank Hsieh.

In the latter part of 2008, as the island's economy began to deteriorate, large anti-Government protests were held. In October an estimated 600,000 Taiwanese attended a rally in Taipei, organized by the opposition DPP, to protest against the policies of President Ma Ying-jeou. The demonstrators were highly critical not only of the President's conduct of the economy but also of his policy of wider engagement with mainland China. In November about 150 police officers and dozens of protesters were reported to have been injured in violent clashes in Taipei during the visit of a senior mainland official, Chen Yunlin, whose presence on the island provoked renewed protests against President Ma Ying-jeou's policy of developing closer relations with the People's Republic.

In July 2008 the 15-year prison sentence imposed on Yen Wan-chin, former Vice-Minister of the Interior in the DPP administration, was reduced by the High Court when one of the bribery charges upon which he had been convicted in September 2007 was successfully challenged. Nevertheless, public concern about the issue of corruption continued to increase. Former Vice-Premier Chiou I-jen was arrested on charges of embezzlement at the end of October 2008; the senior DPP member was accused of having misappropriated diplomatic funds totalling US $500,000 in 2004.

In November 2008 former President Chen Shui-bian was taken into custody on suspicion of having embezzled public funds. After being detained for a month, Chen was formally indicted in December on charges of forgery, corruption, embezzlement and money-laundering. He was returned to prison, after being briefly released from detention. Chen's wife, son, daughter-in-law and 10 former colleagues were indicted on similar charges. In February 2009 Wu Shu-jen, the former President's wife (who owing to ill health had been unable to attend her trial in 2006—see above), pleaded guilty to charges of money-laundering and forgery, but she continued to deny charges of embezzlement. Her son, Chen Chih-chung, and other defendants also pleaded guilty to money-laundering charges. The trial of former President Chen, who had been an outspoken critic of the KMT Government, opened in March 2009, amid suggestions that it was politically motivated and related to his support for the independence of Taiwan. In September Chen was sentenced to life imprisonment upon his conviction by the Taipei District Court on various charges of corruption related to his misuse between 2000 and 2008 of public funds totalling the equivalent of US $15m. The former President's wife, who earlier in September had been found guilty of perjury, also received a life sentence. Chen Chih-chung and the former President's daughter-in-law were found guilty of money-laundering but received relatively short prison terms, while other relatives were given suspended sentences. Two former advisers were sentenced to 16 and 20 years' imprisonment. Following his conviction, Chen made an unsuccessful attempt to claim that technically Taiwan remained under US military occupation and that the island's Government therefore had no legal right to place him on trial. Later in September prosecutors issued a series of new indictments against the former President and four others, including former Vice-Premier Chiou I-jen, alleging that funds allocated to the advancement of diplomatic relations had been embezzled (see Foreign Affairs), but in June 2010 Chen was acquitted on the charge of misappropriating diplomatic funds. However, the pursuit of various other charges against the former President, which included the abetting of his subordinates to give false testimony, continued (see below).

Following the publication in November 2009 of the findings of a new investigation into the apparent attempt to assassinate Chen in 2004, fresh suspicions about the pre-election incident were raised. In addition to the issue of the apparent lack of blood-stains, the Control Yuan's report drew attention to the manner of the suspect's death by drowning, which appeared to be inconsistent with suicide. His widow, moreover, claimed that her confession of her husband's involvement in the alleged shooting had been made under duress. The KMT, which had ordered the new inquiry following its return to office, continued to maintain that the former President had fabricated the incident in order to attract the sympathy of voters. Former Vice-President Annette Lu stated her belief that two gunmen had been responsible and urged the instigation of another inquiry into the affair.

In May 2009, meanwhile, as the first anniversary of President Ma Ying Jeou's assumption of office approached, thousands of protesters again demonstrated on the streets of Taipei against the Government's policy of greater engagement with the mainland. Tsai Ing-wen, Chairwoman of the opposition DPP, claimed that Taiwanese sovereignty was being seriously compromised and stated that the DPP would seek the holding of a referendum on the issue of Ma's plans for a free trade agreement with China. Tsai led a march to the presidential office, where an overnight sit-in protest was held. Thousands more participated in demonstrations in the southern city of Kaohsiung and elsewhere.

In August 2009 Taiwan was devastated by Typhoon Morakot. More than 600 people were killed in the resultant mudslides and flooding. The Government appealed for international assistance, in particular large cargo aircraft capable of transporting digging equipment, cranes and other machinery to the remote mountain areas affected by the typhoon. Although the army was swiftly mobilized, the rescue effort was hampered by the continuation of heavy rain. The Government was subsequently criticized for the shortcomings in its response to the disaster. On 7 September Premier Liu Chao-Shiuan unexpectedly announced that President Ma Ying-jeou had accepted his resignation, submitted in mid-August in order to take responsibility for the failings in the Government's handling of the aftermath of the typhoon. Liu was replaced by Wu Den-yih, hitherto the Secretary-General of the ruling KMT. Chu Li-luan was appointed as Vice-Premier. In a major reorganization of the Executive Yuan, veteran diplomat Timothy Yang replaced Francisco Ou as Minister of Foreign Affairs. Other appointments included that of Jiang Yi-huah as Minister of the Interior and Kao Hua-chu as Minister of National Defense. The Minister of Finance, Li Sush-der, retained his portfolio. The appointment in late September of Shen Lyu-shun as Deputy Minister of Foreign Affairs drew intense criticism from the opposition DPP, owing to his involvement in an embezzlement scandal relating to his tenure during 2003–08 as head of Taiwan's representative office in Switzerland.

In July 2009 President Ma Ying-jeou was elected unopposed by party members as Chairman of the KMT, to replace Wu Po-hsiung in mid-October. As Chairman of the ruling party, therefore, Ma would be in a position to exercise greater control over the legislature, particularly with regard to the approval of appointments. On a party-to-party basis, Ma would also be able to exert more influence over Taiwan's relations with mainland China.

At local elections held in December 2009 the DPP won a much larger percentage of votes than that secured at previous local polls. A significant factor in the decline in support for the KMT was thought to be President Ma's focus on closer relations with mainland China, which many believed would ultimately jeopardize the island's sovereignty as well as lead to job losses. Shortly after the polls, King Pu-tsung replaced Chan Chun-po as Secretary-General of the KMT. Also, having returned to the post only eight months previously, Wu Nai-jen resigned as Secretary-General of the DPP on the grounds of ill health; he was subsequently replaced by Su Jia-chyuan. Amid increasing fears about Taiwan's growing economic dependency on China, later in December an estimated 30,000 Taiwanese joined a march through the city of Taichung to protest against the visit of senior mainland official Chen Yulin, who had travelled from Beijing to attend negotiations on a bilateral trade agreement. The KMT suffered further reverses at by-elections in early 2010, when it lost six of seven seats contested to the DPP. Although the latter's representation in the Legislative Yuan was increased to 33 seats, the KMT nevertheless retained a large majority. In March, however, the KMT also performed less well than anticipated at local elections to choose the speakers and vice-speakers of county and city councils. Nevertheless, in June the KMT fared better than the DPP at local elections in 17 counties and cities.

Wang Ching-feng, the Minister of Justice, unexpectedly resigned in March 2010, owing to her opposition to the removal of the five-year moratorium on the implementation of the death penalty. A former human rights activist, Wang had refused to approve the enforcement of the penalty on 44 prisoners who awaited execution, her stance being at variance with that of the Government. She was replaced by Tseng Yung-fu. Other new appointments to the Executive Yuan included that of Emile Chi-jen Sheng, who assumed the post of Minister of the Council for Cultural Affairs. Also in March, the Minister of the Department of Health, Yaung Chih-liang, withdrew his resignation, submitted earlier in the month but rejected by the Premier, with whom he had disagreed about the scale of increases in health insurance costs.

There were violent scenes in the Legislative Yuan in April 2010, when opponents clashed during a debate on the issue of the opening of Taiwanese institutes of higher education to students from mainland China. In May, in order to pursue his election campaign for a mayoralty, Vice-Premier Eric Chu resigned from the Executive Yuan. He was replaced by Sean Chen, hitherto the Chairman of the Financial Supervisory Commission, who also assumed his predecessor's responsibility for the Consumer Protection Commission. Chen Yu-chang was appointed to chair the Financial Supervisory Commission, and Christina Liu became Minister of the Council for Economic Planning and Development, succeeding Tsai Hsun-hsiung.

In late June 2010 tens of thousands of demonstrators, including former President Lee Teng-hui, rallied in Taipei to protest against the Government's proposals for the new trade agreement with China. The opposition DPP and TSU maintained that the proposed ECFA would not only jeopardize Taiwanese manufacturing industries, by permitting a substantial increase in imports of inexpensive products from the mainland, but also undermine the island's separate political identity; however, the parties' demands for the holding of referendum on the issue of the ECFA were repeatedly rejected. In the following month several members of the Legislative Yuan were injured and the Premier was prevented from delivering his speech when the opposition disrupted the introduction of the law into the chamber. The Speaker then ruled that the bill should proceed directly to its second reading, thereby circumventing the committee stage. In response to this omission of the process of detailed examination, the DPP declared that it would boycott all forthcoming parliamentary proceedings.

Recent developments: further corruption scandals and other events

In July 2010 the President of the Judicial Yuan, Lai In-jaw, and the body's Vice-President resigned in response to the arrest of three high court judges and one prosecutor in connection with a new corruption scandal. It was alleged that the senior judges had collectively accepted bribes, totalling as much as NT $1m., in exchange for the acquittal of a former KMT legislator and county magistrate (whose whereabouts subsequently became unknown) on charges of financial impropriety related to the development of a science park. In August, following an extensive operation by the authorities, several additional suspects were detained in connection with the allegations. In July, meanwhile, with public concern about the involvement of senior functionaries in such cases rising, President Ma announced the establishment of a new agency to combat official corruption. The agency, which was to form part of the Ministry of Justice, was to comprise four departments, one of which was to be responsible for government ethics. Legislation providing for the establishment of the agency received parliamentary approval in April 2011. A human rights commission, headed by Vice-President Vincent Siew, was established in December 2010.

In September 2010 eight incumbent and former members of the Legislative Yuan received prison sentences of between seven and 10 years, following their conviction on charges of bribery. Six of the defendants had been acquitted in a previous trial. In the following month the new President of the Judicial Yuan, Lai Hau-min, expressed his determination to eradicate corruption. In November a total of 13 officials were indicted in connection with the judicial corruption case. In January 2011 the Commander of the Air Force, Gen. Lei Yu-chi, was removed from his post, following the revelation that he had enlisted air force personnel to serve at lavish celebrations for the wedding of his son. Lei was replaced by Gen. Yen Ming. In March impeachment proceedings began against the three high court judges and the prosecutor arrested on charges of bribery.

Former President Chen's appeal against his conviction was rejected by the High Court in June 2010. However, on the basis that the sum involved was less than previously stated, his sentence was reduced from life imprisonment to 20 years, as was that of his wife. In November Chen was acquitted of bribery charges relating to a bank merger and to money-laundering activities. Wen and other family members, along with several others, were also acquitted on related charges. In the same month, however, the Surpreme Court upheld Chen's conviction in connection with two other bribery cases. In December the High Court ruled that the former President serve a maximum combined sentence of 17 years and six months. In February 2011, having recently received an additional sentence upon her conviction of further charges of bribery, the frail Wu Shu-jen was deemed unfit to remain in prison and released from detention. Meanwhile, her husband returned to court to answer new bribery charges.

Campaigning for the mayoral elections of November 2010 was marred by the shooting of Lien Chen-wen, the son of former Vice-President Lien Chan, and the killing of a bystander. Although it was widely believed that the attack was politically motivated, it was subsequently reported that Lien was not the intended target of the assailant, who was apparently involved in a dispute relating to a land transaction. In what was regarded as a major test for President Ma, the KMT won three important mayoralties, including that of Taipei, while the opposition DPP took the southern cities of Kaohsiung and Tainan. The KMT was also successful in elections for local speaker and vice-speaker posts in

December, when the DPP won only that of Tainan. Also in December, having been persuaded to return to the position in May, Wu Nai-jen confirmed his retirement as Secretary-General of the DPP. Su Jia-chyuan agreed to resume the post. The DPP was encouraged by its resounding success at by-elections to fill two vacant seats in the Legislative Yuan, held in Kaohsiung and Tainan in March 2011.

In January 2011 King Pu-tsung resigned as Secretary-General of the KMT, in order to lead President Ma Ying-jeou's campaign for re-election in 2012; King was replaced by Liao Liao-yi. At the beginning of February a minor cabinet reorganization included the appointment of Chiu Wen-ta as Minister of the Department of Health, in place of Yaung chi-liang who had resigned in early January. At the end of April President Ma was nominated unopposed as the KMT's presidential candidate. Meanwhile, Tsai Ing-wen became Taiwan's first female presidential candidate when she defeated former Premier Su Tseng-chang to secure the nomination of the DPP. In a departure from tradition, the next legislative and presidential elections were to be held simultaneously, on 14 January 2012.

Cross-straits Relations

The Government of Taiwan repeatedly rejected offers from the People's Republic to hold discussions on the reunification of China. In 1984, following the agreement between the People's Republic of China and the United Kingdom that China would regain sovereignty over the British colony of Hong Kong in 1997, mainland Chinese leaders urged Taiwan to accept similar proposals for reunification on the basis of 'one country—two systems'. In May 1986 the Government was forced to make direct contact with the Chinese Government for the first time, over the issue of a Taiwanese pilot who had defected to the mainland. In October 1987 the Government announced the repeal of the 38-year ban on visits to the mainland by Taiwanese citizens: only visits by civil servants and military personnel were still prohibited, and this ban was relaxed in November 1998. However, reconciliation initiatives were abruptly halted by the violent suppression of the pro-democracy movement in Beijing in June 1989. In May 1990 a proposal by the President of Taiwan to open direct dialogue on a government-to-government basis with the People's Republic was rejected by China, which continued to maintain that it would negotiate only on a party-to-party basis with the KMT.

In February 1991 the recently formed NUC, under the chairmanship of the President of Taiwan, put forward radical new proposals, whereby Taiwan and the People's Republic of China might recognize each other as separate political entities. In April a delegation from the Straits Exchange Foundation (SEF), established in late 1990 to deal with bilateral issues, travelled to Beijing for discussions, the first such delegation ever to visit the People's Republic. Also in April, Taiwanese President Lee Teng-hui announced the end of the state of war with the People's Republic, and 10 amendments to the Constitution were promulgated. In September the island's President asserted that Taiwan was a de facto sovereign and autonomous country. In December the non-governmental Association for Relations across the Taiwan Straits (ARATS) was established in Beijing. In January 1992 the SEF protested to the People's Republic over the detention of a former pilot of the mainland air force who had defected to Taiwan in 1965 and, upon returning to his homeland for a family reunion in December 1991, had been arrested. He subsequently received a 15-year prison sentence.

In July 1992 President Lee urged the establishment of 'one country, one good system'. Statutes to permit the further expansion of economic and political links with the People's Republic were adopted by the Legislative Yuan. Delegates from the SEF and ARATS met in Hong Kong in October for discussions. However, the Chairman of the Mainland Affairs Council insisted that the People's Republic renounce the use of military force prior to any dialogue on the reunification question.

In 1993 divisions between Taiwan's business sector and political groupings (the former advocating much closer links with the People's Republic, the latter urging greater caution) became evident. In January, and again later in the year, the Secretary-General of the SEF resigned, following disagreement with the Mainland Affairs Council. Historic talks between the Chairmen of the SEF and of the ARATS were held in Singapore in April. Taiwan and the People's Republic agreed on the establishment of a formal structure for negotiations on economic and social issues. Following a series of aircraft hijackings to Taiwan from the mainland, an SEF-ARATS meeting was held in Taiwan in December 1993, in an attempt to address the issue of the repatriation of hijackers. Further meetings between delegates of the SEF and ARATS were held in early 1994. In April, however, 24 Taiwanese tourists were among those robbed and killed on board a pleasure boat plying Qiandao Lake, in mainland China.

The SEF-ARATS talks were resumed in August 1994 when Tang Shubei, Vice-Chairman and Secretary-General of the ARATS, flew to Taipei for discussions with his Taiwanese counterpart, Chiao Jen-ho. The two sides reached tentative agreement on several issues, including the repatriation of hijackers and illegal immigrants from Taiwan to the mainland. Procedures for the settlement of cross-Straits fishing disputes were also established. In mid-November relations were strained once again when, in an apparent accident during a training exercise, Taiwanese anti-aircraft shells landed on a mainland village, injuring several people. Nevertheless, in late November a further round of SEF-ARATS talks took place in Nanjing, at which agreement in principle on the procedure for the repatriation of hijackers and illegal immigrants was confirmed. Further progress was made at meetings in Beijing in January 1995. It was announced in March that the SEF board of directors would henceforth include government officials, while meetings of the Mainland Affairs Council would be attended by officials of the SEF. In the same month the Mainland Affairs Council approved a resolution providing for the relaxation of restrictions on visits by mainland officials and civilians.

In April 1995 President Lee proposed a 'six-point' programme for cross-Straits relations, the objectives of which included unification in accordance with the reality of separate rules and increased trade relations. However, a meeting betweeen the SEF Chairman, Koo Chen-fu, and his mainland counterpart, Wang Daohan, was postponed by the ARATS, in protest at President Lee's recent visit to the USA. In July, furthermore, the People's Republic unexpectedly announced that it was about to conduct an eight-day programme of guided missile and artillery-firing tests off the northern coast of Taiwan. A second series of exercises took place in August. In January 1996 the Taiwanese Premier again urged the early resumption of cross-Straits dialogue, but in March the People's Republic began a new series of missile tests. Live artillery exercises continued in the Taiwan Strait until after the island's presidential election, arousing international concern.

In November 1996 the Mainland Affairs Council announced that the permanent stationing of mainland media representatives in Taiwan was to be permitted. Despite repeated SEF requests, Tang Shubei of the ARATS continued to assert that Taiwan's pursuit of its 'two Chinas' policy (a reference to President Lee's attempts to raise the diplomatic profile of the island) prevented the resumption of cross-Straits discussions. In January 1997, however, shipping representatives of Taiwan and of the People's Republic reached a preliminary consensus on the establishment of direct sea links. Limited services resumed in April, thus ending a ban of 48 years. In July, upon the reversion to Chinese sovereignty of the British colony of Hong Kong, President Lee firmly rejected the concept of 'one country, two systems' and any parallel with Taiwan.

In March 1997 a six-day visit to Taiwan by the Dalai Lama, the first to the island by the exiled spiritual leader of Tibet, was strongly condemned by the People's Republic of China, which denounced a meeting between President Lee and the exiled spiritual leader of Tibet as a 'collusion of splittists'. The Dalai Lama's subsequent visits to Taiwan were similarly criticized by China.

The declaration by an ARATS official in January 1998 that Taiwan did not need to recognize the Government of the People's Republic as the central Government as a precondition for dialogue was regarded as a significant concession on the part of the mainland authorities. However, Taiwan continued to insist that China abandon its demand that talks be conducted under its 'one China' principle. In April a delegation of the SEF visited the People's Republic. Following negotiations with the ARATS, it was announced that the Chairman of the SEF would visit the People's Republic later in 1998 formally to resume the dialogue, suspended since 1995. The arrest on the mainland in May 1998 of four Taiwanese business executives on charges of espionage and their subsequent conviction threatened to reverse the recent improvement in relations, but in July the Chinese Minister of Science and Technology visited Taiwan, the first such visit by a mainland Minister since the civil war. This was followed later in the month by a formal visit to Taiwan by the Deputy Secretary-General of the ARATS. The kidnap and murder in August in the People's Republic of a Taiwanese local government official caused serious concern. In October Koo Chen-fu, the SEF Chairman, travelled to the People's Republic for meetings with his ARATS counterpart, Wang Daohan. Koo's meeting with Chinese President Jiang Zemin represented the highest level of bilateral contact since 1949. Koo also had discussions with other senior officials. A four-point agreement was reached, allowing for increased bilateral communications. In April 1999 President Lee reaffirmed that the People's Republic should recognize Taiwan as being of equal status, that cross-Straits negotiations should concentrate on practical issues and that reunification could take place only if the mainland were to become a democracy. An SEF group went to Beijing in March, but in August the ARATS suspended contacts with the SEF, following President Lee's insistence on the 'two-state theory' (see below).

Meanwhile, China was becoming increasingly demonstrative in its opposition to Taiwan's inclusion in the US-led Theater Missile Defense (TMD) anti-missile system. Ballistic missiles were deployed in mainland coastal regions opposite Taiwan. In July 1999 the People's Republic announced that it had developed a neutron bomb, after declaring itself ready for war should Taiwan attempt to gain independence. This declaration was prompted by a radio interview given by President Lee, during which he asserted that relations with the People's Republic were 'state-to-state'. Chinese military exercises took place in the Taiwan Strait later that month, and in August the USA reaffirmed its readiness to defend Taiwan. Also in August, the ruling KMT incorporated the 'two-state theory' into the party resolution. In September, following a severe earthquake in Taiwan that killed or injured several thousand people, China was among the many countries to offer emergency assistance to the island; however, Taiwan accused the People's Republic of contravening humanitarian principles by trying to force other countries to seek its approval before offering help.

In February 2000 the People's Republic threatened to attack Taiwan if it indefinitely postponed reunification talks. In April the Vice-President-elect, Annette Lu, was denounced by the Chinese media after she made 'separatist' remarks, televised in Hong Kong, declaring that Taiwan was only a 'remote relative and close neighbour' of China. In October China published a policy document on its national defence, which confirmed that the People's Republic would use force to prevent Taiwanese secession. In November, however, Wu Po-hsiung, the Vice-Chairman of the KMT, travelled to Beijing and met unofficially with Chinese Vice-Premier Qian Qichen. Wu was the most senior KMT official to visit mainland China for more than 50 years. Also in November, Taiwan announced that journalists from the People's Republic were to be granted permission to stay in Taiwan for periods of up to one month. In December plans were announced for 'mini three links' with China, providing for direct trade, transport and postal links between the islands of Kinmen and Matsu and the mainland, albeit subject to rigorous security checks. In January 2001 groups sailed from Kinmen and Matsu to Xiamen and Fuzhou, respectively, in the People's Republic. Economic links continued to develop, with many Taiwanese companies investing on the mainland. In August President Chen endorsed a plan to expand commercial links with the People's Republic, a reversal of the previous Government's policy of limiting trade with the mainland.

In October 2001 Taiwan boycotted the APEC summit meeting in Shanghai, following China's refusal to allow Taiwan's chosen delegate, former Vice-President Li Yuan-tsu, to attend, on the grounds that he was not an 'economic' official. Despite this, the opposition DPP deleted from its charter a vow to achieve the island's formal independence, since it was already a de facto separate entity. In January 2002 the Government announced a list of more than 2,000 items that were to be legally importable from the mainland. In March China announced that, for the first time, two Taiwanese banks would be permitted to open offices on the mainland. Taiwan would allow mainland banks to establish offices on the island. The Taiwanese Government also eased restrictions on the island's companies investing in computer-chip manufacturing on the mainland, although controls would remain on the number of plants established and type of chips produced, mainly owing to security concerns.

In July 2002 the Taiwanese Ministry of National Defense warned in a biannual report that China's military spending was accelerating rapidly and that it would possess 600 short-range missiles targeted at the island by 2005. President Chen further antagonized the mainland in August 2002 by supporting demands for a referendum to determine the island's future.

Taiwan then cancelled planned military exercises as a gesture of good faith, but Chen's comments delayed the introduction of direct transport links. At the end of July the Government announced that Chinese products could be advertised on the island and that Chinese employees of Taiwanese or foreign companies would be allowed to work in Taiwan. A Taiwanese semiconductor manufacturer also announced plans to build a new factory on the Chinese mainland, in Shanghai. However, bilateral relations remained volatile, and in September President Chen described China's threats against the island as a form of 'terrorism'. China accused Taiwan of allowing the banned Falun Gong sect to use the island as a base for disrupting Chinese television and satellite broadcasts.

During 2002 Taiwan and China acquired advanced weaponry from the USA and Russia, respectively. In January 2003 President Chen stated that Taiwan was a sovereign state, and would never accept a Hong Kong-style solution nor federate with the mainland. Vice-President Lu described China as being of a 'terrorist nature', referring to its missile build-up across the Taiwan Strait. In late January, none the less, the first Taiwanese airliner in more than 50 years flew to mainland China, via Hong Kong, and landed in Shanghai. The flight was one of 16 charter operations organized by the Taiwanese carrier, China Airlines (CAL), to transport Taiwanese visitors in China home for Chinese New Year celebrations. In February the Minister of National Defense stated that Taiwan would not reduce weapons purchases from the USA in return for the dismantling of Chinese missiles targeting the island. His remarks followed Chinese President Jiang Zemin's offer of such an arrangement, made to US President George W. Bush in October 2002.

An outbreak on the mainland of a pneumonia-like virus, SARS), spread to Taiwan in early 2003. Taiwan accused the Chinese authorities of concealing the seriousness of the outbreak. In August the island's authorities arrested two Taiwanese citizens and a Taiwanese American on charges of spying for China. Also in August, a Chinese surveillance vessel was seen to the north of Taiwan. Military exercises simulating an attack on Taiwan by China were conducted in September. Taiwan's announcement in the same month that it was to issue new passports for its citizens, which for the first time would have 'Taiwan' printed on the front (ostensibly to distinguish Taiwanese passports more clearly from mainland documents), heightened cross-Straits tensions, as did mass protests in Taipei demanding that the name 'Taiwan' be used officially by government agencies and private companies (see Domestic Political Affairs). In October the island's legislature approved the so-called Act Governing Relations between Peoples of the Taiwan Area and the Mainland Area, which was to provide a framework for the regulation of travel and business links between Taiwan and the mainland.

In November 2003 the Taiwanese legislature approved a bill allowing referendums to take place on the island (see Domestic Political Affairs). Although the legislation in its final version prohibited a vote on Taiwan's sovereignty except in the event of an external attack, China feared that the new law might lead to the holding of a vote on Taiwan's independence. An official at China's Taiwan Affairs Office warned that President Chen would be 'risking war' should he initiate any move towards Taiwanese independence. In December the issue of Taiwan dominated a visit by Chinese Premier Wen Jiabao to Washington, DC, with Wen seeking assurance from the USA that it would not support moves towards Taiwanese independence. President Chen defended plans to hold a referendum in March 2004 on the subject of a proposed request to China that it remove hundreds of missiles aimed at the island. In January Chen stated that the referendum might include 'counter-proposals' such as direct transport links between Taiwan and China if the latter were to withdraw its missiles. In February, furthermore, the Taiwanese President suggested the establishment of a demilitarized zone between the mainland and Taiwan in order to facilitate joint discussions. Chen also stated that he would not declare Taiwanese independence, were he to win the forthcoming presidential election, although his attitude to relations with the Chinese mainland, for example in rejecting the 'one country, two systems' model advocated by China, was regarded by some as tantamount to stating that independence already existed.

The Chinese Government did not attempt directly to influence the presidential election held in March 2004, resulting in a narrow victory for Chen. However, following widespread controversy and protests over the election result, the Chinese Government stated that it would not tolerate social instability in

Taiwan. In the event, President Chen's referendum, held concurrently with the presidential election, did not produce a valid result (see Domestic Political Affairs). In August the Taiwanese President cancelled a military exercise scheduled for September, after China removed 3,000 troops from the island of Dongshan owing to a typhoon threat. Anti-secession legislation, drafted with the intention of preventing Taiwan from declaring independence, was approved by the NPC in Beijing in March 2005.

In January 2005 it was announced that for the first time direct flights between Taipei and the Chinese mainland would be permitted over the forthcoming Lunar New Year period. The first direct commercial flights between Taipei and Beijing duly took place at the end of the month. In late April, in the first such visit since 1949, the Chairman of the opposition KMT, Lien Chan, embarked upon an official visit to the mainland, where he and Chinese President Hu Jintao agreed to remain opposed to Taiwanese independence. Following Chan's visit, in May 2005 the Government of the People's Republic offered Taiwan a pair of giant pandas (see below), along with a series of concessions that included the easing of restrictions for mainland Chinese tourists visiting Taiwan. In the same month James Soong, leader of the PFP, an ally of the KMT within the opposition 'pan-blue' alliance, visited the People's Republic and met with President Hu. In June the Chinese Government announced that regulations restricting employment by Chinese companies of residents of Taiwan (and Hong Kong and Macao) were to be relaxed. The approval of a series of constitutional amendments by the Taiwanese National Assembly in June (see Domestic Political Affairs) enabled future constitutional changes, including any declaration of independence, to be endorsed by referendum.

In a New Year speech on 1 January 2006 President Chen reiterated his commitment to achieving a new constitution, ratified by referendum, by 2008, with the implication that this would enshrine Taiwan's independence and sovereignty. This objective was repeated by Chen on the occasion of the Chinese Lunar New Year, when he also proposed the abolition of the NUC, along with the guidelines for unification proposed by the council and accepted by the Executive Yuan in 1991. Furthermore, Chen stated his intention of reapplying for membership of the UN under the name of 'Taiwan', instead of the 'Republic of China'. In March 2006 tens of thousands of protesters participated in a rally in Taipei to protest against the perceived threat of domination by the People's Republic. In April former KMT Chairman Lien Chan made a further controversial trip to Beijing to meet with President Hu Jintao, who urged the restoration of bilateral talks at the highest level. In June it was announced that up to 168 charter passenger flights would operate between the island and the mainland at four important annual holiday periods, and that cargo and humanitarian flights would be licensed on an individual basis. (One month later the first non-stop cargo charter flight was made from Taiwan to Shanghai.) At a two-day Conference on Sustaining Taiwan's Economic Development, held in July, it was decided that investment limits might be relaxed for some Taiwanese companies operating on the mainland. However, during the economic forum President Chen stressed the importance of Taiwan's national development and declared that cross-Straits trade should be viewed as part of the 'entire framework of international trade'. In August the Mainland Affairs Council established the Taiwan Strait Tourism and Travel Association, in response to China's foundation earlier in the month of the Cross-Strait Tourism Exchange Association.

By mid-2006 official Chinese statistics showed that 70,256 Taiwanese companies had invested on the mainland (excluding companies that had invested via third territories, such as Hong Kong). This investment was estimated to have reached a total of US $50,800m., despite measures introduced by the Taiwanese Government in May to ensure stricter supervision. As concerns persisted that many of the island's business people were contravening existing Taiwanese investment regulations, the Government remained under heavy pressure from the business community, which was becoming increasingly frustrated at the inability of Taiwanese companies to deal more directly with China. In September the Mainland Affairs Council announced that it was to raise the limit on the number of Chinese visitors attending business meetings in Taiwan from 30 to 50. By the end of the year, furthermore, tourists from the mainland would be able to visit Taiwan without first passing through a third location. In November a spokesman from the mainland's Taiwan Affairs Office urged the island to reduce its control over cross-Straits tourism.

In a defence document published in December 2006, however, China described Taiwan as a 'major threat'. Cross-Straits relations suffered further in January 2007, when President Chen used his New Year speech to reiterate his views on Taiwan's status, declaring that the island's sovereignty belonged to its people. In the same month Taiwan announced revisions to school history textbooks, in which references to 'the mainland' and 'our country' were to be replaced by simply 'China', thus implying that Taiwan and China were not part of the same country, with a common history. In March the Taiwanese President's confirmation that he wished the island to pursue independence, draft a new constitution and change its official designation from the 'Republic of China' to 'Taiwan' prompted the mainland Chinese Minister of Foreign Affairs to denounce such statements as 'criminal'. On the same day Chinese Premier Wen Jiabao expressed a willingness to open a dialogue with Taiwan on condition that the island recognized the 'one China' principle. In February Taiwan declined to confirm reports that it had test-fired a missile that had a range of 1,000 km (and was therefore capable of reaching Shanghai). In a further development, Taiwan's National Day celebrations in October featured a parade that displayed its military capabilities, including a ship-to-ship missile and an anti-ballistic missile. The event, the first of its kind since the early 1990s, appeared to constitute a response to the perceived threat of military action from the mainland. Also in October 2007, at the 17th Congress of the Chinese Communist Party (CCP) convened in Beijing, President Hu Jintao reaffirmed Premier Wen's position, stressing the need for a dialogue to attain 'peaceful reunification'. Meanwhile, preparations in Beijing for the 2008 Olympic Games were a source of further tension, with Taiwan refusing to accept the proposed route of the Olympic torch in April 2007, based on the implications of an itinerary that sent the torch to Hong Kong and Macao after Taiwan; for Taiwan's Olympic Committee, this 'domestic route' represented an 'attempt to downgrade (Taiwan's) sovereignty'. After several months of difficult discussions, the International Olympic Committee (IOC, see p. 342) announced in September that the route would omit Taiwan completely.

Relations with the People's Republic improved considerably following the election of the KMT candidate, Ma Ying-jeou, as President of Taiwan in March 2008. Ma, who was born in Hong Kong, emphasized the importance of economic and transport links with China and distanced himself from his predecessor's policies, but maintained that a peace treaty could not be agreed while an estimated 1,000 Chinese missiles were directed at Taiwan.

A meeting between the Taiwanese Vice-President-elect, Vincent Siew, and President Hu Jintao, at the Boao Forum for Asia in April 2008, was described as the most senior-level encounter ever to take place between Taiwan and China. In May the Chairman of the KMT, Wu Poh-hsiung, attended an historic meeting with President Hu in China, and formal talks between representatives of the two sides recommenced, following a long hiatus, in June. As a result of these SEF-ARATS negotiations, the two parties agreed to establish offices on each other's territory; to initiate 36 (and eventually 96) regular direct charter flights between China and Taiwan every weekend; and to allow entry to a total of 3,000 tourists per day in each direction. President Ma proposed that bilateral agreements should expand into areas such as taxation and investment, through a process of 'economic normalization'. From late June, banks began offering the conversion of Chinese yuan into New Taiwan dollars.

Emergency aid was swiftly mobilized by Taiwanese charity organizations and religious groups to support the victims of the earthquake in Sichuan Province in May 2008. In the first such cross-Straits relief operation ever mounted, more than 150 metric tons of aid were delivered by air from Taiwan to the mainland within a week. At the end of May the Taiwanese Government announced that it planned to allocate a total of US $67m. in emergency relief funds. In addition, by the end of the month private Taiwanese donations had exceeded US $80m.

In early November 2008 Chiang Pin-kung, Chairman of the SEF, and Chen Yunlin, President of the ARATS, signed a series of agreements in Taipei. Chen was the most senior mainland Chinese official to travel to Taiwan since 1949, although his five-day visit was opposed by demonstrators (see Domestic Political Affairs). The agreements included the expansion of bilateral transport links, permitting the establishment of daily direct flights, shipping and postal services between Taiwan and mainland China. The two sides also agreed, in view of increasing concerns with regard to the safety of Chinese products, to co-operate in the area of food safety. In mid-December 2008 the first regular direct flights and cargo shipping services began. No longer required to operate via an intermediary point such as Hong Kong, about 100 regular passenger flights a week, serving eight cities in Taiwan and more than 20 on the mainland, were envisaged.

Following the return to power of the KMT, negotiations resumed with regard to China's offer of two pandas, traditionally the most esteemed diplomatic gift. The offer had been declined in 2006 on the grounds that Taiwan lacked the requisite facilities for panda care. In December 2008, following the preparation of a special enclosure at Taipei Zoo, amid heavy security two pandas were flown in a specially chartered aircraft to the island. The Taiwanese Government's acceptance of this highly symbolic gift was criticized by the opposition DPP.

As bilateral relations continued to improve, in December 2008 the Taiwanese Government announced that the restrictions hitherto imposed on mainland spouses, notably with regard to issues such as the right to work and the processing of applications for permanent residency on the island, were to be relaxed. At the end of December President Hu Jintao urged the adoption of a more pragmatic approach to the issue of Taiwan. He also indicated some support for Taiwan's ongoing efforts to attain membership of various international organizations. At the annual session of the NPC convened in Beijing in March 2009, Premier Wen Jiabao stated his willingness to negotiate with Taiwan on political and military issues, reiterating that any discussions would be based on the 'one China' principle. In response, the Taiwanese Government expressed its preference to focus on economic matters.

In April 2009 Chiang Pin-kung of the SEF and Chen Yunlin of the ARATS signed agreements to permit further cross-Straits investment. The two sides pledged to 'realize the normalization of cross-strait economic ties'. Also in April, at the third session of discussions between Chiang and Chen, held in Beijing, agreement was reached on several important issues, including the combating of crime, judicial assistance and financial co-operation. A substantial expansion of cross-Straits air transport was also agreed, providing for the addition of six new airport destinations in mainland China and an increase in the number of weekly flights from 108 to 270. By May 2009, one year after President Ma Ying-jeou's assumption of office, a total of nine bilateral agreements on economic co-operation had been signed. Furthermore, in an unprecedented bilateral exchange in late July, President Hu Jintao sent a message of congratulation to President Ma following the latter's election as Chairman of Taiwan's ruling KMT.

However, the Dalai Lama's five-day visit to Taiwan in late August 2009, following the typhoon earlier in the month, provoked condemnation from the mainland. Having stressed the humanitarian nature of his visit, the spiritual leader of Tibet offered comfort to the victims of the disaster, visiting the village of Hsiaolin in southern Taiwan, where almost 500 people had been killed in a mudslide. However, mindful of the importance of the island's economic relations with the People's Republic, President Ma declined to meet the Dalai Lama.

In September 2009 the Taiwanese Government refused entry to Rebiya Kadeer, a Uygur (Uighur) businesswoman who had been imprisoned by the mainland Chinese authorities in 1999; upon her release in 2005 she had gone into exile in the USA. Denounced as a Muslim separatist, more recently Kadeer had been accused of inciting violence in the Chinese autonomous region of Xinjiang, where 200 people had been killed in violence between Uygurs and Han Chinese in July 2009 (see the chapter on The People's Republic of China).

In a report issued in October 2009, the Taiwanese Ministry of National Defense warned that its efforts to improve relations with the Chinese military continued to be impeded by the mainland's confrontational stance. The report urged the withdrawal of missiles aimed at the island (the number of which was estimated by Taiwanese officials to have risen to 1,500) and suggested the establishment of a 'hotline' between Taipei and Beijing. The document also drew attention to the increasing frequency of military exercises being conducted on the mainland. President Ma, meanwhile, remained in favour of a formal peace accord with the mainland.

Despite military tensions, bilateral economic relations continued to expand. In November 2009 Taiwan and China signed a memorandum of understanding that provided for better access to financial services. Negotiations with regard to the conclusion of a free trade pact continued to progress. During four days of discussions held in Taiwan in December Chiang Pin-kung of the SEF and his mainland counterpart concluded a series of economic agreements.

In June 2010 Taiwan and China reached consensus on the details of an historic Economic Co-operation Framework Agreement (ECFA). This major accord provided for the eventual removal of many trade tariffs and permitted wider access to the two respective markets. However, there was much domestic opposition to the agreement in Taiwan, and the passage of the requisite legislation was seriously disrupted (see Domestic Political Affairs). None the less, the legislation was finally approved in August, and the ECFA took effect in the following month.

In May 2010, meanwhile, the first semi-official Taiwanese presence in mainland China was established, when a representative office of the Taiwan Strait Tourism Association, headed by a senior government official, was inaugurated. In the same month the mainland Cross-Strait Tourism Association opened an office in Taipei. In July the KMT and the CCP reached agreement on the expansion of co-operation between the two ruling parties in the areas of culture, education, sports and economic development. In September Cai Wu, the mainland Minister of Culture, undertook an official visit to Taiwan, only the second official of cabinet rank to visit the island. In December a delegation of the ARATS, led by Chen Yunlin, attended the sixth round of bilateral discussions at senior level, convened in Taipei. In February 2011, when Chen returned for a six-day visit at the head of a delegation of more than 50 business people and government officials, his itinerary incorporated major enterprises in southern Taiwan. However, in Kaohsiung his visit prompted protests by pro-independence activists. Nevertheless, bilateral agreement was reached on permitting larger numbers of mainland tourists to visit Taiwan on an individual basis. In April, amid much domestic controversy, the Taiwanese authorities accepted the first applications from mainland students wishing to further their higher education on the island. Following his conviction on charges of espionage, bribery and extortion, at the end of April an intelligence officer at the Taiwanese Ministry of National Defense, Col Lo Chi-cheng, was sentenced to life imprisonment. Col Lo had apparently collaborated with Lo Pin, a Taiwanese businessman based on the mainland, to gather intelligence for the People's Republic of China. In May, following his attendance at a bilateral forum in the Chinese city of Chengdu, Wu Poh-hsiung, honorary Chairman of the KMT, was received in Beijing by President Hu Jintao. In the same month, however, following the revelation by an opposition legislator that China had apparently exerted pressure on WHO to refer to Taiwan as a province of China in its documentation, the Taiwanese President issued a strong protest to China.

Foreign Affairs

Despite the relative lack of formal recognition in the international community, Taiwan's commercial relations with numerous countries continued to flourish, and in 2008 about 50 countries without full diplomatic relations with Taiwan maintained representative offices or visa-issuing centres on the island. In early 2011 the Republic of China was officially recognized by 23 countries.

Relations with the USA

In January 1979 Taiwan suffered a serious set-back when the USA recognized the People's Republic of China. Diplomatic relations with Taiwan were therefore severed, and the USA terminated the 1954 mutual security treaty with Taiwan. However, commercial links were maintained, and Taiwan's purchase of armaments from the USA has remained a controversial issue. In August 1982 a joint Sino-US communiqué was published, in which the USA pledged to reduce gradually its sale of armaments to Taiwan. In September 1992 President George Bush announced the sale of up to 150 F-16 fighter aircraft to Taiwan. In December the US trade representative became the first senior US government official to visit the island since 1979. In September 1994 the USA announced a modification of its policy towards Taiwan, henceforth permitting senior-level bilateral meetings to be held in US government offices. In December the US Secretary of Transportation visited the Ministry of Foreign Affairs in Taipei, the first US official of cabinet rank to visit Taiwan for more than 15 years. In June 1995 President Lee was permitted to make a four-day unofficial visit to the USA, where he met members of the US Congress, following which China recalled its ambassador from Washington.

In March 1996, as China began a new series of missile tests off the Taiwanese coast (see Cross-straits Relations), the USA stationed two naval convoys in waters east of the island. The sale of defensive weapons to Taiwan was agreed. In September President Lee and the US Deputy Treasury Secretary met in Taipei for discussions. In late 1996, however, Taiwanese donors were implicated in reported irregularities in the financing of US President Bill Clinton's re-election campaign and in a large illicit contribution to the US Democratic Party. In early 1997 the first of the *Patriot* anti-missile air defence systems, purchased from the USA under an arrangement made in 1993, were reported to have been deployed on the island. The first of the F-16s were delivered to Taiwan in April 1997. However, in mid-1998 a statement by President Clinton affirming that the USA would not support Taiwan's membership of the UN was sharply criticized. In October the Taiwanese Chief of Staff, Gen. Tang Fei, made a secret two-week visit to the USA. This was regarded as an extremely sensitive matter, in view of the fact that the SEF Chairman had recently met with President Jiang Zemin. In the following month the People's Republic complained to the USA following the US Energy Secretary's visit to Taiwan.

In January 1999 the People's Republic was antagonized by Taiwan's proposed inclusion in the US-led TMD system (see Cross-straits Relations). In August the USA reaffirmed its commitment to defend Taiwan against Chinese military action. In October Taiwan welcomed the adoption, albeit in modified form, of the Taiwan Security Enhancement Act (TSEA), establishing direct military links, by the International Relations Committee of the US House of Representatives, despite opposition from the Clinton Administration. The House of Representatives overwhelmingly approved the Act in February 2000. In April, however, the US Senate postponed consideration of the Act at the behest of the Taiwanese President-elect, Chen Shui-bian, in order not to antagonize China during the sensitive period preceding his inauguration. In the same month the US Government announced that it had decided to defer the sale of four naval destroyers to Taiwan. In September the USA granted a transit visa to Taiwanese Vice-President Annette Lu to stay in New York en route to Central America. In October China condemned a resolution approved by the US Congress that supported Taiwan's participation in the UN and other international organizations.

The election of George W. Bush to the US presidency in late 2000 was widely expected to boost US-Taiwan relations at the expense of the USA's relations with the mainland. Bush's uncompromising stance against China became more apparent after the crisis over the detention of a US reconnaissance plane and its crew following its collision with a Chinese fighter aircraft in April 2001 (see the chapter on The People's Republic of China). The USA subsequently agreed to sell Taiwan military equipment and armaments worth a total of US $4,000m., and President Bush declared that the USA would do whatever was necessary to defend Taiwan, in the event of an invasion by mainland forces. The People's Republic was further antagonized by the visit of President Chen Shui-bian to the USA in May, when he met business leaders and members of the US Congress. Chen's visit was followed by that of his predecessor, Lee Teng-hui, in June, as well as by a group of Taiwanese military and intelligence officials on an exchange programme, the first such exchange since 1979. In August 2001 two US Navy aircraft carrier battle groups conducted a one-day exercise in the South China Sea, coinciding with Chinese military exercises in the Taiwan Strait. In December the US House of Representatives approved the 2002 Defense Authorization Act, which included weapons sales to Taiwan.

In January 2002 a delegation from a US 'think tank', consisting of retired generals and officials, visited the mainland, and subsequently Taiwan, where they met President Chen and other senior officials and discussed the island's security.

In March 2002 the Minister of National Defense, Gen. (retd) Tang Yao-ming, visited the USA to attend a private three-day defence and security conference in Florida, where he met the US Deputy Secretary of Defense, Paul Wolfowitz, and Assistant Secretary of State James Kelly. Tang was the first incumbent official to make a non-transit visit to the USA since 1979. Meanwhile, the scandal in late March concerning former President Lee Teng-hui's co-operation with the island's intelligence services in secretly establishing an unauthorized fund (see above) embarrassed Taiwan and several US lobbying groups, which had received sums of this money. In April, however, the US Under-Secretary of Commerce for International Trade, Grant Aldonas, became the most senior official of George W. Bush's Administration to visit Taiwan, where he had a meeting with President Chen.

In September 2002 the US Congress approved the Foreign Relations Authorization Act, Fiscal Year 2003, which for the first time allowed staff of the US Department of State and other government agencies to work at the American Institute in Taiwan (the unofficial US mission to the island). Previously, US officials were required to embark upon sabbatical leave before serving at the institute. US military officers would also be allowed to work there, albeit not in uniform. Furthermore, the bill recognized Taiwan as a major non-North Atlantic Treaty Organization (NATO) ally of the USA. In August 2003 plans for Taiwan's purchase of four naval destroyers from the USA were finalized. Taiwan also made an advance payment towards the acquisition of eight new diesel submarines from the USA. In November President Chen made a visit to New York, in the course of which he was permitted to make a public speech.

In April 2004 Therese Shaheen, head of the American Institute in Taiwan, resigned after reportedly having misrepresented US policy on Taiwanese independence. Her departure prompted the resignation of the Taiwanese Minister of Foreign Affairs. In June the Executive Yuan approved a special defence budget for the purchase of weapons from the USA, which had been agreed in April 2001 (see above). Following public opposition in Taiwan to the special defence budget, the USA warned that there would be serious implications if the armaments purchase were not approved by the Taiwanese legislature. However, in late 2005 the opposition parties in the Legislative Yuan continued to obstruct the special defence budget, despite significant reductions in the overall scale of the proposed purchase. In January 2006 the US Government described as 'inflammatory' President Chen's proposals for the abolition of the NUC and the reunification guidelines established by it (see Cross-straits Relations). The US Department of State emphasized that it supported the maintenance of the status quo in cross-Straits relations, within the overall framework of a 'one China' policy.

In May 2006 the Deputy US Trade Representative, Karan Bhatia, visited Taiwan to discuss trade issues. In the following month the USA reacted positively to the announcement of a programme of direct charter flights to the mainland (see above). Meanwhile, the USA continued to press Taiwan to purchase its weapons, with US officials expressing 'grave concern' over Taiwan's defence capabilities when two DPP legislators visited Washington, DC, in August. (The remarks followed the Taiwanese opposition's rejection in April, for the 50th time, of the special defence budget to permit the procurement of US weapons.) The two legislators also received a sharp rebuff with regard to Taiwan's renewed request to open negotiations on a bilateral free trade agreement. Nevertheless, the two sides were to continue to focus on discussions under the Taiwan-US Trade and Investment Framework Agreement (TIFA). As President Chen became increasingly embroiled in various scandals, the director of the American Institute in Taiwan, Stephen Young, entered the fray to state that the USA wished Chen to remain in power for the sake of the stability of the island. The USA's commitment to the security of Taiwan was confirmed in February 2007 when the US Department of Defense announced the sale of more than 450 missiles to the island. In May, furthermore, Young reiterated his appeal to the Taiwanese legislature to grant approval to the outstanding defence budget that would permit the purchase of weaponry from the USA (aspects of the sale were expected to proceed following the legislature's approval of an amended budget in June).

The USA continued to exert pressure on Taiwan to give up its efforts to join the UN under the proposed name of Taiwan. In August 2007 the US Deputy Secretary of State, John Negroponte, declared that it would be 'a mistake' if Taiwan were to proceed with a proposal to submit to referendum the issue of UN membership concurrently with the 2008 presidential election, urging the Government to respect the status quo. The referendums were duly conducted in March 2008 (although the required turn-out of 50% was not achieved—see Domestic Political Affairs). The Taiwanese President-elect, Ma Ying-jeou, maintained that he would work to improve relations with the USA. Meanwhile, Taiwan's purchase of various types of US defence equipment, which had been approved by the Taiwan legislature in 2007, made little progress until October 2008, when the Bush Administration confirmed its intention to sell a substantial amount of weaponry, although the agreement excluded the advanced F-16 fighter aircraft and diesel submarines requested by Taiwan. The announcement was welcomed by Senator Barack Obama as being consistent with the USA's obligations under the Taiwan Relations Act of 1979. No immediate change in US policy

TAIWAN

Introductory Survey

towards Taiwan followed Obama's inauguration as US President in early 2009.

In October 2009, upholding a ruling by the US Court of Appeals in April, the US Supreme Court refused to hear a case brought by Roger Lin, a Taiwanese activist who, in the hope that former President Chen Shui-bian's recent conviction on charges of corruption might be quashed, had attempted to argue that the USA remained the principal occupying power of Taiwan and therefore retained control of the island. Chen instigated his own unsuccessful case in the US Court of Appeals for the Armed Forces.

The lack of any reference to the Taiwan Relations Act in a joint statement issued by Presidents Hu Jintao and Barack Obama during the latter's visit to China in November 2009 aroused much concern on the island. Although a reference to the Act was made by Obama at a subsequent press conference in Beijing, President Ma was urged to seek immediate clarification of US policy towards Taiwan. None the less, the USA remained the leading supplier of weaponry to the island, and in January 2010 the Obama Administration's decision to proceed with the sale of defence equipment to the value of US $6,400m., which included 60 helicopters, was welcomed by Taiwan. However, the announcement provoked an unusually strong reaction from the Chinese Government (see the chapter on The People's Republic of China). In May 2011 a KMT member of the Taiwanese legislature appeared to confirm the postponement of the sale of the equipment, ostensibly owing to budget constraints.

Regional relations

Taiwan severed diplomatic relations with Japan in 1972, following the latter's rapprochement with China. Mainland displeasure was incurred in February 1993 when the Taiwanese Minister of Foreign Affairs paid a visit to Japan. In September 1994 pressure from China resulted in the withdrawal of President Lee's invitation to attend the forthcoming Asian Games in Hiroshima. Instead, the Taiwanese Vice-Premier was permitted to visit Japan. Similarly, in July 1995 Japan announced that the Taiwanese Vice-Premier would not be permitted to attend a meeting of APEC members to be held in Osaka in November. Instead, President Lee was represented by Koo Chen-fu, the SEF Chairman. Taiwan's relations with Japan were also strained by the issue of adequate compensation for the thousands of Asian (mostly Korean) women used by Japanese troops for sexual purposes during the Second World War. In October 1996 Taiwan rejected a Japanese offer of nominal compensation for such Taiwanese women.

Taiwan's relations with Japan were also affected by a dispute relating to a group of uninhabited islets in the East China Sea: known as the Tiaoyutai (Diaoyu Dao) in Chinese, or Senkaku in Japanese, the islands were claimed by Taiwan, China and Japan. In July 1996, following the construction of a lighthouse on one of the islands by a Japanese right-wing group, the Taiwanese Ministry of Foreign Affairs lodged a strong protest over Japan's decision to incorporate the islands within its 200-mile (370-km) exclusive economic zone. Further tensions related to the issue of Taiwanese fishing rights within the disputed waters. In October 1997 it was reported that Japanese patrol boats were forcibly intercepting Taiwanese fishing vessels. In November 1999, however, the Governor of Tokyo paid an official visit to Taiwan. In March 2002 it was revealed that Japanese politicians, including former Prime Minister Ryutaro Hashimoto, had received money from an unauthorized fund established by former President Lee Teng-hui in order to procure influence in Japan. However, the incident did not damage commercial relations. In January 2003 Taiwan, along with China, condemned Japan's attempts to assert sovereignty over the Tiaoyutai Islands by renting them out to private companies. In September the second Taiwan-Japan Forum opened in Tokyo, at which issues of mutual concern were discussed. In February 2005, as part of a revised strategic understanding with the USA, Japan identified Taiwan's security as a 'common strategic objective' for the first time. In January 2007 the Taiwanese Government announced that it would designate 2007 as 'Taiwan-Japan Cultural Exchange Year'. In June a visit by former President Lee to the Yasukuni Shrine, a controversial war memorial in Japan, further antagonized the mainland.

The dispute over the sovereignty of the Tiaoyutai Islands, and disagreements over fishing rights, continued, with Taiwanese fishermen repeatedly complaining of harassment by Japanese patrol boats. In June 2005 an armed naval frigate, carrying the Taiwanese Minister of National Defense, the President of the Legislative Yuan and 15 legislators, was dispatched to the region, reportedly in response to these complaints of harassment. Subsequent negotiations between Taiwan and Japan over fishing rights, the 15th round of talks on the issue since 1996, concluded without agreement in July 2005. In September the Taiwanese President's Secretary-General, Yu Shyi-kun, attended a forum on relations between Taiwan and Japan in Tokyo, thus becoming the most senior Taiwanese official to visit Japan since the withdrawal of diplomatic recognition in 1972. In June 2008, following an accident involving a Taiwanese boat and a vessel of the Japanese coastguard off the Tiaoyutai Islands, Taiwanese protesters entered the islands' territorial waters, accompanied by the Taiwanese coastguard. The newly elected President, Ma Ying-jeou, reiterated Taiwan's sovereignty over the islands shortly afterwards.

In July 2009, in a major concession to expatriate Taiwanese, the Japanese legislature approved a revision of immigration law to permit Taiwanese resident in Japan henceforth to declare Taiwan, rather than China, as their nation of citizenship when submitting an application for residence in Japan. The removal of the incumbent Liberal-Democratic Government of Japan at legislative elections in August 2009, after more than 50 years of near-uninterrupted rule, was not expected to have a major impact on Taiwan's relations with Japan. Like its predecessor, the incoming administration of the Democratic Party of Japan did not support Taiwanese independence and opposed the use of force by the People's Republic against the island. With the inauguration of a new air link, in October 2010 Shinzo Abe, the former Japanese Prime Minister, flew to Taiwan, where he had discussions with President Ma. In April 2011 the Taiwanese Government formally protested against Japan's renewal of its claim over the Tiaoyutai Islands.

Despite the lack of formal diplomatic links and repeated obstruction from mainland China, Taiwan continued its attempts to develop good relations with the countries of South-East Asia. In March 1989 President Lee undertook a state visit to Singapore, the first official visit overseas by a Taiwanese head of state for 12 years. (In October 1990, however, Singapore established diplomatic relations with the People's Republic of China.) In February 1994 President Lee embarked upon an eight-day tour of South-East Asia. His itinerary incorporated the Philippines, Indonesia and Thailand, all three of which maintained diplomatic relations with the People's Republic of China. Although the tour was described as informal, President Lee had meetings with the three countries' heads of state, leading to protests from China. In September 1996 the Taiwanese Minister of Foreign Affairs was obliged to curtail an ostensibly private visit to Jakarta (where he was reported to have had discussions with his Indonesian counterpart), following objections from China. The Malaysian and Singaporean Prime Ministers met their Taiwanese counterpart in Taiwan in November 1997. In January 1998 the Taiwanese Premier, Vincent Siew, met senior officials during a visit to the Philippines and Singapore. The Premier's negotiations with the Malaysian Deputy Prime Minister and Minister of Finance, held in Taiwan in February 1998, concentrated on issues. Vincent Siew undertook a reciprocal visit to Malaysia in April. China was highly critical of these visits, accusing Taiwan of seeking to gain political advantage from the regional economic crisis through its offers of financial support. Vice-President Lu also visited Indonesia in August 2002 and met several cabinet ministers. While in Indonesia, Lu discussed possible liquefied natural gas projects, investment and migrant labour. In December, however, President Chen was forced to cancel a trip to Indonesia after that country came under heavy pressure from China.

Taiwan's relations with the Philippines were seriously jeopardized in August 1999 when the Government threatened to refuse entry to Filipino labourers, in apparent retaliation for the Philippine Government's unilateral termination of its aviation agreement with Taipei. Flights to the Philippines were intermittently suspended in subsequent months. In June 2000 the Taiwanese Government imposed a three-month ban on new work permits for Philippine nationals. In September, however, a new aviation agreement was signed. Bilateral relations were severely tested again in February 2011 when, despite Taiwan's request that they be repatriated to their homeland, 14 Taiwanese citizens suspected of fraud were deported to China by the Philippine authorities, along with 10 mainland Chinese alleged to be their accomplices. Taiwan recalled its representative from the Philippines and demanded a formal apology for the incident. A presidential envoy was dispatched to Taipei by the Philippine Government in an attempt to restore good relations.

TAIWAN

The question of the sovereignty of the Spratly Islands, situated in the South China Sea and to which five countries as well as Taiwan laid claim, remained unresolved. Believed to possess petroleum and gas resources, in addition to encompassing rich fishing areas, the grouping comprises more than 100 small islands and reefs. A contingent of Taiwanese marines has been maintained on Taiping Island, the largest of the disputed islands, located some 1,574 km south-west of Taiwan. A satellite telecommunications link between Taiping and Kaohsiung was inaugurated in October 1995. In December 1998 the Legislative Yuan approved the first legal definition of Taiwan's sea borders. The Spratly Islands were claimed, as were the disputed Tiaoyutai Islands (see above), within the 12- and 24-nautical mile zones. In November 2002, in Phnom-Penh, Cambodia, members of the Association of Southeast Asian Nations (ASEAN, see p. 206) signed a 'declaration on the conduct of parties in the South China Sea', which aimed to avoid conflict in the area. Under this agreement, which was similar to one drafted in late 1999 but not implemented, claimants would practise self-restraint in the event of potentially hostile action (such as inhabiting the islands), effect confidence-building measures and give advance notice of military exercises in the region. However, the agreement did not include the Paracel Islands. In August 2003 Minister of the Interior Yu Cheng-hsien visited Taiping Island and reaffirmed Taiwanese sovereignty. In February 2008 President Chen Shui-bian visited Taiwanese forces stationed on Taiping, where he inaugurated a new airstrip and proposed a 'Spratly Initiative', urging claimant countries to disregard the issue of sovereignty and to co-operate in the protection of the islands' environment and resources. The Philippines and Viet Nam had been particularly critical of the construction of the airstrip. (See the chapter on The People's Republic of China for further information.) In April 2011, in response to China's agreement with Viet Nam to co-operate in the area (which prompted an official complaint to the UN from the Philippines), Taiwan announced that it was to reinforce its coastguard deployment in the area of the Spratly Islands.

At the beginning of the 21st century a total of five Pacific nations, namely the Marshall Islands, Nauru, Palau, Solomon Islands and Tuvalu, recognized Taiwan, which was increasingly vying with China for influence in the region. Taiwan maintained several embassies in the Pacific Islands and provided considerable financial support to these nations. In addition, Kiribati granted diplomatic recognition to Taiwan in November 2003. Diplomatic relations were briefly established with Vanuatu in late 2004. In January 2005 President Chen undertook an official visit to Palau, thus becoming the first Taiwanese President to visit the Pacific nation. He also travelled to Solomon Islands and to the US territory of Guam. In May Chen became the first head of any foreign state to visit the Marshall Islands in an official capacity, as part of a diplomatic tour of Pacific nations, during which the Taiwanese President also became the first foreign head of state to visit Kiribati and Tuvalu. However, he controversially altered his published itinerary to visit Fiji, a country that maintained diplomatic relations with the People's Republic of China. Also in May 2005, diplomatic relations with Nauru, which had been terminated in July 2002 after the country established relations with China, were re-established.

As competition with China for diplomatic support in the Pacific region continued, in May 2008 two senior members of the Taiwanese Government, Vice-Premier Chiou I-jen and the Minister of Foreign Affairs, Huang Chih-fang, were forced to resign (see above) over a funding scandal involving an alleged attempt to influence the allegiance of Papua New Guinea, a country with which Taiwan had briefly succeeded in establishing diplomatic relations in 1999. Meanwhile, in June 2007 President Kessai Note of the Marshall Islands embarked upon his sixth visit to Taiwan, and in August 2008 President Ma Ying-jeou received Note's successor, Litokwa Tomeing, in Taipei. During 2009 President Ma held discussions with the heads of government of Palau, Tuvalu and Solomon Islands during their respective state visits to Taiwan. In March 2010 President Ma embarked upon his first official visit to the Pacific Islands. His itinerary incorporated all six diplomatic allies: the Marshall Islands, Kiribati, Tuvalu, Nauru, Solomon Islands and Palau. The Prime Minister of Tuvalu, Apisai Ielemia, undertook an official visit to Taiwan in April. In June the various bilateral projects were also among the topics discussed with their Taiwanese counterpart during the respective visits to Taipei of Kiribati President Anote Tong and Marshallese President Jurelang Zedkaia. In the following month President Ma also received King Mswati III of Swaziland.

In September 2006 a summit meeting attended by the President of Taiwan and the leaders of its six Pacific allies was convened in Palau. The Second Taiwan-Pacific Allies Summit took place in the Marshall Islands in October 2007. The 2008 Summit was cancelled following the recent return to power of the KMT, which had insufficient time to prepare. The meeting scheduled to be held in Solomon Islands in October 2009 was also cancelled, to allow the Taiwanese authorities to focus on addressing the aftermath of Typhoon Morakot.

Other external relations

Taiwan's relations with Africa have been similarly governed by competition with China for influence. In May 1994 President Lee of Taiwan visited South Africa and Swaziland. In January 1997 the Taiwanese Minister of Foreign Affairs embarked upon a tour of seven African nations, including South Africa, in an attempt to consolidate relations. In January 1998, however, South Africa's transfer of diplomatic recognition from Taiwan to China was a major set-back to Taiwan. In February the Minister of Foreign Affairs visited eight African countries, and in April it was announced that Taiwan's overseas aid budget was to be substantially increased, in an attempt to retain diplomatic support. In August 2000 the new Taiwanese President, Chen Shui-bian, embarked upon a tour of diplomatic allies in West Africa. The Taiwanese Vice-President visited The Gambia in December 2001. President Chen completed a four-nation tour of Africa in July 2002, having visited Senegal, São Tomé and Príncipe, Malawi and Swaziland. In subsequent years Taiwan suffered several reverses in Africa. In October 2003 Liberia transferred its diplomatic recognition to the People's Republic of China. Relations with Senegal were also terminated when that country re-established diplomatic links with the People's Republic of China in October 2005. In August 2006, furthermore, Chad also transferred diplomatic recognition to the People's Republic, announcing this decision less than 24 hours before Premier Su Tseng-chang was due to embark upon an official visit to the African nation. Nevertheless, the Taiwanese Minister of Foreign Affairs visited several other African states in 2007, and in September Taiwan hosted the first Taiwan-Africa Summit, which was attended by its five African allies. In January 2008, however, it was announced that Malawi had severed diplomatic relations with Taiwan. President Yahya Jammeh of The Gambia undertook his eighth state visit to Taiwan in April 2009.

Similar trends characterized Taiwan's relations with the countries of Central America and the Caribbean. In July 1997, following the Bahamas' establishment of diplomatic relations with the People's Republic of China, the Taiwanese Minister of Foreign Affairs undertook an extensive tour of the countries of Central America and the Caribbean, in an effort to maintain their support. In September, during a tour of Central America (the six nations of the region having become the core of Taiwan's remaining diplomatic allies), President Lee attended an international conference on the development of the Panama Canal. In May 1998 Vice-President Lien Chan visited Taiwan's Central American and Caribbean allies. In August 2000 the new Taiwanese President, Chen Shui-bian, embarked upon a tour of diplomatic allies in Central America. As Taiwan continued to seek diplomatic recognition in return for aid and investment, in May 2001 President Chen began a tour of five Latin American nations: El Salvador, Guatemala, Panama, Paraguay and Honduras. While in El Salvador, Chen met eight regional leaders, who pledged support for Taiwan. Vice-President Lu visited Nicaragua and Paraguay in January 2002. In March 2004, however, Dominica withdrew its diplomatic recognition of Taiwan, as did Grenada in January 2005. In 2007 Saint Lucia restored recognition in May, but Costa Rica terminated diplomatic links in June. Following his assumption of office in the previous year, in mid-2009 President Ma Ying-jeou undertook official visits to Belize, Guatemala, El Salvador, Panama and Nicaragua. In January 2010 President Ma visited Honduras and the Dominican Republic.

In the 1990s relations with Europe were dominated by the issue of purchases of French defence equipment. In January 1993 official confirmation of Taiwan's purchase of 60 *Mirage* fighter aircraft from France provoked strong protest from China. Taiwan suffered a reverse in January 1994 when (following pressure from the People's Republic) France recognized Taiwan as an integral part of Chinese territory and agreed not to sell weapons to the island. In March 1995, however, it was reported that Taiwan was to purchase anti-aircraft missiles from a French

TAIWAN

company; the sale was subsequently confirmed. In 1996 the first delivery of Mirage aircraft to Taiwan from France took place. It was confirmed that, as agreed in 1991, France would proceed with the sales of six frigates to Taiwan; delivery of these was completed in March 1998. There were tensions in Taiwan's relations with France in early 2004, after President Jacques Chirac expressed his support for China's opposition to a proposed referendum in Taiwan (see Domestic Political Affairs) during a visit by Chinese President Hu Jintao to Paris. Two visits by Taiwanese ministers to France were subsequently cancelled, and joint military exercises between the French and mainland Chinese navies were held in March off Taiwan's northern coast. In May 2010, ruling that the payment of commission to intermediaries involved in the sale of the six French frigates to the island in the 1990s had been a breach of the terms of the contract, an international court of arbitration ordered France and the company concerned to pay the sum of €630m. to Taiwan in compensation. Some of the defendants in the case were subsequently acquitted, although in late 2010 prosecutors declared their intention to continue their pursuit of the bribery charges against a retired naval captain and a weapons dealer.

In January 1997 the Taiwanese Vice-President was received by the Pope during a visit to the Holy See, the only European state that continued to recognize Taiwan. A visit to Europe in October by Vice-President Lien Chan was curtailed when pressure from China forced the Spanish Government to withdraw an invitation. In November 2001 Wu Shu-jen, wife of President Chen, travelled to Strasbourg, France, to accept the 'Prize for Freedom' awarded to her husband by Liberal International, a world grouping of liberal parties. Chen himself had been refused a visa by the European Union (EU). In March 2003 President Chen was again refused a visa by the EU, and was thus unable to travel to Belgium to address members of the European Parliament in Brussels. In early 2010 Taiwan's proposed purchase from the European Aeronautic Defence and Space Company, a corporation based in the Netherlands, of three helicopters attracted some controversy. Although the aircraft were ostensibly being acquired for civilian purposes, observers noted that the Taiwanese air force, rather than the police or coastguard, was to receive the helicopters.

CONSTITUTION AND GOVERNMENT

Under the provisions of the amended 1947 Constitution, the head of state is the President, who is elected by popular vote for a four-year term. There are five Yuans (governing bodies), the highest legislative organ being the Legislative Yuan, to which the Executive Yuan (the Council of Ministers) is responsible. Since the elections of January 2008, the Legislative Yuan has comprised 113 members; 73 chosen by direct election, most of the remainder being appointed from separate lists of candidates on the basis of proportional representation. The Legislative Yuan serves a four-year term. There are also Control, Judicial and Examination Yuans. Their respective functions are: to investigate the work of the executive; to interpret the Constitution and national laws; and to supervise examinations for entry into public offices. In 2000 the role of the National Assembly was revised. The powers to initiate constitutional amendments, to impeach the President or Vice-President, and to approve the appointment of senior officials were transferred to the Legislative Yuan. The National Assembly retained the functions of ratifying constitutional amendments and responsibility for impeachment proceedings, in which case 300 delegates appointed by political parties according to a system of proportional representation were to convene for a session of a maximum duration of one month. In 1997 the National Assembly approved a series of constitutional amendments, in the first stage of the dissolution of the long-standing provincial apparatus. The Fukien (Fujian) Provincial Government has remained responsible for the administration of various islands, including Kinmen (Quemoy) and Matsu.

REGIONAL AND INTERNATIONAL CO-OPERATION

Taiwan is a member of the Asian Development Bank (ADB, see p. 202) and of Asia-Pacific Economic Co-operation (APEC, see p. 197).

The Republic of China was removed from the UN in 1971. In 1992 Taiwan was granted observer status at the General Agreement on Tariffs and Trade (GATT); it became a full member of the successor World Trade Organization (WTO, see p. 430) in 2002.

Introductory Survey

ECONOMIC AFFAIRS

In 2009, according to official figures, Taiwan's gross national income (GNI), at current prices, totalled US $329,350m., equivalent to US $14,271 per head. During 2002–09, it was estimated, the population increased at an average annual rate of 0.4%, while in real terms, on the basis of figures in US dollars, gross domestic product (GDP) per head increased at an average annual rate of 2.1% in 2000–08. In terms of New Taiwan dollars, overall GDP increased at an average annual rate of 3.1% in 2000–09. Compared with the previous year, GDP contracted by 1.9% in 2009, but it expanded by 10.8% in 2010.

Agriculture (including hunting, forestry and fishing) contributed 1.6% of GDP in 2009. The sector engaged 5.3% of the employed labour force in the same year. The principal crops are vegetables, rice, sugar cane and pineapples. Agricultural GDP decreased at an average annual rate of 0.1%, in real terms, during 2000–09. Compared with the previous year, agricultural GDP decreased by 3.0% in 2009 and by 0.9% in 2010, according to the Asian Development Bank (ADB).

Industry (comprising mining, manufacturing, construction and utilities) engaged 35.8% of the employed labour force in 2009, when it provided 30.6% of GDP. Industrial GDP increased, in real terms, at an average rate of 4.1% per year in 2000–09. However, compared with the previous year, industrial GDP decreased by 4.3% in 2009, before increasing by 24.2% in 2010, according to the ADB.

Mining contributed 0.5% of GDP in 2009, employing a negligible percentage of the labour force. Marble, sulphur and dolomite are the principal minerals extracted. The GDP of the mining sector decreased at an average rate of 7.9% per year in 2000–09. Mining GDP was estimated to have declined by 13.9% in 2008 and by 11.8% in 2009.

Manufacturing contributed 25.3% of GDP in 2009 and engaged 27.1% of the employed labour force in that year. The most important branches, measured by gross value of output, are electronics (particularly personal computers), plastic goods, synthetic yarns and the motor vehicle industry. The sector's GDP grew at an average annual rate of 5.1%, in real terms, in 2000–09. Manufacturing GDP was estimated to have decreased by 0.4% in 2008, compared with the previous year, and the sector recorded a decline of 4.8% in 2009.

Construction contributed 2.6% of GDP in 2009 and engaged 7.7% of the employed labour force in that year. The sector's GDP contracted at an average annual rate of 1.7%, in real terms, in 2000–09. The GDP of the construction sector was estimated to have decreased by 5.5% in 2008 and by 6.9% in 2009.

In 2009 52.1% of Taiwan's energy supply was derived from imported petroleum. Imports of crude petroleum accounted for 11.2% of total import expenditure in 2007. In 2009 nuclear power supplied 8.7% of Taiwan's energy requirements. Taiwan has substantial reserves of natural gas.

The services sector contributed 67.8% of GDP in 2009, when it engaged 58.9% of the employed labour force. The number of foreign visitors in 2009 was reported to have increased to almost 4.4m. (of whom nearly 2.8m. were tourists), rising by 27% in 2010 to nearly 5.6m. Travellers from Japan and Overseas Chinese visitors accounted for the majority of arrivals. Tourism receipts reached US $5,936m. in 2008. In 2000–09 the GDP of the services sector increased, in real terms, at an average annual rate of 2.7%. Compared with the previous year, the services sector contracted by 0.3% in 2009, expanding by 4.8% in 2010.

In 2009 Taiwan recorded a visible trade surplus of US $30,553m., and there was a surplus of US $42,056m. on the current account of the balance of payments. In 2009 the principal sources of imports were Japan (accounting for 20.8%), the People's Republic of China (14.0%) and the USA (10.4%). The principal markets for exports in that year were the People's Republic of China (accounting for 26.6% of exports), Hong Kong (14.5%) and the USA (11.6%). Trade with the People's Republic of China (mainly via Hong Kong) has expanded rapidly in recent years. The value of exports to mainland China increased from US $4,391.5m. in 2000 to US $54,248.7m. in 2009. Taiwan's principal imports in 2009 were machinery, mechanical appliances and electrical equipment, crude petroleum, and chemical and allied products. The principal exports in that year were electronic products, base metals and plastics.

The 2010 budget envisaged expenditure of NT $2,460,958m. and revenue of NT $2,113,543m. The budget deficit was projected to be the equivalent of 2.8% of GDP. The 2011 budget projected an operating deficit of NT $139,400m. According to the ADB, Taiwan's external debt amounted to US $81,958m. in 2008, in

TAIWAN

which year the cost of debt-servicing reached the equivalent of 2.7% of the value of exports of goods and services. The annual rate of inflation averaged 0.9% during the period 2000–09. Consumer prices rose by 1.0% in 2010, according to the ADB. The rate of unemployment reached 5.2% of the labour force in 2010.

Owing to its heavy dependence on external trade, Taiwan was badly affected by the global recession of 2008/09. Foreign direct investment declined, and was reported to have decreased from US $7,424m. in 2006 to $2,481m. in 2010. In late 2008 the Government began to implement various fiscal stimulus measures, which included tax concessions for new investment by companies and support for low-income families. In February 2009 details of a two-year stimulus programme, envisaging expenditure of NT $500,000m., notably on infrastructural projects, were announced. Historically, the island has held consistently large reserves of foreign exchange, which in April 2011 stood at US $399,541m., among the largest in the world. The level of inflation remained relatively moderate. In 2010, however, increasing demand for residential property, arising largely from speculative activity, prompted the authorities to restrict lending for the purposes of purchasing a second home. The central bank's interest rate was raised to 1.75% in March 2011. In the same month, in a further effort to curb the housing market, the Government announced plans to impose restrictions on the early resale of such properties and for the introduction of a selective sales tax, to be levied at 10%–15% on luxury items and speculative transactions. Following the exceptional economic growth of 2010, when GDP expanded by more than 10%, the Government forecast a more modest growth rate of 5.0% in 2011. Despite intermittent political tensions, economic links with the People's Republic of China have become increasingly significant, with the value of Taiwan's exports to the mainland rising from less than 8% of total exports in 2002 to more than 26% by 2008. The conclusion with mainland China of the Economic Co-operation Framework Agreement (ECFA) in mid-2010 represented a major development. It was envisaged that this important accord would greatly enhance bilateral trade exchanges, through the reduction of tariffs on hundreds of items, and promote investment in Taiwan. The first tariff reductions were implemented in January 2011, and in March mainland investors were permitted access to a wider range of opportunities, such as those offered by the semiconductor industry.

PUBLIC HOLIDAYS

2012 (provisional): 1–2 January (Founding of the Republic/New Year), 23–25 January (Chinese New Year), 5 April (Ching Ming/Tomb Sweeping Day and Death of President Chiang Kai-shek), 23 June (Dragon Boat Festival), 28 September (Teachers' Day/Birthday of Confucius), 1 October (for Mid-Autumn Moon Festival), 10 October (Double Tenth Day, anniversary of 1911 revolution), 25 October (Retrocession Day, anniversary of end of Japanese occupation), 12 November (Birthday of Sun Yat-sen), 25 December (Constitution Day).

Statistical Survey

Source (unless otherwise stated): Directorate-General of Budget, Accounting and Statistics (DGBAS), 1, Section 1, Jhongsiao East Rd, Taipei 10058; tel. (2) 23803542; fax (2) 23803547; e-mail sicbs@dgbas.gov.tw; internet www.dgbas.gov.tw.

Area and Population

AREA, POPULATION AND DENSITY

Area (sq km)	36,192*
Population (census results)	
16 December 1990	20,393,628
16 December 2000	
Males	11,386,084
Females	10,914,845
Total	22,300,929
Population (official figures at 31 December)	
2007	22,958,360
2008	23,037,031
2009	23,119,772
Density (per sq km) at 31 December 2009	638.8

* 13,974 sq miles.

POPULATION BY AGE AND SEX
(official estimates at 31 December 2009)

	Males	Females	Total
0–14	1,970,302	1,807,716	3,778,018
15–64	8,039,423	7,933,921	15,973,344
65 and over	1,627,009	1,741,401	3,368,410
Total	11,636,734	11,483,038	23,119,772

PRINCIPAL TOWNS
(population at 31 December 2008)

Taipei (capital)	2,622,923	Keelung	388,979
Kaohsiung	1,525,642	Sanchong	384,722
Taichung	1,066,128	Jhongli	362,129
Tainan	768,453	Fongshan	339,240
Banciao	550,767	Sindian	292,693
Jhunghe	412,060	Chiayi	273,793
Hsinchu	405,371	Tucheng	238,230
Sinjhuang	398,317	Jhanghua	236,631
Taoyuan	397,056	Yonghe	236,598

BIRTHS, MARRIAGES AND DEATHS
(registered)

	Live births		Marriages		Deaths	
	Number	Rate (per 1,000)	Number	Rate (per 1,000)	Number	Rate (per 1,000)
2002	247,530	11.02	172,655	7.69	128,636	5.73
2003	227,070	10.06	171,483	7.60	130,801	5.80
2004	216,419	9.56	131,453	5.80	135,092	5.97
2005	205,854	9.06	141,140	6.21	139,398	6.13
2006	204,459	8.96	142,669	6.25	135,839	5.95
2007	204,414	8.92	135,041	5.89	141,111	6.16
2008	198,733	8.64	154,866	6.73	143,624	6.25
2009	191,310	8.29	117,099	5.07	143,582	6.22

Life expectancy (years at birth, 2008, provisional): 78.5 (males 75.5; females 82.0).

TAIWAN

Statistical Survey

ECONOMICALLY ACTIVE POPULATION
(annual averages, '000 persons aged 15 years and over)*

	2007	2008	2009
Agriculture, forestry and fishing	543	535	543
Mining and quarrying	6	6	5
Manufacturing	2,842	2,886	2,790
Construction	846	842	788
Electricity and gas supply	28	28	29
Water supply and remediation services	65	71	73
Services	5,962	6,036	6,051
Trade	1,782	1,770	1,735
Hotels and restaurants	681	687	693
Transport and storage	415	414	402
Information and communication	206	203	207
Finance and insurance	404	411	413
Education	588	605	613
Public administration, defence and compulsory social security	332	343	382
Total employed	10,294	10,403	10,279
Unemployed	419	450	639
Total labour force	10,713	10,853	10,917
Males	6,116	6,173	6,180
Females	4,597	4,680	4,737

* Excluding members of the armed forces and persons in institutional households.

Health and Welfare

KEY INDICATORS

Total fertility rate (children per woman, 2009)	1.0
Under-5 mortality rate (per 1,000 live births, 2006)	6.06
HIV/AIDS (% of persons aged 15–49, 2006)	0.03
Physicians (per 1,000 head, 2008)	1.83
Hospital beds (per 1,000 head, 2009)	6.78
Health expenditure (2007): NT $ per head	33,661
Health expenditure (2007): % of GDP	6.1
Health expenditure (2005): public (% of total)	62.90
Human Development Index (2004): value	0.925

For definitions, see explanatory note on p. vi.

Note: Data are mainly from Directorate-General of Budget, Accounting and Statistics (DGBAS).

Agriculture

PRINCIPAL CROPS
('000 metric tons)

	2006	2007	2008
Potatoes	49.6	47.4	59.7
Rice, paddy	1,558.0	1,363.5	1,457.2
Sweet potatoes	235.2	200.1	212.8
Sorghum	4.7	4.9	2.5
Maize	128.4	118.9	118.1
Tea	19.3	17.5	17.4
Tobacco	2.2	1.7	1.7
Groundnuts	71.6	51.9	55.1
Sugar cane	651.0	720.9	707.1
Vegetables	2,878.0	2,595.2	2,640.7
Fruits	2,743.9	2,654.0	2,577.6
Bananas	214.3	241.7	207.7
Pineapples	491.6	476.8	452.1

LIVESTOCK
('000 head at 31 December)

	2006	2007	2008
Cattle	134.8	137.1	134.0
Buffaloes	3.5	3.5	3.6
Pigs	7,068.6	6,620.8	6,427.6
Goats	267.4	249.4	229.5
Chickens	109,633	103,499	100,298
Ducks	11,912	11,000	9,177
Geese	2,841	2,318	1,990
Turkeys	163	156	147

LIVESTOCK PRODUCTS

	2006	2007	2008
Beef (metric tons)	5,626	5,480	5,683
Pig meat (metric tons)	930,609	913,824	861,836
Sheep and goat meat (metric tons)	3,896	3,548	3,183
Chickens ('000 head)*	346,153	333,504	315,896
Ducks ('000 head)*	37,741	36,862	31,730
Geese ('000 head)*	6,723	5,873	5,149
Turkeys ('000 head)*	335	301	280
Cow's milk (metric tons)	323,165	322,220	315,559
Duck eggs ('000)	466,232	507,328	483,878
Hen eggs ('000)	6,620,415	6,659,584	6,469,671

* Figures refer to numbers slaughtered.

Forestry

ROUNDWOOD REMOVALS
('000 cubic metres)

	2006	2007	2008
Industrial wood	27.0	26.4	25.1
Fuel wood	9.2	7.2	6.1
Mill wood	0.0	1.5	0.0
Total	36.2	35.1	31.2

Fishing
('000 metric tons, live weight)

	2006	2007	2008
Tilapias	72.6	76.1	81.0
Other freshwater fishes	10.2	10.0	n.a.
Japanese eel	23.8	24.8	21.0
Milkfish	56.1	53.2	46.9
Pacific saury	60.6	87.3	139.5
Skipjack tuna	194.4	214.0	168.9
Albacore	40.1	47.5	37.6
Yellowfin tuna	77.7	67.7	71.3
Bigeye tuna	59.1	69.9	53.8
Chub mackerel	54.8	49.9	56.0
Sharks, rays, skates, etc.	49.1	48.6	39.8
Marine shrimps and prawns	37.7	34.4	n.a.
Other crustaceans	7.1	6.7	n.a.
Pacific cupped oyster	28.5	28.1	34.4
Common squids	8.9	7.3	5.0
Argentine shortfin squid	148.1	300.0	240.3
Sailfish	28.6	27.4	24.2
Total catch (incl. others)	1,282.3	1,498.2	1,339.3

Note: Figures exclude aquatic plants, totalling (in '000 metric tons, preliminary): 6.1 in 2006; 9.6 in 2007; n.a. in 2008.

TAIWAN

Mining

(metric tons, unless otherwise indicated)

	2004	2005	2006
Crude petroleum ('000 litres)	44,562	32,389	23,565
Natural gas ('000 cu m)	706,991	486,646	411,524
Sulphur*	222,760	267,790	245,789
Marble (raw material)*	22,970,546	24,069,551	25,492,633
Dolomite*	114,598	173,986	61,224

* Preliminary figures.

Crude petroleum ('000 litres): 17,778 in 2007; 16,097 in 2008; 15,996 in 2009.

Natural gas ('000 cu m): 370,522 in 2007; 317,654 in 2008; 311,701 in 2009.

Industry

SELECTED PRODUCTS
('000 metric tons unless otherwise indicated)

	2007	2008	2009
Carbonated beverages ('000 litres)	336,520	312,115	341,269
Alcoholic beverages—excl. beer ('000 hectolitres)	368.0	361.6	624.6
Paperboard	3,406.5	2,909.6	2,775.3
Spun yarn	223.6	185.1	153.4
Cement	18,957.3	17,330.3	15,918.5
Steel ingots	19,838.7	19,222.1	15,566.4
Sewing machines ('000 units)	1,356.5	1,416.4	1,118.4
Electric fans ('000 units)	7,114.5	5,267.8	4,393.7
Personal computers ('000 units)	1,262.8	760.6	378.7
Mobile phones ('000 units)	22,669.0	25,692.6	15,983.5
LCD displays ('000 units)	1,225.8	849.4	887.4
Integrated circuits (million units)	5,033.4	5,577.6	4,376.7
Electronic condensers (million units)	242,938	252,515	166,372
Global positioning systems	17,784	21,333	20,661
Telephone sets ('000 units)	687.0	514.4	351.8
Passenger motor cars ('000 units)	213.1	137.6	178.2
Trucks, buses and commercial vans ('000 units)	68.8	41.5	46.9
Bicycles ('000 units)	5,120.5	6,131.7	4,778.9
Electric energy (million kWh)	228,806	225,258	n.a.

2006: Wheat flour 784.3; Granulated sugar and molasses 392.3; Cigarettes (million) 22,073.3; Cotton yarn 286.1; Paper 836.0; Sulphuric acid 1,265; Television sets and VCRs 1,829,000; Audio units for cars 682,100; Loudspeakers and microphones 49,038,000; Ships (value of sales, NT $ million) 26,435.5; Refined petroleum (million litres) 59,460.2.

2007: Wheat flour 811.0.

Finance

CURRENCY AND EXCHANGE RATES

Monetary Units
100 cents = 1 New Taiwan dollar (NT $).

Sterling, US Dollar and Euro Equivalents (31 December 2010)
£1 sterling = NT $47.541;
US $1 = NT $30.368;
€1 = NT $40.578;
NT $1,000 = £21.03 = US $32.93 = €24.64.

Average Exchange Rate (NT $ per US $)
2007   32.842
2008   31.517
2009   33.056

Statistical Survey

GENERAL GOVERNMENT BUDGET
(NT $ million, year ending 31 December)

Revenue	2007	2008	2009
Current revenue	2,189,035	2,181,188	2,041,406
Taxes	1,685,875	1,710,617	1,483,518
Income tax	730,160	834,988	640,967
Business tax	246,137	243,961	223,503
Fees	96,579	94,302	91,963
Fines and indemnities	44,646	46,690	41,395
Public enterprise and utilities surplus	291,799	264,918	330,928
Public properties profits	15,103	14,249	14,111
Donations, etc.	7,845	8,862	8,658
Other	47,188	41,550	70,834
Capital revenue	55,724	50,425	72,137
Total	**2,244,758**	**2,231,614**	**2,113,543**

Expenditure	2007	2008	2009
General administration	343,950	350,500	354,981
National defence	255,854	262,150	297,746
Education, science and culture	492,625	495,515	537,310
Economic development	383,298	432,335	445,037
Agriculture	106,788	112,827	133,210
Industry	16,004	34,001	36,071
Transport and communication	218,338	234,604	213,404
Other	42,167	50,902	62,352
Social welfare	372,202	368,136	387,446
Social insurance	162,548	147,651	189,268
Social relief	23,245	25,559	23,333
Benefit service	151,322	158,275	136,719
Employment service	2,480	2,252	2,485
Medical care	32,607	34,400	35,641
Community development and environmental protection	87,282	82,157	86,333
Community development	24,520	13,514	18,941
Environmental protection	62,762	68,643	67,392
Pensions and survivors' benefits	200,677	202,228	205,289
Obligations	139,380	134,697	129,484
Miscellaneous	14,901	15,867	17,331
Total	**2,290,169**	**2,343,585**	**2,460,958**
Current	1,801,511	1,811,308	1,896,804
Capital	488,658	532,278	564,154

INTERNATIONAL RESERVES
(US $ million at 31 December)

	2007	2008	2009
Gold (national valuation)	4,716	4,682	4,769
Foreign exchange	270,311	291,707	348,198
Total	**275,027**	**296,389**	**352,967**

MONEY SUPPLY
(NT $ '000 million at 31 December)

	2007	2008	2009
Currency outside banks	762.6	833.5	912.6
Demand deposits at deposit money banks	7,457.4	7,320.2	9,599.0
Total money	**8,220.0**	**8,153.7**	**10,511.6**

COST OF LIVING
(Consumer Price Index; base: 2006 = 100)

	2007	2008	2009
Food	102.9	111.7	111.2
Clothing	103.0	104.9	104.8
Housing	100.9	102.4	102.1
Transport and communications	101.7	104.1	99.9
Medicines and medical care	103.9	106.2	106.8
Education and entertainment	100.6	101.9	100.1
All items (incl. others)	**101.8**	**105.4**	**104.5**

TAIWAN

Statistical Survey

NATIONAL ACCOUNTS
(NT $ million in current prices)

National Income and Product

	2007	2008	2009
Domestic factor incomes	10,449,317	10,114,244	9,971,899
Consumption of fixed capital	1,742,202	1,905,667	1,919,607
Gross domestic product (GDP) at factor cost	12,191,519	12,019,911	11,891,506
Indirect taxes, *less* subsidies	718,992	678,590	621,172
GDP in purchasers' values	12,910,511	12,698,501	12,512,678
Net factor income from abroad	332,766	314,646	417,723
Gross national product (GNP)	13,243,277	13,013,147	12,930,401
Less Consumption of fixed capital	1,742,202	1,905,667	1,919,607
National income in market prices	11,501,075	11,107,480	11,010,794
Other current transfers from abroad (net)	−125,033	−93,940	−75,016
National disposable income	11,376,042	11,013,540	10,935,778

Gross national product: 12,229,296 in 2006 (revised figure); 12,968,534 in 2007 (revised figure); 12,672,967 in 2008 (preliminary).

Expenditure on the Gross Domestic Product

	2007	2008	2009
Government final consumption expenditure	1,521,102	1,564,394	1,608,957
Private final consumption expenditure	7,506,467	7,626,271	7,610,863
Increase in stocks	14,456	193,546	−164,311
Gross fixed capital formation	2,841,353	2,685,662	2,341,610
Total domestic expenditure	11,883,378	12,069,873	11,397,119
Exports of goods and services	9,304,061	9,226,468	7,826,618
Less Imports of goods and services	8,276,928	8,597,840	6,711,059
GDP in purchasers' values	12,910,511	12,698,501	12,512,678
GDP at constant 2006 prices	12,975,985	13,070,904	12,821,384

Gross Domestic Product by Economic Activity

	2007	2008	2009
Agriculture, hunting, forestry and fishing	191,621	201,950	195,008
Mining and quarrying	58,627	45,912	58,236
Manufacturing	3,405,858	3,162,151	3,097,700
Construction	357,606	363,274	319,655
Electricity, gas and water	208,577	130,643	264,847
Transport, storage and communications	854,421	857,841	852,966
Trade, restaurants and hotels	2,585,113	2,628,326	2,569,954
Finance, insurance and real estate*	2,027,695	2,025,887	1,938,800
Public administration, defence, health and social work	1,277,578	1,330,176	1,532,556
Education	599,751	603,216	615,168
Other services	915,601	954,363	788,561
Sub-total	12,482,448	12,303,739	12,233,451
Value added tax	222,720	221,321	206,237
Import duties	138,047	132,565	117,194
Statistical discrepancy	67,296	40,876	−44,204
GDP in purchasers' values	12,910,511	12,698,501	12,512,678

*Including imputed rents of owner-occupied dwellings.

BALANCE OF PAYMENTS
(US $ million)

	2007	2008	2009
Exports of goods f.o.b.	246,500	254,897	203,399
Imports of goods f.o.b.	−216,055	−236,419	−172,846
Trade balance	30,445	18,478	30,553
Exports of services	31,307	34,770	31,001
Imports of services	−35,102	−35,125	−29,796
Balance on goods and services	26,650	18,123	31,758
Other income received	23,500	23,277	20,338
Other income paid	−13,368	−13,299	−7,827
Balance on goods, services and income	36,782	28,101	44,269
Current transfers received	4,559	5,210	4,753
Current transfers paid	−8,366	−8,189	−6,966
Current balance	32,975	25,122	42,056
Capital account (net)	−96	−334	−96
Direct investment abroad	−11,107	−10,287	−5,868
Direct investment from abroad	7,769	5,432	2,803
Portfolio investment assets	−44,993	3,289	−31,694
Portfolio investment liabilities	4,904	−15,777	21,372
Financial derivatives assets	3,691	7,938	5,344
Financial derivatives liabilities	−3,980	−6,349	−4,492
Other investment assets	−6,847	10,653	25,762
Other investment liabilities	11,585	3,235	364
Net errors and omissions	2,079	3,352	−1,425
Overall balance	−4,020	26,274	54,126

External Trade

PRINCIPAL COMMODITIES
(US $ million)

Imports c.i.f.	2005	2006	2007
Mineral products	29,858.9	38,808.8	45,896.4
Crude petroleum	18,207.0	23,528.5	24,494.8
Products of chemical or allied industries	19,495.1	22,468.4	24,835.1
Organic chemicals	8,566.7	9,742.3	10,236.2
Base metals and articles thereof	18,808.3	23,158.6	26,622.8
Iron and steel products	10,597.3	10,234.3	12,692.7
Machinery and mechanical appliances; electrical equipment; sound and television apparatus	68,832.6	72,541.2	72,528.0
Electronic products	33,345.9	36,773.3	36,331.9
Machinery	17,305.0	17,907.4	17,686.8
Electrical machinery products	6,632.7	6,631.4	7,249.3
Information and communication products	5,546.1	4,957.3	4,851.8
Vehicles, aircraft, vessels and associated transport equipment	6,976.6	4,949.8	5,391.3
Optical, photographic, cinematographic, measuring, precision and medical apparatus; clocks and watches; musical instruments	11,334.7	12,376.5	13,007.7
Total (incl. others)	182,614.4	202,698.3	219,251.9

TAIWAN

Exports f.o.b.	2005	2006	2007
Chemicals	10,126.4	11,268.6	14,866.4
Plastics, rubber and articles thereof	14,732.8	15,908.3	18,925.3
Textiles and textile articles	11,840.1	11,788.8	11,622.6
Fibre and yarn	8,651.0	8,664.6	8,580.4
Base metals and articles thereof	20,467.8	24,010.7	27,752.3
Iron and steel	13,238.1	14,742.4	17,386.8
Machinery and mechanical appliances; electrical equipment; sound and television apparatus	98,268.6	111,592.2	118,031.9
Electronic products	51,008.1	62,822.9	65,551.4
Machinery	13,397.4	14,269.3	15,538.7
Electrical machinery products	9,449.9	10,882.8	14,423.6
Information and communication products	10,973.9	9,883.9	9,552.1
Vehicles, aircraft, vessels and associated transport equipment	7,307.7	7,378.6	8,028.8
Total (incl. others)	**198,431.7**	**224,017.4**	**246,677.3**

2008 (US $ million): *Imports:* Mineral products 65,245.2; Products of chemical or allied industries 26,591.5; Base metals and articles thereof 28,922.4; Machinery and mechanical appliances, electrical equipment, sound and television apparatus 70,575.0; Electronic products; electrical equipment 35,086.1; Machinery 17,657.0; Vehicles, aircraft, vessels and associated transport equipment 4,380.4; Optical, photographic, cinematographic, measuring, precision and medical apparatus; clocks and watches; musical instruments 10,819.3; Total (incl. others) 240,447.8. *Exports:* Chemicals 17,240.6; Plastics, rubber and articles thereof 19,674.0; Textiles and textile articles 10,900.4; Base metals and articles thereof 28,220.5; Machinery and mechanical appliances; electrical equipment; sound and television apparatus 114,246.5; Vehicles, aircraft, vessels and associated transport equipment 9,094.8; Total (incl. others) 255,628.7.

2009 (US $ million): *Imports:* Mineral products 39,335.4; Products of chemical or allied industries 20,424.8; Base metals and articles thereof 15,195.4; Machinery and mechanical appliances, electrical equipment, sound and television apparatus 59,004.6; Electronic products; electrical equipment 31,285.8; Machinery 14,645.2; Vehicles, aircraft, vessels and associated transport equipment 4,175.3; Optical, photographic, cinematographic, measuring, precision and medical apparatus; clocks and watches; musical instruments 7,464.7; Total (incl. others) 174,370.5. *Exports:* Chemicals 13,930.4; Plastics, rubber and articles thereof 16,523.3; Textiles and textile articles 9,344.3; Base metals and articles thereof 19,359.3; Machinery and mechanical appliances; electrical equipment; sound and television apparatus 95,215.0; Vehicles, aircraft, vessels and associated transport equipment 7,727.5; Total (incl. others) 203,674.6.

PRINCIPAL TRADING PARTNERS
(US $ million)

Imports c.i.f.	2005	2006	2007
Angola	983.6	1,866.9	2,118.8
Australia	4,726.4	5,349.5	6,122.1
Chile	1,135.6	1,635.3	1,819.0
China, People's Republic	20,093.7	24,783.1	28,015.0
France	2,544.4	2,220.0	2,381.9
Germany	6,180.3	6,135.2	7,070.0
Hong Kong	2,109.7	1,880.6	1,824.9
India	859.6	1,245.3	2,537.3
Indonesia	4,543.0	5,204.3	5,776.0
Iran	2,468.0	2,906.9	3,260.3
Iraq	732.2	876.2	2,046.8
Japan	46,053.3	46,284.4	45,936.9
Korea, Republic	13,239.2	14,999.6	15,158.4
Kuwait	4,295.8	5,007.8	5,742.7
Malaysia	5,217.2	6,051.6	6,192.4
Netherlands	2,068.7	2,342.6	2,776.8
Philippines	2,794.8	2,775.5	2,277.4
Russia	2,196.4	1,903.0	1,904.3
Saudi Arabia	7,437.2	9,760.2	10,409.6
Singapore	4,960.7	5,105.6	4,791.7
Thailand	2,887.1	3,317.5	3,613.4
United Arab Emirates	1,696.2	3,112.2	3,476.0
United Kingdom	1,714.1	1,781.0	1,920.4
USA	21,170.8	22,664.5	26,508.1
Total (incl. others)	**182,614.4**	**202,698.1**	**219,251.6**

Exports f.o.b.	2005	2006	2007
Australia	2,392.6	2,723.0	3,233.3
China, People's Republic	43,643.7	51,808.6	62,416.8
Germany	4,463.1	5,007.0	5,174.8
Hong Kong*	34,035.6	37,381.2	37,979.7
India	1,582.9	1,471.1	2,342.0
Indonesia	2,358.6	2,499.5	2,910.8
Italy	1,797.5	2,194.7	2,410.4
Japan	15,110.8	16,300.3	15,933.6
Korea, Republic	5,877.4	7,154.2	7,794.0
Malaysia	4,282.6	4,941.5	5,390.2
Netherlands	4,396.2	4,411.6	4,411.5
Philippines	4,324.9	4,484.4	4,921.8
Singapore	8,042.2	9,279.6	10,501.4
Thailand	3,820.3	4,576.6	5,199.6
United Kingdom	3,262.8	3,510.6	3,618.0
USA	29,113.9	32,360.7	32,077.1
Viet Nam	4,102.8	4,869.4	6,860.5
Total (incl. others)	**198,431.7**	**224,017.3**	**246,676.9**

* The majority of Taiwan's exports to Hong Kong are re-exported.

2008 (US $ million): *Imports:* Australia 8,270.6; Brazil 2,192.1; China, People's Republic 31,391.3; France 2,292.8; Germany 7,474.3; Hong Kong 1,492.8; Indonesia 7,289.0; Japan 46,508.0; Korea, Republic 13,168.4; Kuwait 8,074.2; Malaysia 6,762.7; Netherlands 2,354.0; Saudi Arabia 15,172.7; Thailand 3,252.0; United Kingdom 1,917.6; USA 26,326.6; Total (incl. others) 240,447.8. *Exports:* Australia 3,486.6; Brazil 2,744.7; China, People's Republic 66,883.5; Germany 5,729.7; Hong Kong 32,689.9; Italy 2,450.0; Japan 17,556.0; Korea, Republic 8,705.8; Malaysia 5,514.0; Netherlands 4,566.0; Singapore 11,675.8; Thailand 4,906.0; United Kingdom 3,630.5; USA 30,791.0; Viet Nam 7,947.0; Total (incl. others) 255,628.7.

2009 (US $ million): *Imports:* Australia 5,965.9; China, People's Republic 24,423.5; France 1,784.2; Germany 5,672.9; Hong Kong 1,122.6; Indonesia 5,183.7; Japan 36,220.0; Korea, Republic 10,506.8; Malaysia 4,552.6; Netherlands 1,862.8; Thailand 2,681.7; United Kingdom 1,230.3; USA 18,153.9; Total (incl. others) 174,370.5. *Exports:* Australia 2,353.4; Brazil 1,406.5; China, People's Republic 54,248.7; Germany 4,695.9; Hong Kong 29,445.2; Italy 1,786.6; Japan 14,502.3; Korea, Republic 7,302.5; Malaysia 4,060.1; Netherlands 4,229.4; Singapore 8,613.8; Thailand 3,826.8; United Kingdom 2,980.2; USA 23,552.9; Viet Nam 5,987.9; Total (incl. others) 203,674.6.

Transport

RAILWAYS
(traffic)

	2007	2008	2009
Passengers ('000)	602,610	689,880	718,515
Passenger-km ('000)	15,769,121	19,065,567	19,277,397
Freight ('000 metric tons)	17,378	16,583	14,144
Freight ton-km ('000)	889,736	933,341	776,023

ROAD TRAFFIC
(motor vehicles in use at 31 December)

	2007	2008	2009
Passenger cars	5,712,842	5,674,426	5,704,312
Buses and coaches	27,361	27,339	27,667
Goods vehicles	975,650	973,671	986,767
Motorcycles and scooters	13,943,473	14,365,442	14,604,330

SHIPPING

Merchant Fleet
(at 31 December)

	2007	2008	2009
Number of vessels	629	637	641
Total displacement ('000 grt)	2,749.6	2,671.9	2,636.0

Source: IHS Fairplay, *World Fleet Statistics*.

TAIWAN

International sea-borne freight traffic

	2006	2007	2008
Vessels entered ('000 grt)	475,785	480,700	471,040
Vessels cleared ('000 grt)	503,737	498,593	486,700
Goods loaded ('000 metric tons)	47,558	50,810	45,745
Goods unloaded ('000 metric tons)	173,072	191,892	189,261

CIVIL AVIATION
(traffic on scheduled services)

	2007	2008	2009
Passengers carried ('000)	37,142	33,053	32,329
Freight carried ('000 metric tons)	1,231.2	1,072.1	969.9

Tourism

TOURIST ARRIVALS BY COUNTRY OF ORIGIN

	2007	2008	2009
Australia	51,270	57,725	56,697
Canada	56,554	59,605	59,490
Germany	39,372	40,129	39,372
Hong Kong and Macao	79,548	78,628	84,685
Indonesia	95,327	110,017	106,272
Japan	1,164,446	1,084,888	998,973
Korea, Republic	222,347	247,815	164,152
Malaysia	140,720	155,073	166,354
Philippines	80,117	83,056	73,182
Singapore	204,015	204,967	194,129
Thailand	89,137	83,685	77,344
United Kingdom	39,758	48,176	44,619
USA	395,036	383,747	365,266
Total (incl. others)	2,988,815	2,962,536	2,770,082

Note: Figures exclude arrivals of Overseas Chinese (i.e. those bearing Taiwan passports) resident abroad (especially Hong Kong and Macao): 727,248 in 2007; 882,651 in 2008; 1,624,922 in 2009.

Total visitor arrivals: 3,716,063 in 2007; 3,845,187 in 2008; 4,395,004 in 2009.

Tourism receipts (US $ million): 5,136 in 2006; 5,214 in 2007; 5,936 in 2008.

Communications Media

	2007	2008	2009
Book production (titles)	42,018	41,341	40,575
Newspapers (titles)	190	198	189
Magazines	959	982	1,018
Telephone subscribers ('000)	13,302	13,082	12,821
Mobile telephones ('000 in use)	24,287	25,413	26,959
Internet subscribers ('000)	5,974	6,027	5,668
Broadband subscribers ('000)*	4,790	5,024	4,998

*Source: International Telecommunication Union.

Television receivers (2006): 152.3 colour television receivers per 100 households; 79.9 cable television receivers per 100 households.

Education

(2009/10 unless otherwise indicated)

	Schools	Full-time teachers	Students
Pre-school*	3,195	17,369	185,668
Primary	2,658	99,164	1,593,414
Secondary (incl. vocational)	1,226	104,035	1,706,425
Higher	164	50,658	1,336,592
Special*	24	1,734	6,875
Supplementary*	844	1,492	253,275

*2008/09.

Pupil-teacher ratio (primary education, official estimate): 16.1 in 2008/09.

Adult literacy rate (official estimate): 93.0% (males 96.3%; females 89.5%) in 2008.

Directory

Note: the issue of the implementation of a uniform system of romanization of Taiwanese names has remained unresolved; the central Government favours the use of a system of Pinyin similar to that employed in mainland China but with certain differences (Tongyong), while local authorities in Taiwan remain divided between usage of the standard mainland Pinyin system (Hanyu) and a form of the traditional Wade-Giles system.

The Government

HEAD OF STATE

President: MA YING-JEOU (inaugurated 20 May 2008).
Vice-President: VINCENT C. SIEW.
Secretary-General: WU CHIN-LIN.

EXECUTIVE YUAN
(May 2011)

The Government is formed by the Kuomintang.
Premier: WU DEN-YIH.
Vice-Premier and Minister of the Consumer Protection Commission: SEAN C. CHEN.
Secretary-General: LIN JOIN-SANE.

Ministers without Portfolio: YIIN CHII-MING, OVID J. L. TZENG, CHANG JIN-FU, LEE HONG-YUAN, JAMES C. T. HSUEH, LIN JUNQ-TZER, CYRUS C. Y. CHU.
Minister of the Interior: JIANG YI-HUAH.
Minister of Foreign Affairs: TIMOTHY CHIEN-TIEN YANG.
Minister of National Defense: KAO HUA-CHU.
Minister of Finance: LI SUSH-DER.
Minister of Education: WU CHING-JI.
Minister of Justice: TSENG YUNG-FU.
Minister of Economic Affairs: SHIH YEN-SHIANG.
Minister of Transportation and Communications: MAO CHI-KUO.
Minister of the Mongolian and Tibetan Affairs Commission: LUO YING-SHAY.
Minister of the Overseas Compatriot Affairs Commission: WU YING-YIH.
Governor of the Central Bank: PERNG FAI-NAN.
Minister of the Directorate-General of Budget, Accounting and Statistics: SHIH SU-MEI.
Minister of Central Personnel Administration: WU TAI-CHENG.
Minister of the Government Information Office: PHILIP Y. M. YANG.

TAIWAN

Minister of the Department of Health: CHIU WEN-TA.
Minister of the Environmental Protection Administration: STEPHEN SHU-HUNG SHEN.
Director of the National Palace Museum: CHOU KUNG-SHIN.
Minister of the Mainland Affairs Council: LAI SHIN-YUAN.
Minister of the Council for Economic Planning and Development: CHRISTINA LIU.
Minister of the Public Construction Commission: LEE HONG-YUAN.
Minister of the Veterans' Affairs Commission: TSENG JING-LING.
Minister of the National Youth Commission: JACK YUN-JIE LEE.
Minister of the Atomic Energy Council: TSAI CHUEN-HORNG.
Minister of the National Science Council: LEE LOU-CHUANG.
Minister of the Research, Development and Evaluation Commission: CHU CHIN-PENG.
Minister of the Council of Agriculture: CHEN WU-HSIUNG.
Minister of the Council for Cultural Affairs: EMILE CHI-JEN SHENG.
Minister of the Council of Labor Affairs: WANG JU-HSUAN.
Chairperson of the Fair Trade Commission: WU SHIOW-MING.
Minister of the Sports Affairs Council: TAI HSIA-LING.
Minister of the Council of Indigenous Peoples: SUN TA-CHUAN.
Minister of the Coast Guard Administration: WANG GINN-WANG.
Minister of the Council for Hakka Affairs: HUANG YU-CHENG.
Chairperson of the Central Election Commission: CHANG PO-YA.
Minister of the Financial Supervisory Commission: CHEN YUH-CHANG.
Minister of the Aviation Safety Council: CHANG YU-HERN.
Minister of the National Communications Commission: SU HERNG.

MINISTRIES, COMMISSIONS, ETC.

Office of the President: 122 Chungking South Rd, Zhongzheng District, Taipei 10048; tel. (2) 23113731; fax (2) 23311604; e-mail public@mail.oop.gov.tw; internet www.president.gov.tw.

Ministry of Economic Affairs: 15 Foo Chou St, Taipei 10015; tel. (2) 23212200; fax (2) 23919398; e-mail minister@moea.gov.tw; internet www.moea.gov.tw.

Ministry of Education: 5 Chung Shan South Rd, Zhongzheng District, Taipei 10051; tel. (2) 23566051; fax (2) 23976978; internet www.moe.gov.tw.

Ministry of Finance: 2 Ai Kuo West Rd, Taipei 10066; tel. (2) 23228000; fax (2) 23568774; e-mail mof@mail.mof.gov.tu; internet www.mof.gov.tw.

Ministry of Foreign Affairs: 2 Kaitakeland Blvd, Taipei 10048; tel. (2) 23482999; fax (2) 23805678; e-mail eyes@mofa.gov.tw; internet www.mofa.gov.tw.

Ministry of the Interior: 5–9/F, 5 Syujhou Rd, Taipei 10017; tel. (2) 23565005; fax (2) 23566201; e-mail service@minister.moi.gov.tw; internet www.moi.gov.tw.

Ministry of Justice: 130 Chungking South Rd, Sec. 1, Taipei 10048; tel. (2) 23146871; fax (2) 23896274; internet www.moj.gov.tw.

Ministry of National Defense: 2/F, 164 Po Ai Rd, Taipei 10048; tel. (2) 23116117; fax (2) 23144221; internet www.mnd.gov.tw.

Ministry of Transportation and Communications: 50 Ren Ai Rd, Sec. 1, Zhongzheng District, Taipei 10048; tel. (2) 23492900; fax (2) 23492491; e-mail motceyes@motc.gov.tw; internet www.motc.gov.tw.

Mongolian and Tibetan Affairs Commission: 4/F, 5 Hsu Chou Rd, Sec. 1, Taipei 10055; tel. (2) 23566467; fax (2) 23416186; e-mail mtacserv@mtac.gov.tw; internet www.mtac.gov.tw.

Overseas Compatriot Affairs Commission: 15–17/F, 5 Hsu Chou Rd, Taipei 10055; tel. (2) 23272600; fax (2) 23566323; e-mail ocacinfo@mail.ocac.gov.tw; internet www.ocac.gov.tw.

Directorate-General of Budget, Accounting and Statistics: 1 Chung Hsiao East Rd, Sec. 1, Taipei 10058; tel. (2) 33566500; fax (2) 23825267; e-mail sicbs@dgbas.gov.tw; internet www.dgbas.gov.tw.

Government Information Office: 2 Tientsin St, Taipei 10051; tel. (2) 33568888; fax (2) 23568733; e-mail service@mail.gio.gov.tw; internet www.gio.gov.tw.

Council of Indigenous Peoples: 172 Chungking North Rd, Datong District, Taipei 10357; tel. (2) 25571600; fax (2) 23454323; e-mail minister@apc.gov.tw; internet www.apc.gov.tw.

Council of Agriculture: see under Trade and Industry—Government Agencies.

Atomic Energy Council (AEC): 2–8/F, 80 Cheng Kung Rd, Sec. 1, Yonghe City, Taipei County 23452; tel. (2) 82317919; fax (2) 82317833; e-mail public@aec.gov.tw; internet www.aec.gov.tw.

Central Personnel Administration: 10/F, 2-2 Chinan Rd, Taipei 10051; tel. (2) 23979298; fax (2) 23975505; internet www.cpa.gov.tw.

Consumer Protection Commission: 12 Jihe Rd, Taipei 11166; tel. (2) 28863200; fax (2) 28866646; e-mail tcpc@ms1.hinet.net; internet www.cpc.gov.tw.

Council for Hakka Affairs: 8/F, 3 Songren Rd, Taipei 11010; tel. (2) 87894567; fax (2) 87894620; e-mail src@mail.hakka.gov.tw; internet www.hakka.gov.tw.

Council for Cultural Affairs: 30-1 Beiping East Rd, Zhongzheng District, Taipei 10049; tel. (2) 23434000; fax (2) 23216478; e-mail adm@cca.gov.tw; internet www.cca.gov.tw.

Council for Economic Planning and Development: 3 Baocing Rd, Zhongzheng District, Taipei 10020; tel. (2) 23165300; fax (2) 23700415; internet www.cepd.gov.tw.

Environmental Protection Administration: 83 Chung Hua Rd, Sec. 1, Taipei 10042; tel. (2) 23117722; fax (2) 23115486; e-mail umail@epa.gov.tw; internet www.epa.gov.tw.

Public Construction Commission: 9/F, 3 Songren Rd, Taipei 11010; tel. (2) 87897500; fax (2) 87897800; e-mail secr@mail.pcc.gov.tw; internet www.pcc.gov.tw.

Fair Trade Commission: 12–14/F, 2-2 Chi Nan Rd, Sec. 2, Taipei 10051; tel. (2) 23517588; fax (2) 23974997; e-mail ftcpub@ftc.gov.tw; internet www.ftc.gov.tw.

Department of Health: 36 Ta Cheng St, Datong District, Taipei 10341; tel. (2) 85906666; fax (2) 25502052; internet www.doh.gov.tw.

Council of Labor Affairs: 9/F, 83 Yangping North Rd, Sec. 2, Taipei 10346; tel. (2) 85902866; fax (2) 85902960; internet www.cla.gov.tw.

Mainland Affairs Council: 15/F, 2-2 Chi Nan Rd, Sec. 1, Taipei 10051; tel. (2) 23975589; fax (2) 23975300; e-mail macst@mac.gov.tw; internet www.mac.gov.tw.

National Science Council: 17–22/F, 106 Ho Ping East Rd, Sec. 2, Taipei 10622; tel. (2) 27377992; fax (2) 27377566; e-mail nsc@nsc.gov.tw; internet www.nsc.gov.tw.

National Youth Commission: 14/F, 5 Hsu Chou Rd, Taipei 10055; tel. (2) 23566232; fax (2) 23566307; e-mail nycn@nyc.gov.tw; internet www.nyc.gov.tw.

Research, Development and Evaluation Commission: 6/F, 2-2 Chi Nan Rd, Sec. 1, Taipei 10051; tel. (2) 23419066; fax (2) 23969990; e-mail service@rdec.gov.tw; internet www.rdec.gov.tw.

Sports Affairs Council: 20 Zhu Lun St, Taipei 10481; tel. (2) 87711800; fax (2) 27523600; internet www.sac.gov.tw.

Veterans' Affairs Commission: 222 Chung Hsiao East Rd, Sec. 5, Xinyi District, Taipei 11025; tel. (2) 27571750; fax (2) 27230170; e-mail eyes@mail.vac.gov.tw; internet www.vac.gov.tw.

Financial Supervisory Commission: 18/F, 7 Hsien Ming Blvd, Sec. 2, Panchiao City, Taipei County 22041; tel. (2) 89680899; fax (2) 89681215; e-mail fscey@fscey.gov.tw; internet www.fscey.gov.tw.

Coast Guard Administration: 296 Singlong Rd, Taipei 11698; tel. (2) 22399201; fax (2) 22399258; e-mail master@cga.gov.tw; internet www.cga.gov.tw.

President and Legislature

PRESIDENT

Election, 22 March 2008

Candidate*	Votes	% of votes
Ma Ying-jeou (Kuomintang—KMT)	7,659,014	58.45
Frank C. T. Hsieh (Democratic Progressive Party—DPP)	5,444,949	41.55
Total	13,103,963†	100.00

* The vice-presidential candidates were respectively Vincent V. C. Siew of the KMT and Su Tseng-chang of the DPP.
† Not including invalid or spoiled ballot papers.

TAIWAN

LI-FA YUAN
(Legislative Yuan)

President: WANG JIN-PYNG.

Election, 12 January 2008

Party	Seats
Kuomintang (KMT)	81
Democratic Progressive Party (DPP)	27
Non-Partisan Solidarity Union (NPSU)	3
People First Party (PFP)	1
Independents	1
Total	**113**

Election Commission

Central Election Commission: 10/F, 5 Hsu Chou Rd, Taipei 10055; tel. (2) 23565484; fax (2) 23976898; e-mail cec13@cec.gov.tw; internet www.cec.gov.tw; f. 1980; Chair. and 11–19 commrs nominated by Premier and approved by the President; Chair. is also a member of the Exec. Yuan; Chair. CHANG PO-YA; Sec.-Gen. TENG TIEN-YU.

Political Organizations

At August 2006 a total of 109 parties were registered with the Ministry of the Interior.

Democratic Progressive Party (DPP): 10/F, 30 Beiping East Rd, Taipei 10051; tel. (2) 23929989; fax (2) 23930342; e-mail foreign@dpp.org.tw; internet www.dpp.org.tw; f. 1986; advocates 'self-determination' for the people of Taiwan and UN membership; supports establishment of independent Taiwan following plebiscite; 530,975 mems (2004); Chair. Dr TSAI ING-WEN; Sec.-Gen. SU JIA-CHYUAN.

Green Party Taiwan: 5/F, 13 Chung Hsiao East Rd, Zhongzheng District, Taipei 10049; tel. (2) 23920508; fax (2) 23920512; e-mail contact@greenparty.org.tw; internet www.greenparty.org.tw; f. 1996; est. by breakaway faction of DPP.

Jiann Gwo Party (Taiwan Independence Party—TAIP): 9/F, 15-8 Nanjing East Rd, Sec. 5, Taipei 10564; tel. (2) 22800879; f. 1996; est. by dissident mems of DPP; Chair. HUANG CHIEN-MING; Sec.-Gen. LI SHENG-HSIUNG.

Kuomintang (KMT) (Nationalist Party of China): 232–234 Bade Rd, Sec. 2, Taipei 10492; tel. (2) 87711234; fax (2) 23434561; internet www.kmt.org.tw; f. 1894; aims to supplant communist rule in mainland China; supports democratic, constitutional govt, and advocates the unification of China; aims to promote market economy and equitable distribution of wealth; 1.1m. mems; Chair. MA YING-JEOU; Sec.-Gen. LIAO LIAO-YI.

New Party (NP): 4/F, 65 Guangfu South Rd, Taipei 10563; tel. (2) 27562222; fax (2) 27565750; e-mail webmaster@mail.np.org.tw; internet www.np.org.tw; f. 1993 by dissident KMT legislators (hitherto mems of New Kuomintang Alliance faction); merged with China Social Democratic Party in late 1993; advocates co-operation with the KMT and DPP in negotiations with the People's Republic, maintenance of security in the Taiwan Straits, modernization of the island's defence systems, measures to combat govt corruption, support of small and medium-sized businesses and establishment of a universal social security system; 80,000 mems; Chair. YOK MU-MING.

Non-Partisan Solidarity Union: 3/F, 5–1 Zhenjiang St, Taipei 10051; tel. (2) 23585066; f. 2004; Chair. LIN PIN-KUAN.

People First Party (PFP): 2/F, 63 Chang-an East Rd, Sec. 1, Taipei 10455; tel. (2) 25068555; internet www.pfp.org.tw; f. 2000; advocates the unification of China; seeks economic and cultural interaction between Taiwan and the mainland; Chair. JAMES C. Y. SOONG; Sec.-Gen. CHIN CHIN-SHENG.

Taiwan Solidarity Union (TSU): 7/F, Shaoxing North Rd, Zhongzheng District, Taipei; tel. (2) 23940230; fax (2) 23946616; e-mail service@tsu.org.tw; internet www.tsu.org.tw; f. 2001; est. by breakaway faction of KMT; Chair. HUANG HUN-KUI; Sec.-Gen. LIN CHIH-CHIA.

Young China Party (YCP): 12/F, 2 Sinsheng South Rd, Sec. 3, Taipei 10660; tel. (2) 23626715; f. 1923; aims to recover sovereignty over mainland China, safeguard the Constitution and democracy, and foster understanding between Taiwan and the non-communist world; Chair. JEAN JYI-YUAN.

Diplomatic Representation

EMBASSIES IN THE REPUBLIC OF CHINA

Belize: 11/F, 9 Lane 62, Tien Mou West Rd, Taipei 11156; tel. (2) 28760894; fax (2) 28760896; e-mail embelroc@ms41.hinet.net; internet www.embassyofbelize.org.tw; Ambassador EFRAIN RAVEY NOVELO.

Burkina Faso: 6/F, 9-1 Lane 62, Tien Mou West Rd, Taipei 11157; tel. (2) 28733096; fax (2) 28733071; e-mail abftap94@ms17.hinet.net; internet www.ambaburkinataipei.org.tw; Ambassador JACQUES Y. SAWADOGO.

Dominican Republic: 6/F, 9 Lane 62, Tien Mou West Rd, Taipei 11156; tel. (2) 28751357; fax (2) 28752661; e-mail domtaipei@hotmail.com; Ambassador VÍCTOR MANUEL SÁNCHEZ.

El Salvador: 2/F, 9 Lane 62, Tien Mou West Rd, Taipei 11157; tel. (2) 28763606; fax (2) 28763514; e-mail embasal.taipei@msa.hinet.net; Ambassador MARTA CHANG DE TSIEN.

The Gambia: 9/F, 9-1 Lane 62, Tien Mou West Rd, Taipei 11156; tel. (2) 28753911; fax (2) 28752775; e-mail gm.roc@msa.hinet.net; Ambassador Alhaji EBRIMA N. H. JARJOU.

Guatemala: 3/F, 9-1 Lane 62, Tien Mou West Rd, Taipei 11156; tel. (2) 28756952; fax (2) 28740699; e-mail embchina@minrex.gob.gt; Ambassador HÉCTOR IVÁN ESPINOZA FARFÁN.

Haiti: 8/F, 9-1 Lane 62, Tien Mou West Rd, Taipei 11156; tel. (2) 28766718; fax (2) 28766719; e-mail haiti@ms26.hinet.net; Chargé d'affaires MARIO CHOULOUTE.

Holy See: 87 Ai Kuo East Rd, Taipei 10642 (Apostolic Nunciature); tel. (2) 23216847; fax (2) 23911926; e-mail nuntius.taipei@gmail.com; Chargé d'affaires a.i. Mgr PAUL RUSSELL.

Honduras: 9/F, 9 Lane 62, Tien Mou West Rd, Taipei 11156; tel. (2) 28755507; fax (2) 28755726; e-mail honduras@ms9.hinet.net; Ambassador MARLENE VILLELA-TALBOTT.

Marshall Islands: 4/F, 9-1 Lane 62, Tien Mou West Rd, Taipei 11157; tel. (2) 28734884; fax (2) 28734904; e-mail rmiemb.tpe@msa.hinet.net; Ambassador PHILIP K. KABUA.

Nauru: 11/F, 9-1 Lane 62, Tien Mou West Rd, Taipei 11156; tel. (2) 28761950; fax (2) 28761930; Ambassador LUDWIG D. KEKE.

Nicaragua: 3/F, 9-1 Lane 62, Tien Mou West Rd, Taipei 11156; tel. (2) 28749034; fax (2) 28749080; e-mail icaza@ms13.hinet.net; Ambassador WILLIAM TAPIA.

Palau: 5/F, 9 Lane 62, Tien Mou West Rd, Taipei 11156; tel. (2) 28765415; fax (2) 28760436; e-mail palau.embassy@msa.hinet.net; Ambassador JACKSON HENRY.

Panama: 6/F, 111 Sung Kiang Rd, Taipei 10486; tel. (2) 25099189; fax (2) 25099801; Ambassador LUIS CUCALÓN D'ANELLO.

Paraguay: 7/F, 9-1 Lane 62, Tien Mou West Rd, Taipei 11156; tel. (2) 28736310; fax (2) 28736312; e-mail embapartaiwan@embapartwroc.com.tw; internet www.embapartwroc.com.tw; Ambassador CARLOS MARTÍNEZ RUÍZ DIAZ.

São Tomé and Príncipe: 10/F, 9-1 Lane 62, Tien Mou West Rd, Taipei 11156; tel. (2) 28766824; fax (2) 28766984; e-mail stptw@ms69.hinet.net; Ambassador JORGE AMADO.

Solomon Islands: 7/F, 9-1 Lane 62, Tien Mou West Rd, Taipei 11156; tel. (2) 28731168; fax (2) 28735224; e-mail embassy@solomons.org.tw; internet www.solomons.org.tw; Ambassador VICTOR SAMUEL NGELE.

Saint Christopher and Nevis: 5/F, 9-1 Lane 62, Tien Mou West Rd, Taipei 11157; tel. (2) 28733252; fax (2) 28733246; e-mail embskn.tw@msa.hinet.net; Ambassador JASMINE HUGGINS.

Swaziland: 10/F, 9 Lane 62, Tien Mou West Rd, Taipei 11156; tel. (2) 28725934; fax (2) 28726511; e-mail swazitpi@ms41.hinet.net; Ambassador NJABULISO GWEBU.

Judicial System

Judicial Yuan: 124 Chungking South Rd, Sec. 1, Taipei 10048; tel. (2) 23618577; fax (2) 23898923; e-mail judicial@mail.judicial.gov.tw; internet www.judicial.gov.tw; Pres. LAI HAU-MIN; Sec.-Gen. LIN JING-FAN; highest judicial organ; interprets the Constitution and national laws and ordinances; supervises the lower courts.

Supreme Court: 6 Chang Sha St, Sec. 1, Taipei 10048; tel. (2) 23141160; fax (2) 23114246; e-mail tpsemail@mail.judicial.gov.tw; internet tps.judicial.gov.tw; Court of third and final instance for civil and criminal cases; Pres. WU CHII-PIN.

High Court: 124 Chungking South Rd, Sec. 1, Taipei 10048; tel. (2) 23713261; internet tph.judicial.gov.tw; court of second instance for appeals of civil and criminal cases; four branch courts: Taichung, Tainan, Kaohsiung and Hualien.

TAIWAN

District Courts: Courts of first instance in civil, criminal and non-contentious cases.

Supreme Administrative Court: 1 Lane 126, Chungking South Rd, Sec. 1, Taipei 10048; tel. (2) 23113691; fax (2) 23111791; e-mail jessie@judicial.gov.tw; internet tpa.judicial.gov.tw; court of final resort in appeals against rulings of the High Administrative Courts and of the Intellectual Property Court; Pres. PENG FENG-ZHI.

High Administrative Courts: Courts of first instance in cases brought against govt agencies; three courts based in Taipei, Taichung and Kaohsiung.

Intellectual Property Court: 3/F, 7 Citizen Rd Banciao, Sec. 2, Taipei; tel. (2) 22726696; e-mail ipc@mail.judicial.gov.tw; Pres. KAO HSIOW-JEN.

Commission on Disciplinary Sanctions Against Functionaries: 3/F, 124 Chungking South Rd, Sec. 1, Taipei 10048; tel. (2) 23119375; fax (2) 23826255; decides on disciplinary measures against public functionaries impeached by the Control Yuan; Chief Commr LIN KUO-HSIEN.

Religion

According to the Ministry of the Interior, in 2004 35% of the population were adherents of Buddhism, 33% of Daoism (Taoism), 3.5% of I-kuan Tao and 2.6% of Christianity.

BUDDHISM

Buddhist Association of Taiwan: Mahayana and Theravada schools; 1,613 group mems and more than 5.4m. adherents; Leader Ven. CHIN-HSIN.

CHRISTIANITY

The Roman Catholic Church

Taiwan comprises one archdiocese, six dioceses and one apostolic administrative area. In December 2007, according to official figures, there were 299,130 adherents.

Bishops' Conference: Chinese Regional Bishops' Conference, 3 Lane 85, Linsen North Rd, Taipei 10443; tel. (2) 23571776; fax (2) 25231078; e-mail bishconf@ms1.hinet.net; internet www.catholic.org.tw; f. 1967; Pres. Most Rev. JOHN HUNG SHAN-CHUAN (Archbishop of Taipei).

Archbishop of Taipei: Most Rev. JOHN HUNG SHAN-CHUAN, Archbishop's House, 94 Loli Rd, Taipei 10587; tel. (2) 27371311; fax (2) 27373710.

The Anglican Communion

Anglicans in Taiwan are adherents of the Protestant Episcopal Church. In 2004 the Church had 1,000 members.

Bishop of Taiwan: Rt Rev. DAVID JUNG-HSIN LAI, 7 Lane 105, Hangchow South Rd, Sec. 1, Taipei 10060; tel. (2) 23411265; fax (2) 23962014; e-mail skhtpe@ms12.hinet.net; internet www.episcopalchurch.org/taiwan.htm.

Presbyterian Church

Tai-oan Ki-tok Tiu-Lo Kau-Hoe (Presbyterian Church in Taiwan): No. 3, Lane 269, Roosevelt Rd, Sec. 3, Taipei 10647; tel. (2) 23625282; fax (2) 23628096; e-mail pct@mail.pct.org.tw; internet www.pct.org.tw; f. 1865; Gen. Sec. Rev. CHANG TE-CHIEN; 224,679 mems (2000).

DAOISM (TAOISM)

In 2004 there were about 7.6m. adherents. Temples numbered 18,274, and clergy totalled 33,850.

I-KUAN TAO

Introduced to Taiwan in the 1950s, this 'Religion of One Unity' is a modern, syncretic religion, drawn mainly from Confucian, Buddhist and Daoist principles and incorporating ancestor worship. In 2004 there were 3,260 temples. Adherents totalled 810,000.

ISLAM

Leader MOHAMMED NI GUO-AN; 58,000 adherents in 2004.

The Press

In 2010 the number of registered newspapers stood at 2,091. The majority of newspapers are privately owned.

PRINCIPAL DAILIES

Taipei

Apple Daily News: 38, 141 Lane, Xinyi Rd, Taipei 11494; tel. (2) 66013456; fax (2) 66018866; e-mail enquiry@appledaily.com.tw; internet tw.nextmedia.com; jt venture between Hong Kong-based Next Media and several Singapore cos.

The China Post: 8 Fu Shun St, Taipei 10452; tel. (2) 25969971; fax (2) 25957962; e-mail info@mail.chinapost.com.tw; internet www.chinapost.com.tw; f. 1952; morning; English; Publr and Editor JACK HUANG; readership 250,000.

China Times: 132 Da Li St, Taipei 10801; tel. (2) 23087111; fax (2) 23048138; internet www.chinatimes.com; f. 1950; morning; Chinese; Chair. TSAI YAN-MING; Editor-in-Chief WANG MEI-YU; circ. 1.2m.

Commercial Times: 132 Da Li St, Taipei; tel. (2) 66320008; fax (2) 23069456; e-mail service@ctee.com.tw; internet ctee.com.tw; f. 1978; morning; Chinese; Publr PENG CHWEI-MING; Editor-in-Chief SIMON CHENG; circ. 300,000.

Economic Daily News: 369 Datong Rd, Xizhi, Sec. 1, Taipei 22161; tel. (2) 86925588; fax (2) 86925851; internet co.udn.com; f. 1967; morning; Chinese; publ. by United Daily News Group; Chair. ANN WANG.

Liberty Times: 399 Rueiguang Rd, Neihu District, Taipei 11492; tel. (2) 26562828; fax (2) 26561034; e-mail newstips@libertytimes.com.tw; internet www.libertytimes.com.tw; f. 1980; Publr WU A-MING; Editor-in-Chief ROGER CHEN; circ. 682,000 (2009).

Mandarin Daily News: 2 Foo Chou St, Taipei 10078; tel. (2) 23921133; fax (2) 23410203; e-mail feedback@mdnkids.com; internet www.mdnkids.com; f. 1948; children's newspaper; morning; Publr LIN LIANG.

Taipei Times: 14/F, 399 Ruiguang Rd, Neihu District, Taipei 11492; tel. (2) 26561000; fax (2) 26561099; e-mail letters@taipeitimes.com; internet www.taipeitimes.com; f. 1999; English; circ. 700,000 (2007).

Taiwan News: 7/F, 88 Xin Yi Rd, Sec. 2, Taipei 10641; tel. (2) 23517666; fax (2) 23515330; e-mail service@etaiwannews.com; internet www.etaiwannews.com; f. 1949; morning; English; Pres. JACK WONG; Publr LUIS KO.

United Daily News: 369 Datong Rd, Xizhi, Sec. 1, Taipei 22161; tel. (2) 86925588; fax (2) 86925851; e-mail service@udndata.com; internet udn.com; f. 1951; morning; CEO DUNCAN WANG; Editor-in-Chief SUNNY YOU; circ. 1.2m.

Provincial

China Daily News (Southern Edn): 57 Hsi Hwa St, Tainan 70449; tel. (6) 2202691; fax (6) 2201804; f. 1946; morning; Publr C. S. LIU; circ. 670,000.

The Commons Daily: Kaohsiung; tel. (7) 2692121; fax (7) 2692685; e-mail commons911@gmail.com; internet www.thecommonsdaily.tw; f. 1950; fmrly Min Chung Daily News; morning; Executive-in-Chief WANG CHIN-HSIUNG; circ. 148,000.

Keng Sheng Daily News: 36 Wuchuan St, Hualien 97048; tel. (38) 340131; fax (38) 341406; e-mail kengshen@ms6.hinet.net; internet www.ksnews.com.tw; f. 1947; morning; Publr HSIEH LEADER; circ. 50,000.

Taiwan Hsin Wen Daily News: 3 Woo Fu I Rd, Kaohsiung 80252; tel. (7) 2226666; f. 1949; morning; Publr CHANG REI-TE.

Taiwan Times: 32 Kaonan Rd, Renwu Township, Kaohsiung 81453; tel. (7) 3428666; fax (7) 3102828; internet www.twtimes.com.tw; f. 1978; Publr WANG YUH-FA.

SELECTED PERIODICALS

Artist Magazine: 6/F, 147 Chung Ching South Rd, Sec. 1, Taipei 10048; tel. (2) 23866715; fax (2) 23317096; e-mail artvenue@seed.net.tw; f. 1975; monthly; Publr HO CHENG KUANG; circ. 37,600.

Better Life Monthly: 11 Lane 199, Hsin-yih Rd, Sec. 4, Taipei 10685; tel. (2) 27549488; fax (2) 27001516; e-mail bettlife@ms14.hinet.net; f. 1987; Publr JACK S. LIN.

Brain: 12/F, 100 Nanking East Rd, Sec. 2, Taipei 10457; tel. (2) 27132644; fax (2) 25621578; e-mail askbrain@brain.com.tw; internet www.brain.com.tw; f. 1977; media industry; monthly; Publr JOHNSON WU.

Business Next: e-mail service@bxnext.com.tw; internet www.bxnext.com.tw; f. 1999; bi-weekly; circ. 160,000.

Business Weekly: 12/F, 141, Sec. 2, Minsheng East Rd, Taipei 10483; tel. (2) 25056789; fax (2) 27364620; e-mail mailbox@bwnet.com.tw; internet www.businessweekly.com.tw; f. 1987; Publr JIN WEI-TSUN.

Car Magazine: 1/F, 3 Lane 3, Tung Shan St, Taipei 10014; tel. (2) 23218168; fax (2) 23935614; e-mail carguide@ms13.hinet.net; f. 1982; monthly; Publr H. K. LIN; Editor-in-Chief LIN TA-WEI; circ. 85,000.

TAIWAN

Directory

China Times Weekly: 5/F, 25 Min Chuan East Rd, Sec. 6, Taipei 11494; tel. (2) 27936000; fax (2) 87918589; internet www.chinatimes.com; f. 1978; weekly; Chinese; Publr CHANG KUO-LI.

Commonwealth Monthly: 11/F, 139, Sec. 2, Nanking East Rd, Taipei 10553; tel. (2) 26620332; fax (2) 25082941; e-mail cwadmin@cw.com.tw; internet www.cw.com.tw; f. 1981; monthly; business; Pres. CHARLES H. C. KAO; Publr and Editor DIANE YING; circ. 110,000.

CompoTech Asia: Room 3B, 7 Xinyi Rd, Sec. 5, Taipei; tel. (2) 27201789; e-mail carol_liao@computechasia.com; internet www.compotech.com.tw; f. 1999; monthly; computing; Editor-in-Chief CAROL LIAO.

Cosmopolitan: 5/F, 8 Lane 181, Jiou-Tzung Rd, Taipei 11494; tel. (2) 28797890; fax (2) 28797890; e-mail hwaker@ms13.hinet.net; f. 1992; monthly; Publr MINCHUN CHANG.

Crown Magazine: 50 Alley 120, Tun Hua North Rd, Sec. 4, Taipei; tel. (2) 27168888; fax (2) 25148285; internet www.crown.com.tw; f. 1954; monthly; literature and arts; Publr PING HSIN TAO; Editor CHEN LIH-HWA; circ. 76,000.

Defense Technology Monthly: 6/F, 6 Nanking East Rd, Sec. 5, Taipei 10564; tel. (2) 27669628; fax (2) 27666092; e-mail service@dtm.com.tw; internet www.dtmonline.com; f. 1894; Publr J. D. BIH.

Elle Taiwan: 5/F, 9 Lane 130, Minsheng East Rd, Sec. 3, Taipei 10596; tel. (2) 67706168; fax (2) 87706170; e-mail newmedia@hft.com.tw; internet www.elle.com.tw; f. 1991; monthly; women's magazine; Publr JEAN DE WITT; Editors-in-Chief CINDY HU, DORIS LEE; circ. 50,000.

Evergreen Monthly: 11/F, 2 Pa Teh Rd, Sec. 3, Taipei 10558; tel. (2) 25782321; fax (2) 25786838; f. 1983; health care knowledge; Publr LIANG GUANG-MING; circ. 50,000.

Excellence Magazine: 3/F, 15 Lane 2, Chien Kuo North Rd, Sec. 2, Taipei 10487; tel. (2) 25093578; fax (2) 25173607; f. 1984; monthly; business; Man. LIN HSIN-JYH; Editor-in-Chief LIU JEN; circ. 70,000.

Families Monthly: 11/F, 2 Pa Teh Rd, Sec. 3, Taipei 10558; tel. (2) 25785078; fax (2) 25786838; f. 1976; family life; Editor-in-Chief THELMA KU; circ. 155,000.

Foresight Investment Weekly: 7/F, 52 Nanking East Rd, Sec. 1, Taipei 10450; tel. (2) 25512561; fax (2) 25119596; f. 1980; weekly; Dir and Publr SUN WUN HSIUNG; Editor-in-Chief WU WEN SHIN; circ. 55,000.

Global Views Monthly: 2/F, 1 Lane 93, Sungkiang Rd, Taipei 10455; tel. (2) 25173688; fax (2) 25082941; e-mail gvm@cgvm.com.tw; internet www.gvm.com.tw; f. 1986; Editor-in-Chief TIAO MING-FANG.

Gourmet World: 3/F, 53 Jen-Ai Rd, Sec. 1, Taipei 10052; tel. (2) 23972215; fax (2) 23412184; f. 1992; Publr HSU TANG-JEN.

Harvest Farm Magazine: 14 Wenchow St, Taipei 10648; tel. (2) 23628148; fax (2) 23636724; e-mail h3628148@ms15.hinet.net; internet www.harvest.org.tw; f. 1951; every 2 weeks; CEO LIN SHUE-CHENG; Editor-in-Chief YU SHU-LIEN.

Issues and Studies: A Social Science Quarterly on China, Taiwan and East Asian Affairs: Institute of International Relations, National Chengchi University, 64 Wan Shou Rd, Taipei 11666; tel. (2) 82377377; fax (2) 82377231; e-mail issues@nccu.edu.tw; internet iir.nccu.edu.tw/english_web/e_per.htm; f. 1965; quarterly; English; contemporary Chinese studies and East Asian affairs; Editor YEN CHEN-SHEN.

The Journalist: 16/F, 218 Tun Hua South Rd, Sec. 2, Taipei 10669; tel. (2) 23779977; fax (2) 23775850; f. 1987; weekly; Publr WANG SHIN-CHING.

Ladies Magazine: 11/F, 3, 187 Shin Yi Rd, Sec. 4, Taipei 10681; tel. (2) 27026908; fax (2) 27014090; f. 1978; monthly; Publr CHENG CHIN-SHAN; Editor-in-Chief THERESA LEE; circ. 60,000.

Madame Figaro Taiwan: e-mail service@heritage.com.tw; internet www.figaro.tw; f. 2001; fashion; published by Stone Media.

Management Magazine: 14/F, 248 Nan Jing East Rd, Sec. 3, Taipei County 22103; tel. (2) 86471828; fax (2) 86471466; e-mail frankhung@mail.chinamgt.com; internet www.harment.com; f. 1973; monthly; Chinese; Publr and Editor FRANK L. HUNG; Pres. KATHY T. KUO; circ. 65,000.

Money Monthly: 10/F, 289 Chung Hsiao East Rd, Taipei 10696; tel. (2) 25149822; fax (2) 27154657; f. 1986; monthly; personal financial management; Publr PATRICK SUN; Man. Editor JENNIE SHUE; circ. 55,000.

National Geographic/The Earth: 4/F, 319, Sec. 4, Bade Rd, Taipei 10565; tel. (2) 27485698; fax (2) 27480188.

National Palace Museum Monthly of Chinese Art: 221, Sec. 2, Jishan Rd, Taipei 11143; tel. (2) 28821230; fax (2) 28821507; e-mail wyc@npm.gov.tw; f. 1983; monthly in Chinese; Publr CHOU KUNG-SHIN; circ. 3,500.

Nong Nong Magazine: 11/F, 141, Sec. 2, Minsheng East Rd, Taipei 10483; tel. (2) 2502689; fax (2) 25051989; e-mail group@nongnong.com.tw; f. 1984; monthly; women's interest; Publr ANTHONY TSAI; Editor VIVIAN LIN; circ. 70,000.

PC Home: 4/F, 141, Sec. 2, Minsheng East Rd, Taipei 10483; tel. (2) 25000888; fax (2) 25001920; internet www.pchome.com.tw; f. 1996; monthly; Chair. HUNG-TZE JANG; CEO ARTHUR LEE.

PC Office: 11/F, 8 Tun Hua North Rd, Taipei 10547; tel. (2) 25007779; fax (2) 25007903; internet www.pcoffice.com.tw; f. 1997; monthly; Publr HUNG-TZE JANG.

Reader's Digest (Chinese Edn): 2/F, 2 Minsheng East Rd, Sec. 5, Taipei 10572; tel. (2) 82531198; fax (2) 82531211; internet www.readersdigest.com.tw; monthly; Editor-in-Chief VICTOR FUNG.

Studio Classroom: 10 Lane 62, Ta-Chih St, Taipei 10462; tel. (2) 25338082; fax (2) 25326406; internet www.studioclassroom.com; f. 1962; monthly; English teaching magazine; Publr DORIS BROUGHAM.

Taiwan Journal: 2 Tientsin St, Taipei 10051; tel. (2) 23970180; fax (2) 23568233; e-mail tj@mail.gio.gov.tw; internet taiwanjournal.nat.gov.tw; f. 1964; fmrly Free China Journal; weekly; English; news review; Publr VANESSA YEA-PING SHIH; Editor-in-Chief SUSAN YU; circ. 30,000.

Taiwan Panorama: 5/F, 54 Chung Hsiao East Rd, Sec. 1, Taipei 10049; tel. (2) 23922256; fax (2) 23970655; e-mail service@mail.taiwan-panorama.com; internet www.sinorama.com.tw; f. 1976; fmrly *Sinorama*; monthly; bilingual cultural magazine, with edns in Chinese with Japanese or English; Publr PASUYA WEN-CHIH YAO; Editor-in-Chief LAURA LEE; circ. 70,000.

Taiwan Review: 2 Tientsin St, Taipei 100; tel. (2) 23516419; fax (2) 23510829; e-mail tr@mail.gio.gov.tw; internet taiwanreview.nat.gov.tw; f. 1951; fmrly *Taipei Review*, renamed as above March 2003; monthly; English; illustrated; Publr SU JIN-PIN; Editor-in-Chief CHANG HUI-JHEN.

Time Express: B1/F, 205-1 Beisin Rd, Sec. 3, Sinolian City, Taipei County 23143; tel. (2) 89131717; fax (2) 89132232; e-mail timeex@ccw.com.tw; f. 1973; monthly; Publr RICHARD C. C. HUANG.

Unitas: 10/F, 180 Keelung Rd, Sec. 1, Taipei 11006; tel. (2) 27666759; fax (2) 27491208; e-mail unitas@udngroup.com.tw; monthly; Chinese; literary journal; Publr CHANG PAO-CHING; Editor-in-Chief HSU HUI-CHIH.

Vi Vi Magazine: 7/F, 550 Chung Hsiao East Rd, Sec. 5, Taipei 11081; tel. (2) 27275336; fax (2) 27592031; f. 1984; monthly; women's interest; Pres. TSENG CHING-TANG; circ. 60,000.

Vogue/GQ Conde Nast Interculture: 15/F, 51, Sec. 2, Keelung Rd, Sinyi District, Taipei 11082; tel. (2) 27328899; fax (2) 27390504; e-mail vogueeditor@mail.condenast.com.tw; internet www.vogue.com.tw; f. 1996; monthly; Publr BENTHAM LIU.

Wealth Magazine: 7/F, 52 Nanking East Rd, Sec. 1, Taipei 10444; tel. (2) 25512561; fax (2) 25236933; internet www.wealth.com.tw; f. 1974; monthly; finance; Pres. CHIN-HO HSIEH; Editor PHILIP CHEN; circ. 75,000.

Win Win Weekly: 7/F, 52 Nanking East Rd, Sec. 1, Taipei 10444; tel. (2) 25816196; fax (2) 25119596; f. 1996; Publr GIN-HO HSHIE.

Youth Juvenile Monthly: 3/F, 66-1 Chung Cheng South Rd, Sec. 1, Taipei 10045; tel. (2) 23112836; fax (2) 23115368; e-mail customer@youth.com.tw; internet www.youth.com.tw; f. 1965; Publr LEE CHUNG-GUAI.

NEWS AGENCY

Central News Agency (CNA): 209 Sung Chiang Rd, Taipei 10485; tel. (2) 25058379; fax (2) 25023805; e-mail cnamark@mail.cna.com.tw; internet www.cna.com.tw; f. 1924; news service in Chinese, English and Spanish; feature and photographic services; 25 domestic and 32 overseas bureaux; Pres. SU TZEN-PING; Chair. LIU CHIH-TSUNG.

Publishers

There are more than 8,000 publishing houses in Taiwan. In 2007 a total of 42,108 titles were published.

Art Book Co: 1/F, 18 Lane 283, Roosevelt Rd, Sec. 3, Taipei 10647; tel. (2) 23620578; fax (2) 23623594; e-mail artbook@ms43.hinet.net; Publr HO KUNG SHANG.

Cheng Wen Publishing Co: 3/F, 277 Roosevelt Rd, Sec. 3, Taipei 10647; tel. (2) 23628032; fax (2) 23660806; e-mail book@chengwen.com.tw; internet www.chengwen.com.tw; f. 1965; Publr LARRY C. HUANG.

Children's Publication Co Ltd: 7F-1, 314 Neihu Rd, Sec. 1, Taipei 11444; tel. (2) 87972799; fax (2) 87972700; e-mail jay@012book.com.tw; internet www.012book.com.tw; f. 1994.

China Times Publishing Co: 5/F, 240 Hoping West Rd, Sec. 3, Taipei 10803; tel. (2) 23066842; fax (2) 23049302; e-mail jess@

TAIWAN

readingtimes.com.tw; internet www.readingtimes.com.tw; f. 1975; Pres. Mo Chao-ping.

Chinese Culture University Press: 55 Hua Kang Rd, Yangmingshan, Taipei 11114; tel. (2) 28610511, ext. 17503; fax (2) 28617164; e-mail euca@staff.pccu.edu.tw; internet www2.pccu.edu.tw/cuca/ad3.htm; Publr Lee Fu-chen.

Cite Publishing Ltd: 2/F, 141 Minsheng East Rd, Sec. 2, Taipei 10482; tel. (2) 25007088; fax (2) 25007579; e-mail regina@hmg.com.tw; internet www.cite.com.tw; f. 1996.

The Commercial Press Ltd: 37 Chungking South Rd, Sec. 1, Taipei 10046; tel. (2) 23116118; fax (2) 23710274; e-mail ecptw@cptw.com.tw; internet www.cptw.com.tw; f. 1897; Editor Sylvia Wen-i Chen.

Commonwealth Publishing Co: 2/F, 1 Lane 93, Sung Chiang Rd, Taipei; tel. (2) 25173688; fax (2) 25173686; e-mail cwpc@cwgv.com.tw; internet www.bookzone.com.tw; f. 1982.

Crown Publishing Group: 50 Lane 120, Tun Hua North Rd, Taipei 10547; tel. (2) 27168888; fax (2) 27133422; e-mail edit3@crown.com.tw; internet www.crown.com.tw; f. 1954; Publr Philip Ping; 90 employees.

The Eastern Publishing Co Ltd: 4/F, 121 Chungking South Rd, Sec. 1, Taipei 100; tel. (2) 23114514; fax (2) 23317402; e-mail lola@1945.com.tw; f. 1945; Publr Cheng Si-ming.

Elite Publishing Co: 1/F, 33-1 Lane 113, Hsiamen St, Taipei 10048; tel. (2) 23671021; fax (2) 23657047; e-mail elite113@ms12.hinet.net; internet www.elitebooks.com.tw; f. 1975; Publr Ko Ching-hwa.

Far East Book Co: 66 Chungking South Rd, Sec. 1, Taipei 10045; tel. (2) 23118740; fax (2) 23114184; e-mail service@mail.fareast.com.tw; internet eng.fareast.com.tw; art, education, history, physics, mathematics, law, literature, dictionaries, textbooks, language tapes, Chinese-English dictionaries; Publr George C. L. Pu.

Global Group Holding Ltd: 10/F, 15 Lane 174, Hsin Ming Rd, Neihu District, Taipei; tel. (2) 27911197, ext. 208; fax (2) 27918606; e-mail readers@gobooks.com.tw; internet www.gobooks.com.tw; Publr Chu Pao-loung; Dir Kelly Chu.

Hsin Yi Foundation: 75 Chungking South Rd, Sec. 2, Taipei 10015; tel. (2) 23965303; fax (2) 23965015; e-mail arni@hsin-yi.org.tw; internet www.hsin-yi.org.tw; f. 1971; children's education and devt; Exec. Dir Sing-ju Chang.

Kwang Hwa Publishing Co: 5/F, 54 Chung Hsiao East Rd, Sec. 1, Taipei 10049; tel. (2) 23922256; fax (2) 23970655; e-mail service@mail.sinorama.com.tw; internet www.sinorama.com.tw; Publr Cheng Wen-tsang.

Li-Ming Cultural Enterprise Co: 3/F, 49 Chungking South Rd, Sec. 1, Taipei 10045; tel. (2) 23314046; fax (2) 23817230; e-mail liminglf@ms15.hinet.net; internet www.limingco.com.tw; f. 1971; Pres. Shen Fang-shin.

Linking Publishing Co Ltd: 555, Sec. 4, Chung Hsiao East Rd, Taipei 100; tel. (2) 27634300; fax (2) 27567688; e-mail sheh.chang@udngroup.com; internet www.linkingbooks.com.tw/linkingp; Publr Liu Kuo-juei.

Locus Publishing Co: 11/F, 25 Nanking East Rd, Sec. 4, Taipei 10550; tel. (2) 87123898; fax (2) 25453927; e-mail locus@locuspublishing.com; internet www.locuspublishing.com; f. 1996.

San Min Book Co Ltd: 386 Fusing North Rd, Taipei 10476; tel. (2) 25006600; fax (2) 25064000; e-mail editor@sanmin.com.tw; internet www.sanmin.com.tw; f. 1953; literature, history, philosophy, social sciences, dictionaries, art, politics, law; Publr Liu Chen-chiang.

Ta Chien Publishing Co Ltd: 19 Sinheheng Rd, Tainan 70248; tel. (6) 2917489; fax (6) 2921618; e-mail tachiens@ms16.hinet.net; internet www.tachien.com.tw.

Tung Hua Book Co Ltd: 105 Emei St, Taipei 10844; tel. (2) 23114027; fax (2) 23116615; e-mail service@bookcake.com.tw; internet www.bookcake.com.tw; f. 1965; Publr Charles Choh.

The World Book Co: 6/F, 99 Chungking South Rd, Sec. 1, Taipei 10045; tel. (2) 23113834; fax (2) 23317963; e-mail wbc.ltd@msa.hinet.com; internet www.worldbook.com.tw; f. 1921; literature, textbooks; Chair. Yen Feng-chang; Publr Yen Angela Chu.

Youth Cultural Enterprise Co Ltd: 3/F, 66-1 Chungking South Rd, Sec. 1, Taipei 10045; tel. (2) 23112836; fax (2) 23115368; e-mail customer@youth.com.tw; internet www.youth.com.tw; f. 1958; Publr Lee Chung-kuei.

Yuan Liou Publishing Co Ltd: 6/F, 81, Sec. 2, Nanchang Rd, Taipei 10084; tel. (2) 23926899; fax (2) 23926658; e-mail ylib@ylib.com; internet www.ylib.com; f. 1975; fiction, non-fiction, children's; Publr Wang Jung-wen.

Broadcasting and Communications

TELECOMMUNICATIONS

National Communications Commission: 50 Ren-Ai Rd, Sec. 1, Taipei 10052; tel. (2) 33437377; fax (2) 23433994; f. 2006; telecommunications and broadcasting regulatory authority; Chair. Herng Su.

Chunghwa Telecommunications Co Ltd: 21 Hsinyi Rd, Sec. 1, Taipei 10048; tel. (2) 23445385; fax (2) 23919166; e-mail chtir@cht.com.tw; internet www.cht.com.tw; f. 1996; previously state-controlled company, privatization completed in 2005; Chair. and CEO Shyue Ching Lu.

Far EasTone Telecom: 468 Ruei Guang Rd, Neihu District, Taipei 11492; tel. (2) 87935000; e-mail ir@fareastone.com.tw; internet www.fareastone.com.tw; mobile tel. services; Pres. Jan Nilsson.

Taiwan Mobile Co Ltd: 18/F, 172–1, Ji-Lung Rd, Sec. 2, Taipei 106; tel. (2) 66062999; fax (2) 66368669; e-mail ir@taiwanmobile.com; internet www.taiwanmobile.com; f. 1998; est. as Pacific Cellular Corpn; merged with Taiwan Tele-Shop in 2005; mobile telephone and internet services; Chair. Richard Tsai; Pres. Harvey Chang.

BROADCASTING

Radio

In June 2009 there were 172 radio broadcasting corporations in operation.

Broadcasting Corpn of China (BCC): 10/F, 375 Sung Chiang Rd, Taipei 10482; tel. (2) 25019688; fax (2) 25018545; internet www.bcc.com.tw; f. 1928; domestic (5 networks and 1 channel) services; 9 local stations, 131 transmitters; Chair. Jaw Shao-kong.

Central Broadcasting System (CBS): 55 Pei An Rd, Tachih, Taipei 10464; tel. (2) 28856168; fax (2) 28867088; e-mail rti@rti.org.tw; internet www.cbs.org.tw; f. 1928; national broadcasting system of Taiwan; broadcasts internationally in 13 languages via medium and short wave under the call sign Radio Taiwan International (RTI); CEO Kuang Hsiang-hsia.

Cheng Sheng Broadcasting Corpn Ltd: 7/F, 66-1 Chungking South Rd, Sec. 1, Taipei 10045; tel. (2) 23617231; fax (2) 23712715; e-mail csbc_server@csbc.com.tw; internet www.csbc.com.tw; f. 1950; 6 stations, 3 relay stations; Chair. Guo Rong-chang; Pres. Li Yung-guie.

International Community Radio Taipei (ICRT): 19–5F, 107 Jhongshan Rd, Sec. 1, Sinjhuang, Taipei 24250; tel. (2) 85227766; fax (2) 85227077; internet www.icrt.com.tw; f. 1979; predominantly English-language broadcaster.

Kiss Radio: 34/F, 6 Min Chuan 2 Rd, Kaohsiung 80658; tel. (7) 3365888; fax (7) 3364931; e-mail helena@kiss.com.tw; internet www.kiss.com.tw; Pres. Helena Yuan.

M-radio Broadcasting Corpn: 8/F, 1-18 Taichung Kang Rd, Sec. 2, Taichung City 40751; tel. (4) 23235656; fax (4) 23231199; e-mail jason@mradio.com.tw; internet www.mradio.com.tw.

UFO Broadcasting Co Ltd: 25/F, 102 Roosevelt Rd, Sec. 2, Taipei 10084; tel. (2) 23636600; fax (2) 23673083; internet www.ufo.net.tw; Pres. Chang Hsiao-yen.

Voice of Taipei Broadcasting Co Ltd: 10/F, B Rm, 15-1 Han Chou South Rd, Sec. 1, Taipei 10050; tel. (2) 23957255; fax (2) 23947855; internet www.vot.com.tw; Pres. Nita Ing.

Television

China Television Co (CTV): 120 Chung Yang Rd, Nan Kang District, Taipei 11523; tel. (2) 27838308; fax (2) 27896614; e-mail prog@mail.chinatv.com.tw; internet beta.ctv.com.tw; f. 1969; Chinatimes Group; Pres. Jiang Feng-che; Chair. Cheng Su-ming.

Chinese Television System (CTS): 100 Kuang Fu South Rd, Taipei 10694; tel. (2) 27510321; fax (2) 27775414; e-mail public@mail.cts.com.tw; internet www.cts.com.tw; f. 1971; Chair. Louis Chen; Pres. Li Yuan.

Formosa Television Co (FTV): 14/F, 30 Pa Teh Rd, Sec. 3, Taipei 10551; tel. (2) 25786686; fax (2) 25798715; internet www.ftv.com.tw; f. 1997; Chair. Tien Tzai-ting; Pres. Chen Kang-hsing.

Public Television Service Foundation (PTS): 50 Lane 75, Sec. 3, Kang Ning Rd, Neihu, Taipei 11460; tel. (2) 26338037; fax (2) 26301895; e-mail pub@mail.pts.org.tw; internet www.pts.org.tw; some services merged with Chinese Television System July 2006; Chair. Cheng Sheng-fu; Pres. Sylvia Feng.

Taiwan Broadcasting System (TBS): ; tel. (2) 26301003; e-mail prg50044@mail.pts.org.tw; internet www.tbs.org.tw; f. 2006, with the merger of CTS and PTS (see above), and six other channels; Chair. Dr Louis Chen.

Taiwan Television Enterprise (TTV): 10 Pa Teh Rd, Sec. 3, Taipei 10502; tel. (2) 27758888; fax (2) 27758957; internet www.ttv.com.tw; f. 1962; Pres. and Chair. Huang Song.

// TAIWAN

Finance

(cap. = capital; dep. = deposits; m. = million; brs = branches; amounts in New Taiwan dollars unless otherwise stated)

BANKING

In December 2010 there were 67 banks operating in Taiwan. In September 2002 the Ministry of Finance announced plans to privatize state banks by 2006, and to sell the Government's stake in commercial banks by 2010.

Central Bank

Central Bank of the Republic of China (Taiwan): 2 Roosevelt Rd, Sec. 1, Taipei 10066; tel. (2) 23936161; fax (2) 23571974; e-mail adminrol@mail.cbc.gov.tw; internet www.cbc.gov.tw; f. 1928; fmrly Central Bank of China; name changed as above in 2007; bank of issue; cap. and res 1,223,386m., dep. 9,515,944m. (Dec. 2009); Gov. PERNG FAI-NAN; Dir-Gen. JAMES YUE.

Domestic Banks

Bank of Taiwan: 120 Chungking South Rd, Sec. 1, Taipei 10036; tel. (2) 23493456; fax (2) 23315840; e-mail botservice@mail.bot.com.tw; internet www.bot.com.tw; f. 1946; subsidiary of govt-owned Taiwan Financial Holdings Co Ltd (f. 2008 by merger of Bank of Taiwan, Land Bank of Taiwan and Export-Import Bank of China); cap. 45,000m., res 183,393.5m., dep. 3,463.2m. (Dec. 2009); Chair. SUSAN CHANG; Pres. CHANG MING-DAW; 162 domestic brs, 6 overseas brs.

Export-Import Bank of the Republic of China (Eximbank): 8/F, 3 Nan Hai Rd, Taipei 100; tel. (2) 23210511; fax (2) 23940630; e-mail eximbank@eximbank.com.tw; internet www.eximbank.com.tw; f. 1979; merged with Bank of Taiwan and Land Bank of Taiwan in Jan. 2008 to form Taiwan Financial Holding Co, but withdrew from parent co in June; cap. 12,000m., res 757.6m., dep. 38,754.7m. (Dec. 2009); Chair. SHENG YEN LEE; Pres. ROBERT CHU; 3 brs.

Land Bank of Taiwan Co Ltd: 46 Kuan Chien Rd, Taipei 10047; tel. (2) 23483456; fax (2) 23757023; e-mail lbot@landbank.com.tw; internet www.landbank.com.tw; f. 1946; subsidiary of govt-owned Taiwan Financial Holdings Co Ltd (f. 2008 by merger between Land Bank of Taiwan, Bank of Taiwan and Export-Import Bank of China); cap. 50,000m., res 49,741.7m., dep. 1,978,737.3m. (Dec. 2009); Chair. YAO-SHING WANG; Pres. LER-MING SU; 147 domestic brs, 3 overseas brs.

Taiwan Co-operative Bank: 77 Kuan Chien Rd, Taipei 10038; tel. (2) 23118811; fax (2) 23752954; e-mail ib02@tcb-bank.com.tw; internet www.tcb-bank.com.tw; f. 1946; acts as central bank for co-operatives, and as major agricultural credit institution; merged with Farmers Bank of China in May 2006; cap. 54,855m., res 47,505.6m., dep. 2,449,277.3m. (Dec. 2009); Chair. LIU DENG-CHENG; Pres. TSAI CHIU-JUNG; 300 brs.

Commercial Banks

Bank of Kaohsiung: 168 Po Ai 2nd Rd, Zuoying Qu, Kaohsiung 81357; tel. (7) 5570535; fax (7) 5580529; e-mail service@mail.bok.com.tw; internet www.bok.com.tw; f. 1982; cap. 5,257.9m., res 4,099.1m., dep. 172,685.8m. (Dec. 2009); Chair. LEI CHUNG-DAR (acting); Pres. WU CHU HUNG; 33 brs.

Bank of Panhsin: 2/F, 18 Cheng Tu St, Ban Chiau City, Taipei County 220; tel. (2) 29629170; fax (2) 29572011; e-mail 0473@bop.com.tw; internet www.bop.com.tw; f. 1997; cap. 9,557m., res –42.2m., dep. 148,207.6m. (Dec. 2009); Chair. LIU PING-HUI; Pres. CHEN AN-HSIUNG; 48 brs.

Bank SinoPac Co Ltd: 6/F, 306 Sec. 2, Bade Rd, Jhongshan District, Taipei 10492; tel. (2) 25082288; fax (2) 81618485; internet www.banksinopac.com.tw; f. 1992; cap. 48,218.4m., res 12,091.2m., dep. 932,244.5m. (Dec. 2009); Chair. CHIU CHENG-HSIUNG; Pres. and CEO DESMOND JIANG; 46 brs, including 2 overseas.

Cathay United Bank: 1/F, 7 Sungren Rd, Taipei, 110; tel. (2) 87226666; fax (2) 87898789; e-mail webservice@cathaybk.com.tw; internet www.cathaybk.com.tw; f. 1974; merged with United World Chinese Commercial Bank in 2003; cap. 52,277m., res 32,180m., dep. 1,392,407.3m. (Dec. 2009); Chair. GREGORY K. H. WANG; Pres. TSU PEI CHEN; 140 domestic brs, 2 overseas brs.

Chang Hwa Commercial Bank Ltd: 57 Jhongshan N. Rd, Sec. 2, Taipei 10412; tel. (2) 25362951; fax (2) 25114735; e-mail fi@ms1.chb.com.tw; internet www.chb.com.tw; f. 1905; cap. 62,094.8m., res 15,747.8m., dep. 1,384,276.4m. (Dec. 2009); Chair. JULIUS CHEN; Pres. WILLIAM LIN; 184 brs, 7 overseas.

China Development Industrial Bank: F/3, 125 Nanking East Rd, Sec. 5, Taipei 10504; tel. (2) 27638800; fax (2) 27562144; internet www.cdibank.com; f. 1959; cap. 77,604m., res 56,979.5m., dep. 102,587.7m. (Dec. 2009); Chair. TUNG CHAO-CHIN; Pres. SIMON DZENG; 3 brs.

Chinatrust Commercial Bank: 3 SongShou Rd, Taipei 11051; tel. (2) 27222002; fax (2) 27251499; internet www.chinatrust.com.tw; f. 1966; cap. 75,103.2m., dep. 1,515,712.1m. (Dec. 2009); 100% owned by Chinatrust Financial Holding Co; Chair. CHARLES L. F. LO; Pres. JAMES CHEN; 142 brs.

Cosmos Bank: 5–10/F, 39 Tun Hua South Rd, Sec. 2, Taipei 10681; tel. (2) 27011777; fax (2) 27849848; e-mail ibd@cosmosbank.com.tw; internet www.cosmosbank.com.tw; f. 1992; cap. 16,234m., res 12,992.1m., dep. 120,034.6m. (Dec. 2009); Chair. and Pres. PAUL PO; 66 brs.

Cota Commercial Bank: 32-1, Shih Fu Rd, Taichung 40045; tel. (4) 22245161; fax (4) 22275237; internet www.cotabank.com.tw; f. 1999; cap. 3,431m., dep. 95,737m. (Dec. 2006); Chair. LIAO CHUN-TSE; Pres. CHANG CHIN-TING; 18 brs.

DBS Taiwan: 28/F, 7 Xin Yi Rd, Taipei 101 Tower, Taipei 11049; tel. (2) 81010598; fax (2) 81010599; internet www.dbs.com/tw; f. 2008; Chair KOH BOON HWEE; CEO RICHARD B. STANLEY.

E. Sun Commercial Bank: 13/F, 117 Minsheng East Rd, Sec. 3, Taipei 10546; tel. (2) 21751313; fax (2) 87128613; e-mail wulin@email.esunbank.com.tw; internet www.esunbank.com.tw; f. 1992; cap. 33,624m., res 15,790.8m., dep. 880,750.6m. (Dec. 2009); Chair. GARY TSENG; Pres. DUH WU-LIN; 94 domestic brs, 2 overseas brs.

Entie Commercial Bank: 158 Minsheng East Rd, Sec. 3, Taipei 10596; tel. (2) 27189999; fax (2) 27187843; internet www.entiebank.com.tw; f. 1993; cap. 16,796.7m., res 1,480m., dep. 284,818.6m. (Dec. 2009); Chair. MARK ZOLTAN CHIBA; Pres. and CEO JESSE DING; 53 brs.

Far Eastern International Bank: 27/F, 207 Tun Hua South Rd, Sec. 2, Taipei 10602; tel. (2) 23786868; fax (2) 23779000; e-mail secretarial@feib.com.tw; internet www.feib.com.tw; f. 1992; cap. 19,338m., res 9.3m., dep. 347,336.5m. (Dec. 2009); Chair. HOU CHING-ING; Pres. ELI HONG; 36 brs.

First Commercial Bank: 30 Chungking S Rd, Sec. 1, Taipei 10005; tel. (2) 23481111; fax (2) 23892967; e-mail fcb@mail.firstbank.com.tw; internet www.firstbank.com.tw; f. 1899; cap. 46,490m., res 35,108.4m., dep. 1,821,593m. (Dec. 2009); Chair. TSAI CHING-NAIN; Pres. LIN TZUOO-YAU; 187 domestic brs, 15 overseas brs.

Hua Nan Commercial Bank: 38 Chungking S Rd, Sec. 1, Taipei 10006; tel. (2) 23713111; fax (2) 23316741; e-mail service@ms.hncb.com.tw; internet www.hncb.com.tw; f. 1919; cap. 37,809m., res 39,741.6m., dep. 1,685,521m. (Dec. 2009); Chair. LIN MING-CHEN; Pres. WANG JIUNN-CHIH; 183 brs, 6 overseas.

Hwatai Bank: 246 Chang An E Rd, Sec. 2, Taipei 10492; tel. (2) 27525252; fax (2) 87725177; e-mail callcenter@hwataibank.com.tw; internet www.hwataibank.com.tw; f. 1999; cap. 4,499m., res 1,719m., dep. 73,236m. (Dec. 2004); Chair. M. H. LIN; Pres. THOMAS C. W. LEE; 30 brs.

Industrial Bank of Taiwan: 99 Tiding Blvd, Sec. 2, Taipei; tel. (2) 87527000; fax (2) 27985337; internet www.ibt.com.tw; cap. 23,905m., res 397m., dep. 96,906m. (Dec. 2009); Chair. KENNETH C. M. LO; Pres. HENRY PENG.

Jih Sun International Bank: 85 Nanjing E Rd, Sec. 2, Taipei 10407; tel. (2) 25615888; fax (2) 25217698; e-mail planning@jsun.com; internet www.jihsunbank.com.tw; f. 1992 as Baodao Commercial Bank, assumed present name in Dec. 2001; cap. 12,045.5m., res –91.7m., dep. 178,082.3m. (Dec. 2009); Chair. EDWARD CHEN; Pres. DOLLY YANG; 34 brs.

King's Town Bank: 506 His Men Rd, Sec. 1, Tainan 70051; tel. (6) 2139171; fax (6) 2136885; e-mail president@mail.ktb.com.tw; internet www.ktb.com.tw; fmrly Tainan Business Bank; name changed as above in April 2006; cap. 10,512.3m., res 358.1m., 141,794.2m. (Dec. 2009); Chair. DAI CHENG-ZHI; Pres. J. C. SU.

Mega International Commercial Bank Co Ltd (Megabank): 100 Chi Lin Rd, Sec. 2, Jhongshan District, Taipei 10424; tel. (2) 25632614; fax (2) 25611216; e-mail service@megabank.com.tw; internet www.megabank.com.tw; f. 2006; est. from merger of International Commercial Bank of China and Chiao Tung Bank; cap. 64,109.8m., res 81,044.3m., dep. 1,967,058.7m. (Dec. 2009); Chair. MCKINNEY Y. T. TSAI; Pres. SHIU KUANG-SI; 66 domestic brs, 17 overseas brs.

Shanghai Commercial and Savings Bank: 2 Min Chuan East Rd, Sec. 1, Taipei 10452; tel. (2) 25817111; fax (2) 25318501; e-mail service@scsb.com.tw; internet www.scsb.com.tw; f. 1915; cap. 24,723.3m., dep. 535,954.1m. (Dec. 2009); Chair. H. C. YUNG; Pres. Y. P. CHEN; 61 brs.

Standard Chartered Bank (Taiwan) Ltd: 106 Chung Yang Rd, Hsinchu 300; tel. (3) 5245131; fax (3) 5250977; internet www.standardchartered.com.tw; f. 1948; fmrly Hsinchu International Bank; acquired by Standard Chartered Bank in Oct. 2006; cap. 29,105.7m., res 10,553.1m., dep. 546,251.8m. (Dec. 2009); Pres. and CEO SUNIL KAUSHAL; 86 brs.

Sunny Bank: 88 Shih Pai Rd, Sec. 1, Taipei 11271; tel. (2) 28208166; fax (2) 28233414; internet www.esunnybank.com.tw; f. 1997; absorbed Kao Shin Bank in Nov. 2005; cap. 12,248.5m., res 310.3m., dep. 208,488m. (Dec. 2009); Chair. LIN PENG-LANG; Pres. DING WEI-HAO; 96 brs.

TAIWAN

Ta Chong Bank Ltd: 2/F, 2 Xinyi Rd, Sec. 5, Xinyi District, Taipei 11049; tel. (2) 87869888; fax (2) 87869800; e-mail service@tcbank.com.tw; internet www.tcbank.com.tw; f. 1992; cap. 27,293.3m., res −3,872.1m., dep. 343,761.2m. (Dec. 2009); Chair. EDMUND KOH; 52 brs.

Taichung Commercial Bank: 87 Min Chuan Rd, Taichung 40341; tel. (4) 22236021; fax (4) 22240748; e-mail service@ms2.tcbbank.com.tw; internet www.tcbbank.com.tw; f. 1953; cap. 13,719m., res 1,361.4m., dep. 293,210.3m. (Dec. 2009); Chair. HUANG SHIU-NAN; Pres. CHUNG YU-YING; 79 brs.

Taipei Fubon Commercial Bank Co Ltd: 169 Jenai Rd, Sec. 4, Taipei 106; tel. (2) 27716999; fax (2) 66387728; internet www.taipeifubon.com.tw; f. 1969; fmrly City Bank of Taipei; acquired by Fubon Financial Holding in 2002; present name adopted following merger of Taipei Bank and Fubon Commercial Bank in 2005; cap. 47,948.8m., res 28,225.8m., dep. 1,270,093.5m. (Dec. 2009); Chair. DANIEL M. TSAI; Pres. VICTOR KUNG; 125 brs, 3 overseas.

Taishin International Bank: 44 Chung Shan North Rd, Sec. 2, Taipei 104; tel. (2) 25683988; fax (2) 25230539; e-mail pr@taishinbank.com.tw; internet www.taishinbank.com.tw; f. 1992; absorbed Dah An Commercial Bank in Feb. 2002; cap. 49,157.5m., res 3,331.7m., dep. 777,183.8m. (Dec. 2009); Chair. THOMAS T. L. WU; Pres. CHARLES WANG; 24 brs.

Taiwan Business Bank: 30 Tacheng St, Taipei 103; tel. (2) 25597171; fax (2) 25507942; e-mail tbb@mail.tbb.com.tw; internet www.tbb.com.tw; f. 1915; reassumed present name 1976; cap. 38,735.9m., res 1,378m., dep. 1,134,253.7m. (Dec. 2009); Chair. T. C. LO; Pres. LIAO TSAN-CHANG; 128 brs.

Taiwan Shin Kong Commercial Bank: 27–28/F, 66 Chung Hsiao West Rd, Sec. 1, Taipei 100; tel. (2) 23895858; fax (2) 23120164; e-mail service@mail.skbank.com.tw; internet www.skbank.com.tw; f. 2000; cap. 19,577.6m., res 2,125m., dep. 399,499.2m. (Dec. 2009); Chair. PATRICK C. J. LIANG; Gen. Man. LAI JIN-YUAN; 28 brs.

Union Bank of Taiwan: 109 Minsheng East Rd, Sec. 3, Taipei 10544; tel. (2) 27180001; fax (2) 27174093; e-mail 014_0199@email.ubot.com.tw; internet www.ubot.com.tw; f. 1992; cap. 23,188.2m., res −6.3m., dep. 328,887m. (Dec. 2009); Chair. SHIANG-CHANG LEE; Pres. JEFF LIN; 76 brs.

Yuanta Commercial Bank Co Ltd: 66 Tun Hua S Rd, Sec. 1, Taipei 100557; tel. (2) 21736699; fax (2) 23801864; e-mail service@yuanta.com; internet www.yuantabank.com.tw; f. 1992; fmrly Fuhwa Commercial Bank, name changed as above in 2007; cap. 21,500m., res 1,705m., dep. 340,980.2m. (Dec. 2009); Pres. CHIN CHIA-LIN; 88 brs.

There are also a number of Medium Business Banks throughout the country.

Community Financial System

The community financial institutions include both credit co-operatives and credit departments of farmers' and fishermen's associations. These local financial institutions focus upon providing savings and loan services for the community. At the end of 2010 there were 26 credit co-operatives in Taiwan.

Foreign Banks

In December 2010 a total of 28 foreign banks had branches in Taipei.

STOCK EXCHANGE

Under new regulations introduced in 2003, foreign investors were divided into two categories: foreign institutional investors (FINIs) and foreign individual investors (FIDIs). While FIDIs were subject to a US $5m. investment quota, FINIs could benefit from an investment quota with no upper limit. However, some industries continued to impose investment 'ceilings' for foreign investors.

Taiwan Stock Exchange Corpn: 3/F, No. 7, Sec. 5, Xinyi Rd, Taipei 11049; tel. (2) 81013101; fax (2) 81013066; internet www.tse.com.tw; f. 1961; Chair. SCHIVE CHI; Pres. SAMUEL HSU.

Supervisory Body

Securities and Futures Bureau: 85 Hsin Sheng South Rd, Sec. 1, Da-an District, Taipei 106; tel. (2) 87735100; fax (2) 87734143; e-mail sfbmail@sfb.gov.tw; internet www.sfb.gov.tw; Dir-Gen. LEE CHI-HSIEN.

INSURANCE

AIG General Insurance: 16/F, 200 Kee-Lung Rd, Sec. 1, Taipei 110; tel. (2) 37251827; fax (2) 87884338; e-mail aiggeneral@aig.com; internet www.aiggeneral.com.tw.

Allianz President General Insurance Co Ltd: 8/F, 178 Ming Chuan East Rd, Sec. 3, Taipei; tel. (2) 27155888; fax (2) 27176616; e-mail azpl@ms2.seeder.net; internet www.allianz.com.tw; f. 1995; Chair. BRUCE BOWERS.

Bank Taiwan Life Insurance Co Ltd: 6/F, 69 Tun Hua South Rd, Sec. 2, Taipei 10682; tel. (2) 27849151; fax (2) 27052214; internet www.twfhclife.com.tw; f. 1941; life insurance; Dir ZHANG GUOQIN; Gen. Man. FU DENG-HSIEH.

Cathay Life Insurance Co Ltd: 296 Jen Ai Rd, Sec. 4, Taipei 10650; tel. (2) 27551399; fax (2) 27082166; e-mail service@cathaylife.com.tw; internet www.cathaylife.com.tw; f. 1962; Chair. HONG-TU TSAI; Pres. T. K. HUANG.

Central Reinsurance Corpn: 12/F, 53 Nanking East Rd, Sec. 2, Taipei 104; tel. (2) 25115211; fax (2) 25629683; e-mail centralre@centralre.com; internet www.crc.com.tw; f. 1968; Chair. CHENG-TUI YANG; Pres. C. T. JUANG.

China Life Insurance Co Ltd: 5/F, 122 Tun Hua North Rd, Taipei; tel. (2) 27196678; fax (2) 27125966; e-mail services@chinalife.com.tw; internet www.chinalife.com.tw; f. 1963; Chair. CHANG CHING-WANG; Gen. Man. ALAN WANG.

Chung Kuo Insurance Co Ltd: 58 Wucheng St, Sec. 1, Taipei 104; tel. (2) 23812727; fax (2) 23814878; e-mail ckibest@mail.cki.com.tw; internet www.cki.com.tw; f. 1931; Chair. LEON SHEN; Pres. C. Y. LIU.

Far Glory Life Insurance Co Ltd: 18/F, 200 Keelung Rd, Sec. 1, Taipei 110; tel. (2) 27583099; fax (2) 23451635; internet www.fglife.com.tw; f. 1993; Chair. T. S. CHAO; Pres. C. S. TU.

The First Insurance Co Ltd: 54 Chung Hsiao East Rd, Sec. 1, Taipei 100; tel. (2) 23913271; fax (2) 23412864; internet www.firstins.com.tw; f. 1962; Chair. CHENG HANG LEE; Pres. JAMES LAI.

Fubon Insurance Co Ltd: 237 Chien Kuo South Rd, Sec. 1, Da-an District, Taipei 10657; tel. (2) 27067890; fax (2) 27042915; internet www.fubon.com; f. 1961; Chair. DAN CANMING.

Fubon Life Insurance Co Ltd: 14/F, 108 Tun Hua South Rd, Sec. 1, Taipei 105; tel. (2) 87716699; fax (2) 88098889; internet www.fubon.com; f. 1993; Gen. Man. CHENG PENG-YUAN.

Global Life Insurance Co Ltd: 9/F, 50 Chung Hsiao West Rd, Sec. 1, Taipei 10041; tel. (2) 23883399; fax (2) 23887676; e-mail services@globallife.com.tw; internet www.globallife.com.tw; f. 1993; Chair. JOHN TSENG; Pres. LAI YI-MING.

Hontai Life Insurance Co Ltd: 4/F, 156 Minsheng East Rd, Sec. 3, Taipei; tel. (2) 27166888; fax (2) 27166812; e-mail service@hontai.com.tw; internet www.hontai.com.tw; f. 1994; fmrly Hung Fu Life Insurance Co; Chair. DAVID JOU.

Kuo Hua Life Insurance Co Ltd: 277 Song-Ren Rd, Xinyi District, Taipei; tel. (2) 21765166; fax (2) 55519707; internet www.khltw.com; f. 1963; Chair. M. S. HSIA; Pres. CHING JIANG-CHEN.

Mercuries Life Insurance Co Ltd: 6/F, Lane 150, Hsin-Yi North Rd, Sec. 2, Taipei 110; tel. (2) 23455511; fax (2) 23456616; e-mail mmli@mail.mli.com.tw; internet www.mli.com.tw; f. 1993; Chair. HENRY CHEN; Pres. CHUNG-SHIN LU.

MSIG Mingtai Insurance Co Ltd: 1 Jen Ai Rd, Sec. 4, Taipei; tel. (2) 27725678; fax (2) 27726666; internet www.msig-mingtai.com.tw; f. 1961; Chair. LARRY P. C. LIN; Pres. H. T. CHEN.

Nan Shan Life Insurance Co Ltd: 168 Zhuangjing Rd, Xinyi District, Taipei 11049; tel. (2) 87588888; fax (2) 87867087; internet www.nanshanlife.com.tw; f. 1963; Chair. EDMUND TSE; Pres. FRANK CHAN.

Prudential Life Assurance Co Ltd: 10/F, 161 Nanking East Rd, Sec. 5, Taipei; tel. (2) 27678866; fax (2) 27679299; internet www.pcalife.com; f. 1962; Chair. STEPHEN D. JIN.

Shinkong Insurance Co Ltd: 15 Chien Kuo North Rd, Sec. 2, Taipei 104; tel. (2) 25075335; fax (2) 25071645; internet www.skinsurance.com.tw; f. 1963; Chair. ANTHONY T. S. WU; Pres. JUN YU ZHAN.

Shin Kong Life Insurance Co Ltd: 37/F, 66 Chung Hsiao West Rd, Sec. 1, Taipei 100; tel. (2) 23895858; fax (2) 23758688; internet www.skl.com.tw; f. 1963; Chair. EUGENE T. C. WU; Pres. PO TSENG PAN.

Singfor Life Insurance Co Ltd: 8/F, 6 Chung Hsiao West Rd, Sec. 1, Taipei; tel. (2) 23817172; fax (2) 23917176; e-mail sc_lin@singforlife.com.tw; internet www.singforlife.com.tw; f. 1993; Chair. DENG WENCONG; Gen. Man. WEN YEN-CHEN.

South China Insurance Co Ltd: 5/F, 560 Chung Hsiao East Rd, Sec. 4, Xinyi District, Taipei 11071; tel. and fax (2) 27588418; fax (2) 27611069; e-mail ecover@south-china.com.tw; internet www.south-china.com.tw; f. 1963; Chair. JACK E. S. TAI; Pres. KEVIN TU.

Taian Insurance Co Ltd: 59 Kwantsien Rd, Taipei; tel. (2) 23819678; fax (2) 23315332; e-mail eservice@mail.taian.com.tw; internet www.taian.com.tw; f. 1961; Chair. C. H. CHEN; Gen. Man. PATRICK S. LEE.

Taiwan Fire and Marine Insurance Co Ltd: 8–9/F, 49 Kuan Chien Rd, Jungjeng Chiu, Taipei 100; tel. (2) 23821666; fax (2) 23882555; e-mail info@tfmi.com.tw; internet www.tfmi.com.tw; f. 1946; Chair. STEVE LEE; Pres. CHARLES SUNG.

Taiwan Life Insurance Co Ltd: 16–19/F, 17 Hsu Chang St, Taipei; tel. (2) 23116411; fax (2) 23759714; e-mail service1@twlife.com.tw;

TAIWAN

internet www.twlife.com.tw; f. 1947; Chair. PING-YU CHU; Pres. CHENG-TAO LIN.

Tokio Marine Newa Insurance Co Ltd: 7–12/F, 130 Nanking East Rd, Sec. 3, Taipei 104; tel. (2) 87707777; fax (2) 87891190; internet www.tmnewa.com.tw; f. 1999; Chair. HUANG WEN-CHENG; Pres. CHEN REN-TZE.

Union Insurance Co Ltd: 4/F, 219 Chung Hsiao East Rd, Sec. 4, Taipei; tel. (2) 27765567; fax (2) 27737199; internet www.unionins.com.tw; f. 1963; Chair. S. H. CHIN; Gen. Man. FRANK S. WANG.

Zurich Insurance Taiwan Ltd: 9–12/F, 56 Tun Hua North Rd, Taipei 10551; tel. (2) 27752888; fax (2) 27416004; e-mail webmail.twz@zurich.com; internet www.zurich.com.tw; f. 1961; CEO DANIEL RAYMOND.

Trade and Industry

GOVERNMENT AGENCIES

Bureau of Foreign Trade (Ministry of Economic Affairs): 1 Houkow St, Taipei 10066; tel. (2) 23510271; fax (2) 23517080; e-mail boft@trade.gov.tw; internet www.trade.gov.tw; Dir-Gen. CHO SHIH-CHAO.

Council of Agriculture (COA): 37 Nan Hai Rd, Taipei 10014; tel. (2) 23812991; fax (2) 23719233; e-mail coa@mail.coa.gov.tw; internet www.coa.gov.tw; f. 1984; govt agency directly under the Executive Yuan, with ministerial status; a policy-making body in charge of national agriculture, forestry, fisheries, the animal industry and food administration; promotes technology and provides external assistance; Chair. CHEN WU-HSIUNG.

Department of Investment Services (Ministry of Economic Affairs): 8/F, 71 Guancian Rd, Taipei 10047; tel. (2) 23892111; fax (2) 23820497; e-mail generaldois@moea.gov.tw; internet www.dois.moea.gov.tw; f. 1959 to assist investment and planning; Dir-Gen. LING CHIA-YUH.

Industrial Development Bureau (Ministry of Economic Affairs): 41-3 Hsin Yi Rd, Sec. 3, Taipei 10651; tel. (2) 27541255; fax (2) 27030160; e-mail service@moeaidb.gov.tw; internet www.moeaidb.gov.tw; Dir-Gen. DUH TYZZ-JIUN.

CHAMBERS OF COMMERCE

General Chamber of Commerce of the Republic of China: 6/F, 390 Fu Hsing South Rd, Sec. 1, Taipei 10665; tel. (2) 27012671; fax (2) 27555493; e-mail service@roccoc.org.tw; internet www.roccoc.org.tw; f. 1946; 86 group mems, incl. 43 nat. feds of trade asscns, 18 nat. commercial asscns, 22 district export asscns and district chambers of commerce; Chair. CHANG PEN-TSAO; Sec.-Gen. PETER LEE.

Taiwan Chamber of Commerce: 13/F, 168 Sung Chiang Rd, Taipei; tel. (2) 25365455; fax (2) 25211980; e-mail tcoc@tcoc.org.tw; internet www.tcoc.org.tw; f. 1946; 113 mems, comprising 93 provincial trade asscns and 20 local chambers of commerce; Chair. CHANG JONG-WEI.

INDUSTRIAL AND TRADE ASSOCIATIONS

China Productivity Center: 2/F, 79 Hsin Tai 5 Rd, Sec. 1, Hsichih, Taipei County 22101; tel. (2) 26982989; fax (2) 26982976; internet www.cpc.org.tw; f. 1956; management, technology, training, etc.; Pres. CHEN MING-CHANG.

Chinese National Association of Industry and Commerce: 13/F, 390 Fu Hsing South Rd, Sec. 1, Taipei; tel. (2) 27070111; fax (2) 27070977; e-mail service@cnaic.org; internet www.cnaic.org; f. 1975; private, independent, non-profit organization comprising major commercial and industrial firms, financial institutions, business asscns, industrialists and business people; Chair. KENNETH C. M. LO.

Chinese National Federation of Industries (CNFI): 12/F, 390 Fu Hsing South Rd, Sec. 1, Taipei 10665; tel. (2) 27033500; fax (2) 27058317; e-mail cnfi@cnfi.org.tw; internet www.cnfi.org.tw; f. 1948; 152 mem. asscns; Chair. PRESTON W. CHEN; Sec.-Gen. TSAI LIEN-SHENG.

Taiwan External Trade Development Council: 5–7/F, 333 Keelung Rd, Sec. 1, Taipei 11003; tel. (2) 27255200; fax (2) 27576652; e-mail taitra@taitra.org.tw; internet www.taitra.org.tw; trade promotion body; Chair. WANG CHIH-KANG; Pres. and CEO CHAO YUEN-CHUAN.

Taiwan Handicraft Promotion Centre: 1 Hsu Chou Rd, Taipei 10055; tel. (2) 23933655; fax (2) 23937330; e-mail thpc@handicraft.org.tw; internet www.handicraft.org.tw; f. 1957; Pres. J. H. LIN.

Trading Department of Central Trust of China: 49 Wuchang St, Sec. 1, Taipei 10006; tel. (2) 23111511; fax (2) 23821047; f. 1935; export and import agent for private and govt-owned enterprises.

Taiwan Robot Industry Development Asscn (Robotics Association Taiwan): Taichung; tel. (4) 23581866; fax (4) 23581566; e-mail service@roboat.org.tw; internet www.roboat.org.tw; f. 2007; industry promotion body; Chair. ZHOU YONG CHOI.

Taiwan Transportation Vehicle Manufacturers Asscn (TTVMA): 9/F, 390, Sec. 1, Fushing South Rd, Da-an District, Taipei 10656; tel. (2) 27051101; fax (2) 27066440; internet www.ttvma.org.tw; f. 1948; 600 mems; Chair. CHEN KUO-RONG.

UTILITIES

Electricity

Taiwan Power Co (Taipower): 242 Roosevelt Rd, Sec. 3, Taipei 10016; tel. (2) 23651234; fax (2) 23650037; e-mail service@taipower.com.tw; internet www.taipower.com.tw; f. 1946; electricity generation; Chair. EDWARD K. M. CHEN; Pres. HAN SHEN LEE.

Gas

The Great Taipei Gas Corpn: 5/F, Lane 11, 35 Kwang Fu North Rd, Taipei 10577; tel. (2) 27684999; fax (2) 27630480; e-mail k2@taipeigas.com.tw; internet www.taipeigas.com.tw; supply of gas and gas equipment; Chair. LI FENG-YAO.

Hsin Kao Gas Co Ltd: 56 Ta-Yi St, Yen Cheng, Kaohsiung; tel. (7) 5315701; fax (7) 5312932; internet www.hkgas.com.tw; Chair. CHEN TIEN-MIAO; Gen. Man. CHEN CHIEN-TONG.

Shin Shin Natural Gas Co Ltd: 100 Yungho Rd, Sec. 1, Yungho, Taipei; tel. (2) 29217811; fax (2) 29282829; e-mail ssngas11@ms67.hinet.net; internet www.shinshingas.com.tw; f. 1971; supplies natural gas to non-industrial users; Chair. CHEN HO-CHIA; Pres. QI KAM-CHEUNG.

Water

Taiwan Water Corpn: 2-1 Shuangshih Rd, Sec. 2, Taichung 40425; tel. (4) 2224191; fax (4) 2224201; e-mail service@mail.water.gov.tw; internet www.water.gov.tw; f. 1974; supplies water throughout Taiwan Province and Kaohsiung City; Chair. HUANG MIN-KON; Pres. CHEN FU-TIEN.

TRADE UNIONS

Chinese Federation of Labour: 4/F, 177 Roosevelt Rd, Sec. 3, Taipei 10647; tel. (2) 23660111; fax (2) 23696111; e-mail cfl.labor@msa.hinet.net; internet www.cfl.org.tw; f. 1948; mems: 53 feds of unions representing more than 1,000,000 workers; Pres. CHIEH CHEN.

National Federations

Chunghwa Postal Workers' Union: 9/F, 45 Chungking South Rd, Sec. 2, Taipei 10075; tel. (2) 23921380; fax (2) 23563611; e-mail neeko.chang@gmail.com; internet www.cpwu.org.tw; f. 1930; fmrly Chinese Federation of Postal Workers; restructuring completed July 2003; 24,000 mems; Chair. CHIANG TZU-CHEN.

National Chinese Seamen's Union: 8/F, 25 Nanking East Rd, Sec. 3, Taipei 10487; tel. (2) 25150259; fax (2) 25078211; e-mail ncsu.seamen@msa.hinet.net; internet www.ncsu.org.tw; f. 1913; 21,520 mems (June 2005); Pres. SUN ZHEYING.

Taiwan Railway Labor Union: Rm 6044, 6/F, 3 Peiping West Rd, Taipei 10041; tel. (2) 23815226; fax (2) 23896134; e-mail ch.trlu@msa.hinet.net; internet www.trlu.org.tw; f. 1947; 15,579 mems; Pres. CHEN HAN-CHIN.

Regional Federations

Taiwan Federation of Textile and Dyeing Industry Workers' Unions (TFTDWU): 2 Lane 64, Chung Hsiao East Rd, Sec. 2, Taipei 10053; tel. (2) 23415627; fax (2) 23413748; f. 1958; 6,600 mems (July 2005); Chair. ING-JIE CHEN.

Taiwan Federation of Labour: 92 Sungann Rd, Sec.1, Taichung 40650; tel. (4) 22309009; fax (2) 22309012; e-mail tpfl@ms39.hinet.net; internet www.tpfl.org.tw; f. 1948; 49 mem. unions and 1,417,816 individual mems; Pres. CHEN JEA; Sec.-Gen. JING-HUNG CHEN.

Transport

RAILWAYS

Taiwan Railway Administration (TRA): 3 Peiping West Rd, Taipei 10041; tel. (2) 23815226; fax (2) 23831367; internet www.railway.gov.tw; f. 1891; public utility under the Ministry of Transportation and Communications; operates both the west line and east line systems, with a route length of 1,101.5 km; Dir-Gen. FRANK FAN.

TAIWAN

Taipei Rapid Transit Corpn (TRTC): 7 Lane 48, Zhong Shan North Rd, Sec. 2, Taipei 10448; tel. (2) 25363001; fax (2) 25115003; e-mail email@mail.trtc.com.tw; internet www.trtc.com.tw; f. 1994; 90.5 km (incl. 10.5 km medium-capacity rail) open, with further lines under construction; also operates the Maokong Gondola cable car system; Chair. LIN CHUNG-YIH; Pres. Dr TSAY HUEI-SHENG.

Taiwan High Speed Rail Corpn (THSRC): 3/F, 100 Hsin Yi Rd, Taipei 110; tel. (2) 40666600; fax (2) 66268866; internet www.thsrc.com.tw; f. 1996; operates 345-km high-speed rail link between Taipei and Kaohsiung; Chair. and CEO OU CHIN-DER.

An Airport Rail System linking Taipei with Taiwan Taoyuan International Airport is under construction by the Ministry of Transportation and Communications; this is due for completion in 2012.

ROADS

There were 39,286 km of highways in 2006, most of them asphalt-paved. The Sun Yat-sen Freeway, linking Taipei, Keelung and Kaohsiung, was completed in 1978. Construction of a 505-km Second Freeway, which was to extend to Pingtung, in southern Taiwan, was completed in 2004. The Nantou branch, from the Wufeng system interchange of the Second Freeway to Puli in central Taiwan, with a length of 38 km, was completed in 2008. The 31-km Taipei–Ilan freeway and its 24.1-km extension, from Toucheng to Suao, were completed in 2005.

Directorate-General of Highways: 70 Chung Hsiao West Rd, Sec. 1, Taipei 10041; tel. (2) 23113456; fax (2) 23111644; e-mail thbu10z7@ms1.gsn.gov.tw; internet www.thb.gov.tw; Dir-Gen. WU MEN-FENG.

Kuo-Kuang Motor Transport Co Ltd: 4/F, 17 Hsu Chang St, Taipei 10047; tel. (2) 23810731; fax (2) 23810268; internet www.kingbus.com.tw; f. 2001; operates national bus service; Chair. LEE HONG-SEN.

Taiwan Area National Expressway Engineering Bureau: 1 Lane 1, Hoping East Rd, Sec. 3, Taipei 10669; tel. (2) 27078808; fax (2) 27017818; e-mail neebeyes@taneeb.gov.tw; internet www.taneeb.gov.tw; f. 1990; responsible for planning, design, construction and maintenance of provincial and county highways; Dir-Gen. BANE L. B. CHJOU.

Taiwan Area National Freeway Bureau: 70 Banshanya, Liming Village, Taishan Township, Taipei County 24303; tel. (2) 29096141; fax (2) 29093218; e-mail tanfb1@freeway.gov.tw; internet www.freeway.gov.tw; f. 1970; Dir-Gen. TSENG DAR-JEN.

SHIPPING

Taiwan has seven international ports: Anping, Kaohsiung, Keelung, Taichung, Hualien, Suao and Taipei. In December 2009 the merchant fleet comprised 641 vessels, with a total displacement of 2,636,000 grt. Some of the main shipping companies are as follows:

Evergreen International Storage & Transport Corpn: 899 Ching Kuo Rd, Taoyuan 3305; tel. (3) 3252060; fax (3) 3252059; e-mail mgt@evergreen-eitc.com.tw; internet www.evergreen-eitc.com.tw; Chair. YE JIONG-CHAO.

Evergreen Marine Corpn (Taiwan) Ltd: Evergreen Bldg, 166 Minsheng East Rd, Sec. 2, Taipei 10423; tel. (2) 25057766; fax (2) 25058159; e-mail mgt@evergreen-marine.com; internet www.evergreen-marine.com; f. 1968; world-wide container liner services; Chair. CHANG YUNG-FA; Pres. WANG LONG-SHUNG.

Taiwan Navigation Co Ltd: 2–6/F, 29 Chi Nan Rd, Sec. 2, Taipei 10054; tel. (2) 23927177; fax (2) 23936578; e-mail tnctpe@taiwanline.com.tw; internet www.taiwanline.com.tw; Chair. ZHANG YIYUAN; Pres. SHENGQING WU.

U-Ming Marine Transport Corpn: 29/F, Taipei Metro Tower, 207 Tun Hua South Rd, Sec. 2, Taipei 10602; tel. (2) 27338000; fax (2) 27359900; e-mail uming@metro.feg.com.tw; internet www.uming.com.tw; world-wide transportation services; Chair. TSAI HSIUNG CHAN; Pres. C. K. ONG.

Wan Hai Lines Ltd: 10/F, 136 Sung Chiang Rd, Taipei 10485; tel. (2) 25677961; fax (2) 25216000; e-mail serv@wanhai.com.tw; internet www.wanhai.com.tw; f. 1965; regional container liner services; Chair. C. H. CHEN; Pres. P. T. CHEN.

Yang Ming Marine Transport Corpn (Yang Ming Line): 271 Ming De 1st Rd, Keelung 20646; tel. (2) 24559988; fax (2) 24559958; e-mail tara@yml.com.tw; internet www.yml.com.tw; f. 1972; world-wide container liner services, bulk carrier and supertanker services; Chair. FRANK LU; Pres. ROBERT HO.

CIVIL AVIATION

There are two international airports: Taiwan Taoyuan International Airport (formerly known as Chiang Kai-shek) near Taipei, which opened in 1979, a second passenger terminal and expansion of freight facilities being completed in 2000; and Kaohsiung International Airport, which also offers domestic services. There are 16 domestic airports, three of which offer international charter services.

Civil Aeronautics Administration: 340 Tun Hua North Rd, Taipei 10548; tel. (2) 23496000; fax (2) 23496277; e-mail gencaa@mail.caa.gov.tw; internet www.caa.gov.tw; Dir-Gen. YIN CHEN-PONG.

China Airlines Ltd (CAL): 131 Nanjing East Rd, Sec. 3, Taipei 10410; tel. (2) 27151212; fax (2) 25146004; e-mail ju-reng_chen@email.china-airlines.com; internet www.china-airlines.com; f. 1959; international services to destinations in the Far East, Europe, the Middle East, the USA and Australia; Chair. PHILIP HSING-HSIUNG WEI; Pres. SUN HUANG-HSIANG.

EVA Airways (EVA): Eva Air Bldg, 376 Hsin-nan Rd, Sec. 1, Luchu Township, Taoyuan County 33801; tel. (3) 3515151; fax (3) 3510023; e-mail prd@evaair.com; internet www.evaair.com; f. 1989; subsidiary of Evergreen Group; commenced flights in 1991; services to destinations in Asia, the Middle East, Europe, North America, Australia and New Zealand; Chair. LIN BOU-SHIU; Pres. JENG KUNG-YEUN.

Mandarin Airlines (MDA): 13/F, 134 Minsheng East Rd, Sec. 3, Taipei 10596; tel. (2) 27171188; fax (2) 27170716; e-mail mandarin@mandarin-airlines.com; internet www.mandarin-airlines.com; f. 1991; subsidiary of CAL; merged with Formosa Airlines 1999; domestic and regional services; Chair. HARRIS WANG.

TransAsia Airways (TNA): 9/F, 139 Chengchou Rd, Taipei 10341; tel. (2) 25575767; fax (2) 27913318; e-mail tna@tna.com.tw; internet www.tna.com.tw; f. 1951; fmrly Foshing Airlines; domestic and international services; Chair. LIN MING-SHENG; Gen. Man. CHEN JIA.

UNI Airways Corpn (UIA): 9/F, 100 Chang An East Rd, Sec. 2, Taipei 10491; tel. (2) 25135533; fax (2) 25133202; e-mail communication@uniair.com.tw; internet www.uniair.com.tw; f. 1989; fmrly Makung Airlines; merged with Great China Airlines and Taiwan Airlines 1998; domestic flights and international services (to Bali, Indonesia; Seoul, South Korea; Bangkok, Thailand; and Hanoi, Viet Nam); Chair. SU HOMNG-YIH; Pres. PETER CHEN.

Tourism

The attractions of Taiwan include the island's scenery and cultural heritage. In 2010 visitor arrivals (including Overseas Chinese) were estimated to have increased by 27% to reach almost 5.6m. Revenue from tourism in 2008 reached US $5,936m. The relaxation of official restrictions on the numbers of mainland Chinese visitors has led to a substantial increase in arrivals from the People's Republic.

Tourism Bureau, Ministry of Transportation and Communications: 9/F, 290 Chung Hsiao East Rd, Sec. 4, Taipei 10694; tel. (2) 23491500; fax (2) 27717036; e-mail tbroc@tbroc.gov.tw; internet taiwan.net.tw; f. 1972; Dir-Gen. JANICE LAI.

Taiwan Visitors Association: 5/F, 9 Min Chuan East Rd, Sec. 2, Taipei 10470; tel. (2) 25943261; fax (2) 25943265; internet www.tva.org.tw; f. 1956; promotes domestic and international tourism; Chair. CHANG SHUO LAO.

Defence

As assessed at November 2010, the armed forces totalled an estimated 290,000: army 200,000, navy 45,000 (including 15,000 marines), and air force 45,000. Paramilitary forces totalled 17,000. Reserves numbered 1,657,000. Military service is for 12 months.

Defence Expenditure: Budgeted at NT $297,000m. for 2011.

Chief of the General Staff: Adm. LIN CHEN-YI.

Commander of the Army: Gen. YANG TIEN-HSIAO.

Commander of the Navy: Adm. LONG DONG-XIANG.

Commander of the Air Force: Gen. YEN MING.

Education

Pre-school education is optional, although in 2008/09 a total of 185,668 children were attending kindergarten. In 2009/10 1,593,414 pupils attended primary school, and a total of 1,706,425 pupils were enrolled in secondary (including vocational) education. There are three types of secondary school: junior high, senior high and senior vocational. The net enrolment ratio for children between the ages of six and 14 was 100.2% in 2008. In 2009/10 there were 164 universities, junior colleges and independent colleges. Most of these offer postgraduate facilities. A total of 1,336,592 students were enrolled in higher education in 2009/10. The Government's budgetary expenditure on education in 2008 was NT $492,370.1m.

TAJIKISTAN

Introductory Survey

LOCATION, CLIMATE, LANGUAGE, RELIGION, FLAG, CAPITAL

The Republic of Tajikistan is situated in the south-east of Central Asia. To the north and west it borders Uzbekistan, to the north-east Kyrgyzstan, to the east the People's Republic of China and to the south Afghanistan. The climate varies considerably according to altitude. The average temperature in January in Khujand (lowland) is −0.9°C (30.4°F); in July the average is 27.4°C (81.3°F). In the southern lowlands the temperature variation is somewhat more extreme. Rainfall is low in the valleys, in the range of 150–250 mm (6–10 ins) per year. In mountain areas winter temperatures can fall below −45°C (−51°F); the average January temperature in Murgab, in the mountains of south-east Kuhistoni Badakhshon, is −19.6°C (−3.3°F). Levels of rainfall are very low in mountain regions, seldom exceeding 60–80 mm (2–3 ins) per year. The official language is Tajik, a Persian language; the Constitution grants Russian the status of a language of inter-ethnic communication, and all ethnic groups are guaranteed the right to use their native languages freely. The major religion is Islam. Most Tajiks and ethnic Uzbek residents follow the Sunni tradition, but the Pamiris are mostly Isma'ilis, a Shi'ite sect. The national flag (proportions 1 by 2) consists of three horizontal stripes from top to bottom of red, white and green, with a stylized gold crown surmounted by seven gold stars arranged in a semicircle in the centre of the white stripe. The capital is Dushanbe.

CONTEMPORARY POLITICAL HISTORY

Historical Context

In 1918 northern Tajikistan (which had been part of the Russian Empire since the 19th century) was conquered by the Bolsheviks, and the territory was incorporated into the Turkestan Autonomous Soviet Socialist Republic (ASSR). However, Dushanbe and the other southern regions of Tajikistan (subject to the Emirate of Bukhara) did not come under the control of the Bolsheviks until 1921. Opposition to Soviet rule was led by the *basmachis* (local guerrilla fighters) and foreign interventionists. In 1924 the Tajik ASSR was established as a part of the Uzbek Soviet Socialist Republic (SSR), and in January 1925 the south-east of Tajikistan was designated a Special Pamir Region (later renamed the Kuhistoni Badakhshon—Gornyi Badakhshan Autonomous Viloyat) within the Tajik ASSR. On 16 October 1929 the Tajik ASSR became a full Union Republic of the USSR and was slightly enlarged by the addition of the Khujand district from the Uzbek SSR. Soviet rule brought economic and social benefits to Tajikistan, but living standards remained low, and cattle-breeding, the main occupation in the uplands, was severely disrupted by collectivization. During the repressions of the 1930s almost all ethnic Tajiks in the republican Government were replaced by Russians.

During the 1970s increased Islamic influence was reported, as was violence towards non-indigenous nationalities. In 1978 there were reports of an anti-Russian riot, involving some 13,000 people, and after 1979 there were arrests of activists opposed to Soviet intervention in Afghanistan. The first manifestation of the reformist policies of Mikhail Gorbachev, who came to power as Soviet leader in 1985, was a campaign against corruption. Rakhmon Nabiyev, First Secretary of the Communist Party of Tajikistan (CPT) since 1982, was replaced in late 1985 by Kakhar Makhkamov, who accused his predecessor of tolerating nepotism and corruption. Censorship was relaxed, and there was increased debate in the media of perceived injustices—such as alleged discrimination against Tajiks in Uzbekistan, and the legitimacy of the Uzbekistani–Tajikistani boundary. Greater freedom of expression encouraged interest in Tajik and Persian culture and in 1989 Tajik became the state language. In February 1990, following reports that Armenian refugees from the conflict in Nagornyi Karabakh (see the chapter on Azerbaijan) were to be settled in the capital, Dushanbe, violence broke out at a protest rally, when about 3,000 demonstrators clashed with police. A state of emergency was declared, and after troops suppressed the demonstrations, 22 people were reported to have been killed and 565 injured.

Domestic Political Affairs

In 1990 two nascent opposition parties, Rebirth (Rastokhez), which had been involved in the February demonstrations, and the Democratic Party of Tajikistan (DPT), were refused official registration, while the Islamic Rebirth Party (IRP) was denied permission to hold a founding congress. Opposition politicians were barred from contesting the elections to the republic's Supreme Soviet (Supreme Council), held in March; 94% of the deputies elected were members of the CPT. None the less, in an apparent concession, the Supreme Soviet adopted a declaration of sovereignty on 25 August. In November Makhkamov was elected to the new post of executive President of the Republic by the Supreme Soviet; his only opponent was Nabiyev.

The Tajikistani Government displayed enthusiasm for a new Union Treaty (effectively providing for the continuation of the USSR), and 90.2% of eligible voters in the republic were reported to have voted for the preservation of the USSR in a referendum held in March 1991. Makhkamov did not oppose the attempted coup staged by conservative communists in the Soviet and Russian capital, Moscow, in August, and on 31 August, after it had collapsed, he resigned as President, following demonstrations which continued throughout much of September. On 9 September, following the declarations of independence by Uzbekistan and Kyrgyzstan, the Tajikistani Supreme Soviet voted to proclaim an independent Republic of Tajikistan. Kadriddin Aslonov, the Chairman of the Supreme Council and acting President, banned the CPT and nationalized its assets. In response, the communist majority in the Supreme Council demanded Aslonov's resignation, declared a state of emergency in the republic and rescinded the prohibition of the CPT. Aslonov resigned, and was replaced by Nabiyev. Nabiyev was rapidly obliged to make substantial concessions to the opposition, and in early October the Supreme Council revoked the state of emergency, suspended the CPT and legalized the IRP. Shortly afterwards he resigned as acting President, in advance of the presidential election.

Seven candidates contested the direct presidential election, which took place on 24 November 1991. Nabiyev won 57% of the votes cast, compared with 30% for the principal opposition candidate, Davlat Khudonazarov. Nabiyev took office in December. In late December Tajikistan signed the declaration establishing the Commonwealth of Independent States (CIS, see p. 238), the successor body to the USSR. In January 1992 a new Prime Minister, Akbar Mirzoyev, was appointed.

Civil war

Anti-Government demonstrations began in Dushanbe in March 1992, initially prompted by Nabiyev's dismissal of Mamadayez Navzhuvanov from the post of Minister of Internal Affairs. Protests against his dismissal were led by the group Lale Badakhshon, which advocated greater autonomy for the Pamiri peoples of the southern Kuhistoni Badakhshon region (of which Navzhuvanov was a member). It was joined by Rebirth, the IRP and the DPT. Protesters demanding the resignation of Nabiyev and the Government remained encamped in the centre of Dushanbe for nearly two months; in response, the Government organized rival demonstrations, bringing supporters to the capital from the southern region of Kulob (Kulyab) and from Leninabad (later Khujand), in the north—the historic areas of support for the CPT. In April members of the newly formed national guard loyal to Nabiyev opened fire on demonstrators, killing at least eight people. In the following month the National Security Committee (NSC—the successor to the Soviet Committee for State Security—KGB) allegedly distributed weapons to pro-communist supporters, and the ensuing violent clashes escalated into civil war. Fighting in Dushanbe ended after Nabiyev negotiated a truce with opposition leaders and formed a new 'Government of National Reconciliation' led by Mirzoyev, in which eight of the 24 ministers were members of opposition parties. However, violent clashes erupted in Kulob Viloyat between pro-communist forces, who opposed the President's compromise with the opposition, and an informal alliance of Islamist and pro-democracy groups. In late May the conflict spread into Qurgonteppa Viloyat, where a Kulobi militia, the Tajik People's Front (TPF), led by Sangak Safarov, attempted to suppress the local rebel forces. The TPF alleged that their opponents were receiving weapons and assistance from Islamist groups in Afghanistan, and there were reports that Gulbuddin Hekmatyar, the leader of the Afghan *mujahidin* group Hizb-i Islami (Islamic Party), had established training camps in Afghanistan for Tajikistani fighters. The opposition alliance, for its part, claimed that the ex-Soviet (Russian) garrisons were arming the pro-Government militias.

Several members of the DPT and Lale Badakhshon were killed by Kulobi militia forces in Qurgonteppa in August 1992. A violent conflict ensued between local members of the opposition and Kulobis, in which several hundred people were reportedly killed. At the end of August demonstrators entered the presidential palace in Dushanbe and took 30 officials hostage. In September Nabiyev was seized by opposition forces at Dushanbe airport, and was forced to announce his resignation. Akbarsho Iskandarov, the Chairman of the Supreme Council, temporarily assumed the responsibilities of head of state. Mirzoyev also resigned, and Abdumalik Abdullojonov, a communist from Leninabad Viloyat (later Soghd Viloyat), was appointed acting Prime Minister. Iskandarov's administration, however, had little influence outside Dushanbe; much of the south of the country was under the control of the TPF, and some leaders of Leninabad Viloyat threatened to secede from Tajikistan if there was any attempt to introduce an Islamic state. In October the opposition alliance's control of Dushanbe was threatened when forces led by Safarali Kenjayev, a supporter of Nabiyev and a former Chairman of the Supreme Soviet, entered the city and attempted to seize power. Although Kenjayev briefly proclaimed himself head of state, his troops were forced to retreat, despite effectively enforcing an economic blockade of the capital for the following two months.

In November 1992 Iskandarov and the Government resigned. The legislature abolished the office of President, and Emomali Rakhmonov, a collective-farm chairman from Kulob Viloyat, was appointed Chairman of the Supreme Council (Head of State). The legislature appointed a new Government, retaining Abdullojonov as Prime Minister. All opposition representatives lost their portfolios, and the majority of the new ministers were Kulobis or supporters of Nabiyev. The Supreme Council also voted to combine Qurgonteppa and Kulob Viloyats into one unit, Khatlon Viloyat, to be based in Qurgonteppa, in an attempt to secure control of the south of the country by pro-communist forces. In December forces loyal to the new Government captured Dushanbe, hitherto under the control of the Islamist-dominated Popular Democratic Army (PDA).

Between December 1992 and January 1993 some 60,000 Tajikistanis fled to Afghanistan, after reprisals were undertaken against supporters of the PDA. Among those who fled was the influential *qazi* (Islamic judge) of Tajikistan, Akbar Turajonzoda, a senior member of the IRP, whom the new Government accused of seeking to establish an Islamist state. In February he was replaced as spiritual leader of Tajikistan's Muslims by Fatkhullo Sharifzoda, who was given the title of *mufti*.

In February 1993 insurgents in the central region of Garm attempted to declare an 'autonomous Islamic republic', but the Government had secured control of most of the country by March. The Government estimated that 30,000 people had been killed and some 800,000 people displaced during the civil war; however, other sources claimed that as many as 100,000 people had died. Although the civil war effectively ended in early 1993, the continued insurgency by Islamist-dominated forces, notably from across the Afghan border, continued to destabilize the country. In June the Supreme Court formally proscribed the IRP, Lale Badakhshon, Rebirth and the DPT, leaving the CPT as the only legal party. Two new parties established later in the year—the Party of Economic Freedom and the People's Democratic Party of Tajikistan (PDPT)—were founded or sponsored by members of the Government or its associates.

Abdujalil Samadov succeeded Abdullojonov as premier in December 1993, after the latter resigned. From the end of 1993 Rakhmonov, who secured for his own office responsibility for the powerful Ministries of Defence and Internal Affairs, as well as for the NSC (and, in February 1994, operational supervision of the broadcast media), began to show signs of compromise. In March he announced his willingness to negotiate with the opposition, and talks began in April in Moscow, under the auspices of the UN and in the presence of representatives from Iran, Pakistan, Russia and the USA. The negotiations resulted in a protocol on the establishment of a joint commission on refugees. However, from March border incursions from Afghanistan intensified, resulting in clashes with the CIS troops stationed on the frontier (see below), and there was renewed insurgency in Kuhistoni Badakhshon. The continuing conflict along the Tajikistani–Afghan border was interpreted by some observers as being partly a battle for control of drugs-smuggling routes: since securing independence Tajikistan had become a major conduit for illicit drugs (chiefly opium) from Pakistan, Iran and Afghanistan to Russia and Europe.

Emomali Rakhmonov (Rakhmon) elected President

In August 1994 the forthcoming presidential election was postponed, to allow time for opposition candidates to be included in the poll. The implementation of a temporary cease-fire was deferred until October, after rebel forces launched a large-scale offensive in the Tavil Dara region of eastern Tajikistan, which was successfully repelled. In December the UN Security Council authorized the deployment of a Mission of Observers in Tajikistan (UNMOT). When the election was conducted on 6 November, the only two candidates were Rakhmonov and Abdullojonov. Some 85% of eligible voters were reported to have participated in the election, which was won by Rakhmonov, with some 58% of the votes cast; Abdullojonov received about 35% of the votes. The result reflected regional loyalties; Rakhmonov secured most of his support in the south, and Abdullojonov received a large proportion of the votes in Khujand and in Kuhistoni Badakhshon. In a concurrent referendum, some 90% of voters approved a new Constitution. In December Jamshed Karimov was appointed as Chairman of the Council of Ministers.

In February 1995 renewed peace talks, conducted in Almatı, Kazakhstan, proved largely fruitless. In the same month Abdullojonov's newly formed Party of Popular Unity and Accord (PPUA) announced that it would not contest the forthcoming elections to the new Majlisi Oli (Supreme Assembly), after Abdullojonov's candidature was disallowed. The Organization for Security and Co-operation in Europe (OSCE, see p. 385) refused to send observers to the elections, expressing dissatisfaction with the electoral law. Despite the opposition boycott, legislative elections took place on 26 February, with the participation of an estimated 84% of the electorate. In some 40% of constituencies there was only one candidate, and most of those elected were reported to be state officials loyal to the President, largely without party affiliation. A second round of voting was held on 12 March to elect representatives to 19 seats that had not been filled.

In March 1995 the opposition announced a unilateral, 50-day extension of the cease-fire, but later that month there were further attacks on border posts along the Tajikistani–Afghan frontier. In early April there was a serious escalation of the conflict in the region, when 34 border guards and 170 rebel troops were reportedly killed. Nevertheless, the cease-fire was subsequently extended for a further three months, from May, when an exchange of prisoners was also agreed. In August, after Rakhmonov met the leader of the IRP, Sayed Abdullo Nuri, and other opposition leaders for talks in Tehran, Iran, the cease-fire was extended for six months. However, conflict continued in the south of the country and on the border with Afghanistan. In September clashes in Qurgonteppa between two military units, both formerly loyal to the Government, were reported to have resulted in 300 deaths before government forces regained control of the town. The opposition withdrew from peace negotiations, convened under UN auspices, in Aşgabat, Turkmenistan, in November, after the Government refused to accede to demands for the formation of a national reconciliation council to govern the country alongside Rakhmonov during a two-year transition period.

In January 1996 Sharifzoda was killed by gunmen. At the end of January opposition forces began a major offensive in Tavil Dara, and military commanders of the government troops initiated rebellions in two towns, obtaining control of Qurgonteppa and the western town of Tursunzoda. The commanders who led the rebellions (both ethnic Uzbeks) demanded changes to the Government, including the removal of several Kulobi ministers. In early February troops loyal to Makhmoud Khudoberdiyev (who had led the uprising in Qurgonteppa) approached Dushanbe, but retreated when they encountered government forces. Following negotiations, Rakhmonov agreed to the commanders' demands, including the replacement of Karimov as premier with Yakhyo Azimov.

Despite the announcement of an indefinite extension of the cease-fire, fighting intensified in March–May 1996 near Tavil Dara, resulting in the capture of the town itself by opposition forces. Talks resumed in Aşgabat in July. A cease-fire was brokered in Tavil Dara, and agreement was reached on the conduct of further peace negotiations and on a gradual exchange of prisoners of war. However, large-scale hostilities resumed and opposition forces regained control of the Tavil Dara in mid-August; meanwhile, government and rebel troops fought for command of the strategic central regions. A further cease-fire agreement was reached, but was almost immediately violated as fierce fighting continued around Garm. Later that month, meeting in Moscow, Rakhmonov and Nuri agreed to form a National Reconciliation Council (NRC), to be headed by a representative of what had come to be known as the United Tajik Opposition (UTO), and which was to have extensive executive powers over legislation on elections, political parties and the media, constitutional amendments and the monitoring of the implementation of the peace agreement. A general amnesty was agreed, as were terms for an exchange of prisoners and the repatriation of refugees.

Negotiations were held in Tehran in January 1997 to determine the structure and composition of the NRC, and at further UN-mediated peace talks held in Mashhad, Iran, in February, it was agreed that the NRC was to comprise 26 seats divided equally between the Government and the UTO. Negotiations on the reintegration of opposition forces into Tajikistan's military structures, the exchange of prisoners and the legalization of opposition parties were held in Moscow and Tehran throughout March and April. In April Rakhmonov was wounded in an assassination attempt (condemned by the UTO) in Khujand. Following talks held in Tehran later that month, a protocol was signed by government and UTO representatives, which guaranteed the provisions of the December 1996 peace agreement. These were confirmed in the General Agreement on Peace and National Accord in Tajikistan, signed by Rakhmonov and Nuri in Moscow on 27 June 1997, formally ending the five-year civil conflict. In July Nuri was elected Chairman of the NRC, at its inaugural session; a policy of 'mutual forgiveness' and an amnesty to allow UTO fighters to return to Tajikistan were agreed.

The National Reconciliation Council

In September 1997, for the first time in five years, Nuri arrived in Dushanbe, to participate in the NRC. Some 200 UTO fighters were deployed in the capital to guard members of the NRC, sessions of which formally commenced in mid-September. Opposition to the agreement led to a series of minor bomb explosions in Dushanbe in early September. In October at least 14 servicemen were killed following an attack on the barracks of the presidential guard, attributed to Makhmoud Khudoberdiyev. By mid-November some 10,000 Tajikistani refugees had been repatriated from Afghanistan. Meanwhile, negotiations were held between Nuri and Rakhmonov to determine the allocation of portfolios in the new government (under the terms of the peace agreement, the UTO was to receive one-third of posts in both the central and regional administrations). In February 1998 three portfolios, including those of Labour and Employment and of the Economy and Foreign Economic Relations, were formally allocated to UTO members. Following the return of Turajonzoda, the deputy leader of the UTO, from Iran in late February, he was appointed First Deputy Chairman, with responsibility for relations with CIS countries.

In March 1998 several people, including the brother of the former Prime Minister, Abdullojonov, were sentenced to death for their part in the attempt to assassinate Rakhmonov in April 1997. An upsurge in fighting between government and opposition forces, in the vicinity of Dushanbe, resulted in many civilian deaths. In April 1998 Rakhmonov, who had joined the PDPT in March, was elected Chairman of the party. In May a cease-fire was agreed, following renewed fighting between government and opposition forces near Dushanbe. In August Rakhmonov confirmed the appointment of several UTO members to government posts. However, other opposition appointments were rejected by the President, bringing the number of UTO members in the Government to 11, rather than the 14 agreed under the terms of the peace accord. At the end of August five local officials in western Tajikistan were killed; the Government reportedly blamed supporters of Makhmoud Khudoberdiyev. In September the trial of four associates of Khudoberdiyev, accused of attempting to overthrow the Government in August 1997, began in Dushanbe. Also in September 1998 a senior opposition figure, Otakhon Latifi, was assassinated in the capital. Meanwhile, accusations by the Government that the opposition was involved in the deaths of four UNMOT workers in July prompted the UTO to announce its withdrawal from the Government and the NRC at the end of September. The crisis was defused after intensive talks between Rakhmonov and UTO representatives resulted in agreement on a programme to accelerate the peace process.

In October 1998 an operation by government forces against two rebel factions in Dushanbe resulted in 13 deaths and the detention of six rebels. Heavy fighting was reported around Khujand in November, in the most extensive outbreak of violence since the 1997 peace agreement, in which Khudoberdiyev's forces seized police and security headquarters and a nearby airport. An estimated 100–300 people were killed and around 500 were injured. Khudoberdiyev's forces were defeated after five days of fighting. After President Rakhmonov accused Abdullojonov of having instigated the rebellion, criminal proceedings were initiated against the former premier, as well as against Khudoberdiyev and two other prominent figures. In mid-November the Majlisi Oli endorsed the appointment of several UTO members to the Council of Ministers, including Zokir Vazirov as a Deputy Chairman and Davlat Usmon as Minister of the Economy and Foreign Economic Relations. In December 1998 Nuri announced that the UTO would disband its armed forces in early 1999. In March 1999 the re-registration of political parties was effected by the Ministry of Justice: of the eight parties previously registered, only five received new licences. Criminal charges against leading opposition party members, including Nuri and Turajonzoda, were abandoned, in accordance with the 1997 amnesty; 360 UTO members were thus granted immunity from prosecution. At the end of the month the Supreme Court sentenced seven supporters of Khudoberdiyev to 10–14 years' imprisonment, following their conviction on charges of involvement in the attack on government forces in October 1997.

The Majlisi Oli adopted a resolution in mid-May 1999 providing for a general amnesty to be granted to the estimated 5,500 registered opposition fighters. Later in the month the UTO leadership withdrew from the NRC, expressing discontent that several of its demands—including the holding of elections to the Majlisi Oli in 1999, in advance of the presidential election scheduled for November, and further UTO appointments to government posts (so that it held the agreed share of one-third of all government positions) had not been met. In June 1999 President Rakhmonov and Nuri signed an agreement outlining a timetable for the implementation of the remaining provisions of the peace agreement, while an additional four UTO members were appointed to government posts. In July Rakhmonov appointed another five UTO representatives to government positions, and also announced that 21 of the 69 local government posts were to be offered to opposition members. In August the UTO leadership announced that the integration of its fighters into the regular armed forces had been completed. Rakhmonov responded later that month by lifting a ban on opposition parties, and their media, that had been imposed in 1993.

At a referendum held on 26 September 1999, some 72% of the votes cast by an estimated 92% of the electorate approved amendments to the Constitution, proposed by President Rakhmonov, including the formation of a bicameral legislature, the extension of the presidential term from five to seven years and the legalization of religiously based political parties (including the IRP). In October the UTO again temporarily withdrew from the NRC, alleging that pledges made by the Government had not been met and seeking a postponement of the forthcoming presidential election, after three of its candidates were prevented from contesting the presidency. Meanwhile, it was reported in mid-October that Turajonzada had been expelled from both the UTO and its largest constituent party, the IRP, after a policy disagreement.

Constitutional amendments of 1999 and 2003

In the presidential election, held on 6 November 1999, Rakhmonov received some 97.0% of the total votes cast, according to official sources, defeating his only opponent, Usmon. The rate of participation by the electorate was reported to be almost 99%. The opposition demanded that the election (to which the OSCE had again refused to send monitors) be declared invalid, owing to alleged electoral malpractice. Following the inauguration of President Rakhmonov on 16 November, the Government tendered its resignation, although ministers remained in office until the formation of a new Government in late December. Oqil Oqilov was appointed Chairman of the Council of Ministers (Prime Minister).

TAJIKISTAN

In December 1999 the legislature approved the reconstitution of the Majlisi Oli on a bicameral basis. Although six political parties were registered to participate in forthcoming elections to the two chambers, several opposition parties were barred from contesting the poll. In the elections to the new Majlisi Namoyandagon (Assembly of Representatives), the lower chamber of the Majlisi Oli, held on 27 February 2000, Rakhmonov's PDPT (with its allies) was reported to have won 64.5% of the total votes cast and secured 45 of the 63 seats. The CPT won around 20.6% of the votes (13 seats), while the IRP secured about 7.5% (two seats). According to official sources, some 93% of eligible voters participated in the election. The OSCE and opposition parties stated that electoral malpractice had been widespread. Nuri made a formal complaint about the electoral procedures to Rakhmonov, the UN and the OSCE. A second round of voting took place in 11 constituencies on 12 March 2000. Results in three constituencies were declared invalid at the first round of voting; re-elections for two seats took place in April and December, respectively. Meanwhile, on 23 March indirect elections to the Majlisi Milliy (National Assembly), the legislative upper chamber, were held for the first time. Regional deputies elected 25 members of the chamber, and the eight remaining members appointed by the President of the Republic. At the end of the month the NRC was dissolved. In May UNMOT withdrew from the country, its peace-keeping activities having concluded. On 1 June it was succeeded, with the authorization of the UN Security Council, by the UN Tajikistan Office of Peace-building (UNTOP). In October a new currency, the somoni, was introduced, replacing the Tajikistani rouble, which had been in use since May 1995.

In December 2000 the Supreme Court suspended the activities of the Justice (Adolatkhoh) Party for six months; the party claimed that the ruling was a consequence of its opposition to the President during the legislative elections. In August 2001 the party was banned, after it failed to re-register its members during its period of suspension. Meanwhile, in April several bomb attacks took place, as a result of which at least four people were killed. In June some 36 rebels linked with the former UTO field commander, Rakhmon Sanginov, were killed in an operation launched by state security forces near Dushanbe. In August Sanginov was himself killed by security forces, and at the end of the month officials claimed that only about 10 of his supporters remained at large.

In September 2001 the Minister of Culture, Press and Information, Abdurakhim Rakhimov, was assassinated. It was reported in December that 10 men had been sentenced to between eight and 25 years' imprisonment on charges of treason, terrorism and sedition, relating to the November 1998 insurrection in Khujand. In January 2002 two new ministries—of Industry and of State Revenues and Tax Collection—were created. In March a public accord, signed in 1996 by pro-Government political parties and non-governmental organizations to express support for the peace process, and renewed in 1999, was extended indefinitely; the accord was signed by a representative of the IRP for the first time.

Drugs-smuggling remained a significant problem in Tajikistan. In August 2002 a former Deputy Minister of Defence, Col Nikolai Kim, was sentenced to 13 years' imprisonment for drugs-trafficking and embezzlement while in office in 1998. In October 2002 a senior police official was sentenced to 25 years' imprisonment on charges of murder, fraud and extortion. In the same month two men were sentenced to death, and a further six received terms of imprisonment of between two and 25 years, having been found guilty of belonging to an armed grouping loyal to Khudoberdiyev. It was reported that almost 75 supporters of Khudoberdiyev had been convicted since 1999.

In January 2003 President Rakhmonov carried out a major reorganization of the Council of Ministers and other government structures. On 22 June some 96% of the electorate were reported to have participated in a referendum on proposed amendments to the Constitution, which were approved by 93% of the votes cast, according to official figures. Consequently, Rakhmonov would also be permitted to stand for two further seven-year terms of office upon the expiry of his existing mandate in 2006. Among the other amendments approved was the abolition of the constitutional rights to free health care and higher education, and the abolition of a system of categorization under which registered political parties were compulsorily defined as being one of religious, democratic or atheistic in character.

A Deputy Chairman of the IRP, Shamsiddin Shamsiddinov, was arrested in May 2003, and in October he became the first person to be tried on charges relating to the period of civil conflict. Following a closed trial, in January 2004 Shamsiddinov was sentenced to 16 years' imprisonment. Meanwhile, in October 2003 the former commander of the interior ministry rapid-reaction forces, Maj. Shodi Alimadov, was sentenced to eight years in prison, after being convicted on charges of corruption, extortion and abuse of office. In December and in January 2004 Rakhmonov effected a number of high-level government changes.

In September 2004 20 members of the proscribed transnational militant Islamist group Hizb-ut-Tahrir al-Islami (Party of Islamic Liberation—Hizb-ut-Tahrir) were sentenced to prison terms ranging from six months to 15 years, as part of a long-term campaign against the group in Tajikistan. According to the Office of the Prosecutor-General, between 2000 and July 2005 209 people in the country were convicted of membership of Hizb-ut-Tahrir. In January 2006 it was reported that 99 suspected members of the movement had been detained in 2005, of whom 40 had been tried and sentenced.

Rakhmonov undertook a further reorganization of the Government in January–February 2005. Meanwhile, in January the Chairman of the DPT, Makhmadruzi Iskandarov, was denied permission to register as a candidate in the parliamentary elections scheduled for 27 February, owing to the existence of outstanding criminal charges against him; Iskandarov had been arrested in Moscow in December 2004, accused of corruption and involvement in an attack on the offices of a prosecutor and of a regional branch of the Tajikistani Ministry of Internal Affairs in August. Sulton Kuvvatov, the leader of the Union and Development Party (which had been denied registration in March 2004), was also detained and refused permission to register as a candidate in the elections, having been accused of insulting the President and of inciting ethnic hatred. In January 2005 a car bomb explosion outside the Dushanbe offices of the Ministry of Emergency Situations and Civil Defence killed the driver of the vehicle and injured several others. The detonation, in June, of a further bomb outside the same building injured four people. In January 2006, following the completion of an investigation into the two attacks, the Minister of Internal Affairs, Khomiddin Sharipov, announced that, while at least two people suspected of organizing the attacks were still to be apprehended, a number of other suspects, apparently members of the proscribed militant Islamist group, the Islamic Movement of Uzbekistan (IMU), had been imprisoned.

The 2005 legislative elections

Six political parties participated in the elections to the Majlisi Namoyandagon held on 27 February and 13 March 2005. According to the official results, Rakhmonov's PDPT won 74% of the votes cast nation-wide to decide the allocation of seats on the basis of party lists, securing a total of 52 of the 63 seats in the chamber. The CPT won 13% of the national vote on the basis of party lists, obtaining four seats in total, while the IRP secured 8% and two seats. 92.6% of the electorate were reported to have participated in the poll. Both the OSCE and opposition parties claimed that electoral malpractice was widespread and that amendments to the constitutional law on elections adopted in July 2004 had not been fully implemented. Several members of the IRP and other opposition parties received prison sentences after they were found guilty of charges of hooliganism, defamation and embezzlement. The first session of the new Majlisi Namoyandagon was held on 17 March 2005. Indirect elections to the Majlisi Milliy took place on 24 March, and the eight presidential nominees were announced the following day. The first session of the new upper chamber convened on 15 April.

In late April 2005 it was reported that a former Minister of the Interior, Yakub Salimov, who had been extradited from Russia in February 2004, had been sentenced to 15 years' imprisonment for treason after a five-month closed trial. Meanwhile, in early April 2005 the Russian authorities released Iskandarov, owing to a lack of evidence, after refusing a request by Tajikistan for his extradition. However, Iskandarov was arrested in Dushanbe later that month; he claimed to have been kidnapped in Russia and brought to Tajikistan by unidentified persons. After the Russian and Tajikistani authorities failed to clarify the details of Iskandarov's transfer to Tajikistan, the DPT announced in May its temporary withdrawal from the Public Council (a body established in 1994 by Rakhmonov to bring together representatives of social and cultural organizations with those of five of the six officially registered political parties); in addition, the DPT criticized alleged malpractice during the legislative elections. The IRP and CPT subsequently also announced their withdrawal from the Public Council, in protest at the conduct of the elections.

In June 2005 the deputy leader of the Union and Development Party was sentenced to almost six years' imprisonment, having been found guilty of provoking ethnic discord and insulting President Rakhmonov, whom he had accused of genocide. In October the Supreme Court sentenced Iskandarov to 23 years' imprisonment, after he was found guilty on charges of terrorism, embezzlement and the possession of illegal weapons. Iskandarov vehemently denied the charges, but in January 2006 the verdict was upheld by the court of appeal. In March the Chairman of the opposition Social Democratic Party of Tajikistan (SDPT), Rakhmatullo Zoyirov, declared that there were some 1,000 political prisoners in Tajikistan. Also in March the European Union (EU, see p. 270) released a statement in which it expressed concern at the unclear circumstances surrounding Iskandarov's transfer from Russia to Tajikistan, and at his reported mistreatment prior to his trial.

There was considerable concern regarding the freedom of the media in 2005. The authorities reportedly prevented several independent newspapers and printing houses from publishing, and in April a privately owned television station was closed, ostensibly for failing to submit the requisite documentation. Meanwhile, in November two new political parties were registered: the Party of Economic Reforms of Tajikistan (PERT) and the Agrarian Party of Tajikistan (APT). Zoyirov asserted that the organizations were instruments of the Government. In August 2006 the former commander of the presidential guard, Lt-Gen. Gaffor Mirzoyev, was sentenced to life imprisonment, following his conviction on charges of terrorism and of conspiring to overthrow the Government in a closed trial. Also in August Nuri died, and in the following month Muhiddin Kabiri was elected as his successor as Chairman of the IRP.

A presidential election, held on 6 November 2006, was contested by five candidates; Rakhmonov was re-elected to office, with 79.3% of the votes cast, while Olimjon Boboyev of PERT, with 6.2% of votes cast, was the second-placed candidate. The OSCE declared that the elections failed to meet democratic standards. A new Council of Ministers was announced by presidential decree on 1 December and approved by the Majlisi Oliy on 16 December; some 10 ministries and government agencies were either dissolved or merged with other ministries and agencies. Ministers who retained their portfolios from the previous Government included Prime Minister Oqilov (who was appointed, additionally, as Minister of Construction) and the Minister of Defence, Maj.-Gen. Sherali Xayrulloyev. Prominent new appointees included Hamrokhon Zaripov, former ambassador to the USA, as Minister of Foreign Affairs, and Mahmadnazar Solehov as Minister of Internal Affairs. New appointments were also made to the chairmanships of the Constitutional Court and the Supreme Court. In January 2007 an Agency for State Financial Control and the Suppression of Corruption was established by presidential decree. Also in January the Procurator-General announced that 10 allegedly extremist opposition and Islamist organizations had been banned. In February the DPT was refused registration by the Ministry of Justice. In the same month a reorganization of the Ministry of Internal Affairs, including the foundation of a new Migration Service, was announced.

In March 2007 President Rakhmonov declared that he was to remove the Russian-derived '-ov' suffix from his surname and that henceforth he wished to be known as Emomali Rakhmon, on the grounds that it was more authentically Tajik. Minister of Foreign Affairs Zaripov made a similar declaration in April, stating that he wished to be known as Hamrokhon Zarifi, and parents were encouraged to follow these examples when naming their children. Other presidential decrees introduced a new dress-code in schools (reinforcing a prohibition on girls and women wearing headscarves that had been introduced in 2005), and the abolition of numerous Soviet-era holidays. In July the mandate of UNTOP was officially concluded. In November it was reported that the central government office complex in Dushanbe had been damaged by a bomb explosion, as a result of which one civilian was killed; the perpetrators of the attack remained unknown. In January 2008 President Rakhmon removed three ministers in a government reorganization and also replaced a number of public senior state officials, after he criticized their failure to address a series of intermissions in the supply of energy to consumers and institutions across the country. By February a critical humanitarian situation had developed in the country, as a result of severe weather conditions, together with continuing energy shortages, which required substantial humanitarian assistance. In April the authorities ordered the closure of an independent radio station which had commenced broadcasting in the previous year and which was perceived as unusually critical of the authorities, Radio Imruz, purportedly on technical grounds. In September the Tajikistani authorities announced the institution of criminal proceedings against a prominent opposition journalist and leader of the Vatandor (Patriot) Movement, Dodojon Atovullo, on charges of anti-state activities and public defamation of the President; Atovullo, who had been exiled in Moscow since 1992, was reported to have fled to Germany following the issuing of an extradition request to Russia from Tajikistan.

In March 2009 the State Committee for Television and Radio Broadcasting suspended operations of a Russian state television channel, RTR-Planeta (the only terrestrial broadcaster of Russian-language programming operating in Tajikistan), on the grounds that it had accrued debt equivalent to some US $130,000, and announced that a new broadcasting contract would be negotiated; the decision followed a visit by President Rakhmon in Moscow in February (see below) and a significant increase in anti-Russian sentiment in the Tajikistani media. In April the results were announced of an independent audit of the National Bank, conducted by a British company in late 2008 following the discovery that Tajikistan had presented false information to the IMF prior to the receipt of loans from the Fund; it was alleged that Deputy Prime Minister Murodali Alimardon, the Chairman of the National Bank in 1996–2008, was responsible for the misappropriation of at least $856m. of state funds allocated to support the cotton industry, which had been transferred to private enterprises headed by his relatives.

Recent developments: resurgence of Islamist militancy

In May 2009 military and police units carried out large-scale military operations in the Rasht Valley region of eastern Tajikistan. Although official sources stated that the mobilization was associated with an annual anti-narcotics operation, other reports suggested that the operation had been intended to locate an Islamist leader, Mullo Abdullo (Abdullo Rahimov), who had recently returned to Tajikistan from Afghanistan, having reportedly been in the company of numerous militants. Despite initially denying that this was the case, the authorities subsequently stated that Abdullo had proclaimed a *jihad* (Islamic holy war) against the Tajikistani state, and that several of his associates had been arrested. In June a former Minister of Internal Affairs, Lt-Gen. Mahmadnazar Salihov, was reported to have committed suicide, shortly after a warrant for his arrest on charges of abuse of office had been issued. (Members of exiled opposition groups, however, claimed that he had been murdered.)

In mid-July 2009 Lt-Gen. Mirzo Ziyoev (also known as Mirzo Jaga), a UTO commander during the civil war who had subsequently served as Minister of Emergency Situations, and who continued to be regarded as an influential leader of the Islamic opposition, was killed in a gun-fight in the Tavil Dara district, in circumstances that remained obscure. Official reports issued by the Ministry of Internal Affairs attributed his killing to armed militants associated with the IMU, and stated that Ziyoev, having been captured with the militants, had subsequently agreed to reveal the locations of the rebels' arms caches to the authorities, and was negotiating their surrender. Other sources, however, drew into question the credibility of these reports. The security forces had been engaged in operations against insurgents in the region for several weeks; Nemat Azizov, an insurgent leader who was alleged to have led the group of militants who killed Ziyoev, was killed in Tavil Dara later in July. In late July a bomb explosion in a police car in Dushanbe, which injured one officer, was attributed to militant Islamists, while in early August it was reported that 11 IMU fighters had been captured and a further 20 detained in Tavil Dara. In late August four Tajikistani citizens extradited from Afghanistan were sentenced to between eight and 15 years' imprisonment, having been found guilty of engaging in terrorist activities in that country and in Pakistan as members of the transnational militant Islamist al-Qa'ida organization. In October a governmental reorganization was implemented.

In October 2009 an independent newspaper, *Paykon*, was found guilty of libel after it had published an open letter to the President from several businessmen that accused the state standards body, Tajikstandart, of corruption. The newspaper was fined US $40,000; this was confirmed upon appeal in January 2010. In late January the Ministry of Agriculture brought charges of libel against another independent newspaper, *Millat*, in connection with the publication of an article that had documented apparent corruption and misappropriation of funds in the ministry, demanding damages of $150,000m. In early February three senior judges, including two who were members of the Supreme Court, filed a lawsuit urging the closure of three independent newspapers, *Asia Plus*, *Farazh* and *Ozodagon*. The judges alleged that the newspapers had defamed them in the coverage of a controversial trial, as a result of which 31 people had been imprisoned, after they had been found guilty of charges of gangsterism, tax evasion and the misappropriation of funds. These actions were condemned by the international non-governmental organization Reporters Without Borders, while the US embassy in Dushanbe also expressed concern that the lawsuits might cause the newspapers concerned to cease publication, stating that it had urged the Government to ensure that the judiciary not be used to inhibit the operations of the media.

Elections to the Majlisi Namoyandagon were held on 28 February 2010, with repeat voting being required in one constituency on 14 March, when municipal elections were also conducted. The PDPT obtained 55 of the 63 legislative seats, having obtained around 72% of the votes cast to seats awarded on the basis of party lists and some 39 of the 41 seats elected in single-mandate constituencies. The IRP, CPT, the APT and the PERT each obtained two seats. The outgoing President of the Majlisi Namoyandagon, Saidullo Khayrulloyev of the PDPT, did not stand for re-election to the chamber; he was succeeded in that role, from 15 March, by Shukurjon Zuhurov, the hitherto Minister of Labour and Social Welfare. Maxmadamin Maxmadaminov, the hitherto Chairman of the state savings bank, Amonatbonk, assumed the ministerial position formerly held by Zuhurov. Meanwhile, the son of President Rakhmon, Rustami Emomali, was elected to a position on Dushanbe City Council (the President's daughter, Ozoda Rakhmonova, having been appointed as Deputy Minister of Foreign Affairs in September 2009). Earlier in March 2010 Saidi Yokubzod had been dismissed as Minister of Land Reclamation and Water Resources following his election to the Majlisi Namoyandagon; he was replaced by Hidoyatsho Inoyatov. Elections to the new convocation of the Majlisi Milliy were held on 25 March and the eight presidential nominees were announced on 29 March. The chamber convened on 23 April, when Mahmadsaid Ubaidulloyev (concurrently the Mayor of Dushanbe) was re-elected to a second term as President of the chamber.

In mid-August 2010 the Supreme Court convicted 46 people (including nationals of Afghanistan, Russia and Uzbekistan as well as Tajikistan) on charges that included terrorism, planning to stage a coup, and drugs-trafficking. Many of those convicted had been arrested in association with the armed rebellion in Tavil Dara in July 2009. Additionally, among those sentenced was Abdurasoul Mirzoyev (the brother of Gaffor Mirzoyev), who, having been extradited from the United Arab Emirates in January 2010, was sentenced to 30 years' imprisonment for involvement in the coup attempt for which his brother had been imprisoned in 2006. However, later in August 2010 some of those recently convicted (including Abdurasoul Mirzoyev) were among a total of 25 prisoners, including several prominent militant Islamists, who escaped from a gaol in Dushanbe, killing several prison guards in the process, having seized weapons. Several days later President Rakhmon replaced the head of the State Committee for National Security, and other senior security officials were dismissed. (Seven of the escapees had been recaptured by mid-September.) In early September a suicide bomber detonated a car bomb outside a police station in Khujand, injuring at least 25 people in what was believed to be the first suicide attack in Tajikistan. The authorities accused Abdullo of having organized the attack, and also accused militants from Afghanistan, Pakistan and the Russian territory of Chechnya of involvement. In mid-September Islamist militants staged an ambush of soldiers in the Kamarob gorge, in the Rashd district, near Tavil Dara, resulting in the deaths of at least 23 government troops. Further clashes ensued in subsequent weeks, and the security forces announced that at least 15 militants had been killed by the end of the month. In early October militants of the IMU claimed responsibility for bringing down a Tajikistani military helicopter near Rasht (as a result of which 25 soldiers were killed), although official reports attributed the incident to a collision with a power line. In mid-October three armed rebels (who were alleged to have been involved in the attack on soldiers in the Kamarob gorge in the previous month) were shot dead by government troops near Garm.

Amid increasing concern that Tajikistani students were being exposed to radical Islamist ideology while studying at universities or Islamic religious institutes abroad (notably in Iran, Pakistan and several Arab states), in November 2010 President Rakhmon called for students studying abroad to return to Tajikistan, and announced that the Government would operate a stricter system of control and registration of students studying abroad. The Tajikistani authorities also entered into negotiations with the Governments of Egypt, Iran, Pakistan, Saudi Arabia and Yemen on the repatriation of Tajikistani students.

In mid-December 2010 five of those (including three Afghan nationals) who had escaped from the gaol in Dushanbe earlier in the year were arrested in northern Afghanistan; the two Tajikistani citizens were extradited to Tajikistan later in the month, while the three Afghan citizens were to be brought to trial in their country. In early January 2011 Tajikistani government troops killed a militant Islamist leader, Ali Bedak (Aloviddin Davlatov) in an operation in the Rashd district. The authorities accused Bedak of involvement in the ambush of soldiers in the previous September and also described him as a commander of the al-Qa'ida. In mid-April Abdullo (who was also alleged to be associated with al-Qa'ida) was among around 15 militants killed during another major security operation in Rashd.

Controversy was raised, both domestically and internationally, by proposed legislation presented for parliamentary discussion by President Rakhmon in December 2010, which would prohibit those aged under 18 years from visiting any kind of religious institution. In recent months controversy had also resulted from the enforced closure of a number of mosques, including a mosque in Dushanbe closely associated with the IRP, and the dismissal of numerous imams and their replacement by government appointees.

Meanwhile, in early April 2011 the trial, *in camera*, of nine of those men who had escaped from gaol in September 2010, commenced at the Supreme Court, along with that of two accomplices. By this time nine of the escapees remained at liberty, while four had been killed.

Foreign Affairs
Regional relations

After the dissolution of the USSR, Russian troops remained in Tajikistan, officially adopting a neutral stance during the civil war. However, following the communist victory in Dushanbe in December 1992, they openly assisted pro-communist troops in quelling the opposition forces, and the Government became increasingly dependent on Russia, both militarily and economically. In January 1993 Russia, Kazakhstan, Kyrgyzstan and Uzbekistan committed themselves to the defence of Tajikistan's southern frontiers, thereby supporting the Government. In practice, it was mainly Russian troops who were responsible for repelling rebel fighters entering Tajikistan from Afghanistan, with Russia defending the southern CIS border as if it were its own. In August Russia and the Central Asian states (excluding Turkmenistan) signed an agreement establishing a CIS peace-keeping force to police the Tajikistani border with Afghanistan.

Russia also sought to mediate between the Government and the opposition leadership in exile. In 1996–97 Russia hosted several rounds of the UN-sponsored negotiations for a political settlement in Tajikistan, which culminated in the signature of the peace agreement in Moscow in June 1997. In April 1999 an agreement was signed on the establishment of a Russian military base in Tajikistan; in the same month nine major bilateral agreements were signed. In October 2004 Russia officially opened a military base in Tajikistan and took formal control of the Nurek space monitoring centre, after a meeting between the Russian President, Vladimir Putin, and President Rakhmonov; in return, Russia agreed to cancel US $242m. of Tajikistan's $300m. debt to Russia. In February 2009 President Rakhmon (as he had become) held talks with Russian President Dmitrii Medvedev in Moscow, although relations between the two countries were reported to be strained owing to Russian sympathy for the position of the Uzbekistani authorities with regard to their opposition to the construction of a hydroelectric plant at Roghun, in central Tajikistan (see below). Rakhmon notably failed to secure pledges of further financial support from Russia for Tajikistan's hydroelectric sector.

During the civil conflict in Tajikistan, the leadership of Uzbekistan provided military and political support to the Rakhmonov administration. In October 1994 Tajikistan and Uzbekistan signed a Co-operation Agreement that envisaged greater co-ordination in foreign policy and security. However, the Uzbekistani Government criticized the treatment of the Uzbek minority in Tajikistan, alleging that many Uzbeks had been replaced in their posts by Kulobis. None the less, Uzbekistan continued to provide considerable technical and military support for the Tajikistani administration. Following the signature of the peace agreement in June 1997, Uzbekistan expressed renewed concern at the possible growth in influence of Islamist forces in Tajikistan. Further tensions arose in August 1999, when northern Tajikistan came under attack by unidentified aircraft, while an Uzbekistani military contingent was assisting Kyrgyzstan in repelling a group of Islamist militants in that country's nearby Osh region, in the Farg'ona valley. (The Uzbekistani Government subsequently admitted that its forces might accidentally have bombed the territory.) In April 2000 Tajikistan was strongly criticized by Uzbekistan and Kyrgyzstan for having failed to expel the leader of a group of Uzbek anti-Government Islamist rebels, who had allegedly established a permanent base in Tajikistan. Armed incursions into those two countries by insurgents commenced in August. By the end of 2000 hostilities had subsided, although occasional violent incidents continued to be reported. In March 2001, in response to a claim by Kyrgyzstan that Tajikistan harboured some 2,500 international terrorists, the Tajikistani Government declared there to be no members of any militant organization on its territory. The Uzbekistani authorities, which had begun to lay landmines along their country's border with Tajikistan from mid-2000, in an effort to prevent cross-border incursions by Islamist insurgents, officially informed Tajikistan of this only in May 2001, although bilateral relations subsequently improved. President Rakhmonov visited President Islam Karimov of Uzbekistan in December; it was announced that a crossing between the Penjakent region of Tajikistan and Uzbekistan's Samarqand region was to reopen, and the two leaders also agreed to co-operate to combat terrorism, crime and drugs-trafficking. In February 2002, at a meeting of the Tajikistani and Uzbekistani premiers, an agreement on border-crossing procedures was reached. In October a border agreement was signed by Presidents Rakhmonov and Karimov, although four areas in the northern Soghd Viloyat remained in dispute.

Tajikistani–Uzbekistani relations deteriorated sharply following the suspension at the beginning of 2009 of Turkmenistan's electricity exports to Tajikistan, resulting from the continued failure of the Tajikistani and Uzbekistani authorities to agree a transit rate. Tajikistan accused the Uzbekistani state utility company, Uzbekenergo, of interrupting deliveries of Turkmenistani electricity (a complete absence of energy supplies in some regions of Tajikistan was reported), and threatened, in response, to restrict the amount of water flowing downstream to Uzbekistan, in order to maintain levels in its reservoirs. An additional matter of contention was the construction of a hydroelectric plant at Roghun, in central Tajikistan, of critical importance domestically but strongly opposed by Uzbekistan, owing to concerns regarding the potential impact of the project on its own water supplies and status as a major regional energy supplier. Later in January the Uzbekistani and Russian Presidents issued a joint declaration, stating that any hydro-engineering projects with transboundary implications were required to meet international laws and standards. However, in February Karimov unexpectedly announced that Uzbekistan was prepared to reconsider its opposition to the project, provided that international auditors verified its viability. On 19 February Uzbekistani First Deputy Prime Minister Rustam Azimov visited Tajikistan; it was reported that negotiations resulted in agreement on a debt repayment schedule, and on a protocol regarding a reservoir in northern Tajikistan, although a number of the fundamental issues remained unresolved. Electricity supplies from Turkmenistan were subsequently resumed, and in March an agreement was reached on the resumption of direct flights between Dushanbe and the capital of Uzbekistan, Tashkent, which had been suspended in 1992. However, relations with Uzbekistan again deteriorated from late 2009, as rail traffic from Uzbekistan into Tajikistan was repeatedly disrupted.

While the Tajikistani Prime Minister accused Uzbekistan of deliberately causing delays in transit, so as to disrupt Tajikistani agriculture, and as an expression of discontent concerning the construction of the Roghun hydroelectric plant, Uzbekistan maintained that the cause of the delays was technical. However, in April 2010 it was reported that a spokesman for the Uzbekistani state railways company had announced that the Government had issued a secret decree ordering the blocking of passage of Tajikistani transit cargo in Uzbekistan. Moreover, in early 2010 a series of protests was organized in various cities across Uzbekistan, seemingly with official endorsement, ostensibly to protest against pollution allegedly being produced at the Tajikistani state-owned Talco aluminium plant in Tursunzade, western Tajikistan. In mid-April Tajikistan threatened to present a case against Uzbekistan at an international court, in relation to the blockading of railway transport between the two countries. However, following a meeting between the two Presidents, in May several freight trains were permitted to enter Tajikistan. The blockading of railway traffic continued intermittently throughout 2010, with the border between the two countries being completely closed for a period in October, and in January 2011 a senior official of the Tajikistani state railway company announced that the blockade had resulted in the country experiencing losses amounting to an estimated US $20m.

Tajikistan had begun to develop relations outside the USSR before its dissolution in 1991, notably with Iran, with which the Tajiks have strong ethnic and linguistic ties, although the effective collapse of central authority in Tajikistan in 1992 severely hindered further development of foreign relations. The Iranian authorities denied allegations that they were supplying armaments and other goods to Islamist elements in Tajikistan, stating that they were providing only cultural and humanitarian assistance. In July 1995 President Rakhmonov visited Tehran, where a number of agreements on cultural and economic co-operation were signed. Further agreements were signed in late 1996, providing for Iranian investment in Tajikistan's industrial and agricultural sectors, followed by economic, cultural and defence accords in late 1998. In April 2002 Tajikistan and Iran signed nine protocols on co-operation in economic, political and social affairs. In April 2005 the two countries signed a memorandum of understanding on enhanced co-operation in defence matters, and for the provision by Iran of equipment and training to Tajikistani military personnel.

Relations with Afghanistan in the early 1990s were strained by the apparent inability of the Afghan Government to prevent *mujahidin* fighters and consignments of weapons from crossing the frontier into Tajikistan. The widespread victory of the militant Islamist Taliban forces in Afghanistan in 1995 threatened to destabilize the fragile situation in Tajikistan. In July 1998, while heavy fighting occurred close to Tajikistan's border with Afghanistan, the frontier was reinforced by Russian troops. As fighting escalated in Afghanistan in September 2000, the Tajikistani Government closed its border with that country. The Tajikistani President visited Afghanistan for the first time in 2005, meeting with the Afghanistani President, Hamid Karzai, reflecting the improved relations between the two countries following Karzai's appointment in 2004. President Rakhmon visited Afghanistan again in October 2010, when he and President Karzai signed six agreements on co-operation in areas including trade, transport and culture. President Rakhmon also denied press reports that some 150 Islamist militants of the IMU had crossed into Tajikistan from Afghanistan, although both countries were to undertake intensified co-operation in the combat of terrorism.

In the mid-1990s Tajikistan sought to develop relations with other Asian states, in particular the People's Republic of China. In April 1996 Tajikistan signed (together with Russia, Kazakhstan and Kyrgyzstan) a wide-ranging border agreement with China. This was supplemented by a further border accord, signed in August 1999. In January 2002 Tajikistan signed a further treaty with China, resolving contentious issues regarding the two countries' joint border on the edge of Kuhistoni Badakhshon, and in May a border agreement was signed by the two countries, in accordance with which Tajikistan conceded 1,000 sq km of disputed territory to China. This agreement was not, however, ratified by the Tajikistani legislature until January 2011. Meanwhile, in April 1997 an agreement on military confidence-building measures was concluded. Members of the Shanghai Co-operation Organization (SCO, see p. 462), comprising China, Kazakhstan, Kyrgyzstan, Russia, Tajikistan and Uzbekistan, signed the Shanghai Convention on Combating Terrorism, Separatism and Extremism in mid-2001. In October of that year the SCO agreed to establish an anti-terrorism centre. In September 2004 members of the SCO, meeting in Bishkek, Kyrgyzstan, agreed to increase co-operation in trade, science, technology, and humanitarian projects, as well as to strengthen anti-terrorism measures. In November 2010 an SCO summit was held in Dushanbe, on which occasion the Chinese Prime Minister,

TAJIKISTAN

Wen Jiabou, signed seven documents of bilateral co-operation with Tajikistan.

In March 2000 joint military exercises were conducted in southern Tajikistan by Kazakhstan, Kyrgyzstan, Tajikistan, Uzbekistan and Russia. In May 2001 the signatory countries of the Collective Security Treaty—Armenia, Belarus, Kazakhstan, Kyrgyzstan, Russia and Tajikistan—formed a Rapid Reaction Force to combat Islamist militancy in Central Asia; in January 2002 it was announced that the force was ready to undertake combat missions. In March the Central Asian Economic Community, which Tajikistan joined in March 1998, was superseded by the Central Asian Co-operation Organization (CACO). In April 2003 the signatories of the Collective Security Treaty inaugurated a successor organization, the Collective Security Treaty Organization (CSTO). In April 1998 Tajikistan joined a customs union, already comprising Russia, Belarus, Kazakhstan and Kyrgyzstan. In October 2000 a new economic body, the Eurasian Economic Community (EURASEC, see p. 447), was established to supersede the customs union, and this organization merged with CACO in January 2006. In October 2007, meeting in Dushanbe, EURASEC leaders approved the legal basis for the establishment of a new customs union that was initially to comprise Belarus, Kazakhstan and Russia, with Kyrgyzstan, Tajikistan and Uzbekistan expected to join in 2011.

Other external relations

Following the suicide attacks on the USA of 11 September 2001 by the militant Islamist al-Qa'ida organization, Russian troops along the Tajikistani–Afghan border were placed on a state of alert in anticipation of military strikes against Afghanistan by the USA and allied countries. US specialists were granted entry to Tajikistan, initially to oversee the distribution of humanitarian aid to Afghanistan. The Government declared its support for the aerial bombardment of Taliban and al-Qa'ida targets in Afghanistan, which commenced on 7 October, and in early November it was confirmed that Tajikistan had permitted US troops and forces of the North Atlantic Treaty Organization (NATO, see p. 368) to utilize three of its airbases. In January 2002 it was announced that US restrictions on the transfer of defence equipment to Tajikistan, imposed in 1993, had been lifted. In February 2002 Tajikistan joined NATO's 'Partnership for Peace' programme of military co-operation. In October 2004 the Secretary-General of NATO, Jaap de Hoop Scheffer, signed a bilateral transit agreement with Rakhmonov in support of NATO's International Security Assistance Force in Afghanistan. In December Russia began to transfer military control of the Pamir stretch of the Tajikistani–Afghan border to the Tajikistani authorities. The transfer was completed in September 2005, although a Russian task force was to remain in Tajikistan, and Russia was to continue to train Tajikistan's border guards. Throughout the transfer, concern had been expressed at a possible increase in the cross-border smuggling of drugs from Afghanistan, and later in September international donors signed an agreement to provide Tajikistan with installations, equipment and training to help manage its border with Afghanistan. In October the Majlisi Namoyandagon ratified a bilateral security agreement with Afghanistan on co-operation in countering terrorism, extremism and transnational organized crime. In August 2007 the Presidents of Tajikistan and Afghanistan inaugurated a 680m-long bridge (funded principally by the USA) across the river Pyanzh, at the border between the two countries. In February 2009 a potential increase in Tajikistani support for the coalition forces in Afghanistan was discussed with European Commission and NATO officials during a visit by President Rakhmon to Brussels, Belgium, in that month (see below). The first official visit to Tajikistan by a high-level NATO delegation took place in April, when the Government agreed to permit the country to serve as a transit route for non-military supplies to forces operating in Afghanistan and pledged further assistance in stabilization and reconstruction efforts in that country.

Security issues dominated a summit meeting hosted by President Rakhmon in Dushanbe in July 2009 and attended by his Afghan, Pakistani and Russian counterparts, amid concerns that conflict in Afghanistan and Pakistan might be spreading into Tajikistan, following an intensification of activity by Islamist militants in the east of the country.

In February 2009 Rakhmon visited Brussels, for the first time, where he met the President of the European Commission, José Manuel Durão Barroso, to discuss co-operation in a number of areas; Barroso, who welcomed an offer by the Tajikistan Government to support NATO operations in Afghanistan, announced an upgrade in the European Commission's representation in Dushanbe and an increase in EU financial assistance for Tajikistan, in view of its contribution to regional stability.

CONSTITUTION AND GOVERNMENT

Under the Constitution of 1994 (as amended in 1999 and 2003), Tajikistan has a presidential system of government. The President is Head of State and Chairman of the Government. The President appoints a Prime Minister to head the Government (Council of Ministers). Legislative power is vested in the 63-member lower chamber, the Majlisi Namoyandagon (Assembly of Representatives), and the upper chamber, the Majlisi Milliy (National Assembly), which has a minimum of 33 members. Judicial power is exercised by the Constitutional Court, the Supreme Court, the Supreme Economic Court, the Military Court, the Court of Kuhistoni Badakhshon Autonomous Viloyat, and courts of viloyats, the city of Dushanbe, towns and districts. For administrative purposes, the country is divided into two viloyats (regions or oblasts) and the nominally autonomous viloyat of Kuhistoni Badakhshon. These regions are further subdivided into districts and towns. The city of Dushanbe has a separate status. Three cities and 10 districts of central and eastern Tajikistan are not incorporated into any of the viloyats, and are known as the Regions of Republican Subordination.

REGIONAL AND INTERNATIONAL CO-OPERATION

Tajikistan is a member of the Commonwealth of Independent States (CIS, see p. 238), the Eurasian Economic Community (EURASEC, see p. 447) the Shanghai Co-operation Organization (SCO, see p. 462) and the Economic Co-operation Organization (ECO, see p. 264).

Tajikistan joined the UN in 1992. The country was granted observer status at the World Trade Organization (WTO, see p. 430) in 2001.

ECONOMIC AFFAIRS

In 2009, according to estimates by the World Bank, Tajikistan's gross national income (GNI), measured at average 2007–09 prices, was US $4,841m., equivalent to $700 per head (or $1,950 per head on an international purchasing-power parity basis). During 2000–09, it was estimated, the population increased by an annual average of 1.3%, while gross domestic product (GDP) per head increased by an annual average of 6.7%, in real terms. Overall GDP increased, in real terms, by an average of 8.1% per year during 2000–09. According to the Asian Development Bank (ADB, see p. 202), GDP increased by 7.9% in 2008 and by 3.4% in 2009.

Agriculture contributed 21.2% of GDP in 2009, according to preliminary figures from the ADB. The sector provided 66.2% of employment in that year. According to IMF estimates, the rural population accounted for some 72.4% of the total in 2000–03. Only 7% of Tajikistan's land is arable, the remainder being largely mountainous. The principal crop is grain, followed in importance by cotton, vegetables and fruit. Approximately 95% of the country's arable land is irrigated. Although in mid-1998 legislation was passed to establish a centre to aid farm privatization, agricultural reform has proceeded slowly. The IMF estimated that 51% of Tajikistan's arable land was privately owned at the end of 2001. According to the World Bank, during 2000–09 agricultural GDP increased, in real terms, by an average of 7.8% annually. Real agricultural GDP increased by 5.3% in 2009.

Industry (comprising manufacturing, mining, utilities and construction) contributed 24.4% of GDP in 2009, according to preliminary figures from the ADB. In that year the sector provided 7.6% of employment. There is little heavy industry, except for mineral extraction, aluminium production and power generation. Light industry concentrates on food-processing, textiles and carpet-making. According to the World Bank, industrial GDP increased, in real terms, by an average annual rate of 8.8% in 2000–09. Sectoral GDP increased by 8.6% in 2009.

Tajikistan has considerable mineral deposits, including gold, antimony, silver, aluminium, iron, lead, mercury and tin. There are deposits of coal, as well as reserves of petroleum and natural gas. Mineral extraction is hampered by the mountainous terrain.

The GDP of the manufacturing sector increased, in real terms, by an annual average rate of 8.7% in 2000–09, according to the World Bank. Real manufacturing GDP increased by 6.0% in 2008 and 2009.

Construction contributed 10.1% of GDP in 2009, according to preliminary figures from the ADB. The sector provided 2.9% of employment in that year. According to the ADB, construction

GDP increased, in real terms, by an average annual rate of 45.3% in 2001–07. Sectoral GDP increased by 80.3% in 2007.

Although imports of natural gas and petroleum products comprised 13.3% of the value of merchandise imports in 2001 (mainly supplied by Turkmenistan, Uzbekistan, Kazakhstan and Russia), Tajikistan is believed to have sufficient unexploited reserves of petroleum and natural gas to meet its requirements. The mountain river system is widely used for hydroelectric power generation, and Tajikistan is one of the largest producers of hydroelectric power world-wide. In 2007 hydroelectricity accounted for 97.8% of energy production. In January 2005 Tajikistan signed a protocol with Russia and Iran on the construction of two hydroelectric power plants, Sangtuda-1 and Sangtuda-2. In March an agreement was signed with Pakistan on the construction of a 700-km transmission line to transport electricity to Pakistan, from 2009. Construction work on Sangtuda-2 commenced in 2006; Sangtuda-1 was officially launched in July 2009, while Sangtuda-2 was scheduled to begin operations in late 2011. The completion of Sangtuda-1 was fully funded by Russia, and Iran was to provide significant funding for the construction of the Sangtuda-2 plant, ownership of which was to be secured by Tajikistan in 2018. Tajikistan imports some 90% of its gas requirements, principally from Uzbekistan.

The services sector contributed 54.5% of GDP in 2009, according to the preliminary figures from the ADB. The sector provided 26.2% of employment in the same year. The GDP of the services sector increased, in real terms, by an annual average of 8.2% in 2000–07; real services GDP increased by 6.0% in 2007.

In 2009, according to the IMF, Tajikistan recorded a visible trade deficit of US $1,713.9m., and there was a deficit of $179.9m. on the current account of the balance of payments. In 2009 the principal source of imports was Russia (accounting for 19.0% of the total); other important suppliers were the People's Republic of China, Turkey, Iran and Uzbekistan. Russia was also the principal market for exports in that year (accounting for 24.0% of the total); China, Kazakhstan and Turkey were also significant purchasers. The principal exports in 2002 were non-precious metals and mineral products; the principal imports were mineral products and chemicals.

The state budget for 2009 provided for an overall surplus of 1,499.8m. somoni. Tajikistan's general government gross debt was 6,800m. somoni in that year, equivalent to 33.0% of GDP. Tajikistan's total external debt was US $1,466.1m. at the end of 2008, of which $1,356.5m. was public and publicly guaranteed debt. According to the ADB, in 2010 Tajikistan's total external debt was US $1,942m. The cost of debt-servicing in that year was equivalent to 12.3% of the value of exports of goods and services. The average annual rate of inflation was 303.4% in 1990–2000. The rate of inflation was 12.5% in 2001 and 14.5% in 2002. According to the ADB, the rate of inflation was 6.4% in 2009 and 2010, compared to 20.4% in 2008. Official figures indicated that the rate of unemployment was 2.0% in 2009.

The poorest of the republics of the former USSR, the Tajikistani economy was severely affected by the civil war of 1992–97. The country's economic performance improved significantly from 2000, and Tajikistan succeeded in substantially reducing its external debt between 2000 and 2007. Cotton production, a central component of the domestic economy, declined in 2007–09, while a decease in demand for another of the country's principal exports, aluminium, was recorded in 2008–09. Areas previously designated for cotton were increasingly appropriated for other crops, in response to high international food prices. In April 2009 the IMF approved a three-year arrangement to extend some US $120m. under a Poverty Reduction and Growth Facility, thereby granting Tajikistan immediate access to funds of $38.7m. Meanwhile, following high-level discussions, the European Union announced in February that it was to provide some $42.8m. to support the Tajikistani economy. The European Bank for Reconstruction and Development subsequently announced that it was to provide funds totalling some $70m. to finance projects in Tajikistan, particularly in the banking sector, in 2009. The country was severely affected by the international financial crisis, and remittances from abroad declined by around one-third during 2009, having been equivalent to just under one-half of GDP in the previous year. International trade was also affected by the blockade of rail transport at the border with Uzbekistan by the authorities of that country on numerous occasions from 2009. The commencement of operations at the Sangtuda-1 hydropower plant in mid-2009 (together with the eventual completion of the Sangtuda-2 plant, and also of the Roghun plant, should it go ahead) was expected to provide a source of export earnings as well as to constitute a more reliable energy supplies within Tajikistan than had previously existed; frequent critical shortages of energy had previously had a strongly detrimental impact on various areas of the economy, particularly agricultural production. None the less, power shortages continued to be experienced in certain regions of the country, and in November 2010 the rationing of electricity supplies, to no more than 10 hours a day, was introduced in rural areas. In 2010 real GDP growth amounted to 6.5%, reflecting a recovery in industrial output and an increase in remittances received, particularly from Tajikistani citizens resident in Russia. Despite concerns about an increase in inflation, a similar level of economic growth was forecast for 2011.

PUBLIC HOLIDAYS

2012: 1 January (New Year's Day), 8 March (International Women's Day), 21–24 March (Navrus, Spring Holiday), 1 May (International Labour Day), 9 May (Victory Day), 27 June (National Accord Day), 18 August* (Id-al-Fitr, end of Ramadan), 9 September (Independence Day), 25 October* (Id-al-Adha, Feast of the Sacrifice), 6 November (Constitution Day).

* These holidays are dependent on the Islamic lunar calendar and may vary by one or two days from the dates given.

TAJIKISTAN

Statistical Survey

Source (unless otherwise indicated): State Committee for Statistics, 734001 Dushanbe, Kuchai Boxtar 17; tel. (372) 23-25-53; fax (372) 21-43-75; e-mail stat@tojikiston.com; internet www.stat.tj.

Area and Population

AREA, POPULATION AND DENSITY

Area (sq km)	143,100*
Population (census results)†	
12 January 1989	5,092,603
20 January 2000	
Males	3,069,100
Females	3,058,393
Total	6,127,493
Population (estimates at 31 December)	
2007	7,215,700
2008	7,373,800
2009	7,529,600
Density (per sq km) at 31 December 2009	52.6

* 55,251 sq miles.
† Figures refer to *de jure* population. The *de facto* total at the 1989 census was 5,108,576.

POPULATION BY AGE AND SEX
(UN estimates at mid-2011)

	Males	Females	Total
0–14	1,316,082	1,266,713	2,582,795
15–64	2,127,278	2,239,955	4,367,233
65 and over	111,584	142,367	253,951
Total	3,554,944	3,649,035	7,203,979

Source: UN, *World Population Prospects: The 2008 Revision*.

POPULATION BY ETHNIC GROUP
(2000 census)

	Number ('000 persons)	%
Tajik	4,898.4	79.9
Uzbek	936.7	15.3
Russian	68.2	1.1
Kyrgyz	65.5	1.1
Others	158.7	2.6
Total	6,127.5	100.0

ADMINISTRATIVE DIVISIONS
(at 31 December 2009, official estimates)

	Area (sq km)	Population	Density (per sq km)	Capital city
Viloyats				
Khatlon	24,800	2,700,200	108.9	Qurgonteppa
Soghd	25,400	2,216,900	87.3	Khujand
Autonomous Viloyat				
Kuhistoni Badakhshon	64,200	220,600	3.4	Khorog
Capital City				
Dushanbe	100	706,100	7,061.0	—
*Regions of Republican Subordination**	28,600	1,685,800	58.9	—
Total	143,100	7,529,600	52.6	

* The Regions of Republican Subordination comprise three cities (Gissar, Roghun and Vakhdat) and 10 raions or districts (Faizabad, Jirgital, Nurobod, Rasht, Rudaki, Shakhrinav, Tajikabad, Tavildara, Tursunzade and Varzov) in central and eastern Tajikistan, where there is no higher tier of local government.

PRINCIPAL TOWNS
(population at 1 January 2002)

Dushanbe (capital)	575,900	Kanibadam	45,100
Khujand	147,400	Kofarnihon	45,100
Kulob	79,500	Tursunzade	38,100
Qurgonteppa	61,200	Isfara	37,300
Istravshan*	51,700	Panjakent	33,200

* Also known as Urateppa (Ura-Tyube).

Mid-2009 (incl. suburbs, UN estimate): Dushanbe 703,939 (Source: UN, *World Urbanization Prospects: The 2009 Revision*).

BIRTHS, MARRIAGES AND DEATHS*

	Registered live births		Registered marriages		Registered deaths	
	Number	Rate (per 1,000)	Number	Rate (per 1,000)	Number	Rate (per 1,000)
2002	175,600	27.3	32,299	5.0	31,100	4.8
2003	177,900	27.1	39,102	6.0	33,200	5.0
2004	179,600	26.8	47,320	7.1	29,700	4.4
2005	180,800	26.4	52,352	7.6	31,500	4.6
2006	186,500	26.7	57,278	8.2	32,000	4.6
2007	200,000	28.0	97,713	13.7	33,700	4.7
2008	203,300	27.9	106,388	14.6	32,000	4.4
2009	199,800	26.8	100,678	13.5	32,300	4.3

* From 2002 onwards, figures for registered births and deaths are rounded to the nearest 100.

Life expectancy (years at birth, WHO estimates): 67 (males 66; females 69) in 2008 (Source: WHO, *World Health Statistics*).

IMMIGRATION AND EMIGRATION

	2007	2008	2009
Immigrants	24,283	24,419	25,563
Emigrants	38,761	37,651	37,231

ECONOMICALLY ACTIVE POPULATION
(annual averages, '000 persons)

	2007	2008	2009
Activities of the material sphere	1,784	1,800	1,829
Agriculture*	1,430	1,447	1,468
Industry†	114	104	104
Construction	63	65	65
Trade and catering‡	115	113	125
Transport and communications	62	61	58
Activities of the non-material sphere	366	368	390
Housing and municipal services	48	50	55
Health care, social security, physical culture and sports	76	75	81
Education, culture and arts	186	183	180
Science, research and development	4	5	5
Government and finance	34	35	35
Other non-material	18	6	6
Total employed	2,150	2,168	2,219
Unemployed	52	49	45
Total labour force	2,202	2,217	2,264

* Including forestry.
† Comprising manufacturing (except printing and publishing), mining and quarrying, electricity, gas, water, logging and fishing.
‡ Including material and technical supply.

TAJIKISTAN

Health and Welfare

KEY INDICATORS

Total fertility rate (children per woman, 2008)	3.4
Under-5 mortality rate (per 1,000 live births, 2008)	64
HIV/AIDS (% of persons aged 15–49, 2007)	0.3
Physicians (per 1,000 head, 2006)	2.0
Hospital beds (per 1,000 head, 2006)	6.1
Health expenditure (2007): US $ per head (PPP)	93
Health expenditure (2007): % of GDP	5.3
Health expenditure (2007): public (% of total)	21.5
Access to water (% of persons, 2008)	70
Access to sanitation (% of persons, 2008)	94
Total carbon dioxide emissions ('000 metric tons, 2007)	7,221.7
Carbon dioxide emissions per head (metric tons, 2007)	1.1
Human Development Index (2010): ranking	112
Human Development Index (2010): value	0.580

For sources and definitions, see explanatory note on p. vi.

Agriculture

PRINCIPAL CROPS
('000 metric tons)

	2006	2007	2008
Wheat	640	649	659
Rice, paddy	49	52	54
Barley	62	71	58
Maize	139	130	136
Potatoes	574	662	680
Cabbages and other brassicas*	50	54	59
Tomatoes*	221	248	267
Onions, dry*	199	217	236
Carrots and turnips*	124	135	145
Watermelons	218	254	285
Apples*	147	111	186
Apricots*	21	16	26
Peaches and nectarines*	18	14	23
Grapes	105	117	118
Seed cotton	438	420	353
Tobacco, unmanufactured	1.3	0.5	0.2

* Unofficial figures.

2009 (FAO estimates): Wheat 660; Rice, paddy 54; Barley 70; Maize 135; Potatoes 680; Seed cotton 296.

Aggregate production ('000 metric tons, may include official, semi-official or estimated data): 907 in 2007, 909 in 2008, 921 in 2009; Total roots and tubers 662 in 2007, 680 in 2008–09; Total vegetables (incl. melons) 1,089 in 2007, 1,189 in 2008–09; Total fruits (excl. melons) 274 in 2007, 380 in 2008–09.

Source: FAO.

LIVESTOCK
('000 head at 1 January)

	2007	2008	2009
Horses	76	79	77
Asses	169	171	106
Cattle	1,423	1,703	1,800
Camels	63	70	56
Sheep	1,955	2,374	2,579
Goats	1,210	1,424	1,568
Chickens	2,580	3,280	3,682

Source: FAO.

LIVESTOCK PRODUCTS
('000 metric tons)

	2006	2007	2008
Cattle meat	23.7	25.2	25.1
Sheep meat	28.5	30.3	35.6
Chicken meat	0.7	0.7	1.1
Cows' milk*	500	534	548
Goats' milk*	44.7	50.0	53.0
Hen eggs*	5.9	6.2	8.5
Wool, greasy	4.8	5.1	5.2

* Unofficial figures.

2009: Cows' milk 600 (unofficial figure).

Source: FAO.

Forestry

ROUNDWOOD REMOVALS
('000 cubic metres, excluding bark)

	2005*	2006†	2007†
Total (all fuel wood)	90	90	90

* Unofficial estimate.
† FAO estimate.

2008–09: Figures assumed to be unchanged from 2007 (FAO estimates).

Source: FAO.

Fishing

(metric tons, live weight)

	2003	2004	2005*
Capture	158	184	146
Freshwater bream	24	28	22
Common carp	52	45	36
Crucial carp	11	8	6
Silver carp	12	14	11
Sichel	2	10	8
Asp	3	9	7
Other cyprinids	23	32	26
Wels (Som) catfish	9	18	14
Pike-perch	22	20	16
Aquaculture	167	26	26
Common carp	47	12	12
Grass carp (White amur)	30	3	3
Silver carp	88	7	7
Total catch	325	210	172

* FAO estimates.

2006–08: Catch assumed to be unchanged from 2005 (FAO estimates).

Source: FAO.

Mining

(metric tons, unless otherwise indicated)

	2006	2007	2008*
Coal	102,400	81,600	96,200
Crude petroleum	22,300	22,500*	22,500
Natural gas (million cu m)	19.9	19.0*	19.0
Lead concentrate*†	800	800	800
Antimony ore†	3,480	2,000*	2,000
Mercury*†	30	30	30
Silver (kilograms)†	5,000	5,000*	5,000
Gold (kilograms)†	1,920	3,000*	3,000
Gypsum (crude)	8,500	8,500*	8,500

* Estimated production.
† Figures refer to the metal content of ores and concentrates.

Source: US Geological Survey.

2009 ('000 metric tons, unless otherwise indicated): Coal 198; Crude petroleum 26; Natural gas (million cu m) 12 (Source: Asian Development Bank).

TAJIKISTAN

Industry

SELECTED PRODUCTS
('000 metric tons, unless otherwise indicated)

	2007	2008	2009
Cottonseed oil (refined)*	24	17	14
Wheat flour†	470	n.a.	n.a.
Wine (tons)*	24	24	26
Woollen garments ('000)	100	5	4
Woven cotton fabrics (million sq metres)	30.5	30.1	36.5
Rugs and carpets (million sq metres)	0.9	0.9	0.5
Stockings, etc (million pairs)	6.2	5.5	5.7
Fertilizer	24.5	23.0	n.a.
Clay building bricks (million)	48.9	49.4	49.8
Slate (million sheets)	2.7	2.8	2.8
Cement	313.1	190.4	195.0
Electric energy (million kWh)†	17,494	16,147	16,127
Aluminium, unwrought‡	419.1	339.5	n.a.

* Source: FAO.
† Source: Asian Development Bank.
‡ Source: US Geological Survey.

Finance

CURRENCY AND EXCHANGE RATES

Monetary Units
100 diram = 1 somoni.

Sterling, Dollar and Euro Equivalents (30 November 2010)
£1 sterling = 6.832 somoni;
US $1 = 4.400 somoni;
€1 = 5.719 somoni;
100 somoni = £14.64 = $22.73 = €17.49.

Average Exchange Rate (somoni per US $)
2007 3.4425
2008 3.4307
2009 4.1427

Note: The Tajikistani rouble was introduced in May 1995, replacing the Russian (formerly Soviet) rouble at the rate of 1 Tajikistani rouble = 100 Russian roubles. A new currency, the somoni (equivalent to 1,000 Tajikistani roubles), was introduced in October 2000.

BUDGET
(million somoni)*

Revenue†	2007	2008	2009
Tax revenue	2,288.7	3,298.2	3,659.1
Income and profit tax	304.9	454.6	610.2
Social duties	254.8	354.1	494.7
Property taxes	92.3	118.6	142.4
Internal taxes on goods and services	1,278.3	1,859.6	1,915.3
International trade and operations tax	106.3	148.7	165.6
Non-tax revenue	132.2	148.6	210.9
Income from property and enterprise activities	37.5	9.0	40.7
Administrative fees and levies	35.5	32.5	35.4
Total	**2,420.9**	**3,446.8**	**3,869.9**

Expenditure	2007	2008	2009
General government administration	421.1	383.2	376.6
Education	437.0	612.6	845.4
Health	145.2	217.8	287.9
Social security and welfare	355.6	522.1	713.5
Housing and communal services	216.6	230.4	324.7
Sporting, cultural and religious associations	76.2	178.2	177.5
Energy and fuel sector	51.8	286.1	562.6
Agriculture, forestry, fisheries and hunting	76.9	94.8	88.8
Natural resources, mining and construction	27.6	46.1	24.0
Transport and communications	94.3	97.5	94.9
Total (incl. others)	**3,494.8**	**4,823.8**	**5,687.3**

* Figures refer to the consolidated operations of the State Budget, comprising the budgets of the central (republican) Government and local authorities, and the Social Security Fund.
† Excluding grants received (million somoni): 36.5 in 2007; 24.4 in 2008; 317.6 in 2009.

INTERNATIONAL RESERVES
(US $ million at 31 December)

	2004	2005	2006
Gold (national valuation)	14.6	20.7	28.7
IMF special drawing rights	1.3	5.4	3.5
Foreign exchange	156.2	162.8	171.6
Total	**172.1**	**188.9**	**203.8**

2007 (US $ million at 31 December): Gold (national valuation) 44.8; IMF special drawing rights 3.6.
2008 (US $ million at 31 December): Gold (national valuation) 59.3; IMF special drawing rights 15.7.
2009 (US $ million at 31 December): Gold (national valuation) 81.6; IMF special drawing rights 109.5.
2010 (US $ million at 31 December): Gold (national valuation) 160.5; IMF special drawing rights 107.5.
Source: IMF, *International Financial Statistics*.

MONEY SUPPLY
(million somoni at 31 December)

	2006	2007	2008
Currency outside banks	823.7	1,029.9	1,444.7
Demand deposits	146.2	1,174.0	816.3
Total money (incl. others)	**971.5**	**2,226.6**	**2,263.5**

Source: IMF, *International Financial Statistics*.

COST OF LIVING
(Consumer Price Index; base: previous year = 100)

	2007	2008	2009
Food	115.0	126.1	105.3
Non-food	106.4	107.7	105.2
All items	**113.1**	**120.5**	**106.4**

Source: Asian Development Bank.

All items (Consumer Price Index; base: previous year = 100): 106.4 in 2010 (Source: IMF, *International Financial Statistics*).

TAJIKISTAN

NATIONAL ACCOUNTS
(million somoni at current prices)

Expenditure on the Gross Domestic Product

	2006	2007	2008
Government final consumption expenditure	1,036.6	1,140.1	1,293.9
Private final consumption expenditure	7,737.2	10,783.8	15,862.5
Changes in inventories	45.2	180.3	352.5
Gross fixed capital formation	1,445.3	2,973.9	4,341.4
Total domestic expenditure	10,264.3	15,078.1	21,850.3
Exports of goods and services	5,429.0	6,526.2	5,782.4
Less Imports of goods and services	7,748.0	11,044.8	14,004.9
Statistical discrepancy*	1,389.9	2,245.0	4,079.0
GDP in purchasers' values	9,335.2	12,804.5	17,706.9

Gross Domestic Product by Economic Activity

	2007	2008	2009†
Agriculture	2,488.3	3,517.9	3,905.7
Mining, manufacturing and electricity, gas and water	2,349.4	2,515.8	2,629.4
Construction	1,034.6	1,832.6	1,867.9
Trade	2,116.2	3,573.4	4,340.2
Transport and communications	1,221.9	1,782.2	1,315.1
Financial intermediation	255.5	343.1	50.9
Public administration	397.9	406.5	432.9
Other services	1,497.9	1,674.0	3,916.6
Sub-total	11,361.7	15,645.5	18,458.7
Less Financial intermediation services indirectly measured	160.9	174.4	—
Gross value added in basic prices	11,200.8	15,471.1	18,458.7
Indirect taxes, less subsidies	1,603.5	2,235.8	2,163.8
GDP in purchasers' values	12,804.3	17,706.9	20,622.8

*Referring to the difference between the expenditure and production approaches.
†Preliminary figures.

Source: Asian Development Bank.

BALANCE OF PAYMENTS
(US $ million)

	2007	2008	2009
Exports of goods f.o.b.	1,556.9	1,574.9	1,038.5
Imports of goods c.i.f.	−3,115.0	−3,699.0	−2,770.4
Trade balance	−1,558.1	−2,124.2	−1,731.9
Exports of services	148.7	181.4	179.8
Imports of services	−592.1	−455.5	−291.3
Balance on goods and services	−2,001.5	−2,398.3	−1,843.4
Other income received	22.4	19.9	7.2
Other income paid	−73.2	−72.3	−78.5
Balance on goods, services and income	−2,052.3	−2,450.8	−1,914.7
Current transfers received	1,794.3	2,705.2	1,861.8
Current transfers paid	−237.1	−206.8	−126.9
Current balance	−495.1	47.6	−179.9
Capital account (net)	32.8	39.4	120.4
Direct investment (net)	360.0	375.8	15.8
Portfolio investment (net)	0.2	0.1	0.1
Other investment assets	−386.7	−471.9	177.7
Other investment liabilities	837.9	−127.4	−50.0
Net errors and omissions	−362.9	25.6	30.7
Overall balance	−13.8	−111.0	114.8

Source: IMF, *International Financial Statistics*.

External Trade

PRINCIPAL COMMODITIES
(US $ million, excl. alumina and aluminium)

Imports c.i.f.*	2007	2008	2009
Natural gas	65	74	52
Petroleum products	275	413	323
Electricity	66	90	76
Grain and flour	135	207	175
Total (incl. others)	2,547	3,273	2,570

Exports f.o.b.†	2007	2008	2009
Cotton fibre	138	108	100
Electricity	60	62	63
Total (incl. others)	1,468	1,409	1,010

*These figures do not include separate data for imports of alumina, one of Tajikistan's principal import goods. The most recent data available were for 2001, when imports of alumina accounted for US $184m. of $688m. in total imports (c.i.f.).
†These figures do not include separate data for exports of aluminium, Tajikistan's principal export item. The most recent data available were for 2001, when imports of aluminium accounted for US $397m. of $909m. in total exports (f.o.b.).

PRINCIPAL TRADING PARTNERS
(US $ million)

Imports	2007	2008	2009
Azerbaijan	74.1	69.5	61.4
China, People's Rep.	275.3	384.9	667.9
Iran	60.9	120.6	78.4
Kazakhstan	332.8	285.6	252.3
Russia	813.7	1,047.4	672.5
Turkey	72.9	118.1	139.1
Turkmenistan	38.2	67.9	60.0
Ukraine	52.6	101.7	88.4
United Arab Emirates	65.0	106.4	69.2
Uzbekistan	213.9	151.4	133.8
Total (incl. others)	2,537.7	3,245.4	2,796.7

Exports	2007	2008	2009
China, People's Rep.	8.3	81.6	148.6
Iran	75.5	95.6	95.9
Italy	16.3	13.9	31.1
Latvia	31.0	47.3	0.1
Netherlands	570.5	530.1	11.1
Russia	97.3	124.4	154.8
Switzerland	24.4	23.7	19.3
Turkey	477.6	382.4	97.5
Uzbekistan	87.0	73.0	64.5
Total (incl. others)	1,468.1	1,443.8	815.5

Note: Data reflect the IMF's direction of trade methodology and, as a result, the totals may not be equal to those presented for trade in commodities.

Source: Asian Development Bank.

Transport

RAILWAYS

	2007	2008	2009
Passengers (million journeys)	0.8	0.8	0.7
Freight carried ('000 metric tons)	14,529.1	14,544.2	14,546.0

Passenger-km (million): 32 in 2001.

Freight ton-km (million): 1,248 in 2001.

TAJIKISTAN

CIVIL AVIATION
(traffic on scheduled services)

	2004	2005	2006
Kilometres flown (million)	11	9	8
Passengers carried ('000)	498	479	394
Passenger-km (million)	1,000	942	708
Freight carried ('000 metric tons)	4.1	3.7	2.4
Freight ton-km (million)	96	91	69

2007: Passengers carried ('000) 600; Freight carried ('000 metric tons) 2.1.
2008: Passengers carried ('000) 700; Freight carried ('000 metric tons) 2.5.
2009: Passengers carried ('000) 700; Freight carried ('000 metric tons) 2.2.

Source: partly UN, *Statistical Yearbook*.

Communications Media

	2007	2008	2009
Telephones ('000 main lines in use)	292.7	286.9	290.0
Mobile cellular telephones ('000 subscribers)	2,132.8	3,673.5	4,900.0
Internet users ('000)	484.2	600.0	700.0
Broadband subscribers ('000)	3.6	3.7	n.a.

Television receivers ('000 in use): 2,000 in 2000.

Personal computers: 84,591 (12.9 per 1,000 persons) in 2005.

Books published (titles): 150 in 1997.

Books published (copies): 997,000 in 1996.

Daily newspapers (estimates): 2 titles and 120,000 copies (average circulation) in 1996.

Non-daily newspapers: 73 titles and 153,000 copies (average circulation) in 1996.

Other periodicals: 11 titles and 130,000 copies (average circulation) in 1996.

Radio receivers ('000 in use): 850 in 1997.

Sources: UNESCO, *Statistical Yearbook*; International Telecommunication Union.

Education
(2009/10, unless otherwise indicated)

	Males	Females	Total
Pre-primary	32,300	25,800	58,100
Primary			
Secondary:			
Lower	n.a.	n.a.	1,694,900
General			
Vocational	15,800	20,800	36,600
Professional technical*	16,030	5,457	21,487
Higher (incl. universities)	112,000	45,800	157,800

Institutions (2009/10, unless otherwise indicated): Pre-primary 487; Primary 577; Secondary—Lower 782; Secondary—General 2,414; Secondary—Vocational 52; Professional Technical 67*; Higher (incl. universities) 36. Figures exclude 10 schools for pupils with mental or physical disabilities and seven evening schools.

Teachers: Pre-primary 6,615 (1996/97); Primary *and* Secondary—Lower, General *and* Vocational 94,200 (2009/10); Professional Technical n.a.; Higher (incl. universities) 6,100 (2001/02).
* 2008/09 figures.

Pupil-teacher ratio (primary education, UNESCO estimate): 22.7 in 2007/08 (Source: UNESCO Institute for Statistics).

Adult literacy rate (UNESCO estimates): 99.7% (males 99.8%; females 99.5%) in 2008 (Source: UNESCO Institute for Statistics).

Directory

The Government

HEAD OF STATE

President: EMOMALI RAKHMON (elected by popular vote 6 November 1994; re-elected 6 November 1999 and 6 November 2006).

COUNCIL OF MINISTERS
(May 2011)

Chairman of the Government: EMOMALI RAKHMON.
Prime Minister: OQIL OQILOV.
First Deputy Prime Minister: ASADULLO GHULOMOV.
Deputy Prime Minister: RUQIYA QURBONOVA.
Deputy Prime Minister: MURODALI ALIMARDON.
Minister of Justice: BAKHTIYOR XUDOYOROV.
Minister of Agriculture: QOSIM QOSIMOV.
Minister of Internal Affairs: ABDURAHIM QAHHOROV.
Minister of Foreign Affairs: HAMROKHON ZARIFI.
Minister of Education: ABDUJABBOR RAHMONOV.
Minister of Land Reclamation and Water Resources: RAHMAT BOBOKALONOV.
Minister of Labour and Social Welfare: MAXMADAMIN B. MAXMADAMINOV.
Minister of Finance: SAFARALI NAJMIDDINOV.
Minister of Defence: Maj.-Gen. SHERALI XAYRULLOYEV.
Minister of Transport: NIZOM HAKIMOV.
Minister of Economic Development and Trade: FARRUH XAMRALIYEV.
Minister of Health: NUSRATULLO SALIMOV.
Minister of Culture: MIRZOSHOHRUKH ASRORI.
Minister of Energy and Industry: SHERALI GUL.

Note: The Chairmen of the State Committees for National Security, Statistics, and Investment and the Management of State Property are also members of the Council of Ministers.

MINISTRIES

Office of the President: 734023 Dushanbe, Xiyoboni Rudaki 80; tel. (372) 21-25-20; fax (372) 21-18-37; e-mail mail@president.tj; internet www.president.tj.

Secretariat of the Prime Minister: 734023 Dushanbe, Xiyoboni Rudaki 80; tel. (372) 21-18-71; fax (372) 21-51-10.

Ministry of Agriculture: 734025 Dushanbe, Xiyoboni Rudaki 14; tel. (372) 21-15-96; fax (372) 21-57-94.

Ministry of Culture: 734025 Dushanbe, Xiyoboni Rudaki 34; tel. (372) 21-03-05; fax (372) 21-53-07.

Ministry of Defence: 734025 Dushanbe, Kuchai Bokhtar 59; tel. (372) 21-69-83; fax (372) 21-18-97.

Ministry of Economic Development and Trade: 734002 Dushanbe, Kuchai Bokhtar 37; tel. (372) 27-34-34; fax (372) 21-04-04; e-mail info@met.tj; internet www.met.tj.

Ministry of Education: 734025 Dushanbe, Kuchai Chexov 13A; tel. (372) 21-46-05; fax (372) 21-70-41; e-mail mort@maorif.tj; internet www.education.tj.

TAJIKISTAN

Ministry of Energy and Industry: 734025 Dushanbe, Kuchai Boxtar 10; tel. (372) 21-50-64; fax (372) 27-90-10; e-mail energo@rs.tj; internet minenergoprom.tj.

Ministry of Finance: 734067 Dushanbe, Nazarov 64/14; tel. (37) 881-25-79; e-mail nii_finance@mail.tj; internet www.minfin.tj.

Ministry of Foreign Affairs: 734051 Dushanbe, Xiyoboni Rudaki 42; tel. (372) 21-18-08; fax (372) 21-02-59; e-mail info@mfa.tj; internet www.mid.tj.

Ministry of Health: 734025 Dushanbe, Kuchai Shevchenko 69; tel. (372) 21-30-64; fax (372) 21-48-71.

Ministry of Internal Affairs: 734025 Dushanbe, Kuchai Texron 29; tel. (372) 21-17-40; fax (372) 21-26-05.

Ministry of Justice: 734025 Dushanbe, pr. Rudaki 25; tel. (372) 21-00-82; fax (372) 21-80-66.

Ministry of Labour and Social Welfare: 734028 Dushanbe, Kuchai A. Navoi 52; tel. (372) 36-18-37; fax (372) 36-24-15.

Ministry of Land Reclamation and Water Resources: 734001 Dushanbe, Xiyoboni Shamsi 5/1; tel. (372) 35-55-89; e-mail info@mwr.tj; internet www.mwr.tj.

Ministry of Transport: 734042 Dushanbe, Kuchai Aini 14; tel. (372) 21-17-13; fax (372) 221-20-03; e-mail info@mintranscom.tj; internet www.mintranscom.tj.

President

Presidential Election, 6 November 2006*

Candidates	%
Emomali Rakhmonov† (People's Democratic Party of Tajikistan)	79.3
Olimjon Boboyev (Party of Economic Reforms)	6.2
Amirkul Karakulov (Agrarian Party of Tajikistan)	5.3
Ismoil Talbakov (Communist Party of Tajikistan)	5.1
Abdukhalim Gafforov (Socialist Party of Tajikistan)	2.8
Total‡	100.0

* Provisional results.
† Known as Emomali Rakhmon from 2007.
‡ Including invalid votes, equivalent to 1.3% of the total.

Legislature

Constitutional amendments approved by a referendum in September 1999 provided for the establishment of a bicameral legislative body, the Majlisi Oli (Supreme Assembly), comprising a 63-member lower chamber, the Majlisi Namoyandagon (Assembly of Representatives), and an upper chamber, the Majlisi Milliy (National Assembly), which has a minimum of 33 members.

Majlisi Milliy
(National Assembly)

734051 Dushanbe, Xiyoboni Rudaki 42; tel. (372) 23-19-33; fax (372) 21-51-10; e-mail mejparl@parliament.tojikiston.com; internet www.majlisimilli.tj.

President: MAHMADSAID UBAIDULLOYEV.

The Majlisi Milliy has a minimum of 33 members, of whom 25 (five from each of the five administrative regions of Tajikistan) are indirectly elected for a term of five years by regional deputies. Eight members of the chamber, who also serve for a term of five years, are appointed by the President of the Republic. All former Presidents of Tajikistan are also entitled to a seat in the Majlisi Milliy. Elections to the Majlisi Milliy were held on 24 March 2005, and the eight presidential nominees were announced on 25 March. The new chamber convened on 15 April. Elections to the new convocation of the Majlisi Milliy were held on 25 March 2010 and the eight presidential nominees were announced on 29 March. The chamber convened on 23 April.

Majlisi Namoyandagon
(Assembly of Representatives)

734051 Dushanbe, Xiyoboni Rudaki 42; tel. (372) 21-23-66; fax (372) 21-92-81; e-mail mejparl@parliament.tojikiston.com; internet parlament.tj.

President: SHUKURJON ZUHUROV.

Elections, 28 February and 14 March 2010

Parties	%*	A†	B†	Total
People's Democratic Party of Tajikistan	72	16	39	55
Islamic Rebirth Party of Tajikistan	8	2	—	2
Communist Party of Tajikistan	7	2	—	2
Agrarian Party of Tajikistan	5	1	1	2
Party of Economic Reforms of Tajikistan	5	1	1	2
Others	3	—	—	—
Total	**100**	**22**	**41**	**63**

* Percentage refers to the share of the vote cast for seats awarded on the basis of party lists.
† Of the 63 seats in the Majlisi Namoyandagon, 22 (A) are awarded according to proportional representation on the basis of party lists, and 41 (B) are elected in single-mandate constituencies.

Election Commission

Central Commission for Elections and Referenda: 734051 Dushanbe, Xiyoboni Rudaki 42; tel. (372) 21-13-75; comprises Chair., Sec. and 13 mems, elected by the Majlisi Namoyandagon at the proposal of the President of the Republic; Chair. SHERMUHAMAD SHOHIYON.

Political Organizations

In September 2006 there were eight registered parties in Tajikistan.

Agrarian Party of Tajikistan (Agrarnaya partiya Tadzhikistana): 734000 Dushanbe; f. 2005; supports creation of a civil society and aims to protect the interests of the agricultural sector and its workers; Chair. AMIRQUL QARAQULOV; 1,300 mems (Jan. 2005).

Communist Party of Tajikistan (CPT) (Kommunisticheskaya partiya Tadzhikistana): 734002 Dushanbe, Kuchai F. Niyazi 37; tel. (372) 23-29-53; e-mail talbhakov_555@mail.ru; internet www.kpt.freenet.tj; f. 1924; sole registered party until 1991; Chair. SHODI D. SHABDOLOV; Sec. of Central Cttee TUNGUN B. QARIMOV; 60,000 mems (Jan. 2005).

Democratic Party of Tajikistan (DPT) (Xizbi demokrati Tochikiston): 734000 Dushanbe, Kuchai Pushkin 64; tel. (372) 21-77-87; f. 1990; banned in 1993; permitted to re-register 1996 and 1999; secular nationalist and pro-Western; Chair. SAIDJAFAR ISMONOV (acting) (Chair. of Vatan—Fatherland faction registered by the Ministry of Justice in Sept. 2006); Chair. (of unregistered faction) MAHMADRUZI ISKANDAROV; c. 4,500 mems (Jan. 2005).

Islamic Rebirth Party of Tajikistan (IRP): 734000 Dushanbe, pos. Kalinina, Kuchai Tukhagul 55; tel. (372) 27-25-30; fax (372) 27-53-93; f. 1990 by split from the All-Union Islamic Renaissance Party of the USSR; leadership fmrly based in Tehran, Iran; registered in 1991; banned 1993–99; Chair. MUHIDDIN KABIRI; 20,000 mems (Jan. 2005).

Justice (Adolatkoh): 734000 Dushanbe, Kuchai S. Nosirov 41; tel. (372) 24-90-55; f. 1996; campaigns for the establishment of social justice and construction of a state based on the rule of law; registration revoked 2001; Leader ABDURAKHMON KARIMOV.

Party of Economic Reforms (Partiya ekonomicheskikh reform): 734000 Dushanbe; f. 2005; supports establishment of a market economy on the basis of democratic principles; aims to reduce poverty, undertake privatization and increase foreign investment; Chair. OLIMJON BOBOYEV; c. 1,000 mems (2005).

Party of Popular Unity and Accord (PPUA): 734000 Dushanbe; f. 1994; represents interests of northern Tajikistan; banned 1998; Leader ABDUMALIK ABDULLOJONOV.

People's Democratic Party of Tajikistan (PDPT) (Xizbi Xalkii Demokratii Tochikiston): 734000 Dushanbe, Xiyoboni Rudaki 107; tel. (372) 221-05-45; fax (372) 21-25-36; e-mail admin@hhdt.tj; internet www.tribun.tj; f. 1994; campaigns for a united and secular state; Chair. EMOMALI SH. RAKHMON; First Dep. Chair. SAFAR SAFAROV; 100,000 mems (2008).

Social Democratic Party of Tajikistan (SDPT/KhSDT): 734000 Dushanbe, Xiyoboni Rudaki 81/49; tel. (372) 23-47-40; internet www.hsdt-tj.org; f. 1998; registered 2003; fmrly Justice and Progress of Tajikistan; Chair. RAKHMATULLO KH. ZOYIROV; 5,000 mems (Dec. 2004).

Socialist Party of Tajikistan: 734000 Dushanbe, Xiyoboni Rudaki 137; tel. (372) 34-77-11 (officially registered faction led by A. Gaf-

TAJIKISTAN

forov); tel. (372) 27-39-59 (unregistered faction led by M. Narziyev); f. 1996; split into two factions in 2003, only one of which was registered by the Ministry of Justice; Chairmen ABDUKHALIM GAFFOROV (Chair. of faction registered by the Ministry of Justice), MIRKHUSEYN NARZIYEV (Chair. of unregistered faction); 15,000 mems (2003).

Union and Development Party (Hizb-i Ittihod va Taraqqiyot—Taraqqiyot): 734000 Dushanbe; f. 2000; unregistered; fmrly a faction of the Democratic Party of Tajikistan; Chair. SULTON KUVVATOV; 3,000 mems (2001).

Unity Party (Hizb-i-Vahdat): 734000 Dushanbe; f. 2001; unregistered; Leader HIKMATULLO SAIDOV.

The transnational militant Islamist **Hizb-ut-Tahrir al-Islami** (Party of Islamic Liberation—Hizb-ut-Tahrir) was believed to be operative in Tajikistan. As in neighbouring states, the organization was banned in Tajikistan, and a number of people have received gaol sentences for their alleged membership of the group, despite its stated intention of using only peaceful means to pursue its goals, notably the restoration of a caliphate.

Diplomatic Representation

EMBASSIES IN TAJIKISTAN

Afghanistan: 734000 Dushanbe, Kuchai Pushkin 34; tel. (372) 21-67-35; fax (372) 51-00-96; e-mail afghanemintj@yahoo.com; Ambassador SAYED MUHAMMAD KHAIRKHA.

Azerbaijan: 734000 Dushanbe, Kuchai Farhor 1; tel. (372) 27-11-90; fax (372) 27-66-51; e-mail dushanbe@mission.mfa.gov.az; internet www.azembassy.tj; Ambassador MAGERRAM ABYSH OGLŬ ĀLIYEV.

China, People's Republic: 734002 Dushanbe, Xiyoboni Rudaki 143; tel. (372) 24-20-07; fax (372) 51-00-24; e-mail chinaemb_tj@mfa.gov.cn; internet tj.china-embassy.org; Ambassador ZUO XUELIANG.

France: 734025 Dushanbe, Kuchai Rakhimi 17; tel. (372) 21-78-55; fax (372) 51-00-82; e-mail ambassade.douchanbe@diplomatie.gouv.fr; internet ambafrance-tj.org; Ambassador HENRY ZIPPER DE FABIANI.

Germany: 734064 Dushanbe, Kuchai Somoni 59/1; tel. (372) 377-30-00; fax (372) 377-30-81; e-mail info@duschanbe.diplo.de; internet www.duschanbe.diplo.de; Ambassador DORIS HERTRAMPF.

India: 734025 Dushanbe, Kuchai Buxoro 45; tel. (372) 21-71-72; fax (372) 51-00-45; e-mail amb.dushanbe@mea.gov.in; internet www.indianembassy.tj; Ambassador ASITH KUMAR BHATTACHARJEE.

Iran: 734000 Dushanbe, Kuchai Boxtar 18; tel. (372) 21-00-74; fax (372) 51-00-89; e-mail iranembassy.tj@gmail.com; Ambassador ALIASGHAR SHEARDOOST.

Japan: 734000 Dushanbe, Kuchai X. Nazarov 80A; tel. (372) 21-39-70; fax (44) 600-54-78; e-mail embjpn@embjpn.tojikiston.com; Ambassador (vacant).

Kazakhstan: 734000 Dushanbe, Kuchai Xuseinzoda 31/1; tel. (37) 21-89-40; fax (37) 251-01-08; e-mail dipmiskz7@tajnet.com; Chargé d'affaires AYTZHAN AYDASHEV.

Korea, Republic: 734000 Dushanbe, Kuchai Ghani Abdullo 61; fax (37) 221-24-23; e-mail tjkorem@mofat.go.kr; internet tjk.mofat.go.kr; Chargé d'affaires a.i. RO SUNG-MIN.

Kyrgyzstan: 734000 Dushanbe, Kuchai Said-Nusur 56A; tel. and fax (37) 224-26-11; e-mail info@kgembassy.tj; internet www.kgembassy.tj; Ambassador URMAT SARALAYEV (designate).

Pakistan: 734000 Dushanbe, Kuchai Azizbekov 20A; tel. (372) 27-62-55; fax (372) 21-17-29; e-mail parepdushanbe_taj@yahoo.com; internet www.mofa.gov.pk/tajikistan; Ambassador KHALID USMAN QAISER.

Russia: 734026 Dushanbe, Kuchai Abu Ali ibni Sino 29/31; tel. (372) 35-70-65; fax (372) 35-88-06; e-mail rambtadjik@rambler.ru; internet www.rusemb.tj; Ambassador YURII F. POPOV.

Saudi Arabia: Dushanbe.

Turkey: 734019 Dushanbe, Xiyoboni Rudaki 17/2; tel. (372) 21-00-36; fax (372) 51-00-12; e-mail turemdus@tajik.net; internet dushanbe.emb.mfa.gov.tr; Ambassador MEHMET MUNIS DIRIK.

Turkmenistan: 734000 Dushanbe, Kuchai Chexov 22; tel. and fax (372) 21-68-84; e-mail embturkm@tjinter.com; Ambassador NOKERGULY ATAGULYEV.

United Kingdom: 734002 Dushanbe, Kuchai M. Tursunzoda 65; tel. (372) 24-22-21; fax (372) 27-17-26; e-mail dushanbe.reception@fco.gov.uk; internet ukintajikistan.fco.gov.uk; Ambassador TREVOR CHARLES MOORE.

USA: 734019 Dushanbe, Xiyoboni I. Somoni 109A; tel. (372) 29-20-00; fax (372) 29-20-50; e-mail usembassydushanbe@state.gov; internet dushanbe.usembassy.gov; Ambassador KENNETH GROSS.

Uzbekistan: 734003 Dushanbe, Ozodi Zanon 9; tel. (372) 24-76-57; fax (372) 28-99-03; e-mail ruzintaj@rambler.ru; Ambassador SHOQOSIM I. SHOISLOMOV.

Judicial System

Chairman of the Constitutional Court: M. A. MAHMUDOV, 734025 Dushanbe, Kuchai Boxtar 48; tel. (372) 21-61-96; fax (372) 21-29-28; internet www.constcourt.tj.

Chairman of the Supreme Court: NASRATULLO ABDULLOYEV, 734018 Dushanbe, Xiyoboni N. Karabayev 1; tel. (372) 33-48-21; fax (372) 33-93-69.

Chairman of the Supreme Economic Court: AMIRKHOJA GOIBNAZAROV, 734000 Dushanbe, Kuchai F. Niyazi 37; tel. (372) 21-15-58.

Prosecutor-General: BOBOJON BOBOKHONOV, 734000 Dushanbe, Kuchai Abu Ali ibni Sino 126; tel. (372) 35-19-72.

Religion

ISLAM

The majority of Tajiks are adherents of Islam and are mainly Sunnis (Hanafi school). Many of the Pamiri peoples, however, are Isma'ilis (followers of the Aga Khan), a Shi'ite sect. Under the Soviet regime the Muslims of Tajikistan were subject to the Muslim Board of Central Asia and a muftiate, both of which were based in Tashkent, Uzbekistan. The senior Muslim cleric in Tajikistan was the *qazi* (supreme judge). In 1992 the incumbent *qazi* fled to Afghanistan, and in 1993 the Government appointed an independent *mufti* (expert in Islamic law). The Tajikistani Government, however, abolished the post of *mufti* in 1996, following the murder of the incumbent, and established a Council of Islamic Scholars (or *ulema*), as the highest Islamic religious authority in the country.

Council of Islamic Scholars (Ulema): 734000 Dushanbe; Chair. QARI AMANULLOH NEMATZADE.

CHRISTIANITY

Most of the minority Christian population is Slav, the main denomination being the Russian Orthodox Church. There are some Protestant and other groups.

Roman Catholic Church

The Church is represented in Tajikistan by a Mission, established in September 1997. There were 314 adherents at 31 December 2007.

Superior: Rev. CARLOS AVILA, 734006 Dushanbe, Xiyoboni Titova 21/10; tel. (372) 26-75-17; fax (372) 26-76-63; e-mail carlosavila@ive.org; internet www.catholic.tj.

The Russian Orthodox Church (Moscow Patriarchate)

The Church in Tajikistan comes under the jurisdiction of the Eparchy of Tashkent and Central Asia, based in Uzbekistan and headed by the Metropolitan of Tashkent and Central Asia, VLADIMIR (IKIM).

JUDAISM

In the late 2000s there were an estimated 350 Jews in Dushanbe. In 2008 the only synagogue remaining in Tajikistan was demolished by order of the Government, which planned to construct state buildings on its site. A new synagogue was opened elsewhere in Dushanbe in May 2009.

Leader of the Religious Society of Jews of Tajikistan: Rabbi MIHAIL ABURAHMANOV, 734001 Dushanbe, Kuchai N. Xikmata 26; tel. (372) 21-76-58.

The Press

In 2000 there were four national newspapers. In 1996 two daily newspapers and 73 non-daily newspapers and 11 periodicals were published in Tajikistan, although by 2010 all the daily newspapers had ceased publication.

PRINCIPAL NEWSPAPERS

Adabiyet va sanat (Literature and Art): 734001 Dushanbe, Kuchai I. Somoni 8; tel. (372) 24-57-39; f. 1959; weekly; organ of Union of Writers of Tajikistan and Ministry of Culture; in Tajik; Editor GULNAZAR KELDI; circ. 4,000.

Biznes i Politika (Business and Politics): 734025 Dushanbe, Kuchai M. Tursunzoda 30; tel. (372) 23-52-50; e-mail b_p@rambler

.ru; f. 1992; weekly; in Russian; Editor-in-Chief U. RAHMON; circ. 10,000.

Charxi Gardun (Wheel of Fortune): 734016 Dushanbe, Xiyoboni S. Sherozi 16; tel. (372) 33-56-72; e-mail info@gazeta.tj; internet www.gazeta.tj; f. 1996; weekly; in Tajik; general; Editor-in-Chief AKBARALI SATTOROV; circ. 6,000 (2009).

Daijest Press (Press Digest): 734016 Dushanbe, Xiyoboni S. Sherozi 16; tel. (372) 238-53-47; e-mail gazeta@tojikiston.com; f. 1994; weekly; in Russian; overview of world press, incl. economics, popular culture; Editor-in-Chief AKBARALI SATTOROV; circ. 9,750 (2011).

Djavononi Tochikiston (Youth of Tajikistan): 734000 Dushanbe, Kuchai F. Niyazi 32; tel. (372) 23-38-01; f. 1930; weekly; organ of the Union of Youth of Tajikistan; in Tajik; Editor DAVLAT NAZRIYEV; circ. 3,000.

Farazh: Dushanbe; weekly; Chief Editor XURSHED ATOVULLOH.

Ittixod (Unity): 734000 Dushanbe, Xiyoboni Rudaki 137; tel. (372) 34-77-11; organ of the Socialist Party of Tajikistan (q.v.).

Jumhuriyat (Republic): 734018 Dushanbe, Xiyoboni S. Sherozi 16; tel. (372) 33-08-11; e-mail jumhuriyat@tojikiston.com; f. 1925; 3 a week; organ of the Govt and presidential administration; in Tajik; Editor-in-Chief KAMOL ABDURAHIMOV; circ. 8,000.

Kurer Tadzhikistana (Tajikistan Courier): 734018 Dushanbe, Xiyoboni S. Sherozi 16; tel. (372) 33-08-15; e-mail ttemirov@td.silk.org; weekly; independent; in Russian; Editor KH. YUSIPOV; circ. 40,000.

Millat (Nation): 734000 Dushanbe, Xiyoboni S. Sherozi 16/8; tel. (378) 81-11-97; e-mail millat@mail.ru; internet www.millat.tj; f. 2005; in Tajik; independent; Editor ADOLAT UMAROVII.

Minbari Xalk (People's Tribune): 734018 Dushanbe, Xiyoboni S. Sherozi 16; tel. (372) 33-79-07; fax (372) 33-72-10; organ of the People's Democratic Party of Tajikistan (q.v.); Editor MANSUR SAIFIDDINOV; circ. 20,000.

Najot (Salvation): 734000 Dushanbe, Kuchai Toktogul 55; tel. (372) 31-47-38; weekly; organ of the Islamic Rebirth Party of Tajikistan (q.v.); Editor-in-Chief HIKMATULLOH SAIFULLOHZODA.

Narodnaya Gazeta (People's Newspaper): 734018 Dushanbe, Xiyoboni S. Sherozi 16; tel. (372) 33-08-30; e-mail narodnaja@mail.ru; f. 1929; fmrly Kommunist Tadzhikistana (Tajik Communist); weekly; organ of the Govt; in Russian; Editor VLADIMIR VOROBIYEV; circ. 3,000.

Oila: 734018 Dushanbe, Xiyoboni S. Sherozi 16; tel. (372) 33-32-51; e-mail gazeta@tajnet.com; f. 2000; weekly; independent; Editor-in-Chief FIRUZA SATTORI.

Omuzgor (Teacher): 734000 Dushanbe, Kuchai Aini 45; tel. (372) 21-63-36; f. 1932; weekly; organ of the Ministry of Education; in Tajik; Editor-in-Chief SAMIULLO SAIFULLOYEV; circ. 3,000.

Ozodagon (The Independent): Dushanbe; weekly; Editor ZAFAR SUFIEV.

Paykon (Arrowhead): 734000 Dushanbe; internet paikon.wordpress.com; weekly newspaper; Editor-in-Chief JUMABOY TOLIBOV.

Sadoi Mardum (The Voice of the People): 734018 Dushanbe, Xiyoboni S. Sherozi 16; tel. (372) 33-89-22; e-mail sadoimardum@yandex.ru; f. 1991; 3 a week; organ of the legislature; in Tajik; Chief Editor JUMAHON NABOTOV; circ. 8,000.

Tojikiston (Tajikistan): 734018 Dushanbe, Xiyoboni S. Sherozi 16; tel. (372) 34-94-11; e-mail nt@tajnet.com; f. 1938; weekly; social and political; in Tajik; Editor-in-Chief SHARIF HAMDAMOV; circ. (annual) 9,000.

Tribun.tj: 731000 Dushanbe, Xiyoboni Rudaki 107; tel. (372) 21-05-45; fax (372) 24-27-59; e-mail tribun.tj@mail.ru; internet www.tribun.tj; f. 2005; daily; online only; in Russian; organ of the People's Democratic Party of Tajikistan.

Vechernii Dushanbe (Dunshanbe Evening News): 734018 Dushanbe, Xiyoboni S. Sherozi 16; tel. (372) 33-08-15; fax (372) 33-30-25; e-mail anush@tajnet.com; f. 1968; weekly; social and political; in Russian; Editor-in-Chief AKBARALI SATTOROV.

ViD—Den za Dnem (Day After Day): 734018 Dushanbe, Xiyoboni S. Sherozi 16; tel. (372) 38-53-84; general; Editor-in-Chief AKBARALI SATTOROV.

Xalk ovozi (Voice of the People): 734018 Dushanbe, Xiyoboni S. Sherozi 18; tel. (372) 33-05-04; f. 1929; 3 a week; organ of the President; in Uzbek; Editor I. MUKHSINOV; circ. 8,600.

Zindagi (Life): 734000 Dushanbe; f. 2004; weekly; in Tajik; independent; politics; Editor-in-Chief KHURSHED ATOVULLO.

PRINCIPAL PERIODICALS

Monthly, unless otherwise indicated.

Adab: 734025 Dushanbe, Kuchai Chexov 13; tel. (372) 23-49-36; organ of the Ministry of Education; in Tajik; Editor SH. SHOKIRZODA; circ. (annual) 24,000.

Avitsenna: 734018 Dushanbe, Xiyoboni S. Sherozi 16; tel. (372) 34-34-44; e-mail gazeta@tojikiston.com; weekly; in Russian; medicine; Editor-in-Chief AKBARALI SATTOROV.

Bunyod-i Adab (Culture Fund): 734000 Dushanbe; f. 1996 to foster cultural links among the country's Persian-speaking peoples; weekly; Editor ASKAR KHAKIM.

Djashma (Spring): 734018 Dushanbe, Xiyoboni S. Sherozi 16; tel. (372) 33-08-48; f. 1986; journal of the Ministry of Culture; for children; Editor KAMOL NASRULLO; circ. (annual) 10,000.

Farxang (Culture): 734003 Dushanbe, Xiyoboni Rudaki 124; tel. (372) 24-02-39; f. 1991; journal of the Culture Fund and Ministry of Culture; in Tajik; Editor-in-Chief J. AKOBIR; circ. 15,000.

Ilm va khayot (Science and Life): 734025 Dushanbe, Xiyoboni Rudaki 34; tel. (372) 27-48-61; f. 1989; organ of the Academy of Sciences; popular science; Editor T. BOIBOBO; circ. (annual) 12,000.

Istikbol: 734018 Dushanbe, Xiyoboni S. Sherozi 16; tel. (372) 33-14-52; f. 1952; organ of the Ministry of Culture; in Tajik; Chief Editor L. KENJAYEVA; circ. (annual) 10,000.

Marifat: 734024 Dushanbe, Kuchai Aini 45; tel. (372) 23-42-84; organ of the Ministry of Education; in Tajik; Editor O. BOZOROV; circ. (annual) 40,000.

Pamir: 734001 Dushanbe, Kuchai I. Somoni 8; tel. (372) 24-56-56; f. 1949; journal of the Union of Writers of Tajikistan; fiction; in Russian; Editor-in-Chief BORIS PSHENICHNYI.

Sadoi shark (Voice of the East): 734001 Dushanbe, Kuchai I. Somoni 8; tel. (372) 24-56-79; f. 1927; journal of the Union of Writers of Tajikistan; fiction; in Tajik; Editor URUN KUKHZOD; circ. 1,600.

NEWS AGENCIES

Asia-Plus TV-Radio Company: 734002 Dushanbe, Kuchai Boxtar 35/1, 8th Floor; tel. (372) 21-72-20; fax (372) 21-78-63; e-mail agency@asiaplus.tj; internet www.news.tj; f. 2002; independent; reports in Tajik and Russian; Gen. Dir UMED BABAKHANOV.

Avesta News Agency: 734025 Dushanbe, Xiyoboni Sherozi 16A; tel. (372) 27-10-84; e-mail info@avesta.tj; internet www.avesta.tj; f. 2004; Dir ZAFAR ABDULLAYEV.

Khovar (East): 737025 Dushanbe, Xiyoboni Rudaki 40; tel. (372) 21-21-37; fax (372) 23-23-83; e-mail maktub@khovar.tj; internet www.khovar.tj; f. 1925; govt information agency; Dir SADRIDDIN SHAMSIDDINOV.

Varorud: 735700 Soghd Viloyat, Khujand, Kuchai Ferdovsi 123; tel. and fax (3422) 4-09-33; e-mail varorud@varorud.org; f. 2000; independent; Dir ILHOM JAMOLOV.

PRESS ASSOCIATION

Internews Network—Tajikistan: 734025 Dushanbe, Kuchai Ak. Rajabov 7/1/4; tel. (372) 21-99-33; fax (372) 21-99-34; e-mail reception@inewstj.org; internet www.internews.tj; f. 1995; non-governmental org.; provides support and funding to media organizations, and in the training of journalists; Country Dir CHARLES RICE.

Publishers

Adib (Writer): 734018 Dushanbe, Xiyoboni Karabaev 17A; tel. (372) 33-84-35; fax (372) 33-19-73; e-mail karimov-adib@mail.ru; state-owned; publishes in Tajik and Russian; fiction, incl. poetry, and non-fiction, incl. books on Tajikistani and Central Asian culture.

Donish (Knowledge): 734000 Dushanbe, Xiyoboni Akademiya Nauk 33; state-owned; Russian and Tajik; non-fiction, incl. geography, literature, history, and art; associated with the Academy of Sciences.

Irfon (Light of Knowledge) Publishing House: 734018 Dushanbe, Kuchai N. Karabayev 17; tel. (372) 33-39-06; e-mail irfon_company@mail.ru; f. 1925; politics, social sciences, economics, agriculture, medicine and technology; Dir JURA SHARIFOV; Editor-in-Chief ABDURAHMON OLIMOV.

Maorif va Farxang (Education and Culture) Publishing House: 734018 Dushanbe, Kuchai N. Karabayev 17; tel. and fax (372) 33-93-97; e-mail najmidin@netrt.org; f. 1958; educational, academic; Gen. Dir NAJMIDDIN ZAYNIDDINOV.

Sarredaksiyai Ilmii Entsiklopediyai Millii Tajik (Tajik National Scientific Encyclopaedia) Publishing House: 731000 Dushanbe, Kuchai Aini 126; tel. (372) 25-81-55; e-mail encyclopedia@yahoo.com; f. 1969; Editor-in-Chief A. QURBONOV.

Sharki Ozod Publishing House: 734018 Dushanbe, Xiyoboni S. Sherozi 16; tel. (372) 34-94-11; e-mail tadjikis@tajnet.com; state-owned; Dir MANZURHON DODOHONOV.

Surushan Publishing House: 734025 Dushanbe, Xiyoboni Rudaki 37; tel. and fax (372) 21-54-62; e-mail surushan@net.org; f. 1997; literary fiction, educational; Dir NURIDDIN ZAYNIDDINOV.

TAJIKISTAN

Broadcasting and Communications

TELECOMMUNICATIONS

Babilon-Mobil (Babilon-M): 734012 Dushanbe, Kuchai I. Somoni 8; tel. (44) 600-10-10; fax (4) 600-20-20; e-mail info@babilon-m.tj; internet www.babilon-m.com; f. 2002; mobile cellular telecommunications.

Beeline TJ: Dushanbe; e-mail pr@beeline.tj; internet www.beeline.tj; f. 2006; fmrly Tacom; 60% owned by VympelKom-Bilain (Russia); mobile cellular telecommunications services.

Indigo Somonkom (Tcell): 735700 Soghd Viloyat, Khujand, 50 let SSSR 2; tel. (3422) 6-07-50; internet www.somoncom.com; f. 1998; majority share owned by TeliaSonera (Sweden); provides mobile cellular telecommunications in northern regions, particularly Soghd Viloyat; Chair. of Bd of Dirs Mamajon Hamidov; 130,000 subscribers (2006).

Indigo Tajikistan (Tcell): 734000 Dushanbe, Kuchai M. Tursunzoda 23; tel. (372) 23-21-21; fax (372) 23-21-23; e-mail sales@indigo.tajnet.com; internet www.indigo.tj; f. 2001; majority share owned by TeliaSonera (Sweden); mobile cellular telecommunications in central and southern regions of Tajikistan.

MLT (Mobile Lines of Tajikistan): 734025 Dushanbe, Xiyoboni Rudaki 57; tel. (372) 21-42-24; internet www.mlt.tj; f. 2001; fmrly TT Mobile; mobile cellular telecommunications.

Tajiktelecom: 734025 Dushanbe, Xiyoboni Rudaki 57A; tel. (372) 21-31-78; fax (372) 23-21-19; e-mail ttelecom@rs.tj; internet www.tajiktelecom.tj; f. 1996; national telecommunications operator; Dir-Gen. Gulmahmad Kayumov.

BROADCASTING

Regulatory Authority

State Committee for Television and Radio Broadcasting: 734000 Dushanbe; Chair. Asadullo K. Rakhmonov.

Radio

State TV-Radio Broadcasting Co of Tajikistan: 734025 Dushanbe, Kuchai Chapayev 31; tel. (372) 27-75-27; fax (372) 21-34-95; e-mail soro@ctvrtj.td.silk.org; Chair. Abdodzhabbor Rakhmonov.

Asia-Plus: 734018 Dushanbe, Xiyoboni Saadi Sherozi, 13th Floor; tel. and fax (44) 600-71-07; e-mail manager@asiaplus.tj; internet www.asiaplusradio.tj; f. 2002; radio and television station; broadcasts 24 hours a day in Russian and Tajik; Gen. Dir Umed Babakhanov.

Tajik Radio: 734025 Dushanbe, Kuchai Chapayev 31; tel. (372) 27-65-69; broadcasts in Russian, Tajik and Uzbek.

Tiroz: 735716 Soghd Viloyat, Khujand, Mikroraion 27, Kuchai Tiroz 9; tel. (3422) 5-32-94; fax (3422) 5-66-89; e-mail radio@tiroz.org; internet www.tiroz.org; f. 2001; broadcasts music and entertainment and other programming on FM to much of Soghd Viloyat; Dir Khurshed Ulmasov.

Television

State TV-Radio Broadcasting Co of Tajikistan: 734025 Dushanbe, Kuchai Chapayev 31; tel. (372) 27-75-27; fax (372) 21-34-95; e-mail soro@ctvrtj.td.silk.org; Chair. Abdodzhabbor Rakhmonov.

Poitaxt: 734013 Dushanbe, Kuchai Azizbekov 20; tel. (372) 23-26-29; independent; Dir Rakhmon Ostonov.

Tajik Television (TTV): 734013 Dushanbe, Kuchai Behzod 7; tel. (372) 22-43-57.

TV Safina: 734000 Dushanbe, Kuchai Buxoro 43; tel. (372) 27-78-07; fax (372) 27-79-05; e-mail info@safina.tj; internet www.safina.tj; f. 2005; state-owned national TV channel; Dir Lutfullo Davlatov.

Finance

(cap. = capital; res = reserves; dep. = deposits; brs = branches; m. = million; amounts in somoni, unless otherwise stated)

BANKING

Central Bank

National Bank of the Republic of Tajikistan (Bonki Millii Tochikiston): 734003 Dushanbe, Xiyoboni Rudaki 107A; tel. (44) 600-32-27; fax (44) 600-32-35; e-mail info@nbt.tj; internet www.nbt.tj; f. 1991; cap. 0.8m., res 25.4m., dep. 604.8m. (Oct. 2003); Chair. Sharif Rahimzoda.

State Savings Bank

Amonatbonk: 734018 Dushanbe, Kuchai Loxuti 24; tel. (372) 21-70-81; fax (372) 27-38-43; e-mail info@amonatbonk.tj; internet www.amonatbonk.tj; f. 1991; fmrly br. of USSR Sberbank; licensed by presidential decree and not subject to the same controls as the commercial and trading banks; Chair. of Bd Gulnora Hasanova; 58 brs, 480 sub-brs.

Other Banks

In June 2005 President Rakhmonov announced the removal of all restrictions on the activities of foreign banks in Tajikistan. There were reported to be 16 commercial banks in operation in Tajikistan in early 2005, including the following:

Agroinvestbank: 734018 Dushanbe, Xiyoboni S. Sherozi 21; tel. (372) 233-21-14; fax (372) 236-51-66; e-mail info@agroinvestbank.tj; internet www.agroinvestbank.tj; f. 1992; fmrly Agroprombank; open jt-stock co; cap. US $58.3m., res $10.9m., dep. $166.0m. (Jan. 2010); Chair. Niyozmurod M. Saidmurodov; 61 brs.

Orienbank: 734001 Dushanbe, Xiyoboni Rudaki 95/1; tel. (372) 21-05-68; fax (372) 21-18-77; e-mail info@orienbank.com; internet www.orienbank.com; f. 1922; cap. 60m., res 25m., dep. 216m. (Aug. 2008); commercial bank; Chair. of Bd Hasan Asadullozoda; Chair. of Bank Council Shermalik Malikov; 32 brs.

Tajbank: 734064 Dushanbe, Kuchai I. Somoni 59/1; tel. (372) 27-46-54.

Tajprombank (Tajik Joint-Stock Bank for Reconstruction and Development): 734025 Dushanbe, Rudaki 22; tel. (372) 21-27-20; fax (372) 21-25-85; e-mail tpb@tjinter.com; internet www.tajprombank.com; cap. US $1m., res $3m., dep. $4m.; Chair. Dzhamshed Ziyayev; 8 brs.

Tojik Sodiot Bonk (Bank for Foreign Economic Affairs of the Republic of Tajikistan): 734012 Dushanbe, Kuchai X. Dexlavi 4; tel. (372) 21-59-52; fax (372) 21-47-38; e-mail sham@sodirotbonk.com; f. 1990 as a br. of USSR Vneshekonombank; renamed as Tojiksodirotbonk in 1999, and as above in 2009; Chair. I. L. Lalbekov; 10 brs.

COMMODITY EXCHANGE

Tajik Republican Commodity Exchange 'Navruz': 734001 Dushanbe, Kuchai Orjonikidze 37; tel. (372) 23-48-74; fax (372) 27-03-91; f. 1991; Chair. Suleyman Chulebayev.

INSURANCE

Muin Insurance Co: 734025 Dushanbe, Kuchai Sh. Rustaveli 16/1; tel. (372) 21-32-80; fax (372) 21-72-09; e-mail info@muin.tj; internet www.muin.tj; f. 1992; Dir-Gen. Sharifjon Ishakov.

Orien Insurance: 734001 Dushanbe, Xiyoboni Rudaki 100; tel. (44) 600-30-71; fax (372) 21-12-30; e-mail info@orieninsurance.tj; internet www.orieninsurance.tj; f. 2004; life and non-life; Dir Iskandar Kh. Sharipov.

Tojiksurguta State Insurance Co: 734025 Dushanbe, Kuchai Chexov 4A; tel. (372) 21-75-07.

Trud Insurance Co: 734000 Dushanbe, Kuchai Bekzod 70; tel. (372) 27-24-24; fax (372) 21-72-21; e-mail info@trud.tj; internet www.trud.tj; f. 2004; life and non-life.

Trade and Industry

CHAMBER OF COMMERCE

Chamber of Commerce and Industry of the Republic of Tajikistan: 734012 Dushanbe, Kuchai Valamatzade 21; tel. (372) 21-52-84; fax (372) 21-14-80; e-mail chamber@tpp.tj; internet www.tpp.tj; f. 1960; brs in Khujant, Qurgonteppa, Khorog, and Chamber of Services in Dushanbe; Chair. Sharif S. Saidov.

INDUSTRIAL ASSOCIATION

Tajikvneshtorg (Tajik External Trade) Industrial Asscn: 734035 Dushanbe, Xiyoboni Rudaki 25, POB 48; tel. (372) 23-29-03; fax (372) 22-81-20; f. 1988; co-ordinates trade with foreign countries in a wide range of goods; Pres. Abdurakhmon Mukhtashov.

EMPLOYERS' ORGANIZATION

National Asscn of Small and Medium-Sized Businesses of Tajikistan: 734000 Dushanbe, Kuchai Bofanda 9; tel. (372) 27-79-78; fax (372) 21-17-26; f. 1993 with govt support; independent org.; Chair. Matljuba Uljabaeva.

UTILITIES

Electricity

Barqi Tojik (Tajik Electricity): 734000 Dushanbe, Kuchai I. Somoni 64; tel. (372) 35-86-68; fax (372) 35-86-92; e-mail barkitojik@tajnet.com; Gen. Dir Sanat Rakhimov.

TAJIKISTAN

Pamir Energy Co (PamirEnergy): 736100 Kuhistoni Badakhshon, Khorog; tel. (352) 22-33-83; fax (352) 22-25-19; e-mail daler.jumaev@pamirenergy.com; f. 2002; jt venture between Governments of Tajikistan and Switzerland, the Aga Khan Fund for Economic Development, the International Finance Corpn and the International Development Association to provide electricity to Kuhistoni Badakhshon; Gen. Dir DALER JUMAYEV.

Gas

Dushanbegaz: 734000 Dushanbe; tel. (372) 27-89-28; supplies gas to Dushanbe City.

Soghdgaz: 735700 Soghd Viloyat, Khujand, 20 Kvartal; tel. (3422) 2-53-95; fax (3422) 4-35-16; supplies gas to Soghd Viloyat.

Tojikgaz: 734012 Dushanbe, Xiyoboni Rudaki 6; tel. (372) 21-66-68; fax (372) 21-28-16; state-controlled gas utility co.

TRADE UNIONS

Federation of Trade Unions: 734012 Dushanbe, Xiyoboni Rudaki 20; tel. (372) 23-17-79; fax (372) 23-25-06; f. 1926; present name adopted 1992; Chair. MURODALI S. SALIKHOV; 1.3m. mems.

Transport

RAILWAYS

There are few railways in Tajikistan. Lines link the major centres of the country with the railway network of Uzbekistan, connecting Khujand to the Farg'ona (Fergana) valley lines, and the cotton-growing centre of Qurgonteppa to Termiz. A new line, between the town of Isfara, in Soghd Viloyat, and Xavast, in Uzbekistan, was opened in 1995 and in 1997 a passenger route between Dushanbe and Volgograd, Russia, was inaugurated. The first section of a new line between Qurgonteppa and Kulob, in the south-west of Tajikistan, was inaugurated in 1998. In October 2002 a route from Kulob to Astrakhan, Russia, was opened. In 2009 the total length of the rail network in use was 679.9 km.

Tajik Railways: 734012 Dushanbe, M. Nazarshoeva 35; tel. (372) 21-60-59; fax (372) 21-83-34; e-mail tajrwv@rs.tj; Dir AMONULLO KH. KHUKUMATULLO.

ROADS

In mid-2002 Tajikistan's road network totalled an estimated 30,000 km, including 13,747 km of highways. The principal highway links the northern city of Khujand, across the Anzob Pass (3,372 m), with the capital, Dushanbe, continuing to Khorog (Kuhistoni Badakhshon), before wending through the Pamir Mountains, to the east and north, to Osh, Kyrgyzstan, across the Akbaytal Pass (4,655 m). This arterial route exhibits problems common to much of the country's land transport: winter weather is likely to cause the road to be closed by snow for up to eight months of the year. In 2000 Tajikistan and the Asian Development Bank signed a memorandum of understanding for the rehabilitation of the road linking Dushanbe to the south-western cities of Qurgonteppa and Kulob. In the same year a road linking eastern Tajikistan with the People's Republic of China was completed, giving Tajikistan access to the Karakorum highway, which connects China and Pakistan.

CIVIL AVIATION

The main international airport is at Dushanbe, and there is also a major airport at Khujand. The country is linked to cities in Russia and other former Soviet republics, and to a growing number of destinations in Europe and Asia.

TajikAir: 734006 Dushanbe, Kuchai Titova 32/1; tel. (372) 21-21-45; fax (372) 21-86-85; e-mail t.dadadjanova@tajikairlines.com; internet www.tajikair.tj; f. 1924; state-owned; operates flights to 20 international destinations; Dir MUZAFAR ISHAKOV.

Tourism

There was little tourism in Tajikistan even before the 1992–97 civil war. There is some spectacular mountain scenery, hitherto mainly visited by climbers, and, particularly in the Farg'ona (Fergana) valley, in the north of the country, there are sites of historical interest, notably the city of Khujand.

State Committee for Youth, Sports and Tourism: 734000 Dushanbe; f. 2006.

Defence

A Tajikistani Ministry of Defence was established in September 1992; in December it was announced that Tajikistan's national armed forces were to be formed on the basis of the Tajik People's Front and other paramilitary units supporting the Government. Integration of United Tajik Opposition force members into the Tajikistani armed forces took place from 1998. Military service lasts for 24 months. As assessed at November 2010, the armed forces numbered 8,800, comprising an army of 7,300 and an air force of 1,500. There were also 7,500 paramilitary troops, comprising members of the National Guard and of forces answerable to the Ministry of Internal Affairs. Tajikistan became a member of the North Atlantic Treaty Organization's 'Partnership for Peace' programme of military co-operation in February 2002.

Defence Expenditure: Budgeted at 367m. somoni in 2010.

Chief of General Staff: RAMIL NODIROV.

Commander of the Air Force: RAXMONALI D. SAFARALIYEV.

Education

Education is officially compulsory for nine years, to be undertaken between seven and 17 years of age. Primary education begins at seven years of age and lasts for four years. Secondary education, beginning at the age of 11, lasts for as much as seven years, comprising a first cycle of five years and a second of two years. In 2006/07 total enrolment at primary schools included 97% of children in the relevant age-group (males 99%; females 95%). In that year total enrolment at secondary schools included 81% of children in the relevant age-group (males 87%; females 75%).

The majority of pupils receive their education in Tajik. Following the adoption of Tajik as the state language, greater emphasis was placed in the curriculum on Tajik language and literature, including classical Persian literature. However, in 2003 President Emomali Rakhmonov announced that the compulsory teaching of Russian was to be reintroduced to schools from September of that year.

In 2009/10 there were 157,800 students enrolled at 36 institutes of higher education. In 2000 the Presidents of Kazakhstan, Kyrgyzstan and Tajikistan co-signed a charter of foundation for a new University of Central Asia, which was to be established in Khorog (in Kuhistoni Badakhshon Autonomous Viloyat) and administered by the Aga Khan Development Network, based in Geneva, Switzerland. Budgetary expenditure on education by all levels of government was 845.4m. somoni (14.9% of total government budgetary expenditure) in 2009.

TANZANIA

Introductory Survey

LOCATION, CLIMATE, LANGUAGE, RELIGION, FLAG, CAPITAL

The United Republic of Tanzania consists of Tanganyika, on the African mainland, and the nearby islands of Zanzibar and Pemba. Tanganyika lies on the east coast of Africa, bordered by Uganda and Kenya to the north, by Rwanda, Burundi and the Democratic Republic of the Congo (formerly Zaire) to the west, and by Zambia, Malawi and Mozambique to the south. Zanzibar and Pemba are in the Indian Ocean, about 40 km (25 miles) off the coast of Tanganyika, north of Dar es Salaam. The climate varies with altitude, ranging from tropical in Zanzibar and on the coast and plains to semi-temperate in the highlands. The official languages are Swahili and English and there are numerous tribal languages. There are Muslim, Christian and Hindu communities. Many Africans follow traditional beliefs. The national flag (proportions 2 by 3) comprises two triangles, one of green (with its base at the hoist and its apex in the upper fly) and the other of blue (with its base in the fly and its apex at the lower hoist), separated by a broad, yellow-edged black diagonal stripe, from the lower hoist to the upper fly. The administrative capital is Dodoma, although most government offices remain in Dar es Salaam, the commercial capital.

CONTEMPORARY POLITICAL HISTORY

Historical Context

Tanganyika became a German colony in 1884, and was later incorporated into German East Africa, which also included present-day Rwanda and Burundi. In 1918, at the end of the First World War, the German forces in the area surrendered, and Tanganyika was placed under a League of Nations mandate, with the United Kingdom as the administering power. In 1946 Tanganyika became a UN Trust Territory, still under British rule. At a general election in September 1960 the Tanganyika African National Union (TANU) won 70 of the 71 seats in the National Assembly, and the party's leader, Dr Julius Nyerere, became Chief Minister. Internal self-government was achieved in May 1961, when Nyerere became Prime Minister. Tanganyika became independent, within the Commonwealth, on 9 December 1961, but Nyerere resigned as Prime Minister in January 1962, in order to devote himself to the direction of TANU. He was succeeded as premier by Rashidi Kawawa. On 9 December 1962, following elections in November, Tanganyika became a republic, with Nyerere as the country's first President. Kawawa became Vice-President. Zanzibar (including the island of Pemba), a British protectorate since 1890, became an independent sultanate in December 1963. Following an armed uprising by the Afro-Shirazi Party (ASP) in January 1964, the Sultan was deposed and a republic proclaimed. The new Government signed an Act of Union with Tanganyika in April, thus creating the United Republic. The union was named Tanzania in October, and a new Constitution was introduced in July 1965, which provided for a one-party state (although, until 1977, TANU and the ASP remained the respective official parties of mainland Tanzania and Zanzibar, and co-operated in affairs of state). Nyerere was elected President of the United Republic in September 1965, and was subsequently re-elected in 1970, 1975 and 1980.

Despite its incorporation into Tanzania, Zanzibar retained a separate administration, which ruthlessly suppressed all opposition. A separate Constitution for Zanzibar was adopted in October 1979, providing for a popularly elected President and a House of Representatives elected by delegates of the ruling party. The first elections to the 40-member Zanzibar House of Representatives were held in January 1980. Aboud Jumbe won an overwhelming majority at Zanzibar's first presidential election, held in October; however, mounting dissatisfaction among Zanzibaris concerning the union with Tanganyika culminated in the resignation, in January 1984, of Jumbe and three of his ministers. In April Ali Hassan Mwinyi, a former Zanzibari Minister of Natural Resources and Tourism, was elected unopposed as President of Zanzibar, winning 87.5% of the votes cast. A new Constitution for Zanzibar came into force in January 1985, providing for the House of Representatives to be directly elected by universal adult suffrage.

Meanwhile, in February 1977 TANU and the ASP were amalgamated to form Chama Cha Mapinduzi (CCM), the Revolutionary Party of Tanzania. In April the National Assembly approved a permanent Constitution for Tanzania; this provided for the election to the National Assembly of representatives from Zanzibar, in addition to those from the Tanzanian mainland. Major changes to the Constitution were approved by the National Assembly in October 1984, limiting the President's powers and increasing those of the National Assembly.

Domestic Political Affairs

President Nyerere retired in November 1985, and was succeeded by Mwinyi, who, as the sole candidate, had won 96% of the votes cast at a presidential election in October. Elections to the National Assembly were held on the same day, while at presidential and legislative elections in Zanzibar, also held in October, Idris Abdul Wakil (formerly Speaker of the Zanzibar House of Representatives) was elected President of Zanzibar to replace Mwinyi. Nyerere remained Chairman of the CCM until August 1990 when he resigned and Mwinyi was appointed in his place.

In early 1988 tension began to increase in Zanzibar, reflecting underlying rivalries between the inhabitants of the main island and those of the smaller island of Pemba, between Zanzibar's African and Arab populations, and between supporters and opponents of unity with Tanganyika. In January Wakil suspended the islands' Government, the Supreme Revolutionary Council, and assumed control of the armed forces from the office of his main rival, Chief Minister Seif Sharrif Hamad, following earlier claims by Wakil that a group of dissidents, including members of the Council, had been plotting the overthrow of his administration. Hamad was replaced later that month by Dr Omar Ali Juma and in May Hamad and six other officials were expelled from the CCM for allegedly opposing the party's aims and endangering Tanzanian unity.

In October 1990 concurrent parliamentary and presidential elections were held in Zanzibar. Wakil did not stand for re-election; the sole presidential candidate, Dr Salmin Amour, was elected as Wakil's successor by 97.7% of the votes cast. Amour subsequently reappointed Juma as Chief Minister of Zanzibar. At the end of October national parliamentary and presidential elections took place. Mwinyi, the sole candidate in the presidential election, was re-elected for a second term, taking 95.5% of the votes cast.

In February 1992 proposed constitutional amendments, which would establish a multi-party political system, were ratified by a special congress of the CCM, which stipulated that, in order to protect national unity, all new political organizations should command support in both Zanzibar and mainland Tanzania, and should be free of tribal, religious and racial bias. In May the Constitutions of both the United Republic and Zanzibar were amended to enshrine a multi-party system. Several political organizations were officially registered from mid-1992.

In October 1995 multi-party legislative elections were held for the first time, concurrently with presidential elections, both in Zanzibar and throughout the Tanzanian union. At elections on 22 October the CCM secured 26 of the 50 elective seats in the Zanzibari House of Representatives, while the Civic United Front (CUF, campaigning for increased Zanzibari autonomy) took 24 seats. Amour was re-elected President of the islands by 50.2% of the votes cast, only narrowly defeating Hamad, who represented the CUF. Amour appointed a new ruling council, with Dr Mohamed Gharib Bilali, formerly a government official, as Chief Minister. The CUF contested the election results, accusing the Zanzibari authorities of electoral malpractice and refusing to recognize the legitimacy of the new Amour administration, while party delegates initially declined to take up their seats in the House of Representatives. The Tanzanian national elections, on 29 October, were disrupted by a combination of apparent organizational chaos and further allegations by opposition parties of electoral fraud. Administrative inefficiency led to the cancellation of the election results in seven constituencies in

TANZANIA

Introductory Survey

Dar es Salaam; these polls were repeated in mid-November. The opposition parties, alleging that the CCM was manipulating the voting process, refused to re-run, withdrew their candidates from the presidential election, and unsuccessfully petitioned the High Court to declare all results null and void. The Government proceeded to publish the results, whereby the CCM won 186 of the 232 elective seats in the National Assembly, the CUF 24, the National Convention for Construction and Reform (NCCR—Mageuzi) 16, and Chama Cha Demokrasia na Maendeleo (Chadema) and the United Democratic Party (UDP) three seats each. Benjamin Mkapa, hitherto Minister of Science, Technology and Higher Education, was deemed to have been elected President, winning 61.8% of the votes cast. The former Minister of Home Affairs, Augustine Mrema, took 27.8% of the votes. President Mkapa was inaugurated in late November; Juma (hitherto Chief Minister of Zanzibar) was appointed Vice-President. Shortly afterwards Mkapa announced a new Cabinet, with Frederick Sumaye (formerly Minister of Agriculture) as Prime Minister.

In his election campaign Mkapa had pledged to tackle corruption in high public office, and appointed a special presidential commission which in December 1996 issued a report asserting that corruption was widespread in the public sector. In September a parliamentary select committee investigating bribery allegations against the Minister of Finance, Simon Mbilinyi, had published a report recommending that he be made accountable for having illegally granted tax exemptions. Mbilinyi subsequently resigned. In October Mrema unexpectedly won a parliamentary by-election in a Dar es Salaam constituency for NCCR—Mageuzi, of which he had become Chairman following his dismissal from Government in 1995; although his campaign had focused on financial impropriety in government, Mrema had recently been accused of having presented false evidence to the parliamentary select committee on corruption in order to undermine the Government's credibility.

In August 1998 a car bomb exploded outside the US embassy in Dar es Salaam (concurrently with a similar attack at the US mission in Nairobi, Kenya); 11 people were killed in Dar es Salaam and some 75 were injured. The attacks were believed to have been co-ordinated by international Islamist terrorists led by a Saudi-born dissident, Osama bin Laden, and the USA retaliated by launching air-strikes against targets in Afghanistan and Sudan. Four men were convicted of involvement in the bombings by a court in New York, USA, in May 2001 and were later sentenced to life imprisonment.

In April 1999 Mrema and his faction of NCCR—Mageuzi defected to the Tanzania Labour Party (TLP). Mrema initially assumed the chairmanship of the TLP, but in May he was banned by the High Court from holding any official post in that party. There was speculation that the death in October of former President Nyerere might give rise to increased pressure for a restructuring of the United Republic of Tanzania. This was, to some extent, reinforced by the release in December of the report of a committee charged with assessing public opinion on constitutional reform. While it found that some 96.3% of Zanzibaris and 84.8% of mainland Tanzanians favoured a 'two-tier' government for the United Republic, the committee itself recommended the establishment of a 'three-tier' system. In so doing it was adjudged by President Mkapa to have exceeded its mandate. In February 2000 the National Assembly approved draft legislation to amend the Constitution in accordance with citizens' recommendations as reported by the committee. Among these recommendations was one that the President should henceforth be elected by a majority vote.

At a presidential election held on 29 October 2000 Mkapa was re-elected as President, securing 71.7% of votes cast; Prof. Ibrahim Lipumba, the Chairman of the CUF, won 16.3% of the votes cast, Augustine Mrema 7.8% and John Cheyo 4.2%. The participation rate was 84%. In the following month the CUF and Chadema agreed to form a five-year alliance and field joint candidates for the presidential elections in both the United Republic of Tanzania and in Zanzibar. It was agreed that if either candidate (both from the CUF) won, the respective prime minister would be drawn from Chadema. Candidates from the TLP and NCCR—Mageuzi failed to secure the minimum 200 referees and thus were not allowed to stand for election. At legislative elections, held concurrently, the CCM secured 244 seats in the National Assembly. The largest opposition group to obtain representation was the CUF, with 15 seats; the three other opposition parties (Chadema, the TLP and the UDP) won four, three and two seats, respectively. The polls were declared by international observers to have been freely and fairly conducted. In November Mkapa appointed a new Cabinet, reappointing Frederick Sumaye as Prime Minister.

Tensions on Zanzibar

In marked contrast, presidential and legislative elections were also held in Zanzibar and Pemba on 29 October 2000, amid widespread accusations of electoral fraud. Voting in 16 of the islands' 50 constituencies was annulled owing to a lack of ballot papers and voter registration lists. The Zanzibar Electoral Commission (ZEC) announced that new polls would be held in the 16 constituencies (all areas where the CUF enjoyed strong support), and that counting for the presidential elections for both Zanzibar and the United Republic would be delayed until the new results were received. Opposition parties and Commonwealth electoral observers called for a full re-run of the elections, but this was rejected by the ZEC. Following a week of confusion and violent clashes between the police and opposition supporters, the repeated polls were held on 5 November. Accusations of electoral fraud persisted, and the participation rate was reported to be low. Following the poll, the CCM claimed that it had won 67% of the votes cast (thereby winning 34 seats in the House of Representatives). The CUF refused to recognize the results of the ballot. Despite the concerns of the opposition parties and international observers, the ZEC proclaimed Amani Abeid Karume of the CCM as President of Zanzibar. The CUF refused to recognize Karume as President and demanded that a repeat election be held within four months.

In April 2001 an estimated 60,000 supporters of 12 opposition parties gathered peacefully in Dar es Salaam to demand that the Government hold fresh elections in Zanzibar, draft a new Constitution for the United Republic and establish independent electoral commissions. A similar, peaceful demonstration in Zanzibar later that month was attended by an estimated 60,000–85,000 protesters. President Karume, however, continued to reject the opposition's demands. In May 11 members of the Zanzibar House of Representatives and five members of the National Assembly were dismissed from their respective legislatures for having boycotted three successive sittings—their actions were part of the CUF's ongoing refusal to recognize the 2000 election results. The Attorney-General rejected subsequent demands from the CUF for their reinstatement. By-elections were held on 15 May 2003, at which the CUF won every seat it contested (amounting to 15 in the National Assembly and 11 in the Zanzibar House of Representatives). CUF candidates were disqualified from contesting six seats in the House of Representatives; these were won by CCM candidates.

In June 2001 it emerged that, following the violence of the 2000 elections, the CCM and the CUF had been holding a series of secret negotiations intended to resolve the political impasse in Zanzibar. The negotiations concluded with the signing of a *muafaka* (peace accord) between the two parties in Zanzibar in October 2001. Shortly afterwards the State withdrew all legal cases related to the post-election demonstrations.

In accordance with the CCM-CUF accord signed in October 2001, amendments to the Zanzibari Constitution were approved by the House of Representatives in April 2002. The amendments provided for the restructuring of the electoral commission to include opposition representatives (duly appointed in October 2002), the creation of a permanent voters' register and the removal of legislation requiring a person to live in a particular area for five consecutive years in order to qualify as a voter. Also included were the introduction of the right to appeal against High Court decisions and the appointment of a separate director of public prosecutions for Zanzibar.

In late 2003 and early 2004 political tension in Zanzibar intensified ahead of the elections due in late 2005. Supporters of the CUF were keen to avoid a repetition of the irregularities that had marred the elections of 1995 and 2000. Zanzibaris were reportedly particularly anxious as, according to the prevailing custom of the United Republic, they were to elect the next President. However, following remarks from President Mkapa that this custom was not guaranteed by law, many Zanzibaris feared their marginalization. In November 2003 the CUF Chairman, Lipumba, threatened to obtain a court injunction blocking the 2005 elections unless the register of voters was completed in time, and in April 2004 the leader of the Democratic Party made a similar threat, stating his intention to sue the National Electoral Commission (NEC) and the ZEC unless both bodies were reformed to include members of parties other than the CCM and the CUF. Opposition supporters were also concerned that the Government's efforts to encourage mainlanders who had been living in Zanzibar for more than 10 years to register for

Zanzibari citizenship (thus making them eligible to vote in Zanzibar) constituted an attempt to manipulate voter registration in favour of the CCM. The Government, in contrast, deplored the circulation of leaflets throughout Zanzibar urging mainlanders to leave and alleged intimidation of mainlanders.

In early 2004 Islamism appeared to be exerting an increasing influence on politics in Zanzibar. Members of religious groups from Pakistan and Afghanistan were reported to have entered Zanzibar in March 2003 and begun spreading 'seditious teachings'. Moderate Zanzibari Muslim leaders expressed concern about rising extremism, and in March 2004 the island's Mufti, Sheikh Harith bin Kalef, denounced a radical Islamic group, the Zanzibar Union for Awakening and Islamic Forums Community (also known as Uamsho), as a political organization that used religion to disguise its efforts to destabilize Zanzibar. A series of bomb attacks followed, targeting Zanzibari power stations, schools, and other government and private property. In late March two bombs exploded in Stone Town, outside the residences of the Mufti and the Minister of Communications and Transport, Zubeir Ali Maulid, while a third bomb was defused in a bar. A number of Uamsho leaders were subsequently arrested in connection with the bombings.

The 2005 elections

It was reported in February 2004 that the Government was to prepare, for the first time in 10 years, a supplementary budget, in order to cover additional costs associated with the 2005 elections (including the introduction of identity cards and the establishment of a permanent register of voters), as well as to counteract the effects of drought. In August, amid growing tension in Zanzibar, the CUF petitioned the UN to dispatch observers to monitor the 2005 elections. The CUF noted that a permanent voters' register had yet to be established, and that the reformed ZEC still lacked a director. Moreover, the Joint Presidential Supervisory Commission (JPSC), established to implement the 2001 *muafaka*, was being investigated following allegations of embezzlement. The JPSC was partly funded by international donors, who suspended their contributions following the allegations.

In February 2005 Lipumba declared his candidacy for the presidential election, at which he would represent the CUF. The CCM elected Jakaya Mrisho Kikwete as its presidential candidate at its national party congress in May. (Under the terms of the Constitution, Mkapa was prohibited from standing for re-election to the presidency.) There were sporadic outbreaks of civil unrest on Zanzibar during the voter registration period, where new legislation requiring voters to have lived in their constituencies for at least three years resulted in some 32,000 potential voters being disqualified. Hamad, the CUF's presidential candidate in Zanzibar, had initially been barred from registering (which would have disqualified him from standing in the election) but appealed successfully against the decision.

Following the death of a candidate, it was announced in October 2005 that the elections on the mainland would be delayed until December. The elections in Zanzibar proceeded as scheduled on 30 October 2005 at which Karume was elected President, securing 53.2% of the valid votes cast; Hamad received 46.1% and the four other candidates who contested the presidential election received negligible support. In the legislative elections the CCM won 31 seats in the House of Representatives, and the CUF 18. The ballot in the one remaining constituency was re-run on 14 December, although the result was not made available. The ZEC declared the poll to have been free and fair, while observers from the Commonwealth generally agreed, but recommended investigations into violence and irregularities in voting in Stone Town. However, the extreme violence of previous elections was avoided. The CUF accused the authorities of electoral malpractice and announced an indefinite parliamentary boycott. Karume was sworn in as President of Zanzibar on 2 November.

On mainland Tanzania the delayed presidential and legislative elections were held concurrently on 14 December 2005. Turn-out was officially recorded at 72% and voting proceeded without notable incident. Kikwete was elected President with 80.3% of the votes cast, while Lipumba received 11.7%. The CCM won 207 seats in the National Assembly, the CUF 18, Chadema five and the TLP and UDP one seat each. The CCM received a further 59 of the 75 seats reserved for women (of the remainder, the CUF received 10 and Chadema six) and six of the 10 seats reserved for presidential nominees (four remained vacant). Of the five representatives sent from the Zanzibari legislature, three were from the CCM and two from the CUF. The Attorney-General was also a CCM member. Thus, the CCM's final strength in the National Assembly totalled 276 seats and the CUF's 30; Chadema secured 11 seats and the TLP and UDP one each. At his inauguration, on 21 December, Kikwete stated that his main priority as President would be to resolve the tensions on Zanzibar. On 4 January 2006 Kikwete announced his new Cabinet, appointing Edward Lowassa, hitherto the Minister of Water, Livestock and Development, as Prime Minister. In late June Kikwete assumed the chairmanship of the CCM.

The Kikwete administration

In mid-October 2006 Kikwete effected a reshuffle in which 10 cabinet ministers were reassigned to new portfolios. Among those affected by the reorganization was the Minister of Home Affairs, Capt. John Zefania Chiligati, who was replaced by Joseph James Mungai, hitherto the Minister of Agriculture, Food Security and Co-operatives; Chiligati became the new Minister of Labour, Employment and Youth Development, replacing Prof. Jumanne Abdallah Maghembe. Further changes to the Cabinet were implemented in early January 2007, following the death of Juma Akukweti, the Minister of State in the Prime Minister's Office, responsible for Parliamentary Affairs; Dr Batilda Burian was named as his replacement. Bernard Kamillius Membe also assumed the foreign affairs and international co-operation portfolio, after the incumbent, Dr Asha Rose Migiro, was appointed as Deputy Secretary-General of the UN.

In January 2008 President Kikwete dismissed the Governor of the central bank, Daudi Balali, after an external audit revealed that some US $116m. worth of fraudulent payments had been made from the bank's External Payment Arrears account during the 2005/06 financial year. Balali was replaced by his hitherto deputy, Prof. Beno Ndulu and some 20 bank employees and a number of prominent businessmen were arrested in connection with the case. In early February 2008 Prime Minister Lowassa tendered his resignation in response to the findings of a parliamentary investigation into his administration's awarding of a power-generation contract in 2006; the Minister of Energy and Minerals and the Minister of East African Co-operation also resigned as a result of their alleged role. Lowassa denied any wrongdoing and no criminal charges were brought against him. President Kikwete named Mizengo Pinda, hitherto Minister of State in the Prime Minister's Office, as Lowassa's successor. Pinda subsequently named a new Cabinet, which included Membe as Minister of Foreign Affairs and International Co-operation and Hussein Ali Mwinyi as Minister of Defence and National Service. In April Andrew Chenge resigned as Minister of Infrastructure Development, following reports that he was being investigated in relation to corruption inquiries against the British arms manufacturer, BAE Systems. He was replaced the following month by Dr Shukuru Kawambwa, hitherto Minister of Communication, Science and Technology; that portfolio was assumed by Prof. Peter Msolla. Stephen Wassira was named as the new Minister of Agriculture, Food Security and Co-operatives.

Meanwhile, at a meeting of representatives from the ruling CCM and the CUF in Zanzibar in February 2008, a proposed power-sharing accord between the two parties was discussed. However, despite earlier indications of acceptance of the agreement, the CCM rejected the proposal in March, claiming that the issue of power-sharing should be decided at a referendum. In early April the CUF staged demonstrations in opposition to the proposed referendum, in an attempt to exert pressure on the CCM to accept the power-sharing agreement.

In October 2008 a peaceful demonstration was held in Dar es Salaam by albino Tanzanians, in response to an increasing number of murders and mutilations committed against people with albinism over the previous year. President Kikwete announced that there would be a campaign to end these killings, which were carried out by people who believed that the body parts of albinos could be used for ritual medicine and witchcraft. Although government statistics indicated that there were only 8,000 albinos in the country, the Albino Society of Tanzania claimed that the number of albinos totalled more than 150,000; several thousand were believed to be living in hiding. In January 2009 the Government revoked the licences of traditional healers and in March Kikwete ordered a national campaign to identify perpetrators of the murders, whereby the public was encouraged to provide information on those suspected of involvement through an anonymous process. In April at least 11 people were killed and several hundred injured in an explosion at a munitions dump at the Mbagala military base, on the outskirts of

Dar es Salaam. Demands by the NCCR—Mageuzi for the resignation of the President and the Minister of Defence and National Service were rejected, although an official inquiry into the incident was launched. In September the high court in the north-western Shinyanga district sentenced three men to death, after finding them guilty of the killing of an albino boy in December 2008 (the first conviction for the murder of an albino). At that time it was reported that at least 46 murders of albinos had been committed since 2007, and that 173 people had been arrested on suspicion of killing albino people or trading in their body parts. In November 2009 a further four people were sentenced to death in northern Tanzania for killing an albino man and selling his body parts.

In August 2009 the EU and the USA expressed concerns over shortcomings in the process of voter registration in Zanzibar, which had begun in July in preparation for elections in October 2010. The CUF had accused the authorities of preventing its supporters from registering as voters, while protests and clashes between CUF members and security personnel had been reported, particularly on the island of Pemba. In November 2009 the CUF ended its ongoing boycott of the Zanzibar House of Representatives, prior to the forthcoming elections. It was subsequently announced that CCM and CUF politicians had reached agreement on submitting proposals for the formation of a government of national unity at a referendum in Zanzibar. A referendum on the matter was duly held on 31 July: 66.4% of those who voted (some 71.9% of the registered electorate) supported the adoption of constitutional amendments permitting rival parties to form coalition governments.

Recent developments: the 2010 elections

Presidential and legislative elections were conducted in Tanzania and Zanzibar on 31 October 2010, as scheduled. President Kikwete was decisively re-elected, with 62.8% of votes cast, according to official results, while his closest challenger, Willibrod Peter Slaa of Chadema, received 27.1% of the votes. Slaa claimed that the authorities had perpetrated malpractice in some voting districts; however, the Commonwealth Observer Group endorsed the conduct of the elections. In Zanzibar the incumbent Vice-President of Tanzania, Dr Ali Mohammed Shein of the CCM, was elected President by a narrow margin of 50.1% of votes cast, defeating the CUF candidate, Maalim Seif Sharif Hamad, who took 49.1% of the votes. In the legislative elections in Tanzania, the CCM won 251 of the total 335 seats in the National Assembly, while Chadema obtained 45 seats and the CUF 33 seats. The CCM also secured the highest representation in the Zanzibar House of Representatives, with 28 of the 50 elective seats, the CUF taking the remaining 22 seats. On 3 November Shein was inaugurated as President of Zanzibar. On 6 November Kikwete was sworn in for a second term; Dr Mohamed Gharib Bilal became Vice-President of Tanzania, replacing Shein. When the National Assembly was convened on 12 November, Anne Makinda of the CCM was elected as Speaker, becoming the first woman to assume the post. For the first time an albino (a CUF candidate) was elected as a deputy of the National Assembly. On 23 November Kikwete formed a new Government, again under the premiership of Pinda and in which most senior members of the previous administration retained their posts.

Foreign Affairs

Tanzania's relations with Uganda and Kenya were strained throughout the 1970s, particularly after the dissolution of the East African Community (EAC, see p. 447) in 1977. Uganda briefly annexed the Kagera salient from Tanzania in November 1978. In early 1979 Tanzanian troops supported the Uganda National Liberation Front in the overthrow of President Idi Amin Dada. In June 2000 Tanzania called on Uganda to pay 98,500m. shillings to cover the cost of the operation. President Mkapa later stated that the amount was to be regarded as a military debt and not, as some claimed, as compensation for those killed during the war. The Tanzania–Kenya border, closed since 1977, was reopened in November 1983, following an agreement on the distribution of the EAC's assets and liabilities. In the following month Tanzania and Kenya agreed to establish full diplomatic relations. The two countries reached agreement on a trade treaty and on the establishment of a joint co-operation commission in 1986. Tanzania pledged its support for the Government of Yoweri Museveni, which took power in Uganda in January of that year, and in November Tanzania began to send military instructors to Uganda to organize the training of Ugandan government troops. In November 1994, meeting in Arusha, the Presidents of Tanzania, Kenya and Uganda established a commission for co-operation; in March 1996 they met again in Nairobi, Kenya, to inaugurate formally the Secretariat of the Permanent Tripartite Commission for East African Co-operation, which aimed to revive the EAC. A treaty for the re-establishment of the EAC, providing for the creation of a free trade area (with the eventual introduction of a single currency), for the development of infrastructure, tourism and agriculture within the Community, and for the establishment of a regional legislative assembly and court, was formally ratified by the Tanzanian, Kenyan and Ugandan Heads of State in November 1999. The new East African Council of Ministers held its first meeting in Tanzania in January 2001. Talks on integrating the economies of the three EAC members followed, and in March 2004 Mkapa, Museveni, and President Mwai Kibaki of Kenya signed a protocol on the creation of a customs union, eliminating most duties on goods within the EAC, which came into force on 1 January 2005. The EAC was expanded to include Rwanda and Burundi in 2007. In November 2009 the Heads of State of Tanzania, Kenya, Uganda, Rwanda and Burundi signed a common market protocol, allowing the free movement of goods, services, people and capital within the EAC; the protocol entered into force in July 2010.

In August 1993, following a protracted mediation effort by the Mwinyi Government, a peace agreement was signed in Arusha by the Rwandan authorities and the rebel Front patriotique rwandais. In April 1994, however, following the assassination of the Rwandan President, Juvénal Habyarimana, hundreds of thousands of Rwandans fled to Tanzania to escape the atrocities being perpetrated in their homeland. In May the Tanzanian authorities appealed for international emergency aid to assist in the care of the refugees, many of whom were sheltering in makeshift camps in the border region. In March 1995 Tanzania banned the admission of further refugees from both Rwanda and Burundi (where violent unrest had erupted in late 1994); some 800,000 Rwandan and Burundian refugees were reportedly sheltering in Tanzania in September 1995. The International Criminal Tribunal for Rwanda, authorized by the UN to charge and try Rwandan nationals accused of direct involvement in the genocide perpetrated in that country during 1994, was inaugurated in June 1995 in Arusha. After the Tutsi-led military coup, which took place in Burundi in July 1996 (following the failure of peace talks mediated by former President Nyerere), the Mkapa administration imposed economic sanctions against the new regime of President Pierre Buyoya, in co-operation with other regional governments. Relations between Tanzania and Burundi remained strained, owing both to the presence of Burundian rebels in northern Tanzania, which the Buyoya regime accused the Mkapa administration of supporting, and to the increasing numbers of Burundians seeking refuge in Tanzania throughout 1996 and 1997. Talks between the Buyoya Government and opposition politicians, once again mediated by Nyerere, were convened in Arusha in 1998 and early 1999. The regional economic sanctions that were imposed against Burundi in 1996 were suspended in January 1999. In July 2002, following a meeting between President Mkapa and the Burundian Vice-President, Domitien Ndayizeye, the two countries stated that they were to normalize their relations.

In December 1996 some of the Rwandan refugees remaining in Tanzania were repatriated, following the threat of forcible repatriation by the Tanzanian Government; however, 200,000 refugees, unwilling to return to Rwanda, reportedly fled their camps. In March 1997 the Tanzanian Government appealed for further international assistance in coping with the remaining refugees (an estimated 200,000 Burundians and 250,000 Zaireans). In February 2000 the Government announced that nine refugee camps in the Kigoma region of west Tanzania had become saturated. Instability in Burundi and the Democratic Republic of the Congo (DRC—formerly Zaire) had recently led to further heavy influxes of refugees from those countries. At that time the number of officially registered refugees in west Tanzania reportedly totalled 468,000, but it was claimed that an additional 200,000 unregistered refugees were also present in the region. Burundians accounted for 70% of all refugees, and refugees from the DRC for 29%. In May 2001 the United Nations High Commissioner for Refugees (UNHCR) and the Governments of Tanzania and Burundi signed an agreement to establish a tripartite commission for the voluntary repatriation of Burundian refugees in Tanzania. In August 2003 Burundi and Tanzania agreed to open additional border crossings to facilitate the return of refugees. Following the signature of a peace accord in Burundi in August 2004, the UNHCR-assisted repatriation of refugees increased. At the end of 2006 an estimated 352,640 Burundian refugees remained in Tanzania. In February 2004 the remaining Rwandan refugees in Tanzanian camps were repatriated; however, it was reported that an estimated 20,000 Rwandans were illegally resident in Tanzania at this time. In early 2008 the Tanzanian Government announced an initiative (commended by UNHCR), under which the remaining Burundian refugees would be permitted to remain in the country and apply for Tanzanian citizenship or be repatriated; it was reported that some 55,000 had decided to return to Burundi. By October 2009 some 53,500 long-term Burundian refugees had been repatriated under the UNHCR programme since March 2008, following the restoration of peace in Burundi. At January 2010 UNHCR estimated that only about 49,000 officially registered Burundian refugees, including 36,000 refugees in one camp in the north-west (which had been scheduled for closure in mid-2009), and 60,000 refugees from the DRC remained in Tanzania. In April the Government announced that it had granted Tanzanian citizenship to some 162,000 Burundian refugees who had applied.

In January 2009 it was reported that the Tanzanian Government had pledged to contribute troops to reinforce the joint UN-African Union peace-keeping mission in the Darfur region of western Sudan, UNAMID. In August the Government dispatched 275 military personnel to Darfur; a further 600 Tanzanian troops were deployed in Darfur from February 2010. In February 2009 Chinese President Hu Jintao pledged US $22m. in aid to Tanzania during an official visit to the country.

CONSTITUTION AND GOVERNMENT

Under the provisions of the 1977 Constitution, with subsequent amendments, legislative power is held by the unicameral National Assembly, whose members serve for a term of five years. There is constitutional provision for both directly elected members (chosen by universal suffrage) and nominated members (including five members elected by and from the Zanzibar House of Representatives). The number of directly elected members exceeds the number of nominated members. The Electoral Commission may review and, if necessary, increase the number of constituencies before every general election. Executive power lies with the President, elected by popular vote for five years. The President must be at least 40 years of age and his mandate is limited to a maximum of two five-year terms. The President appoints a Vice-President, to assist him in carrying out his functions, and presides over the Cabinet, which is composed of a Prime Minister and other ministers who are appointed from among the members of the National Assembly. In May 1992 the United Republic's Constitution was amended to legalize a multi-party political system.

Zanzibar has its own administration for internal affairs, and the amended Zanzibar Constitution, which came into force in January 1985, provides for the President, elected by universal adult suffrage, to hold office for a maximum of two five-year terms, and for the House of Representatives, of 45–55 members, to be directly elected by universal adult suffrage. The President of Zanzibar appoints the Chief Minister, and the two co-operate in choosing the other members of the Supreme Revolutionary Council, which has a maximum of 20 members.

REGIONAL AND INTERNATIONAL CO-OPERATION

Tanzania is a member of the African Union (see p. 183) and of the Southern African Development Community (see p. 420). Tanzania is a founder member (with Kenya and Uganda) of the restored East African Community (EAC, see p. 447).

Tanzania became a member of the UN in 1964. As a contracting party to the General Agreement on Tariffs and Trade, Tanzania joined the World Trade Organization (WTO, see p. 430) on its establishment in 1995. Tanzania participates in the Group of 77 (G77, see p. 447) developing countries.

ECONOMIC AFFAIRS

In 2009, according to estimates by the World Bank, mainland Tanzania's gross national income (GNI), measured at average 2007–09 prices, was US $21,337m., equivalent to $500 per head (or $1,350 per head on an international purchasing-power parity basis). During 2000–09, it was estimated, the population of the country as a whole increased at an average annual rate of 2.8%, while gross domestic product (GDP) per head increased, in real terms, by an average of 3.8% per year. Overall GDP increased, in real terms, at an average annual rate of 6.7% in 2000–09; growth was 5.5% in 2009.

Agriculture (including hunting, forestry and fishing) contributed an estimated 29.4% of Tanzania's GDP in 2008, according to the African Development Bank (AfDB), and employed some 74.6% of the engaged labour force (including Zanzibar) in 2006. According to FAO estimates, the sector engaged 75.4% of the total labour force in mid-2011. The principal cash crops are coffee (which provided 7.6% of export revenues in 2009), cotton, cashew nuts and cloves (Zanzibar's most important export, cultivated on the island of Pemba—they provided 0.4% of export revenues in 2007). Tobacco farming has increased steadily in recent years, and in 2007 Tanzania had become the third largest producer in Africa, according to official sources. In 2009 exports of tobacco accounted for 3.3% of export revenue. Other cash crops include tea, sisal, pyrethrum, coconuts, sugar and cardamom. Exports of cut flowers (grown in the vicinity of Kilimanjaro Airport and freighted to Europe) commenced in the mid-1990s. Seaweed production is an important activity in Zanzibar. Farmers have been encouraged to produce essential food crops, most importantly cassava and maize. Cattle-rearing is also significant. A large proportion of agricultural output is produced by subsistence farmers. The predominance of illegal logging activities remains a concern, and timber exports have consequently been subject to intermittent bans, owing to the threat of deforestation and lost revenues through unofficial foreign sales. Tanzania's agricultural GDP increased at an average annual rate of 4.9% during 2000–06, according to the World Bank. Agricultural GDP increased by 4.6% in 2008, according to the AfDB.

According to the AfDB, industry (including mining, manufacturing, construction and power) contributed an estimated 22.9% of Tanzania's GDP in 2008; the sector employed 5.0% of the United Republic's working population in 2006. During 2000–06 industrial GDP increased by an average of 9.3% per year, according to the World Bank; growth in 2006 was 8.6%.

Mining provided an estimated 3.7% of Tanzania's GDP in 2008. The sector employed 0.6% of the working population on both Zanzibar and mainland Tanganyika in 2006. Gold, diamonds, other gemstones (including rubies and sapphires), salt, phosphates, coal, gypsum, tin, kaolin, limestone and graphite are mined, and it is planned to exploit reserves of natural gas. Other mineral deposits include nickel, silver, cobalt, copper, soda ash, iron ore and uranium. Petroleum was discovered on Tanzania's coastal belt in the 1960s, but was only recently being considered seriously by companies searching for sources of petroleum outside the Middle East. According to the IMF, the GDP of the mining sector increased by an average of 12.9% per year in 1990–99; it grew by 9.1% in 1999. According to the AfDB, the sector's GDP grew by 10.7% in 2007, and by 2.5% in 2008.

Manufacturing contributed 8.5% of Tanzania's GDP in 2008, according to the AfDB. The sector employed 3.1% of the working population on Zanzibar and mainland Tanganyika in 2006. The most important manufacturing activities are food-processing, textile production, cigarette production and brewing. Pulp and paper, fertilizers, cement, clothing, footwear, tyres, batteries, pharmaceuticals, paint, bricks and tiles and electrical goods are also produced, while other activities include oil-refining, metalworking, vehicle assembly and engineering. Tanzania's manufacturing GDP increased at an average annual rate of 7.7% in 2000–06, according to the World Bank. The sector grew by 9.9% in 2008, according to the AfDB.

According to the AfDB, construction contributed an estimated 8.4% of Tanzania's GDP in 2008. The sector employed 1.2% of the United Republic's working population in 2006. Growth in the construction sector in 2008 was 10.5%.

Energy is derived principally from hydroelectric power, which supplied 60.1% of Tanzania's electricity in 2007; however, dependence upon this source meant that the electricity supply remained vulnerable to drought conditions. The contribution of petroleum to the national grid increased from 1.5% of total supply in 2004 to 38.2% in 2005. In September 2008 a 70-MW gas-fired power plant on Songo Songo Island became operational. Another plant, with a projected capacity of 45 MW, was completed in Tegeta in 2009. Natural gas had not previously been used to generate electricity in any significant quantity in Tanzania. Imports of petroleum and petroleum products accounted for 22.6% of the total value of imports in 2009.

The services sector contributed an estimated 47.7% of Tanzania's GDP in 2008, according to AfDB figures. The sector employed 20.3% of the United Republic's working population

TANZANIA

in 2006. Tourism is an important potential growth sector: tourism receipts were approximately US $1,358m. in 2008. According to the World Bank, the GDP of the services sector increased by an average of 6.3% per year in 2000–06. Growth in the sector was 7.2% in 2006.

In 2009 Tanzania recorded a visible trade deficit of US $2,469.5m., and there was a deficit of $1,816.1m. on the current account of the balance of payments. In 2009 the principal sources of imports were India (providing 11.8% of total imports), the People's Republic of China, South Africa, the United Arab Emirates and Japan. The main markets for exports in that year were Switzerland and Liechtenstein (which, together, purchased 21.1% of total exports), China, Kenya, South Africa, India, the Netherlands and Japan. The principal exports in 2009 were gold, metalliferous ores and metal scrap, coffee and fish and fish products. The principal imports were machinery and transport equipment (largely road vehicles), petroleum and petroleum products, chemicals and related products, food and live animals, and iron and steel.

A budgetary deficit of 3,512,000m. shillings was envisaged for the financial year ending 30 June 2010. Tanzania's general government gross debt was 12,064,300m. shillings in 2009, equivalent to 45.5% of GDP. At the end of 2008 Tanzania's external debt totalled US $5,937.6m., of which $3,710.0m. was public and publicly guaranteed debt. In that year the cost of debt-servicing was equivalent to 1.2% of the value of exports of goods, services and income. The annual rate of inflation for Tanganyika averaged 6.7% in 2000–09; consumer prices there increased by 11.7% in 2009. The annual rate of inflation for Zanzibar averaged 6.4% in 2000–05; consumer prices on the islands increased by 9.8% in 2005.

By the mid-2000s Tanzania had become one of Africa's better-performing economies: from 2000 real GDP growth averaged over 6.0% per year, of which agriculture and services (mostly trade, tourism and hotels) each accounted for about one-third. After the Government launched a major privatization programme, more than 380 of the 410 state-owned companies had been divested by 2003. However, this economic improvement was accompanied by only a slight reduction in poverty, and in terms of GNI per head, Tanzania remained one of the world's poorest countries, with a very high level of external debt and continued dependence on foreign aid. (Tanzania has qualified for debt relief under the IMF's initiative for heavily indebted poor countries.) Following his election in 2005, President Jakaya Kikwete stated that he would continue the free-market policies of his predecessor, and GDP growth subsequently increased.

However, the slowdown in global economic activity from September 2008 caused a severe downturn in foreign direct investment, tourist arrivals and export revenues (which were particularly affected by a sharp decline in the price of cotton and other agricultural exports). In May 2009 the IMF approved a one-year credit arrangement for Tanzania under the Fund's Exogenous Shocks Facility (ESF); funds totalling about US $336m. (of which $244m. was disbursed immediately) were designed to support foreign reserves and balance of payments levels. At the same time the IMF commended the Government's fiscal policies in its fifth review of a Policy Support Instrument (PSI) that had been approved in February 2007, although progress in poverty reduction remained limited. In June 2010, upon completion of its second and final review of economic performance under the ESF, the IMF approved a new three-year PSI to succeed the previous arrangement. Following the establishment of an East African Community (EAC, see p. 447) customs union in 2005, a common market protocol allowing the free movement of goods, services, people and capital between Tanzania and the four other EAC member states (which had been signed in November 2009) entered into force in July 2010. In December the IMF assessed that GDP growth of 6.5% had been achieved in the fiscal year to June (compared with more than 7% prior to the global economic crisis), owing in part to the PSI-supported government economic rescue plan, and that all performance criteria had been met at that time. In March 2011 an IMF mission anticipated that growth, which had continued to recover to about 7% by the end of 2010, would undergo a temporary decline, largely as a result of the adverse effects on output of widespread power shortages caused by unfavourable weather conditions.

PUBLIC HOLIDAYS

2012: 1 January (New Year's Day), 12 January (Zanzibar Revolution Day), 5 February (Chama Cha Mapinduzi Day), 4 February* (Maulid, Birth of the Prophet), 6–9 April (Easter), 26 April (Union Day), 1 May (International Labour Day), 7 July (Saba Saba, Industry's Day), 8 August (Peasants' Day), 18 August* (Id El Fitr, end of Ramadan), 26 August (Sultan's Birthday)†, 26 October* (Id El Haji, Feast of the Sacrifice), 29 October (Naming Day), 15 November* (Muharram, New Year), 9 December (Independence Day), 25–26 December (Christmas).

* These holidays are dependent on the Islamic lunar calendar and may vary by one or two days from the dates given.

† Zanzibar only.

Statistical Survey

Sources (unless otherwise stated): Economic and Research Policy Dept, Bank of Tanzania, POB 2939, Dar es Salaam; tel. (22) 2110946; fax (22) 2113325; e-mail info@hq.bot-tz.org; internet www.bot-tz.org; National Bureau of Statistics, POB 796, Dar es Salaam; tel. (22) 2122722; fax (22) 2130852; e-mail dg@nbs.go.tz; internet www.nbs.go.tz.

Area and Population

AREA, POPULATION AND DENSITY

Area (sq km)	945,087*
Population (census results)	
28 August 1988	23,126,310
25 August 2002	
Males	16,910,321
Females	17,658,911
Total	34,569,232
Population (UN estimates at mid-year)†	
2009	43,739,052
2010	45,039,573
2011	46,385,646
Density (per sq km) at mid-2011	49.1

* 364,900 sq miles. Of this total, Tanzania mainland is 942,626 sq km (363,950 sq miles), and Zanzibar 2,461 sq km (950 sq miles).

† Source: UN, *World Population Prospects: The 2008 Revision*.

POPULATION BY AGE AND SEX
(UN estimates at mid-2011)

	Males	Females	Total
0–14	10,464,946	10,300,599	20,765,545
15–64	12,031,241	12,129,177	24,160,418
65 and over	651,390	808,293	1,459,683
Total	23,147,577	23,238,069	46,385,646

Source: UN, *World Population Prospects: The 2008 Revision*.

ETHNIC GROUPS
(private households, census of 26 August 1967)

African	11,481,595	Others	839
Asian	75,015	Not stated	159,042
Arabs	29,775	**Total**	11,763,150
European	16,884		

TANZANIA

REGIONS
(at census of 25 August 2002)

Arusha	1,292,973	Mwanza	2,942,148
Dar es Salaam	2,497,940	Pwani	889,154
Dodoma	1,698,996	North Pemba†	186,013
Iringa	1,495,333	North Unguja†	136,953
Kagera	2,033,888	Rukwa	1,141,743
Kigoma	1,679,109	Ruvuma	1,117,166
Kilimanjaro	1,381,149	Shinyanga	2,805,580
Lindi	791,306	Singida	1,090,758
Manyara*	603,691	South Pemba†	176,153
Mara	1,368,602	South Unguja†	94,504
Mbeya	2,070,046	Urban West†	391,002
Morogoro	1,759,809	Tabora	1,717,908
Mtwara	1,128,523	Tanga	1,642,015

* Before the 2002 census Manyara was included in the region of Arusha.
† Part of the autonomous territory of Zanzibar.

PRINCIPAL TOWNS
(estimated population at mid-1988)

Dar es Salaam	1,360,850	Mbeya	152,844
Mwanza	223,013	Arusha	134,708
Dodoma	203,833	Morogoro	117,760
Tanga	187,455	Shinyanga	100,724
Zanzibar	157,634		

Source: UN, *Demographic Yearbook*.

Mid-2010 (incl. suburbs, UN estimate): Dar es Salaam 3,349,134 (Source: UN, *World Urbanization Prospects: The 2009 Revision*).

BIRTHS AND DEATHS
(annual averages, UN estimates)

	1995–2000	2000–05	2005–10
Birth rate (per 1,000)	41.9	41.8	41.6
Death rate (per 1,000)	14.7	13.3	11.5

Source: UN, *World Population Prospects: The 2008 Revision*.

Life expectancy (years at birth, WHO estimates): 53 (males 52; females 53) in 2008 (Source: WHO, *World Health Statistics*).

ECONOMICALLY ACTIVE POPULATION
('000 persons aged 15 years and over, labour force survey, 2006)

	Males	Females	Total
Agriculture, hunting and forestry	6,064.8	7,120.3	13,185.1
Fishing	184.6	25.0	209.6
Mining and quarrying	90.8	14.1	104.9
Manufacturing	332.9	232.2	565.1
Electricity, gas and water supply	13.5	3.5	17.0
Construction	204.8	6.7	211.5
Wholesale and retail trade and restaurants and hotels	907.7	665.0	1,572.7
Hotel and restaurants	98.5	279.0	377.5
Transport, storage and communications	245.0	13.1	258.1
Financial intermediation	11.3	6.2	17.5
Real estate, renting and business activities	69.0	13.0	82.0
Public administration and defence; compulsory social security	157.4	27.3	184.7
Education	126.9	98.7	225.6
Health and social work	46.1	59.1	105.2
Community, social and personal services	88.3	38.2	126.5
Households with employed persons	138.2	563.3	701.5
Total employed	**8,779.8**	**9,164.7**	**17,944.6**
Unemployed	274.3	602.7	877.0
Total labour force	**9,054.2**	**9,767.4**	**18,821.5**

Source: ILO.

Mid-2011 (estimates in '000): Agriculture, etc. 17,394; Total labour force 23,070 (Source: FAO).

Health and Welfare

KEY INDICATORS

Total fertility rate (children per woman, 2008)	5.6
Under-5 mortality rate (per 1,000 live births, 2008)	103
HIV/AIDS (% of persons aged 15–49, 2007)	6.2
Physicians (per 1,000 head, 2004)	0.02
Hospital beds (per 1,000 head, 2006)	1.1
Health expenditure (2007): US $ per head (PPP)	63
Health expenditure (2007): % of GDP	5.3
Health expenditure (2007): public (% of total)	65.8
Access to water (% of persons, 2008)	54
Access to sanitation (% of persons, 2008)	24
Total carbon dioxide emissions ('000 metric tons, 2007)	6,038.3
Carbon dioxide emissions per head (metric tons, 2007)	0.1
Human Development Index (2010): ranking	148
Human Development Index (2010): value	0.398

For sources and definitions, see explanatory note on p. vi.

Agriculture

PRINCIPAL CROPS
('000 metric tons)

	2006	2007	2008
Wheat	110.0	82.8	86.4
Rice, paddy	1,206.2	1,341.8	1,341.8*
Maize	3,423.0	3,659.0	3,659.0*
Millet	227.9	219.0*	219.0*
Sorghum	711.6	900.0†	900.0*
Potatoes*	660.0	650.0	650.0
Sweet potatoes	1,396.4	1,322.0	1,322.0*
Cassava (Manioc)	6,158.3	6,600.0*	6,600.0*
Sugar cane*	2,450.0	2,370.0	2,370.0
Beans, dry*	500.0	480.0	480.0
Cashew nuts, with shell	77.4	92.6	99.1
Groundnuts, with shell*	290.0	300.0	300.0
Coconuts*	370.0	370.0	370.0
Oil palm fruit*	65.0	65.0	65.0
Seed cotton*	230.0	320.0	320.0
Tomatoes*	145.0	145.0	145.0
Onions, dry*	51.5	52.0	52.0
Bananas	3,507.5	3,500.0*	3,500.0*
Plantains*	600.0	600.0	600.0
Guavas, mangoes and mangosteens*	400.0	220.0	220.0
Pineapples*	78.0	78.0	78.0
Coffee, green	34.3	54.8	43.1
Tea	30.3	31.3	34.8
Cloves*	9.8	9.9	9.9
Tobacco, unmanufactured	52.0	50.6	50.8

* FAO estimate(s).
† Unofficial figure.

Note: No data were available for individual crops in 2009.

Aggregate production ('000 metric tons, may include official, semi-official or estimated data): Total cereals 5,698.0 in 2006, 6,223.1 in 2007, 6,226.7 in 2008–09; Total roots and tubers 8,222.9 in 2006, 8,580.5 in 2007–09; Total vegetables (incl. melons) 1,242.4 in 2006, 1,242.9 in 2007–09; Total fruits (excl. melons) 4,895.8 in 2006, 4,708.5 in 2007–09.

Source: FAO.

LIVESTOCK
('000 head, year ending September)

	2005	2006	2007
Asses*	182.0	182.0	182.0
Cattle	17,719.1	17,700.0*	18,000.0*
Pigs*	455.0	455.0	455.0
Sheep*	4,000.0	4,000.0	3,550.0
Goats*	12,550.0	12,550.0	12,550.0
Chickens*	32,000	32,500	30,000

* FAO estimate(s).

2008: Figures assumed to be unchanged from 2007 (FAO estimates). Note: No data were available for 2009.

Source: FAO.

TANZANIA

LIVESTOCK PRODUCTS
('000 metric tons, FAO estimates)

	2005	2006	2007
Cattle meat	246.3	247.0	247.0
Sheep meat	11.5	11.5	10.3
Goat meat	30.6	30.6	30.6
Pig meat	13.0	13.0	13.0
Chicken meat	52.3	52.7	45.7
Cows' milk	840.0	840.0	850.0
Goats' milk	104.0	104.0	105.0
Hen eggs	36.7	36.8	36.8
Honey	27.0	27.0	27.0

2008: Production assumed to be unchanged from 2007 (FAO estimates).
2009: Sheep meat 10.3; Goat meat 30.6; Pig meat 13.0; Goats' milk 105.0.
Source: FAO.

Forestry

ROUNDWOOD REMOVALS
('000 cubic metres, excluding bark, FAO estimates)

	2007	2008	2009
Sawlogs, veneer logs and logs for sleepers	317	317	317
Pulpwood	153	153	153
Other industrial wood	1,844	1,844	1,844
Fuel wood	22,127	22,352	22,588
Total	**24,441**	**24,666**	**24,902**

Source: FAO.

SAWNWOOD PRODUCTION
('000 cubic metres, including railway sleepers, FAO estimates)

	1992	1993	1994
Coniferous (softwood)	26	21	13
Broadleaved (hardwood)	22	18	11
Total	**48**	**39**	**24**

1995–2009: Production assumed to be unchanged from 1994 (FAO estimates).
Source: FAO.

Fishing
('000 metric tons, live weight)

	2006	2007	2008
Capture	334.3	328.5	325.5
Tilapias	44.4	38.3	35.6
Nile perch	95.5	95.2	94.2
Dagaas	22.0	17.9	13.0
Other freshwater fishes	130.6	133.0	138.9
Sardinellas	3.1	12.2	11.8
Aquaculture*	0.0	0.0	0.0
Total catch*	**334.3**	**328.5**	**325.5**

* FAO estimates.

Note: Figures exclude aquatic plants ('000 metric tons): 0.6 (capture 0.3, aquaculture 0.3) in 2006; 0.6 (capture 0.2, aquaculture 0.4) in 2007; 0.8 (capture 0.3, aquaculture 0.5) in 2008. Also excluded are crocodiles, recorded by number rather than by weight. The number of Nile crocodiles caught was: 1,100 in 2006; 1,556 in 2007; 1,784 in 2008.
Source: FAO.

Mining
('000 metric tons, unless otherwise indicated)

	2006	2007	2008*
Coal (bituminous)	17.9	27.2	27.0
Diamonds ('000 carats)†	272.2	282.8	180.0
Gold (refined, kilograms)	47,000*	40,193	36,000
Salt	34.8	35.2	35.0
Gypsum and anhydrite	32.6	52.8	53.0
Limestone, crushed	1,607.6	1,322.0	1,300.0
Pozzolanic materials	129.3	184.1	180.0
Sand	7,577.2	8,400.0*	8,400.0

* Estimates.
† Estimated at 85% gem-quality and 15% industrial-quality stones. Excluding smuggled artisanal production.

Source: US Geological Survey.

Industry

SELECTED PRODUCTS
(Tanganyika, '000 metric tons unless otherwise indicated)

	2006	2007	2008
Refined sugar	173.4	251.4	n.a.
Cigarettes (million)	5,095	5,821	6,101
Beer (million litres)	299	310	291
Textiles (million sq m)	147	139	141
Cement	1,422	1,630	1,756
Rolled steel	44	52	40
Iron sheets	30	36	32
Sisal ropes	5.9	9.1	n.a.
Paints ('000 litres)	18,402	17,451	24,857

Selected Products for Zanzibar ('000 metric tons, 2008, unless otherwise indicated): Beverages (million litres) 9.4; Animal feeds (metric tons) 0.2; Coconut oil (metric tons) 77; Bread ('000 loaves, 2007) 77; Copra cake (metric tons, 2007) 49.

Electric energy (Tanganyika and Zanzibar, kWh million): 3,035 in 2005; 2,776 in 2006; 4,175 in 2007 (Source: UN Industrial Commodity Statistics Database).

Finance

CURRENCY AND EXCHANGE RATES

Monetary Units
100 cents = 1 Tanzanian shilling.

Sterling, Dollar and Euro Equivalents (30 November 2010)
£1 sterling = 2,283.42 Tanzanian shillings;
US $1 = 1,470.52 Tanzanian shillings;
€1 = 1,911.38 Tanzanian shillings;
10,000 Tanzanian shillings = £4.38 = $6.80 = €5.23.

Average Exchange Rate (Tanzanian shillings per US $)
2007   1,245.04
2008   1,196.31
2009   1,320.31

BUDGET
('000 million shillings, year ending 30 June)*

Revenue†	2007/08	2008/09	2009/10‡
Tax revenue	3,359	4,044	4,428
Import duties	289	359	367
Value-added tax	1,042	1,231	1,390
Excises	661	762	838
Income tax	984	1,229	1,334
Other taxes	383	463	499
Non-tax revenue	275	249	372
Total	**3,635**	**4,293**	**4,800**

TANZANIA

Statistical Survey

Expenditure	2007/08	2008/09	2009/10‡
Recurrent expenditure	3,398	4,681	5,700
Wages	1,135	1,609	1,723
Interest	265	243	249
Goods, services and transfers	1,998	2,830	3,728
Development expenditure and net lending	1,819	2,226	2,611
Local	567	906	1,005
Foreign	1,252	1,320	1,607
Total	5,217	6,907	8,312

* Figures refer to the Tanzania Government, excluding the revenue and expenditure of the separate Zanzibar Government.
† Excluding grants received.
‡ Budget forecasts.

Source: IMF, *United Republic of Tanzania: First Review Under the Policy Support Instrument and Request for Modification of Assessment Criteria—Staff Report; Press Release on the Executive Board Discussion.* (December 2010).

INTERNATIONAL RESERVES
(excl. gold, US $ million at 31 December)

	2008	2009	2010
IMF special drawing rights	—	248.8	243.8
Reserve position in IMF	15.4	15.7	15.4
Foreign exchange	2,847.5	3,205.9	3,645.4
Total	2,862.9	3,470.4	3,904.6

Source: IMF, *International Financial Statistics*.

MONEY SUPPLY
('000 million shillings at 31 December)

	2008	2009	2010
Currency outside depository corporations	1,438.64	1,566.75	1,897.13
Transferable deposits	2,851.11	3,288.92	4,399.95
Other deposits	3,169.03	3,924.47	4,715.50
Broad money	7,458.78	8,780.14	11,012.59

Source: IMF, *International Financial Statistics*.

COST OF LIVING
(Consumer Price Index)

Tanganyika
(base: 2000 = 100)

	2007	2008	2009
Food (incl. beverages)	152.9	172.2	202.4
Fuel, light and water	170.5	188.7	185.6
Clothing (incl. footwear)	120.9	122.6	130.3
Rent	136.0	139.3	156.7
All items (incl. others)	146.2	161.2	180.8

Source: ILO.

Zanzibar
(base: 2001 = 100)

	2002	2003
Food (incl. beverages)	106.9	116.7
Fuel, light and water	100.0	106.0
Clothing (incl. footwear)	106.7	128.3
Rent	104.9	118.0
All items (incl. others)	105.2	114.7

2004: Food (incl. beverages) 128.6; All items (incl. others) 124.0.
2005: Food (incl. beverages) 143.7; All items (incl. others) 136.1.
Source: ILO.

NATIONAL ACCOUNTS
('000 million shillings at current prices)

Expenditure on the Gross Domestic Product

	2006	2007	2008
Government final consumption expenditure	3,144.9	4,039.0	4,321.7
Private final consumption expenditure	12,195.2	14,231.1	16,432.8
Changes in inventories	74.3	90.7	106.9
Gross fixed capital formation	4,883.5	6,119.0	7,274.3
Total domestic expenditure	20,297.9	24,479.8	28,135.7
Exports of goods and services	4,048.0	5,078.2	6,230.7
Less Imports of goods and services	6,404.6	8,609.7	9,612.1
GDP in purchasers' values	17,941.3	20,948.4	24,754.5

Gross Domestic Product by Economic Activity

	2006	2007	2008
Agriculture, hunting, forestry and fishing	4,950.0	5,690.4	6,671.1
Mining and quarrying	576.4	742.9	839.5
Manufacturing	1,395.3	1,625.5	1,936.0
Electricity, gas and water	352.7	420.9	514.5
Construction	1,399.6	1,641.7	1,904.4
Wholesale and retail trade, hotels and restaurants	2,504.0	2,976.2	3,524.9
Transport and communications	1,144.1	1,374.0	1,649.0
Finance, insurance, real estate and business services	2,023.3	2,327.1	2,782.3
Public administration and defence	1,440.9	1,652.6	1,999.6
Other services	661.6	746.8	863.6
Sub-total	16,447.9	19,198.1	22,684.9
Less Imputed bank service charge	169.7	208.3	260.0
Indirect taxes, less subsidies	1,663.0	1,958.6	2,329.6
GDP in purchasers' values	17,941.3	20,948.4	24,754.5

Source: African Development Bank.

BALANCE OF PAYMENTS
(US $ million)

	2007	2008	2009
Exports of goods f.o.b.	2,226.6	3,578.8	3,364.7
Imports of goods f.o.b.	−4,860.6	−7,012.3	−5,834.1
Trade balance	−2,634.0	−3,433.5	−2,469.5
Exports of services	1,875.7	1,998.8	1,854.6
Imports of services	−1,413.7	−1,648.9	−1,709.1
Balance on goods and services	−2,172.0	−3,083.6	−2,323.9
Other income received	107.3	122.7	161.1
Other income paid	−406.8	−350.5	−336.5
Balance on goods, services and income	−2,471.4	−3,311.5	−2,499.2
Current transfers received	724.0	689.0	751.6
Current transfers paid	−72.5	−79.6	−68.4
Current balance	−1,819.9	−2,702.0	−1,816.1
Capital account (net)	911.7	537.0	493.5
Direct investment from abroad	581.5	400.0	414.5
Portfolio investment liabilities	2.8	2.9	3.0
Other investment assets	34.1	181.7	−333.8
Other investment liabilities	378.9	1,105.5	1,563.6
Net errors and omissions	326.7	584.6	49.2
Overall balance	415.7	109.7	374.0

Source: IMF, *International Financial Statistics*.

TANZANIA

External Trade

PRINCIPAL COMMODITIES
(US $ million)

Imports c.i.f.	2007	2008	2009
Food and live animals	384.9	366.7	402.2
Cereals and cereal preparations	267.1	258.4	281.0
Wheat and meslin, unmilled	233.5	182.0	209.3
Mineral fuels, lubricants, etc.	1,768.6	2,381.0	1,478.2
Petroleum, petroleum products, etc.	1,758.0	2,359.0	1,467.1
Petroleum products, refined	1,740.6	2,337.7	1,430.2
Animal and vegetable oils, fats and waxes	274.3	223.1	130.8
Fixed vegetable oils and fats	247.5	195.0	120.9
Palm oil	227.2	175.5	106.1
Chemicals and related products	682.3	938.2	783.1
Medicinal and pharmaceutical products	172.7	145.3	111.0
Plastics in primary forms	191.6	237.6	218.8
Basic manufactures	805.3	1,244.2	1,014.2
Iron and steel	245.5	399.9	323.5
Other metal manufactures	157.9	255.5	210.7
Machinery and transport equipment	1,627.3	2,488.6	2,295.9
Power generating machinery and equipment	218.2	170.2	111.2
Rotating electric plant, and parts thereof	135.2	98.3	47.8
Machinery specialized for particular industries	220.4	503.2	477.7
General industrial machinery, equipment and parts	169.6	264.7	285.4
Telecommunications, sound recording and reproducing equipment	251.7	306.2	220.1
Telecommunication equipment, parts and accessories	235.7	286.4	200.5
Other electrical machinery, apparatus and appliances, and parts	126.6	206.5	286.0
Road vehicles	502.7	742.4	755.1
Passenger motor vehicles, excl. buses	175.2	222.5	239.2
Lorries and special purpose motor vehicles	158.1	254.0	243.8
Vehicles for the transportation of goods or materials	147.1	237.9	218.4
Miscellaneous manufactured articles	236.4	312.7	294.9
Total (incl. others)	5,919.0	8,087.7	6,530.8

Exports f.o.b.	2007	2008	2009
Food and live animals	570.4	597.2	597.2
Fish, crustaceans, molluscs and preparations thereof	165.6	140.6	127.8
Fish, fresh, chilled or frozen	151.3	119.3	106.8
Fish fillets, fresh or chilled	82.9	61.3	48.7
Fish fillets, frozen	66.9	55.0	55.8
Cereals and cereal preparations	90.9	63.4	22.8
Vegetables and fruit	93.6	157.8	159.4
Fruit and nuts, fresh, dried	60.1	78.7	64.2
Cashew nuts, fresh or dried	27.4	69.4	90.2
Coffee, tea, cocoa, spices, and manufactures thereof	181.3	188.9	227.0
Coffee and coffee substitutes	117.6	105.9	117.4
Coffee, not roasted; coffee husks and skins	113.1	100.0	111.2
Spices	9.3	14.7	21.2
Cloves	8.6	14.3	18.0
Beverages and tobacco	101.8	189.8	106.7
Tobacco and tobacco manufactures	96.7	180.6	97.9
Tobacco, wholly or partly stripped	86.3	171.6	90.0
Crude materials, inedible, except fuels	435.5	643.1	811.7

Exports f.o.b.—continued	2007	2008	2009
Textile fibres (not wool tops) and their wastes (not in yarn)	96.2	138.9	125.3
Raw cotton, excl. linters, not carded or combed	40.4	80.9	89.0
Metalliferous ores and metal scrap	211.9	364.3	507.8
Ores and concentrates of precious metals	201.0	349.5	497.7
Basic manufactures	220.4	362.5	259.3
Non-metallic mineral manufactures	78.8	101.6	63.5
Pearl, precious and semi-precious stones, unworked or worked	61.5	73.5	40.3
Diamonds cut or otherwise worked, but not mounted or set	16.7	20.1	18.4
Gold, non-monetary, unwrought or semi-manufactured	553.8	759.4	818.6
Total (incl. others)	2,139.3	3,121.1	2,982.4

Source: UN, *International Trade Statistics Yearbook*.

PRINCIPAL TRADING PARTNERS
(US $ million)

Imports c.i.f.	2007	2008	2009
Australia	26.8	102.8	125.7
Bahrain	171.9	44.1	36.4
Belgium	109.9	142.5	109.7
Canada	35.9	n.a.	n.a.
China, People's Repub.	415.9	721.3	692.1
France	131.9	162.1	112.2
Germany	156.2	220.7	226.8
India	512.7	865.7	772.9
Indonesia	129.3	94.9	109.3
Italy	83.2	95.6	99.6
Japan	262.8	366.8	422.1
Kenya	103.6	430.7	304.5
Korea, Repub.	75.9	86.9	75.6
Malaysia	148.0	163.0	67.8
Netherlands	85.6	213.0	123.3
Saudi Arabia	220.9	263.4	164.7
Singapore	254.3	441.9	192.0
South Africa	595.6	829.4	686.6
Sweden	104.9	152.0	84.1
Switzerland-Liechtenstein	254.6	139.8	134.6
Thailand	59.4	76.8	71.3
United Arab Emirates	782.5	978.9	631.6
United Kingdom	173.7	175.6	183.2
USA	189.0	224.9	141.0
Total (incl. others)	5,919.0	8,087.7	6,530.8

Exports f.o.b.	2007	2008	2009
Belgium	39.6	50.4	81.5
China, People's Repub.	156.7	270.4	387.3
Congo, Democratic Repub.	83.8	144.6	85.5
France	12.6	27.0	18.0
Germany	100.7	67.1	57.9
Hong Kong	14.5	n.a.	n.a.
India	79.0	173.0	187.8
Italy	57.1	67.6	55.0
Japan	64.2	147.8	178.4
Kenya	123.4	252.7	192.9
Malawi	22.7	49.6	25.6
Netherlands	104.3	163.2	182.4
Saudi Arabia	97.6	16.4	31.9
Singapore	4.8	n.a.	n.a.
South Africa	204.0	265.5	187.9
Switzerland-Liechtenstein	438.0	630.0	630.0
Uganda	46.1	59.8	51.7
United Arab Emirates	97.6	68.1	91.4
United Kingdom	29.5	83.9	32.8
USA	62.5	56.8	47.9
Zambia	30.0	47.1	46.6
Total (incl. others)	2,139.3	3,121.1	2,982.4

Source: UN, *International Trade Statistics Yearbook*.

TANZANIA

Transport

RAILWAYS

	2005	2006	2007
Passengers ('000)	514	594	524
Freight ('000 metric tons)	1,169	775	714

Source: National Bureau of Statistics, *Tanzania in Figures 2008*.

ROAD TRAFFIC
(estimates, '000 motor vehicles in use)

	1994	1995	1996
Passenger cars	28.0	26.0	23.8
Buses and coaches	78.0	81.0	86.0
Lorries and vans	27.2	27.7	29.7
Road tractors	6.7	6.7	6.6

2007: Passenger cars 80,913; Buses and coaches 23,118; Lorries and vans 369,887; Motorcycles and mopeds 52,015.

Source: IRF, *World Road Statistics*.

SHIPPING
Merchant fleet
(registered at 31 December)

	2007	2008	2009
Number of vessels	53	51	75
Displacement ('000 grt)	38.1	40.6	89.4

Source: IHS Fairplay, *World Fleet Statistics*.

International sea-borne traffic

	2005	2006	2007
Vessels docked	3,895	4,154	3,038
Cargo ('000 metric tons)	4,307	6,320	5,703
Passengers ('000)	1,072	664	714

CIVIL AVIATION
(traffic on scheduled services)

	2004	2005	2006
Kilometres flown (million)	5	8	5
Passengers carried ('000)	243	257	221
Passenger-km (million)	216	246	225
Total ton-km (million)	22	24	22

Source: UN, *Statistical Yearbook*.

Tourism

FOREIGN VISITOR ARRIVALS
(by country of origin)

	2006	2007	2008
Burundi	10,631	11,039	11,721
Canada	12,536	15,198	16,482
Congo, Democratic Repub.	9,792	8,372	7,638
France	19,643	21,314	19,598
Germany	19,651	24,468	27,100
India	13,020	14,042	17,530
Italy	50,287	54,194	49,950
Kenya	127,016	130,823	184,269
Malawi	17,247	19,136	21,459
Netherlands	262	18,990	16,945
Rwanda	13,056	14,699	14,394
South Africa	28,961	28,394	28,721
Spain	11,575	11,428	8,470
Uganda	35,521	30,385	31,682
United Kingdom	69,160	55,154	58,245
USA	55,687	58,341	66,953
Zambia	31,132	34,669	37,682
Total (incl. others)	644,124	719,031	770,469

Tourism receipts (US $ million, incl. passenger transport): 986 in 2006; 1,215 in 2007; 1,358 in 2008.

Source: World Tourism Organization.

Communications Media

	2007	2008	2009
Telephones ('000 main lines in use)	163.3	123.8	172.9
Mobile cellular telephones ('000 subscribers)	8,322.9	13,006.8	17,469.5
Internet users ('000)	400	520	678
Broadband Subscribers ('000)	2.5	6.4	6.4

Personal computers: 356,000 (9.1 per 1,000 persons) in 2005.

Source: International Telecommunication Union.

Television receivers ('000 in use, 2000): 700.

Radio receivers ('000 in use, estimate, 1997): 8,800 (Source: UNESCO, *Statistical Yearbook*).

Daily newspapers (2004): 14; average circulation ('000 copies, estimate) 60 (Source: UNESCO Institute for Statistics).

Education

(2008)

	Institutions	Teachers	Students
Primary (state)	15,257	149,433	2,416,000
Primary (private)	416	5,462	29,761
Secondary (state)	3,039	24,971	528,027
Secondary (private)	759	7,864	100,121
Higher (state)*	71	n.a.	64,664
Higher (private)†	51	n.a.	17,865

* Comprising 34 teacher training colleges, 16 technical colleges, 8 full universities, 3 constituent universities and 10 other higher institutions.
† Comprising 40 teacher training colleges and 11 universities.

Pupil-teacher ratio (primary education, UNESCO estimate): 53.7 in 2008/09 (Source: UNESCO Institute for Statistics).

Adult literacy rate (UNESCO estimates): 72.6% (males 79.0%; females 66.3%) in 2008 (Source: UNESCO Institute for Statistics).

Directory

The Government

HEAD OF STATE

President: Lt-Col (Retd) JAKAYA MRISHO KIKWETE (took office 21 December 2005; re-elected 31 October 2010).
Vice-President: Dr MOHAMED GHARIB BILAL.

CABINET
(May 2011)

President and Commander-in-Chief of the Armed Forces: Lt-Col (Retd) JAKAYA MRISHO KIKWETE.
Prime Minister: MIZENGO KAYANZA PETER PINDA.
Ministers of State in the President's Office: HAWA ABDULRAHMAN GHASIA (Public Service Management), MATHIAS CHIKAWE (Good Governance) STEPHEN MASATU WASSIRA (Social Relations and Co-ordination).
Ministers of State in the Vice-President's Office: SAMIA SULUHU (Union Affairs), Dr TEREZYA LUOGA HOVISA (Environment).
Ministers of State in the Prime Minister's Office: GEORGE HURUMA MKUCHIKA (Regional Administration and Local Governments), WILLIAM LUKUVI (Policy, Co-ordination and Parliamentary Affairs) Dr MARY NAGU (Investment and Empowerment).
Minister of Foreign Affairs and International Co-operation: BERNARD KAMILLIUS MEMBE.
Minister of East African Co-operation: SAMWEL JOHN SITTA.
Minister of Finance and Economic Affairs: MUSTAFA MKURO.
Minister of Industry, Trade and Marketing: Dr CYRIL CHAMI.
Minister of Agriculture, Irrigation, Food Security and Co-operatives: Prof. JUMANNE MAGHEMBE.
Minister of Natural Resources and Tourism: EZEKIEL MAIGE.
Minister of Water: Prof. MARK JAMES MWANDOSYA.
Minister of Energy and Minerals: WILLIAM NGELEJE.
Minister of Works: Dr JOHN POMBE MAGUFULI.
Minister of Transport: Eng. OMARI NUNDU.
Minister of Communication, Science and Technology: Prof. MAKAME MNYAA MBARAWA.
Minister of Health and Social Welfare: Dr HAJI HUSSEIN MPONDA.
Minister of Education and Vocational Training: Dr SHUKURU KAWAMBWA.
Minister of Labour and Employment: GAUDENSIA KABAKA.
Minister of Lands, Housing and Human Settlements Development: Prof. ANNA TIBAIJUKA.
Minister of Information, Culture, Youth Affairs and Sports: Dr EMMANUEL NCHIMBI.
Minister of Defence and National Service: Dr HUSSEIN ALI MWINYI.
Minister of Home Affairs: SHAMSI VUAI NAHODHA.
Minister of Justice and Constitutional Affairs: CELINA OMPESHI KOMBANI.
Minister of Community Development, Gender and Children: SOPHIA SIMBA.
Minister of Livestock and Fisheries Development: Dr MATHAYO DAVID MATHAYO.

There were also 20 deputy ministers.

MINISTRIES

Office of the President: State House, POB 2483, Dar es Salaam; tel. (22) 2116538; fax (22) 2113425; e-mail permsec@estabs.go.tz; internet www.tanzania.go.tz/poffice.htm.
Office of the Vice-President: POB 5380, Dar es Salaam; tel. (22) 2113857; fax (22) 2113856; e-mail makamu@twiga.com; internet www.tanzania.go.tz/vpoffice.htm.
Office of the Prime Minister: POB 3021, Dar es Salaam; tel. (22) 2111249; fax (22) 2117266; e-mail ps@pmo.go.tz; internet www.pmo.go.tz.
Ministry of Agriculture, Irrigation, Food Security and Co-operatives: Kilimo I Building, Temeke, POB 9192, Dar es Salaam; tel. (22) 2862480; fax (22) 2865951; e-mail psk@kilimo.go.tz; internet www.kilimo.go.tz.
Ministry of Communication, Science and Technology: Plot 1168/19, Jamhuri St, POB 2645, Dar es Salaam; tel. (22) 2111254; fax (22) 2112533; e-mail mst@mst.go.tz; internet www.mst.go.tz.
Ministry of Community Development, Gender and Children: Kivukoni Front, POB 3448, Dar es Salaam; tel. (22) 2111459; fax (22) 2110933; e-mail info_wic@uccmail.co.tz; internet www.mcdcg.go.tz.
Ministry of Defence and National Service: POB 9544, Dar es Salaam; tel. (22) 2117153; fax (22) 2116719; internet www.modans.go.tz.
Ministry of East African Co-operation: NSSF Water Front Bldg, 5th Floor, POB 9280, Dar es Salaam; tel. (22) 2126660; fax (22) 2120488; e-mail ps@meac.go.tz; internet www.meac.go.tz.
Ministry of Education and Vocational Training: POB 9121, Dar es Salaam; tel. (22) 2120403; fax (22) 2113271; e-mail psmoevt@moe.go.tz; internet www.moe.go.tz.
Ministry of Energy and Minerals: POB 2000, Dar es Salaam; tel. (22) 2112791; fax (22) 2121606; e-mail madini@africaonline.co.tz; internet www.mem.go.tz.
Ministry of Finance and Economic Affairs: POB 9111, Dar es Salaam; tel. (22) 2111174; fax (22) 2110326; internet www.mof.go.tz.
Ministry of Foreign Affairs and International Co-operation: Kivukoni Front, POB 9000, Dar es Salaam; tel. (22) 2111906; fax (22) 2116600; e-mail nje@foreign.go.tz; internet www.mfaic.go.tz.
Ministry of Health and Social Welfare: 36/37 Samore Ave, POB 9083, Dar es Salaam; tel. (22) 2120261; fax (22) 2139951; e-mail moh@moh.go.tz; internet www.moh.gov.tz.
Ministry of Home Affairs: POB 9223, Dar es Salaam; tel. and fax (22) 2119050; e-mail permsec@moha.go.tz; internet www.moha.go.tz.
Ministry of Industry, Trade and Marketing: POB 9503, Dar es Salaam; tel. (22) 2127898; fax (22) 2125832; e-mail tnwinfo@plancom.go.tz; internet www.mitm.go.tz.
Ministry of Information, Culture, Youth Affairs and Sports: Dar es Salaam; internet www.hum.go.tz.
Ministry of Infrastructure Development: Pamba Rd, Tancot House, POB 9144, Dar es Salaam; tel. (22) 2137650; fax (22) 2112751; e-mail permsec@infrastructure.go.tz; internet www.infrastructure.go.tz.
Ministry of Justice and Constitutional Affairs: POB 70069, Dar es Salaam; tel. 2137833; fax (22) 2137831; e-mail katibumkuu@sheria.go.tz; internet www.sheria.go.tz.
Ministry of Labour and Employment: POB 1422, Dar es Salaam; tel. (22) 2120419; fax (22) 2113082; e-mail permsec@kazi.go.tz; internet www.kazi.go.tz.
Ministry of Lands, Housing and Human Settlements Development: Kivukoni Front, Ardhi House, POB 9132, Dar es Salaam; tel. (22) 2121241; fax (22) 2124576; internet www.ardhi.go.tz.
Ministry of Livestock and Fisheries Development: POB 9152, Dar es Salaam; tel. (22) 2861910; fax (22) 2861908; internet www.mifugo.go.tz.
Ministry of Natural Resources and Tourism: POB 9372, Dar es Salaam; tel. (22) 2111061; fax (22) 2110600; e-mail nature.tourism@mnrt.org; internet www.mnrt.org.
Ministry of Water: POB 9153, Dar es Salaam; tel. (22) 2452036; fax (22) 2452037; e-mail dppmaj@raha.com; internet www.maji.go.tz.

ZANZIBAR GOVERNMENT OF NATIONAL UNITY
(May 2011)

The Government is formed by members of Chama Cha Mapinduzi (CCM) and the Civic United Front (CUF).

President: Dr ALI MOHAMMED SHEIN (CCM).
First Vice-President: MAALIM SEIF SHARIF HAMAD (CUF).
Second Vice-President: SEIF ALI IDDI (CCM).
Minister of State in the President's Office and Chairman of the Revolutionary Council: Dr MWINYIHAJI MAKAME (CCM).
Minister of State in the President's Office, in charge of Finance, the Economy and Development Planning: OMAR YUSSUF MZEE (CCM).
Minister of State in the President's Office, in charge of Public Service and Good Governance: HAJI OMAR KHERI (CCM).
Minister of State in the Vice-President's Office: FATMA ABDULHABIB FEREJI (CUF).
Minister of State in the Second Vice-President's Office: MOHAMMED ABOUD MOHAMMED (CCM).
Minister of Constitutional Affairs and Justice: ABOUBAKAR KHAMIS BAKARY (CUF).
Minister of Infrastructure and Communications: HAMAD MASOUD HAMAD (CUF).

TANZANIA

Minister of Education and Vocational Training: RAMADHAN ABDULLA SHAABAN (CCM).
Minister of Health: JUMA DUNI HAJI (CUF).
Minister of Social Welfare, Women Development and Children: ZAINAB OMAR MOHAMMED (CCM).
Minister of Lands, Housing, Water and Energy: ALI JUMA SHAMHUNA (CCM).
Minister of Agriculture and Natural Resources: MANSOOR YUSSUF HIMID (CCM).
Minister of Trade, Industry and Marketing: NASSOR AHMED MAZRUI (CUF).
Minister of Livestock and Fisheries: SAID ALI MBAROUK (CUF).
Minister of Labour, Economic Empowerment and Co-operatives: HAROUN ALI SULEIMAN (CCM).
Members of the Revolutionary Council and Ministers without Portfolio: SULEIMAN OTHMAN NYANGA (CCM), HAJI FAKI SHAALI (CUF), MACHANO OTHMAN SAID (CCM).

There were also six Deputy Ministers.

MINISTRIES

Office of the President: POB 776, Zanzibar; tel. (24) 2230814; fax (24) 2233722.
Office of the Chief Minister: POB 239, Zanzibar; tel. (24) 2311126; fax (24) 233788.
Ministry of Agriculture, Livestock and Co-operatives: Zanzibar; tel. (24) 232662.
Ministry of Communication and Transport: POB 266, Zanzibar; tel. (24) 2232841.
Ministry of Education and Vocational Training: POB 394, Zanzibar; tel. (24) 232827.
Ministry of Employment, Youth, Women and Children: POB 884, Zanzibar; tel. (24) 30808.
Ministry of Finance and Economic Affairs: Vuga St, POB 1154, Zanzibar; tel. (24) 2231169; fax (24) 2230546; e-mail info@mofeaznz.org; internet www.mofeaznz.org.
Ministry of Information, Culture and Sport: POB 236, Zanzibar; tel. (24) 232640.
Ministry of Tourism, Trade and Investment: POB 772, Zanzibar; tel. (24) 232321.
Ministry of Water, Works, Energy and Land: Zanzibar.

President and Legislature

PRESIDENT

Election, 31 October 2010

Candidate	Votes	% of votes
Lt-Col (Retd) Jakaya Mrisho Kikwete (CCM)	5,276,827	62.83
Dr Willibrod Peter Slaa (Chadema)	2,271,941	27.05
Prof. Ibrahim Haruna Lipumba (CUF)	695,667	8.28
Peter Mziray Kuga (APPT-Maendeleo)	96,933	1.15
Hasim Spunda Rungwe (NCCR—Mageuzi)	26,388	0.31
Muttamwega Bhatt Mgaywa (TLP)	17,482	0.21
Yahmi Nassoro Dovutwa (UPDP)	13,176	0.16
Total	**8,398,414***	**100.00**

* According to results released by the National Election Commission of Tanzania, the total number of valid votes cast was 8,398,394. In addition there were 227,889 spoilt ballots.

NATIONAL ASSEMBLY

Speaker: ANNE MAKINDA.
Election, 31 October 2010

Party	Seats*
Chama Cha Mapinduzi (CCM)	251
Chama Cha Demokrasia na Maendeleo (Chadema)	45
Civic United Front (CUF)	33
National Convention for Construction and Reform (NCCR—Mageuzi)	4
Tanzania Labour Party (TLP)	1
United Democratic Party (UDP)	1
Total	**335†**

* In addition to the 239 elective seats and 103 special seats, 10 seats are reserved for presidential nominees and five for members of the Zanzibar House of Representatives; the Attorney-General is also an ex officio member of the National Assembly.
† Voting in seven constituencies was postponed until 14 November. At elections held on that date the CUF and the CCM each secured three seats, while Chadema took one seat.

ZANZIBAR PRESIDENT

Election, 31 October 2010

Candidate	Votes	% of votes
Dr Ali Mohammed Shein	179,809	50.11
Maalim Seif Sharif Hamad	176,338	49.14
Kassim Ali Bakari	803	0.22
Haji Khamis Haji	525	0.15
Juma Ali Khatib	497	0.14
Said Soud Said	480	0.13
Haji Ambar Khamis	363	0.10
Total	**358,815**	**100.00**

ZANZIBAR HOUSE OF REPRESENTATIVES

Speaker: PANDU AMEIR KIFICHO.
Election, 31 October 2010

Party	Seats*
Chama Cha Mapinduzi (CCM)	28
Civic United Front (CUF)	22
Total	**50**

* In addition to the 50 elective seats, 10 seats are reserved for presidential nominees, 20 for women (on a party basis in proportion to the number of elective seats gained) and one for the Attorney-General.

Election Commissions

National Election Commission of Tanzania (NEC): Posta House, POB 10923, Ghana/Ohio St, 6th and 7th Floor, Dar es Salaam; tel. (22) 2114963; fax (22) 2116740; e-mail info@nec.go.tz; internet www.nec.go.tz; f. 1993; Chair. LEWIS M. MAKAME; Dir of Elections R. R. KIRAVU.
Zanzibar Electoral Commission: POB 1001, Zanzibar; tel. (24) 2231489; fax (24) 2233828; e-mail election@zec.go.tz; internet www.zec.go.tz; f. 2007; Chair. KHATIB MWINYI CHANDE.

Political Organizations

African Progressive Party of Tanzania (APPT-Maendeleo): House No. 294, Wibu St, Kinondoni, POB 31932, Dar es Salaam; tel. 754300302 (mobile); f. 2003; Leader PETER MZIRAY KUGA; Sec.-Gen. AHMED HAMAD.
Bismillah Party: Pemba; seeks a referendum on the terms of the 1964 union of Zanzibar with mainland Tanzania.
Chama Cha Amani na Demokrasia Tanzania (CHADETA): House No. 41, Sadan St Ilala, POB 15809, Dar es Salaam; tel. 744889453 (mobile); granted temporary registration in 2003.
Chama Cha Demokrasia na Maendeleo (Chadema—Party for Democracy and Progress): House No. 170 Ufipa St, POB 31191, Dar es Salaam; tel. (22) 2668866; e-mail info@chadema.or.tz; internet www.chadema.or.tz; supports democracy and social development; Chair. FREEMAN MBOWE; Sec.-Gen. WILLIBROD PETER SLAA.
Chama Cha Haki na Usitawi (Chausta—Party for Justice and Development): Drive Inn Oysterbay, POB 5450, Dar es Salaam; tel. 754990228 (mobile); e-mail chausta@yahoo.com; f. 1998; officially regd 2001; Chair. JAMES MAPALALA.
Chama Cha Kijamii (CCJ): Kinondoni, Dar es Salaam; f. 2010; Chair. CONSTANTINE AKITANDA; Sec.-Gen. RENATUS MUHABHI.
Chama Cha Mapinduzi (CCM) (Revolutionary Party of Tanzania): Kuu St, POB 50, Dodoma; tel. 2180575; e-mail katibumkuu@ccmtz.org; internet www.ccmtz.org; f. 1977 by merger of the mainland-based Tanganyika African National Union (TANU) with the Afro-Shirazi Party, which operated on Zanzibar and Pemba; sole legal party 1977–92; socialist orientation; Chair. JAKAYA MRISHO KIKWETE; Vice-Chair. PIUS MSEKWA, AMANI A. KARUME; Sec.-Gen. YUSUF MAKAMBA.
Civic United Front (CUF): Mtendeni St at Malindi, POB 3637, Zanzibar; tel. and fax (24) 2237446; e-mail headquarters@cuftz.org; internet www.cuftz.org; f. 1992 by merger of Zanzibar opposition

party Kamahuru and the mainland-based Chama Cha Wananchi; commands substantial support in Zanzibar and Pemba, for which it demands increased autonomy; Chair. Prof. IBRAHIM HARUNA LIPUMBA; Sec.-Gen. SEIF SHARIF HAMAD.

Democratic Party (DP): Ilala Mchikichini, POB 63102, Dar es Salaam; tel. 713430516; e-mail dp_watanganyika@yahoo.com; f. 2002; Chair. Rev. CHRISTOPHER MTIKILA.

Demokrasia Makini (MAKINI): Mbezi Beach Makonde, nr Nguruko Int. School, POB 75636, Dar es Salaam; tel. 754295670 (mobile); officially regd 2001; Sec.-Gen. DOMINICK LYAMCHAI.

Forum for Restoration of Democracy (FORD): 13 Kibambawe St, Kariakoo, POB 15587, Dar es Salaam; tel. 741292271 (mobile); f. 2002; Chair. RAMADHANI MZEE; Sec.-Gen. EMMANUEL PATUKA.

Movement for Democratic Alternative (MDA): Zanzibar; seeks to review the terms of the 1964 union of Zanzibar with mainland Tanzania; supports democratic institutions and opposes detention without trial and press censorship.

National Convention for Construction and Reform (NCCR—Mageuzi): Plot No. 2 Kilosa St, Ilala, POB 72444, Dar es Salaam; tel. (22) 2111484; f. 1992; Chair. JAMES F. MBATIA; Sec.-Gen. SAMWELI A. RUHUZA.

National League for Democracy (NLD): Plot No. D/73 Sinza, POB 352, Dar es Salaam; tel. 714259442 (mobile); fax (22) 2462180; f. 1993; Chair. EMMANUEL J. E. MAKAIDI; Sec.-Gen. FERUZI MSAMBICHAKA.

National Reconstruction Alliance (NRA): Bububu St, Tandika Kilimahewa, POB 100125, Dar es Salaam; tel. 754496724 (mobile); f. 1993; Chair. RASHID MTUTA; Sec.-Gen. MARSHEED H. HEMED.

Popular National Party (PONA): Plot 104, Songea St, Ilala, POB 21561, Dar es Salaam; Chair. WILFREM R. MWAKITWANGE; Sec.-Gen. NICOLAUS MCHAINA.

Tanzania Democratic Alliance Party (TADEA): Buguruni Malapa, POB 482, Dar es Salaam; tel. (22) 2865244; f. 1993; Pres. JOHN D. LIFA-CHIPAKA; Sec.-Gen. JUMA ALI KHATIB.

Tanzania Labour Party (TLP): Argentina Manzese, POB 7273, Dar es Salaam; tel. (22) 2443237; f. 1993; Chair. AUGUSTINE MREMA; Sec.-Gen. JOHN KOMBA.

Tanzania People's Party (TPP): Mbezi Juu, Kawe, POB 60847, Dar es Salaam; removed from register of political parties 2002; Chair. ALEC H. CHE-MPONDA; Sec.-Gen. GRAVEL LIMO.

United Democratic Party (UDP): Plot No. 34, Block 28, Ilemela St, Mwananyamala, Kinondoni, POB 5918, Dar es Salaam; tel. 784613723 (mobile); f. 1994; Chair. JOHN MOMOSE CHEYO.

Union for Multi-Party Democracy (UMD): House No. 84, Plot No. 630, Block No. 5, Kagera St. Magomeni, POB 2985, Dar es Salaam; tel. 744478153 (mobile); f. 1993; Chair. SALUM S. ALLI; Sec.-Gen. ALI MSHANGAMA ABDALLAH.

United People's Democratic Party (UPDP): 46 Kagera St, POB 11746, Dar es Salaam; tel. 754753075 (mobile); e-mail opodsm@yahoo.com; f. 1993; Chair. YAHMI NASSORO DOVUTWA; Sec.-Gen. ABDALLAH NASSORO ALLY.

Diplomatic Representation

EMBASSIES AND HIGH COMMISSIONS IN TANZANIA

Algeria: 34 Ali Hassan Mwinyi Rd, POB 2963, Dar es Salaam; tel. (22) 2117619; fax (22) 2117620; e-mail algemb@twiga.com; Ambassador ABDELMOUN'AAM AHRIZ.

Angola: Plot 78, Lugalo Rd, POB 20793, Dar es Salaam; tel. (22) 2117674; fax (22) 2132349; Ambassador AMBRÓSIO LUKOKI.

Belgium: 5 Ocean Rd, POB 9210, Dar es Salaam; tel. (22) 2112688; fax (22) 2117621; e-mail daressalaam@diplobel.fed.be; internet www.diplomatie.be/dar-es-salaam; Ambassador PAUL JANSEN.

Burundi: Plot 1007, Lugalo Rd, POB 2752, Upanga, Dar es Salaam; Ambassador (vacant).

Canada: 38 Mirambo St, Garden Ave, POB 1022, Dar es Salaam; tel. (22) 2163300; fax (22) 2116897; e-mail dslam@international.gc.ca; internet www.dfait-maeci.gc.ca/tanzania; High Commissioner ROBERT ORR.

China, People's Republic: 2 Kajificheni Close at Toure Dr., POB 1649, Dar es Salaam; tel. (22) 2668063; fax (22) 2666353; internet tz.chineseembassy.org; Ambassador LIU XISHENG.

Congo, Democratic Republic: 438 Malik Rd, POB 975, Upanga, Dar es Salaam; tel. (22) 2150282; fax (22) 2153341; Ambassador JUMA-ALFANI MPANGO.

Cuba: Plot 313, Lugalo Rd, POB 9282, Upanga, Dar es Salaam; tel. (22) 2115928; fax (22) 2132338; e-mail embajada@ctvsatcom.net; internet emba.cubaminrex.cu/tanzania; Ambassador ERNESTO GÓMEZ DÍAZ.

Denmark: Ghana Ave, POB 9171, Dar es Salaam; tel. (22) 2165200; fax (22) 2116433; e-mail daramb@um.dk; internet www.ambdaressalaam.um.dk; Ambassador BJARNE HENNEBERG SØRENSEN.

Egypt: 24 Garden Ave, POB 1668, Dar es Salaam; tel. (22) 2117622; fax (22) 2112543; e-mail egypt.emb.tz@Cats-net.com; Ambassador WAEL ADEL ABDEL AZEEM NASR.

Finland: cnr Mirambo St and Garden Ave, POB 2455, Dar es Salaam; tel. (22) 2196565; fax (22) 2196573; e-mail sanomat.dar@formin.fi; internet www.finland.or.tz; Ambassador JUHANI TOIVONEN.

France: Ali Hassan Mwinyi Rd, POB 2349, Dar es Salaam; tel. (22) 2198800; fax (22) 2198815; e-mail ambafrance@ctvsatcom.net; internet www.ambafrance-tz.org; Ambassador JACQUES CHAMPAGNE DE LABRIOLLE.

Germany: Umoja House, Mirambo St/Garden Ave, 2nd Floor, POB 9541, Dar es Salaam; tel. (22) 2117409; fax (22) 2112944; e-mail info@daressalam.diplo.de; internet www.daressalam.diplo.de; Ambassador Dr GUIDO HERZ.

Holy See: Oyster Bay, Plot 146, Haile Selassie Rd, POB 480, Dar es Salaam (Apostolic Nunciature); tel. (22) 2666422; fax (22) 2668059; e-mail nunzio@cats-net.com; Apostolic Nuncio Most Rev. JOSEPH CHENNOTH (Titular Archbishop of Milevi).

Indonesia: 299 Ali Hassan Mwinyi Rd, POB 572, Dar es Salaam; tel. (22) 2119119; fax (22) 2115849; e-mail kbridsm@raha.com; internet www.indonesiatz.org; Ambassador SUGANDI YUDHISTIRANO.

Ireland: 353 Toure Dr., POB 9612, Oyster Bay, Dar es Salaam; tel. (22) 2602355; fax (22) 2602362; e-mail embassydaresalaam@dfa.ie; internet www.embassyofireland.or.tz; Ambassador LORCAN FULLAM.

Italy: Plot 316, Lugalo Rd, Upanga, POB 2106, Dar es Salaam; tel. (22) 2115935; fax (22) 2115938; e-mail segr.dar@esteri.it; internet www.ambdaressalaam.esteri.it; Ambassador FRANCESCO CATANIA.

Japan: 1018 Ali Hassan Mwinyi Rd, POB 2577, Dar es Salaam; tel. (22) 2115827; fax (22) 2115830; e-mail embassyofjapan_tz@raha.com; internet www.tz.emb-japan.go.jp; Ambassador HIROSHI NAKAGAWA.

Kenya: Plot 127 Mafinga St, Kinondoni, POB 5231, Dar es Salaam; tel. (22) 2668285; fax (22) 2668213; e-mail info@kenyahighcomtz.org; internet www.kenyahighcomtz.org; High Commissioner MUTINDA MUTISO.

Korea, Democratic People's Republic: Plot 5, Ursino Estate, Kawawa Rd, Msasani, POB 2690, Dar es Salaam; tel. (22) 2775395; fax (22) 2700838; Ambassador SOON CHUN LEE.

Korea, Republic: Plot 97, Msese Rd, Kingsway, Kinondoni, POB 1154, Dar es Salaam; tel. (22) 2668788; fax (22) 2667509; e-mail embassy-tz@mofat.go.kr; internet tza.mofat.go.kr; Ambassador KIM YOUNG-HOON.

Libya: 386 Mtitu St, POB 9413, Dar es Salaam; tel. (22) 2150188; fax (22) 2150068; Secretary of People's Bureau Dr AHMED IBRAHIM EL-ASHHAB.

Malawi: Plot 38, Ali Hassan Mwinyi Rd, POB 7616, Dar es Salaam; tel. (22) 2666284; fax (22) 2668161; e-mail mhc@africaonline.co.tz; High Commissioner (vacant).

Mozambique: 25 Garden Ave, POB 9370, Dar es Salaam; tel. and fax (22) 2124673; fax (22) 2116502; e-mail embamoc.tanzania@minec.gov.mz; High Commissioner ZACARIAS KUPELA.

Netherlands: Umoja House, 4th Floor, Garden Ave, POB 9534, Dar es Salaam; tel. (22) 2110000; fax (22) 2110044; e-mail dar@minbuza.nl; internet tanzania.nlembassy.org; Ambassador Dr KUINDERT ADRIAAN KOEKKOEK.

Nigeria: 83 Haile Selassie Rd, POB 9214, Oyster Bay, Dar es Salaam; tel. (22) 2666000; fax (22) 2668947; e-mail nhc-dsm@raha.com; High Commissioner ISHAYA MAJAMBU.

Norway: 160/50 Mirambo St, POB 2646, Dar es Salaam; tel. (22) 2113366; fax (22) 2116564; e-mail emb.daressalaam@mfa.no; internet www.norway.go.tz; Ambassador INGUNN KLEPSVIK.

Russia: Plot No. 73, Ali Hassan Mwinyi Rd, POB 1905, Dar es Salaam; tel. (22) 2666005; fax (22) 2666818; e-mail embruss@bol.co.tz; Ambassador LEONID SAFANOV.

Rwanda: Plot 32, Ali Hassan Mwinyi Rd, POB 2918, Dar es Salaam; tel. (22) 2120703; fax (22) 2115888; e-mail ambadsm@minaffet.gov.rw; internet www.tanzania.embassy.gov.rw; High Commissioner FATUMA NDANGIZA.

South Africa: Plot 1338/1339, Mwaya Rd, Msaski, POB 10723, Dar es Salaam; tel. (22) 2601800; fax (22) 2600684; e-mail ntombela@foreign.gov.za; High Commissioner S. G. MFENYANA.

Spain: 99B Kinondoni Rd, POB 842, Dar es Salaam; tel. (22) 2666936; fax (22) 2666938; e-mail embesptz@mail.mae.es; Ambassador JUAN MANUEL GONZÁLEZ DE LINARES PALAU.

TANZANIA

Sudan: 'Albaraka', 64 Ali Hassan Mwinyi Rd, POB 2266, Dar es Salaam; tel. (22) 2117641; fax (22) 2115811; e-mail sudan.emb.dar@raha.com; Ambassador ABDELBAGI KABEIR.

Sweden: Mirambo St and Garden Ave, POB 9274, Dar es Salaam; tel. (22) 2196500; fax (22) 2196503; e-mail ambassaden.dar-es-salaam@foreign.ministry.se; internet www.swedenabroad.se/daressalaam; Ambassador LENNARTH HJELMÅKER.

Switzerland: 79 Kinondoni Rd/Mafinga St, POB 2454, Dar es Salaam; tel. (22) 2666008; fax (22) 2666736; e-mail dar.vertretung@eda.admin.ch; internet www.eda.admin.ch/daressalaam; Ambassador ADRIAN SCHLÄPFER.

Syria: 276 Alykhan Rd, Upanga East, POB 2442, Dar es Salaam; tel. (22) 2117656; fax (22) 2115860; Chargé d'affaires a.i. M. B. IMADI.

Uganda: Extelcom Bldg, 7th Floor, Samora Ave, POB 6237, Dar es Salaam; tel. (22) 2116754; fax (22) 2112974; e-mail ugadar@intafrica.com; High Commissioner IBRAHIM MUKIIBI.

United Arab Emirates: 2415 Kaunda Drive House, Dar es Salaam; tel. (22) 2669999; fax (22) 2669996; e-mail uaeembassy@bol.co.tz; Ambassador MALALLAH MUBARAK SUWAID AL-AMIRI.

United Kingdom: Umoja House, Garden Ave, POB 9200, Dar es Salaam; tel. (22) 2110101; fax (22) 2110102; e-mail bhc.dar@fco.gov.uk; internet ukintanzania.fco.gov.uk; High Commissioner DIANE LOUISE CORNER.

USA: 686 Old Bagamoyo Rd, Msasani, POB 9123, Dar es Salaam; tel. (22) 2668001; fax (22) 2668238; e-mail embassyd@state.gov; internet tanzania.usembassy.gov; Ambassador ALFONSO E. LENHARDT.

Yemen: 353 United Nations Rd, POB 349, Dar es Salaam; tel. (22) 2117650; fax (22) 2115924; Chargé d'affaires a.i. MOHAMED ABDULLA ALMAS.

Zambia: 5–6 Ohio St/Sokoine Dr. Junction, POB 2525, Dar es Salaam; tel. and fax (22) 2112977; e-mail zhcd@raha.com; High Commissioner DARIUS STRENBECK BUBALA.

Zimbabwe: 2097 East Upanga, off Ali Hassan Mwinyi Rd, POB 20762, Dar es Salaam; tel. (22) 2116789; fax (22) 2112913; e-mail zimdares@cats-net.com; Ambassador EDZAI CHIMONYO.

Judicial System

Permanent Commission of Enquiry: POB 2643, Dar es Salaam; tel. (22) 2113690; fax (22) 2111533; Chair. and Official Ombudsman Prof. JOSEPH F. MBWILIZA; Sec. A. P. GUVETTE.

Court of Appeal

Consists of the Chief Justice and four Judges of Appeal.

Chief Justice of Tanzania: AUGUSTINO RAMADHANI.

Chief Justice of Zanzibar: HAMID MAHMOUD HAMID.

High Court: headquarters at Dar es Salaam, but regular sessions held in all Regions; consists of a Jaji Kiongozi and 29 Judges.

District Courts: situated in each district and presided over by either a Resident Magistrate or District Magistrate; limited jurisdiction, with a right of appeal to the High Court.

Primary Courts: established in every district and presided over by Primary Court Magistrates; limited jurisdiction, with a right of appeal to the District Courts and then to the High Court.

Attorney-General: FREDERICK WEREMA.

Attorney-General of Zanzibar: OMAR MAKUNGU.

Director of Public Prosecutions: ELIEZER FELESHI.

People's Courts were established in Zanzibar in 1970. Magistrates are elected by the people and have two assistants each. Under the Zanzibar Constitution, which came into force in January 1985, defence lawyers and the right of appeal, abolished in 1970, were reintroduced.

Religion

Religious surveys were eliminated from all government census reports after 1967. However, religious leaders and sociologists generally believe that the country's population is 30%–40% Christian and 30%–40% Muslim, with the remainder consisting of practitioners of other faiths, traditional indigenous religions and atheists. Foreign missionaries operate in the country, including Roman Catholics, Lutherans, Baptists, Seventh-day Adventists, Mormons, Anglicans and Muslims.

ISLAM

The Muslim population is most heavily concentrated on the Zanzibar archipelago and in the coastal areas of the mainland. There are also large Muslim minorities in inland urban areas. Some 99% of the population of Zanzibar is estimated to be Muslim. Between 80% and 90% of the country's Muslim population is Sunni; the remainder consists of several Shi'a groups, mostly of Asian descent. A large proportion of the Asian community is Isma'ili.

Ismalia Provincial Church: POB 460, Dar es Salaam.

National Muslim Council of Tanzania: POB 21422, Dar es Salaam; tel. (22) 234934; f. 1969; supervises Islamic affairs on the mainland only; Chair. Sheikh HEMED BIN JUMA BIN HEMED; Exec. Sec. Alhaj MUHAMMAD MTULIA.

Supreme Muslim Council: Zanzibar; f. 1991; supervises Islamic affairs in Zanzibar; Mufti Sheikh HARITH BIN KALEF.

Wakf and Trust Commission: POB 4092, Zanzibar; f. 1980; Islamic affairs; Exec. Sec. YUSUF ABDULRAHMAN MUHAMMAD.

CHRISTIANITY

The Christian population is composed of Roman Catholics, Protestants, Pentecostals, Seventh-day Adventists, members of the Church of Jesus Christ of Latter-day Saints (Mormons) and Jehovah's Witnesses.

Jumuiya ya Kikristo Tanzania (Christian Council of Tanzania): Church House, POB 1454, Dodoma; tel. (26) 2324445; fax (26) 2324352; f. 1934; Chair. Rt Rev. DONALD LEO MTETEMELA (Bishop of the Anglican Church); Gen. Sec. Rev. Dr LEONARD AMOS MTAITA.

The Anglican Communion

Anglicans are adherents of the Church of the Province of Tanzania, comprising 16 dioceses.

Archbishop of the Province of Tanzania and Bishop of Dar es Salaam: Most Rev. Dr VALENTINO MOKIWA, POB 1028, Iringa; fax (26) 2702479; e-mail ruaha@maf.or.tz.

Provincial Secretary: Dr R. MWITA AKIRI (acting), POB 899, Dodoma; tel. (26) 2321437; fax (26) 2324265; e-mail cpt@maf.org.

Greek Orthodox

Archbishop of East Africa: NICADEMUS OF IRINOUPOULIS (resident in Nairobi, Kenya); jurisdiction covers Kenya, Uganda and Tanzania.

Lutheran

Evangelical Lutheran Church in Tanzania: POB 3033, Boma Rd, Arusha; tel. (27) 2508856; fax (27) 2508858; e-mail elcthq@elct.or.tz; internet www.elct.or.tz; Presiding Bishop ALEX G. MALASUSA; Exec. Sec. AMANI MWENEGOHA; 5.6m. mems (2010).

The Roman Catholic Church

Tanzania comprises five archdioceses and 28 dioceses. Roman Catholics comprised an estimated 28% of the total population.

Tanzania Episcopal Conference

Catholic Secretariat, Mandela Rd, POB 2133, Dar es Salaam; tel. (22) 2851075; fax (22) 2851133; e-mail tec@cats-net.com; internet www.rc.net/tanzania/tec.

f. 1980; Pres. Mgr JUDE THADDAEUS RUWA'ICHI (Bishop of Dodoma).

Archbishop of Arusha: Most Rev. JOSAPHAT LOUIS LEBULU, Archbishop's House, POB 3044, Arusha; tel. (27) 2544361; fax (27) 2548004; e-mail angelo.arusha@habari.co.tz.

Archbishop of Dar es Salaam: Cardinal POLYCARP PENGO, Archbishop's House, POB 167, Dar es Salaam; tel. (22) 2113223; fax (22) 2125751; e-mail nyumba@cats-net.com.

Archbishop of Mwanza: Most Rev. JUDE THADAEUS RUWA'ICHI, Archbishop's House, POB 1421, Mwanza; tel. and fax (28) 2501029; e-mail archmwz@mwanza-online.com.

Archbishop of Songea: Most Rev. NORBERT WENDELIN MTEGA, Archbishop's House, POB 152, Songea; tel. (25) 2602004; fax (25) 2602593; e-mail songea-archdiocese@yahoo.com.

Archbishop of Tabora: PAUL R. RUZOKA, Archbishop's House, Private Bag, PO Tabora; tel. (26) 2605608; fax (26) 2604000; e-mail archbishops-office@yahoo.co.uk.

Other Christian Churches

Baptist Mission of Tanzania: POB 9414, Dar es Salaam; tel. (22) 2170130; fax (22) 2170127; f. 1956; Admin. FRANK PEVEY.

Christian Missions in Many Lands (Tanzania): German Branch, POB 34, Tunduru, Ruvuma Region; f. 1957; Gen. Sec. THOMAS MÜHLING.

Moravian Church in Tanzania: POB 377, Mbeya; 113,656 mems; Gen. Sec. Rev. O. M. T. MPAYO.

Pentecostal Church: POB 34, Kahama.

Presbyterian Church: POB 2510, Dar es Salaam; tel. (22) 229075.

TANZANIA

Directory

BAHÁ'Í FAITH

National Spiritual Assembly: POB 585, Dar es Salaam; tel. and fax (22) 2152766; e-mail bahaitz@cats-net.com; f. 1951; mems resident in 2,301 localities.

OTHER RELIGIONS

Many people follow traditional beliefs. There are also some Hindu communities.

The Press

NEWSPAPERS

Daily

The Citizen: Plot No. 34/35, Mandela Rd, POB 19754, Dar es Salaam; tel. 788455234 (mobile); internet www.thecitizen.co.tz; f. 2004; Man. Editor BAKARI MACHUMU.

Daily News: POB 9033, Dar es Salaam; tel. (22) 2110595; fax (22) 2112881; e-mail newsdesk@dailynews-tsn.com; internet www.dailynews.co.tz; f. 1972; govt-owned; Man. Editor SETHI KAMUHANDA; circ. 50,000.

The Guardian: POB 31042, Dar es Salaam; tel. (22) 275250; fax (22) 273583; e-mail guardian@ipp.co.tz; internet www.ippmedia.com; f. 1994; English and Swahili; Man. Dir KIONDO MSHANA; Man. Editor PASCAL SHIJA.

Kipanga: POB 199, Zanzibar; Swahili; publ. by Information and Broadcasting Services.

Majira: POB 71439, Dar es Salaam; tel. (22) 238901; fax (22) 231104; independent; Swahili; Editor THEOPHIL MAKUNGA; circ. 15,000.

Mwananchi: Plot No. 34/35, Mandela Rd, POB 19754, Dar es Salaam; internet www.mwananchi.co.tz; f. 2000; Swahili; Man. Editor DENNIS MSACKY.

Uhuru: POB 9221, Dar es Salaam; tel. (22) 2182224; fax (22) 2185065; f. 1961; official publ. of CCM; Swahili; Man. Editor SAIDI NGUBA; circ. 100,000.

Weekly

Business Times: POB 71439, Dar es Salaam; tel. (22) 238901; fax (22) 231104; e-mail majira@bcsmedia.com; internet www.bcstimes.com; independent; English; Editor ALLI MWAMBOLA; circ. 15,000.

The Express: POB 20588, Dar es Salaam; tel. (22) 2180058; fax (22) 2182665; e-mail express@raha.com; internet www.theexpress.com; independent; English; Editor FAYAZ BHOJANI; circ. 20,000.

Gazette of the United Republic: POB 9142, Dar es Salaam; tel. (22) 231817; official announcements; Editor H. HAJI; circ. 6,000.

Government Gazette: POB 261, Zanzibar; f. 1964; official announcements.

Kasheshe: POB 31042, Dar es Salaam; Swahili; Editor VENANCE MLAY.

Kiongozi (The Leader): POB 9400, Dar es Salaam; tel. (22) 2851075; fax (22) 2851133; e-mail kiongozinews@yahoo.com; f. 1950; owned by Catholic Publishers Limited; weekly; Swahili; Roman Catholic; Dir JOSEPH MATUMAINI; circ. 33,500.

Mfanyakazi (The Worker): POB 15359, Dar es Salaam; tel. (22) 226111; Swahili; trade union publ; Editor NDUGU MTAWA; circ. 100,000.

Mwanaspoti: POB 19754, Dar es Salaam; tel. (22) 2150312; fax (22) 2180183; e-mail mwanaspoti@mwanaspoti.co.tz; internet www.mwanaspoti.co.tz.

Mzalendo: POB 9221, Dar es Salaam; tel. (22) 2182224; fax (22) 2185065; e-mail uhuru@udsm.ac.tz; f. 1972; publ. by CCM; Swahili; Man. Editor SAIDI NGABA; circ. 115,000.

Nipashe Jumapili: POB 31042, Dar es Salaam; Swahili.

Sunday News: POB 9033, Dar es Salaam; tel. (22) 2116072; fax (22) 2112881; f. 1954; govt-owned; Man. Editor SETHI KAMUCHANDA; circ. 50,000.

Sunday Observer: POB 31042, Dar es Salaam; e-mail guardian@ipp.co.tz; Man. Dir VUMI URASA; Man. Editor PETER MSUNGU.

PERIODICALS

The African Review: POB 35042, Dar es Salaam; tel. (22) 2410130; e-mail mubakar@udsm.ac.tz; 2 a year; journal of African politics, development and international affairs; publ. by the Dept of Political Science, Univ. of Dar es Salaam; Chief Editor Dr MOHAMMED BAKARI; circ. 1,000.

Eastern African Law Review: POB 35093, Dar es Salaam; tel. (22) 243254; f. 1967; 2 a year; Chief Editor N. N. N. NDITI; circ. 1,000.

Elimu Haina Mwisho: POB 1986, Mwanza; monthly; circ. 45,000.

Habari za Washirika: POB 2567, Dar es Salaam; tel. (22) 223346; monthly; publ. by Co-operative Union of Tanzania; Editor H. V. N. CHIBULUNJE; circ. 40,000.

Jenga: POB 2669, Dar es Salaam; tel. (22) 2112893; fax (22) 2113618; journal of the National Development Corpn; circ. 2,000.

Kweupe: POB 222, Zanzibar; weekly; Swahili; publ. by Information and Broadcasting Services.

Mlezi (The Educator): POB 41, Peramiho; f. 1970; every 2 months; Editor Fr DOMINIC WEIS; circ. 8,000.

Mwenge (Firebrand): POB 1, Peramiho; f. 1937; monthly; Editor JOHN P. MBONDE; circ. 10,000.

Nchi Yetu (Our Country): POB 9142, Dar es Salaam; tel. (22) 2110200; f. 1964; govt publ; monthly; Swahili; circ. 50,000.

Nuru: POB 1893, Zanzibar; f. 1992; bi-monthly; official publ. of Zanzibar Govt; circ. 8,000.

Safina: POB 21422, Dar es Salaam; tel. (22) 234934; publ. by National Muslim Council of Tanzania; Editor YASSIN SADIK; circ. 10,000.

Sikiliza: POB 635, Morogoro; tel. and fax (23) 2604374; quarterly; Seventh-day Adventist; Editor MIKA D. MUSA; circ. 100,000.

Tantravel: POB 2485, Dar es Salaam; tel. (22) 2111244; fax (22) 2116420; e-mail safari@ud.co.tz; internet www.tanzaniatouristboard.com; f. 1987; quarterly; publ. by Tanzania Tourist Board; Editor GERVAS TATAH MLOLA.

Tanzania Trade Currents: POB 5402, Dar es Salaam; tel. (22) 2851706; fax (22) 851700; e-mail betis@intafrica.com; bi-monthly; publ. by Board of External Trade; circ. 2,000.

Uhuru na Amani: POB 3033, Arusha; tel. (57) 8855; fax (57) 8858; quarterly; Swahili; publ. by Evangelical Lutheran Church in Tanzania; Editor ELIZABETH LOBULU; circ. 15,000.

Ukulima wa Kisasa (Modern Farming): Farmers' Education and Publicity Unit, POB 2308, Dar es Salaam; tel. (22) 2116496; fax (22) 2122923; e-mail fepu@hotmail.co.uk; f. 1955; bi-monthly; Swahili; publ. by Ministry of Agriculture, Food Security and Co-operatives; Editor LUCAS NYANGI; circ. 15,000.

Ushirika Wetu: POB 2567, Dar es Salaam; tel. (22) 2184081; e-mail ushirika@covision2000.com; monthly; publ. by Tanzania Federation of Co-operatives; Editor SIMON J. KERARYO; circ. 40,000.

NEWS AGENCY

Press Services Tanzania (PST) Ltd: POB 31042, Dar es Salaam; tel. and fax (22) 2119195.

Publishers

Central Tanganyika Press: POB 1129, Dodoma; tel. (26) 2390015; fax (26) 2324565; e-mail ctp@anglican.or.tz; internet www.anglican.or.tz/ctp.htm; f. 1954; religious; Man. PETER MANG'ATI MAKASSI.

DUP (1996) Ltd: POB 7028, Dar es Salaam; tel. and fax (22) 2410137; e-mail director@dup.udsm.ac.tz; f. 1979; educational, academic and cultural texts in Swahili and English; Dir Dr N. G. MWITTA.

Eastern Africa Publications Ltd: POB 1002 Arusha; tel. (57) 3176; f. 1979; general and school textbooks; Gen. Man. ABDULLAH SAIWAAD.

Inland Publishers: POB 125, Mwanza; tel. (68) 40064; general non-fiction, religion, in Kiswahili and English; Dir Rev. S. M. MAGESA.

Oxford University Press: Maktaba Rd, POB 5299, Dar es Salaam; tel. (22) 229209; f. 1969; literature, literary criticism, essays, poetry; Man. SALIM SHAABAN SALIM.

Tanzania Publishing House: 47 Samora Machel Ave, POB 2138, Dar es Salaam; tel. (22) 2137402; e-mail tphhouse@yahoo.com; f. 1966; educational and general books in Swahili and English; Gen. Man. PRIMUS ISIDOR KARUGENDO.

GOVERNMENT PUBLISHING HOUSE

Government Printer: Office of the Prime Minister, POB 3021, Dar es Salaam; tel. (22) 2860900; fax (22) 2866955; e-mail gptz@pmo.go.tz; Dir KASSIAN C. CHIBOGOYO.

Broadcasting and Communications

TELECOMMUNICATIONS

Tanzania Communications Regulatory Authority (TCRA): Mawasiliano Towers, Plot 2005/5/1, Block C, Sam Nujoma Rd, POB 474, Dar es Salaam; tel. (22) 25578455; e-mail dg@tcra.go.tz; internet www.tcra.go.tz; f. 1993; licenses postal and telecommuni-

TANZANIA
Directory

cations service operators; manages radio spectrum; acts as ombudsman; Chair. BUXTON CHIPETA; Dir-Gen. Prof. JOHN S. NKOMA.

Airtel Tanzania: Zain House, Ali Hassan Mwinyi Rd, Dar es Salaam; tel. (22) 2748181; e-mail info.africa@airtel.com; internet africa.airtel.com/tanzania; f. 2001; fmrly Zain Tanzania, present name adopted 2010; Man. Dir SAM ELANGALLOOR.

MIC Tanzania (Mobitel) Ltd: Lugoda St, POB 2929, Dar es Salaam; tel. 713800800 (mobile); fax (22) 2120474; e-mail mobitel@mobitel.co.tz; internet www.tigo.co.tz; operates mobile cellular telecommunications services through Mobitel network; 100% owned by Millicom International Cellular (Luxembourg).

Tanzania Telecommunications Co Ltd (TTCL): Extelcoms House, Samora Ave, POB 9070, Dar es Salaam; tel. (22) 2142000; fax (22) 2113232; e-mail ttcl@ttcl.co.tz; internet www.ttcl.co.tz; 35% sold to consortium of Detecon (Germany) and Mobile Systems International (Netherlands) in Feb. 2001; CEO SAID AMIR SAID.

Vodacom (Tanzania) Ltd: PPF Towers, 14th Floor, Garden Ave/Ohio St, POB 2369, Dar es Salaam; tel. 754705000 (mobile); fax 754704014 (mobile); e-mail feedback@vodacom.co.tz; internet www.vodacom.co.tz; mobile cellular telephone operator; Man. Dir DIETLOF MARE.

Zanzibar Telecom (Zantel): POB 3459, Zanzibar; tel. (24) 2234823; fax (24) 2234850; e-mail customerservices@zantel.co.tz; internet www.zantel.co.tz; f. 1999; mobile cellular telephone operator for Zanzibar; Chair. SALEM AL SHARHAN; CEO NORMAL MOYO.

BROADCASTING
Radio

Parapanda Radio Tanzania: POB 9191, Dar es Salaam; tel. (22) 2860760; e-mail radiotanzania@raha.com; state-run FM station.

Radio 5 Arusha: POB 11843, Arusha; tel. (27) 8052; fax (27) 4201; e-mail impala@cybernet.co.tz.

Radio FM Zenj 96.8: Zanzibar; f. 2005; owned by Zanzibar Media Corpn; broadcasts to 60% of Zanzibar, to be extended to all of Zanzibar and mainland coast from southern Tanzania to Kenya; Gen. Man. AUSTIN MAKANI.

Radio Kwizera: POB 154, N'Gara; tel. and fax (28) 2226079; e-mail rkngara@jrstz.co.tz; internet www.radiokwizera.org; f. 1995; station's objective is to educate, entertain and inform refugee and local communities, with the aim of bringing about peace and reconciliation; Dir DAMAS S. J. MISSANGA.

Radio One: Mikocheni Light Industrial Area, POB 4374, Dar es Salaam; tel. (22) 275914; fax (22) 2775915; e-mail info@itv.co.tz; internet www.ippmedia.com; subsidiary of ITV (see Television).

Radio Tanzania Zanzibar: state-owned.

Radio Tumaini (Hope): 1 Bridge St, POB 9916, Dar es Salaam; tel. (22) 2117307; fax (22) 2112594; e-mail tumaini@cats-net.com; internet radiotumaini.tripod.com; broadcasts in Swahili within Dar es Salaam; operated by the Roman Catholic Church; broadcasts on religious, social and economic issues; Dir ESTHER CHILAMBO.

Sauti Ya Tanzania Zanzibar (The Voice of Tanzania Zanzibar): POB 1178, Zanzibar; f. 1951; state-owned; broadcasts in Swahili on three wavelengths; Dir SULEIMAN JUMA.

Tanzania Broadcasting Corporation (TBC): Broadcasting House, Nyerere Rd, POB 9191, Dar es Salaam; tel. (22) 2860760; fax (22) 2865577; e-mail info@tbcorp.org; internet www.tbcorp.org; f. 2008; incorporates Radio Tanzania Dar es Salaam and the national TV network, Televisheni ya Taifa; Dir-Gen. DUNSTAN TIDO MHANDO.

   Radio Tanzania Dar es Salaam (RTD): POB 9191, Dar es Salaam; tel. (22) 2860760; fax (22) 2865577; e-mail info@tbcorp.org; internet www.tbcorp.org; f. 1951; state-owned; subsidiary of TBC; domestic services in Swahili; external services in English; Gen. Man. EDDA SANGA.

Television

Dar es Salaam Television (DTV): POB 21122, Dar es Salaam; tel. (22) 2116341; fax (22) 2113112; e-mail franco.dtv@raha.com; f. 1994; Man. Dir FRANCO TRAMONTANO.

Independent Television (ITV): Mikocheni Light Industrial Area, POB 4374, Dar es Salaam; tel. (22) 2775914; fax (22) 2775915; e-mail itv@ipp.co.tz; internet www.ippmedia.com; f. 1994; wholly owned by IPP Ltd; 65% of programmes are locally produced and in Kiswahili; Man. Dir JOYCE MHAVILLE.

Star TV: Post Rd, POB 1732, Mwanza; tel. (28) 2503262; fax (28) 2500713; e-mail marketing@startvtz.com; internet www.startvtz.com; f. 2000.

Tanzania Broadcasting Corporation (TBC): see Radio

   Televisheni ya Taifa (TVT): POB 31519, Dar es Salaam; tel. (22) 2700011; fax (22) 2773078; e-mail info@tbcorp.org; internet www.tbc.go.tz; f. 2000; state-owned; subsidiary of TBC since 2008; Gen. Man. CLEMENT MSHANA.

Television Zanzibar: Karume House, POB 314, Zanzibar; tel. and fax (24) 22315951; e-mail karumehouse@tvz.co.tz; internet www.tvz.co.tz; f. 1973; Dir OMAR O. CHANDE.

Finance

(cap. = capital; res = reserves; dep. = deposits; m. = million; brs = branches; amounts in Tanzanian shillings, unless otherwise indicated)

BANKING

In 2010 there were 41 banking institutions in Tanzania: 29 commercial banks, seven regional unit banks and five other financial institutions. Of these, four were fully owned by the Government and the rest were privately owned.

Central Bank

Bank of Tanzania (Benki Kuu Ya Tanzania): 10 Mirambo St, POB 2939, Dar es Salaam; tel. (22) 2110946; fax (22) 2113325; e-mail info@hq.bot-tz.org; internet www.bot-tz.org; f. 1966; bank of issue; cap. 10,000m., res 639,286m., dep. 1,854,572m. (June 2009); Gov. and Chair. Prof. BENNO NDULU; 4 brs.

Principal Banks

Akiba Commercial Bank Ltd: TDFL Bldg, Upanga Rd, POB 669, Dar es Salaam; tel. (22) 2118340; fax (22) 2114173; e-mail akiba@cats-net.com; internet www.acb-bank.com; f. 1997; cap. 8,170.7m., res 4,049.5m., dep. 59,796.2m. (Dec. 2009); Chair. Dr IDRIS RASHIDI; Man. Dir JOHN LWANDE.

Azania Bancorp Ltd: Masdo House, Samora Ave, POB 9271, Dar es Salaam; tel. (22) 2117997; fax (22) 2118010; e-mail info@azaniabank.co.tz; internet www.azaniabank.co.tz; 55% owned by National Social Security Fund, 31% owned by Parastatal Pension Fund, 9% owned by East African Development Bank, 5% owned by individuals; cap. 10,867.6m., res 918,4m., dep. 120,854.0m (Dec. 2009); Chair. WILLIAM E. ERIO; CEO CHARLES SINGILI.

BancABC (Tanzania) Ltd: Barclays House, 1st Floor, Ohio St, POB 31, Dar es Salaam; tel. (22) 2119303; fax (22) 2112402; e-mail abct@africanbankingcorp.com; internet www.africanbankingcorp.com; wholly owned by African Banking Corpn Holdings Ltd; cap. 5,404m. (Dec. 2003); Man. Dir ISRAEL CHASOSA.

Bank M (Tanzania) Ltd: POB 96, 8 Ocean Rd, Dar es Salaam; tel. (22) 2127825; fax (22) 2127824; e-mail ganpath.pillai@bankm.co.tz; internet www.bankm.co.tz; f. 2007; 19.82% owned by Negus Holdings, 17.65% by Equity & Allied Ltd; cap. 10,502.5m., dep. 97,457.6m. (Dec. 2009); Chair. NIMROD MKONO; CEO SANJEEV KUMAR; 4 brs.

Barclays Bank (Tanzania) Ltd: Barclays House, Ohio St, POB 5137, Dar es Salaam; tel. (22) 2136970; fax (22) 2129750; e-mail kihara.maina@barclays.com; internet www.barclays.com/africa/tanzania; 99.9% owned by Barclays PLC (United Kingdom), 0.1% owned by Ebbgate Holdings Ltd; cap. 18,750m. (Dec. 2003); Man. Dir CHRISTOPHER KIHARA MAINA.

BOA Bank (Tanzania) Ltd: NDC Development House, cnr Kivukoni Front and Ohio St, POB 3054, Dar es Salaam; tel. (22) 2111229; fax (22) 2113740; e-mail eab@eurafricanbank-tz.com; internet www.boatanzania.com; f. 1994 as Eurafrican Bank (Tanzania) Ltd, name changed as above in 2007; 36.68% owned by Bank of Africa Kenya Ltd, 25.01% by Aureos Capital East Africa LLC, 25.01% by Belgian Investment Co; total assets 89,486m. (Dec. 2007); Chair. FULGENCE M. KAZAURA; Man. Dir KOBBY ANDAH.

Citibank Tanzania Ltd: Ali Hassan Mwinyi Rd, POB 71625, Dar es Salaam; tel. (22) 2117575; fax (22) 2113910; 99.98% owned by Citibank Overseas Investment Corpn; Chair. EMEKA EMUWA; CEO JAMAL ALI HUSSEIN.

CRDB Bank: Azikiwe St, POB 268, Dar es Salaam; tel. (22) 2117442; fax (22) 2116714; e-mail crdb@crdbbank.com; internet www.crdbbank.com; f. as Co-operative and Rural Development Bank in 1947, transferred to private ownership and current name adopted 1996; 30% owned by DANIDA Investment; cap. 54,413.3m., res 153,209.5m., dep. 1,625,227.7m. (Dec. 2009); Chair MARTIN J. MMARI; Man. Dir Dr CHARLES S. KIMEI; 56 brs.

Dar es Salaam Community Bank Ltd (DCB): Arnautoglu Bldg, Bibi Titi Mohamed St, POB 19798, Dar es Salaam; tel. (22) 2180253; fax (22) 2180239; e-mail dcb@africaonline.co.tz; f. 2001; cap. 1,796m. (Dec. 2003); Chair. PAUL MILVANGE RUPIA; Man. Dir EDMUND PANCRAS MKWAWA.

Diamond Trust Bank Tanzania Ltd: POB 115, 9th Floor, Harbour View Towers, Dar es Salaam; tel. (22) 2114891; fax (22) 2124244; internet www.dtbafrica.com; f. 1946 as Diamond Jubilee Investment Trust; converted to bank and adopted current name in 1996; 55% owned by Diamond Trust Bank Kenya Ltd, 23% owned by Aga Khan Fund for Economic Development SA (Switzerland); cap.

1,550.6m., res 5,452.9m., dep. 176,827.4m. (Dec. 2009); Chair. ABDUL SAMJI; CEO VIJU CHERIAN.

EXIM Bank (Tanzania) Ltd: NIC Investment House, Samora Ave, POB 1431, Dar es Salaam; tel. (22) 2113091; fax (22) 2119737; e-mail marketing@eximbank-tz.com; internet www.eximbank-tz.com; cap. 12,900m., res 15,452m., dep. 462,039m. (Dec. 2009); Chair. YOGESH MANEK; Man. Dir S. M. J. MWAMBENJA.

FBME Bank Ltd: Samora Ave, POB 8298, Dar es Salaam; tel. (22) 2126000; fax (22) 2126006; e-mail headoffice@fbme.com; internet www.fbme.com; f. 1982; cap. US $43.2m., res US $5.9m., dep. US $1,562.8m. (Dec. 2009); Chair. AYOUB-FARID M. SAAB, FADI M. SAAB; Gen. Man. (Tanzania) JOHN LISTER; 5 brs.

Habib African Bank Ltd: Indira Gandhi/Zanaki St, POB 70086, Dar es Salaam; tel. (22) 2111107; fax (22) 2111014; e-mail hasanrizvi@habibafricanbank.co.tz; f. 1998; cap. 7,475m., dep. 65,236m. (Dec. 2009); Chair. HABIB MOHAMMED D. HABIB; Man. Dir SYED HASAN RIZVI; 2 brs.

I & M Tanzania Ltd Bank Ltd: Jivan Hirji Bldg, Indira Gandhi/Mosque St, POB 1509, Dar es Salaam; tel. (22) 2110212; fax (22) 2118750; e-mail cfunionbank@raha.com; internet www.imbank.com; f. 2002 by merger of Furaha Finance Ltd and Crown Finance & Leasing Ltd; present name adopted 2010; cap. 4m. (Dec. 2006); Chair. SARIT S. RAJA SHAH; CEO SUBRAMANIAN GOPALAN.

International Bank of Malaysia (Tanzania) Ltd: Upanga/Kisutu St, POB 9363, Dar es Salaam; tel. (22) 2110518; fax (22) 2110196; e-mail ibm@afsat.com; Chair. JOSEPHINE PREMLA SIVARETNAM; CEO M. RAHMAT.

International Commercial Bank (Tanzania) Ltd: 1st Floor, Jamhuri St/Morogoro Rd, POB 9362, Dar es Salaam; tel. (22) 2134989; fax (22) 2134286; e-mail enquiry@icbank-tz.com; f. 1998; CEO L. K. GANAPATHIRAMANI; 5 brs.

Kenya Commercial Bank (Tanzania) Ltd: National Audit House, Samora/Ohio St, POB 804, Dar es Salaam; tel. (22) 2115386; fax (22) 2115391; internet www.kcb.co.ke; cap. 6,000m. (Dec. 2003); Chair. PETER MUTHOKA; Man. Dir Dr EDMUND BERNARD MNDOLWA.

Mufindi Community Bank: POB 147, Mafinga; tel. and fax (26) 2772165; e-mail mucoba@africaonline.co.tz; cap. 100m. (Dec. 2003); Chair. ATTILIO MOHELE; Gen. Man. DANY MPOGOLE.

Mwanga Community Bank: Mwanga Township, POB 333, Mwanga, Kilimanjaro; tel. and fax (27) 2754235; Man. Dir CHRIS HALIBUT.

National Microfinance Bank Ltd (NMB): Samora Ave, POB 9213, Dar es Salaam; tel. (22) 2124048; fax (22) 2110077; e-mail ceo@nmbtz.com; internet www.nmbtz.com; f. 1997 following disbandment of the National Bank of Commerce; 51% state-owned, 49% owned by a consortium led by Rabobank Group; Chair. MISHECK NGATUNGA; CEO MARK H. WIESSING; 140 brs.

NBC Ltd (National Bank of Commerce Ltd): NBC House, Sokoine Drive, POB 1863, Dar es Salaam; tel. (22) 2112082; fax (22) 2112887; e-mail nbcltd@nbctz.com; internet www.nbctz.com; f. 1997; 55% owned by ABSA Group Ltd (South Africa), 30% by Govt and 15% by International Finance Corpn; cap. 10,000m., res 154,446m., dep. 1,051,393m. (Dec. 2009); Man. Dir LAWRENCE MAFURU; 56 brs.

NIC Bank Ltd: Mezannine Floor, Harbour View Towers, Mission St/Samora Ave, POB 20268, Dar es Salaam; tel. (22) 2118625; fax (22) 2116733; e-mail james.muchiri@nic-bank.com; internet www.sfltz.com; name changed as above in 2010; 51% owned by National Industrial Credit Bank Ltd (Kenya); Chair. ABDULSULTAN HASHAM JAMAL; Man. Dir JAMES MUCHIRI; 4 brs.

People's Bank of Zanzibar Ltd (PBZ): POB 1173, Stone Town, Zanzibar; tel. (24) 2231119; fax (24) 2231121; e-mail pbzltd@zanlik.com; f. 1966; controlled by Zanzibar Govt; cap. 5,000.0m., res 10,785.2m., dep. 99,480.4m. (Dec. 2009); Chair. ABDUL RAHMAN M. JUMBE; Man. Dirs J. M. AMOUR, N. S. NASSOR; 3 brs.

Stanbic Bank Tanzania Ltd: Sukari House, cnr AH Mwinyi/Kinondoni Rd, POB 72647, Dar es Salaam; tel. (22) 2666430; fax (22) 2666301; e-mail tanzaniainfo@stanbic.com; internet www.stanbic.co.tz; f. 1993; wholly owned by Standard Africa Holdings Ltd; cap. 2,000m., res 871m., dep. 230,804m. (Dec. 2005); Chair ARNOLD B. S. KILEWO; Man. Dir BASHIR AWALE; 10 brs.

Standard Chartered Bank Tanzania Ltd: International House, 1st Floor, cnr Shaaban Robert St and Garden Ave, POB 9011, Dar es Salaam; tel. (22) 2122125; fax (22) 2113770; f. 1992; wholly owned by Standard Chartered Holdings (Africa) BV, Netherlands; cap. 15,032.0m., res 2,525.9m., dep. 713,527.3m. (Dec. 2009); Man. Dir JEREMY AWORI; 7 brs.

Tanzania Development Finance Co Ltd (TDFL): TDFL Bldg, Plot 1008, cnr Upanga Rd and Ohio St, POB 2478, Dar es Salaam; tel. (22) 2116417; fax (22) 2116418; e-mail mail@tdfl.co.tz; f. 1962; owned by Govt (32%), govt agencies of the Netherlands and Germany (5% and 26%, respectively), the Commonwealth Development Corpn (26%) and the European Investment Bank (11%); cap. 3,303m. (Dec. 2001); Chair. H. K. SENKORO; CEO J. MCGUFFOG.

Tanzania Investment Bank (TIB): Bldg No. 3, Mlimani City Office Park, Sam Nujoma Rd, POB 9373, Dar es Salaam; tel. (22) 2411101; fax (22) 2411095; e-mail md@tib.co.tz; internet www.tib.co.tz; f. 1970; 99% govt-owned; cap. 7,641m., res 2,823m., dep. 45,746m. (Dec. 2005); Man. Dir PETER E. M. NONI.

Tanzania Postal Bank (TPB): Extelecoms Annex Bldg, Samora Ave, POB 9300, Dar es Salaam; tel. (22) 2112358; fax (22) 2114815; e-mail md@postalbank.co.tz; internet www.postalbank.co.tz; f. 1991; state-owned; cap. 1,041m. (Dec. 2003); Chair. Prof. LETICIA RUTASHOBYA; Man. Dir and CEO ALPHONSE R. KIHWELE; 4 brs and 113 agencies.

United Bank for Africa Tanzania Ltd: 30C/30D Nyerere Rd, POB 80514, Dar es Salaam; tel. (22) 2863452; fax (22) 2863454; e-mail uba@cats-net.com; Chair. N. N. KITOMARI; Man. Dir AYOBOLA ABIOLA.

BANKING ASSOCIATION

Tanzania Bankers Association: 4th Floor, Sukari House, Ohio/Sokoine Dr., POB 70925, Dar es Salaam; tel. (22) 2127764; fax (22) 2124492; e-mail info@tanzaniabankers.org; internet www.tanzaniabankers.org; f. 1995; Chair. BEN CHRISTIAANSE; Exec. Dir PASCAL L. KAMUZORA.

STOCK EXCHANGE

Dar es Salaam Stock Exchange: Twigga Bldg, 4th Floor, Samora Ave, POB 70081, Dar es Salaam; tel. (22) 2135779; fax (22) 2133849; e-mail info@darstockexchange.com; internet www.dse.co.tz; f. 1998; Chair. PETER MACHUNDE; Chief Exec. Dr HAMISI S. KIBOLA.

INSURANCE

In 2010 there were 23 licensed insurance companies in Tanzania, of which two were fully owned by the government.

African Life Assurance Co Ltd: International House, POB 79651, Dar es Salaam; tel. (22) 2122914; fax (22) 2122917; e-mail charlesw@aflife.co.tz; Chair. CHARLES WASHOMA.

Alliance Insurance Corpn Ltd: 7th Floor, Exim Tower, POB 9942, Dar es Salaam; tel. (22) 2139100; fax (22) 2139098; e-mail admin@alliancetz.com; internet www.alliancetz.com; Chair. SHAFFIN JAMAL; Man. Dir K. V. A. KRISHNAN.

Jubilee Insurance Co of Tanzania Ltd (JICT): 4th Floor, Amani Plaza, Ohio St, POB 20524, Dar es Salaam; e-mail jictz@jubileetanzania.com; internet www.jubileetanzania.com; 40% owned by Jubilee Insurance Kenya, 24% by local investors, 15% by the IFC, 15% by the Aga Khan Fund for Economic Devt, 6% by others; cap. US $2m; Prin. Officer S. RAVI.

National Insurance Corporation of Tanzania Ltd (NIC): POB 9264, Dar es Salaam; tel. (22) 2113823; fax (22) 2113403; e-mail info-nic@nictanzania.com; internet www.nictanzania.co.tz; f. 1963; state-owned; all classes of insurance; Chair. Prof. J. L. KANYWANYI; Man. Dir OCTAVIAN W. TEMU; 30 brs.

Niko Insurance (Tanzania) Ltd: PPF House, 8th Floor, Morogoro Rd/Samora Ave, POB 21228, Dar es Salaam; tel. (22) 2120188; fax (22) 2120193; e-mail info@nikoinsurance.co.tz; internet www.nikoinsurance.co.tz; f. 1998; subsidiary of NICO Holdings Ltd (based in Malawi); Gen. Man. MANFRED Z. SIBANDE.

REGULATORY AUTHORITY

Tanzania Insurance Regulatory Authority (TIRA): Block 33, Plot No. 85/2115, Mtendeni St, POB 9892, Dar es Salaam; tel. (22) 2132537; fax (22) 2132539; e-mail coi@tira.go.tz; internet www.tira.go.tz; f. 2009; Chair. Prof. G. M. FIMBO; Commr of Insurance I. L. KAMUZORA.

Trade and Industry

GOVERNMENT AGENCIES

Board of External Trade (BET): POB 5402, Dar es Salaam; tel. (22) 2850238; fax (22) 2850239; e-mail betis@intafrica.com; internet www.bet.co.tz; f. 1978; trade and export information and promotion, market research, marketing advisory and consultancy services; Dir-Gen. MBARUK K. MWANDORO.

Board of Internal Trade (BIT): POB 883, Dar es Salaam; tel. (22) 228301; f. 1967 as State Trading Corpn; reorg. 1973; state-owned; supervises seven national and 21 regional trading cos; distribution of general merchandise, agricultural and industrial machinery, pharmaceuticals, foodstuffs and textiles; shipping and other transport services; Dir-Gen. J. E. MAKOYE.

TANZANIA

Parastatal Sector Reform Commission (PSRC): Sukari House, POB 9252, Dar es Salaam; tel. (22) 2115482; fax (22) 2113065; e-mail masalla@raha.com.

Tanzania Investment Centre (TIC): POB 938, Dar es Salaam; tel. (22) 2116328; fax (22) 2118253; e-mail information@tic.co.tz; internet www.tic.co.tz; f. 1997; promotes and facilitates investment in Tanzania; Chair. E. MTANGO; Exec. Dir EMMANUEL OLE NAIKO.

CHAMBERS OF COMMERCE

Dar es Salaam Chamber of Commerce: Kelvin House, Samora Machel Ave, POB 41, Dar es Salaam; tel. (744) 270438; fax (22) 2112754; e-mail dcc1919@yahoo.com; f. 1919; Exec. Dir Y. P. MSEKWA.

Tanzania Chamber of Commerce, Industry and Agriculture (TCCIA): 2nd Floor, Twiga House, Samora Ave, POB 9713, Dar es Salaam; tel. (22) 2119436; fax (22) 2119437; e-mail info@tccia.com; internet www.tccia.co.tz; f. 1988; Pres. ALOYS MWAMANGA.

Zanzibar Chamber of Commerce: POB 1407, Zanzibar; tel. (24) 2233083; fax (24) 2233349.

DEVELOPMENT CORPORATIONS

Capital Development Authority: POB 1, Dodoma; tel. (26) 2324053; f. 1973 to develop the new capital city of Dodoma; govt-controlled; Dir-Gen. EVARIST BABISI KEWBA.

Economic Development Commission: POB 9242, Dar es Salaam; tel. (22) 2112681; f. 1962 to plan national economic development; state-controlled.

National Development Corporation: Kivukoni Front, Ohio St, POB 2669, Dar es Salaam; tel. (22) 2112893; fax (22) 2113618; e-mail epztz@ndctz.com; internet www.ndctz.com; f. 1965; state-owned; cap. Ts. 30.0m.; promotes progress and expansion in production and investment; Man. Dir GIDEON NASSARI.

Small Industries Development Organization (SIDO): Mfaume/Fire Rd, Upanga, POB 2476, Dar es Salaam; tel. (22) 2151947; fax (22) 2152070; e-mail dg@sido.go.tz; internet www.sido.go.tz; f. 1973; parastatal; promotes and assists development of small-scale enterprises in public, co-operative and private sectors, aims to increase the involvement of women in small businesses; Chair. JAPHET S. MLAGALA; Dir-Gen. MIKE LAISOR.

Sugar Development Corporation: Dar es Salaam; tel. (22) 2112969; fax (22) 230598; Gen. Man. GEORGE G. MBATI.

Tanzania Petroleum Development Corporation (TPDC): POB 2774, Dar es Salaam; tel. (22) 2181407; fax (22) 2180047; internet www.tpdc-tz.com; f. 1969; state-owned; oversees petroleum exploration and undertakes autonomous exploration, imports crude petroleum and distributes refined products; Man. Dir YONA S. M. KILLAGANE.

There is also a development corporation for textiles.

INDUSTRIAL AND TRADE ASSOCIATIONS

Cashewnut Board of Tanzania: POB 533, Mtwara; tel. (23) 2333303; fax (23) 2333536; e-mail info@cashewnut-tz.org; internet www.cashewnut-tz.org; govt-owned; regulates the marketing, processing and export of cashews; Chair. HEMED B. MKALI (acting); Dir-Gen. A. BENO MHAGAMA.

Confederation of Tanzania Industries (CTI): POB 71783, Dar es Salaam; tel. (22) 2114954; fax (22) 2115414; e-mail cti@cti.co.tz; internet www.cti.co.tz; f. 1991; Chair. FELIX MOSHA; Exec. Dir CHRISTINE KILINDU.

National Coconut Development Programme: POB 6226, Dar es Salaam; tel. (22) 2700552; fax (22) 275549; e-mail mari@mari.or.tz; f. 1979 to revive coconut industry; processing and marketing via research and devt in disease and pest control, agronomy and farming systems, breeding and post-harvest technology; based at Mikocheni Agricultural Research Inst; Dir Dr ALOIS K. KULLAYA.

Tanzania Coffee Board (TCB): Kahawa House, POB 732, Moshi; tel. (27) 272324; fax (27) 270998; e-mail enquiries@tanzaniacoffee.co.tz; internet www.tanzaniacoffeeboard.org; Chair. PIUS NGEZE; Dir-Gen. ADOLPH KUMBURU.

Tanzania Cotton Board: Pamba House, Garden Ave, POB 9161, Dar es Salaam; tel. (22) 2122564; fax (22) 2112894; e-mail info@cotton.co.tz; internet www.cotton.or.tz; f. 1984; regulates, develops and promotes the Tanzanian cotton industry; Chair. Dr FESTUS BULUGU LIMBU; Dir-Gen. Dr JOE KABISSA.

Tanzania Exporters' Association: NIC Investment House, 6th Floor, Wing A, Samora Ave, POB 1175, Dar es Salaam; tel. and fax (22) 2125438; e-mail tanexa.exporters@yahoo.com; f. 1994; Exec. Dir MTEMI LAWRENCE NALUYAGA.

Tanzania Horticultural Association (TAHA): Kanisa Rd, House No. 49, POB 16520, Arusha; tel. and fax (27) 2544568; e-mail info@tanzaniahorticulture.com; internet www.tanzaniahorticulture.com; f. 2004; Chair. COLMAN M. NGALO; Exec. Dir JACQUELINE MKINDI.

Tanzania Pyrethrum Board: POB 149, Iringa; f. 1960; Chair. Brig. LUHANGA; CEO P. B. G. HANGAYA.

Tanzania Sisal Board: POB 277, Tanga; tel. and fax (27) 2645060; e-mail tansisal@tsbtz.org; internet www.tsbtz.org; f. 1997; Chair. Prof. JOSEPH SEMBOJA; Dir-Gen. HAMISI MAPINDA.

Tanzania Tobacco Board: POB 227, Mazimbu Rd, Morogoro; tel. (23) 2603364; fax (23) 2604401; Chair. V. KAWAWA; CEO FRANK S. URIO.

Tanzania Wood Industry Corporation: POB 9160, Dar es Salaam; Gen. Man. E. M. MNZAVA.

Tea Association of Tanzania: POB 2177, Dar es Salaam; tel. (22) 2122033; e-mail trit@twiga.com; f. 1989; Chair. Dr NORMAN C. KELLY; Exec. Dir DAVID E. A. MGWASSA.

Tea Board of Tanzania: TETEX House, Pamba Rd, POB 2663, Dar es Salaam; tel. and fax (22) 2114400; Chair. ROSTAM AZIZI; Dir-Gen. MATHIAS ASSENGA BENEDICT.

Zanzibar State Trading Corporation: POB 26, Zanzibar; internet www.zstczanzibar.com; govt-controlled since 1964; sole exporter of cloves, clove stem oil, chillies, copra, copra cake, lime oil and lime juice; Gen. Man. ABDULRAHMAN RASHID.

UTILITIES

Regulatory Authority

Energy and Water Utilities Regulatory Authority (EWURA): 6th Floor, Harbour View Towers, Samora Ave, POB 72175, Dar es Salaam; tel. (22) 2123850; fax (22) 2123180; e-mail info@ewura.go.tz; internet www.ewura.go.tz; f. 2001; technical and economic regulation of the electricity, petroleum, natural gas and water sectors; Chair. SIMON F. SAYORE; Dir-Gen. HARUNA MASEBU.

Electricity

Tanzania Electric Supply Co Ltd (TANESCO): POB 9024, Dar es Salaam; tel. (22) 2451130; fax (22) 2113836; e-mail info@tanesco.com; internet www.tanesco.co.tz; state-owned; placed under private management in May 2002; privatization pending; Chair. PETER J. NGUMBULLU; Man. Dir WILLIAM MHANDO.

Gas

Enertan Corpn Ltd: POB 3746, Dar es Salaam.

Songas Ltd: cnr Nelson Mandela and Morogoro Rds, POB 6342, Dar es Salaam; tel. (22) 2452160; fax (22) 2452161; internet www.songas.com; f. 1998; Gen. Man. JIM MCCARDLE.

Water

Dar es Salaam Water and Sewerage Authority: POB 1573, Dar es Salaam; e-mail dawasapiu@raha.com; privatization pending.

National Urban Water Authority: POB 5340, Dar es Salaam; tel. (22) 2667505.

CO-OPERATIVES

There are some 1,670 primary marketing societies under the aegis of about 20 regional co-operative unions. The Co-operative Union of Tanzania is the national organization to which all unions belong.

Tanzania Federation of Co-operatives Ltd: POB 2567, Dar es Salaam; tel. (22) 2184082; fax (22) 2184081; e-mail ushirika@ushirika.co.tz; internet www.ushirika.coop; f. 1962; Exec. Sec. GERALD P. MALIMA; 700,000 mems.

Department of Co-operative Societies: POB 1287, Zanzibar; f. 1952; promotes formation and development of co-operative societies in Zanzibar.

Principal Societies

Kagera Co-operative Union Ltd: POB 5, Bukoba; tel. (28) 2220229; fax (28) 2221168; e-mail kcu@africaonline.co.tz; internet www.kcu-tz.com; 74 affiliated societies; 75,000 mems.

Kilimanjaro Native Co-operative Union (1984) Ltd: POB 3032, Moshi; tel. (27) 2752785; fax (27) 2754204; e-mail kncu@kilinet.co.tz; f. 1984; represents smallhold farmers and coffee-producers; 68 regd co-operative societies; Gen. Man. TOBIA MASAKI.

Nyanza Co-operative Union Ltd: POB 9, Mwanza.

TRADE UNIONS

Trade Union Congress of Tanzania (TUCTA): Dar es Salaam; f. 2000; Pres. OMARY AYOUB JUMA; Sec.-Gen. NICHOLAS MGAYA.

Zanzibar Trade Union Congress (ZATUC): Zanzibar; f. 2002; Sec.-Gen. MAKAME LAUNI MAKAME.

Transport

RAILWAYS

In 2010 2,707 km of 1,000-mm-gauge railway track were operated by Reli Assets Holding Co Ltd, which develops, promotes and manages rail infrastructure assets. A new railway project linking Tanga with Musoma on Lake Victoria is under consideration. The 1,067-mm-gauge Tazara railway line linking Dar es Salaam with New Kapiri Mposhi, Zambia, has a total length of 1,860 km, of which 969 km are within Tanzania.

Tanzania Railways Corpn (TRC): POB 468, Dar es Salaam; tel. and fax (22) 2110599; e-mail ccm_shamte@trctz.com; internet www.trctz.com; f. 1977 after dissolution of East African Railways; privatization pending; operates 2,600 km of lines within Tanzania; Chair. J. K. CHANDE; Dir-Gen. LINFORD MBOMA.

Tanzania-Zambia Railway Authority (Tazara): Nyerere Rd, POB 2834, Dar es Salaam; tel. (22) 2862191; fax (22) 2862474; e-mail acistz@twiga.com; internet www.tazarasite.com; jtly owned and administered by the Tanzanian and Zambian Govts; operates a 1,860-km railway link between Dar es Salaam and New Kapiri Mposhi, Zambia, of which 969 km are within Tanzania; Chair. SALIM MSOMA; Man. Dir AKASHAMBATWA MBIKUSITA-LEWANIKA; Regional Man. (Tanzania) A. F. S. NALITOLELA.

ROADS

In 2004 Tanzania had an estimated 85,000 km of classified roads, of which some 5,169 km were paved. A 1,930-km main road links Zambia and Tanzania, and there is a road link with Rwanda. A 10-year Integrated Roads Programme, funded by international donors and co-ordinated by the World Bank, commenced in 1991. Its aim was to upgrade 70% of Tanzania's trunk roads and to construct 2,828 km of roads and 205 bridges, at an estimated cost of US $650m.

The island of Zanzibar has 619 km of roads, of which 442 km are bituminized, and Pemba has 363 km, of which 130 km are bituminized.

Tanzania National Roads Agency (TANROADS): Maktaba Building, 3rd Floor, Bibi Titi Mohammed Rd, POB 11364, Dar es Salaam; tel. (22) 2152576; fax (22) 2150022; e-mail tanroadshq@tanroads.org; internet www.tanroads.org; f. 2000; responsible for the maintenance and development of the trunk and regional road network; Chair. ABEL MWAISUMO; CEO EPHRAEM C. M. MREMA.

INLAND WATERWAYS

Steamers connect with Kenya, Uganda, the Democratic Republic of the Congo, Burundi, Zambia and Malawi. A rail ferry service operates on Lake Victoria between Mwanza and Port Bell.

SHIPPING

Tanzania's major harbours are at Dar es Salaam (eight deep-water berths for general cargo, three berths for container ships, eight anchorages, lighter wharf, one oil jetty for small oil tankers up to 36,000 gross tons, offshore mooring for oil supertankers up to 100,000 tons, one 30,000-ton automated grain terminal) and Mtwara (two deep-water berths). There are also ports at Tanga (seven anchorages and lighterage quay), Bagamoyo, Zanzibar and Pemba.

Tanzania Ports Authority (TPA): POB 9184, Dar es Salaam; tel. (22) 2116258; fax (22) 232066; e-mail dp@tanzaniaports.com; internet www.tanzaniaports.com; f. 2005 to replace the Tanzania Harbours Authority, in preparation for privatization; Dir-Gen. EPHRAIM MGAWE.

Chinese-Tanzanian Joint Shipping Co: POB 696, Dar es Salaam; tel. (22) 2113389; fax (22) 2113388; e-mail admin@sinotaship.com; f. 1967; services to People's Republic of China, South East Asia, Eastern and Southern Africa, Red Sea and Mediterranean ports.

National Shipping Agencies Co Ltd (NASACO): POB 9082, Dar es Salaam; f. 1973; state-owned shipping co; Man. Dir D. R. M. LWIMBO.

Tanzania Central Freight Bureau (TCFB): POB 3093, Dar es Salaam; tel. (22) 2114174; fax (22) 2116697; e-mail tcfb@cats-net.com.

Tanzania Coastal Shipping Line Ltd: POB 9461, Dar es Salaam; tel. (22) 237034; fax (22) 2116436; regular services to Tanzanian coastal ports; occasional special services to Zanzibar and Pemba; also tramp charter services to Kenya, Mozambique, the Persian (Arabian) Gulf, Indian Ocean islands and the Middle East; Gen. Man. RICHARD D. NZOWA.

CIVIL AVIATION

There are 53 airports and landing strips. The major international airport is at Dar es Salaam, 13 km from the city centre, and there are also international airports at Kilimanjaro, Mwanza and Zanzibar.

Tanzania Civil Aviation Authority (TCAA): IPS Bldg, cnr Samora Machel Ave and Azikiwe St, POB 2819, Dar es Salaam; tel. (22) 2115079; fax (22) 2118905; e-mail tcaa@tcaa.go.tz; internet www.tcaa.go.tz; f. 2003; replaced Directorate of Civil Aviation (f. 1977); ensures aviation safety and security, provides air navigation services; Dir-Gen. MARGARET T. MUNYAGI.

Air Zanzibar: POB 1784, Zanzibar; f. 1990; operates scheduled and charter services between Zanzibar and destinations in Tanzania, Kenya and Uganda.

New ACS Ltd: Peugeot House, 36 Upanga Rd, POB 21236, Dar es Salaam; fax (22) 237017; operates domestic and regional services; Dir MOHSIN RAHEMTULLAH.

Precision Air Services Ltd: Quality Plaza Bldg, Nyerere Rd, POB 70770, Dar es Salaam; tel. (22) 2168000; fax (22) 2860725; e-mail contactcentre@precisionairtz.com; internet www.precisionairtz.com; f. 1993; operates scheduled and charter domestic and regional services; Man. Dir and CEO ALFONSE KIOKO.

Tanzanair: Julius Nyerere Int. Airport, POB 364, Dar es Salaam; tel. (22) 2843131; fax (22) 2844600; e-mail info@tanzanair.com; internet www.tanzanair.com; f. 1969; operates domestic and regional charter services, offers full engineering and maintenance services for general aviation aircraft; agent for sales of Cessna aircraft; Man. Dir JOHN SAMARAS.

Tourism

Mount Kilimanjaro is a major tourist attraction. Tanzania has set aside about one-quarter of its land area for 12 national parks, 17 game reserves, 50 controlled game areas and a conservation area. Other attractions for tourists include beaches and coral reefs along the Indian Ocean coast, and the island of Zanzibar. Visitor arrivals totalled 770,469 in 2008, and in that year revenue from tourism was US $1,358m.

Tanzania Tourist Board: IPS Bldg, 3rd Floor, POB 2485, Dar es Salaam; tel. (22) 2111244; fax (22) 2116420; e-mail safari@ud.co.tz; internet www.tanzaniatouristboard.com; f. 1993; state-owned; supervises the development and promotion of tourism; Man. Dir PETER J. MWENGUO.

Tanzania Wildlife Co Ltd: POB 1144, Arusha; tel. 787787459 (mobile); e-mail info@tanzaniawildlifecompany.com; internet www.tanzaniawildlifecompany.com; f. 1974; organizes hunting, photographic, horseback and adventure safaris; Man. Dir LEON LAMPRECHT.

Zanzibar Tourist Corporation: POB 216, Zanzibar; tel. (24) 2238630; fax (24) 2233417; e-mail ztc@zanzinet.com; internet www.zanzibartouristcorporation.com; f. 1985; operates tours and hotel services; Gen. Man. SABAAH SALEH ALI.

Defence

As assessed at November 2010, the total armed forces numbered 27,000, of whom an estimated 23,000 were in the army, 1,000 in the navy and 3,000 in the air force. Paramilitary forces comprised a 1,400-strong Police Field Force and an 80,000-strong reservist Citizens' Militia.

Defence Expenditure: Budgeted at 326,000m. shillings in 2009.

Commander-in-Chief of the Armed Forces: President JAKAYA MRISHO KIKWETE.

Chief of Defence Forces: Gen. DAVIS MWAMUNYANGE.

Education

In 2004/05 enrolment at pre-primary level was 23% (23% of both boys and girls). Education at primary level is officially compulsory and is provided free of charge. In secondary schools a government-stipulated fee is paid. Villages and districts are encouraged to construct their own schools with government assistance. Almost all primary schools are government-owned. Primary education begins at seven years of age and lasts for seven years. In 2008/09 enrolment at primary level included 96% of pupils in the appropriate age-group (96% of boys; 97% of girls). Secondary education, beginning at the age of 14, lasts for a further six years, comprising a first cycle of four years and a second of two years. Secondary enrolment in 1999/2000 included only 6% of children in the appropriate age-group (males 6%; females 5%), according to UNESCO estimates. Enrolment at tertiary level included just 1% of those in the relevant age-group in 2004/05 (males 2%; females 1%). There are 10 universities, including one on Zanzibar. Tanzania also has a number of vocational training centres and technical colleges. The 2008/09 budget allocated 19.8% of total government expenditure for education.

THAILAND

Introductory Survey

LOCATION, CLIMATE, LANGUAGE, RELIGION, FLAG, CAPITAL

The Kingdom of Thailand lies in South-East Asia. It is bordered to the west and north by Myanmar (Burma), to the north-east by Laos and to the south-east by Cambodia. Thailand extends southward, along the isthmus of Kra, to the Malay Peninsula, where it borders Malaysia. The isthmus, shared with Myanmar, gives Thailand a short coastline on the Indian Ocean, and the country also has a long Pacific coastline on the Gulf of Thailand. The climate is tropical and humid, with an average annual temperature of 29°C (85°F). There are three main seasons: hot, rainy and cool. Temperatures in Bangkok are generally between 20°C (68°F) and 35°C (95°F). The national language is Thai. There are small minorities of Chinese, Malays and indigenous hill peoples. The predominant religion is Buddhism, mainly of the Hinayana (Theravada) form. About 4% of the population, predominantly Malays, are Muslims, and there is also a Christian minority, mainly in Bangkok and the north. The national flag (proportions 2 by 3) has five horizontal stripes, of red, white, blue, white and red, the central blue stripe being twice as wide as each of the others. The capital is Bangkok.

CONTEMPORARY POLITICAL HISTORY

Historical Context

Formerly known as Siam, Thailand took its present name in 1939. Under the leadership of Marshal Phibul Songkhram, Thailand entered the Second World War (1939–45) as an ally of Japan. Phibul was deposed in 1944, but returned to power in 1947 after a military coup. His influence declined during the 1950s, and in 1957 he was overthrown in a bloodless coup, led by Field Marshal Sarit Thanarat. Elections took place, but in 1958 martial law was declared and all political parties were dissolved. Sarit died in 1963 and was succeeded as Prime Minister by Gen. (later Field Marshal) Thanom Kittikachorn, who had served as Deputy Prime Minister since 1959. Thanom continued the combination of military authoritarianism and economic development instituted by his predecessor. A Constitution was introduced in 1968, and elections to a National Assembly took place in 1969, but in November 1971, following an increase in communist insurgency and internal political unrest, Thanom annulled the Constitution, dissolved the National Assembly and imposed martial law.

Domestic Political Affairs

During 1972 there were frequent student demonstrations against the military regime, and in October 1973 the Government was forced to resign, after the army refused to use force to disperse student protesters, and King Bhumibol withdrew his support from the administration. An interim Government was formed under Dr Sanya Dharmasakti, the President of the Privy Council. In October 1974 a new Constitution, legalizing political parties, was promulgated, and in January 1975 elections were held to the new House of Representatives. A coalition Government was formed in February by Seni Pramoj, the leader of the Democrat Party (DP), but it was defeated by a vote of no confidence in the following month.

A new right-wing coalition Government, headed by the leader of the Social Action Party (SAP), Kukrit Pramoj (brother of Seni), was unable to maintain its unity, and Kukrit resigned in January 1976. After a further general election in April, a four-party coalition Government was formed, with Seni as Prime Minister. However, following the violent suppression of student demonstrations in October, during which the security forces killed hundreds of protesters, the Seni Government was dissolved, and a right-wing military junta, the National Administrative Reform Council (NARC), seized power. Martial law was declared, the Constitution was annulled, political parties were banned and strict press censorship was imposed. A new Constitution was promulgated, and a new Cabinet was announced, with Thanin Kraivixien, a Supreme Court judge, as Prime Minister.

Under the Thanin Government there was considerable repression of students and political activists. In October 1977 the Government was overthrown in a bloodless coup by a Revolutionary Council (later known as the National Policy Council—NPC) of military leaders, most of whom had been members of the NARC. The 1976 Constitution was abrogated, and the Secretary-General of the NPC (who was also the Supreme Commander of the Armed Forces), Gen. Kriangsak Chomanan, became Prime Minister. Many detainees were released, censorship was partially relaxed and the King nominated a National Assembly on the advice of the NPC. In December 1978 the National Assembly approved a new Constitution, and elections to a new House of Representatives were held in April 1979. However, members of the Senate were all nominated by the Prime Minister, and were almost all military officers. Kriangsak remained Prime Minister and formed a new Cabinet, after which the NPC was dissolved. When Kriangsak resigned in March 1980, he was replaced by Gen. Prem Tinsulanonda, the Commander-in-Chief of the Army and the Minister of Defence. A new coalition Government, composed largely of centre-right politicians acceptable to the armed forces, was formed.

Prem's administration survived an abortive coup attempt in April 1981. In December Prem effected a ministerial reorganization, reincorporating members of the SAP (who had been excluded from the Government in March), in order to repulse a challenge from the new National Democracy Party (NDP), established by Kriangsak. In April 1983 no single party won an overall majority in legislative elections, and a coalition Government was formed by the SAP, Prachakorn Thai, the DP and the NDP, despite Chart Thai having won the largest number of seats. Prem was reappointed premier.

In September 1985 an attempted coup by a group of military officers in Bangkok was quickly suppressed by troops loyal to the Government, but at least five people were killed during the fighting. The leader of the revolt, Col Manoon Roopkachorn (who had also led the coup attempt in 1981), fled the country, but 40 others, including Kriangsak, were put on trial in October, accused of inciting sedition and rebellion. Gen. Arthit Kamlang-ek, the Supreme Commander of the Armed Forces and Commander-in-Chief of the Army (who was believed to have been sympathetic to the aims of the coup leaders), was replaced in his posts by Gen. Chavalit Yongchaiyudh, hitherto the army Chief of Staff.

In September 1985 and January 1986 there were extensive changes in the Government, including the replacement of all members of the SAP, following the resignation of Kukrit as the party's leader. In May 1986, after a parliamentary defeat for the Government over proposed vehicle taxation, the House of Representatives was dissolved. At an election for an enlarged legislature in July, the DP won 100 of the 347 seats (compared with 56 of the 324 seats at the previous election). A coalition Government was formed, including members of the DP, Chart Thai, the SAP, Rassadorn and seven 'independent' ministers. Prem remained Prime Minister.

In April 1988 the rejection by dissident members of the DP of proposed legislation on copyright prompted 16 DP ministers to resign from the Government for failing to maintain party unity. The King dissolved the House of Representatives, at Prem's request, and new elections were held in July. Internal disputes weakened support for the DP (25 dissidents had resigned in May), and Chart Thai won the largest number of seats (87). Gen. Chatichai Choonhavan, the leader of Chart Thai, was appointed Prime Minister in August, after Prem declined an invitation to remain in the post. A new Cabinet was formed, comprising members of Chart Thai, the DP, the SAP, Rassadorn, the United Democratic Party and the Muan Chon party. In April 1989 Ruam Thai, the Community Action Party, the Prachachon Party and the Progressive Party merged to form an opposition grouping called Ekkaparb (Solidarity). Nine members of the Prachachon Party subsequently defected to Chart Thai, giving the ruling coalition control of 229 of the 357 seats in the legislature.

In March 1990 Chavalit resigned as acting Supreme Commander of the Armed Forces; he also resigned as Commander-in-Chief of the Army, in which post he was succeeded by Gen. Suchinda Kraprayoon, hitherto his deputy. In July, despite growing criticism of Chatichai's administration, following a number of corruption scandals and labour unrest, the House of Representatives overwhelmingly rejected an opposition motion of no confidence in the Government. In August, however, Chatichai reorganized the Cabinet, incorporating Puangchon Chao Thai in the ruling coalition, and reducing the influence of the SAP, following the implication of many of its members in allegations of corruption.

In November 1990 Chatichai demoted the leader of the Muan Chon party, Chalerm Yoobamrung, an outspoken critic of the armed forces, from his position as Minister to the Prime Minister's Office. The leadership of the armed forces had demanded Chalerm's dismissal, threatening unspecified intervention if government changes did not take place. In early December Chatichai resigned as Prime Minister; he was reappointed on the next day and subsequently formed a coalition Government comprising Chart Thai, Rassadorn, Puangchon Chao Thai and former opposition parties Prachakorn Thai and Ekkaparb, which provided him with reduced support (227 of the 357 seats) in the House of Representatives.

On 23 February 1991 Chatichai's Government was ousted in a bloodless military coup. Gen. Sunthorn Kongsompong, the Supreme Commander of the Armed Forces, assumed administrative power as the Chairman of the newly created National Peace-keeping Council (NPC). The NPC was actually dominated by the effective head of the armed forces, Gen. Suchinda, one of four Deputy Chairmen of the NPC. The coup leaders cited government corruption and abuse of power to justify their action; however, the coup was also widely believed to have been organized in response to the recent erosion of military influence.

Under the NPC, the Constitution was abrogated, the House of Representatives, the Senate and the Cabinet were dissolved, and martial law was imposed. The NPC won unprecedented royal approval, and in March 1991 an interim Constitution was published. Anand Panyarachun, a business executive and former diplomat, was appointed acting Prime Minister pending fresh elections. Anand selected a primarily civilian interim Cabinet, composed mainly of respected technocrats and former ministers. Chatichai and Arthit, who had been arrested at the time of the coup, were released after two weeks. The NPC appointed a 292-member National Legislative Assembly, which included 149 serving or former military personnel, as well as many civilians known to have links to the armed forces.

In May 1991 martial law was repealed in most areas, and political activity was permitted to resume. The New Aspiration Party (NAP—formed in October 1990 by Chavalit) gathered support as the traditional parties were in disarray, largely owing to investigations of corruption by the newly created Assets Examination Committee. In June 1991 the Commander-in-Chief of the Air Force, Air Chief Marshal Kaset Rojananin, sponsored the creation of a new party, Samakkhi Tham, led by Narong Wongwan, a former leader of Ekkaparb. In August Suchinda assumed, in addition to the post of Commander-in-Chief of the Army, the role of Supreme Commander of the Armed Forces.

In November 1991 the Constitution Scrutiny Committee, which had been effectively nominated by the NPC, presented a draft Constitution to the National Legislative Assembly. Following public criticism of the draft (including a demonstration by 50,000 protesters in Bangkok), the document was amended to reduce the number of nominated senators from 360 to 270, and to abolish provisions that allowed the Senate to participate in the selection of the Prime Minister. Opposition parties, including the NAP and Palang Dharma (led by the popular and influential Governor of Bangkok, Maj.-Gen. Chamlong Srimuang), continued to oppose the draft, claiming that it perpetuated the power of the NPC. The National Legislative Assembly approved the new Constitution in December, but concerns remained over certain provisional clauses (which were to remain in effect for four years), under which the NPC was to appoint the Prime Minister and the Senate, and regarding the Senate's right to vote jointly with the elected House on motions of no confidence, thus enabling the Senate to dismiss a government with the support of only 46 elected representatives.

A general election took place on 22 March 1992, when 15 parties contested the 360 seats; 59.2% of the electorate voted. Samakkhi Tham and Chart Thai won the largest number of seats, 79 and 74 respectively. The NAP secured 72 seats and Palang Dharma won 41 seats, 32 of which were in Bangkok. On the day of the election the NPC appointed the 270 members of the Senate, 154 of whom were officers of the armed forces or police. In late March it was announced that Narong Wongwan would lead a coalition government comprising his own party (Samakkhi Tham), Chart Thai, Prachakorn Thai, the SAP and Rassadorn. However, US allegations of Narong's involvement in illicit drugs-trafficking caused the nomination to be rescinded. In early April Suchinda was named as Prime Minister, despite his assurances before the election that he would not accept the post. His accession to the premiership prompted an immediate popular protest by more than 50,000 demonstrators against the appointment of an unelected Prime Minister. Later in April Suchinda appointed eight other unelected members to a new Cabinet, retaining several technocrats from Anand's interim Government.

Constitutional reform

In early May 1992 Chamlong announced, at a rally attended by 100,000 demonstrators, that he would fast until death unless Suchinda resigned. The demonstrations continued uninterrupted for one week until the government parties agreed to amend the Constitution to prevent an unelected Prime Minister (including the incumbent Suchinda) from taking office, and to limit the power of the unelected Senate. However, violent demonstrations erupted in Bangkok when it appeared that the Government might renege on its commitments. The Government declared a state of emergency in Bangkok and neighbouring provinces. Chamlong was arrested and more than 3,000 people were detained by security forces in a brutal attempt to suppress the riots, which continued for several days. Following unprecedented intervention by King Bhumibol, Suchinda ordered the release of Chamlong, announced a general amnesty for those involved in the protests and pledged to introduce amendments to the Constitution. Suchinda resigned on 24 May, after failing to retain the support of the five coalition parties.

On 10 June 1992 the National Assembly approved constitutional amendments, whereby the Prime Minister was required to be a member of the House of Representatives, the authority of the Senate was restricted and the President of the House of Representatives was to be the President of the National Assembly. Contrary to expectations, the King named Anand as Prime Minister. Anand appointed a politically neutral, unelected Cabinet, and dissolved the National Assembly in preparation for a general election. At the end of June the four parties that had opposed the military Government (the DP, the NAP, Palang Dharma and Ekkaparb) formed an electoral alliance, the National Democratic Front. In July Chatichai declined the leadership of Chart Thai and formed a new party, Chart Pattana, which quickly gained widespread support. During mid-1992 Anand introduced measures to curb the political power of the armed forces, reduce military control of state enterprises, and remove the authority of the armed forces to intervene in situations of social unrest. In August Kaset and the Commander-in-Chief of the Army, Issarapong Noonpakdi, were dismissed from their positions and demoted to inactive posts. The new Commander-in-Chief of the Army, Gen. Wimol Wongwanit, pledged that the army would not interfere in politics under his command.

The general election took place on 13 September 1992, when 12 parties contested the 360 seats in the House of Representatives; 62.1% of the electorate voted. 'Vote-buying' and violence persisted, especially in the north-eastern region. The DP won the largest number of seats, taking 79, while Chart Thai and Chart Pattana secured 77 and 60 seats, respectively. The DP was able to form a coalition with its allies, the NAP, Palang Dharma and Ekkaparb, and thus command 185 of the 360 seats. Despite its participation in the previous administration, the SAP (with 22 seats) was also subsequently invited to join the Government. On 23 September Chuan Leekpai, the leader of the DP, was formally approved as Prime Minister. Chuan declared his intention to eradicate corruption, to decentralize government, to enhance rural development and to reduce the powers of the Senate.

Following its announcement in September 1993 that it was to merge with four opposition parties, including Chart Pattana, under the leadership of Chatichai, the SAP (which had been critical of Chuan's style of leadership and alleged indecisiveness) was expelled from the Government and replaced by the Seritham Party. In September 1994 Chamlong resumed the leadership of Palang Dharma in party elections, and subsequently persuaded the party executive committee to approve the replacement of the party's 11 cabinet members. Chamlong's nominations for inclusion in the Cabinet included Thaksin Shinawatra, a prominent business executive, as Minister of Foreign Affairs. Despite some opposition to the selection of unelected candidates, the appointments were confirmed in October, when Chamlong was named a Deputy Prime Minister.

THAILAND

In December 1994 the NAP withdrew from the ruling coalition over a constitutional amendment providing for the future election of local government representatives, including village headmen. The NAP voted against the Government to protect the vested interests of incumbent local administrators who would control many votes at the next election. In order to secure a parliamentary majority, Chuan was obliged to include Chatichai's Chart Pattana in the governing coalition, although this severely compromised the Government's claims to represent honesty and reform.

In January 1995 Chuan finally obtained the approval of the National Assembly for a series of amendments to the Constitution to expand the country's democratic base. The reforms included a reduction in the size of the appointed Senate to two-thirds of that of the elective House of Representatives, the lowering of the eligible voting age from 20 years to 18, equality for women, the establishment of an administrative court, the introduction of parliamentary ombudsmen and the prohibition of senators and members of the Government from holding monopolistic concessions with government or state bodies. This last amendment necessitated the resignation of Thaksin as Minister of Foreign Affairs, owing to his extensive business interests.

In May 1995, dissatisfied with the Government's response to revelations that a land reform programme had been used to benefit wealthy landowners, the opposition tabled a motion of no confidence in the Government. (The scandal had already prompted the resignation of the Minister of Agriculture and Co-operatives in December 1994.) Following an announcement by Chamlong that Palang Dharma would not support the governing coalition in the no confidence vote, Chuan dissolved the House of Representatives on 19 May 1995. Chamlong resigned as leader of Palang Dharma later that month and was replaced by Thaksin, who had relinquished majority control of his company.

At elections to an enlarged 391-seat House of Representatives, which took place on 2 July 1995 and attracted a turn-out of 62.0% of the electorate, Chart Thai won the largest number of seats (92), followed by the DP (86) and the NAP (57). Support for these parties was based on provincial patronage politics, and allegations of 'vote-buying' were widespread. The leader of Chart Thai, Banharn Silpa-archa (who had been accused of 'possessing unusual wealth' by the military junta in 1991), formed a coalition Government comprising Chart Thai, the NAP, Palang Dharma, the SAP, Prachakorn Thai, Muan Chon and later Nam Thai (a business-orientated party established in 1994 by Amnuay Viravan, a former minister). Banharn appointed all the leaders of the coalition parties (except for the Muan Chon party) as Deputy Prime Ministers. The composition of Banharn's Cabinet was widely criticized, owing to the predominance of professional politicians (who were often subject to allegations of corruption and 'vote-buying').

In March 1996 Banharn announced the composition of the new Senate, the first to be appointed by a democratically elected Prime Minister. In contrast to the previous Senate, only 39 active military officers were named as senators; other appointees included academics and business executives. In May 10 government ministers, including the Prime Minister, survived motions of no confidence, despite opposition revelations of financial irregularities at the Bangkok Bank of Commerce, including loans extended without collateral to members of the Thai Cabinet, notably the Deputy Minister of the Interior, Suchart Tancharoen, and the Deputy Minister of Finance, Newin Chidchob, both members of Chart Thai. Palang Dharma refused to support Suchart in the debate. In order to pre-empt the withdrawal of Palang Dharma from the ruling coalition, five members of Chart Thai, including Suchart Sathirathai and Newin, resigned from their government positions. Palang Dharma subsequently agreed to remain in the coalition. A cabinet reorganization at the end of May included the dismissal of Surakiart Surakiart, the Minister of Finance, who had failed to take action to prevent huge losses at the Bangkok Bank of Commerce.

However, Palang Dharma withdrew from the ruling coalition in August 1996, following a cabinet dispute over alleged bribery in the awarding of bank licences, thereby reducing the Government's legislative majority by 23 seats. In September Banharn was able to secure the support of his coalition partners in a scheduled motion of no confidence in his administration only by undertaking to resign from the premiership. However, the inability of the coalition partners to agree on the appointment of a new Prime Minister led to the dissolution of the House of Representatives on 27 September.

In the general election, which was held on 17 November 1996 and was marred by violence and alleged extensive irregularities, the NAP won 125 of the 393 seats, while the DP secured 123 seats. The majority of NAP seats were gained through provincial patronage politics, while the more politically aware electorate of Bangkok returned the DP to 29 of the city's 37 seats. Chavalit, the leader of the NAP, was appointed Prime Minister, heading a coalition that incorporated Chart Pattana, the SAP, Prachakorn Thai, Muan Chon and the Seritham Party. The ruling coalition thus held 221 seats in the House of Representatives. Most major cabinet posts were assigned to members of Chart Pattana and the NAP. Thaksin resigned as leader of Palang Dharma following the party's failure to win more than one seat in the House of Representatives.

The Government's indecisive handling of the economy contributed to a financial crisis in mid-1997, following a series of sustained assaults on the Thai baht by currency speculators, which led to the baht's effective devaluation in July. The deterioration in the state of the economy was reflected in an increase in popular protests. The Government introduced measures in June to constrain media attacks on the authorities and to limit mass protests.

Successive cabinet reorganizations in August and October 1997 failed to restore public or investor confidence in the Government, and the Thai currency continued to depreciate. Chavalit's subsequent announcement that he would resign from the premiership on 6 November, following the adoption of important electoral and financial legislation, caused a slight recovery of the Thai baht. On 9 November Chuan, who maintained his reputation for integrity, assumed the premiership, following the formation of a coalition comprising Chuan's DP, Chart Thai, the SAP, Ekkaparb, the Seritham Party, Palang Dharma and the Thai Party (as well as 12 of the 18 members of Prachakorn Thai), which commanded the support of 210 of the 393 seats in the House of Representatives. The transfer of power to Chuan, under the terms of the new Constitution, without the intervention of the armed forces or resort to a non-elected leader, received widespread approval and represented significant democratic progress. The new Cabinet included Tarrin Nimmanhaeminda as Minister of Finance (a post that he had occupied in Chuan's previous administration) and the former Deputy Prime Minister, Supachai Panichpakdi, as Minister of Commerce. However, the baht continued to depreciate, causing intermittent social unrest.

Meanwhile, in January 1997 an assembly of 99 members was elected by the legislature to draft a new constitution following the unanimous approval of a constitution amendment bill by the National Assembly in September 1996. The draft Constitution included provisions for: a directly elected Senate; the replacement in the House of Representatives of 393 deputies from multi-member constituencies by 400 deputies from single-member constituencies and 100 deputies elected by proportional representation; the resignation of cabinet ministers from the legislature; the establishment of a minimum educational requirement for members of the National Assembly; the formation of an Election Commission to supervise elections (in place of the Ministry of the Interior); the centralization of vote-counting; compulsory voting; and the guarantee of press freedom. Although the draft gained the support of opposition parties and the media, there was considerable opposition to the new charter from within the ruling administration. Chavalit himself reneged on his pledge to support the draft, but then finally gave it his endorsement following the application of pressure by both business representatives and the armed forces. The draft Constitution was approved on 27 September 1997, and was promulgated on 11 October.

In May 1998 new electoral legislation was approved, enabling polls to be held six months later. There were fears that, under the new legislation, the 12 members of the ruling coalition who had defected from Prachakorn Thai to help form the Government in November 1997 might lose their legal status as legislators. (The 12 were formally expelled from Prachakorn Thai in October 1998 but continued to form part of the coalition Government.) In July a new political party, Thai Rak Thai, was established by former Deputy Prime Minister Thaksin.

By August 1998 Thailand's economy appeared to have stabilized, and Chuan received rare public praise from Queen Sirikit. However, the Government was beset by allegations of corruption. In October Chuan reorganized his Government, bringing the Chart Pattana party into the ruling coalition and thereby increasing to 257 the number of seats held by the coalition in the House of Representatives. Five new ministers were appointed to the Cabinet, including the Secretary-General of Chart Pattana, Suwat Liptapanlop, who was assigned the industry portfolio. In December the opposition filed a motion to remove Chuan and Minister of Finance Tarrin from office, on the grounds that they had allegedly acted in breach of the Constitution by submitting four Letters of Intent to the IMF (see p. 143) without first securing the approval of the House of Representatives; the motion was unsuccessful.

In July 1999 the SAP withdrew from the governing coalition, following disputes within the party concerning the allocation of ministerial positions, prompting a reorganization of the Cabinet. By August, however, public approval of the Government appeared to be in decline, and the coalition was placed under increasing pressure from the opposition to dissolve the House of Representatives and call elections. In November Chavalit pledged his willingness to support Thai Rak Thai in the forthcoming general election in the event of his own NAP performing poorly. Meanwhile, in August a report on the state-owned Krung Thai Bank, which exposed the bank's dubious loan policies and other irregularities, led to allegations of corruption being made against Tarrin, whose brother, Sirin Nimmanhaeminda, had been the President of Krung Thai Bank until his resignation in January. Although the Government was reported in October to have exonerated a number of senior Krung Thai executives, including Sirin, of allegations of inefficiency and dishonesty, the controversy surrounding the bank continued and constituted the main focus of a no confidence motion filed by the opposition against the Government in December, in which the ruling coalition was accused of mismanagement of the economy and of condoning corruption. Although the Government survived the censure debate, the proceedings exposed divisions within the governing coalition (particularly between the DP and Chart Thai).

Allegations of corruption against the ruling coalition re-emerged in 2000. In March the Deputy Prime Minister and Minister of the Interior, Maj.-Gen. (retd) Sanan Kajornprasart, was accused by the National Counter Corruption Commission (NCCC) of having falsified his assets declaration statement (recently required of all cabinet ministers). Pending a ruling on the case by the Constitutional Court, Sanan resigned from his ministerial positions, being replaced by Banyat Bantadtan. In August Sanan was convicted of corruption by the Constitutional Court.

On 4 March 2000 elections to the new 200-member Senate were contested by more than 1,500 candidates. The level of voter participation was reported at 70%, with voting being compulsory for the first time. Later in the month the Election Commission disqualified 78 of the 200 winning candidates (including the wives of two cabinet ministers) owing to allegations of electoral fraud. Further allegations of malpractice necessitated four subsequent rounds of polling in April–July. However, on 1 August Thailand's first-ever democratically elected Senate was formally inaugurated. (While the final results of the elections remained in dispute, none of the declared winners had been able to assume their seats as they lacked the necessary quorum, resulting in a backlog of legislation and obliging the outgoing Senate to remain in office in an interim capacity.)

The premiership of Thaksin Shinawatra

In November 2000 it was announced that elections to the House of Representatives would be held in January 2001. In December 2000 the NCCC recommended that Thaksin Shinawatra should be indicted for having violated the Constitution by concealing financial assets and seeking to avoid the payment of taxes. One notable feature of Thai Rak Thai's electoral campaign was its targeting of rural votes by pledging grants of 1m. baht for each of Thailand's 70,000 villages and offering a debt relief scheme for farmers. At the legislative elections held on 6 January 2001 Thai Rak Thai won 248 of the 500 seats in the House of Representatives, thereby almost gaining an unprecedented absolute majority. However, many domestic and international observers declared that, despite the vigilance of the Election Commission, the elections had been the most corrupt ever held in Thailand. In late January repolling was held in more than 60 constituencies where the Election Commission had found evidence of malpractice. In February a new Cabinet nominated by the new Prime Minister, Thaksin, was formally approved by King Bhumibol. All but five of the appointees were members of Thai Rak Thai, with which the Seritham Party had merged since the election, thus affording Thai Rak Thai an absolute majority in the House of Representatives. With the support of its coalition partners, the NAP and Chart Thai, the incoming Thai Rak Thai administration controlled 339 of the 500 seats in the House.

In April 2001 the Constitutional Court formally commenced hearing charges of corruption brought against Thaksin as recommended by the NCCC. In the same month two bombs exploded in southern Thailand, killing a child and injuring 42 people. The involvement of a militant Islamist separatist organization, the Patani United Liberation Organization (PULO), was suspected. The PULO belonged to Bersatu, an umbrella organization of three separatist movements, which, the Government claimed, was seeking to establish a Muslim state in southern Thailand.

On 30 June 2001 by-elections were held in seven constituencies to fill seats in the House of Representatives vacated by members disqualified for breaches of campaign rules after the January elections. However, the polls were again marred by allegations of corruption.

The Prime Minister was acquitted of the charges against him regarding concealment of his assets in August 2001. The judges ruled by a narrow eight-to-seven majority in his favour. Thaksin's exoneration was welcomed by his many supporters, who had conducted a popular campaign that was thought to have exerted some influence over the court's verdict.

In October 2001 the Government introduced a plan to provide low-cost health care for the nation's poorest people, thus implementing one of the Prime Minister's election pledges. Doubts remained over the quality of the service provided. Later in the same month the limits to the Government's reform efforts were highlighted when army Sub-Lt Duangchalerm Yoobamrung (son of Chalerm Yoobamrung) allegedly murdered a police officer during a fight in a night-club. Duangchalerm subsequently fled to Cambodia. As a result of his son's actions and subsequent popular criticism of the Government for its ineffectual attempts to bring him to justice, Chalerm was forced to resign from the deputy leadership of the NAP, although he retained an influential position within the Government. In May 2002 Duangchalerm surrendered himself to the Thai embassy in Malaysia and agreed to return home. In March 2004 Duangchalerm was acquitted of all the charges against him, allegedly owing to insufficient evidence.

Having voted to merge with its coalition partner, Thai Rak Thai, in January 2002, the NAP was legally dissolved in March; the Constitutional Court formally approved the merger in April. Also in March the Government was further strengthened when Chart Pattana joined the ruling coalition; Suwat Liptapanlop, Secretary-General of Chart Pattana, was allocated a ministerial position shortly thereafter. Meanwhile, by-elections were held in 14 constituencies where the January 2001 general election results had been invalidated owing to electoral fraud and corruption. Thai Rak Thai lost five seats as a result, but retained its commanding majority in the National Assembly. Shortly afterwards six policemen died after gunmen attacked security outposts—two in Pattani province and one in Yala province. The attacks were suspected to have been carried out by one of the militant Islamist separatist organizations known to exist in the area. Two bombs later exploded in Yala province, coinciding with a tour of the region by the Minister of the Interior. A Thai military official attributed the attacks to the Gerakan (or Guragan) Mujahideen Islam Pattani, a constituent group of Bersatu thought to be linked to the international terrorist network al-Qa'ida.

In May 2002 the Government defeated no-confidence motions that had been brought by the opposition against 15 of its ministers, including nine members of the Cabinet. In October Thaksin implemented an extensive cabinet reorganization, in which, among other changes, Chavalit Yongchaiyudh was replaced as Minister of Defence by Thammarak Isarangura. Six ministers were appointed to take responsibility for new ministries that had been created as part of the Government's ongoing bureaucratic reforms.

A further redistribution of cabinet portfolios took place in February 2003, in which, inter alia, the Minister of Finance, Somkid Jatusripitak, and the Minister of Justice, Purachai Piemsomboon, were both appointed Deputy Prime Ministers. Meanwhile, the Government announced the commencement of an intensive anti-drugs campaign intended to eliminate Thailand's drug problem within three months. As the campaign progressed, the high number of suspected drug dealers being killed prompted criticism from both local and international human rights groups, which claimed that the Thai authorities were operating an illegal 'shoot to kill' policy and effectively condoning extra-judicial violence. The Government rejected a

THAILAND

request from the Office of the UN High Commissioner for Human Rights (OHCHR, see p. 52) that it be permitted to send a representative to the country to investigate the killings. In March Thaksin acknowledged that mistakes had been made during the campaign, but denied that the police had been responsible for any extra-judicial killings. Later in that month Thaksin ordered that the campaign should henceforth be concentrated upon provinces along the border with Myanmar, where the majority of drugs-smuggling activity was believed to take place. By mid-April 2003, according to a statement issued by police, as a result of the campaign some 2,275 people had been killed, of whom the police admitted to shooting 51 fatally for reasons of self-defence. At the end of April Thaksin claimed that the campaign had eradicated about 90% of the country's drugs problem. Meanwhile, two attacks on army bases in the south of the country were reportedly carried out by the PULO. In May, following the success of the anti-drugs offensive, Thaksin announced the commencement of a 'war on dark influences' intended to eradicate criminal networks operating in the country.

In April 2003 the DP elected Banyat Bantadtan as its new leader, following the retirement of Chuan Leekpai. In May five cabinet ministers evaded censure, following the tabling of an opposition no confidence motion accusing them of corruption. In the following month Thai Rak Thai defeated the DP at a by-election in Si Sa Ket. Later in June three men were arrested on suspicion of being members of the regional terrorist organization Jemaah Islamiah (JI); they later confessed to having plotted to attack embassies and tourist destinations in the country. A further suspect was arrested in July. In the following month, in response to the perceived terrorist threat to Thailand, the Cabinet approved two anti-terrorism laws by decree, circumventing the legislature owing to the reported gravity of the threat. Shortly afterwards, the alleged former operational head of JI, the Indonesian citizen Riduan Isamuddin, also known as Hambali, was apprehended in Thailand; he was later taken into custody by the USA. In September the four suspected members of JI arrested earlier in the year were officially charged with membership of the organization and with plotting terrorist attacks in Thailand. Those charged, together with a fifth man being detained in Singapore, pleaded not guilty to the charges against them. Their trials began in November.

In October 2003, following the conclusion of its anti-drugs offensive five months previously, the Government announced the commencement of a 60-day campaign intended to rid Thailand of 'social evils' such as drug addiction, poverty and organized crime. In November Chart Pattana was removed from the Government upon the ousting from the Cabinet of Deputy Prime Minister Korn Dabbaransi and Minister of Labour and Social Welfare Suwat Liptapanlop.

Escalating violence in the southern provinces

In January 2004 an outbreak of violence in the south of the country, which resulted in the deaths of several members of the security forces and included arson attacks on several schools, prompted the Government to declare martial law in the predominantly Muslim provinces of Pattani, Yala and Narathiwat, on the border with Malaysia. The Government suspected that the violence had been perpetrated by Gerakan Mujahideen Islam Pattani, although involvement by militants affiliated to JI was not discounted as a possibility. Two suspects arrested in January were believed to be members of Bersatu. The unrest continued, resulting in the temporary closure of approximately 1,000 schools in the area. Meanwhile, the Government responded by arresting local Islamic leaders and conducting army raids on *madrasahs* (Islamic religious schools), angering many members of the local Muslim population.

In March 2004 a further cabinet reorganization was implemented, widely believed to be a response to the deterioration in the security situation in the south of the country, together with a decline in the performance of the Stock Exchange of Thailand and public protests at the Government's planned privatization of the Electricity Generating Authority of Thailand. The Ministers of Finance, Defence and the Interior—Suchart Jaovisidha, Thammarak Isarangura and Wan Muhamad Nor Matha—were replaced by, respectively, Somkid Jatusripitak, Chettha Thanajaro and Bhokin Bhalakula, while Korn Dabbaransi returned to the Cabinet as Minister of Science and Technology. In mid-March, following further arson attacks in the south, which destroyed some 36 government buildings, Prime Minister Thaksin dismissed the national police chief and the army commander for the southern region. Later in that month a bomb explosion in Sungai Kolok, in Narathiwat province, which injured 29 people, including 10 Malaysian tourists, prompted the Government to suspend a US $300m. development aid programme intended for Narathiwat, Pattani and Yala.

The violence in the south escalated in April 2004, when more than 100 suspected Islamist militants carried out a series of raids on police and army bases. The security forces suppressed the attacks, killing 108 of the insurgents, including 32 who had taken refuge in a mosque in Pattani. Five security officials also died in the fighting. After the UN, human rights groups and some Muslim leaders had questioned the level of force used by the security forces to quash the attacks, in May the Government established an independent commission to investigate the incident at the mosque. Later in May the body of a Buddhist farmer was found decapitated and a Buddhist shrine in Pattani was ransacked. In June some 3,000 teachers attended a rally in Pattani in support of demands for improved security following the killing of a colleague. At the end of the month more than 4,000 teachers in Narathiwat commenced strike action after a further shooting, but returned to work after two days in response to assurances of increased protection from the security forces.

At the end of June 2004 Chart Pattana rejoined the Government when Suwat Liptapanlop was appointed as a Deputy Prime Minister, in what was regarded as an attempt by Thaksin to consolidate support ahead of the legislative elections due to be held in early 2005. A number of deputies from Chart Thai and the DP subsequently defected to Thai Rak Thai, and in August 2004 Chart Pattana merged into Thaksin's party. Meanwhile, several former senior members of the DP formed a new party, Mahachon. In early August, in its first report since its establishment in 2001, the National Human Rights Commission claimed that human rights violations had increased under Thaksin's administration, notably during the anti-drugs campaign in 2003, and accused the Government of becoming increasingly authoritarian. Thaksin rejected the report's criticisms, and declared a second anti-drugs offensive in October, which was to last for one year. The election of Apirak Kosayodhin of the DP as Governor of Bangkok in late August represented a set-back for Thaksin, who had favoured the candidature of Paveena Hongsakul, the former Secretary-General of Chart Pattana, who had stood as an independent.

More than 300 suspected insurgents had surrendered to the authorities by mid-July 2004 in response to a government campaign; they were transferred to a detention facility at a military camp to undergo a re-education programme. Nevertheless, violent attacks and minor bomb explosions continued to occur in the southern provinces, with killings of public officials, police officers, Buddhist monks and civilians regularly reported. In August the independent commission investigating the deaths at the mosque in April released its report, which criticized the security forces for using grenades and concluded that disproportionate force had been used. The Government announced that unspecified compensation would be paid to the families of those killed. At the end of August Thaksin visited Narathiwat, Pattani and Yala provinces, one day after a bomb had exploded at a market in Sukhirin, in Narathiwat, killing one person and injuring 31. The Government conceded that it had failed to control the violence in the south, and pledged to develop new strategies to quell the unrest.

In October 2004 Thaksin effected a reorganization of the Cabinet, which included the replacement of the Minister of Defence and the Minister of Agriculture and Co-operatives in an apparent response to the ongoing crisis in the south and an outbreak of avian influenza ('bird flu'). In late October troops fired tear gas to disperse more than 2,000 Muslim protesters who were demonstrating in Tak Bai, in Narathiwat province, against the detention of six suspected militants. Seven of the protesters were killed in the ensuing clashes and 78 of 1,300 demonstrators who were arrested later died, many from suffocation, as they were transported in overcrowded trucks to an army barracks. Amid increasing international concern, Thaksin ordered an independent inquiry into the deaths. Most of those detained in connection with the protests were subsequently released. A few days later two people were killed and 20 injured in a bomb attack in Sungai Kolok. The deteriorating security situation in the south prompted rare interventions from the monarchy. King Bhumibol urged the Government to use more restraint, and Queen Sirikit called for an end to the violence. In the first two weeks of November around 30 Buddhists were killed in apparent revenge attacks attributed to the PULO, which had earlier vowed to retaliate in response to the deaths in Tak Bai. Later in that month an alleged leader of Bersatu was killed in a gunfight with the security forces in Panare, in Pattani province.

In December 2004 four Islamic teachers, who were suspected of being leaders of the separatist group Barisan Revolusi Nasional (part of Bersatu), were charged with terrorism and treason. Meanwhile, the inquiry into the incident at Tak Bai in October, in which 85 protesters died, concluded that the deaths had not been caused deliberately, but that the dispersal of the crowd and the transport of the prisoners had been mishandled and that senior officials had been negligent; three army commanders were subsequently transferred to inactive posts. The Cabinet later approved compensation worth more than 30m. baht for families of the dead and those injured. In late December at least two people were killed and several injured when a bomb exploded in Sungai Kolok. Following the fatal shooting of two of their colleagues, thousands of teachers in the south went on strike, urging the authorities to do more to protect them from attacks by Muslim militants.

The west coast of Thailand, in particular the province of Phang Nga, was severely affected by a series of tsunamis caused by a massive earthquake in the Indian Ocean on 26 December 2004. More than 5,300 people, including at least 1,700 foreigners from some 36 countries, were killed, and a further 2,900 were reported missing. The Thai Government largely refused international relief aid, but did accept technical assistance in identifying the dead, a task rendered more difficult by the large number of foreign victims.

In legislative elections held on 6 February 2005 Thai Rak Thai secured a large majority with 377 of the 500 seats in the House of Representatives; the DP took 96 seats, Chart Thai 25 and Mahachon two. The rate of voter participation was reported at 72%. Thai Rak Thai's success, which enabled it to form a single-party government for the first time, was widely attributed to Thaksin's prompt response to the devastation caused by the tsunamis in December and the strong performance of the economy under his premiership. However, as in previous election campaigns, there were numerous allegations of electoral malpractice, including 'vote-buying'. The election results prompted the immediate resignation of Banyat Bantadtan as leader of the DP; Abhisit Vejjajiva was elected as his replacement in March. Prime Minister Thaksin began an unprecedented second consecutive term in office in March, following his formal re-election to the premiership by the House of Representatives. Somkid Jatusripitak was appointed as a Deputy Prime Minister in the new Cabinet, while retaining the finance portfolio, and Kantathee Supamongkol, hitherto a trade representative, was allocated the foreign affairs portfolio, replacing Surakiart Sathirathai, who became a Deputy Prime Minister.

The violence in southern Thailand continued unabated throughout 2005, and by early March more than 690 people had died since January 2004. In February 2005 the Government approved the formation of a new 12,000-strong army regiment to be stationed in the south. The troops were to focus on development work, as well as on improving security, but local Islamic leaders warned that an increased military presence in the region (where Thai Rak Thai had failed to secure a single seat in the recent elections) would only heighten disillusionment with the Government. During a three-day visit to the south in mid-February Thaksin announced controversial proposals to allocate development aid to villages in the region depending on the degree of violence found there. However, the plans were widely criticized, and were subsequently abandoned. As the Prime Minister's visit came to an end, a car bomb in Sungai Kolok killed six people and injured more than 40.

In March 2005 Thaksin appeared to be considering a more moderate approach towards the insurgency in the south. He appointed former premier Anand Panyarachun to chair a 48-member National Reconciliation Commission (NRC), which was charged with restoring peace, and announced his intention to reduce the number of troops deployed in the region. In April two people were killed and more than 60 injured in three bomb explosions in the southern province of Songkhla, the first major attacks to occur outside the provinces of Narathiwat, Pattani and Yala. In November Thaksin extended martial law, already in force in the three southernmost provinces, to encompass the districts of Chana and Thepha in Songkhla province. The state of emergency was subsequently renewed on numerous occasions and remained in place at mid-2011.

In June 2005 a delegation from the Organization of the Islamic Conference (OIC, see p. 400) was dispatched to Thailand on a fact-finding mission, at the invitation of Prime Minister Thaksin.

In their subsequent report, the members of the delegation concluded, contrary to the claims of Islamic nations and rights groups, that religious issues were not the predominant factor in the ongoing militant attacks in the south of the country.

The ousting of Thaksin and imposition of military rule

In January 2006, in the largest corporate take-over in Thailand's history, Thaksin's family sold its 49.6% holding stake in national telecommunications firm Shin Corporation Public Co Ltd (Shin Corp) to Singapore's state investment wing, Temasek Holdings, at a price of 70,000m. baht (US $1,900m.). The transaction took place on the same day on which a new law raising the limit on foreign ownership in telecommunication firms from 25% to 49% took effect. The sale provoked outrage within Thailand, with many people angered by the massive tax-free gains made by the Shinawatra family; there were demands for the Prime Minister to donate to the state the 26,000m. baht that had been waived in tax. Considerable suspicion was also aroused by the fact that Thaksin's son and daughter had purchased shares in Shin Corp from Ample Vision (an investment company established by the Prime Minister in the British Virgin Islands) at a cost of one baht per share and yet had been able to sell them, just three days later, at a price of 49.25 baht per share. Furthermore, there was widespread concern about the sale of a telecommunications firm to a foreign company on account of the potential threat to national security.

In February 2006 the Minister of Culture, Uraiwan Thienthong, tendered her resignation from the Cabinet, citing 'the decline in political morality' as the reason for her decision. Later in that month, and without prior warning, Prime Minister Thaksin announced that the House of Representatives was being dissolved in preparation for an early election; it was subsequently declared that the poll was to be held in early April. However, the three main opposition parties—DP, Chart Thai and Mahachon—all announced that they were to boycott the election, which they argued had been called to divert attention from the Shin Corp scandal. In an attempt to defuse the political tension, Thaksin offered to include the three parties within a national coalition government, regardless of whether or not they participated in the election; however, the offer was rejected. Thaksin also declared his intention to resign if Thai Rak Thai failed to secure more than 50% of the votes cast. During the period prior to the election demonstrators demanded the removal from power of the Prime Minister at numerous protest rallies in the capital, which were organized by the People's Alliance for Democracy (PAD), a loose coalition of anti-Thaksin groups and individuals, popularly known as the 'Yellow Shirts', which had been established in 2005 by Sondhi Limthongkul, the founder of the Manager Media Group. The political tension was accompanied by a further intensification of violence in the southern regions. Hundreds of schools in Yala were closed temporarily following the killing of three Buddhist teachers, allegedly by Muslim militants. In March the Prime Minister's son, Phantongtae Shinawatra, was adjudged to have been guilty of securities violations relating to the sale of Shin Corp, and was fined 5.98m. baht (US $153,000), by the Securities and Exchange Commission (SEC); Phantongtae was deemed to have failed fully to disclose transactions pertaining to his stock-holdings.

On 2 April 2006 legislative elections were held and, as expected, Thai Rak Thai secured victory, winning approximately 57% of votes cast. Turn-out was estimated at 64.8% of the electorate. However, 33.1% of those who voted selected the 'no vote' option on ballot papers. Owing to the boycott of the poll by the three main opposition parties, the House of Representatives was unable to convene by the end of the month as a significant number of seats remained vacant, despite the holding of several by-elections. Soon after the election Thaksin announced that he would not seek to return to the office of Prime Minister on a permanent basis and appointed the Deputy Prime Minister, Gen. Chidchai Wannasathit, to the role in an acting capacity. In May the Constitutional Court annulled the election results, declaring them invalid as the poll had been organized too quickly following the dissolution of the House of Representatives. The Election Commission subsequently announced that a new legislative election would take place in October. At the end of May Thaksin announced that he was returning to the post of interim Prime Minister.

Mounting tension between Thaksin and King Bhumibol, who was becoming increasingly vocal on the subject of the country's troubled political situation, was temporarily alleviated in June 2006 by celebrations to commemorate the 60th anniversary of the King's accession to the throne. In the same month militants carried out a series of co-ordinated attacks over a period of several days, detonating in excess of 50 bombs that targeted more than 30 locations across the three southernmost provinces; the attacks were reported to have killed at least four people and injured more than 20 others. In August almost two dozen bank branches in the province of Yala were targeted in another spate of co-ordinated explosions, which killed two people and injured a further 28. Meanwhile, at the end of June a team of prosecutors from the Office of the Attorney-General urged the disbandment of various parties, including Thai Rak Thai and the DP, on charges related to the April election, the former being accused of funding token opposition candidates, while the latter was alleged to have instigated a boycott of the poll. In July the Chairman of the Election Commission and two commissioners were found guilty of election law contravention and sentenced to four years' imprisonment by the Criminal Court.

On 19 September 2006, while Thaksin was out of the country, the Government was ousted from power in a bloodless military coup led by the Commander-in-Chief of the Army, Gen. Sonthi Boonyaratglin. Gen. Sonthi, acting as part of the so-called Council for Democratic Reform, imposed martial law and suspended the Constitution, the Government and the legislature. In a statement to the media the Council claimed to have the support of King Bhumibol and ordered the cessation of activities by political parties, promising the imminent appointment of an interim Prime Minister with a mandate to oversee fresh elections. Within a week the Council had initiated an investigation into allegations of corruption within the Thaksin Government. At the beginning of October, following the signing of an interim Constitution by King Bhumibol, Gen. (retd) Surayud Chulanont was sworn in as Prime Minister by the military leadership, which had been renamed the Council for National Security and retained significant powers over the Government and the Constitution. Elections were projected for 2007, upon the drafting and approval of a new constitution. The Governor of the Bank of Thailand, Pridiyathorn Devakula, and the chairman of Bangkok Bank, Kosit Panpiemras, were appointed Deputy Prime Ministers in the Cabinet that was subsequently announced, taking additional charge of the finance and industry portfolios, respectively. The National Legislative Assembly, comprising the Council's appointees, was approved by the King and convened in mid-October 2006. In November martial law was rescinded in approximately 40 provinces (although this did not take effect until January 2007). Meanwhile, Thaksin, who had remained overseas since the coup, announced his resignation from Thai Rak Thai in October 2006, following a large number of departures from the party, which were said to have been prompted by the military leadership's assertion that those associated with political organizations guilty of electoral malpractice would be punished. In November Thaksin's son and daughter were ordered to pay tax on their share of the proceeds of the Shin Corp sale.

Hopes of a resolution to the ongoing insurgency in the south were raised by Gen. Sonthi's announcement in October 2006 that the military leadership was willing to engage in dialogue with certain groups. In the following month Prime Minister Surayud apologized for the deaths of the Muslim protesters in Tak Bai in 2004 (see Escalating violence in the southern provinces), and it was later announced that charges against several demonstrators would be rescinded. However, despite the apparent progress towards reconciliation, the violence continued into 2007: by March it was estimated that the conflict had caused more than 2,100 fatalities, of which more than 400 had occurred since the coup. In December 2006 a series of eight bomb explosions in Bangkok killed three people and injured several others; it was implied by some sources that associates of Thaksin were responsible, a claim he subsequently denied. In January 2007 the Government suspended Thaksin's diplomatic passport and requested a media ban on his lawyer's statements. Surayud later affirmed that Thaksin would be permitted to return to Thailand on the condition that he did not engage in political activity. Doubts were expressed in February about the stability of the Government after the Deputy Prime Minister and Minister of Finance, Pridiyathorn Devakula, resigned, citing internal discord among other reasons. The interim Government's economic policies, which were based on a principle of 'self-sufficiency' advocated by the King and had thus far included measures to restrict the movement of foreign capital and foreign ownership of Thai companies, had been widely criticized and had damaged investor confidence. Chalongphob Sussangkarn succeeded Pridiyathorn as Minister of Finance, while the Minister of Social Development and Human Security, Paiboon Wattanasiritham, was promoted to the concurrent position of Deputy Prime Minister. In March Thaksin's wife, Pojaman Shinawatra, was charged with tax evasion in relation to a 1997 share transaction of the company that later became known as Shin Corp. Meanwhile, Gen. Sonthi was reported to have requested the enforcement of emergency rule to address the alleged threat of instability posed by regular anti-coup demonstrations in Bangkok. Surayud denied the request and announced that elections would be held in December 2007, following a constitutional referendum, which was to be conducted by September.

In May 2007 the Constitutional Tribunal (which had replaced the Constitutional Court under the interim Constitution) found Thai Rak Thai guilty of violating electoral legislation prior to the April 2006 poll, but acquitted the DP of all charges of malpractice. The Tribunal ordered the dissolution of Thai Rak Thai and a ban on 111 party members, including Thaksin, from participating in politics for five years. Thai Rak Thai had been accused of funding minor opposition parties to field candidates in constituencies in which it would have been unlikely to achieve the 20% of the vote required to secure election in uncontested seats. A number of demonstrations by the party's supporters in Bangkok followed the verdict. The ban on activities by political organizations was removed in early June 2007 to allow parties to begin campaigning for the forthcoming legislative election. In mid-June the Assets Examination Committee froze bank accounts held by Thaksin (some jointly with Pojaman) containing a total of 52,900m. baht; the Committee later ordered additional assets to be frozen as investigations continued into Thaksin, who remained in self-imposed exile. A week later corruption charges were filed against Thaksin and Pojaman in relation to the latter's purchase in 2003 of a plot of land in Bangkok from a state agency for a sum allegedly far lower than its true value. Thaksin was also accused of concealing assets.

The Constitution Drafting Assembly (the members of which had effectively been appointed by the Council for National Security) approved the final draft of a new constitution in early July 2007. The proposed constitution was designed to curb the powers of the Prime Minister, who would be limited to serving two four-year terms and barred from owning large stakes in private companies. In addition, the threshold for initiating a debate on a motion of no confidence in the Prime Minister would be reduced from two-fifths of the members of the House of Representatives in favour to one-fifth (although such a motion would still require the support of more than one-half of deputies to be endorsed). The Senate would be transformed from a fully elected body of 200 senators to one in which 74 of its 150 senators would be selected by a seven-member committee of judges and other senior state officials (such as the President of the Constitutional Court and the Chairperson of the Election Commission), with the remainder directly elected in each province. The number of deputies in the House of Representatives would be reduced from 500 to 480 (400 to be elected on a multi-member constituency basis and 80 on a proportional representation basis). Further notable provisions committed the state to the implementation of the 'sufficient economy philosophy' and guaranteed an amnesty for those involved in the coup of September 2006. Critics of the draft claimed that it was 'anti-Thaksin' and less democratic than the 1997 Constitution. However, while acknowledging its flaws, the DP and Chart Thai supported the draft in the interest of restoring democracy as swiftly as possible. The draft Constitution was endorsed by 57.8% of those voting in a referendum on 19 August 2007. A relatively low turn-out, of 57.6% of eligible voters, was recorded. More detailed results indicated the country's deep political divisions, with the charter rejected by nearly 63% of voters in the rural north-east, a stronghold of the dissolved Thai Rak Thai, but approved by some 88% of voters in the south. After receiving royal assent, the new Constitution took effect on 24 August. Meanwhile, in July a demonstration against military rule by several thousand people in Bangkok ended in violence, as protesters clashed with police after staging a rally outside the house of former Prime Minister Prem Tinsulanonda, now a senior royal adviser, whom they claimed had been involved in co-ordinating the coup. Nine alleged leaders of the demonstration, reported to be either allies of Thaksin or pro-democracy activists, were subsequently arrested and charged with illegal assembly and inciting violence.

In late July 2007 the National Legislative Assembly adopted legislation prohibiting new political parties from using the same names, logos or acronyms as parties dissolved by the Constitutional Tribunal for a period of five years. Many former Thai Rak

Thai deputies subsequently joined the little-known People's Power Party (PPP), while others participated in the formation of new parties, such as Puea Pandin and Ruam Jai Thai (the latter later merging with Chart Pattana); Samak Sundaravej, a right-wing political veteran and former Governor of Bangkok, was elected leader of the PPP in August. In mid-August the Supreme Court issued arrest warrants for Thaksin and Pojaman after they failed to answer a summons to appear before the Court to answer the corruption charges relating to the land purchase in 2003. Further arrest warrants were issued for the couple by a criminal court in Bangkok in September 2007 in connection with a police inquiry into alleged violations of stock-trading legislation. In late August it was announced that elections to the House of Representatives would be held on 23 December.

Gen. Sonthi was appointed Deputy Prime Minister in charge of Security in early October 2007, having retired as Commander-in-Chief of the Army and resigned as Chairman of the Council for National Security, prompting speculation that he intended to remain in political office beyond the elections scheduled for December. He was replaced as Chairman of the Council for National Security by Air Chief Marshal Chalit Pukpasuk, the Commander-in-Chief of the Air Force. Sonthi's appointment was part of a wider cabinet reorganization necessitated by the recent resignations of five ministers who were under investigation by the NCCC for allegedly breaching a 5% limit on ministerial shareholdings in private companies. Prime Minister Surayud and the Deputy Prime Minister and Minister of Industry, Kosit Panpiemras, assumed additional responsibility for the portfolios of the interior and of information and communications technology, respectively. In late October the Cabinet ordered martial law to be revoked in 221 districts, but maintained in 179 districts in 31 provinces.

The restoration of civilian rule

During the week preceding the 2007 legislative election, amid protests outside the parliament building by students and civil society activists, the National Legislative Assembly adopted many new pieces of legislation, most notably a controversial act giving the Internal Security Operations Command, an agency comprising military and civilian representatives, wide-ranging powers to counter perceived threats to national security. These enhanced powers, which were strongly criticized by human rights groups, included the ability to order curfews, detain suspects without trial, restrict freedom of movement and override the authority of government officials.

Some 74.5% of registered voters participated in the legislative elections, which took place, as scheduled, on 23 December 2007. Polls were repeated in the following month in a number of constituencies where the Election Commission had annulled results owing to 'vote-buying' and other irregularities. The PPP emerged as the largest party in the House of Representatives, securing 233 of the 480 seats, while the DP won 164, Chart Thai 34, Puea Pandin 24, Matchimathipataya 11, Ruam Jai Thai Chart Pattana nine and Pracharaj five. Essentially the successor to Thai Rak Thai, the PPP achieved greatest success in the north and north-east of the country, and its victory was regarded as a rejection of the 2006 coup and the outgoing military leadership. None the less, its failure to secure an outright majority of seats forced the PPP to negotiate with other parties to establish a coalition administration.

In mid-January 2008 the PPP leader, Samak Sundaravej, officially announced the formation of a six-party coalition controlling 316 of the 480 seats in the House of Representatives, leaving the DP as the sole opposition party in the legislature. The new House of Representatives was convened two days later, subsequently electing Yongyuth Tiyapairat, the deputy leader of the PPP, as its new Speaker and Samak as Prime Minister. Meanwhile, the Council for National Security was disbanded. Samak's new Cabinet was sworn in by King Bhumibol in early February. Many strategic posts in the new Government were allocated to personal allies of Thaksin. Samak assumed personal responsibility for the defence portfolio, while Surapong Suebwonglee, the Secretary-General of the PPP, was appointed Deputy Prime Minister and Minister of Finance. Noppadon Pattama, Thaksin's legal adviser, and Chalerm Yoobamrung, another close associate of the deposed Prime Minister, became Minister of Foreign Affairs and Minister of the Interior, respectively. Later in that month the Government announced plans to resume several populist policies initiated by Thaksin and to commence a new anti-drugs campaign, similar to those conducted under the former Prime Minister (which had resulted in some 2,500 deaths). Amendments to the Constitution were also envisaged. Thaksin returned to Thailand in late February after 17 months in exile, insisting that he had retired from active politics. He was immediately taken to hear the corruption charges against him and was granted bail. In mid-March he pleaded not guilty before the Supreme Court to using his influence to assist his wife with her land purchase in 2003. Thaksin's wife, Pojaman, had already returned in January 2008, when she was also granted bail and denied the charges against her. Elections to fill 76 of the 150 seats in the Senate were held on 2 March, the remaining 74 members having been appointed in the previous month by the selection committee. Electoral turn-out was estimated at 55.9%. The appointed senators were considered to be closer to the outgoing military leadership, while many of the elected senators were reported to be allies of Thaksin. Prasobsuk Boondech, an appointed senator and former Chief Justice of the Court of Appeals, was elected Speaker of the Senate in mid-March.

Despite the restoration of civilian rule, political uncertainty persisted in early 2008. In late February the new administration suffered a set-back when the Election Commission voted in favour of disqualifying Speaker Yongyuth from office, concluding that he had bribed local officials in exchange for votes during the general election campaign, and referred the case to the Supreme Court. There was a possibility that the PPP might be disbanded by the Constitutional Court if the Supreme Court were to find Yongyuth guilty and judge that the party was aware of 'vote-buying'. Yongyuth stood down as Speaker pending the Supreme Court's verdict. In mid-April the Election Commission recommended the dissolution of Chart Thai and Matchimathipataya on the grounds of electoral fraud allegedly committed by senior party officials; the case was referred to the Constitutional Court. The Commission was also investigating a complaint that the PPP and Thaksin had violated legislation governing political parties, the former by allegedly acting as a 'nominee' of Thai Rak Thai and the latter through his alleged involvement with the PPP, despite being barred from participating in politics. Meanwhile, the DP accused the coalition Government of self-interest in its plans to revise the Constitution, particularly its desire to amend the article allowing for an entire party to be held responsible for the wrongdoing of a single party executive. In April martial law was rescinded in all areas of the country except for the southern provinces of Narathiwat, Yala, Pattani and part of Songkhla, where the death toll in the ongoing insurgency had recently surpassed 3,000.

Political tensions rose in May 2008, as the PAD (which had led the campaign against Thaksin in 2006) resumed its anti-Government demonstrations in Bangkok, protesting against the plans for constitutional reform. The Minister in the Prime Minister's Office, Chakrapob Penkair, a close ally of Thaksin, was forced to resign from the Cabinet in late May, after it emerged that he was to be charged under *lèse majesté* legislation (prohibiting criticism of the monarch) in connection with a speech that he gave at the Foreign Correspondents' Club in Bangkok in August 2007. Notwithstanding Samak's decision to refer the issue of constitutional change to a parliamentary committee, daily demonstrations continued, albeit on a smaller scale than those of 2006, amid speculation regarding the possibility of another military coup. The Government also provoked criticism by endorsing an application made by the Cambodian Government to UNESCO (see p. 153) seeking World Heritage status for Preah Vihear, an 11th-century temple in an area of disputed sovereignty on the Thai–Cambodian border (see Foreign Affairs). None the less, in June 2008 DP-proposed motions of no confidence in Samak and seven of his ministers were easily defeated in the House of Representatives, owing to the ruling coalition's strong majority. However, the controversy over Preah Vihear persisted, leading to the resignation of the Minister of Foreign Affairs, Noppadon, in July, after the Constitutional Court ruled that he had violated the Constitution by signing an agreement supporting Cambodia's (recently successful) bid without securing legislative approval; Tej Bunnag, hitherto adviser to the Office of His Majesty's Principal Private Secretary, was appointed as Noppadon's replacement. Meanwhile, earlier in July the Supreme Court found Yongyuth guilty of electoral fraud, banning him from participating in politics for five years.

The trial of Thaksin and his wife on charges related to Pojaman's 2003 purchase of a plot of state-owned land commenced in the Supreme Court in July 2008, a fortnight after three of Thaksin's lawyers had been convicted of attempting to bribe Court officials and sentenced to six months' imprisonment. Later in that month the Supreme Court announced that it would also

THAILAND

hear allegations that Thaksin had abused his power by introducing a state lottery in 2003 and by instructing a state-controlled bank to offer a low-interest loan to Myanmar in 2004 for the purchase of telecommunications equipment from a subsidiary of Shin Corp. At the end of July, in a separate case, Pojaman and her brother were convicted of failing to pay tax of 546m. baht on a Shin Corp share transaction in 1997 and sentenced to three years' imprisonment; Pojaman's secretary received a two-year sentence. All three were released on bail, pending an appeal. In mid-August the Supreme Court issued an arrest warrant for Thaksin and Pojaman, who had absconded to the United Kingdom shortly before they were due to appear before the Court; Thaksin announced that he would not return to Thailand, claiming that the charges against him were politically motivated and that he would not be tried fairly. The Supreme Court issued a second arrest warrant for Thaksin in September, after he failed to appear at the beginning of his trial on charges related to the alleged low-interest loan to Myanmar. In October the Supreme Court convicted Thaksin *in absentia* of violating an article of the Constitution concerning conflict of interest in relation to his involvement in his wife's purchase of state land in 2003, sentencing him to two years' imprisonment; Pojaman was acquitted of the corruption charges against her in this case.

Meanwhile, a cabinet reorganization was effected in early August 2008; notable changes included the appointment of Kowit Wattana, the national police chief during 2004–07, as Deputy Prime Minister and Minister of the Interior. Anti-Government protests in Bangkok escalated later that month, with the number of demonstrators rising to an estimated 30,000, as PAD supporters invaded several government buildings and the studios of the state-run National Broadcasting Services of Thailand, before occupying the grounds of Government House and refusing to leave. About 85 people were detained, and arrest warrants were subsequently issued for nine PAD leaders who were accused of illegal assembly and inciting unrest. Samak, who was forced to move his office initially to the military's headquarters and later to the former international airport at Don Muang, rejected demands for his resignation. As well as a change of government, the PAD advocated the introduction of what it termed 'new politics', which would involve a controversial reform of the House of Representatives, whereby 70% of its members would be appointed and only 30% elected. As tensions mounted, with police reportedly using tear gas to repel 2,000 demonstrators attempting to enter the police headquarters in Bangkok, the protests also extended beyond the capital, resulting in the temporary closure of three blockaded regional airports and disruption to rail services. At an emergency session of the National Assembly held at the end of August, Samak maintained his position that he would not resign from office. On 2 September the Prime Minister declared a state of emergency in Bangkok, after one person died in confrontations between rival protesters from the PAD and the United Front for Democracy against Dictatorship (UDD—whose supporters were popularly dubbed 'the Red Shirts'). In a further set-back for the Government, on the following day Tej Bunnag resigned as Minister of Foreign Affairs, just over a month after his appointment. Moreover, the Election Commission recommended that the Constitutional Court dissolve the PPP on the grounds of the electoral fraud committed by former Speaker Yongyuth.

Successive governments

On 9 September 2008 the Constitutional Court ordered Samak Sundaravej and his Cabinet to resign, ruling that the Prime Minister had violated the Constitution by accepting payment for presenting a television cookery programme while in office. After a failed attempt by the PPP to secure the re-election of Samak as Prime Minister, owing to opposition from the party's coalition partners, on 17 September Somchai Wongsawat, a brother-in-law of Thaksin Shinawatra as well as Deputy Prime Minister and Minister of Education in the outgoing Cabinet, was elected to the premiership. A new Cabinet was sworn in on 25 September; Prime Minister Somchai assumed additional responsibility for the defence portfolio, while Sompong Amornwiwat was appointed Deputy Prime Minister and Minister of Foreign Affairs. Somchai replaced Samak as leader of the PPP at the end of the month. Meanwhile, the state of emergency in Bangkok was rescinded on 14 September, but the PAD-led protesters continued their occupation of the Government House compound, vowing to remain as long as the PPP retained power. Two of the nine protest organizers for whom arrest warrants had been issued were detained in early October. Deputy Prime Minister Chavalit Yongchaiyudh, the Government's chief negotiator with the PAD, resigned on 7 October, after two people died and more than 400 were injured during violent clashes that occurred when police used tear gas to disperse several thousand PAD demonstrators who were besieging the legislative building. The remaining seven PAD leaders sought by police surrendered a few days later after treason charges against them were withdrawn; all nine PAD detainees were subsequently released on bail, still charged with lesser offences.

An estimated 40,000 people attended a rally in Bangkok in support of Thaksin and the PPP-led Government at the beginning of November 2008, demonstrating the continued popularity of the former Prime Minister and the deep political divisions within the country. Also in early November two bomb explosions in Narathiwat killed one person and injured more than 70 people. A week earlier Prime Minister Somchai had visited the southern provinces, noting that separatist violence in the region, which had caused more than 3,400 deaths since January 2004, appeared to have eased. The United Kingdom revoked the visas of Thaksin and Pojaman in November 2008, while they were both out of the country; later that month it was announced that the couple had divorced. The Governor of Bangkok, Apirak Kosayodhin of the DP, who had been re-elected to the position in October, resigned in mid-November, after being indicted (together with a number of other officials and former Governor and Prime Minister Samak) in connection with alleged irregularities in the purchase of fire-fighting equipment for the capital; Sukhumbhand Paripatra of the DP was elected to replace Apirak as Governor of Bangkok in January 2009.

Several thousand PAD demonstrators again surrounded the parliament building on 24 November 2008, before moving to the Cabinet's temporary offices at Don Muang airport, in what they described as a 'final battle' to oust the Government. Thousands of PAD protesters then seized control of Suvarnabhumi, Bangkok's main international airport, which led to the cancellation of all flights, severely damaging the tourism industry. The PAD declared that its occupation of Suvarnabhumi would continue until Somchai resigned, prompting the Commander-in-Chief of the Army, Gen. Anupong Paochinda, to suggest that the Prime Minister should relinquish his position and call fresh elections; however, Somchai insisted that he would remain in office. The PAD subsequently also forced the closure of Don Muang airport. On 27 November Somchai declared a state of emergency around Bangkok's two airports, following a meeting of the Cabinet in the northern city of Chiang Mai—where the Prime Minister's flight had been forced to land on his return the previous day from a summit meeting of the Asia-Pacific Economic Co-operation (APEC, see p. 197) in Peru. A stand-off subsequently ensued between police surrounding the airports and the protesters within. At the end of November some 20,000 government supporters attended a rally in the capital. Meanwhile, after three months, PAD protesters began to disperse from their encampment at Government House, where several small bomb attacks in late October and November had resulted in one death and injured around 90 people.

On 2 December 2008 the PAD announced that it was ceasing its protests and airport occupations, after the Constitutional Court ordered the dissolution of the PPP, Chart Thai and Matchimathipataya on the grounds of electoral fraud and barred the executives of the three parties from engaging in politics for five years, thus forcing Somchai to leave office. Many PPP deputies who were not disqualified from participating in politics joined Puea Thai, which had been formed in anticipation of the Court's decision; Yongyuth Wichaidith was elected as the new party's leader. Chart Thai and Matchimathipataya were similarly regrouped, as Chart Thai Pattana and Bhum Jai Thai (BJT), respectively. However, the DP succeeded in securing the support of a significant number of deputies from the dissolved parties, as well as that of several former coalition partners of the PPP, and on 15 December the DP's leader, Abhisit Vejjajiva, was elected as the new Prime Minister by a margin of 37 votes, defeating Pracha Promnok, the leader of Puea Pandin, who was supported by Puea Thai. In response to Abhisit's election, supporters of Somchai's outgoing administration protested outside the parliament building and the DP's headquarters. The new Prime Minister appealed for national unity, pledging to address the country's economic difficulties and to continue some of the more populist policies pursued by previous governments. A new Cabinet took office on 22 December, comprising members of the DP, Friends of Newin (a breakaway faction of the former PPP, led by Newin Chidchob), Chart Thai Pattana, Puea Pandin (12 deputies from which had voted for Abhisit's election as Prime

Minister), Ruam Jai Thai Chart Pattana, BJT and the SAP (which had been revived in mid-2008 by its former leader, Suwit Khunkitti, following his departure from Puea Pandin). Observers expressed concern regarding the lack of experience of several new ministers, while the selection of Kasit Piromya as Minister of Foreign Affairs was also controversial owing to his prominent support for the PAD protests. Thousands of demonstrators loyal to Thaksin and his allies, led by the UDD, took part in protests against the legitimacy of Abhisit's Government in late December, forcing the Prime Minister to make his inaugural policy speech to the National Assembly at the offices of the Ministry of Foreign Affairs; the parliament building was surrounded by protesters for two days.

By-elections were held on 11 January 2009 to fill the seats made vacant by the disqualification of deputies from the parties dissolved in the previous month. The governing coalition increased its majority in the House of Representatives, with the DP winning seven of the 29 seats contested, Chart Thai Pattana 10 and Puea Pandin three, while Puea Thai secured five seats and Pracharaj four. During its first few weeks in office the new Government focused its attention on measures to stimulate the economy, notably securing legislative approval of a 116,700m. baht supplementary budget that included provision for a payment of 2,000 baht to workers earning less than 15,000 baht per month. The new administration also expressed its determination to protect the monarchy, establishing a website urging people to inform on anyone perceived to be criticizing the King, and creating an internet security centre to co-ordinate the blocking of websites deemed to be offensive to the monarchy, with access to about 5,000 sites reportedly being denied during its first day in operation. Also in January the Friends of Newin grouping merged with BJT.

It was reported in January 2009 that the Government intended to appoint a new civilian body to administer the south of the country and supervise military activities in the region. A report published by the human rights organization Amnesty International in that month claimed that the use of torture by the security forces in the counter-insurgency campaign in the southern provinces was widespread. The Thai military was also accused that month of mistreating Myanma and Bangladeshi migrants attempting to reach Thailand (see Foreign Affairs).

The UDD organized several anti-Government rallies at Government House in January–March 2009 in support of its demands for the resignation of Abhisit's Cabinet, the dissolution of the House of Representatives, the organization of new elections, the reinstatement of the 1997 Constitution, and the prosecution of the PAD leadership (for the damage caused to the economy by the occupation of Bangkok's airports in 2008). In March the Government defeated motions of no confidence in Abhisit and five of his ministers, including Kasit and Minister of Finance Korn Chatikavanij, which had been tabled in the House of Representatives by Puea Thai. Meanwhile, the Thai authorities were seeking Thaksin's extradition from Hong Kong, where he was believed to be based.

In April 2009 UDD protesters forced the postponement of an Association of Southeast Asian Nations (ASEAN, see p. 206) summit meeting being held in Pattaya after blocking the route to the conference hall. Abhisit declared an extreme state of emergency as visiting Asian leaders were airlifted from the venue. The Government also invoked the Internal Security Act, affording the authorities additional powers to impose curfews and restrict gatherings. In the same month violent altercations took place in Bangkok between UDD protesters and the authorities, culminating in the death of two protesters, with more than 120 injured. Following the violence, thousands of Thai soldiers were mobilized to implement a security cordon around the demonstrators gathered outside Government House, ultimately prompting protest leaders to appeal for an end to the movement. Arrest warrants were subsequently issued for 13 protest leaders on charges of inciting public disturbance and illegal assembly. Shortly after the ending of the protests, Sondhi Limthongkul, founder of the PAD, was shot in Bangkok in an apparent assassination attempt. Sondhi survived the shooting, in which his driver and aide were also injured, and in October he was selected as leader of the recently established New Politics party.

In September 2009 King Bhumibol was admitted to hospital for apparent respiratory problems; when he was not promptly discharged, considerable speculation emerged with regard to the state of health of the monarch, whom many viewed as the sole unifying figure within the deeply divided country. Concerns were allayed to an extent when the King left hospital in December on the occasion of his 82nd birthday, which he marked by granting a private audience to members of the royal family and senior politicians. In a brief public statement, the King urged the country's leaders to 'clearly understand' the duties of their roles and to 'fulfil it with dedication for the good of the country'. Following the meeting at the royal palace, the King returned to hospital. In August 2010 Queen Sirikit announced that the King's health had 'substantially improved'; however, he remained hospitalized at mid-2011.

Meanwhile, in December 2009 Abhisit was forced to deny claims of a government plot to assassinate Thaksin, following the public disclosure of an ambiguously worded classified document, alleged to have been prepared by the Minister of Foreign Affairs, Kasit Piromya, which referred to Thaksin as a major factor in the destabilization of the Government that 'needed to be tackled'. The Prime Minister adamantly refuted that this was an indirect demand for Thaksin's permanent removal, insisting that the Government wished only to bring Thaksin back to Thailand, using legal means, to serve his two-year prison sentence for corruption.

In early January 2010 DP deputy leader Witthaya Kaewparadai resigned as Minister of Public Health amid allegations of spending irregularities committed by the health ministry. Deputy Minister of Public Health Manit Nop-amornbodi tendered his own resignation a few days later, having been placed under pressure to stand down by Prime Minister Abhisit. Like Witthaya, Nop-amornbodi was being investigated by the National Anti-Corruption Commission (as the NCCC had been renamed in July 2008) for his alleged involvement in the scandal. In mid-January Abhisit announced a government reorganization, which was endorsed by the King from his hospital bed. Among the five changes effected, Jurin Laksanawisit, hitherto Minister of Education, was transferred to the public health portfolio, while the education portfolio was awarded to Chinnaworn Boonyakiat, and Trairong Suwannakhiri replaced Korbsak Sabhavasu as a Deputy Prime Minister.

The UDD protests of 2010

In early February 2010 Maj.-Gen. Khattiya Sawasdipol, an outspoken supporter of former premier Thaksin Shinawatra, was charged with illegal arms possession amid allegations of involvement in a grenade attack on the army headquarters in late January. Khattiya had been suspended a few days prior to the attack for insubordination. A group of about 500 UDD protesters gathered outside the police building in which Khattiya was being questioned, while Prime Minister Abhisit Vejjajiva warned of the potential for more attacks on government buildings; UDD demonstrators had pledged to stage mass protests ahead of a court ruling, due later that month, on the Shinawatra family's assets, which had been frozen in June 2007 (see The ousting of Thaksin and imposition of military rule). The Government moved swiftly to deploy thousands of additional security personnel in 38 provinces across the country in advance of the delivery of the verdict. A minor explosion near the Office of the Prime Minister in mid-February, and the discovery of an unexploded bomb within the compound of the Supreme Court on the following day, resulted in a further elevation of security around the capital. In late February the Supreme Court delivered its verdict in the asset seizure case, ruling that more than half of the Shinawatras' assets had been amassed as a result of Thaksin abusing his authority while Prime Minister in order to benefit Shin Corp—allegations that Thaksin had categorically rebutted throughout the court proceedings—and was therefore to be confiscated. The UDD contended that the ruling had been contrived to punish Thaksin while allowing the Court to maintain the appearance of due adherence to the proper judicial process, despite the judiciary remaining beholden to the agenda of the military-dominated élite. Two bomb attacks at separate branches of Bangkok Bank Public Co Ltd in the capital on the following day were attributed by the authorities to the UDD, which denied any involvement.

The Government invoked the Internal Security Act in Bangkok and seven surrounding provinces, as well as implementing additional security measures, for a two-week period from 11 March 2010 (and subsequently extended) in preparation for the anticipated protests. An estimated 40,000 security troops were deployed, and many checkpoints were erected, in and around the capital. Between 100,000 and 150,000 people attended a UDD mass rally, claiming that Prime Minister Abhisit had come to power illegitimately and demanding his resignation and the holding of fresh elections. The demonstrators marched through the streets of Bangkok, before surrounding Government House, whereupon they demanded that Abhisit tender his resignation and dissolve the House of Representatives by midday on 15 March. Upon learning that Abhisit had been transferred to army barracks in the north of the city (a development that served to reinforce the popular perception that he had come to power as an agent of the military), throngs of protesters gathered at the barracks to demand that the Prime Minister acquiesce to their demands. When the UDD's deadline passed, Abhisit issued a live statement on national television in which he announced that the coalition Government had agreed that it could not meet the UDD's demands.

In mid-March 2010 UDD protesters daubed the gates of Government House with blood, donated by hundreds of UDD supporters, a small number of whom had been allowed to pass through the security cordon around the House, in an indication of the police force's commitment to ensuring a continuation of the hitherto peaceful nature of the protests. UDD leaders described the protest as a symbolic demonstration of the sacrifices that they were prepared to make for democracy, a demonstration designed to express that 'the people's blood is power'. Protesters also threw blood at the headquarters of the DP and the private residence of Abhisit, who remained entrenched in the army barracks. About 65,000 UDD protesters were estimated to have participated in a subsequent mass rally. Thaksin urged the instigation of a campaign of 'civil disobedience', a comment that was criticized by many for appearing to incite further unrest. Towards the end of March Abhisit agreed to meet with UDD leaders for direct talks in order to 'restore peace and minimize the chance of violence'. Earlier that day four soldiers had been injured when grenades were thrown into the compound of the army barracks in which Abhisit was staying. During the direct talks, which were broadcast live on national television, the UDD repeated its demands for fresh elections, while Abhisit highlighted the need to make a decision based on 'a consensus from the entire country' rather than capitulating to the UDD's demands. Abhisit's offer of early elections in 2011 was rejected by the UDD, which continued to press for the immediate dissolution of the legislature.

Mass rallies continued to be held every few days, despite warnings from the authorities that demonstrators would be arrested, as Abhisit came under increasing pressure to adopt a stronger stance and restore order. The non-violent nature of the protests was jeopardized when UDD protesters surrounded the parliamentary compound ine early April 2010, accompanied by thousands of riot police. Legislators were forced to abandon their parliamentary session and were ushered out of the building amid high security, some having to be rescued from the compound by a military helicopter. A small group of protesters then breached security and entered the compound, although there was no report of any violence and the group soon retreated. Later that day Abhisit declared a state of emergency in Bangkok and surrounding areas for a period of three months, the fourth time that a state of emergency had been imposed in the capital since 2008; emergency rule was subsequently extended to encompass 24 of Thailand's 76 provinces. The declaration had no discernible effect on the protesters, who reiterated their resolve to remain encamped in Bangkok until their demands had been met.

Under the new state of emergency laws, the Government shut down the People Channel, a television station that the authorities had accused of inciting violence, on 8 April 2010. On the following day UDD protesters seized control of the station and forced officials to allow the channel to recommence transmissions; the security forces' attempts to repel the demonstrators using water cannons and tear gas—the first time that force had been used during the four weeks of protest—proved unsuccessful. Any hopes of a peaceful resolution to the impasse were quashed when soldiers and police officers clashed violently with demonstrators on 10 April, during an unsuccessful attempt by the Government to reclaim an area of the capital held by the UDD. Security personnel fired tear gas and rubber bullets to disperse the crowds. Furthermore, the UDD alleged that troops had fired live ammunition at the protesters; although this was denied by the authorities, the testimony of independent witnesses to the violence appeared to confirm the veracity of such claims. According to local media, some protesters responded by throwing petrol bombs at advancing soldiers. Nineteen protesters, five soldiers and a Japanese cameraman working for the Reuters news agency were reported to have been killed during the clashes, and more than 800 others were injured in what constituted the worst incident of political violence in Thailand since May 1992. Autopsies carried out on some of the deceased revealed that they had been shot at close range, provoking further condemnation of the authorities. Human Rights Watch urged the Thai Government to establish an independent commission to investigate the fatal clashes.

In mid-April 2010 the Electoral Commission unexpectedly announced that it recommended the dissolution of the ruling DP owing to 'funding irregularities'; UDD leaders welcomed the development but stated that it had no bearing on their protests. An offer from the Government to dissolve the legislature within six months was rejected. Abhisit announced that Gen. Anupong Paojinda, the Commander-in-Chief of the Army, was to assume responsibility for restoring order from Deputy Prime Minister Suthep Thaugsuban. The decision followed a mismanaged attempt, overseen by Suthep, to arrest several UDD leaders, who were filmed escaping from the authorities. The army explicitly stated that live ammunition would be used against protesters in certain circumstances; the UDD abandoned plans to march through Silom later that day, stating that it wished to avoid a confrontation with the army. A series of grenade attacks in the capital's business district resulted in the deaths of three people, with more than 80 others injured; neither side claimed responsibility for the blasts.

The unrest was not restricted to the capital. Several hand grenade attacks were reported in Chiang Mai during March and April 2010, and an improvised explosive device was detonated in the city in late March. Further bomb attacks, targeting the provincial police headquarters and banks, took place in mid-April. Also in mid-April pro-Government protests took place in numerous locations around the country, including Pattaya, Lampang and Ubon Ratchathani; the protests in Pattaya led to violent clashes between pro-Government groups and UDD supporters.

In early May 2010 Abhisit announced his 'road map' for reconciliation, which included the holding of elections in mid-November, subject to certain conditions, if the UDD agreed to call off its protests. The UDD announced that it had accepted the offer of elections in November, but pledged to remain encamped in Bangkok until Deputy Prime Minister Suthep surrendered himself to the police for his involvement, as head of security operations at that time, in the clashes of 10 April that had left 25 people dead. Abhisit withdrew the offer of an election in November, but stated that reconciliation remained a priority; the Prime Minister's Secretary-General, Korbsak Sabhavasu, declared that an election date could only be reconsidered after the UDD had ended its mass protests and dispersed from the streets of Bangkok. In mid-May at least one person was killed and dozens of others were injured during clashes between the UDD and the authorities in which a series of explosions and heavy gunfire was reported. Among the injured was Maj.-Gen. Khattiya, who had been advising the protesters on military strategies since mid-March; Khattiya was admitted to hospital in a critical condition after being shot in the head, and died a few days later. Two journalists were also reported to have been shot. The authorities moved in to seal off the protesters' camp in central Bangkok, allowing people out, but not in, and shutting off the power and water supplies to the area. As the violence escalated, more than 40 people were killed during sporadic altercations, prompting several foreign embassies to close.

An offer extended by the Senate to mediate in talks between the two factions was welcomed by the UDD; however, the Government stated that it would enter into no further negotiations until the protesters had left their camp. On the following day, in response to the UDD's continued refusal to depart, troops were dispatched in armoured vehicles to break through the barricades that the protesters had erected around their camp, as the Government made a decisive effort to regain control; six people were thought to have been killed in the operation. Shortly thereafter, the UDD leaders announced their decision to surrender from a stage erected within the camp, stating that they did not want any more lives to be lost and urging the protesters to go home. Although the majority of the protesters dispersed peacefully from the streets of Bangkok, at least eight people, including an Italian journalist, were killed during exchanges of gunfire between retreating protesters and the authorities; furthermore, more than 30 buildings, including the stock exchange, banks and a shopping centre, were set on fire by protesters, and isolated pockets of resistance remained scattered around central Bangkok. The Government announced an overnight curfew for the capital and 23 provinces, the first time in 15 years that a curfew had been imposed; the curfew remained in place until 29 May, by which time the vast majority of the UDD leadership had been detained by the authorities. The official death toll since the beginning of the protests in March was 91, with a further 1,800 injured. Meanwhile, the High Court approved an application by the Thai police for a warrant to arrest Thaksin on terrorism charges, amid government allegations that the former premier, who remained in self-imposed exile, had provided financial and planning support to the UDD demonstrators.

Recent developments: ongoing discord and UDD rallies

Although the UDD had ultimately failed in its bid to force Abhisit and his Government from office, the protests had served further to highlight the deep political divisions within Thailand. Such divisions were further underscored at the beginning of June 2010 by the results of no-confidence motions lodged by opposition legislators against Abhisit and Deputy Prime Minister Suthep, who were alleged to have abused their respective positions of power and to have authorized the use of excessive force to quell the protest movement. The motion against Abhisit was defeated by 246 parliamentary votes to 186, while that against Suthep was defeated by 245 votes to 187; however, the strength of opposition to both leaders was a cause for concern for the Government. Motions of no confidence were also tabled against Minister of Finance Korn Chatikavanij, Minister of Foreign Affairs Kasit Piromya and Minister of the Interior Chaovarat Chanweerakul, as well as Minister of Transport Sophon Saram, for reasons unrelated to the protests; all survived the action against them, although Chaovarat and Sophon, both of BJT, secured 236 and 234 votes of confidence, respectively, falling just short of the minimum of 238 votes needed to defeat the no-confidence motion outright. However, both ministers retained their posts in a government reorganization effected by Abhisit a few days later. Notable appointments included that of Niphit Intharasombat as Minister of Culture, in place of Teera Slukpetch, and that of Chuti Krairiksh as Minister of Information and Communications, replacing Ranongruk Suwanchawee; Minister of Labour Phaithoon Kaeothong, about whom corruption allegations had been reported and whose performance had been criticized, was replaced by Chalermchai Sri-on, while Chaiwuti Bannawat was awarded the industry portfolio, in place of Charnchai Chairungrueng. Rumours that the reorganization was due to a rift within the DP were denied.

The nomination by Abhisit of Khanit na Nakhon, a former Attorney-General, as the head of an independent fact-finding committee charged with investigating the violence surrounding the UDD protests was approved by the Cabinet in early June 2010. Later in June a bomb exploded outside the headquarters of BJT; it was alleged that the device had exploded prematurely and that the bomber, who was arrested at the scene and was the only person injured in the blast, had intended to plant it within the premises prior to its detonation. Four Thai nationals implicated by the would-be bomber of involvement in the failed attack were arrested in late June, including a man and a woman who were apprehended in Cambodia and deported to Thailand in early July. The five accused, together with a sixth suspect arrested in July, were charged in September in connection with the attack in September.

Meanwhile, prior to the expiry of the three-month state of emergency in July 2010, the Government extended emergency rule in the capital and 19 provinces for a further three months, citing concerns about a renewal of violence; emergency rule was revoked in five other provinces, in three further provinces later in the month and in another three provinces in mid-August. Some opponents of the Government claimed that the attack outside the BJT headquarters in June had been staged so as to provide the Government with a pretext for extending the state of emergency. A bomb explosion in Bangkok in late July, which killed one person and injured 10 others, was attributed by the authorities to elements loyal to the UDD; the attack came a few hours after the closing of polls in a by-election in the capital, in which the DP's candidate defeated Korkaew Pikulthong of Puea Thai, a UDD leader who had been imprisoned since his arrest in late May and had, therefore, been unable to campaign. In mid-August an appeal by Thaksin against the court order in February that more than one-half of the Shinawatras' assets be confiscated (see The UDD protests of 2010) was rejected by the Supreme Court, which ruled that evidence presented by the former premier was not new and a retrial could not therefore be ordered. Also in mid-August 17 of 19 UDD leaders indicted on charges of terrorist activity and inciting violence, including Korkaew, appeared at a preliminary hearing at which they denied the charges against them; Weng Tojirakarn and Nattawut Saikua, former Thai Rak Thai party executives who were prominent members of the UDD leadership, were also among the accused. Their trial commenced in late September.

Tensions in the capital were exacerbated by the discovery in mid-September 2010 of three unexploded bombs in separate locations around Bangkok. Again, critics of the Government alleged that the authorities had fabricated the apparent plot, together with a series of explosions reported in the capital in July–October, in order to justify the continued state of emergency in the capital and surrounding provinces. On 19 September the UDD defied the state of emergency to stage rallies in Bangkok and Thaksin's home town of Chiang Mai to commemorate the fourth anniversary of the coup that had ousted Thaksin from power, as well as to mark four months since the violent suppression of the anti-Government protests on 19 May. Thaksin issued a statement declaring that he would not interfere in the Thai political sphere since he did not wish 'further turmoil for Thailand or its monarchy'; the former premier urged his supporters to 'look to the future, a democratic and free future for all Thailand's people'. An estimated 15,000 UDD supporters attended a further rally in Bangkok on 19 November to commemorate the six-month anniversary of the final suppression of the protests. Later that month the Constitutional Court dismissed a petition filed by the Election Commission appealing for the dissolution of the DP owing to the alleged misuse of a 29m. baht state grant in 2005; the Court ruled that the petition had not been filed within the stipulated time scale and was therefore illegal, prompting anger from opponents of the Government, many of whom questioned why, if the petition were illegal, the Court had allowed the case to proceed in the first place. A second petition, which had been submitted by the Office of the Attorney-General in mid-July and which urged the dissolution of the DP, relating to donations totalling 258m. baht that the party was said to have received illegally through disguised transactions from a cement company in 2005, was also dismissed by the Court on a legal technicality, in early December 2010. The petition had further appealed for party executives who had been aware of the allegedly illicit donations to be banned from political activity for a five-year period. Meanwhile, Abhisit denied rumours that a new party, Thai Khem Khaeng, had been formed as a vehicle for DP members in case the latter were to be dissolved. However, an election commissioner indicated that a new party had been registered under this name in early June.

A report leaked in mid-December 2010, detailing the findings of a preliminary official investigation into the deaths on 19 May of six people, including a volunteer nurse, inside Wat Pathum Wanaram—a Buddhist temple in Bangkok that had been designated a safe zone for women, children, the elderly and the infirm, in which hundreds of people had sought refuge when the authorities moved in to clear the protesters' camp—indicated that security forces had fired into the temple and were responsible for at least three of the six resultant deaths. The report found insufficient evidence to determine the circumstances surrounding the deaths of the remaining three people, although all six were found to have been killed by high-velocity bullets. The Thai Government, which had denied that soldiers were present at the scene of the killings, had previously blamed the deaths on retreating UDD supporters. A separate leaked report in the same month indicated that the death of the Japanese cameraman in April had also been the result of a high-velocity bullet, most likely fired by a member of the security forces. Later in December the state of emergency in Bangkok and surrounding provinces was finally removed; however, it was replaced by the Internal Security Act.

As many as 40,000 people were estimated to have attended the UDD's first rally since the revocation of emergency rule, in mid-January 2011. Thaksin addressed the protesters via a telephone link, praising their dedication to democracy and pledging to 'do everything in his power' to bring 'happiness and prosperity' to the Thai people. The UDD pledged to hold twice-monthly protests appealing for the resignation of Abhisit and the immediate release of UDD members arrested in the aftermath of the protests of 2010. At the end of January 2011 the UDD lodged a formal complaint with the International Criminal Court against Abhisit, claiming that he was guilty of crimes against humanity in his Government's handling of the protests and was criminally liable for the deaths of those killed during the unrest. Meanwhile, in mid-January Gen. Sonthi Boonyaratglin, the leader of the coup that had deposed Thaksin in September 2006 was

THAILAND

elected Leader of the Matubhum Party, which was founded in 2008 and predominantly comprised members of the Muslim Wadah and Pak Nam factions.

In mid-February 2011 constitutional amendments were approved by the legislature providing for a transfer to a single-seat constituency system, and an increase in the number of parliamentary members elected through party-list proportional representation; under the new system there were to be 375 constituency-based members and 125 party-list members. Also in February seven of the UDD leaders on trial for terrorism charges, including Korkaew, Weng and Nattawut, were granted bail on the condition that they refrain from any political activity and remain in Thailand. However, the seven were reported to have attended a UDD rally staged on 10 April to commemorate the anniversary of the clash that had killed 25 people one year previously; while the rally, which was attended by an estimated 20,000 people, passed off peacefully, the seven bailed UDD leaders were alleged to have insulted the monarchy during speeches given at the rally, prompting the police to apply for the revocation of their bail provisions and for their rearrest on charges of *lèse majesté*. In late March a civil court ordered 13 PAD leaders to pay 522m. baht (US $17.2m.) in damages to the operators of the Suvarnabhumi and Don Muang airports that the Alliance had occupied for a week in 2008.

In mid-March 2011 Abhisit announced that he would dissolve the legislature in the first week of May, in advance of early elections expected to be held in July. An estimated 30,000 UDD supporters attended a rally in Bangkok to mark the anniversary of the beginning of their two-month protest in the previous year. Later in March Chart Thai Pattana and BJT announced that they were to form an alliance after the forthcoming polls, pledging to work together in order to 'protect the monarchy' and to 'bring reconciliation' among the Thai people. In the same month it was announced that former Deputy Prime Minister Purachai Piemsomboon, a close ally of Thaksin, was to head the newly formed Pracha Santi Party. However, it was subsequently disclosed that Purachai had instead decided to form his own party, the Rak Santi Party, of which he was selected Chairman in late April. In early April Ruam Chart Pattana and Puea Pandin agreed to merge into a new party, Chart Pattana Puea Pandin. Regardless of the outcome of the election, which was scheduled for 3 July, it appeared certain that Thai politics would continue to be dominated by major rifts and pervasive mistrust. Meanwhile, the insurgency in the south continued unabated. According to a police report published in February 2011, approximately 4,200 people had been killed in 7,499 incidents related to the insurgency since January 2004, with more than 7,750 others injured.

Foreign Affairs

Thailand's former dependence on the USA has been greatly reduced by the increasing importance of regional trade and diplomatic relations. In the late 1980s Prime Minister Chatichai Choonhavan adopted a new business-orientated policy towards Cambodia, Laos, Viet Nam and Myanmar, encouraging investment in their developing economies; this policy was successfully pursued by subsequent premiers. In April 1995, following lengthy discussions with Viet Nam, Cambodia and Laos, the four countries established the Mekong River Commission (see p. 448) to promote the joint development of the Mekong's resources. In September 2008 Thailand ratified the ASEAN Charter, which codified the principles and purposes of the Association and came into effect in December of that year. Relations with the People's Republic of China also improved as Thailand became one of China's most significant trading partners.

Relations with Cambodia

In January 1993, despite its previous reluctance to do so, Thailand officially closed its border with Cambodia to trade with areas controlled by the communist Cambodian insurgent group, the Party of Democratic Kampuchea (known as the Khmers Rouges), in compliance with UN sanctions against the movement. Nevertheless, violations of the embargo (mainly exports of logs and gems from Cambodia through Thailand) were widely reported during 1993. Accusations by representatives of the Cambodian Government that Thai complicity with the Khmers Rouges was undermining Cambodian attempts to end the insurgency were substantiated by reports from UN peace-keeping troops that members of the Thai armed forces were providing transport, medical care and other support for the Khmers Rouges. Official Thai government policy was to support the elected Government of Cambodia, but the armed forces controlled the border and were unwilling to jeopardize their lucrative business relations with the Khmers Rouges.

In January 1994 Chuan Leekpai made an official visit to Cambodia (the first such visit by a Thai premier), following which more strenuous efforts were made to control illicit border trade and to prevent members of the armed forces from co-operating with the Khmers Rouges. However, clashes between Thai and Cambodian troops continued as a result of incursions into Thai territory by Cambodian government forces in pursuit of the Khmers Rouges. In September 1995 Thailand and Cambodia signed an agreement to establish a border co-ordination committee. At its first meeting in November three border checkpoints, which had been closed in April, were reopened. In the latter half of 1997 intense fighting in Cambodia between forces loyal to the First Prime Minister, Hun Sen, and those of the former Second Prime Minister, Prince Norodom Ranariddh, led to further incursions, across Thailand's eastern border with Cambodia, and resulted in an influx of refugees to Thailand. In January 1997, meanwhile, the Thai Government adopted a controversial resolution unilaterally to extend Thailand's maritime jurisdiction over waters that were also claimed by Cambodia and Viet Nam. However, the Thai Government insisted that its decision was legal under international practice.

In January 2003 Thai-Cambodian relations were severely strained when the Thai embassy and several Thai businesses situated in the Cambodian capital, Phnom-Penh, were attacked by Cambodian demonstrators. Those who perpetrated the attacks were protesting against remarks, allegedly made by a Thai actress, claiming that the temples at Angkor Wat in Cambodia in fact belonged to Thailand. In response to the rioting, Prime Minister Thaksin Shinawatra downgraded diplomatic relations with Cambodia and announced plans to evacuate all Thai citizens from the country and to expel illegal Cambodian immigrants living in Thailand; the joint border was subsequently closed. The Cambodian Government issued a formal apology for the incident and promised compensation for those who had been affected by the violence. The Thai Government permitted a limited reopening of the border for commercial reasons in February. In March Cambodia's Prime Minister, Hun Sen, ordered the border to be closed again, owing to alleged security concerns and in protest at the economic inequality between the two countries. However, later in that month the border was fully reopened and, in April, diplomatic relations were upgraded.

Tension arose between Thailand and Cambodia in July 2008, when the Preah Vihear temple, located on the border between the two countries, was declared a World Heritage Site by UNESCO, and both countries subsequently deployed troops to the area. Although the International Court of Justice had awarded ownership of the temple to Cambodia in a ruling in 1962, sovereignty of the surrounding area remained contentious, and the Thai Government's endorsement of Cambodia's application to UNESCO had provoked considerable controversy within Thailand. Bilateral talks aimed at resolving the situation commenced in July 2008, leading to agreement in August on the withdrawal of the majority of the soldiers deployed in the region, but in October at least two Cambodian troops were killed in exchanges of gunfire in the area. In November, following three days of talks, the two Governments agreed on plans for a border demarcation process and a full withdrawal of troops. In February 2009 Prime Minister Abhisit Vejjajiva met with Cambodian Prime Minister Hun Sen in the Thai resort of Hua Hin, to discuss energy co-operation in the Gulf of Thailand, prompting hopes of an improvement in relations. However, four Thai soldiers were reported to have been killed during an exchange of fire across the border in April and, despite both sides subsequently agreeing to plant border posts in July, little discernible progress had been made to this end. A partial withdrawal of troops was reported to have begun in August 2009, but minor skirmishes in the disputed area continued to be reported during the latter half of 2009 and into 2010.

Meanwhile, Thai officials had been angered by Hun Sen at the ASEAN summit meeting, held in Hua Hin, in October 2009; the Cambodian premier had declared that Thaksin (who had been convicted *in absentia* of corruption and sentenced to two years' imprisonment by the Thai Supreme Court in the previous year—see Domestic Political Affairs) was welcome to seek refuge in Cambodia. In late October the Cambodian Government's decision to appoint Thaksin as an economic adviser further escalated the diplomatic dispute. Thailand recalled its ambassador from Phnom-Penh in early November, accusing the Cambodian Government of interfering in Thailand's internal affairs; Cambodia responded by recalling its own ambassador from Bangkok on the following day (see the chapter on Cambodia for more details). In mid-November Thai diplomats presented Cambodian officials with an extradition request for Thaksin, a request that was summarily rejected by the Cambodian Government on the grounds that Thaksin's conviction had been 'politically motivated'. In mid-December a Thai Government spokesman announced that the Thai ambassador would return to Phnom-Penh if Cambodia 'corrected its stated opinions' of Thai politics and of the Thai justice system, and rescinded the appointment of Thaksin as economic adviser. Hun Sen responded by stating that normal bilateral relations would not be restored until Thailand's current Government had been removed from office, accusing the Abhisit Government of using the dispute over Thaksin as a distraction from the more serious issue of border demarcation. In February 2010 Hun Sen paid an official visit to the disputed area around the Preah Vihear temple, during which he accused Thailand of planning to invade Cambodia and urged Cambodian troops to continue to protect the country's borders from 'the enemy'. In March Cambodia was reported to have fired live rounds from rocket launchers in the mountainous province of Kampong Chhnang. ASEAN's Secretary-General expressed deep concern at the development, which, he argued, might be interpreted as a sign of regional instability, but Thailand played down such concerns, dismissing the event as a routine military exercise. An exchange of fire across the border in April was quickly branded by both countries as a 'misunderstanding'; no casualties were reported as a result of the incident. The announcement in August that Thaksin had resigned from his advisory position in Cambodia, citing personal difficulties, led to the restoration of diplomatic relations soon after, and, following several rounds of negotiations between Abhisit and Hun Sen, the two countries announced in December the full restoration of normal relations.

However, tensions once again escalated in mid-October 2010, when a senior Thai investigator alleged that 11 members of the anti-Government Red Shirt movement who had been arrested earlier that month on suspicion of involvement in alleged assassination plots—the intended targets of which had included Abhisit—had received training at a Cambodian military base. The Cambodian Government adamantly denied the claims, which were based on witness statements arising from the arrest in early October of 11 men in Chiang Mai. In December Thailand's Commander-in-Chief of the Army, Gen. Prayuth Chanocha, dismissed Cambodian claims that Thai troops had been withdrawn from the disputed territory around the Preah Vihear site, but did confirm an 'adjustment' of Thai troops in the area, which he stated had been made in response to similar action by Cambodia. However, relations further deteriorated in early 2011. At the beginning of February Veera Somkwamkid, a former leader of the PAD, who had been arrested together with his secretary and five others in December 2010 a short distance inside Cambodian territory, was imprisoned for eight years, after being convicted by a Cambodian court on charges of spying for Thailand and illegally entering Cambodia; his secretary was convicted on the same charges and sentenced to six years' imprisonment. The five other detainees, among them a DP legislator, had been convicted of illegal entry in January 2011, received suspended prison sentences and were deported to Thailand. All seven denied the charges against them. A few days later clashes broke out close to the contested Preah Vihear site; four days of heavy exchanges of gunfire between Thai and Cambodian troops claimed the lives of three Thai nationals (including one civilian) and eight Cambodians (including four civilians). About 30,000 local villagers were reported to have been displaced by the violence. UN Secretary-General Ban Ki-Moon urged both countries to exercise 'maximum restraint', while Hun Sen appealed to Ban to address urgently the issue of 'Thailand's aggression' and claimed that part of the Preah Vihear temple had been damaged by Thai artillery fire, a claim denied by the Thai Government, which insisted that it was merely protecting its own sovereignty.

At a meeting of ASEAN ministers responsible for foreign affairs held in the Indonesian capital, Jakarta, in mid-February 2011, Thailand and Cambodia agreed to allow a team of unarmed Indonesian observers to monitor the disputed border territory. However, tensions were rekindled following the admission by Thailand in early April that Thai soldiers had used cluster bombs during the fighting in February, prompting expressions of outrage from the Cambodian Government and the Cluster Munition Coalition, an international civil society campaign striving to eradicate the use of such weapons. (The Convention on Cluster Munitions, which prohibits the use, stockpiling, production and transfer of cluster munitions, was adopted in May 2008 and entered into force in August 2010, although neither Thailand nor Cambodia was party to the agreement.) Fighting broke out again in contested border areas in mid-April 2011, and by the end of that month at least a dozen Thai and eight Cambodian soldiers were reported to have been killed in the latest bout of violence, prompting Thai Minister of Foreign Affairs Kasit Piromya to declare: 'It is now beyond talks as friendly neighbours.' Kasit also contested that Cambodia was 'the aggressor', a claim that was repudiated by the Cambodian Government, which insisted that its soldiers were acting in self-defence. ASEAN Secretary-General Surin Pitsuwan appealed for the immediate holding of formal dialogue, cautioning that the reputation of the regional bloc would be jeopardized should a complete cessation of hostilities not be swiftly secured. A tentative truce was declared in early May.

Relations with Myanmar

Following a military coup in Burma (now Myanmar) in September 1988, thousands of Burmese students fled to Thailand to avoid government repression. Amnesty International subsequently accused the Thai Government of coercing the students to return (resulting in their arrest and, in some cases, execution). An intensification of Myanma attacks on the strongholds of ethnic minorities along the border resulted in a new influx of Myanma students and members of rebel ethnic groups seeking refuge in Thailand. Not wishing to jeopardize the preferential treatment that it received from the Myanma Government with regard to the exploitation of Myanmar's natural resources, the Thai Government refused to recognize those fleeing from Myanmar as refugees or to offer them aid.

Relations were impeded by sporadic incidents in 1992, including clashes between Thai and Myanmar troops along the border in March. In February 1993 the two countries resolved to demarcate their common border. In April 1994 Thailand invited Myanmar to attend the annual ASEAN meeting of ministers responsible for foreign affairs, in Bangkok. In early 1995, however, relations were tested again by persistent border incursions into Thailand by forces of the Myanma Government during their offensive to capture the headquarters of the rebel Karen (Kayin) National Union (KNU) and subsequent attacks on disarmed Kayin refugees held in Thai camps along the border. In August Myanmar temporarily closed its land border with Thailand in protest at the alleged killing of a substantial number of Myanma seamen by Thai fishermen. In October 1996 the Thai Government approved the opening of three border checkpoints.

In late 1996 and early 1997 attacks allegedly carried out by breakaway Kayin rebels on Kayin refugee camps in Thailand resulted in a number of minor clashes between the Thai army and the rebels. In December 1997 the two countries' Governments agreed jointly to establish a panel to determine the legitimacy of an estimated 98,000 Kayin refugees sheltered along Thailand's border with Myanmar. In the same month, relief agencies operating along the border accused the Thai military authorities of using oppressive tactics to encourage the refugees to return to Myanmar. In March 1998 the Thai Government announced plans for the forced repatriation of several hundred thousand Myanma immigrants working illegally in Thailand, in response to the economic crisis afflicting the country. In the same month one of the largest Kayin refugee camps along the Thai–Myanma border was destroyed in a cross-border attack by the pro-Government Democratic Karen (Kayin) Buddhist Organization.

Bilateral relations were strained in late 1999 when a group of armed Myanma student activists seized control of the Myanma embassy in Bangkok in October, taking 89 people hostage and demanding the release of all political prisoners in Myanmar and the opening of a dialogue between the military Government and the opposition. All the hostages were released within 24 hours, in exchange for the Thai Government's provision of helicopter transport to give the hostage-takers safe passage to the Thai–Myanma border. The Thai Government's release of the assailants angered the ruling military junta in Myanmar, prompting the country to close its border with Thailand. In November Thai forces expelled thousands of illegal Myanma migrant workers from the border town of Mae Sot, despite threats made by Myanma government troops to shoot the returnees. Although the border was reopened to commerce in late November, relations between the two countries remained fraught.

THAILAND

In January 2000 10 armed Myanma rebels took control of a hospital in Ratchaburi, Thailand, holding hundreds of people hostage. The hostage-takers, reported by some sources to be linked to God's Army (a small breakaway faction of the KNU), issued several demands, including that the shelling of their base on the Thai–Myanma border by the Thai military be halted, that co-operation between Thai and Myanma government forces against the Kayins should cease, and that their people be allowed to seek refuge in Thailand. Thai government forces stormed the hospital, killing all 10 of the hostage-takers but releasing all of the hostages unharmed. This uncompromising resolution of the incident was praised by the military Government in Myanmar, and appeared to indicate a strengthening of the Thai authorities' stance on Myanma dissident activity in Thailand. In February 2001 Myanma forces pursued Shan State Army (SSA) rebels into the northern Thai province of Chiang Rai, prompting reprisals by Thai troops. Despite the agreement of a cease-fire, Thailand sealed its border with Myanmar, and the situation was aggravated by Myanmar's assertion that Thailand was assisting the SSA. In April a non-governmental organization in Thailand claimed that, as of that month, the number of refugees of Myanma origin in Thailand totalled almost 131,000. In May the United Wa State Army (UWSA), a Myanma ethnic militia, captured Hua Lone Hill near Chiang Mai; Thai troops recaptured the hill following a four-day battle in which at least 20 members of the UWSA were killed. The Government later lodged a formal protest with the Myanma Government after its forces allegedly bombed a Thai outpost situated near the hill. The Myanma Government responded by accusing the Thai armed forces of having launched air-strikes into its territory.

In June 2001 Thaksin Shinawatra became the first Thai Prime Minister to visit Yangon, the Myanma capital, since 1997. While the subsequent discussions defused the immediate tensions, the two sides failed to come to any firm agreement as to how they would overcome the problems affecting bilateral relations. In January 2002 a joint Thai-Myanma commission met for the first time since 1999 to discuss plans to establish a task force that would aid in the repatriation of illegal Myanma immigrants. Further talks were held in February 2002, intended to facilitate bilateral co-operation in controlling the cross-border narcotics trade.

Relations were placed under severe strain in March 2002 when Thai soldiers clashed with members of the UWSA in Chiang Mai. Following the incident, in which one Thai soldier and 12 UWSA guerrillas were killed, the Thai Government lodged a formal protest with Myanmar's ruling military junta. In April a bomb exploded on the so-called 'Friendship Bridge' linking the two countries, resulting in the deaths of at least seven people. Later in the same month the Vice-Chairman of Myanmar's ruling State Peace and Development Council (SPDC) visited Thailand to hold talks with the Government concerning drugs-smuggling and the continued border tensions. However, in May fresh fighting broke out along the joint border between Myanma government troops, together with their UWSA allies, and the SSA; subsequently, the SPDC again accused the Thai Government of supporting the SSA, following which it closed the shared border. Meanwhile, following the commencement of a Myanma military campaign on the border, intended to reclaim outposts and camps in the country's Shan State, Thai troops fired across the frontier when two Thai soldiers were allegedly injured by Myanma shells. The Government denied that it supported Myanma insurgent ethnic militias but admitted that it had allowed refugees from Myanmar to cross into Thailand. The joint border finally reopened in October following talks aimed at resolving bilateral tensions. Relations continued to improve in 2003. In July of that year the Thai Government announced plans to relocate all Myanma political refugees resident in Thailand to refugee camps near the joint border, where it was believed they could more easily be controlled and would thus present less of a threat to bilateral relations. In June 2004 Myanma Prime Minister Gen. Khin Nyunt visited Thailand and discussed various economic, development and border issues with Thaksin. Following the ousting of Khin Nyunt in October, Thaksin held talks with the new Prime Minister, Lt-Gen. Soe Win, in December. In January 2005 Thailand increased security along the border with Myanmar, amid concerns that fighting between Myanma troops and insurgents might encroach upon Thai territory. At the end of March the Thai Government ordered the relocation of about 3,000 Myanma political refugees to camps near the joint border. However, about 1,000 of the refugees failed to meet a deadline to register with the Thai authorities and were deported to Myanmar. In April Thailand again increased security along the border with Myanmar, in response to renewed fighting between rival Myanma ethnic rebel groups close to Thai territory.

In January 2009 the office of the UN High Commissioner for Refugees (UNHCR, see p. 71) reported that around 110,000 Myanma refugees remained resident in nine camps in Thailand. Also in January UNHCR expressed concern regarding allegations that in the previous month Thai troops had intercepted about 1,000 Rohingya refugees from Myanmar who had been attempting to reach Thailand and forced them back out to sea in boats without engines; about 450 migrants were rescued by the Indonesian navy, but the remainder were unaccounted for. A decision by the Myanma junta in July 2010 to close a border crossing at Myawaddy, adjacent to the Thai border town of Mae Sot, was a source of considerable irritation to the Thai Government; the closure of the crossing was estimated to be costing Thailand nearly US $3m. daily in lost trade. The escalation of tensions in Myanmar's ethnic border areas in the immediate aftermath of the November legislative elections (see the chapter on Myanmar) was reported to have forced more than 20,000 Myanma people to flee into Thailand to escape the violence. Three Thai nationals were injured when mortar and grenade attacks strayed across the Myanma–Thai border during fighting between Myanma government troops and insurgents, causing Mae Sot to be evacuated. Prime Minister Abhisit Vejjajiva announced the deployment of additional Thai troops to the area to reinforce border security, and offered assurances that Myanma refugees fleeing into Thailand would be treated in a humane manner. In early December the Myanma and Thai Ministers of Foreign Affairs met in the Myanma border town of Tachilek, reportedly to discuss the possible reopening of the border crossing at Myawaddy. In an unexpected development a few days later the border crossing at the Three Pagodas Pass, a prominent 'black market' trade route between Thailand and Myanmar, was reopened after a three-year closure. In January 2011 Myanmar eased border control restrictions between Myawaddy and Mae Sot, allowing the transit of goods via cross-border trading posts to resume. Cross-border trade was briefly suspended again in early February, following two bomb explosions in neighbouring Myawaddy on the Myanma side of the border, which reportedly killed three people and injured six others. However, normal service was reported to have resumed later that month, although the land border crossing between Myawaddy and Mae Sot remained closed at mid-2011.

Meanwhile, in January 2011 Human Rights Watch urged Thailand to allow the UNHCR unhindered access to a group of 158 Rohingya asylum-seekers who had fled to Thailand from Myanmar (q.v.) earlier in the month, as well as a further 53 Rohingya asylum-seekers detained in Thailand since 2009. In mid-February 2011 Amnesty International appealed for a full investigation to be launched into claims made by a separate group of 91 Rohingya refugees that they had been intercepted by the Thai navy in January and returned to sea in a boat without an engine and with limited food and water supplies. The Thai authorities denied the accusation, claiming that they had deported the group to Myanmar through official channels.

Relations with Laos

Thai-Laotian relations have been dominated in recent years by the issue of Laotian Hmong refugees living in Thailand. In November 1996 the Thai Government approved a proposal for the establishment of a Joint Thai-Lao Border Committee. In December 1997 it was announced by UNHCR that the review of the status of the last remaining group of Laotian refugees at the Ban Napho refugee camp in the Nakhan Phanom province of Thailand was scheduled to be completed by January 1998, after which the refugees were to be either allowed to settle in a third country or repatriated. In September 1999 282 Laotian refugees who had been residing at the camp were compulsorily repatriated by Thai officials and UNHCR after having been refused refugee status; a further 291 Laotian refugees were repatriated in December. In December 2003 the USA agreed to accept around 15,000 Laotian Hmong refugees living in refugee camps in Thailand. The first group of refugees was resettled in the USA in June 2004, under the aegis of the International Organization for Migration. Meanwhile, in March 2004 the Thai and Laotian Governments held a joint cabinet meeting to discuss bilateral co-operation. In August 2006 the Ministries of Foreign Affairs of Thailand and of Laos indicated that the two countries would co-operate to find a solution to the Hmong refugee issue, although neither side claimed responsibility. Through a joint process, the two countries were later reported to be verifying the origin of the migrants. In December a second bridge connecting Laos and Thailand over the Mekong River was inaugurated. In January 2007 the Thai Government decided against the forcible repatriation to Laos of some 153 Hmong migrants who had been arrested in Bangkok in 2006, following offers of asylum from several Western countries. However, the group of Hmong, now numbering 158, and all recognized as refugees, remained in an immigration detention centre in Thailand until December 2009 (see below). Meanwhile, in February 2008, following a visit to Laos, the Thai Minister of Foreign Affairs announced that the Thai authorities had almost completed the process of verifying the identity of the Hmong remaining in refugee camps in Phetchabun province (estimated at some 7,000). Later in that month 10 Hmong were repatriated to Laos ahead of an official visit to that country by the new Thai Prime Minister, Samak Sundaravej. In June UNHCR expressed concern regarding the conditions under which a group of 837 Hmong had recently been returned to Laos from Ban Huay Nam Khao camp in Phetchabun province, amid reports that they had been forcibly deported following a mass protest at the camp; in July, after a further 391 Hmong were repatriated, UNHCR urged the Thai authorities to allow it access to the camp. A total of 1,809 Hmong were returned to Laos during 2008. In May 2009 the international medical aid organization Médecins Sans Frontières (MSF) announced that it was to withdraw from Ban Huay Nam Khao camp, citing ongoing intimidation and coercive tactics employed by the Thai military. MSF was the sole international agency allowed to operate in the camp and was responsible for providing food and medical treatment to the refugees. In December the Thai Government deported some 4,000 Hmong refugees at the camp back to Laos, including the 158 UNHCR-recognized political refugees, despite protests by UNHCR, the USA and human rights organizations. Following the repatriation, the Thai Government stated that it had concerns for the safety of about 100 of those who had been deported but had been assured by the Laotian Government that they would be granted pardons upon their return to Laos (q.v.). At mid-2011 little was known of their whereabouts.

Meanwhile, in January 2009, in an indication that the new administration in Thailand hoped to strengthen relations with Laos, Thai Prime Minister Abhisit Vejjajiva and Minister of Foreign Affairs Kasit Piromya both chose that country as the destination of their first official foreign visits. Kasit and his Lao counterpart agreed to make efforts to finalize the demarcation of their land border in 2009, followed by that of the maritime border in 2010; however, by mid-2011 the demarcation of neither border had been completed. A rail link constructed on the first Mekong Friendship Bridge was opened in March 2009, connecting Thailand and Laos by rail for the first time. Plans to construct three further bridges over the Mekong were well advanced in 2011 (see the chapter on Laos). Following the meeting of a bilateral commission on co-operation co-chaired in October 2010 by Thai Minister of Foreign Affairs Kasit Piromya and the Laotian Deputy Prime Minister and Minister of Foreign Affairs, Thongloun Sisolit, the two countries reiterated their ongoing commitment to expand bilateral co-operation; Thailand confirmed a prior agreement to purchase 7,000 MW of electricity from Laos by 2015.

Other regional relations

Relations with Malaysia, which had been strained by sporadic incidents in previous years, improved markedly from 1997. In February of that year Malaysia and Thailand established the Kolok River as the border demarcation between the two countries. In January 1998 the Malaysian authorities arrested, and transferred to the Thai authorities, three alleged Muslim separatist leaders wanted in Thailand in connection with terrorist activities in the southern provinces of the country. By April, Prime Minister Chuan Leekpai and his Malaysian counterpart, Mahathir Mohamad, had met five times in as many months to discuss bilateral issues. In April 2001 the two countries agreed to co-operate to find those responsible for two bomb attacks in southern Thailand. In the same month Prime Minister Thaksin paid an official visit to Malaysia, during which the two countries discussed border demarcation issues and agreed that the planned construction of a gas pipeline between Thailand and Malaysia would proceed as originally intended. Relations remained cordial and, in December 2002, the cabinets of the two countries held an historic joint meeting, during which trade and security issues were discussed. In early 2004 the Malaysian Government co-operated with Thailand in efforts to combat violence in the south of the latter country. In February the Thai Government mooted plans to construct a security fence along parts of the joint border, in the hope of preventing militants from seeking refuge in Malaysia. As unrest in southern Thailand continued, Prime Minister Thaksin visited Malaysia in April for talks with his counterpart, Abdullah Badawi, on security along the border and the economic development of the surrounding area. Bilateral relations were strained in December, when the Thai Government claimed to have photographic evidence that militants in southern Thailand had received training in Malaysia. In January 2005 the Malaysian authorities arrested Abdul Rahman Ahmad, whom Thailand held responsible for organizing much of the separatist violence in the south. A diplomatic dispute arose between the two countries in October concerning the fate of 131 Muslim asylum-seekers, who had fled from the violence-stricken southern province of Narathiwat to neighbouring Malaysia (q.v.). Although the issue was eventually resolved in February 2006 when the Thai Government announced that it was to allow the refugees to remain in Malaysia, relations between the two countries had by that stage descended to their lowest point in recent years. In November 2005 former Malaysian Prime Minister Mahathir visited Thailand for discussions with Thaksin, which helped to ease tension that had been caused by Thai security officials' accusations that the Malaysian authorities were failing to prevent insurgents from crossing the border into Thailand, suggestions that were rejected by Malaysia. Thaksin and Mahathir agreed that the two countries should cease their 'war of words' and Mahathir was to stop advocating autonomy for Thailand's southern regions. In December Manasae Saeloh, a suspected leader of PULO, was arrested in Malaysia and relinquished to the Thai authorities, by which he was wanted in connection with numerous bomb attacks and other acts of violence. Relations became more cordial following the ousting from power of Thaksin in 2006. In December 2007 the interim Prime Minister, Gen. (retd) Surayud Chulanont, and Abdullah Badawi officially opened a new bridge across the Kolok River, which it was hoped would lead to a reduction in violence in the border region by improving economic prospects. In December 2009 Malaysian Prime Minister Najib Tun Razak became the first head of government formally to visit Thailand under the administration of Prime Minister Abhisit Vejjajiva. The two countries announced plans to foster closer co-ordination in anti-narcotics operations in June 2010. In November a Thai woman was sentenced to death after being convicted of drugs-trafficking by Malaysia's High Court; the woman had been arrested by the Malaysian authorities in July, when she was found to have ingested a large amount of cocaine that she had smuggled into the country from Argentina.

In 1999 Thailand contributed 1,500 troops to the multinational peace-keeping force in the UN-administered territory of East Timor (now Timor-Leste), following the territory's vote for independence from Indonesia in a referendum held in August. During a visit to Timor-Leste in January 2011 Minister of Foreign Affairs Kasit Piromya pledged Thailand's support for Timorese efforts to join ASEAN; Timor-Leste formally applied for membership of the regional bloc in March of that year.

The country also maintained a cordial bilateral relationship with Indonesia, as well as with the Philippines and Singapore. Under the Singapore-Thailand Third Country Training Programme (TCTP), introduced in 1997, Thailand and Singapore have jointly provided technical assistance to, inter alia, Cambodia, Laos, Myanmar and Viet Nam. In July 2010 Minister of Foreign Affairs Kasit met with his Indonesian counterpart in Jakarta, whereupon the two ministers pledged to extend bilateral co-operation in the fields of agriculture, fisheries, energy and investment; other issues discussed included co-operation on disaster management, and Kasit voiced the appreciation of the Thai Government for Indonesian support for Thailand's successful bid in May to secure election to the UN Human Rights Council.

Other external relations

In December 2001 Prime Minister Thaksin Shinawatra paid an official visit to the USA, during which he met with US President George W. Bush and assured him that Thailand would remain a strong ally in the US-led 'war on terror' following the September terrorist attacks (see the chapter on the USA). The US President praised the Thai Government for its consistent support throughout the campaign. In June 2003 Thaksin met with President Bush again in Washington, DC, to discuss counter-terrorism issues. In October President Bush attended an APEC summit meeting in Bangkok, having paid an official state visit to Thailand in the days preceding the summit. The two heads of state

THAILAND

announced that they were to enter into formal negotiations with regard to the signing of a comprehensive bilateral free trade agreement. However, negotiations were postponed owing to the political upheaval of 2006–08 and remained suspended at mid-2011. None the less, representatives of the two countries convened in Washington, DC, for discussions on trade and investment matters in June 2008 and again in March 2009; among other issues discussed, the USA raised concerns about the deterioration of intellectual property rights protection in Thailand in recent years. Meanwhile, in February 2008, following the return to civilian rule in Thailand, the USA announced the resumption of military aid to Thailand, which it had suspended following the coup of September 2006. Relations were strained in December 2009 by the forced repatriation to Laos of some 4,000 Hmong refugees, which the USA had vehemently opposed (see Relations with Laos). Tensions were further exacerbated by reports in early December 2010 that former premier Thaksin, now a fugitive, had been invited by the US Commission on Security and Co-operation in Europe (CSCE) to Washington, DC, to address a forum entitled 'Thailand: Democracy, Governance and Human Rights'; the Commission's invitation to Thaksin reportedly asked him to offer his perspective on the human rights situation in Thailand, including freedom of the press and of expression, and on the Thai Government's efforts to address the southern insurgency. In mid-December the CSCE announced that the forum had been postponed. In the same month Thai Prime Minister Abhisit was forced to deny claims made by WikiLeaks, an organization publishing leaked private and classified content, that an agreement existed between the respective Governments of Thailand and the USA to exchange Thaksin for Viktor Bout, a Russian businessman accused of supplying weapons to international terrorist organizations, including al-Qa'ida; Bout had been extradited from Thailand to the USA in November 2010, following his arrest in Bangkok in March 2008.

In February 2009 it was announced that a Thai military contingent was to join the African Union/United Nations Mission in Darfur (UNAMID). In November 2010 the first deployment of Thai soldiers, comprising 409 personnel, was dispatched to the Sudanese capital to join the peace-keeping mission; a further 403 Thai troops were deployed in early 2011. (See the chapter on Sudan for details of the Darfur conflict.)

CONSTITUTION AND GOVERNMENT

A new Constitution was adopted in 2007. Thailand is a constitutional monarchy. The King appoints the Prime Minister, who leads the Cabinet. The bicameral National Assembly of Thailand consists of the House of Representatives (Sapha Poothaen Rassadorn) and the Senate (Woothi Sapha). The House of Representatives has 480 members, of whom 400 are directly elected by constituency voting, while the remainder are elected by a party list system of proportional representation. Members are elected for a term of four years. The Senate consists of 150 members, of whom 76 are elected (one from each of Thailand's 76 provinces) and 74 are appointed by a selection committee. Senators serve six-year terms. With the creation of a 77th province in 2011, additional seats were to be created in the legislature.

REGIONAL AND INTERNATIONAL CO-OPERATION

Thailand is a member of the Association of Southeast Asian Nations (ASEAN, see p. 206), the Asia-Pacific Economic Co-operation (APEC, see p. 197), the Asian Development Bank (ADB, see p. 202), the UN's Economic and Social Commission for Asia and the Pacific (ESCAP, see p. 37), the Colombo Plan (see p. 446) and the Mekong River Commission (see p. 448).

Thailand became a member of the UN in 1946. As a contracting party to the General Agreement on Tariffs and Trade, Thailand joined the World Trade Organization (WTO, see p. 430) on its establishment in 1995. The country participates in the Group of 77 (G77, see p. 447) developing countries, and is also a member of the International Labour Organization (ILO, see p. 138) and the Non-aligned Movement (see p. 461).

ECONOMIC AFFAIRS

In 2009, according to estimates by the World Bank, Thailand's gross national income (GNI), measured at average 2007–09 prices, was US $254,690m., equivalent to $3,760 per head (or $7,640 per head on an international purchasing-power parity basis). During 2000–09, it was estimated, the population increased at an average annual rate of 0.9%, while gross domestic product (GDP) per head increased, in real terms, by an average of 3.0% per year. Overall GDP increased, in real terms, at an average annual rate of 3.9% in 2000–09. According to the Asian Development Bank (ADB), GDP decreased by 2.3% in 2009, but increased by 7.8% in 2010.

According to preliminary figures, agriculture (including forestry, hunting and fishing) contributed an estimated 12.4% of GDP in 2010; 40.7% of the employed labour force were engaged in the sector in that year. Thailand's staple crop and principal agricultural export commodity is rice (Thailand became the world's largest exporter of rice in 1981). Rice exports accounted for 3.5% of the total value of exports in 2008. Other major crops include sugar cane, cassava (tapioca), oil palm fruit, maize, natural rubber, bananas, mangoes and pineapples. Fisheries products and livestock (mainly cattle, buffaloes, pigs and poultry) are also important. Thailand is one of the world's largest exporters of farmed shrimp. According to ADB data, during 2000–09 agricultural GDP increased at an estimated average annual rate of 2.3%. Agricultural GDP rose by 1.3% in 2009 but declined by 2.2% in 2010.

According to preliminary figures, industry (including mining, manufacturing, construction and utilities) provided an estimated 44.7% of GDP in 2010. In the same year 19.1% of the employed labour force were engaged in industrial activities. According to figures from the ADB, during 2000–09 industrial GDP increased at an average annual rate of 4.6%. The GDP of the industrial sector declined by 5.0% in 2009, before increasing by 12.8% in 2010.

According to preliminary figures, mining and quarrying contributed an estimated 3.4% of GDP in 2010 and engaged less than 0.1% of the employed labour force in that year. Gemstones, notably diamonds, are the principal mineral export. Natural gas and, to a lesser extent, petroleum are also exploited, and production of these fuels increased substantially from the late 1990s. Tin, lignite, gypsum, tungsten, antimony, manganese, gold, zinc, iron and fluorite are also mined. During 2000–09 the GDP of the mining sector increased at an estimated average annual rate of 4.5%, according to ADB data. Mining GDP increased by an estimated 0.6% in 2008, but decreased by 0.6% in 2009.

Manufacturing provided an estimated 35.6% of GDP in 2010, according to preliminary figures, and engaged 13.4% of the employed labour force in that year. In 1999 manufacturing's contribution to export earnings was 80%. Textiles and garments and electronics and electrical goods (particularly semiconductors) constitute Thailand's principal branches of manufacturing. Other manufacturing activities include the production of cigarettes, chemicals, cement and beer, sugar and petroleum refining, motor vehicle production, rubber production and the production of iron and steel. According to the ADB, during 2000–09 manufacturing GDP increased at an estimated average annual rate of 4.7%. The GDP of the sector increased by an estimated 3.9% in 2008, but decreased by 5.1% in 2009.

According to preliminary figures, construction provided an estimated 2.7% of GDP in 2010 and engaged 5.4% of the employed labour force in that year. According to figures from the ADB, during 2000–09 construction GDP increased at an average annual rate of 2.5%. The sector's GDP decreased by an estimated 5.3% in 2008 but remained constant in 2009.

Energy is derived principally from hydrocarbons. In 2009 56.3m. barrels of crude petroleum and 30,625m. cu m of natural gas were produced. Natural gas production reached 30,904m. cu m. in 2009. In 2007 petroleum accounted for 2.7% of total electricity output, natural gas for 67.3%, coal for 21.4% and hydroelectricity for 5.7%. Solar and wind energy have been introduced, but Thailand remains dependent on imported petroleum and electricity. In 2010 imports of mineral fuels comprised 17.3% of the value of merchandise imports.

Services (including transport and communications, commerce, banking and finance, public administration and other services) contributed an estimated 42.9% of GDP in 2010, according to preliminary figures. In that year 40.1% of the employed labour force were engaged in the services sector. Tourism has become a major source of foreign exchange, although the sector has been intermittently affected by unrest in Bangkok and by the violence in southern Thailand (see Contemporary Political History). Receipts (including passenger transport) totalled US $21,980m. in 2008. According to preliminary estimates, the number of tourist arrivals rose by 11.7% in 2010 to reach almost 15.8m. During 2000–09 the GDP of the services sector expanded at an estimated average annual rate of 3.6%, according to ADB data. The GDP of the sector decreased by 0.2% in 2009 but increased by 4.6% in 2010.

THAILAND

In 2009 Thailand recorded a visible trade surplus of US $32,691m.; in the same year there was a deficit of $21,861m. on the current account of the balance of payments. In 2010 the principal source of imports (20.7%) was Japan; other major suppliers in that year were the People's Republic of China, Malaysia, and the USA. The principal market for exports in 2010 was the People's Republic of China (11.0%); other major purchasers were Japan, the USA, Hong Kong, and Malaysia. The principal imports in 2010 were machinery (35.2%), basic manufactures, mineral fuels and lubricants, and chemical products. The principal exports were machinery (42.2%), food, basic manufactures, chemicals and related products, along with crude materials (inedible) except fuels.

The 2009/10 budget envisaged a deficit of 152,700m. baht, projected to be the equivalent of 1.5% of GDP. According to the ADB, Thailand's external debt totalled US $70,016m. at the end of 2009; in that year the cost of debt-servicing was equivalent to 6.7% of the value of exports of goods and services. The annual rate of inflation averaged 2.6% in 2000–10. Consumer prices decreased by 0.9% in 2009, but increased by 3.3% in 2010. In 2010 only 1.0% of the labour force were unemployed.

The removal of the democratically elected Government in October 2006 and the subsequent political instability (see Contemporary Political History) significantly weakened business confidence. According to the ADB, foreign direct investment (FDI) decreased from US $11,330m. in 2007 to only $4,976m. in 2009. The onset of the global financial crisis in the latter part of 2008 contributed to a sharp reduction in levels of public expenditure and private investment. The overall value of the stock market was reported to have declined by 48% during the course of 2008. In an effort to mitigate the repercussions of global recessionary conditions, in January 2009 the Government announced an economic stimulus plan. The programme envisaged expenditure of 116,700m. baht and included provision for an increase in financial support for the most impoverished of Thai households and low interest loans to small businesses. Although the rate of unemployment remained relatively low, training opportunities for the jobless was also included in the programme. The Bank of Thailand's interest rate was decreased by a total of 2.50 percentage points between December 2008 and April 2009, in which month it stood at 1.25%, remaining unchanged until mid-2010. Thereafter, a series of increases was implemented, and in March 2011 the rate stood at 2.5%. With inflationary pressures rising, in early 2011 the Government announced various subsidies and price controls on energy and other essential commodities, notably food items. The country's resumption of robust growth in 2010 was due largely to the substantial recovery in manufacturing output, higher investment inflows (FDI reaching $6,668m.), an improvement in consumer confidence and increasing external demand. However, a major challenge for the Government was the need to address the widening disparity in income levels and increasing regional inequality. The 11th National Plan, to encompass the 2012–16 period, was expected to place greater emphasis on social welfare. The ADB forecast that GDP would expand by 4.5% in 2011. However, with elections scheduled for mid-2011, economic stability was likely to remain dependent on Thailand's volatile political situation (see Contemporary Political History).

PUBLIC HOLIDAYS

2012: 2 January (for New Year's Day), March* (Makhabuja), 6 April (Chakri Day), 13–15 April (Songkran Festival), May* (Visakhabuja), 1 May (Labour Day), 5 May (Coronation Day), July* (Asalhabuja), July* (Khao Phansa, beginning of Buddhist Lent), 13 August (for Queen's Birthday), 23 October (Chulalongkorn Day), 30 October* (Awk Phansa, end of Buddhist Lent), 5 December (King's Birthday), 10 December (Constitution Day), 31 December (New Year's Eve).

* Regulated by the Buddhist lunar calendar.

Statistical Survey

Source (unless otherwise stated): National Statistical Office, Thanon Larn Luang, Bangkok 10100; tel. (2) 281-0333; fax (2) 281-3815; e-mail onsoadm@nso.go.th; internet www.nso.go.th.

Area and Population

AREA, POPULATION AND DENSITY

Area (sq km)	513,120*
Population (census results)†	
1 April 1990	54,548,530
1 April 2000	
Males	29,844,870
Females	30,762,077
Total	60,606,947
Population (UN estimates at mid-year)†	
2009	67,764,033
2010	68,139,238
2011	68,516,463
Density (per sq km) at mid-2011	133.5

* 198,117 sq miles.
† Source: UN, *World Population Prospects: The 2008 Revision*.

POPULATION BY AGE AND SEX
(UN estimates at mid-2011)

	Males	Females	Total
0–14	7,448,380	7,128,083	14,576,463
15–64	23,821,949	24,726,130	48,548,079
65 and over	2,404,515	2,987,406	5,391,921
Total	33,674,844	34,841,619	68,516,463

REGIONS
(estimates at mid-2008)

	Area (sq km)	Population ('000)	Density (per sq km)
Bangkok	1,568.7	5,711	3,640.4
Central Region	102,336.0	15,616	152.6
Northern Region	169,644.3	11,879	70.0
Northeastern Region	168,855.3	21,443	127.0
Southern Region	70,715.2	8,742	123.6
Total	513,119.5	63,390	123.5

Note: Population data are projected estimates based on results of 2000 census and have not been adjusted for underenumeration; totals may not be equal to the sum of components, owing to rounding.

PRINCIPAL TOWNS
(population at 2000 census)

Bangkok Metropolis*	6,320,174	Pak Kret	141,788
Samut Prakan	378,694	Si Racha	141,334
Nanthaburi	291,307	Khon Kaen	141,034
Udon Thani	220,493	Nakhon Pathom	120,657
Nakhon Ratchasima	204,391	Nakhon Si Thammarat	118,764
Hat Yai	185,557	Thanya Buri	113,818
Chon Buri	182,641	Surat Thani	111,276
Chiang Mai	167,776	Rayong	106,585
Phra Padaeng	166,828	Ubon Ratchathani	106,552
Lampang	147,812	Khlong Luang	103,282

* Formerly Bangkok and Thonburi.

Mid-2010 ('000 persons, incl. suburbs, UN estimate): Bangkok 6,976 (Source: UN, *World Urbanization Prospects: The 2009 Revision*).

THAILAND

BIRTHS, MARRIAGES AND DEATHS*

	Registered live births Number	Rate (per 1,000)	Registered marriages Number	Registered deaths Number	Rate (per 1,000)
2002	782,911	12.5	n.a.	380,364	6.1
2003	742,183	11.8	328,356	384,131	6.1
2004	813,069	13.0	365,721	393,592	6.3
2005	809,485	13.0	345,234	395,374	6.4
2006	793,623	12.7	358,505	391,126	6.2
2007	797,588	12.7	307,910	393,255	6.3
2008	784,256	n.a.	318,496	397,327	n.a.
2009	765,047	n.a.	n.a.	393,916	n.a.

* Registration is incomplete. According to UN estimates, the average annual rates in 1995–2000: Births 16.5 per 1,000; Deaths 7.8 per 1,000; in 2000–05: Births 15.3 per 1,000; Deaths 8.5 per 1,000; in 2005–10: Births 14.6 per 1,000; Deaths 8.9 per 1,000 (Source: UN, *World Population Prospects: The 2008 Revision*).

Source: partly UN, *Demographic Yearbook*.

Life expectancy (years at birth, WHO estimates): 70 (males 66; females 74) in 2008 (Source: WHO, *World Health Statistics*).

ECONOMICALLY ACTIVE POPULATION*
('000 persons aged 15 years and over, July–September of each year)

	2008	2009	2010
Agriculture, hunting and forestry	15,641	15,477	15,406
Fishing	426	458	339
Mining and quarrying	55	48	33
Manufacturing	5,231	5,301	5,189
Electricity, gas and water	103	106	99
Construction	2,012	2,044	2,083
Wholesale and retail trade; repair of motor vehicles, motorcycles and personal and household goods	5,635	5,872	6,110
Hotels and restaurants	2,353	2,557	2,558
Transport, storage and communications	1,091	1,111	1,048
Financial intermediation	396	372	373
Real estate, renting and business activities	717	743	809
Public administration and defence; compulsory social security	1,303	1,366	1,618
Education	1,098	1,167	1,289
Health and social work	720	715	703
Other community, social and personal service activities	819	786	793
Private households with employed persons	196	224	221
Extra-territorial organizations and bodies	1	3	0
Sub-total	37,798	38,351	38,672
Activities not adequately defined	39	21	20
Total employed	37,837	38,372	38,692
Unemployed	451	456	341
Total labour force	38,288	38,828	39,033

* Excluding the armed forces.
Source: partly ILO.

Health and Welfare

KEY INDICATORS

Total fertility rate (children per woman, 2008)	1.8
Under-5 mortality rate (per 1,000 live births, 2008)	14
HIV/AIDS (% of persons aged 15–49, 2007)	1.4
Physicians (per 1,000 head, 2000)	0.4
Hospital beds (per 1,000 head, 2000)	2.2
Health expenditure (2007): US $ per head (PPP)	286
Health expenditure (2007): % of GDP	3.7
Health expenditure (2007): public (% of total)	73.2
Access to water (% of persons, 2008)	98
Access to sanitation (% of persons, 2008)	96
Total carbon dioxide emissions ('000 metric tons, 2007)	277,284.2
Carbon dioxide emissions per head (metric tons, 2007)	4.1
Human Development Index (2010): ranking	92
Human Development Index (2010): value	0.654

For sources and definitions, see explanatory note on p. vi.

Agriculture

PRINCIPAL CROPS
('000 metric tons)

	2007	2008	2009
Rice, paddy	32,099	31,651	31,463
Maize	3,890	4,249	4,616
Sorghum	57	55	54
Cassava (Manioc, Tapioca)	26,916	25,156	30,088
Sugar cane	64,365	73,502	66,816
Beans, dry	113	113*	n.a.
Soybeans (Soya beans)	201	187	188
Groundnuts, with shell	114†	114*	n.a.
Coconuts	1,722	1,484	1,381
Oil palm fruit	6,390	9,271	8,162
Cabbages and other brassicas	489	500	511
Tomatoes	175	194	198
Pumpkins, squash, gourds	177	192	195
Cucumbers and gherkins*	222	222	n.a.
Onions, dry*	280	280	n.a.
Garlic	75	86	71
Maize, green	260	269	268
Watermelons*	432	432	n.a.
Bananas	1,929	1,540	1,528
Oranges*	350	350	n.a.
Tangerines, mandarins, clementines, satsumas*	670	670	n.a.
Mangoes, mangosteens and guavas	2,303	2,374	2,470
Pineapples	2,815	2,279	1,895
Papayas	195	201	207
Tobacco, unmanufactured*	70	70	n.a.
Natural rubber	3,022	3,167	3,090

* FAO estimate(s).
† Unofficial figure.

Aggregate production ('000 metric tons, may include official, semi-official or estimated data): Total cereals 36,193 in 2007, 36,102 in 2008, 36,280 in 2009; Total roots and tubers 27,181 in 2007, 25,410 in 2008, 30,354 in 2009; Total vegetables (incl. melons) 3,718 in 2007, 3,706 in 2008, 3,728 in 2009; Total fruits (excl. melons) 9,466 in 2007, 8,620 in 2008, 8,327 in 2009.

Source: FAO.

THAILAND

LIVESTOCK
('000 head, year ending September)

	2007	2008	2009
Horses	6	4	5
Cattle	6,481	6,700	6,700
Buffaloes	1,744	1,699	1,671
Pigs	8,381	7,845	7,481
Sheep	51	44	40
Goats	445	374	384
Chickens	209,105	219,150	228,207
Ducks	16,351	15,931	16,347
Geese and guinea fowl*	270	270	n.a.

* FAO estimates.
Source: FAO.

LIVESTOCK PRODUCTS
('000 metric tons)

	2007	2008	2009
Cattle meat*	197.0	236.2	212.6
Buffalo meat*	68.1	63.8	61.0
Pig meat*	915.0	864.0	755.8
Chicken meat	986.0	1,018.8	n.a.
Duck meat*	84.9	84.9	n.a.
Cows' milk	729.1	786.2	840.7
Hen eggs*	539.4	562.0	n.a.
Other poultry eggs*	310	310	n.a.

* FAO estimates.
Source: FAO.

Forestry

ROUNDWOOD REMOVALS
('000 cubic metres, excl. bark, FAO estimates)

	2007	2008	2009
Sawlogs, veneer logs and logs for sleepers	300	300	300
Pulpwood	2,900	2,900	2,900
Other industrial wood	5,500	5,500	5,500
Fuel wood	19,615	19,503	19,398
Total	28,315	28,203	28,098

Source: FAO.

SAWNWOOD PRODUCTION
('000 cubic metres, incl. railway sleepers)

	2003	2004	2005
Coniferous (softwood)*	18	18	18
Broadleaved (hardwood)	270*	2,796†	2,850*
Total*	288	2,814	2,868

* FAO estimate(s).
† Unofficial figure.

2006–09: Production assumed to be unchanged from 2005 (FAO estimates).
Source: FAO.

Fishing
('000 metric tons, live weight)

	2006	2007	2008
Capture	2,698.8	2,305.0	2,457.2
Freshwater fishes	208.4	222.2	226.7
Bigeyes	112.9	105.2	94.5
Sardinellas	109.5	97.4	114.5
Anchovies, etc.	157.8	145.6	143.3
Indian mackerels	159.0	136.8	130.5
Other marine fishes	1,507.1	1,337.4	1,574.3
Aquaculture	1,407.0	1,351.1*	1,374.0*
Nile tilapia	205.3	213.8	209.8
Catfish (hybrid)	146.5	136.6	135.5
Whiteleg shrimp	490.0	490.0	498.8
Green mussel	272.9	228.2	243.8
Total catch	4,105.8	3,656.0*	3,831.2*

* FAO estimate.
Source: FAO.

Mining
(metric tons unless otherwise indicated)

	2007	2008	2009*
Lignite ('000 metric tons)	18,239	18,095	20,000
Crude petroleum ('000 barrels)	48,745	52,805	56,302
Natural gas—gross production (million cu m)	28,778	31,157	30,625
Iron ore—gross weight	1,554,860	2,029,100	1,400,800
Iron ore—metal content	779,000	855,000	800,000
Zinc ore—metal content	32,921	17,811	34,000
Tin concentrates—metal content	122	215	153
Manganese ore—metal content	4,550	52,700	50,000
Tungsten concentrates—metal content	477	617	600
Tantalum—metal and oxide powder	142	158	50
Silver (kilograms)	7,727	5,465	15,300
Gold (kilograms)	3,401	2,721	5,400
Marble—dimension stone ('000 cu m)	848.8	664.9	760.0
Granite—dimension stone ('000 cu m)	10.5	10.6	10.0
Granite—industrial ('000 metric tons)	5,229	5,190	5,000
Limestone ('000 metric tons)	151,434	142,118	150,200
Dolomite ('000 metric tons)	1,108.4	1,353.8	1,200.0
Calcite ('000 metric tons)	672.6	823.7	750.0
Silica sand ('000 metric tons)	844.1	495.8	500.0
Ball clay ('000 metric tons)	563.4	1,500.0	1,000.0
Kaolin—marketable production ('000 metric tons)	518.1	479.4	500.0
Phosphate rock, crude	3,550	3,675	3,000
Fluorspar—metallurgical grade ('000 metric tons)	1,820	29,529	20,000
Feldspar ('000 metric tons)	684.7	670.6	600.0
Barite ('000 metric tons)	8.6	9.2	9.0
Perlite	6,400	7,000	7,000
Gypsum ('000 metric tons)	8,643	8,500	8,500
Gemstones ('000 carats)	102	32	30

* Estimates.
Source: US Geological Survey.

THAILAND

Industry

SELECTED PRODUCTS
('000 metric tons, unless otherwise indicated)

	2007	2008	2009*
Raw sugar	7,344	8,194	8,747
Beer (million litres)	2,161	2,160	1,837
Spirits (million litres)	551	631	666
Synthetic fibre	674.6	592.7	601.6
Wood pulp	1,037.4	948.5	880.3
Petroleum products (million litres)	49,856	51,216	53,393
Cement	35,668	31,651	31,180
Galvanized iron sheets	247.2	207.5	169.7
Integrated circuits (million units)	14,334	13,758	13,277
Computer monitors ('000 units)	942	705	660
Computer keyboards ('000 units)	931	633	109
Hard disk drives ('000 units)	205,277	246,986	258,271
Printers ('000 units)	17,439	15,693	8,177

* Provisional.

Source: Bank of Thailand, Bangkok.

Finance

CURRENCY AND EXCHANGE RATES

Monetary Units
100 satangs = 1 baht.

Sterling, Dollar and Euro Equivalents (31 December 2010)
£1 sterling = 47.202 baht;
US $1 = 30.151 baht;
€1 = 40.288 baht;
1,000 baht = £21.19 = $33.17 = €24.82.

Average Exchange Rate (baht per US $)
2008 33.313
2009 34.286
2010 31.686

Note: Figures refer to the average mid-point rate of exchange available from commercial banks. In July 1997 the Bank of Thailand began operating a managed 'float' of the baht. In addition, a two-tier market was introduced, creating separate exchange rates for purchasers of baht in domestic markets and those who buy the currency overseas.

GOVERNMENT FINANCE
(central government transactions, non-cash basis, '000 million baht, year ending 30 September)

Summary of Balances

	2006/07	2007/08*	2008/09*
Revenue	1,659.4	1,828.8	1,686.7
Less Expense	1,502.2	1,655.9	1,778.3
Net operating balance	157.2	172.9	−91.7
Less Net acquisition of non-financial assets	145.9	127.7	184.2
Net lending/borrowing	11.2	45.2	−275.8

Revenue

	2006/07	2007/08*	2008/09*
Taxes	1,374.4	1,493.4	1,371.0
Taxes on income, profits and capital gains	614.9	712.7	638.4
Taxes on goods and services	659.7	674.1	645.4
Social contributions	79.8	84.9	82.8
Grants	1.7	2.1	2.2
Other revenue	203.5	248.4	230.7
Total	1,659.4	1,828.8	1,686.7

Expense/Outlays

Expense by economic type	2006/07	2007/08*	2008/09*
Compensation of employees	559.5	584.5	640.6
Use of goods and services	398.6	447.1	548.3
Consumption of fixed capital	38.5	41.1	47.3
Interest	93.3	89.8	97.6
Subsidies	33.6	69.7	42.4
Grants	205.1	216.6	179.0
Social benefits	170.6	184.1	221.5
Other expense	3.0	23.0	1.6
Total	1,502.2	1,655.9	1,778.3

Outlays by functions of government†	2006/07	2007/08*	2008/09*
General public services	304.7	291.0	274.5
Defence	42.9	114.9	150.0
Public order and safety	136.5	109.4	118.4
Economic affairs	398.6	357.9	400.8
Agriculture, forestry and fishing	109.0	99.9	96.5
Fuel and energy	31.8	18.5	27.9
Transport	55.6	66.2	84.8
Environmental protection	4.8	2.5	4.1
Housing and community amenities	10.6	31.3	50.0
Health	185.6	265.4	281.5
Recreation, culture and religion	14.6	21.1	20.4
Education	334.4	371.4	397.8
Social protection	215.7	218.7	265.0
Total	1,648.2	1,783.6	1,962.5

* Preliminary figures.
† Including net acquisition of non-financial assets.

Source: IMF, *Government Finance Statistics Yearbook*.

INTERNATIONAL RESERVES
(US $ million at 31 December)

	2008	2009	2010
Gold (national valuation)	2,347	2,935	4,599
IMF special drawing rights	131	1,523	1,497
Reserve position in IMF	213	361	377
Foreign exchange	108,317	133,599	165,656
Total	111,008	138,418	172,129

Source: IMF, *International Financial Statistics*.

MONEY SUPPLY
('000 million baht at 31 December)

	2008	2009	2010
Currency outside depository corporations	714.8	804.6	895.1
Transferable deposits	288.9	330.6	365.2
Other deposits	8,283.1	8,726.8	9,482.3
Securities other than shares	620.0	715.7	990.0
Broad money	9,906.8	10,577.6	11,732.7

Source: IMF, *International Financial Statistics*.

COST OF LIVING
(Consumer Price Index; base: 2007 = 100)

	2008	2009	2010
Food (incl. non-alcoholic beverages)	111.6	116.5	122.8
Tobacco and alcoholic beverages	102.9	111.7	117.1
Energy	108.0	93.8	102.9
Clothing (incl. footwear)	100.3	98.1	97.1
Housing and furnishing	96.9	95.2	97.1
All items (incl. others)	105.4	104.5	108.0

Source: Bank of Thailand.

THAILAND

Statistical Survey

NATIONAL ACCOUNTS
(million baht at current prices)

Expenditure on the Gross Domestic Product

	2008	2009*	2010*
Government final consumption expenditure	1,120,842	1,213,928	1,304,640
Private final consumption expenditure	4,999,605	4,993,302	5,428,356
Changes in inventories	152,272	−261,315	128,954
Gross fixed capital formation	2,492,332	2,181,821	2,499,311
Total domestic expenditure	8,765,051	8,127,736	9,361,261
Exports of goods and services	6,941,526	6,180,052	7,203,650
Less Imports of goods and services	6,708,781	5,226,526	6,451,808
Statistical discrepancy	82,670	−39,711	−10,117
GDP in market prices	9,080,466	9,041,551	10,102,986
GDP at constant 1988 prices	4,364,833	4,263,139	4,595,809

Gross Domestic Product by Economic Activity

	2008	2009*	2010*
Agriculture, hunting and forestry	955,710	931,907	1,146,053
Fishing	94,033	104,679	109,136
Mining and quarrying	315,273	306,529	345,923
Manufacturing	3,163,683	3,087,741	3,599,273
Electricity, gas and water	262,027	278,108	296,570
Construction	259,223	246,076	269,273
Wholesale and retail trade; repair of motor vehicles, motorcycles and personal and household goods	1,288,332	1,272,556	1,323,939
Hotels and restaurants	440,173	439,720	479,206
Transport, storage and communications	645,300	647,319	687,678
Financial intermediation	354,619	368,831	410,092
Real estate, renting and business activities	216,681	215,839	228,602
Public administration and defence; compulsory social security	399,094	416,087	439,995
Education	384,444	414,924	433,579
Health and social work	168,839	177,188	185,469
Other community, social and personal service activities	123,353	123,912	138,036
Private households with employed persons	9,682	10,135	10,162
GDP in market prices	9,080,466	9,041,551	10,102,986

* Preliminary figures.

Source: National Economic and Social Development Board, Bangkok.

BALANCE OF PAYMENTS
(US $ million)

	2007	2008	2009
Exports of goods f.o.b.	151,240	175,214	150,713
Imports of goods f.o.b.	−124,479	−157,829	−118,022
Trade balance	26,762	17,385	32,691
Exports of services	30,357	33,383	29,940
Imports of services	−38,425	−46,263	−37,756
Balance on goods and services	18,693	4,504	24,876
Other income received	7,333	8,111	5,880
Other income paid	−14,286	−15,171	−13,378
Balance on goods, services and income	11,740	−2,555	17,377
Current transfers received	4,395	5,324	4,972
Current transfers paid	−457	−558	−488
Current balance	15,678	2,211	21,861
Direct investment abroad	−3,015	−4,089	−4,114
Direct investment from abroad	11,324	8,531	4,976
Portfolio investment assets	−9,638	395	−8,290
Portfolio investment liabilities	2,899	−2,561	2,343
Financial derivatives assets	828	1,385	3,135
Financial derivatives liabilities	−1,143	−2,062	−2,017
Other investment assets	−7,027	11,927	1,962
Other investment liabilities	4,019	−1,660	−771
Net errors and omissions	3,152	10,363	5,045
Overall balance	17,077	24,440	24,131

Source: IMF, *International Financial Statistics*.

External Trade

PRINCIPAL COMMODITIES
(distribution by SITC, '000 million baht)

Imports c.i.f.	2008	2009	2010
Food	228.5	203.5	226.9
Crude materials (inedible) except fuels	219.9	140.6	180.7
Mineral fuels, lubricants, etc.	1,238.4	855.8	1,010.7
Chemicals and related products	657.0	493.3	639.4
Basic manufactures	1,124.3	762.3	1,060.6
Machinery	1,895.4	1,677.4	2,057.6
Total (incl. others)	5,962.5	4,600.5	5,839.4

Exports f.o.b.	2008	2009	2010
Food	736.0	724.9	757.6
Crude materials (inedible) except fuels	309.3	221.6	352.4
Mineral fuels and lubricants	376.0	264.9	304.4
Chemicals and related products	457.6	424.9	536.2
Basic manufactures	734.8	670.8	753.1
Machinery	2,473.4	2,106.0	2,604.0
Miscellaneous manufactured articles	114.2	194.6	204.4
Total (incl. others)	5,851.4	5,194.6	6,176.4

Source: Bank of Thailand, Bangkok.

THAILAND

PRINCIPAL TRADING PARTNERS
('000 million baht)

Imports c.i.f.	2008	2009	2010
Australia	171.7	130.4	188.7
China, People's Republic	670.3	586.1	775.5
France	49.8	63.9	46.2
Germany	150.0	118.3	148.3
Hong Kong	65.2	59.7	58.2
India	87.3	59.4	72.1
Indonesia	180.3	130.9	181.7
Italy	53.8	49.2	46.8
Japan	1,116.5	860.1	1,211.5
Korea, Republic	228.2	186.8	258.4
Malaysia	323.0	295.3	343.2
Philippines	75.7	61.3	76.0
Russia	95.6	57.0	102.7
Singapore	236.1	197.3	201.9
Switzerland	131.7	85.5	166.5
Taiwan	206.9	165.0	218.2
United Arab Emirates	371.6	229.2	276.0
United Kingdom	60.4	60.7	61.2
USA	380.7	288.6	342.1
Total (incl. others)	5,962.5	4,600.5	5,839.4

Exports f.o.b.	2008	2009	2010
Australia	263.2	292.0	297.1
Belgium	55.8	46.0	47.8
Canada	47.1	42.7	45.1
China, People's Republic	532.3	548.8	678.6
France	62.1	52.7	55.7
Germany	105.3	89.5	104.4
Hong Kong	330.8	323.2	413.8
Indonesia	208.0	158.9	232.9
Italy	65.1	44.9	54.1
Japan	661.6	535.9	645.3
Korea, Republic	121.1	96.1	114.3
Malaysia	325.3	260.9	334.6
Netherlands	137.4	106.5	115.3
Philippines	115.2	102.9	154.9
Singapore	332.4	258.0	285.2
Switzerland	66.0	107.8	129.3
Taiwan	88.8	76.7	102.0
United Arab Emirates	92.2	83.9	90.1
United Kingdom	130.9	110.3	115.7
USA	667.7	567.7	638.8
Viet Nam	165.1	159.2	184.5
Total (incl. others)	5,851.4	5,194.6	6,176.4

Source: Bank of Thailand, Bangkok.

Transport

RAILWAYS
(year ending 30 September)

	2005/06	2006/07	2007/08
Passengers carried ('000)	48,867	45,050	47,059
Passenger-kilometres (million)	8,824	8,038	8,225
Freight carried ('000 metric tons)	12,566	11,912	13,541
Freight ton-kilometres (million)	3,508	n.a.	n.a.

ROAD TRAFFIC
('000 motor vehicles in use at 31 December)

	2006	2007	2008
Passenger cars	3,312.9	3,560.2	3,809.1
Buses and trucks	848.8	880.5	905.8
Vans and pick-ups	4,173.6	4,371.5	4,552.3
Motorcycles	15,650.3	15,961.9	16,264.4
Total (incl. others)	24,807.3	25,618.4	26,417.4

SHIPPING
Merchant Fleet
(registered at 31 December)

	2007	2008	2009
Number of vessels	858	879	884
Total displacement ('000 grt)	2,846.9	2,842.4	2,526.1

Source: IHS Fairplay, *World Fleet Statistics*.

International Sea-borne Freight Traffic
(Ports of Bangkok and Laem Chabang, year ending 30 September)

	2004/05	2005/06	2006/07
Goods loaded ('000 metric tons)	21,456	22,401	24,883
Goods unloaded ('000 metric tons)	30,071	32,951	38,024
Vessels entered	7,640	8,975	n.a.

Source: Port Authority of Thailand.

CIVIL AVIATION
(traffic on scheduled services)

	2004	2005	2006
Kilometres flown (million)	223	229	246
Passengers carried ('000)	20,343	18,903	20,102
Passenger-km (million)	51,564	50,809	56,378
Total ton-km (million)	6,579	6,646	7,258

Sources: UN, *Statistical Yearbook*.

2007: Passengers carried ('000) 21,191.7 (Source: World Bank, World Development Indicators database).

2008: Passengers carried ('000) 19,993.1 (Source: World Bank, World Development Indicators database).

Tourism

FOREIGN TOURIST ARRIVALS BY COUNTRY OF RESIDENCE*

Country of origin	2006	2007	2008
Australia	549,547	658,148	693,234
China, People's Republic	949,117	907,117	818,752
France	321,278	373,090	393,013
Germany	516,659	544,495	541,170
Hong Kong	376,636	367,862	334,861
Japan	1,311,987	1,277,638	1,146,633
Korea, Republic	1,092,783	1,083,652	888,344
Malaysia	1,591,328	1,540,080	1,825,379
Singapore	687,160	604,603	570,267
Sweden	306,085	378,387	391,561
Taiwan	475,117	427,474	390,790
United Kingdom	850,685	859,010	822,422
USA	694,258	681,972	663,732
Total (incl. others)	13,821,802	14,464,228	14,536,382

* Includes Thai nationals resident abroad.

Receipts from tourism (US $ million, incl. passenger transport): 16,614 in 2006; 20,623 in 2007; 21,980 in 2008 (Source: World Tourism Organization).

THAILAND

Communications Media

	2007	2008	2009
Telephones ('000 main lines in use)	7,024.0	7,394.3	7,204.9
Mobile cellular telephones ('000 subscribers)	52,974.0	61,837.2	65,952.3
Internet users ('000)	13,416	16,099	17,483
Broadband subscribers ('000)	913	950	994

Personal computers: 4,408,000 (66.8 per 1,000 persons) in 2005.

Radio receivers ('000 in use): 13,959 in 1997.

Television receivers ('000 in use): 18,400 in 2001.

Book production (titles, excluding pamphlets): 8,142 in 1996.

Daily newspapers: 35 (with average circulation of 2,766,000 copies) in 1994; 35 (with average circulation of 2,700,000* copies) in 1995; 30 (with average circulation of 3,808,000 copies) in 1996.

Non-daily newspapers: 280 in 1995; 320 in 1996.

* Provisional.

Sources: International Telecommunication Union; UNESCO, *Statistical Yearbook*; UN, *Statistical Yearbook*.

Education

(2005 unless otherwise indicated)

	Institutions	Teachers	Students
Ministry of Education:			
Office of the Permanent Secretary	3,774	123,486	2,296,415
Office of the Basic Education Commission	32,340	420,965	8,697,983
Office of the Higher Education Commission	156	45,824	1,950,892
Office of Vocational Education Commission	408	16,731	615,548
Mahidol Wittayanusorn School	1	63	704
Mahamakut Buddhist University*	8	150	6,436
Mahachulalongkornrajavidyalaya University*	12	373	8,999
Bangkok Metropolitan Education Department	437	13,196	349,063
Royal Thai Police	192	2,082	29,985
Department of Local Administration	520	18,297	400,361
Ministry of Social Development and Human Security	3	38	407
Ministry of Public Health	39	2,971	17,750
Merchant Marine Training Centre	1	220	918
Civil Aviation Training Centre	1	37	1,052
National Bureau of Buddhism	404	3,188	51,414
Fine Arts Department	16	1,423	10,014
Office of Sports and Recreational Development	28	1,857	13,794
Armed Forces	11	1,400	7,476

* Figures for 2004.

Source: Ministry of Education.

Pupil-teacher ratio (primary education, UNESCO estimate): 16.0 in 2007/08 (Source: UNESCO Institute for Statistics).

Adult literacy rate (UNESCO estimates): 94.1% (males 95.9%; females 92.6%) in 2007 (Source: UNESCO Institute for Statistics).

Directory

The Government

HEAD OF STATE

King: HM King BHUMIBOL ADULYADEJ (King Rama IX—succeeded to the throne June 1946).

PRIVY COUNCIL

The Privy Council comprises a President and not more than 18 Privy Councillors, all of whom are appointed by the King. The Privy Council advises the King on all matters pertaining to his functions.

President: Gen. (retd) PREM TINSULANONDA.

CABINET
(May 2011)

The Cabinet comprises members of the Democrat Party, Bhum Jai Thai, Chart Thai Pattana, Ruam Jai Thai Chart Pattana and the Social Action Party.

Prime Minister: ABHISIT VEJJAJIVA.

Deputy Prime Ministers: SUTHEP THAUGSUBAN, SANAN KAJORN-PRASART, TRAIRONG SUWANNAKHIRI.

Ministers in the Prime Minister's Office: SATIT WONGNONGTAEY, ONG-ART KLAMPAIBOON.

Minister of Defence: Gen. PRAWIT WONGSUWAN.

Minister of Finance: KORN CHATIKAVANIJ.

Minister of Foreign Affairs: KASIT PIROMYA.

Minister of the Interior: CHAOVARAT CHANWEERAKUL.

Minister of Information and Communications Technology: CHUTI KRAIRIKSH.

Minister of Tourism and Sports: CHUMPOL SILPA-ARCHA.

Minister of Commerce: PORNTHIVA NAKASAI.

Minister of Industry: CHAIWUTI BANNAWAT.

Minister of Social Development and Human Security: ISSARA SOMCHAI.

Minister of Agriculture and Co-operatives: THEERA WONGSAMUT.

Minister of Transport: SOPHON SARAM.

Minister of Natural Resources and Environment: SUWIT KHUNKITTI.

Minister of Energy: WANNARAT CHARNNUKUL.

Minister of Justice: PIRAPAN SALIRATHAVIBHAGA.

Minister of Labour: CHALERMCHAI SRI-ON.

Minister of Culture: NIPHIT INTHARASOMBAT.

Minister of Science and Technology: VIRACHAI VIRAMETEEKUL.

Minister of Education: CHINNAWORN BOONYAKIAT.

Minister of Public Health: JURIN LAKSANAWISIT.

MINISTRIES

Office of the Prime Minister: Government House, Thanon Phitsanulok, Dusit, Bangkok 10300; tel. (2) 281-4040; fax (2) 282-5131; e-mail opm@opm.go.th; internet www.opm.go.th.

Ministry of Agriculture and Co-operatives: Thanon Ratchadamnoen Nok, Bangkok 10200; tel. (2) 281-5955; fax (2) 282-1425; e-mail webmaster@moac.go.th; internet www.moac.go.th.

Ministry of Commerce: 44/100 Thanon Nonthaburi 1, Amphur Muang, Nonthaburi, Bangkok 11000; tel. (2) 507-7000; fax (2) 547-5210; e-mail webmaster@moc.go.th; internet www.moc.go.th.

Ministry of Culture: 666 Thanon Borommaratchachonnani, Bang Bumru, Bang Plat, Bangkok 10700; tel. (2) 422-8888; e-mail webmaster@m-culture.go.th; internet www.m-culture.go.th.

Ministry of Defence: Thanon Sanam Chai, Bangkok 10200; tel. (2) 222-1121; fax (2) 226-3117; e-mail webmaster@mod.go.th; internet www.mod.go.th.

Ministry of Education: Wang Chankasem, Thanon Ratchadamnoen Nok, Bangkok 10300; tel. (2) 281-9264; fax (2) 281-1753; e-mail website@emisc.moe.go.th; internet www.moe.go.th.

THAILAND

Ministry of Energy: 17 Kasatsuk Bridge, Thanon Rama I, Rong Muang, Pathumwan, Bangkok 10330; tel. (2) 223-3344; fax (2) 222-4495; e-mail moen@energy.go.th; internet www.energy.go.th.

Ministry of Finance: Thanon Rama VI, Samsennai, Phaya Thai, Rajatevi, Bangkok 10400; tel. (2) 273-9021; fax (2) 273-9408; e-mail webmaster-eng@mof.go.th; internet www.mof.go.th.

Ministry of Foreign Affairs: 443 Thanon Sri Ayudhya, Bangkok 10400; tel. (2) 643-5000; fax (2) 643-5102; e-mail information01@mfa.go.th; internet www.mfa.go.th.

Ministry of Industry: Thanon Rama VI, Ratchathewi, Bangkok 10400; tel. (2) 202-3000; fax (2) 202-3048; e-mail pr@industry.go.th; internet www.industry.go.th.

Ministry of Information and Communications Technology: 120 Moo 3, Government Offices, Bldg B, 6th–9th Floors, Thanon Chaengwattana, Thung Song Hong, Laksi, Bangkok 10210; tel. (2) 141-6747; fax (2) 143-8019; e-mail pr@mict.go.th; internet www.mict.go.th.

Ministry of the Interior: Thanon Atsadang, Bangkok 10200; tel. (2) 222-1141; fax (2) 223-8851; e-mail webmaster@moi.go.th; internet www.moi.go.th.

Ministry of Justice: Thanon Chaengwattana, Pakkred, Nonthaburi, Bangkok 11120; tel. (2) 502-8051; fax (2) 502-8059; e-mail webmaster@moj.go.th; internet www.moj.go.th.

Ministry of Labour: Thanon Mitmaitri, Dindaeng, Bangkok 10400; tel. (2) 232-1421; fax (2) 246-1520; e-mail webmaster@mol.go.th; internet www.mol.go.th.

Ministry of Natural Resources and Environment: 92 Phaholyothin Soi 7, Samsen Nai, Phaya Thai, Bangkok 10400; tel. (2) 278-8500; fax (2) 278-8698; e-mail webmaster@mnre.mail.go.th; internet www.mnre.go.th.

Ministry of Public Health: Thanon Tiwanon, Amphur Muang, Nonthaburi 11000; tel. (2) 590-1000; fax (2) 591-8492; e-mail eng-webmaster@health.moph.go.th; internet www.moph.go.th.

Ministry of Science and Technology: 75/47 Thanon Rama VI, Phaya Thai, Bangkok 10400; tel. (2) 333-3700; fax (2) 333-3833; e-mail webmaster@most.go.th; internet www.most.go.th.

Ministry of Social Development and Human Security: 1034 Thanon Krungkasem, Mahanak, Khet Pom Prab Sattruphai, Bangkok 10100; tel. (2) 659-6399; fax 659-6529; e-mail society@m-society.go.th; internet www.m-society.go.th.

Ministry of Tourism and Sports: 4 Ratchadamnoen Nok, Khet Pom Prab Sattruphai, Bangkok 10100; tel. (2) 283-1500; fax (2) 356-0746; e-mail webmaster@mots.go.th; internet www.mots.go.th.

Ministry of Transport: 38 Thanon Ratchadamnoen Nok, Khet Pom Prab Sattruphai, Bangkok 10100; tel. (2) 283-3000; fax (2) 283-3959; e-mail mot@mot.go.th; internet www.mot.go.th.

Legislature

RATHA SAPHA (NATIONAL ASSEMBLY)

Woothi Sapha (Senate)

The Senate consists of 150 members, of whom 76 members are elected to represent each of Thailand's 75 provinces and Bangkok, and the remainder are selected by a committee consisting primarily of judicial officials. Senators thus selected are drawn from lists of nominees made by organizations in various sectors.

Elections to the Senate were held on 2 March 2008.

Speaker of the Senate: Gen. THEERADET MEEPIAN.

Sapha Poothaen Rassadorn (House of Representatives)

Speaker of the House of Representatives and President of the National Assembly: CHAI CHIDCHOB.

Election, 23 December 2007

Party	Seats
People's Power Party*	233
Democrat Party	164
Chart Thai*	34
Puea Pandin	24
Matchimathipataya*	11
Ruam Jai Thai Chart Pattana	9
Pracharaj	5
Total	**480†**

* Dissolved by the Constitutional Court on 2 December 2008.

† A total of 400 candidates were elected in multi-member constituencies and the remaining 80 through a party-list system. By-elections were held in 29 constituencies on 11 January 2009, following the dissolution in the previous month of the governing People's Power Party, Chart Thai and Matchimathipataya. The Democrat Party was reported to have won seven of the 29 seats contested, with a further 13 being secured by its allies, the newly established Chart Thai Pattana (10 seats) and Puea Pandin (three seats). Puea Thai won five seats and Pracharaj four.

Election Commission

Election Commission of Thailand (ECT): 120 Moo 3, Government Offices, Bldg B, 2nd Floor, Thanon Chaengwattana, Thung Song Hong, Laksi, Bangkok 10210; tel. (2) 141-8888; fax (2) 219-3411; e-mail dav@ect.go.th; internet www.ect.go.th; Chair. APHICHART SUKHAGGANOND.

Political Organizations

Bhum Jai Thai (BJT) (Thai Pride Party): Suite 2159, 11 Thanon Phaholyothin, Chatuchak, Bangkok 10900; tel. (2) 940-6999; internet www.bhumjaithai.com; f. 2008; est. by fmr mems of Matchimathipataya (f. 2006) in anticipation of that party's dissolution, in Dec. 2008, by Constitutional Court; merged in Jan. 2009 with Friends of Newin (f. 2008 by NEWIN CHIDCHOB and other defectors from People's Power Party); announced alliance with Chart Thai Pattana for 2011 elections; Leader CHAOVARAT CHANWEERAKUL; Sec. PORNTIWA NAKASAI.

Chart Pattana Puea Pandin Party: c/o House of Representatives, Bangkok; f. 2007; est. as Ruam Jai Thai Chart Pattana; renamed Ruam Chart Pattana in 2008; above name adopted following merger with Puea Pandin in 2011; Leader WANNARAT CHARNNUKUL.

Chart Thai Pattana (Thai Nation Development): 37/157 Moo 11, Sansab, Minburi, Bangkok; f. 2008; est. by fmr mems of Chart Thai (f. 1981) in anticipation of that party's dissolution, in Dec. 2008, by Constitutional Court; right-wing; announced post-election alliance with Bhum Jai Thai in 2011; Leader CHUMPOL SILPA-ARCHA.

Democrat Party (DP) (Prachatipat): 67 Thanon Setsiri, Samsen Nai, Phaya Thai, Bangkok 10400; tel. (2) 270-0036; fax (2) 279-6086; e-mail public@democrat.or.th; internet www.democrat.or.th; f. 1946; liberal; Leader ABHISIT VEJJAJIVA; Sec.-Gen. SUTHEP THAUGSUBAN.

Karn Muang Mai (New Politics Party—NPP): Phra Nakhon Region, Bangkok 10200; tel. (2) 282-9844; fax (2) 282-9850; internet www.npp.or.th; f. 2009; est. by members of the People's Alliance for Democracy (PAD); Leader SOMSAK KOSAISUK; Sec.-Gen. SURIYASAI KATASILA.

Matubhum Party: Benjamas Bldg, 5th Floor, 555 Soi Ruam Chit, Dusit, Bangkok 10300; tel. (2) 715-3870; fax (2) 715-3790; f. 2008; predominantly comprises members of the Muslim Wadah and Pak Nam factions; Leader Gen. SONTHI BOONYARATGLIN.

Pracharaj (Royal People Party): TPI Tower, 18th Floor, 26/56 Thanon Chan Tat Mai, Tungmahamek, Sathorn, Bangkok 10120; f. 2006; est. by breakaway faction of Thai Rak Thai (f. 1998); Leader SNOH THIENTHONG; Sec.-Gen. CHIENGCHUANG KANLAYANAMITH.

Pracha Santi Party: Thanon Amnuay Songkhram, Bangkok; f. 2011; supports formation of a national govt and eradication of corruption; Leader SERI SUWANNAPHANONT.

Puea Pandin (For the Land): 1 Thanon Witthayu, Lumpini, Pathumwan, Bangkok 10330; tel. (2) 253-0428; e-mail admin@ppd.or.th; internet www.ppd.or.th; f. 2007; most mems left to join the new Chart Pattana Puea Pandin Party in 2011; Sec.-Gen. CHAIYOS JIRAMETHAKORN.

Puea Thai (For Thais): 626 Soi Jinda Tawil, Thanon Rama IV, Bangrak Mahaprutharam, Bangkok 10500; internet www.ptp.or.th; f. 2008; est. by fmr mems of People's Power Party (f. 2007) in anticipation of that party's dissolution, in Dec. 2008, by Constitutional Court; Chair. CHAVALIT YONGCHAIYUDH; Leader YONGYUTH WICHAIDITH.

Rak Santi Party: f. 2011; Chair. PURACHAI PIUMSOMBUN; Sec.-Gen. PORNPEN PHETSUKSIRI.

Social Action Party (SAP) (Kij Sangkhom): 381/28–29 Thanon Mitrapap, Naimuang, Muang, Khon-kaen 40000; tel. and fax (2) 325-2234; f. 1981; disbanded in 2003; revived in mid-2008 by former leader Suwit Khunkitti, following his defection from Puea Pandin; conservative; Sec.-Gen. SUWIT KHUNKITTI.

Other parties that contested the 2007 election included the Artist Party, Farmer Network of Thailand, For our Homeland, Free Thai, Prachamati, Rak Muang Thai, Chart Thai, Matchimathipataya and the People's Power Party. In December 2008 the latter three parties were dissolved by the Constitutional Court.

Two popular movements, which staged large-scale political rallies and became involved in civil unrest from 2008, have emerged in response to the recent political crises: the **People's Alliance for**

THAILAND

Democracy (PAD), a coalition of groups and individuals, including royalists, opposed to Thaksin Shinawatra, established in 2005 by Sondhi Limthongkul and popularly known as the 'Yellow Shirts' (internet www.padnet.net); and the **United Front for Democracy against Dictatorship (UDD)**, a coalition of broadly pro-Thaksin activists, popularly known as the 'Red Shirts', who reject the legitimacy of the Government of Abhisit Vejjajiva (internet www.uddthailand.com).

Groupings in armed conflict with the Government include:

Barisan Revolusi Nasional (BRN) (National Revolutionary Front): Yala; f. 1963; was organized into three principal factions—the BRN Congress (its military wing); the BRN Co-ordinate (its political wing); and the BRN Uram (its religious wing)—in the 1980s; Muslim secessionists.

Bersatu (Council of the Muslim People of Pattani): Pattani; f. 1989; umbrella org. incl. the BRN and the PULO; Pattani secessionists.

Gerakan Mujahidin Islam Patani (GMIP): Pattani; f. 1986; dissolved in 1993 following internal disagreement, but re-formed in 1995; seeks the transformation of Pattani into an Islamic state; Leader KARIM KARUBANG.

Patani United Liberation Organization (PULO): f. 1968; subsequently divided into factions; advocates secession of the five southern provinces (Satun, Narathiwat, Yala, Pattani and Songkhla); Pres. ABU YASIR FIKRI.

Runda Kumpulan Kecil (RKK): Yala; f. 2005; splinter group of the BRN Congress; seeks the implementation of an independent Islamic state in Thailand's southern provinces; Leader USTAZ RORHING AHSONG.

Diplomatic Representation

EMBASSIES IN THAILAND

Argentina: 16th Floor, Suite 1601, Glas Haus Bldg, 1 Soi Sukhumvit 25, Wattana, Bangkok 10110; tel. (2) 259-0401; fax (2) 259-0402; e-mail embtail@csloxinfo.com; Ambassador FELIPE FRYDMAN.

Australia: 37 Thanon Sathorn Tai, Bangkok 10120; tel. (2) 344-6300; fax (2) 344-6593; e-mail austembassy.bangkok@dfat.gov.au; internet www.austembassy.or.th; Ambassador JAMES WISE.

Austria: 14 Soi Nandha, off Thanon Sathorn Tai, Soi 1, Bangkok 10120; tel. (2) 303-6257; fax (2) 303-6260; e-mail bangkok-ob@bmeia.gv.at; internet www.aussenministerium.at/botschaft/bangkok; Ambassador Dr JOHANNES PETERLIK.

Bangladesh: 47/8 Ekamai Soi 30, Thanon Sukhumvit 63, Khlong Tan Nua, Wattana, Bangkok 10110; tel. (2) 390-5107; fax (2) 390-5106; e-mail bdootbkk@truemail.co.th; Ambassador KAZI IMTIAZ HOSSAIN.

Belgium: 17th Floor, Sathorn City Tower, 175 Thanon Sathorn Tai, Tungmahamek, Sathorn, Bangkok 10120; tel. (2) 679-5454; fax (2) 679-5467; e-mail bangkok@diplobel.fed.be; internet www.diplomatie.be/bangkok; Ambassador RUDI VEESTRAETEN.

Bhutan: 375/1 Soi Ratchadanivej, Thanon Pracha-Uthit, Huay Kwang, Bangkok 10320; tel. (2) 274-4740; fax (2) 274-4743; e-mail bht_emb_bkk@yahoo.com; Ambassador TSHERING DORJI.

Brazil: 34th Floor, Lumpini Tower, 1168/101 Thanon Rama IV, Tungmahamek, Sathorn, Bangkok 10120; tel. (2) 679-8567; fax (2) 679-8569; e-mail info@brazilembassy.or.th; internet www.brazilembassy.or.th; Ambassador EDGARD TELLES RIBEIRO.

Brunei: 12 Soi Ekamai 2, Thanon Sukhumvit 63, Prakanong Nua, Wattana, Bangkok 10110; tel. (2) 714-7395; fax (2) 714-7382; e-mail bangkok.thailand@mfa.gov.bn; Ambassador Pengiran Dato' Paduka Haji KAMIS BIN Haji TAMIN.

Bulgaria: 83/24 Soi Witthayu 1, Thanon Witthayu, Lumpini, Pathumwan, Bangkok 10330; tel. (2) 627-3872; fax (2) 627-3874; e-mail bulgemth@csloxinfo.com; internet www.mfa.bg/bangkok; Ambassador KAMEN VELICHKOV.

Cambodia: 518/4 Thanon Pracha Uthit, Ramkhamhaeng Soi 39, Wangtonglang, Bangkok 10310; tel. (2) 957-5851; fax (2) 957-5850; e-mail recbkk@cscoms.com; Ambassador YOU AY.

Canada: Abdulrahim Pl., 15th Floor, 990 Thanon Rama IV, Bangrak, Bangkok 10500; tel. (2) 636-0540; fax (2) 636-0566; e-mail bngkk@international.gc.ca; internet www.canadainternational.gc.ca/thailand-thailande; Ambassador RON HOFFMANN.

Chile: 83/17 Witthayu Pl., Soi Witthayu 1, Thanon Witthayu, Lumpini, Pathumwan, Bangkok 10330; tel. (2) 251-9470; fax (2) 2251-9475; e-mail embajada@chile-thai.com; internet www.chile-thai.com; Ambassador ALBERTO YOACHAM.

China, People's Republic: 57 Thanon Ratchadaphisek, Bangkok 10310; tel. (2) 245-7043; fax (2) 246-8247; e-mail chinaemb_th@mfa.gov.cn; internet www.chinaembassy.or.th/eng; Ambassador GUAN MU.

Cuba: Mela Mansion Apt 7AC, 5 Soi Sukhumvit 27, Klongtoey Nua, Wattana, Bangkok 10110; tel. (2) 665-2803; fax (2) 661-6560; e-mail embajada@th.embacuba.cu; internet embacuba.cubaminrex.cu/tailandiaing; Ambassador LÁZARO HERRERA MARTÍNEZ.

Czech Republic: 71/6 Soi Ruamrudi 2, Thanon Ploenchit, Bangkok 10330; tel. (2) 255-3027; fax (2) 253-7637; e-mail bangkok@embassy.mzv.cz; internet www.mfa.cz/bangkok; Ambassador IVAN HOTĚK.

Denmark: 10 Soi Attakarn Prasit, Thanon Sathorn Tai, Bangkok 10120; tel. (2) 343-1100; fax (2) 213-1752; e-mail bkkamb@um.dk; internet www.ambbangkok.um.dk; Ambassador MIKAEL HEMNITI WINTHER.

Egypt: 6 Las Colinas Bldg, 42nd Floor, Sukhumvit 21, Wattana, Bangkok 10110; tel. (2) 661-7184; fax (2) 262-0235; e-mail egyptemb@loxinfo.co.th; Ambassador MOHAMED ASHRAF MOHAMED KAMAL EL-KHOLY.

Finland: Amarin Tower, 16th Floor, 500 Thanon Ploenchit, Bangkok 10330; tel. (2) 250-8801; fax (2) 250-8802; e-mail sanomat.ban@formin.fi; internet www.finland.or.th; Ambassador SIRPA MÄENPÄÄ.

France: 35 Thanon Charoenkrung, Soi 36, Bangkok 10500; tel. (2) 657-5100; fax (2) 657-5111; e-mail ambassade@ambafrance-th.org; internet www.ambafrance-th.org; Ambassador GILDAS LE LIDEC.

Germany: 9 Thanon Sathorn Tai, Bangkok 10120; tel. (2) 287-9000; fax (2) 287-1776; e-mail info@bangkok.diplo.de; internet www.bangkok.diplo.de; Ambassador Dr HANNS HEINRICH SCHUMACHER.

Greece: Unit 25/5-9, 9th Floor, BKI/YWCA Bldg, 25 Thanon Sathorn Tai, Bangkok 10120; tel. (2) 679-1462; fax (2) 679-1463; e-mail gremb.ban@mfa.gr; internet www.mfa.gr/bangkok; Ambassador NIKOLAOS VAMVOUNAKIS.

Holy See: 217/1 Thanon Sathorn Tai, Bangkok 10120 (Apostolic Nunciature); tel. (2) 212-5853; fax (2) 212-0932; e-mail nuntiusth@csloxinfo.com; Apostolic Nuncio Most Rev. GIOVANNI D'ANIELLO (Titular Archbishop of Montemarano).

Hungary: Oak Tower, 20th Floor, President Park Condominium, 95 Sukhumvit Soi 24, Klongtoey, Prakanong, Bangkok 10110; tel. (2) 661-1150; fax (2) 661-1153; e-mail mission.bgk@kum.hu; internet www.mfa.gov.hu/emb/bangkok; Ambassador Dr ANDRAS BALOGH.

India: 46 Soi Prasarnmitr, 23 Thanon Sukhumvit, Bangkok 10110; tel. (2) 258-0300; fax (2) 258-4627; e-mail indiaemb@mozart.inet.co.th; internet indianembassy.gov.in/bangkok; Ambassador PINAK RANJAN CHAKRAVARTY.

Indonesia: 600–602 Thanon Phetchaburi, Ratchathewi, Bangkok 10400; tel. (2) 252-3135; fax (2) 255-1267; e-mail kukbkk@ksc.th.com; internet www.bangkok.deplu.go.id; Ambassador MOHAMMAD HATTA.

Iran: 215 Thanon Sukhumvit, Soi 49, Klongtan Nua, Wattana, Bangkok 10110; tel. (2) 390-0871; fax (2) 390-0867; e-mail info@iranembassy.or.th; internet www.iranembassy.or.th; Ambassador MAJID BIZMARK.

Israel: Ocean Tower II, 25th Floor, 75 Sukhumvit, Soi 19, Thanon Asoke, Bangkok 10110; tel. (2) 204-9200; fax (2) 204-9255; e-mail info@bangkok.mfa.gov.il; internet bangkok.mfa.gov.il; Ambassador ITZHAK SHOHAM.

Italy: 399 Thanon Nang Linchee, Tungmahamek, Yannawa, Bangkok 10120; tel. (2) 285-4090; fax (2) 285-4793; e-mail ambasciata.bangkok@esteri.it; internet www.ambbangkok.esteri.it; Ambassador MICHELANGELO PIPAN.

Japan: 177 Thanon Witthayu, Lumpini, Pathumwan, Bangkok 10330; tel. (2) 207-8500; fax (2) 207-8510; e-mail jis@eoj.or.th; internet www.th.emb-japan.go.jp; Ambassador SEIJI KOJIMA.

Kazakhstan: Suite 4301, 43rd Floor, JTC Bldg, 919/501 Thanon Silom, Bangrak, Bangkok 10500; tel. (2) 234-6365; fax (2) 234-6368; e-mail mail@kazembassythailand.org; internet www.kazembassythailand.org; Chargé d'affaires a.i. AMIR MUSIN.

Kenya: 62 Thonglor Soi 5, Thanon Sukhumvit 55, Klongtan, Wattana, Bangkok 10110; tel. (2) 712-5721; fax (2) 712-5720; Ambassador RICHARD TITUS EKAI.

Korea, Democratic People's Republic: 14 Mooban Suanlaemthong 2, Soi 28, Thanon Pattanakarn, Suan Luang, Bangkok 10250; tel. (2) 319-2686; fax (2) 318-6333; Ambassador AN SONG NAM.

Korea, Republic: 23 Thanon Thiam-Ruammit, Ratchadaphisek, Huay Kwang, Bangkok 10320; tel. (2) 247-7537; fax (2) 247-7535; e-mail koembth@gmail.com; internet tha.mofat.go.kr; Ambassador CHUNG HAE-MOON.

Kuwait: 100/44 Sathorn Nakhon Tower, Level 24A, Thanon Sathorn Nua, Bangrak, Bangkok 10500; tel. (2) 636-6600; fax (2) 636-7360; e-mail kuembassy@inet.co.th; Ambassador HAFEEZ MOHAMMED SALEM AL-AJMI.

Laos: 502/502/1–3 Soi Sahakarnpramoon, Thanon Pracha Uthit, Wangthonglang, Bangkok 10310; tel. (2) 539-6667; fax (2) 539-3827; e-mail sabaidee@bkklaoembassy.com; internet www.bkklaoembassy.com; Ambassador OUAN PHOMMACHACK.

THAILAND

Luxembourg: Q House Lumpini, 17th Floor, Thanon Sathorn Tai, Tungmahamek, Sathorn, Bangkok 10120; tel. (2) 677-7360; fax (2) 677-7364; e-mail bangkok.amb@mae.etat.lu; internet bangkok.mae.lu; Ambassador MARC UNGEHEUER.

Malaysia: 35 Thanon Sathorn Tai, Tungmahamek, Sathorn, Bangkok 10120; tel. (2) 629-6800; fax (2) 679-2208; e-mail malbangkok@kln.gov.my; internet www.kln.gov.my/web/tha_bangkok; Ambassador Dato' HUSNI ZAI BIN YAACOB.

Mexico: 21/60–62 Thai Wah Tower I, 20th Floor, Thanon Sathorn Tai, Sathorn, Bangkok 10120; tel. (2) 285-0995; fax (2) 285-0667; e-mail consular@mexicanembassythailand.com; internet www.sre.gob.mx/tailandia; Ambassador LUIS ARTURO PUENTE ORTEGA.

Mongolia: 100/3, Soi Ekamai 22, 63 Thanon Sukhumvit, Klongtan Nua, Wattana, Bangkok 10110; tel. (2) 381-1400; fax (2) 392-4199; e-mail mongemb@loxinfo.co.th; Ambassador LUVSANDOOGIIN DASHPÜREV.

Morocco: Sathorn City Tower, 12th Floor, 175 Thanon Sathorn Tai, Sathorn, Bangkok 10120; tel. (2) 679-5604; fax (2) 2679-5603; e-mail sifambkk@samarts.com; internet www.moroccoembassybangkok.org; Ambassador EL HASSANE ZAHID.

Myanmar: 132 Thanon Sathorn Nua, Bangkok 10500; tel. (2) 233-2237; fax (2) 236-6898; e-mail myanmarembassybkk@gmail.com; Ambassador AUNG THEIN.

Nepal: 189 Soi 71, Thanon Sukhumvit, Prakanong, Bangkok 10110; tel. (2) 390-2280; fax (2) 381-2406; e-mail nepembkk@asiaaccess.net.th; Ambassador NAVIN PRAKASH JUNG SHAH.

Netherlands: 15 Soi Tonson, Thanon Ploenchit, Lumpini, Pathumwan, Bangkok 10330; tel. (2) 309-5200; fax (2) 309-5205; e-mail ban@minbuza.nl; internet www.mfa.nl/ban; Ambassador TJACO VAN DEN HOUT.

New Zealand: M Thai Tower, 14th Floor, All Seasons Pl., 87 Thanon Witthayu, Lumpini, Pathumwan, Bangkok 10330; tel. (2) 254-2530; fax (2) 253-9045; e-mail nzembbkk@loxinfo.co.th; internet www.nzembassy.com/thailand; Ambassador BEDE GILBERT CORRY.

Nigeria: 412 Thanon Sukhumvit, Soi 71, Prakanong, Wattana, Bangkok 10110; tel. (2) 711-3076; fax (2) 392-6398; e-mail info@embnigeriabkk.com; Ambassador UMARU A. SULAIMAN.

Norway: UBC II Bldg, 18th Floor, 591 Thanon Sukhumvit, Soi 33, Bangkok 10110; tel. (2) 204-6500; fax (2) 262-0218; e-mail emb.bangkok@mfa.no; internet www.emb-norway.or.th; Ambassador KATJA NORDGAARD.

Oman: Saeng Thong Thani Tower, 32nd Floor, 82 Thanon Sathorn Nua, Bangkok 10500; tel. (2) 639-9380; fax (2) 639-9390; e-mail bangkok@mofa.gov.om; Ambassador HAFEEDH SALIM MOHAMED BA-OMAR.

Pakistan: 31 Soi Nana Nua, Thanon Sukhumvit 3, Bangkok 10110; tel. (2) 253-0288; fax (2) 253-0290; e-mail parepbnk@truemail.co.th; internet www.mofa.gov.pk/thailand; Ambassador SOHAIL MAHMOOD.

Panama: 1168/37 Lumpini Tower, 16th Floor, Tungmahamek, Sathorn, Bangkok 10120; tel. (2) 679-7988; fax (2) 679-7991; e-mail embajada@panathai.com; internet www.panathai.com; Ambassador ISAURO RAMON MORA BORRERO.

Peru: Glas Haus Bldg, 16th Floor, 1 Thanon Sukhumvit, Soi 25, Wattana, Bangkok 10110; tel. (2) 260-6243; fax (2) 260-6244; e-mail peru@peruthai.or.th; Ambassador CARLOS MANUEL VELASCO MENDIOLA.

Philippines: 760 Thanon Sukhumvit, cnr Soi 30/1, Klongtan, Klongtoey, Bangkok 10110; tel. (2) 259-0139; fax (2) 259-2809; e-mail inquiry@philembassy-bangkok.net; internet www.philembassy-bangkok.net; Ambassador ANTONIO V. RODRIGUEZ.

Poland: 100/81–82, Vongvanij Bldg B, 25th Floor, Thanon Rama IX, Huay Kwang, Bangkok 10310; tel. (2) 645-0367; fax (2) 645-0365; e-mail ampolbkk@polemb.or.th; internet www.bangkok.polemb.net; Ambassador JERZY BAYER.

Portugal: 26 Bush Lane, Thanon Charoenkrung, Bangkok 10500; tel. (2) 234-2123; fax (2) 238-4275; e-mail portemb@loxinfo.co.th; Ambassador ANTÓNIO FELIX MACHADO DE FARIA E MAYA.

Qatar: Capital Tower, 14th Floor, All Seasons Pl., 87/1 Thanon Witthayu, Lumpini, Pathumwan, Bangkok 10330; tel. (2) 660-1111; fax (2) 660-1122; e-mail info@qatarembassy.or.th; internet www.qatarembassy.or.th; Ambassador JABOER ALI HUSSEIN AL-DOUSARI.

Romania: 20/1 Soi Rajakhru, Phaholyothin Soi 5, Thanon Phaholyothin, Phaya Thai, Bangkok 10400; tel. (2) 617-1551; fax (2) 617-1113; e-mail romembnk@ksc.th.com; Chargé d'affaires a.i. MIHAI SION.

Russia: 78 Thanon Sap, Bangrak, Bangkok 10500; tel. (2) 234-9824; fax (2) 237-8488; e-mail rusembbangkok@rambler.ru; internet www.thailand.mid.ru; Ambassador ALEKSANDR MARIYASOV.

Saudi Arabia: 82 Saengthong Thani Bldg, 23rd & 24th Floors, Thanon Sathorn Nua, Silom, Bangrak, Bangkok 10500; tel. (2) 639-2999; fax (2) 639-2950; Chargé d'affaires NABIL H. H. ASHRI.

Singapore: 129 Thanon Sathorn Tai, Bangkok 10120; tel. (2) 286-2111; fax (2) 286-6966; e-mail singemb_bkk@sgmfa.gov.sg; internet www.mfa.gov.sg/bangkok; Ambassador PETER CHAN.

Slovakia: 25/9-4, BKI/YWCA Bldg, 9th Floor, Thanon Sathorn Tai, Thungmahamek, Bangkok 10120; tel. (2) 677-3445; fax (2) 677-3447; e-mail slovembassy@bangkok.truemail.co.th; Ambassador VASIL PYTEL.

South Africa: M-Thai Tower, Floor 12A, All Seasons Pl., 87 Thanon Witthayu, Pathumwan, Lumpini, Bangkok 10330; tel. (2) 659-2900; fax (2) 685-3500; e-mail saembbkk@loxinfo.co.th; internet www.saembbangkok.com; Ambassador DOUGLAS HARVEY MONRO GIBSON.

Spain: Lake Rajada Office Complex, 23rd Floor, Suite 98–99, 193 Thanon Ratchadaphisek, Klongtoey, Bangkok 10110; tel. (2) 661-8284; fax (2) 661-9220; e-mail emb.bangkok@maec.es; internet www.maec.es/subwebs/embajadas/bangkok; Ambassador DON IGNACIO SAGAZ.

Sri Lanka: Ocean Tower II, 13th Floor, 75/6–7 Sukhumvit, Soi 19, Klongtoey, Wattana, Bangkok 10110; tel. (2) 261-1934; fax (2) 261-1936; e-mail slemb@ksc.th.com; Ambassador JAYARATNA BANDA DISANAYAKA.

Sweden: First Pacific Pl., 20th Floor, 140 Thanon Sukhumvit, Bangkok 10110; tel. (2) 263-7200; fax (2) 263-7260; e-mail ambassaden.bangkok@foreign.ministry.se; internet www.swedenabroad.com/bangkok; Ambassador LENNART LINNÉR.

Switzerland: 35 Thanon Witthayu Nua, Lumpini, Pathumwan, Bangkok 10330; tel. (2) 253-0156; fax (2) 255-4481; e-mail ban.vertretung@eda.admin.ch; internet www.eda.admin.ch/bangkok; Ambassador CHRISTINE SCHRANER BURGENER.

Timor-Leste: Thanapoom Tower, 7th Floor, 1550 Thanon Petchaburi, Makasan, Ratchathewi, Bangkok 10400; tel. (2) 654-7501; fax (2) 654-7504; e-mail embdrtl_bkk@yahoo.com; Ambassador JOÃO FREITAS DE CÂMARA.

Turkey: 61/1 Soi Chatsan, Thanon Suthisarn, Huay Kwang, Bangkok 10310; tel. (2) 274-7262; fax (2) 274-7261; e-mail tcturkbe@cscoms.com; Ambassador AHMET OĞUZ ÇELIKKOL.

Ukraine: CRC Tower, 33rd Floor, All Seasons Pl., 87 Thanon Witthayu, Lumpini, Pathumwan, Bangkok 10330; tel. (2) 685-3216; fax (2) 685-3217; e-mail emb_th@mfa.gov.ua; internet www.mfa.gov.ua/thailand; Ambassador MARKIIAN CHUCHUK.

United Arab Emirates: CRC Tower, 29th Floor, All Seasons Pl., 87/2 Thanon Witthayu, Pathumwan, Bangkok 10330; tel. (2) 402-4000; fax (2) 402-4005; Ambassador MUHAMMAD ALI AHMAD OMRAN ASH-SHAMSI.

United Kingdom: 14 Thanon Witthayu, Lumpini, Pathumwan, Bangkok 10330; tel. (2) 305-8333; fax (2) 255-8619; e-mail info.bangkok@fco.gov.uk; internet ukinthailand.fco.gov.uk; Ambassador ASIF AHMAD.

USA: 95 Thanon Witthayu, Lumpini, Pathumwan, Bangkok 10330; tel. (2) 205-4000; fax (2) 254-1171; e-mail acsbkk@state.gov; internet bangkok.usembassy.gov; Ambassador ERIC G. JOHN.

Viet Nam: 83/1 Thanon Witthayu, Lumpini, Pathumwan, Bangkok 10330; tel. (2) 251-5836; fax (2) 251-7203; e-mail vnemb.th@mofa.gov.vn; internet www.vietnamembassy-thailand.org; Ambassador NGO DUC THANG.

Judicial System

SUPREME COURT

The Supreme Court (Sarn Dika) is the final court of appeal in all civil, bankruptcy, labour, juvenile and criminal cases. Its quorum consists of three judges. However, the Court occasionally sits in plenary session to determine cases of exceptional importance or where there are reasons for reconsideration or overruling of its own precedents. The quorum, in such cases, is one-half of the total number of judges in the Supreme Court.

President (Chief Justice): SOBCHOK SUKHAROM, 6 Thanon Ratchadamnoen Nai, Bangkok 10200; tel. (2) 221-3161; fax (2) 226-4389; e-mail supremec@judiciary.go.th; internet www.supremecourt.or.th.

Vice-Presidents: PHICHIT KHAMFAENG, THEERARAT PHATTARANWAT, MONGKHOL THAPTHIENG, PANYA SUTHIBODI, WATTANCHAI CHOTICHUTRAKUL, RUNGROJ RUENRENGWONG.

COURT OF APPEALS

The Court of Appeals (Sarn Uthorn) has appellate jurisdiction in all civil, bankruptcy, juvenile and criminal matters. Appeals from all the Courts of First Instance throughout the country, except the central Labour Court, are heard in this Court. Two judges form a quorum.

Chief Justice: KAIT CHATANIBAND, Thanon Ratchadaphisek, Chatuchak, Bangkok 10900.

THAILAND

Deputy Chief Justices: PORNCHAI SMATTAVET, CHATISAK THAMMASAKDI, SOMPOB CHOTIKAVANICH, SOMPHOL SATTAYA-APHITARN.

COURTS OF FIRST INSTANCE

The Courts of First Instance (Sarn Chunton) include the categories of general courts (Civil Courts, Criminal Courts, Provincial Courts and Kwaeng Courts), juvenile and family courts, and specialized courts (Central Labour Court, Central Tax Court, Central Intellectual Property and International Trade Court, Central Bankruptcy Court).

Religion

Buddhism is the predominant religion, professed by more than 95% of Thailand's total population. About 4% of the population are Muslims, being ethnic Malays, mainly in the south. Most of the immigrant Chinese are Confucians. The Christians number about 427,000, mainly in Bangkok and northern Thailand. Brahmins, Hindus and Sikhs number about 85,000.

BUDDHISM

Sangha Supreme Council

The Religious Affairs Dept, Thanon Ratchadamnoen Nok, Bangkok 10300; tel. (2) 281-6080; fax (2) 281-5415.
Governing body of Thailand's 350,000 monks, nuns and novices.

Supreme Patriarch of Thailand: NYANASAMVARA SUVADDHANA.

The Buddhist Association of Thailand: 41 Thanon Phra Aditya, Bangkok 10200; tel. (2) 281-5693; fax (2) 281-9564; f. 1934; under royal patronage; 7,139 mems; Pres. NUTTAPASH INTUPUTI.

CHRISTIANITY

The Roman Catholic Church

For ecclesiastical purposes, Thailand comprises two archdioceses and eight dioceses. At 31 December 2006 there were an estimated 326,978 adherents in the country, representing about 0.5% of the population.

Catholic Bishops' Conference of Thailand

122/11 Soi Naksuwan, Thanon Nonsi, Yannawa, Bangkok 10120; tel. (2) 681-5365; fax (2) 681-5370; e-mail cbct_th@hotmail.com; f. 1969; Pres. Cardinal MICHAEL MICHAI KITBUNCHU (Archbishop of Bangkok).

Archbishop of Bangkok: Cardinal MICHAEL MICHAI KITBUNCHU, Assumption Cathedral, 51 Thanon Oriental, Charoenkrung 40, Bangrak, Bangkok 10500; tel. (2) 237-1031; fax (2) 237-1033; e-mail arcdibkk@loxinfo.co.th.

Archbishop of Tharé and Nonseng: Bishop LOUIS CHAMNIERN SANTISUKNIRAN, POB 6, Amphur Muang, Sakon Nakhon 47000; tel. (42) 711-272; fax (42) 712-023.

The Anglican Communion

Thailand is within the jurisdiction of the Anglican Bishop of Singapore (q.v.).

Other Christian Churches

Baptist Church Foundation (Foreign Mission Board): 90 Soi 2, Thanon Sukhumvit, Bangkok 10110; tel. (2) 252-7078; Mission Admin. TOM WILLIAMS (POB 832, Bangkok 10501).

Church of Christ in Thailand: 328 Thanon Phaya Thai, Phaya Thai, Bangkok 10400; tel. (2) 214-6001; fax (2) 214-6010; e-mail webmaster_cct@cct.or.th; internet www.cct.or.th; f. 1934; c. 100,000 communicants; Moderator Rev. Dr BOONRATNA BOAYEN; Gen. Sec. Rev. Dr SINT KIMHACHANDRA.

ISLAM

Office of the Chularajmontri: 100 Soi Prom Pak, Thanon Sukhumvit, Bangkok 10110; Sheikh Al-Islam (Chularajmontri) Haji ASIS PITHAKKHUMPOL.

BAHÁ'Í FAITH

National Spiritual Assembly: 1415 Sriwara Soi 3/4, Ladprao Soi 94, Wangthonglang, Bangkapi, Bangkok 10310; tel. (2) 530-7417; fax (2) 935-6515; e-mail nsa@bahai.or.th; internet www.thai-bahais.org; f. 1964; c. 15,000 mems resident in 76 provinces.

The Press

DAILIES

Thai Language

Baan Muang: 1 Soi Pluem-Manee, Thanon Vibhavadi Rangsit, Bangkok 10900; tel. (2) 513-3101; fax (2) 513-3106; internet www.banmuang.co.th; f. 1972; Editor MANA PRAEBHAND; circ. 200,000.

Daily News: 1/4 Thanon Vibhavadi Rangsit, Laksi, Bangkok 10210; tel. (2) 561-1456; fax (2) 940-9875; internet www.dailynews.co.th; f. 1964; Editor PRACHA HETRAKUL; circ. 800,000.

Khao Sod (Fresh News): 12 Thanon Tethsaban Naruaman, Prachanivate 1, Chatuchak, Bangkok 10900; tel. (2) 580-0021; fax (2) 580-2301; e-mail matisale@matichon.co.th; internet www.matichon.co.th/khaosod; Editor-in-Chief KIATICHAI PONGPANICH; circ. 650,000.

Kom Chad Luek (Sharp, Clear, Deep): 44 Moo 10, Thanon Bangna Trad, Km 4.5, Bang Na, Bangkok 10260; tel. (2) 325-5555; fax (2) 317-2071; internet www.komchadluek.com; Editor ADISAL LIMPRUNGPATAKIT.

Krungthep Turakij Daily: Nation Multimedia Group Public Co Ltd, 44 Moo 10, Thanon Bangna Trad, Bang Na, Prakanong, Bangkok 10260; tel. (2) 317-0042; fax (2) 317-1489; e-mail kteditor@nationgroup.com; internet www.bangkokbiznews.com; f. 1987; Publr and Group Editor SUTHICHAI YOON; Editor DUANGKAMOL CHOTANA; circ. 75,882.

Manager Daily: Baan Phra Atit, 102/1 Thanon Phra Atit, Phra Nakorn, Bangkok; internet www.manager.co.th; f. 1990; Editor KHUNTHONG LORSERIVANICH.

Matichon: 12 Thanon Tethsaban Naruaman, Prachanivate 1, Chatuchak, Bangkok 10900; tel. (2) 580-0021; fax (2) 580-2301; e-mail matisale@matichon.co.th; internet www.matichon.co.th; f. 1977; Man. Editor PRASONG LERTRATANAVISUTH; circ. 550,000.

Naew Na (Frontline): 96 Moo 3, Thanon Vibhavadi Rangsit, Talaat Bang Khen, Bangkok 10210; tel. (2) 973-4250; fax (2) 552-3800; e-mail naewna@naewna.com; internet www.naewna.com; Editor WANCHAI WONGMEECHAI; circ. 200,000.

Post Today: 136 Thanon Na Ranong, Sonthorn Kosa, Klongtoey, Bangkok 10110; tel. (2) 240-3700; fax (2) 671-3147; e-mail nhakranl@posttoday.com; internet www.posttoday.com; f. 2003; business news; Editor NA KAL LAOHAWILAI; circ. 100,000.

Siam Keela (Siam Sport): 66/26–29, Moo 12, Soi Ram Indra 40, Thanon Ram Indra, Klong Kum, Bueng Kum, Bangkok 10230; tel. (2) 508-8000; e-mail webmaster@siamsport.co.th; internet www.siamsport.co.th; f. 1973.

Siam Rath (Siam Nation): 12 Mansion 6, Thanon Ratchadamnoen, Bangkok 10200; tel. (2) 622-1810; fax (2) 224-1982; e-mail siamrath@siamrath.co.th; internet www.siamrath.co.th; f. 1950; Editor CHACHAWAN KHONGUDOM; circ. 120,000.

Thai Post: 1852 Thanon Kasemrat, Klongtoey, Bangkok 10110; tel. (2) 240-2612; fax (2) 249-0295; internet www.thaipost.net; Editor ROJ NGAMMAEN.

Thai Rath: 1 Thanon Vibhavadi Rangsit, Bangkok 10900; tel. (2) 272-1030; fax (2) 272-1324; e-mail feedback@thairath.co.th; internet www.thairath.co.th; f. 1948; Editor SORAWUT WACHARAPHOL; circ. 800,000.

Than Setakij (Economic Base): 222 Than Setakij Bldg, Thanon Vibhavadi Rangsit, Chatuchak, Bangkok 10900; tel. (2) 513-9896; e-mail webmaster@thannews.th.com; internet www.thannews.th.com.

English Language

Bangkok Post: Bangkok Post Bldg, 136 Soi Na Ranong, Klongtoey, Bangkok 10110; tel. (2) 240-3700; fax (2) 240-3665; e-mail bpadmin@bangkokpost.co.th; internet www.bangkokpost.com; f. 1946; morning; Editor-in-Chief PICHAI CHUENSUKSAWADI.

Business Day: Olympia Thai Tower, 22nd Floor, 444 Thanon Ratchadaphisek, Huay Kwang, Bangkok 10310; tel. (2) 512-3579; fax (2) 512-3565; e-mail info@bday.net; internet www.biz-day.com; f. 1994; business news; Man. Editor CHATCHAI YENBAMROONG.

The Nation: 44 Moo 10, Editorial Bldg, 6th Floor, Thanon Bangna Trad, Km 4.5, Bang Na, Phra Khanong, Bangkok 10260; tel. (2) 338-3333; fax (2) 338-3334; e-mail editor@nationgroup.com; internet www.nationmultimedia.com; f. 1971; morning; Publr and Group Editor SUTHICHAI YOON; Editor TULSATHIT TAPTIM; circ. 55,000.

Chinese Language

Sing Sian Yit Pao Daily News: 267 Thanon Charoenkrung, Talad-Noi, Bangkok 10100; tel. (2) 222-6601; fax (2) 225-4663; e-mail info@singsian.com; internet www.singsian.com; f. 1950; Man. Dir NETRA RUTHAIYANONT; Editor TAWEE YODPETCH; circ. 70,000.

THAILAND

Tong Hua Daily News: 877–879 Thanon Charoenkrung, Talad-Noi, Bangkok 10100; tel. (2) 236-9172; fax (2) 238-5286; Editor CHART PAYONITHIKARN; circ. 85,000.

WEEKLIES
Thai Language

Bangkok Weekly: 533–539 Thanon Sri Ayudhya, Bangkok 10400; tel. (2) 245-2546; fax (2) 247-3410; Editor VICHIT ROJANAPRABHA.

Mathichon Weekly Review: 12 Thanon Tethsaban Naruaman, Prachanivate 1, Chatuchak, Bangkok 10900; tel. (2) 580-0021; fax (2) 580-2301; e-mail weekly@matichon.co.th; internet www.matichon.co.th/weekly; Editor RUANGCHAI SABNIRAND; circ. 300,000.

Sakul Thai: 58 Soi 36, Thanon Sukhumvit, Bangkok 10110; tel. (2) 258-5861; fax (2) 258-9130; internet www.sakulthai.com; Editor SANTI SONGSEMSAWAS.

Siam Rath Weekly Review: 12 Mansion 6, Thanon Rajdamnern, Bangkok 10200; Editor PRACHUAB THONGURAI.

English Language

Bangkok Post Weekly Review: U-Chuliang Bldg, 3rd Floor, 968 Thanon Phra Ram Si, Bangkok 10500; tel. (2) 233-8030; fax (2) 238-5430; f. 1989; Editor ANUSSORN THAVISIN; circ. 10,782.

FORTNIGHTLIES
Thai Language

Darathai: 9-9/1 Soi Sri Ak-Sorn, Thanon Chuapleung, Tungmahamek, Sathorn, Bangkok 10120; tel. (2) 249-1576; fax (2) 249-1575; f. 1954; television and entertainment; Editor USA BUKKAVESA; circ. 80,000.

Dichan: 1400 Thai Bldg, Thanon Phra Ram Si, Bangkok; tel. (2) 249-0351; fax (2) 249-9455; e-mail dichan@pacific.co.th; Man. Editor KHUNYING TIPYAVADI PRAMOJ NA AYUDHYA.

Praew: 65/101–103 Thanon Chaiyaphruk, Taling Chan, Bangkok; tel. (2) 422-9999; fax (2) 434-3555; e-mail chantana@amarin.co.th; internet www.praew.com; f. 1979; women and fashion; Editorial Dir SUPAWADEE KOMARADAT; Editor CHANTANA YUTDHANAPHUM; circ. 150,000.

MONTHLIES

Bangkok 30: 98/5–6 Thanon Phra Arthit, Bangkok 10200; tel. (2) 282-5467; fax (2) 280-1302; f. 1986; Thai; business; Publr SONCHAI LIMTHONGKUL; Editor BOONSIRI NAMBOONSRI; circ. 65,000.

Chao Krung: 12 Mansion 6, Thanon Rajdamnern, Bangkok 10200; Thai; Editor NOPPHORN BUNYARIT.

The Dharmachaksu (Dharma-vision): Foundation of Mahamakut Rajavidyalai, 241 Thanon Phra Sumeru, Bangkok 10200; tel. and fax (2) 629-1391; e-mail books@mahamakuta.inet.co.th; internet www.mahamakuta.inet.co.th; f. 1894; Thai; Buddhism and related subjects; Editor SAENG CHANDR-NGAM; circ. 5,000.

Grand Prix: 4/299 Moo 5, Soi Ladplakhao 66, Thanon Ladplakhao, Bangkhen, Bangkok 10220; tel. (2) 971-6450; fax (2) 971-6469; e-mail pinyo@grandprixgroup.com; internet www.grandprixgroup.com/gpi/maggrandprix/grandprix.asp; f. 1970; Editor PINYO SILPASARTDUMRONG; circ. 80,000.

The Investor: Pansak Bldg, 4th Floor, 138/1 Thanon Phetchaburi, Ratchathawi, Bangkok 10400; tel. (2) 282-8166; f. 1968; English language; business, industry, finance and economics; Editor TOS PATUMSEN; circ. 6,000.

Kasikorn: Dept of Agriculture, Catuchak, Bangkok 10900; tel. (2) 561-2825; fax (2) 579-4406; e-mail pannee.v@doa.in.th; internet www.doa.go.th; f. 1928; Thai; agriculture and agricultural research; Editor-in-Chief SOPIDA HE-MAKOM; Editor PANNEE WICHACHOO.

Look: 1/54 Thanon Sukhumvit 30, Pra Khanong, Bangkok 10110; tel. (2) 258-1265; Editor KANOKWAN MILINDAVANIJ.

Look East: 52/38 Soi Saladaeng 2, Silom Condominium, 12th Floor, Thanon Silom, Bangkok 10500; tel. (2) 235-6185; fax (2) 236-6764; f. 1969; English; Editor ASHA SEHGAL; circ. 30,000.

Metro Magazine: 109 Moo 8, 7th Floor, Srithepthai Bldg, Thanon Bangna Trad, Bang Na, Bangkok 10260; tel. (2) 746-7250; fax (2) 746-7266; e-mail mon@bkkmetro.com; internet www.bkkmetro.com; f. 1996; English language; lifestyle, events listings and consumer-oriented articles; Publr and Editor-in-Chief MUNINTRA SAENGSUVIMOL; circ. 35,000.

Motorcycle Magazine: 4/299 Moo 5, Soi Ladplakhao 66, Thanon Ladplakhao, Anusawari, Bangkhan, Bangkok 10220; tel. (2) 522-1731; fax (2) 522-1730; e-mail webmaster@grandprixgroup.com; internet www.grandprixgroup.com; f. 1972; publ. by Grand Prix Int. Co Ltd; Publr PRACHIN EAMLAMNOW; Editor PRAWIT PRAKEENWINCHA; circ. 55,000.

Saen Sanuk: 50 Soi Saeng Chan, Thanon Sukhumvit 42, Bangkok 10110; tel. (2) 392-0052; fax (2) 391-1486; English; travel and tourist attractions in Thailand; Editor SOMTAWIN KONGSAWATKIAT; circ. 85,000.

Sarakadee Magazine: 28-30 Soi Parinayok, Bangkok 10200; tel. (2) 281-6110; fax (2) 282-7003; e-mail admin@sarakadee.com; internet www.sarakadee.com; Thai; events, culture and nature.

Satawa Liang: 689 Thanon Wang Burapa, Bangkok; Thai; Editor THAMRONGSAK SRICHAND.

Villa Wina Magazine: Chalerm Ketr Theatre Bldg, 3rd Floor, Bangkok; Thai; Editor BHONGSAKDI PIAMLAP.

NEWS AGENCY

Thai News Agency (TNA): 63/1 Thanon Phra Rama 9, Huay Kwang, Bangkok 10320; operated by MCOT PCL; news service in Thai and English.

PRESS ASSOCIATIONS

Confederation of Thai Journalists: 299 Thanon Ratchasima, Dusit, Bangkok 10300; tel. (2) 668-9422; fax (2) 668-7505; internet www.ctj.in.th; Pres. CHATRI LIMCHAROON; Sec.-Gen. NATTAYA CHETCHOTIROS.

Press Association of Thailand: 299 Thanon Ratchasima, Dusit, Bangkok 10300; tel. (2) 537-3777; fax (2) 537-3888; e-mail webmaster@thaipressasso.com; internet www.thaipressasso.com; f. 1941; Pres. MANIT LUEPRAPHAI.

Thai Journalists' Association: 538/1 Thanon Samsen, Dusit, Bangkok 10300; tel. (2) 668-9422; fax (2) 668-7505; e-mail reporter@inet.co.th; internet www.tja.or.th; Pres. PRASONG LERTRATANAWISUTE.

There are also regional press organizations and journalists' organizations.

Publishers

Advance Media: 1400 Rama IV Shopping Centre, Klongtoey, Bangkok 10110; tel. (2) 249-0358; Man. PRASERTSAK SIVASAHONG.

Amarin Printing and Publishing Public Co Ltd: 65/101–103 Moo 4, Thanon Chaiyaphruk, Taling Chan, Bangkok 10170; tel. (2) 422-9999; fax (2) 434-3555; e-mail info@amarin.co.th; internet www.amarin.com; f. 1976; general books and magazines; CEO METTA UTAKAPAN.

Bhannakij Trading: 34 Thanon Nakornsawan, Bangkok 10100; tel. (2) 282-5520; fax (2) 282-0076; Thai fiction, school textbooks; Man. SOMSAK TECHAKASHEM.

Chalermnit Publishing Co Ltd: 108 Thanon Sukhumvit, Soi 53, Bangkok 10110; tel. (2) 662-6264; fax (2) 662-6265; e-mail chalermnit@hotmail.com; internet www.chalermnit.com; f. 1937; dictionaries, history, literature, guides to Thai language, works on Thailand and South-East Asia; Man. Dir Dr PARICHART JUMSAI.

Prae Pittaya Ltd: POB 914, 716–718 Wangburabha, Bangkok 10200; tel. (2) 221-4283; fax (2) 222-1286; general Thai books; Man. CHIT PRAEPANICH.

Praphansarn: 674–676 Thanon Charansanitwong, Bang Yee Khan, Bang Plat, Bangkok 10700; tel. (2) 435-1671; fax (2) 434-6812; e-mail editor@praphansarn.com; internet www.praphansarn.com; f. 1961; Thai pocket books; Man. Dir SUPHOL TAECHATADA.

Ruamsarn (1977): 864 Wangburabha, Thanon Panurangsri, Bangkok 10200; tel. (2) 221-6483; fax (2) 222-2036; f. 1951; fiction and history; Man. PITI TAWEWATANASARN.

Silkworm Books: 6 Thanon Suksasem, T. Suthep, Muang, Chiang Mai 50200; tel. (53) 226-161; fax (53) 226-643; e-mail info@silkwormbooks.com; internet www.silkwormbooks.com; f. 1991; South-East Asian studies; English language.

Suksapan Panit (Business Organization of Teachers' Institute): 128/1 Thanon Ratchasima, Bangkok 10300; tel. (2) 416-7403; internet www.suksapan.or.th; f. 1950; general, textbooks, children's, pocket books; Pres. PANOM KAW KAMNERD.

Thai Watana Panich: 905 Thanon Rama 3, Yannawa, Bangkok 10120; tel. (2) 683-3333; fax (2) 683-2000; e-mail webmaster@twp.co.th; internet www.twp.co.th; children's, school textbooks; Man. Dir INTIRA BUNNAG.

White Lotus Co Ltd: POB 1141, Bangkok 10501; tel. (3) 823-9883; fax (3) 823-9885; e-mail ande@loxinfo.co.th; internet whitelotusbooks.com; f. 1972; regional interests, incl. art and culture, history, sociology and natural history; Publr DIETHARD ANDE.

THAILAND

Directory

PUBLISHERS' ASSOCIATION

Publishers' and Booksellers' Association of Thailand (PUBAT): 83/159 Moo 6, Thanon Ngam Wong Wan, Thung Song Hong, Lak Si, Bangkok 10210; tel. (2) 954-9560; fax (2) 954-9565; e-mail info@pubat.or.th; internet www.pubat.or.th; f. 1960; organizes national book fairs and provides promotional opportunities for publishers; Pres. RITRUAN ARAMCHAROEN; Gen. Sec. SUCHADA SAHATKUL.

Broadcasting and Communications

TELECOMMUNICATIONS

National Telecommunications Commission (NTC): 87 Thanon Phaholyothin, Soi 8, Phayatai, Bangkok 10400; tel. (2) 271-0151; fax (2) 271-3516; e-mail 1200@ntc.or.th; internet www.ntc.or.th; f. 2004; responsible for regulation and administration of telecommunications industry; Chair. Prof. PRASIT PRAPINMONGKOLKARN; Sec.-Gen. TAKORN TANTASITH (acting).

Advanced Info Service Public Co Ltd: 414 Thanon Phaholyothin, Shinawatra Tower I, Phaya Thai, Bangkok 10400; tel. (2) 299-5000; fax (2) 299-5719; e-mail callcenter@ais.co.th; internet www.ais.co.th; mobile telephone network operator providing 3G (third generation) cellular services; Chair. ALLEN LEW KEONG; CEO WICHIAN MEKTRAKARN.

CAT Telecom Public Co Ltd: 99 Thanon Chaengwattana, Moo 3, Laksi, Bangkok 10210-0298; tel. (2) 104-3000; fax (2) 104-3088; e-mail pr@cattelecom.com; internet www.cattelecom.com; f. 2003; est. following division of Communications Authority of Thailand (CAT); originally state-owned; corporatized in 2003; telecommunications and related services; Chair. NATHI PREMRASMI; Pres. JIRAYUT RUNGSRITHONG.

Samart Corpn Public Co Ltd: 99/1 Moo 4, Software Park Bldg, 35th Floor, Thanon Chaengwattana, Pakkred, Nonthaburi, Bangkok 11120; tel. (2) 502-6000; fax (2) 502-6186; e-mail nikhil.a@samartcorp.com; internet www.samartcorp.com; f. 1952; telecommunications installation and distribution; Chair. TONGCHAT HONGLADAROMP; Exec. Chair. and CEO CHAROENRATH VILAILUCK.

Thai Telephone and Telecommunication Public Co Ltd (TT&T): 252/30 Muang Thai Phatra Complex Tower 1, 24th Floor, Thanon Ratchadaphisek, Huay Kwang, Bangkok 10320; tel. (2) 693-2100; fax (2) 693-2124; e-mail icare@ttt.co.th; internet www.ttt.co.th; f. 1992; distributors of telecommunications equipment and services; Chair. SONGRIT KUSOMROSANANAN; Pres. PRACHUAB TANTINONDA.

TOT Public Co Ltd: 89/2 Moo 3, Thanon Chaengwattana, Thung Song Hong, Laksi, Bangkok 10210; tel. (2) 240-0701; e-mail prtot@tot.co.th; internet www.tot.co.th; f. 2002; state-owned; fmrly Telephone Organization of Thailand; name changed as above in 2005; telephone operator; de facto regulator; Chair. AREEPONG BHOOCHA-OOM; Pres. VARUT SUWAKORN.

Total Access Communications Public Co Ltd: 319 Chamchuri Sq. Bldg, 22nd–41st Floors, Thanon Phaya Thai, Pathumwan, Bangkok 10330; tel. (2) 202-8000; fax (2) 202-8929; e-mail ir@dtac.co.th; internet www.dtac.co.th; f. 1989; mobile telephone network operator; 41.46% owned by United Communication Industry Public Co Ltd; 29.94% owned by Telenor Asia Pte Ltd; Chair. BOONCHAI BENCHAROGKUL; CEO TORE JOHNSEN.

True Corpn PCL: 18 True Tower, Thanon Ratchadaphisek, Huay Kwang, Bangkok 10310; tel. (2) 643-1111; fax (2) 643-1651; internet www.truecorp.co.th/eng/index.jsp; f. 1990; est. under the name Telecomasia Corpn PCL; name changed as above in 2004; telecommunications services; Chair. DHANIN CHEARAVANONT; Pres. and CEO SUPHACHAI CHEARAVANONT.

True Move: 18 True Tower, Thanon Ratchadaphisek, Huay Kwang, Bangkok 10310; tel. (2) 647-5000; internet www.truemove.com; f. 2002; fmrly TA Orange Co Ltd; name changed as above in 2005; mobile telephone network operator; Chief Exec. SUPHACHAI CHEARAVANONT.

United Communication Industry Public Co Ltd (UCOM): 333/3 Chai Bldg, 18th Floor, Thanon Vibhavadi Rangsit, Ladyao, Chatuchak, Bangkok 10900; tel. (2) 202-8000; fax (2) 202-8929; e-mail ir.ucom@dtac.co.th; internet www.ucom.co.th; telecommunications service provider; Chair. SRIBHUMI SUKHANETR; Pres. and Chief Exec. BOONCHAI BENCHARONGKUL.

BROADCASTING

Regulatory Authority

Radio and Television Executive Committee (RTEC): Programme, Administration and Law Section, Division of RTEC Works, Government Public Relations Dept, Thanon Ratchadamnoen Klang, Phra Nakhon Region, Bangkok 10200; constituted under Broadcasting and TV Rule 1975, the cttee consists of 17 reps from 14 govt agencies and controls the administrative, legal, technical and programming aspects of broadcasting in Thailand; Dir-Gen. BOWON TECHAINDRA.

Radio

National Broadcasting Services of Thailand (NBT): 236 Thanon Vibhavadi Rangsit, Huay Kwang, Bangkok 10320; tel. (2) 277-8181; fax (2) 277-8182; internet nbt.prd.go.th; f. 1930; govt-controlled; broadcasts educational, entertainment, cultural and news programmes on six national networks; operates more than 150 stations throughout Thailand; external services in French and English commenced in 1938; currently broadcasts in 12 languages; Dir TUENJAI SINTHUVNIK.

Ministry of Education Broadcasting Service: Centre for Innovation and Technology, Ministry of Education, Bangkok; tel. (2) 246-0026; f. 1954; morning programmes for schools (Mon.–Fri.); afternoon and evening programmes for general public (daily); Dir of Centre PISAN SIWAYABRAHM.

Pituksuntirad Radio Stations: stations at Bangkok, Nakorn Ratchasima, Chiang Mai, Pitsanuloke and Songkla; programmes in Thai; Dir-Gen. PAITOON WAIJANYA.

Radio Saranrom: Thanon Ratchadamnoen, POB 2-131, Bangkok 10200; tel. (2) 224-4904; fax (2) 226-1825; internet www.mfa.go.th/web/151.php; f. 1968 as Voice of Free Asia; name changed as above in 1998; operated by the Ministry of Foreign Affairs; broadcasts in Thai; Dir of Broadcasting PAIBOON KUSKUL.

Television

Bangkok Broadcasting & TV Co Ltd (Channel 7): 998/1 Soi Sirimitr, Phaholyothin 18/1, Chatuchak, Bangkok 10900; tel. (2) 610-0777; fax (2) 272-0010; e-mail prdept@ch7.com; internet www.ch7.com; commercial.

Bangkok Entertainment Co Ltd (Channel 3): 3199 Maleenont Tower, Thanon Phra Ram IV, Klong Ton, Klongtoey, Bangkok 10110; tel. (2) 204-3333; fax (2) 204-1384; e-mail info@thaitv3.com; internet www.thaitv3.com; Programme Dir PRAVIT MALEENONT.

MCOT Public Co Ltd: 63/1 Thanon Phra Rama IX, Huay Kuang, Bangkok 10310; tel. (2) 201-6388; fax (2) 245-1855; e-mail ir@mcot.net; internet www.mcot.net; f. 1955; est. as Thai Television Co Ltd; named changed to The Mass Communication Org. of Thailand in 1977; present name adopted 2004; operates Modernine TV (fmrly Channel 9) and a satellite television channel; also operates radio stations and Thai News Agency; Chair. Dr SURAPON NITIKRAIPOJ; Pres. TANAWAT WANSOM.

National Broadcasting Services of Thailand (NBT): internet nbttv.prd.go.th; (see radio); operates TV Channel 11; parent station of eight regional TV networks.

The Royal Thai Army Television HSA-TV (Channel 5): 210 Thanon Phaholyothin, Sanam Pao, Bangkok 10400; tel. (2) 279-2397; fax (2) 271-0930; e-mail webadmin@tv5.co.th; internet www.tv5.co.th; f. 1958; operates channels nation-wide; Dir-Gen. Maj.-Gen. KITTITAT PANECHAPHAN.

Thai Public Broadcasting Service: 1010 Thanon Vibhavadi Rangsit, Chatuchak, Bangkok 10900; tel. (2) 791-1385; fax (2) 791-1383; e-mail people@thaipbs.or.th; internet www.thaipbs.or.th; f. 2008; succeeded the former iTV.

Thai TV Global Network: c/o Royal Thai Army HSA-TV, 210 Thanon Phaholyothin, Phaya Thai, Bangkok 10400; tel. (2) 278-1697; fax (2) 615-2066; e-mail tgn_mail@yahoo.com; internet www.thaitvglobal.com; established with the co-operation of all stations; distributes selected news, information and entertainment programmes from domestic stations for transmission to 170 countries world-wide via six satellite networks; Chair. Maj.-Gen. SOONTHORN SOPHONSIRI.

Finance

(cap. = capital; p.u. = paid up; res = reserves; dep. = deposits; m. = million; brs = branches; amounts in baht)

BANKING

Central Bank

Bank of Thailand: 273 Thanon Samsen, Bangkhunprom, Bangkok 10200; tel. (2) 283-5353; fax (2) 280-0449; e-mail webmaster@bot.or.th; internet www.bot.or.th; f. 1942; bank of issue; cap. 20m., res −74,116.5m., dep. 3,141,445.8m. (Dec. 2009); Gov. PRASARN TRAIRATVORAKUL; 4 brs.

Commercial Banks

Bangkok Bank Public Co Ltd: 333 Thanon Silom, Bangrak, Bangkok 10500; tel. (2) 231-4333; fax (2) 231-4742; e-mail info@

THAILAND

bangkokbank.com; internet www.bangkokbank.com; f. 1944; cap. 19,088.4m., res 241,432.7m., dep. 1,342,977.3m. (Dec. 2009); 49% foreign-owned; Chair. KOSIT PANPIEMRAS; Pres. CHARTSIRI SOPHONPANICH; 656 local brs, 22 overseas brs.

Bank of Ayudhya Public Co Ltd: 1222 Thanon Rama III, Bang Phongphang, Yan Nawa, Bangkok 10120; tel. (2) 296-2000; fax (2) 683-1484; e-mail webmaster@krungsri.com; internet www.krungsri.com; f. 1945; cap. 60,741.4m., res 21,074.3m., dep. 569,987.2m. (Dec. 2009); Pres. MARK JOHN ARNOLD; Chair. VERAPHAN TEEPSUWAN; 384 local brs, 3 overseas brs.

CIMB Thai Bank Public Co Ltd: 44 Thanon Langsuan, Lumpini, Pathumwan, Bangkok 10330; tel. (2) 626-7000; fax (2) 573-3333; e-mail cimbthai.carecenter@cimbthai.com; internet www.cimbthai.com; f. 1998; fmrly BankThai Public Co Ltd, name changed as above 2009; cap. 6,674.7m., res 768.5m., dep. 98,583.2m. (Dec. 2009); Chair. CHAKRAMON PHASUKAVANICH; Pres. SUBHAK SIRAWAKSA; 98 brs.

Kasikorn Bank Public Co Ltd: 1 Soi Ratburana 27/1, Thanon Ratburana, Bangkok 10140; tel. (2) 888-8800; fax (2) 888-8882; e-mail info@kasikornbank.com; internet www.kasikornbank.com; f. 1945; fmrly Thai Farmers Bank PCL; name changed as above April 2003; cap. 23,932.6m., res 33,288m., dep. 1,038,818.8m. (Dec. 2009); 48.98% foreign-owned; Chair. BANYONG LAMSAM; Pres. and CEO BANTHOON LAMSAM; 508 local brs, 4 overseas brs.

Kiatnakin Bank Public Co Ltd: Amarin Tower, 11th Floor, 500 Thanon Ploenchit, Pathumwan, Bangkok 10330; tel. (2) 680-3333; fax (2) 256-9933; internet www.kiatnakinbank.com; f. 1971; est. as Kiatnakin Finance and Securities Co Ltd; name changed in 1999 to Kiatnakin Finance Public Co Ltd following separation of its finance and securities businesses; present name adopted 2005; Chair. SUPOL WATTANAVEKIN; Pres. TAWATCHAI SUDTIKITPISAIN; 16 brs.

Krung Thai Bank Public Co Ltd (State Commercial Bank of Thailand): 35 Thanon Sukhumvit, Klongtoey, Bangkok 10110; tel. (2) 255-2222; fax (2) 255-9391; e-mail call@contactcenter.ktb.co.th; internet www.ktb.co.th; f. 1966; cap. 57,604.0m., res 10,429.3m., dep. 1,283,508.6m. (Dec. 2009); taken under the control of the central bank in 1998, pending transfer to private sector; merged with First Bangkok City Bank PCL in 1999; Chair. DUSIT NONTANAKORN; Pres. APISAK TANTIVORAWONG; 719 local brs, 7 overseas brs.

Siam City Bank Public Co Ltd: 1101 Thanon Phetchaburi Tadmai, Bangkok 10400; tel. (2) 208-5000; fax (2) 253-1240; e-mail scibweb@scib.co.th; internet www.scib.co.th; f. 1941; cap. 21,128m., res 6,595m., dep. 348,137.6m. (Dec. 2009); taken under the control of the central bank in Feb. 1998; merged with Bangkok Metropolitan Bank PCL in April 2002; majority stake acquired by Thanachart Bank Public Co in 2010; Chair. BANTERNG TANTIVIT; Pres. and CEO CHAIWAT UTAIWAN; 387 local brs, 1 overseas br.

Siam Commercial Bank Public Co Ltd: 9 Thanon Ratchadaphisek, Ladyao, Chatuchak, Bangkok 10900; tel. (2) 544-1000; fax (2) 937-7754; e-mail investor.relations@scb.co.th; internet www.scb.co.th; f. 1906; cap. 33,991.9m., res 30,686m., dep. 1,008,332.3m. (Dec. 2009); Exec. Chair. Dr VICHIT SURAPHONGCHAI; Pres. KANNIKAR CHALITAPORN; 987 local brs, 3 overseas brs.

Standard Chartered Bank (Thai) Public Co Ltd: 90 Thanon Sathorn Nua, Silom, Bangkok 10500; tel. (2) 724-6327; fax (2) 724-6121; internet www.standardchartered.co.th; f. 1933 as Wang Lee Bank Ltd, renamed 1985; cap. 14,837m., res 9,571.5m., dep. 194,662m. (Dec. 2009); taken under the control of the central bank in July 1999, 75% share sold to Standard Chartered Bank (United Kingdom); name changed to Standard Chartered Nakornthon Bank PCL in 1999; name changed as above in 2005; Chair. KAIKHUSHRU SHIAVAX NORGALWALA; CEO MEE HAR FOO; 67 brs.

Thanachart Bank Public Co Ltd: 1st, 2nd, 14th and 15th Floors, Thonson Bldg, 900 Thanon Phoenchit, Lumpini, Pathumwan, Bangkok 10330; tel. (2) 655-9000; fax (2) 655-9001; e-mail nfs_rb@nfs.co.th; internet www.thanachartbank.co.th; f. 2002; 49% owned by Bank of Nova Scotia—Scotiabank (Canada); cap. 19,346.1m., res 2,684.4m., dep. 291,004m. (Dec. 2009); Chair. BANTERNG TANTIVIT; Man. Dir SUVARNAPHA SUVARNAPRATHIP.

TMB Bank Public Co Ltd: 3000 Thanon Phaholyothin, Chompon, Chatuchak, Bangkok 10900; tel. (2) 299-1111; fax (2) 273-7121; e-mail ir@tmbbank.com; internet www.tmbbank.com; f. 1957; fmrly Thai Military Bank Public Co Ltd; present name adopted 2005; merged with DBS Thai Danu Bank Public Co Ltd and Industrial Finance Corpn of Thailand in 2004; cap. 24,856.6m., res 971.1m., dep. 181,031.4m. (Dec. 2009); Chair. PHILIPPE DAMAS; CEO BOONTUCK WUNGCHAROEN; 431 local brs, 3 overseas brs.

United Overseas Bank (Thai) Public Co Ltd (UOBT): 191 Thanon Sathorn Tai, Bangkok 10120; tel. (2) 343-3000; fax (2) 287-2973; e-mail webmaster@uob.co.th; internet www.uob.co.th; f. 1998 as the result of the merger of Laem Thong Bank Ltd with Radanasin Bank; name changed to UOB Radanasin Bank Public Co Ltd in Nov. 1999; name changed as above in 2005 following merger with Bank of Asia Public Co Ltd; cap. 24,856.6m., res 973.2m., dep. 180,641m. (Dec. 2009); Chair. WEE CHO YAW; Pres. and CEO WONG KIM CHOONG; 154 brs.

Development Banks

Bank for Agriculture and Agricultural Co-operatives (BAAC): 469 Thanon Nakorn Sawan, Dusit, Bangkok 10300; tel. (2) 280-0180; fax (2) 280-0442; e-mail train@baac.or.th; internet www.baac.or.th; f. 1966 to provide credit for agriculture; cap. and res 49,911m., dep. 431,401m. (March 2006); Chair. KORN CHATIKAVANIJ; Pres. LUCK WAJANANAWAT; 491 brs.

Export-Import Bank of Thailand (EXIM Thailand): EXIM Bldg, 1193 Thanon Phaholyothin, Phaya Thai, Bangkok 10400; tel. (2) 271-3700; fax (2) 271-3204; e-mail info@exim.go.th; internet www.exim.go.th; f. 1993; govt-owned; provides financial services to Thai exporters and Thai investors investing locally and abroad; cap. 12,800m., res 2,614m., dep. 18,655.7m. (Dec. 2009); Chair. NARIS CHAIYASOOT; Pres. KANIT SUKONTHAMAN; 9 brs, 7 sub-brs.

Government Housing Bank: 63 Thanon Rama IX, Huay Kwang, Bangkok 10310; tel. (2) 645-9000; fax (2) 246-1789; e-mail crm@ghb.co.th; internet www.ghb.co.th; f. 1953 to provide housing finance; Chair. AREEPONG BHOOCHA-OOM; Pres. WORAVIT CHAILIMPAMONTRI; 120 brs.

Small and Medium Enterprise Development Bank of Thailand: SME Bank Tower, 310 Thanon Phaholyothin, Phaya Thai, Bangkok 10400; tel. (2) 265-3000; fax (2) 265-4000; e-mail sme@smebank.co.th; internet www.smebank.co.th; fmrly Small Industries Finance Office, which became Small Industrial Finance Co Ltd in 1991; present name adopted 2002; Chair. POONNIS SAKUNTANAGA; Pres. SOROS SAKORNVISAVA.

Savings Bank

Government Savings Bank: 470 Thanon Phaholyothin, Phaya Thai, Bangkok 10400; tel. (2) 299-8000; fax (2) 299-8490; e-mail news@gsb.or.th; internet www.gsb.or.th; f. 1913; cap. 0.1m., res −750.7m., dep. 724,704.3m. (Dec. 2008); Chair. VINAI VITTAVASGARNVEJ; Pres. LERSUK CHULADESA; 578 brs.

Bankers' Association

Thai Bankers' Association: Lake Rachada Office Complex, Bldg 2, 4th Floor, 195/5–7 Thanon Ratchadaphisek, Klongtoey, Bangkok 10110; tel. (2) 264-0883; fax (2) 264-0888; e-mail infodesk@tba.or.th; internet www.tba.or.th; f. 1958; Chair. CHARTSIRI SOPHOPANICH.

STOCK EXCHANGE

Stock Exchange of Thailand (SET): The Stock Exchange of Thailand Bldg, 62 Thanon Ratchadaphisek, Klongtoey, Bangkok 10110; tel. (2) 229-2000; fax (2) 654-5649; e-mail contact.tsd@set.or.th; internet www.set.or.th; f. 1975; 27 mems; Pres. CHARAMPORN JOTIKASTHIRA; Chair. SOMPOL KIATPHAIBOOL.

Securities and Exchange Commission: GPF Witthayu Towers, 15th Floor, 93/1 Thanon Witthayu, Lumpini, Pathumwan, Bangkok 10330; tel. (2) 263-6499; fax (2) 256-7711; e-mail info@sec.or.th; internet www.sec.or.th; f. 1992; supervises new share issues and trading in existing shares; chaired by Minister of Finance; Sec.-Gen. THIRACHAI PHUVANAT NARANUBULA.

INSURANCE

Selected Insurance Companies

Aioi Bangkok Insurance Co Ltd: 22nd Floor, Bangkok Insurance/YWCA Bldg, 25 Thanon Sathorn Tai, Tungmahamek, Sathorn, Bangkok 10120; tel. (2) 620-8000; fax (2) 677-3979; e-mail pr@aioibkkins.co.th; internet www.aioibkkins.co.th; f. 1951; fmrly Wilson Insurance Co Ltd; fire, marine, motor car, general; CEO YOSHIHIKO FUKASAWA; Pres. NOPADOL SANTIPAKORN.

American International Assurance Co Ltd: American International Tower, 181 Thanon Surawongse, Bangrak, Bangkok 10500; tel. (2) 634-8888; fax (2) 236-6452; e-mail th.customer@aia.com; internet www.aia.co.th; f. 1983; ordinary and group life, group and personal accident, credit, life; CEO RON VAN OIJEN.

Ayudhya Insurance Public Co Ltd: 898 Ploenchit Tower, 7th Floor, Thanon Ploenchit, Pathumwan, Bangkok 10330; tel. (2) 263-0335; fax (2) 263-0589; e-mail info@ayud.co.th; internet www.ayud.co.th; non-life; Chair. VERAPHAN TEEPSUWAN; Pres. ROWAN D'ARCY.

Bangkok Insurance Public Co Ltd: Bangkok Insurance Bldg, 25 Thanon Sathorn Tai, Bangkok 10120; tel. (2) 285-8888; fax (2) 610-2100; e-mail corp.comm1@bki.co.th; internet www.bki.co.th; f. 1947; non-life; Chair. and Pres. CHAI SOPHONPANICH.

Bangkok Union Insurance Public Co Ltd: 175–177 Bangkok Union Insurance Bldg, Thanon Surawongse, Bangrak, Bangkok 10500; tel. (2) 233-6920; fax (2) 237-1856; e-mail bui@bui.co.th; internet www.bui.co.th; f. 1929; non-life; Chair. MANU LIEWPAIROT.

THAILAND

Directory

China Insurance Co (Siam) Ltd: 36/68–69, 20th Floor, PS Tower, Thanon Asoke, Sukhumvit 21, Bangkok 10110; tel. (2) 259-3718; fax (2) 259-1402; f. 1948; non-life; Chair. JAMES C. CHENG; Man. Dir FANG RONG-CHENG.

Indara Insurance Public Co Ltd: 364/29 Thanon Sri Ayudhya, Ratchathewi, Bangkok 10400; tel. (2) 247-9261; fax (2) 247-9260; e-mail contact@indara.co.th; internet www.indara.co.th; f. 1949; non-life; Chair. PRATIP WONGNIRUND; Man. Dir SUCHART TRISIRIWE-TAWATTANA.

Mittare Insurance Co Ltd: 295 Thanon Si Phraya, Bangrak, Bangkok 10500; tel. (2) 640-7777; fax (2) 640-7799; internet www.mittare.com; f. 1947; life, fire, marine, health, personal accident, automobile and general; fmrly Thai Prasit Insurance Co Ltd; Chair. SURACHAN CHANSRICHAWLA; Man. Dir SUKHATHEP CHANSRICHAWLA.

Navakij Insurance Public Co Ltd: 90/3–6, 100/50–55 Sathorn Nakorn Tower, Thanon Sathorn Nua, Silom, Bangrak, Bangkok 10500; tel. (2) 664-7777; fax (2) 636-7999; internet www.navakij.co.th; f. 1933; Chair. NIPHON TANGJEERAWONGSA.

Ocean Life Insurance Co Ltd: 170/74–83 Ocean Tower I Bldg, Thanon Ratchadaphisek, Klongtoey, Bangkok 10110; tel. (2) 261-2300; fax (2) 261-3344; e-mail info@ocean.co.th; internet www.ocean.co.th; f. 1949; life; Chair. KIRATI ASSAKUL; Man. Dir DAYANA BUNNAG.

Paiboon Insurance Co Ltd: Thai Life Insurance Bldg, 19th–20th Floors, 123 Thanon Ratchadaphisek, Bangkok 10310; tel. (2) 246-9635; fax (2) 246-9660; f. 1927; non-life; Chair. ANUTHRA ASSAWA-NONDA; Pres. VANICH CHAIYAWAN.

Prudential Life Assurance (Thailand) Public Co Ltd: Sengthong Thani Tower, 28th, 30th and 31st Floors, 82 Thanon Sathorn Nua, Bangkok 10500; tel. (2) 353-4999; fax (2) 353-4888; e-mail customer.service.ptsl@ibm.net; internet www.prudential.co.th; f. 1983; Chair. BURAPHA ATTHAKON; CEO BINAYAK DUTTA.

Siam Commercial New York Life Insurance Public Co Ltd: 4th Floor, SCB Bldg 1, 1060 Thanon Phetchaburi, SCB Chidlom, Ratchathewi, Bangkok 10400; tel. (2) 655-4000; fax (2) 256-1666; e-mail customerservice@scnyl.com; internet www.scnyl.com; f. 1976; life; Chair. and CEO KHUNYING JADA WATTANASIRITHAM.

Southeast Insurance (2000) Co Ltd (Arkanay Prakan Pai Co Ltd): Southeast Insurance Bldg, Unit 315G, 1–3 Thanon Silom, Bangrak, Bangkok 10500; tel. (2) 631-1331; internet www.seic2000.com; f. 1946; life and non-life; Chair. CHAYUT CHIRALERSPONG; Gen. Man. WICHAI INTARANUKULAKIJ.

Syn Mun Kong Insurance Public Co Ltd: 279 Thanon Srinakarin, Bangkapi, Bangkok 10240; tel. (2) 379-3140; fax (2) 377-5043; e-mail info@smk.co.th; internet www.smk.co.th; f. 1951; fire, marine, automobile and personal accident; Chair. RUENGWIT DUSADEESUR-APOJ; Man. Dir RUENGDEJ DUSADEESURAPOJ.

Thai Health Insurance Co Ltd: 31st Floor, RS Tower, 121/89 Thanon Ratchadaphisek, Din-Daeng, Bangkok 10400; tel. (2) 642-3100; fax (2) 642-3130; e-mail care@thaihealth.co.th; internet www.thaihealth.co.th; f. 1979; Chair. APIRAK THAIPATANAGUL; Man. Dir VARANG SRETHBHAKDI.

Thai Insurance Public Co Ltd: 34/3 Soi Lang Suan, Thanon Ploenchit, Lumpini, Pathumwan, Bangkok 10330; tel. (2) 613-0100; fax (2) 652-2870; e-mail tic@thaiins.com; internet www.thaiins.com; f. 1938; non-life; Chair. KAVI ANSVANANDA.

Thai Life Insurance Co Ltd: 123 Thanon Ratchadaphisek, Din-Daeng, Bangkok 10400; tel. (2) 247-0247; fax (2) 246-9946; e-mail thailife@thailife.com; internet www.thailife.com; f. 1942; life; Chair. VANICH CHAIYAWAN; CEO Dr APIRAK THAIPATANAGUL.

ThaiSri Insurance Co Ltd: 126/2 Thanon Krunthonburi, Klongsam, Bangkok 10600; tel. (2) 878-7111; fax (2) 439-4840; e-mail info@thaisri.com; internet www.thaisri.com; f. 1997; personal accident, automobile, fire, marine; jt venture between Thai Metropole Insurance and Zurich Financial Services Group (Switzerland); Chair. TAWEE BUTSUNTORN; CEO NATEE PANICHEWA.

Viriyah Insurance Co Ltd: RS Tower, 121/7 Thanon Ratchadaphisek, Din-Daeng, Bangkok 10320; tel. (2) 239-1000; fax (2) 641-3580; e-mail info@viriyah.co.th; internet www.viriyah.co.th; f. 1947; Chair. JARE CHUTHARATTANAKUL; Man. Dir SUVAPORN THONGTHEW.

Associations

General Insurance Association: 223 Soi Ruamrudee, Thanon Witthayu, Bangkok 10330; tel. (2) 256-6032; fax (2) 256-6039; e-mail general@thaigia.com; internet www.thaigia.com; Pres. JEERAPHAN ASAWATHANAKUL; Sec.-Gen. ANON VANGVASU; 67 mems.

Thai Life Assurance Association: 36/1 Soi Sapanku, Thanon Rama IV, Tungmahamek, Sathorn, Bangkok 10120; tel. (2) 287-4596; fax (2) 679-7100; e-mail tlaa@tlaa.org; internet www.tlaa.org; Pres. SARA LAMSAM; Sec.-Gen. PHERAPONG UNCHIT; 25 mems.

Trade and Industry
GOVERNMENT AGENCIES

Board of Investment (BOI): 555 Thanon Vibhavadi Rangsit, Chatuchak, Bangkok 10900; tel. (2) 553-8111; fax (2) 553-8222; e-mail head@boi.go.th; internet www.boi.go.th; f. 1958; formed to publicize investment potential and encourage economically and socially beneficial investments and also to provide investment information; chaired by the Prime Minister; Sec.-Gen. ATCHAKA SIBUNRUANG BRIMBLE.

Board of Trade of Thailand: 150/2 Thanon Rajbopit, Bangkok 10200; tel. (2) 622-1860; fax (2) 225-3372; internet www.thaichamber.org; f. 1955; mems: chambers of commerce, trade asscns, state enterprises and co-operative societies (large and medium-sized cos have associate membership); Chair. DUSIT NONTANAKORN.

Financial Sector Restructuring Authority (FSRA): 130–132 Tower 3, Thanon Witthayu, Pathumwan, Bangkok 10330; tel. (2) 263-2620; fax (2) 650-9872; f. 1997 to oversee the restructuring of Thailand's financial system; Chair. KAMOL JUNTIMA; Sec.-Gen. MONTRI CHENVIDAYAKAM.

Forest Industry Organization: 76 Thanon Ratchadamnoen Nok, Bangkok 10100; tel. (2) 282-3243; fax (2) 282-5197; e-mail fio@fio.co.th; internet www.fio.co.th; f. 1947; oversees all aspects of forestry and wood industries; Man. MANOONSAK TONTIWIWATTANA.

Office of the Cane and Sugar Board: Ministry of Industry, 6 Thanon Phra Ram Hok, Bangkok 10400; tel. (2) 202-3075; fax (2) 202-3070; e-mail ocsb0601@ocsb.go.th; internet www.ocsb.go.th; Sec.-Gen. PRASERT TAPANEEYANGKUL.

Rubber Estate Organization: 16 Moo, Nabon Station, Nakhon Si Thammarat Province 80220; tel. (75) 491570; fax (75) 491339; e-mail reothai@reothai.co.th; internet www.reothai.co.th; Man. Dir CHAIROJ THAMMARATTANA (acting).

DEVELOPMENT AGENCIES

National Economic and Social Development Board: 962 Thanon Krung Kasem, Bangkok 10100; tel. (2) 280-4085; fax (2) 281-3938; e-mail pr@nesdb.go.th; internet www.nesdb.go.th; economic and social planning agency; Sec.-Gen. AKHOM TERMPITTHAYAPAISIT.

Royal Development Projects Board: Office of the Prime Minister, Government House, Thanon Nakhon Pathom, Bangkok 10300; tel. (2) 280-6193; e-mail rdpbict.g@rdpb.mail.go.th; internet www.rdpb.go.th; Sec.-Gen. SOMPOL PANMANEE.

CHAMBER OF COMMERCE

Thai Chamber of Commerce (TCC): 150 Thanon Rajbopit, Bangkok 10200; tel. (2) 622-1860; fax (2) 225-3372; e-mail tcc@thaichamber.org; internet www.thaichamber.org; f. 1946; Chair. DUSIT NONTANAKORN.

INDUSTRIAL AND TRADE ASSOCIATIONS

The Federation of Thai Industries: Queen Sirikit National Convention Center, Zone C, 4th Floor, 60 Thanon Ratchadaphisek Tadmai, Klongtoey, Bangkok 10110; tel. (2) 345-1000; fax (2) 345-1296; e-mail information@fti.or.th; internet www.fti.or.th; f. 1987; fmrly The Association of Thai Industries; 4,800 mems; Chair. SANTI WILATSAKDANON.

Mining Industry Council of Thailand: Soi 222/2, Thai Chamber of Commerce University, Thanon Vibhavadi Rangsit, Din-Daeng, Bangkok 10400; tel. (2) 275-7684; fax (2) 692-3321; e-mail miningthai@miningthai.org; internet www.miningthai.org; f. 1983; intermediary between govt organizations and private mining enterprises; Chair. YONGYOTH PETCHSUWAN; Sec.-Gen. ORANUCH RAMAKOMUT.

Rice Exporters' Association of Thailand: 37 Soi Ngamdupli, Thanon Phra Rama IV, Tungmahamek, Sathorn, Bangkok 10120; tel. (2) 287-2674; fax (2) 287-2678; e-mail contact@thairiceexporters.or.th; internet www.thairiceexporters.or.th; Pres. KORBSUK IEMSURI; Sec.-Gen. THARNKASEM VANICHJAKVONG.

Sawmills Association: 101 Thanon Amnuaysongkhram, Dusit, Bangkok 10300; tel. (2) 243-4754; fax (2) 243-8629; e-mail info@thaisawmills.com; internet www.thaisawmills.com; Pres. SURASAK IEMDEENGAMLERT.

Thai Coffee Exporters Association: 1302–1306 Thanon Songwad, Samphanthawong, Bangkok 10100; tel. (2) 221-1264; fax (2) 225-1962; e-mail cofexpo@cscoms.com.

Thai Contractors' Association: 2013 Italthai House, 12A Floor, Thanon Petchburi, Huay Kwang, Bangkok 10310; tel. (2) 318-8321; fax (2) 318-8325; e-mail webmaster@tca.or.th; internet www.tca.or.th; f. 1928 under the name The Engineering Association of Siam; name changed to The Engineering Contractors Asscn in 1967 and as

THAILAND

Directory

above in 1983; Pres. POLPAT KARNASUTA; Sec.-Gen. ANGSURAS AREEKUL.

Thai Diamond Manufacturers Association: 87/139–40, Modern Town Bldg, 18th Floor, Soi Ekamai 3, Thanon Sukhumvit 63, Klong Ton Nua, Wattana, Bangkok 10110; tel. (2) 390-0341; fax (2) 711-4039; e-mail odtcbkk@loxinfo.co.th; internet www.thaidiamonds.org; 11-mem. board; Pres. CHIRAKITTI TANGKATHAC.

Thai Food Processors' Association: Tower 1, Ocean Bldg, 9th Floor, 170/21–22 Thanon Ratchadaphisek Tadmai, Klongtoey, Bangkok 10110; tel. (2) 261-2684; fax (2) 261-2996; e-mail thaifood@thaifood.org; internet www.thaifood.org; Pres. NAT ONSRI.

Thai Lac Association: 57/1 Soi Saphantia, Thanon Sipraya, Mahapreuktaram, Bangrak, Bangkok 10500; tel. (2) 233-4583; fax (2) 633-2913.

Thai Maize and Produce Traders' Association: Sathorn Thani II Bldg, 11th Floor, 92/26–27 Thanon Sathorn Nua, Bangrak, Bangkok 10500; tel. (2) 234-4387; fax (2) 667-0178; e-mail thaimaize@tmpta.org; internet www.thaimaizeandproduce.org; Pres. SUNAN SINGSOMBOON.

Thai Pharmaceutical Manufacturers Association: 188/107 Thanon Charan Sanit Wong, Banchanglaw, Bangkoknoi, Bangkok 10700; tel. (2) 863-5106; fax (2) 863-5108; e-mail tpma@truemail.co.th; internet www.tpma.or.th; f. 1969; Pres. CHERNPORN TENGAMNUAY.

Thai Rice Mills Association: 81–81/1 Trok Rongnamkheng, 24 Thanon Charoenkrung, Talad-Noi, Samphanthawong, Bangkok 10100; internet www.thairicemillers.com; tel. (2) 234-7289; fax (2) 234-7286; Pres. CHANCHAI RAKTHANANON.

Thai Rubber Association: 45–47 Thanon Chotivithayakun 3, Hat Yai, Songkhla 90110; tel. (74) 429-011; fax (74) 429-312; e-mail tra@csloxinfo.com; internet www.thainr.com; f. 1951; est. as Thai Rubber Traders' Asscn; Pres. LUKCHAI KITTIPHOL.

Thai Silk Association: Textile Industry Division, Small Industries Bldg, 5th Floor, Soi Trimitr, Thanon Rama IV, Klongtoey, Bangkok 10110; tel. (2) 712-4328; fax (2) 391-2896; e-mail thsilkas@thaitextile.org; internet www.thaitextile.org/tsa; f. 1962; Pres. BUNTOON WONGSEELASHOTE.

Thai Sugar and Bio-energy Producers' Association: SM Tower, 22nd Floor, 979/56 Thanon Phaholyothin, Phaya Thai, Bangkok 10400; tel. (2) 298-0167; fax (2) 298-0169; e-mail tsma2000@cscoms.com; internet www.thaisugar.org.

Thai Sugar Producers' Association: 8th Floor, Thai Ruam Toon Bldg, 794 Thanon Krung Kasem, Pomprap, Bangkok 10100; tel. (2) 282-0990; fax (2) 281-0342.

Thai Tapioca Trade Association: Sathorn Thani II Bldg, 20th Floor, 92/58 Thanon Sathorn Nua, Silom, Bangkok 10500; tel. (2) 234-4724; fax (2) 236-6084; e-mail ttta@loxinfo.co.th; internet www.ttta-tapioca.org; f. 1963; Pres. SEREE DENWORALAK.

Thai Textile Manufacturing Association: Panjit Tower, 4th Floor, 117/7 Thanon Sukhumvit (22), Soi 55, Klongton Nua, Klongtoey, Bangkok 10110; tel. (2) 392-0753-55; fax (2) 712-5440; e-mail ttma@thaitextile.org; internet www.thaitextile.org/ttma; f. 1960; Pres. PHONGSAK ASSAKUL.

Union Textile Merchants' Association (Thai Textile Merchants' Association): 562 Espreme Bldg, 4th Floor, Thanon Rajchawong, Samphanthawong, Bangkok 10100; tel. (2) 622-6711; fax (2) 622-6714; e-mail tma@thaitextile.org; internet www.thaitextile.org/tma; Chair. SUCHAI PORNSIRIKUL.

UTILITIES

Electricity

Electricity Generating Authority of Thailand (EGAT): 53 Moo 2, Thanon Charan Sanit Wong, Bang Kruai, Nothaburi, Bangkok 11130; tel. (2) 436-0000; fax (2) 436-4723; e-mail correspondence@egat.co.th; internet www.egat.co.th; f. 1969; Gov. SUTHAT PATTAMASIRIWAT.

Electricity Generating Public Co Ltd (EGCO): EGCO Tower, 222 Moo 5, Thanon Vibhavadi Rangsit, Thung Song Hong, Laksi, Bangkok 10210; tel. (2) 998-5999; fax (2) 955-0956; e-mail corp_com@egco.com; internet www.egco.com; subsidiary of EGAT; 59% transferred to the private sector in 1994–96; 14.9% owned by China Light and Power Co (Hong Kong); Chair. PORNCHAI RUJIPRAPA; Pres. VINIT TANGNOI.

The Metropolitan Electricity Authority: 30 Soi Chidlom, Thanon Ploenchit, Lumpini, Pathumwan, Bangkok 10330; tel. (2) 254-9550; fax (2) 251-9586; internet www.mea.or.th; f. 1958; one of the two main power distribution agencies in Thailand; Gov. ARTHORN SINSAWAD.

The Provincial Electricity Authority: 200 Thanon Ngam Wongwan, Chatuchak, Bangkok 10900; tel. (2) 589-0100; fax (2) 589-4850; e-mail webmaster@pea.co.th; internet www.pea.co.th; f. 1960; one of the two main power distribution agencies in Thailand; Gov. ADISORN KIERTICHOKWIWAT.

Water

Metropolitan Waterworks Authority: 400 Thanon Prachachuen, Laksi, Bangkok 10210; tel. (2) 504-0123; fax (2) 503-9493; e-mail mwa1125@mwa.co.th; internet www.mwa.co.th; f. 1967; state-owned; provides water supply systems in Bangkok; Gov. CHAROEN PASSARA.

Provincial Waterworks Authority: 72 Thanon Chaengwattana, Don Muang, Bangkok 10210; tel. (2) 551-1020; fax (2) 552-1547; e-mail pr@pwa.co.th; internet www.pwa.co.th; f. 1979; provides water supply systems except in Bangkok Metropolis; Gov. CHAVALIT SARUN; Chair. SURA-AT THONGNIRAMOL.

TRADE UNIONS

Confederation of Thai Labour (CTL): 25/59 Thanon Sukhumvit, Viphavill Village, Tambol Paknam, Amphur Muang, Samutprakarn, Bangkok 10270; tel. (2) 756-5346; fax (2) 755-2165; e-mail ctl_manas@hotmail.com; internet www.ctl.or.th; represents 44 labour unions; Pres. MANAS PHOSORN.

Labour Congress of Thailand (LCT): 420/393–394 Thippavan Village 1, Thanon Teparak, Samrong-Nua, Muang, Samutprakarn, Bangkok 10270; tel. and fax (2) 384-6789; e-mail lct_org@hotmail.com; f. 1978; represents 224 labour unions, four labour federations and approx. 140,000 mems; Pres. CHINCHOTE SAENGSANG; Gen. Sec. SAMAM THOMYA.

National Congress of Private Employees of Thailand (NPET): 142/6 Thanon Phrathoonam Phrakanong, Phrakanong, Klongtoey, Bangkok 10110; tel. and fax (2) 392-9955; represents 31 labour unions; Pres. BANJONG PORNPATTANANIKOM.

National Congress of Thai Labour (NCTL): 1614/876 Samutprakarn Community Housing Project, Sukhumvit Highway Km 30, Tai Baan, Muang, Samutprakarn, Bangkok 10280; tel. (2) 389-5134; fax (2) 385-8975; represents 171 unions; Pres. PANAS THAILUAN.

National Free Labour Union Congress (NFLUC): 277 Moo 3, Thanon Ratburana, Bangkok 10140; tel. (2) 427-6506; fax (2) 428-4543; represents 51 labour unions; Pres. ANUSSAKDI BOONYAPRANAI.

National Labour Congress (NLC): 586/248–250 Moo 2, Mooban City Village, Thanon Sukhumvit, Bang Phu Mai, Mueng, Samutprakarn, Bangkok 10280; tel. and fax (2) 709-9426; represents 41 labour unions; Pres. CHIN THAPPHLI.

Thai Trade Union Congress (TTUC): 420/393–394 Thippavan Village 1, Thanon Teparak, Tambol Samrong-nua, Amphur Muang, Samutprakarn, Bangkok 10270; tel. and fax (2) 384-0438; e-mail thai-tuc@hotmail.com; f. 1983; represents 172 unions; Pres. PANIT CHAROENPHAO.

Thailand Council of Industrial Labour (TCIL): 99 Moo 4, Thanon Sukhaphibarn 2, Khannayao, Bungkum, Bangkok; tel. (2) 517-0022; fax (2) 517-0628; represents 23 labour unions; Pres. TAVEE DEEYING.

Transport

RAILWAYS

Thailand has a railway network of 4,429 km, connecting Bangkok with Chiang Mai, Nong Khai, Ubon Ratchathani, Nam Tok and towns on the isthmus.

State Railway of Thailand: 1 Thanon Rong Muang, Rong Muang, Pathumwan, Bangkok 10330; tel. (2) 220-4567; fax (2) 225-3801; e-mail info@railway.co.th; internet www.railway.co.th; f. 1897; 4,429 km of track in 2007; responsible for licensing a 4,044-km passenger and freight rail system, above ground; Chair. TAWANRAT ORNSIRA; Gov. YUTHANA TUPCHAROEN.

Bangkok Mass Transit System Public Co Ltd: 1000 Thanon Phahonyothin, Chom Phon, Chatuchak, Bangkok 10900; tel. (2) 617-7300; fax (2) 617-7133; e-mail nuduan@bts.co.th; internet www.bts.co.th; f. 1992; responsible for the construction and management of the Skytrain, a two-line, 23.5-km elevated rail system, under the supervision of the Bangkok Metropolitan Area, the initial stage of which was opened in December 1999; Exec. Chair. and CEO KEEREE KANJANAPAS.

Mass Rapid Transit Authority of Thailand (MRTA): 175 Thanon Rama IX, Huay Kwang, Bangkok 10320; tel. (2) 612-2444; fax (2) 612-2436; e-mail pr@mrta.co.th; internet www.mrta.co.th; a 20-km subway system was opened in Bangkok in July 2004; as part of the planned extension of the mass rapid transit system, was charged with the construction of three new lines, totalling 91 km in length: 27-km Blue Line (Hua Lamphong–Bang Khae; Bang Sue–Tha Phra); 24-km Orange Line (Bang Kapi–Bang Bumru); and 40-km Purple Line

THAILAND

(Bang Yai–Rat Burana); Chair. SUPOTH SUBLOM; Gov. CHUKIAT PHOTA-YANUVAT.

ROADS

The total length of the road network was an estimated 180,053 km in 2006. A network of toll roads has been introduced in Bangkok in an attempt to alleviate the city's severe congestion problems.

Bangkok Mass Transit Authority (BMTA): 131 Thanon Thiam Ruammit, Huay Kwang, Bangkok 10310; tel. (2) 246-0973; fax (2) 247-2189; e-mail webmaster@bmta.co.th; internet www.bmta.co.th; controls Bangkok's urban transport system; Chair. PIYAPAN CHAMPASUT; Dir and Sec. PINATE PUAPATANAKUL.

Department of Highways: Thanon Sri Ayudhya, Ratchathewi, Bangkok 10400; tel. (2) 354-6668; e-mail webmaster@doh.go.th; internet www.doh.go.th; Dir-Gen. VEERA RUANGSUKSRIWONG.

Department of Land Transport: 1032 Thanon Phaholyothin, Chatuchak, Bangkok 10900; tel. (2) 272-5671; fax (2) 272-5680; e-mail chairat@dlt.go.th; internet www.dlt.go.th; Dir-Gen. CHAIRAT SANGUANSUE.

Department of Rural Roads: 218/1, Thanon Phra Ram VI, Phaya Thai, Bangkok 10400; tel. (2) 299-4591; fax (2) 299-4606; e-mail webmaster@dor.go.th; internet www.dor.go.th; f. 2002; Dir-Gen. VICHARN KUNAKULSAWAS.

Expressway and Rapid Transit Authority of Thailand (ETA): 2380 Thanon Phaholyothin, Senanikhom, Chatuchak, Bangkok 10900; tel. (2) 579-5380; e-mail webmasters@eta.co.th; internet www.eta.co.th; f. 1972; Dir-Gen. PHACHOEN PHAIROJSAK.

SHIPPING

There is an extensive network of canals, providing transport for bulk goods. The port of Bangkok is an important shipping junction for South-East Asia, and consists of 37 berths for conventional and container vessels. At the end of 2009 the Thai merchant fleet (884 vessels) had a combined displacement totalling 2,526,100 grt.

Marine Department: 1278 Thanon Yotha, Talardnoi, Samphanthawong, Bangkok 10100; tel. (2) 233-1311; fax (2) 236-7148; e-mail marine@md.go.th; internet www.md.go.th; Dir-Gen. TAWALYARAT ONSIRA.

Port Authority of Thailand: 444 Thanon Tarua, Klongtoey, Bangkok 10110; tel. (2) 269-3000; fax (2) 249-0885; e-mail info@port.co.th; internet www.port.co.th; 18 berths at Bangkok Port, 12 berths at Laem Chabang Port; originally scheduled for transfer to private sector in 1999, but plans have been repeatedly delayed; Chair. CHALOR KOTCHARAT; Dir-Gen. SUNIDA SAKULRATTANA.

Principal Shipping Companies

Jutha Maritime Public Co Ltd: Mano Tower, 2nd Floor, 153 Soi 39, Thanon Sukhumvit, Wattana, Bangkok 10110; tel. (2) 260-0050; fax (2) 259-9825; e-mail office@jutha.co.th; internet www.jutha.co.th; services between Thailand, Malaysia, Korea, Japan and Viet Nam; Chair. Rear-Adm. CHANO PHENJATI; Man. Dir CHANET PHENJATI.

Precious Shipping Public Co Ltd: Cathay House, 7th Floor, 8/30 Thanon Sathorn Nua, Bangrak, Bangkok 10500; tel. (2) 696-8800; fax (2) 633-8460; e-mail psl@preciousshipping.com; internet www.preciousshipping.com; Chair. Adm. AMNARD CHANDANAMATTHA; Man. Dir HASHIM KHALID MOINUDDIN.

Regional Container Lines Public Co Ltd: Panjathani Tower, 30th Floor, 127/35 Thanon Ratchadaphisek, Chongnonsee Yannawa, Bangkok 10120; tel. (2) 296-1096; fax (2) 296-1098; e-mail rclbkk@rclgroup.com; internet www.rclgroup.com; Chair. KUA PHEK LONG; Pres. SUMATE TANTHUWANIT.

Thai International Maritime Enterprises Ltd: Sarasin Bldg, 5th Floor, 14 Thanon Surasak, Bangkok 10500; tel. (2) 236-8835; services from Bangkok to Japan; Chair. and Man. Dir SUN SUNDISAMRIT.

Thai Maritime Navigation Co Ltd: Manorom Bldg, 15th Floor, 51 Thanon Rama IV, Klongtoey, Bangkok 10110; tel. (2) 672-8690; fax (2) 249-0108; e-mail tmn@tmn.co.th; internet www.tmn.co.th; f. 1940; state-owned; services from Bangkok to Japan, the USA, Europe and ASEAN countries; Chair. NIPHON CHAKSUDUL; Sec.-Gen. SUWAPHAT SUVANNAKIJBORIHAN.

Thai Mercantile Marine Ltd: 599/1 Thanon Chua Phloeng, Klongtoey, Bangkok 10110; tel. (2) 240-2582; fax (2) 249-5656; e-mail tmmbkk@asiaaccess.net.th; f. 1967; services between Japan and Thailand; Chair. SUTHAM TANPHAIBUL; Man. Dir TANAN TANPHAIBUL.

Thoresen Thai Agencies Public Co Ltd: 26/26–27 Orakarn Bldg, 8th Floor, Soi Chidlom, Thanon Ploenchit, Kwang Lumpinee, Khet Pathumwan, Bangkok 10330; tel. (2) 254-8437; fax (2) 655-5631; e-mail tta@thoresen.com; internet www.thoresen.com; shipowner, liner operator, shipping agent (in Thailand and Viet Nam); ship repairs, offshore and diving services; Chair. M. R. CHANDRAM S. CHANDRATAT; Man. Dir M. L. CHANDCHUTHA CHANDRATAT.

Unithai Group: 11th Floor, 25 Alma Link Bldg, Soi Chidlom, Thanon Ploenchit, Pathumwan, Bangkok 10330; tel. (2) 254-8400; fax (2) 254-8424; e-mail paporn.t@unithai.com; internet www.unithai.com; regular containerized/break-bulk services to Europe, Africa and Far East; also bulk shipping/chartering; Chair. SIVAVONG CHANGKASIRI; CEO NARONG BOONYASAQUAN.

CIVIL AVIATION

Bangkok, Chiang Mai, Chiang Rai, Hat Yai, Phuket and Surat Thani airports are of international standard. U-Tapao is an alternative airport. Suvarnabhumi International Airport, a new facility located south-east of Bangkok, opened in September 2006, with an eventual capacity of 45m. passengers a year. Bangkok's former international airport at Don Muang was subsequently reopened to domestic commercial flights.

Airports of Thailand Public Co Ltd (AOT): 333 Thanon Cherdwutagard, Don Muang, Bangkok 10210; tel. (2) 535-1111; fax (2) 535-4061; e-mail aotpr@airportthai.co.th; internet www.airportthai.co.th; f. 1998; develops and manages airports; Chair. PIYAPAN CHAMPASUT; Pres. SERIRAT PRASUTANOND.

Department of Civil Aviation: 71 Soi Ngarmduplee, Thanon Rama IV, Tung Mahamek, Sathorn District, Bangkok 10120; tel. (2) 287-0320; fax (2) 286-3373; e-mail dca@aviation.go.th; internet www.aviation.go.th; f. 1963; Dir-Gen. VUTICHAI SINGHAMANY.

Bangkok Airways: 99 Moo 14, Thanon Vibhavadi Rangsit, Chom Phon, Chatuchak, Bangkok 10900; tel. (2) 270-6699; fax (2) 265-5522; e-mail reservation@bangkokair.com; internet www.bangkokair.com; f. 1968; est. as Sahakol Air; present name adopted 1989; privately owned; scheduled and charter passenger services to 8 domestic and 8 international destinations; Pres. PUTTIPONG PRASARTTONG-OSOTH; CEO Dr PRASERT PRASARTTONG-OSOTH.

Nok Air: 183 Rajanakarn Bldg, 17th Floor, Thanon Sathorn Tai, Yannawa, Bangkok 10120; tel. (2) 627-2000; fax (2) 627-9830; e-mail public.info@thaiairways.co.th; internet www.nokair.com; f. 2004; 39%-owned by Thai Airways International Public Co Ltd; flights to six domestic destinations; CEO PATEE SARASIN.

Nok Mini Airlines: 19/18–19 Royal City Ave, Blk A, Thanon Phra Ram 9, Bangkapi, Huay Kwang, Bangkok 10310; tel. (2) 641-4190; fax (2) 641-4807; e-mail info@sga.aero; internet www.nokmini.com; f. 2002; est. as SGA Airlines; rebranded 2009; scheduled and chartered domestic services; Chair. Capt. THOM SIRISANT; Pres. JAIN CHARNNARONG.

One-Two-Go: UM Tower Bldg, 21st Floor, 9/211 Thanon Ramkhamhaeng, Suanluang, Bangkok 10250; tel. (2) 229-4260; fax (2) 229-4278; e-mail customer_relation@orient-thai.com; internet www.flyorientthai.com; f. 2003; subsidiary of Orient Thai Airlines; low-cost domestic flights; Chair. UDOM TANTIPRASONGCHAI; CEO MANASNANT TANTIPRASSONGCHAI.

Orient Thai Airlines: UM Tower Bldg, 21st Floor, 9/211 Thanon Ramkhamhaeng, Suanluang, Bangkok 10250; tel. (2) 229-4260; fax (2) 229-4278; e-mail customer_relation@orient-thai.com; internet www.flyorientthai.com; f. 1993; est. as Orient Express Air; domestic and international flights; Chair. UDOM TANTIPRASONGCHAI; CEO MANASSANANT TANTIPRASONGCHAI.

Phuket Air: 1168/71, 25th Floor, Lumpini Tower Bldg, Thanon Rama IV, Tungmahamek, Bangkok 10120; tel. (62) 679-8999; fax (62) 285-6480; e-mail info@phuketairlines.com; internet www.phuketairlines.com; f. 1999; international charter services; Pres. VIKROM AISIRI.

Thai AirAsia Co Ltd: Suvarnabhumi Int. Airport, 999 Moo 1, Departure Hall, 4th Floor, Rm T4-B01/01-04, Bangplee, Samutprakarn 10540; internet www.airasia.com; f. 2004; 50% owned by Asia Aviation, 49% owned by Air Asia Sdn Bhd (Malaysia); low-cost domestic flights; Chair. ARAK CHOLTANON; CEO TASSAPON BIJLEVELD.

Thai Airways International Public Co Ltd (THAI): 89 Thanon Vibhavadi Rangsit, Bangkok 10900; tel. (2) 545-3321; fax (2) 545-3322; e-mail public.info@thaiairways.co.th; internet www.thaiairways.com; f. 1960; 51% owned by Ministry of Finance; shares listed in July 1991, began trading in July 1992; merged with Thai Airways Co in 1988; domestic services from Bangkok to 20 cities; international services to over 50 destinations in Asia, Australasia, Europe and North America; Chair. AMPON KITTIAMPON; Pres. PIYASVASTI AMRANAND.

Tourism

Thailand is a popular tourist destination, noted for its temples, palaces, beaches and islands. Tourist arrivals were provisionally estimated to total 15.8m. in 2010. Revenue from tourism (including passenger transport) was an estimated US $21,980m. in 2008.

THAILAND

Tourism Authority of Thailand (TAT): 1600 Thanon Phetchaburi Tat Mai, Makkasan, Ratchathewi, Bangkok 10400; tel. (2) 250-5500; fax (2) 250-5511; e-mail center@tat.or.th; internet www.tourismthailand.org; f. 1960; Gov. SURAPHON SVETASRENI.

Tourism Council of Thailand: 16th floor, 1600 Thanon Phetchaburi Tat Mai, Makkasan, Ratchathewi, Bangkok 10400; e-mail info@thailandtourismcouncil.org; internet www.thailandtourismcouncil.org; co-ordinates policy and projects between private sector and govt; membership comprises more than 60 tourism asscns; Pres. PIYAMAN TEJAPAIBUL.

Defence

As assessed at November 2010, the total strength of the armed forces was 305,860: army 190,000 (including an estimated 70,000 conscripts), navy 69,860 (25,849 conscripts), air force an estimated 46,000. Paramilitary forces numbered approximately 113,700, including a National Security Volunteer Corps of 45,000. Military service lasts for two years between the ages of 21 and 30 and is compulsory.

Defence Expenditure: Budget for 2011 was estimated at 170,000m. baht.

Chief of the Defence Forces: Gen. SONGKITTI JAGGABATARA.

Chief of Staff of the Royal Thai Armed Forces: Gen. DAPONG RATANASUWAN.

Commander-in-Chief of the Army: Gen. PRAYUTH CHANOCHA.

Commander-in-Chief of the Air Force: Air Chief Marshal ITTHAPORN SUBHAWONG.

Commander-in-Chief of the Navy: Adm. KAMTHORN PHUMPIRUN.

Education

Education in Thailand is free and compulsory for nine years, following the implementation of the Compulsory Education Act of 2003, which extended the period from six years. In 2002 12 years of free basic education was granted to all students throughout the country, and in 2004 this was extended to 14 years, with the two years of pre-primary schooling henceforth also being offered free to all.

Pre-primary education begins at three years and enrolment was equivalent to 80% of the relevant age-group (males 80%, females 80%) in 2007/08. Primary education starts at the age of six and lasts for six years. In 2008/09 enrolment at primary level included 90% (males 91%, females 89%) of the relevant age-group. Secondary education, which also lasts for six years, is divided into two three-year cycles. Enrolment at secondary schools in 2008/09 included 72% (males 68%, females 77%) of students in the relevant age-group. There are numerous public and private universities in Thailand, including 41 Rajabhat Universities (formerly teacher-training colleges) and nine branches of the Rajamangala University of Technology. In 2006 enrolment in tertiary institutions was equivalent to 46% (males 44%, females 47%) of students in the relevant age-group. According to preliminary figures, government expenditure on education amounted to 397,800m. baht (20.2% of total government expenditure) in 2008/09.

TIMOR-LESTE
(EAST TIMOR)
Introductory Survey

LOCATION, CLIMATE, LANGUAGE, RELIGION, FLAG, CAPITAL

The Democratic Republic of Timor-Leste, which is styled Timor Loro Sa'e (Timor of the rising sun) in the principal indigenous language, Tetum, occupies the eastern half of the island of Timor, which lies off the north coast of Western Australia. The western half of the island is Indonesian territory and constitutes part of the East Nusa Tenggara Province. In addition to the eastern half of Timor island, the territory also includes an enclave around Oecusse (Oekussi) Ambeno on the north-west coast of the island, and the islands of Ataúro (Pulo Cambing) and Jaco (Pulo Jako). Timor's climate is dominated by intense monsoon rain, succeeded by a pronounced dry season. The north coast of the island has a brief rainy season from December to February; the south coast a double rainy season from December to June, with a respite in March. The mountainous spine of the island has heavy rains that feed torrential floods. Tetum and Portuguese are the official languages. More than 30 languages are in use in Timor-Leste. The predominant religion is Christianity; 86% of the population were adherents of Roman Catholicism in 1997. Islam and animism are also practised. A national flag was officially adopted on 20 May 2002. The flag (proportions 1 by 2) displays a black triangle at the hoist (approximately one-third of the length of the flag) overlapping a yellow triangle (approximately one-half of the length of the flag) on a red background. The black triangle bears a five-pointed white star with one point aimed at the upper hoist corner. The capital is Dili.

CONTEMPORARY POLITICAL HISTORY
Historical Context

The Portuguese began trading in Timor in about 1520, principally for sandalwood, and they later established settlements and several ports on the island. They were forced to move to the north and east of the island by the Dutch, who had arrived in the early part of the 18th century and had established themselves at Kupana in the south-west. The division of the island between Portugal and the Netherlands was formalized in a treaty of 1859, although the boundaries were modified slightly in 1904. Portuguese Timor and Macao were administered as a single entity until 1896, when Portuguese Timor became a separate province. The eastern half remained a Portuguese overseas province when the Dutch recognized the western area as part of Indonesia in 1949.

The military coup in Portugal in April 1974 was followed by increased political activity in Portuguese Timor. In August 1975 the União Democrática Timorense (UDT—Timorese Democratic Union) demanded independence for Timor. The UDT allied with two other parties, the Associação Popular Democrática de Timor (APODETI—Popular Democratic Association of Timor) and the Klibur Oan Timor Asuwain (KOTA—Association of Timorese Heroes), against the alleged threat of a communist regime being established by the Frente Revolucionária do Timor Leste Independente (Fretilin—Revolutionary Front for an Independent East Timor), and fighting broke out. The UDT forces were supported by the Indonesians. Gains on both sides were uneven, with Fretilin in control of Dili in mid-September. In the same month the Portuguese administration abandoned the capital and moved to the offshore island of Ataúro. A Portuguese attempt to arrange peace talks was rejected in October. The Indonesians intervened directly and by the beginning of December Indonesian troops controlled the capital. In November Portuguese-Indonesian peace talks in Italy were unsuccessful, and diplomatic relations were suspended after Indonesian military involvement. Two meetings of the UN Security Council voted for immediate withdrawal of Indonesian troops. Fretilin's unilateral declaration of independence in November was recognized in December by the People's Republic of China. In December the enclave of Oecusse (Oekussi) Ambeno in West Timor was declared part of Indonesian territory. In May 1976 the People's Representative Council of East Timor voted for integration with Indonesia. However, the UN did not recognize the composition of the Council as being representative, and by mid-1976 the Portuguese had not formally ceded the right to govern, although they had no remaining presence in the territory.

In July 1976 East Timor was declared the 27th province of Indonesia. Human rights organizations claimed that as many as 200,000 people, from a total population of 650,000, might have been killed by the Indonesian armed forces during the annexation. In February 1983 the UN Commission on Human Rights adopted a resolution affirming East Timor's right to independence and self-determination.

Domestic Political Affairs

In September 1983, following a five-month cease-fire (during which government representatives negotiated with Fretilin), the armed forces launched a major new offensive. The rebels suffered a serious set-back in August 1985, when the Australian Government recognized Indonesia's incorporation of East Timor. In November 1988 Gen. Suharto, the President of Indonesia, visited East Timor, prior to announcing that travel restrictions (in force since the annexation in 1976) were to be withdrawn. The territory was opened to visitors in December 1988. In October 1989 the Pope visited East Timor, as part of a tour of Indonesia, and made a plea to the Government to halt violations of human rights. In November 1990 the Government rejected proposals by the military commander of Fretilin, José Alexandre 'Xanana' Gusmão, for unconditional peace negotiations aimed at ending the armed struggle in East Timor.

In 1991 tension in East Timor increased prior to a proposed visit by a Portuguese parliamentary delegation. Some Timorese alleged that the armed forces had initiated a campaign of intimidation to discourage demonstrations during the Portuguese visit. The mission, which was to have taken place in November, was postponed, owing to Indonesia's objection to the inclusion of an Australian journalist who was a prominent critic of Indonesia's policies in East Timor. In November the armed forces fired on a peaceful demonstration (believed to have been originally organized to coincide with the Portuguese visit) at the funeral of a separatist sympathizer in Dili. The Indonesian Armed Forces (ABRI), which admitted killing 20 civilians, claimed that the attack had been provoked by armed Fretilin activists. Independent observers and human rights groups refuted this and estimated the number of deaths at between 100 and 180. There were also subsequent allegations of the summary execution of as many as 100 witnesses. Under intense international pressure, Suharto established a National Investigation Commission. However, the impartiality of the Commission was challenged on the grounds that it excluded non-governmental organizations (NGOs), and Fretilin announced that it would boycott the investigation. Despite this, the Commission's findings received cautious foreign approbation, as they were mildly critical of ABRI and stated that 50 people had died, and 90 disappeared, in the massacre. The senior military officers in East Timor were replaced, and 14 members of the armed forces were tried by a military tribunal. The most severe penalty received by any of the soldiers involved was 18 months' imprisonment; this contrasted with the sentences of convicted demonstrators, which ranged from five years' to life imprisonment.

In July 1992 Indonesia and Portugal agreed to resume discussions on East Timor under the auspices of the UN Secretary-General. In August the UN General Assembly adopted its first resolution condemning Indonesia's violations of fundamental human rights in East Timor. In September the appointment of Abílio Soares as Governor of East Timor provoked widespread criticism in the province; although Soares was a native of East Timor, he was a leading advocate of the Indonesian occupation. In October the US Congress suspended defence training aid to Indonesia, in protest at the killing of separatist demonstrators in November 1991. In October 1992, prior to the anniversary of the massacre, Amnesty International, the human rights organization, reported that hundreds of suspected supporters of independence had been arrested and tortured to prevent a commemorative demonstration.

In November 1992 Xanana Gusmão was arrested. He was subsequently taken to Jakarta, where he was to be tried in February 1993 on charges of subversion and illegal possession of firearms. In May Gusmão was found guilty of rebellion, conspiracy, attempting to establish a separate state and illegal possession of weapons, and was condemned to life imprisonment. The sentence was commuted to 20 years by Suharto in August. During the same month it was announced that all government combat forces were to be withdrawn from East Timor, leaving only troops involved in development projects. In September, however, the acting leader of Fretilin, Konis Santana, declared that, contrary to announcements, the Indonesians were renewing their forces in East Timor and that killings and atrocities continued.

In December 1993 Xanana Gusmão managed to convey letters to the Portuguese Government and the International Commission of Jurists demanding an annulment of his trial, owing to the lack of impartiality of his defence lawyer. The Government subsequently banned Gusmão from receiving visitors. In January 1994 Indonesia announced to the UN Secretary-General's envoy that it would facilitate access to East Timor by human rights and UN organizations. In May, however, a privately organized human rights conference being held in the Philippines, entitled the Asia-Pacific Conference on East Timor, provoked diplomatic tension with the Indonesian Government, which had attempted to force the abandonment of the conference. The outcome of the conference was the establishment of an Asia-Pacific coalition on East Timor, which consisted mainly of NGOs active in the region.

In July 1994 the Indonesian authorities suppressed a demonstration in Dili, following weeks of increasing tension in the capital; at least three people were reportedly killed during the protest. Discussions between the armed forces and Xanana Gusmão in August were reported to have included consideration of the possibility of holding a referendum under the auspices of the UN to determine the future status of the disputed territory. The Indonesian Minister of Foreign Affairs, Ali Alatas, held discussions in October in New York, USA, with José Ramos Horta, the Secretary for International Relations of Fretilin, the first such talks to be officially recognized. At the beginning of November President Suharto agreed to hold talks with exiled East Timorese dissidents. However, the Government's increasingly conciliatory position on East Timor was reported largely to be a superficial attempt to improve Indonesia's human rights image prior to its hosting of the Asia-Pacific Economic Co-operation (APEC, see p. 197) summit meeting in mid-November.

In January 1995 Alatas, the Portuguese Minister of Foreign Affairs and the UN Secretary-General met in Geneva, Switzerland, for the fifth round of talks on East Timor. Agreement was reached to convene a meeting between separatist and pro-integrationist Timorese activists under the auspices of the UN, called the All-Inclusive Intra-East Timorese Dialogue (AETD). The AETD, which was held in June 1995, March 1996 and October 1997, failed to achieve any conclusive progress. The sixth and seventh rounds of talks between the Portuguese and Indonesian ministers responsible for foreign affairs took place in July 1995 and January 1996, again with little progress.

In September 1995 the worst rioting that year took place in protest against Indonesian Muslim immigrants, following an Indonesian prison official's alleged insult to Roman Catholicism. Mosques and Muslim businesses were burned, and some Muslims were forced to flee the island. Further riots erupted in October, in which rival groups of separatists and integrationists clashed on the streets. The Roman Catholic Apostolic Administrator in Dili, the Rt Rev. Carlos Filipe Ximenes Belo, persuaded the rioters to return home following an agreement with ABRI; however, the agreement was subsequently broken by the armed forces, who arrested more than 250 alleged rioters.

From September 1995 East Timorese activists began forcing entry into foreign embassies in Jakarta and appealing for political asylum. They were granted asylum by the Portuguese, who were still officially recognized by the UN as the administrative power in East Timor. The Indonesian Government permitted the asylum-seekers to leave, but denied that there was any persecution in East Timor. The culmination of the successful campaign was the storming by activists of the Dutch and Russian embassies in December. The demonstrators, some of whom were non-Timorese and belonged to a radical group called the People's Democratic Union, demanded unsuccessfully a meeting with the UN High Commissioner for Human Rights (see p. 52), José Ayala Lasso, who was visiting Indonesia and who, following a brief visit to East Timor, confirmed the occurrence of severe violations of human rights in the province.

In February 1996 President Suharto and the Portuguese Prime Minister met in Bangkok, Thailand (the first meeting on the subject of East Timor by heads of government). During the negotiations Portugal offered to re-establish diplomatic links in return for the release of Xanana Gusmão and the guarantee of human rights in East Timor. International awareness of East Timor was heightened in October, when Bishop Belo and José Ramos Horta were jointly awarded the Nobel Prize for Peace. The Indonesian Government, displeased with the Nobel committee's choice, declared that there would be no change in its policy on East Timor. Ramos Horta himself declared that the award should have been made to Xanana Gusmão and invited the Indonesian Government to enter into serious negotiations on the future of East Timor. Four days after the announcement of the award, Suharto visited East Timor for the first time in eight years. Ramos Horta was banned from visiting the Philippines for the duration of an APEC summit meeting that took place there in late 1996; this ban was subsequently extended.

In November 1996 the Indonesian Government withdrew permission for foreign journalists to visit East Timor, where they had planned to attend a press conference conducted by Belo. In December Ramos Horta and Belo attended the Nobel Prize ceremony in Oslo, Norway. Riots in Dili (following a gathering of Belo's supporters to welcome him upon his return) resulted in the death of a member of ABRI; it was reported later in the month that at least one East Timorese citizen had been killed by the Indonesian authorities in a raid to capture those believed to be responsible for the soldier's death.

Following an increase in clashes between resistance forces and ABRI prior to the general election, in June 1997 a military commander of Fretilin, David Alex, was apprehended by the Indonesian armed forces. His subsequent death in custody was highly controversial; resistance groups rejected the official explanation that he had been fatally injured in a clash with security forces and claimed that he had been tortured to death. Guerrilla activity subsequently intensified, and in September at least seven Indonesian soldiers were killed in a clash with resistance forces. Further fighting took place in November and December.

In November 1997 the Australia-East Timor Association released a report cataloguing human rights abuses allegedly perpetrated by members of the Indonesian armed forces against Timorese women; abuses cited in the report included enforced prostitution, rape and compulsory sterilization programmes. Also in November shots were fired when Indonesian troops stormed the campus of the University of East Timor in Dili, following a vigil held by students to commemorate the massacre in Dili in 1991. According to reports, at least one student was killed in the incident, a number of others were injured and many were arrested. Belo accused the Indonesian security forces of having used 'excessive force', and this was confirmed by a report made by the Indonesian National Commission on Human Rights in December 1997. Also in December the Commission demanded the abolition of the country's anti-subversion legislation. In the same month two Timorese were sentenced to death under the legislation for their part in an ambush of election security officials earlier in the year, prompting threats of increased guerrilla activities by separatist forces, and a further four were sentenced to 12 years' imprisonment for taking part in armed resistance operations.

In January 1998 it was announced that a Timorese resistance congress that was due to be held in Portugal in March was to be replaced by a national convention to ensure the participation of the UDT. The convention, held in April, unanimously approved the 'Magna Carta' of East Timor, a charter intended to provide the basis for the constitution of future self-determination within the territory, and ratified plans for the establishment of the Conselho Nacional de Resistência Timorense (National Council of Timorese Resistance), a body intended to give the Timorese resistance movement a single national structure and to bring together representatives of the defunct National Council of Maubere Resistance (Conselho Nacional da Resistência Maubere—CNRM), Fretilin and the UDT. Xanana Gusmão was appointed President of the new Conselho Nacional de Resistência Timorense, and Ramos Horta was named as Vice-

President. In March 1998, meanwhile, Konis Santana, the acting military leader of Fretilin, died following an accident; Taur Matan Ruak was appointed as his successor.

Following his accession to the Indonesian presidency in May 1998, B. J. Habibie publicly suggested that the territory might be given a new 'special' status within Indonesia and that troops might be withdrawn, but there was no initial indication that the Government was contemplating independence for the territory. While a number of prominent political prisoners were released soon after Habibie replaced Suharto as President, Xanana Gusmão's 20-year sentence was reduced by a mere four months. Following the killing of an East Timorese youth by Indonesian soldiers in June, the Government renewed efforts to demonstrate its conciliatory position and, in July, effected a much-publicized withdrawal of a limited number of troops from the territory. However, opposition groups subsequently claimed that fresh troops were being sent by the Indonesian Government to replace those leaving (a claim denied by Indonesian military leaders).

In August 1998 it was announced that Indonesia and Portugal had agreed to hold discussions on the possibility of 'wide-ranging' autonomy for East Timor, and in November the UN was reported to be opening discussions with the two countries regarding a UN plan for extensive autonomy for the territory. Following an outbreak of severe violence in the Alas region of East Timor later that month, in which 82 people were reported to have been killed, Portugal suspended its involvement in the talks; however, in January 1999 it was announced that the talks were to resume. During his visit to East Timor in December 1998, UN special envoy Jamsheed Marker held talks with both Gusmão and Belo; in the same month, Gusmão reportedly advocated that the Timorese people should consider the UN's proposal for autonomy, but only as a transitional stage prior to the holding of a referendum (the possibility of which, in December, was still ruled out by the Indonesian Government).

In January 1999 the Australian Government announced a significant change in its policy on East Timor, stating that it intended actively to promote 'self-determination' in the territory (although the precise intended meaning of 'self-determination' remained unclear). Later in January total independence for East Timor in the near future emerged as an apparent possibility when, in its boldest move to date to appease the East Timorese and the international community, the Indonesian Government suggested that a vote might be held in the national legislature, the Majelis Permusyawaratan Rakyat (MPR, People's Consultative Assembly), following the election to the House of Representatives (the lower chamber of the MPR) scheduled for June, on the issue of Indonesia's granting independence to the territory. As a result of a request from the UN Secretary-General, Kofi Annan, the Government also announced that it was to allow Xanana Gusmão to serve the remainder of his 20-year prison sentence under house arrest in Jakarta. Following the Government's announcement regarding the possibility of independence for East Timor, a number of outbreaks of violence, attributed to supporters of the territory's integration with Indonesia, were reported to have occurred.

The 1999 vote for independence and subsequent events

On 27 January 1999 the Indonesian Government unexpectedly announced that, if the East Timorese voted to reject Indonesia's proposals for autonomy, it would consider granting independence to the province. Although the Indonesian Government was initially opposed to a referendum on the issue of independence for East Timor, it signed an agreement with Portugal on 5 May, giving its assent to a process of 'popular consultation' taking the form of a UN-supervised poll to determine the future status of East Timor. (In an Australian television interview in November 2008, Habibie revealed that his decision to allow a referendum was due to heavy influence from the Australian Prime Minister, John Howard, who had written to Habibie suggesting that East Timor be given the opportunity to vote on independence.) The UN Mission in East Timor (UNAMET) was established by the UN Security Council in June to organize the poll in which the East Timorese could opt for a form of political autonomy or for independence. The 'popular consultation' was initially scheduled to be held on 8 August, and all East Timorese, including those living in exile, were to be allowed to participate in the ballot.

Following the announcement of the scheduled referendum, violence in the territory escalated. In advance of the poll, anti-independence militia groups based within East Timor initiated a campaign of violence and intimidation, which included summary killings, kidnappings, harassment and the forced recruitment of young East Timorese. The Indonesian military itself was discovered to be not only supporting but also recruiting, training and organizing many of the militias. Violence continued to escalate throughout the territory during April and May 1999. In one incident, in April, anti-independence militia members massacred 57 people in a churchyard in the town of Liquiça (Likisia); further massacres were reported to have occurred in other areas, including Dili. Also in April Xanana Gusmão (now under house arrest in Jakarta) responded to the increasing violence from anti-independence militias by reversing his previous position and urging guerrillas in Fretilin's military wing, the Forças Armadas Libertação Nacional de Timor Leste (Falintil), to resume their struggle. Although rival pro-independence and integrationist factions signed a peace accord in June supporting a cease-fire and disarmament in advance of the scheduled referendum, the violence continued unabated.

The escalating violence in the territory, together with logistical difficulties, led the UN to postpone the referendum to 21 August 1999 and then to 30 August. Although intimidation and violence by the militias continued, the referendum proceeded on 30 August. About 98.5% of those eligible to vote participated in the poll, which resulted in an overwhelming rejection, by 78.5% of voters, of the Indonesian Government's proposals for autonomy and in the endorsement of independence for East Timor. However, the announcement of the result of the referendum precipitated a rapid descent into anarchy. Pro-Jakarta militias embarked upon a campaign of murder and destruction in which hundreds of civilians were killed; as many as 500,000 (according to the UN) were forced to flee their homes, and many buildings were destroyed in arson attacks. While many of those who were displaced from their homes sought refuge in the hills, about one-half were estimated by the UN to have left the territory (a large number having entered West Timor), some involuntarily. In one incident during the campaign of extreme violence that followed the announcement of the result of the referendum, anti-independence militia members stormed the residence of Bishop Belo, evicting at gunpoint some 6,000 refugees who had sought shelter in the compound; the home of the bishop was burned down and dozens of East Timorese were reported to have been killed in the attack. Bishop Belo was evacuated to Australia, while Xanana Gusmão (who was released from house arrest in Jakarta by the Indonesian Government on 7 September) took refuge in the British embassy in Jakarta. Thousands of civilians besieged the UN compound in Dili, the premises of other international agencies, churches and police stations, seeking protection from the indiscriminate attacks of the militias. On 7 September martial law was declared in the territory, and a curfew was imposed. However, the violence continued unabated, and in mid-September, following international condemnation of the situation and intense diplomatic pressure, the Indonesian Government reversed its earlier opposition to a proposal by the Australian Government and agreed to permit the deployment of a multinational peace-keeping force. As the massacre of civilians continued, thousands of refugees were airlifted to safety in northern Australia, along with the remaining employees of the UN (many local staff members of UNAMET were among the victims of the violence); shortly after the UN withdrew its staff, anti-independence militia members set fire to the UN compound in Dili. Meanwhile, aid agencies warned that as many as 300,000 East Timorese people would starve if humanitarian assistance were not urgently provided.

The first contingent of several thousand UN peace-keeping troops, forming the International Force for East Timor (Interfet), was deployed in the territory on 20 September 1999. Led by Australia, which committed 4,500 troops, the force gradually restored order. A week later the Indonesian armed forces formally relinquished responsibility for security to the multinational force. At the end of October, after 24 years as an occupying force, the last Indonesian soldiers left East Timor. In late September Indonesia and Portugal reiterated their agreement for the transfer of authority in East Timor to the UN. On 19 October the result of the referendum was ratified by the MPR, thus permitting East Timor's accession to independence to proceed. Shortly thereafter, on 25 October, the UN Security Council established the UN Transitional Administration in East Timor (UNTAET) as an integrated peace-keeping operation fully responsible for the administration of East Timor during its transition to independence. UNTAET, with an initial mandate until 31 January 2001, was to exercise all judicial and executive authority in East Timor, to undertake the establishment and training of a new police force, and to assume responsibility for the co-ordination and provision of humanitarian assistance and emergency rehabilitation; the transfer of command of military operations in the territory from Interfet to the UNTAET peace-keeping force was completed on 23 February 2000. Meanwhile, the UN also began a large-scale emergency humanitarian relief effort; however, many displaced and homeless East Timorese remained without access to adequate food supplies, shelter and basic health care facilities.

Following reports that in mid-October 1999 Indonesian troops and militias had entered the isolated East Timorese enclave of Oecusse (situated within West Timor) and allegedly massacred around 50 people, Interfet troops were deployed in Oecusse; most of the enclave's population of 57,000 were believed to have been removed to refugee camps in West Timor, and by early November only 10,000 of its citizens had been accounted for. Following his popularly acclaimed return to Dili in October, Xanana Gusmão met with the UNTAET Transitional Administrator, Sérgio Vieira de Mello, in November, and reportedly communicated the concerns of local East Timorese organizations that they were being marginalized by UNTAET officials. In late November he visited Jakarta in order to establish relations with the Indonesian Government, and in December he visited Australia, where he met with representatives of the Australian Government to discuss the Timor Gap Treaty. (The Treaty, which had been concluded between Australia and Indonesia in 1991, provided a framework for petroleum and gas exploration in the maritime zone between Australia and East Timor and for the division of any resulting royalties between Australia and Indonesia. However, Indonesia ceased to be party to the original Treaty when it relinquished control of East Timor in October 1999, and the transitional administration in East Timor subsequently expressed a desire to renegotiate the terms of the Treaty, which the UN considered to have no legal standing, as Indonesian sovereignty over East Timor had never been recognized by the international body. In February 2000 a memorandum of understanding (MOU) relating to the Treaty was signed by the Australian Government and East Timor's UN administrators, temporarily maintaining the arrangement for the division of royalties (although between Australia and East Timor rather than Australia and Indonesia). East Timor received its first payment of royalties from Australia under the MOU in October 2000. In the same month, however, the formal renegotiation of the Treaty began, with East Timor requesting the redrawing of the boundaries covered by the Treaty and a larger share of petroleum and gas royalties. Following independence in May 2002, both countries formally signed the Treaty. However, owing to prolonged negotiations over the division of royalties, Australia did not ratify the agreement until March 2003.)

On 1 December 1999 José Ramos Horta returned to East Timor after 24 years of exile. Ramos Horta, who commanded much popular support, urged the East Timorese people to show forgiveness towards their former oppressors and appealed for reconciliation between Indonesia and East Timor. On 11 December Vieira de Mello convened the first meeting of the National Consultative Council (NCC) in Dili; the 15-member Council, comprising members of the Conselho Nacional de Resistência Timorense and other East Timorese political representatives as well as UNTAET officials, was established in late 1999 to advise UNTAET.

A number of mass graves containing the bodies of suspected victims of the violence perpetrated by the anti-independence militias both before and after the holding of the referendum in August 1999 were discovered in East Timor (including two in the Oecusse enclave) in late 1999 and early 2000. In December 1999 Sonia Picado Sotela, the Chair of the International Commission of Inquiry in East Timor, confirmed that the team of UN investigators had discovered evidence of 'systematic killing'.

In January 2000 a panel appointed by the Indonesian Government to investigate human rights abuses in East Timor delivered its report to the Indonesian Attorney-General. The panel reportedly named 24 individuals whom it recommended should be prosecuted for their alleged involvement in violations of human rights in the territory. One of those named was the former Minister of Defence and Security and Commander-in-Chief of the Indonesian armed forces, Gen. Wiranto, who had since been appointed Co-ordinating Minister for Political, Legal and Security Affairs in the Indonesian Government; also named were a number of senior military officers, as well as leaders of the pro-Jakarta militias responsible for the extreme violence perpetrated during the period following the referendum. However, pro-independence leaders in East Timor strongly criticized the report as inadequate. In the same month the International Commission of Inquiry in East Timor recommended that the UN establish an independent international body to investigate allegations of human rights violations in East Timor, and an international tribunal to deal with the cases of those accused by the investigators. In February the recently appointed President of Indonesia, Abdurrahman Wahid, visited East Timor and publicly apologized for the atrocities committed by the Indonesian armed forces during the Republic's occupation of the territory. Wahid reaffirmed the commitment of the Indonesian Government to the prosecution of any individuals implicated in the violation of human rights in East Timor. In the same month Wahid suspended Gen. Wiranto from the Indonesian Government. (Wiranto subsequently resigned in May.) The UN Secretary-General, Kofi Annan, made an official visit to East Timor in mid-February, during which he pledged that investigations into violations of human rights in the territory would be carried out.

In April 2000 UNTAET signed an agreement with the Indonesian Government regarding the extradition to East Timor of Indonesian citizens who were to be charged in connection with the violence of 1999. In July 2000 a team from the Indonesian Attorney-General's Office visited East Timor to investigate a limited number of cases of human rights violations. However, relations between East Timor and Indonesia remained tense, and the introduction in August 2000 (in the closing stages of the annual session of the country's principal legislative body, the MPR) of an amendment to Indonesia's Constitution providing for the exclusion of military personnel from retroactive prosecution prompted fears among many international observers that the possibility of the prosecution of members of the Indonesian military believed responsible for recent human rights abuses in East Timor would be placed in serious jeopardy (despite the suggestions of senior Indonesian legislators that the amendment would probably not apply to crimes such as genocide, war crimes and terrorism). In September the Indonesian Attorney-General's Office named 19 people whom it suspected of involvement in the violence of 1999. While human rights groups in both East Timor and Indonesia welcomed the publication of the list, which included the names of several former high-ranking members of the Indonesian armed forces, there was widespread disappointment that Gen. Wiranto was not among those named.

Progression towards sovereignty

In June 2000 an agreement was reached between UNTAET and East Timorese leaders on the formation of a new transitional coalition Government, in which the two sides were to share political responsibility. The Cabinet of the new transitional Government, which was formally appointed in July, initially incorporated four East Timorese cabinet ministers, including João Carrascalão, President of the UDT and a Vice-President of the Conselho Nacional de Resistência Timorense, who was allocated responsibility for infrastructure, and Mari Alkatiri, Secretary-General of Fretilin, who was appointed Minister of Economic Affairs. The new Cabinet also included four international representatives. Mariano Lopes da Cruz, an East Timorese national, was appointed Inspector-General. It was reported that Xanana Gusmão, while holding no formal position in the new Government, was to be consulted on an informal basis by Sérgio Vieira de Mello (who was to retain ultimate control over the approval of any draft legislation proposed to the Cabinet) with respect to all political decisions. In October the Cabinet was expanded to nine members, with the appointment of José Ramos Horta as Minister of Foreign Affairs and Co-operation.

In July 2000 UNTAET approved the establishment of a 'National Council' to advise the new Cabinet. The East Timorese National Council, the membership of which was expanded from 33 to 36 in October, consisted of a selection of East Timorese representatives from the political, religious and private sectors. The new National Council was inaugurated on 23 October and replaced the 15-member NCC. In the same month Xanana Gusmão was elected to lead the National Council.

In August 2000, meanwhile, Xanana Gusmão retired as the Military Commander of Falintil, in order to concentrate on his political role in the process of guiding East Timor towards full independence, relinquishing control of the guerrilla army to his deputy, Taur Matan Ruak. Initially, the future of Falintil appeared uncertain, and the refusal of the UN to allow the active involvement of the unit in attempts to combat incursions by Indonesian paramilitaries into East Timor led Gusmão to voice indirect criticism of the international organization in his resignation speech. In February 2001, however, a new East Timor Defence Force (Falintil-ETDF) was established, consisting of an initial 650 recruits drawn exclusively from the ranks of Falintil, which was itself to be dissolved. The former Military Commander of the guerrilla army, Taur Matan Ruak, was promoted to the rank of Brigadier-General and appointed to command the new force. Meanwhile, a fund was established to finance the support and retraining of an estimated 1,000 Falintil veterans who were to be demobilized. Training of the new Defence Force was to be conducted by Portugal and Australia; its role was described as that of 'policing', with the defence of the territory remaining the responsibility of UNTAET peace-keeping troops.

In December 2000 four of the five East Timorese members of the transitional Cabinet threatened to resign, reportedly in protest at their treatment by the UN. The ministers, who allegedly claimed that they were merely 'puppet ministers' in the new coalition Government, demanded further clarification of the legal status of the Cabinet and of their authority as individual cabinet ministers, and called for the establishment of a more clearly defined relationship between UNTAET and the Cabinet. Further complaints about UNTAET's treatment of East Timorese officials were voiced at a donors' conference for East Timor held in the same month, and press reports suggested the existence of a level of public resentment of the UN's presence in East Timor. However, in January 2001 Ramos Horta warned that any attempt to scale down the UN's presence in East Timor would destabilize the territory's progression towards independence. In late January 2001 the UN Security Council extended UNTAET's mandate (which had initially been scheduled to expire on 31 January 2001) until 31 January 2002. However, it was acknowledged that modifications of the mandate might be necessary to take into account developments in East Timor's progression towards full independence, and, in January 2002, the mandate was extended until 20 May 2002, the date set for independence. From August 2000, meanwhile, in a move that allowed for greater formal East Timorese influence in the governing of the territory during the period preceding the territory's accession to full independence, a process commenced whereby the transitional Government began to be redefined as the East Timorese Transitional Administration (ETTA). Consisting of both UNTAET and East Timorese staff, ETTA was composed of the transitional Cabinet, the National Council and the judiciary. Final authority over ETTA rested with the Special Representative of the UN Secretary-General and Transitional Administrator, Sérgio Vieira de Mello.

In February 2001 legislation providing for an election to an 88-seat Constituent Assembly, to be conducted on 30 August, was approved. The single chamber was to comprise 75 deputies elected on a national basis, using proportional representation, and one elected delegate from each of East Timor's 13 districts, chosen on a 'first-past-the-post' basis. The members of the Constituent Assembly were to be responsible for the preparation and adoption of a constitution, which would require the endorsement of at least 60 members.

In March 2001 Xanana Gusmão tendered his resignation as Speaker of the National Council, having become disaffected by the stagnation of the political process. At the same time he announced that he would not stand for President in the forthcoming election for the post, despite commanding an overwhelming level of public support for his candidacy. In April UNTAET announced that José Ramos Horta would serve as Gusmão's replacement on the National Council, prompting his resignation as the Minister of Foreign Affairs and Co-operation (the two posts could not be held simultaneously). However, in the 9 April election for the post of Speaker, Manuel Carrascalão emerged victorious, defeating Ramos Horta, and criticized UNTAET for supporting his rival. Two weeks later José Ramos Horta resigned from the National Council and resumed his position in the transitional Cabinet. In June the Conselho Nacional de Resistência Timorense announced its dissolution, reportedly in order to enable the groups of which it was comprised to evolve into fully independent political parties, and, in August, Gusmão finally yielded to immense popular pressure and international encouragement and announced his intention to stand for the presidency in 2002.

On 30 August 2001 91.3% of the eligible populace turned out to vote in the country's first free parliamentary election. Fretilin secured 55 of the 88 seats available in the Constituent Assembly, commanding 57% of the votes cast. In second place, with seven seats, was the Partido Democrático (PD, Democratic Party). The Partido Social Democrata (PSD, Social Democrat Party) and the Associação Social-Democrata Timorense (ASDT, Timor Social Democratic Association) won six seats each. In September Sérgio Vieira de Mello swore in the members of the Constituent Assembly, and five days later the second transitional Government was appointed. Mari Alkatiri of Fretilin was appointed leader of the Cabinet and retained the economy portfolio. José Ramos Horta continued as Minister of Foreign Affairs and Co-operation. Of 20 available government positions, nine were allocated to Fretilin, two to the PD and the remaining nine to independents and various experts. In October the Constituent Assembly appointed a committee to oversee the drafting of the Constitution, taking into account the views of over 36,000 East Timorese summarized in reports presented by 13 constitutional commissions. In November 2001 the Assembly approved the structure of the draft Constitution.

In December 2000 UNTAET issued its first indictments for crimes committed against humanity in connection with the violence that had surrounded the referendum in 1999, charging 11 people (including an officer of the Indonesian special forces) with the murder of nine civilians in September 1999. In January 2001 an East Timor court sentenced a former pro-Jakarta militia member to 12 years' imprisonment for the murder of a village chief in September 1999, marking the first successful prosecution related to the violence of 1999. In September 2001 the UN filed 'extermination' charges against nine militiamen and two Indonesian soldiers accused of murdering 65 people two years previously. In October, in the first civil case of its kind, a US federal court awarded six East Timorese a total of US $66m. in damages after Indonesian Gen. Johny Lumintang was found to bear responsibility for human rights abuses. In December 2001 a UN tribunal took the first step in bringing those responsible for the atrocities committed in 1999 to justice. Of the 11 individuals indicted in December 2000, 10 were convicted of crimes against humanity and sentenced to prison terms of up to 33 years. However, the Jakarta authorities resisted the extradition of the indicted Indonesian Special Forces Officer to stand trial.

In February 2000 the UN expressed its concern that very few of the estimated 90,000 East Timorese refugees remaining in camps across the border in West Timor were returning to East Timor; it had earlier been reported that pro-Jakarta militias had been intimidating the refugees in West Timor and preventing them from returning home. In September the UN temporarily suspended its relief work among East Timorese refugees in West Timor, following the murder by pro-Jakarta militias of three UN aid workers in the territory earlier in the month. The murders prompted international criticism of the Indonesian Government for its failure to control the militia groups operating in West Timor. In November Ramos Horta alleged that estimates of the number of East Timorese refugees residing in West Timor (reported by some sources to be as high as 130,000) were being deliberately exaggerated by the Indonesian Government, and estimated the actual number of refugees to be no higher than 70,000. In December 2000 and January 2001, in an attempt to dispel the fears of refugees remaining in West Timor about the security situation in East Timor, UNTAET arranged for a number of groups of refugees to visit their homeland. The visits resulted in a number of refugees opting to return permanently to East Timor.

In June 2001 refugees from East Timor participated in a process of registration through which they were permitted to decide whether or not they wished to return to the newly independent state. Of the 113,791 refugees who took part, 98% wished to remain in Indonesia. However, it was thought that intimidation by pro-Indonesia militias might have influenced the result and that the survey did not necessarily reflect the participants' long-term intentions. In the same month the six men accused of the murder of the three UN aid workers in September 2000 were found guilty of violence against people and property rather than murder and given light sentences. The UN criticized the verdicts and pressed for a review. Following the formal declaration of the election results, the families of former East Timorese militiamen began returning to their homeland in mid-September 2001. In October the Indonesian authorities announced the imminent halting of aid to an estimated 80,000 East Timorese who remained in refugee camps in West Timor, and in November Gusmão visited West Timor in an effort to promote reconciliation and encourage thousands of the remaining refugees to return home.

In October 2001 the newly elected Constituent Assembly requested that the UN formally grant East Timor independence on 20 May 2002. Gusmão reluctantly lent his support to the request, although he commented that the choice of date was too politically partisan as it commemorated the 28th anniversary of the founding of the country's first political party. However, the UN Security Council endorsed the Assembly's request, and agreed to maintain a peace-keeping presence in the region for between six months and two years after the granting of independence.

On 22 March 2002 the Constituent Assembly finally promulgated East Timor's first Constitution, which was to become effective upon independence on 20 May of that year. The document provided for the adoption of Tetum and Portuguese as the country's official languages. On 14 April East Timor held its first presidential election, which resulted in an overwhelming victory for Gusmão, who secured almost 83% of the votes cast to defeat the only other candidate, Francisco Xavier do Amaral.

On 20 May 2002 East Timor celebrated its formal accession to independence, upon which it became known officially as the Democratic Republic of Timor-Leste. The tenure of the UN interim administration was officially terminated, and UNTAET was replaced by a smaller mission, the UN Mission of Support in East Timor (UNMISET), which was to remain in the country for two years to support administrative development and to assist in the maintenance of law and order, while downsizing its military presence as rapidly as possible. Xanana Gusmão was officially inaugurated as President and swore in the country's first Government. The National Parliament, as the Constituent Assembly had become, then held its inaugural session. Prime Minister Alkatiri stressed that the new Government would give priority to spending on health and education. The President of Indonesia, Megawati Sukarnoputri, attended the independence day celebrations, despite criticism from several members of the Indonesian legislature. On the following day Sérgio Vieira de Mello left the country; he was succeeded by Kamalesh Sharma, the head of UNMISET. Tension developed between Gusmão and Alkatiri after the latter was seen to have used Fretilin's parliamentary majority to secure the passage of a new Constitution that rendered Gusmão a largely symbolic head of state. The ill feeling persisted for several months, but relations between the President and the Prime Minister subsequently appeared to improve somewhat.

Continuing unrest and other concerns

In September 2002 Timor-Leste became the 191st member of the UN. In the same month the Indonesian Government announced that the remaining refugee camps in West Timor would be closed at the end of 2002; Gusmão visited the province in November in an effort to encourage the estimated 30,000 refugees who remained there to return to their homeland. In the following month the Government declared a state of alert in the country following an outbreak of rioting in Dili during which two people were killed. The protests had begun when a police officer allegedly shot at a student participating in a peaceful demonstration outside the police headquarters in the city. The violence was the worst to have occurred in the country since independence. In January 2003 further violence ensued when a group of armed men attacked villages near the town of Atsabe in the Ermera district, resulting in the deaths of five people. In the following month a bus travelling to Dili was ambushed by a group of armed men; two people subsequently died. It was feared that the violence reflected the possible establishment of several militias and insurgent groups intent on undermining the stability of the new nation.

In March 2003 Prime Minister Alkatiri announced the appointment of Ana Pessôa, hitherto Minister of Justice, to the newly created post of Deputy Prime Minister. In the following month, owing to the apparent increase of violence in Timor-Leste in the preceding months, the UN Security Council announced that UNMISET would no longer follow its original downsizing plan (under which the phased withdrawal of UN troops from the country would have commenced in July 2003) and would instead implement an alternative two-phase plan. Under the new strategy, UNMISET would retain primary responsibility for national security until December 2003, maintaining its peace-keeping force at its existing level, before preparing to hand over full responsibility for national defence to Falintil-ETDF on 20 May 2004. In May 2003 the UN Security Council formally extended the mandate of UNMISET until 20 May 2004. In October 2003 the Timorese authorities assumed responsibility for the administration of border crossings in the country from the UN. In May 2004 the UN Security Council voted unanimously to renew UNMISET's mandate, in a modified form and with a reduced military presence, until 20 May 2005. In March 2005 UN Secretary-General Kofi Annan recommended that UNMISET be deployed for an additional year, extending the mandate until 20 May 2006, a suggestion that both the USA and Australia opposed, insisting that peace-keeping forces were no longer required in the country.

From mid-2002, at a specially created court in Jakarta (the Ad Hoc Indonesian Human Rights Tribunal on East Timor), the trials took place of 18 officers, government officials and militiamen believed to have participated in the violence that had surrounded the referendum for independence in 1999. In August 2002 Abílio Soares, the former Governor of East Timor, was found guilty of two charges of 'gross rights violations'; he was sentenced to a three-year prison term. The sentence was widely criticized for its apparent leniency. In the same month the former chief of police in East Timor, Timbul Silaen, was acquitted of charges of failing to control his subordinates; five other Indonesian police and army officers were also acquitted shortly afterwards. In November former Indonesian militia leader Eurico Guterres was sentenced to 10 years in prison, having been convicted of crimes against humanity. In the following month the former military chief of Dili, Lt-Col Soedjarwo, was sentenced to a five-year prison term for his role in the violence. In March 2003 the court sentenced Brig.-Gen. Noer Muis, a former army chief in East Timor, to five years in prison for crimes against humanity. In August Indonesian armed forces officer Maj.-Gen. Adam Damiri, the last and most senior official to be tried by the tribunal, was convicted of having failed to prevent atrocities in East Timor and sentenced to three years in prison. The court was subjected to widespread international criticism, owing to the fact that only six of those tried were convicted of the charges against them. In April 2004, following an appeal, the Indonesian Supreme Court upheld the conviction of Abílio Soares. However, in July the Jakarta High Court overruled the guilty verdicts of Lt-Col Soedjarwo, Brig.-Gen. Muis, Maj.-Gen. Damiri and Col Hulman Gultom (a former Dili police chief), and also halved the sentence of Eurico Guterres to five years. The decision meant that all of the police and military officials indicted by the Tribunal had been released, leaving only the two civilians (Soares and Guterres) serving sentences. The USA and the European Union (EU) denounced the acquittals as massive failings of justice. In November, moreover, Soares was cleared of the charges against him by Indonesia's Supreme Court, leaving only the conviction of Guterres standing. However, having reinstated his 10-year sentence in March 2006, the Supreme Court decided to rescind Guterres' conviction in April 2008, and he was released from prison.

In early 2003 a UN-sponsored Special Panel for Serious Crimes (SPSC) that had been established in Dili began to issue indictments for crimes against humanity against several military officials in relation to the violence surrounding the referendum in 1999, including the former chief of the Indonesian armed forces, Gen. Wiranto, who awaited prosecution for the first time. Wiranto denied the charges against him. However, the Indonesian Government stated that it would refuse to permit the extradition of those charged to face trial. In April 2003 the SPSC sentenced José Cardosa Fereira, an East Timorese militia leader, to a 12-year prison term following his conviction for crimes against humanity. In June Quelo Mauno, a former leader of a pro-Indonesia militia, was convicted of the murder of an independence supporter in Oecusse in 1999 and sentenced to seven years in prison. In the following month the Dili court found a further two former pro-Indonesia militia leaders guilty of crimes against humanity and, by February 2004, some 47 people had been convicted of crimes relating to the referendum period. Meanwhile, the total number of people indicted by the court had risen to approximately 350, many of whom were resident in Indonesia; the Indonesian Government continued to refuse to extradite those indicted to stand trial. In May the SPSC finally issued an arrest warrant for Wiranto, who had been nominated in the previous month as a candidate for Indonesia's presidential election, the first round of which was scheduled for July. Fearing a breach in relations with Indonesia, President Gusmão and the Prosecutor-General, Longuinhos Monteiro, both acted to distance themselves from the warrant, insisting that a good rapport with neighbouring countries should take precedence over court proceedings to hold people accountable for crimes committed during the emergence of their nation. In December Timor-Leste and Indonesia agreed to establish the joint Commission of Truth and Friendship (CTF) to investigate the killings carried out during the period of the Timorese vote for independence, and this was formally approved by their respective Governments in March 2005. However, the CTF was rapidly dismissed by the international community; none of the crimes committed during Indonesian occupation prior to 1999 was to be investigated, and the CTF process was not intended to lead to prosecution. Furthermore, offenders who co-operated 'fully in revealing the truth' were to be guaranteed impunity, irrespective of the nature of their crimes. In August 2005, despite the overwhelmingly negative response to the Commission, the 10-member panel was formally sworn in. Meanwhile, in February of that year the UN established the Commission of Experts, which was to review the judicial processes of the Ad Hoc Indonesian Human Rights Tribunal on East Timor, as well as the Serious Crimes Investigation Unit and the SPSC in Timor-Leste.

In February 2004, as sporadic outbreaks of violence, reportedly perpetrated by rebel militias based in rural areas, continued to occur in Timor-Leste, Cristiano da Costa, the leader of the Conselho Popular pela Defesa da República Democrática de Timor Leste (CPD-RDTL, Popular Council for the Defence of the Democratic Republic of East Timor), announced that his organization intended to challenge the legitimacy of the established Government in Timor-Leste following the planned withdrawal of UNMISET in May of that yar. However, UNMISET's mandate was subsequently extended for an additional year, although its presence was reduced to a mere 604 officers, while responsibility for law and order in the capital and for external security was transferred to the Government in advance of the formal full transfer of power. It was feared that the methods employed by the Government to suppress insurgents might result in further instability in the country. The use of the police to suppress political opposition was a particular cause for concern. In July the National Union of Resistance Staff and Veterans held a rally in Dili, demanding a cabinet reorganization and the dismissal of the unpopular Minister of Interior Affairs, Rogério Lobato. Police officers were drafted in, and resorted to beatings and the use of tear gas to disperse the crowd; some witnesses also claimed that guns were fired. Dili was the scene of another disturbance in December of the same year, when a group of 20 armed soldiers attacked a police station, injuring two officers and causing damage to the premises. There were also numerous reported sightings of alleged ex-militia groups, especially within border areas. In January 2005, in an operation intended to verify the accuracy of one such reported sighting in the Bobonaro district, police encountered six armed men and, following the resultant exchange of gunfire, one of the group was arrested. Prime Minister Alkatiri was quick to assert that it should not be assumed that the men were necessarily acting at the behest of the Indonesian army.

In December 2004 the first local elections since Timorese independence were held in Bobonaro and in the enclave of Oecusse. In order to promote female participation, a minimum of three women were to be elected to each village council. There was a high turn-out, exceeding 90% in some areas, and voters were able to cast their ballots in a calm and orderly manner, free from intimidation. However, there were numerous logistical problems, including errors on the electoral roll, which prohibited some people from casting their vote and delayed the outcome of the elections from being determined. By October 2005 elections had been held in the remaining 11 districts. While local councils held extremely limited authority, the election results revealed a considerable decline in popular support for Fretilin. Timor-Leste's principal party still maintained a sizeable majority, but its share of the vote decreased to less than 50% in some regions, representing a marked decline from previous levels of support.

Meanwhile, on 20 May 2005 the mandate of UNMISET was officially concluded, and the last remaining UN troops were withdrawn from Timor-Leste in the following month. The UN Office in Timor-Leste (UNOTIL) was established to facilitate the transfer of complete power to the Timorese authorities; its mandate was due to be concluded on 19 May 2006.

In July 2005 Prime Minister Alkatiri effected a cabinet reorganization, providing for an enlarged Government comprising 17 ministries, with 15 deputy ministers and 11 state secretaries. Four state secretary portfolios, including those of defence and of public works, were transformed into full ministries. Alkatiri assumed control of the natural resources, minerals and energy policy portfolio, while relinquishing the development portfolio to Abel Ximenes.

In early February 2006 an estimated 400 soldiers (approximately one-quarter of Timor-Leste's 1,600-strong army) staged a protest about living conditions in their barracks and about alleged discrimination against soldiers from western regions of the country; they claimed that army officers, who were predominantly from Timor-Leste's eastern regions, frequently passed over for promotion soldiers from western regions in favour of those from their own localities. Having deserted their duties, the protesting soldiers presented a petition to President Gusmão, who promised a government inquiry into their complaints and urged them to return to their barracks. However, the rebellion escalated in late February when more than 170 additional soldiers deserted their barracks. The military leadership issued an ultimatum, demanding that they return to duty or be dismissed; when they had failed to return by March, the Commander-in-Chief of the Army, Brig.-Gen. Taur Matan Ruak, sanctioned their dismissal. Ruak's action precipitated a series of large-scale protests, which escalated into violence at the end of April, when supporters of the dismissed soldiers clashed with the police. The demonstrations, said to involve gangs, developed into looting, the destruction of property and eventually ethnic violence between eastern and western Timorese, which had claimed at least 37 lives and caused the displacement of an estimated 100,000 people by the following month. Prime Minister Alkatiri was criticized over his Government's handling of the situation, and anti-Government sentiments were increasingly voiced among protesters, who demanded Alkatiri's resignation. The turmoil led to the resignation of the Minister of Development, Abel Ximenes, at the beginning of May. At a Fretilin congress in mid-May, José Luís Guterres, the Timorese ambassador to the USA and Permanent Representative to the UN, withdrew his leadership challenge against Alkatiri after it emerged that the vote was to be determined by a show of hands rather than a secret ballot. At the end of May, in response to a request from Alkatiri, Australia deployed troops to Timor-Leste as part of an international effort to restore stability; Malaysia and New Zealand also contributed troops, while Portugal dispatched a contingent of police officers. The Minister of Foreign Affairs and Co-operation, Ramos Horta, attributed the unrest in part to a 'failure of leadership'; it was reported that Ramos Horta had communicated with Maj. Alfredo Reinado, the leader of the protesting soldiers.

President Gusmão subsequently acted to curb the violence by assuming emergency powers and control of the country's security from the Minister of Defence and Security, Roque Rodrigues, and the Minister of Interior Affairs, Rogério Lobato, both of whom resigned. Gusmão later assigned their portfolios to Ramos Horta, who engaged in dialogue with leaders of the rebel troops. Alkatiri finally yielded to considerable pressure to resign from several quarters, including Gusmão and the protesters, at the end of June 2006, following the resignation of Ramos Horta on the previous day. Ramos Horta was appointed Prime Minister, retaining the defence portfolio, in July, in advance of the swearing in of a new Cabinet comprising several ministers of the previous administration, including the Minister of Agriculture, Forestry and Fisheries, Estanislau Aleixo da Silva, as Deputy Prime Minister. Rui Maria de Araújo retained the health portfolio and was promoted to the position of Deputy Prime Minister, while José Luís Guterres became Minister of Foreign Affairs and Co-operation. The new Government was to remain in power until parliamentary elections, scheduled for mid-2007, were held.

In an indication that the security situation had improved significantly, in July 2006 Australia began to reduce its deployment in Timor-Leste, although some 2,000 personnel were projected to remain; in September Malaysia withdrew its remaining forces. Maj. Reinado was apprehended at the end of July following the expiry of a weapons amnesty, but escaped from prison in August. In the same month UNOTIL was replaced by the UN Integrated Mission in Timor-Leste (UNMIT) for an initial period of six months. With an authorized strength of up to 1,608 police personnel and up to 34 military liaison and staff officers, supported by civilian staff, UNMIT aimed to maintain security and promote reconciliation and good governance. (UNMIT's mandate was later extended—see Recent developments.)

In October 2006 the UN Independent Special Commission of Inquiry for Timor-Leste released its report on the recent unrest: among other conclusions, it found that Rodrigues, Lobato and Ruak had unlawfully transferred weapons to civilians and that, although Alkatiri was not necessarily directly implicated in the transfer, he had failed to denounce it. The Commission consequently recommended further investigation into Alkatiri's involvement. The findings followed allegations that Alkatiri had formed a militia to consolidate his power base and to take action against opponents. Lobato's trial began in January 2007. In March he was found guilty of arming a group of civilians, led by Vicente da Conceição, a former Falintil guerrilla, and was sentenced to seven-and-a-half-years' imprisonment. (In October da Conceição was himself arrested and charged in connection with his role in the unrest.) Although stability had been largely restored, outbursts of violence continued, and the ongoing plight of refugees was highlighted by the Australian Minister of Defence, Dr Brendan Nelson, in November 2006; it was estimated that 70,000 internally displaced people remained in camps. Maj. Reinado continued to elude the security forces, despite the Government's attempts at negotiation, and at the beginning of March 2007 reports of an unsuccessful attempt to capture Reinado prompted protests in Dili.

The 2007 elections and subsequent events

In February 2007 Prime Minister Ramos Horta declared his candidacy for the forthcoming presidential election. In March President Gusmão indicated his desire to become Prime Minister and announced that he intended to join the Congresso Nacional da Reconstrução de Timor-Leste (CNRT—National Congress for the Reconstruction of Timor-Leste), a new political party, following the expiry of his presidential term. The first stage of the presidential election, held on 9 April, was contested by eight candidates. Francisco Guterres, the President of Fretilin, secured 27.9% of the votes cast, followed by Ramos Horta, who was favoured by Gusmão, with 21.8%, and Fernando de Araújo, President of the PD, with 19.2%. An official appeal against the results, lodged by three of the losing candidates, including de Araújo, on the grounds of alleged widespread manipulation of the vote and other serious irregularities, was dismissed. The National Electoral Commission had earlier rejected demands from five of the candidates for a recount of the votes.

As no candidate achieved the requisite overall majority, the two leading contenders proceeded to a second round of voting, which was conducted on 9 May 2007: Ramos Horta received 69.2% of the votes cast. Francisco Guterres duly conceded defeat, promising to support the new President for the sake of the country's development. Unlike the first round, which had been marred by widespread violence and intimidation, the second stage of polling was conducted peacefully with no reports of any serious irregularities. Turn-out was high in both the first and second rounds, at 81.8% and 81.0%, respectively. The election victory of Ramos Horta, who formally took office on 20 May, was attributed to the support of the five non-Fretilin candidates who had been defeated in the first round of voting. Shortly after the inauguration ceremony one man was killed and several others injured in clashes in Dili between supporters of rival political parties. Meanwhile, Estanislau Aleixo da Silva, hitherto the Deputy Prime Minister, assumed the role of Prime Minister in an interim capacity. Among the incoming President's priorities were plans for radical reform of the police force and judiciary. He also intended to address the issue of the nearly 600 so-called 'petitioner soldiers' who had abandoned their barracks in February 2006 in protest at low pay and discrimination (see Continuing unrest and other concerns).

The legislative election held on 30 June 2007 was contested by 14 political organizations and alliances. The number of seats in the National Parliament was reduced from 88 to 65. International observers declared their satisfaction with the conduct of the polls, in which 80.5% of the electorate participated. The electoral campaign had been generally peaceful, with the notable exception of the killing of two CNRT supporters in early June and a few minor clashes between rival supporters. Fretilin remained the largest party in the legislature following the elections, winning 21 seats, although its share of the vote declined to 29%, compared with 57% at the 2001 election. The CNRT came a close second, with 24% of the vote and 18 seats, while an alliance of the ASDT and the PSD took 11 seats and the PD eight. Fretilin's relatively poor performance was attributed to public disillusion with the pace of reform since independence.

As none of the parties had secured sufficient seats to govern alone, talks aimed at forming a coalition government ensued. On 6 July 2007 the CNRT, the ASDT-PSD alliance and the PD announced their intention to establish a coalition. However, Fretilin insisted on its right, as the largest parliamentary party, to participate in government, initially suggesting that it could form a minority administration and later proposing the creation of a 'government of national unity'. After weeks of deadlock, on 6 August Ramos Horta invited the CNRT-led coalition to form a government. The President's decision was denounced as unconstitutional by Fretilin and prompted violent protests by supporters of the party. Nevertheless, Gusmão was inaugurated as Prime Minister on 8 August; his new Cabinet included José Luís Guterres as Deputy Prime Minister. Gusmão pledged to improve security, to combat corruption and to facilitate the return to their homes of the thousands of refugees who remained in camps following their displacement during the unrest of April–May 2006. Meanwhile, Fernando de Araújo was elected Speaker of the National Parliament at its first session at the end of July.

President Ramos Horta held a meeting with Alfredo Reinado in mid-August 2007, under the mediation of the Swiss-based Centre for Humanitarian Dialogue. However, Reinado subsequently rejected attempts by the Timorese Government to initiate further talks aimed at achieving a negotiated settlement. In mid-November another leader of the 'petitioner soldiers', former Lt Gastão Salsinha, announced that the dismissed troops would not engage in dialogue with the Government until they were reinstated into the armed forces. A week later Reinado reiterated this demand for reintegration into the military, threatening to mount further attacks in Dili if the Government did not comply. He also demanded the withdrawal of foreign troops and judges from Timor-Leste. Four former soldiers were convicted of murder and sentenced to up to 12 years' imprisonment in late November for shooting dead eight unarmed police officers in April 2006. Reinado's trial on charges of murder, attempted murder and revolt commenced in absentia in early December 2007, after he refused to surrender to the authorities. None the less, the Government persisted in its efforts to maintain contact with the rebel soldiers.

The UN Secretary-General, Ban Ki-Moon, visited Timor-Leste in mid-December 2007, pledging continued UN assistance for the reform of the security forces and the judiciary. The process of gradually transferring authority from UNMIT to the national police commenced in early February 2008, when local officers assumed control of three police posts in Dili, although they were to remain under UN supervision.

On 11 February 2008 President Ramos Horta was shot by renegade soldiers in an attack on his residence in Dili, during which Reinado and another rebel were killed by presidential guards. Seriously injured, the President was evacuated to Darwin, Australia, for medical treatment. Prime Minister Gusmão, who was reported to have been targeted shortly afterwards in a separate assault reportedly led by Gastão Salsinha, but was unharmed, announced a 48-hour state of emergency in response to what he described as an attempted coup, imposing a night-time curfew in Dili and a ban on public gatherings and protests. Australia swiftly dispatched around 200 additional troops to Timor-Leste following the apparent assassination attempts, amid fears of renewed conflict, although no further violent incidents were reported in the days that followed. Speaker Fernando de Araújo replaced his deputy, Vicente Guterres, as acting President on 13 February after returning from overseas. On the same day arrest warrants were issued for several people suspected of involvement in the shootings, including Salsinha, and a 10-day extension of the state of emergency was approved by the National Parliament. Salsinha subsequently announced that he had assumed the leadership of the group of 'petitioner soldiers' and denied that they had attempted to murder Ramos Horta and Gusmão. Several days later Angelita Pires, reported to be Reinado's legal adviser and former partner, and alleged to have been with the rebel leader in the hours before the attacks, was arrested on suspicion of conspiracy, but was released on bail. Prime Minister Gusmão ordered the Timorese military and police forces temporarily to form a joint command to boost efforts to apprehend the perpetrators of the shootings. Meanwhile, the Prosecutor-General, Longuinhos Monteiro, stated that the authorities now believed that the rebels had intended to kidnap the President and Prime Minister rather than kill them. Three officers from the US Federal Bureau of Investigation were assisting Monteiro with his investigations.

The National Parliament voted to prolong the state of emergency for a further 30 days on 22 February 2008, and later that month UNMIT's mandate was extended for another year. By late February most of the 'petitioner soldiers' had agreed to hold talks with the Government aimed at resolving their situation and were being held in a camp in Dili. In early March Amaro da Costa, a senior rebel leader, was the first of a number of suspects to surrender to the joint command that month, although several others, including Salsinha and Marcelo Caetano, whom Ramos Horta had apparently identified as the gunman who had shot him, remained at large. Having undergone a series of operations in Australia, on 17 April Ramos Horta returned to Dili, where he was welcomed by several thousand supporters, and resumed office immediately, urging Salsinha and his followers to surrender. Four former Timorese soldiers suspected of involvement in the shootings were detained in Indonesia and later extradited to Timor-Leste. In the week after Ramos Horta's return, the National Parliament agreed to his request to rescind the state of emergency, although in the district in which the rebels were believed to be in hiding it was extended for a further month, to 22 May. On 23 April Ramos Horta announced his intention to pardon former government minister Rogério Lobato (see Continuing unrest and other concerns). The decision was widely seen as a tactic to encourage Salsinha and his followers to surrender, and was received with alarm by international groups. In late April, following several days of negotiations with security officials, Salsinha, Caetano and 10 other rebels surrendered, relinquishing their weapons at a formal ceremony in Dili attended by Ramos Horta and Deputy Prime Minister José Luís Guterres. It was hoped that an end to the insurrection would encourage the estimated 100,000 displaced people who remained in camps to return to their homes. Meanwhile, the Australian Government announced the withdrawal of the additional troops that had been deployed to Timor-Leste in February. None the less, some 750 troops from Australia and 170 from New Zealand remained in the country to support UNMIT in its efforts to maintain security.

In late May 2008, on the sixth anniversary of Timor-Leste's accession to independence, President Ramos Horta announced the names of 80 recipients of presidential pardons. Among the recipients was Joni Marques, former leader of the Alfa militia group, who in 2001 had been given a prison sentence of more than 33 years for an attack on a convoy in 1999 in which people, including nuns and priests, had been killed. Ramos Horta's intention to provide amnesty to Timorese perpetrators of violence during the 1999 and 2006 crises was demonstrated further when, in July 2008, he drafted legislation to give criminals the opportunity to avoid court by issuing a public apology, and which allowed for compensation of up to US $10,000 to be paid to the families of victims. International monitoring agencies, including the International Crisis Group, expressed concern at the President's actions, and suggested that such pardons might undermine the rule of law. The draft legislation had yet to be presented to Parliament in mid-2011.

In November 2008, following a legal challenge from the opposition Fretilin, the Constitutional Court ruled that the Government's projected increase of 120% in its budgetary expenditure for 2008/09 was unconstitutional. In January 2009 the legislature approved a reduced budget project. With global commodity prices having risen sharply in the first half of 2008, the Government had intended to allocate much of the additional funding to increases in its subsidies for food and fuel, in order to ease inflationary pressures. An aid agency's report released on World Food Day in October 2008 found that more than 70% of Timorese households surveyed were 'food insecure'; the organization calculated that some families were at risk of severe food shortages for up to five months of each year.

Recent developments

In February 2009 the UN Security Council voted to extend the mandate of UNMIT for a further 12 months. In March the head of UNMIT, Atul Khare, announced that the mission was to begin the phased transfer of responsibility to the Timor-Leste police, stating that in the preceding months significant progress had been made towards the restoration of stability. Longuinhos Monteiro, hitherto the Prosecutor-General, was appointed to command the new police force. (He was replaced as Prosecutor-General by Ana Pessôa, the former Deputy Prime Minister, who had also served as Minister of Justice.) The phased transition commenced in May, in the eastern district of Lautem. At a meeting of the country's development partners in April, Khare acknowledged that, while peace and security had been re-established to an extent during 2008, Timor-Leste still depended on significant, ongoing international aid in order to continue its long-term development. In February 2010 the UN Security Council voted unanimously to extend UNMIT's mandate for a further year and to reduce its police contingent from 1,488 personnel at early 2010 (already reduced from 1,608 in February 2009) to 1,280 by mid-2011. The transition of primary policing responsibilities to the Timorese police force was completed in March 2011; however, UN troops were to remain in the country until 2012 in order to monitor developments and to provide logistical support if necessary. UNMIT's mandate was formally extended for a further year in February 2011.

In March 2009, meanwhile, Timorese investigators and Australian forensic scientists discovered the remains of 16 people in unmarked graves on the outskirts of Dili, believed to be the bodies of protesters killed during the 1991 Dili massacre. In July the trial commenced of 27 people, mostly former members of the army or the police force, charged with involvement in the attempted assassinations of President Ramos Horta and Prime Minister Gusmão in 2008. Ramos Horta was criticized by defence lawyers for refusing to give evidence at the trial despite being the principal witness for the prosecution, contending that this constituted a serious compromise of justice. Following protracted court proceedings, 24 of those charged were convicted in March 2010 and were sentenced to varying prison terms of up to 16 years. Contrary to the expectation of many observers, Australian citizen Angelita Pires was among the five defendants who were acquitted. Despite the conclusion of the trial, significant doubts continued to be expressed by many observers as to the veracity of the official version of events. Particular suspicions were voiced in relation to the apparent attack on Gusmão, which some, notably including former Prime Minister Mari Alkatiri, argued had been fabricated. Furthermore, a report on the autopsy carried out on Reinado's corpse concluded that he had been shot in the back of the head at 'very close range', prompting speculation that he had been executed rather than shot in defence as had been claimed by the authorities.

Local elections were successfully held in October 2009. UN observers noted both the determination of the Timorese population to vote and the generally calm conditions under which people were able to cast their ballots. To encourage voters to focus more on local issues than on existing party allegiances, individuals contesting elections were not permitted to do so under an official party banner. While local councils remained restricted in their remit, it was hoped that the smooth conduct of the polls augured well for the forthcoming presidential and legislative elections, due to be held by April and June 2012, respectively. Amendments to electoral legislation in advance of the presidential and legislative polls were approved by the Cabinet in the latter half of 2010, and were subsequently submitted to the National Parliament to be debated in 2011. Meanwhile, the Government announced in April 2010 that municipal elections, due to be held in late 2010, were to be postponed until 2013 or 2014.

Meanwhile, in February 2009 Prime Minister Gusmão appointed the former Governor of Dili and ex-leader of the PSD, Mário Carrascalão, to the new position of second Deputy Prime Minister. Carrascalão was charged with the task of auditing government departments to identify corruption and financial mismanagement. Later in that month a draft of the World Bank's annual report, obtained by an Australian newspaper, was alleged to have warned that poor decision-making and financial management by the Government, as well as ongoing corruption and the politicization of the security forces and civil service, were undermining Timor-Leste's development and jeopardizing political stability and peace.

The issue of public corruption became increasingly prominent during 2010–11. In January 2010 President Ramos Horta urged Prime Minister Gusmão to reorganize the Cabinet, amid ongoing allegations of rampant government corruption, stating that he did not want to be 'ashamed in the international community'. However, he stressed that he could only recommend, rather than demand, action from Gusmão, whom he would continue to support in whatever decisions he might make as Prime Minister. At the beginning of February Aderito Soares was elected as Timor-Leste's first anti-corruption commissioner, having secured 40 of the 65 votes in the legislature; Soares was sworn in later in that month. Upon assuming his new post, Soares insisted that high-profile prosecutions alone would not be sufficient to address the problem of corruption, stating that a long-term re-education campaign would be required. Shortly thereafter, Gusmão announced that he would not be effecting any changes to his Cabinet, repudiating the claims of corruption within his Government and professing his full confidence in the conduct and integrity of his ministers, thereby prompting scepticism among some observers with regard to the Government's commitment to curbing vice. In September Mário Viegas Carrascalão resigned from the post of Deputy Prime Minister after publicly being described as 'stupid' and 'a liar' by Gusmão; the Prime Minister's comment followed a claim made by Carrascalão that Gusmão had been involved in an alleged corruption scandal at the Ministry of Foreign Affairs and Co-operation. Announcing his resignation, Carrascalão alleged that 'corruption, collusion and nepotism' remained rampant within the Timorese Government, which had fallen short in its efforts to improve the quality of life in Timor-Leste; the outgoing deputy premier further claimed that his own efforts to effect positive changes during his tenure had mostly been met with 'silence, disinterest and passivity'.

Later in September 2010 the Government announced that Deputy Prime Minister José Luis Guterres and Minister of Foreign Affairs and Co-operation Zacarias da Costa had both been formally indicted on corruption charges; Guterres was accused of nepotism and abuse of power in appointing his wife as counsel to the Timorese ambassador to the UN in New York, USA, in 2006 and subsequently authorizing a substantial increase in her salary, an arrangement in which da Costa was alleged to have been complicit. Da Costa was cleared of any wrongdoing by Dili District Court in November 2010. Ramos Horta announced later in that month that he had received instruction from the court to suspend Guterres from the National Parliament in order to remove the deputy premier's parliamentary immunity from prosecution so that he might stand trial; however, no immediate action was taken to this end. In early March 2011 Dili District Court announced that Guterres' trial, scheduled to commence later in the month, had been postponed until April, since his parliamentary immunity remained in place. In early April the legislature approved a resolution suspending Guterres from office for the day of his preliminary hearing. The limited nature of the resolution elicited widespread criticism, with some observers contending that anything less than a full suspension from office until and unless Guterres was exonerated of any wrongdoing was in flagrant violation of the Constitution. In early May the court acquitted Guterres, ruling that the charges were based purely on 'rumours and prejudice'. Critics of the Government claimed that it had interfered in the judicial process.

Nevertheless, in a report published in January 2011 UN Secretary-General Ban-Ki Moon commended the participation of a number of senior-level government and other officials in a seminar convened in December 2010 by the anti-corruption commission on issues relating to the eradication of corruption. The attendance of Prime Minister Gusmão, the Vice-Speaker of the National Parliament, the Prosecutor-General and Arsénio Bano, the Secretary-General of Fretilin, was particularly welcomed by Ban Ki-Moon. The UN Secretary-General also noted the Timorese leadership's 'desire for continued peace, stability and unity' and the achievement of 'further progress towards long-term peace, stability and development'.

In a report published in June 2010, Amnesty International urged the Timorese Government to address a legal loophole that allowed amnesties and presidential pardons to be granted to those convicted of war crimes and/or crimes against humanity, such as Joni Marques in May 2008 (see The 2007 elections and subsequent events), arguing that the authorities' 'routine use' of such action meant that the Government was failing to fulfil its obligations under international law and threatened to create a 'culture of impunity' among the Timorese population. Ramos Horta's decision in October 2010 to grant pardons 'on humanitarian grounds' to the 24 people convicted in March of involvement in the attacks against himself and Gusmão in 2008, appealing to Timorese to 'let the past be the past and look ahead with confidence', prompted concern from the UN Special Representative for Timor-Leste, Ameerah Haq; the men and women had spent less than six months in prison and were reported to have shown no contrition for their part in the apparent assassination attempt. Some observers contended that the pardons indicated that Ramos Horta did not consider those convicted to pose any threat to himself or national security, which, it was argued, appeared to suggest that he might not subscribe to the official version of events that they had attempted to kill him and Gusmão. Some opponents of the Government claimed that the apparent plot had been wholly contrived so as to provide a cover for the execution of Reinado, a claim that was adamantly refuted by the authorities. A draft report released in January 2011 by the UN Development Programme was similarly critical of the Timorese Government's apparent opposition to pursuing the perpetrators of war crimes and of crimes against humanity, while also accusing the Government of failing adequately to address persistently high youth unemployment or to alleviate rural poverty. The Timorese Government rejected the claims made in the report as 'inappropriate' and lacking in objectivity. Meanwhile, in June 2010 the Court of Appeal upheld the acquittal of Angelita Pires in connection with the attempted assassinations of the President and Prime Minister in 2008, concluding that there was not enough evidence to support the Prosecutor-General's case against her.

Regional Affairs
Relations with Indonesia

Following its formal accession to independence in May 2002, Timor-Leste accorded high priority to the development of cordial relations with Indonesia. In July President Xanana Gusmão visited Indonesia on his first official trip abroad since assuming the presidency. In June 2003 Prime Minister Mari Alkatiri paid his first official visit to Indonesia, holding talks with President Megawati Sukarnoputri. However, despite an agreement between the two countries to co-operate in resolving outstanding border demarcation issues, in early 2004 Indonesia caused tensions by announcing that it planned to deploy security forces on the disputed islet of Sinai, located off Oecusse. The Government had previously protested when Indonesia had conducted military exercises on the islet in late 2003. In June 2004 the Timorese Minister of Foreign Affairs and Co-operation, José Ramos Horta, and his Indonesian counterpart, Hassan Wirayuda, signed an agreement that resolved 90% of the border demarcation question. The remaining nine disputed land segments included territory in the Oecusse enclave; however, six of the nine segments were subsequently agreed upon in October, leaving merely three areas still to be resolved. A formal border agreement between the two countries was signed by the respective heads of state during a visit by Indonesian President Susilo Bambang Yudhoyono to Dili in April 2005. During his stay Yudhoyono paid his respects at the cemetery in which victims from the 1991 Dili massacre (see Domestic Political Affairs) were buried. It was hoped that the visit would facilitate the forging of closer relations. In October 2005, however, tensions arose between the two countries after clashes in the Oecusse enclave, allegedly involving gangs that were supported by Indonesian troops. Both the Timorese and the Indonesian Ministers of Foreign Affairs dismissed the violence as mere civilian land disputes arising from confusion over the delineation of the border. In October 2009 nine Indonesian soldiers were detained by Timorese border police after allegedly encroaching upon Timorese territory within the Oecusse enclave; despite all nine soldiers being released later that same day, Timorese media reported that tensions in the border area remained high. During a visit to Indonesia in March 2011, Timorese Minister of Foreign Affairs and Co-operation Zacarias da Costa stated his Government's resolve to conclude the demarcation of the land border before the end of the year.

Meanwhile, relations were further sullied by the final report, published in January 2006, of the Commission for Reception, Truth and Reconciliation (a national body created in 2002, charged with investigating alleged human rights violations during Indonesia's occupation of Timor-Leste). The report documented a catalogue of abuses allegedly carried out by Indonesian security forces in Timor-Leste between April 1974 and October 1999, claiming that as many as 180,000 Timorese civilians had died as a result of the Indonesian army's alleged deliberate policy of starvation. Later in January 2006 a scheduled meeting between Presidents Gusmão and Yudhoyono was cancelled; no official reason was given for the decision, but it was widely perceived to be as a result of Yudhoyono's displeasure with the findings of the report. In February 2007 the CTF (Commission of Truth and Friendship—see Domestic Political Affairs), jointly formed by Indonesia and Timor-Leste in 2004 to establish the truth about the events of 1999, held its first hearing. The CTF held five sessions of hearings between February and September 2007, before retiring to prepare its recommendations. Prominent figures who appeared before the Commission included Gen. Wiranto, Gusmão and Brig.-Gen. Ruak. In July the UN prohibited its officials from testifying, owing to the decision to grant amnesty to perpetrators of serious crimes, while human rights organizations continued to criticize the process, claiming that insufficient numbers of victims had been summoned to give evidence. Meanwhile, in June, some two weeks after taking office as President of Timor-Leste, José Ramos Horta visited Indonesia. Ramos Horta and Indonesian President Yudhoyono reaffirmed their commitment to the CTF, extending its mandate by six months, and emphasized the importance of further improving bilateral relations. In July 2008 the CTF released its report, which found the Indonesian army responsible for the human rights crimes owing to its role in funding the pro-Indonesia militia groups that were the main perpetrators of the violence that occurred. Many international human rights organizations dismissed the report because its remit did not include the prosecution of individuals. The Presidents of Indonesia and Timor-Leste formally accepted the report's findings; however, President Yudhoyono stopped short of an official apology, instead expressing his 'deepest remorse'. In October President Ramos Horta urged the UN, which had boycotted the CTF, to end its ongoing investigation into the crimes committed during and after the 1999 independence vote, reportedly stating that maintaining strong relations with Indonesia was Timor-Leste's first priority.

At a meeting in December 2010 of the Bali Democracy Forum, which had been established by Indonesia in 2008 to promote democracy and enhance the capacity to strengthen democratic institutions in Asia, the Indonesian delegation expressed the willingness of its Government to support Timor-Leste in its bid to become a full member of Association of Southeast Asian Nations (ASEAN, see p. 206) before the end of 2011. This support was reiterated by President Yudhoyono in March 2011 and by Indonesian Minister of Foreign Affairs Dr Raden (Marty) Natalegawa in May 2011. (See also Other regional relations.)

Relations with Australia

Meanwhile, Timor-Leste's relations with Australia were strained by ongoing discussions relating to the Timor Sea Treaty. In November 2003 bilateral negotiations began concerning the demarcation of the maritime boundary between the two countries, an important issue owing to its ramifications for the allocation of revenues from oil and gas fields in the Timor Sea. Australia refused to recognize the boundary delineated by the UN Convention on the Law of the Sea. Prime Minister Mari Alkatiri accused Australia of deliberately attempting to stall the negotiations, following its refusal to agree to the holding of monthly discussions in order to bring about a more rapid resolution to the boundary issues. Months of acrimonious dispute ensued, during which numerous aid agencies, including the British-based Oxfam, accused Australia of pushing Timor-Leste to the point of ruin; Oxfam declared that if a maritime boundary were established between the two countries under international law, 'most, if not all' of the petroleum reserves would be allocated to Timor-Leste. In September 2004 the two countries appeared finally to have agreed upon a revenue-sharing arrangement, which over a period of 30 years would afford Timor-Leste $A5,000m. in tax and royalty payments from the natural gas project in the Timor Sea. However, the negotiations again broke down, principally owing to the two countries' failure to agree on the contentious boundary issues. In February 2005 further acrimony ensued when the Australian Government agreed to a mid-point boundary with New Zealand but still refused to consider a similar arrangement with Timor-Leste, provoking widespread accusations of blatant hypocrisy. Instead, Australia proposed that the decision with Timor-Leste be deferred for up to 100 years while the major petroleum and gas deposits were exhausted, dismissing Timor-Leste's bid for a mid-point boundary as an 'ambit claim'. In November a deal was finally reached, with both countries agreeing to share equally the oil and gas revenues from the disputed region, which included the Greater Sunrise Project; a final decision on the contentious issue of the delineation of a maritime boundary was deferred for 50 years in order to allow petroleum and gas projects to proceed. The agreement was formally signed in the Australian city of Sydney in January 2006 and entered into force in February 2007, following ratification by Timor-Leste's National Parliament. Despite these tensions, the Australian Government remained a major source of financial assistance for Timor-Leste, and announced a $A240m. four-year aid programme in August. After taking office in late 2007, Australian Prime Minister Kevin Rudd visited Dili in February 2008, whereupon he pledged additional support for Timor-Leste in the area of security in order to support long-term reform. Timorese President José Ramos Horta and Prime Minister Xanana Gusmão had both urged Rudd to maintain the presence of Australian troops in Timor-Leste until at least the end of 2008. Australia dispatched additional troops to the country following the attacks on Ramos Horta and Gusmão in February 2008 (see Domestic Political Affairs). In April Ramos Horta requested Australian assistance in investigating the source of a large sum of money that he claimed had been deposited in an Australian bank account held jointly by Alfredo Reinado and his associate, Angelita Pires, as well as a series of telephone calls to Australia apparently made by Reinado. The Australian Minister for Foreign Affairs subsequently rejected Timorese suggestions that Australia was delaying the investigation into the shooting, stating that telecommunications records had already been provided and urging the Timorese authorities to follow the appropriate procedures to gain access to financial records. Pires was charged with conspiracy over the shooting of Ramos Horta and went on trial in July 2009; she was subsequently acquitted, with four other defendants, in March 2010.

In October 2008 the Australian Government recalled 100 troops from Timor-Leste, but reaffirmed its commitment to providing military support until political stability had been achieved. In December the Australian Governor-General, Quentin Bryce, visited Timor-Leste to meet with the President and Prime Minister, and in March 2009 the Australian Minister for Defence opened an Australian-funded specialist military training centre on the outskirts of Dili. In June 2010 the Timorese embassy in the Australian capital, Canberra, moved from its temporary premises to a new, permanent building, construction of which had been funded by charitable fund-raising in Australia. The opening of the new premises was hailed by both sides as a reflection of the consolidation of sound bilateral relations. In the following month the Timorese legislature unanimously rejected a proposal, initiated by Australian Prime Minister Julia Gillard, to open a refugee-processing centre in Timor-Leste. In late October the Timorese Government announced that it was to ask Australia to withdraw its remaining 400 troops from the country after the holding of presidential and parliamentary elections in 2012, citing Timor-Leste's much-improved security situation. A report published by the Australian Strategic Policy Institute in April 2011, in which it was argued that an Australian military presence should remain in Timor-Leste beyond 2012—and possibly until 2020—to prevent or respond to further unrest, was dismissed by Ramos Horta, who maintained that the Australian contingent should leave before the end of 2012; the President contested that a country has to stand 'on its own feet' and that, after 10 years of independence, political tensions in Timor-Leste were now 'almost non-existent'.

Other regional relations

Timor-Leste has continued to strengthen its relations with the rest of the Asia-Pacific region. In September 2007 President José Ramos Horta announced that he had established a task force to prepare for Timor-Leste's anticipated accession to the Association of Southeast Asian Nations (ASEAN, see p. 206), with a view to securing membership within around five years. Timor-Leste submitted its formal application to join the regional grouping in March 2011 and received strong support in its bid from a number of member states, including Indonesia, Cambodia and the Philippines. However, Singapore announced its intention to block the Timorese accession bid, arguing that the plan to create an ASEAN economic community by 2015 would be jeopardized by the inclusion of Timor-Leste, and that the new state lacked the necessary institutions and experienced officials to attend the hundreds of ASEAN meetings held annually.

During a visit to Timor-Leste by the Myanma Minister of Foreign Affairs in August 2010, President Ramos Horta stated that Timor-Leste was keen to expand relations with Myanmar and had urged the Myanma military junta to open a dialogue with detained opposition leader Aung San Suu Kyi (see the chapter on Myanmar). The President welcomed Suu Kyi's release from house arrest shortly after the holding of legislative elections in Myanmar in November, and urged the USA and EU to remove their 'harsh' sanctions against the country.

In October 2008 an agreement was signed to allow the Republic of Korea (South Korea) to import gas from Timor-Leste's Greater Sunrise fields by 2013, the first such energy accord to be concluded by Timor-Leste. In November 2010 it was announced that the two countries had signed an agreement providing for the supply to Timor-Leste of two navy patrol boats, together with an undisclosed quantity of munitions, from South Korea; the agreement was interpreted by some analysts as a reflection of Timor-Leste's resolve to distance itself from Australia's sphere of military influence.

In March 2009 Prime Minister Xanana Gusmão paid a four-day visit to Japan, during which he met with his Japanese counterpart, Taro Aso, and other government officials. President Ramos Horta visited Japan in March 2010, whereupon he met with the new Japanese Prime Minister, Yukio Hatoyama; issues discussed included financial aid, nuclear non-proliferation and climate change.

CONSTITUTION AND GOVERNMENT

In March 2002 the Constituent Assembly promulgated East Timor's first Constitution and, on 14 April, the territory held its

TIMOR-LESTE

first presidential election. The President serves a five-year term. Upon the territory's accession to independence in May 2002, the Constituent Assembly was transformed into the National Parliament. (The number of seats in the National Parliament was reduced from 88 to 65 at the 2007 election.) In 2002 the UN Transitional Administration in East Timor (UNTAET) formally relinquished its responsibility for the administration of the country and was succeeded by the UN Mission of Support in East Timor (UNMISET), which remained in the country, in a supporting role, ultimately for three years. UNMISET was replaced in May 2005 by the UN Office in Timor-Leste (UNOTIL), which was superseded by the UN Integrated Mission in Timor-Leste (UNMIT) in August 2006.

REGIONAL AND INTERNATIONAL CO-OPERATION

Timor-Leste is a member of the Asian Development Bank (ADB, see p. 202), the Comunidade dos Países de Língua Portuguesa (Community of Portuguese-Speaking Countries, see p. 459) and the UN's Economic and Social Commission for Asia and the Pacific (ESCAP, see p. 37). The country has been granted observer status at the Association of Southeast Asian Nations (ASEAN, see p. 206), and submitted a formal application for full membership of the regional grouping in March 2011.

Timor-Leste became a member of the UN in September 2002. The country participates in the Group of 77 (G77, see p. 447) developing nations, and is also a member of the International Labour Organization (ILO, see p. 138) and the Non-aligned Movement (see p. 461).

ECONOMIC AFFAIRS

In 2008, according to estimates by the World Bank, Timor-Leste's gross national income (GNI), measured at average 2006–08 prices, was US $2,706m., equivalent to $2,460 per head (or $4,700 per head on an international purchasing-power parity basis). During 2000–09, it was estimated, the population increased at an average annual rate of 3.7%, while gross domestic product (GDP) per head, in real terms, declined by an annual average of 2.0% in 2000–09. Overall GDP grew, in real terms, at an average annual rate of 1.7% during 2000–08, according to IMF figures. According to the Asian Development Bank (ADB), GDP increased by 12.7% in 2009 and by 9.5% in 2010.

The agricultural sector, according to FAO, in mid-2011 was expected to engage 79.3% of the Timorese labour force. In 2007 the agricultural sector (including forestry and fishing) contributed an estimated 27.5% of non-oil GDP. According to ADB estimates, the sector contributed 30.8% of the GDP in 2009. Coffee is a significant export commodity. However, the coffee sector remains extremely susceptible to climatic conditions, which, combined with poor irrigation systems, are primarily responsible for significant fluctuations in annual output. The value of coffee exports reached an estimated $8.3m. in 2009. There are small plantations of coconuts, cloves and cinnamon. Subsistence crops include rice, maize and cassava. Livestock raised includes cattle and water buffalo. There is some small-scale fishing, and the forestry sector may yield as yet undeveloped potential. According to ADB figures, the GDP of the agricultural sector increased, in real terms, at an average annual rate of 1.2% in 2002–07. Real growth in the sector's GDP was estimated by the ADB at 12.3% in 2009 and at 0.4% in 2010.

The industrial sector (including mining and quarrying, manufacturing, utilities and construction) accounted for an estimated 13.9% of non-oil GDP in 2007. According to ADB estimates, the sector contributed 13.1% of the GDP in 2009. According to figures from the ADB, industrial GDP declined at an average annual rate of 0.3% in 2002–07. The industrial sector's GDP increased by 20.2% in 2009 and by 21.6% in 2010.

In the 1990s sizeable natural gas fields were discovered in and around the Timor Gap zone, and petroleum reserves in the region were estimated by some sources to total a potential 500m. barrels. Although detailed data for the contribution made to GDP by petroleum and gas activities were not available, the IMF estimated that these sectors generated incomes of US $342m. in 2005 and $492m. in 2006 (equivalent to 138% of the value of non-oil GDP in the latter year). The Timor Sea Arrangement, relating to the sharing of petroleum and gas royalties with Australia, was signed in 2002 (see Contemporary Political History). In 2003 a US company was granted permission to develop the Bayu-Undan liquefied natural gas (LNG) field in the Timor Sea. The mining sector, excluding petroleum and gas, was estimated to have contributed only 0.5% of GDP in 2007. In addition to offshore petroleum and gas, mineral resources include high-grade

Introductory Survey

marble. According to the ADB, the GDP of the non-oil mining sector was estimated to have decreased at an average annual rate of 9.9% in 2002–07. However, the sector's GDP increased by 11.8% in 2007.

There is a small manufacturing sector, which is mainly concerned with the production of textiles, the bottling of water and coffee-processing. In 2007 the manufacturing sector provided an estimated 2.3% of non-oil GDP. In May 2004 one of the world's largest wet-processing coffee factories was opened in Estado, which, together with expanded production at the existing Maubisse factory, was expected to increase significantly Timor-Leste's annual coffee output. According to ADB figures, manufacturing GDP declined, in real terms, at an average annual rate of 4.6% in 2002–07. The GDP of the manufacturing sector increased by 10.1% in 2007.

Construction provided an estimated 9.8% of non-oil GDP in 2007. According to ADB figures, construction GDP increased, in real terms, at an average annual rate of 0.1% in 2002–07. The GDP of the sector grew substantially, by 37.4%, in 2007, following a contraction of 14.6% in 2006.

In 2002 the Government elected to transfer control of the national power authority, Electricidade de Timor-Leste (EDTL), to external management. Although the basic rehabilitation of the existing rural power infrastructure was largely complete by 2003, supplies of electricity subsequently remained intermittent. The country's total generating capacity stood at only 40 MW in 2008. In that year a major programme of electrification was announced, and it was envisaged that by the end of 2010 an additional 180 MW would be available following the construction of new power stations, which were to operate with imported oil.

According to ADB estimates, the services sector contributed 56.1% of GDP in 2009. According to ADB figures, the services sector's GDP contracted at an average annual rate of 4.2% in 2002–07. The sector's GDP, in real terms, increased by 11.3% in 2009 and by 11.6% in 2010. In 2007 public administration and defence accounted for an estimated 24.8% of non-oil GDP. Tourism remained negligible, owing to a lack of facilities, as well as to prohibitively high air fares from Indonesia and Australia.

In 2009 Timor-Leste recorded a visible trade deficit of US $375.7m., while there was a surplus of $1,363.2m. on the current account of the balance of payments (largely owing to the allocation of oil and gas export revenues to the income and transfers accounts). The principal source of imports in 2009 was Indonesia, which supplied 32.6%. Other leading suppliers were Singapore, Australia and Viet Nam. The principal destinations for exports (excluding oil and gas) were the USA (which purchased 33.8% of the total) and Germany (27.9%). Reliable data for exports of oil and gas were not available (see above), but these, together with coffee, constituted the most significant merchandise exports in 2009.

According to the IMF, the 2010 budget provided for expenditure of US $625m., with revenue (excluding receipts from government sales of rice) being projected at $2,122m. The ADB estimated the fiscal surplus to be the equivalent of 237.6% of GDP in 2009 and 200.2% in 2010. Australia is a major provider of development assistance, with emphasis on governance, law, training, security and public sector services. Australia's aid budget for Timor-Leste was projected at $A103.0m. in 2010/11. Consumer prices increased at an average annual rate of 4.6% in 2001–09. According to the ADB, the rate of inflation rate declined to 0.7% in 2009, before rising to 6.8% in 2010. In 2001 the rate of unemployment was estimated by the ADB at 5.3%. According to the census of 2004, those recorded as unemployed, or deterred from seeking work, accounted for one-half of Dili residents aged between 15 and 24 years.

Upon independence in 2002 Timor-Leste's first National Development Plan (NDP) was implemented. Its objectives, over an 18-year period, included the reduction of poverty and the introduction of a phased programme of development. External aid remained of vital importance. The agreement signed by Timor-Leste and Australia in January 2006 regarding the allocation of revenue from the Greater Sunrise gas project (see Contemporary Political History) was a major development. Nearly all of the Government's own revenue is derived from its Petroleum Fund. This serves as a long-term repository for all petroleum revenues, most of its assets being invested with offshore institutions. The value of the Petroleum Fund rose to US $5,400m. in December 2009, increasing further to reach $6,900m. by the end of 2010. Timor-Leste benefited greatly from the strength of international oil prices that prevailed until mid-

TIMOR-LESTE

2008 and again from late 2010. Higher petroleum revenues permitted a consolidation of the country's fiscal position. Strong consumer demand sustained the retail sector, supported by increases in workers' wages. Meanwhile, the incidence of poverty was reported to have risen from 36% of the Timorese population in 2001 to 50% in 2007, with the World Food Programme supporting 30% of Timorese. The incidence of poverty was reportedly reduced to 41% in 2009, when inflationary pressures eased considerably. By the latter part of 2010, however, inflationary pressures had begun to re-emerge, mainly as a result of significant increases in food and fuel costs. Although in comparison with the previous year the rate of GDP growth decelerated somewhat in 2010, the ADB projected that the rapid expansion of the economy would continue in 2011, forecasting growth of 10.0%. Economic growth has been bolstered by robust capital expenditure, and spending on infrastructural projects was expected to exceed $3,000m. in 2011–15. However, the Government has encountered difficulties in the implementation of various projects: owing to capacity constraints, budget allocations have not been wholly utilized. A major challenge for the Government remained the provision of basic services, particularly in rural areas, and more than 50% of the capital budget for the period 2009–12 was to be allocated to the programme of electrification (see above).

PUBLIC HOLIDAYS

2012 (provisional): 1 January (New Year's Day), 6 April (Good Friday), 1 May (Labour Day), 20 May (Independence Restoration Day), 7 June (Corpus Christi), 18 August (Id al-Fitr, end of Ramadan), 30 August (Constitution Day), 25 October (Id al-Adha, Feast of the Sacrifice), 1 November (All Saints' Day), 2 November (All Souls' Day), 12 November (National Youth Day), 28 November (Proclamation of Independence Day), 7 December (National Heroes' Day), 8 December (Immaculate Conception), 25 December (Christmas Day).

Statistical Survey

Area and Population

AREA, POPULATION AND DENSITY

Area (sq km)	14,609*
Population (census results)	
31 July 2004	924,642
11 July 2010 (provisional)	
Males	541,147
Females	525,435
Total	1,066,582
Population (UN estimate at mid-year)†	
2011	1,211,190
Density (per sq km) at mid-2011	82.9

*5,641 sq miles.
† Source: UN, *World Population Prospects: The 2008 Revision*.

POPULATION BY AGE AND SEX
(UN estimates at mid-2011)

	Males	Females	Total
0–14	274,542	262,220	536,762
15–64	324,421	313,053	637,474
65 and over	17,541	19,413	36,954
Total	616,504	594,686	1,211,190

Source: UN, *World Population Prospects: The 2008 Revision*.

PRINCIPAL TOWNS
(population at 2010 census, preliminary)

Dili (capital)	234,331		Maliana	24,352
Dare	n.a.		Ermera	33,262
Baucau	46,530			

BIRTHS AND DEATHS
(annual averages, UN estimates)

	1995–2000	2000–05	2005–10
Birth rate (per 1,000)	45.8	40.0	40.2
Death rate (per 1,000)	13.0	10.1	8.8

Source: UN, *World Population Prospects: The 2008 Revision*.

Life expectancy (years at birth, WHO estimates): 62 (males 59; females 64) in 2008 (Source: WHO, *World Health Statistics*).

Health and Welfare

KEY INDICATORS

Total fertility rate (children per woman, 2008)	6.5
Under-5 mortality rate (per 1,000 live births, 2008)	93
Physicians (per 1,000 head, 2004)	0.10
Health expenditure (2007): US $ per head	116
Health expenditure (2007): % of GDP	13.6
Health expenditure (2007): public (% of total)	84.6
Access to water (% of persons, 2008)	69
Access to sanitation (% of persons, 2008)	50
Total carbon dioxide emissions ('000 metric tons, 2007)	183.2
Carbon dioxide emissions per head (metric tons, 2007)	0.2
Human development index (2010): ranking	120
Human development index (2010): value	0.502

For sources and definitions, see explanatory note on p. vi.

Agriculture

PRINCIPAL CROPS
('000 metric tons)

	2005	2006	2007
Maize	92.2	119.0	71.5
Cassava (Manioc)	39.3	39.3	41.2
Rice, paddy	58.9	55.4	60.4
Sweet potatoes	26.9	26.0*	26.0*
Beans, dry*	4.5	4.5	4.5
Groundnuts, with shell*	4.0	4.0	4.0
Coconuts*	14.0	14.0	14.0
Bananas*	2.0	2.0	2.0
Guavas, mangoes and mangosteens*	3.0	3.0	3.0
Coffee, green*	12.0	12.0	12.0

*FAO estimate(s).

2008: Production assumed to be unchanged from 2007 (FAO estimates). Note: No data were available for individual crops in 2009.

Aggregate production ('000 metric tons, may include official, semi-official or estimated data): Total cereals 151.1 in 2005, 174.4 in 2006, 131.9 in 2007–09; Total roots and tubers 111.8 in 2005, 109.3 in 2006, 113.2 in 2007–09; Total vegetables (incl. melons) 18.2 in 2005–09; Total fruits (excl. melons) 7.4 in 2005–09.

Source: FAO.

TIMOR-LESTE

LIVESTOCK
('000 head)

	2006	2007	2008
Cattle	139	142	145
Buffaloes	99	100	102
Pigs	356	373	388
Horses*	48	48	48
Goats	132	135	137
Sheep	40	41	41
Chickens*	1,000	1,000	1,000

* FAO estimates.

2009: Chickens 1,000 (FAO estimate).

Source: FAO.

LIVESTOCK PRODUCTS
('000 metric tons, estimates)

	2006	2007	2008
Cattle meat	0.9	0.9	1.0
Pig meat	8.4	8.8	9.1
Chicken meat	1.0	1.0	1.0
Hen eggs	1.2	1.2	1.2

2009: Figures assumed to be unchanged from 2008 (FAO estimates).

Source: FAO.

Fishing

(metric tons, live weight, FAO estimates)

	2006	2007	2008
Total catch	2,573	2,943	3,176

Source: FAO.

Finance

CURRENCY AND EXCHANGE RATES (US currency is used)

Monetary Units
100 cents (centavos) = 1 United States dollar ($).

Sterling and Euro Equivalents (31 December 2010)
£1 sterling = US $1.565;
€1 = $1.336;
US $100 = £63.88 = €74.84.

BUDGET
(US $ million, central government operations, cash basis)

Revenue	2008	2009*	2010†
Domestic revenue	45	60	67
Direct taxes	19	13	16
Indirect taxes	19	30	34
Non-tax revenues and other	6	16	17
Oil and gas revenues	2,399	1,842	2,055
Oil and gas receipts	2,284	1,660	1,816
Interest	115	182	239
Total	**2,444**	**1,902**	**2,122**

Expenditure	2008	2009*	2010†
Recurrent expenditure	358	363	450
Salaries and wages	53	86	96
Goods and services	154	158	161
Transfers	88	94	161
Subsidies to agencies	63	26	40
Capital expenditure and net lending	175	209	175
Total	**532**	**573**	**625**

* Preliminary figures.
† Projections.

Note: Revenue figures exclude receipts from government rice sales.

Source: IMF, *Democratic Republic of Timor-Leste: 2010 Article IV Consultation—Staff Report; Joint World Bank/IMF Debt Sustainability Analysis; Staff Statement; Public Information Notice on the Executive Board Discussion; and Statement by the Executive Director for Timor-Leste* (March 2011).

INTERNATIONAL RESERVES
(US $ million at 31 December)

	2008	2009	2010
IMF special drawing rights	—	12.115	11.901
Reserve position in IMF	0.002	0.002	0.002
Foreign exchange	210.422	237.812	394.286
Total	**210.424**	**249.929**	**406.189**

Source: IMF, *International Financial Statistics*.

MONEY SUPPLY
(US $ million at 31 December)

	2008	2009	2010
Currency outside depository corporations	2.454	2.801	3.374
Transferable deposits	101.837	154.642	138.012
Other deposits	88.367	110.913	153.637
Broad money	**192.658**	**268.356**	**295.022**

Source: IMF, *International Financial Statistics*.

COST OF LIVING
(Consumer Price Index; base: 2005 = 100)

	2007	2008	2009
All items	114.6	125.0	125.9

Source: IMF, *International Financial Statistics*.

NATIONAL ACCOUNTS
(US $ million at current prices)

Expenditure on Non-oil Gross Domestic Product

	2005	2006	2007
Government final consumption expenditure	157.8	175.9	259.0
Private final consumption expenditure	329.5	301.6	352.2
Change in stocks	6.8	6.8	8.2
Gross fixed capital formation	61.9	61.0	103.0
Total domestic non-oil expenditure	**556.0**	**545.3**	**722.4**
Exports of goods and services	38.3	39.4	43.4
Less Imports of goods and services	262.5	258.0	370.3
Non-oil GDP in purchasers' values	**331.9**	**326.8**	**395.5**
Non-oil GDP at constant 2000 prices	**331.1**	**319.8**	**371.7**

TIMOR-LESTE

Non-oil Gross Domestic Product by Economic Activity

	2005	2006	2007
Agriculture, forestry and fishing	111.3	116.6	124.7
Mining and quarrying (non-oil)	2.9	1.9	2.2
Manufacturing	11.8	8.7	10.2
Electricity, gas and water	5.0	5.0	6.0
Construction	33.4	29.8	44.4
Wholesale and retail trade	24.9	25.4	31.0
Transport and communications	33.8	25.4	31.0
Finance, rents and business services	28.3	28.8	33.6
Public administration and defence	80.5	85.2	112.6
United Nations	18.0	25.6	57.7
Non-oil GDP in purchasers' values	349.9	352.5	453.3

Source: IMF, *Timor-Leste: Selected Issues and Statistical Appendix* (June 2008).

Non-oil GDP in Purchasers' Values (US $ million at current prices): 398.0 in 2007; 499.0 in 2008; 590.0 in 2009 (Source: Asian Development Bank).

BALANCE OF PAYMENTS
(US $ million)

	2007	2008	2009
Exports of goods f.o.b.	6.6	14.1	9.2
Imports of goods f.o.b.	−175.7	−310.9	−384.9
Trade balance	−169.0	−296.9	−375.7
Services and income (net)	1,068.1	1,963.5	1,340.3
Balance on goods, services and income	899.1	1,666.6	964.6
Current transfers (net)	278.1	356.5	398.6
Current balance	1,177.2	2,023.1	1,363.2
Capital account (net)	32.2	17.2	27.3
Direct investment (net)	8.7	39.5	30.4
Portfolio investment (net)	−1,012.1	−2,003.1	−1,325.1
Other investment (net)	−50.6	−94.4	4.2
Net errors and omissions	−8.9	−2.2	−60.5
Overall balance	146.5	−19.9	39.5

Source: Asian Development Bank.

External Trade

SELECTED COMMODITIES
(US $ '000)

Imports c.i.f.	2006*	2008	2009
Meat and edible meat offal	579	3,008	3,919
Dairy and edible products of animal origin	682	2,263	2,662
Cereals	6,516	25,485	35,169
Preparations of cereals, flour, starch or milk; pastry cooks' products	1,609	4,720	4,223
Beverages, spirits and vinegar	1,842	6,749	7,793
Mineral fuels, mineral oils and products of their distillation; bituminous substances; mineral waxes	29,070	71,123	38,040
Boilers, machinery and mechanical appliances; parts thereof	4,512	17,333	22,770
Vehicles, other than railway or tramway rolling stock, and parts thereof	5,830	43,869	58,486
Electrical machinery and equipment and parts thereof; sound recorders and reproducers; televisions, etc.	6,191	17,568	25,198
Pharmaceutical products	1,832	8,100	5,269
Iron or steel articles	1,213	2,304	3,922
Plastics and articles thereof	1,744	2,017	2,643
Total (incl. others)	87,695	258,429	282,594

Exports f.o.b. (excl. oil and gas)	2006*	2008	2009
Coffee	7,999	12,632	8,291
Total (incl. others)	8,455	12,632	8,491

*Comparable data for 2007 were not available.

Re-exports (US $ '000): 52,231 in 2006; 34,199 in 2008; 26,021 in 2009. Note: The significance of re-exports may appear overstated owing to the inclusion of data connected with the outflow of foreign personnel and equipment as peace-keeping operations were scaled down. Note: Comparable data for 2007 were not available.

Source: Ministério do Plano e das Finanças, Dili.

PRINCIPAL TRADING PARTNERS
(US $ '000)

Imports c.i.f.	2006*	2008	2009
Australia	10,951	35,705	47,196
China, People's Republic	2,209	5,363	11,572
Germany	663	2,925	314
Indonesia	37,733	109,840	92,105
Japan	2,183	5,881	7,750
Korea, Republic	98	2,705	1,821
Malaysia	773	11,739	8,052
Portugal	1,946	3,137	9,487
Singapore	17,001	44,112	53,513
Thailand	3,031	5,298	3,346
Viet Nam	4,406	18,099	34,602
Total (incl. others)	87,695	258,429	282,594

Exports f.o.b. (excl. oil and gas)†	2006*	2008	2009
Australia	303	266	250
British Indian Ocean Territory	n.a.	155	142
Canada	n.a.	24	255
Germany	2,042	3,395	2,372
Indonesia	1,146	2,093	412
Japan	119	641	402
Korea, Republic	31	246	106
New Zealand	48	119	86
Portugal	189	808	755
Singapore	642	1,263	289
Taiwan	87	41	33
USA	3,447	3,380	2,873
Total (incl. others)	8,455	12,632	8,491

*Comparable data for 2007 were not available.
† Excluding re-exports (US $ million): 52.2 in 2006; 34.2 in 2008; 26.0 in 2009.
Note: The significance of re-exports may appear overstated owing to the inclusion of data connected with the outflow of foreign personnel and equipment as peace-keeping operations were scaled down.

Source: Ministério do Plano e das Finanças, Dili.

SHIPPING

Merchant Fleet
(registered at 31 December)

	2007	2008	2009
Number of vessels	1	1	1
Total displacement ('000 grt)	1,134	1,134	1,134

Source: IHS Fairplay, *World Fleet Statistics*.

Tourism

TOURIST ARRIVALS
('000 foreign visitors, excl. Indonesians, at classified hotels*)

	1996	1997	1998
Total	0.8	1.0	0.3

*Arrivals at non-classified hotels: 204 in 1996; 245 in 1997; 41 in 1998.

TIMOR-LESTE

Communications Media

	2007	2008	2009
Telephones ('000 main lines in use)	2.4	2.4	2.4
Mobile cellular telephones ('000 subscribers)	78.2	101.0	330.0
Internet users	1,500	1,800	2,100
Broadband subscribers	n.a.	100	200

Daily newspapers: 2 in 2004.

Non-daily newspapers: 3 in 2004.

Source: UNESCO Institute for Statistics and International Telecommunication Union.

Education

(2008/09 unless otherwise indicated)

	Teachers	Students
Pre-primary*	237	6,987
Primary	7,358	213,783
Lower Secondary†	1,359	33,082
Upper Secondary	1,257†	24,808*
Tertiary	1,196	16,727

*2004/05.
† 2007/08 estimates.

Source: UNESCO Institute for Statistics.

Pupil-teacher ratio (primary education, UNESCO estimate): 29.1 in 2008/09 (Source: UNESCO Institute for Statistics).

Adult literacy rate (UNESCO estimate): 58.6% in 2003 (Source: UN Development Programme, *Human Development Report*).

Directory

The Government

HEAD OF STATE

President: JOSÉ RAMOS HORTA (took office 20 May 2007).

CABINET
(May 2011)

The Government is a coalition of Congresso Nacional da Reconstrução de Timor-Leste (CNRT), Associação Social-Democrata Timorense (ASDT), Partido Democrático (PD), Partido Social Democrata Timor Lorosae (PSD) and Partido Unidade Nacional Democrática da Resistência Timorense (UNDERTIM).

Prime Minister and Minister of Defence and Security: KAY RALA (XANANA) GUSMÃO.

Deputy Prime Minister: JOSÉ LUÍS GUTERRES.

Minister of State Administration and Territorial Management: ARCÂNGELO LEITE PINTO.

Minister of Foreign Affairs and Co-operation: ZACARIAS ALBANO DA COSTA.

Minister of Justice: MARIA LÚCIA LOBATO.

Minister of Health: NÉLSON MARTINS.

Minister of Finance: MARIA MADALENA EMÍLIA PIRES.

Minister of Education: JOÃO CÂNCIO FREITAS.

Minister of Economy and Development: JOÃO GONÇALVES.

Minister of Agriculture and Fisheries: MARIANO SABINO LOPES.

Minister of Social Solidarity: MARIA DOMINGAS ALVES.

Minister of Tourism, Trade and Industry: GIL DA COSTA ALVES.

Minister of Infrastructure: PEDRO LAY.

MINISTRIES

Office of the President: Palácio das Cinzas, Caicoli, Dili; tel. 3339011.

Office of the Prime Minister: Palácio do Governo, Av. Presidente Nicolau Lobato, Dili; tel. 7243559; fax 3339503; e-mail mail@primeministerandcabinet.gov.tp; internet www.pm.gov.tp.

Ministry of Agriculture and Fisheries: Edif. 5, Av. Presidente Nicolau Lobato, Dili; tel. 3310418; e-mail agriculture@gov.east-timor.org; internet www.maf.gov.tl.

Ministry of Defence and Security: Palácio do Governo, Edif. 2, 1°, Av. Presidente Nicolau Lobato, Dili; tel. 3331190; e-mail sed-tl@easttimor.minihub.org.

Ministry of Economy and Development: Rua D. Aleixo Corte Real, Edif. Fomento, 2°, Mandarin, Dili; tel. 3339039.

Ministry of Education: Rua de Vila Verde, Dili; tel. 3339654; e-mail education@gov.east-timor.org.

Ministry of Finance: Palácio do Governo, Edif. 5, Av. Presidente Nicolau Lobato, Dili; tel. 3339510; e-mail info@mof.gov.tl; internet www.mof.gov.tl.

Ministry of Foreign Affairs and Co-operation: Av. de Portugal, Praia dos Coqueiros, Dili; tel. 3331234; fax 3339025; e-mail administration@mnec.gov-tl.net.

Ministry of Health: Edif. dos Serviços Centrais do Ministério da Saúde, Rua de Caicoli, POB 374, Dili; tel. 3322467; fax 3325189; e-mail tls_epid@yahoo.com; internet www.moh.gov.tl.

Ministry of Infrastructure: 8 Av. Bispo de Medeiros, Mercado Lama, Dili; tel. 3339355.

Ministry of Justice: Av. Jacinto Candido, Dili; tel. 3331160; e-mail mj@mj.gov.tl; internet www.mj.gov.tl.

Ministry of Social Solidarity: Rua de Caicoli, Dili; tel. 3339582; internet www.mss.gov.tl.

Ministry of State Administration and Territorial Management: Rua Jacinto Candido, Caicoli, Dili; tel. 3339077; e-mail komunikasaun@estatal.gov.tl; internet www.estatal.gov.tl.

Ministry of Tourism, Trade and Industry: Edif. Fomento, Rua Dom Aleixo Corte Real, Mandarin, Dili; tel. 3331202; e-mail mtci.gov.tl@gmail.com; internet www.mtci-timorleste.com.

President and Legislature

PRESIDENT

Presidential Election, First Ballot, 9 April 2007

Candidate	Votes	% of votes
Francisco Guterres (Fretilin)	112,666	27.89
José Ramos Horta (Independent)	88,102	21.81
Fernando de Araújo (PD)	77,459	19.18
Francisco Xavier do Amaral (ASDT)	58,125	14.39
Lucia Maria B. F. Lobato (PSD)	35,789	8.86
Manuel Tilman (KOTA)	16,534	4.09
Avelino Coelho da Silva (PST)	8,338	2.06
João Viegas Carrascalão (UDT)	6,928	1.72
Total	**403,941**	**100.00**

Presidential Election, Second Ballot, 9 May 2007

Candidate	Votes	% of votes
José Ramos Horta	285,835	69.18
Francisco Guterres	127,342	30.82
Total	**413,177**	**100.00**

NATIONAL PARLIAMENT

A single-chamber Constituent Assembly was elected by popular vote on 30 August 2001. Its 88 members included 75 deputies elected under a national system of proportional representation and one representative from each of Timor-Leste's 13 districts, elected under a 'first-past-the-post' system. Upon independence on 20 May 2002 the Constituent Assembly became the National Parliament; it held its inaugural session on the same day. At the election of June 2007 the number of members was reduced from 88 to 65.

Speaker: FERNANDO DE ARAÚJO.

TIMOR-LESTE

General Election, 30 June 2007

	Seats
Frente Revolucionária do Timor Leste Independente (Fretilin)	21
Congresso Nacional da Reconstrução de Timor-Leste	18
Associação Social-Democrata Timorense-Partido Social Democrata Timor Lorosae (ASDT-PSD)	11
Partido Democrático (PD)	8
Partido Unidade Nacional (PUN)	3
Aliança Democrática Klibur Oan Timor Asuwain-Partido do Povo de Timor (AD KOTA-PPT)	2
Partido Unidade Nacional Democrática da Resistência Timorense (UNDERTIM)	2
Total	**65**

Election Commission

National Electoral Commission (CNE): Av. Bispo Medeiros-Kintal, Dili; tel. 3310082; f. 2004; govt body; Chair. Dr FAUSTINO CARDOSO.

Political Organizations

Associação Popular Democrática de Timor Pro Referendo (Apodeti Pro Referendo) (Pro-Referendum Popular Democratic Association of Timor): c/o Frederico Almeida Santos Costa, CNRT Office, Balide, Dili; tel. 3324994; f. 1974; est. as Apodeti; present name adopted Aug. 2000; fmrly supported autonomous integration with Indonesia; Pres. FREDERICO ALMEIDA SANTOS COSTA.

Associação Social-Democrata Timorense (ASDT) (Timor Social Democratic Association): Av. Direitos Humanos Lecidere, Dili; tel. 3983331; f. 2001; Pres. FRANCISCO XAVIER DO AMARAL.

Barisan Rakyat Timor Timur (BRTT) (East Timor People's Front): fmrly supported autonomous integration with Indonesia; Pres. FRANCISCO LOPES DA CRUZ.

Congresso Nacional da Reconstrução de Timor-Leste (CNRT) (National Congress for the Reconstruction of Timor-Leste): Rua Nu Laran, Bairro dos Grilos, Dili; tel. 7358696; internet www.cnrt-timor .org; f. 2007; Pres. KAY RALA 'XANANA' GUSMÃO.

Conselho Popular pela Defesa da República Democrática de Timor Leste (CPD-RDTL) (Popular Council for the Defence of the Democratic Republic of East Timor): opp. the Church, Balide, Dili; tel. 3481462; f. 1999; promotes adoption of 1975 Constitution of Democratic Republic of East Timor; Spokesperson CRISTIANO DA COSTA.

Frente Revolucionária do Timor Leste Independente (Fretilin) (Revolutionary Front for an Independent East Timor): Rua dos Mártires da Pátria, Dili; tel. 3321409; internet fretilin-rdtl.blogspot .com; f. 1974; est. to seek full independence for East Timor; entered into alliance with the UDT in 1986; Pres. VICENTE MAUBOSY.

Klibur Oan Timor Asuwain (KOTA) (Association of Timorese Heroes): Rua dos Mártires da Pátria, Fatuhada, Dili; tel. 3324661; e-mail clementinoamaral@hotmail.com; f. 1974; est. as pro-integration party; supported independence with Timorese traditions; Pres. MANUEL TILMAN.

Partai Democratik Maubere (PDM) (Maubere Democratic Party): Blk B-II, 16 Surikmas Lama Kraik, Fatumeta, Dili; tel. 3184508; e-mail pdm_party@hotmail.com; f. 2000; Pres. PAOLO PINTO.

Partai Liberal (PL) (Liberal Party): Talbessi Sentral, Dili; tel. 3786448; Pres. ARMANDO JOSÉ DOURADO DA SILVA.

Partido Democrata Cristão (PDC) (Christian Democrat Party): Former Escola Cartilha, Rua Quintal Kiik, Bairro Economico, Dili; tel. 3324683; e-mail arlindom@octa4.net.au; f. 2000; Pres. ANTÓNIO XIMENES.

Partido Democrático (PD) (Democratic Party): 1 Rua Democracia, Pantai Kelapa, Dili; tel. 3608421; e-mail flazama@hotmail.com; Pres. FERNANDO DE ARAÚJO.

Partido Nacionalista Timorense (PNT) (Nationalist Party of Timor): Dili; tel. 3323518; internet pnt-timor-leste.planetaclix.pt; Pres. Dr ABÍLIO ARAÚJO.

Partido do Povo de Timor (PPT) (Timorese People's Party): Dili; tel. 3568325; f. 2000; pro-integration; supported presidential candidacy of Xanana Gusmão in 2002 election; Pres. Dr JACOB XAVIER.

Partido Republica National Timor Leste (PARENTIL) (National Republic Party of East Timor): Perumnar Bairopite Bob Madey Ran, Fahan Jalam, Ailobu Laran RTK; tel. 3361393; Pres. FLAVIANO PEREIRA LOPEZ.

Partido Social Democrata Timor Lorosae (PSD) (Social Democrat Party of East Timor): Apdo 312, Correios de Dili, Dili; tel. 3357027; e-mail psdtimor@hotmail.com; f. 2000; Pres. ZACARIAS ALBANO DA COSTA; Sec.-Gen. MARITO MAGONO.

Partido Socialista de Timor (PST) (Socialist Party of Timor): Rua Colegio das Madras, Balide, Dili; tel. 3560246; e-mail kaynaga@ hotmail.com; Marxist-Leninist Fretilin splinter group; Pres. AVELINO COELHO DA SILVA.

Partido Trabalhista Timorense (PTT) (Timor Labour Party): 2B Rua Travessa de Befonte, 2 Bairro Formosa, Dili; tel. 3322807; f. 1974; Pres. PAULO FREITAS DA SILVA.

Partido Unidade Nacional (PUN) (United National Party): c/o National Parliament, Dili; f. 2005; Pres. FERNANDA BORGES.

Partido Unidade Nacional Democrática da Resistência Timorense (UNDERTIM): c/o National Parliament, Dili; Pres. CORNELIO GAMA.

União Democrata-Cristão de Timor (UDC/PDC) (Christian Democratic Union of Timor): 62 Rua Almirante Américo Thomás, Mandarin, Dili; tel. 3325042; f. 1998; Pres. VINCENTE DA SILVA GUTERRES.

União Democrática Timorense (UDT) (Timorese Democratic Union): Palapagoa Rua da India, Dili; tel. 3881453; e-mail joaocarrascalao@email.msn.com; internet fitini.net/udttimor; f. 1974; allied itself with Fretilin in 1986; Pres. GILMAN DOS SANTOS; Sec.-Gen. DOMINGOS OLIVEIRA.

Diplomatic Representation

EMBASSIES IN TIMOR-LESTE

Australia: Av. dos Mártires da Pátria, Dili; tel. 3322111; fax 3322247; e-mail austemb_dili@dfat.gov.au; internet www .easttimor.embassy.gov.au; Ambassador MILES ARMITAGE.

Brazil: Av. Governador Serpa Rosa, POB 157, Farol, Dili; tel. 3324203; fax 3324620; e-mail brasdili@mail.timortelecom.tp; Ambassador EDSON MARINHO DUARTE MONTEIRO.

China, People's Republic: Av. Governador Serpa Rosa, POB 131, Farol, Dili; tel. 3325168; fax 3325166; e-mail chinaembassy2002@ yahoo.com; internet tl.chineseembassy.org; Ambassador FU YUANCONG.

Indonesia: Farol, Palapaco, POB 207, Dili; tel. 3317107; fax 3323684; e-mail kukridil@hotmail.com; internet www.dili.deplu.go .id; Ambassador EDDY SETIABUDHI.

Japan: Av. de Portugal, Pantai Kelapa, POB 175, Dili; tel. 3323131; fax 3323130; e-mail japan.embassy.in.timor-leste@mofa.go.jp; internet www.timor-leste.emb-japan.go.jp; Ambassador KITAHARA IWAO.

Korea, Republic: Av. de Portugal, Campo Alor, Dili; tel. 3321635; fax 3323636; e-mail koreadili@mofat.go.kr; internet tls.mofat.go.kr; Ambassador SEO KYOUNG-SUK.

Malaysia: Av. de Portugal, Praia dos Coqueiros, Dili; tel. 3321804; fax 3321805; e-mail maldili@kln.gov.my; internet www.kln.gov.my/ web/tls_dili; Ambassador NAZARUDIN BIN SALLEH.

New Zealand: Rua Geremias do Amaral, Montael, Dili; tel. 3310087; fax 3324982; e-mail dili@mfat.gov.nz; Ambassador TONY FAUTUA.

Philippines: Av. Governador Serpa Rosa, Farol, Dili; tel. 33310408; fax 3310407; e-mail pe.dili@dfa.gov.ph; Ambassador LEONCIO R. CARDENAS.

Portugal: Edif. ACAIT, Av. Presidente Nicolau Lobato, Dili; tel. 3312533; fax 3312526; e-mail embaixada.portugal@embpor.tp; internet www.embpor.tp; Ambassador LUÍS MANUEL BARREIRA DE SOUSA.

Thailand: Av. de Portugal, Motael, Dili; tel. 3310609; fax 3322179; e-mail thaidli@mfa.go.th; Ambassador WIWAT KUNTHONTHIEN.

USA: Av. de Portugal, Praia dos Coqueiros, Dili; tel. 3324684; fax 3313206; e-mail ConsDili@state.gov; internet timor-leste.usembassy .gov; Ambassador JUDITH R. FERGIN.

Judicial System

Until independence was granted on 20 May 2002 all legislative and executive authority with respect to the administration of the judiciary in East Timor was vested in the UN Transitional Administration in East Timor (UNTAET). During the transitional period of administration a two-tier court structure was established, consisting of District Courts and a Court of Appeal. The Constitution, promulgated in March 2002, specified that Timor-Leste should have three categories of courts: the Supreme Court of Justice and other law courts; the High Administrative, Tax and Audit Court and other administrative courts of first instance; and military courts. The judiciary would be regulated by the Superior Council of the Judiciary, the function of which would be to oversee the judicial sector and, in particular, to control the appointment, promotion, discipline and dismissal of judges. In July 2003 the Court of Appeal was reconstituted. A new penal code was promulgated in March 2009. At that time a code based on Indonesian law remained in place for civil cases, but it was scheduled for replacement by civil codes based on Portuguese law.

Court of Appeal: Caicoli, Dili; tel. 3331149; e-mail tribunal.recurso@tribunais.tl; internet www.tribunais.tl; Pres. CLAUDIO XIMENES.

District Courts: There are four district courts, located in Dili, Baucau, Oecusse and Suai.

Office of the Prosecutor-General: Dili; Prosecutor-General ANA MARIA PESSÔA PEREIRA DA SILVA PINTO.

Religion

In 2009 it was estimated that about 96.5% of the total population were Roman Catholic.

CHRISTIANITY

The Roman Catholic Church

Timor-Leste comprises the dioceses of Dili and Baucau, directly responsible to the Holy See. In December 2007 there were an estimated 958,383 Roman Catholics.

Bishop of Baucau: Most Rev. BASILIO DO NASCIMENTO, Largo da Catedral, Baucau 88810; tel. 4121209; fax 4121380.

Bishop of Dili: Most Rev. ALBERTO RICARDO DA SILVA, Av. dos Direitos Humanos, Bidau Lecidere, CP 4, Dili 88010; tel. 3324850; fax 3321177.

Bishop of Maliana: Fr NORBERTO DO AMARAL.

Protestant Church

Igreja Protestante iha Timor Lorosa'e (Protestant Church in Timor-Leste): Jl. Raya Comoro, POB 1186, Dili 88110; tel. and fax 3323128; f. 1988; est. as Gereja Kristen Timor Timur (GKTT); adopted present name 2000; Moderator Rev. MOISES A. DA SILVA; 30,000 mems.

The Press

The Constitution promulgated in March 2002 guarantees freedom of the press in Timor-Leste.

Guide Post Magazine: Dili; e-mail advertising@guideposttimor.com; internet www.guideposttimor.com; monthly; Editor LEITH CARROLL.

Lalenok (Mirror): Rua Gov. Celestino da Silva, Farol, Dili; tel. 3321607; e-mail lalenok@hotmail.com; f. 2000; publ. by Kamelin Media Group; Tetum; 3 a week; Dir-Gen. and Chief Editor VIRGÍLIO DA SILVA GUTERRES; Editor JOSÉ MARIA POMPELA; circ. 300.

Lian Maubere: Dili; f. 1999; weekly.

Jornal da República (The Official Gazette of Timor-Leste): Dili; e-mail jornal_republica@mj.gov.tl; internet www.jornal.gov.tl; forum for publication of all govt regulations and directives, acts of national organs or institutions, and other acts of public interest requiring general notification; Portuguese.

Suara Timor Lorosae: STL Park, Surik Mas, Dili; tel. 3322824; fax 3322823; e-mail stl_redaksi@yahoo.com; internet suara-timor-lorosae.com; f. 2000; daily; Editor-in-Chief and Publr SALVADOR J. XIMENES SOARES.

Timor Post: 6 Rua Dom Aleixo Corte-Real, Dili; f. 2000; managed by editors and staff of the fmr Suara Timor Timur; Tetum, English, Portuguese and Bahasa Indonesia; daily; Man. Editor OTELIO OTE; Chief Editor and Dir ADERITO HUGO DA COSTA; circ. 600.

PRESS AGENCY

Timornewsline: Rua Sebastian da Costa, Colmera, Dili; tel. 3324475; e-mail alberico@tlmc.org; internet www.timornewsline.com; operated by Timor-Leste Media Development Center.

PRESS ASSOCIATIONS

Sindicato dos Jornalistas de Timor-Leste (SJTL): Rua Dom Aleixo Corte-Real, Bebora, Dili; tel. 7248549; e-mail sjti@yahoo.com; f. 2001; Pres. RODOLFO DE SOUSA.

Timor Lorosae Journalists' Association (TLJA): Rua de Caicoli, Dili; tel. 3324047; fax 3327505; e-mail ajtl_tlja@hotmail.com; f. 1999; Co-ordinator OTELIO OTE; Pres. VIRGÍLIO DA SILVA GUTERRES.

Broadcasting and Communications

TELECOMMUNICATIONS

In July 2002 the Government granted a consortium led by Portugal Telecom a 15-year concession permitting it to establish and operate Timor-Leste's telecommunications systems. Under the terms of the concession, the consortium agreed to provide every district in Timor-Leste with telecommunications services at the most inexpensive tariffs viable within 15 months. At the expiry of the concession in 2017, the telecommunications system was to be transferred to government control.

Timor-Leste Telecom (TT): Sala No. 7, Hotel Timor, Av. dos Mártires da Pátria, POB 135, Dili; tel. 3303000; fax 3303419; e-mail info@timortelecom.tp; internet www.timortelecom.tp; f. 2002; jt venture mainly operated by Portugal Telecom; provides telecommunications services in Timor-Leste; Chair. RUI PEDRO OLIVEIRA SOARES; CEO Capt. MANUEL AMARO; 114 employees.

BROADCASTING

Following independence, the UN Mission of Support in East Timor (UNMISET) transferred control of public television and radio in Timor-Leste to the new Government. In 2003 a Public Broadcasting Service was established, controlled by an independent board of directors.

Radio

There are 18 radio stations operating in Timor-Leste, including community radio stations for each of the country's 13 districts. In addition to the public service, Radio Timor-Leste, the Roman Catholic Church operates a radio station, Radio Kamanak, while a third populist station, Voz Esperança, broadcasts in Dili. A fourth radio station, Radio Falintil FM, also operates in Dili and, in October 2003, the Christian station Voice FM was established. In 2000 the US radio station Voice of America began broadcasting to Timor-Leste seven days a week in English, Portuguese and Bahasa Indonesia.

Radio Timor-Leste (RTL): Rua de Caicoli, Dili; tel. 3321826; e-mail radio@rttl.org; internet www.rttl.org; fmrly Radio UNTAET; name changed as above in 2002; broadcasts mainly in Bahasa Indonesia, but also in English, Portuguese and Tetum, to an estimated 90% of Timor-Leste's population; Man. PAULA RODRIGES.

Television

TV Timor-Leste (TVTL): Rua de Caicoli, Dili; tel. 3321825; e-mail tv@rttl.org; internet www.rttl.org; f. 2000; est. as Televisaun Timor Lorosa'e by UNTAET; adopted present name in May 2002; broadcasts in Tetum and Portuguese; Gen. Man. ANTONIO DIAZ.

Finance

(cap. = capital; res = reserves; dep. = deposits; brs = branches)

BANKING

In February 2001 the East Timor Central Payments Office was officially opened. This was succeeded in November of that year by the Banking and Payments Authority, which was intended to function as a precursor to a central bank.

Banking and Payments Authority (BPA): Av. Bispo Medeiros, POB 59, Dili; tel. 3313712; fax 3313713; e-mail info@bancocentral.tl; internet www.bancocentral.tl; inaugurated Nov. 2001; regulates and supervises Timor-Leste's financial system, formulates and implements payments system policies, provides banking services to Timor-Leste's administration and foreign official institutions, manages fiscal reserves; fmrly Central Payments Office; cap. US $20m., dep. US $191.6m. (June 2009); Chair. and Gen. Man. ABRAÃO F. DE VASCONSELOS; Dep. Gen. Mans MARIA JOSÉ DE JESUS SARMENTO, NUR AINI DJAFAR ALKATIRI.

Instituição de Micro Finanças de Timor-Leste (IMFTL): Av. Martires da Patria, Mandarin, Dili; tel. 3339186; fax 3310444; e-mail smspirito@hotmail.com; f. 2002; microfinance.

Foreign Banks

Australia and New Zealand Banking Group Ltd (ANZ) (Australia): cnr Av. Presidente Nicolau Lobato and Rua Belarmino Lobo, Bidau Lecidere, POB 264, Dili; tel. 3324800; fax 3324822; e-mail easttimor@anz.com; internet www.anz.com/TimorLeste; retail and commercial banking services; Gen. Man. CHRIS DURMAN; Group CEO JOHN MCFARLANE.

Banco Nacional Ultramarino (Portugal): Edif. BNU, 12–13 Av. Presidente Nicolau Lobato, Dili; tel. 3323385; fax 3323678; e-mail cgd.timor@cgd.pt; wholly owned subsidiary of Caixa Geral de Depósitos, Portugal; Gen. Man. Dr CORREIA PINTO; 9 brs.

PT Bank Mandiri (Persero) (Indonesia): 12 Av. Presidente Nicolau Lobato, Colmera, Dili; tel. 3317777; fax 3317444; e-mail dili_timorleste@bankmandiri.co.id; internet www.bankmandiri.co.id; Group Chair. EDWIN GERUNGAN.

Trade and Industry

GOVERNMENT AGENCIES

Autoridade Nacional do Petróleo—ANP (National Petroleum Authority): Ground Floor, East Wing, Pálacio do Governo, POB 113, Farol, Dili; tel. 3324098; fax 3324082; e-mail info@anp-tl.org; internet www.anp-tl.org; f. 2008; responsible for management of govt petroleum revenues; Pres. GUALDINO DO CARMO DA SILVA.

Direcção Nacional Politica do Recursos Naturais: 1st Floor, Fomento Bldg, Mandarin, POB 171, Dili; tel. and fax 3317143; e-mail amandio_gusmao@yahoo.com.au; internet www.timor-leste.gov.tl/EMRD; Dir AMANDIO GUSMÃO SOARES.

TradeInvest Timor-Leste: Memorial Hall, Av. Praia dos Coqueros Farol, Dili 8000; tel. 3331084; fax 3331087; e-mail tradeinvest_tl@yahoo.com; f. 2005; est. to encourage devt of entrepreneurship within Timor-Leste.

UTILITIES

As a result of the civil conflict in 1999, some 13–23 power stations were reported to require repairs ranging from moderate maintenance to almost complete rehabilitation. The rehabilitation of the power sector was funded largely by foreign donors. By July 2003 31 generators had been restored, supplying electricity to Dili, as well as to 12 districts and 33 subdistricts.

Electricidade de Timor-Leste (EDTL): EDTL Bldg, Rua Estrada de Balide, Caicoli, Dili; tel. 3339254; fax 7230095; e-mail virgiliofguterres@hotmail.com; govt dept; responsible for power generation, distribution and financial management of power sector in Timor-Leste; transferred to external management in 2002; Dir VIRGILIO GUTERRES.

CO-OPERATIVES

Cooperativa Café Timor (CCT): 16 Rua Barros Gomes, Dili; tel. 3313139; e-mail boycedjs@gmail.com; f. 2000; est. under the Timor Economic Rehabilitation and Devt Project; produces, markets and distributes organic coffee; also provides information and advisory services for member farmers; Operational Dir SISTO MONIZ PIEDADE; 21,557 mems.

Cooperativa Fera Nakukun: Rua Vila Guico, Loes, Guico, Maubara; tel. 07358236 (mobile); 100% Timor-owned; fresh food supplier.

TRADE UNIONS

Konfederasaun Sindikatu Timor-Leste (KSTL) (Trade Union Confederation of Timor-Leste): Rua Sebastião da Costa, Colmera, Dili; tel. 7239824; e-mail kstl.union@gmail.com; f. 2001; represents nine unions, comprising c. 4,700 workers within the press, teaching, nursing, construction, agricultural, maritime and transport sectors; Pres. JOSÉ DA CONCEIÇÃO DA COSTA.

Labour Advocacy Institute of East Timor (LAIFET): Rua Abílio Monteiro Palapaso, Dili; tel. 3317243; Dir DOMINGOS BAPTISTA DE ARAÚJO.

Serikat Buruh Socialis Timor (SBST) (Timor Socialist Workers' Union): Dili; controlled by Partido Socialista de Timor; Dir Dr LUCIANO DA SILVA.

Transport

ROADS

In December 1999 the World Bank reported that some 57% of the country's 1,414 km of paved roads were in poor or damaged condition. Some repair and maintenance work on the road network was carried out in 2005, using funding supplied by external donors. In 2009 the Asian Development Bank (ADB) approved the Road Network Development Sector Project for Timor-Leste: plans included the rehabilitation of 230 km of national roads and the development of a programme of road maintenance.

SHIPPING

Timor-Leste's maritime infrastructure includes ports at Dili, Carabela and Com, smaller wharves at Oecusse (Oekussi) and Liquiça (Likisia), and slip-landing structures in Oecusse, Batugade and Suai. In November 2001, following its reconstruction, the management of the port at Dili was transferred to the Government.

Port Authority of Timor-Leste (APORTIL): Av. de Portugal, Dili; tel. 3317264; f. 2003.

Principal Shipping Companies

Everise Freight Forwarding Inc: 2 Rua Belarmino Lobo, Dili; tel. 3324844; fax 3312856; e-mail everisedili@yahoo.com.

SDV Logistics (East Timor): Av. Presidente Nicolau Lobato, Bairro dos Grilos, POB 398, Dili; tel. 3322818; fax 3324077; e-mail dili@sdv.com; internet www.sdv.com; f. 1999; freight forwarder, shipping agent and customs broker; Man. Dir JÉRÔME PETIT.

CIVIL AVIATION

Timor-Leste has two international airports and eight grass runways. In June 2001 Dili Express Pte was the first Timor-based company to begin international flights, with a service to Singapore. In 2005 Timor-Leste's first national carrier, Kakoak Air, commenced operations. Air North operates regular flights from Australia (Darwin) to Dili.

Civil Aviation Authority (CAA): Dili; tel. 3317110; fax 3317111; e-mail henriques_sabino@yahoo.com; govt authority responsible for overall planning, implementation and operation of aviation services in Timor-Leste; Dir JULIÃO X. CARLOS.

Air Timor: Aeroporto Presidente Nicolau Lobato, POB 888, Dili; tel. 3312777; fax 3312888; e-mail diliadmin@air-timor.com; internet www.air-timor.com; f. 2008; est. as Austasia Airlines; name changed as above in 2010; operates services between Dili and Singapore in collaboration with SilkAir.

Tourism

In 2009, according to Turismo de Timor-Leste, about 30,000 people visited the country on a tourist visa However, the tourism sector remains relatively undeveloped. The country's first national park, Nino Konis Santana National Park, was established in 2007 and aims to protect a number of endangered species, including 25 endemic birds. The park encompasses more than 123,600 ha, including a marine area of 55,600 ha, which contains a globally important biodiversity of coral and reef fish.

Turismo de Timor-Leste: Apdo 194, Dili; tel. 3310371; fax 3339179; e-mail info@turismotimorleste.com; internet www.turismotimorleste.com; f. 2002; National Dir of Tourism JOSÉ QUINTAS.

Defence

As assessed at November 2010, the East Timor Defence Force (Falintil-ETDF, which replaced the UN Mission of Support in East Timor in 2005) comprised 1,250 army personnel and a naval element of 82. A total of 404 Australian troops and 80 from New Zealand, as well as various international observers, remained in the country.

Commander-in-Chief: Brig.-Gen. TAUR MATAN RUAK.

Education

According to UN estimates, the adult literacy rate was 58.6% in 2003. In 2004/05 there were 6,987 pre-primary school students, 177,970 primary school students, 50,014 lower secondary school students and 24,808 upper secondary school students in the country. By 2008/09 the number of students enrolled in primary schools had increased to 213,783 and primary school teachers numbered 7,358. In 2008/09 there were an estimated 16,727 students engaged in tertiary education, principally at the National University of Timor-Leste. The 2008 budget allocated US $45.3m. to education, equivalent to 13.5% of total government expenditure. In 2007 the Government introduced an Education Reform Plan with the aim of providing nine years of free and compulsory education.

TOGO

Introductory Survey

LOCATION, CLIMATE, LANGUAGE, RELIGION, FLAG, CAPITAL

The Togolese Republic lies in West Africa, forming a narrow strip stretching north from a coastline of about 50 km (30 miles) on the Gulf of Guinea. It is bordered by Ghana to the west, by Benin to the east, and by Burkina Faso to the north. The climate in the coastal area is hot and humid, with an annual average temperature of 27°C (81°F); rainfall in this zone averages 875 mm (34.4 ins) per year, and is heaviest during May–October. Precipitation in the central region is heaviest in May–June and in October, and in the north, where the average annual temperature is 30°C (86°F), there is a rainy season from July to September. The official languages are French, Kabiyé and Ewe. About one-half of the population follows animist beliefs, while about 35% are Christians and 15% Muslims. The national flag (approximate proportions 3 by 5) has five equal horizontal stripes, alternately green and yellow, with a square red canton, containing a five-pointed white star, in the upper hoist. The capital is Lomé.

CONTEMPORARY POLITICAL HISTORY

Historical Context

Togoland, of which modern Togo was formerly a part, became a German colony in 1894. Shortly after the outbreak of the First World War, the colony was occupied by French and British forces. After the war, a League of Nations mandate divided Togoland into two administrative zones, with France controlling the larger eastern section, while the United Kingdom governed the west. The partition of Togoland split the homeland of the Ewe people, who inhabit the southern part of the territory, and this has been a continuing source of friction. After the Second World War, French and British Togoland became UN Trust Territories. In May 1956 a UN-supervised plebiscite in British Togoland produced, despite Ewe opposition, majority support for a merger with the neighbouring territory of the Gold Coast, then a British colony, in an independent state. The region accordingly became part of Ghana in the following year. In October 1956, in another plebiscite, French Togoland voted to become an autonomous republic, with internal self-government, within the French Community. Togo's foremost political parties at that time were the Comité de l'unité togolaise (usually known as the Unité togolaise—UT), led by Sylvanus Olympio, and the Parti togolais du progrès (PTP), led by Nicolas Grunitzky, Olympio's brother-in-law. In 1956 Grunitzky became Prime Minister in the first autonomous Government, but in April 1958 a UN-supervised election was won by the UT. Olympio became Prime Minister and led Togo to full independence on 27 April 1960.

At elections in April 1961 Olympio became Togo's first President, while the UT was elected (unopposed) to all 51 seats in the Assemblée nationale. At the same time a referendum approved a new Constitution. On 13 January 1963 the UT regime was overthrown by a military revolt, in which Olympio was killed. Grunitzky subsequently assumed the presidency on a provisional basis. A referendum in May approved another Constitution, confirmed Grunitzky as President and elected a new legislature from a single list of candidates, giving equal representation to the four main political parties.

Grunitzky was deposed by a bloodless military coup, led by Lt-Col (later Gen.) Etienne (Gnassingbé) Eyadéma, the Army Chief of Staff, on 13 January 1967. Eyadéma, a member of the Kabiyé ethnic group, who had taken a prominent part in the 1963 rising, assumed the office of President in April. Political parties were banned, and the President ruled by decree. In November 1969 a new ruling party, the Rassemblement du peuple togolais (RPT), was founded, led by Eyadéma.

In Togo's first elections for 16 years, held on 30 December 1979, Eyadéma (the sole candidate) was confirmed as President of the Republic for a seven-year term. At the same time a new Constitution was overwhelmingly endorsed, while the list of 67 candidates for a single-party Assemblée nationale was approved by 96% of votes cast. On 13 January 1980 Eyadéma proclaimed the 'Third Republic'. In December 1986 President Eyadéma was re-elected, unopposed, for a further seven-year term.

Domestic Political Affairs

In December 1990 a new constitution was drafted, which envisaged, *inter alia*, a plurality of political parties. Meanwhile, several recently established, unofficial opposition movements formed a co-ordinating organization, the Front des associations pour le renouveau (FAR), led by Yawovi Agboyibo, to campaign for the immediate introduction of a multi-party political system. Eyadéma subsequently agreed to implement a general amnesty for political dissidents and to permit the legalization of political organizations. Following instances of violent unrest in April 1991, Eyadéma, fearing a civil conflict between the Kabiyé and Ewe ethnic groups (the Government and armed forces were composed overwhelmingly of members of the first group, while opposition groups for the most part represented the Ewe people), announced that a new constitution would be introduced within one year, and that multi-party legislative elections would be organized. At the end of the month it was announced that the FAR was to be disbanded. Agboyibo subsequently formed his own party, the Comité d'action pour le renouveau (CAR), which in May became one of 10 parties to enter into a Front de l'opposition démocratique (FOD, later renamed the Coalition de l'opposition démocratique—COD).

Following the organization of a general strike by the FOD, the Government agreed, in June 1991, that a 'national conference' would be held, with the power to choose a transitional Prime Minister and to establish a transitional legislative body. The conference opened in July; however, when it adopted resolutions suspending the Constitution, dissolving the Assemblée nationale and giving the conference sovereign power, government representatives withdrew. Subsequently the conference resolved to freeze the assets of the RPT, to transfer most of the powers of the President to a Prime Minister, and to prevent Eyadéma from contesting future elections. In defiance of a decree issued by Eyadéma temporarily suspending proceedings, the conference elected a Prime Minister, Joseph Kokou Koffigoh (a senior lawyer and prominent human rights activist), announced the dissolution of the RPT and the formation of a transitional legislature, the Haut Conseil de la République (HCR). Eyadéma capitulated, signing a decree that proclaimed Koffigoh as transitional Prime Minister. In September Koffigoh formed a transitional Government, most of the members of which had not previously held office: he himself assumed the defence portfolio.

Following a number of interventions by members of the armed forces, in August 1992 the HCR restored to Eyadéma the power to preside over the Council of Ministers and on 1 September the transitional Government was dissolved. Later that month a new transitional Government, led by Koffigoh, was appointed, including representatives of 10 parties; the most influential ministries were allocated to members of the RPT. On 27 September a new Constitution was approved in a referendum by 98.1% of the votes cast. At the end of the month, however, it was announced that local, legislative and presidential elections, initially scheduled to have been held in June, were to be further postponed. In October eight opposition parties announced the formation of a 'Patriotic Front', to be led by the leader of the Union togolaise pour la démocratie (UTD), Edem Kodjo, and Agboyibo.

In January 1993 Eyadéma dissolved the Government, reappointing Koffigoh as Prime Minister, and stated that he would appoint a new government of national unity to organize elections. His action provoked protests by the opposition parties, who claimed that, according to the Constitution, the HCR should appoint a Prime Minister since the transition period had now expired. In the same month two ministers representing the French and German Governments visited Togo to offer mediation in the political crisis. During their visit at least 20 people were killed when police opened fire on anti-Government protesters. Thousands of Togolese subsequently fled from Lomé, many seeking refuge in Benin or Ghana. In February inter-Togolese discussions organized by the French and German Governments in France failed when the presidential delegation withdrew after one day. In that month the French, German and US Governments suspended their programmes of aid to Togo. A new Government, in which supporters of Eyadéma retained the principal posts, was formed in February.

In April 1993 a new electoral schedule was announced, envisaging elections to the presidency and the legislature in July and August, respectively. The RPT designated Eyadéma as its presidential candidate. In May the COD-2, an alliance of some 25 political parties and trade unions, declared that it would boycott the elections, alleging that they would not be fairly conducted, and that opposition politicians had no guarantee of their safety. In July, however, the Togolese Government and the COD-2 signed an agreement establishing 25 August as the date for the first round of presidential voting. The agreement stipulated that the Togolese armed forces should be confined to barracks during the election period, and that international military observers should be present to confirm this, while international civilian observers should also be present for the election. An independent, nine-member Commission électorale nationale (CEN) was to be established, to include three members nominated by the opposition parties. Later in July the COD-2 nominated Kodjo as its presidential candidate; however, in the same month two other candidates—Agboyibo and Abou Djobo Boukari—were nominated by parties affiliated to the COD-2. Three candidates eventually contested the presidential election held on 25 August at which Eyadéma was reported to have obtained 96.5% of the votes cast. French election observers concluded that the poll had not been satisfactorily conducted; observers from the USA and Germany had withdrawn from Togo shortly before the election took place.

1994 legislative elections

In the legislative elections, finally held on 6 and 20 February 1994, some 347 candidates contested 81 seats. Despite the murder of an elected CAR representative after the first round, and violent incidents at polling stations during the second round, international observers expressed themselves satisfied with the conduct of the elections. The opposition won a narrow victory in the polls, with the CAR winning 36 seats and the UTD seven; the RPT obtained 35 seats and two other smaller pro-Eyadéma parties won three. During March Eyadéma consulted the main opposition parties on the formation of a new government. In late March the CAR and the UTD reached an agreement on the terms of their alliance and jointly proposed the candidacy of Agboyibo for Prime Minister. In March and April the Supreme Court declared the results of the legislative elections invalid in three constituencies (in which the CAR had won two seats and the UTD one) and ordered by-elections. In April Eyadéma nominated Kodjo as Prime Minister. The CAR subsequently declared that it would not participate in an administration formed by Kodjo. Kodjo took office on 25 April; his Government, appointed in May, comprised eight members of the RPT and other pro-Eyadéma parties, three members of the UTD, and eight independents.

At the by-elections, conducted on 4 and 18 August 1996 in the presence of 22 international observers, the RPT won control of all three constituencies. Consequently, the RPT and its allies were able to command a majority in the legislature, thus precipitating the resignation of the Kodjo administration. On 20 August Eyadéma appointed Kwassi Klutse, hitherto Minister of Planning and Territorial Development, as Prime Minister, and the new Council of Ministers, appointed in late August, comprised almost exclusively supporters of Eyadéma. In November the Union pour la justice et la démocratie, which held two seats in the legislature, announced that it was officially to merge with the RPT, thus giving the RPT an overall majority, with 41 seats.

In September 1997 a new electoral code was approved, providing for a CEN comprising nine members, chaired by the President of the Court of Appeal and including four members appointed by the opposition. The CAR, however, boycotted the legislative session in protest at the Government's refusal to reveal the findings of a report by a mission of the European Union (EU, see p. 270) on the country's electoral process. Later that month opposition parties, led by the CAR and the Union des forces de changement (UFC), organized a demonstration in Lomé in protest at the new electoral law and condemned as fraudulent the Government's preparations for the forthcoming presidential election.

Shortly before the presidential election, which was held on 21 June 1998, the Government had refused to permit the presence of 500 national observers trained by the EU. The election proceeded amid accusations of electoral malpractice, and on the following day counting of votes was halted without explanation, reportedly when the early returns showed Eyadéma to be in second place. Four members of the CEN resigned the same day, alleging intimidation. The Minister of the Interior and Security, Gen. Seyi Memene, announced that he had assumed responsibility for the ballot count, and that Eyadéma had been re-elected President with 52.1% of the valid votes cast. Following the announcement of the result, violent protests erupted throughout Lomé. The USA condemned the conduct of the election, and appealed to the Government to respect its own laws and electoral code, while the EU decided not to recognize the result, which was, none the less, confirmed by the Constitutional Court.

In September 1998 Klutse announced his new Council of Ministers. Despite Eyadéma's stated intention to form a government of national unity, no opposition figures were willing to be included. Among the few new appointments was Koffigoh, as Minister of State, responsible for Foreign Affairs and Co-operation.

Elections to the Assemblée nationale took place on 21 March 1999, contested only by the RPT and by two small parties loyal to Eyadéma, including Koffigoh's Coordination nationale des forces nouvelles, as well as by 12 independent candidates. (The principal opposition parties had boycotted the polling.) The Constitutional Court ruled that the RPT had won 77 seats, and that independent candidates had taken two seats. By-elections were to take place in two constituencies in which voting had been invalidated. (Both of these seats were subsequently won by the RPT.) Despite international criticism, Eyadéma rejected demands for fresh elections, declaring that the opposition had been afforded ample opportunity to participate. In April Klutse tendered his Government's resignation; in May Eugene Koffi Adogboli was appointed Prime Minister.

In May 1999 the human rights organization Amnesty International published a report detailing numerous abuses of human rights committed by Togolese security forces, alleging that hundreds of political opponents of Eyadéma had been killed following the 1998 presidential election. In late July 1999 Eyadéma (who rejected the validity of the report) urged the UN and the Organization of African Unity (OAU, now the African Union—AU, see p. 183) to assist in the establishment of an international commission of inquiry into the allegations; such a commission was established in June 2000.

Opposition to Eyadéma

Discussions between the Government and opposition began in Lomé in July 1999, with the assistance of four international facilitators, representing France, Germany, the EU and La Francophonie. Eyadéma's announcement that he would not stand for re-election in 2003 and that new legislative elections would be held was widely credited with breaking the deadlock in negotiations. After the opposition had agreed to accept Eyadéma's victory in the presidential election, an accord was signed on 29 July 1999 by all the parties involved in negotiations. The accord made provision for the creation of an independent electoral body and for the establishment of a code of conduct to regulate political activity.

The first meeting took place in August 1999 of the 24-member Comité paritaire de suivi (CPS) responsible for the implementation of the accord, composed of an equal number of opposition and pro-Eyadéma representatives, and also including intermediaries from the EU. Harry Octavianus Olympio, the Minister for the Promotion of Democracy and the Rule of Law, was appointed to head the CPS. Despite the reservations of the UFC, a compromise agreement on announcing election results was reached in September, and in December agreement was achieved on a revised electoral code, providing for the establishment of an independent electoral commission. In April 2000 Eyadéma obliged the Assemblée nationale to accept the new electoral code. The EU subsequently offered to provide financial support for the elections, which were scheduled to be held later in 2000. The 20 members of the new Commission électorale nationale indépendante (CENI) were named in June, and in July Arthème Ahoomey-Zounou of the Convergence patriotique panafricaine (CPP—formed in 1999 by the amalgamation of the UTD and three smaller parties, and headed by Edem Kodjo) was elected as President of the CENI.

In August 2000 Adogboli was overwhelmingly defeated in a legislative vote of no confidence and resigned. Eyadéma appointed Agbéyomè Kodjo, hitherto President of the Assemblée nationale, and regarded as a close ally of the President, as Prime Minister. A government reorganization was effected in October. In January 2001 the CENI announced that the legislative elections would be held in two rounds, on 14 and 28 October 2001, using the disputed electoral registers from the 1998 presidential election.

In February 2002 the Assemblée nationale approved amendments to electoral legislation; notably, henceforth all candidates for legislative elections were required to have been continuously resident in Togo for six months prior to elections, with presidential candidates to have been resident for a continuous 12 months. The CENI was also to be reduced in size from 20 to 10 members, and decisions were to be taken by a two-thirds' majority, instead of the four-fifths' majority required hitherto. These amendments led to a further postponement of the elections, which had been scheduled to take place in March. These measures attracted international disapproval, notably prompting the EU to suspend aid intended to finance the polls. In February five opposition parties issued a joint communiqué accusing the Government of having broken the conditions of the accord signed in July 1999, and in early March 2002 they rejected an invitation by Kodjo to nominate representatives to the CENI. The Government consequently announced that no date for the legislative elections could be announced until a complete electoral commission had been formed. In late March 10 opposition parties, which had not been party to the accord signed in 1999 and were therefore excluded from the CPS, announced the formation of a Coordination des partis de l'opposition constructive, headed by Harry Octavianus Olympio, who had also assumed the leadership of the Rassemblement pour le soutien de la démocratie et du développement (RSDD). In mid-May 2002 a committee of seven judges (the Comité de sept magistrats—C-7), charged with monitoring the electoral process at the proposed legislative elections, was appointed. At the end of May the EU announced that it would not renew funding for the three facilitators it supported in Togo, in view of the continued lack of progress towards democracy.

In June 2002 Eyadéma dismissed Kodjo as Prime Minister and replaced him with Koffi Sama, the erstwhile Secretary-General of the RPT; a new Government, which included several principal members of the former administration, was appointed in July. Kodjo subsequently issued a statement criticizing the 'monarchic, despotic' regime of Eyadéma, and (in contrast to his former stated position) called for measures to ensure that Eyadéma would be unable to amend the Constitution to stand for a further term of office. The state prosecutor filed a suit against Kodjo on charges of disseminating false information and demeaning the honour of the President; Kodjo was expelled from the RPT and subsequently left Togo, taking up residence in France.

In early October 2002 the Assemblée nationale was dissolved, pending elections on 27 October. Prior to this date nine opposition parties that had declined to participate in the elections announced the formation of a new alliance, the Coalition des forces démocrates (CFD); members of the grouping included the CAR, the CPP and the UFC, in addition to a faction of 'renovators' within the RPT (which subsequently became the Pacte socialiste pour le renouveau—PSR, led by Maurice Dahuku Pere). Meanwhile, a group of 'constructive opposition' parties (including the RSDD), which were prepared to participate in the electoral process and form alliances with the RPT, formed the Coordination des partis politiques de l'opposition constructive (CPOC). The 81 seats of the Assemblée nationale were contested by 118 candidates nominated by 15 parties and eight independent candidates, although the RPT was the sole party to contest every seat. The RPT won 72 seats (46 unopposed) and the RSDD three, while three other parties won a total of five seats, and one independent candidate was elected. The C-7, which now comprised six judges (following the resignation of one member of the committee on the day before the elections), estimated electoral turn-out at 67.4%, although the CFD claimed that only 10% of the electorate had voted. Eyadéma reappointed Sama as Prime Minister in mid-November; a new Government was formed in early December. All ministers were members of the RPT, with the exception of Harry Octavianus Olympio, who was appointed Minister responsible for Relations with Parliament.

In December 2002 the Assemblée nationale approved several constitutional amendments regarding the eligibility of presidential candidates. The restriction that had limited the President to serving two terms of office was removed, and the age of eligibility was reduced from 45 to 35 years. (It was widely believed that these measures were intended to permit Eyadéma to serve a further term of office, and also to permit the possible presidential candidacy of Eyadéma's son, Faure Gnassingbé.) Candidates were henceforth to be required to hold solely Togolese citizenship. In February 2003 the UFC, having opposed the constitutional amendments, announced its withdrawal from the CFD, after other parties within the grouping agreed to appoint representatives to the CENI prior to the holding of a presidential election later in the year. In April Eyadéma confirmed that he was to seek re-election; however, in May the CENI rejected the candidacy of Gilchrist Olympio, the son of the former President who had recently returned to Togo. By mid-May six opposition presidential candidates (including four representatives of the constituent parties of the CFD) had emerged. Emmanuel Bob Akitani, the First Vice-President of the UFC, was announced as his party's candidate, following Olympio's debarment.

Eyadéma was returned to office in the presidential election held on 1 June 2003, receiving 57.8% of the votes cast. His nearest rival was Bob Akitani, with 33.7% of votes. Several of the defeated candidates declared that the election had been conducted fraudulently, although observers from the Economic Community of West African States (ECOWAS), the AU and the Conseil de l'Entente refuted these claims. Eyadéma was inaugurated for a further term of office on 20 June. Sama resigned as Prime Minister later in the month, but was reappointed as premier on 1 July, apparently with instructions from Eyadéma to form a government of national unity. However, most opposition parties reportedly declined representation in the administration, and the new Government, formed on 29 July, included only two representatives of the 'constructive opposition'. Faure Gnassingbé received his first ministerial posting, as Minister of Equipment, Mines, Posts and Telecommunications.

Talks between the EU and the Government on the conditions for a resumption of economic co-operation commenced in April 2004 in Brussels, Belgium; the government delegation, led by Sama, pledged to implement 22 measures, including the introduction of more transparent conditions for elections, the revision of the press code and a guarantee that political parties would be granted the freedom to conduct their activities without fear of harassment. In August the Assemblée nationale adopted amendments to the press code, notably abolishing prison sentences for offences such as defamation and repealing the powers of the Ministry of the Interior, Security and Decentralization to order the closure or seizure of newspapers.

In November 2004 the EU announced that it was to resume partial economic co-operation with Togo, in view of progress towards fulfilment of the 22 conditions established in April. It was emphasized, however, that the full resumption of development aid was dependent on the holding of free and fair elections within six months. In December Eyadéma announced that legislative elections would be held during the first half of 2005. In January 2005 the Assemblée nationale adopted legislation introducing several amendments to the electoral code in accordance with the demands of the EU, notably strengthening the powers of the CENI and increasing its membership to 13, to include two representatives of civil society.

The death of Eyadéma

On 5 February 2005 Prime Minister Sama announced that President Eyadéma had died while being transported out of the country for medical treatment. The Togolese military closed the country's borders, thus preventing Fambaré Natchaba, the President of the Assemblée nationale, who, according to the Constitution, was to assume the functions of head of state pending elections to be held within 60 days, from returning to Togo from a visit to Europe. Hours later it was announced that the Constitution had been suspended and that the armed forces had pledged their allegiance to Eyadéma's son, Faure Gnassingbé, as the new head of state. The following day an extraordinary session of the Assemblée nationale was convened, at which deputies voted to remove Natchaba from his post as President of the legislature and appoint Gnassingbé in his place. The Assemblée also approved a constitutional amendment authorizing an interim President to serve the remainder of the deceased predecessor's term, rather than arranging elections within 60 days (Eyadéma's term was due to expire in June 2008).

Gnassingbé was formally sworn in as President of Togo on 7 February 2005. The circumstances of his succession provoked domestic and international condemnation: the inauguration ceremony was boycotted by diplomats from Nigeria, the EU, the USA and the UN, while the AU and ECOWAS demanded that Gnassingbé stand down to allow fair and democratic elections to be held. Meanwhile, the Togolese opposition called a two-day strike for 8 and 9 February, in protest at the perceived coup; however, the strike was only partially observed. Subsequent protests, concentrated in the Lomé suburb of Bè, reportedly a stronghold of opposition support, resulted in at least four deaths and several injuries from clashes with security forces, who allegedly used tear gas and live ammunition to disperse protesters.

Following intense diplomatic pressure from ECOWAS, and from Nigeria in particular, Gnassingbé announced on 18 February 2005 that elections would be held within 60 days—however, he declined to stand down before that time. Following this announcement, on 21 February the Assemblée nationale voted to reverse the constitutional amendments adopted on 6 February. Judging these concessions to be insufficient, ECOWAS imposed an arms embargo on Togo and travel restrictions on members of the Government, while the ambassadors of ECOWAS states were withdrawn from Lomé. The AU declared its support for the imposition of sanctions, while the USA announced that it would terminate all military assistance to Togo unless Gnassingbé stood down. On 25 February it was revealed that Gnassingbé had been appointed President of the RPT, and endorsed as the party's candidate in the forthcoming presidential election. Later that day Gnassingbé announced that he was resigning from the post of President of the Assemblée nationale, and hence from the position of interim President, stating that he did not wish to compromise the transparency and fairness of the election. Abass Bonfoh, Vice-President of the Assemblée nationale, became the acting head of state. The announcement was welcomed by ECOWAS, which lifted its sanctions.

The date of the election was subsequently set for 24 April 2005, although the opposition protested that it would be impossible to organize fair and transparent elections in such a brief period of time. (The EU also expressed doubts that fair elections could be held so promptly, and declined to send electoral observers.) Nevertheless, the radical opposition, which had grouped itself into a coalition of six parties (including, in addition to the four parties of the Front uni de l'opposition, the PSR and the UFC), subsequently announced that it would present a single candidate, Bob Akitani, to stand against Gnassingbé. Two members of the 'constructive opposition'—Harry Octavianus Olympio and the leader of the Parti du renouveau et de la rédemption, Jean-Nicolas Lawson—announced their candidacies; Gnassingbé's candidature was supported by five small parties of the 'constructive opposition' as well as by the RPT.

On 11 April 2005 a peaceful demonstration in the capital was reported to have been attended by several thousand supporters of the opposition, who demanded that polling be postponed. On 16 April at least seven people were reported to have been killed, and some 150 injured, in clashes between supporters of the opposition and supporters of the youth wing of the RPT in Lomé. On 22 April Bonfoh dismissed the Minister of the Interior, Security and Decentralization, Maj. François Akila Esso Boko, after Boko had appealed for the presidential election to be postponed and for the appointment of a temporary premier from the opposition, citing the risk of civil war if the elections went ahead; Boko sought asylum in the German embassy in Lomé. On 23 April Lawson announced the withdrawal of his candidacy, in protest against Boko's dismissal.

The presidential election was held, as scheduled, on 24 April 2005, amid ongoing tensions. Although widespread violence was not reported on polling day, the seizure of ballot boxes, following the closure of polls, in areas of Lomé in which the opposition was known to have considerable support, and in other areas of the interior, was reported. Preliminary results, issued by the CENI on 26 April, indicated that Gnassingbé had been elected as President by a significant majority. The announcement of Gnassingbé's victory precipitated widespread rioting, particularly in Lomé and in southern regions, with some reports suggesting that as many as 100 people had died in the violence. (According to official figures, 22 people were killed in the rioting.) Meanwhile, Gilchrist Olympio, who had returned to Togo in March, declared that Bob Akitani had been the legitimate winner of polling, claiming that the opposition candidate had received more than 70% of the votes cast. However, on 27 April ECOWAS observers stated that the irregularities in the conduct of the election had not been such as to invalidate the declared results. By early May more than 20,000 Togolese were reported to have fled the country for either Benin or Ghana. On 3 May the Constitutional Court announced the final results of the election, which were not substantially different from the preliminary figures declared by the CENI; Gnassingbé was attributed 60.2% of the votes cast, compared with the 38.3% awarded to Bob Akitani; Lawson (despite the formal withdrawal of his candidacy) and Harry Octavianus Olympio each received around 1%. Some 63% of the electorate were reported to have voted. Gnassingbé was inaugurated as President on 4 May. Although the European Parliament adopted a resolution criticizing the conduct of the election, the election result was generally accepted by the international community.

The Gnassingbé presidency

On 19 May 2005 President Olusegun Obasanjo of Nigeria chaired a reconciliation summit in Abuja, the Nigerian capital, under the aegis of ECOWAS and the AU, which was attended by Gnassingbé, Gilchrist Olympio and other opposition leaders, as well as the heads of state of Benin, Burkina Faso, Gabon, Ghana and Niger. (Bob Akitani was unable to participate owing to ill health.) The talks ended without agreement, however, as the radical opposition continued to reject the legitimacy of Gnassingbé's victory and demanded a full investigation of alleged election irregularities as a precondition for entering into any power-sharing arrangement. None the less, Gnassingbé subsequently held meetings with a number of opposition leaders to discuss the formation of a government of national unity; the UFC upheld its refusal to participate in negotiations. In late May the AU removed sanctions against Togo, declaring that it considered conditions in Togo to be constitutional. Meanwhile, refugees continued to flee Togo, amid reports that opposition supporters were being arrested or kidnapped by the security forces. By late May 34,416 Togolese refugees (19,272 in Benin and 15,144 in Ghana) had been registered by the office of the UN High Commissioner for Refugees (UNHCR). It was estimated that a further 10,000 people had been internally displaced within Togo. Several thousand more people were reported to have fled Togo in subsequent months.

On 8 June 2005 Gnassingbé announced the appointment of former premier Edem Kodjo, regarded as a member of the moderate opposition, as Prime Minister. Negotiations between the President and five radical opposition parties had been unsuccessful, as Gnassingbé refused to accede to several principal opposition demands, including the scheduling of a fresh presidential election and the transfer of some presidential powers to the Prime Minister. Later in June the formation of a 30-member Council of Ministers, dominated by the RPT, but also including several representatives of the opposition and of civil society, was announced. Notably, Tchessa Abi of the PSR was appointed as Keeper of the Seals, Minister of Justice; the other five members of the six-party coalition refused to participate and later condemned Abi's acceptance of a ministerial position, deciding to expel the PSR from the coalition. (The Minister of Culture, Tourism and Leisure, Gabriel Sassouvi Dosseh-Anyroh, was expelled from the UFC, following his acceptance of a post in the administration.) Zarifou Ayéva, the leader of the moderate opposition Parti pour la démocratie et le renouveau (which was absorbed into the RPT later in the year), was appointed as Minister of State, Minister of Foreign Affairs and African Integration, while an elder brother of the President, Kpatcha Gnassingbé, became Minister-delegate at the Presidency of the Republic, responsible for Defence and Veterans.

The return of the refugees was discussed by Gnassingbé and Gilchrist Olympio at a meeting in Rome, Italy, in July 2005, at which the two men also condemned violence and agreed that political prisoners arrested during the electoral process should be released. In September Gnassingbé announced that the holding of legislative elections was to be expedited (although no date was specified), and that, in a measure intended to promote national unity, the country's first President, Sylvanus Olympio, was to be officially rehabilitated. In November some 460 political prisoners were released.

In March 2006 the Government announced that, to encourage Togolese refugees to return to their country, no legal proceedings were to be taken against opposition activists suspected of involvement in the unrest in 2005, excepting those involved in 'bloody crimes'; moreover, President Gnassingbé appealed for a formal resumption of the national dialogue between the authorities and the opposition. The inter-Togolese national dialogue, which had broken down following the death of Eyadéma, finally resumed in Lomé in April 2006, with the participation of six political parties (the CAR, the Convention démocratique des peuples africains—Branche Togolaise, the CPP, the Parti pour la démocratie et le renouveau, the RPT and the UFC), as well as two civil society organizations and the Government.

On 20 August 2006, following negotiations chaired by the President of Burkina Faso, Blaise Compaoré, the Government signed a comprehensive political accord with the main opposition parties in Lomé that provided for the establishment of a transitional government, which would include members of opposition parties. It also called for the re-establishment of the CENI, which would organize and supervise transparent and democratic elections. (In January 2007 the CENI was approved as the official decision-making body for national elections.) Agboyibo replaced Kodjo as Prime Minister in September 2006 and was tasked with forming a government of national unity and organizing elections for 2007. He announced the formation of his new Council of Ministers later that month. In June 2007 the EU agreed to provide funding to support the forthcoming elections (initially scheduled to take place that month but subsequently postponed until August).

After further delays, legislative elections finally took place on 14 October 2007; the RPT secured 50 of the available 81 seats, the UFC took 27 seats and the CAR four. Voter turn-out was estimated at 95%, and international observers declared the election to have been largely free and fair, despite allegations by opposition parties of procedural irregularities. In November Agboyibo, having completed his task of leading the country through legitimate legislative elections, submitted his resignation; Komlan Mally, hitherto Minister of Towns and Town Planning, was appointed Prime Minister in December and named a new 21-member Council of Ministers, including Léopold Messan Gnininvi as Minister of State, Minister of Foreign Affairs and Regional Integration. Notable dismissals included that of Kpatcha Gnassingbé; responsibility for his portfolio was assumed by the presidency. The EU had announced in November its resumption of full co-operation with Togo and granted the country €123m. in development aid.

In April 2008 the UN Office of the High Commissioner for Human Rights initiated the process of establishing a truth and reconciliation commission to investigate the political violence that took place in 2005, following the death of former President Eyadéma. The first stage was to administer surveys to 30,000 people asking how such a commission should be designed; around 23,000 responses were received by September 2008. The commission was finally created by President Gnassingbé in May 2009.

Mally resigned as Prime Minister on 5 September 2008, and two days later Gnassingbé appointed Gilbert Houngbo, who had previously served as the head of the UN Development Programme in Africa, as his replacement. Houngbo formed a new Council of Ministers later that month, in which Mally was appointed to the second most senior cabinet post, that of Minister of State, Minister of Health. There were a number of new additions to the Government, including Kofi Esaw, hitherto the Togolese ambassador to Ethiopia, who was named Minister of Foreign Affairs and Regional Integration, replacing Gnininvi, who was appointed as Minister of State, Minister of Industry, Crafts and Technological Innovation. In October Agboyibo stood down as leader of the CAR, and was replaced by Dodji Apevon.

Kpatcha Gnassingbé was arrested in mid-April 2009 and charged with attempting to overthrow the Government. He had unsuccessfully sought refuge at the US embassy in Lomé after a raid by security forces on his residence, which reportedly resulted in the deaths of two soldiers. In early May 10 civilians were arrested in connection with the coup attempt; 18 soldiers had by this time already been detained. Later that month changes to the Council of Ministers and the leadership of the armed forces were effected. Brig.-Gen. Essofa Ayéva, hitherto Chief of Staff at the Office of the President, was appointed as Chief of General Staff of the armed forces, replacing Gen. Zacharie Nandja, who joined the Government as Minister of State, Minister of Water, Sanitation and Village Hydraulics, while Col Bali Wiyao was named Chief of Staff of the Land Army. Legislation abolishing capital punishment and commuting existing death penalties to life imprisonment was approved by the Assemblée nationale in June.

Recent developments: the 2010 presidential election

Preparations for the presidential election, scheduled to be held in early 2010, dominated political affairs in 2009, and several amendments were made to the electoral law during that year. Some, such as a loosening of the stringent conditions for candidature, were welcomed by the opposition parties, while others, such as the extension, in April, of the mandate of the CENI, were met with considerable disapproval. In a national and international climate very much in favour of arriving at open and democratic elections, President Compaoré of Burkina Faso continued to be much solicited in his role as mediator. In August the Assemblée nationale appointed a newly composed CENI to organize the election; however, the UFC and the CAR contested the manner in which the new commission had been appointed and appealed for popular protests. In October the CENI appointment was annulled and, after lengthy discussions, Issifou Taffa Tabiou was chosen by consensus to preside over the body. The opposition parties then threatened to boycott the election if two rounds of voting were not held, and again called for protests, which duly took place in late November. Gilchrist Olympio appealed for renewed demonstrations in January 2010, following talks between all parties and Compaoré's recommendation that a single round of voting be held; however, despite the announcement of a slight delay to the election (from 28 February to 4 March), it was confirmed that the election was to take place in a single round of voting.

In February 2010 the UFC announced the withdrawal of its three members from the CENI, stating that it did not wish to be associated with an 'electoral masquerade'. The party claimed that large numbers of those ineligible to vote, including minors and foreigners, had been added to the electoral register. In an attempt to alleviate opposition concerns over possible electoral fraud, 40 international observers were deployed by the AU to oversee the election, while the EU sent a 130-strong delegation of monitors, and 150 civilians and 146 soldiers from ECOWAS were also dispatched to Togo. Gilchrist Olympio, who remained in the USA where he was receiving medical treatment, had confirmed in mid-January that he would not stand in the election, and later that month the Secretary-General of the UFC, Jean-Pierre Fabre, was named as the party's candidate.

A total of seven candidates contested the presidential election, which was duly held on 4 March 2010. According to provisional results released by the CENI on 6 March, Gnassingbé, received 60.9% of votes cast, while Fabre was placed second with 33.9%. Agboyibo, representing the CAR, won just 3.0% of the votes. Some 64.5% of the eligible electorate participated in the ballot. The results were immediately contested by Fabre and several days of protests by supporters of both the UFC and the CAR ensued, necessitating the deployment of an estimated 6,000 police officers. Nevertheless, observers from ECOWAS praised the conduct of the election, while those from the EU declared the poll to have been 'free and transparent'. In mid-March the Constitutional Court announced that it had rejected the appeals of five of the defeated candidates and confirmed Gnassingbé's re-election to the presidency. At the end of March the Government issued a decree prohibiting the staging of any further demonstrations against the results of the elections, although this did not prevent 4,000 protesters from demonstrating in April in Lomé.

Gnassingbé was sworn in to serve a second presidential term on 3 May 2010, and two days later Prime Minister Houngbo announced his resignation and that of the Government. On 9 May Houngbo was reappointed to the premiership and was requested to form a new administration. In late May Gilchrist Olympio signed a political accord on behalf of the UFC on the party's participation in Houngbo's Government, a move that was denounced by Fabre. The composition of the new Council of Ministers was announced two days later; the UFC was allocated seven posts, the most senior being that of Minister of State, Minister of Foreign Affairs and Co-operation, to which Elliott Ohin was appointed. In response, the UFC national bureau, in a statement signed by Fabre, claimed that it had not been consulted on the accord and temporarily suspended Olympio and the seven government ministers from the party. The UFC subsequently split into two factions, led by Fabre and Olympio, both of which held separate congresses in August; the Government announced its recognition of the Olympio faction. In October Fabre proceeded to form a new party, the Alliance nationale pour le changement (ANC). In the following month, however, the Constitutional Court ruled that Fabre and eight other deputies belonging to the ANC should relinquish their seats in the Assemblée nationale, based on letters of resignation that they had allegedly sent to the President of the legislature, Abass Bonfoh. Fabre denied the existence of such letters and pledged to challenge the Court's decision.

Col Gnama Latta was appointed as Minister of Security and Civil Protection in February 2011, following the designation of the incumbent, Col Atcha Titikpina, as Chief of General Staff of the armed forces two months earlier. Further government changes were effected in March.

Foreign Affairs

Relations with neighbouring Ghana have frequently become strained, as the common border with Togo has periodically been closed in an effort to combat smuggling and to curb political

TOGO

Introductory Survey

activity by exiles on both sides. In March 1993 and January 1994 the Togolese Government accused Ghana of supporting armed attacks on Eyadéma's residence, reflecting earlier accusations of Ghanaian involvement in unrest in Togo in early 1991. Full diplomatic relations between the two countries, suspended since 1982, were formally resumed in November 1994, and various joint commissions were subsequently reactivated. The newly elected President of Ghana, John Kufuor, visited Togo to mark the celebrations for Liberation Day on 13 January 2001, and a rapprochement in relations between the two countries was subsequently reported. In August 2009, following a visit by President Faure Gnassingbé to Ghana, the two countries agreed to reconvene their Joint Border Demarcation Commission as a matter of urgency to deal with trans-border crime. Following ethnic clashes and land disputes in northern Ghana in May 2010, the Togolese Minister of Security and Civil Protection announced that some 3,500 Ghanaian refugees had fled into Togo and required shelter and food. The UN responded by providing emergency assistance and tents.

Relations with fellow ECOWAS members were jeopardized by the perceived coup by which Gnassingbé assumed power following the death of his father Eyadéma (see The death of Eyadéma). Relations with Nigeria, in particular, were further compromised when the Togolese authorities refused to grant an aeroplane carrying the advance delegation of President Olusegun Obasanjo permission to land in Lomé. Nigeria withdrew its ambassador to Togo and imposed restrictions on visits of Togolese officials to Nigeria following the incident, anticipating the sanctions imposed by ECOWAS after Gnassingbé initially declined to stand down as interim President in advance of a presidential election. Following Gnassingbé's resignation on 25 February 2005, Nigeria and the other ECOWAS member states lifted their sanctions, returned their ambassadors to Lomé and resumed co-operation with Togo, approving the 24 April date for the presidential election and pledging to provide assistance to ensure the fairness and transparency of the poll. In February 2007 Benin, Nigeria and Togo signed a security agreement to promote stability and development within the three countries. An early warning system was to be established and the ECOWAS policy of free movement of goods and persons would be implemented.

In early 2009 Togo deployed 200 soldiers to assist peace-keeping operations with the UN Mission in the Central African Republic and Chad (MINURCAT); in April it was reported that a Togolese officer in Chad had been killed by a French Foreign Legion soldier serving with the EU bridging military operation in Eastern Chad and North Eastern Central African Republic.

In early January 2010 the Togolese association football team travelling to participate in the Africa Cup of Nations in Angola was attacked as it passed through that country's Cabinda province. Three members of the support staff travelling with the Togolese squad were killed, while two players were injured; the Togolese team withdrew from the competition, although all other participants agreed to continue. Days later, two men were arrested in connection with the incident and both the Frente de Libertação do Enclave de Cabinda (FLEC) and the FLEC—Forças Armadas Cabindes claimed responsibility for the shootings, although they maintained that the targets of the ambush were the team's military escorts. By mid-February a further six people had been detained for their role in the attack.

CONSTITUTION AND GOVERNMENT

Under the terms of the Constitution that was approved in a national referendum on 27 September 1992, and modified on 31 December 2002, executive power is vested in the President of the Republic, who is directly elected, by universal adult suffrage, for a period of five years and may serve an unlimited number of terms. The legislature is the unicameral Assemblée nationale, whose 81 members are also elected, by universal suffrage, for a five-year period. The Prime Minister is appointed by the President from among the majority in the legislature, and the Prime Minister, in consultation with the President, nominates other ministers. For administrative purposes, the country is divided into five regions. It is further divided into 30 prefectures and subprefectures.

REGIONAL AND INTERNATIONAL CO-OPERATION

Togo is a member of the African Union (see p. 183), of the Economic Community of West African States (see p. 257) and of the West African organs of the Franc Zone (see p. 332).

Togo became a member of the UN in 1960, and was admitted to the World Trade Organization (WTO, see p. 430) in 1995. Togo participates in the Group of 77 (G77, see p. 447) developing countries and is also a member of the International Cocoa Organization (see p. 443) and of the International Coffee Organization (see p. 443).

ECONOMIC AFFAIRS

In 2009, according to estimates by the World Bank, Togo's gross national income (GNI), measured at average 2007–09 prices, was US $2,883m., equivalent to $440 per head (or $850 on an international purchasing-power parity basis). During 2000–09, it was estimated, the population increased at an average annual rate of 2.6%, while gross domestic product (GDP) per head declined by an average of 0.3% per year. Overall GDP increased, in real terms, at an average annual rate of 2.3% in 2000–09. Real GDP increased by 2.5% in 2009.

Agriculture (including forestry and fishing) contributed 46.4% of GDP in 2009; in mid-2011 52.8% of the working population were employed in the sector, according to FAO estimates. The principal cash crops are cotton (which contributed 8.9% of earnings from merchandise exports in 2007), coffee and cocoa. Togo has generally been self-sufficient in basic foodstuffs: the principal subsistence crops are cassava, yams, maize, sorghum and rice. Imports of livestock products and fish are necessary to satisfy domestic needs. According to the African Development Bank (AfDB), during 2000–07 agricultural GDP increased at an average annual rate of 3.0%; agricultural GDP grew by 7.1% in 2009.

Industry (including mining, manufacturing, construction and power) contributed 20.2% of GDP in 2009, and employed 10.1% of the working population in 1990. During 2000–07, according to the AfDB, industrial GDP increased by an average of 5.0% per year; industrial GDP rose by 2.5% in 2007.

Mining and quarrying contributed 3.3% of GDP in 2009. Togo has the world's richest reserves of first-grade calcium phosphates. Concerns regarding the high cadmium content of Togolese phosphate rock have prompted interest in the development of lower-grade carbon phosphates, which have a less significant cadmium content. Exports of crude fertilizers and crude minerals provided 11.2% of earnings from merchandise exports in 2007. Limestone, diamonds, cement, gold and marble are also exploited. There are, in addition, smaller deposits of iron ore, zinc, rutile and platinum. In 1998 marine exploration revealed petroleum and gas deposits within Togo's territorial waters. In October 2002 the Togolese Government, the Hunt Oil Co of the USA and Petronas Carigali of Malaysia signed a joint-venture oil-production agreement, providing for the first offshore drilling in Togolese territorial waters. In October 2010 the Togolese Government and the Italian hydrocarbons company Eni signed two agreements on the exploration of the offshore area around the Dahomey Basin. The GDP of the mining sector was estimated to have declined at an average annual rate of 3.2% in 1991–95. According to the AfDB, mining GDP decreased by 7.7% in 2008, but increased by 7.9% in 2009.

Manufacturing contributed 9.2% of GDP in 2009. About 6.6% of the labour force were employed in the sector in 1990. Major companies are engaged in agro-industrial activities, the processing of phosphates, steel-rolling and in the production of cement. An industrial 'free zone' was inaugurated in Lomé in 1990, with the aim of attracting investment by local and foreign interests by offering certain (notably fiscal) advantages in return for guarantees regarding export levels and employment; a second 'free zone' was subsequently opened, and provision was made for 'free zone' terms to apply to certain businesses operating outside the regions. According to the AfDB, manufacturing GDP increased by an average of 7.0% per year in 2000–07; manufacturing GDP increased by 5.9% in 2009.

Construction contributed 4.9% of GDP in 2009, and employed 2.5% of the working population according to the 1981 census. The sector's GDP increased by 18.1% in 2009, according to the AfDB.

Togo's dependence on imports of electrical energy from Ghana was reduced following the completion, in 1988, of a 65-MW hydroelectric installation (constructed in co-operation with Benin) at Nangbeto, on the Mono river. In March 2009 the Chinese company Sinohydro signed an agreement in Lomé on the development of a second hydroelectric installation on the Mono river, at Adjarala; the 147-MW plant, again to be operated jointly with Benin, was expected to commence operations in 2013. At the end of 2009 the European Investment Bank granted €32m. for the rehabilitation of the joint Togolese-Beninois electricity network. Meanwhile, a project to construct a pipeline to supply natural gas from Nigeria to Togo (and also to Benin and

Ghana) had suffered numerous delays. In 2007 some 48.0% of electricity produced in Togo was generated from petroleum, while 46.9% was generated from hydroelectric sources. In 2007 fuel imports constituted 27.0% of all merchandise imports by value.

The services sector contributed 33.5% of GDP in 2009, and engaged 24.4% of the employed labour force in 1990. Lomé has been of considerable importance as an entrepôt for the foreign trade of land-locked countries of the region. However, political instability in the early 1990s and in 2005 resulted in the diversion of a large part of this activity to neighbouring Benin and undermined the tourism industry (previously an important source of foreign exchange). According to the AfDB, the GDP of the services sector declined by an average of 0.1% per year in 2000–07; however, services GDP increased by 1.1% in 2007.

In 2008 Togo recorded a visible trade deficit of US $454.6m., and there was a deficit of $222.0m. on the current account of the balance of payments. In 2007 the principal source of imports was France (providing 19.2% of total imports); other major suppliers were the People's Republic of China and the Netherlands. The principal market for exports in that year was Niger (which took 12.7% of Togo's exports); other significant purchasers were Benin, India, Burkina Faso, Mali and Ghana. The principal exports in 2007 were cement, iron and steel, crude fertilizers and minerals, and cotton. The principal imports in that year were refined petroleum products, cement, medicinal and pharmaceutical products, textile yarn and fabrics, and cereals and cereal preparations.

Togo's estimated overall budget deficit for 2009 was 42,100m. francs CFA, equivalent to 2.8% of GDP. Togo's general government gross debt was 818,853m. francs CFA in 2009, equivalent to 55.2% of GDP. Total external debt in 2008 was US $1,573m., of which $1,433m. was public and publicly guaranteed debt. In 2007 the cost of debt-servicing was equivalent to 1.2% of the value of exports of goods, services and income. Consumer prices increased at an average annual rate of 3.0% in 2000–09. Consumer prices increased by 8.7% in 2008, but by only 2.0% in 2009.

From the 1990s Togo's economy was adversely affected by a number of economic and political factors. A sharp and sustained decline in the output of phosphates, historically one of the major sources of export earnings, low international prices for another principal export, cotton, and high international prices for petroleum imports, had a negative impact on the trade balance. The European Union (EU) suspended development aid to Togo in 1993 and 2002, citing dissatisfaction with the democratic system within the country. However, following the holding of free and fair legislative elections in October 2007, the EU agreed to resume development aid. In April 2008 the IMF approved a three-year arrangement for Togo under its Poverty Reduction and Growth Facility (subsequently renamed the Extended Credit Facility); an extension of the arrangement until August 2011 was approved by the Fund in December 2010, by which time some US $133.2m. had been disbursed. Togo also reached the completion point of the heavily indebted poor countries initiative in December 2010, thus qualifying for debt relief of $1,800m., representing an 82% reduction in the country's external debt in nominal terms. The 2011 budget focused on measures to expand economic growth and on investment in the development and rehabilitation of infrastructure. The country continued to rely heavily on external assistance, with non-refundable grants coming from France, the EU and the People's Republic of China. Meanwhile, the European Investment Bank provided funding for the development of the electricity network and for a telecommunications project aimed at increasing access to mobile broadband services, while China and the AfDB invested in the construction of roads to reinforce Togo's position as a trade corridor linking land-locked countries to ports. In 2010 the Government initiated a national strategy for the production the rice, 60% of which was currently imported, amid increasing national consumption. The Government estimated that real GDP rose by 3.4% in 2010, driven by expansions in the mining and construction sectors, as well as a good cereals harvest, and projected growth of 3.7% in 2011.

PUBLIC HOLIDAYS

2012: 1 January (New Year's Day), 13 January (Liberation Day, anniversary of the 1967 coup), 24 January (Day of Victory, anniversary of the failed attack at Sarakawa), 9 April (Easter Monday), 24 April (Day of Victory), 27 April (Independence Day), 1 May (Labour Day), 17 May (Ascension Day), 28 May (Whit Monday), 15 August (Assumption), 18 August* (Id al-Fitr, end of Ramadan), 23 September (anniversary of the failed attack on Lomé), 26 October* (Tabaski, Feast of the Sacrifice), 1 November (All Saints' Day), 25 December (Christmas).

* These holidays are dependent on the Islamic lunar calendar and may vary by one or two days from the dates given.

Statistical Survey

Source (except where otherwise indicated): Direction de la Statistique, BP 118, Lomé; tel. 221-62-24; fax 221-27-75; e-mail dgscn_tg@yahoo.fr; internet www.stat-togo.org.

Area and Population

AREA, POPULATION AND DENSITY

Area (sq km)	56,600*
Population (census results)	
1 March–30 April 1970	1,950,646
22 November 1981	2,719,567
Population (official estimates)	
2007	5,465,000
2008	5,596,000
2009	5,731,000
Density (per sq km) at 2009	101.3

* 21,853 sq miles.

POPULATION BY AGE AND SEX
(UN estimates at mid-2011)

	Males	Females	Total
0–14	1,362,092	1,359,014	2,721,106
15–64	1,966,128	2,004,218	3,970,346
65 and over	110,158	141,296	251,454
Total	3,438,378	3,504,528	6,942,906

Source: UN, *World Population Prospects: The 2008 Revision*.

Population by Age ('000, official estimates at 2009): *0–14* 2,418; *15–64* 3,060; *65 and over* 252; *Total* 5,731 (males 2,810; females 2,921). Note: Totals may not be equal to the sum of components, owing to rounding.

Ethnic Groups (percentage of total, 1995): Kabré 23.7; Ewe 21.9; Kabiye 12.9; Watchi 10.1; Guin 6.0; Tem 6.0; Mobamba 4.9; Gourmantché 3.9; Lamba 3.2; Ncam 2.4; Fon 1.2; Adja 0.9; Others 2.9 (Source: La Francophonie).

TOGO

Statistical Survey

ADMINISTRATIVE DIVISIONS
(2006, official estimates)

Region	Area (sq km)	Population ('000)	Density (per sq km)	Principal city
Centrale	13,317	494	37.1	Sokodé
Kara	11,738	669	57.0	Kara
Maritime	6,100	2,342	384.4	Lomé
Plateaux	16,975	1,222	72.0	Atakpamé
Savanes	8,470	610	72.0	Dapaong
Total	56,600	5,337	94.3	

PRINCIPAL TOWNS
(2005, official estimates)

Lomé (capital)	921,000	Atakpamé	72,700
Golfe Urbain	394,000	Kpalimé	71,400
Sokodé	106,300	Dapaong	51,500
Kara	100,400	Tsevie	46,900

Mid-2009 (incl. suburbs, UN estimate): Lomé 1,593,630 (Source: UN, *World Urbanization Prospects: The 2009 Revision*).

BIRTHS AND DEATHS
(annual averages, UN estimates)

	1995–2000	2000–05	2005–10
Birth rate (per 1,000)	38.4	35.8	33.1
Death rate (per 1,000)	10.0	9.2	8.2

Source: UN, *World Population Prospects: The 2008 Revision*.

Life expectancy (years at birth, WHO estimates): 59 (males 56; females 61) in 2008 (Source: WHO, *World Health Statistics*).

ECONOMICALLY ACTIVE POPULATION
(census of 22 November 1981)

	Males	Females	Total
Agriculture, hunting, forestry and fishing	324,870	254,491	579,361
Mining and quarrying	2,781	91	2,872
Manufacturing	29,307	25,065	54,372
Electricity, gas and water	2,107	96	2,203
Construction	20,847	301	21,148
Trade, restaurants and hotels	17,427	87,415	104,842
Transport, storage and communications	20,337	529	20,866
Financing, insurance, real estate and business services	1,650	413	2,063
Community, social and personal services	50,750	12,859	63,609
Sub-total	470,076	381,260	851,336
Activities not adequately defined	14,607	6,346	20,953
Total employed	484,683	387,606	872,289
Unemployed	21,666	7,588	29,254
Total labour force	506,349	395,194	901,543

Mid-2011 (estimates in '000): Agriculture, etc. 1,475; Total labour force 2,794 (Source: FAO).

Health and Welfare

KEY INDICATORS

Total fertility rate (children per woman, 2008)	4.3
Under-5 mortality rate (per 1,000 live births, 2008)	98
HIV/AIDS (% of persons aged 15–49, 2007)	3.3
Physicians (per 1,000 head, 2004)	0.04
Hospital beds (per 1,000 head, 2005)	0.9
Health expenditure (2007): US $ per head (PPP)	68
Health expenditure (2007): % of GDP	6.1
Health expenditure (2007): public (% of total)	24.9
Access to water (% of persons, 2008)	60
Access to sanitation (% of persons, 2008)	12
Total carbon dioxide emissions ('000 metric tons, 2007)	1,315.4
Carbon dioxide emissions per head (metric tons, 2007)	0.2
Human Development Index (2010): ranking	139
Human Development Index (2010): value	0.428

For sources and definitions, see explanatory note on p. vi.

Agriculture

PRINCIPAL CROPS
('000 metric tons)

	2006	2007	2008
Rice, paddy	76.3	74.8	70.2
Maize	543.3	546.1	595.3
Millet	43.7	45.5	46.4*
Sorghum	221.2	210.3	226.7*
Cassava (Manioc)	767.4	773.2	881.0
Taro (Cocoyam)	13.6	15.5†	15.5*
Yams	621.1	618.2	638.1
Beans, dry	52.8	62.9	71.0
Groundnuts, with shell	39.3	36.0	41.4
Coconuts	14.5*	15.0*	15.0†
Oil palm fruit†	120	120	125
Seed cotton	40.0	48.8	32.5†
Bananas†	18.5	19.0	19.5
Oranges†	12.5	13.0	13.5
Coffee, green	8.9	9.3	9.5†
Cocoa beans*	73.0	78.0	80.0

* Unofficial figure(s).
† FAO estimate(s).

Note: Data for individual crops in 2009 were not available.

Aggregate production ('000 metric tons, may include official, semi-official or estimated data): Total cereals 886 in 2006, 878 in 2007, 940 in 2008–09; Total roots and tubers 1,405 in 2006, 1,411 in 2007, 1,539 in 2008–09; Total vegetables (incl. melons) 140 in 2006, 142 in 2007, 143 in 2008–09; Total fruits (excl. melons) 53 in 2006, 55 in 2007, 56 in 2008–09.

Source: FAO.

LIVESTOCK
('000 head, year ending September)

	2006	2007	2008*
Cattle	344	355	366
Sheep*	1,900	1,950	2,002
Pigs	527	554	582
Goats*	1,490	1,499	1,508
Horses*	2	2	2
Asses*	3	3	3
Chickens	14,487	15,646	16,900

* FAO estimates.

Note: Data for 2009 were not available.

Source: FAO.

TOGO

LIVESTOCK PRODUCTS
('000 metric tons, FAO estimates)

	2006	2007	2008
Cattle meat	8.3	8.5	8.5
Sheep meat	4.2	4.3	4.3
Goat meat	3.8	3.8	3.8
Pig meat	8.1	8.5	9.0
Chicken meat	19.0	20.6	20.6
Game meat	4.5	4.6	4.6
Cows' milk	9.3	9.6	9.9
Hen eggs	7.3	8.1	8.7

2009 (FAO estimates): Cattle meat 8.5; Sheep meat 4.3; Goat meat 3.8; Pig meat 9.0; Chicken meat 20.6; Cows' milk 9.9.

Source: FAO.

Forestry

ROUNDWOOD REMOVALS
('000 cubic metres, excluding bark)

	2003	2004	2005
Sawlogs, veneer logs and logs for sleepers	43	44	86
Other industrial wood	191	210	80
Fuel wood	5,653	4,424	4,424*
Total	5,887	4,678	4,590

*FAO estimate.

2006–09: Production assumed to be unchanged from 2005 (FAO estimates).

Source: FAO.

Fishing

('000 metric tons, live weight)

	2006	2007	2008*
Capture	24.9	19.9	20.0
Tilapias	3.5	3.5	3.5
Other freshwater fishes	1.5	1.5	1.5
West African ilisha	1.1	0.6	0.6
Bigeye grunt	0.8	1.0	1.0
Round sardinella	2.5	1.2	1.2
European anchovy	7.0	2.7	2.7
Atlantic bonito	2.3	0.4	0.4
Jack and horse mackerels	0.7	0.7	0.7
Jacks, crevalles	0.7	2.9	2.9
Aquaculture*	0.1	0.1	0.1
Total catch*	25.0	20.0	20.1

*FAO estimates.

Source: FAO.

Mining

('000 metric tons, unless otherwise indicated)

	2007	2008	2009
Diamonds (carats)	17,362	8,787	125*
Limestone	2,400*	1,824	1,704
Phosphate rock (gross weight)	750*	842	726
Phosphate content*	270	303	260

*Estimated figure(s).

Source: US Geological Survey.

Industry

SELECTED PRODUCTS
('000 metric tons, unless otherwise indicated)

	2005	2006	2007
Palm oil*	7.0	7.0	7.0
Cement	800	800	800
Electric energy (million kWh)	189	221	196

*Unofficial figures.

Cement: 800 in 2008.

Palm oil (FAO estimates): 7.5 in 2008; 7.8 in 2009.

Sources: FAO; US Geological Survey; UN Industrial Commodity Statistics Database.

Finance

CURRENCY AND EXCHANGE RATES

Monetary Units
100 centimes = 1 franc de la Communauté financière africaine (CFA).

Sterling, Dollar and Euro Equivalents (31 December 2010)
£1 sterling = 768.523 francs CFA;
US $1 = 490.912 francs CFA;
€1 = 655.957 francs CFA;
10,000 francs CFA = £13.01 = $20.37 = €15.24.

Average Exchange Rate (francs CFA per US $)
2008   447.81
2009   472.19
2010   495.28

Note: An exchange rate of 1 French franc = 50 francs CFA, established in 1948, remained in force until January 1994, when the CFA franc was devalued by 50%, with the exchange rate adjusted to 1 French franc = 100 francs CFA. This relationship to French currency remained in effect with the introduction of the euro on 1 January 1999. From that date, accordingly, a fixed exchange rate of €1 = 655.957 francs CFA has been in operation.

BUDGET
('000 million francs CFA)

Revenue*	2009	2010†	2011†
Tax revenue	229.0	234.8	269.2
Tax administration	105.7	105.8	118.5
Customs administration	123.3	129.0	150.7
Non-tax revenue	23.4	32.8	51.0
Total	252.4	267.6	320.2

Expenditure‡	2009	2010†	2011†
Current expenditure	235.0	244.3	256.2
Salaries and wages	94.2	91.8	97.5
Goods and services	64.5	64.0	70.6
Transfers and subsidies	51.5	62.6	72.2
Other expenses	7.6	—	3.0
Capital expenditure	82.3	105.2	163.1
Externally financed	44.4	54.2	79.5
Total‡	317.3	349.5	419.3

*Excluding grants received ('000 million francs CFA): 22.8 in 2009; 38.3 in 2010 (projection); 54.7 in 2011 (projection).
† Projections.
‡ Including lending minus repayments.

Source: IMF, *Togo: Fifth Review Under the Three-Year Arrangement Under the Extended Credit Facility, Request for Modification of a Performance Criterion and Request for Extension of the Arrangement—Staff Report; Staff Statement; Press Release on the Executive Board Discussion; and Statement by the Executive Director for Togo* (January 2011).

TOGO

Statistical Survey

INTERNATIONAL RESERVES
(excluding gold, US $ million at 31 December)

	2007	2008	2009
IMF special drawing rights	0.1	0.1	92.9
Reserve position in IMF	0.5	0.5	0.5
Foreign exchange	437.5	581.2	609.8
Total	438.1	581.8	703.2

Source: IMF, *International Financial Statistics*.

MONEY SUPPLY
('000 million francs CFA at 31 December)

	2007	2008	2009
Currency outside banks	122.0	129.2	140.3
Demand deposits at deposit money banks	150.7	200.8	224.5
Total money (incl. others)	278.4	335.9	372.9

Source: IMF, *International Financial Statistics*.

COST OF LIVING
(Consumer Price Index; base: 2000 = 100)

	2007	2008	2009
Food, beverages and tobacco	114.9	138.3	141.7
Clothing	108.8	110.2	109.4
Housing, water, electricity and gas	118.1	121.3	124.9
All items (incl. others)	117.3	127.5	130.0

Source: ILO.

NATIONAL ACCOUNTS
(million francs CFA at current prices)

Expenditure on the Gross Domestic Product

	2007	2008	2009
Government final consumption expenditure	148,789	190,169	170,962
Private final consumption expenditure	1,109,618	1,232,793	1,463,142
Changes in inventories	2,894	47,386	−1,962
Gross fixed capital formation	174,195	203,294	184,816
Total domestic expenditure	1,435,496	1,673,642	1,816,958
Exports of goods and services	451,979	439,517	466,782
Less Imports of goods and services	674,650	685,910	785,732
GDP in purchasers' values	1,212,824	1,427,249	1,498,008

Gross Domestic Product by Economic Activity

	2007	2008	2009
Agriculture, hunting, forestry and fishing	436,667	575,284	640,327
Mining and quarrying	31,818	60,655	44,993
Manufacturing	111,084	120,607	126,598
Electricity, gas and water	38,272	39,012	39,471
Construction	44,855	48,248	67,336
Wholesale and retail trade, restaurants and hotels	135,688	131,138	114,368
Transport and communications	71,267	73,320	75,018
Finance and insurance, real estate and business services	114,022	129,671	135,324
Public administration and defence	94,668	103,069	107,646
Other services	27,660	28,653	29,704
Sub-total	1,106,001	1,309,657	1,380,785
Less Imputed bank service charge	21,643	25,648	26,976
Indirect taxes, less subsidies	128,467	143,240	144,200
GDP in purchasers' values	1,212,824	1,427,249	1,498,008

Source: African Development Bank.

BALANCE OF PAYMENTS
(US $ million)

	2006	2007	2008
Exports of goods f.o.b.	630.4	676.9	852.6
Imports of goods f.o.b.	−949.1	−1,072.0	−1,307.2
Trade balance	−318.7	−395.1	−454.6
Exports of services	200.7	236.0	283.1
Imports of services	−264.1	−305.5	−359.2
Balance on goods and services	−382.1	−464.5	−530.7
Other income received	47.7	61.3	81.1
Other income paid	−85.5	−91.5	−96.2
Balance on goods, services and income	−419.9	−494.8	−545.8
Current transfers received	287.8	328.5	385.2
Current transfers paid	−44.1	−49.5	−61.4
Current balance	−176.3	−215.8	−222.0
Capital account (net)	64.0	73.4	655.8
Direct investment abroad	14.4	0.7	15.9
Direct investment from abroad	77.3	49.2	23.9
Portfolio investment assets	2.0	13.0	−6.8
Portfolio investment liabilities	60.6	6.3	18.9
Financial derivatives (net)	—	−0.1	—
Other investment assets	−48.9	1.1	28.4
Other investment liabilities	144.6	80.4	−824.4
Net errors and omissions	20.0	16.5	8.0
Overall balance	157.8	24.7	−302.2

Source: IMF, International Financial Statistics.

External Trade

PRINCIPAL COMMODITIES
(US $ million)

Imports c.i.f.	2004	2005	2007*
Food and live animals	53.2	62.1	83.6
Fish, crustaceans and molluscs and preparations thereof	4.9	8.6	7.8
Fish, fresh, chilled or frozen	4.0	7.5	5.9
Fish, frozen, excl. fillets	3.9	7.2	5.7
Cereals and cereal preparations	26.4	32.7	40.9
Wheat and meslin, unmilled	17.0	21.0	21.8
Mineral fuels, lubricants, etc.	128.2	171.8	212.8
Petroleum products, refined	127.1	170.4	210.3
Animal and vegetable oils, fats and waxes	14.2	10.5	7.6
Chemicals and related products	53.8	47.8	71.5
Medicinal and pharmaceutical products	24.0	30.4	48.6
Basic manufactures	142.8	136.2	190.2
Textile yarn, fabrics, made-up articles and related products	27.9	26.6	45.5
Cotton fabrics, woven†	11.5	12.6	24.1
Other woven fabrics, 85% plus of cotton, bleached, etc., finished	10.2	10.5	17.3
Non-metallic mineral manufactures	46.5	44.3	74.5
Lime, cement and fabricated construction materials	41.3	39.1	66.4
Cement	39.5	37.3	63.7

TOGO

Imports c.i.f.—continued	2004	2005	2007*
Iron and steel	45.4	41.0	37.4
Iron and steel bars, rods, shapes and sections	25.4	23.3	18.2
Machinery and transport equipment	77.1	95.0	111.2
Telecommunications, sound recording and reproducing equipment	6.8	19.2	24.8
Telecommunication equipment, parts and accessories	3.5	16.4	20.9
Road vehicles	35.7	35.1	37.1
Passenger motor vehicles (excl. buses)	11.9	11.2	18.4
Miscellaneous manufactured articles	39.2	35.9	66.7
Total (incl. others)	557.8	592.6	787.1

Exports f.o.b.	2004	2005	2007*
Food and live animals	74.6	62.6	26.7
Cereals and cereal preparations	9.0	8.5	4.5
Coffee, tea, cocoa, spices, and manufactures thereof	28.1	24.8	9.1
Coffee, not roasted; coffee husks and skins	2.8	4.3	3.7
Crude materials, inedible, except fuels	112.7	70.1	61.7
Textile fibres and their waste‡	60.4	31.1	25.5
Cotton	59.6	30.0	25.0
Raw cotton, excl. linters, not carded or combed	49.0	26.6	25.0
Cotton, carded or combed	10.4	3.3	0.0
Crude fertilizers and crude minerals	48.3	35.9	31.4
Crude fertilizers and crude minerals (unground)	48.1	34.9	31.4
Basic manufactures	150.8	141.8	163.7
Non-metallic mineral manufactures	99.1	98.8	122.7
Cement	98.2	98.6	122.6
Iron and steel	41.3	32.4	35.1
Iron and steel bars, rods, shapes and sections	27.7	14.9	14.8
Machinery and transport equipment	5.1	6.8	1.5
Total (incl. others)	389.6	359.9	280.0

* Data for 2006 not available.
† Excluding narrow or special fabrics.
‡ Excluding wool tops and wastes in yarn.

Source: UN, *International Trade Statistics Yearbook*.

PRINCIPAL TRADING PARTNERS
(US $ million)

Imports c.i.f.	2004	2005	2007*
Belgium	26.9	23.2	29.5
Benin	14.8	12.0	9.9
Brazil	14.0	16.1	15.5
Canada	7.4	9.6	10.0
China, People's Repub.	46.5	78.0	124.0
Côte d'Ivoire	33.8	38.3	20.6
France (incl. Monaco)	108.7	104.3	151.1
Germany	18.3	17.3	15.6
Ghana	9.8	8.0	28.4
Hong Kong	14.3	12.1	4.1
India	9.8	14.0	16.6
Indonesia	11.5	5.8	21.4
Italy	20.8	26.4	17.5
Japan	9.1	10.8	13.7

Imports c.i.f.—continued	2004	2005	2007*
Netherlands	18.7	23.4	87.4
Nigeria	6.3	4.9	12.0
Saudi Arabia	15.0	4.7	0.5
Senegal	4.9	4.6	6.4
South Africa	8.0	11.2	23.6
Spain	16.0	25.0	16.5
Ukraine	12.4	7.6	8.8
United Kingdom	11.4	12.1	6.5
USA	13.5	6.9	33.4
Total (incl. others)	557.8	592.6	787.1

Exports f.o.b.	2004	2005	2007*
Australia	6.5	3.4	0.0
Belgium	10.5	3.2	2.3
Benin	47.5	41.6	30.5
Brazil	4.3	6.3	2.1
Burkina Faso	50.9	66.3	27.3
China, People's Repub.	17.3	7.9	5.1
Côte d'Ivoire	2.6	6.2	9.3
France (incl. Monaco)	15.5	5.0	1.7
Germany	2.0	7.5	0.8
Ghana	46.2	73.0	16.4
India	15.6	21.2	27.4
Indonesia	8.0	1.3	1.9
Italy	3.2	3.1	1.5
Mali	43.5	26.5	19.9
Morocco	3.0	6.5	1.4
Netherlands	15.4	3.9	1.4
New Zealand	7.5	3.1	1.8
Niger	13.1	10.8	35.6
Nigeria	7.3	14.7	0.7
Pakistan	3.5	4.8	0.0
Senegal	14.7	3.2	5.4
Thailand	3.7	1.4	6.5
USA	1.5	4.1	1.6
Total (incl. others)	389.6	359.9	280.0

* Data for 2006 not available.

Source: UN, *International Trade Statistics Yearbook*.

Transport

RAILWAYS
(traffic)

	1997	1998	1999
Passengers carried ('000)	152.0	35.0	4.4
Freight carried ('000 metric tons)	250	759	1,090
Passenger-km (million)	12.7	3.4	0.4
Freight ton-km (million)	28.8	70.6	92.4

Source: Société Nationale des Chemins de Fer du Togo, Lomé.

ROAD TRAFFIC
(motor vehicles registered at 31 December)

	1994	1995	1996*
Passenger cars	67,936	74,662	79,200
Buses and coaches	529	547	580
Goods vehicles	31,457	32,514	33,660
Tractors (road)	1,466	1,544	1,620
Motorcycles and scooters	39,019	52,902	59,000

* Estimates.

2007: Passenger cars 10,611; Buses and coaches 193; Lorries and vans 2,219; Motorcycles and scooters 34,246.

Source: IRF, *World Road Statistics*.

TOGO

SHIPPING

Merchant Fleet
(registered at 31 December)

	2007	2008	2009
Number of vessels	28	50	86
Total displacement ('000 grt)	19.3	74.9	177.8

Source: IHS Fairplay, *World Fleet Statistics*.

International Sea-borne Freight Traffic
('000 metric tons)

Port Lomé	1997	1998	1999
Goods loaded	432.4	794.6	1,021.4
Goods unloaded	1,913.9	1,912.9	1,812.4

Source: Port Autonome de Lomé.

CIVIL AVIATION
(traffic on scheduled services)*

	1999	2000	2001
Kilometres flown (million)	3	3	1
Passengers carried ('000)	84	77	46
Passenger-km (million)	235	216	130
Total ton-km (million)	36	32	19

* Including an apportionment of the traffic of Air Afrique.

Source: UN, *Statistical Yearbook*.

Tourism

FOREIGN TOURIST ARRIVALS*

	2006	2007	2008
Belgium, Luxembourg and the Netherlands	1,073	851	708
Benin	6,495	7,037	5,465
Burkina Faso, Mali and Niger	6,408	6,489	5,104
Côte d'Ivoire	6,181	5,348	3,607
France	24,753	18,114	13,480
Germany	1,102	1,115	1,305
Ghana	2,438	2,090	1,795
Italy	857	1,167	723
Nigeria	3,598	3,445	3,303
United Kingdom	859	1,030	747
USA	2,703	2,200	1,480
Total (incl. others)	94,096	86,165	73,982

* Arrivals at hotels and similar establishments, by country of residence.

Receipts from tourism (US $ million, incl. passenger transport): 27 in 2005; 23 in 2006; 38 in 2007.

Source: World Tourism Organization.

Communications Media

	2007	2008	2009
Telephones ('000 main lines in use)	99.5	140.9	178.7
Mobile cellular telephones ('000 subscribers)	1,190.3	1,549.5	2,187.3
Internet users ('000)	341.3	350.0	356.3
Broadband subscribers ('000)	1.2	1.9	2.7

Television receivers ('000 in use): 150 in 2000.

Radio receivers ('000 in use): 940 in 1997.

Daily newspapers: 1 (average circulation 10,000 copies) in 1999; 1 (average circulation 10,000 copies) in 2000; 1 in 2004.

Book production (number of titles): 5 in 1998.

Personal computers: 185,000 (30.9 per 1,000 persons) in 2005.

Sources: International Telecommunication Union; UNESCO, *Statistical Yearbook*; UNESCO Institute for Statistics; UN, *Statistical Yearbook*.

Education

(2008/09, unless otherwise indicated)

	Institutions*	Teachers	Males	Females	Total
Pre-primary	319*	1,629	20,137	20,920	41,057
Primary	4,701*	28,153	600,458	563,444	1,163,902
Secondary†	n.a.	11,518	267,489	141,475	408,964
Tertiary†	n.a.	470	n.a.	n.a.	32,502

* 1999/2000 figure.
† 2006/07 figures.

Source: UNESCO Institute for Statistics.

Pupil-teacher ratio (primary education, UNESCO estimate): 41.3 in 2008/09 (Source: UNESCO Institute for Statistics).

Adult literacy rate (UNESCO estimates): 64.9% (males 76.6%; females 53.7%) in 2008 (Source: UNESCO Institute for Statistics).

Directory

The Government

HEAD OF STATE

President: Faure Gnassingbé (inaugurated 4 May 2005; re-elected 4 March 2010).

COUNCIL OF MINISTERS
(May 2011)

The Government is formed by the Rassemblement du peuple togolais and the Union des forces de changement.

Prime Minister: Gilbert Fossoun Houngbo.

Minister of State, Minister of the Civil Service and Administrative Reform: Solitoki Magnim Esso.

Minister of State, Minister of Foreign Affairs and Co-operation: Elliott Ohin.

Minister of Health: Komlan Mally.

Minister of Water, Sanitation and Rural Water Supply: Gen. Zakari Nandja.

Minister of Territorial Administration, Decentralization and Local Communities, Government Spokesperson: Pascal Akousoulélou Bodjona.

Minister of the Economy and Finance: Adji Otéth Ayassor.

Minister of Tourism: Batienne Kpabre-Sylli.

Keeper of the Seals, Minister of Justice, responsible for Relations with the Institutions of the Republic: Tchitchao Tchalim.

Minister of Security and Civil Protection: Col Gnama Latta.

Minister of Basic Development, Handicrafts, Youth and Youth Employment: Victoire Sidemeho Tomegah-Dogbe.

Minister of Public Works: Tchamdja Andjo.

TOGO

Minister of Higher Education and Research: FRANÇOIS AGBÉ-VIADÉ GALLEY.
Minister of Social Affairs and National Solidarity: MÉMOUNATOU IBRAHIMA.
Minister of Mines and Energy: DAMMIPI NOUPOKOU.
Minister of Agriculture, Stockbreeding and Fisheries: KOSSI MESSAN EWOVOR.
Minister of Technical Education and Professional Training: HAMADOU BRIM BOURAÏMA-DIABACTE.
Minister to the President of the Republic, responsible for Planning, Development and Land Settlement: DÉDÉ AHOEFA EKOUE.
Minister of Transport: NINSAO GNOFAM.
Minister of the Environment and Forest Resources: KOSSIVI AYIKOE.
Minister of the Promotion of Women: HENRIETTE OLIVIA AMEDJOGBE-KOUEVI.
Minister of Labour, Employment and Social Security: OCTAVE NICOUÉ BROOHM.
Minister of Human Rights, the Consolidation of Democracy and Civic Education: LEONARDINA RITA DORIS WILSON-DE SOUZA.
Minister of Trade and the Promotion of the Private Sector: KWESI SÉLÉAGODJI AHOOMEY-ZUNU.
Minister of Industry, the Free Zone and Technological Innovation: BAKALAWA FOFANA.
Minister of Sport and Leisure: PADUMHÈKOU TCHAO.
Minister of Post and Telecommunications: CINA LAWSON.
Minister of Arts and Culture: YACOUBOU KOUMADJO HAMADOU.
Minister of Town Planning and Housing: KOMLAN NUNYABU.
Minister of Primary and Secondary Education and Literacy: BERNADETTE ESSOZIMNA LEGUEZIM-BALOUKI.
Minister of Communication: DJIMON ORE.
Minister-delegate to the Minister of Agriculture, Stockbreeding and Fisheries, responsible for Rural Infrastructure: GOURDIGOU KOLANI.

MINISTRIES

Office of the President: Palais Présidentiel, ave de la Marina, Lomé; tel. 221-27-01; fax 221-18-97; e-mail presidence@republicoftogo.com; internet www.presidencetogo.com.
Office of the Prime Minister: Palais de la Primature, BP 1161, Lomé; tel. 221-15-64; fax 221-37-53; internet www.primature.gouv.tg.
Ministry of Agriculture, Stockbreeding and Fisheries: 5 ave de Duisburg, BP 385, Lomé; tel. 220-40-20; fax 220-44-99; internet ministereagriculture.com.
Ministry of the Civil Service, Administrative Reform and Relations with the Institutions of the Republic: angle ave de la Marina et rue Kpalimé, BP 372, Lomé; tel. 221-41-83; fax 222-56-85; internet fonctionpubliquetogo.com.
Ministry of Communication and Culture: BP 40, Lomé; tel. 221-29-30; fax 221-43-80; e-mail info@republicoftogo.com.
Ministry of Co-operation, Development and Land Settlement: Lomé; internet ministerecooperation.com.
Ministry of the Economy and Finance: CASEF, ave Sarakawa, BP 387, Lomé; tel. 221-35-54; fax 221-09-05; e-mail eco@republicoftogo.com; internet www.finances.gouv.tg.
Ministry of the Environment and Forest Resources: Lomé; tel. 221-56-58; fax 221-03-33.
Ministry of Foreign Affairs and Regional Integration: pl. du Monument aux Morts, BP 900, Lomé; tel. 221-29-10; fax 221-39-74; e-mail diplo@republicoftogo.com; internet www.togodiplomatie.com.
Ministry of Health: rue Branly, BP 386, Lomé; tel. 221-35-24; fax 222-20-73; internet ministeresante.com.
Ministry of Higher Education and Research: rue Col de Roux, BP 12175, Lomé; tel. 222-09-83; fax 222-07-83; internet www.ministereeducation.org.
Ministry of Human Rights, the Consolidation of Democracy and Civic Education: BP 1325, Lomé; tel. 222-60-63; fax 220-07-74; e-mail mdhdcab@yahoo.fr.
Ministry of Justice: ave de la Marina, rue Colonel de Roux, Lomé; tel. 221-26-53; fax 222-29-06; internet ministerejustice.com.
Ministry of Labour, Employment and Social Security: Lomé.
Ministry of Mines, Energy and Water: Lomé.
Ministry of Post, Telecommunications and Technological Innovation: ave de Sarakawa, BP 389, Lomé; tel. 223-14-00; fax 221-68-12; e-mail eco@republicoftogo.com; internet ministeretelecom.com.

Ministry of Primary and Secondary Education, Technical Education, Professional Training and Literacy: BP 398, Lomé; tel. 221-20-97; fax 221-89-34.
Ministry of Public Works, Transport, Town Planning and Housing: Lomé.
Ministry of Security and Civil Protection: rue Albert Sarraut, Lomé; tel. 222-57-12; fax 222-61-50; e-mail info@republicoftogo.com.
Ministry of Social Affairs, the Promotion of Women, the Protection of Children and the Elderly: Lomé.
Ministry of Sport and Leisure: BP 40, Lomé; tel. 221-22-47; fax 222-42-28.
Ministry of Territorial Administration, Decentralization and Local Communities: Lomé.
Ministry of Trade, Industry, Crafts and Small and Medium-sized Enterprises: 1 ave de Sarakawa, face au Monument aux Morts, BP 383, Lomé; tel. 221-20-25; fax 221-05-72; e-mail ministereducommercetogo@yahoo.fr.

President and Legislature

PRESIDENT

Presidential Election, 4 March 2010

Candidate	Valid votes	% of valid votes
Faure Gnassingbé (RPT)	1,242,409	60.89
Jean-Pierre Fabre (UFC)	692,554	33.94
Yawovi Agboyibo (CAR)	60,370	2.96
Agbéyomé Kodjo (OBUTS)	17,393	0.85
Brigitte Kafui Adjamagbo-Johnson (CDPA—BT)	13,452	0.66
Bassabi Kagbara (PDP)	8,341	0.41
Jean-Nicholas Lawson (PRR)	6,027	0.30
Total	**2,040,546**	**100.00**

LEGISLATURE

Assemblée nationale

Palais des Congrès, BP 327, Lomé; tel. 222-57-91; fax 222-11-68; e-mail assemblee.nationale@syfed.tg.refer.org.

President: El Hadj ABASS BONFOH.

General Election, 14 October 2007

Party	Votes	% of votes	Seats
Rassemblement du peuple togolais (RPT)	922,636	32.71	50
Union des forces de changement (UFC)	867,507	30.75	27
Comité d'action pour le renouveau (CAR)	192,218	6.81	4
Others	838,484	29.72	—
Total	**2,820,845**	**100.00**	**81**

Election Commission

Commission électorale nationale indépendante (CENI): 198 rue des Echis, BP 7005, Lomé; tel. 222-29-51; fax 222-39-61; e-mail info@cenitogo.tg; internet www.cenitogo.tg; 19 mems; Pres. ISSIFOU TAFFA TABIOU.

Political Organizations

Alliance nationale pour le changement (ANC): Lomé; f. 2010; Leader JEAN-PIERRE FABRE; Sec.-Gen. JEAN-CLAUDE CODJO DÉLAVA.
Comité d'action pour le renouveau (CAR): 58 ave du 24 janvier, BP06, Lomé; tel. 222-05-66; fax 221-62-54; e-mail yagboyibo@bibway.com; moderately conservative; Pres. DODJI APEVON; 251,349 mems (Dec. 1999).
Convention démocratique des peuples africains—Branche togolaise (CDPA—BT): 5 rue Djidjollé, BP 13963, Lomé; tel. and fax 225-38-46; e-mail cdpa-bt.cdpa-bt@orange.fr; internet www.cdpa-bt.net; f. 1991; socialist; Gen.-Sec. LÉOPOLD GNININVI; First Sec. Prof. EMMANUEL Y. GU-KONU.

TOGO

Convergence patriotique panafricaine (CPP): BP 12703, Lomé; tel. 221-58-43; f. 1999 by merger of the Parti d'action pour la démocratie (PAD), the Parti des démocrates pour l'unité (PDU), the Union pour la démocratie et la solidarité (UDS) and the Union togolaise pour la démocratie (UTD); did not participate in legislative elections in 2002; Pres. EDEM KODJO; First Vice-Pres. JEAN-LUCIEN SAVI DE TOVÉ.

Coordination nationale des forces nouvelles (CFN): Lomé; f. 1993; centrist; Pres. Me JOSEPH KOKOU KOFFIGOH.

Organisation pour bâtir dans l'union un Togo solidaire (OBUTS): Quartier Djidjole, 686 rue 19 Tosti, Lomé; tel. 226-93-41; internet www.obuts.org; f. 2008; Pres. AGBÉYOMÉ KODJO; Sec.-Gen. YAWOVI BOESSI.

Parti démocratique panafricain (PDP): Lomé; f. 2005; Pres. BASSABI KAGBARA.

Parti démocratique togolais (PDT): Lomé; Leader M'BA KABASSÉMA.

Parti du renouveau et de la rédemption (PRR): Lomé; Pres. NICOLAS LAWSON.

Parti des travailleurs (PT): 49 ave de Calais, BP 13974, Nyékonakpoé, Lomé; tel. 913-65-54; socialist; Co-ordinating Sec. CLAUDE AMEGANVI.

Rassemblement du peuple togolais (RPT): 572 rue Pydal Tokoin Wuiti, BP 1208, Lomé; tel. 226-04-95; fax 261-00-33; internet www.rpt.tg; e-mail rpttogo@yahoo.fr; f. 1969; sole legal party 1969–91; Pres. FAURE GNASSINGBÉ; Sec.-Gen. SOLITOKI ESSO.

Rassemblement pour le soutien de la démocratie et du développement (RSDD): Lomé; tel. 222-38-80; expelled from the CPOC (q.v.) in August 2003; Leader HARRY OCTAVIANUS OLYMPIO.

Union pour la démocratie et le progrès social (UDPS): Lomé; Sec.-Gen. SEKODONA SEGO.

Union des forces de changement (UFC): 59 rue Koudadzé, Lom-Nava, BP 62168, Lomé; tel. and fax 231-01-70; e-mail contact-togo@ufctogo.com; internet www.ufctogo.com; f. 1992; social-democratic; Pres. GILCHRIST OLYMPIO; First Vice-Pres. HAMADOU BRIM BOURAÏMA-DIABACTE; Sec.-Gen. Dr PIERRE JIMONGOU.

Union des libéraux indépendants (ULI): f. 1993 to succeed Union des démocrates pour le renouveau; Leader KWAMI MENSAN JACQUES AMOUZOU.

Diplomatic Representation

EMBASSIES IN TOGO

China, People's Republic: 1381 rue de l'Entente, BP 2690, Lomé; tel. 222-38-56; fax 221-40-75; e-mail chinaemb_tg@mfa.gov.cn; Ambassador WANG ZUOFENG.

Congo, Democratic Republic: Lomé; tel. 221-51-55; Ambassador LOKOKA IKUKELE BOMOLO.

Egypt: 1163 rue de l'OCAM, BP 8, Lomé; tel. 221-24-43; fax 221-10-22; Ambassador MORTADA ALI MOHAMED LASHIN.

France: 13 ave du Golfe, BP 337, Lomé; tel. 223-46-00; fax 223-46-01; e-mail Eric.BOSC@diplomatie.fr; internet www.ambafrance-tg.org; Ambassador DOMINIQUE RENAUX.

Gabon: Lomé; tel. 222-18-93; fax 222-18-92; Ambassador JOSEPH AIMÉ OBIANG NDOUTOUME.

Germany: blvd de la République, BP 1175, Lomé; tel. 223-32-32; fax 223-32-46; e-mail amballtogo@cafe.tg; internet www.lome.diplo.de; Ambassador ALEXANDER BECKMANN.

Ghana: 8 rue Paulin Eklou, Tokoin-Ouest, BP 92, Lomé; tel. 221-31-94; fax 221-77-36; e-mail ghmfa01@cafe.tg; Ambassador JOHN MAXWELL KWADJO.

Guinea: Lomé; tel. 221-74-98; fax 221-81-16.

Holy See: BP 20790, Lomé; tel. 226-03-06; fax 226-68-80; e-mail noncia.tg@gmail.com; Apostolic Nuncio MICHAEL AUGUST BLUME (Titular Archbishop of Alessano).

Korea, Democratic People's Republic: Lomé; Ambassador JONK HAK SE.

Libya: Cite OUA, BP 4872, Lomé; tel. 261-47-08; fax 261-47-10; Ambassador AHMED BALLUZ.

Nigeria: 311 blvd du 13 janvier, BP 1189, Lomé; tel. and fax 221-59-76; Ambassador BABA GANA ZANNA.

USA: Blvd Eyadema, BP 852, Lomé; tel. 261-54-70; fax 261-55-01; e-mail RobertsonJJ2@state.gov; internet togo.usembassy.gov; Ambassador PATRICIA MCMAHON HAWKINS.

Judicial System

Justice is administered by the Constitutional Court, the Supreme Court, two Appeal Courts and the Tribunaux de première instance, which hear civil, commercial and criminal cases. There is a labour tribunal and a tribunal for children's rights. In addition, there are two exceptional courts, the Cour de sûreté de l'Etat, which judges crimes against internal and external state security, and the Tribunal spécial chargé de la répression des détournements de deniers publics, which deals with cases of misuse of public funds.

Constitutional Court: BP 1331, Lomé; tel. 261-06-40; fax 261-05-45; e-mail www.courconstitutionnelle.tg; internet www.courconstitutionnelle.tg; f. 1997; seven mems; Pres. ABOUDOU ASSOUMA.

Supreme Court: BP 906, Lomé; tel. 221-22-58; f. 1961; consists of three chambers (judicial, administrative and auditing); Chair. ABALO PIGNAKIWÉ PETCHELEBIA; Attorney-General KOUAMI AMADOS-DJOKO.

Audit Court (Cour des Comptes): Lomé; f. 2009; Pres. LALLE TANKPANDJA.

State Attorney: ATARA NDAKENA.

Religion

It is estimated that about 50% of the population follow traditional animist beliefs, some 35% are Christians and 15% are Muslims.

CHRISTIANITY

The Roman Catholic Church

Togo comprises one archdiocese and six dioceses. An estimated 25% of the total population was Roman Catholic.

Bishops' Conference

Conférence Episcopale du Togo, 561 rue Aniko Palako, BP 348, Lomé; tel. 221-22-72; fax 222-48-08.

statutes approved 1979; Pres. Most Rev. AMBROISE KOTAMBA DJOLIBA (Bishop of Sokodé).

Archbishop of Lomé: Most Rev. DENIS KOMIVI AMUZU-DZAKPAH, Archevêché, 561 rue Aniko Palako, BP 348, Lomé; tel. 221-22-72; fax 221-02-46; e-mail archlom@yahoo.cfr.

Protestant Churches

There are about 250 mission centres, with a personnel of some 250, affiliated to European and US societies and administered by a Conseil Synodal, presided over by a moderator.

Directorate of Protestant Churches: 1 rue Maréchal Foch, BP 378, Lomé; Moderator Pastor AGBI-AWUME (acting).

Eglise Evangélique Presbytérienne du Togo: 1 rue Tokmake, BP 2, Lomé; tel. 221-46-69; fax 222-23-63; e-mail eeptbs@laposte.tg; internet www.eept-online.org; Moderator Rev. IMANUEL AWANYOH.

Fédération des Evangéliques du Togo: Lomé; Co-ordinator HAPPY AZIADEKEY.

BAHÁ'Í FAITH

Assemblée spirituelle nationale: BP 1659, Lomé; tel. 221-21-99; e-mail asnbaha@yahoo.fr; Sec. ALLADOUM NGOMNA; 19,002 adherents (2006).

The Press

DAILIES

Liberté: BP 80744, Lomé; tel. 336-88-16; fax 222-09-55; internet www.libertetg.com; Dir of Publication ZEUS AZIADOUVO; Editorial Dir MÉDARD AMETEPE.

Togo-Presse: BP 891, Lomé; tel. 221-53-95; fax 222-37-66; internet www.editogo.tg/presse.php; f. 1961; official govt publ; French, Kabiye and Ewe; political, economic and cultural; circ. 8,000.

PERIODICALS

L'Alternative: BP 4132, Lomé; tel. 909-41-33; fax 251-86-94; e-mail info@lalternative-togo.com; internet www.lalternative-togo.com; Dir of Publication FERDINAND MENSAH AYITE; Editor-in-Chief MAXIME DOMEGNI.

L'Aurore: Lomé; tel. 222-65-41; fax 222-65-89; e-mail aurore37@caramail.com; weekly; independent; Editor-in-Chief ANKOU SALVADOR; circ. 2,500.

Carrefour: 596 rue Ablogame, BP 6125, Lomé; tel. 944-45-43; f. 1991; pro-opposition; weekly; Dir HOLONOU HOUKPATI; circ. 3,000 (2000).

TOGO

Cité Magazine: 50 ave Pas de Souza, BP 6275, Lomé; tel. and fax 222-67-40; e-mail citemag@cafe.tg; internet www.cafe.tg/citemag; monthly; Editor-in-Chief GAËTAN K. GNATCHIKO.

Le Citoyen: Lomé; tel. 221-73-44; independent.

La Colombe: Lomé; f. 2001; weekly.

Le Combat du Peuple: 62 rue Blagogee, BP 4682, Lomé; tel. 904-53-83; fax 222-65-89; f. 1994; pro-opposition weekly; Editor LUCIEN DJOSSOU MESSAN; circ. 3,500 (2000).

Le Courrier du Golfe: rue de l'OCAM, angle rue Sotomarcy, BP 660, Lomé; tel. 221-67-92.

Crocodile: 299 rue Kuévidjin, no 27 Bé-Château, BP 60087, Lomé; tel. 221-38-21; fax 226-13-70; f. 1993; pro-opposition; weekly; Dir VIGNO KOFFI HOUNKANLY; Editor FRANCIS-PEDRO AMAZUN; circ. 3,500 (2000).

Le Débat: BP 8737, Lomé; tel. 222-42-84; f. 1991; 2 a month; Dir PROSPER ETEH.

La Dépêche: BP 20039, Lomé; tel. and fax 221-09-32; e-mail ladepeche@hotmail.com; f. 1993; 2 a week; Editor ESSO-WE APPOLINAIRE MÈWÈNAMÈSSÈ; circ. 3,000.

L'Etoile du matin: S/C Maison du journalisme, Casier no 50, Lomé; e-mail wielfridsewa18@hotmail.com; f. 2000; weekly; Dir WIELFRID SÉWA TCHOUKOULI.

Etudes Togolaises (Revue Togolaise des Sciences): Institut National de la Recherche Scientifique, BP 2240, Lomé; tel. 221-01-39; fax 221-21-59; e-mail inrs@tg.refer.org; f. 1965; 2 a year; scientific review, mainly anthropology.

L'Eveil du Peuple: Lomé; weekly; re-established in 2002, having ceased publication in 1999.

L'Evénement: 44–50 rue Douka, Kotokoucondji, BP 1800, Lomé; tel. 222-65-89; f. 1999; independent; weekly; Dir MENSAH KOUDJODJI; circ. 3,000 (2000).

L'Exilé: Maison du journalisme, Casier no 28, Lomé; e-mail jexil@hotmail.com; f. 2000; weekly; independent; Editor HIPPOLYTE AGBOH.

Forum De La Semaine: BP 81129, Lomé; tel. 953-54-55; fax 222-09-51; e-mail forumhebdo7@yahoo.fr; internet www.forumdelasemaine.com; 2 a week; Dir JEAN-BAPTISTE K. D. DZILAN.

Game su/Tev Fema: 125 ave de la Nouvelle Marché, BP 1247, Lomé; tel. 221-28-44; f. 1997; monthly; Ewe and Kabiye; govt publ. for the newly literate; circ. 3,000.

Hébdo-forum: 60 rue Tamakloe, BP 3681, Lomé; weekly.

Journal Officiel de la République du Togo (JORT): BP 891, Lomé; tel. 221-37-18; fax 222-14-89; govt acts, laws, decrees and decisions.

Kpakpa Désenchanté: BP 8917, Lomé; tel. 221-37-39; weekly; independent; satirical.

Kyrielle: BP 823, Lomé; tel. 948-13-69; fax 905-38-35; e-mail kyriellj@yahoo.fr; f. 1999; monthly; culture, sport; Dir CRÉDO TETTEH; circ. 3,000 (2000).

Libre Togovi: BP 81190, Lomé; tel. 904-43-36; e-mail libretogovi@mail.com; 2 a week; pro-democracy, opposed to Govt of fmr Pres. Eyadéma; distributed by the Comité presse et communication de la concertation nationale de la société civile.

La Matinée: Tokoin Nkafu, rue Kpoguédé, BP 30368, Lomé; tel. 226-69-02; f. 1999; monthly; Dir KASSÉRÉ PIERRE SABI.

Le Miroir du Peuple: 48 rue Defale, BP 81231, Lomé; tel. 946-60-24; e-mail nouveau90@hotmail.com; f. 1998; fmrly Le Nouveau Combat; weekly; independent; Dir ELIAS EDOH HOUNKANLY; circ. 1,000 (2000).

Motion d'Information: BP 1251, Lomé; tel. 910-81-15; fax 221-81-95; e-mail motion-info@wanadoo.fr; f. 1997; weekly; pro-opposition; Dir CARLOS KÉTOHOU.

Nouvel Echo: BP 3681, Lomé; tel. 947-72-40; f. 1997; pro-opposition; weekly; Dir ALPHONSE NEVAME KLU; Editor CLAUDE AMEGANVI.

Nouvel Eclat: Lomé; tel. 225-51-60; e-mail charlpass@hotmail.com; f. 2000; weekly; Dir CHARLES PASSOU; circ. 2,500 (2000).

Nouvel Horizon: Maison du journalisme, Casier no. 38, BP 81213, Lomé; tel. 222-09-55; f. 2000; weekly; Dir DONNAS A. AMOZOUGAN; circ. 3,000 (2000).

La Nouvelle République: Lomé; tel. 945-55-43; e-mail nouvelle.republique@caramail.com; f. 1999; Dir WIELFRID SÉWA TCHOUKOULI; circ. 2,500 (2000).

La Parole: Lomé; tel. 221-55-90.

Politicos: Lomé; tel. 905-32-66; fax 226-13-70; e-mail politicos@hotmail.com; f. 1993; weekly; Dir GERMAIN ESSOHANAM POULI; circ. 1,500 (2000).

Le Regard: BP 81213, Lomé; tel. 904-09-09; fax 226-13-70; e-mail leregard13@caramail.com; f. 1996; weekly; pro-opposition; supports promotion of human rights; Editor ABASS DURMAN MIKAÏLA; circ. 3,000 (2000).

Le Reporter des Temps Nouveaux: Maison du journalisme, Casier no 22, BP 1800, Lomé; tel. and fax 226-18-22; e-mail lereporter39@hotmail.com; f. 1998; weekly; independent; political criticism and analysis; Dir AUGUSTIN AMÉGAH; circ. 3,000 (2000).

Le Scorpion—Akéklé: S/C Maison du journalisme, BP 81213, Lomé; tel. 944-43-80; fax 226-13-70; e-mail lescorpion@webmails.com; f. 1998; opposition weekly; Dir DIDIER AGBLETO; circ. 3,500 (2000).

Le Secteur Privé: angle ave de la Présidence, BP 360, Lomé; tel. 221-70-65; fax 221-47-30; monthly; publ. by Chambre de Commerce et d'Industrie du Togo.

Le Soleil: Lomé; tel. 904-41-97; fax 904-89-10; e-mail lesoleil@francemail.com; f. 1999; weekly; Dir YVES LACLÉ; circ. 2,000 (2000).

Témoin de la Nation: Maison du journalisme, Casier no 48, BP 434, Lomé; tel. 221-24-92; f. 2000; weekly; Dir ELIAS EBOH.

Tingo Tingo: 44–50 rue Douka, Kotokoucondji, BP 80419, Lomé; tel. and fax 222-17-53; e-mail jtingo-tingo@yahoo.fr; f. 1996; weekly; independent; Editor AUGUSTIN ASIONBO; circ. 3,500 (2000).

Togo-Images: BP 4869, Lomé; tel. 221-56-80; f. 1962; monthly series of wall posters depicting recent political, economic and cultural events in Togo; publ. by govt information service; Dir AKOBI BEDOU; circ. 5,000.

Togo-Presse: BP 891, Lomé; tel. 221-53-95; fax 22-37-66; f. 1962; publ. by Govt in French, Ewe and Kabré; political, economic and cultural affairs; Dir WIYAO DADJA POUWI; circ. 5,000 (2000).

La Tribune du Peuple: BP 1756, Lomé; tel. 222-65-89; e-mail novapress.tg@assala.com; weekly; pro-opposition; Dir KODJO AFATSAO SILIADIN.

L'Union: Lomé; tel. 226-12-10; e-mail letambour@yahoo.fr; Dir of Publication ERIC JOHNSON.

PRESS ASSOCIATION

Union des Journalistes Indépendants du Togo: BP 81213, Lomé; tel. 226-13-00; fax 221-38-21; e-mail maison-du-journalisme@ids.tg; also operates Maison de Presse; Sec.-Gen. CRÉDO ADJÉ K. TÉTTEH.

NEWS AGENCIES

Agence Togolaise de Presse (ATOP): 35 rue des Medias, BP 2327, Lomé; tel. 221-24-90; fax 222-28-02; e-mail atop.togo@gmail.com; internet www.atoptogo.blogspot.com; f. 1975; Dir-Gen. CLAUDINE ASSIBA AKAKPO.

Savoir News: Lomé; e-mail info@savoirnews.com; internet www.savoirnews.com.

Publishers

Centre Togolais de Communication Evangélique—Editions Haho (CTCE—Editions Haho): 1 rue Sylvanus Olympio, BP 378, Lomé; tel. 221-45-82; fax 221-29-67; e-mail ctce_ctce@yahoo.fr; f. 1983; general literature, popular science, poetry, school textbooks, Christian interest; Dir TOMPY KUDZO NAKOU.

Editions Akpagnon: BP 3531, Lomé; tel. and fax 222-02-44; e-mail yedogbe@yahoo.fr; f. 1978; general literature and non-fiction; Man. Dir YVES-EMMANUEL DOGBÉ.

Editions de la Rose Bleue: BP 12452, Lomé; tel. 222-93-39; fax 222-96-69; e-mail dorkenoo_ephrem@yahoo.fr; general literature, poetry; Dir EPHREM SETH DORKENOO.

Les Nouvelles Editions Africaines du Togo (NEA-TOGO): 239 blvd du 13 janvier, BP 4862, Lomé; tel. and fax 222-10-19; e-mail neatogo@yahoo.fr; general fiction, non-fiction and textbooks; Dir-Gen. KOKOU A. KALIPE; Editorial Dir TCHOTCHO CHRISTIANE EKUE.

Les Presses de l'Université du Lomé: BP 1515, Lomé; tel. 225-48-44; fax 225-87-84.

Société Nationale des Editions du Togo (EDITOGO): BP 891, Lomé; tel. 221-61-06; f. 1961; govt-owned; general and educational; Pres. BIOSSEY KOKOU TOZOUN; Man. Dir WIYAO DADJA POUWI.

Broadcasting and Communications

TELECOMMUNICATIONS

Regulatory Authority

Autorité de Réglementation des Secteurs de Postes et de Télécommunications (ART&P): blvd Léopold Sédar Senghor, Tokoin Tamé Côté Est, S.O.S Village d'Enfants, BP 358, Lomé; tel. 223-63-80; fax 223-63-94; e-mail artp@artp.tg; internet www.artp.tg; Dir-Gen. PALOUKI MASSINA.

TOGO

Service Providers

Moov Togo: 225 blvd du 13 janvier, BP 14511, Lomé; tel. 220-13-20; fax 220-13-23; e-mail moovcontact@moov.tg; internet www.moov.tg; operates mobile cellular telecommunications in 80 localities; Dir-Gen. FRÉDÉRIC FERAILLE.

Togo Télécom: 1 ave N. Grunitzky, BP 333, Lomé; tel. 221-44-01; fax 221-03-73; e-mail contact@togotelecom.tg; internet www.togotelecom.tg; Dir-Gen. PÈTCHÈTIBADI BIKASSAM.

Togo Cellulaire—Togocel: Lomé; tel. 004-05-06; e-mail togocel@togocel.tg; internet www.togocel.tg; f. 2001; provides mobile cellular communications services to more than 70% of the territory of Togo; Dir-Gen. ATCHA-DEDJI AFFOH.

BROADCASTING

Haute autorité de l'Audiovisuel et de la Communication: Lomé; tel. 2501678; e-mail infos@haactogo.tg; internet www.haactogo.tg; Pres. PHILIPPE EVEGNO.

Radio

Radiodiffusion du Togo (Internationale)—Radio Lomé: BP 434, Lomé; tel. 221-24-93; fax 221-24-92; e-mail radiolome@radiolome.tg; internet www.radiolome.tg; f. 1953; state-controlled; radio programmes in French, English and vernacular languages; Dir-Gen. WILLIBRONDE TELOU.

Radiodiffusion du Togo (Nationale): BP 21, Kara; tel. 660-60-60; f. 1974 as Radiodiffusion Kara (Togo); state-controlled; radio programmes in French and vernacular languages; Dir M'BA KPENOUGOU.

Radio Avenir: BP 20183, 76 blvd de la Kara, Doumassessé, Lomé; tel. 221-20-88; fax 221-03-01; f. 1998; broadcasts in French, English, Ewe and Kotokoli; Dir KPÉLE-KOFFI AHOOMEY-ZUNU.

Radio Carré Jeunes: BP 2550, Adidogomé, Lomé; tel. 225-77-44; e-mail carrejeunes@yahoo.fr; f. 1999; community radio station; popular education, cultural information; broadcasts in French, Ewe, Kabiye and other local languages; Dir KOUBATINE MANJAMIE.

Radio de l'Evangile-Jésus Vous Aime (JVA): Klikamé, Bretelle Atikoumé, BP 2313, Lomé; tel. 225-44-95; fax 225-92-81; e-mail radio.jva@fatad.org; f. 1995; owned by the West Africa Advanced School of Theology (Assemblies of God); Christian; education and development; broadcasts on FM frequencies in Lomé and Agou in French, English and 12 local languages; Dir Pastor DOUTI LALLEBILI FLINDJA.

Radio Galaxy: BP 20822, 253 rue 48, Doumassessé, Lomé; tel. and fax 221-63-18; e-mail radiogalaxy@yahoo.fr; f. 1996; broadcasts in French, English, Ewe and Kabiye; Dir PAUL S. TCHASSOUA.

Radio Kanal FM: Immeuble de CAMPOS, ave Champs de Course, BP 61554, Lomé; tel. 221-33-74; fax 220-19-68; e-mail kanalfm@cafe.tg; internet www.kanalfm.tg; f. 1997; broadcasts in French and Mina; independent; Dir MODESTE MESSAVUSSU-AKUE.

Radio Maria Togo: BP 30162, 155 de la rue 158, Hédzranawoé, Lomé; tel. 226-11-31; fax 226-35-00; e-mail info.tog@radiomaria.org; internet www.radiomaria.org; f. 1997; Roman Catholic; broadcasts in French, English and six local languages; Dir YIGBE FAUSTIN.

Radio Nana FM: 29 rue Béeniglato, BP 6212, Lomé; tel. 220-12-02; e-mail nanafm_tg@yahoo.fr; internet www.nanafm.org; f. 1999; broadcasts in French and Mina; community station; political, economic and cultural information; Dir FERDINAND AFFOGNON.

Radio Nostalgie: 14 ave de la Victoire, Quartier Tokoin-Hôpital, BP 13836, Lomé; tel. 222-25-41; fax 221-07-82; e-mail nostalgietogo@yahoo.fr; internet www.nostalgie.tg; f. 1995; broadcasts in French, Ewe and Mina; Pres. and Dir-Gen. FLAVIEN JOHNSON.

Radio Tropik FM: BP 2276, Quartier Wuiti, Lomé; tel. 226-11-11; e-mail tropikfm@nomade.fr; f. 1995; broadcasts in French, Kabyè and Tem; Dir BLAISE YAO AMEDODJI.

Radio Zion: BP 13853, Kpalimé, Lomé; tel. 441-09-15; f. 1999; religious; broadcasts in French, Ewe and Kabiye; Dir EMMANUEL KOUNOUGNA.

Television

Télévision Togolaise: BP 3286, Lomé; tel. 221-53-57; fax 221-57-86; e-mail televisiontogolaise@yahoo.fr; internet www.tvt.tg; f. 1973; state-controlled; three stations; programmes in French and vernacular languages; Dir KUESSAN YOVODEVI.

Broadcasting Association

Organisation Togolaise des Radios et Télévisions Indépendantes (ORTI): Lomé; tel. 221-33-74; e-mail kawokou@syfed.tg.refer.org; Pres. RAYMOND AWOKOU KOUKOU.

Finance

(cap. = capital; res = reserves; dep. = deposits; m. = million; br(s). = branch(es); amounts in francs CFA, unless otherwise indicated)

BANKING

In 2009 there were 11 banks and two other financial institutions in Togo.

Central Bank

Banque centrale des états de l'Afrique de l'ouest (BCEAO): rue Branly, BP 120, Lomé; tel. 221-25-12; fax 221-76-02; e-mail ocourrier@lome.bceao.int; internet www.bceao.int; HQ in Dakar, Senegal; f. 1962; bank of issue for the mem. states of the Union économique et monétaire ouest-africaine (UEMOA, comprising Benin, Burkina Faso, Côte d'Ivoire, Guinea-Bissau, Mali, Niger, Senegal and Togo); cap. 134,120m., res 1,474,195m., dep. 2,124,051m. (Dec. 2009); Interim Gov. JEAN-BAPTISTE MARIE PASCAL COMPAORÉ; Dir in Togo KOSSI TÉNOU; br. at Kara.

Commercial Banks

Banque Internationale pour l'Afrique au Togo (BIA—Togo): 13 rue de Commerce, BP 346, Lomé; tel. 221-32-86; fax 221-10-19; e-mail bia-togo@cafe.tg; internet www.biat.tg; f. 1965; fmrly Meridien BIAO—Togo; 60.2% owned by Banque Belgolaise (Belgium); cap. and res 567m., total assets 51,793m. (Dec. 2003); Pres. VICTOR ALIPUI; Gen. Man. JEAN-PAUL LE CALM; 7 brs.

Banque Togolaise pour le Commerce et l'Industrie (BTCI): 169 blvd du 13 janvier, BP 363, Lomé; tel. 221-46-41; fax 221-32-65; e-mail btci@btci.tg; internet www.btci.tg; f. 1974; 23.8% owned by Groupe BNP Paribas (France), 24.8% owned by Société Financière pour les Pays d'Outre-mer (Switzerland); cap. 1,700m., res 1,706m., dep. 91,564m. (Dec. 2006); Pres. BARRY MOUSSA BARQUÉ; Dir-Gen. YAO PATRICE KANEKATOUA; 9 brs.

Ecobank Togo (EBT): 20 rue du Commerce, BP 3302, Lomé; tel. 221-72-14; fax 221-42-37; e-mail ecobanktg@ecobank.com; internet www.ecobank.com; f. 1988; 80.7% owned by Ecobank Transnational Inc (operating under the auspices of the Economic Community of West African States), 14.0% by Togolese private investors; cap. 5,000.0m., res 7,201.9m., dep. 155,807.2m. (Dec. 2009); Chair. MICHEL KOMLANVI KLOUSSEH; Man. Dir DIDIER ALEXANDRE LAMINE CORREA; 3 brs.

Ecobank Transnational Inc: 2 ave Sylvanus Olympio, BP 3261, Lomé; tel. 221-03-03; fax 221-51-19; e-mail info@ecobank.com; internet www.ecobank.com; f. 1985; holding co for banking cos in Benin, Burkina Faso, Cameroon, Côte d'Ivoire, Ghana, Guinea, Liberia, Mali, Niger, Nigeria, Senegal and Togo, Ecobank Development Corpn and EIC Bourse; cap. and res US $105.5m., total assets $1,523.1m. (Dec. 2003); Chair. KOLAPO LAWSON; CEO ARNOLD EKPE.

Financial Bank Togo: 11 ave du 24 janvier, BP 325, Lomé; tel. 221-62-21; fax 221-62-25; e-mail info-tg@financial-bank.com; internet www.financial-bank.com; f. 2004; 85.3% owned by Financial BC SA Togo; cap. 1,500m., res –558m., dep. 8,763m. (Dec. 2007); Dir-Gen. PATRICK MESTRALLET; 4 brs.

Société Interafricaine de Banque (SIAB): 14 ave Sylvanus Olympio, BP 4874, Lomé; tel. 221-28-30; fax 221-58-29; e-mail info@siabtogo.com; internet www.siabtogo.com; f. 1975; fmrly Banque Arabe Libyenne-Togolaise du Commerce Extérieur; 86% owned by Libyan Arab Foreign Bank, 14% state-owned; cap. and res 181m., total assets 6,999m. (Dec. 2003); Pres. AYAWOVI DEMBA TIGNOKPA; CEO RABIE YOUSSEF ABUSHAWASHI.

Union Togolaise de Banque (UTB): UTB Circulaire, blvd du 13 janvier, Nyékonakpoè, BP 359, Lomé; tel. 223-43-00; fax 221-22-06; e-mail utbsg@cafe.tg; internet www.utb.tg; f. 1964; 100% state-owned; transfer to majority private ownership proposed; cap. and res –12.3m., total assets 49.0m. (Dec. 2003); Chair. BADAWASSO GNARO; Dir-Gen. YAOVI ATTIGBÉ IHOU; 11 brs.

Development Banks

Banque Ouest-Africaine de Développement (BOAD): 68 ave de la Libération, BP 1172, Lomé; tel. 221-42-44; fax 221-72-69; e-mail boadsiege@boad.org; internet www.boad.org; f. 1973; promotes West African economic development and integration; cap. 682,100m., total assets 849,993m. (Dec. 2004); Pres. CHRISTIAN ADOVÈLANDÉ.

Banque Togolaise de Développement (BTD): ave des Nîmes X, angle ave N. Grunitzky, BP 65, Lomé; tel. 221-36-41; fax 221-44-56; e-mail togo_devbank@btd.tg; internet www.btd.tg; f. 1966; 43% state-owned, 20% owned by BCEAO, 13% by BOAD; transfer to majority private ownership pending; cap. 3,065m., res 7,591m., dep. 34,514m. (Dec. 2006); Chair. and Pres. ESSO KANDJA; Dir-Gen. ZAKARI DAROU-SALIM; 8 brs.

Savings Bank

Caisse d'Epargne du Togo (CET): 23 ave de Kléber Dadjo, Lomé; tel. 221-20-60; fax 221-85-83; e-mail cet@ids.tg; internet www.cet.tg; state-owned; privatization proposed; cap. and res 544m., total assets 27,988m. (Dec. 2006); Pres. DJOSSOU SEMONDJI.

Credit Institution

Société Togolaise de Crédit Automobile (STOCA): 3 rue du Mono, BP 899, Lomé; tel. 221-37-59; fax 221-08-28; e-mail stoca@ids.tg; f. 1962; 93.3% owned by SAFCA; cap. and res –112m., total assets 1,677m. (Dec. 2003); Pres. DIACK DIAWAR; Dir-Gen. DÉLALI AGBALE.

Bankers' Association

Association Professionnelle des Banques et Etablissements Financiers du Togo (APBEF): rue Docteur Kaolo-Tokoin Tamé, près de la Résidence du Bénin, BP 4863, Lomé; tel. 226-69-13; fax 221-85-83; e-mail info@apbeftogo.com; internet apbeftogo.com.

STOCK EXCHANGE

Bourse Régionale des Valeurs Mobilières (BRVM): BP 3263, Lomé; tel. 221-23-05; fax 221-23-41; e-mail brvm@brvm.org; internet www.brvm.org; f. 1998; national branch of BRVM (regional stock exchange based in Abidjan, Côte d'Ivoire, serving the member states of UEMOA); Man. in Togo NATHALIE BITHO ATCHOLI.

INSURANCE

In 2009 there were 12 insurance companies in Togo.

Allianz Togo: 21 blvd du 13 janvier, angle ave Duisburg, BP 3703, Lomé; tel. 221-97-73; fax 221-97-75; e-mail allianz.togo@allianz-tg.com; f. 2000; Dir-Gen. ADRIEN COZZA.

Beneficial Life Insurance Togo: BP 1115, Lomé; tel. 222-06-07; fax 222-06-27; f. 2000; Dir-Gen. ALYSON BROWN.

Colina Togo: 10 rue du Commerce, BP 1349, Lomé; tel. 222-93-65; fax 221-73-58; e-mail togo@groupecolina.com; internet www.groupecolina.com; affiliated to Colina SA (Côte d'Ivoire); Dir-Gen. LOUIS KAKRE BADOBRE.

Compagnie Commune de Réassurance des Etats Membres de la CICA (CICA—RE): 43 ave du 24 janvier, 07 BP 12410, Lomé; tel. 223-62-69; fax 261-35-94; e-mail cica-re@cica-re.com; f. 1981; reinsurance co-operating in 12 west and central African states; Pres. ALBERT PAMSY; Dir-Gen. N'GUESSAN JEAN BAPTISTE KOUAME.

Fidelia Assurances: 01 BP 1679, Lomé; tel. 220-74-94; fax 220-76-16; e-mail fideliaass@helim.tg; f. 2004; Dir-Gen. POVI REINHARDT.

Groupement Togolais d'Assurances (GTA): route d'Atakpamé, BP 3298, Lomé; tel. 225-60-75; fax 225-26-78; e-mail gta@laposte.tg; f. 1974; 62.9% state-owned; non-life insurance; Man. Dir GUY CAMARA; also **Groupement Togolais d'Assurances Vie**, life insurance; Man. Dir YAO CLAUDE GBIKPI DATE.

Nouvelle Société Interafricaine d'Assurances Togo (NSIA Togo): rue Brazza, BP 1120, Lomé; tel. 220-81-50; fax 220-81-52; e-mail nsia.tg@groupensia.com; f. 2005; Dir-Gen. JOSÉ KWASSI SYMENOUH.

Sicar Gras Savoye Togo: 140 blvd du 13 janvier, BP 2932, Lomé; tel. 221-35-38; fax 221-82-11; e-mail sicargs@sicargs.tg; internet www.grassavoye.com; affiliated to Gras Savoye (France); Dir GUY BIHANNIC.

Union des Assurances du Togo (UAT): Immeuble BICI, 169 blvd du 13 janvier, BP 495, Lomé; tel. 221-10-34; fax 221-87-24; e-mail unatinfo@cafe.tg; also **Union des Assurances du Togo—Vie (UAT—Vie)**; Dir-Gen. LOCOH THÉOPHILE KODJO.

Trade and Industry

ECONOMIC AND SOCIAL COUNCIL

Conseil Economique et Social: Lomé; tel. 221-53-01; f. 1967; advisory body of 25 mems, comprising five trade unionists, five reps of industry and commerce, five reps of agriculture, five economists and sociologists, and five technologists; Pres. KOFFI GBODZIDI DJONDO.

GOVERNMENT AGENCIES

Direction Générale des Mines et de la Géologie: BP 356, Lomé; tel. 221-30-01; fax 221-31-93; organization and administration of mining in Togo; Dir-Gen. ANKOUME P. AREGBA.

Société d'Administration des Zones Franches (SAZOF): 2564 ave de la Chance, BP 3250, Lomé; tel. 253-53-53; fax 251-43-18; e-mail sazof@zonefranchetogo.tg; internet zonefranchetogo.tg; administers and promotes export processing zones; Dir-Gen. YAZAZ EGBARÉ; Asst Dir-Gen. ATSOUVI YAWO SIKPA.

Société Nationale de Commerce (SONACOM): 29 blvd Circulaire, BP 3009, Lomé; tel. 221-31-18; f. 1972; cap. 2,000m. francs CFA; importer of staple foods; Dir-Gen. JEAN LADOUX.

DEVELOPMENT ORGANIZATIONS

Agricultural development is under the supervision of five regional development authorities, the Sociétés régionales d'aménagement et de développement.

Agence Française de Développement (AFD): 437 ave de Sarakawa, BP 33, Lomé; tel. 221-04-98; fax 221-79-32; e-mail afdlome@groupe-afd.org; internet www.afd.fr; Country Dir PHILIPPE COLLIGNON.

Association Villages Entreprises: BP 23, Kpalimé; tel. and fax 441-00-62; e-mail averafp@hotmail.com; Dir KOMI AFELETE JULIEN NYUIADZI.

France Volontaires: BP 1511, Lomé; tel. 221-09-45; fax 221-85-04; e-mail afvp@togo-imet.com; internet www.france-volontaires.org; f. 1965; fmrly Association Française des Volontaires du Progrès; name changed as above in 2009; Nat. Del. MARC LESCAUDRON.

Office de Développement et d'Exploitation des Forêts (ODEF): 59 QAD rue de la Kozah, BP 334, Lomé; tel. 221-79-86; fax 221-34-91; e-mail kodefly@yahoo.fr; f. 1971; develops and manages forest resources; Man. Dir EDJIDOMÉLÉ GBADOE.

Recherche, Appui et Formation aux Initiatives d'Autodéveloppement (RAFIA): BP 43, Dapaong; tel. 770-80-89; fax 770-82-37; f. 1992; Dir NOIGUE TAMBILA LENNE.

Service de Coopération et d'Action Culturelle: BP 91, Lomé; tel. 221-21-26; fax 221-21-28; e-mail scac-lome@tg.refer.org; administers bilateral aid from the French Ministry of Foreign Affairs; Dir FRÉDÉRIC MERLET.

Société d'Appui a la Filière Café-Cacao-Coton (SAFICC): Lomé; f. 1992; development of coffee, cocoa and cotton production.

CHAMBER OF COMMERCE

Chambre de Commerce et d'Industrie du Togo (CCIT): ave de la Présidence, angle ave Georges Pompidou, BP 360, Lomé; tel. 221-70-65; fax 221-47-30; e-mail ccit@ccit.tg; internet www.ccit.tg; f. 1921; Pres. JONATHAN FIAWOO; Sec.-Gen. DJAHLIN BROOHM; br. at Kara.

EMPLOYERS' ORGANIZATIONS

Association des Grandes Entreprises du Togo (AGET): Lomé; internet www.aget-togo.org; f. 2007; Pres. DAVID ELBEZ; Sec.-Gen. PASCAL COTI.

Conseil National du Patronat du Togo: 60 blvd du Mono, BP 12429, Lomé; tel. 221-08-30; fax 221-71-11; internet www.cnp-togo.tg; f. 1989; Pres. KOSSIVI NAKU.

Groupement Interprofessionnel des Entreprises du Togo (GITO): BP 345, Lomé; Pres. CLARENCE OLYMPIO.

Syndicat des Commerçants Importateurs et Exportateurs du Togo (SCIMPEXTO): BP 1166, Lomé; tel. 222-59-86; Pres. C. SITTERLIN.

Syndicat des Entrepreneurs de Travaux Publics, Bâtiments et Mines du Togo: BP 12429, Lomé; tel. 221-19-06; fax 221-08-30; Pres. JOSÈPHE NAKU.

UTILITIES

Electricity

Communauté Electrique du Bénin: ave de la Kozah, BP 1368, Lomé; tel. 221-61-32; fax 221-37-64; e-mail dg@cebnet.org; f. 1968 as a jt venture between Togo and Benin to exploit the energy resources in the two countries; Chairs TCHAMDJA ANDJO, Z. MARIUS HOUNKPATIN; Man. DJIBRIL SALIFOU.

Togo Electricité: 426 ave du Golfe, BP 42, Lomé; tel. 221-27-43; fax 221-64-98; e-mail m.ducommun@ids.tg; internet www.togoelectricite.com; f. 2000 to replace Compagnie Energie Electrique du Togo; production, transportation and distribution of electricity; Man. Dir MARC DUCOMMUN-RICOUX.

Gas

Société Togolaise de Gaz SA (Togogaz): BP 1082, Lomé; tel. 221-44-31; fax 221-55-30; 71% privatization pending; Dir-Gen. JOËL POMPA.

Water

Société Togolaise des Eaux (STE): 53 ave de la Libération, BP 1301, Lomé; tel. 221-34-81; fax 221-46-13; f. 2003 to replace Régie Nationale des Eaux du Togo; production and distribution of drinking water.

TOGO
Directory

TRADE UNIONS

Collectif des Syndicats Indépendants (CSI): Lomé; f. 1992 as co-ordinating org. for three trade union confederations.

Confédération Nationale des Travailleurs du Togo (CNTT): Bourse du Travail, BP 163, 160 blvd du 13 janvier, Lomé; tel. 222-02-55; fax 221-48-33; f. 1973; Sec.-Gen. DOUEVI TCHIVIAKOU; 35,000 mems (2007).

Confédération Syndicale des Travailleurs du Togo (CSTT): 14 rue Van Lare, BP 3058, Lomé; tel. 222-11-17; fax 222-44-41; e-mail cstt-tg@cstt-togo.org; internet www.csttogo.org; f. 1949, dissolved 1972, re-established 1991; comprises 36 unions and 7 professional federations (Agro-Alimentation, Education, General Employees, Industry, Public Services, Transport, Woodwork and Construction); Sec.-Gen. ADRIEN BÉLÉKI AKOUÉTÉ; 55,266 mems (2007).

Union Nationale des Syndicats Indépendants du Togo (UNSIT): Tokoin-Wuiti, BP 30082, Lomé; tel. 221-32-88; fax 221-95-66; e-mail unsit@netcom.tg; f. 1991; Sec.-Gen. NORBERT GBIKPI-BENISSAN; 17 affiliated unions; 8,061 mems (2007).

Transport

RAILWAYS

Société Nationale des Chemins de Fer du Togo (SNCT): BP 340, Lomé; tel. 221-43-01; fax 221-22-19; e-mail togorail@yahoo.com; f. 1900; owned by West African Cement (Wacem) since Jan. 2003; total length 519 km, incl. lines running inland from Lomé to Atakpamé and Blitta (276 km), and Lomé to Tabligbo (77 km); a coastal line, running through Lomé and Aného, was closed to passenger traffic in 1987 (a service from Lomé to Kpalimé—119 km—has also been suspended); passengers carried (1999): 4,400 (compared with 628,200 in 1990); freight handled (2007): 631,798 metric tons; Gen. Man. M. M. REDDY.

ROADS

In 2000 there were an estimated 7,520 km of roads, of which 2,376 km were paved. The rehabilitation in the late 1990s of the 675-km axis road that links the port of Lomé with Burkina Faso, and thus provides an important transport corridor for land-locked West African countries, was considered essential to Togo's economic competitiveness. Other principal roads run from Lomé to the borders of Ghana, Nigeria and Benin.

Africa Route International (ARI—La Gazelle): Lomé; tel. 225-27-32; f. 1991 to succeed Société Nationale de Transports Routiers; Pres. and Man. Dir BAWA S. MANKOUBI.

SHIPPING

The major port, at Lomé, generally handles a substantial volume of transit trade for the land-locked countries of Mali, Niger and Burkina Faso. There is another port at Kpémé for the export of phosphates.

Conseil National des Chargeurs Togolais (CNCT): BP 2991, Lomé; tel. 223-71-00; fax 227-08-40; e-mail cnct@cnct.tg; internet www.cnct.tg; f. 1980; restructured 2001; Dir-Gen. TOÏ GNASSINGBÉ.

Ecomarine International (Togo): Immeuble Ecomarine, Zone Portuaire, BP 6014, Lomé; tel. 227-48-04; fax 227-48-06; e-mail ecomarineint.com; f. 2001 to develop container-handling facility at Lomé Port; operates maritime transport between Togo, Senegal and Angola; Chair. Alhaji BAMANGA TUKUR.

Port Autonome de Lomé: BP 1225, Lomé; tel. 227-47-42; fax 227-08-18; e-mail togoport@togoport.tg; internet www.togoport.tg; f. 1968; transferred to private management in Jan. 2002; Pres. ASSIBA AMOUSSOU-GUENOU; Man. Dir Adm. ADEGNON KODJO FOGAN; 1,600 employees (2003).

Société Ouest-Africaine d'Entreprises Maritimes Togo (SOAEM—Togo): Zone Industrielle Portuaire, BP 3285, Lomé; tel. 221-07-20; fax 221-34-17; f. 1959; forwarding agents, warehousing, sea and road freight transport; Pres. JEAN FABRY; Man. Dir JOHN M. AQUEREBURU.

Société Togolaise de Navigation Maritime (SOTONAM): pl. des Quatre Etoiles, rond-point du Port, BP 4086, Lomé; tel. 221-51-73; fax 227-69-38; state-owned; privatization pending; Man. PAKOUM KPEMA.

SOCOPAO—Togo: 18 rue du Commerce, BP 821, Lomé; tel. 221-55-88; fax 221-73-17; f. 1959; freight transport, shipping agents; Pres. GUY MIRABAUD; Man. Dir HENRI CHAULIER.

SORINCO—Marine: 110 rue de l'OCAM, BP 2806, Lomé; tel. 221-56-94; freight transport, forwarding agents, warehousing, etc.; Man. AHMED EDGAR COLLINGWOOD WILLIAMS.

Togolaise d'Affrètements et d'Agence de Lignes SA (TAAL): 21 blvd du Mono, BP 9089, Lomé; tel. 223-19-00; fax 221-06-09; e-mail taalsa@togo-imet.com; internet www.taal.tg; f. 1992; shipping agents, haulage management, crewing agency, forwarding agents; Pres. and Man. Dir LAURENT GBATI TAKASSI-KIKPA.

CIVIL AVIATION

There are international airports at Tokoin, near Lomé (Gnassingbé Eyadéma International Airport), and at Niamtougou. In addition, there are smaller airfields at Sokodé, Sansanné-Mango, Dapaong and Atakpamé.

Africa West Cargo: route de l'Aéroport, Zone Franche Aéroportuaire, BP 10019, Lomé; tel. 226-88-10; fax 226-17-49; e-mail info@africawestcargo.com; internet www.africawestcargo.com; f. 1997; air freight operator; CEO YANNICK ERBS.

ASKY Airlines: BP 2988, Lomé; tel. 223-05-10; fax 220-89-00; e-mail headoffice@flyasky.com; internet www.flyasky.com; f. 2008; commenced operations in 2010; 25% owned by Ethiopian Airlines; regional services; Chair. GERVAIS KOFFI DJONDO.

Société aéroportuaire de Lomé-Tokoin (SALT): Aéroport International de Lomé-Tokoin, BP 10112, Lomé; tel. 223-60-60; fax 226-88-95; e-mail salt@cafe.tg; Dir-Gen. Dr AKRIMA KOGOE.

Tourism

Some 73,982 foreign tourist arrivals were reported in 2008. In 2007 receipts from tourism totalled US $38m.

Office National Togolais du Tourisme (ONTT): BP 1289, Lomé; tel. 221-43-13; fax 221-89-27; e-mail angelodjiss@yahoo.fr; internet www.togo-tourisme.com; f. 1963; Dir ANGELO DJISSODEY.

Defence

As assessed at November 2010, Togo's armed forces officially numbered about 8,550 (army 8,100, air force 250, naval force 200). Paramilitary forces comprised a 750-strong gendarmerie. Military service is by selective conscription and lasts for two years. Togo receives assistance with training and equipment from France.

Defence Expenditure: Estimated at 30,000m. francs CFA in 2009.

Chief of General Staff: Col ATCHA MOHAMMED TITIKPINA.

Chief of Staff of the Land Army: Col BALI WIYAO.

Education

Primary education, which begins at six years of age and lasts for six years, is (in theory) compulsory. Secondary education, beginning at the age of 12, lasts for a further seven years, comprising a first cycle of four years and a second of three years. According to UNESCO estimates, in 2008/09 enrolment at primary schools included 94% of children in the relevant age-group (98% of boys; 89% of girls), while in 2006/07 secondary enrolment was equivalent to 41% of the relevant age-group (boys 54%; girls 28%). Proficiency in the two national languages, Ewe and Kabiye, is compulsory. Mission schools are important, educating almost one-half of all pupils. In 2006/07 32,502 students were enrolled in institutions providing tertiary education. The Université du Lomé (formerly the University du Bénin) had about 14,000 students in the early 2000s, and scholarships to French universities are available. A second university opened in Kara, in the north of Togo, in early 2004. In 2002 spending on education represented 13.6% of total budgetary expenditure.

TONGA

Introductory Survey

LOCATION, CLIMATE, LANGUAGE, RELIGION, FLAG, CAPITAL

The Kingdom of Tonga comprises about 170 islands in the south-western Pacific Ocean, about 650 km (400 miles) east of Fiji. The Tonga (or Friendly) Islands are divided into three main groups: Vava'u, Ha'apai and Tongatapu. Only 36 of the islands are permanently inhabited. The climate is mild (16°–21°C or 61°–71°F) for most of the year, though usually hotter (27°C or 81°F) in December and January. The languages are Tongan, which is a Polynesian language, and English. Tongans are predominantly Christians of the Wesleyan faith, although there are some Roman Catholics and Anglicans. The national flag (proportions 1 by 2) is red, with a rectangular white canton, containing a red cross, in the upper hoist. The capital is Nuku'alofa, on Tongatapu Island.

CONTEMPORARY POLITICAL HISTORY

Historical Context

The basis of the constitutional monarchy was established in the 19th century. The kingdom was neutral until 1900, when it became a British Protected State. The treaty establishing the Protectorate was revised in 1958 and 1967, giving Tonga increasing control over its affairs. Prince Tupouto'a Tungi, who had been Prime Minister since 1949, succeeded to the throne as King Taufa'ahau Tupou IV in December 1965 and appointed his brother, Prince Fatafehi Tu'ipelehake, as Prime Minister. Tonga achieved full independence, within the Commonwealth, on 4 June 1970.

Domestic Political Affairs

Elections to the Legislative Assembly held in May 1981 resulted unexpectedly in the new Assembly becoming dominated by traditionalist conservatives. In March 1982 the Minister of Finance, Mahe Tupouniua, resigned at the King's request after refusing to grant him extrabudgetary travel funds. Further elections to the Legislative Assembly took place in May 1984. In September 1985 the King declared his support for the French Government's programme of testing nuclear weapons in the South Pacific, on the grounds that it was in the broader interests of the Western alliance. However, he upheld his former statement of opposition to the tests in French Polynesia.

Elections were held in February 1987 to the nine commoner seats in the Legislative Assembly; among the six newcomers to the legislature were reported to be some of the Government's harshest critics. In July 1988 the Supreme Court awarded 26,500 pa'anga in damages to 'Akilisi Pohiva, the editor of a local independent journal and an elected member of the Legislative Assembly, after the Government had been found guilty of unfairly dismissing him from his post in the Ministry of Education in 1985, because he had reported on controversial issues. The court ruling intensified opposition demands for the abolition of perceived feudal aspects within Tongan society.

In September 1989 the commoner members of the Legislative Assembly (people's representatives) boycotted the Assembly, leaving it without a quorum, in protest at the absence of the Minister of Finance, whom they had wanted to question about the proceeds of the Government's sale of Tongan passports to foreign nationals, a process that had begun in 1983 as a means of acquiring revenue. Upon resuming their seats in the Assembly later in the month, the commoners introduced a motion demanding the reform of the Assembly to make it more accountable to the people. The motion proposed the creation of a more balanced legislature by increasing elected representation from nine to 15 seats and reducing noble representation to three seats (the Cabinet's 12 members were also members of the Assembly). In March 1990 a group of Tongan conservatives submitted an electoral petition, alleging bribery and corruption by Pohiva, the leader of the pro-reform commoners, and his colleagues, who had been re-elected by substantial majorities in the February general election. (In July 1988 the King had indicated his opposition to majority rule, claiming that the monarchical Government reacted more quickly to the needs of the people than the Government of a parliamentary democracy.)

In October 1990 Pohiva initiated a court case against the Government, claiming that its controversial sale of passports to foreign citizens was unconstitutional and illegal. The passports were sold mainly in Hong Kong, for as much as US $30,000 each, allowing the purchasers, in theory, to avoid travel restrictions imposed on mainland Chinese passport-holders. However, in February 1991 a constitutional amendment to legalize the naturalization of the new passport-holders was adopted at an emergency session of the Legislative Assembly, and the case was therefore dismissed. In March a large demonstration was held in protest against the Government's actions, and a petition urging the King to invalidate the 426 passports in question and to dismiss the Minister of Police (who was responsible for their sale) was presented by prominent commoners and church leaders. In the following month the Government admitted that the former President of the Philippines, Ferdinand Marcos, and his family had been given Tongan passports as gifts, after his removal from power in 1986. The events that ensued from the sale of passports were widely viewed as indicative of the growing support for reform and for greater accountability in the government of the country. By 1996 most of the 6,600 passports sold under the scheme had expired.

In August 1991 the Prime Minister, Prince Fatafehi Tu'ipelehake, retired from office, owing to ill health (the Prince died in April 1999), and was succeeded by the King's cousin, Baron Vaea of Houma, who had previously held the position of Minister of Labour, Commerce and Industries.

Pressure for democratic reform

Plans by campaigners for democratic reform to establish a formal political organization were realized in November 1992, when the Pro-Democracy Movement was recognized, the group having been formed in the early 1970s as the Human Rights and Democracy Movement in Tonga. The group, led by Father Seluini 'Akau'ola (a Roman Catholic priest), organized a constitutional convention in the same month, at which options for the introduction of democratic reform were discussed. The Government refused to recognize or to participate in the convention, prohibiting any publicity of the event and denying visas to invited speakers from abroad. Nevertheless, at elections in February 1993 the pro-democracy reformists won six of the nine elective seats in the Legislative Assembly. In August 1994 Tonga's first political party was formed when the Pro-Democracy Movement launched the People's Party, under the chairmanship of a local businessman, Huliki Watab.

Elections took place on 24 January 1996, at which pro-democracy candidates retained six seats in the Legislative Assembly. In March three journalists, including the editor of *The Times of Tonga*, were arrested and imprisoned in connection with an article in the newspaper that criticized the newly appointed Minister of Police, Fire Services and Prisons, Clive Edwards, for unfavourable remarks that he had made regarding the People's Party. All three were subsequently released, but were found guilty in April under a law against angering a civil servant.

In July 1996 the Legislative Assembly voted to resume the sale of Tongan passports to Hong Kong Chinese, despite the controversy caused by the similar scheme operated in the early 1990s. As many as 7,000 citizenships were to be made available for between 10,000 and 20,000 pa'anga, granting purchasers all the rights of Tongan nationality, except ownership of land.

In September 1996 a motion to impeach the Minister of Justice and Attorney-General, Tevita Topou, was proposed in the Legislative Assembly. The motion alleged that Topou had continued to receive his daily parliamentary allowance during an unauthorized absence from the Assembly. Moreover, the publication of details of the impeachment motion, which had been reported to *The Times of Tonga* by Pohiva, before it had been submitted to the Legislative Assembly, resulted in the imprisonment of Pohiva and of the newspaper's editor, Kalafi Moala, and also the deputy editor, Filakalafi Akau'ola, for contempt of parliament. The three were subsequently released, although in October Moala was found guilty on a further charge of contempt. In the same month the King closed the Assembly (which had been expected to sit until mid-November) until further notice. He denied that he had taken this decision in order to prevent further impeachment proceedings against Topou. Furthermore, in February 1997 the Speaker of the Legislative Assembly was found guilty of contempt of court for criticizing the Chief Justice's decision to release the three journalists imprisoned in September of the previous year. The Government rejected accusations made in early 1997 by journalists in Tonga and media organizations throughout the region that it was attempting to force the closure of *The Times of Tonga*, despite forbidding Moala (who was resident in New Zealand) to enter Tonga without written permission from the Government, banning all government-funded advertising in the publication and forbidding all government employees to give interviews to its journalists.

Parliament reopened in late May 1997. In June Akau'ola was arrested once again and charged with sedition for publishing a letter in *The Times of Tonga* that questioned government policy. However, in the same month the Government suffered a significant reverse when the Court of Appeal ruled that the imprisonment of Pohiva and the two journalists in late 1996 had been unlawful. Following an official visit to Tonga by New Zealand Prime Minister Jim Bolger in August 1997, Pohiva, who had unsuccessfully sought a meeting with Bolger, criticized New Zealand's relationship with Tonga, claiming that financial assistance from the country hindered democratic reform.

In September 1997, following a formal apology from Topou, the Legislative Assembly voted to abandon impeachment proceedings against him. In mid-September 1998 the King closed the Legislative Assembly in response to a petition, signed by more than 1,000 people, that sought the removal from office of the Speaker, Eseta Fusitu'a. A parliamentary committee was obliged to conduct an inquiry into the activities of Fusitu'a, who was accused of misappropriating public funds and of abusing his position. Pohiva and other pro-democracy activists commended the King for his decisive action in response to the petition.

At the general election held on 11 March 1999 five members of the reformist Tonga Human Rights and Democracy Movement (formerly the Pro-Democracy Movement/People's Party) were returned to the Legislative Assembly, compared with six at the previous election. In April Veikune was appointed as Speaker and Chairman of the Legislative Assembly, replacing Eseta Fusitu'a, who had lost his seat at the general election.

In January 2000 the King appointed his youngest son, Prince 'Ulukalala-Lavaka-Ata, as Prime Minister, replacing Baron Vaea who had in 1995 announced his desire to retire. It had been expected that Crown Prince Tupouto'a would take up the position, but his support for constitutional reform in Tonga (notably the abolition of life-time terms for the Prime Minister and ministers) contrasted with the King's more conservative approach. In March 2000 a report published by the US Department of State claimed that Tonga's system of Government, whereby most members of the Legislative Assembly were not directly elected, was in breach of UN and Commonwealth human rights guide-lines. The report was welcomed by the leader of the Tonga Human Rights and Democracy Movement, 'Akilisi Pohiva.

In January 2001 the Prime Minister announced a reallocation of cabinet positions in which he assumed responsibility for the newly created telecommunications portfolio. In the same month claims in a newspaper report that members of the pro-democracy movement had been involved in a plot to assist an escape from prison, to seize weapons from the army and to assassinate a cabinet minister were vehemently denied by representatives of the group. Meanwhile, ongoing concerns for the freedom of the media in Tonga were renewed following the arrest of the deputy editor of *The Times of Tonga* on charges of criminal libel.

Financial scandals and other controversy

In September 2000 protests took place in Nuku'alofa, prompted by concerns that Chinese immigrant businesses, encouraged by the Government to establish themselves in Tonga, were creating unfavourable economic conditions for Tongan enterprises. The Tonga Human Rights and Democracy Movement appealed to the Government to cease issuing work permits to foreign (predominantly Chinese) business people and to end the sale of Tongan passports.

In June 1999 Jesse Bogdonoff, a Bank of America employee, successfully sought royal approval to invest the money in a company in the US state of Nevada, Millennium Asset Management, where Bogdonoff was named as the Fund's Advising Officer. The balance of the Fund and the interest it had accrued (totalling some US $40m.) was due to be returned to Tonga in June 2001; instead, the money appeared to have vanished, while the company had seemingly ceased to exist. Bogdonoff denied any wrongdoing, claiming to have been deliberately misled with regard to the value of the funds. In September Princess Pilolevu, acting as Regent in the absence of the King and the Crown Prince, dismissed the Minister of Education, Kinikinilau Tutoatasi Fakafanua, who at the time of the incident had been Minister of Finance, along with the Deputy Prime Minister and Minister of Justice, Tevita Tupou, both of whom were trustees of the Fund. She appointed the Minister of Police, Fire Services and Prisons, Clive Edwards, as Acting Deputy Prime Minister. In October the Acting Deputy Prime Minister denied that the Privy Council had directed the transfers from the Fund or that any ministers were implicated. He stressed that at least $2.1m. of the fund, invested in Tongan banks, was duly accounted for. However, in June 2002 the Government admitted that about $26m. had been lost as a result of Bogdonoff's actions and that legal proceedings had been initiated in the USA. In February 2003 the Legislative Assembly began impeachment proceedings against the ministers implicated in the matter. In February 2004 it was reported that the Government had agreed to settle out of court with Bogdonoff, who was to pay just $1m. in compensation to the Tongan authorities.

In January 2002 Pohiva published allegations that the King held a secret 'offshore' bank account containing US $350m., some of which was believed to be the proceeds of gold recovered from an 18th-century shipwreck. He claimed to possess a letter written to the King from within the palace referring to the account. The Government dismissed the letter as a forgery. Pohiva was briefly held in custody in February, while police searched the offices of the Tonga Human Rights and Democracy Movement and confiscated computer equipment, in an attempt to find the source material of the allegations. New Zealand's Minister of Foreign Affairs and Trade condemned Tonga as being endemically corrupt, implying that New Zealand's annual aid of $NZ6m. profited the élite rather than the Tongan people as a whole. The King admitted that he did possess an overseas account, with the Bank of Hawaii, but claimed that it contained the profits of vanilla sales from his own plantation. Nevertheless, Pohiva was formally charged with the use and publication of a forged document. In May 2002 he was acquitted of charges of sedition.

Increasing criticism of the Government

A general election was held on 6–7 March 2002, at which 52 candidates competed for the nine commoners' seats in the Legislative Assembly. The Tonga Human Rights and Democracy Movement won seven seats. In September, having repeatedly failed since 1998 to secure government approval for the group's registration under this name, the organization once again became known as the Human Rights and Democracy Movement in Tonga (HRDMT). However, in November 2005 the Government gave approval for a licence to be granted under the Incorporated Societies Act as Friendly Islands Human Rights and Democracy Movement Inc (FIHRDM Inc).

In July 2002 it was reported that Pohiva, Moala and Akau'ola were seeking damages from the Tongan Government for wrongful imprisonment, following their incarceration in 1996 on charges of contempt of parliament. Concerns for the freedom of the media re-emerged in February 2003 when the Government declared *The Times of Tonga*, the twice-weekly newspaper printed in New Zealand, to be a 'prohibited import', describing it as a foreign publication with a political agenda. In April Tonga's Chief Justice, Gordon Ward, ruled that it was both illegal and unconstitutional. However, within hours of the ruling the Government ordered a new ban under different legislation. Ward overruled the ban in the following month, describing it as 'an ill-disguised attempt to restrict the freedom of the press', but on arrival from New Zealand 2,000 copies of the paper were seized by the Tongan customs authorities. Moreover, a few days later legislation was proposed that aimed to limit the power of the Supreme Court by excluding laws and ordinances approved by the Legislative Assembly and the Privy Council from judicial review. In early June the Supreme Court granted an injunction to *The Times of Tonga* ordering the Government to allow its distribution. The Government once again defied the order, stating that it would appeal. In mid-June the newspaper (which had been banned in Tonga since February) was finally allowed to go on sale within the country, after Gordon Ward had threatened each individual member of the Cabinet with contempt of court if they did not permit its distribution.

One of the most vocal critics of the affair was the King's nephew, Prince 'Uluvalu Tu'ipelehake, who in June 2003 expressed concern that the attempts to legislate against the freedom of the press and to restrict the right to seek judicial review would bring Tonga into disrepute. In July it was reported that the Government had abandoned its proposals to limit the powers of the Supreme Court, as a result of strong opposition to the plans. However, later that month the Legislative Assembly approved the Media Operators' Bill, which introduced restrictions on the involvement of foreign nationals in Tonga's media. The legislation was widely viewed as a further attempt to ban *The Times of Tonga*, the editor of which resided in New Zealand. In October Tonga's Roman Catholic bishop led a march by some 8,600 people to the government buildings in Nuku'alofa. The demonstration, which was the largest of its kind in Tonga's history, aimed to persuade the Government not to introduce any further restrictions on media freedom in the country. However, a few days later the Legislative Assembly voted in favour of a constitutional amendment allowing for greater control of the media, and shortly afterwards introduced the Newspaper Act, which gave the Government increased powers to regulate the content of newspapers in the country. It was reported that the legislation had been approved by 16 parliamentary votes to 11, with most of the elected members voting against the proposals and most of the appointed members voting in favour.

The failure of Royal Tongan Airlines in early 2004 caused considerable disquiet, particularly in the tourist industry. At the opening session of the Legislative Assembly in late May seven of the nine elected representatives staged a boycott, demanding the resignation of the Prime Minister, who they claimed had allowed millions of pa'anga to be wasted during his tenure as chairman of the airline. A legal challenge to the constitutional amendments governing media freedom, introduced by the Government in 2003, was begun in the Supreme Court in August 2004, and in October the Court declared the Media Operators Act, the Newspaper Act and the associated constitutional amendments invalid. Shortly before the legal hearing began the Prime Minister announced the dismissal of three cabinet ministers, including the Minister of Police, Fire Services and Prisons, Clive Edwards, who had been one of the principal proponents of the constitutional amendments. In November the Prime Minister announced that four new cabinet ministers would be appointed from among the elected members of the Legislative Assembly (two from the nobles and two from the people's representatives) following the elections in March 2005. The announcement, which represented a departure from the usual procedure whereby ministers were selected from outside the legislature, was seen by many, including members of the pro-democracy movement, as a welcome concession towards democratic reform. However, Clive Edwards criticized the proposals, claiming that they were anti-democratic, as they required two members of the Legislative Assembly, elected by the people, to relinquish their seats in order to assume the new positions from which they could be dismissed at the discretion of the King.

Elections for the nine nobles' and nine commoners' seats took place on 16 and 17 March 2005, respectively. The latter were contested by a record number of 60 candidates. Two newly elected members from each group were appointed to positions in the Cabinet, and a by-election for the four vacated seats took place on 3–5 May. The Minister of Defence, 'Aloua Fetu'utolu Tupou, died suddenly in mid-April. One of the new representatives elected at the subsequent by-election was Clive Edwards, under the banner of the People's Democratic Party (PDP). The PDP had been launched in April by a breakaway group from the HRDMT, which had stated its intention to pursue political reform in a more aggressive manner. The new organization was registered in July, despite fears that this might be deemed illegal, as no provision existed in the Constitution for the establishment of political parties.

In late May 2005 some 8,000 people marched to Tonga's Royal Palace in one of the largest demonstrations of its kind to take place in the country. The protesters presented a petition to the King expressing discontent at high electricity prices charged by the Shoreline Power Group and the excessive salaries reportedly paid to the company's executives. Demonstrators urged the Government to renationalize the generation and distribution of power supply in Tonga.

In July 2005 public servants voted to approve the first national strike in Tonga's history, following the Government's rejection of a request by the Public Service Association (PSA) to reconsider large disparities in salary increases awarded to public sector workers in the recent budget. Almost all of the country's teachers, numerous health care workers and employees from many other public services, initially totalling some 3,000 workers, joined the strike. Accusations of government attempts to restrict the PSA's access to the media were made when the power supply of a private television station was cut shortly before a statement by the PSA was due to be broadcast. During the third week of the strike some 10,000 people marched to the Royal Palace in support of the PSA. Striking public servants expressed the hope that the King might overrule the Cabinet, which had hitherto rejected their demands. Subsequent reports of vandalism against school property and government vehicles were received, and an attempt had apparently been made to burn down the house of a senior executive of the Shoreline Power Group. A range of measures, including a new salary scale, subsequently proposed by the Government, was again rejected by the PSA. However, the strike ended in September when the two sides signed an agreement allowing for salary increases of between 60% and 80%. More significantly, the agreement also provided for the establishment of a commission to review the country's Constitution and to examine possibilities for a more democratic form of government. This represented a major victory for the PSA, which had maintained throughout the dispute that the basic cause of its grievances lay in Tonga's political system. Shortly afterwards a further demonstration by more than 10,000 people took place, appealing to the King to dismiss the entire Government and to conduct a constitutional review within 12 months. Protesters also reiterated their demands for the renationalization of former government assets, particularly power generation, but also Tonga's orbital satellite positions and its internet domain address.

Proposals for constitutional change and the riots of 2006

In October 2005 the King agreed to the establishment of a parliamentary committee to examine the issue of constitutional reform. In February 2006, following the Cabinet's consideration of measures to permit a significant reduction in the number of public servants, the PSA threatened further strike action, stating that the Government's proposals breached the agreement signed in September 2005. Also in February 2006, the Prime Minister, Prince 'Ulukalala-Lavaka-Ata, resigned from office, relinquishing all his portfolios. People's Representative Dr Feleti (Fred) Sevele, a commoner and advocate of constitutional reform, was appointed acting Prime Minister. Sevele also assumed temporary responsibility for the Prince's other ministerial portfolios (including civil aviation, telecommunications, marine and ports). Prince 'Ulukalala had confronted increasing demands for his resignation, amid accusations of incompetence and inefficiency. In view of his pro-democracy stance, the appointment of Sevele was widely welcomed. He was expected to be influential in the establishment of democratic government in Tonga, partly owing to his close relationship with the progressive Crown Prince.

In March 2006 the proposals relating to the reduction in the number of government departments were hastily approved by the Cabinet in order to meet final deadlines for submission. It was agreed that most ministries would remain in place, although some were to merge, thereby reducing the existing 16 ministries to 14. Following his confirmation in the position of Prime Minister at the end of March, Sevele retained responsibility for the portfolios of labour, commerce, industries, disaster relief and communications in a reallocation of cabinet portfolios in mid-May. Other changes included the replacement of Cecil Cocker as Deputy Prime Minister by Dr Viliami Tangi and the appointment of 'Alisi Taumoepeau, the country's first female minister, who became Attorney-General and Minister of Justice. During the course of his first official visit to New Zealand, Sevele confirmed that about one-quarter of posts in the civil service were to be abolished, as part of the Government's commitment to the reduction of budgetary expenditure. The National Committee for Political Reform (NCPR) submitted a report detailing its findings in August.

On 11 September 2006, after a protracted illness, King Taufa'ahau Tupou IV died in New Zealand, prompting a month of national mourning. Among those present at the King's funeral were the New Zealand Prime Minister, Helen Clark, and Crown Prince Naruhito of Japan. Crown Prince Tupouto'a succeeded to the throne as King George Tupou V. Two new ministers were later appointed to the Cabinet: Afu'olo Matoto became Minister of Public Enterprises, while Lisiate 'Akolo was named Minister of Labour, Commerce and Small Industries. In October the NCPR's report on political reform was discussed at length by members of the Legislative Assembly. The report envisaged a 26-member legislature, comprising 17 representatives elected by the people and nine representatives elected by nobles; the King would nominate a Prime Minister from the legislature, who would in turn select a cabinet from among the elected representatives. Prime Minister Sevele subsequently stated that the Cabinet had proposed the establishment of a new parliamentary tripartite committee composed of cabinet members and nobles' and people's representatives, which would deliberate on the political reform process and present its conclusions in the following year. As part of its 'roadmap for political reform', the Cabinet made the following recommendations: that the Legislative Assembly should comprise between 23 and 28 representatives, nine of whom would be nobles' representatives and 14 people's representatives, elected according to constituency; the Cabinet should comprise between 12 and 14 members, including two Governors, with at least two-thirds being elected representatives of the Legislative Assembly; the King should appoint two-thirds of the Cabinet on the advice of the Prime Minister and the remaining one-third independently; and the Prime Minister should be an elected representative of the Legislative Assembly, appointed by the King on the advice of the Legislative Assembly, and with responsibility for choosing ministers.

In November 2006 demonstrations in Nuku'alofa against the slow pace of democratic reform developed into riots, with protesters engaging in widespread looting and destruction. Approximately 80% of the buildings in the business area of the city were reported to have been burned down, and police later verified that at least six bodies had been found in the ruins. Responding to Sevele's appeal, security forces from Australia and New Zealand arrived to help restore stability. In the aftermath of the violence hundreds of people were arrested. A modified programme of reform was approved later in the month, apparently in response to the unrest. The new programme envisaged a 30-member legislature comprising 21 people's representatives and nine nobles' representatives, with the Prime Minister to be elected by the legislature. King Tupou V had in fact endorsed the reforms in the previous month, but the final decision had been delayed pending the conclusions of the tripartite committee. In an address to the Legislative Assembly prior to its recess, King Tupou highlighted the reconstruction efforts necessary after the 'shame' of the unrest, and reiterated the importance of democratic reform that was 'appropriate' for Tonga.

In early 2007 five pro-reform people's representatives, including Clive Edwards, were detained on charges that included sedition, in connection with their alleged involvement in the riots of November 2006. In September 2007 other charges against the representatives were abandoned; however, each representative still awaited the outcome of a charge of sedition. The emergency measures proclaimed following the unrest remained in effect during 2007. In June the Minister of Agriculture, Forestry and Fisheries, Peauafi Haukinima, resigned; the Prime Minister assumed responsibility for his portfolios in an acting capacity. Sevele also took charge of finance following the departure of Siosiua 'Utoikamanu in February 2008, but later transferred the portfolio to Afu'alo Matoto, who became Minister of Finance, National Planning, Public Enterprises and Information. In June an independent anti-corruption commission was established to investigate alleged financial wrongdoing within the Government; however, the commission was reportedly criticized by Pohiva, as it did not have the power to investigate the activities of the King. Meanwhile, the formation of the Paati Langafonua Tu'uola (PLT), a new political organization, was announced by its President, Sione Fonua, in August 2007.

The elections of 2008 and subsequent events

On 23 April 2008 29 nobles elected nine representatives to the Legislative Assembly, and on the following day elections were held to determine the nine people's representatives. Approximately 48% of the electorate voted in the latter election, in which 71 candidates participated. Pro-democracy candidates, including several awaiting trial on sedition charges, secured a majority of the commoners' seats, indicating continuing popular support for the reform movement. Although the elections were described as the last to be held under the prevailing system (with forthcoming constitutional changes expected to increase the proportions of democratically elected seats), reformists urged the King to formalize the process at his forthcoming coronation. In early May the King named Tu'ilakepa as the new Speaker of the Assembly. This was followed in July by the approval of legislation providing for the establishment of the Constitutional and Electoral Commission, charged with determining the nature of the country's political reforms. The Commission was to be composed of five commissioners nominated by the Cabinet, nobles, people's representatives and Judicial Services Commission (two), respectively, and was to report to the Government Privy Council and Legislative Assembly. The Commission met for the first time in January 2009, under the chairmanship of the former Chief Justice, Gordon Ward, and conducted a series of public forums throughout the country.

In July 2008, in accordance with the undertaking of King Tupou V to relinquish his private business interests as soon as possible, the Tongan Government agreed to purchase the Shoreline Power Group. The Minister of Finance, National Planning, Public Enterprises and Information, Afu'alo Matoto, confirmed that the Government was to pay US $25m. for ownership of Shoreline, the country's only electric power generation facility, using funds derived from the sale of government shares in the Westpac Bank of Tonga. The new King also undertook to divest himself of his interests in the telecommunications sector and elsewhere.

Shortly before his coronation in August 2008, King Tupou V announced that he was voluntarily surrendering certain powers in favour of the Prime Minister, although the King was to retain judicial powers granting him the right to commute prison sentences and to appoint judges. The King also reiterated his commitment to parliamentary reform.

The emergency regulations imposed following the riots of November 2006 were extended on a monthly basis throughout 2008, in November prompting Clive Edwards to urge Australia and New Zealand to denounce the Government's actions. (The state of emergency remained in place until February 2011—see Recent developments.) In May Prime Minister Sevele dismissed reported criticisms from Edwards that the process of political reform was being obstructed by the Government. Edwards allegedly claimed that the tabling of the Constitutional and Electoral Commission's first report had been delayed, thus ensuring that recommended changes would not be in place in time for the early elections that were scheduled for 2010. Meanwhile, in March 2009 five men (including Sione Teisina Fuko, the President of the PDP) were found not guilty of sedition, having been accused of inciting the unrest of November 2006. In September 2009 five people's representatives were acquitted by the Court of Appeal on charges of seditious conspiracy related to the unrest, but an appeal by Edwards against a conviction of inciting violence was dismissed.

In May 2009 a cabinet reorganization included the resignation of the Minister of Justice and Attorney-General, 'Alisi Taumoepeau, while the Prime Minister assumed responsibility for foreign affairs and defence. John Cauchi, an Australian, was appointed Attorney-General in the same month, the post having been separated from that of the Minister of Justice. In July a new Ministry of Environment and Climate Change was created. In August the Minister of Civil Aviation, Marine and Ports, Paul Karalus, resigned, following the sinking of a ferry, the *Princess Ashika*, with the loss of 74 lives, earlier in that month. A commission of inquiry into the disaster opened in October, and concluded in March 2010 that the Government had been responsible for buying an unseaworthy vessel, and that Karalus had provided false information following the sinking.

Recent developments

In November 2009 the final report of the Constitutional and Electoral Commission was submitted to the Legislative Assembly. The Commission recommended that, effective from the next legislative election, due to take place in late 2010, the elected membership of the Assembly should be increased to 26, of whom nine would be elected by and from among the hereditary nobles (as before), and 17 would be chosen in a general election (compared with nine previously). The term of the legislature was to be increased from three to four years. The executive power of the King was to be considerably reduced. The Prime Minister was to be appointed by the King, but nominated by the legislature, and cabinet ministers were to be selected by the Prime Minister, and not to number more than one-half of the members of the legislature; a maximum of four ministers could be appointed from outside the legislature. The King was to retain the power to approve or veto legislation and to dismiss the legislature. By the end of December the Legislative Assembly had approved most of the recommendations, and in early 2010 it debated the division of the country into 17 constituencies. Some pro-democracy members, including 'Akilisi Pohiva, opposed the adoption of single-member constituencies, arguing that traditional kinship ties might compromise the fairness of the voting system and might encourage bribery. The Assembly gave its approval to the Constitutional Amendment Act and the Constituency Boundaries Act shortly before the close of the 2009/10 legislative session in April 2010.

In late April 2010 the Attorney-General, John Cauchi, resigned, complaining of government interference in the judiciary; it was reported that this referred to judicial appointments, in particular the appointment of two independent prosecutors to investigate the sinking of the *Princess Ashika* (see The elections of 2008 and subsequent events). Cauchi's predecessor in the post, 'Alisi Taumoepeau, then stated that she too had been forced to resign in May 2009 after objecting to political interference in judicial appointments.

The 2011 budget prompted controversy owing to the apparent disclosure that the level of state funding allocated to the King was to increase by nearly 200%, to in excess of US $700,000 annually, with a similar amount reserved each year for the King's travel expenses; a further $7m. was reported to have been allocated to the planned extension and renovation of the royal palace. The revelation provoked considerable consternation among politicians and the general public alike. Isileli Pulu, a member of the newly established Democratic Party of the Friendly Islands (DPFI), argued that such an increase was both morally wrong and financially imprudent, given the beleaguered state of the national economy. In response to the suggestion that about one-half of the proposed increase was to be funded by foreign aid, New Zealand officials stated categorically that no funding provided by the New Zealand Government could be divested to this end. However, the Tongan Government insisted that no such increase was planned and that $700,000 was, in fact, an estimate of the current cost to Tonga of the monarchy. 'Akilisi Pohiva was suspended from parliament for two weeks in August after he queried the sagacity of the costly improvements planned for the royal palace.

In late July 2010 further controversy was caused by the Remuneration Authority Act, which established a five-member authority, to be appointed by the Cabinet on the recommendation of the Minister of Finance, with responsibility for the setting of government salaries. Many expressed the view that such action should have been the responsibility of the government that would be established after the forthcoming legislative election. The Government rejected such criticism, pointing out that the incoming government would be able to repeal the legislation if it so desired.

In a further controversial development that critics argued risked compromising the independence of the judiciary, the Judicial Services Commission Act was repealed in mid-July 2010, thereby abolishing the Commission that hitherto had appointed Tonga's judges, responsibility for which was henceforth to be transferred to the (royally appointed) Lord Chancellor. Further censure was provoked in the same month by what was widely interpreted as a fresh challenge by the Government to the constitutionally enshrined freedom of speech and of the press (see Increasing criticism of the Government). In early August the Government announced the formation by the Privy Council (appointed by the King and including the members of the Cabinet) of a Royal Commission of Inquiry into allegations that the Government had attempted unduly to undermine the independence of the judiciary, prompting the President of the Tongan Law Society to state unequivocally: 'The judiciary is no longer independent in Tonga.'

During a televised interview in July 2010 the Minister of Information and Communication acknowledged that the Government was considering the imposition of a new licensing regime for the print media industry, in line with the system already in place for the broadcasting media industry; however, she denied that the Government was attempting to regulate the print media. Nevertheless, some observers (including the Pacific Freedom Forum, a regional media freedom advocacy network) argued that such action would indeed amount to regulation and that this would be in direct contravention of Clause 7 of the Tongan Constitution, guaranteeing freedom of speech and of the press. The Government denied that it had any intention of amending the clause.

Elections were held for the Legislative Assembly on 25 November 2010; for the first time in Tongan history, the majority of legislators were elected by the general populace. A total of 147 candidates contested the 17 elected seats, of which 12 were secured by DPFI, led by Pohiva, while independent candidates accounted for the remaining five. An opinion poll published shortly before the election suggested that the economy was the principal concern among the majority of the electorate. The nine noble representatives were elected on the same day by 34 nobles (including three of the King's four Law Lords).

On 21 December 2010 former cabinet minister Lord Tu'ivakano, a member of the nobility, was elected Prime Minister, having secured 14 parliamentary votes (including those of the five independent members of the newly elected Legislative Assembly), thereby defeating Pohiva, who was able to muster only 12 votes. On the same day Lord Lasike was appointed as the new parliamentary Speaker. Lord Tu'ivakano announced the composition of the new Cabinet on 4 January 2011. The incoming premier took responsibility for the foreign affairs, defence and information and communication portfolios. Other appointments included that of Samiu Kuita Vaipulu as Deputy Prime Minister and Minister of Justice, Transport and Works, and that of Pohiva as Minister of Health; Sulia Manu Fili was awarded the finance portfolio, while Clive Edwards returned to the Cabinet as Minister of Revenue Services and Public Enterprises. The inclusion within the Cabinet of two non-elected persons—namely, Edwards and the Minister of Education, Women's Affairs and Culture, Dr Ana Maui Taufe'ulungaki—prompted criticism from some observers, who argued that such inclusions were inappropriate and undemocratic. Pohiva resigned as Minister of Health only one week after his nomination, reportedly in protest at the allocation of just two portfolios to members of the DPFI despite its strong performance in the election, and at the inclusion of the two non-elected members; he was subsequently replaced by Uliti Uata, also of the DPFI. Meanwhile, the Prime Minister announced plans to create deputy ministerial posts, in order to prepare legislators for future cabinet roles, and stated that improving the performance of the national economy would be the main priority of his administration.

In early February 2011 the state of emergency, in place since the immediate aftermath of the riots of November 2006, was finally rescinded by the Government, which acknowledged that there remained no significant threats to public order to warrant the continued imposition of emergency rule.

In April 2011 the managing director of Shipping Corporation of Polynesia (the operating firm of the *Princess Ashika*, which sank in August 2009) was convicted on charges of manslaughter, forgery and sending an unseaworthy ship to sea; he was sentenced to five years' imprisonment, and the firm itself was fined US $2m. The captain and a former director at the Ministry of Transport were both convicted of manslaughter and of sending an unseaworthy ship to sea; the captain was sentenced to a four-year prison term, while the latter received a three-year suspended prison sentence. Another senior member of the ferry's crew was convicted of manslaughter and sentenced to five years' imprisonment.

Foreign Affairs

Although never colonized by a European power, Tonga, as a former British protectorate, is a member of the Commonwealth, and belongs to numerous other regional and international organizations (see Regional and International Co-operation). Large numbers of Tongans live and work abroad, mainly in New Zealand, Australia and the USA.

A friendship treaty that Tonga signed with the USA in July 1988 provided for the safe transit within Tongan waters of US ships capable of carrying nuclear weapons. Tonga was virtually alone in the region in failing to condemn the French Government for its decision to resume nuclear weapons tests in the South Pacific in mid-1995. However, in May 1996 it was announced that Tonga was finally to accede to the South Pacific Nuclear-Free Zone Treaty (see p. 414).

Regional relations

Australia and New Zealand are major trading partners and sources of financial and technical assistance for Tonga. Many Tongans are educated in New Zealand, and at the 2006 New Zealand census more than 50,000 residents identified themselves as Tongan. Under a 10-year aid strategy initiated in September 2008, New Zealand agreed to give priority to governance (allocating an initial $NZ5m. to Tonga's police development programme and $1.5m. to finance the work of the Constitutional and Electoral Commission: see Domestic Political Affairs), education, technical and vocational training, and tourism. The New Zealand Tonga Business Council was established in 2010 with a view to promoting and enhancing bilateral business relations; the Council was formally inaugurated in March 2011.

Meanwhile, following the introduction of legislation restricting media freedom in the country in late 2003, the New Zealand Government announced that it was to review its relationship with Tonga. The Tongan Government summoned New Zealand's ambassador to the islands to register its displeasure. However, in January 2004 Prince 'Uluvalu Tu'ipelehake appealed to Australia's Minister for Foreign Affairs, Alexander Downer, to encourage political reform and to support attempts to increase democratic representation in Tonga. In March 2009 Tonga named its first High Commissioner to New Zealand, and the High Commission of Tonga subsequently opened in Wellington. In July an official tour of the Pacific Islands by the New Zealand Minister of Foreign Affairs, Murray McCully, included a visit to Tonga. McCully revisited Tonga in July 2010 to attend a celebration on the occasion of the 40th anniversary of the establishment of diplomatic relations between Tonga and New Zealand; he also met with the King and the Prime Minister during his brief stay.

In November 2008, following the success of a similar scheme in New Zealand, the Australian Government signed a memorandum of understanding with Tonga, Kiribati, Vanuatu and Papua New Guinea, whereby 2,500 Pacific islanders would be permitted to work in Australia, in the horticultural industry, on a seasonal basis. In February 2009 50 Tongans, the first of a projected 800 from the country, arrived in south-eastern Australia to begin work there. An agreement on the Tonga-Australia Partnership for Development was signed by the two countries' Prime Ministers in August: Australian assistance under the programme was to give priority to improving infrastructure, primary health care and training for employment, and to developing a more efficient public sector. Total Australian development assistance for Tonga in the financial year 2010/11 was an estimated $A27.8m. Richard Marles, the Australian Parliamentary Secretary for Pacific Island Affairs, visited Tonga in March 2011, thereby becoming the first foreign politician to be introduced to the new Tongan Prime Minister, Lord Tu'ivakano.

In November 1998 Tonga announced that it had decided to terminate its diplomatic links with Taiwan and to establish relations with the People's Republic of China. Tonga opened a consulate in China in May 2005. Several Chinese businesses were targeted in the Nuku'alofa riots of November 2006, prompting China to evacuate hundreds of its citizens. Tonga renewed a bilateral trade agreement with China in 2005, and an agreement on joint technical and economic co-operation was signed in May 2007. An economic and technical co-operation agreement signed by the two countries in March 2011 provided for US $11m. in Chinese aid to Tonga.

Japan is also an important provider of aid for Tonga. In February 2010 the Japanese Government agreed to fund a project to introduce solar energy to Tonga; the project envisaged the installation of 500 solar home energy units, and was expected to make a sizeable contribution to meeting the Tongan Government's target of deriving 50% of electricity generation from renewable energy sources. Meanwhile, Japan opened an embassy in Tonga in March 2009.

CONSTITUTION AND GOVERNMENT

Tonga is a hereditary monarchy, and the Constitution is based on that of 1875. Under constitutional reforms implemented in 2010, the King remained as head of state but relinquished many of his direct executive powers. Although executive authority has been transferred to the Cabinet, the King retains the power of veto. The King continues to preside over the Privy Council, which has advisory powers. The Legislative Assembly is unicameral. The number of seats determined by direct popular election was increased from a minority of nine People's Representatives to 17 of the 26 seats in 2010. A system of single-seat constituencies, replacing the previous multi-member constituencies, was introduced at the 2010 election. Nine parliamentary seats continue to be reserved for hereditary nobles, chosen as previously from among their peers. In addition to the 26 elected members of the Legislative Assembly, a further four may be nominated by the incoming Prime Minister, who is elected by the Legislative Assembly. The legislature's term of office was increased from three to four years in 2010.

REGIONAL AND INTERNATIONAL CO-OPERATION

Tonga is a member of the Pacific Community (see p. 410), the Pacific Islands Forum (see p. 413), the Asian Development Bank (ADB, see p. 202) and the UN's Economic and Social Commission for Asia and the Pacific (ESCAP, see p. 37). The country is a signatory of the Lomé Conventions and the successor Cotonou Agreement (see p. 327) with the European Union (EU).

Tonga joined the UN in 1999 and was formally admitted to the World Trade Organization (WTO, see p. 430) in July 2007. It is also a member of the Commonwealth.

ECONOMIC AFFAIRS

In 2009, according to estimates by the World Bank, Tonga's gross national income (GNI), measured at average 2007–09 prices, was US $339m., equivalent to $3,260 per head (or $4,580 per head on an international purchasing-power parity basis). During 2000–09, it was estimated, the population increased at an average annual rate of 0.6%, while gross domestic product (GDP) per head increased, in real terms, by an average of 2.8% per year. Overall GDP increased, in real terms, at an average annual rate of 3.4% in 2000–09. GDP was estimated by the Asian Development Bank (ADB) to have decreased by 0.4% in 2009 and by 1.2% in 2010.

Agriculture (including forestry and fishing) contributed 19.0% of GDP in 2009, and the sector was expected by FAO to engage 26.2% of the employed labour force in mid-2011. According to figures from the ADB, agricultural GDP increased at an average annual rate of 0.3% in 2000–09. The principal cash crops are coconuts, squash (pumpkin) and vanilla beans. In 2007 squash accounted for 16.9% of export earnings. Yams, taro, sweet potatoes, watermelons, tomatoes, cassava, lemons and limes, oranges, groundnuts and breadfruit are also cultivated as food crops, while the islanders keep pigs, goats, poultry and cattle. Exports of fish accounted for 27.5% of export receipts in 2007. The ADB estimated that agricultural GDP increased by 0.6% in 2008, but declined by 1.3% in 2009.

Industry (including mining, manufacturing, construction and utilities) provided an estimated 18.0% of GDP in 2009 and engaged 30.6% of the employed labour force in 2003. According to the ADB, industrial GDP declined at an average annual rate of 0.5% in 2000–09. Compared with the previous year, industrial GDP was calculated by the ADB to have increased by 1.7% in 2008 and by 3.0% in 2009.

Mining contributed an estimated 0.3% of GDP in 2009; the sector engaged 0.2% of the employed labour force in 2003. According to figures from the ADB, during 2000–09 the sector's GDP grew, in real terms, at an average annual rate of 0.1%; mining GDP grew by 5.2% in 2008, but fell by 2.9% in 2009. The mining sector is undeveloped, as Tonga possesses no known mineral resources on land. In March 2009, however, it was announced that a company based in Australia was to explore in Tongan waters for undersea deposits of high-grade metals, such as copper, gold, zinc and silver.

Manufacturing contributed an estimated 7.8% of GDP in 2009, and (with mining) engaged 24.7% of the employed labour force in 2003. According to figures from the ADB, during 2000–09 the sector's GDP declined, in real terms, at an average annual rate of 0.9%; manufacturing GDP declined by 6.5% in 2009. Output of food products and beverages dominates the manufacturing sector. Other manufacturing activities include the production of concrete blocks, small excavators, furniture, handicrafts, textiles, leather goods, sports equipment (including small boats), brewing and coconut oil. There is also a factory for processing sandalwood.

Construction contributed an estimated 6.7% of GDP in 2009; the sector engaged 4.2% of the employed labour force in 2003. According to figures from the ADB, during 2000–09 construction GDP declined, in real terms, at an average annual rate of 0.8%; the sector's GDP increased by 3.6% in 2009.

In an attempt to reduce fuel imports, a 2-MW wave-energy power plant was constructed in the early 1990s and would, it was hoped, supply one-third of the islands' total electricity requirements when in full operation. The use of solar power is of increasing significance, and a study of the feasibility of wind power was under way in 2010. Imports of mineral products accounted for 21.7% of total import costs in 2009.

Service industries contributed an estimated 62.9% of GDP in 2009; the sector engaged 37.5% of the employed labour force in 2003. According to ADB figures, the GDP of the services sector increased at an average annual rate of 1.7% in 2000–09. The ADB estimated that the GDP of the services sector expanded by 2.2% in 2008 but contracted by 0.7% in 2009. Tourism makes a significant contribution to the economy. Visitor arrivals rose

TONGA

from 46,040 in 2007 to 49,405 in 2008. Tourism receipts, excluding passenger transport, totalled US $20m. in 2008.

In 2010, according to the ADB, Tonga recorded a visible trade deficit of US $101m., and a deficit of $17m. on the current account of the balance of payments. The latter deficit was equivalent to 5.6% of GDP. In 2009 the principal source of imports was New Zealand (30.4%), other important suppliers were Fiji, the USA, Australia and the People's Republic of China. New Zealand was also the principal market for exports (providing 25.7% of the total). The principal exports in that year were animal and animal products, and vegetable products. The principal imports were mineral products, prepared foodstuffs, animal and animal products, and machinery and transport equipment.

According to the ADB, in the financial year ending 30 June 2009 there was a budgetary surplus of 8.7m. pa'anga, equivalent to 1.3% of GDP. Tonga's total external debt reached US $130m. in 2010. In that year the cost of debt-servicing was equivalent to 8.8% of the total revenue from exports of goods and services. In 2010/11 official development assistance from Australia was projected at $A27.8m. Aid from New Zealand amounted to $NZ17.0m. in 2010/11. The annual rate of inflation averaged 8.2% in 2000–09. Consumer prices increased by an average of 5.0% in 2009 and by 2.0% in 2010, according to the ADB. Some 1.1% of the labour force were unemployed in 2006, according to the ADB.

The constraints on Tonga's economic development have included large-scale emigration and the weakness of international prices for squash, a major export commodity. Riots in the capital of Nuku'alofa in 2006 also had a profound impact on the economy. However, with reconstruction work progressing, financed partly by China, and with new tourism infrastructure projects in the process of implementation, economic growth resumed in 2008. Inflationary pressures moderated in 2009–10 but were expected to re-emerge in 2011, owing to the increased costs of fuel and foodstuffs. Consumer demand weakened, and business conditions remained unfavourable, with insufficient credit facilities being available to private enterprises. Remittances from Tongans resident overseas remained an important source of income. However, the deterioration in the global economy in 2008/09 reduced the availability of employment opportunities in countries such as the USA and New Zealand, leading to a sharp decline in these inflows. Remittances decreased from 200m. pa'anga in 2007/08 to 150m. pa'anga in 2009/10. In May 2011, under a scheme introduced in 2008 (see Contemporary Political History), nearly 1,000 Tongans were reported to be seeking seasonal work in Australia. Although the level of receipts remained stable in 2009/10, the tourism industry had ceased to expand. In comparison with the previous year, visitor arrivals decreased by 10.7% in 2009/10. Observers continued to suggest that Tonga's capacity to service its large public debt might be increased if the country's efforts to reform the public sector and state enterprises were to be more actively pursued. Much of the public debt, which at January 2011 stood at US $303m., was due to the cost of financing reconstruction projects. In a report released in March 2011, the ADB reiterated concerns with regard to the high level of public debt and urged the Government to restrain its expenditure, particularly in relation to civil service salaries. Similar concerns were expressed by the IMF in the same month. While noting that inflows of remittances had begun to stabilize, the IMF also recommended a reduction in government borrowing and in current expenditure. The Government anticipated a third consecutive year of decline in 2010/11, when it expected the economy to contract by 0.5%.

PUBLIC HOLIDAYS

2012: 2 January (for New Year's Day), 6–9 April (Easter), 25 April (ANZAC Day), 4 June (Independence Day), 12 July (Birthday of the Heir to the Crown of Tonga), 1 August (Official Birthday of King Tupou V), 5 November (for Tonga National Day), 4 December (Tupou I Day), 25–26 December (Christmas Day and Boxing Day).

Statistical Survey

Source (unless otherwise indicated): Tonga Government Department of Statistics, POB 149, Nuku'alofa; tel. (676) 23300; fax (676) 24303; e-mail dept@stats.gov.to; internet www.spc.int/prism/country/to/stats.

AREA AND POPULATION

Area: 748 sq km (289 sq miles).

Population: 97,784 at census of 30 November 1996; 101,991 (males 51,772, females 50,219) at census of 30 November 2006. *By Island Group* (2006 census): Tongatapu 72,045; Vava'u 15,505; Ha'apai 7,570; 'Eua 5,206; Niuas 1,665; Total 101,991. *Mid-2011* (Secretariat of the Pacific Community estimate): 103,682 (Source: Pacific Regional Information System).

Density (at mid-2011): 138.6 per sq km.

Population by Age and Sex (Secretariat of the Pacific Community estimates at mid-2011): *0–14:* 39,265 (males 20,452, females 18,813); *15–64:* 58,414 (males 29,487, females 28,927); *65 and over:* 6,003 (males 2,660, females 3,343); *Total* 103,682 (males 52,599, females 51,083) (Source: Pacific Regional Information System).

Principal Towns (population at 2006 census, provisional): Nuku'alofa (capital) 23,658; Neiafu 4,123; Haveluloto 3,405; Tofoa-Koloua 3,213; Vaini 3,091 (Source: Thomas Brinkhoff, *City Population*—internet www.citypopulation.de). *Mid-2009* (incl. suburbs, UN estimate): Nuku'alofa 24,260 (Source: UN, *World Urbanization Prospects: The 2009 Revision*).

Births, Marriages and Deaths (2006 unless otherwise indicated): Registered live births 2,945 (birth rate 28.6 per 1,000); Registered marriages (2004, provisional) 677 (marriage rate 6.6 per 1,000); Registered deaths 709 (death rate 6.9 per 1,000). Source: mainly UN, *Demographic Yearbook* and *Population and Vital Statistics Report*.

Life Expectancy (years at birth, WHO estimates): 71 (males 71; females 70) in 2008. Source: WHO, *World Health Statistics*.

Economically Active Population (persons aged 15 years and over, 2003): Agriculture, forestry and fishing 11,000; Mining and quarrying 60; Manufacturing 8,530; Electricity, gas and water 530; Construction 1,440; Trade, restaurants and hotels 3,560; Transport, storage and communications 1,580; Financing, insurance, real estate and business services 770; Public administration and defence 2,590; Education 1,780; Health and social work 660; Other community, social and personal services 1,330; Private households with employed persons 610; Extra-territorial organizations 90; Not adequately defined 30; *Total employed* 34,560 (males 20,420, females 14,140); Unemployed 1,890 (males 760, females 1,130); *Total labour force* 36,450 (males 21,180, females 15,270). Note: Figures are rounded to the nearest 10 persons. *Mid-2011* (estimates): Agriculture, etc. 11,000; Total labour force 42,000 (Source: FAO).

HEALTH AND WELFARE

Key Indicators

Total Fertility Rate (children per woman, 2008): 4.0.

Under-5 Mortality Rate (per 1,000 live births, 2008): 19.

Physicians (per 1,000 head, 2002): 0.3.

Hospital Beds (per 1,000 head, 2004): 2.9.

Health Expenditure (2007): US $ per head (PPP): 167.

Health Expenditure (2007): % of GDP: 4.4.

Health Expenditure (2007): public (% of total): 70.3.

Access to Sanitation (% of persons, 2008): 97.

Total Carbon Dioxide Emissions ('000 metric tons, 2007): 175.9.

Carbon Dioxide Emissions Per Head (metric tons, 2007): 1.7.

Human Development Index (2010): ranking 85.

Human Development Index (2010): value 0.677.

For sources and definitions, see explanatory note on p. vi.

AGRICULTURE, ETC.

Principal Crops ('000 metric tons, 2008, FAO estimates): Sweet potatoes 6.8; Cassava 9.7; Taro 3.8; Yams 4.7; Other roots and tubers 2.2; Coconuts 58.5; Pumpkins, squash and gourds 21.0; Other vegetables and melons 5.7; Bananas 0.8; Plantains 3.3; Oranges 1.2; Lemons and limes 2.7. Note: No data were available for 2009.

TONGA

Livestock ('000 head, year ending September 2009 unless otherwise indicated, FAO estimates): Pigs 81 (2008); Horses 12 (2008); Cattle 11; Goats 13; Chickens 330 (2008).

Livestock Products (metric tons, 2009 unless otherwise indicated, FAO estimates): Pig meat 1,550 (2008); Hen eggs 300; Honey 13 (2008); Cows' milk 370 (2008).

Forestry ('000 cu m, 2000): *Roundwood Removals* (excl. bark): 4; *Sawnwood Production:* 2 (FAO estimate). *2001–09:* Annual output as in 2000 (FAO estimates).

Fishing (metric tons, live weight, 2008): Marine fishes 1,741 (FAO estimate) (Snappers and jobfishes 162; Albacore 221; Bigeye tuna 81; Yellowfin tuna 291); Marine crustaceans 350 (FAO estimate); Total catch (incl. others, FAO estimate) 2,142.

Source: FAO.

INDUSTRY

Electric Energy (production, million kWh): 55 in 2007; 55 in 2008; 51 in 2009. Source: Asian Development Bank.

FINANCE

Currency and Exchange Rates: 100 seniti (cents) = 1 pa'anga (Tongan dollar or $T). *Sterling, US Dollar and Euro Equivalents* (30 November 2010): £1 sterling = $T2.8644; US $1 = $T1.8447; €1 = $T2.3977; $T100 = £34.91 = US $54.21 = €41.71. *Average Exchange Rate* (pa'anga per US $): 1.9709 in 2007; 1.9424 in 2008; 2.0345 in 2009.

Budget ('000 pa'anga, year ending 30 June 2009): *Revenue:* Taxation 129,096; Non-tax revenue 25,695; Total 154,791 (excl. grants received from abroad 45,503). *Expenditure:* Current expenditure 167,530; Capital expenditure 17,799; Total 185,329 (excl. net lending 6,270). Source: Asian Development Bank.

International Reserves (US $ million at 31 December 2010): IMF special drawing rights 10.90; Reserve position in the IMF 2.64; Foreign exchange 90.99; *Total* 104.53. Source: IMF, *International Financial Statistics*.

Money Supply ('000 pa'anga at 31 December 2010): Currency outside depository corporations 28,388; Transferable deposits 78,699; Other deposits 203,751; *Broad money* 310,838. Source: IMF, *International Financial Statistics*.

Cost of Living (Consumer Price Index, excl. rent; base: 2005 = 100): All items 112.7 in 2007; 124.5 in 2008; 126.2 in 2009. Source: IMF, *International Financial Statistics*.

Gross Domestic Product (million pa'anga at constant 2000/01 prices, year ending 30 June): 372.2 in 2006/07; 379.8 in 2007/08; 378.9 in 2008/09. Source: Asian Development Bank.

Expenditure on the Gross Domestic Product (million pa'anga at current prices, year ending 30 June 2009): Government final consumption expenditure 127.6; Private final consumption expenditure (obtained as residual, incl. statistical discrepancy) 646.8; Gross fixed capital formation 168.7; Change in stocks 0.4; *Total domestic expenditure* 943.5; Exports of goods and services 85.4; *Less* Imports of goods and services 379.4; *GDP in purchasers' values* 649.5. Source: Asian Development Bank.

Gross Domestic Product by Economic Activity (million pa'anga at current prices, year ending 30 June 2009): Agriculture, forestry and fishing 110.7; Mining and quarrying 1.9; Manufacturing 45.6; Electricity, gas and water 18.3; Construction 39.2; Trade, restaurants and hotels 82.5; Transport, storage and communications 26.2; Finance and real estate 63.8; Public administration 79.2; Other services 114.4; *Sub-total* 581.8; *Less* Imputed bank service charges 17.4; *Gross value added in basic prices* 564.4; Indirect taxes, less subsidies 85.1; *GDP at market prices* 649.5. Source: Asian Development Bank.

Balance of Payments (US $ '000, 2008): Exports of goods f.o.b. 10,856; Imports of goods f.o.b. –157,758; *Trade balance* –146,902; Exports of services 38,447; Imports of services –54,937; *Balance on goods and services* –163,393; Other income received 10,628; Other income paid –3,704; *Balance on goods, services and income* –156,469; Current transfers received 109,966; Current transfers paid –13,621; *Current balance* –60,124; Capital account (net) 57,995; Direct investment from abroad 4,166; Financial derivatives assets 16,214; Other investment assets –13,823; Other investment liabilities –19,784; Net errors and omissions 20,109; *Overall balance* 4,753. Source, IMF, *International Financial Statistics*.

EXTERNAL TRADE

Principal Commodities ('000 pa'anga, 2009): *Imports:* Animals and animal products 42,621; Vegetable products 9,854; Prepared foodstuffs 44,820; Mineral products 63,363; Chemical products 13,047; Wood and wood products 6,476; Wood pulp, paper and paperboard 10,987; Base metals and articles thereof 12,916; Machinery, mechanical appliances and electrical equipment 34,358; Transportation equipment 20,257; Miscellaneous manufactured articles 3,661; Works of art, collectors' pieces and antiques 11,875; Total (incl. others) 291,926. *Exports* (including re-exports): Animal and animal products 8,708; Vegetable products 4,716; Chemical products 556; Wood and wood products 213; Total (incl. others) 15,584.

Principal Trading Partners ('000 pa'anga, 2009): *Imports:* Australia 33,497; China, People's Republic 14,845; Fiji 38,796; Japan 10,534; New Zealand 88,853; USA 37,701; Total (incl. others) 291,926. *Exports:* Australia 1,494; Japan 653; New Zealand 4,009; USA 2,265; Total (incl. others) 15,584.

TRANSPORT

Road Traffic (registered motor vehicles, 2004): Passenger cars 6,580; Light goods vehicles 5,183; Heavy goods vehicles 2,698; Buses 114; Taxis 845; Total (incl. others) 16,748.

Shipping: *International Traffic* ('000 metric tons, 1998 unless otherwise indicated): Goods loaded 13.8; Goods unloaded 80.4. Vessels entered ('000 net registered tons) 1,950 in 1991 (Source: UN, *Statistical Yearbook*). *Merchant Fleet* (registered at 31 December 2009): Vessels 50; Total displacement ('000 grt) 68.2 (Source: IHS Fairplay, *World Fleet Statistics*).

Civil Aviation (traffic on scheduled services, 2004): Kilometres flown 1 million; Passengers carried 75,000; Passenger-km 19 million; Total ton-km 2 million. Source: UN, *Statistical Yearbook*.

TOURISM

Foreign Tourist Arrivals (excl. cruise-ship passengers): 39,451 in 2006; 46,040 in 2007; 49,405 in 2008.

Tourist Arrivals by Country (2008): Australia 11,428; New Zealand 22,835; USA 5,836; Total (incl. others) 49,405.

Tourism Receipts (US $ million, excl. passenger transport): 16 in 2006; 14 in 2007; 20 in 2008.

Source: World Tourism Organization.

COMMUNICATIONS MEDIA

Radio Receivers (1997): 61,000 in use.

Television Receivers (1997): 2,000 in use.

Telephones (2009): 31,000 main lines in use.

Mobile Cellular Telephones (2009): 53,000 subscribers.

Personal Computers: 6,000 (58.9 per 1,000 persons) in 2005.

Internet Users (2009): 8,400.

Broadband Subscribers (2009): 1,000.

Daily Newspapers (1996): 1; estimated circulation 7,000.

Non-daily Newspapers (2004 unless otherwise indicated): 3; estimated circulation 13,000 (2001).

Sources: UNESCO, *Statistical Yearbook*; UN, *Statistical Yearbook*; Audit Bureau of Circulations, Australia; and International Telecommunication Union.

EDUCATION

Primary (2006, unless otherwise indicated, provisional): 117 schools (1999); 760 teachers; 16,941 pupils.

General Secondary (2006, unless otherwise indicated, provisional): 39 schools (1999); 999 teachers; 14,311 pupils.

Technical and Vocational: 4 colleges (2001); 45 teachers (1990); 467 students (1999).

Teacher-training (1999, unless otherwise indicated): 1 college; 22 teachers (1994); 288 students.

Universities, etc. (1985): 17 teachers; 85 students.

Other Higher Education: 36 teachers (1980); 620 students (1985); in 1990 230 students were studying overseas on government scholarships.

Pupil-teacher Ratio (primary education, UNESCO estimate): 22.3 in 2005/06 (Source: UNESCO Institute for Statistics).

Adult Literacy Rate: 99.0% (males 99.0%; females 99.1%) in 2006 (Source: UNESCO Institute for Statistics).

TONGA • *Directory*

Directory

The Government

HEAD OF STATE

The Sovereign: HM King GEORGE TUPOU V (succeeded to the throne 11 September 2006).

CABINET
(May 2011)

Prime Minister and Minister of Foreign Affairs, Defence, Information and Communication: Lord TU'IVAKANO.
Deputy Prime Minister and Minister of Justice, Transport and Works: SAMIU KUITA VAIPULU.
Minister of Finance: SUNIA MANU FILI.
Minister of Revenue Services and Public Enterprises: WILLIAM CLIVE EDWARDS.
Minister of Education, Women's Affairs and Culture: Dr ANA MAUI TAUFE'ULUNGAKI.
Minister of Labour, Commerce and Industries: LISIATE 'ALOVEITA 'AKOLO.
Minister of Police, Prisons and Fire Services: Dr VILIAMI LATU.
Minister of Lands, Survey, Natural Resources, Environment and Climate Change: Lord MA'AFU.
Minister of Health: ULITI UATA.
Minister of Training, Employment, Youth and Sports: FE'AOMOEATA VAKATA.
Minister of Agriculture, Food, Forestry and Fisheries: Lord VAEA.
Minister of Tourism: ISILELI PULU.
Attorney-General: (vacant).

GOVERNMENT MINISTRIES AND OFFICES

Office of the Prime Minister: POB 62, Nuku'alofa; tel. 24644; fax 23888; e-mail pmomail@pmo.gov.to; internet www.pmo.gov.to.
Palace Office: Salote Rd, Kolofo'ou, Nuku'alofa; tel. 21000; fax 24102; internet www.palaceoffice.gov.to.
Ministry of Agriculture, Food, Forestry and Fisheries: Administration Office, Vuna Rd, Kolofo'ou, Nuku'alofa; tel. 23038; fax 23039; e-mail pvea@kalianet.to.
Ministry of Education, Women's Affairs and Culture: POB 61, Vuna Rd, Kolofo'ou, Nuku'alofa; tel. 23511; fax 23596; e-mail moe@kalianet.to; internet www.tongaeducation.gov.to.
Ministry of Environment and Climate Change: Nuku'alofa.
Ministry of Finance and National Planning: Treasury Bldg, POB 87, Vuna Rd, Nuku'alofa; tel. 23066; fax 26011; e-mail info@finance.gov.to; internet www.finance.gov.to.
Ministry of Foreign Affairs: National Reserve Bank Bldg, 4th Floor, Salote Rd, Kolofo'ou, Nuku'alofa; tel. 23600; fax 23360; e-mail secfo@candw.to.
Ministry of Health: POB 59, Taufa'ahau Rd, Tofoa, Nuku'alofa; tel. 28233; fax 24921; e-mail tpaea@health.gov.to; internet www.health.gov.to.
Ministry of Information and Communications: POB 1380, Nuku'alofa; tel. 28170; fax 24861; e-mail enquiries@mic.gov.to; internet www.mic.gov.to.
Ministry of Justice: POB 130, Railway Rd, Kolofo'ou, Nuku'alofa; tel. 21055; fax 23098; internet www.justice.gov.to.
Ministry of Labour, Commerce and Industries: POB 110, Nuku'alofa; tel. 23688; fax 23887.
Ministry of Lands, Survey and Natural Resources: POB 5, Vuna Rd, Kolofo'ou, Nuku'alofa; tel. 23611; fax 23216; internet www.lands.gov.to.
Ministry of Police, Prisons and Fire Services: POB 8, Nuku'alofa; tel. 23233; fax 23036; e-mail polcombr@kalianet.to.
Ministry of Public Enterprises: Nuku'alofa.
Ministry of Revenue Services: POB 7, Nuku'alofa; tel. 23444; fax 25018; internet www.revenue.gov.to.
Ministry of Transport: Dupincia Lodge, Ma'ufanga, Nuku'alofa; tel. 24144; fax 24145; e-mail info@mca.gov.to; internet www.mca.gov.to.
Ministry of Works and Disaster Relief Activities: POB 52, Nuku'alofa; tel. 23100; fax 25440; e-mail mowtonga@kalianet.to.

Legislative Assembly

The number of directly elective seats was increased from a minority of nine to a majority of 17 at the 2010 election. The term of the Legislative Assembly was increased from three to four years.
Speaker: Lord LASIKE.

Election, 25 November 2010

Party	Seats
Democratic Party of the Friendly Islands	12
Independents	5
Nobles' Representatives	9
Total	**26**

The nine Nobles' Representatives were elected from among their peers in a separate ballot. An additional four members may be appointed by the Prime Minister

Election Commission

Electoral Commission: Nuku'alofa; f. 2010; Chair. BARRIE SWEETMAN; Supervisor of Elections PITA VUKI.

Political Organizations

Democratic Party of the Friendly Islands (DPFI): c/o Legislative Assembly, Nuku'alofa; f. 2010; est. as electoral vehicle by mems of Human Rights and Democracy Movement; advocates transparent government, further constitutional reform, greater accountability and economic reform; Leader 'AKILISI POHIVA.
Friendly Islands Human Rights and Democracy Movement Inc (FIHRDM Inc): POB 843, Nuku'alofa; tel. 25501; e-mail demo@kalianet.to; f. late 1970s; est. and recognized in 1992 as the Pro-Democracy Movement; application in 1998 for incorporation under new name of Tonga Human Rights and Democracy Movement refused by Govt; reverted to the name of Human Rights and Democracy Movement in Tonga (HRDMT) in 2002; assumed present name in Nov. 2005; advocates democratic reform; Leader ULITI UATA.
Paati Langafonua Tu'uloa (PLT) (Sustainable Nation-Building Party): f. 2007; Pres. SIONE FONUA.
People's Democratic Party: Nuku'alofa; f. 2005; breakaway group from HRDMT; Pres. SIONE TEISINA FUKO; Vice-Pres. SIONE TU'ALAU MANGISI.
Tongan Democratic Labour Party: Nuku'alofa; f. 2010; Chair. Dr PITA TAUFATOFUA.

Diplomatic Representation

EMBASSIES AND HIGH COMMISSIONS IN TONGA

Australia: Salote Rd, Private Bag 35, Nuku'alofa; tel. 23244; fax 23243; e-mail ahctonga@dfat.gov.au; internet www.tonga.embassy.gov.au; High Commissioner THOMAS ROTH.
China, People's Republic: Vuna Rd, POB 877, Nuku'alofa; tel. 24554; fax 24595; e-mail chinaemb_to@mfa.gov.cn; Ambassador WANG DONGHUA.
Japan: 5th Floor, NRBT Bldg, POB 330, Nuku'alofa; tel. 22221; fax 27025; Ambassador YASUO TAKASE.
New Zealand: cnr Taufa'ahau and Salote Rds, POB 830, Nuku'alofa; tel. 23122; fax 23487; e-mail nzhcnuk@kalianet.to; High Commissioner JONATHAN AUSTIN.

Judicial System

There are eight Magistrates' Courts, the Land Court, the Supreme Court and the Court of Appeal. Appeal from the Magistrates' Courts lies to the Supreme Court, and from the Supreme Court and Land Court to the Court of Appeal (except in certain matters relating to hereditary estates, where appeal lies to the Privy Council). The Chief Justice and Puisne Judge are resident in Tonga and are judges of the Supreme Court and Land Court. The Court of Appeal is presided over by the Chief Justice and consists of three judges from other Commonwealth countries. In the Supreme Court, the accused in criminal

TONGA

cases, and either party in civil suits, may elect trial by jury. In the Land Court, the judge sits with a Tongan assessor. Proceedings in the Magistrates' Courts are in Tongan, and in the Supreme Court and Court of Appeal in Tongan and English.

Chief Justice: MICHAEL DISHINGTON SCOTT, Supreme Court, POB 11, Nukuʻalofa; tel. 23599; fax 22380; e-mail cj_tonga@kalianet.to.
Puisne Judge: ROBERT SHUSTER.
Chief Registrar of the Supreme Court: MANAKOVI PAHULU.

Religion

The Tongans are almost all Christians, and about 36% of the population belong to Methodist (Wesleyan) communities. There are also significant numbers of Roman Catholics (15%) and Latter-day Saints (Mormons—15%). Anglicans (1%) and Seventh-day Adventists (5%) are also represented. Fourteen churches are represented in total.

CHRISTIANITY

Kosilio ʻae Ngaahi Siasi ʻi Tonga (Tonga National Council of Churches): POB 1205, Nukuʻalofa; tel. 23291; fax 27506; e-mail tncc@kalianet.to; f. 1973; three mem. churches (Free Wesleyan, Roman Catholic and Anglican); Chair. Rt Rev. ALIFALETI MONE; Gen. Sec. Rev. SIKETI TONGA.

The Anglican Communion

Tonga lies within the diocese of Polynesia, part of the Church of the Province of New Zealand. The Bishop of Polynesia is resident in Fiji.
Archdeacon of Tonga and Samoa: The Ven. SAM KOY, The Vicarage, POB 31, Nukuʻalofa; tel. 22136.

The Roman Catholic Church

The diocese of Tonga, directly responsible to the Holy See, comprises Tonga and the New Zealand dependency of Niue. At 31 December 2007 there were an estimated 15,384 adherents in the diocese. The Bishop participates in the Catholic Bishops' Conference of the Pacific, based in Fiji.
Bishop of Tonga: SOANE PATITA MAFI, Toutaimana Catholic Centre, POB 1, Nukuʻalofa; tel. 23822; fax 23854; e-mail cathbish@kalianet.to.

Other Churches

Church of Jesus Christ of Latter-day Saints (Mormon): Mission Centre, POB 58, Nukuʻalofa; tel. 26007; fax 23763; 53,000 mems; Pres. LYNN C. MCMURRAY.
Church of Tonga: Nukuʻalofa; f. 1928; a branch of Methodism; 6,912 mems; Pres. Rev. FINAU KATOANGA.
Free Church of Tonga: POB 23, Nukuʻalofa; tel. 23896; fax 24458; e-mail kmakakaufaki@yahoo.co.nz; f. 1885; 20,175 mems (2009); brs in Australia, New Zealand and USA; Pres. Rev. SEMISI FONUA.
Free Wesleyan Church of Tonga (Koe Siasi Uesiliana Tauʻataina ʻo Tonga): POB 57, Nukuʻalofa; tel. 23522; fax 24020; e-mail fwc@kalianet.to; internet www.fwc.to; f. 1826; 36,500 mems; Pres. Rev. Dr FINAU ʻAHIO.
Tokaikolo Christian Fellowship: Nukuʻalofa; f. 1978; breakaway group from Free Wesleyan Church; 5,000 mems.

BAHÁʼÍ FAITH

National Spiritual Assembly: POB 133, Nukuʻalofa; tel. 21568; fax 23120; e-mail nsatonga@patco.to; mems resident in 142 localities.

The Press

Eva, Your Guide to Tonga: POB 958, Nukuʻalofa; tel. 25779; fax 24749; e-mail editor@matangitonga.to; internet www.matangitonga.to; f. 1989; 4 a year; publication suspended under media restrictions in Jan. 2004; Publr and Editor PESI FONUA; circ. 4,500.
Ko e Keleʻa (Conch Shell): POB 1567, Nukuʻalofa; tel. 25501; fax 26330; internet www.planet-tonga.com/tongatimes/kelea; f. 1986; monthly; activist-orientated publication, economic and political; Editor MATENI TAPUELUELU; circ. 3,500.
Lali: Nukuʻalofa; f. 1994; monthly; English; national business magazine; Publr KALAFI MOALA.
Lao and Hia: POB 2808, Nukuʻalofa; tel. 14105; weekly; Tongan; legal newspaper; Editor SIONE HAFOKA.
Matangi Tonga: POB 958, Nukuʻalofa; tel. 25779; fax 24749; e-mail editor@matangitonga.to; internet www.matangitonga.to; f. 1986; monthly; national news magazine ceased publication following suspension of licence in Jan. 2004 and subsequently published solely on internet; Man. Editor MARY FONUA.
ʻOfa ki Tonga: c/o Tokaikolo Fellowship, POB 2055, Nukuʻalofa; tel. 24190; monthly; newspaper of Tokaikolo Christian Fellowship; Editor Rev. LIUFAU VAILEA SAULALA.
Taumuʻa Lelei: POB 1, Nukuʻalofa; tel. 27161; fax 23854; e-mail tmlcath@kalianet.to; f. 1931; monthly; Roman Catholic; Editor Dr SOANE LILO FOLIAKI.
The Times of Tonga/Koe Taimiʻo Tonga: POB 880, Nukuʻalofa; tel. 23177; e-mail times@kalianet.to; internet www.taimionline.com; f. 1989; twice-weekly; English edn covers Pacific and world news, Tongan edn covers local news; part of Taimi Media Network; Publr KALAFI MOALA; Editor FAKAʻOSI MAAMA; circ. 8,000.
Tohi Fanongonongo: POB 57, Nukuʻalofa; tel. 26533; fax 24020; e-mail fwctf@kalianet.to; monthly; Wesleyan; Editor Rev. TEVITA PAUKAMEA TIUETI.
Tonga Chronicle/Kalonikali Tonga: POB 197, Nukuʻalofa; tel. 23302; fax 23336; e-mail chroni@kalianet.to; f. 1964; govt-sponsored; weekly; Tongan and English; Editor Josephine LATU; circ. 3,000.

Publisher

Vavaʻu Press Ltd: POB 958, Nukuʻalofa; tel. 25779; fax 24749; e-mail vapress@matangitonga.to; internet www.matangitonga.to; f. 1980; books and magazines; Pres. PESI FONUA.

Broadcasting and Communications

TELECOMMUNICATIONS

Tonga Communications Corporation: Private Bag 4, Nukuʻalofa; tel. 20000; fax 26701; internet www.tcc.to; f. 2000; responsible for domestic and international telecommunications services; Man. Dir TIMOTE KATOANGA.
Digicel Tonga Ltd: Fatafehi Rd, POB 875, Nukuʻalofa; fax 24978; e-mail Paul.Stafford@digicelgroup.com; internet www.digiceltonga.com; f. 2008; CEO PAUL STAFFORD.
Tongasat—Friendly Islands Satellite Communications Ltd: POB 2921, Nukuʻalofa; tel. 24160; fax 23322; e-mail info@tongasat.com; internet www.tongasat.com; f. 1988; 80% Tongan-owned; private co but co-operates with Govt in management and leasing of orbital satellite positions; Chair. Princess SALOTE MAFILEʻO PILOLEVU TUITA; Man. Dir SEMISI PANUVE.

BROADCASTING

Radio

Tonga Broadcasting Commission (TBC): POB 36, Tungi Rd, Fasi-moe-afi, Nukuʻalofa; tel. 23550; fax 28921; internet www.tonga-broadcasting.com; independent statutory board; commercially operated; operates two free-to-air TV channels and three radio stations, with programmes in Tongan and English; Gen. Man. ELENOA AMANAKI.
93FM: Pacific Partners Trust, POB 478, Nukuʻalofa; tel. 23076; fax 24970; broadcasts in English, Tongan, German, Mandarin and Hindi.
A3V The Millennium Radio 2000: POB 838, Nukuʻalofa; tel. 25891; fax 24195; e-mail a3v@tongatapu.net.to; broadcasts on FM; musical programmes; Gen. Man. SAM VEA.
BroadCom—TMN Group: Ngeleʻia; f. 2009; operates one radio station, FM 88.1, and one TV channel, TMN TV2; Founders MAKA TOHI, KATALINA TOHI.
Tonga News Association: Nukuʻalofa; Pres. PESI FONUA.

Television

DigiTV: Fatafehi Rd, POB 875, Nukuʻalofa; tel. 876-1000; fax 24978; e-mail customercaretonga@digicelgroup.com; internet www.digiceltonga.com; fmrly Tonfon TV; acquired by Digicel Group and renamed as above in 2007; operates 20 channels; CEO (Digicel Tonga) PAUL STAFFORD.
Oceania Broadcasting Network: POB 91, Nukuʻalofa; tel. 23314; fax 23658; reportedly ceased operations in late 2006.
Television Tonga: Fasi-moe-afi, Nukuʻalofa; f. 2000; 60% of programmes in English; 40% of programmes in Tongan.

TONGA — Directory

Finance

(cap. = capital; res = reserves; dep. = deposits; m. = million; brs = branches; amounts in Tongan dollars)

BANKING

Central Bank

National Reserve Bank of Tonga: Private Bag 25, Nuku'alofa; tel. 24057; fax 24201; e-mail nrbt@reservebank.to; internet www.reservebank.to; f. 1989; assumed central bank functions of Bank of Tonga; issues currency; manages exchange rates and international reserves; cap. 5.0m., res 13.1m., dep. 101.1m. (June 2009); Gov. SIOSI MAFI; Chair. Princess PILOLEVU TUITA.

Other Banks

Australia and New Zealand Banking Group Ltd: POB 910, Nuku'alofa; tel. 20500; fax 23870; e-mail anztonga@anz.com; internet www.anz.com/Tonga; Gen. Man. ARTHUR HUBBARD.

MBf Bank Ltd: POB 3118, Nuku'alofa; tel. 24600; fax 24662; e-mail info@mbfbank.to; internet www.mbfbank.to; f. 1993; 93.35% owned by MBf Asia Capital Corpn Holdings Ltd, 4.75% owned hitherto by King George Tupou V, 0.95% owned by Tonga Investments Ltd, 0.95% owned by Tonga Co-operative Federation Society; Gen. Man. H. K. YEOH.

Tonga Development Bank: Fatafehi Rd, POB 126, Nuku'alofa; tel. 23333; fax 23775; e-mail ssefanaia@tdb.to; internet www.tdb.to; f. 1977; est. to provide credit for developmental purposes, mainly in agriculture, fishery, tourism and housing; cap. 10.5m., res 9.9m. (Dec. 2007); Man. Dir SIMIONE SEFANAIA; 5 brs.

Westpac Bank of Tonga: POB 924, Nuku'alofa; tel. 23933; fax 25066; e-mail westpactonga@westpac.com.au; internet www.westpac.to; f. 1973; est. as Bank of Tonga; name changed as above in 2002; owned by Westpac Banking Corpn (Australia); cap. 23.5m., res 10.6m., dep. 168.8m. (Sept. 2009); Gen. Man. MISHKA TU'IFUA; 6 brs.

Trade and Industry

DEVELOPMENT ORGANIZATIONS

Tonga Investments Ltd: POB 27, Nuku'alofa; tel. 24388; fax 24313; f. 1992; est. to replace Commodities Board; govt-owned; manages five subsidiary cos; Man. Dir ANTHONY WAYNE MADDEN.

Tonga Association of Small Businesses: Nuku'alofa; f. 1990; est. to cater for the needs of small businesses; Chair. SIMI SILAPELU.

CHAMBER OF COMMERCE

Tonga Chamber of Commerce and Industry: Tungi Arcade, POB 1704, Nuku'alofa; tel. 25168; fax 26039; e-mail chamber@kalianet.to; internet www.tongachamber.org; Pres. PAULA TAUMOEPEAU; CEO 'AINA KAVALIKU (acting).

TRADE ASSOCIATIONS

Tonga Kava Council: Nuku'alofa; promotes the development of the industry both locally and abroad; Chair. TO'IMOANA TAKATAKA.

Tonga Squash Council: Nuku'alofa; promotes the development of the industry; introduced a quota system for exports in 2004; Pres. TSUTOMU NAKAO; Sec. STEVEN EDWARDS.

UTILITIES

Shoreline Power Group: POB 47, Taufa'ahau Rd, Kolofo'ou, Nuku'alofa; tel. 23311; fax 23632; provides electricity via diesel motor generation; took control of operations from the Tonga Electric Power Board in 2004; purchased by Tongan Govt in 2008; CEO SOANE RAMANLAL.

Tonga Water Board: POB 92, Taufa'ahau Rd, Kolofo'ou, Nuku'alofa; tel. 23298; fax 23518; operates four urban water systems, serving about 25% of the population; Man. SAIMONE P. HELU.

TRADE UNIONS

Association of Tongatapu Squash Pumpkin Growers: Nuku'alofa; f. 1998.

Public Servants Association (PSA): Nuku'alofa; Pres. FINAU TUTONE; Gen. Sec. MELE AMANAKI.

Tonga Nurses' Association and Friendly Islands Teachers' Association (TNA/FITA): POB 859, Nuku'alofa; tel. and fax 23972; e-mail fita@candw.to; Pres. FINAU TUTONE; Gen. Sec. TOKANKAMEA PULEIKU.

Transport

ROADS

Total road length was estimated at 680 km in 2000, of which some 27% were all-weather paved roads. Most of the network comprises fair-weather-only dirt or coral roads.

SHIPPING

The chief ports are Nuku'alofa, on Tongatapu, and Neiafu, on Vava'u, with two smaller ports at Pangai and Niuatoputapu.

Shipping Corporation of Polynesia Ltd: Queen Salote Wharf, Vuna Rd, POB 453, Nuku'alofa; tel. 23853; fax 23250; e-mail info@olovaha.com; internet www.olovaha.com; govt-owned; regular inter-islands passenger and cargo services; Chair. 'ALISI TAUMOEPEAU.

Uata Shipping Lines: 'Uliti Uata, POB 100, Nuku'alofa; tel. 23855; fax 23860.

Warner Pacific Line: POB 93, Nuku'alofa; tel. 21088; services to Samoa, American Samoa, Australia and New Zealand; Man. Dir MA'AKE FAKA'OSIFOLAU.

CIVIL AVIATION

Tonga is served by Fua'amotu International Airport, 22 km from Nuku'alofa, and airstrips at Vava'u, Ha'apai, Niuatoputapu, Niuafo'ou and 'Eua. A government agency, Tonga Airports Ltd (TAL), assumed responsibility for the management of all airports in 2007. Air New Zealand provides a regular service to Australia and New Zealand and a regional carrier, Reef Air, operates between Tonga, Niue and Fiji. The New Zealand-based low-cost airline Pacific Blue commenced direct flights to Tonga, from Sydney, Australia, and from Auckland, New Zealand, in 2005.

Airlines Tonga: c/o Teta Tours, cnr of Railway St and Wellington St, Nuku'alofa; tel. 23690; fax 23238; e-mail tetatour@kalianet.to; internet www.airfiji.com.fj/pages.cfm/home/airlines-tonga.html; f. 2006; jt venture between Teta Tours of Tonga and Air Fiji Ltd; sole operator of domestic services in Tonga from Nov. 2006; Man SITAFOOTI 'AHO.

Chathams Pacific (The Friendly Islands Airline): POB 907, Nuku'alofa; tel. 28000; fax 23447; e-mail sales@chathamspacific.com; internet www.chathamspacific.com; f. 2008; owned by Air Chathams (New Zealand); Gen. Man. RUSSELL JENKINS.

Tourism

Tonga's attractions include scenic beauty and a pleasant climate. Visitor arrivals increased from an estimated 46,040 in 2007 to 49,405 in 2008. In 2008 revenue from the industry totalled US $20m. The majority of tourists were from New Zealand, the USA and Australia.

Tonga Tourist Association: POB 74, Nuku'alofa; tel. 23344; fax 23833; e-mail royale@kalianet.to; Pres. PAPILOA FOLIAKI; Sec. KOLOLIANA NAUFAHU.

Tonga Visitors' Bureau: Vuna Rd, POB 37, Nuku'alofa; tel. 25334; fax 23507; e-mail info@tvb.gov.to; internet www.tongaholiday.com; f. 1978; CEO SAKOPO LOLOHEA.

Tourism Tonga Inc: Nuku'alofa; f. 2009.

Defence

Tonga has its own defence force, the Tonga Defence Services, consisting of both regular and reserve units. The island also has a defence co-operation agreement with Australia. Projected government expenditure on defence in 2004/05 was $T3.9m.

Commander of the Tonga Defence Services: Brig.-Gen. TAU'AIKA 'UTA'ATU.

Education

Free state education is compulsory for children between five and 14 years of age, while the Government and other Commonwealth countries offer scholarship schemes enabling students to go abroad for higher education. In 2006 there were 16,941 primary pupils and 14,311 secondary pupils, according to provisional figures. In 1999 a total of 467 students attended technical and vocational colleges, of which there were four in 2001. There was one teacher-training college in 1999, with 288 students. Some degree courses are offered at the university division of 'Atenisi Institute. A new establishment offering higher education, the 'Unuaki 'o Tonga Royal Institute (UTRI), opened in 2004. Recurrent government expenditure on education in 2004/05 was an estimated $T19.0m.

TRINIDAD AND TOBAGO

Introductory Survey

LOCATION, CLIMATE, LANGUAGE, RELIGION, FLAG, CAPITAL

The Republic of Trinidad and Tobago consists of Trinidad, the southernmost of the Caribbean islands, and Tobago, which is 32 km (20 miles) to the north-east. Trinidad, which accounts for 94% of the total area, lies just off the north coast of Venezuela, on the South American mainland, while the country's nearest neighbour to the north is Grenada. The climate is tropical, with a dry season from January to May. Rainfall averages 1,561 mm (61.5 ins) per year. Annual average daytime temperatures range between 32°C (90°F) and 21°C (70°F). The official and main language is English, but French, Spanish, Hindi and Chinese are also spoken. In 2000 some 55% of the population were Christians, mainly Roman Catholics (30%) and Anglicans (25%), while 23% were Hindus and 6% Muslims. The national flag (proportions 3 by 5) is deep red, divided by a white-edged black diagonal stripe from upper hoist to lower fly. The capital is Port of Spain, on the island of Trinidad.

CONTEMPORARY POLITICAL HISTORY

Historical Context

Trinidad was first colonized by the Spanish in 1532, but was ceded to the British in 1802. Africans were transported to the island to work as slaves, but slavery was abolished in 1834. Shortage of labour led to the arrival of large numbers of Indian and Chinese immigrants, as indentured labourers, during the second half of the 19th century. In 1888 the island of Tobago, which had finally been ceded to the British in 1814, was joined with Trinidad as one political and administrative unit, and the territory remained a British colony until its independence on 31 August 1962.

Modern politics emerged in the 1930s with the formation of a trade union movement. The first political party, the People's National Movement (PNM), was founded in 1956 by Dr Eric Williams. It campaigned successfully at the elections to the Legislative Council in September 1956, and Williams became the colony's first Chief Minister in October. In 1958 the territory became a member of the newly established Federation of the West Indies, and in the following year achieved full internal self-government, with Williams as Premier. The Federation collapsed in 1961, however, following the secession of Jamaica and, subsequently, Trinidad and Tobago. After independence, in 1962, Williams was restyled Prime Minister, and the Governor became Governor-General.

Domestic Political Affairs

In April 1970 the Government declared a state of emergency, following several weeks of violent demonstrations by supporters of 'Black Power', protesting against foreign influence in the country's economy and demanding solutions to the problem of unemployment, which was particularly severe among Trinidadians of African descent. On the day that the emergency was proclaimed, part of the Trinidad and Tobago Regiment (the country's army) mutinied, but the mutiny collapsed after only three days. At a general election in May 1971, the PNM won all 36 seats in the House of Representatives.

A new Constitution came into effect on 1 August 1976, whereby Trinidad and Tobago became a republic, within the Commonwealth. At parliamentary elections in September, the PNM won two-thirds of the seats in the House of Representatives. The former Governor-General, Ellis Clarke, was sworn in as the country's first President in December 1976. A parliamentary resolution in 1977 to grant Tobago self-rule resulted, after long resistance from the Government, in the formation in 1980 of a Tobago House of Assembly, giving the island limited autonomy. Tobago was granted full internal self-government in January 1987.

Williams died in March 1981. George Chambers, a deputy leader of the PNM, was formally adopted as party leader in May and confirmed as Prime Minister. The PNM increased its majority in the House of Representatives in a general election in November. The United Labour Front (ULF), the Democratic Action Congress (DAC) and the Tapia House Movement, campaigning jointly as the Trinidad and Tobago National Alliance, succeeded in retaining only 10 seats.

Co-operation between the four opposition parties increased, and, at local elections in August 1983, they successfully combined to inflict electoral defeat on the PNM. In August 1984 the National Alliance and the Organization for National Reconstruction established the National Alliance for Reconstruction (NAR). In September 1985 Arthur Napoleon Raymond (A. N. R.) Robinson, leader of the DAC, was elected leader of the NAR. In 1986 the four parties merged to form one opposition party, still known as the NAR.

The stringent economic policies of the PNM Government provoked labour unrest over wage restraint. The general election of December 1986 resulted in a decisive victory for the NAR. Robinson was appointed Prime Minister. Chambers was among those members of the PNM who lost their seats, and in January 1987 Patrick Manning was appointed parliamentary Leader of the Opposition.

The NAR experienced internal difficulties during 1987–88. In June 1987 former members of the Tapia House Movement announced that they were to leave the NAR. In February 1988 more than 100 NAR members met to discuss the leadership of the alliance and the direction of its policies. Two cabinet ministers (including Basdeo Panday, the Minister of External Affairs) and one junior minister were subsequently dismissed from the Government. All three were former members of the ULF, which derived most of its support from the 'East' Indian community. Despite their accusations of racism against the NAR leadership, they were expelled from the party in October. In April 1989 Panday and the other dissidents announced the formation of a left-wing opposition party, the United National Congress (UNC). Panday was elected leader of the new party; Panday replaced Manning as the Leader of the Opposition in September 1990.

In July 1990 members of the Jamaat al Muslimeen, a small Muslim group led by Yasin Abu Bakr, attempted to seize power. The rebels destroyed the capital's police headquarters and took control of the parliament building and the state television station. Some 45 people were taken hostage, among them Robinson and several cabinet ministers. The rebels demanded Robinson's resignation, elections within 90 days and an amnesty for those taking part in the attempted coup. On 28 July a state of emergency was declared and a curfew was imposed. On 31 July the Prime Minister, who had sustained gunshot wounds, was released from captivity by the rebels. A day later the rebels surrendered unconditionally. An amnesty pardoning them, signed by the President of the Senate, Joseph Emmanuel Carter, in his capacity as acting Head of State, was proclaimed invalid, on the grounds that it had been signed under duress. Bakr and his followers were charged with treason, a capital offence.

In November 1991 the imprisoned Jamaat al Muslimeen rebels won an appeal to the Judicial Committee of the Privy Council in the United Kingdom (the final court of appeal for Trinidad and Tobago), which ruled that the validity of the presidential pardon issued during the attempted coup in July 1990 should be determined before the rebels were brought to trial, and that an application for their release should be heard by the High Court of Trinidad and Tobago immediately. On 30 June 1992 the High Court ruled that the pardon was valid, and ordered the immediate release of the 114 defendants. The Government announced that it would pursue all legal means of appeal against the decision. In October 1993 the Court of Appeal ruled to uphold the decision of the High Court. In October 1994 the Privy Council ruled to overturn the decisions of the High Court and the Court of Appeal, declaring the pardon invalid. As a result, the Jamaat al Muslimeen would be unable to claim compensation for wrongful imprisonment. However, it was also ruled that to rearrest the rebels and try them for offences committed during the insurrection would constitute an abuse of the legal process. The Jamaat al Muslimeen was subsequently awarded some TT $2.1m. in compensation for the destruction of its buildings following the coup attempt.

TRINIDAD AND TOBAGO

1991 election: PNM victorious

A general election, held in December 1991, resulted in a decisive victory for the PNM. The implementation of unpopular austerity measures was widely acknowledged as the main cause of the defeat of the NAR, and Robinson resigned as leader. A notable feature of the elections was the re-emergence of ethnic voting, with the vast majority of the votes divided between the Afro-Trinidadian-orientated PNM and the largely Indo-Trinidadian UNC. Patrick Manning was sworn in as Prime Minister. In spite of the change of government, industrial unrest continued. In February 1993 several thousand public sector employees joined protests against the delay in payments and at the Government's plans to restructure inefficient state enterprises. In early 1994 a government offer of a settlement of the public sector claim was rejected by the majority of employees. In mid-1995 the Government introduced a new plan to settle the claim, involving the issue of bonds with tax credits, which was accepted by the Trinidad and Tobago Unified Teachers' Association. However, industrial action resumed in September in support of demands for a more favourable settlement. Agreement was finally reached on a settlement in March 1996. Meanwhile, industrial unrest persisted in opposition to continuing government plans for the rationalization and privatization of unproductive public utilities.

The NAR retained control of the Tobago House of Assembly following elections in December 1992. In July 1993 the Government and the Tobago House of Assembly agreed to begin discussions concerning the upgrading of Tobago's constitutional status. Measures subsequently submitted for consideration by the legislature included the establishment of an executive council on Tobago and the appointment of an independent senator to represent the island.

Appeals for the restoration of capital punishment, prompted by growing public concern at the increasing rate of murder and violent crime, gained considerable impetus in August 1993 following the murder of the country's Prison Commissioner. In July 1994 Trinidad and Tobago conducted its first execution since 1979. However, the convicted murderer, Glen Ashby, was hanged only minutes before a facsimile transmission from the Privy Council in the United Kingdom was sent to the Court of Appeal in Trinidad granting a stay of execution. Following Ashby's execution, the Privy Council issued a conservatory order whereby, in the case of two men due to be heard by the Trinidad Court of Appeal, should their execution be ordered, it could not be conducted until the case had been heard by the Privy Council itself. This decision provoked protest from the Chief Justice of Trinidad and Tobago, who accused the Privy Council of pre-empting the Court of Appeal's exercise of its jurisdiction. Subsequently, the Government announced its intention to introduce legislation establishing the Court of Appeal as the final appeal court for criminal cases, pending regional agreement on a Caribbean appeal court.

1995 election: coalition Government

A general election was held in November 1995. The PNM and the UNC each secured 17 seats, while the NAR won the remaining two. Following discussions between the leader of the UNC, Basdeo Panday, and Robinson, who had resumed the leadership of the NAR in October, a coalition Government was established, with Panday as Prime Minister. It was widely understood that the NAR's support for the UNC in forming the Government had been dependent on undertakings concerning the prompt upgrading of Tobago's constitutional status. The NAR increased its majority in elections to the Tobago House of Assembly in December 1996.

In January 2000 Hanraj Sumairsingh, a member of the UNC, was found murdered. It was subsequently reported that Sumairsingh had written to the Prime Minister several times regarding threats by the Minister of Local Government, Dhanraj Singh, following Sumairsingh's revelation of alleged corruption in the unemployment relief programme administered by Singh's ministry. In October Singh was dismissed from his government post. Singh was charged with the murder of Sumairsingh, but in October 2003 he was found not guilty of ordering the killing.

In October 1997 it was announced that the Government had approved a proposal by the Attorney-General to expedite executions of persons convicted of murder, whereby the Government would allow only 18 months for completion of a hearing before the UN Human Rights Committee (UNHRC) and the Inter-American Commission on Human Rights (IACHR), in the event of the Privy Council rejecting an appeal. The Government hoped, by imposing a time limit on the UNHRC and the IACHR, to complete the appeals process within the five years allowed by the Privy Council as the maximum length of time between sentencing and execution. In April 1998 the Government refused to grant leave for the hearing of appeals against the death penalty made by nine men convicted of murder (the so-called 'Chadee gang'). The nine subsequently appealed to the UNHRC. In May 1998 the Government announced that it was withdrawing from the UNHRC and the IACHR, as neither body had been able to guarantee the hearing of appeals within the 18 months requested by the Government. Many Caribbean states expressed their support for Trinidad and Tobago, although the PNM criticized the withdrawals as damaging the islands' international reputation. In June 1998 the IACHR ordered Trinidad and Tobago not to execute five people whose cases it had been scheduled to review; however, the authorities announced that the IACHR no longer had any jurisdiction over the cases, and that the executions would be carried out.

In October 1998, in what was considered a landmark case, the Privy Council rejected the appeals of two convicted murderers, who had claimed that their constitutional rights had been infringed by the conditions in which they had been imprisoned. In January 1999, in a further landmark judgment, the Privy Council ruled that, even though Trinidad and Tobago had withdrawn from the IACHR, two convicted killers could not be executed while their appeals were being considered by the Commission, since the appeals had been made prior to the withdrawal. In April the Privy Council ordered the release of three prisoners who had spent almost four years awaiting execution.

In May 1999 the Privy Council rejected an appeal for clemency made by the nine members of the Chadee gang, who had claimed that they were being held in cruel and degrading conditions. However, the Privy Council granted a stay of execution, in order to allow time to consider the legality of hanging as a means of administering the death penalty. At the end of May the Privy Council ruled that Trinidad and Tobago could legally proceed with the nine executions, which, despite international protests, were carried out in June.

In April 2000 the Government announced that it was to withdraw from the first optional protocol to the International Covenant on Civil and Political Rights, following a judgment from the UNHRC that Trinidad and Tobago could not continue to adhere to the resolution while differing on the subject of the death sentence. The announcement attracted widespread international condemnation. The Government, however, stated that the withdrawal was intended purely to prevent condemned murderers from addressing lengthy appeals to the UNHRC. The Government also announced the introduction of a constitutional amendment, which would allow executions to proceed before the IACHR and the UNHRC had ruled on the cases. On 14 February 2001, at a Caribbean Community and Common Market (CARICOM, see p. 219) summit in Barbados, the leaders of 11 Caribbean states signed an agreement to establish the Caribbean Court of Justice (CCJ). The Court was to replace the Privy Council as the final court of appeal, and was to be based in Trinidad and Tobago. The CCJ would be financed by a US $100m. trust fund raised by the Caribbean Development Bank. In February Parliament voted to accept the authority of the new Court to settle CARICOM matters. The Court was eventually inaugurated on 16 April 2005. However, owing to UNC opposition to adopting the appellate jurisdiction of the CCJ, the new Court was only to have jurisdiction in Trinidad and Tobago over CARICOM matters.

Elections of 2000 and 2001

The UNC secured a narrow majority in the House of Representatives at a general election in December 2000. Panday was inaugurated as Prime Minister for the second time. At elections to the Tobago House of Assembly in January 2001 the PNM secured eight of the 12 elective seats, ending the traditional domination of the House by the NAR.

The Government was beset by allegations of corruption in mid-2001 regarding the receipt of payments in exchange for supporting tenders for contracts with the state-owned oil company, Petrotrin, and irregularities in the accounts of the North West Regional Health Authority. A faction within the UNC, Team Unity, emerged in protest at the perceived corruption. Team Unity subsequently gained control of the party's national executive, but despite attempts by Team Unity to prevent UNC constituent elections from taking place in September, supporters of Panday were victorious in 30 of the 34 constituencies. Nevertheless, the Government's legislative majority was effectively lost in October when the three ministers formed a coalition with the PNM and the NAR and obstructed attempts by Panday to approve the budget. Amid increasing pressure from the opposition for his resignation, on 10 October Panday asked the President to dissolve Parliament in preparation for a general election.

In the general election of 10 December 2001 the UNC and the PNM secured an equal number of seats in the House of Representatives. The two party leaders reached an agreement on political collaboration in government, although not a coalition arrangement, that would allow the President to appoint the Prime Minister and Speaker in the House of Representatives and to reform the electoral process. However, following the appointment of Manning as Prime Minister and PNM nominee Max Richards as Speaker of the House of Representatives, the UNC withdrew from the post-election agreement.

Panday's refusal to be sworn in as Leader of the Opposition and to agree to elect a Speaker in the House of Representatives (Richards had withdrawn from the position after his impartiality was questioned) prevented the convening of the new Parliament in January 2002. Panday announced the UNC's intention to prevent Parliament from sitting for the next six months, thereby forcing Manning to call a new election, according to the provisions of the Constitution. Manning and Panday met for discussions at the end of January, but neither these meetings, nor negotiations mediated by CARICOM leaders in February, provided a solution to the dispute. Later in February Manning agreed to put the UNC's proposals for an executive comprising equal numbers of PNM and UNC representatives to the PNM party council. The UNC accused the Prime Minister of deliberately delaying the process. The first session of the new House of Representatives was reconvened in April; however, owing to the failure of the two parties to elect a Speaker, proceedings were adjourned.

Meanwhile, in March 2002 Panday's former finance minister, Brian Kuei Tung, and several senior government officials and prominent businessmen were arrested on charges of fraud and misbehaviour in public office with regard to the construction of a new terminal at Piarco Airport. Manning ordered a Commission of Inquiry into the project. In July the Commission of Inquiry accused two more UNC members of Parliament of criminal activity. Former Minister of Works and Transport Carlos John was accused of ignoring tender procedures during his time in office, and in the same month cocaine worth US $246,000 and two missiles were apparently found at the home of the former housing minister Sadiq Baksh.

A report by the Commission of Inquiry into the Elections and Boundaries Commission in June 2002 documented countless flaws in its practices and recommended that all its members should resign. However, its members failed to relinquish their posts, despite Manning's pledge to implement the recommended reforms. In July Manning announced that if Parliament failed to elect a Speaker by 31 October, further elections would be held. Manning made a final, unsuccessful, attempt to convene Parliament in August before dissolving Parliament and announcing that elections would take place on 7 October.

2002 election: Manning returned to office

The PNM won a small majority in the election of October 2002. Manning again acceded to the office of Prime Minister, stating his intention to seek solutions to issues that divided the nation's political and racial communities. His Cabinet was largely unchanged from the previous administration.

Despite government efforts, in 2003 and 2004 there were increasing concerns over the continuing rise in crime rates, particularly kidnapping and murder. In June 2003 the Senate approved legislation imposing a minimum 25-year prison sentence on those convicted of kidnap. In a landmark ruling, in November 2004 the Privy Council ruled that Trinidad and Tobago's mandatory death sentence for convicted murderers was unconstitutional and inconsistent with the country's international obligations. The ruling followed an appeal brought by Balkissoon Roodal, who had been sentenced to death in July 1999. However, in July 2004 the Privy Council overturned its earlier ruling. A panel of nine judges, rather than the customary five, decreed that the Trinidadian Constitution did not allow outside intervention to abolish the mandatory death penalty. However, the judges further ruled that this would not apply to the estimated 100 prisoners who had benefited from the November judgment.

Despite continuing concerns about the rise in criminal activity and allegations of government corruption, at an election to the Tobago House of Assembly in January 2005 the governing PNM increased its majority.

Allegations of political corruption persisted throughout 2005. In May corruption charges were filed against Panday, his wife, and the former UNC Minister of Works and Transport, Carlos John, in relation to the construction project at Piarco Airport. In November former Minister of Works and Transport Franklin Khan was charged with six counts of corruption, while in January 2006 Minister of Energy and Energy Industries Eric Williams was charged with accepting bribes from a potential contractor. Both Williams and Khan denied the allegations, and the charges against them were dismissed in December 2007 and September 2010, respectively.

In July–October 2005 five bombs exploded in Port of Spain, injuring at least 30 people. The bombs were believed to be criminal, rather than terrorist, attacks; police suggested that they may have been planted to distract attention from drugs-related activities. The authorities' perceived failure to find the perpetrators prompted widespread anger throughout the country. Mounting public pressure on the Government to curb the deterioration in law and order culminated on 22 October in a demonstration in the capital, attended by thousands of protesters.

In September 2005 Manning pledged to reduce unemployment, which, he claimed, was a major cause of the high crime rate. He also announced that he had invited the British Metropolitan Police Service and the USA's Federal Bureau of Investigation to establish specialist units in Trinidad and Tobago. The total number of murders in 2005 rose to 389, while the rate of detection declined from 44% in 2002 to 21% in mid-2005. Some 80% of murders were committed with illegal guns. The number of murders in 2006 stood at 368.

In November 2005 the Government announced a number of initiatives aimed at stemming the rise in violent crime. Proposed reforms to the police force increased Parliament's role in selecting members of the Police Service Commission and the Police Commissioner, while removing the Prime Minister's right to veto the appointment of the latter. The reforms also conferred on the Commissioner of Police greater powers of discipline and management. Another proposal was the establishment of a court expressly for hearing cases involving gun-related crime and kidnapping. Furthermore, legislation would prevent kidnappers and alleged perpetrators of more than three violent crimes from securing bail, and allow suspected kidnappers to be held for up to 60 days before being charged.

In November 2005 Yasin Abu Bakr was arrested and charged with seditious speech, incitement and terrorism, after allegedly preaching a sermon that called for a war on affluent Muslims who refused to pay *zakat*, a tithe for the poor, to his organization. In February 2006 the Attorney-General sought high court authorization for the state to confiscate 12 properties from members of the Jamaat al Muslimeen in compensation for damage caused during the attempted coup in 1990.

In April 2006 Panday was sentenced to two years' imprisonment, after being convicted of failing to make accurate declarations regarding a bank account held in London, United Kingdom. He was released on bail pending an appeal, but suspended as a member of Parliament and removed as Leader of the Opposition. Kamla Persad-Bissessar, a former Attorney-General, replaced him as opposition leader. In September Winston Dookeran, who had succeeded Panday as political leader of the UNC in October 2005, resigned from this post to launch a new political organization, the Congress of the People (COP). Panday's appeal against his conviction was upheld in March 2007 (although a retrial of the case was subsequently ordered), and he was reinstated as UNC political leader in April; however, Persad-Bissessar remained Leader of the Opposition.

2007 election: the PNM re-elected

At a general election held on 5 November 2007 the PNM secured 26 seats in the enlarged 41-seat House of Representatives. The UNC—Alliance, comprising the UNC and several smaller parties, won the remaining 15 seats. Manning continued as Prime Minister but relinquished the finance portfolio, assigning it to Karen Nunez-Tesheira. He committed his administration to diversifying the economy, aiding growth in the commodities, information technology and tourism sectors, in order for Trinidad and Tobago to achieve Developed Nation status by 2020. He was also faced with the problem of increasing public concern over the level of crime; the number of murders in 2007 was subsequently recorded as the highest on record at 395, rising further in 2008, to 550. Following the election, Basdeo Panday, who had been re-elected to Parliament, replaced Persad-Bissessar as Leader of the Opposition.

In April 2008 Manning dismissed Dr Keith Rowley as Minister of Trade and Industry, owing to his 'unacceptable behaviour' at a meeting of the state-owned Urban Development Corporation of Trinidad and Tobago (UDECOTT). However, Rowley claimed that the action had been taken because of his suggestion of possible corruption in UDECOTT's financial operations. A public inquiry into UDECOTT's affairs, chaired by a British lawyer, Prof. John Uff, was established in July. (Uff's report, published in April 2010, recommended the reform of UDECOTT and criticized the board for a lack of transparency, but no evidence of embezzlement was found.)

Elections to the Tobago House of Assembly were held in January 2009, at which the incumbent PNM obtained eight of the 12 seats, while the opposition Tobago Organisation of the People (TOP), formed in 2008, won four seats.

In January 2009 Manning announced plans for significant constitutional reforms, which included the establishment of an executive president as head of government and head of state, an expansion of the Senate (from 31 to 37 members) and a reorganization of the judiciary. The proposals were to undergo a two-year public consultation period before being debated by Parliament. The role of the Integrity Commission was questioned in May when some 10 days after their appointment by the President all five members resigned from the body, citing concerns over the internal organization of the group and public perceptions of its function.

Manning and Panday held discussions on constitutional reform in November 2009, agreeing to continue their collaboration on the issue. However, their views on the amendments required differed substantially, with Panday advocating the direct election of an executive president by the electorate (rather than by the House of Representatives, as proposed by the Government) and the election of a unicameral parliament by a system of proportional representation.

Recent developments: 2010 election

In January 2010 Panday was defeated by Persad-Bissessar in elections to the leadership of the UNC. In the following month, having secured the support of a majority of opposition deputies, Persad-Bissessar also replaced Panday as Leader of the Opposition. Persad-Bissessar proceeded to dismiss five UNC senators who had been appointed by Panday, and in early March filed a motion of no confidence against Manning, accusing the Prime Minister of 'questionable conduct' in a number of matters, including the alleged corruption at UDECOTT. In late March, however, the Prime Minister announced that a general election, which was not constitutionally due to be held until 2012, would take place in 2010, and on 8 April, the day before the no confidence motion was to have been debated, the President dissolved Parliament at Manning's request. The UNC, the COP, the TOP, the Movement for Social Justice and the National Joint Action Committee subsequently formed a coalition, the People's Partnership, to contest the forthcoming election, with Persad-Bissessar as the alliance's prime ministerial candidate.

The People's Partnership secured a comprehensive victory at the general election, which was duly held on 24 May 2010, attracting 60.0% of the votes cast and gaining control of 29 of the 41 seats in the House of Representatives (21 of which were won by the UNC, six by the COP and two by the TOP). The PNM, undermined by persistently high levels of violent crime and allegations of corruption, obtained the remaining 12 seats (down from 26 in 2007). The rate of participation by the electorate, at just under 70%, was the highest on record. Persad-Bissessar was inaugurated as the country's first female Prime Minister on 26 May, and her Cabinet took office two days later. The COP leader Winston Dookeran became Minister of Finance, Surujattan Ranbachan received the foreign affairs portfolio, Jack Warner was appointed as Minister of Works and Transport, and Brig. John Sandy was given responsibility for national security. Manning resigned as PNM leader following the party's poor electoral performance and was replaced by Keith Rowley in June. The People's Partnership strengthened its position further in July, when it overwhelmingly defeated the PNM in local elections, taking control of 11 of the country's 14 local authorities.

In July 2010, on the occasion of the 20th anniversary of the 1990 coup attempt, the Government revealed plans to form a commission to investigate the events surrounding the rebellion. To recover partially the cost of damages incurred during the uprising, in the following month the Government sold nine Jamaat al Muslimeen properties, raising over US $800,000, an act denounced as 'unlawful' by Bakr. The Government announced its intention to seize further property belonging to Jamaat al Muslimeen members involved in the failed coup. The inquiry into the attempted coup commenced proceedings in January 2011.

Legislation that defined the legal parameters for the interception of communications by the security services came into effect in January 2011 following Persad-Bissessar's revelation in November 2010 that the Security Intelligence Agency (SIA), a secretive branch of the Ministry of National Security, had implemented a campaign of illegal wire-tapping operations over the previous five years, seemingly with the approval of the Manning administration. Documents recovered from a police raid of SIA offices revealed that the Agency had unlawfully monitored the telephone calls and e-mails of a wide range of prominent individuals, including Persad-Bissessar, President George Maxwell Richards, PNM leader Keith Rowley, COP leader Winston Dookeran, high-ranking judicial figures, trade union leaders and journalists. Persad-Bissessar accused Manning's Government of an 'abuse of democracy', while Rowley attempted to distance the PNM from the former Prime Minister. In late November Attorney-General Anand Ramlogan announced in the Senate that the former head of the SIA, Nigel Clement, had admitted to receiving direct orders from Manning to carry out certain wire-tapping operations. Manning, who had defended the SIA's actions, denounced Ramlogan's allegation as 'utterly false'. Persad-Bissessar stated her intention of initiating an investigation into the scandal, although progress was expected to be hindered by the reported destruction by SIA operatives of much of the wire-tapping evidence.

With concern over crime still widespread among the public, the Government introduced new proposals in late 2010 to combat gang activity, illegal firearms and corruption within the police force. Moves were also made to abrogate preliminary inquiries in order to expedite criminal trials. The number of murders in 2010 totalled 472, slightly lower than the 506 recorded in 2009, although the number of gangs operating in the country was reported to have increased from 66 in 2005 to over 100 by 2010. A proposed amendment to the Constitution to remove the legal obstacles that prevented the death penalty from being carried out prompted criticism from the United Kingdom and human rights groups in early 2011. The Government argued that capital punishment was necessary to deter criminality. However, PNM opposition to the legislation meant that the Government was unable to secure the three-quarters' majority in the House of Representatives required to modify the Constitution, and the bill was consequently rejected by the lower chamber in March.

Foreign Affairs

In 1991 Trinidad and Tobago ratified with Venezuela a joint declaration on maritime boundaries, under which Trinidad and Tobago's maritime boundary was to be extended from 200 nautical miles (370 km) to 350 nautical miles (648 km). Relations with Venezuela deteriorated in late 1996 and early 1997 owing to a series of incidents involving Trinidadian fishing vessels. In May 1997 a two-year fishing agreement was completed for approval by both Governments. However, tensions were revived later in the month after 15 Trinidadian fishermen were arrested by Venezuelan coast-guards. The Trinidadian Government referred the issue to the Organization of American States (see p. 391). A revised two-year treaty was endorsed in December, permitting an unlimited number of vessels from each country into a shared fishing area. A joint fisheries commission was also re-established. In 2003 the two countries signed a memorandum of understanding on the joint exploitation of cross-border oil and gas fields. Negotiations recommenced in January 2006. The discussions stalled temporarily following Trinidad and Tobago's refusal to sign Venezuela's PetroCaribe energy accord, launched the previous year, which offered oil concessions and favourable financing terms to Caribbean nations. However, in early 2007 an agreement in principle was reached on the division of the cross-border Loran-Manatee natural gas field, which apportioned some 75% of the gas to Venezuela. Negotiations were suspended again later that year, however, and did not resume until 2009. A final agreement on the Loran-Manatee field was concluded in August 2010, and discussions regarding the other fields were ongoing in 2011.

In 2000 talks were held to find a solution to the maritime border dispute between Trinidad and Barbados. Despite further talks being held over the next two years, little progress was

TRINIDAD AND TOBAGO

Introductory Survey

made. Bilateral relations deteriorated in February 2004 after several Barbadian fishermen were arrested in Trinidad and Tobago's waters; Barbados subsequently imposed economic sanctions on imports from Trinidad and Tobago, which they were later ordered to lift by CARICOM's Council for Trade and Economic Development. In April 2006 the UN Convention on the Law of the Sea handed down a decision establishing a median line between the two exclusive economic zones. The UN rejected Trinidad and Tobago's claim to a large area to the south-east of Barbados and instructed the two countries to negotiate a fishing agreement for a large disputed area to the north of Tobago, which would remain in Trinidad and Tobago's possession. Although the Prime Ministers of the two countries expressed their commitment to achieve a resolution, none had been reached by mid-2011. Meanwhile, a treaty on the delimitation of Trinidad and Tobago's maritime border with Grenada was ratified by both nations in April 2010.

Prime Minister Persad-Bissessar generated considerable controversy in November 2010 by implying that assistance to neighbouring Caribbean nations affected by Hurricane Tomas, which had caused widespread damage in Saint Lucia, Saint Vincent and the Grenadines and Barbados during the previous month, would come with preconditions ensuring that companies in Trinidad and Tobago would benefit financially from reconstruction contracts. The outrage caused by this suggestion prompted Persad-Bissessar to retract her statement and issue an apology.

CONSTITUTION AND GOVERNMENT

A new Constitution came into effect on 1 August 1976. Legislative power is vested in the bicameral Parliament, consisting of the Senate, with 31 members, and the House of Representatives, with 41 members. Representatives are elected for a five-year term by universal adult suffrage. The President is a constitutional Head of State, chosen by an electoral college of members of both the Senate and the House of Representatives. Members of the Senate are nominated by the President in consultation with, and on the advice of, the Prime Minister and the Leader of the Opposition. The Cabinet has effective control of the Government and is responsible to Parliament. Tobago Island was granted its own House of Assembly in 1980 and given full internal self-government in 1987. The Tobago House of Assembly has 15 members, of whom 12 are elected; the remaining three members are selected by the majority party.

REGIONAL AND INTERNATIONAL CO-OPERATION

Trinidad and Tobago is a member of the Caribbean Community and Common Market (CARICOM, see p. 219), of the Inter-American Development Bank (see p. 333), of the Latin American Economic System (see p. 448), of the Association of Caribbean States (see p. 445), and of the Organization of American States (see p. 391). Trinidad and Tobago is also host to the Caribbean Court of Justice (see p. 219), although the country retains the Privy Council in the United Kingdom as its final appellate court. Trinidad and Tobago was one of the six founder members of CARICOM's Caribbean Single Market and Economy, which was inaugurated on 1 January 2006. In September 2008 the Organisation of Eastern Caribbean States (see p. 462) approved a proposal for the establishment of an economic union with Trinidad and Tobago by 2011, followed by political union by 2013.

Trinidad and Tobago was admitted to the UN in 1962. As a contracting party to the General Agreement on Tariffs and Trade, Trinidad and Tobago joined the World Trade Organization (see p. 430) shortly after its establishment in 1995. The country is a member of the Commonwealth (see p. 230).

ECONOMIC AFFAIRS

In 2009, according to estimates by the World Bank, Trinidad and Tobago's gross national income (GNI), measured at average 2007–09 prices, was US $22,076m., equivalent to US $16,490 per head (or US $25,100 on an international purchasing-power parity basis). During 2000–09, it was estimated, the population increased at an average annual rate of 0.4%, while gross domestic product (GDP) per head increased, in real terms, by an average of 5.9% per year. Overall GDP increased, in real terms, at an average annual rate of 6.3% in 2000–09; according to the World Bank, the economy grew by 3.5% in 2008, but contracted by 4.4% in 2009.

Agriculture (including forestry, hunting and fishing) contributed 0.6% of GDP in 2009, and employed 3.9% (excluding unclassified activities) of the working population in the same year. The principal cash crops are sugar cane, coffee, cocoa and citrus fruits. The fishing sector is small-scale, but is an important local source of food. During 2000–08, according to the World Bank, agricultural GDP declined by an average of 5.7% per year. According to official figures, the sector expanded by 10.7% in 2008.

Industry (including mining and quarrying, manufacturing, construction and power) provided 62.8% of GDP in 2008, and employed 31.6% (excluding undefined activities) of the working population in 2009. During 2000–08, according to the World Bank, industrial GDP increased at an average annual rate of 10.2%. Industrial GDP increased by 1.4% in 2008.

In 2009 the mining and quarrying sector (including petroleum production) employed some 3.5% of the working population (excluding undefined activities). The petroleum sector provided 35.8% of GDP in 2009. The sector grew by 2.6% in 2009. Trinidad has the world's largest deposits of natural asphalt, and substantial reserves of natural gas. In 2006 Trinidad and Tobago was the world's second largest producer (after Chile) of methanol, a by-product of natural gas. Cement, limestone and sulphur are also mined. According to official figures, the GDP of the energy sector declined by 0.5% in 2008.

Manufacturing contributed 4.7% of GDP in 2008 and employed 8.8% (excluding undefined activities) of the working population in 2009. During 2000–08 manufacturing GDP increased at an average annual rate of 9.8%, according to the World Bank. According to official figures, manufacturing GDP increased by 5.2% in 2008.

Construction contributed 8.7% of GDP in 2008 and engaged 19.3% (excluding undefined activities) of the employed labour force in 2009. According to official figures, sectoral GDP increased by 3.1% in 2008.

Almost all of the country's energy is derived from natural gas (it provided 99.6% of total electricity production in 2007). Natural gas is also used as fuel for the country's two petroleum refineries and several manufacturing plants. Imports of mineral fuels and lubricants comprised 33.0% of the value of merchandise imports in 2009. In the same year exports of mineral fuels accounted for 75.8% of total exports.

The services sector contributed 36.8% of GDP in 2008 and employed some 64.5% (excluding unclassified activities) of the working population in 2009. Tourism is a major source of foreign exchange; in 2008 receipts from tourism totalled US $615m. and some 430,631 tourists visited the islands in 2009. According to the World Bank, the GDP of the services sector increased at an average annual rate of 5.8% in 2000–08. Sectoral GDP increased by 5.2% in 2008.

In 2008 Trinidad and Tobago recorded a visible trade surplus of US $9,064m., and there was a surplus of US $8,519m. on the current account of the balance of payments. In 2008 the principal source of imports was the USA (23.8%); other major suppliers were Canada and Venezuela. The USA was also the principal market for exports (45.0%) in that year. The principal exports in 2009 were mineral fuels and lubricants (75.8% of the total), and chemicals. The principal imports were mineral fuels and lubricants and machinery and transport equipment.

In 2010/11 there was a budgetary deficit of TT $7,732.2m. Trinidad and Tobago's general government gross debt was TT $43,993m. in 2009, equivalent to 32.4% of GDP. At the end of 2004 Trinidad and Tobago's total external debt was US $2,652m., of which US $1,197m. was public and publicly guaranteed debt. In 2004 the cost of debt-servicing was equivalent to 5.4% of the value of exports of goods and services. The annual rate of inflation averaged 6.6% in 2000–09. Retail prices increased by an estimated average of 10.6% in 2010. Some 5.3% of the labour force was unemployed in 2009.

The presence of significant petroleum and natural gas deposits, combined with substantial foreign investment, meant that the energy sector was a major contributor to Trinidad and Tobago's economy. The development of a major liquefied natural gas (LNG) plant at Point Fortin from 2001 would eventually make Trinidad and Tobago one of the world's leading suppliers of LNG. Substantial foreign investment allowed increased industrialization, which, combined with high international fuel prices, contributed to rapid economic expansion and a large trade surplus in 2002–08. However, concerns about rising crime rates damaged investor confidence, increased security costs for businesses and threatened the tourism industry. Furthermore, there was concern over the standard of public services and infrastructure, as well as the increasing public sector debt. In 2009 it was announced that CL Financial Group, Trinidad's largest financial

TRINIDAD AND TOBAGO

conglomerate, would receive government funding to continue its operations, thus confirming that the country's financial sector was not immune to the global credit crisis. Although the energy industry recovered in 2010, activity in the non-energy sector remained stagnant, and zero growth was recorded in that year. Given the economic prominence of the energy sector, dwindling hydrocarbons reserves had become a serious concern; in an attempt to attract foreign investment for new exploration operations, in 2010 the Government lowered industry taxes, although the initial response from investors was disappointing. Despite the sluggish economic environment, inflation increased during 2010—ending the year at over 10%, compared with a record low of 1.3% at the end of 2009. Unemployment continued to rise during 2010, although in early 2011 the Government announced a five-year public works programme, which it claimed would create 27,000 jobs. The IMF forecast real GDP growth of 2.5% in 2011, with rising energy prices and a recovering global economy expected to benefit the country.

PUBLIC HOLIDAYS

2012: 1 January (New Year's Day), 30 March (Spiritual Baptist Shouters' Liberation Day), 6–9 April (Easter), 30 May (Indian Arrival Day), 7 June (Corpus Christi), 19 June (Labour Day), 1 August (Emancipation Day), 18 August* (Id al-Fitr, end of Ramadan), 31 August (Independence Day), 24 September (Republic Day), 13 November† (Diwali), 25–26 December (Christmas).

* These holidays are dependent on the Islamic lunar calendar and may vary by one or two days from the dates given.

† Dependent on lunar sightings.

Statistical Survey

Sources (unless otherwise stated): Central Statistical Office, National Statistics Bldg, 80 Independence Sq., POB 98, Port of Spain; tel. 623-6945; fax 625-3802; e-mail info@cso.gov.tt; internet www.cso.gov.tt; Central Bank of Trinidad and Tobago, POB 1250, Port of Spain; tel. 625-4835; fax 627-4696; e-mail info@central-bank.org.tt; internet www.central-bank.org.tt.

Area and Population

AREA, POPULATION AND DENSITY

Area (sq km)	5,128*
Population (census results)	
2 May 1990	1,213,733
15 May 2000	
Males	633,051
Females	629,315
Total	1,262,366
Population (official estimates at mid-year)	
2008	1,308,600
2009	1,310,100
2010	1,317,714
Density (per sq km) at mid-2010	257.0

* 1,980 sq miles. Of the total area, Trinidad is 4,828 sq km (1,864 sq miles) and Tobago 300 sq km (116 sq miles).

POPULATION BY AGE AND SEX
(UN estimates at mid-2011)

	Males	Females	Total
0–14	140,020	136,162	276,182
15–64	478,493	498,494	976,987
65 and over	36,154	59,465	95,619
Total	654,667	694,121	1,348,788

Source: UN, *World Population Prospects: The 2008 Revision*.

POPULATION BY ETHNIC GROUP
(1990 census*)

	Males	Females	Total	%
African	223,561	221,883	445,444	39.59
Chinese	2,317	1,997	4,314	0.38
'East' Indian	226,967	226,102	453,069	40.27
Lebanese	493	441	934	0.08
Mixed	100,842	106,716	207,558	18.45
White	3,483	3,771	7,254	0.64
Other	886	838	1,724	0.15
Unknown	2,385	2,446	4,831	0.43
Total	560,934	564,194	1,125,128	100.00

* Excludes some institutional population and members of unenumerated households, totalling 44,444.

ADMINISTRATIVE DIVISIONS
(population at 2000 census)

	Population	Capital
Trinidad	1,208,282	Port of Spain
Port of Spain (city, capital)	49,031	—
San Fernando (city)	55,419	—
Arima (borough)	32,278	Arima
Chaguanas (borough)	67,433	Chaguanas
Point Fortin (borough)	19,056	Point Fortin
Diego Martin	105,720	Petit Valley
San Juan/Laventille	157,295	Laventille
Tunapuna/Piarco	203,975	Tunapuna
Couva/Tabaquite/Talparo	162,779	Couva
Mayaro/Rio Claro	33,480	Rio Claro
Sangre Grande	64,343	Sangre Grande
Princes Town	91,947	Princes Town
Penal/Debe	83,609	Penal
Siparia	81,917	Siparia
Tobago	54,084	Scarborough

BIRTHS AND DEATHS
(annual averages, UN estimates)

	1995–2000	2000–05	2005–10
Birth rate (per 1,000)	15.1	14.5	14.8
Death rate (per 1,000)	7.2	7.9	8.0

Source: UN, *World Population Prospects: The 2008 Revision*.

Life expectancy (years at birth, WHO estimates): 70 (males 66; females 73) in 2008 (Source: WHO, *World Health Statistics*).

TRINIDAD AND TOBAGO

ECONOMICALLY ACTIVE POPULATION
('000 persons aged 15 years and over)

	2006	2007	2008
Agriculture, forestry, hunting and fishing	25.8	22.4	22.9
Mining and quarrying	20.4	22.8	21.1
Manufacturing	55.5	54.1	55.1
Electricity, gas and water	7.7	7.2	7.9
Construction	96.7	103.0	108.5
Wholesale and retail trade, restaurants and hotels	106.6	108.3	108.2
Transport, storage and communication	42.7	41.5	41.2
Finance, insurance, real estate and business services	48.1	49.6	52.5
Community, social and personal services	181.1	178.6	179.5
Sub-total	584.6	587.5	596.9
Activities not adequately defined	1.6	0.3	0.7
Total employed	586.2	587.8	597.6
Unemployed	39.0	34.5	29.0
Total labour force	625.2	622.3	626.6
Males	364.9	368.6	n.a.
Females	260.3	253.7	n.a.

Source: ILO.

2009 ('000 persons aged 15 years and over): Total employed 588.3 (Agriculture 23.0; Petroleum and gas 20.5; Construction and utilities 113.4; Manufacturing 51.9); Unemployed 32.6; Total labour force 620.9.

Health and Welfare

KEY INDICATORS

Total fertility rate (children per woman, 2008)	1.6
Under-5 mortality rate (per 1,000 live births, 2008)	35
HIV/AIDS (% of persons, aged 15–49, 2007)	1.5
Physicians (per 1,000 head, 1997)	0.8
Hospital beds (per 1,000 head, 2005)	2.6
Health expenditure (2007): US $ per head (PPP)	1,178
Health expenditure (2007): % of GDP	4.8
Health expenditure (2007): public (% of total)	56.1
Access to water (% of persons, 2008)	94
Access to sanitation (% of persons, 2008)	92
Total carbon dioxide emissions ('000 metric tons, 2007)	37,006.4
Carbon dioxide emissions per head (metric tons, 2007)	27.9
Human Development Index (2010): ranking	59
Human Development Index (2010): value	0.736

For sources and definitions, see explanatory note on p. vi.

Agriculture

PRINCIPAL CROPS
('000 metric tons)

	2005	2006*	2007*
Rice, paddy	2.1	2.3	2.5
Maize*	3.1	3.0	3.0
Taro (Cocoyam)*	4.9	4.9	4.9
Sugar cane	420.0	810.0	810.0
Pigeon peas	1.0	1.0	1.1
Coconuts*	18.0	15.0	15.0
Cabbages*	1.1	1.1	1.1
Lettuce*	1.5	1.5	1.5
Tomatoes	1.6	1.7	1.8
Pumpkins, squash and gourds	2.2	2.2	2.2
Cucumbers and gherkins*	2.0	2.0	2.1
—continued	2005	2006*	2007*
Aubergines*	3.0	3.0	3.0
Watermelons*	1.2	1.2	1.5
Bananas*	7.0	7.0	7.0
Plantains*	4.7	4.7	5.0
Oranges*	5.3	5.3	5.3
Lemons and limes*	1.7	1.7	1.7
Grapefruit and pomelo*	2.8	2.8	2.8
Pineapples*	4.5	4.5	4.5
Coffee, green*	0.4	0.4	0.4
Cocoa beans*	1.4	1.4	1.4

* FAO estimates.

2008: Production assumed to be unchanged from 2007 (FAO estimates). Note: No data were available for individual crops in 2009.

Aggregate production ('000 metric tons, may include official, semi-official or estimated data): Total cereals 5 in 2005–09; Total roots and tubers 9 in 2005–06, 10 in 2007–09; Total vegetables (incl. melons) 18 in 2005, 19 in 2006–09; Total fruits (excl. melons) 85 in 2005, 86 in 2006, 87 in 2007–09.

Source: FAO.

LIVESTOCK
('000 head year ending September, FAO estimates)

	2005	2006	2007
Horses	1.3	1.3	1.3
Asses	2.2	2.2	2.2
Mules	1.9	1.9	1.9
Cattle	29.0	29.0	30.0
Buffaloes	5.7	5.7	5.7
Pigs	43.0	43.0	45.0
Chickens	28,200	28,200	28,500
Sheep	3.4	3.4	3.5
Goats	59.3	59.3	60.0

Source: FAO.

2008: Figures assumed to be unchanged from 2007 (FAO estimates). Note: No data were available for 2009.

LIVESTOCK PRODUCTS
('000 metric tons, FAO estimates)

	2005	2006	2007
Cattle meat	0.8	0.8	0.8
Pig meat	2.9	2.9	3.0
Chicken meat	57.6	57.6	60.0
Cows' milk	10.5	10.5	11.0
Hen eggs	3.8	3.8	3.9

2008: Production assumed to be unchanged from 2007 (FAO estimates). Note: No data were available for 2009.

Source: FAO.

Forestry

ROUNDWOOD REMOVALS
('000 cubic metres, excl. bark)

	2007	2008	2009
Sawlogs, veneer logs and logs for sleepers	65.0	47.0	47.0
Fuel wood*	33.8	33.4	33.1
Total	98.8	80.4	80.1

* FAO estimates.
Source: FAO.

SAWNWOOD PRODUCTION
('000 cubic metres, incl. railway sleepers)

	2007*	2008	2009*
Total (all broadleaved)	41	30	30

* FAO estimate.
Source: FAO.

TRINIDAD AND TOBAGO

Fishing

('000 metric tons, live weight of capture)

	2006	2007	2008
Demersal percomorphs	1.9	1.7	2.0
King mackerel	0.7	0.6	1.0
Serra Spanish mackerel	1.8	1.4	1.5
Tuna-like fishes	0.1	0.1	0.2
Sharks, rays, skates, etc.	0.4	0.4	0.3
Other marine fishes	6.1	6.2	6.3
Penaeus shrimps	0.8	0.7	0.8
Total catch (incl. others)	13.1	13.1	13.8

Source: FAO.

Mining

('000 barrels, unless otherwise indicated)

	2007	2008	2009*
Crude petroleum	43,600	43,799	40,821
Natural gas liquids	12,500	12,500	14,400
Natural gas (million cu m)†	41,766	40,000	42,903

* Estimates.
† Figures refer to the gross volume of output.

Source: US Geological Survey.

Industry

SELECTED PRODUCTS
('000 metric tons, unless otherwise indicated)

	2007	2008	2009
Sugar	67	38	28
Beer ('000 litres)	51,770	50,206	50,377
Fertilizers	5,902	5,599	6,168
Methanol	5,933	5,686	6,111
Cement	902	958	870
Iron (direct reduced)	2,063	1,601	1,182
Steel:			
billets	695	490	417
wire rods	510	272	238
Electric energy (million kWh)	7,704.8	7,759.8	7,873.3

Finance

CURRENCY AND EXCHANGE RATES

Monetary Units
100 cents = 1 Trinidad and Tobago dollar (TT $).

Sterling, US Dollar and Euro Equivalents (31 December 2010)
£1 sterling = TT $10.030;
US $1 = TT $6.407;
€1 = TT $8.561;
TT $100 = £10.0 = US $15.61 = €11.68.

Average Exchange Rate (TT $ per US $)
2008 6.2894
2009 6.3249
2010 6.3614

Statistical Survey

CENTRAL GOVERNMENT BUDGET
(TT $ million)

Revenue	2004/05	2005/06	2006/07
Energy sector	13,961.3	21,416.0	20,079.2
Corporation tax	10,805.6	17,614.8	16,206.2
Withholding tax (oil)	429.2	614.3	928.7
Royalties	1,228.5	1,679.3	1,681.0
Unemployment levy	820.4	1,311.3	1,111.0
Oil impost	42.7	65.9	63.9
Excise duties	634.8	130.4	88.4
Non-energy sector	15,677.4	17,490.9	19,955.6
Taxes	13,878.2	15,414.3	17,266.8
Taxes on income	8,141.2	7,922.5	8,888.1
Taxes on property	62.7	64.4	83.7
Taxes on goods and services	4,200.8	5,591.1	6,288.5
Value-added tax	2,962.5	4,184.2	4,829.0
Taxes on international trade	1,473.5	1,836.3	2,006.5
Non-tax revenue of non-oil sector	1,799.1	2,076.6	2,688.8
Capital revenue and grants	9.1	4.0	29.6
Total	29,647.9	38,910.9	40,064.4

Expenditure	2004/05	2005/06	2006/07
Current expenditure	21,842.4	26,582.6	29,984.0
Wages and salaries	5,309.2	5,455.6	6,221.3
Goods and services	3,170.1	3,843.2	4,283.8
Interest payments	2,541.5	2,453.3	2,698.1
Domestic	1,875.5	1,825.5	2,094.0
External	666.0	600.8	604.1
Transfers and subsidies	10,821.6	14,830.4	16,780.8
Households	2,601.2	4,341.2	8,455.9
Loans and grants to statutory boards and state enterprises	2,481.6	3,805.5	4,916.8
Capital expenditure and net lending	2,798.6	4,615.3	7,781.9
Total	24,641.0	31,197.9	37,765.9

2007/08 (TT $ million): *Revenue:* Energy sector 32,444.3; Non-energy sector 24,403.5; Total 56,847.8. *Expenditure:* Current expenditure 35,030.6; Capital expenditure and net lending 9,684.5; Total 44,715.1.

2008/09 (TT $ million): *Revenue:* Energy sector 19,317.8; Non-energy sector 19,727.0; Total 39,044.8. *Expenditure:* Current expenditure 37,316.9; Capital expenditure and net lending 8,413.9; Total 45,730.8.

2009/10 (TT $ million): *Revenue:* Energy sector 22,597.4; Non-energy sector 20,614.5; Total 43,211.9. *Expenditure:* Current expenditure 37,524.7; Capital expenditure and net lending 5,995.4; Total 43,520.1.

2010/11 (TT $ million, budgeted): *Revenue:* Energy sector 19,367.8; Non-energy sector 21,895.2; Total 41,263.0. *Expenditure:* Current expenditure 41,786.3; Capital expenditure and net lending 7,208.9; Total 48,995.2.

INTERNATIONAL RESERVES
(US $ million at 31 December)

	2007	2008	2009
Gold (national valuation)	51.2	52.9	67.9
IMF special drawing rights	0.9	1.1	431.9
Reserve position in IMF	35.4	61.1	94.4
Foreign exchange	6,657.4	9,380.4	8,651.6
Total	6,744.9	9,495.5	9,245.8

2010: IMF special drawing rights 424.3; Reserve position in IMF 111.2.

Source: IMF, *International Financial Statistics*.

MONEY SUPPLY
(TT $ million at 31 December)

	2007	2008	2009
Currency outside banks	3,182.8	3,433.7	3,850.0
Demand deposits at commercial banks	11,083.6	12,399.9	17,413.3
Total money (incl. others)	16,777.2	19,197.2	26,644.1

Source: IMF, *International Financial Statistics*.

TRINIDAD AND TOBAGO

COST OF LIVING
(Retail Price Index; base: January 2003 = 100)

	2008	2009	2010
Food (incl. non-alcoholic beverages)	274.0	308.7	376.8
Clothing	95.8	95.3	94.4
Transport	117.8	125.5	139.8
Housing and utilities	119.8	125.2	125.6
All items (incl. others)	147.9	158.2	174.9

NATIONAL ACCOUNTS
(TT $ million at current prices)

Expenditure on the Gross Domestic Product

	2006	2007	2008*
Government final consumption expenditure	12,801.9	14,328.1	16,665.2
Private final consumption expenditure	56,339.4	65,690.9	68,668.1
Gross capital formation	18,146.0	17,666.0	19,418.0
Total domestic expenditure	87,287.3	97,685.0	104,751.3
Exports of goods and services	79,417.6	88,792.1	111,688.1
Less Imports of goods and services	44,596.9	49,050.5	64,324.1
GDP in purchasers' values	122,108.0	137,426.7	152,115.2

*Provisional.

Gross Domestic Product by Economic Activity
(revised figures)

	2006	2007	2008
Agriculture, hunting, forestry and fishing	657.3	490.5	576.9
Mining and hydrocarbons	54,517.9	56,833.8	78,412.9
Manufacturing	6,444.6	7,494.1	7,642.6
Electricity and water	981.5	1,534.4	1,526.3
Construction	8,576.9	11,711.2	14,069.5
Transport, storage and communication	4,186.4	7,142.5	7,533.5
Distribution	15,081.2	16,925.1	21,140.0
Finance, insurance and real estate	13,351.5	15,561.8	15,494.7
Government	6,987.5	9,038.3	10,132.6
Other services	4,500.9	4,891.6	5,258.5
Sub-total	115,258.7	131,623.3	161,787.5
Less Financial intermediation services indirectly measured	3,658.6	4,677.8	5,090.7
Value-added tax	4,324.1	5,335.3	6,628.1
GDP in purchaser's values	115,951.2	132,280.8	163,324.9

BALANCE OF PAYMENTS
(US $ million)

	2006	2007	2008
Exports of goods f.o.b.	14,217	13,391	18,686
Imports of goods f.o.b.	−6,517	−7,670	−9,622
Trade balance	7,700	5,721	9,064
Exports of services	814	924	936
Imports of services	−363	−377	−326
Balance on goods and services	8,151	6,268	9,674
Other income received	262	267	310
Other paid	−1,198	−1,231	−1,512
Balance on goods, services and income	7,215	5,304	8,472
Current transfers received	105	121	109
Current transfers paid	−49	−61	−62
Current balance	7,271	5,364	8,519
Direct investment abroad	−370	—	−700
Direct investment from abroad	883	830	2,801
Portfolio investment assets	−200	−252	−82
Other investment assets	−1,009	−12	−1,299
Other investment liabilities	−5,222	−4,063	−6,711
Net errors and omissions	−257	−346	203
Overall balance	1,095	1,521	2,732

Source: IMF, *International Financial Statistics*.

External Trade

PRINCIPAL COMMODITIES
(TT $ million)

Imports c.i.f.	2008	2009
Food and live animals	4,224.8	3,806.1
Beverages and tobacco	324.3	340.2
Crude materials except fuels	3,458.9	1,353.3
Mineral fuels and lubricants	20,897.7	14,481.4
Animal and vegetable oils and fats	290.9	207.3
Chemicals	4,851.1	3,442.5
Manufactured goods	8,272.3	5,744.8
Machinery and transport equipment	14,600.4	12,119.5
Miscellaneous manufactured articles	2,941.0	2,383.5
Total (incl. others)	59,914.8	43,935.7

Exports f.o.b.*	2008	2009
Food and live animals	1,279.3	965.0
Beverages and tobacco	999.8	881.2
Crude materials except fuels	3,214.1	1,750.7
Mineral fuels and lubricants	81,746.4	43,744.9
Animal and vegetable oils and fats	10.7	16.2
Chemicals	21,368.5	5,542.3
Manufactured goods	5,285.6	2,702.2
Machinery and transport equipment	2,241.7	1,661.0
Miscellaneous manufactured articles	513.2	441.8
Miscellaneous transactions and commodities	2.7	2.7
Total	116,662.0	57,708.0

*Including ships' stores and bunkers.

PRINCIPAL TRADING PARTNERS
(TT $ million)

Imports c.i.f.	2006	2007	2008
Barbados	204.1	280.5	n.a.
Canada	911.4	1,981.3	1,636.1
Central and South America*	11,040.0	12,695.8	15,719.6
Venezuela	1,755.0	1,887.3	1,445.5
European Free Trade Association (EFTA)	159.3	162.8	228.2
European Union (EU)†	3,241.1	4,353.0	6,603.3
Guyana	117.5	160.5	n.a.
Jamaica	110.2	99.7	n.a.
United Kingdom	1,072.8	1,342.8	1,368.7
USA	11,152.5	12,000.7	14,299.5
Total (incl. others)	40,934.2	48,329.5	60,197.9

Exports f.o.b.‡	2006	2007	2008
Barbados	2,915.2	1,782.6	n.a.
Canada	1,076.0	854.5	1,205.0
Central and South America*	4,370.3	5,558.8	10,216.8
European Free Trade Association (EFTA)	110.0	505.0	136.7
European Union (EU)†	8,357.2	8,560.3	13,271.8
Guyana	2,089.0	1,466.4	n.a.
Jamaica	5,055.0	3,818.6	n.a.
United Kingdom	759.3	1,348.2	2,093.0
USA	50,553.3	47,338.1	51,832.7
Total (incl. others)	88,275.5	83,897.4	115,093.5

*Excluding Belize, French Guiana, Guyana and Suriname.
†Excluding the United Kingdom, listed separately.
‡Excluding ships' stores and bunkers.

2008 (TT $ million, revised figures): Total imports 59,914.8; Total exports 116,662.0.

2009 (TT $ million): Total imports 43,935.7; Total exports 57,708.0.

TRINIDAD AND TOBAGO

Transport

ROAD TRAFFIC
(motor vehicles in use)

	1997	1998	1999
Passenger cars	194,300	213,400	229,400
Commercial vehicles	47,700	51,100	53,900

Source: UN, *Statistical Yearbook*.

Total number of registered vehicles: 441,541 in 2006; 468,255 in 2007; 471,749 in 2008.

SHIPPING
Merchant Fleet
(registered at 31 December)

	2007	2008	2009
Number of vessels	111	119	119
Total displacement ('000 grt)	51.1	54.3	51.7

Source: IHS Fairplay, *World Fleet Statistics*.

International Sea-borne Freight Traffic
(estimates, '000 metric tons)

	1988	1989	1990
Goods loaded	7,736	7,992	9,622
Goods unloaded	4,076	4,091	10,961

Source: UN, *Monthly Bulletin of Statistics*.

1998: Port of Spain handled 3.3m. metric tons of cargo.

CIVIL AVIATION
(traffic on scheduled services)

	2004	2005	2006
Kilometres flown (million)	28	27	27
Passengers carried ('000)	1,132	1,055	1,024
Passenger-km (million)	3,013	3,100	2,976
Total ton-km (million)	314	328	308

Source: UN, *Statistical Yearbook*.

Tourism

FOREIGN TOURIST ARRIVALS

Country of origin	2006	2007	2008
Barbados	31,218	21,491	19,130
Canada	49,242	51,411	53,647
Germany	6,706	5,422	4,838
Grenada	14,814	10,169	9,017
Guyana	23,673	25,668	24,696
Saint Lucia	8,902	6,006	4,992
Saint Vincent and Grenadines	12,288	8,860	7,931
United Kingdom	58,612	58,660	43,051
USA	170,893	180,557	187,515
Venezuela	9,906	12,392	11,908
Total (incl. others)	457,434	449,453	432,551

Tourism receipts (US $ million, incl. passenger transport): 517 in 2006; 621 in 2007; 615 in 2008.

Source: World Tourism Organization.

Total tourist arrivals: 449,863 in 2008; 430,631 in 2009 (estimate).

Communications Media

	2007	2008	2009
Telephones ('000 main lines in use)	307.3	314.8	303.2
Mobile cellular telephones ('000 subscribers)	1,509.8	1,806.1	1,846.3
Internet users ('000)	429.0	464.0	593.0
Broadband subscribers ('000)	35.5	85.4	125.6

Radio receivers ('000 in use): 680 in 1997.
Personal computers: 175,500 in 2007 (132.1 per 1,000 persons).
Daily newspapers: 4 in 1997 (average circulation: 191,000 in 2001); 3 in 2004 (average circulation: 196,000 in 2003).
Non-daily newspapers: 5 in 1997 (average circulation 167,000 in 2001); 7 in 2004 (average circulation: 170,000 in 2003).
Television receivers ('000 in use): 449 in 2001.

Sources: International Telecommunication Union; UN, *Statistical Yearbook*; UNESCO, *Statistical Yearbook*.

Education

(2007/08, unless otherwise indicated)

	Institutions	Teachers	Males	Females	Total
Pre-primary	50*	2,186	15,021	14,564	29,585
Primary	480†	7,628	67,460	63,420	130,880
Secondary	101†	7,045	46,613	48,662	95,275
Tertiary	3‡	1,800§	7,515§	9,405§	16,920§

* Government schools and assisted schools only, in 1992/93.
† 2001/02.
‡ 2003/04; university and equivalent institutions.
§ 2004/05.

Source: UNESCO Institute for Statistics.

Pupil-teacher ratio (primary education, UNESCO estimate): 17.2 in 2007/08 (Source: UNESCO Institute for Statistics).

Adult literacy rate (UNESCO estimates): 98.7% (males 99.1%; females 98.2%) in 2008 (Source: UNESCO Institute for Statistics).

Directory

The Government

HEAD OF STATE

President: Prof. GEORGE MAXWELL RICHARDS (took office 17 March 2003; re-elected by vote of the Electoral College of the Parliament 11 February 2008).

THE CABINET
(May 2011)

The Government is formed by the People's Partnership coalition, comprising the United National Congress, the Congress of the People and the Tobago Organisation of the People.

Prime Minister: KAMLA PERSAD-BISSESSAR.
Minister of Works and Transport: AUSTIN (JACK) WARNER.
Minister of Finance: WINSTON DOOKERAN.
Minister of National Security: Brig. JOHN SANDY.
Minister of Energy and Energy Affairs: CAROLYN SEEPERSAD-BACHAN.
Minister of Foreign Affairs: Dr SURUJRATTAN RAMBACHAN.
Minister of Public Administration: RUDRAWATEE NAN RAMGOOLAM.
Minister of Science, Technology and Tertiary Education: FAZAL KARIM.
Minister of Health: THERESE BAPTISTE-CORNELIS.
Minister of Public Utilities: EMMANUEL GEORGE.
Minister of Food Production: VASANT BHARATH.
Minister of Planning, Economic and Social Restructuring and Gender Affairs: Dr BHOENDRADATT TEWARIE.
Minister of Local Government: CHANDRESH SHARMA.
Minister of Housing and the Environment: Dr ROODAL MOONILAL.
Minister of Trade and Industry: STEPHEN CADIZ.
Minister of Tourism: Dr RUPERT GRIFFITH.
Minister of Justice: HERBERT VOLNEY.
Minister of the People and Social Development: Dr GLENN RAMADHARSINGH.
Minister of Education: Dr TIM GOPEESINGH.
Minister of Community Development: NIZAM BAKSH.
Minister of Legal Affairs: PRAKASH RAMADHAR.
Minister of Labour and Small and Micro Enterprise Development: ERROL MCLEOD.
Minister of Sport and Youth Affairs: ANIL ROBERTS.
Minister of Tobago Development: VERNELLA ALLEYNE TOPPIN.
Minister of the Arts and Culture: WINSTON PETERS.
Minister in the Ministry of Works and Transport: RUDRANATH INDARSINGH.
Minister in the Ministry of Education: CLIFTON DECOTEAU.
Minister in the Ministry of Tourism: DELMON DEXTER-BAKER.
Ministers of State in the Office of the Prime Minister: COLIN JEFFERSON PARTAP, RODGER DOMINIC SAMUEL.
Attorney-General: ANAND RAMLOGAN.

MINISTRIES

Office of the President: President's House, Circular Rd, St Ann's, Port of Spain; tel. 624-1261; fax 625-7950; e-mail presoftt@carib-link.net.

Office of the Prime Minister: Whitehall, 13–15 St Clair Ave, St Clair, Port of Spain; tel. 622-1625; fax 622-0055; e-mail permsec@opm.gov.tt; internet www.opm.gov.tt.

Ministry of the Arts and Culture: Port of Spain.

Ministry of the Attorney-General: Cabildo Chambers, 23–27 St Vincent St, Port of Spain; tel. 623-7010; fax 624-1986; e-mail communication@ag.gov.tt; internet www.ag.gov.tt.

Ministry of Community Development: ALGICO Bldg, cnr Jerningham Ave and Queens Park East, Belmont, Port of Spain; tel. 623-6621; fax 623-6979; e-mail cdcga@tstt.net.tt; internet www.cdcga.gov.tt.

Ministry of Education: 18 Alexandra St, St Clair; tel. 622-2181; fax 622-4892; e-mail mined@tstt.net.tt; internet www.moe.gov.tt.

Ministry of Energy and Energy Affairs: Energy Tower, Levels 22–26, International Waterfront Centre, 1 Wrightson Rd, Port of Spain; tel. 623-6708; fax 625-6878; e-mail info@energy.gov.tt; internet www.energy.gov.tt.

Ministry of Finance: Eric Williams Finance Bldg, Level 18, Independence Sq., Port of Spain; tel. 627-9700; fax 627-5882; e-mail comm.finance@gov.tt; internet www.finance.gov.tt.

Ministry of Food Production: Port of Spain.

Ministry of Foreign Affairs: Tower C, Levels 10–14, Waterfront Complex, 1 Wrightson Rd, Port of Spain; tel. 623-4116; fax 623-5853; e-mail communications@foreign.gov.tt; internet www.foreign.gov.tt.

Ministry of Health: 63 Park St, Port of Spain; tel. 627-0010; fax 623-9528; e-mail suggestions@health.gov.tt; internet www.health.gov.tt.

Ministry of Housing and the Environment: NHA Bldg, 44–46 South Quay, Port of Spain; tel. 623-4663; fax 625-2793; e-mail info@housing.gov.tt; internet www.mphe.gov.tt.

Ministry of Justice: Cabildo Chambers, 23–27 St Vincent St, Port of Spain; tel. 623-7010; fax 625-0470.

Ministry of Labour and Small and Micro Enterprise Development: Level 11, Riverside Plaza, cnr Besson and Piccadilly Sts, Port of Spain; tel. 623-4241; fax 624-4091; e-mail rplan@tstt.net.tt; internet www.labour.gov.tt.

Ministry of Legal Affairs: Registration House, Huggins Bldg, 72–74 South Quay, Port of Spain; tel. 624-1660; fax 625-9803; e-mail info@legalaffairs.gov.tt; internet www.legalaffairs.gov.tt.

Ministry of Local Government: Kent House, Long Circular Rd, Maraval, Port of Spain; tel. 622-1669; fax 628-7283; e-mail localgovminister@gov.tt; internet www.localgov.gov.tt.

Ministry of National Security: Temple Court, 31–33 Abercromby St, Port of Spain; tel. 623-2441; fax 627-8044; e-mail info@mns.gov.tt; internet www.nationalsecurity.gov.tt.

Ministry of the People and Social Development: St Vincent Court, 45A–C, St Vincent St, Port of Spain; tel. 624-5319; fax 625-5258; e-mail thenry@ssd.gov.tt; internet www.socialservices.gov.tt.

Ministry of Planning, Economic and Social Restructuring and Gender Affairs: Port of Spain.

Ministry of Public Administration: National Library Bldg, Level 7, cnr Hart and Abercromby Sts, Port of Spain; tel. 625-6724; fax 623-6027; e-mail communicationsdivision@mpa.gov.tt; internet www.mpa.gov.tt.

Ministry of Public Utilities: Sacred Heart Bldg, 16–18 Sackville St, Port of Spain; tel. 623-4853; fax 625-7003; e-mail cgeorge@mpu.gov.tt; internet www.mpu.gov.tt.

Ministry of Science, Technology and Tertiary Education: Nahous Bldg, Level 3, cnr Agra and Patna Sts, St James; tel. 622-9922; fax 622-7640; e-mail communicationstte@gov.tt; internet www.stte.gov.tt.

Ministry of Sport and Youth Affairs: 12 Abercromby St, Port of Spain; tel. 625-5622; fax 623-0174; internet www.msya.gov.tt.

Ministry of Tobago Development: Port of Spain.

Ministry of Tourism: Clarence House, 127–129 Duke St, Port of Spain; tel. 624-1403; fax 625-3894; e-mail mintourism@tourism.gov.tt; internet www.tourism.gov.tt.

Ministry of Trade and Industry: Nicholas Tower, Levels 11–17, 63–65 Independence Sq., Port of Spain; tel. 623-2931; fax 627-8488; e-mail info@tradeind.gov.tt; internet www.tradeind.gov.tt.

Ministry of Works and Transport: Main Administrative Bldg, cnr Richmond and London Sts, Port of Spain; tel. 625-1225; fax 625-8070; internet www.mowt.gov.tt.

Legislature

PARLIAMENT

Senate

President: TIMOTHY HAMEL-SMITH.

The Senate consists of 31 members appointed by the President of the Republic.

House of Representatives

Speaker: WADE MARK.

TRINIDAD AND TOBAGO

Election, 24 May 2010

Party	Valid votes	% of valid votes cast	Seats
People's Partnership*	432,026	60.03	29
People's National Movement	285,354	39.65	12
Others	2,347	0.32	—
Total†	719,727	100.00	41

* An electoral alliance comprising the United National Congress, the Congress of the People, the Tobago Organisation of the People, the National Joint Action Committee and the Movement for Social Justice.

† In addition, there were 2,595 invalid votes.

TOBAGO HOUSE OF ASSEMBLY

The House is elected for a four-year term of office and consists of 12 elected members and three members selected by the majority party.

Chief Secretary: ORVILLE LONDON.

Election, 19 January 2009

Party	Seats
People's National Movement	8
Tobago Organisation of the People	4
Total	12

Election Commission

Elections and Boundaries Commission (EBC): Scott House, 134–138 Frederick St, Port of Spain; tel. 623-4622; fax 627-7881; e-mail ebc.research@gmail.com; internet www.ebctt.com; Chair. Dr NORBERT J. MASSON; Chief Election Officer HOWARD CAYENNE.

Political Organizations

Congress of the People (COP): 2 Broome St, Woodbrook, cnr Tragarete Rd, Port of Spain; tel. 622-5817; e-mail secretariat@coptnt.com; internet www.coptnt.com; f. 2006; contested the 2010 general election as a mem. of the People's Partnership coalition; Leader WINSTON DOOKERAN; Chair. JOSEPH TONEY.

Democratic Action Congress: Scarborough; f. Jan. 2003 by faction of National Alliance for Reconstruction (q.v.); only active in Tobago; Leader HOCHOY CHARLES.

Democratic National Assembly (DNA): Port of Spain; f. 2006; Chair. DARA HEALY; Leaders Dr KIRK MEIGHOO (Trinidad), COLLIN COKER (Tobago).

Democratic Party of Trinidad and Tobago (DPTT): Port of Spain; f. 2001; Chair. WAYNE RODRIGUES; Leader STEVE ALVAREZ.

Movement for Social Justice: Port of Spain; contested the 2010 general election as a mem. of the People's Partnership coalition; Chair. ERROL MCLEOD.

National Alliance for Reconstruction (NAR): 37 Victoria Sq. South, Port of Spain; tel. 627-6163; fax 627-4627; e-mail alliancehouse37@gmail.com; f. 1983 as a coalition of moderate opposition parties; reorganized as a single party in 1986; Leader Dr CARSON CHARLES; Chair. HILDA GOODIAL.

National Democratic Party (NDP): Port of Spain; f. 2005; Leader MICHAEL SIMS.

National Joint Action Committee (NJAC): Duke St, Port of Spain; tel. 623-5470; e-mail njaccommunications@gmail.com; internet www.njactt.org; f. 1969; contested the 2010 general election as a mem. of the People's Partnership coalition; Leader MAKANDAL DAAGA.

National Transformation Movement (NTM): Port of Spain; f. 2006; Leader LLOYD ELCOCK.

New National Vision (NNV): Port of Spain; Leader FUAD ABU BAKR.

People's National Movement (PNM): Balisier House, 1 Tranquility St, Port of Spain; tel. 625-1533; fax 627-3311; e-mail info@pnmtt.org; internet www.pnm.org.tt; f. 1956; moderate nationalist party; Leader Dr KEITH ROWLEY; Chair. FRANKLIN KHAN.

The Platform of Truth: Tobago; f. 2011; Leader HOCHOY CHARLES.

Tobago Organisation of the People (TOP): Tobago; internet www.toptobago.com; f. 2007; only active in Tobago; contested the 2010 general election as a mem. of the People's Partnership coalition; Leader ASHWORTH JACK.

United National Congress (UNC): Rienzi Complex, 78–81 Southern Main Rd, Couva; tel. 636-8145; e-mail info@unc.org.tt; internet www.unc.org.tt; f. 1988; contested the 2010 general election as a mem. of the People's Partnership coalition; social democratic; Leader KAMLA PERSAD-BISSESSAR; Chair. JACK WARNER.

Diplomatic Representation

EMBASSIES AND HIGH COMMISSIONS IN TRINIDAD AND TOBAGO

Argentina: TATIL Bldg, 4th Floor, 11 Maraval Rd, POB 162; Port of Spain; tel. 628-7557; fax 628-7544; e-mail etrin@mrecic.gov.ar; internet www.trinidadytobago.embajada-argentina.gov.ar; Chargé d'affaires a.i. EDGARDO GARLOTTI.

Brazil: 18 Sweet Briar Rd, St Clair, POB 382, Port of Spain; tel. 622-5779; fax 622-4323; e-mail brasil@tstt.net.tt; internet www.brazilembtt.org; Chargé d'affaires a.i. ALÍRIO DE OLIVEIRA RAMOS.

Canada: Maple House, 3–3A Sweet Briar Rd, St Clair, POB 1246, Port of Spain; tel. 622-6232; fax 628-1830; e-mail pspan@international.gc.ca; internet www.portofspain.gc.ca; High Commissioner KAREN L. MCDONALD.

China, People's Republic: 39 Alexandra St, St Clair, Port of Spain; tel. 622-6976; fax 622-7613; e-mail chinaembtt@mfa.gov.cn; internet tt.chineseembassy.org; Ambassador YANG YOUMING.

Cuba: 92 Tragarete Rd, 2nd Floor, POB 1779, Port of Spain; tel. 622-6075; fax 628-4186; e-mail embacubatrinidad@tstt.net.tt; internet embacu.cubaminrex.cu/trinidadtobagoing; Ambassador HUMBERTO RIVERO ROSARIO.

Dominican Republic: Suite 101, 10B Queen's Park West, Port of Spain; tel. 624-7930; fax 623-7779; e-mail embdomtrinidadytobago@serex.gov.do; Ambassador JOSÉ A. SERULLE RAMIA.

El Salvador: 29 Long Circular Rd, St James, Port of Spain; tel. 628-4454; fax 622-8314; e-mail elsalvadortt@gmail.com; Chargé d'affaires a.i. JOSÉ ROBERTO GARCÍA PRIETO LEMUS.

France: TATIL Bldg, 6th Floor, 11 Maraval Rd, POB 1242, Port of Spain; tel. 622-7447; fax 628-2632; e-mail cad.port-d-espagne-amba@diplomatie.gouv.fr; internet www.ambafrance-tt.org; Ambassador MICHEL TRINQUIER.

Germany: 7–9 Marli St, Newtown, POB 828, Port of Spain; tel. 628-1630; fax 628-5278; e-mail info@ports.diplo.de; internet www.port-of-spain.diplo.de; Ambassador STEFAN SCHLÜTER.

Guatemala: Regents Towers, Apt 701, Westmoorings-by-the-Sea, Westmoorings; tel. and fax 632-7629; e-mail embtrintobago@minex.gob.gt; Ambassador GUISELA ATALIDA GODÍNEZ SAZO.

Holy See: 11 Mary St, St Clair, POB 854, Port of Spain; tel. 622-5009; fax 628-5457; e-mail apnuntt@googlemail.com; Apostolic Nuncio Most Rev. THOMAS EDWARD GULLICKSON (Titular Archbishop of Bomarzo).

India: 6 Victoria Ave, POB 530, Port of Spain; tel. 627-7480; fax 627-6985; e-mail hc@hcipos.org; internet www.hcipos.org; High Commissioner MALAY MISHRA.

Jamaica: 2 Newbold St, St Clair, Port of Spain; tel. 622-4995; fax 628-9043; e-mail jhctnt@tstt.net.tt; High Commissioner SHARON SAUNDERS.

Japan: 5 Hayes St, St Clair, POB 1039, Port of Spain; tel. 628-5991; fax 622-0858; e-mail embassyofjapan@tstt.net.tt; internet www.tt.emb-japan.go.jp; Ambassador TATSUAKI IWATA.

Korea, Republic: 60 Eagle Crescent, Fairways, Maraval, Port of Spain; tel. 622-9081; fax 627-6317; e-mail koremb.tt@gmail.com; internet tto.mofat.go.kr; Ambassador YONG-KYN KWON.

Mexico: 12 Hayes St, St Clair, Port of Spain; tel. 622-1422; fax 628-8488; e-mail info@mexico.tt; internet www.mexico.tt; Ambassador RICARDO VILLANUEVA-HALLAL.

Netherlands: 69–71 Edward St, POB 870, Port of Spain; tel. 625-1210; fax 625-1704; e-mail por@minbuza.nl; internet tt.nlembassy.org; Ambassador LUCITA MOENIRALAM.

Nigeria: 3 Maxwell-Phillip St, St Clair, POB 140, Newtown, Port of Spain; tel. 622-4002; fax 622-7162; e-mail contact@nigerianhighcommission-tt.org; internet www.nigerianhighcommission-tt.org; High Commissioner MUSA JOHN JEN.

Panama: Suite 6, 1A Dere St, Port of Spain; tel. 623-3435; fax 623-3440; e-mail embapatt@wow.net; Ambassador ARLINE GONZÁLEZ COSTA.

South Africa: 4 Scott St, St Claire, POB 7111, Port of Spain; tel. 622-9869; fax 622-7089; e-mail betsie.erasmus@southafrica.org.tt; Chargé d'affaires a.i. KARABO LETLAKA.

TRINIDAD AND TOBAGO

Directory

Spain: TATIL Bldg, 7th Floor, 11 Maraval Rd, Port of Spain; tel. 625-7938; fax 624-4983; e-mail emb.trinidad@mae.es; Ambassador Joaquín de Arístegui.

Suriname: TATIL Bldg, 5th Floor, 11 Maraval Rd, Port of Spain; tel. 628-0704; fax 628-0086; e-mail surinameembassy@tstt.net.tt; Ambassador Fidelia Graand-Galon.

United Kingdom: 19 St Clair Ave, St Clair, POB 778, Port of Spain; tel. 350-0444; fax 350-0425; e-mail generalenquiries.ptofs@fco.gov.uk; internet ukintt.fco.gov.uk; High Commissioner Arthur Snell.

USA: 15 Queen's Park West, POB 752, Port of Spain; tel. 622-6371; fax 822-5905; e-mail ircpos@state.gov; internet trinidad.usembassy.gov; Ambassador Beatrice Wilkinson Welters.

Venezuela: 16 Victoria Ave, POB 1300, Port of Spain; tel. 627-9821; fax 624-2508; e-mail embaveneztt@tstt.net.tt; Ambassador María Eugenia Marcano Casado.

Judicial System

The Chief Justice, who has overall responsibility for the administration of justice in Trinidad and Tobago, is appointed by the President after consultation with the Prime Minister and the Leader of the Opposition. The President appoints and promotes judges on the advice of the Judicial and Legal Service Commission. The Judicial and Legal Service Commission, which comprises the Chief Justice as chairman, the chairman of the Public Service Commission, two former judges and a senior member of the bar, appoints all judicial and legal officers. The Judiciary comprises the higher judiciary (the Supreme Court) and the lower judiciary (the Magistracy). In February 2005 Parliament voted to accept the authority of the Caribbean Court of Justice to settle international trade disputes. The Court was formally inaugurated in Port of Spain on 16 April 2005.

Chief Justice: Ivor Archie.

Supreme Court of Judicature: Knox St, Port of Spain; tel. 623-2417; fax 627-5477; e-mail ttlaw@wow.net; internet www.ttlawcourts.org; the Supreme Court consists of the High Court of Justice and the Court of Appeal. The Supreme Court is housed in three locations: Port of Spain, San Fernando and Tobago. There are 23 Supreme Court Puisne Judges who sit in criminal, civil, and matrimonial divisions; Registrar Evelyn Ann Petersen.

Court of Appeal: The Court of Appeal hears appeals against decisions of the Magistracy and the High Court. Further appeals are directed to the Judicial Committee of the Privy Council of the United Kingdom, sometimes as of right and sometimes with leave of the Court. The Court of Appeal consists of the Chief Justice, who is President, and six other Justices of Appeal.

The Magistracy and High Court of Justice

The Magistracy and the High Court exercise original jurisdiction in civil and criminal matters. The High Court hears indictable criminal matters, family matters where the parties are married, and civil matters involving sums over the petty civil court limit. High Court judges are referred to as either Judges of the High Court or Puisne Judges. The Masters of the High Court, of which there are four, have the jurisdiction of judges in civil chamber courts. The Magistracy (in its petty civil division) deals with civil matters involving sums of less than TT $15,000. It exercises summary jurisdiction in criminal matters and hears preliminary inquiries in indictable matters. The Magistracy, which is divided into 13 districts, consists of a Chief Magistrate, a Deputy Chief Magistrate, 13 Senior Magistrates and 29 Magistrates.

Chief Magistrate: Patrick Mark Wellington (acting), Magistrates' Court, St Vincent St, Port of Spain; tel. 625-2781.

Director of Public Prosecutions: Roger Gaspard.

Religion

CHRISTIANITY

Caribbean Conference of Churches: POB 876, Curepe; tel. 662-2979; fax 662-1303; e-mail ccchq@tstt.net.tt; internet www.ccc-caribe.org; f. 1973; Pres. Rev. Dr Lesley G. Anderson; Gen. Sec. Gerard A. J. Granado.

Christian Council of Trinidad and Tobago: Hayes Court, 21 Maraval Rd, Port of Spain; tel. 637-9329; f. 1967; church unity org. formed by the Roman Catholic, Anglican, Presbyterian, Methodist, African Methodist, Spiritual Baptist and Moravian Churches, the Church of Scotland and the Salvation Army, with the Ethiopian Orthodox Church and the Baptist Union as observers; Pres. The Rt Rev. Calvin Wendell Bess (Anglican Bishop of Trinidad and Tobago); Sec. Grace Steele.

The Anglican Communion

Anglicans are adherents of the Church in the Province of the West Indies, comprising eight dioceses. The Archbishop of the West Indies is the Bishop of Nassau and the Bahamas. According to figures from the latest available census (2000), some 8% of the population are Anglicans.

Bishop of Trinidad and Tobago: Rt Rev. Calvin Wendell Bess, Hayes Court, 21 Maraval Rd, Port of Spain; tel. 622-7387; fax 628-1319; e-mail diocesett@tstt.net.tt; internet www.trinidad.anglican.org.

Protestant Churches

According to the 2000 census, 7% of the population are (Orthodox) Baptists, 7% are Pentecostalists, 4% are Seventh-day Adventists and 3% are Presbyterians.

Baptist Union of Trinidad and Tobago: 104 High St, Princes Town; tel. 655-2291; e-mail baptuni@tstt.net.tt; f. 1816; Pres. Rev. Francis Ivan Baptiste; Gen. Sec. Rev. Anslem Warrick; 24 churches, 3,600 mems.

Presbyterian Church of Trinidad and Tobago: POB 187, Paradise Hill, San Fernando; tel. and fax 652-4829; e-mail pctt@tstt.net.tt; internet www.presbyterianchurchtt.org; f. 1868; Moderator Rt Rev. Elvis Elahie; Gen. Sec. Alvin Seereeram; 40,000 mems.

The Roman Catholic Church

For ecclesiastical purposes, Trinidad and Tobago comprises the single archdiocese of Port of Spain. According to the 2000 census, 26% of the population are Roman Catholics.

Antilles Episcopal Conference: 9A Gray St, Port of Spain; tel. 622-2932; fax 628-3688; e-mail secretariat@aec.org; internet www.aecrc.org; f. 1975; 21 mems from the Caribbean and Central American regions; Pres. Most Rev. Charles Henry Dufour (Archbishop of Kingston, Jamaica—from 16 June 2011).

Archbishop of Port of Spain: Edward Joseph Gilbert, 27 Maraval Rd, Port of Spain; tel. 622-1103; fax 622-1165; e-mail abishop@carib-link.net.

HINDUISM

Hindu immigrants from India first arrived in Trinidad and Tobago in 1845. The vast majority of migrants, who were generally from Uttar Pradesh, were Vishnavite Hindus, who belonged to sects such as the Ramanandi, the Kabir and the Sieunaraini. The majority of Hindus currently subscribe to the doctrine of Sanathan Dharma, which evolved from Ramanandi teaching. According to the 2000 census, 22% of the population are Hindus.

Arya Pratinidhi Sabha of Trinidad Inc (Arya Samaj): Seereeram Memorial Vedic School, Old Southern Main Rd, Montrose Village, Chaguanas; tel. 663-1721; e-mail president@trinidadaryasamaj.org; Pres. Lakhram Vijay Bachan.

Pandits' Parishad (Council of Pandits): Maha Sabha Headquarters, Eastern Main Rd, St Augustine; tel. 645-3240; works towards the co-ordination of temple activities and the standardization of ritual procedure; affiliated to the Maha Sabha; 200 mems.

Sanathan Dharma Maha Sabha of Trinidad and Tobago Inc: Maha Sabha Headquarters, Eastern Main Rd, St Augustine; tel. 645-3240; e-mail mahasabha@ttemail.com; f. 1952; Hindu pressure group and public org.; organizes the provision of Hindu education; Pres. Dr D. Omah Maharajh; Sec. Gen. Satnarayan Maharaj.

ISLAM

According to the 2000 census, 6% of the population are Muslims.

Muslims of Trinidad and Tobago: Port of Spain; Chair. Imtiaz Mohammed.

The Press

DAILIES

Newsday: 23A Chacon St, Port of Spain; tel. 623-2459; fax 657-5008; internet www.newsday.co.tt; f. 1993; CEO and Editor-in-Chief Therese Mills; circ. 2,200,000.

Trinidad Guardian: 22 St Vincent St, POB 122, Port of Spain; tel. 623-8871; fax 625-5702; e-mail letters@ttol.co.tt; internet guardian.co.tt; f. 1917; morning; independent; Editor-in-Chief Anthony Wilson; circ. 52,617.

Trinidad and Tobago Express: 35 Independence Sq., Port of Spain; tel. 623-1711; fax 627-1451; e-mail express@trinidadexpress.com; internet www.trinidadexpress.com; f. 1967; morning; CEO Ken Gordon; Editor Alan Geere; circ. 55,000.

# TRINIDAD AND TOBAGO

PERIODICALS

The Boca: Crews Inn Marina and Boatyard, Village Sq., Chaguaramas; tel. 634-2055; fax 634-2056; e-mail enquiry@boatersenterprise.com; internet www.theboca.com; monthly; magazine of the sailing and boating community; Man. Dir JACK DAUSEND.

The Bomb: Southern Main Rd, Curepe; tel. 645-2744; weekly; Publr SAT MAHARAJ.

Caribbean Beat Magazine: 6 Prospect Ave, Maraval, Port of Spain; tel. 622-3821; fax 628-0639; e-mail info@meppublishers.com; internet www.caribbean-beat.com; f. 1991; 6 a year; distributed by Caribbean Airlines; Publr JEREMY TAYLOR; Editor JUDY RAYMOND.

Catholic News: 31 Independence Sq., Port of Spain; tel. 623-6093; fax 623-9468; e-mail cathnews@trinidad.net; internet www.catholicnews-tt.net; f. 1892; weekly; Editor JUNE JOHNSTON; circ. 16,000.

Economic Bulletin: Eric Williams Plaza, Independence Sq., POB 1250, Port of Spain; tel. 625-4835; fax 627-4696; e-mail info@central-bank.org.tt; internet www.central-bank.org.tt; f. 1950; issued 3 times a year by the Central Bank; Information Man. KAREN CAMPBELL.

Energy Caribbean: 6 Prospect Ave, Maraval, Port of Spain; tel. 622-3821; fax 628-0639; e-mail dchin@meppublishers.com; internet www.meppublishers.com; f. 2002; bi-monthly; Editor DAVID RENWICK.

Showtime: Cnr 9th St and 9th Ave, Barataria; tel. 674-1692; fax 674-3228; circ. 30,000.

Sunday Express: 35 Independence Sq., Port of Spain; tel. 623-1711; fax 627-1451; e-mail express@trinidadexpress.com; internet www.trinidadexpress.com; f. 1967; circ. 51,405.

Sunday Guardian: 22 St Vincent St, POB 122, Port of Spain; tel. 623-8870; fax 625-7211; e-mail esunday@ttol.co.tt; internet www.guardian.co.tt; f. 1917; independent; morning; Editor-in-Chief DOMINIC KALIPERSAD; circ. 48,324.

Sunday Punch: Cnr 9th St and 9th Ave, Barataria; tel. 674-1692; fax 674-3228; weekly; Editor ANTHONY ALEXIS; circ. 40,000.

Tobago News: Milford Rd, Scarborough; tel. 639-5565; fax 625-4480; e-mail ccngroupc@tstt.net.tt; internet www.thetobagonews.com; f. 1985; weekly; Editor COMPTON DELPH.

Trinidad and Tobago Gazette: 2–4 Victoria Ave, Port of Spain; tel. 625-4139; weekly; official govt paper; circ. 3,300.

Trinidad and Tobago Mirror: Cnr 9th St and 9th Ave, Barataria; tel. 674-1692; fax 674-3228; 2 a week; Editors KEN ALI, KEITH SHEPHERD; circ. 35,000.

Tropical Agriculture: Faculty of Agriculture and Natural Sciences, University of the West Indies, St Augustine; tel. and fax 645-3640; e-mail tropicalagri@fans.uwi.tt; f. 1924; journal of the School of Agriculture (fmrly Imperial College of Tropical Agriculture); quarterly; Editor-in-Chief Prof. FRANK A. GUMBS.

Publishers

Caribbean Children's Press: 7 Coronation St, St James; tel. and fax 628-4248; f. 1987; educational publishers for primary schools.

Caribbean Educational Publishers: Gulf View Link Rd, La Romaine; tel. 657-9613; fax 652-5620; e-mail mbscep@tstt.net.tt; Pres. TEDDY MOHAMMED.

Charran Publishing House Ltd: Wrightson Road, POB 126, Port of Spain; tel. 625-9821; fax 623-6597; e-mail charran_pub@yahoo.com; Man. Dir REGINALD CHARRAN.

Lexicon Trinidad Ltd: Lot 87, Frederick Settlement Industrial Estate, Caroni; tel. 662-1863; fax 663-0081; e-mail lexiconadmin@gmail.com; Dir KEN JAIKARANSINGH.

Morton Publishing: 97 Saddle Rd, Maraval; tel. 348-3777; fax 762-9923; e-mail morton@morton-pub.com; internet www.morton-pub.com; f. 1977; educational books; Pres. DOUG MORTON; Dir JULIE MORTON.

Royards Publishing Co: 7A Macoya Industrial Estate, Macoya; tel. 663-6002; fax 663-3616; e-mail royards@aol.com; internet www.royards.com; f. 1984; educational publishers; Dirs CLIFFORD NARINESINGH, DWIGHT NARINESINGH.

Trinidad Publishing Co Ltd: 22–24 St Vincent St, Port of Spain; tel. 623-8870; fax 625-7211; e-mail business@ttol.co.tt; internet guardian.co.tt; f. 1917; Man. Dir GRENFELL KISSOON; Gen. Man. DOUGLAS WILSON.

Directory

Broadcasting and Communications

TELECOMMUNICATIONS

Regulatory Body

Telecommunications Authority of Trinidad and Tobago (TATT): 5 Eighth Ave Ext., off Twelfth St, Barataria; tel. 675-8288; fax 674-1055; e-mail info@tatt.org.tt; internet www.tatt.org.tt; f. 2001 to oversee the liberalization of the telecommunications sector; Chair. SELBY WILSON.

Major Service Providers

bmobile: 52 Jerningham Ave, Belmont; fax 627-1534; e-mail service@tstt.co.tt; internet www.bmobile.co.tt; f. 1991 as TSTT Cellnet; name changed as above 2006; 51% state-owned, 49% by Cable & Wireless (United Kingdom); mobile cellular telephone operator; Vice-Pres. GARY BARROW.

Columbus Communications Trinidad Ltd (CCTL): Nicholas Towers, Ground Floor, Independence Sq., Port of Spain; tel. 223-3569; fax 624-9584; e-mail getflow@columbustrinidad.com; internet www.flowtrinidad.com; f. 2005; digital cable television, internet and local telephone service providers; mobile cellular telephone licence granted in 2006; Pres. and CEO JOHN REID; 250 employees (2007).

Digicel Trinidad and Tobago: Ansa Centre, 11C Maraval Rd, Port of Spain; tel. 628-7000; fax 628-9540; e-mail tt.customer.care@digicelgroup.com; internet www.digiceltrinidadandtobago.com; owned by an Irish consortium; mobile cellular telephone licence granted in 2005; Chair. DENIS O'BRIEN; CEO NIALL DORRIAN.

One Caribbean Media Ltd (OCM): 35 Independence Sq., Port of Spain; tel. 623-1711; fax 627-4886; e-mail tjohnson@trinidadexpress.com; internet www.onecaribbeanmedia.net; f. 2006 by merger of Caribbean Communications Network (CCN) and The Nation Corpn (Barbados); Chair. Sir FRED GOLLOP.

Open Telecom Ltd: 88 Edward St, Port of Spain; tel. 627-6559; e-mail sales@opentelecom.com; internet www.opentelecomtt.com; f. 1992; Chair. PETER GILLETTE; Chief Operations Man. NICHOLAS LOOK HONG.

Telecommunication Services of Trinidad and Tobago (TSTT) Ltd: 1 Edward St, POB 3, Port of Spain; tel. 625-4431; fax 627-0856; e-mail tsttceo@tstt.net.tt; internet www.tstt.co.tt; 51% state-owned, 49% by Cable & Wireless (United Kingdom); 51% privatization pending; CEO ROBERTO PEÓN.

BROADCASTING

Radio

The Caribbean New Media Group (CNMG): 11A Maraval, Port of Spain; tel. 622-4141; fax 622-0344; e-mail webmaster@ctntworld.com; internet www.ctntworld.com; state-owned; operates three radio stations: Talk City 91.1 FM, Next 99.1 FM and Sweet 100.1 FM; and three television channels: 6 (cable), 9 and 13; CEO INGRID ISAAC.

i95.5 FM: 47 Tragarete Rd, New Town, Port of Spain; tel. 628-4955; fax 628-0251; e-mail info@i955fm.com; internet www.i955fm.com; Exec. Chair. and CEO LOUIS LEE SING.

I.S.A.A.C 98.1 FM: 115A Woodford St, Newtown, Port of Spain; tel. 628-0904; fax 628-3108; e-mail info@isaac981.com; internet www.isaac981.com; f. 2002; 24 hour Christian radio station; CEO MARGARET ELCOCK.

Power 102 FM: Radio Vision Ltd, 88–90 Abercromby St, Port of Spain; tel. 627-6937; fax 627-9320; e-mail power102fm@gmail.com; internet www.power102fm.com; CEO O'BRIAN HAYNES; Man. SHARON PITT.

Radio Jaagriti 102.7 FM: Cnr Pasea Main Rd Ext. and Churchill Roosevelt Hwy, Tunapuna; tel. 645-0613; fax 663-8961; e-mail comments@jaagriti.com; internet www.jaagriti.com; f. 2007; Hindu broadcasting network; Man. Dir SAT MAHARAJ; CEO DEVANT MAHARAJ.

Radio Tambrin 92.7: 3 Picton St, Scarborough, Tobago; tel. 639-3437; fax 660-7351; e-mail tambrin@tstt.net.tt; internet www.tambrintobago.com; f. 1998; CEO GEORGE LEACOCK.

Red 96.7: 47 Tragarete Rd, New Town, Port of Spain; tel. 628-4967; fax 628-0251; e-mail info@citadel.co.tt; internet www.red967fm.com; f. 2005; Exec. Chair. and CEO LOUIS LEE SING.

Soca 91.9 FM (Trini Bashment): 56 A, Maraval Rd, Port of Spain; tel. 628-3460; fax 622-7674; e-mail info@soca919.com; internet www.919socafm.com; Man. Dir ANTHONY DEVON GEORGE.

Telemedia Ltd: Long Circular Mall, 4th Floor, Long Circular Rd, St James; tel. 622-4124; fax 622-6693; operates three commercial radio stations: Music Radio 97 FM (www.musicradio97.com), Ebony Radio 104 FM (www.ebony104.com) and Heartbeat 103.5 FM (www.heartbeatradiott.com); Gen. Man. KIRAN MAHARAJ.

TRINIDAD AND TOBAGO

Directory

Trinidad Broadcasting Co Ltd: Guardian Bldg, 2nd Floor, 22–24 St Vincent St, Port of Spain; tel. 623-9202; fax 623-8972; e-mail tbcnews@ttol.co.tt; operates five radio stations: Inspirational Radio 730 AM, Mix 95.1 FM, Vibe CT 105 FM, Sangeet 106 FM and Aakash Vani 106.5 FM; Gen. Man. BRANDON KHAN.

Trinidad and Tobago Radio Network: 153 Tragarete Rd, Port of Spain; tel. 628-6937; internet www.1077musicforlife.com; operates two stations: 96.1 WEFM and 107.7 FM.

Wack Radio 90.1 FM: 129C Coffee St, San Fernando; tel. 652-9774; fax 657-1888; e-mail contact@wackradio901fm.com; internet www.wackradio901fm.com; CEO KENNY PHILLIPS; Man. Dir DIANNE PHILLIPS.

WMJX 100.5 FM: 9 Long Circular Rd, St James; tel. 628-9516; fax 622-2756; e-mail comments@wmjxfm.com; internet www.wmjxfm.com; Gen. Man. KEITH CADET.

Television

ieTV Channel 1: 76 Tragarete Rd, Port of Spain; tel. 622-3541; fax 622-3097; e-mail ietv@tstt.net.tt; internet www.ietv1.com; owned by CL Communications Group; Indian entertainment programming; CEO ANTHONY MAHARAJ.

TV6: 35 Independence Sq., Port of Spain; tel. 627-8806; fax 623-0785; e-mail enquiries@tv6tnt.com; internet www.tv6tnt.com; f. 1991; operates channels 6 and 18; owned by One Caribbean Media Ltd (OCM); Chair. Sir FRED GOLLOP; Gen. Man. SHIDA BOLAI.

Finance

(cap. = capital; res = reserves; dep. = deposits; m. = million; brs = branches; amounts in TT $)

BANKING

Central Bank

Central Bank of Trinidad and Tobago: Eric Williams Plaza, Brian Lara Promenade, POB 1250, Port of Spain; tel. 625-4835; fax 627-4696; e-mail info@central-bank.org.tt; internet www.central-bank.org.tt; f. 1964; cap. 100.0m., res 100.0m., dep. 29,044.2m. (Sept. 2006); Gov. EWART S. WILLIAMS.

Commercial Banks

Citibank (Trinidad and Tobago) Ltd: 12 Queen's Park East, POB 1249, Port of Spain; tel. 625-1046; fax 627-6128; internet www.citicorp.com; f. 1983; fmrly The United Bank of Trinidad and Tobago Ltd; name changed as above 1989; owned by Citicorp Merchant Bank Ltd; cap. 30.0m., res 14.7m., dep. 455.5m. (Dec. 1996); Chair. SURESH MAHARAJ; Country Man. DENNIS EVANS; 2 brs.

Citicorp Merchant Bank Ltd: 12 Queen's Park East, POB 1249, Port of Spain; tel. 623-3344; fax 624-8131; cap. 57.1m., res 28.5m., dep. 473.6m. (Dec. 2002); owned by Citibank Overseas Investment Corpn; Chair. SURESH MAHARAJ; Man. Dir KAREN DARBASIE.

First Citizens Bank Ltd: 9 Queen's Park East, Port of Spain; tel. 624-3178; fax 627-4548; e-mail enquiries@simplyfirst.net; internet www.firstcitizenstt.com; f. 1993 following merger of National Commercial Bank of Trinidad and Tobago Ltd, Trinidad Co-operative Bank Ltd and Workers' Bank of Trinidad and Tobago; state-owned; cap. 340.0m., res 253.4m., dep. 8,472.1m. (Sept. 2006); Chair. SAMUEL A. MARTIN; CEO LARRY HOWAI; 22 brs.

RBTT Ltd: Royal Court, 19–21 Park St, POB 287, Port of Spain; tel. 623-1322; fax 625-3764; e-mail royalinfo@rbtt.co.tt; internet www.rbtt.com; f. 1972 as Royal Bank of Trinidad and Tobago to take over local brs of Royal Bank of Canada; present name adopted April 2002; bought by Royal Bank of Canada in 2007; cap. 404.0m., res 215.4m., dep. 10,083.1m. (March 2006); Chair. PETER J. JULY; CEO SURESH SOOKOO; 21 brs.

Republic Bank Ltd: 9–17 Park St, POB 1153, Port of Spain; tel. 623-1056; fax 624-1323; e-mail email@republictt.com; internet www.republictt.com; f. 1837 as Colonial Bank; became Barclays Bank in 1972; name changed as above 1981; merged with Bank of Commerce Trinidad and Tobago Ltd 1997; cap. 537.1m., res 951.8m., dep. 28,549.4m. (Sept. 2006); Chair. RONALD F. HARFORD; Man. Dir DAVID DULAL-WHITEWAY; 34 brs.

Republic Finance & Merchant Bank Ltd: 9–17 Park St, POB 1153, Port of Spain; tel. 623-1056; fax 624-1323; e-mail email@republictt.com; internet www.republictt.com; f. 1965; owned by Republic Bank Ltd (q.v.); cap. 30.0m., res 44.5m., dep. 1,836.5m. (Sept. 2004); Chair. RONALD F. HARFORD; Man. Dir CHERYL F. GREAVES.

Scotiabank Trinidad and Tobago Ltd: 56–58 Richmond St, POB 621, Port of Spain; tel. 625-3566; fax 627-5278; e-mail scotiamain@tstt.net.tt; internet www.scotiabankt.com; cap. 267.6m., res 301.2m., dep. 9,588.4m. (Oct. 2007); Chair. ROBERT H. PITFIELD; Man. Dir RICHARD P. YOUNG; 23 brs.

Development Banks

Agricultural Development Bank of Trinidad and Tobago: 87 Henry St, POB 154, Port of Spain; tel. 623-6261; fax 624-3087; e-mail adbceo@tstt.net.tt; f. 1968; provides long-, medium- and short-term loans to farmers and the agri-business sector; Chair. NOEL GARCIA; CEO JACQUELINE RAWLINS.

DFL Caribbean: 10 Cipriani Blvd, POB 187, Port of Spain; tel. 623-4665; fax 624-3563; e-mail dfl@dflcaribbean.com; internet www.dflcaribbean.com; provides short- and long-term finance, and equity financing for projects in manufacturing, agro-processing, tourism, industrial and commercial enterprises; total assets US $84.2m. (Dec. 1998); Chair. AUDLEY WALKER; Man. Dir GERARD M. PEMBERTON.

Credit Unions

Co-operative Credit Union League of Trinidad and Tobago Ltd: 32–34 Maraval Rd, St Clair; tel. 645-6943; fax 645-3130; e-mail culeague@tstt.net.tt; internet www.ccultt.org; Pres. BRIAN MOORE; Chair. CALVIN MOSES.

STOCK EXCHANGE

Trinidad and Tobago Stock Exchange Ltd: Nicholas Tower, 10th Floor, 63–65 Independence Sq., Port of Spain; tel. 625-5107; fax 623-0089; e-mail ttstockx@stockex.co.tt; internet www.stockex.co.tt; f. 1981; 26 cos listed (2011); electronic depository system came into operation in 2003; Chair. ANDREW MCEACHRANE; CEO C. WAINWRIGHT ITON.

INSURANCE

American Life and General Insurance Co (Trinidad and Tobago) Ltd: ALGICO Plaza, 91–93 St Vincent St, POB 943, Port of Spain; tel. 625-4425; fax 623-6218; e-mail algico@wow.net; Man. Dir GORDON DEANE.

Bankers Insurance Co of Trinidad and Tobago Ltd: 5 Mulchan Seuchan Rd, Chaguanas; tel. 672-1057; fax 672-2808; e-mail joan@bankers-tt.com; Man. Dir ZAMANATH ALI.

Barbados Mutual Life Assurance Society: The Mutual Centre, 16 Queen's Park West, POB 356, Port of Spain; tel. 628-1636; Gen. Man. HUGH MAZELY.

Capital Insurance Ltd: 38–42 Cipero St, San Fernando; tel. 657-8077; fax 652-7306; f. 1958; motor and fire insurance; 10 brs and 9 agencies.

CUNA Caribbean Insurance Society Ltd: 37 Wrightson Rd, POB 193, Port of Spain; tel. 623-7963; fax 623-6251; e-mail cunains@trinidad.net; internet www.cunacaribbean.com; f. 1991; marine aviation and transport; motor vehicle, personal accident, property; Gen. Man. ANTHONY HALL; 3 brs.

Furness Anchorage General Insurance Ltd: 11–13 Milling Ave, Sea Lots, POB 283, Port of Spain; tel. 623-0868; fax 625-1243; e-mail furness@wow.net; internet www.furnessgroup.com; f. 1979; general; Chair. IGNATIUS SEVEIRANO FERREIRA; Exec. Chair. WILLIAM A. FERREIRA.

GTM Fire Insurance Co Ltd: 95–97 Queen St, Port of Spain; tel. 623-1525; e-mail gtmis@tstt.net.tt.

Guardian General Insurance Ltd: Princes Court, Keate St, Port of Spain; tel. 623-4741; fax 623-4320; e-mail info@guardiangenerallimited.com; internet www.guardiangenerallimited.com; founded by merger of NEMWIL and Caribbean Home; Chair. HENRY PETER GANTEAUME; CEO RICHARD ESPINET.

Guardian Life of the Caribbean: 1 Guardian Dr., West Moorings, Port of Spain; tel. 625-5433; internet www.guardianlife.co.tt; Chair. ARTHUR LOK JACK; Pres. and CEO DOUGLAS CAMACHO.

Gulf Insurance Ltd: 1 Gray St, St Clair, Port of Spain; tel. 622-5878; fax 628-0272; e-mail info@gulfinsuranceltd.com; internet www.gulfinsuranceltd.com; f. 1974; general; Exec. Chair. GERRARD LEE-INNISS.

Maritime Financial Group: Maritime Centre, 10th Ave, POB 710, Barataria; tel. 674-0130; fax 638-6663; f. 1978; property and casualty; CEO JOHN SMITH.

Motor and General Insurance Co Ltd: 1–3 Havelock St, St Clair, Port of Spain; tel. 622-2637; fax 622-5345.

New India Assurance Co (T & T) Ltd: 22 St Vincent St, Port of Spain; tel. 623-1326; fax 625-0670; e-mail newindia@wow.net; tel. www.newindia.co.in.

Presidential Insurance Co Ltd: 54 Richmond St, Port of Spain; tel. 625-4788; e-mail pic101@tstt.net.tt.

Trinidad and Tobago Export Credit Insurance Co Ltd: 30 Queen's Park West, Port of Spain; tel. and fax 628-2762; e-mail

TRINIDAD AND TOBAGO

eximbank@wow.net; internet www.eximbankt.com; state-owned; CEO Brian Awang; Gen. Man. Josephine Ible.

Trinidad and Tobago Insurance Ltd (TATIL): 11 Maraval Rd, POB 1004, Port of Spain; tel. 622-5351; fax 628-0035; e-mail info@tatil.co.tt; internet www.tatil.co.tt; acquired by ANSA McAL in 2004; Chair. John Jardim; CEO Relna Vire.

United Insurance Co: 30 O'Connor St, Woodbrook, Port of Spain; tel. 628-8343; fax 628-6575; e-mail trinidad@unitedinsure.com; internet unitedinsure.com; 95.0% owned by Barbados Shipping and Trading Co; Gen. Man. Dennis Benisar.

INSURANCE ORGANIZATIONS

Association of Trinidad and Tobago Insurance Companies: 28 Sackville St, Port of Spain; tel. 624-2817; fax 625-5132; e-mail jsc-attic@trinidad.net; internet www.attic.org.tt; Chair. Inez Sinanan.

National Insurance Board: Cipriani Pl., 2A Cipriani Blvd, Port of Spain; tel. 625-2171; fax 627-1787; e-mail nib@nibtt.co.tt; internet www.nibtt.co.tt; f. 1971; statutory corpn; Chair. Calder Hart; Exec. Dir Jeffrey McFarlane.

Trade and Industry

GOVERNMENT AGENCIES

Cocoa and Coffee Industry Board: 27 Frederick St, POB 1, Port of Spain; tel. 625-0298; fax 627-4172; e-mail ccib@tstt.net.tt; f. 1962; marketing of coffee and cocoa beans, regulation of cocoa and coffee industry; Man. Barry Joefield.

Export-Import Bank of Trinidad and Tobago Ltd (EXIM-BANK): 30 Queen's Park West, Port of Spain; tel. 628-2762; fax 622-3545; e-mail eximbank@wow.net; internet www.eximbankt.com; Chair. Clarry Benn; CEO Brian Awang.

Trinidad and Tobago Forest Products Ltd (TANTEAK): Connector Rd, Carlsen Field, Chaguanas; tel. 665-0078; fax 665-6645; f. 1975; harvesting, processing and marketing of state plantation-grown teak and pine; privatization pending; Chair. Ruskin Punch; Man. Dir Clarence Bacchus.

DEVELOPMENT ORGANIZATIONS

National Energy Corporation of Trinidad and Tobago Ltd: PLIPDECO House, Orinoco Dr., POB 191, Point Lisas, Couva; tel. 636-4662; fax 679-2384; e-mail infocent@carib-link.net; internet www.ngc.co.tt; owned by the Nat. Gas Co of Trinidad and Tobago Ltd (q.v.); f. 1979; Chair. Kenneth Birchwood; Pres. Frank Look Kin.

National Housing Authority: 44–46 South Quay, POB 555, Port of Spain; tel. 627-1703; fax 625-3963; e-mail info@housing.gov.tt; internet www.housing.gov.tt; f. 1962; Chair. Andre Monyeil; CEO Noel Garcia.

Point Lisas Industrial Port Development Corporation Ltd (PLIPDECO): PLIPDECO House, Orinoco Dr., POB 191, Point Lisas, Couva; tel. 636-2201; fax 636-4008; e-mail plipdeco@plipdeco.com; internet www.plipdeco.com; f. 1966; privatized in the late 1990s; deep-water port handling general cargo, liquid and dry bulk, to serve adjacent industrial estate, which now includes iron and steel complex, methanol, ammonia, urea and related downstream industries; Chair. Commdr Kayam Mohammed; Pres. Roger Traboulay.

CHAMBERS OF COMMERCE

The Energy Chamber of Trinidad and Tobago: Suite B2.03, Atlantic Plaza, Atlantic Ave, Point Lisas; tel. 652-5613; fax 653-4983; e-mail execoffice@energy.tt; internet www.energy.tt; f. 1956; Pres. Charles Percy; CEO Dr Thackwray Driver.

Trinidad and Tobago Chamber of Industry and Commerce (Inc): Chamber Bldg, Columbus Circle, Westmoorings, POB 499, Port of Spain; tel. 637-6966; fax 637-7425; e-mail chamber@chamber.org.tt; internet www.chamber.org.tt; f. 1891; Pres. Ian Welch; CEO Joan Ferreira; 600 mems.

INDUSTRIAL AND TRADE ASSOCIATIONS

Agricultural Society of Trinidad and Tobago: 52 Penco St, Penco Court, Lange Park, Chaguanas; e-mail agrisocietytt@gmail.com; f. 1839; represents farmers' interests; Pres. Dhano Sookoo.

Coconut Growers' Association (CGA) Ltd: Eastern Main Rd, POB 229, Laventille, Port of Spain; tel. 623-5207; fax 623-2359; e-mail cgaltd@tstt.net.tt; f. 1936; 354 mems; Exec. Chair. Philippe Agostini.

Co-operative Citrus Growers' Association of Trinidad and Tobago Ltd: Eastern Main Rd, POB 174, Laventille, Port of Spain; tel. 623-5127; fax 623-2487; e-mail ccga@wow.net; f. 1932; Gen. Man. Gary Prentice; 437 mems.

Pan Trinbago Inc: Victoria Park Suites, 14–17 Park St, Port of Spain; tel. 623-4486; fax 625-6715; e-mail admin@pantrinbago.co.tt; internet www.pantrinbago.co.tt; f. 1971; official body for Trinidad and Tobago steelbands; Pres. Keith Diaz; Sec. Richard Forteau.

Sugar Association of the Caribbean: Brechin Castle, Couva; tel. 636-2449; fax 636-2847; f. 1942; promotes and protects sugar industry in the Caribbean; Chair. Karl James; 6 mem. asscns.

Trinidad and Tobago Contractors' Association: The Professional Centre, Unit B 203, 11–13 Fitzblackman Dr., Wrightson Rd Extension, Port of Spain; tel. 627-1266; fax 623-2949; e-mail ttcaservice@rave-tt.net; internet www.ttca.com; f. 1968; represents contractors, manufacturers and suppliers to the sector; Pres. Mikey Joseph.

Trinidad and Tobago Manufacturers' Association: 1TTMA Bldg, 42 Tenth Ave, Barataria; tel. 675-8862; fax 675-9000; e-mail info@ttma.com; internet www.ttma.com; f. 1956; Pres. Karen de Montbrun; 260 mems.

EMPLOYERS' ORGANIZATION

Employers' Consultative Association of Trinidad and Tobago (ECA): 23 Chacon St, Port of Spain; tel. 625-4723; fax 625-4891; e-mail ecatt@tstt.net.tt; internet www.ecatt.org; f. 1959; Chair. Clarence Rambharat; CEO Linda Besson; 500 mems.

STATE HYDROCARBONS COMPANIES

National Gas Co of Trinidad and Tobago Ltd (NGC): Orinoco Dr., Point Lisas Industrial Estate, POB 1127, Port of Spain; tel. 636-4662; fax 679-2384; e-mail ngc@ngc.co.tt; internet www.ngc.co.tt; f. 1975; purchases, sells, compresses, transmits and distributes natural gas to consumers; Chair. Keith Awong; Pres. S. Andrew McIntosh.

Petroleum Co of Trinidad and Tobago Ltd (Petrotrin): Petrotrin Administration Bldg, Southern Main Rd, Pointe-à-Pierre; tel. 658-3336; fax 658-2513; e-mail ken.allum@petrotrin.com; internet www.petrotrin.com; f. 1993 following merger between Trinidad and Tobago Oil Co Ltd (Trintoc) and Trinidad and Tobago Petroleum Co Ltd (Trintopec); govt-owned; petroleum and gas exploration and production; operates refineries and a manufacturing complex, producing a variety of petroleum and petrochemical products; Chair. Lindsay Gillette; Pres. Kenneth Allum.

Petrotrin Trinmar Operations: Petrotrin Administration Bldg, Point Fortin; tel. 648-2127; fax 648-2519; f. 1962; owned by Petrotrin; marine petroleum and natural gas co; Gen. Man. Allan Russell; 705 employees.

Trintomar Ltd: Petrotrin Administration Bldg, Pointe-à-Pierre; tel. 647-8861; fax 647-3193; e-mail lisle.ramyad@petrotrin.com; f. 1988; 80% owned by EOG Resources, 20% owned by NGC; develops offshore petroleum sector; Man. Lisle Ramyad.

UTILITIES

Regulatory Authority

Regulated Industries Commission: Furness House, 90 Independence Sq., Port of Spain; tel. 625-5384; fax 624-2027; e-mail complaints@ric.org.tt; internet www.ric.org.tt; Chair. Ian Welch; Exec. Dir Harjinder S. Atwal.

Electricity

Power Generation Co of Trinidad and Tobago (PowerGen): 6A Queen's Park West, Port of Spain; tel. 624-0383; fax 625-3759; f. 1994; 19.5% owned by Taqa (Saudi Arabia), which it planned to sell in 2011; operates 3 generation plants in Point Lisas, Port of Spain and Penal; Gen. Man. Garth Chatoor.

Trinidad and Tobago Electricity Commission (T&TEC): 63 Frederick St, Port of Spain; tel. 623-2611; fax 623-3759; e-mail comments@ttec.co.tt; internet www.ttec.co.tt; state-owned electricity transmission and distribution co; Chair. Prof. Clement Imbert; Gen. Man. Indarjit Singh.

Trinity Power Ltd: Railway Rd, Dow Village, Couva; tel. 679-4542; fax 679-4463; e-mail gthompson@trinitypm.com; f. 1999; fmrly Inncogen Ltd; owned by Trinidad Generation Unlimited; Gen. Man. Jacqueline Look Loy.

Gas

National Gas Co of Trinidad and Tobago Ltd: see State Hydrocarbons Companies.

Water

Water and Sewerage Authority (WASA): Farm Rd, St Joseph; tel. 662-2302; fax 652-1253; e-mail contact@wasa.gov.tt; internet www.wasa.gov.tt; Chair. Dr Rollin Bertrand; CEO Errol Grimes.

TRINIDAD AND TOBAGO — Directory

TRADE UNIONS

Federation of Independent Trade Unions and NGOs (FITUN): Paramount Bldg, 99A Circular Rd, San Fernando; tel. 652-2701; fax 652-7170; e-mail fitun_tt@yahoo.com; f. 2003; Pres. DAVID ABDULLAH; Gen. Sec. MORTON MITCHELL.

National Trade Union Centre (NATUC): 16 New St, Port of Spain; tel. 625-3023; fax 627-7588; e-mail natuc@carib-link.net; f. 1991 as umbrella org. unifying entire trade union movt, incl. fmr Trinidad and Tobago Labour Congress and Council of Progressive Trade Unions; Pres. ROBERT GIUSEPPI; Gen. Sec. VINCENT CARBERA.

Principal Affiliates

Airline Superintendents' Association: c/o Data Centre Bldg, Piarco Int. Airport, Port of Spain; tel. 664-3401; fax 664-3303; Pres. JEFFERSON JOSEPH; Gen. Sec. THEO OLIVER.

All-Trinidad Sugar and General Workers' Trade Union (ATSGWTU): Rienzi Complex, Exchange Village, Southern Main Rd, Couva; tel. 636-2354; fax 636-3372; e-mail atsgwtu@tstt.net.tt; f. 1937; Pres. RUDRANATH INDARSINGH; Gen. Sec. SYLVESTER MARAJH; 2,000 mems.

Amalgamated Workers' Union: 16 New St, Port of Spain; tel. 627-6717; fax 627-8993; f. 1953; Pres.-Gen. CYRIL LOPEZ; Sec. FLAVIUS NURSE; c. 7,000 mems.

Association of Technical, Administrative and Supervisory Staff: Brechin Castle, Couva; Pres. Dr WALLY DES VIGNES; Gen. Sec. ISAAC BEEPATH.

Aviation, Communication and Allied Workers' Union: Aero Services Bldg, Orange Grove Rd, Tacarigua; tel. and fax 640-6518; f. 1982; Pres. CHRISTOPHER ABRAHAM; Gen. Sec. SIEUNARINE BALROOP.

Banking, Insurance and General Workers' Union: 85 Eight St, Barataria, Port of Spain; tel. 675-9135; fax 675-4664; e-mail union@bigwu.org; internet www.bigwu.org; f. 1974 as Bank and General Workers' Union; name changed as above following merger with Bank Employees' Union in 2003; Pres. VINCENT CABRERA; Gen. Sec. TREVOR JOHNSON.

Communication, Transport and General Workers' Trade Union: Aero Services Credit Union Bldg, Orange Grove Rd, Tacarigua; tel. and fax 640-8785; e-mail cattu@tstt.net.tt; Pres. JAGDEO JAGROOP; Gen. Sec. RAYMOND SMALL.

Communication Workers' Union: 146 Henry St, Port of Spain; tel. 623-5588; fax 625-3308; e-mail cwutdad@tstt.net.tt; f. 1953; Pres. PATRICK HALL; Gen. Sec. LYLE TOWNSEND; c. 2,100 mems.

Contractors and General Workers' Trade Union (CAGWTU): 37 Rushworth St, San Fernando; tel. 657-8072; fax 657-6834; e-mail cgtwunion@gmail.com; Pres.-Gen. AYNSLEY MATTHEWS; Vice-Pres. JOSEPH PHILLIP.

Customs and Excise Extra Guard Association: Nicholas Court, Abercromby St, Port of Spain; tel. 625-3311; Pres. ALEXANDER BABB; Gen. Sec. NATHAN HERBERT.

Trinidad and Tobago Fire Service Association (Second Division) (FSA): 127 Edward St, Port of Spain; tel. 627-6700; fax 627-6701; e-mail fsa2@tstt.net.tt; Pres. CHARLES RAMSARROP; Sec. SHARON NICHOLSON-CHARLES.

National General Workers' Union: c/o 143 Charlotte St, Port of Spain; tel. 623-0694; Pres. JIMMY SINGH; Gen. Sec. CHRISTOPHER ABRAHAM.

National Union of Domestic Employees (NUDE): 53 Wattley Circular Rd, Mount Pleasant Rd, Arima; tel. 667-5247; fax 664-0546; e-mail domestic@tstt.net.tt; f. 1982; Gen. Sec. IDA LE BLANC.

National Union of Government and Federated Workers: 145–147 Henry St, Port of Spain; tel. 623-4591; fax 625-7756; e-mail headoffice@nugfw.org.tt; internet nugfw.org.tt; f. 1937; Pres.-Gen. ROBERT GUISEPPI; Gen. Sec. JACQUELINE JACK; c. 20,000 mems.

Oilfield Workers' Trade Union (OWTU): Paramount Bldg, 99A Circular Rd, San Fernando; tel. 652-2701; fax 652-7170; e-mail owtu@owtu.org; internet www.owtu.org; f. 1937; Pres. ANCEL ROGET; Gen. Sec. DAVID ABDULLAH; 9,000 mems.

Public Services Association: 89–91 Abercromby St, POB 353, Port of Spain; tel. 623-7987; fax 627-2980; e-mail psa@tstt.net.tt; f. 1938; Pres. WATSON DUKE; Sec. KAREN FERREIRA; c. 15,000 mems.

Seamen and Waterfront Workers' Trade Union: 1D Wrightson Rd, Port of Spain; tel. 625-1351; fax 625-1182; e-mail swwtu@tstt.net.tt; f. 1937; Pres.-Gen. MICHAEL ANNISETTE; Sec.-Gen. ROSS ALEXANDER; c. 3,000 mems.

Steel Workers' Union of Trinidad and Tobago: c/o ISPAT, Point Lisas, Couva; tel. 679-4666; fax 679-4175; e-mail swutt@tstt.net.tt; Pres. LEX LOVELL; Gen. Sec. PHILIP SANCHO.

Transport and Industrial Workers' Union: 114 Eastern Main Rd, Laventille, Port of Spain; tel. 623-4943; fax 623-2361; e-mail tiwu@tstt.net.tt; f. 1962; Pres. ROLAND SUTHERLAND; Gen. Sec. JUDY CHARLES; c. 5,000 mems.

Trinidad and Tobago Airline Pilots' Association (TTALPA): 35A Brunton Rd, St James; tel. 628-6556; fax 628-2418; e-mail info@ttalpa.org; internet www.ttalpa.org; Chair. Capt. ANTHONY WIGHT; Man. CHRISTINE DAVIS.

Trinidad and Tobago Postal Workers' Union: c/o General Post Office, Wrightson Rd, POB 692, Port of Spain; tel. 625-2121; fax 642-4303; Pres. (vacant); Gen. Sec. EVERALD SAMUEL.

Trinidad and Tobago Unified Teachers' Association: Cnr Fowler and Southern Main Rd, Curepe; tel. 645-2134; fax 662-1813; e-mail generalsecretary@ttuta.org; Pres. ROUSTAN JOB; Gen. Sec. PETER WILSON.

Union of Commercial and Industrial Workers: TIWU Bldg, 114 Eastern Main Rd, POB 460, Port of Spain; tel. and fax 626-2285; f. 1951; Pres. KELVIN GONZALES; Gen. Sec. ROSALIE FRASER; c. 1,500 mems.

Transport

RAILWAYS

In 2005 the Ministry of Works and Transport announced plans to reintroduce a railway service, which had been discontinued in 1968. The design phase of the project began in 2008 and construction was expected to take 10–15 years, costing an estimated TT $15,000m.

ROADS

In 2001 there were 8,320 km (5,170 miles) of roads in Trinidad and Tobago, of which 51.1% were paved. In 2005 the US Agency for International Development allocated US $3.2m. to fund the repair of roads damaged by Hurricane Ivan in 2004.

Public Transport Service Corporation: 60 Railway Bldg, South Quay, POB 391, Port of Spain; tel. 623-2341; fax 625-6502; e-mail ptscpos@ptsc.co.tt; internet www.ptsc.co.tt; f. 1965; national bus services, operates a fleet of buses; Chair. DEVANT MAHARAJ.

SHIPPING

The chief ports are Port of Spain, Pointe-à-Pierre and Point Lisas in Trinidad and Scarborough in Tobago. Port of Spain handles 85% of all container traffic, and all international cruise arrivals. Port of Spain and Scarborough each have a deep-water wharf. Port of Spain possesses a dedicated container terminal, with two large overhead cranes.

Point Lisas Industrial Port Development Corporation Ltd (PLIPDECO): see Trade and Industry—Development Organizations.

Port Authority of Trinidad and Tobago: Dock Rd, POB 549, Port of Spain; tel. 623-2901; fax 627-2666; e-mail vilmal@patnt.com; internet www.patnt.com; f. 1962; Chair. CLIVE SPENCER; CEO CHRISTOPHER MENDEZ.

Shipping Association of Trinidad and Tobago: 15 Scott Bushe St, Port of Spain; tel. 623-3355; fax 623-8570; e-mail satt@wow.net; internet shipping.co.tt; f. 1938; Pres. RHETT CHEE PING; Gen. Man. E. JOANNE EDWARDS-ALLEYNE.

CIVIL AVIATION

Piarco International Airport is situated 25.7 km (16 miles) south-east of Port of Spain and is used by numerous airlines. The airport was expanded and a new terminal was constructed in 2001. Piarco remains the principal air transportation facility in Trinidad and Tobago. However, following extensive aerodrome development at Crown Point Airport (located 13 km from Scarborough) in 1992 the airport was opened to jet aircraft. It is now officially named Crown Point International Airport. There is a domestic service between Trinidad and Tobago.

Airports Authority of Trinidad and Tobago (AATT): Airport Administration Centre, Piarco Int. Airport, South Terminal, Golden Grove Rd, Piarco; tel. 669-5311; fax 669-2319; e-mail aatt@tntairports.com; internet www.tntairports.com; administers Piarco and Crown Point International Airports; Chair. Capt. VARMAN BAJNATH; Gen. Man. LOUIS J. FREDERICK.

Caribbean Airlines: Sunjet House, 30 Edward St, Port of Spain; tel. 625-7200; e-mail mail@caribbean-airlines.com; internet www.caribbean-airlines.com; f. 2007 as successor to BWIA (f. 1940); operates scheduled passenger and cargo services linking destinations in the Caribbean region, South America, North America and Europe; CEO ROBERT CORBIE; Chair. GEORGE M. NICHOLAS, III.

Tourism

The climate and coastline attract visitors to Trinidad and Tobago. The latter island is generally believed to be the more beautiful and is

TRINIDAD AND TOBAGO

less developed. The annual pre-Lenten carnival is a major attraction. Total tourist arrivals numbered an estimated 430,631 in 2009. Tourism receipts were estimated at US $615m. in 2008. There were 3,815 hotel rooms in Trinidad and Tobago in 2008, of which 57.5% were on Tobago.

Tourism Development Co of Trinidad and Tobago (TDC): Maritime Centre, Level 1, 29 Tenth Ave, Barataria; tel. 675-7034; fax 675-7722; e-mail info@tdc.co.tt; internet www.tdc.co.tt; f. 1993 as Tourism and Industrial Devt Co of Trinidad and Tobago; restructured and renamed as above in 2005; Chair. DAVID LEWIS; Pres. ERNEST M. LITTLES.

Trinidad Hotels, Restaurants and Tourism Association (THRTA): c/o Trinidad & Tobago Hospitality and Tourism Institute, Airway Rd, Chaguaramas; tel. 634-1174; fax 634-1176; e-mail info@tnthotels.com; internet www.tnthotels.com; Pres. KEVIN KENNY; Exec. Dir GREER ASSAM.

Tobago Hotel and Tourism Association: Apt 1, Lambeau Credit Union Bldg, Auchenskeoch, Carnbee; tel. and fax 639-9543; e-mail tthtatob@tstt.net.tt; Pres. CAROL ANN BIRCHWOOD-JAMES.

Defence

As assessed at November 2010, the Trinidad and Tobago Defence Force consisted of an army of an estimated 3,000 men and a coastguard of 1,063. Included in the coastguard was an air wing of 50.

Defence Budget: TT $1,120m. (US $177m.) in 2011.

Chief of Defence Staff: Col KENRICK MAHARAJ (acting).

Education

Primary and secondary education is provided free of charge. Many schools are run jointly by state and religious bodies. Attendance at school is officially compulsory for children between five and 12 years of age. Primary education begins at the age of five and lasts for seven years. In 2008 some 92% of children in this age group (males 92%; females 91%) were enrolled at primary schools. Secondary education, beginning at 12 years of age, lasts for up to five years, comprising a first cycle of three years and a second of two years. The ratio for secondary enrolment in 2008 was 74% of those in the relevant agegroup (males 71%; females 76%), according to UNESCO estimates. Entrance to secondary schools is determined by the Common Entrance Examination.

Free tertiary tuition was introduced in 2006. The Trinidad campus of the University of the West Indies (UWI), at St Augustine, offers undergraduate and postgraduate programmes and includes an engineering faculty. The UWI Institute of Business offers postgraduate courses and develops programmes for local companies. Other institutions of higher education are the Eric Williams Medical Sciences Complex, the Polytechnic Institute and the Eastern Caribbean Institute of Agriculture and Forestry. In the late 1990s the Government established the Trinidad and Tobago Institute of Technology and the College of Science, Technology and Applied Arts of Trinidad and Tobago. The University of Trinidad and Tobago was established in 2004. The country has one teacher-training college and three government technical institutes and vocational centres, including the Trinidad and Tobago Hotel School. Budgeted expenditure on education by the central Government in 2009 was TT $7,121.6m., equivalent to some 14.4% of total government expenditure.

TUNISIA

Introductory Survey

LOCATION, CLIMATE, LANGUAGE, RELIGION, FLAG, CAPITAL

The Republic of Tunisia lies in north Africa, bordered by Algeria to the west and by Libya to the south-east. To the north and east, Tunisia has a coastline on the Mediterranean Sea. The climate is temperate on the coast, with winter rain, but hot and dry inland. Temperatures in Tunis are generally between 6°C (43°F) and 33°C (91°F). The country's highest recorded temperature is 55°C. Average annual rainfall is up to 1,500 mm in the north, but less than 200 mm in the southern desert. The official language is Arabic, and there is a small Berber Tamazight-speaking minority. French is widely used as a second language. Islam is the state religion, and almost all of the inhabitants are Muslims. There are small minorities of Christians and Jews. The national flag (proportions 2 by 3) is red, with a white disc, containing a red crescent moon and a five-pointed red star, in the centre. The capital is Tunis.

CONTEMPORARY POLITICAL HISTORY

Historical Context

Formerly a French protectorate, Tunisia was granted internal self-government by France in September 1955 and full independence on 20 March 1956. Five days later elections were held for a Constitutional Assembly, which met in April and appointed Habib Bourguiba as Prime Minister in a Government dominated by members of his Néo-Destour (New Constitution) Party. In July 1957 a republic was established, with Bourguiba as Head of State, and a new Constitution was promulgated in June 1959. At elections held in November, Bourguiba was elected unopposed to the new office of President, and the Néo-Destour Party won all 90 seats in the new National Assembly.

By 1964 the Néo-Destour Party had become the only legal political organization, and in November of that year it was renamed the Parti socialiste destourien (PSD). A moderate socialist economic programme was introduced, which began with the expropriation of foreign-owned lands. However, attempts to introduce agricultural collectivization in 1964–69, under the direction of Ahmad Ben Salah, Minister of Finance and Planning, were abandoned following resistance from the rural population. Ben Salah was dismissed, arrested and subsequently sentenced to 10 years' hard labour. He escaped in 1973 and fled to Europe, from where he organized the radical Mouvement de l'unité populaire (MUP). In 1970 Hédi Nouira, hitherto Governor of the Banque Centrale de Tunisie, was appointed Prime Minister. He began to reverse Ben Salah's socialist economic policies, with the introduction of liberal economic reforms in the sectors of industry and agriculture. Liberalization of the economy was not accompanied by political reform, and the extensive powers of Nouira and Bourguiba were increasingly challenged by younger PSD members in the early 1970s. However, at the 1974 PSD Congress, Bourguiba was elected President-for-Life of the PSD and Nouira was confirmed as Secretary-General. In 1975, after approving the necessary amendments to the Constitution, the National Assembly elected Bourguiba President-for-Life of Tunisia. In 1980 Nouira resigned, owing to ill health, and was succeeded as Prime Minister and Secretary-General of the PSD by Muhammad Mzali.

The one-party system ended in mid-1981, when the Parti communiste tunisien (PCT), which had been proscribed in 1963, was granted legal status. The Government announced that any political group that gained more than 5% of the votes cast in the forthcoming legislative elections would also be officially recognized. Many of the Union générale Tunisienne du travail (UGTT) leaders imprisoned in 1978 after clashes between protesting workers and troops were pardoned. At elections to the National Assembly in November 1981, the PSD and the UGTT formed an electoral alliance, the Front national, which received 94.6% of the total votes cast and won all 126 seats in the new Assembly. In July 1986 Muhammad Mzali was replaced as Prime Minister by Rachid Sfar (hitherto Minister of Finance), and was dismissed as Secretary-General of the PSD. Mzali subsequently fled to Algeria, and was sentenced *in absentia* to terms of imprisonment and hard labour for defamatory comments against Tunisian leaders and mismanagement of public funds. Elections to the National Assembly in November were boycotted by the opposition parties, with the result that the PSD, opposed only by 15 independent candidates, won all 125 seats.

Domestic Political Affairs

During late 1987 President Bourguiba's behaviour became increasingly erratic. In October he revoked several of his recent appointments of leading state officials, and dismissed Sfar from the premiership. Zine al-Abidine Ben Ali was appointed Prime Minister and Secretary-General of the PSD. On 7 November 1987 seven doctors declared that President Bourguiba was unfit to govern, owing to senility and ill health. In accordance with the Constitution, Ben Ali was sworn in as President. Hédi Baccouche (previously Minister of Social Affairs) was appointed Prime Minister, and a new Council of Ministers was formed, which excluded several close associates of Bourguiba. Ben Ali announced plans to reform the Constitution and to permit greater political freedom. In the same month the Government permitted the publication of previously suspended opposition newspapers, and by early 1988 some 3,000 political and non-political detainees had been released. In February the PSD was renamed the Rassemblement constitutionnel démocratique (RCD).

In April 1988 legislation was enacted by the National Assembly to institute a multi-party political system, and in July the Assembly approved a series of proposals to reform the Constitution. The office of President-for-Life was abolished, and the President was, henceforth, to be elected by universal suffrage every five years and limited to two consecutive terms of office. In September two further opposition parties, the left-wing Rassemblement socialiste progressiste and the liberal Parti social pour le progrès (renamed the Parti social libéral—PSL—in 1993) were legalized. In November the Government claimed that there were no longer any political prisoners in Tunisia, a total of 8,000 people having been released during the first year of Ben Ali's regime.

Ben Ali was nominated as the sole candidate (supported by all the officially recognized parties) for the presidential election of 2 April 1989, and was duly elected President, receiving 99.3% of the votes cast. In legislative elections the RCD won all 141 seats in the National Assembly, with some 80% of the votes cast. The fundamentalist Hizb al-Nahdah/Parti de la renaissance (the candidates of which contested the election as independents, since the party was not officially recognized) won some 13% of the votes cast, but failed to win any seats under an electoral system that favoured the ruling party. In September Ben Ali dismissed Prime Minister Baccouche, following a disagreement concerning the Government's economic policy, and appointed Hamed Karoui, the former Minister of Justice, in his place.

In May 1990 the National Assembly approved a reformed electoral code, introducing a system of partial proportional representation for forthcoming municipal elections. The winning party was to receive 50% of the seats, while the remainder were to be distributed among all the parties, according to the number of votes received by each one. However, the six legal opposition parties boycotted the elections, held in June, arguing that they were neither free nor fair. Consequently, the RCD won control of all but one of the 245 municipal councils.

In December 1992 Ben Ali announced a revision of the electoral code, to include the introduction of partial proportional representation at legislative elections scheduled for March 1994. However, this apparent willingness to co-operate with the legalized opposition was accompanied by further repression of the Islamist movement, with increased censorship of publications sympathetic to their cause, and the harassment of suspected activists.

Meanwhile, in March 1992 the human rights organization Amnesty International published a report that detailed the arrests of some 8,000 suspected al-Nahdah members over an 18-month period, and cited 200 cases of the torture and ill-treatment of detainees. It also claimed that at least seven

Islamists had died while in custody. The Government initially denied the allegations, but later conceded that some violations of human rights had occurred. In mid-March it was announced that human rights 'units' were to be established within the Ministries of Foreign Affairs, Justice and the Interior, although new restrictions were imposed on the activities of unofficial, quasi-political groups such as the Ligue tunisienne des droits de l'homme (LTDH). In the same month an amnesty was granted to more than 1,000 detainees. In July and August the trials were held in Tunis of 171 alleged members of al-Nahdah, and of 108 alleged members of the organization's military wing, who were all accused of conspiring to overthrow the Government; 46 of the defendants were sentenced to life imprisonment, 16, including Rachid Ghannouchi, the leader of al-Nahdah, in absentia. (In 1993 Ghannouchi was granted political asylum in the United Kingdom.) Prison sentences of between one and 24 years were imposed on the remainder. In October appeals on behalf of 265 of those convicted were rejected, and another 20 al-Nahdah sympathizers were reportedly arrested in police raids.

There were indications in 1993 of a revival of political activity, and in April a new political organization, the Mouvement du renouveau (MR—Ettajdid, now known as the Mouvement ettajdid), held its first Congress. In November Ben Ali announced that presidential and legislative elections were to take place in March 1994. His candidacy for the presidency was supported not only by the RCD, but also by most of the legal opposition parties. In January 1994 the National Assembly adopted reforms to the electoral code: thenceforth, 19 of the 163 seats in the enlarged Assembly were to be allocated to opposition parties in proportion to their overall national vote. At the presidential election, which took place concurrently with the legislative elections on 20 March 1994, Ben Ali was re-elected President, receiving 99.9% of the votes cast. The RCD received 97.7% of the total votes cast in the legislative elections, securing all 144 seats that were contested under a simple majority system. Of the 19 seats reserved for opposition candidates, the Mouvement des démocrates socialistes (MDS) secured 10, the MR four, the Union démocratique unioniste (UDU) three and the Parti de l'unité populaire (PUP) two.

In October 1995 Muhammad Mouada, the MDS Secretary-General, was arrested and accused of having received money from an unnamed foreign country. The previous day Mouada had, in an open letter to the President, criticized the lack of political freedom in Tunisia; however, government officials denied any connection between the letter and Mouada's arrest. In late October the Tunisian authorities prevented Khemais Chamari, an MDS member of the National Assembly, from travelling to Malta to attend an international conference on human rights. In the following month Chamari's parliamentary immunity was withdrawn, in order to allow judicial charges (relating to Mouada's trial) to be brought against him. In February 1996 Mouada was sentenced to two years' imprisonment for 'illegal detention of currency'. Although a court of appeal subsequently reduced his term by one year, at the end of the month Mouada was sentenced to 11 years' imprisonment for maintaining links with and receiving money from Libya. In July Chamari was sentenced to five years' imprisonment for breaching security proceedings relating to Mouada's trial. Human rights organizations protested at the severity of the sentence and appealed to the Tunisian authorities to release all political detainees. In December Mouada and Chamari were released conditionally on humanitarian grounds.

In December 1996 Ben Ali announced plans to amend the electoral law, which, inter alia, would lower the minimum eligible age of candidates for the National Assembly (from 25 to 23 years) and increase the representation of legal opposition parties in the Assembly and in municipal councils. Political parties would not be permitted to be based on religion, language, race or region, nor to have foreign links. The scope of referendums was also to be widened. In December 1997 the Council of Ministers reached consensus on draft legislation to amend the electoral law.

In January 1999 draft legislation was presented to the National Assembly to introduce extraordinary provisions to the Constitution that would allow pluralism in the presidential election scheduled for that year. The amendments, which were approved in March, allowed for the leaders of all political parties to contest the presidency provided that they had held their current leadership position for at least five consecutive years, and that their party was represented by one or more deputies in the legislature. (Hitherto, opposition parties had been unable to present candidates, owing to the requirement that they be supported by at least 30 deputies in the Assembly.) Despite the new provisions, only two leaders of opposition parties were eligible to contest the presidency, namely Abderrahmane Tlili (UDU) and Muhammad Belhadj Amor (PUP).

The 1999 presidential election

The first contested presidential election since independence was held on 24 October 1999. As expected, Ben Ali comprehensively defeated his two rivals, securing 99.5% of the vote. Voter participation was officially estimated at 91.4%. At concurrent elections to the National Assembly, the RCD won all of the 148 seats contested under a simple majority system. Of the 34 seats reserved for opposition candidates, 13 were won by the MDS, the UDU and the PUP both took seven seats, the MR won five, and the PSL two. Some 91.5% of the electorate voted, according to official sources. In November Hamed Karoui was replaced as Prime Minister by Muhammad Ghannouchi (previously Minister of International Co-operation and Foreign Investment) and Abdallah Kallel succeeded Ali Chaouch as Minister of the Interior.

In June 2000 the President of the Conseil national pour les libertés en Tunisie (CNLT), Moncef Marzouki, visited London, United Kingdom, where he reportedly held talks with the leader of al-Nahdah, Rachid Ghannouchi, and proposed future co-operation between secular and Islamist factions of the Tunisian opposition. In December Marzouki received a one-year prison sentence, having been convicted of belonging to an illegal group and of disseminating false information. His sentence was suspended in September 2001 by the court of appeal, although his civil rights were not restored.

Meanwhile, in November 2000 President Ben Ali announced a number of initiatives aimed at furthering the democratization process and promoting human rights in Tunisia. The measures included: state compensation for detainees held in police custody without reasonable grounds; the transfer of responsibility for the prison system from the Ministry of the Interior to the Ministry of Justice; new legislation to improve conditions in prisons and to reduce censorship of the press; and an increase, by 50%, in government subsidies allocated for other political parties and their publications.

At the fifth congress of the LTDH, held in October 2000, a new executive board was elected, with Mokhtar Trifi, an outspoken critic of the Ben Ali regime, as President. Four former members of the board subsequently filed a suit against the new leadership, claiming that, owing to procedural irregularities, it was invalid, and in November a court imposed a moratorium on the activities of the LTDH. The Tunisian Government denied having ordered the ruling, but was strongly criticized by international and local human rights groups for its perceived role in the affair. Trial proceedings against the LTDH began in January 2001, and in the following month a judgment was issued that the results of the October 2000 congress should be invalidated. In March 2001 Trifi was charged with dissemination of false information and violation of the recent court ruling; however, in June the court of appeal ruled that the LTDH could resume its activities and ordered it to hold another congress within a year.

In March 2001 more than 250 human rights activists in Tunisia produced a petition that demanded wide-ranging democratic reforms in the country prior to the presidential and legislative elections scheduled for 2004. In the same month some 100 moderate figures in civil society signed a separate petition accusing Ben Ali of corruption and nepotism and denouncing his plans to amend the Constitution so as to permit him to seek a fourth term in office. In April al-Nahdah released a joint communiqué with Mouada's faction of the MDS, proposing the formation of an opposition coalition to unite Islamists and liberals against the Ben Ali regime. Later that month the President instructed the Ministry of the Interior to investigate all alleged abuses by the security forces against Tunisian citizens and to ensure that those found guilty were punished; however, the detention and imprisonment of several leading opponents of the regime continued.

The central committee of the ruling RCD announced in September 2001 that it would formally propose changes to the country's Constitution in order to enable Ben Ali to seek a fourth presidential term. In April 2002 members of the National Assembly overwhelmingly approved a constitutional reform bill, and at a referendum held on 26 May, according to official figures, the constitutional changes were approved by 99.5% of voters; the rate of voter participation was officially recorded at 95.6%. The amendments raised the upper age limit for presidential candidates from 70 to 75 years, and removed the limit on the number of terms that could be served by a President. In August 2003 the changes were promulgated and Ben Ali formally announced his intention to stand for a fourth term at elections scheduled for late 2004. Provision was also made for the creation of a second legislative chamber, to be called the Chamber of Advisers, for the establishment of a two-round presidential election system, and for a number of measures that would improve civil liberties and public freedoms.

In April 2002 a tanker lorry exploded outside a synagogue on the island of Djerba, causing the deaths of 21 people, most of whom were German tourists. The driver of the lorry was among those killed. The Tunisian authorities initially claimed that the explosion had been an accident, but a spokesman for the Israeli Ministry of Foreign Affairs insisted that it was an anti-Semitic terrorist attack. The Tunisian authorities subsequently confirmed that the explosion had been a 'premeditated criminal act'. A number of Arabic newspapers immediately carried claims that the al-Qa'ida organization of Osama bin Laden—the principal suspect in the September 2001 attacks on New York and Washington, DC, USA—was responsible. In June 2002 the Qatar-based satellite television station Al Jazeera broadcast a statement by a spokesman for al-Qa'ida, asserting that the attack had been perpetrated in the name of al-Qa'ida in protest against Israel's recent military offensive against Palestinian-controlled areas of the West Bank. In November eight people were arrested in Lyon, France, in connection with the explosion, while in early 2003 several arrests took place in Spain, France and Saudi Arabia. In May 2007 two men were sentenced to five years' imprisonment each by a court in Madrid, Spain, for their role in the financing of the attack; in June the uncle of the lorry driver was sentenced to 20 years in gaol by a court in Tunis for helping to prepare the explosion. The trial of three men (including the principal suspect in the September 2001 attacks, Khalid Sheikh Muhammad) for their alleged involvement in the Djerba synagogue explosion began in France in early January 2009; two of the men were subsequently sentenced to prison sentences of 18 and 12 years. However, it was ordered that a ruling on Sheikh Muhammad, who was in US custody in Guantánamo Bay, Cuba, be postponed until he could appear before the court in person.

In January 2003 Ben Ali announced the merger of a number of ministries, reducing them in number from 29 to 25, in an attempt to improve efficiency in government operations. The most notable changes were the creation of a Ministry of Justice and Human Rights and of a Ministry of Employment. In March 2004 Muhammad Rachid Kechiche was appointed Minister of Finance in place of Munir Jeidan, who assumed Kechiche's previous post of Government Secretary-General in charge of Relations with the Chamber of Deputies and the Chamber of Advisers.

Meanwhile, in July 2003 Abdallah Zouari, an Islamist journalist who had been released from detention in June 2002, having served an 11-year sentence for 'belonging to an illegal organization', was sentenced to four months' imprisonment for libel; in August 2003 Zouari received a further nine-month term for 'failing to obey an administrative order'. Between October and December Radhia Nasraoui, a prominent Tunisian human rights lawyer, undertook a hunger strike in protest against what she alleged was harassment by the authorities, claiming that she had been targeted because she had defended political prisoners and had accused the Government of using torture against opposition activists.

President Ben Ali re-elected

By mid-September 2004 three opposition candidates had officially registered to contest the presidential election scheduled to take place in October—Muhammad Bouchiha of the PUP, Mounir Béji of the PSL and Muhammad Ali Halouani of the MR. The Parti démocrate progressiste (PDP) announced in mid-October that it was withdrawing its candidates for the legislative elections in protest at what it considered an illegitimate electoral process in which it was denied access to the media and faced serious delays in having its manifesto approved. The presidential election took place on 24 October; Ben Ali received 94.5% of the votes cast, while Bouchiha secured 3.8%, Halouani 1.0% and Béji 0.8%. Voter turn-out was officially estimated at 91.5%. At the legislative elections, which took place concurrently, the RCD won all of the 152 seats contested under a simple majority system, 25% of which would be occupied by women under new legislation, while, of the 37 reserved for the opposition, the MDS won 14 seats, the PUP 11, the UDU seven, and the MR and PSL three and two seats, respectively.

A report published in July 2004 by the US-based Human Rights Watch criticized the Government's treatment of political prisoners, many of whom, it claimed, had spent several years in solitary confinement, and urged the Tunisian authorities to allow domestic and international monitors to inspect prison standards. In April, meanwhile, eight young people were arrested and sentenced to between 19 and 26 years' imprisonment for using the internet to plan terrorist activities (although six subsequently had their sentences reduced to 13 years). In June the leader of the UDU, Abderrahmane Tlili, was imprisoned for nine years, after being convicted of abusing his position while he was head of the Office de l'aviation civile et des aéroports. In November President Ben Ali pardoned 80 Islamist prisoners. A further 20 Islamist convicts were freed in July 2007 as part of an amnesty to mark the 50th anniversary of the Tunisian republic, including three former leaders of the banned al-Nahdah party.

At a meeting of the Central Committee of the RCD in February 2005, Ben Ali announced plans to create a national electoral observatory in time for the forthcoming municipal elections. Held on 8 May, the RCD won 4,098 of the 4,366 council seats contested at the municipal elections. In July elections were first held to the new Chamber of Advisers, as provided for by the constitutional amendments of 2002. The new second chamber was composed of 126 members, of whom 43 were indirectly elected by municipal councillors and parliamentary deputies (as representatives of the regions) and 42 by the main professional federations and trade unions; the remaining 41 members were appointed by the President. All 43 regional representatives elected were RCD candidates. The Chamber of Advisers held its inaugural session in October 2005, and Abdullah Kallel was elected as Speaker; however, 14 seats remained vacant after the UGTT refused to elect its members to the new chamber. Meanwhile, in August Ben Ali effected a major reorganization of the Council of Ministers: Abdelwahab Abdallah, a former principal adviser to the President, was appointed Minister of Foreign Affairs and Kamel Morjane received the defence portfolio; Ali Chaouch, the former interior minister, assumed the post of Minister of Social Affairs, Solidarity and Tunisians Abroad and was succeeded as Secretary-General of the RCD by Morjane's predecessor, Hédi M'henni. A further reorganization was announced by Ben Ali in September 2007.

In September and October 2006 the Tunisian authorities increasingly began to take action against the wearing of the Islamic headscarf, following public comments by Ben Ali and other senior politicians that it was a 'sectarian' form of dress that was not native to the country. (President Bourguiba had introduced a ban on headscarves in schools and government offices in 1981.) Also in October 2006 Tunisia closed its embassy in Qatar in protest at an interview with Moncef Marzouki broadcast by Al-Jazeera, in which he spoke against the Government's human rights record and advocated a campaign of civil resistance. In January 2007 the Minister of the Interior and Local Development, Rafik Belhaj Kacem, confirmed that police had shot dead 14 members of a suspected militant Islamist organization and arrested a number of others in Soliman, near Tunis. Two members of the security forces were killed during the operation. Kacem reported that the group, which had been assembled by six militants who had entered the country from Algeria and which was suspected of having links to the Algerian Groupe salafiste pour la prédication et le combat (which in that month restyled itself as the al-Qa'ida Organization in the Land of the Islamic Maghreb—AQIM, see the chapter on Algeria), had been in possession of explosives and details of foreign embassies and diplomatic staff in Tunis. In January 2008 a court in Tunisia issued its judgment on the suspected militants: two of the defendants were handed down death penalties, eight were sentenced to life imprisonment, and a further 20 received prison terms ranging from five to 30 years. The LTDH subsequently issued a statement concluding that, while violence was unacceptable as a means of political expression, the proceedings had lacked the 'minimum conditions' necessary for a fair trial.

In September 2007 two leading members of the PDP went on a hunger strike to protest against legal efforts to evict the party and its official weekly newspaper, Al-Mawkif, from their premises for alleged violation of the lease agreement. PDP Secretary-General Maya Jribi and Al-Mawkif Managing Director Ahmed Néjib Chebbi ended their hunger strike a month later, when the owner of the party offices abandoned a lawsuit against the party and sanctioned a new lease agreement. The outcome was hailed by Jribi as a victory for the Tunisian people in their 'struggle for freedom'. None the less, it was reported in April 2008 that the distribution of *Al-Mawkif* was being prevented by the authorities, with some sources claiming that this apparent official censorship of the newspaper was linked to Chebbi's declared intention to contest the presidential election scheduled for 2009.

Meanwhile, in November 2007 Ben Ali made a speech in front of a large audience in Radès to mark the 20th anniversary of his accession to power, during which he announced a range of measures designed to promote democracy and human rights in the country; these included increasing the level of funding allocated to opposition parties and their press. None the less, in May 2008 the recently founded Syndicat national des journalistes Tunisiens (SNJT—which replaced the pro-Government Association des journalistes Tunisiens) made renewed demands for a review of media regulations in line with international standards of press freedom. This followed the publication of an SNJT report that detailed the various alleged violations of journalists' rights that had occurred in the previous year. The SNJT repeated its demands in early February 2009, after the Government banned an edition of the daily newspaper *Attariq al-Jadid* that reproduced the transcript of a legal case. This, together with the forced closure of a Tunisian radio station a few days earlier, was considered to be further evidence of a significantly compromised level of media freedom in the country. Nevertheless, in a message sent by Ben Ali to the SNJT on the occasion of World Press Freedom Day in early May, the President pledged his commitment to granting 'due attention to the concerns and aspirations of the Tunisian media community'.

In July 2008 President Ben Ali was unanimously re-elected by the RCD congress as Chairman of the party. He thereby effectively became the RCD candidate for the presidential election scheduled to take place in October 2009. Ben Ali's apparent intention to run for a fifth presidential term immediately began to provoke speculation regarding his intention to make himself President-for-Life (a designation abolished in 1988). Also at the congress, the President announced a series of modifications to the structure of the RCD, among them a reduction in the number of vice-chairmen from two to one, and efforts to recruit new, younger members to the party. In August 2008 Ben Ali effected a reorganization of the Council of Ministers, appointing six new ministers. Notably, Slim Tletli, hitherto a presidential adviser, was appointed as Minister of Employment and Professional Integration of Youth, while Abdessalem Mansour, a former banking executive, assumed the post of Minister for Agriculture and Water Resources. Several new secretaries of state were also appointed.

As part of celebrations to mark the 21st anniversary of his accession to the presidency, on 7 November 2008 Ben Ali pardoned 21 imprisoned members of al-Nahdah (said to be the last remaining group of detainees from the banned party); a further 23 prisoners were also reported to have been pardoned. While human rights organizations generally responded with cautious optimism to the release of prisoners, they none the less expressed concerns regarding the infringement of liberties routinely encountered by political prisoners upon their release, and urged a wider amnesty for all detainees imprisoned for non-violent political convictions and practices.

The 2009 presidential and legislative elections

In anticipation of the legislative and presidential elections due later in the year, in March 2009 the National Assembly adopted a series of amendments to the electoral code. The amendments, which were subsequently promulgated by the President in April, were intended to promote greater plurality and ensure increased electoral transparency and participation. Notable among the new measures were an increase in the proportion of seats allocated to the opposition in the Chamber of Deputies from 20% to 25%, and the imposition of a 75% upper limit on the share of seats that could be obtained by any one list in the municipal councils (regardless of the number of votes obtained). The age of eligibility to vote was to be reduced from 20 years to 18.

On 25 August 2009 Ben Ali formally announced his intention to stand for a fifth consecutive elected term of office. The previous day Ahmed Néjib Chebbi had announced that he was withdrawing from the presidential contest, claiming that the process lacked transparency. Chebbi's candidature had been declared illegal in July 2008, when electoral legislation was amended to introduce a requirement for all presidential candidates to have been the elected leader of a recognized party for at least two years prior to the election. Indeed, this amendment rendered the candidatures of all but three potential challengers—the PUP's Muhammad Bouchiha, Ahmed Inoubli of the UDU, and Ahmed Brahim of the Mouvement ettajdid—illegal.

At the presidential election, which was held on 25 October 2009, Ben Ali was overwhelmingly returned to office, winning 89.6% of valid votes cast; Bouchiha was placed second, with 5.0%, while Inoubli secured 3.8% and Brahim 1.6%. The rate of participation by voters was officially estimated at 89.5%. At concurrent legislative elections, the RCD increased its representation, winning 161 of the 214 seats in the Chamber of Deputies (84.6% of valid votes cast). In accordance with the electoral code, the remaining seats were allocated to opposition parties. The MDS obtained 16 seats (4.6% of the vote), the PUP 12 (3.4%), and the UDU nine (2.6%). The remaining 16 seats were divided among the PSL (eight seats), the Parti des verts pour le progrès (six) and the Mouvement ettajdid (two). Turn-out at the legislative elections was officially estimated at 89.4%. Ben Ali was sworn in as President on 12 November 2009. After the ceremony, the President gave a speech in which he vowed to tackle unemployment and develop the media sector to allow for greater freedom of speech; however, he also warned against foreign interference in the country's internal affairs. International observers subsequently declared that the elections had been carried out in a transparent and neutral manner; however, many commentators, including a spokesman of the US Department of State, voiced criticism of the credibility of these observers.

In mid-January 2010 Ben Ali effected a reorganization of the Council of Ministers. Among the most notable appointments were those of Kamel Morjane (hitherto Minister of National Defence) as Minister of Foreign Affairs, and of Lazhar Bououni as Minister of Justice and Human Rights. Muhammad Ridha Chalghoum became Minister of Finance, while Ridha Grira assumed the national defence portfolio vacated by Morjane. At municipal elections held in early May, the RCD won 90.7% of the votes cast, retaining control of all 264 of Tunisia's municipal councils. In October Ben Ali effected a further, minor cabinet reorganization.

Recent developments: the removal from office of Ben Ali

On 17 December 2010 Muhammad Bouazizi set himself alight following the confiscation by the authorities of fruit and vegetable produce that he was selling, without a permit, in the central town of Sidi Bouzid. Upon attempting to pay the required fine, Bouazizi was initially reported to have been assaulted and verbally abused by a police officer. (However, charges brought against the police officer in respect of the incident were later dropped.) The young man's ultimately fatal self-immolation in early January 2011, was widely portrayed as a reflection of the intense frustration and desperation felt by many over Tunisia's continued high rate of youth unemployment, escalating food prices and harassment by the authorities, and the incident prompted angry demonstrations in Sidi Bouzid, which soon spread to neighbouring areas. Hundreds of Tunisians began protesting against the high rate of unemployment, food inflation, poor living standards, perceived state corruption, and a lack of freedom of expression and of other human and political rights. In an attempt to appease the protesters, on 20 December 2010 the Government announced a US $10m. employment programme; however, the announcement bore no tangible results and the demonstrations continued unabated, to which the authorities were widely reported to have responded with significant force and large-scale arrests of protesters. During demonstrations on 22 December in Sidi Bouzid, a 22-year-old man was reported to have shouted 'No to misery, no to unemployment', before fatally electrocuting himself. The incident prompted a further intensification of the unrest, and additional police officers were deployed to a number of cities as the protests continued to spread across the country, including the capital.

On 24 December 2010 one protester was killed, and several others were seriously injured, when police officers shot into a crowd of demonstrators in Menzel Bouzaiene, a town in the Sidi Bouzid governorate; one of those wounded subsequently died of his injuries. The Government claimed that the officers had been acting in self-defence after warning shots had been ignored by protesters, some of whom had thrown petrol bombs at a police station; however, protesters and the opposition accused the police of firing indiscriminately at unarmed protesters who posed no immediate risk. From late December trade union members and lawyers staged rallies, adding their voices to the escalating calls for immediate government action to address the issues raised by the protesters.

On 28 December 2010 President Ben Ali addressed the nation in a televised broadcast, during which he condemned the 'use of violence in the streets by a minority of extremists' and vowed to hold to account all those involved; he also criticized foreign media for broadcasting 'false allegations ... based on dramatization, fermentation and deformation'. Local media made no mention of the unfolding national crisis until 29 December, when a private news television channel first broadcast news and video footage of the protests. Meanwhile, on 28 December Ben Ali dismissed the Ministers of Communication Technologies, of Trade and Handicrafts, of Religious Affairs, and of Youth and Sports, as well as the governors of Sidi Bouzid, Jendouba and Zaghouan provinces, in connection with the unrest.

The protests continued to escalate in early January 2011, spreading to an increasing number of towns and cities across the country and becoming increasingly marred by violence by both the authorities and the protesters. On 3 January police used tear gas to disperse crowds gathered at a peaceful rally in the town of Thala, close to the Algerian border, prompting violent clashes in which nine protesters were reported to have been seriously injured and demonstrators to have attacked local offices of the RCD. On 6 January Tunisian legal professionals staged a general strike in protest at the perceived use of excessive force by the authorities against the protesters. Two days later nine protesters were killed, and many more injured, in clashes between the protesters and authorities in the Kasserine governorate and in Thala; in the latter, police used water cannons and live ammunition after protesters threw petrol bombs and set fire to a government building. On 9 January two protesters were fatally shot by police in Maknassy, in Sidi Bouzid governorate.

Ben Ali dismissed the Minister of the Interior and Local Development, Rafik Belhaj Kacem, on 12 January 2011, and ordered that all protesters within police custody be released; Kacem had been regarded by many to be primarily responsible for the violent police response to the protests. In a second televised speech on 13 January, Ben Ali declared that he would not seek re-election at the next presidential poll, due in 2014; promised to reduce the prices of staple foods, including bread, milk and sugar; pledged to relax censorship so as to allow greater freedoms of speech and of assembly; and announced the creation of a committee of investigation into public corruption and the conduct of certain government officials. The President also pledged to launch a comprehensive investigation into the deaths of protesters, which at that time official estimates put at 23; however, the Paris-based International Freedom for Human Rights claimed on 13 January that at least 66 people had been killed during the protests thus far, including 13 in the past few days alone, and including a further seven who took their own lives in protest at economic hardships and poor living standards. Almost immediately opposition figures were allowed to appear on national television, and blocks on a number of internet sites were removed.

While the political opposition and some protesters cautiously welcomed the unprecedented concessions, Ben Ali's speech did nothing to quell the unrest, with many protesters intensifying their efforts and demanding the immediate resignation of the President. In response, on 14 January 2011 Ben Ali declared the imposition of emergency rule, thereby outlawing gatherings of more than three people, and dismissed the Government, pledging to hold parliamentary elections within six months. Protests outside the Minister of the Interior later that day, during which protesters reiterated their demands for Ben Ali to step down with immediate effect, were dispersed by the police using tear gas. Later that day it was announced that the President had fled the country, and on 15 January Saudi Arabia revealed that it had offered asylum to Ben Ali and his family; it was reported that Ben Ali had intended to fly to France but had been refused entry by the French Government. On 14 January Tunisian Prime Minister Muhammad Ghannouchi, citing Article 56 of the Constitution, had declared himself interim President, a declaration that was met with anger by the protesters, many of whom argued that Ghannouchi and Ben Ali belonged to the same 'corrupt' political élite; however, on 15 January the Constitutional Court ruled that, in the absence of an elected President, the parliamentary Speaker, rather than the Prime Minister, was the legitimate interim head of state; Fouad Mebazaa was duly sworn in as interim President later that day.

The announcement of a new 'national unity' Government on 17 January 2011 provoked further ire, owing to the inclusion of RCD members. However, Ghannouchi defended the appointments, insisting that those ministers who had been retained, who included the ministers responsible for finance, foreign affairs, the interior and defence, had 'clean hands' and had 'managed to reduce certain people's capacity to do harm ... and bought time to preserve the national interest'. As well as former members of the former Ben Ali administration, the new Council of Ministers included representatives of the UGTT, opposition leaders and independents. Opposition leaders named in cabinet included Ahmed Brahim as Minister of Higher Education and Scientific Research, and Dr Mustapha Ben Jaafar, leader of Forum démocratique pour le travail et les libertés, as Minister of Public Health. On the following day, however, it was announced that the UGTT had withdrawn its participation in the Government, while Ben Jaafar also resigned as Minister of Public Health. Following several days of angry protests against the composition of the new cabinet, and demands for the disbandment of the RCD, on 20 January all RCD cabinet ministers resigned from the party. On 27 January Ghannouchi, who a few days previously had stated his intention to resign after the holding of free and fair elections within six months, announced a further cabinet reorganization that was widely interpreted as a bid to appease the protesters: six former RCD members, including, *inter alia*, the Ministers of Finance, Foreign Affairs, the Interior and National Defence, were replaced. On 13 February, however, it was announced that the newly appointed Minister of Foreign Affairs, Ahmed Ounaies, had resigned owing to controversy regarding complimentary comments that he had made to his French counterpart, Michele Alliot-Marie, with the French Government the subject of considerable criticism for offers of support that it had extended to the Ben Ali regime and having suggested that France would be prepared to assist the Tunisian security forces in quelling the protests; Muhammad Mouldi Kéfi was appointed in his place. Meanwhile, in late January and early February about 30 members of Ben Ali's extended family were arrested, together with former Minister of the Interior Kacem, and all 24 regional governors were dismissed.

Violent clashes between protesters and security forces in Tunis in late February prompted Ghannouchi's resignation as Prime Minister on 27 February, and he was replaced later that day by Béji Caïd Essebsi, a former government minister during the presidency of Habib Bourguiba. On 28 February the Minister of Industry and Technology, Muhammad Afif Chelbi, and the Minister of Planning and International Co-operation, Muhammad Nouri Jouini, both of whom had served under Ben Ali, also resigned. On 1 March a further three ministers—including Minister of Higher Education and Scientific Research Brahim and Minister of Regional and Local Development Ahmad Néjib Chebbi—also left the Government. Essebsi named his new Council of Ministers, replacing those who had resigned in the previous week, while retaining ministers from the outgoing interim administration in key posts, on 7 March. On the same day the interim Government announced that the secret police force was to be dissolved, and on 9 March the RCD was formally dissolved, and its assets liquidized, by court order. The party announced its intention to appeal against the ruling prior to the staging of elections to a constituent assembly, which interim President Mebazaa had announced, on 3 March, were to be held on 24 July. Upon its election, one of the immediate priorities for the assembly would be the drafting of a new constitution. In late April it was announced that certain former RCD officials were to be barred from contesting elections for a period of 10 years, following a recommendation by the High Authority for the Achievement of the Objectives of the Revolution, Political Reform and Democratic Transition, formed after Ben Ali's departure to oversee the implementation of reforms during the transitional period. Sporadic unrest continued, however: in early May an evening curfew was imposed in the capital, following renewed protests amid speculation that former supporters of Ben Ali were planning to stage a coup in the event that al-Nahdah emerged victorious at the forthcoming elections.

Foreign Affairs
Regional relations
Relations with the other countries of the Maghreb improved considerably in the 1980s. A meeting between President Bourguiba and President Ben Djedid Chadli of Algeria in March 1983 led to the drafting of the Maghreb Fraternity and Co-operation Treaty, which envisaged the eventual creation of a Greater Maghreb Union, and was signed by Mauritania in December.

In February 1989, at a meeting of North African heads of state in Morocco, a treaty was concluded that proclaimed the Union of the Arab Maghreb (Union du Maghreb arabe—UMA, see p. 450), comprising Algeria, Libya, Mauritania, Morocco and Tunisia. The treaty envisaged: the establishment of a council of heads of state; regular meetings of ministers responsible for foreign affairs; and, eventually, the free movement of goods, people, services and capital throughout the countries of the region.

In 1982 President Bourguiba permitted the Palestine Liberation Organization (PLO) to establish its headquarters near Tunis. In October 1985 Israeli aircraft attacked the PLO headquarters, causing the deaths of some 72 people, including 12 Tunisians. US support for the right of Israel to retaliate (the attack was a reprisal for the murder of three Israeli citizens in Cyprus) severely strained relations between Tunisia and the USA. In April 1988 Abu Jihad, the military commander of the PLO, was assassinated at his home in Tunis. The Tunisian Government blamed Israel for the murder, and complained to the UN Security Council. The PLO transferred its offices to Gaza in mid-1994, following the signing of the PLO-Israeli Cairo Agreement on implementing Palestinian self-rule in the Gaza Strip and Jericho.

In January 1988 the Tunisian Government announced that diplomatic relations with Egypt, which had been severed in 1979, would be resumed. In March 1990 Ben Ali made the first visit to the Egyptian capital, Cairo, by a Tunisian President since 1965, and signed several agreements on bilateral co-operation. In September 1990 a majority of members of the League of Arab States (the Arab League, see p. 361) resolved to move the League's headquarters from Tunis (where it had been established 'temporarily' in 1979) to its original site in Cairo: the Tunisian Government protested at the decision.

Tunisia assumed the annual presidency of the UMA in January 1993. The Government made clear its determination to reactivate the process of Maghreb union, as well as dialogue with the European Community (now European Union—EU, see p. 270). In April 1994 the UMA ratified 11 agreements designed to improve co-operation and trade within the Maghreb. However, tensions between the UMA's member states subsequently undermined the activities of the Union. In March 1999 Ben Ali made his first official visit to Morocco, during which he pledged to strengthen relations with that country, and to revive the UMA. A summit meeting of ministers responsible for foreign affairs of the five UMA member states was arranged, and proceeded in the Algerian capital in March 2001. However, the meeting quickly broke down owing to disagreements between Moroccan and Algerian representatives. Following several further unsuccessful attempts to co-ordinate a summit meeting, in April 2008 celebrations were held in Tangier, Morocco, to mark the 50th anniversary of the summit at which the idea of a union of Arab Maghreb states was first proposed. The event ended with renewed calls for greater regional collaboration and a regalvanized UMA. A year later delegates responsible for foreign affairs from the UMA member states met in Tripoli, Libya, where they reiterated their commitment to improving political and economic co-operation among the countries of North Africa.

Relations with Algeria were threatened in May 2000 when Tunisian security forces responded to an attack by Algerian Islamists; three of the Islamists were killed and two Tunisian soldiers wounded. The attack followed the signing of a bilateral customs agreement aimed at ending cross-border smuggling, considered by the Algerian Government to facilitate the activities of Islamist groups in Algeria. A number of bilateral agreements were signed during a visit to Algeria by Ben Ali in February 2002; most notably, the two countries pledged to formalize delineation of their maritime border. In August 2009, following meetings between Algerian and Tunisian representatives, it was announced that nine co-operation agreements were to be signed between the two countries in the areas of the economy, commerce, culture and education. The Tunisian Secretary of State in charge of Maghreb, Arab and African Affairs, Abdelhafidh Harguem, announced that the introduction of a legal framework to allow for co-operation in the banking and financial sector was to be accelerated. Meanwhile, a preferential trade agreement was signed between Tunisia and Algeria in December 2008, and, following ratification by both countries' legislatures, was implemented in April 2010. The agreement, which was intended further to develop economic and trade co-operation, paved the way for the establishment of a bilateral free trade zone, negotiations on which were ongoing in mid-2011. During a visit to Algeria by Tunisian Prime Minister Essebsi in March of that year, Essebsi announced his intention to 'consolidate the countries' brotherly relations', while the Algerian Government pledged some US $100m. in financial assistance to Tunisia.

Other external relations

In June 1993 President Ben Ali, addressing the European Parliament in Strasbourg, France, advocated the establishment of a Euro-Maghreb Development Bank, which, by stimulating economic growth in North Africa, would alleviate illegal immigration into Europe. In July 1995 Tunisia concluded an association agreement with the EU, designed to foster closer commercial and political co-operation. Several Tunisian deputies demanded a suspension of the association agreement in June 2000, after EU member states, particularly France, criticized the Tunisian authorities' failure to protect human rights. Relations between France and Tunisia deteriorated further during 2001, when the French Government again criticized the growing use of violence against human rights activists and voiced its concern at gaol sentences imposed upon prominent opposition figures. Relations improved, however, during 2002–04, and, during a visit by President Jacques Chirac to Tunisia in December 2003, the two countries signed a number of co-operation agreements relating to tourism and bilateral social security arrangements. In November 2005 the EU made an official complaint to the Tunisian Government days before the UN-sponsored World Summit on the Information Society was scheduled to begin in Tunis. Tunisian security forces had prevented a group of international delegates, including the German ambassador to the UN and representatives of international human rights bodies, from entering the German cultural institute in the Tunisian capital. In April 2008 the French President, Nicolas Sarkozy, made his first state visit to Tunisia since taking office in May 2007. During the visit Sarkozy and Ben Ali supervised the signing of several agreements designed to increase civilian nuclear and aviation co-operation between the two countries. Ben Ali also expressed support for Sarkozy's proposed community of EU member states and countries bordering the Mediterranean Sea. When the Union for the Mediterranean (as it came to be known) was officially inaugurated at a summit meeting in the French capital in July 2008, President Ben Ali was among the many leaders of the 43 member nations to be in attendance.

In March 2010 Tunisia formally applied to the EU for 'advanced partner status', negotiations on which were ongoing in mid-2011. The Tunisian application proved divisive among EU member states, with some, including France and Italy, pledging support to the North African country in recognition of the strengthening economic, political and social partnership, while others argued that Tunisia must do more to improve its human rights record before any such upgrading of relations be conferred. It was not immediately clear whether the ouster of Ben Ali in early 2011 would hinder or help Tunisia's aspirations to this end. Meanwhile, offers of assistance by the French Government to the Tunisian security forces in their efforts to contain the protesters had attracted considerable criticism in January, both within Tunisia and among the international community.

In December 2003 the US Secretary of State, Colin Powell, visited Tunisia for talks with President Ben Ali and the Tunisian Minister of Foreign Affairs, Habib Ben Yahia. Powell praised the excellent relations between the two countries and Tunisia's contribution to the 'war on terror'; however, he urged the Tunisian Government to pursue further political and economic reforms. In February 2004 Ben Ali visited Washington, DC, where he met with the US President, George W. Bush, to discuss a number of trade-related issues. During the talks Bush also stressed that, while the USA applauded Tunisia's efforts to liberalize its society, it remained critical of the country's human rights record and the continued oppression of the Tunisian media. Bilateral relations were further consolidated in September 2008, when US Secretary of State Condoleezza Rice visited Tunisia as part of a tour of Maghreb states. She met with Ben Ali and held discussions with Tunisian officials on issues including counter-terrorism and domestic reform. In a statement to the press, Rice commended the progress that Tunisia had made in promoting women's rights, and urged the authorities to make every effort to ensure that the 2009 elections would be free and fair. In April 2010 Minister of Foreign Affairs Kamel Morjane visited Washington, DC, for talks with US Secretary of State Hillary Clinton.

Despite US support over the years for the Ben Ali regime, in response to the popular protests of early 2011 US President

TUNISIA

Introductory Survey

Barack Obama hailed the courage and dignity of the Tunisian protesters in mid-January, but urged all parties to keep calm and eschew violence. Obama also appealed to the Tunisian Government to respect human rights and to commit to allowing free and fair elections. The US Assistant Secretary of State for Near Eastern Affairs expressed the Obama Administration's hope that the 'example' of Tunisia would bring reform to the rest of the region. In the following month Secretary of State Clinton made an official visit to Tunisia, during which she met with Mebazaa, Prime Minister Essebsi and other members of the interim Government, and pledged US assistance to facilitate the implementation of social and political reforms. Nevertheless, Clinton's visit was marked by protests, with hundreds of people gathering in Tunis to warn against US intervention in Tunisia's internal affairs; crowds were reported to have shouted anti-US slogans.

CONSTITUTION AND GOVERNMENT

Under the terms of the Constitution (promulgated in 1959, with subsequent amendments in 1988 and 2002), legislative power is exercised by a bicameral National Assembly, comprising the Chamber of Deputies and the Chamber of Advisers. The Chamber of Deputies is elected (at the same time as the President) every five years, and has 214 members; 53 seats are reserved for the opposition, allotted according to the proportion of votes received nationally by each party. The Chamber of Advisers currently consists of 126 members, elected for six years (with one-half being replaced every three years). One-third of the members of the Chamber of Advisers is composed of representatives of the main professional unions and federations, one-third by representatives of the 24 governorates (one or two from each governorate, depending on the size of its population), and the remainder are appointed by the President. Executive power is held by the President, elected for five years by popular vote. The President, who is head of state and head of government, appoints a Council of Ministers, led by a Prime Minister, which is responsible to him.

REGIONAL AND INTERNATIONAL CO-OPERATION

Tunisia is a member of the Union of the Arab Maghreb (Union du Maghreb arabe—UMA, see p. 450), the African Union (AU, see p. 183), the League of Arab States (Arab League, see p. 361), and the Community of Sahel-Saharan States (CEN-SAD, see p. 446).

Tunisia joined the UN in November 1956, having gained independence in March of that year. As a contracting party to the General Agreement on Trade and Tariffs, Tunisia became a member of the World Trade Organization (WTO, see p. 430) on its establishment in 1995. The country also participates in the Organization of the Islamic Conference (OIC, see p. 400).

ECONOMIC AFFAIRS

In 2009, according to estimates by the World Bank, Tunisia's gross national income (GNI), measured at average 2007–09 prices, was US $38,845m., equivalent to $3,720 per head (or $7,820 per head on an international purchasing-power parity basis). During 2000–09, it was estimated, the population increased at an average annual rate of 1.0%, while gross domestic product (GDP) per head increased, in real terms, by an average of 3.6%. Overall GDP increased, in real terms, at an average annual rate of 4.6% per year in 2000–09; according to official estimates, it grew by 3.0% in 2010.

Agriculture (including forestry and fishing) contributed 7.9% of GDP and employed 17.7% of the working population in 2010. The principal crops are wheat, barley, potatoes, olives, tomatoes and watermelons. However, Tunisia imports large quantities of cereals, dairy produce, meat and sugar. The country's main agricultural export is olive oil; olives, citrus fruit and dates are also grown for export. During 2000–09, according to the World Bank, agricultural GDP increased at an average annual rate of 2.0%. According to official figures, agricultural GDP increased by 7.6% in 2009, but declined by 8.7% in 2010.

Industry (including mining, manufacturing, construction and power) contributed 31.7% of GDP and engaged 33.0% of the employed labour force in 2010. According to the World Bank, industrial GDP increased by an average of 3.7% per year during 2000–09. According to official figures, industrial GDP increased by 0.5% in 2009 and by 6.8% in 2010.

Mining (excluding hydrocarbons) contributed an estimated 1.1% of GDP in 2010. In 1994 mining (with gas, electricity and water) employed 1.6% of the working population. In 2009 the principal mineral export was petroleum (which accounted for 13.6% of total export earnings). Tunisia's proven published oil reserves at the end of 2009 were estimated at 577m. barrels, sufficient to maintain production (at 2009 levels—averaging an estimated 86,000 barrels per day) for more than 18 years. Iron, zinc, lead, barite, gypsum, phosphate, fluorspar and sea salt are also mined. In addition, Tunisia possesses large reserves of natural gas. The GDP of the mining sector (excluding hydrocarbons) increased by 13.0% in 2010, according to official figures.

Manufacturing (excluding hydrocarbons) contributed 17.7% of GDP in 2010, and employed 19.6% of the working population in 1994. Manufacturing is based on the processing of the country's principal agricultural and mineral products. Other important sectors include textiles, construction materials, machinery, chemicals, and paper and wood. In 2000–09, according to the World Bank, manufacturing GDP increased at an average annual rate of 3.9%. Manufacturing GDP declined by 1.8% in 2009, but grew by 8.5% in 2010.

Construction (including civil engineering) contributed 4.8% of GDP in 2010, and employed 13.2% of the working population in 1994. According to official sources, sectoral GDP grew by 4.3% in 2010.

Energy is derived principally from gas (which contributed 83.1% of total electricity output in 2007) and petroleum (16.2%), although Tunisia also has several hydroelectric plants (which contributed just 0.3% of total output in 2007). Imports of mineral fuels and lubricants comprised 11.5% of the value of total imports in 2009. In the mid-2000s the Tunisian electricity grid was interconnected with that of Libya.

The services sector accounted for 60.4% of GDP and employed 49.3% of the working population in 2010. Tourism represents an important source of revenue: receipts from tourism in 2008 totalled an estimated US $3,909m., and there were 7.0m. tourist arrivals in that year. The GDP of the services sector increased by an average of 5.6% per year in 2000–09, according to the World Bank. Growth in the sector's GDP increased by 5.0% in 2010, according to official figures.

In 2009 Tunisia recorded a visible trade deficit of US $3,699m., and a deficit of $1,234m. on the current account of the balance of payments. In 2009 the principal sources of imports were France, including Monaco (accounting for 20.0% of the total), Italy, Germany and the People's Republic of China. The principal market for Tunisian exports in that year was also France, including Monaco (taking 29.7%); other major purchasers were Italy, Germany and Libya. The member states of the European Union (EU, see p. 270) accounted for 80.5% of Tunisia's exports and 71.4% of its imports in 1999. Tunisia's principal exports in 2009 were miscellaneous manufactured articles, machinery and transport equipment, mineral fuels and lubricants, chemicals and related products, and basic manufactures. The principal imports in that year were machinery and transport equipment, basic manufactures, mineral fuels and lubricants, and chemicals and related products.

In 2009 there was a preliminary budgetary deficit of TD 1,589m. (excluding receipts from privatization). The 2010 budget forecast a deficit of TD 1,864m. (also excluding receipts from privatization). Tunisia's general government gross debt was TD 25,139m. in 2009, equivalent to 42.8% of GDP. At the end of 2008 Tunisia's total external debt was US $20,775.9m., of which $16,448.9m. was public and publicly guaranteed debt. In 2007 the cost of debt-servicing was equivalent to 11.3% of the value of exports of goods, services and income. The average annual rate of inflation was 3.4% in 2000–10; consumer prices increased by 4.1% in 2010. A reported 13.0% of the labour force were unemployed in that year.

As a result of strong growth, low inflation and declining poverty following efforts to restructure and diversify the economy from the mid-1990s, the country was on a strong footing as the world economy began to slow in 2008. In January all trade barriers between Tunisia and the EU were removed when the country formally entered into a free trade agreement with the bloc, which was expected to encourage the inflow of investment capital. However, Tunisia's increased dependence on EU countries, many of which were severely affected by the global economic slowdown, led to reduced external demand. Tunisia's exports (the value of which contracted by 24.8% in 2009), tourist receipts, remittances from migrant workers, and inflows of foreign direct investment (FDI) were all negatively impacted as a result. Despite a recovery in external demand, which led to improved export performance, in the first quarter of 2010, tourism receipts and foreign remittances stagnated, and increased imports led to a widening trade deficit, while the current account

TUNISIA

deficit was forecast by the IMF to increase to 4.5% of GDP. The budgetary deficit was projected to remain broadly stable, at 3.0%–3.5% of GDP, in 2010. FDI inflows were estimated to have decreased from 5.7% in 2008 to 3.3% of GDP in 2009, and were forecast to remain unchanged in 2010, before recovering modestly to 3.9% of GDP in 2011. The rate of inflation decreased from 5.0% in 2008 to 3.7% in 2009, but rose to an estimated 4.8% in 2010 (largely owing to escalating food prices). As part of the Government's privatization programme, Tunisian companies in the agricultural, energy and industrial sectors were due to be sold in 2010–11 with the aim of further diversifying growth; however, progress was reported to be slow. Unemployment remained a serious issue in Tunisia, with the level of joblessness particularly high among the country's youth. One of the principal aims of the Government's development plan (for 2007–16), approved in July 2007, was the reduction of unemployment to 13.4% by 2011, and to 10.4% by 2016; many analysts noted that this would be a difficult challenge in the face of the global economic slowdown. The official rate of unemployment was widely believed significantly to understate the true rate; moreover, in 2010 the rate of youth unemployment (those aged between 18 and 24 years) was estimated at more than double the national average, at 31%. According to a report published by the IMF in September, GDP growth was expected to increase to 3.8% in that year, buoyed by a robust recovery in manufacturing exports (partially offset by a decline in energy and agricultural production), while medium-term growth for the period 2010–14 was provisionally projected at about 5%. However, at mid-2011 it remained to be seen to what extent the civil unrest and installation of a new Government earlier in that year would negatively impact on the national economy.

PUBLIC HOLIDAYS

2012: 1 January (New Year's Day), 20 March (Independence Day), 21 March (Youth Day), 9 April (Martyrs' Day), 1 May (Labour Day), 25 July (Republic Day), 13 August (Women's Day), 18 August* (Aid el-Seghir—Id al-Fitr, end of Ramadan), 15 October (Evacuation of Bizerta), 25 October* (Aid el-Kebir—Id al-Adha, Feast of the Sacrifice).

* These holidays are dependent on the Islamic lunar calendar and may differ by one or two days from the dates given.

Statistical Survey

Source (unless otherwise stated): Institut National de la Statistique, Ministère du Développement Economique, 70 rue al-Cham, 1002 Tunis; tel. (71) 891-002; fax (71) 792-559; e-mail ins@e-mail.ati.tn; internet www.ins.nat.tn.

Area and Population

AREA, POPULATION AND DENSITY

Area (sq km)	
Land	154,530
Inland waters	9,080
Total	163,610*
Population (census results)	
20 April 1994	8,785,364
28 April 2004	
Males	4,965,435
Females	4,945,437
Total	9,910,872
Population (official estimate at 1 July)	
2008	10,328,900
2009	10,439,600
2010	10,549,100
Density (per sq km) at 1 July 2010	68.3†

* 63,170 sq miles.
† Land area only.

POPULATION BY AGE AND SEX
(UN estimates at mid-2011)

	Males	Females	Total
0–14	1,219,117	1,143,122	2,362,239
15–64	3,718,383	3,685,832	7,404,215
65 and over	328,459	381,442	709,901
Total	5,265,959	5,210,396	10,476,355

Source: UN, *World Population Prospects: The 2008 Revision.*

GOVERNORATES
(at 1 July 2010)

	Area (sq km)*	Population (estimates)	Density (per sq km)
Tunis	346	1,000,300	2,891.0
Ariana	498	498,000	1,000.0
Ben Arous	761	577,500	758.9
Manouba	1,060	368,700	347.8
Nabeul	2,788	752,800	270.0
Zaghouan	2,768	170,500	61.6
Bizerte	3,685	546,600	148.3
Béja	3,558	306,200	86.1
Jendouba	3,102	423,200	136.4
Le Kef	4,965	256,600	51.7
Siliana	4,631	234,000	50.5
Kairouan	6,712	559,700	83.4
Kasserine	8,066	432,300	53.6
Sidi Bouzid	6,994	412,500	59.0
Sousse	2,621	611,800	233.4
Monastir	1,019	515,300	505.7
Mahdia	2,966	396,300	133.6
Sfax	7,545	931,000	123.4
Gafsa	8,990	338,100	37.6
Tozeur	4,719	103,500	21.9
Kébili	22,084	150,700	6.8
Gabès	7,175	361,500	50.4
Médenine	8,588	455,900	53.1
Tataouine	38,889	146,200	3.8
Total	**154,530**	**10,549,100**	**68.3**

* Land area only.

Note: Total for population may not be equal to the sum of components, owing to rounding.

TUNISIA

PRINCIPAL TOWNS
(2004, census results)

Tunis (capital)	728,453	Ettadhamen		118,487
Sfax (Safaqis)	265,131	Kairouan (Qairawan)		117,930
Ariana	240,749	Gabès		116,323
Sousse	173,047	Bizerta (Bizerte)		114,371

Source: Thomas Brinkhoff, *City Population* (internet www.citypopulation.de).

Mid-2010 (incl. suburbs, UN estimate): Tunis 766,750 (Source: UN, *World Urbanization Prospects: The 2009 Revision*).

BIRTHS, MARRIAGES AND DEATHS

	Registered live births		Registered marriages		Registered deaths	
	Number	Rate (per 1,000)	Number	Rate (per 1,000)	Number	Rate (per 1,000)
1990	205,345	25.4	55,612	6.8	45,700	5.6
1991	207,455	25.2	59,010	7.1	46,500	5.6
1992	211,649	25.2	64,700	7.6	46,300	5.5
1993	207,786	24.1	54,120	6.3	49,400	5.7
1994	200,223	22.7	52,431	5.9	50,300	5.7
1995	186,416	20.8	53,726	6.0	52,000	5.8
1996	178,801	19.7	56,349	6.2	40,817	5.5
1997	173,757	18.9	57,861	6.3	42,426	5.6

Birth rate (per 1,000): 17.1 in 2006; 17.4 in 2007; 17.7 in 2008–09.

Death rate (per 1,000): 5.6 in 2006; 5.5 in 2007; 5.8 in 2008; 5.7 in 2009.

Life expectancy (years at birth, WHO estimates): 75 (males 73; females 77) in 2008 (Source: WHO, *World Health Statistics*).

EMPLOYMENT
('000 persons aged 15 years and over at 20 April 1994)

	Males	Females	Total
Agriculture, forestry and fishing	393.7	107.3	501.0
Manufacturing	244.7	211.0	455.7
Electricity, gas and water*	34.4	2.4	36.8
Construction	302.6	3.2	305.8
Trade, restaurants and hotels†	277.8	37.8	315.6
Community, social and personal services‡	503.9	163.2	667.1
Activities not adequately defined	28.6	10.0	38.6
Total employed	**1,785.7**	**534.9**	**2,320.6**

* Including mining and quarrying.
† Including financing, insurance, real estate and business services.
‡ Including transport, storage and communications.

2009 (percentage distribution by sector): Agriculture and fishing 18.3; Industry 31.9; Services 49.8.

2010 (percentage distribution by sector): Agriculture and fishing 17.7; Industry 33.0; Services 49.3.

Health and Welfare

KEY INDICATORS

Total fertility rate (children per woman, 2008)	1.8
Under-5 mortality rate (per 1,000 live births, 2008)	21
HIV/AIDS (% of persons aged 15–49, 2007)	0.1
Physicians (per 1,000 head, 2004)	1.3
Hospital beds (per 1,000 head, 2006)	1.9
Health expenditure (2007): US $ per head (PPP)	463
Health expenditure (2007): % of GDP	6.0
Health expenditure (2007): public (% of total)	50.5
Access to water (% of persons, 2008)	94
Access to sanitation (% of persons, 2008)	85
Total carbon dioxide emissions ('000 metric tons, 2007)	23,849.0
Carbon dioxide emissions per head (metric tons, 2007)	2.3
Human Development Index (2010): ranking	81
Human Development Index (2010): value	0.683

For sources and definitions, see explanatory note on p. vi.

Agriculture

PRINCIPAL CROPS
('000 metric tons)

	2007	2008	2009*
Wheat	1,443	919	n.a.
Barley	535	254	n.a.
Potatoes	350	370	370
Broad beans, horse beans, dry	67	59	60
Almonds, with shell	58	52	n.a.
Olives	998	1,183	750
Artichokes	19	18	18
Tomatoes	1,000	1,170	1,200
Pumpkins, squash and gourds	50	44	45
Cucumbers and gherkins	37	34	35
Chillies and peppers, green	278	291	290
Onions and shallots, green	180	185†	180
Onions, dry	160	160†	160
Peas, green*	15	15	n.a.
Carrots and turnips	56	53	55
Watermelons	466	450	n.a.
Oranges	141	171	170
Tangerines, mandarins, clementines and satsumas	35	36	35
Lemons and limes	31	38	38
Grapefruit and pomelos*	72	72	72
Apples	102	110	110
Pears	55	75	75
Apricots	24	27	27
Peaches and nectarines	101	111	111
Grapes	102	132	n.a.
Figs	22	25	25
Dates	124	127	125

* FAO estimates.
† Unofficial figure.

Aggregate production ('000 metric tons, may include official, semi-official or estimated data): Total cereals 2,028 in 2007, 1,228 in 2008–09; Total roots and tubers 350 in 2007, 370 in 2008–09; Total pulses 110 in 2007, 99 in 2008, 101 in 2009; Total vegetables (incl. melons) 2,539 in 2007, 2,700 in 2008, 2,732 in 2009; Total fruits (excl. melons) 1,072 in 2007, 1,196 in 2008, 1,193 in 2009.

Source: FAO.

LIVESTOCK
('000 head, year ending September)

	2007	2008	2009*
Horses	57	57	57
Asses*	240	240	240
Cattle	710	695	700
Camels*	235	235	235
Sheep	7,618	7,301	7,400
Goats	1,551	1,496	1,500
Chickens*	68,000	70,000	70,000
Turkeys*	5,400	5,400	n.a.

* FAO estimates.

Source: FAO.

LIVESTOCK PRODUCTS
('000 metric tons)

	2006	2007	2008
Cattle meat	56.1	60.3	62.1
Sheep meat	55.7	56.6	52.2
Chicken meat	78.8	96.1	102.5
Cows' milk	957	1,006	1,046
Sheep's milk*	18.2	18.5	18.5
Goats' milk*	13.2	13.8	13.2
Hen eggs*	83	87	89
Wool, greasy*	9.0	9.0	9.0

* FAO estimates.

Source: FAO.

TUNISIA

Forestry

ROUNDWOOD REMOVALS
('000 cu m, excl. bark, FAO estimates)

	2007	2008	2009
Sawlogs, veneer logs and logs for sleepers	25	25	25
Pulpwood	75	75	75
Other industrial wood	118	118	118
Fuel wood	2,163	2,170	2,177
Total	2,381	2,388	2,395

Source: FAO.

SAWNWOOD PRODUCTION
('000 cu m, incl. sleepers)

	1992	1993	1994
Coniferous (softwood)	2.2	5.8	6.8
Broadleaved (hardwood)	4.0	13.6	13.6
Total	6.2	19.4	20.4

1995–2009: Production as in 1994 (FAO estimates).
Source: FAO.

Fishing

('000 metric tons, live weight)

	2006	2007	2008
Capture	111.3	103.8	100.2
Mullets	6.2	6.4	6.6
Common pandora	2.4	2.5	2.9
Sargo breams	0.3	0.3	0.3
Bogue	2.9	2.6	2.7
Jack and horse mackerels	7.8	9.5	8.9
Sardinellas	13.6	16.6	16.6
European pilchard	24.8	19.9	18.4
Chub mackerel	4.9	2.8	3.5
Common cuttlefish	6.4	6.7	4.9
Aquaculture	2.6	3.4	3.3
Total catch (incl. others)	113.9	107.2	103.6

Source: FAO.

Mining

('000 metric tons, unless otherwise indicated)

	2007	2008	2009
Crude petroleum	4,608	4,210	4,056
Natural gas (million cu m)	2,062	2,068	2,540
Iron ore: gross weight	180	211	151
Iron ore: metal content*	94	110	79
Phosphate rock†	8,002	7,539	7,298
Salt (marine)	933	1,063	1,395
Gypsum (crude)	157	177	360

* Estimated production.
† Figures refer to gross weight. The estimated phosphoric acid content (in '000 metric tons) was: 1,140 in 2007; 1,009 in 2008; 1,115 in 2009.

Lead concentrates (metric tons): 8,708 in 2005 (figure refers to metal content of concentrates).

Zinc concentrates (metric tons): 15,889 in 2005 (figure refers to metal content of concentrates).

Sources: mostly US Geological Survey.

Industry

SELECTED PRODUCTS
('000 metric tons, unless otherwise indicated)

	2002	2003	2004
Superphosphates	796	875	868
Cement	6,022	6,038	6,662
Beer ('000 hectolitres)	1,100	997	n.a.
Wine ('000 hectolitres)	271	246	n.a.
Olive oil	30	70	n.a.
Flour	753	785	n.a.
Refined sugar	126	131	n.a.
Crude steel	200	86	70
Quicklime	471	446	476
Motor gasoline ('000 barrels)	3,380	3,600	3,450
Kerosene ('000 barrels)	1,590	1,270	1,310
Diesel oil ('000 barrels)	3,500	3,780	3,220
Residual fuel oil ('000 barrels)	4,020	4,050	3,960
Electric energy (million kWh)	11,281	11,829	12,455

2005 ('000 metric tons unless otherwise indicated): Superphosphates 848; Cement 6,691; Crude steel 66; Quicklime 424; Motor gasoline ('000 barrels) 1,840; Kerosene ('000 barrels) 1,770; Diesel oil ('000 barrels) 3,600; Residual fuel oil ('000 barrels) 4,060; Electric energy (million kWh) 13,007.

2006 ('000 metric tons unless otherwise indicated): Superphosphates 800; Cement 6,932; Crude steel 68; Quicklime 401; Motor gasoline ('000 barrels) 1,540; Kerosene ('000 barrels) 1,050; Diesel oil ('000 barrels) 3,780; Residual fuel oil ('000 barrels) 4,020; Electric energy (million kWh) 14,122.

2007 ('000 metric tons unless otherwise indicated): Superphosphates 806; Cement 7,379; Crude steel 61; Quicklime 395; Motor gasoline ('000 barrels) 1,250 (estimate); Kerosene ('000 barrels) 1,000 (estimate); Diesel oil ('000 barrels) 4,140 (estimate); Residual fuel oil ('000 barrels) 4,320 (estimate); Electric energy (million kWh) 14,060.

2008 ('000 metric tons unless otherwise indicated): Superphosphates 863; Cement 7,243; Crude steel 82; Quicklime 369.

2008 ('000 metric tons unless otherwise indicated): Superphosphates 747; Cement 7,181; Crude steel 155; Quicklime 366.

Sources: partly UN Industrial Commodity Statistics Database; US Geological Survey.

Finance

CURRENCY AND EXCHANGE RATES

Monetary Units
1,000 millimes = 1 Tunisian dinar (TD).

Sterling, Dollar and Euro Equivalents (31 December 2010)
£1 sterling = 2.251 dinars;
US $1 = 1.438 dinars;
€1 = 1.921 dinars;
100 Tunisian dinars = £44.42 = $69.55 = €52.05.

Average Exchange Rate (dinars per US $)
2008 1.2321
2009 1.3503
2010 1.4314.

BUDGET
(million dinars)*

Revenue†	2008	2009‡	2010§
Tax revenue	11,331	11,685	12,025
Direct taxes	4,561	4,646	4,918
Trade taxes	585	520	515
Value-added tax (VAT)	3,309	3,400	3,476
Excise	1,465	1,596	1,540
Other taxes	1,412	1,524	1,576
Non-tax revenue	1,826	1,702	2,021
Capital revenue	8	5	10
Total	13,165	13,392	14,056

TUNISIA

Statistical Survey

Expenditure||	2008	2009‡	2010§
Current expenditure	10,495	10,644	11,660
Wages and salaries	5,732	6,269	6,795
Goods and services	881	1,010	1,125
Interest payments	1,143	1,180	1,240
Domestic	563	561	625
External	579	619	615
Transfers and subsidies	2,740	2,186	2,335
Non-allocated	—	—	165
Capital expenditure	3,181	3,866	4,260
Direct investment	1,538	1,862	2,000
Capital transfers and equity	1,643	2,004	1,685
Non-allocated	—	—	575
Total	13,676	14,510	15,920

* Figures refer to the consolidated accounts of the central Government, including administrative agencies and social security funds. The data exclude the operations of economic and social agencies with their own budgets.
† Excluding grants from abroad (million dinars): 192 in 2008; 183 in 2009 (preliminary); 100 in 2010 (projected). Also excluded are receipts from privatization (million dinars): 147 in 2008; 0 in 2009 (preliminary); 200 in 2010 (projected).
‡ Preliminary figures.
§ Projected figures.
|| Excluding net lending (million dinars): 47 in 2008; 654 in 2009 (preliminary); 100 in 2010 (projected).

Source: IMF, *Tunisia: 2010 Article IV Consultation—Staff Report; Public Information Notice on the Executive Board Discussion; and Statement by the Executive Director for Tunisia* (September 2010).

CENTRAL BANK RESERVES
(US $ million at 31 December)

	2008	2009	2010
Gold (national valuation)	3.4	3.3	3.0
IMF special drawing rights	5.2	379.1	372.3
Reserve position in IMF	31.2	31.7	86.6
Foreign exchange	8,812.9	10,646.5	9,000.3
Total	8,852.7	11,060.6	9,462.2

Source: IMF, *International Financial Statistics*.

MONEY SUPPLY
(million dinars at 31 December)

	2008	2009	2010
Currency outside banks	4,400	5,010	5,520
Demand deposits at commercial banks	7,587	8,835	10,020
Total money (incl. others)	12,991	14,874	16,465

Source: IMF, *International Financial Statistics*.

COST OF LIVING
(Consumer Price Index; base: 2000 = 100)

	2008	2009	2010
Food	132.6	138.3	147.2
Electricity, gas and other fuels	146.7	150.0	167.8
Clothing	118.4	121.0	125.3
Rent	131.3	136.1	141.3
All items (incl. others)	128.8	133.6	139.1

Source: ILO.

NATIONAL ACCOUNTS
(million dinars at current prices)

Expenditure on the Gross Domestic Product

	2007	2008	2009
Government final consumption expenditure	8,298.0	8,917.0	9,715.0
Private final consumption expenditure	30,699.5	33,922.3	36,370.4
Gross fixed capital formation	11,490.4	13,060.4	14,310.3
Change in inventories	318.6	998.3	103.2
Total domestic expenditure	50,806.5	56,898.0	60,498.9
Exports of goods and services	25,469.9	30,761.1	26,428.1
Less Imports of goods and services	26,418.8	32,440.3	28,151.6
GDP in purchasers' values	49,857.5	55,218.8	58,775.4
GDP at constant 2005 prices	48,617.5	52,078.1	56,957.3

Gross Domestic Product by Economic Activity

	2008	2009	2010
Agriculture and fishing	4,335.6	4,885.5	4,637.5
Mining (excluding hydrocarbons)	642.7	592.5	618.4
Manufacturing (excluding hydrocarbons)	9,956.2	9,937.5	10,410.8
Hydrocarbons, electricity and water	4,460.1	3,819.5	4,820.8
Construction and public works	2,267.8	2,553.5	2,821.2
Maintenance and repair	198.7	215.8	234.4
Transport and telecommunications	6,800.4	7,283.9	7,780.8
Hotels and restaurants	2,785.1	2,924.7	3,193.3
Trade, finance, etc.	12,359.2	13,494.5	14,641.6
Non-market services	8,273.7	9,002.2	9,697.0
Sub-total	52,079.5	54,709.6	58,855.8
Less Imputed bank service charges	925.1	869.1	937.5
Gross value added at factor cost	51,154.5	53,840.5	57,918.5
Indirect taxes, *less* subsidies	4,064.3	4,934.9	5,445.6
GDP in purchasers' values	55,218.8	58,775.4	63,364.3

BALANCE OF PAYMENTS
(US $ million)

	2007	2008	2009
Exports of goods f.o.b.	15,148	19,184	14,419
Imports of goods f.o.b.	−18,024	−23,194	−18,117
Trade balance	−2,876	−4,010	−3,699
Exports of services	4,909	6,014	5,499
Imports of services	−2,803	−3,370	−2,974
Balance on goods and services	−769	−1,366	−1,174
Other income received	563	522	318
Other income paid	−2,329	−2,789	−2,328
Balance on goods, services and income	−2,536	−3,634	−3,185
Current transfers received	1,650	1,948	1,979
Current transfers paid	−32	−26	−28
Current balance	−917	−1,711	−1,234
Capital account (net)	166	79	164
Direct investment abroad	−17	−38	−70
Direct investment from abroad	1,532	2,638	1,595
Portfolio investment liabilities	30	−39	−89
Other investment assets	−239	−25	−13
Other investment liabilities	170	649	1,217
Net errors and omissions	−37	114	67
Overall balance	689	1,667	1,639

Source: IMF, *International Financial Statistics*.

TUNISIA

External Trade

PRINCIPAL COMMODITIES
(US $ million)

Imports c.i.f.	2007	2008	2009
Food and live animals	1,529.0	1,912.7	1,128.4
Cereal and cereal preparations	941.7	1,229.0	484.0
Mineral fuels, lubricants, etc.	2,442.9	4,151.0	2,178.2
Petroleum and related products	1,990.7	3,299.3	1,686.9
Gas, natural and manufactured	449.1	844.7	487.0
Chemicals and related products	1,898.8	2,345.6	2,065.3
Plastics in primary forms	471.2	531.0	416.7
Basic manufactures	4,798.0	5,598.2	4,334.1
Textile yarn, fabrics and related products	1,997.5	2,087.6	1,749.0
Cotton fabrics, woven	959.0	987.0	829.3
Machinery and transport equipment	5,621.1	6,725.9	6,604.1
General industrial machinery and equipment	860.2	1,048.0	983.0
Electrical machinery, apparatus and appliances	1,568.7	1,920.0	1,756.6
Road vehicles	1,217.8	1,454.4	1,408.4
Miscellaneous manufactured articles	1,656.1	1,778.6	1,684.7
Total	19,099.4	24,638.4	19,096.2

Exports f.o.b.	2007	2008	2009
Food and live animals	687.4	856.6	758.6
Mineral fuels, lubricants, etc.	2,456.1	3,345.2	1,969.2
Petroleum and related products	2,455.8	3,345.0	1,969.0
Petroleum oils and oils obtained from bituminous materials, crude	2,056.3	2,630.8	1,553.1
Animal and vegetable oils	674.1	771.2	1,553.1
Chemicals and related products	1,425.7	2,942.8	1,521.1
Fertilizers	661.7	1,525.4	661.2
Basic manufactures	1,543.6	1,786.1	1,474.0
Machinery and transport equipment	2,910.5	4,044.1	3,624.9
Electrical machinery, apparatus and appliances	1,862.3	2,538.8	2,214.7
Miscellaneous manufactured articles	4,758.7	5,111.4	4,319.1
Articles of clothing and clothing accessories	3,571.1	3,765.6	3,120.3
Men's or boy's outerwear	1,023.1	1,020.7	760.5
Footwear	575.8	608.0	512.3
Total	15,165.4	19,320.0	14,445.1

Source: UN, *International Trade Statistics Yearbook*.

PRINCIPAL TRADING PARTNERS
(US $ million)*

Imports c.i.f.	2007	2008	2009
Algeria	299.8	724.3	501.2
Argentina	208.2	404.5	161.7
Belgium	478.1	444.2	383.1
Brazil	222.2	303.3	197.7
China, People's Republic	654.0	919.6	956.6
Egypt	204.3	249.6	167.8
France (incl. Monaco)	4,082.2	4,546.3	3,832.1
Germany	1,512.7	1,717.0	1,672.5
India	162.6	218.4	223.9
Italy	3,724.2	4,245.4	3,108.9
Japan	289.6	325.9	237.9
Libya	646.3	1,073.7	560.6
Netherlands	277.7	345.0	285.3

Imports c.i.f.—continued	2007	2008	2009
Russia	814.5	1,855.7	688.1
Saudi Arabia	144.2	228.3	107.7
Spain	886.0	951.2	867.0
Sweden	144.8	161.7	153.6
Switzerland (incl. Liechtenstein)	163.2	159.2	171.0
Turkey	496.1	732.3	576.6
Ukraine	305.2	516.4	327.4
United Kingdom	357.2	456.0	341.3
USA	647.2	748.8	764.8
Total (incl. others)	19,099.4	24,638.4	19,096.2

Exports f.o.b.	2007	2008	2009
Algeria	287.0	408.1	451.2
Belgium	358.1	430.0	319.6
France (incl. Monaco)	4,877.6	5,507.5	4,283.3
Germany	1,247.5	1,338.0	1,270.1
India	141.0	595.2	238.3
Iran	66.8	234.7	127.8
Italy	3,531.0	3,991.7	3,038.4
Libya	697.5	871.2	831.8
Morocco	172.9	234.2	209.4
Netherlands	358.5	422.3	232.7
Spain	783.5	946.1	486.9
Switzerland (incl. Liechtenstein)	262.9	456.0	133.3
Turkey	180.8	309.4	170.8
United Kingdom	652.8	898.6	686.7
USA	167.2	323.1	196.8
Total (incl. others)	15,165.4	19,320.0	14,445.1

* Imports by country of production; exports by country of last destination.

Source: UN, *International Trade Statistics Yearbook*.

Transport

RAILWAYS
(traffic)

	2007	2008	2009
Passengers carried ('000)	38,810	39,226	38,576
Passenger-kilometres (million)	1,487	1,494	1,486
Freight carried ('000 metric tons)	11,006	10,528	9,318
Freight net ton-kilometres (million)	2,197	2,073	1,821

ROAD TRAFFIC
(estimates, motor vehicles in use at 31 December)

	2000	2001	2002
Passenger cars	516,525	552,897	585,194
Buses and coaches	11,143	11,973	12,181
Lorries and vans	240,421	253,760	266,499
Road tractors	8,307	9,165	9,605

2007: Passenger cars 746,695; Buses and coaches 10,113; Lorries and vans 300,508; Motorcycles 5,303.

Source: IRF, *World Road Statistics*.

SHIPPING
Merchant Fleet
(vessels registered at 31 December)

	2007	2008	2009
Number of vessels	73	74	75
Total displacement ('000 grt)	140.2	142.2	165.1

Source: IHS Fairplay, *World Fleet Statistics*.

International Sea-borne Freight Traffic
('000 metric tons)

	2007	2008	2009
Goods loaded*	7,986	7,939	7,817
Goods unloaded	16,121	16,520	14,553

* Excluding Algerian crude petroleum loaded at La Skhirra.

CIVIL AVIATION
(traffic on scheduled services)

	2004	2005	2006
Kilometres flown (million)	28	30	31
Passengers carried ('000)	1,940	1,997	2,014
Passenger-km (million)	2,853	2,995	2,976
Total ton-km (million)	299	312	308

Source: UN, *Statistical Yearbook*.

Tourism

FOREIGN TOURIST ARRIVALS BY NATIONALITY
('000)

	2006	2007	2008
Algeria	945.3	980.6	968.5
Austria	92.0	89.2	72.9
Belgium	164.3	167.4	169.1
France	1,234.7	1,335.4	1,395.3
Germany	547.4	514.0	521.5
Italy	464.3	444.5	444.5
Libya	1,472.4	1,544.8	1,766.9
Switzerland	103.1	106.2	105.7
United Kingdom	350.7	312.8	254.9
Total (incl. others)	6,549.5	6,761.9	7,049.0

Receipts from tourism (US $ million, incl. passenger transport): 2,977 in 2006; 3,373 in 2007; 3,909 in 2008.

Source: World Tourism Organization.

Communications Media

	2007	2008	2009
Telephones ('000 main lines in use)	1,273.3	1,239.1	1,278.5
Mobile cellular telephones ('000 subscribers)	7,842.6	8,602.2	9,797.0
Internet users ('000)	1,721.7	2,799.6	3,499.5
Broadband subscribers ('000)	95.9	227.3	372.8

Personal computers: 997,150 (96.6 per 1,000 persons) in 2008.
Radio receivers ('000 in use): 2,060 in 1997.
Book production (titles): 1,260 in 1999.
Daily newspapers (titles): 10 in 2004 (average circulation 219,475 in 2001).
Non-daily newspapers (titles): 39 in 2001 (average circulation 963,861).
Periodicals (titles): 182 in 2000 (average circulation 525,000).
Television receivers ('000 in use): 1,900 in 2000.

Sources: UNESCO, *Statistical Yearbook*; UNESCO Institute for Statistics; UN, *Statistical Yearbook*; and International Telecommunication Union.

Education

(2009/10, unless otherwise indicated)

	Institutions	Teachers	Students
Primary (public)			
1st cycle	4,517	58,567	1,008,600
2nd cycle	1,937*	36,069*	485,860
Secondary (public)	502*	35,812*	481,848
Higher	192*	18,993†	346,079†

* 2008/09.
† Full-time equivalent.

Pupil-teacher ratio (primary education, UNESCO estimate): 17.3 in 2007/08 (Source: UNESCO Institute for Statistics).

Adult literacy rate (UNESCO estimates): 77.6% (males 86.4%; females 71.0%) in 2008 (Source: UNESCO Institute for Statistics).

Directory

The Government

HEAD OF STATE

President: FOUAD MEBAZAA (ad interim; sworn in on 15 January 2011).

COUNCIL OF MINISTERS
(May 2011)

Prime Minister: BÉJI CAÏD ESSEBSI.
Minister of Foreign Affairs: MUHAMMAD MOULDI KÉFI.
Minister of the Interior: HABIB ESSID.
Minister of National Defence: ABDELKARIM ZEBIDI.
Minister of Justice and Human Rights: LAZHAR KAROUI CHEBBI.
Minister of Religious Affairs: LAROUSSI MIZOURI.
Minister of Women's Affairs: LILIA LAABIDI.
Minister of Social Affairs: MUHAMMAD NACEUR.
Minister of Education: TAÏB BACCOUCHE.
Minister of Regional and Local Development: ABDERRAZAK ZOUARI.
Minister of Culture: EZZEDINE BESCHAOUCH.
Minister of Public Health: HABIBA ZÉHI BEN ROMDHANE.
Minister of Youth and Sports: MUHAMMAD ALOULOU.
Minister of Professional Training and Employment: SAID AYDI.
Minister of Finance: JELLOUL AYAD.
Minister of Agriculture and Environment: MOKHTAR JALLALI.
Minister of Transport and Public Works: YACINE IBRAHIM.
Minister of Trade and Tourism: MEHDI HOUAS.
Minister of Planning and International Co-operation: ABDELHAMID TRIKI.
Minister of Higher Education and Scientific Research: RIFAAT CHAABOUNI.
Minister of Industry and Technology: ABDELAZIZ RASSAA.
Minister of State Properties: AHMAD ADHOUM.
Minister-delegate to the Prime Minister: RAFAA BEN ACHOUR.

There are, in addition, nine Secretaries of State. The Governor of the Central Bank also has full ministerial status.

MINISTRIES

Office of the President: Palais de Carthage, 2016 Carthage; internet www.carthage.tn.

Office of the Prime Minister: pl. du Gouvernement, La Kasbah, 1008 Tunis; tel. (71) 565-400; e-mail boc@pm.gov.tn; internet www.pm.gov.tn.

TUNISIA

Ministry of Agriculture, Water Resources and Fisheries: 30 rue Alain Savary, 1002 Tunis; tel. (71) 786-833; fax (71) 780-391; e-mail mag@ministeres.tn.

Ministry of Communications: blvd du 7 novembre 1987, Centre Urbain Nord, 1082 Tunis; tel. (71) 702-288; fax (71) 702–822; e-mail mc@ministeres.tn.

Ministry of Communication Technologies: 3 bis rue d'Angleterre, 1000 Tunis; tel. (71) 359-000; fax (71) 352-353; e-mail info@infocom.tn; internet www.infocom.tn.

Ministry of Culture and Heritage Preservation: 8 rue 2 mars 1934, la Kasbah, 1006 Tunis; tel. (71) 563-006; fax (71) 563-816; e-mail minculture@email.ati.tn; internet www.culture.tn.

Ministry of Development and International Co-operation: pl. Ali Zouaoui, 1069 Tunis; tel. (71) 240-133; fax (71) 351-666; e-mail boc@mdci.gov.tn; internet www.investissement.tn.

Ministry of Education: blvd Bab Benat, 1030 Tunis; tel. (71) 568-768; e-mail med@ministeres.tn; internet www.education.tn.

Ministry of the Environment and Sustainable Development: Centre Urbain Nord, Ariana, 2080 Tunis; tel. (70) 728-455; fax (70) 728-655; e-mail boc@mineat.gov.tn; internet www.environnement.nat.tn.

Ministry of Equipment, Housing and Land Planning: 10 blvd Habib Chrita, Cité Jardin, 1002 Tunis; tel. (71) 842-244; fax (71) 840-495; e-mail brc@mehat.gov.tn; internet www.mehat.gov.tn.

Ministry of Finance: pl. du Gouvernement, La Kasbah, 1008 Tunis; tel. (71) 571-888; fax (71) 572-390; e-mail pcontenu@finances.gov.tn; internet www.portail.finances.gov.tn.

Ministry of Foreign Affairs: ave de la Ligue des états arabes, 1030 Tunis; tel. (71) 847-500; fax (71) 785-025; e-mail mae@ministeres.tn; internet www.diplomatie.gov.tn.

Ministry of Higher Education and Scientific Research: ave Ouled Haffouz, 1030 Tunis; tel. (71) 786-300; fax (71) 786-701; e-mail mes@mes.rnu.tn; internet www.mes.tn.

Ministry of Industry and Technology: Immeuble Beya, 40 rue 8011, Montplaisir, 1002 Tunis; tel. (71) 791-132; fax (71) 782-742; e-mail webmaster@industrie.gov.tn; internet www.industrie.gov.tn.

Ministry of the Interior and Local Development: ave Habib Bourguiba, 1000 Tunis; tel. (71) 333-000; fax (71) 340-888; e-mail mint@ministeres.tn.

Ministry of Justice and Human Rights: 31 ave Bab Benat, 1019 Tunis; tel. (71) 561-440; fax (71) 586-106; e-mail info@e-justice.tn; internet www.e-justice.tn.

Ministry of National Defence: blvd Bab Menara, 1008 Tunis; tel. (71) 560-240; fax (71) 561-804; e-mail defnat@defense.tn; internet www.defense.tn.

Ministry of Professional Training and Employment: 10 ave Ouled Haffouz, 1006 Tunis; tel. (71) 792-432; fax (71) 794-615; e-mail webmaster@email.ati.tn; internet www.emploi.gov.tn.

Ministry of Public Health: Bab Saâdoun, 1006 Tunis; tel. (71) 577-100; fax (71) 567-100; e-mail msp@ministeres.tn; internet www.santetunisie.rns.tn.

Ministry of Religious Affairs: 76 ave Bab Benat, 1009 Tunis; tel. (71) 570-147; fax (71) 572-296; e-mail mar@ministeres.tn; internet www.affaires-religieuses.tn.

Ministry of Social Affairs, Solidarity and Tunisians Abroad: 27 ave Bab Benat, 1019 Tunis; tel. (71) 567-502; fax (71) 568-722; e-mail masste@rnas.gov.tn; internet www.social.tn.

Ministry of State Property and Land Affairs: 19 ave de Paris, 1000 Tunis; tel. (71) 265-340; fax (71) 342-552; e-mail dg.dgomi@mdeaf.gov.tn; internet www.mdeaf.gov.tn.

Ministry of Tourism: 1 ave Muhammad V, 1001 Tunis; tel. (71) 341-077; fax (71) 354-223; e-mail ministere_du_tourisme@email.ati.tn.

Ministry of Trade and Handicrafts: 37 ave Kheireddine Pacha, 1002 Tunis; tel. (71) 904-070; fax (71) 901-324; e-mail mcmr@ministeres.tn; internet www.commerce.gov.tn.

Ministry of Transport: blvd du 7 novembre 1987, 2035 Tunis; tel. (71) 772-110; e-mail mtr@ministeres.tn.

Ministry of Women's, Family, Children's and Elderly Affairs: 2 rue d'Alger, 1001 Tunis; tel. (71) 252-514; fax (71) 349-900; e-mail maffepa@email.ati.tn; internet www.femmes.tn.

Ministry of Youth, Sports and Physical Education: ave Med Ali Akid, Cité El Khadhra, 1003 Tunis; tel. (71) 841-433; fax (71) 800-267; e-mail portail.sport@sport.tn; internet www.sport.tn.

President and Legislature

PRESIDENT

Presidential Election, 25 October 2009

Candidate	Votes	% of votes
Zine al-Abidine Ben Ali	4,238,711	89.62
Muhammad Bouchiha	236,955	5.01
Ahmed Inoubli	176,726	3.80
Ahmed Brahim	74,257	1.57
Total*	**4,729,649**	**100.00**

* Excluding 7,718 invalid votes.

LEGISLATURE

Majlis al-Nuab
(Chamber of Deputies)

Palais du Bardo, 2000 Tunis; tel. (71) 510–200; fax (71) 514-608; e-mail majless@chambre-dep.tn; internet www.chambre-dep.tn.

Election, 25 October 2009

Party	Votes	% of votes	Seats
Rassemblement constitutionnel démocratique	3,754,559	84.59	161
Mouvement des démocrates socialistes	205,374	4.63	16
Parti de l'unité populaire	150,639	3.39	12
Union démocratique unioniste	113,773	2.56	9
Parti social libéral	99,468	2.24	8
Parti des verts pour le progrès	74,185	1.67	6
Mouvement ettajdid	22,206	0.50	2
Others (incl. independents)	18,293	0.41	0
Total*	**4,438,497**	**100.00**	**214†**

* Excluding 8,891 invalid votes.
† Under the terms of an amendment to the electoral code adopted by the National Assembly in 2009, 25% of the seats in the National Assembly (and thus 53 in the current legislature) were reserved for candidates of opposition parties. These were allotted according to the proportion of votes received nationally by each party.

Majlis al-Mustasharin
(Chamber of Advisers)

rue du 2 mars, 1934 Le Bardo, 2000 Tunis; tel. (71) 662-219; fax (71) 662-255; e-mail contact@chambredesconseillers.tn; internet www.chambredesconseillers.tn.

Speaker: ABDULLAH KALLEL.

Election, 10 August 2008

	Seats*
Representatives of the main professional unions and federations†	42
Representatives of the governorates‡	43
Appointed by the President	41
Total	**126**

* Members of the Chamber of Advisers serve a six-year term; one-half of its members are replaced every three years.
† 14 seats are reserved for representatives of the trades unions. However, owing to a boycott by the Union Générale Tunisienne du Travail (UGTT), these seats have remained vacant since the inaugural election in July 2005.
‡ One or two members are elected from each of the 24 governorates, depending on the size of its population.

Political Organizations

Following the removal from office of former President Zine al-Abidine Ben Ali in January 2011, a number of previously outlawed political organizations—including the Islamist Parti de la renaissance/Hizb al-Nahdah—were granted legal status, while several new parties were also expected to participate in elections scheduled for 23 July. In early March the former ruling party, the Rassemblement constitutionnel démocratique, was formally dissolved.

Congrès pour la République: Tunis; e-mail cprtunisie@yahoo.fr; internet www.cprtunisie.net; f. 2001; Leader MONCEF MARZOUKI.

Forum démocratique pour le travail et les libertés (FDTL): Tunis; internet www.fdtl.org; f. 2002; Leader Dr MUSTAPHA BEN JAAFAR.

TUNISIA

Mouvement des démocrates socialistes (MDS): Tunis; in favour of a pluralist political system; participated in 1981 election and was officially recognized in Nov. 1983; 11-mem Political Bureau and 60-mem Nat. Council, normally elected by the party Congress; Sec.-Gen. ISMAIL BOULAHYA.

Mouvement ettajdid: 6 rue Métouia, 1000 Tunis; tel. (71) 256-400; fax (71) 240-981; internet ettajdid.org; f. 1993 as Mouvement du renouveau, successor to Parti communiste tunisien; legal; Sec.-Gen. AHMAD BRAHIM; Pres. of Nat. Council MUHAMMAD ALI HALOUANI.

Parti communiste des ouvriers tunisiens (PCOT): Tunis; e-mail pcot@albadil.org; internet www.albadil.org; illegal; Leader HAMMA HAMMAMI.

Parti démocrate progressiste (PDP): Tunis; tel. (71) 332-194; e-mail admin@pdpinfo.org; internet www.pdpinfo.org; f. 1983 as Rassemblement socialiste progressiste; officially recognized in Sept. 1988; name changed as above in 2001; leftist; Sec.-Gen. MAYA JRIBI.

Parti de la renaissance/Hizb al-Nahdah: Tunis; e-mail nahdha@ezzeitouna.org; fmrly Mouvement de la tendance islamique (banned in 1981); awarded legal status in March 2011; Leader RACHID GHANNOUCHI; Sec.-Gen. Sheikh ABD AL-FATHA MOUROU.

Parti social libéral (PSL): 42 ave Hédi Chaker, 1002 Tunis; tel. (71) 789-089; fax (71) 789-060; e-mail p.s.l@gnet.tn; f. 1988; officially recognized in Sept. 1988 as the Parti social pour le progrès; adopted present name in 1993; liberal; Pres. Dr MONDHER THABET.

Parti de l'unité populaire (PUP): 7 rue d'Autriche, 1002 Tunis; tel. (71) 791-436; fax (71) 835-152; internet www.elwahda.org.tn; breakaway faction from Mouvement de l'unité populaire; officially recognized in Nov. 1983; Sec.-Gen. MUHAMMAD BOUCHIHA.

Parti des verts pour le progrès (PVP): 2 ave de France, bureau 335, 3ème étage, 1000 Tunis; tel. (71) 328-439; fax (71) 328-438; e-mail contact@partivert-tunisie.com; internet www.partivert-tunisie.com; f. 2006; seeks to promote awareness of the environment; Sec.-Gen. MONGI KHAMASSI.

Rassemblement constitutionnel démocratique (RCD): f. 1934 as the Néo-Destour Party, following a split in the Destour (Constitution) Party; renamed Parti socialiste destourien 1964; present name adopted 1988; moderate left-wing republican party, which achieved Tunisian independence; officially dissolved March 2011.

Union démocratique unioniste (UDU): Tunis; officially recognized in Nov. 1988; supports Arab unity; Sec.-Gen. AHMED INOUBLI.

Diplomatic Representation

EMBASSIES IN TUNISIA

Algeria: 18 rue de Niger, 1002 Tunis; tel. (71) 783-166; fax (71) 788-804; e-mail ambalg@gnet.tn; Ambassador MUHAMMAD BEN HASSINE.

Argentina: rue du Lac Victoria, BP 12, 1053 Tunis; tel. (71) 964-871; fax (71) 963-006; e-mail embargentunez@gnet.tn; Chargé d'affaires a.i. FERNANDO JAVIER VALLINA PADRO.

Austria: 16 rue ibn Hamdiss, BP 23, al-Menzah, 1004 Tunis; tel. (71) 239-038; fax (71) 755-427; e-mail tunis-ob@bmeia.gv.at; Ambassador Dr JOHANN FRÖHLICH.

Bahrain: 72 rue Mouaouia ibn Soufiane, BP 79, al-Menzah VIII, 2019 Tunis; tel. (71) 750-865; fax (71) 766-549; e-mail tunis.mission@mofa.gov.bh; Ambassador Sheikh MUHAMMAD BIN ALI AL KHALIFA.

Belgium: 47 rue du 1er juin, BP 24, 1002 Tunis; tel. (71) 781-655; fax (71) 792-797; e-mail tunis@diplobel.fed.be; internet www.diplomatie.be/tunis; Ambassador THOMAS ANTOINE.

Brazil: 5 rue Sufétula, BP 83, 1002 Tunis; tel. (71) 893-569; fax (71) 846-995; e-mail brasemb.tunis@gnet.tn; internet www.ambassadedubresil.com; Ambassador LUIZ ANTONIO FACHINI GOMES.

Bulgaria: 5 rue Ryhane, BP 6, Cité Mahrajène, 1082 Tunis; tel. (71) 798-962; fax (71) 791-667; e-mail amba_bulgarie@hexabyte.tn; internet www.mfa.bg/en/66/; Ambassador PETKO DOYKOV.

Canada: 3 rue du Sénégal, pl. d'Afrique, BP 31, Belvédère, 1002 Tunis; tel. (71) 104-000; fax (71) 104-190; e-mail tunis@international.gc.ca; internet www.canadainternational.gc.ca/tunisia-tunisie; Ambassador ARIEL DELOUYA.

China, People's Republic: 22 rue Dr Burnet, 1002 Tunis; tel. (71) 780-064; fax (71) 792-631; e-mail chinaemb_tn@mfa.gov.cn; Ambassador HUO ZHENGDE.

Congo, Democratic Republic: 11 rue Tertullien, Notre Dame, Tunis; tel. (71) 281-833; Ambassador MBOLADINGA KATAKO.

Côte d'Ivoire: 17 rue el-Mansoura, BP 21, Belvédère, 1002 Tunis; tel. (71) 755-911; fax (71) 755-901; e-mail acitn@ambaci-tunis.org; Ambassador YAPO ATCHAPO THOMAS.

Cuba: 1 rue Amilcar, al-Menzah VIII, 1004 Tunis; tel. (71) 767-235; fax (71) 755-922; e-mail embajador-tunez@topnet.tn; internet emba.cubaminrex.cu/tunezar; Ambassador GABRIEL TIEL CAPOTE.

Czech Republic: 98 rue de Palestine, BP 53, Belvédère, 1002 Tunis; tel. (71) 781-916; fax (71) 793-228; e-mail embassy@embassy.mzv.cz; internet www.mzv.cz/tunis; Ambassador ALEXANDR SLABÝ.

Egypt: ave Muhammad V, Quartier Montplaisir, rue 8007, Tunis; tel. (71) 792-233; fax (71) 794-389; e-mail egyembassy.tunis@planet.tn; Ambassador AHMED CHAFIK ISMAIL ABDELMOTI.

Finland: Dar Nordique, rue du Lac Neuchâtel, Les Berges du Lac, 1053 Tunis; tel. (71) 861-777; fax (71) 961-080; e-mail sanomat.tun@formin.fi; internet www.finlandtunis.org; Ambassador TIINA JORTIKKA-LAITINEN.

France: 2 pl. de l'Indépendance, 1000 Tunis; tel. (71) 105-111; fax (71) 105-100; e-mail courier@ambassadefrance-tn.org; internet www.ambassadefrance-tn.org; Ambassador BORIS BOILLON.

Germany: 1 rue al-Hamra, BP 35, Mutuelleville, 1002 Tunis; tel. (71) 143-200; fax (71) 788-242; e-mail reg1@tunis.diplo.de; internet www.tunis.diplo.de; Ambassador Dr HORST-WOLFRAM KERLL.

Greece: 6 rue Saint Fulgence, Notre Dame, 1082 Tunis; tel. (71) 288-411; fax (71) 789-518; e-mail gremb.tun@mfa.gr; Ambassador DORA GROSOMANIDOU.

Hungary: 12 rue Achtart, BP 572, Nord Hilton, 1082 Tunis; tel. (71) 780-544; fax (71) 781-264; e-mail mission.tun@kum.hu; internet www.mfa.gov.hu/emb/tunis; Ambassador TIBOR KECSKÉS.

India: 4 pl. Didon, Notre Dame, 1002 Tunis; tel. (71) 787-819; fax (71) 783-394; e-mail amb.tunis@mea.gov.in; internet www.indianembassytunis.com; Ambassador PARAMPREET SINGH RANDHAWA.

Indonesia: 15 rue du Lac Malaren, BP 58, 1053 Tunis; tel. (71) 860-377; fax (71) 861-758; e-mail kbritun@gnet.tn; Ambassador MOHAMMAD IBNU SAID.

Iran: 10 rue de Docteur Burnet, Belvédère, 1002 Tunis; tel. (71) 790-084; fax (71) 793-177; Ambassador PEIMAN DJEBELLI.

Iraq: ave Tahar B. Achour, route X2 m 10, Mutuelleville, Tunis; tel. (71) 965-824; fax (71) 964-750; e-mail tunemb@iraqmofamail.net; Ambassador SAAD JASSEM AL-HAYANI.

Italy: 3 rue Gamal Abd al-Nasser, 1000 Tunis; tel. (71) 321-811; fax (71) 324-155; e-mail ambitalia.tunisi@esteri.it; internet www.ambtunisi.esteri.it; Ambassador PIETRO BENASSI.

Japan: 9 rue Apollo XI, BP 163, Cité Mahrajène, 1082 Tunis; tel. (71) 791-251; fax (71) 786-625; e-mail contact.embj@planet.tn; internet www.tn.emb-japan.go.jp; Ambassador TOSHIYUKI TAGA.

Jordan: 10 Nahj al-Shankiti, 1002 Tunis; tel. (71) 785-829; fax (71) 786-461; e-mail emb.jordan@planet.tn; Ambassador SAMIR MUSTAPHA KHALIFA.

Korea, Republic: 3 rue de l'Alhambra, Mutuelleville, Tunis; tel. (71) 799-905; fax (71) 791-923; e-mail tunisie@mofat.go.kr; internet tun.mofat.go.kr; Ambassador SONG BONG-HEON.

Kuwait: 40 route Ariane, al-Menzah, Tunis; tel. (71) 754-811; fax (71) 767-659; e-mail tunis@mofa.gov.kw; Ambassador AHMAD AL-AWADHI.

Lebanon: rue d'Ormia, 1053 Les Berges du Lac, Tunis; tel. and fax (71) 960-001; e-mail ambassadeliban@planet.tn; Ambassador FARID ABBOUD.

Libya: 48 bis rue du 1er juin, Mutuelleville, 1002 Tunis; tel. (71) 780-866; fax (71) 795-338.

Mali: 3 impasse Aboul Atahya, rue Dr Burnet, Mutueville, 1002 Tunis; BP 109, Cité Mahrajène, 1082 Tunis; tel. (71) 792-589; fax (71) 791-453; e-mail ambamali@planet.tn; Ambassador ARAFA M'BARAKOU ASKIA TOURÉ.

Malta: Immeuble Carthage Centre, rue du Lac de Constance, BP 71, Les Berges du Lac, Tunis; tel. (71) 965-811; fax (71) 965-977; e-mail maltaembassy.tunis@gov.mt; Ambassador Dr VICTORIA ANN CREMONA.

Mauritania: 17 rue Fatma Ennechi, BP 62, al-Menzah, Tunis; tel. (71) 234-935; Ambassador CHEIKH EL AFIA OULD KHOUNA.

Morocco: 39 ave du 1er juin, 1002 Tunis; tel. (71) 782-775; fax (71) 787-103; e-mail ambamaroc@sifamatunis.net; Ambassador NAJIB ZEROUALI EL-OUARITI.

Netherlands: 6–8 ave Meycen, BP 47, Belvédère, 1082 Tunis; tel. (71) 155-300; fax (71) 155-335; e-mail tun@minbuza.nl; internet www.hollandembassy-tunisia.com; Ambassador CAROLINE GABRIËLA WEIJERS.

Pakistan: 35 rue Ali Ayari, al-Menzah IX, Tunis; tel. (71) 871-330; fax (71) 871-410; e-mail pareptunis@yahoo.com; Ambassador ATHAR MAHMOUD.

Poland: Le Grand Blvd de la Corniche, 1053 Tunis; tel. (71) 196-191; fax (71) 196-203; e-mail tunis.amb.sekretariat@msz.gov.pl; internet www.tunis.polemb.net; Ambassador KRZYSZTOF OLENDZKI.

Portugal: 2 rue Sufétula, Belvédère, 1002 Tunis; tel. (71) 893-981; fax (71) 791-008; e-mail ambport@hexabyte.tn; Ambassador MARIA RITA DA FRANCA SOUSA FERRO LEVY GOMES.

TUNISIA

Qatar: rue Alhadi Krai, Northern al-Omran Quarter, 1082 Tunis; tel. (71) 849-600; fax (71) 749-073; e-mail tunis@mofa.gov.qa; Ambassador SAAD BIN NASSER AL-HUMAIDI.

Romania: 18 ave d'Afrique, BP 57, al-Menzah V, 1004 Tunis; tel. (71) 766-926; fax (71) 767-695; e-mail amb.roumanie@planet.tn; internet www.ambassade-roumanie.intl.tn; Ambassador SORIN-MIHAIL TĂNĂSESCU.

Russia: 4 rue Bergamotes, BP 48, el-Manar I, 2092 Tunis; tel. (71) 882-446; fax (71) 882-478; e-mail ambrustn@mail.ru; internet www.tunisie.mid.ru; Ambassador ANDREI POLYAKOV.

Saudi Arabia: blvd du 7 novembre 1987, Centre Urbain Nord C, Mahrajène, 1080 Tunis; tel. (70) 233-466; fax (70) 751-441; Ambassador Dr ABDULLAH BIN ABD AL-AZIZ BIN MUAMMAR.

Senegal: 122 ave de la Liberté, Belvédère, Tunis; tel. (71) 802-397; fax (71) 780-770; e-mail ambassene@planet.tn; internet www.ambasenegal.intl.tn; Ambassador SAOUDATOU NDIAYE SECK.

Serbia: 4 rue de Libéria, Belvédère, 1002 Tunis; tel. (71) 783-057; fax (71) 796-482; e-mail amb.serbia@gnet.tn; Ambassador MILICA CUBRILO FILIPOVIC.

Somalia: 6 rue Hadramout, Mutuelleville, Tunis; tel. (71) 289-505; Ambassador AHMAD ABDALLAH MUHAMMAD.

South Africa: 7 rue Achtart, Nord Hilton, 1082 Tunis; tel. (71) 800-311; fax (71) 796-742; e-mail sa@emb-safrica.intl.tn; internet www.southafrica.intl.tn; Ambassador LUCAS DON NGAKANE.

Spain: 22–24 ave Dr Ernest Conseil, Cité Jardin, 1002 Tunis; tel. (71) 782-217; fax (71) 786-267; e-mail emb.tunez@maec.es; Ambassador ANTONIO COSANO PÉREZ.

Sudan: 37 rue d'Afrique, al-Menzah V, 1008 Tunis; tel. (71) 231-322; fax (71) 751-756; e-mail contact@soudanembassy-tn.com; Ambassador ABD AL-BASSET BADAOUI ALI SENOUSSI.

Switzerland: BP 56, Les Berges du Lac, 1053 Tunis; tel. (71) 962-997; fax (71) 965-796; e-mail tun.vertretung@eda.admin.ch; internet www.eda.admin.ch/tunis; Ambassador PIERRE COMBERNOUS.

Syria: 119 Azzouz Ribai-Almanar 3, Tunis; tel. (71) 888-188; Ambassador Dr SAMI GLAIEL.

Turkey: 4 ave Hédi Karay, BP 134, 1082 Tunis; tel. (71) 750-668; fax (71) 767-045; e-mail turkemb.tunis@mfa.gov.tr; internet tunis.emb.mfa.gov.tr; Ambassador AKIN ALGAN.

Ukraine: 7 rue Saint Fulgence, Notre Dame, 1002 Tunis; tel. (71) 845-861; fax (71) 840-866; e-mail emb_tn@mfa.gov.ua; internet www.mfa.gov.ua/tunis; Ambassador VALERII RYLACH.

United Arab Emirates: 9 rue Achtart, Nord Hilton, Belvédère, 1002 Tunis; tel. (71) 788-888; fax (71) 788-777; e-mail emirates.embassy@planet.tn; Ambassador ABDULLAH IBRAHIM GHANIM SULTAN AL-SUWAIDI.

United Kingdom: rue du Lac Windermere, Les Berges du Lac, 1053 Tunis; tel. (71) 108-700; fax (71) 108-749; e-mail TunisConsular.tunis@fco.gov.uk; internet ukintunisia.fco.gov.uk; Ambassador CHRISTOPHER PAUL O'CONNOR.

USA: Les Berges du Lac, 1053 Tunis; tel. (71) 107-000; fax (71) 963-263; e-mail tuniswebsitecontact@state.gov; internet tunisia.usembassy.gov; Ambassador GORDON GRAY.

Yemen: rue Mouaouia ibn Soufiane, al-Menzah VI, Tunis; tel. (71) 237-933; Ambassador HUSSEIN DHAIFULLAH AL-AWADHI.

Judicial System

The **Cour de Cassation** in Tunis has three civil and one criminal sections. There are three **Cours d'Appel** at Tunis, Sousse and Sfax, and 13 **Cours de Première Instance**, each having three chambers, except the **Cour de Première Instance** at Tunis, which has eight chambers. **Justices Cantonales** exist in 51 areas.

Religion

The Constitution of 1959 recognizes Islam as the state religion, with the introduction of certain reforms, such as the abolition of polygamy. An estimated 99% of the population are Muslims. Minority religions include Judaism (an estimated 1,500 adherents in 2008) and Christianity. The Christian population comprises Roman Catholics, Greek Orthodox, and French and English Protestants.

ISLAM

Grand Mufti of Tunisia: Sheikh KAMAL AL-DIN JA'EIT.

CHRISTIANITY

The Roman Catholic Church

There were an estimated 20,500 adherents in Tunisia in December 2007.

Archbishop of Tunis: Most Rev. MAROUN ELIAS LAHHAM, Evêché, 4 rue d'Alger, 1000 Tunis; tel. (71) 335-831; fax (71) 335-832; e-mail eveche.tunisie@evechetunisie.org; internet www.diocesetunisie.org.

The Protestant Church

Reformed Church of Tunisia: 36 rue Charles de Gaulle, 1000 Tunis; tel. (71) 327-886; e-mail eglisereformee@yahoo.fr; f. 1880; c. 220 mems; Pastor WILLIAM BROWN.

The Press

DAILIES

Al-Chourouk (Sunrise): 25 rue Jean Jaurès, BP 36619, Tunis; tel. (71) 331-000; fax (71) 253-024; e-mail directiongenerale@alchourouk.com; internet www.alchourouk.com; Arabic; Dir SLAHEDDINE AL-AMRI; Editor-in-Chief ABD AL-HAMID RIAHI; circ. 70,000.

Essahafa: 6 rue Ali Bach-Hamba, 1000 Tunis; tel. (71) 341-066; fax (71) 349-720; e-mail contact@essahafa.info.tn; internet www.essahafa.info.tn; f. 1936; Arabic; Dir and Editor-in-Chief ABOU ESSAOUD HMIDI.

Al-Horria: 8 rue de Rome, 1000 Tunis; tel. (71) 351-578; fax (71) 350-721; e-mail alhorria@email.ati.tn; internet www.alhorria.info.tn; Arabic; organ of the RCD; Dir and Editor-in-Chief MONGI ZEIDI; circ. 50,000.

La Presse de Tunisie: 6 rue Ali Bach-Hamba, 1000 Tunis; tel. (71) 341-066; fax (71) 349-720; e-mail contact@lapresse.tn; internet www.lapresse.tn; f. 1936; French; Pres. and Dir-Gen. MUHAMMAD GONTARA; circ. 40,000.

Le Quotidien: 25 rue Jean Jaurès, 1000 Tunis; tel. (71) 331-000; fax (71) 253-02; e-mail directiongenerale@lequotidien-tn.com; internet www.lequotidien-tn.com; f. 2001; French; Dir SLAHEDDINE AL-AMRI; Editor-in-Chief CHOUKRY BAKOUCHE; circ. 20,000.

Le Renouveau: 8 rue de Rome, 1000 Tunis; tel. (71) 352-058; fax (71) 352-927; e-mail lerenouveau@lerenouveau.com.tn; internet www.lerenouveau.com.tn; f. 1988; French; organ of the RCD; Dir and Editor-in-Chief NEJIB OUERGHI.

As-Sabah (The Morning): blvd du 7 novembre 1987, BP 441, al-Menzah, 1004 Tunis; tel. (71) 238-222; fax (71) 232-761; e-mail redaction@assabah.com.tn; internet www.assabah.com.tn; f. 1951; Arabic; Dir MUSTAPHA AL-JABER; Editor-in-Chief NOUREDDINE ACHOUR; circ. 50,000.

Le Temps: blvd du 7 novembre 1987, BP 441, al-Menzah, 1004 Tunis; tel. (71) 238-222; fax (71) 232-761; e-mail redaction@letemps.com.tn; internet www.letemps.com.tn; f. 1975; French; Dir MUSTAPHA AL-JABER; Editor-in-Chief RAOUF KHALSI; circ. 42,000.

PERIODICALS

Afrique Economie: 16 rue de Rome, BP 61, 1015 Tunis; tel. (71) 347-441; fax (71) 353-172; e-mail iea@planet.tn; f. 1970; monthly; Dir MUHAMMAD ZERZERI.

Al-Akhbar (The News): 1 passage d'al-Houdaybiyah, 1000 Tunis; tel. (71) 344-100; fax (71) 355-079; internet www.akhbar.tn; f. 1984; weekly; Arabic; general; Dir MUHAMMAD BEN YOUSUF; circ. 75,000.

Journal Les Annonces: 6 rue de Sparte, BP 1343, Tunis; tel. (71) 350-177; fax (71) 347-184; e-mail nejib.azouz@planet.tn; internet www.elilane.com; f. 1978; 2 a week; French and Arabic; Dir MUHAMMAD NEJIB AZOUZ; circ. 170,000.

Al-Anouar al-Tounissia (Tunisian Lights): 25 rue al-Cham, 5000 Tunis; tel. (71) 331-000; fax (71) 253-022; internet www.alanouar.com; Arabic; Dir SLAHEDDINE AL-AMRI; circ. 165,000.

Attariq al-Jadid (New Road): 6 rue Metouia, 1069 Tunis; tel. (71) 256-400; fax (71) 240-981; internet www.attariq.org; f. 1981; weekly; Arabic; organ of the Mouvement ettajdid; Dir MUHAMMAD HARMEL; Editor-in-Chief HICHAM SKIK.

L'Avenir: 26 rue Gamal Abd al-Nasser, BP 1200, Tunis; tel. (71) 258-941; f. 1980; weekly; organ of the Mouvement des démocrates socialistes (MDS).

Al-Bayan (The Manifesto): 61 rue Abderrazek, Chraîbi, 1001 Tunis; tel. (71) 339-633; fax (71) 338-533; e-mail darelbayane@gnet.tn; f. 1976; weekly; general; organ of the Union tunisienne de l'industrie, du commerce et de l'artisanat; Dir HÉDI DJILANI; circ. 100,000.

Al-Biladi (My Country): 15 rue 2 mars 1934, Tunis; f. 1974; Arabic; political and general weekly for Tunisian workers abroad; Dir HÉDI AL-GHALI; circ. 90,000.

TUNISIA

Bulletin Mensuel de Statistiques: Institut National de la Statistique, 70 rue al-Cham, BP 265, 1080 Tunis; tel. (71) 891-002; fax (71) 792-559; e-mail ins@mdci.gov.tn; internet www.ins.nat.tn; monthly.

Conjoncture: 37 ave Kheireddine Pacha, 1002 Tunis; tel. (71) 891-826; fax (71) 200-706; e-mail conjoncture2003@yahoo.fr; f. 1974; monthly; economic and financial surveys; Dir HABIB BEDHIAFI; circ. 5,000.

Démocratie: Tunis; f. 1978; monthly; French; organ of the MDS; Dir HASSIB BEN AMMAR; circ. 5,000.

Dialogue: 15 rue 2 mars 1934, Tunis; tel. (71) 264-899; f. 1974; weekly; French; cultural and political organ of the RCD; Dir NACEUR BECHEKH; circ. 30,000.

L'Economiste Maghrébin: 3 rue el-Kewekibi, 1002 Tunis; tel. (71) 790-773; fax (71) 793-707; e-mail leconomiste@planet.tn; internet www.leconomiste.com.tn; f. 1990; bi-weekly; French; Dir HÉDI MÉCHRI; circ. 30,000.

Etudiant Tunisien: Tunis; f. 1953; French and Arabic; Chief Editor FAOUZI AOUAM.

El-Fallah: 8451 rue Alain Savary, al-Khadra, 1003 Tunis; tel. (71) 806-800; fax (71) 809-181; e-mail utap.tunis@email.ati.tn; internet www.utap.org.tn; weekly; organ of the Union tunisienne de l'agriculture et de la pêche (UTAP); Dir MABROUK BAHRI; Editor GHARBI HAMOUDA; circ. 7,000.

L'Hebdo Touristique: rue 8601, 40, Zone Industrielle, La Charguia 2, 2035 Tunis; tel. (71) 786-866; fax (71) 794-891; e-mail haddad.tijani@planet.tn; f. 1971; weekly; French; tourism; Dir TIJANI HADDAD; circ. 5,000.

IBLA: Institut des Belles Lettres Arabes, 12 rue Jemaâ el-Haoua, 1008 Tunis; tel. (71) 560-133; fax (71) 572-683; e-mail ibla@gnet.tn; internet www.iblatunis.org; f. 1937; 2 a year; French, Arabic and English; social and cultural review on Maghreb and Muslim-Arab affairs; Dir JEAN FONTAINE; circ. 600.

Al-Idhaa wa Talvaza (Radio and Television): 71 ave de la Liberté, Tunis; tel. (71) 782-700; fax (71) 796-691; e-mail revue@ertt.nat.tn; f. 1956; fortnightly; Arabic language broadcasting magazine; Dir MUSTAPHA KHAMMARI; Editor JAMEL KARMAOUI.

Irfane (Children): 6 rue Muhammad Ali, 1000 Tunis; tel. (71) 256-877; fax (71) 351-521; f. 1965; monthly; Arabic; Dir-Gen. RIDHA EL-OUADI; circ. 100,000.

Jeunesse Magazine: 6 rue Muhammad Ali, 1000 Tunis; tel. (71) 256-877; fax (71) 351-521; f. 1980; monthly; Arabic; Dir-Gen. RIDHA EL-OUADI; circ. 30,000.

Journal Officiel de la République Tunisienne: ave Farhat Hached, 2040 Radès; tel. (71) 299-914; fax (71) 297-234; f. 1860; official gazette; Arabic and French; twice-weekly; publ. by Imprimerie Officielle (State Press); Pres. and Dir-Gen. ROMDHANE BEN MIMOUN; circ. 20,000.

Al-Maraa (The Woman): 56 blvd Bab Benat, 1006 Tunis; tel. (71) 567-845; fax (71) 567-131; e-mail unft@email.ati.tn; f. 1961; monthly; Arabic and French; political, economic and social affairs; issued by Union nationale de la femme tunisienne; Pres. AZIZA HABIRA; circ. 10,000.

Al-Mawkif: 10 rue Eve Nohelle, 1001 Tunis; tel. (71) 332-271; fax (71) 332-194; e-mail mawkef_21@yahoo.fr; f. 1984; weekly; organ of the Parti démocrate progressiste; Man. Dir AHMED NÉJIB CHEBBI; Editor-in-Chief RACHID KHECHANA.

Al-Moussawar: 10 rue al-Cham, Tunis; tel. (71) 289-000; fax (71) 289-357; internet www.almoussawar.com; weekly; circ. 75,000.

Mouwatinoun (Citizens): Tunis; internet www.fdtl.org; f. 2007; weekly; Arabic; organ of the Forum démocratique pour le travail et les libertés (FDTL).

Outrouhat: Tunis; monthly; scientific; Dir LOTFI BEN AÏSSA.

Réalités: 6–7 rue de Cameroun, 1002 Tunis; tel. (71) 788-313; fax (71) 787-160; e-mail redaction@realites.com.tn; internet www.realites.com.tn; f. 1979; weekly; Arabic and French; Dir TAÏEB ZAHAR; circ. 25,000.

Tounes el Khadra: 8451 rue Alain Savary, al-Khadra, 1003 Tunis; tel. (71) 806-800; fax (71) 809-181; e-mail utap.tunis@email.ati.tn; internet www.utap.org.tn; f. 1976; bi-monthly; agricultural, scientific and technical; organ of the UTAP; Dir MABROUK BAHRI; Editor GHARBI HAMOUDA; circ. 5,000.

Tunis Hebdo: 1 passage d'al-Houdaybiyah, 1000 Tunis; tel. (71) 344-100; fax (71) 355-079; e-mail tunishebdo@tunishebdo.com.tn; internet www.tunishebdo.com.tn; f. 1973; weekly; French; general and sport; Dir MUHAMMAD BEN YOUSUF; circ. 35,000.

NEWS AGENCY

Tunis Afrique Presse (TAP): 7 ave Slimane Ben Slimane, al-Manar, 2092 Tunis; tel. (71) 889-000; fax (71) 883-500; e-mail desk.inter@email.ati.tn; internet www.tap.info.tn; f. 1961; Arabic, French and English; offices in Algiers (Algeria), Rabat (Morocco), Paris (France) and New York (USA); daily news services; Chair. and Gen. Man. MUHAMMAD BEN EZZEDDINE.

Publishers

Al-Dar al-Arabia Lil Kitab: 4 ave Mohieddine el-Klibi, BP 32, al-Manar 2, 2092 Tunis; tel. (71) 888-255; fax (71) 888-365; e-mail mal@gnet.tn; f. 1975; general literature, children's books, non-fiction; Dir-Gen. MUSTAPHA ATTIA.

Centre de Publications Universitaires: Campus Universitaire, BP 255, 1080 Tunis; tel. (71) 874-000; fax (71) 871-677; e-mail cpu@cpu.rnu.tn; internet www.mes.tn/cpu; educational books, journals.

Cérès Editions: 6 rue Alain Savary, Belvédère, 1002 Tunis; tel. (71) 280-505; fax (71) 287-216; e-mail info@ceres-editions.com; internet www.ceres-editions.com; f. 1964; social sciences, art books, literature, novels; Man. Editor KARIM BEN SMAIL.

Dar Cheraït: Centre Culturel et Touristique Dar Cheraït, Route Touristique, 2200 Tozeur; tel. (76) 452-100; fax (76) 452-329; e-mail darcherait@planet.tn; internet www.darcherait.com.tn.

Dar al-Kitab: 5 ave Bourguiba, 4000 Sousse; tel. (73) 25097; f. 1950; literature, children's books, legal studies, foreign books; Pres. TAÏEB KACEM; Dir FAYÇAL KACEM.

Dar as-Sabah: blvd du 7 Novembre 1987, BP 441, al-Menzah, 1004 Tunis; tel. (71) 717-222; fax (71) 232-761; f. 1951; 200 mems; publishes daily and weekly papers, including the dailies *As-Sabah* and *Le Temps*, which circulate throughout Tunisia, North Africa, France, Belgium, Luxembourg and Germany; Chair. MUHAMMAD SAKHER EL MATERI; Dir-Gen. MUSTAPHA AL-JABER.

Editions Apollonia: 4 rue Claude Bernard, 1002 Tunis; tel. (71) 786-381; fax (71) 799-190; e-mail sales@apollonia.com.tn; internet www.apollonia.com.tn; art, literature, essays, poetry.

Editions Bouslama: 15 ave de France, 1000 Tunis; tel. (71) 243-745; fax (71) 381-100; f. 1960; history, children's books; Man. Dir ALI BOUSLAMA.

Institut National de la Statistique: 70 rue al-Cham, BP 265, 1080 Tunis; tel. (71) 891-002; fax (71) 792-559; e-mail ins@mdci.gov.tn; internet www.ins.nat.tn; publishes a variety of annuals, periodicals and papers concerned with the economic policy and devt of Tunisia.

Librairie al-Manar: 60 ave Bab Djedid, BP 179, 1008 Tunis; tel. (71) 253-224; fax (71) 336-565; e-mail librairie.almanar@planet.tn; f. 1938; general, educational, Islam; Man. Dir HABIB M'HAMDI.

Société d'Arts Graphiques, d'Edition et de Presse (SAGEP): 15 rue 2 mars 1934, La Kasbah, 1000 Tunis; tel. (71) 564-988; fax (71) 569-736; f. 1974; prints and publishes daily papers, magazines, books, etc.; Dir-Gen. MAHMOUD MEFTAH.

Sud Editions: 79 rue de Palestine, 1002 Tunis; tel. (71) 785-179; fax (71) 848-664; e-mail sud.editions@planet.tn; f. 1976; Arab literature, art and art history, history, sociology, religion; Man. Dir MUHAMMAD MASMOUDI.

GOVERNMENT PUBLISHING HOUSE

Imprimerie Officielle de la République Tunisienne: 40 ave Farhat Hached, 2098 Radès; tel. (71) 434-211; fax (71) 434-234; e-mail iort@iort.gov.tn; internet www.iort.gov.tn; f. 1860; Pres. and Dir-Gen. HOSNI TOUMI.

Broadcasting and Communications

TELECOMMUNICATIONS

A consortium formed by France Télécom and a Tunisian investment company, Investec, was awarded a licence to operate fixed and mobile telephone services in June 2009. The new operator, Orange Tunisie, commenced services in May 2010.

Société Tunisienne d'Entreprises des Télécommunications (SOTETEL): rue des Entrepreneurs, Zone Industrielle, BP 640, La Charguia 2, 1080 Tunis; tel. (71) 941-100; fax (71) 940-584; e-mail sotetel@email.ati.tn; internet www.sotetel.com.tn; f. 1981; privatized in 1998; Dir-Gen. HÉDI FRIOUI.

Orange Tunisie: rue du Lac de Côme, Les Berges du Lac, 1053 Tunis; tel. (71) 167-900; fax (71) 961-808; internet www.orange.tn; f. 2010; launched mobile telephone network in May 2010; 49% stake owned by France Télécom; Chair. MARWAN MABROUK.

Orascom Telecom Tunisia (Tunisiana): 11 rue 8607, Zone Industrielle, La Charguia 1, 2035 Tunis; tel. (22) 121-478; e-mail serviceRP@tunisiana.com; internet www.tunisiana.com; f. 2002; Chair. and CEO NAGUIB SAWIRIS.

Tunisie Télécom: Cité Ennassim, ave du Japon, Montplaisir, 1073 Tunis; tel. (71) 901-717; fax (71) 900-777; e-mail actel.virtuelle@ttnet.tn; internet www.tunisietelecom.tn; 65% state-owned, 35% owned by Tecom-Dig (Dubai, United Arab Emirates); CEO RAOUF CHKIR.

TUNISIA   *Directory*

BROADCASTING

Office National de la Télédiffusion (ONT) (National Broadcasting Corporation of Tunisia): Cite Ennasim, 1 Borjel, BP 399, 1080 Tunis; tel. (71) 801-177; fax (71) 781-927; e-mail ont@telediffusion.net.tn; internet www.telediffusion.net.tn; f. 1993; supervision and management of the radio and television broadcasting networks.

Radio

Etablissement de la Radiodiffusion-Télévision Tunisienne (ERTT): 71 ave de la Liberté, 1002 Tunis; tel. (71) 847-300; fax (71) 780-993; e-mail portail@radiotunisienne.tn; internet www.radiotunisienne.tn; govt service; broadcasts in Arabic, French, German, Italian, Spanish and English; radio stations at Gafsa, El-Kef, Monastir, Sfax, Tataouine and Tunis (three); television stations Tunis 7 and Canal 21; Pres. and Dir-Gen. (Radio) CHAOUKI ALAOUI.

Radio Mosaïque: Tunis; tel. (71) 287-246; e-mail dg@mosaiquefm.net; internet www.mosaiquefm.net; f. 2003; first privately owned radio station when launched in 2003; broadcasts in Arabic and French to Tunis and the north-east of the country; Dir-Gen. NOUREDDINE BOUTAR.

Television

Etablissement de la Radiodiffusion-Télévision Tunisienne: e-mail info@tunisiatv.com; internet www.tunisie7.tn; Pres. and Dir-Gen. (Television) MOKHTAR RASSAA (acting); see Radio.

Finance

(cap. = capital; dep. = deposits; res = reserves; m. = million; br(s) = branch(es); amounts in dinars unless otherwise stated)

BANKING

Central Bank

Banque Centrale de Tunisie (BCT): 25 rue Hédi Nouira, BP 777, 1080 Tunis; tel. (71) 340-588; fax (71) 354-214; e-mail boc@bct.gov.tn; internet www.bct.gov.tn; f. 1958; cap. 6m., res 90m., dep. 5,752m. (Dec. 2009); Gov. MUSTAPHA KAMEL NABLI; 12 brs.

Commercial Banks

Amen Bank: ave Muhammad V, 1002 Tunis; tel. (71) 835-500; fax (71) 833-517; e-mail amenbank@amenbank.com.tn; internet www.amenbank.com.tn; f. 1967 as Crédit Foncier et Commercial de Tunisie; name changed as above in 1995; cap. 100m., res 205m., dep. 3,212m. (Dec. 2009); Chair. RACHID BEN YEDDER; Gen. Man. AHMAD EL-KARM; 81 brs.

Arab Banking Corpn Tunisie (ABC Tunisie): Immeuble ABC, rue du Lac d'Annecy, Les Berges du Lac, 1053 Tunis; tel. (71) 861-861; fax (71) 860-921; e-mail abc.tunis@arabbanking.com; internet www.arabbanking.com; f. 2000; cap. 50m., res −22m., dep. 189m. (Dec. 2009); Chair. MUHAMMAD HUSSAIN LAYAS; Pres. and Chief Exec. HASSAN ALI JUMA; 4 brs.

Arab Tunisian Bank: 9 rue Hédi Nouira, BP 520, 1001 Tunis; tel. (71) 351-155; fax (71) 342-852; e-mail atbbank@atb.com.tn; internet www.atb.com.tn; f. 1982; 64.2% owned by Arab Bank PLC (Jordan); cap. 80m., res 183m., dep. 3,494m. (Dec. 2009); Pres. Dr SAMAR EL-MOLLA; Dir-Gen. MUHAMMAD FERID BEN TANFOUS; 107 brs.

Attijari Bank: 14 ave de la Liberté, Tunis; tel. (71) 141-400; fax (71) 782-663; e-mail courrier@attijaribank.com.tn; internet www.attijaribank.com.tn; f. 1968 as Banque du Sud; present name adopted 2006; 37.11% owned by Attijariwafa Bank (Morocco), 17.46% by Banco Santander (Spain); cap. 168m., res 25m., dep. 3,078m. (Dec. 2009); Pres. MONCEF CHAFFAR; CEO MUHAMMAD EL-KETTANI; Dir-Gen. HASSAN BERTAL; 93 brs.

Banque de l'Habitat: 21 ave Kheireddine Pacha, BP 242, 1082 Tunis; tel. (71) 001-800; fax (71) 951-048; e-mail banquehabitat@bh.fin.tn; internet www.bh.com.tn; f. 1984; 32.62% govt-owned; cap. 90m., res 267m., dep. 3,954m. (Dec. 2009); CEO HAJJI BRAHIM; 79 brs.

Banque Internationale Arabe de Tunisie (BIAT): 70–72 ave Habib Bourguiba, BP 520, 1080 Tunis; tel. (71) 340-733; fax (71) 346-454; e-mail correspondent.banking@biat.com.tn; internet www.biat.com.tn; f. 1976; cap. 170m., res 260m., dep. 5,417m. (Dec. 2009); Chair. ISMAIL MABROUK; Gen. Man. SLAHEDDINE LADJIMI; 138 brs.

Banque Nationale Agricole (BNA): rue Hédi Nouira, 1001 Tunis; tel. (71) 831-000; fax (71) 832-807; e-mail bna@bna.com.tn; internet www.bna.com.tn; f. 1989 by merger of Banque Nationale du Développement Agricole and Banque Nationale de Tunisie; cap. 135m., res 317m., dep. 4,979m. (Dec. 2009); Chair. and Gen. Man. MONCEF DAKHLI; 157 brs.

Banque de Tunisie SA: 2 rue de Turquie, BP 289, 1001 Tunis; tel. (71) 332-188; fax (71) 349-401; e-mail finance@bt.com.tn; internet www.bt.com.tn; f. 1884; cap. 112m., res 266m., dep. 2,066m. (Dec. 2009); CEO HABIB BEN SAAD; 100 agencies.

Société Tunisienne de Banque (STB): rue Hédi Nouira, BP 638, 1001 Tunis; tel. (71) 340-477; fax (71) 348-400; e-mail stb@stb.com.tn; internet www.stb.com.tn; f. 1957; 24.81% govt-owned; merged with Banque Nationale de Développement Touristique and Banque de Développement Economique de Tunisie in 2000; cap. 124m., res 349m., dep. 4,475m. (Dec. 2009); Chair. and Gen. Man. HÉDI ZAR; 119 brs.

Union Bancaire pour le Commerce et l'Industrie (UBCI): 139 ave de la Liberté, Belvédère, 1002 Tunis; tel. (71) 842-000; fax (71) 346-737; e-mail saber.mensi@bnpparibas.com; internet www.ubcinet.net; f. 1961; affiliated with, and 50% owned by, BNP Paribas (France); cap. 50m., res 114m., dep. 1,525m. (Dec. 2009); Pres. and Gen. Man. SLAHEDDINE BOUGERRA; 87 brs.

Union Internationale de Banques SA: 65 ave Habib Bourguiba, BP 109, 1000 Tunis; tel. (71) 347-000; fax (71) 353-090; e-mail lilia.meddeb@uib.fin.tn; internet www.uib.com.tn; f. 1963 as a merging of Tunisian interests by the Société Franco-Tunisienne de Banque et de Crédit with Crédit Lyonnais (France) and other foreign banks, incl. Banca Commerciale Italiana; 52.3% owned by Société Générale (France); cap. 196m., res −123m., dep. 2,009m. (Dec. 2009); Chair. DAVID BERNARD; Dir-Gen. KAMEL NEJI; 94 brs.

Merchant Banks

Banque d'Affaires de Tunisie (BAT): 32 rue Hédi Karray, 1082 Tunis; tel. (71) 703-175; fax (71) 703-604; e-mail bat@bat.com.tn; internet www.bat-tunisie.com; f. 1997; cap. 4.5m.; Pres. and Gen. Man. Dir MUHAMMAD HABIB KARAOULI.

International Maghreb Merchant Bank (IM Bank): Immeuble Maghrebia, Bloc B, 3ème étage, Les Berges du Lac, 2045 Tunis; tel. (71) 860-816; fax (71) 860-057; e-mail imbank@imbank.com.tn; internet www.imbank.com.tn; f. 1995; Pres. OLIVIER PASTRÉ; Exec. Dirs NASREDINE DEKLI, AHMED BESBES.

Development Banks

Banque de Tunisie et des Emirats (BTE): 5 bis blvd Muhammad Badra, 1002 Tunis; tel. (71) 112-000; fax (71) 286-409; e-mail dg@bte.com.tn; internet www.bte.com.tn; f. 1982 as Banque de Tunisie et des Emirats d'Investissement; name changed as above in 2005; owned by the Govt of Tunisia and Abu Dhabi Investment Authority; cap. 90m., res 42m., dep. 247m. (Dec. 2009); Chair. SALAM RACHID AL-MOHANNADI; Gen. Man. GOLSOM JAZIRI; 12 brs.

Banque Tunisienne de Solidarité (BTS): 56 ave Muhammad V, 1002 Tunis; tel. (71) 844-040; fax (71) 845-537; e-mail bts@email.ati.tn; internet www.bts.com.tn; f. 1997; provides short- and medium-term finance for small-scale projects; cap. 40m.; Man. Dir LAMINE HAFSAOUI; 25 brs.

Banque Tuniso-Libyenne: 25 ave Kheireddine Pacha, BP 102, Belvédère, 1002 Tunis; tel. (71) 781-500; fax (71) 782-818; f. 1983 as Banque Arabe Tuniso-Libyenne de Développement et de Commerce; present name adopted 2005; promotes trade and devt projects between Tunisia and Libya, and provides funds for investment in poorer areas; cap. 70.0m., res 2.2m., dep. 309.1m. (Dec. 2008); Chair. and Gen. Man. BADREDDINE BARKIA.

Société Tuniso-Séoudienne d'Investissement et de Développement (STUSID): 32 rue Hédi Karray, BP 20, 1082 Tunis; tel. (71) 718-233; fax (71) 719-233; e-mail commercial@stusid.com.tn; internet www.stusid.com.tn; f. 1981; provides long-term finance for devt projects; cap. 100.0m., res 84.4m., dep. 10.5m. (Dec. 2002); Chair. Dr ABD AL-AZIZ A. AL-NASRALLAH; Pres. and Dir-Gen. ABD AL-WAHEB NACHI.

'Offshore' Banks

Albaraka Bank Tunisia: 88 ave Hédi Chaker, 1002 Tunis; tel. (71) 790-000; fax (71) 780-235; e-mail bestbank@planet.tn; f. 1983; as Beit Ettamouil Saoudi Tounsi; name changed to above in 2009; Islamic bank; Chair. ABDELILAH SOUBAHI; Vice-Chair. and Man. Dir AISSA HIDOUSSI.

Alubaf International Bank: 8007 rue Montplaisir, BP 51, Belvédère, 1002 Tunis; tel. (71) 783-500; fax (71) 793-905; e-mail alub@alubaf.com.tn; internet www.alubaf.com.tn; f. 1985; 100% owned by Libyan Arab Foreign Bank; cap. US $25m., res $4m., dep. $195m. (Dec. 2009); Chair. Dr AHMAD MNEISSI ABD EL-HAMID; Gen. Man. ALTAHER M. AL-SHAMES.

North Africa International Bank: ave Kheireddine Pacha, BP 485, 1002 Tunis; tel. (71) 950-800; fax (71) 950-840; e-mail naib@naibank.com; internet www.naibbank.com; f. 1984; cap. US $30m., res $19m., dep. $372m. (Dec. 2009); Chair. and Gen. Man. GIUMA M. WAHEBA; 1 br.

Tunis International Bank: 18 ave des Etats-Unis d'Amérique, BP 81, 1002 Tunis; tel. (71) 782-411; fax (71) 782-479; e-mail tib1.tib@planet.tn; internet www.tib.com.tn; f. 1982; 86.6% owned by United

TUNISIA

Gulf Bank (Bahrain); cap. US $25.0m., res $31.8m., dep. $402.4m. (Dec. 2009); Chair. Masoud J. Hayat; Dep. Chair. and Man. Dir Muhammad Fekih; 3 brs.

STOCK EXCHANGE

Bourse des Valeurs Mobilières de Tunis (Bourse de Tunis): Les Jardins du Lac, Les Berges du Lac, 1053 Tunis; tel. (71) 197-710; fax (71) 197-703; e-mail info@bvmt.com.tn; internet www.bvmt.com.tn; f. 1969; Chair. Yousuf Kortobi; Dir-Gen. Muhammad Bichiou.

INSURANCE

BEST Reinsurance (BEST Re): Rue du Lac de Côme, Les Berges du lac, BP 484, 1080 Tunis; tel. (71) 860-355; fax (71) 861-011; e-mail general@bestre.com.tn; internet www.best-re.com; f. 1985; operates according to Islamic principles; cap. US $100m.; Chair. Dr Saleh J. Malaikah.

Caisse Tunisienne d'Assurances Mutuelles Agricoles—Mutuelle Générale d'Assurances (CTAMA—MGA): 6 ave Habib Thameur, 1069 Tunis; tel. (71) 340-933; fax (71) 332-276; e-mail ctama@planet.tn; internet www.ctamamga.com; f. 1912; Pres. Moktar Bellagha; Dir-Gen. Mezri Jelizi.

Cie d'Assurances Tous Risques et de Réassurance (ASTREE): 45 ave Kheireddine Pacha, BP 780, 1002 Tunis; tel. (71) 792-211; fax (71) 794-723; e-mail courrier@astree.com.tn; internet www.astree.com.tn; f. 1949; cap. 4m.; Pres. and Dir-Gen. Muhammad Habib Ben Saad.

Cie Tunisienne pour l'Assurance du Commerce Extérieur (COTUNACE): ave Muhammad V, Montplaisir I, rue 8006, 1002 Tunis; tel. (71) 783-000; fax (71) 782-539; e-mail cotunace.ddc@planet.tn; internet www.cotunace.com.tn; f. 1984; cap. 5m.; 65 mem. cos; Pres. and Dir-Gen. Moncef Zouari.

Société Tunisienne d'Assurance et de Réassurance (STAR): ave de Paris, 1000 Tunis; tel. (71) 340-866; fax (71) 340-835; e-mail star@star.com.tn; internet www.star.com.tn; f. 1958; Pres. and Dir-Gen. Abdelkrim Merdassi.

Tunis-Ré (Société Tunisienne de Réassurance): 7 rue Borjine, Montplaisir 1, BP 29, 1073 Tunis; tel. (71) 904-911; fax (71) 904-930; e-mail tunisre@tunisre.com.tn; internet www.tunisre.com.tn; f. 1981; various kinds of reinsurance; cap. 45m. (2010); Chair. and Gen. Man. Lamia Ben Mahmoud.

Trade and Industry

GOVERNMENT AGENCIES

Centre de Promotion des Exportations (CEPEX): Centre Urbain, BP 225, 1080 Tunis; tel. (71) 234-200; fax (71) 237-325; e-mail info@cepex.nat.tn; internet www.cepex.nat.tn; f. 1973; state export promotion org.; Pres. and Dir-Gen. Abdellatif Hammem.

Foreign Investment Promotion Agency (FIPA): rue Slaheddine al-Ammami, Centre Urbain Nord, 1004 Tunis; tel. (71) 752-540; fax (71) 231-400; e-mail boc.fipa@mdci.gov.tn; internet www.investintunisia.tn; f. 1995; Dir-Gen. Mongia Khemiri.

Office du Commerce de la Tunisie (OCT): 65 rue de Syrie, 1002 Tunis; tel. (71) 785-619; fax (71) 784-491; e-mail OCT@Email.ati.tn; internet www.infocommerce.gov.tn; f. 1962; Pres. and Dir-Gen. Slaheddine Makhlouf; Sec.-Gen. Mustapha Debbabi.

CHAMBERS OF COMMERCE AND INDUSTRY

Chambre de Commerce et d'Industrie du Centre: rue Chadli Khaznadar, 4000 Sousse; tel. (73) 225-044; fax (73) 224-227; e-mail ccis.sousse@planet.tn; internet www.ccicentre.org.tn; f. 1895; 30 mems; Pres. Néjib Mellouli; Dir Faten Basly.

Chambre de Commerce et d'Industrie du Nord-Est: Tom Bereaux Bizerte Center, angle rues 1er mai, Med Ali, 7000 Bizerte; tel. (72) 431-044; fax (72) 431-922; e-mail ccine.biz@gnet.tn; internet www.ccibizerte.org.tn; f. 1902; 30 mems; Pres. Faouzi Ben Aissa; Dir Moufida Chakroun.

Chambre de Commerce et d'Industrie de Sfax: rue du Lieutenant Hammadi Tej, BP 794, 3000 Sfax; tel. (74) 296-120; fax (74) 296-121; e-mail ccis@ccis.org.tn; internet www.ccis.org.tn; f. 1895; 35,000 mems; Pres. Abdessalem Ben Ayed; Dir Sofiene Sallemi.

Chambre de Commerce et d'Industrie de Tunis: 31 ave de Paris, 1000 Tunis; tel. (71) 247-322; fax (71) 354-744; e-mail ccitunis@planet.tn; internet www.ccitunis.org.tn; f. 1885; 30 mems; Pres. Mounir Mouakhar.

INDUSTRIAL AND TRADE ASSOCIATIONS

Agence des Ports et des Installations de Pêches (APIP): Port de Pêche de La Goulette, BP 64, 2060 Tunis; tel. (71) 736-012; fax (71) 735-396; e-mail apip@apip.com.tn; internet www.apip.nat.tn; fishing ports authority; Pres. and Dir-Gen. Sghaïer Houcine.

Agence de Promotion de l'Industrie (API): 63 rue de Syrie, 1002 Tunis; tel. (71) 792-144; fax (71) 782-482; e-mail api@api.com.tn; internet www.tunisieindustrie.nat.tn; f. 1987 by merger; co-ordinates industrial policy, undertakes feasibility studies, organizes industrial training and establishes industrial zones; overseas offices in Belgium, France, Germany, Italy, Sweden, the United Kingdom and the USA; 24 regional offices; Gen. Man. Muhammad Ben Abdallah.

Centre Technique du Textile (CETTEX): ave des Industries, Zone Industrielle, Bir el-Kassaâ, BP 279, Ben Arous, 2013 Tunis; tel. (71) 381-133; fax (71) 382-558; e-mail cettex@cettex.com.tn; internet www.cettex.com.tn; f. 1991; responsible for the textile industry; Dir-Gen. Samir Haouet.

Cie des Phosphates de Gafsa (CPG): Cité Bayech, 2100 Gafsa; tel. (76) 226-022; fax (76) 224-132; e-mail cpg.gafsa@cpg.com.tn; internet www.gct.com.tn; f. 1897; production and marketing of phosphates; Pres. and Dir-Gen. Muhammad Fadhel Zrelli.

Entreprise Tunisienne d'Activités Pétrolières (ETAP): 27 ave Kheireddine Pacha, BP 83, 1073 Tunis; tel. (71) 902-688; fax (71) 906-141; e-mail dexprom@etap.com.tn; internet www.etap.com.tn; f. 1974; state-owned; responsible for exploration, production, trade and investment in hydrocarbons; Pres. and CEO Khaled Becheikh.

Office des Céréales: Ministry of Agriculture, Water Resources and Fisheries, 30 rue Alain Savary, 1002 Tunis; tel. (71) 780-550; fax (71) 794-152; e-mail office.cereales@email.ati.tn; f. 1962; responsible for the cereals industry; Chair. and Dir-Gen. Yousuf Neji.

Office National des Mines: 24 rue 8601, BP 215, 1080 Tunis; tel. (71) 788-242; fax (71) 794-016; e-mail contact@onm.nat.tn; internet www.onm.nat.tn; f. 1963; mining of iron ores; research and study of mineral wealth; Dir-Gen. Abdelbaki Mansouri.

Office des Terres Domaniales (OTD): 60 rue Alain Savary, 1002 Tunis; tel. (71) 771-086; fax (71) 795-026; e-mail boc@otd.nat.tn; internet www.otd.nat.tn; f. 1961; responsible for agricultural production and the management of state-owned lands; Pres. and Dir-Gen. Abdelhakim Khaldi.

UTILITIES

Electricity and Gas

Société Tunisienne de l'Electricité et du Gaz (STEG): 38 rue Kemal Atatürk, BP 190, 1080 Tunis; tel. (71) 341-311; fax (71) 349-981; e-mail dpsc@steg.com.tn; internet www.steg.com.tn; f. 1962; responsible for generation and distribution of electricity and for production of natural gas; Pres. and Dir-Gen. Othman Ben Arfa; 35 brs.

Water

Société Nationale d'Exploitation et de Distribution des Eaux (SONEDE): ave Slimane Ben Slimane, el-Manar 2, 2092 Tunis; tel. (71) 887-000; fax (71) 871-000; e-mail sonede@sonede.com.tn; internet www.sonede.com.tn; f. 1968; production and supply of drinking water; Pres. and Dir-Gen. Muhammad Ali Khouaja.

TRADE AND OTHER UNIONS

Union Générale des Etudiants de Tunisie (UGET): 11 rue d'Espagne, Tunis; f. 1953; 600 mems; Pres. Mekki Fitouri.

Union Générale Tunisienne du Travail (UGTT): 29 pl. Muhammad Ali, 1000 Tunis; tel. (71) 332-400; fax (71) 354-114; e-mail ugtt.tunis@email.ati.tn; internet www.ugtt.org.tn; f. 1946 by Farhat Hached; affiliated to ITUC; 360,000 mems in 24 affiliated unions; 18-mem. exec. bureau; Gen. Sec. Abdessalem Jerad.

Union Nationale de la Femme Tunisienne (UNFT): 56 blvd Bab Benat, 1008 Tunis; tel. (71) 560-178; fax (71) 567-131; e-mail unft@email.ati.tn; internet www.unft.org.tn; f. 1956; promotes the rights of women; 150,000 mems; 28 regional delegations, 199 professional training centres, 13 professional alliances; Pres. Salwa Terzi Ben Attia; Vice-Pres. Faïza Azouz; 23 brs abroad.

Union Tunisienne de l'Agriculture et de la Pêche (UTAP): rue 8451, ave Alain Savary, 1003 Tunis; tel. (71) 806-800; fax (71) 809-181; internet www.utap.org.tn; f. 1955 as Union Nationale des Agriculteurs Tunisiens (which supplanted the Union Générale des Agriculteurs Tunisiens, f. 1950); name changed as above in 1995; Pres. Mabrouk Bahri.

Union Tunisienne de l'Industrie, du Commerce et de l'Artisanat (UTICA): Cité Administrative, Lot 7, Cité el-Khadhra, 1003 Tunis; tel. (71) 142-000; fax (71) 142-100; internet www.utica.org.tn; f. 1946; mems: 15 national federations and 170 syndical chambers at national levels; Pres. Hédi Djilani.

TUNISIA

Transport

RAILWAYS

In 2007 the total length of railways was 2,167 km; 38.6m. passengers travelled by rail in Tunisia in 2009.

Société Nationale des Chemins de Fer Tunisiens (SNCFT): Gare de Tunis ville, pl. Barcelone, 1001 Tunis; tel. (71) 334-444; fax (71) 254-320; e-mail sncft@sncft.com.tn; internet www.sncft.com.tn; f. 1956; state org. controlling all Tunisian railways; Pres. and Dir-Gen. ABD AL-AZIZ CHABANE.

Société des Transports de Tunis (TRANSTU): 1 ave Habib Bourgiba, BP 660, 1025 Tunis; tel. (71) 259-422; fax (71) 342-727; e-mail contact@snt.com.tn; internet www.snt.com.tn; f. 2003 following merger of the Société Nationale des Transports and the Société du Métro Léger de Tunis; operates 5 light train routes with 136 trains, and 206 local bus routes with 1,050 buses; also operates in the suburbs of Tunis-Goulette-Marsa, with 18 trains; plans approved in 2006 for expansion of the light rail system, with five new express lines; Pres. and Dir-Gen. CHEDLY HAJRI.

ROADS

In 2008 there were 359 km of motorways, 4,738 km of main roads and 6,499 km of secondary roads. The total length of the road network was 19,371 km, of which 75.2% was paved.

Société Nationale de Transport Interurbain (SNTRI): ave Muhammad V, BP 40, Belvédère, 1002 Tunis; tel. (71) 784-433; fax (71) 791-621; e-mail marketing@sntri.com.tn; internet www.sntri.com.tn; f. 1981; Dir-Gen. SASSI YAHIA.

Société des Transports de Tunis: see Railways.

There are 12 **Sociétés Régionales des Transports**, responsible for road transport, operating in different regions in Tunisia.

SHIPPING

Tunisia has seven major ports: Tunis-La Goulette, Radès, Bizerta, Sousse, Sfax, Gabès and Zarzis. There is a special petroleum port at La Skhirra. In April 2009 the Government invited bids for the construction of a new deep-water port at Enfidha.

Port Authority

Office de la Marine Marchande et des Ports: Bâtiment Administratif, Port de la Goulette, 2060 La Goulette; tel. (71) 735-300; fax (71) 735-812; e-mail ommp@ommp.nat.tn; internet www.ommp.nat.tn; maritime port administration; Pres. and Dir-Gen. ALI LABIEDH.

CIVIL AVIATION

There are international airports at Tunis-Carthage, Sfax, Djerba, Monastir, Tabarka, Gafsa and Tozeur. Zine el-Abidine Ben Ali airport, located at Enfidha, 100 km south of Tunis, began operations in December 2009. The airport, with an initial annual capacity of 7m. passengers, was officially inaugurated by Ben Ali in early 2010. However, following Ben Ali's ouster in January 2011, the airport was renamed Enfidha-Hammamet International Airport.

Office de l'Aviation Civile et des Aéroports: BP 137 and 147, Aéroport International de Tunis-Carthage, 1080 Tunis; tel. (71) 755-000; fax (71) 755-133; e-mail relations.exterieures@oaca.nat.tn; internet www.oaca.nat.tn; f. 1970; civil aviation and airport authority; Pres. and Gen. Dir RIDHA ABDELHAFID.

Nouvelair Tunisie: Zone Touristique Dkhila, 5065 Monastir; tel. (73) 520-600; fax (73) 520-650; e-mail info@nouvelair.com.tn; internet www.nouvelair.com.tn; f. 1989 as Air Liberté Tunisie; name changed as above in 1996; Tunisian charter co; flights from Tunis, Djerba and Monastir airports to Scandinavia and other European countries; Chair. AZIZ MILAD; Gen. Man. KAMEL OUERGHEMNI.

Sevenair: 10 rue de l'Artisanat, La Charguia 11, Tunis; tel. (71) 942-323; fax (71) 942-272; e-mail info@sevenair.com.tn; internet www.sevenair.com.tn; f. 1992 as Tuninter; Tunisian charter co; Man. Dir ABD AL-KARIM OUERTANI.

TunisAir (Société Tunisienne de l'Air): blvd du 7 novembre 1987, 2035 Tunis; tel. (71) 700-100; fax (71) 700-897; e-mail Resaonline@tunisair.com.tn; internet www.tunisair.com; f. 1948; 45.2% govt-owned; 20% of assets privatized in 1995; flights to Africa, Europe and the Middle East; Pres. and Dir-Gen. NABIL CHETTAOUI.

Tunisavia (Société de Transports, Services et Travaux Aériens): blvd du leader Yasser Arafat, Tunis-Carthage International Airport, 2035 Tunis; tel. (71) 280-555; fax (71) 281-333; e-mail siege@tunisavia.com.tn; internet www.tunisavia.com.tn; f. 1974; helicopter and charter operator; Pres. AZIZ MILAD; Gen. Man. MOHSEN NASRA.

Tourism

The main tourist attractions are the magnificent sandy beaches, Moorish architecture and remains of the Roman Empire. Tunisia contains the site of the ancient Phoenician city of Carthage. Tourism, a principal source of foreign exchange, has expanded rapidly, following extensive government investment in hotels, improved roads and other facilities. The number of hotel beds increased from 71,529 in 1980 to 188,600 in 1999. There were 7.0m. foreign tourist arrivals in 2008 (compared with 4.7m. in 1998); receipts from tourism were estimated at US $3,909m. 2008.

Office National du Tourisme Tunisien: 1 ave Muhammad V, 1001 Tunis; tel. (71) 341-077; fax (71) 350-997; e-mail ontt@email.ati.tn; internet www.bonjour-tunisie.com; f. 1958; Dir-Gen. KHALED CHEIKH.

Defence

Chief of Staff of the Army: Col RACHID AMMAR.
Chief of Staff of the Navy: Adm. TAREK FAOUZI LARBI.
Chief of Staff of the Air Force: Gen. MAHMOUD BEN MUHAMMAD.
Estimated Defence Budget (2009): TD 718m.
Military Service: 1 year (selective).
Total Armed Forces (as assessed at November 2010): 35,800 (army 27,000; navy 4,800; air force 4,000).
Paramilitary Forces (as assessed at November 2010): 12,000 National Guard.

Education

Education is compulsory in Tunisia for a period of nine years between the ages of six and 16. Primary education begins at six years of age and normally lasts for six years. Secondary education begins at 12 years of age and lasts for seven years, comprising a first cycle of three years and a second cycle of four years. In 2007/08, according to UNESCO estimates, the total enrolment at primary schools included 98% of children in the relevant age-group. In that year the total enrolment at secondary schools included 71% of children in the relevant age-group. In 2010 some TD 2,832.8m. was allocated to education and professional training (equivalent to 15.5% of budgeted government expenditure).

Arabic is the first language of instruction in primary and secondary schools, but French is also used. French is used almost exclusively in higher education. The University of Tunis was opened in 1959/60. In 1988 the university was divided into two separate institutions: one for science, the other for arts. It has 54 faculties and institutes. In 1986 two new universities were opened, at Monastir and Sfax. In 2009/10 the number of full-time students enrolled at higher educational establishments in Tunisia was 346,079.

TURKEY

Introductory Survey

LOCATION, CLIMATE, LANGUAGE, RELIGION, FLAG, CAPITAL

The Republic of Turkey lies partly in south-eastern Europe and partly in western Asia. The European and Asian portions of the country (known, respectively, as Thrace and Anatolia) are separated by the Sea of Marmara, linking the Black Sea and the Aegean Sea. Turkey has an extensive coastline: on the Black Sea, to the north; on the Mediterranean Sea, to the south; and on the Aegean Sea, to the west. Most of Turkey lies in Asia, the vast Anatolian peninsula being bordered to the east by Armenia, Georgia, the Nakhichevan Autonomous Republic (part of Azerbaijan) and Iran, and to the south by Iraq and Syria. The smaller European part of the country is bordered to the west by Greece and Bulgaria. In the Asian interior the climate is one of great extremes, with hot dry summers and cold, snowy winters on the plateau. Temperatures in Ankara are generally between −4°C (25°F) and 30°C (86°F). On the Mediterranean coast it is more equable, with mild winters and warm summers. The principal language is Turkish, spoken by 90% of the population. About 7% speak Kurdish, mainly in the south-east. In 1928 the Arabic characters of the written Turkish language were superseded by Western-style script. Islam is the religion of 99% of the population. The national flag (proportions 2 by 3) is red, with a white crescent and a five-pointed white star to the left of centre. The capital is Ankara.

CONTEMPORARY POLITICAL HISTORY

Historical Context

Turkey was formerly a monarchy, ruled by a Sultan, with his capital in Constantinople (now Istanbul). At its zenith, the Turkish Empire, under the Osmanlı (Ottoman) dynasty, extended from the Persian (Arabian) Gulf to Morocco, including most Arab regions and south-eastern Europe. Following the dissolution of the Ottoman Empire after the First World War, political control of Turkey itself passed to the nationalist movement led by Mustafa Kemal, a distinguished army officer. On 23 April 1920, in defiance of the Sultan, a newly elected assembly established a provisional Government, led by Kemal, in Ankara, then a minor provincial town. Kemal's forces waged war against the Greek army in 1920–22, forcing the Greeks to evacuate Smyrna (İzmir) and eastern Thrace (the European portion of Turkey). The new regime abolished the sultanate in November 1922 and declared Turkey a republic, with Ankara as its capital and Kemal as its first President, on 29 October 1923. The Ottoman caliphate (the former monarch's position as Islamic religious leader) was abolished in March 1924.

Kemal remained President of Turkey, with extensive dictatorial powers, until his death in 1938. He pursued a radical programme of far-reaching reform and modernization, including: secularization of the state (in 1928); abolition of Islamic courts and religious instruction in schools; emancipation of women (enfranchised in 1934); banning of polygamy; development of industry; introduction of a Latin alphabet; adoption of the Gregorian (in place of the Islamic) calendar; and encouragement of European culture and technology. Another Westernizing reform was the introduction of surnames in 1934: Kemal assumed the name Atatürk ('Father of the Turks'). His autocratic regime attempted, with considerable success, to replace the country's Islamic traditions by the principles of republicanism, nationalism, populism and state control.

Following Atatürk's death, his Cumhuriyet Halk Partisi (CHP—Republican People's Party), the only authorized political grouping, remained in power under his close associate, Ismet İnönü, who had been Prime Minister in 1923–24 and 1925–37. İnönü was President from 1938 to 1950, and maintained Turkey's neutrality during most of the Second World War (Turkey declared war on Germany in February 1945). After the war İnönü introduced some liberalization of the regime. The one-party system was ended in 1946, when opposition leaders, including Celâl Bayar and Adnan Menderes, registered the Demokratik Parti (DP—Democratic Party); numerous other parties were subsequently formed. The DP won Turkey's first free election in 1950, and ruled for the next decade. Bayar became President, with Menderes as Prime Minister.

In May 1960 the Government was overthrown by a military coup, led by Gen. Cemal Gürsel, who assumed the presidency, claiming that the DP regime had betrayed Atatürk's principle of secularism. A series of coalition governments, mostly led by İnönü, held office from November 1961 until October 1965, when an election was won by the conservative Adalet Partisi (Justice Party), led by Süleyman Demirel, which appealed to supporters of the former DP. The Demirel Government remained in power until March 1971, when escalating student and labour unrest caused the armed forces to demand its resignation. 'Guided democracy', under military supervision, continued until October 1973, with a succession of right-wing 'non-party' administrations, martial law and the rigorous suppression of all left-wing activities.

Domestic Political Affairs

The return to civilian rule began in April 1973, when the Turkish Grand National Assembly (TGNA—the legislative body established in 1961) chose Adm. Fahri Korutürk as President, in preference to a candidate supported by the armed forces. Military participation in government was ended by an election in October 1973. No single party received sufficient support to form a government, and it was not until January 1974 when Bülent Ecevit, leader of the CHP (which had become a left-of-centre party), took office as Prime Minister, having negotiated a coalition with the Milli Selamet Partisi (MSP—National Salvation Party), a pro-Islamic right-wing group. Deteriorating relations with Greece were exacerbated by the Greek-backed coup in Cyprus (q.v.) in July 1974, when Turkey responded by dispatching troops, and occupying the northern part of the island, to protect the Turkish Cypriot population. Despite the failure of the coup, Turkish forces retained control of northern Cyprus, and the island remained effectively partitioned.

A long period of political instability was fostered by a succession of unsuccessful coalitions, headed by either Ecevit or Demirel, and prompted an escalation in political violence, mainly involving clashes between left-wing and right-wing groups. On 12 September 1980, as the violence neared the scale of a civil war, the armed forces, led by Gen. Kenan Evren, Chief of the General Staff, seized power in a bloodless coup; a five-member National Security Council (NSC) was formed, which appointed a mainly civilian Cabinet. Martial law was declared throughout the country. In December the NSC published a decree endowing the military regime with unlimited powers. During 1981–83 a campaign to eradicate all possible sources of political violence was undertaken. In April 1981 former politicians were banned from future political activity, and in October all political parties were disbanded.

The new Government succeeded in reducing the level of political violence in Turkey and in restoring law and order. However, that this had been achieved at the expense of respect for human rights caused concern among Western governments: Turkey was banned from the Parliamentary Assembly of the Council of Europe (see p. 250), aid from the European Community (EC, now European Union—EU, see p. 270) was suspended, and fellow members of NATO urged Turkey to return to democratic rule as soon as possible. (Although Turkey was readmitted to the Parliamentary Assembly of the Council of Europe in May 1984, the Assembly continued to advocate the establishment of full democracy and political freedom in the country.) In October 1981 a Consultative Assembly was established to draft a new constitution, which was approved by referendum in November 1982; objections were widely expressed that the President was to be accorded excessive powers while judicial powers and the rights of trade unions and the press were to be curtailed. An appended 'temporary article' installed Evren as President for a seven-year term.

In May 1983 the NSC revoked the ban on political organizations, permitting the formation of parties, subject to strict rules, in preparation for the first election to be held under the new Constitution. All the former political parties remained proscribed, and 723 former members of the TGNA and leading party officials were banned from political activity for up to 10 years. Followers of the former parties thus regrouped under new names and with new leaders. However, of the 15 new parties, only three were allowed to take part in the election: the Milliyetçi Demokrasi Partisi (MDP—Nationalist Democracy Party) and the Halkçı Partisi (HP—Populist Party), both of which had the tacit support of the NSC, and the conservative Anavatan Partisi (ANAVATAN—Motherland Party), led by Turgut Özal. In the November election ANAVATAN won 211 of the 400 seats in the unicameral legislature, and Özal was appointed Prime Minister in December. This result, which was followed by the holding of local government elections in March 1984, suggested a decisive rejection of military rule.

In November 1985 the HP and the Sosyal Demokrasi Partisi (Social Democratic Party), respectively the main opposition parties within and outside the National Assembly, merged to form the Sosyal Demokrat Halkçı Parti (SHP—Social Democratic Populist Party). However, the left-wing opposition was split as a result of the immediate formation of the Demokratik Sol Parti (DSP—Democratic Left Party), which drew support from the former CHP. The MDP voted to disband in May 1986.

In July 1987 all martial law decrees were repealed when martial law was replaced with a state of emergency in several provinces. At a national referendum in September 1987 a narrow majority approved the repeal of the ban on participation in political affairs, imposed on more than 200 politicians in 1981. This enabled Ecevit to assume the leadership of the DSP, while Demirel was elected as leader of the Doğru Yol Partisi (DYP—True Path Party). In a general election conducted in November 1987 ANAVATAN obtained 292 of the 450 seats in the enlarged TGNA, while the SHP won 99 seats and the DYP 59.

Özal succeeded Evren as President in November 1989, having secured the support of the simple majority required in a third round of voting by the TGNA in October. Yıldırım Akbulut, the Speaker of the TGNA and a former Minister of the Interior, was subsequently appointed Prime Minister. However, having been defeated by former Minister of Foreign Affairs Mesut Yılmaz in a contest for the ANAVATAN leadership in June 1991, Akbulut subsequently resigned as premier. In accordance with the Constitution, President Özal invited Yılmaz, the leader of the party's liberal faction, to head a new administration.

Legislative elections, October 1991 and April 1995

In a general election held on 20 October 1991 the DYP, under Demirel's leadership, received an estimated 27.3% of the votes cast, narrowly defeating ANAVATAN (with 23.9%) and the SHP (20.6%). Demirel formed a coalition administration with the SHP (which with the DYP accounted for 266 of the 450 newly elected deputies in the TGNA), with Erdal İnönü, the SHP leader, as deputy premier. However, by September 1992, following a succession of political defections from the SHP, the representation of the coalition parties in the TGNA had been reduced to 229. Furthermore, the reactivation of the CHP in September (following a relaxation of guidelines for the formation of political parties) threatened to undermine left-wing support for the Government.

Following the death of President Özal, Süleyman Demirel was elected to the presidency in May 1993. Minister of State Tansu Çiller was elected to the DYP party leadership in June and promptly assumed the premiership. Çiller (Turkey's first female Prime Minister) formed a new Cabinet, retaining the 12 SHP members of the previous Government but replacing 17 former DYP ministers, notably several Demirel loyalists.

The new administration was strained by a sharp escalation of violence on the part of the outlawed Partiya Karkeren Kurdistan (PKK—Kurdistan Workers' Party). Plans to extend cultural and educational rights to the Kurds were abandoned following strong opposition from Demirel, right-wing members of the DYP and military leaders, who, in October 1993, effectively resisted a proposal to discuss the establishment of local autonomy for the Kurdish population in the south-east of the country.

A significant increase in outbreaks of urban terrorism in early 1990, together with a perceived increase in the influence of fundamentalist thought, led to widespread fears of a return to the extremist violence of the late 1970s. The increase in terrorist attacks by Islamist and left-wing groups, especially the Dev-Sol (Revolutionary Left), was exacerbated by the Government's stance in the Gulf crisis of 1990–91, and both factions unleashed a series of attacks against Western targets in Turkey, including US civilians, diplomatic missions and offices of several national airlines and banks in Istanbul and Ankara. The leader of Dev-Sol, Dursun Karatas, was detained in France in September 1994, and diplomatic efforts began to ensure his extradition. Two weeks later a former Minister of Justice, Mehmet Topaç, was shot dead by Dev-Sol members in Ankara. In January 1996 a faction of Dev-Sol, Devrimci Halk Kurtuluş Partisi—Cephesi (DHKP—C, the Revolutionary People's Liberation Party—Front), claimed responsibility for the murder of two leading Turkish business executives in Istanbul. At the end of the year it was reported that Dev-Sol had been subsumed by the DHKP—C.

In February 1995 a special conference of the SHP voted to merge with the CHP, consequently increasing the Government's parliamentary majority but forcing a renegotiation of the conditions of the coalition. Agreement was reached by Çiller and Hikmet Çetin, the CHP leader, in March, and an extensive reorganization of the Government was undertaken in order to accommodate the party. Çetin became Deputy Prime Minister and Minister of State; İsmet İnönü assumed the foreign affairs portfolio. Efforts by the Prime Minister to extend democratic rights within the Constitution encountered considerable opposition, both from conservative elements within her own party and from the fundamentalist Islamist Refah Partisi (RP—Welfare Party). Certain constitutional reforms, including the removal of restrictions on political associations and trade unions, the lowering of the age of eligibility to vote from 21 to 18 years and the expansion of the TGNA by 100 parliamentary seats to 550, were finally approved in July. Yet Çiller failed to obtain sufficient support for the amendment of the 'anti-terrorism' legislation, which was expected to be crucial in securing the European Parliament's ratification of the EU-Turkish customs union (see below).

Deniz Baykal was elected leader of the CHP in September 1995. All CHP ministers subsequently resigned their cabinet positions, and ensuing coalition negotiations with Çiller failed as it became apparent that the political differences between the two leaders were insurmountable. Later in September Demirel was forced to accept the Prime Minister's resignation, but Çiller was immediately invited to form a new government. A DYP-CHP Government, headed by Çiller, with Baykal as Deputy Prime Minister and Minister of Foreign Affairs, took office in November.

At the general election held in December 1995 the RP, which had campaigned to strengthen political and economic relations with other Islamic countries, to withdraw from NATO and the EU customs union, and to increase state involvement in the economy, secured the largest number of parliamentary seats (158), with 21.4% of the votes cast. The DYP won 135 seats, with 19.2% of the votes, while ANAVATAN took 132, with 19.7% of the votes. Since no party had an absolute majority, the two other parties securing parliamentary representation, the DSP and the CHP, were expected to have considerable political leverage in the new parliament. A new administration comprising ANAVATAN, led by Mesut Yılmaz, and the DYP was appointed in March 1996; Çiller conceded the premiership to Yılmaz, under a rotating arrangement. The new Government was soon strained by tensions between the two leaders, and allegations of corruption against Çiller, and at the end of May Çiller announced the withdrawal of her party's support for the Government. In June 1996 Yılmaz announced the resignation of his Government, following a Constitutional Court ruling that annulled the March 1996 parliamentary vote of confidence in his administration.

Erbakan was subsequently invited to form a government, and at the end of June 1996 the RP concluded an agreement with the DYP; Erbakan was to lead the new coalition administration, with Çiller assuming the deputy premiership and foreign affairs portfolio. The leaders asserted that the objective of the new Government was to secure political and economic stability, and they guaranteed that Turkey would adhere to its existing international and strategic agreements. Nevertheless, eight DYP deputies in the TGNA resigned from the party in protest at the coalition with the RP, and a further 15 failed to endorse the new administration in a parliamentary vote of confidence conducted in July; none the less, the new Government secured a narrow majority.

The contradictions inherent in the new RP-DYP administration became evident in many aspects of government policy. In foreign affairs, the Government attempted to reassure its Western allies of its continued support. At the end of July 1996 the mandate for the use of Turkish airbases by allied forces engaged in 'Operation Provide Comfort' in northern Iraq (see Foreign Affairs) was extended, and in August a new military co-operation agreement was signed with Israel, expanding on an accord concluded in February. In addition, there was evidence of the military asserting its authority by dismissing 13 officers in August on disciplinary charges relating to Islamist practices (50 officers had been dismissed on similar grounds in December 1995). At the same time, however, Prime Minister Erbakan embarked on a tour of Asian and Middle Eastern Muslim countries in order to strengthen bilateral relations and co-operation. In August Turkey and Iran finalized an economic agreement, shortly after legislation had been ratified in the USA that threatened punitive measures against countries undertaking investments in Iran. In January 1997 the TGNA cleared Çiller of the final corruption charges against her. In the same month Hüsamettin Cindoruk, who had been expelled from the DYP in October 1995, established a new breakaway party, the Demokrat Türkiye Partisi (Democratic Turkey Party).

In February 1997, following pressure from the military and DYP members of the Government, the RP was forced to withdraw proposals to extend Muslim education and to allow religious garments to be worn by public workers. At a meeting of the NSC held at the end of February, the military leadership presented an 18-point memorandum which set out to ensure the protection of Turkish secular state traditions, including greater supervision of Islamic financial and media operations, the removal of Islamists from public administration and closure of all unauthorized Islamic groupings; the military warned of punitive action if the proposals were not implemented. Political tension was defused when Erbakan, who had initially criticized the NSC for attempting to impose laws on the Government, signed a memorandum endorsing the NSC measures and declared that the leaders of all the main political parties were unanimous in their view that the Constitution must be upheld. The Council of Ministers agreed in March to implement the NSC proposals, but concern subsequently arose over the failure of the Government to act on the measures. At a meeting of the NSC held in April, however, Erbakan agreed to pursue the military's demands, including restrictions on Islamic education. Although the Government defeated an opposition attempt in that month to pursue a censure motion in the TGNA, the political situation remained critical, and charges from the military, opposition parties and dissident members of the DYP that the Government was undermining the modern secular tradition were reinforced when the country's chief prosecutor initiated legal proceedings to ban the RP (on the grounds that the party had violated the Constitution). By June the coalition had lost its majority in the TGNA as a result of defections, principally from the DYP. Erbakan announced that he would seek an early election, but the military continued to exert pressure on the Government, and the Prime Minister finally resigned. President Demirel asked the ANAVATAN leader, Mesut Yılmaz, to form a new administration, and a coalition with the DSP and the Democratic Turkey Party was inaugurated in July; the coalition controlled only a minority of seats in the TGNA, and was dependent on the support of the CHP. The tripartite Government pledged to improve law and order, implement previously proposed changes to the education system, and vigorously pursue EU membership. Defections from the DYP continued, and by the end of July its representation in the TGNA had been reduced from 135 to 93.

In August 1997 the TGNA approved legislation extending compulsory education from five to eight years. This was intended to raise the entry age to Islamic schools from 11 to 14, thus reducing attendance at such schools and lessening Islamic influence. The RP organized popular demonstrations in protest against the legislation (which constituted a principal demand of the military). A further 73 members of the armed forces were expelled, owing to suspected affiliation to Islamist organizations, while further public demonstrations were prompted by the military's insistence on the strict enforcement of the ban on wearing Islamic dress in public buildings, notably educational establishments.

In January 1998 the Constitutional Court ordered the dissolution of the RP on the grounds that it was responsible for undermining the secular regime, and banned seven of its members, including Erbakan, from holding political office for five years. Many former RP deputies joined the Fazilet Partisi (FP—Virtue Party), which had been established in December 1997. By March 1998 the FP's representation in the TGNA had risen to 140 seats, making it the largest parliamentary party (ANAVATAN controlled 139 seats). In April the mayor of Istanbul, Recep Tayyip Erdoğan, who was expected to assume the leadership of the FP, was sentenced to 10 months' imprisonment for inciting hatred; he was released pending an appeal.

The stability of Yılmaz's minority Government was threatened by the demands of the CHP for an early general election. The CHP demonstrated its power in April 1998 by voting with the opposition in favour of an investigation into allegations of corruption against the Prime Minister. Following an agreement signed by Yılmaz and CHP leader Deniz Baykal, the Prime Minister announced in June 1998 that he was to resign at the end of the year; he was to be succeeded by an interim government that would call early elections for April 1999.

In August 1998 12 former RP politicians, including Erbakan and FP leader Recai Kutan, were charged with illegally diverting funds from the party prior to its dissolution. An investigation into Çiller's assets was begun in September. Further investigations were launched in that month into Çiller and the former Minister of Finance for financial irregularities, and the immunity of the former TGNA Speaker was revoked, to allow an investigation, at his request, into his conduct following corruption allegations. Meanwhile, the Court of Appeal upheld the prison sentence on the mayor of Istanbul. As a result of his conviction, Erdoğan was deprived of his position of mayor; he also resigned from the FP. In December new charges were filed against him for insulting the judiciary in a speech following his sentencing. In November 1998 corruption charges against Çiller were dismissed by a parliamentary commission, owing to insufficient evidence, while Erbakan was acquitted on charges of slandering the judiciary.

The April 1999 legislative elections

The Government resigned in November 1998, after the TGNA approved a motion of no confidence submitted by the CHP in response to accusations of corruption against Yılmaz. In January 1999, following protracted political manoeuvring, Bülent Ecevit of the DSP formed a Government, comprising DSP and independent deputies, which was to hold office until the elections in April. In February 1999 the trial began of 79 alleged Islamists, including Erbakan. Meanwhile, the High Election Council ruled that former RP deputies would not be allowed to take part in the forthcoming elections as independent candidates.

Despite pressure to postpone the elections, voting proceeded as scheduled on 18 April 1999. No party secured an outright majority in the TGNA; the DSP won 136 of the 550 seats, and subsequently formed a coalition with the Milliyetçi Hareket Partisi (MHP—Nationalist Movement Party), which had won 129 seats, and ANAVATAN, with 86 seats. The remaining seats in the TGNA were won by the FP (111) and the DYP (85), with three seats won by independent candidates. The pro-Kurdish nationalist Halkın Demokrasi Partisi (HADEP—People's Democracy Party) performed strongly in the south-east, but failed to secure the 10% of the national vote necessary for a seat in the TGNA. The CHP leader, Deniz Baykal, resigned following the poor performance of his party. The new Government, led by Bülent Ecevit, won a parliamentary vote of confidence in June.

Several articles of a political parties act relating to the closure of parties were approved in August 1999: no party would be permitted to re-form, even under a different name; party officials would be prohibited from active politics for five years and would be forbidden from standing as candidates for the party, although they would be permitted to stand as independent candidates. In September the FP submitted its preliminary defence against the motion to ban it. In October the assets of Erbakan and nine other former RP officials were frozen as part of the continuing trial of a case brought by the Treasury demanding the repayment of aid given to the RP in 1997, as well as the repayment of allegedly unregistered party funds. In March 2000 Erbakan was sentenced to one year in prison and a lifetime ban from politics for provoking animosity and hatred in a speech made in 1994. (In January 2001, however, his sentence was suspended, under penal legislation allowing conditional release for certain convictions. Moreover, in July 2006 the European Court of Human Rights—ECHR—ruled that Erbakan had not received a fair trial.) In December 1999, meanwhile, 300 people were detained following protests over the ban on wearing headscarves in universities; the Court of Appeals ruled that the prerogative to wear Islamic headscarves was not a democratic right.

In January 2000, following a lack of agreement within the TGNA on a suitable presidential candidate (Demirel's term of office was to end in May), Ecevit announced plans for a constitutional amendment that would allow Demirel to renew his term. Despite the agreement of the governing coalition for the proposal, a vote in the TGNA failed to achieve the necessary level of support for the amendment to be carried. In April the parties of the governing coalition agreed to nominate the Chairman of the

Constitutional Court, Ahmet Necdet Sezer, as their joint candidate for the presidency; he was elected in a third round of voting.

A major security operation against the fundamentalist guerrilla group Hezbollah (apparently sponsored by fundamentalist elements in Iran, but unrelated to the Lebanese group of the same name) was launched in January 2000. An armed confrontation between police and Hezbollah members resulted in the death of its leader, Hüseyin Velioğlu, and the capture of two of his closest associates; information provided by these associates led to the discovery of the bodies of nine men, believed to have been abducted by the group in İstanbul. In early 2000 the operation resulted in the detention of some 690 suspected Hezbollah members, while the bodies of more than 50 people, believed to have been victims of the group, were discovered. At that time the Government denied that it had tolerated the activities of Hezbollah, owing to its anti-PKK activities, and the office of the Chief of the General Staff strongly denied allegations of links between Hezbollah and the army. In February Çiller denied that the state had supplied weapons to Hezbollah during her time as Prime Minister. In October the Ministry of the Interior reported that since January some 1,600 people with ties to Hezbollah had been arrested. Trial proceedings involving 31 alleged Hezbollah members finally concluded in December 2009; 16 men, including the two close associates of Velioğlu captured in 2000, were sentenced to life imprisonment.

In December 2000 two police officers were killed following an attack on a police bus in İstanbul. In January 2001 the DHKP—C claimed responsibility for a suicide bomb attack on a police building, which killed two people. In April Sahil Izzet Erdis, the leader of the outlawed Great Eastern Islamic Raiders' Front (IBDA—C), was sentenced to death on charges of seeking to overthrow the secular state. In September a suicide bomber, believed to be acting on behalf of the DHKP—C, killed two policemen and a foreign tourist in central İstanbul. In May 2002 the EU designated the DHKP—C as a terrorist organization. Security forces arrested several members of DHKP—C in two attempted military operations during November 2004. In June 2006 four members of the organization were arrested following the shooting of a police officer in İstanbul. In January 2007 a further five DHKP—C members (including Karatas) were detained by the Turkish authorities.

Despite the implementation of structural reform measures by the Ecevit Government, in November 2000 a severe banking crisis was provoked by an investigation by the Banking and Supervision Agency into 10 failed banks. The investigation exposed the vulnerability of the banking sector and the lack of confidence of foreign investors in the Turkish economy, as a result of a widening current account deficit and delays to the structural reform programme. The IMF and the World Bank agreed to emergency loans in order to support the programme. In February 2001 a second economic crisis was precipitated following a dispute between the President and Prime Minister: Sezer had accused Ecevit of not responding adequately to allegations of government corruption. Opposition parties and the business community had demanded the dismissal of Deputy Prime Minister Hüsamettin Özkan, the Minister of Energy and Natural Resources, Cumhur Ersümer, and the Minister of Public Works, Koray Aydin, and the initiation of a parliamentary investigation into the two ministers' affairs. The precarious balance of power within the governing coalition was, however, thought to have dissuaded Ecevit from undertaking any action against the alleged corruption. Later in February Turkey, with the support of the IMF, abandoned its exchange rate controls and allowed the lira to float, while empowering the Central Bank to pursue a rigorous monetary policy to control inflation.

Following the banking crisis, in March 2001 Ecevit replaced the Governor of the Central Bank and appointed Kemal Derviş, a senior economist at the World Bank, as Minister of Finance, in an attempt to salvage Turkey's economic reforms and restore confidence in the financial markets. Derviş announced an emergency plan for economic stabilization, which included the restructuring of three state-owned banks under one supervisory board, and succeeded in securing the financial support of the IMF and the World Bank. Yet the political implications of the financial crisis continued to be felt in April, as anti-Government demonstrations involving tens of thousands of people degenerated into riots in Ankara and İzmir. Ecevit, however, rejected demands for his Government to resign. Later in the month it was announced that 15 officials and business executives were to be tried on conspiracy and bribery charges, following a high-profile investigation into corruption in the state energy sector. The testimonies of the defendants resulted in the resignation of Ersümer, who was succeeded as head of the energy portfolio by Zeki Cakan of ANAVATAN in early May.

In May 2001 the TGNA approved legislation designed to meet conditions demanded by the IMF before the latter was to release US $10,000m. in financial aid. At the end of the month the Minister of State for Privatization, Yuksel Yalova, resigned, owing to disagreements within the Government over the liberalization of the tobacco industry stipulated by the IMF. In July the Minister of Communications, Enis Öksüz, resigned, owing to his opposition to IMF-imposed plans to privatize the telecommunications sector. In September the Minister of Public Works and Housing, Koray Aydin, also resigned from his government post and from the TGNA, after corruption charges were brought against him with regard to his alleged receipt of funds from contracts relating to reconstruction in the aftermath of the 1999 earthquake in İzmit.

The rise to prominence of the AKP

In June 2001 the Constitutional Court banned the FP, on the grounds that it was essentially a continuation of the banned Islamist RP and was thus regarded as seeking to undermine the secular system. The Court expelled two FP members from the TGNA; however, it refrained from ordering the mass expulsions of the 100 remaining FP members from the legislature, who were allowed to remain in place as independents or join two planned successor parties. The ban was, nevertheless, opposed by most TGNA members, who were reportedly concerned that it would lead to more political instability. In July the ECHR upheld the Government's 1998 decision to ban the RP. In July 2001 former FP leader Recai Kutan established a new Islamist party, Saadet Partisi (SP—Felicity Party), incorporating about one-half of the former members of the FP (mainly from the conservative wing); the new party pledged to defend religious rights without challenging the secular state. It was believed that, as with the FP, Erbakan was the main force in the party. In August the remaining members of the FP joined the new reformist Islamist Adalet ve Kalkınma (AKP—Justice and Development Party), established by the former mayor of İstanbul, Recep Tayyip Erdoğan, and FP member Abdullah Gül as an alternative to the SP. Shortly afterwards Erdoğan came under investigation for comments he had reportedly made in 1994 that allegedly insulted the Turkish state.

Meanwhile, in March 2001 the Government had announced a new programme aimed at facilitating EU membership that entailed, *inter alia*, the eventual abolition of the death penalty and ending restrictions on freedom of expression, as well as improving the rights of minorities, but EU officials criticized the programme for its lack of specifics. Despite such plans, the TGNA approved a four-month extension of the state of emergency in the predominantly Kurdish south-east of the country, and in May the Turkish Radio and Television Supreme Council ordered the closure of 89 radio and television stations for broadcasting separatist and disruptive programmes. The TGNA in October overwhelmingly approved a number of constitutional amendments designed to facilitate Turkey's admission to the EU. The changes largely pertained to political freedoms and civil liberties, including minority rights (notably regarding the use of the Kurdish language). Significantly, the number of civilians on the powerful NSC would rise from five to nine, thereby lessening the power of the military (which would retain five members). Improved rights for women were approved in November. In August 2002 the TGNA formally abolished the death penalty in peacetime; in September, however, Amnesty International released a report alleging the widespread use of torture by police, citing testimony from more than 60 individuals during the first half of 2002.

In January 2002 the Constitutional Court imposed restrictions on the political activities of AKP leader Erdoğan, owing to his earlier allegedly seditious activities. The Court banned him from contesting the elections to the TGNA, and ordered his party to remove him from its leadership within six months. In March Ankara's Higher Criminal Court sentenced Erbakan to two years and four months in prison for embezzling party funds. (In December 2003 the Court of Appeals in Ankara upheld this sentence, although it was deferred for one year on medical grounds.)

In February 2002 the TGNA approved additional laws on freedom of thought and expression by means of a 'mini-reform' programme designed to satisfy EU standards. In subsequent weeks the ruling coalition experienced increasing disagreement over the possible execution of PKK leader Abdullah Öcalan, and on broadcasting and education in the Kurdish language, with the MHP taking an uncompromising stance on these issues in opposition to ANAVATAN. In July Prime Minister Ecevit was forced to call early elections to the TGNA for November, after several of his ministers and numerous DSP party legislators resigned, thereby denying the ruling coalition a majority in the TGNA. Notable resignations included those of Deputy Prime Minister and Minister of State Hüsamettin Özkan and Minister of Foreign Affairs İsmail Cem. Cem formed a new party, the Yeni Türkiye Partisi (YTP—New Turkey Party), with 62 defectors from the DSP, whose representation in the TGNA had fallen from 128 seats to 65 seats. Ecevit appointed DSP member Şükrü Sina Gürel as Deputy Prime Minister and Minister of State, and concurrently Minister of Foreign Affairs. In early August the Minister of Finance, Kemal Derviş, resigned, and subsequently agreed to co-operate with the CHP. At the end of the month the notably pro-EU and strongly secularist commander of the army's ground forces, Gen. Hilmi Özkök, was appointed to the powerful position of Chief of the General Staff for a four-year term.

In September 2002 the AKP, which was leading in opinion polls, underwent a reverse, when Turkey's highest election board confirmed the Constitutional Court's decision to ban Erdoğan from holding public office. Although he had publicly professed secular and pro-European views, Erdoğan retained the distrust of the secularist military and judiciary, and in October the chief prosecutor sought to obtain an outright ban on the AKP, although this was not implemented. Attempts by several political parties to delay the elections also failed.

The AKP comes to power

The elections to the TGNA, held on 3 November 2002, significantly transformed the Turkish political landscape. With voter participation of 79.0%, the AKP won 34.3% of the votes cast, securing 363 seats in the TGNA. Only one other party, the CHP, achieved the 10% of the vote required for representation in the TGNA, winning 19.4% of the votes cast and securing 178 seats. Following the election, President Sezer appointed AKP deputy leader Abdullah Gül as Prime Minister, since Erdoğan was ineligible for the position. (None the less, Erdoğan acted as de facto Prime Minister, exerting a strong influence on the new Government and making a number of official foreign visits.) The new Council of Ministers largely consisted of technocrats from the AKP. Three Deputy Prime Ministers were appointed, while Ali Babacan became Minister of State with responsibility for the Economy and Kemal Unakıtan acquired the finance portfolio. Mehmet Vecdi Gönül was appointed Minister of National Defence. Owing to the fact that AKP's representation in the TGNA was only four seats less than the two-thirds' majority needed to amend the Constitution, and the party commanded the support of several independents, in December the legislature approved constitutional reforms allowing Erdoğan to contest a forthcoming by-election. Initially vetoed by Sezer, these changes were subsequently re-endorsed by the TGNA, forcing the President to accept them.

In January 2003 Erdoğan was re-elected leader of the AKP and immediately announced plans to contest the by-election for the TGNA, membership of which would allow him to become Prime Minister. In February the electoral commission endorsed his candidacy, and Erdoğan was elected to the TGNA on 9 March. Two days later President Sezer appointed Erdoğan as Prime Minister. Erdoğan appointed a new Council of Ministers, which retained most ministers from the incumbent Government. Gül replaced Ertuğrul Yalçınbayır as Deputy Prime Minister and also assumed the foreign affairs portfolio.

In March 2003 a ruling by Turkey's Constitutional Court banned HADEP from political activity on the grounds that it had been aiding the PKK (a charge denied by the party). Some 46 members of the party were also subjected to a five-year ban. Shortly afterwards HADEP became reconstituted as the Demokratik Halkın Partisi (DEHAP—Democratic People's Party). In June the TGNA adopted a further series of human rights reforms, including additional legislation to permit education and broadcasting in Kurdish and other minority languages, and to amend the existing legal definition of terrorism, in order to qualify for accession negotiations with the EU. At the end of that month Sezer vetoed one of the amendments, under which peaceful advocacy of an independent Kurdish state would no longer be illegal. However, the TGNA utilized its power to overrule the veto by returning the legislation to the President without amendment. Further reforms approved by the TGNA (in accordance with EU requirements) in July included provisions for the prompt investigation of allegations of torture and for prohibiting the trial of civilians in military courts in peacetime, as well as the reconstitution of the predominantly military NSC as an entirely advisory body and the offer of a qualified amnesty to supporters of KADEK (the Congress for Freedom and Democracy in Kurdistan—see below), with the specific exclusion of those believed to have committed acts of violence; these measures were formally approved by Sezer in August. In September a decision by the Court of Appeals over the November 2002 elections confirming the disqualification of DEHAP for malpractice prompted concern that the results would be annulled, thereby ending the majority of the AKP. However, on 4 October 2003 the High Electoral Council upheld the election results. In the same month an independent parliamentary deputy joined the Liberal Demokratik Parti, which consequently secured one seat in the TGNA.

Some 25 people were killed and about 300 injured in suicide bombings outside two of İstanbul's largest synagogues on 15 November 2003. On 20 November a further two suicide bombs exploded outside the Hong Kong and Shanghai Banking Corporation and the British consulate in İstanbul, killing some 31 people (including the Consul-General) and injuring more than 450. Although several extremist Turkish Islamist groups, including IBDA—C, claimed responsibility for the attacks, the involvement of the militant Islamist al-Qa'ida network led by Osama bin Laden was immediately suspected. Erdoğan condemned all acts of terrorism in a national statement, and demonstrations were staged in Turkey against the bombings, although popular sentiment also attributed blame to the US-led military action in Iraq. By the end of that month a total of 62 had been killed in the four bomb attacks, and 159 had been arrested on suspicion of involvement, of whom a number had been charged. The Turkish authorities announced that the bombings had been organized by a cell of Turkish nationals connected to al-Qa'ida, all of whom had been trained outside Turkey; one principal suspect was repatriated from Syria, while another was arrested on Turkey's south-eastern border with Iran.

Local government elections, which were held on 28 March 2004, resulted in a strong increase in support for the AKP, which secured 42% of the votes cast and 58 of the country's 81 provinces. In May, as part of the series of reforms intended to bring Turkey into conformity with EU human rights and democratic standards, the TGNA adopted draft constitutional amendments to: abolish the death penalty and anti-terrorist state security courts; guarantee equality for women; and establish full parliamentary control over the budget of the armed forces. However, new education legislation, ending restrictions on university entrance for those trained in religious schools, was suspended in early June, following a veto by President Sezer. Security concerns shortly before a NATO summit, attended by US President George W. Bush, in June were heightened by further explosions in İstanbul, including a suicide bombing, in which four people were killed. In the same month Turkey's stated commitment to new human rights standards, in compliance with EU requirements, appeared to be demonstrated by the Supreme Court's decision to order the release of the four Kurdish former parliamentary deputies, who had been sentenced to 15 years' imprisonment in 1994 for supporting the PKK. Following their release, a court in July 2004 overturned their convictions and ordered retrials. In a further significant measure, the TGNA in July authorized the prosecution for corruption of former Prime Minister Mesut Yılmaz and three other former ministers. In August a further three bombs exploded at hotels in İstanbul, killing two people, and were again attributed by the authorities to Kurdish militants.

In January 2005, following the provisional offer by the EU in December 2004 to commence accession negotiations, Islamist party leaders criticized the conditions imposed and demanded that the Government organize a referendum on EU membership; protests were organized in İstanbul and in İzmit. In February 2005 the Chairman of the Human Rights Consultative Council tendered his resignation, citing continuing impediments posed by the Government (which had rejected a previous critical report of the Council over the stance on human rights). Turkey's new penal code, adopted as a precondition for the commencement of EU accession talks (see Foreign Affairs), entered into force at the beginning of June, after a two-month postponement. Sezer subsequently vetoed an amendment reducing the penalties for anti-secular teaching in illegal religious schools; however, the President's veto was overruled by the TGNA later that month.

The murder of a prominent Armenian-Turkish journalist and human rights campaigner, Hrant Dink, in İstanbul in January 2007 provoked considerable outrage among the population.

Eight suspects, some with close links to nationalist organizations, were arrested following Dink's killing, while several local police officers were suspended from duty for allegedly having failed to offer sufficient protection to the journalist after he had received death threats, or for apparently having shown support to the incarcerated principal suspect. A teenage youth suspected of having links with extreme right-wing nationalist organizations had reportedly confessed to Dink's murder. Trial proceedings against the alleged murderer, together with 17 other suspects, commenced in the Turkish capital in July. In September 2010 the ECHR ruled that the Turkish Government had contravened two, three and 13 of the European Convention on Human Rights in relation to Dink's murder and ordered Turkey to compensate Dink's family for its failure to act upon information it had received regarding plots to murder the journalist. At the trial's 15th hearing in October, judges ruled that the alleged murderer should be tried as a minor (the youth had been 17 years of age at the time of the killing); the trial finally commenced at a juvenile court in Istanbul on 28 February 2011.

Meanwhile, in February 2006 Erdoğan criticized the decision of the Council of State to refuse to allow the promotion of a teacher who had worn a headscarf on her way to work. In May an extremist Islamist lawyer, angered at the ruling, entered the Council of State building and assassinated a senior judge. Large demonstrations followed in Ankara, supported by the judiciary and the Chief of the General Staff, Gen. Hilmi Özkök; protesters demanded the protection of secularization in Turkey. (The Islamist lawyer was given two terms of life imprisonment by an Ankara court in February 2008, having been one of four defendants convicted of involvement in the murder.) In August Gen. Yaşar Büyükanıt succeeded Özkök as Chief of the General Staff. In April 2006 the trial of two Syrian nationals, including a suspected member of al-Qa'ida, was merged with that of 71 defendants charged with involvement in the bombings in Istanbul in November 2003. (In February 2007 seven people—six Turks and a Syrian—were sentenced to life imprisonment for their involvement in the attacks; 41 were given prison terms of between four and 18 years, while 26 were acquitted.) In March 2006 three people were killed when a bomb exploded near the Governor's office in the south-eastern town of Van, and in April a further bomb attack was staged at the offices of the AKP in Istanbul. A number of suspected al-Qa'ida militants were detained in south-eastern Turkey in January 2008, on suspicion of plotting large-scale attacks within the country.

In mid-April 2007, as the TGNA began preparations to elect a successor to President Sezer (whose term of office was to end on 16 May), some 300,000 people held a demonstration in Ankara to demand that Turkey remain a secular state. The protest was organized amid strong speculation that Prime Minister Erdoğan was intending to stand for the presidency; many feared that Erdoğan would pursue an Islamist agenda if he became President. In late April, however, the day before the deadline for the registration of candidates, the Prime Minister declared that the Minister of Foreign Affairs, Abdullah Gül, had been chosen as the ruling AKP's candidate. Gül immediately pledged to retain Turkey's secular status should he be elected to the presidency, although there was considerable scepticism about the likelihood of this since Gül's wife chose to wear the Islamic headscarf. The initial round of voting in the TGNA was boycotted by the CHP and other opposition parties, which complained that they had not been consulted about Gül's application; they lodged an appeal with the Constitutional Court for the voting process to be cancelled. Since Gül secured only 357 out of 550 votes at the first round—10 fewer than the requisite number—it was announced at the end of the month that the Constitutional Court had annulled the initial vote. Prime Minister Erdoğan subsequently asked the legislature to approve proposals initiated by his party to endorse a constitutional amendment enabling the President henceforth to be directly elected for a five-year term and that a general election (scheduled for November) be brought forward to June in order to resolve the political crisis. The Higher Council of Elections ruled in May that an election should be held on 22 July. Meanwhile, the AKP's legislation was approved by the TGNA on 11 May, but subsequently vetoed by President Sezer. Following the re-endorsement of the legislation by the TGNA at the end of May, in a final bid to delay its passage the President exercised his right to refer the decision to a referendum.

The elections of 2007 and 2009

The AKP of Prime Minister Erdoğan obtained 46.7% of the votes and 341 seats at the legislative elections, on 22 July 2007, against the CHP's 20.9% and 112 seats. The MHP came third, with 14.3% and 71 seats; however, one of the party's elected representatives died on 26 July, resulting in one seat remaining vacant. Pro-Kurdish deputies entered the TGNA as independents—the first time that there had been Kurdish representation in the legislature for 13 years. In early August Köksal Toptan of the AKP was elected Speaker of the Assembly, in succession to Bülent Arınç. Shortly afterwards Abdullah Gül signalled his desire to remain a candidate for the presidency, and he was endorsed unanimously by his party. The first round of the presidential vote was held on 20 August; Gül failed to secure the required two-thirds' majority to be elected at this stage. However, by the third round of voting, on 28 August, at which a simple majority was required, Gül was chosen as Turkey's 11th President, securing 339 votes. At his inauguration the new President again pledged his commitment to secularism, pluralism and freedom of belief. A new Council of Ministers was approved by President Gül at the end of the month. Among the principal appointees were Ali Babacan as Minister of Foreign Affairs and Chief Negotiator of Turkey for European Union Affairs, and Dr Beşir Atalay as Minister of Internal Affairs. The new Government's programme, which won a vote of confidence in early September, included proposals to reform and modernize the Turkish Constitution, and measures aimed at increasing economic prosperity. Concerns were raised in mid-September when the Prime Minister recommended an amendment to the Constitution specifically to overturn the ban on women wearing the Islamic headscarf in Turkish universities. At the nation-wide referendum held on 21 October, a reported 69.0% of eligible voters approved the constitutional reforms regarding the direct election of future Turkish presidents. The serving term of a president was also reduced from seven to five years (renewable once), while that of TGNA deputies was reduced from five to four years.

In January 2008 the AKP and the MHP together submitted a motion to the TGNA that would end the ban on the wearing of the Islamic headscarf by women at universities. The two constitutional amendments were passed into law by President Gül in February, having received parliamentary approval. The development provoked anger among Turkish secularists, who protested against the decision in Ankara and elsewhere. Two secularist opposition parties, the CHP and the DSP, lodged an appeal with the Constitutional Court on the grounds that the legislation contravened the secular principles of Turkey's Constitution. In March an indictment was filed at the Constitutional Court by Abdurrahman Yalçınkaya, a prosecutor at the Court of Appeals, which presented detailed evidence of alleged 'anti-secular activities' of the AKP and called for the closure of the party and a five-year suspension from politics of 71 senior party officials, including the incumbent President and Prime Minister. The Court voted unanimously to hear the case against the ruling party. The AKP denied the anti-secular charges, and contended that banning the party would amount to overturning the democratic outcome of the legislative elections. In June the Constitutional Court rescinded the recent legislation pertaining to the wearing of headscarves at universities, on the grounds that it was unconstitutional. However, the AKP narrowly avoided disbandment when the verdict was announced at the end of July. A minimum of seven votes from 11 judges was required to effect the closure of a political party: six voted to disband the party; four voted for a financial penalty, and one rejected the case. None the less, the Court found the party guilty of being a 'focal point of anti-secular activity', and ordered that its state funding be halved for a year.

Amid ongoing tension between the Government and its secularist opponents (see also The 'Ergenekon' investigation), Erdoğan publicly declared that the forthcoming municipal elections, scheduled for 29 March 2009, would serve as a referendum on his leadership. The Prime Minister campaigned vigorously, appearing at large political rallies throughout Turkey and exhorting the electorate to reinforce his mandate to lead the country. The AKP won 38.8% of the votes cast, consolidating its position as Turkey's dominant political party. Following evidence of electoral irregularities, the High Electoral Board ordered a rerun of the elections in 30 districts. In the municipal elections, held on 8 June, the AKP won an estimated 42.2% of the votes cast, securing control in 12 of the 30 districts; the CHP won in 10 districts.

Meanwhile, a major reorganization of the Council of Ministers, involving 17 ministerial changes, was announced in May 2009. Ali Babacan, hitherto Minister of Foreign Affairs, was appointed Deputy Prime Minister and accorded responsibility for economic co-ordination; the foreign affairs portfolio was reassigned to

TURKEY

Ahmet Davutoğlu, a foreign affairs adviser to the Prime Minister who had played a central role in Turkey's mediation of indirect peace talks between Israel and Syria during 2008 (see Foreign Affairs). Other significant changes included the appointment of Mehmet Şimşek as Minister of Finance, and Sadullah Ergin as Minister of Justice. On 5 August the TGNA elected the AKP's Mehmet Ali Şahin, a former Minister of Justice, as Speaker of the Assembly, in succession to Toptan.

In November 2009 the merger of ANAVATAN with the Demokrat Parti was announced. Supporters of the two centre-right parties were hopeful that the merger would help to restore their political influence; neither party had secured representation in the TGNA since the success of the AKP at the 2002 legislative elections.

Recent developments: the 'Ergenekon' investigation and referendum on constitutional reform

Following the discovery of a hoard of munitions at a property belonging to a retired army officer in İstanbul in June 2007, an investigation was launched into the existence of a clandestine nationalist organization, known as Ergenekon, with alleged links to senior military, police, judicial and media figures. From early 2008 a series of high-profile arrests were made in connection with the investigation. In July 21 people, including two retired army generals, were detained. In August Gen. İlker Başbuğ succeeded Yaşar Büyükanıt as Chief of the General Staff. Başbuğ was replaced as Ground Forces Commander by Gen. Işık Koşaner, who, in a speech in late August, denied allegations of links between the military and Ergenekon; he also reiterated the army's readiness to take action, if needed, to protect Turkey's secular Constitution. Trial proceedings against 86 suspected members of Ergenekon were initiated in October. Suspects were charged with various offences, which included belonging to a terrorist organization and plotting to overthrow the Government. According to the prosecution, the organization had plotted to foment disorder through a series of violent incidents, including high-profile assassinations, in order to undermine the Government and provoke a military coup. The organization was also indicted with responsibility for several violent incidents, previously attributed to Islamist militants, such as the murder of the judge at the Council of State in May 2006 (see The AKP comes to power) and a bomb attack at the offices of *Cumhuriyet* newspaper in the same month. Among those that Ergenekon allegedly planned to assassinate were the President, the Prime Minister and the internationally renowned Turkish writer Orhan Pamuk. As many as 40 additional suspects, including three retired generals and a former police chief, were arrested in January 2009. In March charges against an additional 56 suspects were appended to the ongoing trial proceedings. In April the Supreme Court of Appeals ordered that the trial relating to the Council of State attack of 2006 be merged with the Ergenekon trial. The proliferation of arrests during 2008–09 prompted some critics to accuse the Government of exploiting the case to discredit their political rivals.

In June 2009 the daily newspaper *Taraf* published a document, purported to have been drafted by a senior naval officer, containing details of a military plot to undermine the Government. Although an internal military inquiry concluded later that month that the document was a forgery, prosecutors assigned to the ongoing Ergenekon investigation none the less ordered the arrest of the accused officer. A significant amendment to Turkey's code of criminal procedure gained parliamentary approval in late June: the new legislation endorsed the holding of civilian trials for military personnel accused of constitutional offences or crimes against national security. (The establishment of civil jurisdiction over the military was an important condition of Turkey's EU accession process.) However, the legislation was referred to the Constitutional Court by the CHP. A second Ergenekon trial, involving 56 suspects including two retired army generals, the highest ranking officials so far to face trial, commenced on 20 July. In January 2010 the Constitutional Court issued an annulment of the legislation concerning civil trials for military personnel. Nevertheless, later that month the 12th High Criminal Court in İstanbul ruled that the Constitutional Court annulment would not affect the conduct of the ongoing Ergenekon trials.

A further series of arrests relating to two alleged coup plots (code-named 'Sledgehammer' and 'Cage') was carried out in early 2010; detainees included former and serving military officers, with around 50 senior officers reported to have been detained on 22 February. In July 196 people—including 30 serving or retired military officers, among them a former army commander, Gen. (retd) Çetin Doğan, who the authorities alleged was the primary orchestrator of the plot—were indicted of conspiracy to overthrow the Government in relation to the Sledgehammer investigation. The 196 defendants, who remained free pending trial, were formally charged during a preliminary hearing in mid-December. The arrest of a number of journalists who had previously been critical of the Government's performance, including Ahmet Şık and Nedim Şener, who were detained in early March 2011 on suspicion of belonging to Ergenekon, heightened concerns that the Government was exploiting the ongoing coup investigations to discredit its critics and the opposition prior to legislative elections due in June. Human Rights Watch noted the arrest of journalists in connection with the investigation as a 'disturbing development'. The most senior Ergenekon prosecutor, Zekeriya Öz, defended the arrests as 'necessary' in light of certain (unspecified) evidence and unrelated to the 'journalistic duties, writings, books and views' of those detained. However, in an unexpected development, Öz was transferred to the position of deputy chief public prosecutor and removed from the Ergenekon investigation in late March, a decision that was widely interpreted as an attempt by the authorities to regain credibility for the ongoing investigation, following widespread criticism of the journalists' detention.

In March 2010 the Government announced a package of proposed constitutional reforms aimed at resolving persistent constitutional disputes between the executive, legislative, judicial and military branches of the Turkish state and at expediting Turkey's accession to the EU. The chief amendments proposed by the Government included: a restructuring of the Supreme Council of Judges and Public Prosecutors that would result in greater government control over the Council's composition and activities; limitations on the judicial powers of the Constitutional Court and the Council of State; revised criteria for the dissolution of political parties and the establishment of a parliamentary commission to oversee closure cases; measures to allow the trial of military personnel in civilian courts (rejected by the Constitutional Court in January) and to limit the jurisdiction of military courts over civilians; and the removal of immunity from prosecution for the instigators of the 1980 military coup. The Government embarked on a series of consultations with opposition parties in an effort to secure the required two-thirds' parliamentary majority for the legislation. However, CHP leader Deniz Baykal rejected the package of reforms, accusing the ruling party of seeking to consolidate its own power base. The Government was forced to abandon a proposal to revise criteria for the dissolution of political parties—which was widely regarded as the AKP's most desired reform, following the party's narrow avoidance of disbandment in 2008—after it failed to secure sufficient backing in a parliamentary vote at the beginning of May 2010.

On 6 May 2010 the TGNA voted, by 336 votes to 72, to approve a revised package of constitutional reforms, thus falling short of the two-thirds' majority required to secure its passage outright, but exceeding the necessary 330 votes to put the legislation to a public referendum. Following the approval of President Gül, it was announced by the High Electoral Board that a public referendum on the reforms was to be held on 12 September, a date of considerable symbolic importance, being the 30th anniversary of the 1980 military coup, an event that had precipitated the drafting of the existing, deeply unpopular Constitution.

In mid-May 2010 the CHP filed a petition with the Supreme Court appealing for the annulment of the package of reforms; the petition cited 'procedural errors', including the claim that the proposals constituted a draft bill and not a parliamentary proposal and that the AKP had failed to honour the rule of secret parliamentary voting, and alleged that the proposals to reform the judicial system were unconstitutional and posed a threat to the independence of the judiciary. Also in mid-May Deniz Baykal was forced to resign as CHP leader following allegations published in the media regarding his private life; Kemal Kılıçdaroğlu was elected unopposed as party leader at a conference in Ankara later that month. In early July the Supreme Court rejected the CHP's bid to have the entire package of reforms annulled, but did overturn some of the proposals relating to the judicial system, including the proposed restructuring of the Supreme Council of Judges and Public Prosecutors. In response, the Government claimed that the Court had exceeded the limitations of its authority by judging the reforms' content 'on merit', rather than ruling on potential procedural violations, but contended that the remaining proposals, if approved by referendum, would still represent significant reform of the Constitution. The CHP expressed disappointment that the Supreme Court ruling did not annul the entire package of reforms, arguing that the remaining proposals, if approved, would provide for an erosion of crucial checks on the Government's authority.

As in the 2009 municipal elections, Erdoğan acknowledged that the referendum on constitutional reform would effectively serve as a vote on his leadership and on the AKP's governance, and branded the AKP's campaign to secure the package of reforms as a 'struggle for democracy'. Keen to secure the backing of the Kurdish minority, which was identified as potentially holding the balance of power in the referendum, in early September 2010 Erdoğan pledged to effect a more comprehensive overhaul of the Constitution after the 2011 legislative elections. However, Kurdish politicians urged Kurds to boycott the referendum in protest at Erdoğan's failure better to protect Kurdish rights.

The referendum was duly held on 12 September 2010, and turn-out was recorded at 73.7% of the registered electorate. The package of reforms was approved by 57.9% of the valid votes cast, a more comfortable margin of victory than had been widely anticipated. Erdoğan welcomed the result as a mandate for deeper reform, declaring that 'the mentality that opposes change has lost' and pledging the Government's commitment to redrafting the reviled 1982 Constitution.

In mid-October 2010 former Prime Minister Erbakan was elected, uncontested, as the new leader of the SP; Erbakan's election followed a court ruling in September that had ordered the party to elect a new administration owing to internal divisions, prompting the resignation as party Chairman of Prof. Dr Numan Kurtulmuş at the beginning of October. Following a period of deteriorating health, Erbakan died in late February 2011; Mustafa Kamalak became party leader in early March. Meanwhile, in November 2010 Kurtulmuş founded a new party, Halkın Sesi Partisi (HSP—People's Voice Party), the stated objectives of which included striving for a 'new era for Turkey' in which 'all people can benefit from justice, prosperity and independence'. In March 2011 the TGNA unanimously approved a proposal submitted by the AKP to set 12 June as the date for the forthcoming legislative elections. Following the official announcement of the election date, on 8 March the Ministers of Justice, the Interior and Transport all resigned from the Government in accordance with the Constitution. Each was succeeded by their deputy, with the portfolios awarded, respectively, to Ahmet Kahraman, Osman Güneş and Mehmet Habib Soluk.

The Kurdish Issue

In 1984 the outlawed PKK, seeking the creation of a Kurdish national homeland in Turkey, launched a violent guerrilla campaign against the Turkish authorities in the south-eastern provinces. The Government responded by arresting suspected Kurdish leaders, sending in more security forces, establishing local militia groups and imposing martial law (and later states of emergency) in the troubled provinces. However, violence continued to escalate, and in April and May 1990 clashes between rebel Kurds, security forces and civilians resulted in the deaths of 140 people. The conflict entered a new phase when, in August and October 1991, and March 1992 (in retaliation for continuing cross-border attacks on Turkish troops), government fighter planes conducted numerous sorties into northern Iraq in order to attack suspected PKK bases there. In the course of these raids many civilians and refugees (including Iraqi Kurds) were reportedly killed, prompting international observers and relief workers publicly to call into question the integrity of the exercises. The Iraqi Government lodged formal complaints with the UN, denouncing Turkish violations of Iraq's territorial integrity.

Violence in the south-eastern provinces, resulting from ethnic tension, persisted throughout 1992 and 1993. In late 1992 Turkish air and ground forces (in excess of 20,000 troops) conducted further attacks upon PKK bases inside northern Iraq. Hopes that a negotiated resolution to the conflict might be achieved, following the unilateral declaration of a cease-fire by the PKK in March 1993, were frustrated by renewed fighting in May and an intensification of the conflict in June. The bombing of several coastal resorts and of tourist attractions in central İstanbul confirmed the PKK's intention to disrupt the country's economy and to attract international attention to the conflict.

In November 1993 a 10,000-strong élite anti-terrorist force was created to counter the PKK forces, in addition to the estimated 150,000–200,000 troops already positioned in the area of conflict. In 1994 the security forces mounted a heavy offensive against the separatists, and again conducted air attacks on suspected PKK strongholds in south-eastern Turkey and in northern Iraq. Reports that an estimated 6,000 Kurds were forcibly displaced into northern Iraq as a result of the destruction of their villages by security forces were denied by the Minister of Foreign Affairs. In November a Kurdish proposal for a cease-fire, accompanied by international mediation, to achieve a peaceful settlement to the conflict was rejected by the Government, which emphasized the success of its anti-terrorist campaign.

On 20 March 1995 a massive offensive, involving 35,000 air and ground force troops, was initiated against PKK targets in northern Iraq. Turkish forces advanced some 40 km across the border, prompting protests from Iraq. Under increasing international pressure, Turkey undertook a complete withdrawal of its troops by May. Official figures stated that 555 Kurdish separatists and 58 Turkish soldiers were killed as a result of the operation. Earlier, in April, the PKK had obtained permission to convene in the Netherlands, in an attempt to establish a Kurdish parliament-in-exile, prompting Turkey temporarily to recall its ambassador to the Netherlands. Fighting was again resumed in the south-east of the country in June, and in July a further week-long offensive was conducted against Kurdish bases in northern Iraq. In December the PKK leader, Abdullah Öcalan, announced a unilateral cease-fire on the part of his organization. By March 1996, having received no assurances of a cease-fire from the Turkish authorities, Öcalan advised tourists against visiting the country, warning of possible renewed attacks against major tourist sites. During April an estimated 400 PKK members were killed in the renewed military operation. In the following months PKK activists were frequently pursued into northern Iraq by Turkish ground and air forces, provoking protests from the Iraqi Government, and fighting in the south-eastern provinces escalated. In June five soldiers were killed in a suicide bomb attack in Tunceli, eastern Turkey. A further two suicide attacks, reportedly by PKK members, were perpetrated in October, killing 10 people. In response, Turkish security forces conducted air raids against PKK targets in northern Iraq, which continued into early 1997. An estimated 2,800 PKK activists were killed during 1996 as a result of the conflict, in addition to 532 members of the security forces and 145 civilians.

In May 1997 Turkey again launched a massive military offensive against the PKK in northern Iraq, involving the mobilization of 50,000 troops. Turkey claimed that the incursion was in response to an appeal by the Iraqi-based Kurdistan Democratic Party (KDP), which co-operated with the Turkish attack. The operation elicited rigorous condemnation from Iraq, Iran and Syria, but the response from members of NATO was muted. By June Turkish military officials claimed that the attack had achieved its objectives of destroying several PKK bases in northern Iraq and estimated that more than 3,000 PKK troops had been killed. A further offensive, launched in September, was speculated to be part of a Turkish plan to establish a security zone in northern Iraq to prevent cross-border attacks by the PKK. This assumption was apparently confirmed by the lifting of the state of emergency in three of the nine south-eastern provinces in October.

Relations with Syria, which had already deteriorated in July 1998 (owing to Syria's repeated claim to the Hatay region of Turkey), worsened in early October, after Turkey threatened the use of force if Syria did not expel Öcalan and close down terrorist training camps in both Syria and the Beqa'a valley in Lebanon. It was reported that 10,000 Turkish troops had been deployed near the border; the Turkish ambassador to Syria was also recalled. Egypt and Iran both attempted to mediate in the dispute, and, following a meeting of Turkish and Syrian officials in late October, an agreement was signed under which Syria would not allow the PKK to operate on its territory; Öcalan was thus forced to leave the country, and he arrived in Italy in November. Turkey had already temporarily recalled its ambassador to Italy in October, after a meeting of the Kurdish parliament-in-exile was hosted there. Relations deteriorated further owing to Italy's refusal to extradite Öcalan and his subsequent application for asylum. However, in January 1999 Öcalan was reported to have left Italy after the application was rejected. In the following month he was captured at the Greek embassy in Kenya and returned to Turkey, prompting protests by Kurdish activists throughout Europe.

At the end of February 1999 Öcalan was formally charged, in the absence of defence counsel, and the first hearing was set for late March. PKK violence in protest at the trial continued in that month, and there were also threats of violence against tourists in

Turkey. In April a further operation was launched against the PKK, involving the deployment of some 15,000 Turkish troops in northern Iraq. Semdin Sakik, a former PKK commander who had been captured in March 1998, was sentenced to death in May 1999. In June Öcalan was convicted on treason charges and sentenced to death; violent demonstrations were held in protest at his sentence. A third PKK leader, Cevat Soysal, was arrested in Moldova in July.

The PKK agreed to a cease-fire in early August 1999, at which time Öcalan announced that the PKK was prepared to surrender its arms in exchange for Kurdish rights; PKK fighters withdrew from Turkey at the end of the month. However, the Government insisted that the PKK cease hostilities entirely in order for Turkey to reassess the situation. Following a statement issued by Öcalan in September in which he urged PKK rebels to show their commitment to the end of hostilities by surrendering to Turkish forces, two eight-member PKK delegations travelled to Ankara, where they were arrested and detained by the authorities.

In September 1999 the Kurdish parliament-in-exile convened in Brussels, Belgium, where it voted to dissolve and to join the Kurdistan National Congress. Following the cease-fire the number of armed confrontations in the south-east had declined substantially and in October the Government reduced the number of checkpoints in the region. In November Öcalan's death sentence was upheld on appeal and the chief prosecutor rejected his application for a final appeal; his lawyers referred the case to the ECHR. A second trial against Öcalan, together with 101 other defendants, began in Ankara in December for a series of offences including extortion and murder allegedly carried out in the 1970s; the trial was adjourned until February 2000. In January 2000 the parties of the governing coalition announced that they had agreed to delay Öcalan's execution until a ruling had been given by the ECHR.

The PKK announced formally the end to its war against Turkey in February 2000, and stated that it would campaign for Kurdish rights within a framework of peace and democracy. In February three HADEP mayors were arrested and charged with aiding the PKK; they were released on bail, following protests both from within Turkey and internationally. Relations with the EU deteriorated further in February, when Turkey denied EU politicians permission to visit Öcalan in prison. At that time 18 people, including the HADEP leader, Ahmet Turan Demir, were sentenced to almost four years' imprisonment for organizing demonstrations in support of Öcalan. Despite the PKK's cease-fire declaration, Turkish troops continued to push into Kurdish strongholds throughout the year, and in early 2001 Turkish troops advanced into northern Iraq in an attempt to suppress PKK activities. Meanwhile, the hearing of the appeal against Öcalan's death sentence began at the ECHR in November 2000. Öcalan's appeal was based on the grounds that he had not received a fair trial in Turkey under the terms of the European Convention on Human Rights.

In April 2002 the PKK formally announced a change of name to the Congress for Freedom and Democracy in Kurdistan (KADEK), under Öcalan's leadership, and asserted its wish to campaign peacefully for Kurdish rights. Although the movement had abandoned its initiative for an independent Kurdish state, the announcement was received with scepticism on the part of the Turkish Government. However, KADEK was not included in the EU's list of organizations designated as 'terrorist', and it was believed that its agenda had been designed to win support from the EU. In November 2002, in a sign that the Government had acknowledged the conversion of the PKK, the state of emergency that prevailed in the two remaining south-eastern provinces of Diyarbakır and Sirnak was finally ended.

In October 2002, meanwhile, the State Security Court officially commuted Öcalan's death sentence to life imprisonment, in accordance with the abolition of the death penalty in peacetime by the TGNA in August. In March 2003 the ECHR issued a non-binding ruling that Öcalan had not received a fair trial, and criticized Turkey for violating some of Öcalan's rights; however, the ECHR rejected accusations by Öcalan's lawyers of inhumane treatment and illegal detention. Turkey immediately appealed against the ECHR, fearing renewed pressure from the EU to hold a retrial if the ruling was upheld. Despite its success in defeating Kurdish separatism, the Government continued to fear the possible emergence of a Kurdish state in northern Iraq after the ouster of Iraqi President Saddam Hussain's regime by US-led coalition forces in March–April 2003. In September, following renewed attacks by the organization in eastern Turkey, KADEK formally ended the cease-fire declared in February 2000, accusing the authorities of failing to address demands for improved Kurdish rights and freedom of expression. In November 2003 KADEK was reconstituted as the Kongreya Gelê Kurdistanê (KONGRA-GEL—Kurdistan People's Congress), which, in January 2004, the US Administration added to its list of designated terrorist organizations.

After revoking its cease-fire, KONGRA-GEL organized sporadic attacks during 2004. In July government troops launched an offensive against KONGRA-GEL positions at the border with Iraq. In late 2004 and early 2005 further clashes erupted between KONGRA-GEL militants and Turkish security forces, and in April the KONGRA-GEL leadership announced that the organization was to revert to its original name, PKK (although it appeared that not all elements of the movement did so). In May the ECHR ruled that the trial of Öcalan had been unfair, on the grounds that he had not been tried by an independent tribunal (owing to the presence of a military judge on the panel); the Turkish Government indicated that a further trial would be conducted.

A series of bomb attacks in July and August 2005 were attributed to Kurdish militants (although the PKK denied responsibility). In September some 88 PKK supporters were arrested in İstanbul, after protesting at being prevented from attending a rally in support of Öcalan (who was said to have been placed in solitary confinement). Despite the PKK's extension until early October of a unilateral cease-fire, which it had declared in August, clashes between rebels and government forces continued in the east of the country. Security forces, meanwhile, staged several operations in eastern Turkey against members of the PKK and its military wing, Hezên Parastina Gel (HPG—People's Defence Forces). In March 2006 some 50 suspected militants were detained after a security operation in central Turkey. Between 28 March and 1 April the funeral of four suspected PKK supporters in the south-eastern town of Viranşehir precipitated large-scale Kurdish rioting in the regional capital, Diyarbakır; some 12 people were killed in the disturbances. In April a series of bomb attacks in İstanbul resulted in three deaths, and in August the coastal resorts of Marmaris and Antalya were also targeted: a further three people were killed in the Antalya blast and in both bombings there were dozens of casualties, including many foreign nationals. Responsibility for the attacks was claimed by a group calling itself Teyrêbazên Azadiya Kurdistan (TAK—Kurdistan Freedom Falcons), which purported to be linked to the PKK. A suicide bomb attack carried out at a shopping centre in Ankara in May 2007 resulted in the deaths of six people. Turkish security officials claimed that the attack had been perpetrated by Kurdish extremists, although spokesmen for the PKK denied responsibility.

Amid the intensification of violence in south-eastern Turkey during 2006, the likelihood grew of a large-scale Turkish military incursion to attempt to defeat PKK rebels in northern Iraq. By July 2007, according to Hoshyar al-Zibari, the Iraqi Minister of Foreign Affairs, Turkish armed forces along the countries' mutual border amounted to some 140,000 personnel. In August, after a reported 12 Turkish soldiers had died during fighting with PKK militants in that month, Erdoğan and the Iraqi Prime Minister, Nuri al-Maliki, reached a memorandum of understanding aimed at ending the 'safe haven' of the PKK in northern Iraq. A further security co-operation pact was signed in late September, although the Iraqi Government refused Turkey's principal demand that its military be permitted to enter Iraqi territory in pursuit of Kurdish fighters. A large number of Turkish soldiers were reported to have been killed during clashes with the PKK in subsequent weeks. In October the TGNA endorsed a decision to allow Turkish military raids into northern Iraq, despite US President George W. Bush and al-Maliki urging the Turkish leadership to show restraint. In November Bush pledged that the USA would increase its military co-operation with Turkey, in an apparent effort to dissuade the Turkish Government from launching a major incursion into Iraqi territory. Nevertheless, in December Turkish troops began an offensive against PKK bases in Iraq's northern region, in response to a series of cross-border raids by armed Kurdish separatists. The Iraqi Government protested to its Turkish counterpart that it had not been consulted over the military action, while the President of the Kurdish Autonomous Region, Masoud Barzani, described Turkey's actions as a violation of Iraqi sovereignty. In late February 2008 it was initially reported that up to 10,000 Turkish troops had entered northern Iraq, in what appeared to be a much larger incursion than that of the previous December, and with the additional launching of air-strikes against PKK militant bases; however, it was reported at the end of February that only several hundred troops had participated in the military campaign. Nevertheless, dozens of PKK militants were killed in the week-long offensive, together with several Turkish soldiers. (The Turkish military claimed by this time to have killed at least 230 PKK fighters, and to have lost 27 of its soldiers; however, PKK sources alleged that around 90 Turkish soldiers had died in the recent incursion.)

Sporadic cross-border clashes between Turkish forces and PKK rebels continued throughout 2008. At least 45 PKK fighters were reportedly killed in air-strikes between March and June. Prime Minister Erdoğan visited Iraq in July, the first visit by a Turkish premier in some 18 years, holding talks with his Iraqi counterpart on strengthening economic and political ties; the Iraqi authorities also indicated their support for Turkey's campaign against the PKK in northern Iraq. The military offensive against PKK positions in northern Iraq intensified following an attack on a Turkish army border camp in the Şemdinli district in early October, in which at least 15 soldiers were killed. In that month the TGNA voted to extend the Government's mandate to launch military operations against targets in northern Iraq. In January 2009 the establishment of a joint command centre to combat PKK operations in northern Iraq was announced, involving Turkish, Iraqi and US intelligence authorities. Despite a decrease in the intensity of the conflict at the beginning of 2009, renewed air-strikes were launched against PKK targets in northern Iraq from early February.

Meanwhile, as many as 10,000 people took part in a demonstration in Istanbul in June 2008 to demand fresh initiatives to resolve the Kurdish conflict. Erdoğan embarked on a tour of the mainly Kurdish south-eastern provinces in early November, calling for national unity and solidarity in the face of separatism and terrorism; his presence provoked violent demonstrations in several towns. According to Turkish military sources, 696 PKK rebels had been killed and 177 captured during the conflict in 2008, while 171 members of the security forces and 51 civilians were killed in that year. In mid-February 2009 at least 50 people were arrested in various south-eastern towns as demonstrations marking the 10th anniversary of the imprisonment of Öcalan escalated into violent clashes with security forces. The Demokratik Toplum Partisi (DTP—Democratic Society Party), a pro-Kurdish political party formed in 2005 to replace DEHAP, performed strongly in south-eastern Turkey in the municipal elections in March 2009, retaining control of local councils in Diyarbakır, Hakkari and Şırnak provinces, and gaining control of Van and Siirt at the expense of the AKP.

Hopes for a breakthrough in the Kurdish conflict were raised significantly in April 2009 when the PKK announced it was suspending all offensive operations until 1 June, in order to facilitate peace negotiations with the Government. In a series of newspaper interviews in May, PKK leaders revealed that the organization was willing to relinquish its demand for an independent Kurdish state and to seek a peaceful settlement to the conflict, in return for the recognition of Kurdish rights and the establishment of a regional legislature. At the beginning of June the PKK extended its truce for a further six weeks; an additional six-week extension was announced in mid-July. Meanwhile, the Turkish authorities refused to recognize the PKK's unilateral cease-fire, and military operations against Kurdish rebels continued. Six Turkish soldiers were killed when a roadside bomb exploded in Hakkari province in late May 2009; in response, the security forces launched air attacks on suspected PKK bases in northern Iraq at the end of May and in June. In July Prime Minister Erdoğan launched a major new initiative aimed at solving the Kurdish conflict. While specific details of the Government's Kurdish initiative were not publicly announced, the plan was believed to encompass greater political and cultural rights for Kurds, as well as incentives for militants to relinquish their armed resistance. In October the TGNA endorsed for a further year the Government's mandate to launch military operations against PKK targets in northern Iraq.

In what was designed to serve as a confidence-building measure, on 19 October 2009 a group of 34 PKK militants and supporters surrendered to a Turkish delegation close to Turkey's border with Iraq; following a brief interrogation all of the group were reported to have been released within 24 hours. On 22 October the returning PKK members were guests of honour at a rally in Diyarbakır attended by up to 100,000 jubilant supporters. The scale of the reception, as well as numerous other public celebrations in Kurdish provinces, provoked strong criticism from nationalist opposition parties, which accused the Government of granting an amnesty to terrorists. Further planned PKK repatriations were postponed, apparently in response to the widespread public outcry against the initiative. In November the Government announced plans to remove long-standing bans on private television channels broadcasting in Kurdish and the use of Kurdish names for towns and villages.

On 11 December 2009 the Constitutional Court ordered the dissolution of the DTP. The ruling stemmed from an indictment, first lodged in mid-2007, that accused the party of promoting separatism and supporting the PKK. According to the ruling, 37 DTP members were banned from political activity for five years. Two DTP parliamentary deputies, Ahmet Türk, the party's Chairman, and Aysel Tuğluk, a senior official, were expelled from the TGNA. The party's leadership initially indicated that the remaining 19 DTP deputies would be withdrawn from the TGNA. However, on 18 December 2009 it was announced that the 19 former DTP deputies were to maintain their parliamentary participation as members of the Barış ve Demokrasi Partisi (BDP—Peace and Democracy Party). The ruling drew expressions of concern from the EU, and Erdoğan stated that he was opposed to the judicial closure of political parties. Meanwhile, the dissolution provoked widespread rioting in south-eastern Kurdish provinces and in cities throughout Turkey.

The security forces mounted renewed operations against suspected Kurdish separatists from December 2009, with more than 30 people, including some municipal officials, arrested on 23 December; more than 140 people were reported to have been detained during further operations in south-eastern provinces on 21 January and 14 February 2010. In April it was reported that state prosecutors in Diyarbakır had filed indictments against 30 of the PKK contingent that had returned in October 2009, accusing them of disseminating propaganda or membership of a terrorist organization.

In July 2010 PKK leader Murat Karayilan declared that he would order his grouping to lay down its weapons under UN supervision if the Turkish Government agreed to a cease-fire and his demands for greater political and cultural rights for Turkey's Kurds. The Turkish Government declined to respond to Karayilan's comments, stating that it was 'not in the habit of commenting on statements made by terrorists'.

Meanwhile, a roadside bomb attack on a police bus in İstanbul in June 2010, which was attributed to Kurdish separatists, was reported to have injured 15 people; a second bomb attack on a military bus later in the month, for which the TAK claimed responsibility, claimed the lives of five people and injured 12 others. A suicide bomb attack on a police post in central Istanbul at the end of October, also thought to have been carried out by Kurdish rebels, injured more than 30 people, including 15 police officers. Sporadic ground- and air-strikes against alleged PKK militants in northern Iraq continued to be reported throughout 2010 and into 2011. On 29 March Erdoğan became the first Turkish premier to visit the Kurdish Autonomous Region of Iraq, where he held talks with the President of the Kurdish Autonomous Region, Masoud Barzani, regarding co-operation in combating the PKK.

Foreign Affairs

Relations with the USA and regional relations

Turkey has been a member of NATO since 1952, and is widely considered to have fulfilled a crucial role in NATO defence strategy in south-eastern Europe. During the 1990s Turkey's importance to its key ally, the USA, increased as its strategic location allowed it to co-operate with the USA in regional security issues. The Turkish Government responded positively to requests from the USA for logistical aid, following the forcible annexation of Kuwait by Iraq in August 1990, and complied with UN proposals for economic sanctions against Iraq by closing its border to all non-essential trade and, later, to traffic. In September Turkey and the USA extended an agreement to allow the USA access to more than 25 military establishments, in return for military and economic aid, that had been initially signed in 1980, and renewed in 1987. In January 1991 a resolution to extend the war powers of the Government and effectively endorse the unrestricted use of Turkish airbases by coalition forces was agreed by the TGNA. US aircraft subsequently embarked upon bombing missions into north-eastern Iraq from NATO bases inside south-eastern Turkey. In February and March the US Government announced substantial increases in military and economic aid to Turkey. In April an estimated 600,000 Kurds attempted to flee northern Iraq into Turkey.

TURKEY

Introductory Survey

Following a massive international relief effort and the subsequent repatriation of the majority of refugees, the Turkish Government agreed to the deployment in south-east Turkey of a 3,000-strong multi-national 'rapid reaction force', which would respond to any further acts of aggression by Iraq against the Kurds in the newly created 'safe havens'. While all ground forces were withdrawn in October, the Turkish Government agreed to the continued use of its airbases by a small allied air-strike force to conduct patrols of northern Iraq under the mandate of 'Operation Provide Comfort'. The mandate was granted six-month extensions, despite increasing unease on the part of the Turkish authorities that the Kurdish enclave was providing a refuge for PKK separatists (see The Kurdish Issue). Difficulties in Turkey's relations with the USA arose in 1994, following a decision by the US Congress to withhold some military and economic aid in order to encourage greater respect for human rights in the Turkish Government's treatment of Kurdish separatists.

In July 1996, in spite of his earlier election pledge to conclude the mandate for the use of Turkish bases for allied aircraft engaged in 'Operation Provide Comfort', the new RP Prime Minister, Necmettin Erbakan, secured a final extension of the operation's mandate until the end of the year. In September the Turkish Government refused permission for the use of its airbases for a US military operation against Iraqi forces that had violated the Kurdish area in northern Iraq. Turkey amassed an estimated additional 20,000 troops along the border and revealed proposals to establish a temporary security zone in the region in order to stem any influx of refugees from Iraq and to prevent the PKK from exploiting the situation. The Government also undertook to relocate the military co-ordination centre of 'Operation Provide Comfort' from Zakho in northern Iraq to Silopi in southeastern Turkey. ('Operation Provide Comfort' was superseded by the more limited aerial surveillance operation 'Northern Watch' in January 1997.) During 1996 Turkey pursued diplomatic efforts to secure the reopening of the petroleum pipeline from Kirkuk in northern Iraq to Yumurtalik in Turkey, which had been closed since August 1990 as a result of UN-imposed economic sanctions. The pipeline was finally reactivated in December, in accordance with a UN agreement permitting the export of US $2,000m. of petroleum by Iraq over a six-month period, in order to fund the purchase of essential medical and other humanitarian supplies. As relations between Iraq and the UN deteriorated from the end of 1997, Turkey announced that it opposed the use of its İncirlik airbase for potential US-led strikes against Iraq and urged a peaceful solution to the crisis. Although Turkey was informed of the air-strikes against Iraq in December, in January 1999 it announced that Turkish airbases would not be used in any new operation against Iraq.

Following the suicide attacks on the USA in September 2001, perpetrated by Osama bin Laden's al-Qa'ida network, Turkey emerged as a crucial ally in the former's 'war on terror', immediately pledging its co-operation. In October the TGNA agreed in principle to send troops to Afghanistan and allow foreign forces to be stationed in Turkey, and in December US Secretary of State Colin Powell visited Turkey to discuss security and bilateral trade issues. Meanwhile, hundreds of Turkish commandos were deployed in Uzbekistan in preparation for possible combat in Afghanistan, and 90 of these entered northern Afghanistan to train the opposition United National Islamic Front for the Salvation of Afghanistan (the United Front—UF, or 'Northern Alliance'). Turkey assumed command of the International Security Assistance Force (ISAF) in Afghanistan in June 2002, raising its troop presence in that country to 1,000. (Turkish command of the ISAF ended in February 2003, whereupon control of the force passed to Germany and the Netherlands.)

In 2002 Turkish leaders became increasingly concerned about the possibility that the USA would open a 'second front' in its military campaign to overthrow the regime of Saddam Hussain. In particular, the Government feared a break-up of the Iraqi state and the creation of a Kurdish state in northern Iraq that could be used to foster Kurdish nationalism in its own territory, and the possible mass exodus of Iraqi Kurds into Turkey. There were also concerns about the disruption to Turkish-Iraqi trade and economic co-operation that any US-led attack would bring. Prime Minister Ecevit's illness and subsequent preparations for elections to the TGNA in November meant that no agreements between Turkey and the USA were reached over the latter's planned invasion of Iraq. Relations between the two countries were further complicated by the victory of the AKP in the elections, and overwhelming public opposition to war against Iraq. By January 2003 a number of senior US officials had visited Turkey to persuade the Government to accept the deployment of 62,000 US troops in the south-east of the country, and the use of the region as a staging post for a 'northern front' in the planned conflict. Following lengthy negotiations, the US Government offered a financial package of US $6,000m. in direct grants and an additional $20,000m. in loans and trade concessions in compensation for any economic losses incurred during the war; however, the Turkish authorities considered this sum to be insufficient. President Sezer warned in February that US forces could only be deployed in Turkey if the USA obtained a second UN resolution from the UN Security Council authorizing the use of force against Iraq.

On 1 March 2003 the TGNA rejected a motion allowing the USA to deploy troops in Turkey. As many as 50 AKP legislators voted against the Government, underscoring the level of opposition to US plans for a military campaign to oust the Iraqi regime. On 20 March the TGNA voted only to allow the use of Turkish airspace for the conflict, but endorsed the deployment of Turkish troops in Iraq if considered necessary. The US-led coalition forces initiated attacks against the Iraqi regime on that day, and shortly thereafter abandoned attempts to negotiate the use of Turkish bases. The aid package was withdrawn following the TGNA vote, but in April the USA offered a new, reduced loan package totalling US $8,500m. in order to repair bilateral relations. US Secretary of State Powell visited Ankara at that time and secured Turkish permission for humanitarian aid and US logistical supplies to be delivered to US and coalition troops in Iraq via Turkish territory. In September the Turkish and US Governments signed an agreement approving the loan to compensate for the adverse effects of the March–April conflict in Iraq. In October a motion proposed by the Council of Ministers in favour of contributing peace-keeping troops to the US-led coalition in Iraq was endorsed by the TGNA. Following widespread protests in both Turkey and Iraq, however, Prime Minister Erdoğan announced that he would consider reversing this decision, and in November the planned deployment of Turkish forces in Iraq was cancelled.

In early October 2007 Turkey temporarily withdrew its ambassador to Washington, DC, in protest against the adoption by the Committee on Foreign Affairs of the US House of Representatives of a non-binding resolution describing as 'genocide' the killing of an estimated 1.5m. Armenians following the First World War. In his first visit to a Muslim country since becoming US President, Barack Obama travelled to Turkey in early April 2009. In a speech to the TGNA he emphasized the importance of US-Turkish ties, and used the platform to address all Muslim nations, declaring that the USA was not 'at war with Islam'. He also urged the EU to admit Turkey as a full member. In a statement issued on Armenian Remembrance Day later that month, Obama described the killing of an estimated 1.5m. Armenians in 1915–23 as a 'great atrocity' but, crucially, refrained from using the term 'genocide', despite a pre-election pledge to do so. The Turkish Ministry of Foreign Affairs issued a statement that described some aspects of the President's statement as 'unacceptable', however, Obama's careful choice of words was widely believed to reflect his Administration's desire to expedite the normalization of Turkish-Armenian ties (see Other external relations).

On 5 March 2010, despite opposition from President Obama and other senior members of his Administration, the US House of Representatives Committee on Foreign Affairs narrowly adopted a further non-binding resolution that called for the formal recognition of the Turkish 'genocide' against the Armenians. In response, Turkey recalled its ambassador from Washington, DC, for consultations, warning that the resolution could be detrimental to US-Turkish relations and to the Turkish-Armenian normalization process. None the less, in April the Turkish authorities expressed their satisfaction with US assurances concerning the 'genocide' dispute, and the Turkish ambassador returned to his post. However, concerned at Turkey's perceived shift closer towards Iran and further away from Israel, in August the US Senate took an unprecedented step when it blocked Obama's ambassadorial nomination to Ankara (together with the nomination for the Azerbaijan ambassadorial post), while the House of Representatives Committee on Foreign Affairs conducted a special hearing on Turkey to discuss whether its oreientation was indeed shifting in ways that might be unfavourable to US-Turkish relations. Later in the month the US Department of State held a rare publicly announced high-level policy discussion on Turkey, chaired by Secretary of State Hillary Clinton and with the participation of senior department officials. Although Obama, capitalizing on a legislative 'loophole', circumvented the Senate and unilaterally installed the two nominees during a congressional recess in late December, the series of events in mid-2010 appeared to indicate a sense of deepening US mistrust of Turkish foreign policy.

In late 1995 a long-standing dispute with Syria and Iraq concerning the water supply from the Euphrates and Tigris rivers re-emerged as a major source of tension in Turkey's external relations. (Hostilities with Syria had already intensified during the year over that country's apparent support for the PKK, with the Turkish Government accusing Syria of supplying armaments to the separatist organization.) In December Syria issued a formal protest at the construction of a new hydroelectric dam on the Euphrates river (as part of the extensive southern Anatolia project—GAP) arguing that it would adversely affect the supply of water flowing into Syria. Further protests by Syria and Iraq that Turkey was storing their share of water from the two rivers and restricting flow, in contravention of previous agreements, resulted in a ruling, in March 1996, by the Council of the Arab League that the waters of the rivers should be shared equally between the three countries. However, in August 1998 the Government refused to revive water talks with Syria and Iraq, citing issues that had first to be improved between the countries, primarily that of terrorism. Relations between Syria and Turkey improved during 1999 and in October officials from the two countries reportedly agreed to open a new border crossing. However, in January 2000 Turkey appealed to the USA not to remove Syria from its list of nations accused of sponsoring terrorism, until such time as all PKK bases had been removed from Syria, and ruled out any concessions on the water issue in order to aid talks between Israel and Syria. In March Turkey and Syria announced a new framework for bilateral relations and discussed the basic principles that would apply to them. A major rapprochement materialized in early 2002 when Turkey signed an agreement with Syria allowing for joint military exercises. President Bashar al-Assad became the first Syrian head of state to undertake an official visit to Turkey in January 2004. Following a meeting of Arab and Turkish ministers in Istanbul in June 2010, an agreement to establish a free trade zone between Turkey, Syria, Jordan and Lebanon was announced.

In July 2008 Erdoğan became the first Turkish premier to visit Iraq in almost 20 years. During the two-day visit the Prime Minister held talks on bilateral trade and regional security issues with his Iraqi counterpart, Nuri al-Maliki, and the establishment of a strategic co-operation council was announced. The Turkish Minister of Foreign Affairs, Ahmet Davutoğlu, acted as a mediator, apparently with some success, during a diplomatic dispute between Iraq and Syria from late August 2009, which resulted from allegations of Syrian involvement in a series of bomb attacks in Baghdad earlier in August. Davutoğlu held meetings with his counterparts in Baghdad and Damascus, and hosted a tripartite summit in Ankara in September aimed at resolving the dispute. Following a meeting of the Turkey-Iraq strategic co-operation council in October in Baghdad, 48 memorandums of understanding on co-operation in areas including trade, security, energy, water resources and agriculture were signed by the Iraqi and Turkish Prime Ministers. However, Prime Minister al-Maliki expressed his concern regarding Turkish military operations against PKK targets in northern Iraq and urged Turkey to respect Iraq's territorial integrity. Furthermore, the dispute concerning the supply of water from the Euphrates to Iraq remained unresolved. Provisional plans to open two new border crossings and to create a free trade and industrial zone inside Iraqi land on the Turkish border were announced in June 2010, and both sides stated their resolve to not allow an escalation in PKK violence to compromise bilateral relations. In late March 2011 Erdoğan led a high-level Turkish delegation on a two-day visit to Iraq, during which he visited the Kurdish Autonomous Region (see The Kurdish Issue), Baghdad and Najaf, holding discussions with al-Maliki and Iraq's most senior Shi'ite cleric, Ayatollah Ali al-Sistani, as well as other Iraqi political and religious figures.

In early 1996 Turkey signed a new military and intelligence co-operation agreement with Israel, which permitted the use of Turkish airbases and airspace for military training purposes. The pact stemmed from common concerns about Iran, Iraq and Syria, and received support from the USA, a strong ally of both Turkey and Israel. The Arab League denounced the agreement as 'an act of aggression'. Business deals quickly followed, especially those concerning the supply of Turkish water to Israel. However, the gradual improvement in Turkey's relations with its Arab neighbours from 2000 made the pact with Israel less significant, and, in response to the increasing violence between Israelis and Palestinians in the West Bank and Gaza, Prime Minister Ecevit in April 2002 accused Israel of 'genocide' against the Palestinians. None the less, in August Turkey signed an agreement with Israel according to which it would sell the latter 50m. cu m of water every year for the next 20 years. In May 2004 relations with Israel became further strained, when Prime Minister Erdoğan condemned an Israeli offensive in Gaza. In January 2005, however, the Turkish Deputy Prime Minister and Minister of Foreign Affairs made an official visit to Israel—the first by a Turkish politician since the AKP Government was elected in November 2002.

Turkey received praise for its role as host and mediator for indirect peace talks between Syria and Israel during 2008. The talks, several rounds of which took place in Istanbul in mid-2008, were believed to be making progress towards a possible settlement of Israel and Syria's territorial dispute over the Golan Heights. However, negotiations were suspended following the launch of Israel's military offensive against Islamic Resistance Movement (Hamas) targets in Gaza in late December (see the chapters on Israel and the Palestinian Autonomous Areas). Turkey, along with most other Muslim countries, voiced strong condemnation of Israel's actions. In late January 2009 there was an angry exchange between Erdoğan and Israeli President Shimon Peres during a debate on Gaza at the World Economic Forum in Davos, Switzerland. Erdoğan accused Israel of having committed crimes against humanity, and walked out when he was not afforded as much time to speak on the matter as the Israeli President. Nevertheless, a meeting between the foreign ministers of Israel and Turkey, which took place in Brussels, Belgium, in early March at the time of a NATO foreign ministers summit, signalled some improvement in relations.

However, relations between Israel and Turkey grew increasingly tense in the months following the formation in March 2009 of a new, predominantly right-wing Israeli Government led by Prime Minister Binyamin Netanyahu. In mid-October Turkey announced the cancellation of Israel's involvement in a major military exercise. Despite initial denials that the cancellation was a political measure, Davutoğlu acknowledged in November that the decision stemmed from Turkish disapproval of Israel's military operation in Gaza. Meanwhile, in response, Netanyahu declared his opposition to Turkey resuming its role as mediator in the stalled Syrian-Israeli peace talks. Relations deteriorated further in January 2010 when Israel's Deputy Minister of Foreign Affairs, Danny Ayalon, was deemed to have 'humiliated' Turkey's ambassador to Israel, Ahmet Çelikkol, during a meeting that was attended by journalists and cameramen. Ayalon had summoned the ambassador officially to complain about the broadcast on Turkish state television of programmes depicting Israeli security forces in a manner considered offensive to Israel. The Turkish authorities summoned the Israeli ambassador in Ankara to protest at the mistreatment of their representative and threatened to suspend bilateral relations unless an unequivocal apology was issued. Following the subsequent issue of two separate apologies, the dispute was declared officially to be finished.

Relations declined markedly in May 2010, following the deaths of nine Turkish citizens during a raid by Israeli troops on a ship that had been chartered by a Turkish charitable organization, as part of a flotilla of vessels attempting to break the Israeli blockade of Gaza and deliver humanitarian supplies to the territory. On the evening of the raid, hundreds of Israelis gathered outside the Turkish embassy in Tel-Aviv to protest at what they perceived to be a Turkish ploy to cast Israel in a negative light, claiming that the flotilla of ships had been dispatched with the express intention of provoking a response from the Israeli military, allegations that were adamantly denied by the Turkish authorities. Although the Israeli Government insisted that its troops had acted in self-defence after being attacked by pro-Palestinian activists on board the ship, Erdoğan branded the incident an act of 'state terror' and in June Turkey suspended its diplomatic and military ties with Israel, withdrawing its ambassador from Tel-Aviv and insisting that it would not restore full relations until Israel publicly apologized for the incident, compensated the relatives of the victims and agreed to the holding of a full and independent international inquiry. Israel refused to acquiesce to the demands. It was reported in July that Davutoğlu and the Israeli Minister of Industry, Trade and Labour, Binyamin Ben-Eliezer, had conducted covert discussions aimed at securing an improvement in relations following the incident, seemingly at the behest of the US Administration; the Israeli Minister of Foreign Affairs, who had not been informed of the discussions, took 'a very serious view' of his exclusion from the proceedings. Reports emerged in December that Israel had proposed to offer financial compensation to relatives of the nine victims of the raid on the condition that Turkey concede that Israel was not legally liable for the incident, although this remained unconfirmed speculation. Talks were ongoing at mid-2011.

In April 1996 the Turkish and Iranian authorities ordered the expulsion of diplomatic personnel following accusations of Iranian involvement in Islamist terrorist attacks committed in Turkey in the early 1990s. In August relations with Iran were strengthened by the conclusion of an agreement providing for the construction of a 320-km pipeline between the two countries and the export of substantial supplies of natural gas from Iran. In December 1996 the Presidents of Turkey and Iran agreed to pursue greater economic and security co-operation. A trade agreement was concluded granting each other the status of most favoured nation. In February 1997 the Iranian ambassador to Turkey provoked a diplomatic crisis by advocating the introduction of Islamic law in Turkey. Criticism of the actions of the Turkish military by an Iranian consul-general later in that month resulted in both men being asked to leave the country. Iran responded by expelling two Turkish diplomats. However, both countries immediately undertook diplomatic initiatives to restore relations, and in March it was agreed that all bilateral agreements were to be pursued. Following negotiations, it was announced in September that full diplomatic relations were to be resumed.

In October 1998 Iran and Turkey established a committee to demarcate their joint border; they later signed a memorandum to increase customs co-operation at their main border crossing. In June 1999 a meeting of the Turkish-Iranian border committee was held for the first time since 1994; a number of issues were discussed and it was agreed that the committee should meet every year. In July, however, the Turkish chargé d'affaires was twice summoned to the Iranian Ministry of Foreign Affairs following the alleged bombing of an Iranian border region by Turkey in which five people died. In October Turkey announced it would contribute to compensation for the Iranian bomb damage; a Turkish report into the incident concluded that Turkey had bombed Iraq not Iran, although some people with Iranian citizenship, living in northern Iraq, might have been affected. However, from 2001 rising tensions between Azerbaijan and Iran over claims to the Caspian Sea, Turkey's strong support for Azerbaijan, its continuing alliance with Israel, and competition for influence in the Caucasus and Central Asia threatened to strain the relationship.

After coming to power in 2002 the AKP Government endeavoured to improve relations with Turkey's Muslim neighbours. This policy encompassed a significant strengthening of ties with Iran. Iranian President Mahmoud Ahmadinejad undertook a working visit to Turkey in August 2008, holding discussions with Prime Minister Erdoğan. In 2009 Turkey represented the largest consumer of Iranian natural gas exports, and negotiations concerning Turkish investment in the development of Iran's South Pars gasfield, which commenced in 2008, were ongoing. Meanwhile, amid growing tensions between Iran and Western nations over Iran's nuclear activities (see the chapter on Iran), Erdoğan made his second official visit to Tehran in October 2009 for further discussions on bilateral trade and energy projects. During the visit Erdoğan emphatically defended Iran's entitlement to pursue a civil nuclear programme and called for the crisis to be resolved through international diplomacy. The Turkish Prime Minister subsequently rejected growing demands from the USA and other Western powers for a new round of UN sanctions in response to Iran's nuclear programme. Nevertheless, during an official visit to Washington, DC, in December Erdoğan indicated to US President Barack Obama his willingness to act as a mediator in the international dispute over Iran's nuclear programme—a proposal that secured Qatari and Syrian support in May 2010. Also in May Turkey and Iran, together with Brazil, signed an agreement under the terms of which Iran was to transfer the majority of its low-enriched uranium stockpiles to Turkey, to be kept under the supervision of the International Atomic Energy Agency and Iran, in exchange for the supply to Iran by Turkey of nuclear fuel rods. In June Turkey and Brazil voted against a UN Security Council resolution to impose fresh sanctions on Iran in response to that country's nuclear programme; however, the resolution was approved, having secured the support of 12 members of the Council. In February 2011 President Gül embarked on his inaugural state visit to Iran, during which he met with Ahmadinejad and reiterated Turkey's continued support for the resolution of the dispute over Iran's nuclear programme through negotiation.

The Cyprus question and relations with Greece

Although Turkey and Greece are both members of NATO, long-standing disputes over sovereignty in the Aegean Sea and concerning Cyprus have strained relations between the two countries, and tension was exacerbated when Turkey granted recognition to the 'Turkish Republic of Northern Cyprus' ('TRNC'), proclaimed in November 1983 (see the chapter on Cyprus). In April 1988 the Greek Prime Minister, Andreas Papandreou, officially accepted Turkey's status as an associate of the EC by signing the Protocol of Adaptation (consequent on Greece's accession to the EC) to the EC-Turkey Association Agreement, which the Greek Government had hitherto refused to do, and in June Turgut Özal became the first Turkish Prime Minister to visit Greece for 36 years. In February 1990 relations deteriorated again, following violent clashes between Christians and the Muslim minority in western Thrace, in Greece. Throughout the early 1990s Turkey and Greece maintained strong support for their respective communities in Cyprus during the ongoing, but frequently interrupted, negotiations to resolve the issue.

The issue of the demarcation of territorial waters in the Aegean re-emerged as a source of tension with Greece in 1994. Turkey insisted that it would retaliate against any expansion of territorial waters in the region, as provided for under the terms of the UN Convention on the Law of the Sea (UNCLOS), which entered into force in November. Bilateral relations deteriorated sharply in early 1996, owing to a series of incidents in the Aegean in which both countries claimed sovereignty of Imia (Kardak), a small, uninhabited island. Turkey's claim was based on a concession granted by Italy prior to the 1947 settlement that awarded the main Dodecanese islands to Greece. The dispute was exploited by nationalist media in both countries; however, the threat of military action was averted in February 1996 when the two sides agreed to a petition of the US Government to withdraw naval vessels from the region and to pursue efforts to conclude a diplomatic solution. Throughout 1996 relations remained strained as a result of several minor confrontations between Greek and Turkish patrol vessels in the Aegean, persistent Greek allegations of violations of its airspace by Turkish aircraft and Turkish concern at the treatment of the ethnic population in western Thrace. From mid-1996 an escalation in intercommunal tension in Cyprus emphasized divisions between the two countries. Turkey remained committed in its support for the 'TRNC' authorities and resolved to respond with military action to the proposed deployment of an anti-aircraft missile system in the Greek Cypriot territory. A joint defence doctrine was agreed by the Turkish and 'TRNC' authorities in January 1997, and in March a co-operation accord, providing for some US $250m. in economic assistance to the 'TRNC', was ratified by the two sides.

In April 1997, following Greece's continued refusal to conduct bilateral discussions with Turkey over sovereignty rights in the Aegean, Turkey presented proposals to refer the dispute over Imia (Kardak) to the International Court of Justice (ICJ). At the end of April the Greek and Turkish ministers responsible for foreign affairs held bilateral talks in Malta under EU auspices, during which it was agreed that each country would establish a committee of experts to help resolve bilateral disputes. In July, at a NATO summit in Madrid, Spain, direct talks took place between Demirel and the Greek Prime Minister, Konstantinos Simitis. The so-called Madrid agreement was signed, in which both sides pledged to respect the other's sovereign rights and to renounce violence, and the threat of violence, in their dealings with each other.

In July 1997 Turkey announced the formation of a joint committee to implement partial integration between Turkey and the 'TRNC', in response to the EU's agreement to commence accession talks with Cyprus. Turkey also declared in September that should the EU continue to conduct membership talks with the Greek Cypriot Government, then it would seek further integration with the 'TRNC'. Shortly afterwards Turkey banned all Greek Cypriot ships from entering Turkish ports.

In early 1999 Greece denied Turkish accusations of Greek support for the PKK, although Öcalan was later captured at the Greek embassy in Kenya. In August relations between the two countries improved markedly, following the Greek response to the earthquake that occurred in north-west Turkey at the end of that month In January 2000 the Greek Minister of Foreign Affairs made the first official visit to Turkey by a Greek foreign minister for 38 years, during which it was agreed that direct talks would be held to reduce military tensions in the Aegean. In February his Turkish counterpart made an equally historic visit, becoming the first Turkish foreign minister to visit Greece in 40 years. In October, however, Greece withdrew from a joint NATO military exercise in the Aegean, after it accused Turkey of preventing Greek aircraft from flying over the disputed islands of Limnos and Ikaria. This followed a joint NATO military exercise with Greek and Turkish troops on a Greek beach in June, which had been considered to be a mark of considerable progress in Greek-Turkish relations. In February 2001 the Greek parliament decreed a 'Genocide Day' to commemorate the Turkish assault on the Greek community in eastern Turkey by Atatürk's forces in 1922. However, in April 2001 both Turkey and Greece announced major reductions in their weapons-procurement programmes, and in May Greece announced measures to improve the rights of its ethnic Turks (mainly in Thrace). In June the two countries discussed the possibility of allowing Turkish nationals to visit Greek islands in the Aegean for day trips without the need for visas, and the Minister of Foreign Affairs, İsmail Cem, received his Greek counterpart, Georgios Papandreou, to discuss friendship-building measures such as the demining of their mutual border and submitting a joint bid to host the 2008 European Football Championship.

None the less, Cyprus continued to overshadow bilateral relations, and in May 2001 Cem warned that there would be 'no limits' to Turkey's response were Cyprus to be admitted to EU membership before a political settlement had been reached; in November Ecevit warned that Turkey could annex the 'TRNC' if this were to occur. In February 2002 the Turkish and Greek foreign ministers recommenced talks, following the resumption of negotiations between the Greek and Turkish Cypriot sides on the island. In mid-March Turkey and Greece discussed ongoing disputes over the Aegean Sea, including the control of the continental shelves and the resources beneath them. Later in the month the two Governments signed an agreement to build a 285-km natural gas pipeline from Ankara to Komotini, Greece, thereby allowing Iranian gas to flow to the EU via the existing Tabriz-Ankara pipeline.

Following the elections to the TGNA in November 2002 (see The AKP comes to power), Recep Tayyip Erdoğan stated that a final peace agreement over Cyprus would accelerate Turkey's chances of joining the EU. Erdoğan, whose political priority was Turkey's EU membership, was increasingly in conflict with Turkish Cypriot leader Rauf Denktaş's unyielding stance on reaching a political solution. In January 2003 Erdoğan publicly criticized Denktaş and stated that he was in favour of a new policy for Cyprus, with a view to achieving a solution by 28 February 2003 in order to allow the 'TRNC' to join the EU in 2004 at the same time as the Greek part of the island. During late 2002 and early 2003 the Turkish- and Greek-Cypriot leaders had made significant progress towards reaching a final agreement, which would permit the entire island to accede to the EU on 1 May 2004. However, negotiations on the peace plan failed in March 2003 (see the chapter on Cyprus). Following further UN-sponsored discussions in New York, on 13 February 2004 agreement was reached on a reunification plan based on proposals drafted by the UN Secretary-General, Kofi Annan. The Greek Cypriot President, Tassos Papadopoulos, and Denktaş resumed UN-sponsored negotiations in the Cypriot capital, Nicosia, on 19 February. Greece and Turkey joined the negotiations later in March; however, both Papadopoulos and Denktaş subsequently opposed a final resolution, which was to be submitted for approval by both the Greek- and Turkish-Cypriot communities at a referendum. On 24 April the reunification plan was endorsed by Turkish Cypriots by 64.9% of votes cast at the referendum, but rejected by Greek Cypriots by an overwhelming majority of 75.8% of the votes; consequently, only the Greek part of Cyprus was admitted to the EU on 1 May.

In April 2005 the Turkish Cypriot Prime Minister, Mehmet Ali Talat, who strongly supported reunification of the island and full participation in the EU, was elected to the 'TRNC' presidency, replacing Denktaş. In late January 2008 the Greek Prime Minister, Dr Konstantinos (Kostas) Karamanlis, undertook an official three-day visit to Turkey—the first such visit by a Greek premier since 1959. In February 2008 Papadopoulos was defeated at the first round of the Greek Cypriot presidential elections, and at the second round Demetris Christofias was elected to succeed him. It was strongly hoped that the election of Christofias would facilitate the procurement of a swift and lasting resolution to Cyprus's long-running division, and, therefore, prove advantageous to Turkish hopes of EU accession. UN-sponsored reunification talks involving Christofias and Talat commenced in Nicosia in March, during which convergence was reached on a number of issues, including arrangements for the opening of a Green Line crossing-point in the heart of Nicosia as a symbol of reconciliation between their two communities (this occurred on 3 April). By August 2009 the two leaders had held 40 meetings and a second round of negotiations commenced in September.

In his first overseas visit since becoming Prime Minister of Greece, Georgios Papandreou visited Turkey on 9 October 2009 for a meeting of the South-East European Cooperation Process. During his visit Papandreou held discussions encompassing bilateral relations and the Cyprus dispute with Turkey's Prime Minister and Minister of Foreign Affairs. Nevertheless, in mid-October Papandreou declared that the withdrawal of Turkish troops from Cyprus remained a precondition for Turkey's accession to the EU. Talks on the reunification of Cyprus continued in early 2010; however, although agreement had been reached on several technical aspects of the negotiations, as well as various confidence-building initiatives, several core issues remained unresolved and, following the victory of Dr Derviş Eroğlu—who was regarded as an opponent of reunification—at the 'TRNC' presidential election in April, the prospect of a settlement appeared to be receding.

During a visit by Erdoğan to Greece in May 2010, an unprecedented joint cabinet meeting was held by the Greek Government and the Turkish Prime Minister and 10 ministers accompanying him on the visit, and 21 bilateral accords providing for increased mutual co-operation in the fields of, inter alia, energy, technology, tourism and transportation, were signed. During the meeting, the two sides were reported to have discussed a reduction in arms spending, including a proposal suggested by Erdoğan for both countries to disarm in the Aegean, a suggestion that the Greek Government claimed it would seriously consider when Turkey proved that it was no longer a military threat. In November, following a request from the Greek Government, the European Commission dispatched more than 150 border guards from EU member countries to assist in controlling Greece's border with Turkey, in response to an increasing flow of migrants into the former country. (In early 2011 the Council of Europe and other bodies criticized the Greek authorities' treatment of immigrants, including chronically poor conditions in detention centres at the border.) In March the Turkish Minister of Foreign Affairs, Ahmet Davutoğlu, travelled to the Greek capital, Athens, where he met his Greek counterpart; both sides pledged to strive for a continued improvement in bilateral relations.

Turkey's application for membership of the European Union

Following the 1980 military coup, the EC-Turkish Association Council (which had been established in 1963) was suspended, together with all community aid to the country. Turkey was readmitted to associate membership of the EC in September 1986, but failed to gain access to the suspended EC aid or to extend the rights of the large number of Turkish workers in Europe. In April 1987 Turkey made a formal application to become a full member of the EC. In December 1989 the application was effectively rejected, at least until 1993, by the Commission of the European Communities. The Commission cited factors including Turkey's unsatisfactory human rights record, high rate of inflation, dependence upon the rural population and inadequate social security provisions as falling short of EC expectations.

The Turkish Government began to implement measures to construct a customs union with the EU, which was to become effective on 1 January 1995. Human rights issues remained the main obstacle to securing an agreement, and in December 1994 the customs union was postponed on these grounds. In February 1995 Greece withdrew its veto on the customs union, having received assurance on the accession of Cyprus to the EU, and the agreement was signed in March. The Turkish Government subsequently pursued efforts to introduce new democratization legislation and to secure the support of European leaders for the customs union by extending guarantees on human rights and treatment of its Kurdish population. The final terms of the arrangement were agreed at a meeting of the EU-Turkish

Association Council in October, and were approved by the European Parliament in December. The EU was expected to provide a total of ECU 1,800m. over a five-year period, in order to assist the implementation of the new trade regime and to alleviate any initial hardships resulting from the agreement. The customs union came into effect on 1 January 1996. Its implementation was, however, delayed, owing to Greek opposition to the release of ECU 375m. in aid, claiming that Turkish action in the Aegean was a violation of the agreement. In July Greece withdrew its opposition to Turkey's participation in an EU-Mediterranean assistance programme, although the block on funds from the customs union remained in effect. Throughout 1996 the Turkish Government criticized the EU for its failure to adhere to the terms of the economic agreement. In January 1997 Turkey warned that it would disrupt any expansion of NATO if the EU refused to consider the Turkish membership application. Previously, Turkey had prevented the use of NATO facilities by members of Western European Union, owing to Greek opposition to Turkey's full participation in the regional defence grouping.

Relations with the EU were tense in 1997 as the next group of EU applicants was selected. In December, following EU announcements that Turkey would not be invited to join the EU, but that it would be invited to a newly created EU Conference, which was to include both EU and non-EU states, Turkey stated that it would not attend such a conference and that it would also cease negotiations on Cyprus, human rights and the Aegean disputes. It further threatened to boycott EU goods and to withdraw its application to the EU if it was not included in a list of candidates by June. On 20 December Turkey announced a six-month freeze in relations with the EU, which later announced it was withholding all aid to Turkey for the following year, owing to the situation in the south-east of the country and its human rights problems. Turkey officially declined its invitation to the EU Conference in March 1998 and in May also declined to attend a scheduled meeting of the EU-Turkish Association Council. Relations with France deteriorated in May when the French National Assembly adopted a motion recognizing the Turkish 'genocide' against the Armenians in 1915–23; a number of bilateral military and commercial contracts were suspended as a result.

In October 1999 an EU report declared Turkey to be a suitable candidate to join the union, although Turkey stated that it would not accept any extraordinary conditions attached to such a candidacy, particularly with relation to Öcalan and the Kurdish problem. A number of EU member states offered their support to Turkey in late 1999, including Greece and Italy. In December Turkey was invited to attend the EU summit in Helsinki, Finland, and to accept formal status as a candidate for membership. The Government initially objected, owing to attached conditions concerning Cyprus and the Aegean dispute with Greece, but following a visit to Turkey by Javier Solana, the Secretary-General of the Council of the European Union, decided to accept. It announced at that time that it would seek an end to its territorial disputes with Greece by 2004, the deadline set by the EU for a review.

In August 2000 Turkey signed the International Covenant of Civil and Political Rights and the International Covenant on Economic, Social and Cultural Rights. This was described as a positive step by the EU in its progress to accession report on Turkey in November, although it pointed out that Turkey had not yet acceded to a number of other major human rights instruments, such as the abolition of the death penalty and the Convention on the Elimination of All Forms of Racial Discrimination. The report concluded that Turkey did not yet meet the Copenhagen criteria (which state that a country must have achieved 'stability of institutions guaranteeing democracy, the rule of law, human rights and respect for and protection of minorities'), thus making accession negotiations impossible, and described the overall human rights record in Turkey as worrying. It also stated that although Turkey had the basic features of a democratic system, it was slow to implement institutional reforms. Accession was also conditional on a satisfactory settlement of the Cyprus problem. This condition led to the Turkish withdrawal from the UN-sponsored proximity talks in protest. Prime Minister Ecevit accused the EU of 'deception' over Turkey's membership application, stating that it had reneged on a promise not to link Turkey's application to a resolution of the Cyprus problem and disputes with Greece over territorial rights in the Aegean Sea. A rewording of the Cyprus condition was later approved by Turkey; however, further tension was caused by Turkey's obstruction of an EU-NATO agreement enabling the EU's planned Rapid Reaction Force to use NATO assets, despite Turkey's offer to contribute up to 6,000 troops to the force.

Meanwhile, the Armenian 'genocide' question continued to provoke tension between Turkey and the EU. The European Parliament adopted a resolution in November 2000 that formally accused Turkey of genocide against Armenians in 1915 (at the same time it also called on Turkey to pull its forces out of the 'TRNC'). Turkey reacted angrily, with the Fazilet Partisi (FP—Virtue Party) proposing a legislative investigation 'with the aim of removing wrong and biased opinions'. Relations with France were, however, more seriously damaged in January 2001, after the French National Assembly unanimously voted to recognize the 1915–23 massacre of Armenians under the Ottoman Empire as 'genocide', against the wishes of the Government. In November 2000 the French Senate had already voted to recognize the massacre as 'genocide'; none the less, the French Government attempted to reassure Turkey that bilateral relations remained intact. Following the National Assembly vote, however, Ecevit stated that the French action would damage relations and recalled Turkey's ambassador to France immediately after the vote for consultations. The Government further announced plans to erect a 'genocide' monument to the 1.5m. Algerians killed in the 1954–62 war of independence against the French. Relations received a further setback in early May 2001 when the ECHR ruled that Turkey had grossly violated the human rights of thousands of Greek Cypriots during the 1974 invasion, and its subsequent occupation, of northern Cyprus. The court highlighted the failure of the Turkish Government to investigate the fate of missing Greek Cypriots, and their forcible eviction from the north and the subsequent confiscation of their property.

In late May 2001 Turkey nominally agreed to grant the EU's Rapid Reaction Force access to NATO assets for future operations. Although Turkey would be consulted on such matters, it would not have the same participation rights or veto powers as the existing 15 EU members. However, Turkish officials remained dissatisfied at the arrangements, having lobbied strongly for a greater influence in EU security planning. Turkey also feared that an upsurge of violence in Cyprus would necessitate the deployment of the Rapid Reaction Force on the island, placing the EU directly against itself, and had unsuccessfully sought guarantees against such an eventuality. In December Turkey finally reached agreement with the EU regarding the Rapid Reaction Force after months of British diplomacy.

In August 2001, meanwhile, the ECHR ruled that the Government's decision to ban the Islamist FP did not violate human rights laws. In October the TGNA passed constitutional amendments designed to facilitate EU membership but stopped short of abolishing the death penalty, a crucial EU demand. The issue of capital punishment placed the EU at odds with the ultra-nationalist MHP in the ruling coalition, which had pledged to exact the death penalty imposed on PKK leader Abdullah Öcalan. In August 2002 the EU welcomed the TGNA's vote to abolish the death penalty in peacetime, as part of a broader package of reforms. The new AKP Government elected in November pledged to accelerate efforts to join the EU. However, in that month Valéry Giscard d'Estaing, the Chairman of the Convention on the Future of Europe, stated publicly that Turkey should never be allowed to join the EU, and that its accession would mean the 'end of the European Union'. Senior EU officials distanced themselves from the remarks, which were also dismissed by Erdoğan. At the EU summit in Copenhagen, Denmark, in December, EU leaders agreed to delay negotiations on Turkish membership until after December 2004, and to resume discussions then only if Turkey had fulfilled all the entry obligations. Several EU members, notably France and Germany, remained less enthusiastic about Turkish membership, citing its poor human rights record, which Turkey again pledged to improve.

A further complication to Turkish ambitions for EU membership emerged with the failure of a UN plan for the reunification of Cyprus in April 2004 (see The Cyprus question and relations with Greece). The resultant accession of only Greek Cypriot Cyprus to the EU on 1 May presented complications for Turkey's EU aspirations, although the Greek Cypriot Government declared that it would not veto Turkey's membership application, provided that it met the standards stipulated by the EU. An official visit to Greece by Erdoğan in May—the first by a Turkish premier in 16 years—reflected the improvement in relations between the two countries.

In May 2004 the TGNA approved a number of constitutional amendments, in accordance with EU requirements, which included the removal of references to the death penalty and the abolition of the country's system of State Security Courts (which was used to try dissidents). An EU summit in Brussels in June reaffirmed that a decision would be taken in December on whether Turkey had made sufficient progress on the EU's criteria for membership and that formal accession negotiations would be initiated if standards were considered to have been met. However, severe doubts about Turkey's qualifications had been presented in a European Parliament resolution, which had been adopted overwhelmingly in April, drawing attention to Turkey's continued use of torture, to the persecution of minorities and other contraventions.

Nevertheless, in October 2004 the European Commission announced its approval of Turkey's qualification for accession negotiations, on condition that reforms continued. In many EU member states, however, there was increasing opposition to the admission of Turkey, especially in Germany and France, where the opposition was believed to reflect concern over the accession of a predominantly Muslim country; some favoured an option that Turkey be offered 'privileged member' status, rather than full membership. On 17 December the EU extended a provisional invitation to Turkey to commence accession negotiations on 3 October 2005, subject to the Turkish Government's fulfilment of a number of criteria, including continued progress in political and economic reforms. Erdoğan accepted an EU requirement to sign a customs accord with member states by that date, but insisted that the protocol would not constitute official Turkish recognition of the authorities of Greek Cyprus; instead he agreed to a compromise arrangement, whereby Turkey made a commitment for future recognition. The British Prime Minister welcomed the agreement; however, both the French and Austrian Governments pledged to conduct national referendums on Turkish entry, while a demonstration in protest at Turkish membership was conducted in Italy. In June 2005 the German Bundestag (Federal Assembly) became the latest EU legislature to attract Turkish anger by condemning the Armenian 'genocide' and accusing the Turkish Government of failing to address the issue.

In July 2005, pending an EU decision on the opening of accession negotiations in October, the Turkish Government signed the requisite customs protocol with Cyprus and the other nine new EU member states, but appended a declaration reaffirming that the accord did not constitute official recognition of Greek Cyprus. In September EU member states adopted a draft declaration stating that Turkish recognition of Cyprus was necessary to the accession process, but without stipulating a date for this (thereby posing no obstacle to the beginning of negotiations). At the beginning of October intensive debate took place between EU member states to resolve the impasse over Austria's insistence that Turkey be offered the lesser option of 'privileged partnership' (to which the Turkish Government remained opposed), rather than full membership. Austria withdrew its veto to the admission of Turkey, after Croatia was unexpectedly declared eligible to enter into membership negotiations (see the chapter on Croatia). Turkey's accession negotiations with the EU were officially approved on 3 October, and opened on the following day.

In early November 2005 an EU report, while welcoming Turkey's economic performance, criticized a lack of progress in political reforms, citing continued human rights violations, including torture, and the necessity for further judicial reforms. Furthermore, the subsequent reluctance of the Turkish authorities to open ports and airports to Greek Cypriot-registered traffic by the end of 2006, in adherence to the customs protocol and as a condition to progress in the accession negotiations, prompted criticism from EU officials and repeated threats from the Greek Cypriot Government to veto Turkey's membership. Nevertheless, EU ministers responsible for foreign affairs formally opened the first chapter of accession negotiations with Turkey in June. Attempts by the Finnish presidency of the EU to broker a deal under which the EU would take charge of the port of Famagusta in the 'TRNC' while the nearby town of Varosha would be returned to Greek Cypriot control were eventually abandoned in late November. Meanwhile, relations with France worsened in October 2006, when the French National Assembly endorsed a bill making it a crime to deny that Armenians suffered genocide at the hands of Turks in 1915–23; the vote was criticized by the EU. In the same month the EU advised Turkey that safeguarding freedom of expression in the country was to be regarded as a matter of urgency. During 2005–06 court proceedings were initiated against several prominent novelists who were accused of 'insulting Turkishness' under Article 301 of the penal code.

In November 2006 the European Commission recommended the suspension of negotiations on eight of 35 chapters of the accession talks (these included trade, financial services and transport), a decision that was endorsed at the summit meeting of the European Council in early December. At the end of December Turkey pledged to implement a six-year 'roadmap' and reform programme and to continue implementing all the required judicial and military reforms, even in those areas where negotiations had been suspended. In March 2007 the EU resumed negotiations with Turkey on the accession chapter relating to enterprise and industry. However, in June, following the inauguration as French President of Nicolas Sarkozy in the previous month, France blocked the commencement of negotiations on the accession chapter relating to economic and monetary union, apparently in a further move to prevent Turkey's eventual accession to the EU. (French officials later asserted that they were not opposed to the commencement of further negotiating chapters with Turkey, but that they believed that all options, including that of 'preferential partnership', should be considered.) Later in June the EU did extend membership discussions with Turkey on two new, smaller chapters concerning financial controls and statistics. In November the European Commission urged the Turkish Government to accelerate its political and social reform process, citing the treatment of the minority Kurdish population and Article 301 as particular areas where further progress was required. Accession talks concerning health and consumer affairs, as well as inter-European transport links, were initiated in mid-December. The TGNA approved amendments to Article 301 at the end of April 2008, although critics of the Government countered that the changes were not as far-reaching as they had hoped. Under the newly revised legislation, it would become a crime to insult 'the Turkish nation' rather than 'Turkishness', while the maximum sentence for someone convicted of such a crime was to be shortened from three to two years.

Despite the European Commission expressing concern at the lack of progress on key reforms in Turkey, two new negotiating chapters, concerning free movement of capital, and information and media, commenced in December 2008. Turkey created its first post within the Council of Ministers dedicated exclusively to EU negotiations in January 2009. Egemen Bağış, a former AKP Vice-Chairman in charge of Foreign Affairs, was appointed Minister of State and Chief Negotiator for EU Affairs, the responsibilities of which role had hitherto been undertaken by the Minister of Foreign Affairs. During a Franco-German summit in Berlin in May, President Sarkozy and German Chancellor Angela Merkel reiterated their opposition to Turkey's full membership of the EU, stating their preference for the negotiation of a 'privileged partnership' arrangement. Turkish officials again rejected this proposal and urged all European states to adhere to the ongoing accession process. An additional negotiating chapter, concerning taxation, commenced in June.

In its latest progress report on Turkey's EU accession, published in November 2009, the European Commission recognized that substantial progress had been made on judicial reform, civil-military relations and Kurdish rights. However, the report highlighted continuing concerns with regard to freedom of expression and referred specifically to tax fines levied against Doğan Media Holding, Turkey's largest media group, which it described as disproportionate and potentially politically motivated. (Critical coverage of the Government in newspapers and television stations owned by the Doğan group had led to increasing tensions with the AKP; in 2008 the Prime Minister called for a boycott of the media group.) A new negotiating chapter, concerning environmental issues, opened in December 2009, bringing to 12 the number of chapters under discussion. In January 2010 the European Parliament adopted a resolution on the 2009 progress report that called on Turkey to begin withdrawing its troops from northern Cyprus in order to facilitate reunification negotiations.

The approval by referendum of the Government's package of constitutional reforms in September 2010 (see Domestic Political Affairs) was expected to bolster Turkish hopes of acceding to the EU. However, while the EU had expressed support for the reforms, on the grounds that they afforded the democratically elected Turkish Government greater control over the military, the Union also voiced concern that the reforms gave the Government excessive control over the judiciary.

Meanwhile, in a two-day state visit to Turkey in March 2010 Chancellor Merkel reiterated her support for a 'privileged partnership' arrangement; however, she insisted that negotiations on Turkey's EU accession were 'open-ended'. During a visit to Berlin intended to strengthen Turkey's EU accession bid in February 2011, Erdoğan issued an unexpectedly stern rebuke to the German Government's efforts to integrate Turkish immigrants into German society, arguing that 'any policy which seeks to revoke the language and culture of migrants violates international law'. The criticism appeared to have been in retaliation for a comment made by a senior German government official urging that the Turkish accession bid be suspended owing to the failure of the Erdoğan Government to protect religious freedoms. Erdoğan also accused Merkel of using 'stalling tactics' to appease those among the German electorate who were opposed to Turkey's bid to join the EU. During a visit to Ankara by Sarkozy later in February, the French President reiterated his Government's opposition to Turkish accession.

Other external relations

Following the formal dissolution of the USSR in December 1991, the Turkish Government sought to further its political, economic and cultural influence in the Caucasus and Central Asia, in particular with Azerbaijan, Kazakhstan, Kyrgyzstan, Turkmenistan and Uzbekistan, all of which share ethno-linguistic ties with Turkey. Following the outbreak of war between Armenia and Azerbaijan in 1991, Turkey blockaded Armenia and provided support to its 'Turkic' ally, Azerbaijan. In April 1992 Prime Minister Demirel undertook an official visit to several former Soviet republics, pledging aid of more than US $1,000m. in the form of credits for the purchase of Turkish goods and contracts. At the same time programmes broadcast by the Turkish national television company began to be relayed, by satellite, to the region. In June leaders of 11 nations, including Turkey, Greece, Albania and six former Soviet republics, established the Organization of the Black Sea Economic Co-operation (BSEC, see p. 398). In October 1994 a meeting of the heads of state of Turkey, Azerbaijan, Turkmenistan, Uzbekistan, Kazakhstan and Kyrgyzstan took place in İstanbul, in an effort to develop and improve relations among the 'Turkic' republics. Summit meetings have subsequently been convened each year. In the late 1990s Turkey sought to encourage Western firms to build a new petroleum pipeline from Baku, Azerbaijan, to the Turkish port of Ceyhan, thereby allowing the transportation of petroleum from the Caspian Sea to the Mediterranean, via Azerbaijan and Georgia. Such a scheme would also increase Turkey's importance to the EU by making it the centre of the Transport Corridor Europe–Caucasus–Asia (TRACECA) project. Despite the cost of the pipeline, construction began in June 2002.

In mid-2001 work began on a new natural gas pipeline from Dzhubga, Russia, to Samsun, Turkey, beneath the Black Sea, which would increase Turkey's dependency on Russian natural gas. During a significant visit to Turkey in December 2004 the Russian President, Vladimir Putin, signed co-operation agreements in the fields of trade, defence and finance. In May 2009 Prime Minister Erdoğan visited Russia and held talks with his counterpart, Putin, on energy co-operation and regional affairs. The premiers announced the extension of a contract for the supply of Russian natural gas to Turkey. In May 2010 the two countries signed a US $20,000m. agreement under the terms of which Russia was to construct Turkey's first nuclear energy plant, in Akkuyu, Mersin province, comprising four 1,200-MW reactors, and was to hold a controlling stake in the project. During a state visit to Russia in March 2011, Erdoğan met with President Dmitrii Medvedev and Prime Minister Putin, and reaffirmed Turkish commitment to the project; construction was expected to commence by 2012 and the first reactor was expected to become operational in 2018.

Diplomatic relations between Turkey and Armenia, which had been suspended since Turkey closed its border with Armenia in 1993, in response to Armenia's conflict with Azerbaijan, remained suspended in 2008. However, following the installation of Serge Sarkissian as President of Armenia in April of that year, there were renewed hopes of a rapprochement. President Gül accepted an invitation from President Sarkissian to attend the first football match between the national teams in the Armenian capital, Yerevan, in September and, in doing so, became the first Turkish head of state to visit Armenia. In July, meanwhile, officials of Turkey's Ministry of Foreign Affairs confirmed speculation that Turkish and Armenian delegations had met in Switzerland for informal discussions on bilateral relations. However, the Armenian 'genocide' question (see Relations with the USA and regional relations) remained a critical obstacle to the restoration of normal relations. Turkey's Minister of Foreign Affairs, Ali Babacan, held direct talks on bilateral relations with his Armenian counterpart in mid-April 2009 during a BSEC conference in Yerevan. Moreover, in the same month the Ministry of Foreign Affairs announced that the Swiss-mediated negotiations had resulted in an agreement on a comprehensive framework for the normalization of bilateral ties.

In May 2009, during a visit to Baku, Azerbaijan, Prime Minister Erdoğan insisted that the reopening of the Turkish–Armenian border was conditional on Armenia withdrawing its troops from the Nagornyi Karabakh region. (Nagornyi Karabakh is the subject of a long-standing territorial dispute between Armenia and Azerbaijan.) Erdoğan's statement was widely interpreted as an attempt to appease Azerbaijan, which is a major supplier of natural gas to Turkey. Despite this apparent setback, the US Administration actively fostered Turkish-Armenian reconciliation efforts in the following months and, at the end of August, agreement was reached on two protocols regarding bilateral relations, providing for a six-week period of consultation following which normalization agreements would be presented to the respective legislatures for ratification. The initiative also provided for the establishment of an impartial commission to examine historical disputes involving the two nations. The protocols were signed according to schedule in Zürich, Switzerland, on 10 October, with US Secretary of State Hillary Clinton in attendance. However, a ruling by the Armenian Constitutional Court in January 2010 concerning the irrevocability of the term 'genocide' in reference to the Turkish massacre of Armenians after the First World War, and Turkey's continuing attempts to link the normalization process to the Nagornyi Karabakh issue, represented critical obstacles to normalization. In April the Armenian legislature suspended ratification of the protocols 'until the Turkish side is prepared to continue the process without preconditions'. By mid-2011 the protocols had yet to be ratified. In April of that year Turkish Deputy Prime Minister Bülent Arınç referred to ties with Armenia as 'the only missing part in our diplomatic relations'.

CONSTITUTION AND GOVERNMENT

In October 1981 the National Security Council (NSC), which took power in September 1980, announced the formation of a Consultative Assembly to draft a new constitution, replacing that of 1961. The Assembly consisted of 40 members appointed directly by the NSC and 120 members chosen by the NSC from candidates put forward by the governors of the 67 provinces; all former politicians were excluded. The draft Constitution was approved by the Assembly in September 1982 and by a national referendum in November. Under the terms of the Constitution approved in 1982 (with subsequent amendments), legislative power is vested in the unicameral Turkish Grand National Assembly (TGNA), with 550 deputies, who are elected by universal adult suffrage for a four-year term. Executive power is vested in the President of the Republic, to be elected by universal adult suffrage for a term of five years (although no one candidate may serve more than two terms of office). The President is empowered to appoint a Prime Minister and senior members of the judiciary, the Central Bank and broadcasting organizations; to dissolve the TGNA; and to declare a state of emergency entailing rule by decree. Further changes to the Constitution were approved at a national referendum in September 2010 (see Contemporary Political History). For administrative purposes, Turkey comprises 81 provinces and 2,935 municipalities.

REGIONAL AND INTERNATIONAL CO-OPERATION

Turkey is a member of several regional organizations, including the Economic Co-operation Organization (ECO, see p. 264), and the Organization of the Black Sea Economic Co-operation (BSEC, see p. 398), which has its headquarters in İstanbul. Turkey also adheres to both the Council of Europe (see p. 250) and the Organisation for Security and Co-operation in Europe (OSCE, see p. 385), and in December 1999 was accepted as a candidate for membership of the European Union (EU, see p. 270). (For details regarding Turkey's accession negotiations with the EU, see Contemporary Political History.)

Turkey was a founder member of the UN in October 1945. As a contracting party to the General Agreement on Tariffs and Trade, Turkey joined the World Trade Organization (WTO, see p. 430) on its establishment in 1995. It became a member of the North Atlantic Treaty Organization (NATO, see p. 368) in 1952. Turkey participates in the Organisation of the Islamic

TURKEY

Conference (OIC, see p. 400), as well as several development and economic co-operation bodies, including the Organisation for Economic Co-operation and Development (OECD, see p. 376), the Group of 20 (G20, see p. 451), and the Developing Eight (D-8, see p. 446).

ECONOMIC AFFAIRS

In 2009, according to estimates by the World Bank, Turkey's gross national income (GNI), measured at average 2007–09 prices, was US $653,096m., equivalent to $8,730 per head (or $13,730 per head on an international purchasing-power parity basis). During 2000–09, it was estimated, the population increased at an average annual rate of 1.3%, while gross domestic product (GDP) per head rose, in real terms, by an average of 2.0% per year. Overall GDP increased, in real terms, by an annual average of 3.3% in 2000–09. According to official figures, GDP decreased by 4.8% in 2009, before expanding by 8.9% in 2010.

Agriculture (including forestry and fishing) contributed 9.4% to GDP and engaged 25.2% of the employed population in 2010. The country is self-sufficient in most basic foodstuffs. The principal agricultural exports are cotton, tobacco, wheat, fruit and nuts. Other important crops are barley, maize, sugar beet, potatoes and onions. The raising of sheep, goats, cattle and poultry is also an important economic activity. During 2000–10 agricultural GDP increased by an annual average rate of 1.2%; the agricultural sector grew by 1.6% in 2010.

Industry (including mining, manufacturing, construction and power) contributed 26.1% to GDP and engaged 26.2% of the employed population in 2010. During 2000–10 industrial GDP increased by an annual average rate of 4.0%; the industrial sector contracted by 8.6% in 2009, before expanding by 13.6% in 2010.

Mining contributed 1.6% to GDP and engaged 0.5% of the employed population in 2010. Chromium, copper and borax are the major mineral exports. Coal, petroleum, natural gas, bauxite, iron ore, manganese and sulphur are also mined. The development and expansion of Turkey's gold-mining facilities was in progress in the mid-2000s. During 2000–10 mining GDP increased by an annual average rate of 1.7%; mining GDP contracted by 6.7% in 2009, but expanded by 4.7% in 2010.

Manufacturing contributed 17.3% to GDP and employed 18.7% of the employed population in 2010. The most important branches, measured by gross value of output, are textiles, food-processing, petroleum refineries, iron and steel, and industrial chemicals. During 2000–10 manufacturing GDP increased by an annual average rate of 4.2%; sectoral GDP declined by 7.2% in 2009, but grew by some 13.6% in 2010.

Construction contributed 4.6% to GDP and engaged 6.3% of the employed population in 2010. During 2000–10 construction GDP increased by an annual average rate of 3.6%; the construction sector contracted by some 16.1% in 2009, but increased by 17.1% in 2010.

Energy is derived principally from thermal power plants. In 2007 49.6% of energy was derived from natural gas, 27.9% from coal, 18.7% from hydroelectric power and a further 3.4% from petroleum. The energy sector (including water) contributed 2.6% to GDP and employed 0.4% of the employed population in 2010. Total domestic output of crude petroleum and natural gas accounts for some 12% of the country's hydrocarbon requirements. Imports of petroleum and its products comprised 11.3% of the value of total imports in 2010. A major development project for south-eastern Anatolia, initially scheduled for completion in 2010, was expected to increase Turkey's energy production by 70% and to irrigate 1.6m. ha of uncultivable or inadequately irrigated land, by constructing dams and hydroelectric plants on the Tigris and Euphrates rivers and their tributaries. However, progress was delayed by the withholding of funding by the World Bank owing to the lack of an official agreement between Turkey, Iraq and Syria on water-sharing pertaining to the Tigris and Euphrates rivers, and the anticipated completion date was revised to 2013. Meanwhile, in July 2006 the second largest petroleum pipeline in the world—transporting oil between Baku, Azerbaijan, and the Turkish terminal at Ceyhan, via Tbilisi, Georgia—was formally inaugurated. In March 2010 parliamentary approval was granted for the construction by a multilateral European consortium, including a subsidiary of Turkey's Türkiye Petrolleri Anonim Ortaklığı, of a 3,300-km pipeline from Erzurum in eastern Turkey to Austria; the US $10,700m. Nabucco project was designed to transport natural gas from the Caspian Sea region to central Europe, thus reducing Europe's dependency on gas supplies from Russia. Construction of the project was due to commence in early 2012 and it was expected to become operational in late 2015. Work on Turkey's first nuclear power plant, at Akkuyu, in Mersin province, with Russian involvement (see Contemporary Political History), was expected to commence in 2012; two other nuclear plants, in the Black Sea province of Sinop and at Iğneada, in Kırklareli province, were scheduled to be built by 2023.

The services sector contributed 64.5% of GDP and engaged 48.6% of the employed population in 2010. Tourism is one of Turkey's fastest growing sources of revenue. Total tourist arrivals increased to more than 28.6m. in 2010 and tourists generated some US $20,807m. in revenue in that year. Remittances from Turkish workers abroad also make an important contribution to the economy, amounting to $1,936m. in 2002. During 2000–10 the GDP of the services sector increased by an annual average rate of 4.2%; services GDP contracted by 3.3% in 2009, but expanded by 6.9% in 2010.

In 2010 Turkey recorded a visible trade deficit of US $56,354m., and there was a deficit of $48,561m. on the current account of the balance of payments. In 2010 the principal source of imports (11.6% of the total) was Russia; other major suppliers were Germany, the People's Republic of China, the USA and Italy. Germany was the principal market for exports in that year (10.1% of the total); other important purchasers were the United Kingdom, Italy, France and Iraq. Exports in 2010 were dominated by basic manufactures (mainly textiles), machinery and transport equipment, miscellaneous manufactured articles, food and live animals and chemicals and related products. In that year the principal imports were machinery and transport equipment, mineral fuels (particularly petroleum), basic manufactures, chemical products, crude materials (inedible) except fuels and miscellaneous manufactured articles.

In 2010 there was an overall budgetary deficit of 39,600m. Turkish liras. Turkey's general government gross debt was 433,428m. Turkish liras in 2009, equivalent to 45.5% of GDP. Turkey's external debt at the end of 2008 was US $277,277m., of which $77,945m. was public and publicly guaranteed debt. In that year the cost of debt-servicing was equivalent to 29.5% of the value of exports of goods, services and income. The annual rate of inflation averaged 8.6% in 2003–10. Consumer prices increased by 6.2% in 2009 and 8.6% in 2010. In 2010 the rate of unemployment was 11.9%.

The Government's national development plan for 2007–13 had as its principal aim the achievement of the levels of macroeconomic stability required for attaining membership of the European Union (EU, see p. 270). At the beginning of 2005 the Government established a new monetary unit, the 'new' Turkish lira, as part of ongoing efforts to restrain inflation. (The name of the currency reverted to Turkish lira from 1 January 2009, although 'new' Turkish lira notes and coins remained in circulation until the beginning of 2010, when a phased withdrawal of the currency commenced, which was completed by the end of that year.) During 2003–07 Turkey's GDP, supported by an extensive programme of economic reform, grew at an average annual rate of almost 7% and the public debt was reduced significantly. However, from the latter part of 2008 the impact of the global financial crisis resulted in negative growth and a sharp decline in output, particularly in the manufacturing sector. The contraction worsened in early 2009, exacerbated by declining export revenues owing to the effects of adverse economic conditions on Turkey's main trading partners. In September the Government announced its medium-term macroeconomic programme, which aimed to promote private sector activity and halt the deterioration in the public finances. In the final quarter of 2009 the economy returned to growth, although GDP in 2009 as a whole declined by 4.8%. Owing in part to regulatory reforms introduced after the financial crises in the early 2000s, the Turkish banking sector proved particularly resilient in the face of the global financial crisis, with net profits for the sector increasing by more than 40% in 2009. Negotiations with the IMF for a new stand-by arrangement to support Turkey's economic recovery programme commenced in October 2008. However, in a sign of growing domestic confidence in the recovery, the Government withdrew from the negotiations in March 2010, with Prime Minister Recep Tayyip Erdoğan declaring that the country could henceforth 'stand on its own feet'. GDP growth in 2010 increased to an impressive 8.9%—comfortably exceeding government forecasts—buoyed by structural reforms to increase productivity and create new jobs. Unemployment had reached a record annual average of 14.0% in 2009, having peaked at 16.1% in February of

TURKEY

Statistical Survey

that year. However, the unemployment rate had fallen to 11.4% by December 2010 and averaged 11.9% for the year as a whole, while the budgetary deficit declined by 24.9% year-on-year in 2010. Controversial draft employment legislation under debate in the Turkish Grand National Assembly provoked protests in the capital, Ankara, in February 2011, which were dispersed by the authorities using tear gas and water cannons; thousands of workers and students had gathered to demonstrate against the bill, which they claimed would reduce workers' rights and allow employers to exploit unregulated labour. According to the Organisation for Economic Co-operation and Development, GDP was expected to remain robust, at 5.3% and 5.4%, in 2011 and 2012, respectively, owing to the Government's 'prudent' fiscal and monetary policy.

PUBLIC HOLIDAYS

2012: 1 January (New Year's Day), 23 April (National Sovereignty and Children's Day), 1 May (Labour and Solidarity Day), 19 May (Commemoration of Atatürk, and Youth and Sports Day), 18–20 August* (Ramazan Bayram—End of Ramadan), 30 August (Victory Day), 25–28 October* (Kurban Bayram—Feast of the Sacrifice), 29 October (Republic Day).

* These holidays are dependent on the Islamic lunar calendar and may vary by one or two days from the dates given.

Statistical Survey

Source (unless otherwise stated): T. C. Başbakanlık Türkiye İstatistik Kurumu (Turkish Statistical Institute), Necatibey Cad. 114, 06580-Yücetepe/Ankara; tel. (312) 400410; internet www.turkstat.gov.tr.

Area and Population

AREA, POPULATION AND DENSITY

Area (sq km)	
Land	769,604
Inland water	13,958
Total	783,562*
Population (periodic census results)	
21 October 1990	56,473,035
22 October 2000	
Males	34,346,735
Females	33,457,192
Total	67,803,927
Population (annual census results at 31 December)†	
2008	71,517,100
2009	72,561,312
2010	73,722,988
Density (per sq km) at 31 December 2010	94.1‡

* 302,535 sq miles.
† In accordance with new methodology employing Address Based Population Registration System introduced in 2007.
‡ Land area only.

POPULATION BY AGE AND SEX
(annual population census at 31 December 2010)

	Males	Females	Total
0–14	9,691,297	9,187,285	18,878,582
15–64	25,020,856	24,495,814	49,516,670
65 and over	2,331,029	2,996,707	5,327,736
Total	37,043,182	36,679,806	73,722,988

PROVINCES
(annual population census at 31 December 2010)

	Area (sq km)	Population	Density (per sq km)
Adana	14,046	2,085,225	148.5
Adıyaman	7,606	590,935	77.7
Afyon	14,719	697,559	47.4
Ağrı	11,499	542,022	47.1
Aksaray	7,966	377,505	47.4
Amasya	5,704	334,786	58.7
Ankara	25,402	4,771,716	187.8
Antalya	20,791	1,978,333	95.2
Ardahan	4,968	105,454	21.2
Artvin	7,367	164,759	22.4
Aydın	7,904	989,862	125.2
Balıkesir	14,473	1,152,323	79.6
Bartın	2,080	187,758	90.3
Batman	4,659	510,200	109.5
Bayburt	3,739	74,412	19.9
Bilecik	4,307	225,381	52.3
Bingöl	8,254	255,170	30.9
—continued	Area (sq km)	Population	Density (per sq km)
Bitlis	7,095	328,767	46.3
Bolu	8,323	271,208	32.6
Burdur	7,135	258,868	36.3
Bursa	10,886	2,605,495	239.3
Çanakkale	9,950	490,397	49.3
Çankırı	7,492	179,067	23.9
Çorum	12,796	535,405	41.8
Denizli	11,804	931,823	78.9
Diyarbakır	15,204	1,528,958	100.6
Düzce	2,593	338,188	130.4
Edirne	6,098	390,428	64.0
Elazığ	9,281	552,646	59.5
Erzincan	11,728	224,949	19.2
Erzurum	25,331	769,085	30.4
Eskişehir	13,902	764,584	55.0
Gaziantep	6,845	1,700,763	248.5
Giresun	6,832	419,256	61.4
Gümüşhane	6,437	129,618	20.1
Hakkari	7,179	251,302	35.0
Hatay	5,831	1,480,571	253.9
Iğdır	3,588	184,418	51.4
Isparta	8,871	448,298	50.5
İstanbul	5,315	13,255,685	2,494.0
İzmir	12,016	3,948,848	328.6
Kahramanmaraş	14,457	1,044,816	72.3
Karabük	4,109	227,610	55.4
Karaman	8,869	232,633	26.2
Kars	10,139	301,766	29.8
Kastamonu	13,158	361,222	27.5
Kayseri	17,109	1,234,651	72.2
Kırıkkale	4,570	276,647	60.5
Kırklareli	6,300	332,791	52.8
Kırşehir	6,530	221,876	34.0
Kilis	1,428	123,135	86.2
Kocaeli	3,625	1,560,138	430.4
Konya	40,814	2,013,845	49.3
Kütahya	12,014	590,496	49.2
Malatya	12,103	740,643	61.2
Manisa	13,229	1,379,484	104.3
Mardin	8,806	744,606	84.6
Mersin	15,512	1,647,899	106.2
Muğla	12,949	817,503	63.1
Muş	8,067	406,886	50.4
Nevşehir	5,392	282,337	52.4
Niğde	7,365	337,931	45.9
Ordu	5,952	719,183	120.8
Osmaniye	3,196	479,221	149.9
Rize	3,922	319,637	81.5
Sakarya	4,880	872,872	178.9
Samsun	9,364	1,252,693	133.8
Siirt	5,473	300,695	54.9
Sinop	5,817	202,740	34.9
Sivas	28,567	642,224	22.5
Şanlıurfa	19,336	1,663,371	86.0
Şırnak	7,152	430,109	60.1
Tekirdağ	6,342	798,109	125.8
Tokat	10,073	617,802	61.3

TURKEY

—continued

	Area (sq km)	Population	Density (per sq km)
Trabzon	4,664	763,714	163.7
Tunceli	7,686	76,699	10.0
Uşak	5,363	338,019	63.0
Van	22,983	1,035,418	45.1
Yalova	850	203,741	239.7
Yozgat	14,074	476,096	33.8
Zonguldak	3,310	619,703	187.2
Total	783,562	73,722,988	94.1

PRINCIPAL TOWNS
(population at annual census of 31 December 2010)

İstanbul	13,120,596	Hatay		743,439
Ankara (capital)	4,641,256	Balıkesir		694,926
İzmir (Smyrna)	3,606,326	Eskişehir		681,854
Bursa	2,308,574	Sakarya		646,899
Adana	1,836,432	Denizli		641,093
Gaziantep	1,501,566	Kahramanmaraş		636,828
Konya	1,486,653	Aydın		588,552
Kocaeli	1,459,772	Tekirdağ		545,481
Antalya	1,392,974	Van		539,619
Mersin	1,281,048	Erzurum		489,486
Diyarbakır	1,090,172	Malatya		480,144
Kayseri	1,064,164	Sivas		433,932
Manisa	924,267	Mardin		428,899
Şanlıurfa	922,539	Trabzon		415,652
Samsun	816,576			

BIRTHS, MARRIAGES AND DEATHS

	Live births Number	Rate (per 1,000)	Marriages Number	Rate (per 1,000)	Deaths Number*	Rate (per 1,000)
2003	1,193,154	17.8	565,468	8.1	430,000	6.1
2004	1,213,545	17.9	615,357	8.6	433,000	6.1
2005	1,231,678	18.0	641,241	8.9	436,000	6.1
2006	1,238,725	17.8	636,121	8.7	440,000	6.0
2007	1,266,503	18.0	638,311	8.6	447,000	6.1
2008	1,262,333	17.8	641,973	9.0	454,000	6.4
2009	1,270,000	17.7	591,742	8.2	461,000	6.4

* Figures are estimates derived from address-based population registration.

Sources: partly UN, *Demographic Yearbook* and *Population and Vital Statistics Report*.

Recorded deaths (province and district centres only): 197,520 in 2005; 210,146 in 2006; 212,731 in 2007; 215,562 in 2008.

Life expectancy (years at birth, WHO estimates): 74 (males 72; females 77) in 2007 (Source: WHO, *World Health Statistics*).

ECONOMICALLY ACTIVE POPULATION*
(sample surveys, '000 persons aged 15 years and over)

	2006	2007	2008
Agriculture, hunting, forestry and fishing	6,088	4,867	5,016
Mining and quarrying	128	128	115
Manufacturing	4,186	4,089	4,235
Electricity, gas and water	93	97	92
Construction	1,267	1,231	1,241
Wholesale and retail trade; repair of motor vehicles, motorcycles and personal and household goods	3,729	3,569	3,575
Hotels and restaurants	1,001	989	998
Transport, storage and communications	1,163	1,136	1,089
Financial intermediation	238	248	260
Real estate, renting and business activities	772	807	910
Public administration and defence; compulsory social security	1,225	1,260	1,265
Education	907	868	921
Health and social work	591	560	594
Other services	942	889	883
Total employed	22,330	20,738	21,194
Unemployed	2,446	2,376	2,611
Total labour force	24,776	23,114	23,805
Males	18,297	17,098	17,475
Females	6,480	6,016	6,329

* Excluding armed forces.
Source: ILO.

2009 (sample surveys, '000 persons aged 15 years and over): Agriculture, hunting, forestry and fishing 5,254; Mining and quarrying 103; Manufacturing 3,949; Electricity, gas and water 78; Construction 1,249; Wholesale and retail trade, hotels and restaurants 4,542; Transport, communications and storage 1,081; Finance, insurance, real estate and business services 1,339; Community, social and other personal services 3,682; Total employed 21,277; Unemployed 3,471; Total labour force 24,748.

2010 (sample surveys, '000 persons aged 15 years and over): Agriculture, hunting, forestry and fishing 5,683; Mining and quarrying 115; Manufacturing 4,216; Electricity, gas and water 165; Construction 1,431; Wholesale and retail trade, hotels and restaurants 4,410; Transport, communications and storage 1,213; Finance, insurance, real estate and business services 1,529; Public administration and defence 1,292; Community, social and other personal services 2,542; Total employed 22,594; Unemployed 3,046; Total labour force 25,641.

WORKERS ABROAD

	2000	2001	2002
Turkish citizens working abroad (number)	1,170,226	1,178,412	1,200,725
Workers' remittances from abroad (US $ million)	4,560	2,786	1,936

Turkish citizens working abroad (number): 1,197,968 in 2003; 1,195,612 in 2004.

Sources: Undersecretariat of the Prime Ministry for Foreign Trade; Secretariat of the State Planning Organization.

Health and Welfare

KEY INDICATORS

Total fertility rate (children per woman, 2008)	2.1
Under-5 mortality rate (per 1,000 live births, 2008)	22
HIV/AIDS (% of persons aged 15–49, 2001)	<0.1
Physicians (per 1,000 head, 2006)	1.6
Hospital beds (per 1,000 head, 2006)	2.7
Health expenditure (2007): US $ per head (PPP)	677
Health expenditure (2007): % of GDP	5.0
Health expenditure (2007): public (% of total)	69.0
Access to water (% of persons, 2008)	99
Access to sanitation (% of persons, 2008)	90
Total carbon dioxide emissions ('000 metric tons, 2007)	288,444.7
Carbon dioxide emissions per head (metric tons, 2007)	4.0
Human Development Index (2010): ranking	83
Human Development Index (2010): value	0.679

For sources and definitions, see explanatory note on p. vi.

TURKEY

Agriculture

PRINCIPAL CROPS
('000 metric tons)

	2007	2008	2009
Wheat	17,234	17,782	20,600
Rice, paddy	648	753	750
Barley	7,307	5,923	7,300
Maize	3,535	4,274	4,250
Rye	241	247	343
Oats	189	196	218
Potatoes	4,246	4,225	4,398
Sugar beet	12,415	15,488	17,275
Beans, dry	154	155	181
Chick peas	505	518	563
Lentils	535	131	n.a.
Walnuts	173	171	177
Hazelnuts, with shell	530	801	500
Olives	1,076	1,464	1,291
Sunflower seed	854	992	1,057
Cabbages and other brassicas	648	675	707
Lettuce and chicory	428	440	438
Spinach	236	226	225
Tomatoes	9,945	10,985	10,746
Cauliflowers and broccoli	135	151	157
Pumpkins, squash and gourds	338	379	412
Cucumbers and gherkins	1,675	1,679	1,735
Aubergines (Eggplants)	863	814	816
Chillies and peppers, green	1,759	1,796	1,837
Onions and shallots, green	185	168	169
Onions, dry	1,859	2,007	1,850
Garlic	98	105	105
Beans, green	520	563	604
Carrots and turnips	642	592	594
Watermelons	3,797	4,002	3,810
Cantaloupes and other melons	1,661	1,750	1,679
Bananas	189	201	205
Oranges	1,427	1,427	1,690
Tangerines, mandarins, etc.	744	756	846
Lemons and limes	652	672	784
Grapefruit and pomelos	163	168	191
Apples	2,458	2,504	2,782
Pears	356	355	384
Quinces	95	95	96
Apricots	558	716	661
Sweet cherries	398	338	418
Sour cherries	181	185	193
Peaches and nectarines	539	552	547
Plums and sloes	241	248	246
Strawberries	250	261	292
Grapes	3,613	3,918	4,265
Figs	210	205	244
Tea	206	1,100	1,986
Anise, badian, fennel and coriander	8	9	9
Tobacco, unmanufactured	75	93	85

Aggregate production ('000 metric tons, may include official, semi-official or estimated data): Total cereals 29,250 in 2007, 29,280 in 2008, 33,570 in 2009; Total roots and tubers 4,246 in 2007, 4,197 in 2008, 4,398 in 2009; Total pulses 1,385 in 2007, 960 in 2008, 1,066 in 2009; Total vegetables (incl. melons) 25,625 in 2007, 27,164 in 2008, 26,733 in 2009; Total fruits (excl. melons) 12,287 in 2007, 12,830 in 2008, 14,081 in 2009.

Source: FAO.

LIVESTOCK
('000 head, year ending September)

	2007	2008	2009
Horses	204	189	180
Asses	296	296*	n.a.
Cattle	10,871	11,037	10,860
Buffaloes	101	85	86
Camels	1	1	1
Pigs	1	2	2
Sheep	25,617	25,462	23,975
Goats	6,643	6,286	5,594
Chickens	344,820	269,368	244,280
Ducks	525	482	470
Geese and guinea fowls	830	1,023	1,063
Turkeys	3,227	2,675	3,230

* FAO estimate.
Source: FAO.

LIVESTOCK PRODUCTS
('000 metric tons)

	2007	2008	2009
Cattle meat	431.9	370.6	325.3
Buffalo meat	2.0	1.3	1.0
Sheep meat*	280	278	262
Goat meat*	43	42	37
Horse meat*	2.0	2.0	2.0
Chicken meat	1,068.5	1,087.7	1,293.3
Cows' milk	11,279.3	11,255.2	11,583.3
Buffalo milk	30.4	31.4	32.4
Sheep milk	782.6	746.9	734.2
Goats' milk	237.5	209.6	192.2
Hen eggs	795.3	824.4	864.5
Honey	73.9	81.4	82.0

* FAO estimates.
Source: FAO.

Forestry

ROUNDWOOD REMOVALS
('000 cubic metres, excl. bark)

	2007	2008	2009
Sawlogs, veneer logs and logs for sleepers	7,898	8,126	7,935
Pulpwood	5,560	6,154	6,200
Other industrial wood	216	182	247
Fuel wood	4,645	4,958	5,048
Total	18,319	19,420	19,430

Source: FAO.

SAWNWOOD PRODUCTION
('000 cubic metres, incl. railway sleepers)

	2007	2008	2009
Coniferous (softwood)	4,226	4,076	3,777
Broadleaved (hardwood)	2,373	2,099	2,076
Total	6,599	6,175	5,853

Source: FAO.

TURKEY

Fishing

('000 metric tons, live weight)

	2006	2007	2008
Capture	533.0	632.5	494.1
Common carp	12.1	12.3	11.6
Tarek	12.0	11.6	11.8
Whiting (incl. Poutassou)	12.6	16.3	13.5
Mullets	13.7	13.3	8.4
European pilchard	15.6	20.9	17.5
European sprat	7.3	11.9	39.3
European anchovy	270.0	385.0	251.7
Atlantic bonito	29.7	6.0	6.4
Bluefish	8.4	6.9	4.0
Atlantic horse mackerel	11.8	9.0	10.0
Mediterranean horse mackerel	14.1	23.0	22.1
Sand smelts (Silversides)	7.7	7.5	7.8
Striped venus	48.3	47.2	36.9
Marine molluscs	73.9	67.0	52.7
Aquaculture	129.0	140.0	152.3
Trout	57.7	61.2	68.6
Gilthead seabream	28.5	33.5	31.7
Seabasses	38.4	41.9	49.3
Total catch	662.1	772.5	646.4

Source: FAO.

Mining

('000 metric tons unless otherwise indicated)

	2007	2008	2009
Hard coal	3,233	3,343	3,774
Lignite	70,606	85,953	82,263
Iron ore: gross weight	4,849	4,697	4,170
Iron ore: metal content[1]	2,600	2,500	2,200
Copper[1,2]	81	100	105
Bauxite	1,265.9	818.9	1,473.0
Lead: mine output[2]	32	25[1]	26[1]
Lead: concentrates[1,2]	30	24	25
Chromium[3]	1,678.9	1,885.7	1,573.9
Silver (kilograms)	198,000	294,000	351,600
Gold (kilograms)[1,2,4]	9,920	11,016	14,469
Marble ('000 cu m)	2,801.8	2,262.5	2,715.6
Limestone[5]	7,171	7,200[1]	7,000[1]
Quartzite	2,147.0	1,762.9	1,943.9
Dolomite	15,672.2	16,440.3	11,152.1
Bentonite	1,742.5	1,553.5	932.4
Kaolin	914.1	792.0	727.6
Silica sand[6]	4,998.0	2,422.5	4,499.1
Gypsum	3,241.2	7,338.1	4,369.5
Magnesite: mine output	802.4	677.8	861.2
Feldspar: mine output	6,548.8	6,767.5	4,212.5
Borate minerals: mine output	4,407.0	4,897.9	3,923.5
Borate minerals: concentrates	2,127.8	2,139.2	1,800.0[1]
Nitrogen[7]	n.a.	50.0[1]	100.0[1]
Perlite: mine output	478.6	551.3	522.8
Pumice	3,995.4	3,449.7	4,322.5
Pyrites[6]	109.1	116.1	124.1
Sodium sulphate: concentrates	1,121.0	961.3	4,592.0

[1] Estimated production.
[2] Figures refer to metal content of ores and concentrates.
[3] Figures refer to gross weight of ores.
[4] Figures include estimated output from the by-products of refining other base metals.
[5] Excluding production used for making cement.
[6] Figures refer to gross weight of minerals.
[7] Nitrogen content of ammonia.

Source: US Geological Survey.

2010 ('000 metric tons unless otherwise indicated, provisional): Hard coal 3,667; Lignite 74,437; Iron ore (gross weight) 5,188.

Crude petroleum ('000 metric tons, provisional): 2,131.3 in 2007; 2,222.6 in 2008; 2,489.9 in 2009; 2,602 in 2010.

Natural gas (million cu metres, provisional): 839.8 in 2007; 894.7 in 2008; 660.4 in 2009; 625.7 in 2010.

Industry

SELECTED PRODUCTS
('000 metric tons unless otherwise indicated)

	2008	2009	2010*
Margarine	619.3	702.9	599.7
Flour	3,934.9	4,194.8	4,460.0
Sugar	2,132.2	2,522.4	2,465.6
Beer (million litres)	1,030.8	1,009.3	1,024.0
Alcoholic spirits (million litres)	71.0	68.9	72.2
Cigarettes (with filter)	134.9	132.9	115.2
Cotton yarn	677.1	619.1	711.4
Wool yarn	41.4	32.5	34.8
Products of the paper industry	4,303.2	4,190.9	5,001.9
Wood block flooring ('000 sq m)	30,739.8	44,498.7	64,801.8
Crude steel	26,809.1	25,303.7	29,029.8
Cement	54,027.3	55,741.2	60,580.7
Sulphuric acid	843.1	n.a.	n.a.
Motor oil	6,819.3	4,769.8	4,976.2
Motor gasoline	4,509.1	3,878.3	3,882.8
Liquefied petroleum gas	n.a.	621.8	683.3
Asphalt	2,241.9	2,056.7	2,789.0
Fuel oil (No. 6)	n.a.	2,730.2	n.a.
Kerosene	80.9	13.5	n.a.
Fertilizers (incl. mineral or chemical)	2,994.6	2,957.1	3,551.7
Domestic refrigerators and freezers ('000)	5,640.6	5,348.5	7,161.5
Domestic washing machines ('000)	4,791.3	4,804.3	5,167.8
Ovens ('000)	7,688.0	7,439.5	8,301.0
Vacuum cleaners ('000)	1,819.6	1,633.3	2,249.3
Television receivers ('000, colour)	9,287.4	9,144.9	9,209.6
Tyres for automobiles ('000 units)	16,813.9	15,373.9	17,991.2
Tractors (number)	31,016	21,041	43,406
Passenger motor cars (number)	899,338	752,365	885,135
Pick-up trucks (number)	162,742	84,243	n.a.
Buses and minibuses (number)	42,376	22,500	28,463
Electric energy (gross production, million kWh)	198,418.0	194,812.9	n.a.

* Provisional figures.

Finance

CURRENCY AND EXCHANGE RATES

Monetary Units
100 kuruş = 1 Turkish lira.

Sterling, Dollar and Euro Equivalents (31 December 2010)
£1 sterling = 2.413 liras;
US $1 = 1.541 liras;
€1 = 2.059 liras;
100 Turkish liras = £41.44 = US $64.88 = €48.56.

Average Exchange Rate (Turkish liras per US $)
2008 1.3015
2009 1.5500
2010 1.5028

Note: A new currency, the new Turkish lira, equivalent to 1,000,000 of the former units, was introduced on 1 January 2005. Figures in this survey have been converted retrospectively to reflect this development. (The name of the currency reverted to Turkish lira on 1 January 2009, although new Turkish lira banknotes and coins remained in circulation for a further year.).

TURKEY

CONSOLIDATED BUDGET
(million Turkish liras)

Revenue	2001	2002	2003
General budget	50,890.5	74,603.7	98,558.7
Taxation	39,735.9	59,631.9	84,316.2
Taxes on income	15,647.6	19,343.2	25,716.0
Taxes on wealth	433.3	734.3	2,092.1
Taxes on goods and services	18,103.2	30,064.0	43,927.0
Taxes on foreign trade	5,551.1	9,487.2	12,578.7
Non-tax revenue	7,418.4	10,874.5	10,222.8
Special revenue and funds	3,736.2	4,097.3	4,019.8
Annexed budget revenues	652.5	988.6	1,691.7
Total	**51,543.0**	**75,592.3**	**100,250.4**

Expenditure	2001	2002	2003
Current expenditure	20,448.0	31,108.0	38,513.9
Personnel	15,211.9	23,089.2	30,209.5
Other current expenditure	5,236.1	8,018.8	8,304.4
Investment expenditure	4,149.6	6,891.8	7,179.7
Transfers	55,981.5	77,682.6	94,761.3
Interest payments	41,062.2	51,870.7	58,609.2
Domestic debt interest	37,494.3	46,807.0	52,718.9
Foreign debt interest	3,567.9	5,063.6	5,890.3
Transfers to state-owned economic enterprises	1,107.1	2,170.0	1,881.0
Tax rebates	2,918.2	5,665.8	8,335.9
Social security payments	5,112.0	11,205.0	15,922.0
Other transfers	5,268.8	6,746.1	9,973.2
Total	**80,579.1**	**115,682.4**	**140,454.8**

2004 (million Turkish liras): Total revenue 121,869.9; Total expenditure 152,169.9.

2005 (million Turkish liras): Total revenue 150,462.7; Total expenditure 158,579.4.

2006 (million Turkish liras): Total revenue 173,483.4; Total expenditure 178,126.0.

2007 (million Turkish liras): Total revenue 190,359.8; Total expenditure 204,067.7.

2008 (million Turkish liras): Total revenue 209,598.5; Total expenditure 227,030.6.

2009 (million Turkish liras): Total revenue 215,458.3; Total expenditure 268,219.2.

2010 (million Turkish liras): Total revenue 254,028.5; Total expenditure 293,628.2.

Source: Ministry of Finance, Ankara.

INTERNATIONAL RESERVES
(US $ million at 31 December)

	2008	2009	2010
Gold (national valuation)	3,229	4,121	5,367
IMF special drawing rights	23	1,519	1,494
Reserve position in IMF	174	177	174
Foreign exchange	70,231	69,178	79,046
Total	**73,657**	**74,995**	**86,081**

Source: IMF, *International Financial Statistics*.

MONEY SUPPLY
(million Turkish liras at 31 December)

	2007	2008	2009
Currency outside depository corporations	24,357	28,554	33,845
Transferable deposits	71,996	76,068	95,503
Other deposits	273,335	356,962	391,069
Broad money	**369,689**	**461,584**	**520,417**

Source: IMF, *International Financial Statistics*.

COST OF LIVING
(Consumer Price Index; base: 2003 = 100)

	2008	2009	2010
Food and non-alcoholic beverages	155.9	168.4	186.2
Alcoholic beverages and tobacco	192.5	216.9	292.4
Clothing and footwear	118.2	119.2	124.6
Housing, water, electricity, gas and other fuels	179.9	195.7	208.0
Household goods	138.0	139.2	142.3
Health	123.0	126.7	127.6
Transport	155.6	155.9	171.0
Communications	108.6	112.4	112.1
Recreation and culture	129.9	142.7	146.0
Education	166.7	176.4	185.9
Restaurants and hotels	191.7	209.3	229.1
Miscellaneous goods and services	158.6	179.2	191.7
All items	**154.7**	**164.3**	**178.4**

NATIONAL ACCOUNTS
(million Turkish liras at current prices)

Expenditure on the Gross Domestic Product

	2008	2009	2010
Government final consumption expenditure	121,681.1	140,028.9	157,451.3
Private final consumption expenditure	663,944.3	680,768.3	786,079.2
Increase in stocks	17,949.5	−18,427.3	15,646.8
Gross fixed capital formation	189,094.3	160,718.0	206,879.6
Total domestic expenditure	**992,669.1**	**963,087.9**	**1,166,056.9**
Exports of goods and services	227,252.9	222,102.6	233,076.6
Less Imports of goods and services	269,387.8	232,632.1	294,032.4
GDP in purchasers' values	**950,534.3**	**952,558.6**	**1,105,101.1**
GDP at constant 1998 prices	**101,921.7**	**97,003.1**	**105,680.1**

Gross Domestic Product by Economic Activity

	2008	2009	2010
Agriculture, forestry and fishing	72,274.6	78,775.9	92,803.6
Mining and quarrying	13,458.5	14,235.4	15,785.4
Manufacturing	153,721.5	144,992.2	170,744.9
Electricity, gas and water	20,637.5	22,818.1	25,467.9
Construction	44,657.6	36,577.6	45,239.6
Wholesale and retail trade	116,297.1	103,452.3	123,997.6
Hotels and restaurants	21,034.5	23,714.1	25,589.6
Transport, storage and communications	135,030.2	127,283.5	147,131.1
Financial institutions	33,036.6	42,687.8	41,550.3
Ownership of dwellings	106,137.8	117,287.0	124,667.7
Real estate, renting and business activities	40,670.6	45,167.5	52,710.1
Public administration and defence; compulsory social security	36,436.7	41,270.6	46,028.0
Education	27,878.1	31,813.4	36,796.5
Health and social work	15,577.7	16,448.8	17,933.8
Other community, social and personal services	16,030.8	16,078.2	18,515.2
Private households with employed persons	1,705.4	1,847.3	2,095.6
Sub-total	**854,585.2**	**864,449.7**	**987,056.7**
Taxes, *less* subsidies	110,876.6	109,817.0	137,671.7
Less Financial intermediation services indirectly measured	14,927.5	21,708.1	19,627.3
GDP in purchasers' values	**950,534.3**	**952,558.6**	**1,105,101.1**

TURKEY

BALANCE OF PAYMENTS
(US $ million)

	2008	2009	2010
Exports of goods f.o.b.	140,800	109,647	120,923
Imports of goods f.o.b.	−193,821	−134,497	−177,277
Trade balance	−53,021	−24,850	−56,354
Exports of services	35,243	33,655	33,913
Imports of services	−17,932	−16,906	−19,668
Balance on goods and services	−35,710	−8,101	−42,109
Other income received	6,889	5,164	3,975
Other income paid	−15,251	−13,353	−11,791
Balance on goods, services and income	−44,072	−16,290	−49,925
Current transfers received	2,791	2,833	1,987
Current transfers paid	−678	−534	−623
Current balance	−41,959	−13,991	−48,561
Direct investment abroad	−2,549	−1,553	−1,777
Direct investment from abroad	19,504	8,409	8,931
Portfolio investment assets	−1,244	−2,711	−3,326
Portfolio investment liabilities	−3,770	2,938	19,617
Other investment assets	−12,058	10,985	9,033
Other investment liabilities	34,675	−8,311	27,061
Net errors and omissions	4,696	5,195	4,019
Overall balance	−2,765	919	14,961

Source: IMF, *International Financial Statistics*.

External Trade

PRINCIPAL COMMODITIES
(distribution by SITC, US $ million, excl. military goods)

Imports c.i.f.	2008	2009	2010
Crude materials (inedible) except fuels	16,199.5	9,936.1	15,392.6
Metalliferous ores and metal scrap	9,865.7	5,236.2	8,199.9
Mineral fuels, lubricants, etc.	48,281.0	29,905.1	38,496.1
Petroleum, petroleum products, etc.	27,034.4	15,171.8	21,037.2
Chemicals and related products	25,541.7	20,265.7	25,446.4
Organic chemicals	4,168.6	3,127.7	4,172.3
Medicinal and pharmaceutical products	4,738.4	4,418.9	4,777.7
Plastics in primary forms	7,321.0	5,306.1	7,650.0
Basic manufactures	36,295.0	23,186.6	31,801.9
Textile yarn, fabrics, etc.	5,801.5	4,879.7	6,701.8
Iron and steel	15,033.7	7,680.3	9,720.7
Machinery and transport equipment	51,594.8	41,055.1	53,875.3
Power-generating machinery and equipment	6,236.3	5,585.6	6,716.9
Machinery specialized for particular industries	5,315.0	3,271.0	5,138.4
General industrial machinery, equipment and parts	7,899.8	5,848.2	6,873.1
Road vehicles	12,358.4	8,744.7	13,174.4
Miscellaneous manufactured articles	11,486.3	9,324.8	11,638.1
Non-monetary gold, unwrought or semi-manufactured	4,991.0	1,632.4	2,523.5
Total (incl. others)	201,963.6	140,928.4	185,541.0

Exports f.o.b.	2008	2009	2010
Food and live animals	9,155.0	9,126.0	10,507.4
Vegetables and fruit	5,308.0	5,353.8	6,157.0
Chemicals and related products	6,121.8	5,293.0	6,807.2
Basic manufactures	40,595.3	28,599.9	33,213.8
Textile yarn, fabrics, etc.	9,406.9	7,733.3	8,973.4
Non-metallic mineral manufactures	3,987.8	3,512.3	3,708.5
Iron and steel	16,841.6	9,081.1	10,224.9
Machinery and transport equipment	39,147.4	28,789.0	31,821.5
Road vehicles	17,991.1	11,891.2	13,524.1
Miscellaneous manufactured articles	20,796.9	17,580.7	19,780.3
Clothing and accessories (excl. footwear)	13,589.4	11,553.5	12,760.2
Total (incl. others)	132,027.2	102,142.6	113,979.5

PRINCIPAL TRADING PARTNERS
(US $ million, excl. military goods*)

Imports c.i.f. (excl. grants)	2008	2009	2010
Algeria	3,262.2	2,028.1	2,274.9
Austria	1,525.5	1,203.6	1,439.3
Belgium	3,150.7	2,371.5	3,213.7
China, People's Republic	15,658.2	12,676.6	17,180.8
France	9,022.0	7,091.8	8,176.6
Germany	18,687.2	14,097.0	17,549.2
India	2,457.9	1,902.6	3,409.9
Iran	8,199.7	3,406.0	7,644.8
Italy	11,011.5	7,673.4	10,203.7
Japan	4,026.8	2,782.0	3,297.8
Korea, Republic	4,091.7	3,118.2	4,764.0
Libya	336.3	402.6	425.7
Netherlands	3,056.3	2,543.1	3,156.0
Romania	3,547.8	2,258.0	3,449.2
Russia	31,364.5	19,450.0	21,599.6
Saudi Arabia	3,322.4	1,686.7	2,437.2
Spain	4,548.2	3,776.9	4,840.1
Sweden	1,908.9	1,891.0	1,922.8
Switzerland	5,588.4	1,999.4	3,153.7
Ukraine	6,106.3	3,156.7	3,832.7
United Kingdom	5,324.0	3,473.4	4,680.6
USA	11,975.9	8,575.7	12,318.8
Total (incl. others)	201,963.6	140,928.4	185,541.0

Exports f.o.b.	2008	2009	2010
Algeria	1,613.6	1,777.2	1,506.6
Austria	991.0	807.1	834.9
Belgium	2,122.4	1,795.7	1,961.2
Bulgaria	2,151.5	1,385.5	1,497.8
China, People's Republic	1,437.2	1,600.3	2,259.8
Denmark	953.4	690.9	766.0
Egypt	1,426.5	2,599.0	2,260.8
France	6,617.5	6,211.4	6,055.1
Germany	12,951.8	9,793.0	11,486.8
Greece	2,430.0	1,629.6	1,456.2
Iran	2,029.8	2,024.5	3,043.4
Iraq	3,916.7	5,123.4	6,041.9
Israel	1,935.2	1,522.4	2,083.0
Italy	7,819.0	5,889.0	6,508.6
Netherlands	3,143.8	2,127.3	2,462.2
Poland	1,586.8	1,322.2	1,504.5
Romania	3,987.5	2,201.9	2,599.0
Russia	6,483.0	3,189.6	4,631.5
Saudi Arabia	2,201.9	1,768.2	2,219.4
Spain	4,047.3	2,818.5	3,563.5
Switzerland	2,856.8	3,935.1	2,057.1
United Arab Emirates	7,975.4	2,896.6	3,337.7
United Kingdom	8,158.7	5,938.0	7,238.4
USA	4,299.9	3,240.6	3,770.8
Total (incl. others)	132,027.2	102,142.6	113,979.5

* Imports by country of origin, exports by country of last consignment.

TURKEY

Transport

RAILWAYS
(traffic)

	2007	2008	2009
Passengers carried ('000)	81,260	79,187	80,092
Passenger-km (million)	5,553	5,097	5,374
Freight carried ('000 metric tons)*	20,849	22,870	21,270
Freight ton-km (million)	9,921	10,739	10,326

*Excluding parcels and departmental traffic.

ROAD TRAFFIC
(motor vehicles by use)

	2007	2008	2009
Passenger cars	6,472,156	6,796,629	7,093,964
Minibuses	372,601	383,548	384,053
Buses and coaches	189,128	199,934	201,033
Small trucks	1,890,459	2,066,007	2,204,951
Trucks	729,202	744,217	727,302
Motorcycles and mopeds	2,003,492	2,181,383	2,303,261
Special purpose vehicles	38,573	35,100	34,104

SHIPPING

Merchant Fleet
(registered at 31 December)

	2007	2008	2009
Number of vessels	1,252	1,301	1,344
Total displacement ('000 grt)	4,995.1	5,181.0	5,450.5

Source: IHS Fairplay, *World Fleet Statistics*.

International Sea-borne Traffic

	1999	2000	2001
Vessels entered (number)	23,097	25,199	20,431
Passengers disembarked (number)	482,715	600,948	590,454
Goods unloaded ('000 metric tons)*	71,453	79,337	68,342
Vessels cleared (number)	18,097	18,385	18,916
Passengers embarked (number)	484,244	593,493	599,474
Goods loaded ('000 metric tons)*	25,075	25,477	34,137

*Including timber.

2004: Passengers disembarked (number) 688,965; Goods unloaded ('000 metric tons, incl. timber) 105,941; Passengers embarked (number) 701,250; Goods loaded ('000 metric tons, incl. timber) 39,946.

2005: Passengers disembarked (number) 698,915; Goods unloaded ('000 metric tons, incl. timber) 107,526; Passengers embarked (number) 705,937; Goods loaded ('000 metric tons, incl. timber) 36,601.

CIVIL AVIATION
(scheduled services)

	2003	2004	2005
Domestic services:			
Kilometres flown ('000)	28,180	28,489	35,886
Number of passengers	4,991,517	5,805,291	7,151,491
Passenger-km ('000)	2,751,910	3,223,299	3,991,885
Freight handled (metric tons)	29,146	30,710	31,504
Total ton-km ('000)	275,681	321,118	392,055
International services:			
Kilometres flown ('000)	101,738	109,038	122,899
Number of passengers	4,802,897	5,617,506	6,486,320
Passenger-km ('000)	12,223,997	14,227,375	16,359,597
Freight handled (metric tons)	88,993	93,736	87,851
Total ton-km ('000)	1,617,729	1,849,177	2,104,407

Passengers carried (million): 58.8 in 2006; 66.5 in 2007; 75.0 in 2008; 78.7 in 2009.

Freight handled ('000 metric tons): 1,279.3 in 2006; 1,447.6 in 2007; 1,534.6 in 2008; 1,597.7 in 2009.

Tourism

VISITOR ARRIVALS BY NATIONALITY
(provisional)

Country	2008	2009	2010
Austria	520,334	548,117	500,321
Azerbaijan	459,593	424,155	486,381
Belgium	596,442	592,078	543,003
Bulgaria	1,255,343	1,406,604	1,433,970
France	885,006	932,809	928,376
Georgia	830,184	995,381	1,112,193
Germany	4,415,525	4,488,350	4,385,263
Greece	572,212	616,489	670,297
Iran	1,134,965	1,383,261	1,885,097
Israel	558,183	311,582	109,559
Italy	600,261	634,886	671,060
Netherlands	1,141,580	1,127,150	1,073,064
Russia	2,879,278	2,694,733	3,107,043
Sweden	404,092	401,740	447,270
Ukraine	730,689	574,700	568,227
United Kingdom	2,169,924	2,426,749	2,673,605
USA	679,445	667,159	642,768
Total (incl. others)	26,336,677	27,077,114	28,632,204

Tourism receipts (million US $, excl. passenger transport, incl. expenditure of Turkish nationals residing abroad): 21,950.8 in 2008; 21,249.3 in 2009; 20,806.7 in 2010.

Communications Media

	2007	2008	2009
Telephones ('000 main lines in use)	18,201.0	17,502.2	16,534.4
Mobile cellular telephones ('000 subscribers)	61,975.8	65,824.1	62,779.6
Internet users ('000)*	20,901.0	25,404.3	27,232.9
Broadband subscribers ('000)	4,753.8	5,749.9	6,386.3

*Estimates.

Personal computers: 4,400,000 (61.0 per 1,000 persons) in 2006.
Radio receivers ('000 in use): 11,300 in 1997.
Television receivers ('000 in use): 21,152 in 2001.
Book production (titles): 2,920 in 1999.
Daily newspapers (number): 588 in 2004.
Non-daily newspapers (number): 1,771 in 2004.

Sources: International Telecommunication Union; UNESCO Institute for Statistics; UN, *Statistical Yearbook*.

Education

(2010/11, unless otherwise indicated, provisional figures)

	Institutions	Teachers	Students
Pre-primary	27,606	47,289	1,115,818
Primary	32,797	503,328	10,981,100
Secondary:			
general	4,102	118,378	2,676,123
vocational and teacher training	5,179	104,327	2,072,487
Higher*	1,306	84,785	2,181,217

*Figures for 2005/06.

Adult literacy rate (UNESCO estimates): 88.7% (males 96.2%; females 81.3%) in 2007 (Source: UNESCO Institute for Statistics).

TURKEY

Directory

The Government

HEAD OF STATE

President: ABDULLAH GÜL (took office 28 August 2007).

COUNCIL OF MINISTERS
(May 2011)

The executive is formed by the Adalet ve Kalkınma Partisi (AKP).

Prime Minister: RECEP TAYYIP ERDOĞAN.
Deputy Prime Ministers: BÜLENT ARINÇ, ALI BABACAN, CEMIL ÇIÇEK.
Minister of Foreign Affairs: Prof. Dr AHMET DAVUTOĞLU.
Minister of Justice: AHMET KAHRAMAN.
Minister of National Defence: MEHMET VECDI GÖNÜL.
Minister of Internal Affairs: OSMAN GÜNEŞ.
Minister of Finance: MEHMET ŞIMŞEK.
Minister of National Education: NIMET ÇUBUKÇU.
Minister of Public Works and Settlement: FARUK MUSTAFA DEMIR.
Minister of Health: Prof. Dr RECEP AKDAĞ.
Minister of Transport: MEHMET HABIB SOLUK.
Minister of Agriculture and Rural Affairs: Dr MEHMET MEHDI EKER.
Minister of Labour and Social Security: ÖMER DINÇER.
Minister of Industry and Trade: NIHAT ERGÜN.
Minister of Energy and Natural Resources: Dr TANER YILDIZ.
Minister of Culture and Tourism: ERTUĞRUL GÜNAY.
Minister of the Environment and Forestry: Prof. Dr VEYSEL EROĞLU.
Minister of State and Chief Negotiator of Turkey for European Union Affairs: EGEMEN BAĞIŞ.
Ministers of State: Prof. Dr MEHMET AYDIN, MEHMET ZAFER ÇAĞLAYAN, FARUK ÇELIK, SELMA ALIYE KAVAF, FARUK NAFIZ ÖZAK, HAYATI YAZICI, CEVDET YILMAZ.

MINISTRIES

President's Office: Cumhurbaşkanlığı Köşkü, 06689 Çankaya, Ankara; tel. (312) 4702345; fax (312) 4701316; e-mail cumhurbaskanligi@tccb.gov.tr; internet www.cankaya.gov.tr.
Prime Minister's Office: Başbakanlık, Bakanlıklar, Ankara; tel. (312) 4137000; fax (312) 4180476; e-mail bimer@basbakanlik.gov.tr; internet www.basbakanlik.gov.tr.
Deputy Prime Ministers' Office: Başbakan yard. ve Devlet Bakanı, Bakanlıklar, Ankara; tel. (312) 4191621; fax (312) 4191547.
Ministry of Agriculture and Rural Affairs: Tarım ve Köyişleri Bakanlığı, Kampüsü Eskişehir Yolu 9km Lodumlu, Ankara; tel. (312) 2873360; fax (312) 2863964; e-mail admin@tarim.gov.tr; internet www.tarim.gov.tr.
Ministry of Culture and Tourism: Kültür ve Turizm Bakanlığı, Atatürk Bul. 29, 06050 Opera, Ankara; tel. (312) 3090850; fax (312) 3124359; e-mail info@kulturturizm.gov.tr; internet www.kultur.gov.tr.
Ministry of Energy and Natural Resources: Enerji ve Tabii Kaynaklar Bakanlığı, İnönü Bul. 27, Bahçelievler, Ankara; tel. (312) 2126420; fax (312) 2156586; e-mail bilgi@enerji.gov.tr; internet www.enerji.gov.tr.
Ministry of the Environment and Forestry: Çevre ve Orman Bakanlığı, Söğütözü Cad. 14E, Ankara; tel. (312) 2075000; fax (312) 2150094; e-mail webmaster@cevreorman.gov.tr; internet www.cevreorman.gov.tr.
Ministry of Finance: Maliye Bakanlığı, Dikmen Cad., Ankara; tel. (312) 4250018; fax (312) 4257816; e-mail bshalk@maliye.gov.tr; internet www.maliye.gov.tr.
Ministry of Foreign Affairs: Dişişleri Bakanlığı, Dr Sadık Ahmet Cad. 12, 06100 Balgat, Ankara; tel. (312) 2921000; fax (312) 2873869; e-mail info@mfa.gov.tr; internet www.mfa.gov.tr.
Ministry of Health: Sağlık Bakanlığı, Mithatpasa Cad. 3 Sihhiye, 06434 Ankara; tel. (312) 5852250; fax (312) 4339885; e-mail info@saglik.gov.tr; internet www.saglik.gov.tr.
Ministry of Industry and Trade: Sanayi ve Ticaret Bakanlığı, Eskişehir Yolu üzeri 7 km, Ankara; tel. (312) 2015000; fax (312) 2196738; e-mail webmaster@sanayi.gov.tr; internet www.sanayi.gov.tr.
Ministry of Internal Affairs: Içişleri Bakanlığı, Bakanlıklar, Ankara; tel. (312) 4224000; fax (312) 4181795; e-mail basin@icisleri.gov.tr; internet www.icisleri.gov.tr.
Ministry of Justice: Adalet Bakanlığı, 06659 Kizilay, Ankara; tel. (312) 4177770; fax (312) 4193370; e-mail info@adalet.gov.tr; internet www.adalet.gov.tr.
Ministry of Labour and Social Security: Çalışma ve Sosyal Güvenlik Bakanlığı, İnönü Bul. 42, 06100 Emek, Ankara; tel. (312) 2966000; fax (312) 4179765; e-mail iletisim@csgb.gov.tr; internet www.csgb.gov.tr.
Ministry of National Defence: Milli Savunma Bakanlığı, 06100 Ankara; tel. (312) 4026100; fax (312) 4184737; internet www.msb.gov.tr.
Ministry of National Education: Milli Eğitim Bakanlığı, Atatürk Bul., Bakanlıklar, Ankara; tel. (312) 4191410; fax (312) 4177027; e-mail meb@meb.gov.tr; internet www.meb.gov.tr.
Ministry of Public Works and Settlement: Bayındırlık ve İskan Bakanlığı, Vekaletler Cad. 1, 06100 Ankara; tel. (312) 4186443; fax (312) 4251288; e-mail bilgiedinme@bayindirlik.gov.tr; internet www.bayindirlik.gov.tr.
Ministry of Transport: Ulaştırma Bakanlığı, Hakkı Turayliç Cad. 5, 06338 Emek, Ankara; tel. (312) 2031116; fax (212) 2124930; e-mail okm@ubak.gov.tr; internet www.ubak.gov.tr.

Legislature

Büyük Millet Meclisi
(Grand National Assembly)

TBMM 06543, Bakanlıklar, Ankara; tel. (312) 4205151; fax (312) 4206756; e-mail gensek@tbmm.gov.tr; internet www.tbmm.gov.tr.

Speaker: MEHMET ALI ŞAHIN.

General Election, 22 July 2007

Party	Valid votes cast	% of valid votes	Seats
Adalet ve Kalkınma Partisi (AKP)	16,340,534	46.66	341
Cumhuriyet Halk Partisi (CHP)	7,300,234	20.85	112
Milliyetçi Hareket Partisi (MHP)	5,004,003	14.29	70
Independents	1,822,253	5.20	26
Demokrat Parti (DP)	1,895,807	5.41	0
Genç Parti (GP)	1,062,352	3.03	0
Saadet Partisi (SP)	817,843	2.34	0
Others	774,289	2.21	0
Total	35,017,315*	100.00	549†

* Excluding 870,653 invalid votes.
† One of the elected representatives of the MHP died on 26 July 2007, thus one seat remained vacant.

Election Commission

Yüksek Seçim Kurulu (YSK) (High Electoral Board): Kızılırmak Cad. 9, 06640 Küçükesat, Ankara; tel. (312) 4191040; fax (312) 4195308; e-mail bilgiedinme@ysk.gov.tr; internet www.ysk.gov.tr; independent; Chair. ALI EM.

Political Organizations

Political parties were banned from 1980–83. Legislation enacted in March 1986 stipulated that a party must have organizations in at least 45 provinces, and in two-thirds of the districts in each of these provinces, in order to take part in an election. A political party is recognized by the Government as a legitimate parliamentary group only if it has at least 20 deputies in the Grand National Assembly.

In mid-1992, following the adoption of less restrictive legislation concerning the formation of political parties, several new parties were established, and the left-wing CHP, dissolved in 1981, was reactivated.

In December 2009 the Kurdish nationalist Demokratik Toplum Partisi (DTP—Democratic Society Party) was banned by the Constitutional Court due to its alleged links to the proscribed Partiya Karkeren Kurdistan (PKK—Kurdistan Workers' Party).

TURKEY

Adalet ve Kalkınma Partisi (AKP) (Justice and Development Party): Söğütözü Cad. 6, Çankaya, Ankara; tel. (312) 2045000; fax (312) 2045020; e-mail rte@akparti.org.tr; internet www.akparti.org.tr; f. 2001; Islamist-orientated; Leader Recep Tayyip Erdoğan.

Bağımsız Türkiye Partisi (BTP) (Independent Turkey Party): Bestekar Sok. 45 Kavaklıdere, Ankara; tel. (312) 4269146; fax (312) 4262908; e-mail btp@btp.org.tr; internet www.btp.org.tr; f. 2001; Chair. Prof. Dr Haydar Baş.

Barış ve Demokrasi Partisi (BDP) (Peace and Democracy Party): Ankara; internet www.bdp.org.tr; f. 2008; Kurdish nationalist, social democratic; following the dissolution of the pro-Kurdish Demokratik Toplum Partisi (DTP), its representatives in the Grand National Assembly and some elected officials at the provincial and local levels joined the BDP; Chair. Selahattin Demirtaş, Gülten Kışanak.

Büyük Birlik Partisi (BBP) (Great Unity Party): Tuna Cad. 28, Yenişehir, Ankara; tel. (312) 4340923; fax (312) 4355818; e-mail iletisim@bbp.org.tr; internet www.bbp.org.tr; f. 1993; Chair. Yalçın Topçu.

Cumhuriyet Halk Partisi (CHP) (Republican People's Party): Anadolu Bul. 12, Söğütözü, Ankara; tel. (312) 2074000; fax (312) 2074039; e-mail halklailiskiler@chp.org.tr; internet www.chp.org.tr; f. 1923 by Mustafa Kemal (Atatürk); dissolved in 1981 and reactivated in 1992; merged with Sosyal Demokrat Halkçı Parti (Social Democratic Populist Party) in Feb. 1995 and with the Yeni Türkiye Partisi in Oct. 2004; left-wing; Chair. Kemal Kılıçdaroğlu; Sec.-Gen. Önder Sav.

Demokrat Parti (DP) (Democratic Party): Akay Cad. 16, Kızılay, Ankara; tel. (312) 4441946; fax (312) 4168683; e-mail dp@dp.org.tr; internet www.dp.org.tr; f. 1983 as Doğru Yol Partisi (True Path Party); renamed as above in May 2007; merged with Anavatan Partisi (Motherland Party) in Nov. 2009; centre-right; Chair. Namık Kemal Zeybek.

Demokratik Sol Parti (DSP) (Democratic Left Party): Mareşal Fevzi Çakmak Cad. 17, Ankara; tel. (312) 2124950; fax (312) 2124188; e-mail dsp@dsp.org.tr; internet www.dsp.org.tr; f. 1985, drawing support from mems of the fmr Republican People's Party; centre-left; Chair. Masum Türker.

Emek Partisi (EMEP) (Labour Party of Turkey): Tarlabasi Bul., Kamerhatun Mah., Alhatun Sok. 25/1, Beyoglu, Istanbul; tel. (212) 3612508; fax (212) 3612512; e-mail info@emep.org; internet www.emep.org; f. 1996; advocates scientific socialism; Pres. Levent Tüzel.

Genç Parti (GP) (Youth Party): İller Sok. 7, Mebusevleri, 06580 Tandoğan, Ankara; fax (312) 2969757; internet www.gencpartiankara.com; f. 2002; populist, nationalist; Leader Cem Uzan.

Halkın Sesi Partisi (HAS Parti) (People's Voice Party): Oğuzlar Mah. 1397, Sok. 14, 06520 Balgat, Ankara; tel. (312) 2852484; fax (312) 2852480; e-mail iletisim@hasparti.org.tr; internet www.hasparti.org.tr; f. 2010 by fmr Chair. of Saadet Partisi; Chair. Prof. Dr Numan Kurtulmuş.

Halkın Yükselişi Partisi (HYP) (People's Ascent Party): Filistin Sok. 30, Gaziosmanpaşa, Ankara; tel. (312) 4480621; fax (312) 4476968; e-mail hypgenelmerkez@hyp.org.tr; internet www.hyp.org.tr; f. 2005; advocates social democratic principles; Leader Prof. Dr Yaşar Nuri Öztürk.

İşçi Partisi (IP) (Workers' Party): Toros Sok. 9, Sıhhıye, Ankara; tel. (312) 2318111; fax (312) 2292994; e-mail int@ip.org.tr; internet www.ip.org.tr; f. 1992; Chair. Doğu Perinçek.

Liberal Demokratik Parti (LDP) (Liberal Democratic Party): İstanbul; tel. (212) 2546860; fax (212) 2550291; e-mail ldp@liberal.tc; internet www.ldp.org.tr; f. 1994; Chair. Cem Toker.

Millet Partisi (MP) (Nation Party): Atatürk Bul. 72/37, Kızılay, Ankara; tel. (312) 4194060; fax (312) 3127651; e-mail milletpartisi@hotmail.com; internet www.milletpartisi.org; f. 1992; Chair. Aykut Edibali.

Milliyetçi Hareket Partisi (MHP) (Nationalist Action Party): Ceyhun Atif Kansu Cad. 128, Balgat, Ankara; tel. (312) 4725555; fax (312) 4731544; e-mail bilgi@mhp.org.tr; internet www.mhp.org.tr; f. 1983; fmrly the Democratic and Conservative Party; Leader Devlet Bahçeli; Sec.-Gen. Faruk Bal.

Özgürlük ve Dayanisma Partisi (ODP) (Freedom and Solidarity Party): GMK Bul. 87/18, Maltepe, Ankara; tel. (312) 2317232; fax 2320347; e-mail odp@odp.org.tr; internet www.odp.org.tr; f. 1996; Chair. Alper Taş.

Özgür Toplum Parti (OTP) (Free Society Party): f. June 2003; associated with Halkın Demokrasi Partisi; Leader Ahmet Turan Demir.

Saadet Partisi (SP) (Felicity Party): Ziyabey Cad. 2, Sok. 15, 06520 Balgat, Ankara; tel. (312) 2848800; fax (312) 2856246; e-mail bilgi@saadet.org.tr; internet www.saadet.org.tr; f. 2001; replaced conservative wing of Islamist fundamentalist and free-market advocating Fazilet Partisi (Virtue Party), which was banned in that year; Chair. Prof. Dr Mustafa Kamalak.

Türkiye Komünist Partisi (TKP) (Communist Party of Turkey): Osmanağa Mah. Nüzhet Efendi Sok. 4, Kadıköy, İstanbul; tel. (216) 3455480; fax (216) 3461137; e-mail tkp@tkp.org.tr; internet www.tkp.org.tr; f. 1981 as the Party of Socialist Power; name changed as above in 2001; Chair. Erkan Baş.

Yurt Partisi (Homeland Party): Meşrutiyet Cad. Bayındır 2, Sok. 59/5, Kızılay, Ankara; tel. (312) 4189034; fax (312) 4189364; e-mail iletisim@yurtpartisi.org.tr; internet www.yurtpartisi.org.tr; f. 2002; nationalist and conservative party; Leader Saadettin Tantan.

The following proscribed organizations were engaged in an armed struggle against the Government:

Devrimci Halk Kurtuluş Partisi—Cephesi (DHKP—C) (Revolutionary People's Liberation Party—Front): e-mail dhkc@ozgurluk.org; faction of Dev-Sol; subsumed parent org. in 1996.

Partiya Karkeren Kurdistan (PKK) (Kurdistan Workers' Party): internet www.pkkonline.net; f. 1978; 57-mem. directorate; launched struggle for an independent Kurdistan in 1984; declared cease-fire 2000; renamed Congress for Freedom and Democracy in Kurdistan (KADEK) April 2002 and KONGRA-GEL Nov. 2003; return to fmr name, PKK, announced April 2005, following resumption of armed struggle; name KONGRA-GEL continued to be used by some elements; military wing, Hezên Parastina Gel (HPG—People's Defence Forces), re-emerged 2004; Chair. Murat Karayilan; Leader Abdullah Öcalan.

Diplomatic Representation

EMBASSIES IN TURKEY

Afghanistan: Cinnah Cad. 88, 06551 Çankaya, Ankara; tel. (312) 4422523; fax (312) 4426256; Ambassador Salahuddin Rabbani.

Albania: Ebu Ziya Tevfik Sok. 17, Çankaya, Ankara; tel. (312) 4416103; fax (312) 4416109; e-mail embassy.ankara@mfa.gov.al; Ambassador Altin Kodra.

Algeria: Şehit Ersan Cad. 42, 06680 Çankaya, Ankara; tel. (312) 4687719; fax (312) 4687593; e-mail cezayirbe@yahoo.fr; Ambassador Mouloud Hamai.

Argentina: Uğur Mumcu Cad. 60/1, 06700 Gaziosmanpaşa, Ankara; tel. (312) 4462062; fax (312) 4462063; e-mail embargturquia@yahoo.com.ar; Ambassador Armando Juan José Maffei.

Australia: Uğur Mumcu Cad. 88, 7th Floor, 06700 Gaziosmanpaşa, Ankara; tel. (312) 4599500; fax (312) 4464827; e-mail info-ankara@dfat.gov.au; internet www.turkey.embassy.gov.au; Ambassador Ian Biggs.

Austria: Atatürk Bul. 189, 06680 Kavaklıdere, Ankara; tel. (312) 4055190; fax (312) 4189454; e-mail ankara-ob@bmeia.gv.at; internet www.aussenministerium.at/botschaft/ankara.html; Ambassador Dr Heidemaria Gürer.

Azerbaijan: Diplomatik Site, Bakü Sok. 1, 06450 Oran, Ankara; tel. (312) 4911681; fax (312) 4920430; e-mail azer-tr@tr.net; Ambassador Faig Bagirov.

Bahrain: İlkbahar Mah. 612, Sok. 10, Oran-Çankaya, Ankara; tel. (312) 4912656; fax (312) 4912676; e-mail bahrainembassyank@bahembassyank.com; Ambassador Ibrahim Yousuf al-Abdullah.

Bangladesh: Birlik Mah. 391, Cad. 16, 06610 Çankaya, Ankara; tel. (312) 4952719; fax (312) 4952744; e-mail bdootankara@ttmail.com; Ambassador Zulfiqur Rahman.

Belarus: Abidin Daver Sok. 17, 06550 Çankaya, Ankara; tel. (312) 4416769; fax (312) 4416674; e-mail turkey@belembassy.org; Ambassador Valery Kolesnik.

Belgium: Mahatma Gandhi Cad. 55, 06700 Gaziosmanpaşa, Ankara; tel. (312) 4056166; fax (312) 4468251; e-mail ankara@diplobel.fed.be; internet www.diplomatie.be/ankara; Ambassador Pol de Witte.

Bosnia and Herzegovina: Turan Emeksiz Sok., Park Bloklan, B Blok 3/9–10, Gaziosmanpaşa, Ankara; tel. (312) 4273602; fax (312) 4273604; e-mail bh_emba@ttmail.com; Ambassador Dragoljub Ljepoja.

Brazil: Reşit Galip Cad., İlkadım Sok. 1, 06700 Gaziosmanpaşa, Ankara; tel. (312) 4481840; fax (312) 4481838; e-mail brasemb@brasembancara.org; internet www.brasembancara.org; Ambassador Marcelo Jardim.

Bulgaria: Atatürk Bul. 124, 06680 Kavaklıdere, Ankara; tel. (312) 4672071; fax (312) 4672074; e-mail bulankemb@ttmail.com; internet www.mfa.bg/en/67/; Ambassador Krasimir Tulechki.

Canada: Cinnah Cad. 58, 06690 Çankaya, Ankara; tel. (312) 4092700; fax (312) 4092811; e-mail ankra@international.gc.ca; internet www.turkey.gc.ca; Ambassador Mark Edward Bailey.

TURKEY

Chile: Reşit Galip Cad., İrfanli Sok. 14/1–3, 06700 Gaziosmanpaşa, Ankara; tel. (312) 4473418; fax (312) 4474725; e-mail embassy@chile.org.tr; internet www.chile.org.tr; Ambassador Luis Kenneth Palma Castillo.

China, People's Republic: Gölgeli Sok. 34, 06700 Gaziosmanpaşa, Ankara; tel. (312) 4360628; fax (312) 4464248; e-mail chinaemb_tr@mfa.gov.cn; internet www.chinaembassy.org.tr; Ambassador Gong Xiaosheng.

Croatia: Kelebek Sok. 15/A, 06700 Gaziosmanpaşa, Ankara; tel. (312) 4469460; fax (312) 4464700; e-mail ankara@mvpei.hr; internet tr.mvp.hr; Ambassador Dražen Hrastić.

Cuba: Şölen Sok. 8, 06550 Çankaya, Ankara; tel. (312) 4428970; fax (312) 4414007; e-mail embacubatur@tr.net; Ambassador Jorge Quesada Concepcion.

Czech Republic: Kaptanpaşa Sok. 15, 06700 Gaziosmanpaşa, Ankara; tel. (312) 4056139; fax (312) 4463084; e-mail ankara@embassy.mzv.cz; internet www.mzv.cz/ankara; Ambassador Václav Hubinger.

Denmark: Mahatma Gandhi Cad. 74, 06700 Gaziosmanpaşa, Ankara; tel. (312) 4466141; fax (312) 4472498; e-mail ankamb@um.dk; internet www.ambankara.um.dk; Ambassador Ole Egberg Mikkelsen.

Ecuador: Kelebek Sok. 21/1, Ankara; tel. (312) 4460160; fax (312) 4460173; e-mail eecuturquia@mmrree.gov.ec; Ambassador Saa Augusto Corriere.

Egypt: Atatürk Bul. 126, 06680 Kavaklıdere, Ankara; tel. (312) 4261026; fax (312) 4270099; e-mail ankara@egyptturkey.com; internet www.egyptturkey.com; Ambassador Abd al-Rahman Salah el-Din.

Estonia: Gölgeli Sok. 16, 06700 Gaziosmanpaşa, Ankara; tel. (312) 4056970; fax (312) 4056976; e-mail embassy.ankara@mfa.ee; internet www.estemb.org.tr/embassy; Ambassador Aivo Orav.

Ethiopia: Uğur Mumcu Sok. 74/1–2, 06700 Gaziosmanpaşa, Ankara; tel. (312) 4360400; fax (312) 4481938; e-mail ethembank@ttnet.net.tr; Ambassador Mulatu Teshome Wirtu.

Finland: Kader Sok. 44, 06700 Gaziosmanpaşa, Ankara; tel. (312) 4574400; fax (312) 4680072; e-mail sanomat.ank@formin.fi; internet www.finland.org.tr; Ambassador Kirsti Eskelinen.

France: Paris Cad. 70, 06540 Kavaklıdere, Ankara; tel. (312) 4554545; fax (312) 4554527; e-mail ambaank@yahoo.fr; internet www.ambafrance-tr.org; Ambassador Bernard Jean M. Emié.

The Gambia: Hilal Mah. 31, Yıldız, Ankara; Ambassador Gibril Joof.

Georgia: Kılıç Ali Sok. 12, Oran, Ankara; tel. (312) 4918030; fax (312) 4918032; e-mail ankara.emb@mfa.gov.ge; internet www.turkey.mfa.gov.ge; Ambassador Tariel Lebanidze.

Germany: Atatürk Bul. 114, 06690 Kavaklıdere, Ankara; tel. (312) 4555100; fax (312) 4555337; e-mail german.embassyank@anka.diplo.de; internet www.ankara.diplo.de; Ambassador Dr Eckart Cuntz.

Greece: Zia ür-Rahman Cad. 9–11, 06670 Gaziosmanpaşa, Ankara; tel. (312) 4480873; fax (312) 4463191; e-mail gremb.ank@mfa.gr; Ambassador Fotios-Jean Xydas.

Holy See: Apostolic Nunciature, Birlik Mah. 3, Cad. 37, PK 33, 06552 Çankaya, Ankara; tel. (312) 4953514; fax (312) 4953540; e-mail vatican@tr.net; Apostolic Nuncio Most Rev. Antonio Lucibello (Titular Archbishop of Thurio).

Hungary: Sancak Mah. Layoş, Koşut Cad. 2, Yıldız, Çankaya, Ankara; tel. (312) 4422273; fax (312) 4415049; e-mail mission.ank@kum.hu; internet www.mfa.gov.hu/kulkepviselet/TR/hu; Ambassador István Szabó.

India: Cinnah Cad. 77, 06680 Çankaya, Ankara; tel. (312) 4382195; fax (312) 4403429; e-mail chancery@indembassy.org.tr; internet www.indembassy.org.tr; Chargé d'affaires a.i. Dr A. V. S. Ramesh Chandra.

Indonesia: Abdullah Cevdet Sok. 10, 06680 Çankaya, Ankara; tel. (312) 4382190; fax (312) 4382193; e-mail indoank@indoank.org; Ambassador Nahari Agustini.

Iran: Tahran Cad. 10, 06700 Kavaklıdere, Ankara; tel. (312) 4682821; fax (312) 4682823; e-mail iranembassy_ankara@hotmail.com; Ambassador Bahman Hosseinpour.

Iraq: Turan Emeksiz Sok. 11, 06700 Gaziosmanpaşa, Ankara; tel. (312) 4687421; fax (312) 4684832; e-mail ankemb@iraqmofamail.com; Ambassador Abd al-Amir Kamal Abu Tabikh.

Ireland: Uğur Mumcu Cad. 88, MNG Binası B Blok Kat 3, 06700 Gaziosmanpaşa, Ankara; tel. (312) 4466172; fax (312) 4468061; e-mail ankaraembassy@dfa.ie; internet www.embassyofireland.org.tr; Ambassador Thomas Russell.

Israel: Mahatma Gandhi Cad. 85, 06700 Gaziosmanpaşa, Ankara; tel. (312) 4597500; fax (312) 4597555; e-mail info@ankara.mfa.gov.il; internet ankara.mfa.gov.il; Ambassador Gabby Levy.

Italy: Atatürk Bul. 118, 06680 Kavaklıdere, Ankara; tel. (312) 4574200; fax (312) 4574280; e-mail ambasciata.ankara@esteri.it; internet www.ambankara.esteri.it; Ambassador Gianpaolo Scarante.

Japan: Reşit Galip Cad. 81, 06692 Gaziosmanpaşa, Ankara; tel. (312) 4460500; fax (312) 4371812; e-mail culture@jpn-emb.org.tr; internet www.tr.emb-japan.go.jp; Ambassador Kiyoshi Araki.

Jordan: Dede Korkut Sok. 18 Mesnevi, 06690 Çankaya, Ankara; tel. (312) 4402054; fax (312) 4404327; e-mail jordembank@superonline.com; Ambassador Faris Shawkat al-Mufti.

Kazakhstan: Kılıç Ali Sok. 6, Oran Sitesi, Çankaya, Ankara; tel. (312) 4919100; fax (312) 4904455; e-mail kazank@kazakhstan.org.tr; internet www.kazakhstan.org.tr; Ambassador Zhanseit Tuimebayev.

Korea, Republic: Cinnah Cad., Alaçam Sok. 5, 06690 Çankaya, Ankara; tel. (312) 4684822; fax (312) 4267872; e-mail turkey@mofat.go.kr; internet tur-ankara.mofat.go.kr; Ambassador Bae Jae-Hyun.

Kosovo: Hirfanli Sok. 14/2, Gaziosmanpaşa, Ankara; tel. (312) 4467054; fax (312) 4467055; e-mail embassy.turkey@ks-gov.net; Ambassador Bekim Sejdiu.

Kuwait: Reşit Galip Cad., Kelebek Sok. 110, Gaziosmanpaşa, Ankara; tel. (312) 4450576; fax (312) 4462826; e-mail kuwait@ada.net.tr; Ambassador Abdullah Abd al-Aziz al-Duwaikh.

Kyrgyzstan: Turan Güneş Bul. 15 Cad. 21, Yıldız Oran, Ankara; tel. (312) 4913506; fax (312) 4913513; e-mail kirgiz-o@tr.net; Chargé d'affaires a.i. Ramaza Dyryldaev.

Latvia: Reşit Galip Cad. 95, Çankaya, Ankara; tel. (312) 4056136; fax (312) 4056137; e-mail embassy.turkey@mfa.gov.lv; Ambassador Aivars Vovers.

Lebanon: Kızkulesi Sok. 44, Gaziosmanpaşa, 06700 Ankara; tel. (312) 4467485; fax (312) 4461023; e-mail lebembas@ttnet.net.tr; Chargé d'affaires Wajib Abd al-Samad.

Libya: Cinnah Cad. 60, 06690 Çankaya, Ankara; tel. (312) 4381110; fax (312) 4403862; e-mail ashaabiankara@hotmail.com; Ambassador Ziad Adham al-Muntasir.

Lithuania: Mahatma Gandhi Cad. 17/8–9, 06700 Gaziosmanpaşa, Ankara; tel. (312) 4470766; fax (312) 4470663; e-mail amb.tr@urm.lt; internet tr.mfa.lt; Chargé d'affaires a.i. Jolanda Kriškovieciené.

Macedonia, former Yugoslav republic: Karaca Sok. 24/5–6, 06700 Gaziosmanpaşa, Ankara; tel. (312) 4399204; fax (312) 4399206; e-mail ankara@mfa.gov.mk; Ambassador Goran Taskovski.

Malaysia: Mahatma Gandhi Cad. 58, 06700 Gaziosmanpaşa, Ankara; tel. (312) 4463547; fax (312) 4464130; e-mail malankara@kln.gov.my; internet www.kln.gov.my/perwakilan/ankara; Ambassador Dato' Saipul Anwar Abd al-Muin.

Mauritania: Oran Mah. Şemsettin Bayramoğlu Sok. 7, Çankaya, Ankara; tel. (312) 4917063; fax (312) 4917064; Ambassador Ould Elemine Muhammad Ahmad.

Mexico: Kırkpınar Sok. 18/6, 06540 Çankaya, Ankara; tel. (312) 4423033; fax (312) 4420221; e-mail mexico@embamextur.com; internet www.mexico.org.tr; Ambassador Jaime García Amaral.

Moldova: Kaptanpaşa Sok. 49, 06700 Gaziosmanpaşa, Ankara; tel. (312) 4465627; fax (312) 4465816; e-mail ankara@mfa.md; Chargé d'affaires a.i. Alexei Ţurcan.

Mongolia: Koza Sok. 109, 06700 Gaziosmanpaşa, Ankara; tel. (312) 4467977; fax (312) 4467791; e-mail mogolelc@ttnet.net.tr; internet web.ttnet.net.tr/mogolelc; Ambassador Ochir Ochirjav.

Montenegro: Büyükesat, Gökçek Sok. 11, 06700 Ankara; tel. (312) 4364698; fax (312) 4361546; e-mail turkey@mfa.gov.me; Ambassador Ramo Bralić.

Morocco: Reşit Galip Cad., Rabat Sok. 11, 06700 Gaziosmanpaşa, Ankara; tel. (312) 4376020; fax (312) 4468430; e-mail sifamatr@tr.net; Ambassador Muhammad Lotfi Aouad.

Netherlands: Hollanda Cad. 5, 06550 Yıldız, Ankara; tel. (312) 4091800; fax (312) 4091898; e-mail ank@minbuza.nl; internet www.nl.org.tr; Ambassador Jan Paul Dirkse.

New Zealand: PK 162, İran Cad. 13/4, 06700 Kavaklıdere, Ankara; tel. (312) 4679054; fax (312) 4679013; e-mail nzembassyankara@ttmail.com; internet www.nzembassy.com/turkey; Ambassador Andrea Joan Smith.

Nigeria: Uğur Mumcu Sok. 56, 06700 Gaziosmanpaşa, Ankara; tel. (312) 4481077; fax (312) 4481082; e-mail nigeriaembassyturkey@yahoo.co.uk; Ambassador Ahmed Abdulhamid.

Norway: Kirkpinar Sok. 18/3–4, 06540 Çankaya, Ankara; tel. (312) 4058010; fax (312) 4430544; e-mail emb.ankara@mfa.no; internet www.norway.org.tr; Ambassador Cecilie Landsverk.

Oman: İlkbahar Mah. Cad. 63, 06700 Gaziosmanpaşa, Ankara; tel. (312) 4910940; fax (312) 4900682; e-mail omanembassy@yahoo.com; Ambassador Sayyid Qais bin Salim bin Ali al-Said.

TURKEY

Pakistan: İran Cad. 37, 06700 Gaziosmanpaşa, Ankara; tel. (312) 4271410; fax (312) 4671023; e-mail perepankhara@yahoo.com; internet www.pakembassyankara.com; Ambassador TARIQ AZIZUDDIN.

Peru: Reşit Galip Cad. 70/1, 06700 Ankara; e-mail ambassador@embassyofperu-ankara.org; Ambassador JORGE ABARCA DEL CARPIO.

Philippines: Mahatma Gandhi Cad. 56, 06700 Gaziosmanpaşa, Ankara; tel. (312) 4465831; fax (312) 4465733; e-mail ankarape@dfa.gov.ph; Ambassador PEDRO O. CHAN.

Poland: Atatürk Bul. 241, 06650 Kavaklıdere, Ankara; tel. (312) 4572048; fax (312) 4678963; e-mail embpl.ankara@ada.net.tr; internet www.ankara.polemb.net; Ambassador MARCIN WILCZEK.

Portugal: Kuleli Sok. 26, 06700 Gaziosmanpaşa, Ankara; tel. (312) 4056028; fax (312) 4463670; e-mail embaixada@portugal.org.tr; internet www.portugalembassy.org.tr; Ambassador LUISA BASTOS DE ALMEIDA.

Qatar: Bakü Sok. 6, Diplomatik Site, Oran, Ankara; tel. (312) 4907274; fax (312) 4906757; e-mail ankara@mofa.gov.qa; Ambassador ABD AL-RAZAK ABD AL-GHANI.

Romania: Bükreş Sok. 4, 06680 Çankaya, Ankara; tel. (312) 4663706; fax (312) 4271530; e-mail romania@attglobal.net; internet www.ankara.mae.ro; Ambassador ION PASCU.

Russia: Karyağdı Sok. 5, 06692 Çankaya, Ankara; tel. (312) 4392122; fax (312) 4383952; e-mail rus-ankara@yandex.ru; internet www.turkey.mid.ru; Ambassador VLADIMIR E. IVANOVSKII.

Saudi Arabia: Turan Emeksiz Sok. 6, 06700 Gaziosmanpaşa, Ankara; tel. (312) 4685540; fax (312) 4274886; e-mail tremb@mofa.gov.sa; Chargé d'affaires a.i. ABDULLAH M. A. AL-GHAMDI.

Senegal: Kızkulesi Sok. 1, Gaziosmanpaşa, Ankara; tel. (312) 4460932; fax (312) 4465375; e-mail senegalbuyukelciligi@yahoo.com; Ambassador ISSAKHA MBACKE.

Serbia: Paris Cad. 47, 06691 Kavaklıdere, Ankara; tel. (312) 4260236; fax (312) 4278345; e-mail embserank@tr.net; Ambassador DUŠAN SPASOJEVIĆ.

Slovakia: Atatürk Bul. 245, 06692 Kavaklıdere, Ankara; tel. (312) 4675075; fax (312) 4682689; e-mail emb.ankara@mzv.sk; Ambassador VLADIMÍR JAKABČÍN.

Slovenia: Kırlangıç Sok. 36, 06700 Gaziosmanpaşa, Ankara; tel. (312) 4054221; fax (312) 4260216; e-mail van@gov.si; Ambassador MILAN JAZBEC.

Somalia: Rabat Sok. 24/2, 06700 Gaziosmanpaşa, Ankara; tel. (312) 4364028; fax (312) 4364029; Ambassador HILAL MOHAMED ADEN.

South Africa: Filistin Sok. 27, 06700 Gaziosmanpaşa, Ankara; tel. (312) 4056861; fax (312) 4466434; e-mail general.ankara@foreign.gov.za; internet www.southafrica.org.tr; Ambassador TEBOGO JOSEPH SEOKOLO.

Spain: Abdullah Cevdet Sok. 8, 06680 Çankaya, Ankara; tel. (312) 4380392; fax (312) 4426991; e-mail emb.ankara@mae.es; Ambassador CRISTOBAL GONZALEZALLER JURADO.

Sudan: Mahatma Gandhi Cad. 48, Gaziosmanpaşa, Çankaya, Ankara; tel. (312) 4466327; fax (312) 4468506; e-mail ankara@mfa.gov.sd; Ambassador OMER HAIDAR ABU ZAID.

Sweden: Katip Çelebi Sok. 7, 06692 Kavaklıdere, Ankara; tel. (312) 4554100; fax (312) 4554120; e-mail ambassaden.ankara@foreign.ministry.se; internet www.swedenabroad.com/ankara; Ambassador HÅKAN ÅKESSON.

Switzerland: Atatürk Bul. 247, 06692 Kavaklıdere, Ankara; tel. (312) 4573100; fax (312) 4671199; e-mail ank.vertretung@eda.admin.ch; internet www.eda.admin.ch/ankara; Ambassador RAIMUND KUNZ.

Syria: Sedat Simavi Sok. 40, 06550 Çankaya, Ankara; tel. (312) 4409657; fax (312) 4385609; Ambassador Dr NIDAL KABALAN.

Tajikistan: Ferit Recai Ertuğrul Cad. 20, 25009 Oran, Ankara; tel. (312) 4911607; fax (312) 4911603; e-mail tajemb_turkey@inbox.ru; Ambassador FARRUH SHARIPOV.

Thailand: Koza Sok. 87, 06700 Gaziosmanpaşa, Ankara; tel. (312) 4374318; fax (312) 4378495; e-mail thaiank@ttmail.com; Ambassador ARBHOR MANASVANICH.

Tunisia: Ferit Recai Ertuğrul Cad. 19, Oran Diplomatic Site, Ankara; tel. (312) 4919635; fax (312) 4919634; e-mail at.ankara@superonline.com; Ambassador HAJ GLEY.

'Turkish Republic of Northern Cyprus': Rabat Sok. 20, 06700 Gaziosmanpaşa, Ankara; tel. (312) 4461036; fax (312) 4465238; e-mail info@kktcbe.org; internet www.kktcbe.org; Ambassador MUSTAFA LAKADAMYALI.

Turkmenistan: Koza Sok. 28, 06700 Gaziosmanpaşa, Ankara; tel. (312) 4416122; fax (312) 4417125; e-mail tmankara@ttnet.net.tr; Ambassador MAKSAT DOVLETSAHEDOV.

Ukraine: Sancak Mah. 512 Sok. 17, 06550 Çankaya, Ankara; tel. (312) 4415499; fax (312) 4406815; e-mail emb_tr@mfa.gov.ua; internet www.mfa.gov.ua/turkey; Ambassador SERGEI KORSUNSKII.

United Arab Emirates: Turan Güneş Bul. 15, Cad. 290, Sok. 3, Sancak Mah., Çankaya, Ankara; tel. (312) 4901414; fax (312) 4912333; e-mail uaeemb@uaeemb.net; internet www.uaeemb.net; Ambassador KHALID KHALIFA A. RASHED AL-MU'ALLA.

United Kingdom: Şehit Ersan Cad. 46/A, 06680 Çankaya, Ankara; tel. (312) 4553344; fax (312) 4553320; e-mail britembinf@fco.gov.uk; internet ukinturkey.fco.gov.uk; Ambassador DAVID REDDAWAY.

USA: Atatürk Bul. 110, 06100 Kavaklıdere, Ankara; tel. (312) 4555555; fax (312) 4670019; e-mail webmaster_ankara@state.gov; internet turkey.usembassy.gov; Ambassador FRANCIS J. RICCIARDONE, Jr.

Uzbekistan: Sancak Mah. 549 Sok. 3, Yıldız, 06550 Çankaya, Ankara; tel. (312) 4413871; fax (312) 4427058; e-mail embankara@post.mfa.uz; Ambassador ULFAT S. KADYROV.

Venezuela: Koza Sok. 91/3, 06700 Gaziosmanpaşa, Ankara; tel. (312) 4478131; fax (312) 4470711; e-mail mision-ankara@embavenez-turquia.com; Ambassador RAÚL JOSÉ BETANCOURT SEELAND.

Viet Nam: Koza Sok. 109, Gaziosmanpaşa, Çankaya, Ankara; tel. (312) 4468049; fax (312) 4465623; e-mail dsqvnturkey@yahoo.com; internet www.vietnamembassy-turkey.org; Ambassador LAP DUONG HUYNG.

Yemen: Fethiye Sok. 2, 06700 Gaziosmanpaşa, Ankara; tel. (312) 4462637; fax (312) 4461778; e-mail yemenemb@superonline.com; Ambassador ABD AL-QUAWI ABD AL-WASA A. AL-ERYANI.

Judicial System

Until the foundation of the Turkish Republic, a large part of the Turkish civil law—the laws affecting the family, inheritance, property, obligations, etc.—was based on the Koran, and this holy law was administered by special religious (*Shari'a*) courts. The legal reform of 1926 was not only a process of secularization, but also a radical change of the legal system. The Swiss Civil Code and the Code of Obligation, the Italian Penal Code and the Neuchâtel (Cantonal) Code of Civil Procedure were adopted and modified to fit Turkish customs and traditions.

According to current Turkish law, the power of the judiciary is exercised by judicial (criminal), military and administrative courts. These courts render their verdicts in the first instance, while superior courts examine the verdict for subsequent rulings.

SUPERIOR COURTS

Constitutional Court: Consists of 11 regular and four substitute members, appointed by the President. Reviews the constitutionality of laws, at the request of the President of the Republic, parliamentary groups of the governing party or of the main opposition party, or of one-fifth of the members of the National Assembly, and sits as a high council empowered to try senior members of state. The rulings of the Constitutional Court are final. Decisions of the Court are published immediately in the Official Gazette, and shall be binding on the legislative, executive and judicial organs of the state; Chief Justice HAŞIM KILIÇ.

Court of Appeals: The court of the last instance for reviewing the decisions and verdicts rendered by judicial courts. It has original and final jurisdiction in specific cases defined by law. Members are elected by the Supreme Council of Judges and Public Prosecutors; Chief Justice HASAN GERÇEKER.

Council of State: An administrative court of the first and last instance in matters not referred by law to other administrative courts, and an administrative court of the last instance in general. Hears and settles administrative disputes and expresses opinions on draft laws submitted by the Council of Ministers. Three-quarters of the members are appointed by the Supreme Council of Judges and Public Prosecutors; the remaining quarter is selected by the President of the Republic.

Military Court of Appeals: A court of the last instance to review decisions and verdicts rendered by military courts, and a court of first and last instance with jurisdiction over certain military persons, stipulated by law, with responsibility for the specific trials of these persons. Members are selected by the President of the Republic from nominations made by the Military Court of Appeals.

Supreme Military Administrative Court: A military court for the judicial control of administrative acts concerning military personnel. Members are selected by the President of the Republic from nominations made by the Court.

Court of Jurisdictional Disputes: Settles disputes among judicial, administrative and military courts arising from disagreements on jurisdictional matters and verdicts.

TURKEY

Court of Accounts: A court charged with the auditing of all accounts of revenue, expenditure and government property, which renders rulings related to transactions and accounts of authorized bodies on behalf of the National Assembly.

Supreme Council of Judges and Public Prosecutors: The Minister of Justice serves as the President of the Supreme Council, while the Under-Secretary to the Minister of Justice is an ex officio member. The remaining 20 members of the Council comprise four appointed directly by the President of the Republic, three nominated by the Court of Appeals, two by the Council of State, one by the Justice Academy and 10 elected by judges and prosecutors; each of these members is appointed for a four-year term. Decides all personnel matters relating to judges and public prosecutors.

Public Prosecutor: The law shall make provision for the tenure of public prosecutors and attorneys of the Council of State and their functions. The Chief Prosecutor of the Republic, the Chief Attorney of the Council of State and the Chief Prosecutor of the Military Court of Appeals are subject to the provisions applicable to judges of higher courts.

Military Trial: Military trials are conducted by military and disciplinary courts. These courts are entitled to try the military offences of military personnel and those offences committed against military personnel or in military areas, or offences connected with military service and duties. Military courts may try non-military persons only for military offences prescribed by special laws.

Religion

ISLAM

More than 99% of the Turkish people are Muslims. However, Turkey is a secular state. Although Islam was stated to be the official religion in the Constitution of 1924, an amendment in 1928 removed this privilege. Since 1950 subsequent Governments have tried to re-establish links between religion and state affairs, but secularity was protected by the revolution of 1960, the 1980 military takeover and the 1982 Constitution.

Diyanet İşleri Başkanlığı (Presidency of Religious Affairs): Eskişehir Yolu 9 km Çankaya, Ankara; tel. (312) 2957000; e-mail protokol@diyanet.gov.tr; internet www.diyanet.gov.tr; Pres. Prof. Dr ALI BARDAKOĞLU.

CHRISTIANITY

The town of Antioch (now Antakya) was one of the earliest strongholds of Christianity, and by the 4th century had become a patriarchal see. Formerly in Syria, the town was incorporated into Turkey in 1939. Constantinople (now İstanbul) was also a patriarchal see, and by the 6th century the Patriarch of Constantinople was recognized as the Ecumenical Patriarch in the East. Gradual estrangement from Rome developed, leading to the final breach between the Catholic West and the Orthodox East, usually assigned to the year 1054.

There are estimated to be about 100,000 Christians in Turkey.

The Orthodox Churches

Armenian Patriarchate: Ermeni Patrikliği, Sevgi Sok. 20, 34130 Kumkapı, İstanbul; tel. (212) 5170970; fax (212) 5164833; e-mail haybadtivan@gmail.com; internet www.lraper.org; f. 1461; 100,000 adherents (incl. workers from Armenia—2007); Patriarch MESROB II; Deputy Patriarch ARAM ATESHIAN.

Bulgarian Orthodox Church: Bulgar Ortodoks Kilisesi, Halâskâr Gazi Cad. 319, Şişli, İstanbul; Rev. Archimandrite GANCO ÇOBANOF.

Greek Orthodox Church: The Ecumenical Patriarchate (Rum Ortodoks Patrikhanesi), Sadrazam Ali Paşa Cad. 35, 34220 Fener-Haliç, İstanbul; tel. (212) 5255416; fax (212) 5316533; e-mail patriarchate@ec-patr.org; internet www.ec-patr.org; Archbishop of Constantinople (New Rome) and Ecumenical Patriarch BARTHOLOMEW I.

The Roman Catholic Church

At 31 December 2007 there were an estimated 34,540 adherents in the country. Of these, an estimated 23,345 were adherents of the Latin Rite and 6,450 of the Armenian Rite.

Bishops' Conference: Conferenza Episcopale di Turchia, Satırcı Sok. 2, Harbiye, 34373 İstanbul; tel. (212) 2307312; fax (212) 2303195; f. 1987; Pres. Most Rev. RUGGERO FRANCESCHINI (Archbishop of İzmir).

Armenian Rite

Patriarchate of Cilicia: f. 1742; Patriarch NERSES BEDROS TARMOUNI XIX (resident in Beirut, Lebanon).

Archdiocese of İstanbul: Sakızağacı Cad. 31, PK 183, 80072 Beyoğlu, İstanbul; tel. (212) 2441258; fax (212) 2432364; f. 1928; Archbishop HOVHANNES TCHOLAKIAN.

Byzantine Rite

Apostolic Exarchate of İstanbul: Hamalbaşı Cad. 44, PK 259, 80070 Beyoğlu, İstanbul; tel. (212) 2440351; fax (212) 2411543; f. 1911; Apostolic Admin. LOUIS PELÂTRE (Titular Bishop of Sasima).

Bulgarian Catholic Church: Bulgar Katolik Kilisesi, Eski Parmakkapı Sok. 15, Galata, İstanbul.

Latin Rite

Metropolitan Archdiocese of İzmir: Church of St Polycarp, Necatibey Bul. 2, PK 267, 35210 İzmir; tel. (232) 4840531; fax (232) 4845358; e-mail curiaves@yahoo.it; f. 1818; Archbishop of İzmir Most Rev. RUGGERO FRANCESCHINI.

Apostolic Vicariate of Anatolia: Mithat Paša Cad. 5, PK 75, 31200 Iskenderum; tel. (326) 6175916; fax (326) 6139291; e-mail curiaves@yahoo.it; f. 1990; Vicar Apostolic LUIGI PADOVESE (Titular Bishop of Monteverde).

Apostolic Vicariate of İstanbul: Papa Roncalli Sok. 83, 80230 Harbiye, İstanbul; tel. (212) 2480775; fax (212) 2411543; e-mail vapostolique@yahoo.fr; f. 1742; Vicar Apostolic LOUIS PELÂTRE (Titular Bishop of Sasima).

Maronite Rite

The Maronite Patriarch of Antioch, Cardinal Nasrallah Pierre Sfeir, is resident in Bkerké, Lebanon.

Melkite Rite

The Greek Melkite Patriarch of Antioch, Grégoire III Laham, is resident in Damascus, Syria.

Syrian Rite

The Syrian Catholic Patriarch of Antioch, Ignace Pierre VIII Abdel Ahad, is resident in Beirut, Lebanon.

Patriarchal Exarchate of Turkey: Sarayarkası Sok. 15, PK 84, 34437 Ayazpaşa, İstanbul; tel. (212) 2432521; fax (212) 2490261; e-mail info@suryanikatolikkilisesi.com; f. 1908; Patriarchal Exarch Fr YUSUF SAĞ.

The Anglican Communion

Within the Church of England, Turkey forms part of the diocese of Gibraltar in Europe. The Bishop is resident in the United Kingdom.

Anglican Chaplaincy in İstanbul: Christ Church, Serdar Ekram Sok. 82, Karaköy, İstanbul; tel. (212) 2515616; fax (212) 2435702; e-mail parson@tnn.net; internet www.anglicanistanbul.com; Chaplain Rev. Canon IAN SHERWOOD.

JUDAISM

There are estimated to be about 23,000 Jews in Turkey.

Jewish Community of Turkey: Türkiye Hahambaşılığı, Yemenici Sok. 21, Beyoğlu, 34430 Tünel, İstanbul; tel. (212) 2938794; fax (212) 2441980; e-mail info@musevicemaati.com; internet www.musevicemaati.com; Chief Rabbi ISAK HALEVA.

The Press

Almost all İstanbul papers are also printed in Ankara and İzmir on the same day, and some in Adana. The most popular national dailies are *Zaman*, *Posta*, *Hürriyet* and *Sabah*; *Yeni Asır*, published in İzmir, is the best-selling quality daily of the Aegean region. There are numerous provincial newspapers with a limited circulation.

PRINCIPAL DAILIES

Akşam (Evening): Davutpaşa Cad. 34, 34020 Zeytinburnu, İstanbul; tel. (212) 4493000; fax (212) 4819561; e-mail editor@aksam.com.tr; internet www.aksam.com.tr; publ. by Türkmedya AŞ; Man. Dir MUSTAFA DOLU; circ. 150,053 (April 2009).

Bugün (Today): Meliha Avni Sozen Cad. 17, Block B, Mecidiyeköy, Sisli, İstanbul; tel. (212) 3558580; fax (212) 2730954; e-mail bugun@bugun.com.tr; internet www.bugun.com.tr; f. 2003; publ. by Koza Davetiye; Editor-in-Chief SELAHATTIN SADIKOĞLU; circ. 60,770 (April 2009).

Cumhuriyet (Republic): Prof. Nurettin Mazhar Öktel Sok. 2, 34381 Şişli, İstanbul; tel. (212) 3437274; fax (212) 2914976; e-mail portal@cumhuriyet.com.tr; internet www.cumhuriyet.com.tr; f. 1924; morning; left-wing; nationalist; Editor-in-Chief IBRAHIM YILDIZ; circ. 65,132 (April 2009).

TURKEY

Fotomaç: Barbaros Bul. 153, Cam Han, Beşiktaş, İstanbul; tel. (212) 3543368; fax (212) 3543557; e-mail spor@fotomac.com.tr; internet www.fotomac.com.tr; f. 1991; sport; publ. by Turkuvaz Radyo Televizyon Gazetecilik ve Yayıncılık AŞ (a subsidiary of Çalık Holding); Editor-in-Chief ZEKI UZUNDURUKAN; circ. 214,441 (April 2009).

Gazete Haberturk: Abdülhakhamit Cad. 25, Beyoğlu, İstanbul; tel. (212) 3136000; fax (212) 3136590; internet www.htgazete.com; f. March 2009; publ. by Ciner Yayın Holding; Editor-in-Chief FATIH ALTAYLI; weekly circ. 297,709 (April 2009).

Güneş (Sun): Merkezefendi Mah. Davutpaşa Cad. 34, 34020 Zeytinburnu, İstanbul; tel. (212) 4493010; fax (212) 4819571; internet www.gunes.com; f. 1997; publ. by Türkmedya AŞ; Editor-in-Chief MURAT BÜYÜKÇELEBI; circ. 128,619 (April 2009).

Hürriyet (Freedom): Hürriyet Medya Towers, 34212 Güneşli, İstanbul; tel. (212) 6770000; fax (212) 6770846; e-mail interneteditor@hurriyet.com.tr; internet www.hurriyet.com.tr; f. 1948; morning; political; independent; publ. by Doğan Yayın Holding (Doğan Media Group); Chief Editor ENIS BERBEROĞLU; circ. 495,567 (April 2009).

Hürriyet Daily News and Economic Review: Sogutozu Mah., Dumlupinar Bul. 102, 06510 Çankaya, Ankara; tel. (312) 2070090; fax (312) 2070094; e-mail hdn@hurriyet.com.tr; internet www.turkishdailynews.com; f. 1961 as Daily News; later renamed Turkish Daily News; renamed as above 2008; English language; publ. by Doğan Yayın Holding (Doğan Media Group); CEO RAGIP NEBIL İLSEVEN; Editor-in-Chief DAVID JUDSON; circ. 6,106 (April 2009).

Milliyet: Doğan Medya Center, Bağcılar, 34204 İstanbul; tel. (212) 5056111; fax (212) 5056233; e-mail webadmin@milliyet.com.tr; internet www.milliyet.com.tr; f. 1950; morning; political; publ. by Doğan Yayın Holding (Doğan Media Group); Editor-in-Chief DERYA SAZAK; circ. 200,532 (April 2009).

Posta (Post): Yüzyıl Mah., Doğan Medya Center, 34204 Bağcılar, İstanbul; tel. (212) 5056111; fax (212) 5056520; e-mail internet@posta.com.tr; internet www.posta.com.tr; f. 1995; publ. by Doğan Yayın Holding (Doğan Media Group); Editor-in-Chief RIFAT ABABAY; circ. 516,136 (April 2009).

Radikal: Hürriyet Medya Towers, 34212 Güneşli, İstanbul; tel. (212) 6770000; fax (212) 4496047; e-mail iletisim@radikal.com.tr; internet www.radikal.com.tr; f. 1996; liberal; merged with economics and business daily *Referans* in 2010; publ. by Doğan Yayın Holding (Doğan Media Group); Man. Editor EYÜP CAN SAĞLIK.

Sabah (Morning): Barbaros Bul. 153, Cam Han, Beşiktaş, İstanbul; tel. (212) 3543000; e-mail editor@sabah.com.tr; internet www.sabah.com.tr; publ. by Turkuvaz Radyo Televizyon ve Gazetecilik AŞ (a subsidiary of Çalık Holding); Exec. Editor ERDAL ŞAFAK; circ. 380,851 (April 2009).

Star: Yeni Bosna Merkez Mah., Kavak Sok. 3/2, Ser Plaza, İstanbul; tel. (212) 4962020; fax (212) 4962179; e-mail editor@stargazete.com; internet www.stargazete.com; f. 1999; Man. Editor MUSTAFA KARAALIOĞLU; circ. 102,706 (April 2009).

Takvim (Calendar): Barbaros Bul. 153, Cam Han 5, Beşiktaş, İstanbul; tel. (212) 3543000; fax (212) 3470677; e-mail takvim@takvim.com.tr; internet www.takvim.com.tr; lifestyle, entertainment and sport; publ. by Turkuvaz Radyo Televizyon Gazetecilik AŞ (a subsidiary of Çalık Holding); Man. Editor ERGÜN DILER; circ. 150,053 (April 2009).

Today's Zaman: Ahmet Taner Kışlalı Cad. 6, 34194 Yenibosna, İstanbul; tel. (212) 4541454; fax (212) 4541497; e-mail editor@todayszaman.com; internet www.todayszaman.com; f. 2007; English language; publ. by Zaman Media Group; Editor-in-Chief BÜLENT KENES; circ. 4,677 (April 2009).

Türkiye (Turkey): Ekim Cad. 29, 34197 Yenibosna, İstanbul; tel. (212) 4543000; fax (212) 4543100; e-mail info@tg.com.tr; internet www.turkiyegazetesi.com.tr; f. 1970; nationalist, pro-Islamic; Editor-in-Chief NUH ALBAYRAK; circ. 141,313 (April 2009).

Vakit: Cağaloğlu: Ada 55, İstoç Bağcılar, İstanbul; tel. (212) 6592056; fax (212) 4474209; e-mail haber@vakit.com.tr; internet www.vakit.com.tr; f. 1978; Editor-in-Chief AHMET KARAHASANOĞLU; circ. 52,204 (April 2009).

Vatan (Homeland): Büyükdere Cad. 123, 34349 Gayrettepe, İstanbul; tel. (212) 3545454; internet www.gazetevatan.com; f. 2002; publ. by Doğan Yayın Holding (Doğan Media Group); Man. Editor ISMAIL YUVACAN; circ. 204,819 (April 2009).

Yeni Asır (New Century): Gaziosmanpaşa Bul. 5, 35260 Çankaya, İzmir; tel. (232) 4415000; fax (232) 4464222; e-mail yasir@yeniasir.com.tr; internet www.yeniasir.com.tr; f. 1895; political; publ. by Turkuvaz İzmir Gazete Dergi Basın Yayın AŞ (subsidiary of Çalık Holding); Chair. AHMET ÇALIK; Man. Editor ŞEBNEM BURSALI; circ. 38,760 (April 2009).

Yeni Çağ (New Age): Çobançeşme Mah., Kalender Sok. 12, 34550 Yenibosna, İstanbul; tel. (212) 4524040; fax (212) 4524055; e-mail yenicag@yenicaggazetesi.com.tr; internet www.yg.yenicaggazetesi.com.tr; f. 2002; nationalist; Man. Editor HAYRI KÖKLÜ; circ. 51,190 (April 2009).

Yeni Şafak (New Dawn): Yenidoğan Mah., Kızılay Sok. 39, Bayrampaşa, İstanbul; tel. (212) 6122930; fax (212) 6121903; e-mail halklailiskiler@yenisafak.com.tr; internet yenisafak.com.tr; f. 1995; Editor-in-Chief YUSUF ZIYA CÖMERT; circ. 103,598 (April 2009).

Zaman (Era): Ahmet Taner Kislali Cad. 6, 34194 Yenibosna, İstanbul; tel. (212) 4541454; fax (212) 4541467; e-mail h.dikmen@zaman.com.tr; internet www.zaman.com.tr; f. 1962; morning; Man. Editor EKREM DUMANLI; circ. 773,228 (April 2009).

WEEKLIES

Aksiyon: Fevzi Çakmak Mah., A. Taner Kışlalı Cad. 6, 34194 Yenibosna, İstanbul; tel. (212) 4541400; fax (212) 4548625; e-mail okur@aksiyon.com.tr; internet www.aksiyon.com.tr/aksiyon; f. 1994; news, politics, economics; Man. Editor BÜLENT KORUCU; circ. 38,184 (Nov. 2009).

BusinessWeek Türkiye: Ebulula Mardin Cad. 4, Gazeteciler Sitesi A8-1, 34330 Akatlar, İstanbul; tel. (212) 3245515; fax (212) 3245505; internet www.businessweek.com.tr; business and economics; publ. by Infomag Publishing Ltd and Bloomberg LP (USA); Man. Editor SERDAR TURAN.

Ekonomist: Hürriyet Medya Towers, 34212 Güneşli, İstanbul; tel. (212) 4103256; fax (212) 4103255; e-mail ekonomist@doganburda.com; internet www.ekonomist.com.tr; f. 1991; business and economics; publ. by Doğan Burda Dergi Yayıncılık ve Pazarlama AŞ; Man. Editor TALAT YEŞILOĞLU; circ. 9,505 (Nov. 2009).

Newsweek Türkiye: Abdülhakhamit Cad. 25, Beyoğlu, İstanbul; tel. (212) 3136000; fax (212) 3137455; internet www.newsweek.com.tr; news, business, economics; publ. by Ciner Gazete Dergi Basım Yayıncılık Sanayi ve Ticaret AŞ; Man. Editor SELÇUK TEPELI; circ. 4,500 (Nov. 2009).

Para: Toprak Center, Ihlamur Yıldız Cad. 10, 34353 Beşiktaş, İstanbul; tel. (212) 3263333; fax (212) 3543792; e-mail para@paradergi.com.tr; internet www.paradergi.com.tr; business and economics; publ. by Turkuvaz Gazete Dergi Basım AŞ; Man. Editor OĞUZ DEMIR; circ. 8,380 (Nov. 2009).

Tempo: Hürriyet Medya Towers, 34212 Güneşli, İstanbul; tel. (212) 4103282; fax (212) 4103311; internet www.tempoonline.com.tr; f. 1987; celebrity gossip, lifestyle; publ. by Doğan Burda Dergi Yayıncılık ve Pazarlama AŞ; Editor-in-Chief AYŞEGÜL SAVUR.

Yeni Aktüel: Toprak Center, Ihlamur Yıldız Cad. 10, 34353 Beşiktaş, İstanbul; tel. (212) 3263334; fax (212) 3543792; internet www.yeniaktuel.com.tr; culture; publ. by Turkuvaz Gazete Dergi Basım AŞ; Man. Editor DEFNE ASAL ER; circ. 6,381 (Nov. 2009).

PERIODICALS

Atlas: Hürriyet Medya Towers, 34212 Güneşli, İstanbul; tel. (212) 4103566; fax (212) 4103564; e-mail atlas@doganburda.com; internet www.kesfetmekicinbak.com; f. 1993; monthly; archaeology, geography; publ. by Doğan Burda Dergi Yayıncılık ve Pazarlama AŞ; Man. Editor ÖZCAN YÜKSEK.

Capital: Hürriyet Medya Towers, 34212 Güneşli, İstanbul; tel. (212) 4103228; fax (212) 4103227; e-mail capital@doganburda.com; internet www.capital.com.tr; f. 1993; monthly; business, economics; publ. by Doğan Burda Dergi Yayıncılık ve Pazarlama AŞ; Man. Editor SEDEF SEÇKIN BÜYÜK.

Chip: Hürriyet Medya Towers, 34212 Güneşli, İstanbul; tel. (212) 4103200; fax (212) 4103357; internet www.chip.com.tr; f. 1996; monthly; computing; publ. by Doğan Burda Dergi Yayıncılık ve Pazarlama AŞ; Man. Editor MAHMUT KARSLIOĞLU.

Global: Büyükdere Cad. 65, Saadet Apt 8/15, Mecidiyeköy, İstanbul; tel. (212) 2133881; fax (212) 2133884; e-mail info@globaldergisi.com; internet www.globaldergisi.com; business, economics; Man. Editor MÜGE MEŞE.

Güncel Hukuk: Hürriyet Medya Towers, 34212 Güneşli, İstanbul; tel. (212) 4103534; fax (212) 4103531; e-mail guncelhukuk@doganburda.com; internet www.guncelhukuk.com.tr; monthly; law; publ. by Doğan Burda Dergi Yayıncılık ve Pazarlama AŞ; Man. Editor Prof. Dr KÖKSAL BAYRAKTAR.

Infomag: Ebulula Mardin Cad. 4, Gazeteciler Sitesi A-8/1, Akatlar 1, Levent, İstanbul; tel. (212) 3245515; fax (212) 3245505; e-mail info@infomag.com.tr; internet www.infomag.com.tr; monthly; business; Man. Editor SERDAR TURAN.

Platin: Davutpaşa Cad. 34, 34020 Topkapı, İstanbul; tel. (212) 4493400; fax (212) 4819581; e-mail info@platinonline.com; internet www.platinonline.com; monthly; business, economics; publ. by Türkmedya AŞ; Editor LEVENT ERTEM.

TURKEY

NEWS AGENCIES

Anadolu Ajansı: Mustafa Kemal Bul. 128/C, Tandoğan, Ankara; tel. (312) 2317000; fax (312) 2312174; e-mail ozelbulten@aa.com.tr; internet www.aa.com.tr; f. 1920; Chair. and Dir-Gen. S. HILMI BENGI.

ANKA Ajansı: Cinnah Cad. 11/5 Kavaklıdere, Ankara; tel. (312) 4682500; fax (312) 4268471; e-mail anka@ankaajansi.com.tr; internet www.ankaajansi.com.tr; Dir-Gen. VELI ÖZDEMIR.

Bagımsiz Basın Ajansı (BBA): Saglam Fikir Sok. 9, Esentepe, 34394 İstanbul; tel. (212) 2122936; fax (212) 2122940; e-mail bba@bba.tv; internet www.bba.tv; f. 1971; provides camera crewing, editing and satellite services in Turkey, the Balkans, the Middle East and the former Soviet republics to broadcasters world-wide; Pres. BEDRI KAYABAL.

Cihan News Agency: Çobançeşme Mah. Kalender Sok. 16, 34530 Yenibosna, Bahçelievler, İstanbul; tel. (212) 5524057; fax (212) 4541456; e-mail newssales@cihan.com.tr; internet www.cihanmedia.com; f. 1992; part of Feza Media Corpn; Production Man. ZEKI SAATÇI.

Doğan Haber Ajansı (Doğan News Agency): Doğan TV Center, 34204 Bağcılar, İstanbul; tel. (212) 4135555; fax (212) 4135598; internet www.dha.com.tr; f. 1999 by merger of Hürriyet Haber Ajansı and Milliyet Haber Ajansı; subsidiary of Doğan Yayın Holding (Doğan Media Group); 34 bureaux world-wide; Dir-Gen. UĞUR ÇEBECI.

İKA Haber Ajansı (Economic and Commercial News Agency): Atatürk Bul. 199/A-45, Kavaklıdere, Ankara; f. 1954; Dir ZIYA TANSU.

TEBA—Türk Ekonomik Basın Ajansı (Turkish Economic Press Agency): Süleyman Hacı Abdullahoğlu Cad. 5, D3 Balgat, Ankara; tel. (312) 2842006; fax (312) 2840638; e-mail teba@tebahaber.com.tr; internet www.tebahaber.com.tr; f. 1981; private economic news service; Propr YELDA CALTAS; Editor AKIN TOKATLI.

Ulusal Basın Ajansı (UBA): Meşrutiyet Cad. 5/10, Ankara; Man. Editor OĞUZ SEREN.

JOURNALISTS' ASSOCIATION

Türkiye Gazeteciler Cemiyeti: Türkocağı Cad. 1, Cağaloğlu, İstanbul; tel. (212) 5138300; fax (212) 5268046; e-mail tgc@tgc.org.tr; internet www.tgc.org.tr; f. 1946; Pres. ORHAN ERINÇ; Sec.-Gen. CELAL TOPRAK.

Publishers

Altın Kitaplar Yayınevi Anonim ŞTİ: Göztepe Mah. Kazım Karabekir Cad., İstanbul; tel. (212) 4463888; e-mail uyelik@altinkitaplar.com.tr; internet www.altinkitaplar.com.tr; f. 1959; fiction, non-fiction, biography, children's books, encyclopaedias, dictionaries; Publrs FETHI UL, TURHAN BOZKURT; Chief Editor MÜRSIT UL.

Arkadas Co Ltd: Yuva Mah. 3702, Sok. 4, Yenimahalle, Ankara; tel. (312) 3960111; fax (312) 3960121; e-mail arops@arkadas.com.tr; internet www.arkadas.com.tr; f. 1980; fiction, educational and reference books; Gen. Man. CUMHUR OZDEMIR.

Arkeoloji ve Sanat Yayınları (Archaeology and Art Publications): Hayriye Cad. 3/4 Çorlu Apt., 34425 Beyoğlu, İstanbul; tel. (212) 2932003; fax (212) 2456877; e-mail info@arkeolojisanat.com; internet www.arkeolojisanat.com; f. 1978; classical, Byzantine and Turkish studies, art and archaeology, numismatics and ethnography books; Publr NEZIH BASGELEN; Senior Editor BRIAN JOHNSON.

Bilgi Yayınevi: Meşrutiyet Cad. 46/A, Yenişehir, 06420 Ankara; tel. (312) 4318122; fax (312) 4317758; e-mail info@bilgiyayinevi.com.tr; internet www.bilgiyayinevi.com.tr.

Doğan Burda Dergi Yayıncılık ve Pazarlama AŞ: Hürriyet Medya Towers, 34212 Güneşli, İstanbul; tel. (212) 4780300; fax (212) 4103581; e-mail dalan@doganburda.com; internet www.doganburda.com; jt venture between Doğan Yayın Holding (Doğan Media Group) and Hubert Burda Media Holding GmbH & Co KG (Germany); publishes 27 magazines and periodicals; Man. Dir MEHMET ALI YALÇINDAĞ.

IKI NOKTA (Research Press & Publications Industry & Trade Ltd): Eğitim M. Kasap İsmail S. Öğün İş Merkezi 5/2, 34722 Kadıköy, İstanbul; tel. (216) 3490141; fax (216) 3376756; e-mail info@ikinokta.com.tr; internet www.ikinokta.com; humanities; Pres. YÜCEL YAMAN.

Iletisim Yayınları: Binbirdirek Meydanı Sok., Iletisim Han 7/2, 34122 Cağaloğlu, İstanbul; tel. (212) 5162260; fax (212) 5161258; e-mail iletisim@iletisim.com.tr; internet www.iletisim.com.tr; f. 1984; fiction, non-fiction, encyclopaedias, reference; Gen. Man. NIHAT TUNA.

Inkilap Kitabevi: Çobançeşme Mah. Altay Sok. 8 Yenibosna, İstanbul; tel. (212) 4961111; fax (212) 4961112; e-mail posta@inkilap.com; internet www.inkilap.com; f. 1935; general reference and fiction; Man. Dir A. FIKRI; Dir of Foreign Rights S. DIKER.

Kabalci Yayınevi: Ankara Cad. 47, Cağaloğlu, İstanbul; tel. (212) 5226305; fax (212) 5268495; e-mail info@kabalci.com.tr; internet www.kabalci.com.tr; art, history, literature, social sciences; Pres. SABRI KABALCI.

Metis Yayınları: Ipek Sok. 5, 34433 Beyoğlu, İstanbul; tel. (212) 2454696; fax (212) 2454519; e-mail rights@metisbooks.com; internet www.metisbooks.com; f. 1982; fiction, literature, non-fiction, social sciences; Dir SEMIH SÖKMEN.

Nobel Medical Publishing: Millet Cad. 111 Çapa, İstanbul; tel. (212) 6328333; fax (212) 5870217; e-mail destek@nobeltip.com; internet www.nobeltip.com; f. 1974; medical books and journals; CEO ERSAL BINGÖL.

Nurdan Yayınları Sanayi ve Ticaret Ltd Sti: Prof. Kâzim Ismail Gürkan Cad. 13, Kati 1, 34410 Cağaloğlu, İstanbul; tel. (212) 5225504; fax (212) 5125186; e-mail nurdan@nurdan.com.tr; internet www.nurdan.com.tr; f. 1980; children's and educational; Dir NURDAN TÜZÜNER.

Parantez Yayınları AŞ: Istikal Cad. 212 Alt Kat 8, Beyoğlu, İstanbul; tel. and fax (212) 2526516; e-mail parantez@yahoo.com; internet www.parantez.net; f. 1991; Publr METIN ZEYNIOĞLU.

Payel Yayınevi: Cağaloğlu Yokusu Evren han Kat 3/51, 34400 Cağaloğlu, İstanbul; tel. (212) 5284409; fax (212) 5124353; f. 1966; science, history, literature; Editor AHMET ÖZTÜRK.

Remzi Kitabevi AŞ: Akmerkez E3 Blok Kat. 14, Etiler, İstanbul; tel. (212) 2822080; fax (212) 2822090; e-mail post@remzi.com.tr; internet www.remzi.com.tr; f. 1927; general and educational; Dirs EROL ERDURAN, ÖMER ERDURAN, AHMET ERDURAN.

Seckin Yayınevi: Saglik Sok. 19B, 06410 Sihhiye, Ankara; tel. (312) 4353030; fax (312) 4355088; e-mail satis@seckin.com.tr; internet www.seckin.com.tr; f. 1959; accounting, computer science, economics, law; Dir KORAY SEÇKIN.

Türk Dil Kurumu (Turkish Language Institute): Atatürk Bul. 217, 06680 Kavaklıdere, Ankara; tel. (312) 4575200; fax (312) 4680783; e-mail bilgi@tdk.org.tr; internet tdk.gov.tr; f. 1932; non-fiction, research, language; Pres. Prof. Dr ŞÜKRÜ HALUK AKALIN.

Varlık Yayınları AŞ: Ayberk Ap. Piyerloti Cad. 7–9, Çemberlitaş, 34400 İstanbul; tel. (212) 5162004; fax (212) 5162005; e-mail varlik@varlik.com.tr; internet www.varlik.com.tr; f. 1933; fiction and non-fiction books, and cultural monthly review; Dirs FILIZ NAYIR DENIZTEKIN, OSMAN DENIZTEKIN.

GOVERNMENT PUBLISHING HOUSE

Ministry of Culture and Tourism: Directorate of Publications, Necatibey Cad. 55, 06440 Kızılay, Ankara; tel. (312) 2315450; fax (312) 2315036; e-mail yayimlar@kutuphanelergm.gov.tr; internet www.kultur.gov.tr; f. 1973; Dir ALI OSMAN GÜZEL.

PUBLISHERS' ASSOCIATION

Türkiye Yayıncılar Birliği Derneği (Publishers' Association of Turkey): Kazım Ismail Gürkan Cad. 12/3, Ortaklar Han, 34440 Cağaloğlu, İstanbul; tel. (212) 5125602; fax (212) 5117794; e-mail info@turkyayibir.org.tr; internet www.turkyayibir.org.tr; f. 1985; Pres. ÇETIN TÜZÜNER; Sec. METIN CELÂL ZEYNIOĞLU; 300 mems.

Broadcasting and Communications

TELECOMMUNICATIONS

Regulatory Authorities

Bilgi Teknolojileri ve İletişim Kurumu (Information and Communication Technologies Authority): Yeşilırmak Sok., 16 Demirtepe, 06430 Ankara; tel. (312) 2947200; fax (312) 2947145; e-mail info@tk.gov.tr; internet www.tk.gov.tr; f. 2000; Chair. Dr TAYFUN ACARER.

General Directorate of Communications: Hakkı Turayliç Cad. 5 Kat 7–8, Emek, Ankara; tel. (312) 2031000; fax (312) 2121775; e-mail soytas@ubak.opr.tr; internet hgm.ubak.gov.tr; Dir-Gen. ALI ZOR.

Principal Operators

Avea İletişim Hizmetleri AŞ: Abdi İpekçi Cad. 75, 34367 Maçka, İstanbul; tel. (212) 4601500; internet www.avea.com.tr; f. Feb. 2004 as TT&TIM İletişim Hizmetleri AŞ; present name adopted Oct. 2004; 81.13% stake owned by Türk Telekom, 18.87% owned by İş Bankası; provides mobile cellular telecommunications services; 11.4m. subscribers in 2010; Chair. MUHAMMAD HARIRI; CEO ERKAN AKDEMIR.

Turkcell İletişim Hizmetleri AŞ: Turkcell Plaza, Mesrutiyet Cad. 71, 34430 Tepebaşi, İstanbul; tel. (212) 3131000; fax (212) 2925393; e-mail musteri.hizmetleri@turkcell.com.tr; internet www.turkcell.com.tr; f. 1994; provides mobile cellular telecommunications ser-

TURKEY

vices; 13.07% by TeliaSonera AB (Sweden); 33.9m. subscribers at Sept. 2010; Chair. COLIN J. WILLIAMS; CEO SÜREYYA CILIV.

Türksat AŞ: Konya Yolu 40 km, Gölbaşı, Ankara; tel. (312) 6153000; fax (312) 4995115; e-mail info@turksat.com.tr; internet www.turksat.com.tr; satellite and cable telecommunications services; CEO ÖZKAN DALBAY.

Türk Telekomünikasyon AŞ (Türk Telekom): Turgut Özal Bul., 06103 Aydınlıkevler, Ankara; tel. (312) 3060733; fax (312) 3245311; e-mail iletisim@turktelekom.com.tr; internet www.turktelekom.com.tr; 55% owned by Oger Telecoms Joint Venture Group, 30% by Turkish Govt and 15% by private investors; fixed-line telecommunications services; Chair. MUHAMMAD HARIRI; CEO Dr K. GÖRKHAN BOZKURT.

Vodafone Telekomünikasyon AŞ (Vodafone Türkiye): Vodafone Plaza, Büyükdere Cad. 67, 34398 Maslak, İstanbul; tel. (212) 3670000; fax (212) 3670010; internet www.vodafone.com.tr; f. 1994 as Telsim; name changed 2006, following acquisition by Vodafone Group PLC (United Kingdom); offers mobile cellular telecommunications services; CEO SERPIL TIMURAY.

BROADCASTING

Regulatory Authority

Radyo ve Televizyon Üst Kurulu (RTÜK) (Radio and Television Supreme Council): Bilkent Plaza B2 Blok, Bilkent, 06530 Ankara; tel. (312) 2975000; fax (312) 2661985; e-mail rtuk@rtuk.org.tr; internet www.rtuk.org.tr; f. 1994; responsible for assignment of channels, frequencies and bands, controls transmitting facilities of radio stations and TV networks, draws up regulations on related matters, monitors broadcasting and issues warnings in case of violation of the Broadcasting law; Pres. DAVUT DURSUN.

Radio

Türkiye Radyo ve Televizyon Kurumu (TRT) (Turkish Radio and Television Corpn): Turan Güneş Bul., 06450 Oran, Ankara; tel. (312) 4632330; fax (312) 4632335; e-mail aktifhat@trt.net.tr; internet www.trt.net.tr; f. 1964; controls Turkish radio and television services, incl. four national radio channels; Dir-Gen. İBRAHIM ŞAHIN; Head of Radio ÇETIN TEZCAN.

Voice of Turkey: PK 333, 06443 Yenişehir, Ankara; tel. (312) 4633270; fax (312) 4633277; e-mail tsr@trt.net.tr; internet www.trt.net.tr; f. 1937; external service of the TRT; Head of Dept SULEYMAN KOKSOY.

There are also more than 50 local radio stations, an educational radio service for schools and a station run by the Turkish State Meteorological Service. The US forces have their own radio and television service.

Television

Digitürk: tel. (212) 4737373; fax (212) 3260099; e-mail destek@digiturk.com.tr; internet www.digiturk.gen.tr; f. 1999; subsidiary of Çukurova Holding; subscription-based satellite television service offering 170 channels; also internet service provider; CEO ERTAN ÖZERDEM.

Türkiye Radyo ve Televizyon Kurumu (TRT): (Turkish Radio and Television Corpn): Oran Sitesi Turan Güneş Bul. A Blk Kat 6, 06450 Oran, Ankara; tel. (212) 2597275; e-mail aktifhat@trt.net.tr; internet www.trt.net.tr; four national, one regional and two international channels in 2008; launched Kurdish-language channel (TRT 6) January 2009; Arabic-language service (TRT 7) launched April 2010; Dir-Gen. İBRAHIM ŞAHIN; Head of Television NILGÜN ARTUN; Dir Ankara TV GÜRKAN ELÇI.

As of 2008 there were 23 national, 16 regional and 212 local terrestrial television broadcasters. There are also cable and satellite channels.

Finance

(cap. = capital; res = reserves; dep. = deposits; m. = million; br(s) = branch(es); amounts in Turkish liras unless otherwise indicated; note: figures have been converted retrospectively to reflect the introduction on 1 January 2005 of the new unit of currency, equivalent to 1,000,000 of the old Turkish lira)

The Central Bank of the Republic of Turkey (Türkiye Cumhuriyet Merkez Bankası AŞ) was founded in 1931, and constituted in its present form in 1970. The Central Bank is the bank of issue and is also responsible for the execution of monetary and credit policies, the regulation of the foreign and domestic value of the Turkish lira jointly with the Government, and the supervision of the credit system. In 1987 a decree was issued to bring the governorship of the Central Bank under direct government control. In 2001 the Central Bank was granted policy independence.

In June 1999 an independent supervisory body, the Regulatory and Supervisory Board for Banking, was established by law to monitor the financial sector. The treasury, the Ministry of Finance, the Central Bank, the state planning organization, the Capital Markets Board and the Banks' Association of Turkey were each to nominate one member to the Board for a six-year term. The Board was operational from mid-2000. Other legislation passed in June 1999 incorporated core principles of the Basle Committee on Banking Supervision relating to risk-based capital requirements, loan administration procedures, auditing practices and credit risk issues.

The largest of the private-sector Turkish banks is the Türkiye İş Bankası AŞ, which operates 1,088 branches in the country.

There are several credit institutions in Turkey, including the Türkiye Sınai Kalkınma Bankası AŞ (Industrial Development Bank of Turkey), which was founded in 1950, with the assistance of the World Bank, to encourage private investment in industry by acting as underwriter in the issue of share capital.

There are numerous co-operative organizations, including agricultural co-operatives in rural areas. There are also a number of savings institutions.

In 1990 the Turkish Government announced plans to establish a structure for offshore banking. A decree issued in October of that year exempted foreign banks, operating in six designated free zones, from local banking obligations.

At the end of 1999 the number of banks operating in Turkey (excluding the Central Bank) totalled 81, of which seven were state owned. Following a number of liquidations, mergers and acquisitions in the banking system after 2000, the number of banks had been reduced to 43 by the end of 2008. Of this total, 13 were development and investment banks; the number of state-owned banks had been reduced to three, with the control of Birleşik Fon Bankası AŞ (formerly Bayindirbank) passing to the Savings Deposit Insurance Fund. There were 11 private commercial banks and 16 foreign-owned banks.

BANKING

Regulatory Authority

Bancacılık Düzenleme ve Denetleme Kurumu (BDDK) (Banking Regulation and Supervisory Agency): Atatürk Bul. 191, 06680 Kavaklidere, Ankara; tel. (312) 4556500; fax (312) 4240879; e-mail bilgi@bddk.org.tr; internet www.bddk.org.tr; Chair. TEVFIK BILGIN.

Central Bank

Türkiye Cumhuriyet Merkez Bankası AŞ (Central Bank of the Republic of Turkey): Head Office, İstiklal Cad. 10 Ulus, 06100 Ankara; tel. (312) 5075000; fax (312) 5075640; e-mail iletisimbilgi@tcmb.gov.tr; internet www.tcmb.gov.tr; f. 1931; bank of issue; cap. 46.2m., res 3,691.2m., dep. 89,359.6m. (Dec. 2009); Gov. DURMUŞ YILMAZ; 21 brs.

State Banks

Türkiye Cumhuriyeti Ziraat Bankası (Agricultural Bank of the Turkish Republic): Doğanbey Mah., Atatürk Bul. 8, 06107 Ulus, Ankara; tel. (312) 5842000; fax (312) 5844053; e-mail zbmail@ziraatbank.com.tr; internet www.ziraat.com.tr; f. 1863; absorbed Türkiye Emlâk Bankası AŞ (Real Estate Bank of Turkey) in July 2001; cap. 2,500m., res 4,343m., dep. 110,919m. (Dec. 2009); Chair. MUHARREM KARSLI; Gen. Man. CAN AKIN ÇAĞLAR; 1,225 brs in Turkey, 11 brs abroad.

Türkiye Halk Bankası AŞ: Esikişehir Yolu, 2 Cad. 63, Söğütözü, 06520 Ankara; tel. (312) 2892000; fax (312) 2893575; e-mail info@halkbank.com.tr; internet www.halkbank.com.tr; f. 1938; absorbed Türkiye Öğretmenler Bankası TAŞ in 1992; acquired 96 brs of Türkiye Emlak Bankası in 2001; merged with Pamukbank TAŞ in 2004; cap. 1,250m., res 2,878m., dep. 51,116m. (Dec. 2009); Chair. HASAN CEBECI; Gen. Man. HÜSEYIN AYDIN; 705 brs in Turkey, 4 brs abroad.

Türkiye Vakıflar Bankası TAO (Vakifbank) (Foundation Bank of Turkey): Camlik Cad. Cayir Cimen Sok. 2, 34330 1 Levent, İstanbul; tel. (212) 3167116; fax (212) 3167126; e-mail international@vakifbank.com.tr; internet www.vakifbank.com.tr; f. 1954; cap. 3,300.1m., res 1,558.0m., dep. 51,161.8m. (Dec. 2009); Dep. Chair. AHMET CANDAN; Gen. Man. SÜLEYMAN KALKAN; 603 brs in Turkey, 2 brs abroad.

Principal Commercial Banks

Akbank TAŞ: Sabancı Center, 34330 4 Levent, 80745 İstanbul; tel. (212) 3855555; fax (212) 2697787; e-mail investor.relations@akbank.com; internet www.akbank.com; f. 1948; absorbed Ak Uluslararası Bankası AŞ in Sept. 2005; 20% owned by Citigroup; cap. 5,029m., res 2,238m., dep. 79,283m. (Dec. 2009); Chair. SUZAN SABANCI DINÇER; Gen. Man. ZIYA AKKURT; 867 brs in Turkey, 1 br. abroad.

TURKEY

Alternatifbank AŞ: Cumhuriyet Cad. 22–24, Elmadağ, 34367 İstanbul; tel. (212) 3156500; fax (212) 2331500; e-mail kalite@abank.com.tr; internet www.abank.com.tr; f. 1991; 95.6% owned by Anadolu Group; cap. 300.0m., res 144.1m., dep. 2,658.4m. (Dec. 2009); Chair. TUNCAY ÖZILHAN; CEO HAMIT AYDOĞAN; 56 brs.

ING Bank AS: Eski Büyükdere Cad., Ayazaga Köyyolu 6, Maslak, 34398 İstanbul; tel. and fax (212) 4440600; internet www.ingbank.com.tr; f. 1990; fmrly Oyak Bank; owned by ING Groep NV (Netherlands); name changed as above in 2008; cap. 1,735m., res 28m., dep. 10,132m. (Dec. 2009); Chair. JOHN T. MCCARTHY; CEO WILFRED NAGEL; 365 brs in Turkey, 1 br. in Bahrain.

Şekerbank TAŞ: Büyükdere Cad. 171, Metrocity İş Merkezi, A-Blok 34330 1 Levent, İstanbul; tel. (212) 3440737; fax (212) 3197162; e-mail intdiv@sekerbank.com.tr; internet www.sekerbank.com.tr; f. 1953; 33.98% owned by TuranAlem Securities (Kazakhstan); cap. 500m., res 140m., dep. 7,142m. (Dec. 2009); Chair. HASAN BASRI GÖKTAN; Gen. Man. MERIÇ ULUŞAHIN; 250 brs.

Tekstil Bankasi AŞ (Tekstilbank): Büyükdere Cad. 63, 34398 Maslak, İstanbul; tel. (212) 3355335; fax (212) 3281328; e-mail ir@tekstilbank.com.tr; internet www.tekstilbank.com.tr; f. 1986; cap. 420.0m., res 48.8m. dep. 1,469.6m. (Dec. 2009); 75.4% owned by GSD Holdings; Chair. AKGÜN TÜRER; Gen. Man. ÇIM GÜZELAYDINLI; 44 brs.

Türk Ekonomi Bankası AŞ (TEB): Meclisi Mebusan Cad. 57, 34427 Fındıklı, İstanbul; tel. (212) 2512121; fax (212) 2525058; internet www.teb.com.tr; f. 1927; fmrly Kocaeli Bankası TAŞ; jt venture between Colakoğlu Group and BNP Paribas SA (France); in Feb. 2011 Fortis Bank AŞ merged into the above; cap. 1,100.0m., res 679.9m., dep. 11,566.7m. (Dec. 2009); Chair. YAVUZ CANEVI; Exec. Dir and Gen. Man. VAROL CIVIL; 275 brs in Turkey, 1 br. in Bahrain.

Türkiye Garanti Bankası AŞ (Garantibank): Nispetiye Mah, Aytar Cad. 2, 34340 Levent Beşiktaş, İstanbul; tel. (212) 3181818; fax (212) 3181888; e-mail mutlus@garanti.com.tr; internet www.garantibank.com; f. 1946; owned by Doğuş Group; cap. 5,146.4m., res 1,788.7m., dep. 79,546.1m. (Dec. 2009); Chair. FERIT FAIK ŞAHENK; Pres. and CEO ERGUN ÖZEN; 808 brs in Turkey, 2 brs abroad.

Türkiye İş Bankası AŞ (İşbank): İş Kuleleri, 34330 Levent, İstanbul; tel. (212) 3160000; fax (212) 3160900; e-mail halkla.iliskiler@isbank.com.tr; internet www.isbank.com.tr; f. 1924; cap. 5,057.1m., res 1,663.2m., dep. 83,734.6m. (Dec. 2009); Chair. ERSIN ÖZINCE; CEO and Dir ADNAN BALI; 1,088 brs in Turkey, 15 abroad.

Yapı ve Kredi Bankası AŞ: Yapı Kredi Plaza, Blok D, 80620 İstanbul; tel. (212) 3397000; fax (212) 3396000; internet www.ykb.com.tr; f. 1944; cap. 4,347.0m., res 711.2m., dep. 46,984.1m. (Dec. 2009); merged with Koçbank AŞ in 2006; Exec. Dir and Dep. CEO CARLO VIVALDI; CEO FAIK AÇIKALIN; 838 brs.

Development and Investment Banks

İller Bankasi Genel Müdürülüğü: Atatürk Bul. 21, 06053 Opera, Ankara; tel. (312) 5087000; fax (312) 5087399; e-mail ilbank@ilbank.gov.tr; internet www.ilbank.gov.tr; Chair. and Gen. Man. HIDAYET ATASOY; 19 brs.

Türkiye Kalkınma Bankası (Development Bank of Turkey): İzmir Cad. 35, 06440 Kızılay Ankara; tel. (312) 4179200; fax (312) 4183967; e-mail rkalkinmahaberlesme@kalkinma.com.tr; internet www.kalkinma.com.tr; cap. 160m., res 313m. (Dec. 2009); Chair. AHMET YAMAN (acting); Gen. Man. METIN PEHLIVAN (acting).

Türkiye Sınai Kalkınma Bankası AŞ (Industrial Development Bank of Turkey): Meclisi Mebusan Cad. 81, Findikli, 34427 İstanbul; tel. (212) 3345050; fax (212) 3345234; e-mail info@tskb.com.tr; internet www.tskb.com; f. 1950; cap. 613.5m., res 58.0m., dep. 1,395.6m. (Dec. 2009); Chair. ADNAN BALI; Pres. HALIL EROĞLU; 2 brs.

Savings Deposit Insurance Fund Bank

Birleşik Fon Bankasi AŞ: Büyükdere Cad. 143, 34394 Esentepe, İstanbul; tel. (212) 3401000; fax (212) 3473217; e-mail callcenter@fonbank.com.tr; internet www.fonbank.com.tr; fmrly Bayindirbank; name changed as above 2005; control passed to Savings Deposit Insurance Fund in 2001; Chair. SALIM ALKAN; Gen. Man. RECEP SÜLEYMAN ÖZDIL.

Banking Organization

Banks' Association of Turkey: Nıspetıye Cad. Akmerkez B3 Blok. Kat 13–14, 34340 Etiler, İstanbul; tel. (212) 2820973; fax (212) 2820946; e-mail gensek@tbb.org.tr; internet www.tbb.org.tr; f. 1958; Chair. HUSEYIN AYDIN.

STOCK EXCHANGE

İstanbul Menkul Kıymetler Borsası (İMKB): Resitpaşa Mah., Tuncay Artun Cad., 34467 Emirgan, İstanbul; tel. (212) 2982100; fax (212) 2982500; e-mail international@imkb.gov.tr; internet www.ise.org; f. 1866; revived in 1986 after being dormant for about 60 years; 104 mems of stock market, 132 mems of bond and bills market (April 2008); Chair. and CEO HÜSEYIN ERKAN; Senior Vice-Chair. ARIL SEREN.

INSURANCE
Principal Companies

AKSigorta AŞ: Meclis-i Mebusan Cad. 67, 34427 Fındıklı, İstanbul; tel. (212) 3934300; fax (212) 3343900; e-mail info@aksigorta.com.tr; internet www.aksigorta.com.tr; f. 1960; life and non-life; Chair. AHMET CEMAL DÖRDÜNCÜ; Gen. Man. UĞUR GÜLEN.

Allianz Sigorta AŞ: Bağlarbaşı, Kısıklı Cad. 13, 34662 Altunizade, İstanbul; tel. (216) 5566666; fax (216) 5566777; e-mail info@allianz.com.tr; internet www.allianz.com.tr; f. 1923; general, non-life; also offers life insurance through its subsidiary, Allianz Hayat ve Emeklilik AŞ; fmrly Koç Allianz Sigorta AŞ; 84% owned by Allianz AG (Germany); Chair. Dr RÜŞDÜ SARAÇOĞLU; CEO GEORGE D. SARTOREL.

Anadolu Sigorta TAŞ (Anadolu Insurance Co): Büyükdere Cad. İş Kuleleri Kule 2 Kat. 23–26 34330 4 Levent, İstanbul; tel. (212) 3500350; fax (212) 3500355; e-mail bilgi@anadolusigorta.com.tr; internet www.anadolusigorta.com.tr; f. 1925; life and non-life; 35.53% owned by Türkiye İş Bankası AŞ; Chair. BURHAN KARAGÖZ; CEO MUSTAFA ALI SU.

AvivaSA Emeklilik ve Hayat AŞ (AvivaSA): İnkılap Mah., Küçüksu Cad., Akçakoca Sk. 8, 34768 Ümraniye, İstanbul; tel. (216) 6333333; fax (216) 6343888; e-mail musteri@avivasa.com.tr; internet www.aviva.com.tr; f. 2007 by merger of Aviva Hayat ve Emeklilik and AK Emeklilik; life; 49.7% stakes owned by AK Sigorta AŞ and Aviva PLC (United Kingdom); Chair. HAKAN AKBAŞ; Gen. Man. MERAL EGEMEN.

AXA Sigorta AŞ: Meclis-i Mebusan Cad. Oyak İş Hanı 15, 34427 Salıpazarı, İstanbul; tel. (212) 3342424; fax (212) 2521515; e-mail iletisim@axasigorta.com.tr; internet www.axasigorta.com.tr; life and non-life; Chair. and CEO HAKKI CEMAL ERERDI; 10 brs.

ERGO Sigorta AŞ: Saray Mah., Dr Adnan Büyükdeniz Cad. 4, Akkom Ofis Park, Blok Kat. 10–14, Ümraniye, İstanbul; tel. (216) 5548100; fax (216) 6667777; e-mail ergoisvicre@ergoisvicre.com.tr; internet www.ergoturkiye.com; f. 1926 as La Suisse Umum Sigorta, acquired by İsviçre in 1981; acquired by ERGO Versicherungsgrüppe AG (Germany) in 2008; name changed as above 2010; fire, accident, marine, engineering, agricultural; Chair. AKIN KOZANOĞLU; Gen. Man. Dr THOMAS BARON; 11 regional brs.

Eureko Sigorta: Büyükdere Cad., Nurol Plaza 257, 34398 Maslak, İstanbul; tel. (212) 3041000; fax (212) 2854424; e-mail esmusterihizmetleri@eurekosigorta.com.tr; internet www.eurekosigorta.com.tr; f. 1989 as Garanti Sigorta; renamed as above in Oct. 2007; 80% owned by Eureko BV (Netherlands) and 20% by Türkiye Garanti Bankası AŞ; non-life; Chair. ERGUN ÖZEN; CEO OKAN UTKUERI.

Groupama Sigorta AŞ: Groupama Plaza, Eski Büyükdere Cad. 2, 34398 Maslak, İstanbul; tel. (212) 3676767; fax (212) 3676868; e-mail sigorta@groupama.com.tr; internet www.groupama.com.tr; f. 1959 as Başak Sigorta; 56.67% stake acquired by Groupama SA (France) in 2006; adopted present name 2009, following merger with Güven Sigorta TAŞ; life and non-life; Chair. PIERRE LEFEVRE; Gen. Man. ALAIN BAUDRY.

Güneş Sigorta: Güneş Plaza, Büyükdere Cad. 110, 34394 Esentepe-Şişli, İstanbul; tel. (212) 4441957; fax (212) 3556464; e-mail gunes@gunessigorta.com.tr; internet www.gunessigorta.com.tr; f. 1957; non-life; 51.3% stake owned by Türkiye Vakıflar Bankası TAO, 45% owned by Groupama (France); Chair. BILAL KARAMAN; Gen. Man. MEHMET İLKER AVCI.

Yapı Kredi Sigorta AŞ: Yapı Kredi Plaza, A Blok, Büyükdere Cad., 34330 Levent, İstanbul; tel. (212) 3360606; fax (212) 3360808; e-mail yksigorta@yksigorta.com.tr; internet www.yksigorta.com.tr; f. 1943 as Halk Sigorta; present name adopted 2000; life and non-life; 53.1% stake owned by Yapı ve Kredi Bankası AŞ; Chair. TAYFUN BAYAZIT; Gen. Man. Dr S. GIRAY VELIOĞLU.

Insurance Organization

Türkiye Sigorta ve Reasürans Şirketleri Birliği (Asscn of the Insurance and Reinsurance Companies of Turkey): Büyükdere Cad., Büyükdere Plaza 195, 1-2, 34394 Levent, İstanbul; tel. (212) 3241950; fax (212) 3256108; e-mail genel@tsrsb.org.tr; internet www.tsrsb.org.tr; f. 1954 by merger of the Association of the Insurance Companies of Turkey and the Central Office of Insurers; present name adopted 1975; 57 mems (2009); Pres. HULUSI TAŞKIRAN; Sec.-Gen. ERHAN TUNÇAY.

Trade and Industry

GOVERNMENT AGENCIES

Özelleştirme İdaresi Başkanlığı (ÖİB) (Privatization Administration): Ziya Gökalp Cad. 80, Kurtuluş, 06600 Ankara; tel. (312)

TURKEY

Directory

4304560; fax (312) 4359342; e-mail info@oib.gov.tr; internet www.oib.gov.tr; co-ordinates privatization programme; Pres. METIN KILCI.

Rekabet Kurumu (Turkish Competition Authority): Bilkent Plaza B3 Blok, 06800 Bilkent, Ankara; tel. (312) 2914444; fax (312) 2667920; e-mail rek@rekabet.gov.tr; internet www.rekabet.gov.tr; f. 1997; prevents restriction of competition, oversees mergers and monitors state aid; Pres. and Chair. Prof. Dr NURETTIN KALDIRIMCI.

Türkiye Atom Enerjisi Kurumu (Turkish Atomic Energy Authority): Eskişehir Yolu 9km, 06530 Lodumlu, Ankara; tel. (312) 2958700; fax (312) 2878761; e-mail bilgi_taek@taek.gov.tr; internet www.taek.gov.tr; f. 1956; controls the development of peaceful uses of atomic energy; 7 mems; Pres. Prof. Dr ÜNER ÇOLAK.

CHAMBERS OF COMMERCE AND INDUSTRY

Türkiye Odalar ve Borsalar Birliği (TOBB) (Union of Chambers and Commodity Exchanges of Turkey): Dumlupınar Bul. 252, Eskişehir Yolu 9 Km, 06530 Ankara; tel. (312) 2182000; fax (312) 2194090; e-mail info@tobb.org.tr; internet www.tobb.org.tr; f. 1950; represents 365 chambers and commodity exchanges; Pres. RIFAT HISARCIKLIOĞLU.

Ankara Sanayi Odası (ASO) (Ankara Chamber of Industry): Atatürk Bul. 193, Kavaklıdere, Ankara; tel. (312) 4171200; fax (312) 4175205; e-mail aso@aso.org.tr; internet www.aso.org.tr; f. 1963; Pres. M. NURETTIN ÖZDEBIR.

Ankara Tabip Odası (ATO) (Ankara Chamber of Commerce): Mithatpaşa Cad. 62/18 Kızılay, 06420 Ankara; tel. (312) 4188700; fax (312) 4187794; e-mail ato@ato.org.tr; internet www.ato.org.tr; Pres. Prof. Dr GÜLRIZ ERSÖZ.

İstanbul Sanayi Odası (İSO) (İstanbul Chamber of Industry): Meşrutiyet Cad. 62, 34430 Tepebaşi, İstanbul; tel. (212) 2522900; fax (212) 2495084; e-mail info@iso.org.tr; internet www.iso.org.tr; f. 1952; more than 12,500 mems (2006); Chair. C. TANIL KÜÇÜK; Gen. Sec. METE MELEKSOY.

İstanbul Ticaret Odası (İstanbul Chamber of Commerce): Reşadiye Cad. 34112 Eminönü, İstanbul; tel. (212) 4556000; fax (212) 5131565; e-mail info@us-istanbul.com; internet www.ito.org.tr; f. 1952; more than 300,000 mems; Pres. MURAT YALÇINTAŞ.

EMPLOYERS' ASSOCIATIONS

Türk Sanayicileri ve İşadamları Derneği (TÜSİAD) (Turkish Industrialists' and Businessmen's Association): Meşrutiyet Cad. 74, 34420 Tepebaşi, İstanbul; tel. (212) 2491929; fax (212) 2491350; e-mail tusiad@tusiad.org; internet www.tusiad.org; f. 1971; c. 600 mems; Chair. ÜMIT BOYNER; Sec.-Gen. ZAFER ALI YAVAN.

Türkiye İşveren Sendikaları Konfederasyonu (TİSK) (Turkish Confederation of Employer Associations): Hoşdere Cad. Reşat Nuri Sok. 108, 06540 Çankaya, Ankara; tel. (312) 4397717; fax (312) 4397592; e-mail tisk@tisk.org.tr; internet www.tisk.org.tr; f. 1962; represents (on national level) 23 employers' asscns; official representative in labour relations; Pres. TUĞRUL KUDATGOBILIK; Sec.-Gen. BÜLENT PIRLER.

UTILITIES

Plans for the privatization of the electricity distribution grid were announced in 2004. Following numerous delays, the privatization process resumed in 2008, under the supervision of the Privatization Administration.

Electricity

Elektrik Üretim Anonim Şirketi (EÜAŞ) (Electricity Generation Co Inc): İnönü Bul. 27, Bahçelievler, 06490 Ankara; tel. (312) 2126900; fax (312) 2130103; e-mail basinhalk@euas.gov.tr; internet www.euas.gov.tr; f. 2001, following devolution of responsibilities of fmr Elektrik Üretim-İletim AŞ into separate entities for generation, transmission and wholesale activities; responsible for electricity generation; Chair. SEFER BÜTÜN.

Türkiye Elektrik Dağıtım AŞ (TEDAŞ): İnönü Bulv. 27, Bahçelievler, 06490 Ankara; tel. (312) 2126915; fax (312) 2138873; e-mail bilgi@tedas.gov.tr; internet www.tedas.gov.tr; privatization pending; responsible for distribution and sale of electricity; owns 20 regional distribution cos; Pres. and Man. Dir HAŞIM KEKLIK.

Türkiye Elektrik İletim Anonim Şirketi (TEIAŞ) (Turkish Electricity Transmission Company): İnönü Bul. 27, Bahçelievler, 06490 Ankara; tel. (312) 2038061; fax (312) 2228160; e-mail basinmail@teias.gov.tr; internet www.teias.gov.tr; f. 2001 (see EÜAŞ, above); responsible for electricity transmission; Chair. and Gen. Man. KEMAL YILDIR (acting).

Water

Devlet Su İşleri Genel Müdürlüğü (DSİ) (General Directorate of State Hydraulic Works): İnönü Bul., Yücetepe, 06100 Ankara; tel. (312) 4178300; fax (312) 4182498; e-mail idarim@dsi.gov.tr; internet www.dsi.gov.tr; f. 1954; controlled by the Ministry of Energy and Natural Resources; responsible for the planning and devt of water resources; Dir-Gen. HAYDAR KOÇAKER.

TRADE UNIONS

(Note: Statistics correct to July 2009)

Confederations

DİSK (Türkiye Devrimci İşçi Sendikaları Konfederasyonu) (Confederation of Progressive Trade Unions of Turkey): Cad. Abide-I Hürriyet 117, Nakiye Elgün Sok. 91, Şişli, İstanbul; tel. (212) 2910005; fax (212) 2342075; e-mail disk@disk.org.tr; internet www.disk.org.tr; f. 1967; member of ITUC and European Trade Union Confed; Pres. SÜLEYMAN ÇELEBI; Sec.-Gen. TAYFUN GÖRGÜN; 17 affiliated unions with 400,000 mems.

Hak-İş (Hak İşçi Sendikaları Konfederasyonu) (Confederation of Turkish Real Trade Unions): Tunus Cad. 37, 06680 Kavaklıdere, Ankara; tel. (312) 4178002; fax (312) 4250552; e-mail hakis@hakis.org.tr; internet www.hakis.org.tr; f. 1976; mem. of ITUC and European Trade Union Confed; Pres. SALIM USLU; Gen. Sec. FEUDUN TANKUT; 8 affiliated unions with 400,000 mems.

KESK (Kamu Emekçileri Sendikaları Konfederasyonu) (Confederation of Public Employees' Trade Unions): Çehre Sok. 6/1, Gaziosmanpaşa, Ankara; tel. (312) 4367111; fax (312) 4367470; e-mail kesk@kesk.org.tr; internet www.kesk.org.tr; f. 1995; mem. of ITUC and European Trade Union Confed; Pres. SAMI DÖNDÜ TAKA ÇINAR; Gen. Sec. KASIM BIRTEK; 11 affiliated unions with 224,413 mems.

Memur-Sen (Memur Sendikaları Konfederasyonu) (Confederation of Public Servants' Trade Unions): Özveren Sok. 9, 4 Demirtepe, Ankara; tel. (312) 2304898; fax (312) 2303989; e-mail info@memursen.org.tr; internet www.memursen.org.tr; f. 1995; Pres. AHMET GÜNDOĞDU; Gen. Sec. MAHMUT KAÇAR; 12 affiliated unions with 376,355 mems.

Türk-İş (Türkiye İşçi Sendikaları Konfederasyonu) (Confederation of Turkish Trade Unions): Bayındır Sok. 10, 06410 Kizilay, Ankara; tel. (312) 4333125; fax (312) 4336809; e-mail turkis@turkis.org.tr; internet www.turkis.org.tr; f. 1952; mem. of ITUC, European Trade Union Confed. and OECD/Trade Union Advisory Cttee; Pres. MUSTAFA KUMLU; Gen. Sec. (vacant); 33 affiliated unions and federations with 2.2m. mems.

Türkiye Kamu-Sen (Türkiye Kamu Çalışanları Sendikaları Konfederasyonu) (Confederation of Turkish Public Employees' Unions): Dr Mediha Eldem Sok. 85, Kocatepe, Çankaya, Ankara; tel. (312) 4242200; fax (312) 4242208; e-mail kamusen@kamusen.org.tr; internet www.kamusen.org.tr; f. 1992; Pres. BIRCAN AKYILDIZ; Gen. Sec. ISMAIL KONCUK; 12 affiliated unions with 375,990 mems.

Principal Affiliated Trade Unions

Belediye-İş (Türkiye Belediyeler ve Genel Hizmetler İşçiler Sendikası) (Municipal and Public Services Workers): Necatibey Cad. 59, Kızılay, Ankara; tel. (312) 2318343; fax (312) 2320874; internet www.belediyeis.org.tr; f. 1983; affiliated to Türk-İş; Pres. NIHAT YURDAKUL; Gen. Sec. NIHAT AYÇIÇEK; 205,666 mems.

Genel-İş (Türkiye Genel Hizmetler İşçileri Sendikası) (Municipal Workers): Çankırı Cad. 28, Kat. 5–9, Ulus, Ankara; tel. (312) 3091547; fax (312) 3091046; e-mail bilgi@genel-is.org.tr; internet www.genel-is.org.tr; f. 1983; affiliated to DISK; Pres. EROL EKICI; Gen. Sec. KANI BEKO; 83,976 mems.

Hizmet-İş Sendikası (Municipal and Public Service Workers): Gazi Mustafa Kemal Bul. 86, Maltepe, 06570 Çankaya, Ankara; tel. (312) 2318710; fax (312) 2319889; e-mail hizmet-is@hizmet-is.org.tr; internet www.hizmet-is.org.tr; f. 1979; affiliated to Hak-İş; Pres. MAHMUT ARSLAN; Gen. Sec. DEVLET SERT; 130,942 mems.

Petrol-İş (Türkiye Petrol, Kimya ve Lastik İşçileri Sendikası) (Petroleum, Chemicals and Rubber Industry): Altunizade Mah., Kuşbakışı Cad. 23, Üsküdar, İstanbul; tel. (212) 4749870; fax (212) 4749867; e-mail merkez@petrol-is.org.tr; internet www.petrol-is.org.tr; f. 1954; affiliated to Türk-İş; Pres. MUSTAFA ÖZTAŞKIN; Gen. Sec. MUSTAFA ÇAVDAR; 89,442 mems.

Sağlık-Sen (Sağlık ve Sosyal Hizmet Çalışanları Sendikası) (Health and Social Workers): GMK Bul., Özveren Sok. 9/2, Demirtepe, Ankara; tel. (312) 444 1995; fax (312) 2308365; internet www.sagliksen.org.tr; f. 1995; affiliated to Memur-Sen; Pres. MAHMUT KAÇAR; Gen. Sec. MENDERES TURBAY; 103,500 mems.

Tarım-İş (Türkiye Orman, Topraksu, Tarım ve Tarım Sanayii İşçileri Sendikası) (Forestry, Agriculture and Agricultural Industry Workers): Bankacı Sok. 10, 06700 Kocatepe, Ankara; tel. (312) 4190456; fax (312) 4193113; e-mail info@tarimis.org.tr; internet www.tarimis.org.tr; f. 1961; affiliated to Türk-İş; Pres. BEDRETTIN KAYKAÇ; Gen. Sec. MUSTAFA ÇARDAKÇI; 43,337 mems.

Tekgıda-İş (Türkiye Tütün, Müskirat Gıda ve Yardımcı İşçileri Sendikası) (Tobacco, Drink, Food and Allied Workers): 4

TURKEY

Levent Konaklar Sok. 1, İstanbul; tel. (212) 2644996; fax (212) 2789534; e-mail bilgi@tekgida.org.tr; internet www.tekgida.org.tr; f. 1952; affiliated to Türk-İş; Pres. MUSTAFA TÜRKEL; Gen. Sec. MECIT AMAÇ; 191,641 mems.

Teksif (Türkiye Tekstil, Örme ve Giyim Sanayii İşçileri Sendikası) (Textile, Knitting and Clothing Workers): Ziya Gökalp Cad. Aydoğmuş Sok. 1, 06600 Ankara; tel. (312) 4312170; fax (312) 4357826; e-mail teksif@oda.net.tr; internet www.teksif.org.tr; f. 1951; affiliated to Türk-İş; Pres. NAZMI IRGAT; Gen. Sec. MEHMET ÇAKAN; 338,835 mems.

Tes-İş (Türkiye Enerji, Su ve Gaz İşçileri Sendikası) (Electricity, Water and Gas Workers): Meriç Sok. 23, 06510 Beştepeler, Ankara; tel. (312) 2126510; fax (312) 2126552; e-mail info@tes-is.org.tr; internet www.tes-is.org.tr; f. 1963; affiliated to Türk-İş; Pres. MUSTAFA KUMLU; Gen. Sec. MUSTAFA ŞAHIN; 122,350 mems.

Türk Eğitim-Sen (Türkiye Eğitim ve Öğretim Bilim Hizmetleri Kolu Kamu Çalışanları Sendikası) (Teachers and University Lecturers): Bayındır 2., Sok. 46, Kızılay, Ankara; tel. (312) 4240960; fax (312) 4240968; e-mail gds@turkegitimsen.org.tr; internet www.turkegitimsen.org.tr; affiliated to Türkiye Kamu-Sen; Pres. İSMAIL KONCUK; Gen. Sec. MUSA AKKAŞ; 155,021 mems.

Türk Maden-İş (Türkiye Maden İşçileri Sendikası) (Mining): Strazburg Cad. 7, Sıhhiye, Ankara; tel. (312) 2317355; fax (312) 2298931; e-mail genelmerkez@madenis.org.tr; internet www.madenis.org.tr; affiliated to Türk-İş; Pres. İSMAIL ARSLAN; Gen. Sec. VEDAT ÜNAL; 58,591 mems.

Türk-Metal (Türkiye Metal, Çelik, Mühimmat, Makina ve Metalden Mamul, Eşya ve Oto, Montaj ve Yardımcı İşçileri Sendikası) (Auto, Metal and Allied Workers): Kızılırmak Mah., Adalararası Sok. 3, Eskişehir Yolu 1 km, 06560 Söğütözü, Ankara; tel. (312) 2926400; fax (312) 2844018; e-mail bilgiislem@turkmetal.org.tr; internet www.turkmetal.org.tr; f. 1963; affiliated to Türk-İş; Pres. PEVRUL KAVLAK; Gen. Sec. MUHARREM ASLIYÜCE; 343,263 mems.

Türkiye Çimse-İş (Türkiye Çimento, Seramik, Toprak ve Cam Sanayii İşçileri Sendikası) (Cement, Ceramics, Clay and Glass Industries): Esat Cad. 43, Küçükesat, Çankaya, Ankara; tel. (312) 4195830; fax (312) 4251335; internet www.cimse-is.org.tr; f. 1963; affiliated to Türk-İş; Pres. RAMAZAN ŞAFAK; Gen. Sec. YUSUF ÇIRAK; 71,510 mems.

Yol-İş (Türkiye Yol, Yapı ve İnşaat İşçileri Sendikası) (Road, Construction and Building Workers): Sümer 1 Sok. 18, Kızılay, Ankara; tel. (312) 2324687; fax (312) 2324810; e-mail yildirimkoc@yol-is.org.tr; internet www.yol-is.org.tr; f. 1963; affiliated to Türk-İş; Pres. RAMAZAN ADAR; Gen. Sec. TEVFIK ÖZÇELIK; 165,505 mems.

Transport

RAILWAYS

The total length of the railways in operation within the national frontiers was 11,405 km in 2009, of which 9,080 km were main lines. There are direct rail links with Bulgaria, Iran and Syria. Construction work on a new line connecting Turkey with Georgia and Azerbaijan commenced in late 2007. However, construction was temporarily suspended in August 2008, owing to military conflict between Georgia and Russia in the Georgian secessionist region of South Ossetia. Environmental concerns further delayed the project, which consequently was not expected to be completed until 2012, two years later than originally envisaged. Construction work on a 533-km high-speed rail link between Ankara and İstanbul commenced in 2003. A 245-km section of the line between Ankara and Eskişehir became operational in March 2009; the line was scheduled to be fully operational by 2013. Construction work on the Marmaray Project, a 76-km suburban line between the European and Asian sections of İstanbul, incorporating a 13.6-km tunnel under the Bosphorus strait, commenced in 2004. The project was scheduled for completion by 2012. İstanbul operates a two-line, 34.7-km light railway system and a 15-km metro line. Ankara, Adana, Bursa and İzmir also operate metro and light railway systems.

Türkiye Cumhuriyeti Devlet Demiryolları (TCDD) (Turkish State Railways): Talatpaşa Bul., 06330 Gar, Ankara; tel. (312) 3090515; fax (312) 3126247; e-mail byhim@tcdd.gov.tr; internet www.tcdd.gov.tr; f. 1924; operates all railways and connecting ports of the State Railway Admin., which acquired the status of a state economic enterprise in 1953, and a state economic establishment in 1984; 494 main-line diesel locomotives, 64 main-line electric locomotives, 995 passenger coaches and 17,079 freight wagons (2008); Chair. of Bd and Dir-Gen. SÜLEYMAN KARAMAN.

ROADS

In January 2011 the total road network was estimated at 64,865 km of classified roads, of which 2,080 km were motorways, 31,395 km were highways and 31,390 km were secondary roads.

Karayolları Genel Müdürlüğü (KGM) (General Directorate of Highways): İnönü Bul., Yücetepe, 06100 Ankara; tel. (312) 4157000; fax (312) 4172851; e-mail info@kgm.gov.tr; internet www.kgm.gov.tr; f. 1950; Dir-Gen. MEHMET CAHIT TURHAN.

SHIPPING

At the end of 2009 Turkey's merchant fleet comprised 1,344 vessels and had an aggregate displacement of 5,450,500 grt.

The ports of Bandırma, Derince, Haydarpaşa (İstanbul), İskenderun and İzmir, all of which are connected to the railway network, are operated by Turkish State Railways (TCDD), while the port of İstanbul and five smaller ports are operated by the Turkish Maritime Organization. Responsibility for some 13 ports, including those of Antalya and Trabzon, was transferred from the Turkish Maritime Organization to private companies under separate 30-year agreements in 1997–2003. In 2007 control of the port of Mersin was transferred from TCDD to the private sector under a 36-year concession agreement. A similar arrangement involving the port of Samsun commenced in April 2010. In late April 2011 Prime Minister Recep Tayyip Erdoğan announced plans to construct a 50-km canal through the European portion of the country, connecting the Black and Mediterranean Seas. The 'Canal İstanbul' project was intended to relieve congestion on the Bosphorus Strait.

Regulatory and Port Authorities

Turkish Maritime Organization (TDI): Genel Müdürlüğü, Rıhtım Cad. Merkez Han 32, 34425 Karaköy, İstanbul; tel. (212) 2515000; fax (212) 2495391; e-mail tdibasin@tdi.gov.tr; internet www.tdi.com.tr; Gen. Man. BURHAN KÜLÜNK.

Port of Bandırma: TCDD Liman İşletme Müdürlüğü, Bandırma; tel. (266) 7187530; fax (266) 7136011; e-mail bandirmaliman@tcdd.gov.tr; Port Man. OKKES DEMIREL; Harbour Master RUSEN OKAN.

Port of Derince: TCDD Liman İşletme Müdürlüğü, Derince; tel. (262) 2399021; e-mail derinceliman@tcdd.gov.tr; Port Man. ALI ARIF AYTAÇ; Harbour Master HAYDAR DOĞAN.

Port of Haydarpaşa (İstanbul): TCDD Liman İşletme Müdürlüğü, Haydarpaşa, İstanbul; tel. (216) 3488020; fax (216) 3451705; e-mail haydarpasaliman@tcdd.gov.tr; Port Man. NEDIM OZCAN; Harbour Master İSMAIL SAFAER.

Port of İskenderun: TCDD Liman İşletme Müdürlüğü, İskenderun; tel. (326) 6140044; fax (326) 6132424; e-mail iskenderunliman@tcdd.gov.tr; Port Man. HILMI SÖNMEZ; Harbour Master İSHAK ÖZDEMIR.

Port of İzmir: TCDD Liman İşletme Müdürlüğü, İzmir; tel. (232) 4631600; fax (232) 4632248; e-mail izmirliman@tcdd.gov.tr; Port Man. GÜNGÖR ERKAYA; Harbour Master MEHMET ONGEL.

Port of Mersin: Yeni Mah. 101, Cad. 5307, Sok. 5, 33100 Mersin; tel. (324) 2412920; fax (324) 2290849; e-mail marketing@mersinport.com.tr; internet www.mersinport.com.tr; f. 2007; managed by a consortium of PSA Int. (Singapore) and Akfen (Turkey) under a 36-yr concession; Gen. Man. JOHN PHILLIPS; Harbour Master RACI TARHUSOĞLU.

Port of Samsun: TCDD Liman İşletme Müdürlüğü, Samsun; tel. (362) 2332293; fax (362) 4451626; e-mail samsunliman@tcdd.gov.tr; managed since April 2010 by Cey Group (Turkey) under a 36-year concession; Port Man. SAFFET YAMAK; Harbour Master Capt. ARIF H. UZUNOĞLU.

Principal Shipping Companies

Akmar Shipping Group: Küçükbakkalköy Mah. Cicek Sok. 4, Aksoy Plaza, 34750 Kadıköy, İstanbul; tel. (216) 5762666; fax (216) 5727195; e-mail info@akmar.com.tr; internet www.akmar.com.tr; f. 2004; Chair. NECDET AKSOY.

Deniz Nakliyatı TAŞ (Turkish Cargo Lines): Fahrettin Kerim Gökay Cad. Denizciler İş Merkezi No. 18, 1A Blok Kat. 1, Altunizade/Üsküdar, İstanbul; tel. (216) 4747400; fax (216) 4747430; e-mail tcl@tcl.com.tr; internet www.tcl.com.tr; f. 1955; bulk carriers; Chair. M. GÜNDÜZ KAPTANOĞLU; Gen. Man. CEMIL GÜCÜYENER; 2 large and 2 small handy bulk/ore carriers.

İstanbul Deniz Otobusleri Sanayi ve Ticaret AŞ: Kennedy Cad., Hizli Feribot Iskelesi Yenikapi, İstanbul; tel. (212) 4556900; fax (212) 5173958; e-mail info@ido.com.tr; internet www.ido.com.tr; f. 1987; state-owned; ferry co; scheduled for privatization; Chair. HUSEYIN EREN; Gen. Man. Dr AHMET PAKSOY; 90 vessels.

Kiran Group of Shipping Companies: Fahrettin Kerim Gorkay Cad. 18, Denizciler İş Merkezi B Blok Kat. 2, 34662 Altunizade, İstanbul; tel. (216) 5541400; fax (216) 5541414; e-mail kiran@kiran.com.tr; internet www.kiran.com.tr; f. 1959; Chair. TURGUT KIRAN; Man. Dir TAMER KIRAN; 19 vessels.

Ozsay Seatransportation Co Inc: Güzelyalı, E-5 Üzeri 18, 34903 Pendik, İstanbul; tel. (216) 4933610; fax (216) 4930306; e-mail ozsay@tnn.net; internet www.ozsay.com; Pres. RECEP KALKAVAN; Man. Dir OMER KALKAVAN; 10 vessels.

TURKEY

Directory

Türkiye Denizcilik İşletmeleri Denizyolları İşletmesi Müdürlüğü (TDI): Meclısı Mebusan Cad. 18, 80040 Salıpazarı, İstanbul; tel. (212) 2521700; fax (212) 2515767; e-mail bilgiedinme@tdi.gov.tr; internet www.tdi.com.tr; ferry co; Chair. ERKAN ARIKAN; Man. Dir KADIR KURTOĞLU; 5 vessels.

Yardimci Shipping Group of Companies: Aydintepe Mah. Tersaneler Cad. 50 Sok. 7, 34947 Tuzla, İstanbul; tel. (216) 4938000; fax (216) 4928080; e-mail info@yardimci.gen.tr; internet www.yardimci.gen.tr; f. 1976; Chair. KEMAL YARDIMCI; Man. Dir HUSEYIN YARDIMCI; 9 vessels.

CIVIL AVIATION

There are 40 airports for international and domestic flights in Turkey. The largest of these are Atatürk and Sabiha Gökçen (both serving İstanbul), Esenboğa (Ankara), Adnan Menderes (İzmir), Antalya, Dalaman, Milas–Bodrum, Adana, Trabzon, Isparta Süleyman Demirel and Nevşehir–Kapadokya. A second terminal building at Sabiha Gökçen International Airport was inaugurated in October 2009. Earlier that year plans were announced to increase total passenger capacity at the airport to 20m. by 2018.

Devlet Hava Meydanları İşletmesi Genel Müdürlüğü (General Directorate of State Airports Authority): Konya Yolu Üzeri No. 66, 06330 Etiler, Ankara; tel. (312) 2042000; fax (312) 2123917; e-mail dhmi@dhmi.gov.tr; internet www.dhmi.gov.tr; f. 1984; manages 36 airports nation-wide; responsible for air traffic control in Turkish airspace; Chair. of Bd and Dir-Gen. ORHAN BIRDAL.

Sivil Havacılık Genel Müdürlüğü (Directorate General of Civil Aviation): Bosna Hersek Cad. 5, 06510 Emek, Ankara; tel. (312) 2036000; fax (312) 2124684; internet web.shgm.gov.tr; Dir-Gen. Dr ALI ARIDURU.

Atlasjet Havacilik AŞ: Yeşilyurt Mah. Eski Halkali Yolu Alacati Evleri Yani 5B, 34153 Florya, İstanbul; tel. (212) 6632000; fax (212) 6632751; e-mail info@atlasjet.com; internet www.atlasjet.com; f. 2001; passenger and cargo; 17 aircraft; Chair. TUNCAY DOĞANER; CEO ORHAN COŞKUN.

Onur Air Taşımacılık AŞ: Senlikköy Mah., Çatal Sok. 3, 34153 Florya, İstanbul; tel. (212) 6632300; fax (212) 6632319; e-mail info@onurair.com.tr; internet www.onurair.com.tr; f. 1992; international and domestic passenger and cargo charter services; 22 aircraft; Chair. CANKUT BAGANA.

Pegasus Hava Taşımacılığı AŞ (Pegasus Airlines): Basın Ekspres Yolu 2, Halkalı, İstanbul; tel. (212) 6977777; fax (212) 6939777; internet www.flypgs.com; f. 1990; domestic and international scheduled and charter services; 23 aircraft; Chair. ALI SABANCI; Gen. Man. SERTAÇ HAYBAT.

SunExpress (Güneş Ekspres Havacilik AŞ): Mehmetçik Mah. Aspendos Bul. Aspendos İş Merkezi 63/1–2, 07300 Antalya; tel. (242) 3102626; fax (242) 3102650; e-mail travelcenter@sunexpress.com; internet www.sunexpress.com; f. 1989; 50% owned by Deutsche Lufthansa AG (Germany) and 50% by Turkish Airlines; charter and scheduled passenger and freight; serves European destinations; 26 aircraft; Man. Dir PAUL SCHWAIGER.

TAV Havalimanları Holding AŞ: İstanbul Atatürk Havalimanı, Dış Hatlar Terminali, 34149 Yeşilköy, İstanbul; tel. (212) 4633000; fax (212) 4655050; e-mail info@tav.aero; internet www.tavairports.com; f. 1997; construction and management of airport facilities; manages Atatürk (İstanbul), Esenboğa (Ankara), Adnan Menderes (İzmir) and Gazipaşa (Antalya) airports, as well as airports in Georgia and Tunisia; Chair. HAMDI AKIN; Pres. and CEO Dr MUSTAFA SANI ŞENER.

Türk Hava Yolları AO (THY) (Turkish Airlines Inc): Genel Müdürlük Binas, Atatürk Hava Limani, 34830 Yeşilköy, İstanbul; tel. (212) 4636363; fax (212) 4652121; e-mail customer@thy.com; internet www.thy.com.tr; f. 1933; 49.12% state-owned; extensive internal network and scheduled and charter flights to destinations in the Middle East, Africa, the Far East, Cen. Asia, the USA and Europe; 133 aircraft; Chair. HAMDI TOPÇU; Gen. Man. TEMEL KOTIL.

Tourism

Visitors to Turkey are attracted by the climate, fine beaches and ancient monuments. With government investment, the country has rapidly become a leading holiday destination for European tourists (particularly from the United Kingdom and Germany). According to provisional data, in 2010 the number of tourists increased to 28.6m. (compared with 7.5m. in 1999); receipts from tourism reached US $20,807m. in 2010.

Ministry of Culture and Tourism: See The Government—Ministries; Dir-Gen. of Information MUSTAFA SYAHHAN; Dir-Gen. of Investments and Establishments KUDRET ASLAN.

Defence

Chief of the General Staff: Gen. IŞIK KOŞANER.
Ground Forces Commander: Gen. ERDAL CEYLANOĞLU.
Navy Commander: Adm. UĞUR YIĞIT.
Air Force Commander: Gen. HASAN AKSAY.
Gendarmerie Commander: Gen. ATILA IŞIK.
Defence Budget (2010): estimated at TL 15,800m.
Military Service: 15 months.
Total Armed Forces (as assessed at November 2010): 510,600 (including an estimated 359,500 conscripts): army 402,000, navy 48,600, air force 60,000.
Paramilitary Forces (as assessed at November 2010): 153,250: 150,000 gendarmerie, 3,250 coast guard.

Education

When the Turkish Republic was formed, the Ministry of Education became the sole authority in educational matters, replacing the dual system of religious schools and other schools. One of the main obstacles to literacy was the Arabic script, which required years of study before proficiency could be attained. In 1928, therefore, a Turkish alphabet was introduced, using Latin characters. At the same time the literary language was simplified, and purged of some of its foreign elements. In 2004 government expenditure on education was budgeted at about US $6,700m.

PRIMARY EDUCATION

Primary education may be preceded by an optional pre-school establishment for children between three and six years of age. In the 2010/11 academic year, according to provisional figures, there were 27,606 such schools, with 47,289 teachers. In the same year 1,115,818 children were enrolled at pre-schools.

According to the 'Basic Law of National Education', the education of children between the ages of six and 14 is compulsory. The transition from a five-year cycle of primary schools, followed by a three-year cycle of middle schools, to that of a single eight-year basic education system was introduced throughout the country from September 1997.

Primary education is now entirely free, and co-education is the accepted basis for universal education. According to provisional figures, the number of primary schools has risen from 12,511 in 1950 to 32,797 in 2010/11, and the number of teachers from 27,144 to 503,328. In the same year 10,981,100 children were enrolled at primary schools. In 2007/08, according to UNESCO estimates, 95% of children in the relevant age-group were enrolled in primary education.

SECONDARY EDUCATION

Secondary education lasts for a minimum of three years after primary education, and provides for students intending to proceed to higher educational institutions. The secondary education system encompasses general high schools, and vocational and technical high schools. In addition, since 1992/93 'open' high schools have provided secondary education opportunities to young working people through the media and other new technologies.

Those students who wish to proceed to an institute of higher education must pass the state matriculation examination. The study of a modern language (English, French or German) is compulsory. In 2010/11, according to provisional figures, there were 4,102 general high schools, with 118,378 teachers. In that year 2,676,123 children were enrolled in general secondary education. In 2007/08, according to UNESCO estimates, 74% of children in the relevant age-group were enrolled in secondary education.

VOCATIONAL EDUCATION

In 2010/11, according to provisional figures, a total of 2,072,487 students attended 5,179 vocational and teacher training high schools, with 104,327 teachers. In addition, there are colleges for commerce, tourism, communication, local administration and secretarial skills.

HIGHER EDUCATION

Higher educational institutions in Turkey were established, and are administered, by the state. In 2005/06, according to provisional figures, Turkey had 1,306 institutes of higher education, including some 69 universities of various types, with 84,785 teachers. The main university at İstanbul, originally established in 1453, was attended by 73,061 students in 2003. A total of 2,181,217 students were enrolled at institutes of higher education in the 2005/06 academic year.

TURKMENISTAN

Introductory Survey

LOCATION, CLIMATE, LANGUAGE, RELIGION, FLAG, CAPITAL

Turkmenistan is situated in the south-west of Central Asia. It is bordered to the north by Uzbekistan, to the north-west by Kazakhstan, to the west by the Caspian Sea, to the south by Iran and to the south-east by Afghanistan. The climate is severely continental, with extremely hot summers and cold winters. The average temperature in January is −4°C (25°F), but winter temperatures can fall as low as −33°C (−27°F). In summer temperatures often reach 50°C (122°F) in the south-eastern Kara-Kum desert; the average temperature in July is 28°C (82°F). Precipitation is slight throughout much of the country: average annual rainfall ranges from only 80 mm (3.1 ins) in the north-west to about 300 mm (11.8 ins) in mountainous regions. Turkmen, a member of the Southern Turkic group, is the official language. Most of the population are Sunni Muslims. Islam in Turkmenistan has traditionally featured elements of Sufi mysticism and shamanism, and pilgrimages to local religious sites are reported to be common. The national flag (proportions 2 by 3) consists of a maroon stripe bearing a vertical design of five different carpet patterns above a wreath of olive branches on a green background, with five white, five-pointed stars framed by a narrow white crescent moon, in its upper dexter corner. The capital is Aşgabat.

CONTEMPORARY POLITICAL HISTORY

Historical Context

In 1877 Russia began a campaign against the Turkmen, which culminated in the battle of Gök Tepe in 1881, at which some 20,000 Turkmen are estimated to have been killed. In 1895 the Russian conquest was confirmed by agreement with the British; the international boundary thus established divided some Turkmen under Russian rule from others in the British sphere of influence. In 1917 the Bolsheviks attempted to take power in the region, but found limited local support. An anti-Bolshevik Russian Provisional Government of Transcaspia was formed, and a Turkmen Congress was also established. Soviet forces were sent to Aşgabat, and a Turkestan Autonomous Soviet Socialist Republic was declared on 30 April 1918. In July nationalists, aided by British forces, ousted the Bolshevik Government and established an independent Government in Aşgabat, protected by a British garrison. After the British withdrew, however, the Government was soon removed, and by 1920 Red Army troops were in control of Aşgabat. A Turkmen Soviet Socialist Republic (SSR) was established on 27 October 1924. In May 1925 it became a constituent republic of the USSR, and political power in the republic became the preserve of the Communist Party of Turkmenistan (CPT).

In 1928 all Islamic institutions in Turkmenistan were closed. A programme of agricultural collectivization, which was begun in 1929 and entailed the forcible settlement of traditionally nomadic people in collective farms, provoked military resistance, and guerrilla warfare against Soviet power continued until 1936. In the early 1930s many Turkmen intellectuals were imprisoned or executed. The scope of the purges widened in the late 1930s to include government and CPT officials. The immigration of Russians into the urban areas of Turkmenistan, from the 1920s, gradually diminished the proportion of Turkmen in leading posts in the republic. The development of extensive irrigation projects enabled rapid development of cotton-growing, particularly after 1945.

In the late 1980s Turkmenistan's role as a provider of raw materials (mainly natural gas and cotton) to more developed regions of the USSR provoked strong criticism of the relationship between the republican and the all-Union authorities, while concerns were expressed in the republican media about the environmental and health hazards associated with intensive agriculture. The geographical remoteness of the republic inhibited its involvement in the political changes occurring in some other Soviet republics, and the CPT dominated the republic's elections to the all-Union Congress of People's Deputies in the Soviet and Russian capital, Moscow, in early 1989. A 'popular front' organization concerned with the status of Turkmen language and culture and environmental matters, Unity (Agzybirlik), was formed in September; despite initially gaining official registration, it was banned in January 1990. Only the CPT and its approved organizations were permitted to participate in elections to the republican Supreme Soviet on 7 January. When the new Supreme Soviet convened, Saparmyrat Niyazov, the First Secretary of the CPT since 1985, was elected Chairman of the Supreme Soviet, the highest government office in the republic.

In May 1990 Turkmen officially became the state language, replacing Russian. On 22 August the Turkmenistani Supreme Soviet adopted a declaration of sovereignty. On 27 October Niyazov was elected, unopposed, by direct ballot, to the new post of executive President of Turkmenistan, reportedly receiving 98.3% of the votes cast. In late 1990 and early 1991 Turkmenistan participated in negotiations towards a new Union Treaty, which was to provide a new framework for the continuation of the USSR. The republic's dependence on the central Government for subsidies, ensured that the republic's leadership was one of the most enthusiastic proponents of the preservation of the USSR. At the referendum on the status of the USSR in March 1991, 95.7% of eligible voters in Turkmenistan—a higher proportion than in any other Soviet republic—approved the preservation of the USSR as a 'renewed federation'.

Domestic Political Affairs

President Niyazov made no public announcements either opposing or supporting the attempted coup by conservative communists in Moscow of August 1991. However, opposition groups, including Unity, publicly opposed the coup, which led to the arrest of several of their leaders. On 18 October Turkmenistan was among the signatories of the treaty establishing an economic community of eight republics. This was followed on 26 October by a national referendum, at which, according to the official results, 94.1% of the electorate voted for independence. On the following day the Turkmenistani Supreme Council adopted a law on independence. The name of the republic was changed from the Turkmen SSR to Turkmenistan. In December the CPT changed its name to the Democratic Party of Turkmenistan (DPT), with Niyazov as its Chairman. On 21 December Turkmenistan was one of 11 republics to sign the Almaty (Alma-Ata) Declaration, which formally established the Commonwealth of Independent States (CIS, see p. 238); this decision was subsequently ratified by the Turkmenistani Supreme Council.

The DPT and Niyazov came to dominate independent Turkmenistan. Although Niyazov reportedly continued to enjoy widespread popular support, there was some criticism of his authoritarian leadership, rigid control of the media and the restriction of opposition activity. The promotion of a presidential 'cult of personality' was reported to have prompted the resignation, in mid-1992, of the Minister of Foreign Affairs, Abdy Kuliyev. The new Constitution, adopted on 18 May, further enhanced presidential authority, making Niyazov Chairman of the Government (prime minister), as well as Head of State, and giving him certain legislative prerogatives. In June Niyazov was re-elected, again unopposed, to the presidency, receiving a purported 99.5% of the votes cast in a direct ballot.

Other significant structural changes were introduced under the new Constitution. The Supreme Council was to be replaced as Turkmenistan's legislature by a 50-member Majlis (Assembly); however, until the expiry of its five-year term, the Supreme Soviet elected in 1990 (although renamed the Majlis) was to be retained as the republican legislature. The Khalk Maslakhaty (People's Council) was established as the 'supreme representative body of popular power', and was to act in a supervisory capacity; it was to debate and decide important political and economic issues, and would be empowered to demand changes to the Constitution and to vote to express no confidence in the President, if it found his actions to be at variance with the law. The Khalk Maslakhaty was to comprise the 50 deputies of the Majlis in addition to 50 elected and 10 appointed representatives from the electoral districts of Turkmenistan (the former were

TURKMENISTAN

directly elected in November–December 1992); it was also to include other members of local government and prominent figures, including the members of the Government and the Chairman of the Supreme Court, and was to be headed by the President.

After the new Constitution was adopted, there were fears that the rights of members of Turkmenistan's minority ethnic groups (the most numerous of which, Russians and Uzbeks, represented some 10% and 9%, respectively, of the total population in the early 1990s) were in jeopardy, as the document stipulated that only ethnic Turkmen would be eligible for employment in state enterprises, and removed the status of 'language of inter-ethnic communication' hitherto granted to Russian. The Constitution guaranteed state secularism.

The presidential personality cult was strengthened during 1993, with numerous institutions, streets and public buildings being named after Niyazov, while the Caspian Sea port of Krasnovodsk was renamed Türkmenbaşi ('Head of the Turkmen', a recently introduced mode of address for Niyazov). In December the Majlis voted to extend Niyazov's term of office until 2002, a decision that was endorsed by a reported 99.99% of the electorate in a referendum held on 15 January 1994.

Elections to the new, 50-member Majlis were held in December 1994, officially with the participation of 99.8% of the registered electorate. It was reported that 49 of the 50 deputies had been elected unopposed. The Majlis convened later in the month; the overwhelming majority of the deputies were believed to be members of the DPT.

Despite the result of the referendum of January 1994, elements of opposition to Niyazov were believed to be active in Turkmenistan, as well as in exile in other republics of the CIS, in particular Russia, where Abdy Kuliyev led an opposition group, the Turkmenistan Foundation. In June 1995 the Turkmenistani Supreme Court sentenced two opposition leaders to respective terms of 12 and 15 years' imprisonment in a labour colony, having found them guilty of involvement in an alleged plot to assassinate Niyazov. In July 1995 a protest rally took place in Aşgabat (reportedly the first to be held in Turkmenistan since independence), at which up to 1,000 demonstrators criticized Niyazov's leadership and the continuing economic hardships. In August, in what was interpreted as a response to the previous month's unrest, Niyazov dismissed 10 of Turkmenistan's 50 local etrap (district or raion) administrative leaders. In October the President dismissed several senior members of the Council of Ministers.

In 1996 and 1997 Niyazov effected widespread dismissals of government officials, as well as local administrative leaders and members of the judiciary. In February 1998 the President revealed that he planned to amend the Constitution after the legislative elections of December 1999, devolving certain presidential powers to the Majlis and relinquishing the premiership (although in the event he retained the latter position). In April 1998 elections to the Khalk Maslakhaty were held, with the reported participation of 99.5% of the electorate.

Turkmenistan continued to attract the censure of international human rights organizations during the late 1990s. In April 1998 a delegation of the Organization for Security and Co-operation in Europe (OSCE, see p. 385) appealed to Niyazov to release eight political prisoners who had been detained since the July 1995 demonstration. Niyazov agreed to their release, following which he made his first official visit to the USA where he met President Bill Clinton. Niyazov's systematic purging of government and other officials continued in May 1998. An attempted military rebellion in western Turkmenistan in September was followed by the dismissal of the Minister of Defence, and the comprehensive reorganization of senior personnel of the armed forces.

The promotion of the presidential cult of personality appeared to intensify during 1998: in December a giant ceremonial arch, surmounted by a revolving gold-plated statue of the President, was inaugurated in central Aşgabat. In what was interpreted as an effort to counter growing international accusations of dictatorial methods, the President declared, in December, that the elections to the Majlis scheduled for late 1999 would be contested on a multi-party basis, and that the establishment of new political parties would be permitted in advance of the poll. In December the Khalk Maslakhaty voted to abolish the death penalty; Turkmenistan thus became the first state in post-Soviet Central Asia to proscribe capital punishment.

Extension of Niyazov's presidential term

Elections to the Majlis were conducted on 12 December 1999. According to official reports, some 99% of the registered electorate participated in the poll. In the event, the DPT was the only party represented and the OSCE declined an invitation to monitor the poll. In late December the new Majlis approved an amendment to the Constitution, extending Niyazov's presidential term indefinitely. Niyazov had made repeated claims that the success of democratic and economic reform would be dependent on the continuity of successive 10-year plans. Niyazov subsequently announced that the creation of opposition political parties would not be contemplated before 2010. These developments further aroused the concerns of the international community, and there was considerable outrage when, in March 2000, the leader of the unofficial popular opposition front, Unity, Nurberdi Nurmämmet, was sentenced to five years' imprisonment on charges of 'hooliganism and intent to murder', after he protested that the constitutional amendment was undemocratic.

On 1 January 2000 Turkmenistan formally adopted a revised form of the Latin script for the Turkmen language, replacing the Cyrillic script introduced in the 1920s. In July Niyazov issued an order declaring that, henceforth, knowledge of the Turkmen language would be a mandatory requirement for all government officials. Furthermore, all candidates for leadership posts were to have their genealogies over the previous three generations verified.

In January and June 2000 President Niyazov dismissed a number of prominent government officials. Niyazov also instructed Turkmenistani citizens and government organizations to close any bank accounts held abroad, so as to curtail the outflow of capital from Turkmenistan. In July the President dismissed Boris Shikhmuradov, the Minister of Foreign Affairs; he was succeeded by Batyr Berdyyev. It was also announced that all officials, including government ministers, would henceforth be appointed for a six-month probationary period, prior to being confirmed in office.

In the early 2000s Niyazov oversaw the introduction of a number of policies intended to develop a strong Turkmen national identity, including the closure of the opera and ballet theatre in Aşgabat, which Niyazov denounced as 'alien' to Turkmen culture. A principal element of Niyazov's proposals to promote a Turkmen national culture was the publication of the *Ruhnama*, or national code of spiritual conduct purportedly written by the President. The *Ruhnama* became a key element of the school curriculum, and was in effect elevated to the status of a holy text, with display of the volume required in mosques, citations from the work included in inscriptions in religious and public buildings, and with knowledge of the text, moreover, becoming a prerequisite for entry into various professions. (A second volume of the *Ruhnama* was published in September 2004.)

In July 2001 Berdyyev was dismissed as Minister of Foreign Affairs, and replaced by Rashid Meredov. In late October Shikhmuradov was dismissed as ambassador to the People's Republic of China. He fled to exile in Moscow from where, in November, he issued a statement condemning Niyazov's rule. Meanwhile, the Prosecutor-General, Gurbanbibi Atajanova, issued a warrant for Shikhmuradov's arrest on charges of the misappropriation of state property, along with a request for his extradition from Russia, amid widespread speculation that Shikhmuradov (who denied the charges against him) intended to replace Niyazov by means of a coup. In January 2002 he established the People's Democratic Movement of Turkmenistan. In early February Nurmukhammet Hanamov resigned as ambassador to Turkey in order to join the opposition movement. In mid-February a former deputy premier, Hudayberdy Orazov, announced his support for the opposition-in-exile. The Turkmenistani authorities subsequently issued a request for the extradition of Hanamov and accused Orazov of embezzling state funds. Meanwhile, in March Niyazov dismissed a number of senior officials from the defence, intelligence and security services (including the Minister of Defence), whom he accused of plotting to remove him from power. In addition, the State Border Service was placed under the direct control of the President. A new Minister of Internal Affairs was appointed in May, and in the same month Seitbay Gandimov was dismissed as Deputy Chairman and Chairman of the Central Bank, following allegations that he had links with Orazov. A further cabinet reorganization followed in August. Government changes in September included the appointment of three new ministers and the creation of a Ministry of National Security, led by Batyr Busakov, to replace the Committee for National Security. In September the newly appointed Chairman of the Central Bank was dismissed, following the theft from the bank of US $41.5m. In the same month Niyazov announced the creation of so-called 'labour armies', comprising 20,000 men under the age of 35, which were to be drafted to work without remuneration on public projects; the term of service was to be two years, irrespective of previous army service. Further government changes took place in mid-November, when Ovezgeldy Atayev was elected Chairman of the Majlis.

On 25 November 2002 an assassination attempt was made against the presidential motorcade, as it travelled through Aşgabat. An emergency cabinet meeting was held, and Niyazov publicly accused Shikhmuradov and Hanamov, among others, of involvement in the organization of what they termed an attempted coup. On the same day Shikhmuradov, who had clandestinely returned to Turkmenistan, was arrested in Aşgabat. An official announcement, made one day later, reported that 16 suspects had been arrested, although international human rights organizations reported that hundreds of people were detained in subsequent days. Following a televised confession, a one-day trial at the Supreme Court on 30 December found Shikhmuradov guilty of the attempt on Niyazov's life, and he was sentenced to 25 years' imprisonment (subsequently increased to a life sentence by the Majlis). Orazov and Hanamov were also convicted in absentia, and another former Minister of Foreign Affairs, Berdyyev, was detained and sentenced in early 2003 to 25 years' imprisonment for his involvement in the assassination attempt; the opposition-in-exile subsequently indicated that both Shikhmuradov and Berdyyev may have died while in detention, although these claims remained unconfirmed. Meanwhile, opposition leader Murad Esenov, in exile in Sweden, claimed that the assassination attempt had been staged as a pretext for the arrest of Shikhmuradov and other members of the opposition, and the OSCE, concerned at the circumstances surrounding Shikhmuradov's trial and confession, sent a fact-finding mission to Aşgabat. In late December the Uzbekistani ambassador to Turkmenistan (the embassy of which country had been searched, in violation of the Vienna Convention on Diplomatic Relations) was expelled from the country, having been accused of harbouring Shikhmuradov immediately after the attack. In June 2003 Orazov reportedly stated that Shikhmuradov and his opposition allies had intended to stage a coup, but that they had no intention of killing Niyazov.

In February 2003 Niyazov issued decrees that temporarily reinstated the requirement for exit visas (which had been abolished in December 2001), and imposed severe restrictions on the exchange of Turkmenistani currency. (The requirement for exit visas was abolished again in March 2004.) The import of foreign periodicals was prohibited, and the restrictions imposed on journalists were intensified. On 6 April 2003 elections to the Khalk Maslakhaty and to district and village councils took place, with the participation of some 89.3% of the electorate. The OSCE, which had accused the authorities of widespread human rights abuses in a report issued in March, questioned the legitimacy of the electoral process.

Constitutional amendments

On 15 August 2003 amendments to the Constitution elevated the Khalk Maslakhaty, which was henceforth to comprise 2,507 members, to the status of a 'permanently functioning supreme representative body of popular authority', and required it to remain in continuous session. The Khalk Maslakhaty was also accorded a number of legislative powers, which enabled it to adopt constitutional laws, thus effectively displacing the Majlis as the country's leading legislative body. Other changes to the Constitution forbade Turkmenistani citizens from holding dual nationality, superseding an agreement on dual nationality reached with Russia in December 1993.

Government changes in September 2003 included the appointment of Maj.-Gen. Agageldy Mamatgeldiyev as Minister of Defence. As part of further restructuring in November, two new Deputy Chairmen and a new Minister of National Security were appointed. In the same month a new law came into force, which severely restricted the activities of non-governmental organizations, imposing fines, prison sentences and periods of 'corrective labour' for those convicted under the new guidelines. Also in November a new law was approved, restricting the activities of religious groups by criminalizing any confession not registered with the Ministry of Justice (at that time the only state-registered faiths were Sunni Islam and Russian Orthodox Christianity). The formation of political parties on religious grounds was also prohibited. (These laws were revised in March 2004.) In late November the UN General Assembly adopted a resolution (which was, notably, supported by Russia), expressing grave concerns over human rights violations in Turkmenistan. At the end of the month Niyazov pardoned more than 7,000 prisoners.

In February 2004 President Niyazov replaced 15,000 medical workers with army conscripts in an attempt to reduce government expenditure on health care. In April the Minister of the Economy and Finance, the Minister of Education and the heads of two state-controlled banks were dismissed. In May Niyazov signed a decree prohibiting the use of child labour in the cotton industry. A further presidential decree, issued in June, invalidated all higher-education degrees received abroad; all teachers with such degrees were to be dismissed. In August Geldymuhammet Ashirkulov was appointed Minister of Internal Affairs, although he only remained in office until December, when he was succeeded by Akmamed Rahmanov. Meanwhile, in October Niyazov removed Enebai Atayeva as Deputy Chairman and Governor of the cotton-producing Ahal Velayat (Region). This dismissal reportedly reflected dissatisfaction with the nationwide cotton harvest; the regional deputy governor and four heads of cotton-producing associations were also replaced. In the same month the UN General Assembly adopted a second resolution criticizing human rights violations in Turkmenistan; on this occasion, Russia abstained from voting, while Uzbekistan voted against the resolution, despite its explicit condemnation of discrimination by the Government of Turkmenistan against Russians, Uzbeks and other minority groups in the country.

Elections to the Majlis were conducted on 19 December 2004. According to official reports, 76.9% of the registered electorate participated in the poll, at which the DPT was the only party represented. (A second round of voting took place on 9 January 2005 in seven districts where candidates had failed to obtain the required 50% plus one of the votes cast.) In February 2005 Niyazov announced plans to close all hospitals outside Aşgabat, stating that the provision of hospitals outside the capital was unnecessary. Niyazov also ordered the closure of rural libraries, asserting that the rural Turkmenistani population was largely illiterate and therefore made limited use of the existing facilities. In April the President prohibited the import and circulation of all foreign print media and refused to renew the licences of international shipping firms and express couriers operating in Turkmenistan. In June a report published by the London School of Hygiene and Tropical Medicine (United Kingdom) expressed concern at the 'systematic dismantling' of Turkmenistan's health care system; the report urged the international community to apply pressure on Turkmenistan to improve services.

Throughout 2005 and early 2006 President Niyazov frequently replaced state officials; many of those dismissed were accused of corruption or other abuses of office, and were sentenced to long custodial terms. Notably, in late May 2005 the deputy prime minister for the Fuel and Energy Sector, Yolly Gurbanmuradov, was dismissed, after being accused of abusing his former position (in 1993–2001) as head of the State Bank for Foreign Economic Activities in 1993–2001. In July 2005 Gurbanmuradov was sentenced to 25 years' imprisonment. Meanwhile, in May 2005 Niyazov dismissed the Chairman of the Central Bank, who was accused of corruption. Niyazov further reorganized the energy sector in August and September of that year. In mid-April 2006 Niyazov appointed Muhammetguly Ogshukov, previously First Deputy Prosecutor-General, to succeed Atajanova as Prosecutor-General. Although Niyazov initially stated that Atajanova was to retire (having occupied the post since 1997), later in the month Atajanova admitted that accusations, made by Niyazov, to the effect that she had taken bribes and stolen state property, were true. In early May Niyazov declared invalid the presidential decree relieving Atajanova of her post in connection with her retirement, instead decreeing that she had been relieved of her duties for having committed 'shameful' deeds and having damaged the reputation of the office of Prosecutor-General. In the same month work was completed on a palace made of ice, the construction of which had cost some US $21.5m., in Aşgabat, ordered by the President. Elections to the 625 municipal councils (gengeşes) took place on 23 July.

Death of President Niyazov

On 21 December 2006 President Niyazov died, after he suffered a heart attack. Under the terms of the Constitution, the role of acting President should have been assumed by the Chairman of the Majlis, Ovezgeldy Atayev; however, Atayev was dismissed from his post shortly after Niyazov's death, when state prosecutors announced they would be investigating criminal charges against Atayev. Subsequently, the State Security Council appointed the Deputy Chairman of the Government and Minister of Health and the Medical Industry, Gurbanguly Berdymuhamedov, to act as acting President, while Akja Nurberdiyeva succeeded Atayev as Chairman of the Majlis. Six candidates contested the presidential elections held on 11 February 2007. Berdymuhamedov won by an overwhelming majority, receiving 89.2% of the votes cast; the rate of participation by the electorate was officially recorded at 98.6%. Berdymuhamedov was inaugurated as President on 14 February. From mid-February the appointment of government ministers and other senior state officials was announced, including several ministers who had served under Niyazov. Among the principal appointments were those of Rashid Meredov as deputy premier and Minister of Foreign Affairs, Mamatgeldiyev as Minister of Defence and Myrat Karryyev as Minister of Justice; Muhammetgeldy Annaamanov was appointed Minister of Education, replacing Hydyr Saparliyev, who was promoted to the position of deputy premier. New appointments were also made to regional governorships and to the chairmanship of the Supreme Court and to the Office of the Prosecutor-General.

The most significant of President Berdymuhamedov's early decrees was the Code of Social Guarantees, signed into law on 19 March 2007, which restored pension rights that had been removed from an estimated 100,000 senior citizens in the previous year. In a speech to the Khalk Maslakhaty, President Berdymuhamedov announced a programme of agricultural reforms and plans to extend public access to the internet, which hitherto had been severely restricted in Turkmenistan. (The first public access point to the internet in the country had been opened in February in Aşgabat.) In April the recently appointed Minister of Internal Affairs was dismissed, reportedly on the grounds that he had failed to address corruption within the ministry and to combat an increase in drug abuse within the country; he was succeeded by Khodjamyrat Annagurbanov. In July Berdymuhamedov effected a minor government reorganization. In early October Berdymuhamedov dismissed Minister of Internal Affairs Annagurbanov and the Minister of National Security, both of whom, according to an official announcement, were to be subject to criminal proceedings on undisclosed charges. Charymyrat Amanov was appointed to the Ministry of National Security, while Orazgeldy Amanmyradov received the internal affairs portfolio. On 9 December elections were conducted to councils in each of Turkmenistan's velayats. In April 2008 Hojamyrat Geldimyradov, hitherto Minister of Finance, was appointed as Deputy Chairman of the Government, responsible for Economic Affairs, while the Chairman of the Central Bank was also replaced. Later in April Berdymuhamedov established a special commission to revise the Constitution, and officially abolished the names of the months introduced by Niyazov (which had included various titles of Niyazov and his parents). On 21 July the text of a new draft constitution was announced.

New Constitution

On 26 September 2008 the new Constitution was approved at an extraordinary session of the Khalk Maslakhaty; it provided, *inter alia*, for the dissolution of the Khalk Maslakhaty, and the division of its powers between the President and the Majlis, which was to be enlarged to number 125 deputies. The President was henceforth to be responsible for appointing regional governors and mayors directly. Elections to the expanded 125-member Majlis were conducted on 14 December, with a second round of voting following in one district on 28 December. A CIS observer mission stated that the poll had been conducted in accordance with the country's legislation and democratic standards. However, human rights groups and the OSCE, which had also dispatched a small monitoring mission to Turkmenistan, criticized the absence of democratic alternatives for the electorate. Opposition parties disputed the official voter participation figure of 93.8%, and claimed that participation amounted to only about 30% of the electorate. The new Majlis was convened on 9 January 2009; Nurberdiyeva was re-elected as its Chairman. Reports stated that around 90% of the elected deputies were members of the DPT, and that the remainder were independent candidates endorsed by the party.

In January 2009 Tuvakmammed Japarov, hitherto the head of the Supreme Control Chamber of Turkmenistan (a financial regulatory body created in 2007), was appointed Deputy Chairman of the Government, responsible for Economic Affairs, following the resignation of Geldimyradov on grounds of ill health. Berdymuhamedov also replaced a number of ministers, governors and senior managers of state concerns; these included the Minister of Energy and Industry and the Chairman of government petroleum agency Turkmenneft, after investigations conducted by the Supreme Control Chamber and the Office of the Prosecutor-General were reported to have revealed financial irregularities. Later that month Mamatgeldiyev tendered his resignation as Minister of Defence, on grounds of ill health; Yalym Berdyyev, hitherto Secretary of the State Security Council, was appointed to succeed him. In March the head of the presidential administration was replaced. In April Berdymuhamedov dismissed the Editor-in-Chief of the leading government newspaper *Türkmenistan*. In May it was announced that Berdymuhamedov had ordered the release of large numbers of prisoners, including Muhammetguly Aymuradov, who had served more than 14 years' imprisonment for anti-state crimes. In February 2010 the Turkmenistan Independent Lawyers Association and the Initiative for Human Rights issued the first report on Turkmenistan's prisons, detailing human rights abuses in a number of institutions.

Recent developments: ministerial changes

In late May 2009 Berdymuhamedov dismissed Amanmyradov as Minister of Internal Affairs, with the stated intention of addressing endemic corrupt practices within interior ministry bodies; Iskander Mulikov, hitherto head of a regional police department in the north of the country, was appointed to the post. A number of ministerial changes were effected in July; notably, Baymyrat Hojamuhammedov, hitherto Chairman of the state natural gas agency Türkmengaz, was appointed to replace Tachberdy Tagiyev as Deputy Chairman of the Government, responsible for Petroleum and Natural Gas. In August Berdymuhamedov signed a decree providing for the establishment of a naval force, which was to be based at the port of Türkmenbaşi by 2015 (the existing maritime contingent comprising only coastal guard units). In January 2010 Berdymuhamedov announced a number of appointments to state enterprises and to the Government; the Mayor of Aşgabat was removed and Shamuhammet Durdylyev (hitherto the Minister of Construction) appointed in his stead, while the Minister of the Petroleum and Gas Industry and Mineral Resources was also replaced. Also in January Berdymuhamedov's order that the giant ceremonial arch surmounted by a statue of Niyazov, which had been constructed in 1998, be removed from central Aşgabat was widely viewed as a further disassociation from the former regime. (The statue was duly dismantled in August 2010.) In February Bayar Abayev, previously the Chairman of the Association of Food Industry of Turkmenistan, was appointed as the new Minister of Trade and Foreign Economic Relations. In March it was reported that Mulikov had been severely reprimanded by Berdymuhamedov for ineffective management. In early April Berdymuhamedov carried out a further reorganization of government and other state officials. In mid-September the Government announced the publication of the inaugural edition of what was deemed to be the first nominally independent newspaper in Turkmenistan since the early 1990s. However, the publication, *Rysgal* (Welfare), was published by the Union of Industrialists and Entrepreneurs, an organization regarded as closely allied with President Berdymuhamedov, and the first edition of the publication included an editorial feature written by the President.

In mid-February 2011 Saparliyev was removed as deputy premier, in connection with his appointment as the Rector of the national polytechnic institute. In early April Berdymuhamedov dismissed Charymyrat Amanov as Minister of National Security, after an investigation by the office of the Prosecutor-General had apparently revealed shortcomings in his work. Amanov was succeeded by the hitherto Minister of Defence, Yilym Berdyyev, who was, in turn, replaced by his hitherto deputy, Begench Gundogdyyev. Later in April it was announced that the examination based on knowledge of the *Ruhnama*, which had formed a compulsory part of the curriculum at all state secondary schools, had been abolished, while compulsory courses on the text at universities were also to be withdrawn.

Foreign Affairs

Regional relations

One of the fundamental, constitutionally enshrined, principles of Turkmenistan's foreign policy is that of 'permanent neutrality'. The republic's neutral status was recognized by the UN General Assembly in December 1995, two months after Turkmenistan became the first of the former Soviet republics to join the Non-aligned Movement (see p. 461). Turkmenistan has also adopted a somewhat equivocal attitude towards its membership of the CIS. President Niyazov consistently expressed opposition to centralized structures within the Commonwealth, preferring to regard it as a 'consultative body'. Moreover, the republic refused to sign a number of CIS agreements on closer political, military and economic integration, and at the beginning of September 2005 Niyazov confirmed that Turkmenistan intended to withdraw from full membership of the CIS, but would remain an associate member of the organization.

None the less, Turkmenistan's most important political ally and economic partner remains Russia. In December 1993 Turkmenistan became the first of the former Soviet republics to sign an agreement on dual citizenship with Russia; it was hoped that this would further strengthen bilateral relations, while helping to stem the exodus of ethnic Russians from the republic. However, at a meeting in Moscow in April 2003, Niyazov and President Vladimir Putin of Russia agreed to rescind the agreement. In the same month Niyazov decreed that the estimated 95,000 dual passport holders in Turkmenistan should renounce either their Russian or Turkmenistani citizenship within two months, prompting protests from the Russian Ministry of Foreign Affairs, which insisted that the new agreement was not meant to apply with retroactive effect and, moreover, had not yet been ratified by Russia. In June the lower chamber of the Russian legislature, the Gosudarstvennaya Duma (State Duma), adopted a resolution condemning Niyazov's unilateral revocation of dual citizenship. Nevertheless, in August the Khalk Maslakhaty adopted constitutional amendments forbidding Turkmenistani citizens from holding dual citizenship, and placing any dual citizens remaining in the country in breach of the law.

Meanwhile, Turkmenistan's natural gas exports were a persistent cause of friction between Turkmenistan and Russia. The transport of natural gas from Turkmenistan was dependent on the use of the former Soviet pipeline system, which remained largely under Russian control. In 1993 Turkmenistan's access to European markets through this system was effectively curbed by Russia's decision to direct Turkmenistani gas exports to Ukraine and the South Caucasus. However, as a result of the recipient countries' delay in paying for their gas imports, Turkmenistan suspended all deliveries in 1993–95, a measure that proved severely detrimental to the Turkmenistani economy. Although gas exports to Ukraine and the South Caucasus were resumed in 1996, in the following year Niyazov announced the dissolution of the Turkmenistani-Russian company Türkmenrosgaz (which held a monopoly on the sale and export of Turkmenistani gas) because the company was in severe debt. In response, the Russian Government denied Turkmenistan access to the regional pipeline system. In subsequent years, delivery of natural gas supplies to both Russia and Ukraine has been interrupted on numerous occasions, as a result of disputes over tariffs and payments.

In September 2006 President Niyazov declared that Russia and the People's Republic of China were priority customers for gas, while casting doubts on the prospects for the proposed trans-Caspian and trans-Afghanistan pipelines. Turkmenistan's success in convincing Russia to agree to a substantial price increase for gas in the same month underscored the latter's need to continue to exert control over Turkmenistani gas supplies, on which it was dependent in order to meet its own export commitments to Western Europe and elsewhere. Following Niyazov's death in December 2006, in May 2007 President Berdymuhamedov met Presidents Putin of Russia and Nursultan Nazarbayev of Kazakhstan in Türkmenbaşi, where an agreement was reached to export Turkmenistani gas to Russia by way of Kazakhstan; Russia accepted a 40% price increase for imports of Turkmenistani gas over the following year. In March 2009 Berdymuhamedov met Putin (who, following the expiry of his second term as President in 2008, had become Russian premier) during an official visit to Moscow; however, discussions failed to result in the signature of an agreement on a proposed pipeline across Turkmenistan. In early April 2009 the Turkmenistani Government accused the Russian state-controlled natural gas monopoly Gazprom of having caused an explosion on a natural gas pipeline in Turkmenistan (thereby disrupting the country's exports), by unexpectedly reducing the flow of imported gas; Russian energy officials claimed that the blast had resulted from negligence on the part of the Turkmenistani authorities. Berdymuhamedov ordered that an investigation be conducted into the explosion, which had significantly strained relations between the two states, while Gazprom suspended gas imports from Turkmenistan. At an energy security conference, convened in Aşgabat later in April, Berdymuhamedov declared that Turkmenistan would seek to diversify the country's export partners for gas and that it intended to increase co-operation with the countries of Europe (thereby appearing to assert an energy policy independent of that of Russia). The dispute was resolved in December, when Russian President Dmitrii Medvedev and Berdymuhamedov, meeting in Aşgabat, signed a further agreement, under which Gazprom was to purchase reduced quantities of natural gas from Turkmenistan (amounting to annual imports of 30,000m. cu m, compared with 50,000m. cu m previously); the two Heads of State also signed an accord to expand bilateral strategic energy co-operation. Exports of Turkmenistani gas to Russia resumed in January 2010.

Turkmenistan has also concentrated on developing closer relations with Kazakhstan, Kyrgyzstan, Tajikistan and Uzbekistan. Turkmenistan remained neutral regarding the civil war in Tajikistan (q.v.), and it did not contribute troops to the joint CIS peace-keeping forces in the region, although it did host some of the Tajikistani peace negotiations. In September 2000 Turkmenistan and Uzbekistan had signed a treaty defining their common border, and, under President Niyazov's orders, a 1,700-km fence was installed along the border in 2001. Relations with Uzbekistan deteriorated sharply in late 2002, following the alleged coup attempt in Turkmenistan on 25 November (see above). In December the Uzbekistani embassy in Aşgabat was searched for evidence of complicity in the plot, and Uzbekistan's ambassador to Turkmenistan was subsequently declared *persona non grata*. The Uzbekistani authorities reacted with hostility, and troops from both countries were deployed along their common border. Stricter border controls were subsequently implemented. In November 2004 President Niyazov and President Islam Karimov of Uzbekistan met for their first presidential summit in more than four years in Buxoro, Uzbekistan, where they signed three bilateral agreements, pledging friendship between the two countries, mutual trust, and co-operation, and agreeing the simplification of cross-border travel regulations for residents of border zones and establishing a framework for the sharing of regional water resources. The Presidents declared that all bilateral issues had been resolved, and in early December they celebrated the demarcation of the border between the two countries. A new Uzbekistani ambassador to Turkmenistan was appointed in January 2005.

The legal status of the Caspian Sea, and the ownership of the extensive deposits of petroleum and natural gas beneath it, provoked controversy from the mid-1990s between all five of the littoral states (Turkmenistan, Azerbaijan, Iran, Kazakhstan and Russia). At a special conference on the Sea's status, held in Aşgabat in November 1996, the Ministers of Foreign Affairs of all five countries established a working group to formulate the demarcation of national boundaries. Nevertheless, in early 1997 Turkmenistan and Azerbaijan were engaged in a dispute over the status of two Caspian oilfields (the Azeri and Çıraǧ fields—known as the Khazar and Kaverochkin fields in Turkmenistan), which were being developed by Azerbaijan and a consortium of international companies. The situation deteriorated in July 1997, when Azerbaijan announced its intention to develop, in conjunction with a consortium of Russian companies, a third oilfield, which both countries laid claim to, known as Kyapaz to the Azeris and as Serdar to the Turkmen. Although Russia subsequently withdrew from the project, Azerbaijan refused to abandon its claim to the field. Apparently in response, in September Turkmenistan launched its first international tender for petroleum and gas exploration in the Caspian Sea, and announced that it expected Azerbaijan to compensate it for developing the Azeri and Çıraǧ fields. The commercial exploitation of the latter field began in November. Although Kazakhstan and Russia signed an agreement in October 2000 defining the legal status of the Caspian Sea, the remaining littoral states made limited progress. In November 2003 representatives of the five littoral states, meeting in Tehran, Iran, signed a UN-sponsored framework Convention for the Protection of the Marine Environment of the Caspian Sea. In mid-January 2005 President Niyazov approved a proposal from a Canadian company, Buried Hill Energy and Petroleum, to develop the Serdar oilfield, prompting protests from Azerbaijan. In June 2008 President Berdymuhamedov and his Azerbaijani counterpart, meeting in St Petersburg, Russia, reached agreement on the reopening of the Turkmenistani embassy in the Azerbaijani capital, Baku (Bakı), which had been closed since 2001, and announced the establishment of an intergovernmental commission on bilateral

TURKMENISTAN

Introductory Survey

co-operation. In July 2009 negotiations began between Turkmenistan and Azerbaijan, in an attempt to resolve ownership of energy resources in the Caspian Sea, but were rapidly abandoned, causing Berdymuhamedov to announce his intention to refer the dispute to an international arbitration court. In August plans by the Turkmenistani Government to establish a naval base at the Caspian Sea port of Türkmenbaşi prompted criticism from Azerbaijani officials. In October Berdymuhamedov indicated that dialogue on the issue was to continue in an effort to reach a compromise agreement.

Iran plays the most important role in Turkmenistan's foreign relations outside the CIS. In 1992 a number of agreements on closer political, economic and cultural integration were signed, including an accord to construct a railway line between Iran and Turkmenistan. The line, which linked the Turkmenistani city of Tejen with the northern Iranian city of Mashad, was opened in May 1996, thus affording Turkmenistan access both to the Persian (Arabian) Gulf and to Istanbul, Turkey. Turkmenistan and Iran also signed an agreement on the construction of a 140-km gas pipeline between the Korpeje natural gas deposit in south-western Turkmenistan and the city of Kord Kuy in northern Iran. The pipeline was to be the first segment on a route that, it was envisaged, would eventually transport Turkmenistani gas via Iran to Turkey and thence to Western Europe. The inauguration of the pipeline in December 1997 opened the first alternative export route for Turkmenistan's natural gas, and thus promised greater economic independence for the republic from Russia. In January 2008 Turkmenistan temporarily suspended supplies of gas to Iran, owing to disagreements over the price. Following an agreement in July 2009, a second gas pipeline connecting Turkmenistan and Iran, which was to increase the volume of natural gas exports to Iran to 20,000m. cu m annually, entered into operation in January 2010.

In March 2003 work on a project, initially proposed in 1999, to construct an underwater trans-Caspian gas export pipeline to Turkey, via Azerbaijan and Georgia, was suspended indefinitely, owing to disagreement between Turkmenistan and Azerbaijan over the division of the pipeline's anticipated throughput. Meanwhile, in late April 2002 President Niyazov requested UN support for the construction of a proposed 1,680-km gas pipeline from Dauletabad in Turkmenistan to Fazilka, on the Pakistan–India border, via Afghanistan, led by the US company Unocal. In December an agreement was signed on the construction of the pipeline, which was expected to be able to carry some 708,000m. cu m of gas per year. The project was subject to prolonged delays, and in December 2010 it was announced that construction of the pipeline would commence in 2012, with completion forecast for 2016.

In April 2006 Turkmenistan and the People's Republic of China signed an agreement to construct a natural gas pipeline between the two countries, by way of Uzbekistan and Kazakhstan; China was to purchase 30,000m. cu m of Turkmenistani gas each year for a period of 30 years from 2009. In August 2007 the Turkmenistani Government awarded China rights to develop gas reserves in the east of Turkmenistan in association with this project. Chinese President Hu Jintao made an official visit to Turkmenistan in August 2008, and in June 2009 the Turkmenistani and Chinese Governments signed an agreement increasing the amount of natural gas China would purchase annually from Turkmenistan over a 30-year period to 40,000m. cu m. The new pipeline was officially inaugurated in December, at a ceremony attended by Berdymuhamedov, Hu Jintao, and the Presidents of Kazakhstan and Uzbekistan; it was expected to reach its full capacity by 2012.

President Niyazov maintained the country's neutrality in the civil war in Afghanistan following the large-scale suicide attacks in the USA in September 2001 by the Islamist militant al-Qa'ida organization of Osama bin Laden, who had developed a close association with the Taliban. None the less, Niyazov gave his consent to the use of Turkmenistan's ground and air transport 'corridors' for the delivery of humanitarian aid to Afghanistan during air-strikes against al-Qa'ida and its Taliban hosts; Niyazov refused US troops access to Turkmenistan's military bases, however, reaffirming the country's policy of non-interference. In December 2010 President Berdymuhamedov, President Hamid Karzai of Afghanistan, President Asif Ali Zardari of Pakistan and the Indian Minister of Petroleum of Natural Gas, Murli Deora, meeting in Aşgabat, signed a framework agreement on the construction of a pipeline, known as Tapi (Turkmenistan–Afghanistan–Pakistan–India), to carry Turkmenistani natural gas to the other countries represented at the meeting. Work on the project, which had been initially proposed in 1995, but had been delayed as a result of ongoing insecurity in Afghanistan and the border regions of Pakistan, was to be developed by the Asian Development Bank, and was also supported by the USA.

Other external relations

In September 2007 President Berdymuhamedov, addressing the UN General Assembly, announced that he planned to develop co-operation with the international community in all areas of activity; he and other members of the Turkmenistani Government also met with US officials to discuss reforms and private investment. At the end of February 2008 further discussions on energy co-operation were conducted during a visit to Aşgabat by a senior US official. In November 2010 the Government pledged to supply gas for the EU's planned Nabucco Turkey–Austria pipeline project, which was expected to commence operations in 2015. On 22 April 2009 the European Parliament approved the conclusion of an interim trade agreement with Turkmenistan, stating that this might be used to influence the authorities in strengthening the reform process. (The agreement, which had been advocated by the European Commission and the majority of EU member states, had previously been delayed by the European Parliament, owing to concern over the human rights situation in Turkmenistan.)

CONSTITUTION AND GOVERNMENT

Under the terms of the 2008 Constitution, the President of the Republic is directly elected, by universal adult suffrage, for five years, for a maximum of two terms. The President is both Head of State and Head of Government (Prime Minister in the Council of Ministers), holding executive power in conjunction with the Council of Ministers (which is appointed by the President), and is concurrently Supreme Commander of the Armed Forces. The supreme legislative body is the Majlis (Assembly), which is directly elected for a term of five years. Judicial power is exercised by the Supreme Court, the High Commercial Court, and military and other courts. Judges, who are independent, are appointed by the President for a term of five years. Turkmenistan is divided into five velayats (regions), which are subdivided into 50 etraps (districts) and 625 gengeşes (municipalities).

REGIONAL AND INTERNATIONAL CO-OPERATION

Turkmenistan is a member of the Non-aligned Movement (see p. 461), the European Bank for Reconstruction and Development (EBRD, see p. 265), the Economic Co-operation Organization (ECO, see p. 264) and the Organization of the Islamic Conference (OIC, see p. 400). Turkmenistan is an associate member of the Commonwealth of Independent States (CIS, see p. 238).

Turkmenistan was admitted to the UN in 1992. In May 1994 Turkmenistan became the first Central Asian republic of the former USSR to join the 'Partnership for Peace' programme (see p. 371) of the North Atlantic Treaty Organization (NATO, see p. 368). The country's constitutional principle of 'permanent neutrality' was recognized by the UN General Assembly in December 1995.

ECONOMIC AFFAIRS

In 2009, according to estimates by the World Bank, Turkmenistan's gross national income (GNI), measured at average 2007–09 prices, was US $17,498m., equivalent to $3,420 per head (or $6,990 on an international purchasing-power parity basis). During 2000–09, it was estimated, the population increased at an average annual rate of 1.4%. Gross domestic product (GDP) per head increased, in real terms, by an average of 12.3% per year in 2000–09. Overall GDP increased, in real terms, at an average annual rate of 13.9% per year in 2000–09, according to the World Bank. GDP increased by 10.5% in 2008 and by 8.0% in 2009.

Agriculture contributed 22.6% of GDP in 2008, according to the Asian Development Bank (ADB, see p. 180). The sector employed 48.2% of the labour force in 2004 and, according to FAO, was forecast to employ an estimated 29.3% of the total economically active population at mid-2011. Although the Kara-Kum desert covers some 80% of the country's territory, widespread irrigation has enabled rapid agricultural development; however, over-intensive cultivation of the principal crop, cotton, together with massive irrigation projects, have led to serious ecological damage. In 1996 cotton contributed an estimated 11.5% of GDP, although the Government subsequently planned to reduce cotton production in favour of food production. Other important crops include grain, vegetables and fruit (in particular grapes and melons), although the country remains heavily dependent on imports of foodstuffs. Livestock husbandry (including the production of astrakhan and karakul wools) plays a central role in the sector, and silkworms are bred. According to the ADB, agricultural GDP increased, in real terms, at an average annual rate of 6.0% in 2000–08. Real agricultural GDP increased by 9.3% in 2008.

Industry (including mining, manufacturing, construction and power) contributed 41.9% of GDP in 2008, according to the ADB. In 2004 13.8% of the employed labour force were engaged in the sector. During 2000–08 industrial GDP increased, in real terms, at an average annual rate of 6.2%. Real industrial GDP increased by 11.0% in 2008.

Turkmenistan is richly endowed with mineral resources, in particular natural gas and petroleum (recoverable reserves of which were estimated at some 8,104,000m. cu m and 600m. barrels, respectively, at the end of 2009). In 2009 Turkmenistan produced approximately 36,400m. cu m of gas, and production of petroleum averaged 206,000 barrels per day. A new power installation, constructed at a cost of US $120m. in the town of Daşoguz, commenced production in December 2007; it was expected to generate more than 1,500m. kWh of electricity per year. In addition, Turkmenistan has large deposits of iodine, bromine, sodium sulphate, clay, gypsum and different types of salt.

The manufacturing sector contributed 46.7% of GDP in 2009, according to the World Bank. The principal branches of manufacturing are the processing of mineral resources (predominantly petroleum and natural gas) and textiles (mainly cotton products). Petroleum is refined at three refineries, at Türkmenbaşi, Seidi and Türkmenabat. According to the World Bank, manufacturing GDP increased by 24.0% in 1998–2003. Sectoral growth was estimated at 25.6% in 2002 and 34.7% in 2003.

The construction sector contributed 4.3% of GDP in 2008, according to the ADB. Construction GDP increased by 0.4% in 2000–08. Sectoral growth reached some 16.6% in 2008.

In 2007 an estimated 14,880m. kWh of electricity was produced domestically; of electricity produced in 1994, some 20% was reported to have been exported, while a proportion of the remainder was distributed free of charge to domestic users. (Some charges for domestic electricity use were introduced in 1996; however, the 2006 budget provided for free distribution.) In 2003 mineral fuels accounted for just 0.7% of the value of merchandise imports, according to ADB estimates.

The services sector provided 35.5% of GDP in 2008, according to the ADB. The sector employed some 38.0% of the working population in 2004. Services GDP increased, in real terms, at an average annual rate of 6.4% in 2000–08. Real services GDP increased by 7.8% in 2008.

According to the ADB, in 2009 Turkmenistan recorded a trade surplus of US $5,300.0m. In 2007 there was a trade surplus of $5,216.1m. and and a surplus of $4,524.7m. on the current account of the balance of payments. In 2009 the principal source of imports (accounting for 18.1% of the total) was the People's Republic of China; other major suppliers were Turkey, Russia, Germany, the United Arab Emirates (UAE), Ukraine and the USA. The principal markets for exports were Ukraine (22.3%); other notable buyers were Turkey, Hungary, Poland, the UAE, Afghanistan and Iran. In 2003 the principal exports were basic manufactures. The principal imports in that year were machinery and transport equipment, basic manufactures, chemicals, miscellaneous manufactured articles, and food and live animals.

In 2006 Turkmenistan recorded an overall budgetary surplus of an estimated 5,843,000m. manats (equivalent to some 5.9% of GDP). Turkmenistan's general government gross debt was 1,403m. manats in 2009, equivalent to 2.7% of GDP. At the end of 2008 total external debt was US $638m., of which $587m. was public and publicly guaranteed debt. The annual average inflation rate declined from 1,748% in 1994 to 24.2% in 1999. According to the ADB, inflation averaged 8.8% per year in 2000–09. Consumer prices increased by an annual average of 5.5% in 2009. In 2004 some 62,000 people were registered as unemployed (about 2.6% of the labour force); however, unofficial sources estimated the rate to be considerably higher.

The opening of a new gas pipeline to Iran in 1997 contributed to a revival in the economically crucial gas sector, which had been adversely affected by the dissolution of the USSR. In 2003 Turkmenistan concluded major agreements with both Russia and Ukraine to supply them with natural gas for 25 years. In late 2006 the discovery of a major new gas field, at South Yolöten, near Mari, in south-eastern Turkmenistan, was announced. In late 2009 the Government announced that contracts to develop the field had been awarded to the China National Petroleum Co (of the People's Republic of China), Hyundai and LG Corpn (both of the Republic of Korea), and Petrofac International (of the UAE). The construction of a pipeline to supply natural gas to Afghanistan, Pakistan and India, agreed in principle in December 2010, would further benefit Turkmenistan's gas sector, although concerns about continuing insecurity in both Afghanistan and Pakistan threatened to delay the implementation of the project. Moreover, any further expansion of gas exports would require the expansion and modernization of the pipeline infrastructure within Turkmenistan. Following the death of President Niyazov in 2006, there were signs that the country's new leadership intended to pursue significant economic reforms and greater international integration. In June 2008 restrictions on foreign exchange transactions were ended. In September a new Constitution that protected private property rights and committed the country to the principles of the market economy was adopted. The suspension of exports of gas to Russia in April 2009–January 2010 (see Foreign Affairs) had a negative impact on government revenue and the balance of payments on the current account in 2009. In October of that year an IMF delegation stated that Turkmenistan had remained largely unaffected by the international financial crisis, owing to its substantial international reserves and lack of external debt. A major natural gas pipeline from Turkmenistan to the People's Republic of China entered into operation in December, followed by a second gas pipeline to Iran in January 2010, and steady GDP growth, of around 9.4% (according to IMF projections), occurred in that year. The IMF projected growth of 11.5% in 2011.

PUBLIC HOLIDAYS

2012: 1 January (New Year's Day), 12 January (Memorial Day), 19 February (Flag Day), 8 March (International Women's Day), 21 March (Novrus Bairam, Spring Holiday), 9 May (Victory Day), 18 May (Constitution Day), 18 August* (Oraza Bairam—Id al-Fitr, end of Ramadan), 6 October (Remembrance Day), 25 October* (Kurban Bairam—Id al-Adha, Feast of the Sacrifice), 27 October (Independence Day), 12 December (Neutrality Day).

* These holidays are dependent on the Islamic calendar and may vary by one or two days from the dates given.

TURKMENISTAN

Statistical Survey

Principal sources (unless otherwise stated): IMF, *Turkmenistan, Economic Review, Turkmenistan—Recent Economic Developments* (December 1999); World Bank, *Statistical Handbook: States of the Former USSR*.

Area and Population

AREA, POPULATION AND DENSITY

Area (sq km)	488,100*
Population (census results)	
12 January 1989	3,533,925
10 January 1995	
Males	2,225,331
Females	2,257,920
Total	4,483,251
Population (UN estimates at mid-year)†	
2009	5,109,880
2010	5,176,502
2011	5,243,476
Density (per sq km) at mid-2011	10.7

* 188,456 sq miles.
† Source: UN, *World Population Prospects: The 2008 Revision*; these estimates are substantially lower than those produced by the state statistics institute (see below).

Population (official estimate): 6,800,200 at 1 April 2006 (Source: National Institute of State Statistics and Information).

POPULATION BY AGE AND SEX
(UN estimates at mid-2011)

	Males	Females	Total
0–14	762,121	740,963	1,503,084
15–64	1,734,511	1,790,725	3,525,236
65 and over	85,777	129,379	215,156
Total	2,582,409	2,661,067	5,243,476

Source: UN, *World Population Prospects: The 2008 Revision*.

POPULATION BY ETHNIC GROUP
(official estimates at 1 January 1993)

	Number	%
Turkmen	3,118,000	73.3
Russian	419,000	9.8
Uzbek	382,000	9.0
Kazakh	87,000	2.0
Others	248,000	5.8
Total	4,254,000	100.0

Ethnic groups (percentage of total, at census of 1995): Turkmen 77.0; Uzbek 9.2; Russian 6.7; Kazakh 2.0; Others 5.1 (Source: US embassy in Turkmenistan).

PRINCIPAL TOWNS
(estimated population at 1 January 1999)

Aşgabat (capital)	605,000	Türkmenbaşi‡	70,000
Türkmenabat*	203,000	Bayramaly	60,000
Daşoguz	165,000	Tejen	54,000
Mari	123,000	Serdar§	51,000
Balkanabat†	119,000		

* Formerly Charjew (Chardzhou).
† Formerly Nebit-Dag.
‡ Formerly Krasnovodsk.
§ Formerly Gyzylarbat (Kizyl-Arvat).

1 July 2002 (official estimate): Aşgabat 743,000.

Mid-2009 (incl. suburbs, UN estimate): Aşgabat 637,238 (Source: UN, *World Urbanization Prospects: The 2009 Revision*).

BIRTHS, MARRIAGES AND DEATHS

	Registered live births		Registered marriages		Registered deaths	
	Number	Rate (per 1,000)	Number	Rate (per 1,000)	Number	Rate (per 1,000)
1987	126,787	37.2	31,484	9.2	26,802	7.9
1988	125,887	36.0	33,008	9.4	27,317	7.8
1989	124,992	34.9	34,890	9.8	27,609	7.7

Registered deaths: 25,755 (death rate 7.0 per 1,000) in 1990; 27,403 (7.3 per 1,000) in 1991; 27,509 (6.8 per 1,000) in 1992; 31,171 (7.2 per 1,000) in 1993; 32,067 (7.3 per 1,000) in 1994.

1998 (provisional): Live births 98,461 (birth rate 20.3 per 1,000); Marriages 26,361 (marriage rate 5.4 per 1,000); Deaths 29,628 (death rate 6.1 per 1,000).

Source: UN, *Demographic Yearbook*.

Births (annual averages, UN estimates): Birth rate (per 1,000): 24.5 in 1995–2000; 23.3 in 2000–05; 22.0 in 2005–10 (Source: UN, *World Population Prospects: The 2008 Revision*).

Deaths (annual averages, UN estimates): Death rate (per 1,000): 7.7 in 1995–2000; 7.7 in 2000–05; 7.7 in 2005–10 (Source: UN, *World Population Prospects: The 2008 Revision*).

2008: Birth rate 21.9 per 1,000; death rate 7.7 per 1,000 (Source: UN, *Statistical Yearbook for Asia and the Pacific*).

Life expectancy (years at birth, WHO estimates): 63 (males 60; females 67) in 2008 (Source: WHO, *World Health Statistics*).

EMPLOYMENT
('000 persons at 31 December)

	1996	1997	1998*
Agriculture	769.8	778.8	890.5
Forestry	2.5	2.9	1.9
Industry†	172.0	188.1	226.8
Construction	136.2	122.8	108.2
Trade and catering	91.8	101.2	115.8
Transport and communications	77.7	77.9	90.7
Information-computing services	1.3	1.0	1.2
Housing and municipal services	50.2	46.8	48.3
Health care and social security	97.4	100.4	89.2
Education, culture and arts	183.8	185.9	190.5
Science, research and development	9.2	6.9	5.2
General administration	24.7	25.3	28.8
Finance and insurance	8.7	9.6	12.6
Other activities	41.5	28.3	29.0
Total	1,666.8	1,675.9	1,838.7

* Provisional.
† Comprising manufacturing (except printing and publishing), mining and quarrying, electricity, gas, water, logging, and fishing.

2004 ('000 persons at 31 December, estimates): Employed 2,110 (Agriculture 1,017, Industry 291, Other 802); Unemployed 62; Total labour force (incl. those not registered) 2,389 (Source: Asian Development Bank, *Key Indicators of Developing Asian and Pacific Countries*).

Mid-2011 ('000 persons, estimates): Agriculture, etc. 732; Total (incl. others) 2,497 (Source: FAO).

TURKMENISTAN

Health and Welfare

KEY INDICATORS

Total fertility rate (children per woman, 2008)	2.5
Under-5 mortality rate (per 1,000 live births, 2008)	48
HIV/AIDS (% of persons aged 15–49, 2007)	<0.1
Physicians (per 1,000 head, 2006)	2.5
Hospital beds (per 1,000 head, 2006)	4.3
Health expenditure (2007): US $ per head (PPP)	153
Health expenditure (2007): % of GDP	2.6
Health expenditure (2007): public (% of total)	52.1
Access to water (% of persons, 2004)	71
Access to sanitation (% of persons, 2008)	98
Total carbon dioxide emissions ('000 metric tons, 2007)	45,770.7
Carbon dioxide emissions per head (metric tons, 2007)	9.2
Human Development Index (2010): ranking	87
Human Development Index (2010): value	0.669

For sources and definitions, see explanatory note on p. vi.

Agriculture

PRINCIPAL CROPS
('000 metric tons)

	2006	2007	2008
Wheat	3,260*	2,700*	2,700†
Rice, paddy	135*	111*	111†
Barley	78*	59*	59†
Potatoes	175†	185†	240
Sugar beet†	235	234	234
Seed cotton	700*	946	850*
Cabbages and other brassicas*	58	52	64
Tomatoes	282*	256†	310*
Onions, dry	96*	95†	106*
Carrots and turnips	60*	60†	66*
Watermelons	250†	240†	254
Grapes†	175	175	175
Apples	43*	42†	62*

* Unofficial figure(s).
† FAO estimate(s).

Note: No data were available for individual crops in 2009.

Aggregate production ('000 metric tons, may include official, semi-official or estimated data): Total cereals 3,489 in 2006, 2,886 in 2007–09; Total roots and tubers 175 in 2006, 185 in 2007, 240 in 2008–09; Total vegetables (incl. melons) 814 in 2006, 763 in 2007, 875 in 2008–09; Total fruits (excl. melons) 282 in 2006, 277 in 2007, 326 in 2008–09.

Source: FAO.

LIVESTOCK
('000 head at 1 January)

	2006	2007	2008
Horses*	17	16	16
Asses*	25	25	25
Camels*	41	40	40
Cattle	2,065†	1,948†	1,948*
Pigs*	29	30	30
Sheep	15,694†	15,500†	15,500*
Goats	904†	900†	900*
Chickens*	7,500	7,000	7,000
Turkeys*	200	200	200

* FAO estimate(s).
† Unofficial figure.

Note: No data were available for 2009.

Source: FAO.

LIVESTOCK PRODUCTS
('000 metric tons, FAO estimates)

	2005	2006	2007
Cattle meat	100	102	102
Sheep meat	90	93	93
Goat meat	7	7	6
Chicken meat	12	14	13
Cows' milk	1,140	1,197	1,333
Hen eggs	35	37	34
Honey	8	9	9
Wool, greasy	20	20	20

2008: Figures assumed to be unchanged from 2007 (FAO estimates). Note: No data were available for 2009.

Source: FAO.

Fishing

(metric tons, live weight)

	2003	2004	2005*
Capture	14,543	14,992	15,000
Azov sea sprat	14,276	14,674	14,680
Aquaculture	24	16	16
Total catch	14,567	15,008	15,016

* FAO estimates.

2006–08: Catch assumed to be unchanged from 2005 (FAO estimates).

Source: FAO.

Mining

('000 metric tons unless otherwise indicated)

	2005	2006	2007
Crude petroleum*	9,500	9,200	9,800
Natural gas (million cu metres)*	57,000	60,400	65,400
Bentonite†	1.4	2.0	2.0
Salt (unrefined)†	4.8	5.0	5.2
Gypsum (crude)†	1.6	3.0	3.3

* Source: BP, *Statistical Review of World Energy*.
† Estimates from US Geological Survey.

2008 ('000 metric tons unless otherwise indicated): Crude petroleum 10,200; Natural gas (million cu metres) 66,100 (Source: BP, *Statistical Review of World Energy*).

2009 ('000 metric tons unless otherwise indicated): Crude petroleum 10,200; Natural gas (million cu metres) 36,400 (Source: BP, *Statistical Review of World Energy*).

TURKMENISTAN

Industry

SELECTED PRODUCTS
('000 metric tons unless otherwise indicated)

	2000	2001	2002
Cottonseed oil	48	45	26
Wheat flour	544	561	537
Woven cotton fabrics (million sq metres)	34	61	78
Woven silk fabrics ('000 sq metres)	216	115	283
Blankets	14	7	10
Knotted wool carpets and rugs ('000 sq metres)	1,040	1,434	1,475
Footwear, excl. rubber ('000 pairs)	478	444	253
Nitric acid (100%)	192	151	212
Ammonia (nitrogen content)	117	99	130
Nitrogenous fertilizers (a)*	89	72	103
Phosphate fertilizers (b)*†	11	11	17
Soap	3.0	2.5	1.6
Motor spirit (petrol)	1,132	1,283	1,292
Gas-diesel (distillate fuel) oil	2,247	2,547	2,360
Residual fuel oils	1,536	1,586	1,640
Clay building bricks (million)	309	269	279
Quicklime	17	17	15
Cement	420	448	486
Electric energy (million kWh)	9,845	10,610	10,700

* Production in terms of (a) nitrogen or (b) phosphoric acid.
† Official figures.

Electric energy (million kWh): 12,820 in 2005; 13,650 in 2006; 14,880 in 2007.

Motor spirit (petrol) ('000 metric tons): 1,313 in 2005; 1,564 in 2006; 1,464 in 2007.

Gas-diesel (distillate fuel) oil ('000 metric tons): 2,607 in 2005 3,105 in 2006; 2,908 in 2007.

Woven woollen fabrics (million sq metres): 2.8 in 1996; 3.2 in 1997; 2.5 in 1998.

Ethyl alcohol ('000 hectolitres): 2 in 1997; 1 in 1998; 1 in 1999.

Source: mainly UN Industrial Commodity Statistics Database.

2003 ('000 metric tons, unless otherwise indicated, estimates): Wheat flour 503; Nitrogenous fertilizers 96 (Source: Asian Development Bank, *Key Indicators of Developing Asian and Pacific Countries*).

Cement ('000 metric tons, estimates): 450 in 2003; 550 in 2004; 650 in 2005; 1,000 in 2006; 1,500 in 2007 (Source: US Geological Survey).

Finance

CURRENCY AND EXCHANGE RATES

Monetary Units
100 tenge = 1 Turkmen manat.

Sterling, Dollar and Euro Equivalents (31 December 2011)
 £1 sterling = 4.462 new manats;
 US $1 = 2.850 new manats;
 €1 = 3.808 new manats;
 100 new manats = €22.41 = $35.09 = €26.26.

Note: The Turkmenistani manat was introduced on 1 November 1993, replacing the Russian (formerly Soviet) rouble at a rate of 1 manat = 500 roubles. Following the introduction of the Turkmenistani manat, a multiple exchange rate system was established. The foregoing information refers to the official rate of exchange. This rate was maintained at US $1 = 4,165 manats between May 1997 and April 1998. It was adjusted to $1 = 5,200 manats in April 1998. In addition to the official rate, there was a commercial bank rate of exchange until this market was closed in December 1998. There is also a 'parallel' market rate, which averaged $1 = 6,493 manats in 1998 and reached $1 = 14,200 manats at mid-1999. A new manat, equivalent to 5,000 of the former currency, was introduced on 1 January 2009.

BUDGET
('000 million manats)

Revenue*	1997	1998	1999†
State budget	2,067.3	1,867.5	2,382.3
Personal income tax	108.3	157.4	224.9
Profit tax	579.6	412.0	422.0
Value-added tax	797.9	714.9	946.3
Natural resources tax	231.2	43.1	201.1
Excise tax	92.4	221.3	377.8
Other receipts*	257.9	318.8	210.1
Pension and Social Security Fund	471.0	711.0	832.5
Medical Insurance Fund	32.7	8.2	0.0
Repayments on rescheduled gas debt	246.6	474.1	478.3
Total	**2,817.6**	**3,060.8**	**3,693.1**

Expenditure	1997	1998	1999‡
National economy	843.9	461.1	623.3
Agriculture	632.5	331.4	223.2
Transport and communications	121.1	63.4	190.0
Other	90.3	66.3	210.1
Socio-cultural services†	975.7	1,850.0	1,907.9
Education	435.3	919.2	1,048.7
Health	443.1	493.8	550.6
Communal services	9.1	337.9	188.6
Culture, recreation and other purposes	88.2	99.1	120.0
Defence§	440.2	435.8	582.0
Pension and Social Security Fund	387.8	511.5	605.9
Interest payments	72.1	11.1	18.0
Public administration and other purposes	94.3	153.4	157.2
Total	**2,814.0**	**3,422.8**	**3,894.3**

* Including grants received and road fund revenues.
† Approved budget.
‡ Excluding expenditure of the Pension and Social Security Fund.
§ Variable coverage, owing to changes in classification.

2007 ('000 million manats): Revenue 23,390; Expenditure 18,117 (Source: Asian Development Bank).

2008 ('000 million manats): Revenue 63,897; Expenditure 33,302 (Source: Asian Development Bank).

2009 ('000 million manats): Revenue 66,619; Expenditure 41,837 (Source: Asian Development Bank).

INTERNATIONAL RESERVES
(US $ million at 31 December)

	2005	2006	2007
Total	4,457.0	8,059.2	13,221.5

Source: Asian Development Bank.

MONEY SUPPLY
('000 million manats at 31 December)

	1996	1997	1998
Currency in circulation	270.2	407.7	1,040.2
Demand deposits at banks	130.0	423.4	259.8

Total money ('000 million manats at 31 December): 2,552 in 1999; 4,965 in 2000; 5,792 in 2001; 5,877 in 2002; 7,840 in 2003; 8,906 in 2004; 9,405 in 2005; 10,411 in 2006; 20,448 in 2007; 18,894 in 2008 (Source: Asian Development Bank).

TURKMENISTAN

COST OF LIVING
(Consumer Price Index; base: 2000 = 100)

	2007	2008	2009
All items	180.4	202.1	213.2

Source: Asian Development Bank.

NATIONAL ACCOUNTS
('000 million manats at current prices)

Expenditure on the Gross Domestic Product

	2006	2007	2008
Government final consumption expenditure	14,384.4	17,541.2	21,125.6
Private final consumption expenditure	62,549.5	74,251.0	84,853.4
Changes in inventories / Gross fixed capital formation	27,033.5	31,703.4	38,123.0
Total domestic expenditure	103,967.4	123,495.6	144,102.0
Exports of goods and services	71,573.0	86,203.4	104,215.3
Less Imports of goods and services	62,079.3	73,602.1	85,225.4
Statistical discrepancy	138.2	221.1	353.4
GDP in purchasers' values	113,599.2	136,318.0	163,445.3

Gross Domestic Product by Economic Activity

	2006	2007	2008
Agriculture	23,651.9	28,578.6	34,123.9
Mining and quarrying / Manufacturing / Electricity, gas and water	39,473.1	47,339.5	56,717.6
Construction	4,367.0	5,135.0	6,538.3
Trade, hotels and restaurants	2,147.2	2,700.6	3,126.8
Transport and communications	3,347.0	3,967.7	4,798.6
Finance / Public administration / Other activities	32,053.2	38,915.4	45,656.5
Sub-total	105,039.4	126,636.8	150,961.7
Taxes, less subsidies, on products	8,559.9	9,681.2	12,483.6
GDP in purchasers' values	113,599.2	136,318.0	163,445.3

Note: Deduction for financial intermediation services indirectly measured and adjustment for indirect taxes assumed to be distributed at origin.

Source: Asian Development Bank.

BALANCE OF PAYMENTS
(US $ million)

	1996	1997	1998
Exports of goods f.o.b.	1,692.0	774.0	614.1
Imports of goods f.o.b.	−1,388.3	−1,005.0	−1,137.1
Trade balance	303.7	−230.9	−523.0
Services (net)	−323.4	−402.5	−471.0
Balance on goods and services	−19.7	−633.5	−994.0
Other income (net)	16.7	84.8	32.6
Balance on goods, services and income	−3.0	−548.7	−961.4
Current transfers (net)	4.8	−31.2	26.9
Current account	1.8	−579.9	−934.5
Direct investment	108.1	102.4	64.1
Trade credit (net)	60.8	−266.5	56.5
Other (net)	−211.6	1,035.9	749.7
Net errors and omissions	46.4	−71.4	33.9
Overall balance	5.4	220.6	−30.3

Current balance (US $ million): 4,036.0 in 2007; 3,560.0 in 2008; 5,300.0 in 2009 (Source: Asian Development Bank).

External Trade

PRINCIPAL COMMODITIES
(US $ million)

Imports c.i.f.	2001	2002	2003
Food and live animals	129.4	114.3	130.3
Beverages and tobacco	56.8	70.1	67.4
Mineral fuels, lubricants, etc.	39.1	25.7	17.7
Chemicals	178.6	210.8	271.2
Basic manufactures	448.7	394.2	487.7
Machinery and transport equipment	1,204.7	857.6	1,125.6
Miscellaneous manufactured articles	128.1	112.7	165.2
Total (incl. others)	2,348.8	2,119.4	2,450.0*

Exports f.o.b.	2001	2002	2003
Food and live animals	4.7	3.4	2.9
Beverages and tobacco	—	0.6	0.3
Mineral fuels, lubricants, etc.	123.7	83.8	152.4
Chemicals	7.0	28.4	55.0
Basic manufactures	141.6	150.6	169.6
Machinery and transport equipment	14.5	17.1	16.9
Miscellaneous manufactured articles	52.8	74.1	80.8
Total (incl. others)	2,620.2	2,855.6	3,320.0*

*Estimate.

2004 (US $ million): Total imports 2,678.1; Total exports 3,519.0.
2005 (US $ million): Total imports 2,626.9; Total exports 4,997.4.
2006 (US $ million): Total imports 2,553.5; Total exports 5,617.4.
2007 (US $ million): Total imports 3,331.7; Total exports 6,247.9.
2008 (US $ million): Total imports 5,291.3; Total exports 9,923.7.
2009 (US $ million): Total imports 6,307.5; Total exports 2,925.0.

Source: Asian Development Bank.

PRINCIPAL TRADING PARTNERS
(US $ million)

Imports	2007	2008	2009
China, People's Repub.	332.5	883.3	1,140.8
France	55.9	135.6	272.2
Germany	238.2	290.7	372.3
Iran	201.3	263.5	175.9
Russia	422.6	891.3	1,033.8
Turkey	372.9	729.2	1,039.4
Ukraine	216.4	414.6	357.7
United Arab Emirates	411.6	538.9	359.8
USA	203.2	65.7	341.1
Total (incl. others)	3,331.7	5,291.3	6,307.5

Exports	2007	2008	2009
Afghanistan	169.8	193.8	171.2
Azerbaijan	36.6	46.9	31.3
Hungary	0.3	797.0	197.8
Iran	170.0	222.6	148.6
Italy	216.9	275.6	56.0
Poland	1.2	988.3	180.3
Turkey	360.8	353.9	300.7
Ukraine	3,878.7	5,119.7	653.0
United Arab Emirates	205.5	269.0	179.6
Total (incl. others)	6,247.9	9,923.7	2,925.0

Note: Data reflect the IMF's direction of trade methodology, and, as a result, the totals may not be equal to those presented for trade in commodities.

Source: Asian Development Bank.

TURKMENISTAN

Transport

RAILWAYS
(traffic)

	1996	1997	1999*
Passenger journeys (million)	7.8	6.4	3.1
Passenger-km (million)	2,104	958	701
Freight transported (million metric tons)	15.9	18.5	17.2
Freight ton-km (million)	6,779	7,445	7,337

* Data for 1998 were not available.

Source: *Railway Directory*.

SHIPPING

Merchant Fleet
(registered at 31 December)

	2007	2008	2009
Number of vessels	53	55	56
Total displacement ('000 grt)	51.9	53.6	63.1

Source: IHS Fairplay, *World Fleet Statistics*.

CIVIL AVIATION
(estimated traffic on scheduled services)

	2004	2005	2006
Kilometres flown (million)	17	16	17
Passengers carried ('000)	1,612	1,654	1,843
Passenger-km (million)	1,916	1,905	2,072
Total ton-km (million)	182	182	197

Source: UN, *Statistical Yearbook*.

Tourism

FOREIGN VISITOR ARRIVALS*

Country of nationality	2005	2006	2007
France	683	398	682
Germany	1,028	870	1,338
Iran	7,173	1,478	2,133
Japan	428	523	537
Netherlands	453	328	402
Russia	13	6	80
USA	332	441	566
Total (incl. others)	11,611	5,620	8,177

* Arrivals of non-resident tourists at national borders.

Tourism receipts (US $ million): 66 in 1996; 74 in 1997; 192 in 1998.

Source: World Tourism Organization.

Communications Media

	2007	2008	2009
Telephones ('000 main lines in use)	458.2	477.7	478.0
Mobile cellular telephones ('000 subscribers)	381.7	1,135.2	1,500.0
Internet users ('000)	70.0	75.0	80.4

Television receivers ('000 in use): 880 in 2001.

Book production (including pamphlets): 450 titles (5,493,000 copies) in 1994.

Radio receivers ('000 in use): 1,225 in 1997.

Personal computers: 347,991 (71.9 per 1,000 persons) in 2005.

Sources: International Telecommunication Union; UNESCO, *Statistical Yearbook*.

Education

1990/91: 76,000 students at higher schools (Source: UNESCO, *Statistical Yearbook*).

Institutions (2005): Secondary schools 1,704; Secondary specialized schools 15; Higher schools (incl. universities) 16 (Source: Permanent Mission of Turkmenistan to the United Nations).

Students enrolled at universities (2003): 14,859 (Source: UNICEF).

Adult literacy rate (UNESCO estimates): 99.5% (males 99.7%; females 99.3%) in 2008 (Source: UNESCO Institute for Statistics).

Directory

The Government

HEAD OF STATE

President of the Republic: GURBANGULY BERDYMUHAMEDOV (elected 11 February 2007; inaugurated 14 February 2007).

COUNCIL OF MINISTERS
(May 2011)

Chairman of the Government: GURBANGULY BERDYMUHAMEDOV.
Deputy Chairman, responsible for Construction: DERIYAGELDI ORAZOV.
Deputy Chairman, responsible for Petroleum and Natural Gas: BAYMYRAT HOJAMUHAMMEDOV.
Deputy Chairman, responsible for Transport and Communications: NAZARGULY SHAGULYYEV.
Deputy Chairman, responsible for Economic Affairs: TUVAKMAMMED JAPAROV.
Deputy Chairman and Minister of Foreign Affairs: RASHID MEREDOV.
Deputy Chairman, responsible for the Textile Industry, Trade and the Chamber of Commerce and Industry: HOJAMUHAMMET MUHAMMEDOV.
Deputy Chairman: MAISA YAZMUHAMMEDOVA.
Deputy Chairman: MYRATGELDY AKMAMMEDOV.
Minister of National Security: YILYM BERDYYEV.
Minister of Defence: BEGENCH GUNDOGDYYEV.
Minister of Justice: MYRAT KARRYYEV.
Minister of Internal Affairs: ISKANDER MULIKOV.
Minister of Finance: ANNAMUHAMMET GOCHIYEV.
Minister of Social Security: BEKMYRAT SHAMYRADOV.
Minister of Construction: JUMAGELDY BAYRAMOV.
Minister of the Construction Materials Industry: YAZMYRAT HOMMADOV.
Minister of Culture, Television and Radio: GULMYRAT MYRADOV.

TURKMENISTAN

Minister of Energy and Industry: YARMUKHAMMED ORAZGULYYEV.
Minister of Railways: ROZYMYRAT SEYITKULIYEV.
Minister of Communications: OVLIYAGULY JUMAGULYYEV.
Minister of Road Transport: GURBANMYRAT HANGULYYEV.
Minister of the Petroleum and Gas Industry and Mineral Resources: BAYRAMGELDI NEDIROV.
Minister of Trade and Foreign Economic Relations: BAYAR ABAYEV.
Minister of the Textile Industry: AYNABAT BABAYEVA.
Minister of Health and the Medical Industry: GURBANMAMMET ELYASOV.
Minister of Education: GULSHAT MAMMEDOVA.
Minister of Water Resources: ANNAGELDY YAZMYRADOV.
Minister of Agriculture: MERDAN BAYRAMOV.
Minister of the Economy and Development: BYASHIMMYRAT HOJAMAMMEDOV.
Minister of Environmental Protection: BABAGELDY ANNABAYRAMOV.

Note: The following positions also form part of the Council of Ministers: the Prosecutor-General; the Chairmen of three state concerns, Türkmennebit/Turkmenneft (Turkmen Oil), Türkmengaz/Turkmengaz (Turkmen Gas) and Türkmennebitgazgurlushyk/Turkmenneftegazstroi (Turkmen Oil and Gas Construction), and of the state joint-stock corporation Türkmenhaky/Turkmenkover (Turkmen Carpets); the Chairmen of the Board of the Central Bank of Turkmenistan and of Türkmenvnesheconombank (State Bank for Foreign Economic Affairs of Turkmenistan); and the Chairman of the following bodies: the Supreme Court; the Supreme Economic Court; the State Borders Service; the State Customs Service; and the National Committee for Hydrometeorology at the Council of Ministers.

MINISTRIES

Office of the President and the Council of Ministers: 744000 Aşgabat, Presidential Palace; tel. (12) 35-45-34; fax (12) 35-51-12; e-mail nt@online.tm; internet www.turkmenistan.gov.tm.
Ministry of Agriculture: 744000 Aşgabat, Azad köç. 63; tel. (12) 35-66-91; fax (12) 35-05-18; e-mail selhoz2004@mail.ru.
Ministry of Communications: 744000 Aşgabat, Asudalyk köç. 36; tel. (12) 35-21-53; fax (12) 21-04-19; e-mail mincom@online.tm; internet www.mincom.gov.tm.
Ministry of Construction: 744000 Aşgabat, 2049 köç.; tel. (12) 35-60-60; fax (12) 39-35-90; e-mail mpsmt@online.tm.
Ministry of the Construction Materials Industry: Aşgabat.
Ministry of Culture, Television and Radio: 744000 Aşgabat, Puşkin köç. 14; tel. (12) 35-41-05; fax (12) 35-35-00.
Ministry of Defence: 744000 Aşgabat, Galkynyş köç. 4; tel. (12) 40-27-64; fax (12) 39-14-44.
Ministry of the Economy and Development: 744000 Aşgabat, 2008 köç. 4/1; tel. (12) 51-11-34; fax (12) 35-09-39; e-mail minekonom@online.tm.
Ministry of Education: 744000 Aşgabat, Gurungan köç. 2; tel. (12) 35-58-03; fax (12) 39-88-11.
Ministry of Energy and Industry: 744000 Aşgabat, 2008 köç. 6; tel. (12) 35-38-70; fax (12) 39-35-12; e-mail kuwwat@online.tm.
Ministry of Environmental Protection: 744000 Aşgabat, Kemine köç. 102; tel. (12) 35-43-17; fax (12) 39-31-84; e-mail makhtum@untuk.org.
Ministry of Finance: 744000 Aşgabat, 2008 köç. 4; tel. (12) 51-05-63; fax (12) 51-06-87; e-mail omeft@online.tm.
Ministry of Foreign Affairs: 744000 Aşgabat, Magtymguly Şaýoly 83; tel. (12) 39-21-54; fax (12) 35-42-41; e-mail mfatm@online.tm.
Ministry of Health and the Medical Industry: 744000 Aşgabat, Magtymguly Şaýoly 90; tel. (12) 40-04-46; fax (12) 40-04-16; e-mail healthtm@online.tm.
Ministry of Internal Affairs: 744000 Aşgabat, Magtymguly Şaýoly 85; tel. (12) 35-13-28; fax (12) 39-37-39.
Ministry of Justice: 744000 Aşgabat, 2022 köç. 86; tel. (12) 38-04-11; fax (12) 39-44-10.
Ministry of National Security: 744000 Aşgabat, Magtymguly Şaýoly 91; tel. (12) 39-71-58; fax (12) 51-07-55.
Ministry of the Petroleum and Gas Industry and Mineral Resources: 744000 Aşgabat, Gurungan köç. 28; tel. (12) 40-30-01; fax (12) 40-30-44; e-mail ministryoilgas@online.tm.
Ministry of Railways: 744000 Aşgabat, S. Türkmenbaşi köç. 9; tel. (12) 39-43-34; fax (12) 39-28-74; e-mail tde@online.tm.
Ministry of Road Transport: 744000 Aşgabat, Baba Annanov köç. 2; tel. (12) 47-49-92; fax (12) 47-03-91; e-mail tcentr@online.tm.
Ministry of Social Security: 744007 Aşgabat, 2003 köç. 3; tel. (12) 25-30-03.
Ministry of the Textile Industry: 744000 Aşgabat, Annadurdiyev köç. 52; tel. (12) 21-03-03; fax (12) 35-54-42; e-mail textile@online.tm.
Ministry of Trade and Foreign Economic Relations: 744000 Aşgabat, Gurungan köç. 1; tel. (12) 35-10-47; fax (12) 39-51-08; e-mail mtfer@online.tm.
Ministry of Water Resources: 744000 Aşgabat, 2005 köç. 1; tel. (12) 39-06-15; fax (12) 39-85-39.

President

Following the death of President Gen. SAPARMYRAT NIYAZOV on 21 December 2006, the hitherto Deputy Chairman of the Government and Minister of Health and the Medical Industry, GURBANGULY BERDYMUHAMEDOV, assumed the presidency in an acting capacity, before being elected President in an election held on 11 February 2007. BERDYMUHAMEDOV was elected by 89.2% of votes cast, with a participation rate of some 98.6% of registered voters, according to official results; he was inaugurated on 14 February.

Legislature

Majlis (Assembly)
744000 Aşgabat, Bitarap Türkmenistan köç. 17; tel. (12) 39-59-58; fax (12) 35-31-47.
Chairman: AKJA NURBERDIYEVA.

The Majlis is directly elected for a term of five years. Elections to an expanded 125-member Majlis were conducted on 14 December 2008, with a second round of voting following in one district on 28 December. It was reported that about 90% of the elected deputies were members of the ruling Democratic Party of Turkmenistan, while the remainder were independent candidates endorsed by the party. Following the resignation of a deputy, a poll was repeated in one district on 8 February 2009.

Election Commission

Central Commission for Elections and Referendums: Aşgabat; comprises a chairman, two vice-chairmen, a secretary and 12 mems, all appointed by the President of the Republic; Chair. ORAZMYRAT NYYAZLYEV; Sec. JEREN TAIMOVA.

Political Organizations

Democratic Party of Turkmenistan: 744014 Aşgabat, Gurungan köç. 28; tel. (12) 25-12-12; name changed from Communist Party of Turkmenistan in 1991; Chair. GURBANGULY BERDYMUHAMEDOV; Sec. ONJIK MUSAYEV.

Unity (Agzybirlik): 744000 Aşgabat; e-mail agzybirlik@hotmail.com; internet www.agzybirlik.com; f. 1989; unregistered popular front organization; Leader NURBERDI NURMÄMMET.

Turkmenistan is effectively a one-party state, with the Democratic Party of Turkmenistan (led by the President of the Republic) dominant in all areas of government. The President of the Republic is also the leader of the **Galkynyş National Revival Movement of Turkmenistan**. There are, however, several unregistered opposition groups, such as **Unity (Agzybirlik)**. A **Social Democratic Party** was reportedly established in Aşgabat in August 1996, upon the merger of several small unofficial groups.

Other opposition elements are based in other republics of the Commonwealth of Independent States, in particular Russia. A leading opposition figure in exile is a former Minister of Foreign Affairs, ABDY KULIYEV, whose **United Democratic Opposition of Turkmenistan (ODOT)** is based in Moscow, Russia, while the **Movement for Democratic Reform**, founded in 1996, is based in Sweden. The **Fatherland (Watan)** movement is also based in Sweden (e-mail info@watan.ru; internet watan.ru) and comprises Turkmen and other Central Asian oppositionists. In January 2002 a former Minister of Foreign Affairs, BORIS SHIKHMURADOV, established the opposition **People's Democratic Movement of Turkmenistan** (PDMT; internet gundogar.org); however, he was imprisoned in December, having been convicted of orchestrating the attempted assassination of President Saparmyrat Niyazov in November. Another opposition leader accused of conspiring with Shikhmuradov was NURMUKHAMMET HANAMOV, founder of the **Republican Party of Turkmenistan**

TURKMENISTAN

(RPT; internet tmrepublican.org; Co-Chair. NURMUKHAMMET HANA-MOV, SAPAR YKLYMOV).

Opposition leaders met in Prague, Czech Republic, in September 2003 and announced the formation of the **Union of Democratic Forces of Turkmenistan (UDFT)**, comprising four main groups: the RPT; Fatherland; the ODOT; and the **Revival Social Political Movement**.

Diplomatic Representation

EMBASSIES IN TURKMENISTAN

Afghanistan: 744000 Aşgabat, Gerogly köç. 14; tel. (12) 39-58-21; fax (12) 39-58-20; e-mail eira.tm@gmail.com; Ambassador Dr MOHAMMDA FASEL SAIFI.

Armenia: 744000 Aşgabat, Gerogly köç. 14; tel. (12) 35-44-18; fax (12) 33-14-19; e-mail eat@online.tm; Ambassador VLADIMIR BADALIAN.

Azerbaijan: 744020 Aşgabat, M. Kosayev köç. 44; tel. (12) 36-46-08; fax (12) 36-46-10; e-mail azsefir_ashg@online.tm; internet www.azembassyashg.com; Ambassador VAHDET SULTANZADE.

Belarus: 744000 Aşgabat, Gorky köç. 51; tel. (12) 33-11-83; fax (12) 33-11-85; e-mail turkmenistan@belembassy.org; internet www.turkmenistan.belembassy.org; Ambassador YURIY H. MALUMOV.

China, People's Republic: 744036 Aşgabat, Archabil köç. 45; tel. (12) 48-01-70; fax (12) 21-06-70; e-mail chinaemb_tkm@mfa.gov.cn; internet tm.china-embassy.org; Ambassador XIAO QINGHUA.

France: 744000 Aşgabat, Esgerler köç. 35; tel. (12) 36-35-50; fax (12) 36-35-46; e-mail cad.achgabat-amba@diplomatie.gouv.fr; internet www.ambafrance-achgabat.org; Ambassador PIERRE LEBOVICS.

Georgia: 744000 Aşgabat, Azad 1 köç. 39A; tel. (12) 33-02-48; fax (12) 33-03-65; e-mail ashgabat.emb@mfa.gov.ge; internet www.turkmenistan.mfa.gov.ge; Ambassador IOSEB CHAKHVASHVILI.

Germany: 744000 Aşgabat, Hydyr Derzhazhev köç., Hotel 'Ak Altin'; tel. (12) 36-35-15; fax (12) 36-35-22; e-mail info@aschgabat.diplo.de; Ambassador REINER MORELL.

Holy See: 744000 Aşgabat, Merkezi Poçta, POB 98; tel. (12) 39-11-40; fax (12) 35-36-83; e-mail aszomi@gmail.ru; Apostolic Nuncio ANTONIO LUCIBELLO (Titular Archbishop of Thurio) (resident in Ankara, Turkey).

India: 744000 Aşgabat, Yu. Emre köç. 2/1, Imperial International Business Centre; tel. (12) 45-81-52; fax (12) 45-61-56; e-mail indembhoc@online.tm; internet www.indianembassy-tm.org; Ambassador SUNIL JAIN.

Iran: 744000 Aşgabat, 2072 köç. 3; tel. (12) 34-93-61; fax (12) 35-05-65; Ambassador MOHAMMAD-MOUSA HASHEMI GOLPAYEGANI.

Israel: Aşgabat; Ambassador REUVEN DINAL (designate).

Japan: 744000 Aşgabat, 1945 köç. 60, Paytagt Trading Centre; tel. (12) 47-70-82; fax (12) 47-70-83; e-mail embassy@japan-tm.ru; internet www.tm.emb-japan.go.jp; Ambassador (vacant).

Kazakhstan: 744036 Aşgabat, Garaşyslyk köç. 11/13; tel. (12) 48-04-68; fax (12) 48-04-75; e-mail emb@kaztm.info; Ambassador ASKHAT OAZBAY.

Korea, Democratic People's Republic: 744000 Aşgabat; Ambassador KIM YON CHJE.

Korea, Republic: 744000 Aşgabat, Berzengi köç. 25; tel. (12) 48-97-61; fax (12) 48-97-60; e-mail korembtm@mofat.go.kr; internet tkm.mofat.go.kr; Ambassador AHN MYUNG-SOO.

Kyrgyzstan: 744000 Aşgabat, Gerogly köç. 85; tel. and fax (12) 35-55-06; e-mail kg@online.tm; Ambassador BAZARBAY MAMBETOV.

Libya: 744000 Aşgabat, Azad köç. 17A; tel. (12) 35-49-17; fax (12) 39-35-26; Ambassador ZIAD ADHAM AL-MUNTASIR.

Poland: 744005 Aşgabat, Azad köç. 17A; tel. (12) 27-40-35; fax (12) 27-31-22; e-mail aszchabad.amb.sekretariat@msz.gov.pl; internet www.aszchabad.polemb.net; Ambassador STEFAN RADOMSKI.

Romania: 744000 Aşgabat, Kusayev köç. 122; tel. (12) 34-76-55; fax (12) 34-76-20; e-mail ashabat@mae.ro; Ambassador RADU LIVIU HORUMBA.

Russia: 744005 Aşgabat, S. Türkmenbaşi Şayoly 11; tel. (12) 35-39-57; fax (12) 39-84-66; e-mail emb-rus@online.tm; internet www.turkmenistan.mid.ru; Ambassador ALEKSANDR BLOKHIN.

Saudi Arabia: 744000 Aşgabat, Yu. Emre köç. 2/1, Imperial International Business Centre; tel. (12) 45-49-63; fax (12) 45-49-70; e-mail tmemb@mofa.gov.sa; Ambassador TURKI BIN KHALID BIN FAISAL AL-HASHR.

Tajikistan: 744000 Aşgabat, Gurungan köç. 19; tel. (12) 35-56-96; fax (12) 39-31-74; e-mail tadjemb_tm@mail.ru; internet www.tajembassy-tm.com; Ambassador ABDURAHIM ASHUR.

Turkey: 744000 Aşgabat, Şevçenko köç. 9; tel. (12) 35-41-18; fax (12) 39-19-14; e-mail askabat.be@mfa.gov.tr; internet ashgabat.emb.mfa.gov.tr; Ambassador ŞEVKI MÜTEVELLIOĞLU.

Ukraine: 744001 Aşgabat, Azad köç. 49; tel. (12) 39-13-73; fax (12) 39-10-28; e-mail emb_tm@mfa.gov.ua; internet www.mfa.gov.ua/turkmenistan; Ambassador VALENTIN SHEVALEV.

United Arab Emirates: 744000 Aşgabat, Archabil 41/1; tel. (12) 48-10-28; fax (12) 48-10-29; e-mail uaembassy@online.tm; Ambassador HASSAN ABDULLAH AL-ADHAB.

United Kingdom: 744001 Aşgabat, Four Points Ak Altin Hotel, 3rd Floor, Offices 301–308; tel. (12) 36-34-62; fax (12) 36-34-65; e-mail beasb@online.tm; internet ukinturkmenistan.fco.gov.uk; Ambassador KEITH RENNIE ALLAN.

USA: 744000 Aşgabat, Puşkin köç. 9; tel. (12) 35-00-45; fax (12) 39-26-14; e-mail irc-ashgabat@iatp.edu.tm; internet turkmenistan.usembassy.gov; Ambassador ROBERT PATTERSON.

Uzbekistan: 744006 Aşgabat, Gerogly köç. 50A; tel. (12) 33-10-55; fax (12) 33-10-57; e-mail embashgabat@yahoo.com; Ambassador SHERZOD FAYZIYEV.

Judicial System

Judicial power is exercised by the Supreme Court, the High Commercial Court, and military and other courts. Judges are appointed by the President for a term of five years.

Chairman of the Supreme Court: YARANMYRAT YAZMYRADOV; tel. (12) 39-02-31; fax (12) 35-50-50.

Prosecutor-General: CHARY HOJAMYRADOV, 744000 Aşgabat, Seidi köç.; fax (12) 35-44-82.

Religion

The majority of the population are adherents of Islam. In June 1991 the Supreme Soviet of the Turkmen SSR adopted a Law on Freedom of Conscience and Religious Organizations. In April 1994 a council (gengeş) for religious affairs was established, within the office of the President; it was chaired by the qazi (supreme Islamic judge) of Turkmenistan, with the head of the Orthodox Church in Turkmenistan serving as Deputy Chairman. In November 2003 new legislation, replacing that of 1991, was approved, restricting the activities of religious groups, although registration requirements for religious communities were made more flexible by a presidential decree, issued in early 2004. Further legislation, approved in March of that year, reduced the membership threshold required for a group to register from 500 to five. Prior to these amendments, only Sunni Muslim and Russian Orthodox Christian groups had been permitted to register. By mid-2004 groups of Seventh-day Adventist and Baptist Christians, Hare Krishnas, and Bahá'ís had also registered.

ISLAM

Turkmen are traditionally Sunni Muslims, but with elements of Sufism. Islam was severely persecuted by the Soviet regime from the late 1920s. Until July 1989 Aşgabat was the only Central Asian capital without a functioning mosque. The Muslims of Turkmenistan are officially under the jurisdiction of the Muslim Board of Central Asia, based in Tashkent, Uzbekistan, but, in practice, the Government permits little external influence in religious affairs. The Board is represented in Turkmenistan by a qazi, who is responsible for appointing Muslim clerics in all rural areas.

Qazi of Turkmenistan: ROVSHEN ALLABERDIYEV.

CHRISTIANITY

The Russian Orthodox Church (Moscow Patriarchate)

The Church in Turkmenistan comes under the jurisdiction of the Eparchy of Tashkent and Central Asia, headed by the Metropolitan of Tashkent and Central Asia, VLADIMIR (IKIM), based in Uzbekistan.

Roman Catholic Church

The Church is represented in Turkmenistan by a Mission, established in September 1997. There were 85 adherents at 31 December 2007.

Superior: Fr ANDRZEJ MADEJ, 744000 Aşgabat, Gerogly köç. 20A, POB 98; tel. (12) 39-11-40; fax (12) 35-36-83; e-mail amadej@oblaci.pl.

The Press

In July 2010 some 25 newspapers and 15 periodicals, all of which were state-owned, were published in Turkmenistan. The first pri-

TURKMENISTAN

vately owned publication in the country, *Rysgal*, was launched in September of that year. All publications listed below are in Turkmen, except where otherwise stated.

PRINCIPAL NEWSPAPERS

Adalat (Justice): 744005 Aşgabat, 2033 köç. 1/4; tel. (12) 39-79-04; weekly; Editor-in-Chief Dovlet H. Gurbangeldiyev; circ. 84,051.

Beyik Türkmenbaşiyn Nesli (Generation of Türkmenbaşi the Great): 744064 Aşgabat, Galkynyş köç. 20; tel. (12) 22-33-78; f. 1922; 3 a week; for young people; Editor Annagul Narlieva; circ. 21,591.

Edebiyat we sungat (Literature and Art): 744004 Aşgabat, Galkynyş köç. 20; tel. (12) 35-30-34; f. 1958; weekly; Editor Annamyrat Poladov; circ. 19,111.

Esger (Soldier): 744004 Aşgabat, 2038 köç. 29; tel. (12) 35-68-09; f. 1993; weekly; organ of the Council of Ministers; military newspaper; Editor-in-Chief Agamyrat Geldyev; circ. 40,200.

Galkynyş (Revival): 744604 Aşgabat, Galkynyş köç. 20; tel. (12) 22-34-23; weekly; organ of the Democratic Party of Turkmenistan (q.v.); Editor-in-Chief Khudaiberdi Divanguliyev; circ. 44,586.

Habarlar: 744004 Aşgabat, Galkynyş köç. 20; tel. (12) 46-84-70; weekly; in Russian and Turkmen; television and radio; business; advertisements; Editor-in-Chief R. Balaban; circ. 3,596.

Mugallymlar gazeti (Teachers' Newspaper): 744004 Aşgabat, G. Kuliyev köç. 20; tel. (12) 38-61-45; f. 1952; 3 a week; organ of the Ministry of Education; Editor Rejepnur Gurbannazarov; circ. 75,226.

Neitralnyi Turkmenistan (Neutral Turkmenistan): 744004 Aşgabat, Galkynyş köç. 20; tel. and fax (12) 39-42-76; e-mail nt@online.tm; f. 1924; 6 a week; organ of the Majlis and the Council of Ministers; in Russian; Editor-in-Chief Bekdurdy Amansariyev; circ. 30,091.

Novosti Turkmenistana (Turkmenistan News): 744000 Aşgabat, Bitarap Turkmenistan köç. 24A; tel. (12) 39-12-21; fax (12) 51-02-34; e-mail tpress@online.tm; f. 1994; weekly; in Russian, English and Turkmen; publ. by Türkmen Dowlet Khabarlar Gullugy news agency; Chair. Bekdurdy T. Amansariyev; circ. 500.

Syyasy sokhbetdeş (Political Symposium): 744604 Aşgabat, Galkynyş köç. 20; tel. (12) 25-10-84; f. 1992; weekly; organ of the Democratic Party of Turkmenistan; Editor Akbibi Yusupova; circ. 14,500.

Türkmening yupekyoli (Turkmen Railwayman): 744007 Aşgabat, Chary Nurymov köç. 3; tel. and fax (12) 35-06-52; f. 1936; weekly; organ of the Turkmenistan State Railways; covers transport and communications; Editor Bayram Sahedov; circ. 11,500 (March 2010).

Türkmenistan—Altyn Asar/ Turkmenistan—Zolotoi Vek/ Turkmenistan—The Golden Age: 744004 Aşgabat, Galkynyş köç. 20; tel. (12) 22-33-38; e-mail nt@online.tm; internet turkmenistan.gov.tm/_tm; f. 2003; online only; publ. by Govt and President; in Turkmen, Russian and English.

Watan (Fatherland): 744604 Aşgabat, Galkynyş köç. 20; tel. (12) 22-34-56; f. 1925; 3 a week; Editor-in-Chief Amanmuhammet Repow; circ. 25,419.

PRINCIPAL PERIODICALS

Monthly, unless otherwise indicated.

Diyar: 744604 Aşgabat, Galkynyş köç. 20; tel. (12) 35-53-97; f. 1992; foreign policy and international relations; publ. by the President of the Republic and the Council of Ministers; Editor-in-Chief Ashirberdy Gurbanov; circ. 12,881.

Garagum (Kara-Kum): 744005 Aşgabat, Galkynyş köç. 20; tel. (12) 35-11-15; f. 1928; literary; Editor Sapar Orayev; circ. 2,546.

Guneş (The Sun): 744000 Aşgabat, Galkynyş köç. 20; tel. (12) 22-33-05; for children; Editor-in-Chief Shadurdy Charygyllyev; circ. 44,696.

Obrazovaniye (Education): Aşgabat; f. 2010; six a year; in Russian; organ of the Office of the Deputy Chairman, responsible for Education, Science, Health, Culture, Sport, the Mass Media and Social Organizations and of the Ministry of Education.

Rysgal (Welfare): 744000 Aşgabat, Ostrovsky köç. 26, Union of Industrialists and Entrepreneurs; f. 2010; in Turkmen and Russian; publ. by Union of Industrialists and Entrepreneurs; business.

Saglyk (Health): 744000 Aşgabat, Kerbabayev köç. 39/57; tel. (12) 39-16-21; f. 1990; 6 a year; publ. by the Ministry of Health and the Medical Industry (q.v.); Editor-in-Chief Bayramammed Tachmamedov; circ. 35,071.

Taze oba (New Countryside): 744000 Aşgabat, Azad köç. 63; tel. (12) 35-19-38; f. 1929; fmrly *Türkmenistanyň oba khozhalygy*; monthly; Editor Byashim Tallykov; circ. 9,450.

Türkmen dunyasi: 744004 Aşgabat, Azad köç. 20; tel. (12) 47-81-18; monthly; organ of the Humanitarian Association of World Turkmen; Editor-in-Chief Annaberdy Agabayev; circ. 11,956.

Türkmen medeniyeti (Turkmen Culture): 744007 Aşgabat, O. Kuliyev köç. 21; tel. (12) 25-37-22; f. 1993; 2 a year; publ. by the Ministry of Culture, Television and Radio; Editor Geldymyrat Nurmukhammedov.

Türkmen sporty/Sport Turkmenistana (Turkmen Sport): 744004 Aşgabat, Galkynyş köç. 20; tel. (12) 22-33-72; weekly; in Turkmen and Russian; Editor-in-Chief Viktor Mihaylov; circ. 2,500.

Turkmenistanda Ylym We Tekhnika (Science and Engineering of Turkmenistan): 744000 Aşgabat, Azad köç. 59; f. 1995 as *Izvestiya Akademii Nauk Turkmenistana*; 6 a year; in Russian and Turkmen.

Türkmenistanyň Lukmancykygy: 744004 Aşgabat, A. Gulmammedov köç. 4A; tel. (12) 35-25-40; f. 2002; every two months; health policy; Editor-in-Chief O. Serdarov.

Türkmenistanyň Mejlisining Maglumatlary (Bulletin of the Majlis of Turkmenistan): 744004 Aşgabat, Garaşyslyk köç. 110; tel. (12) 35-50-39; fax (12) 35-31-47; e-mail mejlis@online.tm; f. 1960; 4 a year; proceedings of the Turkmenistan Parliament; in Russian and Turkmen.

Vozrozhdeniye (Rebirth): 744604 Aşgabat, Galkynyş köç. 20; tel. (12) 35-10-84; f. 1937; fmrly *Politicheskii sobesednik* (Political Colloquium); in Russian; publ. by the Democratic Party of Turkmenistan (q.v.); circ. 2,300.

Zenan Kalby (Women's Soul): 744604 Aşgabat, Galkynyş köç. 20; tel. (12) 22-33-09; f. 1931; fmrly *Ovadan* (Beautiful), then *Gurbansoltan Eje* (Mother of Türkmenbaşi); for women; Editor Akbibi Yusubova; circ. 56,626.

NEWS AGENCY

Türkmen Dowlet Khabarlar Gullugy (Turkmen State News Service): 744000 Aşgabat, Bitarap Türkmenistan köç. 24A; tel. (12) 39-12-21; fax (12) 51-02-34; e-mail tpress@online.tm; f. 1967; Dir Jeren Taimova.

Publishers

Magaryf Publishing House: 744000 Aşgabat; Dir N. Atayev.

Turkmenistan State Publishing Service: 744000 Aşgabat, Galkynyş köç. 20; tel. (12) 46-90-13; f. 1965; politics, science and fiction; Chair. Annanur Charyyarov.

Ylym Publishing House: 744000 Aşgabat, Azad köç. 59; tel. (12) 29-04-84; f. 1952; desert devt, science; Dir N. I. Faizulayeva.

Broadcasting and Communications

TELECOMMUNICATIONS

The principal provider of telecommunications services is the state-owned Türkmentelekom, while mobile cellular communications are provided by its subsidiary company, Altyn Asyr. A local subsidiary of the Russian company MTS provided mobile communications and internet services in Turkmenistan from 2007, but was obliged to withdraw from the country following the expiry of its contract at the end of 2010.

Altyn Asyr: 744000 Aşgabat, Chary Nuriev köç. 3; tel. (12) 39 88 26; fax (12) 39 88 91; e-mail altynasyrgsm@online.tm; f. 2004; subsidiary of Türkmentelekom (q.v.); provides mobile communications services.

Türkmentelekom: 744000 Aşgabat, Asudalyk köç. 36; tel. (12) 51-12-77; fax (12) 51-02-40; e-mail admin@telecom.tm; internet www.telecom.tm; f. 1993; state-owned; subsidiary co, Altyn Asyr, provides mobile telecommunication services; Dir-Gen. Annaly Ch. Berdinobatov.

BROADCASTING

In 2009 there were five state television channels and four state radio stations.

Turkmen State Information Agency (Türkmen Dovlet Habarlary): 744004 Aşgabat, Gurungan köç.; tel. (12) 39-12-21; fax (12) 51-02-34; e-mail tpress@online.tm; Head Jeren Taimova.

Radio

Turkmen National Radio Co: 744000 Aşgabat, Navoi köç. 5; tel. (12) 39-25-20; Chair. Murad Orazov.

    Char Tarapdan (From All Sides): tel. (12) 39-86-72; Dir Berdimyrat Abdyyev.

    Miras (Heritage): tel. (12) 35-68-50; Dir Gurbandurdy Rejepov.

    Watan (Fatherland): tel. (12) 51-12-96; Dir Nurberdi Dadebayev.

TURKMENISTAN

Television

Turkmen National Television Co: 744000 Aşgabat, Navoi köç. 5; tel. (12) 39-25-20; Chair. MURAD ORAZOV.

Altyn Asar (Golden Age): tel. (12) 39-85-06; Dir SHADURDY ALOVOV (acting).

Miras (Heritage): tel. (12) 35-20-43; Dir BYAGUL CH. NURMURADOVA.

Türkmenistan: tel. (12) 35-00-86; Dir MURAD A. ORAZOV.

Yaşlyk (Youth): tel. (12) 35-00-86.

Finance

(cap. = capital; res = reserves; dep. = deposits; m. = million; brs = branches; amounts in Turkmen manats)

BANKING

In late 2002 there were 12 commercial banks operating in Turkmenistan. The state retains substantial interests and involvement in banking.

Central Bank

Central Bank of Turkmenistan (Türkmenistanyň Merkezi Banky): 744000 Aşgabat, Bitarap Türkmenistan köç. 36; tel. (12) 38-10-27; fax (12) 51-08-12; e-mail merkezb2@online.tm; internet www.cbt.tm; f. 1991; central monetary authority, issuing bank and supervisory authority; Chair. of Bd GUVANCHMYRAT GEKLENOV; 5 brs.

Other Banks

Daihanbank: 744000 Aşgabat, 2067 köç. 60; tel. and fax (12) 41-98-68; e-mail daybank@online.tm; f. 1989 as independent bank, Agroprombank, reorganized 1999; specializes in agricultural sector; Chair. of Bd TUMAR MAMMEDOV; 70 brs.

Garagum International Joint-Stock Bank: 744000 Aşgabat, O. Kuliyev köç. 3; tel. (12) 35-22-01; fax (12) 35-38-54; e-mail garagum@telekom.tm; f. 1993 as International Bank for Reconstruction, Development and Support of Entrepreneurship, name changed 2000; Chair. BEGENCH CHOPANOV.

Garaşyslyk Bank: 744000 Aşgabat, Gerogly köç. 30A; tel. (12) 35-48-75; fax (12) 39-01-24; e-mail garash@cbtm.net; f. 1999 following merger of Gas Bank and Aşgabat Bank; cap. US $5m. (Oct. 2003); Chair. (vacant); 5 brs.

Kreditbank: 744000 Aşgabat, Magtymguly Şayoly; tel. (12) 35-02-22; fax (12) 35-03-09; e-mail kreditbank@online.tm; f. 1995; fmrly Rossiiskii Kredit; Chair. BATYR BAYRIYEV.

President Bank of Turkmenistan (Türkmenistanyň Prezidentbank): 744005 Aşgabat, 1932 köç. 132; tel. (12) 27-19-90; fax (12) 27-20-10; e-mail presidentbank@cbtm.net; internet www.presidentbank.gov.tm; f. 2000; cap. US $60m.; state-owned; Chair. of Bd NURGELDI SAZAKOV.

Savings Bank of Turkmenistan (Sberbank): 744000 Aşgabat, Magtymguly Şayoly 86; tel. (12) 35-46-71; fax (12) 35-40-04; f. 1923, reorganized 1989; wholly state-owned; Chair. BEGENCH BAYMUKHAMEDOV; 120 brs.

Senagatbank: 744013 Aşgabat, S. Türkmenbaşi Şayoly 42; tel. (12) 45-31-33; fax (12) 45-44-09; e-mail senagat@online.tm; f. 1989; cap. 31,200m., res 1,394m., dep. 32,547m. (Feb. 2005); Chair. AKMYRAT ORAZOV; 5 brs.

Turkmen-Turkish Joint-Stock Commercial Bank (Türkmen-Türk paýdarlar täjirçilik banky): 744000 Aşgabat, Magtymguly Şayoly 111/2, POB 15; tel. (12) 51-10-09; fax (12) 51-11-23; e-mail ttcb@online.tm; internet www.turkmenturkbank.com; f. 1993; 50% owned by Türkiye Cumhuriyeti Ziraat Bankasi, AŞ (Turkey), and 50% by Daihanbank; cap. 26,000.0m., res 2,220.8m., dep. 34,463.5m. (Dec. 2005); Gen. Man. AVNI DEMIRCI.

Türkmenbank—State Commercial Bank 'Türkmenistan': 744000 Aşgabat, Gurungan köç. 10A; tel. (12) 51-07-21; fax (12) 39-67-35; e-mail turkmenbank@ctbm.net; f. 1992; Chair. ATAMYRAT ATALYKOV.

Türkmenbaşi Bank: 744000 Aşgabat, Annadurdiyev köç. 4/20–26; tel. (12) 51-24-50; fax (12) 51-11-11; e-mail mail@investbank.org; f. 1992 as Investbank, renamed in 2000; Chair. BATIR DURDUMAMMADOV; 23 brs.

Türkmenvnesheconombank—State Bank for Foreign Economic Affairs of Turkmenistan: 744000 Aşgabat, Garaşyslyk Şayoly 32; tel. (12) 40-60-40; fax (12) 40-65-63; e-mail tveb@online.tm; internet www.tfeb.gov.tm; f. 1992 as independent bank, from Soviet Vneshekonombank; wholly state-owned; cap. 353,735m., dep. 1,219,725m., total assets 5,130,275m. (Dec. 2007); Chair. of Bd RAHYMBERDI JEPBAROV.

COMMODITY EXCHANGE

State Commodity and Raw Materials Exchange of Turkmenistan (GTSBT): 744000 Aşgabat, Arçabil Şayoly 52; tel. (12) 44-66-30; fax (12) 44-66-16; e-mail info@exchange.gov.tm; internet www.exchange.gov.tm; f. 1994; Chair. ŞABERDY MEREDOV.

Trade and Industry

GOVERNMENT AGENCIES

National Institute of State Statistics and Information on Turkmenistan (Türkmenmillihasabat): 744000 Aşgabat, 2033 köç. 72; tel. (12) 39-42-65; fax (12) 35-43-79; e-mail staff@natstat.gov.tm; f. 1997; Dir KAKAMYRAT MOMMADOV.

State Agency for Foreign Investment (SAFI): 744000 Aşgabat, Azad köç. 53; tel. and fax (12) 35-04-16; e-mail saffi@online.tm; f. 1996; monitors and regulates all foreign investment in Turkmenistan; registers foreign cos in Turkmenistan; Dir (vacant).

DEVELOPMENT ORGANIZATION

Small and Medium Enterprise Development Agency (SMEDA): 744000 Aşgabat, 2015 köç. 8; tel. (12) 34-42-59; fax (12) 34-51-49; e-mail smeda@cat.glasnet.ru; jt venture between Govt and the European Union; Dir SERDAR BABAYEV.

CHAMBER OF COMMERCE

Chamber of Commerce and Industry of Turkmenistan: 744000 Aşgabat, 2037 köç. 17; tel. (12) 35-47-17; fax (12) 35-13-52; e-mail mission@online.tm; internet cci.gov.tm; f. 1959; Chair. ARSLAN F. NEPESOV.

EMPLOYERS' ORGANIZATION

Union of Industrialists and Entrepreneurs: 744000 Aşgabat, Ostrovsky köç. 26; f. 2008; Dir ALEKSANDR DADAYEV.

UTILITIES

Electricity

Kuvvat Turkmen State Energy Technology Corpn: 744000 Aşgabat, 2008 köç. 6; tel. (12) 35-68-04; fax (12) 39-06-82; e-mail kuvvat@online.tm; state electrical power generation co and agency; Chair. YUSUP DAVYDOV.

STATE HYDROCARBONS COMPANIES

Türkmenbaşi Complex of Oil-refining Plants (TKNPZ): 745000 Balkan Velayat, Türkmenbaşi, POB 5; tel. (222) 7-45-45; fax (222) 7-45-44; production and refining of petroleum; sales of petroleum and liquefied natural gas; Dir-Gen. SAHETMYRAT MAMMEDOV.

Türkmengaz/Turkmengaz (Turkmen Gas): 744036 Aşgabat, 1939 köç. 56; tel. (12) 40-32-00; fax (12) 40-32-54; e-mail annam@online.tm; f. 1996; govt agency responsible for natural gas operations, incl. development of system of extraction, processing of gas and gas concentrate, and gas transportation and sale; Chair. AMANALI HANALIYEV.

Türkmengeologiya: 744000 Aşgabat, 2023 köç. 7/32; tel. (12) 35-13-46; fax (12) 35-50-15; govt agency responsible for natural gas and petroleum exploration; Chair. TORE YAGSHIMURAADOV.

Türkmennebit/Turkmenneft (Turkmen Oil): 745100 Balkan Velayat, Balkanabat, Magtymguly Şayoly 49; tel. (243) 2-19-45; govt agency responsible for petroleum operations and production; Chair. ANNAGULY DERYAYEV.

Türkmennebitgazgurlushyk/Turkmennefftegazstroi (Turkmen Oil and Gas Construction): 744036 Aşgabat, Arçabil köç. 56; tel. (12) 40-35-01; fax (12) 40-35-01; e-mail tngg@online.tm; govt agency for construction projects in the hydrocarbons sector; Chair. AKMYRAT YEGELEYEV.

TRADE UNIONS

Federation of Trade Unions of Turkmenistan: 744000 Aşgabat, S. Türkmenbaşi Şayoly 13; tel. (12) 35-62-08; fax (12) 35-21-30; Chair. ENEBAY G. ATAYEVA.

Committee of Trade Unions of Ahal Velayat: 744000 Ahal Velayat, pos. Anau, Gyaver etrap; tel. 41-39-19; Dir A. TAGANOV.

Committee of Trade Unions of Daşoguz Velayat: 746311 Daşoguz Velayat, Niyazovsk, S. Türkmenbaşi Şayoly 8; Dir SH. IGAMOV.

TURKMENISTAN

Transport

RAILWAYS

The main railway line in the country runs from Türkmenbaşi (formerly Krasnovodsk), on the Caspian Sea, in the west, via Aşgabat and Mari, to Türkmenabat (formerly Charjew) in the east. From Türkmenabat, one line runs further east, to the other Central Asian countries of the former USSR, while another runs north-west, via Uzbekistan and Kazakhstan, to join the Russian rail network. In 2007 the total length of rail track in use in Turkmenistan was 2,523 km. A 203-km rail link from Türkmenabat to Atamarut was opened in 1999. In 1996 a rail link was established with Iran (on the route Tejen–Serakhs–Mashad), thus providing the possibility of rail travel and transportation between Turkmenistan and Istanbul, Turkey, as well as giving access to the Persian (Arabian) Gulf. A 540-km railway line, running south–north across the country from Aşgabat to Daşoguz, via Garagum, was completed in early 2006.

Turkmenistan State Railways (Türkmendemorjollari): 744007 Aşgabat, S. Türkmenbaşi Şaýoly 7; tel. (12) 35-55-45; fax (12) 51-06-32; f. 1992; Pres. B. P. REDJEPOV.

ROADS

In 1999 there was an estimated total of 24,000 km of roads, of which some 19,500 km were hard-surfaced. In early 2008 construction was under way on a principal road of 1,200 km, which was to link Türkmenbaşi with the eastern town of Farap.

SHIPPING

Shipping services link Türkmenbaşi (formerly Krasnovodsk) with Baku (Bakı, Azerbaijan), Makhachkala (Dagestan, Russia) and the major Iranian ports on the Caspian Sea. The Amu Dar'ya river is an important inland waterway. From 2000 Türkmenbaşi port was undergoing an extensive process of modernization.

Shipowning Companies

Neftec: 745100 Balkan Velayat, Türkmenbaşi; tel. (2) 765-81; fax (2) 766-89.

Turkmen Maritime Steamship Co: 745100 Balkan Velayat, Türkmenbaşi, Şagadam köç. 8; tel. (2) 767-34.

Turkmen Shipping Co: 745100 Balkan Velayat, Türkmenbaşi, Şagadam köç. 8; tel. (2) 972-67; fax (2) 767-85.

Türkmenderyayollary: 746000 Lebap Velayat, Türkmenabat, ul. Gyamichiler 8; tel. (2) 223-12; fax (2) 23-46-88; f. 1992 as Turkmen River Shipping Co; renamed as above in 1998.

Türkmennefteflot: 745100 Balkan Velayat, Türkmenbaşi, POB 6; tel. (2) 762-62.

CIVIL AVIATION

Turkmenistan's principal international airport is at Aşgabat. A second international airport, at Türkmenbaşi, opened in April 2010.

National Civil Aviation Authority of Turkmenistan (Türkmenhovayollary): 744000 Aşgabat, 2007 köç. 3 A; tel. (12) 35-10-52; fax (12) 35-44-02; e-mail aviahead@online.tm; f. 1992; Dir-Gen. BATYR KAKALIEV.

Türkmenhovayollary—Turkmenistan Airlines: 744000 Aşgabat, Magtymguly köç. 80; tel. (12) 35-10-52; fax (12) 35-44-02; f. 1992; state-owned; domestic and international scheduled and charter passenger flights, incl. services to Europe, Central and South-East Asia, and the Middle East; three divisions: Ahal Air Co, Khazar Air Co and Lebap Air Co; Chair. IMAMBERDY IMAMBERDYYEVA (acting).

Tourism

Although the tourism sector in Turkmenistan remains relatively undeveloped, owing, in part, to the vast expanse of the Kara-Kum desert (some 80% of the country's total area), the Government has made efforts to improve the standard of visitor accommodation (there are a number of new luxury hotels in Aşgabat) and to improve the capacity and efficiency of the capital's international airport. The scenic Kopet Dagh mountains, the Caspian Sea coast, the archaeological sites and mountain caves of Kugitang, and the hot subterranean mineral lake at Kov-Ata are among the country's natural attractions, while the ancient cities of Mari and Nisa—former capitals of the Seljuk and Parthian empires, respectively—are of considerable historical interest. In addition, Kunya-Urgench is an important site of Muslim pilgrimage. In 2007, according to the World Tourism Organization, there were 8,177 visitors from abroad; receipts from tourism totalled US $192m. in 1998.

State Committee for Tourism and Sport: 744000 Aşgabat, ul. Puşkin köc. 17; tel. (12) 35-47-77; fax (12) 39-67-40; e-mail turkmentan@online.tm; internet www.tourism-sport.gov.tm; founded in 2000 on the basis of the State Tourist Corpn Turkmensyyakhat; Chair. YALKAPBERDY ATALYYEV.

Defence

The National Armed Forces of Turkmenistan began to be formed in mid-1992, initially under joint Turkmen and Russian command. As assessed at November 2010, the estimated strength of the armed forces was 22,000, consisting of an army of 18,500, an air force of 3,000 and a navy of 500. Military service is for a period of 24 months. In August 2009 President Gurbanguly Berdymuhamedov signed a decree providing for the establishment of a naval force by 2015 (the existing navy comprised only coastguard units). In May 1994 Turkmenistan became the first Central Asian republic of the former USSR to join the North Atlantic Treaty Organization's 'Partnership for Peace' programme.

Defence Expenditure: Budgeted at 744m. manats in 2010.

Chief of the General Staff: BEGENCH GUNDOGDIYEV.

Commander of the Ground Forces: BATIR MOLLAYEV.

Education

In September 2005 it was reported that all former Russian-language schools had adopted Turkmen as the main language of instruction, although one class with instruction in Russian was to be maintained in each school. In 2004 there was also one Turkish university and 14 Turkish schools. In 1995 34.4% of 15-to-18-year-olds were enrolled in general secondary education; in 1997 7.9% of those aged between 15 and 18 years were enrolled in technical and vocational schools. In 1997 83.1% of children aged between seven and 15 years were enrolled in basic education. The 1999 budget allocated 26.9% of total expenditure (1,048,700m. manats) to education.

From the second half of the 1990s reform of the education system left many children without access to free education, and free education at Turkmenistan's 16 universities was reportedly abolished from 2003. In 2004 a presidential decree invalidating all higher-education degrees received abroad came into effect; all teachers with such degrees were to be dismissed. Between 2002 and 2005 more than 12,000 teachers were removed from their posts. In March 2007 the new President, Gurbanguly Berdymuhamedov, increased the period of compulsory primary and secondary education from nine to 10 years and extended the period of higher education from two to five years (effective from the beginning of the 2007/08 school year). Students were no longer required to complete two years of practical work experience before applying to universities, and foreign degrees were given recognition. Some 13,800 students were enrolled at the country's 18 institutions of higher education in 2007/08.

TUVALU

Introductory Survey

LOCATION, CLIMATE, LANGUAGE, RELIGION, FLAG, CAPITAL

Tuvalu is a scattered group of nine small atolls (five of which enclose sizeable lagoons), extending about 560 km (350 miles) from north to south, in the western Pacific Ocean. Its nearest neighbours are Fiji to the south, Kiribati to the north and Solomon Islands to the west. The climate is warm and pleasant, with a mean annual temperature of 30°C (86°F), and there is very little seasonal variation. The average annual rainfall is about 3,500 mm (140 ins), the wettest months being November to February. The inhabitants speak Tuvaluan and English. Almost all of them profess Christianity, and about 98% are Protestants. The national flag (proportions 1 by 2) is light blue with the United Kingdom flag as a rectangular canton in the upper hoist, occupying one-quarter of the area, and nine five-pointed yellow stars (arranged to symbolize a map of the archipelago) in the fly. The flag was reintroduced in February 1997 to replace a design, adopted in October 1995, omitting the British union flag. The capital is on Funafuti Atoll.

CONTEMPORARY POLITICAL HISTORY

Historical Context

Tuvalu was formerly known as the Ellice (or Lagoon) Islands. Between about 1850 and 1875 many of the islanders were captured by slave-traders and this, together with European diseases, reduced the population from about 20,000 to 3,000. In 1877 the United Kingdom established the Western Pacific High Commission (WPHC), with its headquarters in Fiji, and the Ellice Islands and other groups were placed under its jurisdiction. In 1892 a British protectorate was declared over the Ellice Islands, and the group was linked administratively with the Gilbert Islands to the north. In 1916 the United Kingdom annexed the protectorate, which was renamed the Gilbert and Ellice Islands Colony (GEIC). During the Japanese occupation of the Gilbert Islands in 1942–43, the administration of the GEIC was temporarily moved to Funafuti in the Ellice Islands. (For more details of the history of the GEIC, see the chapter on Kiribati.)

A series of advisory and legislative bodies prepared the GEIC for self-government. In May 1974 the last of these, the Legislative Council, was replaced by the House of Assembly, with 28 elected members (including eight Ellice Islanders) and three official members. A Chief Minister was elected by the House and chose between four and six other ministers, one of whom had to be from the Ellice Islands.

In January 1972 the appointment of a separate GEIC Governor, who assumed most of the functions previously exercised by the High Commissioner for the Western Pacific, increased the long-standing anxiety of the Ellice Islanders over their minority position as Polynesians in the colony, dominated by the Micronesians of the Gilbert Islands. In a referendum held in the Ellice Islands in August and September 1974, more than 90% of the voters favoured separate status for the group, and in October 1975 the Ellice Islands, under the old native name of Tuvalu ('eight standing together', which referred to the eight populated atolls), became a separate British dependency. The Deputy Governor of the GEIC took office as Her Majesty's Commissioner for Tuvalu. The eight Ellice representatives in the GEIC House of Assembly became the first elected members of the new Tuvalu House of Assembly. They elected one of their number, Toaripi Lauti, to be Chief Minister. Tuvalu was completely separated from the GEIC administration in January 1976. The remainder of the GEIC was renamed the Gilbert Islands and achieved independence, as Kiribati, in July 1979.

Domestic Political Affairs

Tuvalu's first separate elections took place in August 1977, when the number of elective seats in the House of Assembly was increased to 12. An independence Constitution was finalized at a conference in the United Kingdom in February 1978. After five months of internal self-government, Tuvalu became independent on 1 October 1978, with Lauti as the first Prime Minister. The pre-independence House of Assembly was redesignated Parliament. In September 2000 Tuvalu was formally admitted to the UN.

In 1983 the USA formally renounced its claim, dating from 1856, to the four southernmost atolls. Following elections to Parliament in September 1981, Lauti was replaced as Prime Minister by Dr Tomasi (later Sir Tomasi) Puapua. Puapua was re-elected Prime Minister following subsequent elections in September 1985.

In February 1986 a nation-wide poll was conducted to establish public opinion as to whether Tuvalu should remain an independent constitutional monarchy, with the British monarch at its head, or become a republic. Only on one atoll did the community appear to be in favour of the adoption of republican status. In March Tupua (later Sir Tupua) Leupena, a former Speaker of Parliament, was appointed Governor-General, replacing Sir Penitala Teo, who had occupied the post since independence in 1978.

At a general election in September 1989 supporters of Puapua were reported to have been defeated in the election, and an opponent, Bikenibeu Paeniu (who had been appointed Minister of Community Services within the previous year), was elected Prime Minister. In October 1990 Toaripi Lauti succeeded Sir Tupua Leupena as Governor-General.

Legislation approved by Parliament in mid-1991, which sought to prohibit all new religions from the islands and to establish the Church of Tuvalu as the State Church, caused considerable controversy and extensive debate. A survey showed the population to be almost equally divided over the matter, although Paeniu firmly opposed the motion, describing it as incompatible with basic human rights.

In August 1991 the Government announced that it was to prepare a compensation claim against the United Kingdom for the allegedly poor condition of Tuvalu's economy and infrastructure at the time of the country's achievement of independence in 1978. Moreover, Tuvalu was to seek additional compensation for damage caused during the Second World War when the United Kingdom gave permission for the USA to build airstrips on the islands (some 40% of Funafuti was uninhabitable because of large pits created by US troops during the construction of an airstrip on the atoll). Relations with the United Kingdom deteriorated further in late 1992, when the British Government harshly criticized the financial policy of Paeniu's Government. Paeniu defended his Government's policies, and stated that continued delays in the approval of aid projects from the United Kingdom meant that Tuvalu would not be seeking further development funds from the British Government.

The two elections of 1993 and subsequent events

At a general election held in September 1993, three of the 12 incumbent members of Parliament lost their seats. However, at elections to the premiership held in the same month, Paeniu and Puapua received six votes each. When a second vote produced a similar result, the Governor-General dissolved Parliament, in accordance with the Constitution. Paeniu and his Cabinet remained in office until the holding of a further general election in November. At elections to the premiership in the following month Kamuta Latasi defeated Paeniu by seven votes to five. Puapua, who had agreed not to challenge Paeniu in the contest in favour of supporting Latasi, was elected Speaker of Parliament. In June 1994 Latasi removed the Governor-General, Toomu Malaefono Sione, from office, some seven months after he had been appointed to the position, and replaced him with Tulaga (later Sir Tulaga) Manuella. Latasi alleged that Paeniu's appointment of Sione had been politically motivated.

In December 1994, in what was widely regarded as a significant rejection of its political links with the United Kingdom, the Tuvaluan Parliament voted to remove the British union flag from the Tuvaluan national flag. A new design was selected and the new flag was inaugurated in October 1995. Speculation that the British monarch would be removed as Head of State intensified during 1995, following the appointment of a committee to review the Constitution. The three-member committee was to examine the procedure surrounding the appointment and removal of the Governor-General, and, particularly, to consider the adoption of a republican system of government.

In late 1996 the Deputy Prime Minister, Otinielu Tausi, and the parliamentary Speaker, Dr Tomasi Puapua, both announced their decision to withdraw their support for Latasi's Government, thereby increasing the number of opposition members in Parliament from five to seven. The reversal appeared to be in response to increasing dissatisfaction among the population with Latasi. This had been initially prompted by his unpopular initiative to replace the country's national flag, and was exacerbated by revelations that the leasing of Tuvalu's telephone code to a foreign company had resulted in the use of the islands' telephone system for personal services considered indecent by the majority of islanders. (The lease was subsequently terminated by the Government.) Opponents of the Prime Minister submitted a parliamentary motion of no confidence in his Government in December, which was approved by seven votes to five. Paeniu subsequently defeated Latasi, by a similar margin, to become Prime Minister, and a new Cabinet was appointed. The new premier acted promptly to restore the country's original flag, by proposing a parliamentary motion in February 1997, which was approved by seven votes to five.

A total of 35 candidates contested a general election on 26 March 1998. The period prior to the election had been characterized by a series of bitter disputes between Paeniu and Latasi, in which both had made serious accusations of sexual and financial misconduct against the other. Five members of the previous Parliament were returned to office, although Latasi unexpectedly failed to secure re-election. Paeniu was subsequently re-elected Prime Minister by 10 votes to two. In June the new Government announced a series of development plans and proposals for constitutional reform, including the introduction of a code of conduct for political leaders and the creation of an ombudsman's office. Paeniu stated that his administration intended to consult widely with the population before any changes were implemented. Also in 1998 Puapua was appointed Governor-General, replacing Manuella.

On 13 April 1999 Paeniu lost a parliamentary vote of confidence and was forced to resign. Later in the month Ionatana Ionatana, hitherto the Minister of Health, Education, Culture, Women and Community Affairs, was elected by Parliament as the new Prime Minister. On his appointment Ionatana immediately effected a reorganization of the Cabinet.

It was announced in February 2000 that a US $50m. agreement on the sale of the country's national internet '.tv' suffix had been concluded with a US company, which intended to market the internet address to international television companies. The sale was expected to generate some $10m. annually in revenue for Tuvalu. The funds generated from the sale enabled Tuvalu officially to join the UN, and participate in the 55th annual UN General Assembly Meeting, held in September 2000. Proceeds from the internet domain sale were also used to develop the islands' infrastructure.

In December 2000 Prime Minister Ionatana Ionatana died unexpectedly. The Deputy Prime Minister, Lagitupu Tuilimu, was immediately appointed as interim Prime Minister, pending the election of a replacement. In February 2001 Parliament elected as Prime Minister the Minister of Internal Affairs and Rural and Urban Development, Faimalaga Luka; he assumed responsibility for the additional portfolios of foreign affairs, finance and economic planning, and trade and commerce, and immediately named a new Cabinet. A vote of no confidence was upheld against Luka in December while he was away in New Zealand, undergoing a medical examination. Koloa Talake, a former Minister of Finance, was elected Prime Minister in the same month, winning eight of the 15 votes cast (the number of parliamentary seats having been increased from 12 to 15). He appointed an entirely new Cabinet.

Talake announced in March 2002 that lawyers were preparing evidence for further legal action against the United Kingdom, seeking compensation for the alleged inequality of the division of assets between Tuvalu and Kiribati when the two nations had achieved independence in the late 1970s. Following the general election held on 25 July 2002, Saufatu Sopoanga, a former Minister of Finance, defeated Amasone Kilei, the opposition candidate, by eight votes to seven to become the new Prime Minister. Sopoanga subsequently announced his intention to hold a referendum on the adoption of a republican system of government in Tuvalu.

In May 2003 two by-elections resulted in the loss of the Government's one-seat majority. The Government's subsequent refusal to convene Parliament (allegedly in order to evade a vote of no confidence) was strongly criticized by the opposition. The Government maintained that it would regain its majority with an imminent defection from the opposition and would then convene Parliament. In July, however, the situation remained unchanged and the opposition consequently sought a court order obliging Sopoanga to convene Parliament. The appointment, in early September, of Faimalaga Luka, hitherto Speaker and a member of Parliament, as the country's new Governor-General necessitated an additional by-election, which resulted in a further delay to Parliament's being convened. However, following the success of its candidate at the by-election, and (as anticipated) the defection of an opposition member, the Government regained its majority in October. Parliament was finally convened in November. In April 2004 the Government announced that a team of officials was touring the outer islands to canvas opinion on the adoption of republican status for Tuvalu.

In August 2004 the Prime Minister, Saufatu Sopoanga, was ousted by nine parliamentary votes to five in a vote of no confidence after a member of the Government crossed the floor to vote with the opposition and was joined by the Speaker. However, the election of a new Prime Minister was delayed by Sopoanga's decision to relinquish his seat, thus necessitating the organization of a by-election before Parliament could select a premier. Deputy Prime Minister Maatia Toafa assumed the role of acting Prime Minister in the interim. Sopoanga regained his seat in a by-election in early October, and on 11 October acting Prime Minister Maatia Toafa was elected to the premiership, defeating Sopoanga by eight votes to seven.

In April 2005 it was announced that Sio Patiale, a member of Parliament, was to resign on grounds of ill health. The consequent by-election was expected to be very significant, owing to the possibility that it might result in a majority for the opposition in Parliament. In the same month the Governor-General, Faimalaga Luka, resigned, having reached the maximum permitted age for the post of 65, and was replaced by Filoimea Telito. Luka died in August of that year. A further by-election in September, caused by the resignation of another member of Parliament, was won by a candidate who decided to support the Government, thus consolidating its majority.

Recent developments

The legislative election held on 3 August 2006 resulted in major changes to the composition of Parliament, with the entry of eight new members. Maatia Toafa was the only cabinet member to retain a seat, and was subsequently replaced as Prime Minister by Apisai Ielemia in mid-August. Ielemia assumed additional responsibility for the foreign affairs portfolio, while Taavau Teii was appointed Deputy Prime Minister and Minister of Natural Resources and Environment. Other appointments to the new Government included Lotoala Metia as Minister of Finance, Economic Planning and Industries and Willie Telavi as Minister of Home Affairs and Rural Development.

On 30 April 2008 a referendum on Tuvalu's system of government was conducted. The level of participation was reportedly low, at approximately 21% of the electorate. The majority of voters rejected proposals for a republican system, with a president as head of state: according to reports, 1,260 voters (or 65%) out of a total of 1,939 preferred the retention of the existing system of constitutional monarchy.

The issue of the lack of female members in Parliament came to the fore in May 2010 when a consultation group, arranged by the Department of Women with support from the Pacific Islands Forum Secretariat and other regional organizations, recommended the creation of two seats specifically to be reserved for women.

Parliament was dissolved in mid-August 2010 in advance of legislative elections to be held on 16 September. A total of 26 candidates registered to contest the 15 available seats. Ten incumbent legislators, including Prime Minister Ielemia and the Speaker, former premier Kamuta Latasi, were returned to office; however, Deputy Prime Minister and Minister of Natural Resources and Environment Teii unexpectedly lost his seat. On 29 September Maatia Toafa was elected Prime Minister, narrowly defeating Kausea Natano, the Minister for Public Utilities and Industries in the outgoing Government, by eight votes to seven. Toafa's Cabinet included Enele Sopoaga as Deputy Prime Minister and Minister of Foreign Affairs, Environment and Labour, and Monise Laafai as Minister of Finance. Isaia Taeia was appointed parliamentary Speaker.

On 22 December 2010 Prime Minister Toafa was removed from office following his defeat, by eight votes to seven, in a parliamentary motion of no confidence, reportedly filed in response to members' concerns about Toafa's management of the budget, a particular issue being indications that the Government was no longer to fund the cost of medical treatment abroad for Tuvaluans. The Minister of Home Affairs, Willie Telavi, had withdrawn his support for Toafa and defected to the opposition, reportedly in exchange for support for his candidacy for the premiership. Telavi was sworn in as the new Prime Minister on 24 December, having defeated Enele Sopoaga in the contest for the premiership, securing eight votes to Sopoaga's seven. Telavi appointed his Cabinet on the same day, allocating himself the home affairs portfolio, while former premier Ielemia was appointed Minister for Foreign Affairs, Environment, Trade, Labour and Tourism; Lotoala Metia was returned to the finance portfolio.

Following a demonstration by about 50 residents on Funafuti, a state of emergency, limiting meetings to a maximum of 10 people, was declared on 13 January 2011. The protesters, members of the Nukufetau community, demanded the resignation of their parliamentary representative, Minister of Finance Metia. A challenge to the Government's invocation of emergency rule lodged with the magistrate's court by local village leaders was dismissed in the following week. Prime Minister Telavi subsequently claimed that the state of emergency had been declared in response to the authorities' fears that the homes of parliamentary members might be targeted in arson attacks; constituents were alleged to have sent an intimidatory letter to Metia demanding his immediate resignation and threatening to do all in their power to remove him from office should he refuse to step down. The restriction on public gatherings was eased in late January to allow people to apply for approval from the police commissioner for gatherings of more than 10 people. The state of emergency was rescinded in February amid opposition claims that it had been imposed in order to silence dissenters, rather than in response to any genuine security concerns.

Environmental Concerns

In 1989 a UN report on the greenhouse effect (the anthropomorphic heating of the earth's atmosphere) listed Tuvalu as one of the island groups that would completely disappear beneath the sea in the 21st century, unless drastic action were taken. At the UN World Climate Conference, held in Switzerland in late 1990, Paeniu appealed for urgent action by developed nations to combat the environmental changes caused by the greenhouse effect, which were believed to include a 10-fold increase in cyclone frequency (from two in 1940 to 21 in 1990), an increase in salinity in ground water and a considerable decrease in the average annual rainfall. However, the Government remained critical of the inertia with which it considered certain countries had reacted to its appeal for assistance and reiterated the Tuvaluan people's fears of physical and cultural extinction. The subsequent Prime Minister, Kamuta Latasi, was similarly critical of the industrial world's apparent disregard for the plight of small island nations vulnerable to the effects of climate change, particularly when Tuvalu was struck by tidal waves in 1994 (believed to be the first experienced by the islands). The Government of Tuvalu was strongly critical of Australia's refusal to reduce its emission of pollutant gases (known to contribute to the greenhouse effect) at the Conference of the Parties to the UN Framework Convention on Climate Change (UNFCCC—UN Environment Programme, see p. 65) in Kyoto, Japan, in late 1997. In August 2001 Tuvalu was one of six members of the Pacific Islands Forum to demand a meeting with US President George W. Bush to try to enlist his support for the Kyoto Protocol. Although the USA produced nearly one-third of the industrialized countries' carbon dioxide emissions, it had repeatedly refused to adopt the Kyoto Protocol, which urged industrial nations to reduce carbon dioxide emissions by 5.2% from 1990 levels by 2012.

The installation of a new sea-level monitoring station began in December 2001 as part of the South Pacific Sea Level and Climate Monitoring Project administered by the Australian aid agency, AusAID. In January 2002 it was reported that the Government had engaged a US law firm to prosecute the USA and other nations for failing to meet their commitments to the UNFCCC. In September 2003 Tuvalu's Prime Minister addressed the 58th session of the UN General Assembly in New York, USA, and appealed for collective action to mitigate the impact of climate change and rising sea-levels on the islands. He once again urged all industrialized nations, particularly the USA, to sign the Kyoto Protocol. The option of resettlement on neighbouring islands, including Fiji, was under consideration, but only as a last resort, and the Government was also considering the purchase of land in other countries, while declaring that this might be a useful long-term solution should the problems caused by climate change worsen. In December 2007 it was reported that water from wells was becoming increasingly unsuitable for consumption, while high tides were causing frequent flooding.

Although the Kyoto Protocol was finally ratified by Australia in December 2007, in April 2010 Tuvalu expressed its profound disappointment at the delay in Australia's plans to implement a carbon emissions trading scheme, owing to the Government's parliamentary difficulties in enacting the requisite legislation (see the chapter on Australia). At a climate change convention held in the Australian town of Cairns in April 2011, the Tuvaluan delegate stated that Tuvalu was experiencing flooding from high tides more frequently each year and asked for regional assistance in addressing the issue. At a UN climate change convention held in Bangkok, Thailand, later in April, the Tuvaluan delegate warned that discussions on climate change were becoming stagnant and urged those in attendance to make securing an extension to the Kyoto Protocol beyond its scheduled expiry in 2012 their principal priority.

Foreign Affairs

Tuvalu has been subject to considerable international criticism regarding its stance on whaling. Its decision in mid-2004 to join the International Whaling Commission (IWC, see p. 439) was met with considerable disappointment. Environmental and animal welfare groups accused the Tuvaluan Government of accepting financial incentives from Japan in return for agreeing to use its vote to support a removal of the ban on commercial whaling at the commission's annual meeting in Italy in July 2004. In early 2006 the US ambassador to Tuvalu, Larry Dinger, received a petition from Greenpeace, the international environmentalist group, urging Tuvalu to cease voting with Japan at the IWC. In May of the same year, however, prior to the IWC's annual meeting in Japan, Tuvalu reiterated its stance. Tuvalu later denied that Japan had secured its vote at the meeting through its financing of infrastructure projects in Tuvalu after IWC delegates voted narrowly in favour of the resolution calling for a resumption of commercial whaling. In June 2010 the Tuvaluan Government was again forced to deny allegations that it had accepted financial assistance from Japan in return for voting, at that month's annual meeting of the IWC, in favour of an end to the moratorium on commercial whaling.

In July 2009 the New Zealand Minister of Foreign Affairs, Murray McCully, undertook a visit to the Pacific islands, his itinerary including Tuvalu. It was reported in September 2010 that a new four-year fisheries initiative, intended to facilitate the management and development of the Tuvaluan fisheries industry in order to ease the problem of food security, was expected to be funded by New Zealand.

In September 2010 the US Secretary of State, Hillary Clinton, sent a message on the occasion of the 32nd anniversary of Tuvaluan independence, in which she noted the co-operation enjoyed between Tuvalu and the USA in a range of fields, including combating climate change and protecting the environment. Clinton pledged the US Administration's commitment to further enhancing bilateral links.

During a visit to Taiwan in December 2006 Prime Minister Apisai Ielemia declared that Tuvalu was Taiwan's staunchest international ally and would continue to offer its support to Taiwanese efforts to secure international recognition. During another visit to Taiwan in February 2009, Ielemia held discussions with Taiwanese President Ma Ying-jeou, following which the two leaders pledged their commitment to the development of bilateral relations. President Ma also expressed Taiwan's support for Tuvalu in addressing the problems arising from global warming (see Environmental Concerns). On his tour of Taiwan's six Pacific allies in March 2010, President Ma included a brief stop in Tuvalu; the focus of the visit was vocational training, and President Ma reiterated support for Tuvalu in its efforts to address the increasingly pressing issue of rising sea-levels.

CONSTITUTION AND GOVERNMENT

Tuvalu is a constitutional monarchy. Under the Constitution of 1978, executive authority is vested in the British sovereign, as Head of State, and is exercisable by her representative, the Governor-General, who is appointed on the recommendation of the Prime Minister and acts, in almost all cases, on the advice of

TUVALU

the Cabinet. Legislative power is vested in the unicameral Parliament, with 15 members elected by universal adult suffrage for four years (subject to dissolution). The Cabinet is led by the Prime Minister, who is elected by and from the members of Parliament. On the Prime Minister's recommendation, other ministers are appointed by the Governor-General. The Cabinet is responsible to Parliament. Judicial power is exercised by Magistrates' and Island Courts and the High Court. Each of the inhabited atolls has its own elected Island Council, which is responsible for local government.

REGIONAL AND INTERNATIONAL CO-OPERATION

Tuvalu is a member of the Pacific Community (see p. 410), the Pacific Islands Forum (see p. 413) and the UN's Economic and Social Commission for Asia and the Pacific (ESCAP, see p. 37). In 1993 the country was admitted to the Asian Development Bank (ADB, see p. 202).

Tuvalu joined the UN in 2000. The country is also a member of the Commonwealth (see p. 230) and joined the International Monetary Fund (IMF, see p. 143) in June 2010.

ECONOMIC AFFAIRS

In 2008 the UN's Economic and Social Commission for Asia and the Pacific (ESCAP) estimated Tuvalu's gross domestic product (GDP) at current prices to be US $31.8m.; GDP per head was estimated at some $2,811 in 2007. During 2000–08, it was estimated, the population increased at an average annual rate of 0.5%. According to figures from ESCAP, overall GDP increased, in real terms, at an average annual rate of 4.2% in 2000–08. Compared with the previous year, GDP contracted by 1.7% in 2009, and there was no discernible growth in 2010, according to the Asian Development Bank (ADB).

Agriculture (including fishing) is, with the exception of copra production, of a basic subsistence nature. According to UN estimates, the sector contributed some 16.6% of GDP in 2008; the GDP of the agricultural sector increased at an average annual rate of 1.6% in 2000–08. Compared with the previous year, agricultural GDP increased by 0.4% in 2008, according to the ADB. In mid-2011, according to FAO estimates, the sector was expected to engage some 25% of the labour force. Coconuts (the source of copra) are the only cash crop. Pulaka, taro, papayas, the screw-pine (*Pandanus*) and bananas are cultivated as food crops, and honey is produced. From the 1990s agriculture was increasingly affected by climate change and rising sea-levels. More frequent high tides caused flooding and damaged crops, particularly the important taro crop; such floods have also killed tree roots, which reduced the harvest of coconuts and other fruits. Livestock comprises pigs, poultry and goats. Fish and other sea products are staple constituents of the islanders' diet. The sale of fishing licences to foreign fleets is an important source of income and earned $A11.8m. in 2001 (compared with $A3.6m. in 1997), equivalent to 50.3% of current revenue. However, revenue from this source declined in subsequent years, owing to decreases in catches.

Industry (including mining, manufacturing, construction and utilities) accounted for 13.7% of GDP in 2008, according to UN estimates. In 2000–08, according to the same source, industrial GDP expanded at an average annual rate of 3.7%. Compared with the previous year, the sector's GDP decreased by 8.2% in 2008, according to the ADB. Manufacturing is confined to the small-scale production of coconut-based products, soap and handicrafts. According to UN estimates, the manufacturing sector contributed some 3.4% of GDP in 2008. In the same year, the construction sector contributed some 4.6% of GDP. According to the UN, between 2000 and 2008 the construction sector increased by an average annual rate of 2.8%.

Energy is derived principally from a power plant (fuelled by oil) and, on the outer islands, solar power. Tuvalu has announced its intention to reduce its carbon output to zero by 2020 through increased use of solar and wind power. In 2009 it was reported that the commencement of a programme to install solar power had resulted in a significant reduction in the country's fuel imports.

The Government is an important employer (engaging 1,185 people in 2001, equivalent to about one-half of the labour force), and consequently the services sector makes a relatively large contribution to Tuvalu's economy (providing some 69.7% of GDP in 2008, according to UN estimates). The GDP of the services sector increased at an average annual rate of 3.4% in 2000–08. Compared with the previous year, the sector's GDP expanded by 3.9% in 2008, according to the ADB. The islands' remote situation and lack of amenities have hindered the development of a tourist industry. Visitor arrivals were reported to total 1,130 in 2007. In 2001 receipts from the leasing of the islands' internet domain address reached US $1.6m., while revenue from telecommunication licence fees totalled $0.31m.

Tuvalu recorded a visible trade deficit of $A29.0m. in 2003, in which year the deficit on the balance of payments reached $A18.0m. In 2009, according to the ADB, the cost of imports totalled US $129.4m., while export revenue reached US $2.4m. The principal source of imports in 2009 were Japan (44.2%) and Fiji. The principal markets for exports were Australia and India (each accounting for 25%). The principal imports in 2005 were mineral products, prepared foodstuffs, machinery, mechanical appliances and electrical equipment, and transport equipment. An important source of support for the balance of payments has been remittances from Tuvaluan emigrant workers. Remittances from Tuvaluan seafarers employed on foreign vessels were estimated at $A4m. in 2006. However, such inflows were reported to have weakened in subsequent years.

According to ADB figures, the 2008 budget allowed for expenditure of $A42.9m., while revenue (including grants of $A28.6m.) totalled $A45.4m. (in comparison with $A19.1m. in 2007). A budget deficit of $A7.6m. was projected for 2010. None the less, with the support of the Consolidated Investment Fund (CIF, a depository of the Tuvalu Trust Fund—TTF), the budget deficit was reduced to $A4.6m. in 2007, equivalent to an estimated 14.3% of GDP. The TTF was established in 1987, with assistance from New Zealand, Australia and the United Kingdom, to generate funding, through overseas investment, for development projects. By September 2006 the assets of the TTF were estimated to total $A77m. In 2006 the TTF contributed more than $A11m. to the CIF. In 2010/11 New Zealand budgeted for bilateral assistance worth $NZ3.5m. Aid from Australia was budgeted at $A8.9m. for 2010/11. Tuvalu has also received significant financial assistance from Taiwan. Other donors have included Japan and the European Union. The annual rate of inflation averaged 2.6% in 2000–08; according to the ADB, consumer prices decreased by 0.1% in 2009 and by 1.9% in 2010.

Tuvalu has continued to suffer from the increasing impact of climate change. However, in an attempt to turn the arrival of the annual high tide to the islands' advantage by raising awareness of the issue of rising sea-levels, in February 2010 Tuvalu held its first King Tide Festival; through initiatives such as this, the Government hoped to increase revenue from tourism. Receipts from the sale of fishing licences have become more vulnerable to variations in fish stocks. Income from fishing licence fees rose by 19% in 2008, before weakening in tandem with the increasing strength of the Australian dollar. Amid reports that in the previous year Tuvalu had received only 5% of the revenue derived from local fishing activities, in late 2010 New Zealand expressed its support for a four-year fisheries programme that was expected to require funding of nearly US $3m. Having remained steady in 2007–08, revenues from the '.tv' internet domain facility were also reported to have declined in subsequent years. In 2010, as the country continued its attempts to secure a greater portion of revenue from VeriSign, the company to which the '.tv' facility had been leased, an international internet consultant stated that he expected its value to decline, owing to the emergence of more generic domain names. The agreement with VeriSign, whereby Tuvalu received US $3m. annually, was scheduled to expire in 2016. Despite Tuvalu's vulnerability to increases in the costs of imports of essential commodities, consumer prices declined in 2009 and again in 2010, mainly owing to Tuvalu's use of the Australian dollar. With numerous Tuvaluan seafarers having lost their jobs as a result of the global economic downturn, remittances were subdued, and the level of household poverty was reported to have increased to 20% in 2010. A priority for successive governments has been the need to reduce the disparities in living standards between Funafuti and the outer islands. The high level of public debt, estimated by the ADB at 44% of GDP in 2010, has become an issue of some concern. A continued stagnation in GDP was forecast by the ADB for 2011.

PUBLIC HOLIDAYS

2012 (provisional): 2 January (for New Year's Day), 12 March (Commonwealth Day), 6–9 April (Easter), 11 June (Queen's Official Birthday), 6 August (National Children's Day), 1–2 October (Tuvalu Day, anniversary of independence), 12 November (for Prince of Wales's Birthday), 25–26 December (Christmas).

Statistical Survey

Source (unless otherwise indicated): Central Statistics Division, Ministry of Finance, Economic Planning and Industries, PMB, Vaiaku, Funafuti; tel. 20107; fax 21210; e-mail statistics@tuvalu.tv; internet www.spc.int/prism/country/tv/stats/.

AREA AND POPULATION

Land Area: 25.6 sq km (9.9 sq miles).

Population: 9,043 at census of 17 November 1991; 9,561 (males 4,729, females 4,832) at census of 1 November 2002 (*By Atoll:* Funafuti 4,492; Vaitupu 1,591; Nanumea 664; Niutao 663; Nanumaga 589; Nukufetau 586; Nui 548; Nukulaelae 393; Niulakita 35). *Mid-2011* (Secretariat of the Pacific Community estimate): 11,206 (Source: Pacific Regional Information System).

Density (at mid-2011): 437.7 per sq km.

Population by Age and Sex (Secretariat of the Pacific Community estimates at mid-2011): *0–14:* 3,553 (males 1,840, females 1,713); *15–64:* 7,060 (males 3,501, females 3,560); *65 and over:* 593 (males 240, females 353); *Total* 11,206 (males 5,582, females 5,626) (Source: Pacific Regional Information System).

Principal Towns (population at 2002 census): Alapi 1,024; Fakaifou 1,007; Senala 589; Teone 540; Vaiaku (capital) 516; Motufoua 506. Source: Thomas Brinkhoff, *City Population* (internet www.citypopulation.de).

Births and Deaths (2007): Registered live births 155; Registered deaths 47 (provisional).

Life Expectancy (years at birth, WHO estimates): 64 (males 64; females 63) in 2008. Source: WHO, *World Health Statistics*.

Economically Active Population: In 1979 there were 936 people in paid employment, 50% of them in government service. In 1979 114 Tuvaluans were employed by the Nauru Phosphate Co, with a smaller number employed in Kiribati and about 255 on foreign ships. At the 1991 census the total economically active population (aged 15 years and over) stood at 2,383 (males 1,605, females 778). *Mid-2011* (estimates): Agriculture, etc. 1,000; Total labour force 4,000 (Source: FAO).

HEALTH AND WELFARE
Key Indicators

Total Fertility Rate (children per woman, 2008): 3.2.

Under-5 Mortality Rate (per 1,000 live births, 2008): 36.

Physicians (per 1,000 head, 2003): 0.9.

Hospital Beds (per 1,000 head, 2001): 5.6.

Health Expenditure (2007): US $ per head (PPP): 150.

Health Expenditure (2007): % of GDP: 9.8.

Health Expenditure (2007): public (% of total): 99.8.

Access to Sanitation (% of persons, 2008): 81.

For sources and definitions, see explanatory note on p. vi.

AGRICULTURE, ETC.

Principal Crops (metric tons, 2008, FAO estimates): Coconuts 1,700; Roots and tubers 150; Vegetables 540; Bananas 280. Note: No data were available for 2009.

Livestock ('000 head, year ending September 2008, FAO estimates): Pigs 13.6; Chickens 45; Ducks 15. Note: No data were available for 2009.

Livestock Products (metric tons, 2008, unless otherwise indicated, FAO estimates): Chicken meat 45; Pig meat 95; Hen eggs 22 (2009); Honey 3.

Fishing (metric tons, live weight, 2008, FAO estimates): Total catch 2,200 (Skipjack tuna 1,000; Yellowfin tuna 900).

Source: FAO.

FINANCE

Currency and Exchange Rates: Australian and Tuvaluan currencies are both in use. Australian currency: 100 cents = 1 Australian dollar ($A). *Sterling, US Dollar and Euro Equivalents* (31 December 2010): £1 sterling = $A1.540; US $1 = $A0.984; €1 = $A1.315; $A100 = £64.92 = US $101.63 = €76.06. *Average Exchange Rate* ($A per US dollar): 1.1922 in 2008; 1.2822 in 2009; 1.0901 in 2010.

Budget ($A '000, 2008): Current revenue 16,790 (Revenue from taxation 6,772, Non-tax revenue 10,018); Grants 28,567; Total revenue and grants 45,357; Total expenditure 42,936.

Official Development Assistance (US $ million, 2002): Bilateral 11.2; Multilateral 0.5; Total 11.7 (all grants). *2007:* Total assistance 11.7. Source: UN, *Statistical Yearbook for Asia and the Pacific*.

Cost of Living (Consumer Price Index; base: November 2006 = 100): All items 98.7 in 2006; 99.2 in 2007; 100.2 in 2008. Source: Asian Development Bank.

Gross Domestic Product (US $ million at constant 2005 prices): 23.6 in 2007; 24.1 in 2008; 24.6 in 2009. Source: UN Statistics Division, National Accounts Main Aggregates Database.

Expenditure on the Gross Domestic Product (US $ million at current prices, 2008): Government final consumption expenditure 17.2; Private final consumption expenditure 28.9; Gross fixed capital formation 17.7; *Total domestic expenditure* 63.8; Exports of goods and services 4.0; *Less* Imports of goods and services 36.2; *GDP in purchasers' values* 31.8. Source: UN Statistics Division, National Accounts Main Aggregates Database.

Gross Domestic Product by Economic Activity (US $ million at current prices, 2008): Agriculture, hunting, forestry and fishing 5.8; Mining, manufacturing and utilities 3.2 (Manufacturing 1.2); Construction 1.6; Trade, restaurants and hotels 4.4; Transport, storage and communications 3.9; Other services 16.0; *Gross value added* 34.9; Net taxes on products –3.1 (obtained as residual); *GDP in purchasers' values* 31.8. Source: UN Statistics Division, National Accounts Main Aggregates Database.

Balance of Payments ($A '000, 2003): Exports of goods f.o.b. 444; Imports of goods f.o.b. –28,995; *Trade balance* –28,552; Exports of services and other income 7,403; Imports of services and other income –17,687; *Balance on goods, services and income* –38,836; Current transfers (net) 20,833; *Current balance* –18,003. Source: Asian Development Bank.

EXTERNAL TRADE

Principal Commodities ($A '000, 2005): *Imports:* Animals and animal products 1,473.8; Vegetable products 1,224.2; Prepared foodstuffs 2,385.1; Mineral products 3,661.2; Chemical products 734.5; Textiles and textile articles 759.2; Base metals and articles thereof 695.1; Machinery, mechanical appliances and electrical equipment 2,318.9; Transportation equipment 884.8; Total (incl. others) 16,908.3. *Exports:* Mineral products 5.9; Wood and wood products 10.0; Base metals and articles thereof 12.3; Machinery, mechanical appliances and electrical equipment 13.9; Transportation equipment 9.3; Instruments—measuring, musical 14.9; Total (incl. others) 80.0. *2006:* Total imports 17,903.0; Total exports 130.0. *2007:* Total imports 18,503.0; Total exports 120.0. Source: Asian Development Bank.

Principal Trading Partners (US $ million, 2009): *Imports*: Australia 2.59; China, People's Republic 13.50; Fiji 24.96; India 5.70; Japan 57.21; New Zealand 1.57; Norway 2.07; Total (incl. others) 129.35. *Exports*: Australia 0.62; Denmark 0.03; Fiji 0.31; Germany 1.59; India 0.59; Indonesia 0.37; Italy 0.02; Japan 0.20; Total (incl. others) 2.40.

Source: Asian Development Bank.

TRANSPORT

Shipping: *Merchant Fleet* (registered at 31 December 2009): Vessels 181; Total displacement ('000 grt) 1,098.2. Source: IHS Fairplay, *World Fleet Statistics*.

TOURISM

Tourist Arrivals: 1,085 in 2005; 1,135 in 2006; 1,130 in 2007.

Tourist Arrivals by Country of Residence (2007): Australia 138; Fiji 218; Japan 227; New Zealand 105; United Kingdom 35; USA 54; Total (incl. others) 1,130.

Source: World Tourism Organization.

COMMUNICATIONS MEDIA

Non-daily Newspapers (2004 unless otherwise stated): 1; Estimated circulation 300 in 1996*.

Telephones (main lines, 2009): 1,700 in use†.

Mobile Cellular Telephones (subscribers, 2009): 2,000.

Internet Users (2009): 4,300.

Radio Receivers (1997): 4,000 in use*.

TUVALU

*Source: UNESCO, *Statistical Yearbook*.
†Source: International Telecommunication Union.

EDUCATION

Pre-school (2005/06 unless otherwise indicated): 57 teachers (2004/05); 711 pupils.

Primary (2001 unless otherwise indicated): 9 government schools, 1 private school; 103 teachers (2006); 2,093 pupils (2007).

General Secondary (2005): 2 government schools; 56 teachers; 593 pupils. **Pupil-teacher Ratio** (primary education, UNESCO estimate): 19.2 in 2003/04. Source: UNESCO Institute for Statistics.

Directory

The Government

HEAD OF STATE

Sovereign: HM Queen ELIZABETH II.
Governor-General: Sir IAKOBA TAEIA ITALELI (took office May 2010).

CABINET
(May 2011)

Prime Minister and Minister of Home Affairs: WILLIE TELAVI.
Minister of Foreign Affairs, Environment, Trade, Labour and Tourism: APISAI IELEMIA.
Minister of Finance: LOTOALA METIA.
Minister of Communications: KAUSEA NATANO.
Minister of Education and Sports: FALESA PITOI.
Minister of Health: TAOM TANUKALE.
Minister of Natural Resources: ISAIA ITALELI TAEIA.

MINISTRIES

Office of the Prime Minister: PMB, Vaiaku, Funafuti; tel. 20101; fax 20820.
Ministry of Education, Sports and Health: POB 37, Vaiaku, Funafuti; tel. 20405; fax 20832.
Ministry of Finance, Economic Planning and Industries: PMB, Vaiaku, Funafuti; tel. 20202; fax 20210.
Ministry of Foreign Affairs: Vaiaku, Funafuti; tel. 20102; fax 20820.
Ministry of Home Affairs and Rural Development: PMB, Vaiaku, Funafuti; tel. 20172; fax 20821.
Ministry of Natural Resources and Environment: PMB, Vaiaku, Funafuti; tel. 20827; fax 20826.
Ministry of Public Utilities and Industries: PMB, Vaiaku, Funafuti.
Ministry of Works, Communications and Transport: PMB, Vaiaku, Funafuti; tel. 20052; fax 20772; e-mail tuvmet@tuvalu.tv.

Legislature

PARLIAMENT

Parliament has 15 members, who hold office for a term of up to four years. At the general election held on 16 September 2010, 10 of the 15 previous incumbents were re-elected. There are no political parties.
Speaker: ISAIA TAEIA.

Diplomatic Representation

There are no embassies or high commissions in Tuvalu. The British High Commissioner in Fiji is also accredited as High Commissioner to Tuvalu. Other Ambassadors or High Commissioners accredited to Tuvalu include the Australian, New Zealand, US, French and Japanese Ambassadors in Fiji.

Judicial System

The Supreme Law is embodied in the Constitution. The High Court is the superior court of record, presided over by the Chief Justice, and has jurisdiction to consider appeals from judgments of the Magistrates' Courts and the Island Courts. Appeals from the High Court have traditionally been heard by the Court of Appeal in Fiji or, in the ultimate case, with the Judicial Committee of the Privy Council in the United Kingdom.

There are eight Island Courts with limited jurisdiction in criminal and civil cases.

Chief Justice of the High Court: GORDON WARD, Vaiaku, Funafuti; tel. 20837.
Attorney-General: ESELEALOFA APINELU, Funafuti; tel. 20823; fax 20819; e-mail agoffice@tuvalu.tv.

Religion

CHRISTIANITY

Te Ekalesia Kelisiano Tuvalu (The Christian Church of Tuvalu): POB 2, Funafuti; tel. 20755; fax 20651; f. 1861; autonomous since 1968; derived from the Congregationalist foundation of the London Missionary Society; some 91% of the population are adherents; Pres. Rev. TOFIGA FALANI; Gen. Sec. Rev. KITIONA TAUSI.
Roman Catholic Church: Catholic Centre, POB 58, Funafuti; tel. and fax 20527; e-mail cathcent@tuvalu.tv; 131 adherents (31 Dec. 2006); Superior Fr CAMILLE DESROSIERS.

Other churches with adherents in Tuvalu include the Church of Jesus Christ of Latter-day Saints (Mormons), the Jehovah's Witnesses, the New Apostolic Church and the Seventh-day Adventists.

BAHÁ'Í FAITH

National Spiritual Assembly: POB 48, Funafuti; tel. 20860; mems resident in 8 localities.

The Press

Te Lama: Ekalesia Kelisiano Tuvalu, POB 2, Valuku, Funafuti; tel. and fax 20755; e-mail gs_ekt@yahoo.com; quarterly; religious; Pres. Rev. TOFIGA FALANI; Editor Rev. KITIONA TAUSI; circ. 1,000.
Tuvalu Echoes: Broadcasting and Information Office, Vaiaku, Funafuti; tel. 20138; fax 20732; f. 1984; fortnightly; English; Editor MELAKI TAEPE; circ. 250.

Broadcasting and Communications

TELECOMMUNICATIONS

Tuvalu Telecommunications Corporation: Vaiaku, Funafuti; tel. 20001; fax 20800; f. 1994; Gen. Man. SIMETI LOPATI.

BROADCASTING

Tuvalu Media Corporation: PMB, Vaiaku, Funafuti; tel. 20731; fax 20732; e-mail media@tuvalu.tv; internet www.tuvalu-news.tv/tmc; f. 1999; govt-owned; Chief Broadcasting and Information Officer PUSINELLI LAAFAI.

Radio

Radio Tuvalu: Broadcasting and Information Office, PMB, Vaiaku, Funafuti; tel. 20138; fax 20732; f. 1975; daily broadcasts in Tuvaluan and English, 43 hours per week; Programme Producer RUBY S. ALEFAIO.

Finance

BANKS
(cap. = capital; dep. = deposits; m. = million)

Development Bank of Tuvalu: POB 9, Vaiaku, Funafuti; tel. 20199; fax 20850; f. 1993; replaced the Business Development Advisory Bureau; Gen. Man. TAUKAVE POOLO.
National Bank of Tuvalu: POB 13, Vaiaku, Funafuti; tel. 20803; fax 20802; e-mail nbt@tuvalu.tv; f. 1980; commercial bank; govt-

owned; ($A '000) cap. 471.0, dep. 23,725 (Dec. 2008); Chair. AUNESE SIMATI; Gen. Man. SIOSE P. TEO; brs on all atolls.

Trade and Industry

GOVERNMENT AGENCIES

National Fishing Corporation of Tuvalu (NAFICOT): POB 93, Funafuti; tel. 20724; fax 20152; fishing vessel operators; seafood-processing and -marketing; agents for diesel engine spare parts, fishing supplies and marine electronics; Gen. Man. SEMU SOPOANGA TAAFAKI.

Tuvalu Philatelic Bureau: POB 24, Funafuti; tel. 20224; fax 20712.

CHAMBER OF COMMERCE

Tuvalu Chamber of Commerce: POB 27, Vaiaku, Funafuti; tel. 20846; fax 20800; Chair. MATANILE IOSEFA; Sec. TEO PASEFIKA.

UTILITIES

Electricity

Tuvalu Electricity Corporation (TEC): POB 32, Vaiaku, Funafuti; tel. 20352; fax 20351; Gen. Man. MAFALU LOTOLUA.

CO-OPERATIVE

Tuvalu Co-operative Society Ltd: POB 11, Funafuti; tel. 20747; fax 20748; e-mail mlaafai@tuvalu.tv; f. 1979; est. by amalgamation of the eight island socs; controls retail trade in the islands; Gen. Man. MONISE LAAFAI; Registrar AUNESE MAKOI.

TRADE UNION

Tuvalu Overseas Seamen's Union (TOSU): POB 99, Funafuti; tel. 20609; fax 20610; e-mail tosu@tuvalu.tv; f. 1988; Sec.-Gen. FEPUALI KITISENI.

Transport

ROADS

Funafuti has some impacted-coral roads totalling some 8 km in length; elsewhere, tracks exist.

SHIPPING

There is a deep-water lagoon at the point of entry, Funafuti, and ships are able to enter the lagoon at Nukufetau. Irregular shipping services connect Tuvalu with Fiji and elsewhere. The Government operates an inter-island vessel.

CIVIL AVIATION

In 1992 a new runway was constructed with aid from the European Union to replace the grass landing strip on Funafuti. Air Marshall Islands operates a three-weekly service between Funafuti, Nadi (Fiji) and Majuro (Marshall Islands). The Government of Tuvalu purchased a substantial shareholding in Air Fiji in 2001, but the carrier terminated all operations in 2009. Air Pacific commenced a twice-weekly service from Fiji in August 2008.

Tourism

In 2004 there was one hotel, with 16 rooms, on Funafuti and three guest houses. Visitor arrivals were estimated to total 1,130 in 2007. The majority of visitors are from Fiji, Australia, Japan and New Zealand. In a new initiative to attract tourists, in February 2010 Tuvalu held its first King Tide Festival, celebrating the arrival of the annual high tide.

Tuvalu Tourism Office: Ministry of Finance, Economic Planning and Industries, PMB, Funafuti; tel. 20055; fax 20722; e-mail tourism@tuvalu.tv; internet www.timelesstuvalu.com; Tourism Officer LONO LENEUOTI.

Education

Education is provided by the Government, and is compulsory between the ages of six and 15 years. In 2001 there were nine government and one private primary schools, with a total of 2,093 pupils in 2007 and 103 teachers in 2006. There were two secondary schools with 56 teachers and 593 pupils in 2005. The only tertiary institution is the Maritime Training School at Amatuku on Funafuti, with vocational, technical and commerce-related courses. About 60 people graduate from the school annually. Further training or vocational courses are available in Fiji and Kiribati. The University of the South Pacific (based in Suva, Fiji) has an extension centre on Funafuti offering diploma and vocational courses and the first two years of degree courses (the latter requiring completion in Suva). A programme of major reforms in the education system in Tuvalu, begun in the early 1990s, resulted in the lengthening of primary schooling (from six to eight years) and a compulsory two years of secondary education, as well as the introduction of vocational, technical and commerce-related courses at the Maritime Training School. Total government expenditure on education in 2001 was equivalent to some 35% of total budgetary expenditure.

UGANDA

Introductory Survey

LOCATION, CLIMATE, LANGUAGE, RELIGION, FLAG, CAPITAL

The Republic of Uganda is a land-locked equatorial country in East Africa, bordered by Sudan to the north, the Democratic Republic of the Congo to the west, Kenya to the east and Rwanda, Tanzania and Lake Victoria to the south. The climate is tropical, with temperatures, moderated by the altitude of the country, varying between 15°C and 30°C. The official language is English and there are many local languages, the most important of which is Luganda. About 75% of the population follow Christian beliefs, while some 15% are Muslims. The national flag (proportions 2 by 3) has six horizontal stripes: black, gold, red, black, gold and red. In the centre is a white disc containing a crested crane. The capital is Kampala.

CONTEMPORARY POLITICAL HISTORY

Historical Context

Formerly a British protectorate, Uganda became an independent member of the Commonwealth on 9 October 1962. The Government was led by Dr Milton Obote, leader of the Uganda People's Congress (UPC) from 1960 and Prime Minister from April 1962. At independence the country comprised four regions, including the kingdom of Buganda, which had federal status. Exactly one year after independence Uganda became a republic, with Mutesa II, Kabaka (King) of Buganda, as first President. In February 1966 Obote led a successful coup against the Kabaka, and in April he became executive President. In September 1967 a new Constitution was introduced, establishing a unitary republic, and Buganda was brought under the control of the central Government. In 1969 all opposition parties were banned.

Obote was overthrown in January 1971 by the army, led by Maj.-Gen. (later Field Marshal) Idi Amin Dada, who assumed full executive powers and suspended political activity. Amin declared himself Head of State, took over legislative powers and suspended parts of the 1967 Constitution. In August 1972 Amin, proclaiming an 'economic war' to free Uganda from foreign domination, undertook a mass expulsion of non-citizen Asians (who comprised the majority of the resident Asian population), thereby incurring widespread international condemnation.

Amin's regime was characterized by the ruthless elimination of suspected opponents, mass flights of refugees to neighbouring countries and periodic purges of the army (which, in turn, perpetrated numerous atrocities). In February 1976 Amin claimed that large areas of western Kenya were historically part of Uganda, and in November 1978 Uganda annexed the Kagera salient from Tanzania. In early 1979 an invasion force comprising Tanzanian troops and the Uganda National Liberation Army (UNLA) gained control of the southern region of Uganda. Amin's forces capitulated, and in April a Tanzanian assault force entered Kampala. The remaining pro-Amin troops were defeated in June. Amin fled initially to Libya and in 1980 took up permanent residence in Saudi Arabia. He remained in exile there until his death in August 2003.

Domestic Political Affairs

A provisional Government, the National Executive Council (NEC), was established in April 1979 from the ranks of the Uganda National Liberation Front (UNLF, a coalition of 18 previously exiled groups), with Dr Yusuf Lule, a former vice-chancellor of Makerere University, as President. Lule was succeeded in June by Godfrey Binaisa (a former Attorney-General), who was, in turn, overthrown by the Military Commission of the UNLF in May 1980, after he had decided to allow only UNLF members to stand in parliamentary elections and attempted to reorganize the leadership of the UNLA. The elections, in December, were contested by four parties and won by the UPC, with Obote, who remained its leader, becoming President for the second time. The defeated parties complained of gross electoral malpractice by UPC supporters.

The Obote Government was subject to constant attack from guerrilla groups operating inside the country. Hundreds of Obote's opponents were detained, including Democratic Party (DP) members of the National Assembly. Following the withdrawal of Tanzanian troops in June 1981, there were reports from the West Nile Region of further atrocities by Ugandan soldiers. In January 1982 the Uganda Popular Front was formed to co-ordinate, from abroad, the activities of the main opposition groups in exile: the Uganda Freedom Movement (UFM), the Uganda National Rescue Front and the National Resistance Movement (NRM), led by Lule and his former Minister of Defence, Lt-Gen. (later Gen.) Yoweri Museveni. The NRM had a military wing, the National Resistance Army (NRA), led by Museveni. Lule died in 1985, whereupon Museveni became sole leader of the NRM and NRA.

In July 1985 Obote was overthrown in a military coup, led by Brig. (later Lt-Gen.) Basilio Okello. (Obote was subsequently granted political asylum by Zambia.) A Military Council, headed by Lt-Gen. (later Gen.) Tito Okello, the Commander-in-Chief of the army, was established to govern the country, pending elections to be held one year later. In subsequent months groups that had been in opposition to Obote, with the exception of the NRA and the NRM (see below), reached agreement with the new administration and accepted positions on the Military Council. An amnesty was declared for exiles who had supported Amin.

In August 1985 the NRA, led by Museveni, entered into negotiations with the Government (under the auspices of President Daniel arap Moi of Kenya), while conducting a simultaneous military campaign to overthrow Okello. During the following two months the NRA gained control of large areas of the country and in January 1986 the NRA took control of Kampala by force and dissolved the Military Council. Okello fled to Sudan, and then to Tanzania. On 29 January Museveni was sworn in as President, and in February he announced the formation of a new Cabinet, comprising mainly members of the NRA and NRM, but also representatives of other political groups including the DP, the UPC, the UFM, the Federal Democratic Movement (FEDEMO), and three members of the previous administration. A National Resistance Council (NRC) was formed to act in place of a legislature for an indefinite period. All party political activity was banned in March, although political organizations were not proscribed. At a summit meeting in March the Heads of State of all the countries adjoining Uganda pledged their support for Museveni.

The most widespread source of disruption during 1987 was a rebellion that had arisen in northern and eastern Uganda in late 1986 by the cultish 'Holy Spirit' movement; between December 1986 and November 1987 some 5,000 ill-equipped 'Holy Spirit' fighters were reportedly killed in clashes with the NRA. By December 1987 the rebellion had been suppressed and its leader had escaped to Kenya. Surviving members of the movement, however, regrouped as the Lord's Resistance Army (LRA—see below).

In February 1989 the first national election since 1980 was held. The NRC, hitherto composed solely of presidential nominees, was expanded from 98 to 278 members, to include 210 elected representatives. While 20 ministerial posts were reserved for nominated members of the NRC, 50 were allocated to elected members. Also in February Museveni appointed a Constitutional Commission to assess public opinion on Uganda's political future and to draft a new constitution.

In October 1989 (despite opposition from the DP) the NRC approved draft legislation to prolong the Government's term of office by five years from January 1990 (when its mandate had been due to expire): the NRM justified seeking to extend its rule by claiming that it required further time in which to prepare a new constitution, organize elections, eliminate guerrilla activity, improve the judiciary, police force and civil service and rehabilitate the country's infrastructure. In March 1990 the NRM extended the national ban on party political activity (imposed in March 1986) for a further five years. In May 1991 Museveni formally invited all former resident Asians expelled at the time of the Amin regime to return, pledging the restitution of expropriated property.

In December 1992 the Constitutional Commission presented its draft constitution to the Government. The draft was published in March 1993, and in the following month the NRC approved legislation authorizing the establishment of a Constituent Assembly (see below). In July the NRC adopted a constitutional amendment revoking the abolition of traditional rulers, as provided for under the 1967 Constitution. Restored traditional rulers would, however, have only ceremonial significance.

In January 1994 the Ugandan National Democratic Alliance and the Ugandan Federal Army agreed to suspend their armed struggle, under the provisions of a government amnesty, and in March the surrender of senior members of the Ruwenzururu Kingdom Freedom Movement in the south-west signified the end of a conflict dating from independence. During January the Government took part in negotiations with the LRA. However, following the collapse of the discussions, the LRA intensified guerrilla activities in northern Uganda. From 1994 large numbers of security forces were deployed in the region, representing a considerable burden on national resources; they failed, however, to suppress the rebellion (see below).

At elections to the 288-member Constituent Assembly, which took place on 28 March 1994, more than 1,500 candidates contested the 214 elective seats. Although the elections were officially conducted on a non-party basis, NRM members were believed to have secured the majority of votes in the centre, west and south-west of the country, whereas UPC and DP members, who advocated an immediate return to multi-party politics, secured the most seats in the north and east. The Constituent Assembly, which also comprised nominated representatives of the armed forces, political parties, trade unions, and youth and disabled organizations, debated and amended the draft constitution, finally enacting it in September 1995. The Constitution, under the terms of which a national referendum on the future introduction of a multi-party political system took place in 2000 (see below), was promulgated in October 1995.

A presidential election took place in May 1996, at which Museveni was returned to office, winning 74.2% of the votes cast. The election was pronounced free and fair by international observers. Legislative elections took place in June at which the total membership of the NRC, redesignated the Parliament under the new Constitution, was reduced from 278 to 276, comprising 214 elected and 62 nominated representatives.

During 1993–98 the LRA was alleged to have killed as many as 10,000 people, while some 220,000 sought refuge in protected camps; economic activity in the region was devastated. The LRA's use of abducted children as soldiers (reportedly some 10,000 by early 1999) attracted widespread international condemnation. The Government strongly resisted pressure to resume negotiations with the LRA, prompting some speculation that Museveni (a southerner) might be prepared to profit from the disablement of opposition strongholds in the northern region. In May 1999, however, the Government appeared to modify its policy towards the LRA by offering it an amnesty and promising its leader, Joseph Kony, a cabinet post in the event of his being democratically elected. In the west, meanwhile, the Uganda People's Defence Forces (UPDF, as the NRA had been restyled) fought intermittently with two rebel groups: the Allied Democratic Forces (ADF), mainly comprising Ugandan Islamist fundamentalist rebels, exiled Rwandan Hutu militiamen and former soldiers from Zaire (which became the Democratic Republic of the Congo—DRC—in May 1997), and the West Nile Bank Front (WNBF). Although WNBF activities subsided in mid-1997, following the killing of several hundred of its members by Sudanese rebels, the ADF mounted a persistent terror campaign from mid-1997 against western Ugandan targets, threatening tourism to the region and disrupting economic activity.

Towards multi-party politics

In July 1999 legislation was enacted providing for a referendum on a multi-party political system to take place in the following year. However, most political parties announced that they would boycott the referendum on the grounds that it would be manipulated by the NRM for its own objectives. Ugandan political leaders had criticized the readiness of some Western donors (in particular those that formed the Referendum 2000 Group in December 1999) to support the referendum process, claiming that by so doing they were legitimizing the prevailing suspension of active political opposition. In February 2000 Uganda's Multi-Party National Referendum Committee appealed for a postponement of the referendum on the grounds that the Electoral Commission had not made funds available to some advocates of a return to political pluralism. In the same month the Referendum 2000 Group expressed concern at the Government's failure to implement measures on which it had made conditional its support of the referendum process. At the referendum, which proceeded on 29 June, 90.7% of participants voted in favour of retaining the existing 'no-party' political system. However, the result was effectively nullified by the Constitutional Court in 2004 (see below).

A presidential election was held on 12 March 2001. The election had been scheduled for 7 March, but was delayed after it was revealed that the electoral register contained some 2.5m. more voters than there were citizens eligible to vote. At the election, which had a participation rate of 70%, Museveni was re-elected President, winning 69.3% of the votes cast. His main challenger, Kizza Besigye, won 27.8%.

Legislative elections were held on 26 June 2001, at which 50 parliamentarians, including 10 ministers, failed to secure re-election. The rate of voter participation was reported as being low. The total number of seats in Parliament was increased to 292 (comprising 214 elected and 78 nominated representatives), of which the NRM reportedly secured more than 70%. In July Museveni appointed a new Cabinet, again under the premiership of Apollo Nsibambi, Prime Minister since April 1999, and including the 10 ministers who had failed to retain their parliamentary seats in June 2001. Notably, Amama Mbabazi was appointed as Minister of Defence, a portfolio hitherto held by Museveni.

In May 2002 Parliament approved the Political Parties and Organizations Act 2002, which severely curtailed the activities of political parties, while classifying the NRM as a 'political system' rather than a party. The Act also provided for the dissolution of all parties not registered by 17 January 2003. However, in March 2003 opposition leaders successfully challenged two clauses of the Act in the Constitutional Court, which ruled that the NRM was not a system, but a political party, and suspended the section of the Act that required parties to register, pending the outcome of a further petition against the Act. (The Attorney-General later clarified that parties would still be obliged to register, but not by a particular time.) The ruling allowed political parties to operate nationally for the first time in 17 years. The NRM became the first party to apply for registration, in June 2003. Meanwhile, in late May Museveni effected a cabinet reorganization, notably appointing Prof. Gilbert Bukenya as Vice-President, following the resignation of the incumbent, Dr Speciosa Kazibwe, and dismissing a number of ministers who had recently expressed opposition to a proposal to revoke the current two-term limit on the presidential mandate. This proposal was endorsed by the Cabinet in August. By April 2004 some 60 new political parties had emerged, although only 13 had applied for registration.

In June 2004 the Constitutional Court issued a ruling that annulled the Referendum (Political System) Act of 2000 and effectively nullified the June 2000 referendum at which a return to a multi-party system had been rejected. Thus, legislative elections, scheduled to be held concurrently with the presidential election in 2006, would be held under the new system—subject to approval at a referendum, which was to be held in July 2005 (see below). In November 2004 the Constitutional Court repealed legislation preventing political parties from contesting elections. The Court also rejected an appeal from opposition parties against mandatory registration and ruled that parties would have six months to register prior to the 2006 elections. Meanwhile, it was reported in August 2004 that a new opposition party, the Forum for Democratic Change (FDC), had been formed by a merger of the Reform Agenda, the Parliamentary Advocacy Forum and the National Democratic Forum. Several parliamentarians affiliated to the UPC had apparently joined the new party.

In February 2005 the Constitution (Amendment) Bill, which provided for a return to multi-party democracy, was presented to the Parliament. The Bill also contained a provision for the removal of the two-term limit on the presidency. Parliament approved the removal of the two-term limit on the presidency in June, and voted in favour of the holding of a national referendum on the restoration of multi-party democracy. At the referendum, which took place on 28 July, 92.5% of participants approved the motion. The rate of voter participation was low, however, at just 47%.

The 2006 presidential election

In October 2005 Besigye returned from four years of self-imposed exile in South Africa in order to contest the presidential election as the FDC's candidate. (He had left Uganda following the presidential election of 2001 claiming to fear for his safety.) Besigye was arrested in November 2005 and charged with rape and treason and later that month also appeared before a military tribunal on charges of terrorism and illegally possessing weapons. In January 2006 the High Court ruled that the military tribunal's authority to detain Besigye had expired and ordered his release; his trial was adjourned until after the election.

At the presidential election on 23 February 2006, Museveni, securing 59.3% of votes cast, was elected for a third term. Besigye was the only other candidate to mount a credible challenge, receiving 37.4% of the votes. While international observers did not condemn the process outright, they reported a number of serious flaws and concluded that a law adopted in 1997 that effectively granted the NRM access to public funds for campaigning did not provide a fair basis for multi-party elections. Legislative elections were held concurrently with the presidential election; the NRM secured 191 seats in the 319-member Parliament, while the FDC took 37 seats.

In March 2006 Besigye was acquitted of rape. The military conceded that Besigye would not have to face a court martial while on trial for treason, but did not drop the charges against him and appealed against the ruling that the terrorism and weapons charges must be heard in the High Court. In April Besigye challenged the results of the presidential election in the Supreme Court. The Court unanimously decided that the Electoral Commission had not conducted the election in compliance with the Constitution and other relevant legislation. However, it further ruled (by four votes to three) that this had not substantially affected the final outcome of the election. Besigye's trial for treason commenced in April; he and his 22 co-defendants denied the charges. In late May Museveni named his new Cabinet, again under the premiership of Nsibambi. Most notably, Gen. Ali Moses was replaced as First Deputy Prime Minister by Eriya Kategaya.

In March 2007 security agents raided the High Court and arrested six supporters of Besigye who had been granted bail. One lawyer was beaten unconscious during the heavily armed raid. In response, the judiciary commenced industrial action and only agreed to return to work after Museveni expressed regret for the incident one week later. In April violence erupted in Kampala during protests against plans to allocate one-third of the Mabira forest to an Asian-owned sugar company, forcing police to protect Asian businesses and a Hindu temple; three people, including one Asian, were killed. In October Besigye announced that he was to relinquish the presidency of the FDC in 2010, allowing sufficient time for a new leader to be selected ahead of the presidential election scheduled for 2011. In February 2009, however, Besigye was re-elected as President of the FDC, and it was widely believed that he would once again challenge Museveni for the presidency in the forthcoming election. (In October 2010 the Constitutional Court dismissed the charges of treason against Besigye and 10 others, on the grounds that their fundamental rights had been violated by state agents.)

In February 2009 Museveni reorganized his Cabinet, replacing the Minister of Finance, Planning and Economic Development, Ezra Suruma, with Sydda Bbumba, who had previously held the gender, labour and social services portfolio. There were several new additions to the Government, including Gabriel Opio, who was named as the new Minister of Gender and Social Affairs, while Hope Mwesigye became the Minister of Agriculture, Animal Industry and Fisheries. Other notable changes included the appointment of Museveni's wife, Janet Museveni, as Minister of State for the Karamoja region.

In September 2009 tensions arose between President Museveni and Ronald Muwenda Mutebi II, the Kabaka (King) of Buganda (a region bordering Lake Victoria in southern Uganda) after the President prohibited Mutebi from visiting an area of the region inhabited by ethnic minorities and closed the operations of four vernacular radio stations. The President's decision to prevent the visit, based on Mutebi's hard-line stance on controversial issues, including land settlement and relations with ethnic minorities, prompted violence in Buganda and also in Kampala, where it was reported that at least 21 people had been killed and almost 100 people had been injured. Many of the Baganda people had withdrawn their support for Museveni's presidency as they sought greater autonomy under a regional federal-style government. In November the Government approved land legislation that it claimed would grant greater rights to long-standing tenants in Buganda. The people of Buganda, however, were opposed to the decision, claiming that the new laws prevented them from developing the land and that its value would diminish. In late April 2010 Central Broadcasting Service was finally permitted to recommence broadcasting. (Two of the other proscribed radio stations had their bans lifted in November 2009, while the third station was again permitted to transmit programmes in January 2010.)

Meanwhile, with divisions emerging within the NRM, in December 2009 four opposition parties (the UPC, the Justice Forum, the Conservative Party and the FDC) launched a 'Change 2011' strategy and pledged to field single presidential and parliamentary candidates in the 2011 elections in an attempt to remove Museveni from power. The DP did not join the alliance as a result of disagreements among its senior members, and in February 2010 Norbert Mao was elected as the new party President. Museveni had been confirmed as the NRM's presidential candidate in January, and in April the FDC selected Besigye to contest the presidential election on behalf of the opposition coalition. However, in August the UPC withdrew from the alliance and threatened to boycott the elections, owing to dissatisfaction with the Electoral Commission.

On 11 July 2010 at least 74 people were killed and a further 70 injured in two bomb attacks in Kampala. Suicide attackers were believed to have detonated their bombs at a rugby club and an Ethiopian restaurant while those attending were watching broadcasts of the Fédération Internationale de Football Association World Cup. The insurgent Islamist movement al-Shabaab claimed responsibility for the attacks, stating that they were in response to Uganda's support for the Somali Transitional Federal Government and the presence of Ugandan armed forces in Somalia. In January 2011 Human Rights Watch urged the Government to organize an independent investigation into the killing of a prominent homosexual rights activist, David Kato, who had suffered severe harassment and threats following his successful legal appeal against the anti-homosexual campaigning of a local newspaper. (In October 2009 proposed legislation seeking to increase the punishments for homosexuality, and including provision for the death penalty for the offence of 'aggravated homosexuality', had provoked international criticism and concern from donor Governments.) In early February 2011 the police announced the arrest of a suspect in Kato's murder, which was reported to have been motivated by a personal dispute.

Recent developments: the 2011 elections

In January 2011 Besigye threatened to withdraw from the presidential poll, owing to suspicions that its conduct would be fraudulent. The presidential and legislative elections took place on 18 February 2011, as scheduled. Museveni was re-elected for a fourth term with about 68.4% of votes cast, while Besigye received 26.0% of the votes, according to official results. In the elections to the Parliament, the NRM secured 164 of the 238 directly elected seats; the FDC received 24 seats, the DP 11 seats and the UPC only seven seats. A voter turn-out of about 59% of the registered electorate was recorded. However, Commonwealth observers reported both bias during the electoral campaign and irregularities in the conduct of the voting, while a European Union (EU) monitoring group stated that the process had been marred by administrative failures. Besigye subsequently released a statement rejecting the results and complaining of widespread malpractice perpetrated by the authorities, and several opposition leaders declared support for him. Later in February Besigye, together with Mao and a further prominent opposition leader, Olara Otunnu, announced a campaign of peaceful protests against Museveni's Government; however, the Inspector General of Police announced that such demonstrations would be regarded as illegal. In the same month Museveni signed into force legislation authorizing the clandestine surveillance of telephones and other private communications for security purposes. At the end of February Prime Minister Nsibambi suspended from office nine government members who had contested the legislative elections as independent candidates, following a ruling by the Constitutional Court that it was illegal for party members to do so; a Minister of State subsequently resigned.

In early April 2011 Besigye was arrested in Kampala, after participating in a prohibited 'walk to work' campaign, which had been organized by the opposition leaders in protest against sharp price rises in fuel and commodities. Nevertheless, a further civil protest proceeded as planned a few days later, and was violently suppressed by the military police, prompting demonstrations in several towns; it was reported that 49 people, including Besigye, had been injured and some 220 demonstrators, among them a number of opposition leaders, arrested.

Foreign Affairs

In March 1996 Museveni, Moi and President Benjamin Mkapa of Tanzania, meeting in Nairobi, Kenya, formally inaugurated the Secretariat of the Permanent Tripartite Commission for East African Co-operation, which aimed to revive the East African Community (EAC, see p. 447). A treaty for the re-establishment of the EAC, providing for the creation of a free trade area (with the eventual introduction of a single currency), for the development of infrastructure, tourism and agriculture within the Community and for the establishment of a regional legislature and court was ratified by the three Heads of State in November 1999. Museveni, Mkapa and President Mwai Kibaki of Kenya signed a protocol in March 2004 on the creation of a customs union, whereby most duties on goods within the EAC would be eliminated. The customs union was established on 1 January 2005. Following a two-day summit in Nairobi in December 2006, the Presidents of Burundi, the DRC, Kenya, Zambia, Tanzania and Uganda signed a regional security, stability and development treaty. The EAC was expanded to include Rwanda and Burundi in 2007. In November 2009 the Heads of State of Tanzania, Kenya, Uganda, Rwanda and Burundi signed a common market protocol, allowing the free movement of goods, services, people and capital within the EAC; the protocol entered into force in July 2010.

During 1988 tension arose along Uganda's border with Zaire (now the DRC—see above), owing to a number of attacks by Zairean troops on NRA units; further border clashes occurred in 1992. In November 1996 Ugandan rebels were reportedly operating from within Zaire with the support of Zairean troops. In late 1996 and early 1997 the Ugandan authorities repeatedly denied allegations that Ugandan forces were occupying territory in eastern Zaire; however, it was widely reported that the Museveni Government supplied armaments and tactical support to Laurent-Désiré Kabila's Alliance des forces démocratiques pour la libération du Congo-Zaïre, which took power in Zaire in May 1997. The Museveni administration, however, subsequently withdrew its support from the new regime in the DRC, as President Kabila made no attempt to sever the ongoing supply of armaments to Ugandan guerrilla groups operating in the DRC–Uganda border region. In November 1998 the Museveni administration, in co-operation with the Rwandan Government, formed a joint military command. The Kabila regime accused Uganda and Rwanda of creating, with DRC rebels, a Tutsi-dominated alliance with expansionist ambitions; it was also alleged that the DRC's two eastern neighbours were illegally exploiting mineral interests in the area occupied by their forces. In July 1999 a comprehensive cease-fire agreement was concluded in Lusaka, Zambia, by the Heads of State of all the countries engaged militarily in the civil war in the DRC, including those of Angola, Namibia and Zimbabwe, who had supported the DRC Government. In August tensions escalated into hostilities between Ugandan and Rwandan armed forces around the city of Kisangani. In May 2000 the DRC Government signed an agreement consenting to the deployment of the UN Mission in the Democratic Republic of the Congo (MONUC, see p. 94), to monitor the frequently violated cease-fire that had been inaugurated by the Lusaka accord. After further clashes, Uganda and Rwanda withdrew their troops from Kisangani to allow its eventual cession to the control of MONUC. Following the publication of a UN report in April 2001, alleging that Burundi, Rwanda and Uganda were illegally exploiting the DRC's mineral reserves, Museveni announced that Uganda would withdraw its remaining troops from the DRC and pull out of the UN-sponsored Lusaka accord. Despite the redeployment of Ugandan troops in the north-east of the DRC in January 2002, to prevent escalating fighting between the rebel factions from reaching the border with Uganda, negotiations between Uganda and Rwanda continued, with British mediation, and in April the two countries signed a peace agreement in Kigali, Rwanda. In September a peace accord was signed by Uganda and the DRC in Luanda, Angola, providing for the normalization of relations between the two countries and the complete withdrawal of Ugandan troops from the DRC. Uganda subsequently began the withdrawal of its troops, although the UN permitted some of them to remain near the north-eastern town of Bunia to assist with maintaining security. In March 2003 the Governments of Uganda and the DRC and local rebel groups signed a cease-fire agreement. In response to the continuing violence around Bunia, the UN Security Council issued a resolution appealing for increased numbers of military and humanitarian observers to be stationed in the DRC under the MONUC mandate, and the immediate withdrawal of Ugandan troops. The Ugandan Government subsequently pledged to withdraw forces from the DRC, and all remaining Ugandan troops left the north-east of the country in May. In December 2005 the International Court of Justice (ICJ, see p. 23), in The Hague, Netherlands, upheld an appeal by the DRC against Uganda, submitted in April, and ordered the Ugandan Government to pay reparations for violations of international law perpetrated by its forces deployed in the country during 1998–2003.

From the late 1980s Sudanese troops reportedly made repeated incursions into Ugandan territory in pursuit of Sudanese rebels. Relations between the two countries deteriorated seriously in 1994, when each Government accused the other of harbouring and supporting their respective outlawed guerrilla groups; in April 1995 Uganda severed diplomatic relations with Sudan. Relations between the two countries remained strained: in September 1996 and in February 1997 it was alleged that Sudanese aircraft had attacked northern Uganda, and in April, despite a continuing dialogue mediated by Iran and Libya, the Sudanese authorities claimed that their forces had killed several hundred Ugandan soldiers who had been assisting Sudanese rebels from within Sudanese territory. In February 1998 Uganda deployed troops along the Uganda–Sudan border, with the aim of preventing LRA rebels from taking captives over the frontier into Sudan. In December, in Kenya, the Presidents of Uganda and Sudan unexpectedly signed an accord that set out a comprehensive resolution of the two countries' differences. The Nairobi Agreement committed Uganda and Sudan to the renunciation of force as a means of settling disputes; to the disarmament and disbandment of terrorist groups and the cessation of support for rebel groups; to the repatriation of prisoners of war; and to the restoration of full diplomatic relations by the end of February 2000. Joint committees were to be established to oversee the implementation of the Agreement from January 2000. In September Uganda and Sudan agreed to disarm the LRA, which had been active throughout 2000, and to relocate it at least 1,000 km deeper within Sudanese territory. It was also agreed that the Governments of Uganda, Sudan, Libya and Egypt, in collaboration with the Carter Center, Canada, the UN Children's Fund (UNICEF) and the office of the UN High Commissioner for Refugees (UNHCR), would set up a body to find and repatriate all children abducted from Sudan by rebel groups. Rebel attacks continued in northern Uganda, however, and in January 2001 President Museveni threatened to send troops to pursue rebel groups into Sudanese territory. Following a Libyan diplomatic initiative in that month, Sudan and Uganda agreed to restore diplomatic relations. In August the Ugandan embassy reopened in the Sudanese capital, Khartoum, and a chargé d'affaires was appointed; relations were upgraded to ambassadorial level in April 2002. In August 2001 the Sudanese President, Lt-Gen. Omar Hassan Ahmad al-Bashir, announced that his Government would no longer provide support for the LRA, and in December bank accounts used by the LRA in London, United Kingdom, were frozen. Negotiations between Sudan and Uganda continued successfully throughout early 2002, with both countries remaining committed to implementing the Nairobi Agreement. In March it was announced that Sudan was to allow the UPDF to deploy forces within its borders in order to pursue operations against the LRA, and later that month the Ugandan Government announced that its troops had captured all four main bases in Sudan belonging to the LRA. In November the Sudanese authorities agreed to extend permission for Ugandan troops to remain on its territory for as long as Uganda deemed necessary.

In early 2003 Museveni agreed to a cease-fire and appointed a delegation to commence peace negotiations with the LRA, but these soon collapsed. The Government ordered 800,000 people in northern Uganda to enter refugee camps for their protection; however, the LRA continued to attack the camps. In October LRA attacks, which had begun to spread further south and east, intensified, and a counter-offensive by the UPDF in December had little success. In February 2004 the LRA massacred more than 200 civilians sheltering in a refugee camp near Lira, in northern Uganda. Thousands demonstrated in Lira against the Government's failure to protect civilians, and the protests rapidly became violent. The UPDF commenced a new offensive in southern Sudan, and in March killed more than 50 rebels entering Uganda from Sudan. Despite the UPDF's continued claims of imminent victory, the LRA attacks continued unabated. The Government introduced legislation in mid-2004 that allowed the prosecution by the International Criminal

Court (ICC, see p. 340) of Ugandans suspected of war crimes. In June it was reported that at least 12 high-ranking LRA commanders had taken advantage of an amnesty offered by the Government and surrendered; among them was Kony's personal secretary.

In November 2004 an LRA spokesman stated that the group no longer believed a military end to the conflict was possible, and that the LRA was thus willing to negotiate towards a peace accord. A cease-fire was agreed, although fighting continued outside the cease-fire zone. Although there were indications at the end of December that the Government and LRA were close to agreeing a permanent truce, the LRA postponed the signing of a memorandum of understanding in order to continue internal consultations. Shortly afterwards a UPDF force was ambushed, for which Museveni blamed the LRA. The Government refused to extend the cease-fire, and UPDF troops re-occupied the cease-fire zone in order to prevent attacks on civilians. A cease-fire was agreed in February 2005, during which an amnesty was offered to LRA fighters who wished to surrender. Later that month Brig. Sam Kolo, the LRA's chief negotiator in the recent peace talks, escaped an attack by LRA combatants with the help of the UPDF, to whom he surrendered. The UPDF stated that Kolo's life was in danger following a dispute with the LRA's deputy leader, Vincent Otti. The Government's chief negotiator confirmed that Otti would take Kolo's place in any future negotiations. In March, following a government request, the ICC agreed to delay issuing arrest warrants for LRA commanders after concerns were raised that they would be reluctant to negotiate if they feared arrest once peace had been established. The cease-fire agreed in February lapsed in March and fighting resumed. The UPDF began an offensive against LRA bases, while the LRA, in turn, attacked villages and resumed its abduction of children.

In September 2005 two groups of LRA fighters, one led by Otti, entered the DRC from southern Sudan. Representatives of the UN met for first time with the LRA and urged the group to disarm. The meeting was also attended by senior members of the DRC military. In October the ICC issued arrest warrants for Kony, Otti and three other LRA commanders. Kony was indicted on 12 counts of crimes against humanity, including sexual enslavement, and 21 counts of war crimes. The UPDF claimed to have recently killed one of the five indicted LRA commanders. Shortly after the warrants were issued the LRA altered its tactics and began to attack humanitarian workers. In November it killed two UN mine clearance experts in southern Sudan. Later that month Otti offered to enter into peace negotiations, stating he was willing to be tried by the ICC, but added that the UPDF had also committed crimes during the conflict for which the Government should be tried. In April 2006 it was announced that refugee camps in the Lango and Teso sub-regions were to close (but not those in the Acholi sub-region). Also in that month the Ugandan Parliament approved legislation that enabled the Government to exclude Kony and others from the amnesty offered to the LRA.

In July 2006 peace talks between the LRA and the Government commenced in Juba, southern Sudan. On 26 August both sides agreed on a truce and a cease-fire came into force on 29 August. However, it emerged in October that both the Ugandan army and the LRA had violated the terms of their truce, according to a report by a peace process monitoring team. In December President Museveni held direct talks with a member of the LRA for the first time when he spoke by satellite telephone with Otti. A cessation of hostilities agreement, signed by both sides, was also extended in the same month for a second time, until 28 February 2007. However, the LRA withdrew from the talks in January, citing security fears after al-Bashir apparently indicated that he sought to eradicate the LRA from Sudan. Following a meeting between the UN Special Envoy for areas affected by the LRA, the former President of Mozambique, Joaquim Chissano, and Kony in mid-March, the LRA agreed to resume negotiations on condition that other African mediators join the talks along with Sudan. In mid-April the LRA signed a new cease-fire with the Government. Under the new agreement the LRA was granted six weeks in which to assemble its fighters at Ri-Kwangba near the border with the DRC. Peace talks resumed in Juba at the end of May. In November Kony appointed Okot Odhiambo as deputy leader of the LRA, amid unconfirmed reports that Otti had been executed alongside his family and several commanders who remained loyal to him. In January 2008 Otti's death was confirmed, although the cause of death remained unclear. A new cease-fire was agreed between the Government and the LRA in late January, ahead of peace talks that were to resume at the end of the month. Violence had largely subsided during the latest round of peace negotiations and refugees had begun to return home. Negotiations were ongoing in March to determine a timescale for demobilization; however, mediators were confident that they were close to agreeing a final peace deal to end the conflict.

In April 2008, however, peace talks collapsed when Kony failed to appear at a meeting between LRA and government negotiators, held on the border between Sudan and the DRC; Kony indicated that he was not ready to sign a full peace agreement until the ICC arrest warrant for him was lifted, and later dismissed his chief negotiator. In May a new court was established to deal specifically with human rights violations committed during the LRA insurgency in northern Uganda. The War Crimes Court was set up as a special division of the Uganda High Court, in what was widely regarded as an attempt to persuade the ICC to drop indictments against LRA commanders, following the recent breakdown in negotiations. (In March President Museveni had refused to hand over LRA leaders to stand trial at the ICC, stating that they should instead be tried by northern Uganda's traditional justice system.) In May a report by Human Rights Watch claimed that the LRA had taken advantage of the recent cease-fire to resume abduction and enslavement of civilians, including children, from neighbouring countries; Kony was believed to be rearming and preparing for a renewed conflict. In July the Sudanese Government ordered UPDF troops to withdraw from southern Sudan, claiming that they were responsible for recent attacks on civilians. In the following month Chissano reported that Kony had been in contact with him and was now willing to sign a final peace deal; however, this failed to materialize, and attacks on civilians in Sudan and the DRC continued. In late 2008 the situation deteriorated further after Kony once again failed to appear at a meeting having committing himself to a peace agreement, effectively ending any hope of a negotiated settlement. In December Ugandan, Sudanese and Congolese forces launched a joint offensive against LRA positions in north-eastern DRC. The LRA launched attacks on Congolese villages in response; by March 2009 as many as 1,000 civilians were believed to have been killed in reprisal for the offensive. In March a senior LRA commander, Thomas Kwoyelo, was captured in eastern DRC, while later that month Ugandan troops began to withdraw from the country as the joint offensive came to an end.

During the late 1980s an estimated 250,000 Rwandan refugees were sheltering in Uganda. Relations with Rwanda deteriorated in October 1990, following the infiltration of northern Rwanda by an invasion force of some 4,000 Rwandan rebels who had been based in Uganda. In February 1991 a conference was held on the Rwandan security situation; an amnesty was agreed for all Rwandans who were exiled abroad, and the rebels were urged to observe a cease-fire. Nevertheless, the allegedly Ugandabased Rwandan rebels continued to operate in northern Rwanda during 1991–93. The victory in Rwanda of the Front patriotique rwandais (FPR) in mid-1994 brought about a significant change in bilateral relations; Maj.-Gen. Paul Kagame, Rwandan Vice-President and Minister of National Defence, had previously served in the Ugandan NRA, as had other members of the FPR administration. In August 1995 Museveni made an official visit to Rwanda, and both countries made commitments to enhance economic and social co-operation. In August 1998 Uganda and Rwanda jointly deployed troops in the DRC (see above). Relations between the two countries worsened again during their involvement in the hostilities in the DRC; there were frequent reports of fighting, especially around the town of Kisangani. However, this tension eased when both armies withdrew from Kisangani during May 2000 (see above), and in July Museveni and Kagame met to discuss relations between their respective countries. In July 2003 the Rwandan Government signed a tripartite agreement with the Ugandan authorities and UNHCR, providing for the voluntary repatriation of some 26,000 Rwandans resident in refugee camps in western Uganda. In February 2004 an improvement in diplomatic relations between Rwanda and Uganda (following progress in the situation in the DRC) was demonstrated by a bilateral agreement to strengthen co-operation in several fields. Relations with the DRC became strained in 2007 due to a dispute over the ownership of Rukwanzi island in Lake Albert, on the border between the two countries; tension had increased in the area following the recent discovery of petroleum in the Lake Albert basin. In August a British national working for a Canadian oil company was killed in a clash involving Congolese and Ugandan security forces, and in

UGANDA

Introductory Survey

the following month Museveni and the DRC President, Joseph Kabila, held a meeting in which they agreed to carry out a joint demarcation of the border. None the less, there were further violent incidents in late 2007, and in May 2008 Congolese troops occupied a disputed border area; Museveni and Kabila subsequently agreed to implement joint administration of Rukwanzi island. However, in September a spokesman for the UPDF claimed that a survey had been conducted that found the island was in Ugandan territory.

In November 2009 the Ugandan army claimed to have killed one of the principal commanders of the LRA, Lt-Col Okello Ogutti. Shortly after the announcement, the US Senate approved the LRA Disarmament and Northern Uganda Recovery Act of 2009, which outlined the provision of military, intelligence and humanitarian assistance to countries in the region in support of the fight against the LRA. The UN Security Council also condemned the rising number of LRA attacks across the region, but praised regional governments' efforts at co-operation, encouraging leaders to co-ordinate security and defence strategies. Meanwhile, defence officials from Uganda and the DRC pledged to resume cross-border patrols in an attempt to suppress rebel activity and tighten security.

In the late 2000s LRA operations caused further displacement of civilians from neighbouring countries. At the beginning of 2010, according to UNHCR, the number of refugees in Uganda totalled about 139,000, most of whom were from the DRC. In early 2011 some 5,200 Ugandan troops were deployed in Somalia as part of the African Union (see p. 183) Mission in Somalia (AMISOM, then numbering more than 8,300), which was mandated to assist in peace-keeping operations in that country.

CONSTITUTION AND GOVERNMENT

Amendments to the Constitution of October 1995, introducing a multi-party political system and removing the two-term limit on the President, were endorsed at a national referendum held on 28 July 2005. Under the amended Constitution, the President (who had an unlimited number of mandates) and the unicameral legislature, the Parliament, were directly elected for a five-year term. Following elections in February 2011, the number of seats in Parliament totalled 375, comprising 238 directly elected representatives and 137 nominated members, including 112 women.

For the purposes of local administration, Uganda is divided into four regions and 80 districts.

REGIONAL AND INTERNATIONAL CO-OPERATION

Uganda is a member of the African Union (see p. 183), of the Common Market for Eastern and Southern Africa (COMESA, see p. 228), and the East African Community (EAC, see p. 447).

Uganda became a member of the UN in 1962. As a contracting party to the General Agreement on Tariffs and Trade, Uganda joined the World Trade Organization (WTO, see p. 430) on its establishment in 1995. Uganda participates in the Group of 77 (G77, see p. 447) developing countries. In October 2008 Uganda was elected as a non-permanent member of the UN Security Council for 2009 and 2010.

ECONOMIC AFFAIRS

In 2009, according to estimates by the World Bank, Uganda's gross national income (GNI), measured at average 2007–09 prices, was US $15,036m., equivalent to $460 per head (or $1,190 per head on an international purchasing-power parity basis). During 2000–09, it was estimated, the population increased at an average annual rate of 3.3%, while gross domestic product (GDP) per head increased, in real terms, by an average of 3.9% per year. Overall GDP increased, in real terms, at an average annual rate of 7.3% in 2000–09; growth was 7.1% in 2009.

Agriculture (including hunting, forestry and fishing) contributed 24.3% of GDP in 2009 and engaged 68.7% of the employed labour force in 2003. According to FAO estimates, the sector employed 74.2% of the total labour force in 2011. The principal cash crops are coffee, tobacco, tea and cotton. Cassava, sweet potatoes, maize, sugar cane and cocoa are also cultivated, and the production of cut flowers is an important activity. Together, coffee, tea, cocoa and spices provided 27.8% of export earnings in 2008. The main subsistence crops are plantains, cassava, sweet potatoes, maize, millet, sorghum, beans, groundnuts and rice. In addition, livestock (chiefly cattle, goats, sheep and poultry) are reared, and freshwater fishing is an important rural activity. Agricultural GDP increased by an average of 2.0% per year in 2000–09, according to the World Bank; it increased by 9.1% in 2008, but decreased by 1.8% in 2009.

Industry (including mining, manufacturing, construction and power) contributed 24.7% of GDP in 2009, and employed 7.8% of the working population in 2003. Industrial GDP increased at an average annual rate of 9.8% in 2000–09, according to the World Bank; it increased by 11.5% in 2009.

Mining has made a negligible contribution to GDP since the 1970s (0.2% in 2009) and in 2003 it employed just 0.3% of the working population. The Government aims to encourage renewed investment in the sector. Output of copper, formerly an important export, virtually ceased during the late 1970s. However, the state-owned Kilembe copper mine in western Uganda was transferred to private ownership and the first phase of preparations to reopen the mine was expected to be completed during 2005; the second phase was expected to take a further 10 months to complete. In 2006 Uganda Gold Mining Ltd (UGM) signed an agreement with Kilembe Mines Ltd transferring ownership of 70% of the Kilembe copper mine to UGM. The production of cobalt from stockpiled copper pyrites commenced in 1999. Uganda is believed to possess the world's second largest deposit of gold, which began to be exploited again in the mid-1990s, and in mid-2010 a Russian-owned gold refinery, capable of refining 60 kg of gold per day, commenced operation. Apatite and limestone are also mined, while petroleum production—initially of some 500–1,000 barrels per day (b/d), but projected to reach 150,000 b/d by 2013—was expected to commence in late 2010. There are, in addition, reserves of iron ore, magnetite, tin, tungsten, beryllium, bismuth, asbestos, graphite, phosphate and tantalite.

Manufacturing contributed 8.1% of GDP in 2009 and in 2003 it employed 6.1% of the working population. The most important manufacturing activities are the processing of agricultural commodities, brewing, vehicle assembly and the production of textiles, cement, soap, fertilizers, paper products, metal products, shoes, paints, matches and batteries. Manufacturing GDP increased by an average of 6.2% per year in 2000–09, according to the World Bank. The sector's GDP increased by 2.5% in 2009.

Construction contributed 12.2% of GDP in 2009, and employed 1.3% of the working population in 2003. Construction GDP increased at an average annual rate of 13.3% in 2004–08; it increased by 10.7% in 2008.

Energy is derived principally from hydroelectric power, although Uganda generates only about two-thirds of national energy requirements. Significant investment has, however, been made in hydroelectric power projects in recent years: in August 2007 construction of a hydroelectric power station at Bujagali with financial assistance from the World Bank began and construction of a further hydroelectric power station at Karuma commenced in mid-2009. Imports of petroleum and petroleum products accounted for 18.5% of the value of Uganda's merchandise imports in 2008.

The services sector contributed 51.0% of GDP in 2009, and engaged 23.5% of the employed labour force in 2003. Trade is the most important aspect of the sector. Services GDP increased by an average of 8.6% per year in 2000–09, according to the World Bank. Services GDP increased by 13.0% in 2008, but decreased by 2.2% in 2009.

In 2009 Uganda recorded a visible trade deficit of US $799.7m., and there was a deficit of $451.1m. on the current account of the balance of payments. In 2008 the principal sources of imports were the United Arab Emirates (UAE, 11.4%), Kenya, India, the People's Republic of China, South Africa and Japan. Sudan (14.3%), Kenya, the UAE, Rwanda, the Democratic Republic of the Congo and Switzerland-Liechtenstein were the main markets for exports in that year. COMESA and the EU (see p. 270) are important trading partners: in 2003 they took 28.3% and 17.7%, respectively, of total imports and provided 27.7% and 26.3%, respectively, of total exports. The principal exports in 2008 were coffee, fish and tobacco; the main imports in that year were machinery and transport equipment, non-metallic mineral manufactures, petroleum products, road vehicles, and medical and pharmaceutical products.

In the financial year ending 30 June 2010 Uganda's central government budgetary deficit was projected at 113,600m. shillings. Uganda's general government gross debt was 6,689.78m. shillings in 2009, equivalent to 22.2% of GDP. Uganda's external debt totalled US $2,249m. at the end of 2008, of which $1,781m. was public and publicly guaranteed debt. In that year the cost of debt-servicing was equivalent to 1.7% of the value of exports of

UGANDA

goods, services and income. The annual average rate of inflation was 6.4% in 2000–10; consumer prices increased by 4.0% in 2010.

Uganda is regarded as having an open, deregulated economy, with conditions favourable to investment. As such, the country has enjoyed good relations with international donors, and during 1998–2000 Uganda secured international aid and debt-relief, including assistance under the IMF's initiative for heavily indebted poor countries. Following the conclusion of an IMF arrangement in 2005, the IMF announced that Uganda's economy had improved to the point where it no longer qualified for aid. In December 2006 Uganda was granted a three-year Policy Support Instrument (PSI), an IMF non-lending programme. Nevertheless, Uganda remained one of the poorest nations in the world, and faced two main challenges: to sustain growth (which continued to be largely dependent on agricultural exports) at a sufficient level to enable the reduction of poverty; and to reduce its reliance on foreign aid, which financed around one-half of the country's expenditure. In early 2009 the discovery of large onshore reserves of petroleum in the western Lake Albert region was announced. Following several years of high economic growth and low inflation, the global economic crisis began to affect Uganda from mid-2008. Along with a series of tax-reducing measures, a key priority of the 2009/10 budget was investment in agriculture with the aim of modernizing the sector and improving production levels: an Agricultural Credit Facility was established to provide low-cost loans for up to eight years and increase spending within the agriculture sector. A five-year National Development Programme, which emphasized investment in public infrastructure, was introduced by the Government in April 2010. In May the IMF, having completed the seventh review of Uganda's economic performance under the PSI, cancelled the existing arrangement and approved a new three-year programme. Despite the slowdown in economic activity in 2009, GDP growth remained relatively strong and had begun to recover rapidly to pre-crisis levels. The new PSI was to support the strengthening of the country's institutions prior to anticipated large-scale petroleum production and Uganda's participation in the common market established by the East African Community (EAC, see p. 447), which subsequently entered into force in July 2010. In early 2011 a rapid rise in inflation, owing in part to higher international food and fuel prices, increased social discontent at alleged electoral malpractice perpetrated by the authorities in February and prompted civil protests.

PUBLIC HOLIDAYS

2012: 1 January (New Year's Day), 26 January (Liberation Day), 8 March (International Women's Day), 6–9 April (Easter), 1 May (Labour Day), 3 June (Martyrs' Day), 9 June (National Heroes' Day), 18 August* (Id al-Fitr, end of Ramadan), 9 October (Independence Day), 26 October* (Id al-Adha, Feast of the Sacrifice), 25 December (Christmas), 26 December (Boxing Day).

* These holidays are dependent on the Islamic lunar calendar and the exact dates may vary by one or two days from those given.

Statistical Survey

Sources (unless otherwise stated): Uganda Bureau of Statistics, POB 13, Entebbe; tel. (41) 320165; fax (41) 320147; e-mail ubos@infocom.co.ug; internet www.ubos.org; Statistics Department, Ministry of Finance, Planning and Economic Development, POB 8147, Kampala.

Area and Population

AREA, POPULATION AND DENSITY

Area (sq km)	
Land	197,323
Inland water and swamp	44,228
Total	241,551*
Population (census results)	
12 January 1991	16,671,705
12 September 2002	
Males	11,929,803
Females	12,512,281
Total	24,442,084
Population (official estimates at mid-year)	
2008	29,592,600
2009	30,661,300
2010	31,784,600
Density (per sq km) at mid-2010	131.6

* 93,263 sq miles.

POPULATION BY AGE AND SEX

('000, official projections at mid-2010)

	Males	Females	Total
0–14	7,962	8,042	16,003
15–64	7,372	7,979	15,350
65 and over	186	249	431
Total	15,517	16,268	31,785

Note: Totals may not be equal to the sum of components, owing to rounding.

PRINCIPAL ETHNIC GROUPS

(at census of 12 September 2002)*

Acholi	1,145,357	Basoga	2,062,920
Baganda	4,126,370	Iteso	1,568,763
Bagisu	1,117,661	Langi	1,485,437
Bakiga	1,679,519	Lugbara	1,022,240
Banyakole	2,330,212		

* Ethnic groups numbering more than 1m. persons, excluding population enumerated in hotels.

DISTRICTS

(population, official estimates at mid-2004)

Central	7,015,300	Northern	5,812,700
Kalangala	41,400	Adjumani	225,100
Kampala	1,290,500	Apac	716,800
Kayunga	306,800	Arua	915,500
Kiboga	249,200	Gulu	491,000
Luwero	496,100	Kitgum	307,500
Masaka	777,300	Kotido	705,400
Mpigi	424,300	Lira	805,200
Mubende	742,400	Moroto	185,500
Mukono	845,800	Moyo	229,800
Nakasongola	129,200	Nakapiripirit	170,500
Rakai	485,700	Nebbi	453,500
Sembabule	190,700	Pader	315,300
Wakiso	1,035,800	Yumbe	291,500
Eastern	6,712,400	Western	6,761,500
Bugiri	464,800	Bundibugyoi	232,900
Busia	239,500	Bushenyi	746,400
Iganga	757,300	Hoima	380,000
Jinja	436,100	Kabale	479,400
Kaberamaido	130,600	Kabarole	368,300
Kamuli	753,200	Kamwenge	312,300
Kapchorwa	208,600	Kanungu	212,300
Katakwi	343,800	Kasese	568,600
Kumi	417,500	Kibaale	454,100
Mayuge	346,800	Kisoro	224,300
Mbale	760,800	Kyenjojo	405,700
Pallisa	552,000	Masindi	512,900
Sironko	305,700	Mbarara	1,142,500
Soroti	406,800	Ntungamo	400,000
Tororo	589,300	Rukungiri	322,000

2010 (official estimates at mid-year): Central 8,220,800; Eastern 8,301,800; Northern 7,283,300; Western 7,978,700.

UGANDA

PRINCIPAL TOWNS
(population according to provisional results of census of 12 September 2002)*

Kampala (capital)	1,208,544	Entebbe	57,518
Gulu	113,144	Kasese	53,446
Lira	89,971	Njeru	52,514
Jinja	86,520	Mukono	47,305
Mbale	70,437	Arua	45,883
Mbarara	69,208	Kabale	45,757
Masaka	61,300	Kitgum	42,929

* According to administrative divisions of 2002.

Mid-2010 ('000, incl. suburbs, UN estimate): Kampala 1,598 (Source: UN, *World Urbanization Prospects: The 2009 Revision*).

BIRTHS AND DEATHS
(annual averages, UN estimates)

	1995–2000	2000–05	2005–10
Birth rate (per 1,000)	48.3	47.4	46.3
Death rate (per 1,000)	17.3	15.2	12.9

Source: UN, *World Population Prospects: The 2008 Revision*.

2006: Birth rate 46.7 per 1,000; Death rate 13.6 per 1,000 (Source: African Development Bank).

2007: Birth rate 46.5 per 1,000; Death rate 13.1 per 1,000 (Source: African Development Bank).

2008: Birth rate 46.2 per 1,000; Death rate 12.7 per 1,000 (Source: African Development Bank).

2009: Birth rate 45.8 per 1,000; Death rate 12.3 per 1,000 (Source: African Development Bank).

Life expectancy (years at birth, WHO estimates): 52 (males 51; females 53) in 2008 (Source: WHO, *World Health Statistics*).

EMPLOYMENT
(persons aged 10 years and over, census of 12 September 2002)*

	Males	Females	Total
Agriculture, hunting and forestry	2,545,962	2,649,779	5,195,741
Fishing	102,043	16,743	118,786
Mining and quarrying	13,613	6,127	19,740
Manufacturing	108,653	45,594	154,247
Electricity, gas and water supply	12,860	1,509	14,369
Construction	105,769	2,939	108,708
Wholesale and retail trade, repair of motor vehicles, motorcycles and personal and household goods	191,191	143,145	334,336
Hotels and restaurants	23,741	64,099	87,840
Transport, storage and communications	119,437	5,798	125,235
Financial intermediation / Real estate, renting and business activities	14,539	7,562	22,101
Public administration and defence, compulsory social security	146,319	27,278	173,597
Education	124,167	85,015	209,182
Health and social work	54,327	53,108	107,435
Other community, social and personal service activities	22,736	26,734	49,470
Private households with employed persons	14,019	19,115	33,134
Not classifiable by economic activity	120,219	76,167	196,386
Total employed	3,719,595	3,230,712	6,950,307

* Excluding population enumerated at hotels.

2003 ('000 persons aged 10 years and over): Agriculture, hunting and forestry 6,278.3; Fishing 83.3; Mining and quarrying 27.8; Manufacturing 564.9; Electricity, gas and water supply 9.3; Construction 120.4; Wholesale and retail trade, repair of motor vehicles, motorcycles and personal and household goods 1,074.2; Hotels and restaurants 240.8; Transport, storage and communications 175.9; Real estate, renting and business activities 37.0; Public administration and defence, compulsory social security 74.1; Education 240.8; Health and social work 74.1; Other community, social and personal service activities 148.2; Private households with employed persons 111.1; *Total employed* 9,260.0; Unemployed 346.0; *Total labour force* 9,606.0 (Source: ILO).

Mid-2011 ('000, estimates): Agriculture, etc. 11,450; Total labour force 15,435 (Source: FAO).

Health and Welfare

KEY INDICATORS

Total fertility rate (children per woman, 2008)	6.3
Under-5 mortality rate (per 1,000 live births, 2008)	135
HIV/AIDS (% of persons aged 15–49, 2007)	5.4
Physicians (per 1,000 head, 2004)	0.1
Hospital beds (per 1,000 head, 2006)	1.1
Health expenditure (2007): US $ per head (PPP)	74
Health expenditure (2007): % of GDP	6.3
Health expenditure (2007): public (% of total)	26.2
Access to water (% of persons, 2008)	67
Access to sanitation (% of persons, 2008)	48
Total carbon dioxide emissions ('000 metric tons, 2007)	3,202.3
Carbon dioxide emissions per head (metric tons, 2007)	0.1
Human Development Index (2010): ranking	143
Human Development Index (2010): value	0.422

For sources and definitions, see explanatory note on p. vi.

Agriculture

PRINCIPAL CROPS
('000 metric tons)

	2007	2008	2009
Rice, paddy	162	171	181
Maize	1,262	1,266	1,272
Millet	732	783	841
Sorghum	456	477	497
Potatoes	650	670	689
Sweet potatoes	2,602	2,707	2,766
Cassava (Manioc)	4,456	5,072	5,179
Sugar cane*	2,350	2,350	n.a.
Beans, dry	435	440	452
Cow peas, dry	75	79	84
Pigeon peas	89	90	91

UGANDA

—continued	2007	2008	2009
Soybeans	176	178	180
Groundnuts, with shell	165	173	185
Sesame seed	168	173	178
Seed cotton*	40	75	66
Onions, dry*	147	147	n.a.
Bananas*	615	615	n.a.
Plantains	9,231	9,371	9,512
Coffee, green	175	212	196
Tea	45	43	49
Tobacco, unmanufactured	26	29	19

* FAO estimates.

Aggregate production ('000 metric tons, may include official, semi-official or estimated data): Total cereals 2,631 in 2007, 2,716 in 2008, 2,811 in 2009; Total roots and tubers 7,708 in 2007, 8,449 in 2008, 8,634 in 2009; Total vegetables (incl. melons) 556 in 2006–09; Total fruits (excl. melons) 9,899 in 2007, 10,039 in 2008, 10,180 in 2009.

Source: FAO.

LIVESTOCK
('000 head, year ending September)

	2006	2007	2008
Asses*	18	18	18
Cattle	6,973	7,182	7,398
Sheep	1,648	1,697	1,748
Goats	8,034	8,275	8,523
Pigs	2,060	2,122	2,186
Chickens	22,849	26,950	27,508

* FAO estimates.

Note: No data were available for 2009.

Source: FAO.

LIVESTOCK PRODUCTS
('000 metric tons, FAO estimates)

	2005	2006	2007
Cattle meat	106	106	106
Sheep meat	6	6	6
Goat meat	29	29	29
Pig meat	98	60	60
Chicken meat	38	38	38
Cows' milk	735	735	735
Hen eggs	20	20	21

2008: Production assumed to be unchanged from 2007 (FAO estimates).

2009: Cows' milk 735 (FAO estimate).

Source: FAO.

Forestry

ROUNDWOOD REMOVALS
('000 cubic metres, excl. bark)

	2006	2007	2008
Sawlogs, veneer logs and logs for sleepers	1,283*	1,369*	1,369†
Other industrial wood†	2,120	2,120	2,120
Fuel wood†	37,343	37,900	38,468
Total†	40,746	41,389	41,957

* Unofficial figure.
† FAO estimate(s).

2009: Figures assumed to be unchanged from 2008 (FAO estimates).

Source: FAO.

SAWNWOOD PRODUCTION
('000 cubic metres, incl. railway sleepers)

	2004	2005	2006
Coniferous (softwood)	67	24	24
Broadleaved (hardwood)	197	101	93
Total	264	125	117

2007–09: Figures assumed to be unchanged from 2006 (FAO estimates).

Source: FAO.

Fishing

('000 metric tons, live weight)

	2006	2007	2008*
Capture	367.1	500.0	450.0
Cyprinids	22.7	30.9	27.8
Tilapias	137.0	186.7	168.0
African lungfishes	12.8	17.4	15.7
Characins	19.8	26.9	24.3
Nile perch	154.3	210.2	189.0
Aquaculture	32.4	51.1	52.3
Total catch	399.5	551.1	502.3

* FAO estimates.

Note: Figures exclude aquatic animals, recorded by number rather than weight. The number of Nile crocodiles captured was: n.a. in 2006; n.a. in 2007; 290 in 2008 (FAO estimate).

Source: FAO.

Mining

('000 metric tons, unless otherwise indicated)

	2006	2007	2008
Cement (hydraulic)*	630.0	650.0	650.0
Tantalum and niobium (columbium) concentrates (kilograms)	275	275*	275*
Cobalt (metric tons)	689	698	663
Gold (kilograms)	22	20*	20*
Limestone	425.6	450.0*	450.0*
Salt (unrefined)*	2	2	2

* Estimate(s).

Source: US Geological Survey.

Industry

SELECTED PRODUCTS
('000 metric tons, unless otherwise indicated)

	2003	2004	2005
Soft drinks (million litres)	78.5	111.5	163.5
Sugar	139.5	189.5	182.9
Soap	101.3	93.4	127.6
Cement	507.1	559.0	692.7
Paint (million litres)	1.9	2.2	8.2
Edible oil and fat	56.0	58.1	43.3
Animal feed	20.9	19.6	17.3
Footwear (million pairs)	3.4	3.6	46.3
Wheat flour	42.2	25.7	20.3
Processed milk (million litres)	14.9	19.6	18.5
Cotton and rayon fabrics (million sq m)	11.1	10.1	13.6
Clay bricks, tiles, etc.	33.3	15.4	36.2
Corrugated iron sheets	39.2	48.8	61.6

Source: Bank of Uganda.

UGANDA

Statistical Survey

Finance

CURRENCY AND EXCHANGE RATES

Monetary Units
100 cents = 1 new Uganda shilling.

Sterling, Dollar and Euro Equivalents (31 August 2010)
£1 sterling = 3,496.7 new Uganda shillings;
US $1 = 2,270.0 new Uganda shillings;
€1 = 2,878.4 new Uganda shillings;
10,000 new Uganda shillings = £2.86 = $4.41 = €3.47.

Average Exchange Rate (new Uganda shillings per US $)
2007 1,723.5
2008 1,720.4
2009 2,030.3

Note: Between December 1985 and May 1987 the official exchange rate was fixed at US $1 = 1,400 shillings. In May 1987 a new shilling, equivalent to 100 of the former units, was introduced. At the same time, the currency was devalued by 76.7%, with the exchange rate set at $1 = 60 new shillings. Further adjustments were implemented in subsequent years. Foreign exchange controls were mostly abolished in 1993.

BUDGET
('000 million new shillings, year ending 30 June)

Revenue	2007/08	2008/09	2009/10*
Taxes	3,161.1	3,662.3	4,315.5
Grants	738.5	884.8	924.6
Other revenue	85.7	124.3	82.2
Total	3,985.3	4,671.4	5,322.3

Expenditure	2007/08	2008/09	2009/10*
Compensation of employees	471.8	591.4	675.2
Consumption of goods and services	1,049.4	1,300.7	1,453.6
Interest payments	309.4	357.9	356.0
Domestic	271.4	310.3	305.2
External	38.0	47.6	50.8
Subsidies	87.4	92.0	92.0
Grants	1,747.3	1,692.7	2,334.0
Social benefits	78.5	79.0	227.0
Other expenses	16.0	60.0	70.3
Total	3,759.8	4,173.7	5,208.1

* Projections.

INTERNATIONAL RESERVES
(US $ million at 31 December)

	2008	2009	2010
IMF special drawing rights	0.2	225.2	220.8
Foreign exchange	2,300.3	2,769.3	2,739.6
Total	2,300.5	2,994.5	2,960.4

Source: IMF, *International Financial Statistics*.

MONEY SUPPLY
('000 million new shillings at 31 December)

	2008	2009	2010
Currency outside depository corporations	1,254.52	1,329.75	1,776.68
Transferable deposits	2,525.60	3,071.25	4,135.07
Other deposits	2,005.60	2,396.74	3,442.96
Broad money	5,785.73	6,797.75	9,354.71

Source: IMF, *International Financial Statistics*.

COST OF LIVING
(Consumer Price Index for all urban households; base: 2000 = 100)

	2008	2009	2010
Food	171.1	213.9	218.4
Clothing	121.5	131.3	135.1
Rent, fuel and light	181.1	193.2	203.1
All items (incl. others)	158.5	179.2	186.3

Source: ILO.

NATIONAL ACCOUNTS
('000 million new shillings at current prices)

Expenditure on the Gross Domestic Product

	2007	2008	2009
Government final consumption expenditure	2,609	2,814	2,926
Private final consumption expenditure	17,970	22,900	26,662
Increase in stocks	62	77	93
Gross fixed capital formation	5,304	5,672	7,100
Total domestic expenditure	25,945	31,463	36,781
Exports of goods and services	4,405	5,625	8,094
Less Imports of goods and services	7,000	8,912	10,710
GDP in purchasers' values	23,351	28,176	34,166
GDP at constant 2002 prices	17,138	18,924	19,918

Gross Domestic Product by Economic Activity

	2007	2008	2009
Agriculture, hunting, forestry and fishing	4,827	6,083	7,774
Mining and quarrying	67	81	80
Manufacturing	1,616	2,041	2,581
Electricity and water	1,062	1,172	1,363
Construction	2,840	3,458	3,895
Wholesale and retail trade	3,286	4,140	5,450
Hotels and restaurants	954	1,149	1,379
Transport, storage and communications	1,474	1,772	2,129
Financial intermediation	683	856	1,019
Real estate	1,645	1,873	2,126
Business services	359	410	498
Public administration and defence	747	845	940
Education	1,474	1,568	1,734
Health	307	302	324
Other services	506	614	727
Sub-total	21,847	26,364	32,019
Less Financial intermediation services indirectly measured	408	512	651
Gross value added at basic prices	21,439	25,852	31,368
Net taxes on products	1,911	2,326	2,799
GDP at market prices	23,351	28,176	34,166

BALANCE OF PAYMENTS
(US $ million)

	2007	2008	2009
Exports of goods f.o.b.	1,999.0	2,703.5	2,987.7
Imports of goods f.o.b.	−2,958.2	−4,038.9	−3,787.3
Trade balance	−959.2	−1,335.4	−799.7
Exports of services	594.6	802.4	966.3
Imports of services	−977.0	−1,256.1	−1,422.3
Balance on goods and services	−1,341.5	−1,789.1	−1,255.8
Other income received	97.1	130.2	41.9
Other income paid	−339.8	−374.8	−370.5
Balance on goods, services and income	−1,584.2	−2,033.8	−1,584.4
Current transfers received	1,311.0	1,564.0	1,512.6
Current transfers paid	−203.2	−323.7	−379.4
Current balance	−476.4	−793.4	−451.1
Direct investment from abroad	792.3	728.9	603.7
Portfolio investment assets	—	−12.1	—
Portfolio investment liabilities	44.9	29.7	20.0
Financial derivatives liabilities	1.4	6.9	−6.2
Other investment assets	26.2	54.8	37.4
Other investment liabilities	511.5	364.4	782.8
Net errors and omissions	−230.7	−440.9	−701.7
Overall balance	669.2	−61.8	285.0

Source: IMF, *International Financial Statistics*.

UGANDA

External Trade

PRINCIPAL COMMODITIES
(distribution by SITC, US $ million)

Imports c.i.f.	2006	2007	2008
Food and live animals	233.7	277.6	303.6
Cereals and cereal preparations	156.8	158.8	173.2
Crude materials (inedible) except fuels	54.7	59.7	80.2
Mineral fuels, lubricants, etc.	539.6	654.0	863.6
Petroleum, petroleum products and related materials	526.6	645.6	837.1
Animal and vegetable oils, fats and waxes	89.7	125.1	227.4
Chemicals and related products	337.5	443.1	639.3
Medicinal and pharmaceutical products	123.1	175.8	246.2
Plastics in primary forms	70.6	96.1	117.8
Basic manufactures	430.3	570.9	812.7
Non-metallic mineral manufactures	662.8	955.0	1,252.0
Iron and steel	141.6	173.4	309.5
Machinery and transport equipment	662.8	955.0	1,252.0
Telecommunications and sound recording/reproducing apparatus	137.0	246.5	297.6
Electrical machinery, apparatus, etc.	76.9	109.2	134.4
Road vehicles (incl. air-cushion vehicles) and parts (excl. tyres, engines and electrical parts)	216.4	294.2	338.4
Miscellaneous manufactured articles	186.9	251.9	293.7
Total (incl. others)	2,557.3	3,493.4	4,525.9

Exports f.o.b.	2006	2007	2008
Food and live animals	462.0	572.0	735.1
Fish, crustaceans, molluscs and preparations thereof	140.7	117.7	118.7
Cereals and cereal preparations	36.7	43.1	49.6
Coffee, tea, cocoa, spices and manufactures	225.8	336.2	478.6
Beverages and tobacco	38.9	98.2	121.6
Tobacco and tobacco manufactures	27.7	67.3	69.4
Crude materials (inedible) except fuels	100.8	115.7	130.6
Textile fibres (not wool tops) and their wastes (not in yarn)	26.8	29.6	21.1
Crude animal and vegetable materials n.e.s.	41.1	50.2	58.2
Mineral fuels, lubricants and related materials	42.2	49.0	61.6
Petroleum, petroleum products and related materials	37.3	40.3	50.6
Basic manufactures	57.8	133.1	241.8
Iron and steel	31.3	63.1	102.5
Machinery and transport equipment	89.5	169.9	187.2
Miscellaneous manufactured articles	16.0	31.4	95.6
Gold, non-monetary (excl. gold ores and concentrates)	122.6	65.0	43.0
Total (incl. others)	962.2	1,336.7	1,724.3

Source: UN, *International Trade Statistics Yearbook*.

PRINCIPAL TRADING PARTNERS
(US $ million)

Imports c.i.f.	2006	2007	2008
Bahrain	85.8	61.7	46.8
Belgium	35.8	48.5	52.8
China, People's Repub.	138.3	274.3	365.8
France (incl. Monaco)	37.4	101.0	179.6
Germany	74.9	81.6	88.4
Hong Kong	20.5	40.1	46.9
India	209.0	345.0	470.5
Italy	33.1	44.7	87.5
Japan	174.5	233.0	268.7
Kenya	401.0	472.4	511.3
Malaysia	48.9	63.2	146.0
Netherlands	51.7	55.8	75.5
Saudi Arabia	52.3	47.4	115.7
Singapore	37.3	60.2	94.2
South Africa	156.3	207.2	305.2
Sweden	31.9	98.7	96.5
Tanzania	28.7	29.2	55.5
United Arab Emirates	325.3	420.5	515.5
United Kingdom	124.0	117.8	137.6
USA	89.7	101.9	117.4
Total (incl. others)	2,557.3	3,493.4	4,525.9

Exports f.o.b.	2006	2007	2008
Belgium	39.6	52.8	63.7
Burundi	20.6	42.7	45.4
Congo, Democratic Repub.	44.8	100.0	125.0
Congo, Republic	8.1	42.3	22.0
France (incl. Monaco)	38.4	32.7	33.7
Germany	41.9	65.1	75.0
Hong Kong	12.4	10.3	16.1
India	1.8	4.3	18.7
Italy	14.6	13.3	33.6
Japan	3.9	5.3	8.2
Kenya	88.0	118.2	164.6
Netherlands	61.9	66.6	81.8
Rwanda	30.5	83.3	136.9
Singapore	34.5	22.5	26.0
South Africa	10.9	10.7	14.9
Spain	19.3	26.6	26.9
Sudan	91.7	157.1	245.9
Switzerland-Liechtenstein	45.4	86.6	155.7
Tanzania	13.7	30.6	30.5
United Arab Emirates	186.3	177.9	128.1
United Kingdom	30.0	53.3	118.4
USA	14.2	19.6	15.7
Total (incl. others)	962.2	1,336.7	1,724.3

Source: UN, *International Trade Statistics Yearbook*.

Transport

RAILWAYS
(traffic)

	1994	1995	1996
Passenger-km (million)	35	30	28
Freight ton-km (million)	208	236	187

Freight traffic ('000 ton-km): 212,616 in 2003; 229,439 in 2004; 185,559 in 2005.

UGANDA

ROAD TRAFFIC
(vehicles in use)

	2006	2007	2008
Passenger cars	70,652	81,320	90,856
Buses and coaches	32,863	40,471	50,472
Lorries and vans	73,633	79,273	86,818
Motorcycles	133,985	176,516	236,452

Source: Bank of Uganda.

CIVIL AVIATION
(traffic on scheduled services)

	2004	2005	2006
Kilometres flown (million)	3	3	3
Passengers carried ('000)	46	49	55
Passenger-km (million)	272	302	327
Total ton-km (million)	50	55	61

Source: UN, *Statistical Yearbook*.

Tourism

FOREIGN TOURIST ARRIVALS

Country of residence	2007	2008	2009
India	12,408	16,236	12,946
Kenya	199,598	249,786	261,329
Rwanda	123,262	181,339	199,530
Sudan	10,299	16,169	15,088
Tanzania	55,435	45,276	48,948
United Kingdom	38,667	51,812	35,716
USA	32,344	42,418	37,971
Total (incl. others)	641,743	843,864	806,655

Tourism receipts (US $ million): 449 in 2007; 590 in 2008; 564 in 2009.

Communications Media

	2007	2008	2009
Telephones ('000 main lines in use)	165.8	168.5	233.5
Mobile cellular telephones ('000 subscribers)	4,195.3	8,554.9	9,383.7
Internet users ('000)	1,125	2,500	3,200
Broadband subscribers	1,900	4,800	6,000

Source: International Telecommunication Union.

Personal computers: 500,000 (16.9 per 1,000 persons) in 2006.

Television receivers ('000 in use, 2000): 610.

Radio receivers ('000 in use, 1997): 2,600.

Book production (titles, excl. pamphlets and govt publications, 1996): 288.

Daily newspapers: 2 titles (average circulation 40,000 copies) in 1996; 7 titles in 2004.

Non-daily newspapers: 10 titles in 2004.

Sources: mainly UNESCO, *Statistical Yearbook*; UN, *Statistical Yearbook*; UNESCO Institute for Statistics.

Education

(2007/08 unless otherwise indicated)

	Institutions	Teachers	Students
Pre-primary	n.a.	10,519	417,386
Primary*	n.a.	168,376	8,297,780
Secondary*	n.a.	65,045	1,194,454
Tertiary	n.a.	3,581	107,728
Teacher training colleges†	10	n.a.	16,170
Technical schools and institutes†	25	n.a.	7,999
Universities†	18	n.a.	58,823

* 2008/09.
† 2003/04.

Source: mainly UNESCO Institute for Statistics.

Pupil-teacher ratio (primary education, UNESCO estimate): 49.3 in 2008/09 (Source: UNESCO Institute for Statistics).

Adult literacy rate (UNESCO estimates): 74.6% (males 82.4%; females 66.8%) in 2008 (Source: UNESCO Institute for Statistics).

Directory

The Government

HEAD OF STATE

President: Gen. (retd) YOWERI KAGUTA MUSEVENI (took office 29 January 1986; elected 9 May 1996; re-elected 12 March 2001, 23 February 2006 and 18 February 2011).

Vice-President: Prof. GILBERT BALIBASEKA BUKENYA.

On 24 May President Museveni nominated Edward Ssekandi and Amama Mbabzi for the positions of Vice-President and Prime Minister, respectively. Parliament approved the nominations the following day.

THE CABINET
(May 2011)

Prime Minister: Prof. APOLO NSIBAMBI.

First Deputy Prime Minister and Minister in Charge of East African Affairs: ERIYA KATEGAYA.

Second Deputy Prime Minister and Minister of Public Service: HENRY MUGANWA KAJURA.

Third Deputy Prime Minister and Minister of Internal Affairs: KIRUNDA KIVEJINJA.

Minister of Security: AMAMA MBABAZI.

Minister in Charge of the Presidency: BEATRICE WABUDEYA.

Minister in the Office of the Prime Minister, in charge of General Duties: JANAT MUKWAYA.

Minister of Agriculture, Animal Industry and Fisheries: HOPE MWESIGYE.

Minister of Defence: CRISPUS KIYONGA.

Minister of Relief and Disaster Preparedness: Prof. TARSIS KABWEGYERE.

Minister of Education and Sports: GERALDINE BITAMAZIRE.

Minister of Energy and Mineral Development: HILLARY ONEK.

Minister of Information and National Guidance: KABAKUMBA L. MATSIKO.

Minister of Finance, Planning and Economic Development: SYDDA BBUMBA.

Minister of Works and Transport: JOHN NASASIRA.

Minister of Justice and Constitutional Affairs, and Attorney-General: GERALD KIDDU MAKUBUYA.

Minister of Gender, Labour and Social Development: GABRIEL OPIO.

Minister of Tourism, Trade and Industry: KAHINDA OTAFIIRE.

Minister of Water and Environment: MARIA MUTAGAMBA.

UGANDA

Minister of Lands, Housing and Urban Development: OMARA ATUBO.
Minister of Health: Dr STEPHEN MALLINGA.
Minister of Foreign Affairs: SAM KUTESA.
Minister of Information Communication Technology: AGGREY AWORI.
Minister of Local Government: ADOLF MWESIGYE.
Minister without Portfolio: DOROTHY HYUHA.

In addition to the Cabinet Ministers, there were 44 Ministers of State. The Chief Whip is also a member of the Cabinet.

MINISTRIES

Office of the President: Parliament Bldg, POB 7168, Kampala; tel. (41) 4258441; fax (41) 4256143; e-mail aak@statehouse.go.ug; internet www.statehouse.go.ug.

Office of the Prime Minister: Post Office Bldg, Yusuf Lule Rd, POB 341, Kampala; tel. (41) 4236252; fax (41) 4341139; e-mail ps@opm.go.ug; internet www.opm.go.ug.

Ministry of Agriculture, Animal Industry and Fisheries: POB 102, Entebbe; tel. (41) 4320987; fax (41) 4321255; e-mail mosagr@hotmail.com; internet www.agriculture.go.ug.

Ministry of Defence: Bombo, POB 7069, Kampala; tel. (41) 4270331; fax (41) 4245911; e-mail spokesman@defenceuganda.mil.ug; internet www.defence.go.ug.

Ministry of Education and Sports: Embassy House and Development Bldg, Plot 9/11, Parliament Ave, POB 7063, Kampala; tel. (41) 4234451; fax (41) 42230437; e-mail pro@education.go.ug; internet www.education.go.ug.

Ministry of Energy and Mineral Development: Amber House, Kampala Rd, Kampala; tel. (41) 4311111; fax (41) 4234732; e-mail psmemd@energy.go.ug; internet www.energyandminerals.go.ug.

Ministry of Finance, Planning and Economic Development: Appollo Kaggwa Rd, Plot 2-12, POB 8147, Kampala; tel. (41) 4707000; fax (41) 4230163; e-mail webmaster@finance.go.ug; internet www.finance.go.ug.

Ministry of Foreign Affairs: Embassy House, POB 7048, Kampala; tel. (41) 4345661; fax (41) 4258722; e-mail info@mofa.go.ug; internet www.mofa.go.ug.

Ministry of Gender, Labour and Social Development: Plot 2, Lumumba Ave, Simbamanyo House, POB 7136, Kampala; tel. (41) 347854; fax (41) 256374; e-mail ps@mglsd.go.ug; internet www.mglsd.go.ug.

Ministry of Health: Plot 6, Lourdel Rd, Wandegeya, POB 7272, Kampala; tel. (41) 4340884; fax (41) 4340887; e-mail info@health.go.ug; internet www.health.go.ug.

Ministry of Information Communication Technology: NSSF House, Jinja Rd, POB 7817, Kampala; tel. (41) 4236262; fax (41) 4231314; internet www.ict.go.ug.

Ministry of Information and National Guidance: Kampala.

Ministry of Internal Affairs: Plot 75, Jinja Rd, POB 7191, Kampala; tel. (41) 4258355; fax (41) 4343088; e-mail info@mia.go.ug; internet www.mia.go.ug.

Ministry of Justice and Constitutional Affairs: Plot 1, Parliament Ave, Queens Chambers, POB 7183, Kampala; tel. (41) 4230538; fax (41) 4254829; e-mail mojca@africaonline.co.ug; internet www.justice.go.ug.

Ministry of Lands, Housing and Urban Development: Kampala; internet www.mlhud.go.ug.

Ministry of Local Government: Uganda House, 8/10 Kampala Rd, POB 7037, Kampala; tel. (41) 4341224; fax (41) 4258127; e-mail info@molg.go.ug; internet www.molg.go.ug.

Ministry of Relief and Disaster Preparedness: POB 341, Kampala; tel. (41) 4236967.

Ministry of Security: Kampala.

Ministry of Tourism, Trade and Industry: 6/8 Parliament Ave, POB 7103, Kampala; tel. (41) 4314000; fax (41) 4347286; e-mail mintrade@mtti.go.ug; internet www.mtti.go.ug.

Ministry of Water and Environment: POB 7096, Kampala; tel. (41) 4342931; e-mail mwle@mwle.go.ug; internet www.mwle.go.ug.

Ministry of Works and Transport: Plot 4/6, Airport Rd, POB 10, Entebbe; tel. (42) 4320101; fax (42) 4321364; e-mail mowt@works.go.ug; internet www.works.go.ug.

President and Legislature

PRESIDENT

Election, 18 February 2011

Candidate	Votes	% of votes
Gen. (Retd) Yoweri Kaguta Museveni (NRM)	5,428,368	68.38
Kizza Besigye (FDC)	2,064,963	26.01
Norbert Mao (DP)	147,917	1.86
Olara Otunnu (UPC)	125,059	1.58
Beti Olive Namisango Kamya (UFA)	52,782	0.66
Abed Bwanika (PDP)	51,708	0.65
Jaberi Bidandi Ssali (PPP)	34,688	0.44
Samuel Lubega Walter Mukaaku (Ind.)	32,726	0.41
Total	**7,938,211**	**100.00**

PARLIAMENT

Speaker: REBECCA KADAGA.
Deputy Speaker: JACOB OULANYAH.

General Election, 18 February 2011

Party	Directly elected seats	Women members	Total seats
National Resistance Movement (NRM)	164	85	249
Forum for Democratic Change (FDC)	24	11	35
Democratic Party (DP)	11	1	12
Uganda People's Congress (UPC)	7	3	10
Conservative Party (CP)	1	—	1
Justice Forum (JEEMA)	1	—	1
Ind.	30	12	42
Others*	—	—	25
Total	**238**	**112**	**375**

* Comprises 10 nominated representatives from the Uganda People's Defence Forces, five nominated representatives for young people (four from the NRM and one independent), five nominated representatives for people with disabilities (all from the NRM) and five nominated representatives for workers (four from the NRM and one independent).

Election Commission

Electoral Commission: 53–56 Jinja Rd, POB 22678, Kampala; tel. (41) 4337500; fax (41) 4337595; e-mail info@ec.or.ug; internet www.ec.or.ug; f. 1997; independent; Chair. Dr BADRU M. KIGGUNDU.

Political Organizations

Political parties were ordered to suspend active operations, although not formally banned, in March 1986. At a referendum on the future restoration of a plural political system, which took place on 29 June 2000, the retention of the existing 'no-party' system was overwhelmingly endorsed by voters. However, the result was nullified by the Constitutional Court in mid-2004. Following a successful challenge to the Political Parties and Organizations Act 2002, political parties were permitted to resume their activities nationally from March 2003. Discussions on a proposed transition to multi-party politics commenced in 2004. By April of that year some 60 new political parties had emerged, but only 13 had sought registration. In mid-2005 legislation was adopted allowing for a return to full multi-party democracy; the legislation was approved by 92.5% of voters in a national referendum held on 28 July 2005. A total of 38 political parties had been officially registered by 2011.

Conservative Party (CP): POB 5145, Kampala; f. 1979; Leader KEN LUKYAMUZI.

Democratic Party (DP): City House, Plot 2/3, William St, POB 7098, Kampala; tel. and fax (41) 4252536; e-mail info@dpuganda.org; internet www.dpuganda.org; f. 1954; main support in southern Uganda; seeks a multi-party political system; Pres. NORBERT MAO; Vice-Pres. ZACHARY OLUM.

Forum for Democratic Change (FDC): FDC Villas, Entebbe Rd, Plot no. 109, Najjanankumbi, POB 26928, Kampala; tel. (41) 4267920; fax (41) 4267918; e-mail info@fdcuganda.org; internet www.fdcuganda.org; f. 2004 by a merger of the Reform Agenda, the

UGANDA

Parliamentary Advocacy Forum and the National Democratic Forum; Leader KIZZA BESIGYE.

Forum for Integrity in Leadership (FIL): Plot 48B, Ntinda Rd, POB 7606, Kampala; Chair. EMMANUEL TUMUSIIME.

Justice Forum (JEEMA): POB 3999, Kampala; Leader MUHAMMAD KIBIRIGE MAYANJA; Sec.-Gen. HUSSEIN KYANJO.

Movement for Democratic Change (MDC): Balintuma Rd, Nakulabye, POB 70952, Kampala.

National Peasant Party (NPP): Plot 123, Katwe Rd, Sapoba House, POB 20692, Kampala.

National Resistance Movement (NRM): Plot 10, Kyadondo Rd, POB 7778, Kampala; tel. (41) 346295; e-mail info@nrm.ug; internet www.nrm.ug; f. as National Resistance Movement to oppose the UPC Govt 1980–85; also opposed the mil. Govt in power from July 1985 to Jan. 1986; its fmr mil. wing, the National Resistance Army (NRA), led by Lt-Gen. (later Gen. retd) Yoweri Kaguta Museveni, took power in Jan. 1986; name changed as above on registration in 2003; Chair. YOWERI MUSEVENI; Sec.-Gen. AMAMA MBABAZI.

People's Development Party (PDP): Makerere Hill Rd, Relief Bldg (Opp. LDC), POB 25765, Kampala; f. 2007; Pres. Dr ABED BWANIKA.

People's Progressive Party (PPP): Plot 6, Commercial St, Luzira, POB 9252, Kampala; tel. (41) 4505178; internet www.ppp.ug; f. 2004; Chair. JABERI BIDANDI SSALI.

Uganda Federal Alliance (UFA): POB 14196, Kampala; internet www.ugandafederalalliance.com; f. 2010; Leader BETI OLIVE NAMIS-SANGO KAMYA.

Uganda Patriotic Movement (UPM): POB 2083, Kampala; f. 1980; Sec.-Gen. JABERI SSALI.

Uganda People's Congress (UPC): Plot 8–10, Kampala Rd, Uganda House, POB 37047, Kampala; tel. and fax (41) 236748; e-mail upcsecretariat@upcparty.net; internet www.upcparty.net; f. 1960; socialist-based philosophy; ruling party 1962–71 and 1980–85, sole legal political party 1969–71; Pres. OLARA OTUNNU; Sec.-Gen. JOSEPH BOSSA.

The following organizations are in armed conflict with the Government:

Allied Democratic Forces (ADF): active since 1996 in south-eastern Uganda; combines Ugandan Islamic fundamentalist rebels, exiled Rwandan Hutus and guerrillas from the Democratic Republic of the Congo; Pres. Sheikh JAMIL MUKULU.

Lord's Resistance Army (LRA): f. 1987; claims to be conducting a Christian fundamentalist 'holy war' against the Govt; forces est. to number up to 1,500, operating mainly from bases in Sudan; Leader JOSEPH KONY; a breakaway faction (LRA—Democratic) is led by RONALD OTIM KOMAKECH.

Uganda People's Freedom Movement (UPFM): based in Tororo and Kenya; f. 1994 by mems of the fmr Uganda People's Army; Leader PETER OTAI.

West Nile Bank Front (WNBF): operates in northern Uganda.

Diplomatic Representation

EMBASSIES AND HIGH COMMISSIONS IN UGANDA

Algeria: 14 Acacia Ave, Kololo, POB 4025, Kampala; tel. (41) 4232918; fax (41) 4341015; e-mail ambalgka@imul.com; Ambassador ABDERRAHMANE BENMOKHTAR.

Belgium: Rwenzori House, 3rd Floor, Plot 1, Lumumba Ave, POB 7043, Kampala; tel. (41) 4349559; fax (41) 4347212; e-mail kampala@diplobel.fed.be; internet www.diplomatie.be/kampala; Ambassador MARC GEDOPT.

China, People's Republic: 37 Malcolm X Ave, Kololo, POB 4106, Kampala; tel. (41) 4259881; fax (41) 4235087; e-mail chinaemb_ug@mfa.gov.cn; internet ug.china-embassy.org; Ambassador SUN HEPING.

Congo, Democratic Republic: 20 Philip Rd, Kololo, POB 4972, Kampala; tel. (41) 4250099; fax (41) 4340140; Ambassador JEAN-CHARLES OKOTO LOLAKOMBE.

Cuba: KAR Dr., 16 Lower Kololo Terrace, POB 9226, Kampala; tel. (41) 4233742; fax (41) 4233320; e-mail ecuba@africaonline.co.ug; Ambassador MARIANO L. BETANCOURT.

Denmark: Plot 3, Lumumba Ave, POB 11243, Kampala; tel. (31) 2263211; fax (31) 2264624; e-mail kmtamb@um.dk; internet www.ambkampala.um.dk; Ambassador NATHALIA FEINBERG.

Egypt: 33 Kololo Hill Dr., POB 4280, Kampala; tel. (41) 4254525; fax (41) 4232103; e-mail egyembug@utlonline.co.ug; Ambassador SABRI MAGDI.

Ethiopia: 3L Kitante Close, off Kira Rd, POB 7745, Kampala; tel. (41) 4348340; fax (41) 4341885; Ambassador ATO TERFA MENEGESHA.

France: 16 Lumumba Ave, Nakasero, POB 7212, Kampala; tel. (41) 4304500; fax (41) 4304520; e-mail ambafrance.kampala@diplomatie.gouv.fr; internet www.ambafrance-ug.org; Ambassador ALINE KUSTER-MÉNAGER.

Germany: 15 Philip Rd, Kololo, POB 7016, Kampala; tel. (41) 4501111; fax (41) 4501115; e-mail info@kampala.diplo.de; internet www.kampala.diplo.de; Ambassador KLAUS DIETER DÜXMANN.

Holy See: Chwa II Rd, Mbuya Hill, POB 7177, Kampala (Apostolic Nunciature); tel. (41) 4505619; fax (41) 4441774; e-mail nuntius@imul.com; Apostolic Nuncio PAUL TSCHANG IN-NAM (Titular Archbishop of Amanzia).

India: 11 Kyaddondo Rd, Nakasero, POB 7040, Kampala; tel. (41) 4257368; fax (41) 4254943; e-mail hoc@hicomindkampala.org; High Commissioner S. N. RAY.

Iran: 9 Bandali Rise, Bugolobi, POB 24529, Kampala; tel. (41) 4441689; fax (41) 4443590; Ambassador ALI A. DABIRAN.

Ireland: 25 Yusuf Lule Rd, Nakasero, POB 7791, Kampala; tel. (41) 7713000; fax (41) 4344353; e-mail kampalaembassy@dfa.ie; internet www.embassyofireland.ug; Ambassador KEVIN KELLY.

Italy: 11 Lourdel Rd, Nakasero, POB 4646, Kampala; tel. (41) 4250442; fax (41) 4250448; e-mail segreteria.kampala@esteri.it; internet www.ambkampala.esteri.it; Ambassador PIETRO BALLERO.

Japan: Plot 8, Kyaddondo Rd, Nakasero, POB 23553, Kampala; tel. (41) 4349542; fax (41) 4349547; e-mail jembassy@jembassy.co.ug; Ambassador KATO KEIICHI.

Kenya: 41 Nakasero Rd, POB 5220, Kampala; tel. (41) 4458235; fax (41) 4458239; e-mail kenyahicom@africaonline.co.ug; High Commissioner Maj.-Gen. (retd) GEOFFREY OKANGA LUKALE.

Korea, Democratic People's Republic: 10 Prince Charles Dr., Kololo, POB 5885, Kampala; tel. (41) 4546033; fax (41) 4450224; Ambassador JONG THAE YANG.

Libya: 26 Kololo Hill Dr., POB 6079, Kampala; tel. (41) 4344924; fax (41) 4344969; Sec. of People's Bureau ABDALLA ABDULMAULA BUJELDAIN.

Netherlands: Rwenzori Courts, 4th Floor, Plot 2, Nakasero Rd, POB 7728, Kampala; tel. (41) 2346000; fax (41) 2231861; e-mail kam@minbuza.nl; internet www.netherlandsembassyuganda.org; Ambassador JEROEN VERHEUL.

Nigeria: 33 Nakasero Rd, POB 4338, Kampala; tel. (41) 4433691; fax (41) 4432543; e-mail nighicom-sgu@africaonline.co.ug; High Commissioner FIDEL AYOGU.

Norway: 18B Akii-Bua Rd, Nakasero, POB 22770, Kampala; tel. (41) 7112000; fax (41) 4343936; e-mail emb.kampala@mfa.no; internet www.norway.go.ug; Ambassador BJØRG SCHONHOWD LEITE.

Russia: 28 Malcolm X Ave, Kololo, POB 7022, Kampala; tel. (41) 4433676; fax (41) 4345798; Ambassador SERGEI SHISHKIN.

Rwanda: 2 Nakaima Rd, POB 2468, Kampala; tel. (41) 4344045; fax (41) 4458547; e-mail Ambakampala@minaffet.gov.rw; internet www.uganda.embassy.gov.rw; High Commissioner Maj.-Gen. FRANK MUGAMBAGE.

Saudi Arabia: 3 Okurut Close, Kololo, POB 22558, Kampala; tel. (41) 4340614; fax (41) 4454017; Ambassador AHMAD BIN MUHAMMAD AL-BAHLAL.

South Africa: Plot 15A, Nakasero Rd, POB 22667, Kampala; tel. (41) 4343543; fax (41) 4348216; e-mail kampala.sahc@foreign.gov.za; High Commissioner THANDUYISE HENRY CHILIZA.

Sweden: 24 Lumumba Ave, Nakasero, POB 22669, Kampala; tel. (41) 7700800; fax (41) 7700801; e-mail ambassaden.kampala@foreign.ministry.se; internet www.swedenabroad.com/kampala; Ambassador ANDERS JOHNSON.

Tanzania: 6 Kagera Rd, Nakasero, POB 5750, Kampala; tel. (41) 4456272; fax (41) 4343973; High Commissioner RAJAB H. GAMAHA.

United Kingdom: Plot 4, Windsor Loop Rd, POB 7070, Kampala; tel. (31) 2312000; fax (41) 4257304; e-mail bhcinfo@starcom.co.ug; internet ukinuganda.fco.gov.uk; High Commissioner MARTIN SHEARMAN.

USA: Plot 1577, Ggaba Rd, POB 7007, Kampala; tel. (41) 4259791; fax (41) 4259794; e-mail kampalawebcontact@state.gov; internet kampala.usembassy.gov; Ambassador JERRY P. LAINER.

Judicial System

Courts of Judicature: High Court Bldg, POB 7085, Kampala; tel. (41) 4233420; fax (41) 4344116; e-mail info@judicature.go.ug; internet www.judicature.go.ug.

UGANDA

The Supreme Court
Plot 10, Upper Koloko, Seenu Awasthi Terrace, Mengo, Kampala. Hears appeals from the Court of Appeal. Also acts as a Constitutional Court.

Chief Justice: BENJAMIN ODOKI.
Deputy Chief Justice: L. E. M. MUKASA-KIKONYOGO.
The Court of Appeal: 5 Parliament Ave, Kampala; hears appeals from the High Court; the Court of Appeal consists of the Deputy Chief Justice and no fewer than seven Justices of Appeal, the number thereof being prescribed by Parliament.

The High Court
POB 7085, Kampala; tel. (41) 4233422.
Has full criminal and civil jurisdiction and also serves as a Constitutional Court. The High Court consists of the Principal Judge and 27 Puisne Judges.

Principal Judge: JAMES OGOOLA.
Magistrates' Courts: These are established under the Magistrates' Courts Act of 1970 and exercise limited jurisdiction in criminal and civil matters. The country is divided into magisterial areas, presided over by a Chief Magistrate. Under the Chief Magistrate there are two categories of Magistrates. The Magistrates preside alone over their courts. Appeals from the first category of Magistrates' Court lie directly to the High Court, while appeals from the second categories of Magistrates' Court lie to the Chief Magistrate's Court, and from there to the High Court. There are 27 Chief Magistrates' Courts, 52 Magistrates' Grade I Courts and 428 Magistrates' Grade II Courts.

Religion

Christianity is the majority religion—its adherents constitute approximately 75% of the population. Muslims account for approximately 15% of the population. A variety of other religions, including traditional indigenous religions, several branches of Hinduism, the Bahá'í Faith and Judaism, are practised freely and, combined, make up approximately 10% of the population. There are few atheists in the country. In many areas, particularly in rural settings, some religions tend to be syncretistic: deeply held traditional indigenous beliefs are blended into or observed alongside the rites of recognized religions, particularly in areas that are predominantly Christian. Missionary groups of several denominations are present and active in the country, including the Pentecostal Church, the Baptist Church, the Episcopal Church/Church of Uganda, the Church of Christ and the Mormons.

CHRISTIANITY
The Roman Catholic and Anglican Churches claim approximately the same number of followers, accounting for 90% of the country's professed Christians. The Seventh-day Adventist Church, the Church of Jesus Christ of Latter-day Saints (Mormons), the Orthodox Church, Jehovah's Witnesses, the Baptist Church, the Unification Church and the Pentecostal Church, among others, are also active.

The Anglican Communion
Anglicans are adherents of the Church of the Province of Uganda, comprising 29 dioceses. In 2002 there were about 8m. adherents.

Archbishop of Uganda and Bishop of Kampala: Most Rev. LIVINGSTONE MPALANYI-NKOYOYO, POB 14123, Kampala; tel. (41) 4270218; fax (41) 4251925; e-mail couab@uol.co.ug.

Greek Orthodox Church
Archbishop of East Africa: NICADEMUS OF IRINOUPOULIS (resident in Nairobi, Kenya); jurisidiction covers Kenya, Tanzania and Uganda.

The Roman Catholic Church
Uganda comprises four archdioceses and 15 dioceses. An estimated 43% of the total population was Roman Catholic.

Uganda Episcopal Conference
Uganda Catholic Secretariat, POB 2886, Kampala; tel. (41) 4510398; fax (41) 4510545.
f. 1974; Pres. Most Rev. MATTHIAS SSEKAMANYA (Archbishop of Lugazi).

Archbishop of Gulu: Most Rev. JOHN BAPTIST ODAMA, Archbishop's House, POB 200, Gulu; tel. (47) 4132026; fax (47) 4132860; e-mail metrog@archdioceseofgulu.org.

Archbishop of Kampala: CYPRIAN KIZITO LWANGA, Archbishop's House, POB 14125, Mengo, Kampala; tel. (41) 4270183; fax (41) 4345441; e-mail klarchdioc@utlonline.co.ug.

Archbishop of Mbarara: Most Rev. PAUL BAKYENGA, POB 150, Mbarara; tel. (48) 5420052; fax (48) 5421249; e-mail mbarchd@utlonline.co.ug.

Archbishop of Tororo: Most Rev. DENIS KIWANUKA LOTE, Archbishop's House, Plot 17 Boma Ave, POB 933, Mbale; tel. (45) 4433269; fax (45) 4433754; e-mail tororoad@africaonline.co.ug.

ISLAM
Muslims are mainly Sunni, although there are Shi'a followers of the Aga Khan among the Asian community.

The Uganda Muslim Supreme Council: POB 1146, Kampala; tel. (41) 4344499; fax (41) 4256500; Mufti of Uganda Sheikh SHABAN MUBAJJE; Chief Kadi and Pres. of Council HUSAYN RAJAB KAKOOZA.

BAHÁ'Í FAITH
National Spiritual Assembly: Kikaaya Hill Mile 4, Gayaza Rd, Kawempe Division, POB 2662, Kampala; tel. (31) 2262681; e-mail ugandabahai@gmail.com; mems resident in 2,721 localities.

JUDAISM
There is a small Jewish community, the Abayudaya, in central Uganda, with some 600 members and six synagogues.

The Press

DAILY AND OTHER NEWSPAPERS

The Citizen: Kampala; internet www.theugandacitizen.com; f. 2007; English.

The Daily Monitor: Plot 29–35, 8th St, POB 12141, Kampala; tel. (41) 4232367; fax (41) 4232369; e-mail editorial@monitor.co.ug; internet www.monitor.co.ug; f. 1992; daily; English; Man. Editor DAVID KALINAKI; circ. 22,000 (Mon.–Sat.), 24,000 (Sun.).

The Economy: POB 6787, Kampala; weekly; English; Editor ROLAND KAKOOZA.

Financial Times: Plot 17/19, Station Rd, POB 31399, Kampala; tel. (41) 4245798; bi-weekly; English; Editor G. A. ONEGI OBEL.

Focus: POB 268, Kampala; tel. (41) 4235086; fax (41) 4242796; f. 1983; publ. by Islamic Information Service and Material Centre; 4 a week; English; Editor HAJJI KATENDE; circ. 12,000.

Guide: POB 5350, Kampala; tel. (41) 4233486; fax (41) 4268045; f. 1989; weekly; English; Editor-in-Chief A. A. KALIISA; circ. 30,000.

Mulengera: POB 6787, Kampala; weekly; Luganda; Editor ROLAND KAKOOZA.

Munnansi News Bulletin: POB 7098, Kampala; f. 1980; weekly; English; owned by the Democratic Party; Editor ANTHONY SGEKWEYAMA.

Munno: POB 4027, Kampala; f. 1911; daily; Luganda; publ. by the Roman Catholic Church; Editor ANTHONY SSEKWEYAMA; circ. 7,000.

New Vision: POB 9815, Kampala; tel. (41) 4337000; fax (41) 4232050; e-mail editorial@newvision.co.ug; internet www.newvision.co.ug; f. 1986; official govt newspaper; daily; English; Editor-in-chief BARBARA KAIJA; Man. Editor BEN OPOLOT; circ. 34,000 (Mon.–Sat.), 42,000 (Sun.).

Bukedde: e-mail bukeddekussande@newvision.co.ug; daily; Luganda; Editor MAURICE SSEKWAUNGU; circ. 16,000.

Etop: e-mail etop@newvision.co.ug; weekly; vernacular; Editor KENNETH OLUKA; circ. 5,000.

Orumuri: tel. (48) 5421265; internet www.orumuri.co.ug; weekly; vernacular; Editor JOSSY MUHANGI; circ. 11,000.

Rupiny: e-mail rupiny@newvision.co.ug; weekly; vernacular; Editor CHRIS BANYA; circ. 5,000.

Ngabo: POB 9362, Kampala; tel. (41) 4242637; f. 1979; daily; Luganda; Editor MAURICE SEKAWUNGU; circ. 7,000.

The Star: POB 9362, Kampala; tel. (41) 4242637; f. 1980; revived 1984; daily; English; Editor SAMUEL KATWERE; circ. 5,000.

Taifa Uganda Empya: POB 1986, Kampala; tel. (41) 4254652; f. 1953; daily; Luganda; Editor A. SEMBOGA; circ. 24,000.

Weekly Topic: POB 1725, Kampala; tel. (41) 4233834; weekly; English; Editor JOHN WASSWA; circ. 13,000.

PERIODICALS

Eastern Africa Journal of Rural Development: Dept of Agricultural Economics and Agribusiness, Makerere University, POB 7062, Kampala; tel. 772616540 (mobile); fax (41) 4530858; e-mail bkiiza@infocom.co.ug; annual; Editor BARNABAS KIIZA; circ. 800.

UGANDA

The Exposure: POB 3179, Kampala; tel. (41) 4267203; fax (41) 4259549; monthly; politics.

The Independent: Kampala; internet www.independent.co.ug; f. 2007; weekly; Editor ANDREW MWENDA.

Leadership: POB 2522, Kampala; tel. (41) 4422407; fax (41) 4421576; f. 1956; 11 a year; English; Roman Catholic; circ. 7,400; Editor Fr CARLOS RODRÍGUEZ.

Mkombozi: c/o Ministry of Defence, Republic House, POB 3798, Kampala; tel. (41) 4270331; f. 1982; military affairs; Editor A. OPOLOTT.

Musizi: POB 4027, Mengo, Kampala; f. 1955; monthly; Luganda; Roman Catholic; Editor F. GITTA; circ. 30,000.

Pearl of Africa: POB 7142, Kampala; monthly; govt publ.

Uganda Confidential: POB 5576, Kampala; tel. (41) 4250273; fax (41) 4255288; e-mail ucl@swiftuganda.com; internet www.swiftuganda.com/~confidential; f. 1990; monthly; Editor TEDDY SSEZI-CHEEYE.

NEWS AGENCY

Uganda News Agency (UNA): POB 7142, Kampala; tel. (41) 4232734; fax (41) 4342259; Dir CRISPUS MUNDUA (acting).

Publishers

Centenary Publishing House Ltd: POB 6246, Kampala; tel. (41) 4241599; fax (41) 4250427; f. 1977; religious (Anglican); Man. Dir Rev. SAM KAKIZA.

Fountain Publishers Ltd: POB 488, Kampala; tel. (41) 4259163; fax (41) 4251160; e-mail fountain@starcom.co.ug; internet www.fountainpublishers.co.ug; f. 1989; general, school textbooks, children's books, academic, scholarly; Man. Dir JAMES TUMUSIIME.

Longman Uganda Ltd: POB 3409, Kampala; tel. (41) 4242940; f. 1965; Man. Dir M. K. L. MUTYABA.

Uganda Printing and Publishing Corporation (UPPC): POB 33, Entebbe; tel. (41) 4220639; fax (41) 4220530; e-mail info@uppc.co.ug; internet www.uppc.co.ug; f. 1993; Man. Dir BAKAAWA ELIZABETH.

Broadcasting and Communications

TELECOMMUNICATIONS

Airtel Uganda Ltd: Celtel House, 40 Wampewo Ave, Kololo, POB 6771, Kampala; tel. 752230110 (mobile); fax (41) 4230106; e-mail info.africa@airtel.com; internet africa.airtel.com/uganda; f. 1995; fmrly Celtel Uganda, subsequently Zain Uganda, present name adopted 2010; Man. Dir V. G. SOMASEKHAR.

MTN Uganda Ltd: MTN Towers, 22 Hannington Rd, POB 24624, Kampala; tel. and fax (31) 2212333; e-mail mtn@mtn.co.ug; internet www.mtn.co.ug; f. 1998.

Orange Uganda: Plot 28–30, Clement Hill Rd, POB 24144, Kampala; tel. 790000100 (mobile); e-mail care@orange.co.ug; internet www.orange.ug; f. 2009 following acquisition by France Telecom of a 53% stake in the Ugandan mobile phone operator Hits Telecom Uganda Ltd; provides mobile cellular telecommunications services; CEO PHILIPPE LUXCEY.

Uganda Communications Commission: Communications House, 12th Floor, 1 Colville St, POB 7376, Kampala; tel. (41) 4339000; fax (41) 4348832; e-mail ucc@ucc.co.ug; internet www.ucc.co.ug; f. 1998; regulatory body; Chair. Dr A. M. S. KATAHOIRE; Exec. Dir PATRICK MASAMBU.

Uganda Telecom Ltd (UTL): Rwenzori Courts, Plot 2/4A, Nakasero Rd, POB 7171, Kampala; tel. (41) 4333200; fax (41) 4345907; e-mail info@utlonline.co.ug; internet www.utl.co.ug; f. 1998; state-owned; privatization pending; Man. Dir ABDULBASET ELAZZABI.

WARID Telecom: Plot 16A, Clement Hill Rd, POB 70665, Kampala; tel. 700100100 (mobile); fax 200221111; e-mail customercare@waridtel.co.ug; internet waridtel.co.ug; f. 2006; CEO MADHUR TANEJA.

BROADCASTING

Regulatory Body

Uganda Broadcasting Council (UBC): Broadcasting Council Secretariat, Worker's House, Northern wing, 6th Floor, Plot 1, Pilkington Rd, POB 27553, Kampala; tel. (41) 4251452; fax (41) 4250612; e-mail info@broadcastug.com; internet www.broadcastug.com; f. 1998; statutory body enacted by the Electronic Media Act of 2000; main functions include licensing and regulating radio and television stations, video and cinema operators and libraries for hiring out video recordings or cinema films; consists of 12 mems appointed by the Minister of Information Communication Technology; Chair. GODFREY MUTABAAZI; Dir-Gen. EDGAR TABAARO.

Radio

91.3 Capital FM: POB 7638, Kampala; tel. (41) 4235092; fax (41) 4344556; f. 1993; independent music station broadcasting from Kampala, Mbarara and Mbale; Chief Officers WILLIAM PIKE, PATRICK QUARCOO.

Central Broadcasting Service (CBS): POB 12760, Kampala; tel. (41) 4272993; fax (41) 4340031; f. 1996; independent station broadcasting in local languages and English to most of Uganda; Man. Dir KAAYA KAVUMA.

Radio One: Duster St, POB 4589, Kampala; tel. (41) 4348211; fax (41) 4344385; e-mail info@radioonefm90.com; internet www.radioonefm90.com.

Sanyu Radio: Katto Plaza, Nkrumah Rd, Kampala; f. 1993; independent station broadcasting to Kampala and its environs.

UBC Radio: Plot 17/19, Nile Ave, POB 2038, Kampala; tel. (41) 4257257; fax (41) 4257252; e-mail ubc@ubconline.co.ug; internet ubconline.co.ug; f. 1954; state-controlled; under Uganda Broadcasting Corpn (UBC), formed by merger of Radio Uganda and Uganda Television in 2005; broadcasts in 23 languages, including English and Ugandan vernacular languages, through four stations, Red, Blue, Butebo and Star FM; Man. Dir EDWARD MUKASA.

Voice of Toro: POB 2203, Kampala.

Television

Sanyu Television: Naguru; f. 1994; independent station broadcasting to Kampala and its environs.

UBC TV: Plot 17/19, Nile Ave, POB 2038, Kampala; tel. (41) 4257897; fax (41) 4257252; e-mail ubc@ubconline.co.ug; internet ubconline.co.ug; f. 1962; state-controlled commercial service; under Uganda Broadcasting Corpn (UBC), formed by merger of Radio Uganda and Uganda Television in 2005; programmes mainly in English, also in Swahili and Luganda; transmits over a radius of 320 km from Kampala; five relay stations are in operation, others are under construction; Man. Dir EDWARD MUKASA.

Finance

(cap. = capital; res = reserves; dep. = deposits; m. = million; brs = branches; amounts in new Uganda shillings, unless otherwise indicated)

BANKING

In August 2010 there were 22 commercial banks, three credit institutions and three microfinance deposit-taking institutions in Uganda.

Central Bank

Bank of Uganda: 37–43 Kampala Rd, POB 7120, Kampala; tel. (41) 4258441; fax (41) 4230878; e-mail info@bou.or.ug; internet www.bou.or.ug; f. 1966; bank of issue; cap. 20,000m., res 1,099,687m., dep. 5,416,569m. (June 2009); Gov. EMMANUEL TUMUSIIME-MUTEBILE; Dep. Gov. DAVID G. OPIOKELLO (acting).

State Bank

Uganda Development Bank Ltd (UDBL): 15A Clement Hill Rd, Ruth Towers, POB 7210, Kampala; tel. (41) 4355555; fax (41) 4355556; e-mail info@udbl.co.ug; internet www.udbl.co.ug; f. 1972; state-owned; reorg. 2001; cap. 11m. (Dec. 1993); CEO GABRIEL OTUDA ETOU.

Commercial Banks

ABC Capital Bank (U) Ltd: Colline House, Plot 4, Pilkington Rd, POB 21091, Kampala; tel. (41) 4345200; fax (41) 4258310; e-mail abc@abccapitalbank.com; f. 2009.

Bank of Africa—Uganda Ltd: Plot 45, Jinja Rd, POB 2750, Kampala; tel. (41) 4302001; fax (41) 4230902; e-mail boa@boa-uganda.com; internet www.boa-uganda.com; f. 1986 as Allied Bank International (Uganda); name changed as above in 2005; 47.7% owned by Bank of Africa—Kenya, 21.9% by Aureos East Africa Fund, 19.8% by The Netherlands Development Finance Co, 10.6% by Central Holdings Ltd; cap. 7,508m., res 9,599m., dep. 174,631m. (Dec. 2009); Chair. JOHN CARRUTHERS; Man. Dir MICHEL KAHN; 5 brs.

Cairo International Bank: 30 Kampala Rd, POB 7052, Kampala; tel. (41) 4230132; fax (41) 4230130; e-mail moona@cib.co.ug; internet www.cairointernationalbank.co.ug; 44.4% owned by Banque du Caire, 36.1% owned by Kato Aromatics SAE, 6.5% each owned by Bank of Egypt, Bank Misr and Bank of Alexandria; cap. 7,135m. (Dec. 2003); Chair. JOHN ELANGOT; Man. Dir NABIL GHANEM.

UGANDA

Crane Bank Ltd: Crane Chambers, 38 Kampala Rd, POB 22572, Kampala; tel. (41) 4345345; fax (41) 4231578; e-mail cranebank@cranebanklimited.com; internet www.cranebanklimited.com; f. 1995; wholly owned by various private investors; cap. 50,000m., res 9,948m., dep. 418,768m. (Dec. 2009); Chair. J. BIRIBONWA; Man. Dir A. R. KALAN.

DFCU Bank Ltd: Plot 2, Jinja Rd, POB 70, Kampala; tel. (41) 4256891; fax (41) 4231687; e-mail dfcubank@dfcugroup.com; internet www.dfcugroup.com; f. 1984 as Gold Trust Bank Ltd; current name adopted 2000; 60.02% owned by Commonwealth Development Corpn; total assets US $114.3m. (Dec. 2006); Chair. NKOSANA MOYO; Man. Dir GEORGE E. MORTIMER.

Diamond Trust Bank (Uganda) Ltd: Diamond Trust Bldg, Plot 17–19, Kampala Rd, POB 7155, Kampala; tel. (41) 4259331; fax (41) 4342286; e-mail info@dtbuganda.co.ug; internet www.dtbafrica.com; f. 1995; 40% owned by The Diamond Jubilee Investment Trust, 33.3% owned by Aga Khan Fund for Economic Development, 26.7% owned by Diamond Trust Bank Kenya Ltd; cap. 6,000m., res 3,400m., dep. 182,961m. (Dec. 2009); Chair. MAHMOOD MANJI; CEO VARGHESE THAMBI.

Ecobank Uganda Ltd: Plot 4, Parliament Ave, POB 7368, Kampala; tel. (41) 7700231; fax (31) 2266079; e-mail ecobankug@ecobank.com; internet www.ecobank.com; f. 2008; Chair. DAVID TWAHIRWA; Man. Dir OLADELE ADEBIYI ALABI.

Equity Bank Uganda Ltd: Plot 390, Muteesa 1 Rd, Katwe, POB 10184, Kampala; tel. (31) 2262437; fax (31) 2262436; e-mail info@equitybank.co.ug; internet www.equitybank.co.ug; Chair. PETER MUNGA; Exec. Dir APOLLO N. NJOROGE.

Fina Bank Uganda Ltd: Plot 7, Buganda Rd, POB 7323, Kampala; tel. (41) 4237305; fax (41) 4237305; e-mail banking@finabank.co.ug; internet www.finabank.com/ug; f. 2008; Chair. DHANU HANSRAJ CHANDARIA; CEO CHARLES NALYAALI.

Global Trust Bank (U) Ltd: Plot 2A, Kampala Rd, POB 72747, Kampala; tel. (41) 7100700; fax (41) 4254007; e-mail globaltrust@bankglobaltrust.com; internet www.bankglobaltrust.com; Chair. PETER KABATSI; Man. Dir CHARLES AJAEGBU (acting).

Mercantile Credit Bank Ltd: Plot 10, Old Port Bell Rd, POB 620, Kampala; tel. and fax (41) 4235967; e-mail mcb@afsat.com; cap. 1,000m. (Dec. 2003); Chair. PALLE MOELLER; Man. NELSON LUGOLOBI.

National Bank of Commerce (Uganda) Ltd: Cargen House, Plot 13A, Parliament Ave, POB 23232, Kampala; tel. (41) 2347699; fax (41) 2347701; e-mail nbc@swiftuganda.com; cap. 4,631m. (Dec. 2003); Chair. AMOS NZEYI; Man. Dir G. BANGERA.

Orient Bank Ltd: Orient Plaza, Plot 6/6A, Kampala Rd, POB 3072, Kampala; tel. (41) 4236012; fax (41) 4236066; e-mail mail@orient-bank.com; internet www.orient-bank.com; f. 1993; cap. 5,000m., res 2,440m., dep. 205,920m. (Dec. 2009); Chair. MICHAEL COOK; CEO MAXWELL IBEANUSI; 6 brs.

Post Bank Uganda Ltd: Plot 11/13, Nkrumah Rd, POB 7189, Kampala; tel. (41) 4258551; fax (41) 4347107; e-mail postbank@imul.com; wholly state-owned; cap. 2,000m. (Dec. 2003); Chair. STEPHEN MWANJE.

Development Banks

Capital Finance Corpn Ltd: 4 Pilkington Rd, POB 21091, Kampala; tel. (41) 4345200; fax (41) 4258310; 70% owned by City Credit Bank Ltd; Chair. KEMAL LALANI; Man. Dir and CEO GHULAM HAIDER DAUDANI.

Centenary Rural Development Bank: 7 Entebbe Rd, POB 1892, Kampala; tel. (41) 4251276; fax (41) 4251273; e-mail info@centenarybank.co.ug; internet www.centenarybank.co.ug; cap. 4,020.5m., res 6,675.5m., dep. 448,308.5m. (Dec. 2009); Chair. Dr JOHN DDUMBA SSENTAMU; Man. Dir FABIAN KASI.

Development Finance Co of Uganda Ltd: Rwenzori House, 1 Lumumba Ave, POB 2767, Kampala; tel. (41) 4231215; fax (41) 4259435; e-mail dfcu@dfcugroup.com; internet www.dfcugroup.com; owned by Commonwealth Devt Corpn (60%), Uganda Devt Corpn (18.5%) and International Finance Corpn (21.5%); cap. 3,978m. (Dec. 2003); Chair. WILLIAM S. KALEMA; Man. Dir C. MCCORMACK.

East African Development Bank (EADB): East African Development Bank Bldg, 4 Nile Ave, POB 7128, Kampala; tel. (41) 4230021; fax (41) 4259763; e-mail admin@eadb.org; internet www.eadb.org; f. 1967; majority stake held by the Govts of Kenya, Tanzania and Uganda; provides financial and tech. assistance to promote industrial development within Uganda, Kenya, Rwanda and Tanzania; regional offices in Nairobi (Kenya), Kigali (Rwanda) and Dar es Salaam (Tanzania); cap. US $99.8m., res US $11.1m., dep. US $118.7 (Dec. 2009); Dir-Gen. APOPO VIVIENNE.

Housing Finance Bank Ltd: Investment House, 25 Kampala Rd, POB 1539, Kampala; tel. (41) 4259651; fax (41) 4341429; internet www.housingfinance.co.ug; f. 1967; 45% owned by Govt, 50% owned by National Social Security Fund, 5% owned by National Housing and Construction Corpn; cap. 61,000.0m., res 6,475.4m., dep. 109,411.7m. (Dec. 2009); Chair. KEITH MUHAKANIZI; Man. Dir NICHOLAS OKWIR.

Foreign Banks

Bank of Baroda (Uganda) Ltd (India): 18 Kampala Rd, POB 7197, Kampala; tel. (41) 4233680; fax (41) 4230781; e-mail bobho@spacenet.co.ug; internet www.bankofbaroda.com; f. 1953; 80% owned by Bank of Baroda (India); cap. 4,000m., res 5,647m., dep. 126,995m. (Dec. 2004); Chair. and Man. Dir M. D. MALLYA; 6 brs.

Barclays Bank of Uganda Ltd (United Kingdom): Barclay House, Plot 4, Hannington Rd, POB 7101, Kampala; tel. (31) 4218300; fax (31) 4259467; e-mail barclays.uganda@barclays.com; internet www.barclays.com; f. 1969; wholly owned by Barclays Bank PLC (United Kingdom); cap. 4,000m., res 15,236m., dep. 328,553m. (Dec. 2005); Chair. GEORGE EGADU; Man. Dir CHARLES ONGWAE; 4 brs.

Citibank (Uganda) Ltd (USA): Plot 4, Centre Court, Ternan Ave, Nakasero, POB 7505, Kampala; tel. (41) 4305500; fax (41) 4340624; internet www.citibank.com/eastafrica/uganda.htm; 99.9% owned by Citicorp Overseas Investment Corpn, 0.1% owned by Foremost Investment; cap. 21,285m. (Dec. 2003); Chair. Prof. J. M. L. SSEBUWUUFU; Man. Dir SHIRISH BHIDE.

Stanbic Bank Uganda Ltd (United Kingdom): Crested Towers, Short Tower, 17 Hannington Rd, POB 7131, Kampala; tel. (31) 4224111; fax (41) 4231116; e-mail ugandainfo@stanbic.com; internet www.stanbicbank.co.ug; f. 1906 as National Bank of India Uganda; adopted present name 1993; 80% owned by Stanbic Africa Holdings Ltd (United Kingdom); merged with Uganda Commercial Bank Ltd 2002; cap. 5,119m., res 67,880m., dep. 1,539,873m. (Dec. 2009); Chair. Dr MARTIN ALIKER; Man. Dir KITILI MBATHI; 2 brs.

Standard Chartered Bank Uganda Ltd (United Kingdom): 5 Speke Rd, POB 7111, Kampala; tel. (41) 44258211; fax (41) 44231473; e-mail scb.uganda@ug.standardchartered.com; internet www.standardchartered.com/ug; f. 1912; wholly owned by Standard Chartered Bank PLC; cap. 4,000m., res 22,806m., dep. 604,380m. (Dec. 2006); Chair. JAMES MULWANA; Man. Dir LAMIN MANJANG; 7 brs.

Tropical Bank (Libya): Plot 27, Kampala Rd, POB 9485, Kampala; tel. (41) 4313100; fax (31) 2264494; e-mail admin@trobank.com; internet www.trobank.com; f. 1972; 99.7% owned by Libyan Arab Foreign Bank; cap. 30,000m., res 8,433m., dep. 125,314m. (Dec. 2009); Chair. GERALD SENDAULA; Man. Dir PRINCE KASSIM NAKIBINGE.

United Bank for Africa (Uganda) Ltd: Spear House, Plot 22, Jinja Rd, POB 7396, Kampala; tel. (41) 7715122; fax (41) 7715117; f. 2008; CEO MARGARET MWANAKATWE; 5 brs.

STOCK EXCHANGE

Uganda Securities Exchange: Workers' House, 2nd Floor, Northern Wing, 1 Pilkington Rd, POB 23552, Kampala; tel. (41) 4343297; fax (41) 4343841; internet www.use.or.ug; f. 1997; Chair. CHARLES MBIRE; Chief Exec. JOSEPH S. KITAMIRIKE.

INSURANCE

In March 2011 there were 22 insurance companies licensed to operate in Uganda.

APA Insurance (Uganda) Ltd: Crown House, 1st Floor, Plot 4A, Kampala Rd, POB 7651, Kampala; tel. (41) 4250087; e-mail apa.uganda@apainsurance.org.

Chartis Uganda Insurance Co Ltd: Plot 60, Bombo Rd, POB 7077, Kampala; tel. (41) 4533781; fax (41) 4541572; internet www.chartisinsurance.com/ug-about-us_918_210594.html; f. 1962; fmrly AIG Uganda Insurance Co Ltd; name changed as above in 2009; Man. Dir ALEX WANJOHI; 3 brs.

East Africa General Insurance Co Ltd: Plot 14, Kampala Rd, POB 1392, Kampala; tel. (31) 22262221; fax (41) 4343234; e-mail vkrishna@eagen.co.ug; internet www.eagen.co.ug; f. 1949; public shareholding co; fire, life, motor, marine and accident; CEO VYASA KRISHNA.

Excel Insurance Co Ltd: Crest House, Plot 2D, Nkurumah Rd, POB 7213, Kampala; tel. (41) 4348595; fax (41) 4342304; e-mail excelins@infocom.co.ug; internet www.excelinsurance.co.ug; Man. Dir JOHN SSENTAMU DDUMBA.

First Insurance Co Ltd: King Fahd Plaza, 2nd Floor, Plot 52, Kampala Rd, POB 5254, Kampala; tel. (41) 4342863; fax (41) 345923.

GoldStar Insurance Co Ltd: Plot 38, Kampala Rd, Crane Chambers, POB 7781, Kampala; tel. (41) 4250110; fax (41) 4254956; e-mail goldstar@goldstarinsurance.com; Man. Dir AZIM THARANI.

Lion Assurance Co Ltd: Tall Tower, 12th Floor, Crested Towers Bldg, POB 7658, Kampala; tel. (41) 4341450; fax (41) 4257027; e-mail insure@lion.co.ug; fmrly Pan World Insurance Co Ltd; Chair. OWEK. GODFREY K. KAVUMA; Gen. Man. GEORGE ALANDE.

National Insurance Corporation: Plot 3, Pilkington Rd, POB 7134, Kampala; tel. (41) 4258001; fax (41) 4259925; e-mail nic@nic.co.ug; internet www.nic.co.ug; f. 1964; 60% owned by IGI PLC, Nigeria; general and life; Chair. REMI OLOWUDE; Man. Dir SAM JEFF NJOROGE.

NICO Insurance (Uganda) Ltd: 3rd Floor, Greenland Towers, Kampala Rd, Opposite Bank of Uganda, POB 24256, Kampala; tel. (31) 2264720; fax (31) 2264723; internet www.nicomw.com; subsidiary of NICO Holdings Ltd (based in Malawi); Man. Dir RONALD ZAKE.

Phoenix of Uganda Assurance Co Ltd: Workers House, Northern Wing, 8th Floor, Pilkington Rd, POB 70149, Kampala; tel. (41) 349664; fax (41) 349662; e-mail info@phoenixuganda.com; internet phoenixassurancegroup.com; f. 2003; Chair. MAHEBOOB ALIBHAI; Gen. Man. V. PARTHASARATHI.

Rio Insurance Co Ltd: Plot 20, Kampala Rd, POB 5710, Kampala; tel. (41) 4341264; fax (41) 4235292.

Statewide Insurance Co Ltd (SWICO): Sure House, Plot 1, Bombo Rd, POB 9393, Kampala; tel. (41) 4345996; fax (41) 4343403; e-mail swico@infocom.co.ug; internet www.swico.co.ug; f. 1982; Man. Dir JOSEPH KIWANUKA.

TransaAfrica Assurance Co Ltd: Impala House, Plot 13/15, Kimathi Ave, POB 7601, Kampala; tel. (41) 4251411; fax (41) 4254511; e-mail taacl@spacenet.co.ug.

UAP Insurance Co Ltd: Plot 1, Kimathi Ave, POB 7185, Kampala; tel. (41) 4234190; fax (41) 4256388; e-mail uac@starcom.co.ug; internet www.uap.co.ug; Chair. RONALD KALYANGO.

Uganda Co-operative Insurance Ltd: Plot 10, Bombo Rd, POB 6176, Kampala; tel. (41) 4241836; fax (41) 4258231; f. 1982; general; Chair. EPHRAIM KAKURU; Gen. Man. (vacant).

Regulatory Authority

Uganda Insurance Commission: NIC Building Annexe, 3rd Floor, Plot 3, Pilkington Rd, POB 22855; tel. (41) 4346712; fax (41) 4349260; e-mail uic@uginscom.go.ug; Chair. ELIAS B. KASOZI.

Insurance Association

Uganda Insurers Association: Plot 24A, Acacia Ave, Kololo, POB 8912, Kampala; tel. (41) 4230469; fax (41) 4500944; internet www.uia.co.ug; f. 1965; Chair. SOLOMON RUBONDO.

Trade and Industry

GOVERNMENT AGENCIES

Capital Markets Authority: 8th Floor, Jubilee Insurance Centre, 14 Parliament Ave, POB 24565, Kampala; tel. (41) 4342788; fax (41) 4342803; e-mail info@cmauganda.co.ug; internet www.cmauganda.co.ug; f. 1996 to develop, promote and regulate capital markets sector; Chair. HAJI TWAHA KAWASSE; CEO JAPHETH KATTO.

Enterprise Development Unit (EPD): Kampala; oversees privatization programme; Exec. Dir LEONARD MUGANWA.

Export and Import Licensing Division: POB 7000, Kampala; tel. (41) 4258795; f. 1987; advises importers and exporters and issues import and export licences; Prin. Commercial Officer JOHN MUHWEZI.

Uganda Advisory Board of Trade: POB 6877, Kampala; tel. (41) 4233311; f. 1974; issues trade licences and services for exporters.

Uganda Export Promotion Board: POB 5045, Kampala; tel. (41) 4230233; fax (41) 4259779; e-mail uepc@starcom.co.ug; internet www.ugandaexportsonline.com; f. 1983; provides market intelligence, organizes training, trade exhibitions, etc.; Exec. Dir FLORENCE KATE.

Uganda Investment Authority: Investment Centre, TWED Plaza, Plot 22, Lumumba Ave, POB 7418, Kampala; tel. (41) 4301000; fax (41) 4342903; e-mail info@ugandainvest.com; internet www.ugandainvest.com; f. 1991; promotes foreign and local investment, assists investors, provides business information, issues investment licences; Exec. Dir Dr MAGGIE KIGOZI.

DEVELOPMENT ORGANIZATIONS

National Housing and Construction Corpn: Crested Towers, POB 659, Kampala; tel. (41) 4330002; fax (41) 4258708; e-mail sales@nhcc.co.ug; internet www.nhcc.co.ug; f. 1964; govt agent for building works; also develops residential housing; Chair. Dr COLIN SENTONGO; Gen. Man. M. S. KASEKENDE.

Uganda Industrial Development Corpn Ltd: 9–11 Parliament Ave, POB 7042, Kampala; tel. (41) 4234381; fax (41) 4241588; f. 1952; Chair. SAM RUTEGA.

CHAMBER OF COMMERCE

Uganda National Chamber of Commerce and Industry: Plot 2, 1st Floor, Parliament Ave, Jumbo Plaza, POB 3809, Kampala; tel. (41) 4503024; fax (41) 4230310; e-mail info@chamberuganda.com; internet www.chamberuganda.com; Chair. OLIVE Z. KIGONGO.

INDUSTRIAL AND TRADE ASSOCIATIONS

CMB Ltd (Coffee Marketing Board): POB 7154, Kampala; tel. (41) 4254051; fax (41) 4230790; state-owned; privatization pending; purchases and exports coffee; Chair. Dr DDUMBA SSENTAMU; Man. Dir SAM KIGGUNDU.

Cotton Development Organization: POB 7018, Kampala; tel. (41) 4232968; fax (41) 4232975; Man. Dir JOLLY SABUNE.

Produce Marketing Board: Plot 15, Clement Hill Rd, POB 3705, Kampala; tel. (41) 232968; fax (41) 232975; internet cdouga.org; Gen. Man. ESTHER KAMPAMPARA.

Uganda Coffee Development Authority (UCDA): Coffee House, Plot 35, Jinja Rd, POB 7267, Kampala; tel. (41) 4256940; fax (41) 4256994; e-mail ucdajc@ugandacoffee.org; internet www.ugandacoffee.org; f. 1991; enforces quality control and promotes coffee exports, maintains statistical data, advises Govt on local and world prices and trains processors and quality controllers; Chair. FABIANO R. TIBEITA; Man. Dir HENRY A. NGABIRANO.

Uganda Manufacturers' Association (UMA): Lugogo Show Grounds, POB 6966, Kampala; tel. (41) 4221034; fax (41) 4220285; e-mail administration@uma.or.ug; internet www.uma.or.ug; f. 1988; promotes mfrs' interests; Chair. KADDU KIBERU.

Uganda Tea Authority: POB 4161, Kampala; tel. (41) 4231003; state-owned; controls and co-ordinates activities of the tea industry; Gen. Man. MIRIA MARGARITA MUGABI.

EMPLOYERS' ORGANIZATION

Federation of Uganda Employers: Plot 60, Veron House, Ntinda, POB 3820, Kampala; tel. (41) 4220201; fax (41) 4286290; e-mail fue@infocom.co.ug; internet www.employers.co.ug; f. 1958; Chair. ALOYSIUS K. SSEMMANDA; Exec. Dir ROSEMARY N. SSENABULYA.

UTILITIES

Electricity

Electricity Regulatory Authority (ERA): ERA House, Plot 15, Shimon Rd, Nakasero, POB 10332, Kampala; tel. (41) 4341852; fax (41) 4341624; e-mail era@africaonline.co.ug; internet www.era.or.ug; f. 1999; CEO Eng. Dr F. B. SEBBOWA.

Uganda Electricity Distribution Co Ltd: Plot 29/33, Amber House, Kampala Rd, POB 7390, Kampala; tel. (31) 2330300; fax (41) 4255600; e-mail contact@uedcl.co.ug; internet www.uedcl.com; f. 2001 as one of the successor bodies of the Uganda Electricity Board; privatized and operations handed over to UMEME Uganda Ltd in 2005 under a 20-year concession agreement; functions as a statutory body overseeing the operations of UMEME Uganda Ltd; Chair. GAD GASAATURA.

  UMEME Uganda Ltd: Rwenzori House, Plot 1, 2nd Floor, Lumumba Ave, POB 23841, Kampala; tel. (41) 2360600; e-mail info@umeme.co.ug; internet www.umeme.co.ug; f. 2005; develops, operates and maintains the electricity distribution network on behalf of Uganda Electricity Distribution Co Ltd; Man. Dir CHARLES CHAPMAN.

Uganda Electricity Generation Co Ltd: Plot 2–8, Faraday Rd, Ambercourt, POB 1001, Jinja; tel. (43) 4120891; fax (43) 4123064; f. 2001 as one of the successor bodies of the Uganda Electricity Board; Man. Dir JOHN MUGYENZI.

Uganda Electricity Transmission Co Ltd: Plot 10, Hannington Rd, POB 7625, Kampala; tel. (41) 4233433; fax (41) 3441789; e-mail transco@uetcl.com; internet www.uetcl.com; f. 2001; as one of the successor bodies of the Uganda Electricity Board; Man. Dir E. KIYEMBA.

Water

National Water & Sewerage Corpn: Plot 39, Jinja Rd, POB 7053, Kampala; tel. (41) 4315100; fax (41) 4258299; e-mail info@nwsc.co.ug; internet www.nwsc.co.ug; f. 1972; serves 22 towns; privatization pending; Man. Dir WILLIAM TSIMWA MUHAIRWE.

CO-OPERATIVES

In 2000 there were 6,313 co-operative societies, grouped in 34 unions. There is at least one co-operative union in each administrative district.

Uganda Co-operative Alliance: Plot 47/49, Nkurumah Rd, Kampala; tel. (41) 4258898; e-mail ucainfocen@uca.co.ug; internet www.uca.co.ug; co-ordinating body for co-operative unions, of which the following are among the most important:

UGANDA

Bugisu Co-operative Union Ltd: Palisa Rd, Private Bag, Mbale; tel. (45) 4233027; f. 1954; processors and exporters of Bugisu Arabica coffee; 226 mem. socs; Gen. Man. WOMUTU.

East Mengo Growers' Co-operative Union Ltd: POB 7092, Kampala; tel. (41) 4270383; fax (41) 4243502; f. 1968; processors and exporters of coffee and cotton; 280 mem. socs; Chair. FRANCIS MUKAMA; Man. JOSEPH SSEMOGERERE.

Kakumiro Growers' Co-operative Union: POB 511, Kakumiro; processing of coffee and cotton; Sec. and Man. TIBIHWA-RUKEERA.

Kimeeme Livestock Co-operative Society: Mwanga II Rd, POB 6670, Kampala; f. 1984; farming and marketing of livestock; Chair. SAMUSI LUKIMA.

Lango Co-operative Union: POB 59, Lira; f. 1956; ginning and exporting of conventional and organic cotton produce; Chair. JOHNSON ENGOLE.

Masaka Co-operative Union Ltd: POB 284, Masaka; tel. (48) 1420260; f. 1951; coffee, dairy farming, food processing, carpentry; 245 primary co-operative socs; Chair. J. M. KASOZI; Gen. Man. EDWARD C. SSERUUMA.

Nyakatonzi Growers Co-operative Union: Fort Portal Rd, POB 32, Kasese; tel. (48) 3444370; fax (48) 3444135; f. 1957; processors and exporters of coffee and cotton; Gen. Man. ADAM BWAMBALE.

South Bukedi Co-operative Union: 6 Busia Rd, POB 101, Tororo; tel. (45) 4244327; f. 1952; ginning and export of cotton lint; Gen. Man. MICHAEL O. OGUNDY.

South-west Nile Co-operative Union: POB 33, Pakwach, Nebbi; f. 1958; ginning and export of cotton; Gen. Man. PHILIP UPAKRWOTH.

Uganda Co-operative Savings and Credit Society: 62 Parliament Ave, POB 9452, Kampala; tel. (41) 4257410; f. 1973; Chair. PATRICK KAYONGO.

Uganda Co-operative Transport Union: 41 Bombo Rd, POB 5486, Kampala; tel. and fax (41) 4567506; e-mail uctultd@infocom.co.ug; f. 1971; general transport, imports of motor vehicles, vehicle repair and maintenance; Gen. Man. NUWAGIRA NABOTH MWEJUNE.

Wamala Growers' Co-operative Union Ltd: POB 99, Mityana; tel. (46) 4442036; e-mail kizitoherbert@yahoo.com; f. 1968; coffee and cotton growers, real estate agents, cattle ranchers, printers, mfrs of edible oils, bricks, tiles and clay products; 250 mem. socs; Gen. Man. HERBERT KIZITO.

West Mengo Growers' Co-operative Union Ltd: POB 7039, Kampala; tel. (41) 4567511; f. 1948; cotton growing and buying, coffee buying and processing, maize milling; 250 mem. socs; Chair. H. E. KATABALWA MIIRO.

West Nile Tobacco Co-operative Union: Wandi, POB 71, Arua; f. 1965; growing, curing and marketing of tobacco; Gen. Man. ANDAMAH BABWA.

TRADE UNIONS

National Organization of Trade Unions (NOTU): Plot 64, Ntinda Rd, POB 2150, Kampala; tel. (41) 4256295; fax (41) 4259833; e-mail notu@ifocom.co.ug; internet www.notu.or.ug; f. 1973; Chair. OWERE USHER WILSON; Sec.-Gen. PETER CHRISTOPHER WERIKHE; 89,500 mems (2007).

Amalgamated Transport and General Workers' Union: POB 30407, Kampala; tel. (41) 232508; fax (41) 341541; e-mail atgwu@utlonline.co.ug; internet www.atgwu.or.ug; f. 1938.

Transport

RAILWAYS

In 2002 there were 260 km of track in operation. A programme to rehabilitate the railway network is under way. A 725-km railway project to link Gulu in northern Uganda with Juba, South Sudan, has been under consideration since 2004. There are also plans to upgrade and re-open the 333-km Kampala–Kasese railway line.

Uganda Railways Corporation (URC): Plot 53, 1st Floor, Nasser Rd, POB 7150, Kampala; tel. (41) 4254961; fax (41) 4344405; f. 1977 following the dissolution of East African Railways; management of operations assumed by Rift Valley Railways consortium in Nov. 2006; CEO I. IYAMULEMYE.

ROADS

In 2006 Uganda's road network consisted of approximately 10,800 km of national or trunk roads (of which some 2,200 km were bituminized, the rest being gravel), 27,500 km of district or feeder roads, 4,300 km of urban roads (comprising roads in Kampala City, the 13 municipal councils and the 50 town councils in the country) and 30,000 km of community roads. There are also private roads, some of which are open to the general travelling public. Road transport remains the dominant mode of transport in terms of scale of infrastructure and the volume of freight and passenger movement. The National (Trunk) Road Network carries 80% of Uganda's passenger and freight traffic and includes international routes linking Uganda to neighbouring countries and to the sea (via Kenya and Tanzania), and internal roads linking areas of high population and large administrative and commercial centres. It provides the only form of access to most rural communities. The Government is implementing a programme of continuous upgrading of key gravel roads to bitumen standard.

INLAND WATERWAYS

A rail wagon ferry service connecting Jinja with the Tanzanian port of Tanga, via Mwanza, was inaugurated in 1983, thus reducing Uganda's dependence on the Kenyan port of Mombasa. In 1986 the Uganda and Kenya Railways Corporations began the joint operation of Lake Victoria Marine Services, to ferry goods between the two countries via Lake Victoria.

CIVIL AVIATION

The international airport is at Entebbe, on Lake Victoria, some 40 km from Kampala. There are also several small airfields.

Civil Aviation Authority (CAA): POB 5536, Kampala; Passenger Terminal Bldg, 2nd floor, Entebbe International Airport; tel. (41) 4352000; fax (41) 4321401; e-mail aviation@caa.co.ug; internet www.caa.co.ug; Man. Dir RAMA MAKUZA.

Principal Airlines

Air Uganda (AU): Plot 11/13, Lower Kololo Terrace, POB 36591, Kampala; tel. (41) 4258262; fax (41) 4500932; e-mail info@air-uganda.com; internet www.air-uganda.com; f. 2007; services to Africa; CEO HUGH FRASER.

Dairo Air Cargo Services: 24 Jinja Rd, POB 5480, Kampala; tel. (41) 4257731.

Eagle Air Ltd: Adam House, Plot 11, Portal Ave, POB 7392, Kampala; tel. (41) 4344292; fax (41) 4344501; e-mail admin@eagleair-ug.com; internet www.flyeagleuganda.com; f. 1994; domestic services, charter flights to neighbouring countries; Man. Dir Capt. ANTHONY RUBOMBORA.

Royal Daisy Airlines: Plot 13, Buganda Rd, POB 35177, Kampala; tel. (41) 4256213; fax (41) 4256137; e-mail admin@royaldaisy.com; internet www.royaldaisy.com; f. 2005.

Tourism

Uganda's principal attractions for tourists are the forests, lakes, mountains and wildlife and an equable climate. A programme to revive the tourist industry by building or improving hotels and creating new national parks began in the late 1980s. There were 806,655 tourist arrivals in 2009 (compared with 12,786 in 1983). Revenue from the sector in 2009 was estimated at US $564m., including revenue from the transport of passengers.

Uganda Tourist Board: Impala House, 13/15 Kimatti Ave, POB 7211, Kampala; tel. (41) 4342196; fax (41) 4342188; e-mail utb@visituganda.com; internet www.visituganda.com; Chair. PETER KAMYA; Gen. Man. IGNATIUS NAKISHERO.

Defence

As assessed at November 2010, the Uganda People's Defence Forces (UPDF, formerly the National Resistance Army) was estimated to number 45,000 men, including paramilitary forces (a border defence unit of about 600 men, a police air wing of about 800 men, about 400 marines and local defence units totalling about 3,000 men). The Lord's Resistance Army was thought to have over 1,500 members, with about 600 in Uganda and the remainder in Sudan.

Defence Expenditure: Budgeted at Us. 464,000m. in 2009.
Chief of Defence Forces: Gen. ARONDA NYAKARIMA.
Commander of the Air Force: Maj.-Gen. JIM OWOYESIGIRE.
Commander of the Land Forces: Lt-Gen. KATUMBA WAMALA.

Education

Education is not compulsory. Most schools are supported by the Government, although a small proportion are sponsored by missions. Traditionally, all schools have charged fees. In 1997, however, the Government introduced an initiative known as Universal Primary

Education (UPE), whereby free primary education was to be phased in for up to four children per family. In January 2007 the Government initiated free secondary school education in 700 public schools as part of a phased programme to introduce universal free education. Primary education begins at six years of age and lasts for seven years. Secondary education, beginning at the age of 13, lasts for a further six years, comprising a first cycle of four years and a second of two years. In 2008/09, according to UNESCO, enrolment at primary level included 98% (males 96%; females 99%) of children in the relevant age-group. However, in 2007/08 enrolment at secondary schools included just 22% of children (males 22%; females 21%) in the relevant age-group, while in 2004/05 just 3.5% of those in the relevant age-group (males 4.3%; females 2.7%) were enrolled in tertiary education. In addition to Makerere University in Kampala, there is a university of science and technology at Mbarara, and a small Islamic university is located at Mbale. In 2004 58,823 students were enrolled in Ugandan universities. In 2009 spending on education represented 15.6% of total budgetary expenditure.

UKRAINE

Introductory Survey

LOCATION, CLIMATE, LANGUAGE, RELIGION, FLAG, CAPITAL

Ukraine is situated in east-central Europe. It is bordered by Poland, Slovakia, Hungary, Romania and Moldova to the west, by Belarus to the north, and by Russia to the north-east and east. To the south lie the Black Sea and the Sea of Azov. The climate is temperate, especially in the south. The north and north-west share many of the continental climatic features of Poland or Belarus. Average temperatures in Kyiv (Kiev) range from −6.1°C (21°F) in January to 20.4°C (69°F) in July, and average annual rainfall is 615 mm (24 ins). The official state language is Ukrainian, although Russian is widely spoken, except in the west. Most of the population are adherents of Orthodox Christianity, and there are many adherents of the Catholic Church (mostly followers of Eastern rites), predominantly in western regions. There are also a number of Protestant churches and small communities of Jews and Muslims, the latter principally comprising Crimean Tatars. The national flag (proportions 2 by 3) has two equal horizontal stripes, of pale blue over yellow. The capital is Kyiv.

CONTEMPORARY POLITICAL HISTORY

Historical Context

The original East Slavic state, Kyivan (Kievan) Rus, founded in the late 10th century, was based in what is now Ukraine, and is claimed as the precursor of Russia, Belarus and Ukraine. Following the fall of the Rus principalities, in the 13th and 14th centuries, during the Mongol invasions, the Ukrainians (sometimes known as Little Russians or Ruthenians), mainly under Polish and Lithuanian rulers, developed distinctively from the other Eastern Slavs. Ukrainians first entered the Russian Empire in 1654, when a Cossack state east of the Dnipro (Dniepr) River, led by Hetman Bohdan Khmelnytsky, sought Russian protection from Polish invasion. In 1667 Ukraine was divided: the regions east of the Dnipro became part of Russia, while Western Ukraine was annexed by Poland. Russia gained more Ukrainian lands as a result of subsequent partitions of Poland (1793 and 1795) and, in the south, from the Ottoman Empire; the western regions were acquired by Austria.

When the Russian Empire collapsed, in 1917, Ukrainian nationalists set up a central Rada (council or soviet) in Kyiv and demanded autonomy from the Provisional Government in Petrograd (St Petersburg). After the Bolshevik coup, in November, the Rada proclaimed a Ukrainian People's Republic. In December the Bolsheviks established a rival Government in Kharkiv, and by February 1918 much of Ukraine was occupied by Soviet forces. In March, however, the Bolsheviks were forced to cede Ukraine to Germany, under the terms of the Treaty of Brest-Litovsk. Ukraine was the battleground for much of the fighting in the Civil War over the next two years, but in December 1920 a Ukrainian Soviet Socialist Republic (SSR) was established.

The Treaty of Riga, which formally ended the Soviet–Polish War in 1921, assigned territories in western Ukraine to Poland, Czechoslovakia and Romania. Eastern and central lands formed the Ukrainian SSR, one of the founding members of the Union of Soviet Socialist Republics (USSR), in December 1922. The collectivization of agriculture from 1929 had severe consequences for the republic; at least 5m. Ukrainians were estimated to have died in a famine in 1933, which resulted from collectivization. In the 1930s advocates of wider cultural or political autonomy were arrested, and by the late 1930s almost the entire Ukrainian cultural and political élite had been imprisoned, killed or exiled. Ukraine also suffered greatly during the Second World War, which resulted in an estimated 6m. deaths in the republic. Soviet victory in the war, and the annexing of territories from Czechoslovakia, Poland and Romania resulted in the uniting of western and eastern Ukraine. In 1954 Crimea (formerly part of Russia), the Tatar inhabitants of which had been deported *en masse* to Soviet Central Asia in 1944, was transferred to Ukrainian control. During the 1960s there was an increase in covert opposition to the regime. In 1973 Petro Shelest, the First Secretary (leader) of the Communist Party of Ukraine (CPU), was dismissed and replaced by Vladimir Shcherbitsky, a loyal ally of the Soviet leader, Leonid Brezhnev, whose conservatism was such that the accession of the reformist Mikhail Gorbachev to the Soviet leadership, in 1985, had little initial effect in Ukraine.

On 26 April 1986 a serious explosion occurred at the Chornobyl (Chernobyl) nuclear power station, in northern Ukraine. Only after high levels of radiation were reported in other European countries did Soviet officials admit that large amounts of radioactivity had leaked into the atmosphere. Some 135,000 people were evacuated from a 50-km (30-mile) exclusion zone around Chornobyl (much of which was within Belarus). Thirty-one people were killed in the initial explosion, but in 1996 it was reported that an estimated 2,500 deaths in Ukraine may have been caused by the accident, while a further 3.2m. people had been affected by the disaster, as a result of increased numbers of cancers and other related illnesses. Official secrecy surrounding the Chornobyl accident led to greater public support for Ukrainian opposition movements, such as the liberal nationalist Ukrainian People's Movement for Restructuring (Rukh), founded in 1988 by a group of prominent writers and intellectuals. Meanwhile, economic problems contributed to a growing militancy among mining communities in the Donbass region (around Donetsk, in eastern Ukraine) in early 1999, and the revival of hitherto 'underground' religious groups resulted in the re-legalization, in December 1989, of the Ukrainian Byzantine rite Catholic Church, which had been suppressed in 1946.

Shcherbitsky was dismissed in September 1989; he was replaced by Volodymyr Ivashko. In local and republican elections, held on 4 March 1990, candidates supported by the Democratic Bloc, led by Rukh, won 108 of the 450 seats in the Verkhovna Rada (Supreme Council—republican legislature). Independents supported by the Bloc won about 60 seats, although an estimated 280 independent candidates supported the CPU leadership. In June Ivashko was elected Chairman of the Verkhovna Rada (the highest state post in the Republic); he resigned later in the month as First Secretary of the CPU. On 16 July the Verkhovna Rada adopted a declaration of sovereignty. Later in the month Ivashko resigned as Chairman of the Verkhovna Rada, following his appointment as Deputy General Secretary of the Communist Party of the Soviet Union; he was replaced by Leonid Kravchuk, hitherto Second Secretary of the CPU. In October Vitold Fokin, a moderate reformist, succeeded Vitaliy Masol as Chairman of the Council of Ministers (Prime Minister).

The Government participated in negotiations on a new union treaty and signed the protocol to a draft treaty in March 1991. The Government also agreed to conduct the all-Union referendum on the future of the USSR (see the chapter on the Russian Federation), but appended a further question, asking if Ukraine's declaration of sovereignty should form the basis for participation in a renewed federation. Of the electorate, 84% participated in the referendum, 70% of whom approved Gorbachev's proposal to preserve the USSR as a 'renewed federation'. However, Ukraine's own question received greater support (80%), and an additional question in certain western regions, which asked voters if they supported a fully independent Ukraine, secured the support of 90% of those voting.

Domestic Political Affairs

Following the attempted coup by conservative communists in Moscow, the Russian and Soviet capital, on 19 August 1991, the Verkhovna Rada, on 24 August, adopted a declaration of independence, pending confirmation by a referendum on 1 December, when a direct presidential election was also scheduled. The CPU was banned in late August. Kravchuk was elected as President of the Republic on 1 December, with 62% of the votes cast. In the referendum, some 90% of votes were cast in favour of independence (84% of the electorate participated), which thereby took effect. In early December an independent Ukrainian armed forces was established. In January 1992 a new interim currency coupon, which retained the Ukrainian name of the Soviet currency, the karbovanets, was introduced.

UKRAINE

The Government was subject to intense criticism as inflation increased sharply in mid-1992, and resigned in September, having been conclusively defeated in a vote of no confidence. In October Leonid Kuchma, hitherto director-general of a missile factory in Dnipropetrovsk, was appointed Prime Minister, and a new Government was formed. Kuchma proposed a programme of economic reform, which was strongly opposed by left-wing groups, including the Socialist Party of Ukraine (SPU), which had been formed from elements of the CPU. As Ukraine began to experience 'hyperinflation', more than 2m. miners and factory workers, mainly in the Donbass region, joined a strike, in June 1993, demanding a referendum of confidence in the President and in the Verkhovna Rada. In September Kuchma tendered his resignation, which was accepted by the legislature; Yufym Zvyahylsky was appointed as Prime Minister, in an acting capacity, although after several days President Kravchuk assumed direct control of the Government.

Elections to the new, 450-member Verkhovna Rada were held on 27 March 1994, with two subsequent rounds of voting in constituencies where candidates had failed to secure at least 50% of the votes cast. The CPU was permitted to contest the elections and won 86 seats, more than any other group, and, in alliance with the SPU and the Peasants' Party of Ukraine (PPU), formed the largest bloc in the Verkhovna Rada; 170 nominally independent candidates were elected. A notable political division between eastern (where left-wing parties obtained greater support) and western (where moderate nationalist parties won the greatest share of the votes) regions was evident in the election results. Further rounds of voting, held in late 1994 to fill the 112 vacant seats, failed to elect candidates in more than 50 seats. In May Oleksandr Moroz, the leader of the SPU, was elected Chairman of the Verkhovna Rada, which in June elected Masol as Prime Minister.

A presidential election held on 26 June 1994 was inconclusive, as no candidate secured the minimum 50% of the votes necessary for election. Kravchuk received the greatest share of votes cast, with 37.7%, followed by Kuchma, with 31.3%. In a second round of voting, held on 10 July, Kuchma was elected President, securing 52.1% of the votes. A continuing polarity in voting patterns was recorded between the east, where voters largely supported Kuchma, and the west, where Kravchuk secured a majority of votes cast. In March 1995 Masol resigned as Prime Minister and was replaced, in an acting capacity, by Yevhen Marchuk. In June the President and the Verkhovna Rada granted the President additional powers, including the right to issue decrees with the force of legislation, until a new constitution was adopted. Additionally, the President was to retain the prerogative to legislate on economic reform until the expiry of his term in 1999.

In May 1996 Kuchma dismissed Marchuk as premier, appointing Pavlo Lazarenko in his place. The new Constitution, providing extensive powers of appointment to the President, was adopted on 28 June. In July the Cabinet of Ministers resigned; Lazarenko retained the premiership in the new Government. The Government commenced a structural reorganization of the coal-mining sector, and in mid-July an agreement was reached with the trade unions to end an ongoing strike. The attempted assassination of Lazarenko, shortly after the signing of the agreement, was linked by some observers to his role in resolving the dispute. Lazarenko resigned in July 1997. In mid-July the legislature approved Valeriy Pustovoytenko as Prime Minister. In September the legislature approved a new electoral law, which provided for 225 seats in the 450-member Verkhovna Rada to be allocated by proportional representation on the basis of party lists, subject to a minimum threshold of 4% of the total votes cast, and for the remaining 225 to be elected from single-seat constituencies. Meanwhile, it was announced that Lazarenko was to be prosecuted on charges of embezzlement.

Some 30 parties and blocs contested the legislative elections held on 29 March 1998, in which 70.8% of the electorate participated. The CPU obtained 123 seats, becoming the largest party in the legislature. Eight parties secured representation on the basis of party lists, and 136 independent deputies were elected. Oleksandr Tkachenko, the leader of the PPU, was elected as legislative Chairman in July. Lazarenko was arrested in December as he attempted to enter Switzerland, and charged with money-laundering (he was later released on bail). In February 1999 the Verkhovna Rada endorsed a resolution allowing for Lazarenko to be charged, and shortly afterwards he was detained in the USA. (In June 2004 Lazarenko was convicted of money-laundering, fraud and extortion by a federal court in Los Angeles, California, USA, and in August 2006 a US court sentenced Lazarenko to nine years' imprisonment.)

Kuchma is re-elected

In the first round of voting in the presidential election, held on 31 October 1999, Kuchma was placed first, with 36.5% of the votes cast; his opponent in the second round was to be Petro Symonenko of the CPU, who had obtained 22.2% of the first round votes. In early November Kuchma undertook a number of measures that were regarded as being intended to ensure his re-election, including the dismissal of governors of three oblasts (regions) in which he not been the first-placed candidate. In the second ballot, on 14 November, Kuchma retained the presidency, receiving some 57.7% of the votes cast; he was inaugurated on 30 November. In December the Verkhovna Rada endorsed the nomination of Viktor Yushchenko (Governor of the National Bank of Ukraine—NBU—since 1993) as premier. In January 2000 left-wing factions in the legislature prevented a vote on Tkachenko's dismissal as legislative Chairman, compelling the new centrist parliamentary majority led by Kravchuk to hold a session in a separate building, where it voted unanimously to remove Tkachenko and his deputy from the chairmanship of the legislature. In February the majority faction elected Ivan Plyushch, an ally of Pustovoytenko, as legislative Chairman. After several days, deputies of the majority grouping gained entry to the parliamentary building, and normal activity resumed.

Meanwhile, a presidential decree, issued in January 2000, scheduled a referendum on proposed constitutional amendments for 16 April, although two of the six questions initially intended to feature in the referendum were excluded from the plebiscite by the Constitutional Court. The four remaining questions—on the dissolution of the Verkhovna Rada should deputies fail to approve the state budget within three months of its submission; the reduction of the number of deputies from 450 to 300; the establishment of a bicameral legislature; and the placing of limitations on the immunity enjoyed by deputies—were approved by a majority of the 81% of the electorate that participated in the referendum. However, as no proposal to implement these decisions ensued, it appeared that the referendum had served primarily to increase the President's authority over the legislature.

In July 2000 the Deputy Prime Minister, responsible for Energy Issues, Yuliya Tymoshenko, a prominent instigator of reforms in the energy sector and the leader of the Fatherland party, was charged with corruption, as a result of investigations into her former ally, Lazarenko, in the USA. In early November a decapitated corpse, believed to be that of an investigative opposition journalist, Heorhiy Gongadze, missing since September, was discovered near Kyiv, by police. In late November Moroz released audio recordings of a discussion, allegedly between Kuchma, the head of the presidential administration, Volodymyr Lytvyn, and the Minister of Internal Affairs, Yuriy Kravchenko, on possible means of killing Gongadze. Controversy surrounded the authenticity of the recordings, which a former presidential security adviser, Maj. Mykola Melnychenko, had made over a period of several months, prior to fleeing Ukraine.

In January 2001 Kuchma dismissed Tymoshenko, as an investigation into her alleged involvement in tax evasion and the smuggling of Russian gas proceeded. After further audio recordings were made public, in February, Kuchma admitted that the recordings were of his voice, but stated that they had been edited in an attempt to incriminate him. Demonstrations in Kyiv to demand Kuchma's resignation continued for several weeks, of which Tymoshenko, leading a loose coalition of opposition movements, the National Salvation Forum (NSF), became the most prominent leader. In February Kuchma dismissed the head of the national security service, Gen. Leonid Derkach, and the head of the presidential bodyguard. In mid-February Tymoshenko was arrested on charges of tax evasion. In late February Gongadze's body was formally identified by the Prosecutor-General's office, and a murder inquiry was opened. In May Gongadze's death was officially attributed to a criminal attack, and it was announced that the investigation into his death was to be closed. Meanwhile, in March a demonstration by up to 18,000 anti-Kuchma protesters in Kyiv degenerated into violent clashes and was dispersed by police; several prominent members of the extreme nationalist Ukrainian National Assembly-Ukrainian National Self-Defence Organization (UNA-UNSO) were arrested and charged with provoking unrest. In the same month Kuchma dismissed Kravchenko as Minister of Internal Affairs, replacing him with Yuriy Smirnov. At the end of March

Tymoshenko was released from prison, although the charges against her remained under investigation.

In April 2001 the Verkhovna Rada approved a motion of no confidence in the Prime Minister and his Cabinet of Ministers, despite the economic growth that had been achieved during Yushchenko's premiership—the first growth recorded since independence. In May Anatoliy Kinakh, hitherto First Deputy Prime Minister, responsible for Economic Policy, was appointed to succeed Yushchenko as Prime Minister. In September Tymoshenko issued an appeal for other opposition groupings to join the NSF, but rejected the suggestion that the group unite with the Our Ukraine bloc of centrist and nationalist parties headed by Yushchenko; her supporters subsequently became known as the Yuliya Tymoshenko Bloc (YuTB). Meanwhile, in advance of forthcoming legislative elections, supporters of Kuchma formed the For a United Ukraine (FUU) bloc, headed by Lytvyn.

In February 2002 Ukrainian prosecutors charged Lazarenko, *in absentia*, with having ordered the murders of two parliamentary deputies in 1996 and 1998; in March 2002 the Government's director of arms exports, Valeriy Malev, was killed in an automobile collision. It subsequently emerged that several days before Malev's death Kuchma had been informed of the discovery of audio recordings made by Melnychenko, in which Kuchma and Malev were allegedly heard to discuss the sale of air-defence equipment to Iraq, in violation of UN sanctions.

The 2002 legislative elections

In the legislative elections, held on 31 March 2002, Our Ukraine, then comprising 10 parties, obtained both the largest share of the votes (23.6%) and the largest number of seats to be won by any party (112); FUU received the second largest number of seats (101), but only 11.8% of the votes cast. The CPU obtained 20.0% of the votes cast, but received only 66 seats. The Social-Democratic Party of Ukraine—United (SDPU—U) received 24 seats and 6.3% of the votes cast, the SPU 23 seats and 6.9% of the votes, and the YuTB 22 seats and 7.3% of the votes. Ninety-three independent candidates were elected. A report by observers from the Organization for Security and Co-operation in Europe (OSCE, see p. 385) indicated 'important flaws' in the organization of the elections. After the elections, Viktor Medvedchuk, the Chairman of the SDPU—U, was appointed to head the presidential administration, replacing Lytvyn, who was elected Chairman of the Verkhovna Rada.

In August 2002 Kuchma announced that a Constitutional Commission was to be formed to investigate the possibility of introducing constitutional reforms. In October a senior judge in Kyiv opened a criminal investigation into Kuchma, who was charged with violating 11 articles of the criminal code. However, in November an ally of Kuchma was elected as Chairman of the Supreme Court, and in late December the Court ruled that the investigation into Kuchma had been opened illegally.

Meanwhile, on 16 November 2002, following the dismissal of Kinakh, Kuchma appointed Viktor Yanukovych of the Party of the Regions (PR—one of the parties affiliated to FUU), latterly Governor of Donetsk Oblast, as Prime Minister. A new Government, in which several principal positions remained unchanged, was appointed later in the month. In December a stable pro-presidential majority was finally established in the Verkhovna Rada.

In February 2003 Yushchenko issued a public statement, addressed to Kuchma, Yanukovych and Lytvyn, urging an end to what he described as 'political terror', including physical assaults against a number of political activists and the unsolved murders of several journalists. Later in the month anti-Kuchma demonstrations were held in several major cities. In mid-February the Verkhovna Rada rejected draft legislation on constitutional reform presented by deputies of the SDPU—U and the SPU, providing for the election of all 450 deputies by proportional representation on the basis of party lists; the Verkhovna Rada again rejected the draft in April. Meanwhile, in March Kuchma submitted a draft on constitutional reform to the legislature, providing for the replacement of the unicameral legislature with a 300-seat State Assembly elected under a party list system and an 81-member House of the Regions; the parliament was to be granted the power to dismiss the Prime Minister, and the President the power to dissolve parliament. In April the two highest-ranking members of the Government were elected to senior positions in the PR: Yanukovych was elected as Chairman, while the First Deputy Prime Minister and Minister of Finance, Mykola Azarov, became the Chairman of the Political Council. Following the failure of the Verkhovna Rada to support either of the constitutional amendments proposed, the President stated in June that he was prepared to co-operate with members of the legislative opposition. In September a new draft, prepared by members of the pro-presidential and CPU legislative factions (widely known as the Medvedchuk-Symonenko draft), was presented to the Verkhovna Rada; the text envisaged the extension of the mandate of the existing legislature by one year, until 2007, when its replacement would be elected by a system of proportional representation. The draft also provided for the direct election, in 2004, of an interim President with reduced powers, until 2006, when a President would be elected by the Verkhovna Rada.

In September 2003 Anatoliy Zlenko retired as Minister of Foreign Affairs. He was replaced by Kostyantyn Hryshchenko, hitherto ambassador to the USA. In October Kuchma dismissed the Prosecutor-General, Svyatoslav Pyskun, nominating Hennadiy Vasilyev, a former Chief Prosecutor in Donetsk Oblast, as his replacement; the legislature approved the appointment in November. There were renewed concerns about the use of force to inhibit political debate, after Our Ukraine was prevented from holding a conference in Donetsk at the end of October. Reports stated that as many as 2,000 people had prevented members and supporters of the grouping from entering the building where the meeting was to have been held, and that material that presented Yushchenko as a sympathizer with Nazi ideology had been widely disseminated around the city. Our Ukraine, the YuTB and the SPU subsequently issued a statement accusing the Kuchma administration of dictatorial methods. Also in October Kuchma had ordered the Ministry of Internal Affairs and the State Security Service to investigate allegations made by Yushchenko that he was the target of an assassination plot.

In late December 2003 the Verkhovna Rada provisionally approved the Medvedchuk-Symonenko draft on constitutional reform (however, the 274 votes cast in favour of the proposals, although sufficient to enable the bill to receive a second reading in the legislature, fell short of the 300 votes required for its approval), although the leadership of the Our Ukraine, YuTB and SPU factions did not support the proposals. On 30 December the Constitutional Court declared that Kuchma would be eligible to seek re-election upon the expiry of his term of office in October 2004. On 3 February 2004 the Verkhovna Rada voted to amend the Medvedchuk-Symonenko draft on constitutional reform, removing those proposals pertaining to the election of the President by the legislature. The SPU supported this amendment, which was approved by 304 votes. In March the Verkhovna Rada approved legislation, supported by the SPU and the CPU, introducing a proportional representation system for the election of all 450 parliamentary deputies; the percentage of the votes required for a party to obtain election was to be reduced from 4% to 3%. The legislation was signed into law by Kuchma in early April. (The Our Ukraine and YuTB factions had boycotted the votes on both of these proposals.) Also in March legislation was approved to modify the presidential election procedure, reducing the number of signatures of eligible voters required of a candidate to 500,000 from 1m. (as had been the case since 1999). On 7 April the Verkhovna Rada failed to approve the the amended Medvedchuk-Symonenko draft. In accordance with the Constitution, the draft could not be reintroduced to the legislature for the period of one year.

The 'orange revolution'

Politics in 2004 were dominated by preparations for the presidential election. In April Yanukovych was named as the candidate for the pro-presidential bloc, while Yushchenko's candidacy was officially registered in August; 24 candidates registered to contest the poll. On 20 August two bombs exploded in a Kyiv market, and a further explosion occurred on 3 September; the authorities suggested that the explosions were connected to members of Our Ukraine, while the opposition claimed that the secret services had orchestrated the attacks in an attempt to discredit them. In September Yushchenko was admitted to a clinic in Vienna, Austria, subsequently emerging with his face (and other regions of his skin) severely scarred by lesions; it appeared that this resulted from his poisoning during a meal with senior members of the secret services, and Yushchenko himself accused the incumbent administration of seeking to murder him. Shortly before the first round of the election Yanukovych, in his capacity as Prime Minister, announced that the rate of state pensions was to be increased. In his capacity as presidential candidate, meanwhile, Yanukovych pledged to grant Russian the status of a joint official language and work towards permitting dual Ukrainian-Russian citizenship.

Yushchenko, conversely, made it clear that he would, if elected, seek the closer integration of Ukraine into the European Union (EU, see p. 270) and the North Atlantic Treaty Organization (NATO, see p. 368).

At the first round of voting, held on 31 October 2004, Yushchenko received 39.9% of the votes cast, and Yanukovych 39.3% of the votes, according to results released by the Central Electoral Commission (CEC); Yushchenko and Yanukovych consequently proceeded to a second round on 21 November. The CEC initially indicated that Yanukovych led by nearly 3% in the second round, with more than 99% of the votes counted, contradicting several exit polls endorsed by the opposition. Large-scale protests at the allegedly fraudulent conduct of the count, and in support of both Yushchenko and Tymoshenko, commenced in central Kyiv on 22 November, focused around Maidan Nezalezhnosti (Independence Square). The youth group Pora! (Enough!) played a major role in the organization of the protests. The demonstrators established a tent settlement along Kyiv's main thoroughfare, and adopted the colour orange as a unifying symbol, leading what became known as the 'orange revolution'. Protests were almost entirely peaceful, with several hundred thousand people reportedly present at the height of the demonstrations. Meanwhile, a number of local administrations, including the city councils of Kyiv and Lviv, declared that they did not accept the results announced by the CEC and that they regarded Yushchenko as the legitimate Head of State. The OSCE condemned the conduct of both rounds of voting. On 23 November Yushchenko took a symbolic oath of office in front of the Verkhovna Rada. On 24 November the CEC officially announced the preliminary results of the second round: Yanukovych was declared the winner, with 49.5% of the votes cast, while Yushchenko was deemed to have received 46.6%. Opposition protests persisted, however, with demands for a general strike the following day, and speeches and demonstrations, led by Yushchenko and Tymoshenko, continued in freezing conditions in central Kyiv, and protesters blockaded numerous government buildings. In eastern Ukraine the administrations of several oblasts (notably Donetsk and Luhansk) threatened to hold referendums on autonomy or secession should Yushchenko be declared president.

Following an appeal to the Supreme Court regarding the conduct of the second round of voting, on 25 November 2004 the Court announced that it would suspend the publication of the election results until the opposition's complaints could be considered. A significant shift in the allegiances of the state-owned broadcasting outlets, which had hitherto demonstrated a pro-Yanukovych bias, was also observed. On 27 November the Verkhovna Rada voted to declare the 21 November ballot invalid and to express a lack of confidence in the CEC, while a subsequent motion of no confidence in Yanukovych's Government was adopted on 1 December (these resolutions, however, carried no legal force, as they required the signature of President Kuchma to be binding). On 29 November Serhiy Tihipko resigned as NBU Governor and as the manager of Yanukovych's presidential campaign. Meanwhile, Polish President Aleksander Kwaśniewski, Lithuanian President Valdas Adamkus and the EU High Representative for Common Foreign and Security Policy, Javier Solana, arrived in Kyiv to attempt mediation between Yushchenko and Yanukovych, in the presence of Kuchma. On 3 December the Supreme Court ruled that the declared results of the second round of voting were invalid, and ordered that a repeat election be conducted within three weeks.

Viktor Yushchenko becomes President

On 8 December 2004, following extensive negotiations, the Verkhovna Rada voted to support a series of amendments to the Constitution and electoral law, with 420 deputies voting in favour of the proposals. The constitutional amendments provided for the transfer of several powers of appointment from the President to the Prime Minister and the legislature and for the expulsion from the legislature of any deputy who left the party or bloc on whose list he had been elected. Kuchma signed the amendments into law, although they were not fully to take effect until after the legislative elections due to be held in March 2006. Kuchma also announced the dismissal of the Prosecutor-General, Hennadiy Vasilyev (who was replaced by his predecessor, Pyskun, after he won a court case declaring his dismissal in 2003 to be illegal), and approved a substantial reconstitution of the CEC. Yanukovych was granted leave from his position as Prime Minister in order to campaign for the repeated second round of voting; he was replaced in an acting capacity by Azarov. The repeat ballot was held on 26 December 2004. After preliminary results suggested a victory for Yushchenko, Yanukovych lodged complaints against the conduct of the election with the CEC and, subsequently, the Supreme Court, causing the official publication of the results to be delayed. Meanwhile, on 27 December Minister of Transport and Communications Heorhiy Kirpa was found dead, as a result of multiple bullet wounds. Earlier in the month Yuriy Lyakh, Chairman of the Ukrainian Credit Bank, had been found dead in his office, from neck wounds apparently inflicted with a paper knife. Both cases were officially described as suicide, despite widespread speculation that both deaths had been political assassinations. On 31 December Yanukovych resigned as Prime Minister, and on 6 January 2005 Kuchma signed a decree dismissing the Cabinet of Ministers. On that date Yanukovych's complaints were rejected by the Supreme Court, and four days later Yushchenko was officially declared to have won the ballot of 26 December 2004, receiving 51.99% of the votes cast, compared with the 44.2% awarded to Yanukovych. A clear regional divide was evident in the results, with Yushchenko obtaining more than 75% of the votes cast in 12 administrative divisions of western and central Ukraine, including Kyiv City, while Yanukovych received similarly overwhelming majorities in four divisions of eastern Ukraine and Crimea. Following the Supreme Court's rejection of Yanukovych's final appeal, Yushchenko was inaugurated as President on 23 January.

On 4 February 2005 the Verkhovna Rada approved Yushchenko's nomination of Tymoshenko as Prime Minister and a new Cabinet of Ministers was announced, notably including Kinakh as First Deputy Prime Minister. Other ministerial appointments included Yuriy Lutsenko as Minister of Internal Affairs and Anatoliy Hrytsenko as Minister of Defence. Yushchenko also appointed many new regional governors, and named Petro Poroshenko, a prominent business executive, as Chairman of the National Security and Defence Council. Yanukovych, meanwhile, expressed his intention of leading a 'harsh opposition' to Yushchenko's administration. The new Government declared combating corruption to be a priority, and several privatizations conducted during Kuchma's presidency were targeted for investigation; the extent to which they should be investigated became a significant source of tension between the various parties and elements represented within the new administration. Similar tensions existed over other policy matters between the three main political groupings represented within the Government: nationalists and populists, associated chiefly with Tymoshenko; statist socialists linked with the SPU; and those elements regarded as more sympathetic to business interests, associated more closely with Yushchenko. The latter formed a new political party, People's Union Our Ukraine; Yushchenko was named as the Honorary Chairman of the party, Roman Bezsmertny (Yushchenko's electoral campaign manager and a Deputy Prime Minister) became the Chairman of the party's Council, and Yuriy Yekhanurov (a former First Deputy Prime Minister and Minister of the Economy, and the recently appointed Governor of Dnipropetrovsk Oblast) the Chairman of the party's Executive Committee.

Yushchenko also endorsed a reopening of the investigation into the death of Gongadze. On 4 March 2005 former Minister of Internal Affairs Kravchenko, who was alleged to be one of the officials who had discussed the killing of Gongadze on the audio recordings released in 2000, was found dead, reportedly as the result of suicide, shortly before he had been due to be questioned at the office of the Prosecutor-General. It was subsequently announced that four people were to be charged in connection with Gongadze's death. The trial of three men, all former police officers, commenced in January 2006; the fourth man, suspected of being Gongadze's killer, was believed to have fled Ukraine. (In March 2008 the three men were found guilty of murdering Gongadze, each receiving custodial sentences of 12–13 years, although the investigations failed to discover who had ordered the killing.)

Meanwhile, it soon became apparent that some of the new administration's policy decisions had been instrumental in reducing the hitherto strong rate of economic growth. Increases in social spending (introduced by both the new Government, and by the Yanukovych administration prior to the first round of voting in late 2004) led to heightened inflation. Moreover, Tymoshenko's decision, in April 2005, to maintain at existing levels the retail prices of petroleum (for which Ukraine was heavily dependent on Russia) resulted in several Russian companies limiting their supplies to Ukraine, causing a severe shortfall relative to demand. In May Yushchenko issued a decree criticizing the Government's action in restraining prices, ordering

UKRAINE

that the restraints be removed as a matter of urgency. Meanwhile, inter-factional disagreements in the Verkhovna Rada meant that several items of legislation, which had been intended to expedite Ukraine's application for membership of the World Trade Organization (WTO, see p. 430), were not approved by the legislature before the beginning of its summer recess.

The collapse of the orange coalition

The growing tensions between the constituent groupings that had supported the 'orange revolution' resulted in a series of resignations in early September 2005. On 1 September an adviser to Tymoshenko, Mykola Brodsky, alleged that elements close to Yushchenko were engaged in corrupt practices; one day later the Chief of the Presidential Staff, Oleksandr Zinchenko, announced his resignation, criticizing the actions of Poroshenko, in particular. On 8 September Mykola Tomenko announced his resignation as Deputy Prime Minister. Later the same day Yushchenko dismissed Tymoshenko and her Government, and also announced that Poroshenko had resigned from the National Security and Defence Council. Tymoshenko stated that, as a result of her dismissal, the YuTB would effectively go into opposition and present its own list of candidates at the 2006 elections to the Verkhovna Rada. Meanwhile, on 20 September 2005 the Verkhovna Rada narrowly failed to approve Yushchenko's nomination of Yekhanurov as Prime Minister. Consequently, in order to obtain support for Yekhanurov's nomination from the sizeable PR faction within the legislature, Yushchenko and Yanukovych agreed a 10-point memorandum; among the controversial measures provided for by the document were an amnesty for all those involved in electoral fraud at the annulled second round of presidential voting in 2004, and an extension of the immunity from prosecution enjoyed by legislative deputies to members of regional and local councils. On 22 September 2005 Yekhanurov was confirmed as Prime Minister, having received 289 votes in favour of his nomination in the Verkhovna Rada, compared with the 223 votes obtained prior to the signature of the memorandum. Several ministers holding principal positions in the former administration retained their portfolios. New appointments included that of Arseniy Yatsenyuk as Minister of the Economy, and Stanislav Stashevsky as First Deputy Prime Minister, replacing Kinakh, who became the Chairman of the National Security and Defence Council. The dismissal of Pyskun as Prosecutor-General, on 14 October, was a further significant personnel charge; his replacement, in an acting capacity, was Serhiy Vynokurov, who subsequently announced that all criminal charges against Poroshenko had been abandoned. On 31 October the Verkhovna Rada approved the appointment of Oleksandr Medvedko as Prosecutor-General.

New arrangements for the purchase of natural gas (following a dispute with Russia—see below) were a source of considerable controversy within Ukraine and were instrumental in bringing about a vote of no confidence in the Government on 10 January 2006, which was approved by 250 votes to 50 against. (Tymoshenko stated that she would withdraw from the agreement on gas purchases in the event of her again becoming Prime Minister.) However, the constitutional position at this time was obscure (the transfer of many of the powers of appointment from the President to the Prime Minister and the Chairman of the Verkhovna Rada, agreed in late 2004, had taken effect on 1 January 2006), and in the absence of a functioning Constitutional Court, President Yushchenko requested that the Yekhanurov administration remain in office until after the forthcoming legislative elections.

The legislative elections proceeded, as scheduled, on 26 March 2006, contested by 45 parties and blocs. With the introduction of a system of full proportional representation and the exclusion of nominally independent deputies, the new Verkhovna Rada had a very different composition to the one that it replaced. The results of voting confirmed the persistence of the regional division in support for parties. Yanukovych's PR became the largest party in the new Verkhovna Rada, with 32.1% of the total votes cast, receiving 186 seats. The YuTB was placed second, with 22.3% and 129 seats, while the Our Ukraine bloc (comprising several smaller, generally liberal or nationalist parties, in addition to Our Ukraine) obtained 14.0% and 81 seats. The SPU, with 5.7% (33 seats), and the CPU, with 3.7% (21 seats), also surpassed the 3% quota required for representation. Although there were some suspicions of malpractice in the concurrent elections to the Crimean Supreme Council (see below), the elections to the Verkhovna Rada were described by international monitors as free and fair. However, the formation of a coalition administration that would enjoy a parliamentary majority proved protracted. In late June it was announced that Our Ukraine, the YuTB and the SPU were to form a governing coalition supportive of Yushchenko, with Tymoshenko as premier. However, when the coalition declined to nominate Moroz as legislative Chairman, the SPU announced its withdrawal from the coalition, which thereby ceased to hold a majority of legislative seats. The SPU subsequently announced that it would support a so-called 'anti-crisis coalition' headed by Yanukovych and the PR and also comprising the CPU and the SPU; these three parties controlled 240 of the 450 parliamentary seats. Subsequently, the anti-crisis coalition was also dissolved, and at the end of July a 'national unity coalition' was formed after Yushchenko and leaders of four of the five parliamentary parties (with the YuTB the exception) signed a document that outlined various domestic and foreign policy aims, including the retention of Ukrainian as the sole official language (outwith Crimea) and the eventual incorporation of Ukraine into European and Atlantic organizations (subject to approval by national referendums).

On 4 August 2006 the Verkhovna Rada approved the nomination of Yanukovych as Prime Minister and the formation of a new Government, comprising representatives of the PR, Our Ukraine, the SPU and the CPU. This was the first Government in post-Soviet Ukraine to include members of the CPU. Our Ukraine did not enter officially into the coalition, although four members of the new Government belonged to the bloc, as did non-party allies of Yushchenko, while the YuTB remained in opposition.

Tensions between President Yushchenko and Prime Minister Yanukovych continued to be evident, while the balance of powers between the President, Prime Minister and Verkhovna Rada, following the enactment of the 2004 constitutional amendments, remained uncertain; in particular, several of Yanukovych's actions as Prime Minister appeared to exceed the responsibilities of that office. In September 2006 Yanukovych refused to sign several presidential decrees (which, in order to become valid, require the approval of the Prime Minister and Chairman of the Verkhovna Rada). In the same month Yanukovych expressed Ukraine's unpreparedness to enter into a closer relationship with NATO at a meeting of the Alliance in Brussels, Belgium (see below), despite such remarks being contrary to the terms of the coalition policy document. Later that month the Verkhovna Rada voted to abolish the prohibition on parliamentary deputies switching party allegiance or becoming independent. At the end of September Yanukovych demanded the dismissal of the governors of five eastern regions who were members of Our Ukraine, a demand that required presidential endorsement. In early October Our Ukraine announced its decision to withdraw its members from the Government and enter into the opposition; however, both Yushchenko and Yanukovych refused to accept the ministers' resignations.

On 1 December 2006 the Verkhovna Rada voted in favour of the dismissal of the Minister of Foreign Affairs Borys Tarasyuk and the Minister of Internal Affairs Lutsenko; Tarasyuk subsequently had his dismissal overturned by a district court (on the grounds that his post was one answerable to the President, rather than to the Verkhovna Rada and the Government), although his dismissal was upheld by the appeals court in Kyiv in January 2007. Consequently, on 30 January Tarasyuk resigned from the Government. On 20 March the Verkhovna Rada rejected Yushchenko's nomination of Volodymyr Ohryzko as Minister of Foreign Affairs. The legislature approved the appointment of Yatsenyuk to that position on the following day, as well as several other ministerial appointments. Later in the month a group of deputies hitherto loyal to Yushchenko, including Kinakh, announced that they would henceforth form part of the PR faction in the Verkhovna Rada.

The 2007 pre-term legislative elections

Frustrated at the inability to govern effectively, on 2 April 2007 Yushchenko issued a decree dissolving the Verkhovna Rada and scheduling pre-term parliamentary elections for 27 May. Yanukovych initially refused to accept the presidential decree and asked the Constitutional Court to rule on the constitutionality of the dissolution of parliament. Meanwhile, the Verkhovna Rada continued to meet, refusing to recognize the legitimacy of its dissolution. On 25 April Yushchenko announced that the parliamentary elections were to be delayed until 24 June. On 30 April the Verkhovna Rada approved a resolution calling for the concurrent holding of fresh presidential and legislative elections, to be held no later than December and subject to the introduction of a number of constitutional amendments. Yushchenko continued to insist, however, that the Constitution required any pre-term elections to be held no later than 60 days after the dissolution of the Verkhovna Rada. Meanwhile, the Constitutional Court had failed to issue any ruling on the legitimacy of the dissolution of the legislature within one month, as required; the acting Chairman of the Court resigned in May, while several other judges of the Court were absent, resigned, or were dismissed, effectively rendering the Court unable to conduct its work. On 1 June Yushchenko again dismissed Pyskun, who had been reappointed to the Office of Prosecutor-General in April, and replaced him, again, with Medvedko. On 5 June Yushchenko rescheduled the legislative elections to 30 September, following the agreement of a compromise arrangement with Yanukovych and Moroz. Our Ukraine and YuTB deputies subsequently withdrew from the Verkhovna Rada. In early July Our Ukraine formed an electoral alliance with the People's Self-Defence group of Lutsenko and several smaller parties, which became known as the Our Ukraine-People's Self-defence bloc. Tymoshenko demanded that a national referendum to resolve the constitutional impasse be conducted to coincide with the elections, and began to organize a petition to that end. In August the YuTB succeeded, after a legal appeal, in reversing a decision by the CEC to refuse to register it for the elections, on the grounds that it had submitted incomplete documentation.

According to official results of the legislative elections on 30 September 2007, released by the CEC in mid-October, Yanukovych's PR won 34.4% of the votes and 175 seats, the YuTB 30.7% and 156 seats, the Our Ukraine-People's Self-defence bloc 14.2% and 72 seats, the CPU 5.4% and 27 seats, and the Lytvyn bloc 4.0% and 20 seats. The SPU, with 2.9% of the votes, narrowly failed to secure representation. Tymoshenko and the leader of the Our Ukraine-People's Self-defence bloc, Vyacheslav Kyrylenko, subsequently announced their intention to sign a coalition agreement, which would allow the two groupings a narrow parliamentary majority; Tymoshenko would be returned to the office of Prime Minister, while ministerial portfolios were to be divided equally between the two blocs. Although the elections were regarded by international observers to have met democratic standards, the official publication of the final results was delayed, pending the outcome of a legal challenge. The Verkhovna Rada was convened on 23 November, when Yanukovych formally relinquished the premiership. Yatsenyuk was appointed legislative Chairman on 4 December. Following further protracted negotiations, the coalition agreement announced in October was finalized; on 18 December, after two failed attempts, Tymoshenko's nomination as Prime Minister was finally approved by 226 votes in the Verkhovna Rada. The Government additionally comprised 12 representatives of the YuTB and 11 of the Our Ukraine-People's Self-defence bloc; the new Minister of Foreign Affairs, Volodymyr Ohryzko, who, together with the Minister of Defence, had been nominated by the President in accordance with the Constitution, was independent.

In January 2008 it was reported that Lutsenko, who had been reappointed Minister of Internal Affairs, had assaulted the Mayor of Kyiv, Leonid Chernovetsky, following an altercation over allegedly corrupt agreements relating to the transfer of land ownership in the city. In March a largely defunct political party, supportive of Yushchenko, United Centre, chaired by a strenuous opponent of Tymoshenko, Ihor Kril, was effectively re-established; tensions between the President and Prime Minister were heightened, as Yushchenko criticized the Government's economic policies and accused Tymoshenko of permitting corrupt practices in land auctions. Lutsenko announced that his parliamentary People's Self-defence bloc would form the basis for a new party. In April the Constitutional Court ruled that the constitutional system could be amended by a national referendum (although the Verkhovna Rada would first be required to amend certain aspects of the existing Constitution). Following continued denunciations of Tymoshenko by Yushchenko, in May YuTB deputies blockaded the Verkhovna Rada, preventing Yushchenko from making his annual parliamentary address.

Continuing tensions between Our Ukraine and the Tymoshenko Bloc

On 6 June 2008 the coalition of the YuTB and the Our Ukraine-People's Self-defence bloc lost its narrow parliamentary majority, after two deputies, one from each faction, resigned. A parliamentary motion expressing no confidence in Tymoshenko's Government was defeated in early July. Following Russia's military action in Georgia in early August, a presidential aide accused Tymoshenko (who had refrained from criticizing Russia while Yushchenko had demonstrated strong support for Georgian President Mikheil Saakashvili—see below) of having reached a clandestine agreement with Russia that would result in the Russian authorities providing her with support at the next presidential election. On 1 September PR parliamentary faction leader Raisa Bohatyryova, who had been appointed National Security and Defence Council Secretary in December 2007, was expelled from the party, after refusing to endorse Yanukovych's support for the declared independence of South Ossetia and Abkhazia from Georgia. On the following day Yushchenko announced the withdrawal of the Our Ukraine-People's Self-defence bloc from the ruling coalition, after the YuTB supported the PR in voting for a parliamentary motion approving legislation that strengthened the powers of the Government, while reducing those of the President. On 16 September 2008 Yatsenyuk officially declared that the governing coalition had failed and subsequently tendered his resignation as Chairman of the Verkhovna Rada; in the event that no new coalition was formed within 30 days, the President was required, under the Constitution, to schedule new elections. On 8 October Yushchenko officially dissolved the Verkhovna Rada and announced that further legislative elections would take place on 7 December. Following a legal challenge by Tymoshenko, he subsequently rejected a ruling by a regional court against his election decree and dismissed its judge. Later in October Yushchenko reconvened the Verkhovna Rada to debate financial austerity measures required for the disbursement of IMF assistance (following the onset of the international financial crisis—see Economic Affairs) and rescheduled the elections for 14 December. The Verkhovna Rada accepted Yatsenyuk's resignation on 12 November; after attempts to adopt legislation allocating funds to the organization of the elections failed, Yushchenko announced that it would not be possible to organize legislative elections in 2008, as had been envisaged.

On 9 December 2008 Lytvyn was elected as Chairman of the Verkhovna Rada (having held the post in 2002–06), prior to the formal signature of a further coalition agreement between Our Ukraine-People's Self-defence bloc, the YuTB and the Lytvyn bloc on 16 December. However, Kyrylenko withdrew from Our Ukraine-People's Self-defence bloc in protest against its joining the new coalition and, together with a further 17 former members, subsequently formed a breakaway movement, For Ukraine. Yushchenko attributed responsibility for the increasing adverse effects on the economy, including a sharp decline in the value of the currency, to the Government, while Tymoshenko demanded that both the President and the Governor of the NBU, Volodymyr Stelmakh, resign from office. Later in December the Verkhovna Rada adopted a motion expressing no confidence in Stelmakh. In early February 2009 Viktor Pynzenyk, who had expressed opposition to the Government's plan for economic recovery, resigned as Minister of Finance. In the same month the Ministry of Foreign Affairs threatened to expel the Russian ambassador in Ukraine (and former Russian premier), Viktor Chernomyrdin, following a newspaper interview in which he made a number of disparaging comments about the Ukrainian political leadership. In early March the Verkhovna Rada voted in favour of removing Ohryzko from the post of Minister of Foreign Affairs, on grounds of mismanagement of government policy.

In April 2009 the Verkhovna Rada voted in favour of scheduling the first round of the forthcoming presidential election for 25 October (rather than on 17 January 2010, at the end of the existing presidential term, favoured by Yushchenko, and as provided for by the Constitution). Yushchenko also proposed constitutional amendments for the creation of a second parliamentary chamber and an increase in presidential powers to allow him to veto certain government decisions. In early May 2009, following a challenge by Yushchenko, the Constitutional Court overturned the proposed rescheduling of the election. Also in May Lutsenko offered his resignation from the post of Minister of Internal Affairs, at the request of Yushchenko, after he had been detained by police at the airport of Frankfurt, Germany, for allegedly intoxicated and violent behaviour. After parliamentary deputies belonging to the YuTB bloc opposed the acceptance of his resignation (which was likely to precipitate the collapse of the ruling coalition), the Verkhovna Rada voted in favour of a motion requesting his suspension for the duration of an investigation into the incident. In early June the Verkhovna Rada approved the dismissal of Yekhanurov as Minister of Defence, a development strongly supported by Tymoshenko. On 7 June negotiations between the PR and the YuTB on the formation of a parliamentary 'grand coalition' failed when Yanukovych withdrew, rejecting a proposal for constitutional reform that would have provided for the election of the President by the Verkhovna Rada, rather than by direct popular vote. Later that month the Minister of Transport and Communications resigned, citing disagreements with Tymoshenko.

In July 2009 Oleksiy Pukach, the former head of the interior ministry's external surveillance directorate, was arrested for suspected involvement in the murder in 2000 of journalist Heorhiy Gongadze (after being charged *in absentia* in 2003). (He remained in custody, pending the conclusion of an official investigation.) In early September 2009 PR deputies began a blockade of parliamentary sessions (thereby preventing voting from taking place), after the Verkhovna Rada rejected a PR proposal for increases in salaries and pensions. Also in September Lutsenko (who remained in post as Minister of the Interior) claimed that senior NBU officials had been involved in plans to weaken the national currency, on the instructions of the Ukrainian presidency, in order to damage Tymoshenko's Government. The deputy head of the NBU, Oleksandr Savchenko, a supporter of Tymoshenko, resigned, accusing his colleagues of pursuing the monetary policies that had previously caused the currency to decrease in value; he was subsequently appointed Deputy Minister of Finance. At the end of September the privatization of one of Ukraine's largest petrochemical factories, the Odesa Portside Plant, which had been strenuously opposed by Yushchenko and suspended by a court in Kyiv, was invalidated by the State Property Fund, on the grounds that the highest tendered price represented an undervaluing of the factory. In October President Yushchenko's nomination of his close associate, Poroshenko, as Minister of Foreign Affairs, was approved by the Verkhovna Rada (the position having remained vacant since March). In November, despite the continued opposition of Tymoshenko's Government, budgetary amendments providing for increases in salaries and pensions were approved by the Verkhovna Rada, resulting in the suspension of IMF lending.

Viktor Yanukovych elected President

At the first round of the presidential election, which was contested by 18 candidates on 17 January 2010, Yanukovych won 35.3% of the votes cast and Tymoshenko 25.1%; Tihipko (contesting the election as an independent candidate) received 13.1%, ahead of Yatsenyuk, with 7.0%, and Yushchenko, who received only 5.5% of the votes. Some 70.4% of the electorate participated in the poll. On 28 January the Verkhovna Rada voted in favour of removing Lutsenko as interior minister, on the grounds that police had disrupted voting (while he claimed that members of the police service had intervened to prevent electoral malpractice); on the following day Tymoshenko reinstated him as acting Minister of Internal Affairs, although his reinstatement was subsequently suspended by a Kyiv court. In early February Yushchenko signed into law amendments to electoral legislation, which had been proposed by the PR and approved in the Verkhovna Rada, abolishing the requirement for representatives of both candidates to endorse vote counts at polling stations. These amendments would thereby apply with effect from the second round of the presidential election.

The second round of the presidential election, which was conducted on 7 February 2010, was narrowly won by Yanukovych, with 49.0% of votes cast, compared with the 45.5% awarded to Tymoshenko (4.4% of votes cast were against both candidates). Although OSCE observers declared that the poll had been fair, Tymoshenko claimed that widespread malpractice had been perpetrated and submitted a legal challenge against the election results to the Supreme Administrative Court. She withdrew her case a few days later but stated that she continued to refuse to recognize the legitimacy of Yanukovych's election as President and boycotted his inaugural ceremony, which took place on 25 February. After Tymoshenko refused to resign as Prime Minister, the Verkhovna Rada adopted a motion of no confidence in her Government on 3 March. A new parliamentary coalition was negotiated on 11 March between the PR, the Lytvyn bloc and the CPU, which (following a number of defections) controlled 235 of the 450 seats in the Verkhovna Rada. On the same day the legislature voted to approve the nomination of Azarov as Prime Minister; a new Government, dominated by the PR, was formed. A former deputy premier in the Yanukovych administrations, Andriy Klyuyev, became the First Deputy Prime Minister. Tihipko (who had recently announced the revival of the Working Ukraine political party that he headed, under the new name, A Strong Ukraine) became Deputy Prime Minister, responsible for Economic Affairs. Five other Deputy Prime Ministers were prominent members of the PR. Other appointments included that of Anatoliy Mohilyov, a senior police official as the new Minister of Internal Affairs, while Hryshchenko returned to the position of Minister of Foreign Affairs that he had held in 2003–05. In late March an opposition motion of no confidence in the Minister of Education and Science, Dmytro Tabachnyk, who was widely regarded as being dismissive of Ukrainian cultural aspirations and identity, was defeated in the Verkhovna Rada. In early April the Constitutional Court rejected an opposition appeal against the formation of the pro-presidential coalition in the Verkhovna Rada, ruling that individual deputies were entitled to leave their existing parliamentary caucuses; a further six deputies had defected from the Our Ukraine-People's Self-defence and YuTB blocs to the ruling coalition, which consequently increased in size to 241 deputies. Following discussions between Azarov and an IMF delegation on conditions for the resumption of the IMF credit agreement, the CPU indicated that it would withdraw from the ruling coalition if the Government adopted economic austerity measures (see Economic Affairs). On 23 April Azarov was elected Chairman of the PR.

An agreement was reached with Russia on 21 April 2010, whereby Ukraine was to obtain natural gas at reduced prices, and consequently much needed support for the state budget, in exchange for the extension of the lease on the base of the Black Sea Fleet in the Crimean peninsula (due to expire in 2017) for a further 25 years. Large protests outside the building of the Verkhovna Rada ensued, while Tymoshenko attempted to muster opposition to the treaty on the grounds that it violated national sovereignty. Despite violent disturbances by opposition deputies, who sought to obstruct the parliamentary session, the agreement was approved by 236 votes in favour in the Verkhovna Rada on 27 April (when it was also ratified by the Russian Duma). Tymoshenko denounced the agreement and urged a mass opposition protest outside the Verkhovna Rada in early May to demand the removal of Yanukovych and early elections. In May the Office of the Prosecutor-General announced the resumption of a 2004 criminal case against Tymoshenko relating to the alleged bribery of Supreme Court judges, which had been abandoned with her installation as premier in January 2005. In early June 2010 a US law firm commissioned by Azarov began an investigation into spending by the previous Government.

Meanwhile, in May 2010, a new Chief of the General Staff and Commander-in-Chief of the land forces was appointed. On 2 July the Verkhovna Rada voted to dismiss Volodymyr Semynozhenko as Deputy Prime Minister, responsible for Humanitarian Affairs, in response to a motion proposed by a YuTB deputy. (Semynozhenko was appointed later in the month as an adviser to the Prime Minister.) Viktor Boiko was also removed as Minister of the Environment; he was succeeded in that post by Mykola Zlochevsky. In the same month President Yanukovych appointed a close ally, Nestor Shufrych, hitherto the Minister of Emergency Situations, as Deputy Chairman of the National Security Council. Later in July the IMF approved the resumption of lending to Ukraine, after the Government pledged to adhere to fiscal austerity measures. In early August the International Press Institute, in an open letter to Yanukovych, urged him to address what it described as the significant deterioration in press freedom since his election. In the same month the Minister of Internal Affairs expressed concern over the disappearance, in the Kharkiv region, of the editor of newspaper *Novyy Styl*, Vasyl Klymentyev, who had received threats after refusing to withdraw an article in which a local prosecutor was accused of corruption. In September the Office of the Prosecutor-General announced that the official investigation into the killing of Gongadze in 2000 had concluded that former Minister of Internal Affairs Kravchenko had ordered his murder.

Recent developments: Yanukovych consolidates power

On 1 October 2010 the Constitutional Court ruled that the constitutional amendments agreed in December 2004 were unlawful; consequently, the powers to appoint the Prime Minister and other members of the Government, which since 2006 had been shared between the President, Prime Minister and the Verkhovna Rada, were to resume being the sole responsibility of the President. On 13 October Yanukovych dismissed Viktor Slauta as Deputy Prime Minister, responsible for the Agro-Industrial Complex and Volodymyr Sivkovych as Deputy Prime Minister, responsible for Security Affairs; Slauta became an adviser to the President, while Sivkovych was appointed to a position on the National Security Council. On 31 October local elections were conducted, on the basis of a mixed single-mandate and proportional representation electoral system, under new regulations, which had been adopted by the Verkhovna Rada on 10 July; parties that had been established less than one year beforehand and political alliances (notably the YuTB) were prohibited from contesting the elections. International election monitors concluded that the organization of the elections failed to meet the democratic standards of the previous presidential election and cited numerous procedural violations, many of which were related to the new electoral regulations. A low voter turn-out, of about 50%, was recorded; the PR secured 11 of the 24 contested mayoral posts, while Fatherland (which effectively contested the elections in place of the YuTB) obtained only two. In early November Yanukovych appointed Viktor Pshonka as Prosecutor-General, replacing Medvedko. At the end of that month Yanukovych vetoed legislation providing for reforms to the tax code and returned it to the Verkhovna Rada for revision, in response to large-scale protests in Kyiv and other towns that had been organized by owners of small and medium-sized enterprises (who would be disadvantaged by tax rises under the changes). Amended legislation on a new tax code was adopted by the Verkhovna Rada on 2 December. On 9 December Yanukovych signed a decree effecting a government reorganization and a further rationalization of the central administration, which included the abolition of several ministries; Viktor Baloha was appointed Minister of Emergency Situations.

On 20 December 2010 Tymoshenko was formally charged with abuse of power during her term as premier; she denied all charges, which related to the misappropriation of carbon credit funds amounting to €320m. Five YuTB parliamentary deputies, having staged a protest in the Verkhovna Rada, were slightly injured in an ensuing clash with PR deputies. A number of former members of Tymoshenko's administration were also accused of abuse of office, including Lutsenko, who was arrested later that month. In January 2011 former Minister of the Economy in the Tymoshenko Government Bohdan Danylyshyn, who had been arrested in the Czech Republic in October 2010 in response to an international arrest warrant, was granted political asylum by the Czech Government and released from custody, amid concerns that the charges against him and other opposition members were politically motivated. Also in January 2011 Yanukovych appointed an associate, Dmytro Salamatin, to head Ukroboronprom, a new state concern that had been established by the amalgamation of seven state-owned defence companies.

On 1 February 2011 the Verkhovna Rada approved, by 310 votes, legislation scheduling the next parliamentary elections (which had been due in March) for 28 October 2012, thereby substantially extending its mandate, while the the next presidential election was scheduled for March 2015. (Seven YuTB deputies who had voted in favour of the motion were expelled from the party.) Fifty-three parliamentary deputies subsequently submitted a challenge to the legislation at the Constitutional Court, claiming that the requisite majority had been obtained by fraudulent voting practices in the Verkhovna Rada. While the rescheduling of the elections had been proposed on grounds of cost, it was also expected to benefit the PR. In March 2011 the Government delayed the proposal of legislation on pensions reform, which included a proposed increase in the age of retirement, owing to concerns that it would precipitate further social unrest; following pressure from the IMF (see Economic Affairs), however, the adoption of the legislation by June was required. Meanwhile, on 22 March former President Kuchma was officially charged with abuse of office in connection with the killing of Gongadze; it was subsequently reported that the prominent US lawyer Alan Dershowitz was to defend him. The trial of Pukach on charges related to the murder of Gongadze began in April.

Crimea

Despite the political differences between the Ukrainian-speaking western regions and the Russian-speaking eastern regions that were evident during the 1990s and 2000s, only in the Crimean peninsula did any significant movement for reunification with Russia emerge. The situation was further complicated by the status of the Crimean Tatars, who had been forcibly deported to Soviet Central Asia in 1944, and who began to return to Crimea from late 1989. In a referendum held in January 1991, residents of Crimea (which then had the status of an ordinary oblast) voted to restore it to the status of a nominally autonomous republic. The decision, although it had no legal basis, was ratified by the Verkhovna Rada. In June Crimean Tatars established 'parallel' institutions to those of the state, without any constitutional or legal status. The Kurultay (Assembly) was a popular assembly that was intended to convene once a year, the Qırımtatar Milly Meclisi (Crimean Tatar National Assembly) was to meet throughout the year, and a number of local assemblies were also established. In February 1992 the Crimean Supreme Council, the regional legislature, voted to transform the region into the Republic of Crimea, and in May declared Crimea an independent state, adopting a new Constitution. However, following threats from the Verkhovna Rada to impose an economic blockade and direct rule on Crimea, this declaration was rescinded. In June the Ukrainian Government confirmed the status of Crimea (except for Sevastopol city) as an autonomous republic within Ukraine. Meanwhile, relations between the local leadership and Crimean Tatars, some 250,000 of whom had returned to Crimea by late 1992, deteriorated steadily, primarily as a result of disputes over the ownership of land and property, and the right to gain Ukrainian citizenship. In October a Tatar encampment was dispersed on the orders of the Crimean Government, and in response some 6,000 Tatars stormed the Crimean parliament building.

With the election of Yurii Meshkov as President of Crimea in January 1994, it appeared likely that the region would renew efforts towards sovereignty, as well as establishing closer links with Russia. In response, the Verkhovna Rada approved constitutional amendments, according to which the Ukrainian President could nullify any measures taken by the Crimean authorities he deemed to be illegal. In March a referendum was held in Crimea, simultaneously with the Ukrainian legislative elections; 70% of those voting in the referendum supported broader autonomous powers for Crimea. In May, following a vote by the Crimean parliament to restore the suspended Constitution of May 1992, the Ukrainian Government ordered the Crimean legislature to rescind its decision. In September 1994 the Crimean legislature voted to restrict the Crimean President's executive authority. Meanwhile, the Verkhovna Rada approved a constitutional amendment, permitting it to nullify any legislation adopted by the Crimean parliament that contravened the Ukrainian Constitution. In March 1995 the Ukrainian legislature voted to abolish both the Crimean Constitution of May 1992 and the Crimean presidency, and in April 1995 Kuchma imposed direct rule on Crimea.

In October 1995 the Crimean legislature approved a new Constitution. Before its final adoption by the Verkhovna Rada in December 1996, the Constitution underwent several amendments; notably, Ukrainian was recognized as the state language, although Russian was to be the language of all official correspondence of the autonomous republic. In February 1997, contrary to national law, which stipulates that the appointment of the Crimean Prime Minister is the prerogative of the Ukrainian President, the Crimean parliament arrogated to itself the power to appoint the regional Government. In April it appointed Anatolii Franchuk as the new Crimean premier, in place of Arkadii Demydenko. Kuchma suspended this resolution, declaring it to be a violation of the Ukrainian Constitution, but, following the approval of a second motion of no confidence in Demydenko, in June Kuchma consented to his dismissal. The Crimean legislature subsequently approved a new Council of Ministers headed by Franchuk. In October Kuchma exercised his veto over items of legislation approved by the Crimean Supreme Council—the adoption of Russian as the peninsula's official language of business communication, and the realignment of Crimea's time zone with that of Moscow—that were regarded as an assertion of the primacy of Crimea's links with Russia. Further conflict arose between the national Government and the Crimean legislature in February 1998, following the approval of legislation by the Verkhovna Rada, whereby all Ukrainian citizens were to be eligible to contest the seats in the Crimean legislature—hitherto, only citizens resident in Crimea had been eligible. In addition, the new legislation stated that elections to the Crimean parliament were to be held simultaneously with the elections to the Verkhovna Rada in March and not in September, as had previously been decided by the Crimean Supreme Council.

Elections to the Crimean legislature in March 1998 brought the issue of the status of the Crimean Tatars to the fore, when demonstrations were staged by Tatars appealing for the right to vote. The OSCE estimated that about one-half of the 165,000 Tatars resident in Crimea did not have Ukrainian citizenship and were, therefore, ineligible to vote. Leonid Grach, the leader of the CPU in Crimea, was elected Chairman of the new Crimean Supreme Council. In May a new Council of Ministers was appointed, with Sergei Kunitsyn as Chairman. In January

1999 a new Crimean Constitution came into effect. Although citizenship had recently been granted to a number of Crimean Tatars, representatives of the group held a demonstration in May in Simferopol, demanding constitutional changes to ensure better representation and rights for Crimean Tatars and for the Crimean Tatar language to be recognized as a state language; subsequent protests culminated in a 20,000-strong demonstration in Simferopol in May 2000. In July 2001 the Supreme Council dismissed Kunitsyn from the premiership for the third time. Although Kuchma had refused to recognize the previous dismissals, in late July Kuchma accepted Kunitsyn's removal from office, and expressed support for the new premier elected by the Crimean Supreme Council, Valerii Gorbatov.

As campaigning for the concurrent elections to the Verkhovna Rada and the Crimean Supreme Council, to be held on 31 March 2002, commenced, controversy was provoked at the end of February by the invalidation of Grach's candidacy for a seat in the Supreme Council, on technical grounds. Despite his disqualification, Grach's name appeared on ballot papers, and he was re-elected to the Supreme Council in defiance of the decision of the Crimean Court of Appeal. The elections to the Crimean Supreme Council demonstrated a sizeable shift in support away from the communists, towards the centrist Kunitsyn Team, named after its leader, which won 39 of the 100 seats in the Council; a pro-communist electoral alliance, the Grach bloc, received 28 seats. Three other parties obtained representation, and 29 independent candidates were elected. In late April the Ukrainian Supreme Court approved Grach's appeal, thereby serving to legitimize his status as a deputy of the Crimean legislature, although he failed to be re-elected as Chairman of the Crimean legislature. The new parliament also voted for the dismissal of Gorbatov and the reappointment of Kunitsyn as Prime Minister, and allies of Kunitsyn established a legislative majority. None the less, in the concurrent elections to the Verkhovna Rada, the CPU remained the most popular party on the peninsula. For the first time, Crimean Tatar deputies were elected to the Verkhovna Rada, within the Our Ukraine bloc.

In early 2004 concern was expressed by ethnic Russians resident in Crimea that a measure, approved by the Crimean Government in 2000, ordering foreign citizens to pay higher rates for utilities and accommodation than those paid by Ukrainian citizens, was being applied to Russian citizens. Meanwhile, an increase in ethnic tensions between Crimean Tatars and the Slavic inhabitants of the peninsula was reported in early 2004. Although it appeared that disputes over land were the principal source of tensions, some reports suggested that violence had been provoked by groups of Russian extremist nationalists and Cossack groups resident in neighbouring regions of Russia. In the first few months of the year, in advance of the 60th anniversary of the deportation of the Tatars from the peninsula, several clashes and violent incidents occurred, and in early April a petition, signed by over 35,000 Crimean Tatars, which alleged that the police force in Crimea were ignoring incidents of inter-ethnic violence against Tatars, was presented to President Kuchma. The continuing tension in Crimean society was reflected in the allegiances displayed in the presidential election of late 2004, when the peninsula's Russophone majority overwhelmingly supported Yanukovych, while the Crimean Tatar minority was reported to have voted principally for the victorious candidate, Yushchenko. In April 2005 Kunitsyn resigned as Prime Minister of Crimea, following his appointment as an adviser to President Yushchenko; the Crimean Supreme Council voted to approve Anatolii Matviyenko as his replacement. Following the dismissal of Tymoshenko as Prime Minister of Ukraine, in early September, the Crimean Supreme Council voted to dismiss the republican Government; Matviyenko duly resigned on 20 September. On 23 September the Crimean Supreme Council approved the appointment of Anatolii Burdyugov, the leader of the Crimean branch of Yushchenko's People's Union Our Ukraine party, as Prime Minister, and a new Government was formed at the end of the month. In late February 2006 the Crimean legislature voted to hold a referendum on the proposed introduction of Russian as a state language within the peninsula; however, President Yushchenko stated that the referendum would be unconstitutional, and this ruling was subsequently confirmed by the CEC.

Elections to the Crimean Supreme Council, held concurrently with local elections and with those to the Verkhovna Rada on 26 March 2006, were marred by allegations of electoral fraud; moreover, one candidate was killed on polling day. At the end of March the President's Representative in Crimea, Volodomyr Kulich, announced that a commission comprising senior officials of several ministries and law-enforcement bodies was to be established to investigate the apparent electoral violations. Meanwhile, protesters outside the Crimean Parliament demanded that elections in districts where violations were found be declared null and void. The national Prosecutor-General and Matviyenko (in his role as deputy head of the presidential secretariat, to which he had been appointed in November 2005) also became involved in the investigation of the alleged irregularities. The results of the elections were finally announced on 19 April. The For Yanukovych bloc (principally comprising the PR) obtained the largest proportion of the votes cast, with 32.6%; it was awarded 44 of the 100 seats in the Supreme Council. The second-placed party was the pro-Russian Union party, with 7.6% of the votes and 10 seats. The Kunitsyn bloc obtained 10 seats, the CPU nine, the People's Movement of Ukraine-Rukh and the YuTB each obtained eight seats, the far left Nataliya Vitrenko People's Opposition bloc obtained seven seats, and the 'Ne Tak' Opposition bloc (which comprised several centrist parties associated with allies of former President Kuchma) obtained four. In early June Viktor Plakyda, a former energy sector executive and a member of the PR, was elected Prime Minister by the Supreme Council.

In late May 2006 the proposed staging of military exercises off the coast of Crimea, under the aegis of NATO and with the participation of the defence forces of 12 countries, was a focus for protests in the port of Feodosiya, in the east of Crimea, principally by Russian nationalists opposed to Ukrainian involvement with NATO. It was also reported that the local branches of the CPU and the PR supported the protests. Although similar exercises had taken place in the region on an annual basis since 1997, on each occasion, in accordance with the national Constitution, they had required the specific approval of the Verkhovna Rada. As the outgoing Verkhovna Rada had failed to vote to approve the exercises on three occasions, and the prolonged coalition negotiations following the elections to that body on 26 March 2006 had prevented the new legislature from convening, it became apparent that the forthcoming exercises had no legal standing. In early June the Crimean Supreme Council was reported to have voted to approve a statement declaring the peninsula a 'NATO-free territory'. On 11 June some 200 US reserve troops began to leave Crimea, having been prevented from undertaking the construction work for which they had been contracted, and the proposed exercises were abandoned. Meanwhile, there were heightened ethnic tensions on the peninsula during 2006, mostly relating to questions of land ownership. In the first half of the year clashes broke out on several occasions in protest against the operations of a market located on a traditional Crimean Tatar burial site. (The market was moved to a new location later in the year.) In December the Crimean branch of the CPU organized a 'people's referendum' on the peninsula (which was not, however, recognized as having any official status) on Ukraine's aspirations towards NATO membership. According to the results of the poll issued by the CPU, some 58% of eligible voters participated in the 'referendum', of whom almost 99% rejected the notion of Ukrainian accession to NATO.

Following the dissolution of the Verkhovna Rada and scheduling of pre-term elections for 30 September 2007, it was announced in July that Kunitsyn was again to head the pro-presidential coalition, reconstituted as Our Ukraine-People's Self-defence bloc, in Crimea. A number of electoral irregularities were reported in the Republic on 30 September; at the elections to the Verkhovna Rada, Yanukovych's PR secured some 61.0% of votes cast in the Republic, followed by the Our Ukraine-People's Self-defence bloc, with only 8.2%, the CPU, with 7.6%, and the YuTB, with about 6.9%. Following the elections, a temporary ban on demonstrations was ended by the Crimean authorities; in mid-October some 2,000 Crimean Tatars demonstrated in Simferopol to demand land for resettlement, and a further series of protests was planned.

Russia's military operation in Georgia in early August 2008, staged with the stated aim of seeking to protect those to whom it had recently granted citizenship in South Ossetia, and recognition of the separatist regimes in South Ossetia and Abkhazia on 26 August increased domestic and international fears of a similar conflict eventually breaking out in Crimea. In early September the Ukrainian Government expressed concern that Russian passports had been issued to (ethnically Russian) residents of Crimea, and accused Russia of encouraging instability. The Ukrainian authorities formally protested to the Russian consulate in Sevastopol; however, the Representative of the President of Ukraine in Crimea, Leonid Zhunko, denied that a large-scale issuance of Russian passports had been conducted. On 17 September the Crimean legislature approved an appeal to the Ukrainian Verkhovna Rada for the recognition of the independence of Abkhazia and South Ossetia, while pro-Russian groups demonstrated outside the parliamentary building in support of the separatist authorities in those territories.

The election of Viktor Yanukovych to the presidency in early 2010 was reported to have encouraged separatist sentiments in Crimea; in February the republican legislature voted to adopt the Russian, rather than Ukrainian, variant of its name as its official designation, in infringement of the Ukrainian Constitution. In mid-March premier Plakyda and the parliamentary Chairman submitted their resignations. On 17 March the Supreme Council elected the leader of the PR in Crimea, Vladimirr Konstantinov, as the new Chairman. With the agreement of Yanukovych, Konstantinov's nomination of Vasilii Dzharty, also a prominent local member of the PR, as Prime Minister was approved by 82 deputies in the legislature on the same day. Yanukovych subsequently appointed Kunitsyn as his representative in the Republic. In May the Crimean legislature adopted a resolution stating that the Russian language was to be used, together with Ukrainian, in official processes in the peninsula. Elections to the Supreme Council were conducted concurrently with local elections throughout Ukraine, on 31 October, under a new mixed single-mandate and proportional representation electoral system. The PR markedly strengthened its position in the Republic, obtaining 48.9% of the votes cast on the basis of party list votes and a total of 80 seats in the legislature, ahead of the CPU, with only 7.4% of the votes cast and five seats. The other parties represented in the new Crimean Supreme Council were the People's Movement of Ukraine-Rukh (with 7.0% of the votes cast and five seats), Union (5.3%, five seats), Russian Unity (4.0%, three seats) and A Strong Ukraine (3.6%, two seats). Konstantinov was re-elected as legislative Chairman.

Foreign Affairs
Regional relations

Following the collapse of the USSR in 1991, the Ukrainian leadership was notably reluctant to sign any union agreement with the other former Soviet republics that might compromise its declaration of independence. It was this reluctance to enter into a renewed political union that led to the establishment of the Commonwealth of Independent States (CIS, see p. 238) by President Kravchuk, and the leaders of Russia and Belarus, on 8 December. Uniquely among the states associated with the organization, Ukraine declined to ratify the agreement providing for its membership of the CIS. Although relations with Russia, as Ukraine's major trading partner and a country with close ethnic, historic, cultural and familial links with Ukraine, remained generally good following independence, tensions existed between those who sought to renew closer relations with Russia and countries of 'Eurasia', and those who sought to emphasize Ukraine's independence and 'European' status. Ukraine agreed to a unified command for the strategic (principally nuclear-armed) forces of the former USSR, but began to establish its own conventional armed forces. In January 1994 a trilateral agreement on the removal of nuclear weapons from Ukraine was signed by Ukraine, Russia and the USA, and in November the Verkhovna Rada voted to ratify the Treaty on the Non-Proliferation of Nuclear Weapons (see p. 118). In December Kuchma formally signed the Treaty, and the Strategic Arms' Reduction Treaty (START) I entered into force. The transfer to Russia of Ukraine's nuclear weapons was completed by June 1996.

Throughout the 1990s Ukraine consistently refused to participate in organizations that it perceived as being dominated by Russia, although it became an associate member of the CIS Air Defence Agreement in 1995. In 1997 Ukraine initiated the establishment of the GUAM (Georgia-Ukraine-Azerbaijan-Moldova) grouping. In 2001 a permanent office of the grouping (known as GUUAM in 1999–2005, when Uzbekistan was also a member) was opened in Yalta, Crimea. In 2006, at a summit held in Kyiv, the grouping was formally inaugurated as a full international organization concerned with the promotion of democracy, energy security and strengthening relations; it was also redesignated as the Organization for Democracy and Economic Development—GUAM (see p. 462). As the Kuchma administration became increasingly isolated internationally in the early 2000s, particularly in response to allegations that it had illegally sold military equipment to the Iraqi regime of Saddam Hussain, Ukraine's relationship with Russia appeared to strengthen. In January 2003 Kuchma was elected as Chairman of the CIS, becoming the first non-Russian to hold that post. (He was, however, replaced by Russian President Vladimir Putin in 2004.) Later in 2003 proposals to form a 'single economic zone' with Belarus, Kazakhstan and Russia became increasingly popular, and were approved by the Verkhovna Rada in September, on the condition that participation did not contravene the Ukrainian Constitution, although interest in Ukraine's participation in such a zone waned following the election of Yushchenko as President in late 2004. In August 2005 Yushchenko and President Mikheil Saakashvili of Georgia, meeting in Borjomi, Georgia, signed a declaration on the creation of a nine-country Community of Democratic Choice. The alliance was officially launched in December, at a meeting in Kyiv.

The principal controversy between Ukraine and Russia concerned ownership of the former Soviet Black Sea Fleet, based in Sevastopol, on the Crimean peninsula. Although both countries agreed in July 1992 to exercise joint control over the fleet for a transitional period of three years, in April 1995 the Russian parliament imposed a moratorium on plans to divide the fleet. Nevertheless, in June Russian President Boris Yeltsin and Kuchma agreed to the equal division of the fleet, with separate Ukrainian and Russian bases. The main Russian base was to be at Sevastopol, although the exact legal status of the city was left unresolved. Yeltsin and Kuchma signed an agreement on 31 May 1997, in accordance with which the Russian fleet was to lease three bays in Sevastopol for 20 years, while the Ukrainian fleet was to use the remainder. Upon expiry, the treaty could be renewed for five years, but would then be subject to renegotiation. A bilateral Treaty of Friendship, Co-operation and Partnership was also signed, in which Russia for the first time recognized the sovereignty of Ukraine. Russia finally ratified the treaty in February 1999, and later that year and in March 2000 further agreements were signed between Russia and Ukraine pertaining to the fleet. In January 2003 a treaty delineating the land boundary between Russia and Ukraine (which remained largely unmarked and unregulated) was signed by Kuchma and Putin, although discussions on the status of the Sea of Azov, which lies between the two countries, remained unresolved. Work on the construction of a Russian dam in the Sea precipitated considerable controversy, and raised concerns that the territorial integrity of Ukraine was being violated. In December Presidents Kuchma and Putin signed an agreement on the use of the Sea of Azov, the entirety of which was defined as comprising the internal waters of both countries. Agreement was also reached on the maritime state boundary of Russia and Ukraine in the region.

The Ukrainian presidential election of 2004 caused considerable upheaval in diplomatic relations with Russia. During the course of the campaign, the Russian Government was accused of interference in favour of Yanukovych; notably, President Putin visited Ukraine before each round of voting to appear publicly with Yanukovych and Kuchma, and telephoned Yanukovych to congratulate him on his apparent victory after the second round before the official (and subsequently annulled) results had been announced. Putin described the demonstrations that resulted in the election being repeated as constitutionally illegitimate. Symbolically, and in accordance with promises made during his election campaign, President Yushchenko visited Moscow one day after his inauguration in January 2005, and emphasized the importance of maintaining co-operative relations with Russia. However, further diplomatic tension was caused by the appointment of Tymoshenko as Prime Minister in February, in part as a result of a warrant existing in Russia for her arrest on charges of the attempted bribery of Russian officials during her time as head of a Ukrainian natural gas trading company in the 1990s. In late 2005 the Russian state-controlled gas monopoly, Gazprom, issued demands that Ukraine pay market prices for the supply of natural gas, rather than the heavily subsidized rate (of US $50 per 1,000 cu m) that it had paid hitherto. Following the failure of the Ukrainian authorities and Gazprom to reach agreement, on 1 January 2006 Gazprom suspended supplies to Ukraine, a measure that caused considerable hardship in Ukraine, as well as resulting in the loss of supplies to other European countries that received gas from pipelines traversing Ukraine. On 4 January supplies of natural gas to Ukraine were restored, after Ukraine agreed to pay $95 per 1,000 cu m for a mixture of Russian and Turkmenistani natural gas, which was to be supplied to Ukraine by a Swiss-registered company, RosUkrEnergo.

The appointment of Yanukovych as Prime Minister in August 2006 facilitated an improvement in relations between Ukraine and Russia: on 15 August Yanukovych met Chairman of the Government Mikhail Fradkov of Russia at the Black Sea port of Sochi, and on 22 December President Putin visited Ukraine for the first time since Yushchenko's election. On 3 October Gazprom threatened again to suspend natural gas supplies to Ukraine, on the grounds that it was owed US $1,300m.; on 9 October, however, it was announced that a compromise agreement had been reached, whereby Ukraine was to repay $1,200m. by transferring gas from underground storage facilities in Ukraine to Gazprom for further export. Tymoshenko, who had recently returned to the office of Prime Minister, strenuously criticized an agreement reached between Russia and Ukraine, which retained the intermediary trading company in gas supplies to Ukraine, RosUkrEnergo (jointly owned by Gazprom and a consortium of Ukrainian businessmen). Meanwhile, Russia strongly opposed Ukraine's formal request for NATO membership (see below). Putin subsequently warned that, in the event that Ukraine joined NATO and agreed to the deployment on its territory of elements of the planned US national missile defence system, Russia would be prepared to target its missiles at Ukraine. In February 2008 Gazprom warned that it would reduce supplies to Ukraine, in response to debts incurred during the previous month; it was subsequently announced that Ukraine and Russia had reached a debt settlement, and also agreed to discontinue use of RosUkrEnergo as an intermediary. Later in February, however, Gazprom claimed that Ukraine had failed to sign the negotiated agreements. After further discussions, in April the Ukrainian Government announced that agreement had been reached on a new payment scheme; at the insistence of the Russian authorities, RosUkrEnergo was to remain the intermediary company, operating within Russia.

Following Russia's military operation against Georgia in early August 2008, Yushchenko, together with the Presidents of Estonia, Lithuania and Poland, and the Prime Minister of Latvia, visited Georgia in a demonstration of solidarity, where he attended a rally in support of President Saakashvili in Tbilisi, the Georgian capital. On 13 August Yushchenko issued a ruling, based on a resolution by the National Security and Defence Council, requiring Russia to request prior permission for movements of its Black Sea Fleet based at Sevastopol (after Russian vessels belonging to the Fleet participated in the conflict). Later in August he officially ended a bilateral agreement reached in 1992 (which had been abrogated by Russia in February) on Russian use of two Ukrainian radar stations, and offered to make them available to European nations.

In December 2008 a further dispute erupted with Russia, after Gazprom demanded some US $2,100m. owed by Ukraine for the non-payment of natural gas and incurred fines; although Ukrainian state utility Naftogaz Ukrainy announced at the end of that month that it was to pay $1,500m., continuing disagreement over the price Ukraine would pay for Russian gas and the level of transit fees to be paid by Gazprom during 2009 resulted in Russia's suspension of gas supplies to Ukraine on 1 January. After accusing Ukraine of abstracting gas intended for export to Europe flowing through Russian-owned pipelines in Ukraine, Russia also halted supplies to Europe by way of Ukraine on 7 January (resulting in severe disruptions to supplies to some 18 European countries). Following intensive EU mediation and emergency discussions between Gazprom and Naftogaz, on 19 January Putin (as Russian premier) and Tymoshenko signed an agreement in Moscow whereby Ukraine would pay an average price for Russian gas in 2009 that would be 20% lower than that charged to European countries, while the transit price would remain unchanged (with both converging to market levels in 2010). Gas supplies to Europe by way of Ukraine were finally restored on 21 January. Following further discussions between Putin and Tymoshenko in Moscow at the end of April, it was agreed that Gazprom would not penalize Ukraine for failure to accept the contracted amount of gas in 2009 and would assist in payment of the transit fee to ensure supply, while Russia was invited to participate in an EU-supported programme to modernize Ukraine's gas transportation system (which had been announced in March).

In February 2009 Ukraine threatened to expel the Russian ambassador, former Russian premier Viktor Chernomyrdin, after he criticized the Ukrainian authorities; Chernomyrdin was transferred from the post in June. In an open letter in August, Russian President Dmitrii Medvedev accused Yushchenko of pursuing 'anti-Russian' policies and of supplying armaments to Georgian forces in the conflict of the previous year, and attributed responsibility to Ukraine for the periodic disruption of Russian gas supplies to Europe via Ukraine; Medvedev also stated that he would postpone the dispatch of a new Russian ambassador to Ukraine. Later in August the Russian Prosecutor-General's Office announced that it had located evidence suggesting that Ukrainian troops had supported Georgian forces in the fighting in South Ossetia. At the beginning of September discussions between Tymoshenko and Putin resulted in a concession to allow Ukraine to pay only for the natural gas it consumed, rather than the amount that it was contracted to import from Russia. In November, following discussions in Yalta between Tymoshenko and Putin, it was confirmed that the gas transit fees paid by Russia to Ukraine would be increased significantly in the following year, while Ukraine would be charged the European market price for Russian gas. In January 2010, shortly after the defeat of Yushchenko in the first round of a presidential election, Medvedev finalized the appointment of a new Russian ambassador to Ukraine. Following his election to the presidency in February, Yanukovych pledged to restore cordial relations between Ukraine and Russia and to end the recurrent disputes over gas supplies. In mid-February Medvedev invited Yanukovych to Moscow. In March the new Ukrainian Prime Minister, Mykola Azarov, met Putin and Gazprom officials for discussions in Moscow, when Putin consented to conduct further negotiations on gas prices. On 21 April Medvedev and Yanukovych, meeting in Kharkiv, reached an agreement whereby Russia was to grant Ukraine a substantial discount on the price of Russian gas, while Ukraine was to extend the lease on the base of the Black Sea Fleet in the Crimean peninsula (due to expire in 2017) for a further 25 years. (The Verkhovna Rada ratified the agreement on 27 April.) Following a meeting in Sochi between Azarov and Putin at the end of April, Putin announced proposals for the merger of Gazprom and Naftogaz Ukrainy, and the integration of the two countries' nuclear industries. In May, during Medvedev's first official state visit to Ukraine, he signed a number of further agreements with Yanukovych, including one confirming the border between the two countries.

In August 2010 the Ukrainian Government conducted discussions with Gazprom regarding a possible arrangement whereby Ukraine would purchase gas at Russian domestic prices, which was dependent on Ukrainian approval of the proposed sale of Naftogaz Ukrainy to Gazprom. In November a settlement was reached in a significant dispute between Naftogaz and RosUkrEnergo, which had won an international arbitration case that 12,000m. cu m of gas had been illegally expropriated from it, after being transferred to Naftogaz Ukrainy as part of an agreement to resolve the gas crisis in early 2009; the equivalent amount of gas was returned to RosUkrEnergo, which was to pay about one-half of its market value. In March 2011 the Verkhovna Rada established a commission to investigate the agreement between Naftogaz Ukrainy and Gazprom reached by the Tymoshenko administration. In April it was reported that the Ukrainian Government had failed to respond to an invitation, extended by Putin during a visit to Ukraine, to join Russia's newly established customs union with Belarus and Kazakhstan; in his annual address to the legislature earlier that month, President Yanukovych had indicated that he favoured closer co-operation with the customs union, in conjunction with the establishment of a free trade agreement with the EU (see below).

Other external relations

Ukraine sought to counterbalance its close relations with Russia during the 1990s by a policy of engagement with Western nations and organizations, as part of what was termed a 'multi-vector' foreign policy. In 1994 Ukraine joined NATO's 'Partnership for Peace' (see p. 371) programme; a 'Charter on a Distinctive Relationship' was signed with the Organization in 1997, envisaging enhanced co-operation with the Alliance. In April 1999, in protest against NATO air-strikes against Yugoslavia (Serbia and Montenegro), the Verkhovna Rada voted to withdraw from the 'Partnership for Peace' programme; Ukraine rejoined the programme when the conflict ended in June.

The 'orange revolution' that brought Yushchenko to power was generally regarded favourably in the USA; in early April 2005 he visited the USA, meeting President George W. Bush and addressing the US Senate. Later that month Yushchenko authorized the withdrawal of Ukrainian peace-keeping troops from Iraq by the end of the year, as had been approved by the Verkhovna Rada in the previous year. During a visit to Kyiv in July 2009, US Vice-President Joseph Biden reaffirmed US support for Ukraine's aspirations for integration into Western

UKRAINE

institutions, emphasizing that this would not be affected by recent US efforts to achieve a rapprochement with Russia, but also urged reform of the energy sector.

Ukraine signed a trade agreement with the EU in June 1995, and was formally admitted to the Council of Europe (see p. 250) in November. The Ukrainian leadership had long expressed an intention to pursue full membership of the EU; however, the failure to abolish capital punishment (which is prohibited by the conditions of membership of the organization) before March 2000 was a source of tension, as was the slow pace of political and economic reform and, in particular, concerns that President Kuchma may have been implicated in the murder of investigative journalist Heorhiy Gongadze in 2000. President Yushchenko, who was elected in late 2004, emphasized in his earliest diplomatic pronouncements that he regarded the integration of Ukraine into both the EU and NATO as fundamental goals of his presidency. However, the return of Yanukovych as Prime Minister in August 2006 proved detrimental to Ukraine's attempts to enter into a Membership Action Plan with NATO. Ukraine's membership application to the World Trade Organization (WTO, see p. 430), submitted in 1993, was formally approved on 5 February 2008, and was ratified by the legislature in April. Ukraine's accession to the WTO was expected to allow discussions on a free trade agreement with the EU to proceed. In January 2008 the Ukraine Government formally requested a NATO Membership Action Plan (MAP), which was regarded as preparatory to membership. (Opposition parties, notably the PR and the CPU, strongly criticized Ukraine's request for NATO membership.) At a NATO summit meeting, which was convened in Bucharest, Romania, on 2 April, Ukraine and Georgia were not offered a MAP, although the Alliance made clear that it welcomed a closer relationship with both countries. Following Russia's military action in Georgia in early August, an EU summit meeting on Ukraine, which was conducted in Paris, France, on 9 September, resulted in an offer of an Association Agreement, replacing a 10-year Partnership and Co-operation Agreement and providing for trade benefits and increased energy co-operation; negotiations on visa-free entry to EU states for Ukrainian citizens began in late October. In May 2009 Ukraine, together with Armenia, Azerbaijan, Belarus, Georgia and Moldova, was included in the EU's Eastern Partnership programme, which envisaged enhanced free trade and visa arrangements for those countries. In January 2010 Ukraine became the first non-member state to contribute forces to the multinational NATO Response Force. Following his inauguration on 25 February, Yanukovych's first state visit at the beginning of March was to Brussels, Belgium, where he discussed with EU officials a programme for the adoption of the Association Agreement, including the establishment of a free trade area. In July the Verkhovna Rada approved legislation, which was subsequently signed into force by Yanukovych, defining Ukrainian foreign policy as being based upon the 'non-bloc' status of the country (thereby excluding it from NATO membership), while emphasizing that it would seek to maintain constructive co-operation with a range of partners, including NATO, the EU, the CIS and Russia. The first summit meeting between the EU and Ukraine under the Government of Yanukovych took place in Brussels in November, when the President issued assurances that Ukraine's closer relations with Russia would benefit Euro-Atlantic security and also sought to allay concerns regarding a perceived deterioration in democratic conditions in the country (see above).

CONSTITUTION AND GOVERNMENT

Executive power is vested in the President and the Prime Minister, and legislative power is the prerogative of the 450-member Verkhovna Rada (Supreme Council), which is directly elected for a five-year term. The President is elected by direct, popular vote for a five-year term. The President appoints the Prime Minister and the members of the Cabinet of Ministers and may, in certain circumstances, order the dissolution of the legislature. Judicial power is exercised by the Supreme Court and by courts of general jurisdiction. Ukraine is a unitary state, divided for administrative purposes into 24 oblasts (regions), one autonomous republic (Crimea), and two metropolitan areas (Kyiv and Sevastopol). The Constitution guarantees local self-government to regions, cities, settlements and villages. Regional governors are appointed by the President.

REGIONAL AND INTERNATIONAL CO-OPERATION

Ukraine is a founder member of the Commonwealth of Independent States (CIS, see p. 238), but has not ratified the CIS Charter. Ukraine is a member of the European Bank for Reconstruction and Development (EBRD, see p. 265), the Organization of the Black Sea Economic Co-operation (see p. 398) and the Organization for Democracy and Economic Development—GUAM (see p. 462). In June 1994 Ukraine signed an agreement of partnership and co-operation with the European Union (EU, see p. 270), which was ratified in 1998. Ukraine was admitted to the Organization for Security and Co-operation in Europe (OSCE, see p. 385) and the Council of Europe (see p. 250) in 1995. In 1994 Ukraine joined the 'Partnership for Peace' (see p. 371) programme of the North Atlantic Treaty Organization (NATO, see p. 368).

Ukraine was, as the Ukrainian Soviet Socialist Republic, a founder member of the UN. Prior to the dissolution of the USSR in 1991, both Ukraine and Belarus had formally separate UN membership from that of the USSR, despite both republics forming integral parts of the Union. Ukraine acceded to the World Trade Organization (see p. 430) in 2008.

ECONOMIC AFFAIRS

In 2009, according to the World Bank, Ukraine's gross national income (GNI), measured at average 2007–09 prices, was US $128,848m., equivalent to $2,800 per head (or $6,190 per head, on an international purchasing-power parity basis). During 2000–09 gross domestic product (GDP) per head increased, in real terms, at an average annual rate of 5.0% per year, while the population decreased by an average annual rate of 0.7%. Ukraine's GDP increased, in real terms, at an average annual rate of 4.2% in 2000–09. Real GDP increased by 2.1% in 2008, but decreased by 15.1% in 2009.

Agriculture (including forestry and fishing) contributed 7.8% of GDP in 2010, and the sector provided 15.8% of employment in 2008. Ukraine has large areas of extremely fertile land, forming part of the 'black earth' belt, and the country is self-sufficient in almost all aspects of agricultural production. The principal crops are grain, potatoes, sugar beet and other vegetables. A programme to transfer state collective farms to private ownership was initiated in 1991, although by 1997 only 14% of land was managed by private farms, which, in that year, contributed some 46% of total agricultural output. During 2000–09, according to the World Bank, agricultural GDP increased at an average annual rate of 3.5%, in real terms. In 2008 the GDP of the sector decreased by 15.0% and remained constant in 2009.

Industry (including mining, manufacturing, construction and power) contributed an estimated 29.5% of GDP in 2010, and the sector provided 23.4% of employment in 2008. Heavy industry dominates the sector, particularly metal-working, mechanical engineering, chemicals and machinery products. According to the World Bank, industrial GDP increased by an average of 8.4% annually, in real terms, in 2000–09. Real industrial GDP increased by 20.0% in 2009.

In 2003 some 3.7% of the work-force were engaged in mining and quarrying; the sector contributed 6.3% of GDP in 2010. Ukraine has large deposits of coal (mainly in the huge Donbass coal basin) and high-grade iron ore, and there are also significant reserves of manganese, titanium, graphite, natural gas and petroleum. Production of coal declined by some 53% in 1989–95, and in 1996 the Government implemented a major reorganization of the coal-mining industry, including the closure of several loss-making mines. According to UN estimates, during 2000–09, the GDP of the mining sector (including utilities) increased at an average annual rate of 0.4%, in real terms; however the GDP of the sector (including utilities) decreased by 10.0% in 2009.

The manufacturing sector provided 17.6% of employment in 2003, and the sector contributed 16.5% of GDP in 2010. During 2000–09 real manufacturing GDP increased by an average annual rate of 6.8%. The GDP of the sector increased by 4.0% in 2008, but decreased by 17.0% in 2009.

The construction sector contributed some 3.2% of GDP in 2010, and the sector provided 5.0% of employment in 2008. According to UN estimates, during 2000–09 construction GDP increased, in real terms, at an average annual rate of 2.9%; however, the sector's GDP decreased by 17.5% in 2008 and further decreased by 3.6% in 2009.

Ukraine is highly dependent on imports of energy products, of which Russia and Turkmenistan are the principal suppliers. Imports of mineral fuels comprised 34.8% of the value of total imports in 2010. Ukraine is also vitally important as an energy transit country, situated as it is between the mineral resource-rich countries of the former USSR and the developed economies of Europe. A pipeline from a new oil terminal at Odesa, on the Black Sea coast, to Brody, near the border with Poland, which was originally intended to carry petroleum from the Caspian Sea to Central and Western Europe, was completed in 2001; however, following Ukraine's failure to secure petroleum suppliers from the Caspian region, the pipeline entered operation in reverse direction, permitting Russian companies to pump their petroleum to the Black Sea for export. Two new nuclear reactors began energy production in 2004. In 2007 nuclear power accounted for 47.2% of Ukraine's electricity production; coal accounted for 34.2% and natural gas for 13.0%.

The services sector contributed 62.7% of GDP in 2010, and the sector engaged 60.7% of the employed labour force in 2008. During 2000–09 the GDP of the sector decreased, in real terms, by an average annual rate of 0.1%; the sector's GDP increased by 4.3% in 2008, but saw a sharp decline of 42.3% in 2009. A significant event for the development of the tourist sector in Ukraine was the announcement, in April 2007, that the country was to co-host, with Poland, the 2012 football European Championship finals.

In 2009 Ukraine recorded a trade deficit of US $4,307m., while there was a deficit of $1,732m. on the current account of the balance of payments. In 2010 the principal market for exports was Russia (accounting for 26.1% of the value of total exports). Other important markets for exports included Turkey and Italy. Russia was also the principal source of imports in 2010, providing 36.5% of all imports. Other significant suppliers of imports were the People's Republic of China and Germany. The principal exports in 2010 were base metals and products of base metals (some 33.7% of the total, comprising principally iron and steel), mineral products, machinery, mechanical and electrical equipment, vegetable products and chemical products. The principal imports in that year were mineral products (which accounted for 34.8% of total imports), machinery, mechanical and electrical equipment, chemical products, vehicles and transportation equipment, and plastics and rubber.

In 2009 a consolidated budgetary deficit of 44,781m. hryvnyas was recorded, equivalent to 4.9% of GDP in that year. Ukraine's general government gross debt was 316,883m. hryvnyas in 2009, equivalent to 34.6% of GDP. Ukraine's total external debt was US $92,479m. at the end of 2008, of which $10,726m. was public and publicly guaranteed debt. In that year the cost of debt-servicing was equivalent to 19.4% of the value of exports of goods, services and income. According to ILO estimates, in 2000–09 the average annual inflation rate was 11.3%. According to official figures, consumer prices increased by 25.2% in 2008 and by 15.9% in 2009. Some 8.1% of the labour force were unemployed in 2010.

The economy showed significant signs of improvement from 2000. Ukraine's reliance on imported energy supplies, principally from Russia, and its economy's overdependence on steel exports, along with a rapid growth in exposure to credit and increases in wage payments in the mid-2000s, were among the principal reasons that the country was severely affected by the international financial crisis from late 2008. In November the IMF agreed to lend some US $16,400m. to Ukraine under a two-year emergency stand-by arrangement to help restore financial stability, subject to the fulfilment of a number of budgetary and supervisory measures. However, by February 2009 Ukraine had failed to meet the stipulated conditions amid the continued economic downturn, causing the IMF to withhold funds; credit was resumed in May, after the Government agreed a revised commitment to a budgetary deficit of no more than 4% of GDP for that year. Meanwhile, a dispute with the Russian state-controlled company Gazprom over the non-payment of gas supplies and associated fines, and over the rate of transit fees charged by Ukraine, resulted in the temporary suspension of gas supplies to Ukraine in January. Antagonistic relations between President Yushchenko and the Government of premier Yuliya Tymoshenko further obstructed the adoption of economic policies agreed with the IMF during 2009; in November budget amendments providing for increases in salaries and pensions were approved by the legislature, resulting in the suspension of IMF credit. Effective governance with regard to economic reforms improved following the election to the presidency of Viktor Yanukovych in February 2010 and the establishment of a majority parliamentary coalition. On 21 April President Yanukovych reached an agreement with his Russian counterpart, whereby Russia was to grant Ukraine a substantial discount on the price of Russian gas, in exchange for the extension of the lease on the base of the Black Sea Fleet in the Crimean peninsula. In June Yanukovych announced an extensive programme of economic reforms, which included revision of the tax system, completion of the privatization programme, the introduction of pension reforms, and the adoption of price increases for domestic energy consumption. Consequently, in late July the IMF approved a new stand-by credit agreement for Ukraine, totalling $15,100m. over a period of 29 months, and disbursed the first tranche of $1,890m. In November legislation providing for reforms to the tax code prompted large-scale protests, organized by owners of small and medium-sized enterprises (who would be disadvantaged by tax rises under the changes); amended legislation on the new tax code was finally adopted by the Verkhovna Rada in early December. The Government negotiated with the IMF for a more gradual increase in gas tariffs for the population than had been originally agreed (after a 50% rise imposed in August). Later in December the IMF completed its first review of Ukraine's economic performance under the reform programme, and approved a disbursement of about $1,500m. Following a contraction of GDP of some 15.1% in 2009, the IMF projected growth of 3.7% for 2010. Meanwhile, in late 2010 the Ukrainian and Russian Governments conducted negotiations regarding a possible arrangement whereby Ukraine would purchase gas at Russian domestic prices, which was dependent on Ukrainian approval of the proposed sale of Ukrainian state utility Naftogaz Ukrainy to Gazprom (see Regional relations). The Ukrainian Government also envisaged the establishment of a free trade agreement with the European Union (see p. 270) by the end of 2011. In March the Ukrainian authorities again postponed the approval of legislation providing for pension reform. As a result of this and the Government's failure to implement other reforms, notably to reduce sufficiently the deficit of Naftogaz Ukrainy through the gas tariff increases, in April the IMF delayed the disbursement of a tranche of funds under the stand-by agreement (although it was expected that this would be forthcoming by mid-2011).

PUBLIC HOLIDAYS

2012: 1 January (New Year), 7 January (Orthodox Christmas), 8 March (International Women's Day), 16 April (Orthodox Easter Monday), 1 May (Labour Day), 9 May (Victory Day), 13 June (Pentecost Monday), 28 June (Constitution Day), 24 August (Independence Day).

UKRAINE

Statistical Survey

Principal source (unless otherwise stated): State Committee for Statistics, 01023 Kyiv, vul. Sh. Rustaveli 3; tel. (44) 226-20-21; fax (44) 235-37-39; e-mail info@ukrstat.gov.ua; internet www.ukrstat.gov.ua.

Area and Population

AREA, POPULATION AND DENSITY

Area (sq km)	603,700*
Population (census results)	
12 January 1989	51,706,742
5 December 2001	
Males	22,441,344
Females	26,015,758
Total	48,457,102
Population (official estimates at 1 January, rounded)	
2009	46,143,700
2010	45,962,900
2011	45,778,500
Density (per sq km) at 1 January 2011	75.8

* 233,090 sq miles.

POPULATION BY AGE AND SEX
(UN estimates at mid-2011)

	Males	Females	Total
0–14	3,248,817	3,078,347	6,327,164
15–64	15,245,456	16,593,000	31,838,456
65 and over	2,323,456	4,678,031	7,001,487
Total	20,817,729	24,349,378	45,167,107

Source: UN, *World Population Prospects: The 2008 Revision*.

POPULATION BY ETHNIC GROUP
(permanent inhabitants, census of 5 December 2001)

	'000	%
Ukrainian	37,541.7	78.13
Russian	8,334.1	17.34
Belarusian	275.8	0.57
Moldovan	258.6	0.54
Crimean Tatar	248.2	0.52
Others	1,393.9	2.90
Total	48,052.3	100.00

ADMINISTRATIVE DIVISIONS

	Area ('000 sq km)	Population (at 1 January 2011)*	Density (per sq km)
Regions			
Cherkasy	20.9	1,285,400	61.5
Chernihiv	31.9	1,098,200	34.4
Chernivtsi	8.1	904,300	111.6
Dnipropetrovsk	31.9	3,336,500	104.6
Donetsk	26.5	4,433,000	167.3
Ivano-Frankivsk	13.9	1,379,800	99.3
Kharkiv	31.4	2,755,100	87.7
Kherson	28.5	1,088,200	38.2
Khmelnytsky	20.6	1,326,900	64.4
Kirovohrad	24.6	1,010,000	41.1
Kyiv	28.1	1,717,600	61.1
Luhansk	26.7	2,291,300	85.8
Lviv	21.8	2,544,700	116.7
Mykolayiv	24.6	1,183,300	48.1
Odesa	33.3	2,388,700	71.7
Poltava	28.8	1,487,800	51.7
Rivne	20.1	1,152,500	57.3
Sumy	23.8	1,161,500	48.8
Ternopil	13.8	1,084,100	78.6
Transcarpathia	12.8	1,247,400	97.5
Vinnytsyia	26.5	1,641,200	61.9
Volyn	20.2	1,037,200	51.3
Zaporizhzhya	27.2	1,801,300	66.2
Zhytomyr	29.9	1,279,000	42.8
—continued	Area ('000 sq km)	Population (at 1 January 2011)*	Density (per sq km)
Cities			
Kyiv	0.8	2,799,200	3,499.0
Sevastopol	0.9	380,800	423.1
Autonomous Republic			
Crimea	26.1	1,963,500	75.2
Total	603.7	45,778,500	75.8

* Official estimates, rounded.

PRINCIPAL TOWNS
(population at census of 5 December 2001, rounded figures)

Kyiv (Kiev, capital)	2,611,000	Poltava	318,000
Kharkiv	1,470,000	Chernihiv	305,000
Dnipropetrovsk	1,065,000	Cherkasy	295,000
Odesa	1,029,000	Sumy	293,000
Donetsk	1,016,000	Horlivka	292,000
Zaporizhzhya	815,000	Zhytomyr	284,000
Lviv	733,000	Dniprodzerzhynsk	256,000
Kryvyi Rih	669,000	Khmelnytsky	254,000
Mykolayiv	514,000	Kirovohrad	254,000
Mariupol	492,000	Rivne	249,000
Luhansk	463,000	Chernivtsi	241,000
Makiyivka	390,000	Kremenchuk	234,000
Vinnytsya	357,000	Ternopil	228,000
Simferopol	344,000	Ivano-Frankivsk	218,000
Sevastopol	342,000	Lutsk	209,000
Kherson	328,000	Bila Tserkva	200,000

2010 ('000, official estimates at 1 January): Kyiv (Kiev, capital) 2,785; Kharkiv 1,452; Dnipropetrovsk 1,011; Odesa 1,010.

BIRTHS, MARRIAGES AND DEATHS

	Registered live births		Registered marriages		Registered deaths	
	Number	Rate (per 1,000)	Number	Rate (per 1,000)	Number	Rate (per 1,000)
2002	390,687	8.1	317,228	6.6	754,911	15.7
2003	408,591	8.5	370,966	7.8	765,408	16.0
2004	427,259	9.0	278,230	5.9	761,263	16.0
2005	426,085	9.0	332,138	7.1	781,964	16.6
2006	460,368	9.8	354,959	7.6	758,093	16.2
2007	472,657	10.2	416,427	9.0	762,877	16.4
2008	510,588	11.0	321,992	7.0	754,462	16.3
2009	512,526	11.1	318,199	6.9	706,740	15.3

Life expectancy (years at birth, WHO estimates): 68 (males 62; females 74) in 2008 (Source: WHO, *World Health Statistics*).

IMMIGRATION AND EMIGRATION

	2008	2009	2010
Immigrants	37,281	32,917	30,810
Emigrants	22,402	19,470	14,677

UKRAINE

ECONOMICALLY ACTIVE POPULATION
(annual averages, '000 persons aged 15–70 years)

	2006	2007	2008
Agriculture, hunting, forestry and fishing	3,649.1	3,484.5	3,322.1
Mining and quarrying; manufacturing; electricity, gas and water supply	4,036.9	3,973.0	3,871.4
Construction	987.1	1,030.2	1,043.4
Wholesale and retail trade; repair of motor vehicles, motorcycles and personal and household goods; hotels and restaurants	4,406.9	4,564.4	4,744.4
Transport, storage and communications	1,428.8	1,451.9	1,465.8
Financial intermediation	286.0	344.4	394.9
Real estate, renting and business activities	1,041.9	1,134.7	1,150.4
Public administration and defence; compulsory social security	1,033.7	1,036.4	1,067.5
Education	1,690.5	1,693.7	1,702.4
Health and social work	1,356.7	1,359.0	1,369.9
Other community, social and personal service activities; private households with employed persons; extra-territorial organizations and bodies	812.8	832.5	840.1
Total employed	20,730.4	20,904.7	20,972.3
Total unemployed	1,515.0	1,417.6	1,425.1
Total labour force	22,245.4	22,322.3	22,397.4

Source: ILO.

2009 (annual averages, '000 persons aged 15–70 years): Total employed 20,191.5; Unemployed 1,958.8; Total labour force 22,150.3.
2010 (annual averages, '000 persons aged 15–70 years): Total employed 20,266.0; Unemployed 1,785.6; Total labour force 22,051.6.

Health and Welfare

KEY INDICATORS

Total fertility rate (children per woman, 2008)	1.3
Under-5 mortality rate (per 1,000 live births, 2008)	15
HIV/AIDS (% of persons aged 15–49, 2007)	1.6
Physicians (per 1,000 head, 2006)	3.1
Hospital beds (per 1,000 head, 2006)	8.7
Health expenditure (2007): US $ per head (PPP)	475
Health expenditure (2007): % of GDP	6.9
Health expenditure (2007): public (% of total)	57.6
Access to water (% of persons, 2008)	98
Access to sanitation (% of persons, 2008)	95
Total carbon dioxide emissions ('000 metric tons, 2007)	317,276.8
Carbon dioxide emissions per head (metric tons, 2007)	6.8
Human Development Index (2010): ranking	69
Human Development Index (2010): value	0.710

For sources and definitions, see explanatory note on p. vi.

Agriculture

PRINCIPAL CROPS
('000 metric tons)

	2007	2008	2009
Wheat	13,937.7	25,885.4	20,886.4
Barley	5,980.8	12,611.5	11,833.1
Maize	7,421.1	11,446.8	10,486.3
Rye	562.5	1,050.8	9,535.0
Oats	544.4	944.4	730.7
Millet	84.3	220.7	139.3
Buckwheat	217.4	240.6	188.6
Potatoes	19,102.0	19,545.4	19,666.1
Sugar beet	16,977.7	13,437.7	10,067.5
Peas, dry	268.1	454.9	493.6
Sunflower seed	4,174.4	6,526.0	6,360.6

—continued	2007	2008	2009
Cabbages and other brassicas	1,309.5	1,677.3	1,509.3
Tomatoes	1,269.6	1,492.1	2,040.8
Pumpkins, squash and gourds	524.7	533.4	559.9
Cucumbers and gherkins	599.2	751.5	883.0
Chillies and peppers, green	134.0	146.0	155.3
Onions, dry	721.7	1,049.2	875.6
Garlic	131.5	136.8	150.1
Carrots and turnips	597.1	739.6	686.4
Watermelons	391.1	426.6	531.0
Apples	754.9	719.3	853.4
Pears	139.5	126.3	145.9
Apricots	55.6	88.9	115.8
Sweet cherries	68.2	74.7	53.0
Sour (Morello) cherries	134.6	129.2	n.a.
Plums and sloes	109.6	135.5	136.7
Grapes	359.7	415.3	468.7

Aggregate production ('000 metric tons, may include official, semi-official or estimated data): Total cereals 28,938 in 2007, 52,740 in 2008, 45,406 in 2009; Total roots and tubers 19,102 in 2007, 19,545 in 2008, 19,666 in 2009; Total vegetables (incl. melons) 7,064 in 2007, 8,520 in 2008, 9,009 in 2009; Total fruits (excl. melons) 1,760 in 2007, 1,851 in 2008, 2,066 in 2009.

Source: FAO.

LIVESTOCK
('000 head at 1 January)

	2007	2008	2009
Horses	534	498	466
Cattle	6,175	5,491	5,079
Pigs	8,055	7,020	6,526
Sheep	925	1,034	1,096
Goats	693	645	631
Chickens	145,600	148,800	158,800
Ducks	9,700	10,150	8,720
Geese and guinea fowls	8,600	7,700	6,820
Turkeys	2,250	2,100	2,200

Source: FAO.

LIVESTOCK PRODUCTS
('000 metric tons)

	2007	2008	2009
Cattle meat	546.1	479.7	453.5
Pig meat	634.7	589.9	526.5
Chicken meat	689.4	794.0	894.2
Cows' milk	12,002.9	11,523.6	11,363.5
Sheep's milk	24.5	23.9	27.9
Goats' milk	234.7	213.8	218.2
Poultry eggs	814.8	868.5	924.7
Hen eggs	807.2	855.2	910.6
Honey	67.7	74.9	74.0

Source: FAO.

Forestry

ROUNDWOOD REMOVALS
('000 cubic metres, excl. bark)

	2005	2006	2007
Sawlogs, veneer logs and logs for sleepers	4,632	4,891	5,337
Pulpwood	953	1,000	1,059
Other industrial wood*	876	1,016	968
Fuel wood*	8,146	8,942	9,520
Total	14,606	15,849	16,884

* Unofficial figures.

2008–09: Production assumed to be unchanged from 2007 (FAO estimates).
Source: FAO.

UKRAINE

SAWNWOOD PRODUCTION
('000 cubic metres, incl. railway sleepers)

	2007	2008	2009
Coniferous (softwood)	1,817	1,817	1,817
Broadleaved (hardwood)	708	650	508
Total	2,525	2,467	2,325

Source: FAO.

Fishing

('000 metric tons, live weight)

	2006	2007	2008
Capture	238.7	213.5	195.4
Azov sea sprat	11.7	12.9	12.1
Blue grenadier	7.5	n.a.	n.a.
Gobies	9.9	7.7	8.7
Snoek	9.2	—	—
Sardinellas	12.9	12.0	5.9
European pilchard (sardine)	51.5	29.5	27.6
European sprat	21.3	18.0	21.1
European anchovy	7.0	8.8	11.0
Greenback horse mackerel	20.6	n.a.	n.a.
Other jack and horse mackerels	3.9	9.2	0.5
Other mackerels	6.6	9.5	0.3
Antarctic krill	15.2	n.a.	8.1
Wellington flying squid	12.9	n.a.	n.a.
Aquaculture	4.0	27.8	15.4
Common carp	0.1	23.0	11.1
Silver carp	2.4	3.1	2.8
Total catch	242.8	241.3	210.8

Source: FAO.

Mining

('000 metric tons unless otherwise indicated)

	2006	2007	2008
Coal (Anthracite)	13,444	13,000*	14,000*
Coal (Bituminous)	66,600	62,255	63,400*
Coal (Lignite)	231	182	200*
Crude petroleum	4,506	4,459	4,240
Natural gas (million cu m)	21.1	21.1	21.4
Iron ore: gross weight	74,000	77,900	72,700
Manganese ore†	1,606.4	1,719.6	1,446.6
Ilmenite concentrate*	470	500	520
Rutile concentrate*	60	60	60
Zirconium concentrates*	35	35	35
Uranium concentrate (metric tons)†	800	800	830
Bentonite*	300	300	200
Kaolin	251	244	245
Potash salts (crude)‡	8.1	11.9*	12.0*
Native sulphur*	133	135	135
Salt (unrefined)	5,996	5,548	4,425
Graphite (metric tons)	5,800	5,800*	5,800*
Peat	462	395	358

* Estimated production.
† Figures refer to the metal content of ores and concentrates.
‡ Figures refer to potassium oxide content.

Source: US Geological Survey.

2009 ('000 metric tons unless otherwise indicated): Coal (available) 55,000; Crude petroleum 2,900; Natural gas (million cu m) 20,700; Iron ore (gross weight) 66,500; Salt (unrefined) 5,395.

Industry

SELECTED PRODUCTS
('000 metric tons unless otherwise indicated)

	2007	2008	2009
Flour	2,908	3,030	2,735
Margarine, etc.	317	316	353
Sunflower oil (unrefined)	2,228	1,867	2,796
Fruit and vegetable juices	1,077	977	733
Sugar (white, crystalline)	1,867	1,571	1,275
Vodka and similar spirits ('000 hectolitres)	3,720	4,000	4,230
Beer ('000 hectolitres)	31,600	32,000	30,000
Soft drinks ('000 hectolitres)	19,600	17,300	14,700
Cigarettes (million)	129,000	130,000	114,000
Cotton yarn	12.7	10.4	6.7
Textiles (million sq m)	114.0	109.0	86.8
Coats for women and girls ('000)	2,541	2,512	1,783
Jackets, blazers, pullovers, etc. for women and girls ('000)	3,725	2,527	2,036
Trousers for men and boys ('000)	6,436	5,513	4,671
Trousers for women and girls ('000)	5,988	5,207	3,255
Knitted outerwear ('000 pieces)	4,174	4,421	3,119
Footwear (million pairs)	22.5	22.2	20.4
Particle board (unprocessed, '000 cu m)	1,641	1,622	1,295
Paper for household, sanitary and hygiene purposes	122	125	120
Boxes, cabinets and bags from paper and cardboard (million sq m)	857	856	783
Coke-oven coke	20,600	19,500	17,400
Coal-tar pitch	934	881	785
Motor spirit (petrol)	4,161	3,223	3,259
Gas-diesel (distillate fuel) oil	4,147	3,659	3,903
Residual fuel (Mazout) oils	3,477	2,460	2,600
Ammonia (synthetic)	5,139	4,890	3,033
Sulphuric acid	1,657	1,479	890
Nitric mineral or chemical fertilizers	2,840	2,689	2,166
Caustic soda (Sodium hydroxide)	135	88	78
Rubber tyres ('000)	7,411	6,631	4,805
Quicklime	5,688	5,128	4,101
Cement	15,000	14,900	9,500
Ceramic building bricks (million)	2,312	2,183	1,109
Cement building blocks (million)	2,225	2,077	1,057
Cast iron	35,600	31,000	25,700
Steel (incl. semi-finished products)	43,700	38,100	30,300
Finished rolled ferrous metals	24,500	20,500	16,100
Pipes of ferrous metals	2,811	2,542	1,742
Tractors (number)	5,282	6,339	1,445
Household refrigerators ('000)	310	222	157
Household washing machines ('000)	173	230	164
AC motors and generators, universal motors, etc. ('000)	670	602	460
Electrical transformers ('000)	19,500	17,400	12,200
Low-tension electrical facilities ('000)	75,900	67,400	51,200
Television receivers ('000)	507	558	238
Passenger motor cars ('000)	380	402	66
Buses (number)	9,100	10,200	1,500
Trucks (incl. other than self-propelled, number)	42,900	42,000	15,200
Trailers and semi-trailers (number)	30,800	32,700	23,100
Electric energy ('000 million kWh)	196	193	174

UKRAINE

Finance

CURRENCY AND EXCHANGE RATES

Monetary Units
100 kopiykas = 1 hryvnya.

Sterling, Dollar and Euro Equivalents (31 December 2010)
£1 sterling = 12.464 hryvnyas;
US $1 = 7.962 hryvnyas;
€1 = 10.638 hryvnyas;
100 hryvnyas = £8.02 = $12.56 = €9.40.

Average Exchange Rate (hryvnyas per US $)
2008   5.2672
2009   7.7912
2010   7.9356

Note: Following the dissolution of the USSR in December 1991, Russia and several other former Soviet republics retained the rouble (known as the karbovanets—KRB in Ukraine) as their monetary unit. In November 1992 this currency ceased to be legal tender in Ukraine, and was replaced (initially at par) by a currency coupon, also known as the karbovanets, or kupon, for a transitional period. Following the introduction of the transitional currency, Ukraine operated a system of multiple exchange rates, but in October 1994 the official and auction rates were merged. The unified exchange rate at 31 December 1995 was US $1 = 179,400 KRB. On 2 September 1996 Ukraine introduced a new currency, the hryvnya, at a rate of 100,000 KRB per hryvnya (1.750 hryvnyas per $).

GOVERNMENT FINANCE
(general government transactions, million hryvnyas)

Summary of Balances

	2007	2008	2009
Revenue	301,218	409,061	384,910
Less Expense	292,533	407,205	429,691
Net operating balance	8,685	1,857	−44,781
Less Net acquisition of non-financial assets	12,903	17,306	8,111
Net lending/borrowing	−4,218	−15,449	−52,891

Revenue

	2007	2008	2009
Taxes	161,594	224,918	204,280
Taxes on income, profits and capital gains	70,915	95,736	79,423
Taxes on goods and services	77,575	113,616	114,741
Social contributions	93,467	123,848	118,802
Grants	118	154	677
Other revenue	46,039	60,140	61,151
Total	301,218	409,061	384,910

Expense/Outlays

Expense by economic type	2007	2008	2009
Compensation of employees	74,454	100,433	108,768
Use of goods and services	47,328	61,878	69,979
Interest	4,063	4,906	10,644
Subsidies	20,684	35,315	27,799
Grants	249	177	119
Social benefits	125,040	185,199	202,796
Other expense	20,715	19,296	9,587
Total	292,533	407,205	429,691

Outlays by functions of government*	2007	2008	2009
General public services	23,882	30,534	33,164
Defence	9,481	11,307	10,463
Public order and safety	16,357	24,393	21,747
Economic affairs	42,234	54,344	42,103
Environmental protection	2,052	2,365	2,301
Housing and community amenities	6,228	9,103	7,316
Health	28,220	35,451	38,563
Recreation, culture and religion	5,919	8,142	8,560
Education	43,697	60,108	65,778
Social protection	133,740	195,467	211,460
Total	311,810	431,213	441,455

* Including net acquisition of non-financial assets.

Source: IMF, *Government Finance Statistics Yearbook*.

Consolidated budget (million hryvnyas): *Total revenue:* 171,812 in 2006, 219,937 in 2007, 297,845 in 2008. *Total expenditure:* 175,284 in 2006, 226,054 in 2007, 309,216 in 2008 (Source: Ministry of Finance, Kyiv).

INTERNATIONAL RESERVES
(US $ million at 31 December)

	2008	2009	2010
Gold (national valuation)	742.7	948.2	1,249.0
IMF special drawing rights	8.6	63.6	8.0
Foreign exchange	30,791.9	25,493.3	33,319.4
Total	31,543.2	26,505.1	34,576.4

Source: IMF, *International Financial Statistics*.

MONEY SUPPLY
(million hryvnyas at 31 December)

	2008	2009	2010
Currency outside depository corporations	154,758.5	157,029.4	182,989.9
Transferable deposits	105,371.5	118,161.9	148,469.2
Other deposits	252,396.9	209,580.6	265,381.7
Securities other than shares	3,200.2	2,526.3	1,030.7
Broad money	515,727.1	487,298.2	597,871.6

Source: IMF, *International Financial Statistics*.

COST OF LIVING
(Consumer Price Index at December; base: December previous year = 100)

	2008	2009	2010
Food and non-alcoholic beverages	124.5	110.9	110.6
Alcoholic and tobacco products	122.7	138.4	122.1
Clothing and footwear	104.6	107.6	102.2
Housing, water, electricity, gas and other fuels	128.2	108.2	113.8
Furnishings, household equipment and routine maintenance of the house	116.2	114.3	101.2
Health	121.9	126.3	105.8
Transport	122.5	119.2	106.6
Communication	105.0	104.3	91.1
Recreation and culture	117.1	111.8	102.5
Education	129.2	115.1	110.3
Restaurants and hotels	127.9	110.0	107.4
Miscellaneous goods and services	130.4	119.1	108.7
All goods and services	122.3	112.3	109.1

UKRAINE

Statistical Survey

NATIONAL ACCOUNTS
(million hryvnyas at current prices)

National Income and Product

	2007	2008	2009
Compensation of employees	351,936	470,464	451,343
Net operating surplus and mixed income	207,883	272,896	239,472
Domestic primary incomes	559,819	743,360	690,815
Consumption of fixed capital	73,071	87,914	107,204
Gross domestic product (GDP) at factor cost	632,890	831,274	798,019
Taxes on production and imports	101,230	142,599	134,842
Less Subsidies	13,389	25,817	19,516
GDP in market prices	720,731	948,056	913,345
Primary incomes received from abroad	18,410	28,304	35,938
Less Primary incomes paid abroad	21,735	37,004	54,977
Gross national income (GNI)	717,406	939,356	894,306
Less Consumption of fixed capital	73,071	87,914	107,204
Net national income	644,335	851,442	787,102
Current taxes and transfers from abroad	20,829	21,240	34,967
Less Current transfers paid abroad	2,437	4,221	4,701
Net national disposable income	662,727	868,461	817,368

Expenditure on the Gross Domestic Product

	2008	2009	2010
Final consumption expenditure	758,902	772,826	913,313
Gross capital formation	264,883	155,815	211,801
Gross fixed capital formation	250,158	167,644	208,288
Changes in inventories	14,379	−12,274	3,131
Acquisitions, less disposals, of valuables	346	445	382
Total domestic expenditure	1,023,785	928,641	1,125,114
Exports of goods and services	444,859	423,564	549,365
Less Imports of goods and services	520,588	438,860	579,872
GDP in market prices	948,056	913,345	1,094,607

Gross Domestic Product by Economic Activity

	2008	2009	2010
Agriculture, hunting, forestry and fishing	65,148	65,758	78,963
Mining and quarrying	54,337	40,676	63,831
Manufacturing	164,735	141,878	167,150
Electricity, gas and water supply	28,800	31,804	35,656
Construction	29,185	21,528	32,466
Wholesale and retail trade; repair of motor vehicles, motorcycles and personal goods	131,261	129,997	152,596
Transport, storage and communication	87,078	97,050	122,468
Education	43,520	49,239	57,649
Health and social work	29,209	34,573	42,090
Other economic activities	227,441	234,827	259,449
Sub-total	860,714	847,330	1,012,318
Less Financial intermediation services indirectly measured	36,538	50,849	45,814
Gross value added in basic prices	824,176	796,481	966,504
Taxes on products	126,425	119,988	130,958
Less Subsidies on products	2,545	3,124	2,855
GDP in market prices	948,056	913,345	1,094,607

BALANCE OF PAYMENTS
(US $ million)

	2007	2008	2009
Exports of goods f.o.b.	49,840	67,717	40,394
Imports of goods f.o.b.	−60,412	−83,808	−44,701
Trade balance	−10,572	−16,091	−4,307
Exports of services	14,161	17,895	13,859
Imports of services	−11,741	−16,154	−11,505
Balance on goods and services	−8,152	−14,350	−1,953
Other income received	3,656	5,419	4,624
Other income paid	−4,315	−6,959	−7,064
Balance on goods, services and income	−8,811	−15,890	−4,393
Current transfers received	4,147	4,165	3,460
Current transfers paid	−608	−1,038	−799
Current balance	−5,272	−12,763	−1,732
Capital account (net)	3	5	595
Direct investment abroad	−673	−1,010	−162
Direct investment from abroad	9,891	10,913	4,816
Portfolio investment assets	−29	12	−8
Portfolio investment liabilities	5,782	−1,292	−1,551
Other investment assets	−22,838	−22,884	−10,822
Other investment liabilities	22,994	23,425	−3,157
Net errors and omissions	−452	569	306
Overall balance	9,406	−3,025	−11,715

Source: IMF, *International Financial Statistics*.

External Trade

PRINCIPAL COMMODITIES
(distribution by Harmonized System, US $ million)

Imports f.o.b.	2008	2009	2010
Prepared food, beverages, spirits, tobacco	2,679.2	2,034.3	2,504.9
Mineral products	25,441.3	15,695.1	21,127.9
Mineral fuels, oils, waxes and bituminous substances	22,832.0	14,638.7	19,602.7
Crude petroleum	4,513.7	2,989.6	4,171.3
Natural gas	9,438.8	7,979.4	9,392.9
Chemicals and related products	6,959.1	5,319.3	6,441.7
Pharmaceutical products	2,433.3	2,130.3	2,445.8
Plastics, rubbers, and articles thereof	4,476.6	2,663.8	3,661.4
Plastic and articles thereof	3,519.2	2,141.6	2,867.3
Textiles and textile articles	2,099.2	1,416.9	1,974.8
Base metals and articles thereof	6,390.0	2,676.6	4,128.0
Iron and steel	3,299.3	1,117.5	1,921.4
Machinery and mechanical appliances, electrical equipment and appliances, parts and accessories	13,379.8	6,257.0	8,167.0
Machinery and mechanical appliances, computers, etc.	9,571.5	3,947.8	4,563.8
Electrical machinery, equipment and parts, etc.	3,808.4	2,309.3	3,603.2
Vehicles, aircraft, vessels and associated transportation equipment	12,091.4	2,163.8	3,664.3
Vehicles other than railway or tramway rolling stock	11,370.3	1,963.2	3,320.6
Total (incl. others)	85,535.4	45,435.6	60,740.0

UKRAINE

Statistical Survey

Exports f.o.b.	2008	2009	2010
Vegetable products	5,577.4	5,034.9	3,976.3
Cereals	3,703.8	3,556.2	2,467.1
Animal or vegetable fats and oils, etc.	1,945.8	1,796.0	2,617.3
Prepared food, beverages, spirits, tobacco	2,518.2	2,088.0	2,571.1
Mineral products	7,046.1	3,900.1	6,731.3
Ores, slag and ash	2,153.6	1,340.1	2,576.2
Mineral fuels, oils, waxes and bituminous substances	4,109.2	2,130.8	3,661.4
Chemicals and related products	5,045.4	2,515.2	3,479.2
Base metals and articles thereof	27,594.0	12,816.8	17,332.5
Iron and steel	22,954.6	10,252.5	14,626.6
Articles of iron and steel	3,533.1	1,946.9	1,993.7
Machinery and mechanical appliances, electrical equipment and appliances, parts and accessories	6,341.1	5,014.3	5,670.4
Machinery and mechanical appliances, computers, etc.	3,497.8	2,787.0	3,135.3
Electrical machinery, equipment and parts, etc.	2,843.4	2,227.4	2,535.1
Vehicles, aircraft, vessels and associated transportation equipment	4,321.3	5,014.3	3,262.4
Railway or tramway locomotives, rolling stock, track fixtures and fittings, signals, etc.	2,653.2	777.1	2,400.9
Total (incl. others)	66,954.4	39,702.9	51,430.5

PRINCIPAL TRADING PARTNERS
(US $ million)

Imports f.o.b.	2008	2009	2010
Austria	1,031.2	612.2	697.6
Belarus	2,809.6	1,692.8	2,567.6
China, People's Republic	5,601.5	2,734.3	4,700.4
Czech Republic	1,376.0	622.1	747.9
France (incl. Monaco)	1,682.5	971.1	1,106.7
Germany	7,165.2	3,852.1	4,603.1
Hungary	1,282.7	678.3	1,214.3
Italy	2,432.1	1,139.8	1,390.3
Japan	2,795.8	519.5	801.8
Kazakhstan	3,118.9	2,033.9	766.2
Korea, Republic	2,046.2	567.6	786.0
Netherlands	1,283.7	677.5	837.9
Poland	4,280.3	2,170.3	2,788.8
Romania	1,171.1	488.1	682.2
Russia	19,414.2	13,235.8	22,198.0
Sweden	696.2	451.3	358.9
Switzerland	1,171.6	438.0	508.2
Turkey	1,950.3	952.2	1,298.3
Turkmenistan	5,631.7	718.3	31.4
United Kingdom	1,375.8	651.1	821.0
USA	2,808.2	1,286.3	1,766.8
Uzbekistan	2,118.3	1,640.8	81.7
Total (incl. others)	85,535.4	45,435.6	60,740.0

Exports f.o.b.	2008	2009	2010
Algeria	345.0	266.8	159.3
Azerbaijan	910.5	546.6	610.8
Belarus	2,105.6	1,258.9	1,899.2
British Virgin Islands	862.0	378.5	379.1
Bulgaria	1,106.0	395.5	450.9
China, People's Republic	547.5	1,434.4	1,316.6
Czech Republic	670.8	340.7	626.2
Egypt	1,560.3	1,013.3	1,328.0
Germany	1,837.1	1,248.1	1,499.5
Hungary	1,367.1	730.2	860.1
India	1,005.6	1,152.5	1,426.1
Iran	859.2	755.8	1,030.7
Italy	2,911.7	1,227.6	2,412.3
Jordan	998.4	474.5	519.0
Kazakhstan	1,832.6	1,418.4	1,300.5

Exports f.o.b.—continued	2008	2009	2010
Moldova	1,172.0	693.6	713.5
Netherlands	1,118.0	594.9	563.2
Poland	2,338.3	1,213.1	1,787.2
Romania	670.8	319.5	705.9
Russia	15,735.6	8,495.1	13,431.9
Saudi Arabia	956.4	498.2	644.5
Slovakia	910.2	433.7	568.2
Spain	870.0	570.4	411.7
Switzerland	831.3	453.3	472.2
Syria	1,037.4	753.3	646.8
Turkey	4,633.4	2,126.5	3,026.7
United Arab Emirates	898.8	318.6	277.3
United Kingdom	640.6	346.3	506.5
USA	1,949.1	250.6	812.2
Total (incl. others)	66,954.4	39,702.9	51,430.5

Transport

RAILWAYS
(traffic)

	2008	2009	2010
Passengers carried ('000 journeys)	445,466	425,900	426,600
Freight carried ('000 metric tons)	498,800	391,200	432,500
Passenger-km (million)	53,225	48,274	50,038
Freight ton-km (million)	256,868	195,979	218,038

ROAD TRAFFIC
(motor vehicles in use)

	2006	2007	2008
Passenger cars	5,603,629	5,939,598	6,393,903
Motorcycles and mopeds	821,903	714,345	650,938
Buses and coaches	180,010	185,503	188,008
Lorries and vans	n.a.	406,441	451,106

Source: IRF, *World Road Statistics*.

INLAND WATERWAYS

	2008	2009	2010
Passengers carried ('000 journeys)	8,900	7,800	7,600
Freight carried ('000 metric tons)	19,500	9,800	11,100
Passenger-km (million)	123	123	95
Freight ton-km (million)	15,842	7,927	9,015

SHIPPING

Merchant Fleet
(registered at 31 December)

	2007	2008	2009
Number of vessels	655	644	622
Total displacement ('000 grt)	1,144.6	1,087.7	905.0

Source: IHS Fairplay, *World Fleet Statistics*.

International Sea-borne Freight Traffic
('000 metric tons)

	2007	2008	2009
Goods loaded	63,857.0	76,330.6	88,081.9
Goods unloaded	18,333.9	21,145.2	12,839.4

UKRAINE

CIVIL AVIATION
(traffic on scheduled services)

	2008	2009	2010
Passengers carried ('000)	6,200	5,100	6,100
Passenger-km (million)	10,777	9,021	10,969

Total ton-km (million): 378.4 in 2008; 350.3 in 2009; 378.2 in 2010.

Kilometres flown (million): 54 in 2004; 56 in 2005; 62 in 2006 (Source: UN, *Statistical Yearbook*).

Tourism

TOURIST ARRIVALS

Country of residence	2008	2009	2010
Belarus	3,407,064	2,984,672	3,058,023
Hungary	1,033,376	814,790	944,777
Moldova	4,418,821	4,339,138	4,063,459
Poland	5,242,980	2,546,132	2,089,647
Romania	1,440,466	1,077,299	910,450
Russia	7,638,222	6,964,435	7,900,436
Slovakia	644,918	537,511	609,994
Total (incl. others)	25,449,078	20,798,342	21,203,327

Receipts from tourism (US $ million, incl. passenger transport): 4,597 in 2007; 5,768 in 2008; 3,576 in 2009 (provisional) (Source: World Tourism Organization).

Communications Media

	2007	2008	2009
Book production (titles)	17,987	24,040	22,491
Newspapers (titles)	2,885	2,647	2,499
Magazines and other periodicals (titles)	2,420	2,422	2,515
Telephones ('000 main lines in use)	12,905.9	13,176.9	13,026.3
Mobile cellular telephones ('000 subscribers)	55,240.4	55,694.5	55,333.2
Internet users ('000)	6,400*	10,400*	7,770
Broadband subscribers ('000)	800	1,600	1,908

* Estimate.

Radio receivers ('000 in use): 45,050 in 1997.

Television receivers ('000 in use): 23,000 in 2000.

Personal computers: 2,121,200 (45.3 per 1,000 persons) in use in 2006.

Sources: mainly UNESCO, *Statistical Yearbook*; International Telecommunication Union.

Education

(2010/11 unless otherwise indicated)

	Institutions	Teachers	Students
Pre-primary	15,600*	191,500†	1,273,000
Primary *and* General secondary	20,300	515,000	4,299,000
Specialized secondary: vocational	976	265,100‡	433,500
Higher	854	121,300†	2,491,300

* Including some 900 with activities suspended.
† 1993/94 figure.
‡ 2008/09 figure.

Pupil-teacher ratio (primary education, UNESCO estimate): 15.6 in 2008/09 (Source: UNESCO Institute for Statistics).

Adult literacy rate (UNESCO estimates): 99.7% (males 99.8%; females 99.6%) in 2008 (Source: UNESCO Institute for Statistics).

Directory

The Government

HEAD OF STATE

President: VIKTOR F. YANUKOVYCH (elected 7 February 2010; inaugurated 25 February).

CABINET OF MINISTERS
(May 2011)

The administration principally comprises representatives of the Party of the Regions (PR).

Prime Minister: MYKOLA YA. AZAROV (PR).
First Deputy Prime Minister and Minister of Economic Development and Trade: ANDRIY P. KLYUYEV (PR).
Deputy Prime Minister and Minister of Infrastructure: BORYS V. KOLESNIKOV (PR).
Deputy Prime Minister and Minister of Social Policy: SERHIY L. TIHIPKO (A Strong Ukraine).
Deputy Prime Minister and Minister of Regional Development, Construction and Communal Services and Municipal Economy: VIKTOR M. TYKHONOV (PR).
Minister of Justice: OLEKSANDR V. LAVRYNOVYCH (PR).
Minister of Education and Science, and Youth and Sport: DMYTRO V. TABACHNYK (PR).
Minister of Agrarian Policy and Production: MYKOLA V. PRYSYAZHNYUK (PR).
Minister of Energy and the Coal Industry: YURIY A. BOIKO (PR).
Minister of Defence: MYKHAILO B. YEZHEL (PR).
Minister of Foreign Affairs: KOSTYANTYN I. HRYSHCHENKO (PR).
Minister of Culture: MYKHAILO A. KULYNYAK (PR).
Minister of the Protection of Health: (vacant).
Minister of Ecology and Natural Resources: MYKOLA V. ZLOCHEVSKY (PR).
Minister of Emergency Situations: VIKTOR I. BALOHA (United Centre).
Minister of Internal Affairs: ANATOLIY V. MOHILYOV (PR).
Minister of Finance: FEDIR O. YAROSHENKO (PR).
Minister of the Cabinet of Ministers: ANATOLIY V. TOLSTOUKHOV.

MINISTRIES

Office of the President: 01220 Kyiv, vul. Bankova 11; tel. (44) 255-71-40; fax (44) 255-78-44; e-mail press@stpu.gov.ua; internet www.president.gov.ua.

Office of the Cabinet of Ministers: 01008 Kyiv, vul. M. Hrushevskoho 12/2; tel. and fax (44) 254-05-84; e-mail web@kmu.gov.ua; internet www.kmu.gov.ua.

Ministry of Agrarian Policy and Production: 01001 Kyiv, vul. Khreshchatik 24; tel. (44) 278-71-18; fax (44) 229-87-56; e-mail ministr@minapk.gov.ua; internet www.minagro.gov.ua.

Ministry of Culture: 01030 Kyiv, vul. Ivana Franka 19; tel. (44) 235-23-78; fax (44) 235-32-57; e-mail ministr@mincult.gov.ua; internet www.mincult.gov.ua.

Ministry of Defence: 01021 Kyiv, vul. M. Hrushevskoho 30/1; tel. (44) 253-11-56; fax (44) 226-20-15; e-mail webmaster@mil.gov.ua; internet www.mil.gov.ua.

Ministry of Ecology and Natural Resources: 03035 Kyiv, vul. Uritskoho 35; tel. (44) 206-31-15; fax (44) 206-31-07; e-mail press@menr.gov.ua; internet www.menr.gov.ua.

UKRAINE

Ministry of Economic Development and Trade: 01008 Kyiv, vul. M. Hrushevskoho 12/2; tel. (44) 253-93-94; fax (44) 226-31-81; e-mail meconomy@me.gov.ua; internet www.me.gov.ua.
Ministry of Education and Science, and Youth and Sport: 01135 Kyiv, pr. Peremohi 10; tel. (44) 486-24-42; fax (44) 236-10-49; e-mail ministry@mon.gov.ua; internet www.mon.gov.ua.
Ministry of Emergency Situations: 01030 Kyiv, vul. O. Honchara 55A; tel. (44) 247-31-91; e-mail oper@mns.gov.ua; internet www.mns.gov.ua.
Ministry of Energy and the Coal Industry: 01601 Kyiv, vul. Khreshchatik 30; tel. (44) 206-38-00; fax (44) 462-05-61; e-mail kanc@mintop.energy.gov.ua; internet mpe.kmu.gov.ua.
Ministry of Finance: 01008 Kyiv, vul. M. Hrushevskoho 12/2; tel. (44) 253-54-28; fax (44) 425-90-26; e-mail infomf@minfin.gov.ua; internet www.minfin.gov.ua.
Ministry of Foreign Affairs: 01018 Kyiv, pl. Mykhailivska 1; tel. (44) 238-15-50; fax (44) 226-31-69; e-mail zsmfa@mfa.gov.ua; internet www.mfa.gov.ua.
Ministry of Infrastructure: 01135 Kyiv, pr. Peremohy 14; tel. (44) 226-22-04; fax (44) 486-72-06; e-mail com@mintrans.gov.ua; internet www.mintrans.gov.ua.
Ministry of Internal Affairs: 01024 Kyiv, vul. Ak. Bohomoltsya 10; tel. (44) 256-03-33; fax (44) 256-16-33; e-mail mail@centrmia.gov.ua; internet mvs.gov.ua.
Ministry of Justice: 01001 Kyiv, vul. Horodetskoho 13; tel. and fax (44) 228-37-23; e-mail themis@minjust.gov.ua; internet www.minjust.gov.ua.
Ministry of the Protection of Health: 01021 Kyiv, vul. M. Hrushevskoho 7; tel. (44) 253-24-39; fax (44) 226-22-05; e-mail moz@moz.gov.ua; internet www.moz.gov.ua.
Ministry of Regional Development, Construction and Communal Services: 01205 Kyiv, vul. V. Zhytomyrska 9; tel. (44) 278-82-90; fax (44) 278-83-90; e-mail komitet@build.gov.ua; internet www.minregionbud.gov.ua.
Ministry of Social Policy: 01001 Kyiv, vul. Esplanadna 8/10; tel. (44) 226-24-45; fax (44) 289-00-98; e-mail info@mlsp.gov.ua; internet www.mlsp.gov.ua.

President

Presidential Election, First Ballot, 17 January 2010

Candidates	Votes	%
Viktor F. Yanukovych (Party of the Regions)	8,686,751	35.33
Yuliya V. Tymoshenko (Fatherland)	6,159,829	25.05
Serhiy L. Tihipko (Independent)	3,211,257	13.06
Arseniy P. Yatsenyuk (Independent)	1,711,749	6.96
Viktor A. Yushchenko (Independent)	1,341,539	5.46
Petro M. Symonenko (Bloc of the Left for Left-of-Centre Forces*)	872,908	3.55
Volodymyr M. Lytvyn (People's Party)	578,886	2.35
Oleh Ya. Tyahnibok (Freedom)	352,282	1.43
Anatoliy S. Hrytsenko (Independent)	296,413	1.21
Others	428,277	1.74
Against all candidates	542,824	2.21
Total†	24,588,257	100.00

* An electoral alliance comprising the Communist Party of Ukraine, Justice, the Union of Leftist Forces and the Social Democratic Party (United).
† Including 405,542 invalid votes (1.65% of the total).

Second Ballot, 7 February 2010

Candidates	Votes	%
Viktor F. Yanukovych (Party of the Regions)	12,481,266	48.96
Yuliya V. Tymoshenko (Fatherland)	11,593,357	45.48
Against all candidates	1,113,069	4.37
Total*	25,493,529	100.00

* Including 305,837 invalid votes (1.20% of the total).

Legislature

Verkhovna Rada
(Supreme Council)

01008 Kyiv, vul. M. Hrushevskoho 5; tel. (44) 255-21-15; fax (44) 253-32-17; e-mail umz@rada.gov.ua; internet www.rada.gov.ua.

Chairman: VOLODYMYR M. LYTVYN.

General Election, 30 September 2007

Parties and blocs	Votes	%	Seats
Party of the Regions	8,013,895	34.37	175
Yuliya Tymoshenko bloc*	7,162,193	30.72	156
Our Ukraine-People's Self-defence bloc†	3,301,282	14.16	72
Communist Party of Ukraine	1,257,291	5.39	27
Lytvyn bloc‡	924,538	3.97	20
Socialist Party of Ukraine	668,234	2.87	—
Others	970,936	4.16	—
Total§	23,315,257	100.00	450

* Electoral bloc comprising Fatherland, the Reforms and Order Party and the Ukrainian Social Democratic Party.
† Electoral bloc comprising nine parties, including Our Ukraine People's Union, the 'Enough!' Civic Party, the People's Movement of Ukraine-Rukh, the Synod Ukrainian Republican Party and the Ukrainian People's Party.
‡ Electoral bloc comprising the People's Party and the Labour Party of Ukraine.
§ The total number of votes cast was 23,315,257, including 637,185 votes 'against all lists' (2.73% of the total) and 379,703 invalid votes (representing 1.63% of the total).

Election Commission

Central Electoral Commission of Ukraine (CEC) (Tsentralna vyborcha Komisiya Ukrainy): 01196 Kyiv, pl. L. Ukrainky 1; tel. (44) 286-84-62; e-mail post@cvk.gov.ua; internet www.cvk.gov.ua; Head VOLODYMYR SHAPOVAL.

Political Organizations

Since the 1990s Ukrainian politics has been characterized by frequent changes of formation and allegiance within and between various factions or blocs. At the end of September 2010 there were 185 political parties registered in Ukraine, of which the following were the most important:

Communist Party of Ukraine (CPU) (Komunistychna Partiya Ukrainy): 04070 Kyiv, vul. Borysohlibska 7; tel. (44) 425-54-87; e-mail press@kpu.net.ua; internet www.kpu.net.ua; banned 1991–93; advocates state control of economy and confederation with Russia; Sec. of Cen. Cttee PETRO M. SYMONENKO.

'Enough!' Civic Party (Hromadyanska Partiya 'Pora!'): 01025 Kyiv, vul. Desyatynna 1/3; tel. (44) 583-55-72; e-mail porapress@gmail.com; f. 2005 on the basis of the 'Yellow Pora' civil organization; supports expansion of democratic freedoms and greater integration with the West; contested 2006 legislative elections as mem. of the Enough!-Party of Reforms and Order civic bloc and 2007 legislative elections as mem. of the Our Ukraine-People's Self-defence bloc; Chair. of Political Council VLADYSLAV V. KASKIV.

Fatherland (Batkivshchyna): 01133 Kyiv, bulv. Lesi Ukrainky 26/615; tel. (44) 286-42-36; fax (44) 285-69-07; e-mail sector@byti.org.ua; internet www.tymoshenko.com.ua; f. 1999; merged with Conservative Republican Party in 2002, and with Yabluko party in 2004; nationalist, populist, supportive of socially orientated economics; contested 2006 and 2007 legislative elections as mem. of Yuliya Tymoshenko bloc; Chair. YULIYA V. TYMOSHENKO; 275,000 mems (2005).

Freedom (Svoboda): 02140 Kyiv, vul. Vyshnyakivska 6A/70; e-mail vo@svoboda.org.ua; f. 1995; nationalist; Chair. OLEH YA. TYAHNIBOK.

Front of Changes (Front Zmin): 04071 Kyiv, vul. Verkhniy Val 4A/17; tel. (44) 220-07-73; fax (44) 220-07-72; e-mail office@frontzmin.org; internet frontzmin.org; f. 2007; Pres. ARSENIY P. YATSENYUK.

Green Party of Ukraine (Partiya Zelenykh Ukrainy): 01001 Kyiv, vul. Chapayeva 2/16, POB 535B; e-mail sekretariat@greenparty.ua; internet www.greenparty.ua; f. 1990; Pres. TETYANA V. KONDRATYUK.

Our Ukraine (Nasha Ukraina): 04070 Kyiv, vul. Borychiv Tik 22A; tel. (44) 569-75-36; internet www.razom.org.ua; f. 2005 as People's Union Our Ukraine to support administration of Pres. Viktor Yushchenko; renamed Our Ukraine People's Union 2007; present name adopted 2009; contested 2006 legislative elections as mem. of the Our Ukraine bloc and 2007 legislative elections as mem. of Our Ukraine-People's Self-defence bloc; Chair. VIKTOR A. YUSHCHENKO; Chair. of Council VIRA I. ULYANCHENKO.

Party of the Regions (PR) (Partiya Rehioniv): 01021 Kyiv, vul. Lypska 10; tel. (44) 594-95-31; fax (44) 594-74-30; e-mail partreg@ln.ua; internet www.partyofregions.org.ua; f. 1997 as the Workers'

UKRAINE

Solidarity Party of Regional Rebirth of Ukraine; present name adopted 2001; Chair. MYKOLA AZAROV.

People's Movement of Ukraine-Rukh (PMU-R) (Narodnyi Rukh Ukrainy): 01034 Kyiv, vul. O. Honchara 33; tel. (44) 246-47-67; fax (44) 531-30-42; e-mail info@nru.org.ua; internet www.nru.org.ua; f. 1989 as popular movement (Ukrainian People's Movement for Restructuring); registered as political party in 1993; contested 2006 legislative elections as mem. of Our Ukraine bloc and 2007 legislative elections as mem. of Our Ukraine-People's Self-defence bloc; national democratic party; Chair. BORYS I. TARASYUK.

People's Party (Narodna Partiya): 01601 Kyiv, vul. Reitarska 6 A; tel. (44) 270-61-86; fax (44) 270-65-91; e-mail info@narodna.org.ua; internet narodna.org.ua; f. 1996 as Agrarian Party of Ukraine; renamed People's Agrarian Party of Ukraine in 2004; present name adopted 2005; contested 2006 legislative elections as mem. of Lytvyn's People's bloc and 2007 legislative elections as mem. of Lytvyn bloc; centrist; Leader VOLODYMYR M. LYTVYN.

People's Self-defence (Narodna Samooborona): 01133 Kyiv, vul. Lesi Ukrainky 10A; tel. (44) 224-54-58; fax (44) 451-47-29; e-mail edit@samooborona.in.ua; internet www.nso.org.ua; f. 1999 as Forward, Ukraine!; present name adopted 2010; Leader YURIY V. LUTSENKO.

Progressive Socialist Party of Ukraine (Prohresyvna Sotsialistychna Partiya Ukrainy): 01011 Kyiv, vul. P. Mirnoho 27/51; tel. and fax (44) 483-32-57; e-mail pspu@tsu.net.ua; internet www.vitrenko.org; f. 1996 by members of the Socialist Party of Ukraine; contested 2006 legislative elections as mem. of the Nataliya Vitrenko People's Opposition bloc; favours extension of Belarus-Russia Union to incorporate Ukraine; opposed to Ukraine seeking membership of NATO; Chair. NATALIYA M. VITRENKO.

Reforms and Order Party (Partiya 'Reformy i poryadok'): 01021 Kyiv, vul. Institutska 28; tel. (44) 536-91-26; fax (44) 536-91-27; e-mail ref_ord@i.com.ua; internet www.prp.org.ua; f. 1997 as Reforms and Order Party; changed name to Our Ukraine in mid-2004; in July 2005 the Ministry of Justice ruled that the party had acted unlawfully in adopting the name 'Our Ukraine', and the party reverted to its original name; contested 2006 legislative elections as part of the Enough!-Party of Reforms and Order civic bloc and 2007 legislative elections as part of the Yuliya Tymoshenko bloc; Chair. SERHIY V. SOBOLYEV.

Socialist Party of Ukraine (SPU) (Sotsialistychna Partiya Ukrainy): 02100 Kyiv, vul. Bazhova 12; tel. and fax (44) 296-68-27; e-mail zegal@socialist.in.ua; internet www.spu.in.ua; f. 1991; formed as partial successor to the CPU; advocates democratic socialism; Leader and Gen. Sec. OLEKSANDR O. MOROZ.

A Strong Ukraine (Sylna Ukraina): 01033 Kyiv, vul. Haydara 50B; tel. (44) 523-52-00; fax (44) 523-52-02; e-mail n.secretariat@silnaukraina.com; internet silnaukraina.com; f. 1999 as Working Ukraine; present name adopted 2009; supports economic reform and closer relations with Western European countries; Leader SERHIY L. TIHIPKO.

Ukrainian People's Party (UPP) (Ukrainska Narodna Partiya): 01601 Kyiv, vul. Pushkinska 28 A; tel. and fax (44) 234-59-17; e-mail analit@unp.ua; internet www.unp.ua; f. 1999 as breakaway faction of People's Movement of Ukraine-Rukh by fmr leader Vyacheslav Chornovil; fmrly Ukrainian People's Movement-Rukh; present name adopted 2003; contested 2006 legislative elections as mem. of Kostenko and Plyushch's Ukrainian People's bloc and 2007 legislative elections as mem. of Our Ukraine-People's Self-defence bloc; Chair. YURIY I. KOSTENKO.

Ukrainian Social Democratic Party (Ukrainska Sotsial-demokratychna Partiya): 01001 Kyiv, vul. Antonovycha 18/6; tel. (44) 495-64-60; fax (44) 495-64-62; e-mail kmpousdp@ukr.net; internet www.usdp.kiev.ua; f. 1998; contested 2007 legislative elections as mem. of the Yuliya Tymoshenko bloc; Chair. YEVHEN V. KORNIYCHUK.

United Centre (Yedyny Tsentr): 04071 Kyiv, vul. Yaroslavska 56A; tel. (44) 207-44-77; fax (44) 207-44-72; e-mail press@edc.org.ua; internet www.edc.org.ua; f. 1999; fmrly Party of Private Property; Chair. VIKTOR BALOHA.

Diplomatic Representation

EMBASSIES IN UKRAINE

Afghanistan: 03069 Kyiv, vul. Yaslynska 9/7; tel. and fax (44) 275-58-93; e-mail afembkiev@yahoo.com; Ambassador MOHAMMED ASEF DELAWAR.

Algeria: 01014 Kyiv, vul. Zvirenetska 76 A; tel. (44) 286-76-88; fax (44) 286-76-78; e-mail ambalgkiev@bigmir.net; Ambassador MOHAMED BACHIR MAZOUZ.

Argentina: 01901 Kyiv, vul. Fedorova 12; tel. (44) 581-33-27; fax (44) 238-69-22; e-mail eucra@mrecic.gov.ar; Ambassador LILA ROLDÁN VÁZQUEZ DE MOINE.

Armenia: 01901 Kyiv, vul. Volodymyrska 45; tel. (44) 234-90-05; fax (44) 235-43-55; e-mail despanut@voliacable.com; Ambassador ANDRANIK MANOUKIAN.

Austria: 01901 Kyiv, vul. Ivana Franka 33; tel. (44) 277-27-90; fax (44) 230-23-52; e-mail kiew-ob@bmeia.gv.at; internet www.bmeia.gv.at/kiew; Ambassador WOLF DIETRICH HEIM.

Azerbaijan: 04050 Kyiv, vul. Hlubochytska 24; tel. (44) 484-69-32; fax (44) 484-69-46; e-mail embass@faust.kiev.ua; internet www.azembassy.com.ua; Ambassador EYNULLA YADULLA OĞLU MADATLI.

Belarus: 01901 Kyiv, vul. M. Kotsyubynskoho 3; tel. (44) 537-52-00; fax (44) 537-52-13; e-mail ukr@belembassy.org; internet www.ukraine.belembassy.org; Ambassador VALENTYN V. VELICHKO.

Belgium: 01030 Kyiv, vul. Leontovicha 4; tel. (44) 238-26-00; fax (44) 238-26-01; e-mail ambabel@kiev.farlep.net; internet www.diplomatie.be/kiev; Ambassador JANA ZIKMUNDOVA.

Brazil: 01010 Kyiv, vul. Suvorova 14/12, POB 471; tel. (44) 280-63-01; fax (44) 280-95-68; e-mail kievbrem@brasil.kiev.ua; internet brasil.kiev.ua; Ambassador ANTÔNIO FERNANDO CRUZ DE MELLO.

Bulgaria: 01023 Kyiv, vul. Hospitalna 1; tel. (44) 246-72-37; fax (44) 235-51-19; e-mail embuln@i.kiev.ua; Ambassador DIMITAR VLADIMIROV.

Canada: 01901 Kyiv, vul. Yaroslaviv Val 31; tel. (44) 590-31-00; fax (44) 590-31-34; e-mail kyiv@international.gc.ca; Ambassador DANIEL CARON.

China, People's Republic: 01901 Kyiv, vul. M. Hrushevskoho 32; tel. and fax (44) 253-81-31; internet ua.china-embassy.org; Ambassador ZHANG XIYUN.

Croatia: 01901 Kyiv, vul. Artema 51/50; tel. (44) 486-21-22; fax (44) 484-69-43; e-mail vrhukr@mvpei.hr; internet ua.mvp.hr; Ambassador ŽELJKO KIRINČIĆ.

Cuba: 01901 Kyiv, prov. Byekhtyerevsky 5; tel. (44) 486-57-43; fax (44) 486-19-07; e-mail embacuba@embcuba.com.ua; Ambassador FÉLIX LEÓN CARBALLO.

Czech Republic: 01901 Kyiv, vul. Yaroslaviv Val 34A; tel. (44) 272-21-10; fax (44) 272-62-04; e-mail kiev@embassy.mzv.cz; internet www.mzv.cz/kiev; Chargé d'affaires a.i. VÍTĚZSLAV PIVOŇKA.

Denmark: 01901 Kyiv, vul. B. Khmelnytskoho 56; tel. (44) 200-12-60; fax (44) 200-12-81; e-mail ievamb@um.dk; internet www.ambkyiv.um.dk; Ambassador MICHAEL BORG-HANSEN.

Egypt: 01901 Kyiv, vul. Observatorna 19; tel. (44) 212-13-27; fax (44) 486-94-28; e-mail eg.emb_kiev@mfa.gov.eg; Ambassador YASER ATEPH.

Estonia: 01901 Kyiv, vul. Volodymyrska 61/11; tel. (44) 590-07-80; fax (44) 590-07-81; e-mail embassy.kiev@mfa.ee; internet www.estemb.kiev.ua; Ambassador JAAN HEIN.

Finland: 01901 Kyiv, vul. Striletska 14; tel. (44) 278-70-49; fax (44) 278-20-32; e-mail sanomat.kio@formin.fi; internet www.finland.org.ua; Ambassador CHRISTER MICHELSSON.

France: 01901 Kyiv, vul. Reitarska 39; tel. (44) 590-36-00; fax (44) 590-36-24; internet www.ambafrance-ua.org; Ambassador JACQUES FAURE.

Georgia: 01032 Kyiv, bulv. T. Shevchenko 25; tel. (44) 220-03-40; fax (44) 220-03-48; e-mail kyiv.emb@mfa.gov.ge; internet www.ukraine.mfa.gov.ge; Ambassador GRIGOL KATAMADZE.

Germany: 01901 Kyiv, vul. B. Khmelnytskoho 25; tel. (44) 247-68-00; fax (44) 247-68-18; e-mail info@kiew.diplo.de; internet kiew.diplo.de; Ambassador Dr HANS-JÜRGEN HEIMSOETH.

Greece: 01901 Kyiv, vul. Panfilovtsiv 10; tel. (44) 254-54-71; fax (44) 254-39-98; e-mail greece@kiev.relc.com; internet www.mfa.gr/kiev; Ambassador GEORGIOS GEORGOUNTZOS.

Holy See: 01901 Kyiv, vul. Turhenyevska 40; tel. (44) 482-35-57; fax (44) 482-35-53; e-mail nuntiusua@gmail.com; internet www.nuntiatura.kiev.ua; Apostolic Nuncio (vacant).

Hungary: 01034 Kyiv, vul. Reitarska 33; tel. (44) 230-80-01; fax (44) 272-20-90; e-mail mission.kev@kum.hu; internet www.mfa.gov.hu/emb/kiev; Ambassador MIHÁLY BAYER.

India: 01901 Kyiv, vul. Teryokhina 4; tel. (44) 468-66-61; fax (44) 468-66-19; e-mail india@public.ua.net; internet www.indianembassy.org.ua; Ambassador (vacant).

Indonesia: 04107 Kyiv, vul. Nahirna 27B; tel. (44) 206-54-46; fax (44) 206-54-40; e-mail kbri@indo.ru.kiev.ua; internet www.indonesianembassy.kiev.ua; Ambassador NINING SUNINGSIH ROCHADIAT.

Iran: 01901 Kyiv, vul. Kruhlouniversytetska 12; tel. (44) 253-85-43; fax (44) 254-02-53; internet www.iranembassy.com.ua; Ambassador AKBAR QASEMI-ALIABADI.

UKRAINE

Iraq: 01014 Kyiv, vul. Zvirynetska 35; tel. (44) 268-04-40; fax (44) 286-04-45; e-mail kefemb@iraqmofamail.com; Ambassador SHORSH KHALID SAID.

Israel: 01901 Kyiv, bulv. L. Ukrainky 34; tel. (44) 586-15-00; fax (44) 586-15-55; e-mail info@kiev.mfa.gov.il; internet ukraine.mfa.gov.il; Ambassador ZINA KALAY-KLEITMAN.

Italy: 01901 Kyiv, vul. Yaroslaviv Val 32B; tel. (44) 230-31-00; fax (44) 230-31-03; e-mail ambasciata.kiev@esteri.it; internet www.ambkiev.esteri.it; Ambassador PETRO GIOVANNI DONNICI.

Japan: 01901 Kyiv, prov. Muzeiniy 4; tel. (44) 490-55-00; fax (44) 490-55-02; e-mail jpembua7f@sovamua.com; internet www.ua.emb-japan.go.jp; Ambassador TADASHI IDZAVA.

Kazakhstan: 04050 Kyiv, vul. Melnykova 26; tel. (44) 489-18-58; fax (44) 483-11-98; e-mail admin@kazemb.kiev.ua; internet www.kazembassy.com.ua; Ambassador AMANGELDY ZH. ZHUMABAYEV.

Korea, Republic: 01034 Kyiv, vul. Volodymyrska 43; tel. (44) 246-37-59; fax (44) 246-37-57; e-mail koremb@mofat.go.kr; internet ukr.mofat.go.kr; Ambassador PAK RO-BYOK.

Kuwait: 04210 Kyiv, vul. Obolonska nab. 19; tel. (44) 391-51-60; fax (44) 391-51-64; e-mail kiev@mofa.gov.kw; Ambassador YOUSEF HUSSAIN AL-GABANDI.

Kyrgyzstan: 01901 Kyiv, vul. Malo—kitayevska 48A; tel. and fax (44) 524-09-24; e-mail embassy.kg.kiev@silvercom.net; internet kyrgyzembassy.com.ua; Ambassador (vacant).

Latvia: 01901 Kyiv, vul. I. Mazepy 6B; tel. (44) 490-70-30; fax (44) 490-70-35; e-mail embassy.ukraine@mfa.gov.lv; internet www.latemb.kiev.ua; Ambassador ATIS SJANITS.

Lebanon: 01030 Kyiv, vul. Chapayeva 4/3; tel. (44) 234-15-91; fax (44) 234-15-65; e-mail embassy_lebanon_kiev@yahoo.com; Ambassador YOUSSEF SADAKA.

Libya: 04050 Kyiv, vul. Ovrutska 6; tel. (44) 238-60-70; fax (44) 238-60-68; Ambassador FEISAL AL-SHAARI.

Lithuania: 01901 Kyiv, vul. Buslivska 21; tel. (44) 254-09-20; fax (44) 254-09-28; e-mail amb.ua@urm.lt; internet ua.mfa.lt; Ambassador PETRAS VAITIEKŪNAS.

Macedonia, former Yugoslav republic: 03150 Kyiv, vul. I. Fedorova 12; tel. (44) 238-66-16; fax (44) 238-66-17; e-mail embmac@carrier.kiev.ua; Ambassador ACO SPASENOVSKI.

Malaysia: 01001 Kyiv, vul. Buslivksa 25; tel. (44) 286-89-40; fax (44) 286-89-42; e-mail malkiev@kln.gov.my; internet www.kln.gov.my/perwakilan/kiev; Ambassador CHUAH TEONG BAN.

Mexico: 01033 Kyiv, vul. Volodymyrska 63; tel. (44) 251-29-44; fax (44) 251-29-33; e-mail embamexucrania@mexico.kiev.ua; Ambassador BERENICE RENDON TALAVERA.

Moldova: 01901 Kyiv, vul. Yagotinska 2; tel. (44) 521-22-80; fax (44) 521-22-72; e-mail kiev@mfa.md; internet www.ucraina.mfa.md; Ambassador ION STĂVILĂ.

Morocco: 03680 Kyiv, vul. I. Fedorova 12; tel. (44) 284-33-26; fax (44) 568-58-84; e-mail morocco@kiev.farlep.net; Ambassador ABDELJALIL SAUBRY.

Netherlands: 01901 Kyiv, Kontraktova pl. 7; tel. (44) 490-82-00; fax (44) 490-82-09; e-mail kie@minbuza.nl; Ambassador PIETER JAN WOLTHERS.

Nigeria: 01015 Kyiv, bulv. Panfilovtsiv 36; tel. (44) 254-58-50; fax (44) 254-53-71; e-mail nigeriakyiv@yahoo.com; internet www.nigeriaembassy.org.ua; Ambassador IBRAHIM PADA KASAI.

Norway: 01034 Kyiv, vul. Striletska 15; tel. (44) 590-04-70; fax (44) 234-06-55; e-mail emb.kiev@mfa.no; internet www.norway.com.ua; Ambassador OLAV BERSTAD.

Pakistan: 01015 Kyiv, pr. Panfilovtsiv 7; tel. (44) 280-25-77; fax (44) 254-45-30; e-mail parepkyiv@mail.kar.net; Ambassador AHMAD NAWAZ SALIM MELA.

Poland: 01034 Kyiv, vul. Yaroslaviv Val 12; tel. (44) 230-07-00; fax (44) 270-63-36; e-mail kijow.amb.sekretariat@msz.gov.pl; internet www.kijow.polemb.net; Chargé d'affaires DARIUSZ GÓRCZYŃSKI.

Portugal: 01901 Kyiv, vul. I. Fedorova 12; tel. (44) 287-58-61; fax (44) 230-26-25; e-mail geral@embport.kiev.ua; Ambassador MÁRIO JESUS DOS SANTOS.

Romania: 01030 Kyiv, vul. M. Kotsyubynskoho 8; tel. (44) 234-00-40; fax (44) 235-20-25; e-mail romania@adamant.net; internet www.kiev.mae.ro; Ambassador CORNEL IONESCU.

Russia: 03049 Kyiv, Povitroflotskyi pr. 27; tel. (44) 244-09-63; fax (44) 246-34-69; e-mail rusemb@kv.ukrtel.net; internet www.embrus.org.ua; Ambassador MIKHAIL YU. ZUBAROV.

Serbia: 04070 Kyiv, vul. Voloska 4; tel. (44) 425-60-60; fax (44) 417-55-10; e-mail ambars@ukr.net; Ambassador DUŠAN LAZIĆ.

Slovakia: 01901 Kyiv, vul. Yaroslaviv Val 34; tel. (44) 272-03-10; fax (44) 272-32-71; e-mail emb.kiev@mzv.sk; internet www.slovakia.kiev.ua; Ambassador PAVOL HAMŽÍK.

Slovenia: 01030 Kyiv, vul. B. Khmelnytskoho 48; tel. (44) 585-23-31; fax 585-23-43; e-mail vki@gov.si; internet www.kijev.veleposlanistvo.si; Chargé d'affaires a.i. NATAŠA PRAH.

South Africa: 01004 Kyiv, vul. V. Vasylkivska 9/2, POB 7; tel. (44) 287-71-72; fax (44) 287-72-06; e-mail saemb@utel.net.ua; Ambassador ANDRIES VENTER.

Spain: 01901 Kyiv, vul. Khoriva 46; tel. (44) 492-73-20; fax (44) 492-73-27; e-mail embespua@mail.mae.es; Ambassador JOSÉ RODRÍGUEZ MOYANO.

Sweden: 01901 Kyiv, vul. Ivana Franka 34/33; tel. (44) 494-42-70; fax (44) 494-42-71; e-mail ambassaden.kiev@foreign.ministry.se; internet www.swedenabroad.com/kiev; Ambassador STEFAN GULLGREN.

Switzerland: 01015 Kyiv, vul. Kozyatynska 12, POB 114; tel. (44) 281-61-28; fax (44) 280-14-48; e-mail kie.vertretung@eda.admin.ch; internet www.eda.admin.ch/kiev; Ambassador GEORG ZUBLER.

Syria: 04050 Kyiv, vul. Biloruska 5; tel. (44) 489-55-51; fax (44) 483-97-88; e-mail syrian-emb@ukr.net; Ambassador MUHAMMAD SAID AKIL.

Turkey: 01901 Kyiv, vul. Arsenalna 18; tel. (44) 281-07-51; fax (44) 285-64-23; e-mail turkemb.kiev@mfa.gov.tr; internet kiev.emb.mfa.gov.tr; Ambassador AHMET BÜLENT MERIÇ.

Turkmenistan: 01901 Kyiv, vul. Pushkinska 6; tel. (44) 279-34-49; fax (44) 279-30-34; e-mail ambturkm@ukrpack.net; Ambassador NURBERDI AMANMYRADOV.

United Kingdom: 01025 Kyiv, vul. Desyatynna 9; tel. (44) 490-36-60; fax (44) 490-36-62; e-mail ukembinf@gmail.com; internet ukinukraine.fco.gov.uk; Ambassador ROBERT LEIGH TURNER.

USA: 01901 Kyiv, vul. Yu. Kotsyubynskoho 10; tel. (44) 490-40-00; fax (44) 490-40-85; e-mail press@usembassy.kiev.ua; internet kiev.usembassy.gov; Ambassador JOHN F. TEFFT.

Uzbekistan: 01901 Kyiv, vul. Volodymyrska 16; tel. (44) 501-50-00; fax 501-50-01; e-mail embassy@uzbekistan.org.ua; internet www.uzbekistan.org.ua; Ambassador (vacant).

Viet Nam: 01011 Kyiv, vul. Tovarna 51A; tel. (44) 284-57-40; fax (44) 284-55-42; e-mail vnemb.ua@mofa.gov.vn; Ambassador NGUYET HO DAC MINH.

Judicial System

Constitutional Court of Ukraine (Konstytutsiynyi Sud Ukrayiny): 01033 Kyiv, vul. Zhylianska 14; tel. (44) 289-05-53; fax (44) 287-20-01; e-mail idep@ccu.gov.ua; internet www.ccu.gov.ua; f. 1996; Chair. ANATOLIY S. HOLOVIN.

Supreme Court (Verkhovnyi sud Ukraini): 01024 Kyiv, vul. P. Orlyka 4; tel. (44) 253-63-08; internet www.scourt.gov.ua; Chair. VASYL V. OPONENKO; Chair. of Civil Chamber ANDRIY V. HNATENKO; Chair. of Criminal Chamber MYKOLA YE. KOROTKEVYCH; Chair. of Economic Chamber VALENTYN P. BARBARA; Chair. of Administrative Chamber VIKTOR V. KRYVENKO; Chair. of Military Judicial Commission OLEKSANDR F. VOLKOV.

Supreme Economic Court (Vyshyi hospodarskyi sud Ukraini): 01011 Kyiv, vul. Kopylenka 6; tel. (44) 536-05-00; fax (44) 536-18-18; e-mail kantselariya@vasu.arbitr.gov.ua; internet www.arbitr.gov.ua; Chair. VIKTOR I. TATKOV.

Office of the Prosecutor-General: 01011 Kyiv, vul. Riznytska 13/15; tel. (44) 226-20-27; fax (44) 280-28-51; e-mail ilrd@gp.gov.ua; internet www.gp.gov.ua; Prosecutor-General VIKTOR P. PSHONKA.

Religion

State Department for Ethnic and Religious Affairs (Derzhavnyi departament u spravakh nationalnostei ta religii): 01025 Kyiv, vul. Volodymyrska 9; tel. (44) 278-17-18; e-mail mail@scnm.gov.ua; internet www.scnm.gov.ua; Chair. YURIY YE. RESHETNIKOV.

CHRISTIANITY

The Eastern Orthodox Church

Eastern Orthodoxy is the principal religious affiliation in Ukraine. Until 1990 all legally constituted Orthodox church communities in Ukraine were part of the Ukrainian Exarchate of the Russian Orthodox Church (Moscow Patriarchate). In that year the Russian Orthodox Church in Ukraine was renamed the Ukrainian Orthodox Church (UOC), partly to counter the growing influence of the previously prohibited Ukrainian Autocephalous Orthodox Church (UAOC). A new ecclesiastical organization was formed in June 1992, when Filaret (Denisenko), the former Metropolitan of Kyiv, united with a faction of the UAOC to form the Kyiv Patriarchate. In July 1995 Filaret was elected as Patriarch, prompting some senior

UKRAINE

clergy to leave the church and join the UAOC. In the late 2000s the UOC (Moscow Patriarchate) remained the largest church organization in Ukraine.

Ukrainian Autocephalous Orthodox Church: 01001 Kyiv, vul. Andriyivsky uzviz 23; e-mail uaocinfo@ukr.net; internet www.uaoc.info; f. 1921; forcibly incorporated into the Russian Orthodox Church (Moscow Patriarchate) in 1930; continued to operate clandestinely; formally revived in 1990; 1,219 parishes in 2009; Metropolitan of Kyiv and all Ukraine Archbishop MEFODIY (KUDRYAKOV).

Ukrainian Orthodox Church (Kyiv Patriarchate): 01004 Kyiv, vul. Pushkinska 36; tel. (44) 234-10-96; fax (44) 234-30-55; e-mail patb@ukrpack.net; internet www.cerkva.info; f. 1992 by factions of the Ukrainian Orthodox Church (Moscow Patriarchate) and Ukrainian Autocephalous Orthodox Church; 4,221 parishes in 2009; Patriarch of Kyiv and all Rus-Ukraine FILARET (DENISENKO).

Ukrainian Orthodox Church (Moscow Patriarchate): 01015 Kyiv, vul. Sichnevoho Povstannya 25/34; tel. (44) 255-12-04; fax (44) 254-53-01; e-mail press@orthodox.org.ua; internet www.pravoslavye.org.ua; exarchate of the Russian Orthodox Church (Moscow Patriarchate) in 2009; 11,738 parishes in 2009; Metropolitan of Kyiv and All-Ukraine VLADIMIR (SABODAN).

Russian Orthodox Old Belief (Old Ritual) Church (Russkaya Pravoslavnaya Staroobryadcheskaya Tserkov): 49017 Dnipropetrovsk, pr. K. Marksa 60/8; tel. (562) 52-17-75; internet www.staroobryad.narod.ru; f. 1652 by separation from the Moscow Patriarchate; divided into two main branches: the *popovtsi* (which have priests) and the *bezpopovtsi* (which reject the notion of ordained priests and the use of all sacraments, other than that of baptism). Both branches are further divided into various groupings. The largest group of *popovtsi* are those of the Belokrinitskii Concord; there were 56 parishes of the Belokrinitskii Concord in Ukraine in 2009, and 10 parishes of *bezpopovtsi* at that time; Bishop of Kyiv and all Ukraine SAVVAYIYE.

The Roman Catholic Church

Most Catholics in Ukraine are adherents of the Byzantine rites observed by the so-called 'Greek' Catholic Church, which is based principally in western Ukraine and Transcarpathia. In 2005 the seat of the head of the Byzantine-rite Church was relocated from Lviv to Kyiv. In 2009 there were 3,728 parishes of the Byzantine rites in Ukraine, 1,064 parishes of the Latin rite and 27 parishes of the Armenian rite. Ukraine comprises one archbishopric-major (of the Byzantine rite), three archdioceses (including one each for Catholics of the Latin, Byzantine and Armenian rites), three archiepiscopal exarchates, eight dioceses of the Byzantine rite (of which one is directly responsible to the Holy See) and six dioceses of the Latin rite. At 31 December 2007 there were an estimated 4,801,879 adherents (excluding adherents of the Armenian rite, for whom figures were not available), equivalent to some 8.8% of the population. Of that number, around 83% followed the Byzantine rite.

Bishops' Conference of Ukraine: 79008 Lviv, pl. Katedralna 1; tel. (32) 276-94-15; fax (32) 296-61-14; f. 1992; Pres. Most Rev. MIECZYSŁAW MOKRZYCKI (Latin Rite Archbishop of Lviv).

Byzantine Ukrainian Rite

Archbishop-Major of Kyiv and Halych: Most Rev. SVIATOSLAV SHEVCHUK, 01000 Kyiv, vul. Riznytska 11 B/28–29; tel. and fax (44) 254-56-10; e-mail arkyrparh-kv@voliacable.com; internet www.ugcc.org.ua; head of Ukrainian Greek Catholic Church; established in 1596 by the Union of Brest; forcibly integrated into the Russian Orthodox Church (Moscow Patriarchate) in 1946, but continued to function in an 'underground' capacity; relegalized in 1989; in 2005 the seat of the head of the Church was relocated from Lviv, in western Ukraine, to Kyiv.

Byzantine Ukrainian Rite Archbishop of Lviv: Most Rev. IHOR VOZNIAK, 79000 Lviv, pl. Sv. Yura 5; tel. and fax (32) 261-08-94; e-mail cerkvalviv@ugcc.org.ua.

Latin Rite

Latin Rite Archbishop of Lviv: Most Rev. MIECZYSŁAW MOKRZYCKI, 79011 Lviv, vul. Samchuka 14 A; tel. (32) 240-37-47; fax (32) 240-37-48; e-mail rka@lviv.farlep.net; internet www.rkc.lviv.ua.

Armenian Rite

Armenian Rite Archbishop of Lviv: (vacant).

Protestant Churches

There were 9,069 Protestant communities registered in Ukraine in 2009.

All-Ukrainian Union of Associations of Evangelical Christians-Baptists: 01004 Kyiv, vul. L. Tolstoho 3B; tel. (44) 234-82-41; fax (44) 234-16-76; e-mail office@ecbua.info; internet www.ecbua.info; 2,391 churches in Ukraine (2010); the Baptist Union of Ukraine is a part of the Euro-Asiatic Baptist Federation; Pres. VYACHESLAV V. NESTERUK.

All-Ukrainian Union of Christians of the Evangelical Faith—Pentecostalists: 03115 Kyiv, vul. Oniskevycha 3; tel. (44) 452-21-40; fax (44) 424-25-80; e-mail mail@uupc.org; internet uupc.org; 1,553 parishes in 2009; Pres. MYKHAILO S. PANOCHKO.

Embassy of the Blessed Kingdom of God for All Nations: 02152 Kyiv, vul. Tychchyny 18, Legkoatletletichesky manezh; tel. (44) 553-15-38; e-mail mail@godembassy.org; internet www.godembassy.org; f. 1994 as Word of Faith (Slovo Very); Pastor SUNDAY ADELAJA; 25,000 mems (2005).

Ukrainian Lutheran Church: 01004 Kyiv, vul. V. Vasylkivska 14/15; tel. (44) 235-77-21; fax (44) 234-08-00; e-mail vhorpynchuk@yahoo.com; internet www.ukrlc.org; 43 parishes in 2009; Leader of Church Bishop Dr VYACHESLAV HORPYNCHUK.

ISLAM

In 2009 there were 535 Islamic communities officially registered in Ukraine, of which 352 were members of the Religious Administration of Muslims of Crimea. An Islamic University was established in Donetsk in 1998.

All-Ukrainian Association of Muslim Social Organizations (Arraid): 04119 Kyiv, vul. Dekhtyarivska 25A; tel. (44) 490-99-00; fax (44) 490-99-22; e-mail office@arraid.org; internet www.arraid.org; f. 1997; brs in Dnipropetrovsk, Donetsk, Kharkiv, Luhansk, Lviv, Odesa, Simferopol, Vinnytsya and Zaporizhzhya; publishes periodical *Arraid (Pioneer)* in Arabic and Russian and educational material in Russian, Tatar and Ukrainian; undertakes charitable and educational work; Chair. ISMAIL KADI.

Religious Administration of Muslims of Crimea: 95000 Crimea, Simferopol, Kebir Çami Mosque; 352 communities in 2009; Mufti AJE NURALI ABLAIYEV.

Religious Administration of Muslims of Ukraine: 04071 Kyiv, vul. Lukyanovska; tel. (44) 465-18-77; fax (44) 456-17-70; e-mail islam@i.kiev.ua; internet www.islamyat.org; f. 1992; 112 communities in 2009; Mufti Sheikh AKHMED TAMIM.

JUDAISM

In 2001 there were 103,600 Jews in Ukraine (according to census results), despite high levels of emigration from the 1970s. From 1989 there was a considerable revival in the activities of Jewish communities. In 2009 there were 295 Jewish religious communities registered in Ukraine (of which 124 were members of the Chabad-Lubavitch sect), compared with 12 synagogues in 1989.

All-Ukrainian Jewish Congress: 01023 Kyiv, vul. Mechnykova 14/1; tel. (44) 235-71-20; fax (44) 235-10-67; e-mail vek@i.kiev.ua; internet www.jewish.kiev.ua; f. 1997; affiliated to the Federation of Jewish Communities of the CIS and the Baltic states; unites 183 communities; Chief Rabbi of Ukraine AZRIEL CHAIKIN.

Jewish Confederation of Ukraine: 04071 Kyiv, vul. Shekavystka 29; tel. (44) 463-70-75; fax (44) 463-70-88; e-mail eku@jewukr.org; internet www.jewukr.org; f. 1999; Chief Rabbi of Kyiv and All Ukraine YAAKOV DOV BLEICH.

The Press

In 2009 there were a total of 2,499 newspapers and 2,515 periodicals published in Ukraine. In addition to newspapers published in Ukraine, several newspapers and magazines published in Russia have a large circulation in Ukraine.

The publications listed below are in Ukrainian, except where otherwise stated.

PRINCIPAL NEWSPAPERS

Demokratychna Ukraina (Democratic Ukraine): 03047 Kyiv, pr. Peremohy 50; tel. (44) 454-88-30; fax (44) 456-91-21; e-mail dua@dua.com.ua; internet www.dua.com.ua; f. 1918; fmrly *Radyanska Ukraina* (Soviet Ukraine); 4 a week; Editor VITALIY ADAMENKO; circ. 62,400 (2005).

Den (The Day): 04212 Kyiv, vul. Marshala Tymoshenka 2L; tel. (44) 414-40-66; fax (44) 414-49-20; e-mail master@day.kiev.ua; internet www.day.kiev.ua; f. 1998; in Ukrainian and Russian; 5 a week; publ. by the Presa Ukrainy (Press of Ukraine) Publishing House; Editor-in-Chief LARYSA IVSHYNA.

Fakty i Kommentarii (Facts and Commentaries): 04116 Kyiv, vul. V. Vasylevskoy 27–29; tel. (44) 484-17-81; fax (44) 482-05-50; e-mail info@fakty.ua; internet www.facts.kiev.ua; f. 1997; daily; politics, economics, sport, law, culture; in Russian; Chief Editor ALEKSANDR SHVETS.

UKRAINE

Gazeta po-Kiyevski (Kyiv Newspaper): 04080 Kyiv, vul. Frunze 104A; tel. (44) 205-43-85; e-mail online@pk.kiev.ua; internet pk.kiev.ua; in Russian; 6 a week; Chief Editor SERGEI TIKHII.

Holos Ukrayiny/Golos Ukrayiny (Voice of Ukraine): 03047 Kyiv, vul. Nesterova 4; tel. (44) 503-68-72; fax (44) 224-72-54; e-mail mail@golos.com.ua; internet www.golos.com.ua; f. 1990; organ of the Verkhovna Rada; in Ukrainian and Russian; 5 a week; Editor ANATOLIY F. GORLOV; circ. 150,000 (2011).

Kommersant-Ukrayina (Businessman-Ukraine): 01011 Kyiv, vul. Rybalska 22; tel. and fax (44) 497-37-20; internet www.kommersant.ua; f. 2005; owned by Kommersant Publishing House (Russia); in Russian; Dir-Gen. and Chief Editor ANDREI GOGOLEV.

Kyiv Post: 01034 Kyiv, vul. Prorizna 22B; tel. (44) 234-65-00; fax (44) 234-30-62; e-mail letters@kyivpost.com; internet www.kyivpost.com; f. 1995; weekly; in English; Chief Editor BRIAN BONNER; circ. 25,000 (2010).

Literaturna Ukrayina (Literary Ukraine): 01061 Kyiv, bulv. L. Ukrainky 20; tel. (44) 286-36-39; e-mail lit_ukraine@ukr.net; f. 1927; weekly; organ of Union of Writers of Ukraine; Editor PETRO PEREBYJNIS; circ. 7,150 (2007).

Molod Ukrayiny (The Youth of Ukraine): 03047 Kyiv, pr. Peremohy 50; tel. (44) 454-83-90; fax (44) 235-31-52; e-mail mu@pressa.kiev.ua; f. 1925; 3 a week; Editor-in-Chief T. M. FEDORENKO; circ. 8,000 (2010).

Pravda Ukrayiny (The Truth of Ukraine): 01032 Kyiv, vul. Starovokzalna 17; tel. (44) 270-62-16; e-mail vyasnopolska@pravda-ua.info; internet www.pravda-ua.info; f. 1938; weekly; in Russian; Editor-in-Chief VIKTORIYA YASNOPOLSKAYA; circ. 187,000.

Robitnycha Hazeta/Rabochaya Gazeta (Workers' Gazette): 03047 Kyiv, pr. Peremohy 50; tel. (44) 454-84-94; fax (44) 456-68-85; e-mail mail@rg.kiev.ua; internet www.rg.kiev.ua; f. 1957; 5 a week; publ. by the Cabinet of Ministers and Inter-regional Association of Manufacturers; Ukrainian and Russian edns; Dir-Gen. and Chief Editor ANATOLIY KRYVOLAPOV.

Silski Visti (Rural News): 03047 Kyiv, pr. Peremohy 50; tel. (44) 441-86-32; fax (44) 446-93-71; e-mail ssk@silvist.kiev.ua; internet www.silskivisti.kiev.ua; f. 1920; 3 a week; Chief Editor V. D. HRUZIN.

Ukrayina Moloda (Ukraine The Young): 03047 Kyiv, pr. Peremohy 50; tel. and fax (44) 454-83-92; e-mail natali@umoloda.kiev.ua; internet www.umoloda.kiev.ua; f. 1991; 5 a week; independent; Editor MYKHAYLO DOROSHENKO; circ. 131,657 (2008).

Ukrayinska Pravda (Ukrainian Truth): Kyiv; e-mail ukrpravda@gmail.com; internet www.pravda.com.ua; online only; in Russian and Ukrainian; Editor-in-Chief OLENA PRYTULA.

Ukrayinske Slovo (The Ukrainian Word): 01010 Kyiv, vul. I. Mazepy 6; tel. (44) 280-70-59; fax (44) 280-62-65; e-mail ukrslovo@ukr.net; internet www.ukrslovo.com.ua; f. 1933; weekly; nationalist; Editor-in-Chief HRYHORIY KRYMCHUK.

Uryadoviy Kuryer (Official Courier): 01008 Kyiv, vul. Sadova 1; tel. (44) 253-12-95; fax (44) 253-39-50; e-mail letter@ukcc.com.ua; f. 1990; 5 a week; organ of the Cabinet of Ministers; Editor-in-Chief ALLA KOVTUR; circ. 83,000 (2008).

Vechirniy Kyiv (Evening Kyiv): 04136 Kyiv, vul. Marshala Hrechka 13; tel. (44) 434-61-09; fax (44) 443-96-09; f. 1932; 5 a week; Editor-in-Chief OLEKSANDR BALABKO; circ. 45,000 (2005).

PRINCIPAL PERIODICALS

Avto-Tsentr (Autocentre): 03047 Kyiv, pr. Peremohy 50, POB 2; tel. (44) 206-56-01; fax (44) 458-44-04; e-mail editor@autocentre.ua; internet www.autocentre.ua; f. 1997; weekly; motoring; in Russian; Editor-in-Chief SERGEI TARNAVSKII; circ. 200,000.

Barvinok (Periwinkle): 04119 Kyiv, vul. Dekhtyarivska 38–44; tel. (44) 213-99-13; fax (44) 211-04-36; e-mail barvinok@kievweb.com.ua; f. 1928; fortnightly; illustrated popular fiction for school-age children; in Ukrainian; Editor VASYL VORONOVYCH; circ. 40,000.

Berezil: 61002 Kharkiv, vul. Chernyshevskoho 59; tel. (57) 700-32-23; fax (57) 700-54-37; e-mail berezil@ukr.net; f. 1956; fmrly Prapor; monthly; journal of Union of Writers of Ukraine; fiction and socio-political articles; Editor-in-Chief VOLODYMYR NAUMENKO; circ. 5,000.

Delovaya Stolitsya (Capital City Business): 01135 Kyiv, vul. Pavlovska 29; tel. (44) 502-02-21; fax (44) 502-02-27; e-mail editor@dsnews.ua; internet www.dsnews.ua; f. 2001; weekly; in Russian; Editor-in-Chief INNA KOVTUN; circ. 67,500 (2008).

Dnipro (The Dnieper): 04119 Kyiv, vul. Dekhtyarivska 38–44; tel. (44) 446-11-42; f. 1927; 2 a month; novels, short stories, essays, poetry, social and political topics; Editor MYKOLA LUKIV.

Dzerkalo Tyzhnya/Zerkalo Nedyeli (Mirror of the Week): 03150 Kyiv, vul. Tverska 6; tel. (44) 529-78-22; fax (44) 269-74-52; e-mail info@mirror.kiev.ua; internet www.mw.ua; f. 1994; weekly; politics, economics, the arts; Ukrainian and Russian edns; also English edition (online only); Editor-in-Chief VLADIMIR MOSTOVOI; circ. 57,000 (2006).

Kompanyon (Companion): 01010 Kyiv, vul. I. Mazepy 10A; tel. (44) 494-25-01; fax (44) 494-25-05; e-mail administrator@companion.ua; internet www.companion.ua; f. 1996; weekly; in Russian; economics, politics, business; Editor-in-Chief A. POHORELOV; circ. 25,000 (2004).

Kyiv: 01025 Kyiv, vul. Desyatinna 11; tel. (44) 229-02-80; f. 1983; monthly; journal of the Union of Writers of Ukraine and the Kyiv Writers' Organization; fiction; Editor-in-Chief PETRO M. PEREBYJNIS.

Malyatko (Child): 04119 Kyiv, vul. Dekhtyarivska 38–44; tel. (44) 483-96-26; fax (44) 483-98-91; e-mail malyatko_1@online.com.ua; f. 1960; monthly; illustrated; for pre-school children; Editor-in-Chief ZINAIDA LESHENKO; circ. 35,780 (2005).

Nataly: 02156 Kyiv, vul. Kyoto 25; tel. (44) 593-05-85; e-mail natali@blitz.kiev.ua; internet www.nataly.com.ua; monthly; women's interest; Editor-in-Chief ZHANNA LAVROVA; circ. 679,115 (2002).

Natsionalna Bezpeka i Oborona (National Security and Defence): 01015 Kyiv, vul. Lavrska 18, Oleksander Razumkov Ukrainian Centre for Economic and Political Studies; tel. (44) 201-11-95; fax (44) 201-11-99; e-mail info@uceps.com.ua; internet www.uceps.com.ua; f. 2000; monthly; politics, economics, international relations; in Russian and English; Chief Editor LYUDMYLA SHANHINA.

Perets (Pepper): 03047 Kyiv, pr. Peremohy 50; tel. (44) 454-82-14; fax (44) 234-35-82; e-mail prudnyk@bigmir.net; f. 1922; monthly; publ. by the Presa Ukrainy Publishing House; satirical; Editor MYKHAYLO PRUDNYK; circ. 14,000 (2011).

Politychna Dumka/Politicheskaya Mysl/Political Thought: 01030 Kyiv, vul. Leontovycha 5; tel. and fax (98) 413-62-17; e-mail politdumka@bigmir.net; internet www.politdumka.kiev.ua; f. 1993; current affairs and political analysis; Ukrainian, Russian and English edns; Editor MARINA PYROZHUK.

Vitchyzna (Fatherland): 01021 Kyiv, vul. M. Hrushevskoho 34; tel. (44) 253-28-51; internet www.vitchyzna.ukrlife.org; f. 1933; 6 a year; Ukrainian prose and poetry; Editor OLEKSANDR HLUSHKO; circ. 50,100.

Vsesvit (The Universe): 01021 Kyiv, vul. M. Hrushevskoho 34/1; tel. (44) 253-13-18; fax (44) 253-06-13; e-mail myk@vsesvit-review.kiev.ua; internet www.vsesvit-journal.com; f. 1925; monthly; foreign fiction, literary criticism and reviews of foreign literature and art; Exec. Editor OLEH MYKYTENKO; circ. 2,000–3,000 (2007).

Yi (Ji): Lviv; e-mail info@ji.lviv.ua; internet www.ji-magazine.lviv.ua; f. 1989; independent; literature and literary criticism, culture, politics, philosophy; Chief Editor IRYNA MAGDYSH.

Zhinka (Woman): 03047 Kyiv, pr. Peremohy 50; tel. (44) 226-30-55; fax (44) 456-36-94; e-mail zhinka@cki.ipri.kiev.ua; f. 1920; monthly; publ. by Presa Ukrainy Publishing House; social and political subjects, fiction; for women; Editor LIDIYA MAZUR; circ. 55,000.

NEWS AGENCIES

Interfax-Ukrayina (Interfax-Ukraine): 01034 Kyiv, vul. Reitarska 8/5 A; tel. (44) 270-74-65; fax (44) 270-65-69; e-mail pr@interfax.kiev.ua; internet www.interfax.kiev.ua; f. 1992; Dir OLEKSANDR MARTYNENKO.

Respublika Ukrainian Independent Information Agency (UNIAR): 02005 Kyiv, vul. Mechnykova 14/1; tel. (44) 246-46-34; e-mail naboka@uniar.kiev.ua; internet www.uniar.com.ua; independent press agency; Dir S. NABOKA.

Ukrainian Independent Information and News Agency (UNIAN): 01001 Kyiv, vul. Khreshchatyk 4; tel. (44) 279-31-31; fax (44) 461-91-11; e-mail iviu@unian.net; internet www.unian.net; f. 1993; press agency and monitoring service; selected services are provided in Ukrainian, Russian and English; Gen. Dir OLEH I. NALIVAIKO; Editor-in-Chief OLEKSANDR A. KHARCHENKO.

Ukrayinski Novyni Informatsyonnoye Ahentstvo (Ukrainian News Information Agency): 01033 Kyiv, vul. Volodymyrska 61/11/41; tel. (44) 494-31-60; fax (44) 494-31-67; e-mail office@ukranews.com; internet www.ukranews.com; f. 1993; economic and political news; in Ukrainian, Russian and English.

UkrInform–Ukrainian National Information Agency: 01001 Kyiv, vul. B. Khmelnytskoho 8/16B; tel. (44) 279-81-52; fax (44) 279-86-65; e-mail office@ukrinform.com; internet news.ukrinform.com.ua; f. 1918; Dir-Gen. VIKTOR CHAMARA.

Publishers

In 1996 there were 6,460 book titles (including pamphlets and brochures) published in Ukraine (total circulation 50.9m.). By 2009 the number of book titles published in Ukraine had increased to 22,491.

Donbas: 83015 Donetsk, vul. B. Khmelnytskoho 102; tel. (62) 304-01-56; fiction and criticism; in Ukrainian and Russian; Dir A. I. YEZHEL.

Folio: 61002 Kharkiv, vul. Chubarya 11; tel. (57) 700-42-29; fax (57) 715-64-92; e-mail trade@folio.com.ua; internet folio.com.ua; f. 1992; classic and contemporary fiction in Russian, Ukrainian and French; Gen. Man. OLEKSANDR V. KRASOVYTSKIY.

Kamenyar (Stonecrusher): 79008 Lviv, vul. Pidvalna 3; tel. and fax (32) 235-59-49; e-mail vyd_kamenyar@mail.lviv.ua; internet www.kamenyar.com.ua; f. 1939; state-owned; fiction and criticism; in Ukrainian, Russian and Polish; Dir DMYTRO I. SAPIGA.

Karpaty (The Carpathians): 88000 Transcarpathian obl., Uzhhorod, pl. Zhupanatska 3; tel. (312) 23-23-66; fiction and criticism; Dir V. V. BRASLAVETS.

Lybid (Swan): 01004 Kyiv, vul. Pushkinska 32; tel. and fax (44) 279-11-71; e-mail info@lybid.org.ua; internet www.lybid.org.ua; f. 1835; University of Kyiv press; Dir OLENA A. BOIKO.

Medytsyna Svitu (Medicines of the World): 79071 Lviv, vul. Kulparkivska 131, POB 3566; tel. (32) 224-47-15; fax (32) 224-47-15; e-mail msvitu@mail.lviv.ua; internet www.msvitu.lviv.ua; f. 1997; medical journals, history, art and religion; Dir ZINOVIY MATCHAK.

Molod (Youth): 04119 Kyiv, vul. Dekhtyarivska 38–44; tel. (44) 211-02-18; in Ukrainian; Dir OLHA I. POLONSKA.

Muzichna Ukraina (Musical Ukraine): 01034 Kyiv, vul. Pushkinska 32; tel. (44) 225-63-56; fax (44) 224-63-00; f. 1966; books on music; in Ukrainian; Dir ANATOLIY K. ANDRIYCHUK.

Mystetstvo: 01034 Kyiv, vul. Zolotovoritska 11; tel. (44) 235-53-92; fax (44) 279-05-64; e-mail mystetstvo@ukr.net; f. 1932; fine art criticism, theatre and screen art, tourism, Ukrainian culture; in Ukrainian, Russian, English, French and German; Dir NINA D. PRYBEHA.

Naukova Dumka (Scientific Thought): 01601 Kyiv, vul. Tereshchenkivska 3; tel. (44) 234-40-68; fax (44) 234-70-60; e-mail ndumka@i.kiev.ua; internet www.ndumka.kiev.ua; f. 1922; scientific books and periodicals; research monographs; Ukrainian literature; dictionaries and reference books; in Ukrainian, Russian and English; Dir IHOR R. ALEKSEYENKO.

Osvita (Education): 04053 Kyiv, vul. Yu. Kotsyubynski 5; tel. and fax (44) 486-54-44; e-mail osvita@kv.ukrtel.net; internet www.osvitapublish.com.ua; f. 1920; state-owned; educational books for schools of all levels; Dir-Gen. BORYS MAKSYMETS.

Prapor (Flag): 61002 Kharkiv, vul. Chubarya 11; tel. (57) 247-72-52; fax (57) 243-07-21; fmrly Berezil; general; in Ukrainian and Russian; Dir S. A. YEFYMENKO.

Prosvita (Enlightenment): 01032 Kyiv, bulv. Shevchenka 46; tel. (44) 234-15-86; fax (44) 234-95-23; e-mail office@prosvita.kiev.ua; internet www.prosvita.kiev.ua; f. 1990; textbooks for all levels of education from pre-school to higher education.

Sich (Camp): 49070 Dnipropetrovsk, pr. K. Marksa 60; tel. (562) 45-22-01; fax (562) 45-44-04; f. 1964; fiction, juvenile, socio-political, criticism; in Ukrainian, English, German, French and Russian; Dir YU. A. SKALOZUB.

Tavria: 95000 Crimea, Simferopol, vul. Gorkogo 5; tel. (652) 27-45-66; fax (652) 27-65-74; e-mail ingvi@ukr.net; fiction, criticism, folklore and geography; in Ukrainian, Russian and Crimean Tatar; Dir YU. YA. IVANICHENKO.

Tekhnika (Technology): 04053 Kyiv, vul. Observatorna 25; tel. (44) 212-10-90; f. 1930; industry and transport books, popular science, posters and booklets; in Ukrainian and Russian; Dir YURIY YU. KOSTRYTSYA.

Ukrainska Ensyklopedia im. M. P. Bazhana (Ukrainian M. P. Bazhan Encyclopedia): 01004 Kyiv, vul. Pushkinska 32 A; tel. (44) 235-11-08; encyclopedias, dictionaries and reference books; Dir MYKHAILO P. ZYABLYUK.

Ukrainskiy Pysmennyk (Ukrainian Writer): 01054 Kyiv, vul. O. Honchara 52; tel. and fax (44) 216-25-92; e-mail ukps@ln.ua; f. 1933; publishing house of the National Union of Writers of Ukraine; fiction; in Ukrainian; Dir OLEKSANDR A. SAVCHUK.

Urozhai (Harvest): 03035 Kyiv, vul. Uritskoho 45; tel. (44) 245-09-95; f. 1925; books and journals about agriculture; Dir LILIYA A. PILKEVYCH.

Veselka (Rainbow): 04050 Kyiv, vul. Melnikova 63; tel. (44) 213-95-01; fax (44) 483-33-59; e-mail veskiev@iptelecom.net.ua; internet www.veselka-ua.com; f. 1934; books for pre-school and school-age children; in Ukrainian and foreign languages; Dir YAREMA P. HOYAN.

Zdorovya (Health): 01054 Kyiv, vul. Vorovskoho 32B; tel. (44) 216-89-08; books on medicine, physical fitness and sport; in Ukrainian; Dir VALERIY P. SYTNYK.

Znannya Ukrainy (Knowledge of Ukraine): 01034 Kyiv, vul. Striletska 28; tel. (44) 234-80-43; fax (44) 238-82-65; e-mail znannia@society.kiev.ua; internet www.znannia.com.ua; f. 1948; general non-fiction; Dir VOLODYMYR I. KARASOV.

Broadcasting and Communications

TELECOMMUNICATIONS

Regulatory Authority

State Committee for Communication and Information: 01001 Kyiv, vul. Khreshchatyk 22; tel. (44) 228-15-00; fax (44) 228-61-41; e-mail mailbox@stc.gov.ua; internet www.stc.gov.ua; Chair. YURIY O. PLAKSYUK.

Major Service Providers

Astelit: 03110 Kyiv, vul. Solomyanska 11 A; tel. (44) 233-31-31; internet www.life.com.ua; f. 2005; 51% owned by TurkCell (Turkey); provides mobile cellular telecommunications services under the brand name 'Life'.

Golden Telecom GSM: 01021 Kyiv, vul. Khreshchatyk 19 A; tel. (44) 490-00-90; fax (44) 490-00-70; e-mail info@goldentele.com; internet www.goldentele.com; mobile cellular telephone services; Gen. Man. YURIY BEZBORODIV.

KyivStar GSM: Kyiv, vul. I. Mazepy 24; tel. (44) 466-04-66; internet www.kyivstar.net; f. 1997; 54.2% owned by Telenor (Norway); provides mobile cellular telecommunications services under the brand names 'Ace & Base' and 'Djuice' in major cities and other regions across Ukraine; Pres. IHOR LITOVCHENKO; 15.1m. subscribers (May 2006).

MTS Ukraina: 01015 Kyiv, vul. Leiptsizka 15; fax (44) 230-02-56; e-mail slavik@umc.com.ua; internet www.umc.com.ua; f. 1991; fmrly Ukrainian Mobile Communications; present name adopted 2007; 100% owned by MTS (Russia); Gen. Man. ANDRIY DUBOVSKOV.

UkrTelecom: 01030 Kyiv, bulv. Shevchenka 18; tel. (44) 226-25-41; fax (44) 234-39-57; e-mail ukrtelecom@ukrtelecom.net; internet www.ukrtelecom.ua; f. 1993; national fixed telecommunications network operator; provides national and international telecommunications services; Chair. of Bd HEORHIY B. DZEKON.

BROADCASTING

Regulatory Authorities

National Television and Radio Broadcasting Council of Ukraine: 01601 Kyiv, vul. Prorizna 2; tel. (44) 278-68-32; fax (44) 278-74-90; e-mail pressa@nrada.gov.ua; f. 1994; monitoring and supervisory; issues broadcasting licences; Chair. VOLODYMYR A. MANZHOSOV.

State Committee for Television and Radio Broadcasting (Derzhavnyi komitet telebachennya i radiomovlennya Ukrainy): 01001 Kyiv, vul. Khreshchatyk 26/206; tel. (44) 239-63-89; internet comin.kmu.gov.ua; responsibilities include the supervision of 27 state-controlled television and radio companies; Chair. EDUARD PRUTNIK.

Radio

Hromadske (Community) Radio: 01025 Kyiv, vul. Volodymyrska 61/11/50; tel. (44) 494-40-14; information, news and discussion programmes.

National Radio Co of Ukraine-Ukrainian Radio (Natsionalna Radiokompaniya Ukrainy-Ukrainske Radio): 01001 Kyiv, vul. Khreshchatyk 26; tel. (44) 239-61-03; fax (44) 279-11-70; e-mail krutouz@nrcu.gov.ua; internet www.nrcu.gov.ua; state-owned; domestic broadcasts; also international broadcasts in English, German, Romanian and Ukrainian; Gen. Dir. TARAS AVRAKHOV.

Several independent radio stations broadcast to the major cities of Ukraine.

Television

Ukrainian State Television and Radio Co (Derzhavna Teleradiomovna Kompaniya Ukrainy): 01001 Kyiv, vul. Khreshchatyk 26; tel. (44) 481-43-86; Chair. VITALIY DOKALENKO.

1+1: 01001 Kyiv, vul. Khreshchatyk 7/11; tel. and fax (44) 490-01-01; e-mail contact@1plus1.tv; internet www.1plus1.tv; f. 1995; independent; broadcasts for 24 hours daily to 95% of Ukrainian population; Chair. of Bd of Dirs OLEKSANDR YU. RODNYANSKY.

5 Kanal: 04176 Kyiv, vul. Elektrykiv 26; tel. (44) 239-16-86; internet 5.ua; terrestrial broadcasts to 14 cities, and cable and satellite broadcasts; 24-hour news broadcasts; Dir-Gen. IVAN ADAMCHUK.

Inter: 01601 Kyiv, vul. Dmitriyevska 30; tel. and fax (44) 490-67-65; e-mail pr@inter.ua; internet www.inter.kiev.ua; f. 1996.

Novy Kanal (New Channel): 04107 Kyiv, vul. Nahorna 24/1; tel. (44) 238-80-28; fax (44) 238-80-20; e-mail post@novy.tv; internet www.novy.tv; f. 1998; broadcasts in Ukrainian and Russian; Chair. OLEKSANDR M. TKACHENKO.

STB: 03113 Kyiv, vul. Shevtsova 1; tel. (44) 501-98-99; e-mail y@stb.ua; internet stb.ua; Chair. of Bd VOLODYMYR BORODYANSKY.

UKRAINE   *Directory*

Finance

(cap. = capital; res = reserves; dep. = deposits; brs = branches;
m. = million; amounts in hryvnyas, unless otherwise indicated)

BANKING

Central Bank

National Bank of Ukraine (Natsionalny Bank Ukrainy): 01601 Kyiv, vul. Institutska 9; tel. (44) 253-01-80; fax (44) 230-20-33; e-mail webmaster@bank.gov.ua; internet www.bank.gov.ua; f. 1991; cap. 100m., res 89,871m., dep. 39,308m. (Dec. 2008); Gov. SERHIY H. ARBUZOV.

Other State Banks

Republican Bank of Crimea: 95000 Crimea, Simferopol, ul. Gorkogo; tel. (652) 51-09-46; e-mail webmaster@rbc.crimea.ua.

UkrExImBank—State Export-Import Bank of Ukraine: 03150 Kyiv, vul. Horkoho 127; tel. (44) 247-89-48; fax (44) 247-80-82; e-mail bank@eximb.com; internet www.eximb.com; f. 1992; fmrly br. of USSR Vneshekonombank (External Trade Bank); cap. 3,775.9m., res 655.3m., dep. 42,397.7m. (Dec. 2008); Chair. of Bd IHOR SOTULENKO; 29 brs.

Commercial Banks

Aktyv-Bank (Active-Bank): 03127 Kyiv, vul. Borysohlibska 3; tel. (44) 207-45-84; fax (44) 390-25-72; e-mail bank@activebank.com.ua; internet www.activebank.com.ua; f. 2002; cap. 312.7m., res 124.8m., dep. 1,490.2m. (Dec. 2008); Chair. of Managing Bd LYUDMYLA V. RASPUTNAYA.

Alfa-Bank (Ukraine): 01025 Kyiv, vul. Desyatinna 4/6; tel. (44) 490-46-00; fax (44) 490-46-01; e-mail ccd@alfabank.kiev.ua; internet www.alfabank.com.ua; f. 1993; cap. US $272.6m., res $25.0m., dep. $1,552.2m. (Dec. 2007); Pres. and CEO OLEKSANDR LUKANOV; Chair. of Bd MYKHAILO VIKTORIYA.

Bank Kredyt Dnipro/ Bank Kredit Dnepr (Credit Dnepr Bank): 49600 Dnipropetrovsk, vul. Pysarzhevskoho 1A; tel. (562) 36-73-16; fax (562) 33-39-77; e-mail info@creditdnepr.com; internet creditdnepr.com.ua; f. 1993; 99.99% owned by Brancroft Enterprises (Cyprus); cap. 298.7m., res 72.3m., dep. 3,213.6m. (Dec. 2008); Chair. PAVEL MAKAROV.

Brokbiznesbank: 03057 Kyiv, pr. Peremohy 41; tel. (44) 206-22-06; fax (44) 459-67-80; e-mail bank@bankbb.com; internet www.bankbb.com; f. 1991; cap. 1,852.2m., res 217.8m., dep. 9,427.3m. (Dec. 2007); Chair. of Council MYKOLA STRILA; Chair. of Bd SERHIY P. MISHTA; 235 brs.

Calyon Bank Ukraine: 01034 Kyiv, vul. Volodymyrska 23A; tel. (44) 490-14-00; fax (44) 490-14-02; e-mail ukr-general@ua.calyon.com; internet www.calyon.kiev.ua; f. 1993; 100% owned by Crédit Agricole (France); cap. 172.9m., res 163.4m., dep. 4,300.0m. (Dec. 2008); Pres. and Dir-Gen. JACQUES MOUNIER.

Dongorbank: 83086 Donetsk, vul. Artema 38; tel. and fax (62) 332-73-00; e-mail bank@dongorbank.com; internet www.dongorbank.com; f. 1992; cap. 805.9m., res 76.1m., dep. 6,103.6m. (Dec. 2008); Chair. of Bd NATALIYA F. KOSENKO.

Finance and Credit Bank (Bank 'Financy ta Kredyt'): 04050 Kyiv, vul. Artema 60; tel. (44) 495-29-07; fax (44) 238-24-65; e-mail info.contactcenter@fcbank.com.ua; internet www.fc.kiev.ua; f. 1990; res 79.8m., dep. 12,701.2m., total assets 14,536.7m. (Dec. 2007); Chair. VLADIMIR H. KHLYVNYUK; 11 brs.

First Ukrainian International Bank/Pershyi Ukrainskyi Mizhnarodnyi Bank (FUIB): 83001 Donetsk, vul. Universitetska 2A; tel. (623) 32-45-00; fax (623) 32-47-00; e-mail info@fuib.com; internet www.fuib.com; f. 1991; cap. US $344.8m., res $88.8m., dep. $1,314.1m. (Dec. 2008); Chair. of Bd KONSTANTYN VAISMAN.

Forum Bank (Bank Forum): 02100 Kyiv, bulv. Verkhovnoi Rady 7; tel. (44) 206-63-03; fax (44) 554-70-90; e-mail info@forum.ua; internet www.forum.ua; f. 1994; 94.5% owned by Commerzbank (Germany); cap. 1,639.7m., res 33.2m., dep. 15,254.5m. (Dec. 2008); Chair. YAROSLAV V. KOLESNYK; 194 brs (Dec. 2010).

Indeks Bank: 01004 Kyiv, vul. Pushkinska 42/4; tel. (44) 581-07-00; fax (44) 581-07-76; e-mail liudmyla.leonova@indexbank.ua; internet indexbank.ua; f. 1993; 99.98% owned by Crédit Agricole (France); cap. 400.0m., res 30.9m., dep. 3,647.8m. (Dec. 2008); Chief Exec. and Chair. of Bd PHILIPPE GUIDEZ.

Khreshchatyk Bank: 01001 Kyiv, vul. Khreshchatyk 8A; tel. (44) 490-25-00; e-mail bank@xbank.com.ua; internet www.xcitybank.com.ua; f. 1993; present name adopted 1998; 23.7% owned by Kyiv City Administration; cap. US $72.5m., res $-41.5m., dep. $528.1m. (Dec. 2008); Chair. of Bd DMYTRO M. GRYDZHYK; 160 brs.

Klyrynhovy Dom AB (Clearing House Joint-Stock Bank): 04070 Kyiv, vul. Borysohlibska 5A; tel. (44) 593-10-30; fax (44) 593-10-31; e-mail info@clhs.kiev.ua; internet www.clhs.kiev.ua; f. 1996; cap. 418.0m., dep. 1,722.2m., total assets 2,198.5m. (Dec. 2007); Chair. of Bd VIKTORIYA ANDREYIVSKA.

Kredobank: 79026 Lviv, vul. Sakharova 78; tel. (32) 297-23-20; fax (32) 297-08-37; e-mail office@kredobank.com.ua; internet www.kredobank.com.ua; f. 1990; present name adopted 2006; 98.6% owned by PKO Bank Polski SA (Poland); cap. 580.9m., dep. 5,317.6m., total assets 5,753.7m. (Dec. 2008); Chair. IVAN FESKIV.

Kredytprombank: 01014 Kyiv, bulv. Druzhby Narodiv 38; tel. (44) 490-27-77; fax (44) 490-72-28; e-mail kpb@kreditprombank.com; internet www.kreditprombank.com; f. 1997; cap. 877.2m., res 78.4m., dep. 10,310.7m. (Dec. 2007); Chair. of Bd VIKTOR D. LEONIDOV.

Kyivska Rus Bank: 04071 Kyiv, vul. Khoryva 11A; tel. (44) 467-64-95; fax (44) 467-78-17; e-mail info@kruss.kiev.ua; internet www.kruss.kiev.ua; f. 1996; 47.7% owned by Sharp Arrow Holdings (Cyprus); cap. 282.1m., res 68.7m., dep. 3,771.1m. (Dec. 2008); Chair. VIKTOR BRATKO.

Megabank: 61002 Kharkiv, vul. Artema 30; tel. (572) 14-33-63; fax (572) 47-20-78; e-mail mega@megabank.net; internet www.megabank.net; f. 1990; present name adopted 2001; cap. 250.1m., res 34.9m., dep. 2,494.5m. (Dec. 2008); Chair. of Supervisory Council VIKTOR G. SUBOTIN; Chair. of Bd OLENA ZHUKOVA; 8 brs.

OTP Bank: 01033 Kyiv, vul. Zhylyanska 43; tel. (44) 490-05-00; fax (44) 490-05-01; e-mail office@otpbank.com.ua; internet www.otpbank.com.ua; f. 1998; present name adopted 2006; 100% owned by OTP Bank plc (Hungary); cap. 2,088.3m., dep. 30,106.3m., total assets 34,566m. (Dec. 2008); Chair. of Bd DMITRII ZINKOV.

Pivdennyi Bank: 65059 Odesa, vul. Krasnova 6/1; tel. and fax (482) 30-70-30; e-mail in@pivdenny.ua; internet www.bank.com.ua; f. 1993; cap. 655.4m., res 510.5m., dep. 9,866.9m. (Dec. 2008); Chair. of Bd VADYM V. MOROKHOVSKIY; 16 brs.

PrivatBank: 49094 Dnipropetrovsk, nab. Peremohy 50; tel. (562) 716-10-00; fax (56) 716-12-71; e-mail privatbank@pbank.dp.ua; internet www.privatbank.ua; f. 1992; cap. 5,939.0m., res 1,700.0m., dep. 74,487.0m. (Dec. 2008); Chair. of Bd ALEKSANDR V. DUBILET; 51 brs.

ProCredit Bank Ukraine (ProKredyt Bank Ukraine): 03115 Kyiv, pr. Peremohy 107A; tel. (44) 590-10-00; fax (44) 590-10-01; e-mail info@procreditbank.com.ua; internet www.procreditbank.com.ua; f. 2000; present name adopted 2003; 60% owned by ProCredit Holding AG (Germany), 20% by Western NIS Enterprise Fund (Germany), 20% by European Bank for Reconstruction and Development (United Kingdom); cap. US $19.4m., res $0.1m., dep. $182.1m. (Dec. 2008); Gen. Man. SUSANNE DECKER.

Prominvestbank (Industrial-Investment Bank): 01001 Kyiv, prov. Shevchenka 12; tel. (44) 201-51-20; fax (44) 201-50-44; e-mail bank@pib.com.ua; internet www.pib.com.ua; f. 1922 as Stroibank, name changed 1992; cap. 2,232.9m., res 1,547.5m., dep. 22,060.5m. (Dec. 2008); Chair. VIKTOR BASHKIROV; 600 brs.

Raiffeisen Bank Aval: 01011 Kyiv, vul. Leskova 9; tel. (44) 490-88-88; fax (44) 490-87-55; e-mail info@aval.ua; internet www.aval.ua; f. 1992 as Aval Bank; present name adopted 2006; 95.93% owned by Raiffeisen International Bank Holding AG (Austria); cap. US $324.7m., res $-65.0m., dep. $7,502.8m. (Dec. 2008); Pres. VOLODYMYR I. LAVRENCHUK; 1,400 brs and sub-brs.

Sberbank Rossii (Ukraine): 01034 Kyiv, vul. Volodymyrska 46; tel. and fax (44) 247-45-45; e-mail sbrf@sbrf.com.ua; internet www.sbrf.com.ua; f. 2001; fmrly Bank NRB, present name adopted 2008; 100% owned by Sberbank—Savings Bank of the Russian Federation; cap. 839.9m., res 117.0m., dep. 3,545.0m. (Dec. 2008); Chair. of Bd IGOR YUSHKO.

Swedbank: 01032 Kyiv, vul. Kominterna 30; tel. (44) 481-48-67; fax (44) 481-48-85; e-mail info@swedbank.ua; internet www.swedbank.ua; f. 1991; present name adopted 2007; wholly owned by Swedbank (Sweden); cap. US $405.3m., res $-134.5m., dep. $1,954.9m. (Dec. 2008); Chair. of Bd RAINER MULLER-HANKO.

Ukrgazbank: 01004 Kyiv, vul. Chervonoarmiyska 39; tel. (44) 494-46-50; fax (44) 239-28-44; e-mail office@ukrgasbank.com; internet www.ukrgasbank.com; f. 1993; cap. 512.8m., res 339.8m., dep. 8,903.1m. (Dec. 2007); Chair. OLEKSANDR MOROZOV.

UkrSibbank: 04070 Kyiv, vul. Andriyevksa 2/12; tel. (44) 590-06-75; fax (44) 230-48-98; e-mail info@ukrsibbank.com; internet www.ukrsibbank.com; f. 1990; commercial and investment banking, non-banking financial services; 81.42% owned by BNP Paribas SA (France); cap. 4,005.0m., res -14.0m., dep. 44,668.9m. (Dec. 2008); Gen. Man. SERGIY NAUMOV; 1,000 brs and sub-brs.

UkrSotsBank—Bank for Social Development: 03150 Kyiv, vul. Kovpaka 29; tel. (44) 230-32-99; fax (44) 529-13-07; e-mail info@ukrsotsbank.com; internet www.usb.com.ua; f. 1990; cap. 1,196.6m., res 1,977.6m., dep. 42,622.9m. (Dec. 2008); Chair. of Supervisory Council WILLIBALD CERNKO; Chair. of Bd BORIS TIMONKIN; over 500 brs.

VAB Bank-Vseukrainsky Aktsionerny Bank (All-Ukrainian Share Bank): 04119 Kyiv, vul. Zoolohichna 5; tel. (44) 496-33-96;

UKRAINE

Directory

fax (44) 489-01-45; e-mail info@vab.ua; internet www.vab.ua; f. 1992; present name adopted 2007; cap. US $52.5m., res $22.6m., dep. $2.2m. (2008); CEO Peter Baron; 170 brs.

VTB Bank: 01004 Kyiv, vul. Pushkinska 8/26; tel. (44) 486-04-90; e-mail info@vtb.com.ua; internet www.vtb.com.ua; f. 2005; present name adopted 2007; cap. 2,187.9m., res 115.1m., dep. 24,351.4m. (Dec. 2008); Chair. of Bd Vadym Pushkarov; 20 brs.

Savings Bank

State Savings Bank of Ukraine—Oschadbank (Derzhavnyi Oshchadnyi Bank Ukrainy): 01023 Kyiv, vul. Hospitalna 12 G; tel. (44) 247-85-69; fax (44) 247-85-68; e-mail council@oschadnybank.com; internet www.oschadnybank.com; f. 1991; cap. 878.5m., res 484.7m., dep. 7,400m. (2006); Chair. Anatoliy Guley; 6,300 brs.

Banking Association

Association of Ukrainian Banks (Asotsiatsiya Ukrainskykh Bankiv): 02002 Kyiv, vul. M. Raskova 15/703; tel. (44) 516-87-75; fax (44) 516-87-76; e-mail kanc@aub.com.ua; internet www.aub.org.ua; f. 1990; fmrly Commercial Bank Asscn; Pres. Oleksandr Sugoniako.

COMMODITY EXCHANGES

Carpathian Commodity Exchange: 78200 Ivano-Frankivsk obl., Kolomiya, vul. Vahylevycha 1, POB 210; tel. and fax (343) 32-19-61; f. 1996; Gen. Man. Ivan P. Vatutin.

Crimea Universal Exchange: 95050 Crimea, Simferopol, vul. L. Chaikinoy 1/421; tel. (652) 22-04-32; fax (652) 22-12-73; f. 1923 as Simferopol Commodity Exchange; present name adopted 1991; Pres. Nataliya S. Syumak.

Pridniprovska Commodity Exchange: 49000 Dnipropetrovsk, vul. Nab. Lenina 15A; tel. (562) 35-77-11; fax (56) 35-77-45; e-mail ptb@pce.dp.ua; internet pce.co.ua; originally founded 1908 as Katerinoslav Commodity Exchange; re-established with present name in 1991; brs in Dniprodzerzhynsk, Kryvyi Rih, Marhanets, Pavlohrad and Synelnykove; Dir-Gen. Vadym F. Kameko.

Donetsk Commodity Exchange: 83086 Donetsk, vul. Pershotravnevska 12; tel. (62) 338-10-93; fax (62) 335-92-91; e-mail oltradex@pub.dn.ua; f. 1991; Gen. Man. Petro O. Vyshnevskyi.

Kharkiv Commodity Exchange: 61058 Kharkiv, vul. Lenina 5; tel. (57) 701-36-02; fax (57) 701-37-03; e-mail ss@htb.kharkov.ua; f. 1993; Pres. Ihor V. Zotov.

Kyiv Universal Exchange: 01103 Kyiv, Zaliznychne shose 57; tel. and fax (44) 295-11-29; e-mail nva@iptelecom.net.ua; internet www.kue.kiev.ua; f. 1990; Pres. Konstantin Lapushen.

Odesa Commodity Exchange: 65114 Odesa, vul. Lyustdorfska doroha 140A; tel. (482) 61-89-92; fax (482) 47-72-84; e-mail yuri@oce.odessa.ua; f. 1796; re-established 1990; Gen. Man. Mykola O. Nikolishen.

Ukrainian Universal Commodity Exchange: 03680 Kyiv, pr. Akadmika Hlushkova 1/6; tel. (44) 596-94-94; fax (44) 251-95-40; e-mail birga@uutb.kiev.ua; internet www.uutb.com.ua; f. 1991; Gen. Man. A. A. Kazakov.

Zaporizhzhya Commodity Exchange 'Hileya': 69037 Zaporizhzhya, vul. 40 rokiv Radyanskoyi Ukrainy 41; tel. (612) 33-32-73; fax (612) 34-76-62; f. 1991; re-established 1996; Gen. Man. Anton A. Khulakhsiz.

INSURANCE

State Insurance Companies

Crimean Insurance Co: 99011 Sevastopol, vul. Butakov 4; tel. (692) 55-30-28; fax (692) 54-23-00; e-mail ksk@ksk.in.ua; internet www.ksk.in.ua; f. 1993; Dir Isabella Bilder.

DASK UkrinMedStrakh: 01601 Kyiv, vul. O. Honshara 65; tel. (44) 216-30-21; fax (44) 216-96-92; e-mail ukrmed@ukrpack.com; f. 1999; provides compulsory medical insurance to foreigners and stateless persons temporarily resident in Ukraine.

Oranta Insurance Co: 01015 Kyiv, vul. Zhylyanska 75; tel. (44) 537-58-00; fax (44) 537-58-83; e-mail oranta@oranta.ua; internet www.oranta.ua; f. 1921; Chair. of Bd Oleg Spilka.

Commercial Insurance Companies

AKB Garant Insurance Co: 03062 Kyiv, pr. Peremohy 67; tel. (44) 454-75-25; e-mail akb@garant.kiev.ua; internet www.garant.kiev.ua; f. 1994; general insurance services; Gen. Man. Oleksandr I. Dyachenko.

ECCO Insurance Co: 01034 Kyiv, vul. Prorizna 4/23; tel. (44) 278-40-84; fax (44) 278-10-82; e-mail insurance@ecco-alpha.kiev.ua; internet www.ecco-insurance.at; f. 1991; affiliated to ECCO (Austria); life and non-life insurance; Chair. Jacob Kuess.

EnergoPolis Insurance Co: 01033 Kyiv, vul. Sh. Rustaveli 39–41; tel. (44) 244-02-36; fax (44) 244-05-94; e-mail office@enpolis.com.ua; internet www.enpolis.com.ua; Chair. Viktor V. Protsenko (acting).

Galinstrakh Insurance Co: 04054 Kyiv, Kudryavskyi uzviz; tel. (44) 502-99-61; fax (44) 417-86-34; e-mail postbox@inserv.kiev.ua; f. 1991; general insurance services; Chair. of Bd Stephan Sovinskiy.

HDI Insurance: 03150 Kyiv, vul. Chervonoarmiyska 102; tel. (44) 247-44-77; fax (44) 529-08-94; e-mail hdi@hdi.ua; internet www.hdi.ua; f. 1992; fmrly Alkona Insurance Co, present name adopted 2008; insurance and reinsurance; Chair. Kostyantyn Ksyenich.

Ingo Ukraina Insurance Co: 01054 Kyiv, vul. Vorovskogo 33; tel. (44) 490-27-44; fax (44) 490-27-48; e-mail office@ingo.ua; internet www.ingo.com.ua; f. 1994; fmrly Ostra-Kyiv Insurance Co; re-insurance, medical, travel, property and cargo insurance; Chair. of Bd Ihor N. Hordyenko.

Inter-Policy Insurance Co: 01033 Kyiv, vul. Volodymyrska 69; tel. (44) 465-30-48; fax (44) 289-14-84; e-mail info@inter-policy.com; internet www.inter-policy.com; f. 1993.

Kyiv Insurance Co: 04053 Kyiv, vul. Yu. Kotsubynskoho 20; tel. (44) 461-92-41; fax (44) 461-92-43; f. 1998.

Ostra Insurance Co: 65026 Odesa, vul. Pushkinska 13; tel. (48) 724-68-30; fax (48) 724-38-41; e-mail main@ostra.com.ua; internet www.ostra.com.ua; f. 1990; non-life; Chair. Khyrach Mahdyev.

PZU Ukraine Insurance Co: 04112 Kyiv, vul. Dehtyarivska 62; tel. (44) 238-62-38; fax (44) 581-04-55; e-mail mail@pzu.com.ua; internet www.pzu.com.ua; 100% owned by PZU (Poland); 4 subsidiary cos; life and non-life; Pres. Ireneusz Wesołowski.

QBE Ukraina Insurance: 04070 Kyiv, vul. Illinska 8; tel. (44) 537-53-90; fax (44) 537-53-99; e-mail info.ukraine@qbe.com; internet www.qbeeurope.com/ukraine; f. 1998; affiliate of QBE Insurance (New Zealand); Gen. Dir Oleh Sosnovsky.

Skide Insurance Co: 04050 Kyiv, vul. Hlybochytska 72; tel. (44) 417-40-04; fax (44) 228-40-33; e-mail skide@iptelecom.net.ua; f. 1991; Pres. Volodymyr Besarab.

Sun Life Ukraine: 01032 Kyiv, vul. Starovokzalna 17; tel. (44) 235-20-02; fax (44) 235-89-17; e-mail office@sunlife.com.ua; f. 1993; life; Pres. Rostyslav B. Talskyi.

UkrGazPromPolis Insurance Co: 01034 Kyiv, vul. O. Honshara 41; tel. (44) 235-25-00; fax (44) 235-31-13; e-mail office@ugpp.com.ua; internet www.ugpp.com.ua; f. 1996; jointly owned by UkrGazProm, UkrGazPromBank and KyivTransGaz; Pres. Konstantyn O. Yefymenko.

Insurance Association

League of Insurance Organizations of Ukraine: 02660 Kyiv, vul. M. Roskovoyi 11; tel. and fax (44) 516-82-30; e-mail liga@uainsur.com; internet www.uainsur.com; f. 1992; non-profit asscn of insurance cos; Pres. Nataliya Hudyma.

Trade and Industry

GOVERNMENT AGENCY

State Property Fund of Ukraine (Fond Derzhavnoho Maina Ukrainy): 01133 Kyiv, vul. Kutuzova 18/9; tel. (44) 200-33-33; fax (44) 286-79-85; e-mail marketing@spfu.kiev.ua; internet www.spfu.gov.ua; Head Oleksandr V. Ryabchenko (acting).

NATIONAL CHAMBER OF COMMERCE

Ukrainian Chamber of Commerce and Industry (Torgovo-Promyslova Palata Ukrainy/Torgovo-Promyshlennaya Palata Ukrainy): 01601 Kyiv, vul. V. Zhytomyrska 33; tel. (44) 272-29-11; fax (44) 272-33-53; e-mail ucci@ucci.org.ua; internet www.ucci.org.ua; f. 1972; Pres. Serhiy P. Skrypchenko; 27 regional brs with a total of c. 9,000 mems.

REGIONAL CHAMBERS OF COMMERCE

Chambers of Commerce are located in every administrative region of Ukraine, including the following:

Chamber of Commerce and Industry of Crimea: 95013 Crimea, Simferopol, ul. Sevastopolskaya 45; tel. (652) 49-33-46; fax (652) 44-58-13; e-mail cci@cci.crimea.ua; internet www.cci.crimea.ua; f. 1974; sub-brs in Armyansk, Dzhankoi, Feodosiya, Kerch, Yalta and Yevpatoriya; Pres. Neonila M. Gracheva.

Dnipropetrovsk Chamber of Commerce: 49044 Dnipropetrovsk, vul. Shevchenka 4; tel. (562) 36-22-58; fax (562) 36-22-59; e-mail dcci@dcci.org.ua; internet www.dcci.org.ua; f. 1995; brs at Kryvyi Rih and Dniprodzerzhynsk; Pres. Vytaliy H. Zhmurenko.

Donetsk Chamber of Commerce: 83007 Donetsk, pr. Kyivsky 87; tel. (62) 387-80-00; fax (62) 387-80-01; e-mail info@dttp.donetsk.ua;

UKRAINE

internet www.cci.donbass.com; f. 1964; brs at Artemovsk, Horlivka, Kramatorsk, Makiyivka and Mariupol; Pres. GENNADII D. CHIZHIKOV.

Kharkiv Chamber of Commerce: 61037 Kharkiv, pr. Moskovksky 122; tel. (57) 714-96-90; fax (57) 738-64-79; e-mail info@kcci.kharkov.ua; internet www.kcci.kharkov.ua; Pres. VIKTOR I. LOBODA.

Kyiv Chamber of Commerce and Industry: 01504 Kyiv-54, vul. B. Khmelnytskoho 55; tel. (44) 246-83-01; fax (44) 246-99-66; e-mail info@kiev-chamber.org.ua; internet www.kiev-chamber.org.ua; Pres. MYKOLA V. ZASULSKIY.

Lviv Chamber of Commerce and Industry: 79011 Lviv, Stryiskiy park 14; tel. and fax (32) 276-46-11; e-mail lcci@cci.com.ua; internet www.lcci.com.ua; f. 1850; Pres. DMYTRO D. AFTANAS.

Odesa Chamber of Commerce and Industry: 65125 Odesa, vul. Bazarna 47; tel. (48) 38-04-82; fax (482) 49-63-07; e-mail orcci@orcci.odessa.ua; internet www.orcci.odessa.ua; f. 1924; brs at Illichivsk, Izmayil and Reni; Pres. SERHIY SHUVALOV.

Sevastopol Chamber of Commerce and Industry: 99011 Sevastopol, ul. B. Morskaya 34; tel. (692) 54-35-36; fax (692) 54-06-44; e-mail members@stpp.org.ua; internet www.stpp.org.ua; f. 1963; Pres. LYUDMILA I. VISHNYA.

Transcarpathian (Zakarpatska) Chamber of Commerce and Industry: 88015 Transcarpathian obl., Uzhhorod, vul. Hrushevskoho 62; tel. (312) 66-94-50; fax (312) 66-94-60; e-mail tpp@tpp.uzhgorod.ua; internet www.tpp.uzhgorod.ua; br. at Mukachevo; Pres. OTTO O. KOVCHAR.

Zaporizhzhya Chamber of Commerce: 69000 Zaporizhzhya, bulv. Tsentralnyi 4; tel. (612) 13-50-24; fax (612) 33-11-72; e-mail cci@cci.zp.ua; internet www.cci.zp.ua; brs at Berdyansk and Melitopol; Pres. VOLODOMYR I. SHAMYLOV.

EMPLOYERS' ORGANIZATION

Congress of Business Circles of Ukraine: 01061 Kyiv, vul. Prorizna 15; tel. (44) 228-64-81; fax (44) 229-52-84; Pres. VALERIY G. BABICH.

UTILITIES

Regulatory Bodies

National Electricity Regulatory Commission of Ukraine: 03057 Kyiv, vul. Smolenska 19; tel. (44) 241-90-01; fax (44) 241-90-47; e-mail box@nerc.gov.ua; f. 1994; promotion of competition and protection of consumer interests; Chair. YURIY PRODAN.

State Committee for Nuclear Regulation (Derzhavnyi komitet yadernoho rehulyuvannya Ukrainy): 01011 Kyiv, vul. Arsenalna 9/11; tel. (44) 254-33-47; fax (44) 254-33-11; e-mail pr@hq.snrc.gov.ua; internet www.snrc.gov.ua; Chair. OLENA A. MYKOLAICHUK.

Electricity

EnergoAtom: 01032 Kyiv, vul. Vetrova 3; tel. (44) 281-48-83; e-mail pr@nae.atom.gov.ua; internet www.energoatom.kiev.ua; f. 1996; responsible for scientific and technical policy within the nuclear power industry; manages all five nuclear power producing installations in Ukraine; Pres. ANDRIY L. DERKACH.

Kyivenergo: 01001 Kyiv, pl. Ivana Franka 5; tel. (44) 201-58-67; fax (44) 239-47-06; e-mail pubrel@kievenergo.com.ua; internet www.kievenergo.com.ua; power generation and distribution; Chair. SERHIY M. TITENKO.

Zakhidenergo (West Energy): 79026 Lviv, vul. Kozelnytska 15; tel. (322) 39-07-10; fax (322) 39-07-17; e-mail kanc@gwce.energy.gov.ua; internet www.zakhidenergo.ua; f. 1995; power generation; Dir-Gen. PETRO I. OMELYANOVSKIY.

Gas

Naftogaz Ukrainy (Oil and Gas of Ukraine): 01001 Kyiv, vul. B. Khmelnytskoho 6B; tel. (44) 461-25-37; fax (44) 220-15-26; e-mail ngu@naftogaz.net; internet www.naftogaz.com; f. 1998; state-owned; production and distribution of gas and petroleum; storage of gas; gas- and condensate-processing; Chair. of Bd OLEH DUBYNA.

TRADE UNION FEDERATIONS

Confederation of Free Trade Unions of Ukraine (CFTUU) (Konfederatsiya Vilnykh Profspilok Ukrainy—KVPU): 03150 Kyiv, vul. V. Vasylkivska 54; tel. (44) 287-33-38; fax (44) 287-72-83; e-mail info@kvpu.org.ua; internet www.kvpu.org.ua; f. 1997; independent; Chair. MYKHAYLO YA. VOLYNETS.

Federation of Trade Unions of Ukraine: 01012 Kyiv, Maidan Nezalezhnosti 2; tel. (44) 278-87-88; fax (44) 278-87-98; e-mail fpsu@fpsu.org.ua; internet www.fpsu.org.ua; f. 1990; fmr Ukrainian branch of General Confederation of Trade Unions of the USSR; 46 sectoral and 27 regional member bodies; Chair. VASYL KHARA.

Transport

RAILWAYS

In 2002 there were 22,078 km of railway track in use, of which more than 9,000 km were electrified.

State Railway Transport Administration—Ukrzaliznytsia: 03680 Kyiv, vul. Tverska 5; tel. (44) 223-00-10; fax (44) 258-80-11; e-mail ci@uz.gov.ua; internet www.uz.gov.ua; Dir-Gen. MYLHAILO KOSTYUK.

Ukrreftrans: 03049 Kyiv, vul. Furmanova 1/7; tel. (44) 245-47-22; e-mail sekretar@intertrans.com.ua; internet www.intertrans.com.ua; state-owned freight transportation service.

Dnipropetrovsk Metro: 49038 Dnipropetrovsk, vul. Kurchatova 8; tel. (562) 42-37-68; fax (56) 778-65-33; e-mail metrodp@ukr.net; internet gorod.dp.ua/metro/; f. 1995; one line with six stations; total length 8 km; total planned network of 74 km.

Kharkiv Metro: 61052 Kharkiv, vul. Engelsa 29; tel. (57) 731-59-83; fax (57) 731-21-41; e-mail s@metro.kharkov.ua; internet www.metro.kharkov.ua; f. 1975; three lines with 28 stations; total length 35.5 km; Gen. Man. SERHIY Z. MUSYEYEV.

Kyiv Metro: 03055 Kyiv, pr. Peremohy 35; tel. (44) 238-44-21; fax (44) 238-44-46; e-mail nto@metro.kiev.ua; internet www.metro.kiev.ua; f. 1960; three lines with 42 stations; Dir MYKOLA M. SHAVLOVSKIY.

ROADS

At 31 December 2002 there were 169,678 km of roads, of which 96.8% were paved.

INLAND WATERWAYS

The Dnipro (Dniepr—Dnieper) River is the most important route for river freight.

SHIPPING

The main ports are Yalta and Yevpatoriya in Crimea, and Odesa. In addition to long-distance international shipping lines, there are services to Russia and Georgia. At December 2009 Ukraine's merchant fleet (622 vessels) had a total displacement of 905,000 grt.

Port Authority

Odesa Commercial Sea Port: 65026 Odesa, pl. Mytna 1; tel. (48) 729-35-55; fax (48) 729-36-27; e-mail welcome@port.odessa.ua; internet www.port.odessa.ua; f. 1794; state-owned; cargo handling and storage, marine passenger terminal services; Gen. Man. MYKOLA P. PAVLYUK.

Shipping Companies

Azov Shipping Co: 87510 Donetsk obl., Mariupol, pr. Admirala Lunina 89; tel. (629) 31-15-00; fax (629) 31-12-25; e-mail admin@c2smtp.azsco.anet.donetsk.ua; f. 1871; Pres. SERHIY V. PRUSIKOV.

State Black Sea Shipping Co: 65026 Odesa, vul. Lanzheronovska 1; tel. (482) 25-21-60; fax (482) 60-57-33; Pres. BORIS SCHERBAK.

Ukrainian Danube Shipping Co: 68600 Odesa obl., Izmayil, vul. Chervonoflotska 28; tel. (4841) 2-55-50; fax (4841) 2-53-55; e-mail udp_t@udp.izmail.uptel.net; f. 1944; cargo and passenger services; Pres. PETR S. SUVOROV.

Ukrainian Shipping Co (UkrShip): 65014 Odesa, vul. Marazlyevska 8; tel. (48) 734-73-50; fax (48) 777-07-00; e-mail admin@ukrship.odessa.ua; f. 1996; Pres. A. SAVITSKIY.

Ukrrechflot Co: 04071 Kyiv, Nizhny val. 51; tel. and fax (44) 490-66-48; e-mail info@ukrrichflot.com.ua; f. 1992; jt-stock co; Dir-Gen. MIKHAILO CHUBAI.

Yugreftransflot: 99014 Crimea, Sevastopol, ul. Rybakov 5; tel. (692) 41-25-41; fax (692) 42-39-19; e-mail jsc@urtf.com; jt-stock co; Chair. VOLODYMYR ANDREYEV.

CIVIL AVIATION

The principal international airport is at Boryspil (Kyiv), but several other airports, including those at Dnipropetrovsk and Odesa, also service international flights.

AeroSvit Airlines: 01032 Kyiv, bulv. Shevchenko 58A; tel. (44) 246-50-70; fax (44) 246-50-46; e-mail av@aswt.kiev.ua; internet www.aerosvit.com; f. 1994; operates scheduled and charter passenger services to domestic and international destinations; Chief Exec. and Dir-Gen. GRYGORIY GURTOVOY.

ARP 410: 03151 Kyiv, Vozdukhoflotsky pr. 94; tel. (44) 246-26-64; fax (44) 243-40-33; e-mail arp410-cs@svitonline.com; f. 1999; domestic passenger and international cargo flights; Dir-Gen. ANATOLIY P. KUDRIN.

Donbassaero Airlines (Donbass-Vostochnye Aviyalinii Ukrainy—Donbassaero): 83021 Donetsk, vul. Vzlyotna 1, Donetsk International Airport; tel. (62) 388-51-03; fax (62) 332-00-55; e-mail info@donbass.aero; internet www.donbass.aero; f. 1933 as Donetsk State Airline; present name adopted 2007; passenger and cargo flights between Donetsk and domestic and international destinations; Dir-Gen. ALEKSANDR HRECHKO.

Khors Air Company: 01133 Kyiv, vul. L. Ukrainki 34; tel. (44) 294-94-11; fax (44) 573-86-72; e-mail aircargo@khors.com.ua; internet www.khors.com.ua; f. 1990; operates international, regional and domestic cargo and passenger services; Gen. Dir ANATOLIY VYSOCHANSKIY.

Ukraine International Airlines (Mizhnarodni Avialinyi Ukraini): 01054 Kyiv, vul. B. Khmelnytskoho 63A; tel. (44) 461-56-56; fax (44) 230-88-66; e-mail uia@ps.kiev.ua; internet www.ukraine-international.com; f. 1992; 61.6% state-owned; operates domestic services, and international services to European and Middle Eastern destinations from Kyiv, Dnipropetrovsk, Kharkiv, Lviv, Odesa and Simferopol; Pres. VITALIY M. POTEMSKIY.

Tourism

The Black Sea coast of Ukraine has several popular resorts, including Odesa and Yalta. The Crimean peninsula is a popular tourist centre in both summer and winter, owing to its temperate climate. Kyiv, Lviv and Odesa have important historical attractions, and there are many archaeological monuments on the Black Sea coast, including the remains of ancient Greek and Ottoman settlements. However, the tourist industry remains relatively undeveloped. There were 21.2m. foreign tourist arrivals in Ukraine in 2010; receipts from tourism in 2009 (including passenger transport) totalled US $3,576m., according to provisional figures.

Ministry of Culture: see The Government (Ministries).

Ministry of Health Resorts and Tourism of the Autonomous Republic of Crimea: 95005 Crimea, Simferopol, pr. Kirova 13; tel. (652) 54-46-68; fax (652) 25-94-38; e-mail tourism_crimea@ukr.net; internet www.tourism.crimea.ua; Minister ANDREW A. SUMTSOV.

State Tourism Administration of Ukraine (Derzhavna turystychna administratsiya Ukrainy): 01034 Kyiv, vul. Yaroslaviv val 36; tel. (44) 272-42-15; fax (44) 272-42-77; e-mail info@tourism.gov.ua; internet www.tourism.gov.ua; f. 1999; Chair. VALERIY I. TSYBUKH.

Defence

In December 1991 an independent Ukrainian military was established. As assessed at November 2010, there were an estimated 129,925 active personnel in the Ukrainian Armed Forces (excluding the Black Sea Fleet), including 70,753 ground forces, an air force of 45,240 and a navy of an estimated 13,932. There were also paramilitary forces, comprising some 45,000 in the Border Guard and 39,900 serving under the Ministry of Internal Affairs. In addition, some 9,500 were serving in civil defence troops. There were, additionally, some 1m. reserves. Military service is compulsory for males over 18 years of age, for a period of 18 months in the ground forces and air forces, and for 24 months in the navy.

In 1993–94 a programme of nuclear disarmament was agreed with the USA and Russia, involving the dismantling and surrender of the ex-Soviet warheads. The transfer of strategic nuclear weapons to Russia for dismantling was completed in mid-1996. On 31 May 1997 Ukraine and Russia signed an agreement on the division of the Soviet Black Sea Fleet, on the terms of its deployment and on the status of its base, Sevastopol. In 2010 an agreement was reached to extend Russia's lease on the Black Sea Fleet base for a further 25-year period from 2017.

Defence Expenditure: Budgeted at an estimated 13,200m. hryvnyas in 2011.

Chief of the General Staff and Commander-in-Chief of the Land Forces: Col-Gen. HRYHORIY PEDCHENKO.

Commander-in-Chief of the Air Defence: Col-Gen. IVAN S. RUSNAK.

Commander-in-Chief of the Land Forces: Col-Gen. HENNADIY VOROBYOV.

Commander-in-Chief of the Navy: Vice-Adm. VIKTOR MAKSIMOV.

Education

The reversal of the 'Russification' of the education system was one of the principal demands of the opposition movements that emerged in the late 1980s. In the early 1990s there were significant changes to the curriculum, with greater emphasis on Ukrainian history and literature, while some religious and private educational institutions were established.

Education is compulsory between seven and 15 years of age. Primary education lasts for four years, while secondary education comprises two cycles, of five years and two years, respectively. In 2010/11 there were 15,600 pre-primary educational establishments in Ukraine (although 900 of these had their operations suspended), providing for 1,273,000 students. Some 4,299,000 students attended 20,300 primary and general secondary institutions, and 433,500 students attended 976 vocational secondary educational institutions. In 2006/07 some 89% of children in the relevant age-group were enrolled in primary education, while enrolment at secondary level included 84% of children in the relevant age-group. In 2010/11 there were 2,491,300 students enrolled in higher education. Government expenditure on education in 2009 was 65,778m. hryvnyas (14.9% of total budgetary expenditure).

THE UNITED ARAB EMIRATES

Introductory Survey

LOCATION, CLIMATE, LANGUAGE, RELIGION, FLAG, CAPITAL

The United Arab Emirates (UAE) lies in the east of the Arabian peninsula. It is bordered by Saudi Arabia to the west and south, and by Oman to the east. In the north the UAE has a short frontier with Qatar and a coastline of about 650 km on the southern shore of the Persian (Arabian) Gulf, separated by a detached portion of Omani territory from a small section of coast on the western shore of the Gulf of Oman. The climate is exceptionally hot in summer, with average maximum temperatures exceeding 40°C, and humidity is very high. Winter is mild, with temperatures ranging from 17°C to 20°C. Average annual rainfall is very low: between 100 mm and 200 mm. The official language is Arabic, spoken by almost all of the native population. Arabs are, however, outnumbered by non-Arab immigrants, mainly from India, Pakistan, Bangladesh and Iran. According to official census results, UAE nationals represented about 20% of the total population in 2005. Official figures published in late 2008 indicated that non-nationals made up more than 80% of the UAE's population and constituted over 90% of the work-force. Most of the inhabitants are Muslims, mainly of the Sunni sect. The national flag (proportions 1 by 2) has three equal horizontal stripes, of green, white and black, with a vertical red stripe at the hoist. The capital is Abu Dhabi.

CONTEMPORARY POLITICAL HISTORY

Historical Context

Prior to independence the UAE was Trucial Oman, also known as the Trucial States, and the component sheikhdoms of the territory were under British protection. Although from 1892 the United Kingdom assumed responsibility for the sheikhdoms' defence and external relations, they were otherwise autonomous and followed the traditional form of Arab monarchy, with each ruler having virtually absolute power over his subjects.

In 1952 the Trucial Council, comprising the rulers of the seven sheikhdoms, was established in order to encourage the adoption of common policies in administrative matters. Petroleum, the basis of the area's modern prosperity, was first discovered in 1958, when deposits were located beneath the coastal waters of Abu Dhabi, the largest of the sheikhdoms. Onshore petroleum was found in Abu Dhabi in 1960, and commercial exploitation of petroleum began in 1962, providing the state with greatly increased revenue. However, Sheikh Shakhbut bin Sultan Al Nahyan, the Ruler of Abu Dhabi since 1928, failed to use the income from petroleum royalties to develop his domain. As a result, the ruling family deposed him in August 1966 and installed his younger brother, Sheikh Zayed bin Sultan. Under the rule of Sheikh Zayed, Abu Dhabi was transformed, with considerable income from the petroleum industry allocated for public works and the provision of welfare services. In 1966 petroleum was discovered in neighbouring Dubai (the second largest of the Trucial States), which also underwent a rapid development.

In January 1968 the United Kingdom announced its intention to withdraw British military forces from the area by 1971. In March 1968 the Trucial States formed the Federation of Arab Emirates, along with nearby Bahrain and Qatar. However, both Bahrain and Qatar seceded from the Federation in August 1971 to become separate independent states. In July six of the Trucial States (Abu Dhabi, Dubai, Sharjah, Umm al-Qaiwain, Ajman and Fujairah) had agreed on a federal Constitution for achieving independence as the United Arab Emirates (UAE). The United Kingdom accordingly terminated its special treaty relationship with the States, and the UAE became independent on 2 December 1971. The remaining sheikhdom, Ras al-Khaimah, joined the UAE in February 1972. At independence Sheikh Zayed of Abu Dhabi took office as the first President of the UAE. Sheikh Rashid bin Said Al Maktoum, the Ruler of Dubai since 1958, became Vice-President, while his eldest son, Sheikh Maktoum bin Rashid Al Maktoum (Crown Prince of Dubai), became Prime Minister in the federal Council of Ministers. A 40-member consultative assembly, the Federal National Council (FNC), was also inaugurated.

Domestic Political Affairs

In January 1972 the Ruler of Sharjah, Sheikh Khalid bin Muhammad al-Qasimi, was killed by rebels under the leadership of his cousin, Sheikh Saqr bin Sultan, who had been deposed as the sheikhdom's Ruler in June 1965. However, the rebels were defeated, and Sheikh Khalid was succeeded by his brother, Sheikh Sultan bin Muhammad al-Qasimi.

Sheikh Zayed, disappointed with progress towards centralization, reportedly announced in August 1976 that he was not prepared to accept another five-year term as President. In November, however, the highest federal authority, the Supreme Council of Rulers (comprising the Rulers of the seven emirates), re-elected him unanimously, following agreements granting the federal Government greater control over defence, intelligence services, immigration, public security and border control.

Owing to a dispute over a senior appointment in February 1978, the forces of Dubai and Ras al-Khaimah refused to accept orders from the Federal Defence Force. Although Ras al-Khaimah later reintegrated with the Federal Defence Force, Dubai's armed forces effectively remained a separate entity. In March 1979 a 10-point memorandum from the National Council, containing proposals for increased unity, was rejected by Dubai, which, together with Ras al-Khaimah, boycotted a meeting of the Supreme Council. In April Sheikh Maktoum resigned as Prime Minister; he was replaced by his father, Sheikh Rashid, who formed a new Council of Ministers in July, while retaining the post of Vice-President. Sheikh Ahmad bin Rashid al-Mu'alla, the Ruler of Umm al-Qaiwain (the smallest of the emirates) since 1929, died in February 1981, and was succeeded by his son, Rashid. Sheikh Rashid bin Humaid al-Nuaimi, the Ruler of Ajman since 1928, died in September 1981, and was succeeded by his son, Humaid.

There was an attempted coup in Sharjah in June 1987, when Sheikh Abd al-Aziz, a brother of Sheikh Sultan, announced (in his brother's absence) the abdication of the Ruler, on the grounds that he had mismanaged the economy. The Supreme Council of Rulers intervened to endorse Sheikh Sultan's claim to be the legitimate Ruler of Sharjah, effectively restoring him to power. Sheikh Abd al-Aziz was given the title of Crown Prince and was granted a seat on the Supreme Council. In February 1990, however, Sheikh Sultan removed his brother from the post of Crown Prince and revoked his right to succeed him as Ruler. In July Sheikh Sultan appointed Sheikh Ahmad bin Muhammad al-Qasimi, the head of Sharjah's petroleum and mineral affairs office, as Deputy Ruler of Sharjah, although he was not given the title of Crown Prince.

The UAE became involved in a major international financial scandal in July 1991, when regulatory authorities in seven countries abruptly closed down the operations of the Bank of Credit and Commerce International (BCCI), in which the Abu Dhabi ruling family and agencies had held a controlling interest (77%) since April 1990. The termination of the bank's activities followed the disclosure of systematic, large-scale fraud by BCCI authorities prior to April 1990. By July 1991 BCCI's activities had been suspended in all 69 countries in which it had operated. At the conclusion of fraud trials in May 1994 all but one of the defendants were sentenced to terms of imprisonment ranging from three to 14 years. (In June 1995 a court of appeal overturned the guilty verdicts of two of those imprisoned.) New legislation was subsequently prepared to strengthen the role of the Central Bank and to enforce stricter regulation of the Emirates' financial sector.

Meanwhile, in October 1990, upon the death of his father, Sheikh Maktoum acceded to the positions of Ruler of Dubai and Vice-President and Prime Minister of the UAE. In January 1995 Sheikh Maktoum issued a decree naming Sheikh Muhammad bin Rashid Al Maktoum as Crown Prince, and Sheikh Hamdan bin Rashid Al Maktoum as Deputy Ruler of Dubai. In June 1996 legislation designed to make the provisional Constitution permanent was endorsed by the FNC, following its approval by the

Supreme Council of Rulers. At the same time Abu Dhabi was formally designated capital of the UAE.

In October 2003 Sheikh Zayed appointed Sheikh Hamdan bin Zayed Al Nahyan as a Deputy Prime Minister, in addition to his existing responsibilities as Minister of State for Foreign Affairs. In the following month Sheikh Zayed issued a decree installing Sheikh Muhammad bin Zayed Al Nahyan, the Chief of Staff of Federal Armed Forces, as Deputy Crown Prince of Abu Dhabi. Meanwhile, in June Sheikh Saqr bin Muhammad al-Qasimi, the ruler of Ras al-Khaimah, deposed his eldest son, Khalid, as Crown Prince and appointed a younger son, Saud, in his place. Tanks from the federal UAE armed forces arrived in Ras al-Khaimah city, apparently in an attempt to prevent supporters of Sheikh Khalid from demonstrating against the decision. Tension in the emirate quickly eased, however, after the departure of Sheikh Khalid to Oman. In January 2004 Sheikh Saud ordered the release of 124 prisoners, including several of the protesters who had demonstrated against his appointment.

Sheikh Khalifa succeeds Sheikh Zayed as President

Sheikh Zayed died on 2 November 2004, following several years of ill health. His son, Sheikh Khalifa bin Zayed Al Nahyan, automatically succeeded him as Ruler of Abu Dhabi and was elected by the Supreme Council to the presidency the following day. The day before Sheikh Zayed's death a restructuring had been implemented of the Council of Ministers (the first such reorganization since 1997). The most significant changes were the appointment as Minister of Economy and Planning of Sheikha Lubna bint Khalid al-Qasimi, who became the first woman to hold a cabinet position in the UAE, and the combining of the petroleum and mineral resources ministry with the electricity and water portfolio to form a new Ministry of Energy, headed by Muhammad bin Dhaen al-Hamili. In December Sheikh Khalifa announced a similarly rare restructuring of the Abu Dhabi Executive Council, to be chaired by the new Crown Prince, Sheikh Muhammad, who also remained the Chief of Staff of Federal Armed Forces.

Sheikh Maktoum, who had reportedly suffered from heart problems, died suddenly in January 2006. He was immediately succeeded as Ruler of Dubai by his brother, Sheikh Muhammad bin Rashid Al Maktoum, who had been Dubai's Crown Prince since 1995. Sheikh Muhammad replaced Sheikh Maktoum as Vice-President and Prime Minister of the UAE, while also retaining control of the Ministry of Defence, a position he had held since 1971.

In December 2005 Sheikh Khalifa announced tentative proposals to open one-half of the 40 seats in the FNC to indirect election via new national councils in each of the emirates. The President envisaged that this represented the first step towards wider participatory democracy and the federation's first general election. Officials indicated that the gradual democratization of the Co-operation Council for the Arab States of the Gulf (the Gulf Co-operation Council—GCC, see p. 243) states had created both external and internal pressure on the Government to adopt constitutional change. The partial elections to the FNC were held on 16, 18 and 20 December 2006: four members of the Council were elected from each of Abu Dhabi and Dubai, three each from Sharjah and Ras al-Khaimah, and two each from Fujairah, Umm al-Qaiwain and Ajman. The 20 seats were contested by 450 candidates, including 65 women. Just 6,689 selected UAE nationals (among them 1,189 women) were eligible to participate in the polls as members of the new electoral colleges (these had been chosen by the National Electoral Committee, established in August). The elected members included one woman, selected in Abu Dhabi. Overall voter turn-out in the seven emirates was reported to be 74.4%. The new FNC was inaugurated in February 2007. (Of its 20 appointed members, nine were women.) At the opening session, Abd al-Aziz Abdullah al-Ghurair was elected Speaker.

In February 2008 Sheikh Muhammad issued a decree appointing his son, Sheikh Hamdan bin Muhammad bin Rashid Al Maktoum, as Crown Prince of Dubai. The new Crown Prince and his younger brother, Sheikh Maktoum, were also named as Deputy Rulers of Dubai. (Sheikh Hamdan had been appointed Chairman of the Dubai Executive Council in September 2006.) The appointments were followed in the same month by a reorganization of the federal Council of Ministers. While the strategic portfolios of energy, foreign affairs and defence remained unchanged, other appointments were regarded as reflecting Sheikh Muhammad's policy priorities in further developing the business sector. Sheikha Lubna al-Qasimi was transferred from the post of Minister of Economy to the new position of Minister of Foreign Trade; she was replaced in her former role by Sultan bin Said al-Mansour. The appointment of Saqr Ghobash Said Ghobash, hitherto ambassador to the USA, as Minister of Labour was interpreted as a significant indicator that Sheikh Muhammad was seeking to address perceived international concerns regarding workers' rights in the UAE.

A new draft media law was adopted by the FNC in January 2009. The law stipulated that journalists could not be imprisoned for carrying out their duties, nor could they be forced to reveal the identity of confidential sources. However, journalists and media organizations would be liable to large fines and possible revocation of their licence if found guilty of publishing information deemed harmful to the state, untruthful, or damaging to the national economy. The latter provisions prompted criticism from international press and human rights organizations, including Human Rights Watch, which published a report in April which considered that the authorities were seeking to stifle legitimate criticism of the Government. In early 2011 the law was awaiting ratification by the President.

The UAE's record on human rights was reviewed under the UN Human Rights Council's Universal Periodic Review (UPR) process during 2008. A national report, outlining the Emirates' achievements and plans regarding human rights, with contributions from several government ministries and domestic non-governmental organizations, was published in September. At a Council session in Geneva, Switzerland, in December, the UAE's Minister of State for Foreign Affairs announced that the UAE had agreed to adopt 36 recommendations on human rights made by other member states: these included proposals on human-trafficking, working conditions, freedom of the press and children's rights; 21 recommendations were rejected, including those on corporal and capital punishment, trade unions, and women's rights; while a further 17 recommendations were reserved for further review. Of these last, nine had been rejected and eight either accepted or placed under consideration by the time of the final UPR session in March 2009, at which the Human Rights Council voted unanimously to endorse the UAE's national report. Nevertheless, the US Department of State's 2008 Human Rights Report on the UAE, published in February 2009, contained several negative observations on the human rights situation in the UAE, including its record on issues such as the mistreatment of prisoners, media censorship, people-trafficking and working conditions, as well as the allegation that a member of the royal family had tortured a foreign national because of a business dispute. The Ministry of Foreign Affairs issued a statement rejecting much of the criticism in the report, which, it claimed, contained 'generalities and unsubstantiated statements', and was the result of the application of a foreign value system to an Islamic state. In April a US television channel broadcast segments of a video recording, which, it claimed, showed the alleged torture incident, and named the royal family member as Sheikh Issa bin Zayed Al Nahyan, a brother of Sheikh Khalifa. In May Sheikh Issa was detained in connection with the investigation into the incident. At his trial, which began in December, Sheikh Issa pleaded not guilty to all charges; his lawyer alleged that his client was the victim of a conspiracy and that the video recording had been manipulated. In January 2010 Sheikh Issa was acquitted on all charges, although full details of the judge's decision were not published. Two US-Lebanese brothers, who had been involved in recording the incident and smuggling the tape to the USA, were convicted, in absentia, on charges of blackmail and of drugging the prince; each was sentenced to five years' imprisonment.

A number of constitutional amendments were endorsed by the Supreme Council of Rulers in December 2008 and approved by the FNC in January 2009, including the extension of the FNC's legislative term from two to four years and an article prohibiting FNC members from conducting business arrangements with government agencies during their legislative term.

Sheikh Rashid bin Ahmad al-Mu'alla, Ruler of Umm al-Qaiwain since 1981, died in January 2009. His son, Sheikh Saud bin Rashid al-Mu'alla, was immediately appointed to succeed him. Sheikh Rashid bin Saud bin Rashid al-Mu'alla was appointed Crown Prince.

Impact of the global economic downturn

In late 2008 and early 2009 the negative impact of the global economic downturn on the UAE's economy, particularly in the construction, property, financial services and tourism sectors, began to result in job losses, the cancellation of thousands of work permits for foreign workers, and the postponement or scaling down of numerous infrastructure projects. Dubai's highly ser-

THE UNITED ARAB EMIRATES

vice-based economy was considered to be particularly vulnerable, and in February 2009 it was announced that the Central Bank of the UAE was to purchase some US $10,000m. of Dubai-issued bonds in order to enable Dubai to meet its debt-servicing obligations.

In May 2009 there was some uncertainty regarding the future of plans to create a GCC monetary union, with a common currency, by 2010, after the UAE announced that it was to withdraw from the project. The UAE's apparent abandonment of proposed monetary union arose from a recent decision of the GCC to locate key financial institutions, including the future central bank, in the Saudi Arabian capital, Riyadh, rather than in the UAE.

Sheikh Khalifa effected a reorganization of the Council of Ministers in May 2009. Lt-Gen. Sheikh Saif bin Zayed Al Nahyan, the Minister of the Interior, and Sheikh Mansour bin Zayed Al Nahyan, the Minister of Presidential Affairs, were both appointed Deputy Prime Ministers, in addition to their existing responsibilities. Humaid Muhammad Obaid al-Qattami, hitherto Minister of Health, was accorded the education portfolio, replacing Dr Hanif Hassan Ali, who assumed the health portfolio. The former Deputy Prime Ministers, Sheikh Sultan bin Zayed Al Nahyan and Sheikh Hamdan bin Zayed Al Nahyan, both left the Government. In November the members of the Supreme Council of Rulers re-elected Sheikh Khalifa as President for a further five-year term.

In late November 2009 Dubai World, the government-owned investment company that controls a large proportion of Dubai's state investments in real estate, shipping and other sectors, announced a six-month moratorium on debt repayments, prompting a slump in international share prices, as investors feared that Dubai might default on billions of dollars of sovereign debt held abroad. The company was reported to hold debts worth up to US $59,000m. The crisis provoked protracted international scrutiny of the heavily service-based and debt-laden economic model that had underpinned Dubai's recent burgeoning economic growth. However, the acquisition by Abu Dhabi-controlled banks of a further $10,000m. of Dubai-issued bonds in November and December enabled Dubai to meet its most urgent financial obligations. From late 2009 the authorities in Dubai introduced a number of administrative reforms in an effort to prevent a recurrence of the debt crisis. In December new legislation was introduced requiring state-owned companies to transfer surplus revenue to the emirate's treasury. In January 2010 Sheikh Hamdan, the Crown Prince, announced a significant reorganization of Dubai's Executive Council, involving the establishment of new committees to oversee government policy in five key sectors: economic development; security and justice; infrastructure and environment; social development; and health and safety. Several analysts suggested that Dubai's debt crisis, and Abu Dhabi's role in stabilizing its neighbour's economy, could lead to increased economic and administrative integration between the seven emirates. In mid-May Dubai World announced that it had achieved approval 'in principle' from its main creditors for a proposed restructuring of its outstanding debt.

The assassination in Dubai of a senior member of the Palestinian Islamic Resistance Movement (Hamas), Mahmoud al-Mabhouh, on 19 January 2010 provoked an international diplomatic dispute, after Hamas accused the Israeli intelligence service, Mossad, of involvement in al-Mabhouh's death. In mid-February the Dubai authorities issued details of 11 individuals suspected of carrying out the assassination, all of whom had travelled to the emirate using false British, Australian, Irish, French and German passports. The head of Dubai's police force subsequently stated that he was '99%' certain that Mossad was responsible for the killing. Nevertheless, the Israeli Government insisted that there was no proof that its intelligence service had been involved in the killing (see the chapters on Israel and the Palestinian Autonomous Areas for further details).

Recent developments: succession in Ras al-Khaimah and reaction to regional unrest in 2011

In late October 2010 Sheikh Saqr bin Muhammad al-Qasimi, the Ruler of Ras al-Khaimah since 1948, died. He was immediately succeeded by Crown Prince Sheikh Saud, despite a counter-claim by Sheikh Khalid, who had been deposed as Crown Prince in 2003.

In mid-March 2011 it was announced that indirect elections for one-half of the 40 seats in the FNC would take place on 24 September. The previous month the membership of the electoral colleges used to allocate those 20 seats had been expanded to include around 12,000 people. The announcement of the election date followed an online petition submitted to the President in early March by 133 academics, journalists and political activists, in which they called for the introduction of direct elections and for the advisory FNC to be given full legislative powers. Amid anti-Government protests and unrest across the Middle East and North Africa from January 2011, it was reported in April that five signatories to the petition—including the organizer of an online forum promoting political reforms and a lecturer in economics at the Abu Dhabi branch of the Université Paris-Sorbonne—had been arrested by the UAE authorities.

Foreign Affairs

Regional relations

Conflict arose between the UAE and Iran in 1992 concerning the sovereignty of Abu Musa, an island situated between the states in the Persian (Arabian) Gulf. The island had been administered since 1991 under a joint agreement between Iran and Sharjah, in accordance with which an Iranian garrison was stationed on the island. In that year Iran had also seized the smaller neighbouring islands of Greater and Lesser Tunb. In April 1992 the Iranian garrison on Abu Musa was said to have seized civilian installations on the island. There were further allegations that Iranian officials were attempting to force expatriate workers employed by the UAE to leave the island, preventing the entry of other expatriates, and increasing the number of Iranian nationals there. However, in April 1993 all those who had been expelled from or refused entry to Abu Musa in 1992 were reportedly permitted to return. In October 1993 Sheikh Zayed announced the introduction of a federal law standardizing the limits of the UAE's territorial waters to 12 nautical miles (22.2 km) off shore, in response to a similar announcement by the Iranian authorities. In December 1994 the UAE announced its intention to refer the dispute to the International Court of Justice (ICJ) in The Hague, Netherlands, and in February 1995 it was alleged that Iran had deployed air defence systems on the islands.

In March–April 1996 bilateral relations deteriorated further when Iran opened an airport on Abu Musa and a power station on Greater Tunb. In February 1999 the UAE protested at the construction by Iran of municipal facilities on Abu Musa and at recent Iranian military exercises near the disputed islands. Iran subsequently complained to the UN that, in disputing the location of its military exercises, the UAE was interfering in Iranian internal affairs. In November a tripartite committee, established by the GCC and comprising representatives of Oman, Qatar and Saudi Arabia, announced that it would continue efforts to facilitate a settlement. However, no significant progress had been reached concerning a resolution of the territorial dispute by mid-2011.

Commercial links between the two countries remained strong, meanwhile, with the UAE having particular importance as the largest supplier of imports to Iran. President Mahmoud Ahmadinejad of Iran made the first visit to the UAE by an Iranian head of state in May 2007. Sheikh Muhammad visited Iran in February 2008 (he was the most senior UAE official to visit the country since the Iranian Revolution in 1979). However, reports in August that Iran had established two maritime administrative offices on Abu Musa provoked strong condemnation from the UAE authorities and the GCC. None the less, an official visit to the Iranian capital, Tehran, in late October by the UAE's Minister of Foreign Affairs, Sheikh Abdullah bin Zayed Al Nahyan, culminated in the signing of an agreement to establish a joint UAE-Iran commission to promote bilateral relations. While both countries were committed to the advancement of their political and economic ties, neither side showed any inclination to retreat from their stance on the disputed islands. In March 2009 a spokesman for Iran's Ministry of Foreign Affairs, in response to repeated GCC statements on the UAE's claims to sovereignty over the islands, described them as 'inseparable parts of Iran'. This duly provoked further condemnation from the UAE and the GCC, as well as renewed calls for the issue to be referred to the ICJ. The dispute was revived in April 2010 when, during a meeting with the Executive President of the Palestinian (National) Authority, Mahmud Abbas, in the West Bank, Minister of Foreign Affairs Sheikh Abdullah alluded to the Iranian 'occupation' of the contested islands, comparing it with the situation in the Israeli Occupied Territories. The UAE's envoy in Tehran was summoned by the Iranian Ministry of Foreign Affairs to receive an official complaint concerning Sheikh Abdullah's remarks. In July relations appeared to be strained further, following reports that the UAE's ambassador to the USA had stated his support for the use of military force to prevent Iran from acquiring nuclear weapons during a discussion at a conference in Colorado, USA.

Meanwhile, relations between the UAE and Saudi Arabia had also become strained by the UAE's trade negotiations with the USA (see below); Saudi Arabia considered that the GCC should negotiate any trade agreement as a single body. In December 2005 the relationship was weakened further in relation to a long-standing border dispute between the UAE and Saudi Arabia concerning the Shaybah oilfield in the Rub al-Khali desert region.

In response to Iraq's occupation of Kuwait in August 1990, the UAE (which supported the US-led multinational effort against Iraq) announced that foreign armed forces opposing the Iraqi invasion would be provided with military facilities in the Emirates. By the mid-1990s, however, the UAE was among those states questioning the justification for the continued maintenance of international sanctions (imposed in 1990) against Iraq, in view of the resultant humanitarian consequences for the Iraqi population. Following the restoration of diplomatic ties with Iraq in 1998, the UAE's embassy in the Iraqi capital was reopened in April 2000. Although Iraq's Minister of Trade visited Abu Dhabi in December, where he was received by Sheikh Zayed, the UAE lent its support to a declaration of the GCC annual summit meeting that urged Iraq to conform with UN resolutions: it was generally considered that the UAE had been compelled to endorse the declaration in return for GCC support in its territorial dispute with Iran. Addressing the Arab Inter-Parliamentary Union in February 2001, Sheikh Zayed none the less urged Arab states to work jointly towards an end to the sanctions regime in force against Iraq. In November the UAE and Iraq signed a free trade agreement, which was ratified by Sheikh Zayed in May 2002.

At the summit meeting of the Council of the League of Arab States (the Arab League, see p. 361) convened in Beirut, Lebanon, in March 2002, the Minister of State for Foreign Affairs, Sheikh Hamdan bin Zayed Al Nahyan, declared the UAE to be opposed to any future US-led campaign to oust the regime of Saddam Hussain in Iraq as a potential second phase in the USA's declared 'war on terror'. The UAE continued to urge a diplomatic solution to the crisis, and promoted a plan for the Iraqi leader to go into exile in order to prevent a war to oust his regime; however, in March 2003 the UAE disregarded appeals by some members of the Arab League to refuse to provide facilities for military action in Iraq. At the commencement of the conflict later in that month some 3,000 US air force personnel and 72 combat aircraft were stationed in the UAE. Following the overthrow of Iraq's Baathist regime by the US-led coalition in early April and the subsequent announcement that US forces were to be withdrawn from Saudi Arabia, the USA stated that it would develop the al-Dhafra airport in Abu Dhabi for use by its military aircraft. In the immediate aftermath of the ousting of the regime of Saddam Hussain, the UAE provided significant humanitarian aid to Iraq, and made clear its intention to participate in the reconstruction of the country. In early 2004 the UAE agreed to write off most of Iraq's bilateral debt. Following the kidnap of a member of its diplomatic staff in Iraq in May 2006, the UAE withdrew its chargé d'affaires from Baghdad. In June 2008, however, the UAE's Minister of Foreign Affairs visited Baghdad, becoming the first senior government official from a GCC country to do so since the US-led invasion of Iraq in 2003. This was followed, in July 2008, by the visit of Iraqi Prime Minister Nuri al-Maliki to Abu Dhabi, during which Sheikh Khalifa announced plans to reinstate full diplomatic relations and approved the cancellation of some US $7,000m. of Iraqi debt. A new UAE ambassador to Iraq, the first since 1990, took up his post in September.

In mid-March 2011 a contingent of 500 UAE police officers was deployed to Bahrain as part of a GCC 'Peninsula Shield' force, which also comprised 1,000 troops from Saudi Arabia. The deployment was effected in response to a request from King Hamad bin Isa Al Khalifa of Bahrain and followed several weeks of unrest and anti-Government protests in the kingdom.

Other external relations

In common with other GCC members, the UAE pledged support for the USA in its efforts to bring to justice the perpetrators of terrorism, following the suicide attacks against New York and Washington, DC, USA, on 11 September 2001. (Hitherto, the UAE had been one of only three states to maintain official relations with the Taliban regime in Afghanistan.) None the less, the UAE emphasized that the success of the US-led 'coalition against terror' must be linked to a resumption of the Arab-Israeli peace process, and expressed concerns that military action should not target any Arab state. The UAE's banking sector came under international scrutiny after US investigators claimed to have evidence of transactions between banks in the UAE and the USA linking bin Laden with the suicide attacks. At the end of September the Emirates' Central Bank ordered that the assets in the UAE of 27 individuals and organizations accused by the USA of involvement in terrorism be frozen; in November the Central Bank reportedly ordered a freeze on the assets of a further 62 entities. In November 2002 the Central Bank tightened regulations on the informal money-transfer system known as *hawala*, after the practice was criticized by Western law enforcement agencies as an important element in the financing of terrorism.

In July 2004 the UAE signed a Trade and Investment Framework Agreement with the USA—regarded as a preliminary step towards a bilateral free trade agreement. Free trade negotiations with the USA duly commenced in March 2005. However, the talks were postponed in March 2006, as a result of a disagreement between the two countries regarding the acquisition by the state-owned Dubai Ports World (DP World) of a British-based ports and ferries operator, P&O, the holdings of which included six major US ports. DP World agreed to sell the six US ports after the House Appropriations Committee of the US House of Representatives, in opposition to the US executive, adopted an amendment that would prevent the operation of the US ports by DP World; it was considered a risk to US security that the ports should be held by UAE interests. DP World reached an agreement to sell the US ports to a US company in December of that year. Trade negotiations meanwhile resumed. In late 2007, however, the Office of the US Trade Representative announced that the two countries had agreed that they would be unable to conclude a free trade accord during the tenure of the incumbent US Administration. However, despite the inauguration of Barack Obama as the new US President in January 2009, substantive negotiations on a free trade agreement had not recommenced by mid-2011.

In January 2008 US President George W. Bush delivered the key address of his first tour of the Middle East from Abu Dhabi. In April the UAE's Minister of Foreign Affairs, Sheikh Abdullah bin Zayed Al Nahyan, and the US Secretary of State, Condoleezza Rice, meeting in Bahrain in advance of a GCC-US summit, signed a memorandum of understanding governing co-operation in the peaceful use of nuclear energy. Prior to this agreement, the UAE (which had in January ratified the International Convention for the Suppression of Acts of Nuclear Terrorism) issued a policy document regarding plans for the potential development of nuclear energy for civilian use, including a commitment to forgo any domestic enrichment or reprocessing capability in exchange for the long-term supply of fuel from external sources. Military co-operation with the USA increased in December with the signing of a contract, worth over US $3,000m., for the provision of a US-made medium-range defensive missile system. This was followed, in mid-January 2009, by the signing of an agreement, subject to US congressional approval, on civilian nuclear co-operation, which brought the UAE a step closer to its ambition of developing the Gulf's first nuclear power network. Statements released by both parties expressed the hope that the UAE's nuclear energy programme would serve as a model for similar projects throughout the region. In September Sheikh Muhammad bin Zayed Al Nahyan, Crown Prince of Abu Dhabi, held talks on bilateral relations and civil nuclear co-operation with President Obama in Washington, DC. Having achieved congressional approval, the US-UAE civil nuclear co-operation agreement, the so-called 123 Agreement, entered into effect in December. In the same month the contract to construct four civil nuclear power plants in the UAE, at a reported cost of some $40,000m., was awarded to a South Korean consortium.

Bilateral co-operation accords signed during the course of a visit to the UAE by President Nicolas Sarkozy of France in January 2008 included an arrangement whereby France would assist in the development of a civilian nuclear energy programme in the UAE. Agreement was also reached on the establishment by France of a permanent military base in Abu Dhabi, capable of accommodating some 500 armed forces personnel. The base was officially inaugurated by Sarkozy during a visit to the UAE in May 2009.

THE UNITED ARAB EMIRATES

Introductory Survey

CONSTITUTION AND GOVERNMENT

A provisional Constitution for the UAE took effect in December 1971. This laid the foundation for the federal structure of the Union of the seven emirates, previously known as the Trucial States. In July 1975 a committee was appointed to draft a permanent federal constitution, but in 1976 the provisional document was extended for five years. The provisional Constitution was extended for for further five-year periods in 1981, 1986 and 1991. Legislation designed to make the provisional Constitution permanent was endorsed in June 1996, after it had been approved by the Supreme Council of Rulers.

The highest federal authority is the Supreme Council of Rulers, comprising the hereditary rulers of the seven emirates, each of whom is virtually an absolute monarch in his own domain. Decisions of the Supreme Council require the approval of at least five members, including the rulers of both Abu Dhabi and Dubai. From its seven members, the Supreme Council elects a President and a Vice-President. The President appoints the Prime Minister and the federal Council of Ministers, responsible to the Supreme Council, to hold executive authority. The legislature is the Federal National Council (FNC), a consultative assembly that considers laws proposed by the Council of Ministers. The FNC comprises 40 members, of whom one-half are appointed by the emirates and the remainder are chosen by electoral colleges. A constitutional amendment extending the FNC's term from two to four years was endorsed by the Supreme Council of Rulers in December 2008 and approved by the FNC in January 2009. Partial elections to the FNC were scheduled to take place on 24 September 2011. There are no political parties.

REGIONAL AND INTERNATIONAL CO-OPERATION

The UAE was a founder member of the Co-operation Council for the Arab States of the Gulf (the Gulf Co-operation Council—GCC, see p. 243) in May 1981. GCC member states established a unified regional customs tariff in January 2003, and agreed to create a single market and currency. The economic convergence criteria for the monetary union were agreed at a GCC summit in Abu Dhabi in December 2005, and in January 2008 the GCC common market was launched. However, there was doubt regarding prospects for monetary union after the UAE announced in May 2009 that it was to withdraw from the project. The country also participates in the League of Arab States (Arab League) and the Organization of the Arab Petroleum Exporting Countries (OAPEC, see p. 397).

The UAE joined the UN in December 1971 and became a member of the World Trade Organization (WTO, see p. 430) in 1996. It is also a participant in the Organization of the Islamic Conference (OIC, see p. 400). The International Renewable Energy Agency (IRENA, see p. 457), established in 2009, has its headquarters in Abu Dhabi.

ECONOMIC AFFAIRS

In 2004, according to estimates by the World Bank, the UAE's gross national income (GNI), measured at average 2002–04 prices, was US $103,692m., equivalent to $26,270 per head (or $45,510 on an international purchasing-power parity basis). During 2000–09, it was estimated, the population increased by an average annual rate of 4.0%. Gross domestic product (GDP) per head decreased, in real terms, by an average of 1.8% per year during 2000–09. Overall GDP increased, in real terms, by an average annual rate of 5.9% in 2000–09. According to World Bank estimates, real GDP increased by an estimated 5.1% in 2008, before declining by 0.7% in 2009.

According to official estimates, agriculture (including livestock and fishing) contributed 0.9% of GDP in 2008, and engaged 6.9% of the employed population in that year. The principal crops are dates, tomatoes, aubergines, and pumpkins, squash and gourds. The UAE imports some 70% of food requirements. Some agricultural products are exported on a small scale. Livestock-rearing and fishing are also important. During 2001–08 agricultural GDP, according to official estimates, decreased, in real terms, at an average annual rate of 1.0%; the GDP of the sector increased by 0.2% in 2008.

Industry (including mining, manufacturing, construction and power) contributed 56.7% of GDP in 2008, according to official estimates, and engaged 37.5% of the working population in the same year. During 2001–08, according to official estimates, industrial GDP increased by an average of 13.7% per year; the GDP of the sector expanded by 9.7% in 2008.

Mining and quarrying contributed 36.2% of GDP in 2008, according to official estimates, and employed only 1.4% of the working population in that year. Petroleum production is the most important industry in the UAE, with balance of payments data as published by the IMF indicating that exports of crude petroleum and related products contributed 38.0% of total export revenues in 2008. At the end of 2009 the UAE's proven recoverable reserves of petroleum were 97,800m. barrels, representing 7.3% of world reserves. Production levels in 2009 averaged 2.60m. barrels per day (b/d). As a member of the Organization of the Petroleum Exporting Countries (OPEC, see p. 405), the UAE is subject to production quotas agreed by the Organization's Conference. The UAE has large natural gas reserves, estimated at 6,430,000m. cu m at the end of 2009 (3.4% of world reserves). Most petroleum and natural gas reserves are concentrated in Abu Dhabi. Dubai is the UAE's second largest producer of petroleum. Marble and sand are also quarried. According to official estimates, the GDP of the mining sector increased by an average annual rate of 15.7% during 2001–08; mining GDP increased by 12.1% in 2008.

Manufacturing contributed 11.8% of GDP in 2008, according to official estimates, and employed 12.7% of the working population in that year. The major heavy industries in the UAE are related to hydrocarbons, and activities are concentrated in the Jebel Ali Free Zone (in Dubai) and the Jebel Dhanna-Ruwais industrial zone in Abu Dhabi. The most important products are liquefied petroleum gas, distillate fuel oils and jet fuels. There are two petroleum refineries in Abu Dhabi, and the emirate has 'downstream' interests abroad. The most important activities in the non-hydrocarbons manufacturing sector are aluminium, steel and chemicals. During 2001–08, according to official estimates, manufacturing GDP increased at an average annual rate of 9.6%; the GDP of the sector increased by 4.5% in 2008.

Construction contributed 7.2% of GDP in 2008, according to official estimates, and engaged 22.3% of the working population in that year. During 2001–08, according to official estimates, the GDP of the construction sector increased by an average of 12.9% per year; the construction sector grew by 6.7% in 2008.

Each of the emirates is responsible for its own energy production. Electric energy is generated largely by thermal power stations, utilizing the UAE's own hydrocarbons resources. In December 2009 an agreement with the USA regarding co-operation in the development of a civilian nuclear power programme entered into effect. In the same month the contract to construct four civil nuclear power plants was awarded to a South Korean consortium.

The services sector contributed 42.4% of GDP in 2008, according to official estimates, and engaged 55.7% of the working population in that year. The establishment of the Jebel Ali Free Zone in 1985 enhanced Dubai's reputation as a well-equipped entrepôt for regional trade, and significant growth in both re-exports and tourism has been recorded in recent years. The financial services and real estate sectors have also expanded rapidly as the UAE has pursued economic diversification. During 2001–08, according to official estimates, the GDP of the services sector increased by an average of 6.5% per year; the sector's GDP increased by 3.5% in 2008.

In 2009, according to preliminary Central Bank figures, the UAE recorded a visible trade surplus of AED 154,760m., and there was a surplus of AED 28,820m. on the current account of the balance of payments. In 2009 the principal source of imports was the India, which supplied 13.8% of total imports; other important suppliers were the People's Republic of China, the USA, Germany and Japan. India was also the principal market for non-petroleum exports in that year, taking 21.8% of the total. The other member states of the Co-operation Council for the Arab States of the Gulf (the Gulf Co-operation Council—GCC, see p. 243) together took 15.6% of non-petroleum exports in that year. Largely through its re-export trade, the UAE is of particular importance as a supplier of goods to Iran. Excluding hydrocarbons and free trade exports, the principal exports in 2009 were base metals and articles of base metal, plastics, rubber and related articles, prepared foodstuffs, beverages, spirits and tobacco, and mineral products. The principal imports in that year were machinery and electrical equipment, pearls, precious or semi-precious stones and precious metals, vehicles and other transport equipment, base metals and articles of base metal, and chemical products.

Preliminary Central Bank figures for 2007 indicated a surplus of AED 69,024m. on the consolidated government budget, equivalent to 9.5% of GDP. Including oil and gas revenues from other government entities, the IMF put the overall surplus in 2009 at AED 3,600m. (equivalent to 0.4% of GDP). The federal

THE UNITED ARAB EMIRATES

budget, to which Abu Dhabi is the major contributor, represents about one-quarter of the country's total public expenditure, as the individual emirates have their own budgets for municipal expenditure and local projects. In 2009 the UAE's gross government debt was AED 222,989m., equivalent to 27.1% of GDP. According to ILO figures, annual inflation averaged 6.5% in 2000–08. Consumer prices increased by an annual average of just 1.5% in 2009, compared with 12.3% in 2008. Some 4% of the labour force were recorded as unemployed in 2008. More than 90% of the work-force are estimated to be non-UAE nationals.

The sustained high level of international petroleum prices contributed substantially to very high rates of economic growth and strong fiscal and balance of payments surpluses in the UAE in 2003–07. None the less, successful efforts at diversification of economic activity, hitherto particularly in Abu Dhabi and Dubai, resulted in less reliance on the hydrocarbons sector than in many other petroleum-producing countries. Highly developed infrastructure and low import tariffs have enhanced the UAE's position as a centre for regional trade. Meanwhile, the tourism, real estate and financial services sectors also grew rapidly, and the strong performance of the construction sector reflected the rapid expansion of infrastructure. The economy of the UAE was negatively affected by the international financial crisis and the sharp decline in international oil prices from late 2008. By the final quarter of the year, the impact of the global economic downturn was particularly pronounced in Dubai, the heavily services-based economic model of which came under intense scrutiny. In February 2009 the Central Bank acquired US $10,000m. of a sovereign bond issue by the Government of Dubai (one-half of the total issue), thereby assisting Dubai in meeting its debt-servicing obligations for that year. Earlier in the same month the Government of Abu Dhabi made available some $4,300m. to five of its banks, in order to increase their capital and enhance lending capacity. Federal intervention in the economy was particularly notable in view of the traditional autonomy retained by each emirate in its economic affairs. Prospects for economic recovery were threatened in late November, following the announcement of a six-month postponement of repayments on the estimated $59,000m. of debt held by the government-owned investment company Dubai World. The announcement provoked fears of a major default on the emirate's sovereign debt, leading to a sharp decline in international share prices. In response, the Central Bank introduced additional liquidity facilities to support the banking sector, while Dubai World announced plans to restructure some $23,000m. of its liabilities. However, the authorities in Abu Dhabi and Dubai declined to offer state guarantees for Dubai World's debt. In mid-December the acquisition by Abu Dhabi-controlled institutions of the remaining $10,000m. of Dubai's sovereign bond issue was completed, while the provision in March 2010 of a $9,500m. fund to support Dubai World's debt-servicing obligations provided further reassurance to the company's creditors. Meanwhile, economic growth in Abu Dhabi, supported by strong public sector investment, remained resilient throughout the global economic crisis. Analysts predicted increased economic growth in Dubai in 2011, citing improvements in the tourism and trade sectors: the IMF indicated that it expected the emirate's GDP to grow by 3.0% in that year, compared with just 0.5% in 2010. In December 2010, meanwhile, the Federal National Council approved a federal budget for 2011–13. A deficit of AED 3,000m. was projected for 2011, despite a reduction in expenditure of 6.0%. According to the IMF, GDP growth for the UAE was expected to reach 3.2% in 2010 and 3.3% in the following year.

PUBLIC HOLIDAYS

2012: 1 January (New Year's Day), 4 February* (Mouloud, Birth of Muhammad), 16 June* (Leilat al-Meiraj, Ascension of Muhammad), 18 August* (Id al-Fitr, end of Ramadan), 25 October* (Id al-Adha, Feast of the Sacrifice), 14 November* (Muharram, Islamic New Year), 2 December (National Day).

* These holidays are dependent on the Islamic lunar calendar and may vary slightly from the dates given.

Statistical Survey

Source (unless otherwise stated): Central Bank of the UAE, POB 854, Abu Dhabi; tel. (2) 6652220; fax (2) 6652504; e-mail admin@cbuae.gov.ae; internet www.centralbank.ae; National Bureau of Statistics, POB 93000, Abu Dhabi; tel. (2) 6271100; fax (2) 6261344; e-mail contactus@nbs.gov.ae; internet www.uaestatistics.gov.ae.

Area and Population

AREA, POPULATION AND DENSITY

Area (sq km)	77,700*
Population (census results)	
17 December 1995	2,411,041
5 December 2005	
UAE nationals	825,495
Males	417,917
Females	407,578
Non-UAE nationals	3,280,932
Total	4,106,427
Population (official estimates at mid-year)	
2007	4,488,000
2008	4,765,000
2009	5,066,000
Density (per sq km) at mid-2009	65.2

* 30,000 sq miles.

POPULATION BY AGE AND SEX
(official estimates at mid-2009)

	Males	Females	Total
0–14	501,235	458,498	959,733
15–64	2,977,717	1,085,556	4,063,273
65 and over	25,048	17,946	42,994
Total	**3,504,000**	**1,562,000**	**5,066,000**

POPULATION BY EMIRATE
(official estimates at mid-2009)

	Area (sq km)	Population ('000)	Density (per sq km)
Abu Dhabi	67,340	1,628	24.2
Dubai	3,885	1,722	443.2
Sharjah	2,590	1,017	392.7
Ajman	259	250	965.3
Ras al-Khaimah	1,684	241	143.1
Fujairah	1,166	152	130.4
Umm al-Qaiwain	777	56	72.1
Total	**77,700**	**5,066**	**65.2**

PRINCIPAL TOWNS
(estimated population at mid-2003)

Dubai	1,171,000		Ras al-Khaimah	102,000
Abu Dhabi (capital)	552,000		Fujairah	54,000
Sharjah	519,000		Umm al-Qaiwain	38,000
Al-Ain	348,000		Khor Fakkan	32,000
Ajman	225,000			

2010 (official estimate at 31 December): Dubai 1,905,476 (Source: Statistics Centre, Municipality of Dubai, *Dubai in Figures*).

THE UNITED ARAB EMIRATES

BIRTHS, MARRIAGES AND DEATHS

	Live births Number	Rate (per 1,000)	Marriages* Number	Rate (per 1,000)	Deaths Number	Rate (per 1,000)
2001	56,136	16.1	9,697	2.8	5,758	1.8
2002	58,070	15.5	11,285	3.0	5,994	1.6
2003	61,165	15.1	12,277	3.0	6,002	1.5
2004	63,113	14.6	12,794	2.9	6,123	1.4
2005	64,623	15.7	12,984	3.2	6,361	1.5
2006	62,969	14.9	13,190	3.1	6,483	1.5
2007	67,689	15.1	12,987	2.9	7,414	1.7
2008	68,779	14.4	15,041	3.2	7,755	1.6

* Muslim marriages only.

Life expectancy (years at birth, WHO estimates): 78 (males 77; females 80) in 2008 (Source: WHO, *World Health Statistics*).

EMPLOYMENT
(persons aged 15 years and over)

	2005	2006*	2007
Agriculture, hunting, forestry and fishing	193,044	209,066	225,499
Mining and quarrying	38,694	41,906	45,199
Oil and gas	33,200	35,956	38,783
Manufacturing	336,585	364,521	393,173
Electricity, gas and water supply	34,207	37,046	39,958
Construction	534,398	578,753	624,242
Wholesale and retail trade; repair of motor vehicles, motorcycles and personal and household goods	502,427	544,129	586,897
Hotels and restaurants	116,615	126,294	136,220
Transport, storage and communications	162,768	176,278	190,133
Financial intermediation	31,015	33,589	36,229
Real estate, renting and business activities	77,858	84,320	90,947
Public administration and defence; compulsory social security	286,105	309,851	334,207
Community, social and personal service activities	114,736	124,259	134,026
Private households with employed persons	222,506	240,975	259,916
Total employed	2,650,958	2,870,987	3,096,646

* Preliminary figures.
† Estimates.

2008 ('000 persons aged 15 years and over): Agriculture, hunting, forestry and fishing 233; Mining and quarrying 47 (Oil and gas 40); Manufacturing 431; Electricity, gas and water 39; Construction 757; Wholesale and retail trade; repair of motor vehicles, motorcycles and personal and household goods 643; Hotels and restaurants 146; Transport, storage and communications 204; Financial intermediation 42; Real estate, renting and business activities 97; Public administration and defence; compulsory social security 353; Community, social and personal service activities 142; Private households with employed persons 264; *Total employed* 3,397.

Health and Welfare

KEY INDICATORS

Total fertility rate (children per woman, 2008)	1.9
Under-5 mortality rate (per 1,000 live births, 2008)	8.0
HIV/AIDS (% of persons aged 15–49, 1994)	0.18
Physicians (per 1,000 head, 2004)	2.0
Hospital beds (per 1,000 head, 2005)	1.8
Health expenditure (2007): US $ per head (PPP)	982
Health expenditure (2007): % of GDP	2.7
Health expenditure (2007): public (% of total)	70.5
Access to sanitation (% of persons, 2008)	97
Total carbon dioxide emissions ('000 metric tons, 2007)	135,428.8
Carbon dioxide emissions per head (metric tons, 2007)	31.0
Human Development Index (2010): ranking	32
Human Development Index (2010): value	0.815

For sources and definitions, see explanatory note on p. vi.

Agriculture

PRINCIPAL CROPS
('000 metric tons)

	2005	2006	2007*
Potatoes	7.1	7.1	7.9
Cabbages	16.0*	9.3	17.5
Lettuce*	1.0	1.2	1.3
Spinach*	0.9	1.0	1.2
Tomatoes	240.0*	202.1	215.0
Cauliflowers and broccoli	13.0*	10.0	11.5
Pumpkins, squash and gourds*	21.5	20.0	20.0
Cucumbers and gherkins	26.5*	17.4	17.2
Aubergines (Eggplants)	20.5*	6.9	22.0
Chillies and peppers, green*	6.0	5.5	5.6
Onions and shallots, green*	16.0	16.5	16.5
Beans, green	1.2*	3.1	1.2
Carrots and turnips	2.2*	8.5	2.4
Watermelons	3.0*	3.0	3.9
Cantaloupes and other melons	7.0*	4.5	8.0
Lemons and limes	11.5*	4.4	12.3
Mangoes, mangosteens and guavas	5.0*	6.2	5.7
Dates	750.0*	757.6	755.0

* FAO estimate(s).

2008: Production assumed to be unchanged from 2007 (FAO estimates). Note: No data were available for individual crops in 2009.

Aggregate production ('000 metric tons, may include official, semi-official or estimated data): Total fruits (excl. melons) 778 in 2005; 780 in 2006; 785 in 2007–09.

Source: FAO.

LIVESTOCK
('000 head, year ending September, FAO estimates)

	2006	2007	2008
Cattle	120	125	125
Camels	342	260	260
Sheep	600	615	615
Goats	1,550	1,570	1,570
Chickens	14,000	14,000	15,500

Note: No data were available for 2009.

Source: FAO.

THE UNITED ARAB EMIRATES

LIVESTOCK PRODUCTS
('000 metric tons, FAO estimates)

	2006	2007	2008
Cattle meat	11.0	10.0	10.0
Camel meat	21.5	19.9	19.9
Sheep meat	11.1	7.0	7.0
Goat meat	29.4	15.2	15.2
Chicken meat	28.8	26.4	36.0
Cows' milk	12.0	12.0	12.0
Camels' milk	40.0	40.0	40.0
Sheep's milk	12.0	12.0	12.0
Goats' milk	36.0	36.0	36.0
Hen eggs	17.0	17.2	17.2

2009: Cattle meat 10.0; Camel meat 19.9; Sheep meat 7.0; Goat meat 15.2; Chicken meat 36.0.

Source: FAO.

Fishing
('000 metric tons, live weight)

	2006*	2007*	2008
Capture	82.5	78.3	74.1
Groupers and seabasses	12.7	10.8	9.0
Grunts and sweetlips	2.9	2.1	1.3
Emperors (Scavengers)	20.8	21.4	22.0
King soldier bream	5.0	4.2	3.4
Sardinellas	4.8	4.5	4.1
Stolephorus anchovies	2.0	0.5	n.a.
Narrow-barred Spanish mackerel	4.6	4.0	3.3
Jacks and crevalles	1.6	1.6	1.6
Carangids	4.0	6.0	7.9
Indian mackerel	2.4	1.5	0.6
Aquaculture	0.6	0.6	1.2
Total catch (incl. others)	83.1	78.9	75.3

* FAO estimates.

Source: FAO.

Mining
(estimated production)

	2007	2008	2009
Crude petroleum (million metric tons)	135.1	137.3	120.6
Natural gas (million cu metres)*	50,340	50,235	48,840

* Excluding gas flared or recycled.

Source: BP, *Statistical Review of World Energy*.

Industry

SELECTED PRODUCTS
('000 barrels, unless otherwise indicated, estimates)

	2007	2008	2009
Cement ('000 metric tons)	12,000	21,885	18,997
Aluminium ('000 metric tons)	890	945	955
Motor spirit (petrol)	20,000	18,000	16,000
Kerosene	31,000	37,000	42,000
Gas-diesel (distillate fuel) oil	20,000	28,000	32,000
Residual fuel oils	2,000	5,000	7,000
Liquefied petroleum gas	2,000	3,600	5,800

Source: US Geological Survey.

Electric energy (million kWh): 60,698 in 2005; 66,768 in 2006; 76,106 in 2007 (Source: UN Industrial Commodity Statistics Database).

Finance

CURRENCY AND EXCHANGE RATES

Monetary Units
100 fils = 1 UAE dirham (AED).

Sterling, Dollar and Euro Equivalents (31 December 2010)
£1 sterling = 5.749 dirhams;
US $1 = 3.673 dirhams;
€1 = 4.907 dirhams;
100 UAE dirhams = £17.39 = $27.23 = €20.38.

Exchange Rate: The Central Bank's official rate was set at US $1 = 3.671 dirhams in November 1980. This remained in force until December 1997, when the rate was adjusted to $1 = 3.6725 dirhams.

BUDGET OF THE CONSOLIDATED GOVERNMENTS
(million UAE dirhams)

Revenue	2005	2006	2007
Tax revenue	6,810	8,027	13,833
Custom revenue	3,852	4,461	8,020
Non-tax revenue	137,095	193,139	214,917
Revenue from petroleum and natural gas	111,377	164,775	176,265
Profit of joint stock corporations	4,624	9,478	6,613
Total	143,905	201,166	228,750

Expenditure	2005	2006	2007
Current expenditure	84,255	103,907	121,314
Salaries and wages	16,654	17,693	21,265
Goods and services	24,383	26,177	35,420
Subsidies and transfers	18,916	30,806	29,692
Development expenditure	14,042	15,225	17,271
Loans and equity	6,133	6,845	21,141
Total	104,430	125,977	159,726

Consolidated government finances (consolidated accounts of the federal governments of Abu Dhabi, Dubai and Sharjah, '000 million UAE dirhams, 2008): *Revenue* (including IMF estimates of revenues from other government entities operating in the oil and gas sector): Total 450.3 (Hydrocarbons 362.1, Non-hydrocarbon 88.2). *Expenditure and grants:* Total 254.0 (Current 166.8, Development 31.5, Loans and equity 51.8, Foreign grants 3.6) (Source: IMF, *United Arab Emirates: 2009 Article IV Consultation—Staff Report; Public Information Notice; and Statement by the Executive Director for United Arab Emirates*—February 2010).

Consolidated government finances (consolidated accounts of the federal governments of Abu Dhabi, Dubai and Sharjah, '000 million UAE dirhams, 2009, estimates): *Revenue* (including IMF estimates of revenues from other government entities operating in the oil and gas sector): Total 292.6 (Hydrocarbons 217.5, Non-hydrocarbon 75.0). *Expenditure and grants:* Total 289.0 (Current 196.7, Development 37.9, Loans and equity 52.1, Foreign grants 2.4) (Source: IMF, *United Arab Emirates: 2009 Article IV Consultation—Staff Report; Public Information Notice; and Statement by the Executive Director for United Arab Emirates*—February 2010).

INTERNATIONAL RESERVES
(excluding gold, US $ million at 31 December)

	2008	2009	2010
IMF special drawing rights	17.1	848.2	833.5
Reserve position in IMF	120.8	185.6	200.8
Foreign exchange*	31,556.6	35,070.4	41,750.9
Total	31,694.5	36,104.2	42,785.2

* Figures exclude the Central Bank's foreign assets and accrued interest attributable to the governments of individual emirates.

Source: IMF, *International Financial Statistics*.

THE UNITED ARAB EMIRATES

MONEY SUPPLY
(million UAE dirhams at 31 December)

	2008	2009	2010
Currency outside banks	36,967	37,217	38,560
Demand deposits at commercial banks	171,171	186,265	194,401
Total money	208,138	223,482	232,961

Source: IMF, *International Financial Statistics*.

COST OF LIVING
(Consumer Price Index; base: 2007 = 100)

	2008	2009
Food, beverages and tobacco	116.3	117.2
Clothing and footwear	119.9	114.1
Housing (incl. rent)	113.4	113.9
Furniture, etc.	107.2	113.6
Medical care and health services	107.8	106.2
Transport	106.3	110.8
Communication	101.0	104.2
Recreation and education	105.2	104.4
Education	108.6	119.3
All items (incl. others)	112.3	114.0

NATIONAL ACCOUNTS
(million UAE dirhams at current prices)

Gross Domestic Product by Emirate

	2006	2007*	2008†
Abu Dhabi	341,286	400,047	519,921
Dubai	224,344	264,174	301,485
Sharjah	49,406	59,682	71,994
Ajman	7,428	9,583	11,549
Ras al-Khaimah	11,435	13,400	15,895
Fujairah	7,122	8,134	9,843
Umm al-Qaiwain	2,482	3,006	3,576
Total	643,503	758,026	934,263

* Preliminary figures.
† Estimates.

Expenditure on the Gross Domestic Product

	2006	2007*	2008†
Government final consumption expenditure	57,961	76,190	86,570
Private final consumption expenditure	312,804	350,347	425,183
Increase in stocks	6,663	7,435	15,235
Gross fixed capital formation	120,999	248,562	300,427
Total domestic expenditure	498,427	682,534	827,415
Exports of goods and services	559,813	685,620	913,748
Less Imports of goods and services	414,737	610,128	806,901
GDP in purchasers' values	643,503	758,026	934,263
GDP at constant 2000 prices	470,214	498,302	535,354

* Preliminary figures.
† Estimates.

Gross Domestic Product by Economic Activity

	2006	2007*	2008†
Agriculture, livestock and fishing	8,671	8,692	8,852
Mining and quarrying	221,656	255,130	345,800
Oil and gas	220,499	253,767	344,132
Manufacturing	84,610	96,634	113,245
Electricity and water	10,019	11,566	13,579
Construction	43,525	54,882	69,218
Wholesale and retail trade, and repairs	99,381	125,022	148,415
Restaurants and hotels	11,001	12,631	14,533
Transport, storage and communications	36,169	41,219	46,973
Financial institutions and insurance	46,411	54,065	62,648
Real estate and business services	56,424	68,676	78,497
Government services	29,171	34,196	37,857
Community, social and personal services	9,480	10,780	12,390
Private households with employed persons	3,264	3,674	4,014
Sub-total	659,782	777,167	956,021
Less Imputed bank service charge	16,279	19,141	21,759
GDP in purchasers' values	643,503	758,026	934,263

* Preliminary figures.
† Estimates.

BALANCE OF PAYMENTS
('000 million UAE dirhams)

	2007	2008	2009*
Exports of goods f.o.b.	656.02	878.51	705.83
Imports of goods f.o.b.	−485.17	−647.42	−551.07
Trade balance	170.85	231.09	154.76
Services (net)	−95.36	−124.24	−100.35
Income (net)	30.75	13.97	11.80
Balance on goods, services and income	106.24	120.82	66.21
Current transfers (net)	−34.11	−39.00	−37.40
Current balance	72.13	81.82	28.82
Capital and financial accounts (net)	105.42	−203.06	8.41
Net errors and omissions	5.68	−50.76	−59.75
Overall balance	183.24	−172.00	−22.52

* Preliminary estimates.

External Trade

PRINCIPAL COMMODITIES
(distribution by HS, million UAE dirhams)

Imports c.i.f.	2007	2008	2009
Vegetable products	6,224.3	8,775.3	8,318.6
Prepared foodstuffs, beverages, spirits and tobacco	8,763.6	9,406.0	8,868.2
Chemical products, etc.	21,716.6	26,630.2	24,063.4
Plastics, rubber and articles thereof	14,303.2	17,842.3	13,720.2
Textiles and textile articles	17,490.6	20,067.6	17,494.7
Pearls, precious or semi-precious stones, precious metals, etc.	76,894.1	121,688.8	101,497.7
Base metals and articles of base metal	45,507.1	82,724.4	41,206.3
Machinery and electrical equipment	89,128.8	120,435.5	108,134.3
Vehicles and other transport equipment	51,307.0	80,777.1	57,205.1
Total (incl. others)	388,356.8	565,719.8	447,393.8

THE UNITED ARAB EMIRATES

Exports f.o.b.*	2007	2008	2009
Vegetable products	241.1	345.4	300.7
Prepared foodstuffs, beverages, spirits and tobacco	3,024.4	3,596.4	4,265.1
Mineral products	4,349.7	4,994.4	3,713.3
Chemical products, etc.	1,141.7	1,425.7	1,692.9
Plastics, rubber and articles thereof	3,762.5	5,534.7	5,211.4
Textiles and textile articles	1,183.9	1,365.9	1,005.0
Stone, plaster, cement, ceramic and glassware	2,056.7	9,652.4	1,903.6
Base metals and articles of base metal	5,230.2	5,215.0	8,019.5
Machinery and electrical equipment	924.0	1,007.7	1,386.9
Vehicles and other transport equipment	635.3	405.9	1,718.4
Total (incl. others)†	36,262.3	60,359.1	65,278.9

*Excluding petroleum exports and excluding re-exports; re-exports amounted to 128,338.4m. dirhams in 2007; 162,844.6m. dirhams in 2008; and 147,693.4m. dirhams in 2009.
† Excluding free zone exports.

SELECTED MAJOR TRADING PARTNERS
(million UAE dirhams)

Imports	2007	2008	2009
Australia	9,774.3	12,241.6	6,365.4
Belgium	6,971.1	9,767.5	6,496.8
Brazil	4,736.3	4,295.6	3,750.2
Canada	2,417.4	4,575.0	4,323.7
China, People's Republic	45,201.1	63,740.2	47,825.6
Finland	2,226.4	3,584.1	1,836.4
France (incl. Monaco)	11,375.7	14,072.3	14,027.1
GCC countries	17,831.4	25,694.0	21,537.6
Germany	26,398.8	37,098.2	29,998.0
Hong Kong	2,685.0	4,877.8	4,054.6
India	44,977.3	61,968.6	61,564.8
Italy (incl. San Marino)	17,263.0	21,735.6	17,417.6
Japan	29,650.8	42,638.6	26,903.7
Korea, Republic	10,337.0	15,583.0	16,899.2
Netherlands	4,084.8	5,258.7	4,800.7
South Africa	4,835.2	12,531.5	2,477.8
United Kingdom	16,996.6	28,000.7	18,762.4
USA	30,891.9	44,946.0	41,524.9
Total (incl. others)	388,356.8	565,719.8	447,393.8

Exports*	2007	2008	2009
Australia	463.2	541.8	503.4
Belgium	3,115.5	4,755.3	3,451.2
Brazil	143.2	105.3	256.7
Canada	171.8	1,063.6	316.1
GCC countries	22,719.5	32,064.1	33,311.3
Germany	924.0	1,871.0	1,033.1
India	34,615.7	55,977.2	46,497.0
New Zealand	179.6	177.7	169.1
United Kingdom	1,350.0	1,846.3	1,551.2
USA	2,180.3	4,011.1	3,323.1
Total (incl. others)	164,600.7	223,203.6	212,972.3

*Data for non-petroleum exports and all re-exports.

Transport

ROAD TRAFFIC
('000 registered motor vehicles in use)

	2000	2001	2002
Passenger cars (incl. taxis)	561.9	654.2	606.1
Trucks (incl. public)	83.3	66.2	66.2
Buses (incl. public)	14.7	13.3	16.0
Other	13.2	11.2	13.1

Total vehicles in use: 767 in 2002; 792 in 2003.

2007 (motor vehicles registered at 31 December 2007): Passenger cars 1,279,098; Buses and coaches 48,205; Vans and lorries 39,424; Motorcycles and mopeds 13,639 (Source: IRF, *World Road Statistics*).

SHIPPING
Merchant Fleet
(registered at 31 December)

	2007	2008	2009
Number of vessels	446	469	489
Total displacement ('000 grt)	807.2	1,075.0	1,083.5

Source: IHS Fairplay, *World Fleet Statistics*.

International Sea-borne Shipping
(estimated freight traffic, '000 metric tons)

	1988	1989	1990
Goods loaded	63,380	72,896	88,153
Crude petroleum	54,159	63,387	78,927
Other cargo	9,221	9,509	9,226
Goods unloaded	8,973	8,960	9,595

Source: UN, *Monthly Bulletin of Statistics*.

CIVIL AVIATION
(traffic on scheduled services)*

	2004	2005	2006
Kilometres flown (million)	277	321	382
Passengers carried ('000)	14,314	16,210	19,102
Passenger-km (million)	54,703	65,121	79,704
Total ton-km (million)	8,979	10,669	12,903

*Figures include an apportionment (one-quarter) of the traffic of Gulf Air, a multinational airline with its headquarters in Bahrain.

Source: UN, *Statistical Yearbook*.

Tourism

FOREIGN TOURIST ARRIVALS*

Country	2002	2003	2004
Canada	95,878	55,297	57,718
Egypt	111,822	121,221	131,635
France	90,735	98,624	112,429
Germany	236,660	235,147	337,594
India	336,046	357,941	356,446
Iran	270,350	334,453	336,734
Jordan	73,140	76,553	76,308
Lebanon	74,225	83,137	90,409
Pakistan	154,711	183,724	173,152
Russia	267,655	324,484	340,716
United Kingdom	491,604	496,147	644,688
USA	123,112	175,116	192,948
Total (incl. others)†	5,445,367	5,871,023	6,195,006

*Figures refer to international arrivals at hotels and similar establishments.
† Total includes domestic tourists.

Receipts from tourism (US$ million, incl. passenger transport): 4,972 in 2006; 6,072 in 2007; 7,162 in 2008.

Source: World Tourism Organization.

THE UNITED ARAB EMIRATES

Communications Media

	2007	2008	2009
Telephones ('000 main lines in use)	1,385.5	1,508.3	1,561.2
Mobile cellular telephones ('000 subscribers)	7,731.5	9,357.7	10,671.9
Internet users ('000)	2,662.0	3,229.2	3,449.0
Broadband subscribers ('000)	379.8	557.6	690.4

Personal computers: 1,400,000 (330.8 per 1,000 persons) in 2006.
Daily newspapers (titles): 9 in 2004.
Radio receivers ('000 in use): 820 in 1997.
Television receivers ('000 in use): 780 in 2001.
Sources: partly UNESCO, *Statistical Yearbook*; UN, *Statistical Yearbook*; International Telecommunication Union.

Education

(Government schools only)

	2004/05	2005/06	2006/07
Institutions	758	759	744
Teachers*	28,191	27,982	27,737
Students			
Pre-primary	20,318	20,750	22,506
Primary	197,148	189,024	186,093
Secondary	65,456	64,727	63,767
Other schools	4,061	2,870	2,254

* Includes administrative and technical staff.

Pupil-teacher ratio (primary education, UNESCO estimate): 15.6 in 2008/09 (Source: UNESCO Institute for Statistics).
Adult literacy rate (UNESCO estimates): 90.4% (males 90.9%; females 89.2%) in 2007 (Source: UNESCO Institute for Statistics).

Directory

The Government

HEAD OF STATE

President: Sheikh KHALIFA BIN ZAYED AL NAHYAN (Ruler of Abu Dhabi, elected by the Supreme Council of Rulers as President of the UAE on 3 November 2004; re-elected 3 November 2009).
Vice-President: Sheikh MUHAMMAD BIN RASHID AL MAKTOUM (Ruler of Dubai).

SUPREME COUNCIL OF RULERS
(with each Ruler's date of accession)

Ruler of Abu Dhabi: Sheikh KHALIFA BIN ZAYED AL NAHYAN (2004).
Ruler of Dubai: Sheikh MUHAMMAD BIN RASHID AL MAKTOUM (2006).
Ruler of Sharjah: Sheikh SULTAN BIN MUHAMMAD AL-QASIMI (1972).
Ruler of Ras al-Khaimah: Sheikh SAUD BIN SAQR AL-QASIMI (2010).
Ruler of Umm al-Qaiwain: Sheikh SAUD BIN RASHID AL-MU'ALLA (2009).
Ruler of Ajman: Sheikh HUMAID BIN RASHID AL-NUAIMI (1981).
Ruler of Fujairah: Sheikh HAMAD BIN MUHAMMAD AL-SHARQI (1974).

COUNCIL OF MINISTERS
(May 2011)

Prime Minister and Minister of Defence: Sheikh MUHAMMAD BIN RASHID AL MAKTOUM.
Deputy Prime Minister and Minister of the Interior: Lt-Gen. Sheikh SAIF BIN ZAYED AL NAHYAN.
Deputy Prime Minister and Minister of Presidential Affairs: Sheikh MANSOUR BIN ZAYED AL NAHYAN.
Minister of Finance: Sheikh HAMDAN BIN RASHID AL MAKTOUM.
Minister of Foreign Affairs: Sheikh ABDULLAH BIN ZAYED AL NAHYAN.
Minister of Higher Education and Scientific Research: Sheikh NAHYAN BIN MUBARAK AL NAHYAN.
Minister of Public Works: Sheikh HAMDAN BIN MUBARAK AL NAHYAN.
Minister of Economy: SULTAN BIN SAID AL-MANSOURI.
Minister of Foreign Trade: Sheikha LUBNA BINT KHALID AL-QASIMI.
Minister of Justice: Dr HADIF JOWAN AL-DHAHIRI.
Minister of Energy: MUHAMMAD BIN DHAEN AL-HAMILI.
Minister of Labour: SAQR GHOBASH SAID GHOBASH.
Minister of Social Affairs: Dr MARIAM MUHAMMAD KHALFAN AL-ROUMI.
Minister of Education: HUMAID MUHAMMAD OBAID AL-QATTAMI.
Minister of Health: Dr HANIF HASSAN ALI.
Minister of the Environment and Water: Dr RASHID AHMAD AL-FAHD.
Minister of Culture, Youth and Community Development: ABD AL-RAHMAN MUHAMMAD AL-OWAIS.
Minister of Cabinet Affairs: MUHAMMAD BIN ABDULLAH AL-GARGAWI.
Minister of State for Financial Affairs: OBAID HUMAID AL-TAYER.
Minister of State for Foreign Affairs and for Federal National Council Affairs: Dr ANWAR MUHAMMAD GARGASH.
Ministers of State: REEM IBRAHIM AL-HASHEMI, Dr MAITHA SALIM AL-SHAMSI.

FEDERAL MINISTRIES

Office of the Prime Minister: POB 12848, Dubai; tel. (4) 3534550; fax (4) 3530111; e-mail info@primeminister.ae; internet www.uaepm.ae.
Office of the Deputy Prime Minister: POB 831, Abu Dhabi; tel. (2) 4451000; fax (2) 4450066.
Ministry of Cabinet Affairs: POB 899, Abu Dhabi; tel. (2) 6811113; fax (2) 6812968; e-mail moca@uae.gov.ae; internet www.moca.gov.ae.
Ministry of Culture, Youth and Community Development: POB 17, Abu Dhabi; tel. (2) 4453000; fax (2) 4452504; e-mail mcycd@mcycd.ae; internet www.mcycd.ae.
Ministry of Defence: POB 46616, Abu Dhabi; tel. (4) 4461300; fax (4) 4463286; internet www.mod.gov.ae.
Ministry of Economy: POB 901, Abu Dhabi; tel. (2) 3161111; fax (2) 6260000; e-mail economy@economy.ae; internet www.economy.ae.
Ministry of Education: POB 295, Abu Dhabi; tel. (2) 6213800; fax (2) 6313778; e-mail moe@uae.gov.ae; internet www.moe.gov.ae.
Ministry of Energy: POB 59, Abu Dhabi; tel. (2) 6671999; fax (2) 6664573; e-mail mopmr@uae.gov.ae; internet www.moenr.gov.ae.
Ministry of the Environment and Water: POB 213, Abu Dhabi; tel. (2) 4495100; fax (2) 4495150; e-mail archives@moew.gov.ae; internet www.moew.gov.ae.
Ministry of Finance: POB 433, Abu Dhabi; tel. (2) 6726000; fax (2) 6768414; e-mail webmaster@mof.gov.ae; internet www.mof.gov.ae.
Ministry of Foreign Affairs: POB 1, Abu Dhabi; tel. (2) 4444488; fax (2) 4449200; e-mail mofa@mofa.gov.ae; internet www.mofa.gov.ae.
Ministry of Foreign Trade: POB 110555, Abu Dhabi; tel. (2) 4956000; fax (2) 4499164; e-mail info@moft.gov.ae; internet www.moft.gov.ae.
Ministry of Health: POB 848, Abu Dhabi; tel. (2) 6330000; fax (2) 6726000; e-mail info@moh.gov.ae; internet www.moh.gov.ae.
Ministry of Higher Education and Scientific Research: POB 45253, Abu Dhabi; tel. (2) 6428000; fax (2) 6428778; e-mail mohe@uae.gov.ae; internet www.mohesr.ae.
Ministry of the Interior: POB 398, Abu Dhabi; tel. (2) 4414666; fax (2) 4022776; e-mail info@moi.gov.ae; internet www.moi.gov.ae.
Ministry of Justice: POB 260, Abu Dhabi; tel. (2) 6814000; fax (2) 6810680; e-mail moj@uae.gov.ae; internet ejustice.gov.ae.
Ministry of Labour: POB 809, Abu Dhabi; tel. (2) 6671700; fax (2) 6665889; e-mail minister@mol.gov.ae; internet www.mol.gov.ae.
Ministry of Presidential Affairs: POB 208, Abu Dhabi; tel. (2) 6222221; fax (2) 6222228; e-mail webmaster@mopa.gov.ae; internet www.mopa.ae.

THE UNITED ARAB EMIRATES

Ministry of Public Works: POB 878, Abu Dhabi; tel. (2) 6260606; fax (2) 6260026; e-mail info@mopw.gov.ae; internet www.mopw.gov.ae.

Ministry of Social Affairs: POB 809, Abu Dhabi; tel. (4) 2637777; fax (4) 2633525; e-mail info@msa.gov.ae; internet www.msa.gov.ae.

Ministry of State for Federal National Council Affairs: POB 130000, Abu Dhabi; tel. (2) 4041000; fax (2) 4041155; e-mail mfnca@mfnca.gov.ae; internet www.mfnca.gov.ae.

Ministry of State for Financial Affairs: POB 433, Abu Dhabi; tel. (2) 771133; fax (2) 793255.

Ministry of State for Foreign Affairs: POB 1, Abu Dhabi; tel. (2) 6660888; fax (2) 6652883.

Legislature

Federal National Council

POB 836, Abu Dhabi; tel. (2) 6812000; fax (2) 6812846; e-mail fncuae@emirates.net.ae; internet www.almajles.gov.ae.

Formed under the provisional Constitution, the Council is composed of 40 members from the various emirates (eight each from Abu Dhabi and Dubai, six each from Sharjah and Ras al-Khaimah, and four each from Ajman, Fujairah and Umm al-Qaiwain). Each emirate appoints its own representatives separately. The Council studies laws proposed by the Council of Ministers and can reject them or suggest amendments. In December 2005 Sheikh Khalifa announced that elections would be introduced to choose one-half of the members of the FNC, which would also be expanded and granted enhanced powers. In August 2006 a National Electoral Committee was established to preside over the elections, which were held during 16–20 December. A constitutional amendment extending the Council's term from two to four years was endorsed by the Supreme Council of Rulers in December 2008 and approved by the FNC in January 2009.

Speaker: ABD AL-AZIZ ABDULLAH AL-GHURAIR.

Diplomatic Representation

EMBASSIES IN THE UNITED ARAB EMIRATES

Afghanistan: POB 5687, Abu Dhabi; tel. (2) 6655560; fax (2) 6655576; e-mail info@afghanembassy-uae.com; internet www.afghanembassy-uae.eedevelopment.com; Ambassador FARID ZIKRIA.

Algeria: POB 3070, Abu Dhabi; tel. (2) 448949; fax (2) 4470686; Ambassador HAMID CHEBIRA.

Angola: Abu Dhabi; Ambassador RUI JORGE CARNEIRO MANGUEIRA.

Argentina: POB 3325, Abu Dhabi; tel. (2) 4436838; fax (2) 4431392; e-mail info@argentinauae.ae; Ambassador RUBÉN EDUARDO CARO.

Armenia: POB 6358, Abu Dhabi; tel. (2) 4444196; fax (2) 4444197; e-mail armemiratesembassy@mfa.am; Ambassador VAHAGN MELIKIAN.

Australia: POB 32711, al-Muhairy Centre, 14th Floor, Sheikh Zayed I St, Abu Dhabi; tel. (2) 6346100; fax (2) 6393525; e-mail abudhabi.embassy@dfat.gov.au; internet www.uae.embassy.gov.au; Ambassador DOUG TRAPPETT.

Austria: POB 35539, al-Khazna Tower, 7th Floor, Najda St, Abu Dhabi; tel. (2) 6766611; fax (2) 6715551; e-mail abu-dhabi-ob@bmeia.gv.at; internet www.austrianembassy.ae; Ambassador Dr JULIUS LAURITSCH.

Azerbaijan: POB 45766, Plot N-297, W-16, al-Bateen Area, Abu Dhabi; tel. (2) 6662848; fax (2) 6663150; e-mail abudhabi@mission.mfa.gov.az; internet www.azembassy.ae; Ambassador ELKHAN GAHRAMANOV.

Bahrain: Villa 173, W-16, Paynoonah Rd, Abu Dhabi; tel. (2) 6657500; fax (2) 6674141; e-mail abudhabi.mission@mofa.gov.bh; Ambassador MUHAMMAD SAQR AL-MAAWDA.

Bangladesh: POB 2504, Villa 21, Delma St, al-Rowdha, Abu Dhabi; tel. (2) 668375; fax (2) 667324; e-mail embassy@bdembassyuae.org; internet www.bdembassyuae.org; Ambassador MUHAMMAD NUZMUL QAWNAIN.

Belarus: POB 30337, Villa 434, 26th St, al-Rouda Area, Abu Dhabi; tel. (2) 4453399; fax (2) 4451131; e-mail belembas@emirates.net.ae; internet uae.belembassy.org; Ambassador ALEXANDER SEMESHKO.

Belgium: POB 3686, al-Masood Tower, 6th Floor, Hamdan St, Abu Dhabi; tel. (2) 6319449; fax (2) 6319353; e-mail abudhabi@diplobel.fed.be; internet www.diplomatie.be/abudhabi; Ambassador ANICK VAN CALSTER.

Bosnia and Herzegovina: POB 43362, Abu Dhabi; tel. (2) 6444164; fax (2) 6443619; e-mail ambassador.rk@bhmc.ae; internet www.bhmc.ae; Ambassador RADOMIR KOSIĆ.

Brazil: POB 3027, Villa 3, St 5, Madinat Zayed, Abu Dhabi; tel. (2) 6320606; fax (2) 6327727; e-mail abubrem@emirates.net.ae; internet www.brazilembuae.ae; Ambassador RAUL CAMPOS DE CASTRO.

Brunei: POB 5836, Plot 8, Villa 1, St 27, E-33, Abu Dhabi; tel. (2) 4486999; fax (2) 4486333; e-mail abudhabi.uae@mfa.gov.bn; Ambassador Dato Paduka Haji ADNAN BIN Haji ZAINAL.

Canada: POB 6970, Abu Dhabi Trade Towers, West Tower, 9th and 10th Floors, Abu Dhabi; tel. (2) 6940300; fax (2) 6940399; e-mail abdbi@international.gc.ca; internet www.dfait-maeci.gc.ca/abudhabi; Ambassador KEN LEWIS.

Chile: St 4, nr St 23, al-Mushrif, Abu Dhabi; tel. (2) 4472022; fax (2) 4472023; e-mail info@chile-uae.com; internet chile-uae.com; Ambassador JEAN-PAUL TARUD KUBORN.

China, People's Republic: POB 2741, Plot 26, W-22, Abu Dhabi; tel. (2) 4434276; fax (2) 4436835; e-mail chinaemb_ae@mfa.gov.cn; internet ae.chineseembassy.org; Ambassador GAO YUNSHENG.

Cyprus: POB 63013, 426 al-Khaleej al-Arabi St, Abu Dhabi; tel. (2) 6654480; fax (2) 6657870; e-mail cyembadb@eim.ae; Ambassador COSTAS PAPADEMAS.

Czech Republic: POB 27009, City Bank Bldg, Corniche Plaza, Abu Dhabi; tel. (2) 6782800; fax (2) 6795716; e-mail abudhabi@embassy.mzv.cz; internet www.mzv.cz/abudhabi; Ambassador JAROSLAV LUDVA.

Denmark: Abu Dhabi; e-mail auhamb@um.dk; Ambassador POUL O. G. HOINESS.

Egypt: POB 4026, Abu Dhabi; tel. (2) 4445566; fax (2) 4449878; e-mail egemb_abudhabi@mfa.gov.eg; Ambassador TAMER MANSOUR.

Eritrea: POB 2597, Abu Dhabi; tel. (2) 6331838; fax (2) 6346451; Ambassador OSMAN MUHAMMAD OMAR.

Finland: POB 3634, al-Masood Tower, Hamdan St, Abu Dhabi; tel. (2) 6328927; fax (2) 6325063; e-mail sanomat.abo@formin.fi; internet www.finland.ae; Ambassador MATTI LASSILA.

France: POB 4014, Abu Dhabi; tel. (2) 4435100; fax (2) 4434158; e-mail contact@ambafrance.ae; internet www.ambafrance-eau.org; Ambassador ALAIN AZOUAOU.

The Gambia: Abu Dhabi; tel. (2) 6678030; Ambassador MAMBURY NJIE.

Germany: POB 2591, Abu Dhabi Mall, West Tower, 14th Floor, Abu Dhabi; tel. (2) 6446693; fax (2) 6446942; e-mail info@abu-dhabi.diplo.de; internet www.abu-dhabi.diplo.de; Ambassador KLAUS-PETER BRANDES.

Greece: POB 5483, Plot 141, Villa 1, E-48, Moroor, Abu Dhabi; tel. (2) 4492550; fax (2) 4492455; e-mail gremb.abd@mfa.gr; Ambassador DIONISIOS ZOIS.

Hungary: POB 44450, Abu Dhabi; tel. (2) 6766190; fax (2) 6766215; e-mail mission.abu@kum.hu; Ambassador JÁNOS GÖNCI.

India: POB 4090, Abu Dhabi; tel. (2) 4492700; fax (2) 4444685; e-mail indiauae@indembassyuae.org; internet www.indembassyuae.org; Ambassador M. K. LOKESH.

Indonesia: POB 7256, Abu Dhabi; tel. (2) 4454448; fax (2) 4455453; e-mail indoemb@emirates.net.ae; internet www.indoemb.org/kbri; Ambassador WAHID SUPRIYADI.

Iran: POB 4080, Abu Dhabi; tel. (2) 4447618; fax (2) 4448714; e-mail iranemb@eim.ae; internet www.iranembassy.org.ae; Ambassador MUHAMMAD REZA FAYYAZ.

Iraq: Manhal St, Haoudh 55, St 32, Abu Dhabi; tel. (2) 6655215; fax (2) 6655214; e-mail adbemb@iraqmofamail.net; Ambassador FARES UJAIL AL-YAWER.

Ireland: 1–2 Khalifa al-Suwaidi Development, 19th St (off 32nd St), al-Bateen Area, Abu Dhabi; tel. (2) 4958200; fax (2) 6819233; e-mail irishvisaofficedubai@gmail.com; Ambassador CIARÁN MADDEN.

Italy: POB 46752, Villa 438–439, St 26, al-Manaseer Area, Abu Dhabi; tel. (2) 4435622; fax (2) 4434337; e-mail italianembassy.abudhabi@esteri.it; internet www.ambabudhabi.esteri.it; Ambassador GIORGIO STARACE.

Japan: POB 2430, Abu Dhabi; tel. (2) 4435696; fax (2) 4434219; e-mail embjpn@japanembassyauh.com; internet www.uae.emb-japan.go.jp; Ambassador TATSUO WATANABE.

Jordan: POB 4024, Abu Dhabi; tel. (2) 4447100; fax (2) 4449157; e-mail embjord1@emirates.net.ae; Ambassador NAYEF ZEIDAN.

Kazakhstan: POB 39556, al-Mushrif, W-52, Villa 61B, Abu Dhabi; tel. (2) 4498778; fax (2) 4498775; e-mail kazemb@emirates.net.ae; internet www.kazembemirates.net; Ambassador ASKAR A. MUSSINOV.

Kenya: POB 3854, Abu Dhabi; tel. (2) 6666300; fax (2) 6652827; e-mail kenyarep@emirates.net.ae; internet www.kenyaembassy.ae; Ambassador MUHAMMED ABDI GELLO.

Korea, Republic: POB 3270, Abu Dhabi; tel. (2) 4435337; fax (2) 4435348; e-mail keauhlee@emirates.net.ae; Ambassador CHUNG YONG-CHIL.

THE UNITED ARAB EMIRATES

Kuwait: POB 926, Abu Dhabi; tel. (2) 4446888; fax (2) 4444990; e-mail abudhabi@mofa.gov.kw; Ambassador Saleh Muhammad al-Buaijan.

Lebanon: POB 4023, Abu Dhabi; tel. (2) 4492100; fax (2) 4493500; e-mail libanamb@emirates.net.ae; Ambassador Fauzi Yousuf Fawaz.

Libya: POB 5739, Abu Dhabi; tel. (2) 4450030; fax (2) 4450033; e-mail sunnylib@eim.ae; Ambassador Muhammad al-Buaishi.

Malaysia: POB 3887, Abu Dhabi; tel. (2) 4482775; fax (2) 4482779; e-mail admin@malaysianembassy.ae; internet www.kln.gov.my/perwakilan/abudhabi; Ambassador Dato' Yahaya Abdul Jabar.

Mauritania: POB 2714, Abu Dhabi; tel. (2) 4462724; fax (2) 4465772; Ambassador Bebaha Ould Ibrahim Khalil.

Morocco: POB 4066, Abu Dhabi; tel. (2) 4433973; fax (2) 4433917; e-mail sifmabo@yahoo.com; internet www.moroccan-emb.ae; Ambassador Muhammad Boudrif.

Nepal: POB 38282, Abu Dhabi; tel. (2) 6344385; fax (2) 6344469; e-mail nepemuae@emirates.net.ae; internet www.nepembassyuae.ae; Ambassador Arjun Bahadur Thapa.

Netherlands: POB 46560, al-Masood Tower, 6th Floor, Suite 6, Abu Dhabi; tel. (2) 6321920; fax (2) 6313158; e-mail abu@minbuza.nl; internet www.netherlands.ae; Ambassador Dr Gerald Michels.

Nigeria: POB 110171, Abu Dhabi; tel. (2) 4431503; fax (2) 4431792; e-mail nigerabudhabi@yahoo.co.uk; Ambassador Alhaji Bashir Yoguda Gusau.

Norway: POB 47270, Abu Dhabi; tel. (2) 6211221; fax (2) 6213313; e-mail emb.abudhabi@mfa.no; internet www.norway.ae; Ambassador Åse Elin Bjerke.

Oman: POB 2517, Said bin Tahnon Sq., al-Mushraf Area, Abu Dhabi; tel. (2) 4463333; fax (2) 4464633; e-mail omanemb@emirates.net.ae; Ambassador Sheikh Muhammad bin Abdullah Ali al-Qatabi.

Pakistan: POB 846, Abu Dhabi; tel. (2) 4447800; fax (2) 4447172; e-mail pakisuae@emirates.net.ae; internet www.pakistanembassy.ae; Ambassador Khurshid Ahmad Junejo.

Philippines: POB 3215, Plot 97, Villa 2, St 5, E-18/02, Abu Dhabi; tel. (2) 6415922; fax (2) 6412559; e-mail auhpe@philembassy.ae; internet philembassy.ae; Ambassador Grace Relucio Princesa.

Poland: POB 2334, Abu Dhabi; tel. (2) 4465200; fax (2) 4462967; e-mail polonez@emirates.net.ae; internet www.abuzabi.polemb.net; Ambassador Adam Krzymowski.

Qatar: POB 3503, 26th St, al-Minaseer, Abu Dhabi; tel. (2) 4493300; fax (2) 4493311; e-mail abudhabi@mofa.gov.qa; Ambassador Abdullah M. al-Uthman.

Romania: 9 POB 70416, Abu Dhabi; tel. (2) 4459919; fax (2) 4461143; e-mail romaniae@emirates.net.ae; Ambassador Nikolai Goia.

Russia: POB 8211, Abu Dhabi; tel. (2) 6721797; fax (2) 6728713; e-mail uaeruss@hotmail.com; internet www.uae.mid.ru; Ambassador Andrei V. Andreyev.

Saudi Arabia: POB 4057, Abu Dhabi; tel. (2) 4445700; fax (2) 4448491; e-mail aeemb@mofa.gov.sa; Ambassador Ibrahim al-Saad al-Ibrahim.

Somalia: POB 4155, Abu Dhabi; tel. (2) 6669700; fax (2) 6651580; e-mail somen@emirates.net.ae; internet www.uae.somaligov.net; Ambassador Ahmed Mohammed Ajal.

South Africa: POB 29446, Abu Dhabi; tel. (2) 4473446; fax (2) 4473031; e-mail saemb@emirates.net.ae; internet www.southafrica.ae; Ambassador Yacoob Abba Omar.

Spain: POB 46474, al-Saman Tower, Hamdam St, Abu Dhabi; tel. (2) 6269544; fax (2) 6274978; e-mail emb.abudhabi@maec.es; Ambassador Gonzalo de Benito Secades.

Sri Lanka: POB 46534, Abu Dhabi; tel. (2) 6316444; fax (2) 6331661; e-mail lankemba@emirates.net.ae; Ambassador Sarath Wijesinghe.

Sudan: POB 4027, Abu Dhabi; tel. (2) 6666788; fax (2) 6654231; e-mail sudembll@emirates.net.ae; Ambassador Ahmed al-Siddiq Abd al-Hai.

Sweden: POB 31867, Abu Dhabi; tel. (2) 6210162; fax (2) 6394941; e-mail ambassaden.abudhabi@foreign.ministry.se; internet www.swedenabroad.com/abudhabi; Ambassador Magnus Schöldtz.

Switzerland: POB 46116, Abu Dhabi; tel. (2) 6274636; fax (2) 6269627; e-mail adh.vertretung@eda.admin.ch; internet www.eda.admin.ch/uae; Ambassador Wolfgang Amadeus Bruelhart.

Syria: POB 4011, Abu Dhabi; tel. (2) 4448768; fax (2) 4449387; Ambassador Dr Abd al-Latif al-Dabbagh.

Thailand: POB 47466, Abu Dhabi; tel. (2) 6421772; fax (2) 6421773; e-mail thaiauh@emirates.net.ae; internet www.thaiembassy.ae; Ambassador Somchai Charanasomboon.

Tunisia: POB 4166, Abu Dhabi; tel. (2) 6811331; fax (2) 6812707; e-mail pol_ambtunad@eim.ae; Ambassador Muhammad al-Sediri.

Turkey: POB 3204, Abu Dhabi; tel. (2) 4454864; fax (2) 4452522; e-mail tcadbe@eim.ae; internet abudhabi.emb.mfa.gov.tr; Ambassador Ş. Vural Altay.

Uganda: Abu Dhabi; Ambassador Semakula Kiwanuka.

Ukraine: POB 35572, Abu Dhabi; tel. (2) 6327586; fax (2) 6327506; e-mail embua@embukr.ae; internet www.oae.mfa.gov.ua/oae; Ambassador Yuriy V. Polurez.

United Kingdom: POB 248, Abu Dhabi; tel. (2) 6101100; fax (2) 6101586; e-mail information.abudhabi@fco.gov.uk; internet ukinuae.fco.gov.uk; Ambassador Dominic Jermey.

USA: POB 4009, Abu Dhabi; tel. (2) 4142200; fax (2) 4142469; e-mail webmasterabudhabi@state.gov; internet abudhabi.usembassy.gov; Chargé d'affaires a.i. Douglas C. Greene.

Yemen: POB 2095, Abu Dhabi; tel. (2) 4448457; fax (2) 4447978; e-mail yemenemb@emirates.net.ae; Ambassador Abdullah Hussain Muhammad al-Defae'.

Judicial System

The 95th article of the Constitution of 1971 provided for the establishment of the Union Supreme Court and Union Primary Tribunals as the judicial organs of State.

The Union has exclusive legislative and executive jurisdiction over all matters that are concerned with the strengthening of the federation, such as foreign affairs, defence and Union armed forces, security, finance, communications, traffic control, education, currency, measures, standards and weights, matters relating to nationality and emigration, Union information, etc.

The late President Sheikh Zayed signed the law establishing the new federal courts on 9 June 1978. The new law effectively transferred local judicial authorities into the jurisdiction of the federal system.

Primary tribunals in Abu Dhabi, Sharjah, Ajman and Fujairah are now primary federal tribunals, and primary tribunals in other towns in those emirates have become circuits of the primary federal tribunals.

The primary federal tribunals may sit in any of the capitals of the four emirates and have jurisdiction on all administrative disputes between the Union and individuals, whether the Union is plaintiff or defendant. Civil disputes between Union and individuals will be heard by primary federal tribunals in the defendant's place of normal residence.

The law requires that all judges take a constitutional oath before the Minister of Justice and that the courts apply the rules of *Shari'a* (Islamic religious law) and that no judgment contradicts the *Shari'a*. All employees of the old judiciaries will be transferred to the federal authority without loss of salary or seniority.

In February 1994 President Sheikh Zayed ordered that an extensive range of crimes, including murder, theft and adultery, be tried in *Shari'a* courts rather than in civil courts.

Chief Shari'a Justice: Ahmad Abd al-Aziz al-Mubarak.

FEDERAL SUPREME COURT

President and Chief Justice: Abd al-Wahab Abdul.

Religion

ISLAM

Most of the inhabitants are Sunni Muslims, while about 16% of Muslims are Shi'ites.

CHRISTIANITY

Roman Catholic Church

Apostolic Vicariate of Southern Arabia: POB 54, Abu Dhabi; tel. (2) 4461895; fax (2) 4465177; e-mail vicapar@eim.ae; internet www.stjosephsabudhabi.org; f. 1889; fmrly Apostolic Vicariate of Arabia; renamed as above, following reorganization in 2011; responsible for most of the Arabian peninsula (incl. the UAE, Oman and Yemen), containing an estimated 650,000 Catholics (31 December 2010); Vicar Apostolic Bishop Paul Hinder (Titular Bishop of Macon, Georgia, resident in the UAE).

The Anglican Communion

Within the Episcopal Church in Jerusalem and the Middle East, the UAE forms part of the diocese of Cyprus and the Gulf. The Anglican congregations in the UAE are entirely expatriate. The Bishop in Cyprus and the Gulf resides in Cyprus, while the Archdeacon in the Gulf is resident in Bahrain.

THE UNITED ARAB EMIRATES

The Press

The state regulator for the sector is the National Media Council, under the Chairmanship of SAQR GHOBASH SAID GHOBASH (Minister of Labour).

ABU DHABI

Abu Dhabi Magazine: POB 662, Abu Dhabi; tel. (2) 6214000; fax (2) 6348954; f. 1969; Arabic, some articles in English; monthly; Editor ZUHAIR AL-QADI; circ. 18,000.

Abu Dhabi Official Gazette: POB 19, Abu Dhabi; tel. (2) 6688413; fax (2) 6669981; e-mail gazette@ecouncil.ae; f. 1965; Arabic; daily; official reports and papers.

Abu Dhabi Tempo: POB 33760, Abu Dhabi; tel. (2) 6673349; fax (2) 6673389; e-mail info@abudhabitempo.com; internet www.abudhabitempo.com; f. 2009; monthly; local community news; distributed free of charge; publ. by BrandMoxie; Editor SANA BAGERSH; circ. 30,000.

Al-Ain Times: POB 15229, al-Ain; tel. (3) 7671995; fax (3) 7671997; e-mail alaintimes@gmail.com; internet www.alaintimesuae.com; f. 2006; English and Arabic; weekly; publ. by Alpha Beta Publrs and Media Consultants; Chief Editor FADWA M. B. AL-MUGHARIBI.

Akhbar al-Arab: POB 54040, Abu Dhabi; tel. (2) 4486000; e-mail info@akhbaralarab.ae; internet www.akhbaralarab.co.ae; f. 1999; daily; political; circ. 50,000.

Alrroya Aleqtisadiya (Economic Vision): POB 112494, Abu Dhabi; tel. (2) 6517777; fax (2) 6517772; internet www.alrroya.com; f. 2009; Arabic; business daily; publ. by Imedia LLC; Man. Editor REFAAT JAAFAR.

Hiya (She): POB 2488, Abu Dhabi; tel. (2) 4474121; Arabic; weekly for women; publ. by Dar al-Wahdah.

Al-Ittihad (Unity): POB 791, Abu Dhabi; tel. (2) 4455555; fax (2) 4455126; e-mail editor@alittihad.co.ae; internet www.alittihad.ae; f. 1972; Arabic; daily and weekly; publ. by Abu Dhabi Media Co; Man. Editor ALI ABU AL-RISH; circ. 58,000 daily, 60,000 weekly.

Majid: POB 791, Abu Dhabi; tel. (2) 4451804; fax (2) 4451455; e-mail majid-magazine@emi.co.ae; internet www.majid.ae; f. 1979; Arabic; weekly; children's magazine; publ. by Abu Dhabi Media Co; Man. Editor AHMAD OMAR; circ. 164,000.

The National: Abu Dhabi Media Co, 4th St, Sector 18, Zone 1, Abu Dhabi; tel. (2) 4144000; fax (2) 4144001; internet www.thenational.ae; f. 2008; English; daily; publ. by Abu Dhabi Media Co; Editorial Dir MARTIN NEWLAND; Editor-in-Chief HASSAN FATTAH.

Zahrat al-Khaleej (Splendour of the Gulf): POB 791, Abu Dhabi; tel. (2) 4461600; fax (2) 4451653; e-mail abedrabbo@admedia.ae; f. 1979; Arabic; weekly; women's magazine; publ. by Abu Dhabi Media Co; Editor-in-Chief TALAL TOHME; circ. 10,000.

DUBAI

Al-Bayan (The Official Report): POB 2710, Dubai; tel. (4) 3444400; fax (4) 3447846; e-mail readers@albayan.ae; internet www.albayan.ae; f. 1980; Arabic; daily; publ. by Awraq Publishing, a subsidiary of Arab Media Group; CEO SAMI AL-QAMZI; Editor-in-Chief DA'EN SHAHIN; circ. 82,575.

Emarat Al-Youm: POB 502012, Dubai; e-mail 1971ey@gmail.com; internet www.emaratyoum.com; Arabic; business daily; publ. by Awraq Publishing, a subsidiary of Arab Media Group; Editor SAMI AL-RIYAMI.

Emirates 24/7: POB 191919, Dubai; tel. (4) 3062222; fax (4) 3407698; e-mail news@emirates247.com; internet www.emirates247.com; f. 2005; English; online; Editor-in-Chief RIYAD MICKDADY.

Emirates Woman: POB 2331, Dubai; tel. (4) 2824060; fax (4) 2827593; e-mail faye@motivate.co.ae; f. 1981; English; monthly; fashion, health and beauty; publ. by Motivate Publishing; Editor FAYE JAMES; circ. 20,324.

Gulf News: Sheikh Zayed Rd, POB 6519, Dubai; tel. (4) 3447100; fax (4) 3441627; e-mail editor@gulfnews.com; internet www.gulfnews.com; f. 1978; English; daily; two weekly supplements, *Junior News* (Wed.), *Gulf Weekly* (Thur.); publ. by Al-Nisr Publishing; Editor-in-Chief ABD-AL HAMID AHMAD; circ. 103,000.

Al-Jundi (The Soldier): POB 2838, Dubai; tel. (4) 3532222; fax (4) 3744272; e-mail mod5@eim.ae; f. 1973; Arabic; monthly; military and cultural; Editor-in-Chief Brig. MUHAMMAD ALI ABDULLAH AL-EASSA; circ. 10,000.

Khaleej Times: POB 11243, Dubai; tel. (4) 3383535; fax (4) 3383345; e-mail ktimes@emirates.net.ae; internet www.khaleejtimes.com; f. 1978; a Galadari enterprise; English; daily; distributed throughout the region and in India, Pakistan and the United Kingdom; free weekly supplement, *Weekend* (Fri.); Publr and Editor-in-Chief MUHAMMAD A. R. GALADARI; Man. Dir QASSIM MUHAMMAD YOUSUF; circ. 70,000.

Al-Manara: Office 129, Bldg 10, Dubai Media City; tel. (4) 3901777; fax (4) 3904554; e-mail dar@almanaramagazine.ae; internet www.almanaramagazine.ae; Arabic; lifestyle; Editor WALID AL-SAADI.

Trade and Industry: POB 1457, Dubai; tel. (4) 2280000; fax (4) 2211646; e-mail dcciinfo@dcci.org; internet www.dubaichamber.ae; f. 1975; Arabic and English; monthly; publ. by Dubai Chamber of Commerce and Industry; circ. 26,000.

UAE Digest: POB 500595, Dubai; tel. (4) 3672245; fax (4) 3678613; e-mail info@sterlingp.ae; internet www.sterlingp.ae; English; monthly; publ. by Sterling Publications; current affairs; Man. Editor K. RAVEENDRAN.

Viva: POB 500024, Dubai; tel. (4) 2108000; fax (4) 2108080; e-mail vivaletters@itp.com; internet www.vivamagazine.ae; f. 2004; publ. by ITP; Editor MANDIE GOWER; circ. 23,000.

What's On: POB 2331, Dubai; tel. (4) 2824060; fax (4) 2827593; e-mail editor-wo@motivate.co.ae; internet www.whatsonlive.com; f. 1979; English; monthly; publ. by Motivate Publishing; Group Editor and Man. Partner IAN FAIRSERVICE; circ. 31,055.

Xpress: POB 6519, Dubai; tel. (4) 3447100; fax (4) 3420433; e-mail editor@alnisrmedia.com; internet www.xpress4me.com; f. 2007; English; weekly; publ. by Al-Nisr Publishing; Editor NIRMALA JANSSEN.

RAS AL-KHAIMAH

Akhbar Ras al-Khaimah (Ras al-Khaimah News): POB 87, Ras al-Khaimah; Arabic; monthly; local news.

Al-Ghorfa: POB 87, Ras al-Khaimah; tel. (7) 2333511; fax (7) 2330233; f. 1970; Arabic and English; free monthly; publ. by Ras al-Khaimah Chamber of Commerce and Industry; Editor ZAKI H. SAQR.

Ras al-Khaimah Magazine: POB 200, Ras al-Khaimah; Arabic; monthly; commerce and trade; Chief Editor AHMAD AL-TADMORI.

SHARJAH

Al-Azman al-Arabia (Times of Arabia): POB 5823, Sharjah; tel. (6) 5356034.

The Gulf Today: POB 30, Sharjah; tel. (6) 5591919; fax (6) 5532737; e-mail nilofer@godubai.com; internet www.godubai.com/gulftoday; f. 1995; English; daily; circ. 38,000.

Al-Khaleej (The Gulf): POB 30, Sharjah; tel. (6) 5625304; fax (6) 5598547; e-mail kh_readers@alkhaleej.ae; internet www.alkhaleej.co.ae; f. 1970; Arabic; daily; political; independent; Editor GHASSAN TAHBOUB; circ. 82,750.

Al-Sharooq (Sunrise): POB 30, Sharjah; tel. (6) 5598777; fax (6) 5599336; f. 1970; Arabic; weekly; general interest; Editor YOUSUF AL-HASSAN.

Al-Tijarah (Commerce): Sharjah Chamber of Commerce and Industry, POB 580, Sharjah; tel. (6) 5116600; fax (6) 5681119; e-mail scci@sharjah.gov.ae; internet www.sharjah.gov.ae; f. 1970; Arabic/English; monthly magazine; circ. 50,000; annual trade directory; circ. 100,000.

NEWS AGENCY

Emirates News Agency (WAM): POB 3790, Abu Dhabi; tel. (2) 4454545; fax (2) 4044200; e-mail wamnews@eim.ae; internet www.wam.org.ae; f. 1977; operated by the Govt; Dir-Gen. IBRAHIM AL-ABED; Chief Editor JAMAL NASSER.

Publishers

All Prints: POB 857, Abu Dhabi; tel. (2) 6336999; fax (2) 6320844; e-mail allprints@allprints.co.ae; internet web.allprints.ae; f. 1968; publishing and distribution; Partners BUSHRA KHAYAT, TAHSEEN S. KHAYAT.

ITP: POB 500024, Dubai; tel. (4) 2108000; fax (4) 2108080; e-mail info@itp.com; internet www.itp.com; f. 1987; publishes more than 60 magazines, incl. *Ahlan!*, *Arabian Business*, *Time Out Dubai*, *Viva*; CEO WALID AKAWI.

Kalimat Publishing and Distribution: POB 21969, Sharjah; tel. (6) 5566696; fax (6) 5566691; e-mail info@kalimat.ae; internet www.kalimat.ae; f. 2007; children's books; CEO Sheikha BODOUR AL-QASIMI.

Motivate Publishing: POB 2331, Dubai; tel. (4) 2824060; fax (4) 2820428; e-mail motivate@motivate.ae; internet www.motivatepublishing.com; f. 1979; books and magazines; Man. Partner and Group Editor IAN FAIRSERVICE.

Sterling Publications: POB 500595, Dubai; tel. (4) 3672245; fax (4) 3678613; e-mail info@sterlingp.ae; internet www.sterlingp.ae; publs include *UAE Digest*, *Banking*, *Business Review* and *Ajman Today*;

THE UNITED ARAB EMIRATES

Publr and Man. Dir Sankara Narayanan; Man. Editor K. Raveendran.

Broadcasting and Communications

TELECOMMUNICATIONS
Regulatory Authority

Telecommunications Regulatory Authority (TRA): POB 26662, Abu Dhabi; tel. (2) 6269999; fax (2) 6118209; e-mail info@tra.ae; internet www.tra.ae; f. 2004; Chair. Muhammad bin Ahmad al-Qamzi; Dir-Gen. Muhammad al-Ghanem.

Principal Operators

Emirates Integrated Telecommunications Co (du): POB 502666, Dubai; tel. (4) 3600000; fax (4) 3604440; e-mail talk-to-us@du.ae; internet www.du.ae; f. 2006; commenced operations under the brand name *du* in Feb. 2007; 40% owned by the federal Govt, 20% by TECOM Investment, 20% by Mubadala Devt Co and 20% by public shareholders; provides telecommunications services throughout the UAE; Chair. Ahmad bin Byat; CEO Osman Sultan.

Emirates Telecommunications Corpn (Etisalat): POB 3838, Abu Dhabi; tel. (2) 6182091; fax (2) 6334448; e-mail prd@etisalat.co.ae; internet www.etisalat.co.ae; f. 1976; provides telecommunications services throughout the UAE; Chair. Muhammad Hassan Omran; CEO Muhammad al-Qamzi.

BROADCASTING
Radio

Abu Dhabi Radio: Abu Dhabi Media Co, 4th St, Sector 18, Zone 1, Abu Dhabi; tel. (2) 4144000; fax (2) 4144001; internet www.admedia.ae; f. 1969; broadcasts in Arabic over a wide area; also broadcasts in French, Bengali, Filipino and Urdu; affiliated channels include Emarat FM, Quran Kareem Radio, Sawt Al Musiqa; owned and operated by Abu Dhabi Media Co; Dir-Gen. Abd al-Wahab al-Radwan.

Arabian Radio Network: POB 502012, Dubai; tel. (4) 3912000; fax (4) 3912007; e-mail info@arnonline.com; internet www.arnonline.com; f. 2001; owned by Arab Media Group; operates nine stations; CEO Abd al-Latif al-Sayegh.

Capital Radio: POB 63, Abu Dhabi; tel. (2) 4451000; fax (2) 4451155; govt-operated; English-language FM music and news station; Station Man. Aida Hamza.

Channel 4 Radio Network: POB 442, Ajman; tel. (6) 7461444; e-mail chris@channel4fm.com; internet www.channel4fm.com; operates 89.1 FM, 104.8 FM and 107.8 Radio Al Rabia stations; owned by Ajman Independent Studios LLC; Head Chris Rose.

Ras al-Khaimah Broadcasting Station: POB 141, Ras al-Khaimah; tel. (7) 2851151; fax (7) 2352300; five transmitters broadcast in Arabic, Urdu, Malayalam, Telugu, Tamil and Bangla; Chair. Abd al-Malik bin Kayed al-Qassimi.

Sharjah Radio and Television: POB 111, Sharjah; tel. (6) 5661111; fax (6) 5669999; e-mail info@sharjahtv.ae; internet www.sharjahtv.ae; Dir Amna Khamis Gharib al-Nakhi.

Umm al-Qaiwain Broadcasting Station: POB 444, Umm al-Qaiwain; tel. (6) 7666044; fax (6) 7666055; e-mail uaqfm@emirates.net.ae; f. 1978; broadcasts music and news in Arabic, Malayalam, Sinhala and Urdu; Gen. Man. Ali Jassem.

Television

Abu Dhabi Television: Abu Dhabi Media Co, 4th St, Sector 18, Zone 1, Abu Dhabi; tel. (2) 4144000; fax (2) 4144001; internet www.adtv.ae; f. 1969; reorg. 2008; broadcasts entertainment and news programmes; affiliated channels include Emirates Channel, Abu Dhabi Sports; owned by Abu Dhabi Media Co; Exec. Dir Karim Sarkis.

Ajman Television Network: POB 442, Ajman; tel. (6) 7465000; fax (6) 7465135; e-mail progajtv@ajmantv.com; internet www.ajmantv.com; f. 1996; broadcasts in Arabic and English; Chair. Abdullah Muhammad.

Arabian Television Network: Arab Media Group, POB 500666, Dubai; tel. (4) 3062222; fax (4) 3479965; e-mail info@arabmediagrouponline.com; internet www.arnonline.com; f. 2007; broadcasts own entertainment channels, incl. SHOOFtv and Noor Dubai TV; also adapts international brands for Arab market, such as MTV Arabia; owned by Arab Media Group; Gen. Man. Maryam al-Falasi.

City 7 Television: POB 502209, Bldg 4, Dubai Media City, Dubai; tel. (4) 3678147; fax (4) 3678060; e-mail info@city7tv.com; internet www.city7tv.com; Chair. Mohi el-Din bin Hendi.

Dubai Media Inc: POB 835, Dubai; tel. (4) 3369999; fax (4) 3360060; e-mail info@dmi.ae; internet www.dmi.gov.ae; f. 2004; channels include Dubai Television, Dubai One, Sama Dubai, Dubai Sports; state-owned; Chair. Sheikh Maktoum bin Muhammad bin Rashid Al Maktoum; Man. Dir Ahmad Abdullah al-Sheikh.

Middle East Broadcasting Center (MBC): POB 76267, Dubai; tel. (4) 3919999; fax (4) 3919900; e-mail infotv@mbc.ae; internet www.mbc.net; f. 1991; broadcasts throughout region via satellite; channels include Al-Arabiya News Channel, MBC Persia (Farsi service), MBC 1, 2, 3 and 4 (entertainment); Chair. Sheikh Walid al-Ibrahim.

Sharjah Radio and Television: see Radio.

Finance

(cap. = capital; res = reserves; dep. = deposits; m. = million; brs = branches; amounts in dirhams, unless otherwise indicated)

BANKING
Central Bank

Central Bank of the United Arab Emirates: POB 854, Abu Dhabi; tel. (2) 6652220; fax (2) 6652504; e-mail admin@cbuae.gov.ae; internet www.centralbank.ae; f. 1973; acts as issuing authority for local currency; superseded UAE Currency Bd in Dec. 1980; cap. 300m., res 1,200m., dep. 156,274m. (Dec. 2009); Chair. Muhammad Sharif Foulathi; Gov. Sultan bin Nasser al-Suwaidi; 5 brs.

Principal Banks

Abu Dhabi Commercial Bank (ADCB): POB 939, Abu Dhabi; tel. (2) 6962222; fax (2) 6450384; e-mail info@adcb.com; internet www.adcb.com; f. 1985 by merger; 65% govt-owned, 35% owned by private investors; cap. 4,810.0m., res 12,743.0m., dep. 91,038.1m. (Dec. 2009); Chair. Muhammad Ghanim al-Suwaidi; CEO Ala'a Muhammad Khalil Eraiqat; 40 brs in the UAE, 2 in India.

Abu Dhabi Islamic Bank: POB 313, Abu Dhabi; tel. (2) 6100600; fax (2) 6656028; e-mail adib@adib.co.ae; internet www.adib.ae; f. 1997; cap. 1,970.0m., res 4,446.4m., dep. 49,498.1m. (Dec. 2009); Chair. Jawan Awaidha Suhail al-Khaili; CEO Tirad Mahmoud; 60 brs.

Ajman Bank PJSC: POB 7770, Block C, 13th Floor, al-Mina Rd, Ajman Free Zone, Ajman; tel. (6) 7479999; fax (6) 7479990; e-mail info@ajmanbank.ae; internet www.ajmanbank.ae; f. 2008; 25% owned by Govt of Ajman; *Shari'a*-compliant services; cap. 1,000m., res 2m., dep. 867m. (Dec. 2009); Chair. Sheikh Ammar bin Humaid al-Nuaimi; CEO Mubasher Hanif Khokhar; 2 brs.

Arab Emirates Investment Bank PJSC: POB 5503, Office 904, Twin Towers, Baniyas St, Deira, Dubai; tel. (4) 2328080; fax (4) 2328134; e-mail aeibank@emirates.net.ae; internet www.aeibank.com; f. 1976 as Arab Emirate Investment Bank Ltd; name changed as above in 2000; cap. 44m., res 9m., dep. 518m. (Dec. 2009); Chair. Omar Abdullah al-Futtaim.

Bank of Sharjah: POB 1394, Sharjah; tel. (6) 5694411; fax (6) 5694422; e-mail bankshj@emirates.net.ae; internet www.bankofsharjah.com; f. 1973; cap. 2,000m., res 1,503m., dep. 12,616m. (Dec. 2009); Chair. Ahmad al-Noman; Exec. Dir and Gen. Man. Varoujan Nerguizian; 2 brs.

Commercial Bank of Dubai PSC: POB 2668, Mankhool St, Dubai; tel. (4) 2121000; fax (4) 2121911; e-mail cbd-ho@cbd.ae; internet www.cbd.ae; f. 1969; 20% owned by Govt of Dubai; cap. 1,764.8m., res 3,002.0m., dep. 28,695.0m. (Dec. 2009); Chair. Ahmad Humaid al-Tayer; CEO Peter Baltussen; 24 brs.

Commercial Bank International PSC: POB 4449, al-Riqah St, Dubai; tel. (4) 2275265; fax (4) 2279038; e-mail cbiho@emirates.net.ae; internet www.cbiuae.com; f. 1991; cap. 1,340m., res 212m., dep. 8,621m. (Dec. 2009); Chair. Hamad Abdullah al-Mutawaa; CEO Douwe J. Oppedijk; 9 brs.

Dubai Bank PJSC: POB 65555, Sheikh Zayed Rd, Dubai; e-mail info@dubaibank.ae; internet www.dubaibank.ae; tel. (4) 3328989; fax (4) 3290071; f. 2002 by Emaar Properties, a real estate developer; cap. 1,500m., res 113m., dep. 15,306m. (Dec. 2009); Chair. Fadel al-Ali; CEO Salaam al-Shaksi.

Dubai Islamic Bank PJSC: POB 1080, Airport Rd, Deira, Dubai; tel. (4) 2953000; fax (4) 2954111; e-mail contactus@dib.ae; internet www.alislami.ae; f. 1975; cap. 3,617.5m., res 4,536.1m., dep. 69,397.1m. (Dec. 2009); Chair. Dr Muhammad Ebrahim al-Shaibani; CEO Abdullah al-Hamli; 44 brs.

Emirates Islamic Bank PJSC: POB 5547, Beniyas Rd, Deira, Dubai; tel. (4) 2287474; fax (4) 2272172; e-mail info@emiratesislamicbank.ae; internet www.emiratesislamicbank.ae;

f. 1976 as Middle East Bank; became a Public Joint Stock Co (PJSC) in 1995; present name adopted 2004; subsidiary (99.8% owned) of Emirates Bank Int; cap. 2,314.6m., res 300.5m., dep. 20,625.6m. (Dec. 2009); CEO Ibrahim Fayez al-Shamsi; 32 brs.

Emirates NBD PJSC: POB 2923, Beniyas Rd, Deira, Dubai; tel. (4) 2256256; fax (4) 2227662; e-mail ibrahims@emiratesbank.com; internet www.emiratesnbd.com; f. 2007 by merger of Emirates Bank Int. PJSC with Nat. Bank of Dubai PJSC; 56% owned by Govt of Dubai; cap. 5,557.7m., res 20,328.9m., dep. 214,772.8m. (Dec. 2009); Chair. Ahmad Humaid al-Tayer; CEO Rick Pudner; 132 brs.

First Gulf Bank: POB 6316, Sheikh Zayed St, Abu Dhabi; tel. (2) 6816666; fax (2) 6814282; e-mail info@fgb.ae; internet www.fgb.ae; f. 1979; cap. 1,375.0m., res 14,307.9m., dep. 88,362.4m. (Dec. 2009); Chair. Sheikh Mansour bin Zayed Al Nahyan; Man. Dir Abd al-Hamid Said; 19 brs.

Investbank PSC: POB 1885, Sharjah; tel. (6) 5694440; fax (6) 5694442; e-mail custserv@invest-bank.ae; internet www.investbank.ae; f. 1975; cap. 1,155m., res 490m., dep. 7,360m. (Dec. 2009); Chair. Dr Abdullah Omran Taryam; Gen. Man. Sami R. Farhat; 12 brs.

Mashreqbank PSC: POB 1250, Omer bin al-Khattab St, Deira, Dubai; tel. (4) 2223333; fax (4) 2226061; internet www.mashreqbank.com; f. 1967 as Bank of Oman; present name adopted 1993; cap. 1,610.2m., res 812.3m., dep. 69,098.2m. (Dec. 2009); Chair. Abdullah bin Ahmad al-Ghurair; CEO Abd al-Aziz Abdullah al-Ghurair; 57 brs in the UAE, 22 abroad.

Al-Masraf: POB 46733, ARBIFT Bldg, Hamdan St, Tourist Club Area, Abu Dhabi; tel. (2) 6721900; fax (2) 6777550; e-mail arbiftho@emirates.net.ae; internet www.arbift.com; f. 1976 as Arab Bank for Investment and Foreign Trade; renamed as above in 2007; jointly owned by the UAE Federal Govt, the Libyan Arab Foreign Bank and the Banque Extérieure d'Algérie; cap. 1,500.0m., res 972.4m., dep. 8,275.6m. (Dec. 2009); Pres. and Chair. Dr Abd al-Hafid M. Zlitni; Gen. Man. Ibrahim Nasser Rashid Lootah; 7 brs in the UAE.

National Bank of Abu Dhabi (NBAD): POB 4, Tariq ibn Ziad St, Abu Dhabi; tel. (2) 6111111; fax (2) 6275738; e-mail CustomerSupport@nbad.com; internet www.nbad.com; f. 1968; 73% owned by Abu Dhabi Investment Council, 3% by foreign institutions and the remainder by UAE citizens; issued Islamic bonds for the first time in June 2010; cap. 2,174.2m., res 15,098.1m., dep. 154,727.2m. (Dec. 2009); Chair. Nasser Ahmad Khalifa al-Suwaidi; Chief Exec. Michael H. Tomalin; 73 brs in the UAE, 31 abroad.

National Bank of Fujairah PSC: POB 2979, Dubai; tel. (4) 3971700; fax (4) 3973922; e-mail nbfho@nbf.ae; internet www.nbf.ae; f. 1982; owned jointly by Govt of Fujairah (36.78%), Govt of Dubai (9.78%), and UAE citizens and cos (51.25%); cap. 1,100m., res 354m., dep. 8,799m. (Dec. 2009); Chair. Sheikh Saleh bin Muhammad al-Sharqi; CEO Steve Mullins; 11 brs.

National Bank of Ras al-Khaimah PSC (RAKBANK): POB 5300, Rakbank Bldg, Oman St, al-Nakheel, Ras al-Khaimah; tel. (7) 2281127; fax (7) 2283238; e-mail nbrakho@emirates.net.ae; internet www.rakbank.ae; f. 1976; 52.75% owned by Govt of Ras al-Khaimah; cap. 962.0m., res 1,278.1m., dep. 13,953.4m. (Dec. 2009); Chair. Sheikh Omar bin Saqr al-Qasimi; Gen. Man. Graham Honeybill; 16 brs.

National Bank of Umm al-Qaiwain PSC: POB 800, Umm al-Qaiwain Private Properties Dept Bldg, King Faisal St, Umm al-Qaiwain; tel. (6) 7655225; fax (6) 7655440; e-mail nbuq@nbq.ae; internet www.nbq.ae; f. 1982; cap. 1,452m., res 1,021m., dep. 9,169m. (Dec. 2009); Chair. Sheikh Saud bin Rashid al-Mu'alla; Man. Dir and CEO Sheikh Nasser bin Rashid al-Mu'alla; 16 brs.

Noor Islamic Bank PJSC: POB 8822, Dubai; tel. (4) 4268888; fax (4) 3456789; internet www.noorbank.com; f. 2008; Shari'a-compliant services; 25% owned by Investment Corpn of Dubai, 25% by Dubai Group, 5% by UAE Federal Govt, 45% by private investors; total assets 22,000m.; Chair. Sheikh Ahmad bin Saeed Al Maktoum; CEO Hussain al-Qemzi; 10 brs.

Sharjah Islamic Bank: POB 4, Al-Borj Ave, Sharjah; tel. (6) 5115123; fax (6) 5681699; e-mail contact.center@sib.ae; internet www.sib.ae; f. 1976 as Nat. Bank of Sharjah; present name adopted 2005, reflecting the bank's conversion to Shari'a-compliant operations; commercial bank; cap. 2,310.0m., res 1,533.0m., dep. 10,503.9m. (Dec. 2009); Chair. Sheikh Sultan bin Muhammad bin Sultan al-Qassimi; CEO Muhammad Ahmad Abdullah; 13 brs.

Union National Bank (UNB): POB 3865, Salam St, Abu Dhabi; tel. (2) 6741600; fax (2) 6786080; e-mail feedback@unb.co.ae; internet www.unb.co.ae; f. 1983; fmrly Bank of Credit and Commerce (Emirates); cap. 2,062.5m., res 4,302.4m., dep. 54,476.0m. (Dec. 2009); Chair. Sheikh Nahyan bin Mubarak Al Nahyan; CEO Muhammad Nasr Abdeen; 26 brs in the UAE.

United Arab Bank: POB 25022, 6th Floor, HE Sheikh Abdullah bin Salem al-Qassimi Bldg, al-Qassimi St, Sharjah; tel. (6) 5733900; fax (6) 5733907; e-mail uarbae@emirates.net.ae; internet www.uab.ae; f. 1975; affiliated to Société Générale, France; 35% owned by Commercial Bank of Qatar; cap. 996m., res 590m., dep. 5,196m. (Dec. 2009); Chair. Sheikh Faisal bin Sultan bin Salem al-Qassimi; CEO Paul Trowbridge; 9 brs.

Development Bank

Emirates Industrial Bank: POB 2722, 6th Floor, Arab Monetary Fund Bldg, Corniche Rd, Abu Dhabi; tel. (2) 6339700; fax (2) 6319191; e-mail projects_auh@emiratesindustrialbank.net; internet www.eib.ae; f. 1982; offers low-cost loans to enterprises with at least 51% local ownership; 100% state-owned; cap. 200m.; Chair. Obaid Humaid al-Tayer; Gen. Man. Muhammad Abd al-Baki Muhammad.

Bankers' Association

United Arab Emirates Bankers' Association: POB 44307, Abu Dhabi; tel. (2) 4467706; fax (2) 4463718; e-mail ebauae@emirates.net.ae; internet www.eba-ae.com; f. 1983; Chair. Ahmad Humaid al-Tayer (Chair., Commercial Bank of Dubai); Gen. Man. Fathi M. Skaik.

SOVEREIGN WEALTH FUNDS

Abu Dhabi Investment Authority (ADIA): 211 Corniche, POB 3600, Abu Dhabi; tel. (2) 4150000; fax (2) 4151000; internet www.adia.ae; f. 1976; manages Govt of Abu Dhabi's investment portfolio; Chair. Sheikh Khalifa bin Zayed Al Nahyan (President of the UAE and Ruler of Abu Dhabi); Man. Dir Sheikh Hamad bin Zayed Al Nahyan.

Abu Dhabi Investment Company (Invest AD): POB 46309, Abu Dhabi; tel. (2) 6658100; fax (2) 6650575; e-mail info@investad.ae; internet www.investad.ae; f. 1977; investment of govt funds, and advisory activities in the UAE and the Middle East; 98% owned by Abu Dhabi Investment Council and 2% by Nat. Bank of Abu Dhabi; Chair. Khalifa M. al-Kindi; CEO Nazem Fawwaz al-Kudsi.

Emirates Investment Authority: POB 3235, Abu Dhabi; e-mail careers@eia.gov.ae; internet www.eia.gov.ae; f. 2007; federal sovereign wealth fund; Chair. Sheikh Mansour bin Zayed Al Nahyan (Deputy Prime Minister and Minister of Presidential Affairs); CEO Mubarak Rashid al-Mansouri.

Investment Corporation of Dubai: POB 333888, Dubai International Financial Center, 6th Floor, DIFC Gate Village, Dubai; tel. (4) 7071333; fax (4) 7071444; e-mail info@icd.gov.ae; internet www.icd.gov.ae; f. 2006; manages Govt of Dubai's investment portfolio; Chair. Sheikh Muhammad bin Rashid Al Maktoum (Ruler of Dubai); Exec. Dir and CEO Muhammad I. al-Shaibani.

RAK Investment Authority: POB 31291, Ras al-Khaimah; tel. (7) 2446533; fax (7) 2447202; e-mail gm@rakinvestmentauthority.com; internet www.rak-ia.com; f. 2005; sovereign wealth fund of Ras al-Khaimah Govt; cap. US $1,200m. (2009); CEO Dr Khater Masaad.

STOCK EXCHANGES

Abu Dhabi Securities Exchange (ADX): POB 54500, Abu Dhabi; tel. (2) 6277777; fax (2) 6128728; e-mail info@adx.ae; internet www.adx.ae; f. 2000 as Abu Dhabi Securities Market, renamed as above 2008; 67 listed cos (Jan. 2010); Chair. Nasser Ahmad al-Suwaidi; Dir-Gen. Tom Healy.

Dubai Financial Market (DFM): POB 9700, Dubai; tel. (4) 3055555; fax (4) 3314924; e-mail helpdesk@dfm.co.ae; internet www.dfm.co.ae; f. 2000; restructured to comply with Shari'a principles in 2006; 63 listed cos, seven bonds, 15 mutual funds (Sept. 2008); market capitalization AED 61,370m. (Feb. 2004); Chair. Abd al-Jalil Yousuf; CEO and Man. Dir Essa Abd al-Fattah Kazim.

NASDAQ Dubai: POB 53536, Level 7, The Exchange Bldg, Gate District, Dubai International Financial Centre, Dubai; tel. (4) 3612222; fax (4) 3612130; e-mail corpcomm@nasdaqdubai.com; internet www.nasdaqdubai.com; f. 2005 as Dubai Int. Financial Exchange; renamed as above 2008; Chair. Abd al-Wahed al-Fahim; CEO Jeffrey H. Singer.

Regulatory Authority

Securities and Commodities Authority: POB 33733, Abu Dhabi; tel. (2) 6277888; fax (2) 6274600; e-mail contactus@sca.ae; internet sca-mo1.sca.ae; f. 2000; Chair. Sultan bin Said al-Mansouri (Minister of Economy); CEO Abdullah Salem al-Turifi.

INSURANCE

Abu Dhabi National Insurance Co (ADNIC): POB 839, Abu Dhabi; tel. (2) 8040100; fax (2) 6268600; e-mail adnic@adnic.ae; internet www.adnic.ae; f. 1972; subscribed 25% by the Govt of Abu Dhabi and 75% by UAE nationals; all classes of insurance; Chair. Khalifa Muhammad al-Kindi.

Al-Ahlia Insurance Co: POB 128, Ras al-Khaimah; tel. (7) 2221479; e-mail contactus@alahli.com; internet www.alahli.com;

THE UNITED ARAB EMIRATES

f. 1977; Chair. ABDULLAH S. BAHAMDAN; Gen. Man. YAHYA NOUR ED-DIN; 3 brs.

Al-Ain Ahlia Insurance Co: POB 3077, Abu Dhabi; tel. (2) 4459900; fax (2) 4456685; e-mail alainins@emirates.net.ae; internet www.alaininsurance.com; f. 1975; Chair. MUHAMMAD BIN J. R. AL-BADIE AL-DHAHIRI; Gen. Man. MUHAMMAD MAZHAR HAMADEH; brs in Dubai, Sharjah, Tarif, Ghouifat and al-Ain.

Dubai Insurance Co PSC: POB 3027, Dubai; tel. (4) 2693030; fax (4) 2693727; e-mail info@dubins.ae; internet www.dubins.ae; f. 1970; Chair. BUTI OBAID AL-MULLA.

Al-Fujairah National Insurance Co PSC: POB 277, Fujairah; tel. (9) 2233355; fax (9) 2224344; e-mail ho@fujinsco.ae; internet www.afnic.ae; f. 1976; 84.75% owned by Govt of Fujairah; cap. 75m.; Chair. ABD AL-GHAFOUR BAHROUZIAN; Gen. Man. ANTOINE MAALOULI.

Sharjah Insurance Co: POB 792, Sharjah; tel. (6) 5686690; fax (6) 5686545; e-mail sico@emirates.net.ae; internet www.shjins.com; f. 1970; Chair. Sheikh MUHAMMAD BIN SAOUD AL-QASSIMI; Gen. Man. AHMED KHATER.

Union Insurance Co PSC: POB 1225, Ajman; tel. (6) 7466996; fax (6) 7466997; e-mail unins@emirates.net.ae; internet www.unioninsuranceuae.com; national insurance co of Ajman emirate; Chair. ABDULLAH HUMAID AL-MAZROUI; Gen. Man. SAMER S. BUSHNAQ.

Trade and Industry

DEVELOPMENT ORGANIZATIONS

Abu Dhabi Fund for Development (ADFD): POB 814, al-Salam St, Abu Dhabi; tel. (2) 6441000; fax (2) 6440800; e-mail ifo@adfd.ae; internet www.adfd.ae; f. 1971; offers economic aid to other Arab states and other developing countries in support of their development; cap. AED 4,000m.; Dir-Gen. SAID KHALFAN MATAR AL-ROMAITHI.

Abu Dhabi Investment Council (ADIC): POB 3600, Abu Dhabi; tel. (2) 4150000; fax (2) 4151000; f. 2006 as successor to Abu Dhabi Investment Authority (f. 1976); responsible for co-ordinating Abu Dhabi's investment policy; Chair. Sheikh KHALIFA BIN ZAYED AL NAHYAN; 1 br. overseas.

Department of Economic Development Abu Dhabi: POB 12, Abu Dhabi; tel. (2) 6727200; fax (2) 6727749; e-mail ier@adeconomy.ae; internet www.adeconomy.ae; f. 1974; supervises Abu Dhabi's Economic Vision 2030 programme; Chair. NASSER AL-SOWAIDI; Under-Sec. MUHAMMAD OMAR ABDULLAH.

General Holding Corpn (GHC): POB 4499, Abu Dhabi; tel. (2) 6144444; fax (2) 6312857; e-mail info@ghc.ae; internet www.ghc.ae; f. 1979 as Gen. Industry Corpn; name changed as above 2004; responsible for the promotion of non-petroleum-related industry; Chair. Sheikh HAMAD BIN ZAYED AL NAHYAN; Vice-Chair. NASSER AHMAD AL-SOWAIDI.

CHAMBERS OF COMMERCE

Federation of UAE Chambers of Commerce and Industry: POB 3014, Abu Dhabi; tel. (2) 6214144; fax (2) 6339210; POB 8886, Dubai; tel. (4) 2955500; fax (4) 2941212; e-mail info@fcciuae.ae; internet www.fcciuae.ae; f. 1976; seven mem. chambers; Chair. SALAH SALEM BIN OMAIR AL-SHAMSI; Sec.-Gen. ABDULLAH SULTAN ABDULLAH.

Abu Dhabi Chamber of Commerce and Industry: POB 662, Abu Dhabi; tel. (2) 6214000; fax (2) 6215867; e-mail services@adcci.gov.ae; internet www.abudhabichamber.ae; f. 1969; 45,000 mems; Pres. SALAH SALEM BIN OMAIR AL-SHAMSI; Dir-Gen. MUHAMMAD RASHID AL-HAMELI.

Ajman Chamber of Commerce and Industry: POB 662, Ajman; tel. (6) 7422177; fax (6) 7471666; e-mail info@ajcci.gov.ae; internet www.ajcci.gov.ae; f. 1977; Chair. OBEID BIN ALI AL-MUHAIRI; Dir-Gen. MUHAMMAD AL-HAMRANI.

Dubai Chamber of Commerce and Industry: POB 1457, Dubai; tel. (4) 2280000; fax (4) 2211646; e-mail customercare@dubaichamber.ae; internet www.dubaichamber.ae; f. 1965; 108,000 mems (2007); Chair. ABD AL-RAHMAN SAIF AL-GHURAIR; Dir-Gen. HAMAD BUAIMIM.

Fujairah Chamber of Commerce, Industry and Agriculture: POB 738, Fujairah; tel. (9) 2222400; fax (9) 2221464; internet www.fujcci.ae; Pres. SAID ALI KHAMAS; Dir-Gen. MUHAMMAD KHALID AL-JASSEM.

Ras al-Khaimah Chamber of Commerce and Industry: POB 87, Ras al-Khaimah; tel. (7) 2260000; fax (7) 2260112; e-mail rcci@rakchamber.ae; internet www.rakchamber.ae; f. 1967; 17,840 mems (Dec. 2007); Chair. YOUSUF AL-NEAIMI; Dir-Gen. Dr NASER AHMED SALMEEN.

Sharjah Chamber of Commerce and Industry: POB 580, Sharjah; tel. (6) 5116600; fax (6) 5681119; e-mail scci@sharjah.gov.ae; internet www.sharjah.gov.ae; f. 1970; 33,500 mems; Chair. AHMAD MUHAMMAD AL-MIDFA'A; Dir-Gen. SAID OBAID AL-JARWAN.

Umm al-Qaiwain Chamber of Commerce and Industry: POB 436, Umm al-Qaiwain; tel. (6) 7651111; fax (6) 7657056; e-mail uaqcci@emirates.net.ae; Pres. ABDULLAH RASHID AL-KHARJI; Man. Dir SHAKIR AL-ZAYANI.

STATE HYDROCARBONS COMPANIES

Abu Dhabi

Supreme Petroleum Council: POB 898, Abu Dhabi; tel. (2) 602000; fax (2) 6023389; f. 1988; assumed authority and responsibility for the administration and supervision of all petroleum affairs in Abu Dhabi; Chair. Sheikh KHALIFA BIN ZAYED AL NAHYAN; Sec.-Gen. YOUSUF BIN OMEIR BIN YOUSUF.

Abu Dhabi National Oil Co (ADNOC): POB 898, Abu Dhabi; tel. (2) 6020000; fax (2) 6023389; e-mail adnoc@adnoc.com; internet www.adnoc.ae; f. 1971; cap. AED 7,500m.; state co; deals in all phases of oil industry; owns two refineries: one on Umm al-Nar island and one at Ruwais; Habshan Gas Treatment Plant (scheduled for partial privatization); gas pipeline distribution network; a salt and chlorine plant; holds 60% participation in operations of ADMA-OPCO and ADCO, and 88% of ZADCO; has 100% control of Abu Dhabi Nat. Oil Co for Oil Distribution (ADNOC-FOD), Abu Dhabi Nat. Tanker Co (ADNATCO), Nat. Drilling Co (NDC) and interests in numerous other cos, both in the UAE and overseas; ADNOC is operated by Supreme Petroleum Council, Chair. Sheikh KHALIFA BIN ZAYED AL NAHYAN; CEO YOUSUF BIN OMEIR BIN YOUSUF.

Subsidiaries include:

Abu Dhabi Co for Onshore Oil Operations (ADCO): POB 270, Abu Dhabi; tel. (2) 6040000; fax (2) 6665523; e-mail webmaster@adco.ae; internet www.adco.ae; f. 1978; shareholders are ADNOC (60%), BP, Shell and Total (9.5% each), ExxonMobil (9.5%) and Partex (2%); oil exploration, production and export operations from onshore oilfields; average production (1990): 1.2m. b/d; Chair. YOUSUF BIN OMEIR BIN YOUSUF; Gen. Man. ABD AL-MUNIM SAIF AL-KINDI.

Abu Dhabi Drilling Chemicals and Products Ltd (ADDCAP): POB 46121, Abu Dhabi; tel. (2) 6029000; fax (2) 6029010; e-mail addcap@emirates.net.ae; f. 1975; production of drilling chemicals and provision of marine services; wholly owned subsidiary of ADNOC; Chair. YOUSUF BIN OMEIR BIN YOUSUF; Gen. Man. MAHFOUD A. DARBOUL AL-SHEHHI.

Abu Dhabi Gas Industries Co (GASCO): POB 665, Abu Dhabi; tel. (2) 6030000; fax (2) 6037414; e-mail info@gasco.ae; internet www.gasco.ae; f. 1978; started production in 1981; recovers condensate and LPG from Asab, Bab and Bu Hasa fields for delivery to Ruwais natural gas liquids fractionation plant; capacity of 22,000 metric tons per day; 68% owned by ADNOC; Total, Shell Gas and Partex have a minority interest; Chair. YOUSUF OMEIR BIN YOUSUF; Gen. Man. MUHAMMAD SAHOO AL-SUWAIDI.

Abu Dhabi Gas Liquefaction Co (ADGAS): POB 3500, Abu Dhabi; tel. (2) 6061111; fax (2) 6065500; e-mail info@adgas.com; internet www.adgas.com; f. 1973; 70% owned by ADNOC, 15% by Mitsui and Co, 10% by BP, 5% by Total; operates LGSC and the LNG plant on Das Island, which uses natural gas produced in association with oil from offshore fields and has a design capacity of approx. 2.3m. metric tons of LNG per year and 1.29m. tons of LPG per year; the liquefied gas is sold to the Tokyo Electric Power Co, Japan; Chair. ABDULLAH NASSER AL-SUWAIDI; Gen. Man. SAIF AHMAD AL-GHAFLI.

Abu Dhabi Marine Operating Co (ADMA-OPCO): POB 303, Abu Dhabi; tel. (2) 6060000; fax (2) 6064888; e-mail webmaster@adma.ae; internet www.adma-opco.com; operates a concession 60% owned by ADNOC, 40% by Abu Dhabi Marine Areas Ltd (BP, Total and Japan Oil Devt Co); f. 1977 as an operator for the concession; production (1984): 67,884,769 barrels (8,955,721 metric tons); Chair. YOUSUF BIN OMEIR BIN YOUSUF; Gen. Man. ALI R. AL-JARWAN.

Abu Dhabi Oil Refining Co (TAKREER): POB 3593, Abu Dhabi; tel. (2) 6027000; fax (2) 6027001; e-mail publicrelation@takreer.com; internet www.takreer.com; refining of crude petroleum; production of chlorine and related chemicals; Chair. YOUSUF BIN OMEIR BIN YOUSUF; Gen. Man. JASIM ALI AL-SAYEGH.

ADNOC Distribution: POB 4188, Abu Dhabi; tel. (2) 6771300; fax (2) 6722322; e-mail Information@adnoc-dist.ae; internet www.adnoc-dist.co.ae; 100% owned by ADNOC; distributes petroleum products in UAE and world-wide; Chair. YOUSUF BIN OMEIR BIN YOUSUF; Gen. Man. JAMAL JABER AL-DHAREEF.

National Drilling Co (NDC): POB 4017, Abu Dhabi; tel. (2) 6776100; fax (2) 6779937; e-mail webmaster@ndc.ae; internet www.ndc.ae; drilling operations; Chair. ABDULLAH NASSER AL-SUWAIDI; Gen. Man. ABDALLAH SAEED AL-SUWAIDI.

National Petroleum Construction Co (NPCC): POB 2058, Abu Dhabi; tel. (2) 5549000; fax (2) 5549111; e-mail npccnet@eim.ae;

THE UNITED ARAB EMIRATES

internet www.npcc.ae; f. 1973; 'turnkey' construction and maintenance of offshore facilities for the petroleum and gas industries; cap. AED 100m.; Chair. HUSSAIN JASEM AL-NOWAIS; CEO AQEEL A. MADHI.

Ajman

Ajman National Oil Co (AJNOC): POB 410, Ajman; tel. (6) 7421218; f. 1983; 50% govt-owned, 50% held by Canadian and private Arab interests.

Dubai

Dubai Petroleum Establishment: POB 2222, Dubai; tel. (4) 3432222; fax (4) 3012200; internet www.dubaipetroleum.ae; f. 1963 as Dubai Petroleum Co; reorg. and renamed as above 2007; wholly owned by Dubai authorities; responsible for managing Dubai's offshore petroleum assets; Gen. Man. JEFF SEVERIN.

DUGAS (Dubai Natural Gas Co Ltd): POB 4311, Dubai (Location: Jebel Ali); tel. (4) 8846000; fax (4) 8846118; wholly owned by Dubai authorities; Dep. Chair. and Dir SULTAN AHMAD BIN SULAYEM.

Emarat: POB 9400, Dubai; tel. (4) 3434444; fax (4) 3433393; e-mail info@emarat.ae; internet www.emarat.ae; f. 1981 as Emirates General Petroleum Corpn, renamed as above 1996; wholly owned by Ministry of Finance; marketing and distribution of petroleum; Chair. MUHAMMAD BIN DHAEN AL-HAMILI (Minister of Energy); Gen. Man. JAMAL AL-MIDFA.

Emirates National Oil Co (ENOC): POB 6442, ENOC Complex, Sheikh Rashid Rd, Dubai; tel. (4) 3374400; fax (4) 3134702; e-mail webmaster@enoc.com; internet www.enoc.com; f. 1993; responsible for management of Dubai-owned cos in petroleum-marketing sector; Chief Exec. SAEED KHOORY.

Emirates Petroleum Products Co Pvt. Ltd (EPPCO): POB 5589, Dubai; tel. (4) 372131; fax (4) 3031605; e-mail f&e@eppcouae.com; internet www.eppcouae.com; f. 1980; jt venture between Govt of Dubai and Caltex Alkhaleej Marketing; sales of petroleum products, bunkering fuel and bitumen; Chair. Sheikh HAMDAN BIN RASHID AL MAKTOUM.

Sedco-Houston Oil Group: POB 702, Dubai; tel. (4) 3224141; holds onshore concession of over 400,000 ha as well as the offshore concession fmrly held by Texas Pacific Oil; Pres. CARL F. THORNE.

Sharjah

A Supreme Petroleum Council was established in Sharjah in 1999; it was to assume the responsibilities of the Petroleum and Mineral Affairs Department.

Petroleum and Mineral Affairs Department: POB 188, Sharjah; tel. (6) 5541888; Dir ISMAIL A. WAHID.

Sharjah Liquefied Petroleum Gas Co (SHALCO): POB 787, Sharjah; tel. (6) 5286333; fax (6) 5286111; e-mail shalco@shalco.ae; f. 1984; 100% owned by Sharjah authorities; gas-processing; producer of liquified commercial propane and commercial butane; Dir-Gen. SALEH AL-ALI.

Umm al-Qaiwain

Petroleum and Mineral Affairs Department: POB 9, Umm al-Qaiwain; tel. (6) 7666034; Chair. Sheikh SULTAN BIN AHMAD AL-MU'ALLA.

UTILITIES

Abu Dhabi

Regulation and Supervision Bureau: POB 32800, Abu Dhabi; tel. (2) 4439333; fax (2) 4439334; e-mail bureau@rsb.gov.ae; internet www.rsb.gov.ae; f. 1998; regulatory authority; Chair. MUHAMMAD AHMAD AL-BOWARDI; Dir-Gen. NICK CARTER.

Abu Dhabi Water and Electricity Authority (ADWEA): POB 6120, Abu Dhabi; tel. (2) 6943333; fax (2) 6943192; e-mail pr@adwea.gov.ae; internet www.adwea.gov.ae; f. 1998 to manage the water and electricity sectors and oversee the privatization process; Chair. Dr AHMAD BIN MUBARAK AL-MAZROUI.

Abu Dhabi Distribution Co: POB 219, Abu Dhabi; tel. (2) 6423000; fax (2) 6426033; e-mail contactcentre@addc.ae; internet www.addc.ae; f. 1998; distribution of water and electricity; Chair. Sheikh DIAB BIN ZAYED AL NAHYAN.

Abu Dhabi National Energy Co (TAQA): POB 55224, Abu Dhabi; tel. (2) 6943662; fax (2) 6422555; e-mail info@taqa.ae; internet www.taqa.ae; f. 2005; 51% owned by ADWEA; owns assets in power, water, petroleum and mineral sectors in the UAE and abroad; provides more than 85% of the water and electricity produced in Abu Dhabi; Chair. HAMAD AL-HURR AL-SUWAIDI; Gen. Man. CARL SHELDON.

Abu Dhabi Transmission and Dispatch Co: POB 173, Abu Dhabi; tel. (2) 6414000; fax (2) 6426333; internet www.transco.ae; f. 1999; operation and devt of the transmission network for water and electricity; Chair. Dr ABDULLAH AL-SUWAIDI; Man. Dir DAVID COPESTAKE.

Abu Dhabi Water and Electricity Co (ADWEC): POB 51111, Abu Dhabi; tel. (2) 6943333; fax (2) 6425773; e-mail webmaster@adwec.ae; internet www.adwec.ae; f. 1999; responsible for forecasting and managing the supply and demand of electricity and water; Chair. AHMAD SAIF AL-DARMAKI; Man. Dir GERHARDT GLEISSNER.

Al-Ain Distribution Co: POB 1065, al-Ain; tel. (3) 7636000; fax (3) 7629949; e-mail customercare@aadc.ae; internet www.aadc.ae; f. 1999; distribution of water and electricity; Chair. Sheikh DIAB BIN ZAYED AL NAHYAN.

Bayounah Power Co: POB 33477, Abu Dhabi; tel. (2) 6731100; fax (2) 6730403; e-mail webmaster@adwea.gov.ae; internet www.bpc.ae; f. 1999; operates two power stations at Abu Dhabi (also water desalination) and Al-Ain; Chair. AHMAD HILAL AL-KUWAITI; Man. Dir ABD AL-JALEEL AL-KHOURY.

Al-Mirfa Power Co: POB 32277, Abu Dhabi; tel. (2) 8833044; fax (2) 8833011; e-mail info@ampc.ae; internet www.ampc.ae; f. 1999 to control Mirfa and Madinat Zayed plants; capacity 300 MW electricity per day, 37m. gallons water per day; Chair. MUHAMMAD FOULAD; Gen. Man. PHILIP GRAHAM TILSON.

As part of the privatization programme, several independent power and water projects (IWPPs) have been established, including Arabian Power Co, Emirates CMS Power Co, Gulf Total Tractebel Power Co, Shuweihat CMS International Power Co, and Taweelah Asia Power Co (TAPCO). In each IWPP, ADWEA retains a 60% shareholding while the remaining 40% is owned by private investors.

Dubai

Dubai Electricity and Water Authority (DEWA): POB 564, Dubai; tel. (4) 3244444; fax (4) 3248111; e-mail customercare@dewa.gov.ae; internet www.dewa.gov.ae; f. 1992 following merger of Dubai Electricity Co and Dubai Water Dept; management and devt of the water and electricity sectors; CEO and Man. Dir SAID MUHAMMAD AHMAD AL-TAYER.

Northern Emirates (Ajman, Fujairah, Ras al-Khaimah and Umm al-Qaiwain)

Federal Water and Electricity Authority: POB 1672, Dubai; tel. (4) 2315555; fax (4) 2809977; e-mail cs@fewa.gov.ae; internet www.fewa.gov.ae; generation and distribution of electricity and water in the northern emirates; operates six power-generating plants and three water desalination plants; scheduled for part-privatization; Gen. Man. MUHAMMAD MUHAMMAD SALEH.

Sharjah

Sharjah Electricity and Water Authority (SEWA): Sharjah; tel. (2) 5288888; fax (2) 5288000; e-mail contactus@sewa.gov.ae; internet www.sewa.gov.ae; Chair. Sheikh SULTAN BIN MUHAMMAD AL-QASSIMI.

Transport

RAILWAYS

The first phase of an urban light-railway system, Dubai Metro—with 10 of the 29 planned stations in operation on the Red Line—opened in September 2009. By May 2011 27 stations had been opened. Construction work on the 23-km Green Line was due for completion in August 2011, while work on the Purple Line—linking Dubai International Airport with the new Al Maktoum International Airport (see below)—was expected to open in 2012. A fourth line was also planned. In 2006 the Abu Dhabi authorities announced plans for the construction of a 130-km metro system, projected for completion by 2015. The project formed an integral part of Abu Dhabi's Surface Transport Masterplan, which was to allocate up to US $20,000m. to road, rail and marine transport infrastructure up to 2030. Plans for the construction of a federal railway network for passengers and freight, linking the seven emirates, gained final government approval in March 2009. The 1,000-km network was to be constructed in two phases, with the first phase, involving freight and industrial services, expected to take five years to complete. It was anticipated that the federal network would eventually be linked to a planned railway for the member countries of the GCC.

Etihad Rail: f. 2009 as Union Railway Co; current name adopted 2011; charged with construction of, and eventual operations of, a federal railway network for both passengers and freight, to extend throughout the UAE; first phase of construction—comprising a 264-km freight line between Ruwais and Habshan and Shah in Abu Dhabi—expected to commence in 2011; wholly state-owned; Chair. NASIR AL-SUWAIDI; CEO RICHARD BOWKER.

THE UNITED ARAB EMIRATES

ROADS

The road network in the UAE is undergoing rapid development. Abu Dhabi and Dubai are linked by a good road that is dual carriageway for most of its length. This road forms part of a west coast route from Shaam, at the UAE border with the northern enclave of Oman, through Dubai and Abu Dhabi to Tarif. An east coast route links Dibba with Muscat, Oman. Other roads include the Abu Dhabi–al-Ain highway and roads linking Sharjah and Ras al-Khaimah, and Sharjah and Dhaid. An underwater tunnel links Dubai Town and Deira by dual carriageway and pedestrian subway. Plans for the construction of a causeway between the UAE and Qatar were announced in December 2004; however, the project was subsequently delayed owing to objections from Saudi Arabia. An extensive development plan announced in July 2006, the Dubai Strategic Plan, was to allocate AED 44,000m. to road infrastructure up to 2020 and to include the construction of 500 km of new roads, more than 95 new interchanges, and upgrades of the emirate's existing road network. In addition, contracts for the construction of a 327-km Mafraq–Ghoueifat highway, linking the UAE with Qatar and Saudi Arabia, were awarded in December 2010. In 2008 there was a total paved road network of 4,080 km.

SHIPPING

Dubai has been the main commercial centre in the Gulf for many years. Abu Dhabi has also become an important port since the opening of the first section of its artificial harbour, Port Zayed. Abu Dhabi's port capacity is to be greatly expanded with the construction of Khalifa Port and Industrial Zone; construction work on the offshore facility near Taweelah began in mid-2008. There are smaller ports in Sharjah, Fujairah, Ras al-Khaimah and Umm al-Qaiwain. Dubai possesses two docks capable of handling 500,000-metric-ton tankers, seven repair berths and a third dock able to accommodate 1,000,000-ton tankers. The Dubai port of Mina Jebel Ali, which was to be expanded at a cost of some US $1,362m., has the largest man-made harbour in the world. An expansion of facilities at Sharjah's Khor Fakkan Port was completed in mid-2009, while plans were also under way to expand Ras al-Khaimah's Mina Saqr Port. The first phase of the Mina Saqr project was completed in 2007, increasing the port's annual capacity to 350,000 20-ft equivalent units (TEU); upon completion of the second phase, capacity would increase to 1.7m. TEUs per year.

Abu Dhabi

Abu Dhabi Ports Co (ADPC): Mina Zayed, Abu Dhabi; tel. (2) 6952000; fax (2) 6952111; e-mail info@adpc.ae; internet www.adpc.ae; responsible for the devt and regulation of Abu Dhabi's ports and related industrial zones; Chair. Dr SULTAN AHMAD AL-JABER; CEO TONY DOUGLAS.

Abu Dhabi Terminals: POB 422, Port Zayed, Abu Dhabi; tel. (2) 6730600; fax (2) 6731023; e-mail info@adterminals.ae; internet www.adterminals.ae; f. 2006; replaced Abu Dhabi Seaports Authority (f. 1972); administers Port Zayed, Musaffah port and Freeport; facilities at Port Zayed include 21 deep-water berths and five container gantry cranes of 40 metric tons capacity; cold storage 20,500 tons; handled a total of 390,087 TEUs in 2008; jt venture between ADPC and Mubadala; Chair. Sheikh SAID BIN ZAYED AL NAHYAN; CEO MUHAMMAD AL-MANNAEI.

Abu Dhabi National Tanker Co (ADNATCO): POB 2977, 11th and 12th Floors, Takreer Tower, Khalifa St, Abu Dhabi; tel. (2) 6028400; fax (2) 6723999; e-mail info@adnatcongsco.com; internet www.adnatco.com; f. 1975; subsidiary of ADNOC, operating owned and chartered tankships, and transporting crude petroleum, refined products and sulphur; Chair. NASSER AHMAD AL-SUWAIDI; Gen. Man. ALI OBAID AL-YABHOUNI.

Abu Dhabi Petroleum Ports Operating Co (IRSHAD): POB 61, Abu Dhabi; tel. (2) 6028000; fax (2) 6742094; e-mail info@irshad.ae; internet www.irshad.ae; f. 1979; 60% owned by ADNOC, 40% by LAMNALCO Kuwait; manages Jebel Dhanna, Ruwais, Das Island, Umm al-Nar and Zirku Island SPM terminal, Mubarraz; operates fleet of 36 vessels; cap. AED 50m.; Chair. YOUSUF BIN OMEIR BIN YOUSUF; Gen. Man. KHALIFA M. AL-GOBAISI.

National Marine Services Co (NMS): POB 7202, Abu Dhabi; tel. (2) 6339800; fax (2) 6211239; 60% owned by ADNOC, 40% by Jackson Marine Corpn, USA; operates, charters and leases specialized offshore support vessels; cap. AED 25m.; Chair. SOHAIL FARES AL-MAZRUI; Gen. Man. Capt. HASSAN A. SHARIF.

Dubai

Dubai Ports World (DP World): POB 17000, 5th Floor, JAFZA 17, Dubai; tel. (4) 8811110; fax (4) 48811331; e-mail info@dpworld.com; internet www.dpworld.ae; f. 2005 by merger of Dubai Ports Authority (f. 1991 by merger of Mina Jebel Ali and Mina Rashid) and Dubai Ports Int. (f. 1999); subsidiary of state-controlled Dubai World; 23% sold via initial public offering Nov. 2007; storage areas and facilities for loading and discharge of vessels; operates ports of Mina Jebel Ali and Mina Rashid in Dubai, Port Zayed in Abu Dhabi, Fujairah Port and numerous other international facilities; handled 42m. TEUs world-wide in 2006; CEO MUHAMMAD SHARAF; Sr Vice-Pres. and Man. Dir, UAE Region MUHAMMAD AL-MUALLEM.

Drydocks World—Dubai: POB 8988, Dubai; tel. (4) 3450626; fax (4) 3450116; e-mail faxop@drydocks.gov.ae; internet www.drydocks.gov.ae; f. 1983; state-owned; dry-docking and repairs, tank cleaning, construction of vessels and floating docks, conversions, galvanizing, dredging, etc.; Man. Dir NAWAL AJUDHIANATH SAIGAL.

Sea Bridge Shipping: POB 8458, Dubai; tel. (4) 3379858; fax (4) 3358226; e-mail adm.sbs@transworld.co; internet www.sbshipping.com; f. 1988; shipping and freight agency; Chair. S. RAMAKRISHNAN; Man. Dir S. MAHESH.

Vela International Marine: POB 26373, City Towers 2, Sheikh Zayed Rd, Dubai; tel. (4) 3123100; fax (4) 3310585; internet www.vela.ae; subsidiary of Saudi Arabian Oil Co; operates tankers; Pres. and CEO SALEH B. K'AKI.

Fujairah

Fujairah Port: POB 787, Fujairah; tel. (9) 2228800; fax (9) 2228811; e-mail info@fujairahport.ae; internet www.fujairahport.ae; f. 1982; operated by Dubai Ports World; offers facilities for handling container, general cargo and roll on, roll off (ro-ro) traffic; handled 565,723 TEUs in 1999; Chair. Sheikh SALEH BIN MUHAMMAD AL-SHARQI; Gen. Man. Capt. MOUSA MURAD.

Ras al-Khaimah

Saqr Port Authority: POB 5130, Ras al-Khaimah; tel. (7) 2668444; fax (7) 2668533; e-mail info@saqrport.ae; internet www.saqrport.ae; govt-owned; port operators handling bulk cargoes, containers, general cargo and ro-ro traffic; Gen. Man. Capt. COLIN CROOKSHANK.

Sharjah

Department of Seaports and Customs: POB 510, Sharjah; tel. (6) 5281327; fax (6) 5281425; e-mail shjports@eim.ae; internet www.sharjahports.ae; the authority administers Port Khalid, Hamriyah Port and Port Khor Fakkan and offers specialized facilities for container and ro-ro traffic, reefer cargo and project and general cargo; in 2003 Port Khalid handled 145,482 TEUs of containerized shipping, and Port Khor Fakkan 1,444,451 TEUs; Port Khalid and Hamriyah Port together handled over 4m. metric tons of non-containerized cargo; Chair. (Ports and Customs) Sheikh KHALID BIN ABDULLAH AL-QASIMI; Dir-Gen. ISSA JUMA AL-MUTAWA.

Fal Shipping Co Ltd: POB 6600, Sharjah; tel. (6) 5286666; fax (6) 5280861; e-mail osman@faloil.co.ae; internet www.falgroup.com/htm/shipping.htm; operates a fleet of 21 tankships; Chair. ABDULLAH JUMA AL-SARI; Gen. Man. MUHAMMAD OSMAN FADUL.

Umm al-Qaiwain

Ahmed bin Rashid Port and Free Zone Authority: POB 279, Umm al-Qaiwain; tel. (6) 7655882; fax (6) 7651552; e-mail abrpaftz@emirates.net.ae; Pres. KHALID BIN RASHID AL-MU'ALLA; Gen. Man. MURTAZA K. MOOSAJEE.

CIVIL AVIATION

There are seven international airports, two in Dubai, and one in each of Abu Dhabi, al-Ain, Fujairah and Ras al-Khaimah, as well as a smaller one at Sharjah, which forms part of Sharjah port, linking air, sea and overland transportation services. The second airport in Dubai, Al Maktoum International Airport—construction of which had commenced, at Jebel Ali, in 2005, owing to space constraints at the existing Dubai International Airport (DIA)—was officially inaugurated in June 2010. Initially, the airport was open exclusively to cargo carriers; passenger services were scheduled to commence in late 2011. Part of the Dubai World Central commercial and residential infrastructure development, the new airport was expected, upon completion of a secondary phase of construction, to have five runways, four terminal buildings and an annual capacity of 160m. passengers and 12m. metric tons of freight, rendering it the largest airport world-wide. Meanwhile, an expansion project at DIA, to increase annual capacity from 30m. to 75m. passengers, was scheduled for completion in 2011. As part of this project, a new third terminal began operating in late 2008 and plans for a fourth terminal, which would expand passenger capacity to 80m., were announced in early 2009. In that year a record 41m. passengers were reported to have used DIA. An expansion project at Abu Dhabi was expected to increase annual passenger capacity there to 20m. in 2012; a new runway became operational during 2008 and the following year a third terminal was opened. Plans to construct a new terminal at Sharjah International Airport, at a cost of US $354m., were announced in late 2008.

THE UNITED ARAB EMIRATES

General Civil Aviation Authority: POB 6558, Abu Dhabi; tel. (2) 4447666; fax (2) 4054535; e-mail info@gcaa.ae; internet www.gcaa.ae; f. 1996; responsible for all aspects of civil aviation; Chair. SULTAN BIN SAID AL-MANSOURI (Minister of Economy); Dir-Gen. MUHAMMAD ABDULLAH AL-SALAMI.

Abu Dhabi Aviation: POB 2723, Abu Dhabi; tel. (2) 5758000; fax (2) 5757775; e-mail adava@abudhabiaviation.com; internet www.adaviation.com; f. 1976; domestic charter flights; Chair. Sheikh TAHNOON BIN ZAYED AL NAHYAN; Gen. Man. MUHAMMAD IBRAHIM AL-MAZROUI.

Air Arabia: POB 132, Sharjah; tel. (6) 5088888; fax (6) 5580244; e-mail hraydan@airarabia.com; internet www.airarabia.com; f. 2003; 55% owned by private investors, 45% by the Sharjah Govt; low-fare airline; serves 46 destinations across the Middle East, N Africa, S and Cen. Asia, and Europe; handled 3.6m. passengers in 2008; Chair. Sheikh ABDULLAH BIN MUHAMMAD AL THANI; CEO ADEL ALI.

Emirates Airline: POB 686, Dubai; tel. (4) 2951111; fax (4) 2955817; e-mail corpcom@emiratesairline.com; internet www.emirates.com; f. 1985; owned by the Dubai Govt; operates services to over 100 destinations in 61 countries; carried 21.2m. passengers and 1.3m. metric tons of freight in 2007/08; Chair. and CEO Sheikh AHMAD BIN SAID AL MAKTOUM; Exec. Vice-Chair. MAURICE FLANAGAN.

Etihad Airways: POB 35566, Abu Dhabi; tel. (2) 5058000; fax (2) 5058111; internet www.etihadairways.com; f. 2003; owned by the Abu Dhabi Govt; operates 37 aircraft serving more than 50 short- and long-haul destinations; carried 4.6m. passengers in 2007; Chair. Sheikh HAMAD BIN ZAYED AL NAHYAN; CEO JAMES HOGAN.

Falcon Express Cargo Airlines (FECA): Dubai International Airport, POB 93722, Dubai; tel. (4) 2826886; fax (4) 2823125; e-mail admin@feca.bz; internet www.falcongroup.bz; f. 1995; dedicated courier freight.

RAK Airways: POB 31457, Ras al-Khaimah; tel. (7) 2075000; fax (7) 2447387; e-mail info@rakairways.com; internet www.rakairways.com; f. 2006; flights commenced 2007; owned by Govt of Ras al-Khaimah; operates from Ras al-Khaimah Int. Airport; serves destinations in Bangladesh, Egypt, India and Saudi Arabia; Chair. Sheikh OMAR BIN SAQR AL-QASIMI; CEO OMAR JAHAMEH.

Tourism

Each emirate develops and promotes its tourist attractions separately, although a federal tourism authority, the National Council for Tourism and Antiquities, commenced operations in late 2009. Dubai is the UAE's most popular tourist destination; its wide range of luxury hotels and resorts, and entertainment and shopping facilities attracted around 7m. visitors in 2008. Abu Dhabi is developing its tourism industry, with an emphasis on leisure, heritage and cultural facilities, as well as luxury hotels and resorts. An extensive commercial, residential and leisure project is being developed at Saadiyat Island, which will incorporate beaches, hotels, golf courses and a cultural district that will accommodate branches of the Louvre and Guggenheim museums, as well as the Sheikh Zayed National Museum. There are established tourism sectors in Sharjah and Ras al-Khaimah, and plans are being implemented to foster tourism in Ajman and Fujairah. In 2004 foreign visitors to the UAE totalled almost 6.2m., compared with 616,000 in 1990. Receipts from tourism totalled US $7,162m. in 2008.

National Council of Tourism and Antiquities (NCTA): Abu Dhabi; f. 2008; commenced operations Nov. 2009; Dir-Gen. MUHAMMAD KHAMIS BIN HARIB AL-MUHAIRI.

Abu Dhabi Tourism Authority (ADTA): POB 94000, Abu Dhabi; tel. (2) 4440444; fax (2) 4440400; e-mail contact@abudhabi.ae; internet www.abudhabitourism.ae; f. 2004; Chair. Sheikh SULTAN BIN TAHNUN AL NAHYAN; Dir-Gen. MUBARAK HAMAD AL-MUHEIRI.

> **Tourism Development and Investment Authority (TDIC):** POB 126888, Abu Dhabi; tel. (2) 4061400; e-mail info@tdic.ae; internet www.tdic.ae; 100% owned by ADTA; responsible for the devt of a range of major projects incl. Saadiyat Island; CEO LEE TABLER.

Dubai Department of Tourism and Commerce Marketing: POB 594, Dubai; tel. (4) 2230000; fax (4) 2230022; e-mail info@dubaitourism.co.ae; internet www.dubaitourism.co.ae; 18 offices abroad; Chair. Sheikh MUHAMMAD BIN RASHID AL MAKTOUM (Ruler of Dubai); Dir-Gen. KHALID A. BIN SULAYEM.

Fujairah Tourism and Antiquities Authority: POB 829, Fujairah; tel. (9) 2231554; fax (9) 2231006; e-mail fujtourb@emirates.net.ae; internet fujairah-tourism.gov.ae; f. 1995; Chair. Sheikh SAEED BIN SAEED AL-SHARQI; Gen. Man. SAEED AL-SAMAHI.

National Corporation for Tourism and Hotels (NCTH): POB 6942, Abu Dhabi; tel. (2) 4099999; fax (2) 4099990; e-mail ncth@emirates.net.ae; internet www.ncth.com; 20% owned by Govt of Abu Dhabi; Chair. HAMDAN BIN MUBARAK AL-NAYHAN.

Ras al-Khaimah Tourism Promotion Board: POB 31219, Ras al-Khaimah; tel. (7) 2445125; fax (7) 2447463; internet www.raktourism.com; f. 2006; Chair. Sheikh ABD AL-AZIZ BIN HUMAID AL-QASIMI; CEO Dr KHATER MASSAAD.

Sharjah Commerce and Tourism Development Authority: POB 26661, 9th Floor, Crescent Tower, Buheirah Corniche, Sharjah; tel. (6) 5566777; fax (6) 5563000; e-mail sctda@sharjah.org; internet www.sharjahtourism.ae; f. 1996; Dir-Gen. MUHAMMAD ALI AL-NOMAN.

Defence

The Union Defence Force and the armed forces of the various emirates were formally merged in May 1976. Abu Dhabi and Dubai retain a degree of independence. Military service is voluntary.

Chief of Staff of the Federal Armed Forces: Lt-Gen. HAMAD MUHAMMAD THANI AL-RUMAITHI.

Defence Budget (2010): est. AED 29,200m.; federal expenditure on defence has been substantially reduced since the early 1980s, but procurement and project costs are not affected, as individual emirates finance these separately.

Total armed forces (as assessed at November 2010): 51,000 (army 44,000; navy est. 2,500; air force 4,500).

In May 2009 a French military base, comprising naval, air force and army facilities for up to 500 personnel, was inaugurated in Abu Dhabi; at November 2010, a force numbering 86 was deployed at the base.

Education

Primary education is compulsory, beginning at six years of age and lasting for six years. Secondary education, starting at the age of 12, also lasts for six years, comprising two equal cycles of three years. According to UNESCO estimates, enrolment at primary schools included 90% of children in the relevant age-group in 2008/09, while the comparable ratio for secondary enrolment was 83%. In 2006/07 a total of 22,506 children attended government pre-primary schools, and 186,093 attended primary schools in the UAE. In the same year secondary enrolment in government schools totalled 63,767. There are primary and secondary schools in all the emirates, and further education in technical fields is available in the more advanced areas. Many students receive higher education abroad. The UAE has 14 universities. A branch of the Université Paris-Sorbonne opened in Abu Dhabi in October 2006, while a branch of New York University opened in 2009. Two American Universities are in operation, in Sharjah and Dubai. A British University and a Canadian University operate in Dubai, which also hosts branches of universities from Australia, the United Kingdom and the USA. Four higher colleges of technology (two for male and two for female students) in Abu Dhabi opened in 1988. According to UNESCO, in 2008/09 87,006 students were enrolled in university and other higher education; some 60% of students in tertiary education in that year were females. Budgeted federal government expenditure by the Ministries of Education and of Higher Education and Scientific Research in the 2009/10 fiscal year totalled an estimated AED 9,706m. (23.0% of total expenditure by the central Government).

THE UNITED KINGDOM

Introductory Survey

LOCATION, CLIMATE, LANGUAGE, RELIGION, FLAG, CAPITAL

The United Kingdom of Great Britain and Northern Ireland lies in north-western Europe, occupying the major portion of the British Isles. It is separated from the coast of Western Europe by the English Channel to the south and by the North Sea to the east. The United Kingdom comprises four countries: England, Scotland and Wales, which constitute the island of Great Britain; and Northern Ireland, situated in the north-east of the island of Ireland (comprising six of the nine counties in the historic Irish province of Ulster), which borders the state of Ireland and provides the United Kingdom with its only land boundary. The climate of the United Kingdom is generally temperate but variable. The average temperature is about 15°C (59°F) in summer and about 5°C (41°F) in winter. The annual average rainfall is 1,125 mm (44.3 ins). The principal language is English, but Welsh also has official status in Wales, where it is spoken by about one-fifth of the population. The Church of England is the established church in England. Other large Christian denominations are Roman Catholicism, Methodism, the United Reformed Church and the Baptists. The national flag (proportions 1 by 2), known as the Union Jack, is a superimposition of the red cross of Saint George of England, the white saltire of Saint Andrew of Scotland and the red saltire of Saint Patrick of Ireland, all on a blue background. The capital is London.

CONTEMPORARY POLITICAL HISTORY

Historical Context

The United Kingdom of Great Britain and Ireland was established in 1801 by the union of the Parliament of Ireland (hitherto in personal union with the British crown) with that of Great Britain. Throughout the 19th century the United Kingdom's imperial expansion across the globe consolidated its dominance in world affairs. Increasing demands from the Roman Catholic population in Ireland for home rule were eventually conceded to after the First World War, following a guerrilla campaign waged by the clandestine Irish Republican Army (IRA) in an attempt to force British withdrawal. In 1920 two parliaments were created in Ireland: one in Belfast, for the six Protestant-dominated counties in the north-east (Northern Ireland), and one in Dublin for the rest of the island. The Parliament of Northern Ireland subsequently chose to remain an integral part of the United Kingdom when the Irish Free State (now Ireland) acceded to dominion status in 1922.

Following the Second World War, successive British Governments, in response both to nationalist aspirations and world pressure, gradually granted independence to the remaining overseas colonies; almost all of these became members of the Commonwealth (see p. 230). The United Kingdom's dominance diminished over the Commonwealth, which became a free association of states, and the country looked increasingly to the North Atlantic Treaty Organization (NATO, see p. 368) and to the European Community (EC, now European Union—EU, see p. 270) for its future security.

Domestic Political Affairs

Following the general election of 1945, the Labour Party formed a Government under Clement Attlee. The general election of 1951 was won by the Conservative Party, which remained in power for 13 years. The election of 1964 gave a small parliamentary majority to the Labour Party, led by Harold Wilson. The Labour Party was re-elected in 1966, but in 1970 a Conservative Government, under Edward Heath, was returned. After the general election of February 1974 Wilson formed a minority Government; at a further election in October the Labour Party achieved a small majority in the House of Commons. Wilson resigned as Prime Minister in April 1976, and was succeeded by James Callaghan. His Labour Government immediately encountered a serious monetary crisis and, following a series of by-election defeats, became a minority Government again.

At the general election of May 1979 the Conservative Party won a parliamentary majority. A Government was formed under Margaret Thatcher, who became the United Kingdom's first woman Prime Minister. Thatcher's policies proved controversial, owing to the austerity of certain economic measures and an accompanying increase in unemployment. New legislation restricted the power of the trade unions. Meanwhile, the Labour Party became increasingly divided, and in March 1981 four former ministers from the right wing of the party formed the Social Democratic Party (SDP). The SDP formed a political alliance with the Liberals later that year. (The two parties formally merged in 1988 as the Social and Liberal Democrats, and became the Liberal Democrats in the following year.)

In April 1982 Argentine forces invaded the British dependency of the Falkland Islands (q.v.). The successful military campaign to recover the islands in June increased the Government's popularity, despite rising unemployment and strict monetary control of the economy. In the general election of June 1983 the Conservative Party increased its majority in the House of Commons to 146 seats. The Labour Party's parliamentary representation fell and Neil Kinnock subsequently replaced Michael Foot as the Labour leader. In June 1987 the Conservative Government was again re-elected, winning a majority of 102 seats in the House of Commons.

In mid-1990 the introduction of a local tax, the community charge (or 'poll tax'), in conjunction with an economic recession, contributed to considerable national dissatisfaction with the Thatcher administration. The Cabinet was also divided, chiefly over policy on integration with the EC. In November the Deputy Prime Minister, Sir Geoffrey Howe, resigned from the Government in protest against Thatcher's hostility towards economic and political union within the EC. Michael Heseltine (who had resigned as Secretary of State for Defence in 1986) announced that he would challenge Thatcher for the leadership of the Conservative Party. In the first ballot of the leadership election (conducted among Conservative Members of Parliament—MPs) Thatcher failed to achieve an outright victory and subsequently withdrew her candidacy. John Major, Chancellor of the Exchequer since October 1989, finally won the contest and was officially appointed Prime Minister in November 1990. (The community charge was replaced with a local council tax, based on property values, in April 1993.)

In a general election held in April 1992 the Conservative Party was re-elected with an overall, but substantially reduced, majority in the House of Commons. Economic recession continued and the Government's economic policies were criticized by political opponents and by industrial and business leaders. Divisions within the Conservative Party over the provisions of the Treaty on European Union (the Maastricht Treaty) were exacerbated by the United Kingdom's departure from the exchange rate mechanism (ERM) of the European Monetary System (see p. 311) in September.

John Smith replaced Kinnock as leader of the Labour Party in July 1992. Prior to his death, in May 1994, Smith reformed the relationship between the Labour Party and the trade unions, reducing the unions' influence over policy formulation and the election of party chiefs and parliamentary candidates. In July 1994 Tony Blair, Labour's parliamentary spokesman on home affairs, was elected leader by the party's electoral college. Blair's initiative to abandon Labour's socialist commitment to common ownership of the means of production provoked a much-publicized reassessment of party ideology, and became a test of support for the new leadership. In April 1995 a special party conference endorsed a draft text to replace the relevant clause of the party's constitution.

In June 1995 Major announced his resignation as leader of the Conservative Party, asserting that speculation regarding a challenge to his leadership was undermining both his authority as Prime Minister and that of the Government. The Secretary of State for Wales, John Redwood, resigned from the Cabinet in order to challenge Major as party leader. In the ballot for the leadership, held in July, Major was endorsed by a large majority of the parliamentary party. However, Major's authority within the party continued to be challenged by those MPs demanding a limitation in the country's convergence with the EU. In April

Major committed a future Conservative administration to conducting a popular referendum on the country's participation in a European single currency, but in June more than 70 Conservative MPs declared their support for a wider referendum on EU membership, demonstrating the increasing prominence of the so-called Eurosceptic faction of the party.

The Government of Tony Blair

At a general election held on 1 May 1997 the Labour Party secured an overwhelming victory, winning 418 of the 659 parliamentary seats. The Conservative Party won only 165 seats and failed to win any parliamentary representation in Scotland or Wales for the first time in its history. Major immediately announced his resignation as leader of the Conservative Party: William Hague, hitherto Secretary of State for Wales, was elected to the post (and thus as Leader of the Opposition) by Conservative MPs in June. In the new Labour Government Gordon Brown, who had been instrumental in Blair's modernization of the Labour Party, was named as Chancellor of the Exchequer and Robin Cook became Secretary of State for Foreign and Commonwealth Affairs. The new administration set out a series of radical policy proposals and government reforms, including a transfer of operational responsibility for monetary policy to the Bank of England, legislation intended to improve standards in education, the adoption of a national minimum wage, and constitutional reform.

In July 1997 the Government formally published its proposals for the establishment of devolved legislative authorities in Scotland and Wales. For Scotland a proposed new elected Parliament was envisaged as having powers to legislate on all domestic matters, including education, health, local government, law and order, and the possible mandate to vary the rate of income tax set by the United Kingdom Government. An executive level of government was to be headed by a First Minister. The National Assembly for Wales, like the Scottish body, was envisaged as assuming control of the annual block grant for the region from central government, and as undertaking responsibility for issues covered by the Welsh Office. In a referendum held in Scotland in September, 74.3% of those voting supported a new Parliament, while 63.5% approved its having tax-varying powers. The referendum in Wales, held one week later, was less conclusive, with only 50.3% of participants (or some 25% of eligible voters) endorsing the National Assembly; none the less, the Government declared its intention to implement the majority decision. Elections to the new legislative authorities were held in May 1999, and powers were transferred to both the Scottish and the Welsh legislatures on 1 July.

In October 1998 the Government announced that legislation was to be introduced to remove the voting rights of hereditary peers in the House of Lords, and that a Royal Commission was to be appointed to consider options for a definitive reform of the non-elected second chamber. Opposition from within the House of Lords was appeased in December when a compromise agreement was reached under which 92 hereditary peers were to retain their seats in an interim second chamber pending the definitive reform. Legislation for the abolition of hereditary peerages and the establishment of an interim chamber was approved by the Lords in October 1999 and received royal assent in November. In January 2000 the Royal Commission published its proposals for the definitive reform of the upper house, recommending that the new chamber should comprise some 550 members, the majority of whom would be chosen by an independent commission, while a 'significant minority' (between 65 and 195) would be elected by regional proportional representation.

In February 2001 an outbreak of foot-and-mouth disease among British livestock prompted the European Commission to impose a temporary ban on the export of live animals, meat and dairy products from the United Kingdom. The rapid spread of the disease throughout the country, mounting pressure from agricultural interest groups and popular opposition to the timing of the polls led the Government to announce in April that emergency legislation would be introduced to provide for a five-week postponement of the local elections due to be held in May. Blair later confirmed that an early general election (which, prior to the epidemic, had been widely expected to be held concurrently with the local elections) would also be conducted in June. The last case of foot-and-mouth disease was identified in September, and in February 2002 the European Commission lifted remaining restrictions on the import and export of British meat and livestock.

At the general election, held on 7 June 2001, the Labour Party won a further comprehensive victory, securing 412 of the 659 parliamentary seats. The Conservative Party won 166 seats, while the Liberal Democrats increased their parliamentary representation to 52 seats. Following his party's poor performance, Hague announced his intention to resign the leadership of the Conservative Party; in September Iain Duncan Smith, hitherto the Conservative Party's parliamentary spokesman on defence, was elected to replace him. Meanwhile, in a major reorganization of the Cabinet, Jack Straw, hitherto Secretary of State for the Home Department, replaced Cook as Secretary of State for Foreign and Commonwealth Affairs and David Blunkett assumed Straw's portfolio. The Ministry of Agriculture, Fisheries and Food, which had been heavily criticized for its handling of the foot-and-mouth outbreak, was replaced by the Department for the Environment, Food and Rural Affairs.

Upon their release in November 2001, the Government's proposals for further reform of the House of Lords encountered fierce opposition from both Labour and opposition MPs concerning the number of directly elected members envisaged in the plans. A public consultation process on the proposals ended in January 2002. In May the Government effectively abandoned the recommendations, and in December a new joint committee of MPs and peers presented seven options for the future proportion of elected members in the House of Lords, ranging from a wholly elected chamber to a wholly appointed house. However, in February 2003 all seven options were rejected by MPs voting in the House of Commons.

Blair's support for the US-led campaign to oust the regime of Saddam Hussain in Iraq in 2003 (see Foreign Affairs) provoked considerable public opposition and caused division within the Labour Party and the Government. In February increasing popular opposition to military action against Iraq precipitated nation-wide anti-war demonstrations, including a march in London reportedly attended by some 1m. people. Following the failure to secure a second UN resolution authorizing military action in Iraq and the announcement in March that British troops would be deployed as part of the US-led coalition, Cook resigned as Leader of the House of Commons, citing his unwillingness to accept collective responsibility for the decision to commit the United Kingdom to military action without international agreement or domestic support. However, despite the opposition of a significant number of Labour MPs, Blair's strategy was supported by the Conservative Party, and a motion endorsing military action was approved by a large majority in the Commons. In May Clare Short, the Secretary of State for International Development, also resigned from the Cabinet, accusing Blair of reneging on assurances he had made to her concerning the need for a UN mandate to establish a legitimate Iraqi government. The British Broadcasting Corporation (BBC) came into conflict with the Government in the same month, when a BBC journalist alleged that a dossier, published by the Government in September 2002 to explain the case for the removal of the Iraqi regime, had made exaggerated claims concerning Iraq's possession of chemical and biological weapons: he claimed that the Prime Minister's Director of Communications and Strategy, Alastair Campbell, was responsible for including misleading information in the dossier, against the wishes of the intelligence agencies. In July 2003 a parliamentary committee concluded that Campbell had not exerted improper influence on the drafting of the publication; the BBC, however, while refusing to reveal its source, rejected Campbell's demand that it retract the story. The Ministry of Defence subsequently confirmed that Dr David Kelly, a senior adviser to the ministry, was the source of the BBC's story. Later in July Dr Kelly committed suicide. An independent judicial inquiry into his death, under Lord Hutton, which reported in January 2004, concluded that there had been no duplicitous strategy on the part of the Government to reveal Kelly's name to the media, but that the Ministry of Defence's treatment of him after his public exposure had been unsatisfactory. The report criticized the management and editorial systems of the BBC, whose Director-General, together with the Chairman of the Board of Governors, then resigned. A further inquiry, under Lord Butler of Brockwell, was established in February 2004 to investigate the accuracy of the intelligence gathered on Iraqi weapons of mass destruction; in July 2004 it reported that intelligence surrounding the compilation of the September 2002 dossier was 'seriously flawed' and criticized the intelligence services for using unreliable sources of information within Iraq.

In June 2003, meanwhile, an extensive reorganization of the Cabinet included plans to effect major changes to the British legal and judicial system. Under the proposals the post of Lord

THE UNITED KINGDOM

Chancellor was to be abolished and a supreme court was to replace the judicial function of the House of Lords as the United Kingdom's highest court of appeal. The Lord Chancellor's Office was replaced by a newly created Department for Constitutional Affairs, which also incorporated the Scotland and Wales Offices. Lord Falconer of Thoroton was appointed to head the new department, while also assuming temporarily the functions of the Lord Chancellor—although he would not sit as a judge—pending the full implementation of the reforms. The decision to abolish such an historic position without prior consultation was heavily criticized by a number of parliamentarians, and in July the clause of the Constitutional Reform Bill providing for the removal of the Lord Chancellor was rejected by the House of Lords. The Government subsequently agreed only to modify the Lord Chancellor's role, while retaining the office. The Constitutional Reform Act finally received royal assent in March 2005 and came into force in April, when the Lord Chief Justice of England and Wales assumed control of the judiciary in England and Wales from the Lord Chancellor; in January 2006 the House of Lords formally agreed to elect a Speaker, the Lord Chancellor having hitherto traditionally presided over debates. The new Supreme Court commenced operations in October 2009.

At the general election on 5 May 2005 the Labour Party was re-elected for a third term, albeit with a substantially reduced majority, securing 355 of the 645 parliamentary seats contested. The Conservative Party and the Liberal Democrats both increased their representation in the House of Commons, securing 197 and 62 seats, respectively. The Labour Party's loss of popularity was attributed principally to a decline in personal support for Blair and the ongoing military action in Iraq. Following the election, the Conservative leader, Michael Howard, who had replaced Iain Duncan Smith in October 2003 after the latter lost a vote of confidence among Conservative MPs, announced his resignation; in December David Cameron was elected by the party membership to succeed him.

The London bombings

On 7 July 2005 52 people were killed and more than 700 injured in four attacks—three on London Underground trains and one on a bus—perpetrated by suicide bombers in London. Of the four bombers, all of whom also died in the attacks, three were subsequently discovered to have been native British Muslims of Pakistani descent, while the fourth was a convert to Islam of Jamaican origin. In September Al-Jazeera, a Qatar-based television station, broadcast a videotaped communiqué, supplied to it by the militant Islamist al-Qa'ida organization, in which Mohammad Sidique Khan, who had been identified as one of the four bombers, cited the United Kingdom's participation in the invasion of Iraq in 2003 as one of the motivations for the attacks. On 21 July 2005 at least four further attempts to attack London Underground trains and a bus with bombs were unsuccessful owing to the failure of the bombs to explode. By the end of the month four men suspected of involvement in the 21 July attacks had been arrested in the United Kingdom, while two further suspects were extradited from Italy and Ethiopia during the remainder of the year. The trial of the six men on charges of conspiracy to murder commenced in January 2007. In July four of the defendants were found guilty and were each sentenced to life imprisonment. A retrial was expected to take place in the case of the two remaining defendants after the jury failed to reach a verdict; however, in November the two men each admitted lesser charges, and both received prison terms. Inquests into the deaths of the 52 people killed in the bombings were conducted from October 2010 to March 2011, notably hearing evidence from officers of the Security Service (MI5).

In response to the attacks, the Government published a new Terrorism Bill in September 2005. The draft legislation sought to establish new offences of preparing, assisting in, encouraging or exalting terrorist acts, and proposed that the maximum period for which suspected terrorists could be detained without charge should be extended from 14 to 90 days. While a number of the bill's provisions were supported by both the Conservatives and the Liberal Democrats, representatives of those parties claimed that the Government had failed to justify the proposed extension of the maximum period of detention without charge, while civil liberties organizations claimed that such an extension would infringe suspects' human rights. In November the 90-day extension was emphatically rejected by the House of Commons. The rejection of the proposed legislation, which 49 Labour MPs had also refused to support, marked the first defeat that the Labour Government had suffered in the Commons since it assumed power in 1997. The defeat was followed by a vote in favour of

Introductory Survey

extending the maximum permissible period of detention of terrorist suspects without charge to 28 days. In late March 2006 the House of Lords finally approved the legislation, which came into force in April.

In March 2006, after the House of Lords Appointments Commission had expressed concern over a number of Labour nominations for peerages, it was revealed that four of the nominees had made unpublicized loans totalling at least £4.5m. to the Labour Party. A police investigation was subsequently launched into whether, effectively, the Labour Party had illegally sold 'titles of honour'. Although the police investigation was widened to examine the funding of both the Conservatives and the Liberal Democrats, the nominations called into question the Labour Party's commitment to transparency in political party funding, the reform of which it had begun after its election in 1997. Labour had in fact been under no legal obligation—as it would have been had they been donations—to declare the loans, but the fact that the party's treasurer had been unaware of them strengthened the impression of duplicity. In July 2006 the Labour Party's principal fund-raiser, Lord Levy, was arrested in the course of the investigation, while during the year the Prime Minister was among about 90 others (including members of all three main political parties) who were interviewed by the police. However, in July 2007 the Crown Prosecution Service announced that no charges would be brought in relation to the allegations.

New legislative proposals on the reform of the House of Lords, published in February 2007, suggested the abolition (over a transitional period) of all hereditary and life peerages and the reduction of the total membership of the upper house to 540, while MPs were to choose between a range of options on the proportion of members that would be elected and appointed. In a non-binding vote on these options, conducted in March, a majority of MPs favoured an upper house that would be entirely elected, while a smaller majority voted for one with 80% elected and 20% appointed members; in the House of Lords itself all the options were rejected and the house voted to retain a non-elected upper chamber.

At local and regional elections on 4 May 2007 the Labour Party incurred considerable losses. In Scotland the Scottish National Party (SNP), which favoured independence for Scotland, gained 20 new seats, thus obtaining 47 of the 129 seats in the legislature, while Labour won 46, the Conservatives 17, the Liberal Democrats 16 and the Scottish Green Party two; the complexity of the voting procedure was blamed for the fact that about 7% of the ballot papers were declared invalid. On 16 May 2007 members of the Scottish Parliament elected the SNP leader, Alex Salmond, as First Minister, at the head of a minority SNP administration (with partial support from the Green members). In the election to the National Assembly for Wales Labour lost four seats, but remained the largest party in the legislature with 26 of the 60 seats, while the Welsh nationalist Plaid Cymru won 15, the Conservative Party 12 and the Liberal Democrats six. In June Labour and Plaid Cymru finally agreed to form a coalition administration, in which Rhodri Morgan remained as First Minister and Plaid Cymru leader Ieuan Wyn Jones became his Deputy. (Morgan retired in December 2009 and was replaced as leader of Welsh Labour and First Minister by Carwyn Jones.)

The Government of Gordon Brown

In May 2007 Blair made the long-anticipated announcement that he would resign as leader of the Labour Party, with effect from 27 June. As the sole candidate, Gordon Brown, Chancellor of the Exchequer since 1997, was confirmed as the new leader of the party on 24 June. Brown assumed the role of Prime Minister three days later, following Blair's resignation, and subsequently announced an extensive reorganization of the Cabinet. Alistair Darling, previously the Secretary of State for Trade and Industry, replaced Brown as Chancellor of the Exchequer, while David Miliband was appointed Secretary of State for Foreign and Commonwealth Affairs. Jack Straw was appointed Secretary of State for Justice (a new cabinet post created in the previous month) and Lord Chancellor, and Jacqui Smith was named as Secretary of State for the Home Department.

The first week of Brown's premiership was marked by two failed bomb attacks perpetrated by Islamist extremists. At the end of June 2007 two car bombs placed in central London failed to detonate, while a day later two men were arrested after driving a vehicle containing explosive materials into a terminal building at Glasgow Airport. (One of the men arrested in Glasgow died in August, having sustained severe injuries during the attack.) The trials of two men suspected of plotting the two attacks began in October 2008, and in December one of the men, Bilal Abdulla, was sentenced to 32 years' imprisonment; the other defendant, Muhammad Asha, was acquitted of all charges.

Despite widespread cross-party opposition, in June 2008 the Government's controversial Counter-Terrorism Bill, which contained provisions for the extension of the maximum period of detention for terrorist suspects from 28 to 42 days in exceptional circumstances, was narrowly approved by the House of Commons, with the support of members of the Democratic Unionist Party. The following day David Davis, the Conservative Party's spokesman on home affairs, unexpectedly announced his resignation from the Commons in order to prompt a by-election, citing his desire to focus attention on the issue of civil liberties. The Labour Party and the Liberal Democrats declined to nominate candidates for the by-election, which took place in July; Davis was re-elected by a large majority. In October 2008 the House of Lords overwhelmingly rejected the proposals for an extension of the detention period for terrorist suspects, which were subsequently omitted from the Counter-Terrorism Bill; the bill was given royal assent in November.

Support for Brown's leadership within the parliamentary party declined further in July 2008, following the loss to the SNP of a by-election in Glasgow East, a constituency the Labour Party had won by a large majority at the general election of 2005. Media speculation regarding a potential leadership challenge, notably by Miliband, extended until the Labour Party conference in September, where Brown's speech was well received. In October, in a cabinet reorganization, Brown unexpectedly appointed Peter Mandelson to succeed John Hutton as Secretary of State for Business, Enterprise and Regulatory Reform. (Mandelson, a former close associate of Blair, had served in the former Prime Minister's Cabinet from 1997–98 and 1999–2001, but had been forced to resign on two occasions owing to impropriety; since 2004 he had been a European Commissioner.) Hutton, in turn, was appointed as Secretary of State for Defence, in place of Des Browne. The Prime Minister's political reputation was enhanced in late 2008 by his response to the global financial crisis, as he played a significant role in international efforts to co-ordinate measures to address the global economic downturn.

Meanwhile, from early 2008 a campaign by sections of the media to force the disclosure of MPs' claims for parliamentary allowances began increasingly to damage the reputation of ministers and other parliamentarians. In 2005 a group of journalists had requested the disclosure of claims made by 14 prominent politicians, including Brown, Blair and Cameron, under the 2000 Freedom of Information Act; this request was endorsed by the Information Tribunal in February 2008, and in May the High Court of Justice rejected an appeal against this decision by the Speaker of the House of Commons, Michael Martin. The details of these expense claims were disclosed later that month, and the Commons authorities consequently prepared to publish details of claims made by all MPs since 2004. Meanwhile, successive revelations throughout 2008 and early 2009 regarding allowances for secondary residences implicated senior Conservative and Labour politicians (notably including Jacqui Smith, the Secretary of State for the Home Department) and precipitated calls for a comprehensive reform of the system of parliamentary expenses. New regulations requiring the submission of receipts for all items included in expense claims, as well as the publication of details regarding income earned by MPs from activities separate from their parliamentary role, were approved by the Commons in May 2009; however, no agreement was reached over a reform of second home allowances, which were the subject of an ongoing inquiry by the independent public advisory body, the Committee on Standards in Public Life.

In May 2009 a national newspaper, *The Daily Telegraph*, disclosed that it had covertly obtained a copy of the digital file in preparation by the House of Commons authorities that was to detail the expense claims made by all MPs between 2004 and 2008, and which had been scheduled for official publication in July. The newspaper published excerpts from the file over the course of the month, revealing what was commonly perceived to be extensive and widespread abuse of the parliamentary allowance system by MPs from all three main parties, and prompting intense public criticism of the members concerned. In particular, a number of MPs were criticized for their allegedly excessive claims for the upkeep of a second home, or for the practice of swapping their designated primary and secondary residences in order to claim additional allowances. Later in May 2009 a substantial number of MPs from all three main parties expressed support for a proposed motion of no confidence in the Speaker, Martin, who had been heavily criticized for his handling of the issue. The following day Martin announced his resignation both as Speaker of the Commons and as an MP. Meanwhile, the details of all MPs' allowance claims were officially released ahead of schedule in late June; on the same day the Commons authorities announced that, since April, MPs had voluntarily repaid a total of nearly £500,000 arising from dubious expense claims.

The extent of public disaffection with the Government, and the established political parties in general, was highlighted by the results of elections to local councils in England and to the European Parliament, held concurrently on 4 June 2009. In the local elections the Labour Party lost control of the four remaining county councils it had held, while the Conservative Party emerged with control of 30 of the 34 councils contested. In the European Parliament election the Labour Party won just 15.7% of the votes cast in Great Britain and 13 of the 69 available seats (compared with 19 in 2004); the UK Independence Party, which advocated British withdrawal from the EU, won 16.5% of the votes and also took 13 seats, while the Conservatives won 27.7% (25 seats) and the Liberal Democrats 13.7% (11 seats). The extreme right-wing British National Party secured representation for the first time at national or European level, winning two seats in the north of England. Participation in the European election was recorded at just 34.7% of electors in the United Kingdom. Brown effected a government reorganization shortly after the elections, in response to the Labour Party's poor performance; his authority had been weakened in the preceding days by a series of ministerial resignations, including those of Smith (who had announced her intention to leave the Government on 2 June, as a result of the criticism she had received over her expense claims) and James Purnell (who resigned as Secretary of State for Work and Pensions shortly before polling closed on 4 June, urging Brown also to step down in order to improve Labour's chances of winning the forthcoming general election). Alan Johnson was appointed to replace Smith as Secretary of State for the Home Department, while Purnell was replaced by Yvette Cooper. Among other changes, Mandelson was appointed First Secretary of State, Secretary of State for Business, Innovation and Skills and Lord President of the Council, thus gaining additional responsibilities including higher education.

In late June 2009 the Government introduced emergency legislation to effect a partial reform of the parliamentary allowances system: the Parliamentary Standards Act, which received cross-party support and came into force in July, introduced an Independent Parliamentary Standards Authority (IPSA) to regulate MPs' allowances, and made it a criminal offence for an MP to provide false or misleading information about a claim for expenses. In November the Committee on Standards in Public Life published the results of its inquiry into MPs' allowances: among its recommendations were that members should be compensated only for rental of a second home, rather than for mortgage payments. The proposals were largely adopted by IPSA, which published its new rules on parliamentary expenses (which were to take effect after the forthcoming general election) in March 2010. Meanwhile, in February Sir Thomas Legg, a former senior civil servant who had conducted an audit of the expenses disclosed in May and June 2009, published his report: 390 current and former MPs who were judged to have made excessive claims under the second homes allowance were asked to make repayments totalling some £1.1m. (including the Prime Minister, who was asked to return more than £12,000 claimed for home maintenance costs). During 2010 six parliamentarians were charged with false accounting in relation to their expense claims. By late April 2011 one serving and two former Labour MPs had pleaded guilty to the charges against them, while another former MP and a former Conservative peer had been convicted, having denied the charges against them; three of the five convicted had been sentenced by this time, receiving prison terms ranging from 12 to 18 months, and the trial of a second former Conservative peer was expected to take place in May. Meanwhile, the implementation of the new rules on parliamentary allowances proved controversial among legislators, despite further minor changes to the system announced in September 2010, with some claiming that they were being prevented from obtaining legitimate expenses.

Meanwhile, in June 2009, following the withdrawal of British troops from Iraq in April (see below), Brown announced the establishment of a long-awaited independent inquiry into the invasion and occupation of that country, which was to report on the lessons to be learned from the United Kingdom's involvement in the conflict. The public hearings of the inquiry, chaired by Sir John Chilcot, commenced in November and were concluded in

February 2011; the inquiry was not expected to submit its final report for several months. In January 2010 the inquiry heard evidence from senior ministers and government advisers in office at the time of the invasion, including Blair, who defended his decision to participate in the US-led military action. Brown also testified before the inquiry in March, when he insisted that, as Chancellor of the Exchequer, he had not denied any request for funding of the military campaign. Blair appeared before the inquiry for a second time in January 2011, largely reiterating the arguments he had made during his first testimony, although he conceded that his assertion in the House of Commons in January 2003 that a second UN resolution was not required to authorize the use of military force in Iraq was inconsistent with the legal advice that he was receiving at that time from the Attorney-General (who later decided, however, that a second resolution was, in fact, not essential). A few days earlier Chilcot had expressed disappointment at a decision made by the Cabinet Secretary, Sir Gus O'Donnell, following consultation with Blair, not to allow the inquiry to publish correspondence and records of discussions between the former Prime Minister and the US President in the period preceding the invasion of Iraq.

Recent developments: the 2010 election and the coalition Government

The general election of 6 May 2010 was the first since February 1974 at which no party won an outright majority in the House of Commons. The Conservative Party became the largest grouping in the House, winning 305 of the 649 contested seats with 36.1% of the votes cast. The Labour Party secured 258 seats with 29.0% of the votes, while the Liberal Democrats took 57 seats with 23.0% of the votes, thus holding the balance of power. Analysts had widely predicted that the Liberal Democrats' representation would increase significantly, as opinion polls had indicated a large increase in support for the party as a result of Nick Clegg's strong performance in three televised debates, held in the weeks prior to the election, between the leaders of the three main parties; however, the party's share of the votes was only marginally higher than the 22.0% it received at the previous general election, and it emerged with five fewer seats than in 2005. The rate of participation was 65.1%.

Following the election, Clegg declared that the Conservatives, as the party with the greatest number of seats and votes, had the right to seek to form a government first (contrary to the existing constitutional convention, which favoured the incumbent Prime Minister, and despite the fact that the Liberal Democrats were considered ideologically closer to the Labour Party). Accordingly, the Conservatives and the Liberal Democrats entered into negotiations with a view to forming a government that would command the support of the House of Commons. On 10 May 2010 Liberal Democrat negotiators began formal parallel talks with the Labour Party, following an announcement by Brown that he intended to resign as party leader by September; it was widely speculated that the Liberal Democrats would be more amenable to forming a coalition government with Labour (which would nevertheless require the support of smaller parties to pass legislation) if Brown were replaced as Prime Minister. However, on 11 May, following the collapse of negotiations between Labour and the Liberal Democrats, Brown resigned as both Prime Minister and Labour leader. He was succeeded as Prime Minister by the Conservative leader, David Cameron, who announced that the Conservatives and the Liberal Democrats had agreed to form a coalition Government (the United Kingdom's first since the Second World War). The composition of the Cabinet was announced the following day; Clegg became Deputy Prime Minister and Lord President of the Council, while the majority of ministerial roles were assigned to Conservatives. Notably, William Hague, the former party leader, was appointed First Secretary of State and Secretary of State for Foreign and Commonwealth Affairs, George Osborne became Chancellor of the Exchequer, and Theresa May was named Secretary of State for the Home Department and Minister for Women and Equalities. In addition to Clegg, four Liberal Democrats were appointed to the Cabinet, including Dr Vincent Cable as Secretary of State for Business, Innovation and Skills and Chris Huhne as Secretary of State for Energy and Climate Change. The Labour leadership was assumed on an interim basis by Harriet Harman, hitherto deputy leader of the party, until September, when Ed Miliband, Secretary of State for Energy and Climate Change in Brown's administration, was elected leader of the Labour Party by the party's electoral college, only narrowly defeating his brother, David, the former Secretary of State for Foreign and Commonwealth Affairs, with strong support from trade union voters.

Shortly after taking office the Conservative-Liberal Democrat coalition published a document outlining its agreed programme for government, which included a commitment to reduce public expenditure by some £6,200m. in the current financial year as part of urgent measures to reduce the structural deficit, as well as proposals for parliamentary and electoral reform, a banking levy, an annual limit on immigration from outside the EU, education reforms and the cancellation of the previous Government's plans to introduce identity cards. The resignation of David Laws, the Liberal Democrat Chief Secretary to the Treasury, in late May 2010, after he admitted impropriety in relation to his claims for parliamentary allowances, necessitated an early, but minor, reorganization of the Cabinet: Laws was succeeded by Danny Alexander, hitherto Secretary of State for Scotland, who was replaced in that post by Michael Moore.

With the primary focus of the Government being to eliminate the public deficit within five years, in June 2010 Osborne presented an emergency budget, providing for a combination of real-terms reductions in expenditure, to affect all areas with the exception of health and overseas development aid, and measures to increase revenue, including, from January 2011, a rise in the rate of value-added tax and the introduction of the banking levy. Meanwhile, an independent Office for Budget Responsibility was created to provide official growth and budget forecasts and to assess the Government's progress in achieving its fiscal targets. Also in June 2010, Osborne announced the Government's intention to reform the regulatory framework of the financial sector, with far greater responsibility in this area to be granted to the Bank of England. A comprehensive spending review presented in October expanded on the Government's plans to reduce expenditure: the budgets of all government departments (other than health and overseas aid) would be cut by an average of 19% over a period of four years, with a particular focus on reducing the cost of social welfare payments, where net savings of some £7,000m. per year were envisaged, through, for example, the withdrawal, from 2013, of child benefit from families with a higher-rate taxpayer and the introduction of a limit on the amount a non-working household could receive in benefits. Overall, the reductions in expenditure were to amount to £81,000m. by 2014/15. Under his 'Big Society' initiative, Prime Minister Cameron aimed to decentralize the provision of many public services away from central government to voluntary groups and individuals, as well as to local authorities. Also published in October was a strategic defence and security review, which included provision for a reduction of 25,000 in the number of civilian staff employed by the Ministry of Defence.

In July 2010 Clegg announced the details of the Government's proposals for parliamentary and electoral reform: the introduction of fixed five-year parliamentary terms; a reduction in the number of seats in the House of Commons from 650 to 600 and amendments to the boundaries of constituencies in order to make them more equal in terms of the size of their electorate; and the organization of a national referendum in May 2011 on whether the alternative vote (AV) model should replace the current 'first-past-the-post' voting system in general elections. The two coalition parties were divided over the issue of electoral reform. The Conservatives strongly favoured the retention of existing voting procedures, while the Liberal Democrats advocated the AV system (whereby voters rank candidates in order of preference and the first candidate to secure 50% of the vote wins the seat), considering it to be a compromise that might eventually lead to a full version of proportional representation. Although the Labour Party had supported a referendum on AV during the election campaign, it opposed a reduction in the number of legislative seats and changes to constituency boundaries. As these measures were contained in the same bill, Labour peers sought to impede its passage through the House of Lords in early 2011. However, the proposed legislation was finally approved on 16 February, the legal deadline for it to be possible to organize a referendum on the planned date of 5 May. A separate bill on fixed five-year parliamentary terms remained under consideration in the House of Lords in May 2011.

In November 2010 the Government proposed an annual limit of 21,700 on the number of skilled workers permitted to enter the United Kingdom from outside the European Economic Area (comprising the EU, Iceland, Norway and Liechtenstein) from April 2011. However, in an apparent concession to opponents of a fixed limit both within the coalition and within the business sector, intra-company transfers of personnel with annual salaries exceeding £40,000 would be exempt. The Secretary of State for Business, Innovation and Skills, Vincent Cable, had notably raised concerns in September that an interim limit imposed in June was too restrictive and was damaging the economy. Immigration policy again prompted tensions within the Government in April 2011, when Cable publicly criticized a pledge by Cameron to reduce net migration levels from hundreds of thousands of people per year to tens of thousands, noting that such a target was Conservative, rather than coalition, policy and 'risked inflaming extremism'; the Prime Minister rejected this charge. Meanwhile, in December 2010 Cable was stripped of responsibility for overseeing competition and policy issues relating to the media, broadcasting and telecommunications sectors, after making injudicious comments to journalists posing as constituents regarding a takeover bid by News Corporation for British Sky Broadcasting Group (BSkyB) that he had the power to block.

Government plans to raise the state-imposed limit on the tuition fees that universities in England could charge domestic students for undergraduate courses from £3,000 per year to £9,000 from September 2012 provoked significant opposition in late 2010. A series of demonstrations against the proposal took place in university towns nation-wide; one of these, held in central London on 10 November, escalated into rioting at the Conservative Party's headquarters. More than 120 people were arrested in connection with the violence and with further disorder that occurred at a second major protest later that month. Considerable anger was directed towards the Liberal Democrats, who had pledged not to increase tuition fees during the campaign for the May elections. None the less, the legislation on tuition fees was adopted by Parliament in December, albeit by a majority of only 21 votes in the House of Commons, with 21 Liberal Democrat and six Conservative MPs voting against the bill and a further 10 from both parties abstaining. While the debate on the measure was in progress in the Commons, further protests were held in central London, again leading to violent clashes with the police.

Following a review of counter-terrorism policy, in January 2011 the Secretary of State for the Home Department, Theresa May, confirmed that the maximum period for which suspected terrorists could be detained without charge had reverted from 28 days to 14 days and announced the Government's intention to abolish control orders, which had been introduced in 2005 to place restrictions on the movements of terrorism suspects who could not be prosecuted owing to the sensitivity of the evidence against them. However, proposed new 'terrorism prevention and investigation measures' were deemed by civil liberties campaigners to be only slightly less restrictive than the control orders, which critics had claimed were effectively a form of house arrest and had been subject to several legal challenges.

Also in January 2011 the Secretary of Health, Andrew Lansley, presented a bill for major reform of the National Health Service in England, which provided for a drastic reduction in the number of health bodies, in order to lower administration costs, and an increase in the powers of general practitioners (family doctors) to commission medical services for their patients. However, amid mounting criticism of the proposals, notably from the British Medical Association and the Royal College of Nursing (the two main organizations representing doctors and nurses), in April Lansley announced a 'pause' to allow further consultation on the bill.

The Labour Party comfortably retained two seats in the House of Commons at by-elections held in January and March 2011; the second ballot was notable for the poor performance of the Liberal Democrats, whose share of the vote declined to 4.1% from 17.2% at the general election in May 2010. In early March 2011, at a referendum held in Wales, 63.5% of those participating (35.3% of the electorate) voted in favour of the Welsh National Assembly being granted full legislative powers over domestic matters, without the need to seek the consent of the United Kingdom Parliament. The transfer of additional, mainly fiscal, powers to the Scottish Parliament was also under consideration. More than 250,000 people participated in a march organized by the Trades Union Congress later that month in central London in protest against reductions in public spending; although the demonstration was largely peaceful, some 200 arrests were made after small groups of protesters attacked shops and banks, clashing with police officers.

On 5 May 2011 local and regional elections took place, together with a national referendum on the replacement of the first-past-the-post electoral system with AV. The change in the voting system, which had been advocated by the Liberal Democrats, was defeated by a significant margin, with 67.9% of the valid votes cast against the proposal and only 32.1% in favour. The Liberal Democrats also performed poorly at the local elections, where they lost almost one-half of their incumbent councillors whose seats were contested. The Conservatives, by contrast, (who had campaigned against the adoption of AV) slightly increased their already high number of councillors and won control of two further councils. The Labour Party, which had been divided over support for AV, gained more than 800 council seats in England and won a plurality of seats in the Welsh Assembly, missing a majority by just one seat, but suffered serious losses in the election to the Scottish Assembly. The SNP, led by Alex Salmond, became the first party to win an overall majority in the Scottish Assembly, taking 69 seats (an increase of 22 seats from the previous election), compared with 37 seats for the Labour Party (a loss of nine seats). While the Conservatives only lost one seat in Scotland, leaving its total at 15 seats, the Liberal Democrats' representation declined from 16 seats to five. Salmond, who was re-elected as First Minister later in May, announced that a referendum on Scottish independence would take place in the second half of the new parliamentary term.

Allegations of Complicity in Torture

Following the NATO-led invasion in Afghanistan in October 2001, the United Kingdom became subject to allegations that its airspace and air transport facilities had been used in the transfer ('extraordinary rendition') of detainees, in particular terrorist suspects, by the US Central Intelligence Agency (CIA) to third countries where it was possible that they might be subjected to torture during interrogation. In December 2005 Blair dismissed calls by human rights organizations for an inquiry into the so-called rendition flights and insisted that he had no evidence to suggest that anything illegal had occurred. However, in February 2008 David Miliband, the Secretary of State for Foreign and Commonwealth Affairs, admitted to the House of Commons that the US military base on Diego Garcia in the British Indian Ocean Territory had, in fact, been used in the rendition of detainees.

In October 2008 the Secretary of State for the Home Department asked the Attorney-General, Baroness Scotland of Asthal, to investigate allegations made by Binyam Mohamed, an Ethiopian national resident in the United Kingdom who had been detained in Afghanistan by the US authorities in 2002. Mohamed claimed that members of the British intelligence services had colluded in his torture during a period of detention in Morocco, prior to being transferred to the US camp for detained 'enemy combatants' at Guantánamo Bay, Cuba, in 2005; Miliband denied that the British authorities had been complicit in torture. Mohamed returned to the United Kingdom in February 2009, following his release from Guantánamo Bay, where all charges against him had been dropped. In March Scotland asked the Commissioner of the Metropolitan Police to investigate the allegations relating to Mohamed. Although human rights groups and lawyers welcomed the investigation, they continued to demand a judicial inquiry to establish the full extent of British collusion in acts of torture. In February 2010 the Court of Appeal ordered Miliband to authorize the publication of a document summarizing information, given to MI5 by the CIA, on Mohamed's treatment while in US custody. The information, which was subsequently released, indicated that MI5 had, at the very least, been aware of 'cruel, inhuman and degrading treatment' by the US authorities. In early May, moreover, the Court of Appeal overturned a High Court ruling, made the previous November, that evidence could be withheld from claimants seeking compensation for alleged British complicity in their mistreatment by foreign countries if disclosure would compromise national security. Later in May the new Secretary of State for Foreign and Commonwealth Affairs, William Hague, promised that an independent inquiry would be conducted into all unresolved allegations of British complicity in the torture of terrorist suspects abroad. The inquiry, headed by Sir Peter Gibson, the Intelligence Services Commissioner, was established in July, although it was not to commence work until all police investigations into the allegations had been completed. In November the Lord Chancellor and Secretary of State for Justice, Kenneth Clarke, announced that out-of-court settlements had been reached with 16 former detainees at Guantánamo Bay claiming to have been victims of British complicity in torture; no admission of culpability was made.

THE UNITED KINGDOM

Northern Ireland
Towards a peace settlement

During the late 1960s an active civil rights movement sought to end discrimination against Roman Catholics in Northern Ireland, where the Protestant-supported Ulster Unionist Party (UUP) had remained in permanent control of the Parliament and Government since the partition of Ireland in 1922. However, Protestant extremists viewed the non-violent movement as a republican threat, and resorted to violence against Catholic activists. The IRA was originally a small element in the civil rights movement, but, after increasingly serious disturbances, a breakaway group, calling itself the Provisional IRA (generally known simply as the IRA), embarked on a campaign of violence with the aim of reuniting Ireland on its own terms. In April 1969 the Northern Ireland Government requested that British army units be assigned to protect important installations and in August the British and Northern Ireland Governments agreed that all security forces in the territory would be placed under British command. In March 1972, as a result of increased violence, the British Government assumed direct responsibility for law and order. Finding this unacceptable, the Northern Ireland Government resigned. The British Government prorogued the Northern Ireland Parliament and introduced direct rule from London, thus alienating many Protestants.

In 1973 new legislation abolished the office of Governor (the British monarch's representative) and the Northern Ireland Parliament, and provided for new constitutional arrangements. In June elections were conducted for a 78-member Northern Ireland Assembly, and an Executive was subsequently constituted from its members. An important part of this new 'power-sharing' arrangement was the establishment of a limited role for the Irish Government in Northern Ireland's affairs. Accordingly, in December, at Sunningdale (in southern England), the British and Irish Governments and the Northern Ireland Executive finalized an agreement to form a Council of Ireland (with members drawn from the Governments of Northern Ireland and Ireland), which would have a range of economic and cultural responsibilities in both parts of Ireland. However, the Sunningdale Agreement and the new devolved authority in Northern Ireland were rejected by many Protestants, and led, in 1974, to a general strike. A state of emergency was declared and the Executive was forced to resign. The Assembly was prorogued, and Northern Ireland returned to direct rule by the British Government. The collapse of the Sunningdale Agreement led to a rise in popularity of the more extreme Democratic Unionist Party (DUP—founded in 1971, and led by Rev. Dr Ian Paisley), which established itself as the main rival to the UUP.

Throughout the 1970s and 1980s the IRA and the Irish National Liberation Army (INLA, which emerged in 1975) continued their terrorist attacks on British military and civilian targets both in Northern Ireland and in England and continental Europe, while Protestant 'loyalist' paramilitary groups engaged in attacks on Roman Catholics.

Discussions between the Governments of the United Kingdom and Ireland in 1984–85 culminated in the signing of the Anglo-Irish Agreement in November 1985. The Agreement established the Intergovernmental Conference, through which British and Irish ministers were to meet regularly to discuss political, security, legal and cross-border matters relating to Northern Ireland. While giving the Irish Government a formal consultative role in Northern Ireland affairs, the Agreement recognized that the constitutional status of Northern Ireland remained unchanged and would not be altered without the consent of a majority of Northern Ireland's population. The Agreement had the support of the predominantly Roman Catholic Social Democratic and Labour Party (SDLP), and was approved by the Irish and British Parliaments. However, it was strongly opposed by most unionist politicians, who organized mass demonstrations and violent protests against the Agreement. In June 1986 the Northern Ireland Assembly was dissolved.

In January 1990 the British Government launched an initiative to convene meetings between representatives from the major political parties in Northern Ireland and the British and Irish Governments to discuss devolution in Northern Ireland and the future of its relations with Ireland. Sinn Féin (the political wing of the IRA) was to be excluded from the talks because of its refusal to denounce the IRA's campaign of violence. Bilateral discussions between the British Government and the DUP, the UUP, the SDLP and the non-sectarian Alliance Party eventually began in April 1991, and talks subsequently commenced between all the Northern Ireland parties and the Irish Government. The principal point of contention was the unionists' demand that Ireland hold a referendum on Articles 2 and 3 of its Constitution, which laid claim to the territory of Northern Ireland. The Irish Government, however, remained unwilling to make such a concession except as part of an overall settlement. In the absence of an agreement, the negotiations formally ended in November 1992, and the Anglo-Irish Conference resumed.

In December 1993 the British and Irish Prime Ministers, John Major and Albert Reynolds, made a joint declaration, known as the Downing Street Declaration (after the British Prime Minister's official residence in London), which provided a specific framework for a peace settlement. The initiative, which was widely supported by opposition parties in the United Kingdom and Ireland, referred to the possibility of a united Ireland and accepted the legitimacy of self-determination, while insisting on majority consent within Northern Ireland. The DUP, the UUP and Sinn Féin rejected the document, which effectively removed any confidence of achieving an imminent peace settlement. However, the British and Irish Governments reiterated their intention to pursue the peace process.

In August 1994 the IRA announced 'a complete cessation of violence'. In October the loyalist paramilitary groups declared a suspension of military activity, which was effectively to be linked to that of the IRA. Later that month Major announced new measures to restart the peace process, adopting the 'working assumption' that the IRA cease-fire was permanent. The first public meeting between Sinn Féin and government officials was held in December, marking the start of exploratory talks between the two sides. In February 1995 Major and the new Irish Prime Minister, John Bruton, presented a Framework Document containing proposals for cross-border co-operation, together with a separate British government paper outlining a new Northern Ireland Assembly with wide legislative and executive authority. Both Governments emphasized that any final agreement about the proposals was to be subject to parliamentary approval and popular consent by means of a referendum. Despite a positive Sinn Féin response to the Framework Document, the issue of decommissioning paramilitary weapons remained the major obstacle to peace negotiations: the British Government objected to Sinn Féin's linking of IRA decommissioning with the demilitarization of Northern Ireland, while Sinn Féin rejected the Government's insistence that decommissioning by paramilitary organizations be a precondition to conducting all-party negotiations.

In November 1995 the British and Irish Governments agreed to initiate preliminary talks with all the parties in Northern Ireland. An international commission to assess the practicalities of the decommissioning of armaments and other aspects of the peace process, chaired by George Mitchell, an adviser to US President Bill Clinton, began meetings with all sides involved in the peace process in December. The commission's final report, issued in January 1996, recommended proceeding with all-party talks on the condition that all sides endorse the eventual complete disarmament of paramilitary organizations, the renunciation of violence and the cessation of paramilitary 'punishment' attacks. According to the report, arms decommissioning was to be considered in parallel with the negotiations, while the eventual surrender of weaponry was to be conducted under international supervision, with those involved being free from prosecution. The report was generally supported by all sides.

In February 1996 the IRA abruptly terminated its cease-fire by exploding a large bomb in London. The organization blamed the British Government for the resumption of hostilities, citing its inflexible response to the Mitchell report. Bruton and Major declared that they would suspend all ministerial dialogue with Sinn Féin, but would intensify efforts to achieve a peaceful settlement. At the end of the month the leaders announced an initiative to pursue the peace process, involving the election of a forum for intersectoral dialogue that would subsequently engage in comprehensive political negotiations, to be based on the 1995 Framework Document. The election to the 110-member Northern Ireland Forum, under an electoral system intended to ensure a wide representation of the region's political groupings, was held in May; the UUP secured the largest number of seats, followed by the DUP, the SDLP and Sinn Féin. The Alliance Party and five smaller parties also won representation. The multi-party discussions, which commenced in June, were undermined by Sinn Féin's exclusion, in the absence of a new IRA cease-fire declaration, and by unionist opposition to the appointment of Mitchell as Chairman, which they claimed was part of a nationalist agenda. Further political uncertainty followed an

THE UNITED KINGDOM

IRA bomb attack in Manchester in June. Moreover, sectarian disputes regarding the organization of traditional Protestant marches in July prompted the SDLP to withdraw from the Forum.

The election of the Labour Government in May 1997 generated renewed optimism that a peace settlement could be achieved. The Prime Minister, Tony Blair, proposed a timetable for the talks, and reiterated that he envisaged their conclusion no later than May 1998, when the results were to be put to a popular referendum. In June 1997 the British and Irish Governments announced a new initiative to accelerate the peace process, whereby the decommissioning of paramilitary weapons, together with other confidence-building measures, would be undertaken concurrently with political negotiations, in an attempt to facilitate Sinn Féin's participation in the process, and clarified that Sinn Féin would be eligible to join substantive negotiations six weeks after a new IRA cease-fire announcement.

In July 1997 the IRA announced a restoration of its cease-fire. A few days later the Irish and British Governments jointly declared that the all-party negotiations would commence in September, with the participation of Sinn Féin. Accordingly, in September Sinn Féin endorsed the so-called 'Mitchell principles', which committed participants to accepting the outcome of the peace process and renouncing violence as a means of punishment or resolving problems. The UUP, together with the DUP and the United Kingdom Unionist Party (UKUP), which had already declared their boycott of any discussions with Sinn Féin, and other loyalist representatives, failed to attend the opening session of the talks when they resumed in September, owing partly to a statement by the IRA that undermined Sinn Féin's endorsement of the Mitchell principles. Nevertheless, the UUP rejoined the peace negotiations a few days later, and in late September all eight parties to the talks signed a procedural agreement to pursue substantive negotiations. At the same time the Independent International Commission on Decommissioning (IICD) was inaugurated, under the chairmanship of the former head of the Canadian armed forces, Gen. John de Chastelain.

The Good Friday Agreement

In January 1998 Blair and the Irish Prime Minister, Bertie Ahern, published a document outlining a framework for negotiations: this envisaged 'balanced constitutional change' by both Governments and proposed a devolved form of government within Northern Ireland. After intensive negotiations, on 10 April a settlement was announced. The Good Friday Agreement (or Belfast Agreement) envisaged radical reform of the political structures of Northern Ireland, its relations with Ireland, and its constitutional standing within the United Kingdom. The main provisions of the Agreement were as follows: the establishment of a 108-member elected Northern Ireland Assembly, with authority to legislate on all domestic matters currently administered by the Northern Ireland Office; an Executive Committee, to be elected by the Assembly and headed by a First Minister and Deputy First Minister; an obligation that the Assembly establish, within one year, a North/South Ministerial Council at which representatives of the Irish Government and the executive authority in Northern Ireland might consider issues of cross-border concern; regular meetings of representatives of the Irish Government with members of the British Parliament, the Northern Ireland Assembly and other regional assemblies of the United Kingdom, under a new British-Irish Council, with the objective of promoting co-operation, information exchange and agreement on issues of mutual interest; amendment of Articles 2 and 3 of the Irish Constitution; replacement of the 1985 Anglo-Irish Agreement with a new bilateral accord, incorporating a British-Irish Intergovernmental Council to oversee the Assembly and North/South Council; and a commitment by all parties to achieve the decommissioning of paramilitary weapons within two years. The UUP, the SDLP, Sinn Féin and most of the smaller parties approved the settlement, although several dissident UUP politicians later joined the DUP and UKUP in their campaign to prevent an endorsement of the accord, and the Protestant Orange Order urged its members to oppose the Agreement. Some 71.1% of voters in Northern Ireland approved the proposed peace settlement in a referendum conducted on 22 May, while in a concurrent referendum in Ireland 94.4% of voters approved the proposed amendments to the Constitution.

The first election to the Northern Ireland Assembly was conducted on 25 June 1998, with the UUP and the SDLP emerging as the largest parties. At the inaugural meeting of the Assembly in July, Trimble was elected as First Minister of the executive body, while Seamus Mallon of the SDLP was elected as Deputy First Minister. Sectarian violence soon threatened to disrupt the peace process following confrontations between the security forces and members of the Orange Order who, in defiance of the newly established Parades Commission, sought to march its traditional route along the predominantly Roman Catholic-inhabited Garvaghy Road in Portadown to the church at nearby Drumcree. In August the peace process again came under threat when 29 people in Omagh, Co Tyrone, were killed by an explosive device planted by a dissident republican group, the Real IRA, representing the single largest toll of deaths in any incident since the onset of sectarian unrest in the 1960s.

Progress in the peace process continued to be obstructed throughout late 1998 by a dispute between unionists and Sinn Féin concerning the decommissioning of paramilitary weapons, with Trimble insisting that the admittance of Sinn Féin representatives to the Executive Committee be conditional on progress in the demilitarization of the IRA. For its part, Sinn Féin insisted that the Good Friday Agreement did not specify when decommissioning should begin, only that it should be completed by May 2000. As a result of the dispute the deadline of 21 October 1998 for the formation of the Executive Committee and the North/South bodies was not met. In December agreement was finally reached on the responsibilities of the 10 government departments of the Executive Committee and of six North/South 'implementation' bodies. This was endorsed by the Northern Ireland Assembly in February 1999.

During 1999 the date for the devolution of powers to the new Northern Ireland institutions, envisaged as 10 March in the Good Friday Agreement, was postponed several times, and negotiations were halted in July when Trimble announced that the UUP would not participate in a devolved administration with Sinn Féin until some decommissioning had taken place. A review of the peace process, headed by George Mitchell, began in September. In that month the former Chairman of the Conservative Party, Chris Patten, who had been appointed in April 1998 to head an independent commission charged with conducting a review of policing in Northern Ireland, published his report. Recommended changes to the Royal Ulster Constabulary (RUC) included the establishment of an elected body of representatives, drawn from all sections of the community, to which the new force would be accountable, the active recruitment of Roman Catholic officers in order that the force should achieve a balanced representation, and a reduction in the number of serving officers from 13,500 to 7,500, subject to the successful conclusion of the peace process. The report provoked anger from unionists, who particularly objected to plans to change the force's name, oath and symbols. Sinn Féin, meanwhile, renewed its demand that the force be disbanded.

In November 1999 Mitchell concluded the review of the peace process, producing an agreement providing for the devolution of powers to the Executive Committee. The agreement followed a statement by the IRA that it would appoint a representative to enter discussions with the IICD. Trimble persuaded his party to approve the agreement. On 29 November the Northern Ireland Assembly convened to appoint the 10-member Executive Committee. On 2 December power was officially transferred from London to the new Northern Ireland executive and, in accordance with the Good Friday Agreement, the Irish Government removed from the Irish Constitution its territorial claim over Northern Ireland. The North/South Ministerial Council and the British-Irish Council both held their inaugural meetings in that month. In late December the British Government announced a review of security procedures in Northern Ireland and the withdrawal of some 2,000 troops from Northern Ireland, and in January 2000 it adopted the majority of the recommendations contained in the Patten report, provoking an angry response from unionists. In that month the Sinn Féin President, Gerry Adams, dismissed the possibility of immediate IRA decommissioning, and a report by the IICD confirmed that there had been no disarmament. With the prospect of the collapse of the peace process, the British and Irish Governments engaged in intensive negotiations. On 1 February the IRA released a statement giving assurances that its cease-fire would not be broken and expressing support for the peace process. However, it failed to comply with an 11 February deadline to begin decommissioning, and legislation came into effect on that day suspending the new executive, legislative and co-operative institutions and returning Northern Ireland to direct rule. The IRA subsequently announced its withdrawal from discussions with the IICD.

Adams refused to participate in any further review of the peace process until the suspended institutions had been restored.

Continuing impasse over decommissioning

Direct talks between the British and Irish Governments and the principal parties resumed in early May 2000, with the Government promising to restore the Northern Ireland institutions on 22 May and postpone the deadline for decommissioning until June 2001, subject to a commitment by the IRA on the arms issue. On 6 May the IRA responded by offering to 'initiate a process that will completely and verifiably put arms beyond use'. Under the offer a number of IRA arms depositories were to be regularly inspected by two independent international figures, Martti Ahtisaari, the former President of Finland, and Cyril Ramaphosa, a principal figure in the South African peace process. Trimble narrowly succeeded in securing the approval of the UUP of a return to power sharing, and on 30 May power was once again transferred from London to the new Northern Ireland institutions. In accordance with their continued policy of attempting to impede the functioning of the Assembly, DUP ministers agreed to retake their places in the Assembly but announced their intention periodically to resign their posts in order to disrupt parliamentary business. In June the IRA allowed three arms depositories to be inspected by Ramaphosa and Ahtisaari and announced that it had also resumed contact with the IICD.

In July 2000 the decision again to prohibit the Orange Order from marching along the Garvaghy Road in Portadown provoked renewed sectarian violence and numerous attacks on the security forces. Later in that month, under the terms of the Good Friday Agreement, the final group of 86 convicted terrorists was freed from prison in Northern Ireland. Their release was widely criticized as it had been conditionally linked to the commencement of IRA arms decommissioning, which had yet to begin. Feuding between loyalist paramilitary groups led to violent unrest in the second half of 2000, and in August troops were once again deployed on the streets of Belfast. In an attempt further to disrupt the peace process, the dissident Real IRA exploded two bombs outside the BBC's Television Centre building in London in March and April 2001. Meanwhile, in March the IRA unexpectedly announced that it had re-established contact with the IICD.

On 1 July 2001 Trimble resigned as First Minister, fulfilling a pledge to step down if the IRA had not commenced a process of decommissioning by that date. (Mallon's position of Deputy First Minister also became vacant, although he continued to exercise the functions of his office.) Trimble's resignation triggered a six-week period at the end of which, barring the resolution of the impasse between the parties and the election of a First Minister and Deputy First Minister, new elections to the Assembly would have to be held. Later in July the IICD stated that the IRA had yet to decommission a single weapon, and had failed to outline how it intended to put its arms beyond use.

In August 2001 the British and Irish Governments published their joint 'Proposals for the Implementation of the Good Friday Agreement'. The proposals stipulated that while decommissioning was not a precondition of the Agreement, it remained indispensable to a political resolution and must be resolved in a manner 'acceptable to and verified by the IICD'. However, Trimble remained adamant that in the continued absence of IRA decommissioning of weapons there would be no progress. A few days later both the IICD and the IRA confirmed that they had agreed upon a confidential decommissioning scheme, and de Chastelain announced that he was satisfied that the IRA had begun a process that would put arms 'completely and verifiably' beyond use. Trimble described the announcement as a 'step forward', but insisted that it was not sufficient for him to retract his resignation and demanded evidence of the destruction of weapons. Faced with the impending collapse of the Northern Ireland institutions, on 10 August the British Government suspended the Northern Ireland institutions for a 24-hour period. Under a legal loophole contained within the Good Friday Agreement, this decision allowed for a six-week extension to the previously imposed deadline for the election of a First Minister and Deputy. In response to the suspension, the IRA withdrew the offer to commence the process of decommissioning. A further 24-hour suspension was effected on 22 September, thus granting the parties a further six weeks in which to overcome the continuing impasse.

Also in August 2001 the British Government announced revised policing proposals, which envisaged the equal division of recruitment to the police force between Protestants and Roman Catholics and allowed for the possibility of ex-paramilitary prisoners sitting on the 29 District Police Partnership Boards, providing they relinquished their support for terrorist organizations. Sinn Féin had rejected the proposals before their publication and insisted that they would refuse to nominate members to the new 19-member Northern Ireland Policing Board (NIPB), which would be responsible for overseeing the police. In November the RUC was officially renamed the Police Service of Northern Ireland (PSNI) and the NIPB held its inaugural meeting. The two vacant Sinn Féin seats on the board were allocated to the DUP and the UUP.

In September 2001 Trimble announced that the UUP would introduce a motion in the Assembly to exclude the two Sinn Féin ministers from the Executive, and that if, as was almost certain, the motion was defeated and there was still no progress on the decommissioning issue by the IRA, UUP ministers would begin to withdraw from the Executive, thus precipitating its collapse. The UUP exclusion motion was duly defeated in October and the three UUP ministers and the two DUP ministers resigned. Later that month the IRA and the IICD issued separate statements, which affirmed that the IRA had taken the unprecedented step of putting a significant quantity of arms, ammunition and explosives beyond use. The announcement prevented the imminent collapse of the Northern Ireland institutions and was widely welcomed by all pro-Agreement parties. Trimble immediately announced that he would seek re-election to the post of First Minister, and the UUP and DUP ministers subsequently resumed their posts. On 2 November, however, Trimble failed in his attempt to be re-elected as First Minister. Although he secured a majority of the total votes cast (including all 38 nationalist votes), two anti-Agreement members of the UUP voted against Trimble, thus preventing him from obtaining the constitutionally required majority of unionists in favour of his re-election. Following intensive negotiations, four members of non-aligned parties agreed to redesignate themselves temporarily as unionists, and on 6 November Trimble finally regained the post of First Minister. The new SDLP leader, Mark Durkan, was elected Deputy First Minister.

In mid-2002, despite the announcement in April that the IRA had put a further quantity of arms, ammunition and explosives beyond use, the fragility of the peace process was underscored by unprecedented levels of street violence in Belfast, for which the UUP maintained that the IRA was primarily responsible. Adams' refusal to testify before a US investigation into alleged IRA links with left-wing rebels in Colombia, allied with allegations of IRA involvement in the theft of documents from PSNI Special Branch offices in Belfast in March 2002 and the discovery, in June, of an IRA intelligence database listing details of more than 200 judges, politicians and members of the security forces, provoked unionist demands that Sinn Féin ministers be removed from the power-sharing Executive and further 'crisis' meetings between the British and Irish Governments. In August the Real IRA was suspected to have been responsible for a bomb attack in which a Protestant man was killed—the first fatality caused by the organization since the Omagh bombing in August 1998—and a Roman Catholic was murdered in an apparent revenge act for the earlier wounding of a young Protestant. The situation was exacerbated by the escalation of a feud between rival loyalist paramilitary groups, which resulted in a number of shootings.

In October 2002 Sinn Féin's offices at the Northern Ireland Assembly were raided by police, who, as part of a major investigation into intelligence-gathering by republicans, suspected that the IRA had infiltrated the Northern Ireland Office and gained access to large numbers of confidential documents. Trimble accused Sinn Féin of a 'massive political conspiracy' and threatened to withdraw from the Executive unless the British Government proposed the expulsion of Sinn Féin from the Assembly. Emergency talks between the British and Irish Governments and the Northern Ireland political leaders followed; however, Blair's demands for IRA concessions on the arms issue were not met. The two DUP ministers resigned from the Executive, and on 14 October the Assembly was suspended and direct rule imposed. In a joint statement, Blair and Ahern announced that the devolved institutions would only be restored if Sinn Féin ended its link with paramilitary organizations. Later that month the IRA announced the suspension of all contact with the IICD and claimed that the British Government was to blame for the current crisis, having failed to honour its commitments under the Good Friday Agreement.

THE UNITED KINGDOM

In May 2003 the British and Irish Governments published a Joint Declaration, which included plans to reduce the security forces from 14,500 to 5,000 by April 2005, to repeal anti-terrorist legislation specific to Northern Ireland, to establish an independent international monitoring body to assess any breaches of the Good Friday Agreement, and to transfer policing and judicial powers to a devolved government. The Declaration also urged a full and permanent cessation of all paramilitary activity. Talks between the British and Irish Governments and the major Northern Ireland political parties continued during late 2003, and in September the four members of the International Monitoring Commission (IMC) were appointed. In an attempt to restart the process of devolution, Trimble and Adams met with Ahern and Blair in London in October, and it was revealed that elections to the Northern Ireland Assembly would take place in November. However, later on the same day Trimble declared that the acts of decommissioning of IRA weapons, witnessed by de Chastelain earlier that day, were not sufficiently transparent, and that the UUP was to withdraw from the peace process. The British Government later acknowledged that the devolved institutions would not be restored following the elections, and that a review of the Good Friday Agreement would take place in early 2004.

At the election to the Northern Ireland Assembly in November 2003 the DUP, which remained opposed to the Good Friday Agreement, secured 30 of the 108 seats, thus becoming the largest party in the Assembly. The UUP won 27 seats, while Sinn Féin increased its parliamentary representation to 24 seats. The SDLP suffered a significant loss of support, winning just 18 seats. The election results increased the pressure on Trimble from anti-Agreement factions of the UUP, which called for his resignation. Furthermore, the DUP demanded a full renegotiation of the Good Friday Agreement. However, both Ahern and Blair reiterated that the 'principles and values' of the Agreement would not be changed.

The review of the Good Friday Agreement commenced in February 2004 with Paisley setting out his party's own proposals for power sharing. While acknowledging that the proposals signalled progress on the part of the DUP, they were generally negatively received by Sinn Féin, which feared that they would lead to a return to unionist majority rule. In March Trimble withdrew his party in protest at the alleged IRA involvement in the recent kidnapping of a dissident republican in Belfast. Further negotiations at Leeds Castle in England in September ended with no agreement. In November the Ulster Defence Association (UDA) indicated its intention to end violence and demilitarize following an announcement by the British Government that it would officially recognize the loyalist paramilitary group's February cease-fire. Later in the month Paisley stated that the disarming of the IRA would only be an acceptable starting point for the power-sharing agreement if it was verified by photographic evidence. Paisley later issued an ultimatum to the IRA to the effect that if the peace accord were not restored in the current situation it would become an almost impossible task in the future, and demanded that the IRA repent of its past actions. Adams declared Paisley's comments to be offensive and stated that Sinn Féin would go no further in negotiations. In December, despite being resigned to the collapse of the peace process, Blair and Ahern met in Belfast to reveal their final proposals to restore devolution. On the following day the IRA declared that photographic proof of decommissioning had never been an option and that although the IRA was committed to the peace process, it would not be subjected to a process of humiliation.

In December 2004 an estimated £26.5m. was stolen from the Belfast headquarters of Northern Bank. The PSNI immediately set up an investigation into the incident and later stated that the IRA had been responsible for the robbery. In a report published in February 2005 the IMC implicated not only the IRA but also Sinn Féin leaders (these accusations were vehemently denied by Adams). In early February Ahern and Blair warned the IRA that its failure to demilitarize was the only obstacle to an agreement on power sharing; on the following day the IRA withdrew its commitment to decommissioning. In April, in an initiative that aimed to break the deadlock over the restoration of devolution, Adams urged the IRA to embrace the political alternative to armed struggle that now existed.

At the general election to the British Parliament in May 2005 the UUP recorded its worst electoral performance since the formation of Northern Ireland's first government in 1921, retaining only one of the five seats it had previously held. Following the election, in which he had himself lost his seat, Trimble resigned as leader of the UUP; in June the party elected Sir Reg Empey as its new leader.

The IRA renounces violence

In July 2005 the IRA issued a communiqué in which it formally renounced its armed struggle and committed itself to the pursuit of its objectives, including the goal of a united Ireland, through peaceful means only. At the same time the IRA undertook to conclude the process of comprehensive, verifiable weapons decommissioning. The communiqué was cautiously welcomed by Blair and Ahern, as well as by leading unionists, including Paisley and Empey; however, the DUP condemned the Government's decision to begin removing security facilities in South Armagh on the day after it had been issued. In September the IRA formally declared that it had completed the process of weapons decommissioning. De Chastelain, who, together with two clergymen, one Roman Catholic and one Protestant, had witnessed the decommissioning, announced at the same time that he was satisfied that the arms decommissioned represented the totality of the IRA's arsenal. In the following month the proscribed Loyalist Volunteer Force (LVF) responded to weapons decommissioning by the IRA by disbanding all of its paramilitary units. In December, in a further response to the IRA's abandonment of its armed struggle, the Government announced that British military strength in Northern Ireland would be reduced to below 9,000 in the following month.

The Northern Ireland Assembly was recalled on 15 May. The Assembly's primary responsibility was to elect a First Minister and a Deputy First Minister as soon as possible, to allocate ministerial portfolios, and to make other preparations for government. Once the Assembly had elected a First Minister and a Deputy First Minister on a cross-community basis and formed an Executive, power would automatically be devolved to the Assembly and at that point the British Government's power to suspend the Assembly would lapse definitively. In the event of the Assembly's being unable to elect First and Deputy First Ministers within the normal six-week period, Blair and Ahern stated that they would be prepared to allow a further period of 12 weeks after the summer recess for the formation of an Executive. However, if by 24 November the Assembly had failed to achieve this, the Prime Ministers' joint view was that no further purpose would be served by another election at that point or in May 2007. They would be obliged, therefore, to cancel salaries and allowances payable to members of the Assembly and to defer restoration of the Assembly and the Executive until a clear political willingness to exercise devolved power existed.

In October 2006 discussions took place at St Andrews, in Scotland, between Blair, Ahern and the leaders of the principal Northern Ireland parties. The ensuing St Andrews Agreement declared the parties' commitment to stable power-sharing government, the rule of law (including support for the PSNI), and human rights and equality issues, and established a schedule for the restoration of devolved government by March 2007 and the devolution of criminal justice and policing by 2008. It also provided for changes to the functioning of the Northern Ireland Assembly and Executive, including the introduction of a statutory ministerial code and amendments to the procedure for the election of the First Minister and Deputy First Minister. Following qualified approval of the St Andrews Agreement by Sinn Féin and the DUP, legislation giving effect to the accord was adopted by Parliament in November 2006. The new law provided for the Northern Ireland Assembly to be redesignated as a transitional assembly and to be dissolved in January 2007, pending an election in March, after which parties would nominate assembly members to positions in a devolved executive, to take office on 26 March. In January Sinn Féin held a special party conference, at which delegates voted to support the PSNI and to take up the party's allocated places on the NIPB, thereby reversing the party's long-standing policy and removing the last obstacle to the process of devolution. In February the UDA announced that it would accept the participation of Sinn Féin in a future government, while in May the loyalist Ulster Volunteer Force (UVF) announced that it had renounced paramilitary activity.

At the election to the Assembly, held on 7 March 2007, the DUP won 36 of the 108 seats, Sinn Féin 28, the UUP 18, the SDLP 16 and the Alliance Party seven. On 26 March Paisley and Adams committed themselves to forming a new power-sharing executive by 8 May, on which date Paisley was duly sworn in as First Minister and McGuinness as Deputy First Minister. The remaining 10 ministries were allocated using the so-called 'D'Hondt method', in proportion to the number of seats obtained by each party in the Assembly.

During 2007 relations between the two main parties within the Executive were cordial. However, by 2008 the issue of the devolution of powers over the justice system and policing to the Executive had led to renewed disagreements between the DUP and Sinn Féin. Paisley insisted that the IRA disband its army council, that arson attacks on Orange Order buildings cease and that financing measures be agreed by the Executive and the British Government before powers could be transferred. Adams, however, welcomed the British Government's proposals to transfer powers by the end of the year and accused the DUP of reneging on its commitment to the St Andrews Agreement. In March a cross-party Assembly committee failed to reach an agreement over the devolution of powers.

In March 2008 Paisley announced his intention to resign as leader of the DUP and, thus, as First Minister at the end of May. At a meeting of the party's executive committee the following month, the Minister of Finance and Personnel, Peter Robinson, was nominated to succeed Paisley as party leader. Paisley duly resigned from both posts and in June Robinson, having assumed the party leadership, was elected as First Minister by the Assembly. (McGuinness was concurrently re-elected as Deputy First Minister.) However, continued disagreements between the DUP and Sinn Féin, most notably regarding devolution, precipitated the latter's refusal to attend meetings of the Executive from June. In November, following the conclusion of protracted discussions between the two main parties, Robinson and McGuinness announced the details of an initial agreement outlining the process by which the transfer of powers over justice and policing to the Northern Ireland institutions could take place. Under the terms of the agreement, a temporary arrangement for the devolution of powers would be invoked, allowing the Assembly to elect by cross-community vote a single minister responsible for justice until May 2012, upon which date a permanent settlement would be enacted. The agreement also included the appointment of an independent Attorney-General for Northern Ireland (a role currently held by the Attorney-General for England and Wales). None the less, the parties failed to agree a timetable for devolution to take place.

In early 2009 a series of attacks against police officers and military personnel prompted concerns over the increased security threat from armed dissident republican groups. In March two British soldiers were shot dead at a barracks in Co Antrim, while two days later a police officer was killed in Co Armagh; representatives of all the parties engaged in the democratic process condemned the killings, responsibility for which was claimed by two dissident republican groups, the Real IRA and the Continuity IRA. Later that month a prominent republican opponent of Sinn Féin's participation in the power-sharing arrangements, Colin Duffy, was charged with murder in relation to the deaths of the two soldiers. In May the IMC published a report in which it stated that the threat from dissident republican paramilitaries remained 'serious'. Incidents of violence and attempted bomb attacks attributed to dissident republican groups occurred throughout the remainder of 2009; notably, in November a large car bomb was placed outside the headquarters of the NIPB in Belfast but failed to explode fully, while on the same day police exchanged gunfire with dissident republican paramilitaries in Co Fermanagh. Meanwhile, the IICD confirmed in June that the UVF and a related loyalist paramilitary organization, the Red Hand Commando, had completed the decommissioning of their weapons; the other main loyalist armed group, the UDA, completed its decommissioning process in January 2010. In October 2009 the republican INLA, which had declared a cease-fire in 1998, announced that its armed struggle was over; in February 2010 it announced that it had disposed of its arsenal, just one day before the mandate of the IICD was due to expire (and, with it, the immunity from prosecution for possession of weapons afforded to armed groups). The Official IRA (which had maintained a cease-fire since 1972) and a dissident faction of the UDA also completed their decommissioning on the same day.

Disagreements between the DUP and Sinn Féin over a timetable for the devolution of policing and justice powers continued to hinder the functioning of the Executive during 2009. Legislation providing for the appointment of a Minister of Justice within the Executive was approved by the Assembly in December; however, the DUP insisted on the establishment of measures to improve unionist 'community confidence', including the abolition of the Parades Commission, before it would agree to an immediate transfer of powers. The political turmoil was exacerbated in January 2010 by the emergence of a scandal concerning the personal and financial affairs of Robinson's wife, Iris (herself a DUP MP and member of the Assembly), in which the First Minister himself was implicated. Peter Robinson denied any wrongdoing in relation to the affair; however, he temporarily relinquished the post of First Minister in order to attend to his personal affairs, resuming his role in early February. None the less, during January Robinson continued to lead the DUP delegation in negotiations with Sinn Féin over the transfer of policing and justice powers. After talks collapsed later in January, Brown and the Irish Prime Minister, Brian Cowen, held discussions in Belfast with all the Northern Irish parties, following which the two Prime Ministers declared that they would publish their own proposals for devolution if substantial progress had not been reached within 48 hours. The DUP and Sinn Féin finally reached an agreement on 4 February, which, subject to approval by the Assembly, would lead to the transfer of powers and the appointment of a Minister of Justice (who would not be nominated by either party) on 12 April. As well as detailing the relationship between the Minister of Justice and the rest of the Executive, the agreement also provided for the establishment of a new mechanism to resolve disputes over marches by Protestant orders, which would replace the Parades Commission; in addition, the agreement contained further measures aimed at improving the working relationship between the parties of the Executive. The proposed timetable for devolution was approved by the Assembly in March. On 12 April David Ford, the leader of the Alliance Party, was elected Minister of Justice in a cross-community vote in the Assembly—despite the opposition of the UUP, which remained opposed to the immediate transfer of powers, and of the SDLP, which maintained that it was entitled to the ministerial post under the D'Hondt method.

At the general election to the House of Commons on 6 May 2010 Robinson unexpectedly lost his seat to the Alliance Party, which gained representation in the Commons for the first time. The DUP retained its remaining eight seats, while Sinn Féin and the SDLP also emerged with their representation unchanged, at five and three seats, respectively. The UUP, which contested the election in a controversial alliance with the Conservative Party as Ulster Conservatives and Unionists—New Force, failed to win any seats; however, one former UUP MP, Lady Silvia Hermon, was re-elected as an independent, having resigned from the party in protest against the alliance with the Conservatives. Despite Robinson's personal defeat in the election, on 10 May he was endorsed as leader of the DUP and First Minister by the party's Assembly members. Following the UUP's poor electoral performance, Empey announced that he would resign as leader of the party later that year; in September Tom Elliott was elected as his successor.

The proposals of a working group established by the DUP and Sinn Féin to draft a new framework for resolving disputes over marches by Protestant orders were published in April 2010. Under the plan, the Parades Commission would be replaced by two new bodies: one to consider applications for permission to hold a parade or protest, and a second to adjudicate in the event of a dispute. A proposed code of conduct would enshrine the right to live in freedom from sectarian harassment, but would also make it an offence to prevent or disrupt a lawful public assembly or parade. However, at a meeting in early July, the Grand Orange Lodge of Ireland voted in favour of rejecting the draft legislation. Later that month sectarian violence surrounding the Orange Order parades was described as the worst for a number of years, with the most serious rioting occurring in the Ardoyne district of north Belfast. In September Robinson announced that the bill on the marches had been put on hold, in view of the opposition of the Orange Order, and in December new members were appointed to the Parades Commission (with which the Order refused to engage).

Meanwhile, in June 2010 the report was finally published of an inquiry established in 1998 into the fatal shooting of 14 republican demonstrators by the security forces in Londonderry (Derry) on 30 January 1972 ('Bloody Sunday'). Conducted by Lord Saville of Newdigate, the inquiry, which had begun hearing evidence in March 2000 and concluded in November 2004, was the longest running and most expensive, at a cost of some £195m., in British history. The Saville report exonerated the civilians who were killed or wounded, noting that none of those shot was armed with a firearm or posed a threat of causing death or serious injury, and that some had been attempting to flee or aid others when shot. Contrary to the findings of a previous inquiry carried out by Lord Widgery of South Molton in 1972, the

Saville report concluded that the deaths of the demonstrators resulted from a 'serious and widespread loss of discipline among the soldiers', who gave no warning before firing unjustifiably, and that some soldiers had knowingly given false evidence to seek to justify their actions. As regards allegations surrounding the IRA's involvement in events, the inquiry found that although there had been some firing by republican paramilitaries, the soldiers had fired first, and that Martin McGuinness, who had admitted being the IRA's adjutant (effectively second-in-command) in Londonderry in January 1972, had not 'engaged in any activity that provided any of the soldiers with any justification for opening fire', despite the unconfirmed possibility that he might have fired a weapon on the day. In a statement to the House of Commons on the day of the publication of the report, the Prime Minister, David Cameron, apologized, on behalf of the Government, for the conduct of the armed forces on 'Bloody Sunday'. In August a report issued by the Police Ombudsman for Northern Ireland on an investigation concerning a bombing in Claudy, Co Londonderry, in July 1972, in which nine people were killed, concluded that the RUC had colluded with the British Government and the Roman Catholic Church to conceal the suspected involvement of a priest in the bombing by transferring him to a parish in the Republic of Ireland, amid fears that an arrest would provoke a deterioration in the security situation.

Attacks by dissident republicans in Northern Ireland increased in 2010, amid indications of greater co-operation between the various groups and their development of enhanced technical capabilities, leading the British authorities to raise the official threat level to Great Britain from Northern Irish-related terrorism from moderate to substantial in September. In a report presented in November, the IMC also stated that the threat posed by dissident republican paramilitary groups, particularly to the security forces, remained 'substantial and potentially lethal', noting an increase in the number of improvised explosive devices deployed during the six-month period under review (March–August) and identifying the two factions of the Real IRA as being the most active. The Commission reiterated concerns, first raised in a report submitted in September, regarding the commitment of the UVF to its stated aim of becoming a civilian organization; these concerns had been prompted by the murder, in Belfast in May, allegedly by members of the UVF, of Bobby Moffet, an associate of both that organization and the related Red Hand Commando. However, the Commission also recorded a substantial rise in the number of dissidents arrested and charged with terrorist offences and declines in the number of casualties from shootings and assaults. The IMC completed its mission in March 2011. In the following month the killing of a Roman Catholic police officer in a car bombing in Omagh was attributed to dissident republicans, although no group claimed responsibility for the incident; the murder provoked widespread cross-community condemnation.

In November 2010 Adams announced his resignation as a member of the Assembly in order to contest the forthcoming general election in the Republic of Ireland; he also relinquished his seat in the House of Commons in January 2011 and was duly elected to the Irish legislature in February. At the election to the Northern Ireland Assembly on 5 May the DUP and Sinn Féin retained their positions as the two principal parties in the legislature, winning 38 and 29 seats, respectively.

Foreign Affairs

Regional relations

The United Kingdom became a full member of the EC in January 1973. A referendum in 1975 endorsed British membership by a large majority. During the 1980s the Thatcher Government demanded controls on spending by the EC, and particularly reform of the Common Agricultural Policy (CAP), and expressed scepticism regarding proposals for greater European economic unity, on the grounds that this was likely to entail a loss of national sovereignty. Following Major's assumption of the British premiership, relations with individual members of the EC (particularly Germany) improved, and the Government adopted a more pragmatic approach towards European developments. Nevertheless, the British Government agreed to the terms of the Maastricht Treaty in 1992 only after substantial concessions had been granted for the United Kingdom. In particular, the United Kingdom's participation in the final stage of European Economic and Monetary Union (EMU), including the adoption of a single EC currency by 2000, was made optional.

On its election in May 1997, the Blair administration announced its intention to withdraw the country's option not to participate in the 'social chapter' of the Maastricht Treaty, and to promote completion of the internal economic market and enlargement of the EU. However, the new Government remained opposed to greater EU authority over national borders and immigration controls, and its demands for reform of the CAP. In June 1997 EU heads of state and of government signed the Treaty of Amsterdam, amending the Maastricht Treaty. The new agreement incorporated the social chapter, given the Labour Government's willingness to subscribe to the protocol. The United Kingdom, together with Ireland, secured an exemption from obligations with regard to immigration, asylum and visa policies; however, Blair negotiated an option to participate in certain co-operative aspects of the border arrangements.

In October 1997 the Chancellor of the Exchequer, Gordon Brown, attempted to clarify the Government's stance on the European single currency. He identified five key principles for participation in EMU, relating to its impact on the British economy and employment, and insisted that membership would have to be preceded by a sustained period of economic stability. In May 1999 Blair expressed his intention to end what he termed the United Kingdom's 'ambivalence' towards the EU and to make the country a 'leading partner' in the bloc. Earlier in the year he had predicted that the relevant conditions for participation in EMU would be in place shortly after the next general election. In June 2003 Brown announced that four of the five key principles for deciding British participation in EMU had not yet been fulfilled. Nevertheless, he stated that the Government remained in favour of joining the single currency once the conditions were in place.

A bill was published in January 2005 to allow for a referendum on a draft EU constitutional treaty, which had been approved by the leaders of the 25 member states of the EU in June 2004. In June 2005, however, following the failure of the French and Dutch electorates to endorse the treaty in referendums, the Government announced that it would not proceed with a second reading of the bill in the House of Commons. In December 2007 the Reform Treaty (later known as the Treaty of Lisbon), which replaced the defunct constitutional treaty, was signed in Lisbon, Portugal. A motion by the Conservative Party to ratify the treaty by national referendum was rejected by the House of Commons in March 2008. (Prior to the 2005 general election, all three main political parties had promised to ratify the constitutional treaty by means of a referendum.) The treaty was ratified by parliamentary vote in June 2008. In October the Conservative Party promised to conduct a national referendum on ratification of the Treaty of Lisbon, should the party take office before the treaty entered into effect. However, in November 2009, following ratification of the treaty by all 27 EU member states, the party announced that a future Conservative administration would not seek a referendum on the treaty (which entered into force in December).

The coalition Government that took office under David Cameron in May 2010 pledged that, during the current parliamentary term, no further powers would be transferred to the EU and that the United Kingdom would not adopt or prepare to adopt the European single currency. In November 2010 the Government introduced a bill to Parliament that would notably incorporate a sovereignty clause into the European Communities Act of 1972 affirming that ultimate legal authority remains with the British Parliament rather than with the EU and provide for a national referendum on any proposed new EU treaty or amendment to an existing EU treaty that would transfer powers from the United Kingdom to the EU. The bill was due to have its second reading in the House of Commons in January 2012. Meanwhile, in late 2010 Cameron failed to secure sufficient support from other member states for his demand that there should be no expansion in the EU budget for 2011, but succeeded in limiting the increase in expenditure from an initially proposed 5.9% to 2.9%. The Prime Minister also persuaded his French and German counterparts to join him in declaring their opposition to any rise in the EU budget in real terms in 2014–20 compared with expenditure in 2013. The British Government came into conflict with the European Court of Human Rights in early 2011 over its reluctance to comply with a 2005 ruling by the Court that the United Kingdom was in breach of the European Convention on Human Rights by disenfranchising all prisoners. In February 2011 the House of Commons overwhelmingly voted in favour of a non-binding motion to retain the current ban preventing convicted prisoners from voting, but in April the Court rejected an attempt by the Government to overturn the 2005 ruling, insisting that the United Kingdom draft proposals to grant prisoners the right to vote within six months.

The long-standing dispute with Spain over the sovereignty of Gibraltar has frequently strained relations between the two countries (see the chapters on Spain and Gibraltar). In November 2001 the British Government announced that it would be willing to consider joint sovereignty of the territory with Spain, and at subsequent talks the British and Spanish Governments concluded that they would reach an agreement on the future of the territory by mid-2002. Despite widespread public opposition in Gibraltar, in March 2002 both the Spanish and British Governments reiterated their determination to proceed with plans for a joint sovereignty agreement. However, in April the Spanish Prime Minister stated that Spain would never cede its claim to sovereignty over the territory. In response to the joint sovereignty proposals, the Gibraltarian authorities organized a referendum which explicitly asked if Gibraltarians approved of 'the principle that Britain and Spain should share sovereignty over Gibraltar'. The referendum, held on 7 November, resulted in an overwhelming rejection of the Spanish and British proposals. Although both Spain and the United Kingdom condemned the referendum and refused to recognize its validity, the British Government subsequently acknowledged that any arrangements for joint sovereignty were practically unenforceable due to the strength of public opposition in Gibraltar. In June 2003 the Government announced that talks with Spain regarding the possibility of sharing the sovereignty of Gibraltar had failed and suspended any further negotiations over the issue indefinitely. In December 2004 a tripartite meeting between the United Kingdom, Spain and Gibraltar was held in the United Kingdom, and it was subsequently announced that, henceforth, decisions on the territory's future must be agreed by all three parties. In March 2006 the British Government sought to reassure Spain that, in its view, Spanish rights over Gibraltar would not be affected by a proposed new constitution for the territory, despite the inclusion of references to the right to self-determination of Gibraltarians. The new Constitution was approved in a referendum in November and entered into force in January 2007. Meanwhile, in September agreements were signed by representatives of the three Governments allowing easier border crossings in and out of Gibraltar, direct commercial flights to Gibraltar from Spain, and improved telecommunications links.

Other external relations

Following Iraq's forcible annexation of Kuwait in August 1990, the British Government promptly supported the efforts of the USA in defending Saudi Arabia from potential Iraqi aggression and deployed some 42,000 personnel in the subsequent engagement in hostilities against Iraq, under the auspices of the UN. British troops also participated in subsequent humanitarian efforts to protect the Kurdish population within Iraq from persecution by the Iraqi armed forces. In January 1993 British fighter aircraft participated in US-led attacks on military targets in Iraq, launched in response to renewed Iraqi incursions into Kuwait and obstruction of a UN investigation into a suspected Iraqi nuclear weapons programme. In September 1996 the British Government gave political and logistical support to a series of air-strikes by the USA against targets in Iraq. In December 1998, following Iraq's refusal to co-operate with weapons inspections by the UN Special Commission (UNSCOM), the USA and the United Kingdom conducted a further series of air-strikes in an effort to 'degrade' Iraq's military capabilities. Further airborne attacks were conducted in early 1999 and mid-2000 in response to alleged violations by Iraq of the UN air exclusion zone. In February 2001 the United Kingdom and the USA were again involved in the bombardment of a number of targets in Iraq, in response to a reportedly increased threat to aircraft from those countries in the preceding weeks. The action was, however, condemned by several Western and Arab countries.

In July 2002, as speculation mounted about the possibility of further military action against Iraq, Blair indicated that he had concerns about any possible military strikes and subsequently announced his support for the UN Security Council's proposal that UN weapons inspectors be readmitted to Iraq. He did, however, stress in August that the British Government was determined to deal with the threat posed by Iraq's possession of weapons of mass destruction. In September, following a meeting with the US President, George W. Bush, Blair announced that the United Kingdom and the USA would attempt to secure a new UN Security Council resolution that would approve military action in Iraq, should that country fail to comply with UN weapons inspectors. Both British and US officials greeted with scepticism Iraq's declaration of its willingness to readmit weapons inspectors 'without conditions'. In September the British Government published a dossier outlining its case against the Iraqi regime and the perceived threat posed by that country's 'illicit weapons programmes' to the security of both the West and the Middle East. However, it appeared that the United Kingdom and the USA were becoming increasingly isolated in their attempts to secure approval for the use of military force against Iraq. In November, after a compromise had been reached between the five permanent members, the UN Security Council unanimously adopted Resolution 1441, which demanded, *inter alia*, that Iraq permit weapons inspectors from UNSCOM's replacement, the UN Monitoring, Verification and Inspection Commission (UNMOVIC), and the International Atomic Energy Agency (IAEA, see p. 118) unrestricted access to sites suspected of holding illegal weapons, and required the Iraqi leadership to make a full declaration of its chemical, biological, nuclear and ballistic weapons, as well as related materials used in civilian industries, within 30 days.

During January 2003 Blair, while asserting that conflict was not inevitable if Iraq complied with the UN's disarmament terms and insisting that UNMOVIC and the IAEA be granted sufficient time in order to complete their inspections, ordered large numbers of troops to the Persian (Arabian) Gulf region to join the increasing number of US forces already in position there. As the likelihood of a US-led military response to the crisis increased, the United Kingdom was one of eight European countries to sign a joint statement expressing support for the USA's stance on Iraq. Despite signs of progress being reported by UNMOVIC, on 24 February the United Kingdom, the USA and Spain presented a draft resolution to the Security Council effectively authorizing a US-led military campaign against Saddam Hussain's regime, in response to what the USA claimed was overwhelming evidence of Iraq's possession of weapons of mass destruction, its attempts to conceal such weapons from the UN inspectorate and its links with international terrorism, including the al-Qa'ida network. Officials from France, Russia and Germany responded to the draft resolution by presenting an alternative proposal involving an extended timetable of weapons inspections in order to avert a war. On 7 March the United Kingdom submitted an amended draft resolution to the Security Council, which demanded that Iraq demonstrate 'full, unconditional, immediate and active co-operation with its disarmament obligations under resolution 1441' by 17 March.

On 16 March 2003 Blair attended a summit meeting in the Azores, Portugal, along with President Bush and the Spanish Prime Minister, José María Aznar. The following day the United Kingdom, the USA and Spain withdrew their resolution from the UN, stating that they reserved the right to take their own action to ensure Iraqi disarmament. Later that day Bush issued an ultimatum giving Saddam Hussain and his two sons 48 hours to leave Baghdad or face military action. Shortly after the expiry of Bush's 48-hour deadline, on 19 March US and British armed forces launched a campaign (code-named 'Operation Iraqi Freedom') to oust the regime of Saddam Hussain. British troops were principally engaged in securing towns in southern Iraq, including Iraq's second largest city, Basra, after the US-led coalition had seized control of the key southern port of Umm Qasr and the Al-Faw Peninsula. Baghdad was captured by US forces on 9 April and, following the collapse of the Iraqi regime, on 1 May President Bush officially declared an end to 'major combat operations' in Iraq.

On 22 May 2003 the UN Security Council approved Resolution 1483, which recognized the US- and British-led Coalition Provisional Authority (CPA) as the legal occupying power in Iraq, and mandated the CPA to establish a temporary Iraqi governing authority. UN sanctions imposed on Iraq in 1990 were also lifted. However, armed resistance to coalition forces continued unabated. In July 2003 the British Government formally assumed command of the multinational task force for south-eastern Iraq, with its headquarters in Basra, comprising some 16,000 troops, of whom 11,000 were British. In September the British Government agreed to dispatch a further 1,200 troops to Iraq while placing another 1,800 soldiers on stand-by. Meanwhile, there appeared to be little sign of the chemical, biological and nuclear weapons that had been the *raison d'être* of the US-led campaign. In September Blair apologized for the intelligence claim that Iraq possessed weapons of mass destruction; however, he refused to apologize for sending British troops to Iraq, stating that the removal of Saddam Hussain was sufficient justification.

THE UNITED KINGDOM

In June 2004 the USA formally transferred sovereignty to the new Iraqi authorities. By the end of 2006 responsibility for two of the four provinces supervised by British forces had been transferred to the Iraqi security forces; responsibility for Maysan province was transferred in April 2007, and the withdrawal from Al-Basrah (Basra) province was completed in December 2008. However, in April the British Government confirmed the postponement of further troop withdrawals, citing an increase in attacks on coalition and Iraqi forces by insurgents. The complete withdrawal of British troops commenced in March 2009, when responsibility for operations in the south of the country were transferred to US forces, and the British mission in Iraq formally ended on 30 April.

In early 1999 the United Kingdom was one of the principal participants in a NATO air offensive against the Federal Republic of Yugoslavia (now Serbia). The campaign, which began in March, was intended to end the atrocities committed by Serb forces against ethnic Albanians in the Serbian province of Kosovo. As the military campaign developed Blair was perceived as the most determined of NATO's leaders in his effort to force the Yugoslav President, Slobodan Milošević, to accept the alliance's terms for a cessation of hostilities. In June Milošević conceded to these demands, and by the end of that month Serb forces had withdrawn from Kosovo. British troops formed part of the force that entered the province to enforce the peace process. In November diplomatic relations with Yugoslavia were restored. The United Kingdom was one of the first countries to afford diplomatic recognition to Kosovo following its declaration of independence from Serbia in February 2008.

The terrorist attacks on New York and Washington, DC, on 11 September 2001, for which the USA held the al-Qa'ida organization of Osama bin Laden responsible and in which 78 British citizens were killed, were denounced by Blair as an attack on the democratic world. The Prime Minister pledged that the United Kingdom would stand 'shoulder to shoulder' with the USA in its quest to bring the perpetrators of the attacks to justice and offered to provide military and diplomatic assistance to the US Administration. Blair, who by late October had held talks with more than 50 foreign heads of government, played a significant role in strengthening the international coalition against terrorism and obtaining support for military action against the Islamist Taliban regime in Afghanistan, which was suspected of harbouring senior al-Qa'ida figures, including bin Laden.

In October 2001 US and British armed forces commenced the aerial bombardment of suspected al-Qa'ida camps and strategic Taliban positions in Afghanistan, and in the following month British troops began ground operations in the country. In December it was announced that the United Kingdom had agreed to lead the International Security Assistance Force (ISAF), which was granted a six-month mandate by the UN to provide security in Kabul and its environs. ISAF was expected to comprise as many as 5,000 troops from 17 countries, some 2,000 of whom would be from the United Kingdom. The first British peace-keeping troops arrived in Afghanistan later in December. In March 2002 a separate force of 1,700 British combat troops was deployed in Afghanistan to assist US special forces with their pursuit of the remaining Taliban and al-Qa'ida fighters. By the end of 2006 around 5,300 British troops remained stationed in Afghanistan, either participating in ISAF or assisting US special forces. In mid-2007 an additional 1,400 troops were deployed to Afghanistan. In June 2008 the Secretary of State for Defence, Des Browne, announced an increase in the number of British troops in Afghanistan, from 7,800 to 8,030, to take effect by mid-2009. The Prime Minister visited Afghanistan in April 2009, where he announced an increase in the size of the British contingent, to 9,000 troops, to take effect from August. An additional 500 troops were deployed to Afghanistan in December. At a NATO summit meeting in November 2010, at which a framework for transferring full military control of Afghanistan's national security to Afghan forces by the end of 2014 was endorsed, the British Prime Minister, David Cameron, stated that all British combat troops would be withdrawn from the country by 2015. The transition process was scheduled to commence in 2011, and in March of that year the President of Afghanistan identified seven areas from which foreign troops would withdraw in July. Some 9,500 British troops remained stationed in Afghanistan in March.

In November 1991 the United Kingdom and the USA demanded that Libya extradite for trial, either in the United Kingdom or the USA, two suspected intelligence agents who were alleged to be responsible for an explosion that destroyed a US passenger aircraft over Lockerbie, Scotland, in 1988. The United Kingdom subsequently supported the imposition, by the UN, of economic and political sanctions against Libya. In view of Libya's continued refusal to allow the suspects to be tried in Scotland, in August 1998 the United Kingdom and the USA conceded to a Libyan proposal, subsequently endorsed by the UN Security Council, that they be tried on neutral territory in the Netherlands. In March 1999 Libya finally agreed to the extradition of the suspects. The UN sanctions against Libya were subsequently suspended. The trial of Abd al-Baset Ali Muhammad al-Megrahi and Al-Amin Khalifa Fhimah, which was heard under Scottish law by a panel of Scottish judges in the presence of international observers, commenced in May 2000. At the end of January 2001 the judges announced that they had unanimously found al-Megrahi guilty of the murder of 270 people and sentenced him to life imprisonment. Fhimah was, however, acquitted, owing to lack of evidence of his involvement in the bombing, and freed to return to Libya. Despite mounting pressure from Arab states, the United Kingdom maintained that sanctions against Libya would not be permanently revoked until Libya accepted responsibility for the bombing and paid 'substantial' compensation. In March 2002, following an appeal that was unanimously rejected by the five judges, al-Megrahi was transferred to a prison in Scotland to begin his sentence; it was ruled in November 2003 that he would serve 27 years in prison before becoming eligible for parole. Also in March 2002 Libya appointed an ambassador to the United Kingdom for the first time in 17 years.

In March 2003 it was reported that, following negotiations in London, Libya had agreed to accept civil responsibility for the actions of its officials in the Lockerbie case and would pay compensation to the families of the victims, in stages, conditional upon the removal of UN and US sanctions. In August Libya informed the UN Security Council that it accepted 'responsibility for the actions of its officials' in the Lockerbie bombing; agreed to pay compensation to the families of the victims; pledged co-operation in any further Lockerbie inquiry; and agreed to continue its co-operation in the 'war against terror' and to take practical measures to ensure that such co-operation was effective. Following the transfer of US $2,700m. in compensation to the International Bank of Settlements, the United Kingdom submitted a draft resolution to the Security Council requesting the formal lifting of UN sanctions against Libya, which was approved by the Security Council in September.

In December 2003 Blair announced that Libya had agreed to disclose and dismantle its programme to develop weapons of mass destruction and long-range ballistic missiles. The statement was the culmination of nine months of clandestine negotiations between Libyan, British and US diplomats, during which the Libyan authorities had reportedly shown evidence of a 'well advanced' nuclear weapons programme, as well as the existence of large quantities of chemical weapons and bombs designed to carry poisonous gas. In March 2004 Blair visited Tripoli and held talks with Libyan leader Col Muammar al-Qaddafi, after which the British Prime Minister stated that there was genuine hope for a 'new relationship', while Qaddafi insisted that he was willing to join the international 'war against terror'. In September Qaddafi announced that Libya had dismantled its weapons of mass destruction programme and in December, with the unilateral sanctions imposed upon Libya by the USA having consequently been lifted, Libya paid the second instalment of its compensation to the families of those killed in the Lockerbie bombing. In May 2006 Libya was removed from the US list of states deemed to support international terrorism, the condition for the payment of the final instalment of compensation. In October 2005 a memorandum of understanding signed by Libya and the United Kingdom guaranteed that Libya would not subject to torture or execute any person who was repatriated to it from the United Kingdom. A further memorandum of understanding was signed by Qaddafi and Blair in May 2007, which provided for negotiations on the transfer of prisoners, extradition and mutual assistance in criminal law. A final agreement was signed in November 2008 and ratified by the British Government in April 2009.

A second appeal against al-Megrahi's conviction opened at the High Court in Edinburgh in April 2009, in accordance with a recommendation made by the Scottish Criminal Cases Review Commission in June 2007. In May 2009 the Scottish Government rejected a request from the Libyan authorities to transfer al-Megrahi to Libya under the terms of the recently ratified prisoner transfer agreement, on the grounds that such a transfer could not take place while an appeal was in progress. However, in July al-Megrahi, who was suffering from a terminal illness, asked the Scottish Cabinet Secretary for Justice, Kenny MacAskill, to release him from gaol on compassionate grounds. Al-Megrahi's request was duly granted in August and he returned to Libya, where he was publicly welcomed by Qaddafi's son, Seif al-Islam. The news of his return caused considerable controversy in the United Kingdom and strained relations with the USA, especially after allegations emerged that the British Government had exerted pressure on the Scottish authorities to release him as part of a secret agreement with Libya. In September Brown insisted that no such assurances had been made to Libya and maintained that the decision to release al-Megrahi had been taken entirely by the Scottish Government. None the less, it was reported that the Secretary of State for Justice, Jack Straw, had informed MacAskill in December 2007 that it would be contrary to British interests to seek to exclude al-Megrahi from the terms of the pending prisoner transfer agreement. Confidential US diplomatic cables published in December 2010 by WikiLeaks, an organization disseminating leaked private and classified content, claimed that Qaddafi had threatened a range of repercussions against the United Kingdom, including an immediate cessation of all British commercial activity in Libya, if al-Megrahi were not released. However, in February 2011 a report on al-Megrahi's release prepared by the Cabinet Secretary, Sir Gus O'Donnell, concluded that although the British Government had done 'all it could' to facilitate a Libyan appeal for al-Megrahi's transfer or release, there was no evidence that it had exerted pressure on the Scottish authorities to respond favourably to such an appeal.

The British Government arranged the voluntary evacuation of its nationals from Libya in February 2011, amid a series of violent clashes in that country between anti-Government protesters and armed forces loyal to Qaddafi. In early March six British soldiers and two officials from the Foreign and Commonwealth Office, who had been dispatched to eastern Libya to make contact with leading opponents of the Qaddafi regime, were seized by rebel fighters and held for two days. Meanwhile, following the adoption in late February of a resolution by the UN Security Council that demanded an end to the violence and the use of force against civilians in Libya, and imposed an embargo on the supply of arms to Libya, together with other sanctions against Qaddafi, his family and associates, the British Prime Minister, David Cameron, confirmed that assets held in the United Kingdom by the Libyan leader and his family had been frozen and their diplomatic immunity had been revoked. Cameron also strongly advocated the imposition of a no-fly zone over Libya, which was approved on 17 March by the UN Security Council in a resolution that also authorized member states to take 'all necessary measures' to enforce the ban on flights and to protect civilians under threat of attack, but excluded 'a foreign occupation force of any form on any part of Libyan territory'. Two days later, as part of a multinational coalition under US command, British, French and US forces commenced missile strikes against Libyan air defence systems. The House of Commons voted overwhelmingly in support of military action in Libya on 21 March, and on 27 March NATO member states agreed to assume full command of UN-authorized military operations in Libya from the USA. At the end of the month Musa Kusa, hitherto Libyan Secretary for Foreign Liaison and International Co-operation, arrived in the United Kingdom and resigned from the Libyan Government. Kusa, a former head of the Libyan intelligence agency and the most high-profile minister to defect from the Libyan Government, was questioned in April by Scottish police investigating the Lockerbie bombing; after resigning as Libyan Secretary for Justice in February, in protest against the violence used to quell anti-Government demonstrations, Moustafa Abd al-Jelil had claimed that Qaddafi had personally ordered the bombing. NATO-led operations to enforce the no-fly zone and to protect Libyan civilians continued during April and May.

Diplomatic relations with Argentina, which had been severed in 1982 following the invasion of the Falkland Islands, were restored in 1990. While both countries continued to indicate that their respective claims to sovereignty over the Falkland Islands were not negotiable, political dialogue was able to proceed under a mutual arrangement to circumvent the issue of sovereignty. In September 1995 the two sides concluded an accord to allow exploration for offshore petroleum and gas deposits in the disputed waters around the Islands. A joint commission was to be established to supervise licensing and revenue sharing. (The first licences were awarded in October 1996.) In October 1995 Major met with the Argentine President, Carlos Menem, at the UN headquarters in New York, USA (the first meeting at this level since the 1982 war). In October 1998 Menem made an official visit to the United Kingdom, the first by an Argentine President in almost 40 years, and in July 2001 Blair became the first serving British Prime Minister to visit Argentina. Tensions between the two countries increased in the late 2000s; in March 2007 Argentina withdrew from the 1995 agreement on petroleum exploration, arguing that the United Kingdom had used it to justify its sovereignty claim. In February 2010 the commencement of prospecting operations in Falklands waters by a British oil company provoked strong protests from the Argentine Government, which asked the UN to initiate negotiations between the two countries on the sovereignty issue. The British Government defended the Islands' right to develop its petroleum industry and declared that the United Kingdom would take all necessary measures to defend the Islands. In October the Argentine Government formally protested to the British Government and to the UN, after the United Kingdom announced that it was to conduct military exercises, including the firing of missiles, off the coast of the Falklands; the British Government insisted that the manoeuvres were 'routine'.

Relations with Iran were strained from 1989 as a result of the *fatwa* (edict) issued by the Iranian spiritual leader, Ayatollah Ruhollah Khomeini, demanding the execution of the British author Salman Rushdie for his novel *The Satanic Verses*, which contained material deemed to be blasphemous against Islam. Although tensions eased in the late 1990s following the establishment of a more moderate Government in Iran, relations came under further strain in the mid-2000s. In May 2004 demonstrators in the Iranian capital, Tehran, demanded the closure of the British embassy in the city and the removal of the ambassador, in protest against British policy in Iraq, and threw petrol bombs at the building. Diplomatic relations deteriorated further in June when three British patrol crafts and eight Royal Navy personnel were captured on the Shatt al-Arab waterway by Iranian authorities who claimed the servicemen had entered Iranian territorial waters. After intense negotiations between British and Iranian diplomats, the men were released four days later and claimed that they had been forcibly escorted into Iranian waters. In October 2005 Blair warned Iran against supporting rebel factions in Iraq. The Iranian Government denied that it was doing so, and accused British forces stationed in Iraq of assisting Arab separatists responsible for recent bomb explosions in the Iranian city of Ahvaz. The United Kingdom, together with the USA and other Western governments, expressed suspicion during the early 2000s that Iran's programme of uranium enrichment was not, as Iran claimed, purely for peaceful purposes. In November 2004, after discussions with representatives of France, Germany and the United Kingdom, acting on behalf of the EU, Iran agreed to suspend its uranium enrichment programme, but in January 2006 it announced that it was resuming nuclear research and development. In December and again in March 2007, March 2008 and June 2010 the UN Security Council imposed sanctions on Iran for refusing to comply with requests to desist from uranium enrichment. Meanwhile, in March 2007 the Iranian navy arrested 15 British naval personnel whom it accused of intruding into Iranian territorial waters; they were released after almost two weeks in captivity. Relations between Iran and the United Kingdom deteriorated further in mid-June 2009, when the Iranian authorities alleged British involvement in fomenting the civil unrest that followed a disputed presidential election held in Iran that month. Two British diplomats were expelled from Iran on the grounds that they had engaged in activities 'inconsistent with their diplomatic status', and the British Government responded with the expulsion of two Iranian diplomats. In late June nine Iranian employees of the United Kingdom's embassy in Tehran were arrested for their alleged role in the post-election disturbances. Although the majority were released without charge in July, Hossein Rassam, a senior political analyst, was convicted of espionage in October and sentenced to four years' imprisonment. An appeals court overturned the espionage conviction in October 2010, however, reducing Rassam's sentence to a one-year suspended prison term for the dissemination of propaganda against the authorities. Talks on Iran's nuclear programme involving the participation of the United Kingdom, the other four permanent members of the UN Security Council and Germany, as well as Iran, remained at an impasse in early 2011; a new round of discussions began in Turkey in May.

THE UNITED KINGDOM

Introductory Survey

CONSTITUTION AND GOVERNMENT

The United Kingdom is a constitutional monarchy. However, it has no written Constitution; its constitutional principles are determined by an accumulation of statutes, common law, convention and precedent. Among the most important statutes in the evolution of the British Constitution may be cited: Magna Carta of 1215, which began the process by which the law acquired a status of its own, independent of the Crown; the Bill of Rights of 1689, which established the rights of the people and Parliament in relation to the Crown; the Reform Act of 1832, the first in a series of Acts widening the electoral franchise, culminating in the Representation of the People Act of 1928, which granted universal suffrage; and the Parliament Act of 1911, which established the supremacy in Parliament of the elected House of Commons.

The sovereign is the head of state and the monarchy is hereditary. Parliament consists of the House of Commons and the House of Lords. The 650 members of the Commons are elected for a maximum of five years by direct suffrage by all citizens of 18 years and over, using single-member constituencies. The House of Lords is composed of hereditary Peers of the Realm and Life Peers created by the sovereign for outstanding public service. (Legislation providing for the abolition of all but 92 hereditary peers and the establishment of an interim second chamber pending a definitive reform of the House of Lords took effect in 1999.) Legislation may be initiated in either House but it usually originates in the Commons. Each bill has three readings in the Commons and it is then passed to the Lords, who may return it to the Commons with amendments or suggestions. The Lords may delay, but cannot prevent, any bill from becoming law once it has been passed by the Commons. Executive power is held by the Cabinet, headed by the Prime Minister. The Cabinet is responsible to the House of Commons.

The 108-member Northern Ireland Assembly was established in 1998, as part of the multi-party agreement on the future governance of Northern Ireland. An Executive Committee, headed by a First Minister, was constituted from among the legislative members. Responsibility for all matters formerly implemented by the Northern Ireland Office was transferred to the devolved authority under new parliamentary legislation implemented in December 1999. The 1998 Agreement also provided for the establishment of a North/South Ministerial Council, to facilitate co-operation between the Irish Government and representatives of the Northern Ireland Executive on specific cross-border and all-island concerns, and of a British-Irish Council, comprising representatives of British and Irish Governments, members of the devolved authorities in Northern Ireland, Scotland and Wales, and representatives of the Isle of Man and the Channel Islands. The new Northern Ireland institutions were suspended during 2000 and again from 2002 until 2007, when devolved government was restored. Full devolution under the terms of the agreement was completed in April 2010 with the transfer of powers over policing and justice.

In 1999 devolved legislative authorities were established in Scotland and Wales. In Scotland a new elected Parliament, based in Edinburgh, was established with powers to legislate on all domestic matters (including education, health, local government and law and order) and with a mandate to vary taxes set by the Government of the United Kingdom by 3%. The Scottish Parliament has 129 members, elected every four years by a combined system of direct voting and a form of proportional representation, whereby additional members are elected at large from a party list. In November 2010 a bill providing for the transfer of additional, mainly fiscal, powers to the Scottish Parliament was introduced in the House of Commons; the bill remained under consideration in May 2011. The National Assembly for Wales, located in Cardiff, undertook responsibility for issues covered by the Welsh Office of the Government of the United Kingdom. The 60-member National Assembly is elected under the same system as in Scotland. In November 2009, in a report submitted to the Welsh First Minister, a 16-member All Wales Convention, appointed in mid-2008, concluded that the devolution of full legislative powers over domestic matters to the National Assembly for Wales would be desirable. In a referendum held in Wales on 3 March 2011, 63.5% of those participating (35.3% of the electorate) voted in favour of the Assembly being granted direct law-making powers in the currently devolved areas. Later that month the Welsh First Minister signed a commencement order giving the Assembly direct law-making powers, following its approval by the Assembly's members.

REGIONAL AND INTERNATIONAL CO-OPERATION

The United Kingdom is a member of the European Union (EU, see p. 270), but declined to participate in economic and monetary union, which introduced the single currency, or the Schengen Agreement on open borders. It is a member of the Council of Europe (see p. 250) and the Organization for Security and Co-operation in Europe (OSCE, see p. 385).

The United Kingdom joined the UN on its foundation in 1945, and is a permanent member of the UN Security Council. As a contracting party to the General Agreement on Tariffs and Trade, it joined the World Trade Organization (WTO, see p. 430) on its establishment in 1995. It was a founder member of the North Atlantic Treaty Organization (NATO, see p. 368). The Commonwealth (see p. 230), which developed as an association of the United Kingdom and its former dependencies, has its Secretariat in London. The United Kingdom also participates in the Organisation for Economic Co-operation and Development (OECD, see p. 376), the Group of Eight major industrialized nations (G8, see p. 460) and the Group of 20 major industrialized and systemically important emerging market nations (G20, see p. 451).

ECONOMIC AFFAIRS

In 2009, according to estimates by the World Bank, the United Kingdom's gross national income (GNI), measured at average 2007–09 prices, was US $2,567,480m., equivalent to $41,520 per head (or $37,360 per head on an international purchasing-power parity basis). During 2000–09, it was estimated, the population increased at an average annual rate of 0.5%, while gross domestic product (GDP) per head increased, in real terms, by an average of 0.9% per year over the same period. According to UN estimates, overall GDP increased, in real terms, at an average annual rate of 1.4% in 2000–09. Real GDP increased by 2.7% in 2007, but declined by 0.1% in 2008, and by 5.0% in 2009.

Agriculture (including hunting, forestry and fishing) contributed 0.7% of GDP in 2009, according to UN estimates, and accounted for 1.5% of work-force jobs in 2010. The principal crops include wheat, sugar beet, potatoes and barley. Livestock-rearing (particularly poultry and cattle) and animal products are important, as is fishing. The GDP of the agricultural sector decreased, in real terms, by an average of 0.2% per year during 2000–09; it declined by 5.0% in 2009.

Industry (including mining, manufacturing, construction and power) contributed 21.1% of GDP in 2009, according to UN estimates, and accounted for 16.3% of work-force jobs in 2010. Industrial GDP decreased, in real terms, at an average annual rate of 1.3% during 2000–09; it declined by 10.1% in 2009.

Mining (including petroleum and gas extraction) contributed 2.9% of GDP in 2008, according to official figures, and the sector accounted for 0.2% of work-force jobs in 2010. Natural gas, sand and gravel, limestone, crude petroleum, igneous rock and coal are the principal minerals produced. The GDP of the mining sector (together with utilities) decreased, in real terms, at an average annual rate of 3.4% during 2000–09, according to UN estimates; the GDP of extractive and utilities industries decreased by 6.9% in 2009.

Manufacturing provided 11.1% of GDP in 2009, according to UN estimates, and accounted for 8.2% of work-force jobs in 2010. The principal branches of manufacturing include transport equipment, food products, machinery, chemical products, and metals and metal products. In real terms, the GDP of the manufacturing sector decreased at an average annual rate of 1.5% during 2000–09; manufacturing GDP declined by 10.7% in 2009.

Construction provided 6.1% of GDP in 2009, according to UN estimates, and accounted for 6.9% of work-force jobs in 2010. In real terms, the GDP of the construction sector increased at an average annual rate of 0.8% during 2000–09; construction GDP declined by 10.6% in 2009.

Energy is derived principally from natural gas, petroleum and, to a lesser degree in recent years, coal. Of the United Kingdom's total consumption of energy in 2009, 47.5% was derived from petroleum, 30.5% was from natural gas, 18.1% from electricity (including nuclear and hydroelectric power), 1.4% was from renewable and waste sources (including geothermal and solar heat) and 1.1% was from coal. At the end of 2010 19 nuclear power reactors were operating in the United Kingdom (a further 26 had been permanently shut down). In 2010 mineral fuels accounted for about 12.5% of the value of total merchandise imports.

THE UNITED KINGDOM

Services accounted for 78.2% of GDP in 2009, according to UN estimates, and accounted for 82.2% of work-force jobs in 2010. The United Kingdom is an important international centre for business and financial services. Financial intermediation and other business services (including renting and real estate) contributed 32.4% of GDP in 2008. Receipts from tourism totalled £16,592m. in 2009. Wholesale and retail trade (including the motor trade) and repairs (11.4% of GDP in 2008) and transport and communications (7.1% of GDP in 2008) are also major contributors to the economy. In real terms, the GDP of the services sector increased at an average annual rate of 2.3% during 2000–09; the sector's GDP declined by 3.3% in 2009.

In 2009 the United Kingdom recorded a visible trade deficit of £81,875m., and there was a deficit of £15,506m. on the current account of the balance of payments. In 2010 the principal source of imports (12.5%) was Germany, while the principal market for exports in that year was the USA (14.4%). Other major trading partners include the People's Republic of China, France, the Netherlands, Ireland and Norway. The principal imports in 2010 were machinery and transport equipment (including road vehicles), mineral fuels (especially petroleum and petroleum products), road vehicles and miscellaneous manufactured articles (notably clothing and footwear). Machinery and transport equipment were the principal exports in that year, followed by chemicals and chemical products (notably medicinal products) and petroleum and petroleum products.

There was a budgetary deficit of £106,900m. in the financial year ending 31 March 2010, equivalent to 7.6% of GDP for the same period. At the end of December 2010 general government debt was £1,105,800m. (equivalent to 76.1% of GDP). The annual rate of inflation, according to the retail price index, averaged 2.8% in 2000–10; retail prices decreased by 0.5% in 2009, but increased by 4.6% in 2010, while consumer prices (excluding owner-occupier housing costs and council tax) increased by 2.1% in 2009 and by 3.3% in 2010. The rate of unemployment averaged 7.9% in October–December 2010.

Following a period of recession in the early 1990s, the British economy experienced a prolonged period of expansion, with sustained growth in GDP accompanied by declining unemployment and low rates of inflation. However, the world-wide economic crisis that began in 2007 had a severe effect on the British economy. The shortage of credit in the global financial system caused substantial losses in the British financial sector, and led to significant government intervention in the banking sector. As the availability of credit contracted, house prices and consumer spending declined and redundancies increased. In a bid to encourage spending and ease pressure on businesses, the Bank of England lowered its official interest rate from 5.0% in September 2008 to an historic low of 0.5% in March 2009. This policy was augmented by 'quantitative easing', in which the Bank increased the money supply by some £200,000m. between March 2009 and January 2010 through the purchase of government and corporate bonds. None the less, the United Kingdom GDP contracted by 5.0% in 2009, while the budget deficit increased to 7.6% of GDP in 2009/10, with net borrowing rising to 11.1% of GDP and public sector net debt reaching 52.7% of GDP. The coalition Government that took office in May 2010 declared that it would implement a 'significantly accelerated' reduction of the deficit, to be achieved principally through reduced spending, and presented an emergency budget in June and a comprehensive spending review in October. With the aim of balancing the budget by 2015/16, expenditure by government departments (other than health and overseas aid) would be reduced by an average of 19% in real terms over four years, while tax-related measures included an increase in the rate of value-added tax from 17.5% to 20% from January 2011. GDP increased by an estimated 1.3% in 2010, although there was a contraction, of 0.5%, in the final quarter. In March 2011 the Office for Budget Responsibility forecast GDP growth of 1.7% for that year. The Bank of England's official interest rate remained at 0.5% in May 2011, but (modest) increases were anticipated later that year, amid concerns regarding the inflation rate, which stood at 4.5% in April 2011, according to the consumer price index, the 17th consecutive month that it had exceeded the target of 2%. Meanwhile, the unemployment rate remained high, averaging 7.8% in the three months to February 2011 (compared with 5.2% for the same period in 2008).

PUBLIC HOLIDAYS

2012: 1 January (New Year's Day), 2 January* (Scotland only), 17 March (St Patrick's Day, Northern Ireland only), 6 April (Good Friday), 9 April† (Easter Monday), 7 May* (May Bank Holiday), 4 June (Spring Bank Holiday), 5 June (Bank Holiday, Queen's Diamond Jubilee), 12 July (Battle of the Boyne, Northern Ireland only), 6 August* (Summer Bank Holiday, Scotland only), 27 August† (Summer Bank Holiday), 25 December (Christmas Day), 26 December* (Boxing Day).

Additional public holidays may be established by local authorities in Scotland.

* Bank Holidays but not national holidays in Scotland.
† Excluding Scotland.

Statistical Survey

Source (unless otherwise stated): Office for National Statistics, 1 Drummond Gate, London, SW1V 2QQ; internet www.statistics.gov.uk.

Area and Population

AREA, POPULATION AND DENSITY

Land area (sq km)	242,495*
Population usually resident (census results)	
21 April 1991	56,466,700
29 April 2001	
Males	28,581,233
Females	30,207,961
Total	58,789,194
Population (official estimates at mid-year)	
2007	60,985,700
2008	61,398,200
2009	61,792,000
Density (per sq km) at mid-2009	254.8

* 93,628 sq miles.

POPULATION BY AGE AND SEX
('000, official estimates at mid-2009)

	Males	Females	Total
0–14	5,525.6	5,270.0	10,795.6
15–64	20,425.9	20,464.7	40,890.4
65 and over	4,422.4	5,683.4	10,105.8
Total	30,374.0	31,417.9	61,792.0

Note: Totals may not be equal to the sum of components, owing to rounding.

DISTRIBUTION OF POPULATION
('000 at mid-2009)

	Land area (sq km)	Population	Density (per sq km)
Great Britain	228,919	60,003.1	262.1
England	130,279	51,809.7	397.7
Wales	20,733	2,999.3	144.7
Scotland	77,907	5,194.0	66.7
Northern Ireland	13,576	1,788.9	131.8
Total	242,495	61,792.0	254.8

THE UNITED KINGDOM

ADMINISTRATIVE AREAS
('000, population estimates at mid-2009)

England

Greater London	7,753.6	Redcar and Cleveland	137.5
		Rutland	38.4

Metropolitan Counties:

Greater Manchester	2,600.9	Shropshire[6]	291.8
Merseyside	1,350.6	Slough	128.4
South Yorkshire	1,317.3	South Gloucestershire	262.2
Tyne and Wear	1,106.3	Southampton	236.7
West Midlands	2,638.7	Southend-on-Sea	164.2
West Yorkshire	2,226.7	Stockton-on-Tees	191.1
		Stoke-on-Trent	238.9
		Swindon	198.8

Unitary Authorities:

Bath and North East Somerset	177.7	Telford and Wrekin	162.3
Bedford[1]	158.0	Thurrock	157.2
Blackburn with Darwen	139.9	Torbay	134.0
Blackpool	140.0	Warrington	197.8
Bournemouth	164.9	West Berkshire	153.0
Bracknell Forest	115.1	Windsor and Maidenhead	143.8
Brighton and Hove	256.3	Wiltshire[7]	456.1
Bristol	433.1	Wokingham	161.9
Central Bedfordshire[1]	252.9	York	198.8

Non-Metropolitan Counties:

Cheshire East[2]	362.7	Buckinghamshire	494.7
Cheshire West and Chester[2]	326.6	Cambridgeshire	607.0
Cornwall[3]	531.1	Cumbria	495.0
Darlington	100.4	Derbyshire	760.2
Derby	244.1	Devon	747.4
Durham[4]	506.4	Dorset	404.0
East Riding of Yorkshire	337.0	East Sussex	512.1
Halton	118.7	Essex	1,399.0
Hartlepool	90.9	Gloucestershire	589.1
Herefordshire	179.1	Hampshire	1,289.4
Isle of Wight	140.2	Hertfordshire	1,095.5
Isles of Scilly[3]	2.2	Kent	1,411.1
Kingston upon Hull	262.4	Lancashire	1,165.8
Leicester	304.7	Leicestershire	644.7
Luton	194.3	Lincolnshire	697.9
Medway	254.8	Norfolk	853.4
Middlesbrough	140.5	North Yorkshire	597.7
Milton Keynes	236.7	Northamptonshire	683.8
North Lincolnshire	161.0	Nottinghamshire	776.6
North Somerset	209.1	Oxfordshire	640.3
North East Lincolnshire	157.1	Somerset	523.5
Northumberland[5]	311.1	Staffordshire	828.7
Nottingham	300.8	Suffolk	714.0
Peterborough	171.2	Surrey	1,113.1
Plymouth	256.7	Warwickshire	535.1
Poole	141.2	West Sussex	792.9
Portsmouth	203.5	Worcestershire	556.5
Reading	151.8		

Wales

		Isle of Anglesey	68.8

Unitary Authorities:

Blaenau Gwent	68.6	Merthyr Tydfil	55.7
Bridgend	134.2	Monmouthshire	88.0
Caerphilly	172.7	Neath Port Talbot	137.4
Cardiff	336.2	Newport	140.4
Carmarthenshire	180.8	Pembrokeshire	117.4
Ceredigion	76.4	Powys	131.7
Conwy	111.4	Rhondda, Cynon, Taff	234.4
Denbighshire	96.7	Swansea	231.3
Flintshire	149.9	Torfaen	90.7
Gwynedd	118.8	Vale of Glamorgan	124.6
		Wrexham	133.2

Scotland

		Glasgow City	588.5

Unitary Authorities:

Aberdeen City	213.8	Highland	220.5
Aberdeenshire	243.5	Inverclyde	80.2
Angus	110.3	Midlothian	80.8
Argyll and Bute	90.0	Moray	87.7
Clackmannanshire	50.5	North Ayrshire	135.5
Comhairle nan Eilean Siar (Western Isles)	26.2	North Lanarkshire	326.3
		Orkney Islands	20.0
Dumfries and Galloway	148.5	Perth and Kinross	145.9
Dundee City	143.4	Renfrewshire	169.9
East Ayrshire	120.2	Scottish Borders	112.7
East Dunbartonshire	104.7	Shetland Islands	22.2
East Lothian	96.8	South Ayrshire	111.4
East Renfrewshire	89.2	South Lanarkshire	310.9
Edinburgh, City of	477.7	Stirling	88.7
Falkirk	152.5	West Dunbartonshire	90.9
Fife	363.5	West Lothian	171.0

Northern Ireland

		Derry	109.6

Unitary Authorities:

Antrim	54.0	Down	70.3
Ards	78.1	Dungannon	56.4
Armagh	58.8	Fermanagh	62.4
Ballymena	63.2	Larne	31.4
Ballymoney	30.4	Limavady	34.0
Banbridge	47.6	Lisburn	116.5
Belfast	268.4	Magherafelt	44.2
Carrickfergus	40.1	Moyle	16.9
Castlereagh	66.8	Newry and Mourne	98.7
Coleraine	57.1	Newtownabbey	83.4
Cookstown	36.3	North Down	79.6
Craigavon	92.4	Omagh	52.4
		Strabane	39.9

PRINCIPAL LOCALITIES*
('000, population estimates at mid-2009)

Greater London (capital)	7,753.6	Wigan	306.5
Birmingham	1,028.7	Leicester	304.7
Leeds	787.7	Nottingham	300.8
Glasgow City	588.5	Sandwell	291.0
Sheffield	547.0	Doncaster	290.1
Bradford	506.8	Newcastle upon Tyne	284.3
Manchester	483.8	Stockport	283.7
Edinburgh	477.7	Sunderland	281.7
Liverpool	442.3	Sefton	273.3
Bristol	433.1	Belfast	268.4
Kirklees	406.8	Bolton	265.1
Fife	363.5	Kingston upon Hull	262.4
East Riding of Yorkshire	337.0	South Gloucestershire	262.2
Cardiff	336.2	Plymouth	256.7
North Lanarkshire	326.3	Brighton and Hove	256.3
Wakefield	323.9	Walsall	255.9
Coventry	312.8	Medway	254.8
South Lanarkshire	310.9	Rotherham	253.9
Wirral	308.5	Central Bedfordshire	252.9
Dudley	306.6		

* Local authority areas with populations greater than 250,000.

---

[1] Formerly part of Non-Metropolitan County of Bedfordshire; became two new unitary authorities of Bedford and Central Bedfordshire on 1 April 2009.

[2] Formerly part of Non-Metropolitan County of Cheshire; became two new unitary authorities of Cheshire East and Cheshire West and Chester on 1 April 2009.

[3] Formerly part of Non-Metropolitan County of Cornwall/Isles of Scilly; became two new unitary authorities of Cornwall and Isles of Scilly on 1 April 2009.

[4] Formerly Non-Metropolitan County of Durham; became new unitary authority of Durham on 1 April 2009.

[5] Formerly Non-Metropolitan County of Northumberland; became new unitary authority of Northumberland on 1 April 2009.

[6] Formerly Non-Metropolitan County of Shropshire; became new unitary authority of Shropshire on 1 April 2009.

[7] Became new unitary authority of Wiltshire on 1 April 2009.

THE UNITED KINGDOM

BIRTHS, MARRIAGES AND DEATHS*

	Registered live births Number	Rate (per 1,000)	Registered marriages† Number	Rate (per 1,000)	Registered deaths Number	Rate (per 1,000)
2002	668,777	11.3	293,021	4.9	608,045	10.3
2003	695,549	11.7	308,620	5.1	612,085	10.3
2004	715,996	12.0	313,550	5.2	583,082	9.8
2005	722,549	12.0	286,826	4.8	582,964	9.7
2006	748,563	12.4	277,600‡	n.a.	572,224	9.4
2007	772,245	12.7	273,900‡	n.a.	574,685	9.4
2008	794,383	12.9	270,403	n.a.	579,697	9.4
2009	790,200‡	12.8	n.a.	n.a.	559,600‡	9.1

* In England and Wales, figures for births are tabulated by year of occurrence, while figures for Scotland and Northern Ireland are tabulated by year of registration. Births to non-resident mothers in Northern Ireland are excluded from the figures for the United Kingdom.
† Figures exclude civil partnerships (figures are rounded to nearest 10): 1,950 in 2005; 16,110 in 2006; 8,730 in 2007; 7,170 in 2008; 6,280 in 2009 (provisional).
‡ Provisional figure, rounded to nearest 100.

Sources: Office for National Statistics; General Register Office for Scotland; Northern Ireland Statistics and Research Agency.

Life expectancy (years at birth, WHO estimates): 80 (males 78; females 82) in 2008 (Source: WHO, *World Health Statistics*).

IMMIGRATION AND EMIGRATION*

Immigrants
('000)

Origin†	2007	2008	2009
EU‡	220	224	198
Commonwealth countries	200	196	204
Australia, New Zealand, Canada	47	48	45
Australia	31	29	29
South Africa	17	20	11
Other African Commonwealth	24	31	31
Bangladesh, India, Pakistan, Sri Lanka	95	80	101
Other	16	17	16
Other territories‡	154	171	164
USA	23	28	31
Middle East	23	30	26
Total	**574**	**590**	**567**

Emigrants
('000)

Destination†	2007	2008	2009
EU‡	131	202	144
Commonwealth countries	127	119	127
Australia, New Zealand, Canada	83	79	82
Australia	58	55	57
South Africa	11	7	6
Other African Commonwealth	5	8	8
Bangladesh, India, Pakistan, Sri Lanka	18	17	23
Other	9	9	8
Other territories‡	83	105	97
USA	18	23	27
Middle East	11	21	15
Total	**341**	**427**	**368**

* For 2007 figures were compiled in accordance with the Long-term International Migration (LTIM) methodology, which supplements International Passenger Survey (IPS) data (whereby small samples of detailed passenger numbers are extrapolated according to a weighting system) with estimates of migration between the UK and Ireland (agreed between the Irish Central Statistics Office and the UK Office for National Statistics), and with Home Office data on asylum seekers and their dependents. In addition, two adjustments were estimated to account for 'visitor switchers' (who stay longer than their stated intention) and 'migrant switchers' (who stay for less time than intended). From 2008 an amended methodology was introduced whereby data for migration between the UK and the Republic of Ireland were included in the IPS data; the new methodology also incorporated data on migration between the UK and Northern Ireland supplied by the Northern Ireland Statistics and Research Agency (NISRA), which had previously been supplied by IPS.
† Figures refer to the country of immigrants' last permanent residence or emigrants' intended future residence.
‡ Figures for all years show the EU as it was constituted at 31 December of year shown, therefore figures for 'EU' and for 'Other territories' may not be comparable for all years.

WORK-FORCE JOBS BY INDUSTRY
('000, annual averages, seasonally adjusted)

	2008	2009	2010
Agriculture, hunting, forestry and fishing	412	405	463
Mining and quarrying	68	62	60
Manufacturing	2,872	2,640	2,557
Construction	2,304	2,240	2,158
Electricity, gas and water	255	277	301
Wholesale and retail trade; repair of motor vehicles and motorcycles	5,046	4,871	4,755
Hotels and restaurants	2,012	1,960	1,904
Transport, storage and communications	2,736	2,693	2,591
Real estate, renting and other business activities	5,279	5,088	5,128
Banking, finance, insurance, etc.	1,189	1,180	1,125
Public administration and defence; compulsory social security	1,750	1,769	1,757
Education	2,610	2,712	2,719
Human health and social work	3,751	3,887	4,027
Other services	1,778	1,683	1,656
Total	**32,063**	**31,466**	**31,201**

Note: Since data correspond to jobs rather than employees, a single worker may be counted more than once; figures include armed forces personnel.

Economically active population (labour force survey, '000 persons aged 16 years and over, excl. armed forces, October–December 2010): Total employed 29,121; Unemployed 2,492; Total labour force 31,613 (males 17,096, females 14,517).

THE UNITED KINGDOM

Statistical Survey

Health and Welfare

KEY INDICATORS

Total fertility rate (children per woman, 2008)	1.8
Under-5 mortality rate (per 1,000 live births, 2008)	6
HIV/AIDS (% of persons aged 15–49, 2007)	0.2
Physicians (per 1,000 head, 2004)	2.3
Hospital beds (per 1,000 head, 2004)	3.9
Health expenditure (2007): US $ per head (PPP)	2,992
Health expenditure (2007): % of GDP	8.4
Health expenditure (2007): public (% of total)	81.7
Total carbon dioxide emissions ('000 metric tons, 2007)	539,175.9
Carbon dioxide emissions per head (metric tons, 2007)	8.8
Human Development Index (2010): ranking	26
Human Development Index (2010): value	0.849

For sources and definitions, see explanatory note on p. vi.

Agriculture

PRINCIPAL CROPS
('000 metric tons)

	2006	2007	2008
Wheat	14,747	13,221	17,227
Barley	5,239	5,079	6,144
Oats	728	712	784
Rye	43	38	32
Triticale (wheat-rye hybrid)	61	65	81
Potatoes	5,864	5,635	5,999
Sugar beet	7,400	6,733	7,500
Rapeseed	1,890	2,108	1,973
Peas, dry	145	130*	91
Broad beans, dry*	150	160	160
Onions, dry	359	304	349
Mushrooms and truffles	68	72	44
Carrots and turnips	701	752	719
Cabbages and other brassicas	300	254	254*
Cauliflower and broccoli	196	186	186*
Peas, green	300	244	244*
Linseed	49	23	29
Lettuce and chicory	135	117	124
Tomatoes	84	86	89
Cucumbers and gherkins	57	49	49
Apples	269	263	243
Pears	28	21	20
Strawberries	74	87	87*

*FAO estimate(s).

2009: Wheat 14,379; Barley 6,969; Oats 757; Rye 36; Triticale (wheat-rye hybrid) 66; Potatoes 6,423; Sugar beet 8,330; Rapeseed 1,951; Peas, dry 132; Broad beans, dry 160 (FAO estimate).

Aggregate production (may include official, semi-official or estimated data): Total cereals 20,832 in 2006, 19,128 in 2007, 24,282 in 2008, 22,237 in 2009; Total pulses 795 in 2006, 745 in 2007, 863 in 2008, 424 in 2009; Total roots and tubers 5,864 in 2006, 5,635 in 2007, 5,999 in 2008, 6,423 in 2009; Total vegetables (incl. melons) 2,505 in 2006, 2,368 in 2007, 2,348 in 2008–09; Total fruits (excl. melons) 422 in 2006, 420 in 2007, 412 in 2008–09.

Source: FAO.

LIVESTOCK
('000 head, year ending September)

	2007	2008	2009
Cattle	10,304	10,107	9,901
Sheep	33,946	33,131	30,783
Pigs	4,834	4,714	4,601
Chickens	157,513	154,180	170,000*
Ducks and geese	2,520	2,339	n.a.
Turkeys	3,832	5,514	5,600

*FAO estimate.
Source: FAO.

LIVESTOCK PRODUCTS
('000 metric tons unless otherwise indicated)

	2007	2008	2009
Cattle meat	882	862	850
Sheep meat	325	326	303
Pig meat	739	740	720
Chicken meat	1,270	1,259	1,463
Cows' milk	14,023	13,719	13,237
Butter and ghee	120	122	118
Cheese	374	343	322
Hen eggs	579	600	n.a.
Wool, greasy*	62	62	n.a.

*FAO estimates.
Source: FAO.

Forestry

ROUNDWOOD REMOVALS
('000 cubic metres, excl. bark)

	2007	2008	2009
Sawlogs, veneer logs and logs for sleepers	5,716	5,095	5,226
Pulpwood	2,396	2,258	1,737
Other industrial wood	450	506	546
Fuel wood	459	557	988
Total	9,021	8,416	8,497

Source: FAO.

SAWNWOOD PRODUCTION
('000 cubic metres, incl. railway sleepers)

	2007	2008	2009
Coniferous (softwood)	3,100	2,771	2,824
Broadleaved (hardwood)	45	44	48
Total	3,145	2,815	2,871

Source: FAO.

Fishing

('000 metric tons, live weight)

	2006	2007	2008
Capture	624.4	619.7	596.0
Haddock	39.8	33.5	33.1
Blue whiting	82.1	56.5	38.2
Atlantic herring	109.6	91.1	67.1
Atlantic mackerel	103.0	133.7	124.9
Edible crab	22.9	31.1	22.7
Norway lobster	41.3	44.5	43.5
Aquaculture	171.8	174.2	179.2
Atlantic salmon	132.0	130.1	128.7
Blue mussel	24.0	25.4	28.2
Total	796.2	793.9	775.2

Note: Figures exclude aquatic mammals, recorded by number rather than weight. The number of whales and porpoises caught was: 54 in 2006; 55 in 2007; 28 in 2008.

Source: FAO.

THE UNITED KINGDOM

Mining and Quarrying

('000 metric tons, unless otherwise indicated)

	2007	2008	2009*
Hard coal (incl. slurries)	17,007	18,054	17,874
Natural gas and petroleum:			
Methane—colliery	62	55	n.a.
Methane—onshore	104	101	59,640
Methane—offshore	71,959	69,517	
Crude petroleum	70,357	66,745	62,627
Onshore	1,271	1,248	n.a.
Offshore	69,086	65,497	n.a.
Condensates and others[1]	6,475	6,201	5,377
China clay (sales)[2]	1,671	1,355	1,060
Ball clay (sales)	1,022	1,020	727
Fireclay[3]	338	180	180
Common clay and shale[3]	10,104	8,459	8,000
Slate[4]	1,428	1,058	1,100
Limestone	83,491	74,143	59,700
Dolomite	7,622	5,509	
Chalk[3]	7,566	5,874	6,000
Sandstone	16,806	12,255	9,200
Common sand and gravel[5]	93,236	85,471	65,800
Igneous rock[6]	58,909	53,489	40,100
Gypsum*	1,700	1,700	1,700
Rock salt*	1,900	1,900	2,000
Salt from brine*	1,000	1,000	1,000
Salt in brine*[7]	2,800	2,800	2,800
Fluorspar*	45	37	19
Barytes	53	43	36
Talc	3	2	3
Potash[8]	712	673	600

* Estimates.
[1] Includes ethane, propane and butane, in addition to condensates (pentane and hydrocarbons).
[2] Dry weight.
[3] Excluding production in Northern Ireland.
[4] Including waste used for constructional fill and powder and granules used in industry.
[5] Including marine-dredged sand and gravel for both home consumption and export.
[6] Excluding production in Northern Ireland and the Channel Islands.
[7] Used for purposes other than salt-making.
[8] Chloride (K$_2$O content).

Source: British Geological Survey.

Industry

SELECTED PRODUCTS

('000 metric tons unless otherwise indicated)

	2006	2007	2008
Flour of wheat and meslin[1]	4,433	4,509	n.a.
Beer ('000 hectolitres)	53,768	51,341	49,611
Cigarettes ('000 million)	44.4	42.0	42.1
Butane and propane[2]	2,105	2,259	2,248
Petroleum naphtha[2]	2,734	2,561	1,863
Motor spirit (petrol)[2]	21,443	21,313	20,319
Aviation turbine fuel[2]	6,261	6,176	6,549
Burning oil[2]	3,374	2,968	3,092
Diesel fuel and gas oil[2]	26,037	26,452	26,971
Fuel oil[2]	11,279	10,433	10,496
Lubricating oils[2]	617	547	514
Petroleum bitumen (asphalt)[2]	1,749	1,628	1,485
Cement[3]	11,470	11,890	10,070

Statistical Survey

—continued	2006	2007	2008
Pig-iron[4]	10,696	10,960	10,137
Crude steel (usable)	13,905	14,392	13,521
Aluminium—(wrought remelt)	565.0	572.7	654.5
Refined lead—unwrought[5]	245.9	304.4	318.7
Electric energy (million kWh)	397,292	397,044	389,649

[1] Source: UN Industrial Commodity Statistics Database.
[2] Refinery production only (excluding supplies from other sources).
[3] Excluding production in Northern Ireland.
[4] Including blast-furnace ferro-alloys.
[5] Lead reclaimed from secondary and scrap material, and lead refined from bullion and domestic ores; includes antimonial lead.

Passenger motor cars 1,442,100 in 2006.

Road goods vehicles 206,800 in 2005.

2009: Beer ('000 hectolitres) 45,141; Cigarettes ('000 million) 44.0.

Finance

CURRENCY AND EXCHANGE RATES

Monetary Units
100 pence (pennies) = 1 pound sterling (£).

Dollar and Euro Equivalents (31 December 2010)
US $1 = 63.88 pence;
€1 = 85.35 pence;
£10 = $15.65 = €11.72.

Average Exchange Rate (pound sterling per US $)
2008   0.5440
2009   0.6419
2010   0.6472

BUDGET

(general government transactions, year ending 31 March, £ '000 million)

Current Revenue

	2007/08	2008/09	2009/10
Income tax (net)	147.4	147.8	147.5
National insurance contributions	100.4	96.9	96.6
Value-added tax	80.6	78.4	73.5
Corporation tax	46.4	43.1	36.5
Petroleum revenue tax	1.7	2.6	0.9
Fuel duties	24.9	24.6	26.2
Capital gains tax	5.3	7.9	2.5
Inheritance tax	3.9	2.8	2.4
Stamp duties	14.1	8.0	7.9
Tobacco duty	8.1	8.2	8.8
Spirits duties	2.4	2.4	2.7
Wine duties	2.6	2.7	3.0
Beer and cider duties	3.3	3.4	3.5
Air passenger duty	2.0	1.9	1.9
Insurance premium tax	2.3	2.3	2.3
Climate change levy	0.7	0.7	0.7
Business rates	21.4	22.9	23.4
Council tax	23.4	24.4	25.3
Other HMRC taxes	5.2	5.5	5.4
Other taxes and royalties	20.1	21.7	19.3
Vehicle excise duty (VED)	5.4	5.6	5.6
Interest and dividends	9.0	9.0	3.4
Gross operating surplus and rent	25.0	24.7	23.3
Other receipts and adjustments	−0.9	−7.9	−3.7
Total current revenue	**549.2**	**533.8**	**513.3**

Source: HM Treasury, *Budget 2011* (March 2011).

THE UNITED KINGDOM

Statistical Survey

Expenditure*

By function of government	2007/08	2008/09	2009/10
General public services	50.7	52.8	53.4
International services	6.7	7.3	8.1
Public sector debt interest	31.4	31.6	31.4
Public and common services	12.6	13.9	13.9
Defence	33.6	36.7	38.2
Public order and safety	31.7	33.6	35.0
Economic affairs	38.9	48.1	45.6
Enterprise and economic development	6.9	15.6	9.1
Science and technology	3.2	3.2	3.5
Employment policies	3.3	3.1	3.8
Agriculture, fisheries and forestry	5.0	5.4	6.1
Transport	20.5	20.8	23.1
Environment protection	9.5	9.6	11.4
Housing and community amenities	12.9	15.0	15.6
Health	102.2	110.0	119.8
Recreation, culture and religion	12.2	13.1	14.1
Education	78.1	82.6	88.3
Social protection	187.5	203.6	222.5
EU transactions	−1.5	−2.9	0.0
Unallocated	—	—	−2.5
Accounting adjustments	26.7	27.7	27.8
Less Public sector net investment	28.8	46.4	49.0
Total current expenditure	**553.7**	**583.5**	**620.2**

* Including depreciation.

Source: HM Treasury, *Public Expenditure Statistical Analyses 2010* (July 2010).

Budget forecasts (general government transactions, year ending 31 March, £ '000 million): *Total current revenue:* 548.5 in 2010/11; 588.6 in 2011/12. *Total current expenditure (incl. depreciation):* 653.3 in 2010/11; 678.6 in 2011/12 (Source: HM Treasury, *Budget 2011*—March 2011).

OFFICIAL RESERVES
(US $ million at 31 December)*

	2008	2009	2010
Gold	8,628	11,012	14,067
IMF special drawing rights	448	14,344	14,118
Foreign currencies†	40,487	35,618	43,489
Reserve position in IMF	2,350	3,333	4,892
Other reserve assets	−2,939	−169	1,303
Total	**48,974**	**64,138**	**77,869**

* Reserves are revalued at 31 March each year.
† Excluding unsettled trades (US $ million): −138 in 2008; 0 in 2009; 0 in 2010.

Source: Bank of England.

MONEY SUPPLY
(£ million at 31 December)

	2009	2010
Retail deposits and cash	1,187,097	1,234,496
Notes and coin in private sector	50,284	51,772
Bank deposits	923,205	1,182,724
Building society deposits	213,609	
Wholesale deposits	854,774	921,063
Bank deposits	824,023	n.a.
Building society deposits	30,750	n.a.
Total broad money	**2,041,871**	**2,155,558**

Source: Bank of England.

COST OF LIVING
(General Index of Retail Prices, annual averages; base: January 1987 = 100)

	2008	2009	2010
Food	179.5	189.1	195.0
Catering	264.2	271.4	279.8
Alcoholic drink	227.7	236.0	244.3
Tobacco	377.6	392.6	422.6
Housing	339.9	305.6	313.7
Fuel and light	253.6	269.4	262.1
Household goods	155.6	162.7	169.8
Household services	203.7	208.8	217.3
Clothing and footwear	90.3	86.4	91.9
Personal goods and services	222.3	228.7	237.1
Motoring expenditure	195.1	193.7	219.1
Fares and other travel costs	261.1	273.4	287.6
Leisure goods	87.2	85.8	86.5
Leisure services	287.2	302.3	317.6
All items	**214.8**	**213.7**	**223.6**

NATIONAL ACCOUNTS
(£ million at current prices)

National Income and Product

	2008	2009	2010
Compensation of employees	769,191	774,035	796,128
Gross operating surplus	424,804	382,852	389,359
Mixed income	84,884	84,243	86,906
Gross domestic product (GDP) at factor cost	**1,278,879**	**1,241,130**	**1,272,393**
Taxes on production and imports *Less* Subsidies	166,701	154,891	179,007
Statistical discrepancy	—	−1,032	2,216
GDP at market prices	**1,445,580**	**1,394,989**	**1,453,616**
Primary incomes received from abroad *Less* Primary incomes paid abroad	26,178	19,722	29,777
Gross national income	**1,471,758**	**1,414,711**	**1,483,393**
Less Consumption of fixed capital	151,370	n.a.	n.a.
Net national income	**1,320,388**	n.a.	n.a.
Current transfers from abroad *Less* Current transfers paid abroad	−12,196	n.a.	n.a.
Net national disposable income	**1,308,192**	n.a.	n.a.

Expenditure on the Gross Domestic Product

	2008	2009	2010
Final consumption expenditure	1,242,070	1,237,535	1,289,433
Households (incl. non-profit institutions serving households)	928,026	910,632	954,830
General government	314,044	326,903	334,603
Gross capital formation	241,270	188,594	216,056
Gross fixed capital formation	240,361	203,619	212,215
Changes in inventories	295	−15,602	3,596
Acquisitions, less disposals of valuables	614	577	245
Total domestic expenditure	**1,483,340**	**1,426,129**	**1,505,489**
Exports of goods and services	422,905	390,893	428,259
Less Imports of goods and services	460,665	420,580	476,713
Statistical discrepancy	—	−1,453	−3,419
GDP in purchasers' values	**1,445,580**	**1,394,989**	**1,453,616**

THE UNITED KINGDOM

Statistical Survey

Gross Domestic Product by Economic Activity

	2006	2007	2008
Agriculture, hunting, forestry and fishing	7,788	8,628	9,715
Mining and quarrying	31,752	30,849	37,718
Manufacturing	151,455	154,726	150,298
Electricity, gas and water supply	20,279	21,884	21,342
Construction	74,619	80,675	80,756
Wholesale and retail trade; repair of motor vehicles, motorcycles and personal and household goods	135,366	141,735	147,159
Hotels and restaurants	34,594	35,962	36,427
Transport, storage and communication	83,655	88,280	91,347
Financial intermediation	90,806	103,730	116,801
Real estate, renting and business activities	276,109	296,956	303,179
Public administration and defence	62,224	63,308	65,090
Education	68,926	72,766	76,493
Health and social work	85,965	89,381	93,775
Other community, social and personal services*	60,166	62,824	65,563
Gross value added at basic prices	1,183,704	1,251,704	1,295,663
Value-added taxes on products	87,758	92,017	91,952
Other taxes on products	62,869	66,787	63,188
Less Subsidies on products	5,968	5,663	5,223
GDP in purchasers' values	1,328,363	1,404,845	1,445,580

* Including private households with employees, and extra-territorial organizations.

BALANCE OF PAYMENTS
(£ million)

	2007	2008	2009
Exports of goods f.o.b.	220,858	252,086	227,537
Imports of goods f.o.b.	−310,612	−345,202	−309,412
Trade balance	−89,754	−93,116	−81,875
Exports of services	153,145	170,819	159,111
Imports of services	−106,347	−115,463	−109,259
Balance on goods and services	−42,956	−37,760	−32,023
Other income received	292,602	262,013	174,044
Other income paid	−272,582	−233,978	−142,762
Balance on goods, services and income	−22,936	−9,725	−741
Current transfers received	13,877	16,321	16,623
Current transfers paid	−27,423	−30,372	−31,388
Current balance	−36,482	−23,776	−15,506
Capital account (net)	2,566	3,241	3,219
Direct investment abroad	−162,639	−87,608	−30,116
Direct investment from abroad	100,344	49,767	14,759
Portfolio investment abroad	−92,015	123,545	−154,145
Portfolio investment from abroad	217,850	200,531	188,980
Financial derivatives (net)	−26,990	−121,684	29,104
Other investment abroad	−742,391	599,133	330,996
Other investment from abroad	731,822	−739,211	−368,218
Net errors and omissions	9,126	−5,276	6,690
Overall balance	1,191	−1,338	5,763

GROSS PUBLIC EXPENDITURE ON OVERSEAS AID
(£ million, year ending 31 March)

	2007/08	2008/09	2009/10
Total bilateral aid	3,517.4	4,334.0	4,765.7
DFID* bilateral programmes	2,957.9	3,284.0	3,958.3
Poverty reduction budget support	635.1	648.7	634.1
Other financial aid	456.7	516.4	518.8
Technical co-operation	474.3	514.2	419.9
Grants and other aid in kind	889.7	1,136.1	1,898.8
Humanitarian assistance	430.8	449.2	434.6
DFID debt relief	71.4	19.4	52.1

—continued	2007/08	2008/09	2009/10
Other bilateral programmes	559.5	1,050.0	807.5
CDC investments	360.8	436.0	354.4
Debt relief	3.8	280.3	7.2
Other	194.9	333.7	445.9
Total multilateral aid	2,247.0	2,600.4	2,748.8
European Commission	1,200.3	1,407.9	1,424.1
World Bank Group	493.4	573.7	559.8
UN agencies	296.9	308.2	278.6
Other	256.3	310.7	486.3
Administrative costs	262.7	249.0	252.1
Total gross expenditure on aid	6,027.1	7,183.3	7,766.6

* Department for International Development (DFID).

Source: Department for International Development, *Statistics on International Development*.

External Trade

(Note: Figures include the Isle of Man and the Channel Islands)

PRINCIPAL COMMODITIES
(£ million, seasonally adjusted)

Imports c.i.f.	2008	2009	2010
Food and live animals	25,307	26,338	27,034
Mineral fuels, lubricants, etc.	48,589	35,113	45,418
Petroleum, petroleum products, etc.	38,021	27,682	36,530
Chemicals and related products	37,955	38,944	44,656
Basic manufactures*	41,934	35,910	43,520
Machinery and transport equipment	121,078	107,440	128,516
Mechanical machinery and equipment	28,932	24,271	28,381
Electrical machinery, apparatus, etc.	47,611	44,917	51,137
Road vehicles and parts†	33,952	26,156	33,181
Other transport equipment	10,583	12,096	15,817
Miscellaneous manufactured articles	50,940	49,974	54,624
Clothing and footwear	16,054	16,970	18,401
Scientific and photographic apparatus	8,447	8,486	9,076
Total (incl. others)	345,202	310,010	363,278

Exports f.o.b.	2008	2009	2010
Food and live animals	8,703	9,167	10,092
Mineral fuels, lubricants, etc.	35,762	27,033	36,154
Petroleum, petroleum products, etc.	32,212	24,671	32,316
Chemicals and related products	43,866	46,929	50,947
Organic chemicals	8,405	9,093	8,938
Medicinal products	17,258	20,387	22,227
Basic manufactures*	32,451	24,559	29,140
Machinery and transport equipment	89,328	79,638	92,836
Mechanical machinery and equipment	32,315	29,371	32,921
Electrical machinery, apparatus, etc.	25,325	24,232	25,937
Road vehicles and parts†	22,517	17,046	23,338
Other transport equipment	9,171	8,989	10,640
Miscellaneous manufactured articles	28,512	27,755	31,353
Scientific and photographic apparatus	8,073	8,303	9,285
Total (incl. others)	252,086	227,645	266,079

* Sorted industrial diamonds, usually classified with natural abrasives (under 'crude materials'), are included with 'basic manufactures'.
† Excluding tyres, engines and electrical parts.

THE UNITED KINGDOM

PRINCIPAL TRADING PARTNERS
(£ million, seasonally adjusted)

Imports c.i.f.	2008	2009	2010
Belgium-Luxembourg	17,344	15,748	17,974
Canada	5,824	4,528	5,908
China, People's Republic	23,175	24,300	30,429
Czech Republic	3,580	3,342	4,020
Denmark	3,924	3,849	4,104
Finland	2,787	2,117	2,198
France	23,199	20,472	21,704
Germany	44,689	39,827	45,256
Hong Kong	8,080	7,661	8,128
India	4,490	4,560	5,781
Ireland	12,250	12,457	12,942
Italy	14,160	12,108	13,898
Japan	8,547	6,659	8,160
Korea, Republic	3,510	2,857	2,574
Netherlands	25,840	21,952	26,408
Norway	21,609	15,913	20,785
Poland	4,312	4,679	6,038
Russia	6,928	4,608	5,240
Singapore	4,007	3,541	4,127
South Africa	4,739	3,800	4,127
Spain (excl. Canary Is)	10,783	9,450	10,303
Sweden	6,808	5,493	6,590
Switzerland	5,256	5,232	7,351
Turkey	4,874	4,582	5,288
USA	26,009	24,604	27,658
Total (incl. others)	345,202	310,010	363,278

Exports f.o.b.	2008	2009	2010
Australia	3,103	2,953	3,354
Belgium-Luxembourg	13,619	11,060	13,653
Canada	3,266	3,335	4,142
China, People's Republic	5,084	5,399	7,607
Denmark	2,593	2,473	2,775
France	18,168	17,171	19,290
Germany	27,970	24,195	27,957
Hong Kong	3,676	3,735	4,460
India	4,135	2,949	4,071
Ireland	19,124	15,917	16,928
Italy	9,399	8,282	8,782
Japan	3,908	3,562	4,331
Netherlands	19,905	18,179	21,559
Norway	2,849	2,805	3,055
Poland	3,014	2,793	3,785
Russia	4,274	2,403	3,596
Singapore	2,820	2,958	3,450
Spain (excl. Canary Is)	10,230	9,194	9,881
Sweden	5,213	4,210	5,534
Switzerland	4,656	3,938	5,170
United Arab Emirates	3,833	3,634	4,027
USA	35,471	33,979	38,272
Total (incl. others)	252,086	227,645	266,079

Transport

RAILWAYS

	2006/07	2007/08	2008/09
Passenger journeys (million):			
National railways	1,151	1,232	1,274
Underground railways (London and Glasgow)	1,053	1,110	1,103
Light rail	192	201	203
Passenger-km (million):			
National railways	46,218	49,007	50,698
Underground railways (London and Glasgow)	7,989	8,398	8,691
Light rail	1,120	1,185	1,191
Freight carried (million metric tons)*	108	102	103
Freight ton-km ('000 million)*	22	21	21

* Great Britain only. Figures exclude parcels and materials for rail infrastructure.

ROAD TRAFFIC
('000 licensed vehicles in Great Britain at 31 December)

	2006	2007	2008
Private motor cars	26,508	26,878	27,021
Motorcycles, scooters and mopeds	1,094	1,133	1,160
Light goods vehicles*	3,137	3,261	3,303
Heavy goods vehicles	446	446	436
Public passenger vehicles	107	109	111
Crown property and tax exempt	1,991	2,043	2,091

* Goods vehicles less than 3,500 kg in weight.

SHIPPING

Merchant Fleet
(registered at 31 December)

	2007	2008	2009
Number of vessels	1,637	1,676	1,697
Total displacement ('000 grt)	13,443.8	15,246.9	16,958.0

Source: IHS Fairplay, *World Fleet Statistics*.

International Sea-borne Freight Traffic
('000 metric tons)

	2004	2005	2006
Goods imported	342,425	354,391	365,112
Goods exported	230,645	230,529	218,627

Source: Department for Transport.

CIVIL AVIATION
(United Kingdom airlines)

	2007	2008	2009
All scheduled services:			
Aircraft stage flights (number)	1,052,799	1,056,298	1,001,504
Aircraft-km flown (million)	1,474	1,508	1,444
Passengers carried (million)	102	105	103
Passenger-km flown (million)	227,720	232,592	230,588
Total cargo carried (metric tons)	941,421	979,791	900,668
Total metric ton-km (million)	6,311	6,383	5,952
Freight metric ton-km (million)	6,199	6,284	5,864
Mail metric ton-km (million)	112	99	89
Domestic scheduled services:			
Aircraft stage flights (number)	383,591	369,499	341,207
Aircraft-km flown (million)	140	173	123
Passengers carried (million)	22	21	20
Passenger-km flown (million)	9,449	8,952	8,326
Total cargo carried (metric tons)	7,099	6,125	5,202
Total metric ton-km (million)	3	2	2
Freight metric ton-km (million)	2	2	2
Mail metric ton-km (million)	1	0	1
International scheduled services:			
Aircraft stage flights (number)	669,208	686,799	660,027
Aircraft-km flown (million)	1,333	1,371	1,320
Passengers carried (million)	80	84	83
Passenger-km flown (million)	218,271	233,640	222,262
Total cargo carried (metric tons)	934,323	973,665	895,466
Total metric ton-km (million)	6,308	6,381	5,951
Freight metric ton-km (million)	6,197	6,282	5,862
Mail metric ton-km (million)	111	99	89

THE UNITED KINGDOM

Tourism

FOREIGN VISITORS BY REGION OF ORIGIN
('000 unless otherwise indicated)

	2007	2008	2009
Europe	23,887	23,666	22,083
North America	4,403	3,806	3,564
Other countries	4,488	4,416	4,242
Total	32,778	31,888	29,889
Total expenditure (£ million)	15,960	16,323	16,592

Source: International Passenger Survey, Office for National Statistics, *Travel Trends*.

VISITS BY COUNTRY OF PERMANENT RESIDENCE
('000)

	2007	2008	2009
Australia	941	955	912
Belgium	995	970	903
Canada	852	857	687
France	3,404	3,636	3,784
Germany	3,376	2,900	2,780
Ireland	2,970	3,070	2,948
Italy	1,615	1,639	1,221
Netherlands	1,823	1,818	1,715
Norway	609	688	573
Poland	1,294	1,492	1,041
Spain	2,227	1,974	2,164
Sweden	748	743	604
Switzerland	738	702	701
USA	3,551	2,950	2,877
Total (incl. others)	32,778	31,888	29,889

Source: International Passenger Survey, Office for National Statistics, *Travel Trends*.

Communications Media

	2007	2008	2009
Telephones ('000 main lines in use)	33,814.7	33,209.2	33,614.5
Mobile cellular telephones ('000 subscribers)	73,836.2*	77,360.8	80,375.4
Internet users ('000)†	45,729.2	47,998.9	51,442.1
Broadband subscribers ('000)	15,606‡	17,276‡	18,354§

* At September.
† Estimates.
‡ Excluding corporate connections.
§ At December.

Personal computers: 48,600,000 (801.9 per 1,000 persons) in 2006.

1997: Radio receivers ('000 in use) 84,500.

1999: Book production (titles) 110,965.

2000: Daily newspapers 108 (average circulation 19,159,000); Non-daily newspapers 467 (average circulation 6,246,000).

Sources: UNESCO, *Statistical Yearbook*; UN, *Statistical Yearbook* and International Telecommunication Union.

Statistical Survey

Education

PRE-PRIMARY, PRIMARY AND SECONDARY EDUCATION

	2006/07	2007/08*	2008/09
Schools	33,892	33,661	33,396
Public sector mainstream	29,526	29,250	28,960
Nursery[1]	3,326	3,273	3,209
Primary	21,968	21,768	21,568
Secondary (incl. specialist)	4,232	4,209	4,183
Modern	113	172	169
Selective (Grammar)	233	233	233
City Technology Centres	10	5	3
Academies	46	83	133
Comprehensive	3,398	3,304	3,247
Not applicable	432	412	398
Middle deemed secondary	248	243	231
Non-maintained mainstream	2,486	2,527	2,547
Special schools	1,391	1,378	1,378
Maintained	1,285	1,264	1,264
Non-maintained	106	114	114
Pupil referral units	489	506	511
Teachers ('000):[2]	520.6	520.6	n.a.
Maintained nursery and primary schools	207.0	206.3	n.a.
Maintained secondary schools	234.4	231.7	n.a.
Non-maintained mainstream	58.7	62.0	n.a.
All special schools	20.5	20.6	n.a.
Full-time and part-time pupils ('000):	9,813.0	9,741.7	9,691.3
Maintained schools	9,136.5	9,113.3	9,064.2
Nursery	157.1	151.1	150.3
Primary	4,921.9	4,891.9	4,868.8
Nursery classes	316.8	320.1	294.8
Other classes	4,605.0	4,571.8	4,574.0
Secondary	3,941.6	3,953.4	3,928.5
Special schools	100.2	100.1	100.9
Pupil referral units[3]	15.7	16.7	15.7
Non-maintained schools	676.5[4]	628.4	627.1
Special schools	5.8	5.8	5.7
Other	670.7	622.5	621.5

* Includes some provisional figures.
[1] Excluding pre-school education centres not in partnership with a local authority.
[2] Qualified teachers only. Full-time teachers and the full-time equivalent of part-time teachers. Excluding Pupil Referral Unit teachers.
[3] England and Wales only; excluding pupils registered elsewhere.
[4] Including City Technology Colleges (CTCs) and Academies in England, which were subsequently transferred to state-funded secondary.

Source: Department for Children, Schools and Families, London.

POST-COMPULSORY EDUCATION

	2005/06	2006/07	2007/08
Universities	119	120	120
Other higher education institutes	47	48	49
Further education institutes/colleges	476	476	444
Sixth-form colleges	102	102	95
Full-time teaching and research staff ('000)*	171	173	175
Students (incl. from overseas) taking higher education courses:			
full-time students ('000)	1,055.0	1,046.6	1,053.3
part-time students ('000)	3,395.4	2,593.6	2,415.7

* In addition there were an estimated 132,000 part-time academic staff in further and higher education institutes in 2006/07.

Note: Figures for institutions include, but for teaching staff exclude, the Open University.

Source: Department for Children, Schools and Families, London.

THE UNITED KINGDOM

Directory

The Government

HEAD OF STATE

Queen: HM Queen Elizabeth II (succeeded to the throne 6 February 1952).

THE MINISTRY
(May 2011)

A coalition of the Conservative Party (Con.) and the Liberal Democrats (LD).

The Cabinet

Prime Minister, First Lord of the Treasury and Minister for the Civil Service: David Cameron (Con.).
Deputy Prime Minister and Lord President of the Council (with special responsibility for political and constitutional reform): Nick Clegg (LD).
First Secretary of State and Secretary of State for Foreign and Commonwealth Affairs: William Hague (Con.).
Chancellor of the Exchequer: George Osborne (Con.).
Lord Chancellor and Secretary of State for Justice: Kenneth Clarke (Con.).
Secretary of State for the Home Department and Minister for Women and Equalities: Theresa May (Con.).
Secretary of State for Defence: Dr Liam Fox (Con.).
Secretary of State for Business, Innovation and Skills: Dr Vincent (Vince) Cable (LD).
Secretary of State for Work and Pensions: Iain Duncan Smith (Con.).
Secretary of State for Energy and Climate Change: Chris Huhne (LD).
Secretary of State for Health: Andrew Lansley (Con.).
Secretary of State for Education: Michael Gove (Con.).
Secretary of State for Communities and Local Government: Eric Pickles (Con.).
Secretary of State for Transport: Philip Hammond (Con.).
Secretary of State for Environment, Food and Rural Affairs: Caroline Spelman (Con.).
Secretary of State for International Development: Andrew Mitchell (Con.).
Secretary of State for Northern Ireland: Owen Paterson (Con.).
Secretary of State for Scotland: Michael Moore (LD).
Secretary of State for Wales: Cheryl Gillan (Con.).
Secretary of State for Culture, Olympics, Media and Sport: Jeremy Hunt (Con.).
Chief Secretary to the Treasury: Danny Alexander (LD).
Leader of the House of Lords and Chancellor of the Duchy of Lancaster: Lord Strathclyde (Con.).
Minister without Portfolio (Minister of State): Baroness Warsi (Con.).

Also attending Cabinet

Minister for the Cabinet Office and Paymaster General: Francis Maude (Con.).
Minister of State, Cabinet Office: Oliver Letwin (Con.).
Minister of State for Universities and Science, Department for Business, Innovation and Skills: David Willetts (Con.).
Leader of the House of Commons and Lord Privy Seal: Sir George Young (Con.).
Parliamentary Secretary to the Treasury and Chief Whip: Patrick McLoughlin (Con.).

Attending Cabinet when required

Attorney-General: Dominic Grieve (Con.).

Ministers not in the Cabinet

Ministers of State, Foreign and Commonwealth Office: David Lidington (Con.), Jeremy Browne (LD).
Financial Secretary to the Treasury: Mark Hoban (Con.).
Economic Secretary to the Treasury: Justine Greening (Con.).
Exchequer Secretary to the Treasury: David Gauke (Con.).
Minister of State, Ministry of Justice: Lord McNally (LD).
Minister of State, Ministry of Justice and Home Office: Nick Herbert (Con.).
Ministers of State, Home Office: Baroness Browning (Con.), Damian Green (Con.).
Minister of State for the Armed Forces, Ministry of Defence: Nick Harvey (LD).
Ministers of State, Department for Business, Innovation and Skills: Lord Green (Con.), Mark Prisk (Con.), John Hayes (Con.).
Ministers of State, Department for Work and Pensions: Chris Grayling (Con.), Steve Webb (LD).
Ministers of State, Department of Energy and Climate Change: Charles Hendry (Con.), Gregory Barker (Con.).
Ministers of State, Department of Health: Paul Burstow (LD), Simon Burns (Con.).
Ministers of State, Department for Education: Sarah Teather (LD), Nick Gibb (Con.).
Ministers of State, Department for Communities and Local Government: Greg Clark (Con.), Grant Shapps (LD).
Minister of State, Department for Transport: Theresa Villiers (Con.).
Minister of State, Department for Environment, Food and Rural Affairs: James Paice (Con.).
Minister of State, Department for International Development: Alan Duncan (Con.).
Minister of State, Northern Ireland Office: Hugo Swire (Con.).
Solicitor-General: Edward Garnier (Con.).
Lords Chief Whip and Captain of the Honourable Corps of Gentlemen at Arms: Baroness Anelay of St Johns (Con.).

MINISTRIES

Prime Minister's Office: 10 Downing St, London, SW1A 2AA; tel. (20) 7270-3000; fax (20) 7925-0918; internet www.number10.gov.uk.

Cabinet Office: 70 Whitehall, London, SW1A 2AS; tel. (20) 7276-1234; e-mail pscorrespondence@cabinet-office.x.gsi.gov.uk; internet www.cabinetoffice.gov.uk.

Department for Business, Innovation and Skills: 1 Victoria St, London, SW1H 0ET; tel. (20) 7215-5000; fax (20) 7215-0105; internet www.bis.gov.uk.

Department for Communities and Local Government: Eland House, Bressenden Place, London, SW1E 5DU; tel. (20) 7944-4400; fax (20) 7944-4101; e-mail contactus@communities.gov.uk; internet www.communities.gov.uk.

Department for Culture, Media and Sport: 2–4 Cockspur St, London SW1Y 5DH; tel. (20) 7211-6000; fax (20) 7211-6032; e-mail enquiries@culture.gov.uk; internet www.culture.gov.uk.

Ministry of Defence: Main Bldg, 5th Floor, Whitehall, London, SW1A 2HB; tel. (20) 7218-9000; e-mail ministerial-correspondence@mod.uk; internet www.mod.uk.

Department for Education: Sanctuary Bldgs, Great Smith St, London, SW1P 3BT; tel. (870) 000-2288; fax (1928) 794248; internet www.education.gov.uk.

Department of Energy and Climate Change: 3–8 Whitehall Place, London, SW1A 2HH; tel. (300) 060-4000; e-mail correspondence@decc.gsi.gov.uk; internet www.decc.gov.uk.

Department for Environment, Food and Rural Affairs: Nobel House, 17 Smith Sq., London, SW1P 3JR; tel. (20) 7238-6000; fax (20) 7238-2188; e-mail helpline@defra.gsi.gov.uk; internet www.defra.gov.uk.

Foreign and Commonwealth Office: King Charles St, London, SW1A 2AH; tel. (20) 7008-1500; internet www.fco.gov.uk.

Government Equalities Office: Eland House, 9th Floor, Bressenden Place, London SW1E 5DU; tel. (20) 7944-0601; e-mail enquiries@geo.gsi.gov.uk; internet www.equalities.gov.uk.

Department of Health: Richmond House, 79 Whitehall, London, SW1A 2NS; tel. (20) 7210-4850; fax (20) 7210-5523; e-mail dhmail@dh.gsi.gov.uk; internet www.dh.gov.uk.

Home Office: 2 Marsham St, London, SW1P 4DF; tel. (20) 7035-4848; fax (20) 7035-4745; e-mail public.enquiries@homeoffice.gsi.gov.uk; internet www.homeoffice.gov.uk.

Department for International Development: 1 Palace St, London, SW1E 5HE; tel. (20) 7023-0000; fax (20) 7023-0019; e-mail enquiry@dfid.gov.uk; internet www.dfid.gov.uk.

THE UNITED KINGDOM

Ministry of Justice: 102 Petty France, London, SW1H 9AJ; tel. (20) 3334-3555; fax (20) 3334-4455; e-mail general.queries@justice.gsi.gov.uk; internet www.justice.gov.uk.

Leader of the House of Commons: 26 Whitehall, London SW1A 2WH; tel. (20) 7276-1005; e-mail leader@commonsleader.x.gsi.gov.uk; internet www.commonsleader.gov.uk.

Northern Ireland Office: 11 Millbank, London, SW1P 4PN; tel. (28) 9052-0700; e-mail info@nio.gov.uk; internet www.nio.gov.uk.

Scotland Office: Dover House, Whitehall, London, SW1A 2AU; tel. (20) 7270-6754; fax (20) 7270-6812; e-mail scottish.secretary@scotland.gsi.gov.uk; internet www.scotlandoffice.gov.uk.

Department for Transport: Great Minster House, 76 Marsham St, London, SW1P 4DR; tel. (20) 7944-8300; fax (20) 7944-9643; e-mail fax9643@dft.gsi.gov.uk; internet www.dft.gov.uk.

HM Treasury: 1 Horse Guards Rd, London, SW1A 2HQ; tel. (20) 7270-4558; fax (20) 7270-4861; e-mail ministers@hm-treasury.gov.uk; internet www.hm-treasury.gov.uk.

Wales Office: Gwydyr House, Whitehall, London, SW1A 2NP; tel. (20) 7270-0534; fax (20) 7270-0578; e-mail wales.office@walesoffice.gsi.gov.uk; internet www.walesoffice.gov.uk.

Department for Work and Pensions: Caxton House, Tothill St, London, SW1H 9DA; tel. (20) 7340-4000; e-mail enquiries@dwp.gsi.gov.uk; internet www.dwp.gov.uk.

Legislature

PARLIAMENT

House of Commons

House of Commons Information Office, Norman Shaw North, London, SW1A 2TT; tel. (20) 7219-4272; e-mail hcinfo@parliament.uk; internet www.parliament.uk.

Speaker: JOHN BERCOW.

Chairman of Ways and Means and Deputy Speaker: LINDSAY HOYLE.

General Election, 6 May 2010

	Votes	% of votes	Seats
Conservative Party	10,703,754	36.05	306*
Labour Party	8,609,527	29.00	258
Liberal Democrats	6,836,824	23.03	57
Democratic Unionist Party	168,216	0.57	8
Scottish National Party	491,386	1.65	6
Sinn Féin	171,942	0.58	5
Plaid Cymru	165,394	0.56	3
Social Democratic and Labour Party	110,970	0.37	3
Others	2,433,367	8.20	4†
Total	29,691,380	100.00	650*

* Including the representative for the Thirsk and Malton constituency, for which the election was postponed until 27 May 2010, owing to the death of a candidate.
† Including the Speaker.

House of Lords
(May 2011)

Lord Speaker: Baroness HAYMAN.

Lord Chairman of Committees and Deputy Speaker: Lord BRABAZON OF TARA.

Distribution of seats at 3 May 2011

	Life Peers	Hereditary Peers	Archbishops and Bishops	Total
Labour Party	239	4	—	243
Conservative Party	170	48	—	218
Liberal Democrats	88	4	—	92
Crossbench	152	30	—	182
Others	27	2	25	54
Total	676	88	25	789*

* Excluding 23 members on leave of absence, two who are suspended, 15 disqualified as senior members of the judiciary and one disqualified as a member of the European Parliament.

The Legislative Authorities and Executive Bodies of Northern Ireland, Scotland and Wales

New constitutional arrangements for Northern Ireland entered into force in 1998, following their approval in a popular referendum. Responsibility for all matters formerly implemented by the Northern Ireland Office was transferred to the new devolved institutions in 1999; however, the institutions were suspended and direct rule by the British Government was reimposed in 2000 and from 2002–07, owing to a series of political impasses. Responsibility for justice and policing was transferred to the devolved institutions in April 2010. The 108-member Northern Ireland Assembly is elected for a term of four years under a form of proportional representation by means of the single transferable vote in multi-member constituencies. Members are required to designate themselves as 'Nationalist', 'Unionist', or 'Other', and certain decisions of the Assembly must be approved by a majority both of Nationalist and Unionist members. A power-sharing Executive Committee, headed by a First Minister and a Deputy First Minister (who must represent the largest party in each of the two main communities, respectively), is elected from among the Assembly members.

Devolved legislative authorities for Scotland and Wales were established in 1999. An executive level of government, headed by a First Minister, was also established for each country. The Scottish Parliament has powers to legislate on all domestic matters, including education, health, local government and law and order. It is also empowered to vary the rate of income tax set by the United Kingdom Government by up to 3%. The National Assembly for Wales (Cynulliad Cenedlaethol Cymru) exercises responsibility for issues formerly covered by the Wales Office of the United Kingdom Government. Initially the Assembly could only initiate secondary legislation in areas under its control, but in 2007 it was granted powers to initiate primary legislation—known as Assembly Measures—in its fields of competence, subject to prior approval by the British Parliament. At a referendum held in Wales on 3 March 2011, 63.5% of those participating (35.3% of the electorate) voted in favour of the Assembly being granted direct law-making powers in the currently devolved areas, including education, health and local government. Later that month the Welsh First Minister signed a commencement order giving the Assembly direct law-making powers, following its approval by the Assembly's members. In November 2010 a bill providing for the transfer of additional, mainly fiscal, powers to the Scottish Parliament was introduced in the House of Commons; the bill remained under consideration in May 2011. Both the Scottish Parliament and the National Assembly for Wales are elected, for a term of four years, by a combined system of direct voting in single-member constituencies and a form of proportional representation, whereby additional members are elected from a party list on the basis of larger, multi-member constituencies.

NORTHERN IRELAND

Northern Ireland Assembly

Parliament Bldgs, Ballymiscaw, Belfast, BT4 3XX; tel. (28) 9052-1333; fax (28) 9052-1961; e-mail info.office@niassembly.gov.uk; internet www.niassembly.gov.uk.

Presiding Officer (Speaker): WILLIAM HAY.

Election, 5 May 2011

	First preference votes	% of first preference votes	Seats
Democratic Unionist Party	198,436	29.98	38
Sinn Féin	178,222	26.93	29
Ulster Unionist Party	87,531	13.23	16
Social Democratic and Labour Party	94,286	14.24	14
Alliance Party	50,875	7.69	8
Traditional Unionist Voice	16,480	2.49	1
Green Party	6,031	0.91	1
Independents	3,003	0.45	1
Total (incl. others)	670,778	100.00	108

Executive Committee
(May 2011)

A power-sharing executive, comprising the Democratic Unionist Party (DUP), Sinn Féin (SF), the Ulster Unionist Party (UUP), the Social Democratic and Labour Party (SDLP) and the Alliance Party (AP).

THE UNITED KINGDOM

First Minister: PETER ROBINSON (DUP).
Deputy First Minister: MARTIN MCGUINNESS (SF).
Minister of Finance and Personnel: SAMMY WILSON (DUP).
Minister of Education: JOHN O'DOWD (SF).
Minister of Enterprise, Trade and Investment: ARLENE FOSTER (DUP).
Minister of Health, Social Services and Public Safety: EDWIN POOTS (DUP).
Minister for Social Development: NELSON MCCAUSLAND (DUP).
Minister for Regional Development: DANNY KENNEDY (UUP).
Minister of the Environment: ALEX ATTWOOD (SDLP).
Minister of Agriculture and Rural Development: MICHELLE O'NEILL (SF).
Minister of Culture, Arts and Leisure: CARÁL NÍ CHUILÍN (SF).
Minister for Employment and Learning: Dr STEPHEN FARRY (AP).
Minister of Justice: DAVID FORD (AP).

SCOTLAND

Scottish Parliament

Edinburgh, EH99 1SP; tel. (131) 348-5000; fax (131) 348-5601; e-mail sp.info@scottish.parliament.uk; internet www.scottish.parliament.uk.

Presiding Officer: TRICIA MARWICK.

Election, 5 May 2011

	Total votes	%	Seats
Scottish National Party	1,779,336	44.70	69
Labour Party	1,154,020	28.99	37
Conservative Party	522,619	13.13	15
Liberal Democrats	261,186	6.56	5
Others	263,112	6.61	3*
Total	3,980,273	100.00	129

Note: Table includes constituency and regional results
* Comprises two seats for the Scottish Green Party and one for an independent candidate.

Scottish Government
(May 2011)

The Government is formed by the Scottish National Party.

First Minister: ALEX SALMOND.
Deputy First Minister and Cabinet Secretary for Health, Wellbeing and Citizens Strategy: NICOLA STURGEON.
Cabinet Secretary for Finance, Employment and Sustainable Growth: JOHN SWINNEY.
Cabinet Secretary for Education and Lifelong Learning: MICHAEL RUSSELL.
Cabinet Secretary for Parliament and Government Strategy: BRUCE CRAWFORD.
Cabinet Secretary for Justice: KENNY MACASKILL.
Cabinet Secretary for Rural Affairs and the Environment: RICHARD LOCHHEAD.
Cabinet Secretary for Culture and External Affairs: FIONA HYSLOP.
Cabinet Secretary for Infrastructure and Capital Investment: ALEX NEIL.
Minister for Commonwealth Games and Sport: SHONA ROBISON.
Minister for Public Health: MICHAEL MATHESON.
Minister for Energy, Enterprise and Tourism: FERGUS EWING.
Minister for Local Government and Planning: AILEEN CAMPBELL.
Minister for Children and Young People: ANGELA CONSTANCE.
Minister for Learning and Skills, with responsibility for Gaelic and Scots: ALASDAIR ALLAN.
Minister for Parliamentary Business and Chief Whip: BRIAN ADAM.
Minister for Community Safety and Legal Affairs, with responsibility for tackling sectarianism: ROSEANNA CUNNINGHAM.
Minister for Environment and Climate Change: STEWART STEVENSON.
Minister for Housing and Transport: KEITH BROWN.
Lord Advocate: FRANK MULHOLLAND.
Solicitor-General: LESLEY THOMSON.

WALES

National Assembly for Wales
(Cynulliad Cenedlaethol Cymru)

Cardiff Bay, Cardiff, CF99 1NA; tel. (800) 010-5500; internet www.assemblywales.org.

Presiding Officer: ROSEMARY BUTLER.

Election, 5 May 2011

	Total votes	%	Seats
Labour Party	751,612	39.58	30
Conservative Party	451,161	23.76	14
Plaid Cymru	352,706	18.58	11
Liberal Democrats	176,608	9.30	5
Others	166,553	8.77	0
Total	1,898,640	100.00	60

Note: Table includes constituency and regional results

Welsh Government
(May 2011)

The Government is formed by the Welsh Labour Party

First Minister: CARWYN JONES.
Minister for Finance and Leader of the House: JANE HUTT.
Minister for Business Enterprise and Technology: EDWINA HART.
Minister for Health and Social Services: LESLEY GRIFFITHS.
Minister for Environment and Sustainable Development: JOHN GRIFFITHS.
Minister for Education and Skills: LEIGHTON ANDREWS.
Minister for Local Government and Communities: CARL SARGEANT.
Minister for Housing, Regeneration and Heritage: HUW LEWIS.

Election Commission

The Electoral Commission: 3 Bunhill Row, London EC1Y 8YZ; tel. (20) 7271-0500; fax (20) 7271-0505; e-mail info@electoralcommission.org.uk; internet www.electoralcommission.org.uk; f. 2000; Chair. JENNY WATSON; Chief Exec. PETER WARDLE.

Political Organizations

Alliance Party of Northern Ireland: 88 University St, Belfast, BT7 1HE; tel. (28) 9032-4274; fax (28) 9033-3147; e-mail alliance@allianceparty.org; internet www.allianceparty.org; f. 1970; non-sectarian and non-doctrinaire party of the centre, attracting support from within both Catholic and Protestant sections of the community in Northern Ireland; 1,500 mems; Leader DAVID FORD.

British National Party: POB 14, Welshpool, SY21 0WE; tel. (20) 7078-3269; e-mail enquiries@bnp.org.uk; internet www.bnp.org.uk; f. 1982 as a breakaway faction from the National Front; Leader NICK GRIFFIN.

Conservative Party (Conservative and Unionist Party): 30 Millbank, London, SW1P 4DP; tel. (20) 7222-9000; fax (20) 7222-1135; internet www.conservatives.com; f. 1870 as Conservative Central Office; mem. of the International Democrat Union and the European Democrat Union; in the European Parliament part of the European Conservatives and Reformists; 320,000 mems (adherent on a local, rather than national, basis); Leader DAVID CAMERON; Co-Chairs Baroness WARSI, ANDREW FELDMAN.

  Conservative Party in Northern Ireland: Unit 5F, Weavers Court Business Park, Linfield Rd, Belfast, BT12; tel. (28) 9033-3381; party has no Assembly members, but is represented at council level; formed electoral alliance with the Ulster Unionist Party, as Ulster Conservatives and Unionists—New Force, in 2009.

  Scottish Conservative & Unionist Party: 67 Northumberland St, Edinburgh EH3 6JG; tel. (131) 524-0030; fax (131) 524-0049; e-mail info@scottishconservatives.com; internet www.scottishconservatives.com; Chair. ANDREW FULTON; Leader ANNABEL GOLDIE.

  Welsh Conservative Party: 4 Pennline Rd, Whitchurch, Cardiff, CF14 2XS; tel. (29) 2061-6031; fax (29) 2061-0544; e-mail ccowales@tory.org; internet www.welshconservatives.com; Chair. CATRIN EDWARDS; Interim Assembly Leader PAUL DAVIES.

THE UNITED KINGDOM

Co-operative Party: 77 Weston St, London, SE1 3SD; tel. (20) 7367-4150; fax (20) 7407-4476; e-mail mail@party.coop; internet www.party.coop; f. 1917; under an Agreement with the Labour Party it is recognized as the political party representing the co-operative movement, and fields candidates, jointly with the Labour Party, who are Labour and Co-operative candidates at local and British parliamentary elections; promotes the principles of the co-operative movement; seeks to extend co-operative enterprise and cares for the interests of the consumer; individual mems in 200 brs; 47 societies are affiliated; Chair. GARETH THOMAS; Gen. Sec. MICHAEL STEPHENSON.

Democratic Unionist Party (DUP): 91 Dundela Ave, Belfast, BT4 3BU; tel. (28) 9047-1155; fax (28) 9052-1289; e-mail info@dup.org.uk; internet www.dup.org.uk; f. 1971 as the successor to the Protestant Unionist Party; upholds the union of Northern Ireland with the United Kingdom; Leader PETER ROBINSON; Party Sec. MICHELLE MCILVEEN.

Green Party: 56–64 Development House, Leonard St, London EC2A 4LT; tel. (20) 7549-0310; fax (20) 7549-0318; e-mail office@greenparty.org.uk; internet www.greenparty.org.uk; f. 1973 as People, adopted the name Ecology Party in 1975; present name adopted 1985; campaigns for the protection of the environment and the promotion of social justice; approx. 12,000 mems; Leader CAROLINE LUCAS; Chair. JAYNE FORBES.

Labour Party: 39 Victoria St, London, SW1H 0HA; tel. (8705) 900200; fax (20) 7802-1234; e-mail info@new.labour.org.uk; internet www2.labour.org.uk; f. 1900; affiliated to the Socialist International and the Party of European Socialists; 15 trade unions are affiliated to the party through the Trade Union and Labour Party Liaison Organisation; Leader ED MILIBAND; Deputy Leader and Chair. HARRIET HARMAN; Gen. Sec. RAY COLLINS.

  Scottish Labour: John Smith House, 145 West Regent St, Glasgow, G2 4RE; tel. (141) 572-6900; fax (141) 572-2566; e-mail scotland@new.labour.org.uk; internet www.scottishlabour.org.uk; Leader IAIN GRAY; Gen. Sec. COLIN SMYTH.

  Welsh Labour: 1 Cathedral Rd, Cardiff, CF11 9HA; tel. (29) 2087-7700; internet www.welshlabour.org.uk; Leader CARWYN JONES.

Liberal Democrats: 4 Cowley St, London, SW1P 3NB; tel. (20) 7222-7999; fax (20) 7799-2170; e-mail info@libdems.org.uk; internet www.libdems.org.uk; f. 1988, following the merger of the Liberal Party (f. 1877) and the Social Democratic Party (f. 1981, disbanded 1990); c. 65,000 mems; Leader NICK CLEGG; Pres. TIM FARRON.

  Scottish Liberal Democrats: 4 Clifton Terrace, Edinburgh, EH12 5DR; tel. (131) 337-2314; fax (131) 337-3566; e-mail administration@scotlibdems.org.uk; internet www.scotlibdems.org.uk; Leader WILLIE RENNIE.

  Welsh Liberal Democrats: 7 Blake Court, Schooner Way, Butetown, Cardiff, CF10 4DW; tel. (29) 2031-3400; fax (29) 2031-3401; e-mail enquiries@welshliberaldemocrats.org.uk; internet www.welshlibdems.org.uk; Leader KIRSTY WILLIAMS.

Plaid Cymru—Party of Wales: Tŷ Gwynfor, Marine Chambers, Anson Court, Atlantic Wharf, Cardiff, CF10 4AL; tel. (29) 2047-2272; fax (29) 2064-6001; e-mail post@plaidcymru.org; internet www.plaidcymru.org; f. 1925; promotes Welsh interests and seeks independence for Wales; 10,000 mems; Leader (vacant); Pres. DAFYDD IWAN.

Progressive Unionist Party: 299 Newtownards Rd, Belfast, BT4 1AG; tel. (28) 9022-5040; fax (28) 9022-5041; internet progressiveunionistparty.org; loyalist party in Northern Ireland; Leader BRIAN ERVINE.

Respect: POB 167, Manchester, M19 0AH; tel. (7794) 192-670; e-mail admin@respectparty.org; internet www.therespectparty.net; f. 2004; left-wing; Chair. KAY PHILLIPS.

Scottish Green Party: 20 Graham St, Edinburgh, EH6 5QR; tel. (870) 0772207; internet www.scottishgreens.org.uk; f. 1990; ecologist; Co-convenors PATRICK HARVIE, ELEANOR SCOTT.

Scottish National Party (SNP): Gordon Lamb House, 3 Jackson's Entry, Edinburgh, EH8 8PJ; tel. (800) 633-5432; fax (131) 525-8901; e-mail snp.hq@snp.org; internet www.snp.org; f. 1934; advocates independence for Scotland as a member of the EU and Scottish control of national resources; Leader ALEX SALMOND.

Scottish Socialist Party (SSP): Suite 308, 93 Hope St, Glasgow, G2 6LD; tel. (141) 221-7470; e-mail ssp.glasgow@btconnect.com; internet www.scottishsocialistparty.org; f. 1998; Convener COLIN FOX; Nat. Sec. KEVIN MCVEY.

Sinn Féin (We Ourselves): 53 Falls Rd, Belfast, BT12 4PD; tel. (28) 9034-7350; fax (28) 9022-3001; e-mail sfadmin@eircom.net; internet www.sinnfein.ie; f. 1905; seeks the reunification of Ireland and the establishment of a 32-county democratic socialist state; engages in community politics; Pres. GERRY ADAMS; Chair. DECLAN KEARNEY; Gen. Sec. DAWN DOYLE.

Social Democratic and Labour Party (SDLP): 121 Ormeau Rd, Belfast, BT7 1SH; tel. (28) 9024-7700; fax (28) 9023-6699; e-mail info@sdlp.ie; internet www.sdlp.ie; f. 1970; radical, left-of-centre principles with a view to the eventual reunification of Ireland by popular consent; Leader MARGARET RITCHIE.

Socialist Labour Party: POB 112, Leigh, WN7 4WS; tel. and fax (1942) 603335; e-mail info@socialist-labour-party.org.uk; internet www.socialist-labour-party.org.uk; f. 1996; supports renationalization of industry, constitutional reform, withdrawal from the European Union; Leader ARTHUR SCARGILL; Pres. ANDREW JORDAN; Gen. Sec. IAN JOHNSON.

Socialist Party: POB 24697, London, E11 1YD; tel. (20) 8988-8777; e-mail info@socialistparty.org.uk; internet www.socialistparty.org.uk; f. 1991 as Militant Labour by fmr members of the Militant tendency (an extreme-left faction within the Labour Party); present name adopted 1997; registered with the Electoral Commission under the name Socialist Alternative; mem. of the Committee for a Workers' International (CWI); Gen. Sec. PETER TAAFFE.

Socialist Workers' Party (SWP): POB 42184, London, SW8 2WD; tel. (20) 7819-1170; fax (20) 7819-1179; e-mail enquiries@swp.org.uk; internet www.swp.org.uk; f. 1950; advocates workers' control through revolution, not reform; Nat. Sec. MARTIN SMITH.

Solidarity—Scotland's Socialist Movement: POB 7565, Glasgow, G42 2DN; e-mail info@solidarityscotland.org; internet www.solidarityscotland.org; f. 2006 by disaffected members of the Scottish Socialist Party; Leaders TOMMY SHERIDAN, ROSEMARY BYRNE.

Traditional Unionist Voice (TUV): 39 Holywood Rd, Belfast, BT4 3BE; tel. (28) 9065-5011; internet www.tuv.org.uk; f. 2007 by fmr members of Democratic Unionist Party opposed to power sharing in Northern Ireland; Leader JIM ALLISTER.

UK Independence Party (UKIP): POB 408, Newton Abbot, Devon, TQ12 9BG; tel. (1626) 831290; fax (1626) 831348; e-mail mail@ukip.org; internet www.ukip.org; f. 1994; advocates withdrawal from the European Union; 27,000 mems; Leader NIGEL FARAGE; Exec. Chair. STEVE CROWTHER.

Ulster Unionist Party: First Floor, 174 Albertbridge Rd, Belfast, BT5 4GS; tel. (28) 9046-3200; fax (28) 9045-6899; e-mail uup@uup.org; internet www.uup.org; f. 1905; governed Northern Ireland 1921–72; supports parity and equality for Northern Ireland within the United Kingdom; formed electoral alliance with the Conservative Party in Northern Ireland, as Ulster Conservatives and Unionists—New Force, in 2009; Leader TOM ELLIOTT.

Veritas: Office 404, 4th Floor, Albany House, 324–326 Regent St, London, W1B 3HH; tel. (870) 7606148; e-mail office@veritas-party.com; internet www.veritasparty.com; f. 2005; advocates withdrawal from the European Union; Leader THERESE MUCHEWICZ.

Diplomatic Representation

EMBASSIES AND HIGH COMMISSIONS IN THE UNITED KINGDOM

Afghanistan: 31 Prince's Gate, London, SW7 1QQ; tel. (20) 7589-8891; fax (20) 7584-4801; e-mail contacts@afghanistanembassy.org.uk; internet www.afghanistanembassy.org.uk; Ambassador (vacant).

Albania: 33 St George's Drive, London, SW1V 4DG; tel. (20) 7828-8897; fax (20) 7828-8869; e-mail embassy.london@mfa.gov.al; internet www.albanianembassy.co.uk; (vacant).

Algeria: 54 Holland Park, London, W11 3RS; tel. (20) 7221-7800; fax (20) 7221-0448; e-mail info@algerianembassy.org.uk; internet www.algerianembassy.org.uk; Ambassador AMAR ABBA.

Angola: 22 Dorset St, London, W1U 6QY; tel. (20) 7299-9850; fax (20) 7486-9397; e-mail embassy@angola.org.uk; internet www.angola.org.uk; Ambassador ANA MARIA TELES CARREIRA.

Antigua and Barbuda: 2nd Floor, 45 Crawford Pl., London, W1H 4LP; tel. (20) 7258-0070; fax (20) 7258-7486; e-mail enquiries@antigua-barbuda.com; internet www.antigua-barbuda.com; High Commr Dr CARL ROBERTS.

Argentina: 65 Brook St, London, W1K 4AH; tel. (20) 7318-1300; fax (20) 7318-1301; e-mail info@argentine-embassy-uk.org; internet www.argentine-embassy-uk.org; Chargé d'affaires a.i. OSVALDO MÁRSICO.

Armenia: 25A Cheniston Gdns, London, W8 6TG; tel. (20) 7938-5435; fax (20) 7938-2595; e-mail armemb@armenianembassyuk.com; internet www.armenianembassy.org.uk; Ambassador (vacant).

Australia: Australia House, Strand, London, WC2B 4LA; tel. (20) 7379-4334; fax (20) 7240-5333; internet www.uk.embassy.gov.au; High Commr JOHN DAUTH.

Austria: 18 Belgrave Mews West, London, SW1X 8HU; tel. (20) 7344-3250; fax (20) 7344-0292; e-mail london-ob@bmeia.gv.at; internet www.bmeia.gv.at/london; Ambassador Dr EMIL BRIX.

THE UNITED KINGDOM

Azerbaijan: 4 Kensington Court, London, W8 5DL; tel. (20) 7938-3412; fax (20) 7937-1783; e-mail london@mission.mfa.gov.az; internet www.azembassy.org.uk; Ambassador FAKHRADDIN GURBANOV.

Bahamas: 10 Chesterfield St, London, W1J 5JL; tel. (20) 7408-4488; fax (20) 7499-9937; e-mail information@bahamashclondon.net; internet www.bahamashclondon.net; High Commr PAUL H. FARQUHARSON.

Bahrain: 30 Belgrave Sq., London, SW1X 8QB; tel. (20) 7201-9170; fax (20) 7201-9183; e-mail information@bahrainembassy.co.uk; internet www.bahrainembassy.co.uk; Ambassador Sheikh KHALIFA BIN ALI AL-KHALIFA.

Bangladesh: 28 Queen's Gate, London, SW7 5JA; tel. (20) 7584-0081; fax (20) 7581-7477; e-mail info@bhclondon.org.uk; internet www.bhclondon.org.uk; High Commr Dr MOHAMMAD SAYEEDUR RAHMAN KHAN.

Barbados: 1 Great Russell St, London, WC1B 3ND; tel. (20) 7299-7150; fax (20) 7323-6872; e-mail london@foreign.gov.bb; High Commr HUGH ANTHONY ARTHUR.

Belarus: 6 Kensington Court, London, W8 5DL; tel. (20) 7937-3288; fax (20) 7361-0005; e-mail uk@belembassy.org; internet www.uk.belembassy.org; Ambassador ALEKSANDR MIKHNEVICH.

Belgium: 17 Grosvenor Cres., London, SW1X 7EE; tel. (20) 7470-3700; fax (20) 7470-3795; e-mail london@diplobel.fed.be; internet www.diplomatie.be/london; Ambassador JOHAN VERBEKE.

Belize: 45 Crawford Pl., 3rd Floor, London, W1H 4LP; tel. (20) 7723-3603; fax (20) 7723-9637; e-mail bzhc-lon@btconnect.com; internet www.belizehighcommission.com; High Commr KAMELA PALMA.

Bolivia: 106 Eaton Sq., London, SW1W 9AD; tel. (20) 7235-4255; fax (20) 7235-1286; e-mail bolivianembassy@yahoo.co.uk; Ambassador MARÍA BEATRIZ SOUVIRON CRESPO.

Bosnia and Herzegovina: 5–7 Lexham Gdns, London, W8 5JJ; tel. (20) 7373-0867; fax (20) 7373-0871; e-mail embassy@bhembassy.co.uk; internet www.bhembassy.co.uk; Ambassador JADRANKA NEGODIĆ.

Botswana: 6 Stratford Pl., London, W1C 1AY; tel. (20) 7499-0031; fax (20) 7495-8595; e-mail bohico@govbw.com; High Commr ROY BLACKBEARD.

Brazil: 32 Green St, London, W1K 7AT; tel. (20) 7399-9000; fax (20) 7399-9100; e-mail info@brazil.org.uk; internet www.brazil.org.uk; Ambassador ROBERTO JAGUARIBE.

Brunei: 19–20 Belgrave Sq., London, SW1X 8PG; tel. (20) 7581-0521; fax (20) 7235-9717; e-mail bhcl@brunei-high-commission.co.uk; High Commr MOHD AZIYAN bin ABDULLAH.

Bulgaria: 186–188 Queen's Gate, London, SW7 5HL; tel. (20) 7584-9400; fax (20) 7584-4948; e-mail ambass.office@bulgarianembassy.org.uk; internet www.bulgarianembassy-london.org; Ambassador LYUBOMIR NEDKOV KYUCHUKOV.

Cambodia: 64 Brondesbury Park, Willesden Green, London, NW6 7AT; tel. (20) 8451-7850; fax (20) 8451-7594; e-mail cambodianembassy@btconnect.com; internet www.cambodianembassy.org.uk; Ambassador HOR NAMBORA.

Cameroon: 84 Holland Park, London, W11 3SB; tel. (20) 7727-0771; fax (20) 7792-9353; e-mail highcom@cameroonhighcommission.co.uk; internet www.cameroonhighcommission.co.uk; High Commr NKWELLE EKANEY.

Canada: MacDonald House, 1 Grosvenor Sq., London, W1K 4AB; tel. (20) 7258-6600; fax (20) 7258-6533; e-mail ldn@international.gc.ca; internet www.london.gc.ca; High Commr JAMES R. WRIGHT.

Chile: 37–41 Old Queen St, London, SW1H 9JA; tel. (20) 7580-6392; fax (20) 7436-5204; e-mail embachile@embachile.co.uk; Ambassador TOMAS MÜLLER.

China, People's Republic: 49–51 Portland Pl., London, W1B 4JL; tel. (20) 7299-4049; fax (20) 7636-5578; e-mail press@chinese-embassy.org.uk; internet www.chinese-embassy.org.uk; Ambassador LIU XIAOMING.

Colombia: 3 Hans Cres., London, SW1X 0LN; tel. (20) 7589-9177; fax (20) 7589-4718; e-mail mail@colombianembassy.co.uk; internet www.colombianembassy.co.uk; Ambassador JOSÉ MAURICIO RODRÍGUEZ MÚNERA.

Congo, Democratic Republic: 281 Gray's Inn Rd, London, WC1X 8QF; tel. (20) 7278-9825; fax (20) 7833-9967; e-mail info@ambardc-londres.gov.cd; Ambassador BARNABE KIKAYA BIN KARUBI.

Costa Rica: Flat 1, 14 Lancaster Gate, London, W2 3LH; tel. (20) 7706-8844; fax (20) 7706-8655; e-mail costarica@btconnect.com; Ambassador PILAR SABORÍO DE ROCAFORT.

Côte d'Ivoire: 2 Upper Belgrave St, London, SW1X 8BJ; tel. (20) 7235-6991; fax (20) 7259-5320; e-mail info@ambaci-uk.org; internet www.ambaci-uk.org; Chargé d'affaires a.i. KONE TOURE MAMAN.

Croatia: 21 Conway St, London, W1T 6BN; tel. (20) 7387-2022; fax (20) 7387-0310; e-mail croemb.london@mvpei.hr; internet uk.mfa.hr; Ambassador Dr IVICA TOMIĆ.

Cuba: 167 High Holborn, London, WC1V 6PA; tel. (20) 7240-2488; fax (20) 7836-2602; e-mail embacuba@cubaldn.com; internet www.cubaldn.com; Ambassador ESTHER ARMENTEROS.

Cyprus: 13 St James' Sq., London, SW1Y 4LB; tel. (20) 7321-4100; fax (20) 7321-4164; e-mail cyphclondon@dial.pipex.com; internet www.mfa.gov.cy/highcomlondon; High Commr ALEXANDROS N. ZENON.

Czech Republic: 26 Kensington Palace Gdns, London, W8 4QY; tel. (20) 7243-1115; fax (20) 7727-9654; e-mail london@embassy.mzv.cz; internet www.mzv.cz/london; Ambassador MICHAEL ŽANTOVSKÝ.

Denmark: 55 Sloane St, London, SW1X 9SR; tel. (20) 7333-0200; fax (20) 7333-0270; e-mail lonamb@um.dk; internet www.amblondon.um.dk; Ambassador BIRGER RIIS-JØRGENSEN.

Dominica: 1 Collingham Gdns, London, SW5 0HW; tel. (20) 7370-5194; fax (20) 7373-8743; e-mail info@dominicahighcommission.co.uk; internet www.dominicahighcommission.co.uk; High Commr AGNES ADONIS (acting).

Dominican Republic: 139 Inverness Terrace, London, W2 6JF; tel. (20) 7727-7091; fax (20) 7727-3693; e-mail info@dominicanembassy.org.uk; internet www.dominicanembassy.org.uk; Ambassador ANIBAL DE CASTRO.

Ecuador: Flat 3B, 3 Hans Cres., Knightsbridge, London, SW1X 0LS; tel. (20) 7584-1367; fax (20) 7590-2509; e-mail eecugranbretania@mmrree.gov.ec; Ambassador ANA ALBÁN MORA.

Egypt: 26 South St, London, W1K 1DW; tel. (20) 7499-3304; fax (20) 7491-1542; e-mail eg.emb_london@mfa.gov.eg; internet www.egyptianconsulate.co.uk; Ambassador HATEM SEIF EN-NASR.

El Salvador: 8 Dorset Sq., 1st and 2nd Floors, London, NW1 6PU; tel. (20) 7224-9800; fax (20) 7224-9878; e-mail elsalvador.embassy@gmail.com; Ambassador WERNER MATIAS ROMERO.

Equatorial Guinea: 13 Park Pl., St James's, London, SW1A 1LP; tel. (20) 7499-6867; fax (20) 7499-6782; e-mail embarege-londres@embarege-londres.org; internet www.embarege-londres.org; Ambassador AGUSTIN NZE NFUMU.

Eritrea: 96 White Lion St, London, N1 9PF; tel. (20) 7713-0096; fax (20) 7713-0161; e-mail paamba@erimbauk.com; Ambassador TESFAMICAEL GERAHTU OGBAGHIORGHIS.

Estonia: 16 Hyde Park Gate, London, SW7 5DG; tel. (20) 7589-3428; fax (20) 7589-3430; e-mail london@mfa.ee; internet www.estonia.gov.uk; Ambassador Dr AINO von WIRÉN.

Ethiopia: 17 Prince's Gate, London, SW7 1PZ; tel. (20) 7589-7212; fax (20) 7584-7054; e-mail info@ethioembassy.org.uk; internet www.ethioembassy.org.uk; Ambassador BERHANU KEBEDE.

Fiji: 34 Hyde Park Gate, London, SW7 5DN; tel. (20) 7584-3661; fax (20) 7584-2838; e-mail mail@fijihighcommission.org.uk; internet www.fijihighcommission.org.uk; High Commr (vacant).

Finland: 38 Chesham Pl., London, SW1X 8HW; tel. (20) 7838-6200; fax (20) 7235-3680; e-mail sanomat.lon@formin.fi; internet www.finemb.org.uk; Ambassador PEKKA HUHTANIEMI.

France: 58 Knightsbridge, London, SW1X 7JT; tel. (20) 7073-1000; fax (20) 7073-1004; e-mail presse.londres-amba@diplomatie.gouv.fr; internet www.ambafrance-uk.org; Ambassador BERNARD EMIÉ.

Gabon: 27 Elvaston Pl., London, SW7 5NL; tel. (20) 7823-9986; fax (20) 7584-0047; Ambassador OMER PIANKALI.

The Gambia: 57 Kensington Court, London, W8 5DG; tel. (20) 7937-6316; fax (20) 7937-9095; e-mail gambiahighcomuk@btconnect.com; High Commr ELIZABETH YA ELI HARDING.

Georgia: 4 Russell Gdns, London, W14 8EZ; tel. (20) 7348-1941; fax (20) 7603-6682; e-mail embassy@geoemb.plus.com; internet www.uk.mfa.gov.ge; Ambassador GIORGI BADRIDZE.

Germany: 23 Belgrave Sq., London, SW1X 8PZ; tel. (20) 7824-1300; fax (20) 7824-1435; e-mail info@london.diplo.de; internet www.london.diplo.de; Ambassador GEORG BOOMGAARDEN.

Ghana: 13 Belgrave Sq., London, SW1X 8PN; tel. (20) 7235-5900; fax (20) 7245-9552; e-mail information@ghanahighcommissionuk.com; internet www.ghanahighcommissionuk.com; High Commr KWAKU DANSO-BOAFO.

Greece: 1A Holland Park, London, W11 3TP; tel. (20) 7229-3850; fax (20) 7229-7221; e-mail political@greekembassy.org.uk; internet www.greekembassy.org.uk; Ambassador ARISTIDIS C. SANDIS.

Grenada: The Chapel, Archel Rd, West Kensington, London, W14 9QH; tel. (20) 7385-4415; fax (20) 7381-4807; e-mail office@grenada-highcommission.co.uk; internet www.grenadahclon.org.uk; High Commr RUTH ELIZABETH ROUSE.

Guatemala: 13A Fawcett St, London, SW10 9HN; tel. (20) 7351-3042; fax (20) 7376-5708; e-mail inglaterra@minex.gob.gt; Ambassador ACISCLO VALLADARES MOLINA.

THE UNITED KINGDOM

Guinea: 258 Belsize Rd, London, NW6 4BT; tel. (20) 7316-1861; e-mail ambaguineeuk@yahoo.co.uk; Ambassador (vacant).

Guyana: 3 Palace Court, Bayswater Rd, London, W2 4LP; tel. (20) 7229-7684; fax (20) 7727-9809; e-mail guyanahc1@btconnect.com; internet www.guyanahclondon.co.uk; High Commr LALESHWAR K. N. SINGH.

Holy See: 54 Parkside, London, SW19 5NE (Apostolic Nunciature); tel. (20) 8944-7189; fax (20) 8947-2494; e-mail nuntius@globalnet.co.uk; Apostolic Nuncio Most Rev. ANTONIO MENNINI (Titular Archbishop of Ferentium).

Honduras: 115 Gloucester Pl., London, W1U 6JT; tel. (20) 7486-4880; fax (20) 7486-4550; e-mail hondurasuk@lineone.net; internet www.hondurasembassy.co.uk; Ambassador IVÁN ROMERO-MARTÍNEZ.

Hungary: 35 Eaton Pl., London, SW1X 8BY; tel. (20) 7201-3440; fax (20) 7823-1348; e-mail office.lon@kum.hu; internet www.mfa.gov.hu/emb/london; Ambassador JÁNOS CSÁK.

Iceland: 2A Hans St, London, SW1X 0JE; tel. (20) 7259-3999; fax (20) 7245-9649; e-mail icemb.london@utn.stjr.is; internet www.iceland.org/uk; Ambassador BENEDIKT JÓNSSON.

India: India House, Aldwych, London, WC2B 4NA; tel. (20) 7836-8484; fax (20) 7836-4331; e-mail administrativewing@hcilondon.in; internet www.hcilondon.in; High Commr NALIN SURIE.

Indonesia: 38 Grosvenor Sq., London, W1X 2HW; tel. (20) 7499-7661; fax (20) 7491-4993; e-mail kbri@btconnect.com; internet www.indonesianembassy.org.uk; Ambassador YURI OCTAVIAN THAMRIN.

Iran: 16 Prince's Gate, London, SW7 1PT; tel. (20) 7225-3000; fax (20) 7589-4440; e-mail info@iran-embassy.org.uk; internet www.iran-embassy.org.uk; Ambassador (vacant).

Iraq: 4 Elvaston Pl., London, W14 8BP; tel. (20) 7602-8456; fax (20) 7371-1652; e-mail lonemb@iraqmofamail.net; internet www.iraqembassy.org.uk; Chargé d'affaires a.i. ABD AL-MUHAIMEN AL-ORAIBI.

Ireland: 17 Grosvenor Pl., London, SW1X 7HR; tel. (20) 7235-2171; fax (20) 7201-6961; internet www.embassyofireland.co.uk; Ambassador BOBBY McDONAGH.

Israel: 2 Palace Green, Kensington, London, W8 4QB; tel. (20) 7957-9500; fax (20) 7957-9555; e-mail public@london.mfa.gov.il; internet london.mfa.gov.il; Ambassador RON PROSOR.

Italy: 14 Three Kings Yard, London, W1K 4EH; tel. (20) 7312-2200; fax (20) 7312-2230; e-mail emblondon@embitaly.org.uk; internet www.amblondra.esteri.it; Ambassador ALAIN GIORGIO MARIA ECONOMIDES.

Jamaica: 1–2 Prince Consort Rd, London, SW7 2BZ; tel. (20) 7823-9911; fax (20) 7589-5154; e-mail jamhigh@jhcuk.com; internet www.jhcuk.com; High Commr ANTHONY JOHNSON.

Japan: 101–104 Piccadilly, London, W1J 7JT; tel. (20) 7465-6500; fax (20) 7491-9347; e-mail info@ld.mofa.go.jp; internet www.uk.emb-japan.go.jp; Ambassador KEIICHI HAYASHI.

Jordan: 6 Upper Phillimore Gdns, London, W8 7HA; tel. (20) 7937-3685; fax (20) 7937-8795; e-mail london@fm.gov.jo; internet www.jordanembassy.org.uk; Ambassador (vacant).

Kazakhstan: 33 Thurloe Sq., London, SW7 2SD; tel. (20) 7581-4646; fax (20) 7584-8481; e-mail london@kazakhstan-embassy.org.uk; internet www.kazakhstanembassy.org.uk; Ambassador KAIRAT ABUSSEITOV.

Kenya: 45 Portland Pl., London, W1N 4AS; tel. (20) 7636-2371; fax (20) 7323-6717; e-mail info@kenyahighcommission.net; internet www.kenyahighcommission.net; High Commr EPHRAHIM W. NGARE.

Korea, Democratic People's Republic: 73 Gunnersbury Ave, London, W5 4LP; tel. (20) 8992-4965; fax (20) 8992-2053; e-mail dprkrepmission@yahoo.co.uk; Ambassador JA SONG NAM.

Korea, Republic: 60 Buckingham Gate, London, SW1E 6AJ; tel. (20) 7227-5500; fax (20) 7227-5503; internet www.koreanembassy.org.uk; Ambassador CHOO KYU-HO.

Kosovo: 100 Pall Mall, London SW1Y 5NQ; tel. (20) 7659-6140; fax (20) 7659-6137; e-mail embassy.uk@ks-gov.net; Ambassador Dr MUHAMET HAMITI.

Kuwait: 2 Albert Gate, London, SW1X 7JU; tel. (20) 7590-3400; fax (20) 7823-1712; e-mail kuwait@dircon.co.uk; internet www.kuwaitinfo.org.uk; Ambassador KHALID AL-DUWAISAN.

Kyrgyzstan: Ascot House, 119 Crawford St, London, W1U 6BJ; tel. (20) 7935-1462; fax (20) 7935-7449; e-mail mail@kyrgyz-embassy.org.uk; internet www.kyrgyz-embassy.org.uk; Ambassador BAKTYGUL KALAMBEKOVA.

Latvia: 45 Nottingham Pl., London, W1U 5LY; tel. (20) 7312-0041; fax (20) 7312-0042; e-mail embassy.uk@mfa.gov.lv; internet www.london.mfa.gov.lv; Ambassador EDUARDS STIPRAIS.

Lebanon: 21 Palace Gardens Mews, London, W8 4RB; tel. (20) 7227-6696; fax (20) 7243-1699; e-mail emb.leb@btinternet.com; Ambassador INAAM OSSEIRAN.

Lesotho: 7 Chesham Pl., London, SW1 8HN; tel. (20) 7235-5686; fax (20) 7235-5023; e-mail lhc@lesotholondon.org.uk; internet www.lesotholondon.org.uk; High Commr Prince SEEISO BERENG SEEISO.

Liberia: 23 Fitzroy Sq., London, W1T 6EW; tel. (20) 7388-5489; fax (20) 7380-1593; e-mail info@embassyofliberia.org.uk; internet www.embassyofliberia.org.uk; Ambassador WESLEY MOMO JOHNSON.

Libya: 15 Knightsbridge, London, SW1X 7LY; tel. (20) 7201-8280; fax (20) 7245-0588; internet www.libyan-embassy.co.uk; Ambassador (vacant).

Lithuania: 84 Gloucester Pl., London, W1U 6AU; tel. (20) 7486-6401; fax (20) 7486-6403; e-mail amb.uk@urm.lt; internet uk.mfa.lt; Ambassador Dr OSKARAS JUSYS.

Luxembourg: 27 Wilton Cres., London, SW1X 8SD; tel. (20) 7235-6961; fax (20) 7235-9734; e-mail londres.amb@mae.etat.lu; internet londres.mae.lu; Ambassador HUBERT WURTH.

Macedonia, former Yugoslav republic: Suites 2.1 and 2.2, 2nd Floor, Buckingham Court, Buckingham Gate, London, SW1E 6PE; tel. (20) 7976-0535; fax (20) 7976-0539; e-mail info@macedonianembassy.org.uk; internet www.macedonianembassy.org.uk; Ambassador MARIJA EFREMOVA.

Malawi: 70 Winnington Rd, London, N2 0TX; tel. (20) 8455-5624; fax (20) 3235-1066; e-mail malawihighcom@btconnect.com; internet www.malawihighcommission.co.uk; High Commr (vacant).

Malaysia: 45–46 Belgrave Sq., London, SW1X 8QT; tel. (20) 7235-8033; fax (20) 7235-5161; e-mail mwlon@btconnect.com; internet www.kln.gov.my/web/uki_london; High Commr Datuk ZAKARIA SULONG.

Maldives: 22 Nottingham Pl., London, W1U 5NJ; tel. (20) 7224-2135; fax (20) 7224-2157; e-mail info@maldiveshighcommission.org; internet www.maldiveshighcommission.org; High Commr Dr FARAHANAZ FAIZAL.

Malta: Malta House, 36–38 Piccadilly, London, W1J 0LE; tel. (20) 7292-4800; fax (20) 7734-1831; e-mail maltahighcommission.london@gov.mt; High Commr JOSEPH ZAMMIT TABONA.

Mauritius: 32–33 Elvaston Pl., London, SW7 5NW; tel. (20) 7581-0294; fax (20) 7823-8437; e-mail londonmhc@btinternet.com; High Commr ABHIMANU MAHENDRA KUNDASAMY.

Mexico: 16 St George St, Hanover Sq., London, W1S 1FD; tel. (20) 7499-8586; fax (20) 7495-4035; e-mail mexuk@sre.gob.mx; internet www.sre.gob.mx/reinounido; Ambassador EDUARDO MEDINA-MORA ICAZA.

Moldova: 5 Dolphin Sq., Edensor Rd, London, W4 2ST; tel. (20) 8995-6818; fax (20) 8995-6927; e-mail embassy.london@mfa.md; internet www.britania.mfa.gov.md; Chargé d'affaires a.i. MIHAELA MANOLI.

Monaco: 7 Upper Grosvenor St, London, W1K 2LX; tel. (20) 7318-1081; fax (20) 7493-4563; e-mail embassy@gouv.mc; Ambassador EVELYNE GENTA.

Mongolia: 7–8 Kensington Court, London, W8 5DL; tel. (20) 7937-0150; fax (20) 7937-1117; e-mail office@embassyofmongolia.co.uk; internet www.embassyofmongolia.co.uk; Ambassador BULGAAGIIN ALTANGEREL.

Montenegro: Trafalgar House, 5th Floor, 11–12 Waterloo Pl., London, SW1Y 4AU; tel. (20) 7863-8806; e-mail dragisa_burzan@yahoo.com; fax (20) 7863-8807; Ambassador LJUBIŠA STANKOVIĆ.

Morocco: 49 Queen's Gate Gdns, London, SW7 5NE; tel. (20) 7581-5001; fax (20) 7225-3862; e-mail ambalondres@maec.gov.ma; internet www.moroccanembassylondon.org.uk; Ambassador Princess CHRIFA LALLA JOUMALA ALAOUI.

Mozambique: 21 Fitzroy Sq., London, W1T 6EL; tel. (20) 7383-3800; fax (20) 7383-3801; e-mail helga@mozambiquehc.co.uk; internet www.mozambiquehighcommission.org.uk; High Commr ANTÓNIO GUMENDE.

Myanmar: 19A Charles St, London, W1J 5DX; tel. (20) 7499-4340; fax (20) 7409-7043; e-mail melondon@btconnect.com; Ambassador Maj. Gen. NAY WIN.

Namibia: 6 Chandos St, London, W1G 9LU; tel. (20) 7636-6244; fax (20) 7637-5694; e-mail info@namibiahc.org.uk; internet www.namibiahc.org.uk; High Commr GEORGE MBANGA LISWANISO.

Nepal: 12A Kensington Palace Gdns, London, W8 4QU; tel. (20) 7229-1594; fax (20) 7792-9861; e-mail eon@nepembassy.org.uk; internet www.nepembassy.org.uk; Ambassador Dr SURESH CHANDRA CHALISE.

Netherlands: 38 Hyde Park Gate, London, SW7 5DP; tel. (20) 7590-3200; fax (20) 7225-0947; e-mail london@netherlands-embassy.org.uk; internet www.netherlands-embassy.org.uk; Ambassador PIETER WILLEM (PIM) WALDECK.

New Zealand: New Zealand House, 80 Haymarket, London, SW1Y 4TQ; tel. (20) 7930-8422; fax (20) 7839-4580; e-mail aboutnz@newzealandhc.org.uk; internet www.nzembassy.com/uk; High Commr DEREK WILLIAM LEASK.

THE UNITED KINGDOM

Nicaragua: Vicarage House, Suite 31, 58–60 Kensington Church St, London, W8 4DP; tel. (20) 7938-2373; fax (20) 7937-0952; e-mail embaniclondon@btconnect.com; Ambassador Carlos Argüello Gómez.

Nigeria: Nigeria House, 9 Northumberland Ave, London, WC2N 5BX; tel. (20) 7839-1244; fax (20) 7839-8746; e-mail chancery@nigeriahc.org.uk; internet www.nigeriahc.org.uk; High Commr Dr Dalhatu Sarki Tafida.

Norway: 25 Belgrave Sq., London, SW1X 8QD; tel. (20) 7591-5500; fax (20) 7245-6993; e-mail emb.london@mfa.no; internet www.norway.org.uk; Ambassador Kim Traavik.

Oman: 167 Queen's Gate, London, SW7 5HE; tel. (20) 7225-0001; fax (20) 7589-2505; Ambassador Abd al-Aziz al-Hinai.

Pakistan: 34–36 Lowndes Sq., London, SW1X 9JN; tel. (20) 7664-9200; fax (20) 7664-9224; internet www.pakmission-uk.gov.pk; High Commr Wajid Shamsul Hasan.

Panama: 40 Hertford St, London, W1J 7SH; tel. (20) 7493-4646; fax (20) 7493-4333; e-mail panama1@btconnect.com; Ambassador Gilberto Arias.

Papua New Guinea: 3rd Floor, 14 Waterloo Pl., London, SW1R 4AR; tel. (20) 7930-0922; fax (20) 7930-0828; e-mail kunduldn3@btconnect.com; High Commr Jean L. Kekedo.

Paraguay: 3rd Floor, 344 Kensington High St, London, W14 8NS; tel. (20) 7610-4180; fax (20) 7371-4297; e-mail embapar@btconnect.com; internet www.paraguayembassy.co.uk; Ambassador Miguel Angel Solano Lopez Casco.

Peru: 52 Sloane St, London, SW1X 9SP; tel. (20) 7235-1917; fax (20) 7235-4463; e-mail postmaster@peruembassy-uk.com; internet www.peruembassy-uk.com; Ambassador Hernán Couturier.

Philippines: 6–8 Suffolk St, London, SW1Y 4HG; tel. (20) 7451-1800; fax (20) 7930-9787; e-mail embassy@philemb.co.uk; internet www.philemb.org.uk; Ambassador (vacant).

Poland: 47 Portland Pl., London, W1B 1JH; tel. (20) 7291-3520; fax (20) 7291-3575; e-mail london@msz.gov.pl; internet www.london.polemb.net; Ambassador Barbara Tuge-Erecińska.

Portugal: 11 Belgrave Sq., London, SW1X 8PP; tel. (20) 7235-5331; fax (20) 7235-0739; e-mail london@portembassy.co.uk; Ambassador João de Vallera.

Qatar: 1 South Audley St, London, W1K 1NB; tel. (20) 7493-2200; fax (20) 7493-2661; Ambassador Khalid bin Rashid bin Salim al-Hamoudi al-Mansouri.

Romania: Arundel House, 4 Palace Green, London, W8 4QD; tel. (20) 7937-9666; fax (20) 7937-8069; e-mail roemb@roemb.co.uk; internet londra.mae.ro; Ambassador Ion Jinga.

Russia: 13 Kensington Palace Gdns, London, W8 4QX; tel. (20) 7229-6412; fax (20) 7727-8625; e-mail office@rusemblon.org; internet www.rusemb.org.uk; Ambassador Aleksandr Yakovenko.

Rwanda: 120–122 Seymour Pl., London, W1H 1NR; tel. (20) 7724-9832; fax (20) 7724-8642; e-mail uk@ambarwanda.org.uk; internet www.ambarwanda.org.uk; High Commr Ernest Rwamulyo.

Saint Christopher and Nevis: 2nd Floor, 10 Kensington Court, London, W8 5DL; tel. (20) 7937-9718; fax (20) 7937-7484; e-mail sknhighcomm@btconnect.com; High Commr Kevin Monroe Isaac.

Saint Lucia: 1 Collingham Gdns, London, SW5 0HW; tel. (20) 7370-7123; fax (20) 7370-1905; e-mail enquiries@stluciahcuk.org; High Commr Eldridge Stephens.

Saint Vincent and the Grenadines: 10 Kensington Court, London, W8 5DL; tel. (20) 7565-2874; fax (20) 7937-6040; e-mail info@svghighcom.co.uk; High Commr Cenio E. Lewis.

Saudi Arabia: 30 Charles St, London, W1J 5DZ; tel. (20) 7917-3000; fax (20) 7917-3330; e-mail ukemb@mofa.gov.sa; internet www.saudiembassy.org.uk; Ambassador Prince Muhammad bin Nawaf bin Abd al-Aziz.

Senegal: 39 Marloes Rd, London, W8 6LA; tel. (20) 7937-7237; fax (20) 7938-2546; e-mail senegalembassy@hotmail.co.uk; internet www.senegalembassy.co.uk; Ambassador Abdou Sourang.

Serbia: 28 Belgrave Sq., London, SW1X 8QB; tel. (20) 7235-9049; fax (20) 7235-7092; e-mail london@serbianembassy.org.uk; internet www.serbianembassy.org.uk; Ambassador Dr Dejan Popovic.

Seychelles: 18 Hanover St, London, W1S 1YN; High Commr Patrick Pillay.

Sierra Leone: 41 Eagle St, London, WC1R 4TL; tel. (20) 7404-0140; fax (20) 7430-9862; e-mail info@slhc-uk.org.uk; internet www.slhc-uk.org.uk; High Commr Edward Mohamed Turay.

Singapore: 9 Wilton Cres., London, SW1X 8SP; tel. (20) 7235-8315; fax (20) 7245-6583; e-mail singhc_lon@sgmfa.gov.sg; internet www.mfa.gov.sg/london; High Commr Michael Eng Cheng Teo.

Slovakia: 25 Kensington Palace Gdns, London, W8 4QY; tel. (20) 7313-6470; fax (20) 7313-6481; e-mail emb.london@mzv.sk; internet www.slovakembassy.co.uk; Chargé d'affaires a.i. Milan Vojtko.

Slovenia: 10 Little College St, London, SW1P 3SH; tel. (20) 7222-5700; fax (20) 7222-5277; e-mail vlo@gov.si; internet london.embassy.si; Ambassador Iztok Jarc.

South Africa: South Africa House, Trafalgar Sq., London, WC2N 5DP; tel. (20) 7451-7299; fax (20) 7451-7283; e-mail london.general@foreign.gov.za; internet www.southafricahouse.com; High Commr Dr Zola Sidney Themba Skweyiya.

Spain: 39 Chesham Pl., London, SW1X 8SB; tel. (20) 7235-5555; fax (20) 7259-5392; e-mail emb.londres@maec.es; internet www.maec.es/embajadas/londres; Ambassador Carles Casajuana Palet.

Sri Lanka: 13 Hyde Park Gdns, London, W2 2LU; tel. (20) 7262-1841; fax (20) 7262-7970; e-mail mail@slhc-london.co.uk; internet www.slhclondon.org; High Commr (vacant).

Sudan: 3 Cleveland Row, St James's, London, SW1A 1DD; tel. (20) 7839-8080; fax (20) 7839-7560; e-mail admin@sudanembassy.co.uk; internet www.sudanembassy.co.uk; Ambassador Abdullahi Hamad Ali.

Swaziland: 20 Buckingham Gate, London, SW1E 6LB; tel. (20) 7630-6611; fax (20) 7630-6564; e-mail enquiries@swaziland.org.uk; High Commr Dumsile T. Sukati.

Sweden: 11 Montagu Pl., London, W1H 2AL; tel. (20) 7917-6400; fax (20) 7724-4174; e-mail ambassaden.london@foreign.ministry.se; internet www.swedenabroad.com/london; Ambassador Nicola Clase.

Switzerland: 16–18 Montagu Pl., London, W1H 2BQ; tel. (20) 7616-6000; fax (20) 7724-7001; e-mail lon.swissembassy@eda.admin.ch; internet www.swissembassy.org.uk; Ambassador Anton Thalmann.

Syria: 8 Belgrave Sq., London, SW1X 8PH; tel. (20) 7245-9012; fax (20) 7235-4621; e-mail embassy@syrianembassy.co.uk; internet www.syrianembassy.co.uk; Ambassador Dr Sami Khiyami.

Tajikistan: Grove House, 27 Hammersmith Grove, London, W6 0NE; tel. (20) 8600-2520; fax (20) 8600-2501; e-mail info@tajembassy.org.uk; internet www.tajembassy.org.uk; Ambassador Erkin S. Kasymov.

Tanzania: 3 Stratford Pl., London, WIC 1AS; tel. (20) 7569-1470; fax (20) 7495-8817; e-mail tanzarep@tanzania-online.gov.uk; internet www.tanzania-online.gov.uk; Ambassador Peter Kallaghe.

Thailand: 29–30 Queen's Gate, London, SW7 5JB; tel. (20) 7589-2944; fax (20) 7823-9695; e-mail csinfo@thaiembassyuk.org.uk; internet www.thaiembassyuk.org.uk; Ambassador Kitti Wasinondh.

Tonga: 36 Molyneux St, London, W1H 5BQ; tel. (20) 7724-5828; fax (20) 7723-9074; e-mail office@tongahighcom.co.uk; High Commr Dr Sione Ngongo Kioa.

Trinidad and Tobago: 42 Belgrave Sq., London, SW1X 8NT; tel. (20) 7245-9351; fax (20) 7823-1065; e-mail tthc@btconnect.com; High Commr Garvin Nicholas.

Tunisia: 29 Prince's Gate, London, SW7 1QG; tel. (20) 7584-8117; fax (20) 7584-3205; e-mail london@tunisianembassy.co.uk; Ambassador Hatem Atallah.

Turkey: 43 Belgrave Sq., London, SW1X 8PA; tel. (20) 7393-0202; fax (20) 7393-0066; e-mail turkish.emb@btclick.com; internet www.turkishembassylondon.org; Ambassador Ünal Çeviköz.

Turkmenistan: 2nd Floor South, St George's House, 14–17 Wells St, London, W1T 3PD; tel. (20) 7255-1071; fax (20) 7323-9184; Ambassador Yazmurad Seryaev.

Uganda: Uganda House, 58–59 Trafalgar Sq., London, WC2N 5DX; tel. (20) 7839-5783; fax (20) 7839-8925; e-mail info@ugandahighcomission.co.uk; internet www.ugandahighcommission.co.uk; High Commr Joan Kakima Nyakatuura Rwabyomere.

Ukraine: 60 Holland Park, London, W11 3SJ; tel. (20) 7727-6312; fax (20) 7792-1708; e-mail emb_gb@mfa.gov.ua; internet www.ukremb.org.uk; Ambassador Volodymyr Khandogiy.

United Arab Emirates: 30 Princes Gate, London, SW7 1PT; tel. (20) 7581-1281; fax (20) 7581-9616; e-mail informationuk@mofa.gov.ae; internet www.uae-embassy.ae/uk; Ambassador Abd al-Rahman Ghanim al-Mutaiwee.

USA: 24–32 Grosvenor Sq., London, W1A 1AE; tel. (20) 7499-9000; internet london.usembassy.gov; Ambassador Louis B. Susman.

Uruguay: 125 Kensington High St, London, W8 5SF; tel. (20) 7937-4170; fax (20) 7376-0502; e-mail emburuguay@emburuguay.org.uk; Ambassador Julio Moreira Morán.

Uzbekistan: 41 Holland Park, London, W11 3RP; tel. (20) 7229-7679; fax (20) 7229-7029; e-mail info@uzbekembassy.org; internet www.uzbekembassy.org; Ambassador Otabek H. Akbarov.

Venezuela: 1 Cromwell Rd, London, SW7 2HW; tel. (20) 7584-4206; fax (20) 7589-8887; e-mail info@venezlon.co.uk; internet www.embavenez-uk.org; Ambassador Dr Samuel Moncada.

Viet Nam: 12–14 Victoria Rd, London, W8 5RD; tel. (20) 7937-1912; fax (20) 7937-6108; e-mail embassy@vietnamembassy.org.uk;

THE UNITED KINGDOM

internet www.vietnamembassy.org.uk; Ambassador QUANG HOANG TRAN.

Yemen: 57 Cromwell Rd, London, SW7 2ED; tel. (20) 7584-6607; fax (20) 7589-3350; e-mail yemenembassy@btconnect.com; internet www.yemenembassy.org.uk; Ambassador ABDULLAH AL-RADHI.

Zambia: Zambia House, 2 Palace Gate, London, W8 5NG; tel. (20) 7589-6655; fax (20) 7581-1353; e-mail immzhcl@btconnect.com; internet www.zhcl.org.uk; High Commr Prof. ROYSON MUKWENA.

Zimbabwe: Zimbabwe House, 429 Strand, London, WC2R 0QE; tel. (20) 7836-7755; fax (20) 7379-1167; e-mail zimlondon@yahoo.co.uk; Ambassador GABRIEL MHARADZE MACHINGA.

Judicial System

There are, historically, three sources of the law as administered in the law courts of England and Wales: Statute Law, which is a written law and consists mainly of Acts of Parliament; Common Law, which originated in ancient usage and has not been formally enacted; and Equity, which was the system evolved by the Lord Chancellor's court (Court of Chancery) to mitigate the strictness of some of the common law rules. The law of the European Union has been added to these.

Scottish common and statute law differ in some respects from that current in England and Wales, owing to Scotland's retention of its own legal system under the Act of Union with England of 1707. Northern Ireland also retains a separate judicial structure, which closely resembles the English system.

Judicial independence is guaranteed by the Constitutional Reform Act 2005, which states that ministers of the Crown may not seek to influence judicial decisions through any special access to the judiciary. According to the Act of Settlement 1701, senior judges in England and Wales are appointed for life and can be removed from office only after an address from Parliament to the Sovereign. The participation of private citizens in all important criminal and some civil cases, in the form of a summoned jury of 12 persons, who judge, if necessary by a majority, the facts of a case (questions of law being decided by the judge), also helps to ensure a fair trial.

THE SUPREME COURT

The Supreme Court (which assumed the judicial functions formerly exercised by the House of Lords in 2009) is the final court of appeal for the whole of the United Kingdom in civil cases, and for England, Wales and Northern Ireland in criminal cases. It hears appeals from the Court of Appeal in England and Wales, the Court of Appeal in Northern Ireland and the Court of Session in Scotland, and in some limited cases from the High Court of Justice in England and Wales and the High Court in Northern Ireland. It also exercises jurisdiction in relation to devolution matters: that is, it decides on whether the actions of the legislative and executive bodies of Northern Ireland, Scotland and Wales are within their respective competencies.

The Justices of the Supreme Court additionally constitute the Judicial Committee of the Privy Council. This is the final court of appeal for appeals from the Overseas Territories and Crown Dependencies, and from certain Commonwealth countries; it also exercises domestic jurisdiction in ecclesiastical matters and appeals from disciplinary tribunals of certain professions.

Supreme Court: Parliament Sq., London, SW1P 3BD; tel. (20) 7960-1500; fax (20) 7960-1901; e-mail enquiries@supremecourt.gsi.gov.uk; internet www.supremecourt.gov.uk.

Justices of the Supreme Court: Lord PHILLIPS OF WORTH MATRAVERS (President), Lord HOPE OF CRAIGHEAD (Deputy President), Lord SAVILLE OF NEWDIGATE, Lord RODGER OF EARLSFERRY, Lord WALKER OF GESTINGTHORPE, Baroness HALE OF RICHMOND, Lord BROWN OF EATON-UNDER-HEYWOOD, Lord MANCE, Lord COLLINS OF MAPESBURY, Lord KERR OF TONAGHMORE, Lord CLARKE OF STONE-CUM-EBONY, Sir JOHN ANTHONY DYSON.

JUDICIAL SYSTEM OF ENGLAND AND WALES

The criminal courts of lowest jurisdiction in England and Wales are the magistrates' courts (or petty sessions), presided over by Justices of the Peace, who are unpaid lay citizens. They have power to try all non-indictable offences, and may try some of the less serious indictable offences if the defendant agrees. More serious criminal cases are heard initially in the magistrates' courts, whence they are committed for trial in the Crown Court. In London and in certain other large towns there are a small number of professional salaried magistrates, known as District Judges (Magistrates' Court), who sit alone, whereas lay justices normally sit in threes when acting judicially. Youth Courts, composed of specially trained justices, have power to try most charges against children aged under 18 years.

More serious criminal cases are tried by jury in the Crown Court, which sits at various centres throughout England and Wales. Court centres are administratively divided into three tiers. The most serious offences are tried at first and second tier centres presided over by High Court Judges, Circuit Judges or Recorders. Circuit Judges or Recorders preside over third tier centres, where the less serious offences are tried. The Crown Court also hears appeals from the magistrates' courts.

Most civil actions are tried in the county courts, which have unlimited jurisdiction in civil matters. They are presided over by a Circuit Judge, or, in some cases, a District Judge, sitting alone.

Certain important civil cases are heard in the High Court of Justice, which has three divisions—Chancery, Queen's Bench and Family. The Chancery Division deals with litigation about property, patents, family trusts, companies, dissolution of partnerships and disputed estates. The Queen's Bench Division hears cases involving damage to property, personal injuries, etc., and also includes the Administrative, Commercial, Admiralty, and Technology and Construction Courts. The Family Division hears contested or complex divorce and separation cases and matters relating to children such as adoption, wardship or guardianship of minors.

The Court of Appeal hears appeals in civil cases from County Courts and the High Court of Justice and in criminal cases from the Crown Courts. Appeals from the High Court that involve important points of law occasionally go direct to the Supreme Court.

Court of Appeal

The Royal Courts of Justice, Strand, London, WC2A 2LL; tel. (20) 7947-6000.

The Court of Appeal consists of a Civil Division and a Criminal Division, headed respectively by the Master of the Rolls and the Lord Chief Justice (who is also the head of the judiciary). The Master of the Rolls is the effective head of the court. The presidents of the three divisions of the High Court are also ex officio members of the Court of Appeal.

Master of the Rolls and Head of Civil Justice: Lord NEUBERGER OF ABBOTSBURY.

Lord Chief Justice of England and Wales and Head of Criminal Justice: Lord JUDGE.

Lords Justices of Appeal: Sir MALCOLM THOMAS PILL, Sir ALAN HYLTON WARD, Sir MATHEW ALEXANDER THORPE, Sir GEORGE MARK WALLER, Sir JOHN FRANK MUMMERY, Sir JOHN GRANT MCKENZIE LAWS, Sir STEPHEN JOHN SEDLEY, Sir BERNARD ANTHONY RIX, Dame MARY HOWARTH ARDEN, Dame JILL MARGARET BLACK, Sir ANDREW CENTLIVRES LONGMORE, Sir ROBERT JOHN ANDERSON CARNWATH, Dame JANET HILARY SMITH, Sir ROGER JOHN LAUGHARNE THOMAS, Sir ROBERT RAPHAEL HAYIM (ROBIN) JACOB, Sir MAURICE RALPH KAY, Sir ANTHONY HOOPER, Sir TIMOTHY ANDREW WIGRAM LLOYD, Sir MARTIN JAMES MOORE-BICK, Sir NICHOLAS ALLAN ROY WILSON, Sir ALAN GEORGE MOSES, Sir STEPHEN PRICE RICHARDS, Dame HEATHER CAROL HALLETT, Sir ANTHONY PHILLIP GILSON HUGHES, Sir BRIAN HENRY LEVESON, Sir ROGER GRENFELL TOULSON, Sir COLIN PERCY FARQUHARSON RIMER, Sir STANLEY JEFFREY BURNTON, Sir TERRENCE MICHAEL ELKAN BARNET ETHERTON, Sir RUPERT MATTHEW JACKSON, Sir JOHN BERNARD GOLDRING, Sir RICHARD PEARSON AIKENS, Sir JEREMY MIRTH SULLIVAN, Sir PATRICK ELIAS, Sir NICOLAS JOHN PATTEN, Sir JAMES LAWRENCE MUNBY, Sir CHRISTOPHER JOHN PITCHFORD, Dame JILL MARGARET BLACK, Sir STEPHEN MILES TOMLINSON, Sir PETER HENRY GROSS.

High Court of Justice

The Royal Courts of Justice, Strand, London, WC2A 2LL; tel. (20) 7947-6000.

Chancellor of the High Court (President of the Chancery Division): Sir ROBERT ANDREW MORRITT.

President of the Queen's Bench Division and Judge in Charge of the Administrative Court: Sir ANTHONY TRISTRAM KENNETH MAY.

President of the Family Division and Head of Family Justice: Sir NICHOLAS PETER RATHBONE WALL.

JUDICIAL SYSTEM OF NORTHERN IRELAND

The judicial system of Northern Ireland closely resembles that of England and Wales. The senior courts, as in England and Wales, are the Court of Appeal, the High Court (which hears certain civil cases) and the Crown Court (which has jurisdiction in criminal matters). The county court system also corresponds to its English counterpart, with minor variations. County court judges share with the judges of the High Court the exercise of the jurisdiction of the Crown Court. The jurisdiction of the magistrates' courts (courts of summary jurisdiction) is exercised by a permanent judiciary of legally qualified resident magistrates. The Supreme Court in London is the final court of appeal for civil and criminal cases.

Lord Chief Justice of Northern Ireland: Sir DECLAN MORGAN, Royal Courts of Justice, Chichester St, Belfast, BT1 3JF; tel. (28) 9023-5111; fax (28) 9031-3508; e-mail adminoffice@courtsni.gov.uk; internet www.courtsni.gov.uk.

Judges of the Court of Appeal: Sir MALACHY HIGGINS, Sir PAUL FREDERICK GIRVAN, Sir PATRICK COGHLIN.

THE UNITED KINGDOM

Judges of the High Court: Sir JOHN GILLEN, Sir RICHARD MCLAUGHLIN, Sir RONALD WEATHERUP, Sir REGINALD WEIR, Sir CHARLES MORGAN, Sir DONNELL DEENY, Sir ANTHONY RONALD HART, Sir WILLIAM BENJAMIN SYNGE STEPHENS, Sir SEAMUS TREACY, Sir BERNARD MCCLOSKEY.

SCOTTISH JUDICIAL SYSTEM

Minor criminal offences are dealt with in the Justice of the Peace courts (formerly district courts), each headed by a lay Justice of the Peace assisted by a legally qualified Clerk. Most criminal actions, including all but the most serious offences, are tried in the Sheriff courts. Cases are usually heard by a Sheriff and a jury, but may be heard by a Sheriff alone. Sheriff courts also hear civil cases, in which they have practically unlimited jurisdiction. There are 49 Sheriff courts grouped in six regional sheriffdoms, each headed by a Sheriff Principal, to whom decisions of the Sheriffs in civil cases may be appealed.

The highest criminal court is the High Court of Justiciary, which sits in various locations around Scotland. It acts as a court of first instance for the most serious cases, which are tried by a judge and a jury of 15 members. It also functions as the supreme court of appeal in criminal matters, in which capacity it sits only in Edinburgh; appeal may be made to it from the Sheriff courts and from the Justice of the Peace courts. There is no further appeal to the Supreme Court in London.

The Court of Session is the supreme civil court in Scotland. It has an Inner House and an Outer House. The latter deals with the major civil cases and divorce actions, usually at first instance. The Inner House is mainly an appeal court, whence further appeal may be made to the Supreme Court in London.

The most senior members of the Scottish judiciary are the Senators of the College of Justice. They sit both in a criminal capacity as judges of the High Court of Justiciary, where they are known as Lords Commissioners of the Justiciary, and in a civil capacity as judges of the Court of Session, where they are known as Lords of Council and Session.

Court of Session

Parliament House, Parliament Sq., Edinburgh, EH1 1RQ; tel. (131) 225-2595; fax (131) 240-6755; e-mail supreme.courts@scotcourts.gov.uk; internet www.scotcourts.gov.uk.

The Court of Session comprises an Inner House and an Outer House. The Inner House has two divisions of equal standing, each consisting of five judges and headed by the Lord President and the Lord Justice Clerk, respectively.

Lord President of the Court of Session and Lord Justice General: Lord HAMILTON.

Lord Justice Clerk: Lord GILL.

Judges of the Inner House (First Division): Lord HARDIE, Lord REED, Lord EASSIE, Lord BONOMY.

Judges of the Inner House (Second Division): Lord OSBORNE, Lord MACKAY OF DRUMADOON, Lady PATON, Lord CARLOWAY, Lord CLARKE.

Judges of the Outer House: Lord MENZIES, Lord DRUMMOND YOUNG, Lord EMSLIE, Lady SMITH, Lord BRODIE, Lord BRACADALE, Lady DORRIAN, Lord HODGE, Lord GLENNIE, Lord KINCLAVEN, Lord TURNBULL, Lady CLARK OF CALTON, Lord BRAILSFORD, Lord UIST, Lord MALCOLM, Lord MATTHEWS, Lord WOOLMAN, Lord PENTLAND, Lord BANNATYNE, Lady STACEY, Lord TYRE, Lord DOHERTY, Lord STEWART.

High Court of Justiciary

Lawnmarket, Edinburgh, EH1 2PE; tel. (131) 225-2595; fax (131) 240-6915; e-mail supreme.courts@scotcourts.gov.uk; internet www.scotcourts.gov.uk.

The head of the High Court of Justiciary is the Lord Justice General, who is also Lord President of the Court of Session. The Lord Justice Clerk is the deputy head of the court. The ordinary judges are those of the Court of Session, sitting in a criminal capacity as Lords Commissioners of Justiciary.

Religion

CHRISTIANITY

Churches Together in Britain and Ireland: 39 Eccleston Sq., London, SW1V 1BX; tel. (20) 7901-4890; fax (20) 7901-4894; e-mail info@ctbi.org.uk; internet www.ctbi.org.uk; f. 1990 as successor to the British Council of Churches; co-ordinates the activities of its 38 member churches and liaises with ecumenical bodies in Britain and Ireland; provides a forum for joint decision-making and enables the churches to take action together; Gen. Sec. Rev. Canon BOB FYFFE.

Action of Churches Together in Scotland (ACTS): Inglewood House, Alloa, FK10 2HU; tel. (1259) 216980; fax (1259) 215964; e-mail ecumenical@acts-scotland.org; internet www.acts-scotland.org; aims to encourage and express unity of Christian Churches in Scotland; 9 mem. churches; Convener Rt. Rev. PHILLIP KERR; Gen. Sec. STEPHEN SMYTH.

Churches Together in England (CTE): 27 Tavistock Sq., London, WC1H 9HH; tel. (20) 7529-8131; fax (20) 7529-8134; e-mail office@cte.org.uk; internet www.churches-together.org.uk; f. 1990; 32 mem. bodies; Pres Most Rev. Dr ROWAN WILLIAMS, Most Rev. VINCENT NICHOLS, ELIZABETH MATEAR; Gen. Sec. Rev. DAVID CORNICK.

Churches Together in Wales (Cytûn): 58 Richmond Rd, Cardiff, CF24 3UR; tel. (29) 2046-4375; e-mail post@cytun.org.uk; internet www.cytun.org.uk; fmrly the Council of Churches for Wales; Chief Exec. Rev. ALED EDWARDS.

Irish Council of Churches: Inter-Church Centre, 48 Elmwood Ave, Belfast, BT9 6AZ; tel. (28) 9066-3145; fax (28) 9066-4160; e-mail info@irishchurches.org; internet www.irishchurches.org; f. 1922 (present name adopted 1966); 14 mem. churches; the organization of the churches in Ireland takes no account of the partition of the island into two separate political entities, with Ireland and Northern Ireland thus subject to a unified jurisdiction for ecclesiastical purposes; Pres. Most Rev. RICHARD CLARKE; Gen. Sec. MICHAEL EARLE.

The Anglican Communion

The Church of England

The Church of England is the Established Church, and as such acknowledges the authority of Parliament in matters in which secular authority is competent to exercise control. Queen Elizabeth I was declared 'Supreme Governor on Earth' of the Church of England, and the Sovereign is consecrated to this office at coronation.

In England there are two Provinces, Canterbury and York. The former contains 30, the latter 14, dioceses. Each Province has its ancient Convocations, the Upper and Lower House. By the Enabling Act the Constitution of the National Assembly of the Church of England ('Church Assembly') received statutory recognition in 1920, with power, subject to the control and authority of Parliament, of initiating legislation on all matters concerning the Church of England. Measures passed by the Assembly and approved by Parliament were submitted for the Royal Assent, having the force of Acts of Parliament.

In 1970, by the Synodical Government Measure (1969), the Church Assembly was reconstituted as the General Synod and was also given authority to exercise most of the functions of the Convocations. The House of Bishops consists of members of the Upper House of the Convocations (53 persons). The House of Clergy consists of the Lower Houses (a maximum of 259 persons). The House of Laity consists almost entirely of representatives of the dioceses elected by the deanery synods (a maximum of 258 persons).

In 2001 there were 1,372,000 people on the Church's electoral rolls.

The Archbishops and the 24 senior Bishops sit in the House of Lords.

Archbishop of Canterbury, Primate of All England and Metropolitan: Most Rev. Dr ROWAN WILLIAMS, Lambeth Palace, London, SE1 7JU; tel. (20) 7898-1200; fax (20) 7261-9836; internet www.archbishopofcanterbury.org.

Archbishop of York, Primate of England and Metropolitan: Most Rev. Dr JOHN SENTAMU, Bishopthorpe Palace, Bishopthorpe, York, YO23 2GE; tel. (1904) 707021; fax (1904) 709204; e-mail office@archbishopofyork.org; internet www.archbishopofyork.org.

General Synod of the Church of England: Church House, Great Smith St, London, SW1P 3AZ; tel. (20) 7898-1000; e-mail cofe.comms@churchofengland.org; internet www.churchofengland.org; Sec.-Gen. WILLIAM FITTALL.

The Church of Ireland

The See House, Cathedral Close, Armagh, BT61 7EE; tel. (28) 3752-7144; fax (28) 3752-7823; e-mail enquiries@ireland.anglican.org; internet www.ireland.anglican.org.

Ireland (including Northern Ireland) comprises two archdioceses and 10 dioceses; in 2006 there were 275,000 members of the Church of Ireland in Northern Ireland.

Archbishop of Armagh and Primate of All Ireland: Most Rev. ALAN HARPER, The See House, Cathedral Close, Armagh, BT61 7EE; tel. (28) 3752-7144; fax (28) 3752-7823; e-mail archbishop@armagh.anglican.org.

The Church in Wales

39 Cathedral Rd, Cardiff, CF11 9XF; tel. (29) 2034-8200; fax (29) 2038-7835; e-mail information@churchinwales.org.uk; internet www.churchinwales.org.uk.

The Province of Wales was created as a result of the Welsh Church Act of 1914, which took effect on 31 March 1920 and separated the four Welsh dioceses from the Province of Canterbury. It is divided into six dioceses served by 620 stipendiary clerics. The number of

THE UNITED KINGDOM

Easter communicants is 68,837 (2007). The Church in Wales has an administrative governing body which is a legislative assembly composed of bishops, clergy and laity, and a representative body incorporated by Royal Charter, which holds and manages the property and central funds of the Church; Provincial Sec. JOHN SHIRLEY.

Archbishop of Wales: Most Rev. BARRY C. MORGAN, Llys Esgob, Cathedral Green, Llandaff, Cardiff, CF5 2YE; tel. (29) 2056-2400; fax (29) 2056-8410; e-mail archbishop@churchinwales.org.uk.

The Scottish Episcopal Church

21 Grosvenor Cres., Edinburgh, EH12 5EE; tel. (131) 225-6357; fax (131) 346-7247; e-mail office@scotland.anglican.org; internet www.scotland.anglican.org.

Formerly the Established Church of Scotland, was disestablished and disendowed in 1689; is in full communion with all branches of the Anglican Communion; seven dioceses: Aberdeen and Orkney, Argyll and The Isles, Brechin, Edinburgh, Glasgow and Galloway, Moray, Ross and Caithness, and St Andrews, Dunkeld and Dunblane. There is a Bishop in each diocese; one of them is elected by the other Bishops as the Primus; Churches, mission stations, etc. 310, clergy 402, communicants 29,810; Sec.-Gen. to the General Synod JOHN STUART.

Primus: Most Rev. DAVID CHILLINGWORTH (Bishop of St Andrew's, Dunkeld and Dunblane), The Diocesan Centre, 5 St Vincent Pl., Glasgow, G1 2DH; tel. (141) 2215720; fax (141) 2217014; e-mail office@glasgow.anglican.org; internet www.glasgow.anglican.org.

The Roman Catholic Church

For ecclesiastical purposes Great Britain comprises seven archdioceses and 23 dioceses. There is also an apostolic exarchate for the Ukrainian Rite. Ireland (including Northern Ireland) comprises four archdioceses and 22 dioceses. The dioceses of Down and Connor and Dromore are completely in Northern Ireland, while the archdiocese of Armagh and the dioceses of Derry and Clogher are partly in Northern Ireland and partly in Ireland. At 31 December 2006 there were an estimated 4,097,772 adherents in England and Wales, of whom about 50,000 were of the Ukrainian Rite, and an estimated 702,890 adherents in Scotland. At the 2001 census 40.3% of the population of Northern Ireland gave their religion as Catholic or Roman Catholic.

Latin Rite

Bishops' Conference of England and Wales

39 Eccleston Sq., London, SW1V 1BX; tel. (20) 7630-8220; fax (20) 7901-4821; e-mail secretariat@cbcew.org.uk; internet www.catholic-ew.org.uk; President Most Rev. VINCENT NICHOLS (Archbishop of Westminster); Gen. Sec. Rt. Rev. MARCUS STOCK.

Archbishop of Westminster: Most Rev. VINCENT NICHOLS, Archbishop's House, Vaughan House, 46 Francis St, London SW1P 1QN; tel. (20) 7798-9033; fax (20) 7798-9077; e-mail archbishop@rcdow.org.uk; internet www.rcdow.org.uk/archbishop.

Archbishop of Birmingham: Most Rev. BERNARD LONGLEY, Archbishop's House, 8 Shadwell St, Queensway, Birmingham, B4 6EY; tel. (121) 236-9090; fax (121) 212-0171; e-mail archbishop@rc-birmingham.org; internet www.birminghamdiocese.org.uk.

Archbishop of Liverpool: Most Rev. PATRICK ALTHAM KELLY, Archbishop's House, Lowood, Carnatic Road, Mossley Hill, Liverpool, L18 8BY; tel. (151) 724-6398; fax (151) 724-6405; e-mail archbishop.liverpool@rcaolp.co.uk; internet www.liverpoolcatholic.org.uk.

Archbishop of Southwark: Most Rev. PETER DAVID SMITH, Archbishop's House, 150 St George's Rd, Southwark, London, SE1 6HX; tel. (20) 7928-2495; fax (20) 7928-7833; e-mail secswk@rcsouthwark.co.uk; internet www.rcsouthwark.co.uk.

Archbishop of Cardiff: GEORGE STACK, Archbishop's House, 41–43 Cathedral Rd, Cardiff, South Glamorgan, CF11 9HD; tel. (29) 2022-0411; fax (29) 2037-9036; e-mail arch@rcadc.org; internet www.rcadc.org.

Archbishop of Armagh and Primate of All Ireland: Cardinal SEÁN B. BRADY, Ara Coeli, Cathedral Rd, Armagh, BT61 7QY; tel. (28) 3752-2045; fax (28) 3752-6182; e-mail admin@aracoeli.com; internet www.armagharchdiocese.org.

Bishops' Conference of Scotland

64 Aitken St, Airdrie, ML6 6LT; tel. (1236) 764061; fax (1236) 762489; e-mail gensec@bpsconfscot.com; internet www.bpsconfscot.com; President HE Cardinal KEITH MICHAEL PATRICK O'BRIEN (Archbishop of St Andrews and Edinburgh); Gen. Sec. Rev. PAUL M. CONROY.

Archbishop of St Andrews and Edinburgh: HE Cardinal KEITH MICHAEL PATRICK O'BRIEN, Archbishop's House, 42 Greenhill Gdns, Edinburgh, EH10 4BJ; tel. (131) 447-3337; fax (131) 447-0816; e-mail cardinal@staned.org.uk; internet www.archdiocese-edinburgh.com.

Archbishop of Glasgow: Most Rev. MARIO JOSEPH CONTI, Curial Offices, 196 Clyde St, Glasgow, G1 4JY; tel. (141) 226-5898; fax (141) 225-2600; e-mail info@rcag.org.uk; internet www.rcag.org.uk.

Ukrainian Rite

Apostolic Administrator: Rt Rev. HLIB LONCHYNA, Bishop's House, 21 and 22 Binney St, London, W1Y 1YN; tel. (20) 7629-1534; fax (20) 7355-3314; e-mail frben@catholic.org; internet www.cerkva.org.uk.

Protestant Churches

Association of Baptist Churches in Ireland: 19 Hillsborough Rd, Moira, Craigavon, County Armagh, BT67 0HG; tel. (28) 9261-9267; e-mail abc@thebaptistcentre.org; internet www.baptistsinireland.org; 115 churches; 93 ministers; 8,500 mems; Pres. Pastor DEREK BAXTER; Dir Pastor WILLIAM COLVILLE.

Baptist Union of Great Britain: Baptist House, POB 44, 129 Broadway, Didcot, Oxfordshire, OX11 8RT; tel. (1235) 517700; fax (1235) 517715; e-mail info@baptist.org.uk; internet www.baptist.org.uk; f. 1813; the Baptist form of church government is congregational; baptism by immersion of believers is practised; the churches are grouped in associations; 142,000 mems (2006); Gen. Sec. Rev. JONATHAN P. EDWARDS.

Church of Scotland: 121 George St, Edinburgh, EH2 4YN; tel. (131) 225-5722; fax (131) 220-3113; e-mail lturnbull@cofscotland.org.uk; internet www.churchofscotland.org.uk; the national Church of Scotland was reformed in 1560, and became Presbyterian in doctrine and constitution. In 1921 the Church of Scotland Act was passed, by which the articles declaring the full spiritual freedom of the Church are recognized as lawful. In 1925 the Church of Scotland (Property and Endowments) Act became law, and made over to the Church of Scotland places of worship, manses and endowments in absolute property, vesting the future control of them in Trustees. The union of the Church of Scotland and the United Free Church was effected in 1929; Moderator of the General Assembly (2010/11) Rt Rev. JOHN CAIRNS CHRISTIE; 600,000 mems.

Elim Pentecostal Church: De Walden Rd, West Malvern WR14 4DF; tel. (845) 3026750; fax (1242) 3026752; e-mail info@elimhq.net; internet www.elim.org.uk; f. 1915; c. 550 churches and 60,000 adherents in Great Britain; Gen. Superintendent Rev. JOHN GLASS.

Free Church of Scotland: 15 North Bank St, The Mound, Edinburgh, EH1 2LS; tel. (131) 226-5286; fax (131) 220-0597; e-mail offices@freechurchofscotland.org.uk; internet www.freechurch.org; f. 1843; 103 congregations; Principal Clerk of Assembly Rev. JAMES MACIVER.

Free Churches Group, Churches Together in England: 27 Tavistock Sq., London, WC1H 9HH; tel. (20) 7529-8131; fax (20) 7529-8134; e-mail office@cte.org.uk; internet www.churches-together.net; central body for the co-ordination of the work of the Free Churches throughout England and Wales; Moderator Cmmr ELIZABETH MATEAR; Exec. Sec. Rev. MARK FISHER.

Lutheran Council of Great Britain: 30 Thanet St, London, WC1H 9QH; tel. (20) 7554-2900; fax (20) 7383-3081; e-mail enquiries@lutheran.org.uk; internet www.lutheran.org.uk; 10 mems; Chair. Rev. TORBJØRN HOLT; Gen. Sec. Rev. THOMAS BRUCH.

Methodist Church: Methodist Church House, 25 Marylebone Rd, London, NW1 5JR; tel. (20) 7486-5502; fax (20) 7224-5228; e-mail helpdesk@methodistchurch.org.uk; internet www.methodist.org.uk; f. 1739 by Rev. John Wesley, a priest of the Church of England; the governing body of the Church is the Annual Conference, which consists of ministers and lay representatives. The Church throughout Great Britain is divided into 31 Districts, and these hold their Synod Meetings in the autumn and the spring. The Districts are divided into Circuits, which hold regular Circuit Meetings, made up of representatives from the churches within the Circuit. There are also local Church Councils; 265,000 mems (2009); Pres. of the Methodist Conference (2009/10) Rev. DAVID GAMBLE; Gen. Sec. Dr MARTYN ATKINS.

Methodist Church in Ireland: 1 Fountainville Ave, Belfast, BT9 6AN; tel. (28) 9032-4554; fax (28) 9023-9467; e-mail secretary@irishmethodist.org; internet www.irishmethodist.org; 230 churches; 207 ministers; 51,425 mems; Pres. Rev. IAN D. HENDERSON.

Moravian Church: 5 Muswell Hill, London, N10 3TJ; tel. (20) 8883-3409; fax (20) 8365-3371; e-mail office@moravian.org.uk; internet www.moravian.org.uk; f. 1457; Sec. Provincial Board JACKIE MORTEN.

Moravian Church in Ireland: 5 Locksley Park, Belfast BT10 0AR; tel. (28) 9061-9755; e-mail paul.holdsworth@moravian.org.uk; f. 1746; Chair. of Conf. PAUL M. HOLDSWORTH.

Non-Subscribing Presbyterian Church of Ireland: 41A Rosemary St, Belfast, BT1 1QB; e-mail info@nspresbyterian.org; internet www.nspresbyterian.org; Moderator Rt. Rev. SAM PEDEN; Clerk Rev. NORMAN HUTTON.

THE UNITED KINGDOM

Presbyterian Church in Ireland: Church House, Fisherwick Pl., Belfast, BT1 6DW; tel. (28) 9032-2284; fax (28) 9041-7301; e-mail info@presbyterianireland.org; internet www.presbyterianireland.org; 549 churches; 381 ministers; 258,000 mems, 27,000 in 550 Sunday Schools; Moderator of the Gen. Assembly Rev. Dr NORMAN HAMILTON; Clerk of Assembly and Gen. Sec. Rev. Dr DONALD WATTS.

Presbyterian Church of Wales: Tabernacle Chapel, 81 Merthyr Rd, Whitchurch, Cardiff, CF14 1DD; tel. (29) 2062-7465; fax (29) 2061-6188; e-mail swyddfa.office@ebcpcw.org.uk; internet www.ebcpcw.org.uk; f. 1811; 832 churches, 77 full-time ministers, 34,819 mems (2005); Moderator of General Assembly Rev. GWENDA RICHARDS; Gen. Sec. Rev. IFAN RH ROBERTS.

Salvation Army: 101 Newington Causeway, London, SE1 6BN; tel. (20) 7367-4500; fax (20) 7367-4728; e-mail info@salvationarmy.org.uk; internet www.salvationarmy.org.uk; f. 1865; Territorial Commdr JOHN MATEAR.

Union of Welsh Independents: Tŷ John Penri, 5 Axis Court, Riverside Business Park, Swansea Vale, Swansea, SA7 0AJ; tel. (1792) 795888; fax (1792) 795376; e-mail undeb@annibynwyr.org; internet www.annibynwyr.org; f. 1872; Pres. ANDREW LENNY; Gen. Sec. Rev. Dr GERAINT TUDUR.

United Free Church of Scotland: 11 Newton Pl., Glasgow, G3 7PR; tel. (141) 332-3435; fax (141) 333-1973; e-mail office@ufcos.org.uk; internet www.ufcos.org.uk; f. 1900; 62 congregations, 29 ministers and pastors, 3,394 mems; Moderator Rev. ROBERT OWENS; Gen. Sec. Rev. JOHN O. FULTON.

United Reformed Church: United Reformed Church House, 86 Tavistock Pl., London, WC1H 9RT; tel. (20) 7916-2020; fax (20) 7916-2021; e-mail urc@urc.org.uk; internet www.urc.org.uk; f. 1972 by union of the Congregational Church in England and Wales and the Presbyterian Church of England; joined by the Churches of Christ 1981 and by the Scottish Congregational Church 2000; approx. 1,800 churches, 700 ministers and 250,000 mems; Moderator Rev. VAL MORRISON; Gen. Sec. Rev. Dr ROBERTA ROMINGER.

Orthodox Churches

Council of Oriental Orthodox Churches in the United Kingdom and the Republic of Ireland: 97 Cadogan Gdns, London E18 1LY; e-mail freldhose@hotmail.com; comprises the Armenian, Coptic, Ethiopian, Eritrean, Indian and Syrian Orthodox Churches; Pres. Bishop ANGAELOS.

Armenian Community and Church Council of Great Britain: POB 46207, London, W5 1XX; e-mail info@accc.org.uk; internet www.accc.org.uk.

Greek Orthodox Church (Archdiocese of Thyateira and Great Britain of the Ecumenical Patriarchate): Thyateira House, 5 Craven Hill, London, W2 3EN; tel. (20) 7723-4787; fax (20) 7224-9301; e-mail mail@thyateira.org.uk; internet www.thyateira.org.uk; f. 1922; Archbishop of Thyateira and Great Britain GREGORIOS; Chancellor Bishop ATHANASIOS OF TROPAEOU.

Russian Orthodox Patriarchal Church in Great Britain (Moscow Patriarchate): Cathedral of the Dormition of the Mother of God and All Saints, Ennismore Gdns, London, SW7 1NH; tel. (20) 7584-0096; fax (20) 7584-9864; e-mail sourozh@mail.ru; internet www.sourozh.org; Archbishop ELISEY OF SOUROZH.

Serbian Orthodox Church: 131 Cob Lane, Bournville, Birmingham, B30 1QE; tel. (121) 458-5273; fax (121) 458-4986; Patriach Bishop IRINEJ GAVRILOVICA.

Other Christian Churches

First Church of Christ, Scientist: 8 Wright's Lane, Kensington, London, W8 6TA; tel. (20) 7937-3389; fax (20) 7937-3341; e-mail fccslon@tiscali.co.uk; internet www.ccs.org.uk; f. 1879; the Mother Church is the First Church of Christ, Scientist, in Boston, MA (USA); approx. 150 churches in Great Britain; District Man. for Great Britain and Ireland TONY LOBL.

Church of Jesus Christ of Latter-day Saints (Mormon): Press Office, 751 Warwick Rd, Solihull, West Midlands, B91 3DQ; tel. (121) 712-1161; fax (121) 712-1126; e-mail adcockmp@ldschurch.org; internet www.lds.org.uk; f. 1830; c. 186,082 mems; Area Pres. ELDER KENNETH JOHNSON.

General Assembly of Unitarian and Free Christian Churches: Essex Hall, 1–6 Essex St, London, WC2R 3HY; tel. (20) 7240-2384; fax (20) 7240-3089; e-mail info@unitarian.org.uk; internet www.unitarian.org.uk; f. 1928; 200 congregations; Pres. NEVILLE KENYON.

Jehovah's Witnesses: Watch Tower House, The Ridgeway, London, NW7 1RN; tel. (20) 8906-2211; fax (20) 8371-0051; internet www.watchtower.org; f. 1900; there were an estimated 130,000 Jehovah's Witnesses in the UK in 2007.

The Religious Society of Friends (Quakers) in Britain: Friends House, 173 Euston Rd, London, NW1 2BJ; tel. (20) 7663-1000; fax (20) 7663-1001; e-mail enquiries@quaker.org.uk; internet www.quaker.org.uk; f. mid-17th century by George Fox; the Quakers have 15,800 mems and 8,400 'attenders' in Great Britain; Asst. Recording Clerk MICHAEL HUTCHINSON.

Seventh-day Adventist Church Headquarters: Stanborough Park, Watford, Herts, WD25 9JZ; tel. (1923) 672251; fax (1923) 893212; e-mail info@adventist.org.uk; internet www.adventist.org.uk; f. 1863; there were 30,000 mems. in approx. 340 congregations across the UK and Ireland in late 2009; Communication Dir VICTOR HULBERT.

Spiritualists' National Union: Redwoods, Stansted Hall, Stansted Mountfitchet, Essex, CM24 8UD; tel. (845) 458-0768; fax (1279) 812034; e-mail charles.coulston@snu.org.uk; internet www.snu.org.uk; f. 1891 (and inc. 1901); for the advancement of Spiritualism as a religion and a religious philosophy, it is a trust corporation officially recognized as the central and national body representing the Spiritualists of Great Britain; manages the Arthur Findlay College of Psychic Science; c. 400 Spiritualist churches, societies and 20,000 individual mems; Pres. DAVID BRUTON; Gen. Sec. CHARLES S. COULSTON.

ISLAM

The Muslim community in the United Kingdom, which according to the 2001 census numbered 1.59m., consists mainly of people from the Indian sub-continent and their British-born descendants. The chief concentrations of Muslims are in London, the Midlands, South Wales, Lancashire and Yorkshire.

London Central Mosque Trust and Islamic Cultural Centre: 146 Park Rd, London, NW8 7RG; tel. (20) 7725-2213; fax (20) 7724-0493; e-mail info@iccuk.org; internet www.iccuk.org; Dir-Gen. Dr AHMAD AL-DUBAYAN.

Muslim Council of Britain: POB 57330, London, E1 2WJ; tel. (845) 2626786; fax (20) 7247-7079; e-mail admin@mcb.org.uk; internet www.mcb.org.uk; f. 1997; Sec.-Gen. FAROOQ MURAD.

SIKHISM

According to the 2001 census, there were 336,000 Sikhs in the United Kingdom, who originally came from the Punjab region of the Indian sub-continent as well as from East Africa, although many are now British-born. Each gurdwara (temple) is independent, and there is no central national body.

Sikh Missionary Society, UK: 10 Featherstone Rd, Southall, Middx, UB2 5AA; tel. (20) 8574-1902; fax (20) 8574-1912; e-mail info@sikhmissionarysociety.org; internet www.sikhmissionarysociety.org; promotes Sikhism and acts as a resource centre for information and literature; Hon. Gen. Sec. SURINDER SINGH PUREWAL.

HINDUISM

According to the 2001 census, there were 559,000 Hindus in the United Kingdom, with their origins in India, East Africa and Sri Lanka, although many are now British by birth. Hindus in the United Kingdom are concentrated in London, the Midlands and Yorkshire.

JUDAISM

The Jewish community in the United Kingdom numbered 267,000, according to the 2001 census. Jewish congregations are concentrated in London and the South-East. The Chief Rabbi of the United Hebrew Congregations of the Commonwealth is the spiritual leader of United Synagogue, which is the largest synagogue organization and represents the mainstream Orthodox branch of Judaism in the United Kingdom. Other organizations represent the various other Jewish denominations.

Chief Rabbi of the United Hebrew Congregations of the Commonwealth: Lord SACKS, 305 Ballards Lane, London N12 8GB; tel. (20) 8343-6301; fax (20) 8343-6310; e-mail info@chiefrabbi.org; internet www.chiefrabbi.org.

Assembly of Masorti Synagogues: Alexander House, 3 Shakespeare Rd, Finchley, London, N3 1XE; tel. (20) 8349-6650; e-mail enquiries@masorti.org.uk; internet www.masorti.org.uk; 15 synagogues and communities; Senior Rabbi JONATHAN WITTENBERG.

Liberal Judaism: The Montagu Centre, 21 Maple St, London, W1T 4BE; tel. (20) 7580-1663; fax (20) 7631-9838; e-mail montagu@liberaljudaism.org; internet www.liberaljudaism.org; f. 1902; 9,300 mems, 31 affiliated synagogues, 3 assoc. communities; Chief Exec. Rabbi DANNY RICH.

Movement for Reform Judaism: The Sternberg Centre for Judaism, 80 East End Rd, Finchley, London, N3 2SY; tel. (20) 8349-5640; fax (20) 8349-5699; e-mail admin@reformjudaism.org.uk; internet www.reformjudaism.org.uk; Head Rabbi Dr TONY BAYFIELD.

Spanish and Portuguese Jews' Congregation: 2 Ashworth Rd, London, W9 1JY; tel. (20) 7289-2573; fax (20) 7289-2709; e-mail howardmiller@spsyn.org.uk; internet www.sandp.org; f. 1657; Pres. of the Bd of Elders ALFRED MAGNUS; Chief Exec. HOWARD MILLER.

THE UNITED KINGDOM

Union of Orthodox Hebrew Congregations (UOHC): 140 Stamford Hill, London, N16 6QT; tel. (20) 8802-6226; fax (20) 8809-6590; e-mail ck@uohc.co.uk; f. 1926; over 100 affiliated synagogues in the United Kingdom and other Commonwealth countries; Gen. Sec. CHAYIM SCHNECK.

United Synagogue: 305 Ballards Lane, London, N12 8GB; tel. (20) 8343-8989; fax (20) 8343-6262; internet www.theus.org.uk; f. 1870 by Act of Parliament; Pres. Dr SIMON HOCHHAUSER; Chief Exec. JEREMY JACOBS.

BUDDHISM

According to the 2001 census, the Buddhist community in the United Kingdom numbered 152,000.

Buddhist Society: 58 Eccleston Sq., London, SW1V 1PH; tel. (20) 7834-5858; e-mail info@thebuddhistsociety.org; internet www.thebuddhistsociety.org; f. 1924; Registrar LOUISE MARCHANT.

BAHÁ'Í FAITH

National Spiritual Assembly of the Bahá'ís of the United Kingdom: 27 Rutland Gate, London, SW7 1PD; tel. (20) 7584-2566; fax (20) 7584-9402; e-mail nsa@bahai.org.uk; internet www.bahai.org.uk; f. 1923; Sec. Dr KISHAN MANOCHA.

The Press

The United Kingdom has some of the highest circulation figures in the world for individual newspapers (*News of the World* and *The Sun* both 2.8m., and *Daily Mail* 2.1m. at April 2009). At 1 January 2004 there were more than 2,600 regional and local daily and weekly newspapers (including free titles) in the United Kingdom and the total weekly circulation of all newspapers was 136.4m.

There is no law which specifies the operations of the press, but several items of legislation bear directly on press activities. Although exact reporting of legal proceedings appearing at the time of trial is protected from later charges of defamation, the freedom to report cases is subject to certain restrictions. The strict laws of contempt of court and of libel somewhat limit the scope of the press. Libel cases can involve the awarding of punitive damages against the press. The Official Secrets Act of 1911 prohibits the publication of secret information where this is judged not to be in the national interest.

The Press Complaints Commission, which replaced the Press Council in 1991, has an independent chairman and 16 members, drawn from the lay public and the press. It deals with complaints from the public and upholds a 16-point Code of Practice.

Among the most influential newspapers may be included: *The Times*, *The Guardian*, *The Independent*, *Daily Telegraph* and *Financial Times* (daily), *The Observer*, *The Independent on Sunday*, *The Sunday Times* and *Sunday Telegraph* (Sunday newspapers). Prominent among the popular press are: *Daily Express*, *Daily Mail*, *Daily Mirror* and *The Sun* (daily); *News of the World* and *Sunday Mirror* (Sunday newspapers).

No important newspaper is directly owned by a political party. The industry has fostered the growth of large national groups or chains of papers controlled by a single organization or individual. The largest of these are as follows:

Daily Mail and General Trust PLC: Northcliffe House, 2 Derry St, London, W8 5TT; tel. (20) 7938-6000; fax (20) 7938-4626; e-mail webmaster@dmgt.co.uk; internet www.dmgt.co.uk; controls through Associated Newspapers 1 national daily, *Daily Mail*, 1 national Sunday, *The Mail on Sunday*, 1 London daily, the *Metro*; through Northcliffe Media controls 18 daily titles, 28 weekly titles and 50 free newspapers; Group Chair. Viscount ROTHERMERE; Group CEO MARTIN MORGAN.

Guardian Media Group PLC: Kings Pl., 90 York Way, London, N1 9GU; tel. (20) 3353-2000; internet www.gmgplc.co.uk; f. 1821; owned by the Scott Trust Ltd; subsidiary publishing cos include Guardian Newspapers Ltd (controls *The Guardian*, *The Observer*) and GMG Regional Media (controls *Manchester Evening News*); Chair. AMELIA FAWCETT; CEO ANDREW MILLER.

Independent News and Media (UK) Ltd: 2 Derry St, London, W8 5HF; tel. (20) 7005-2000; internet www.inmplc.com; British subsidiary of Ireland's Independent News & Media PLC; publishes 2 national dailies, *The Independent* and a concise version, *i*, and one national Sunday paper, *The Independent on Sunday*; also publishes *Belfast Telegraph* and *Sunday Life* in Northern Ireland; Group Chief Exec. GAVIN O'REILLY; Chief Exec., United Kingdom I. G. FALLON.

News International PLC: 3 Thomas More Sq., London, E98 1XY; tel. (20) 7782-6000; fax (20) 7782-6097; internet www.newsint.co.uk; British subsidiary of USA's News Corporation; subsidiary cos: News Group Newspapers Ltd (controls *The Sun* and *News of the World*), Times Newspapers Ltd (controls *The Times* and *The Sunday Times*); CEO REBEKAH BROOKS.

Trinity Mirror PLC: 1 Canada Sq., Canary Wharf, London, E14 5AP; tel. (20) 7293-3000; fax (20) 7293-3280; internet www.trinitymirror.com; f. 1999; by merger of Mirror Group Newspapers Ltd and Trinity International Holdings; controls a total of over 200 newspapers, including 1 national daily paper, *Daily Mirror*, 2 national Sunday papers, *The People*, *Sunday Mirror*, 2 Scottish national papers, *Daily Record* and *Sunday Mail*, and numerous regional and local papers; Chair. Sir IAN GIBSON; Chief Exec. SYLVIA (SLY) BAILEY.

United Business Media Ltd: Ludgate House, 245 Blackfriars Rd, London, SE1 9UY; tel. (20) 7921-5000; e-mail communications@ubmgroup.biz; internet www.ubmgroup.biz; f. 1996 by merger of United Newspapers and MAI group; international media and information group; three core business divisions—professional media, market research, news distribution; Chair. JOHN BOTTS; CEO DAVID LEVIN.

PRINCIPAL NATIONAL DAILIES
(average net circulation figures, in the United Kingdom only, as at April 2009, unless otherwise stated)

Daily Express: The Northern & Shell Bldg, 10 Lower Thames St, London, EC3R 6EN; tel. (871) 4341010; e-mail expressletters@express.co.uk; internet www.express.co.uk; f. 1900; Propr Northern and Shell Group; Editor HUGH WHITTOW; circ. 690,217.

Daily Mail: Northcliffe House, 2 Derry St, London, W8 5TT; tel. (20) 7938-6000; fax (20) 7937-4463; e-mail news@dailymail.co.uk; internet www.dailymail.co.uk; f. 1896; inc. *News Chronicle* (1960) and *Daily Sketch* (1971); Propr Associated Newspaper Holdings; Editor-in-Chief PAUL DACRE; Man. Dir GUY ZITTER; circ. 2,051,478.

Daily Mirror: 1 Canada Sq., Canary Wharf, London, E14 5AP; tel. (20) 7293-3000; fax (20) 7293-3280; e-mail mailbox@mirror.co.uk; internet www.mirror.co.uk; f. 1903; Propr Trinity Mirror PLC; Editor RICHARD WALLACE; circ. 1,218,460.

Daily Sport: 19 Gt Ancoats St, Manchester, M60 4BT; tel. (161) 236-4466; fax (161) 236-4535; internet www.dailysport.net; f. 1988; Propr Sport Media Group; Editor PAM MCVITIE; (Jan. 2009) circ. 72,592 (Mon.–Fri.); 47,551 (Sat.).

Daily Star: The Northern & Shell Bldg, 10 Lower Thames St, London, EC3R 6EN; tel. (8714) 341010; fax (20) 7922-7960; e-mail news@dailystar.co.uk; internet www.dailystar.co.uk; f. 1978; Propr Express Newspapers PLC; Editor DAWN NEESOM; circ. 287,609.

Daily Telegraph: 111 Buckingham Palace Rd, London, SW1W 0DT; tel. (20) 7931-2000; e-mail dtletters@telegraph.co.uk; internet www.telegraph.co.uk; *Daily Telegraph*, f. 1855, *Morning Post*, f. 1772; amalgamated 1937; Propr Press Acquisitions Ltd; Chief Exec. MURDOCH MACLENNAN; Editor TONY GALLAGHER; circ. 778,273.

Financial Times: Number One Southwark Bridge, London, SE1 9HL; tel. (20) 7873-3000; fax (20) 7873-3076; internet www.ft.com; f. 1880; Propr Pearson PLC; CEO JOHN RIDDING; Editor LIONEL BARBER; circ. 118,043.

The Guardian: Kings Pl., 90 York Way, London, N1 9GU; and 164 Deansgate, Manchester, M3 3GG; tel. (20) 3353-2000; fax (20) 7837-2114; e-mail userhelp@guardian.co.uk; internet www.guardian.co.uk; tel. (161) 832-7200; fax (161) 832-5351; f. 1821; Propr Guardian Newspapers Ltd; Editor ALAN RUSBRIDGER; circ. 300,879.

i: 2 Derry St, London, W8 5HF; tel. (20) 7005-2000; fax (20) 7005-2999; e-mail i@independent.co.uk; internet www.independent.co.uk/i; f. 2010; concise version of *The Independent*; Editor SIMON KELNER; circ. 133,472 (Jan. 2011).

The Independent: 2 Derry St, London, W8 5HF; tel. (20) 7005-2000; fax (20) 7005-2999; e-mail customerservices@independent.co.uk; internet www.independent.co.uk; f. 1986; Editor SIMON KELNER; circ. 157,777.

Racing Post: 1 Canada Sq., Canary Wharf, London, E14 5AP; tel. (20) 7293-3000; fax (20) 7293-3758; e-mail editor@racingpost.co.uk; internet www.racingpost.co.uk; f. 1986; covers national and international horse racing, greyhound racing, general sport and betting; Editor BRUCE MILLINGTON; circ. 57,751.

The Sun: 3 Thomas More Sq., London E98 1XY; tel. (20) 7782-4000; fax (20) 7782-4108; e-mail corporate.info@the-sun.co.uk; internet www.thesun.co.uk; f. 1921 as *Daily Herald*; present name since 1964; Propr News International PLC; Editor DOMINIC MOHAN; Man. Dir MIKE ANDERSON; circ. 2,822,917.

The Times: 1 Virginia St, London E98 1RL; tel. (20) 7782-5000; fax (20) 7782-5046; internet www.timesonline.co.uk; f. 1785; Propr News International PLC; Editor JAMES HARDING; circ. 563,426.

LONDON DAILIES
(average net circulation figures as at April 2009, unless otherwise stated)

London Evening Standard: Northcliffe House, 2 Derry St, London, W8 5EE; tel. (20) 3367-7000; fax (20) 7937-2648; internet www

THE UNITED KINGDOM

.standard.co.uk; f. 1827; merged with *Evening News* 1980; Mon.–Fri.; evening; distributed free of charge; 75% stake acquired by Evening Standard Ltd in Jan. 2009; Editor GEORDIE GREIG; Man. Dir ANDREW MULLINS; circ. 600,000.

Metro: Northcliffe House, 2 Derry St, London, W8 5TT; tel. (20) 7651-5200; fax (20) 7806-8338; e-mail mail@ukmetro.co.uk; internet www.metro.co.uk; f. 1999; Mon.–Fri.; morning; distributed free of charge; also distributed in Bath, Birmingham, Brighton, Bristol, Cardiff, Derby, Edinburgh, Glasgow, Leeds, Leicester, Liverpool, Manchester, Newcastle, Nottingham and Sheffield; Propr Associated Newspaper Holdings PLC; Editor KENNY CAMPBELL; Man. Dir STEVE AUCKLAND; circ. 734,488 (London); 1,332,225 (total UK).

PRINCIPAL PROVINCIAL DAILIES
(average net circulation figures as at December 2008, unless otherwise stated)

Aberdeen

Evening Express: Aberdeen Journals Ltd, Lang Stracht, Mastrick, Aberdeen, AB15 6DF; tel. (1224) 690222; fax (1224) 699575; e-mail ee.news@ajl.co.uk; internet www.eveningexpress.co.uk; f. 1879; Editor DAMIAN BATES; circ. 52,029.

Press and Journal: Aberdeen Journals Ltd, Lang Stracht, Mastrick, Aberdeen, AB15 6DF; tel. (1224) 690222; fax (1224) 663575; e-mail pj.newsdesk@ajl.co.uk; internet www.pressandjournal.co.uk; f. 1747; morning; Editor DAMIAN BATES; circ. 72,767.

Belfast

Belfast Telegraph: 124–144 Royal Ave, Belfast, BT1 1EB; tel. (28) 9026-4000; fax (28) 9055-4506; e-mail newseditor@belfasttelegraph.co.uk; internet www.belfasttelegraph.co.uk; f. 1870; independent; evening; Proprs Independent News and Media PLC; Editor MIKE GILSON; circ. 69,457.

Irish News: 113–117 Donegall St, Belfast, BT1 2GE; tel. (28) 9032-2226; fax (28) 9033-7505; e-mail newsdesk@irishnews.com; internet www.irishnews.com; f. 1855; Irish nationalist; morning; Editor NOEL DORAN; circ. 47,819.

News Letter: 2 Esky Drive, Carn Industrial Estate, Craigavon, BT63 5YY; tel. (28) 9089-7700; fax (28) 9066-9910; e-mail darwin.templeton@jpress.co.uk; internet www.newsletter.co.uk; f. 1737; unionist; morning; Editor DARWIN TEMPLETON; circ. 25,253.

Birmingham

Birmingham Mail: 6th Floor, Fort Dunlop, Fort Parkway, B24 9FF; tel. (121) 236-3366; fax (121) 233-0271; e-mail steve_dyson@birminghammail.net; internet www.birminghammail.net; f. 1870; morning; independent; Propr Trinity Mirror PLC; Editor DAVID BROOKES; circ. 61,526.

Bradford

Telegraph & Argus: Hall Ings, Bradford, BD1 1JR; tel. (1274) 729511; fax (1274) 723634; e-mail newsdesk@bradford.newsquest.co.uk; internet www.telegraphandargus.co.uk; f. 1868; evening; Editor PERRY AUSTIN-CLARKE; circ. 34,042.

Brighton

The Argus: Argus House, Crowhurst Rd, Hollingbury, Brighton, BN1 8AR; tel. (1273) 544544; fax (1273) 566114; e-mail editor@theargus.co.uk; internet www.theargus.co.uk; f. 1880; Propr Newsquest Media Group; Editor MICHAEL BEARD; circ. 30,070.

Bristol

Evening Post: Temple Way, Bristol, BS99 7HD; tel. (117) 934-3000; fax (117) 934-3575; e-mail epnews@bepp.co.uk; internet www.thisisbristol.co.uk; f. 1932; inc. the *Evening World*; Propr Northcliffe Newspapers; independent; Editor-in-Chief MIKE NORTON; circ. 46,522.

Western Daily Press: Temple Way, Bristol, BS99 7HD; tel. (117) 934-3000; fax (117) 934-3574; e-mail wdnews@bepp.co.uk; internet www.westerndailypress.co.uk; f. 1858; Propr Northcliffe Newspapers; morning; independent; Editor ANDY WRIGHT; circ. 38,211.

Cardiff

South Wales Echo: Six Park St, Cardiff, CF10 1XR; tel. (29) 2022-3333; fax (29) 2058-3624; e-mail mike.hill@mediawales.co.uk; internet www.walesonline.co.uk; f. 1884; Propr Trinity Mirror PLC; evening; independent; Editor MIKE HILL; circ. 41,550.

The Western Mail: Six Park St, Cardiff, CF10 1XR; tel. (29) 2022-3333; fax (29) 2058-3652; e-mail alan.edmunds@mediawales.co.uk; internet www.walesonline.co.uk; f. 1869; independent; Editor ALAN EDMUNDS; circ. 33,693.

Coventry

Coventry Telegraph: Corporation St, Coventry, CV1 1FP; tel. (24) 7663-3633; fax (24) 7655-0869; e-mail alan.kirby@coventrytelegraph.net; internet www.coventrytelegraph.net; f. 1891 as *Midland Daily Telegraph*; Propr Trinity Mirror PLC; independent; morning; Editor DAVID BROOKES; circ. 43,594.

Darlington

Northern Echo: POB 14, Priestgate, Darlington, Co Durham, DL1 1NF; tel. (1325) 505065; e-mail newsdesk@nne.co.uk; internet www.thenorthernecho.co.uk; f. 1869; morning; independent; Editor PETER BARRON; circ. 48,783.

Derby

Derby Evening Telegraph: Northcliffe House, Meadow Rd, Derby, DE1 2DW; tel. (1332) 291111; fax (1332) 253027; e-mail newsdesk@derbytelegraph.co.uk; internet www.thisisderbyshire.co.uk; f. 1932; inc. *Derby Daily Telegraph*, f. 1879, *Derby Daily Express*, f. 1884; Editor STEVE HALL; circ. 39,152.

Dundee

Courier and Advertiser: Albert Sq., Dundee, DD1 9QJ; tel. (1382) 223131; fax (1382) 225511; e-mail editor@thecourier.co.uk; internet www.thecourier.co.uk; f. 1810; morning; Editor WILLIAM HUTCHEON; circ. 69,414.

Edinburgh

Edinburgh Evening News: 108 Holyrood Rd, Edinburgh, EH8 8AS; tel. (131) 620-8703; fax (131) 620-8696; e-mail jmclellan@edinburghnews.com; internet www.edinburghnews.com; f. 1873; Propr Johnston Press PLC; Editor JOHN MCLELLAN; circ. 47,129.

The Scotsman: 108 Holyrood Rd, Edinburgh, EH8 8AS; tel. (131) 620-8620; fax (131) 620-8616; e-mail enquiries@scotsman.com; internet www.scotsman.com; f. 1817; morning; Propr Johnston Press PLC; Editor MIKE GILSON; circ. 48,135 (April 2009).

Glasgow

Daily Record: 1 Central Quay, Glasgow, G3 8DA; tel. (141) 309-3000; fax (141) 309-3340; internet www.dailyrecord.co.uk; f. 1895; morning; independent; Propr Trinity Mirror PLC; Editor-in-Chief BRUCE WADDELL; circ. 341,275 (April 2009).

Glasgow Evening Times: 200 Renfield St, Glasgow, G2 3Q3; tel. (141) 302-7000; fax (141) 302-6600; e-mail times@eveningtimes.co.uk; internet www.eveningtimes.co.uk; f. 1876; Propr Newsquest; Editor-in-Chief DONALD MARTIN; circ. 68,422.

The Herald: 200 Renfield St, Glasgow, G2 3QB; tel. (141) 302-7000; fax (141) 302-7171; e-mail news@theherald.co.uk; internet www.theherald.co.uk; f. 1783; morning; independent; Propr Newsquest; Editor-in-Chief DONALD MARTIN; circ. 58,704 (April 2009).

Scottish Daily Express: Citypoint Z, 25 Tyndrum St, Glasgow, G4 0JY; tel. (141) 332-9600; fax (141) 332-2555; e-mail scot.news@express.co.uk; internet www.express.co.uk/scottish; morning; regional edition of *Daily Express*; Propr Northern and Shell Group; Editor DAVID HAMILTON.

Grimsby

Grimsby Telegraph: 80 Cleethorpe Rd, Grimsby, DN31 3EH; tel. (1472) 360360; fax (1472) 372257; e-mail newsdesk@grimsbytelegraph.co.uk; internet www.thisisgrimsby.co.uk; f. 1898; evening; Editor MICHELLE LALOR; circ. 31,538.

Ipswich

East Anglian Daily Times: 30 Lower Brook St, Ipswich, IP4 1AN; tel. (1473) 230023; e-mail news@eadt.co.uk; internet www.eadt.co.uk; morning; Editor TERRY HUNT; circ. 32,208.

Kingston upon Hull

Hull Daily Mail: Blundell's Corner, Beverley Rd, Kingston upon Hull, HU3 1XS; tel. (1482) 327111; fax (1482) 584353; e-mail news@mailnewsmedia.co.uk; internet www.thisishullandeastriding.co.uk; f. 1885; evening; Editor JOHN MEEHAN; circ. 51,886.

Leeds

Yorkshire Evening Post: POB 168, Wellington St, Leeds, LS1 1RF; tel. (113) 243-2701; fax (113) 238-8536; e-mail eped@ypn.co.uk; internet www.yorkshireeveningpost.co.uk; f. 1890; Propr Johnston Press PLC; Editor PAUL NAPIER; circ. 49,064.

Yorkshire Post: POB 168, Wellington St, Leeds, LS1 1RF; tel. (113) 243-2701; fax (113) 244-3430; e-mail yp.newsdesk@ypn.co.uk;

THE UNITED KINGDOM

internet www.yorkshirepost.co.uk; f. 1754; morning; Propr Johnston Press PLC; Editor Peter Charlton; circ. 45,718.

Leicester
Leicester Mercury: St George St, Leicester, LE1 9FQ; tel. (116) 251-2512; fax (116) 253-0645; e-mail newsdesk@leicestermercury.co.uk; internet www.thisisleicestershire.co.uk; f. 1874; evening; Editor Nick Carter; circ. 64,919.

Liverpool
Liverpool Echo: POB 48, Old Hall St, Liverpool, L69 3EB; tel. (151) 227-2000; fax (151) 472-2474; e-mail letters@liverpoolecho.co.uk; internet www.liverpoolecho.co.uk; f. 1879; evening; independent; Propr Trinity Mirror PLC; Editor Alastair Machray; circ. 97,779.

Manchester
Manchester Evening News: 1 Scott Pl., Hardman St, Manchester, M3 3RN; tel. (161) 832-7200; fax (161) 211-2034; e-mail newsdesk@men-news.co.uk; internet www.manchestereveningnews.co.uk; f. 1868; independent; Editor Paul Horrocks; circ. 153,724.

Middlesbrough
Evening Gazette: Borough Rd, Middlesbrough, TS1 3AZ; tel. (1642) 245401; fax (1642) 210565; e-mail darren.thwaites@eveninggazette.co.uk; internet www.gazettelive.co.uk; f. 1869; Propr Trinity Mirror PLC; Editor Darren Thwaites; circ. 46,320.

Newcastle upon Tyne
Evening Chronicle: Groat Market, Newcastle upon Tyne, NE1 1ED; tel. (191) 232-7500; fax (191) 232-2256; e-mail ec.news@ncjmedia.co.uk; internet www.chroniclelive.co.uk; f. 1885; Propr Trinity Mirror PLC; Editor Paul Robertson; circ. 67,103.

The Journal: Groat Market, Newcastle upon Tyne, NE1 1ED; tel. (191) 232-7500; fax (191) 230-4144; e-mail jnl.newsdesk@ncjmedia.co.uk; internet www.journallive.co.uk; f. 1832; morning; Propr Trinity Mirror PLC; Editor Brian Aitken; circ. 32,859.

Norwich
Eastern Daily Press: Prospect House, Rouen Rd, Norwich, NR1 1RE; tel. (1603) 628311; fax (1603) 623872; e-mail edp@archant.co.uk; internet www.edp24.co.uk; f. 1870; independent; Propr Archant Regional Ltd; Editor Peter Franzen; circ. 61,143.

Nottingham
Nottingham Evening Post: Castle Wharf House, Nottingham, NG1 7EU; tel. (115) 948-2000; fax (115) 964-4032; e-mail newsdesk@nottinghameveningpost.co.uk; internet www.thisisnottingham.co.uk; f. 1878; Editor Malcolm Pheby; circ. 51,526.

Plymouth
Western Morning News: 17 Brest Rd, Derriford Business Park, Plymouth, PL6 5AA; tel. (1752) 765500; fax (1752) 765535; e-mail wmnnewsdesk@westernmorningnews.co.uk; internet www.westernmorningnews.co.uk; f. 1860; Editor Alan Qualtrough; circ. 37,819.

Portsmouth
The News: The News Centre, London Rd, Hilsea, Portsmouth, PO2 9SX; tel. (23) 9266-4488; e-mail newsdesk@thenews.co.uk; internet www.portsmouth.co.uk; f. 1877; evening; Editor Mark Waldron; circ. 49,628.

Sheffield
The Star: York St, Sheffield, S1 1PU; tel. (114) 276-7676; fax (114) 272-5978; e-mail starnews@sheffieldnewspapers.co.uk; internet www.thestar.co.uk; f. 1887; evening; independent; Propr Johnston Press PLC; Editor Alan Powell; circ. 47,216.

Southampton
Southern Daily Echo: Newspaper House, Test Lane, Redbridge, Southampton, SO16 9JX; tel. (23) 8042-4777; fax (23) 8042-4545; e-mail newsdesk@dailyecho.co.uk; internet www.dailyecho.co.uk; f. 1888; Propr Newsquest; Editor Ian Murray; circ. 36,906.

Stoke-on-Trent
The Sentinel: Sentinel House, Etruria, Stoke-on-Trent, ST1 5SS; tel. (1782) 602525; fax (1782) 602616; e-mail newsdesk@thesentinel.co.uk; internet www.thisisthesentinel.co.uk; f. 1854; Editor-in-Chief Mike Sassi; circ. 58,049.

Sunderland
Sunderland Echo: Echo House, Pennywell, Sunderland, Tyne and Wear, SR4 9ER; tel. (191) 501-5800; fax (191) 534-3807; e-mail echo.news@northeast-press.co.uk; internet www.sunderlandecho.com; f. 1873; evening; Editor Rob Lawson; circ. 39,159.

Swansea
South Wales Evening Post: Adelaide St, Swansea, SA1 1QT; tel. (1792) 510000; fax (1792) 514197; e-mail postnews@swwmedia.co.uk; internet www.thisissouthwales.co.uk; f. 1930; Editor Spencer Feeney; circ. 47,875.

Telford
Shropshire Star: Waterloo Rd, Ketley, Telford, Shropshire, TF1 5HU; tel. (1952) 242424; fax (1952) 254605; e-mail newsroom@shropshirestar.co.uk; internet www.shropshirestar.com; f. 1964; evening; Propr Shropshire Newspapers Ltd; Editor Sarah-Jane Smith; circ. 67,726.

Wolverhampton
Express and Star: 51–53 Queen St, Wolverhampton, West Midlands, WV1 1ES; tel. (1902) 313131; fax (1902) 710106; e-mail newsdesk@expressandstar.co.uk; internet www.expressandstar.co.uk; f. 1874; evening; Propr The Midland News Association Ltd; Editor Adrian Faber; circ. 130,216.

York
The Press: POB 29, 76–86 Walmgate, York, YO1 9YN; tel. (1904) 653051; fax (1904) 612853; e-mail newsdesk@ycp.co.uk; internet www.thepress.co.uk; morning; Editor Kevin Booth; circ. 31,569.

PRINCIPAL WEEKLY NEWSPAPERS
(average net circulation figures as at April 2009, unless otherwise stated)

Asian Times: Ethnic Media Group, Whitechapel Technology Centre, Unit 2, 65 Whitechapel Rd, London, E1 1DU; tel. (20) 7650-2000; fax (20) 7650-2001; internet www.asiantimesonline.co.uk; Editor Hamant Verma; Man. Dir Wayne Bower.

Daily Star Sunday: Ludgate House, 245 Blackfriars Rd, London, SE1 9UX; tel. (20) 7928-8000; fax (20) 7633-0244; e-mail dailystarnewsdesk@dailystar.co.uk; internet www.dailystar.co.uk/sunday; f. 1978; Propr Express Newspapers PLC; Editor Gareth Morgan; circ. 287,609.

The Independent on Sunday: 2 Derry St, London, W8 5HF; tel. (20) 7005-2000; fax (20) 7005-2627; internet www.independent.co.uk; f. 1990; Propr Independent Newspapers UK; Editor-in-Chief Simon Kelner; Editor John Mullin; circ. 119,919.

The Mail on Sunday: Northcliffe House, 2 Derry St, London, W8 5TS; tel. (20) 7938-6000; fax (20) 7937-3829; internet www.mailonsunday.co.uk; f. 1982; Propr Associated Newspapers Ltd; Editor Peter Wright; Man. Dir Stephen Miron; circ. 1,876,015.

News of the World: 1 Virginia St, London, E1 9XR; tel. (20) 7782-1000; fax (20) 7583-9504; e-mail newsdesk@notw.co.uk; internet www.notw.co.uk; f. 1843; Propr News International; Sun.; Editor Colin Myler; Man. Dir Mike Anderson; circ. 2,751,320.

The Observer: Kings Pl., 90 York Way, London, N1 9GU; tel. (20) 3353-2000; fax (20) 7713-4250; e-mail userhelp@guardian.co.uk; internet observer.guardian.co.uk; f. 1791; owned by Guardian Newspapers Ltd; Sun.; Editor John Mulholland; circ. 375,183.

The People: 1 Canada Sq., Canary Wharf, London, E14 5AP; tel. (20) 7293-3000; fax (20) 7293-3887; internet www.people.co.uk; f. 1881; Propr Trinity Mirror PLC; Editor Lloyd Embley; circ. 533,531.

Scotland on Sunday: Barclay House, 108 Holyrood Rd, Edinburgh, EH8 8AS; tel. (131) 620-8620; fax (131) 620-8491; e-mail letters_sos@scotlandonsunday.com; internet scotlandonsunday.scotsman.com; f. 1988; Propr Johnston Press PLC; Editor Les Snowdon; circ. 60,296.

Sunday Express: The Northern & Shell Bldg, 10 Lower Thames St, London, EC3R 6EN; tel. (871) 434-1010; fax (871) 520-7766; e-mail sunday.exletters@express.co.uk; internet www.express.co.uk; f. 1918; inc. *Sunday Despatch* 1961; independent; Propr Northern and Shell Group; Editor-in-Chief Martin Townsend; circ. 597,083.

Sunday Herald: 200 Renfield St, Glasgow, G2 3QB; tel. (141) 302-7800; e-mail editor@sundayherald.com; internet www.sundayherald.com; f. 1999; Propr Newsquest Media Group; Editor Richard Walker; circ. 40,298.

Sunday Life: 124–144 Royal Ave, Belfast, BT1 1EB; tel. (28) 9026-4300; fax (28) 9054-4507; e-mail writeback@belfasttelegraph.co.uk; internet www.sundaylife.co.uk; f. 1988; Editor Martin Lindsay; circ. 63,528 (June–Dec. 2008).

THE UNITED KINGDOM

Directory

Sunday Mail: 1 Central Quay, Glasgow, G3 8DA; tel. (141) 309-3000; fax (141) 242-3587; e-mail mailbox@sundaymail.co.uk; internet www.sundaymail.co.uk; Propr Trinity Mirror PLC; Editor ALLAN RENNIE; circ. 421,147.

Sunday Mercury: Weaman St, Birmingham, B4 6AZ; tel. (121) 234-5567; e-mail sundaymercury@mrn.co.uk; internet www.icbirmingham.co.uk; Propr Trinity Mirror PLC; f. 1918; Editor STEVE DYSON; circ. 54,375 (June–Dec. 2008).

Sunday Mirror: 1 Canada Sq., Canary Wharf, London, E14 5AP; tel. (20) 7293-3000; fax (20) 7822-3587; e-mail mailbox@mirror.co.uk; internet www.sundaymirror.co.uk; f. 1915; Propr Trinity Mirror PLC; independent; Editor TINA WEAVER; circ. 1,146,601.

The Sunday Post: 2 Albert Sq., Dundee, DD1 9QJ; tel. (1382) 223131; fax (1382) 201064; e-mail mail@sundaypost.com; internet www.sundaypost.com; f. 1919; D.C. Thomson & Co. Ltd; Editor DONALD MARTIN (acting); circ. 356,724.

Sunday Sport: 19 Gt Ancoats St, Manchester, M60 4BT; tel. (161) 236-4466; fax (161) 236-4535; f. 1986; Propr Sport Media Group; Editor-in-Chief MURRAY MORSE; circ. 70,796 (Jan. 2009).

Sunday Sun: Groat Market, Newcastle upon Tyne, NE1 1ED; tel. (191) 201-6299; fax (191) 230-0238; e-mail colin.patterson@ncjmedia.co.uk; internet www.sundaysun.co.uk; f. 1919; Propr Trinity Mirror PLC; independent; north-east England; Editor COLIN PATTERSON; circ. 61,869 (June–Dec. 2008).

Sunday Telegraph: 111 Buckingham Palace Rd, London, SW1W 0DT; tel. (20) 7931-2000; e-mail stletters@telegraph.co.uk; internet www.telegraph.co.uk; f. 1961; Propr Press Acquisitions Ltd; Editor IAN MCGREGOR; circ. 559,090.

The Sunday Times: 1 Virginia St, London E98 1RL; tel. (20) 7782-5000; fax (20) 7782-5658; internet www.sunday-times.co.uk; f. 1822; Propr News International; Editor JOHN WITHEROW; circ. 1,049,095.

Wales on Sunday: Media Wales Ltd, Six Park St, Cardiff, CF10 1XR; tel. (29) 2022-3333; e-mail tim.gordon@mediawales.co.uk; internet www.walesonline.co.uk; f. 1991; Editor ALISON GOW; circ. 35,955 (June–Dec. 2008).

SELECTED PERIODICALS

Arts and Literature

Apollo: 22 Old Queen St, London, SW1H 9HP; tel. (20) 7961-0150; fax (20) 7961-0110; e-mail editorial@apollomag.com; internet www.apollo-magazine.com; f. 1925; owned by Press Holdings; monthly; fine and decorative art; Editor OSCAR HUMPHRIES.

Architects' Journal: Greater London House, Hampstead Rd, London, NW1 7EJ; tel. (20) 7728-4573; fax (20) 7391-3435; e-mail crystal.bennes@emap.com; internet www.architectsjournal.co.uk; f. 1895; Thurs.; Editor CHRISTINE MURRAY; circ. 13,491 (July 2005).

Architectural Review: Greater London House, Hampstead Rd, London, NW1 7EJ; tel. (20) 7728-4589; e-mail paul.finch@emap.com; internet www.arplus.com; f. 1896; monthly; Editor CATHERINE SLESSOR; circ. 18,544 (May 2007).

The Artist: Caxton House, 63–65 High St, Tenterden, Kent, TN30 6BD; tel. (1580) 763673; fax (1580) 765411; e-mail sally@tapc.co.uk; internet www.painters-online.co.uk; f. 1931; monthly; Man. Editor SALLY BULGIN.

ArtReview: 1 Sekforde St, London, EC1R 0BE; tel. (20) 7107-2760; fax (20) 7107-2761; e-mail editorial@artreview.com; internet www.art-review.com; f. 1949; monthly; Editor MARK RAPPOLT.

BBC Music Magazine: 14th Floor, Tower House, Fairfax St, Bristol, BS1 3BN; tel. (117) 314-7355; fax (117) 934-9008; e-mail music@bbcmagazines.com; internet www.classical-music.com; f. 1992; monthly; classical music; Editor OLIVER CONDY; circ. 42,834 (Dec. 2010).

The Bookseller: Endeavour House, Shaftesbury Ave, London, WC2H 8TJ; tel. (20) 7420-6006; fax (20) 7420-6103; e-mail letters.to.editor@bookseller.co.uk; internet www.thebookseller.com; f. 1858; incorporates *Bent's Literary Advertiser* (f. 1802); Fri.; Propr VNU Entertainment Media UK Ltd; Editor NEILL DENNY.

The Burlington Magazine: 14–16 Dukes Rd, London, WC1H 9SZ; tel. (20) 7388-8157; fax (20) 7388-1230; e-mail burlington@burlington.org.uk; internet www.burlington.org.uk; f. 1903; monthly; all forms of art, ancient and modern; Editor RICHARD SHONE.

Classical Music: Rhinegold Publishing Ltd, 241 Shaftesbury Ave, London, WC2H 8TF; tel. (20) 7333-1742; fax (20) 7333-1769; e-mail classical.music@rhinegold.co.uk; internet www.rhinegold.co.uk; f. 1976; fortnightly; Editor KEITH CLARKE; circ. 18,000 (July 2005).

Dancing Times: 45–47 Clerkenwell Green, London, EC1R 0EB; tel. (20) 7250-3006; fax (20) 7253-6679; e-mail dt@dancing-times.co.uk; internet www.dancing-times.co.uk; f. 1910; monthly; ballet, modern dance and musical theatre; Editor JONATHAN GRAY.

Empire: Endeavour House, Shaftesbury Ave, WC2H 8JG; tel. (20) 7182-8781; internet www.empireonline.co.uk; monthly; film; Editor MARK DINNING; circ. 172,639 (July–Dec. 2010).

Film Review: Visual Imagination Ltd, 9 Blades Court, Deodar Rd, London, SW15 2NU; tel. (20) 8875-1520; fax (20) 8875-1588; e-mail filmreview@visimag.com; internet www.visimag.com/filmreview; f. 1955; monthly.

Folklore: The Folklore Society, c/o The Warburg Institute, Woburn Sq., London, WC1H 0AB; tel. (20) 7862-8564; e-mail enquiries@folklore-society.com; internet www.folklore-society.com; f. 1878; 3 a year; Editor Prof. PATRICIA LYSAGHT.

Gramophone: Teddington Studios, Broom Rd, Teddington, Middlesex, TW11 9BE; tel. (20) 8267-5000; fax (20) 8267-5844; e-mail gramophone@haymarket.com; internet www.gramophone.co.uk; f. 1923; monthly; Publr SIMON TEMLETT; Editor JAMES JOLLY; circ. 36,817 (2007).

Granta: 12 Addison Ave, London, W11 4QR; tel. (20) 7605-1360; fax (20) 7704-1361; e-mail editorial@granta.com; internet www.granta.com; f. 1889; quarterly; Editor JOHN FREEMAN; circ. 80,000 (2005).

Index on Censorship: Free Word Centre, 60 Farringdon Rd, London EC1R 3GA; tel. (20) 7324-2522; fax (20) 7278-1878; e-mail contact@indexoncensorship.org; internet www.indexoncensorship.org; f. 1972; four a year; concerned with freedom of expression throughout the world; Editor JO GLANVILLE.

Jazz Journal: Jazz Journal, The Invicta Press, Queen's Rd, Ashford, TN24 8HH; tel. (20) 8516-0456; e-mail editor@jazzjournal.co.uk; internet www.jazzjournal.co.uk; f. 1948; owned by JJ Publishing Ltd; monthly; Editor MARK GILBERT.

Language Learning Journal: Association for Language Learning, University of Leicester, University Rd, Leicester, LE1 7RH; tel. (116) 2297453; fax (116) 2297456; e-mail info@all-languages.org.uk; internet www.all-languages.org.uk; f. 1990; 2 a year; Editors Dr NORBERT PACHLER, Dr DOUGLAS ALLFORD, ELSPETH BROADY.

mixmag: 90–92 Pentonville Rd, London, N1 9HS; tel. (20) 7078-8400; fax (20) 7833-9900; e-mail mixmag@mixmag.net; internet www.mixmag.net; f. 1983; publ. by Development Hell Ltd; monthly; dance music and club culture; Editor NICK DE COSEMO; circ. 34,073 (2008).

Mojo: Endeavour House, 189 Shaftesbury Ave, London, WC2H 8JG; tel. (20) 7208-3443; fax (20) 7182-8596; internet www.mojo4music.com; f. 1993; monthly; popular music; Editor PHIL ALEXANDER; circ. 94,617 (2010).

NME: IPC Media Ltd, The Blue Fin Bldg, 110 Southwark St, London, SE1 0SU; tel. (20) 3148-5000; e-mail krissi_murison@ipcmedia.com; internet www.nme.com; f. 1952; Wed.; popular music; Editor KRISSI MURISON; circ. 56,284.

Opera: 36 Black Lion Lane, London, W6 9BE; tel. (20) 8563-8893; fax (20) 8563-8635; e-mail editor@opera.co.uk; internet www.opera.co.uk; f. 1950; monthly; Editor JOHN ALLISON.

Poetry Review: 22 Betterton St, London, WC2H 9BX; tel. (20) 7420-9883; fax (20) 7240-4818; e-mail poetryreview@poetrysociety.co.uk; internet www.poetrysociety.org.uk; f. 1909; quarterly; Editor FIONA SAMPSON; circ. 4,500 (2008).

Q Magazine: Endeavour House, 189 Shaftesbury Ave, London, WC2H 8JG; tel. (20) 7182-8000; fax (20) 7182-8547; internet www.q4music.com; f. 1986; monthly; music, general features; Editor PAUL REES; circ. 88,240 (2010).

Sight and Sound: British Film Institute, 21 Stephen St, London, W1T 1LN; tel. (20) 7255-1444; fax (20) 7436-2327; e-mail s&s@bfi.org.uk; internet www.bfi.org.uk/sightandsound; f. 1932; monthly; international film review; Editor NICK JAMES; circ. 20,283 (2007).

The Stage: Stage House, 47 Bermondsey St, London, SE1 3XT; tel. (20) 7403-1818; fax (20) 7357-8478; e-mail editor@thestage.co.uk; internet www.thestage.co.uk; f. 1880; Thurs.; theatre, light entertainment, television, opera, dance; Man. Dir CAROLINE COMERFORD; circ. 34,000 (2008).

The Times Literary Supplement: Times House, 1 Pennington St, London, E98 1BS; tel. (20) 7782-5000; fax (20) 7782-4966; e-mail letters@the-tls.co.uk; internet www.the-tls.co.uk; f. 1902; Fri.; weekly journal of literary criticism; Editor Sir PETER STOTHARD; circ. 36,535 (2008).

Top of the Pops: Media Centre, 201 Wood Lane, London, W12 7TQ; tel. (20) 8433-1201; e-mail totp.magazine@bbc.co.uk; internet www.totpmag.com; monthly; popular music; Editor PETER HART; circ. 119,739 (2009).

Current Affairs and History

Antiquity: King's Manor, York, YO1 7EP; tel. and fax (1904) 433994; e-mail editor@antiquity.ac.uk; internet antiquity.ac.uk; f. 1927; quarterly; archaeology; Editor Prof. MARTIN CARVER.

The Big Issue: 1–5 Wandsworth Rd, London, SW8 2LN; tel. (20) 7526-3200; fax (20) 7526-3201; e-mail info@bigissue.com; internet

THE UNITED KINGDOM

www.bigissue.com; also offices based in Bristol, Cardiff, Glasgow, Manchester and the Midlands producing regional weekly editions; f. 1991; weekly; current affairs, social issues; Editor-in-Chief A. JOHN BIRD; total circ. 134,456 (2008).

Classical Quarterly: Journals Group, Cambridge University Press, The Edinburgh Bldg, Shaftesbury Rd, Cambridge, CB2 2RU; tel. (1223) 326070; fax (1223) 325150; e-mail journals@cambridge.org; internet journals.cambridge.org/jid_caq; f. 1906; 2 a year; language, literature, history and philosophy; Editors BRUCE GIBSON, JOHN WILKINS.

Contemporary Review: POB 1242, Oxford, OX1 4FJ; tel. and fax (1865) 201529; e-mail editorial@contemporaryreview.co.uk; internet www.contemporaryreview.co.uk; f. 1866; quarterly; publ by Contemporary Review Co Ltd; politics, international affairs, social subjects, the arts; Editor Dr RICHARD MULLEN.

English Historical Review: Faculty of History, Old Boys' High School, George St, Oxford, OX1 2RL; e-mail ehr@history.ox.ac.uk; internet ehr.oxfordjournals.org; f. 1886; 6 a year; learned articles and book reviews; Editors G. W. BERNARD, MARTIN CONWAY.

The Historian: The Historical Association, 59A Kennington Park Rd, London, SE11 4JH; tel. (20) 7735-3901; fax (20) 7582-4989; e-mail enquiry@history.org.uk; internet www.history.org.uk; f. 1906; 4 a year; Editors Prof. BILL SPECK, IAN MASON; circ. 3,500 (2005).

History Today: 25 Bedford Ave, London WC1B 3AT; tel. (20) 3219-7810; fax (20) 3219-7829; e-mail admin@historytoday.com; internet www.historytoday.com; f. 1951; monthly; illustrated general historical magazine; Editor PAUL LAY; circ. 25,274 (2007).

International Affairs: Royal Institute of International Affairs, Chatham House, 10 St James's Sq., London, SW1Y 4LE; tel. (20) 7957-5724; fax (20) 7957-5710; e-mail csoper@chathamhouse.org.uk; internet www.chathamhouse.org.uk; f. 1922; 6 a year; owned by Royal Institute of International Affairs; publ. by Wiley-Blackwell; original articles, and reviews of publications on international affairs; Editor CAROLINE SOPER.

Journal of Contemporary History: Unit 24, The Bardfield Centre, Great Bardfield, Essex, CM7 4SL; tel. (1371) 811608; fax (870) 288-9730; e-mail office@jch.org.uk; internet www.jch.org.uk; f. 1966; quarterly; publ. by SAGE Publications Ltd; Editors RICHARD J. EVANS, STANLEY G. PAYNE.

London Gazette: POB 7923, London, SE1 5ZH; tel. (20) 7394-4517; fax (20) 7394-4572; e-mail london.gazette@tso.co.uk; internet www.london-gazette.co.uk; f. 1665; 5 a week; the oldest continuously published newspaper in the UK; government journal of official, legal and public notices.

New Left Review: 6 Meard St, London, W1F 0EG; tel. (20) 7734-8830; fax (20) 7439-3869; e-mail mail@newleftreview.org; internet www.newleftreview.org; f. 1960; 6 a year; international politics, economics and culture; Editor SUSAN WATKINS.

New Statesman: 7th Floor, John Carpenter House, 7 Carmelite St, Blackfriars EC4Y 0BS; tel. (20) 7936-6400; fax (20) 7936-6501; e-mail info@newstatesman.co.uk; internet www.newstatesman.com; f. 1913; weekly; current affairs, politics and the arts; publ. by Progressive Media Group; Editor JASON COWLEY; circ. 26,208 (2007).

People in Power: Cambridge International Reference on Current Affairs Ltd (CIRCA), 13–17 Sturton St, Cambridge, CB1 2SN; tel. (1223) 564334; fax (1223) 354643; e-mail pip@circaworld.com; internet www.peopleinpower.com; f. 1987; bi-monthly; current worldwide government listings and health contacts; owned by CIRCA Ltd; Man. Dir ROGER EAST; Producer ROSEMARY PAYNE.

The Political Quarterly: Wiley-Blackwell, 9600 Garsington Rd, Oxford, OX4 2DQ; tel. (1865) 476303; fax (1865) 476770; internet www.wiley.com; f. 1930; Editors ANDREW GAMBLE, ANTHONY WRIGHT.

Private Eye: 6 Carlisle St, London, W1D 3BN; tel. (20) 7437-4017; fax (20) 7437-0705; e-mail strobes@private-eye.co.uk; internet www.private-eye.co.uk; f. 1961; fortnightly; satirical; Editor IAN HISLOP; circ. 205,231 (2008).

Prospect: 2 Bloomsbury Pl., London, WC1A 2QA; tel. (20) 7255-1281; fax (20) 7255-1279; e-mail editorial@prospect-magazine.co.uk; internet www.prospect-magazine.co.uk; f. 1995; monthly; political and cultural; Editor BRONWEN MADDOX; circ. 27,552.

Race & Class: The Institute of Race Relations, 2–6 Leeke St, London, WC1X 9HS; tel. (20) 7837-0041; fax (20) 7278-0623; e-mail info@irr.org.uk; internet www.irr.org.uk; f. 1959; quarterly; journal on racism, empire and globalization; Editors A. SIVANANDAN, HAZEL WATERS.

The Spectator: 22 Old Queen St, London, SW1H 9HP; tel. (20) 7961-0200; fax (20) 7961-0058; e-mail editor@spectator.co.uk; internet www.spectator.co.uk; f. 1828; Propr Press Holdings; Thurs.; independent political and literary review; Editor FRASER NELSON; circ. 76,952 (2008).

Tribune: 9 Arkwright Rd, London, NW3 6AN; tel. (20) 7433-6410; fax (20) 7433-6419; e-mail mail@tribunemagazine.co.uk; internet www.tribuneweb.co.uk; f. 1937; Fri.; Labour's independent weekly; politics, current affairs, arts; Editor CHRIS McLAUGHLIN.

Economics and Business

Accountancy Age: Incisive Media, 32–34 Broadwick St, London, W1A 2HG; tel. (20) 7316-9000; fax (20) 7316-9250; e-mail news@accountancyage.com; internet www.accountancyage.co.uk; f. 1969; weekly; Editor GAVIN HINKS; circ. 60,337 (2007).

The Banker: Number One Southwark Bridge, London, SE1 9HL; tel. (20) 7873-3000; e-mail stephen.timewell@ft.com; internet www.thebanker.com; f. 1926; monthly; monetary and economic policy, international and domestic banking and finance, banking technology, country surveys; Propr Pearson PLC; Editor-in-Chief STEPHEN TIMEWELL; circ. 28,771 (2008).

Campaign: Haymarket Marketing Publications Ltd, 174 Hammersmith Rd, London, W6 7JP; tel. (20) 8267-4656; fax (20) 8267-4915; e-mail campaign@haymarket.com; internet www.brandrepublic.com/campaign; f. 1968; advertising, marketing and media; Thurs.; Editor CLAIRE BEALE; circ. 10,012 (June 2008).

Crops: Farmers Weekly Group, Quadrant House, The Quadrant, Sutton, Surrey, SM2 5AS; tel. (20) 8652-4934; fax (20) 8652-8928; e-mail crops@rbi.co.uk; internet www.fwi.co.uk; f. 1984; fortnightly; publ. by Reed Business Information; Editor ROBERT HARRIS; circ. 14,792 (June 2008).

The Economic Journal: Wiley-Blackwell, 9600 Garsington Rd, Oxford, OX4 2DQ; tel. (1865) 776868; fax (1865) 714591; e-mail rchandler@wiley.com; internet www.wiley.com; f. 1891; 9 a year; owned by Royal Economic Society; Editors ANTONIO CICCONE, JÖRN-STEFFEN PISCHKE, STEVE MACHIN, ANDREW SCOTT, DAVID MYATT.

The Economist: 25 St James's St, London, SW1A 1HG; tel. (20) 7830-7000; fax (20) 7839-2968; e-mail letters@economist.com; internet www.economist.com; f. 1843; 50% owned by Pearson PLC, 50% by individual shareholders; Fri.; Editor JOHN MICKLETHWAIT; CEO ANDREW RASHBASS; circ. 182,539 (June 2008).

Euromoney: Nestor House, Playhouse Yard, London, EC4V 5EX; tel. (20) 7779-8888; fax (20) 7779-8653; e-mail hotline@euromoneyplc.com; internet www.euromoney.com; f. 1969; monthly; Editor CLIVE HORWOOD; circ. 25,368 (June 2008).

Farmers Weekly: Farmers Weekly Group, Quadrant House, The Quadrant, Sutton, Surrey, SM2 5AS; tel. (20) 8652-4911; fax (20) 8652-4005; e-mail farmers.weekly@rbi.co.uk; internet www.fwi.co.uk; f. 1934; Fri.; publ. by Reed Business Information; Editor JANE KING; circ. 68,897 (June 2008).

Investors Chronicle: Number One Southwark Bridge, London, SE1 9HL; tel. (20) 7382-3000; e-mail ic.cs@ft.com; internet www.investorschronicle.co.uk; f. as *Money Market Review* 1860; amalgamated with *Investors Chronicle* 1914; amalgamated with the *Stock Exchange Gazette* 1967; Fri.; independent financial and economic review; Editor JONATHAN ELEY; circ. 30,027.

Management Today: 174 Hammersmith Rd, London, W6 7JP; tel. (20) 8267-4967; fax (20) 8267-4680; e-mail editorial@mtmagazine.co.uk; internet www.managementtoday.co.uk; f. 1966; monthly; Editor MATTHEW GWYTHER; circ. 100,002 (June 2008).

Education

Higher Education Quarterly: Wiley-Blackwell, 9600 Garsington Rd, Oxford, OX4 2DQ; tel. (1865) 776868; fax (1865) 714591; internet www.blackwellpublishing.com/hequ; f. 1946; Editors LEE HARVEY, CELIA WHITCHURCH.

The Teacher: Hamilton House, Mabledon Pl., London, WC1H 9BD; tel. (20) 7380-4708; fax (20) 7387-8458; e-mail teacher@nut.org.uk; internet www.teachers.org.uk/theteacher; f. 1872; magazine of the NUT; news, comments and articles on all aspects of education; 6 a year; Editor ELLIE CAMPBELL-BARR.

The Times Educational Supplement (TES): 26 Red Lion Sq., London, WC1R 4HQ; tel. (20) 3194-3000; fax (20) 3194-3333; e-mail letters@tes.co.uk; internet www.tes.co.uk; f. 1910; Fri.; Editor GERARD KELLY; circ. 57,714.

Times Higher Education (THE): 26 Red Lion Sq., London, WC1R 4HQ; tel. (20) 3194-3000; fax (20) 3194-3300; e-mail editor@thes.co.uk; internet www.timeshighereducation.co.uk; f. 1971 as *The Times Higher Education Supplement*; Thurs.; Editor ANN MROZ; circ. 21,140 (Dec. 2007).

Home, Fashion and General

Bella: H. Bauer Publishing Ltd, 1st Floor, 24–28 Oval Rd, London, NW1 7DT; tel. (20) 7241-8000; fax (20) 7241-8030; internet www.bauer.co.uk; f. 1987; Tues.; fashion, beauty, health, cookery, handicrafts; Editor JULIA DAVIS; circ. 246,446 (2010).

Best: National Magazine Company, 72 Broadwick St, London, W1F 9EP; tel. (20) 7439-5000; fax (20) 7439-4580; e-mail best@acp-natmag

THE UNITED KINGDOM

.co.uk; internet www.natmags.co.uk; f. 1987; weekly; women's interest; Editor JACKIE HATTON; circ. 302,309 (2010).

Chat: IPC Connect Ltd, The Blue Fin Bldg, 110 Southwark St, London, SE1 0SU; tel. (20) 3148-6153; fax (20) 3148-8111; e-mail ben_gelblum@ipcmedia.com; internet www.ipcmedia.com; weekly; women's interest; Editor GILLY SINCLAIR; circ. 430,674 (2010).

Company: National Magazine House, 72 Broadwick St, London, W1F 9EP; tel. (20) 7439-5000; fax (20) 7439-6886; e-mail company.mail@natmags.co.uk; internet www.natmags.co.uk; monthly; Editor VICTORIA WHITE; circ. 217,324 (2010).

Cosmopolitan: National Magazine House, 72 Broadwick St, London, W1F 9EP; tel. (20) 7439-5000; fax (20) 7439-5016; e-mail contact@natmags.co.uk; internet www.cosmopolitan.co.uk; f. 1972; monthly; women's interest; Editor LOUISE COURT; circ. 401,750 (2010).

Elle: 64 North Row, London, W1K 7LL; tel. (20) 7150-7000; fax (20) 7150-7001; e-mail lorraine.candy@hf-uk.com; internet www.elleuk.com; f. 1985; monthly; women's interest; Editor-in-Chief LORRAINE CANDY; circ. 195,625 (2010).

Esquire: National Magazine House, 72 Broadwick St, London, W1F 9EP; tel. (20) 7439-5601; fax (20) 7439-5675; e-mail info@esquire.co.uk; internet www.esquire.co.uk; f. 1991; monthly; men's interest; Editor ALEX BILMES; circ. 52,705 (2009).

FHM: Endeavour House, 189 Shaftesbury Ave, London, WC2H 8JG; tel. (20) 7436-8534; fax (20) 7182-8021; e-mail help@fhm.com; internet www.fhm.com; f. 1987; monthly; men's interest; Editor JOE BARNES; circ. 192,586 (2010).

Glamour: Vogue House, Hanover Sq., London, W1S 1JU; tel. (20) 7499-9080; e-mail glamoureditorialmagazine@condenast.co.uk; internet www.glamour.com; f. 2001; monthly; women's interest; Editor JO ELVIN; circ. 526,216 (2010).

Good Housekeeping: National Magazine House, 72 Broadwick St, London, W1F 9EP; tel. (20) 7439-5000; fax (20) 7437-6886; e-mail goodh.mail@natmags.co.uk; internet www.goodhousekeeping.co.uk; f. 1922; monthly; Editor-in-Chief LINDSAY NICHOLSON; circ. 422,496 (2010).

GQ: The Condé Nast Publications Ltd, Vogue House, Hanover Sq., London, W1S 1JU; tel. (20) 7499-9080; fax (20) 7495-1679; internet www.gq-magazine.co.uk; f. 1988; monthly; Editor DYLAN JONES; circ. 120,019 (2009).

Grazia: Endeavour House, 189 Shaftesbury Ave, London, WC2H 8JG; tel. (20) 7437-9011; e-mail graziadaily@graziamagazine.co.uk; internet www.graziamagazine.co.uk; f. 2005; weekly; Editor JANE BRUTON; circ. 224,421 (2010).

Harper's Bazaar: National Magazine House, 72 Broadwick St, London, W1F 9EP; tel. (20) 7439-5000; fax (20) 7437-6886; internet www.harpersbazaar.co.uk; f. 1929; Propr National Magazine Co Ltd; monthly; international fashion, beauty, general features; Editor LUCY YEOMANS; circ. 109,646 (2009).

Heat: Endeavour House, 189 Shaftesbury Ave, London, WC2H 8JG; tel. (20) 7437-9011; internet www.heatworld.com; f. 1999; Tues.; celebrity news, TV, radio, films; Editor LUCIE CAVE (acting); circ. 370,132 (2010).

Hello!: Hello! Ltd, Wellington House, 69–71 Upper Ground, London, SE1 9PQ; tel. (20) 7667-8700; fax (20) 7667-8716; e-mail hello@hellomagazine.com; internet www.hellomagazine.com; Propr. Hola, SA (Spain); weekly; Publishing Dir CHARLOTTE STOCKTING; Editor KAY GODDARD; circ. 412,195 (2010).

Homes and Gardens: The Blue Fin Bldg, 110 Southwark St, London, SE1 0SU; tel. (20) 7261-6202; fax (20) 7261-6247; e-mail homesandgardens@ipcmedia.com; internet www.homesandgardens.com; f. 1919; monthly; Editor DEBORAH BARKER; circ. 136,136 (2010).

House & Garden: The Condé Nast Publications Ltd, Vogue House, Hanover Sq., London, W1S 1JU; tel. (20) 7499-9080; fax (20) 7629-2907; e-mail harriet.bindloss@condenast.co.uk; internet www.houseandgarden.co.uk; f. 1920; monthly; Editor SUSAN CREWE; circ. 130,781 (2010).

Ideal Home: IPC Media Ltd, The Blue Fin Bldg, 110 Southwark St, London, SE1 0SU; tel. (20) 3148-5000; e-mail ideal_home@ipcmedia.com; internet www.idealhomemagazine.co.uk; f. 1920; 11 a year; Editor ISOBEL MCKENZIE-PRICE; circ. 205,659 (2010).

InStyle: The Blue Fin Bldg, 110 Southwark St, London, SE1 0SU; tel. (20) 7261-4747; fax (20) 7261-6664; internet www.instylemagazine.co.uk; f. 2001; monthly; fashion, beauty; Editor EILIDH MACASKILL; circ. 186,251 (2010).

The Lady: 39–40 Bedford St, London, WC2E 9ER; tel. (20) 7379-4717; fax (20) 7497-2137; e-mail admin@lady.co.uk; internet www.lady.co.uk; f. 1885; Tues.; Editor RACHEL JOHNSON; circ. 29,095.

Marie Claire: IPC Media Ltd, The Blue Fin Bldg, 110 Southwark St, London, SE1 0SU; tel. (20) 3148-7664; e-mail marieclaire@ipcmedia.com; internet www.marieclaire.co.uk; f. 1988; monthly; women's interest; Man. Editor TRISH HALPIN; circ. 280,021 (2010).

My Weekly: D. C. Thomson & Co Ltd, 80 Kingsway East, Dundee, DD4 8SL; tel. (1382) 223131; fax (1382) 452491; e-mail myweekly@dcthomson.co.uk; f. 1910; Thurs.; women's interest; Editor SALLY HAMPTON; circ. 134,393 (2010).

Now: The Blue Fin Bldg, 110 Southwark St, London, SE1 0SU; tel. (20) 3148-6373; fax (20) 3148-8110; internet www.nowmagazine.co.uk; weekly; celebrity news, TV, radio, films; Editor SALLY EYDEN; circ. 338,080 (2010).

Nuts: The Blue Fin Bldg, 110 Southwark St, London, SE1 0SU; tel. (20) 7261-6174; e-mail nutsmagazine@ipcmedia.com; internet www.nutsmag.co.uk; f. 2004; weekly; Editor DOMINIC SMITH; circ. 147,134 (2010).

OK!: The Northern & Shell Bldg, 10 Lower Thames St, London, EC3R 6EN; tel. (871) 434-1010; e-mail editor@ok-magazine.com; internet www.ok-magazine.co.uk; weekly; Editor LISA BYRNE; circ. 478,878 (2010).

The People's Friend: D. C. Thomson & Co Ltd, 80 Kingsway East, Dundee, DD4 8SL; tel. (1382) 223131; fax (1382) 452491; e-mail peoplesfriend@dcthomson.co.uk; f. 1869; Wed.; women's fiction, home, crafts, general; Editor ANGELA GILCHRIST; circ. 330,093.

Prima: 72 Broadwick St, London, W1F 9EP; tel. (20) 7439-5000; fax (20) 7312-4100; e-mail prima@natmags.co.uk; internet www.allaboutyou.com/prima; f. 1986; monthly; Editor MAIRE FAHEY; circ. 282,544.

Reader's Digest: 157 Edgware Rd, London, W2 2HR; tel. (20) 7715-8000; fax (20) 7053-4500; e-mail theeditor@readersdigest.co.uk; internet www.readersdigest.co.uk; f. 1938; monthly; Editor GILL HUDSON; circ. 403,458 (2010).

The Scots Magazine: D. C. Thomson & Co. Ltd, 80 Kingsway East, Dundee, DD4 8SL; tel. (1382) 223131; fax (1382) 322214; e-mail mail@scotsmagazine.com; internet www.scotsmagazine.com; f. 1739; monthly; Scottish interest; Editor PHIL SMITH; circ. 36,049 (2008).

She: 72 Broadwick St, London, W1F 9EP; tel. (20) 7439-5000; fax (20) 7437-6886; e-mail sian.rees@natmags.co.uk; internet www.natmags.co.uk; f. 1955; monthly; Editor CLAIRE IRVIN; circ. 144,228 (2010).

Take a Break: H. Bauer Publishing Ltd, 24–28 Oval Rd, London, NW1 7DT; tel. (20) 7241-8000; fax (20) 7241-8052; e-mail tab.features@bauer.co.uk; internet www.bauer.co.uk; f. 1990; Thurs.; Editor REBECCA FLEMING; circ. 855,372 (2010).

Tatler: The Condé Nast Publications Ltd, Vogue House, Hanover Sq., London, W1S 1JU; tel. (20) 7499-9080; fax (20) 7409-0451; internet www.tatler.co.uk; f. 1709; monthly; Man. Editor KAREN HODKINSON; circ. 85,064 (2010).

That's Life!: H. Bauer Publishing Ltd, 24–28 Oval Rd, London, NW1 7DT; tel. (20) 7241-8000; fax (20) 7241-8008; e-mail sales@tpc-london.com; internet www.bauer.co.uk; f. 1995; Thurs.; Editor SOPHIE HEARSEY; circ. 341,545 (2010).

Vanity Fair: The Condé Nast Publications Ltd, Vogue House, Hanover Sq., London, W1S IJU; tel. (20) 7499-9080; fax (20) 7499-4415; internet www.vanityfair.com; monthly; Editor HENRY PORTER; circ. 102,471 (2010).

Viz: Dennis Publishing Ltd, 30 Cleveland St, London, W1T 4JD; tel. (20) 7907-6000; fax (20) 7907-6020; e-mail viz@viz.co.uk; internet www.viz.co.uk; f. 1979; monthly; Editor SIMON DONALD; circ. 88,165 (2007).

Vogue: The Condé Nast Publications Ltd, Vogue House, Hanover Sq., London, W1S 1JU; tel. (20) 7499-9080; fax (20) 7408-0559; e-mail vogue.com.editor@condenast.co.uk; internet www.vogue.co.uk; f. 1916; monthly; Editor ALEXANDRA SHULMAN; circ. 210,561 (2010).

The Voice: GV Media Group Ltd, Northern & Shell Tower, 6th Floor, 4 Selsdon Way, London, E14 9GL; tel. (20) 7510-0340; fax (20) 7510-0341; e-mail letters@gvmedia.com; internet www.voice-online.co.uk; f. 1982; Mon.; black interest; Editor STEVE POPE.

Wallpaper*: 7th Floor, The Blue Fin Bldg, 110 Southwark St, London, SE1 0SU; tel. (20) 3148-5000; fax (20) 3148-8119; e-mail contact@wallpaper.com; internet www.wallpaper.com; f. 1996; monthly; Editor TONY CHAMBERS; circ. 108,050 (2008).

Woman: The Blue Fin Bldg, 110 Southwark St, London, SE1 0SU; tel. (20) 3148-6491; e-mail woman@ipcmedia.com; internet www.ipcmedia.com/brands/woman; f. 1937; Tues.; Editor KAREN LIVERMORE; circ. 338,577 (2010).

Woman and Home: The Blue Fin Bldg, 110 Southwark St, London, SE1 0SU; tel. (20) 3148-7836; e-mail woman&home@ipcmedia.com; internet www.ipcmedia.com/brands/womanhome; f. 1926; monthly; Editor SUE JAMES; circ. 369,321 (2010).

Woman's Own: The Blue Fin Bldg, 110 Southwark St, London, SE1 0SU; tel. (20) 3148-6552; fax (20) 3148-8112; internet www.ipcmedia.com/brands/womansown; f. 1932; Tues.; Editor-in-Chief VICKY MAYER; circ. 272,376 (2010).

Woman's Weekly: The Blue Fin Bldg, 110 Southwark St, London, SE1 0SU; tel. (20) 3148-6628; internet www.ipcmedia.com/brands/

THE UNITED KINGDOM

womansweekly; f. 1911; Wed.; Editor DIANE KENWOOD; circ. 38,577 (2010).

Zoo: Mappin House, 4 Winsley St, London, W1W 8HF; tel. (20) 7182-8000; internet www.zootoday.com; f. 2004; weekly; Editor TOM ETHERINGTON; circ. 68,610 (2010).

Law

Law Quarterly Review: 100 Avenue Rd, London, NW3 3PF; tel. (20) 7393-7000; fax (20) 7393-7010; internet www.sweetandmaxwell.co.uk; f. 1885; quarterly; Editor Prof. FRANCIS M. B. REYNOLDS.

Law Society's Gazette: 113 Chancery Lane, London, WC2A 1PL; tel. (20) 7242-1222; e-mail gazette-editorial@lawsociety.org.uk; internet www.lawgazette.co.uk; f. 1903; weekly; Editor-in-Chief PAUL ROGERSON; circ. 118,927.

The Lawyer: St Giles House, 50 Poland St, London, W1V 7AX; tel. (20) 7970-4614; fax (20) 7970-4640; e-mail catrin.griffiths@thelawyer.com; internet www.thelawyer.com; weekly; Editor CATRIN GRIFFITHS; circ. 31,571 (June 2008).

Leisure Interests and Sport

Autocar Magazine: Haymarket Publishing, Teddington Studios, Broom Rd, Teddington, Middx, TW11 9BE; tel. (20) 8267-5630; fax (20) 8267-5759; e-mail editorial@autocar.co.uk; internet www.autocar.co.uk; f. 1895; Wed.; Editor CHAS HALLETT; circ. 58,091 (2008).

Autosport: Haymarket Consumer Media, Broom Rd, Teddington, Middx, TW11 9BE; tel. (20) 8267-5118; e-mail rob.aherne@haymarket.com; internet www.autosport.com; f. 1950; Thurs.; covers all aspects of motor sport; Editor-in-Chief ANDY VAN DE BURGT; circ. 38,324 (2007).

Car: Media House, Lynchwood Business Park, Lynchwood, Peterborough, PE2 6EA; tel. (1733) 468485; fax (1733) 468660; e-mail car@bauermedia.co.uk; internet www.carmagazine.co.uk; f. 1962; monthly; Editor PHIL MCNAMARA; circ. 58,380 (2010).

Country Life: 9th Floor, The Blue Fin Bldg, 110 Southwark St, London, SE1 0SU; tel. (20) 3148-4435; fax (20) 3148-8129; e-mail milly_cumming@ipcmedia.com; internet www.countrylife.co.uk; f. 1897; Thurs.; Editor MARK HEDGES; circ. 40,821 (2007).

The Countryman: The Water Mill, Broughton Hall, Skipton, BD23 3AG; tel. (1756) 701381; fax (1756) 701326; e-mail editorial@thecountryman.co.uk; internet www.thecountryman.co.uk; f. 1927; monthly; independent; Editor PAUL JACKSON; circ. 19,817 (2007).

FourFourTwo: Haymarket Consumer Media, Broom Rd, Teddington, TW11 9BE; tel. (20) 8267-5848; fax (20) 8267-5354; e-mail martyn.jones@haymarket.com; internet www.fourfourtwo.com; f. 1994; monthly; football; Editor DAVID HALL; circ. 107,987 (2008).

BBC Gardeners' World Magazine: BBC Worldwide Ltd, Room AG193, 80 Wood Lane, London, W12 0TT; tel. (20) 8433-3959; fax (20) 8433-3986; e-mail gweditorial@bbc.co.uk; internet www.gardenersworld.com; f. 1991; monthly; Editor ADAM PASCO; circ. 260,133 (2010).

Golf Monthly: The Blue Fin Bldg, 110 Southwark St, London, SE1 0SU; tel. (20) 7148-4530; e-mail golfmonthly@ipcmedia.com; internet www.golf-monthly.co.uk; f. 1911; monthly; Editor MICHAEL HARRIS; circ. 82,264 (2008).

BBC Good Food: BBC Worldwide Ltd, 80 Wood Lane, London, W12 0TT; tel. (20) 8433-1316; fax (20) 8433-1277; e-mail goodfoodrs@galleon.co.uk; internet www.bbcmagazines.com/goodfood; f. 1989; monthly; Editor GILLIAN CARTER; circ. 305,825 (2010).

Hi-Fi News: Leon House, 10th Floor, 233 High St, Croydon, Surrey, CR9 1HZ; tel. (20) 8726-8310; fax (20) 8726-8397; e-mail hi-finews@ipcmedia.com; internet www.hifinews.co.uk; f. 1956; monthly; all aspects of high quality sound reproduction, record reviews; Editor PAUL MILLER; circ. 11,353 (2008).

Men's Health: 72 Broadwick St, London, W1F 9EP; tel. (20) 7339-4400; fax (20) 7339-4444; e-mail nicky.williams@natmag-rodale.co.uk; internet www.menshealth.co.uk; f. 1995; monthly; lifestyle, health, general features; Editor MORGAN REES; circ. 245,754 (2010).

Practical Photography: Media House, Lynchwood Business Park, Lynchwood, Peterborough, PE2 6EA; tel. (1733) 468546; fax (1733) 468387; e-mail practical.photography@bauerconsumer.co.uk; internet www.photoanswers.co.uk; monthly; Editor-in-Chief ANDREW JAMES; circ. 62,303 (2007).

Radio Times: BBC Worldwide Ltd, Media Centre, White City, 201 Wood Lane, London, W12 7TS; tel. (870) 608-4455; fax (20) 8433-3160; e-mail radio.times@bbc.com; internet www.radiotimes.com; f. 1923; weekly; programme guide to television and radio broadcasts; Editor BEN PRESTON; circ. 947,131 (2010).

Rugby World: The Blue Fin Bldg, 110 Southwark St, London, SE1 0SU; tel. (20) 3148-4702; e-mail paul_morgan@ipcmedia.com; internet www.rugbyworld.com; monthly; Editor PAUL MORGAN; circ. 48,381 (2007).

Time Out: Time Out Magazine Ltd, Universal House, 251 Tottenham Court Rd, London, W1T 7AB; tel. (20) 7813-3000; fax (20) 7813-6001; e-mail net@timeout.co.uk; internet www.timeout.com; f. 1968; weekly; listings and reviews of events in London; Time Out Group also publishes city guides and specialized London guides; Editor MARK FRITH; circ. 76,356 (2008).

TVTimes: The Blue Fin Bldg, 110 Southwark St, London, SE1 0SU; tel. (20) 3148-5570; e-mail tvtimes_letters@ipcmedia.com; internet www.ipcmedia.com/brands/tvtimes; f. 1955; features and listings of all television broadcasts; Editor IAN ABBOTT; circ. 290,686 (2010).

What Car?: Teddington Studios, Broom Rd, Teddington, Middx, TW11 9BE; tel. (20) 8267-5688; fax (20) 8267-5750; e-mail whatcar@haymarket.com; internet www.whatcar.com; f. 1973; 13 a year; Group Editor STEVE FOWLER; circ. 83,102 (2009).

What's On TV: The Blue Fin Bldg, 110 Southwark St, London, SE1 0SU; tel. (20) 3148-5928; e-mail wotv-postbag@ipcmedia.com; internet www.ipcmedia.com/brands/whatsontv; f. 1991; weekly; television programme guide and features; Editor COLIN TOUGH; circ. 1,209,018 (2010).

The Wisden Cricketer: Wisden Cricketer Publishing Ltd, 2nd Floor, 123 Buckingham Palace Rd, London, SW1W 9SL; tel. (20) 7705-4911; e-mail twc@wisdencricketer.com; internet wisdencricketer.com; f. 1921; monthly; Propr BSkyB Publications; Editor JOHN STERN; circ. 34,559 (2007).

Zest: 72 Broadwick St, London, W1F 9EP; tel. (20) 7439-5000; fax (20) 7437-6886; e-mail contact@zest.co.uk; internet www.zest.co.uk; health, beauty, fitness and nutrition; Editor MANDIE GOWER; circ. 104,636 (2008).

Medicine, Science and Technology

Biochemical Journal: Portland Press Ltd, 3rd Floor, Eagle House, 16 Procter St, London, WC1V 6NX; tel. (20) 7280-4110; fax (20) 7280-4169; e-mail editorial@portlandpress.com; internet www.biochemj.org; f. 1906; 2 a month; publ. by Portland Press on behalf of the Biochemical Society; Chair., Editorial Board PETER R. SHEPHERD.

British Journal of Psychiatry: 17 Belgrave Sq., London, SW1X 8PG; tel. (20) 7235-2351; fax (20) 7259-6507; e-mail bjp@rcpsych.ac.uk; internet bjp.rcpsych.org; monthly; original articles, reviews and correspondence; publ. by the Royal College of Psychiatrists; Editor PETER TYRER; circ. 14,100 (2005).

British Journal of Psychology: St Andrew's House, 48 Princess Rd East, Leicester, LE1 7DR; tel. (116) 254-9580; fax (116) 227-1314; e-mail journals@bps.org.uk; internet www.bpsjournals.co.uk; f. 1904; quarterly; publ. by the British Psychological Society; Editor Prof. PETER MITCHELL.

British Journal of Sociology: Wiley-Blackwell, 9600 Garsington Rd, Oxford, OX4 2DQ; tel. (1865) 776868; fax (1865) 714591; internet www.blackwellpublishing.com/bjos; f. 1950; quarterly; Editor RICHARD WRIGHT.

BMJ: BMA House, Tavistock Sq., London, WC1H 9JP; tel. (20) 7387-4410; fax (20) 7383-6418; e-mail editor@bmj.com; internet www.bmj.com; f. 1840; Sat.; 10 overseas editions; Editor Dr FIONA GODLEE; circ. 120,606 (2008).

Computer Weekly: Reed Business Information, Quadrant House, The Quadrant, Sutton, Surrey, SM2 5AS; tel. (20) 8652-8642; fax (20) 8652-8979; e-mail cwnews@rbi.co.uk; internet www.computerweekly.com; f. 1966; Tues.; Editor BRIAN MCKENNA.

Computing: Incisive Media, 32–34 Broadwick St, London, W1A 2HG; tel. (20) 7316-9000; fax (20) 7316-9160; e-mail computing@vnu.co.uk; internet www.computing.co.uk; f. 1973; Thurs.; Editor ABIGAIL WARAKER; circ. 115,000 (2005).

Flight International: Reed Business Information, Quadrant House, The Quadrant, Sutton, Surrey, SM2 5AS; tel. (20) 8652-3842; fax (20) 8652-3840; e-mail flight.international@rbi.co.uk; internet www.flightinternational.com; f. 1909; Tues.; Editor MURDO MORRISON.

Geographical Magazine: Circle Publishing, 1 Victoria Villas, Richmond, Surrey, TW9 2GW; tel. (20) 8332-2713; fax (20) 8332-9307; e-mail magazine@geographical.co.uk; internet www.geographical.co.uk; f. 1935; monthly; Editor GEORDIE TORR; circ. 21,684 (2008).

The Lancet: 32 Jamestown Rd, London, NW1 7BY; tel. (20) 7424-4910; fax (20) 7424-4911; e-mail editorial@lancet.com; internet www.thelancet.com; f. 1823; Sat.; medical; Editor Dr RICHARD HORTON.

Nature: Macmillan Magazines Ltd, 4 Crinan St, London, N1 9XW; tel. (20) 7833-4000; fax (20) 7843-4640; e-mail nature@nature.com; internet www.nature.com/nature; f. 1869; Thurs.; scientific; Editor-in-Chief Dr PHILIP CAMPBELL.

New Scientist: Lacon House, 84 Theobald's Rd, London, WC1X 8NS; tel. (20) 7611-1200; fax (20) 7611-1250; e-mail news@newscientist.com; internet www.newscientist.com; f. 1956; Thurs.;

science and technology; Editor ROGER HIGHFIELD; circ. 144,401 (2010).

Nursing Times: Emap Inform, Greater London House, Hampstead Rd, London, NW1 7EJ; tel. (20) 728-3702; fax (20) 7874-0505; e-mail nt@emap.com; internet www.nursingtimes.net; f. 1905; Tues.; professional nursing journal; Editor JENNI MIDDLETON; circ. 35,754 (2008).

The Practitioner: Ludgate House, 245 Blackfriars Rd, London, SE1 9UY; tel. (20) 7921-8113; e-mail editor@thepractitioner.co.uk; internet www.thepractitioner.co.uk; f. 1868; monthly; medical journal for General Practitioners; Editor CORINNE SHORT.

Religion and Philosophy

Catholic Herald: Herald House, 15 Lamb's Passage, Bunhill Row, London, EC1Y 8TQ; tel. (20) 7448-3602; fax (20) 7256-9728; e-mail editorial@catholicherald.co.uk; internet www.catholicherald.co.uk; f. 1888; Catholic weekly newspaper; Fri.; Editor LUKE COPPEN.

Church Times: 13–17 Long Lane, London, EC1A 9PN; tel. (20) 7776-1060; fax (20) 7776-1086; e-mail editor@churchtimes.co.uk; internet www.churchtimes.co.uk; f. 1863; owned by Hymns Ancient & Modern Trust; Church of England and world-wide Anglican news; Fri.; Man. Editor PAUL HANDLEY.

Jewish Chronicle: 25 Furnival St, London, EC4A 1JT; tel. (20) 7415-1500; fax (20) 7405-9040; e-mail editorial@thejc.com; internet www.thejc.com; f. 1841; Fri.; Editor STEPHEN POLLARD; circ. 32,875 (June 2008).

Methodist Recorder: 122 Golden Lane, London, EC1Y 0TL; tel. (20) 7251-8414; fax (20) 7251-8600; e-mail editorial@methodistrecorder.co.uk; internet www.methodistrecorder.co.uk; f. 1861; Thurs.; Man. Editor MOIRA SLEIGHT.

New Blackfriars: Blackfriars, Oxford, OX1 3LY; tel. (1865) 776868; fax (1865) 714591; e-mail fergus.kerr@english.op.org; internet www.wiley.com; f. 1920; 6 a year; religious and cultural; Editor Rev. FERGUS KERR.

Philosophy: Royal Institute of Philosophy, 14 Gordon Sq., London, WC1H 0AR; tel. (20) 7387-4130; e-mail editor@royalinstitutephilosophy.org; internet www.royalinstitutephilosophy.org; f. 1925; quarterly; Editor Prof. ANTHONY O'HEAR.

The Universe: The Universe Media Group Limited, 4th Floor, Landmark House, Station Rd, Cheshire SK8 7JH; tel. (161) 488-1700; e-mail newsdesk@totalcatholic.com; internet www.totalcatholic.com; f. 1860; Sun.; illustrated Catholic newspaper and review; publ. by Gabriel Communications Ltd; Editorial Dir JOSEPH KELLY.

Woman Alive: Christian Publishing and Outreach, Garcia Estate, Canterbury Rd, Worthing, West Sussex, BN13 1BW; tel. (1903) 604352; e-mail womanalive@cpo.org.uk; internet www.womanalive.co.uk; f. 1982; monthly; Editor JACKIE STEAD.

PRESS ORGANIZATION

Press Complaints Commission: Halton House, 20–23 Holborn, London, EC1 2JD; tel. (20) 7831-0022; fax (20) 7831-0025; e-mail complaints@pcc.org.uk; internet www.pcc.org.uk; f. 1991 to replace the Press Council, following the report of the Committee on Privacy and Related Matters; an independent organization established by the newspaper and magazine industry through the Press Standards Board of Finance to deal with complaints from the public about the contents and conduct of newspapers and magazines; the Commission has an independent chairman and 16 members, drawn from the lay public (who are in the majority) and the press. It upholds a 16-point Code of Practice, agreed by a committee of editors representing the newspaper and magazine industry. It aims to ensure that the British press maintains the highest professional standards, having regard to generally established press freedoms; Chair. Baroness BUSCOMBE; Dir STEPHEN ABELL.

NEWS AGENCIES

Press Association Ltd: 292 Vauxhall Bridge Rd, London, SW1V 1AE; tel. (870) 120-3200; fax (870) 120-3201; e-mail info@pa.press.net; internet www.pa.press.net; f. 1868; national news agency of the United Kingdom and Ireland; Exec. Chair. PAUL POTTS; Man. Dir TONY WATSON; Editor JONATHAN GRUN.

Thomson Reuters: The Thomson Reuters Bldg, 30 The South Colonnade, Canary Wharf, London, E14 5EP; tel. (20) 7250-1122; fax (20) 7324-5000; e-mail editor@reuters.com; internet uk.reuters.com; f. 2008 by merger of Reuters Group PLC (f. 1851) and Thomson Corpn; world-wide news and information service to media and business clients in 57,900 organizations and media clients in 157 countries; over 55,000 employees; Chair. DAVID THOMSON; CEO THOMAS GLOCER.

INSTITUTIONS

Chartered Institute of Journalists: 2 Dock Offices, Surrey Quays Rd, London, SE16 2XU; tel. (20) 7252-1187; fax (20) 7232-2302; e-mail memberservices@cioj.co.uk; internet www.cioj.co.uk; f. 1884; Pres. JOHN THORPE; Gen. Sec. DOMINIC COOPER.

The Journalists' Charity (Newspaper Press Fund): Dickens House, 35 Wathen Rd, Dorking, Surrey, RH4 1JY; tel. (1306) 887511; fax (1306) 888212; e-mail enquiries@journalistscharity.org.uk; internet www.journalistscharity.org.uk; f. 1864; charity for journalists and their dependants; Chair. ROBERT WARREN; Dir DAVID ILOTT.

Newspaper Publishers' Association (NPA): St Andrew's House, 8th Floor, 18-20 St Andrew St, London, EC4A 3AY; tel. (20) 7636-7014; fax (20) 7631-5119; f. 1906; comprises 8 national newspaper groups; Chair. TIM BROOKS; Dir DAVID NEWELL.

Newspaper Society (NS): St Andrew's House, 8th Floor, 18-20 St Andrew St, London, EC4A 3AY; tel. (20) 7632-7400; fax (20) 7632-7401; e-mail ns@newspapersoc.org.uk; internet www.newspapersoc.org.uk; f. 1836; represents the regional and local press; Pres. MICHAEL PELOSI; Dir DAVID NEWELL.

Professional Publishers' Association: Queen's House, 28 Kingsway, London, WC2B 6JR; tel. (20) 7404-4166; fax (20) 7404-4167; e-mail info@ppa.co.uk; internet www.ppa.co.uk; f. 1913; trade association for the British magazine industry; Chair. CHARLES REED; Chief Exec. BARRY MCILHENEY; more than 200 mems.

Association of Publishing Agencies (APA): Queen's House, 3rd Floor, 55–56 Lincoln's Inn Fields, London, WC2A 3LJ; tel. (20) 7404-4166; fax (20) 7404-4167; e-mail info@apa.co.uk; internet www.apa.co.uk; f. 1993; trade association for the customer publishing industry; Chair. MARTIN MACCONNOL; CEO PATRICK FULLER.

UK Association of Online Publishers (AOP): Queen's House, 55–56 Lincoln's Inn Fields, London, WC2A 3LJ; tel. (20) 7404-4166; fax (20) 7404-4167; e-mail lee.baker@ukaop.org.uk; internet www.ukaop.org.uk; f. 2002; represents the interests of online content providers; Chair. TIM FAIRCLIFF; Dir LEE BAKER.

Scottish Newspaper Society: 21 Lansdowne Cres., Edinburgh, EH12 5EH; tel. (131) 535-1064; fax (131) 535-1063; e-mail info@scotns.org.uk; f. 2010 following merger of Scottish Daily Newspaper Society and Scottish Newspaper Publishers Association; Dir JAMES RAEBURN.

See also under Employers' Organizations and Trade Unions.

Principal Publishers

Publishing firms in the United Kingdom are mainly located in London and many are members of large publishing groups, notably Random House, Reed Elsevier, the Pearson Group and Thomson Reuters. Fiction remains the largest category. The United Kingdom publishes more new titles every year than any other European country. In 2009 133,224 new and revised titles were issued.

Anova Books Group Ltd: The Old Magistrates Court, 10 Southcombe St, London, W14 0RA; tel. (20) 7605-1400; fax (20) 7605-1401; e-mail info@anovabooks.com; internet www.anovabooks.com; f. 2005; fmrly Chrysalis Books; imprints: Batsford, Collins & Brown, Conway, National Trust Books, Paper Tiger, Pavilion, Portico, Robson, Salamander; Man. Dir POLLY POWELL; Chief Exec. ROBIN WOOD.

Asean Academic Press Ltd: POB 13945, London, E5 0XY; fax (20) 8533-5856; e-mail aapub@attglobal.net; internet www.aseanacademicpress.com; educational, technical, professional and scientific books on Asia.

Ashgate Publishing Ltd: Wey Court East, Union Rd, Farnham, Surrey, GU9 7PT; tel. (1252) 736600; fax (1252) 736736; e-mail ashgate.online@ashgate.com; internet www.ashgate.com; f. 1967; social sciences and humanities, art, business and public sector management books; imprints: Ashgate, Gower, Lund Humphries, Variorum; Chair. N. FARROW.

Atlantic Books: Ormond House, 26-27 Boswell St, London, WC1N 3JZ; tel. (20) 7269-1610; fax (20) 7430-0916; e-mail enquiries@groveatlantic.co.uk; internet www.atlantic-books.co.uk; f. 2000; subsidiary of Grove/Atlantic, Inc (USA); mem. of Independent Alliance; imprints: Guardian Books, Observer Books, Portobello Press; CEO and Publr TOBY MUNDY.

Berlitz Publishing: 58 Borough High St, London, SE1 1XF; tel. (20) 7403-0284; fax (20) 7403-0290; e-mail publishing@berlitz.co.uk; internet www.berlitzpublishing.com; f. 1970; travel, languages, reference, leisure, children's books; owned by Apa Publications UK Ltd; Man. Dir KATHARINE LECK.

A. & C. Black Publishers Ltd: 37 Soho Sq., London, W1D 3QZ; tel. (20) 7758-0200; fax (20) 7758-0222; e-mail enquiries@acblack.com;

THE UNITED KINGDOM

internet www.acblack.com; f. 1807; inc. Adlard Coles Nautical, Christopher Helm, Herbert Press, Pica Press, T & AD Poyser, Thomas Reed, Methuen Drama, Wisden; children's and educational books, music, arts and crafts, drama, reference, sport, theatre, travel, sailing, ornithology; owned by Bloomsbury Publishing PLC; Chair. NIGEL NEWTON; Editorial Dir JANET MURPHY.

Bloomsbury Publishing PLC: 36 Soho Sq., London, W1D 3QY; tel. (20) 7494-2111; fax (20) 7434-0151; e-mail csm@bloomsbury.com; internet www.bloomsbury.com; f. 1986; fiction, non-fiction and children's; Chair. JEREMY WILSON; CEO NIGEL NEWTON.

Bowker (UK) Ltd: St Andrew's House, 18-20 St Andrew's St, London, EC4A 3AG; tel. (20) 7832-1770; fax (20) 7832-1710; e-mail sales@bowker.co.uk; internet www.bowker.co.uk; owned by the Cambridge Information Group; bibliographic information, catalogue enrichment and general information; Man. Dir DOUG MCMILLAN.

Marion Boyars Publishers Ltd: 26 Parke Rd, London SW13 9NG; tel. (20) 8788-9522; fax (20) 8789-8122; e-mail catheryn@marionboyars.com; internet www.marionboyars.co.uk; f. 1975; fiction, plays, cinema, music, translations, literary criticism, sociology; Man. Dir CATHERYN KILGARRIFF.

Boydell & Brewer Ltd: Whitwell House, St Audry's Park Rd, Suffolk IP12 1SY; tel. (1394) 610600; fax (1394) 610316; e-mail editorial@boydell.co.uk; internet www.boydellandbrewer.com; f. 1978; literature, art, history; Editorial Dir CAROLINE PALMER; Sr Commissioning Editor MICHAEL MIDDEKE.

Calder Publications (UK) Ltd: London House, 243-253 Lower Mortlake Rd, Richmond, Surrey, TW9 2LL; tel. (20) 8948-9550; fax (20) 8948-5599; e-mail info@oneworldclassics.com; internet www.calderpublications.com; f. 1949; acquired by Oneworld Publications in 2007; fiction, plays, music, opera, European classics, translations, general books, social sciences, politics; Calderbooks, Journal of Beckett Studies, English National Opera guides; Man. Dir ALESSANDRO GALLENZI.

Cambridge University Press: The Edinburgh Bldg, Shaftesbury Rd, Cambridge, CB2 2RU; tel. (1223) 312393; fax (1223) 315052; e-mail information@cambridge.org; internet www.cambridge.org; f. 1534; academic and scientific monographs and textbooks, educational, English language teaching materials, microsoftware, Bibles, prayer books and academic journals; Chief Exec. STEPHEN R. R. BOURNE.

Canongate Books: 14 High St, Edinburgh, EH1 1TE; tel. (131) 557-5111; fax (131) 557-5211; e-mail info@canongate.co.uk; internet www.canongate.net; f. 1973; general, fiction, non-fiction; mem. of Independent Alliance; Chair. JAMIE BYNG.

Jonathan Cape Ltd: Random House, 20 Vauxhall Bridge Rd, London, SW1V 2SA; tel. (20) 7840-8606; fax (20) 7233-6117; e-mail enquiries@randomhouse.co.uk; internet www.randomhouse.co.uk; f. 1921; imprint of The Random House Group Ltd; general, biography, travel, belles-lettres, fiction, history, poetry; subsidiary imprint: The Bodley Head (biography, current affairs, humour); Publishing Dir DAN FRANKLIN.

Carlton Books: 20 Mortimer St, London W1T 3JW; tel. (20) 7612-0418; fax (20) 7612-0401; e-mail sales@carltonbooks.co.uk; internet www.carltonbooks.co.uk; f. 1992; Man. Dir JONATHAN GOODMAN.

Century: Random House, 20 Vauxhall Bridge Rd, London, SW1V 2SA; tel. (20) 7840-8569; fax (20) 7233-6127; e-mail enquiries@randomhouse.co.uk; internet www.randomhouse.co.uk; f. 1987; imprint of The Random House Group Ltd; general, biography, travel, current affairs, fiction, memoirs, music, philosophy; Man. Dir RICHARD CABLE.

Chatto and Windus: 20 Vauxhall Bridge Rd, London, SW1V 2SA; tel. (20) 7840-8745; fax (20) 7233-6117; internet www.randomhouse.co.uk; imprint of The Random House Group Ltd; general, academic, biography, memoirs, politics, history, literary criticism, current affairs, cultural studies and fiction; imprint: Hogarth Press; Dir CLARA FARMER.

Church House Publishing: Church House, Great Smith St, London, SW1P 3AZ; tel. (20) 7898-1451; fax (20) 7898-1449; e-mail publishing@c-of-e.org.uk; internet www.chpublishing.co.uk; Publ. Man. Dr THOMAS ALLAIN-CHAPMAN.

James Clarke and Co Ltd: POB 60, Cambridge, CB1 2NT; tel. (1223) 350865; fax (1223) 366951; e-mail publishing@jamesclarke.co.uk; internet www.jamesclarke.co.uk; f. 1859; academic and reference, history, philosophy, religion, theology; imprints: Acorn Editions, Lutterworth Press, Patrick Hardy Books; acquired James Nisbet & Co in 2008; Man. Dir ADRIAN BRINK.

Collins Bartholomew: Westerhill Rd, Bishopbriggs, Glasgow, G64 2QT; tel. (141) 306-3606; fax (141) 306-3245; e-mail collinsbartholomew@harpercollins.co.uk; internet www.bartholomewmaps.com; f. 1826; cartographic division of HarperCollins Publishers; maps, atlases, bespoke mapping services and data; Man. Dir SHEENA BARCLAY.

Conran Octopus: Endeavour House, 189 Shaftesbury Ave, London WC2H 8JY; tel. (20) 7632-5400; fax (20) 7531-8627; e-mail info@octopus-publishing.co.uk; internet www.octopusbooks.co.uk; illustrated reference books; imprint of Octopus Publishing Group Ltd; Group CEO ALISON GOFF.

Constable and Robinson Ltd: 3 The Lanchesters, 162 Fulham Palace Rd, London, W6 9ER; tel. (20) 8741-3663; fax (20) 8748-7562; e-mail enquiries@constablerobinson.com; internet www.constablerobinson.com; biography and autobiography, general and military history, current affairs, psychology and self-help, health, popular science, and crime fiction; Man. Dir NICHOLAS ROBINSON.

Continuum International Publishing Group: The Tower Bldg, 11 York Rd, London, SE1 7NX; tel. (20) 7922-0880; fax (20) 7922-0881; e-mail info@continuumbooks.com; internet www.continuumbooks.com; f. 1994; popular culture, religion, humanities, social sciences, philosophy and education; imprints: Burns & Oates, Continuum, T&T Clark, Thoemmes Continuum, Hambledon Continuum and Network Continuum; Chair. PATRICK AUSTEN; CEO OLIVER GADSBY.

Darton, Longman and Todd Ltd: 1 Spencer Court, 140–142 Wandsworth High St, London, SW18 4JJ; tel. (20) 8875-0155; fax (20) 8875-0133; e-mail info@darton-longman-todd.co.uk; internet www.darton-longman-todd.co.uk; f. 1959; theology, spirituality, religious biography and history, Bibles; Editorial Dir BRENDAN WALSH.

David & Charles Ltd: Brunel House, Forde Close, Newton Abbot, Devon, TQ12 4PU; tel. (1626) 323200; fax (1526) 323319; e-mail postmaster@davidandcharles.co.uk; internet www.davidandcharles.co.uk; f. 1960; owned by F+W Publications, Inc. (USA); general, trade and reference; Group Chair. and CEO DAVID NUSSBAUM.

André Deutsch Ltd: 20 Mortimer St, London, W1T 3JW; tel. (20) 7612-0400; fax (20) 7612-0401; e-mail enquiries@carltonbooks.co.uk; internet www.carltonbooks.co.uk; f. 1950; biography, memoirs, humour, art, politics, history, travel, sport; imprint of Carlton Books.

Dorling Kindersley PLC: 80 Strand, London, WC2R 0RL; tel. (20) 7010-3000; fax (20) 7010-6060; e-mail customerservice@dk.com; internet www.dorlingkindersley-uk.co.uk; f. 1974; holding co Pearson PLC; illustrated reference books; CEO PETER FIELD.

Gerald Duckworth and Co Ltd: 1st Floor, East Wing, Greenhill House, 90–93 Cowcross St, London, EC1M 6BF; tel. (20) 7490-7300; fax (20) 7490-0080; e-mail info@duckworth-publishers.co.uk; internet www.ducknet.co.uk; f. 1898; trade, academic; Propr PETER MAYER.

Edinburgh University Press: 22 George Sq., Edinburgh, EH8 9LF; tel. (131) 650-4218; fax (131) 650-3286; e-mail editorial@eup.ed.ac.uk; internet www.euppublishing.com; learned books and journals; Chair. IVON ASQUITH; Chief Exec. TIMOTHY WRIGHT.

Edward Elgar Publishing Ltd: The Lypiatts, 15 Lansdown Rd, Cheltenham, GL50 2JA; tel. (1242) 226934; fax (1242) 262111; e-mail info@e-elgar.com; internet www.e-elgar.com; f. 1986; economics, law, business and management, public and social policy; Man. Dir E. ELGAR.

Elsevier Ltd: The Boulevard, Langford Lane, Kidlington, Oxford, OX5 1GB; tel. (1865) 843000; fax (1865) 843010; internet www.elsevier.com; f. 1958; academic and professional reference books; imprints: Academic Press, Architectural Press, Bailliere Tindall, Butterworth-Heinemann, Churchill Livingstone, Digital Press, Elsevier, Elsevier Advanced Technology, Focal Press, Gulf Professional, Made Simple Books, Morgan Kaufmann, Mosby, Newnes, North-Holland, Pergamon, Saunders; part of Reed Elsevier Group PLC; Man. Dir ANNA MOON.

Encyclopaedia Britannica UK Ltd: 2nd Floor, Unity Wharf, Mill St, London, SE1 2BH; tel. (20) 7500-7800; fax (20) 7500-7878; e-mail enquiries@britannica.co.uk; internet www.britannica.co.uk; f. 1768; publs Encyclopaedia Britannica, Britannica Book of the Year, Great Books of the Western World, Britannica Learning Library, Britannica Almanac; Man. Dir IAN GRANT.

Euromonitor International: 60–61 Britton St, London, EC1M 5UX; tel. (20) 7251-8024; fax (20) 7608-3149; e-mail info@euromonitor.com; internet www.euromonitor.com; f. 1972; business and commercial reference; Chair. R. N. SENIOR; Man. Dir T. J. FENWICK.

Evans Publishing Group: 2A Portman Mansions, Chiltern St, London, W1U 6NR; tel. (20) 7487-0920; fax (20) 7487-0921; e-mail sales@evansbrothers.co.uk; internet www.evansbooks.co.uk; f. 1906; educational, children's, general and overseas books; Man. Dir BRIAN JONES; Publr SU SWALLOW.

Everyman's Library: Northburgh House, 10 Northburgh St, London, EC1V 0AT; tel. (20) 7566-6350; fax (20) 7490-3708; e-mail books@everyman.uk.com; internet www.randomhouse.com/knopf/classics; f. 1906; publ. in United Kingdom by The Random House Group Ltd.

Faber and Faber Ltd: Bloomsbury House, 74–77 Great Russell St, London, WC1B 3DA; tel. (20) 7927-3800; fax (20) 7927-3801; internet www.faber.co.uk; f. 1929; biography, autobiography, children's, film, drama, popular science, economics, fiction, history, music, poetry; mem. of Independent Alliance; Man. Dir STEPHEN PAGE.

The Folio Society Ltd: 44 Eagle St, London, WC1R 4FS; tel. (20) 7400-4200; fax (20) 7400-4242; internet www.foliosociety.com; f. 1947; fine illustrated editions of children's, fiction, food, gardening, history, biographies, poetry and travel books; Publishing Dir DAVID HAYDEN.

Footprint Handbooks Ltd: 6 Riverside Court, Lower Bristol Rd, Bath, BA2 3DZ; tel. (1225) 469141; fax (1225) 469461; e-mail discover@footprintbooks.com; internet www.footprintbooks.com; Publr ALAN MURPHY; Dirs ANDY RIDDLE, PATRICK DAWSON.

W. Foulsham & Co Ltd: The Oriel, Capital Point, 33 Bath Rd, Slough SL1 3UF; tel. (1753) 526769; fax (1753) 535003; e-mail reception@foulsham.com; internet www.foulsham.com; f. 1819; finance, reference; Man. Dir BARRY BELASCO.

Fourth Estate: 77–85 Fulham Palace Rd, London, W6 8JB; tel. (20) 8741-7070; fax (20) 8307-4440; e-mail general@4thestate.co.uk; internet www.4thestate.co.uk; f. 1984; literature, humour, general reference, current affairs, literary and commercial fiction, cookery; imprint of HarperCollins Publishers; Pub. Dir NICHOLAS PEARSON.

Samuel French Ltd: 52 Fitzroy St, London, W1T 5JR; tel. (20) 7387-9373; fax (20) 7387-2161; e-mail theatre@samuelfrench-london.co.uk; internet www.samuelfrench-london.co.uk; f. 1830; drama; Chair. (vacant); Man. Dir VIVIEN GOODWIN.

Granta Books: 12 Addison Ave, London, W11 4QR; tel. (20) 7605-1360; fax (20) 7605-1361; e-mail publicity@granta.com; internet www.granta.com; fiction, political non-fiction; mem. of Independent Alliance; Publr SIGRID RAUSING.

Gresham Books Ltd: 19–21 Sayers Lane, Tenterden, Kent, TN30 6BW; tel. (1580) 767596; fax (1580) 764142; e-mail info@gresham-books.co.uk; internet www.gresham-books.co.uk; f. 1978; hymn books, school histories, music folders; Chief Exec. NICHOLAS OULTON.

Guinness World Records Ltd: 184-192 Drummond St, 3rd Floor, London, NW1 3HP; tel. (20) 7891-4567; fax (20) 7891-4501; internet www.guinnessworldrecords.com; f. 1954; acquired by Jim Pattison Group in 2008; music and general interest; Man. Dir ALISTAIR RICHARDS.

Hachette UK: 338 Euston Rd, London, NW1 3BH; tel. (20) 7873-6000; fax (20) 7873-6124; internet www.hachette.co.uk; f. 1993 as Hodder Headline; acquired by Hachette Livre (France) in 2004; present name adopted 2008; divisions: Hodder Education, John Murray Ltd, Headline Publishing Group, Hodder and Stoughton Ltd, Hachette Children's Books, Orion, Octopus Publishing Group, Little, Brown Book Group, Chambers Harrap; Group Chief Exec. TIM HELY HUTCHINSON.

Robert Hale Ltd: Clerkenwell House, 45–47 Clerkenwell Green, London, EC1R 0HT; tel. (20) 7251-2661; fax (20) 7490-4958; e-mail enquire@halebooks.com; internet www.halebooks.com; f. 1936; memoirs, biography, travel, sport, fiction, belles-lettres, general non-fiction; Man. Dir JOHN HALE.

Hamlyn: Endeavour House, 189 Shaftesbury Ave, London WC2H 8JY; tel. (20) 7632-5400; fax (20) 7531-8650; e-mail info@octopus-publishing.co.uk; internet www.hamlyn.co.uk; imprint of Octopus Publishing Group Ltd; cookery, DIY, gardening, sports, health, animals; Man. Dir DAVID INMAN.

Harlequin Mills and Boon Ltd: Eton House, 18–24 Paradise Rd, Richmond, Surrey, TW9 1SR; tel. (20) 8288-2800; fax (20) 8288-2899; internet www.millsandboon.co.uk; f. 1908; romantic fiction; Man. Dir MANDY FERGUSON.

HarperCollins Publishers Ltd: 77–85 Fulham Palace Rd, London, W6 8JB; tel. (20) 8307-4000; fax (20) 8307-4440; e-mail contact@harpercollins.co.uk; internet www.harpercollins.co.uk; f. 1819; owned by News International; fiction and non-fiction of all classes, including biographies, history, travel, nature, sport, art, children's, classics, atlases, reference, religion; imprints: Armada, Bartholomew, Collins, Collins Bibles, Collins Cartographic, Collins Classics, Collins Crime, Collins English Dictionaries, Collins Liturgical, Flamingo, Fontana, HarperCollins, HarperCollins Audio, HarperCollins Paperbacks, HarperCollins Science Fiction and Fantasy, Jets, Lions, Marshall Pickering, Nicholson, Times Books, Tolkien, Tracks, Young Lions; CEO and Publr VICTORIA BARNSLEY.

Harvill Secker: The Random House Group Ltd, 20 Vauxhall Bridge Rd, London, SW1V 2SA; tel. (20) 7840-8540; fax (20) 7233-6117; e-mail enquiries@randomhouse.co.uk; internet www.randomhouse.co.uk/harvillsecker; fiction, non-fiction, illustrated books; imprint of The Random House Group Ltd.

Haynes Publishing: Sparkford, Yeovil, Somerset, BA22 7JJ; tel. (1963) 440635; fax (1963) 440001; e-mail sales@haynes.co.uk; internet www.haynes.co.uk; f. 1960; transport, manuals etc.; Chair. J. H. C. HAYNES; CEO E. OAKLEY.

Headline Publishing Group: 338 Euston Rd, London, NW1 3BH; tel. (20) 7873-6000; fax (20) 7873-6124; e-mail enquiries@headline.co.uk; internet www.headline.co.uk; f. 1986; division of Hachette UK; fiction, autobiography, biography, food and wine, gardening, popular science, sport and TV tie-ins; Man. Dir JANE MORPETH; CEO KATE WILSON.

Heinemann: Halley Court, Jordan Hill, Oxford, OX2 8EJ; tel. (1865) 311366; fax (1865) 310043; e-mail enquiries@pearson.com; internet www.heinemann.co.uk; imprint of Pearson Education; educational textbooks for UK and abroad; Man. Dir JOHN FALLON.

William Heinemann: Random House, 20 Vauxhall Bridge Rd, London, SW1V 2SA; tel. (20) 7840-8707; fax (20) 7233-6127; e-mail enquiries@randomhouse.co.uk; internet www.randomhouse.co.uk; arts, biography, fiction, history, science, travel; imprint of The Random House Group Ltd.

Hodder Education: 338 Euston Rd, London, NW1 3BH; tel. (20) 7873-6000; fax (20) 7873-6299; e-mail educationenquiries@hodder.co.uk; internet www.hoddereducation.co.uk; f. 1906; imprints: Hodder Arnold, Hodder Gibson, Hodder Murray and Teach Yourself; division of Hachette UK; Chief Exec. THOMAS WEBSTER.

Hodder and Stoughton: 338 Euston Rd, London, NW1 3BH; tel. (20) 7873-6000; fax (20) 7873-6024; e-mail websiteadministrator@hodder.co.uk; internet www.hodder.co.uk; f. 1868; division of Hachette UK; imprints: Mobius, Sceptre; general, biography, travel, fiction, current affairs; Man. Dir JAMIE HODDER-WILLIAMS.

Icon Books Ltd: Omnibus Business Centre, 39–41 North Rd, London, N7 9DP; tel. (20) 7697-9695; fax (20) 7697-9501; e-mail info@iconbooks.co.uk; internet www.iconbooks.co.uk; f. 1991; non-fiction; mem. of Independent Alliance; Man. Dir SIMON FLYNN.

Informa PLC: Informa House, 30–32 Mortimer St, London, W1W 7RE; tel. (20) 7017-5000; internet www.informa.com; journals and books; commercial, professional, academic and scientific, reference; Chair. DEREK MAPP; Chief Exec. PETER RIGBY.

IOP Publishing: Dirac House, Temple Back, Bristol, BS1 6BE; tel. (117) 929-7481; fax (117) 929-4318; e-mail custserv@iop.org; internet publishing.iop.org; f. 1874; scientific and technical publishers; Man. Dir STEVEN HALL.

Jane's Information Group Ltd: Sentinel House, 163 Brighton Rd, Coulsdon, Surrey, CR5 2YH; tel. (20) 8700-3700; fax (20) 8763-1006; e-mail info.uk@janes.com; internet www.janes.com; owned by IHS, Inc (USA); intelligence and analysis on national and international defence, security and risk developments; Pres. and COO SCOTT KEY.

Jordan Publishing Ltd: 21 St Thomas St, Bristol, BS1 6JS; tel. (117) 923-0600; fax (117) 923-0486; e-mail achim.bosse@jordanpublishing.co.uk; internet www.jordanpublishing.co.uk; f. 1863; practical law books covering family law, litigation, company, property and private client law; Man. Dir CAROLINE VANDRIDGE-AMES.

Michael Joseph Ltd: 80 Strand, London, WC2R 0RL; tel. (20) 7010-3000; fax (20) 7010-6060; internet www.penguin.co.uk; f. 1936; general, fiction, non-fiction; division of Penguin; Publishing Dir LOUISE MOORE.

Richard Joseph Publishers Ltd: POB 15, Torrington, EX38 8ZJ; tel. (1805) 625750; fax (1805) 625376; e-mail info@sheppardsconfidential.com; internet www.sheppardsconfidential.com; f. 1990; reference and directories; publishes the weekly journal *Sheppard's Confidential*; Man. Dir RICHARD JOSEPH.

Kenyon-Deane: 10 Station Rd, Industrial Estate, Malvern, Worcs., WR13 6RN; tel. and fax (1684) 540154; e-mail simon@cressrelles.co.uk; internet www.cressrelles.co.uk; f. 1971; owned by Cressrelles Publishing Company Ltd; incorporates Kenyon House Press, H. F. W. Deane Ltd; plays and drama textbooks, specialists in all-women plays and plays for young people; Man. Dir LESLIE SMITH.

Kingfisher Publications PLC: New Penderel House, 283–288 High Holborn, London, WC1V 7HZ; tel. (20) 7903-9999; fax (20) 7242-4979; e-mail sales@kingfisherpub.com; internet www.kingfisherpub.com; children's books; imprints: Kingfisher; owned by Pan Macmillan Ltd; Man. Dir JOHN PICKETT.

Kogan Page Ltd: 120 Pentonville Rd, London, N1 9JN; tel. (20) 7278-0433; fax (20) 7837-6348; e-mail kpinfo@koganpage.com; internet www.koganpage.co.uk; f. 1967; business, management, accountancy, textbooks, transport, careers, personal development, training, marketing, consumer, reference; Man. Dir HELEN KOGAN.

Lawrence and Wishart Ltd: 99A Wallis Rd, London, E9 5LN; tel. (20) 8533-2506; fax (20) 8533-7369; e-mail info@lwbooks.co.uk; internet www.lwbooks.co.uk; f. 1936; politics, history, feminism, race, economics, Marxist theory, cultural studies; Man. Editor SALLY DAVISON.

Letts and Lonsdale: Letts and Lonsdale, HarperCollins Publrs Ltd, Westerhill Rd, Bishopbriggs, Glasgow, G64 2QT; tel. (844) 576-

8126; fax (844) 576-8131; e-mail education@harpercollins.co.uk; internet www.lettsandlonsdale.com; a division of HarperCollins Ltd; children's, educational, textbooks; Man. Dir ANDREW WARE.

LexisNexis Butterworths: Halsbury House, 35 Chancery Lane, London, WC2A 1EL; tel. (20) 7400-2500; fax (20) 7400-2842; internet www.lexisnexis.co.uk; f. 1818; part of Reed Elsevier PLC; law, tax, accountancy, banking books and journals; Group Man. Dir CHRISTIAN FLECK.

Frances Lincoln: 4 Torriano Mews, Torriano Ave, London, NW5 2RZ; tel. (20) 7485-0409; fax (20) 7485-0490; e-mail reception@frances-lincoln.com; internet www.franceslincoln.com; f. 1977; illustrated non-fiction, children's fiction and non-fiction; Man. Dir JOHN NICOLL.

Little, Brown Book Group UK: 100 Victoria Embankment, London, EC4Y 0DY; tel. (20) 7911-8000; fax (20) 7911-8100; e-mail info@littlebrown.co.uk; internet www.littlebrown.co.uk; imprints: Abacus, Virago, Sphere, Orbit, Little Brown, Piatkus, Atom; division of Hachette UK; CEO and Publr URSULA MACKENZIE.

Liverpool University Press: 4 Cambridge St, Liverpool, L69 7ZU; tel. (151) 794-2233; fax (151) 794-2235; e-mail lup@liv.ac.uk; internet www.liverpool-unipress.co.uk; f. 1899; European and American literature, social, political, economic and natural history, planning, hispanic studies, population studies, architecture, art, art history, cultural studies, science fiction criticism series; Dir ANTHONY COND.

Lonely Planet Publications: 2nd Floor, 186 City Rd, London, EC1V 2NT; tel. (20) 7106-2100; fax (20) 7106-2101; internet www.lonelyplanet.com; f. 1973; travel, languages; 100% stake acquired by BBC Worldwide in 2011; Publr STEPHEN PALMER.

Lund Humphries: Wey Court East, Union Rd, Farnham, Surrey, GU9 7PT; tel. (1252) 736600; fax (1252) 736736; e-mail ashgate.online@ashgate.com; internet www.lundhumphries.com; f. 1967; arts, graphic arts, design, architecture, photography, scholarly, Arabic language; Chair. NIGEL FARROW.

McGraw-Hill Education: McGraw-Hill House, Shoppenhangers Rd, Maidenhead, Berks., SL6 2QL; tel. (1628) 502500; fax (1628) 635895; e-mail helpme@mcgraw-hill.com; internet www.mcgraw-hill.co.uk; f. 1909; technical, scientific, computer studies, professional reference, general and medical books; Pres. ROBERT BAHASH.

Macmillan Education Ltd: Between Towns Rd, Oxford, OX4 3PP; tel. (1865) 405700; fax (1865) 405701; e-mail help@macmillan.com; internet www.macmillaneducation.com; a division of Macmillan Publishers Ltd; English Language Teaching and educational books; Chief Exec. SIMON ALLEN; Man. Dir SUE JONES.

Manchester University Press: Oxford Rd, Manchester, M13 9NR; tel. (161) 275-2310; fax (161) 274-3346; e-mail d.rodgers@manchester.ac.uk; internet www.manchesteruniversitypress.co.uk; f. 1904; humanities and social sciences; Chief Exec. DAVID RODGERS.

Methuen Publishing Ltd: 8 Artillery Row, London, SW1P 1RZ; tel. (20) 7802-0018; fax (20) 7828-1244; e-mail info@methuen.co.uk; internet www.methuen.co.uk; f. 1889; literature, fiction, non-fiction, biography, sport, theatre, drama, humour, music; imprint: Politico's Publishing; Man. Dir PETER TUMMONS.

Mitchell Beazley: Endeavour House, 189 Shaftesbury Ave, London WC2H 8JY; tel. (20) 632-5400; fax (20) 7531-8650; e-mail info@mitchell-beazley.co.uk; internet www.mitchell-beazley.co.uk; f. 1969; imprint of Octopus Publishing Group Ltd; Miller's antiques, arts and design, interiors and style, gardening, reference, wine and food; Publr DAVID LAMB.

John Murray Publishers: 338 Euston Rd, London, NW1 3BH; tel. (20) 7873-6000; fax (20) 7873-6446; internet www.hachette.co.uk; f. 1768; division of Hachette UK; biography, autobiography, memoir, history, travel, fiction, current affairs; Man. Dir ROLAND PHILIPPS.

Nelson Thornes Ltd: Delta Pl., 27 Bath Rd, Cheltenham, GL53 7TH; tel. (1242) 267287; fax (1242) 253695; e-mail csupport@nelsonthornes.com; internet www.nelsonthornes.com; educational; Man. Dir PAUL HOWARTH.

Novello and Co Ltd: 14–15 Berners St, London, W1T 3LJ; tel. (20) 7612-7400; fax (20) 7612-7545; e-mail promotion@musicsales.co.uk; internet www.chesternovello.com; music; Man. Dir JAMES RUSHTON.

Octopus Publishing Group Ltd: Endeavour House, 189 Shaftesbury Ave, London WC2H 8JY; tel. (20) 632-5400; fax (20) 7531-8650; e-mail info@octopus-publishing.co.uk; internet www.octopus-publishing.co.uk; division of Hachette UK; imprints: Bounty, Cassell Illustrated, Conran Octopus, Gaia Books, Godsfield Press, Hamlyn, Miller's, Mitchell Beazley, Philip's, Spruce; Chief Exec. ALISON GOFF.

Open University Press, McGraw-Hill Education: Shoppenhangers Rd, Maidenhead, Berkshire, SL6 2QL; tel. (1628) 502500; fax (1628) 635895; e-mail enquiries@openup.co.uk; internet www.openup.co.uk; academic, study skills, politics, sociology, psychology, education, higher education, media, film and cultural studies, health and social welfare, counselling and psychotherapy, management and public policy; Man. Dir SHONA MULLEN.

Orion Publishing Group: Orion House, 5 Upper St Martin's Lane, London, WC2H 9EA; tel. (20) 7240-3444; fax (20) 7240-4822; e-mail info@orionbooks.co.uk; internet www.orionbooks.co.uk; f. 1991; division of Hachette UK; imprints: Gollancz, Orion, Orion Children's, Phoenix, Weidenfeld & Nicolson; CEO PETER ROCHE.

Peter Owen Publishers: 20 Holland Park Ave, London W11 3QU; tel. (20) 7373-5628; fax (20) 7221-0931; e-mail admin@peterowen.com; internet www.peterowen.com; f. 1951; general publishers of fiction, autobiography, biography, translations, history, the arts, etc.; Man. Dir PETER OWEN; Editorial Dir ANTONIA OWEN.

Oxford University Press: Great Clarendon St, Oxford, OX2 6DP; tel. (1865) 556767; fax (1865) 556646; e-mail webenquiry.uk@oup.com; internet www.oup.com; f. c. 1478; Bibles, prayer books, the *Oxford English Dictionary*, the *Oxford Dictionary of National Biography* and many other dictionaries and books of reference, learned and general works from the humanities to the sciences, educational, electronic, music and children's books and audio-visual and English language teaching material; Sec. to the Delegates of the Press and Chief Exec. NIGEL PORTWOOD.

Palgrave Macmillan Ltd: Houndmills, Basingstoke, Hants., RG21 6XS; tel. (1256) 329242; fax (1256) 479476; e-mail palgrave@palgrave.com; internet www.palgrave.com; academic, professional, textbooks and journals; Man. Dir DOMINIC KNIGHT.

Pan Macmillan Ltd: 20 New Wharf Rd, London, N1 9RR; tel. (20) 7014-6000; fax (20) 7014-6001; e-mail sales@macmillan.co.uk; internet www.panmacmillan.com; fiction and non-fiction, children's, general reference; imprints: Macmillan, Pan, Picador, Sidgwick & Jackson, Boxtree, Tor, Macmillan Children's Books, Campbell Books, Young Picador, Rodale; Man. Dir ANTHONY FORBES WATSON.

Pearson Education Ltd: Edinburgh Gate, Harlow, Essex, CM20 2JE; tel. (1279) 623623; fax (870) 850-5255; e-mail enquiries@pearson.com; internet www.pearsoned.co.uk; Propr Pearson PLC; acquired Harcourt Education International in 2007; imprints include: Ginn, Heinemann, Longman, Payne-Gallway, Prentice Hall, Raintree, Rigby and Scott Prentice; CEO JOHN FALLON.

Pearson Publishing Group: Pearson Publishing Group, Chesterton Mill, French's Rd, Cambridge, CB4 3NP; tel. (1223) 350555; fax (1223) 356484; e-mail info@pearson.co.uk; internet www.pearson.co.uk; f. 1991; Chair. GEORGE PEARSON.

Penguin Books Ltd: 80 The Strand, London, WC2R 0RL; tel. (20) 7010-3000; fax (20) 7416-3099; e-mail editor@penguin.co.uk; internet www.penguin.co.uk; f. 1936; holding co Pearson PLC; paperback imprints: Penguin and Puffin; reprints and original works of fiction and non-fiction including travel, biography, science and social studies, reference books, handbooks, plays, poetry, classics and children's books; Penguin Group UK is made up of Penguin Press (Allen Lane, Reference, Penguin Classics and Penguin Modern Classics), Penguin General (imprints: Viking, Hamish Hamilton, Fig Tree and Penguin Ireland), Michael Joseph and the children's division (imprints: Puffin, Ladybird, Frederick Warne and BBC Children); Chair. and Chief Exec. JOHN MAKINSON; CEO (UK) TOM WELDON.

Phaidon Press Ltd: Regent's Wharf, All Saints St, London, N1 9PA; tel. (20) 7843-1000; fax (20) 7843-1010; e-mail enquiries@phaidon.com; internet www.phaidon.com; art, architecture, children's, contemporary culture, cookery, design, decorative arts, fashion, photography and music, film, fine art; Chair. RICHARD SCHLAGMAN.

Philip's: 2–4 Heron Quays, London, E14 4JP; tel. (20) 7644-6940; fax (20) 7644-8464; e-mail philips@philips-maps.co.uk; internet www.philips-maps.co.uk; imprint of Octopus Publishing Group Ltd; maps, atlases, astronomy, encyclopaedias; Man. Dir JOHN GAISFORD.

Pluto Press: 345 Archway Rd, London, N6 5AA; tel. (20) 8348-2724; fax (20) 8348-9133; e-mail pluto@plutobooks.com; internet www.plutobooks.com; academic, scholarly, and current affairs; Chair. ROGER VAN ZWANENBERG; Man. Dir ANNE BEECH.

Profile Books Ltd: 3A Exmouth House, Pine St, Exmouth Market, London, EC1R 0JH; tel. (20) 7841-6300; fax (20) 7833-3969; e-mail info@profilebooks.co.uk; internet www.profilebooks.com; f. 1996; fiction, non-fiction; imprints: Economist Books, GreenProfile, Profile Business, Serpent's Tail; mem. of Independent Alliance; Man. Dir ANDREW FRANKLIN.

ProQuest Information and Learning: The Quorum, Barnwell Rd, Cambridge, CB5 8SW; tel. (1223) 215512; fax (1223) 215514; e-mail marketing@proquest.co.uk; internet www.proquest.com; f. 1973 as Chadwyck-Healey Ltd; changed name as above in 2001; academic; CEO MARTY KAHN.

Quercus Publishing PLC: 21 Bloomsbury Sq., London, WC1A 2NS; tel. (20) 7291-7200; e-mail richard.arcus@quercusbooks.co.uk; internet www.quercusbooks.co.uk; f. 2004; fiction, non-fiction; mem. of Independent Alliance; CEO MARK EVANS.

THE UNITED KINGDOM

The Random House Group Ltd: Random House, 20 Vauxhall Bridge Rd, London, SW1V 2SA; tel. (20) 7840-8400; fax (20) 7840-8778; e-mail enquiries@randomhouse.co.uk; internet www.randomhouse.co.uk; imprints: Arrow, Jonathan Cape, Cedar, Century, Chatto & Windus, Ebury Press, Everyman, Harvill Secker, William Heinemann, Hutchinson, Mainstream, Pimlico, Random House Children's Books, Rider, Vermilion, Vintage, Yellow Jersey; Chair. and CEO MARKUS DOHLE.

Reader's Digest Association Ltd: 157 Edgware Rd, London, W2 2HR; tel. (20) 7053-4500; internet www.readersdigest.co.uk; various non-fiction, condensed and series fiction; Chair. RANDALL CURAN; CEO TOM WILLIAMS.

Reed Business Information: Quadrant House, The Quadrant, Sutton, Surrey, SM2 5AS; tel. (20) 8652-3500; fax (20) 8652-8932; e-mail rbi.subscriptions@qss-uk.com; internet www.reedbusiness.co.uk; f. 1866; business directories and online services; CEO MARK KELSEY.

Reed Elsevier Group PLC: 1–3 Strand, London, WC2N 5JR; tel. (20) 7930-7077; fax (20) 7166-5799; e-mail london@reedelsevier.com; internet www.reedelsevier.com; f. 1992; books, journals, magazines and electronic resources; divisions: science and medical, education, legal and business; Chair. ANTHONY HABGOOD; CEO ERIK ENGSTROM.

Routledge: 2 Park Sq., Milton Park, Abingdon, Oxfordshire, OX14 4RN; tel. (20) 7017-6000; fax (20) 7017-6699; e-mail webmaster.books@tandf.co.uk; internet www.routledge.com; f. 1988; imprint of Taylor and Francis Group; professional, academic, reference; Man. Dir JEREMY NORTH.

SAGE Publications Ltd: 1 Oliver's Yard, 55 City Rd, London, EC1Y 1SP; tel. (20) 7324-8500; fax (20) 7324-8600; e-mail info@sagepub.co.uk; internet www.sagepub.co.uk; f. 1971; academic and professional social sciences, sciences and humanities; imprint: Sage Education; Pres. STEPHEN BARR.

Schofield and Sims Ltd: Dogley Mill, Penistone Rd, Fenay Bridge, Huddersfield, West Yorks., HD8 0NQ; tel. (1484) 607080; fax (1484) 606815; e-mail post@schofieldandsims.co.uk; internet www.schofieldandsims.co.uk; f. 1901; educational; Chair. NICK PLATTS.

Scholastic Ltd: Villiers House, Clarendon Ave, Leamington Spa, Warwickshire, CV32 5PR; tel. (1926) 887799; fax (1926) 883331; e-mail enquiries@scholastic.co.uk; internet www.scholastic.co.uk; f. 1964; direct marketing, educational and children's books; Group Man. Dir ALAN HURCOMBE.

SCM-Canterbury Press Ltd: 13–17 Long Lane, London, EC1A 9PN; tel. (1603) 785925; fax (1603) 785915; e-mail admin@norwichbooksandmusic.co.uk; internet www.canterburypress.co.uk; f. 1929; imprint of Hymns Ancient and Modern Ltd; religious, theological; Group CEO DOMINIC VAUGHAN.

Scripture Union: 207–209 Queensway, Bletchley, Milton Keynes, Bucks, MK2 2EB; tel. (1908) 856000; fax (1908) 856111; e-mail info@scriptureunion.org.uk; internet www.scriptureunion.org.uk; f. 1867; Christian education and Bible reading guides; Nat. Dir Rev. TIM HASTIE-SMITH.

Short Books: 3A Exmouth House, Pine St, London, EC1R 0JH; tel. (20) 7833-9429; e-mail info@shortbooks.co.uk; internet www.shortbooks.co.uk; f. 2001; biography, fiction, non-fiction; mem. of Independent Alliance; Man. Dirs REBECCA NICOLSON, AUREA CARPENTER.

Simon and Schuster: 1st Floor, 222 Gray's Inn Rd, London, WC1X 8HB; tel. (20) 7316-1900; fax (20) 7316-0332; e-mail enquiries@simonandschuster.co.uk; internet www.simonandschuster.co.uk; f. 1986; owned by CBS Corpn (USA); fiction, non-fiction, music, travel; imprints: Pocket Books, Touchstone, Scribner, Free Press; Man. Dir IAN S. CHAPMAN.

Society for Promoting Christian Knowledge: 36 Causton St, London, SW1P 4ST; tel. (20) 7592-3900; fax (20) 7592-3939; e-mail spck@spck.org.uk; internet www.spck.org.uk; f. 1698; religious; imprints: SPCK, Azure, Sheldon Press; Publishing Dir JOANNA MORIARTY.

Souvenir Press Ltd: 43 Great Russell St, London, WC1B 3PD; tel. (20) 7580-9307; fax (20) 7580-5064; e-mail souvenirpress@ukonline.co.uk; general; Man. Dir ERNEST HECHT.

The Stationery Office: St Crispins, Duke St, Norwich, NR3 1PD; tel. (1603) 622211; e-mail customer.services@tso.co.uk; internet www.tso.co.uk; f. 1786 as His Majesty's Stationery Office (govt publishing house); privatized in 1996; acquired by Williams Lea in 2007; business and publishing services; publishes *Hansard*, *Highway Code*, *British Pharmacopoeia*; Chief Exec. RICHARD DELL.

Sweet and Maxwell Ltd: 100 Avenue Rd, London, NW3 3PF; tel. (20) 7393-7000; fax (20) 7393-7010; e-mail customer.services@sweetandmaxwell.co.uk; internet www.sweetandmaxwell.co.uk; f. 1799; imprints: Stevens and Sons Ltd, W. Green, Round Hall, ESC Publishing, the European Law Centre; holding co Thomson Reuters; law books; Pres. MARK SCHLAGETER.

Directory

Taylor and Francis Group Ltd: 2 Park Sq., Milton Park, Abingdon, Oxfordshire, OX14 4RN; tel. (20) 7017-6000; fax (20) 7017-6699; e-mail info@tandf.co.uk; internet www.taylorandfrancisgroup.com; division of Informa PLC; imprints: Taylor and Francis, Routledge, Garland Science, CRC Press and Psychology Press; professional, academic, scientific, technical, reference; books and journals; Chief Exec. ROGER HORTON.

Thames and Hudson Ltd: 181A High Holborn, London, WC1V 7QX; tel. (20) 7845-5000; fax (20) 7845-5050; e-mail sales@thamesandhudson.co.uk; internet www.thamesandhudson.com; f. 1949; art, archaeology, history, etc.; Chair. THOMAS NEURATH; Man. Dir JAMIE CAMPLIN.

Thomson Reuters: The Thomson Reuters Bldg, South Colonnade, Canary Wharf, London, E14 5EP; tel. (20) 7250-1122; e-mail general.info@thomsonreuters.com; internet thomsonreuters.com; f. 2008 by merger of Thomson Corpn and Reuters Group PLC (f. 1865); legal, financial; also owns Reuters news agency; Chair. DAVID THOMSON; CEO THOMAS H. GLOCER.

Transworld Publishers Ltd: 61–63 Uxbridge Rd, London, W5 5SA; tel. (20) 8579-2652; fax (20) 8579-5479; e-mail info@transworld-publishers.co.uk; internet www.booksattransworld.co.uk; imprints: Corgi, Bantam Books, Black Swan, Bantam Press, Doubleday, Expert Books, Eden Project Books, Channel 4 Books; all types of fiction and non-fiction; division of The Random House Group Ltd; Publishing Dir SELINA WALKER.

University of Wales Press: 10 Columbus Walk, Brigantine Pl., Cardiff, CF10 4UP; tel. (29) 2049-6899; fax (29) 2049-6108; e-mail press@press.wales.ac.uk; internet www.uwp.co.uk; f. 1922; academic and educational (Welsh and English); Dir HELGARD KRAUSE.

Usborne Publishing: Usborne House, 83–85 Saffron Hill, London, EC1N 8RT; tel. (20) 7430-2800; fax (20) 7430-1562; e-mail mail@usbornebooksathome.co.uk; internet www.usborne.com; f. 1973; educational and children's publishing; Man. Dir T. P. USBORNE.

Virgin Books: 20 Vauxhall Bridge Rd, London, SW1V 2SA; tel. (20) 7840-8400; e-mail editorial@virgin-books.co.uk; internet www.virginbooks.com; 90% owned by The Random House Group Ltd; general, popular culture, film, music, humour, biography, fiction, non-fiction, erotica; imprints: Virgin, Black Lace and Nexus; Chair. RICHARD CABLE.

Frederick Warne (Publishers) Ltd: 80 Strand, London, WC2R 0RL; tel. (20) 7010-3000; fax (20) 7010-6707; e-mail peterrabbit@uk.penguingroup.com; internet www.peterrabbit.com; f. 1865; a division of Penguin Books since 1983; classic illustrated children's books (including Beatrix Potter); Man. Dir STEPHANIE BARTON.

Wiley-Blackwell: 9600 Garsington Rd, Oxford, OX4 2DQ; tel. (1865) 776868; fax (1865) 714591; e-mail customer@wiley.co.uk; internet www.wiley.com; f. 2001 as Blackwell Publishing Ltd, by merger of Blackwell Publishing and Blackwell Science; acquired by John Wiley & Sons, Inc. (USA) in 2007; academic, professional, business, medical and science books and journals; Pres. and CEO WILLIAM J. PESCE.

The Women's Press: 27 Goodge St, London, W1T 2LD; tel. (20) 7636-3992; fax (20) 7637-1866; e-mail david@the-womens-press.com; internet www.the-womens-press.com; f. 1978; feminist; Man. Dir CHARLOTTE GASCOIGNE.

Yale University Press: 47 Bedford Sq., London, WC1B 3DP; tel. (20) 7079-4900; fax (20) 7079-4901; e-mail sales@yaleup.co.uk; internet www.yalebooks.co.uk; f. 1973; the only US university press to operate a separate publishing co in Europe; Man. Dir ROBERT BALDOCK.

Zed Books Ltd: 7 Cynthia St, London, N1 9JF; tel. (20) 7837-0384; fax (20) 7833-3960; e-mail editorial@zedbooks.net; internet www.zedbooks.co.uk; f. 1977; academic, current affairs; Editor TAMSINE O'RIORDAN.

PUBLISHERS' ORGANIZATIONS

Booktrust: Book House, 45 East Hill, London, SW18 2QZ; tel. (20) 8516-2977; fax (20) 8516-2978; e-mail query@booktrust.org.uk; internet www.booktrust.org.uk; non-profit-making organization funded by voluntary donations and membership fees; f. 1945; originally f. 1925 as The National Book Council to extend the use and enjoyment of books; renamed Book Trust 1986; publishes annotated book lists; postal book information service; administers book prizes, including the Orange Prize for Fiction and the John Llewellyn Rhys Prize; runs www.booktrusted.com, a website dedicated to children's books; Chair. SUE HORNER; Exec. Dir VIV BIRD.

The Publishers' Association: 29B Montague St, London, WC1B 5BW; tel. (20) 7691-9191; fax (20) 7691-9199; e-mail mail@publishers.org.uk; internet www.publishers.org.uk; f. 1896; represents book, journal and electronic publishers in the UK and seeks to promote the sales of British books; Pres. VICTORIA BARNSLEY; Chief Exec. RICHARD MOLLET; 127 mems.

THE UNITED KINGDOM

Publishing Scotland: Scottish Book Centre, 137 Dundee St, Edinburgh, EH11 1BG; tel. (131) 228-6866; fax (131) 228-3220; e-mail enquiries@publishingscotland.org; internet www.publishingscotland.co.uk; f. 1973 as Scottish Publishers' Assen; present name adopted 2007; assists member publishers in the promotion and marketing of their books; offers export services, seminars, events and training; Chair. CAROLINE GORHAM; Chief Exec. MARION SINCLAIR.

Broadcasting and Communications

REGULATORY AUTHORITY

Office of Communications (Ofcom): Riverside House, 2A Southwark Bridge Rd, London, SE1 9HA; tel. (20) 7981-3000; fax (20) 7981-3333; e-mail contact@ofcom.org.uk; internet www.ofcom.org.uk; f. 2003 to replace the Office of Telecommunications, the Broadcasting Standards Commission, the Radio Authority, the Radiocommunications Agency and the Independent Television Commission; the independent regulator for the British communications industries, with responsibilities across television, radio, telecommunications and wireless communications services; promotes choice, quality and value in electronic communications services, where appropriate, by encouraging competition between the providers of those services; ensures the most efficient use of the radiocommunications spectrum (the airwaves used for the transmission of all non-military wireless communications services); ensures that a wide range of electronic communications services, including broadband, is available across the United Kingdom; ensures that a wide range of television and radio programmes of high quality and wide appeal are broadcast; maintains plurality in the media by ensuring a sufficiently broad range of ownership; protects audiences against offensive or harmful material, unfairness or the infringement of privacy on television and radio; Chair. COLETTE BOWE; Chief Exec. ED RICHARDS.

TELECOMMUNICATIONS

Arqiva Ltd: Crawley Court, Winchester, Hampshire, SO21 2QA; tel. (1962) 823434; internet www.arqiva.com; f. 2005; Chair. PETER SHORE; CEO JOHN CRESSWELL.

British Telecommunications PLC: BT Centre, 81 Newgate St, London, EC1A 7AJ; tel. (20) 7356-5000; fax (20) 7356-6630; e-mail btgroup@bt.com; internet www.bt.com; wholly owned subsidiary of BT Group PLC; Chair. Sir MICHAEL RAKE; Chief Exec. IAN LIVINGSTON.

Cable and Wireless Communications: 26 Red Lion Sq., 3rd Floor, London, WC1R 4HQA; tel. (20) 7315-4000; internet www.cwc.com; fixed-line, mobile and broadband services; Chair. Sir RICHARD LAPTHORNE; Chief Exec. TONY RICE.

Hutchison 3G UK Ltd (3): Star House, 20 Grenfell Rd, Maidenhead, Berkshire, SL6 1EH; tel. (1628) 765000; internet www.three.co.uk; f. 2003; mobile cellular telecommunications; owned by Hutchison Whampoa Ltd (Hong Kong); CEO KEVIN RUSSELL.

KCOM Group PLC: 37 Carr Lane, Hull, HU1 3RE; tel. (1482) 602100; fax (1482) 219289; e-mail me@kcom.com; internet www.kcom.com; f. 1904; fmrly Kingston Communications; Chair. BILL HALBERT.

Orange: St James Court, Gt Park Rd, Almondsbury Park, Bradley Stoke, Bristol, BS32 4QJ; tel. (870) 376-8888; internet www.orange.co.uk; f. 1994; acquired by France Telecom in 2000; part of the Orange SA (France) group; merged with T-Mobile (UK) Ltd in July 2010 to form Everything Everywhere Ltd; Chief Exec. TOM ALEXANDER; Group Chair. DIDIER LOMBARD.

TalkTalk Telecom Group PLC: 11 Evesham St, London, W11 4AR; tel. (20) 3417-1000; fax (20) 3417-1001; internet www.talktalkgroup.com; TalkTalk demerged from Carphone Warehouse in 2010 to become TalkTalk Telecom Group PLC; acquired AOL's UK broadband business in 2007 and Tiscali UK in 2009; provides fixed-line telecommunications, digital television services and broadband internet access; markets under the TalkTalk and AOL brands to residential customers and the Opal brand to business customers; Chair. CHARLES DUNSTONE; CEO DIDO HARDING.

Telefónica O$_2$ UK: 260 Bath Rd, Slough, Berks, SL1 4DX; tel. (113) 2722000; e-mail feedback@o2.com; internet www.o2.co.uk; f. 2001 after demerging from BT Group as O$_2$; formerly BT Cellnet; acquired by Telefónica, SA (Spain) in March 2006; CEO RONAN DUNNE.

THUS: 1–2 Berkeley Sq., 99 Berkeley St, Glasgow, G3 7HR; tel. (141) 567-1234; fax (141) 566-3035; e-mail thus.enquiries@thus.net; internet www.thus.net; f. 1994 as Scottish Power Telecommunications Holdings; demerged from ScottishPower and renamed THUS Group PLC 2002; acquired by Cable and Wireless 2008; offers fixed-line telecommunications services to business customers; also internet service provider; Man. Dir STEWART SMYTHE.

T-Mobile (UK) Ltd: Hatfield Business Park, Hatfield, Herts, AL10 9BW; tel. (1707) 315000; internet www.t-mobile.co.uk; owned by Deutsche Telekom AG (Germany); fmrly One2One; merged with Orange in July 2010 to form Everything Everywhere Ltd; Man. Dir RICHARD MOAT.

Virgin Media: Media House, Bartley Wood Business Park, Bartley Way, Hook, Reading, RG27 9UP; tel. (1256) 752000; fax (1256) 752100; internet www.virginmedia.com; f. 2007 by merger of NTL Inc and Virgin Mobile; Chair. JAMES F. MOONEY; CEO NEIL BERKETT.

Vodafone Group PLC: Vodafone House, The Connection, Newbury, Berks, RG14 2FN; tel. (1635) 33251; fax (1635) 676147; internet www.vodafone.com; Chair. Sir JOHN BOND; Group Chief Exec. VITTORIO COLAO.

BROADCASTING

British Broadcasting Corporation (BBC): Broadcasting House, Portland Pl., London, W1A 1AA; tel. (20) 7580-4468; fax (20) 7637-1630; internet www.bbc.co.uk; f. 1922; operates under Royal Charter; financed by the television licence fees; governed by BBC Trust, which replaced fmr Board of Governors in 2007; Chair. of BBC Trust Lord PATTEN; Dir-Gen. MARK THOMPSON; Deputy Dir-Gen. MARK BYFORD; Dir of Vision JANA BENNETT; Dir of Audio and Music TIM DAVIE; Dir of Future Media RALPH RIVERA; Dir of Marketing, Communications and Audiences SHARON BAYLAY; Dir of BBC People LUCY ADAMS; Chief Financial Officer ZARIN PATEL; CEO of BBC Worldwide JOHN SMITH; COO CAROLINE THOMSON.

Radio

British Broadcasting Corporation

BBC Radio provides a service of five national networks throughout the United Kingdom, 40 local radio stations in England and the Channel Islands, Radio Scotland, Radio Wales, Radio Cymru, broadcasting in Welsh, and Radio Ulster and Radio Foyle (in Northern Ireland); it also offers a number of specialist digital services; Dir of Audio and Music TIM DAVIE.

Radio 1: broadcasts 24 hours a day of contemporary music programmes; Controller ANDY PARFITT.

Radio 2: broadcasts popular music and culture; Controller BOB SHENNAN.

Radio 3: provides 24-hour broadcasts of classical music, drama, talks and documentaries; Controller ROGER WRIGHT.

Radio 4: broadcasts news and current affairs and also provides a wide range of features, drama and discussions; Controller GWYNETH WILLIAMS.

Radio 5 Live: began broadcasting in March 1994, replacing Radio 5; provides a 24-hour service of news and sports programmes; also operates **5 Live Sports Extra**, a part-time digital network for sports events not broadcast elsewhere on BBC Radio; Controller ADRIAN VAN KLAVEREN.

6 Music: began broadcasting in 2002, digital station playing pop and rock music; Controller BOB SHENNAN.

1Xtra: began broadcasting in 2002; digital station playing contemporary urban music for a young audience; Controller ANDY PARFITT.

Asian Network: began broadcasting in 2002, digital station aimed at the Asian communities in the United Kingdom; Controller ANDY PARFITT.

BBC Radio 4 Extra: began broadcasting in 2002; digital radio station featuring archive material and original spoken-word programming; Controller GWYNETH WILLIAMS.

BBC World Service: Bush House, Strand, London, WC2B 4PH; tel. (20) 7240-3456; fax (20) 7557-1258; e-mail worldservice@bbc.co.uk; internet www.bbc.co.uk/worldservice; the World Service in English is broadcast for 24 hours daily and is directed to all areas of the world. In addition, there are special services to: the Far East (in Cantonese, Burmese and Thai); the Indian sub-continent (in Bengali, Sinhala, Tamil and Urdu); the Caucasus and Central Asia (in Uzbek); the Middle East and North Africa (in Arabic, Pashto, Farsi and Turkish); Europe (in Romananian); and Africa (in Arabic, English, French, Hausa, Somali and Swahili); Dir PETER HORROCKS.

Independent Radio

Absolute Radio: 1 Golden Sq., London, W1F 9DJ; tel. (20) 7434-1215; fax (20) 7434-1197; internet www.absoluteradio.co.uk; began broadcasting April 1993 as Virgin Radio; present name adopted 2008; popular music; also operates two digital stations, **Absolute Classic Rock** and **Absolute Xtreme**; Propr TIML Radio Ltd; Chief Exec. DONNACH O'DRISCOLL.

Global Radio: 30 Leicester Sq., London, WC2H 7LA; tel. (20) 7766-6000; fax (20) 7766-6111; e-mail info@thisisglobal.com; internet www.thisisglobal.com; owns and operates radio stations across the United Kingdom, incl. 95.8 Capital FM, Choice FM, Classic FM,

THE UNITED KINGDOM

Galaxy, Gold, Heart, LBC and Xfm; Chair. CHARLES ALLEN; CEO STEPHEN MIRON.

Independent Radio News (IRN): Mappin House, 4 Winsley St, London W1W 8HF; tel. (20) 7182-8591; fax (20) 7182-8594; e-mail news@irn.co.uk; internet www.irn.co.uk; f. 1973; produced by ITN Radio; news agency for the independent local radio network; Chair. TERRY SMITH; Man. Dir TIM MOLLOY.

The Local Radio Company PLC: Carn Brea Studios, Barncoose Industrial Estate, Redruth, Cornwall TR15 3RQ; tel. (1209) 310435; fax (1209) 310406; internet www.thelocalradiocompany.com; f. 2004 to purchase the entire share capital of Radio Investments Ltd; owns and operates 21 local radio licences across the United Kingdom; Chief Exec. WILLIAM ROGERS.

TalkSport UK: 18 Hatfields, London, SE1 8DJ; tel. (20) 7959-7800; fax (20) 7959-7808; internet www.talksport.net; began broadcasting February 1995 as Talk Radio UK; name changed as above January 2000; Propr UTV PLC; Man. Dir SCOTT TAUNTON.

Television

There are five principal television channels: BBC One and BBC Two, controlled by the British Broadcasting Corporation; and Channel 3 (ITV), Channel 4 and Five, operated by commercial broadcasters licensed by the Office for Communications (Ofcom). Channel 3 comprises 16 franchises allocated by a system of competitive tendering (15 on a regional basis—including one for the Channel Islands, q.v.—and one for the nation-wide breakfast-time programme), the majority of which are owned by ITV PLC. The central co-ordinating body for Channel 3 is ITV Network Ltd.

Digital television broadcasting in the United Kingdom began in 1998. In 2005 Ofcom published a timetable outlining plans for the country to switch entirely from analogue to digital television on a region-by-region basis. The transition to digital television began in 2008 and was scheduled to be completed across the whole of the United Kingdom in 2012.

British Broadcasting Corporation

BBC Television: Television Centre, Wood Lane, London, W12 7RJ; tel. (20) 8743-8000; internet www.bbc.co.uk; operates BBC One, BBC Two, BBC Three, BBC Four, CBeebies, CBBC, BBC News and BBC Parliament; Dir of Vision JANA BENNETT.

BBC One: internet www.bbc.co.uk/bbcone; Controller DANNY COHEN.

BBC Two: internet www.bbc.co.uk/bbctwo; began broadcasting in 1964; Controller JANICE HADLOW.

BBC Three: internet www.bbc.co.uk/bbcthree; launched in 2003; digital entertainment channel; Controller ZAI BENNETT.

BBC Four: internet www.bbc.co.uk/bbcfour; digital channel showing in-depth cultural programmes, dramas, documentaries, current affairs, etc.; Controller RICHARD KLEIN.

CBBC: internet www.bbc.co.uk/cbbc; digital service for children aged six to 13; Controller DAMIAN KAVANAGH.

CBeebies: internet www.bbc.co.uk/cbeebies; digital service aimed at under-fives; Controller KAY BENBOW.

BBC News: internet www.bbc.co.uk/news; 24-hour digital news service; Dir of News HELEN BOADEN; Controller KEVIN BAKHURST.

BBC Parliament: internet www.bbc.co.uk/parliament; provides coverage from the Houses of Parliament and the devolved Parliament and Assemblies in Scotland, Wales and Northern Ireland; Controller PETER KNOWLES.

BBC Alba: c/o MG Alba, Seaforth Rd, Stornoway, Isle of Lewis, HS1 2SD; tel. (1851) 705550; fax (1851) 706432; e-mail fios@mgalba.com; internet www.bbc.co.uk/alba; f. 2008 to provide radio and television programming in Scottish Gaelic; operates a free-to-air digital television channel, **BBC Alba**, and a radio station, **BBC Radio nan Gàidheal**; jtly managed by BBC and MG Alba (Gaelic Media Service); Chief Exec. DONALD CAMPBELL; Head of Content ALAN ESSLEMONT; Head of Service MARGARET MARY MURRAY.

Channel 3 (ITV)

ITV Network Ltd: ITV Network Centre, 200 Gray's Inn Rd, London, WC1V 8HF; tel. (20) 7156-6000; fax (20) 7843-8158; e-mail info@itv.co.uk; internet www.itv.com; f. 1956 as Independent Television Association; from 1992 the central co-ordinating body for Channel 3 (ITV); Dir of Television PETER FINCHAM.

ITV PLC: The London Television Centre, Upper Ground, London SE1 9LT; tel. (20) 7157-3000; internet www.itvplc.com; f. 2004 following the merger of Carlton and Granada; through its subsidiary ITV Broadcasting Ltd, owns all of the regional Channel 3 licences in England, Wales and the border region of Scotland, comprising Anglia (East of England), Border (Northern England, Southern Scotland and Isle of Man), Central (East, West and South Midlands), Granada (North-West England), London (London Weekday), LWT (London Weekend), Meridian (South and South-East England), Tyne Tees (North-East England), Wales and West, Westcountry (South-West England), Yorkshire (Yorkshire and Lincolnshire) and ITV Breakfast Ltd (national breakfast-time service); broadcasts on Channel 3 as ITV1; its subsidiary ITV Digital Channels Ltd operates 5 free-to-air digital channels: ITV2, ITV3, ITV4, ITV1 HD and CITV; Chair. ARCHIE NORMAN; Chief Exec. ADAM CROZIER.

STV Group PLC: Pacific Quay, Glasgow, G51 1PQ; tel. (141) 300-3300; e-mail communication@stv.tv; internet www.stvplc.tv; fmrly SMG PLC; owns the Channel 3 licences for Central and Northern Scotland; broadcasts as STV; Chair. RICHARD FINDLAY; Chief Exec. ROB WOODWARD; Man. Dir, Broadcasting Services and Regulatory Affairs BOBBY HAIN.

UTV PLC (Ulster Television): Havelock House, Ormeau Rd, Belfast, BT7 1EB; tel. (28) 9032-8122; fax (28) 9024-6695; e-mail info@u.tv; internet www.u.tv; started transmission 1959; owns Channel 3 licence for Northern Ireland; Chair. JOHN B. MCGUCKIAN; Chief Exec. JOHN MCCANN; Man. Dir, Television MICHAEL WILSON.

Other Independent Television Broadcasters

Channel 4 Television: 124 Horseferry Rd, London, SW1P 2TX; tel. (20) 7306-8333; internet www.channel4.com; f. 1980; began broadcasting 1982; national television service; also operates 4 free-to-air digital channels: E4, Film4, More4 and 4Music; financed by advertising; a publicly owned corporation with a remit to provide public-service broadcasting that demonstrates innovation, experiment and creativity, appeals to the tastes and interests of a culturally diverse society, includes programmes of an educational nature and exhibits a distinctive character; Chair. LUKE JOHNSON; Chief Exec. DAVID ABRAHAM.

Five: 22 Long Acre, London, WC2E 9LY; tel. (8457) 050505; e-mail customerservices@five.tv; internet www.five.tv; awarded licence for fifth national terrestrial channel in October 1995; commenced broadcasting on 30 March 1997 as Channel 5; renamed as above in 2002; also operates 2 digital channels: Fiver and Five USA; owned by Northern & Shell; Chair. and Chief Exec. DAWN AIREY; Dir of Programmes RICHARD WOOLFE.

Freeview: DTV Services Ltd, Broadcast Centre, 27–29 Cursitor St, London, EC4A 1LT; tel. (8708) 809980; internet www.freeview.co.uk; f. 2002; a consortium of the BBC, Arqiva, ITV PLC, Channel 4 and BSkyB providing Freeview, a digital service offering more than 40 television stations and additional interactive services; commenced transmission in late 2002; Man. Dir ILSE HOWLING.

Independent Television News Ltd (ITN): 200 Gray's Inn Rd, London, WC1X 8XZ; tel. (20) 7833-3000; fax (20) 7430-4305; internet www.itn.co.uk; f. 1955; ITV PLC holds a 40% stake, with Daily Mail and General Trust PLC, Thomson Reuters and United Business Media each holding a 20% stake; provides all national and international news programming for ITV1 and the London region, plus news programming for Channel 4 and Independent Radio News (IRN); also operates the ITN Archive, ITN Factual, ITN On and ITN Source; became a profit-making company in 1993; Chair. MAGGIE CARVER; Chief Exec. JOHN HARDIE.

Sianel Pedwar Cymru (S4C) (Channel Four Wales): Parc Tŷ Glas, Llanishen, Cardiff, CF14 5DU; tel. (29) 2074-7444; fax (29) 2075-4444; e-mail helo@s4c.co.uk; internet www.s4c.co.uk; f. 1980; commenced broadcasting in 1982; Welsh-language television service for Wales; English-language programming ceased in 2010 following the extension of Channel 4 programming to Wales; regulated by the Welsh Fourth Channel Authority, a public body appointed by the UK Secretary of State for Culture, Media and Sport; financed by Dept for Culture, Media and Sport and advertising revenue; Chair. JOHN WALTER JONES; Chief Exec. ARWEL ELLIS OWEN (acting).

Satellite and Cable Broadcasting

By the end of 2008 12.8m. households in the United Kingdom paid to subscribe to multi-channel satellite or cable television services. Of these, 8.9m. subscribed to digital satellite television with a further 3.4m. households subscribing to cable television (digital 3.3m.; analogue 100,000). Some 10.1m. households received free-to-view digital satellite television services. The major satellite and cable television companies are listed below.

BBC Worldwide Television: Media Centre, 201 Wood Lane, London, W12 7TQ; tel. (20) 8433-2000; fax (20) 8749-0538; internet www.bbcworldwide.com; began broadcasting in 1991; part of BBC Worldwide Ltd; broadcasts 24-hour news and information ('BBC World') and light entertainment programmes to Europe ('BBC Prime'); other news programmes broadcast to Africa, Asia (including a Japanese-language service to Japan), the Middle East, North America, Australia and New Zealand; Chief Exec. JOHN SMITH.

British Sky Broadcasting Group PLC (BSkyB): Grant Way, Isleworth, Middlesex, TW7 5QD; tel. (20) 7705-3000; fax (20) 7705-3030; internet www.sky.com; f. 1990 by merger of British Satellite Broadcasting (BSB) and Sky TV PLC (a subsidiary of News

THE UNITED KINGDOM

International); satellite broadcaster and programme provider; multi-channel digital television service SkyDigital (see below); Chair. JAMES MURDOCH; CEO JEREMY DARROCH.

SkyDigital: 6 Centaurs Business Park, Grant Way, Isleworth, Middlesex, TW7 5QD; tel. (20) 7705-3000; fax (20) 7705-3030; internet www.sky.com; owned by British Sky Broadcasting Group PLC; CEO JEREMY DARROCH.

Eurosport UK: 55 Drury Lane, London, WC2B 5SQ; tel. (20) 7468-7777; fax (20) 7468-0023; e-mail dorman@eurosport.com; internet www.eurosport.co.uk; began broadcasting in 1989; broadcasts sport events, sport news; Man. Dir SIMON CRANE.

Freesat: POB 6296, London, W1A 3FF; tel. (845) 313-0051; internet www.freesat.co.uk; f. 2007; commenced broadcasting in May 2008; free-to-air digital satellite service, offering more than 130 digital television and radio channels; jointly owned by the BBC and ITV PLC; Man. Dir EMMA SCOTT.

MTV Networks UK and Ireland: 17–29 Hawley Cres., London, NW1 8TT; tel. (20) 7284-7513; fax (20) 7284-7511; e-mail pressuk@mtvne.com; internet www.mtvnetworks.co.uk; began broadcasting in 1987; popular music; Man. Dir DAVID LYNN.

UKTV: 160 Great Portland St, London, W1W 5QA; tel. (20) 7299-6200; fax (20) 7299-6000; internet www.uktv.co.uk; f. 1997; 10 channels: Alibi, Blighty, Dave, Eden, G.O.L.D., Home, UKTV Food, UKTV Gardens, Watch and Yesterday; satellite, cable and DTT; co-owned by BBC Worldwide Ltd and Virgin Media; CEO DAVID ABRAHAM; Controller MATTHEW LITTLEFORD.

Finance

BANKING
(cap. = capital; res = reserves; dep. = deposits; m. = million; brs = branches; amounts in pounds sterling)

Central Bank

Bank of England: Threadneedle St, London, EC2R 8AH; tel. (20) 7601-4444; fax (20) 7601-5460; e-mail enquiries@bankofengland.co.uk; internet www.bankofengland.co.uk; inc by Royal Charter in 1694, and nationalized by Act of Parliament on 1 March 1946; under the 1998 Bank of England Act, the Bank's Monetary Policy Committee is responsible for formulating monetary policy within the framework of maintaining price stability and supporting the Government's economic policies; ensures the stability of the financial markets and acts as a lender of last resort; mem. of the Cheque and Credit Clearing Company; office in Leeds; 12 regional agencies assess economic conditions and contribute to the formulation of monetary policy; cap. 15m., res 558m., dep. 143,438m. (Feb. 2009); Gov. MERVYN KING; Dep. Govs PAUL TUCKER, CHARLES BEAN.

Principal Banks Incorporated in the United Kingdom

Alliance & Leicester: Carlton Park, Narborough, Leicester, LE19 0AL; tel. (116) 201-1000; fax (116) 200-4040; internet www.alliance-leicester.co.uk; fmrly a building society; assumed banking status in 1997; broad-based financial services provider incl. business banking services through wholly owned subsidiary, Girobank; acquired by Banco Santander, SA (Spain) in 2008; cap. 1,519m., res 199m., dep. 106,156m. (Dec. 2009); Chair. ALAN GILLESPIE; Chief Exec. DAVID BENNETT; 256 brs.

Barclays Bank PLC: 1 Churchill Place, London, E14 5HP; tel. (20) 7116-1000; fax (20) 7699-3463; internet group.barclays.com; inc. 1896; clearing bank; principal operating co of Barclays PLC (group holding co); cap. 2,853m., res 1,719m., dep. 1,957,523m. (Dec. 2009); Group Chair. MARCUS AGIUS; Chief Exec. ROBERT E. DIAMOND, Jr.

Clydesdale Bank PLC: 30 St Vincent Pl., Glasgow, G1 2HL; tel. (141) 248-7070; fax (141) 204-0828; internet www.cbonline.co.uk; f. 1838; wholly-owned by National Australia Bank Ltd; clearing bank; cap. 632m., res 702m., dep. 37,444m. (Dec. 2009); Chair. MALCOLM WILLIAMSON; Chief Exec. (Europe) DAVID THORBURN; 150 brs.

The Co-operative Bank PLC: POB 101, 1 Balloon St, Manchester, M60 4EP; tel. (161) 832-3456; fax (161) 829-4475; e-mail customerservice@co-operativebank.co.uk; internet www.co-operativebank.co.uk; f. 1872; clearing bank; merger with Britannia Building Society approved April 2009; cap. 55m., res 51m., dep. 13,667m. (Jan. 2009); Chair. PAUL FLOWER; Chief Exec. NEVILLE RICHARDSON; 158 brs.

Coutts and Co: 440 Strand, London, WC2R 0QS; tel. (20) 7753-1000; fax (20) 7753-1050; internet www.coutts.com; f. 1692; private clearing bank and asset management; parent co Royal Bank Of Scotland Group PLC; Chair. DAVID DOUGLAS-HOME, Earl of Home; Chief Exec. MICHAEL MORLEY; 24 brs.

First Trust Bank: 4 Queens Sq., Belfast, BT1 3DJ; tel. (28) 9032-5599; fax (28) 9032-1754; internet www.firsttrustbank.co.uk; f. 1991 following merger of Northern Ireland operations of AIB Group, Ireland and TSB Northern Ireland; trading name of AIB Group (UK) PLC in Northern Ireland; Group Chair. (UK) DAVID PRITCHARD; Man. Dir TERRY MCDAID; 57 brs.

HSBC Bank PLC: 8 Canada Sq., London, E14 5HQ; tel. (20) 7991-8888; fax (20) 7992-4880; internet www.hsbc.co.uk; f. 1836; from 1992 subsidiary of HSBC Holdings PLC; clearing bank; cap. 797m., res 18,855m., dep. 687,176m. (Dec. 2008); Chair. DOUGLAS FLINT; CEO STUART GULLIVER; 1,700 brs.

Lloyds Banking Group PLC: 25 Gresham St, London, EC2V 7HN; tel. (20) 7626-1500; fax (20) 7356-2494; internet www.lloydsbankinggroup.com; f. 2009 by merger of Lloyds TSB Bank PLC and HBOS PLC; owns and operates Bank of Scotland, Cheltenham and Gloucester, Halifax and Lloyds TSB; 44.3% stake owned by UK Govt; cap. 1,513m., res −380m., dep. 347,316m. (Dec. 2008); Chair. Sir WINFRIED BISCHOFF; Group Chief Exec. ANTÓNIO HORTA OSÓRIO.

National Westminster Bank PLC (NatWest): 135 Bishopsgate, London, EC2M 3UR; tel. (20) 7726-1000; fax (20) 7375-5050; internet www.natwest.com; f. 1968; clearing bank; acquired by The Royal Bank of Scotland Group PLC in 2000; cap. 1,678m., res 3,817m., dep. 279,295m. (Dec. 2008); Group Chair. Sir PHILIP HAMPTON; Group Chief Exec. STEPHEN HESTER; 1,631 brs.

Northern Bank Limited: Donegall Sq. West, Belfast, BT1 6JS; tel. (28) 9004-5000; fax (28) 9089-3214; internet www.northernbank.co.uk; f. 1960; owned by Danske Bank Group; cap. 88m., res 20.7m., dep. 3,831.2m. (Dec. 2005); Chair. PETER STRAARUP; CEO GERRY MALLON; 94 brs.

Northern Rock PLC: Northern Rock House, Gosforth, Newcastle upon Tyne, NE3 4PL; tel. (191) 285-7191; fax (191) 284-8470; internet www.northernrock.co.uk; taken under state ownership in Feb. 2008; cap. 124m., res −462m., dep. 100,888m. (Dec. 2008); Exec. Chair. RON SANDLER; 90 brs.

The Royal Bank of Scotland PLC: POB 1000, Gogaburn, Edinburgh, EH12 1HQ; tel. (131) 556-8555; fax (131) 557-6565; internet www.rbs.co.uk; f. 1985 as result of merger of Royal Bank of Scotland and Williams & Glyn's Bank. The Royal Bank of Scotland (est. by Royal Charter in 1727) merged with National Commercial Bank of Scotland in 1969. Williams & Glyn's Bank was result of merger of Glyn Mills & Co (est. 1753) and Williams Deacon's Bank (est. 1771); 57.9% stake acquired by UK Govt in Oct. 2008; cap. 14,630m., res 50,972m., dep. 1,448,055m. (Dec. 2009); Chair. Sir PHILIP HAMPTON; Group Chief Exec. STEPHEN HESTER; 639 brs.

Santander UK PLC: Abbey National House, 2 Triton Sq., Regent's Pl., London, NW1 3AN; tel. (870) 607-6000; e-mail feedback@abbey.com; internet www.santander.co.uk; f. 1944 as Abbey National Building Society; current status assumed in 1989; owned by Banco Santander, SA (Spain); cap. 1,148m., res 1,857m., dep. 215,753m. (Dec. 2008); Chair. Lord BURNS; Chief Exec. ANA BOTÍN; 793 brs.

Standard Chartered Bank: 1 Basinghall Ave, London, EC2V 5DD; tel. (20) 7885-9999; fax (20) 7885-8888; internet www.standardchartered.com; f. 1853; holding co Standard Chartered PLC; cap. US $948m., res $8,339m., dep. $372,617m. (Dec. 2008); Chair. JOHN PEACE; Group Chief Exec. PETER SANDS; 570 brs.

Ulster Bank Ltd: 11–16 Donegall Sq. East, Belfast, BT1 5UB; tel. (28) 9027-6000; fax (28) 9027-5661; e-mail morrow@ulsterbank.com; internet www.ulsterbank.co.uk; f. 1836; mem. of Royal Bank of Scotland Group; cap. 717m., res 2,053m., dep. 52,817m. (Dec. 2008); Chair. SEAN DORGAN; Group Chief Exec. CORMAC MCCARTHY; 214 brs.

Yorkshire Bank: 30 St Vincent Pl., Glasgow, G1 2HL; tel. (113) 247-2000; fax (113) 242-0733; internet www.ybonline.co.uk; f. 1859; wholly owned by National Australia Bank Ltd; Chief Exec. (Europe) DAVID THORBURN; 260 brs.

Principal Merchant Banks

Ansbacher & Co: 2 London Bridge, London, SE1 9RA; tel. (20) 7089-4700; fax (20) 7089-4850; e-mail info@ansbacher.com; internet www.ansbacher.com; f. 1894; subsidiary of Qatar National Bank SAQ; cap. 59m., res 0.9m., dep. 420m. (Dec. 2008); Chair. and CEO (vacant).

Barclays Capital: 5 The North Colonnade, Canary Wharf, London, E14 4BB; tel. (20) 7623-2323; e-mail publisher@barclayscapital.com; internet www.barcap.com; investment banking division of Barclays PLC; Chief Exec. ROBERT E. DIAMOND, Jnr.

Brown, Shipley & Co Ltd: Founders Court, Lothbury, London, EC2R 7HE; tel. (20) 7606-9833; fax (20) 7282-3399; e-mail info@brownshipley.co.uk; internet www.brownshipley.com; f. 1810; owned by KBC Group NV (Belgium); cap. issued 86.4m., dep. 573.7m. (Dec. 2001); Chair. STEPHEN BLANEY; Man. Dir IAN SACKFIELD.

Butterfield Bank (UK) Ltd (Butterfield Private Bank): 99 Gresham St, London, EC2V 7NG; tel. (20) 7776-6700; fax (20) 7776-6701; e-mail info@uk.butterfieldgroup.com; internet www.uk.butterfieldgroup.com; f. 1919; acquired by Bermuda's Bank of

THE UNITED KINGDOM

Butterfield 2004; cap. 20m., res 14m., dep. 806m. (Dec. 2008); Man. Dir GEORGE BOGUCKI.

Cater Allen Private Bank: Abbey House, 9 Nelson St, Bradford, BD1 5AN; tel. (114) 228-2407; e-mail info@caterallen.co.uk; internet www.caterallen.co.uk; f. 1981 by merger of Cater Ryder and Co Ltd (f. 1816) and Allen Harvey and Ross Ltd (f. 1888); part of Santander Private Banking UK; Chair. MALCOLM MILLINGTON; Man. Dir RICHARD J. DUNN.

Citibank International PLC: POB 242, Citigroup Centre, 33 Canada Sq., Canary Wharf, London, E14 5LB; tel. (20) 7500-5000; fax (20) 7500-1695; internet www.citibank.co.uk; f. 1972; cap. 1,757m., res 620m., dep. 42,221m. (Dec. 2008); Chair. and Chief Exec. WILLIAM J. MILLS.

Citigroup: 33 Canada Sq., Canary Wharf, London, E14 5LB; tel. (20) 7986-4000; internet www.citigroup.com; f. 2000 by merger of J. Henry Schroder & Co Ltd and Salomon Smith Barney; present name adopted 2001; Chair RICHARD PARSONS.

Close Brothers Ltd: 10 Crown Pl., London, EC2A 4FT; tel. (20) 7426-4000; fax (20) 7426-4044; e-mail cblbank@closebrothers.co.uk; internet www.closebrothers.co.uk; cap. 82m., res 238m., dep. 4,437m. (July 2008); Man. Dir STEPHEN HODGES.

Commerzbank: 30 Gresham St, London, EC2V 7PG; tel. (20) 7623-8000; fax (20) 7623-4069; internet www.commerzbank.com; f. 1958; acquired Dresdner Kleinwort Ltd in 2009; share cap. 548.6m., res 67.5m., dep. 602.2m. (Dec. 2005); Chair. and CEO MARTIN BLESSING.

DB UK Bank Limited: 23 Great Winchester St, London, EC2P 2AX; tel. (20) 7545-8000; fax (20) 7545-6155; internet www.db.com/unitedkingdom; f. 1838; as George Peabody & Co; renamed Morgan Grenfell & Co Ltd in 1910; present name adopted 2004; acquired by Deutsche Bank Group in 1989; cap. 385m., res 3m., dep. 4,347m. (Dec. 2008); Chair. JOSEF ACKERMANN; Chief Exec. COLIN GRASSIE; 1 br.

Investec Bank (UK) Ltd: 2 Gresham St, London, EC2V 7QP; tel. (20) 7597-4000; fax (20) 7597-4070; internet www.investec.com; f. 1977 as Allied Arab Bank Ltd, name changed as above 1997; acquired Guinness Mahon & Co Ltd 1998; cap. 655m., res 60m., dep. 11,479m. (March 2009); Chair. HUGH HERMAN; CEO STEPHEN KOSEFF.

Rothschild: New Court, St Swithin's Lane, London EC4P 4DU; tel. (20) 7280-5000; fax (20) 7929-1643; internet www.rothschild.com; f. 1804; cap. 50m., res −2m., dep. 3,653m. (March 2007); Chair. Baron DAVID DE ROTHSCHILD; 4 brs.

UBS Limited (UBS Investment Bank): 100 Liverpool St, London, EC2M 2RH; tel. (20) 7567-8000; fax (20) 7568-4800; internet www.ubs.com/investmentbank; Group Chair. KASPER VILLIGER; CEO ALEX WILMOT-SITWELL, CARSTEN KENGETER.

Savings Organization

National Savings & Investments: 375 Kensington High St, London, W14 8SD; tel. (845) 9645-0000; e-mail pressoffice@nationalsavings.co.uk; internet www.nsandi.com; govt department and Executive Agency of the Chancellor of the Exchequer; money placed in National Savings and Investments is used by the Treasury to help cost-effectively manage the national debt and contribute towards the Government's financing needs; Chair. MARTIN GRAY; Chief Exec. JANE PLATT.

National Savings regional offices: Glasgow, G58 1SB; Durham, DH99 1NS; Blackpool, FY3 9ZW; Lytham St Annes, FY0 1YN; f. 1861; Chief Exec. PETER BAREAU.

Credit Institutions

ECI Ventures: 1st Floor, Brettenham House, Lancaster Pl., London, WC2E 7EN; tel. (20) 7606-1000; fax (20) 7240-5050; e-mail enquiries@ecipartners.com; internet www.eciv.co.uk; f. 1976; advises and manages ECI5 (£78m. UK Ltd Partnership), ECI6 (£100m. UK Ltd Partnership) and EC17 (£175m. UK Ltd Partnership) to provide equity capital, mainly for management buy-outs; Chair. STEPHEN DAWSON.

Permira: 80 Pall Mall, London, SW1Y 5ES; tel. (20) 7632-1000; fax (20) 7930-3185; e-mail chris.davison@permira.com; internet www.permira.com; fmrly Schroder Ventures Europe; present name adopted 2001; advises 19 Permira Funds world-wide to provide equity capital for financial acquisitions, leveraged buy-outs and buy-ins, growth buy-outs, public-to-private transactions, 'turnarounds'; Chair. DAMON BUFFINI.

3i Group PLC: 16 Palace St, London, SW1E 5JD; tel. (20) 7975-3456; fax (20) 7928-0058; e-mail general_enquiries@3i.com; internet www.3i.com; f. 1945 as the Industrial and Commercial Finance Corpn Ltd by the English and Scottish clearing banks, renamed Finance for Industry PLC, renamed Investors in Industry Group PLC in 1983, and renamed as above in 1988; provides long-term and permanent financial advice; Chair. Baroness HOGG; Chief Exec. MICHAEL QUEEN.

Banking and Finance Organizations

Association for Financial Markets in Europe: 1 George Yard, St Michael's House, London, EC3V 9DH; tel. (20) 7743-9300; fax (20) 7743-9301; e-mail info@afme.eu; internet www.afme.eu; f. 2009 with the merger of London Investment Banking Asscn and Financial Market Asscn; approx. 150 mems include British and foreign banks and securities houses; CEO SIMON LEWIS.

Association of Foreign Banks (AFB): 1 Bengal Ct, London, EC3V 9DD; tel. (20) 7283-8300; fax (20) 7283-8302; e-mail secretariat@foreignbanks.org.uk; internet www.foreignbanks.org.uk; f. 1947; incorporated mems of the British Overseas and Commonwealth Banks' Association (f. 1917) in 1996; name changed as above in 2002; approx. 185 mem. banks; Chair. ROGER GIFFORD; Man. Dir JOHN TREADWELL.

British Bankers' Association (BBA): Pinners Hall, 105–108 Old Broad St, London, EC2N 1EX; tel. (20) 7216-8800; fax (20) 7216-8811; e-mail info@bba.org.uk; internet www.bba.org.uk; f. 1919; 225 mems; Chair. STEPHEN GREEN; Chief Exec. ANGELA KNIGHT.

Building Societies Association (BSA): 6th Floor, York House, 23 Kingsway, London, WC2B 6UJ; tel. (20) 7520-5900; fax (20) 7240-5290; e-mail simon.rex@bsa.org.uk; internet www.bsa.org.uk; represents building societies; Dir-Gen. ADRIAN COLES.

The Chartered Institute of Bankers in Scotland: Drumsheugh House, 38B Drumsheugh Gardens, Edinburgh, EH3 7SW; tel. (131) 473-7777; fax (131) 473-7788; e-mail info@charteredbanker.com; internet www.charteredbanker.com; f. 1875; professional examinations, courses and publications; approx. 13,000 mems; Pres. PHILIP GRANT; Chief Exec. SIMON THOMPSON.

Lending Standards Board: Level 17, City Tower, 40 Basinghall St, London, EC2V 5DE; tel. (845) 230-9694; fax (20) 7374-4414; e-mail info@lstdb.org.uk; internet www.lendingstandardsboard.org.uk; self-regulatory body which monitors and enforces Banking Code (for personal customers) and Business Banking Code; fmrly known as Banking Code Standards Bd; name changed to present in 2009; Chair. GERARD LEMOS; Chief Exec. ROBERT SKINNER.

London Money Market Association: 2 Gresham St, London, EC2V 7QP; tel. (20) 7597-4492; fax (20) 7597-4491; e-mail richard.vardy2@btinternet.com; internet www.lmma.org.uk; f. 1997; 22 mems include international banks, securities houses, building societies; Chair. IAN MAIR; Dep. Chair. R. J. VARDY.

STOCK EXCHANGE

The London Stock Exchange: 10 Paternoster Sq., London, EC4M 7LS; tel. (20) 7797-1000; fax (20) 7334-8916; e-mail enquiries@londonstockexchange.com; internet www.londonstockexchange.com; had its origins in the coffee houses of 17th-century London; formally constituted in 1801; became a public limited company in 2000; merged with TMX Group, operator of the Toronto Stock Exchange, in 2011; 55% shares held by The London Stock Exchange; 2,682 listed cos with a total value of £3,779,699m. (Sept. 2010); Chair. CHRIS GIBSON-SMITH; Chief Exec. XAVIER ROLET.

SUPERVISORY BODIES

The Financial Ombudsman Service: South Quay Plaza, 183 Marsh Wall, London, E14 9SR; tel. (20) 7964-1000; fax (20) 7964-1001; e-mail complaint.info@financial-ombudsman.org.uk; internet www.financial-ombudsman.org.uk; f. 2001 to replace The Personal Investment Authority Ombudsman Bureau, The Insurance Ombudsman Bureau, The Office of the Banking Ombudsman, The Office of the Building Societies Ombudsman, The Office of the Investment Ombudsman, The Securities and Futures Authority Complaints Bureau, The Financial Services Authority Complaints Unit and The Personal Insurance Arbitration Service; Chair. Sir CHRISTOPHER KELLY; Chief Ombudsman NATALIE CEENEY.

Financial Services Authority (FSA): 25 The North Colonnade, Canary Wharf, London, E14 5HS; tel. (20) 7066-1000; fax (20) 7066-1099; e-mail consumerhelp@fsa.gov.uk; internet www.fsa.gov.uk; f. 1998 to undertake supervision, regulation and market surveillance of all areas of financial activity as defined under the 2000 Financial Services and Markets Act; single statutory regulator responsible for promoting orderly, efficient and fair markets, promoting public understanding of the financial system and reducing financial crime; Chair. Lord TURNER OF ECCHINSWELL; Chief Exec. HECTOR SANTS.

Securities & Investment Institute: 8 Eastcheap, London, EC3M 1AE; tel. (20) 7645-0600; fax (20) 7645-0601; e-mail info@sii.org.uk; internet www.sii.org.uk; f. 1992; aims to promote professional standards and ethics in the securities industry; Chair. SCOTT DOBBIE; Chief Exec. SIMON CULHANE.

INSURANCE

Lloyd's: 1 Lime St, London, EC3M 7HA; tel. (20) 7327-1000; fax (20) 7327-2389; e-mail enquiries@lloyds.com; internet www.lloyds.com; had its origins in the coffee house opened c. 1688 by Edward Lloyd

THE UNITED KINGDOM

and was incorporated by Act of Parliament (Lloyd's Acts 1871 and 1982); an international insurance market and Society of Underwriters, consisting of individual members ('Names') and corporate members grouped into syndicates who accept risks on the basis of unlimited and limited liability, respectively; business is effected through firms of brokers who are permitted to place insurances either directly or by way of reinsurance; administered by the Corporation of Lloyd's through an 18-member Council, mostly elected by and from the underwriting membership; regulated by the Financial Services Authority (FSA), under the Financial Services and Markets Act of 2000; capacity to accept insurance premiums of more than £17,000m. in 2009; 80 syndicates underwriting insurance in 2009, covering all classes of business from more than 200 countries and territories world-wide; Chair. Lord LEVENE; CEO RICHARD WARD.

Principal Insurance Companies

AEGON UK PLC: Edinburgh Park, Edinburgh, EH12 9SE; tel. (870) 600-0337; fax (131) 549-4188; e-mail louise.sutherland@aegon.co.uk; internet www.aegon.co.uk; f. 1831 as Scottish Equitable Life Assurance Society; restyled Scottish Equitable PLC in 1994; acquired by AEGON NV (Netherlands) in 1998 and present name adopted 1999; Chief Exec. OTTO THORESEN.

Allianz Insurance PLC: 57 Ladymead, Guildford, Surrey, GU1 1DB; tel. (1483) 568161; fax (1483) 300952; internet www.allianz.co.uk; part of the Allianz Group (Germany); f. 1905, fmrly Cornhill Insurance Co PLC; Chair. CLEMENT B. BOOTH; Chief Exec. ANDREW TORRANCE.

Aviva PLC: POB 420, St Helen's, 1 Undershaft, London, EC3P 3DQ; tel. (20) 7283-2000; e-mail aviva_info@aviva.com; internet www.aviva.com; formed by merger of Commercial Union and General Accident in 1998; merged with Norwich Union PLC in 2000; renamed as above in 2002; Chair. Lord SHARMAN OF REDLYNCH; Group Chief Exec. ANDREW MOSS.

AXA Insurance PLC: 1 Aldgate, London, EC3N 1RE; tel. (20) 7702-3109; fax (20) 7369-3909; e-mail customerservice@axa-insurance.co.uk; internet www.axa-insurance.co.uk; f. 1903; Chair. ANTHONY HAMILTON; Group CEO NICOLAS MOREAU.

The Co-operative Insurance: Miller St, Manchester, M60 0AL; tel. (161) 832-8686; fax (161) 837-4048; e-mail ibis@co-operativeinsurance.co.uk; internet www.co-operativeinsurance.co.uk; f. 1867; Chair. BOB BURLTON; Chief Exec. NEVILLE RICHARDSON.

Direct Line Group: 3 Edridge Rd, Croydon, Surrey, CR9 1AG; tel. (20) 8686-3313; fax (20) 8681-0512; internet www.directline.com; wholly owned by The Royal Bank of Scotland; Man. Dir CHRIS MOAT.

Ecclesiastical Insurance Office PLC: Beaufort House, Brunswick Rd, Gloucester, GL1 1JZ; tel. (1452) 528533; fax (1452) 423557; e-mail information@eigmail.com; internet www.ecclesiastical.co.uk; f. 1887; Chair. WILL SAMUEL; Chief Exec. MICHAEL TRIPP.

Equitable Life Assurance Society: Walton St, Aylesbury, Buckinghamshire, HP21 7QW; tel. (845) 603-6771; fax (1296) 386383; e-mail enquiries@equitable.co.uk; internet www.equitable.co.uk; f. 1762; Chair. IAN BRIMECOME; Chief Exec. CHRIS WISCARSON.

Friends Provident PLC: 100 Wood St, London, EC2V 7AN; tel. (845) 641-7825; fax (1306) 740150; e-mail customer.services@friendsprovident.co.uk; internet www.friendsprovident.co.uk; f. 1832; Exec. Chair. Sir MALCOLM WILLIAMSON; CEO TREVOR MATTHEWS.

Legal and General Group PLC: 1 Coleman St, London, EC2R 5AA; tel. (20) 3124-2000; fax (20) 7528-6222; internet www.legalandgeneral.com; f. 1836; Group CEO TIM BREEDON; Group Chair. ROB MARGETTS; Sec. DAVID BINDING.

    Legal and General Insurance Ltd: 1 Coleman St, London, EC2R 5AA; tel. (20) 3124-2000; fax (20) 7528-6222; f. 1946 as British Commonwealth Insurance Co; Chair. TIM BREEDON; Sec. JEAN WEBB.

Liverpool Victoria (LV): County Gates, Bournemouth, BH1 2NF; tel. (1202) 292333; fax (1202) 292253; internet www.lv.com; f. 1843; Chair. DENNIS HOLT; Group Chief Exec. MICHAEL (MIKE) ROGERS.

MGM Advantage: MGM House, Heene Rd, Worthing, Sussex, BN11 3AT; tel. (1903) 836067; fax (1903) 836004; e-mail customercentre@mgmadvantage.com; internet www.mgmadvantage.com; f. 1852; Chair. WILLIAM PROBY; CEO CHRIS EVANS.

The National Farmers Union Mutual Insurance Society Ltd: Tiddington Rd, Stratford upon Avon, Warwicks., CV37 7BJ; tel. (1789) 204211; fax (1789) 298992; internet www.nfumutual.co.uk; f. 1910; Chair. Sir DONALD CURRY; Group Chief Exec. LINDSAY SINCLAIR.

Pearl: The Pearl Centre, Lynch Wood, Peterborough, Cambridgeshire, PE2 6FY; tel. (1733) 470470; fax (1733) 472300; e-mail customersupport@pearl.co.uk; internet www.pearl.co.uk; f. 1864; part of Phoenix Group of Cos; present name adopted Dec. 2003; Chair. JONATHAN EVANS.

Phoenix Life Ltd: 1 Wythall Green Way, Wythall Green, Birmingham, B47 6WG; tel. (845) 002-0036; internet www.phoenixlifegroup.co.uk; f. 2005 by a merger of Swiss Life UK and Royal & Sun Alliance UK life business; merged with Britannic Assurance PLC in 2007; subsidiary of Resolution PLC; Chair. RON SANDLER; Group CEO JONATHAN MOSS.

The Prudential Assurance Co Ltd: 250 Euston Rd, London, NW1 2PQ; tel. (20) 7405-9222; fax (20) 7548-3465; e-mail media.relations@prudential.co.uk; internet www.prudential.co.uk; f. 1848; holding co: Prudential Corpn PLC; Group Chair. HARVEY MCGRATH; CEO TIDJANE THIAM.

Royal Liver Assurance Ltd: Royal Liver Bldg, Pier Head, Liverpool, L3 1HT; tel. (151) 236-1451; fax (151) 236-2122; e-mail info@royallivergroup.com; internet www.royallivergroup.com; f. 1850; Chair. DAVID E. WOODS; Chief Exec. BILL CONNOLLY (acting).

The Royal London Mutual Insurance Society Ltd: 55 Gracechurch St, London, EC3V 0RL; tel. (8450) 502020; fax (1625) 605400; e-mail info@royal-london.co.uk; internet www.royal-london.co.uk; f. 1861; Chair. TIM MELVILLE-ROSS; CEO MIKE YARDLEY.

    Scottish Life: St Andrew House, 1 Thistle St, Edinburgh, EH2 1DG; tel. (845) 605-0050; fax (131) 456-7880; e-mail e-face@scottishlife.co.uk; internet www.scottishlife.co.uk; f. 1881; re-inc as a Mutual Company 1968; became part of Royal London Mutual Insurance Society in July 2001; Chief Exec. JOHN DEANNE.

RSA Insurance Group PLC: 9th Floor, 1 Plantation Place, 30 Fenchurch St, London, EC3M 3BD; tel. (20) 7111-7000; internet www.rsagroup.com; f. 1996 by merger of Royal Insurance Holdings PLC (f. 1845) and Sun Alliance Group PLC; present name adopted 2008; Chair. JOHN NAPIER; CEO ANDY HASTE.

Scottish Widows PLC: 69 Morrison St, Edinburgh EH3 8YF; tel. (845) 608-0371; fax (131) 662-4053; e-mail cameron.walker@scottishwidows.co.uk; internet www.scottishwidows.co.uk; f. 1815 as Scottish Widows' Fund and Life Assurance Society; name changed as above March 2000 following acquisition by Lloyds TSB; mem. of Lloyds Banking Group; Chair. Lord LEITCH; Group Exec. Dir ARCHIE KANE.

Standard Life PLC: Standard Life House, 30 Lothian Rd, Edinburgh, EH1 2DH; tel. (131) 225-2552; e-mail customer_service@standardlife.com; internet www.standardlife.com; f. 1825; present name adopted 2006; assets under management £156,800m. (2009); Chair. GERRY GRIMSTONE; Group CEO DAVID NISH.

Swiss Re UK Ltd: 30 St Mary Axe, London, EC3A 8EP; tel. (20) 7933-3000; fax (20) 7933-5000; internet www.swissre.com; f. 1863; Chair. WALTER B. KIELHOLZ; CEO STEFAN LIPPE.

Wesleyan Assurance Society: Colmore Circus, Birmingham, B4 6AR; tel. (121) 335-3487; fax (121) 200-2971; internet www.wesleyan.co.uk; f. 1841; Chair. LOWRY D. MACLEAN; CEO CRAIG ERRINGTON.

Zurich Assurance Ltd: UK Life Centre, Station Rd, Swindon, SN1 1EL; tel. (1793) 511227; fax (1793) 506625; internet www.zurich.co.uk; f. 1872; Group Chair. MANFRED GENTZ; CEO JAMES SCHIRO.

Insurance Associations

Associated Scottish Life Offices: POB 25, Craigforth, Stirling, FK9 4UE; tel. (1786) 448844; fax (1786) 450427; constituted 1841 as an Association of General Managers of Scottish Offices transacting life assurance business; 7 full mems; Chair. GRAHAM POTTINGER; Dep. Chair. DAVID HENDERSON.

Association of British Insurers: 51 Gresham St, London, EC2V 7HQ; tel. (20) 7600-3333; fax (20) 7696-8999; e-mail info@abi.org.uk; internet www.abi.org.uk; f. 1985; principal trade association for insurance companies; protection, promotion, and advancement of the common interests of all classes of insurance business; c. 390 mems; Chair. ARCHIE KANE; Dir-Gen. KERRIE KELLY.

British Insurance Brokers' Association (BIBA): 8th Floor, John Stow House, 18 Bevis Marks, London, EC3A 7JB; tel. (870) 950-1790; fax (20) 7626-9676; e-mail enquiries@biba.org.uk; internet www.biba.org.uk; f. 1977; Chair. PATRICK SMITH; Chief Exec. ERIC GALBRAITH.

Chartered Insurance Institute: 42–48 High Rd, South Woodford, London, E18 2JP; tel. (20) 8989-8464; fax (20) 8530-3052; e-mail customer.serv@cii.co.uk; internet www.cii.co.uk; f. 1897; inc 1912; approx. 90,000 mems; Pres. BARRY SMITH; CEO Dr ALEXANDER SCOTT.

Fire Protection Association: London Rd, Moreton-in-Marsh, Gloucestershire, GL56 0RH; tel. (1608) 812500; fax (1608) 812501; e-mail fpa@thefpa.co.uk; internet www.thefpa.co.uk; f. 1946; Man. Dir JONATHAN O'NEILL.

Insurance Institute of London: 5th Floor, 20 Aldermanbury, London, EC2V 7HY; tel. (20) 7600-1343; fax (20) 7600-6857; e-mail iii.london@cii.co.uk; internet www.iilondon.co.uk; f. 1907; Pres. STEPHEN CATLIN.

THE UNITED KINGDOM

International Underwriting Association (IUA): London Underwriting Centre, 3 Minster Ct, Mincing Lane, London, EC3R 7DD; tel. (20) 7617-4444; fax (20) 7617-4440; e-mail info@iua.co.uk; internet www.iua.co.uk; f. 1998; Chair. STEPHEN RILEY; Chief Exec. DAVE J. MATCHAM.

Associations of Actuaries

Faculty of Actuaries: 18 Dublin St, Edinburgh, EH1 3PP; tel. (20) 7632-2100; fax (131) 240-1313; e-mail faculty@actuaries.org.uk; internet www.actuaries.org.uk; f. 1856; 1,275 Fellows, 13 Honorary Fellows; Pres. RONNIE BOWIE; Chief Exec. CAROLINE INSTANCE.

Institute of Actuaries: Staple Inn Hall, High Holborn, London, WC1V 7QJ; tel. (20) 7632-2100; fax (20) 7632-2111; e-mail institute@actuaries.org.uk; internet www.actuaries.org.uk; f. 1848; Royal Charter 1884; 16,287 mems (May 2008); Pres. JANE CURTIS (designate); Chief Exec. CAROLINE INSTANCE.

Trade and Industry

GOVERNMENT AGENCIES

Advisory, Conciliation and Arbitration Service (Acas): Brandon House, 180 Borough High St, London, SE1 1LW; tel. (20) 7210-3613; fax (20) 7210-3615; internet www.acas.org.uk; f. 1975; an independent organization, under the direction of a council comprising employers, trade union representatives and independent members, appointed by the Secretary of State for Business, Innovation and Skills; aims to improve organizations and working life through good employment relations; provides collective conciliation, arbitration, mediation, advisory, training and information services, and conciliates in individual employment rights issues; Chair. ED SWEENEY; Chief Exec. JOHN TAYLOR.

Central Arbitration Committee: 22nd Floor, Euston Tower, 286 Euston Rd, London, NW1 3JJ; tel. (20) 7904-2300; fax (20) 7904-2301; e-mail enquiries@cac.gov.uk; internet www.cac.gov.uk; f. 1976 as an independent body under the 1975 Employment Protection Act, in succession to Industrial Court/Industrial Arbitration Board; adjudicates on claims for statutory trade union recognition and derecognition under the 1999 Employment Relations Act; determines disclosure of information complaints and considers applications and complaints received under the Information and Consultation of Employees Regulations 2004; considers applications in relation to the establishment and operation of European Works Councils, European Companies and European Co-operative Societies; Chair. Sir MICHAEL BURTON; Chief Exec. SIMON GOULDSTONE.

Competition Appeal Tribunal: Victoria House, Bloomsbury Pl., London, WC1A 2EB; tel. (20) 7979-7979; fax (20) 7979-7978; e-mail info@catribunal.org.uk; internet www.catribunal.org.uk; f. 2002; a specialist tribunal established to hear certain cases in the sphere of British competition and economic regulatory law; hears appeals against decisions of the Office of Fair Trading and the regulators in the telecommunications, electricity, gas, water, railways and air traffic services sectors under the Competition Act of 1998; reviews decisions of the Office of Fair Trading, the Competition Commission and the Secretary of State made pursuant to the merger control and market investigation provisions of the Enterprise Act of 2002; also has jurisdiction, under the Competition Act of 1998, to award damages in respect of infringements of EC or British competition law and, under the Communications Act of 2003, to hear appeals against decisions of Ofcom; headed by the President and a panel of Chairmen and 14 mems with backgrounds in law, economics, business, accountancy and regulation who sit with the President or a mem. of the panel of Chairmen to hear cases; Pres. Sir GERALD BARLING; Registrar CHARLES DHANOWA.

Competition Commission: Victoria House, Southampton Row, London, WC1B 4AD; tel. (20) 7271-0100; fax (20) 7271-0367; e-mail info@cc.gsi.gov.uk; internet www.competition-commission.org.uk; conducts in-depth inquiries into mergers, markets and the regulation of the major regulated industries; Chair. PETER FREEMAN; Chief Exec. DAVID SAUNDERS.

Competition Service: Victoria House, Bloomsbury Pl., London, WC1A 2EB; tel. (20) 7979-7979; fax (20) 7979-7978; e-mail info@catribunal.org.uk; internet www.catribunal.org.uk; f. 2003 under the Enterprise Act 2002; a corporate and executive non-departmental public body, whose purpose is to fund and provide support services to the Competition Appeal Tribunal.

Consumer Focus: 4th Floor, Artillery House, Artillery Row, London, SW1P 1RT; tel. (20) 7799-7900; fax (20) 7799-7901; e-mail contact@consumerfocus.org.uk; internet www.consumerfocus.org.uk; f. 2008 by merger of Postwatch, energywatch and the National Consumer Council; Advocacy body for consumer rights; Chair. CHRISTINE FARNISH.

Forestry Commission: Silvan House, 231 Corstorphine Rd, Edinburgh, EH12 7AT; tel. (131) 334-0303; fax (131) 334-3047; e-mail enquiries@forestry.gsi.gov.uk; internet www.forestry.gov.uk; government department responsible for protecting and expanding the forests and woodlands of England, Scotland and Wales and increasing their value to society and the environment; implements the Government's forestry policy within the framework of the Forestry Acts, administers the Woodland Grant Scheme, controls tree-felling through the issue of licences, administers plant health regulations to protect woodlands against tree pests and diseases, and conducts research; responsible for the management of the national forests; Chair. PAMELA WARHURST; Dir-Gen. TIM ROLLINSON.

GLE oneLondon: New City Court, 20 St Thomas St, London, SE1 9RS; tel. (20) 7403-0300; fax (20) 7940-1742; e-mail info@gle.co.uk; internet www.one-london.com; f. 2001 following merger between London Enterprise Agency and Greater London Enterprise; jointly owned by all 33 London borough councils; Man. Dir NICHOLAS NICOLAOU.

Natural England: 1 East Parade, Sheffield, S1 2ET; tel. (114) 241-8920; fax (114) 241-8921; e-mail enquiries@naturalengland.org.uk; internet www.naturalengland.org.uk; f. 2006 by merger of English Nature, landscape, access and recreation sections of the Countryside Agency and the environmental land management functions of the Rural Development Service; advises Government and acts on issues relating to the conservation and enhancement of the environmental, economic and social well-being of the English countryside; Chair. POUL CHRISTENSEN; Chief Exec. Dr HELEN PHILLIPS.

Office of Fair Trading: Fleetbank House, 2–6 Salisbury Sq., London, EC4Y 8JX; tel. (20) 7211-8000; fax (20) 7211-8800; e-mail enquiries@oft.gsi.gov.uk; internet www.oft.gov.uk; f. 1973; monitors consumer affairs, competition policy, consumer credit, estate agencies, etc.; Chair. PHILIP COLLINS; Chief Exec. JOHN FINGLETON.

Postal Services Commission (Postcomm): Hercules House, 6 Hercules Rd, London, SE1 7DB; tel. (20) 7593-2100; fax (20) 7593-2142; e-mail info@psc.gov.uk; internet www.psc.gov.uk; f. 2000 under the Postal Services Act of 2000 as an independent regulator for postal services in the UK; duties include ensuring the provision of a universal postal service, licensing postal operators, introducing competition into mail services, regulating Royal Mail and advising the Govt on the Post Office network; Chair. NIGEL STAPLETON; Chief Exec. TIM BROWN.

Skills Funding Agency: Cheylesmore House, Quinton Rd, Coventry, CV1 2WT; tel. (845) 377-5000; e-mail info@skillsfundingagency.bis.gov.uk; internet skillsfundingagency.bis.gov.uk; f. 2010; agency of the Department for Business, Innovation and Skills; funds and regulates adult further education and skills training in England; Chief Exec. GEOFF RUSSELL.

United Kingdom Atomic Energy Authority: Culham Science Centre, Abingdon, Oxfordshire, OX14 3DB; tel. (1235) 528822; internet www.uk-atomic-energy.org.uk; f. 1954 to take responsibility for British research and development into all aspects of atomic energy; fmr commercial division responsible for managing decommissioning of nuclear reactors, UKAEA Ltd, transferred to private sector in 2009; a non-departmental public body within the Department for Business, Innovation and Skills; carries out nuclear fusion research on behalf of the Government at the Culham Centre for Fusion Energy; Chair. Lady BARBARA JUDGE; Chief Exec. Prof. STEVEN COWLEY.

DEVELOPMENT ORGANIZATIONS

Economic Research Institute of Northern Ireland (ERINI): Floral Buildings, 2–14 East Bridge St, Belfast, BT1 3NQ; tel. (28) 9072-7350; fax (28) 9031-9003; e-mail contact@erini.ac.uk; internet www.erini.ac.uk; f. 2004 by merger of Northern Ireland Economic Research Centre and Northern Ireland Economic Council; provides independent economic research, analysis and advice aimed at challenging and developing public policy-making and strategic thinking on issues facing Northern Ireland society; 15 mems representing trade union, employer and independent interests; Chair. (vacant); Dir VICTOR HEWITT.

Invest Northern Ireland (Invest NI): Bedford Sq., Bedford St, Belfast, BT1 7ES; tel. (28) 9023-9090; fax (28) 9043-6536; e-mail eo@investni.com; internet www.investni.com; f. 2002; Invest NI is the main economic development agency in Northern Ireland and, sponsored by the Dept of Enterprise, Trade and Investment, aims to strengthen the Northern Ireland economy; Chair. STEPHEN KINGON; Chief Exec. ALASTAIR HAMILTON.

London First: 3 Whitcomb St, London, WC2H 7HA; tel. (20) 7665-1500; fax (20) 7665-1501; e-mail staff@london-first.co.uk; internet www.london-first.co.uk; promotes London as a business centre; Chair. Sir ADRIAN MONTAGUE; Chief Exec. Baroness JO VALENTINE.

Overseas Development Institute: 111 Westminster Bridge Rd, London, SE1 7JD; tel. (20) 7922-0300; fax (20) 7922-0399; e-mail odi@odi.org.uk; internet www.odi.org.uk; f. 1960; independent policy unit

THE UNITED KINGDOM

on international development and humanitarian issues; Chair. Dr DALEEP MUKARJI; Dir Dr ALISON EVANS.

Scottish Enterprise: Atrium Court, 50 Waterloo St, Glasgow, G2 6HQ; tel. (141) 204-1111; fax (141) 248-1600; e-mail enquiries@scotent.co.uk; internet www.scottish-enterprise.com; economic development agency for lowland Scotland; Chair. CRAWFORD GILLIES; Chief Exec. LENA C. WILSON.

CHAMBERS OF COMMERCE

British Chambers of Commerce (BCC): 65 Petty France, London, SW1H 9EU; tel. (20) 7654-5800; fax (20) 7654-5819; e-mail info@britishchambers.org.uk; internet www.britishchambers.org.uk; f. 1860; in January 1993 subsumed National Chamber of Trade (f. 1897); represents the new Approved Chamber Network in the United Kingdom (comprising 58 Chambers at June 2007); Pres. NEVILLE RAYNER; Dir-Gen. DAVID FROST.

International Chamber of Commerce (ICC) United Kingdom: 12 Grosvenor Pl., London, SW1X 7HH; tel. (20) 7838-9363; fax (20) 7235-5447; e-mail info@iccorg.co.uk; internet www.iccuk.net; f. 1920; British affiliate of the world business org.; Dir ANDREW HOPE.

London Chamber of Commerce and Industry: 33 Queen St, London, EC4R 1AP; tel. (20) 7248-4444; fax (20) 7489-0391; e-mail lc@londonchamber.co.uk; internet www.londonchamber.co.uk; f. 1881; Pres. STEPHEN GREENE; Chief Exec. COLIN STANBRIDGE.

Northern Ireland Chamber of Commerce (NICC): Chamber of Commerce House, 22 Great Victoria St, Belfast, BT2 7BJ; tel. (28) 9024-4113; fax (28) 9024-7024; e-mail mail@northernirelandchamber.com; internet www.nicci.co.uk; f. 1783; Pres. BRO MCFERRAN; Chief Exec. ANN MCGREGOR; 4,000 mems.

INDUSTRIAL AND TRADE ASSOCIATIONS

ADS: Salamanca Sq, 9 Albert Embankment, London, SE1 7SP; tel. (20) 7091-4500; fax (20) 7091-4545; e-mail enquiries@adsgroup.org.uk; internet www.adsgroup.org.uk; f. 2009 by merger of Asscn of Police and Public Security Suppliers, Defence Mfrs Asscn and Soc. of British Aerospace Cos; national trade asscn for the British aerospace, defence and security industries; Chair. IAN GODDEN; CEO REES WARD.

Aluminium Federation: National Metalforming Centre, 47 Birmingham Rd, West Bromwich, B70 6PY; tel. (121) 601-6363; fax (870) 138-9714; e-mail alfed@alfed.org.uk; internet www.alfed.org.uk; f. 1962; Pres. COLIN DAVIES; Chief Exec. WILL SAVAGE.

Association of the British Pharmaceutical Industry: 12 Whitehall, London, SW1A 2DY; tel. (20) 7930-3477; fax (20) 7747-1414; e-mail abpi@abpi.org.uk; internet www.abpi.org.uk; f. 1930; Pres. CHRIS BRINSMEAD; Dir-Gen. Dr RICHARD BARKER.

Association of Manufacturers of Domestic Appliances: Rapier House, 40–46 Lamb's Conduit St, London, WC1N 3NW; tel. (20) 7405-0666; fax (20) 7405-6609; e-mail info@amdea.org.uk; internet www.amdea.org.uk; f. 1969; 32 mem. cos; Chief Exec. DOUGLAS HERBISON.

BFM (British Furniture Manufacturers Association): Wycombe House, 9 Amersham Hill, High Wycombe, Bucks, HP13 6NR; tel. (149) 4523-021; fax (149) 4474-270; e-mail info@bfm.org.uk; internet www.bfm.org.uk; merged in January 1993 with BFM Exhibitions and BFM Exports; Man. Dir JACKIE BAZELEY.

British Beer and Pub Association: Market Towers, 1 Nine Elms Lane, London, SW8 5NQ; tel. (20) 7627-9191; fax (20) 7627-9123; e-mail web@beerandpub.com; internet www.beerandpub.com; f. 1904; trade association for British brewing industry and multiple pub operators; Chair. MICHAEL TURNER; Chief Exec. DAVID LONG (acting).

British Cable Association: 3–30 Lingfield Rd, Wimbledon, SW19 4PU; tel. and fax (20) 8946-6978; e-mail peter.smeeth@btconnect.com; internet www.bcauk.org; f. 1903; fmrly British Cable Makers' Confederation; Sec.-Gen. PETER SMEETH.

British Cement Association: Riverside House, 4 Meadows Business Park, Station Approach, Blackwater, Camberley, Surrey, GU17 9AB; tel. (1276) 608700; fax (1276) 608701; e-mail info@bca.org.uk; internet www.bca.org.uk; Chair. CLIVE JAMES; Chief Exec. PAL CHANA.

British Ceramic Confederation: Federation House, Station Rd, Stoke-on-Trent, Staffs., ST4 2SA; tel. (1782) 744631; fax (1782) 744102; e-mail bcc@ceramfed.co.uk; internet www.ceramfed.co.uk; f. 1984; 100 mems; Chief Exec. Dr LAURA COHEN.

British Clothing Industry Association (BCIA): 5 Portland Pl., London, W1B 1PW; tel. (20) 7636-7788; fax (20) 7636-7515; e-mail bcia@dial.pipex.com; f. 1980; Chair. PETER LUCAS; Dir JOHN R. WILSON.

British Electrotechnical and Allied Manufacturers' Association (BEAMA Ltd): Westminster Tower, 3 Albert Embankment, London, SE1 7SL; tel. (20) 7793-3000; fax (20) 7793-3003; e-mail info@beama.org.uk; internet www.beama.org.uk; f. 1905 as British Electrical and Allied Manufacturers' Association Ltd, present name from 2002; 460 mems; Pres. and Chair. RICHARD DICK; CEO DAVID DOSSETT.

British Exporters' Association: Broadway House, Tothill St, London, SW1H 9NQ; tel. (20) 7222-5419; fax (20) 7799-2468; e-mail hughbailey@bexa.co.uk; internet www.bexa.co.uk; Pres. Sir RICHARD NEEDHAM; Chair. SUSAN ROSS; Dir HUGH BAILEY.

British Footwear Association: 3 Burystead Place, Wellingborough, Northants, NN8 1AH; tel. (1933) 229005; fax (1933) 225009; e-mail info@britfoot.com; internet www.britfoot.com; f. 1898; Sec. ELAINE DAVIES.

British Glass: 9 Churchill Way, Chapeltown, Sheffield, S35 2PY; tel. (114) 290-1850; fax (114) 290-1851; e-mail info@britglass.co.uk; internet www.britglass.org.uk; over 100 mems; Dir-Gen. DAVID WORKMAN.

British Hospitality Association: Queen's House, 55/56 Lincoln's Inn Fields, London, WC2A 3BH; tel. (845) 880-7744; fax (20) 7404-7799; e-mail bha@bha.org.uk; internet www.bha.org.uk; f. 1907; Pres. Sir DAVID MICHELS; Chief Exec. ROBERT COTTON.

The British Precast Concrete Federation Ltd: 60 Charles St, Leicester, LE1 1FB; tel. (116) 253-6161; fax (116) 251-4568; e-mail info@britishprecast.org; internet www.britishprecast.org; f. 1918; approx. 125 mems; Chief Exec. MARTIN A. CLARKE.

British Printing Industries Federation: Farringdon Point, 29–35 Farringdon Rd, London, EC1M 3JF; tel. (870) 240-4085; fax (20) 7405-7784; e-mail andrew.brown@bpif.org.uk; internet www.britishprint.com; f. 1900; 2,500 mems; Pres. MIKE TAYLOR; Chief Exec. MICHAEL JOHNSON.

British Rubber Manufacturers' Association: 6 Bath Pl., Rivington St, London, EC2A 3JE; tel. (20) 7457-5040; fax (20) 7972-9008; e-mail mail@brma.co.uk; internet www.brma.co.uk; f. 1968; Pres. JAMES RICKARD; Dir A. J. DORKEN.

The Carpet Foundation: MFC Complex, 60 New Rd, Kidderminster, Worcs., DY10 1AQ; tel. (1562) 755568; fax (1562) 865405; internet www.comebacktocarpet.com; 11 manufacturer and 1,100 retailer mems; Chair. JOHN DUNCAN; Chief Exec. MIKE HARDIMAN.

CBI: Centre Point, 103 New Oxford St, London, WC1A 1DU; tel. (20) 7379-7400; fax (20) 7240-1578; internet www.cbi.org.uk; f. 1965 as the Confederation of British Industry; adopted current name in 2001; acts as a national point of reference for all seeking views of industry and is recognized internationally as the representative organization of British industry and management; advises the Government on all aspects of policy affecting the interests of industry; has a direct corporate membership employing more than 4m., and a trade association membership representing more than 6m. of the workforce; Pres. HELEN ALEXANDER; Dir-Gen. JOHN CRIDLAND.

Chemical Industries Association: King's Buildings, Smith Sq., London, SW1P 3JJ; tel. (20) 7834-3399; fax (20) 7834-4469; e-mail enquiries@cia.org.uk; internet www.cia.org.uk; Chief Exec. STEVE ELLIOTT.

Construction Confederation: 55 Tufton St, London, SW1P 3QL; tel. (870) 898-9090; fax (870) 898-9095; e-mail enquiries@thecc.org.uk; internet www.thecc.org.uk; f. 1878; 5,000 mems; Chair. JAMES WATES; Chief Exec. STEPHEN RATCLIFFE.

Dairy UK: 93 Baker St, London, W1U 6QQ; tel. (20) 7486-7244; fax (20) 7487-4734; e-mail info@dairyuk.org; internet www.dairyuk.org; f. 1933; Chair. MARK ALLEN; Dir-Gen. JIM BEGG.

Electrical Contractors' Association: ESCA House, 34 Palace Court, London, W2 4HY; tel. (20) 7313-4800; fax (20) 7221-7344; e-mail info@eca.co.uk; internet www.eca.co.uk; f. 1901; Pres. ALLAN LITTLER; Dir DAVID R. J. POLLOCK.

Energy Networks Association: 6th Floor, Dean Bradley House, 52 Horseferry Rd, London, SW1P 2AF; tel. (20) 7706-5100; e-mail info@energynetworks.org; internet www.energynetworks.org; f. 2003; represents British gas and electricity transmission and distribution licence holders; Chair. MARK MATHIESON; Chief Exec. DAVID SMITH.

EEF—The Manufacturers' Organization: Broadway House, Tothill St, London, SW1H 9NQ; tel. (20) 7222-7777; fax (20) 7222-2782; e-mail enquiries@eef-fed.org.uk; internet www.eef.org.uk; f. 1896 as Engineering Employers' Federation; 6,000 mems through 14 associations; Pres. ALAN WOOD; CEO GILBERT TOPPIN.

Farmers' Union of Wales: Llys Amaeth, Plas Gogerddan, Aberystwyth, Ceredigion, SY23 3BT; tel. (1970) 820820; fax (1970) 820821; e-mail head.office@fuw.org.uk; internet www.fuw.org.uk; f. 1955; 14,000 mems; Pres. GARETH VAUGHAN.

Food and Drink Federation: 6 Catherine St, London, WC2B 5JJ; tel. (20) 7836-2460; fax (20) 7836-0580; e-mail generalenquiries@fdf.org.uk; internet www.fdf.org.uk; Dir-Gen. MELANIE LEECH.

Glass and Glazing Federation: 44–48 Borough High St, London, SE1 1XB; tel. (870) 042-4255; fax (870) 042-4266; e-mail info@ggf.org.uk; internet www.ggf.org.uk; f. 1977; trade organization for

THE UNITED KINGDOM

employers and cos in the flat glass, glazing, home improvement, plastic and window film industries; Chief Exec. NIGEL REES.

Institute of Export: Export House, Minerva Business Park, Lynch Wood, Peterborough, PE2 6FT; tel. (1733) 404400; fax (1733) 404444; e-mail institute@export.org.uk; internet www.export.org.uk; f. 1935; professional educational organization devoted to the development of British export trade and the interests of those associated with it; more than 6,000 mems; Pres. JAMES DAVIES; Chair. LESLEY BATCHELOR; Dir ANDY GIBSON.

Labour Relations Agency: 2-8 Gordon St, Belfast, BT1 2LG; tel. (28) 9032-1442; fax (28) 9033-0827; e-mail info@lra.org.uk; internet www.lra.org.uk; f. 1976; provides an impartial and confidential employment relations service to those engaged in industry, commerce and the public services in Northern Ireland; provides advice on good employment practices and assistance with the development and implementation of employment policies and procedures; also active in resolving disputes through its conciliation, mediation and arbitration services.

National Association of British and Irish Millers Ltd: 21 Arlington St, London, SW1A 1RN; tel. (20) 7493-2521; fax (20) 7493-6785; e-mail info@nabim.org.uk; internet www.nabim.org.uk; trade assoc. of the British flour milling industry; f. 1878; Dir-Gen. ALEXANDER WAUGH; Sec. NIGEL BENNETT.

National Farmers' Union: Agriculture House, Stoneleigh Park, Warwickshire CV8 2TZ; tel. (24) 7685-8500; fax (24) 7685-8501; e-mail nfu@nfu.org.uk; internet www.nfuonline.com; f. 1908; Pres. PETER KENDALL; Dir-Gen. KEVIN ROBERTS.

National Metal Trades Federation: Savoy Tower, 77 Renfrew St, Glasgow, G2 3BZ; tel. (141) 332-0826; fax (141) 332-5788; e-mail alex.shaw@nmtf.org.uk; Sec. ALEX SHAW.

Northern Ireland Hotels Federation: Midland Bldg, Whitla St, Belfast, BT15 1JP; tel. (28) 9035-1110; fax (28) 9035-1509; e-mail office@nihf.co.uk; internet www.nihf.co.uk; Pres. ISSAM HORSHI; Chief Exec. JANICE GAULT.

Northern Ireland Textiles and Apparel Asscn: 5c The Square, Hillsborough, BT26 6AG; tel. (28) 9268-9999; fax (28) 9268-9968; e-mail info@nita.co.uk; internet www.nita.co.uk; f. 1993; Dir LINDA MACHUGH; 30 mems.

Producers Alliance for Cinema and Television (PACT) Ltd: 2nd Floor, 1 Procter St, London, WC1V 6DW; tel. (20) 7067-4367; fax (20) 7067-4377; e-mail enquiries@pact.co.uk; internet www.pact.co.uk; film and TV producers; represents 1,000 companies; Chief Exec. JOHN MCVAY; Chair. CHARLES WACE.

Quarry Products Association: Gillingham House, 38–44 Gillingham St, London, SW1V 1HU; tel. (20) 7963-8000; fax (20) 7963-8001; e-mail info@qpa.org; internet www.qpa.org; fmrly British Ready Mixed Concrete Asscn, and the British Aggregate Construction Materials Industry Ltd; Chair LYNDA THOMPSON; Dir SIMON VAN DER BYL.

Scottish Building Federation: Crichton House, Crichton's Close, Edinburgh, EH8 8DT; tel. (131) 556-8866; fax (131) 558-5247; e-mail info@scottish-building.co.uk; internet www.scottish-building.co.uk; Pres. BILL IMLACH; Gen. Man. DOUGLAS FERGUS.

Scottish Enterprise—Textiles: Apex House, 99 Haymarket Terrace, Edinburgh, EH12 5DH; tel. (131) 313-6243; fax (131) 313-4231; internet www.scottish-textiles.co.uk; present name since 1991.

Sea Fish Industry Authority (Seafish): 18 Logie Mill, Logie Green Rd, Edinburgh, EH7 4HS; tel. (131) 558-3331; fax (131) 558-1442; e-mail seafish@seafish.co.uk; internet www.seafish.org; non-departmental public body sponsored by the four United Kingdom Government fisheries departments and funded by a levy on seafood; works with all sectors of the British seafood industry to satisfy consumers, raise standards, improve efficiency and secure a sustainable future; Chair. CHARLES HOWESON; Chief Exec. JOHN RUTHERFORD.

Society of Motor Manufacturers and Traders: Forbes House, Halkin St, London, SW1X 7DS; tel. (20) 7235-7000; fax (20) 7235-7112; e-mail membership@smmt.co.uk; internet www.smmt.co.uk; f. 1902; Pres. JOE GREENWELL; Chief Exec. PAUL EVERITT.

The Sugar Bureau: 25 Floral St, London, WC2E 9DS; tel. (20) 7189-8301; fax (20) 7031-8101; e-mail info@sugar-bureau.co.uk; internet www.sugar-bureau.co.uk; f. 1964; represents sugar companies in the UK, provides technical, educational and consumer information about sugar and health; Dir Dr ALISON BOYD.

Timber Trade Federation: Building Centre, 26 Store St, London, WC1E 7BT; tel. (20) 3205-0067; fax (20) 7291-5379; e-mail ttf@ttf.co.uk; internet www.ttf.co.uk; Chief Exec. JOHN WHITE.

Ulster Chemists' Asscn: 5 Annadale Ave, Belfast, BT7 3JH; tel. (28) 9069-0456; fax (28) 9069-0457; e-mail adrienne@uca.org.uk; internet www.uca.org.uk; f. 1901; promotion and protection of interests of community pharmacies in Northern Ireland; Pres. JONATHAN LLOYD.

Ulster Farmers' Union: Dunedin, 475 Antrim Rd, Belfast, BT15 3DA; tel. (28) 9037-0222; fax (28) 9037-1231; e-mail info@ufuhq.com; internet www.ufuni.org; f. 1918; Pres. GRAHAM FUREY; Chief Exec. CLARKE BLACK; 12,500 mems.

United Kingdom Petroleum Industry Association: Quality House, Quality Court, Chancery Lane, London, WC1A 1HP; tel. (20) 7269-7600; e-mail info@ukpia.com; internet www.ukpia.com; f. 1978; Pres. Dr BRIAN WORRALL; Dir-Gen. CHRIS HUNT.

EMPLOYERS' ASSOCIATIONS

British Retail Consortium: 21 Dartmouth St, London, SW1H 9BP; tel. (20) 7854-8900; fax (20) 7854-8901; e-mail info@brc.org.uk; internet www.brc.org.uk; f. 1975; represents retailers; Chair. LUKE MAYHEW; Dir-Gen. STEPHEN ROBERTSON.

Chartered Management Institute: Management House, Cottingham Rd, Corby, NN17 1TT; tel. (1536) 204222; fax (1536) 201651; e-mail enquiries@managers.org.uk; internet www.managers.org.uk; f. 1992 as the Institute of Management by amalgamation of British Institute of Management (f. 1947) and Institution of Industrial Managers (f. 1931); changed name as above in 2002; represents 86,000 individual mems and 450 corporate mems; Pres. Sir DAVID HOWARD; Chief Exec. RUTH SPELLMAN.

Federation of Small Businesses: Sir Frank Whittle Way, Blackpool Business Park, Blackpool, Lancashire FY4 2FE; tel. (1253) 336000; fax (1253) 348046; e-mail membership@fsb.org.uk; internet www.fsb.org.uk; f. 1974; represents the interests of British small businesses and the self-employed; 213,000 mems; Nat. Chair. JOHN WRIGHT.

Institute of Directors: 116 Pall Mall, London, SW1Y 5ED; tel. (20) 7839-1233; fax (20) 7766-8833; e-mail enquiries@iod.com; internet www.iod.com; f. 1903; 45,000 mems; Chair. Dr NEVILLE BAIN; Dir-Gen. MILES TEMPLEMAN.

UTILITIES

Electricity and Gas

Regulatory Authorities

Northern Ireland Authority for Utility Regulation (Utility Regulator): Queens House, 14 Queens St, Belfast, BT1 6ED; tel. (28) 9031-1575; fax (28) 9031-1740; e-mail info@uregni.gov.uk; internet www.uregni.gov.uk; name changed from Northern Ireland Authority for Energy Regulation to present in 2007; independent public body to regulate the electricity, water, sewage, and natural gas industries in Northern Ireland; Chair. PETER MATTHEWS; Chief Exec. IAIN OSBORNE.

Office of Gas and Electricity Markets (Ofgem): 9 Millbank, London, SW1P 3GE; tel. (20) 7901-7000; fax (20) 7901-7066; e-mail consumeraffairs@ofgem.gov.uk; internet www.ofgem.gov.uk; f. 1999 following merger of Offer and Ofgas; regulates the gas and electricity industries in England, Scotland and Wales and aims to promote the interests of all gas and electricity customers by promoting competition and regulating monopolies; Chair. Lord MOGG; Chief Exec. ALISTAIR BUCHANAN.

Principal Companies

British Energy: GSO Business Park, East Kilbride, G74 5PG; tel. (1355) 846000; fax (1355) 846001; e-mail john.mcnamara@british-energy.com; internet www.british-energy.com; production of electricity; operates 8 nuclear power stations and 1 coal-fired power station in the United Kingdom; acquired by EDF (France) Jan. 2009; 20% stake held by Centrica; Chief Exec. BILL COLEY.

British Gas: Centrica PLC, Millstream, Maidenhead Rd, Windsor, Berkshire, SL4 5GD; tel. (1753) 494000; fax (1753) 494001; e-mail house@britishgas.co.uk; internet www.britishgas.co.uk; part of Centrica Group; Chair. ROGER CARR; Man. Dir PHIL BENTLEY.

CE Electric UK: 98 Aketon Rd, Castleford, WF10 5DS; tel. (1977) 605934; fax (1977) 605944; e-mail cus.serv@ce-electricuk.com; internet www.ceelectricuk.com; subsidiary of MidAmerican Energy Holdings Co; delivers electricity to 3.6m. homes in the north-east of England, Yorkshire and Humberside; Dir J. M. FRANCE.

Central Networks: Herald Way, Pegasus Business Park, East Midlands Airport, Castle Donington, DE74 2TU; tel. (800) 0963080; internet www.central-networks.co.uk; distribution of electricity; subsidiary of E.ON UK PLC; fmrly East Midlands Electricity PLC; merged with Midlands Electricity PLC in 2004 and name changed to above; Man. Dir JOHN CRACKETT.

EDF Energy: 40 Grosvenor Pl., London, SW1X 7GN; tel. (20) 7242-9050; e-mail info@edfenergy.com; internet www.edfenergy.com; producer and supplier of electricity and gas; Chair. HENRI PROGLIO; Chief Exec. VINCENT DE RIVAZ.

E.ON UK PLC: Westwood Way, Westwood Business Park, Coventry, CV4 8LG; tel. (24) 7642-4000; fax (24) 7642-5432; e-mail email.queries@eonenergy.com; internet www.eon-uk.com; f. 2004; fmrly

THE UNITED KINGDOM

Powergen UK PLC; supplies, distributes and sells electricity; also retailer of gas; subsidiary of E.ON AG (Germany); bought by PPL Corpn (USA) in March 2011; Chair. Dr WULF H. BERNOTAT; Chief Exec. Dr PAUL GOLBY.

Green Energy (UK) PLC: 23 Baldock St, Ware Herts SG12 9DH; tel. (1920) 486156; fax (1920) 484268; e-mail help@greenenergyuk.com; internet www.greenenergyuk.com; Chair. Sir PETER THOMPSON; CEO DOUGLAS STEWART.

National Grid PLC: 1–3 Strand, London, WC2N 5EH; tel. (20) 7004-3000; fax (20) 7004-3004; internet www.nationalgrid.com; Chair. Sir JOHN PARKER; Chief Exec. STEVE HOLLIDAY.

Northern Ireland Electricity PLC (NIE): 120 Malone Rd, Belfast, BT9 5HT; tel. (28) 9066-1100; e-mail customercontact@nie.co.uk; internet www.nie.co.uk; holding co Viridian Group; sale to Electricity Supply Board (ESB—Ireland) agreed July 2010; transmission and distribution of electricity in Northern Ireland; associated co NIE Energy supplies electricity; Man. Dir HARRY MCCRACKEN.

npower: Oak House, Bridgwater Rd, Warndon, Worcester, WR4 9FP; tel. (1793) 877777; fax (1793) 892525; internet www.npower.com; f. 1999 to combine the electricity and gas supply business of six companies; launched in 2000; retail arm of RWE npower PLC; CEO VOLKER BECKERS.

Phoenix Natural Gas Ltd: 197 Airport Rd West, Belfast, BT3 9ED; tel. (28) 9055-5555; fax (28) 9055-5500; e-mail info@phoenix-natural-gas.com; internet www.phoenix-natural-gas.com; f. 1997; CEO PETER DIXON.

RWE npower plc: Windmill Hill Business Park, Whitehill Way, Swindon, Wiltshire, SN5 6PB; tel. (1793) 877777; fax (1793) 893955; internet www.rwenpower.com; Group CEO VOLKER BECKERS.

Scottish and Southern Energy PLC: Inveralmond House, 200 Dunkeld Rd, Perth, PH1 3AQ; tel. (1738) 456660; fax (1738) 455281; e-mail info@scottish-southern.co.uk; internet www.scottish-southern.co.uk; Chair. Lord SMITH OF KELVIN; CEO IAN MARCHANT.

Scottish Power Ltd: Corporate Office, 1 Atlantic Quay, Glasgow, G2 8SP; tel. (141) 248-8200; fax (141) 248-8300; internet www.scottishpower.com; subsidiary of Iberdrola, SA (Spain); Chair. JOSÉ IGNACIO SÁNCHEZ GALÁN.

South Wales Electricity PLC: POB 7506, Perth, PH1 3QR; tel. (800) 052-5252; internet www.swalec.co.uk; part of Scottish and Southern Energy Group; CEO JOHN ROBINS.

Southern Electric: 55 Vastern Rd, Reading, Berks, RG1 8BU; internet www.southern-electric.co.uk; part of Scottish and Southern Energy Group; Group CEO IAN MARCHANT.

Water

Regulatory Authority

Water Services Regulation Authority (Ofwat): Centre City Tower, 7 Hill St, Birmingham, B5 4UA; tel. (121) 644-7500; fax (121) 644-7699; e-mail enquiries@ofwat.gsi.gov.uk; internet www.ofwat.gov.uk; independent economic regulator of the water and sewerage cos in England and Wales; ensures compliance with the functions specified in the Water Industry Act of 2003; Chair. PHILIP FLETCHER; Chief Exec. REGINA FINN.

Principal Companies

Anglian Water Services Ltd: POB 770, Lincoln, LN5 7WX; tel. (8457) 919155; fax (1480) 326981; internet www.anglianwater.co.uk; Chair. Sir ADRIAN MONTAGUE; Man. Dir PETER SIMPSON.

Northern Ireland Water: Northland House, 3 Frederick St, Belfast, BT1 2NR; tel. (8457) 440088; e-mail waterline@niwater.com; internet www.niwater.com; Chief Exec. TREVOR HASLETT (interim).

Northumbrian Water Ltd: Abbey Rd, Pity Me, Durham, DH1 5FJ; tel. (870) 608-4820; fax (191) 301-6202; internet www.nwl.co.uk; Chair. Sir DEREK WANLESS; CEO HEIDI MOTTRAM.

Scottish Water: Castle House, 6 Castle Drive, Carnegie Campus, Dunfermline, KY11 8GG; tel. (845) 601 8855; e-mail customer.service@scottishwater.co.uk; internet www.scottishwater.co.uk; f. 2002; Chair. RONNIE MERCER; Chief Exec. RICHARD K. ACKROYD.

Severn Trent Water Ltd: 2297 Coventry Rd, Birmingham, B26 3PU; tel. (121) 722-4000; fax (121) 722-4800; internet www.stwater.co.uk; Chair. Sir JOHN EGAN; Chief Exec. TONY WRAY.

South East Water Ltd: Rocfort Rd, Snodland, Kent, ME6 5AH; tel. (845) 301-8045; e-mail contactcentre@southeastwater.co.uk; internet www.southeastwater.co.uk; merged with Mid Kent Water 2007; owned by Hastings Diversified Utilities Fund and the Utilities Trust of Australia; Chair. GORDON MAXWELL; Man. Dir PAUL BUTLER.

South Staffordshire Water PLC: POB 63, Walsall, WS2 7PJ; tel. (1922) 616239; internet www.south-staffs-water.co.uk; Exec. Chair. DAVID SANKEY; Man. Dir Dr JACK CARNELL.

South West Water Ltd: Peninsula House, Rydon Lane, Exeter, EX2 7HR; tel. (1392) 446688; fax (1392) 434966; internet www.southwestwater.co.uk; part of Pennon Group; Chair. KENNETH HARVEY; CEO CHRISTOPHER LOUGHLIN.

Southern Water PLC: POB 41, Worthing, West Sussex, BN13 3NZ; tel. (1903) 264444; fax (1903) 691435; e-mail customerservices@southernwater.co.uk; internet www.southernwater.co.uk; Chair. MIKE WELTON; CEO LES DAWSON.

Thames Water Utilities Ltd: POB 286, Swindon, SN38 2RA; tel. (845) 920-0888; internet www.thameswater.co.uk; acquired by Kemble Water Ltd in 2006; Chair. Sir PETER MASON; CEO MARTIN BAGGS.

United Utilities PLC: Haweswater House, Lingley Mere Business Park, Great Sankey, Warrington, WA5 3LW; tel. (1925) 237000; fax (1925) 237066; internet www.uuplc.co.uk; Chair. Dr JOHN MCADAM; CEO PHILIP GREEN.

Veolia Water Central Limited: Tamblin Way, Hatfield, Hertfordshire, AL10 9EZ; tel. (845) 782-3333; internet central.veoliawater.co.uk; fmrly known as Three Valley Waters PLC; name changed as above in 2009; Chair. FREDERIC DEVOS; Man. Dir RICHARD BIENFAIT.

Welsh Water (Dwr Cymru Cyfyngedig): Pentwyn Rd, Nelson, Treharris, Mid Glamorgan, CF46 6LY; tel. (1443) 452300; fax (1443) 452809; e-mail enquiries@dwrcymru.com; internet www.dwrcymru.com; f. 1989; Chair. BOB AYLING (designate); Man. Dir NIGEL ANNETT.

Wessex Water Services Ltd: Claverton Down Rd, Bath, BA2 7WW; tel. (1225) 526000; e-mail info@wessexwater.co.uk; internet www.wessexwater.co.uk; Propr YTL (Malaysia); Chair. and CEO COLIN SKELLETT.

Yorkshire Water Services Ltd: POB 52, Bradford, BD6 2SZ; tel. (845) 124-2424; fax (1274) 372800; internet www.yorkshirewater.com; Chair. KEVIN WHITEMAN; Chief Exec. RICHARD FLINT.

CO-OPERATIVE ORGANIZATIONS

Co-operatives UK: Holyoake House, Hanover St, Manchester, M60 0AS; tel. (161) 246-2900; fax (161) 831-7684; e-mail info@cooperatives-uk.coop; internet www.cooperatives-uk.coop; f. 1869; co-ordinates, informs and advises the 45 retail consumer co-operative societies and 700 worker co-operatives and employee-owned businesses; Chair. DAVID BUTTON; Society Sec. ED MAYO; Chief Exec. Dame PAULINE GREEN.

Co-operative Group Ltd: New Century House, POB 53, Manchester, M60 4ES; tel. (161) 834-1212; fax (161) 834-4507; e-mail customer.relations@co-op.co.uk; internet www.co-operative.co.uk; f. 1863; merged with United Co-operatives in 2007; Chair. LEN WARDLE.

National Association of Co-operative Officials (NACO): 6A Clarendon Pl., Hyde, Cheshire, SK14 2QZ; tel. (161) 351-7900; fax (161) 366-6800; e-mail info@nacoco-op.org; internet www.naco.coop; f. 1918; Nat. Pres. KAREN FROGGATT.

TRADE UNIONS

Central Organizations

Trades Union Congress (TUC): Congress House, Great Russell St, London, WC1B 3LS; tel. (20) 7636-4030; fax (20) 7636-0632; e-mail info@tuc.org.uk; internet www.tuc.org.uk; f. 1868; 58 affiliated unions, with a total membership of 6.2m. (2010); affiliated to the ITUC and the European Trade Union Confederation; nominates the British Workers' Delegate to the International Labour Organization; Gen. Sec. BRENDAN BARBER.

Irish Congress of Trade Unions (Northern Ireland Committee): 4–6 Donegall Street Pl., Belfast, BT1 2FN; tel. (28) 9024-7940; fax (28) 9024-6898; e-mail info@ictuni.org; internet www.ictuni.org; 32 affiliated unions in Northern Ireland, with a membership of 231,451 (2011); Gen. Sec. DAVID BEGG.

Scottish Trades Union Congress: 333 Woodlands Rd, Glasgow, G3 6NG; tel. (141) 337-8100; fax (141) 337-8101; e-mail info@stuc.org.uk; internet www.stuc.org.uk; f. 1897; 655,192 individual mems affiliated through 37 trade unions and 22 trades union councils (2009); Gen. Sec. GRAHAME SMITH.

Wales Trades Union Council: 1 Cathedral Rd, Cardiff; tel. (29) 2034-7010; fax (29) 2022-1940; e-mail wtuc@tuc.org.uk; internet www.wtuc.org.uk; f. 1973; Gen. Sec. MARTIN MANSFIELD.

Principal Trade Unions Affiliated to the TUC

Includes all affiliated unions whose membership is in excess of 10,000.

ACCORD: Simmons House, 46 Old Bath Rd, Charvil, Reading, Berks, RG10 9QR; tel. (118) 934-1808; fax (118) 932-0208; e-mail info@accordhq.org; internet www.accord-myunion.org; Gen. Sec. GED NICHOLS; 30,415 mems (2008).

THE UNITED KINGDOM

Associated Society of Locomotive Engineers and Firemen (ASLEF): 9 Arkwright Rd, London, NW3 6AB; tel. (20) 7317-8600; fax (20) 7794-6406; e-mail info@aslef.org.uk; internet www.aslef.org.uk; f. 1880; Gen. Sec. KEITH NORMAN; 18,033 mems (2008).

Association of Teachers and Lecturers (ATL): 7 Northumberland St, London WC2N 5RD; tel. (20) 7930-6441; fax (20) 7930-1359; e-mail info@atl.org.uk; internet www.atl.org.uk; f. 1978; Pres. ANDY BALLARD; Gen. Sec. Dr MARY BOUSTED; 120,534 mems.

Bakers, Food and Allied Workers' Union (BFAWU): Stanborough House, Great North Rd, Stanborough, Welwyn Garden City, Herts., AL8 7TA; tel. (1707) 260150; fax (1707) 261570; e-mail info@bfawu.org; internet www.bfawu.org; f. 1861; Pres. RONNIE DRAPER; Gen. Sec. JOSEPH MARINO; 28,426 mems.

Broadcasting, Entertainment, Cinematograph and Theatre Union (BECTU): 373–377 Clapham Rd, London, SW9 9BT; tel. (20) 7346-0900; fax (20) 7346-0901; e-mail info@bectu.org.uk; internet www.bectu.org.uk; f. 1991 as a result of merger between Asscn of Cinematograph, Television and Allied Technicians (f. 1933) and the Broadcasting and Entertainment Trades Alliance (f. 1984); Pres. TONY LENNON; Gen. Sec. GERRY MORRISSEY; 26,210 mems (2008).

Chartered Society of Physiotherapy (CSP): 14 Bedford Row, London, WC1R 4ED; tel. (20) 7306-6666; fax (20) 7306-6611; e-mail enquiries@csp.org.uk; internet www.csp.org.uk; f. 1894; Pres. Baroness FINLAY OF LLANDAFF; Chief Exec. PHIL GRAY; 49,000 mems (2010).

Communications Workers' Union (CWU): 150 The Broadway, Wimbledon, London, SW19 1RX; tel. (20) 8971-7200; fax (20) 8971-7300; e-mail info@cwu.org; internet www.cwu.org; f. 1995 by merger of the National Communications Union and the Union of Communication Workers; Pres. DAVIE BOWMAN; Gen. Sec. BILLY HAYES; 236,679 mems.

Community: 67/68 Long Acre, Covent Gdn, London WC2E 9FA; tel. (20) 7420-4000; fax (20) 7420-4085; e-mail info@community-tu.org; internet www.community-tu.org; f. 2004 by the merger of the Iron and Steel Trades Confed. and the National Union of Knitwear, Footwear and Apparel Trades; Gen. Sec. MICHAEL J. LEAHY; 25,000 mems.

Connect: 30 St George's Rd, Wimbledon, London, SW19 4BD; tel. (20) 8971-6000; fax (20) 8971-6002; e-mail union@connectuk.org; internet www.connectuk.org; trade union for professionals in the communications industry; fmrly Society of Telecom Executives, name changed as above in 2000; Pres. DENISE MCGUIRE; Gen. Sec. ADRIAN ASKEW; 19,472 mems (2009).

Educational Institute of Scotland (EIS): 46 Moray Pl., Edinburgh, EH3 6BH; tel. (131) 225-6244; fax (131) 220-3151; e-mail enquiries@eis.org.uk; internet www.eis.org.uk; f. 1847; professional and trade union org. for teachers and lecturers in schools, colleges and universities; Pres. DAVID DREVER; Gen. Sec. RONALD A. SMITH; 59,539 mems (2008).

Equity: Guild House, Upper St Martin's Lane, London, WC2H 9EG; tel. (20) 7379-6000; fax (20) 7379-7001; e-mail info@equity.org.uk; internet www.equity.org.uk; represents artists and performers; Pres. HARRY LANDIS; Gen. Sec. CHRISTINE PAYNE; 35,527 mems (2008).

FDA: 8 Leake St, London, SE1 7NN; tel. (20) 7401-5555; fax (20) 7401-5550; e-mail info@fda.org.uk; internet www.fda.org.uk; f. 1919; public sector managers and professionals; Pres. DAVID WATTS; Gen. Sec. JONATHAN BAUME; 20,544 mems.

Fire Brigades Union (FBU): Bradley House, 68 Coombe Rd, Kingston upon Thames, Surrey, KT2 7AE; tel. (20) 8541-1765; fax (20) 8546-5187; e-mail office@fbu.org.uk; internet www.fbu.org.uk; f. 1918; Pres. MICK SHAW; Gen. Sec. MATT WRACK; 47,071 mems.

GMB—Britain's General Union: 22–24 Worple Rd, Wimbledon, London, SW19 4DD; tel. (20) 8947-3131; fax (20) 8944-6552; e-mail info@gmb.org.uk; internet www.gmb.org.uk; f. 1982; Pres. MARY TURNER; Gen. Sec. PAUL KENNY; 601,131 mems (2009).

Musicians' Union (MU): 60–62 Clapham Rd, London, SW9 0JJ; tel. (20) 7582-5566; fax (20) 7582-9805; e-mail info@themu.org; internet www.theMU.org; f. 1893; Gen. Sec. JOHN SMITH; 30,000 mems (2009).

National Association of Schoolmasters Union of Women Teachers (NASUWT): Hillscourt Education Centre, Rose Hill, Rednal, Birmingham, B45 8RS; tel. (121) 453-6150; fax (121) 457-6208; e-mail nasuwt@mail.nasuwt.org.uk; internet www.nasuwt.org.uk; f. 1919; merged with UWT 1976; Pres. JOHN MAYES; Gen. Sec. CHRIS KEATES; 265,202 mems (2008).

National Union of Journalists (NUJ): Headland House, 308-312 Gray's Inn Rd, London, WC1X 8DP; tel. (20) 7278-7916; fax (20) 7837-8143; e-mail info@nuj.org.uk; internet www.nuj.org.uk; f. 1907; Pres. CHRIS MORLEY; Gen. Sec. JEREMY DEAR; 32,409 mems (2008).

National Union of Rail, Maritime and Transport Workers (RMT): 39 Chalton Rd, London, NW1 1JD; tel. (20) 7387-4771; fax (20) 7387-4123; e-mail info@rmt.org.uk; internet www.rmt.org.uk; f. 1990 through merger of National Union of Railwaymen (f. 1872) and National Union of Seamen (f. 1887); Pres. JOHN LEACH; Gen. Sec. BOB CROW; 75,906 mems (2008).

National Union of Teachers (NUT): Hamilton House, Mabledon Pl., London, WC1H 9BD; tel. (20) 7388-6191; fax (20) 7387-8458; internet www.teachers.org.uk; Pres. MARTIN REED; Gen. Sec. CHRISTINE BLOWER (acting); 366,657 mems (2008).

Nationwide Group Staff Union (NGSU): Middleton Farmhouse, 37 Main Rd, Middleton Cheney, Banbury, OX17 2QT; tel. (1295) 710767; fax (1295) 712580; e-mail ngsu@ngsu.org.uk; internet www.ngsu.org.uk; Gen. Sec. TIM POIL; 13,892 mems (2008).

Nautilus International: 1–2, The Shrubberies, George Lane, South Woodford, London E18 1BD; tel. (20) 8989-6677; fax (20) 8530-1015; e-mail enquiries@nautilusint.org; internet www.nautilusint.org; f. 1936; as the National Union of Marine, Aviation and Shipping Transport Officers; renamed Nautilus UK in 2006, and as above in 2009; Sec. MARK DICKINSON; 16,274 mems (2008).

Prison Officers' Association (POA): Cronin House, 245 Church St, London, N9 9HW; tel. (20) 8803-0255; fax (20) 8803-1761; internet www.poauk.org.uk; f. 1939; Chair. COLIN MOSES; Gen. Sec. BRIAN CATON; 36,172 mems (2008).

Prospect: New Prospect House, 8 Leake St, London, SE1 7NN; tel. (20) 7902-6600; fax (20) 7902-6667; e-mail enquiries@prospect.org.uk; internet www.prospect.org.uk; f. 1919 as the Institution of Professionals, Managers and Specialists; name changed as above in 2001; Pres. CATHARINE DONALDSON; Gen. Sec. PAUL NOON; 102,702 mems (2008).

Public and Commercial Services Union (PCS): 160 Falcon Rd, London, SW11 2LN; tel. (20) 7924-2727; fax (20) 7924-1847; internet www.pcs.org.uk; f. 1998 by merger of Civil and Public Services Asscn (f. 1903) and Public Services, Tax and Commerce Union (f. 1996); Pres. JANICE GODRICH; Gen. Sec. MARK SERWOTKA; 300,000 mems.

Society of Radiographers (SoR): 207 Providence Sq., Mill St, London, SE1 2EW; tel. (20) 7740-7200; fax (20) 7740-7233; e-mail info@sor.org; internet www.sor.org; f. 1920; Pres. SANDIE MATHERS; Chief Exec. RICHARD EVANS; 23,817 mems.

Transport Salaried Staffs' Association (TSSA): Walkden House, 10 Melton St, London, NW1 2EJ; tel. (20) 7387-2101; fax (20) 7383-0656; internet www.tssa.org.uk; f. 1897; Pres. ANDY BAIN; Gen. Sec. GERRY DOHERTY; 29,102 mems (2008).

Union of Construction, Allied Trades and Technicians (UCATT): UCATT House, 177 Abbeville Rd, Clapham, London, SW4 9RL; tel. (20) 7622-2442; fax (20) 7720-4081; e-mail info@ucatt.org.uk; internet www.ucatt.info; f. 1971; Pres. JOHN THOMPSON; Gen. Sec. ALAN RITCHIE; 129,065 mems (2008).

Union of Shop, Distributive and Allied Workers (USDAW): 188 Wilmslow Rd, Manchester, M14 6LJ; tel. (161) 224-2804; fax (161) 257-2566; e-mail enquiries@usdaw.org.uk; internet www.usdaw.org.uk; Pres. JEFF BROOME; Gen. Sec. JOHN HANNETT; 356,046 mems (2008).

UNISON: 1 Mabledon Pl., London, WC1H 9AJ; tel. (845) 355-0845; fax (20) 7551-1101; e-mail direct@unison.co.uk; internet www.unison.org.uk; f. 1993 through merger of Confederation of Health Service Employees (COHSE—f. 1910), National and Local Government Officers Asscn (NALGO—f. 1905) and National Union of Public Employees (NUPE—f. 1888); Pres. SUE HIGHTON; Gen. Sec. DAVE PRENTIS; 1,343,000 mems (2008).

Unite—The Union: 35 King St, London, WC2E 8JG; tel. (20) 7420-8900; fax (20) 7420-8998; internet www.unitetheunion.com; f. 2007 by merger of Amicus and Transport and General Workers' Union; Gen. Sec. LEN MCCLUSKEY; 1,952,510 mems (2008).

United Road Transport Union (URTU): Almond House, Oak Green, Stanley Green Business Park, Cheadle Hulme, SK8 6QL; tel. (800) 526639; fax (161) 861-0976; e-mail info@urtu.com; internet www.urtu.com; f. 1890 as United Carters' Asscn; present name adopted 1964; Gen. Sec. ROBERT MONKS; 16,800 mems.

University and College Union (UCU): Carlow St, London, NW1 7LH; tel. (20) 7756-2500; fax (20) 7756-2501; e-mail hq@ucu.org.uk; internet www.ucu.org.uk; f. 2006 by merger of the Association of University Teachers and NATFHE—The University & College Lecturers' Union; Pres. SASHA CALLAGHAN; Gen. Sec. SALLY HUNT; 117,028 mems (2008).

Unions not affiliated to the TUC

Irish National Teachers' Organization (INTO): 23 College Gardens, Belfast, BT9 6BS (headquarters in Dublin); tel. (28) 9038-1455; fax (28) 9066-2803; e-mail infoni@into.ie; internet www.into.ie; f. 1868; affiliated to the Irish Congress of Trade Unions (Northern Ireland Committee); Northern Sec. FRANK BUNTING; 6,149 mems (Dec. 2006).

National Farmers' Union (NFU): see Industrial and Trade Associations.

THE UNITED KINGDOM

Northern Ireland Public Service Alliance: Harkin House, 54 Wellington Park, Belfast, BT9 6DP; tel. (28) 9066-1831; fax (28) 9066-5847; e-mail info@nipsa.org.uk; internet www.nipsa.org.uk; affiliated to the Irish Congress of Trade Unions; Pres. (2008/09) BRIAN MOORE; Gen. Sec. JOHN COREY; 44,500 mems.

Services Industrial Professional Technical Union (SIPTU): 3 Antrim Rd, Belfast, BT15 2BE; tel. (28) 9031-4000; fax (28) 9031-4044; e-mail athompson@siptu.ie; internet www.siptu.ie; affiliated to the Irish Congress of Trade Unions (Northern Ireland Committee); Regional Sec. JOE CUNNINGHAM; 7,000 members.

Ulster Teachers' Union: 94 Malone Rd, Belfast, BT9 5HP; tel. (28) 9066-2216; fax (28) 9068-3296; e-mail office@utu.edu; internet www.utu.edu; f. 1919; affiliated to the Irish Congress of Trade Unions (Northern Ireland Committee); Pres. MELANIE HOUSTON; Gen. Sec. AVRIL HALL-CALLAGHAN; 6,700 mems (Dec. 2006).

Union of Democratic Mineworkers (UDM): The Miners' Offices, Berry Hill Lane, Mansfield, Nottinghamshire, NG18 4JU; tel. (1623) 626094; fax (1623) 642300; e-mail enquiries@udmoffices.co.uk; internet www.unionofdemocraticmineworkers.co.uk; f. 1986; Pres. and Gen. Sec. NEIL GREATREX; c. 1,500 mems.

National Federations

Confederation of Shipbuilding and Engineering Unions: 5th Floor, 35 King St, London, WC2E 8JG; tel. (20) 7420-8988; fax (20) 7420-1488; 750,000 mems in 6 affiliated trade unions; Gen. Sec. HUGH SCULLION.

Federation of Entertainment Unions: 1 Highfield, Twyford, Hampshire, SO21 1QR; tel. and fax (1962) 713134; e-mail harris.s@btconnect.com; f. 1990; 6 affiliated unions; Sec. PAUL EVANS.

General Federation of Trade Unions (GFTU): Central House, Upper Woburn Pl., London, WC1H 0HY; tel. (20) 7387-2578; fax (20) 7383-0820; e-mail gftuhq@gftu.org.uk; internet www.gftu.org.uk; f. 1899; represents specialist unions; Pres. DOUG NICHOLLS; Gen. Sec. MIKE BRADLEY; 34 affiliated unions with total membership of 225,687 (Dec. 2006).

Transport

RAILWAYS

The Railways Act 1993, providing for a process of rail privatization, received royal assent in November 1993. A separate, government-owned company, Railtrack, was set up on 1 April 1994 to take responsibility for infrastructure (track, signals and stations) and levy charges on train operators for track access. As a result of the 1993 Railways Act, 25 Train Operating Units (TOUs) came into being on 1 April 1994. The Director of Passenger Rail Franchises was responsible for awarding franchises for the 25 TOUs as early as practicable and was to monitor the franchises to ensure compliance with the agreed contracts. The first passenger train franchises were awarded in 1995, and two TOUs were transferred to private operators in 1996; the final TOU transferred to the private sector the following year. Railtrack was transferred to the private sector in 1996. In October 2001 the Government placed the heavily indebted Railtrack in administration. Railtrack remained in administration until October 2002, when Network Rail, a 'not-for-profit' government-supported company, completed a takeover.

In February 1986 the Treaty of Canterbury was signed between the Governments of France and the United Kingdom, providing the constitutional basis for the construction of a tunnel between the two countries under the English Channel. The Channel Tunnel opened in May 1994, at an estimated cost of £4,700m., and comprises a fixed link of two rail tunnels and one service tunnel. Of the total length of 31 miles (50 km), 24 miles (38 km) are under the seabed. The rail services provider, Eurostar UK, moved all London operations from Waterloo International to St Pancras station in 2007.

DfT Rail Group: Department for Transport, Great Minster House, 76 Marsham St, London SW1P 4DR; tel. (20) 7944-8300; fax (20) 7944-9643; e-mail rail@dft.gsi.gov.uk; internet www.dft.gov.uk/pgr/rail; f. 2005 to assume many functions of the dissolved Strategic Rail Authority (SRA); has strategic and financial responsibility for the railways; Dir-Gen. MIKE MITCHELL.

Office of Rail Regulation: 1 Kemble St, London, WC2B 4AN; tel. (20) 7282-2000; fax (20) 7282-2040; e-mail rail.library@orr.gsi.gov.uk; internet www.rail-reg.gov.uk; f. 2004; Chair. CHRIS BOLT.

Network Rail Ltd: 40 Melton St, London, NW1 2EE; tel. (20) 3356-9595; fax (20) 3356-9245; internet www.networkrail.co.uk; f. 2002 as a 'not-for-profit' company by train operators, rail unions and passenger groups to take over responsibility for running the UK rail network from Railtrack PLC; Chair. RICK HAYTHORNWAITE; Chief Exec. DAVID HIGGINS.

Northern Ireland Railways Co Ltd: Central Station, East Bridge St, Belfast, BT1 3PB; tel. (28) 9089-9400; fax (28) 9089-9401; internet www.nirailways.co.uk; f. 1967; subsidiary of Northern Ireland Transport Holding Co (see under Roads) and part of the Translink rail and bus network; operates rail services for passenger traffic over 342 km and for freight traffic over 268 km of railway track; a high-speed passenger service between Belfast and Dublin, launched in co-operation with Irish Rail, began operations in 1997; Chief Exec. CATHERINE MASON; Gen. Man., Rail Services MALACHY MCGREEVY.

Channel Tunnel Rail Link

Eurotunnel Group: UK Terminal, Ashford Rd, Folkestone, Kent, CT18 8XX; tel. (1303) 282222; fax (1303) 850360; e-mail press@eurotunnel.com; internet www.eurotunnel.com; f. 1986; Anglo-French consortium contracted to design, finance and construct the Channel Tunnel under a concession granted for a period up to 2052 (later extended to 2086); receives finance exclusively from the private sector; operates a service of road vehicle 'shuttle' trains and passenger and freight trains through the Channel Tunnel; Chair. and Chief Exec. JACQUES GOUNON.

Eurostar UK Ltd/Eurostar Group: Times House, Bravingtons Walk, Regent Quarter, London, N1 9AW; tel. (20) 7902-3658; e-mail press.office@eurostar.co.uk; internet www.eurostar.com; commenced international high-speed passenger rail services in 1994; provides services from London, and Ebbsfleet and Ashford (both in Kent), direct to Paris, Brussels, Lille, Calais-Frethun, Disneyland Paris, Avignon and Bourg St Maurice; Chair. GUILLAUME PEPY; CEO RICHARD BROWN.

Associations

Railway Industry Association: 22 Headfort Pl., London, SW1X 7RY; tel. (20) 7201-0777; fax (20) 7235-5777; e-mail ria@riagb.org.uk; internet www.riagb.org.uk; f. 1875; represents UK-based railway suppliers, with a free sourcing service for products and services; Chair. COLIN WALTON; Dir-Gen. JEREMY CANDFIELD; 160 mems.

Association of Train Operating Companies: 3rd Floor, 40 Bernard St, London, WC1N 1BY; tel. (20) 7841-8000; e-mail atocnews@atoc.org; internet www.atoc.org; f. 1994; Chair. MIKE ALEXANDER; Dir-Gen. MICHAEL ROBERTS.

ROADS

Total road length in Great Britain in 2006 was 398,351 km (247,523 miles), of which 3,556 km (2,210 miles) was motorway. In 2005 there were 24,930 km (15,491 miles) of roads of all classes in Northern Ireland, including some 110 km (68 miles) of motorway.

Highways Agency: 123 Buckingham Palace Rd, London, SW1W 9HA; tel. and fax (8459) 556575; e-mail ha_info@highways.gsi.gov.uk; internet www.highways.gov.uk; executive agency of the Department for Transport; responsible for maintaining, operating and improving the motorway and trunk road network in England; Chief Exec. GRAHAM DALTON.

Northern Ireland Transport Holding Co: Chamber of Commerce House, 22 Great Victoria St, Belfast, BT2 7LX; tel. (28) 9024-3456; fax (28) 9033-3845; internet www.translink.co.uk/nithco.asp; publicly owned; owns Metro, Northern Ireland Railways Co Ltd and Ulsterbus, all part of the Translink rail and bus network; Chair. VERONICA PALMER; Chief Exec. CATHERINE MASON.

Ulsterbus: Milewater Rd, Belfast, BT3 9BG; Central Station, Belfast, BT1 3PB; tel. (28) 9089-9400; fax (28) 9035-1474; internet www.translink.co.uk/atulsterbus.asp; responsible for almost all bus transport in Northern Ireland, except Belfast city; services into Ireland; assoc. co Flexibus Ltd (minibus contract hire); Chief Exec. CATHERINE MASON; Gen. Man., Bus Services FRANK CLEGG (acting).

METROPOLITAN TRANSPORT

Metro: Milewater Rd, Belfast, BT3 9BG; tel. (28) 9035-1201; fax (28) 9035-1474; internet www.translink.co.uk/metro.asp; responsible for operating municipal transport in the City of Belfast; subsidiary of Northern Ireland Transport Holding Co (see under Roads); Chief Exec. CATHERINE MASON.

Metrolink: Metrolink House, Queens Rd, Manchester, M8 0RY; tel. (161) 205-2000; e-mail customerservices@metrolink.co.uk; internet www.metrolink.co.uk; opened 1992; owned by the Greater Manchester Passenger Transport Executive (GMPTE); operated by Serco Metrolink; 37-station hybrid tram and rail network in Greater Manchester, bounded by Altrincham, Bury, Eccles and Manchester Piccadilly; construction of 4 new lines expected to be completed in 2012; Dir PHILIP PURDY.

Transport for London (TfL): Windsor House, 42–50 Victoria St, London, SW1H 0TL; tel. (20) 7941-4500; fax (20) 7649-9121; e-mail enquire@tfl.gov.uk; internet www.tfl.gov.uk; f. 2000; executive arm of Greater London Authority (GLA), responsible for activities of former London Transport; Chair. BORIS JOHNSON (Mayor of London); Commr PETER HENDY.

THE UNITED KINGDOM

Directory

Docklands Light Railway: POB 154, Castor Lane, London, E14 0DS; tel. (20) 7363-9700; fax (20) 7363-9532; e-mail cservice@dlr.co.uk; internet www.dlr.co.uk; opened 1987; operations franchised to a private co., Serco Docklands; 34-km, 40-station system in east London; construction of an extension from Canning Town to Stratford International scheduled for completion in early 2011; Dir JONATHAN FOX.

London Underground: 55 Broadway, London, SW1H 0BD; tel. (20) 7222-5600; internet www.tfl.gov.uk/tube; f. 1985; however, underground railway network dates back to 1863; responsible for providing and securing the services of underground rail in Greater London; Man. Dir RICHARD PARRY (acting).

SPT Subway: Consort House, 12 West George St, Glasgow, G2 1HN; tel. (141) 332-6811; e-mail enquiry@spt.co.uk; internet www.spt.co.uk/subway; f. opened 1896; electrified in 1923; owned and operated by Strathclyde Partnership for Transport (SPT); 10-km, 15-station underground rail network in central Glasgow; Dir, Subway Operations DAVID WALLACE.

Tyne and Wear Metro: Nexus House, St James' Blvd, Newcastle upon Tyne, NE1 4AX; tel. (191) 203-3333; fax (191) 203-3180; e-mail metro.communications@nexus.org.uk; internet www.tyneandwearmetro.co.uk; opened 1980; 77.5-km, 60-station light rail network serving Newcastle, Gateshead, North Tyneside, South Tyneside and Sunderland; owned and operated by Tyne and Wear Passenger Transport Executive (Nexus); Dir-Gen. BERNARD GARNER.

INLAND WATERWAYS

There are some 3,541 km (2,200 miles) of inland waterways in Great Britain under the control of British Waterways, varying from the river navigations and wide waterways accommodating commercial craft to canals taking small holiday craft.

British Waterways: 6 Clarendon Rd, Watford, Hertfordshire, WD17 1DA; tel. (1923) 201120; fax (1923) 201400; e-mail enquiries.hq@britishwaterways.co.uk; internet www.britishwaterways.co.uk; f. 1963; Chair. TONY HALES; Chief Exec. ROBIN EVANS.

SHIPPING

There are more than 400 ports in the United Kingdom, of which Grimsby and Immingham, the Tees and Hartlepool ports, London (Tilbury), Southampton, Milford Haven, Liverpool, the Forth ports, Felixstowe, Dover and Sullom Voe are the largest (in terms of the tonnage of goods traffic handled). Twenty-one ports, including Grimsby and Immingham, Hull, Southampton and five ports in South Wales, are owned and administered by Associated British Ports. The majority of the other large ports are owned and operated by public trusts, including London, which is administered by the Port of London Authority, and Belfast, administered by the Belfast Harbour Commissioners.

Britain is linked to the rest of Europe by an extensive passenger and vehicle ship ferry service.

Associated British Ports (ABP): 150 Holborn, London, EC1N 2LR; tel. (20) 7430-1177; fax (20) 7430-1384; e-mail pr@abports.co.uk; internet www.abports.co.uk; f. 1983; controls 21 UK ports; Chair. CHRIS CLARK; Chief Exec. PETER JONES.

The Baltic Exchange Ltd: 38 St Mary Axe, London, EC3A 8BH; tel. (20) 7623-5501; fax (20) 7369-1622; e-mail enquiries@balticexchange.co.uk; internet www.balticexchange.com; world market for chartering ships, charters aircraft, buys and sells ships and aircraft; Chair. MICHAEL DRAYTON; Chief Exec. JEREMY PENN.

British Ports Association (BPA): 4th Floor, Carthusian Court, 12 Carthusian St, London, EC1M 6EZ; tel. (20) 7260-1780; fax (20) 7260-1784; e-mail info@britishports.org.uk; internet www.britishports.org.uk; promotes and protects the general interests of port authorities, comments on proposed legislation and policy matters; Dir DAVID WHITEHEAD.

Port of London Authority: London River House, Royal Pier Rd, Gravesend, Kent, DA12 2BG; tel. (1474) 562200; fax (1474) 562281; internet www.portoflondon.co.uk; Chair. SIMON SHERRARD; Chief Exec. RICHARD EVERITT.

Principal Shipping Companies

Bibby Line Ltd: 105 Duke St, Liverpool, L1 5JQ; tel. (151) 708-8000; fax (151) 794-1000; e-mail enquiries@bibbyline.co.uk; internet www.bibbyline.co.uk; f. 1807; various shipping operations incl. chemical carriage and shallow water accommodation; Chair. S. P. SHERRARD; Man. Dir SIMON KITCHEN.

Boyd Line: The Orangery, Hesslewood Country Office Park, Ferriby Rd, Hessle, HU13 0LH; tel. (1482) 324024; fax (1482) 323737; e-mail jon.carden@boydline.co.uk; internet www.boydline.co.uk; vessel owners and managers; Man. Dir JONATHAN CARDEN; 2 vessels.

BP Shipping Ltd: Chertsey Rd, Sunbury on Thames, Middlesex, TW16 7LN; tel. (1932) 771652; internet www.bpshipping.co.uk; f. 1915; division of BP PLC; Group Vice-Pres. and Chief Exec. DAVID BALDRY; 56 vessels.

CalMac Ferries Ltd (Caledonian MacBrayne): The Ferry Terminal, Gourock, Renfrewshire, PA19 1QP; tel. (1475) 650100; fax (1475) 637607; e-mail info@calmac.co.uk; internet www.calmac.co.uk; f. 1851; fmrly Caledonian MacBrayne Ltd; adopted current name 2006; owned by Scottish Govt; extensive car and passenger services on Firth of Clyde and to Western Isles of Scotland; 29 ro-ro vessels; Chair. PETER TIMMS; Man. Dir PHILIP PRESTON.

Coastal Container Line Ltd: Coastal House, Victoria Terminal 3, West Bank Rd, Belfast, BT3 9JL; tel. (28) 9037-3200; fax (28) 9037-1333; internet www.coastalcontainer.co.uk; container services from Belfast and Dublin to Cardiff and Liverpool; Operations Dir JOHN FORRESTER.

James Fisher & Sons PLC: Fisher House, POB 4, Barrow-in-Furness, Cumbria, LA14 1HR; tel. (1229) 615400; fax (1229) 836761; e-mail b.reception@james-fisher.co.uk; internet www.james-fisher.co.uk; f. 1847; provider of marine services operating in all sectors; also supplier of engineering services to the nuclear energy industry; Exec. Chair. TIMOTHY C. HARRIS; CEO NICHOLAS P. HENRY.

Fyffes Group Ltd: Houndmills Rd, Houndmills Industrial Estate, Basingstoke, Hampshire, RG21 6XL; tel. (1256) 383200; fax (1256) 383259; e-mail info@fyffes.com; internet www.fyffes.com; f. 1901.

Geest Line: 3700 Parkway, Whiteley, Fareham, PO15 7AL; tel. (1489) 873575; fax (1489) 873562; e-mail quotes@geestline.com; internet www.geestline.com; container cargo transportation between the UK and the Caribbean; Man. Dir BILL SALMOND.

Goulandris Brothers (Chartering) Ltd: 34A Queen Anne's Gate, London, SW1H 9AB; tel. (20) 7222-5244; fax (20) 7222-6817; e-mail chartering@goulanbros.co.uk; internet www.goulanbros.co.uk; f. 1968; ship chartering and brokerage; Man. Dir BASIL GOULANDRIS.

Heyn Shipping Solutions: 1 Corry Pl., Belfast Harbour, Belfast, BT3 9AH; tel. (28) 9035-0035; fax (28) 9035-0011; e-mail info@heyn.co.uk; internet www.heyn.co.uk; liner and port agency; Man. Dir DAVID CLARKE.

Holbud Ship Management Ltd: Hydery House, 66 Leman St, London, E1 8EU; tel. (20) 7488-4901; fax (20) 7265-0654; ship agents; Dir B. D. SABARWAL.

Norfolkline Irish Sea Ferries: 12 Quays Terminal, Tower Rd, Birkenhead, Wirral, CH41 1FE; tel. (151) 906-2700; fax (151) 906-2718; internet www.norfolkline.com; fmrly Norse Merchant Ferries; owned by Norfolk Line BV (Netherlands); ro-ro freight, car and passenger services from Birkenhead–Belfast and Dublin, and Dover–Dunkirk (France).

OSG Ship Management (UK) Ltd: Moreau House, 116 Brompton Rd, London, SW3 1JJ; tel. (20) 7591-6660; fax (870) 607-9546; internet www.osg.com; bulk carriers, parcels tankers, conventional tankers; transportation of crude petroleum, petroleum products and liquified natural gas; Man. Dir Capt. IAN T. BLACKLEY.

P & O Ferries: Channel House, Channel View Rd, Dover, Kent, CT17 9TJ; tel. (1304) 863000; fax (1304) 863223; e-mail customer.services@poferries.com; internet www.poferries.com; car and passenger services across the English Channel and North Sea; subsidiary of DP World (Dubai, UAE); parent co of P&O Irish Sea Ferries; fmrly P&O Stena Line; CEO HELEN DEEBLE.

Shell International Trading and Shipping Co Ltd: Shell Centre, York Rd, London, SE1 7NA; tel. (20) 7934-1234; e-mail shelltradingcommunications@shell.com; internet www.shell.com/shipping; world-wide operations trading and transporting crude petroleum and supplying petroleum products; incorporates Shell Tankers (UK) Ltd.

Stena Line Ltd: Stena House, Station Approach, Holyhead, Anglesey, LL65 1DQ; tel. (8705) 707070; e-mail info.uk@stenaline.com; internet www.stenaline.com; parent co Stena AB (Sweden); services from Great Britain to Northern Ireland, Ireland and the Netherlands; Group CEO GUNNAR BLOMDAHL; Area Dir, Irish Sea MICHAEL MCGRATH.

Stephenson Clarke Shipping Ltd: Eldon Court, Percy St, Newcastle upon Tyne, NE99 1TD; tel. (191) 232-2184; fax (191) 261-1156; e-mail all@scsbulk.co.uk; internet www.scsbulk.com; f. 1730; ship operators, agency and management services; Man. Dir TREVOR KINGSLEY-SMITH.

Andrew Weir & Co Ltd: Dexter House, 2 Royal Mint Court, London, EC3N 4XX; tel. (20) 7575-6000; fax (20) 7481-4784; e-mail aws@aws.co.uk; internet www.aws.co.uk; f. 1885; shipowners, ship managers; Man Dir STEVE CORKHILL.

Shipping Associations

Chamber of Shipping Ltd: Carthusian Court, 12 Carthusian St, London, EC1M 6EZ; tel. (20) 7600-1534; fax (20) 7726-2080; e-mail postmaster@british-shipping.org; internet www.british-shipping.org; Pres. MARTIN WATSON; Dir-Gen. MARK BROWNRIGG.

THE UNITED KINGDOM

Passenger Shipping Association Ltd (PSA): 1st Floor, 41–42 Eastcastle St, London W1W 8DU; tel. (20) 7436-2449; fax (20) 7636-9206; e-mail h.tapping@psa-psara.org; internet www.the-psa.co.uk; fmrly Ocean Travel Development (f. 1958); 50 mems; Chair. LARS OLSSON; Dir WILLIAM GIBBONS.

CIVIL AVIATION

In addition to many international air services into and out of the country, an internal air network operates from more than 20 main commercial airports.

The principal airports are Heathrow, Gatwick and Stansted serving London, and Manchester, Birmingham and Glasgow, which in 2007 handled 67.9m., 35.2m., 23.8m., 21.9m., 9.1m. and 8.7m. passengers, respectively. In 2008 London City Airport handled 3.3m. passengers. In March 2008 a fifth terminal building opened at Heathrow, increasing capacity at the airport to some 90m. passengers a year.

BAA PLC: 130 Wilton Rd, London, SW1V 1LQ; tel. (20) 7834-9449; fax (20) 7932-6699; e-mail baamediacentre@baa.com; internet www.baa.com; f. 1966 as British Airports Authority; privatized in 1987; propr of Heathrow, Stansted, Southampton, Glasgow, Aberdeen and Edinburgh airports; Chair. Sir NIGEL RUDD; CEO COLIN MATTHEWS.

Civil Aviation Authority (CAA): CAA House, 45–59 Kingsway, London, WC2B 6TE; tel. (20) 7379-7311; e-mail infoservices@caa.co.uk; internet www.caa.co.uk; f. 1972; public service enterprise and a regulatory body responsible for economic and safety regulation of civil aviation; advises Govt on aviation issues; conducts economic and scientific research; produces statistical data; regulates British airspace; represents consumer interests and manages airspace users' needs; Chair. Dame DEIRDRE HUTTON.

NATS Ltd: Corporate and Technical Centre, 4000 Parkway, Whiteley, Fareham, Hants, PO15 7FL; tel. (1489) 616001; fax (1489) 615734; internet www.nats.co.uk; f. 1960 as National Air Traffic Control Services; name changed as above in 1972 when the org. became part of the CAA (q.v.); public-private partnership between the Airline Group (a consortium of British Airways, BMI, easyJet, Monarch, MyTravel, Thomsonfly and Virgin Atlantic), BAA PLC, NATS employees and the British Govt; provides air traffic control services over the UK and North Atlantic, at 15 British airports and at Gibraltar Airport. It operates and maintains a nation-wide communications, surveillance and navigation network; Chair. JOHN DEVANEY; CEO PAUL BARRON.

Principal Private Airlines

Air Southwest: Plymouth City Airport, Crownhill, Plymouth, PL6 8BW; tel. (870) 043-4553; e-mail other-queries@airsouthwest.com; internet www.airsouthwest.com; f. 2003; scheduled flights from Plymouth, Newquay and Bristol to destinations in the UK, France and Ireland; owned by Sutton Harbour Group; Group Man. Dir NIGEL GODEFROY.

British Airways PLC: Waterside, POB 365, Harmondsworth, Middlesex, UB7 0GB; tel. (845) 779-9977; internet www.britishairways.com; f. 1972; operates extensive domestic, European and world-wide services, scheduled services to more than 250 destinations in 99 countries; British Airways and Iberia (Spain) merged to form International Airlines Group (IAG) in Jan. 2011; Chair. MARTIN BROUGHTON; Chief Exec. KEITH WILLIAMS.

bmi: Donington Hall, Castle Donington, Derby, DE74 2SB; tel. (1332) 854000; fax (1332) 854662; internet www.flybmi.com; f. 1938 as Air Schools Ltd; name changed to British Midland Airways Ltd in 1964 and as above in 2002; 35% owned by Deutsche Lufthansa AG (Germany), through LHBD Holding Ltd; scheduled services to over 40 destinations world-wide; cargo and charter flights; Chair. Sir MICHAEL BISHOP; CEO NIGEL TURNER.

bmibaby: Donington Hall, Castle Donington, Derby, DE74 2SB; tel. (1332) 854000; internet www.bmibaby.com; f. 2002; low-cost passenger services to 30 European destinations; Man. Dir CRAWFORD RIX.

easyJet PLC: Hangar 89, London Luton Airport, Luton, Bedfordshire, LU2 9LS; tel. (1582) 445566; fax (1582) 443355; internet www.easyjet.co.uk; f. 1995; low-cost scheduled domestic and European passenger services from 17 UK airports; Chair. Sir MICHAEL RAKE; CEO CAROLYN MCCALL.

First Choice Airways: Commonwealth House, Chicago Ave, Manchester Airport, M90 3DP; tel. (161) 489-0321; fax (161) 908-2275; e-mail eteam@firstchoice.co.uk; internet www.firstchoice.co.uk/flights; f. 1987 as air2000; present name adopted 2004; scheduled services from 26 airports in the United Kingdom to 80 destinations world-wide; subsidiary of TUI Travel PLC; Man. Dir, UK and Ireland DERMOT BLASTLAND.

Flybe: Jack Walker House, Exeter International Airport, Exeter, EX5 2HL; tel. (1392) 366669; fax (1392) 366151; e-mail corporate@flybe.com; internet www.flybe.com; f. 1979 as Jersey European Airways; name changed as above 2002; acquired BA Connect in 2007; independent regional airline providing low-cost domestic and European services; Chair. and CEO JIM FRENCH.

flyglobespan: Atlantic House, 38 Gardners Cres., Edinburgh, EH3 8DQ; tel. (870) 556-1522; internet www.flyglobespan.com; f. 2003; low-cost scheduled lights to 23 destinations world-wide, operating from 9 UK airports; entered administration in Dec. 2009; Chair. TOM DALRYMPLE.

Loganair Ltd: St Andrews Drive, Glasgow Airport, Abbotsinch, Paisley, Renfrewshire, PA3 2TG; tel. (141) 848-7594; fax (141) 887-6020; internet www.loganair.co.uk; f. 1962; signed franchise agreement with Flybe in 2008; Scottish domestic services and flights to Belfast, Birmingham, Londonderry and the Isle of Man; Chair. SCOTT GRIER; Chief Exec. PETER TIERNEY.

Monarch Airlines: Prospect House, Prospect Way, London Luton Airport, Luton, Bedfordshire, LU2 9NU; tel. (1582) 400000; fax (1582) 411000; internet www.flymonarch.com; f. 1967; scheduled and charter services to the Mediterranean; CEO PETER BROWN.

Thomsonfly: London Luton Airport, Luton, Bedfordshire, LU2 9ND; tel. (870) 190-0737; e-mail lynn.houghton@thomson.co.uk; internet www.thomsonfly.com; f. 2004; propr TUI AG (Germany); operates scheduled services from 20 UK airports to 80 destinations world-wide; Man. Dir COLIN MITCHELL.

Virgin Atlantic Airways: Manor Royal, Crawley, West Sussex, RH10 2NU; tel. (1293) 562345; fax (1293) 561721; internet www.virgin-atlantic.com; f. 1984; operates services to destinations in the USA, Africa, the Caribbean and the Far East; Chair. Sir RICHARD BRANSON; Chief Exec. STEVE RIDGWAY.

Tourism

In 2009 there were 31.9m. arrivals by foreign visitors to the United Kingdom; receipts from tourism totalled £16,592m. in that year.

Northern Ireland Tourist Board: St Anne's Court, 59 North St, Belfast, BT1 1NB; tel. (28) 9023-1221; fax (28) 9024-0960; e-mail info@nitb.com; internet www.discovernorthernireland.com; Chair. HOWARD HASTINGS; Chief Exec. ALAN CLARKE.

VisitBritain: Thames Tower, Black's Rd, London, W6 9EL; tel. (20) 8846-9000; fax (20) 8563-0302; e-mail corporatepr@visitbritain.org; internet www.visitbritain.com; markets Great Britain overseas; Chair. CHRISTOPHER RODRIGUES; CEO SANDIE DAWE.

VisitEngland: Thames Tower, Black's Rd, London, W6 9EL; tel. (20) 8846-9000; fax (20) 8563-0302; internet www.visitengland.com; f. 2009; promotes tourism in England to domestic visitors; Chair. Lady COBHAM; CEO JAMES BERRESFORD.

Visit London: 6th Floor, 2 More London Riverside, London, SE1 2RR; tel. (20) 7234-5800; fax (20) 7378-6525; e-mail enquiries@visitlondon.com; internet www.visitlondon.com; f. 1963; promotes London to leisure and business visitors; Chair. TAMARA INGRAM; Interim CEO SALLY CHATTERJEE.

VisitScotland: Ocean Point One, 94 Ocean Drive, Leith, Edinburgh, EH6 6JH; tel. (131) 472-2207; e-mail info@visitscotland.com; internet www.visitscotland.com; Chair. PETER LEDERER; Chief Exec. PHILIP RIDDLE.

Visit Wales: Brunel House, 2 Fitzalan Rd, Cardiff, CF24 0UY; tel. (845) 010-3300; fax (29) 2048-5031; e-mail info@visitwales.co.uk; internet www.visitwales.co.uk; Dir, Tourism and Marketing JONATHAN JONES.

Defence

The United Kingdom is a member of the North Atlantic Treaty Organization (NATO) and maintains a regular army. As assessed at November 2010, the total strength of the armed forces, including those enlisted outside Britain (3,520), was 178,470 (army 102,600, navy 35,480, air force 40,390). There was also a reserve force of 195,795. There is no compulsory military service. In November 2004 the EU ministers responsible for defence agreed to create a number of 'battlegroups' (each numbering about 1,500 men), which could be deployed at short notice to crisis areas around the world. The EU battlegroups, two of which were to be ready for deployment at any one time, following a rotational schedule, reached full operational capacity from 1 January 2007. The United Kingdom was the sole contributor to one battlegroup and also participated in another in conjunction with the Netherlands. The United Kingdom possesses its own nuclear weapons.

Defence Expenditure: £38,200m. in 2009/10.
Chief of Defence Staff: Gen. Sir DAVID RICHARDS.
Vice-Chief of Defence Staff: Gen. Sir NICHOLAS HOUGHTON.
First Sea Lord and Chief of Naval Staff: Adm. Sir MARK STANHOPE.

THE UNITED KINGDOM

Chief of General Staff: Gen. Sir PETER WALL.
Chief of Air Staff: Air Chief Marshal Sir STEPHEN DALTON.

Education

Education is compulsory for all children between the ages of five (four in Northern Ireland) and 16, and is provided free of charge between the ages of three and 18 years. (Under the Education and Skills Act 2008, from 2015 pupils in England will be compelled to remain in full-time education or training until the age of 18 years.) In Northern Ireland, Scotland and Wales the devolved authorities are responsible for all levels of education. In England the Department for Education is responsible for schools, whereas responsibility for further and higher education rests with the Department for Business, Innovation and Skills. For historical reasons, the education system in Scotland differs considerably from that current in the rest of the United Kingdom.

All state schools in England, Wales and Northern Ireland must conform to the national curriculum, which is set by the competent government authority. Compulsory education in the state sector England and Wales comprises four Key Stages. Primary schools cover Key Stages 1 and 2, catering for children aged from five to seven years and seven to 11 years, respectively, while Key Stages 3 (ages 11–14) and 4 (14–16) are covered in secondary schools. (In some areas, middle schools, which may be classified as either primary or secondary, cater for various age ranges between eight and 14 years.) A similar system prevails in Northern Ireland, where the stages at primary level are designated Foundation Stage (ages 4–6), Key Stage 1 (6–8) and Key Stage 2 (8–11). Various provisions exist for pre-school education in nursery schools and playgroups, which may be state-run or provided by voluntary or private organizations. Most children in England and Wales enter primary school at the age of four and are grouped in reception classes (part of the Early Years Foundation Stage in England), where they receive up to one year of schooling prior to Key Stage 1. At secondary level, the system of comprehensive (mixed-ability) schools prevails in most areas; however, some localities (including Northern Ireland) additionally retain grammar schools, to which admission is determined through a test of ability. At the end of compulsory education at the age of 16 years, most pupils in England, Wales and Northern Ireland take examinations for the General Certificate of Secondary Education (GCSE). Thereafter, pupils may remain in secondary school for a further two years, where they may take the General Certificate of Education Advanced Level (A Level) in the subjects of their choice; alternatively, they may attend a sixth-form or further education college, where they may study for A Levels or vocational awards. The A Level consists of two units: the Advanced Subsidiary (AS) Level, examinations for which are taken after one year of study (at the age of 17 years); and the A2, which is taken after two years of study (aged 18 years). From 2008 pupils aged 14 years have been able to undertake a Diploma, comprising up to three stages, lasting up to five years, in one of five vocational subject areas in place of GCSE and A Level examinations. Further education colleges offer a wide range of vocational courses for students aged 16 years and over; among the most prominent of these are National Vocational Qualifications (NVQs), which consist of five defined levels of achievement.

In Scotland the curriculum in state schools is not prescribed by statute; however, the Scottish Government issues advice and guidance to schools and Scottish Local Authorities. From August 2010 all schools were expected to follow the Scottish Government's new curriculum for education at ages 3–18, known as the Curriculum for Excellence. Primary education begins at the age of five and lasts for seven years, with pupils entering secondary school at the age of 12. At the age of 16 most pupils are examined for Standard Grades, part of the system of National Qualifications (NQs). Some schools offer NQ Intermediate 1 and 2 qualifications as an alternative to Standard Grades; as part of the Curriculum for Excellence, Standard Grades and Intermediate awards were to be replaced by National awards from 2014. Pupils remaining at secondary school for post-compulsory education take the NQ Higher award (typically in up to five or six subjects) after one further year of study, after which they are eligible for higher education in Scotland; they may subsequently remain in school for an additional year and study for the NQ Advanced Higher award, which is generally required for entry into universities in England and Wales. As in the rest of the United Kingdom, further education colleges provide a variety of vocational qualifications; the Scottish equivalent of the NVQ is the Scottish Vocational Qualification (SVQ).

In 2006/07 there were 124 publicly funded universities (including the Open University) and 45 other higher education institutions offering courses of higher education in the United Kingdom. There is also one privately funded university, the University of Buckingham. The Open University provides degree and other courses predominantly through distance learning methods, and requires no formal qualifications for entry to its courses. The first degree course normally lasts for three years (four in Scotland) and leads to a Bachelor of Arts or Sciences (BA or BSc) degree. The second degree course lasts for one or two years and leads to a master's degree; the third lasts three years and leads to a doctoral degree. Many higher education institutions also offer a range of vocational qualifications below degree level, including the Higher National Diploma (HND), which requires two years of study. Publicly funded universities in England, Wales and Northern Ireland may charge domestic students tuition fees for undergraduate courses, subject to a state-imposed limit. Eligible full-time Scottish-domiciled or non-British EU students who are studying in Scotland are not required to pay tuition fees. University fees for postgraduate courses, and those charged to foreign students, are unregulated.

Schools in the United Kingdom are administered and financed in several ways. Most schools are controlled by local authorities (Education and Library Boards in Northern Ireland). Academies are publicly funded schools within the state sector in England that receive direct funding from the Department of Education and have considerable operational autonomy. Alongside the state system, there are independent schools, which do not receive grants from public funds but are financed by fees and endowments; many of these schools are administered by charitable trusts and church organizations. Budgetary expenditure on education and training in 2007/08 totalled an estimated £78,800m., representing 14.1% of total current expenditure.

UNITED KINGDOM CROWN DEPENDENCIES

The Channel Islands and the Isle of Man lie off shore from the United Kingdom but are not integral parts of the country. They are dependencies of the British Crown and have considerable self-government in internal affairs.

THE CHANNEL ISLANDS

The Channel Islands lie off the north-west coast of France to the west of Normandy, in the English Channel (la Manche). The bailiwicks of the Channel Islands (Guernsey and its dependencies, and Jersey) are the remnants of the Duchy of Normandy, which was in permanent union with the English (now British) Crown from 1106. They do not, however, form part of the United Kingdom. The islands have their own legislative assemblies and legal and administrative systems, their laws depending for their validity on Orders made by the Queen in Council. Her Majesty's Government in the United Kingdom is responsible for the defence and international relations of the islands, and the Crown is ultimately responsible for their good government. The bailiwicks do not form part of the European Union.

Guernsey

Introduction

The civil flag of Guernsey is white, bearing a red cross of St George, with a yellow couped cross superimposed on the cross. The capital is St Peter Port. English is the language in common use, but the Norman *patois* is spoken in some rural parishes.

The sovereign is represented in Guernsey by the Lieutenant-Governor, appointed by the Crown. Executive power is exercised by the Policy Council, headed by the Chief Minister. The legislature, the States of Deliberation, comprises the Bailiff, appointed by the Crown, who is President ex officio; HM Procureur and HM Comptroller, Law Officers of the Crown (who are entitled to speak, but not to vote); 45 People's Deputies, elected by popular franchise; and two Alderney Representatives, elected by the States of Alderney. Dependencies of Guernsey are Alderney, Brecqhou, Herm, Jethou, Lihou and Sark.

In addition to the British public holidays, Guernsey celebrates 9 May (Liberation Day).

Statistical Survey

(including Herm and Jethou)

Source (unless otherwise stated): Policy and Research Unit, Sir Charles Frossard House, La Charroterie, St Peter Port, Guernsey, GY1 1FH; tel. (1481) 717012; fax (1481) 717157; internet www.gov.gg.

AREA AND POPULATION

Area: 63.6 sq km (24.6 sq miles).

Population: 59,807 (males 29,138, females 30,669) at census of 29 April 2001. *2009* (official estimate at 31 March): 62,274 (males 30,777, females 31,497).

Density (at 31 March 2009): 979.2 per sq km.

Population by Age and Sex (official estimates at 31 March 2009): *0–14:* 9,470 (males 4,873, females 4,597); *15–64:* 42,780 (males 21,507, females 21,273); *65 and over:* 10,024 (males 4,397, females 5,627); *Total* 62,274 (males 30,777, females 31,497).

Parishes (2001 census): St Peter Port 16,488; Vale 9,573; Castel 8,975; St Sampson 8,592; St Martin 6,267; St Saviour 2,696; St Andrew 2,409; St Pierre du Bois 2,188; Forest 1,549; Torteval 973; Herm 95; Jethou 2; Total 59,807.

Births and Deaths (2008): Live births 631; Deaths 476.

Immigration and Emigration (2008): Immigrants 5,531; emigrants 4,894.

Economically Active Population (at 31 December 2010): Horticulture and other primary 434; Manufacturing 717; Construction 3,166; Utilities 427; Transport and storage 1,035; Information and communication 1,042; Hostelry 1,887; Wholesale, retail and repairs 4,456; Finance 6,817; Real estate activities 207; Professional, business, scientific and technical activities 1,987; Administrative and support service activities 1,319; Public administration 5,493; Education 465; Human health, social and charitable work activities 1,629; Arts, entertainment and recreation 410; Other services 753; *Total employed* 32,244 (males 17,473, females 14,771); Unemployed 420; *Total labour force* 32,664.

AGRICULTURE

The principal crops are flowers, much of which are grown under glass. About 16.3 sq km (6.2 sq miles) are cultivated.

MINING

Production ('000 metric tons): Igneous rock 129 in 2005; 136 in 2006; 180 in 2007.

FINANCE

Currency and Exchange Rates: 100 pence = 1 pound sterling (£). *Dollar and Euro Equivalents* (31 December 2010): US $1 = 63.88 pence; €1 = 85.35 pence; £10 = $15.65 = €11.72.

Note: Guernsey is in monetary union with the United Kingdom. It has its own coins and notes but United Kingdom coins and notes are also legal tender.

Budget (£ million, 2009): General revenue income 341 (Income tax 273); General revenue expenditure 326 (Education 72; Health and Social Services 107).

Cost of Living: (Retail Price Index at mid-year; base: 31 December 1999 = 100) All items 141.5 in 2008; 139.6 in 2009; 142.8 in 2010.

Gross Domestic Product (£ million at current prices): 1,787 in 2007 (provisional); 1,902 in 2008 (estimate); 1,903 in 2009 (forecast).

Gross Domestic Product by Economic Activity (£ '000 at current prices, 2007, provisional): Horticulture 11,974; Other primary 11,267; Manufacturing 41,120; Construction 131,430; Utilities 12,467; Transport 33,098; Hostelry 48,232; Wholesale 34,608; Retail 118,022; Recreation 14,514; Information 41,766; Financial services 527,537; Legal, business and personal services 232,997; Health, education and public administration 231,808; Non-profit 6,711; *Total factor incomes* 1,497,551; *Less* Pensions 34,206; Other income 193,650; *Less* Adjustment to profit account 1,405; *Total* 1,655,590.

EXTERNAL TRADE

Principal Commodities: *Imports* (1999): Petroleum and oil 168,026,000 litres. *Exports* (1998, £ million): Light industry 47.0; Total flowers 34.0; Total vegetables 5.0.

TRANSPORT

Road Traffic (vehicles registered, 2009): Private vehicles 61,661; Commercial vehicles 14,030; Motorcycles 11,069.

Shipping (2009): Passenger movements 327,528.

Civil Aviation (2009): Passenger movements 905,717.

UNITED KINGDOM CROWN DEPENDENCIES

TOURISM

Number of Visitors (2009): 304,000.

COMMUNICATIONS MEDIA

Telephones (2009): 45,100 main lines in use.
Mobile Cellular Telephones (2004): 43,800.
Internet Users (2009): 48,300.
Source: International Telecommunication Union.

EDUCATION

Primary (at January 2010): 4,406 pupils (males 2,266, females 2,140).

Secondary (incl. further education, at January 2010): 4,292 pupils (males 2,098, females 2,194).

Higher (2008/09): 889 students.

Directory

The Government

HEAD OF STATE

Queen: HM Queen ELIZABETH II.
Lieutenant-Governor and Commander-in-Chief of the Bailiwick of Guernsey: Air Marshal PETER WALKER.

POLICY COUNCIL
(May 2011)

Chief Minister: LYNDON TROTT.
Deputy Chief Minister and Minister of Public Services: BERNARD FLOUQUET.
Minister of the Treasury and Resources: CHARLES PARKINSON.
Minister of the Home Department: GEOFF MAHY.
Minister of Education: CAROL STEERE.
Minister of Health and Social Services: HUNTER ADAM.
Minister of Housing: DAVID JONES.
Minister of Commerce and Employment: CARLA MCNULTY BAUER.
Minister of Social Security: MARK DOREY.
Minister of the Environment: PETER SIRETT.
Minister of Culture and Leisure: MIKE O'HARA.

OTHER OFFICIALS

Bailiff of Guernsey: Sir GEOFFREY ROBERT ROWLAND.
Deputy Bailiff: RICHARD JOHN COLLAS.
HM Procureur (Attorney-General): HOWARD EDWARD ROBERTS.
HM Comptroller (Solicitor-General): RICHARD JAMES MCMAHON.

GOVERNMENT OFFICE

States of Guernsey: Sir Charles Frossard House, La Charroterie, St Peter Port, GY1 1FH; tel. (1481) 717000; internet www.gov.gg.

Judicial System

Justice is administered in Guernsey by the Royal Court, which consists of the Bailiff and the 12 Jurats. The Royal Court also deals with a wide variety of non-contentious matters. A Stipendiary Magistrate deals with minor civil and criminal cases. The Guernsey Court of Appeal deals with appeals from the Royal Court.

Religion

CHRISTIANITY

The Church of England

The Church of England in Guernsey is the established church. The Deanery includes the islands of Alderney, Sark, Herm and Jethou; it forms part of the diocese of Winchester.

Dean of Guernsey: Very Rev. Canon PAUL MELLOR, The Deanery, Cornet St, St Peter Port, GY1 1BZ; tel. (1481) 720036; fax (1481) 722948; e-mail paul@townchurch.org.gg.

The Roman Catholic Church

The diocese of Portsmouth includes the Channel Islands and part of southern England. In Guernsey there are three Roman Catholic churches, of which the senior is St Joseph and St Mary, Cordier Hill, St Peter Port.

Catholic Dean of Guernsey: Fr MICHAEL HORE, Ampthill House, Cordier Hill, St Peter Port, GY1 1JH; tel. (1481) 720196; fax (1481) 711247; e-mail sjoss.guernsey@virgin.net; internet catholic.org.gg.

Other Christian Churches

The Presbyterian Church and the Church of Scotland are represented by St Andrew's Church, The Grange, St Peter Port. The Baptist, Congregational, Elim and Methodist Churches are also represented in the island.

The Press

Guernsey Press and Star: The Guernsey Press Co, POB 57, Braye Rd, Vale, GY1 3BW; tel. (1481) 240240; fax (1481) 240235; e-mail newsroom@guernsey-press.com; internet www.thisisguernsey.com/guernsey-press; f. 1897; daily; independent; Editor RICHARD DIGARD; circ. 15,780 (Dec. 2008).

Guernsey Weekly Press: The Guernsey Press Co, POB 57, Braye Rd, Vale, GY1 3BW; tel. (1481) 240240; fax (1481) 240235; e-mail editorial@thisisguernsey.com; internet www.thisisguernsey.com; f. 1902; Thursday; independent; Editor RICHARD DIGARD.

Publishers

Toucan Press: The White Cottage, route de Carteret, Castel, GY5 7YG; tel. (1481) 257017; f. 1850; history, Thomas Hardy, Channel Islands; Man. Dir G. STEVENS COX.

Broadcasting and Communications

TELECOMMUNICATIONS

Airtel-Vodafone (Guernsey): 45 The High Street, St Peter Port GY1 2JT; tel. 7839700121 (mobile); e-mail 121@airtel-vodafone.gg; internet www.airtel-vodafone.com; mobile phone services; jt venture between Bharti Airtel Ltd (India) and Vodafone PLC (United Kingdom); mobile telecommunications services; Chief Exec. IAIN WILLIAMS.

Cable and Wireless Guernsey Ltd: POB 3, Telecoms House, Upland Rd, St Peter Port, GY1 3AB; tel. (1481) 700700; fax (1481) 724640; e-mail contact@surecw.com; internet www.surecw.com/guernsey; operates under brand name Sure; fixed-line and mobile telecommunications services, as well as broadband internet services; Chief Exec. DENIS MARTIN.

Wave Telecom: 24 High St, St Peter Port, GY1 2JU; tel. (1481) 818152; internet www.wavetelecom.com; f. 2002; subsidiary of Jersey Telecom; offers fixed-line and mobile telecommunications services; Man. Dir TIM RINGSDORE.

BROADCASTING

Radio

BBC: Radio and Television (see United Kingdom).

BBC Radio Guernsey: Television House, Bulwer Ave, St Sampson, GY2 4LA; tel. (1481) 200600; fax (1481) 200361; e-mail radio.guernsey@bbc.co.uk; internet www.bbc.co.uk/guernsey; f. 1982; Man. Editor DAVID MARTIN.

Island FM: 12 Westerbrook, St Sampson, GY2 4QQ; tel. (1481) 242000; fax (1481) 241120; e-mail studio@islandfm.com; internet www.islandfm.com; Programme Controller EDDIE CARTER.

Television

Channel Television: Television House, Bulwer Ave, St Sampson, GY2 4LA; tel. (1481) 241888; fax (1481) 241889; e-mail broadcast.gsy@channeltv.co.uk; internet www.channelonline.tv; Exec. Chair. MICK DESMOND.

(See also under Jersey.)

Finance

(cap. = capital; res = reserves; dep. = deposits; brs = branches; amounts in pounds sterling, unless otherwise indicated.)

Guernsey Financial Services Commission: POB 128, La Plaiderie Chambers, La Plaiderie, St Peter Port, GY1 3HQ; tel. (1481) 712706; fax (1481) 712010; e-mail info@gfsc.gg; internet www.gfsc.gg; f. 1988; regulates banking, investment, insurance and fiduciary

UNITED KINGDOM CROWN DEPENDENCIES

activities; Chair. PETER HARWOOD; Dir-Gen. JOHN NIKOLAS (NIK) VAN LEUVEN.

BANKING

At December 2009 total bank deposits in Guernsey were £117,400m. in 44 financial institutions.

Adam and Company International Ltd: POB 402, Royal Bank Pl., 1 Glategny Esplanade, St Peter Port, GY1 3GB; tel. (1481) 715055; fax (1481) 726919; e-mail john.judge@adambank.com; internet www.adambank.com; f. 1990; cap. 0.5m., res 13m., dep. 187m. (Dec. 2008); Chair. S. FLETCHER; Man. Dir J. JUDGE.

Bank Sarasin (CI) Ltd: POB 348, Park Court, Park St, St Peter Port, GY1 3UY; tel. (1481) 725147; fax (1481) 725157; e-mail ken.gibbs@sarasin.gg; internet www.sarasin.co.uk; owned by Bank Sarasin & Co Ltd (Switzerland); Chair. FIDELIS GOETZ; Man. Dir KEN A. GIBBS.

Butterfield Bank (Guernsey) Ltd: POB 25, Regency Court, Glategny Esplanade, St Peter Port, GY1 3AP; tel. (1481) 711521; fax (1481) 714533; e-mail info@butterfield.gg; internet www.butterfieldbank.gg; f. 1989; subsidiary of Bank of N. T. Butterfield & Son Ltd (Bermuda); cap. 40m., res –2m., dep. 898m. (Dec. 2008); Man. Dir ROBERT MOORE.

Close Bank Guernsey Ltd: POB 116, Trafalgar Court, Admiral Park, St Peter Port, GY1 3EZ; tel. (1481) 726014; fax (1481) 727645; e-mail bankinggsy@closewm.com; internet www.closewm.com; f. 1965 as Rea Brothers (Guernsey) Ltd; present name adopted 1999; cap. 1m., dep. 350m. (July 2009); Chair. STRONE MACPHERSON; Man. Dir PHIL O'SHEA.

Crédit Suisse (Guernsey) Ltd: POB 368, Helvetia Court, South Esplanade, St Peter Port, GY1 3JY; tel. (1481) 719000; fax (1481) 724676; e-mail csguernsey.info@credit-suisse.com; internet www.credit-suisse.com/guernsey; f. 1986; cap. US $6m., res $307m., dep. $5,952m. (Dec. 2008); CEO R. MCGREGOR.

EFG Private Bank (Channel Islands) Ltd: POB 603, EFG House, St Julian's Ave, St Peter Port, GY1 4NN; tel. (1481) 723432; fax (1481) 723488; internet www.efggroup.com; f. 1992 as The Private Bank & Trust Co (Guernsey) Ltd; present name adopted 1997; cap. 5m., res 33m., dep. 819m. (Dec. 2006); Man. Dir D. G. GARDNER.

SG Hambros Bank (Channel Islands) Ltd: POB 6, Hambro House, St Julian's Ave, St Peter Port, GY1 3AE; tel. (1481) 726521; fax (1481) 727139; e-mail channelislands@sghambros.com; internet www.sghambros.com; f. 1967; formerly SG Hambros Bank and Trust (Guernsey) Ltd; name changed in 2005 following merger with SG Hambros Bank and Trust (Jersey) Ltd; merchant bankers; cap. 5m., res 162m., dep. 5,716m. (Dec. 2008); Chair. WARWICK J. NEWBURY; Chief Exec. RICHARD A. OLLIVER.

HSBC Private Bank (CI) Ltd: HSBC Private Bank Bldg, Park Pl., Park St, St Peter Port, GY1 1EE; tel. (1481) 759000; fax (1481) 759020; internet www.hsbcprivatebank.com; f. 1985; present name adopted 2008, following merger with HSBC Private Bank (Jersey) Ltd; cap. US $25m., res $555m., dep. $23,469m. (Dec. 2008); CEO GARY MILLER.

Investec Bank (Channel Islands) Ltd: POB 188, La Vieille Cour, St Peter Port, GY1 3LP; tel. (1481) 711500; fax (1481) 741147; e-mail enquiries@investec-ci.com; internet www.investec.com; f. 1977 as Guinness Mahon Guernsey Ltd; present name adopted 1999; cap. 15m., res 113m., dep. 1,909m. (March 2009); Chair. A. TAPNACK; Gen. Man. MORT MIRGHAVAMEDDIN.

Lloyds TSB Offshore Ltd Private Banking Office: POB 136, Sarnia House, Le Truchot, St Peter Port, GY1 4EN; tel. (1481) 708000; fax (1481) 727416; e-mail pvtbankingg@lloydstsb-offshore.com; internet www.privatebanking.lloydstsb-offshore.com; Head of Sales and Relationships GARY BROWNBRIDGE.

Rothschild Bank International Ltd: St Julian's Court, St Peter Port, GY1 3BP; tel. (1481) 713713; fax (1481) 727705; e-mail private.banking@rothschild.com; internet www.rothschild.gg; f. 1967; present name adopted 2007; subsidiary of N. M. Rothschild & Sons Ltd, London; cap. 5m., res 72m., dep. 765m. (March 2010); Chair. CHRISTOPHER COLEMAN; Man. Dir PETER ROSE.

Royal Bank of Canada (Channel Islands) Ltd: POB 48, Canada Court, St Peter Port, GY1 3BQ; tel. (1481) 744000; fax (1481) 744001; e-mail infogpb@rbc.com; internet www.rbcprivatebanking.com; f. 1973; subsidiary of Royal Bank of Canada; cap. 5m., res 387m., dep. 7,027m. (Oct. 2009); Chair. DAVID P. O'BRIEN; Man. Dir C. C. BLAMPIED.

Schroders (CI) Ltd: POB 334, Regency Court, Glategny Esplanade, St Peter Port, GY1 3UF; tel. (1481) 703700; fax (1481) 703600; internet www.schroders.com/ci; f. 1992; cap. 0.5m., res 5m., dep. 716m. (Dec. 2009); Chief Exec. JULIAN WINSER.

Banking Organization

Association of Guernsey Banks: c/o Butterfield Bank (Guernsey) Ltd, St Peter Port, GY1 3AP; tel. (1481) 711521; fax (1481) 714533;

e-mail John.Robinson@gg.butterfieldgroup.com; internet www.agb.org.gg; f. 1988; 37 mems; Chair. JOHN ROBINSON.

STOCK EXCHANGE

Channel Islands Stock Exchange (CISX): 1 Lefebvre St, St Peter Port, GY1 4PJ; tel. (1481) 713831; fax (1481) 714856; e-mail info@cisx.com; internet www.cisx.com; Chair. JONATHAN HOOLEY; Chief Exec. TAMARA MENTESHVILI.

INSURANCE

At 31 March 2010 there were 351 international insurers and 21 domestic insurers operating in Guernsey.

Generali Worldwide Insurance Co Ltd: POB 613, Generali House, Hirzel St, St Peter Port, GY1 4PA; tel. (1481) 715400; fax (1481) 715390; e-mail enquiries@generali-guernsey.com; internet www.generali-gw.com; Chair. CHRISTOPHER SPENCER; CEO GAVIN TRADELIUS.

Heritage Group: POB 225, Heritage Hall, Le Marchant St, St Peter Port, GY1 4HY; tel. (1481) 716000; fax (1481) 712357; e-mail info@heritage.co.gg; internet www.heritage.co.gg; CEO RICHARD TEE.

Insurance Corpn of the Channel Islands Ltd: POB 160, Dixcart House, Sir William Pl., St Peter Port, GY1 4EY; tel. (1481) 707551; e-mail icci@insurancecorporation.com; internet www.insurancecorporation.com; mem. of the RSA Insurance Group; Man. Dir GLYN SMITH.

Islands' Insurance Brokers Ltd: Lancaster Court, Forest Lane, St Peter Port, GY1 1WJ; tel. (1481) 710731; fax (1481) 712223; e-mail insure@islandsinsurance.com; internet www.islands-insurance.com; f. 1978; insurance broker; owned by National Farmers' Union Mutual Insurance Society Ltd; Dir PETER ROWE.

Trade and Industry

CHAMBER OF COMMERCE

Guernsey Chamber of Commerce: Suite 1, 16 Glategny Esplanade, St Peter Port, GY1 1WN; tel. (1481) 727483; fax (1481) 710755; e-mail office@guernseychamber.com; internet www.guernseychamber.com; f. 1808; Pres. JULIAN WINSER; Dir BARRY CASH.

UTILITIES

Electricity

Guernsey Electricity: POB 4, Electricity House, Northside, Vale, GY1 3AD; tel. (1481) 200700; fax (1481) 246942; e-mail admin@electricity.gg; internet www.electricity.gg; Chair. KEN GREGSON; Man. Dir ALAN BATES.

Gas

Guernsey Gas: The Energy Centre, Admiral Park, St Peter Port, GY1 2BB; tel. (1481) 724811; internet www.gsygas.com; Dir PAUL GARLICK.

Water

Guernsey Water: POB 30, South Esplanade, St Peter Port, GY1 3AS; tel. (1481) 724552; fax (1481) 715094; e-mail customer.service@water.gg; internet www.water.gg; fmrly States of Guernsey Waterboard; name changed as above 2004; Dir of Water Services ANDREW REDHEAD.

Transport

SHIPPING

Alderney Shipping Co Ltd: POB 77, White Rock, St Peter Port, GY1 4BN; tel. (1481) 724810; fax (1481) 712081; e-mail annika@aldshp.co.uk; internet www.aldshp.co.uk.

Condor Ltd: 3rd Floor, La Plaiderie House, La Plaiderie, St Peter Port, GY1 1WD; tel. (1481) 729666; fax (1481) 712555; internet www.condorferries.co.uk; f. 1964; regular passenger service operating between the Channel Islands and St Malo (France), and between the Channel Islands and Poole, Weymouth and Portsmouth; Man. Dir ROBERT PROVAN; Gen. Man. NICK DOBBS.

Condorferries Freight: 3rd Floor, La Plaiderie House, La Plaiderie, St Peter Port, GY1 1WD; tel. (1481) 728620; fax (1481) 728521; e-mail jeff.vidamour@condorferries.co.uk; internet www.condorferries.co.uk; regular ro-ro freight services between Portsmouth, Guernsey, Jersey and St Malo (France); Freight Dir JEFF VIDAMOUR.

Herm Seaway Express: Albert Pier, St Peter Port; tel. (1481) 724161; fax (1481) 700226; Contact PETER WILCOX.

Isle of Sark Shipping Co Ltd: White Rock, St Peter Port, GY1 2LN; tel. (1481) 724059; fax (1481) 713999; e-mail info@sarkshipping.info; internet www.sarkshipping.info; operates daily services between Guernsey and Sark.

Trident Charter Co Ltd: Woodville, Les Dicqs, Vale, GY6 8JW; tel. (1481) 245253; fax (1481) 700226; e-mail peterwilcox@cwgsy.net; internet www.herm-island.com; f. 1968; Man. PETER WILCOX.

CIVIL AVIATION

Aurigny Air Services Ltd: States Airport, La Planque Lane, Forest, GY8 0DT; tel. (1481) 266444; fax (1481) 266446; e-mail customerrelations@aurigny.com; internet www.aurigny.com; f. 1968; scheduled passenger services from Guernsey to Alderney, Jersey, Bristol, East Midlands, London Gatwick, London Stansted, Manchester, Southampton and Dinard (France); freight services, tour operation, ambulance charters and third party handling; owned by the States of Guernsey; Man. Dir MALCOLM HART.

Blue Islands: Century House, 12 Victoria St, St Anne, Alderney, GY9 3UF; tel. (1481) 711321; fax (1481) 735235; e-mail enquiries@blueislands.com; internet www.blueislands.com; f. 1999 as Le Cocqs Air Link; name changed as above in 2006; scheduled passenger flights between Alderney, Guernsey and Jersey, and to Southampton, the Isle of Man, Geneva and Zürich (both Switzerland); Chair. DEREK COATES; Man. Dir PAUL SABIN.

Tourism

A total of 304,000 tourists visited Guernsey during 2009.

VisitGuernsey: POB 459, Raymond Falla House, Longue Rue, St Martin, GY1 6AF; tel. (1481) 234567; fax (1481) 238755; e-mail enquiries@visitguernsey.com; internet www.visitguernsey.com; Dir, Marketing and Tourism CHRIS ELLIOTT.

Islands of the Bailiwick of Guernsey

Alderney

The area of Alderney is 7.9 sq km (3.1 sq miles) and at the 2001 census the population was 2,294. The principal town is St Anne's.

The President, who is elected for a four-year term, is the civic head of Alderney and has precedence on the island over all persons except the Lieutenant-Governor of Guernsey, and the Bailiff of Guernsey or his representative. He presides over meetings of the States of Alderney, which are responsible for the administration of the island with the exception of policing, public health and education, which are administered by the States of Guernsey. The States consist of 10 members who hold office for four years and are elected by universal suffrage of residents.

President of the States: Sir NORMAN BROWSE.

Chief Executive of the States: DAVID JEREMIAH.

Greffier: SARAH KELLY.

States of Alderney: POB 1, Alderney, GY9 3AA; tel. (1481) 822811; fax (1481) 822436; e-mail states@alderney.net; internet www.alderney.gov.gg.

Brecqhou and Lihou

Brecqhou (measuring 1.2 km by 0.5 km) is a dependency of Sark. Lihou (area 0.2 sq km) is, for administrative purposes, part of Guernsey.

Herm

Herm is held on a 100-year lease from the States of Guernsey by Wood of Herm Island Ltd, with a duty to preserve the island's outstanding natural beauty and peacefulness. Farming and tourism are the chief sources of income. The island has an area of 2.0 sq km (0.8 sq miles). At the 2001 census the population of Herm was 95.

Herm Island Administration Office: Herm Island, Guernsey, GY1 3HR; tel. (1481) 722377; fax (1481) 700334; e-mail admin@herm-island.com; internet www.herm-island.com; Admin. Dir ANDREW BAILEY.

Jethou

Jethou has an area of 0.2 sq km (0.07 sq miles) and is leased by the Crown to a tenant who has no official functions. At the 2001 census the population of Jethou was two.

Sark

The area of the island is 5.5 sq km (2.1 sq miles) and at the 2001 census the population was 589. No motor vehicles are permitted apart from a small number of tractors. In summer a daily boat service runs between Guernsey and Sark, and in winter a limited service is provided. There are two harbours on the island.

The Seigneur of Sark is the hereditary civic head of the island and thereby entitled to certain privileges. The Seigneur is a member of the Chief Pleas of Sark, the island's parliament, and has a suspensory veto on its ordinances. The Seigneur has the right, subject to the approval of the Lieutenant-Governor of Guernsey, to appoint the Seneschal of Sark, who is President of the Chief Pleas and Chairman of the Seneschal's Court, which is the local Court of Justice.

In March 2006 the Chief Pleas voted in favour of reducing the number of its members from 52 (comprising the owners of the island's 40 tenements—known as tenants—and 12 elected 'deputies of the people') to 28, of whom 14 were to be tenants and the remaining 14 residents. Under the reformed system the members of the Chief Pleas would be elected by universal suffrage of residents. An official opinion poll on the composition of the Chief Pleas was conducted between mid-August and early September. Some 56.0% of the valid votes cast (234 of a total of 418) supported open elections for all 28 seats in the Chief Pleas, while 44.0% of voters favoured the option of reserving 12 of the 28 seats specifically for residents and eight for tenants. A participation rate of 89.5% was recorded for the opinion poll, which was subsequently approved by the Chief Pleas. In February 2008 the Chief Pleas ratified the reform law, which would allow for the introduction of an elected chamber. The Privy Council of the United Kingdom approved the proposed changes in April and elections for a fully elected, 28-member Chief Pleas duly took place in December.

Seigneur of Sark: JOHN MICHAEL BEAUMONT.

Seneschal: Lt-Col REGINALD J. GUILLE.

Greffier: TREVOR J. HAMON.

Sark Committee Office: La Chasse Marette, GY9 0SF; tel. (1481) 832118; fax (1481) 833086; e-mail seigneur@gov.sark.gg; internet www.gov.sark.gg.

Sark Tourism: Harbour Hill, Sark, GY9 0SB; tel. (1481) 832345; fax (1481) 832483; e-mail contact@sark.info; internet www.sark.info.

UNITED KINGDOM CROWN DEPENDENCIES

The Channel Islands (Jersey)

JERSEY

Introduction

Jersey, the largest of the Channel Islands, is situated to the southeast of Guernsey, from which it is separated by 27 km (17 miles) of sea. The official language of Jersey is English (since 1960), although French is still used in the courts. The state and civil flag is white with a red saltire and coat of arms bearing three yellow lions and surmounted by a yellow crown. The capital is St Helier.

The sovereign is represented in Jersey by a Lieutenant-Governor, appointed by the Crown. Executive power is exercised by the Council of Ministers, headed by the Chief Minister, who is elected by the Assembly of the States (the insular legislature). The Assembly of the States is presided over by the Bailiff, appointed by the Crown, who does not have a vote. It consists of 12 Senators (elected for six years, six retiring every third year), 12 Connétables (triennial), and 29 Deputies (triennial), all elected by universal suffrage. The Dean of Jersey, the Attorney-General and Solicitor-General are appointed by the Crown and are entitled to sit and speak in the States, but not to vote.

In addition to the British public holidays, Jersey celebrates 9 May (Liberation Day).

Statistical Survey

Source (unless otherwise stated): States of Jersey Statistics Department, Cyril Le Marquand House, POB 140, JE4 8QT; tel. (1534) 440426; fax (1534) 440409; e-mail statistics@gov.je; internet www.gov.je/statistics.

AREA AND POPULATION

Area: 118.2 sq km (45.6 sq miles).

Population (census of 11 March 2001): 87,186 (males 42,484, females 44,702). *2009* (official estimate at 31 December, provisional): 92,500.

Density (at 31 December 2009, provisional): 782.6 per sq km.

Population by Age and Sex (census of 11 March 2001): *0–14:* 14,767 (males 7,588, females 7,179); *15–64:* 60,089 (males 29,653, females 30,436); *65 and over:* 12,330 (males 5,243, females 7,087); *Total* 87,186 (males 42,484, females 44,702) (Source: UN, *Demographic Yearbook*).

Principal Towns (2001): St Helier 28,310; St Saviour 12,491; St Brelade 10,134; St Clement 8,196.

Births and Deaths (2009): Live births 1,005 (10.9 per 1,000); Deaths 760 (8.2 per 1,000). *2010:* Live births 1,066; Deaths 797.

Employment (private sector employees at December 2010, rounded estimates): Agriculture and fishing 1,530; Manufacturing and utilities 1,840; Construction and quarrying 5,300; Wholesale and retail 8,690; Hotels, restaurants etc. 4,560; Transport, storage and communication 2,660; Financial services 12,680; Miscellaneous business activities (incl. computers) 4,140; Education, health and other services 5,290; *Total employed* 46,690. Note: In addition 6,780 employees were engaged in the public sector. *February 2011:* Registered unemployed and actively seeking work 1,470.

AGRICULTURE, ETC.

Principal Crops: Some 57% of total land area was classified as agricultural in 2009. The principal crops are potatoes, cauliflowers and tomatoes.

Livestock (2009): Cattle 5,090 (including 2,980 heifers in milk); Poultry 20,560.

Livestock Product (2008): Cows' milk 12.6m. litres.

Fishing (metric tons, 2009): Capture 1,254 (Skates and rays 23, Other wet fish 49, Brown crab 361, Lobster 177, Spider crab 177, Scallops 361, Whelk 104, Others 2); Aquaculture 1,007 (Oysters 903, Scallops 3, Mussels 101); *Total catch* 2,261.

MINING

Production ('000 metric tons): Igneous rock 305 in 2005; 286 in 2006; 295 in 2007.

FINANCE

Currency and Exchange Rates: 100 pence = 1 pound sterling (£). *Dollar and Euro Equivalents* (31 December 2010): US $1 = 63.88 pence; €1 = 85.35 pence; £10 = $15.65 = €11.72.

Note: Jersey is in monetary union with the United Kingdom. It has its own coins and notes but United Kingdom coins and notes are also legal tender.

Budget (£ million, 2009): Net consolidated fund income 674 (Tax 507); Consolidated fund expenditure 594 (Recurrent expenditure 564, Capital 30).

Money Supply (currency in circulation, £ million at 31 December 2009): Notes 83.4; Coins 7.3; *Total* 90.7.

Cost of Living (Retail Price Index at December; base June 2000 = 100, all items): 137.7 in 2008; 140.0 in 2009; 143.2 in 2010.

Gross National Income (£ million at current prices): 3,730 in 2007; 4,000 in 2008 (provisional); 3,700 in 2009 (provisional).

Gross Value Added by Economic Activity (£ million at current prices, 2009, provisional): Agriculture 62; Manufacturing 53; Electricity, gas and water 37; Construction 226; Wholesale and retail trade 257; Hotels, restaurants and bars 121; Transport, storage and communications 167; Finance 1,550; Other business activities 845; Public administration 304; *Total* 3,621.

TRANSPORT

Road Traffic (vehicles registered at 31 December 2001): Motor cars 71,059; Motorcycles 5,676; Mopeds 2,200; Buses and minibuses 691; Tractors 2,369; Vans 7,562; Trucks 3,617; Total (incl. others) 94,538. *2010* (vehicles registered at 31 December): Total 115,198.

Shipping (2010): Passenger movements 756,000; Containerized freight ('000 metric tons handled) 338.

Civil Aviation (2005): Aircraft movements 70,012; Total passengers carried 1,483,477 (Arrivals 741,969, Departures 741,508). *2009:* Total passenger arrivals 720,249 (from UK 609,234).

TOURISM

Tourist Arrivals (2004): *Holiday and Leisure Visitors* (staying in paid accommodation): 377,820 (UK mainland 301,460; Other Channel Islands 14,900; France 29,380; Germany 10,060); *Total Arrivals*: 731,310. *2010:* Total visitor arrivals 685,20000 (number staying in paid accommodation 335,150); Total revenues £230m.

COMMUNICATIONS MEDIA

Telephones (2009): 73,900 main lines in use.

Mobile Cellular Telephones (2006, estimate): 102,000.

Internet Users (2009): 29,500.

Source: partly International Telecommunication Union.

EDUCATION

Pupils (2010): Primary 6,896 (state schools 5,602, private 1,294); Secondary 6,365 (state schools 5,189, private 1,176).

Directory

The Government

HEAD OF STATE

Queen: HM Queen ELIZABETH II.

Lieutenant-Governor and Commander-in-Chief of Jersey: Lt-Gen. ANDREW RIDGEWAY.

COUNCIL OF MINISTERS
(May 2011)

Chief Minister: TERENCE (TERRY) LE SUEUR.
Minister for the Treasury and Resources: PHILIP OZOUF.
Minister for Home Affairs: IAN LE MARQUAND.
Minister for Education, Sport and Culture: JAMES REED.
Minister for Health and Social Services: ANNE PRYKE.
Minister for Social Security: IAN GORST.
Minister for Economic Development: ALAN MACLEAN.
Minister for Transport and Technical Services: MIKE JACKSON.

UNITED KINGDOM CROWN DEPENDENCIES

Minister for Housing: ANDREW KENNETH FRANCIS GREEN.
Minister for Planning and the Environment: FREDDIE COHEN.

OTHER OFFICIALS

Bailiff: MICHAEL CAMERON ST JOHN BIRT.
Deputy Bailiff: WILLIAM JAMES BAILHACHE.
Dean of Jersey: Very Rev. ROBERT FREDERICK KEY.
Attorney-General: TIMOTHY LE COCQ.
Solicitor-General: HOWARD SHARP.

GOVERNMENT OFFICES

Chief Minister's Department: POB 140, Cyril Le Marquand House, St Helier, JE4 8QT; tel. (1534) 445500; fax (1534) 440409; e-mail cmdept@gov.je; internet www.gov.je.
Economic Development Department: Jubilee Wharf, Esplanade, JE1 1BB; tel. (1534) 448100; fax (1534) 448170; e-mail economicdevelopment@gov.je.
Education, Sport and Culture Department: POB 142, Highlands Campus, JE4 8QJ; tel. (1534) 445504; fax (1534) 445524; e-mail esc@gov.je.
Health and Social Services Department: Peter Crill House, Gloucester St, St Helier, JE1 3QS; tel. (1534) 442000; fax (1534) 444216; e-mail healthandsocialservicesdepartment@gov.je.
Home Affairs Department: 11 Royal Sq., St Helier, JE2 4WA; tel. (1534) 445507; fax (1534) 447933; e-mail homeaffairs@gov.je.
Housing Department: POB 587, Jubilee Wharf, 24 Esplanade, St Helier, JE4 8XT; tel. (1534) 445510; fax (1534) 445530; e-mail socialhousing@gov.je.
Planning and Environment Department: South Hill, St Helier, JE2 4US; tel. (1534) 445508; fax (1534) 445528; e-mail planning@gov.je.
Social Security Department: POB 55, La Motte St, St Helier, JE4 8PE; tel. (1534) 445505; fax (1534) 445525; e-mail socialsecurity@gov.je.
Transport and Technical Services Department: POB 412, States Offices, Southern Hill, St Helier, JE4 8UY; tel. (1534) 445509; fax (1534) 445529; e-mail tts@gov.je.
Treasury and Resources Department: POB 353, Cyril Le Marquand House, St Helier, JE4 8UL; e-mail treasury@gov.je.
States of Jersey Assembly: Morier House, St Helier, JE1 1DD; tel. (1534) 441020; fax (1534) 441098; e-mail m.delahaye@gov.je; internet www.statesassembly.gov.je.

Judicial System

Justice is administered in Jersey by the Royal Court, which consists of the Bailiff or Deputy Bailiff and 12 Jurats elected by an Electoral College. There is a Court of Appeal, which consists of the Bailiff (or Deputy Bailiff) and two judges, selected from a panel appointed by the Crown. A final appeal lies to the Privy Council in certain cases.

A Stipendiary Magistrate deals with minor civil and criminal cases. He also acts as an Examining Magistrate in some criminal matters.

Religion

CHRISTIANITY

The Church of England

The Church of England is the established church. The Deanery of Jersey is an Ecclesiastical Peculiar, governed by its own canons, the Dean being the Ordinary of the Island; it is attached to the diocese of Winchester for episcopal purposes.

Dean of Jersey: Very Rev. ROBERT FREDERICK KEY, The Deanery, David Place, St Helier, JE2 4TE; tel. (1534) 720001; fax (1534) 617488; e-mail deanofjersey@jerseymail.co.uk.

The Roman Catholic Church

The diocese of Portsmouth includes the Channel Islands and part of southern England. The Episcopal Vicar for the Channel Islands resides at St Peter Port, Guernsey. In Jersey there are 12 Roman Catholic churches, including St Mary and St Peter's, Wellington Rd, St Helier (English), and St Thomas's, Val Plaisant, St Helier (French).

Catholic Dean of Jersey: Fr NICHOLAS FRANCE, 17 Val Plaisant, St Helier, JE2 4TA; tel. (1534) 720235; fax (1534) 607991.

Other Christian Churches

The Baptist, Congregational New Church, Methodist and Presbyterian churches are also represented.

The Channel Islands (Jersey)

The Press

Jersey Evening Post: Guiton House, Five Oaks, St Saviour, JE4 8XQ; tel. (1534) 611611; fax (1534) 611622; e-mail news@jerseyeveningpost.com; internet www.jerseyeveningpost.com; f. 1890; independent; Propr The Guiton Group; Editor CHRIS BRIGHT; circ. 20,070 (2008).
Jersey Weekly Post: POB 582, Guiton House, Five Oaks, St Saviour, JE4 8XQ; tel. (1534) 611611; fax (1534) 611622; e-mail news@jerseyeveningpost.com; internet www.thisisjersey.com; Thurs; Propr The Guiton Group; Editor CHRIS BRIGHT; circ. 1,200.

Publishers

Ashton & Denton Publishing Co (CI) Ltd: 3 Burlington House, St Saviour's Rd, St Helier, JE2 4LA; tel. (1534) 735461; fax (1534) 875805; e-mail asden@supanet.com; f. 1957; local history, holiday guides, financial; Man. Dir A. MACKENZIE.
Barnes Publishing Ltd: 18 Great Union Rd, St Helier, JE2 3YA; tel. (1534) 618166; e-mail ian@barnespublishing.com; internet barnespublishing.com; f. 1992 as Apache Publishing; present name adopted 1998; Man. Dir IAN BARNES.

Broadcasting and Communications

TELECOMMUNICATIONS

Airtel-Vodafone (Jersey): 26 Queen St, St Helier, JE2 4WD; tel. 7829700121 (mobile); e-mail 121@airtel-vodafone.je; internet www.airtel-vodafone.com; f. 2007; mobile cellular telecommunications; jt venture between Bharti Airtel Ltd (India) and Vodafone PLC (United Kingdom); Chief Exec. DAVID WATSON.
Cable and Wireless Jersey: King St, St Helier, JE2 4WE; tel. (1534) 888291; fax (1534) 888292; e-mail hello@surecw.com; internet www.surecw.com/jersey; offers mobile cellular telecommunications under brand name Sure Mobile; Chief Exec., Sure Jersey GRAHAM HUGHES.
Jersey Telecom: POB 53, No. 1 The Forum, Grenville St, St Helier, JE4 8PB; tel. (1534) 882882; fax (1534) 882883; e-mail enquiries@jerseytelecom.com; internet www.jerseytelecom.com; Chair. JOHN BOOTHMAN; CEO GRAEME MILLAR.

BROADCASTING

Radio

BBC: Radio and Television (see United Kingdom).
BBC Jersey: 18 and 21 Parade Rd, St Helier, JE2 3PL; tel. (1534) 870000; e-mail jersey@bbc.co.uk; internet www.bbc.co.uk/jersey; f. 1982; broadcasts 78 hours a week; Editor JON GRIPTON.
Channel 103 FM: 6 Tunnell St, St Helier, JE2 4LU; tel. (1534) 888103; fax (1534) 877177; e-mail info@channel103.com; internet www.channel103.com; f. 1992; Man. Dir LINDA BURNHAM.

Television

Channel Television: Television Centre, La Pouquelaye, St Helier, JE1 3ZD; tel. (1534) 816816; fax (1534) 816777; e-mail broadcast@channeltv.co.uk; internet www.channelonline.tv; f. 1962; privately owned regional licence-holder for Channel 3 (ITV1) in the United Kingdom; daily transmissions; Exec. Chair. MICK DESMOND.

Programmes are also received from the BBC, Channel 4 and Five in the United Kingdom and also from France.

Finance

Jersey Financial Services Commission: POB 267, 14–18 Castle St, St Helier, JE4 8TP; tel. (1534) 822000; fax (1534) 822002; e-mail info@jerseyfsc.org; internet www.jerseyfsc.org; f. 1998; financial services regulator; Dir-Gen. JOHN HARRIS.

BANKING

(cap. = capital; auth. = authorized; res = reserves; dep. = deposits; m. = million; br./brs = branch(es); amounts in pounds sterling, unless otherwise indicated)

In 2009 total bank deposits in Jersey were £165,220m. in 47 institutions.

Banks

ABN AMRO Private Banking: POB 255, 7 Castle St, St Helier, JE4 8TB; tel. (1534) 604000; fax (1534) 759041; e-mail pbclients@uk.abnamro.com; internet www.abnamroprivatebanking.com/jersey; f. 1997; Head of Private Banking PATRICK CROWLEY.

The Channel Islands (Jersey)

AIB Bank (CI) Ltd: POB 468, AIB House, 25 Esplanade, St Helier, JE1 2AB; tel. (1534) 883000; fax (1534) 883112; e-mail one@aib.je; internet www.aib.je; f. 1981; cap. 3m., res 6m., dep. 2,607m. (Dec. 2008); CEO D. J. MOYNIHAN.

Bank Leumi (Jersey) Ltd: POB 510, 2 Hill St, St Helier, JE4 5TR; tel. (1534) 702525; fax (1534) 617446; e-mail info@leumijersey.com; internet www.bankleumi.co.uk; f. 1993; cap. 15m., res 6m., dep. 363m. (Dec. 2008).

Bank of Scotland International Ltd: Halifax House, 31–33 New St, St Helier, JE4 8YW; tel. (1534) 613500; fax (1534) 759280; e-mail enquiry@bankofscotlandint.co.uk; internet www.bankofscotland-international.com; cap. 15.0m., dep. 822.8m. (Feb. 2001); f. 1986; Man. Dir TONY WILCOX.

Bank Julius Baer (Jersey) Ltd: 3rd Floor, Forum House, Grenville St, St Helier, JE2 4UF; tel. (1534) 880888; fax (1534) 880777; internet www.ing.je; fmrly ING Bank (Jersey) Ltd; name changed as above in 2010 after acquisition by Bank Julius Baer; Man. Dir PAUL VAN NESTE.

Citibank (Channel Islands) Ltd: POB 104, 38 The Esplanade, St Helier, JE4 8QB; tel. (1534) 608000; fax (1534) 608190; internet www.citibank.com/privatebank/index.htm; f. 1969; cap. US $0.9m., res $7.6m., dep. $216.4m. (Dec. 2005); Chair. RICHARD D. PARSONS.

Deutsche Bank International Ltd: POB 727, St Paul's Gate, New St, St Helier, JE4 8ZB; tel. (1534) 889900; fax (1534) 889911; internet www.dboffshore.com; f. 1972; cap. 15m., res 223m., dep. 4,582m. (Dec. 2008); Chief Country Officer ANDREAS TAUTSCHER.

Dexia Private Bank Jersey Ltd: POB 12, 2–6 Church St, St Helier, JE4 9NE; tel. (1534) 834400; fax (1534) 834411; e-mail dexiapbjsy@localdial.com; internet www.dexia-privatebank.je; f. 1996; Man. Dir DAVID G. SMITH.

Fairbairn Private Bank Ltd: Fairbairn House, 31 The Esplanade, St Helier, JE1 1FB; tel. (1534) 887889; fax (1534) 509725; e-mail jer@fairbairnpb.com; internet www.fairbairnpb.com; f. 1994 as Flemings (Jersey) Ltd, name changed as above in 2004; cap. 0.4m., res 13m., dep. 942m. (Dec. 2008); Man. Dir G. J. HORTON.

SG Hambros Bank (Channel Islands) Ltd: POB 197, SG Hambros House, 18 The Esplanade, St Helier, JE4 8PR; tel. (1534) 815555; fax (1534) 815640; e-mail channelislands@sghambros.com; internet www.sghambros.com; f. 1967 as Hambros (Jersey) Ltd; previously SG Hambros Bank and Trust (Jersey) Ltd; name changed in 2005 following merger with SG Hambros Bank and Trust (Guernsey) Ltd; subsidiary of SG Hambros Bank and Trust Ltd, London; cap. 4.5m., res 162.1m., dep. 5,717m. (Dec. 2008); Chair. WARWICK J. NEWBURY; Man. Dir RICHARD A. OLLIVER.

HSBC Bank International Ltd: HSBC House, St Helier, JE1 1HS; tel. (1534) 616111; fax (1534) 616001; e-mail offshore@hsbc.com; internet www.offshore.hsbc.com; f. 1967 as Midland Bank Finance Corpn (Jersey) Ltd; cap. 1m., res 70m, dep. 7,229m. (Dec. 2009); Chief Exec. MARTIN DAVID SPURLING.

HSBC Bank Middle East Ltd: POB 315, HSBC House, The Esplanade, St Helier, JE4 8UB; tel. (1534) 606512; fax (1534) 606149; e-mail chris.keirle@hsbc.com; internet www.middleeast.hsbc.com; cap. US $631m., res $47m., dep. $36,209m. (Dec. 2008); Chair. YOUSSEF NASR.

Kleinwort Benson (Channel Islands) Ltd: POB 76, Kleinwort Benson House, Wests Centre, St Helier, JE4 8PQ; tel. (1534) 613000; fax (1534) 613141; internet www.kleinwortbenson.com; f. 1962; mem. of the Dresdner Bank Group; cap. 5m., res 20m., dep. 1,910m. (Dec. 2008); Man. Dir MARTIN ANGUS TAYLOR.

Lloyds TSB Offshore Ltd: POB 160, 25 New St, St Helier, JE4 8RG; tel. (1534) 854144; fax (1534) 503215; e-mail jerseyoffc@lloydstsb-offshore.com; internet www.lloydstsb-offshore.com; part of Lloyds TSB banking group; cap. 208m., res 287m., dep. 8,283m. (Dec. 2009); Chair. MARTIN FREDERICK FRICKER.

JPMorgan Chase Bank: POB 127, JPMorgan House, Grenville St, St Helier, JE4 8QH; tel. (1534) 626262; fax (1534) 626301; Gen. Man. L. C. WORTHAM.

JP Morgan Trust Co (Jersey): POB 127, JPMorgan House, Grenville St, St Helier; tel. (1534) 626262; fax (1534) 626300; Chair. T. TODMAN; Man. Dir L. C. WORTHAM.

RBS Coutts Channel Islands: POB 6, 23–25 Broad St, St Helier, JE4 8ND; tel. (1534) 282345; fax (1534) 282199; e-mail info@rbscoutts.com; internet www.rbscoutts.com.

The Royal Bank of Scotland International Ltd: POB 64, 71 Bath St, St Helier, JE4 8PJ; tel. (1534) 285200; fax (1534) 285588; internet www.rbsint.com; f. 1966; cap. 86.5m., res 686.3m., dep. 14,216.7m. (Dec. 2002); Chief Exec. ADRIAN GILL.

Standard Bank Jersey Ltd: POB 583, Standard Bank House, 47–49 La Motte St, St Helier, JE4 8XR; tel. (1534) 881188; fax (1534) 881199; e-mail sboff@standardbank.com; internet www.standardbank.com/wealth; f. 1977 as Brown Shipley (Jersey); present name adopted 2000; cap. 14m., res 0.3m., dep. 1,238m. (Dec. 2008); Chair. R. A. G. LEITH; CEO IAN GIBSON.

Standard Chartered (Jersey) Ltd: POB 80, 15 Castle St, St Helier, JE4 8PT; tel. (1534) 704000; fax (1534) 704600; internet www.standardchartered.com/je; f. 1966 as Julian S. Hodge Bank (Jersey) Ltd; present name adopted 2004; cap.US $7m., res $84m., dep. $4,896m. (Dec. 2009); CEO RICHARD INGLE.

INSURANCE

Jersey Mutual Insurance Soc.: 74 Halkett Pl., St Helier, JE1 1BT; tel. (1534) 734246; fax (1534) 733381; e-mail info@jerseymutual.com; internet www.jerseymutual.com; f. 1869; general and household; Pres. A. MOLLET; Gen. Man. R. A. JEANNE.

Trade and Industry

CHAMBER OF COMMERCE

Jersey Chamber of Commerce: Chamber House, 25 Pier Rd, St Helier, JE1 4HF; tel. (1534) 724536; fax (1534) 734942; e-mail admin@jerseychamber.com; internet www.jerseychamber.com; f. 1768; Pres. RAY SHEAD; Head, Marketing and Operations CATHERINE HARGREAVES; 500 mems.

Utilities

Electricity

Jersey Electricity Co Ltd: The Powerhouse, POB 45, Queen's Rd, St Helier, JE4 8NY; tel. (1534) 505460; fax (1534) 505565; e-mail jec@jec.co.uk; internet www.jec.co.uk; f. 1924; Chair. GEOFFREY GRIME; CEO CHRIS AMBLER.

Gas

Jersey Gas Co Ltd: POB 169, Tunnell St, St Helier, JE4 8RE; tel. (1534) 755500; fax (1534) 769822; e-mail jerseygas@jsy-gas.com; internet www.jsygas.com; Man. Dir PAUL GARLICK.

Water

Jersey New Waterworks Co Ltd (Jersey Water): Mulcaster House, Westmount Rd, St Helier, JE1 1DG; tel. (1534) 707300; fax (1534) 707400; e-mail info@jerseywater.je; internet www.jerseywater.je; 73.9% stake owned by States of Jersey; Chair. KEVIN KEEN; Man. Dir HOWARD SNOWDEN.

Transport

SHIPPING

The harbour of St Helier has 1,400 m of cargo working quays, with 10 berths in dredged portion (2.29 m) and eight drying berths.

Condor Jersey Ltd: Elizabeth Terminal and Albert Quay, St Helier; tel. (1534) 607080; fax (1534) 280767; e-mail reservations@condorferries.co.uk; internet www.condorferries.co.uk; head office in Guernsey; daily services to mainland Britain; also regular services to Guernsey and St Malo (France); Gen. Man. NICK DOBBS.

CIVIL AVIATION

The States of Jersey Airport is at St Peter, Jersey.

Tourism

In 2009 Jersey recorded some 685,200 tourist arrivals; 335,150 visitors stayed in paid accommodation. Tourist receipts in that year were £230m.

Jersey Tourism: Liberation Sq., St Helier, JE1 1BB; tel. (1534) 448800; fax (1534) 448898; e-mail info@jersey.com; internet www.jersey.com; Dir DAVID DE CARTERET.

THE ISLE OF MAN

Introduction

The Isle of Man lies in the Irish Sea between the Cumbrian coast of England and Northern Ireland. It is a dependency of the Crown and does not form part of the United Kingdom or the European Union. It has its own legislative assembly and legal and administrative systems, its laws depending for their validity on Orders made by the Queen in Council. Her Majesty's Government in the United Kingdom is responsible for the defence and international relations of the island, and the Crown is ultimately responsible for its good government. However, control of direct taxation is exercised by the Manx Government and, although most rates of indirect taxation are the same on the island as in the United Kingdom, there is some divergence of rates. The capital is Douglas.

The head of state of the Isle of Man is the British monarch as the Lord of Mann. The Lieutenant-Governor, who is the Crown's personal representative on the island, is appointed by the head of state for a five-year term. The legislature is Tynwald, comprising two branches, the Legislative Council and the House of Keys, sitting together as one body, but voting separately on all questions except in certain eventualities. The House of Keys, the lower chamber, has 24 members, who represent single member and multi-member constituencies and are elected by adult suffrage for five years. Eight of the 11 members of the Legislative Council are elected by the House of Keys. The remainder are ex officio members: the Lord Bishop of Sodor and Man, the Attorney-General, and the President of Tynwald, who is elected by all the members of Tynwald.

In addition to the British public holidays, the Isle of Man also celebrates Senior Race Day of the annual Isle of Man Tourist Trophy (TT) Races (which, in 2012, falls on 8 June) and Tynwald Day (5 July).

Statistical Survey

Source: Isle of Man Government Offices, Bucks Rd, Douglas; tel. (1624) 685711; internet www.gov.im.

AREA AND POPULATION

Area: 572 sq km (221 sq miles).

Population (census, 23–24 April 2006): 80,058 (males 39,523, females 40,535).

Density (at 2006 census): 140.0 per sq km.

Population by Age and Sex (census, 23–24 April 2006): *0–14:* 13,537 (males 7,048, females 6,489); *15–64:* 52,834 (males 26,503, females 26,331); *65 and over:* 13,687 (males 5,972, females 7,715); *Total* 80,058 (males 39,523, females 40,535).

Principal Localities (2006 census): Douglas (capital) 26,218; Onchan 9,172; Ramsey 7,309; Peel 4,280; Port Erin 3,575; Braddan 3,151; Castletown 3,109.

Births and Deaths (2005): Live births 901 (birth rate 11.3 per 1,000); Deaths 775 (death rate 10.5 per 1,000). *2009:* Live births 1,015; Deaths 816.

Economically Active Population (2006 census): Agriculture, etc. 642; Manufacturing 2,248; Electricity, gas and water 603; Transport and communication 3,171; Wholesale and retail trade 4,550; Entertainment, catering and tourist accommodation 2,259; Banking and finance 7,010; Real estate and renting 1,072; Other professional, business and scientific services 3,741; Education 2,805; Medical and health services 3,316; Public administration 2,898; Other services 3,075; *Sub-total* 40,764; Activities not adequately defined 19; *Total employed* 40,783 (males 22,020, females 18,763); Unemployed 1,010 (males 634, females 376); *Total labour force* 41,793 (males 22,654, females 19,139). *2009* (at December): Unemployed 878.

AGRICULTURE, ETC.

Crops (area in acres, 2009): Cereals and potatoes 11,522; Grass 68,486; Rough grazing 32,193.

Livestock (2009): Cattle 33,989; Sheep 144,919; Pigs 710; Poultry 17,409.

Fishing (2009 unless otherwise indicated): *Amount Landed* (metric tons): Scallops 1,578; Queen scallops 1,473; Lobsters 38. *Value of Landings* (2008): Scallops £2.3m.; Queen scallops £0.3m.; Lobsters £0.4m.

FINANCE

Currency and Exchange Rates: 100 pence = 1 pound sterling (£). *Dollar and Euro Equivalents* (31 December 2010): US $1 = 63.88 pence; €1 = 85.35 pence; £10 = $15.65 = €11.72.

Note: The Isle of Man is in monetary union with the United Kingdom. It has its own coins and notes, but United Kingdom coins and notes are also legal tender.

Budget: (£ million, 2009/10, estimates): *Total Revenue* 572.3 (Customs and excise 398.6; Income and other taxes 160.5); *Total Expenditure* 541.2 (Health and social security 246.8).

Cost of Living: (Retail Price Index; base: January 2000 = 100) All items 134.6 in 2008; 135.4 in 2009; 142.2 in 2010.

Gross National Income (GNI) (£ million at current factor cost): 3,412.1 in 2007/08; 3,418.3 in 2008/09.

GDP by Economic Activity (£ million at current factor cost, 2008/09): Agriculture, hunting, forestry and fishing 23.8; Mining and quarrying 15.4; Manufacturing 146.3; Electricity, gas and water supply 40.7; Construction 173.7; Wholesale and retail trade, repair of motor vehicles, motorcycles and personal and household goods 187.7; Transport and communications 216.3; Catering and entertainment and tourist accommodation 48.2; Financial services, real estate, renting and business activities 1,205.1; Other professional, educational, scientific and medical service activities 874.2; Public administration 130.4; Other services 102.7; *Sub-total* 3,164.6; Imputed rents, less adjustments for financial intermediation services indirectly measured, government depreciation of fixed assets and non-profit institutions serving households 5.6; *Total* 3,170.1.

TRANSPORT

Road Traffic (registered vehicles, 2001): Private 45,195; Engineering 385; Goods 4,489; Agricultural 931; Hackney 790; Public service 146; Motorcycles, scooters and tricycles 4,519.

Shipping (at 31 December 2009 unless otherwise indicated): Passengers handled 638,505 (2008/09); General freight handled 127,599 metric tons (2008/09); Registered merchant vessels 339; Other registered vessels 708; Total displacement ('000 grt) 10,737.

Civil Aviation: Passengers handled 721,620 (2009); Freight carried 4,594 metric tons (2003).

TOURISM

Tourist Arrivals (2009): Staying visitors 205,256; Day visitors 3,319; Business travellers 78,549.

COMMUNICATIONS MEDIA

Telephone Connections (2001): Fixed 56,000; Mobile 32,000.

Television Licences (2000): 28,601.

EDUCATION

State Primary: 35 schools (2007/08), 6,564 students (2008/09).

State Secondary: 5 schools (2007/08), 4,719 students (2008/09).

Further and Higher Education (2008/09): 1 college, 1,429 students.

There are, in addition, two private schools.

Directory

The Government

HEAD OF STATE

Lord of Mann: HM Queen ELIZABETH II.
Lieutenant-Governor: ADAM WOOD.

COUNCIL OF MINISTERS
(May 2011)

Chief Minister: TONY BROWN.
Minister of Community, Culture and Leisure: DAVID CRETNEY.
Minister of Economic Development: ALLAN BELL.
Minister of Education and Children: EDDIE TEARE.

UNITED KINGDOM CROWN DEPENDENCIES

Minister of Environment, Food and Agriculture: JOHN SHIMMIN.
Minister of Health: DAVID ANDERSON.
Minister of Home Affairs: ADRIAN EARNSHAW.
Minister of Infrastructure: PHIL GAWNE.
Minister of Social Care: MARTYN QUAYLE.
Minister of the Treasury: ANNE CRAINE.

GOVERNMENT OFFICES

Isle of Man Government: Government Office, Bucks Rd, Douglas, IM1 3PN; tel. (1624) 6856711; fax (1624) 685710; e-mail enquiries.cso@gov.im; internet www.gov.im.

Department of Community, Culture and Leisure: St Andrew's House, Douglas, IM1 2PX; tel. (1624) 686817; e-mail enquiries@dccl.gov.im; internet www.gov.im/tourism.

Department of Economic Development: Hamilton House, Peel Rd, Douglas, IM1 5EP; tel. (1624) 682354; fax (1624) 682355; e-mail dti@gov.im; internet www.gov.im/dti.

Department of Education and Children: St George's Court, Upper Church St, Douglas, IM1 2SG; tel. (1624) 685820; fax (1624) 685834; e-mail admin@doe.gov.im; internet www.gov.im/education.

Department of Environment, Food and Agriculture: Thie Slieau Whallian, Foxdale Rd, St Johns, IM4 3AS; tel. (1624) 685835; fax (1624) 685851; e-mail daff@gov.im; internet www.gov.im/defa.

Department of Health: Markwell House, Market St, Douglas, IM1 2RZ; tel. (1624) 685004; fax (1624) 685130; e-mail ceo@dhss.gov.im; internet www.gov.im/dhss.

Department of Home Affairs: Homefield, 88 Woodbourne Rd, Douglas, IM2 3AP; tel. (1624) 694300; fax (1624) 621298; e-mail generalenquiries.dha@gov.im; internet www.gov.im/dha.

Department of Infrastructure: Sea Terminal, Douglas, IM1 2RF; tel. (1624) 686600; e-mail enquiries@dot.gov.im; internet www.gov.im/transport.

Department of Social Care: Markwell House, Market St, Douglas, IM1 2RZ; tel. (1624) 685004; fax (1624) 685130; e-mail ceo@dhss.gov.im; internet www.gov.im/health/.

Department of the Treasury: Government Office, Bucks Rd, Douglas, IM1 3PZ; tel. (1624) 685586; e-mail treasuryadmin@gov.im; internet www.gov.im/treasury.

External Relations Division: Government Office, Bucks Rd, Douglas, IM1 3PN; tel. (1624) 685703; fax (1624) 685710; e-mail enquiries.cso@gov.im; internet www.gov.im/cso/externalrelations.

Legislature

TYNWALD

President: NOEL QUAYLE CRINGLE.
Deputy President: STEPHEN CHARLES RODAN.

Legislative Council (Upper House)

President of the Council: NOEL QUAYLE CRINGLE.
Lord Bishop of Sodor and Man: Rt Rev. ROBERT M. E. PATERSON.
Attorney-General: WILLIAM JOHN HOWARTH CORLETT.
Members appointed by the House of Keys: ROBERT PHILIP BRAIDWOOD, EDWARD ALAN CROWE, EDWARD GEORGE LOWEY, CLARE MARGARET CHRISTIAN, DAVID ALEXANDER CALLISTER, DUDLEY MICHAEL WILLIAM BUTT, ALEXANDER FRANK DOWNIE, JUAN RICHARD TURNER.
Clerk: JONATHAN KING.

House of Keys (Lower House)

Speaker: STEPHEN CHARLES RODAN.
Clerk of Tynwald, Secretary of the House and Counsel to the Speaker: ROGER IAN SEXTON PHILLIPS.

The House of Keys consists of 24 members, elected by adult suffrage for five years—eight for Douglas, three for Onchan, two for Ramsey, one each for Peel and Castletown, and nine for rural districts. The last general election took place on 23 November 2006. Most members of the House of Keys are elected as independents. However, a small number are affiliated to political parties.

Political Organizations

Liberal Vannin: White Cot, King Edward's Rd, Onchan; tel. (1624) 853352; fax (1624) 852977; e-mail office@liberalvannin.org; internet www.liberalvannin.org; f. 2006; Chair. ROY REDMAYNE; Leader PETER KARRAN.

Manx Labour Party: f. 1918; Spokesperson DAVID CRETNEY.

Mec Vannin: internet www.mecvannin.im; f. 1962; advocates the establishment of the Isle of Man as a sovereign republic; Pres. BERNARD MOFFATT; Chair. MARK KERMODE.

Judicial System

The Isle of Man is, for legal purposes, an autonomous sovereign country under the British Crown, with its own legislature and its own independent judiciary administering its own common or customary and statute law. The law of the Isle of Man is, in most essential matters, the same as the law of England and general principles of equity administered by the English Courts are followed by the Courts of the Isle of Man unless they conflict with established local precedents. Her Majesty's High Court of Justice of the Isle of Man is based upon the English system but modified and simplified to meet local conditions. Justices of the Peace are appointed by the Lord Chancellor of Great Britain usually on the nomination of the Lieutenant-Governor. The Deemsters (see below), the High Bailiff, the Mayor of Douglas, and the Chairmen of the Town and Village Commissioners are all ex officio Justices of the Peace. The Manx Court of Appeal consists of the Deemsters and the Judge of Appeal.

First Deemster and Clerk of the Rolls: DAVID DOYLE.
Second Deemster: ANDREW CORLETT.
Deemster: ALASTAIR MONTGOMERIE.
Judge of Appeal: GEOFFREY TATTERSALL.

Religion

CHRISTIANITY

The Church of England

The Isle of Man forms the diocese of Sodor and Man, comprising 28 parishes. The parish church of St German at Peel was designated a cathedral in 1980.

Lord Bishop of Sodor and Man: Rt Rev. ROBERT M. E. PATERSON, Bishop's House, The Falls, Tromode Road, Douglas, IM4 4PZ; tel. (1624) 622108; fax (1624) 672890; e-mail bishop-sodor@iommail.net; internet www.gumbley.net/diocese.htm.

Roman Catholic Church

The deanery of the Isle of Man is part of the archdiocese of Liverpool. There are six Catholic churches on the island.

Dean of the Isle of Man: Very Rev. Canon BRENDAN ALGER, St Mary of the Isle, Hill St, Douglas, IM1 3EG; tel. (1624) 675509; fax (1624) 674359; e-mail bjpalger@yahoo.co.uk.

Other Churches

There are also congregations of the following denominations: Baptist, Bethel Non-Denominational, Christadelphian, Congregational, Greek Orthodox, Independent Methodist, Methodist, Presbyterian, Elim Pentecostal, United Reformed, and Religious Society of Friends (Quakers); also Christian Science, Jehovah's Witnesses and the Church of Jesus Christ of Latter-day Saints.

There are small Bahá'í, Jewish and Muslim communities on the island.

The Press

Isle of Man Courier: Publishing House, Peel Rd, Douglas, IM1 5PZ; tel. (1624) 695695; fax (1624) 661041; e-mail john.sherrocks@newsiom.co.im; internet www.iomonline.co.im; f. 1884; weekly; Editor RICHARD BUTT; circ. 37,102 (2009).

Isle of Man Examiner: Publishing House, Peel Rd, Douglas, IM1 5PZ; tel. (1624) 695695; fax (1624) 661041; e-mail john.sherrocks@newsiom.co.im; internet www.iomonline.co.im; f. 1880; weekly; Editor RICHARD BUTT; circ. 12,057 (2009).

The Manx Independent: Publishing House, Peel Rd, Douglas, IM1 5PZ; tel. (1624) 695695; fax (1624) 661041; e-mail john.sherrocks@newsiom.co.im; internet www.iomonline.co.im; f. 1987; Fri; Editor RICHARD BUTT; circ. 11,002 (2009).

Manx Tails Magazine: Media House, Cronkbourne, Douglas, IM4 4SB; tel. (1624) 696565; fax (1624) 625623; e-mail mail@manninmedia.co.im; f. 1982 as in-flight magazine of Manx Airlines; launched as an all-island publication in 2002; monthly; distributed free of charge; Editor SIMON RICHARDSON; circ. 36,400.

Sea Breezes Magazine: Media House, Cronkbourne, Douglas, IM4 4SB; tel. (1624) 696573; fax (1624) 661655; e-mail sb.enquiries@seabreezes.co.im; internet www.seabreezes.co.im; f. 1919; Editor STEVE ROBINSON.

UNITED KINGDOM CROWN DEPENDENCIES   *The Isle of Man*

Publishers

Amulree Publications: Lossan y Twoaie, Glen Rd, Laxey, IM4 7AN; tel. (1624) 862238; e-mail amulree@mcb.net; internet www.manxshop.com; f. 1993; Propr BILL SNELLING.

Electrochemical Publications Ltd: Asahi House, 10 Church Rd, Port Erin, IM9 6AQ; tel. (1624) 834941; fax (1624) 835400; Man. Dir WILLIAM GOLDIE.

Lily Publications Ltd: POB 33, Ramsey, IM99 4LP; tel. (1624) 898446; fax (1624) 898449; e-mail sales@lilypublications.co.uk; internet www.lilypublications.co.uk; f. 1991; Man. Dir MILES COWSILL.

Mannin Media Group Ltd: Media House, Cronkbourne, Douglas, IM4 4SB; tel. (1624) 696565; fax (1624) 625623; e-mail mail@manninmedia.co.im; internet www.manninmedia.co.im; Chief Exec. STEVEN BROWN.

The Manx Experience: Sunnybank Ave, Birch Hill, Onchan, IM3 3BW; tel. (1624) 627727; fax (1624) 663627; e-mail mail@manxexperience.co.uk; Man. Dir GWYNNETH BROWN, STEVEN BROWN.

Pines Press: The Pines, Ballelin, Maughold, Ramsey, IM7 1HJ; tel. (1624) 862030; f. 1987; Dir B. CLYNE.

Keith Uren Publishing: 12 Manor Lane, Farmhill, Braddan, IM2 2NX; tel. and fax (1624) 611100; e-mail portfolio@manxe.net; internet keithurenpublishing.com; magazines.

Vathek Publishing Ltd: Bridge House, Dalby, IM5 3BP; tel. (1624) 844056; fax (1624) 845043; e-mail mlw@vathek.com; internet www.vathek.com; legal journals; Man. Dir MAIRWEN LLOYD-WILLIAMS.

Broadcasting and Communications

Isle of Man Communications Commission: 2nd Floor, St Andrew's House, Doughlas, IM1 2PX; tel. (1624) 677022; fax (1624) 626499; e-mail margaret.king@cc.gov.im; internet www.gov.im/government/boards/cc.xml; appointed by the Isle of Man Govt to represent the island's interests in all matters of telecommunications, radio and television; Chair. ADRIAN EARNSHAW (Minister of Home Affairs); Dir CARMEL MCLAUGHLIN.

TELECOMMUNICATIONS

Cable & Wireless Communications: 14 Athol St, Douglas IM1 1JA; tel. (1624) 247247; e-mail talk@surecw.com; internet www.surecw.com; mobile, broadband and fixed-line services; operates under the brand name of Sure Mobile; Chair. Sir RICHARD LAPTHORNE.

Manx Telecom Ltd: Isle of Man Business Park, Cooil Rd, Braddan, IM99 1HX; POB 100, Douglas, IM99 1HX; tel. (1624) 624624; fax (1624) 636011; e-mail mail@manx-telecom.com; internet www.manx-telecom.com; f. 1986; subsidiary of Telefónica O_2 UK PLC; Man. Dir CHRIS HALL.

BROADCASTING
Radio and Television

BBC: Radio and Television (see United Kingdom).

Energy FM: 100 Market St, Douglas, IM1 2PH; tel. (1624) 611936; fax (1624) 664699; internet www.energyfm.net; f. 2001.

ITV Border: Television (see United Kingdom).

Manx Radio: Broadcasting House, POB 1368, Douglas, IM99 1SW; tel. (1624) 682600; fax (1624) 682604; e-mail reception@manxradio.com; internet www.manxradio.com; f. 1960; commercial station operated (by agreement with the Isle of Man Government) by Radio Manx Ltd; Chair. DAVID NORTH; Man. Dir ANTHONY PUGH.

3FM: 45 Victoria St, Douglas, IM1 3RS; tel. (1624) 616333; fax (1624) 614333; internet www.three.fm; music.

The Isle of Man also receives television programmes from Channel 4 and Five.

Finance

Financial Supervision Commission: POB 58, Finch Hill House, Bucks Rd, Douglas, IM99 1DT; tel. (1624) 689300; fax (1624) 689399; e-mail fsc@gov.im; internet www.fsc.gov.im; f. 1983; responsible for the licensing, authorization and supervision of banks, building societies, investment businesses, collective investment schemes and fiduciary service providers; Chair. ROSEMARY PENN; Chief Exec. JOHN ASPDEN.

Treasury: Government Office, Bucks Rd, Douglas, IM1 3PU; tel. (1624) 685586; fax (1624) 685662; e-mail treasuryadmin@gov.im; internet www.gov.im/treasury; Minister ANNE CRAINE; Chief Financial Officer P. M. SHIMMIN.

BANKING

(cap. = capital; res = reserves; dep. = deposits; m. = million; brs = branches; amounts in pounds sterling)

At 30 June 2009 there were 38 licensed banks and building societies in the Isle of Man. At 31 December 2009, total bank deposits amounted to some £51,950m. The Financial Supervision Commission may allow a major bank to establish a presence on the island on a managed bank basis, by awarding an 'offshore' banking licence.

AIB Bank (CI) Ltd: 10 Finch Rd, Douglas, IM1 2PT; tel. (1624) 639639; fax (1624) 639636; e-mail one@aib.im; internet www.aib.im; f. 1977; cap. 10m., dep. 2,268m. (Dec. 2007); Dir CHRISTOPHER HOWLAND.

Alliance & Leicester International Ltd: POB 226, 19–21 Prospect Hill, Douglas, IM99 1RY; tel. (1624) 641888; fax (1624) 663577; internet www.alil.co.im; owned by Banco Santander, SA (Spain); Jt Man. Dirs SIMON NUTTALL (acting), SIMON RIPTON (acting).

Anglo Irish Bank Corpn (International) PLC: Jubilee Bldgs, Victoria St, Douglas, IM1 2SH; tel. (1624) 698000; fax (1624) 698001; e-mail enquiries@angloirishbank.co.im; internet www.angloirishbank.co.im; f. 1988; Man. Dir DAVID MACGREGOR.

Bank of Ireland (IOM) Ltd: POB 246, Christian Rd, Douglas, IM99 1XF; tel. (1624) 644222; fax (1624) 644298; e-mail info@boioffshore.com; internet www.boioffshore.com; f. 1981; cap. 25m., res 0.06m., dep. 3,243m. (March 2008); Chair. J. L. M. QUINN; Man. Dir MICHAEL MCKAY.

Barclays Private Bank and Trust (Isle of Man) Ltd: POB 48, Queen Victoria House, Victoria St, Douglas, IM99 1DF; tel. (1624) 682828; fax (1624) 620905; internet www.barclays.co.uk/privatebank; Man. Dir ALAN R. PATRICK.

Barclays Private Clients International Ltd: POB 213, Eagle Court, 25 Circular Rd, Douglas, IM99 1RH; tel. (1624) 684000; fax (1624) 684321; international banking services; Man. Dir GREG ELLISON; 6 brs.

Britannia International Ltd: POB 231, Britannia House, Athol St, Douglas, IM99 1SD; tel. (1624) 681100; fax (1624) 681105; e-mail enquiries@britanniainternational.com; internet www.britanniainternational.com; f. 1988; 'offshore' subsidiary of The Co-operative Bank PLC; Man. Dir MARK BERESFORD.

Cayman National Bank and Trust Co (Isle of Man) Ltd: Cayman National House, 4–8 Hope St, Douglas, IM1 1AQ; tel. (1624) 646900; fax (1624) 662192; e-mail banking@caymannationalwealth.com; internet www.caymannationalwealth.com; f. 1985; subsidiary of Cayman National Corpn, Cayman Islands; cap. 4m., dep. 58m (Sep. 2009); Man. Dir IAN BANCROFT.

Celtic Bank Ltd: POB 114, Celtic House, Victoria St, Douglas, IM99 1JW; tel. (1624) 622856; fax (1624) 620926; f. 1977; issued cap. 7m., res 11m., dep. 500m. (March 2009); Chair. RICHARD G. DANIELSON; Chief Exec. SIMON YOUNG.

Close Bank (Isle of Man) Ltd: POB 203, St George's Court, Upper Church St, Douglas, IM99 1RB; tel. (1624) 643200; fax (1624) 622039; e-mail infoiom@closepb.com; internet www.closepb.com; f. 1976 as Rea Brothers (Isle of Man) Ltd; present name adopted 1999; merchant bank; cap. 5m., dep. 307m. (July 2008); Man. Dir GRAHAM SHEWARD.

Conister Bank Ltd: Conister House, Isle of Man Business Park, Cooil Rd, Braddan, IM2 2QZ; tel. (1624) 694694; fax (1624) 624278; e-mail info@conistertrust.com; internet www.conistertrust.com; f. 1935; specializes in asset finance; cap. 7m., dep. 53m. (Dec. 2005); Chair. PETER HAMMONDS; Man. Dir SIMON HULL; 1 br.

Duncan Lawrie (IOM) Ltd: 14–15 Mount Havelock, Douglas, IM1 2QG; tel. (1624) 620770; fax (1624) 676315; e-mail iom@duncanlawrie.com; internet www.duncanlawrie.com; cap. 6m., dep. 165m. (Dec. 2008); Chair. P. J. FIELD; Man. Dir ALAN M. MOLLOY.

Fairbairn Private Bank (IOM) Ltd: St Mary's Court, 20 Hill St, Douglas, IM1 1EU; tel. (1624) 645000; fax (1624) 627218; e-mail iom@fairbairnpb.com; internet www.fairbairnpb.com; f. 1987 as Robert Fleming (IOM) Ltd; present name adopted 2004; cap. 5m., res 4m., dep. 559m. (Dec. 2008); Chair. H. ASKARI; Man. Dir G. J. HORTON.

Habib European Bank Ltd: 14 Athol St, Douglas, IM1 1JA; tel. (1624) 622554; fax (1624) 627135; e-mail habibbank@manx.net; internet www.habibbank.com; f. 1982; subsidiary of Habib Bank AG (Switzerland); cap. 5m., dep. 98m. (Dec. 2008); Sr Vice-Pres. A. SHAIKH.

Nationwide International Ltd: POB 217, 5–11 St George's St, Douglas, IM99 1RN; tel. (1624) 696000; fax (1624) 696001; internet www.nationwideinternational.com; f. 1990; Chair. CARL GANDY; Man. Dir PHILIP DUNNE.

Standard Bank Isle of Man Ltd: Standard Bank House, 1 Circular Rd, Douglas, IM1 1SB; tel. (1624) 643643; fax (1624) 643800; e-mail sbiom@standardbank.com; internet www.sboff.com; f. 1972 as Standard Chartered Bank (Isle of Man) Ltd; present name adopted

1995; cap. 5m., res −0.8m., dep. 1,154m. (Dec. 2008); Man. Dir J. COYLE.

Zurich Bank International Ltd: POB 422, Lord St, Douglas, IM99 3AF; tel. (1624) 671666; fax (1624) 627526; e-mail relationship.banking@zurich.com; internet www.zurichbankinternational.com; f. 1983 as Dunbar International Ltd; present name adopted 2003; Chair. RICHARD DESMOND; Man. Dir DAVID PEACH.

'Offshore' Banks

Bank of Scotland International Ltd: POB 19, Evergreen House, 43 Circular Rd, Douglas, IM99 1AT; tel. (1624) 613500; fax (1624) 759280; e-mail enquiry@bankofscotlandint.com; internet www.bankofscotland-international.com; f. 1976; part of Lloyds Banking Group (United Kingdom); Chair. PETER JACKSON.

Bradford & Bingley International Ltd: 30 Ridgeway St, Douglas, IM1 1TA; tel. (1624) 695000; fax (1624) 695001; e-mail enquiries@bbi.co.im; internet www.bbi.co.im; f. 1989; subsidiary of Abbey National PLC; cap. and res 266m. (Dec. 2006); Man. Dir JOHN PEARSON.

Isle of Man Bank Ltd: POB 13, 2 Athol St, Douglas IM99 1AN; tel. (1624) 637000; fax (1624) 624686; internet www.iombank.com; f. 1865; cap. 8m., res 139m., dep. 1,644m. (Dec. 2008); bankers to Isle of Man Govt; mem. of the Royal Bank of Scotland Group; Chair. JAMES MORRIS; 11 brs.

RBS Coutts Isle of Man: POB 59, Royal Bank House, 2 Victoria St, Douglas, IM99 INJ; tel. (1624) 632222; fax (1624) 620988; e-mail info@rbscoutts.com; internet www.rbscoutts.com.

The Royal Bank of Scotland International Ltd: POB 151, Royal Bank House, 2 Victoria St, Douglas, IM99 1NJ; tel. (1624) 646464; fax (1624) 646497; e-mail marketingiom@rbsint.com; internet www.rbsinternational.com; Chief Exec. IAN HENDERSON.

Restricted Banks

Merrill Lynch Bank and Trust Co (Cayman) Ltd: Belgravia House, 34–44 Circular Rd, Douglas, IM1 1QW; tel. (1624) 688600; fax (1624) 688601; internet www.ml.com; Man. N. ORDERS.

INSURANCE

There were 173 authorized insurance companies in the Isle of Man at 31 December 2008, including:

Canada Life International Ltd: St Mary's, The Parade, Castletown, IM9 1RJ; tel. (1624) 820200; fax (1624) 820201; e-mail customer.support@canadalifeint.com; internet www.canadalifeint.com; f. 1987; Man. Dir TONY PARRY.

Castletown Insurance Services Ltd: Compton House, Parliament Sq., Castletown, IM9 1LA; tel. (1624) 827710; fax (1624) 827709; e-mail rdrinkwater@castletowninsurance.com; internet www.castletowninsurance.com; f. 1998; Jt Man. Dirs CHRISTINE CROWTHER, RICHARD DRINKWATER.

CMI Insurance Co Ltd: Clerical Medical House, Victoria Rd, Douglas, IM99 1LT; tel. (1624) 638888; fax (1624) 625900; e-mail iom.policyadministration1@clericalmedical.com; internet www.offshore.clericalmedical.com; part of Lloyds Banking Group (United Kingdom).

Friends Provident International Ltd: Royal Court, Castletown, IM9 1RA; tel. (1624) 821212; fax (1624) 824405; e-mail rowservicing@fpiom.com; internet www.fpinternational.com; Man. Dir PAUL QUIRK.

Hansard International Ltd: POB 192, Harbour Court, Lord St, Douglas, IM99 1QL; tel. (1624) 688000; fax (1624) 688008; e-mail enquiries@hansard.com; internet www.hansard.com; Exec. Chair. Dr LEONARD S. POLONSKY.

Isle of Man Assurance Ltd: IOMA House, Hope St, Douglas, IM1 1AP; tel. (1624) 681200; fax (1624) 681391; e-mail info@ioma.co.im; internet www.ioma.co.im; Chair. ROBIN BIGLAND; Man. Dir NIGEL WOOD.

Royal Insurance Service Co (IOM) Ltd: Jubilee Bldgs, 1 Victoria St, Douglas, IM99 1BF; tel. (1624) 645947; fax (1624) 620934; Man. DAVID STACEY.

Royal London 360°: Royal London House, Isle of Man Business Park, Cooil Rd, Douglas, IM2 2SP; tel. (1624) 681681; fax (1624) 677336; e-mail csc@royallondon360.com; internet www.royallondon360.com; f. 2008 by merger of Scottish Life International Insurance Co Ltd and Scottish Provident International Life Assurance Ltd; subsidiary of Royal London Mutual Insurance Society Ltd; Dir MIKE CRELLIN.

Royal Skandia Life Assurance Ltd: POB 159, Skandia House, King Edward Rd, Onchan, IM99 1NU; tel. (1624) 655555; fax (1624) 611715; e-mail support@royalskandia.com; internet www.royalskandia.com.

Tower Insurance Co Ltd: POB 27, Jubilee Bldgs, 1 Victoria St, Douglas, IM99 1BF; tel. (1624) 645900; fax (1624) 663864; e-mail tower.insurance@uk.rsagroup.com; internet www.towerinsurance.co.im; subsidiary of RSA Insurance Group PLC (United Kingdom); Dir DAVID STACEY.

Zurich International Life Ltd: 43–51 Athol St, Douglas, IM99 1EF; tel. (1624) 662266; fax (1624) 662038; e-mail client.services@zurich.com; internet www.zurichintlife.com.

Supervisory Authority

Insurance and Pensions Authority: 4th Floor, HSBC House, Ridgeway St, Douglas, IM1 1ER; tel. (1624) 646000; fax (1624) 646001; e-mail ipa@gov.im; internet www.gov.im/ipa; Chief Exec. DAVID VICK.

Trade and Industry

CHAMBER OF COMMERCE

Isle of Man Chamber of Commerce: 17 Drinkwater St, Douglas, IM1 1PP; tel. (1624) 674941; fax (1624) 663367; e-mail enquiries@iomchamber.org.im; internet www.iomchamber.org.im; f. 1956; 400 mems; Pres. NICK VERARDI; Chair. MIKE SHAW; Chief Exec. MIKE HENNESSY.

UTILITIES
Electricity

Manx Electricity Authority: POB 177, Douglas, IM99 1PS; tel. (1624) 687687; fax (1624) 687612; e-mail mea@gov.im; internet www.gov.im/mea; Chair. QUINTIN GILL; Chief Exec. ASHTON LEWIS.

Gas

Manx Gas Ltd: Murdoch House, South Quay, Douglas, IM1 5PA; tel. (1624) 644444; fax (1624) 626528; e-mail info@manxgas.com; internet www.manxgas.com; f. 1999 by merger of Douglas Gas and Calor Manx Gas; Man. Dir ALAN BATES.

Water

Isle of Man Water Authority: Drill Hall, Tromode Rd, Douglas, IM2 5PA; tel. (1624) 695949; fax (1624) 695956; e-mail water@gov.im; internet www.gov.im/water; Chair. TIM CROOKALL; Chief Exec. JOHN SMITH.

TRADE UNIONS

In 1991 the Trade Union Act was approved by Tynwald, providing for the registration of trade unions. Although trade unions had been active previously on the Isle of Man, they had not received legal recognition.

Manx Fish Producers' Organization Ltd: Heritage Centre, The Quay, Peel, IM5 1TA; tel. (1624) 842144; fax (1624) 844395; e-mail manx.fa@lineone.net; Chair. MICHAEL MOORE.

Manx National Farmers' Union: Agriculture House, Ballafletcher Farm Rd, Tromode, IM4 4QE; tel. (1624) 662204; e-mail gensec@manx-nfu.org; internet www.manx-nfu.org; Pres. HOWARD QUAYLE; Gen. Sec. BELINDA LEACH.

Unite: 25 Fort St, Douglas, IM2 2LJ; tel. (1624) 621156; fax (1624) 673115.

Transport

RAILWAYS

Isle of Man Transport: Transport Headquarters, Banks Circus, Douglas, IM1 5PT; tel. (1624) 662525; fax (1624) 663637; e-mail info@busandrail.dtl.gov.im; internet www.iombusandrail.info; 29 km (18 miles) of electric track; also 25 km (16 miles) of steam railway track, and Snaefell Mountain Railway (7 km of electric track); 85 buses; Head of Rail Services JOHN KENNAUGH; Head of Bus Services DAVE KINRADE.

ROADS

There are over 805 km (500 miles) of roads on the Isle of Man.

Dept of Transport: Sea Terminal, Douglas, IM1 2RF; tel. (1624) 686600; fax (1624) 686617; e-mail enquiries@dot.gov.im; internet www.gov.im/transport; Chief Exec. IAN THOMPSON.

SHIPPING

Döhle (IOM) Ltd: Fort Anne, Douglas, IM1 5PD; tel. (1624) 649649; e-mail info@doehle-iom.com; internet www.doehle-iom.com; fmrly Midocean Maritime Ltd; present name adopted 2001; part of Peter Döhle Group (Germany); ship management; Chair. JÖRG VANSELOW; COO CLIFF DAVIES.

Isle of Man Steam Packet Co Ltd: Imperial Bldgs, Douglas, IM1 2BY; tel. (1624) 645645; fax (1624) 645609; internet www.steam-packet.com; f. 1830; daily services operate all the year round between Douglas and Heysham and Liverpool; during the summer there are frequent services between the island and Dublin and Belfast; Chair. ROBERT QUAYLE; Chief Exec. MARK WOODWARD.

Mezeron Ltd: East Quay, Ramsey, IM8 1BG; tel. (1624) 812302; fax (1624) 815613; e-mail info@mezeron.com; internet www.mezeron.com; f. 1983; cargo services; acquired by Döhle (IOM) Ltd in 2008; Operations Dir NORMAN LEECE.

Ramsey Steamship Co Ltd: 8 Auckland Terrace, Parliament St, Ramsey, IM8 1AF; tel. (1624) 816202; fax (1624) 816206; e-mail tony@ramsey-steamship.com; internet www.ramsey-steamship.com; f. 1913; cargo services; Man. Dir A. G. KENNISH.

Tufton Oceanic Investments Ltd: 2nd Floor, St George's Court, Upper Church St, Douglas, IM1 1EE; tel. (1624) 663616; fax (1624) 663918; e-mail tufton@tuftonoceanic.com; internet www.tuftonoceanic.com; Chair. TAKIS KLERIDES; Man. Dir CATO BRAHDE.

CIVIL AVIATION

Island Aviation and Travel Ltd: Ronaldsway Airport, Ballasalla, IM9 2AS; tel. (1624) 824300; fax (1624) 824946; e-mail enquiries@iaat.co.uk; internet www.iaat.co.uk; provides executive charters to world-wide destinations, runs air-ambulance services, aircraft management, handling; Man. Dir JOHN CRITCHLEY.

Manx2 Ltd: Ronaldsway Airport, Ballasalla, IM9 2AS; tel. (1624) 822111; e-mail customer.services@manx2.com; internet www.manx2.com; scheduled passenger flights to Belfast City and Belfast International, Blackpool, East Midlands, Gloucestershire, Jersey and Leeds/Bradford; Chair. NOEL HAYES; Gen. Man. DYLAN EVANS.

Tourism

In 2009 a total of 205,256 tourists stayed at least one night on the Isle of Man.

Dept of Tourism and Leisure, Tourism Division: St Andrew's House, Douglas, IM1 2PX; tel. (1624) 686801; fax (1624) 686800; e-mail tourism@gov.im; internet www.visitisleofman.com; responsibilities of tourist board, also operates modern and vintage transport systems, a Victorian theatre and an indoor and outdoor sport and leisure complex; f. 1896; Dir of Tourism GEOFF LE PAGE.

UNITED KINGDOM OVERSEAS TERRITORIES

From February 1998 the British Dependent Territories were referred to as the United Kingdom Overseas Territories, following the announcement of the interim findings of a British government review of the United Kingdom's relations with the Overseas Territories. In March 1999 draft legislation confirming this change was published by the British Government: under the proposed legislation, the citizens of Overseas Territories would be granted the rights, already enjoyed by the citizens of Gibraltar and the Falkland Islands, to British citizenship and of residence in the United Kingdom. These entitlements were not reciprocal, and British citizens would not enjoy the same rights with regard to the Overseas Territories. The British Overseas Territories Act entered effect in May 2002. The British Government meanwhile announced its determination to ensure that legislation in the Overseas Territories adhered to British and European Union standards, particularly in the areas of financial regulation and human rights.

ANGUILLA

Introductory Survey

LOCATION, CLIMATE, LANGUAGE, RELIGION, FLAG, CAPITAL

Anguilla, a coralline island, is the most northerly of the Leeward Islands, lying 113 km (70 miles) to the north-west of Saint Christopher (St Kitts) and 8 km (5 miles) to the north of St Maarten/St Martin. Also included in the territory are the island of Sombrero, 48 km (30 miles) north of Anguilla, and several other uninhabited small islands. The climate is sub-tropical, the heat and humidity being tempered by the trade winds. Temperatures average 27°C (80°F) and mean annual rainfall is 914 mm (36 ins), the wettest months being September to December. English is the official language. Many Christian churches are represented, the principal denominations being the Anglican and Methodist Churches. The flag (proportions 3 by 5 on land, 1 by 2 at sea) has a dark blue field with the Union flag in the upper hoist corner and, in the centre of the fly, a white shield bearing three orange circling dolphins above a light blue base. The capital is The Valley.

CONTEMPORARY POLITICAL HISTORY

Historical Context

Anguilla, previously inhabited by Arawaks and Caribs, was a British colony from 1650 until 1967. From 1825 the island became increasingly associated with Saint Christopher (St Kitts) for administrative purposes (see chapter on Saint Christopher and Nevis). The inhabitants of Anguilla petitioned for separate status in 1875 and 1958. In February 1967, however, St Christopher-Nevis-Anguilla assumed the status of a State in Association with the United Kingdom, as did four other former British colonies in the Eastern Caribbean. These Associated States became independent internally, while the British Government retained responsibility for external affairs and defence.

Domestic Political Affairs

In May 1967 the Anguillans, under the leadership of Ronald Webster, a local businessman and head of the only political party, the People's Progressive Party (PPP), repudiated government from Saint Christopher. After attempts to repair the breach between Saint Christopher and Anguilla had failed, British security forces were deployed in Anguilla in March 1969 to install a British Commissioner. Members of London's Metropolitan Police Force remained on the island until the Anguilla Police Force was established in 1972. In July 1971 the British Parliament approved the Anguilla Act, one clause of which stipulated that, should Saint Christopher-Nevis-Anguilla decide to end its associated status, Anguilla could be separated from the other islands. In August the British Government's Anguilla Administration Order 1971 determined that the British Commissioner would continue to be responsible for the direct administration of the island, with the co-operation of a local elected council. The terms of this Order were superseded by the introduction of a new Constitution in February 1976. Anguilla formally separated from Saint Christopher-Nevis-Anguilla on 19 December 1980, assuming the status of British Dependent Territory. In accordance with the terms of the British Government's Anguilla Constitution Order of 1982, a new Constitution came into operation in Anguilla on 1 April 1982.

Legislative elections were held in March 1976, and Webster was appointed Chief Minister. In February 1977, following his defeat on a motion of confidence, he was replaced by Emile Gumbs as Chief Minister and as leader of the PPP (renamed the Anguilla National Alliance—ANA—in 1980). Webster was returned to power, to lead the recently formed Anguilla United Party (AUP), at a general election in May 1980. Webster's administration collapsed in May 1981 and Webster subsequently formed a new political party, the Anguilla People's Party (APP), which won a general election in June. An early general election in March 1984, however, resulted in a conclusive defeat for the APP. Gumbs became Chief Minister, and pursued a policy of revitalizing the island's economy, mainly through tourism and attracting foreign investment. Webster resigned as leader of the APP, which was renamed the Anguilla Democratic Party (ADP).

The majority of the population expressed no desire for independence, but the new Government appealed for wider powers for the Executive Council, and for more aid and investment from the United Kingdom in the island's economy and infrastructure. In October 1985 the Governor appointed a committee to review the Constitution, in response to an earlier unanimous request from the House of Assembly for modifications, particularly concerning the status of women and of persons born overseas of Anguillan parents. The amendments, which provided for the appointment of a Deputy Governor and designated international financial affairs (the 'offshore' banking sector) as the Governor's responsibility, came into effect in May 1990.

Gumbs remained Chief Minister following a general election in February 1989. In May 1991 the British Government abolished capital punishment for the crime of murder in Anguilla (as well as in several other British Dependent Territories).

A general election in March 1994 failed to produce a clear majority for any one party, and a coalition was subsequently formed by the ADP and the AUP. The AUP leader, Hubert Hughes, was subsequently appointed Chief Minister, replacing Sir Emile Gumbs (as he had become). On assuming the post, Hughes stated that he might seek Anguilla's independence from the United Kingdom.

In October 1995 the island suffered severe damage from Hurricane Luis. Destruction of buildings and infrastructure, as well as damage to the agricultural sector, was estimated to be worth some EC $72m. Hughes was highly critical of the British Government's response to the hurricane, which he alleged was inadequate.

The announcement by the British Government in January 1997 that it was considering the extension of its powers in the Dependent Territories of the Caribbean attracted further criticism from Hughes. The proposed reintroduction of reserve powers, whereby the Governor (with the consent of the British Government) can amend, veto or introduce legislation without the agreement of the local legislature, provoked accusations from Hughes that the United Kingdom hoped to create a situation in which territories would be forced to seek independence. The British Government, however, maintained that the initiative had been prompted largely by a desire to secure Anguilla's financial services sector from exploitation by criminal organizations, particularly drugs-traffickers (which had remained a problem, owing to the territory's bank secrecy laws).

In May 1998 Hughes announced that public consultations would be undertaken on a proposal to reform Anguilla's constitutional status in the hope that a reformed Constitution could be in place before the general election, scheduled for March 1999. Hughes criticized the current Constitution for vesting executive authority in the Governor rather than in locally elected ministers. Hughes ruled out any prospect of creating a Senate on the grounds of the cost involved. In September 1998, however, the British Government announced that its Overseas Dependencies were to be renamed United Kingdom Overseas Territories. In March 1999 the British Government issued a policy document confirming the change of name, and guaranteeing citizens of Overseas Dependencies the right to British citizenship. The proposals also included the requirement that the Constitutions of Overseas Territories should be revised in order to conform to British and international standards. The process of revision of the Anguillan Constitution began in September 1999.

Following the general election of 4 March 1999 the composition of the legislature remained unaltered. The AUP-ADP coalition therefore kept control of the House of Assembly, and the four members of the Executive Council retained their portfolios.

In May 1999 the two ADP ministers threatened to withdraw from the coalition Government, accusing Hughes of excluding them from the decision-making process, and in June the ADP leader, Victor Banks, resigned his post as Minister of Finance and Economic Development, and withdrew from the ruling coalition. The other ADP minister, Edison Baird, refused, however, to resign his post, and was subsequently expelled from the party. Although Banks' resignation deprived the AUP-ADP coalition of its majority in the House of Assembly, Hughes announced that he did not intend to resign his position. Banks and the three members of the opposition ANA therefore withdrew from the House, demanding that fresh elections be held. Lacking the necessary quorum in the legislature, the Government was unable to implement policy or to introduce a budget for 1999/2000.

In January 2000 legal proceedings begun by Hughes, in an attempt to compel the Speaker to convene the House of Assembly, were rejected by the High Court. Hughes therefore announced that he would hold legislative elections in March. At the elections, held on 3 March, the ANA won three seats, the AUP two, and the ADP one, while Edison Baird was elected as an independent. The ANA and the ADP, which had formed an electoral alliance, known as the Anguilla United Front, prior to the elections, therefore gained control of the House of Assembly. The leader of the ANA, Osbourne Fleming, was subsequently appointed the Chief Minister of an Executive Council that included two other ANA ministers.

Following Anguilla's inclusion on an Organisation for Economic Co-operation and Development (OECD, see p. 376) 'black list' of tax havens in 2000, the Government introduced a number of articles of legislation to combat money-laundering on the island, including the establishment of a Money Laundering Reporting Authority. OECD removed Anguilla from the list in 2002, declaring that the Government had made sufficient commitments to improve transparency and effective exchange of information on tax matters by the end of 2005. In late 2002, however, the burgeoning financial sector faced further disruption when the United Kingdom, under pressure from the European Union (EU, see p. 270), as part of its effort to investigate tax evasion, demanded that Anguilla disclose the identities and account details of Europeans holding private savings accounts on the island. Anguilla, along with some other British Overseas Territories facing similar demands, claimed it was being treated unfairly compared with more powerful European countries, such as Switzerland and Luxembourg. In February 2004 a new financial regulatory body, the Anguilla Financial Services Commission, commenced operations. The Commission replaced the Financial Services Department of the Ministry of Finance and represented a further commitment to transparency within the sector. Nevertheless, in April 2009 Anguilla was included on OECD's so-called 'grey list' of territories that had committed to improving transparency in the financial sector but had not yet substantially implemented such change. In March 2010 OECD announced that Anguilla had 'substantially implemented' international financial standards by signing tax-sharing agreements with 13 other countries in the previous 12 months.

In May 2002 the British Overseas Territories Act, having received royal assent in the United Kingdom in February, came into force and granted British citizenship to the people of its Overseas Territories, including Anguilla. Under the new law Anguillans would be able to hold British passports and work in the United Kingdom and anywhere else in the EU.

In May 2004 Edison Baird replaced Hubert Hughes as Leader of the Opposition after Albert Hughes resigned from the AUP and transferred his support to Baird. Baird later formed a new political party, the Anguilla National Strategic Alliance (ANSA), in advance of the 2005 general election.

At the general election, which was held on 21 February 2005, the Anguilla United Front (the AUF, comprising the ANA and the ADP) secured four seats; the remaining three seats were shared by the Anguilla United Movement (AUM—as the AUP had been renamed, with one seat) and the ANSA (two seats). Analysts were surprised by the scale of the AUF's victory; a closer contest had been expected, but the alliance campaigned strongly on the success of its infrastructural improvements, particularly the expansion of Anguilla's airport, during its previous administration.

Constitutional reform

In December 2005 the Government announced its intention to establish a new Constitutional and Electoral Reform Commission, to build on the work done by the previous electoral commission in 2001–04 in ascertaining the views of the people of Anguilla. The Commission began work in February 2006; key issues to be addressed were the fundamental rights and freedoms outlined in the Constitution, the powers of the Governor and the size of the House of Assembly. The Commission's recommendations were submitted to the Governor in August. It was announced in March 2007 that the Government was to receive a delegation from the British Foreign and Commonwealth Office (FCO) in July to facilitate discussions towards constitutional reform. This necessitated a preliminary review of the Commission's recommendations, together with public consultations, prior to the FCO representatives' arrival. The first in an extensive series of such reviews was convened in early March and attended by parliamentary representatives and the Chairman of the Constitutional and Electoral Reform Commission. While several sections of the extant Constitution were regarded by the Commission as still relevant and adequate, areas identified as problematic and in most urgent need of amendment included the administration of justice—particularly to reflect the abolition of the death penalty—transparency in judicial proceedings, enforcement of constitutional rights, and the appointment of the island Governor and deputies.

In addition, concern had been expressed that the existing number of ministers in the Executive Council (or Cabinet, in accordance with the Commission's proposals) was insufficient for the dispatch of governmental responsibilities and should be increased, but that the ratio of ministers to non-ministerial representatives in the House of Assembly should not exceed 50%; it was proposed that members of the Council be increased from three to five ministers, in addition to the Chief Minister (or Premier under the recommendations). The Cabinet would comprise these six members, each awarded a vote, together with the Deputy Governor and the Attorney-General, who would remain without voting authority. The Premier would replace the Governor as chairman of the Cabinet, although the latter would retain the right to be informed by, consult and advise the Cabinet. Further, it was suggested that the size of the Assembly be increased from seven elected members to 13. (Should it be concluded that seven ministers be appointed in addition to the Chief Minister, the Assembly should grow to 15 members in order to accommodate the recommended majority of non-ministerial members.) An expanded Assembly, it was suggested, would also obviate the need for a Parliamentary Secretary. It was also proposed that, in the event of a motion of no confidence being brought in the Assembly, there would be recourse to the pre-1982 Constitution, whereby the Governor would exercise discretion as to whether to call a general election. Such a motion might be upheld by a simple majority vote, as opposed to the existing two-thirds' majority requirement. An existing provision, reportedly not yet exercised, affording the Governor alternative powers to force legislation through the House of Assembly was considered a threat to democracy and the Commission urged for its repeal; similarly, the rescision of powers previously vested in the Secretary of State to disallow legislation passed by the Governor was advised, on the basis that such a provision was no longer required.

The Commission also proposed extensive electoral reform: *inter alia*, the institution of an independent Boundaries Commission was put forward, as was thorough revision of the Election Act. The abolition of the Judicial Services Commission and establishment of a Judicial and Legal Services Commission as its successor, endowed with powers to influence the Governor's judicial appointments, was also suggested and constituted a measure more consistent with other Caribbean states under the jurisdiction of the Eastern Caribbean Supreme Court. The embedding of the Financial Services Commission and its regulatory authority within the constitution was also promulgated in order to enhance supervision of the financial services industry in Anguilla.

Interpreted broadly, the Commission's recommendations sought to advance Anguilla's ambitions towards greater self-determination and the democratic, inclusive administration of its own affairs, gradually reducing the influence of the Government of the United Kingdom—upon whose unilateral authority so many of its existing constitutional statutes were premised. The institution of independent public service and advisory bodies was intended to equip a future government with the appropriate consultative resources to generate more comprehensive and effective legislative proposals for the advancement of Anguilla and the protection of its people.

The proposed visit by an FCO delegation to discuss constitutional reform was postponed in July 2007 by the Anguillan Government in order that further public consultations might be conducted. The Government confirmed, however, that it would be seeking 'full internal self-government' for Anguilla, and at the end of April 2008 it announced the commencement of work on a draft constitution. The proposed document was scheduled for completion in mid-2009, after which consultations between representatives of the Governments of Anguilla and the United Kingdom were to begin, although the change of government in early 2010 meant discussions were delayed.

The 2010 election

A general election was held on 15 February 2010. The AUM, led by former Chief Minister Hubert Hughes, won four of the seven elected seats in the House of Assembly. The AUF's parliamentary represen-

UNITED KINGDOM OVERSEAS TERRITORIES

tation was reduced to two seats while the remaining seat was secured by the APP. The AUF leader, Victor Banks, lost his seat in the Valley South constituency. Hughes' new administration included Edison Baird as Deputy Chief Minister and Minister of Social Development and Walcott Richardson in the key post of Minister of Home Affairs, including Labour, Natural Resources, Lands, Physical Planning and Immigration. Hughes took on the finance portfolio. Lowering the unemployment rate was one of the stated priorities of the new Council. In the following month the Chief Minister and the Governor announced the formation of a government task force further to improve financial transparency in Anguilla. The territory had recently been removed from OECD's 'grey list' of jurisdictions that failed to meet international tax standards (see above). One of the AUM's electoral pledges had been to strengthen the economically important financial sector. The financial task force was inaugurated in September.

Recent developments: relations with the United Kingdom

A political dispute arose in January 2011, when Governor Alistair Harrison rejected the 2011 budget on the grounds that it failed to address adequately the territory's precarious fiscal position. Harrison had urged the Government to increase taxes and to reduce drastically the number of public sector workers in order to return government finances to a sustainable level by 2013. Hughes claimed that these austerity measures would inflict unprecedented suffering upon the local population and demanded independence from the United Kingdom. Financial consultants, hired by the British Government, were sent to Anguilla in February 2011 to assist with the modification of the budget, which was finally approved in early April. Hughes declared that the delayed approval had led to the loss of a number of important revenue streams, prompting him to reiterate his desire for independence for Anguilla. Later in April relations between Anguilla and the United Kingdom deteriorated further when the Government accused the Governor of exceeding his powers after Harrison had instructed the Minister of Home Affairs, Walcott Richardson, to stop issuing visa vaivers. The Governor claimed that too many waivers had been granted since Richardson took office and that the matter was a security concern.

Foreign Affairs

In July 2005 the Governments of Anguilla and the British Virgin Islands announced the formal establishment of the maritime boundary between the two territories. The boundary had been agreed in 2002 following discussions facilitated by the British Government. Co-operation between British Virgin Islands customs officials and their Anguillan counterparts enabled the recovery of a substantial quantity of drugs from a container vessel impounded in Anguilla in July 2006; the haul was thought to be the largest ever seized on the island and an indication of the success of joint law enforcement initiatives in the region.

CONSTITUTION AND GOVERNMENT

The Constitution vests executive power in a Governor, appointed by the British monarch. The Governor is responsible for external affairs, international financial affairs, defence and internal security. In most other matters the Governor acts on the advice of the Executive Council, led by the Chief Minister. Legislative power is held by the House of Assembly, comprising 11 members: two ex officio, two nominated by the Governor, and seven elected for five years by universal adult suffrage. The Executive Council is responsible to the House. A review of the Constitution was ongoing in 2011.

REGIONAL AND INTERNATIONAL CO-OPERATION

In 1987 Anguilla became the eighth member of the Eastern Caribbean Central Bank (see p. 451) and in 2001 joined the regional stock exchange, the Eastern Caribbean Securities Exchange (based in Saint Christopher and Nevis), established in the same year. The territory is also a member of the Organisation of Eastern Caribbean States (OECS, see p. 462) and an associate member of the Economic Community for Latin America and the Caribbean (see p. 41). In December 2009 Anguilla was a signatory to the Treaty of the OECS, establishing an Economic Union among member states. The Economic Union, which involved the removal of barriers to trade and the movement of labour as a step towards a single financial and economic market, came into effect on 21 January 2011. Anguilla required British consent to join the grouping, which was pending in early 2011. In July 2007 the country joined the single market component of CARICOM's Single Market and Economy, full implementation of which was expected by 2015. The territory is a member of the Commonwealth (see p. 230). As a dependency of the United Kingdom, Anguilla has the status of Overseas Territory in association with the EU (see p. 270). In 1999 Anguilla was granted associate membership of the Caribbean Community and Common Market (CARICOM, see p. 219).

Anguilla

ECONOMIC AFFAIRS

In 2008 the gross national income (GNI) of Anguilla, measured at current prices, was EC $798.2m., equivalent to EC $51,743 per head. During 2001–09, it was estimated, the population increased at an average annual rate of 3.9%, while gross domestic product (GDP) per head increased, in real terms, by an average of 6.1% per year during 2001–08. Overall GDP increased, in real terms, at an average annual rate of 10.5% in 2001–08; real GDP increased by 1.3% in 2008.

Agriculture (including crops, livestock and fishing) contributed 1.4% of GDP in 2008 and agriculture, fishing and mining engaged 3.2% of the employed labour force in 2001. Smallholders grow vegetables and fruit for domestic consumption; the principal crops are pigeon peas, sweet potatoes and maize. Livestock-rearing traditionally supplies significant export earnings, but the principal productive sector is the fishing industry (which is also a major employer). Real agricultural GDP increased by an annual average of 6.4% during 2001–08; growth was 4.3% in 2008.

Industry (including mining, manufacturing, construction and power), which accounted for 33.9% of GDP in 2008 and (not including the small mining sector) engaged 18.8% of the employed labour force in 2001, is traditionally based on salt production and shipbuilding, although the construction sector grew strongly in recent years. Real industrial GDP increased by an annual average of 20.3% in 2001–08; the sector expanded by 13.5% in 2008.

The mining and quarrying sector, contributed 2.0% of GDP in 2008 and engaged only 0.2% of the working population in 1992. Anguilla's principal mineral product is salt. Mining GDP increased by an annual average of 26.8% during 2001–08; growth was 7.0% in 2008.

The manufacturing sector, accounting for 2.4% of employment in 2003 and for only 1.9% of GDP in 2008, consists almost entirely of boat-building and fisheries-processing. Real manufacturing GDP increased by an annual average of 15.8% in 2001–08. Sectoral GDP increased by 29.3% in 2007, but declined by 2.3% in 2008.

The construction industry, which engaged 14.9% of the employed labour force in 2001, accounted for 26.5% of GDP in 2008. GDP in the construction sector increased at an annual average of 22.5% during 2001–08. The sector expanded by 17.4% in 2008. Imported hydrocarbon fuels meet most energy needs.

The services sector accounted for 64.7% of GDP in 2008 and engaged 77.9% of the employed labour force in 2001. Tourism is increasingly the dominant industry of the economy, and is a catalyst for growth in other areas. The hotel and restaurant sector is the largest contributor to GDP, accounting for 16.5% of GDP in 2008. The hotel and restaurant sector decreased by 12.1% in 2008. Tourism expenditure totalled a preliminary EC $229.1m. in 2009. The USA provided 29.7% of visitors (including excursionists) in that year. The 'offshore' financial institutions are also important contributors to the GDP of the services industry, with the banking and insurance sector contributing 12.1% of GDP in 2008 and employing some 7.7% of the economically active population in 2001. The real GDP of the services sector increased at an annual average of 7.5% in 2001–08; growth was 2.5% in 2008.

According to IMF estimates, in 2010 Anguilla recorded a merchandise trade deficit of EC $332.9m., and a deficit on the current account of the balance of payments of EC $204.6m. The trade deficit was partly offset by receipts from the 'invisibles' sector: tourism, financial services, remittances from Anguillans abroad and official assistance. The principal sources of imports are the USA (51.2% in 2008), Trinidad and Tobago and Puerto Rico. The principal markets for exports are Guyana (38.4% in 2008) and the USA (14.8%). The main commodity exports are lobsters, fish, livestock and salt. Imports, upon which Anguilla is highly dependent, consist of machinery and transport equipment, manufactures, foodstuffs and construction materials.

In 2009, according to the Eastern Caribbean Central Bank (see p. 451), a budgetary deficit of EC $64.7m. was estimated. Anguilla's total public sector debt was an estimated EC $171m. at the end of 2008. Consumer prices increased by an annual average of 4.1% in 2000–09; consumer prices fell by 0.7% in 2009. Some 7.8% of the labour force were unemployed in July 2002.

Following several years of robust growth, Anguilla's economy contracted by a preliminary 25.5% in 2009. The island's two most important sectors, tourism and construction, both declined as a direct consequence of the global economic downturn. The economies of Anguilla's two most significant sources of visitors, the USA and the United Kingdom, continued to be in recession in that year, leading to a fall in tourist numbers and revenues. Fuelled by the tourism sector, construction has expanded considerably in recent years; however, growth decelerated significantly in 2008, owing to financing difficulties on several major private sector projects, and the sector contracted by 55.0% in 2009. Official forecasts indicated that GDP contracted again in 2010. Although a modest recovery in the tourism sector was evident in that year, a lack of investment in new developments meant that the construction industry remained depressed. Meanwhile, in an attempt to stabilize the fiscal position, a temporary 6% income tax was introduced in April 2011.

Anguilla

PUBLIC HOLIDAYS

2012: 1 January (New Year's Day), 2 March (Birthday of James Ronald Webster), 6 April (Good Friday), 9 April (Easter Monday), 1 May (Labour Day), 28 May (Whit Monday), 30 May (Anguilla Day), 11 June (Queen's Official Birthday—provisional), 6 August (August Monday), 7 August (Constitution Day), 9 August (August Thursday), 19 December (National Heroes' and Heroines' Day), 25–26 December (Christmas).

Statistical Survey

Source (unless otherwise stated): Government of Anguilla, The Secretariat, The Valley; tel. 497-2451; fax 497-3389; e-mail stats@gov.ai; internet gov.ai/statistics.

AREA AND POPULATION

Area (sq km): 96 (Anguilla 91, Sombrero 5).

Population: 11,430 (males 5,628, females 5,802) at census of 9 May 2001. *Mid-2009* (official estimate): 15,962.

Density (at mid-2009): 166.3 per sq km.

Population by Age and Sex (at 2001 census): *0–14:* 3,202 (males 1,590, females 1,612); *15–64:* 7,356 (males 3,632, females 3,724); *65 and over:* 872 (males 406, females 466); *Total* 11,430 (males 5,628, females 5,802).

Principal Towns (population at 2001 census): South Hill 1,495; North Side 1,195; The Valley (capital) 1,169; Stoney Ground 1,133. *Mid-2009* (UN estimate, incl. suburbs): The Valley 1,635 (Source: UN, *World Urbanization Prospects: The 2009 Revision*).

Births, Marriages and Deaths (2009): Registered live births 181 (birth rate 11.3 per 1,000); Registered marriages 58 (marriage rate 3.6 per 1,000); Registered deaths 46 (death rate 2.9 per 1,000). *2010:* Registered live births 186; Registered marriages 62; Registered deaths 66.

Life Expectancy (years at birth): 80.8 (males 78.2; females 83.4) in 2010 (Source: Pan American Health Organization).

Economically Active Population (persons aged 15 years and over, census of 9 May 2001): Agriculture, fishing and mining 183; Manufacturing 135; Electricity, gas and water 81; Construction 830; Trade 556; Restaurants and hotels 1,587; Transport, storage and communications 379; Finance, insurance, real estate and business services 433; Public administration, social security 662; Education, health and social work 383; Other community, social and personal services 164; Private households with employed persons 164; Activities not stated 871; *Total employed* 5,644 (males 3,014, females 2,630); Unemployed 406 (males 208, females 198); *Total labour force* 6,050 (males 3,222, females 2,828). *July 2002:* Total employed 5,496 (males 3,009, females 2,487); Unemployed 465 (males 204, females 261); Total labour force 5,961 (Source: ILO).

HEALTH AND WELFARE

Total Fertility Rate (children per woman, 2010): 1.8.

Under-5 Mortality Rate (per 1,000 live births, 1997): 34.0.

Physicians (per 1,000 head, 2003): 1.2.

Hospital Beds (per 1,000 head, 2009): 2.2.

Health Expenditure (% of GDP, 2007): 3.0.

Access to Water (% of persons, 2004): 60.

Access to Sanitation (% of persons, 2004): 99.

Sources: Caribbean Development Bank, *Social and Economic Indicators 2004* and Pan American Health Organization.

For definitions, see explanatory note on p. vi.

AGRICULTURE, ETC.

Fishing (metric tons, live weight, 2008): Marine fishes 460; Caribbean spiny lobster 232; Stromboid conchs 9; Total catch 701. Source: FAO.

INDUSTRY

Electric Energy ('000 kWh): 88,999 in 2007; 89,728 in 2008; 80,755 in 2009. Source: Eastern Caribbean Central Bank.

FINANCE

Currency and Exchange Rates: 100 cents = 1 Eastern Caribbean dollar (EC $). *Sterling, US Dollar and Euro Equivalents* (31 December 2010): £1 sterling = EC $4.227; US $1 = EC $2.700; €1 = EC $3.608; EC $100 = £23.66 = US $37.04 = €227.72. *Exchange Rate:* Fixed at US $1 = EC $2.70 since July 1976.

Budget (EC $ million, 2009): *Revenue:* Tax revenue 111.6 (Taxes on domestic goods and services 44.7, Taxes on international trade and transactions 65.4, Taxes on property 1.5); Non-tax revenue 36.7; Total 148.3. *Expenditure:* Current expenditure 202.4 (Personal emoluments 90.7, Other goods and services 48.4, Transfers and subsidies 55.0, Interest payments 8.3); Capital expenditure 10.6; Total 213.0. Source: Eastern Caribbean Central Bank, *Annual Economic and Financial Review 2009*.

Cost of Living (Consumer Price Index; base: 2005 = 100): All items 113.9 in 2007: 121.7 in 2008; 120.8 in 2009. Source: IMF, *International Financial Statistics*.

Gross Domestic Product (EC $ million at constant 1990 prices): 397.90 in 2006; 470.82 in 2007; 477.07 in 2008. Source: Eastern Caribbean Central Bank.

Expenditure on the Gross Domestic Product (EC $ million at current prices, 2008): Government final consumption expenditure 114.75; Private final consumption expenditure 690.48; Gross fixed capital formation 491.98; *Total domestic expenditure* 1,297.21; Exports of goods and services 366.85; *Less* Imports of goods and services 879.84; *GDP in purchasers' values* 784.22. Source: Eastern Caribbean Central Bank.

Gross Domestic Product by Economic Activity (EC $ million at current prices, 2008): Agriculture (including crops, livestock and fishing) 9.35; Mining and quarrying 13.42; Manufacturing 12.60; Electricity and water 23.84; Construction 179.70; Wholesale and retail trade 31.58; Hotels and restaurants 111.90; Transport and Communications 89.18; Banks and insurance 82.01; Real estate and housing 10.28; Government services 104.44; Other services 9.35; *Sub-total* 677.65; *Less* Financial intermediation services indirectly measured 48.08; *Gross value added in basic prices* 629.57; Taxes, *less* subsidies, on products 154.65; *GDP in purchasers' values* 784.22. Source: Eastern Caribbean Central Bank.

Balance of Payments (EC $ million, 2010): Goods (net) –332.88; Services (net) 143.73; *Balance on goods and services* –189.15; Income (net) –23.79; *Balance on goods, services and income* –212.94; Current transfers (net) 8.39; *Current balance* –204.55; Capital account (net) 43.73; Direct investment (net) 66.59; Portfolio investment (net) 5.85; Other investments (net) 128.13; Net errors and omissions 95.02; *Overall balance* 134.77. Source: Eastern Caribbean Central Bank.

EXTERNAL TRADE

Principal Commodities (EC $ million, 2008): *Imports:* Food and live animals 56.4; Beverages and tobacco 39.7; Mineral fuels, lubricants, etc. 104.7; Chemicals and related products 53.2; Basic manufactures 215.1; Machinery and transport equipment 156.5; Miscellaneous manufactured articles 87.6; Total (incl. others) 733.7. *Exports* (incl. re-exports): Food and live animals 0.2; Beverages and tobacco 12.7; Basic manufactures 8.0; Machinery and transport equipment 8.1; Miscellaneous manufactured articles 0.2; Total (incl. others) 31.0.

Principal Trading Partners (EC $ million, 2008): *Imports:* Barbados 4.7; Guyana 14.6; Puerto Rico 56.2; Trinidad and Tobago 106.2; United Kingdom 5.5; USA 375.9; US Virgin Islands 3.9; Total (incl. others) 733.7. *Exports* (incl. re-exports): British Virgin Islands 0.1; Guyana 11.9; United Kingdom 0.6; USA 4.6; Total (incl. others) 31.0.

TRANSPORT

Road Traffic (motor vehicles in use at 31 December 2006): Passenger cars 4,155; Vans and lorries 92; Motorcycles and mopeds 22; Total 4,269 (Source: IRF, *World Road Statistics*).

Shipping: *Merchant Fleet* (registered at 31 December 2009): 4; Total displacement 805 grt. Source: IHS Fairplay, *World Fleet Statistics*.

TOURISM

Visitor Arrivals: 164,067 (stop-overs 77,652, excursionists 86,415) in 2007; 127,862 (stop-overs 68,284, excursionists 59,578) in 2008; 109,159 (stop-overs 55,848, excursionists 53,311) in 2009.

Visitor Arrivals by Place of Residence (2009): Canada 1,820; Caribbean 12,819; United Kingdom 2,921; USA 32,393; Total (incl. others) 109,159.

Tourism Receipts (EC $ million): 309.2 in 2007; 275.6 in 2008; 229.1 in 2009. Source: Eastern Caribbean Central Bank, *Annual Economic and Financial Review 2009*.

COMMUNICATIONS MEDIA

Radio Receivers (1997): 3,000 in use.

Television Receivers (1999): 1,000 in use.

UNITED KINGDOM OVERSEAS TERRITORIES

Telephones (2009): 6,300 main lines in use.
Mobile Cellular Telephones (2009): 27,000 subscribers.
Internet Users (2009): 3,700.
Broadband Subscribers (2009): 3,700.
Sources: partly UN, *Statistical Yearbook*; International Telecommunication Union.

EDUCATION

Pre-primary (2007/08, unless otherwise indicated): 11 schools (2003); 43 teachers; 450 pupils (males 221, females 229).
Primary (2007/08, unless otherwise indicated): 8 schools (2003); 114 teachers; 1,610 pupils (males 817, females 793).
Secondary (2007/08, unless otherwise indicated): 1 school (2002/03); 96 teachers (2006/07); 1,008 pupils (males 505, females 503).
Tertiary (2007/08): 14 teachers; 54 students (9 males, 45 females).
Pupil-teacher Ratio (primary education, UNESCO estimate): 14.1 in 2007/08 (Source: UNESCO Institute for Statistics).
Adult Literacy Rate (UNESCO estimates): 95.4% (males 95.1%; females 95.7%) in 1995. Source: UNESCO, *Statistical Yearbook*.

Source (unless otherwise indicated): UNESCO Institute for Statistics.

Directory

The Government

HEAD OF STATE

Queen: HM Queen ELIZABETH II.
Governor: WILLIAM ALISTAIR HARRISON (took office 21 April 2009).

EXECUTIVE COUNCIL
(May 2011)

The Government is formed by the Anguilla United Movement.

Chief Minister and Minister of Finance, Economic Development, Investments and Tourism: HUBERT B. HUGHES.
Deputy Chief Minister and Minister of Social Development: EDISON BAIRD.
Minister of Home Affairs, including Labour, Natural Resources, Lands, Physical Planning and Immigration: WALCOTT RICHARDSON.
Minister of Infrastructure, Communications, Utilities, Housing, Agriculture and Fisheries: EVAN GUMBS.
Parliamentary Secretary with responsibility for Tourism: HAYDN HUGHES.
Deputy Governor: STANLEY EVERTON REID.
Attorney-General: WILHELM C. BOURNE.

MINISTRIES

Office of the Governor: Government House, POB 60, The Valley; tel. 497-2622; fax 497-3314; e-mail governorsoffice@gov.ai.
Office of the Chief Minister: The Secretariat, POB 60, The Valley; tel. 497-2518; fax 497-3389; e-mail chief-minister@gov.ai.

All ministries are based in The Valley, mostly at the Secretariat (tel. 497-2451; internet www.gov.ai).

Legislature

HOUSE OF ASSEMBLY

Speaker: BARBARA WEBSTER-BOURNE.
Clerk to House of Assembly: ADELLA RICHARDSON.
Election, 15 February 2010

Party	% of votes	Seats
Anguilla United Movement (AUM)	32.67	4
Anguilla United Front (AUF)	39.39	2
Anguilla Progressive Party (APP)	14.71	1
Independent candidates	13.24	—
Total	**100.00**	**7**

There are also two ex officio members and two nominated members.

Political Organizations

Anguilla Progressive Party (APP): The Valley; Leader BRENT DAVIS.
Anguilla United Front (AUF): The Valley; internet www.unitedfront.ai; f. 2000 by the alliance of the Anguilla Democratic Party and the Anguilla National Alliance; Leader VICTOR F. BANKS.
Anguilla United Movement (AUM): The Valley; f. 1979; revived 1984; previously known as the Anguilla United Party—AUP; conservative; Leader HUBERT B. HUGHES.

Judicial System

Justice is administered by the High Court, Court of Appeal and Magistrates' Courts. Anguilla is under the jurisdiction of the Eastern Caribbean Supreme Court (ECSC). One of the ECSC's High Court Judges arbitrates in sittings of the territory's High Court.

High Court Judge: LOUISE BLENMAN.
Registrar: PATRICIA HARDING.

Religion

CHRISTIANITY

The Anglican Communion

Anglicans in Anguilla are adherents of the Church in the Province of the West Indies, comprising nine dioceses. Anguilla forms part of the diocese of the North Eastern Caribbean and Aruba. According to figures from the last census (2001), 29% of the population are Anglican.

Bishop of the North Eastern Caribbean and Aruba: Rt Rev. LEROY ERROL BROOKS, St Mary's Rectory, POB 180, The Valley; tel. 497-2235; fax 497-8555; e-mail brookx@anguilla.net.com.

The Roman Catholic Church

The diocese of St John's-Basseterre, suffragan to the archdiocese of Castries (Saint Lucia), includes Anguilla, Antigua and Barbuda, the British Virgin Islands, Montserrat and Saint Christopher and Nevis. The Bishop resides in St John's, Antigua. Some 5.7% of the population are Roman Catholic, according to census figures.

Roman Catholic Church: St Gerard's, POB 47, The Valley; tel. 497-2405; e-mail info@stgerards-anguilla.org; internet stgerards-anguilla.org; Pastor PAUL CZOCH.

Other Christian Churches

According to the last census, 24% of the population are Methodist.

Methodist Church: Epworth Manse, POB 5, 2640 The Valley; tel. 497-2612; fax 497-8460; e-mail methodism@anguillanet.com; internet www.lidmethodist.org; Supt Minister Rev. E. DUNSTAN RICHARDSON.

The Seventh-day Adventist, Baptist, Church of God, Pentecostal, Apostolic Faith and Jehovah's Witnesses Churches and sects are also represented.

The Press

Anguilla Life Magazine: POB 1622, The Valley; tel. 497-3080; fax 497-4196; e-mail anguillalife@anguillanet.com; 3 a year; Publr and Editor CLAIRE DEVENER; circ. 10,000.
Anguilla Official Gazette: House of Assembly, POB 60, The Valley; tel. 497-5081; fax 498-2210; internet gazette.gov.ai; monthly; govt news-sheet.
The Anguillian Newspaper: POB 98, The Valley; tel. 497-3823; fax 497-8706; e-mail theanguillian@anguillanet.com; internet www.anguillian.com; weekly; Editor A. NAT HODGE.
The Light: Sandy Hill, POB 1373, The Valley; tel. 497-5058; fax 497-5641; e-mail thelight@anguillanet.com; f. 1993; owned by Hodgeco Publishing Inc; weekly; newspaper; Editor GEORGE C. HODGE.
What We Do in Anguilla: Sandy Hill, POB 1373, The Valley; tel. 497-5641; e-mail thelight@anguillanet.com; f. 1987; monthly; tourism; Editor GEORGE C. HODGE; circ. 20,000.

Broadcasting and Communications

TELECOMMUNICATIONS

LIME: POB 77, The Valley; tel. 804-2994; e-mail customerservice@time4lime.com; internet www.time4lime.com; fmrly Cable & Wireless (Anguilla) Ltd; name changed as above 2008; contact centres in Jamaica and Saint Lucia; CEO DAVID SHAW; Exec. Vice-Pres. (Leeward Islands) DAVIDSON CHARLES.

UNITED KINGDOM OVERSEAS TERRITORIES

Anguilla

Wireless Ventures (Anguilla) Ltd: Babrow Bldg, The Valley; tel. 498-7500; fax 498-7510; e-mail customercareanguilla@digicelgroup.com; internet www.digicelanguilla.com; owned by Digicel Ltd (Bermuda); fmrly AT&T Wireless; Country Man. STEPHENIE BROOKS.

BROADCASTING

Radio

The Caribbean Beacon: Long Rd, POB 690, The Valley; Head Office: POB 7008, Columbus, GA 31908, USA; tel. 497-4340; fax 497-4311; f. 1981; privately owned and operated; religious and commercial; broadcasts 24 hours daily; Pres. MELLISA SCOTT; CEO B. MONSELL HAZELL.

Klass 92.9 FM: POB 339, The Valley; tel. 497-3791; e-mail request@klass929.com; internet www.klass929.com; f. 2006; commercial; Owner ABNER BROOKS, Jr.

Kool FM: North Side, The Valley; tel. 497-0103; fax 497-0104; e-mail kool@koolfm103.com; internet www.koolfm103.com; commercial; Man. ASHLEY BROOKS.

Radio Anguilla: Dept of Information and Broadcasting, Secretariat, POB 60, The Valley; tel. 497-2218; fax 497-5432; e-mail radioaxa@anguillanet.com; internet www.radioaxa.com; f. 1969; owned and operated by the Govt of Anguilla since 1976; 250,000 listeners throughout the north-eastern Caribbean; broadcasts 17 hours daily; Dir FARRAH BANKS; Programme Man. KEITH STONE GREAVES.

UP Beat Radio 97.7 FM: Cedar Ave, Rey Hill, POB 5045, The Valley, AI 2640; tel. 498-3354; fax 497-5995; e-mail info@hbr1075.com; internet hbr1075.com; f. 2001; commercial; music and news programmes.

ZJF FM: POB 333, The Valley; tel. 497-3919; fax 497-3909; f. 1989; commercial; Man. SELWYN BROOKS.

Television

Anguilla TV: tel. 662-7365; e-mail donna@islandeyetv.com; internet www.islandeyetv.com; operated by Eye TV; terrestrial channels 3 and 9; 24-hour local and international English language programming; Exec. Producer DONNA DAVIS.

Caribbean Cable Communications (Anguilla): Edwin Wallace Rey Dr., POB 336, The Valley; tel. 497-3600; fax 497-3602; e-mail customersupport@caribcable.com; internet www.caribcable.com; also broadcasts to Nevis; Pres. LEE BERTMAN.

Finance

(cap. = capital; res = reserves; dep. = deposits; m. = million; amounts in EC dollars)

CENTRAL BANK

Eastern Caribbean Central Bank: Fairplay Commercial Complex, POB 1385, The Valley; tel. 497-5050; fax 497-5150; e-mail eccbaxa@anguillanet.com; internet www.eccb-centralbank.org; HQ in Basseterre, Saint Christopher and Nevis; bank of issue and central monetary authority for Anguilla, Antigua and Barbuda, Dominica, Grenada, Montserrat, Saint Christopher and Nevis, Saint Lucia and Saint Vincent and the Grenadines; Gov. Sir K. DWIGHT VENNER; Country Man. MARILYN BARTLETT-RICHARDSON.

COMMERCIAL BANKS

Caribbean Commercial Bank (Anguilla) Ltd: POB 23, The Valley; tel. 497-3917; fax 497-3570; e-mail service@ccb.ai; internet www.ccb.ai; f. 1976; Chair. OSBOURNE B. FLEMING; Man. Dir STARRY WEBSTER-BENJAMIN.

FirstCaribbean International Bank Ltd: POB 140, The Valley; tel. 497-2301; fax 497-2980; e-mail care@firstcaribbeanbank.com; internet www.firstcaribbeanbank.com; f. 2002 following merger of Caribbean operations of Barclays Bank PLC and CIBC; Exec. Chair. MICHAEL MANSOOR; CEO JOHN D. ORR.

National Bank of Anguilla Ltd (NBA): POB 44, The Valley; tel. 497-2101; fax 497-3310; e-mail nbabankl@anguillanet.com; internet www.nba.ai; f. 1985; 5% owned by Govt of Anguilla; cap. 30.7m., res 69.2m., dep. 928.1m. (March 2008); CEO E. VALENTINE BANKS.

Scotiabank Anguilla Ltd: Fairplay Commercial Centre, POB 250, The Valley; tel. 497-3333; fax 497-3344; e-mail bns.anguilla@scotiabank.com; internet www.scotiabank.com; Man. Dir KERWIN BAPTISTE.

There are 'offshore' foreign banks based on the island, but most are not authorized to operate in Anguilla. There is a financial complex known as the Caribbean Commercial Centre in The Valley.

TRUST COMPANIES

Barwys Trust Anguilla Ltd: Caribbean Suite, The Valley; tel. 497-2189; fax 497-5007; e-mail info@barwys.com; internet www.barwys.com; Man. JOSEPH BRICE.

Codan Trust Co (Anguilla) Ltd: Mitchell House, POB 147, The Valley; tel. 498-6789; fax 498-8423; e-mail anguilla@conyersdill.com; internet www.conyersdill.com; subsidiary of Conyers, Dill and Pearman, Bermuda; Man. GARETH THOMAS.

First Anguilla Trust Co Ltd: Mitchell House, POB 174, The Valley, AI 2640; tel. and fax 498-8800; e-mail information@firstanguilla.com; internet www.firstanguilla.com; owned by Webster Dyrud Mitchell; f. 1995; Dir PAM WEBSTER.

GenevaTrust: National Bank Corporate Bldg, Caribbean Suite, Airport Rd, The Valley; tel. 870-3178; fax 870-3949; e-mail geneva@genevatrust.com; internet www.genevatrust.com; f. 2005; as the GenevaTrust Corpn; subsidiary of Geneva Assurance Ltd; CEO NADINE DE KOKER.

Global Trustees (Anguilla) Ltd: 201 The Rogers Office Bldg, Edwin Wallace Rey Dr., George Hill; tel. 498-5858; fax 497-5504; e-mail anguilla@gcsl.info; internet www.gcsl.info; fmrly Hansa Bank and Trust Co; Man. Dir CARLYLE K. ROGERS.

Intertrust (Anguilla) Ltd: National Bank Corporate Bldg, Airport Rd, POB 1388, The Valley; tel. 497-2189; fax 497-5007; e-mail toni.niekoop@intertrustgroup.com; internet www.intertrustgroup.com; fmrly Fortis Intertrust (Anguilla) Ltd; Dir TONI NIEKOOP.

Lutea (Anguilla) Ltd: S1 South, Auckland House, POB 1533, The Quarter; tel. 498-0340; fax 498-0341; e-mail acharles@lutea.com; internet www.lutea.com; owned by the Lutea Group of Cos, administered in Jersey (United Kingdom); Man. AINE CHARLES.

Mossack Fonseca & Co (British Anguilla) Ltd: Quantum Bldg, Suite 29, Caribbean Commercial Centre, The Valley; tel. 498-7777; fax 497-3727; e-mail britishanguilla@mossfon.com; internet www.mossfon.com; Administrator CUTELYN CARTY.

Sinel Trust (Anguilla) Ltd: POB 821, The Valley; fax 497-8289; e-mail arichardson@sineltrust.com; CEO ALEX RICHARDSON.

REGULATORY AUTHORITIES

Anguilla Financial Services Commission: The Secretariat, POB 1575, The Valley; tel. 497-5881; fax 497-5872; e-mail info@fsc.org.ai; internet www.fsc.org.ai; f. 2004 to replace the Financial Services Dept of the Ministry of Finance, Economic Development, Investment, Tourism and Commerce; Chair. HELEN HATTON.

Financial Services Regulatory Commission: The Valley; internet www.fsrc.gov.ag; f. 2002; responsible for the regulation and supervision of all institutions licensed under the International Business Corpns Act of 2002; CEO JOHN BENJAMIN.

STOCK EXCHANGE

Eastern Caribbean Securities Exchange: Bird Rock, Basseterre, Saint Christopher and Nevis; tel. (869) 466-7192; fax (869) 465-3798; e-mail info@ecseonline.com; internet www.ecseonline.com; f. 2001; regional securities market designed to facilitate the buying and selling of financial products for the eight member territories—Anguilla, Antigua and Barbuda, Dominica, Grenada, Montserrat, Saint Christopher and Nevis, Saint Lucia, and Saint Vincent and the Grenadines; Chair. Sir K. DWIGHT VENNER; Gen. Man. TREVOR E. BLAKE.

INSURANCE

A-Affordable Insurance Services Inc: Old Factory Plaza, POB 6, The Valley; tel. 497-5757; fax 497-2122.

Caribbean Alliance Insurance Co Ltd: POB 1377, The Valley; tel. 497-3525; fax 497-3526; e-mail info@d3ent.com.

D-3 Enterprises Ltd: Caribbean Commercial Complex, POB 1377, The Valley; tel. 497-3525; fax 497-3526; e-mail d3ent@anguillanet.com; internet www.d-3enterprises.com; Man. Dir CLEMENT RUAN.

Gulf Insurance Ltd: c/o Ferry Boat Inn, POB 189, Blowing Point; tel. 497-6613; fax 497-6713; e-mail ferryb@anguillanet.com; internet www.gulfinsuranceltd.com; Contact MARJORIE MCCLEAN.

Malliouhana-Anico Insurance Co Ltd (MAICO): Herbert's Commercial Centre, POB 492, The Valley; tel. 497-3712; fax 497-3710; e-mail maico@anguillanet.com; Man. MONICA HODGE.

National Caribbean Insurance Co Ltd: Caribbean Commercial Complex, POB 323, The Valley; tel. 497-2865; fax 497-3783.

National General Insurance Co N.V. (NAGICO): c/o Fairplay Management Services, POB 79, The Valley; tel. 497-2976; fax 497-3303; e-mail fairplay@anguillanet.com; internet www.nagico.com.

UNITED KINGDOM OVERSEAS TERRITORIES

Trade and Industry

DEVELOPMENT ORGANIZATION

Anguilla Development Board: Cannon Ball Office Complex, Wallblake Rd, POB 285, The Valley; tel. 497-2595; fax 497-2959; f. 1979; provides financial and technical assistance to fishing, agriculture, tourism and industry; Gen. Man. ALTHEA HODGE.

CHAMBER OF COMMERCE

Anguilla Chamber of Commerce and Industry: POB 321, The Valley; tel. and fax 497-3880; e-mail acoci@caribcable.com; internet www.anguillachamber.com; Pres. JOHN BENJAMIN; Exec. Dir CALVIN BARTLETT.

INDUSTRIAL AND TRADE ASSOCIATION

Anguilla Financial Services Association (AFSA): POB 1071, The Valley; tel. 498-4224; fax 498-4220; e-mail support@anguillafsd.com; internet www.anguillafsc.com; Pres. JOHN D. K. LAWRENCE.

UTILITIES

Electricity

Anguilla Electricity Co Ltd: POB 400, The Valley; tel. 497-5200; fax 497-5440; e-mail info@anglec.com; internet www.anglec.com; f. 1991; operates a power station and 12 generators; Chair. RODNEY REY; Gen. Man. THOMAS HODGE.

Transport

ROADS

Anguilla has 175 km (108 miles) of roads, of which 46.9% is paved.

SHIPPING

There are three main seaports. The principal port of entry is Sandy Ground on Road Bay. The Corito Bay port is used by two oil companies for the import of petroleum products and propane. The Blowing Point port is the passenger terminal for ferries operating between Anguilla and Marigot (St Martin). The other areas of entry are Cove, Forest, Island Harbour and Little Harbour.

Anguilla Air and Seaports Authority: C/O Permanent Secretary, MICUHAF, POB 60, The Valley; tel. 497-3476; fax 497-5258; e-mail larry.franklin@gov.ai; f. 2009; Supt. EDWIN HARRIS.

Link Ferries: Little Harbour; tel. 497-2231; fax 497-3290; e-mail fbconnor@anguillanet.com; internet www.link.ai; f. 1992; daily services to Julianna International Airport (St Martin) and charter services to neighbouring islands and offshore quays; Capt. and Owner FRANKLYN CONNOR.

CIVIL AVIATION

Clayton J. Lloyd International Airport (known as Wallblake Airport until July 2010), 3.2 km (2 miles) from The Valley, has an asphalt-surfaced runway with a length of 1,665 m (5,462 ft). Reconstruction and expansion of the airport was completed in 2004. Most of the cost of the EC $49.2m. project was allocated to the extension of the runway to accommodate mid-range aircraft. LIAT and Winair regional airlines also operate from Clayton J. Lloyd International Airport.

American Eagle: POB 659, Clayton J. Lloyd International Airport; tel. 497-3131; fax 497-3502; regional partner co of American Airlines; operates scheduled flights from Puerto Rico 3 times a day (December to April) and once daily (May to November); Regional Man. EVETTE NEGRON.

Anguilla Air Services: POB 559, Clayton J. Lloyd International Airport; tel. 498-5922; fax 498-5921; e-mail info@anguillaairservices.com; internet www.anguillaairservices.com; f. Dec. 2006; operates passenger and cargo charter flights from Anguilla to neighbouring islands; official carrier for Winair (Winward Islands Airways) in Anguilla; Man. Dir CARL THOMAS.

Trans Anguilla Airways (2000) Ltd (TAA): POB 1329, Clayton J. Lloyd International Airport; tel. 497-8690; fax 497-8689; e-mail transang@anguillanet.com; internet www.transanguilla.com; f. 1996; air charter service in the Eastern Caribbean; Chair. JOSHUA GUMBS.

Tourism

Anguilla's sandy beaches and unspoilt natural beauty attract tourists and also day visitors from neighbouring St Martin/St Maarten. Tourism receipts totalled an estimated EC $229.1m. in 2009, and there were 746 hotel rooms on the island in 2005. Visitor arrivals totalled 109,159 in 2009.

Anguilla Hotel and Tourism Association: Coronation Ave, POB 1020, The Valley; tel. 497-2944; fax 497-3091; e-mail ahtaadmin@anguillanet.com; internet www.anguillahta.com; f. 1981; Pres. SHERILLE HUGHES; Exec. Dir GILDA GUMBS-SAMUEL.

Anguilla Tourist Board: Coronation Ave, POB 1388, The Valley, AI 2640; tel. 497-2759; fax 497-2710; e-mail atbtour@anguillanet.com; internet www.anguilla-vacation.com; Dir CANDIS NILES.

Defence

The United Kingdom is responsible for the defence of Anguilla. According to the 2008 budget address, proposed recurrent expenditure on the Royal Anguilla Police Force was EC $10.9m. (equivalent to 5.5% of total recurrent expenditure), representing a 26% increase on the allocation for 2007.

Education

Education is free and compulsory between the ages of five and 16 years. Primary education begins at five years of age and lasts for six years. Secondary education, beginning at 11 years of age, lasts for a further six years. There are six government primary schools and one government secondary school. According to UNESCO estimates, in 2007/08 enrolment at primary schools included 93% of children in the relevant age-group, while in 2004/05 enrolment at secondary schools included 91% of pupils in the relevant age-group. A 'comprehensive' secondary school education system was introduced in 1986. Post-secondary education is undertaken abroad. A new five-year strategic Education Development Plan was being discussed by the Government in 2010. According to the 2008 budget address, government expenditure on education was to total EC $22m. in that year, equivalent to 11% of proposed recurrent expenditure and an increase of 21% on the allocation for 2007.

BERMUDA

Introductory Survey

LOCATION, CLIMATE, LANGUAGE, RELIGION, FLAG, CAPITAL

The Bermudas or Somers Islands are an isolated archipelago, comprising about 138 islands, in the Atlantic Ocean, about 917 km (570 miles) off the coast of South Carolina, USA. Bridges and causeways link seven of the islands to form the principal mainland. The climate is mild and humid. Temperatures are generally between 8°C (46°F) and 32°C (90°F), with an average annual rainfall of 1,470 mm (58 ins). The official language is English, but there is a small community of Portuguese speakers. Most of the inhabitants profess Christianity, and numerous denominations are represented, the principal one being the Anglican Church. The flag (proportions 1 by 2) is the British 'Red Ensign' (this usage being unique among the British colonies), with, in the fly, the colony's badge: a seated red lion holding a shield (with a gold baroque border), which depicts the wreck off Bermuda of the ship of the first settlers. The capital is Hamilton.

CONTEMPORARY POLITICAL HISTORY

Historical Context

Bermuda was first settled by the British in 1609. It has had a representative assembly since 1620 (and thus claims one of the oldest parliaments in the world), and became a British crown colony in 1684. Bermuda was granted internal self-government by the Constitution introduced in 1968, although the British Government retains responsibility in certain matters. Various amendments to the 1968 Constitution were made in 1973, the most important being the establishment of the Governor's Council, through which the Governor exercises responsibility for external affairs, defence, internal security and the police. In 1974 the Government Leader was restyled Premier and the Executive Council became the Cabinet.

UNITED KINGDOM OVERSEAS TERRITORIES

Bermuda

Domestic Political Affairs

The first general election under the new Constitution, which took place in May 1968 against a background of rioting and racial tension (some 60% of the population are of African origin, the rest mostly of European extraction), was won by the United Bermuda Party (UBP), a moderate, multi-racial party whose policies were based on racial co-operation and continued support for dependent status. The underlying racial tensions were emphasized in 1972 and 1973 by shooting incidents which resulted in the deaths of the Governor, the Commissioner of Police and three others. In December 1977 the Governor's assassin and another convicted murderer were executed, and further rioting ensued. A state of emergency was declared, and British troops were flown to Bermuda to restore order.

At the general election of May 1976, the UBP was returned to power with a decreased majority. The mainly black, left-wing Progressive Labour Party (PLP), which campaigned for independence increased its legislative presence. In August 1977 Sir John Sharpe, Premier and leader of the UBP since December 1975, resigned both posts and was succeeded by David Gibbons, the Minister of Finance.

In February 1978 a Royal Commission was established to investigate the causes of racial violence, and in August the Commission published a report which suggested the redrawing of constituency boundaries to improve the PLP's prospects for winning seats. Despite this, the UBP won the December 1980 election. Gibbons resigned as Premier and was succeeded by John Swan, the Minister of Home Affairs. At a general election in February 1983, the UBP increased its majority in the House of Assembly. Internal divisions within the PLP led to the expulsion from the party of four PLP deputies. These members, after sitting as independents, formed a new centre party, the National Liberal Party (NLP), in August 1985. In October Swan called an early general election, hoping to take advantage of the divided opposition. The UBP was decisively returned to power. Following a general election in February 1989, the UBP remained in power, but with a reduced legislative representation.

Constitutional amendments introduced in 1979 included provision for closer consultation between the Premier and the Leader of the Opposition on the appointment of members of the Public Service Commission and the Boundaries Commission, and on the appointment of the Chief Justice. The 1978 Royal Commission recommended early independence for Bermuda, but the majority of the population at that time seemed to oppose such a policy. Swan had declared himself in favour of eventual independence for the colony, but only with the support of the Bermudian people.

The UBP was returned to power at a general election in October 1993. In February 1994 legislation providing for the organization of a referendum on independence for Bermuda was narrowly approved in the House of Assembly. The debate on independence was believed to have intensified as a result of the announcement in late 1993 that British and US forces would close their facilities and withdraw permanently from the island by April 1995 and September 1995, respectively. The PLP, which advocates independence for Bermuda, consistently opposed the organization of a referendum on the subject, believing that the independence issue should be determined by a general election. In May 1994 a PLP legislative motion to reject a proposed government inquiry into the possibilities for independence was narrowly approved, effectively halting further progress towards a referendum. However, the debate continued, and further legislation regarding the proposed referendum was narrowly approved in March 1995. It was subsequently announced that a vote would be held in August. The PLP encouraged its supporters to boycott the poll, which required not only a majority of votes, but also the approval of 40% of eligible voters in order to achieve a pro-independence result.

The referendum took place on 16 August 1995. Some 59% of eligible voters participated in the poll (a relatively low level for Bermuda), of which 74% registered their opposition to independence from the United Kingdom, and 26% expressed their support for it. The following day Swan resigned as Premier and as leader of the UBP. Factions within the governing party were perceived to have become considerably polarized during the independence debate, which had resulted in the division of opinion along racial lines. The Minister of Finance, David Saul (who had remained neutral on the independence issue), was subsequently elected leader of the UBP, and therefore became Premier. Saul stated that his principal objectives were to re-establish a climate of political stability, to encourage the continued development of the financial services and tourism sectors and to reunite the UBP. However, under his leadership divisions within the party appeared to deepen. In March 1997 Saul announced his resignation as Premier and as leader of the UBP. He was replaced by Pamela Gordon, who was elected to the party leadership (and thus as Premier) unopposed.

The PLP in power

Elections to the House of Assembly took place in November 1998. The PLP won its first ever majority in the House of Assembly. A new Cabinet was appointed and party leader Jennifer Smith was sworn in as Bermuda's first PLP Premier. She sought to reassure the international business community that her Government would seek to enhance Bermuda's attractiveness as an international business centre, and that she would resist any attempts to alter the island's tax status. Smith further promised that, although independence for Bermuda remained a stated aim of her party, no immediate moves in that direction were planned.

In October 2000 the opposition UBP boycotted the opening of parliament in protest at government plans to reduce the number of seats in the House of Assembly. Pamela Gordon claimed that there had not been adequate public consultation on the matter. Premier Smith had rejected calls for a constitutional conference or a referendum on the proposals, which included replacing the two-member constituencies with single-member ones, although she did announce that the Government would hold a public meeting to discuss the issue. The PLP believed that the existing system was weighted in favour of the UBP, which was considered the party of the white population. In December the House of Assembly approved a motion requesting the British Government approve the establishment of a boundaries commission. Any changes would be subject to ratification by the United Kingdom's Foreign and Commonwealth Office (FCO). In January 2001 the UBP submitted an 8,500-signature petition to the British Government, demanding a constitutional conference or referendum before any changes were made. Gordon also claimed that some Bermudians had refused to sign the petition, fearing recriminations. The FCO, however, stated that a constitutional conference was unnecessary, and in April it began consultations over the proposed changes. The commission recommended reducing the number of seats in the House of Assembly by four, to 36. In addition, whereas deputies had previously been elected from 20 two-member constituencies, under the proposed scheme each member of parliament would be elected by a separate constituency. The FCO approved the changes before the July 2003 general election.

In March 1999 the British Government published draft legislation redesignating its Dependencies as United Kingdom Overseas Territories, and guaranteeing their citizens' rights to a British passport and to residence in the United Kingdom. The document also stated, however, that the Overseas Territories would be obliged to reform their legislation to ensure compliance with European standards on human rights and on financial regulation. In October it was announced that in accordance with the proposed reforms, corporal and capital punishment were to be removed from the statute book. In May 2002 the British Overseas Territories Act, having received royal assent in the United Kingdom in February, came into force and granted British citizenship to the people of its Overseas Territories, including Bermuda. Under the new law Bermudians would be able to hold British passports and work in the United Kingdom and anywhere else in the European Union (see p. 270).

At an election to the smaller 36-seat House of Assembly in July 2003, the PLP retained its parliamentary majority, securing 22 seats, but its share of the popular vote was reduced to 52% (compared with 48% for the UBP). Smith resigned as Premier after it emerged that she had retained her seat, in what was regarded as a 'safe' PLP constituency, by just eight votes. She was replaced by William Alexander Scott. Scott's first Cabinet, announced a few days after the elections, consisted of 12 members, despite the PLP's pre-election pledge to reduce the size of the executive to eight in order to reduce costs.

In July 2005 the Misuse of Drugs Amendment Act introduced legislation allowing courts to fine those convicted of drugs offences up to US $1m. and to impose prison sentences of between 10 years and life. Despite the designation of a dedicated cabinet minister and employment of an eminent British police officer as Assistant Commissioner specializing in drugs crime prevention, drugs-related violent crime escalated during 2006.

In November 2005 a Bermuda Independence Commission, established by Scott in order to foment debate regarding the island's future, submitted its report. However, its findings were criticized for being biased, as they failed to include contributions from the UBP, including only the ruling PLP's submission. In an attempt to quell the criticism, Scott declared that discussions would take place in 2006 regarding the future status of Bermuda. However, public opinion remained strongly in favour of maintaining links with the United Kingdom. In March both the UN and the British Government indicated their support for a referendum on the issue; however, Scott maintained that the question of independence should be decided at the next general election, constitutionally due by 2008. The issue of independence created political tension between the population's black majority, from which the PLP drew much of its support, and the white minority.

Scott's premiership was abruptly curtailed on 27 October 2006 after he was defeated in a PLP leadership contest; former Deputy Premier Ewart Brown succeeded him. Demonstrating his intention to compete for the party leadership, Brown had resigned from his ministerial responsibilities earlier in the month. Brown pledged to invest substantially in the country's care system and confirmed his commitment to addressing disruptive racial tensions among the island's communities by creating a ministerial post for matters of social rehabilitation. Racial tensions proved of particular pertinence to the opposition UBP, embroiled as it was in an internal racial discrimination controversy which, in January 2007, precipitated the resignations of House of Assembly member Jamahl Simmons and party Chairwoman Gwyneth Rawlins. Both alleged serious charges of racial discrimination against factions within the party. Simmons claimed that a white élite within the UBP was attempting to remove him from his seat; the departure of two black party members only exacerbated public scepticism about the party's professed allegiance to an integrated Bermudian society.

The unauthorized disclosure, from a source within the Bermuda police, of documents implicating the Premier and a number of other high-ranking government officials in a corruption scandal, served to compromise relations with the United Kingdom in May 2007. Brown maintained that a previous inquiry, in 2004, into the alleged dubious arrangement between government personnel (including himself) and the state-owned Bermuda Housing Corporation—whereby considerable public funds were appropriated for private enrichment—had discharged him of any misconduct.

At a general election held on 18 December 2007 the PLP secured a third consecutive term in office with 52.5% of the votes cast, while the UBP won 47.3% of the ballot. The parties' representation in the legislature remained as at the 2003 election: 22 seats for the PLP and 14 seats for the UBP. Allegations of corruption and issues of race featured prominently in the election campaign, with PLP candidates employing inflammatory rhetoric to suggest that the UBP, if elected, would install a regime oppressive to the black population. After failing to win the constituency seat he contested, Michael Dunkley was replaced as leader of the UBP by Kim Swan.

A political dispute developed in June 2009 after it was revealed that the PLP Government had agreed with US authorities to allow four Chinese Uygur (Uighur) Muslim separatists to settle in Bermuda following their release from the US detention centre at Guantánamo Bay, Cuba. The UBP claimed that Premier Brown had acted 'autocratically' by accepting the former detainees without consultation with either the Cabinet, the Governor or the British Government. On 20 June the Government survived a motion of no confidence in the House of Assembly,. Following the vote, the Minister of Culture and Social Rehabilitation, Dale Butler, resigned in protest at the Premier's handling of the affair. The FCO also remonstrated with the Government for its lack of consultation, claiming that the matter fell outside the Bermudian authorities' remit.

Recent developments: a new Premier

Brown resigned as Premier, and PLP leader, on 28 October 2010 in accordance with an earlier pledge to serve only one four-year term. Deputy Premier and Minister of Finance Paula Cox won the PLP leadership election on the same day, and was inaugurated as the new Premier on 29 October. Cox reorganized the Cabinet in November. Notably, Derrick Burgess, who succeeded Cox as Deputy Premier, was given responsibility for public works (one of several newly created portfolios), former Premier Dame Jennifer Smith was appointed as Minister of Education, David Burch took control of the new Ministry of National Security, and Michael Scott became Attorney-General and Minister of Justice; Cox retained the finance portfolio. Promoting fiscal discipline and economic recovery were declared to be the main aims of the new Government. Wayne Perinchief, a former Deputy Police Commissioner, was appointed as Minister of National Security in April 2011, following Burch's resignation earlier that month.

The 'Offshore' Financial Sector

In February 1999 Premier Smith met members of the Organisation for Economic Co-operation and Development (OECD, see p. 376) to reassure them that Bermuda was determined to improve regulation of the 'offshore' financial services sector. A report by the Financial Action Task Force on Money Laundering (see p. 451) concluded in June 2000 that Bermuda appeared 'to have effective regulations and supervision' in place in its financial services sector. In the same month the Government agreed to co-operate with OECD in an international effort to reduce tax evasion, promising to end within five years the 'harmful' practices that had given the island a reputation as a tax haven. Measures included a pledge to exchange information about tax in Bermuda with other nations, the introduction of legislation for companies to audit accounts and for these to be made available to the Bermudian authorities, and in the opening up of previously sheltered sectors of the economy to international companies. The Government had, however, pledged to maintain its existing tax system, which included no income tax. In December the members of the House of Assembly agreed, for the first time, to declare their assets and financial interests.

In mid-2002 the issue of financial transparency and corporate governance in Bermuda re-emerged following the disastrous collapse of several US multinationals. The indictment on tax evasion charges of Dennis Kozlowski, the former CEO of Tyco International Ltd, a manufacturer of electronic security systems with a nominal headquarters on the island, fuelled a growing campaign in the US media and the US Congress against the perceived lack of financial scrutiny in Bermuda. The USA's Corporate Patriot Enforcement Act of 2005 sought to discourage US corporations to relocate their headquarters from the USA to offshore sites such as Bermuda, by making them still liable to pay tax in the USA.

The arrest in Bermuda of Dutch businessman and oil magnate, John Deuss, in October 2006 attracted considerable local and international media interest; Deuss was compelled to resign as Chairman and Chief Executive Officer of Bermuda Commercial Bank (BCB) following allegations of money-laundering, among other illegal practices, and extradited to the Netherlands. Despite these troubling developments, in December the House of Assembly ratified the Investment Funds Act 2006, designed to facilitate the registration and license of investment funds in the territory by eliminating 'unnecessary' administrative protocols and to encourage further expansion in a sector already attractive to international fund operators. Bermuda's financial sector was criticized in February 2007 for its resistance to regulatory mechanisms and reluctance to engage in transparency exercises. In April 2009 OECD included Bermuda on its 'grey list' of tax havens that had committed to, but not implemented, an internationally agreed standard of transparency measures. However, Bermuda was the first jurisdiction to be removed from the list two months later after it signed its 12th tax information-sharing agreement. By March 2011 the Government had signed a further 10 accords.

CONSTITUTION AND GOVERNMENT

The Constitution was introduced on 8 June 1968 and amended in 1973 and 1979. An appointed Governor, responsible for external affairs, defence and internal security, represents the British monarch. The bicameral legislature comprises the Senate (11 nominated members) and the House of Assembly, with 36 members representing separate constituencies elected for five years by universal adult suffrage. The Governor appoints the majority leader in the House as Premier, and the latter nominates other ministers. The Cabinet is responsible to the legislature. For the purposes of local government, the island has long been divided into nine parishes (originally known as 'tribes', except for the 'public land' of St George's, the capital until 1815). The town of St George's and the city of Hamilton constitute the two municipalities of the territory.

REGIONAL AND INTERNATIONAL CO-OPERATION

Bermuda, the oldest colony of the United Kingdom, has the status of Overseas Territory in association with the European Union (EU, see p. 270) and has also been granted Designated Territory status by the British Government (this allows Bermudian-based funds and unit trusts access to the British market). Bermuda's financial services also benefit from a special tax treaty with the USA. A similar agreement was signed in November 2005 with Australia, in which both parties would share tax information on a specific subject under investigation or audit. In 2000 Bermuda joined the Caribbean Tourism Organization. In July 2003 Bermuda became an associate member of the Caribbean Community and Common Market (CARICOM, see p. 219). The territory is a member of the Commonwealth (see p. 230).

ECONOMIC AFFAIRS

In 1997, according to estimates by the World Bank, Bermuda's gross national income (GNI), measured at average 1995–97 prices, was US $2,128m. During 2000–09, it was estimated, the population increased at an average annual rate of 0.4%. Overall gross domestic product (GDP) increased, in real terms, at an average annual rate of 3.6% in 2000–08. Real GDP increased by 0.7% in 2008, but decreased by 8.1% in 2009.

Agriculture (including forestry, fishing, and mining and quarrying) engaged only 1.8% of the employed labour force in 2008. Agriculture, forestry and fishing contributed 0.8% of GDP in 2009. The principal crops were potatoes, carrots, bananas, vegetables and melons. Flowers are grown for export. Other vegetables and fruit are also grown, but Bermuda remains very dependent upon food imports, which, with beverages and tobacco, accounted for 17.1% of total imports in 2008. There is a small fishing industry, mainly for domestic consumption. In 2004–09, according to official figures, agricultural GDP increased by an annual average of 2.4%; the sector declined by 0.4% in 2009.

Industry (including manufacturing, construction, quarrying and public utilities) contributed 8.3% of GDP in 2009 and engaged 12.4% of the employed labour force in 2008. The principal industrial sector is construction. Industrial GDP decreased by an average of 2.0% per year in 2004–09; the sector decreased by 13.0% in 2009.

Manufacturing contributed 1.3% of GDP in 2009 and employed 2.3% of the active labour force in 2008. The main activities include

UNITED KINGDOM OVERSEAS TERRITORIES — Bermuda

ship repairs, boat-building and the manufacture of paints and pharmaceuticals. According to official figures, in real terms, the manufacturing sector declined at an average rate of 4.3% per year during 2004–09; the sector increased by 0.7% in 2008, but decreased by 17.2% in 2009.

The construction (including quarrying) sector contributed 5.4% of GDP in 2009 and engaged 9.1% of the employed labour force in 2008. In real terms, the construction sector decreased at an average rate of 0.4% per year during 2004–09; sectoral GDP decreased by 16.0% in 2009.

Energy requirements are met mainly by the import of mineral fuels (fuels accounted for 11.0% of total imports in 2009). Most of Bermuda's water is provided by privately collected rainfall.

Bermuda is overwhelmingly a service economy, with service industries contributing 90.9% of GDP in 2009 and engaging 85.8% of the employed labour force in 2008. There is a significant commercial and 'offshore' financial sector. An estimated 31.1% of the employed labour force were engaged directly in the finance, insurance, real estate and business sectors in 2008. International business was estimated to account for 25.3% of GDP in 2009. At the end of 2010 the number of companies registered in Bermuda totalled 15,091, a 3.6% decline on the previous year's total. Another important source of income is the 'free-flag' registration of shipping, giving Bermuda one of the largest fleets in the world. Tourism is estimated to account for some 60% of all employment, directly and indirectly. The total number of tourists, particularly of cruise ship passengers, is strictly controlled, in order to maintain Bermuda's environment and its market for wealthier visitors. Most tourists come from the USA (some 73.2% of total arrivals by air in 2009). In 2010 some 580,193 tourists visited Bermuda, a 4.7% increase on the previous year's figure, although this was owing to a rise in the number of cruise ship visitors rather than the higher-spending arrivals by air. Tourism revenues fell in 2009, to US $331.3m. The GDP of the hotel and restaurants sector contracted by 23.9% in 2009. In 2004–09 the GDP of the services sector increased by an annual average of 2.2%; services GDP decreased by 10.4% in 2009.

Bermuda is almost entirely dependent upon imports, has very few commodity exports and, therefore, consistently records a large visible trade deficit (B $1,046m. in 2009, according to preliminary figures). Receipts from the service industries normally ensure a surplus on the current account of the balance of payments (recorded at $615m. in 2009). The USA is the principal source of imports (providing 68.6% of total imports in 2009) and the principal market for exports. Other important trading partners include Canada and the United Kingdom. The main exports are rum, flowers, medicinal and pharmaceutical products and the re-export of petroleum products. In 2009 the principal imports were machinery and transport equipment and basic manufactures.

In 2010/11 there was an estimated budgetary deficit of some B $11.3m. (excluding capital expenditure). The average annual rate of inflation was 3.1% in 2000–10. The rate averaged 2.3% in 2010. In May 2009 the official unemployment rate was recorded at 4.5%.

Bermudians enjoy a high standard of living, although there is considerable inequality in the distribution of wealth. There is also local disquiet at the cost of property. Proximity to the USA and the parity of the US and Bermuda dollars help both tourism and financial industries, and Bermuda's status as a United Kingdom Overseas Territory remains a perceived contributor to political stability and financial integrity. The international business sector was the most significant component of the territory's economy, contributing about one-quarter of GDP. Following several years of rapid expansion, this sector contracted in 2008–10 owing to the global economic downturn. The international recession also had a negative impact on the tourism sector, which relied heavily on visitors from the USA, although the opening of a mega-cruise port in early 2009 resulted in an 11.2% increase in cruise ship arrivals in that year and a further rise of 9.2% in 2010. The economy as a whole contracted by 8.1% in 2009 and, according to government estimates, contracted by a further 4%–5% in 2010. A revival in the tourism and international business sectors was expected in 2011. Nevertheless, the Ministry of Finance forecast another decline in GDP (of 0.5%–1.0%) for that year, although a return to growth was expected by mid-2012. Owing to the islands' heavy dependence on the tourism and 'offshore' finance sectors, this was conditional on the continued recovery of the US economy.

PUBLIC HOLIDAYS

2012: 2 January (for New Year's Day), 6 April (Good Friday), 24 May (Bermuda Day), 18 June (National Heroes' Day), 26 July (Emancipation Day), 27 July (Somers' Day), 3 September (Labour Day), 12 November (for Remembrance Day), 26–26 December (Christmas).

Statistical Survey

Source: Dept of Statistics, Cabinet Office, POB HM 3015, Hamilton HM MX; tel. 297-7761; fax 295-8390; e-mail statistics@gov.bm; internet www.statistics.gov.bm.

AREA AND POPULATION

Area: 53.3 sq km (20.59 sq miles).

Population (civilian, non-institutional): 58,460 at census of 20 May 1991; 62,059 (males 29,802, females 32,257) at census of 20 May 2000. *Mid-2011* (official projection): 64,722.

Density (mid-2011): 1,214.3 per sq km.

Population by Age and Sex (official projections at mid-2011): *0–14:* 11,093 (males 5,646, females 5,447); *15–64:* 45,063 (males 21,670, females 23,393); *65 and over:* 8,566 (males 3,482, females 5,084); *Total* 64,722 (males 30,798, females 33,924).

Principal Town (2009, UN estimate): Hamilton (capital) 11,535. Source: UN, *World Urbanization Prospects: The 2009 Revision*.

Births, Marriages and Deaths (2009 unless otherwise indicated): Live births 819 (birth rate 12.7 per 1,000); Marriages 721 in 2008 (marriage rate 11.2 per 1,000); Deaths 470 (death rate 7.3 per 1,000) (Sources: UN, *Population and Vital Statistics Report*; UN, *Demographic Yearbook*). *2010:* Birth rate 11.5; Death rate 7.4 (Source: Pan American Health Organization).

Life Expectancy (years at birth, 2010): 80.6 (males 77.4; females 83.9). Source: Pan American Health Organization.

Employment (excluding unpaid family workers, 2008): Agriculture, forestry, fishing, mining and quarrying 717; Manufacturing 915; Electricity, gas and water 412; Construction 3,649; Wholesale and retail trade 4,766; Hotels and restaurants 4,869; Transport and communications 2,602; Financial intermediation 2,907; Real estate 625; Business activities 4,326; Public administration 4,223; Education, health and social services 3,279; Other community, social and personal services 2,162; International business activity 4,761; *Total employed* 40,213. *2009:* Total employed 36,549; Unemployed 1,714; Total labour force 38,263.

HEALTH AND WELFARE

Total Fertility Rate (children per woman, 2010): 2.0.

Physicians (per 1,000 head, 2005): 2.1.

Hospital Beds (per 1,000 head, 2008): 6.7.

Health Expenditure (% of GDP, 2004): 4.3.

Health Expenditure (public, % of total, 1995): 53.2.

Total Carbon Dioxide Emissions ('000 metric tons, 2007): 513.0.

Carbon Dioxide Emissions Per Head (metric tons, 2007): 8.0.

Source: partly Pan American Health Organization.

For other sources and definitions, see explanatory note on p. vi.

AGRICULTURE, ETC.

Principal Crops (metric tons, 2008, FAO estimates): Potatoes 1,100; Carrots and turnips 380; Vegetables and melons 3,009; Bananas 363. Note: No data were available for 2009.

Livestock (2008, FAO estimates): Cattle 650; Horses 1,000; Pigs 800. Note: No data were available for 2009.

Livestock Products (metric tons, 2008, FAO estimates): Cows' milk 1,550; Hen eggs 300. Note: No data were available for 2009.

Fishing (metric tons, live weight, 2008): Groupers 54; Snappers and jobfishes 37; Wahoo 117; Yellowfin tuna 15; Carangids 49; Caribbean spiny lobster 34; Total catch (incl. others) 400.

Source: FAO.

INDUSTRY

Electric Energy (production, million kWh): 617 in 2005; 631 in 2006; 643 in 2007. Source: UN Industrial Commodity Statistics Database.

FINANCE

Currency and Exchange Rates: 100 cents = 1 Bermuda dollar (B $). *Sterling, US Dollar and Euro Equivalents* (31 December 2010): £1 sterling = B $1.565; US $1 = B $1.000; €1 = B $1.336; B $100 = £63.88 = US $100.00 = €74.84. *Exchange Rate:* The Bermuda dollar is at par with the US dollar. Note: US and Canadian currencies are also accepted.

UNITED KINGDOM OVERSEAS TERRITORIES

Bermuda

Budget (B $ million, 2010/11): Total current account revenue 977.2; Total current account expenditure 988.5; Total capital expenditure 127.7.

Cost of Living (Consumer Price Index; base: 2000 = 100): All items 130.0 in 2008; 132.4 in 2009, 135.5 in 2010. Source: ILO.

Gross Domestic Product (US $ million at constant 1996 prices): 4,174.4 in 2007; 4,161.4 in 2008; 3,826.3 in 2009.

Expenditure on the Gross Domestic Product (B $ million at current prices, 2008, UN estimates): Government final consumption expenditure 1,284.3; Private final consumption expenditure 4,811.6; Gross fixed capital formation 1,219.4; Change in inventories 63.3; *Total domestic expenditure* 7,378.6; Exports of goods and services 2,626.6; *Less* Imports of goods and services 3,573.1; *GDP in purchasers' values* 6,432.1. Source: UN Statistics Division, National Accounts Main Aggregates Database.

Gross Domestic Product by Economic Activity (B $ million at current prices, 2009): Agriculture, forestry and fishing 45.3; Manufacturing 76.9; Electricity, gas and water 96.7; Construction and quarrying 317.0; Wholesale and retail trade and repair services 421.3; Restaurants and hotels 243.5; Transport and communications 281.8; Financial intermediation 684.3; Real estate and renting activities 810.5; Business activities 571.5; Public administration 337.2; Education, health and social work 399.9; Other community, social and personal services 118.5; International business activity 1,489.8; *Sub-total* 5,894.3; *Less* Imputed bank service charges 407.7; Taxes and duties on imports 228.7; *GDP in purchasers' values* 5,715.3.

Balance of Payments (B $ million, 2009): Exports of goods f.o.b. 21; Imports of goods f.o.b. –1,067; *Trade Balance* –1,046; Receipts from services and income 3,028; Payments on services and income –1,355; *Balance on goods, services and income* 627; Current transfers (net) –13; *Current balance* 615; Direct investment (net) –88; Portfolio investment (net) –1,691; Other investments (net) 2,203; Reserve assets (net) –18; *Overall balance* 1,021.

EXTERNAL TRADE

Principal Commodities (US $ million, 2009): *Imports:* Food and live animals 122.0; Beverages and tobacco 50.3; Mineral fuels and lubricants 113.1 (Petroleum and petroleum products 110.6); Chemicals and related products 71.9 (Medicinal and pharmaceutical products 30.6); Basic manufactures 133.8; Machinery and transport equipment 195.4; Total (incl. others) 1,028.1. *Exports:* Total 28.7.

Principal Trading Partners (US $ million): *Imports* (2009): Canada 69.6; Caribbean countries 9.7; United Kingdom 46.7; USA 705.5; Total (incl. others) 1,028.1. *Exports* (1995): France 7.5; United Kingdom 3.9; USA 31.3; Total (incl. others) 62.9. *2009:* Total exports 28.7.

Source: partly UN, *International Trade Statistics Yearbook*.

TRANSPORT

Road Traffic (vehicles in use, 2008): Private cars 22,730; Motorcycles 15,089; Buses, taxis and limousines 759; Trucks and tank wagons 4,196; Other 5,797; *Total* 48,571.

Shipping: *Ship Arrivals* (2004): Cruise ships 161; Cargo ships 186; Oil and gas tankers 21. *Merchant Fleet* (registered at 31 December 2009): 155; Total displacement 9,705,967 grt (Source: IHS Fairplay, *World Fleet Statistics*). *International Freight Traffic* ('000 metric tons, 1990): Goods loaded 130; Goods unloaded 470 (Source: UN, *Monthly Bulletin of Statistics*).

Civil Aviation (2008): Aircraft arrivals 15,347; Passengers 442,821; Air cargo 4,766,331 kg; Air mail 159,718 kg.

TOURISM

Visitor Arrivals: 550,021 (arrivals by air 263,613, cruise ship passengers 286,408) in 2008; 554,394 (arrivals by air 235,866, cruise ship passengers 318,528) in 2009; 580,193 (arrivals by air 232,262, cruise ship passengers 347,931) in 2010.

Tourism Receipts (US $ million, incl. passenger transport): 513.2 in 2007; 401.8 in 2008; 331.3 in 2009.

COMMUNICATIONS MEDIA

Radio Receivers (1997): 82,000 in use.
Television Receivers (1999): 70,000 in use.
Telephones (2009): 57,700 main lines in use.
Mobile Cellular Telephones (2009): 85,000 subscribers.
Personal Computers: 14,250 (225 per 1,000 persons) in 2004.
Internet Users (2009): 54,000.
Broadband Subscribers (2009): 40,000.

Daily Newspapers (2004): 1 (estimated circulation 16,708).
Non-daily Newspapers (2004): 2 (estimated circulation 22,650).

Sources: mainly UNESCO, *Statistical Yearbook*; UN, *Statistical Yearbook*; International Telecommunication Union.

EDUCATION

Pre-primary (1999, unless otherwise indicated): 12 schools (2006); 191 teachers; 429 pupils.

Primary: 17 (and 5 middle) schools (2006); 608 teachers (2009/10); 4,473 pupils (2009/10) (Source: partly UNESCO Institute for Statistics).

Senior: 18 schools (1999); 825 teachers (2009/10); 4,418 pupils (2009/10)*.

Higher: 1 institution (2002); 83 teachers (2008/09); 1,366 students (2008/09).

* Including 7 private schools.

2004: Local student enrolment 10,594 (government schools including pre-school 6,370, private schools excluding pre-school 3,512, Bermuda College 712); Teachers 1,310.

Pupil-teacher Ratio (primary education, UNESCO estimate): 8.3 in 2005/06. Source: UNESCO Institute for Statistics.

Adult Literacy Rate (UNESCO estimates): 99% (males 98%; females 99%) in 1998 (Source: UNESCO, *Statistical Yearbook*).

Directory

The Government

HEAD OF STATE

Queen: HM Queen ELIZABETH II.
Governor and Commander-in-Chief: Sir RICHARD HUGH GOZNEY (took office 12 December 2007).
Deputy Governor: DAVID ARKLEY.

CABINET
(May 2011)

The Government is formed by the Progressive Labour Party.

Premier and Minister of Finance: PAULA A. COX.
Deputy Premier, Minister of Public Works: DERRICK BURGESS.
Minister of Economy, Trade and Industry: KIM WILSON.
Minister of Health: ZANE DESILVA.
Minister of the Environment, Planning and Infrastructure Strategy: WALTER ROBAN.
Minister of Education: Dame JENNIFER SMITH.
Minister of National Security: WAYNE PERINCHIEF.
Minister of Business Development and Tourism: PATRICE MINORS.
Minister of Youth, Families, Sports and Community Development: GLENN BLAKENEY.
Minister of Public Information Services: NELETHA BUTTERFIELD.
Minister of Transport: TERRY LISTER.
Attorney-General and Minister of Justice: MICHAEL SCOTT.
Minister without Portfolio: MICHAEL WEEKS.

MINISTRIES

Office of the Governor: Government House, 11 Langton Hill, Pembroke HM 13; tel. 292-3600; fax 292-6831; e-mail executiveofficer@gov.bm; internet www.gov.bm.

Office of the Premier: Cabinet Office, Cabinet Bldg, 105 Front St, Hamilton HM 12; tel. 292-5501; fax 292-0304; e-mail premier@gov.bm; internet www.gov.bm.

Ministry of Business Development and Tourism: Global House, 43 Church St, Hamilton HM 12; tel. 295-3130; fax 295-1013; e-mail wgriffith@gov.bm; internet www.bermudatourism.com.

Ministry of Economy, Trade and Industry: Hamilton.

Ministry of Education: Dundonald Pl., 14 Dundonald St, POB HM 1185, Hamilton HM EX; tel. 278-3300; fax 278-3348; e-mail reve@gov.bm; internet www.moed.bm.

Ministry of the Environment, Planning and Infrastructure Strategy: Dame Lois Browne-Evans Bldg, 5th Floor, 58 Court St, Hamilton HM 12; tel. 297-7590; fax 292-2349; e-mail aftodd@gov.bm.

UNITED KINGDOM OVERSEAS TERRITORIES
Bermuda

Ministry of Finance: Government Administration Bldg, 30 Parliament St, Hamilton HM 12; tel. 295-5151; fax 295-5727.

Ministry of Health: Continental Bldg, 25 Church St, Hamilton HM 12; tel. 278-4900; fax 292-2622; e-mail wjones@gov.bm; internet www.health.gov.bm.

Ministry of Justice and Attorney-General's Chambers: Penthouse Floor, Global House, 43 Church St, Hamilton HM 12; tel. 292-2463; fax 292-3608; e-mail agc@gov.bm.

Ministry of National Security: Government Administration Bldg, 1st Floor, 30 Parliament St, POB HM 1364, Hamilton HM 12; tel. 297-7819; fax 295-4780; e-mail mtelemaque@gov.bm.

Ministry of Public Information Services: Hamilton.

Ministry of Public Works: General Post Office Bldg, 56 Church St, Hamilton HM 12; tel. 297-7699; fax 295-0170; e-mail nfox@bdagov.bm.

Ministry of Transport: Global House, 43 Church St, Hamilton HM12; tel. 295-3130; fax 295-1013; e-mail clwhitter@gov.bm.

Ministry of Youth, Families, Sports and Community Development: F. B. Perry Bldg, 40 Church St, Hamilton; tel. 295-0855; fax 295-6292; e-mail info@youthandsport.bm; internet www.youthandsport.bm.

Legislature

SENATE

President: CAROLANNE MARIE BASSETT.

Vice-President: Dr IDWAL WYN (WALWYN) HUGHES.

There are 11 nominated members.

HOUSE OF ASSEMBLY

Speaker: STANLEY W. LOWE.

Deputy Speaker: WAYNE N. M. PERINCHIEF.

Clerk to the Legislature: SHERNETTE WOLFE; tel. 292-7408; fax 292-2006; e-mail smwolffe@gov.bm.

General Election, 18 December 2007

Party	% of votes	Seats
Progressive Labour Party	52.5	22
United Bermuda Party	47.3	14
Total (incl. others)	100.0	36

Political Organizations

Bermuda Democratic Alliance (BDA): Hamilton; e-mail info@thealliance.bm; internet www.thealliance.bm; f. 2009 by fmr mems of the United Bermuda Party; Leader CRAIG CANNONIER; Chair. MICHAEL FAHY; Sec. TONI DANIELS.

Progressive Labour Party (PLP): Alaska Hall, 16 Court St, POB 1367, Hamilton HM 17; tel. 292-2264; fax 295-7890; e-mail info@plp.bm; internet www.plp.bm; f. 1963; advocates the 'Bermudianization' of the economy, more equitable taxation, a more developed system of welfare and preparation for independence; Leader PAULA A. COX; Chair. ANTHONY SANTUCCI; Sec.-Gen. JAMAINE SMITH.

United Bermuda Party (UBP): Central Office, 3rd Floor, Bermudiana Arcade, 27 Queen St, Hamilton HM 11; tel. 295-0729; fax 292-7195; e-mail info@ubp.bm; internet www.ubp.bm; f. 1964; policy of participatory democracy, supporting system of free enterprise; Leader KIM SWAN; Chair. JEANNE ATHERDEN; Sec. JANET BRIDGEWATER.

Judicial System

Chief Justice: RICHARD GROUND.

President of the Court of Appeal: EDWARD ZACCA.

Registrar of Supreme Court: CHARLENE A. SCOTT.

Director of Public Prosecutions: RORY FIELD.

The Court of Appeal was established in 1964, with powers and jurisdiction of equivalent courts in other parts of the Commonwealth. The Supreme Court has jurisdiction over all serious criminal matters and has unlimited civil jurisdiction. The Court also hears civil and criminal appeals from the Magistrates' Courts. The three Magistrates' Courts have jurisdiction over all petty offences, and have a limited civil jurisdiction.

Religion

CHRISTIANITY

The Anglican Communion

According to the latest available census figures (2000), some 23% of the population are Anglicans. The Anglican Church of Bermuda consists of a single, extra-provincial diocese, directly under the metropolitan jurisdiction of the Archbishop of Canterbury, the Primate of All England.

Bishop of Bermuda: Rt Rev. PATRICK WHITE, Bishop's Lodge, 18 Ferrar's Lane, Pembroke HM 08, POB HM 769, Hamilton HM CX; tel. 292-6987; fax 292-5421; internet www.anglican.bm.

The Roman Catholic Church

According to the latest available census figures (2000), some 15% of the population are Roman Catholics. Bermuda forms a single diocese, suffragan to the archdiocese of Kingston in Jamaica. The Bishop participates in the Antilles Episcopal Conference (currently based in Port of Spain, Trinidad and Tobago).

Bishop of Hamilton in Bermuda: ROBERT JOSEPH KURTZ, 2 Astwood Rd, POB HM 1191, Hamilton HM EX; tel. 232-4414; fax 232-4447; e-mail rjkurtz@northrock.bm.

Protestant Churches

According to the 2000 census, 11% of the population are African Methodist Episcopalians, 7% are Seventh-day Adventists, 4% are Pentecostalists and 4% are Wesleyan Methodists. The Presbyterian Church, the Church of God, the Salvation Army, the Brethren Church and the Baptist Church are also active in Bermuda.

Baptist Church: Emmanuel Baptist Church, 35 Dundonald St, Hamilton HM 10; tel. 295-6555; fax 296-4491; Pastor RONALD K. SMITH.

Wesley Methodist Church: 41 Church St, Hamilton HM 12; tel. 292-0418; fax 295-9460; e-mail info@wesley.bm; internet www.wesley.bm; Rev. CALVIN STONE.

The Press

Bermuda Magazine: POB HM 283, Hamilton HM HX; tel. 295-0695; fax 295-8616; e-mail cbarclay@ibl.bm; f. 1990; quarterly; Editor-in-Chief CHARLES BARCLAY.

The Bermuda Sun: 19 Elliott St, POB HM 1241, Hamilton HM FX; tel. 295-3902; fax 292-5597; e-mail feedback@bermudasun.bm; internet www.bermudasun.bm; f. 1964; 2 a week; official govt gazette; Publr RANDY FRENCH; Editor TONY MCWILLIAM; circ. 12,500.

The Bermudian: POB HM 283, Hamilton HM AX; tel. 232-7041; fax 232-7042; e-mail info@thebermudian.com; internet www.thebermudian.com; f. 1930; monthly; pictorial and lifestyle magazine; Editor TINA STEVENSON; circ. 7,500.

Bermuda Business Online: POB HM 283, Hamilton HM AX; tel. 232-7041; fax 232-7042; e-mail info@thebermudian.com; internet www.bermudianbusiness.com; f. 1996; publ. by The Bermudian Publishing Co Ltd; Publr TINA STEVENSON; circ. 2,500.

Preview Bermuda: 19 Elliott St, POB HM 3273, Hamilton HM PX; tel. 292-4155; fax 292-4156; e-mail info@previewbermuda.com; internet www.previewbermuda.com; monthly magazine; caters to tourists and visitors to Bermuda; Publr JACKIE STEVENSON; circ. 15,000 per month.

The Royal Gazette: 2 Par-la-Ville Rd, POB HM 1025, Hamilton HM DX; tel. 295-5881; fax 292-2498; e-mail letters@royalgazette.bm; internet www.theroyalgazette.com; f. 1828; morning daily; incorporates *The Colonist* and *Daily News* (f. 1866); Editor WILLIAM J. ZUILL; Man. Dir KEITH JENSEN; circ. 17,500.

TV Week: 2 Par-la-Ville Rd, Hamilton HM 08; tel. 295-5881.

The Worker's Voice: 49 Union Sq., Hamilton HM 12; tel. 292-0044; fax 295-7992; e-mail biu@ibl.bm; fortnightly; organ of the Bermuda Industrial Union; Editor-in-Chief CALVIN SMITH.

Publishers

Bermudian Publishing Co Ltd: POB HM 283, Hamilton HM AX; tel. 232-7041; fax 232-7042; e-mail info@thebermudian.com; internet www.thebermudian.com; social sciences, sociology, sports; Editor TINA STEVENSON.

MediaHouse Ltd: 19 Elliot St, Hamilton HM 10; tel. 295-1944; e-mail rfrench@mediahouse.com; internet www.mediahouse.com; f. 1959 as Island Press; rebranded as above in 2005; newspapers, magazines, directories; CEO RANDY FRENCH.

UNITED KINGDOM OVERSEAS TERRITORIES — Bermuda

Broadcasting and Communications

TELECOMMUNICATIONS

Bermuda Digital Communications/CellularOne: 22 Reid St, Hamilton HM 11; tel. 296-4010; fax 296-4020; e-mail info@cellularone.bm; internet www.cellularone.bm; f. 1998; mobile cellular telephone operator; CEO KURT EVE.

Bermuda Telephone Co (BTC): 30 Victoria St, POB 1021, Hamilton HM DX; tel. 295-1001; fax 295-1192; e-mail customersupport@btc.bm; internet www.btc.bm; f. 1987; Pres. and CEO FRANCIS R. MUSSENDEN.

Cable & Wireless (Bermuda) Ltd: 1 Middle Rd, Smith's FL 03, POB HM 151, Hamilton HM AX; tel. 497-7000; fax 297-7159; e-mail helpdesk@bda.cwplc.com; internet www.cw.com/bermuda; new fibre-optic submarine cable, Gemini Bermuda, replaced satellite dish in 2007 as facilitator of Cable & Wireless' global communications services; acquired by the Bragg Group, Canada, in 2011; CEO ANN PETLEY-JONES.

Digicel Bermuda: Washington Mall, 22 Church St, Phase II, POB 896, Hamilton HM 11; tel. 500-5000; fax 295-3235; e-mail info.bermuda@digicelgroup.com; internet www.digicelbermuda.com; f. 2005; CEO (Bermuda) WAYNE MICHAEL CAINES.

TeleBermuda International Ltd (TBI): Victoria Pl., 1st Floor, 31 Victoria St, POB HM 3043, Hamilton HM 10; POB HM 3043, Hamilton HM NX; tel. 296-9000; fax 296-9010; e-mail business@telebermuda.com; internet www.telebermuda.com; f. 1997; a division of GlobeNet Communications, provides an international voice and data service; owns a fibre-optic network connecting Bermuda, Cayman Islands and the USA; Pres. and COO GREGORY SWAN.

BROADCASTING
Radio

Bermuda Broadcasting Co: POB HM 452, Hamilton HM BX; tel. 295-2828; fax 295-4282; e-mail zbmzfb@bermudabroadcasting.com; f. 1982 as merger of ZBM (f. 1943) and ZFB (f. 1962); operates 4 radio stations; Man. Dir ULRIC P. (RICK) RICHARDSON; Comptroller MALCOLM R. FLETCHER.

DeFontes Broadcasting Co Ltd (VSB): 94 Reid St, POB HM 1450, Hamilton HM FX; tel. 292-0050; fax 295-1658; e-mail news@vsbbermuda.com; internet www.vsbbermuda.com; f. 1981 as St George's Broadcasting Co; commercial; 4 radio stations; Pres. KENNETH DEFONTES; Station Man. MIKE BISHOP.

Television

Bermuda Broadcasting Co: see Radio; operates 2 TV stations (Channels 7 and 9).

Bermuda Cablevision Ltd: 19 Laffan St, POB 1642, Hamilton HM GX; tel. 292-5544; fax 295-3023; e-mail info@cablevision.bm; internet www.cablevision.bm; f. 1988; 180 channels; Pres. DAVID LINES; Gen. Man. TERRY ROBERSON.

DeFontes Broadcasting Co Ltd (VSB): see Radio; operates 1 TV station.

Finance

(cap. = capital; res = reserves; dep. = deposits; m. = million; brs = branches; amounts in Bermuda dollars)

BANKING
Central Bank

Bermuda Monetary Authority: BMA House, 43 Victoria St, Hamilton HM 12; tel. 295-5278; fax 292-7471; e-mail info@bma.bm; internet www.bma.bm; f. 1969; central issuing and monetary authority; cap. 20.0m., res 22.5m., total assets 188.1m. (Dec. 2008); Chair. ALAN COSSAR; CEO JEREMY COX.

Commercial Banks

Bank of N. T. Butterfield & Son Ltd: 65 Front St, POB HM 195, Hamilton HM 12; tel. 298-4691; fax 292-4365; e-mail contact@bntb.bm; internet www.bm.butterfieldgroup.com; f. 1858; inc 1904; cap. 98.4m., res 455.0m., dep. 9,801.2m. (Dec. 2008); Chair. ROBERT MULDERIG; Pres. and CEO BRADFORD KOPP; 4 brs.

Bermuda Commercial Bank Ltd: Bermuda Commercial Bank Bldg, 19 Par-la-Ville Rd, POB 1748, Hamilton HM GX; tel. 295-5678; fax 295-8091; e-mail enquiries@bcb.bm; internet www.bermuda-bcb.com; f. 1969; cap. 13.8m., res 18.2m., dep. 407.6m. (Sept. 2008); COO HORST E. FINKBEINER, II; Chief Financial Officer GREG REID.

HSBC Bank Bermuda Ltd: 6 Front St, POB HM 1020, Hamilton HM 11; tel. 295-4000; fax 295-7093; e-mail customer.care@hsbc.bm; internet www.hsbc.bm; f. 1889; fmrly Bank of Bermuda Ltd; 100% acquired by HSBC Asia Holdings BV (Netherlands) in Feb. 2004; name changed as above in May 2010; cap. 30.0m., res 309.0m., dep. 8,134.7m. (Dec. 2008); Chair. JOHN D. CAMPBELL; CEO PHILIP BUTTERFIELD; 6 brs.

STOCK EXCHANGE

Bermuda Stock Exchange: 3rd Floor, Washington Mall, Church St, POB 1369, Hamilton HM FX; tel. 292-7212; fax 292-7619; e-mail info@bsx.com; internet www.bsx.com; f. 1971; 707 listed equities, funds, debt issues and depositary programmes; Chair. DAVID BROWN; Pres. and CEO GREG WOJCIECHOWSKI.

INSURANCE

Bermuda had a total of some 1,600 registered insurance companies in 2002, the majority of which are subsidiaries of foreign insurance companies, or owned by foreign industrial or financial concerns. Many of them have offices on the island.

Bermuda Insurance Market Information Office: Cedarpark Centre, 48 Cedar Ave, POB HM 2911, Hamilton HM LX; tel. 292-9829; fax 295-3532; e-mail biminfo@bii.bm; internet www.bermuda-insurance.org; division of the Bermuda Insurance Development Council; Dir DAVID FOX.

Major Companies

ACE Bermuda: ACE Global HQ, 17 Woodbourne Ave, POB HM 1015, Hamilton HM DX; tel. 295-5200; fax 298-9620; e-mail info@acebermuda.com; internet www.acebermuda.com; total revenue $14,154m. (Dec. 2007); Pres. and CEO G. REES FLETCHER; Chair. EVAN G. GREENBERG; Regional Exec. ALLISON TOWLSON.

Argus Insurance Co Ltd: Argus Insurance Bldg, 14 Wesley St, POB HM 1064, Hamilton HM EX; tel. 295-2021; fax 292-6763; e-mail insurance@argus.bm; internet www.argus.bm; Pres. and CEO GERALD D. E. SIMONS; Chair. SHEILA E. NICOLL.

Bermuda Insurance Development Council (IDC): c/o Bermuda Insurance Institute, The Cedar Parkade Bldg, 48 Cedar Ave, POB HM 2911, Hamilton HM LX; tel. 292-9829; fax 296-3840; e-mail fox@bii.bm; internet www.bermuda-insurance.org; sub-cttee of the Insurance Advisory Council; Chair. ROGER GILLETT.

Bermuda Insurance Management Association (BIMA): POB HM 2993, Hamilton HM HX; tel. 279-7925; fax 2962-8846; e-mail peter.willitts@libertybermuda.com; f. 1978; manages over 1,200 insurance and reinsurance cos; liaises with govt and other financial orgs with regard to insurance industry issues; Pres. PETER WILLITTS.

Paumanock Insurance Co Ltd: Windsor Place, 3rd Floor, 18 Queen St, Hamilton; tel. 292-2404; fax 292-2648.

XL Insurance Co Ltd: XL House, 1 Bermudiana Rd, Hamilton HM 08; tel. 292-8515; fax 292-5280; e-mail contact.xli@xlgroup.com; internet www.xlinsurance.com; CEO DAVID B. DUCLOS.

Trade and Industry

GOVERNMENT AGENCY

Bermuda Registrar of Companies: Government Administration Bldg, 30 Parliament St, Hamilton HM HX; tel. 294-9244; fax 292-6640; e-mail jfsmith@gov.bm; internet www.roc.gov.bm; Registrar of Companies STEPHEN LOWE.

DEVELOPMENT ORGANIZATION

Bermuda Small Business Development Corpn (BSBDC): Sofia House, 48 Church St, POB HM 637, Hamilton HM CX; tel. 292-5570; fax 295-1600; e-mail bdasmallbusiness@gov.bm; internet www.bsbdc.bm; f. 1980; funded jtly by the Govt and private banks; guarantees loans to small businesses; responsible for establishing economic empowerment zones; Gen. Man. MICHELLE KHALDUN.

CHAMBER OF COMMERCE

Bermuda Chamber of Commerce: 1 Point Pleasant Rd, POB HM 655, Hamilton HM CX; tel. 295-4201; fax 292-5779; e-mail info@bermudacommerce.com; internet www.bermudacommerce.com; f. 1907; Pres. STEPHEN W. G. TODD; Exec. Dir DIANE GORDON; 750 mems.

INDUSTRIAL AND TRADE ASSOCIATION

Bermuda International Business Association (BIBA): The Windsor Place, 1st Floor, 22 Queen St, Hamilton HM 12; tel. 292-0632; fax 292-1797; e-mail info@biba.org; internet www.biba.org; Chair. VICKI COELHO; CEO CHERYL PACKWOOD.

EMPLOYERS' ASSOCIATIONS

Bermuda Employers' Council: 4 Park Rd, Hamilton HM 11; tel. 295-5070; fax 295-1966; e-mail mlaw@bec.bm; internet www.bec.bm;

f. 1960; advisory body on employment and labour relations; Pres. WILLIAM DESILVA; Exec. Dir MARTIN LAW; 420 mems.

Construction Association of Bermuda: POB HM 238, Hamilton HM AX; tel. 292-0633; fax 292-0564; e-mail caob@logic.bm; internet www.constructionbermuda.com; f. 1968; Pres. J. ANDREW PEREIRA; 90 mems.

Hotel Employers of Bermuda: c/o Bermuda Hotel Asscn, 'Carmel', 61 King St, Hamilton HM 19; tel. 295-2127; fax 292-6671; e-mail jharvey@bdahotels.bm; f. 1968; Pres. JONATHAN CRELLIN; CEO JOHN HARVEY; 8 mems.

UTILITY

BELCO Holdings Ltd: 27 Serpentine Rd, POB HM 1026, Hamilton HM DX; tel. 295-5111; fax 292-8975; e-mail info@belco.bhl.bm; internet www.belcoholdings.bm; f. 1906; holding co for Bermuda Electric Light Co Ltd, and Bermuda Gas and Utility Co Ltd; Chair. J. MICHAEL COLLIER; Pres. and CEO A. L. VINCENT INGHAM.

TRADE UNIONS

In 2007 trade union membership was estimated at approximately 9,140. There are nine registered trade unions, eight of which profess membership of the Bermuda Trades Union Congress.

Bermuda Industrial Union: 49 Union Sq., Hamilton HM 12; tel. 292-0044; fax 295-7992; e-mail biu@biu.bm; f. 1946; Pres. CHRIS FURBERT; Gen. Sec. HELENA BURGESS; 5,202 mems.

Bermuda Trades Union Congress (BTUC): POB 2080, Hamilton HM HX; tel. 292-6515; fax 292-0697; e-mail mcharles@ibl.bm; Pres. ANTHONY WOLFFE; Gen. Sec. MICHAEL CHARLES; principal mems of the BTUC include:

Bermuda Federation of Musicians and Variety Artists: Reid St, POB HM 6, Hamilton HM AX; tel. 291-0138; Sec.-Gen. LLOYD H. L. SIMMONS; 318 mems.

Bermuda Public Services Union: POB HM 763, Hamilton HM CX; tel. 292-6985; fax 292-1149; e-mail osimmons@bpsu.bm; internet www.bpsu.bm; re-formed 1961; Pres. ARMELL L. THOMAS; Gen. Sec. EDWARD G. BALL, Jr; c. 3,500 mems.

Bermuda Union of Teachers: 72 Church St, POB HM 726, Hamilton HM CX; tel. 292-6515; fax 292-0697; e-mail butunion@ibl.bm; internet www.bermudaunionofteachers.org; f. 1919; Pres. KEISHA DOUGLAS; Gen. Sec. MICHAEL A. CHARLES; 700 mems.

Transport

ROADS

There are some 225 km (140 miles) of public highways and 222 km of private roads, with almost 6 km reserved for cyclists and pedestrians. Each household is permitted only one passenger vehicle, and visitors may only hire mopeds, to limit traffic congestion.

SHIPPING

The chief port of Bermuda is Hamilton, followed by St George's and King's Wharf. All three are used by freight and cruise ships. There is also a 'free' port, Freeport, on Ireland Island. In 2000 it was proposed to enlarge Hamilton docks in order to accommodate larger cruise ships. There remained, however, fears that such an enlargement would place excessive strain on the island's environment and infrastructure. Bermuda is a 'free-flag' nation, and at December 2009 the shipping register comprised 155 vessels, totalling 9,705,967 grt.

Department of Marine and Ports Services: POB HM 180, Hamilton HM AX; tel. 295-6575; fax 295-5523; e-mail marineports@bolagov.bm; internet www.marineandports.bm; Dir of Marine and Ports Services FRANCIS RICHARDSON; Harbour Master DAVID SIMMONS.

Department of Maritime Administration: Magnolia Pl., 2nd Floor, 45 Victoria St, POB HM 1628, Hamilton HM GX; tel. 295-7251; fax 295-3718; e-mail maradros@gov.bm; Chief Surveyor (vacant); Registrar of Shipping ANGELIQUE BURGESS.

Principal Shipping Companies

B & H Ocean Carriers Ltd: Par-la-Ville Pl., 3rd Floor, 14 Par-la-Ville Rd, POB HM 2257, Hamilton HM JX; tel. 295-6875; fax 295-6796; e-mail info@bhcousa.com; internet www.bhocean.com; f. 1988; Chair. MICHAEL S. HUDNER.

Benor Tankers Ltd: Cedar House, 41 Cedar Ave, Hamilton HM 12; Pres. CARL-ERIK HAAVALDSEN; Chair. HARRY RUTTEN.

Bermuda Forwarders Ltd: 2 Mill Creek Park, POB HM 511, Hamilton HM CX; tel. 292-4600; fax 292-1859; e-mail info@bermudaforwarders.com; internet www.bermudaforwarders.com; international import and export handlers; Pres. TOBY KEMPE.

Bernhard Schulte Shipmanagement (Bermuda) Ltd Partnership: Richmond House, 12 Par-la-Ville Rd, POB HM 2089, Hamilton HM HX; tel. 295-0614; fax 292-1549; e-mail management@amlp.bm; internet www.bs-shipmanagement.com; f. 2008 by the merger of Hanseatic Shipping, Dorchester Atlantic Marine, Eurasia Group and Vorsetzen Bereederungs- und Schiffahrtskontor; owned by the Schulte Group; CEO ANDREAS DROUSSIOTIS; Man. Dir JENS ALERS.

BEST Shipping: 6 Addendum Lane South, POB HM 335, Hamilton HM BX; tel. 292-8080; fax 295-1713; e-mail dsousa@best.bm; internet www.best.bm; f. 1987 as Bermuda Export Sea Transfer Ltd; sea and air freight services; Pres. and Man. Dir DAVID SOUSA.

Container Ship Management Ltd: 14 Par-la-Ville Rd, POB HM 2266, Hamilton HM JX; tel. 295-1624; fax 295-3781; e-mail csm@csm.bm; internet www.bcl.bm; f. 1980; privately owned; Pres. and CEO GEOFFREY FRITH.

Gearbulk Holding Ltd: Par-la-Ville Pl., 14 Par-la-Ville Rd, POB HM 2257, Hamilton HM JX; tel. 295-2184; fax 295-2234; internet www.gearbulk.com; f. 1968; Pres. ARTHUR E. M. JONES.

Golden Ocean Group Ltd: Par-la-Ville Pl., 14 Par-la-Ville Rd, POB HM 1593, Hamilton HM 08; tel. 295-6935; fax 295-3494; e-mail tor@frontmgt.no; internet www.goldenocean.no; Chair. and Pres. JOHN FREDRIKSON.

Meyer Shipping: Waverley Bldg, 35 Church St, Hamilton HM 12; tel. 296-9798; fax 295-4556; e-mail shipping@meyer.bm; internet www.meyer.bm; f. 1867; subsidiary of the Meyer Group of Companies; CEO J. HENRY HAYWARD.

Norwegian Cruise Line: 3rd Floor, Reid House, Church St, POB 1564, Hamilton; internet www.ncl.com; Chair. EINAR KLOSTER.

Shell Bermuda (Overseas) Ltd: Shell House, Ferry Reach, POB 2, St George's 1.

Unicool Ltd: POB HM 1179, Hamilton HM EX; tel. 295-2244; fax 292-8666; Pres. MATS JANSSON.

Worldwide Shipping Ltd: 22 Church St, Suite 412, POB HM 1862, Hamilton HM 11; tel. 295-3770; fax 295-3801.

CIVIL AVIATION

The former US Naval Air Station (the only airfield) was returned to the Government of Bermuda in September 1995, following the closure of the base and the withdrawal of US forces from the islands. Bermuda does not have its own airline. The L. F. Wade International Airport is served by Air Canada, American Airlines, British Airways, Continental Airlines, Delta Airlines, JetBlue, USA3000 and US Airways.

Department of Civil Aviation: Channel House, Suite 2, 12 Longfield Rd, Southside, St. David's DD 03, POB GE 218, St George's GE BX; tel. 293-1640; fax 293-2417; e-mail info@dca.gov.bm; internet www.dca.gov.bm; responsible for all civil aviation matters; Dir of Civil Aviation THOMAS DUNSTAN.

L.F. Wade International Airport: 3 Cahow Way, St George's GE CX; tel. 293-2470; e-mail dao@gov.bm; internet www.bermudaairport.aero; fmrly Bermuda International Airport, adopted present name 2007; Gen. Man. AARON ADDERLEY.

Tourism

Tourism is the principal industry of Bermuda and is government-sponsored. The great attractions of the islands are the climate, scenery, and facilities for outdoor entertainment of all types. In 2010 a total of 580,193 tourists (including 347,931 cruise ship passengers) visited Bermuda. In 2009 the industry earned an estimated US $331m. In 2006 there were 56 licensed hotels, 2,824 rooms and 5,698 beds.

Bermuda Department of Tourism: Global House, 43 Church St, Hamilton; tel. 292-0023; fax 292-7537; e-mail webmaster@bermudatourism.com; internet www.bermudatourism.com; Dir of Tourism BILLY GRIFFITH.

Bermuda Hotel Association: 'Carmel', 61 King St, Hamilton HM 19; tel. 295-2127; fax 292-6671; e-mail jharvey@bdahotels.bm; internet www.experiencebermuda.com; Pres. FRANK STOCEK; Exec. Dir JOHN HARVEY; 37 mem. hotels.

Defence

The local defence force is the Bermuda Regiment, with a strength of some 630 men and women in 1999. The Regiment employs selective conscription. According to the 2011/12 budget statement, the Government of Bermuda allocated B $8.6m. of its current account expenditure to defence and $60.5m. to the police force for the fiscal year 2010/11. It was expected to provide $8.3m. and $65.7m. to those departments, respectively, in 2011/12.

UNITED KINGDOM OVERSEAS TERRITORIES

Education

There is free compulsory education in government schools between the ages of five and 16 years, and a number of scholarships are awarded for higher education and teacher training. There are also seven private secondary schools, which charge fees. In 2005/06 enrolment at primary and secondary level institutions was equivalent to an estimated 92% of children in the relevant age-groups. The Bermuda College accepts students over the age of 16, and is the only post-secondary educational institution. Extramural degree courses are available through Queen's University, Canada, and Indiana and Maryland Universities, USA. A major public education reform programme was scheduled to be implemented in 2010–15.

THE BRITISH ANTARCTIC TERRITORY

The British Antarctic Territory lies within the Antarctic Treaty area (i.e. south of latitude 60° S). The territory, created by an Order in Council which came into force on 3 March 1962, consists of all islands and territories south of latitude 60° S, between longitudes 20° W and 80° W, and includes the South Orkney Islands, the South Shetland Islands, the Antarctic Peninsula and areas south and east of the Weddell Sea. With the island of South Georgia and the South Sandwich Islands (now forming a separate territory, q.v.), this area had been constituted by the United Kingdom as the Falkland Islands Dependencies in 1908. The flag of the British Antarctic Territory (proportions 1 by 2) has a white field bearing the union flag of the United Kingdom in the canton and, in the centre of the fly half of the flag, the arms of the territory, which consists of a white shield with three wavy blue horizontal lines at the top overlapped by a red triangle, apex downwards, bearing a brown and yellow torch with red-bordered yellow flames framed by golden rays, the shield supported by a golden lion and a black and white penguin with a yellow throat, both supporters surmounted by a scroll of yellow and light blue with a red reverse and the red inscription 'Research and Discovery'; above the shield, a helmet of grey, light blue and white supporting a torse, alternately of white and light blue, is depicted below a sailing ship of black flying the British Blue Ensign at the gaff. The territory has its own legal system and postal administration, and is financially self-sufficient owing to revenue derived from income tax and the sale of postage stamps.

Area: Land covers about 1,709,400 sq km (660,003 sq miles).

Population: There is no permanent population, but scientists and support personnel staff the British Antarctic Survey stations. *2005/06:* Summer 200 (Rothera 148, Halley 37, Signy 15); Winter 37.

Commissioner, Head of Overseas Territories Directorate: COLIN ROBERTS, Overseas Territories Directorate, Foreign and Commonwealth Office, King Charles St, London, SW1A 2AH, United Kingdom; tel. (20) 7008-2743; internet www.fco.gov.uk.

Administrator: ROB BOWMAN, Polar Regions Unit, Overseas Territories Directorate, Foreign and Commonwealth Office, King Charles St, London, SW1A 2AH, United Kingdom; tel. (20) 7008-2617; fax (20) 7008-2086; e-mail polarregions@fco.gov.uk.

British Antarctic Survey: High Cross, Madingley Rd, Cambridge, CB3 0ET, United Kingdom; tel. (1223) 221400; fax (1223) 362616; e-mail basweb@bas.ac.uk; internet www.antarctica.ac.uk; f. 1962 to replace Falkland Islands Dependencies Survey; responsible for almost all British scientific activities in Antarctica; operates two ice-strengthened ocean-going vessels (RRS *Ernest Shackleton* and RRS *James Clark Ross*), four de Havilland Twin Otter and one Dash-7 aircraft; Total Budget £47.1m. in 2009/10; Dir Prof. NICHOLAS OWENS.

RESEARCH STATIONS

	Latitude	Longitude
Halley	75° 35' S	26° 34' W
King Edward Point	54° 17' S	36° 30' W
Rothera	67° 34' S	68° 08' W
Signy (summer only)	60° 43' S	45° 36' W

THE BRITISH INDIAN OCEAN TERRITORY (BIOT)

The British Indian Ocean Territory (BIOT) was formed in November 1965, through the amalgamation of the former Seychelles islands of Aldabra, Desroches and Farquhar with the Chagos Archipelago, a group of islands 1,930 km north-east of Mauritius, previously administered by the Governor of Mauritius. Aldabra, Desroches and Farquhar were ceded to Seychelles when that country was granted independence in June 1976. Since then BIOT has comprised only the Chagos Archipelago, including the coral atoll Diego Garcia, with a total land area of 60 sq km (23 sq miles).

BIOT was established to meet British and US defence requirements in the Indian Ocean. Following the purchase of the islands by the British Crown in 1967, the coconut plantations (production of copra was previously the principal economic function of the islands) ceased to operate and the inhabitants were offered the choice of resettlement in Mauritius or in Seychelles. The majority (which numbered about 1,200) went to Mauritius, the resettlement taking place during 1969–73, prior to the construction of the military facility. Mauritius subsequently campaigned for the immediate return of the Territory, and received support from the Organization of African Unity (now the African Union) and from India. A protracted dispute with the United Kingdom over compensation for those displaced ended in 1982 when the British Government agreed to an *ex-gratia* payment of £4m. In July 2000 a judicial review of the validity of the Immigration Ordinance of 1971, under which the islanders were removed from BIOT, and which continued to prevent them from resettling in the Territory, was instigated. Meanwhile, in March 1999 it was disclosed that the displaced islanders and their families, then estimated to number up to 4,000, were not to be included in the offer of full British citizenship with the right of abode in the United Kingdom, that was to be extended to residents of other United Kingdom Overseas Territories by legislation pending in the British Parliament.

In November 2000 the British High Court ruled that the Chagos islanders (Ilois) had been illegally evicted from the Chagos Archipelago, and quashed Section 4 of the 1971 Ordinance, which prevented the return of the Ilois to BIOT. During the case it transpired that the British Government had received a subsidy of US $11m. on the purchase of Polaris submarines in the 1960s from the USA, in return for the lease of Diego Garcia for the US military. Furthermore, the Government had apparently termed the Ilois 'contract workers' in order to persuade the UN that the islanders were not an indigenous population with democratic rights. However, memoranda of the Foreign and Commonwealth Office (FCO) revealed government knowledge of some of the Ilois living in the Chagos Archipelago for two generations. The British Secretary of State for Foreign and Commonwealth Affairs declined an appeal, thereby granting the islanders an immediate right to return to BIOT. Despite this, a new ordinance, issued in January 2001, allowed the residents to return to any of the islands in the Archipelago, except Diego Garcia. The British Overseas Territories Act came into effect in May 2002, allowing the displaced islanders to apply for British citizenship. In October 2003 the High Court ruled that although the islanders could claim to have been ill-treated, the British Government had not known at the time that its actions were unlawful and their claims for compensation were dismissed. Many of the islanders subsequently moved to the United Kingdom.

In June 2004 the British Government issued two decrees explicitly stating the country's control of immigration services within the archipelago and banning the Ilois from returning. On 11 May the British High Court ruled that the exclusion of the islanders from their territory was irrational and unlawful. The British Government commenced proceedings to overturn the May ruling at the Court of Appeal in February 2007; however, in May that court confirmed that the residents of the Chagos Archipelago had been unlawfully removed and upheld the displaced islanders' immediate right to return. In November the House of Lords granted the British Government the right to appeal against the Court of Appeal's decision, on the condition that the Chagossians' costs were met by the British Government. The appeal was heard in mid-2008 and in November the House of Lords ruled in favour of the British Government, thus denying the Chagossians the right to return, and citing as its main reason the fact that the United Kingdom would have been obliged to meet the costs of economic, social and educational advancement of the residents. The ruling also stated that fair compensation had been agreed and paid, and that the British Government had no further obligations towards the Chagossians. Having exhausted the appeals process in the United Kingdom, the Chagossians announced that they would take their case to the European Court of Human Rights (ECHR); however, it was estimated that only approximately 700 of the 2,000 deported during the 1960s and 1970s were still alive.

In April 2010 the British Government announced that it had designated the Chagos archipelago a marine protection area (MPA), within which all fishing and other activities were to be prohibited. The conservation area, covering some 544,000 sq km, was to be patrolled by a ship vested with the powers to arrest fleets caught fishing illegally, to impose fines of up to £100,000 and to confiscate boats and fishing equipment. These plans were expected to have an impact on the Chagossians' hearing at the ECHR as the ban on fishing would remove the legal means by which they could sustain their standard of living. In December the Mauritian Government announced that it had taken a case against the United Kingdom to the UN International Tribunal for the Law of the Sea on the grounds that the MPA was not compatible with the UN Convention on the Law of the Sea. Furthermore, the Chagossians also appealed for a judicial review of the decision to create the MPA, although this was not to take place until after the ECHR had delivered its verdict.

A 1966 agreement between the United Kingdom and the USA provided for BIOT to be used by both countries over an initial period of 50 years, with the option of extending this for a further 20 years. The United Kingdom undertook to cede the Chagos Archipelago to Mauritius when it was no longer required for defence purposes. Originally the US military presence was limited to a communications centre on Diego Garcia. In 1972, however, construction of a naval support facility was begun, apparently in response to the expansion of the Soviet maritime presence in the Indian Ocean. Diego Garcia has frequently been used as a base for US aircraft carrying out air strikes on Iraq and Afghanistan. In March–April 2003 the base was used to launch bombing raids on Iraq in the US-led military campaign to oust the regime of Saddam Hussain. In February 2008 the British Secretary of State for the Foreign and Commonwealth Office admitted that, contrary to previous government statements, a number of so-called rendition flights (the transfer of detainees, in particular terrorist suspects, by the US Central Intelligence Agency to third countries where it was possible that they might be subjected to torture during interrogation) had used facilities at Diego Garcia.

In December 2000, following the British High Court's ruling, Mauritius again staked its claim for sovereignty over the Chagos Archipelago. In April 2004 Paul Bérenger, the recently installed Prime Minister of Mauritius, renewed the campaign to reclaim sovereignty after specialists in international law advised him that the decree by which the United Kingdom separated the Chagos Archipelago from Mauritius was illegal. An attempt was made to block the Mauritian Government from pursuing the case at the International Court of Justice on the basis of a long-standing ruling, whereby members of the Commonwealth could not take the United Kingdom to court; in July the ruling was extended to former members of the Commonwealth, in order to prevent Mauritius from circumventing the obstacle by withdrawing from that organization. Mauritius announced that it would pursue the matter at the General Assembly of the UN.

The civil administration of BIOT is the responsibility of a non-resident commissioner in the FCO in London, United Kingdom, represented on Diego Garcia by a Royal Navy commander and a small British naval presence. A chief justice, a senior magistrate and a principal legal adviser (who performs the functions of an attorney-general) are resident in the United Kingdom.

Land Area: about 60 sq km.

Population: There are no permanent inhabitants. In November 2004 there were about 4,000 US and British military personnel and civilian support staff stationed in the Territory.

Currency: The official currency is the pound sterling, but the US dollar is also accepted.

Commissioner: COLIN ROBERTS, Head of Overseas Territories Dept, Foreign and Commonwealth Office, King Charles St, London, SW1A 2AH, United Kingdom; tel. (20) 7008-2890.

Administrator: JOANNE YEADON, Overseas Territories Dept, Foreign and Commonwealth Office, King Charles St, London, SW1A 2AH, United Kingdom; tel. (20) 7008-2890.

Commissioner's Representative: Commdr SIMON C. L. NICHOLSON, RN, Diego Garcia, c/o BFPO Ships.

THE BRITISH VIRGIN ISLANDS

Introductory Survey

LOCATION, CLIMATE, LANGUAGE, RELIGION, FLAG, CAPITAL

The British Virgin Islands consist of more than 60 islands and cays, of which only 16 are inhabited. The islands, most of which are mountainous and of volcanic origin (the only exception of any size is the coralline island of Anegada), lie at the northern end of the Leeward Islands, about 100 km (62 miles) to the east of Puerto Rico and adjoining the United States Virgin Islands. The climate is subtropical but extremes of heat are relieved by the trade winds. The average annual rainfall is 1,000 mm (39 ins). The official language is English. Most of the inhabitants profess Christianity. The flag is the British 'Blue Ensign', with the territory's badge (a green shield, with a white-clad virgin and 12 oil lamps, above a scroll bearing the motto 'vigilate') in the fly. The capital, Road Town, is situated on the island of Tortola.

CONTEMPORARY POLITICAL HISTORY

Historical Context

Previously peopled by Caribs, and named by the navigator Christopher Colombus after St Ursula and her 11,000 fellow-martyrs, the islands were settled by buccaneers and the Dutch, but were finally annexed by the British in 1672. In 1872 they became part of the British colony of the Leeward Islands, which was administered under a federal system. The federation was dissolved in July 1956, but the Governor of the Leeward Islands continued to administer the British Virgin Islands until 1960, when an appointed Administrator (restyled Governor in 1971) assumed direct responsibility. Unlike the other Leeward Islands, the British Virgin Islands did not join the Federation of the West Indies (1958–62), preferring to develop its links with the US Virgin Islands.

Domestic Political Affairs

A new Constitution was introduced in April 1967, when H. Lavity Stoutt became the islands' first Chief Minister. He was later replaced by Willard Wheatley. At an election in September 1975 Stoutt's Virgin Islands Party (VIP) and the United Party (UP) each won three of the seven elective seats on the Legislative Council. Wheatley, sitting as an independent member, held the balance of power and he continued in office, with Stoutt as Deputy Chief Minister.

An amended Constitution took effect in June 1977, giving more extensive internal self-government. In an election in November 1979 independent candidates won five of the nine elective seats on the enlarged Legislative Council, with the VIP winning the remainder. Stoutt secured enough support to be reinstated as Chief Minister. In the November 1983 election the VIP and the UP each secured four seats. The one successful independent candidate, Cyril Romney, became Chief Minister and formed a coalition Government with members of the UP.

In August 1986 the Governor dissolved the Legislative Council six days before a scheduled council debate on a motion of no confidence against Romney (who had allegedly been involved with a company under investigation by the British police and the US Department of Justice's Drug Enforcement Administration). At a general election in the following month the VIP won a majority of seats and Stoutt was appointed Chief Minister. The VIP increased its majority at a general election in 1990.

The principal concern of the Stoutt administration in the early 1990s was the trade in, and increasing local use of, illicit drugs. In late 1990 the Stoutt administration introduced legislation to impose more stringent regulations governing the 'offshore' financial sector, while plans to review immigration policy were under discussion, in an attempt to reduce the number of illegal immigrants entering the territory. Both areas had previously been considered to be insufficiently protected from exploitation by traffickers seeking to introduce illicit drugs into the islands or to divert funds from their sale through the financial sector.

In August 1993 the British Government appointed three commissioners to review the territory's Constitution at the request of the Legislative Council. Proposed changes included the introduction of direct elections for the position of Chief Minister, the enlargement of the Legislative Council and the adoption of a bill of rights. The British Government's decision in 1994 to accept the commission's proposal to enlarge the Legislative Council to 13 seats (by the creation of four seats representing the territory 'at large') was strongly criticized by Stoutt.

At elections to the legislature in February 1995 the VIP won six seats, the UP and the Concerned Citizens' Movement (CCM) each secured two seats and independent candidates won the remaining three seats. One of the successful independents subsequently gave his support to the VIP, thus providing the party with the majority required to form a Government, again headed by Stoutt. In May the Deputy Chief Minister, Ralph O'Neal, was appointed Chief Minister, following Stoutt's sudden death.

Elections to the Legislative Council took place in May 1999. The VIP retained control of the legislature, increasing its representation to seven seats. The recently founded National Democratic Party (NDP) took five seats, while the CCM retained one seat. O'Neal subsequently re-appointed the members of the previous Executive Council.

Relationship with the United Kingdom and financial transparency

In March 1999 the Government of the United Kingdom published draft legislation pertaining to its relationship with its Overseas Dependencies, which were to be renamed United Kingdom Overseas Territories (and had been referred to as such since February 1998). The legislation proposed the extension of British citizenship to the citizens of Overseas Territories, although it also required its Overseas Territories to amend their legislation on human rights and on the regulation of the financial services sector to meet international standards. In July the British Government appointed a consultant, Alan Hoole, a former Governor of Anguilla, to review the Constitution of the British Virgin Islands. In September Hoole proposed several changes to the Constitution, including the introduction of more frequent meetings of the Legislative Council and the removal of the Governor's powers to veto legislation. Under the terms of the proposed changes, the Governor was also to be obliged to consult with the Executive Council before implementing policy in his areas of special responsibility (foreign affairs, the civil service and defence). It was also suggested that members of the Legislative Council and senior civil servants should be obliged to declare their interests. In August the Governor outlined the Government's legislative programme. The main aim of the proposed legislation was to ensure that the regulation of the financial services sector conformed to international standards.

In September 2000 the Legislative Council passed legislation abolishing judicial corporal punishment on the British Virgin Islands, in keeping with the United Kingdom's acceptance of the European Convention of Human Rights.

The Organisation for Economic Co-operation and Development (OECD, see p. 376) announced in April 2002 that the British Virgin Islands had made sufficient commitments to improve the transparency of its tax and regulatory systems to be removed from an updated list of 'unco-operative' tax havens. In the same month, the financial secretary, L. Allen Wheatley, was arrested in connection with the mishandling of government contracts relating to the Beef Island Airport development project, and in May the Government survived a motion of no confidence brought against it in connection with the airport development project. The trial of Wheatley and four other men began in November 2003; four of the five defendants pleaded guilty to approving an airport telecommunications contract based on inflated prices that cost the Government some US $450,000. In January 2004 Wheatley was sentenced to nine months in gaol; in return for the guilty pleas, prosecutors withdrew theft charges, which carried much harsher jail terms. (Wheatley had already been sentenced to five years' imprisonment on separate corruption charges in February 2003.)

In late 2002 the recovering financial sector faced further disruption when the United Kingdom, under pressure from a European Union (EU, see p. 270) investigation into tax evasion, demanded that the British Virgin Islands disclose the identities and account details of Europeans holding private savings accounts on the islands. The British Virgin Islands, along with some other British Overseas Territories facing similar demands, claimed it was being treated unfairly compared with more powerful European countries, such as Switzerland and Luxembourg. In January 2005 the Business Companies Act came into force, which eliminated the distinction between laws governing local and 'offshore' businesses. Further reform to the tax system also took place.

In May 2002 the British Overseas Territories Act, having received royal assent in the United Kingdom in February, came into force and granted British citizenship to the people of its Overseas Territories, including the British Virgin Islands. Under the new law British Virgin Islanders would be able to hold British passports and work in the United Kingdom and anywhere else in the EU.

A commission for constitutional review was appointed in April 2004, which was to consider, *inter alia*, the criteria for qualification for residency status, the reserve powers of the Governor, the duties of the Attorney-General and the introduction of an article relating to human rights into the Constitution. A Constitutional Review Report was released in 2005, based on the commission's findings. Among the suggestions included in the report were the reform of the legal system, and a move towards a cabinet system of government, with the title of Chief Minister changing to Premier. The possibility of renaming the Legislative Council a Parliament was also examined. A first round of negotiations to discuss the proposed constitutional reform, between representatives of the British Government and the Chief Minister, was held in Barbados in March 2006. Negotiations continued throughout that year. A final forum, conducted in the United Kingdom in February 2007, sought to examine the provisions of a draft constitution document prepared by the Constitutional Review Commission and conclude debate upon the proposed new statutes. The British Foreign and Commonwealth Office endorsed the successful completion of negotiations, announcing the formulation of a new constitution for the territory that would simultaneously afford greater autonomy to the country while maintaining harmonious relations with the United Kingdom; Chief Minister Smith expressed his satisfaction that '95 per cent' of the Review Commission's stated objectives for constitutional reform had been achieved.

The principal features of the proposed constitution included the institution of a cabinet system of government (whereby the Executive Council would be renamed 'the Cabinet'), within which the Premier (formerly Chief Minister) would command influence in the determination of the cabinet agenda, previously the subject of the Governor's sole arbitration, and a Cabinet Secretary would be appointed to set the Cabinet's agenda; the establishment of a National Security Council—to be comprised of the Governor, the Premier, a named government minister, the Attorney-General and the Commissioner of Police—conferring matters of internal security and policing of the islands from the sole remit of the British Government to that of the British Virgin Islands also, and upon whose recommendations the Governor would be obliged to act; the institution of an Office for Public Prosecutions; a reduction in the Governor's powers of veto; the inclusion of a Fundamental Rights Chapter to ensure the promotion and protection of citizens' human rights and freedoms; and provision for the creation of a sixth government ministry to accommodate the requirements of the territory's expanding population. The United Kingdom would retain some residual authority in order to regulate the development of the British Virgin Islands, embracing issues such as the observation of international standards in relation to the burgeoning financial services sector and the islands' natural disaster preparedness. After being approved by the United Kingdom Privy Council on 14 June, the Virgin Islands Constitutional Order 2007 became effective on 15 June, subsequent to the dissolution of the Legislative Council.

The NDP in power

A general election was held on 16 June 2003. The NDP secured eight seats compared with the VIP's five after a campaign that was dominated by the issues of alleged corruption, management of public sector capital projects, and relations with the United Kingdom. Orlando Smith became the new Chief Minister.

Proposals for the liberalization of the telecommunications sector featured in parliamentary discussion during 2006 and, in October, some tangible progress was made towards ending the 'three-way monopoly' within the territory's communications and broadcasting market, with the establishment of a Telecommunications Regulatory Commission (TRC). The authority, a statutory body affiliated to the Ministry of Communications and Works, was instituted under the Telecommunications Act 2006, which was effected in October. It was proposed that three or four operators would be awarded licences for the provision of a comprehensive range of telecommunications services and, in March 2007, the sole mobile provider in the British Virgin Islands, Cable & Wireless, signed a memorandum of understanding with CCT Global Communications (operating locally as CCT Boatphone). In April the Government announced that it was inviting licence applications—permitting operation in all sectors of the telecommunications market for 15 years—from only the three current providers. After its licence application was rejected, Digicel appealed the decision. The High Court ruled in favour of the company, which was granted a mobile services licence in December 2007. Digicel launched its mobile service in November 2008, providing coverage to 98% of the population.

Recent developments: the VIP in power

The VIP achieved a convincing victory at a general election held on 20 August 2007, securing 10 seats while the NDP won two. An independent candidate won the remaining seat in the renamed legislature, the House of Assembly. The leader of the VIP, Ralph

O'Neal, became the British Virgin Islands' first Premier, the title accorded to him under the terms of the new Constitution. O'Neal assumed responsibilities for the portfolios of finance and tourism, and Dancia Penn Sallah became the Deputy Premier and Minister of Health and Social Development. On assuming office, O'Neal pledged to address the increase in serious crime by reviewing levels of funding for the police force and the customs and immigration departments, and to enact a period of fiscal transparency and responsibility, particularly with regard to construction projects, owing to a predicted budget deficit of US $13m. for 2007.

It was announced in April 2009 that the Eastern Caribbean Supreme Court (ECSC) was to establish a new division of the court, based on Tortola, to preside over all stages of litigation concerning major domestic, international or cross-border commercial claims. Tortola had been chosen as the location for this new body because of its important role in the region's 'offshore' financial sector and because a number of multi-million dollar cases had been brought by commercial interests in the territory in recent years. Justice Edward Alexander Banner was sworn in on 30 March to preside over the new court, which came into effect in May.

The British Virgin Islands was, in April 2009, included in OECD's (see p. 376) so-called 'grey list' of of territories that had yet substantially to implement moves towards transparency in the financial sector. The territory consequently increased efforts to reach internationally agreed standards of financial openness by signing tax information sharing agreements with other countries. In August, after reaching its 12th such accord, the British Virgin Islands was removed from the OECD list. By March 2011 the jurisdiction had secured a further eight agreements.

In February 2010 the Government awarded a 16-year contract to supply drinking water on the islands to the British company Biwater. The contract, worth US $43m., included the construction of a desalination plant and two sewage treatment plants, as well as a pipeline network and resevoirs. The opposition claimed that the terms of the contract were too generous to Biwater and that the Government was guaranteeing a loan to the company; these claims were denied by the Minister of Communications and Works, Julian Fraser, who insisted the contract would only be beneficial to the islands' economy and quality of life. In June the NDP demanded that an official inquiry be established to investigate the controversy surrounding the contract; the opposition were particularly concerned about the lack of a tender process. In October Minister of Education and Culture Andrew Fahie also publicly expressed reservations about the deal. Nevertheless, the Government and the Governor continued to resist this pressure and reiterated their support for Biwater.

William Boyd McCleary was inaugurated as the territory's new Governor in August 2010, following the retirement of David Pearey.

CONSTITUTION AND GOVERNMENT

Under the provisions of the 2007 Constitution, the Governor is appointed by the British monarch and is responsible for external affairs, defence and internal security, terms and conditions of service of public officers, and the administration of the Courts. The Governor also fulfils the role of Presiding Officer at meetings of the Cabinet, which comprises the Premier and five other members. The House of Assembly comprises 15 members: a Speaker, one ex officio member, and 13 members elected by universal adult suffrage.

REGIONAL AND INTERNATIONAL CO-OPERATION

The British Virgin Islands became an associate member of the Caribbean Community and Common Market (CARICOM, see p. 219) in 1991; it is a member of CARICOM's Caribbean Development Bank (see p. 224) and an associate member of the Organisation of Eastern Caribbean States (OECS, see p. 462). In December 2009 the British Virgin Islands were a signatory to the Treaty of the OECS, establishing an Economic Union among member states. The Economic Union, which involved the removal of barriers to trade and the movement of labour as a step towards a single financial and economic market, came into effect on 21 January 2011. To join the Economic Union, the British Virgin Islands required British consent, which was pending in early 2011. The territory is also an associate member of the Economic Community for Latin America and the Caribbean (see p. 41). In economic affairs the territory has close affiliations with the neighbouring US Virgin Islands, and uses US currency. The territory is a member of the Commonwealth (see p. 230). As a dependency of the United Kingdom, the islands have the status of Overseas Territory in association with the European Union (EU, see p. 270).

ECONOMIC AFFAIRS

In 2009, according to UN estimates, the British Virgin Islands' gross domestic product (GDP) was US $1,328m., equivalent to some $57,626 per head. During 2000–08, according to official estimates, the population increased at an average annual rate of 2.9%. GDP increased, in real terms, by 2.2% per year during 2000–09, according to UN estimates; growth was estimated at 2.3% in 2009.

Agriculture (including forestry and fishing) contributed 0.9% of GDP in 2009, and engaged 0.6% of the employed labour force in 2005. The islands produce fruit and vegetables for domestic consumption or export to the US Virgin Islands, and some sugar cane (for the production of rum). Food imports accounted for 18.9% of total import costs in 1997. The fishing industry caters for local consumption and export, and provides a sporting activity for tourists. According to UN estimates, in 2000–09 agriculture GDP declined, in real terms, at an average annual rate of 1.1%; however, the sector registered strong growth, of 27.1%, in 2008, but decreased by 8.4% in 2009.

Industry (including mining, manufacturing, construction and public utilities) accounted for 10.7% of GDP in 2009 and engaged 11.4% of the employed labour force in 2005. The mining sector is negligible, consisting of the extraction of materials for the construction industry and of some salt. Manufacturing, which provided 2.6% of GDP in 2009, consists mainly of light industry; there is one rum distillery, two factories for the production of ice, some plants producing concrete blocks and other construction materials, small boat manufacture and various cottage industries. Most energy requirements must be imported (mineral fuels accounted for an estimated 8.5% of total imports in 1997). According to UN estimates, in 2000–09 GDP of the industrial sector increased, in real terms, at an average annual rate of 0.9%; industrial GDP declined by 1.0% in 2009.

The construction sector contributed 5.9% of GDP in 2009, according to UN estimates, and engaged 7.8% of the employed labour force in the same year. During 2000–09, the GDP of the sector increased at an average annual rate of 0.6%. However, construction GDP declined by 11.1% in 2008, but increased by 1.1% in 2009.

Services, primarily tourism and financial services, constitute the principal economic sector of the British Virgin Islands, contributing 88.4% of GDP in 2009, and accounting for the same proportion of employment in 2005. The tourism industry earned some US $437m. in 2005, and employed about one-third of the working population, directly or indirectly. The British Virgin Islands is the largest 'bareboat' chartering centre in the Caribbean, and approximately 60% of stop-over visitors stay aboard yachts. Nevertheless, in 2008 the restaurants and hotels sector contributed about 16% of GDP. The number of stop-over visitors was 308,793 in 2009 (most of whom were from the USA), a 10.7% decrease on the previous year's total. The financial services sector contributed about 60% of overall revenue in 2008. By 2009 the number of International Business Companies (IBC) registered was estimated at more than 700,000, although there was a 20% fall in the number of IBC registrations in 2008. The islands have recorded significant growth in the establishment of mutual funds and of insurance companies, although the rate of growth for this sector also declined in 2008.

In 2003, according to the Caribbean Development Bank (CDB), the British Virgin Islands recorded a trade deficit of US $158.1m. The trade deficit is normally offset by receipts from tourism, development aid, remittances from islanders working abroad (many in the US Virgin Islands) and, increasingly, from the 'offshore' financial sector. The principal sources of imports (most of the islands' requirements must be imported) are the USA (which provided 56.9% of imports in 1997), Trinidad and Tobago, Antigua and Barbuda, and also the United Kingdom. The principal markets for the limited amount of exports are the US Virgin Islands and the USA and Puerto Rico; rum is exported to the USA. Machinery and transport equipment are the principal imports (accounting for 40.4% of total imports in 1997), and fruit and vegetables, rum, sand and gravel are the main exports.

The budget for the 2007 financial year projected revenue at US $265.0m. against recurrent and capital expenditure of $267.9m. In 1996/97 there was a surplus of $56m. on the current account of the balance of payments. In 2004 total external debt was calculated to be $44.1m. In 1998 the territory received $1.2m. in development assistance. Central government debt to GDP ratio was estimated at below 10% in 2007, according to CDB estimates. The average annual rate of inflation was 2.8% in 2000–08; consumer prices increased by an average 2.5% in 2007 and by 7.1% in 2008. The rate of unemployment was estimated to be 3.1% in 2008.

The economy of the British Virgin Islands is largely dominated by tourism and by the provision of international financial services. The 'offshore' financial sector is an important source of employment and the single most important source of government revenue. International attempts, notably by the Organisation for Economic Co-operation and Development (OECD, see p. 376), to encourage the reform of 'offshore' financial centres are therefore of great concern to the British Virgin Islands, particularly as IBCs, which are not taxed and which are not obliged to disclose their directors or shareholders, have been singled out for particular criticism. The Government has expressed a desire to achieve greater diversification of the economy, in order to reduce reliance on tourism and financial services, both of which remained vulnerable to external pressures, in particular the performance of the US economy. The global economic downturn led to a fall in visitor numbers to the islands in 2008 and 2009, which in turn affected other sectors of the economy, notably construction and retail. Financial services experienced a more significant decline during those years as a result of the world-wide recession, which was compounded by the greater scrutiny of the sector from OECD and other international bodies. The economy as a whole expanded by 2.3% in 2009, but the Government projected growth of some 6% in 2010, fuelled by a recovery in the key tourism and financial services sectors. Further growth of 4%–5% was forecast for 2011, driven by the improving economic situation in the USA and expectations of a continued upsurge in the number of tourist arrivals and company incorporations.

PUBLIC HOLIDAYS

2012: 2 January (for New Year's Day), 5 March (H. Lavity Stoutt's Birthday), 12 March (Commonwealth Day), 6 April (Good Friday), 9 April (Easter Monday), 28 May (Whit Monday), 9 June (Queen's Official Birthday), 1 July (Territory Day), 6–8 August (Festival Monday, Tuesday and Wednesday), 22 October (for Saint Ursula's Day), 25–26 December (Christmas).

Statistical Survey

Source: Development Planning Unit, Central Administrative Complex, Road Town, Tortola VG1110; tel. 494-3701; fax 494-3947; e-mail dpu@dpu.org; internet dpu.gov.vg.

AREA AND POPULATION

Area: 153 sq km (59 sq miles). *Principal Islands* (sq km): Tortola 54.4; Anegada 38.8; Virgin Gorda 21.4; Jost Van Dyke 9.1.

Population: 16,115 at census of 12 May 1991; 23,161 (males 11,436, females 11,725) at census of 21 May 2001; 29,537 (official projection) in 2010; *By Island* (2001 census): Tortola 19,282; Virgin Gorda 3,203; Anegada 250; Jost Van Dyke 244; Other 182 (Other islands 86, Boats 96); Total 23,161.

Density (2010): 193.1 per sq km.

Population by Age (official projections, 2010): *0–14:* 7,404; *15–64:* 20,368; *65 and over:* 1,765; *Total* 29,537.

Principal Town: Road Town (capital), population 9,384 (UN estimate, incl. suburbs, mid-2009). Source: UN, *World Urbanization Prospects: The 2009 Revision*.

Births, Marriages and Deaths (2007 unless otherwise indicated): 279 live births (birth rate 10.1 per 1,000); 419 marriages (marriage rate 15.2 per 1,000); 109 deaths (2008—death rate 3.9 per 1,000). *2009:* Crude birth rate 14.6 per 1,000; Crude death rate 4.4 per 1,000 (Source: Pan American Health Organization).

Life Expectancy (years at birth, estimates): 77.5 (males 76.2; females 78.8) in 2010. Source: Pan American Health Organization.

Employment (2005): Agriculture, hunting and forestry 78; Fishing 14; Mining and quarrying 37; Manufacturing 404; Electricity, gas and water supply 145; Construction 1,260; Wholesale and retail trade 1,624; Hotels and restaurants 2,573; Transport, storage and communications 454; Financial intermediation 797; Real estate, renting and business activities 1,307; Public administration and social security 5,142; Education 1,119; Health and social work 141; Other community, social and personal service activities 724; Private households with employed persons 404; *Sub-total* 16,223; Not classifiable by economic activity 9; *Total* 16,232. 2010: Total employed 18,796.

HEALTH AND WELFARE

Total Fertility Rate (children per woman, 2010): 1.7.

Physicians (per 1,000 head, 1999): 1.15.

Hospital Beds (per 1,000 head, 2006): 1.8.

Health Expenditure (% of GDP, 1995): 3.9. *2004* (public expenditure only): 2.3.

Health Expenditure (public, % of total, 1995): 36.5.

Source: Pan American Health Organization.

For definitions, see explanatory note on p. vi.

AGRICULTURE, ETC.

Livestock ('000 head, 2008, FAO estimates): Cattle 2.4; Sheep 6.1; Goats 10.0; Pigs 1.5. Note: No data were available for 2009.

Fishing (metric tons, live weight, 2008, FAO estimates): Snappers 320; Boxfishes 30; Jacks and crevalles 25; Caribbean spiny lobster 40; Marine fishes 770; Total catch (incl. others) 1,200.

Source: FAO.

INDUSTRY

Electric Energy (production, million kWh): 45 in 2005; 48 in 2006–07. Source: UN Industrial Commodity Statistics Database.

FINANCE

Currency and Exchange Rate: United States currency is used: 100 cents = 1 US dollar ($). *Sterling and Euro Equivalents* (31 December 2010): £1 sterling = US $1.565; €1 = US $1.336; US $100 = £63.88 = €74.84.

Budget (US $ million, 2006): *Revenue:* Total recurrent revenue 247.9. *Expenditure:* Recurrent expenditure 222.6; Capital expenditure 38.6; Total expenditure 261.2. *2007* (US $ million, projections): Total recurrent revenue 265.0; Total expenditure 267.9 (Recurrent expenditure 221.5, Capital expenditure 46.4).

Cost of Living (Consumer Price Index; base: 1995 = 100): All items 139.4 in 2006; 142.9 in 2007; 153.1 in 2008.

Gross Domestic Product (US $ million at constant 2005 prices): 971 in 2007; 996 in 2008; 1,018 in 2009. Source: UN Statistics Division, National Accounts Main Aggregates Database.

Expenditure on the Gross Domestic Product (US $ million at current prices, 2009): Government final consumption expenditure 119; Private final consumption expenditure 485; Gross fixed capital formation 319; Changes in inventories –22; *Total domestic expenditure* 901; Exports of goods and services 1,456; *Less* Imports of goods and services 1,029; *GDP in purchasers' values* 1,328. Source: UN Statistics Division, National Accounts Main Aggregates Database.

Gross Domestic Product by Economic Activity (US $ million at current prices, 2009): Agriculture, hunting, forestry and fishing 12; Mining, manufacturing and utilities 65 (Manufacturing 35); Construction 79; Wholesale, retail trade, restaurants and hotels 400; Transport, storage and communication 165; Other activities 627; *Total gross value added* 1,348; Net taxes on products –20 (figure obtained as a residual); *GDP in purchasers' values* 1,328 (Source: UN Statistics Division, National Accounts Main Aggregates Database).

EXTERNAL TRADE

Principal Commodities (US $ '000): *Imports c.i.f.* (1997): Food and live animals 31,515; Beverages and tobacco 8,797; Crude materials (inedible) except fuels 1,168; Mineral fuels, lubricants, etc. 9,847; Chemicals 8,816; Basic manufactures 31,715; Machinery and transport equipment 47,019; Total (incl. others) 116,379. *Exports f.o.b.* (1996): Food and live animals 368; Beverages and tobacco 3,967; Crude materials (inedible) except fuels 1,334; Total (incl. others) 5,862. *2001* (exports, US $ million): Animals 0.1; Fresh fish 0.7; Gravel and sand 1.4; Rum 3.6; Total 28.13.

Principal Trading Partners (US $ '000): *Imports c.i.f.* (1997): Antigua and Barbuda 1,807; Trinidad and Tobago 2,555; United Kingdom 406; USA 94,651; Total (incl. others) 166,379. *Exports f.o.b.* (1996): USA and Puerto Rico 1,077; US Virgin Islands 2,001; Total (incl. others) 5,862. *1999:* Imports 208,419; Exports 2,081.

Source: mainly UN, *International Trade Statistics Yearbook*.

TRANSPORT

Road Traffic (motor vehicles registered and licensed, 2005): 13,392 (Private vehicles 9,201, Commercial vehicles 2,102, Rental vehicles 1,196, Taxis 483, Government 275, Motorcycles 135).

Shipping: *International Freight Traffic* ('000 metric tons, 2002): Goods unloaded 145.6. *Cargo Ship Arrivals* (2002): 2,027. *Merchant Fleet* (vessels registered, at 31 December 2009): 18; Total displacement 19,421 grt (Sources: British Virgin Islands Ports Authority; IHS Fairplay, *World Fleet Statistics*).

Civil Aviation (passenger arrivals): 153,391 in 2003; 220,239 in 2004 (estimate); 220,116 in 2005 (estimate).

TOURISM

Visitor Arrivals ('000): 358.1 stop-over visitors, 575.2 cruise ship passengers in 2007; 345.9 stop-over visitors, 571.7 cruise ship passengers in 2008; 308.8 stop-over visitors, 530.3 cruise ship passengers in 2009.

Tourism Revenue (US $ million, incl. passenger transport): 342 in 2003; 393 in 2004; 437 in 2005. Source: World Tourism Organization.

COMMUNICATIONS MEDIA

Radio Receivers (1997): 9,000 in use.

Television Receivers (1999): 4,000 in use.

UNITED KINGDOM OVERSEAS TERRITORIES

Telephones (2009): 20,100 main lines in use.
Mobile Cellular Telephones (2009): 24,000 subscribers.
Daily Newspapers (2004): 1.
Non-daily Newspapers (2004, unless otherwise indicated): 8 (estimated circulation 4,000 in 1996).

Sources: UNESCO, *Statistical Yearbook*; UN, *Statistical Yearbook*; International Telecommunication Union.

EDUCATION

Pre-primary: 5 schools (1994/95); 45 teachers (2005/06); 653 pupils (2005/06).
Primary: 21 schools (2006); 215 teachers (2006/07); 3,044 pupils (2006/07).
Secondary: 7 schools (2006); 223 teachers (2006/07); 1,921 pupils (2006/07).
Tertiary (2004/05): 110 teachers; 1,200 pupils.
Pupil-teacher Ratio (primary education, UNESCO estimate): 14.2 in 2006/07.

Sources: UNESCO Institute for Statistics; Caribbean Development Bank, *Social and Economic Indicators*.

Directory

The Government

HEAD OF STATE

Queen: HM Queen ELIZABETH II.
Governor: WILLIAM BOYD MCCLEARY (assumed office 20 Aug. 2010).
Deputy Governor: INEZ ARCHIBALD.

CABINET
(May 2011)

The Government is formed by the Virgin Islands Party.

Premier and Minister of Finance and Tourism: RALPH TELFORD O'NEAL.
Deputy Premier and Minister of Health and Social Development: DANCIA PENN-SALLAH.
Minister of Natural Resources and Labour: OMAR HODGE.
Minister of Education and Culture: ANDREW FAHIE.
Minister of Communications and Works: JULIAN FRASER.
Attorney-General: BABA AZIZ (acting).

MINISTRIES

Office of the Governor: 20 Waterfront Dr., POB 702, Road Town, Tortola VG1110; tel. 494-2345; fax 494-5582; e-mail bvigovernor@gov.vg; internet www.bvi.gov.vg.
Office of the Deputy Governor: Central Administration Bldg, West Wing, 33 Admin Dr., Road Town, Tortola VG1110; tel. 494-3701; fax 494-6481; e-mail webmaster@dgo.gov.vg; internet www.dgo.gov.vg.
Office of the Premier: 33 Admin Dr., Wickham's Cay 1, Road Town, Tortola VG1110; tel. 468-0026; fax 468-6413; e-mail premieroffice@gov.vg.
Ministry of Communications and Works: 33 Admin Dr., Wickham's Cay 1, Road Town, Tortola VG1110; tel. 468-2183; fax 494-3873; e-mail mcw@gov.vg.
Ministry of Education and Culture: 33 Admin Dr., Wickham's Cay 1, Road Town, Tortola VG1110; tel. 468-2036; fax 468-0021; e-mail bvimecgov@hotmail.com.
Ministry of Finance and Tourism: 33 Admin Dr., Wickham's Cay 1, Road Town, Tortola VG1110; tel. 494-3701; fax 494-6180; e-mail finance@gov.vg; internet www.finance.gov.vg.
Ministry of Health and Social Development: 33 Admin Dr., Wickham's Cay 1, Road Town, Tortola VG1110; tel. 468-3701; fax 494-5018; e-mail ministryofhealth@gov.vg.
Ministry of Natural Resources and Labour: 33 Admin Dr., Wickham's Cay 1, Road Town, Tortola VG1110; tel. 468-2147; fax 494-4283; e-mail nrl@gov.vg.

The British Virgin Islands

HOUSE OF ASSEMBLY

Speaker: ROY HARRIGAN.
Clerk: PHYLLIS EVANS, Richard C. Stoutt Bldg, Wickham's Cay I, POB 2390, Road Town, Tortola VG1110; tel. 494-4757; fax 494-4544; e-mail JHodge@gov.vg; internet www.legco.gov.vg.

General Election, 20 August 2007

Party	% of vote	Seats
Virgin Islands Party	45.2	10
National Democratic Party	39.6	2
Independent	15.2	1
Total	**100.0**	**13**

Election Commission

Office of the Supervisor of Elections: Ulric Dawson Bldg, 6 Russell Hill Rd, Road Town, Tortola VG1110; tel. 494-6842; fax 468-2779; e-mail electionsoffice@gov.vg; Supervisor of Elections JULIETTE PENN.

Political Organizations

National Democratic Party (NDP): Road Town, Tortola VG1110; f. 1998; Chair. RUSSELL HARRIGAN; Leader ORLANDO SMITH.
People's Party (POP): Road Town, Tortola; f. 2011; Leader ALLEN WHEATLEY.
United Party (UP): POB 3068, Road Town, Tortola VG1110; tel. 495-2656; fax 494-1808; e-mail liberatebvi@msn.com; f. 1967; Chair. CONRAD MADURO.
Virgin Islands Party (VIP): Road Town, Tortola VG1110; e-mail info@viparty.com; internet www.viparty.com; Chair. RALPH T. O'NEAL.

Judicial System

Justice is administered by the Eastern Caribbean Supreme Court (ECSC), based in Saint Lucia, which consists of two divisions: the High Court of Justice and the Court of Appeal. There are two resident High Court Judges, as well as an Acting High Court Judge. A visiting Court of Appeal, comprised of the Chief Justice and two Judges of Appeal, sits twice a year in the British Virgin Islands. There is also a Magistrates' Court, which hears prescribed civil and criminal cases. The final Court of Appeal is the Privy Council in the United Kingdom. Under the terms of the 2007 Constitution, a Judicial and Legal Services Commission, chaired by the Chief Justice, was established to counsel the Governor in matters relating to judicial appointments and regulation of the territory's legal system. In April 2009 the ECSC announced the establishment of a new division of the court, based on Tortola, to preside over all stages of litigation concerning major domestic, international or cross-border commercial claims. Justice Edward Alexander Banner was to preside over the new Commercial Court, which became operational in June 2009.

High Court Judges: INDRA HARIPRASHAD-CHARLES, RITA JOSEPH-OLIVETTI, EDWARD BANNISTER (acting).
Registrar: PAULA AJARIE.
Magistrate's Office: Magistrates Court, POB 140, Road Town, Tortola VG1110; tel. 494-3460; fax 494-2499; e-mail magistrate@vigilate.org; Magistrate VALERIE R. STEPHENS.

Religion

CHRISTIANITY

The Roman Catholic Church

The diocese of St John's-Basseterre, suffragan to the archdiocese of Castries (Saint Lucia), includes Anguilla, Antigua and Barbuda, the British Virgin Islands, Montserrat and Saint Christopher and Nevis. The Bishop is resident in St John's, Antigua. According to official estimates from 2005, 10% of the population are Roman Catholics.

The Anglican Communion

The British and US Virgin Islands form a single, missionary diocese of the Episcopal Church of the United States of America. The Bishop of the Virgin Islands is resident on St Thomas in the US Virgin Islands. According to official estimates from 2005, 17% of the population are Anglicans.

Protestant Churches

Various Protestant denominations are represented, principally the Methodist Church (an estimated 33% of the population in 2005).

UNITED KINGDOM OVERSEAS TERRITORIES

The British Virgin Islands

Others include the Church of God (9%), Seventh-day Adventist (6%), and Baptist Churches (5%).

The Press

The BVI Beacon: 10 Russell Hill Rd, POB 3030, Road Town, Tortola VG1110; tel. 494-3434; fax 494-6267; e-mail bvibeacn@surfbvi.com; internet www.bvibeacon.com; f. 1984; Thurs; covers local and international news; also operates from the US Virgin Islands; Editor LINNELL M. ABBOTT; circ. 3,400.

The BVI StandPoint: Wickham's Cay, POB 4311, Road Town, Tortola VG1110; tel. 494-8106; fax 494-8647; e-mail editorial@vistandpoint.com; internet www.vistandpoint.com; fmrly *BVI PennySaver*, adopted current name in 2001; Tues. and Fri.; covers local and international news; Publr ELTON CALLWOOD; Editor CARMILITA JAMIESON; circ. 18,000.

The Island Sun: 112 Main St, POB 21, Road Town, Tortola VG1110; tel. 494-2476; fax 494-5854; e-mail issun@candwbvi.net; internet islandsun.com; f. 1962; Fri.; publ. by Sun Enterprises (BVI) Ltd; Editor VERNON W. PICKERING; circ. 3,000.

The Welcome (The British Virgin Islands Welcome Tourist Guide): POB 133, Road Town, Tortola; tel. 494-2413; fax 494-4413; e-mail jim@bviwelcome.com; internet www.bviwelcome.com; f. 1971; every 2 months; general, tourist information; Publr and Editor CLAUDIA COLLI; annual circ. 176,000.

Publishers

aLookingGlass: 7 Road Reef Plaza, POB 3895, Sea Cow's Bay, Tortola, VG1110; tel. 494-7788; fax 494-8777; e-mail info@alookingglass.com; internet alookingglass.com; f. 2002; publishes *The BVI Property & Yacht* monthly; Man. Dir OWEN WATERS; Gen. Man. COLIN RATHBUN.

Global Directories (BVI) Ltd: Wickhams Cay 1, POB 3403, Road Town, Tortola VG1110; tel. 494-2060; fax 494-3060; e-mail bvi-sales@globaldirectories.com; internet bviyp.com; fmrly Caribbean Publishing Co (BVI) Ltd; subsidiary of MediaHouse Ltd, Bermuda; Gen. Man. MICHAEL ARNOLD.

Island Publishing Services Ltd: Pasea Estate, POB 133, Road Town, Tortola VG1110; tel. 494-2413; fax 494-4413; e-mail info@bviwelcome.com; internet www.caribbeanprinting.com; publishes *The British Virgin Islands Welcome Tourist Guide* (q.v.), *BVI Restaurant and Food Guide* (annual), *The Limin' Times* (weekly entertainment guide), and *The British Virgin Islands Cruise Ship Visitors' Guide* (annual); Gen. Man. PAUL BACKSHALL; Publr CLAUDIA COLLI.

Broadcasting and Communications

TELECOMMUNICATIONS

A Telecommunications Regulatory Commission was established under the Telecommunications Act 2006 in October to facilitate the liberalization of the telecommunications sector, which had commenced earlier that year. In April 2007 a Telecommunications Liberalization Act was ratified by the Government; the legislation prepared the market for the addition of further operators after a period of three years, until which time the market would be restricted to the existing three service providers. However, the market was subsequently opened to applications from alternative operators after Digicel pursued a successful lawsuit against the restriction: the first unitary licences were issued in June 2007, and Digicel was granted a mobile licence in December.

Regulatory Bodies

Telecommunications Regulatory Commission: LM Business Centre, 3rd Floor, 27 Fish Lock Rd, Road Town, POB 4401, Tortola; tel. 468-4165; fax 494-6786; e-mail contact@trc.vg; internet www.trc.vg; f. Oct. 2006; regulatory body; Chair. COLLIN SCATLIFFE; CEO TOMAS LAMANAUSKAS.

Telephone Services Management Unit: Deputy Governor's Office, Central Administration Bldg, 2nd Floor, West Atrium, Road Town, Tortola VG1110; tel. 494-4728; fax 494-6551; e-mail tsmu@bvigovernment.org; govt agency; Man. REYNELL FRASER.

Principal Companies

Caribbean Cellular Telephone (CCT Global Communications): Geneva Pl., 333 Waterfront Dr., POB 267, Road Town, Tortola VG1110; tel. 494-3825; fax 494-4933; internet www.cctwireless.com; f. 1986 as CCT Boatphone; mobile cellular telephone operator; Gen. Man. JOSE LUIS FERNANDEZ.

Digicel: POB 4168, Road Town, Tortola VG1110; tel. 494-2048; fax 494-0111; e-mail bvicustomercare@digicelgroup.com; internet www.digicelbvi.com; granted licence to operate mobile cellular telephone network in British Virgin Islands in Dec. 2007; CEO ALAN BATES (British Virgin Islands).

LIME: Cutlass Bldg, Wickham's Cay 1, POB 440, Road Town, Tortola VG1110; tel. 494-4444; fax 494-2506; e-mail support@candwbvi.net; internet www.time4lime.com; f. 1967 as Cable & Wireless (WI) Ltd; name changed as above 2008; Exec. Vice-Pres. (British Virgin Islands) JOEL ABDINOOR; Country Man. VANCE LEWIS.

BROADCASTING

Radio

Virgin Islands Broadcasting Ltd—Radio ZBVI: Baughers Bay, POB 78, Road Town, Tortola VG1110; tel. 494-2250; fax 494-1139; e-mail zbvi@caribsurf.com; internet www.zbvi.vi; f. 1965; commercial; Gen. Man. HARVEY HERBERT; Operations Man. SANDRA POTTER WARRICAN.

Television

BVI Cable TV: Fishlock Rd, POB 644, Road Town, Tortola VG1110; tel. 494-3831; fax 494-3205; operated by Innovative Communication Corporation, based in the US Virgin Islands; programmes from US Virgin Islands and Puerto Rico; secured a licence to compete in the newly liberalized telecommunications market in June 2007; 53 channels; Gen. Man. LUANNE HODGE.

Finance

BANKING

Regulatory Authority

Financial Services Commission: Pasea Estate, POB 418, Road Town, Tortola VG1110; tel. 494-1324; fax 494-5016; e-mail enquiries@bvifsc.vg; internet www.bvifsc.vg; f. 2002; independent financial services regulator; Chair. ROBIN GAUL; Man. Dir and CEO ROBERT MATHAVIOUS.

Commercial Banks

Ansbacher (BVI) Ltd: International Trust Bldg, POB 659, Road Town, Tortola VG1110; tel. 494-3215; fax 494-3216.

Banco Popular de Puerto Rico: POB 67, Road Town, Tortola VG1110; tel. 494-2117; fax 494-5294; e-mail internet@bppr.com; internet www.bancopopular.com; Pres. and CEO RICHARD L. CARRIÓN; Man. SANDRA SCATLIFFE.

Bank of Nova Scotia (Canada): Wickham's Cay 1, POB 434, Road Town, Tortola VG1110; tel. 494-2526; fax 494-4657; e-mail joycelyn.murraine@scotiabank.com; internet www.bvi.scotiabank.com; f. 1967; Man. Dir JOYCELYN MURRAINE.

DISA Bank (BVI) Ltd: POB 985, Road Town, Tortola VG1110; tel. 494-4977; fax 494-4980; Man. ROSA RESTREPO.

First Bank Virgin Islands: Road Town Business Centre, Wickham's Cay 1, Road Town, POB 435, Tortola VG1110; tel. 494-2662; fax 494-3863; e-mail e-firstbank@firstbankpr.com; internet www.firstbankvi.com; f. 1994; est. as a commercial bank in Puerto Rico; CEO AURELIO ALEMÁN-BERMUDEZ.

FirstCaribbean International Bank Ltd: Wickham's Cay 1, POB 70, Road Town, Tortola VG1110; tel. 852-9900; fax 494-4315; e-mail barcbvi@surfbvi.com; internet www.firstcaribbeanbank.com; f. 2003 following merger of Caribbean operations of Barclays Bank PLC and CIBC; Barclays relinquished its stake in 2006; CEO JOHN D. ORR; Man. MICHAEL SPENCER; 2 brs.

Rathbone Bank (BVI) Ltd: POB 986, Road Town, Tortola VG1110; tel. 494-6544; fax 494-6532; e-mail rathbone@surfbvi.com; Man. Dir CORNEL BAPTISTE.

VP Bank (BVI) Ltd: 3076 Sir Francis Drake's Highway, POB 3463, Road Town, Tortola VG1110; tel. 494-1100; fax 494-1199; e-mail info.bvi@vpbank.com; internet www.vpbank.vg; Man. Dir Dr PETER REICHENSTEIN.

Development Bank

National Bank of the Virgin Islands Ltd: New Social Security Bldg, Wickham's Cay 1, POB 275, Road Town, Tortola VG1110; tel. 494-3737; fax 494-3119; e-mail admin@natbankvi.com; internet www.natbankvi.com; f. 1976; fmrly Development Bank of the British Virgin Islands; state-owned; Chair. KENNETH HODGE.

TRUST COMPANIES

Abacus Trust and Management Services Ltd: 333 Waterfront Dr., Road Town, Tortola VG1110; tel. 494-4388; fax 494-3088; e-mail info@mwmabacus.com; internet www.mwmabacus.com; f. 1994; Man. MEADE MALONE.

UNITED KINGDOM OVERSEAS TERRITORIES   The British Virgin Islands

Aleman, Cordero, Galindo and Lee Trust (BVI) Ltd: POB 3175, Road Town, Tortola VG1110; tel. 494-4666; fax 494-4679; e-mail alcogalbvi@alcogal.com; Man. GABRIELLA CONTE.

AMS Trustees Ltd: Sea Meadow House, POB 116, Road Town, Tortola VG1110; tel. 494-3399; fax 494-3041; e-mail enquiries@amsbvi.com; internet www.amsbvi.com; f. 1985; privately owned; subsidiary of the AMS Group (British Virgin Islands); Man. Dir NICHOLAS CLARK.

Belmont Trust Ltd: Belmont Chambers, Tropic Isle Bldg, Nibbs St, POB 3443, Road Town, Tortola VG1110; tel. 494-5800; fax 494-2545; e-mail info@belmontbvi.net; internet www.belmontbvi.com; Man. Dir ANDREA DOUGLAS.

CCP Financial Consultants Ltd: Ellen Skelton Bldg, Fishers Lane, POB 681, Road Town, Tortola VG1110; tel. 494-6777; fax 494-6787; e-mail ccp@surfbvi.com; internet www.ccpbvi.com; Man. JOSEPH ROBERTS.

Citco BVI Ltd: Wickham's Cay, POB 662, Road Town, Tortola VG1110; tel. 494-2217; fax 494-3917; e-mail bvi-trust@citco.com; internet www.citco.com; Man. NICOLA GILLESPIE.

HSBC International Trustee (BVI) Ltd: Woodbourne Hall, POB 916, Road Town, Tortola VG1110; tel. 494-5414; fax 494-2417; e-mail kenneth.morgan@htvg.vg; Dir KENNETH MORGAN.

Hunte & Co Services Ltd: Omar Hodge Bldg, 3rd Floor, Wickham's Cay I, POB 3504, Road Town, Tortola; tel. 495-0232; fax 495-0229; internet www.hunteandco.com; Office Man. DEBORAH BLANFORD.

Maples and Calder BVI: Sea Meadow House, POB 173, Road Town, Tortola VG1110; tel. 852-3000; fax 852-3097; e-mail bviinfo@maplesandcalder.com; internet www.maplesandcalder.com; Managing Partners CLINTON HEMPEL, ARABELLA DI LORIO.

Midocean Management and Trust Services (BVI) Ltd: 9 Columbus Centre, Pelican Dr., POB 805, Road Town, Tortola VG1110; tel. 494-4567; fax 494-4568; e-mail midocean@maitlandbvi.com; owned by Maitland Group; Man. ELIZABETH WILKINSON.

Moore Stephens International Services (BVI) Ltd: Palm Grove House, Wickham's Cay I, POB 3186, Road Town, Tortola VG1110; tel. 494-3503; fax 494-3592; e-mail moorestephens@moorestephensbvi.com; internet www.moorestephens.com; Man. NICHOLAS LANE.

TMF (BVI) Ltd: POB 964, Road Town, Tortola VG11900; tel. 494-4997; fax 494-4999; e-mail bvi@tmf-group.com; internet www.tmf-group.com; Man. GRAHAM COOK.

Totalserve Trust Company Ltd: 197 Main St, POB 3540, Road Town, Tortola VG1110; tel. 494-6900; fax 494-6990; e-mail bvi@totalserve.eu; internet www.totalservecy.com; Man. DENESHAR MEADE.

Tricor Services (BVI) Ltd: POB 3340, Road Town, Tortola VG1110; tel. 494-6004; fax 494-6404; e-mail info@bvi.tricorglobal.com; internet www.bvi.tricorglobal.com; Man. PATRICK A. NICHOLAS.

Trident Trust Company (BVI) Ltd: Trident Chambers, Wickham's Cay, POB 146, Road Town, Tortola VG1110; tel. 494-2434; fax 494-3754; e-mail bvi@tridenttrust.com; internet www.tridenttrust.com; Man. BARRY R. GOODMAN.

At the beginning of 2007 there were some 2,600 active mutual and hedge funds registered with the British Virgin Islands International Finance Centre.

INSURANCE

ALTA Insurance Management (BVI) Ltd: POB 4623, Road Town, Tortola VG1110; tel. 494-9670; fax 494-9690; e-mail gtaylor@altaholdings.com; internet www.altaholdings.com; Man. GREGORY TAYLOR.

AMS Insurance Management Services Ltd: Sea Meadow House, POB 116, Road Town, Tortola VG1110; tel. 494-4078; fax 494-8589; e-mail dlloyd@amsbvi.com; internet www.amsbvi.com; Man. DEREK LLOYD.

Belmont Insurance Management Ltd: Belmont Chambers, Tropic Isle Bldg, Nibbs St, POB 3443, Road Town, Tortola VG1110; tel. 494-5800; fax 494-2545; e-mail info@belmontbvi.com; internet www.belmontbvi.com; Man. Dir ANDREA DOUGLAS.

Caledonian Insurance Services (BVI) Ltd: 4th Floor, Rodus Bldg, Road Town, Tortola VG1110; tel. 949-0050; fax 814-4875; e-mail insurance@caledonian.com; internet www.caledonian.com; f. 2005; Dir HARRY THOMPSON.

Captiva Global Ltd: Columbus Centre, POB 4428, Road Town, Tortola VG1110; tel. 494-4111; fax 494-4222; e-mail info@captiva.vg; internet www.captiva.vg; Man. Dir HARRY J. THOMPSON.

Caribbean Insurers Ltd (CIL): Mirage Bldg, POB 129, Road Town, Tortola VG1110; tel. 494-2728; fax 494-4393; e-mail info@caribbins.com; internet www.caribbeaninsurers.com; f. 1973; part of the Caribbean Insurers Group; Chair. and CEO JOHN WILLIAMS.

HWR Insurance Management Services Ltd (Harneys Insurance): Craigmuir Chambers, POB 71, Road Town, Tortola VG1110; tel. 494-2233; fax 494-3547; e-mail bvi@harneys.com; internet www.harneys.com; Man. Dir DAVID SPYER.

Marine Insurance Office (BVI) Ltd (MIO): Mill Mall, Wickham's Cay 1, POB 874, Road Town, Tortola VG1110; tel. 494-3795; fax 494-4540; e-mail info@mioinsurance.com; internet mioinsurance.com; f. 1985; Man. WESLEY WOOLHOUSE.

Osiris Insurance Management Ltd: Coastal Bldg, Wickham's Cay 11, POB 2221, Road Town, Tortola VG1110; tel. 494-9820; fax 494-6934; e-mail info@osiristrust.com; internet osiristrust.com; Man. Dir MILES WALTON.

Trident Insurance Management (BVI) Ltd: POB 146, Road Town, Tortola VG1110; tel. 494-4078; fax 494-2519; e-mail trident@surfbvi.com; Man. DEREK LLOYD.

TSA Insurance Management Ltd: POB 3443, Road Town, Tortola VG1110; tel. 494-5800; fax 494-6563; e-mail jwilliams@surfbvi.com; Man. JOHN WILLIAMS.

USA Risk Group (BVI) Inc: 30 Main St, Suite 450, Burlington, VT05401; tel. 371-2225; fax 371-2220; e-mail info@usarisk.com; internet www.usarisk.com; Pres. STUART H. GRAYSTON.

Several US and other foreign companies have agents in the British Virgin Islands. In 2006 57 new 'captive' insurers were registered by the British Virgin Islands International Financial Centre, increasing the total such registered to more than 400.

Trade and Industry

GOVERNMENT AGENCY

Trade and Investment Promotion Department: Chief Minister's Office, Central Administration Bldg, 33 Administration Dr., Road Town, Tortola VG1110; tel. 494-5007; fax 494-5657; e-mail trade@bvigovernment.org.

CHAMBER OF COMMERCE

British Virgin Islands Chamber of Commerce and Hotel Association: Tropic Aisle Bldg, Wickham's Cay 1, POB 376, Road Town, Tortola VG1110; tel. 494-3514; fax 494-6179; e-mail info@bviccha.org; internet www.bviccha.org; f. 1986; Chair. BIRNEY M. HARRIGAN; Pres. (Business and Commerce) DEBORAH O'NEAL; Pres. (Hotels and Tourism) ROMNEY PENN; 250 mems.

UTILITIES

Electricity

British Virgin Islands Electricity Corpn (BVIEC): Long Bush, POB 268, Road Town, Tortola VG1110; tel. 494-3911; fax 494-4291; e-mail bviecgm@bvielectricity.com; internet www.bvielectricity.com; f. 1979; privatization pending; Chair. MARGARET PENN; Gen. Man. LEROY ABRAHAM.

Water

Water and Sewerage Dept: Water & Sewerage Compound, Baughers Bay, Road Town, POB 130, Tortola VG1110; tel. 468-3416; fax 494-6746; e-mail wsd@gov.vg; f. 1980; publs quarterly newsletter *The Vapour*; Dir. JULIAN WILLOCK.

Transport

ROADS

In 2002 there were 132 km (82 miles) of access roads, 77 km of primary roads, 37 km of secondary roads and 90 km of tertiary roads. In 2005 13,392 vehicles were licensed, 9,201 of which were private vehicles.

Public Works Department: Baughers Bay, POB 284, Tortola VG1110; tel. 494-2722; fax 494-4740; e-mail pwd@bvigovernment.org; responsible for road maintenance; Dir DREXEL GLASGOW (acting).

SHIPPING

There are two direct steamship services, one from the United Kingdom and one from the USA. Motor launches maintain daily mail and passenger services with St Thomas and St John, US Virgin Islands. A new cruise ship pier, built at a cost of US $6.9m. with assistance from the Caribbean Development Bank, was opened in Road Town in 1994 and was later expanded. Further expansion work was completed in December 2008.

British Virgin Islands Ports Authority: Port Purcell, POB 4, Road Town, Tortola VG1110; tel. 494-3435; fax 494-2642; e-mail bviports@bviports.org; internet www.bviports.org; f. 1991; Chair. CARL DAWSON; Man. Dir VINCENT VICTOR O'NEAL.

UNITED KINGDOM OVERSEAS TERRITORIES

Tropical Shipping: Port Purcell Seaport, Island Shipping and Trading, POB 250, Road Town, Tortola VG1110; tel. 494-2674; fax 494-3505; e-mail lmoses@tropical.com; internet www.tropical.com; Man. LEROY MOSES.

CIVIL AVIATION

Terrance B. Lettsome (formerly Beef Island) Airport, about 16 km (10 miles) from Road Town, has a runway with a length of 1,500 m (4,921 ft). A new US $65m. airport terminal was opened at the airport in March 2002. Captain Auguste George Airport on Anegada has been designated an international point of entry and was resurfaced in the late 1990s. In June 2008 the Government signed an agreement with Halcrow Group Ltd of the United Kingdom to develop the airport on Virgin Gorda, including an extension to the runway to allow larger aircraft to land.

British Virgin Islands Airports Authority: POB 4416, Road Town, Tortola VG1110; tel. 852-9000; fax 852-9045; internet www.bviaa.com; f. 2005; Man. Dir DENNISTON FRASER.

Tourism

The main attraction of the islands is their tranquillity and clear waters, which provide excellent facilities for sailing, fishing, diving and other water sports. In 2004 there were an estimated 1,370 hotel rooms. There are also many charter yachts offering overnight accommodation. There were some 308,800 stop-over visitors and 530,300 cruise ship passengers in 2009. The majority of tourists are from the USA. Receipts from tourism totalled some US $437m. in 2005.

British Virgin Islands Chamber of Commerce and Hotel Association: see Chamber of Commerce.

British Virgin Islands Tourist Board: 2nd Floor, AKARA Bldg, DeCastro St, Road Town, Tortola VG1110; tel. 494-3134; fax 494-3866; e-mail info@bvitourism.com; internet www.bvitourism.com; Chair. NEIL BLYDEN.

Defence

The United Kingdom is responsible for the defence of the islands.

Education

Primary education is free, universal and compulsory between the ages of five and 11. Secondary education is also free and lasts from 12 to 16 years of age. In 2005/06 some 653 pupils were attending pre-primary schools; in 2006/07, according to UNESCO estimates, enrolment at primary schools included 93% of children in the relevant age-group, while enrolment at secondary schools included 84% of pupils in the relevant age category. Higher education is available at the University of the Virgin Islands (St Thomas, US Virgin Islands) and elsewhere in the Caribbean, in North America and in the United Kingdom. Central government expenditure on education in 2008 was estimated at US $40.4m. (equivalent to 14.2% of total expenditure).

THE CAYMAN ISLANDS

Introductory Survey

LOCATION, CLIMATE, LANGUAGE, RELIGION, FLAG, CAPITAL

The Cayman Islands lie about 290 km (180 miles) west-north-west of Jamaica and consist of three main islands: Grand Cayman and, to the north-east, Little Cayman and Cayman Brac. The climate is tropical but is tempered by the trade winds, with a cool season between November and March, when temperatures average 24°C (75°F). The rainy season lasts from May until October. Mean annual rainfall is 1,524 mm (60 ins). The official language is English. Many Christian churches are represented. The flag is the British 'Blue Ensign', with the islands' coat of arms (a golden lion on a red background above three stars in green, representing the three main islands, superimposed on wavy lines of blue and white, the shield surmounted by a torse of white and blue bearing a yellow pineapple behind a green turtle, and with the motto 'He hath founded it upon the seas' on a scroll beneath) on a white roundel in the fly. The capital is George Town, on the island of Grand Cayman.

CONTEMPORARY POLITICAL HISTORY

Historical Context

The Cayman Islands came under acknowledged British rule in 1670 and were settled mainly from Jamaica and by privateers and buccaneers. The islands of Little Cayman and Cayman Brac were permanently settled only in 1833, and until 1877 there was no administrative connection between them and Grand Cayman. A representative assembly first sat in 1832. The islands formed a dependency of Jamaica until 1959, and the Governor of Jamaica held responsibility for the Cayman Islands until Jamaican independence in 1962, when a separate administrator was appointed (the title was changed to that of Governor in 1971). The 1959 Constitution was revised in 1972, 1992 and 1994.

Domestic Political Affairs

For many years there have been no formal political parties on the islands, despite the emergence of a nascent party political system during the 1960s with the formation, in 1961, of the National Democratic Party (NDP), as part of a campaign for self-government. The Christian Democratic Party was formed as a conservative opposition. Both parties disappeared within a few years despite the electoral success of the NDP, largely owing to the system of gubernatorial nomination to the Executive Council. In the 1970s elections for the 12 elective seats in the Legislative Assembly came to be contested by 'teams' of candidates, as well as by independents. Two such teams were formed, Progress and Dignity (the more conservative) and Unity, but all candidates were committed to augmenting the economic success of the Caymans, and favoured continued dependent status. There are no plans for independence, and the majority of the population wish to maintain the islands' links with the United Kingdom.

At elections in 1980 the Unity team won a legislative majority. This majority was overturned in 1984, owing to public disquiet at the rapid growth of the immigrant work-force, and the implications of the recent US challenges to the Cayman Islands' bank secrecy laws. In 1987 the Legislative Assembly successfully sought stricter regulations of status and residency for those able to participate in elections, in an attempt to protect the political rights of native Caymanians (in view of the very large immigrant population). Prior to the November 1988 election the teams regrouped into more informal coalitions, indicating the primacy of personal over 'party' affiliations.

In July 1990 the Legislative Assembly approved proposals to review the Constitution. The implementation of most recommendations, including the appointment of a Chief Minister, was postponed pending a general election. One of the amendments, however, which involved increasing the number of elective seats in the Legislative Assembly to 15, was adopted in March 1992. The proposed reforms had prompted the formation, in mid-1991, of the territory's first political organization since the 1960s, the Progressive Democratic Party, later renamed the National Team. National Team members secured a majority in the Legislative Assembly in the November 1992 general election. In the same month James Ryan was appointed Chief Secretary, following the retirement of Lemuel Hurlston.

At a general election in November 1996 the governing National Team remained in power, although with a reduced majority. Two new groupings, the Democratic Alliance and Team Cayman (which had formed in opposition to the Government's alleged mismanagement of the public debt and of Cayman Airways) won parliamentary representation.

Emergence of new political parties

In a general election held on 8 November 2000 the governing National Team suffered a heavy defeat, losing six of its nine seats. The newly elected Legislative Assembly appointed Kurt Tibbetts of the Democratic Alliance as Leader of Government Business.

In an unprecedented development in November 2001, several members of the Legislative Assembly, dissatisfied with the Government's leadership during the economic slowdown, formed the United Democratic Party (UDP). McKeeva Bush, the leader of the new party and Deputy Leader of Government Business and Minister of Tourism, Environment and Transport, claimed that at least 10 members of the 15-member Assembly were UDP supporters. Subsequently, the passing of a motion of no confidence against the Leader of Government Business resulted in Tibbetts and Edna Moyle, the Minister of Community Development, Women's Affairs, Youth and Sport, leaving the Executive Council. Bush became the new Leader of Government Business, while two other legislators, Gilbert McLean and Frank McField, both members of the UDP, joined the Cabinet. In

May 2002 it was announced that the five opposition members of the legislative assembly had formed a new political party, the People's Progressive Movement (PPM), led by Tibbetts.

The financial sector

In March 1999 the Government of the United Kingdom published draft legislation pertaining to its relationship with its Overseas Dependencies, which were to be renamed United Kingdom Overseas Territories (and had been referred to as such since February 1998). The legislation proposed the extension of British citizenship to the citizens of Overseas Territories, although it also required the Territories to amend their legislation on human rights and on the regulation of the financial services sector to meet international standards. The Cayman Islands were praised for the introduction in 1998 of laws on tax evasion, and for strengthening the regulatory powers of the Monetary Authority.

In late April 1999 representatives of the European Union (EU, see p. 270) held meetings with the overseas territories of member states to discuss proposed reforms of legislation relating to the financial services sector. The Cayman Islands delegation defended the islands' standards of regulation, arguing that the islands had implemented some of the strictest laws in the world against money-laundering, and that proposals to abolish the Cayman Islands' laws on banking secrecy would place the islands at a disadvantage, compared with the financial centres of Switzerland and Luxembourg. In early June the Cayman Islands announced that it was to seek certification under the UN's Offshore Initiative, and that consequently a UN agency, the Global Programme against Money Laundering, was to undertake a review of the islands' financial systems and regulations.

In January 2003 Bush accused the United Kingdom of undermining the course of Cayman Islands' justice, after a routine money-laundering case was dismissed amid allegations of espionage and obstruction of justice by British intelligence agents. The trial collapsed after it was alleged that the Director of the Cayman Islands Financial Reporting Unit (and a key witness in the trial) had passed information about the case to an unnamed agency of the British Government, understood to be the Secret Intelligence Service (MI6). It was claimed that MI6 wished to protect the names of its sources within the Caribbean 'offshore' banking community. Bush demanded the British Government pay for the failed trial, estimated to cost some US $5m., and for any negative repercussions the affair might have for the reputation of the islands' banking sector. The United Kingdom, however, refused to compensate the Cayman Islands and maintained that although its intelligence agencies might have helped in the investigation, they had never interfered in the case. In March the Attorney-General, David Ballantyne, resigned amid accusations that he was aware that British intelligence agents were working covertly in the Cayman Islands; Samuel W. Bulgin, the erstwhile Solicitor-General, was appointed as Ballantyne's successor in July.

The US Senate Finance Committee reported in June 2007 that it had identified more than 14,000 registered companies purportedly maintaining headquarters at a single address in the Cayman Islands, and subsequently commissioned an inquiry into the anomaly by the Government Accountability Office. It was estimated that evasion of US tax obligations by such entities—achieved by establishing 'offshore' subsidiaries on the islands—had resulted in a US $100,000m. shortfall in tax-based revenue and precipitated a growing sentiment of hostilities between the two nations' respective regulatory authorities. The inquiry reported its findings in July 2008: it concluded that although the Cayman Islands adhered to international financial standards, the use of the islands by US citizens (5% of companies registered at the address were entirely US-owned and a further 40%–50% had a US billing address) was often indicative of illegal tax activities. The collapse in 2008 of several Cayman Island-based hedge funds, exacerbating the global financial crisis, caused increased attention to be focused on the territory's financial institutions. US President Barack Obama announced in May 2009 that he intended to implement stringent new laws governing tax havens, and called for more transparency from the 'offshore' sector.

The Cayman Islands' inclusion, in April 2009, on an Organisation for Economic Co-operation and Development (OECD, see p. 376) so-called 'grey list' of territories that had yet substantially to implement moves towards transparency in the financial sector was a set-back for the jurisdiction's reputation. However, in August the territory was removed from the list after signing 12 tax information sharing agreements with other countries. By March 2011 the Cayman Islands had signed a further 10 accords. In October 2010 the territory received a broadly favourable assessment under OECD's Global Forum on Transparency and Exchange of Information for Tax Purposes peer review mechanism, although the need for further reform was highlighted.

Constitutional reform

In March 2002 a three-member Constitutional Review Commission, appointed by the Governor in May 2001, submitted a new draft constitution. The proposed document had to be debated by the Legislative Assembly and then approved by the British Parliament before being formally adopted. The draft constitution included the creation of the office of Chief Minister, proposed a full ministerial government, and incorporated a bill of rights. The opposition demanded a referendum on the recommendations, on the grounds that the UDP had rejected several of the proposals, despite strong public support for the changes, but Bush forwarded the proposals to the British Foreign and Commonwealth Office (FCO), via the Governor's office. In December Bush and the leader of the opposition, Tibbetts, travelled to the United Kingdom in order to review the proposed constitution with FCO officials. Consensus, however, proved impossible to achieve. While the PPM called for a public referendum on issue, the UDP announced in February 2004 that it would not participate in the constitutional review process before the next election. In March 2006 an FCO delegation visited the Cayman Islands for informal discussions aimed at restarting the process of constitutional reform.

In May 2002 the British Overseas Territories Act, having received royal assent in the United Kingdom in February, came into force and granted British citizenship to the people of its Overseas Territories, including the Cayman Islands. Under the new law Caymanians would be able to hold British passports and work in the United Kingdom and elsewhere in the EU.

The opposition PPM won a resounding victory at the general election of May 2005. The outgoing UDP Government had been criticized for its handling of the aftermath of Hurricane Ivan, which had caused an estimated CI $2,800m. of damage in September 2004, and also for its decision, in the same month, to grant 'belonger' status to some 3,000 people, a move interpreted by many as an attempt to increase the party's electoral support. The Leader of Government Business, Kurt Tibbetts, pledged to hold a referendum on increased autonomy for the islands. In November he announced a Freedom of Information Bill, to be debated in the Legislative Assembly, prior to a public consultation exercise. The proposed legislation was intended to promote government transparency and accountability, thus increasing constitutional democracy. Following several delays, the legislation was finally approved at the end of August 2006 and in the following month the Freedom of Information Unit was officially opened. The law finally became effective on 5 January 2009.

In mid-February 2007 the Government announced the establishment of a Constitutional Review Secretariat to initiate renewed efforts towards constitutional reform in the territory from March. The mandate of the government-administered body, to be presided over by Cabinet Secretary Orrett Connor, was stated as promoting public awareness, disseminating information and expediting the public consultation process through education and the institution of an effective communication framework. Formal embarkation upon constitutional modernization—facilitated by the counsel of a British constitutional lawyer, Professor Jeffrey Jowell—was expected to commence once the Secretariat became fully operational, entailing a national referendum and negotiations with the United Kingdom in the advanced stages. In January 2008 the Government launched a series of public consultations ahead of a referendum scheduled to be held in May. The FCO affirmed in early April that the new Constitution must include a bill of rights and, in response, the Government postponed the referendum to allow a longer period of public deliberation. Discussions resumed in January 2009, and on 6 April it was announced that the referendum would be held on 20 May, at the same time as the legislative election.

Recent developments: 2009 election and referendum

At the general election in May 2009, the opposition UDP defeated the incumbent PPM, securing nine of the 15 available seats. The PPM secured five seats and the remaining one was taken by an independent candidate. The rate of voter participation was 80.6% of the electorate. McKeeva Bush was subsequently sworn in as Leader of Government Business on 27 May.

In the concurrent referendum on the draft constitution some 62% of voters supported the changes, which was more than the 50% plus one required for the result to be binding. As a result, on 10 June 2009 the Privy Council approved the new charter. It came into force on 6 November. The new Constitution gave greater autonomy to the Cabinet, replacing the Governor-appointed Financial Secretary with an elected Minister of Finance (a portfolio assumed by Premier Bush). Although the Governor retained overall control of foreign affairs, certain aspects of external dealings were delegated to the Cabinet. A Bill of Rights, Freedom and Responsibilities was also scheduled to come into effect in November 2012.

Tibbetts resigned as leader of the opposition and PPM leader in February 2011. He was succeeded by Alden McLaughlin in the same month.

CONSTITUTION AND GOVERNMENT

A new Constitution was adopted in 2009, granting greater autonomy to Cayman Islanders, although it extended many of the terms of the

UNITED KINGDOM OVERSEAS TERRITORIES

The Cayman Islands

previous 1959 charter. The Governor, who is appointed by the British monarch, is responsible for external affairs, defence, internal security and the public service. The Governor is Chairman of the Cabinet, comprising three members appointed by the Governor and five members elected by the Legislative Assembly. The Legislative Assembly comprises three official members and 15 members elected by universal adult suffrage for a period of four years.

REGIONAL AND INTERNATIONAL CO-OPERATION

The Cayman Islands has been an associate member of the Caribbean Community and Common Market (CARICOM, see p. 219) since 2002; the territory is also a member of CARICOM's Caribbean Development Bank (CDB, see p. 224). The Cayman Islands has the status of Overseas Territory in association with the European Union (EU, see p. 270). The territory is a member of the Commonwealth (see p. 230).

ECONOMIC AFFAIRS

In 2007, according to UN estimates, the Cayman Islands' gross domestic product (GDP) was CI $2,493.0m., equivalent to some US $54,827 per head. During 2000–09, according to official estimates, the population increased at an average annual rate of 3.5%, while GDP increased, in real terms, by 1.6% per year during 2000–09, according to UN estimates; overall GDP grew by 1.1% in 2008, but fell by 6.6% in 2009.

Agriculture (which engaged only 1.9% of the employed labour force in 2009 and accounted for 0.3% of value added in the same year) is limited by infertile soil, low rainfall and high labour costs. The principal crops are citrus fruits and bananas, and some other produce for local consumption. Flowers (particularly orchids) are produced for export. Livestock-rearing consists of beef cattle, poultry (mainly for eggs) and pigs. The traditional activity of turtle-hunting has virtually disappeared; the turtle farm (the only commercial one in the world) now produces mainly for domestic consumption (and serves as a research centre), following the imposition of US restrictions on the trade in turtle products in 1979. Fishing is mainly for lobster and shrimp.

Industry, engaging 18.5% of the employed labour force in 2009 and, according to the UN, accounting for 9.1% of value added in 2009, consists mainly of construction and related manufacturing, some food-processing and tourism-related light industries. The construction sector contributed 4.6% of value added in 2009, while manufacturing activities accounted for only about 0.9% of the total in that year. Energy requirements are satisfied by the import of petroleum products and gas (15.5% of total imports in 2008).

Service industries dominate the Caymanian economy, accounting for 79.7% of employment (excluding unclassified activities) in 2009 and contributing 90.5% of value added in the same year. The tourism industry is the principal economic activity, and in 1991 accounted for 22.9% of GDP and employed, directly and indirectly, some 50% of the working population. The industry earned US $479m. in 2007, before declining to $353m. in 2008. Most visitors are from the USA (78.5% of tourist arrivals in 2009). The Cayman Islands is one of the largest 'offshore' financial centres in the world; in March 2010 there were 333 banks and trust companies and 8,819 mutual funds on the islands, according to the Cayman Islands Monetary Authority. In 2008 the financial services sector engaged 10.2% of the working population, and in 1999 contributed about 36.0% of GDP.

In 2008 the Cayman Islands recorded a trade deficit of CI $862.7m. Receipts from tourism and the financial sector, remittances and capital inflows normally offset the trade deficit. The principal source of imports is the USA (which provided some 75.7% of total imports in 2009). Other major trading partners in 2009 included the Netherlands Antilles. The principal imports in 2009 were miscellaneous manufactured articles, food and live animals, petroleum products and gas, machinery and transport equipment and basic manufacturers.

An estimated government budget deficit of CI $149.4m. was recorded in 2009. In 1998 official development assistance totalled US $0.2m. At the end of 1999 the public debt stood at US $114.8m. The average annual rate of inflation was 2.2% in 2000–10; consumer prices declined by an annual average of 1.3% in 2009, but it increased by 0.1% in 2010. According to official census figures, only 59% of the resident population of the islands were Caymanian in 2009 (compared with 79% in 1980). Some 6.0% of the labour force were unemployed in 2008.

Both the principal economic sectors, 'offshore' finance and tourism, benefit from the Cayman Islands' political stability, good infrastructure and extensive development. The financial sector, which benefits from an absence of taxation and of foreign exchange regulations, as well as enjoying strict confidentiality laws, recorded consistently high levels of growth during the 1990s, and provided an estimated 54% of GDP in 2007. The jurisdiction dominated the hedge fund sector; in March 2011 some 9,261 hedge funds were registered in the islands. Nevertheless, the sector contracted during 2009, following the onset of the global financial crisis in the previous year. Tourist arrivals also declined in 2009 (by 3.4%), owing to the ongoing economic downturn. With North America and Europe accounting for 92% of total air arrivals in 2009, the recession in those regions was particularly detrimental to the Cayman Islands: real GDP contracted by 6.6% in that year, according to government estimates. In spite of the downturn, the Government ruled out the introduction of direct taxes in its 2009/10 budget. Instead, it announced rises in work permit, transaction and banking licence fees, as well as cuts in public sector salaries and the divestment of several assets. The British Government also pledged a loan of CI $225m. The Government estimated that real GDP contracted by around 4.0% in 2010. The financial sector remained subdued in that year, and activity in the construction industry, which had been particularly badly affected by the recession, declined further. However, there was an increase in air arrivals and cruise ship visitors, indicating a recovery in the tourism sector, and renewed GDP growth of 2.2% was projected for 2011.

PUBLIC HOLIDAYS

2012: 2 January (for New Year's Day), 23 January (National Heroes' Day), 22 February (Ash Wednesday), 6 April (Good Friday), 9 April (Easter Monday), 21 May (Discovery Day), 9 June (Queen's Official Birthday), 2 July (Constitution Day), 13 November (Remembrance Day), 25–26 December (Christmas),

Statistical Survey

Sources: Government Information Services, Cricket Sq., Elgin Ave, George Town, Grand Cayman; tel. 949-8092; fax 949-5936; The Information Centre, Economic and Statistics Office, Government Administration Bldg, Grand Cayman; tel. 949-0940; fax 949-8782; e-mail infostats@gov.ky; internet www.eso.ky.

AREA AND POPULATION

Area: 262 sq km (102 sq miles). The main island of Grand Cayman is about 197 sq km (76 sq miles), about one-half of which is swamp. Cayman Brac is 39 sq km (15 sq miles); Little Cayman is 26 sq km (11 sq miles).

Population: 39,410 (males 19,311, females 20,099) at census of 10 October 1999 (Grand Cayman 37,473, Cayman Brac 1,822, Little Cayman 115); 54,878 at census of 10 October 2010 (preliminary).

Density (at 2010 census): 209.5 per sq km.

Population by Age and Sex (official estimates at 31 December 2008): *0–14:* 10,633 (males 5,247, females 5,386); *15–64:* 43,502 (males 21,741; females 21,761); *65 and over:* 2,874 (males 1,275, females 1,599); *Total* 57,009 (males 28,263, females 28,746). Note: Estimates not adjusted to take account of results of 2010 census.

Principal Towns (at 2010 census, preliminary): George Town (capital) 27,704; West Bay 11,269; Bodden Town 10,341.

Births, Marriages and Deaths (2009): Live births 824 (birth rate 15.0 per 1,000); Marriages 554 (marriage rate 10.5 per 1,000); Deaths 152 (death rate 2.8 per 1,000).

Life Expectancy (years at birth, 2010): 80.6 (males 77.9; females 83.3). Source: Pan American Health Organization.

Economically Active Population (sample survey, persons aged 15 years and over, October–November 2009): Agriculture and fishing 630; Manufacturing, mining, printing and publishing 745; Construction 5,018; Electricity, gas and water supply 499; Wholesale and retail trade 4,563; Restaurants and hotels 3,307; Transport, post and telecommunication 1,710; Financial services 3,185; Public administration, education, health and social work 5,050; Other community, social and personal service activities 1,774; Private households with employed persons 3,095; Real estate, renting and business services 4,308; *Sub-total* 33,884; Not classifiable by economic activity 33; *Total employed* 33,917; Unemployed 2,183; *Total labour force* 36,100 (Caymanian 18,165, non-Caymanian 17,935).

HEALTH AND WELFARE

Total Fertility Rate (children per woman, 2010): 1.9.

Physicians (per 1,000 head, 2008): 2.7.

Health Expenditure: % of GDP (1997): 4.2.

Health Expenditure: public (% of total, 1997): 53.2.

Total Carbon Dioxide Emissions ('000 metric tons, 2007): 538.6.

Total Carbon Dioxide Emissions Per Head (metric tons, 2007): 10.1.

Source: mainly Pan American Health Organization.

For definitions, see explanatory note on p. vi.

AGRICULTURE, ETC.

Livestock ('000 head, 2009, FAO estimates): Cattle 1.3; Goats 0.3; Pigs 0.4; Chickens 6.

Fishing (metric tons, live weight, 2008): Total catch 125 (all marine fishes).

Source: FAO.

INDUSTRY

Electric Energy (production, million kWh): 584.4 in 2007; 596.8 in 2008; 608.8 in 2009.

FINANCE

Currency and Exchange Rates: 100 cents = 1 Cayman Islands dollar (CI $). *Sterling, US Dollar and Euro Equivalents* (31 December 2010): £1 sterling = CI $1.305; US $1 = 0.833 CI cents; €1 = CI $1.113; CI $100 = £76.65 = US $120.00 = €89.81. *Exchange rate:* Fixed at CI $1 = US $1.20.

Budget (CI $ million, 2009): *Revenue:* Taxes on international trade and transactions 155.3 Taxes on other domestic goods and services 235.9; Taxes on property 22.6; Other tax revenue 2.4; Non-coercive revenue 54.4 (Sales of goods and services 47.0); Total 470.6. *Expenditure:* Current expenditure 478.1 (Personnel costs 222.6, Supplies and consumable goods 86.4, Subsidies 119.3, Transfer payments 30.3, Interest payments 19.5); Extraordinary expenses 18.0; Other executive expenses 14.3; Capital expenditure and net lending 109.6; Total 620.0.

Cost of Living (Consumer Price Index; base: June 2008 = 100): All items 100.1 in 2008; 98.8 in 2009; 98.9 in 2010.

Gross Domestic Product (CI $ million at constant 2007 prices): 2,569.5 in 2007; 2,598.8 in 2008; 2,427.3 in 2009.

Gross Domestic Product by Economic Activity (CI $ million in current prices, 2007): Agriculture 8.2; Fishing 2.2; Mining and quarrying 29.6; Manufacturing 29.5; Electricity and water supply 82.4; Construction 139.3; Wholesale and retail trade 236.4; Hotels and restaurants 96.3; Transport, storage and communication 175.5; Finance and insurance 1,374.9; Real estate, renting and business services 532.3; Public administration and defence 169.4; Education 62.7; Health and social work 69.8; Other services 93.5; *Sub-total* 3,102.0; *Less* Financial intermediation services indirectly measured 532.5; *GDP in purchasers' values* 2,569.5. *2008:* GDP in purchasers' values 2,704.4. *2009* (preliminary): GDP in purchasers' values 2,493.0.

EXTERNAL TRADE

Principal Commodities (CI $ million, 2009): *Imports c.i.f.:* Food and live animals 94.4; Beverages and tobacco 33.7; Petroleum products and gas 88.0; Chemicals and related products 27.0; Basic manufactures 47.3; Machinery and transport equipment 66.4; Miscellaneous manufactured articles 324.8; Total (incl. others) 735.9. *Exports f.o.b.:* Total 16.0.

Principal Trading Partners (CI $ million, 2009): *Imports c.i.f.:* Jamaica 6.3; Japan 2.2; Netherlands Antilles 84.6; United Kingdom 3.9; USA 556.8; Total (incl. others) 735.9. *Exports f.o.b.:* Total 16.0.

TRANSPORT

Road Traffic ('000 motor vehicles in use, 2002): Passenger cars 23.8; Commercial vehicles 6.4.

Shipping: *International Freight Traffic* ('000 metric tons): Goods loaded 735 (1990); Goods unloaded 239,138 (2000). *Cargo Vessels* (2007): Vessels 10, Calls at port 551. *Merchant Fleet* (vessels registered at 31 December 2009): 150; Total displacement 2,912,275 grt. (Source: IHS Fairplay, *World Fleet Statistics*).

TOURISM

Visitor Arrivals ('000): 2,007.2 (arrivals by air 291.5, cruise ship passengers 1,715.7) in 2007; 1,855.9 (arrivals by air 302.9, cruise ship passengers 1,553.1) in 2008; 1,792.4 (arrivals by air 272.0, cruise ship passengers 1,520.4) in 2009.

Stay-over Arrivals by Place of Origin ('000, 2009): Canada 17.3; Europe 19.1; USA 215.0; Total (incl. others) 273.9. Source: Cayman Islands Tourism Department, George Town.

Tourism Receipts (US $ million, incl. passenger transport): 513 in 2006; 479 in 2007; 353 in 2008. Source: World Tourism Organization.

COMMUNICATIONS MEDIA

Radio Receivers: 36,000 in use in 1997.

Television Receivers: 23,239 in use in 1999.

Telephones: 38,000 main lines in use in 2009.

Mobile Cellular Telephones (subscribers): 108,700 in 2009.

Fixed and Mobile Telecommunication Lines (number in service): 110,656 in 2005.

Internet Users: 24,000 in 2009.

Daily Newspapers: 2 (circulation 15,400) in 2004.

Source: mainly International Telecommunication Union.

EDUCATION
(30 September 2009)

Institutions (excl. Lighthouse School): Government 16; Private 10; Total 26.

Enrolment: *Government:* Primary 2,378; Middle 1,151; Secondary 1,132; Total 4,661. *Private:* Total 2,976. *Total:* 7,637 (excl. Lighthouse School 61).

Pupil-teacher Ratio (primary education, UNESCO estimate): 12.1 in 2007/08. Source: UNESCO Institute for Statistics.

Adult Literacy Rate: 98.9% in 2007 (males 98.7%, females 99.0%). Source: UNESCO Institute for Statistics.

Directory

The Government

HEAD OF STATE

Queen: HM Queen Elizabeth II.
Governor: Duncan Taylor (assumed office 15 January 2010).

CABINET
(May 2011)

The Government is formed by the United Democratic Party.

Chairman: Duncan Taylor (The Governor).
Premier and Minister of Finance, Tourism and Development: W. McKeeva Bush.
Deputy Governor and Minister of Internal and External Affairs*: Donovan Ebanks.
Attorney-General and Minister of Legal Affairs*: Samuel Bulgin.
Cabinet Secretary*: Orrett Connor.
Minister of Health, Environment, Youth, Sports and Culture: Mark Scotland.
Minister of Education, Training and Employment: Rolston Anglin.
Deputy Premier and Minister of District Administration, Works, Lands and Agriculture: Juliana O'Connor-Connolly.
Minister of Community Affairs, Gender and Housing: Michael (Mike) Adam.

A District Commissioner, Ernie Scott, represents the Governor on Cayman Brac and Little Cayman.

*Appointed by the Governor.

GOVERNMENT OFFICES

Office of the Governor: The Professional Centre, Suite 202, 2nd Floor, Smith Rd, POB 10261, George Town, Grand Cayman KY1-1003; tel. 244-2401; fax 945-4131; e-mail staffoff@candw.ky; internet www.ukincayman.fco.gov.uk.

All official government offices and ministries are located in the Government Administration Bldg, Elgin Ave, George Town, Grand Cayman.

Ministry of Community Affairs, Gender and Housing: tel. 244-2424; fax 949-3896; e-mail dorine.whittaker@gov.ky.

Ministry of District Administration, Works, Lands and Agriculture: tel. 244-2412; fax 945-2922; e-mail foi.mpc@gov.ky; internet www.dapah.gov.ky.

Ministry of Education, Training and Employment: tel. 244-2417; fax 949-9343; e-mail brighterfutures@gov.ky; internet www.education.gov.ky.

Ministry of Finance, Tourism and Development: tel. 244-2458; fax 945-1746; e-mail tedc@gov.ky; internet www.caymanislands.ky (Dept of Tourism).

Ministry of Health, Environment, Youth, Sports and Culture: tel. 244-2318; fax 949-1790; e-mail h&hs@gov.ky; internet www.hsa.ky (Health Services Authority).

UNITED KINGDOM OVERSEAS TERRITORIES   *The Cayman Islands*

Ministry of Internal and External Affairs: tel. 244-3179; fax 946-5453; e-mail foi.pie@gov.ky; internet www.pie.gov.ky.

Ministry of Legal Affairs: tel. 244-2405; fax 949-6079; e-mail agc@gov.ky; internet www.caymanjudicial-legalinfo.ky.

LEGISLATIVE ASSEMBLY

Legislative Assembly: 33 Fort St, POB 890, George Town, Grand Cayman KY1-1103; tel. 949-4236; fax 949-9514; internet www.legislativeassembly.ky; Clerk ZENA MERREN-CHIN.

Members: The Deputy Governor, the Attorney-General, and 15 elected members. According to the terms of the 2009 Constitution, the number of elected members was to be increased to 18 at the next dissolution of the Legislative Assembly, when the Deputy Governor was to give up his seat. An Electoral Boundaries Commission also was to be established to review constituency boundaries. The most recent election to the Assembly was on 20 May 2009.

Speaker: MARY LAWRENCE.

Election Commission

Elections Office: Smith Road Professional Centre, 2nd Floor, 150 Smith Rd, George Town, Grand Cayman; tel. 949-8047; fax 949-2977; e-mail electionsoffice@candw.ky; internet www.electionsoffice.ky; Supervisor of Elections KEARNEY SIDNEY GOMEZ.

Political Organizations

People's Progressive Movement (PPM): POB 10526 APO, Grand Cayman; tel. 945-1776; f. 2002; Leader ALDEN MCLAUGHLIN; Chair. ANTONY DUCKWORTH.

United Democratic Party (UDP): Godfrey Nixon Rd, George Town, Grand Cayman; tel. 943-3338; e-mail info@udp.ky; internet www.udp.ky; tel. 943-3338; fax 943-3339; f. 2001; Leader W. MCKEEVA BUSH; Gen. Sec. ROLSTON ANGLIN.

Judicial System

There is a Grand Court of the Islands (with Supreme Court status), a Summary Court, a Youth Court and a Coroner's Court. The Grand Court has jurisdiction in all civil matters, admiralty matters, and in trials on indictment. Appeals lie to the Court of Appeal of the Cayman Islands and beyond that to the Privy Council in the United Kingdom. The Summary Courts deal with criminal and civil matters (up to a certain limit defined by law) and appeals lie to the Grand Court.

Chief Justice: ANTHONY SMELLIE.
Director of Public Prosecutions: CHERYLL RICHARDS.
President of the Court of Appeal: EDWARD ZACCA.
Clerk of the Courts of the Islands: VALDIS FOLDATS, Court's Office, Edward St, George Town, Grand Cayman KY1-1106; tel. 949-4296; fax 949-9856; e-mail valdis.foldats@gov.ky.

Religion

CHRISTIANITY

The oldest established denominations are (on Grand Cayman) the United Church of Jamaica and Grand Cayman (Presbyterian), and (on Cayman Brac) the Baptist Church. Anglicans are adherents of the Church in the Province of the West Indies (Grand Cayman forms part of the diocese of Jamaica). Within the Roman Catholic Church, the Cayman Islands forms part of the archdiocese of Kingston in Jamaica. According to the latest available census figures (1999), some 26% of the population are adherents of the Church of God, 12% belong to the United Church, 11% are Roman Catholics, 9% are Baptists, 8% are Seventh-day Adventists, 6% are Anglicans and 5% are Pentecostalists.

The Press

The Cayman Islands Journal: The Compass Centre, Shedden Rd, POB 1365, George Town, Grand Cayman; tel. 949-5111; fax 949-7675; internet www.compasscayman.com/journal; publ. by Cayman Free Press; monthly; broadsheet business newspaper; Publr BRIAN UZZELL.

Cayman Net News: 85 North Sound Rd, Alisста Towers, POB 10707, Grand Cayman; tel. 946-6060; fax 949-0679; e-mail news@caymannetnews.com; internet www.caymannetnews.com; internet news service; publishes weekly newspaper (f. 2006); Publr and Editor-in-Chief DESMOND SEALES.

Caymanian Compass: The Compass Centre, Shedden Rd, POB 1365, George Town, Grand Cayman; tel. 949-5111; fax 949-7675; internet www.compasscayman.com; f. 1965; publ. by the Cayman Free Press; 5 a week; Publr BRIAN UZZELL; circ. 10,000.

The Chamber: POB 1000, George Town, Grand Cayman; tel. 949-8090; fax 949-0220; e-mail info@caymanchamber.ky; internet www.caymanchamber.ky; f. 1965; monthly; newsletter of the Cayman Islands Chamber of Commerce; Editor WIL PINEAU; circ. 5,000.

Christian Lifestyle: Bldg G, Unit 3, Countryside Shopping Village, POB 1217, Grand Cayman KY1 1108; tel. 926-2507; fax 947-2228; e-mail editor@cstylemagazine.com; internet www.christianlifestylemagazine.com; f. 2008; publ. every 2 months; Editor KAREN CHIN.

Gazette: Gazette Office, Government Information Service, Cayman Islands Government, Aqua World Mall, Merrendale Dr., Grand Cayman; tel. 949-8092; fax 949-5936; e-mail caymangazette@gov.ky; internet www.gazettes.gov.ky; official govt newspaper; publ. fortnightly on Mon; Editor-in-Chief PATRICIA EBANKS.

Key to Cayman: The Compass Centre, Shedden Rd, POB 1365 George Town, Grand Cayman KY1 1108; tel. 949-5111; fax 949-7675; e-mail cfp@candw.ky; internet keytocayman.com; 2 a year; free tourist magazine; publ. by the Cayman Free Press; Cayman Free Press also publs *Caymanian Compass* newspaper and accompanying supplements, *Cayman Islands Journal*, *Cayman Islands Yearbook & Business Directory*, *Cayman Islands Map*, and *Inside Out*, a home and living magazine; Publr BRIAN UZZELL.

Publishers

Cayman Free Press Ltd: The Compass Centre, Shedden Rd, POB 1365, George Town, Grand Cayman, KY1-1108; tel. 949-5111; fax 949-7675; e-mail info@cfp.ky; internet www.caymanfreepress.com; f. 1965; Gen. Man. BRIAN UZZELL.

CLM Publishing: POB 1217, Grand Cayman, KY1-1108; tel. 926-2507; fax 947-2228; e-mail clmpublishing@officeliveusers.com; internet clmpublishing.books.officelive.com; publishes *Christian Lifestyle Magazine*; Chair. and CEO KAREN E. CHIN.

Global Directories (Cayman) Ltd: 62 Form Lane, 3rd Floor, Camana Bay, POB 688, George Town, Grand Cayman; tel. 949-7027; fax 949-8366; e-mail caysales@globaldirectories.com; internet caymanislandsyp.com; f. 1978; fmrly Caribbean Publishing Co (Cayman) Ltd; Dir LESTER GARNETT.

Government Information Service: Gazette Office, Cayman Islands Govt, Aqua World Mall, 2nd Floor, Merrendale Dr., Grand Cayman; tel. 949-8092; fax 949-5936; e-mail caymangazette@gov.ky; internet www.gazettes.gov.ky; publr of official govt releases, *Gazette*.

Progressive Publications Ltd: Economy Printers Bldg, POB 764, George Town, Grand Cayman; tel. 949-5780; fax 949-7674.

Tower Marketing: Grand Cayman; tel. 623-6700; fax 769-6700; e-mail lynne@tower.com.ky; internet www.tower.com.ky; f. 1999; Man. Dir LYNNE BYLES.

Broadcasting and Communications

REGULATORY AUTHORITY

Information and Communications Technology Authority (ICTA): Alisста Towers, 3rd Floor, 85 North Sound Rd, POB 2502, Grand Cayman KY1-1104; tel. 946-4282; fax 945-8284; e-mail info@icta.ky; internet www.icta.ky; f. 2002; responsible for the regulation and licensing of telecommunications, broadcasting, and all forms of radio which includes ship, aircraft, mobile and amateur radio and the management of the Cayman Islands internet domain; Chair. GLEN DAYKIN; Man. Dir DAVID ARCHBOLD.

TELECOMMUNICATIONS

Digicel Cayman: Cayman Financial Centre, 36A Roys Dr., 3rd Floor, POB 700, George Town, Grand Cayman; tel. 623-3444; fax 623-3329; e-mail caycustomercare@digicelgroup.com; internet www.digicelcayman.com; f. 2003; owned by an Irish consortium; acquired the operations of Cingular Wireless (fmrly those of AT&T Wireless) in the country in 2005 (www.cingular.ky); CEO VICTOR CORCORAN.

LIME: Anderson Sq. Bldg, Anderson Sq., Shedden Rd, POB 293, George Town, Grand Cayman; tel. 949-7800; fax 949-7962; e-mail cs@candw.ky; internet www.time4lime.com; f. 1966 as Cable & Wireless (Cayman Islands) Ltd; name changed as above 2008; Cable & Wireless' monopoly over the telecommunications market ended in 2004; Exec. Vice-Pres.(Cayman Islands) JOEL ABDINOOR; Country Man. ANTHONY RITCH.

Logic Communications: Governors Sq., West Bay Rd, Seven Mile Beach, POB 31112, Grand Cayman, KY1-1205; tel. 743-4300; fax 743-4301; e-mail support@logic.ky; internet www.logic.ky; f. 2003 as WestTel Ltd; name changed as above in 2010; wholly owned subsidiary of KeyTech Ltd, Bermuda; provides telephone and internet services; CEO MICHAEL EDENHOLM.

UNITED KINGDOM OVERSEAS TERRITORIES

The Cayman Islands

TeleCayman: Cayman Corporate Centre, 27 Hospital Rd, 4th Floor, POB 704 GT, Grand Cayman; tel. 769-1000; fax 769-0999; e-mail customer@telecayman.com; internet www.telecayman.com; f. 2003; provides telephone and internet services; Business Man. CHRIS HAYDON.

BROADCASTING

Radio

Radio Cayman: Elgin Ave, POB 1110 GT, George Town, Grand Cayman KY1-1102; tel. 949-7799; fax 949-6536; e-mail radiocayman@gov.ky; internet www.radiocayman.gov.ky; started full-time broadcasting 1976; govt-owned commercial radio station; service in English; operates Radio Cayman One and Breeze FM; Dir NORMA MCFIELD.

Radio Heaven 97 FM: Hurst Rd, Newlands, POB 31481, Grand Cayman, KY1-1206; tel. and fax 938-1082; e-mail pam@heaven97.com; internet www.heaven97.com; f. 1997; owned by Christian Communications Asscn; commercial station; Christian broadcasting, music and news; Man. Dir STEPHEN FAUCETTE.

Radio ICCI-FM: International College of the Cayman Islands, 595 Hirst Rd, POB 136, Grand Cayman KY1-1501; tel. 947-1100; fax 947-1210; e-mail info@myicci.com; internet www.icci.edu.ky; f. 1973; radio station of the International College of the Cayman Islands; educational and cultural; Pres. JOHN H. CUMMINGS.

Radio Vibe: 21 Eclipse Dr., POB 10236, George Town, Grand Cayman KY1-1002; tel. 949-8423; fax 946-9867; e-mail info@vibefm.ky; internet www.vibefm.ky; operated by Paramount Media Services, in addition to Spin FM; Man. KENNETH G. RANKINE.

Radio Z99.9 FM: Grand Harbour, Suite 21 and 22, Shamrock Rd, POB 30110, George Town, Grand Cayman KY1-1201; tel. 945-1166; fax 945-1006; e-mail info@z99.ky; internet www.z99.ky; owned by Hurley's Entertainment Corpn Ltd; Operations Man. J. B. WEBB.

Television

Cayman Adventist Television Network (CATN/TV): 209 Walkers Rd, POB 515, George Town, Grand Cayman KY1-1106; tel. 949-8167; fax 949-6167; e-mail mission@candw.ky; internet caymanadventist.org; f. 1996; local and international programmes, mainly religious; Pres. ERIC D. CLARKE.

Cayman Christian TV Ltd: POB 964, Grand Cayman KY1-1102; tel. 947-2599; relays Christian broadcasting from the Trinity Broadcasting Network (USA); Vice-Pres. FRED RUTTY.

CITN Cayman 27: 45 Eclipse Way, POB 30563, Grand Cayman KY1-1203; tel. 745-2739; fax 749-1002; e-mail hlofters@weststartv.com; internet www.cayman27.com.ky; f. 1992 as Cayman International Television Network; 24 hrs daily; local and international news and US entertainment; 10-channel cable service of international programmes by subscription; Gen. Man. and Dir MIKE MARTIN; Station Man. RICK ALPERT.

WestStar TV Ltd: 45 Eclipse Way, POB 31117, Grand Cayman KY1-1205; tel. 745-5555; e-mail info@weststartv.com; internet www.weststartv.com; f. 1993; operates wireless cable television service; affiliated to WestTel Ltd; CEO RODNEY HANSEN; Operations Man. TRACI BRADLEY.

Finance

(cap. = capital; res = reserves; dep. = deposits; m. = million; brs = branches)

Banking facilities are provided by commercial banks. The islands have become an important centre for 'offshore' companies and trusts. In 2008 there were 93,693 companies registered in the Cayman Islands. At the end of March 2011 there were 246 licensed banks and trusts and a total of 9,261 registered mutual (including hedge) funds. The islands are well-known as a tax haven because of the absence of any form of direct taxation. In September 2010 assets held by banks registered in the Cayman Islands totalled US $1,725,000m.

Cayman Islands Monetary Authority (CIMA): 80E Shedden Rd, Elizabethan Sq., POB 10052 APO, George Town, Grand Cayman KY1-1001; tel. 949-7089; fax 946-4230; e-mail contactpublicrelations@cimoney.com.ky; internet www.cimoney.com.ky; f. 1997; responsible for managing the territory's currency and reserves and for regulating the financial services sector; cap. CI $10m., res CI $20.3m., dep. CI $83.6m. (Jun. 2009); Chair. GEORGE MCCARTHY; Man. Dir CINDY SCOTLAND.

PRINCIPAL BANKS AND TRUST COMPANIES

AALL Trust and Banking Corpn Ltd: AALL Bldg, POB 1166, George Town, Grand Cayman; tel. 949-5588; fax 945-5772; internet www.aall.com; Chair. ERIK MONSEN; Man. Dir KEVIN DOYLE.

Appleby Trust (Cayman) Ltd: Clifton House, 75 Fort St, POB 190, Grand Cayman KY1-1104; tel. 949-4900; fax 949-4901; e-mail cayman@applebyglobal.com; internet www.applebyglobal.com; f. 2006 following acquisition of business interests of Ansbacher (Cayman) Ltd; offices in Bermuda; Man. Dir HUW ST J. MOSES.

Atlantic Security Bank: POB 10340, George Town 1097, Grand Cayman; internet www.asbnet.com; f. 1981 as Banco de Crédito del Perú International, name changed as above 1986; Chair. DIONISIO ROMERO; Pres. CARLOS MUÑOZ.

Julius Baer Bank and Trust Co Ltd: Windward Bldg 3, Suite 310, Regatta Office Park, West Bay Rd, POB 1100, George Town, Grand Cayman; tel. 943-2237; fax 949-6096; e-mail charles.farrington@juliusbaer.com; internet www.juliusbaer.ch; f. 1974; 100% owned by Julius Baer Holding Ltd (Switzerland); Man. Dir CHARLES FARRINGTON.

Banco Português do Atlântico: POB 30124, Grand Cayman; tel. 949-8322; fax 949-7743; e-mail bcpjvic@candw.ky; Gen. Man. HELENA SOARES CARNEIRO.

Banco Safra (Cayman Islands) Ltd: c/o Bank of Nova Scotia, POB 501, George Town, Grand Cayman; tel. 949-2001; fax 949-7097; f. 1993; res US $124.5m., dep. US $268.8m. (Dec. 2007).

BANIF-Banco Internaçional do Funchal (Cayman) Ltd: Genesis Bldg, 3rd Floor, POB 32338 SMB, George Town, Grand Cayman; tel. 945-8060; fax 945-8069; e-mail banifcay@candw.ky; internet www.banif.pt; Chair., Exec. Bd Dr JOAQUIM FILIPE MARQUES DOS SANTOS; Chair., Admin. Bd HORÁCIO DA SILVA ROQUE.

Bank of Bermuda (Cayman) Ltd: British American Tower, 3rd Floor, POB 513, George Town, Grand Cayman; tel. 949-9898; fax 949-7959; internet www.bankofbermuda.bm; f. 1968 as a trust; converted to a bank in 1988; total assets US $1,041m. (July 2001); Chair. HENRY B. SMITH; Man. Dir ALLEN BERNARDO.

Bermuda Trust (Cayman) Ltd: 5th Floor, Bermuda House, POB 513, George Town, Grand Cayman; tel. 949-9898; fax 949-7959; internet www.bankofbermuda.bm; f. 1968 as Arawak Trust Co; became subsidiary of Bank of Bermuda in 1988; bank and trust services; Chair. JOHN CAMPBELL; Man. Dir KENNETH GIBBS.

Butterfield Bank (Cayman) Ltd: Butterfield House, 68 Fort St, POB 705, George Town, Grand Cayman KY1-1107; tel. 949-7055; fax 949-7004; e-mail info@ky.butterfieldbank.com; internet www.ky.butterfieldgroup.com; f. 1967; name changed as above in 2004, fmrly Bank of Butterfield International (Cayman) Ltd; subsidiary of Bank of N. T. Butterfield & Son Ltd, Bermuda; cap. US $16.5m., dep. US $3,116.8m. (Dec. 2008); Exec. Vice-Pres. (Int.) GRAHAM BROOKS; Man. Dir CONOR J. O'DEA; 3 brs.

Caledonian Bank and Trust Ltd: Caledonian House, 69 Dr Roy's Dr., POB 1043, George Town, Grand Cayman KY1-1102; tel. 949-0050; fax 949-8062; e-mail info@caledonian.com; internet www.caledonian.com; f. 1970; Chair. WILLIAM S. WALKER; Man. Dir DAVID WALKER.

Cayman National Bank Ltd: Cayman National Bank Bldg, 4th Floor, 200 Elgin Ave, POB 1097, George Town, Grand Cayman; tel. 949-4655; fax 949-7506; e-mail cnb@caymannational.com; internet www.caymannational.com; f. 1974; subsidiary of Cayman National Corpn; cap. CI $2.4m., res CI $42.7m., dep. CI $776.6m. (Sept. 2008); Chair. BENSON O. EBANKS; Pres. STUART DACK; 6 brs.

CITCO Bank and Trust Co Ltd: 89 Nexus Way, 2nd Floor, Camana Bay, POB 31105, Grand Cayman KY1-1205; tel. 945-3838; fax 945-3888; e-mail cayman-bank@citco.com; internet www.citco.com; Man. Dir ROBERT THOMAS.

Deutsche Bank (Cayman) Ltd: Boundary Hall, Cricket Sq., 171 Elgin Ave, POB 1984, George Town, Grand Cayman KY1-1104; tel. 949-8244; fax 949-8178; e-mail dmg-cay@candw.ky; internet www.dboffshore.com; f. 1983 as Morgan Grenfell (Cayman) Ltd; name changed to Deutsche Morgan Grenfell (Cayman) Ltd in 1996; name changed as above in 1998; cap. US $5.0m., res US $20.3m., dep. US $129.3m. (Dec. 1998); Chair. MARK HIRST; Regional Head JANET HISLOP.

Deutsche Bank International Trust Co (Cayman) Ltd: POB 1984, George Town, Grand Cayman; tel. 949-8244; fax 949-7866; f. 1999; Regional Man. TIM GODBER.

Deutsche Girozentrale Overseas Ltd: POB 694, George Town, Grand Cayman; tel. 914-9483; fax 949-0626; Man. Dir RAINER MACH.

Fidelity Bank (Cayman) Ltd: POB 914, George Town, Grand Cayman KY1-1103; tel. 949-7822; fax 949-6064; e-mail bank@fidelitycayman.com; internet www.fidelitycayman.com; f. 1979; Pres. and CEO BRETT HILL.

FirstCaribbean International Bank Ltd: POB 68, 25 Main St, George Town, Grand Cayman KY1-1102; tel. 949-7300; fax 949-7179; internet www.firstcaribbeanbank.com; f. 2002 following merger of Caribbean operations of Barclays Bank PLC and CIBC; Barclays relinquished its stake to CIBC in June 2006; Exec. Chair. MICHAEL MANSOOR; CEO JOHN D. ORR; Cayman Islands Contact MARK MCINTYRE.

UNITED KINGDOM OVERSEAS TERRITORIES

The Cayman Islands

Fortis Bank (Cayman) Ltd: Grand Pavilion Commercial Centre, 802 West Bay Rd, POB 2003, George Town, Grand Cayman; tel. 949-7942; fax 949-8340; e-mail phil.brown@ky.fortisbank.com; internet www.fortis.com; f. 1984 as Pierson, Heldring & Pierson (Cayman) Ltd; name changed to Mees Pierson (Cayman) Ltd in 1993; present name adopted in June 2000; Man. Dir ROGER HANSON.

HSBC Financial Services (Cayman) Ltd: HSBC House, 68 West Bay Rd, POB 1109, George Town, Grand Cayman KY1-1102; tel. 949-7755; fax 949-7634; e-mail hbky.information@ky.hsbc.com; internet www.hsbc.ky; f. 1982; CEO GONZALO JALLES.

Merrill Lynch Bank and Trust Co (Cayman) Ltd: Harbour Centre, 4th Floor, North Church St, George Town, Grand Cayman; tel. 814-6405; fax 949-8895; internet www.ml.com.

RBS Coutts (Cayman) Ltd: Coutts House, 1446 West Bay Rd, POB 707, George Town, Grand Cayman KY1-1107; tel. 945-4777; fax 945-4799; e-mail info@rbscoutts.com; internet www.rbscoutts.com; f. 1967; fmrly NatWest International Trust Corpn (Cayman) Ltd; 100% owned by Royal Bank of Scotland International (Holdings) Ltd (Jersey); CEO GERHARD H. MÜLLER.

Royal Bank of Canada: 24 Shedden Rd, POB 245, Grand Cayman KY1-1104; tel. 949-4600; fax 949-7396; internet www.royalbank.com; Vice-Pres. and Country Head JASON K. WATERS.

Royal Bank of Canada Trust Co (Cayman) Ltd: 24 Shedden Rd, POB 1586 GT, Grand Cayman KY1-1110; tel. 949-9107; fax 949-5777; internet www.rbcprivatebanking.com/cayman-islands.html; Man. Dir DEANNA BIDWELL.

Scotiabank and Trust (Cayman) Ltd: Scotia Centre, 6 Cardinal Ave, POB 689, George Town, Grand Cayman KY1-1107; tel. 949-2001; fax 949-7097; e-mail scotiaci@candw.ky; internet www.cayman.scotiabank.com; f. 1968; fmrly Bank of Nova Scotia Trust Company (Cayman) Ltd; present name adopted Dec. 2003; Man. Dir FARRIED SULLIMAN.

UBS Fund Services (Cayman Islands) Ltd: UBS House, 227 Elgin Ave, POB 852, George Town, Grand Cayman KY1-1103; tel. 914-1060; fax 914-4060; internet www.ubs.com/cayman-funds; Man. Dir DARREN STAINROD.

Development Bank

Cayman Islands Development Bank: Cayman Financial Centre, 36B Dr Roy's Dr., POB 1271 GT, George Town, Grand Cayman; tel. 949-7511; fax 949-6168; e-mail angela.miller@gov.ky; f. 2002; replaced the Housing Devt Corpn and the Agricultural and Industrial Devt Bd; under the jurisdiction of the Ministry of Finance, Tourism and Development; Devt Finance Institution Gen. Man. RALPH LEWIS.

Banking Association

Cayman Islands Bankers' Association: Macdonald Sq., Fort St, POB 676, George Town, Grand Cayman; tel. 949-0330; fax 945-1448; e-mail ciba@candw.ky; internet www.cibankers.org; Pres. DAVID WALKER; Sec. GARY DARWENT; 86 full mems, 250 assoc. mems.

STOCK EXCHANGE

Cayman Islands Stock Exchange (CSX): 4th Floor, Elizabethan Sq., POB 2408, George Town, Grand Cayman KY1-1105; tel. 945-6060; fax 945-6061; e-mail csx@csx.com.ky; internet www.csx.com.ky; f. 1996; more than 3,000 cos listed (Feb. 2011); Chair. ANTHONY B. TRAVERS; CEO VALIA THEODORAKI.

INSURANCE

Several foreign companies have agents in the islands. A total of 720 insurance companies were registered as of March 2011. In particular, the islands are a leading international market for health insurance. Locally incorporated companies include the following:

BAF Insurance Co (Cayman) Ltd: POB 10389, Grand Cayman KY1–1004; tel. 949-5089; fax 949-7192; e-mail spars-myles@mybafsolutions.com; Man. SANDRA PARS MYLES.

Cayman First Insurance Co Ltd: POB 2171, Grand Cayman KY1-1105; tel. 815-0869; fax 949-7457; e-mail michael.gayle@caymanfirst.com; internet www.caymanfirst.com; Man. MICHAEL GAYLE.

Cayman Islands National Insurance Co Ltd (CINICO): Cayman Centre, 1st Floor, Dorcy Dr, Airport Rd, George Town, POB 10112, Grand Cayman KY1-1001; tel. 949-8101; fax 949-8226; e-mail ltibbetts@cinico.ky; internet www.cinico.ky; govt-owned; Chair. DALE CROWLEY; Man. LONNY TIBBETTS.

Insurance Company of the West Indies (Cayman) Ltd (ICWI): 93 Hospital Rd, POB 461, Grand Cayman KY1-1106; tel. 949-6970; fax 949-6929; e-mail icwi@candw.ky; internet www.icwi.com/cayman; subsidiary of Insurance Company of the West Indies, Jamaica; Pres. PAUL LABOR; Man. HEATHER LANIGAN.

Island Heritage Insurance Co Ltd: Atlantic Star House, 128 Lawrence Blvd, POB 2501, Grand Cayman KY1-1104; tel. 949-7280; fax 945-6765; e-mail info@islandheritage.com.ky; internet www.islandheritageinsurance.com; general insurance; Chair. and CEO GARTH MACDONALD.

Sagicor Life of the Cayman Islands Ltd: 198 North Church St, POB 1087, George Town, Grand Cayman KY1-1102; tel. 949-8211; fax 949-8262; e-mail customerservice@sagicor.com; internet www.sagicor.com; f. 2004 by merger between Global Life and Capital Life; Man. NORMAN WILSON.

Sagicor General Insurance (Cayman) Ltd: 3rd Floor, Harbour Pl., 103 South Church St, POB 701, Grand Cayman KY1-1107; tel. 949-0579; fax 949-0624; e-mail abogle@bogleins.com; internet www.sagicor.ky; fmrly Cayman General Insurance Co Ltd; renamed as above in 2006 following acquisition of 51% interest by Sagicor Life of the Cayman Islands Ltd (q.v.); Man. ARTHUR BOGLE.

Trade and Industry

GOVERNMENT AGENCY

National Investment Council: Cayman Corporate Centre, 1st Floor, Hospital Rd, POB 10087 APO, Grand Cayman KY1-1001; tel. 945-0943; fax 945-0941; e-mail info@investcayman.gov.ky; internet www.investcayman.ky; f. 2003 as Cayman Islands Investment Bureau; renamed 2010 and merged into Dept of Commerce and Investment.

CHAMBER OF COMMERCE

Cayman Islands Chamber of Commerce: Macdonald Sq., 2nd Floor, Fort St, POB 1000, George Town, Grand Cayman KY1-1102; tel. 949-8090; fax 949-0220; e-mail info@caymanchamber.ky; internet www.caymanchamber.ky; f. 1965; Pres. STEWART BOSTOCK; CEO WIL PINEAU; 594 corporate mems and 78 associates.

TRADE ASSOCIATION

Cayman Finance: POB 11048, Grand Cayman; tel. 946-6000; fax 946-6001; e-mail info@caymanfinances.com; internet www.caymanfinances.com; f. 2003 as Cayman Islands Financial Services Association; name changed as above in Oct. 2009; aims to promote the integrity and transparency of the financial services sector; Chair. RICHARD COLES.

EMPLOYERS' ORGANIZATION

Human Resources Department: 4th Floor, Tower Bldg, Grand Cayman; tel. 949-0941; fax 945-6057; Dir DALE M. BANKS.

UTILITIES

Electricity

Electricity Regulatory Authority: Grand Pavilion, Suite 2, West Bay Rd, POB 10189, Grand Cayman KY1-1002; tel. 949-8372; fax 947-9598; e-mail general@caymanera.com; internet caymanera.com; f. 2005; Chair. SHERRI BODDEN-COWAN; Man. Dir PHILIP THOMAS.

Caribbean Utilities Co Ltd (CUC): Corporate HQ & Plant, 457 North Sound Rd, POB 38, George Town, Grand Cayman; tel. 949-5200; fax 949-5203; e-mail service@cuc.ky; internet www.cuc-cayman.com; Pres. and CEO J. F. RICHARD HEW; Chair. DAVID RITCH.

Cayman Brac Power and Light Co Ltd (CBP&L): Stake Bay Point, POB 95, Stake Bay, Cayman Brac; tel. 948-2224; fax 948-2204; e-mail braclite@candw.ky; Gen. Man. JONATHAN TIBBETTS.

Water

Cayman Islands Water Authority: 13G Red Gate Rd, POB 1104 GT, George Town, Grand Cayman KY1-1102; tel. 949-2837; fax 949-0094; e-mail info@waterauthority.ky; internet www.waterauthority.ky; Dir Dr GELIA FREDERICK-VAN GENDEREN; Chair. JONATHAN PIERCY.

Consolidated Water Co Ltd (CWCO): Windward 3, 4th Floor, Regatta Office Park, POB 1114, George Town, Grand Cayman KY1-1102; tel. 945-4277; fax 949-2957; e-mail info@cwco.com; internet ir.cwco.com; f. 1973; Pres. and CEO FREDERICK W. MCTAGGART; Dir and Chair. WILMER F. PERGANDE.

Transport

ROADS

There are some 406 km (252 miles) of motorable roads, of which 304 km are surfaced with tarmac. The road network connects all districts on Grand Cayman and Cayman Brac (which has 76 km of motorable road), and there are 43 km of motorable road on Little Cayman (of which about 18 km are paved). According to the 2009 budget address, US $5.3m. was to be allocated for ongoing improvements to the islands' road network.

UNITED KINGDOM OVERSEAS TERRITORIES

SHIPPING

George Town is the principal port. An agreement to build a new port facility in George Town was signed in April 2010. Cruise liners, container ships and smaller cargo vessels ply between the Cayman Islands, Florida, Jamaica and Costa Rica. There is no cruise ship dock in the Cayman Islands. Ships anchor off George Town and ferry passengers ashore to the North or South Dock Terminals in George Town. The number of cruise ship passengers is limited to 6,000 per day. The port of Cayman Brac is Creek; there are limited facilities on Little Cayman. In December 2009 the shipping register comprised 150 vessels, with combined displacement totalling 2,912,275 grt.

Maritime Authority of Cayman Islands (MACI): Strathvale House, 2nd Floor, 90 North Church St, POB 2256, Grand Cayman KY1-1107; tel. 949-8831; fax 949-8849; e-mail maci.consulting@cishipping.com; internet www.cishipping.com; f. 2005; wholly govt-owned; legal entity responsible for: enforcement of international maritime laws and conventions; implementation of maritime safety and security, Cayman Islands marine environment laws; formation of national maritime policy; representation and protection of national maritime interests at international forums; also undertakes vessel and mortgage registration, advisory and marine survey and audit services fmrly administered by CISR; Chair. SHARON E. ROULSTONE; CEO A. JOEL WALTON.

Port Authority of the Cayman Islands: Harbour Dr., POB 1358 GT, George Town, Grand Cayman KY1-1108; tel. 949-2055; fax 949-5820; e-mail support@caymanport.com; internet www.caymanport.com; Chair. STEFAN BARAUD.

Principal Shipping Companies

Cayman Islands Shipping Registry: Strathvale House, 2nd Floor, 90 North Church St, POB 2256, Grand Cayman KY1-110; tel. 949-8831; fax 949-8849; e-mail cisrky@cishipping.com; internet www.cishipping.com; f. 1993; division of Maritime Authority of Cayman Islands (MACI); Dir A. JOEL WALTON.

Seaboard Marine (Cayman): Mirco Commerce Centre, 2nd Floor, Industrial Park, POB 1372, George Town, Grand Cayman KY1-1108; tel. 949-4977; fax 949-8402; e-mail info@seaboardcayman.com; internet www.seaboardcayman.com; Man. Dir ROBERT FOSTER.

Thompson Shipping Co Ltd: Cayman Shipping Centre, 2nd Floor, 432 Eastern Ave, POB 188, George Town, Grand Cayman KY1-1004; tel. 949-8044; fax 949-8349; e-mail info@thompsonshipping.com; internet www.thompsonshipping.com; f. 1977; agent for Thompson Line, a div. of Tropical Shipping; Contact Person SUSAN GABRUCH.

CIVIL AVIATION

There are two international airports in the Territory: Owen Roberts International Airport, 3.5 km (2 miles) from George Town, and Gerrard Smith International Airport on Cayman Brac. Both are capable of handling jet-engined aircraft. Edward Bodden Airport on Little Cayman can cater for light aircraft. Several scheduled carriers serve the islands.

Civil Aviation Authority of the Cayman Islands (CAACI): Unit 2, Cayman Grand Harbour Complex, Shamrock Rd, POB 10277, George Town, Grand Cayman KY1-1003; tel. 949-7811; fax 949-0761; e-mail civil.aviation@caacayman.com; internet www.caacayman.com; f. 1987; Dir-Gen. RICHARD SMITH; Chair. SHERIDAN BROOKS-HURST.

Cayman Airways Ltd: 91 Owen Roberts Dr., POB 10092, Grand Cayman KY1-1001; tel. 949-8200; fax 949-7607; e-mail customerrelations@caymanairways.net; internet www.caymanairways.com; f. 1968; wholly govt-owned since 1977; operates local services and scheduled flights to Jamaica, Honduras and the USA; Pres. and CEO FABIAN WHORMS.

Island Air: Airport Rd, POB 2433, George Town, Grand Cayman KY1-1105; tel. 949-5252; fax 949-1073; e-mail res@islandair.ky; internet islandair.ky; f. 1987; operates daily scheduled services between Grand Cayman, Cayman Brac and Little Cayman; Man. Dir MARCUS CUMBER.

Tourism

The Cayman Islands are a major tourist destination, the majority of visitors coming from North America. The beaches and opportunities for diving in the offshore reefs form the main attraction for most tourists. In 2007 there were an estimated 4,484 hotel rooms. In 2009 there were 272,000 arrivals by air (compared with 302,900 in 2008) and some 1,520,400 cruise visitors (compared with 1,553,100 in 2008). The USA remained the core market for stay-over visitors to the islands (78.5% in 2009). In 2008 the tourism industry earned an estimated US $353m.

Cayman Islands Department of Tourism: Cricket Sq., POB 67, George Town, Grand Cayman KY1-1102; tel. 949-0623; fax 949-4053; internet www.caymanislands.ky; f. 1965; Dir SHOMARI SCOTT (acting).

Cayman Islands Tourism Association (CITA): Largatos Bldg, 73 Lawrence Blvd, POB 31086 SMB, Grand Cayman; tel. and fax 949-8522; e-mail info@cita.ky; internet www.cita.ky; f. 2001 as a result of the amalgamation of the Cayman Tourism Alliance and the Cayman Islands Hotel and Condominium Asscn; Pres. KARIE BERGSTROM; Exec. Dir KEN THOMPSON.

Sister Islands Tourism Association (SITA): POB 187, Cayman Brac KY2-2101; tel. and fax 948-1345; e-mail sita@candw.ky; internet www.sisterislands.com; Pres. PETER HILLENBRAND (acting).

Defence

The United Kingdom is responsible for the defence of the Cayman Islands.

Education

Schooling is compulsory for children between the ages of five and 15 years. It is provided free in 16 government-run schools, and there are also 10 private schools. Primary education, from five years of age, lasts for six years; in 2007/08 enrolment at primary schools included an estimated 85% of pupils in the relevant age-group. Secondary education is for seven years; enrolment at secondary-level institutions in 2007/08 included an estimated 81% of students in the relevant age-group. There were also 381 children enrolled at pre-primary schools in 2008. The Cayman Islands Law School, Community College of the Cayman Islands, University College of the Cayman Islands and the International College of the Cayman Islands number among providers of tertiary level education in the territory. Budgetary spending on education in 2009/10 was approved at US $176.3m.

THE FALKLAND ISLANDS

Introductory Survey

LOCATION, CLIMATE, LANGUAGE, RELIGION, FLAG, CAPITAL

The Falkland Islands, comprising two large islands and about 200 smaller ones, are in the south-western Atlantic Ocean, about 770 km (480 miles) north-east of Cape Horn, South America. The climate is generally cool, with strong winds (mainly westerly) throughout the year. The mean annual temperature is 6°C (42°F), while average annual rainfall is 635 mm (25 ins). The language is English. Most of the inhabitants profess Christianity, with several denominations represented. The flag is the British 'Blue Ensign', with the territory's coat of arms (a shield showing a white and violet ram standing in green grass, on a blue background, above a sailing ship bearing red crosses on its pennants and five six-pointed stars on its central sail, on three white horizontal wavy lines, with the motto 'Desire the Right' on a scroll beneath) on a white disc in the centre of the flag. The capital is Stanley, on East Falkland Island.

CONTEMPORARY POLITICAL HISTORY

Historical Context

The first recorded landing on the islands was made from a British ship in 1690, when the group was named after Viscount Falkland, then Treasurer of the Royal Navy. French sailors named the islands 'Les Malouines' (after their home port of Saint-Malo), from which the Spanish name 'Islas Malvinas' is derived. A French settlement was established in 1764 on the island of East Falkland, but in 1767 France relinquished its rights to the territory to Spain, which then ruled the adjacent regions of South America. Meanwhile, a British expedition annexed West Falkland in 1765, and a garrison was established. The British settlement, formed in 1765–66, was recognized by Spain in 1771 but withdrawn in 1774. The Spanish garrison was withdrawn in 1811.

When the United Provinces of the River Plate (now Argentina) gained independence from Spain in 1816, the Falkland Islands had no permanent inhabitants, although they provided temporary bases for sealing and whaling activities by British and US vessels. In 1820 an Argentine ship was sent to the islands to proclaim Argentine sovereignty as successor to Spain. An Argentine settlement was founded in 1826 but most of its occupants were expelled by a US warship in 1831. The remaining Argentines were ejected by a British expedition in 1832, and British sovereignty was established in 1833.

Domestic Political Affairs
Conflict with Argentina

The islands became a Crown Colony of the United Kingdom, administered by a British-appointed Governor. However, Argentina did not relinquish its claim, and negotiations to resolve the dispute began in 1966 at the instigation of the UN. The inhabitants of the islands, nearly all British by descent, consistently expressed their desire to remain under British sovereignty.

After routine talks between delegations of the British and Argentine Governments in New York in February 1982, the Argentine foreign ministry announced that it would seek other means to resolve the dispute. Argentina's military regime took advantage of a British protest at the presence of a group of Argentine scrap merchants, who had made an unauthorized landing on South Georgia in March and had raised an Argentine flag, to invade the Falkland Islands on 2 April. A small contingent of British marines was overwhelmed, the British Governor was expelled and an Argentine military governorship was established. The USA and the UN attempted (unsuccessfully) to mediate, in an effort to prevent military escalation. British forces, which had been dispatched to the islands immediately after the Argentine invasion, recaptured South Georgia on 25 April. The Argentine forces on the Falklands formally surrendered on 14 June, after a conflict in the course of which about 750 Argentine, 255 British and three Falklanders' lives were lost.

The Governor returned to the islands as Civil Commissioner on 25 June 1982, and the United Kingdom established a 'protection zone' around the islands, extending 150 nautical miles (278 km) off shore, as well as a garrison of about 4,000 troops. The British Government began an investigation into the possibilities of developing the islands' economy, and in November agreed to grant the Falkland Islanders full British citizenship. In November 1983 the post of Chief Executive of the Falkland Islands Government was created, in combination with the executive vice-chairmanship of the newly formed Falkland Islands Development Corporation.

The issue of the sovereignty of the Falkland Islands remained a major impediment to the normalization of relations between Argentina and the United Kingdom. The Argentine Government refused to agree to a formal declaration that hostilities were ended until the United Kingdom agreed to participate in negotiations over sovereignty, while the United Kingdom refused to negotiate until Argentina had formally ended hostilities. In October 1984 the Argentine Government removed restrictions on British companies and interests in Argentina as a possible prelude to resuming negotiations. However, the British Government's refusal to discuss the issue of sovereignty, and its insistence on the paramountcy of the Falkland Islanders' wishes, were reflected in the new Constitution for the Falklands (approved by the islands' Legislative Council in January 1985), which guaranteed the islanders' right to self-determination.

The number of British troops stationed on the islands was reduced, following the opening, in mid-1985, of a new military airport at Mount Pleasant, about 30 km south-west of Stanley, enabling rapid reinforcement of the garrison, if necessary. In October elections took place on the Falklands for a new Legislative Council.

In 1986 parliamentary delegations from the United Kingdom and Argentina conducted exploratory talks. However, the British Government remained intransigent on the issue of sovereignty. In early 1986 Argentina's continued claim to the naval 'protection zone' was manifested in attacks on foreign fishing vessels by Argentine gunboats. In October the United Kingdom unilaterally declared a fisheries conservation and management zone extending 150 nautical miles (278 km) around the islands, with effect from February 1987, to prevent the over-fishing of the waters. The imposition of this zone, whose radius coincided with that of the naval protection zone, was condemned by the majority of UN members, as was the United Kingdom's rejection, in November 1986, of an offer by Argentina to declare a formal end to hostilities in exchange for the abolition of the protection zone.

Beginning in 1982 the UN General Assembly voted annually, by an overwhelming majority, in favour of the resumption of negotiations between Argentina and the United Kingdom. The British Government consistently declined to engage in such dialogue. However, relations between Argentina and the United Kingdom improved, following the election, in May 1989, of a new Argentine President, Carlos Saúl Menem, who initially indicated that his country would be willing to suspend temporarily its demand that the issue of the sovereignty of the Falkland Islands be discussed, in the interests of the restoration of full diplomatic and commercial relations with the United Kingdom. In October a meeting of British and Argentine representatives, which took place in Madrid, Spain, culminated in the formal cessation of all hostilities, and the re-establishment of diplomatic relations at consular level. Restrictions on Argentine merchant vessels with regard to the naval protection zone around the Falkland Islands were also eased. In the following month, however, the United Kingdom announced that it was to increase the extent of its territorial waters around the islands from three to 12 nautical miles, in spite of protests from the Argentine authorities. In February 1990 Argentina and the United Kingdom conducted further negotiations in Madrid, as a result of which the two countries re-established full diplomatic relations. It was also announced that the naval protection zone around the Falkland Islands was to be modified in March, and that mutually agreed military procedures, which would ensure the security of the region, would take effect.

Following successful negotiations between Argentina and the United Kingdom in Madrid in November 1990, an agreement regarding the protection and conservation of the South Atlantic fishing area was announced. The two sides also agreed to establish a South Atlantic Fisheries Commission, to discuss fishing activity and conservation in the region.

In December 1993 the Argentine Government indicated its acceptance of the United Kingdom's proposed extension of fishing rights around the Falkland Islands from 150 to 200 miles, in order to allow the islanders to fulfil an annual squid-fishing quota of 150,000 metric tons. In August 1994 the British Government unilaterally decided to extend its fisheries conservation zone north of the islands, thereby annexing a small but lucrative fishing ground (not previously protected by British or Argentine legislation) that was being plundered by foreign fishing vessels. In January 1997 the United Kingdom and Argentina agreed to resume negotiations on a long-term fisheries agreement that would include the disputed waters around the islands. Following the release of a Joint Declaration between the two Governments on 14 July 1999, both Governments agreed to co-operate to combat illegal fishing in the South West Atlantic and to ensure the sustainability of fish stocks in the region.

In November 1991 the Governments of both Argentina and the United Kingdom claimed rights of exploration and exploitation of the sea-bed and the subsoil of the continental shelf around the Falkland Islands (which were believed to be rich in petroleum reserves). In April 1992 the Falkland Islands Government invited tenders for seismic reports of the region. In December 1993 the British Geological Survey reported that preliminary seismic investigations indicated deposits in excess of those located in British North Sea oilfields. A bilateral agreement on petroleum and gas exploration in an area of 18,000 sq km, south-west of the islands, was concluded in New York, USA, in September 1994. A joint hydrocarbons commission would regulate licensing in the area, examining bids from Anglo-Argentine joint ventures (in which case taxes would be levied on operators by the respective Governments) or by third countries (from which royalties on revenues would be exacted by the Falkland Islands Government at a rate expected to approach 9%). The successful conclusion of the agreement appeared to dissipate Argentine objections, voiced earlier in the year, to the Falkland Islands' unilateral offer of rights to drill in 19 areas (comprising 44,000 sq km not covered by the Anglo-Argentine agreement) to the north and south of the islands. Licences to explore for hydrocarbons were awarded to five international consortia in October 1996. The possibility that commercial quantities of petroleum might be discovered prompted renewed discussion as to the amount of any future royalties exacted by the Falkland Islands Government that should be returned to the Government of the United Kingdom. In early 1997 the British Government indicated that it expected to benefit considerably from any such royalties, while the Falkland Islands administration proposed that some of the revenue could be used to finance the islands' defence expenditure (currently funded by the United Kingdom). Meanwhile, the Argentine Government claimed that it should be entitled to benefit from the discovery of petroleum in the region: draft legislation presented to Congress provided for the imposition of sanctions on petroleum companies and fishing vessels operating in Falkland Islands waters without Argentine authorization, in addition to the levying of 3% royalties from the sale of petroleum discovered in the area.

In May 1999 formal negotiations between the Falkland Islands and Argentina took place in the United Kingdom. Issues under discussion included co-operation in fishing and petroleum exploration, Argentine access to the islands and the resumption of air links with mainland South America. (In March Chile had ended its country's regular air services to the islands in protest at the British Government's continued detention of the former Chilean President, Gen. Augusto Pinochet; Uruguay subsequently agreed not to establish an air link with the islands unless flights were routed via the Argentine capital.) The sovereignty of the Falkland Islands was not scheduled for discussion. Four of the islands' councillors also attended the three days of talks, thereby occasioning the first direct talks between Falkland Islanders and the Argentine Government. The dialogue continued in July in New York and London. On 14 July a joint Argentine-British declaration was issued that eliminated the restrictions on travel by Argentine citizens to the Falkland Islands and re-established airline services by the Chilean carrier LanChile between South America and the Falkland Islands (with a stop-over in Argentina). It was also agreed to increase bilateral co-operation between Argentina and the Falkland Islands on combating illegal fishing and conservation of fish stocks. Symbolic gestures included allowing the construction of a monument to the Argentine war dead at their cemetery on the islands (permission was finally granted in March 2002), while in return the Argentine Government would cease to use the Spanish names given to Falklands locations during the 1982 occupation. The agreement did not affect claims to sovereignty. Even so, the round of talks provoked demonstrations by an estimated 500 people on the Falkland Islands. The protests resumed on 16 October when the first flights carrying Argentine visitors arrived in the Falklands. In July 2000 the Anglo-Argentine dialogue on joint petroleum and gas exploration was suspended by mutual agreement for an indefinite period of time.

In May 2003 the new Argentine President, Néstor Carlos Kirchner, reiterated his country's claim to the Falkland Islands. In November Argentina began to demand that the increasingly frequent air charter services flying from the Falkland Islands to Chile obtain permission to use Argentine airspace. The decision was intended to exert pressure on the British Government into reversing its policy of not allowing Argentine airlines to fly to the Falkland Islands. The services were suspended in January 2004 after the British Government lodged objections to the Argentine demands; the situation seemed likely to damage the territory's burgeoning tourism trade. In March a British proposal for the resumption of direct charter flights from Argentina to the Falkland Islands was rejected by the Kirchner Government, which continued to demand that an Argentine carrier be authorized to benefit from the increased passenger traffic between the Falkland Islands and mainland South America. A reference to the islands was included in a draft of the constitutional treaty of the European Union, to which Argentina strongly objected. At a meeting of the UN's Special Committee on Decolonization, held in mid-2005, the Falkland Islands appealed for the right to self-determination; the Committee requested that the Governments of Argentina and the United Kingdom resume negotiations.

The Argentine Government formed a Congressional Observatory in June 2006 with the express function of actively reclaiming the Falkland Islands, which it continued to refer to as Argentine territory. In January 2007 the Argentine Minister of Foreign Affairs, International Trade and Worship, Jorge Taiana, had sought to enlist the support of the UN Secretary-General, Ban Ki-Moon, asserting that the United Kingdom had seized the archipelago by illegal means. President Kirchner maintained that the islanders possessed no right to self-determination, contending that the present population displaced indigenous Argentine residents upon settlement in 1833 with the intention of establishing a British colonial state, a claim strenuously refuted by the United Kingdom. In February Argentina rejected an invitation by the British Government to participate in joint commemorative celebrations to mark the 25th anniversary of the conflict's end. A joint hydrocarbon exploratory contract between Argentina and the United Kingdom was abandoned in the following month; the Argentine Government accused the British of pursuing a 'unilateral' approach to oil exploration initiatives and averred that there would be no further developments on the matter until the United Kingdom had agreed to resume negotiations over the islands' sovereignty. The original agreement, signed by former Argentine President Carlos Saúl Menem in 1995, followed the restoration of diplomatic relations between the two countries in 1990 and had been regarded as Argentine acknowledgment of the United Kingdom's claim to the sea floor surrounding the Falkland Islands. In April 2007 the Kirchner administration reiterated its claim to the territory and enjoined the British Government to cede to international demands to engage in dialogue over the future of the islands. The United Kingdom stated that it would not consider amendments to the governance or affiliations of the Falkland Islands unless and until a request to this effect was registered by the populace; it was asserted that no such request had been expressed by the islanders and, further, that they opposed Argentina's territorial offensive.

New legislation approved by the Argentine legislature on 11 April 2007 effectively required fishing companies wishing to operate in the maritime exclusion zone surrounding the islands to choose between Argentine or British authorities when making permit applications, and included restrictions against fishing in Argentine jurisdictional waters where a permit issued by the corresponding issuing authority was not held. A recent decision by the Falkland Islands authorities to begin issuing 25-year licences—as opposed to the one-year permits issued previously—had provoked protest from Argentina, which claimed its territorial rights had been disregarded.

During her inauguration speech in December 2007, the new President of Argentina, Cristina Fernández de Kirchner, stated that she was not prepared to make concessions in sovereignty claims, and her Government once again urged the United Kingdom to relaunch the negotiations process. However, in October 2007 the British Government announced its intention to submit a claim to the UN Commission on the Limits of the Continental Shelf for Atlantic seabed territory around the Falkland Islands. Argentine foreign minister Taiana insisted that his Government would challenge any such claim made by the United Kingdom. Furthermore, tensions between the two countries were exacerbated in early May 2008 when Taiana accused the British Government of 'illegitimately' issuing licences for hydrocarbon exploration and extraction activities in an area north of the Falkland Islands, part of the Argentine continental shelf. The British Government refused to concede to any of the claims made by its Argentine counterpart and maintained that it held sovereignty over the disputed area. On 24 April 2009 Argentina lodged a hostile claim before the UN Commission to some 1.7m. sq km (660,000 sq miles) of seabed surrounding the territory, as well as an area north of Antarctica. This was formally countered by the United Kingdom, which presented its own claim to the disputed region. Tensions between Argentina and the United Kingdom rose further in September after a British company, Desire Petroleum, announced plans to commence drilling in an area north of the Falklands in 2010. In the weeks preceding the start of the operation in February, the Argentine Government asserted that the drilling was illegal, and reiterated its claim on the seabed surrounding the islands. In mid-February President Kirchner decreed that all ships sailing through Argentine waters must hold a permit, effectively blockading the area around the islands and at the end of the month US Secretary of State Hillary Clinton appeared to support Argentina's position by pledging to help 'resolve' the sovereignty issue. Despite the escalation of the dispute, drilling went ahead as planned (although by April 2011 Desire had yet to produce petroleum from any of the wells drilled). In May 2010 Rockhopper Exploration of the United Kingdom announced that it had discovered oil in an offshore bloc to the north of the islands, prompting renewed Argentine criticism of the drilling operations. After further analysis of the deposit, Rockhopper Exploration confirmed in March 2011 the presence of a 'significant' amount of petroleum, which was 'highly likely to prove commercially viable'.

In May 2010 Argentina expressed dissatisfaction that the new British Government had rejected a proposal to restart sovereignty discussions. An escalating British naval presence in the region, as part of 'routine military exercises' in Falkland waters, including the firing of missiles, attracted criticism from Argentina, Brazil, Paraguay, Uruguay and Venezuela in October. In support of neighbouring Argentina's position on the Falklands Islands, in September Uruguay had refused to allow a British naval vessel, which was en route to the disputed archipelago, to refuel at a Uruguayan port. In a similar incident, Brazil also denied a British naval ship permission to dock in January 2011.

A new Constitution

A new Constitution came into force on 1 January 2009. The charter was a culmination of a constitutional review process initiated by the British Government's Department of Overseas Territories in 1997, with the aim of according greater self-governance to the islands. A number of changes to the administration of the territory had been proposed; a Constitutional Select Committee was convened in February 2007 to complete the review discussions, and final proposals were submitted to the British Foreign and Commonwealth Office (FCO) for deliberation in June. Most notable among the amendments proposed were the insertion of the citizens' right to self-determination within the main body of the Constitution, the updating of provisions in accordance with the United Kingdom's obligations under the European Convention on Human Rights, and clarification of the Governor's and Chief Executive's roles as head of the Public Service and head of the Civil Service, respectively. Proposals for the establishment of a Complaints Commissioner and a Public Accounts Committee, the consolidation of electoral districts into a single constituency and the determination of the extent of self-government to be exercised by the territory were designated as matters requiring further consultation with the FCO before being written into statute. Officials from the FCO held two rounds of talks with the Constitutional Select Committee in December 2007 and February 2008 to discuss the draft new constitution. Following further public consultation, the new Constitution came into force in 2009. It asserted the islanders' right to self-determination and contained amendments to the rules under which British citizens would be eligible for Falklands Islands status, as well as provisions for a Public Accounts Committee and a Complaints Commissioner to improve transparency in the territory. It also provided further clarification of the division of powers between the Executive Council and the Governor, stating that the Governor must abide by the advice of the Executive Council on domestic policies, though not in matters of external affairs, defence and the administration of justice.

Recent developments: landmine-clearing

In enforcing the statutes of the Ottawa Convention, adopted under the Landmines Act 1998, the United Kingdom was required to identify and eliminate all mine devices within its territory and overseas jurisdictions within 10 years of the Convention's enactment. The resultant deadline for the destruction of all anti-personnel landmines in the Falkland Islands was established as March 2009.

UNITED KINGDOM OVERSEAS TERRITORIES

The Falkland Islands

An assessment of the feasibility of eliminating the remaining landmines was conducted in October 2007 and revealed that the process would be technically possible but was expected to require a considerable amount of funding. At a meeting of Ottawa Convention signatories in Geneva, Switzerland, in November 2008, the United Kingdom was granted a 10-year extension to the March 2009 deadline, with the proviso that research into modern methods of mine-clearing be undertaken. An operation, begun in 2009, to remove some 1,250 landmines from four minefields was completed successfully in June 2010. However, the British Government estimated in February 2011 that over 15,000 mines, in 83 minefields, were still deployed in the territory. An FCO contingent travelled to the islands in the same month to discuss the implementation of a new mine-clearing programme. The operation was expected to commence in November following a bidding process and would focus on demining affected areas in Stanley, opening up previously inaccessible parts of the capital to residents and tourists.

CONSTITUTION AND GOVERNMENT

A new Constitution came into force on 1 January 2009. Administration is conducted by the appointed Governor (who is the personal representative of the British monarch), aided by the Executive Council, comprising two ex officio members and three members elected by the Legislative Assembly. The Legislative Assembly is composed of the Governor, two ex officio members and eight elected members. Voting is by universal adult suffrage.

REGIONAL AND INTERNATIONAL CO-OPERATION

The Falkland Islands are a member of the Commonwealth (see p. 230).

ECONOMIC AFFAIRS

According to government estimates, gross domestic product (GDP) was some £104m. in 2007. In 2001 GDP per head was put at £24,030 and annual growth was estimated at 2%.

Most of the agricultural land on the Falkland Islands is devoted to the rearing of sheep. However, the land is poor and more than four acres are required to support one animal. In the late 1990s annual exports of wool were valued at some £3.5m. Declining international wool prices encouraged agricultural diversification, such as the pursuit of organic farming, the breeding of cashmere goats and also the development of meat production (an abattoir was constructed to meet European Union standards, incurring expenditure of £372,332 in 2002 and a further £678,371 in 2003). Some vegetables are produced (notably in a hydroponic market garden), and there are small dairy herds (384 dairy cows in 2009/10). From 1987, when a licensing system was introduced for foreign vessels fishing within a 150-nautical-mile conservation and management zone (see Contemporary Political History), the economy was diversified and the islands' annual income increased considerably. Although revenue from the sale of licences declined in the 1990s following the Argentine Government's commencement of the sale of fishing licences in 1993, licences (and transshipments) totalled £18.0m. in 2009/10, equivalent to 42.5% of total budget revenue in that year. The revenue funds social provisions and economic development programmes. In the late 1980s about one-third of the world's total catch of *illex* and *loligo* squid was derived from this fishing zone. However, over-fishing in the area surrounding the conservation zone had a detrimental effect on stocks of fish in the islands' waters. The sector contracted in 2009. A recovery was evident in 2010, but squid numbers remained relatively low.

Manufacturing activity on the islands reflects the predominance of the agricultural sector: a wool mill on West Falkland produces yarns for machine knitting, hand knitting and weaving. Several small companies in the Falklands produce garments for local and export sales. Some fish-processing also takes place on East Falkland.

The Falkland Islands are heavily dependent on imports of all fuels, except peat; households primarily depend on kerosene and diesel for heating purposes. Wind power is used in many remote locations to offset this dependence and reduce pollution of the atmosphere. Two British prospecting companies were granted exploration licences to explore for hydrocarbons in waters to the north of the islands in 2010; in May one of the companies, Rockhopper Exploration, announced it had made a 'significant' discovery of petroleum.

The Falkland Islands Development Corporation oversees the islands' economic development on behalf of the Government. Since the 1980s the Government has sought to promote the development of the tourism sector. Tourism, and in particular eco-tourism, developed rapidly in the 2000s, and the number of visitors staying on the Falklands Islands had grown to some 3,000 a year, while around 40,000 tourists a year sailed through Stanley harbour on their way to Antarctica and sub-Antarctic islands such as South Georgia. In 2009/10 some 62,500 cruise ship passengers visited the Falkland Islands. The sale of postage stamps and coins represents a significant source of income; the value of sales of the former was £296,229 in 1996/97, while the value of sales of the latter totalled £49,351 in 1995/96.

In 2000 the islands recorded an estimated trade surplus of £28,041,897. Fish, most of which is purchased by the United Kingdom, Spain and Chile, is the islands' most significant export. The principal imports are fuel, provisions, alcoholic beverages, building materials and clothing. In 2001 the Government brought 100 reindeer from the South Georgia Islands (with the aim of increasing the number to 10,000 over the following 20 years) in order to export venison to Scandinavia and Chile.

The budget for the financial year 2009/10 provided for revenue of £42.4m. and expenditure of £47.6m. The islands are generally self-sufficient in all areas of the economy (although expenditures associated with defence are the responsibility of the British Government). The annual rate of inflation averaged 2.5% in 1995–2003; consumer prices increased by 0.7% in 2002 and by 1.2% in 2003. There is a significant shortage of local labour on the islands.

The economy of the Falkland Islands enjoyed a period of strong and sustained growth from the 1980s, partly owing to substantial investment by the British Government, but primarily as a result of the introduction of the fisheries licensing scheme in 1987. The sector accounted for about 60% of GDP. The area around the islands had been overfished both by Falkland Islanders and, from 2005 (when Argentina withdrew from the South Atlantic Fishing Commission, which manages fisheries), by Argentine vessels. The precarious nature of the fishing licence sector increased hopes that exploitation of hydrocarbons in the waters around the islands would yield positive results. Seismic surveys conducted in the waters around the Falkland Islands in 2008 suggested the area could yield as much as 18,000m. barrels of petroleum. Drilling began in early 2010; confirmation in early 2011 of a 'significant' petroleum deposit raised expectations of further oil reserves being uncovered. Nevertheless, the exploration of hydrocarbons in the area threatened other sectors of the economy. Argentina imposed several economic sanctions on the Falklands, including a ban on oil companies working in that country from any involvement in oil exploration around the Falkland Islands. It also prohibited Chilean flights to the islands from using Argentine airspace, a move that threatened the Falkland Islands' burgeoning tourism sector. Tourism numbers decreased slightly in 2010 following a sharper decline in 2009, although the sector was forecast to recover in 2011. According to government figures, the economy was expected to expand by 5.3% in 2010. This followed a drastic contraction of about 9.0%, according to preliminary estimates, in 2009, mainly owing to the fall in the squid catch and a reduction in tourist numbers.

PUBLIC HOLIDAYS

2012: 1 January (New Year's Day), 6 April (Good Friday), 23 April (for HM the Queen's Birthday), 14 June (Liberation Day), 1 October (Spring Holiday), 10 December (for Anniversary of the Battle of the Falkland Islands in 1914), 25–27 December (Christmas).

Statistical Survey

Source (unless otherwise stated): The Treasury of the Falkland Islands Government, Stanley, FIQQ 1ZZ; tel. 27143; fax 27144; internet www.falklands.gov.fk.

AREA AND POPULATION

Area: approx. 12,173 sq km (4,700 sq miles): East Falkland and adjacent islands 6,760 sq km (2,610 sq miles); West Falkland and adjacent islands 5,413 sq km (2,090 sq miles).

Population: 2,478 at census of 8 October 2006. Note: Figure excludes military personnel and civilians based at Mount Pleasant military base and the 84 residents absent on the night of the census.

Density (2006 census): 0.20 per sq km.

Population by Age and Sex (at 2006 census): *0–14:* 458 (males 222, females 236); *15–64:* 1,755 (males 903, females 852); *65 and over:* 265 (males 135, females 130); *Total* 2,478 (males 1,260, females 1,218).

Principal Town (2006 census): Stanley (capital), population 2,115.

Births and Deaths (2006): Live births 27; Deaths 20. Source: UN, *Population and Vital Statistics Report*.

Economically Active Population (persons aged 15 years and over, 2001 census): 2,475 (males 1,370, females 1,105).

AGRICULTURE, ETC.

Livestock (2010, official figures at 31 May): Sheep 478,525; Cattle 4,738; Goats 149; Reindeer 184; Horses 519; Poultry 1,870.

Livestock Products (metric tons, 2009 unless otherwise indicated, FAO estimates): Cattle meat 156; Sheep meat 810; Cows' milk 1,600 (2008); Wool, greasy 2,400 (2008). Source: FAO.

Fishing ('000 metric tons, live weight of capture, 2008): Southern blue whiting 1.8; Argentine hake 3.9; Patagonian grenadier 4.1; Patagonian squid 45.7; Argentine shortfin squid 4.0; Total catch (incl. others) 81.7. Source: FAO.

FINANCE

Currency and Exchange Rates: 100 pence (pennies) = 1 Falkland Islands pound (FI £). *Sterling, Dollar and Euro Equivalents* (31 December 2010): £1 sterling = FI £1.00; US $1 = 63.88 pence; €1 = 85.35 pence; FI £100 = £100.00 sterling = $156.55 = €117.16. *Average Exchange Rate* (FI £ per US dollar): 0.5440 in 2008; 0.6419 in 2009; 0.6472 in 2010. Note: The Falkland Islands pound is at par with the pound sterling.

Budget (FI £ million, 2009/10): *Revenue:* Sales and services 9.7; Fishing licences and transshipment 18.0; Investment income 4.5; Taxes and duties 10.2; Total 42.4 *Expenditure:* Operating expenditure 38.9 (Public works 8.5, Fisheries 5.2, Health care 7.5, Education 5.3, Aviation 2.5, Police and justice 1.5, Agriculture 1.0, Central administration 3.5 Other 3.9); Capital expenditure 8.7; Total 47.6.

Cost of Living (Consumer Price Index for Stanley; base: 2000 = 100): All items 101.3 in 2001; 102.0 in 2002; 103.2 in 2003. Source: ILO.

EXTERNAL TRADE

2000 (estimates): Total imports £18,958,103; Total exports £47,000,000. Fish is the principal export. Trade is mainly with the United Kingdom, Spain and Chile.

TRANSPORT

Shipping: *Merchant Fleet* (at 31 December 2009): Vessels 26; Displacement 47,231 grt. Source: IHS Fairplay, *World Fleet Statistics*.

Road Traffic: 3,065 vehicles in use in 1995.

TOURISM

Day Visitors (country of origin of cruise ship excursionists, 2006/07 season): Canada 4,862; United Kingdom 6,736; USA 21,298; Total (incl. others) 51,282. *2008/09:* Total 62,600 (Source: Falkland Islands Tourist Board).

EDUCATION

2003 (Stanley): *Primary:* Teachers 18; Pupils 203. *Secondary:* Teachers 18; Pupils 160.

Directory

The Government

(May 2011)

HEAD OF STATE

Queen: HM Queen ELIZABETH II.
Governor: NIGEL ROBERT HAYWOOD (took office 16 October 2010).

HEAD OF GOVERNMENT

Chief Executive of the Falkland Islands Government: Dr TIM THOROGOOD.

TERRITORIAL ADMINISTRATION

Government Secretary: PETER T. KING.
Attorney-General: DAVID PICKUP.
Commander, British Forces South Atlantic Islands: Cdre PHILIP THICKNESSE.

EXECUTIVE COUNCIL

The Council consists of six members.

GOVERNMENT OFFICES

Office of the Governor: Government House, Stanley, FIQQ 1ZZ; tel. 27433; fax 27434; e-mail gov.house@horizon.co.fk.
London Office: Falkland Islands Government Office, Falkland House, 14 Broadway, London, SW1H 0BH, United Kingdom; tel. (20) 7222-2542; fax (20) 7222-2375; e-mail reception@falklands.gov.fk; internet www.falklands.gov.fk; f. 1983.

LEGISLATIVE ASSEMBLY

Comprises the Governor, two ex officio (non-voting) members and eight elected members. Elections to the Legislative Assembly are held every four years. The last election was held on 5 November 2009.
Speaker: KEITH BILES.
Office of the Legislative Assembly: Legislature Dept, Gilbert House, Stanley, FIQQ 1ZZ; tel. 27455; e-mail assembly@sec.gov.fk; internet www.falklands.gov.fk.

Judicial System

The judicial system of the Falkland Islands is administered by the Supreme Court (presided over by the non-resident Chief Justice), the Magistrate's Court (presided over by the Senior Magistrate) and the Court of Summary Jurisdiction. The Court of Appeal for the Territory sits in England and appeals therefrom may be heard by the Judicial Committee of the Privy Council.

Chief Justice of the Supreme Court: CHRISTOPHER GARDNER, QC.
Judge of the Supreme Court and Senior Magistrate: JOHN TREVASKIS (acting).
Registrar to the Supreme Court and Courts Administrator: CHERILYN KING, Town Hall, Ross Rd, Stanley, FIQQ 1ZZ; tel. 27271; fax 27270.

FALKLAND ISLANDS COURT OF APPEAL

President: Judge BRIAN APPLEBY.
Registrar: MICHAEL J. ELKS.

Religion

CHRISTIANITY

The Anglican Communion, the Roman Catholic Church and the United Free Church predominate. Also represented are the Evangelist Church, Jehovah's Witnesses, the Lutheran Church, Seventh-day Adventists and the Bahá'í faith.

The Anglican Communion

The Archbishop of Canterbury, the Primate of All England, exercises episcopal jurisdiction over the Falkland Islands and South Georgia.
Rector: Rev. Dr RICHARD HINES, The Deanery, Christ Church Cathedral, Stanley, FIQQ 1ZZ; tel. 21100; fax 21842; e-mail deanery@horizon.co.fk.

The Roman Catholic Church

Prefect Apostolic of the Falkland Islands: MICHAEL BERNARD MCPARTLAND, St Mary's Presbytery, 12 Ross Rd, Stanley, FIQQ 1ZZ; tel. 21204; fax 22242; e-mail stmarys@horizon.co.fk; internet www.southatlanticrcchurch.com; f. 1764; 300 adherents (2006).

The Press

Falkland Islands Gazette: Cable Cottage, POB 587, Stanley, FIQQ 1ZZ; tel. 28460; fax 27276; e-mail bsteen@sec.gov.fk; internet www.falklands.gov.fk; govt publ; Editor BARBARA STEEN.

Falkland Islands News Network: POB 141, Stanley, FIQQ 1ZZ; tel. and fax 21182; e-mail finn@horizon.co.fk; internet www.falklandnews.com; relays news daily online and via fax as FINN(COM) Service; Man. JUAN BROCK; publishes *Teaberry Express* (weekly).

Penguin News: Ross Rd, Stanley, FIQQ 1ZZ; tel. 22709; fax 22238; e-mail adverts@penguinnews.co.fk; internet www.penguin-news.com; f. 1979; weekly (Fri.); independent newspaper; Man. FRAN BIGGS; circ. 1,450.

Broadcasting and Communications

TELECOMMUNICATIONS

In 1989 Cable & Wireless PLC installed a £5.4m. digital telecommunications network covering the entire Falkland Islands. The Government contributed to the cost of the new system, which provides international services as well as a new domestic network. Further work to improve the domestic telephone system was completed in the late 1990s at a cost of £3.3m. The first mobile telephone network was introduced in 2005 and a broadband internet service in 2006.

Cable & Wireless South Atlantic Ltd: Ross Rd, POB 584, Stanley, FIQQ 1ZZ; tel. 20834; fax 20811; e-mail info@cwfi.co.fk; internet www.cwfi.co.fk; f. 1989; exclusive provider of national and international telecommunications services in the Falkland Islands under a licence issued by the Falkland Islands Govt; CEO Justin McPhee.

BROADCASTING

Radio

British Forces Broadcasting Service (BFBS): BFBS Falkland Islands, Mount Pleasant, BFPO 655; tel. 32179; fax 32193; e-mail falklands@bfbs.com; internet www.bfbs-radio.com; 24-hour satellite service from the United Kingdom; Station Man. Chris Pearson; Sr Engineer Adrian Almond.

Falkland Islands Radio Service: Broadcasting Studios, John St, Stanley, FIQQ 1ZZ; tel. 27277; fax 27279; e-mail cgoss@firs.co.fk; internet www.firs.co.fk; f. 1929; fmrly Falklands Islands Broadcasting Station; 24-hour service, partly financed by local Govt; broadcasts in English; Station Man. Ailie Biggs (acting); Programme Controller Liz Elliot.

Television

British Forces Broadcasting Service (BFBS): BFBS Falkland Islands, Mount Pleasant, BFPO 655; tel. 32179; fax 32193; internet www.bfbs.com/tv; daily four-hour transmissions of taped broadcasts from BBC and ITV of London, United Kingdom; Sr Engineer Colin McDonald.

KTV: Dean St, POB 68, Stanley, FIQQ 1ZZ; tel. 22349; fax 21049; e-mail kmzb@horizon.co.fk; internet www.ktv.co.fk; satellite television broadcasting services; Man. Dirs Mario Zuvic Bulic, Sharon Zuvic Bulic.

Finance

BANK

Standard Chartered Bank: Ross Rd, POB 597, Stanley, FIQQ 1ZZ; tel. 22220; fax 22219; e-mail bank.info@sc.com; internet www.standardchartered.com/fk; branch opened in 1983; Man. Rino Donosepoetro.

INSURANCE

The British Commercial Union, Royal Insurance and Norman Tremellen companies maintain agencies in Stanley.

Consultancy Services Falklands Ltd: 44 John St, Stanley, FIQQ 1ZZ; tel. 22666; fax 22639; e-mail consultancy@horizon.co.fk; Man. Alison Baker.

Trade and Industry

DEVELOPMENT ORGANIZATION

Falkland Islands Development Corporation (FIDC): Shackleton House, West Hillside, Stanley, FIQQ 1ZZ; tel. 27211; fax 27210; e-mail dwaugh@fidc.co.fk; internet www.fidc.co.fk; f. 1983; provides loans and grants; encourages private sector investment, inward investment and technology transfer; Gen. Man. David Waugh.

CHAMBER OF COMMERCE

Chamber of Commerce: West Hillside, POB 378, Stanley, FIQQ 1ZZ; tel. 22264; fax 22265; e-mail commerce@horizon.co.fk; internet www.falklandislandschamberofcommerce.com; f. 1993; promotes private industry; operates DHL courier service; runs an employment agency; Pres. Roger Spink; 87 mems.

TRADING COMPANIES

Falkland Islands Co Ltd (FIC): Crozier Pl., Stanley, FIQQ 1ZZ; tel. 27600; fax 27603; e-mail fic@horizon.co.fk; internet www.the-falkland-islands-co.com; f. 1851; part of Falkland Islands Holding PLC; the largest trading co; retailing, wholesaling, shipping, insurance and Land Rover sales and servicing; operates as agent for Lloyd's of London and general shipping concerns; travel services; wharf owners and operators; Dir and Gen. Man. Roger Kenneth Spink.

Falkland Islands Meat Co Ltd: Sand Bay, East Falklands, FIQQ 1ZZ; tel. 27013; fax 27113; e-mail info@falklandmeat.co.fk; internet www.falklands-meat.com; exporters of lamb, mutton and beef meat; Gen. Man. John Ferguson.

Falkland Oil and Gas Ltd (FOGL): 56 John St, Stanley, F1QQ 1ZZ; e-mail info@fogl.co.uk; internet www.fogl.co.uk; f. 2004; shareholders include Falkland Islands Holdings PLC (16%), Global Petroleum (14%) and RAB Capital PLC (33%); operates an offshore petroleum exploration programme with 8 licences covering 65,354 sq km; Chair. Richard Liddell; CEO Tim Bushell.

EMPLOYERS' ASSOCIATION

Sheep Owners' Association: Coast Ridge Farm, Fox Bay, FIQQ 1ZZ; tel. 42094; fax 42084; e-mail n.knight.coastridge@horizon.co.fk; f. 1967; asscn for sheep station owners; limited liability private co; Company Sec. N. Knight.

TRADE UNION

Falkland Islands General Employees Union: Ross Rd, Stanley, FIQQ 1ZZ; tel. 21151; e-mail geu@horizon.co.fk; f. 1943; Chair. Gavin Short; 100 mems.

Transport

RAILWAYS

There are no railways on the islands.

ROADS

There are 29 km (18 miles) of paved road in and around Stanley. There are 54 km of all-weather road linking Stanley and the Mount Pleasant airport (some of which has been surfaced with a bitumen substance), and a further 37 km of road as far as Goose Green. There are 300 km of arterial roads in the North Camp on East Falkland linking settlements, and a further 197 km of road on West Falkland. Where roads have still not been built, settlements are linked by tracks, which are passable by all-terrain motor vehicles or motorcycles except in the most severe weather conditions.

SHIPPING

There is a ship on charter to the Falkland Islands Co Ltd, which makes the round trip to the United Kingdom four or five times a year, carrying cargo. A floating deep-water jetty was completed in 1984. The British Ministry of Defence charters ships, which sail for the Falkland Islands once every three weeks. There are irregular cargo services between the islands and southern Chile and Uruguay. The Falkland Islands Development Corpn commissioned a port development plan in February 2007 for the upgrade of existing facilities to reflect growth in containerized traffic and cruise ship arrivals, and to accommodate proposed further oil exploration in territorial waters.

The Falkland Islands merchant fleet numbered 26 vessels, with a total displacement of 47,231 grt, at December 2009; the majority of vessels registered are deep-sea fishing vessels.

Stanley Port Authority: c/o Dept of Fisheries, POB 598, Stanley, FIQQ 1ZZ; tel. 27260; fax 27265; e-mail jclark@fisheries.gov.fk; Marine Officer and Harbour Master Jon Clark.

Private Companies

Byron Marine Ltd: 3 H Jones Rd, Stanley, FIQQ 1ZZ; tel. 22245; fax 22246; e-mail info@byronmarine.com; internet www.byronmarine.com; f. 1992; additional activites include offshore oil and gas exploration support services, deep-sea fishing and property; contracted managers of the Falkland Islands Government Port Facility; island-wide pilotage services; vessel and port agency; Man. Dir Lewis Clifton.

Darwin Shipping Ltd: Stanley, FIQQ 1ZZ; tel. 27600; fax 27603; e-mail darwin@horizon.co.fk; internet www.the-falkland-islands-co.com; subsidiary of the Falkland Islands Co Ltd (q.v.); Man. Andy Watson.

Falkland Islands Co Ltd (FIC): see Trade and Industry—Trading Companies.

Seaview Ltd: 37 Fitzroy Rd, POB 215, Stanley, FIQQ 1ZZ; tel. 22669; fax 22670; e-mail seaview.agent@horizon.co.fk; internet www.fis.com/polar; operates subsidiary co, Polar Ltd (f. 1989); Man. Dir Alex Reid.

Sulivan Shipping Services Ltd: Davis St, POB 159, Stanley, FIQQ 1ZZ; tel. 22626; fax 22625; e-mail sulivan@horizon.co.fk; internet www.sulivanshipping.com; f. 1987; provides port agency and ground-handling services; Man. Dir John Pollard; Operations Man. Migs Cofré.

CIVIL AVIATION

There are airports at Stanley and Mount Pleasant; the latter has a runway of 2,590 m (8,497 ft), and is capable of receiving wide-bodied jet aircraft. The British Royal Air Force operates two weekly flights from the United Kingdom. The Chilean carrier LAN Airlines operates weekly return flights from Punta Arenas. An 'air bridge', operated by charter carriers subcontracted to the British Ministry of Defence, provides a link via Ascension Island between the Falkland Islands and the United Kingdom.

Falkland Islands Government Air Service (FIGAS): Stanley Airport, Stanley, FIQQ 1ZZ; tel. 27219; fax 27309; e-mail operations@figas.gov.fk; internet www.visitorfalklands.com/contents/view/116; f. 1948 to provide social, medical and postal services between the settlements and Stanley; aerial surveillance for

UNITED KINGDOM OVERSEAS TERRITORIES

Dept of Fisheries since 1990; operates five nine-seater aircraft to over 35 landing strips across the islands; Gen. Man. SHAUN MINTO.

Tourism

During the 2008/09 season some 62,600 day visitors from cruise ships visited the islands. US citizens constitute the primary visitor group. Wildlife photography, bird-watching and hiking are popular tourist activities. The Falkland Islands Development Corpn (FIDC) plans to develop the sector in collaboration with the Government and tourism operators in the territory.

Falkland Islands Tourist Board: POB 618, Stanley, FIQQ 1ZZ; tel. 22215; fax 27020; e-mail info@visitorfalklands.com; internet www.falklandislands.com; Gen. Man. JAKE DOWNING.

Defence

As assessed at November 2010, there were approximately 1,520 British troops stationed on the islands (420 army, 680 air force and 420 navy). The annual cost of maintaining the garrison is approximately £65m. There is a Falkland Islands Defence Force, composed of 75 islanders.

Education

Education is compulsory, and is provided free of charge, for children between the ages of five and 16 years. Facilities are available for further study beyond the statutory school-leaving age. In 2003 203 pupils were instructed by 18 teachers at the primary school in Stanley, while 160 pupils received instruction from 18 teachers at the secondary school in the capital; further facilities existed in rural areas, with six peripatetic teachers visiting younger children for two out of every six weeks (older children boarded in a hostel in Stanley). Total expenditure on education was estimated at £5.3m. for 2009/10 (equivalent to 11.1% of total government expenditure).

GIBRALTAR

Introductory Survey

LOCATION, CLIMATE, LANGUAGE, RELIGION, FLAG

The city of Gibraltar lies in southern Europe. The territory consists of a narrow peninsula of approximately 4.8 km (3 miles) in length, running southwards from the south-west coast of Spain, to which it is connected by an isthmus. About 8 km (5 miles) across the bay, to the west, lies the Spanish port of Algeciras, while 32 km (20 miles) to the south, across the Strait of Gibraltar, is Morocco. The Mediterranean Sea lies to the east. The climate is temperate, and snow or frost are extremely rare. The mean minimum and maximum temperatures during the winter are 13°C (55°F) and 18°C (65°F), respectively, and during the summer they are 13°C (55°F) and 29°C (85°F), respectively; the average annual rainfall is 890 mm (35 ins). The official language is English, although most of the population is bilingual in English and Spanish. More than three-quarters of the population are Roman Catholic. The flag (proportions 1 by 2) bears the arms of Gibraltar (a red castle with a pendant golden key) on a background, the upper two-thirds of which are white and the lower one-third red.

CONTEMPORARY POLITICAL HISTORY

Historical Context

Since the Second World War, this Overseas Territory has achieved considerable social and economic progress, through intensive development of its social and economic infrastructure, and by the expansion of commerce and the encouragement of tourism. Gibraltar has exercised control over most internal matters since 1969.

The Spanish Government lays claim to Gibraltar as a part of its territory, while the United Kingdom maintains that the Treaty of Utrecht (1713) granted sovereignty over Gibraltar to the United Kingdom in perpetuity (with the stipulation that, if the United Kingdom relinquished the colony, it would be returned to Spain). In 1963 the Spanish Government began a campaign, through the UN, for the cession of Gibraltar to Spain. It also imposed restrictions against Gibraltar, culminating in the closure of the frontier in 1969, the withdrawal of the Spanish labour force, and the severing of transport and communication links with Spain.

Following a referendum held in the territory in 1967, in which the overwhelming majority voted in favour of retaining British sovereignty, a new Constitution, promulgated in 1969, contained a provision that the British Government undertook never to enter into arrangements whereby the people of Gibraltar would pass under the sovereignty of another state against their freely and democratically expressed wishes. Gibraltar joined the European Community (EC, now European Union—EU, see p. 270) with the United Kingdom in 1973.

By 1977, a more flexible attitude by Spain towards Gibraltar became apparent. At talks held between Spanish and British ministers in November representatives of the Gibraltar Government were included for the first time as part of the British delegation. Further negotiations took place in 1979 and 1980. In October 1980 the British Parliament granted Gibraltarians the right to retain full British citizenship. Negotiations for the reopening of the frontier continued in 1982, but a change of attitudes in both countries, following the war between the United Kingdom and Argentina over the sovereignty of the Falkland Islands (q.v.), resulted in an indefinite postponement. In December Spain reopened the border to pedestrians of Spanish nationality and to British subjects resident in Gibraltar.

Domestic Political Affairs

At the general election held in January 1984 the Gibraltar Labour Party—Association for the Advancement of Civil Rights (GLP—AACR), led by Sir Joshua Hassan, retained a majority of one seat in the House of Assembly. The Gibraltar Socialist Labour Party (GSLP), led by Joe Bossano, secured the remaining seven seats, replacing the Democratic Party of British Gibraltar as the opposition party in the House of Assembly. (Under the terms of the Constitution, the party with the largest share of the vote obtained a maximum of eight seats in the House of Assembly.)

In November 1984 the British and Spanish Governments agreed to provide equal rights for Spaniards in Gibraltar and for Gibraltarians in Spain; to allow free movement for all traffic between Gibraltar and Spain; and to conduct negotiations on the future of the territory, including (for the first time) discussions on sovereignty. Border restrictions were finally ended in February 1985, and negotiations took place between the British and Spanish Governments to improve cross-border co-operation, especially in tourism and civil aviation. In December, however, Spanish proposals for an interim settlement of the territory's future were rejected by the British Government as unacceptable since they implied the eventual automatic cession of Gibraltar to Spain. Subsequent discussions concerning principally Spain's demands for access to the Gibraltar airport (which the Spanish Government claimed was situated on land not covered by the terms of the Treaty of Utrecht) were inconclusive, owing to the Gibraltar Government's insistence that the airport remain exclusively under the control of the British and Gibraltar authorities. In December 1987 negotiators concluded an agreement that recommended increased co-operation between Spain and Gibraltar in the area of transport, in particular the joint administration of Gibraltar's airport. It was announced that Gibraltar's inclusion in an EC directive concerning air transport regulation was subject to the Gibraltar Government's approval of the British-Spanish agreement. However, the House of Assembly rejected the agreement, on the grounds that it would represent an infringement of British sovereignty, and voted unanimously to contest Gibraltar's exclusion from the EC directive.

The Government of Joe Bossano

At a general election held in March 1988, the GSLP received 58.2% of the votes cast, obtaining eight seats in the House of Assembly, and the GLP—AACR received 29.3% of the vote, securing seven seats. Bossano became Chief Minister, at the head of Gibraltar's first socialist Government. Bossano announced that he would not participate in British-Spanish negotiations concerning Gibraltar, on the grounds that the territory's sovereignty was not a matter for negotiation between Spain and the United Kingdom, and that the December 1987 agreement would, in his view, result in the absorption of Gibraltar into Spain.

In February 1990 the British and Spanish Governments agreed to contest a legal action that was to be brought by Gibraltar in the European Court of Justice against Gibraltar's exclusion from measures adopted to liberalize European air transport, which prevented the territory from expanding its air links with Europe. The decision to contest the action was considered to be a further attempt by the United Kingdom to persuade Gibraltar to co-operate with Spain. In

UNITED KINGDOM OVERSEAS TERRITORIES

Gibraltar

March 1991 the United Kingdom withdrew the majority of British army personnel from Gibraltar, although the Royal Navy and Royal Air Force detachments remained.

In May 1991 the Spanish Prime Minister made an official visit to the United Kingdom, and was reported to have proposed a plan for joint sovereignty over Gibraltar, whereby the dependency would become effectively autonomous, with the British and Spanish monarchs as joint heads of state. Although it represented a significant concession by the Spanish Government, the plan was rejected by the Gibraltar Government. At the EC summit meeting held at Maastricht, Netherlands, in December, Spain continued to refuse to recognize Gibraltar's status as part of the EC, and remained determined to exclude it from the External Frontiers Convention (EFC), which was designed to strengthen common controls on entry into countries belonging to the EC. The continued failure to reach an agreement, particularly concerning the administration of Gibraltar airport, prevented the ratification of the EFC.

At a general election held in January 1992 the GSLP retained eight seats in the House of Assembly, and Bossano was returned for a second term as Chief Minister. The Gibraltar Social Democrats (GSD), which supported Gibraltar's participation in British-Spanish negotiations, secured the remaining seven seats. In February 1992, prior to discussions with British ministers in London, Bossano announced that Gibraltar was to attempt to obtain a revision of the 1969 Constitution, with the aim of achieving self-determination within four years. The British Government, however, stated that it would not consider granting independence to Gibraltar, unless the Spanish Government was prepared to accept the agreement, and excluded the possibility of formal negotiations on the issue.

In January 1993 Gibraltarians lodged a formal protest after increasingly stringent monitoring of vehicles by Spanish customs officials resulted in severe delays at the frontier. In March an official meeting between the foreign ministers of the United Kingdom and Spain achieved little progress; it was agreed, however, that contacts between British and Spanish officials were to be maintained. In early 1994 Bossano accused the British Government of subordinating the interests of Gibraltar to the promotion of harmonious relations with Spain, and demanded a renegotiation of the 1987 airport agreement on the grounds that its provisions had subsequently become redundant and contrary to EU law.

In late 1994 Spain alleged that insufficient action was being taken by Gibraltar to curtail the smuggling of tobacco from Gibraltar to Spain and of illegal narcotics between Morocco and Spain by Gibraltar-based speedboats. The imposition in October of stringent border inspections by Spain prompted a protest by the British Government. These border checks were eased following assurances that measures were being taken against those involved in smuggling. Spain reimposed frontier controls in March 1995, precipitating further criticism by the British Government.

In July 1995, following the confiscation of more than 60 speedboats, alleged to be used in the transport of contraband, the Spanish Government eased frontier controls. The seizures provoked two days of riots and looting in Gibraltar, followed by a peaceful mass demonstration organized by Gibraltar business interests and trade unions in support of the continuing implementation of anti-smuggling measures. Although the British and Spanish Governments jointly agreed in September that the anti-smuggling measures were proving effective, the death of a Spanish civil guard in pursuit of smugglers in April 1996 led to the renewal of border controls by Spain.

Caruana becomes Chief Minister

Campaign debates in advance of legislative elections in May 1996 focused on Gibraltar's external relations. Bossano and the GSLP proposed that the territory's status be replaced before the year 2000 by a form of 'free association' with the United Kingdom, while the GSD declared as its aims the achievement of improved relations with both Spain and the United Kingdom and the modernization of Gibraltar's Constitution. The election attracted an unusually high turn-out (87.7% of eligible voters), and resulted in the GSD receiving 48% of the vote and the maximum of eight seats in the House of Assembly; the GSD leader, Peter Caruana, became Chief Minister. The GSLP received 39% of the vote and the Gibraltar National Party obtained 13%.

In November 1996 Caruana renewed his demand that Gibraltar be accorded equal status with the United Kingdom in future negotiations concerning the territory's interests. In January 1997 Caruana refused to attend discussions on Gibraltar, held in Madrid, Spain, between the United Kingdom and Spain, on the grounds that Gibraltar would not be granted power of veto. A suggestion by Spain that sovereignty over Gibraltar be shared between Spain and the United Kingdom for a 100-year period, with full control then passing to Spain, was rejected by the British Government.

In October 1997 Caruana informed the Decolonization Committee of the UN General Assembly that he was to seek from the British Government an extensive review of the territory's 1969 Constitution. It was to be proposed that Gibraltar would obtain additional autonomy in the conduct of its affairs while remaining in a close political and constitutional relationship with the United Kingdom, similar to that held by the Crown Dependencies of the Channel Islands and the Isle of Man (q.v.). During 1997 new tensions arose between the United Kingdom and Spanish Governments over the long-standing refusal by Spain to permit military aircraft from the United Kingdom and the North Atlantic Treaty Organization (NATO, see p. 368) to cross Spanish airspace on their approach to Gibraltar airport. In July the British Government indicated that it would oppose the full incorporation of Spain into NATO unless the ban was lifted. An indication by Spain of its willingness to open its airspace to these flights in return for joint military control of the airport was strongly opposed by Caruana and rejected by the British Government. In July 1998 Spain reversed its long-standing refusal to participate in NATO manoeuvres that were based in, or passed through, Gibraltar. In that month the Spanish Government unsuccessfully requested the British Government to consider a revived proposal for the shared sovereignty of Gibraltar for a period of 50 years, to be followed by the territory's full integration into Spain.

In November 1998 complaints by the Gibraltar Government arose over the conduct of Spanish fishing vessels in the Bay of Gibraltar, which were stated to be operating in violation of the territory's nature protection ordinance. In January 1999 a Spanish trawler was impounded by the Gibraltar authorities, and Spain began to intensify delays in road traffic crossing the frontier. An agreement reached in February between the Gibraltar authorities and the Spanish fishermen was not recognized by the Spanish Government.

At the general election held in February 2000 the GSD secured 58.7% of the vote, against 40.8% obtained by an electoral coalition of the GSLP and the Gibraltar Liberal Party (GLP). Caruana was reconfirmed as Chief Minister, and the GSD retained its eight seats in the House of Assembly. The rate of participation was again high, at 83.6%.

Extended negotiations between the Spanish and British Governments were concluded in April 2000 with a compromise agreement whereby Spain was to recognize the validity of Gibraltar identity cards and of the territory's financial institutions, provided that the 'competent authority' responsible for their supervision was the United Kingdom rather than the Gibraltar Government. It was also agreed that the British authorities would provide a facility, based in London, through which the Spanish and Gibraltar authorities could have indirect communication. An incidental effect of the agreement was to terminate the long-standing refusal by Spain to adopt any legislation by the EU that might have required it to deal directly with Gibraltar's police or financial regulatory authorities.

In March 2001 the Gibraltar political parties reached an agreement to request the previously proposed reforms to the 1969 Constitution, allowing self-determination, and to hold a referendum on decolonization. However, the move was condemned by Spain as a breach of the Treaty of Utrecht.

British-Spanish sovereignty negotiations

In July 2001 the British and Spanish Governments renewed discussions on Gibraltar's future status for the first time since 1998. In response, the Gibraltarian legislature requested that a UN decolonization mission visit the territory. At a subsequent meeting in October, the British Secretary of State for Foreign and Commonwealth Affairs, Jack Straw, and his Spanish counterpart, Josep Piqué i Camps, agreed to work towards achieving a settlement on the issue by December 2002 (this was later modified to September 2002). Amid public criticism of proposals of joint British-Spanish sovereignty, Caruana rebuffed an invitation to attend the next round of negotiations, claiming that he would not be accorded equal status in the discussions. The Chief Minister also stated that the territory would not accept any change in sovereignty, the sharing of responsibility for its external affairs between Spain and the United Kingdom, nor Spanish military presence.

At the negotiations in November 2001, Piqué announced that Spain was prepared to increase the number of telephone lines available to Gibraltar from 35,000 to 100,000 and provide greater access to the Spanish health care system. However, the issue of the right of the citizens of Gibraltar to vote on the terms of an agreement regarding the future status of the territory remained a point of contention between Spain and the United Kingdom. At the end of the month the British Government announced that Gibraltarians would be given the right to vote in elections to the European Parliament, but ruled out the possibility of the territory's further integration into the United Kingdom. In an open letter published in the local press, Piqué attempted to allay Gibraltarians' fears of the implications of Spanish rule and urged Caruana to attend the negotiations. The following month, however, most of the territory's 300,000 citizens took part in a public demonstration against the proposals. Following further public protests in March 2002, EU leaders agreed to a joint British-Spanish request for a grant of £37m. to fund the development of Gibraltar's port, infrastructure and airport. Caruana rejected the proposals and threatened to organize a referendum.

Shortly before negotiations on the sovereignty issue were due to resume in May 2002, the Spanish Prime Minister, José María Aznar, asserted that Spain would never withdraw its territorial claim to Gibraltar. During a subsequent visit, Straw's efforts to persuade Gibraltar of the benefits of joint sovereignty, and to reassure its residents that any such agreement would be subject to approval by referendum, were met with scepticism. Also in May, the Overseas Territories Act, having received royal assent in the United Kingdom in February, came into force, granting British citizenship rights to the people of its Overseas Territories, including Gibraltar. Under the new law Gibraltarians would be able to hold British passports and work in the United Kingdom and other EU countries.

Negotiations between the Spanish and British Governments progressed in mid-2002, although discussions stalled over Spain's claims to eventual sovereignty rather than permanent co-sovereignty and its refusal to allow British control over the military base. In response, Caruana called a referendum for November 2002. Talks recommenced in September, but with no certain deadline. The referendum, held on 7 November, in which 87.9% of the electorate voted, demonstrated overwhelming (98.97%) opinion against joint sovereignty with Spain; it was, however, not recognized by either Spain or the United Kingdom. In January 2003 Caruana proposed constitutional reforms that would establish a decolonized status for the enclave but maintain its links with the United Kingdom.

At a general election held on 28 November 2003 the GSD secured 51.5% of the vote, a significant decrease from the 2000 election, against 39.7% secured by the GSLP-GLP coalition; 79.2% of the electorate participated. The balance of seats in the House of Assembly, however, remained unchanged, with the GSD holding eight seats and the opposition seven seats. Caruana remained as Chief Minister.

For the purposes of the 2004 elections to the European Parliament, in late 2003 the British Parliament adopted legislation incorporating Gibraltar into the south-west region of the United Kingdom; for the first time, Gibraltarians were thus eligible to vote in European elections. Approximately 58% of the Gibaltarian electorate participated in the elections. In June 2006 the European Court of Justice rejected a complaint submitted by the Spanish Government, which insisted that Gibraltarians were ineligible to vote in European elections.

Trilateral talks and constitutional reform

In October 2004 Straw and his recently appointed Spanish counterpart, Miguel Angel Moratinos, held discussions in Madrid, at which they addressed the issue of the future format for talks on Gibraltar, which were to include Gibraltarian representation for the first time. Talks involving the three parties took place in the United Kingdom in December further to define this new forum, and in February 2005 the first official trilateral session took place in Málaga, Spain. As a result, a number of Technical Working Groups were established to focus on the most significant issues: the airport, border control, nuclear submarines, telecommunications and pensions. Following several further rounds of discussions, in September 2006 Caruana, Moratinos and the British Minister of State for Europe, Geoff Hoon, signed a series of agreements in Córdoba, Spain: allowing for the operation of flights from Spain and the rest of Europe to Gibraltar; increasing the number of telephone lines to the territory; addressing the issue of outstanding pension payments to Spaniards formerly employed in Gibraltar; and easing border restrictions. Moratinos also stated that the Spanish Government had received written assurances from the United Kingdom that nuclear submarines would no longer be docked in Gibraltar. The question of sovereignty was not addressed.

Meanwhile, following lengthy negotiations between the United Kingdom and Gibraltar, it was announced in March 2006 that agreement had been reached on the main provisions of a new draft constitution for the territory. The British authorities stressed that the proposals did not diminish British sovereignty over Gibraltar, which would remain a United Kingdom Overseas Territory. The preamble to the new constitution also made clear that the British Government would never enter into arrangements under which the people of Gibraltar would pass under the sovereignty of another state against their freely and democratically expressed wishes. The draft constitution confirmed that the people of Gibraltar had the right of self-determination (according to the provisions of the UN Charter); this right was not constrained by the Treaty of Utrecht, except in so far as Spain would have the right of refusal should Britain ever renounce sovereignty. Thus, Gibraltarian independence would be an option only with Spanish consent. The remainder of the text introduced substantial reforms. The main elements included limiting the responsibilities of the Governor to the areas of external affairs, defence, internal security and public services, thereby reversing the existing practice and giving Gibraltar much greater control over its internal affairs. The House of Assembly was to be restyled the Gibraltar Parliament and would be allowed to determine its own size. The Governor's powers to withhold assent to legislation approved by the Gibraltarian authorities would be streamlined and his power to disallow proposed new laws would be removed (although his mandate to make Orders in Council would be retained). New commissions were to be created to deal with appointments to the judiciary and to public services, and a new Police Authority for Gibraltar was to be established. In a referendum held on 30 November 2006 the Constitution was approved by 60.2% of the valid votes cast, with 37.8% votes against, 1.7% blank ballots, and a participation rate of 60.4%. The new Constitution entered into force on 2 January 2007 (except for those provisions relating to the Parliament, which were to take effect following legislative elections).

In February 2007 Caruana created two new ministries, the Ministry of Finance and the Ministry of Justice. The Chief Minister, who already had responsibility for financial affairs, formally became Minister of Finance and also assumed ministerial responsibility for justice, which had been the preserve of the unelected Attorney-General under the previous Constitution. The approval of legislation, in July, that provided for transfer of the post of head of the judiciary from the Chief Justice to the President of the Court of Appeal, as provided for by the new Constitution, provoked some controversy. The Chief Justice, Derek Schofield, opposed the reform, stating that it threatened the independence of the judiciary. Schofield was suspended from office in September, following accusations of misconduct. In December 2008 a tribunal of three retired senior British judges recommended that Schofield be removed from office. The case was subsequently referred to the Privy Council of the United Kingdom, which confirmed the tribunal's recommendation in November 2009. The Governor, Sir Adrian Johns, subsequently dismissed Schofield from his post. In February 2010 Anthony Dudley, who had served as Acting Chief Justice during Schofield's suspension, was appointed to the position.

At the general election held on 11 October 2007 the GSD remained the largest party in the legislature, holding 10 of the 17 seats, having obtained 49.3% of the votes cast; 81.4% of the electorate voted. The only other grouping to obtain representation was the GSLP-GLP alliance, with seven seats and 45.5% of the votes cast. Caruana reassumed office as Chief Minister and Minister of Finance, but appointed Daniel Feetham as Minister of Justice as part of an extensive government reorganization. Upon his inauguration, Caruana made a speech to Parliament in which he described the new constitutional arrangements as having 'placed Gibraltar and the United Kingdom in a constitutional relationship with each other that is modern and non-colonial in nature', and pledged to explore the possibility of implementing further democratic reforms.

Recent developments: dispute over territorial waters

A ministerial meeting of the trilateral Forum of Dialogue (which had continued to hold regular discussions since 2005) took place in Gibraltar in July 2009 between Caruana, Moratinos, and the British Secretary of State for Foreign and Commonwealth Affairs, David Miliband. Moratinos thus became the first Spanish minister to visit Gibraltar. The three ministers agreed to increase co-operation in matters including environmental protection, taxation, crime prevention, education, and maritime communication and safety; by mutual agreement, the issue of sovereignty was not raised. The meeting was overshadowed by a dispute between Gibraltar and Spain concerning the waters surrounding the territory, which Spain had recently designated a Site of Community Importance in accordance with EU legislation and with the approval of the European Commission. In May the Gibraltar Government had initiated proceedings against the Commission at the European Court of Justice, claiming that waters within three nautical miles of the territory were under British sovereignty and that Spain thus had no right to make such a designation; Spain maintained that none of its territorial waters other than those within the port of Gibraltar had been ceded to the United Kingdom under the Peace of Utrecht. In March 2010 the Government of the United Kingdom filed a separate case before the Court of Justice against the Commission's decision to publish an updated list of Sites of Community Importance that maintained Spain's contested designation.

Further tensions arose between Gibraltar and Spain in September 2010, when the Gibraltar Government accused the Spanish Civil Guard of forcibly preventing Gibraltarian police officers from exercising their powers by facilitating the escape of a suspected Spanish drugs-trafficker that they had arrested in the waters surrounding the territory. Describing the incident as 'wholly unacceptable', in mid-October Caruana stated that technical discussions on matters relating to the waters surrounding Gibraltar would be 'pointless and inappropriate' and challenged Moratinos to agree to refer the dispute over sovereignty of these waters to the International Court of Justice. Later that month the participants in the trilateral Forum of Dialogue agreed to proceed with a series of technical meetings in five areas— visas; financial services and taxation; maritime communications and safety; environmental protection; and education—but that the issue of police, judicial and customs co-operation would be addressed at a more senior, political level.

CONSTITUTION AND GOVERNMENT

Gibraltar is a United Kingdom Overseas Territory. The first Constitution, promulgated in 1969, was replaced by a new Constitution in 2007. Executive authority is vested in the British Sovereign and is exercised by the Council of Ministers, presided over by the Chief Minister, except in areas reserved to the Governor. These are defined by the Constitution as external affairs, defence, internal security and public offices. The Gibraltar Parliament comprises the Speaker (who is elected by, but not from, the Parliament) and 17 members who are elected for a four-year term. The Parliament elects and appoints the Mayor, who represents the City of Gibraltar in a ceremonial capacity.

REGIONAL CO-OPERATION

Gibraltar joined the European Community, now European Union (EU, see p. 270), with the United Kingdom in 1973. However, Gibraltar is outside the customs union, is exempted from the Common Agricultural Policy and is not a signatory to the Schengen Agreement on border controls, although police co-operation rules apply.

ECONOMIC AFFAIRS

In 2008/09, according to preliminary official estimates, Gibraltar's gross domestic product (GDP), measured at current prices, was £850.0m. equivalent to some £29,024 per head. Gibraltar's population totalled some 27,495 at the census of May 2001; in 2009 it was estimated at 29,431.

Gibraltar lacks agricultural land and natural resources, and the territory is dependent on imports of foodstuffs and fuels. Foodstuffs were estimated to account for 6% of total imports (excluding petroleum products) in 2004.

The industrial sector (including manufacturing, construction and power) employed 16.3% of the working population at October 2008.

Manufacturing employed 2.3% of the working population at October 2008. The most important sectors are shipbuilding and ship-repairs, and small-scale domestic manufacturing (mainly bottling, coffee-processing, pottery and handicrafts).

Gibraltar is dependent on imported petroleum for its energy supplies. Mineral fuels (excluding petroleum products) accounted for about 55% of the value of total imports in 2004.

Tourism and banking make a significant contribution to the economy. In 2009 revenue from tourism was estimated at G£257.6m. Visitor arrivals by air in 2009 totalled some 160,713, according to official figures. The number of visitor arrivals via the land frontier also reached a record high in 2009; 10,302,238 people crossed into Gibraltar during that year. Many cross-border day visitors come to the country with the purpose of shopping. At October 2009 the financial sector employed about 9.1% of the working population. Several Spanish banks have established offices in Gibraltar, encouraging the growth of the territory as an 'offshore' banking centre, while the absence of taxes for non-residents has also encouraged the use of Gibraltar as a financial centre. By March 2009 there were 19 banks and 63 licensed insurance companies operating in Gibraltar. In November 2002, however, the European Commission ruled that Gibraltar's tax-free status was illegal and ordered Gibraltar to end its system of granting tax exemption to companies, which was unique in the European Union (EU, see p. 270). In March 2005 the Commission ruled that Gibraltar could extend the tax-exempt status of 8,464 companies registered in the territory until December 2010.

In 2008 Gibraltar recorded a visible trade deficit of £295.8m. In 2009 the principal sources of imports in that year (excluding petroleum products) were the United Kingdom (accounting for 25.4% of the total) and Spain. The principal imports in 2004 were mineral fuels and manufactured goods. The principal re-exports in that year were petroleum products, manufactured goods and wines, spirits, malt and tobacco.

According to official estimates, the budgetary surplus was estimated to reach £13.2m in 2011. The annual rate of inflation averaged 2.4% during 2000–10. Retail prices increased by 3.5% in 2010. Less than 5.0% of the labour force was unemployed in 2004.

The Gibraltar economy is based on tourism, shipping, and banking and finance. From the late 1980s the Gibraltar Government focused on developing the territory as an 'offshore' financial centre, stimulating private investment and promoting the tourism sector. A project to build a new financial district on land reclaimed from the sea commenced in 1990. Following the reduction in British military personnel in Gibraltar in the early 1990s, revenue from the British defence forces (which had accounted for some 60% of the economy in 1985) declined sharply. After 1999 there was a significant increase in gambling outlets in Gibraltar, as operations transferred from the United Kingdom. By October 2010 the Government had issued 19 remote gambling licences, the territory having become a major centre for online gambling firms. In a list published in May 2009, the Organisation for Economic Co-operation and Development (OECD, see p. 376) continued to define Gibraltar as a tax haven, noting that it had committed to internationally agreed tax standards in 2002, but had not yet substantially implemented them. However, in October the signature of Gibraltar's 12th bilateral agreement on the exchange of information regarding taxation ensured the territory's removal from the OECD list, and by March 2011 Gibraltar had signed tax information exchange agreements with a total of 19 jurisdictions (although notably not Spain). In January 2011, as the tax-exempt status previously enjoyed by many companies registered in Gibraltar expired, the corporate tax rate was reduced from 22% to 10% in an effort to encourage businesses, particularly in the financial services sector, to locate in the territory. In December 2008 the European Court of First Instance (now General Court) had upheld Gibraltar's autonomy from the United Kingdom with regard to fiscal policy, rejecting a complaint submitted by the European Commission, although an appeal against this ruling, by both the Commission and Spain, was being considered by the European Court of Justice in early 2011. Meanwhile, Gibraltar's economy continued to expand in 2008–10, recording fiscal surpluses and maintaining low levels of public debt and high employment, despite less favourable global economic conditions.

PUBLIC HOLIDAYS

2012: 1 January (New Year's Day), 12 March (Commonwealth Day), 6 April (Good Friday), 9 April (Easter Monday), 2 May (May Day), 4 June (Spring Bank Holiday), 11 June (Queen's Official Birthday), 27 August (Late Summer Bank Holiday), 10 September (Gibraltar National Holiday), 25–26 December (Christmas).

Statistical Survey

Source (unless otherwise indicated): Statistics Office, 99 Harbours Walk, The New Harbours, Gibraltar; tel. 20075515; fax 20051160; e-mail gibstats@gibtelecom.net; internet www.gibraltar.gov.gi.

AREA AND POPULATION

Area: 6.5 sq km (2.5 sq miles).

Population (excl. armed forces): 27,495 (males 13,644, females 13,851) at census of 12 November 2001 (Gibraltarians 22,882, Other British 2,627, Non-British 1,986). *2009* (official figure): 29,431 (Gibraltarians 23,907, Other British 3,129, Non-British 2,395).

Density (2009): 4,527.8 per sq km.

Population by Age and Sex (at 2001 census): *0–14:* 5,062 (males 2,655, females 2,407); *15–64:* 18,127 (males 9,229, females 8,898); *65 and over:* 4,306 (males 1,760, females 2,546); *Total* 27,495 (males 13,644, females 13,851) (Source: UN, *Demographic Yearbook*).

Births, Marriages and Deaths (2009, excl. armed forces): Live births 417 (birth rate 14.2 per 1,000); Marriages 966 (residents 188) (marriage rate for residents 6.4 per 1,000); Deaths 234 (death rate 8.0 per 1,000).

Life Expectancy (years at birth at census of 2001): Males 78.5; Females 83.3.

Employment (October 2009): Manufacturing 473 (Shipbuilding 279); Construction 2,557; Electricity, gas and water 299; Wholesale and retail trade, and repair of goods 2,943; Restaurants and hotels 1,133; Transport, storage and communications 1,172; Financial intermediation 1,870; Real estate, renting and business activities 2,693; Public administration and defence 1,975; Education 871; Health and social work 1,650; Other community, social and personal services 2,814; Total 20,450 (males 12,025, females 8,425). Figures cover only non-agricultural activities, excluding mining and quarrying.

INDUSTRY

Electric Energy (2009): 174.1m. kWh.

FINANCE

Currency and Exchange Rates: 100 pence (pennies) = 1 Gibraltar pound (G£). *Sterling, Dollar and Euro Equivalents* (31 December 2010): £1 sterling = G£1.0000; US $1 = 63.88 pence; €1 = 85.35 pence; G£10 = £10.00 sterling = $15.65 = €11.72. *Average Exchange Rate* (G£ per US dollar): 0.5440 in 2008; 0.6419 in 2009; 0.6472 in 2010. Note: The Gibraltar pound is at par with sterling.

Budget (G£ '000, year ending 31 March 2010, forecasts): *Recurrent Revenue:* Taxes 143,500; Duties 68,955; Gambling fees 12,320; Rates 16,572; Departmental fees and receipts 17,911; Government earnings 5,192; Total 264,450. *Recurrent Expenditure:* Education, employment and training 25,290; Heritage, culture, youth and sport 4,166; Housing 10,075; Environment and tourism 21,742; Social and civic affairs 26,050; Trade, industry, communications and transport 25,414; Health and civil protection 33,416; Administration 8,584; Finance 14,717; Employment, labour and industrial relations 2,319; Justice 13,903; Immigration and civil status 2,647; House of Assembly 1,314; Office of Principal Auditor 689; Consolidated fund charges 40,187; Contribution to social insurance funds 8,500; Total 239,013. *2010/11* (estimates): Revenue 276,748; Expenditure 263,500..

UNITED KINGDOM OVERSEAS TERRITORIES

Gibraltar

Cost of Living (Retail Price Index at January; base: April 1998 = 100): 120.8 in 2008; 124.1 in 2009; 128.4 in 2010.

Gross National Product (G£ million, at factor cost): 657.61 in 2006/07; 697.86 in 2007/08; 748.56 in 2008/09 (estimate).

Gross Domestic Product (G£ million, at factor cost): 804.36 in 2007/08; 868.69 in 2008/09 (estimate); 914.00 in 2009/10 (provisional estimate).

EXTERNAL TRADE

Imports c.i.f. (G£ million, excluding petroleum products): 425.7 in 2007; 449.8 in 2008; 479.3 in 2009.

Exports f.o.b. (G£ million, excluding petroleum products): 151.8 in 2007; 154.0 in 2008; 169.5 in 2009.

Principal Trading Partners (G£ '000, 2009, excluding petroleum products): *Imports:* Denmark 2,871; Germany 12,538; Japan 2,102; Netherlands 12,576; Spain 110,995; United Kingdom 121,686; USA 4,564; Total (incl. others) 479,286. Note: Figures for exports are not available.

TRANSPORT

Road Traffic (licences current at 31 December 2009): Private vehicles 15,667; Commercial vehicles 1,927; Motorcycles 8,564.

Shipping (merchant fleet registered at 31 December 2009): Vessels 278; Displacement 2,026,782 grt. Source: IHS Fairplay, *World Fleet Statistics*.

Civil Aviation (2009): Passenger arrivals ('000) 183.9; Passenger departures ('000) 186.2; Freight loaded 11 metric tons; Freight unloaded 134 metric tons. Figures exclude military passengers and freight.

TOURISM

Visitor Arrivals ('000): 9,430.1 in 2007; 10,155.0 in 2008; 10,302.2 in 2009.

Tourism Receipts (G£ million): 230.58 in 2007; 247.50 in 2008; 257.59 in 2009.

COMMUNICATIONS MEDIA

Radio Receivers (1997): 37,000 in use (Source: UNESCO, *Statistical Yearbook*).

Television Licences (2005): 5,965.

Daily Newspapers (1999): 1.

Telephone Stations (2004): 34,476.

Telephones (main lines in use, 2009): 24,000 (Source: International Telecommunication Union).

Mobile Cellular Telephones (2009): 28,600 subscribers (Source: International Telecommunication Union).

Internet Connections (31 March 2009): 20,200.

EDUCATION

Primary (state schools, 2009, unless otherwise indicated): 11 schools (1999), 2,926 pupils.

Secondary (state schools, 2009, unless otherwise indicated): 2 schools (1999), 2,180 pupils.

Total Teaching Staff at Primary and Secondary Schools (state schools, 2009): 375.

Technical and Vocational (1999): 1 college, 201 full-time students.

Pupil-teacher Ratio (primary education, UNESCO estimate): 16.0 in 2008/09 (Source: UNESCO Institute for Statistics).

Directory

The Government

HEAD OF STATE

Queen: HM Queen Elizabeth II.

Governor and Commander-in-Chief: Vice-Adm. Sir Adrian Johns (took office 26 October 2009).

COUNCIL OF MINISTERS
(May 2011)

Chief Minister and Minister of Finance: Peter Caruana.
Deputy Chief Minister and Minister for Enterprise, Development, Technology and Transport: Joe J. Holliday.
Minister of Justice: Daniel Feetham.
Minister for Education and Training: Clive Beltran.
Minister for Health and Civil Protection: Yvette Del Agua.
Minister for Housing: Fabian Vinet.
Minister for Employment, Labour and Industrial Relations: Luis Montiel.
Minister for Family, Youth and Community Affairs: James (Jaime) Netto.
Minister for the Environment and Tourism: Ernest Britto.
Minister of Culture, Heritage, Sport and Leisure: Edwin Reyes.

MINISTRIES

Office of the Governor: The Convent, Main St; tel. 20045440; fax 20047823; e-mail enquiry.gibraltar@fco.gov.uk.

Office of the Chief Minister: 6 Convent Pl.; tel. 20070071; fax 20076396.

Ministry of Culture, Heritage, Sport and Leisure: 310 Main St; tel. 20041687; fax 20052589; e-mail minculture@gibtelecom.net.

Ministry of Education and Training: 23 Queensway; tel. 20077486; fax 20071564; e-mail info.det@gibraltar.gov.gi.

Ministry of Employment, Labour and Industrial Relations: Unit 76/77, Harbours Walk, New Harbours; tel. 20040408; fax 20073981; e-mail employment.service@gibraltar.gov.gi.

Ministry of Enterprise, Development, Technology and Transport: Suite 771, Europort; tel. 20052052; fax 20047677; e-mail info.medt@gibraltar.gov.gi.

Ministry of the Environment and Tourism: Joshua Hassan House, Secretary's Lane; tel. 20059801; fax 20076223; e-mail met@gibraltar.gov.gi.

Ministry of Family, Youth and Community Affairs: 14 Governor's Parade; tel. 20044070; fax 20074941; e-mail kerenza.baker@gibraltar.gov.gi.

Ministry of Finance: 6 Convent Pl.; tel. 20070071; fax 20076396; e-mail financeministry@gibtelecom.net.

Ministry of Health and Civil Protection: Gibraltar Health Authority, 17 Johnstone's Passage; e-mail info@gha.gi.

Ministry of Housing: City Hall, John Mackintosh Sq.; tel. 20075603; fax 20052947; e-mail gibhouse@gibtelecom.net.

Ministry of Justice: 6 Convent Pl.; tel. 20059267; fax 20059271; e-mail moj@gibraltar.gov.gi.

Legislature

Gibraltar Parliament

156 Main St; tel. 20078420; fax 20042849; e-mail parliament@gibtelecom.net; internet www.gibraltar.gov.gi.

Speaker: Haresh K. Budhrani.

General Election, 11 October 2007

Party	Votes*	% of votes	Seats
Gibraltar Social Democrats	76,334	49.3	10
Gibraltar Socialist Labour Party }	70,397	45.5	7
Gibraltar Liberal Party }			
Progressive Democratic Party	5,799	3.7	—
New Gibraltar Democracy	1,210	0.8	—
Independent	1,003	0.6	—
Total	**154,743**	**100.0**	**17**

*Each voter was permitted to vote for a maximum of 10 candidates. The total number of ballots cast was 16,004.

Political Organizations

All political organizations in Gibraltar advocate self-determination for the territory.

Gibraltar Liberal Party (GLP): 95 Irish Town; tel. and fax 20076959; e-mail info@liberal.gi; internet www.liberal.gi; f. 1991 as the Gibraltar National Party; Leader Dr Joseph García; Sec.-Gen. Steven Linares.

UNITED KINGDOM OVERSEAS TERRITORIES

Gibraltar

Gibraltar Social Democrats (GSD): College Lane; tel. and fax 20044105; e-mail info@gsd.gi; internet www.gsd.gi; f. 1989; holds a majority of seats in the House of Assembly; absorbed the Gibraltar Labour Party in 2005; Leader PETER CARUANA.

Gibraltar Socialist Labour Party (GSLP): Suite 16, Block 3, Watergardens; tel. 20050700; fax 20078983; e-mail hqgslp@gibtelecom.net; internet www.gslp.gi; f. 1976; Leader JOSEPH (JOE) BOSSANO.

New Gibraltar Democracy (NGD): f. 2005; Christian democratic; Leader CHARLES GOMEZ.

Progressive Democratic Party (PDP): POB 1373; tel. and fax 20049000; e-mail info@pdp.gi; internet www.pdp.gi; f. 2006; Leader KEITH AZOPARDI.

Judicial System

The 2006 Constitution provides for the protection of the fundamental rights and freedoms of the individual and the maintenance of a Supreme Court with unlimited jurisdiction to hear and determine any civil or criminal proceedings under any law. The Courts of Law of Gibraltar comprise a Court of Appeal, the Supreme Court and the Magistrates' Court.

The substantive law of Gibraltar is contained in Orders in Council which apply to Gibraltar, enactments of the Parliament of the United Kingdom which apply to or have been extended or applied to Gibraltar, locally enacted acts and subsidiary legislation, and common law and the rules of equity from time to time in force in England so far as they may be applicable and subject to all necessary modification.

Court of Appeal

The Law Courts, 277 Main St.

Holds three sessions each year; the Justices of Appeal are drawn from the English Court of Appeal.

President: Sir MURRAY STUART-SMITH.

Justices of Appeal: Sir PHILIP OTTON, Sir WILLIAM ALDOUS, Sir JONATHAN PARKER, Sir SIMON TOCKEY.

Supreme Court

The Law Courts, 277 Main St; tel. 20078808; fax 20077118.
Includes the office of Admiralty Marshal.

Chief Justice: ANTHONY E. DUDLEY.

Magistrates' Court

The Law Courts, 277 Main St; tel. 20075671; fax 20040483.

Stipendiary Magistrate: CHARLES PITTO.

Religion

At the 2001 census 78.1% of the population were Roman Catholic, 7.0% Church of England, 4.0% Muslim, 2.1% Jewish and 1.8% Hindu.

CHRISTIANITY

The Roman Catholic Church

Gibraltar forms a single diocese, directly responsible to the Holy See. At 31 December 2006 there were an estimated 21,470 adherents in the territory (78.1% of the total population).

Bishop of Gibraltar: Rt Rev. RALPH HESKETT, 215 Main St; tel. 20076688; fax 20043112; e-mail epis.carroca@gibnynex.gi; internet www.catholicdiocese.gi.

The Church of England

The diocese of Gibraltar in Europe, founded in 1980, has jurisdiction over the whole of continental Europe, Turkey and Morocco.

Bishop of Gibraltar in Europe: Rt Rev. GEOFFREY ROWELL, Bishop's Lodge, Church Rd, Worth, RH10 7RT, United Kingdom; tel. (1293) 883051; fax (1293) 884479; e-mail bishop@dioceseineurope.org.uk; internet europe.anglican.org.

Dean of the Cathedral of the Holy Trinity: Very Rev. JOHN PADDOCK, The Deanery, Bomb House Lane; tel. 20078377; fax 20078463; e-mail deangib@gibnet.gi; internet www.gibconnect.com/~holytrinity.

Other Christian Churches

Church of Scotland: St Andrew's Manse, 29 Scud Hill; tel. and fax 20077040; e-mail scotskirk@gibraltar.gi; internet www.scotskirkgibraltar.com; f. 1800; Minister Rev. EWEN MACLEAN; 50 mems.

Gibraltar Methodist Church: 297 Main St; tel. and fax 20040870; e-mail minister@methodist.org.gi; internet www.methodist.org.gi; f. 1769; Minister Rev. FIDEL PATRON; 80 mems.

ISLAM

A mosque to serve the Islamic community in Gibraltar and financed by the Government of Saudi Arabia was constructed in the late 1990s.

JUDAISM

Jewish Community: Managing Board, 91 Irish Town; tel. 20072606; fax 20040487; e-mail mbjc@gibtelecom.net; internet www.jewishgibraltar.com; Pres. H. J. M. LEVY; Admin. Sec. S. LEVY; 600 mems.

The Press

Gibraltar Chronicle: POB 27, Watergate House, Casemates; tel. 20078589; fax 20079927; e-mail management@chronicle.gi; internet www.chronicle.gi; f. 1801; daily (except Sun.); English; Man. Editor DOMINIQUE SEARLE; circ. 6,000.

Gibraltar Gazette: Ministry of Justice, Legislation Support Unit, Treasury Bldg, 23 John Mackintosh Sq.; tel. 20051246; fax 20041822; f. 1949; weekly; publ. by *Gibraltar Chronicle*; official notices; circ. 375.

Gibraltar Magazine: PMB 1124, 17 Turnbull's Lane; tel. and fax 20077748; e-mail gibmag@gibnet.gi; internet www.thegibraltarmagazine.com; f. 1995; monthly; English; business and leisure; Editor ANDREA MORTON.

Insight: tel. 40913; fax 48665; e-mail insight@gibtelecom.net; internet www.insightgibraltar.com; f. 1992; print and internet magazine; circ. 6,000.

Panorama: 75–77 Irish Town; tel. 79797; fax 74664; e-mail contacts@panorama.gi; internet www.panorama.gi; f. 1975; weekly, Mon.; English; news and features; Editor JOE GARCÍA; circ. 4,000.

The New People: Suite No. 6/608, ICom House, 1–5 Irish Town; tel. 54374000; e-mail thenewpeople@gibtelecom.net; internet www.thenewpeople.net; f. 1996; weekly; English with Spanish section; Editor JUAN CARLOS PÉREZ; circ. 1,000.

Vox: Unit 91, Harbours Walk, New Harbours, POB 306; tel. 20077417; fax 20072531; e-mail editor@vox.gi; internet www.vox.gi; f. 1955; weekly; independent; in English and Spanish; Editor DEREK MCGRAIL; circ. 1,800.

Broadcasting and Communications

TELECOMMUNICATIONS

Gibraltar Regulatory Authority (GRA): Suite 603, Europort; tel. 20074636; fax 20072166; e-mail info@gra.gi; internet www.gra.gi; f. 2000; statutory body responsible for the regulation of the radio spectrum and data protection; Chief Exec. PAUL CANESSA.

CTS Gibraltar Ltd: 48 Royal Ocean Ave, Royal Ocean Plaza; tel. 21651500; fax 21651502; e-mail customerservices@cts-europe.com; internet www.cts-europe.com; part of CTS Group; mobile and broadband internet services.

Gibtelecom: 15/21 John Mackintosh Sq., POB 929; tel. 20052200; fax 20071673; e-mail info@gibtele.com; internet www.gibtele.com; f. 1990; jointly owned by Govt of Gibraltar and Telekom Slovenije (Slovenia); operates local and international telephone and telecommunications services; provides a range of digital, satellite, mobile and internet services; Chair. JOE J. HOLLIDAY (Minister of Enterprise, Development, Technology and Transport); CEO TIM BRISTOW.

Sapphire Networks: Suite 303, Eurotowers, POB 797; tel. 20047200; fax 20047272; e-mail info@sapphire.gi; internet www.sapphire.gi; f. 2005; internet service provider; Man. Dir LAWRENCE ISOLA.

BROADCASTING

Gibraltar Broadcasting Corporation (GBC): Broadcasting House, 18 South Barrack Rd; tel. 20079760; fax 20078673; e-mail gbc@gibraltar.gi; internet www.gbc.gi; f. 1963; responsible for television and radio broadcasting; Chair. ANTHONY PROVASOLI; CEO ALLAN KING.

Radio

GBC—Radio (Radio Gibraltar): 24 hours daily in English and Spanish, including commercial broadcasting. In addition to local programmes, the BBC World Service programme is relayed.

Television

GBC—TV: operates in English for 24 hours daily; GBC and relayed BBC programmes are transmitted.

Finance

(cap. = capital; res = reserves; dep. = deposits; m. = million; brs = branches; amounts in G£)

BANKING

In March 2010 there were 19 banks operating in Gibraltar.

Regulatory Authority

Financial Services Commission: POB 940, Suite 943, Europort; tel. 20040283; fax 20040282; e-mail info@fsc.gi; internet www.fsc.gi; f. 1991; regulates the activities of the financial sector; CEO Marcus Killick.

Banks

Barclays Private Clients International (Gibraltar) Ltd: 1st Floor, Regal House, 3 Queensway, POB 187; tel. 20078565; fax 20079509; e-mail gibraltar@barclays.com; Chief Man. Douglas Reyes.

Credit Suisse (Gibraltar) Ltd: 1st Floor, Neptune House, Marina Bay, POB 556; tel. 20078399; fax 20076027; e-mail csg.mail@credit-suisse.com; f. 1987; Chair. Hans-Ulrich Doerig; Man. Dir Thomas Westh Olsen.

EFG Bank (Gibraltar) Ltd: Eurolife Bldg, 1 Corral Rd, POB 561; tel. 20040117; fax 20040110; e-mail atlaco@gibnet.gi; formerly Banco Atlántico (Gibraltar) Ltd; Man. Emilio Martínez Priego.

SG Hambros Bank (Gibraltar) Ltd: Hambro House, 32 Line Wall Rd, POB 375; tel. 20002000; fax 20079037; e-mail gibraltar@sghambros.com; internet www.sghambros.com; f. 1981; acquired ABN AMRO Private Banking in 2008; owned by Société Générale (France); cap. 1.5m., res 10.2m., dep. 245.0m. (June 2005); Chair. Warwick J. Newbury; Man. Dir Emma Perez.

Jyske Bank (Gibraltar) Ltd: 76 Main St, POB 143; tel. 20072782; fax 20072732; e-mail jyskebank@jyskebank.gi; internet jyskebank.gi; f. 1855 as Galliano (A. L.) Bankers; in 1988 name changed as above; cap. 26.5m., res 0.9m., dep. 1,788.4m. (Dec. 2004); Chair. Jens Lauritzen; Man. Dir Christian Bjørløw.

Lloyds TSB Bank PLC: 1st Floor, Royal Ocean Plaza, Ocean Village, POB 482; tel. 20077373; fax 20070023; internet www.lloydstsb.gi; f. 1986; Man. Albert Douglas Langston.

Lombard Odier Darier Hentsch Private Bank Ltd: Suite 921, Europort, POB 407; tel. 20073350; fax 20073475; e-mail gibraltar@lombardodier.com; internet www.lombardodier.com; Man. Dir Javier de Mendieta.

NatWest Offshore Ltd: NatWest House, 57 Line Wall Rd, POB 707; tel. 20077737; fax 20074557; e-mail natwestgib@gibnynex.gi; internet www.natwestoffshore.com; f. 1988.

Royal Bank of Scotland (Gibraltar) Ltd: 1 Corral Rd, POB 766; tel. 20073200; fax 20070152; e-mail marvincartwright@rbsint.com; internet www.rbsinternational.com; Country Man. Marvin Cartwright.

Turicum Private Bank Ltd: Turicum House, 315 Main St, POB 619; tel. 20044144; fax 20044145; e-mail info@turicum.com; internet www.turicumprivatebank.com; f. 1993; cap. and res €5.0m., dep. €15.7m. (Dec. 2003); Chair. Dr Raymond Bisang; CEO Urs Hüni.

Savings Bank

Gibraltar Savings Bank: Treasury Dept, Treasury Bldg, 23 John Mackintosh Sq.; tel. 20048396; fax 20077147; e-mail treasury@gibtelecom.net; dep. 242.2m. (March 2007); Dir C. Victory.

Association

Gibraltar Bankers' Association (GBA): POB 380; tel. 20073200; fax 20070152; e-mail langham@mercuryin.es; internet www.gba.gi; f. 1982; Pres. Thomas Westh Olsen; 16 mem. banks.

INSURANCE

There were 63 licensed insurance companies operating in Gibraltar in March 2010.

BMI Insurance Services Limited: Unit 7, Portland House, Glacis Rd, POB 469; tel. 20051010; e-mail info@bmigroup.gi; internet www.bmigroup.gi.

Capurro Insurance and Investments Ltd: 20 Line Wall Rd, POB 130; tel. 20040850; fax 20040851; e-mail info@capurroinsurance.com; internet www.capurroinsurance.com; Man. Dir Belen S. Capurro.

Castiel Winser Insurance and Financial Consultants: Natwest House, 57/63 Line Wall Rd, POB 464; tel. 20077723; fax 20079257; e-mail financialservices@castielwinser.com; f. 1985; Man. Dir Sydney Isaac Attias.

Eurolife Assurance (International) Ltd: 6A Queensway, POB 64; tel. 20045502; fax 20051071; e-mail eurolife@gibnet.gi; Man. A. Smith.

Eurolinx (Gibraltar) Ltd: Suites 21–22, Victoria House, 26 Main St, POB 671; tel. 20040240; fax 20040241; e-mail eurolinx@sapphirenet.gi; internet www.eurolinx.gi; f. 1990; Dir Alan Joseph Montegriffo.

Gibro Insurance Services Ltd: Gibro House, 4 Giro's Passage, POB 693; tel. 20076222; fax 20071423; e-mail gibro@gibro.com; internet www.gibro.com; f. 1994; Chair. Hon. John Brian Perez.

Middle Sea Insurance PLC: Suite 1A, 143 Main St, POB 502; tel. 20076434; fax 20076741; f. 2000.

Ophir Insurance Services Ltd: 123 Main St, POB 914; tel. 20073871; fax 20050411; e-mail ophir@gibtelecom.net; internet www.ois-insurance.com; Dirs Geoff Holt, Terry Breedon.

Association

Gibraltar Insurance Association: c/o POB 371, 2nd Floor, 85 Main St; tel. 20045578; fax 20045579; f. 1995; Pres. Penny Hudson.

Trade and Industry

GOVERNMENT AGENCY

InvestGibraltar: Suite 771, Europort; tel. 20052634; fax 20052635; e-mail info@investgibraltar.gov.gi; internet www.investgibraltar.gov.gi.

CHAMBER OF COMMERCE

Gibraltar Chamber of Commerce: Watergate House, 2–6 Casemates Sq., POB 29; tel. 20078376; fax 20078403; e-mail info@gibraltarchamberofcommerce.com; internet www.gibraltarchamberofcommerce.com; f. 1882; Pres. Nicholas Russo; 300 mems.

EMPLOYERS' ORGANIZATIONS

Gibraltar Federation of Small Businesses: GFSB House, POB 211, 112 Irish Town; tel. 20047722; fax 20047733; e-mail gfsb@gfsb.gi; internet www.gfsb.gi; f. 1996; Chair. Charles Serruya.

Gibraltar Hotel Association: c/o Caleta Hotel; tel. 20076501; fax 20071050; e-mail caleta@gibnynex.gi; internet www.caletahotel.com; f. 1960; Chair. Franco Ostuni; 7 mems.

Gibraltar Licensed Victuallers' Association: c/o Watergate Restaurant, Queensway Quay; tel. 20074195; f. 1976; Chair. Michael Oton; 120 mems.

Gibraltar Motor Traders' Association: POB 167; tel. 20079004; f. 1961; Gen. Sec. G. Bassadone; 6 mems.

Hindu Merchants' Association: POB 357; tel. 20079000; fax 20071966; e-mail vikram.nagrani@hassans.gi; f. 1979; Pres. Vikram Nagrani; 600 mems.

PRINCIPAL TRADE UNIONS

Gibraltar Taxi Association: 19 Waterport Wharf; tel. 20070052; fax 20076986; e-mail gibtaxiass@gibtelecom.net; internet www.gibtaxi.com; f. 1957; Pres. Ronald Ignacio; 100 mems.

Gibraltar Trades Council: 7 Hargraves Ramp, POB 279; tel. 20076930; fax 20079646; e-mail ggca@gibtelecom.net; comprises unions representing 70% of the working population; affiliated to the United Kingdom Trades Union Congress; Sec. Michael J. A. Tampin; Pres. Joseph J. Cortes.

Affiliated unions:

Gibraltar General and Clerical Association (GGCA): 7 Hargrave's Ramp, POB 279; tel. 20076930; fax 20079646; e-mail ggca@gibtelecom.net; internet www.ggca.gi; f. 1947; Pres. José Luis García; Gen. Sec. Michael J. A. Tampin; 1,205 mems (2009).

NASUWT (Gibraltar): 98 Harbours Walk, New Harbours; tel. 20076308; fax 77608; e-mail gtateachers@gibtelecom.net; f. 1962; fmrly the Gibraltar Teachers' Association; Pres. Stuart Borastero; 350 mems.

Unite (United Kingdom) (Gibraltar District): tel. 20074185; fax 20071596; f. 1924; Dist. Officer Sukh Khaira; 4,239 mems.

UTILITIES

Electricity

Gibraltar Electricity Authority: Gibelec House, North Mole Rd; tel. 20048908; fax 20077408; e-mail enquiries@gibelec.gi; internet www.gibelec.gi; govt-owned; generation, distribution and supply of electricity.

UNITED KINGDOM OVERSEAS TERRITORIES

Water

AquaGib Ltd: Suite 10B, Leanse Pl., 50 Town Range; tel. 20040880; fax 20040881; e-mail main.office@aquagib.gi; internet www.aquagib.gi; fmrly known as Lyonnais des Eaux (Gibraltar) Ltd; present name adopted 2003; f. 1991; 66.67% owned by Northumbrian Water Group (United Kingdom), 33.33% govt-owned; Man. Dir P. LATIN.

Transport

There are no railways in Gibraltar. There is a total road length of 53.1 km, including 12.9 km of highways and 6.8 km of footpaths.

ROADS

Ministry of Enterprise, Development, Technology and Transport: see Ministries.

SHIPPING

The Strait of Gibraltar is a principal ocean route between the Mediterranean and Black Sea areas and the rest of the world.

Gibraltar is used by many long-distance liners, and has dry dock facilities and a commercial ship-repair yard. Tax concessions are available to ship owners who register their ships in Gibraltar.

A new passenger ferry service between Gibraltar and the Spanish port of Algeciras, across the Bay of Gibraltar, began operating in December 2009.

Gibdock Limited: Main Wharf Rd, The Dockyard; tel. 20059400; fax 20044404; e-mail mail@gibdock.com; internet www.gibdock.com; f. 1998; drydock facilities and general ship-repairing; CEO JOSEPH CORVELLI.

Gibraltar Maritime Administration: Watergate House, 2/8 Casemate Sq.; tel. 20047771; fax 20047770; e-mail maritadmin@gibtelecom.net; internet www.gibmaritime.com; Administrator ALAN CUBBIN.

Gibraltar Port Authority: Port Office, North Mole; tel. 20046254; fax 20051513; e-mail gpa.enquiries@portofgibraltar.gi; internet www.gibraltarport.com; CEO Capt. PETER W. HALL.

M. H. Bland & Co Ltd: Cloister Bldg, Market Lane, POB 554; tel. 20079478; fax 20071608; internet www.mhbland.com; f. 1810; ship agents, stevedoring, warehousing; also operates cable-car service to peak of the Rock of Gibraltar; Chair. JOHN A. GAGGERO.

Association

Gibraltar Shipping Association: c/o Inchcape Shipping Services, POB 194; tel. 20046315; fax 20046316; e-mail mark.porral@iss-shipping.com; f. 1957; Sec. P. L. IMOSSI; 11 mems.

CIVIL AVIATION

The airport is at North Front, on the isthmus, 2.5 km from the city centre. An agreement reached in September 2006 between Gibraltar, the United Kingdom and Spain allowed for the operation of flights from Spain and the rest of Europe to Gibraltar. Hitherto Spain had blocked direct air links between Gibraltar and European countries other than the United Kingdom. Commercial flights between Gibraltar and Spain began in December 2006. In accordance with the 2006 agreement, plans were announced in 2007 for a new airport terminal adjoining the border with Spain.

Gibraltar Civil Aviation Advisory Board: Air Terminal, Winston Churchill Ave; tel. 20073026; fax 20073925; e-mail info@gibraltar-airport.com; Sec. JOHN GONÇALVES.

Tourism

Gibraltar's tourist attractions include its climate, beaches and a variety of amenities. Following the reopening of the border with Spain in February 1985, the resumption of traffic by day-visitors contributed to the expansion of the tourist industry. In 2009 visitor arrivals numbered some 10.3m., while revenue from tourism totalled G£257.8m.

Gibraltar Tourist Board: Duke of Kent House, Cathedral Sq.; tel. 20074950; fax 20074943; e-mail tourism@gibraltar.gi; internet www.gibraltar.gov.gi; CEO NICHOLAS GUERRERO.

Defence

There is a local defence force, the Gibraltar Regiment, which, following the abolition of conscription, was reorganized as a predominantly volunteer reserve unit; as assessed at November 2010 it comprised 175 members. British army personnel stationed in Gibraltar numbered 95 and there were about 70 Royal Air Force personnel. There is one Royal Navy base located in Gibraltar.

Commander-in-Chief: Vice-Adm. Sir ADRIAN JOHNS.

Education

Education is compulsory between the ages of five and 15 years, and is provided free in government schools. The language of instruction is English. There are four nursery schools, 11 primary schools (of which one is private), one Service school (administered by the Ministry of Defence for the children of military personnel), two secondary comprehensive schools—one for boys and one for girls and one college of further education. In 2009 there were 2,926 pupils in state primary schools, 2,180 pupils in state secondary schools and 375 teaching staff in state primary and secondary schools. Higher national diploma and degree courses are offered by the universities in the United Kingdom. Scholarships for students in higher education are provided by both government and private sources. There is also one college providing technical and vocational training, and a school for children with special needs. Government expenditure on education, employment and training in 2008/09 was forecast at G£21.7m. (equivalent to 10.8% of total spending).

MONTSERRAT

Introductory Survey

LOCATION, CLIMATE, LANGUAGE, RELIGION, FLAG, CAPITAL

Montserrat is one of the Leeward Islands in the West Indies. A mountainous, volcanic island, it lies about 55 km (35 miles) north of Basse-Terre, Guadeloupe, and about 43 km south west of Antigua. The climate is generally warm, with a mean maximum temperature of 30°C (86°F) and a mean minimum of 23°C (73°F), but the island is fanned by sea breezes for most of the year. The average annual rainfall is about 1,475 mm (58 ins), although there is more rain in the central and western areas. English is the official language. Many Christian churches are represented, but the principal denominations are the Anglican, Roman Catholic and Methodist Churches. The flag is the British 'Blue Ensign', with the island's badge (a shield depicting a woman dressed in green holding a harp and a cross) on a white roundel in the fly. The capital is Plymouth.

CONTEMPORARY POLITICAL HISTORY

Historical Context

Montserrat was first settled by the British (initially Roman Catholic exiles) in 1632, by which time the few original Carib inhabitants had disappeared. It formed part of the federal colony of the Leeward Islands from 1871 until 1956, when the federation was dissolved and the presidency of Montserrat became a separate colony. Montserrat participated in the short-lived Federation of the West Indies (1958–62) and, from 1960, the island had its own Administrator (the title was changed to that of Governor in 1971). The Constitution (see below) came into force in 1960.

Domestic Political Affairs

The first priority of successive legislatures has been to improve infrastructure and maintain a healthy economy. Between 1952 and 1970 William Bramble dominated island politics. His son, Austin Bramble, leader of the Progressive Democratic Party (PDP), opposed and succeeded him as Chief Minister. In November 1978 the People's Liberation Movement (PLM) won all seven elective seats in the Legislative Council, and the PLM's leader, John Osborne, became Chief Minister. In the general election of February 1983 the PLM was returned to government.

Attempts to form an opposition alliance between the PDP and the National Development Party (formed by business interests and former members of the PDP) were unsuccessful. Against a divided opposition, the PLM won the general election of August 1987. Osborne was returned to office as Chief Minister.

Osborne was an advocate of independence from the United Kingdom, despite the apparent lack of popular support for this policy. A referendum on the issue was planned for 1990, but the devastation caused by Hurricane Hugo in September 1989 meant that any plans for independence were postponed. Furthermore, the Osborne Government and the British authorities were embarrassed by controversy surrounding the hitherto lucrative 'offshore' financial sector. In 1989 the Governor's office announced that the British police were investigating serious allegations against certain banks (involving the processing of illegal funds from a variety of criminal activities). Registration was suspended, several people were charged with criminal offences and most banking licences were revoked. The Montserrat Government agreed to introduce recommended provisions for the regulation of the financial services industry and responsibility for the sector was transferred from the Chief Minister to the Governor. In December 1991 the Legislative Council approved legislation allowing the re-establishment of a comprehensive 'offshore' financial centre. However, despite considerably improved regulation, more than 90% of the island's 'offshore' and commercial banks were again closed following further investigations by British inspectors in mid-1992.

The resignation of the Deputy Chief Minister, Benjamin Chalmers, in September 1991, following a dispute with Osborne, resulted in the loss of the Government's majority in the Legislative Council. This prompted an early election in the following month, when the National Progressive Party (NPP), formed only two months prior to the election, secured a majority of seats. The NPP leader, Reuben Meade, became Chief Minister.

Volcanic eruption

The eruption of Chances Peak volcano in July 1995, which had been dormant for more than 100 years, caused severe disruption to the island and threatened to devastate Plymouth and surrounding areas in southern Montserrat. In late August the threat of a more serious eruption prompted the evacuation of some 5,000 people to the north of the island, and the declaration by the Government of a state of emergency and a night curfew. As volcanic activity subsided in September, evacuated islanders returned to Plymouth and villages near the volcano. However, by December the area was again deemed to be unsafe, and 4,000 people were evacuated for a period of several weeks. The Governor and Chief Minister secured an agreement from the British Government for the provision of assistance with evacuation and rehabilitation programmes. A third evacuation took place in April 1996, following another series of eruptions, and it was announced that some 5,000 evacuees living in 'safe areas' would remain there at least until the end of the year. In that month the British Government announced that Montserratians would be granted residency and the right to work in the United Kingdom for up to two years. In August the British Government announced that it was to provide assistance worth £25m. to finance housing construction projects, infrastructure development, the provision of temporary health and education facilities and other public services in the northern 'safe areas' of the island. By the end of 1996 it was estimated that some 5,000 islanders had left the territory since the onset of volcanic activity in mid-1995.

In September 1996 the Deputy Chief Minister, Noel Tuitt, resigned from his post and from the NPP, stating that he was disillusioned with Meade's leadership. Disagreement over the Government's management of the volcano crisis and its handling of aid funds led to the proposal, by an opposition member in October, of a motion of no confidence in the Chief Minister. Meade, however, avoided a vote on the motion by dissolving the Legislative Council.

No party won an overall majority at a general election in November 1996. A four-member coalition cabinet was subsequently formed under the leadership of Bertrand Osborne, who was sworn in as Chief Minister on 13 November.

In June 1997 the scale of volcanic activity on the island increased dramatically with the eruption of the Soufrière Hills volcano, which left some two-thirds of the island uninhabitable, destroyed the capital and resulted in 19 deaths. Islanders were evacuated to 'safe areas' in the north of the country. The British Government released emergency aid to finance the construction of emergency shelters for evacuees, and for repairs to temporary hospital facilities. In July it was announced that a package of options for Montserratians was being formulated, which would offer islanders resettlement grants and assisted passage either to other islands within the Caribbean or to the United Kingdom. The 'safe area' in the north was to be developed for those wishing to remain on the island. By the end of July the population of Montserrat was estimated to have declined to 5,800; in the month since the eruption of the Soufrière Hills volcano some 800 islanders had moved to Antigua, bringing the total number who had moved there since the onset of volcanic activity in 1995 to some 3,000. Many more had resettled on other Caribbean islands or in the United Kingdom.

In August 1997 Bertrand Osborne resigned as Chief Minister following four days of public demonstrations in protest at his handling of the volcano crisis, in particular at uncertainty surrounding the future of the islanders and at poor conditions in emergency shelters. On the same day the British Government announced the financial details of its voluntary evacuation scheme for those wishing to leave Montserrat. The offer, which comprised a relocation grant of £2,400 for adults and £600 for minors, in addition to travel costs, provoked an angry response from islanders, who protested that the grants were severely inadequate. Osborne's successor as Chief Minister, David Brandt, an independent member of the Legislative Council, criticized the British Government's offer while also accusing it of attempting to depopulate Montserrat by showing insufficient commitment to the redevelopment of the island. The British Secretary of State for International Development, Clare Short, accused the island's leaders of making unreasonable demands, causing considerable offence to the island Government. The controversy was assuaged only when the British Secretary of State for Foreign and Commonwealth Affairs, Robin Cook, announced the formation of a special inter-departmental committee charged with co-ordinating assistance to Montserrat. At the end of August a five-year sustainable development plan for the north of the island was announced, to include finance for new housing, social services and improved infrastructure.

In January 1998 Brandt renewed his accusations that the British Government was attempting to depopulate Montserrat by delaying the release of development funds. It was subsequently announced that the United Kingdom would provide further finance of £4.8m. for housing on the island. The new funding brought the total amount committed by the British Government in 1995–98, since the beginning of the volcano crisis, to £59m. In May the British Government announced that all citizens of Montserrat, except those already resident in other countries, would be entitled to settle in the United Kingdom. The estimated 3,500 refugees already in the United Kingdom on temporary visas were to be allowed to apply for permanent residency. In early July the Soufrière Hills volcano erupted again, covering much of the island in ash, and postponing plans to reopen parts of Plymouth to residents. In August part of the central zone of Montserrat was reopened, following operations to remove ash and debris.

In January 1999 an inquest into the 19 deaths during the eruptions found that in nine cases the British Government was in part to blame for the deaths. The jury criticized the public shelters provided, where conditions were described as 'deplorable', and the Government's failure to provide farming land in the 'safe area', which had led to some farmers choosing to risk their lives rather than abandon their farms. The Department for International Development denied culpability for the deaths, and announced that it was to spend a further £75m. on a three-year redevelopment programme in the north of the island.

In February 1999 studies were published confirming that the volcanic ash covering much of Montserrat contained significant amounts of silica, the cause of the lung disease silicosis. It was suggested that the threat to health from long-term exposure to the ash might further limit the number of areas of the island suitable for redevelopment. Further explosions of ash and minor eruptions of lava continued throughout the rest of the year.

In September 1999 public consultations took place to discuss government proposals to establish a new capital at Little Bay, in the north-west of the island. The new town would take an estimated 10 years to construct. Progress on the project was finally achieved with the establishment of the Montserrat Development Corporation in 2007, whose mandate included the advancement of plans for the construction of the new capital, and the issuing of a contract to a local company to develop the infrastructure. Also in September 1999 the British Government announced further assistance for the construction of housing and expressed support for Government plans to establish Montserrat as a centre for international financial services. In March 2000 the dome of lava, which had been covering the Soufrière Hills volcano, collapsed, producing lava flows and mudslides in the west of the island, and covering much of the 'safe zone' with ash.

In July 2001 there was a further partial collapse of the dome of lava covering the Soufrière Hills volanco. In the following month Montserrat signed up to a British mortgage assistance programme, which would provide housing subsidies and loans to residents who had been made homeless as a result of volcanic activity. Many residents were still paying mortgages on homes in an off-limits zone of the island as well as paying rent for new accommodation.

In February 2001 Chief Minister Brandt's coalition Government collapsed, following the resignations of two members. A general election, under a new, nine-member single constituency system, was held on 2 April. Former Chief Minister John Osborne's newly formed New People's Liberation Movement (NPLM) won most seats. Osborne was sworn in as Chief Minister on 5 April.

A massive volcanic eruption, the largest since 1995, occurred on 12 July 2003, causing infrastructural damage, and the destruction of numerous buildings in Salem, which was on the edge of the 'safe zone'. Further minor eruptions occurred in April 2005 and May 2006.

In July 2007 the exclusion zone around the Soufrière Hills volcanic dome, which had been expanded to include settlements bordering Belham Valley to the north following recent volcanic activity, was reduced to its extent at the start of the year. In July 2008 the dome again partially collapsed, leading to the temporary evacuation of nearby residents.

Coalition government

No party won an overall majority in the general election of 31 May 2006. The Movement for Change and Prosperity (MCAP) secured the largest representation, with four seats, followed by the NPLM with three seats. The Montserrat Democratic Party (MDP) won one seat, as did former Chief Minister David Brandt, again standing as an independent. Lowell Lewis of the MDP assembled a coalition Government, which was sworn in on 2 June. Allegations of corruption and mismanagement levelled against candidates from both the former government and opposition overshadowed the election process and doubts were expressed about the new administration's compositional stability.

Lewis disbanded the coalition Government on 21 February 2008 and formed a new political alliance with the MCAP. Two NPLM ministers were replaced by MCAP members. At the end of March Lewis also ousted John Osborne, Minister of Education, Health and Community Services, assigning his portfolio to a member of the MCAP, and giving the new coalition Government a majority in the Legislative Council, with six seats.

In October 2008 opposition leader David Brandt filed a motion of no confidence against Chief Minister Lewis as a result of his perceived mismanagement of the island's economic affairs. Lewis avoided the motion by relinquishing the portfolios for finance and economic development to fellow minister Meade. However, in June 2009, faced with continuing dissatisfaction within the Council from MCAP members, Lewis dismissed Meade from government, as well as Roselyn Cassell-Sealy, the Minister of Education, Labour, Health and Community Services. Cassell-Sealy was succeeded by Osborne, whom she had replaced. The following day Lewis requested a dissolution of the Legislative Council so that a general election could be held, two years before it was constitutionally due.

In the general election of 8 September 2009 MCAP secured a majority in the Legislative Council, winning six of the nine seats and over 52% of the votes cast. Independent candidates were elected to the other three seats. One of these was outgoing Chief Minister Lewis, who contested the election as an independent after his party, the MDP, did not field any candidates. MCAP leader Reuben Meade was sworn in as Chief Minister on 10 September. He identified economic revival as the main priority of the new administration.

Recent developments: a new Constitution

Concerns emerged in November 2006 relating to the ongoing constitutional revision process, which had been under negotiation with the Government of the United Kingdom since 1997. A series of Legislative Council debates examining a report of the Constitutional Review Commission, first submitted in 2002, and negotiations with Ian Hendry of the British Constitutional Review Team, provoked an angry response from some members of the Chief Minister's Constitutional Advisory Committee. They alleged that Montserrat's increased reliance upon budgetary assistance from the United Kingdom—necessitated by volcanic disruption—was being exploited as a 'coercive tool' in the reform process. While the United Kingdom had encouraged Montserrat to express its preferences and recommendations towards the drafting of a new constitution, it was emphasized that ultimate authority would reside with the British Government, eliciting accusations that only a token democracy was being offered, disregarding Montserratian public consultations. Requests for a system of 'free association', permitting self-determination from the United Kingdom—drafting its own constitution without recourse to the administering nation, but retaining links with that country—and the appointment of an indigenous Deputy Governor who would assume some of the responsibilities of the British Governor in Montserrat, were similarly declined. That other former British colonial territories, including Bermuda, had been granted associated statehood instigated a consultation of the former Saint Christopher and Nevis-United Kingdom Associated Statehood Constitution as a template for Montserrat's submission to the British Constitutional Review Team. However, it was advised that any recommendations found not to concur with the United Kingdom's objective of securing the removal of Montserrat from the UN's Special Committee on Decolonization's list of prospective colonies would be rejected.

Further meetings to discuss the constitutional reform process were conducted during 2009. In May 2010 a contingent of British government officials travelled to the island, and a final draft of the charter was agreed. The new Constitution was approved by the Legislative Council on 7 October and by the Privy Council in the United Kingdom on 13 October, and was scheduled to come into effect on 1 September 2011. Under the terms of the new Constitution, *inter alia*, the Chief Minister would be redesignated as the Premier and a National Advisory Council would be created, giving the Government and the leader of the opposition the opportunity to present the Governor with recommendations on foreign affairs, defence and security, although the Governor would still retain overall responsibility for these areas.

Foreign Affairs

Following a Cuban Government-sponsored diplomatic excursion to Havana by Chief Minister Lowell in January 2007, Montserrat and Cuba pledged to strengthen bilateral relations, particularly in consideration of the burgeoning threat posed by the Soufrière Hills volcanic dome, which had been expanding consistently in the preceding months.

In July 2008 the Jamaican Prime Minister, Bruce Golding, visited Montserrat and signed a memorandum of understanding between the two countries. This pledged Jamaican support in areas such as cultural enhancement, tourism, economic development, education and health.

CONSTITUTION AND GOVERNMENT

Under the provisions of the 1960 Constitution and subsequent legislation, the Governor is appointed by the British monarch and is responsible for defence, external affairs and internal security. The Governor is President of the seven-member Executive Council. The Legislative Council comprises 12 members: nine elected members, two ex officio members and a Speaker. Following a constitutional review, in October 2010 the Legislative Council approved a new Constitution, scheduled to be promulgated on 1 September 2011.

REGIONAL AND INTERNATIONAL CO-OPERATION

Montserrat is a member of the Eastern Caribbean Central Bank (ECCB) and the Organisation of Eastern Caribbean States (OECS, see p. 462). The territory is also a member of the regional stock exchange, the Eastern Caribbean Securities Exchange (based in Saint Christopher and Nevis), established in 2001. Montserrat is a founder member of the Caribbean Community and Common Market (CARICOM, see p. 219). In October 2003 the British Government formally backed plans for Montserrat to participate fully in the Caribbean Single Market and Economy (CSME) proposed by the CARICOM. The CSME came into force at the beginning of 2006, although Montserrat was not a founding member. In December 2009 Montserrat was a signatory to the Treaty of the OECS, establishing an Economic Union among member states. The Economic Union, which involved the removal of barriers to trade and the movement of labour as a step towards a single financial and economic market, came into effect on 21 January 2011. To join the Economic Union, Montserrat required British consent, which was pending in early 2011.

The territory is a member of the Commonwealth (see p. 230). As a dependency of the United Kingdom, Montserrat has the status of Overseas Territory in association with the European Union (EU, see p. 270).

ECONOMIC AFFAIRS

In 2008 Montserrat's gross domestic product (GDP) at market prices was an estimated EC $135.16m., equivalent to approximately EC $27,725.1 per head. In 2001–08 real GDP decreased by an annual average of 1.7%; GDP increased by 1.5% in 2007 and by 6.7% in 2008.

Agriculture (including forestry and fishing) contributed an estimated 1.2% of GDP in 2008, and engaged 6.6% of the employed labour force in 1992. The sector was almost destroyed by the volcanic eruptions of 1997, which caused an 81.3% decline in agricultural production, and a return to subsistence farming. The sector's GDP fluctuated thereafter. Prior to the volcanic eruption the principal crops grown were white potatoes, onions, rice and sea-island cotton. Cattle, goats, sheep and poultry were also farmed. Montserrat's fisheries are under-exploited, owing to the absence of a sheltered harbour. The agriculture sector grew by 24.5% in 2008.

Industry (including mining, manufacturing, construction and public utilities) contributed some 16.0% to GDP in 2008, and engaged some 30.9% of the employed labour force in 1987. Mining and quarrying contributed 1.2% of GDP in 2008. Manufacturing contributed 0.7% of GDP in 2008 and engaged 5.6% of the employed labour force (together with mining) in 1992. Many industrial sites were destroyed in 1997, causing a decline in real manufacturing GDP of 45.2% in that year. The sector declined by an average of 1.4% annually in 2001–08. Light industries comprise the processing of agricultural produce (also cotton and tropical fruits), as well as spring water bottling and the manufacture of garments and plastic bags. In 2006 the Government signed a 25-year contract with a British plastics recycling company to supply volcanic ash, to be used in the blending of recycled plastics.

Construction contributed an estimated 8.0% of GDP in 2008 and employed 17.5% of the working population in 1988. The sector enjoyed growth in the mid-1990s, owing to reconstruction programmes following the volcanic eruptions. The sector declined at an average annual rate of 5.1% between 2001 and 2008. Energy requirements are dependent upon the import of mineral fuels (26.8% of total imports in 2009).

It is hoped to re-establish Montserrat as a centre for financial services, which previously provided an important source of govern-

UNITED KINGDOM OVERSEAS TERRITORIES

Montserrat

ment revenue. The tourism sector, which in 2009 contributed EC $16.8m. in receipts, remains important to the island, and it is hoped to establish Montserrat as a centre for environmental tourism, with the volcano itself as the premier attraction. The GDP of the hotel and restaurant sector increased by an annual average of 4.9% between 2001–08. The sector grew by 9.2% in 2008. The real GDP of the services sector increased by an annual average of 4.0% during 2001–08, rising by 5.8% in 2008. Services contributed 82.8% of GDP in 2008.

In 2010 Montserrat recorded an estimated trade deficit of EC $62.5m. Earnings from the services sector, mainly tourism receipts and net transfers (in particular, the remittances from Montserratians abroad and the income of foreign retired people), generally offset persistent trade deficits. There was an estimated deficit on the current account of the balance of payments of EC $33.9m. in 2010. The principal trading partner is the USA (providing 68.5% of imports and receiving 12.2% of exports in 2009). Other trading partners of importance include Anguilla, Trinidad and Tobago, Saint Christopher and Nevis, the United Kingdom and Antigua and Barbuda. The export of rice and of electrical components, previously the most important of the island's few exports, ceased in 1998 following further volcanic activity. However, export receipts increased to some US $3.1m. by 2009. In addition to mineral fuels, the other principal imports were vehicles and nuclear reactors, boilers and machinery.

In 2009 there was a budgetary surplus of EC $5.9m (including grants of $100.2m.). The capital budget is funded almost entirely by overseas aid, notably from the United Kingdom and Canada. Financial assistance from the United Kingdom for 2010–11 was put at £18m., with a further £2m. available for capital projects. Montserrat's total external public debt was estimated at EC $8.8m. in 2009, according to figures from the Eastern Caribbean Central Bank (ECCB). Consumer prices increased by 2.5% in 2009. The Caribbean Development Bank (see p. 224) estimated the unemployment rate to stand at some 13% of the labour force in 2001.

Montserrat's economic prospects depended entirely on the activity of the Soufrière Hills volcano. Its eruption in 1997, and subsequent volcanic activity, destroyed much of the country's infrastructure, and devastated the island's agricultural heartland. The implications for the island's principal industry, tourism, were extremely severe. It was anticipated that the ongoing reconstruction efforts and the development of the island as a centre for environmental tourism would stimulate short-term economic growth, while in the long term it was hoped to re-establish Montserrat as a centre for international financial services. However, Montserrat's inclusion, in April 2009, on an Organisation for Economic Co-operation and Development's (OECD, see p. 376) so-called 'grey list' of territories that had yet substantially to implement moves towards transparency in the financial sector was a set-back for this aim. By April 2011 Montserrat had signed 11 tax information sharing agreements with other jurisdictions, one short of the 12 accords needed to secure removal from the OECD list. While most of the Caribbean region was struggling with recession in 2009, in Montserrat real GDP increased by 3.8%, according to the ECCB. However, the ECCB estimated that the economy contracted in 2010 owing to the weak performance of the construction sector, which in turn negatively affected the quarrying industry. With the island suffering from drought during that year, agricultural activity was also subdued, although the tourism industry showed signs of recovery.

PUBLIC HOLIDAYS

2012: 1 January (New Year's Day), 17 March (St Patrick's Day), 6 April (Good Friday), 9 April (Easter Monday), 7 May (Labour Day), 28 May (Whit Monday), 9 June (Queen's Official Birthday), 6 August (August Monday), 23 November (Liberation Day), 25–26 December (Christmas), 31 December (Festival Day).

Statistical Survey

Sources (unless otherwise stated): Government Information Service, Media Centre, Chief Minister's Office, Old Towne; tel. 491-2702; fax 491-2711; Eastern Caribbean Central Bank, POB 89, Basseterre, Saint Christopher; internet www.eccb-centralbank.org; OECS Economic Affairs Secretariat, *Statistical Digest*.

AREA AND POPULATION

Area: 102 sq km (39.5 sq miles).

Population: 10,639 (males 5,290, females 5,349) at census of 12 May 1991; 4,491 at census of 12 May 2001 (Source: UN, *Population and Vital Statistics Report*). *2009* (projected estimate at mid-year): 4,932.

Population by Age and Sex (at 2001 census): *0–14:* 869 (males 454, females 415); *15–64:* 2,910 (males 1,599, females 1,311); *65 and over:* 689 (males 344, females 345); *Total* 4,468 (males 5,628, females 5,802). Note: Total includes persons of unknown age.

Density (mid-2009): 48.4 per sq km.

Principal Towns: Plymouth, the former capital, was abandoned in 1997. Brades is the interim capital.

Births and Deaths (1999): 45 live births (birth rate 9.4 per 1,000); 59 deaths (death rate 12.4 per 1,000) (Source: UN, *Population and Vital Statistics Report*). *2003:* Crude birth rate 9.6 per 1,000; Crude death rate 12.3 per 1,000 (Source: Caribbean Development Bank, *Social and Economic Indicators*). *2010:* Crude birth rate 12.1 per 1,000; Crude death rate 7.6 per 1,000 (Source: Pan American Health Organization).

Life Expectancy (years at birth, estimates): 72.9 (males 74.8; females 70.9) in 2010. Source: Pan American Health Organization.

Employment (1992): Agriculture, forestry and fishing 298; Mining and manufacturing 254; Electricity, gas and water 68; Wholesale and retail trade 1,666; Restaurants and hotels 234; Transport and communication 417; Finance, insurance and business services 242; Public defence 390; Other community, social and personal services 952; *Total* 4,521 (Source: *The Commonwealth Yearbook*). *1998* (estimate): Total labour force 1,500.

HEALTH AND WELFARE

Physicians (per 1,000 head, 1999): 0.18.

Hospital Beds (per 1,000 head, 2009): 6.0.

Health Expenditure (public, % of GDP, 2000): 7.7.

Health Expenditure (public, % of total, 1995): 67.0.

Source: Pan American Health Organization.

For sources and definitions, see explanatory note on p. vi.

AGRICULTURE, ETC.

Principal Crops (metric tons, 2009, FAO estimates): Vegetables 495; Fruit (excl. melons) 735.

Livestock ('000 head, 2008, FAO estimates): Cattle 9.9; Sheep 4.8; Goats 7.1; Pigs 1.2. Note: No data were available for 2009.

Livestock Products ('000 metric tons, 2009, FAO estimates): Cattle meat 0.7; Cows' milk 2.3.

Fishing (metric tons, live weight, 2008, FAO estimate): Total catch 50 (all marine fishes).

Source: FAO.

INDUSTRY

Electric Energy (million kWh): 11.6 in 2007; 11.7 in 2008; 11.8 in 2009.

FINANCE

Currency and Exchange Rates: 100 cents = 1 East Caribbean dollar (EC $). *Sterling, US Dollar and Euro Equivalents* (31 December 2010): £1 sterling = EC $4.227; US $1 = EC $2.700; €1 = EC $3.608; EC $100 = £23.66 = US $37.04 = €27.72. *Exchange Rate:* Fixed at US $1 = EC $2.70 since July 1976.

Budget (EC $ million, 2009): *Revenue:* Revenue from taxation 35.8 (Taxes on income and profits 16.8, Taxes on property 1.1, Taxes on domestic goods and services 3.7, Taxes on international trade and transactions 14.2); Non-tax revenue 4.3; Total 40.1 (excl. grants 100.2). *Expenditure:* Current expenditure 97.3 (Personal emoluments 41.4, Goods and services 23.9, Interest payments 0.1, Transfers and subsidies 31.9); Capital expenditure 37.1; Total 134.4.

International Reserves (US $ million at 31 December 2010): Foreign exchange 16.82. Source: IMF, *International Financial Statistics*.

Money Supply (EC $ million at 31 December 2010): Currency outside depository corporations 15.97; Transferable deposits 33.35; Other deposits 140.39; *Broad money* 189.71. Source: IMF, *International Financial Statistics*.

Cost of Living (Consumer Price Index at December; base: December 1982 = 100): All items 226.4 in 2007; 236.6 in 2008; 242.4 in 2009.

Gross Domestic Product (EC $ million at constant 1990 prices): 67.18 in 2006; 68.16 in 2007; 72.71 in 2008.

Expenditure on the Gross Domestic Product (EC $ million at current prices, 2008): Government final consumption expenditure 75.82; Private final consumption expenditure 126.49; Gross fixed capital formation 36.78; *Total domestic expenditure* 239.09; Export of

UNITED KINGDOM OVERSEAS TERRITORIES

goods and services 48.42; *Less* Imports of goods and services 152.35; *GDP at market prices* 135.16.

Gross Domestic Product by Economic Activity (EC $ million at current prices, 2008): Agriculture, forestry and fishing 1.60; Mining and quarrying 1.62; Manufacturing 0.87; Electricity and water 7.80; Construction 10.43; Wholesale and retail trade 5.76; Restaurants and hotels 1.40; Transport 9.26; Communications 3.90; Banks and insurance 13.97; Real estate and housing 15.86; Government services 48.14; Other services 9.11; *Sub-total* 129.72; *Less* Financial intermediation services indirectly measured 12.47; *Gross value added at basic prices* 117.28; Taxes, less subsidies, on products 17.87; *GDP at market prices* 135.16.

Balance of Payments (EC $ million, 2010): Goods (net) −62.51; Services (net) −16.31; *Balance on goods and services* −78.82; Income (net) −9.57; *Balance on goods, services and income* −88.39; Current transfers (net) 54.49; *Current balance* −33.90; Capital account (net) 39.33; Direct investment (net) 5.83; Public sector long-term investment −0.62; Commercial banks −2.31; Other investment assets 10.17; Other investment liabilities −20.82; Net errors and omissions 5.80; *Overall balance* 3.49.

EXTERNAL TRADE

Principal Commodities (US $ '000, 2009): *Imports c.i.f.*: Meat and edible meat offal 914; Beverages, spirits and vinegar 1,285; Mineral fuels, oils, distillation products, etc. 7,943 (Petroleum oils, not crude 7,444); Nuclear reactors, boilers, machinery, etc. 2,067; Electrical, electronic equipment 1,295; Vehicles other than railway, tramway 2,432 (Cars, incl. station wagon 1,445); Total (incl. others) 29,605. *Exports f.o.b.*: Salt, sulphur, earth, stone, plaster, lime and cement 1,404; Nuclear reactors, boilers, machinery, etc. 957; Electrical, electronic equipment 189; Optical, photo, technical, and medical apparatus 299; Total (incl. others) 3,148.

Principal Trading Partners (US $ '000, 2009): *Imports c.i.f.*: Barbados 128; Canada 415; China, People's Repub. 237; Dominican Republic 237; Jamaica 654; Japan 1,520; Netherlands 309; St Vincent and the Grenadines 295; Trinidad and Tobago 1,803; United Kingdom 1,666; USA 20,272; Total (incl. others) 29,605. *Exports f.o.b.*: Anguilla 480; Antigua and Barbuda 77; British Virgin Islands 208; Dominica 381; France (incl. Monaco) 133; Netherlands Antilles 211; New Zealand 247; St Christopher and Nevis 366; Trinidad and Tobago 481; United Kingdom 153; USA 384; Total (incl. others) 3,148.

Source: UN, *International Trade Statistics Yearbook*.

TOURISM

Tourist Arrivals (2009): Stay-over arrivals 6,311 (USA 1,606, Canada 367, United Kingdom 1,864, Caribbean 2,267, Others 207); Excursionists 1,024; Total visitor arrivals (incl. others) 8,864.

Tourism Receipts (EC $ million): 20.1 in 2007; 19.0 in 2008; 16.8 in 2009.

TRANSPORT

Road Traffic (vehicles in use, 1990): Passenger cars 1,823; Goods vehicles 54; Public service vehicles 4; Motorcycles 21; Miscellaneous 806.

Shipping: ('000 metric tons, 1990): *International Freight Traffic*: Goods loaded 6; Goods unloaded 49. Source: UN, *Monthly Bulletin of Statistics*.

Civil Aviation (1985): Aircraft arrivals 4,422; passengers 25,380; air cargo 132.4 metric tons.

COMMUNICATIONS MEDIA

Radio Receivers (1997): 7,000 in use.
Television Receivers (1999): 3,000 in use.
Telephones (2009): 2,700 main lines in use.
Mobile Cellular Telephones (2000): 3,000 subscribers.
Broadband Subscribers: 600 in 2009 (estimate).
Non-daily Newspapers (1996): 2 (estimated circulation 3,000).

Sources: UNESCO, *Statistical Yearbook*; International Telecommunication Union.

EDUCATION

Pre-primary: 11 schools (1999); 11 teachers (2006/07); 116 pupils (2006/07).

Primary: 2 schools (1999); 31 teachers (2006/07); 497 pupils (2006/07).

Secondary: 1 school (1999); 29 teachers (2006/07); 347 pupils (2006/07).

Sources: UNESCO, *Statistical Yearbook*; UNESCO Institute for Statistics.

Directory

The Government

HEAD OF STATE

Queen: HM Queen ELIZABETH II.
Governor: ADRIAN DEREK DAVIS (took office 8 April 2011).
Deputy Governor: SARITA FRANCIS.

EXECUTIVE COUNCIL
(May 2011)

The Government is formed by the Movement for Change and Prosperity.

President: ADRIAN DEREK DAVIS (The Governor).
Official Members:
Attorney-General: JAMES WOOD.
Financial Secretary: JOHN SKERRITT.
Chief Minister and Minister of Finance with responsibility for Local Government, Immigration, Information Communication, Regional and International Affairs, Economic Development, Tourism and Trade: REUBEN T. MEADE.
Minister of Agriculture, Lands, Housing, the Environment, Consumer Affairs and Ecclesiastical Affairs: EASTON TAYLOR-FARRELL.
Minister of Communication, Works and Labour: CHARLES KIRNON.
Minister of Education, Health, Community Services, Youth Affairs, Sports and Culture: COLLIN RILEY.
Clerk to the Executive Council: JUDITH JEFFERS.

MINISTRIES

Office of the Governor: Unit 8, Farara Plaza, Brades; tel. 491-2688; fax 491-8867; e-mail govoffice.montserrat@fco.gov.uk; internet ukinmontserrat.fco.gov.uk.

Office of the Deputy Governor: No. 3, Farara Plaza, Brades; tel. 491-6524; fax 491-9202; e-mail odg@gov.ms; internet odg.gov.ms.

Office of the Attorney-General: POB 129, Valley View; tel. 491-4686; fax 491-4687; e-mail legal@gov.ms; internet agc.gov.ms.

Office of the Chief Minister: Govt HQ, POB 292, Brades; tel. 491-3378; fax 491-6780; e-mail ocm@gov.ms; internet ocm.gov.ms.

Ministry of Agriculture, Lands, Housing and the Environment: Govt HQ, POB 272, Brades; tel. 491-2546; fax 491-9275; e-mail malhe@gov.ms; internet www.malhe.gov.ms.

Ministry of Communications and Works: Woodlands; tel. 491-2521; fax 491-3475; e-mail comworks@gov.ms.

Ministry of Education: Govt HQ, POB 103, Brades; tel. 491-2541; fax 491-6941; e-mail deped@gov.ms.

Ministry of Finance: Govt HQ, POB 292, Brades; tel. 491-2777; fax 491-2367; e-mail minfin@gov.ms; internet www.finance.gov.ms.

Ministry of Health and Community Services: Govt HQ, POB 24, Brades; tel. 491-2880; fax 491-3131; e-mail mehcs@gov.ms; internet moh.gov.ms.

LEGISLATIVE COUNCIL

Speaker: TERESINA BODKIN.
Election, 8 September 2009

Party	Seats
Movement for Change and Prosperity	6
Independent	3
Total	**9**

There are also two ex officio members (the Attorney-General and the Financial Secretary).

Political Organizations

Montserrat Democratic Party (MDP): c/o Kelsick & Kelsick, Woodlands Main Rd, POB 185, Brades; tel. 491-2102; e-mail lowell@mdp.ms; internet www.mdp.ms; f. 2006; Leader Dr LOWELL LEWIS.

Montserrat Labour Party (MLP): Brades; f. 2009 by fmr mems of the NPLM (q.v.); Leaders MARGARET DYER-HOWE, IDABELLE MEADE.

Montserrat Reformation Party (MRP): Brades; f. 2009; Leaders ADELINA TUITT, ALRIC TAYLOR.

Movement for Change and Prosperity (MCAP): POB 419, Brades; e-mail mail@mcap.ms; internet www.mcap.ms; f. 2005 by fmr mems of the National Progressive Party (NPP); Leader REUBEN T. MEADE; Chair. RANDOLPH RILEY.

New People's Liberation Movement (NPLM): f. 1997 as successor party to People's Progressive Alliance and the Movement for National Reconstruction (MNR); opposition party; Leader DAVID OSBORNE.

Judicial System

Justice is administered by the Eastern Caribbean Supreme Court (based in Saint Lucia—comprised of the Court of Appeal and the High Court), the Court of Summary Jurisdiction and the Magistrate's Court. A revised edition of the Laws of Montserrat came into force in April 2005, following five years of preparation by a Law Revision Committee.

Registrar: AMILA DALEY.

Magistrate: CLIFTON WARNER, Govt HQ, Brades; tel. 491-4056; fax 491-8866; e-mail magoff@gov.ms.

Religion

CHRISTIANITY

The Montserrat Christian Council: St Peter's, POB 227; tel. 491-4864; fax 491-2139; Chair. Rev. B. RUTH ALLEN.

The Anglican Communion

Anglicans are adherents of the Church in the Province of the West Indies, comprising eight dioceses. Montserrat forms part of the diocese of the North Eastern Caribbean and Aruba. The Bishop is resident in The Valley, Anguilla.

The Roman Catholic Church

Montserrat forms part of the diocese of St John's-Basseterre, suffragan to the archdiocese of Castries (Saint Lucia). The Bishop is resident in St John's, Antigua and Barbuda.

Other Christian Churches

There are Baptist, Methodist, Pentecostal and Seventh-day Adventist churches and other places of worship on the island.

The Press

Montserrat Newsletter: Farara Plaza, Unit 8, Brades; tel. 491-2688; fax 491-8867; e-mail richard.aspin@fco.gov.uk; f. 1998; 6 a year; govt information publ; Publicity Officer RICHARD ASPIN.

The Montserrat Reporter: POB 306, Davy Hill; tel. 491-4715; fax 491-2430; e-mail editor@themontserratreporter.com; internet www.themontserratreporter.com; f. 1984; acquired by Montserrat Printing and Publishing Inc in 1994; weekly on Fri.; Editor BENNETTE ROACH; circ. 2,000.

Broadcasting and Communications

TELECOMMUNICATIONS

Cable & Wireless (West Indies) Ltd: POB 219, Sweeney's; tel. 491-1000; fax 491-3599; e-mail venus.george@cwni.cwplc.com; internet www.cwmontserrat.com.

BROADCASTING

Radio

Radio Antilles: POB 35/930, Plymouth; tel. 491-2755; fax 491-2724; f. 1963; in 1989 the Govt of Montserrat, on behalf of the Org. of Eastern Caribbean States, acquired the station; has one of the most powerful transmitters in the region; commercial; regional; broadcasts in English and French; Chair. Dr H. FELLHAUER; Man. Dir KRISTIAN KNAACK; Gen. Man. KEITH GREAVES.

Radio Montserrat (ZJB): POB 51, Sweeney's; tel. 491-2885; fax 491-9250; e-mail zjb@gov.ms; internet www.zjb.gov.ms; f. 1952; first broadcast 1957; govt station; CEO LOWELL MASON.

Television

Television services can also be obtained from Saint Christopher and Nevis, Puerto Rico and from Antigua and Barbuda.

Cable Television of Montserrat Ltd: POB 447, Olveston; tel. 491-2507; fax 491-3081; Man. SYLVIA WHITE.

People's Television (PTV): POB 82, Brades; tel. 491-5110; Man. DENZIL EDGECOMBE.

Finance

The Eastern Caribbean Central Bank, based in Saint Christopher and Nevis, is the central issuing and monetary authority for Montserrat.

Eastern Caribbean Central Bank—Montserrat Office: 2 Farara Plaza, POB 484, Brades; tel. 491-6877; fax 491-6878; e-mail eccbmni@candw.ms; internet www.eccb-centralbank.org; Resident Rep. CHARLES T. JOHN.

Financial Services Commission: Phoenix House, POB 188, Brades; tel. 491-6887; fax 491-9888; e-mail fscmrat@candw.ms; internet www.fscmontserrat.org; f. 2001; the Commission consists of the Commissioner and 4 other mems appointed by the Governor; Head DULCIE JAMES.

BANKING

Bank of Montserrat Ltd: Hilltop, POB 10, St Peters; tel. 491-3843; fax 491-3163; e-mail bom@candw.ag; Man. ANTON DOLDRON.

Montserrat Building Society: POB 101, Brades Main Rd, Brades; tel. 491-2391; fax 491-6127; e-mail mbsl@candw.ms.

St Patrick's Co-operative Credit Union Ltd: POB 337, Brades; tel. 491-3666; fax 491-6566; e-mail monndf@candw.ms; Exec. Dir ROSELYN CASSELL-SEALY.

STOCK EXCHANGE

Eastern Caribbean Securities Exchange: based in Bird Rock, Basseterre, Saint Christopher and Nevis; tel. (869) 466-7192; fax (869) 465-3798; e-mail info@ecseonline.com; internet www.ecseonline.com; f. 2001; regional securities market designed to facilitate the buying and selling of financial products for the 8 mem. territories—Anguilla, Antigua and Barbuda, Dominica, Grenada, Montserrat, Saint Christopher and Nevis, Saint Lucia and Saint Vincent and the Grenadines; Chair. Sir K. DWIGHT VENNER; Gen. Man. TREVOR E. BLAKE.

INSURANCE

Insurance Services (Montserrat) Ltd: POB 185, Brades; tel. 491-2103; fax 491-6013; e-mail ismcall@candw.ag; Gen. Man. STEPHEN FRANCOIS.

NAGICO: Ryan Investments, Brades; tel. 491-3403; fax 491-7307; e-mail talicj@yahoo.com.

N. E. M. (West Indies) Insurance Ltd (NEMWIL): POB 287, Brades; tel. 491-3813; fax 491-3815.

United Insurance Co Ltd: Jacquie Ryan Enterprises Ltd, POB 425, Brades; tel. 491-2055; fax 491-3257; e-mail united@candw.ms; CEO JACQUIE RYAN.

Trade and Industry

GOVERNMENT AGENCIES

Montserrat Development Corporation (MDC): Brades; internet www.mdc.ms; f. 2007; overseeing plans for new capital in Little Bay; promotes private sector investment and economic growth; Chair. KENNETH SCOTLAND; CEO COLIN HEARTWELL.

Montserrat Economic Development Unit: Govt HQ, POB 292, Brades; tel. 491-2066; fax 491-4632; e-mail devunit@gov.ms; internet www.devunit.gov.ms.

CHAMBER OF COMMERCE

Montserrat Chamber of Commerce and Industry (MCCI): Ryan's Court, POB 384, Brades; tel. 491-3640; fax 491-3599; e-mail chamber@candw.ms; refounded 1971; 31 company mems, 26 individual mems; Pres. FLORENCE GRIFFITH JOSEPH; Vice-Pres. GRACELYN CASSELL.

UTILITIES

Electricity and Water

Montserrat Utilities Ltd (MUL): POB 324, Davy Hill; tel. 491-2538; fax 491-4904; e-mail mul@mul.ms; internet www.mul.ms; f. 2008 by merger of Montserrat Electricity Services Ltd and Montserrat Water Authority; domestic electricity generation and

UNITED KINGDOM OVERSEAS TERRITORIES

supply; domestic water supply; Man. Dir Peter White; Man. of Water and Sewerage Emile Duberry.

Gas

Grant Enterprises and Trading: POB 350, Brades; tel. 491-9654; fax 491-4854; e-mail granten@candw.ms; domestic gas supplies.

TRADE UNIONS

Montserrat Allied Workers' Union (MAWU): POB 245, Dagenham, Plymouth; tel. 491-5049; fax 491-6145; e-mail bramblehl@candw.ag; f. 1973; private sector employees; Pres. Charles Ryan; Gen. Sec. Hylroy Bramble; 1,000 mems.

Montserrat Civil Service Association: POB 468, Plymouth; tel. 491-6797; fax 491-5655; e-mail lewisp@gov.ms; Pres. Paul Lewis.

Montserrat Union of Teachers: POB 460, Plymouth; tel. 491-4382; fax 491-5779; f. 1978; Pres. Herman Francis; Gen. Sec. Hyacinth Bramble-Browne; 46 mems.

Transport

ROADS

Prior to the 1997 volcanic eruption, Montserrat had an extensive and well-constructed road network. There were 203 km (126 miles) of good surfaced main roads, 24 km of secondary unsurfaced roads and 42 km of rough tracks. Government expenditure on road rehabilitation works in 2006 amounted to more than US $3m., while a further US $0.5m. was allocated to the maintenance budget of the Public Works Department for surfacing of the secondary road network. The 2007 budget allocated funds of over US $5m. for continued road and infrastructure improvements, particularly in areas to become more densely populated through resettlement. In 2008 a $5.9m. road reinstatement project from Salem to St John funded by the British Department for International Development was begun and was expected to be completed by 2012.

SHIPPING

Following the destruction of the principal port at Plymouth in 1997, an emergency jetty was constructed at Little Bay in the north of the island. In 2010 the European Union-funded Little Bay Port Development Project was begun. The project was to be executed in two phases, at an estimated cost of US $40m. A daily ferry service with Antigua, which had been suspended in 2005, was reinstated in 2008.

Port Authority of Montserrat: Little Bay, POB 383, Plymouth; tel. 491-2791; fax 491-8063; e-mail monpa@candw.ms; Man. Shawn O'Garro.

Montserrat Shipping Services: POB 46, Brades; tel. 491-3614; fax 491-3617; e-mail customerservice@monship.org.

CIVIL AVIATION

The main airport, Blackburne at Trants, 13 km (8 miles) from Plymouth, was destroyed by the volcanic activity of 1997. A helicopter port at Gerald's in the north of the island was completed in 2000. A new, temporary international airport at Gerald's, financed at a cost of EC $51.95m. by the European Union and the British Department for International Development, was completed in 2005. In the longer term, the Government intended to construct a permanent international airport at Thatch Valley. Montserrat is linked to Antigua by a helicopter service, which operates three times a day. The island is also a shareholder in the regional airline, LIAT (based in Antigua and Barbuda). In 2008 LIAT and Carib Aviation (also based in Antigua and Barbuda) entered into an agreement to operate scheduled flights into and out of the airport at Gerald's, renamed the John A. Osborne Airport, in the same month.

Montserrat Airways Ltd: John A. Osborne Airport, POB 225, Gerald's; tel. 491-3434; e-mail info@flymontserrat.com; internet www.flymontserrat.com; charter services; subsidiary of Love Air, United Kingdom; Chair. Capt. Nigel Harris.

FlyMontserrat: John A. Osborne Airport, POB 225, Gerald's; tel. 491-3434; e-mail info@flymontserrat.com; internet www.flymontserrat.com; f. 2009; flights between Montserrat and Antigua; subsidiary of Montserrat Airways; Chair. Capt. Nigel Harris.

Tourism

Since the 1997 volcanic activity, Montserrat has been marketed as an eco-tourism destination. Known as the 'Emerald Isle of the Caribbean', Montserrat is noted for its Irish connections, and for its range of flora and fauna. In 2009 there were a preliminary 6,311 stay-over tourist arrivals. In that year some 37% of total tourist arrivals were from Caribbean countries, 28% from the United Kingdom and 25% from the USA. In addition there were 1,024 excursionists. A large proportion of visitors are estimated to be Montserrat nationals residing overseas. Tourism earnings totalled EC $16.8m. in 2009.

Montserrat Tourist Board: 7 Farara Plaza, POB 7, Brades; tel. 491-2230; fax 491-7430; e-mail info@montserrattourism.ms; internet www.visitmontserrat.com; f. 1993; Chair. John Ponteen; Dir of Tourism Ernestine Cassell.

Defence

The United Kingdom is responsible for the defence of Montserrat.

Education

Education, beginning at five years of age, is compulsory up to the age of 14. In 1993 there were 11 primary schools, including 10 government schools, but this was reduced to just two in 1999. Secondary education begins at 12 years of age, and comprises a first cycle of five years and a second, two-year cycle. In 1999 there was one government secondary school. In 2007 enrolment in primary education included an estimated 92% of children in the relevant age-group, while the comparable ratio for secondary education was an estimated 96%. In 1999 there were 11 nursery schools, sponsored by a government-financed organization, and a Technical College, which provided vocational and technical training for school-leavers. There was also an extra-mural department of the University of the West Indies in Plymouth. Construction of the Montserrat Community College was completed in 2003. Three 'offshore' medical schools were licensed in 2003. The Ministry of Education was allocated a total of EC $8.3m. in the 2008 budget.

THE PITCAIRN ISLANDS

Introductory Survey

LOCATION, CLIMATE, LANGUAGE, RELIGION, CAPITAL

The Pitcairn Islands consist of Pitcairn Island and three uninhabited islands, Henderson, Ducie and Oeno. Pitcairn, situated in the Pacific Ocean about midway between Panama and New Zealand, has an area of less than 4.5 sq km (1.75 sq miles) and had a population of 53 permanent residents at the end of 2008. Mean monthly temperatures range from 19°C (66°F) in August to 24°C (75°F) in February, and average annual rainfall is 2,000 mm. The official language is English, but most of the islanders use Pitcairnese or Pitkern, a dialect based on 18th-century seafarers' English and Tahitian. The islanders are adherents of the Seventh-day Adventist Church. The chief settlement is Adamstown on Pitcairn Island.

CONTEMPORARY POLITICAL HISTORY

Discovered in 1767 and first settled by mutineers of *HMS Bounty* in 1790, Pitcairn officially became a British settlement in 1887. In 1893 a parliamentary form of government was adopted, and in 1898 responsibility for administration was assumed by the High Commissioner for the Western Pacific. Pitcairn came under the jurisdiction of the Governor of Fiji in 1952. In 1970 Pitcairn was placed within the remit of the British High Commissioner in New Zealand acting as Governor, in consultation with an Island Council, presided over by the Island Magistrate (elected triennially) and comprising one ex-officio member (the Island Secretary), five elected and three nominated members. The British Overseas Territories Act, which took effect in May 2002, granted citizenship rights in the United Kingdom to residents of the Overseas Territories, including Pitcairn. The legislation also entitled Pitcairn Islanders to hold British passports and to work in the United Kingdom and elsewhere in the European Union.

In 1987 the British High Commissioner in Fiji, acting on behalf of Pitcairn, the United Kingdom's last remaining dependency in the South Pacific, joined representatives of the USA, France, New Zealand and six South Pacific island states in signing the South Pacific Regional Environment Protection Convention, the main objective of which was to prevent the dumping of nuclear waste in the region.

In early 2000 British detectives began an investigation into an alleged rape case on the island. The British team was joined by the New Zealand police force in early 2001, when the case was widened to include 15 alleged sexual assaults, amid reports claiming that sexual abuse, particularly of children, was commonplace on the island. In November 2000 Crown Solicitor Simon Moore, based in Auckland, New Zealand, was appointed Pitcairn's first Public Prosecutor, with the task of deciding whether to bring charges against 20 Pitcairn Islanders. His decision was delayed by the fact that many of the complainants now lived in New Zealand and by the logistical problems of a trial that could potentially involve the entire populace. However, in April 2003 a judicial delegation of eight people visited Pitcairn, and nine men on the island were charged with a total of 64 offences. Many islanders expressed serious concern that their community would not be able to function if the men (who constituted virtually the entire male work-force) were extradited to New Zealand to stand trial. In early June a further four men, who had all become resident in New Zealand, were charged with a total of 32 offences, including 10 charges of rape, which were alleged to have taken place on Pitcairn between five and 40 years previously. In April 2004 the Supreme Court of Pitcairn (sitting for only the second time in its history, at a special session in Auckland) rejected the accused men's application to be tried on Pitcairn, reiterating that they should stand trial in New Zealand. However, in late June Pitcairn's Court of Appeal (sitting for the first time in its history) overruled this decision and stated that, despite the logistical problems involved, the trial would be conducted on Pitcairn. Meanwhile, lawyers for the accused men argued that the trial should be abandoned as the islanders were all descendants of the *Bounty* mutineers, who had renounced all allegiance to the British Crown. Their claims that Pitcairn Islanders were not subject to British jurisdiction appeared to be supported by historical documents discovered in London. Moreover, a group of women from Pitcairn issued a public statement claiming that sexual relations between men and girls below the British legal age of consent were commonplace on the island, and not considered to be a criminal offence by either party or by the community as a whole. However, in late September 2004 the trial of seven of the defendants began in converted school premises on Pitcairn. Some 25 lawyers, police officers and journalists travelled to the island, and witnesses in New Zealand gave evidence via live satellite video link. The trial concluded in late October. Six of the seven defendants were found guilty of many of the 51 charges against them. One islander was acquitted of the charges against him. Among those convicted was the Mayor of Pitcairn, Steve Christian, who was found guilty of five counts of rape.

The convicted men, four of whom were given prison sentences of between two and six years while two received non-custodial sentences, began a legal challenge against their convictions in February 2005. Their defence was based on a previous claim that Pitcairn Islanders were not subject to British jurisdiction. In May their appeal was rejected by the Pitcairn Supreme Court, sitting in Auckland, New Zealand. In 2006 the men took their appeal to the United Kingdom's highest court, the Privy Council, arguing that they were not British subjects and that English law did not apply on Pitcairn. In October the judges rejected their appeal, declaring that Pitcairn had been ruled by the Crown as a British possession for more than 100 years, and was thus unable to reject a law affirming it as such. Furthermore, the judges decided that there was absolutely no doubt that the laws on sexual offences applied to the six men. The convicted men helped to build a new prison. Seven New Zealand prison officers were dispatched to staff the new facility.

In October 2008 the Foreign and Commonwealth Office announced that the victims of sexual abuse would be eligible to apply for compensation. The compensation paid would be comparable to amounts awarded in similar cases in the United Kingdom. The closing date for the submission of applications for compensation was 31 March 2009.

Meanwhile, following some structural changes in the local government of Pitcairn, in December 1999 the position of Mayor, who was to preside over the Island Council, was created. The role had been fulfilled hitherto by the Island Magistrate, a post held by Jay Warren since 1991. The islands' first Mayor, Steve Christian, was dismissed in October 2004, following his conviction on charges of rape (see above). At elections to the Island Council in December five new Council members were elected. Jay Warren, the only defendant to be acquitted in the recent trials, was elected as the island's Mayor for a three-year term. In April 2006 George Fergusson, the newly appointed British High Commissioner to New Zealand, replaced Richard Fell as Governor of Pitcairn, Henderson, Ducie and Oeno Islands. Michael Warren was elected Mayor in December 2007, defeating the incumbent Jay Warren and one other candidate. Michael Warren was re-elected in December 2010. In the same month, however, it was reported that he had been charged with possession of child pornography.

In April 2009, after the majority of islanders voted in favour of the proposal, the Governor signed a law to remove the ban on the consumption of alcohol, subject to various caveats. The prohibition had remained in force since the 1830s.

Consultations on amendments to the Constitution, which were explicitly to state Pitcairn Islanders' rights and responsibilities, commenced in 2009. Emphasis was to be placed on partnership values as the basis of Pitcairn's relationship with the United Kingdom. Advice on human rights and other constitutional matters was provided by the Commonwealth Foundation, and islanders' comments on the proposed revisions were to be submitted to the Governor by the end of October. Video-conference facilities were used during the consultation process, enabling the islanders to discuss the proceedings with officials in the United Kingdom and New Zealand. The constitutional amendments were enacted in February 2010. New provisions included: the formal incorporation of the Island Council into the Constitution; a requirement that the Island Council be consulted with regard to all draft legislation; the creation of the role of Ombudsman, who was to be responsible for investigating any complaints of government maladministration; the establishment of a Supreme Court; and the appointment of an independent attorney-general. In March, at a ceremony in Adamstown attended by the Governor, the new Constitution was duly proclaimed. Victoria Treadell, the incoming British High Commissioner to New Zealand, replaced George Fergusson as Governor of Pitcairn in May.

ECONOMIC AFFAIRS

The economy has traditionally been based on subsistence gardening, fishing, handicrafts and the sale of postage stamps. Attempts to increase revenue from the island's agricultural output by producing dried fruits (notably bananas, mangoes and pineapples) began in 1999. Diversification of this sector to include production of jam, dried fish and coffee was subsequently under consideration. In early 1999 the Pitcairn Island police and customs office requested that no honey or beeswax be sent to the Territory in order to protect from disease the island's growing honey industry, which was being developed as a source of foreign exchange. Pitcairn honey, which was pronounced to be 'exceptionally pure' by the New Zealand Ministry of Agriculture, began to be exported, largely through internet sales, in late 1999. A new stamp was issued to commemorate the launch of the industry. The British Government subsequently provided funding for a bee-keeping expert to spend six months on Pitcairn and assist the islanders with the expansion of their honey industry. By 2010 the number of beehives had been increased to 150, and it was reported that the product was being supplied to exclusive food retailers in the United Kingdom.

A reafforestation scheme, begun in 1963, concentrated on the planting of miro trees, which provide a rosewood suitable for handicrafts. An exclusive economic zone (EEZ) extending 370 km (200 nautical miles) off shore was designated in 1980 and officially declared in 1992. In 1987 the Governor of the islands signed a one-year fishing agreement with Japan, whereby the Japan Tuna Fisheries Co-operative Association was granted a licence to operate vessels within Pitcairn's EEZ. The agreement was subsequently renewed, but lapsed in 1990.

In 1992 it was reported that significant mineral deposits, formed by underwater volcanoes, had been discovered within the islands' EEZ. The minerals, which were believed to include manganese, iron, copper, zinc, silver and gold, could (if exploited) dramatically affect the Territory's economy.

Development projects have been focused on harbour improvements, power supplies, telecommunications and road-building. A new health clinic was established, with British finance, in 1996. Major improvements to the jetty and slipway at Bounty Bay and to the Hill of Difficulty road, which leads to the landing area, were carried out in 2005.

Pitcairn's first radio-telephone link was established in 1985, and a new telecommunications unit was installed in 1992. It was hoped that Pitcairn might find an additional source of revenue through the sale of website addresses in early 2000 when the island won a legal victory to gain control of its internet domain name suffix '.pn'. In 2008 television services became available for the first time, and the telephone system was upgraded to give islanders constant internet access. In March of that year, however, an international software security company reported that in per caput terms Pitcairn had become one of the world's worst offenders with regard to the relaying of unsolicited e-mails.

A steady decline in the population, owing mainly to emigration to New Zealand, has been a major problem. In March 2001 a New Zealand company expressed an interest in acquiring development rights on Pitcairn with the intention of establishing fishing and tourism projects. In May 2002 the company's director reportedly announced that the development would begin within the next 12 months, describing plans for a lodge on Pitcairn and for a floating hotel off Oeno Island. However, the British High Commission in Wellington emphasized that any such developments remained subject to the approval of the Pitcairn Island Council, but that the company was welcome to submit proposals.

UNITED KINGDOM OVERSEAS TERRITORIES — The Pitcairn Islands

In August 2004 the British Government announced the provision of US $6.5m. in emergency assistance for the Territory in order to avert a financial crisis. The aid programme included a grant (partly financed by the European Union) to fund improvements to the road between Bounty Bay and Adamstown, which were carried out in mid-2005. In 2006 the British Government provided £1.9m. for a project to repair local infrastructure. Plans for infrastructural development included the building of a breakwater at Bounty Bay. It was hoped that the project, jointly funded by the British Government and the European Development Fund, would make the island more accessible to passenger and cargo ships. Proposals for the use of wind power as an alternative energy source were also discussed.

New Zealand currency is used. There is no taxation (except for small licensing fees on guns and vehicles), and government revenue has been derived mainly from philatelic sales (one-half of current revenue in 1992/93), and from interest earned on investments. In 1998/99 revenue totalled $NZ492,000 and expenditure $NZ667,000. In the early 2000s revenue was estimated to total about $NZ415,000 annually. Capital assistance worth an average of £100,000 annually is received from the United Kingdom. In 2010 exports from Pitcairn to New Zealand were worth $NZ137,800, while imports from that country cost $NZ626,10000. Pitcairn's imports from the USA totalled US $3,700 in 2010, while exports to the USA were worth US $4,100.

Hopes have been expressed that the development of the tourism sector might provide some impetus to economic growth. In 2005 a museum was constructed on the island to house some of Pitcairn's historical artefacts, including the *Bounty* cannon, which was raised from Bounty Bay with assistance from an Australian team in 1999 and returned to the island in 2009. Other initiatives included the improvement of ship berthing facilities, and in August 2010 it was reported that Pitcairn had begun to derive much economic benefit from the increase in arrivals of cruise-ships, bringing hundreds of tourists. It was hoped that this revitalization of the economy would encourage islanders resident overseas to return to Pitcairn. The islands' potential for eco-tourism, to include activities such as whale-watching, has also been identified as a possible source of revenue. In 1988, meanwhile, uninhabited Henderson Island, the largest of the island grouping, was included on the UNESCO World Heritage List. The island, 168 km (104 miles) east-north-east of Pitcairn, was to be preserved as a bird sanctuary. There are five species of bird unique to the island: the flightless rail or Henderson chicken, the green Henderson fruit dove, the Henderson crake, the Henderson warbler and the Henderson lorikeet. However, concern was expressed in 1994 following claims by scientists studying the island that its unique flora and fauna were threatened by the accidental introduction of foreign plant species by visitors and by an increase in the rat population. In August 2010, with rats now estimated to number 30,000, UNESCO emphasized the need for urgent action to address the rodent issue and warned of the possibility of the removal of Henderson Island's World Heritage status.

PUBLIC HOLIDAYS

2012 (provisional): 2 January (for New Year's Day), 23 January (Bounty Day), 6–9 April (Easter), 4 June (Queen's Birthday), 25 December (Christmas).

Statistical Survey

Source: Office of the Governor of Pitcairn, Henderson, Ducie and Oeno Islands, c/o British Consulate-General, Pitcairn Islands Administration, Private Box 105-696, Auckland, New Zealand; tel. (9) 366-0186; fax (9) 366-0187; e-mail pitcairn@iconz.co.nz.

AREA AND POPULATION

Area: 35.5 sq km. *By Island:* Pitcairn 4.35 sq km; Henderson 30.0 sq km; Oeno is less than 1 sq km and Ducie is smaller.
Population: 66 at census of 31 December 1991. *31 December 2010* (annual census): 58. Note: Figure excludes 10 off-island residents.
Density (Pitcairn only, 31 December 2010): 13.3 per sq km.
Employment (able-bodied men, 2002): 9.

FINANCE

Currency and Exchange Rates: 100 cents = 1 Pitcairn dollar. The Pitcairn dollar is at par with the New Zealand dollar ($NZ). New Zealand currency is usually used.
Budget ($NZ, 1998/99): Revenue 492,000; Expenditure 667,000.

EXTERNAL TRADE

Trade with New Zealand ($NZ '000): *Imports:* 791.4 in 2008; 1,253.3 in 2009; 626.1 in 2010. *Exports:* 45.4 in 2008; 88.8 in 2009; 137.8 in 2010.
Trade with the USA (US $ '000): *Imports:* 0.0 in 2008; 568.2 in 2009; 3.7 in 2010. *Exports:* 0.8 in 2008; 26.0 in 2009; 4.1 in 2010.

TRANSPORT

Road Traffic (motor vehicles, 2002): Passenger vehicles 30 (two-wheeled 1, three-wheeled 6, four-wheeled 23); Tractors 3; Bulldozer 1; Digger 1.
Shipping: *Local Vessels* (communally owned open surf boats, 2000): 3. *International Shipping Arrivals* (visits by passing vessels, 1996): Ships 51; Yachts 30.

COMMUNICATIONS

Telephones (2002): a party-line service with 15 telephones in use; 2 public telephones; 2 digital telephones. Most homes also have VHF radio.

Directory

The Government

Governor of Pitcairn, Henderson, Ducie and Oeno Islands: VICTORIA TREADELL (British High Commissioner in New Zealand—took office May 2010).
Office of the Governor of Pitcairn, Henderson, Ducie and Oeno Islands: c/o British High Commission, 44 Hill St, POB 1812, Wellington 6011, New Zealand; tel. (4) 924-2888; fax (4) 473-4982; e-mail ppa.mailbox@fco.gov.uk; Gov. VICTORIA TREADELL.
Pitcairn Islands Office: Private Box 105-696, Auckland, New Zealand; tel. (9) 366-0186; fax (9) 366-0187; e-mail admin@pitcairn.gov.pn; internet www.government.pn.

ISLAND COUNCIL
(May 2011)

Mayor: MICHAEL WARREN.
Deputy Mayor: SIMON YOUNG.
Governor's Representative (ex officio): LUCY FOSTER.
Other Members: DAVE BROWN, LEA BROWN, BRENDA CHRISTIAN, JAY WARREN, PAUL WARREN.

Elections to the Island Council take place each December. Meetings are held at the Court House in Adamstown.

Office of the Island Secretary: The Square, Adamstown.

Judicial System

The constitutional amendments enacted in February 2010 provided for the establishment of the Pitcairn Supreme Court and for the appointment of an independent Attorney-General.

Chief Justice: CHARLES BLACKIE.
Island Magistrate: SIMON YOUNG.
Public Prosecutor: SIMON MOORE.
Public Defender: PAUL DACRE.
Attorney-General: PAUL RISHWORTH.

Religion

CHRISTIANITY

Since 1887 many of the islanders have been adherents of the Seventh-day Adventist Church.

Pastor: JOHN O'MALLEY, SDA Church, The Square, POB 24, Adamstown; fax 872-7620/9763.

The Press

Pitcairn Miscellany: e-mail admin@miscellany.pn; internet www.miscellany.pn; monthly four-page mimeographed news sheet; f. 1959; edited by the Education Officer; Editor P. FOLEY; circ. 1,400 (2002).

Finance, Trade and Industry

There are no formal banking facilities. A co-operative trading store was established in 1967. Industry consists of handicrafts, and the production of honey and dried fruit.

Transport

ROADS

There are approximately 14 km (9 miles) of dirt road suitable for two-, three- and four-wheeled vehicles. In 2002 Pitcairn had one conventional motor cycle, six three-wheelers and 22 four-wheeled motor cycles, one four-wheel-drive motor car, three tractors, a five-ton digger and a bulldozer; traditional wheelbarrows are used occasionally. In 1995 a total of £79,000 was received from individual donors for work to improve the road leading to the jetty at Bounty Bay. Work to concrete the road, known as the Hill of Difficulty, was completed in mid-2006.

SHIPPING

No passenger ships have called regularly since 1968, and sea communications are restricted to cargo vessels operating between New Zealand and Panama, which make scheduled calls at Pitcairn three times a year, as well as a number of unscheduled calls. A shipping route between French Polynesia and Pitcairn was opened in 2006. There are also occasional visits by private yachts. The number of cruise ships calling at Pitcairn increased in the late 1990s, and 10 such vessels visited the island in 2000 (compared with just two or three annually in previous years). Two cruise ships called at Pitcairn in April 2005 before stopping at Oeno Island for the tourists to witness a solar eclipse near the island. Bounty Bay, near Adamstown, is the only possible landing site, and there are no docking facilities; in mid-2007 plans to build a breakwater at Bounty Bay were announced. In 1993 the jetty derrick was refitted with an hydraulic system. The islanders have three aluminium open surf boats. Major work to repair the slipway and jetty was carried out by the islanders in mid-2005.

Tourism

The tourism sector has yet to be developed. The development of eco-tourism, to include activities such as whale-watching, has been identified as offering particular potential for the islands. Henderson Island was declared a UNESCO World Heritage Site in 1988 and has been designated as a bird sanctuary.

Pitcairn Island Tourism Dept: Adamstown; e-mail tourism@pitcairn.pn; internet www.visitpitcairn.pn; Co-ordinator HEATHER MENZIES.

Education

Free primary education is provided on the island under the direction of a qualified schoolteacher, recruited in New Zealand. Scholarships, provided by the Pitcairn Government, are available for post-primary education or specialist training in New Zealand. In February 2004 there were seven children (four primary and three secondary) being educated on Pitcairn.

SAINT HELENA, ASCENSION AND TRISTAN DA CUNHA

Introductory Survey

LOCATION, CLIMATE, LANGUAGE, RELIGION, FLAG, CAPITAL

Saint Helena lies in the South Atlantic Ocean, about 1,930 km (1,200 miles) from the south-west coast of Africa, while the island of Ascension lies 1,131 km (703 miles) north-west of Saint Helena. The island of Tristan da Cunha lies 2,800 km (1,740 miles) west of Cape Town, South Africa: Saint Helena is 2,300 km (1,430 miles) to the north-east. Also in the group are Inaccessible Island, 37 km (23 miles) west of Tristan; the three Nightingale Islands, 37 km (23 miles) south; and Gough Island (Diego Alvarez), 425 km (264 miles) south. Saint Helena has a sub-tropical and mild climate, with a mean maximum temperature of 24°C (75°F) and a mean minimum of 19°C (66°F). The average annual rainfall is 113 mm (4.5 ins). The mean maximum temperature on Ascension is 30°C (86°F), while the mean minimum temperature is 24°C (75°F). Average annual rainfall is about 2,252 mm (89 ins). The climate on Tristan da Cunha is typically oceanic and temperate with rainfall averaging 1,675 mm (66 ins) per year. English is the official language. The majority of the population of the islands are Anglicans. The flag (proportions 1 by 2) is the British 'Blue Ensign' with the Saint Helena shield (depicting a ship of the British East India Co approaching the rocky shores of the island, above which in the yellow chief is a Saint Helena plover) in the fly. The capital is Jamestown, on Saint Helena.

SAINT HELENA

Contemporary Political History

Governed by the British East India Co from 1673, the island was brought under the direct control of the British Crown in 1834. At general elections held in September 1976, the Saint Helena Progressive Party, advocating the retention of close economic links with the United Kingdom, won 11 of the 12 elective seats in the Legislative Council. This policy has been advocated by almost all members of the Legislative Council brought to office at subsequent general elections (normally held every four years) up to and including that held in November 2009.

In October 1981 a commission was established by the Governor to review the island's constitutional arrangements. The commission reported in 1983 that it was unable to identify any proposal for constitutional change that would command the support of the majority of the islanders. In 1988, however, a formal Constitution was introduced to replace the Order in Council and Royal Instructions under which Saint Helena had been governed since 1967. The Constitution entered into force on 1 January 1989.

Owing to the limited range of economic activity on the island (see below), Saint Helena is dependent on development and budgetary aid from the United Kingdom. Since 1981, when the United Kingdom adopted the British Nationality Act, which effectively removed the islanders' traditional right of residence in Britain, opportunities for overseas employment have been limited to contract work, principally in Ascension and the Falkland Islands. In 1992 an informal 'commission on citizenship' was established by a number of islanders to examine Saint Helena's constitutional relationship with the United Kingdom, with special reference to the legal validity of the 1981 legislation as applied to Saint Helena. In April 1997 the commission obtained a legal opinion from a former Attorney-General of Saint Helena to the effect that the application of the Act to the population of Saint Helena was in contravention of the Royal Charter establishing British sovereignty in 1673. The commission indicated that it intended to pursue the matter further. In July 1997 private legislation was introduced in the British Parliament to extend full British nationality to 'persons having connections with' Saint Helena. In the following month the British Government indicated that it was considering arrangements under which islanders would be granted employment and residence rights in the United Kingdom. In February 1998, following a conference held in London of representatives of the British Dependent Territories, it was announced that a review was to take place of the future constitutional status of these territories, and of means whereby their economies might be strengthened. It was subsequently agreed that the operation of the 1981 legislation in relation to Saint Helena would also be reviewed. As an immediate measure to ameliorate the isolation of Saint Helena, the British Government conceded permission for civilian air landing rights on Ascension Island, which, with the contemplated construction of a small airstrip on Saint Helena, could facilitate the future development of the island as a tourist destination.

In March 1999 the British Government published draft legislation proposing that full British nationality, including the right of abode in the United Kingdom, was to be restored to the population of Saint Helena and its dependencies, under the reorganization of the British Dependent Territories as the United Kingdom Overseas Territories. However, this had still not been implemented by July 2000, when the citizens took their case to the UN Committee on Decolonization, seeking British passports, a new constitution and administration as a Crown dependency rather than as a colony. In May 2002 the British Overseas Territories Act, which granted British citizenship to the people of the Overseas Territories, including Saint Helena and dependencies, came into effect, having received royal assent in February. Under the new legislation these citizens acquired the right to hold a British passport and to work in the United Kingdom, but not the other benefits of citizenship (such as reduced fees for education). The Act restored those rights removed by the British

Nationality Act of 1981. In September 2002 an independent constitutional adviser visited Saint Helena and consulted extensively with the island's residents on the options for future constitutional development. A consultative poll on the draft for a new constitution, which, *inter alia*, proposed the creation of a ministerial form of government, took place on 25 May 2005. The draft document was rejected by 52.6% of voters. Concern was expressed at the low rate of voter participation, recorded at 43% of registered voters. Nevertheless, it was indicated that elements of the rejected constitution were expected to be adopted, including a change to the number of constituencies on Saint Helena. The British Government subsequently stated that it wished to identify any possible improvements to the existing Constitution in conjunction with the new Executive Council, which took office following the elections held on 31 August 2005. In April 2008 Governor Andrew Gurr outlined proposals for a new constitution that would be drafted following a full consultation process, which he envisaged would be completed by mid-2009. He suggested that the previous draft constitution had been rejected due to the proposed introduction of ministerial government, and that consequently a number of potential improvements in other areas had been lost.

On 1 September 2009 the Saint Helena, Ascension and Tristan da Cunha Constitution Order 2009 entered into force. Under the new Constitution, Ascension and Tristan da Cunha were no longer referred to as 'Dependencies' and the territory was henceforth to be known as Saint Helena, Ascension and Tristan da Cunha. The new Constitution also established fundamental rights and freedoms for each of the three islands, which were to share the same Governor, Attorney-General, Supreme Court and Court of Appeal. Saint Helena was to be represented by an eight-member Executive Council and a 17-member Legislative Council, while Ascension and Tristan da Cunha were to be represented by Island Councils. Legislative elections were held in early November following which the new councils were formed. The Legislative Council subsequently appointed chairmen to head the eight Council Committees responsible for overseeing policy formation.

Meanwhile, in February 2002 a referendum was held by the Government in Saint Helena, Ascension Island, the Falkland Islands and on RMS *Saint Helena* on future access to the island; 71.6% of the votes cast were in favour of the construction of an airport (28.4% opting for a shipping alternative). The project was expected to cost some £40m., of which the British Government was reported to have agreed to contribute some £26.3m., approximately equal to the cost of replacing the mail ship in 2010. In July 2003 a public consultation procedure was undertaken on new draft tourism and investment policies, which were intended to provide a framework for private sector investment and tourism development, to maximize the opportunities that air access would bring to Saint Helena. However, in mid-2006 all three of the final contractors for the project declared that some of the commercial risks associated with the terms of the tender were unfeasible. A procurement review was commissioned immediately, and later that year three new potential contractors were shortlisted and invited to develop their proposals for the provision of air services to the island. By February 2007 four contractors had expressed formal interest in bringing air access to Saint Helena, and towards the end of that year two bids were received for the design, build and operation contract for the airport. However, in February 2008 it was revealed that none of the shortlisted companies had provided an appropriate solution, and further negotiations would be necessary for the commencement of the project. Despite an initial commitment to bringing the airport into operation by 2012, in April 2009 the British Department for International Development (DfID), in response to the worsening of the United Kingdom's economic climate, announced a further consultation on future access to Saint Helena. The consultation process lasted until July and an initial report was delivered in late September. In December Douglas Alexander, the British Secretary of State for International Development, announced that as a result of 'current economic conditions' the British Government had decided it would not be appropriate to proceed with the project 'at this time'. However, a further analysis of potential cost savings to the airport contract which might be enabled by recent technological developments, and of options for funding the capital cost of the airport through a public-private partnership, was to be carried out during 2010. In July it was decided that construction of the airport would proceed, although no details on the budget or timescale for completion were made immediately available. In December the DfID and the Saint Helena Government signed a memorandum of understanding detailing the reforms required in order to prepare for the construction of the airport.

In May 2008 it was reported that the United Kingdom Government had registered claims with the UN Commission for the Limits of the Continental Shelf to extend its territorial waters surrounding Saint Helena, Ascension Island and Tristan da Cunha. It was hoped that these areas of seabed could be secured with the possibility of drilling for petroleum, gas and mineral resources in future years.

Economic Affairs

The economy of Saint Helena is heavily reliant on British aid. In 2006/07 the assistance totalled £14.76m. and consisted of direct budgetary aid (£6.9m.), an annual subsidy for the operation of the RMS *St Helena* (£3.1m.) and support for bilateral development assistance. Total United Kingdom assistance to St Helena was to £20.6m. in 2009/10 (direct budgetary aid was £7.7m., a decrease from £8.7m. in 2008/09). Local budget revenues totalled £9.4m. in 2009/10. According to official estimates, Saint Helena's gross national product (GNP) totalled £19.0m. in 2009/10; per caput GNP was estimated at £4,761 in the same financial year. Gross domestic product (GDP) was estimated to have decreased, in real terms, by an annual average of 1.6% during 1999/2000–2005/06; a decline of 10.1%, in real terms, was recorded for 2005/06. The population declined by an annual average of 3.2% during 1999/2000–2005/06, and, largely as a result of this, per caput GDP increased, in real terms, by an annual average of 1.9% over the same period. The annual rate of inflation, according to retail prices, averaged 4.4% in 2000–09, and the rate, influenced to a large extent by the prevailing rates in its two most important trading partners, South Africa and the United Kingdom, had remained relatively stable (around 3%–5%) during 2003–07, although consumer prices increased by 8.0% in both 2008 and 2009. In 2004 the rate of unemployment (including community work scheme placements) was estimated at 7.6%, but by November 2008 this rate was estimated to have fallen to 2.3% of the labour force.

Saint Helena's traditionally high rate of unemployment resulted in widespread reliance on welfare benefit payments and a concurrent decline in living standards for the majority of the population (although an increase in economic migration in recent years has done much to alleviate this situation). Evidence of underlying social discontent emerged in April 1997, when minor public disorders broke out in Jamestown following the refusal of the Governor (who exercises full executive and legislative authority in Saint Helena) to accept the nomination of a prominent critic of government policy to the post of Director of the Department of Social Welfare. Two members of the Executive Council (which acts in an advisory capacity) resigned in protest at the action of the Governor, who subsequently announced that elections to the Legislative Council were to take place in July. Following the elections, held on 9 July, the Governor agreed to the nomination as Chairman of the Education Committee of the candidate he had previously refused to nominate to the Social Welfare Directorate. The newly elected Legislative Council became the first in which members were to receive a fixed salary to serve on a full-time basis, relinquishing any other employment during their term of office.

At the 2008 census 7.3% of the employed labour force were engaged in agriculture and fishing, 20.0% in industry (predominantly construction) and 72.7% in services. Employment in the public sector was estimated to account for 60% of employment in the late 2000s. There is a significant visible trade deficit (£9.9m. in 2009/10), with the cost of imports amounting to £10.3m. (including almost 26% spent on importing food and live animals), compared with export revenues of just £321,000 (derived almost entirely from fish). In 2000 exports of fish (which, apart from a small quantity of coffee, is the only commodity exported) totalled 43.1 metric tons (compared with 27.2 tons in 1985). Improvements in vessel capacity have helped increase fish exports in recent years. An increase in overseas philatelic sales has also generated significant revenues (£89,000 in 2008/09), as has a fledgling tourist industry (£707,000 in 2009/10). However, a large proportion of the labour force (approximately 1,000) must seek employment overseas, principally on Ascension and the Falkland Islands. In March 2001 551 Saint Helenians were working on Ascension, and in December 1999 371 were working on the Falkland Islands; according to the British Foreign and Commonwealth Office, approximately 1,700 members of the work-force were employed offshore at the beginning of 2005. Remittances from overseas contributed an estimated £3.4m. in 2009/10.

Saint Helena is of interest to naturalists for its rare flora and fauna. The island has about 40 species of flora that are unique to Saint Helena.

ASCENSION

Discovered by Portuguese navigators in 1501, the island is a semibarren, rocky peak of purely volcanic origin. Britain took possession of Ascension in 1815, in connection with Napoleon's detention on Saint Helena. The island is famous for green turtles, and is also a breeding ground for the sooty tern. Under an agreement with the British Government, US forces occupy Wideawake Airfield, which is used as a tracking station for guided missiles. Ascension has no indigenous population, being inhabited by British and US military personnel, *émigré* workers and government administrative staff from Saint Helena. There are also a number of expatriate civilian personnel of Merlin Communications International (MCI), which operates the British Broadcasting Corporation (BBC) Overseas World Service Atlantic relay station, Cable and Wireless PLC, which provides international communications services and operates the

'Ariane' satellite tracking station of the European Space Agency, and staff providing the island's common services. The island is an important communications centre. Ascension does not raise its own finance; the costs of administering the island are borne collectively by the user organizations, supplemented by income from philatelic sales. The island is developing a modest eco-tourism sector. Some revenue, which is remitted to the Saint Helena administration, is derived from fishing licences (estimated to be around £1m. in 1999). Facilities on Ascension underwent rapid development in 1982 to serve as a major staging post for British vessels and aircraft on their way to the Falkland Islands (q.v.), and the island has continued to provide a key link in British supply lines to the South Atlantic.

Dissent developed among the resident population in June 2002, following the decision of the Foreign and Commonwealth Office to impose taxes for the first time on the island (including income tax, property tax and tax on alcohol and tobacco). The primary objection of the population was that this was 'taxation without representation', as the islanders do not possess the right to vote, to own property or even to live on the island. The Governor responded with plans to introduce a democratically elected council that would have a purely advisory function and no decision-making powers, claiming that the islanders initially needed to acquire experience of governance. On 22–23 August a vote on the democratic options took place on the island, with 95% of the votes cast being in favour of an Island Council, rather than an Inter-Island Council plus Island Council structure; 50% of those eligible to vote did so. The Council was to be chaired by the Administrator, on behalf of the Governor, and was to comprise seven elected members, the Attorney-General, the Director of Finance and one or two appointed members. Elections for councillors took place in October, and the Island Council was inaugurated in the following month. A joint consultative council was also to be established, with representatives from both Ascension and Saint Helena, in order to develop policy relating to economic development and tourism common to both islands.

The British Government subsequently stated its intention to enact legislation granting the islanders right of abode and the right to own property. However, following a visit to the island by a delegation of British officials in November 2005, it was announced that the proposed reforms would not be carried out. The British Government cited its reluctance fundamentally to change the nature of the territory and also maintained that granting such rights would impose greater financial liabilities on British taxpayers and would bring an unacceptable level of risk to the United Kingdom. In January 2006 The Island Council announced that it intended to seek clarification regarding the legality of the British Government's decision and reiterated its commitment to securing the islanders' right to abode and the right to purchase property.

In May 2007 the Island Council was suspended and the Ascension Island Advisory Group was established to provide advice to the Administrator on certain policy issues. The suspension was expected to remain in place until May 2008, after which elections would be held. It was anticipated that the Advisory Group would meet on a monthly basis, to be supplemented by informal meetings as necessary. Consultation papers were to be issued to encourage the people of Ascension to participate in the decision-making process. In October elections were held and a new Island Council was sworn in later that month. Meanwhile, in May it was reported that the United Kingdom Government had submitted a claim to the UN Commission for the Limits of the Continental Shelf regarding the extension of its territorial waters around Ascension Island (see Saint Helena).

As of early 2004 Ascension Island had a balanced fiscal budget, although with minimal reserves. Government expenditure funds one school, one hospital (offering limited services), police and judicial services; these services are provided without charge to local taxpayers. The Saint Helena-based firm Solomons has a primary role in the incipient private sector and a sports-fishing industry was in the process of being established. In early 2009 the European Development Fund was considering awarding a grant of some €16.6m. to Saint Helena and its dependencies for infrastructure and economic development projects, including a road improvement initiative for Ascension Island.

TRISTAN DA CUNHA

Tristan da Cunha was discovered in 1506, but remained uninhabited until occupied by US whalers during 1790–1811. The British Navy took possession of the island in 1817. Tristan's population was evacuated in 1961, after volcanic eruptions, but was resettled in 1963. The island's major source of revenue derives from a royalty for a crayfishing concession, supplemented by income from the sale of postage stamps and other philatelic items, and handicrafts. The fishing industry and the administration employ all of the working population. Some 20 power boats operating from the island land their catches to a fish-freezing factory built by the Atlantic Islands Development Corpn, whose fishing concession was transferred in January 1997 to a new holder, Premier Fishing (Pty) Ltd, of Cape Town, and later to another South African company, Ovenstone (Pty) Ltd. In February 2008 a fire destroyed the factory, along with the island's power plant; a new factory was opened in July 2009. The island's harbour was also renovated in 2008, in a project paid for by the British Department for International Development (DfID), and undertaken with the help of Royal Engineers from the United Kingdom. Budget estimates for 2005/06 projected a deficit of £147,507. Development aid from the United Kingdom ceased in 1980; since then the island has financed its own projects. In April 2008, prompted by concerns surrounding the island's dwindling capital reserves, Administrator David Morley warned that the island could be bankrupt within four years unless economic austerity measures were implemented immediately. Chief among these proposals was the introduction, with effect from 1 June 2008, of an incremental system of income tax (with a maximum rate of 13%). In June 2001 a hurricane in the main settlement of Edinburgh of the Seven Seas destroyed the hospital, community centre and numerous homes, and also killed many cattle; the satellite phone link was lost and the island was without electricity for one week, although no serious injuries were sustained. DfID granted a £75,000 emergency aid package in response to the disaster. However, the cost of repairs surpassed that figure considerably. Furthermore, the problem of poaching in the island's waters resulted in much of Tristan da Cunha's limited resources being used to fund fishing patrols rather than swiftly restoring the damaged infrastructure. It was reported in May 2008 that the United Kingdom Government had registered a claim with the UN Commission for the Limits of the Continental Shelf to extend its territorial waters around Tristan da Cunha (see Saint Helena).

Statistical Survey

Sources (unless otherwise indicated): Development and Economic Planning Dept, Government of Saint Helena, Saint Helena Island, STHL 1ZZ; tel. 2777; fax 2830; e-mail depd@helanta.sh; Saint Helena Development Agency (SHDA), POB 117, No 2 Main St, Jamestown, Saint Helena Island, STHL 1ZZ; tel. 2920; fax 2166; e-mail enquiries@shda.co.sh; internet www.shda.co.sh.

Note: Unless otherwise indicated, figures in this Statistical Survey relate only to the island of Saint Helena.

AREA AND POPULATION

Area: 411 sq km (159 sq miles). St Helena 121 sq km (47 sq miles); Ascension Island 88 sq km (34 sq miles); Tristan da Cunha 98 sq km (38 sq miles); Inaccessible Island 10 sq km (4 sq miles); Nightingale Islands 2 sq km (1 sq mile); Gough Island 91 sq km (35 sq miles).

Population: 5,157 at census of 8 March 1998; 4,257 (enumerated total) at census of 10 February 2008, 3,981 (resident population) at census of 10 February 2008. *Ascension Island* (enumerated total at 2008 census): 710. *Tristan da Cunha* (enumerated total at 2008 census): 264. Note: There are no indigenous inhabitants on Ascension Island, but several hundred personnel and employees and their families are permanently resident (mostly nationals of Saint Helena, with some 200 UK nationals and 150 US nationals). There is a small weather station on Gough Island, staffed, under agreement, by personnel employed by the South African Government.

Density (at 2008 census): 35.2 per sq km.

Population by Age and Sex (resident population at 2008 census): *0–14:* 600 (males 317, females 283); *15–64:* 2,677 (males 1,378, females 1,299); *65 and over:* 703 (males 326, females 377); *Total* 3,981 (males 2,022, females 1,959). Note: Total includes one male of undetermined age.

Principal Town (UN estimate, incl. suburbs): Jamestown (capital), population 699 in mid-2009 (Source: UN, *World Urbanization Prospects: The 2009 Revision*).

Births and Deaths (2009): Registered live births 35 (8.7 per 1,000); Registered deaths 41 (11.2 per 1,000).

Employment (2008 census): Agriculture, hunting and related activities 122; Fishing 33; Mining and quarrying 8; Manufacturing 115; Electricity, gas and water 113; Construction 190; Wholesale and retail trade, etc. 385; Hotels and restaurants 36; Transport, storage and communications 237; Financial intermediation 20; Real estate, renting and business activities 185; Public administration and defence 157; Education 112; Health and social work 178; Other community services 217; Private household 17; Extra-territorial organizations 5; *Total employed* 2,130 (males 1,174; females 956) (Source: ILO). *Unemployed* (2007/08, incl. community work scheme) 66.

UNITED KINGDOM OVERSEAS TERRITORIES

AGRICULTURE, ETC.

Livestock (livestock census, 2009): Cattle 598; Sheep 651; Pigs 386; Goats 773; Asses 46; Chickens 4,421 (Source: FAO).

Livestock Products (metric tons, 2009): Cattle meat 40.9; Pig meat 67.2; Sheep meat 0.8.

Fishing (metric tons, live weight, including Ascension and Tristan da Cunha, 2008): Skipjack tuna 45; Yellowfin tuna 97; Tristan da Cunha rock lobster 406; Total catch (incl. others) 794. Figures include catches of rock lobster from Tristan da Cunha during the 12 months ending 30 April of the year stated (Source: FAO).

INDUSTRY

Electric Energy (production, kWh million): 8.5 in 2007; 8.5 in 2008; 8.8 in 2009.

FINANCE

Currency and Exchange Rate: 100 pence (pennies) = 1 Saint Helena pound (£). *Sterling, Dollar and Euro Equivalents* (31 December 2010): £1 sterling = Saint Helena £1; US $1 = 63.88 pence; €1 = 85.35 pence; £10 = $15.65 = €11.72. *Average Exchange Rate* (£ per US dollar): 0.5440 in 2008; 0.6419 in 2009; 0.6472 in 2010. Note: The Saint Helena pound is at par with the pound sterling.

Budget (£ million, 2009/10): Total revenue 9.4 (excluding United Kingdom budgetary aid 7.7); Total expenditure (incl. trading accounts) 23.4. *Ascension Island* (£ million, year ending 31 March 2004, estimates): Total revenue 4.3; Total expenditure 4.0 (recurrent 3.3, capital 0.7). *Tristan da Cunha* (£ million, 2005/06, estimates): Total revenue 0.7; Expenditure 0.9 (with excess expenditure financed from capital reserves of 1.2).

Gross National Product (£ million at current prices): 20.32 in 2007/08; 21.47 in 2008/09; 19.04 in 2009/10.

Gross Domestic Product (£ million at current prices): 17.28 in 2007/08; 17.39 in 2008/09; 15.55 in 2009/10.

Expenditure on the Gross Domestic Product (£ million at current prices, 2009/10): Government expenditure 20.22; Private expenditure 14.25; Changes in stocks 0.21; Total domestic expenditure 34.68; Exports of goods and services 1.19; *Less* Imports of goods and services 20.32; *GDP in purchasers' values* 15.55.

Money Supply (£ '000, 2006/07): Currency in circulation 3,618 (excl. commemorative coins valued at 514).

Cost of Living (Retail Price Index; base: February 2002 = 100): 121.6 in 2007; 131.3 in 2008; 141.8 in 2009 (Source: ILO).

EXTERNAL TRADE

Principal Commodities (£ '000, 2009/10): *Imports:* Total 10,267 (Food and live animals 2,617; Mineral fuels, lubricants, etc. 1,349; Machinery and transport equipment 1,896). *Exports:* Total 321 (mostly fish). Note: Trade is mainly with the United Kingdom (imports 4,732 in 2009/10) and South Africa (imports 5,431 in 2009/10).

TRANSPORT

Road Traffic (2009): 2,391 licensed vehicles (incl. 1,459 passenger motor cars).

Shipping: *Vessels Entered* (2009): 235. *Merchant Fleet* (31 December 2009): 2 vessels; Total displacement 2,232 grt (Source: IHS Fairplay, *World Fleet Statistics*).

TOURISM

Visitor Arrivals: 2,595 (tourists 1,113) in 2007; 2,589 (tourists 825) in 2008; 2,452 (tourists 847) in 2009.

Receipts from Tourism (£ '000, estimates): 414 in 2007/08; 320 in 2008/09; 707 in 2009/10.

COMMUNICATIONS MEDIA

Radio Receivers ('000 in use, 1997): 3 (Source: UNESCO, *Statistical Yearbook*).

Television Subscribers (April 2007): 1,161.

Telephones (main lines in use, 2009): 2,300 (Source: International Telecommunication Union).

EDUCATION

Primary (2006/07): 2 schools; 14 teachers; 115 pupils.

Amalgamated School (2006/07): 1 school; 15 teachers; 116 pupils.

Saint Helena, Ascension and Tristan da Cunha

Intermediate (2006/07): 2 schools; 17 teachers; 119 pupils.
Secondary (2006/07): 1 school; 42 teachers; 324 pupils.
2009/10 (all levels): 7 schools; 88 teachers; 516 enrolled pupils.

Directory

The Government

HEAD OF STATE

Queen: HM Queen ELIZABETH II.
Governor: ANDREW GURR.

The Governor of Saint Helena, in his capacity as Governor of Ascension and Tristan da Cunha, is represented by an Administrator on those islands. The Governor, either directly, or through the Administrator, exercises executive authority on behalf of Her Majesty Queen Elizabeth II. The Governor, acting after consultation with the Island Councils, whose advice he or she is not obliged to follow, may make laws for the peace, order and good government of Ascension and Tristan da Cunha.

Administrator of Ascension: ROSS DENNY.
Administrator of Tristan da Cunha: SEAN BURNS.

EXECUTIVE COUNCIL
(May 2011)

President: ANDREW GURR (The Governor).
Chief Secretary: ANDREW WELLS.
Financial Secretary: PAUL BLESSINGTON.
Attorney-General: KENNETH BADDON.
Elected Members: RODNEY BUCKLEY, CYRIL GUNNELL, MERVYN YON, TARA THOMAS, ANTHONY GREEN.

LEGISLATIVE COUNCIL
(May 2011)

The Legislative Council consists of the Speaker, the Deputy Speaker, 12 elected members and three ex officio members (the Chief Secretary, the Financial Secretary and the Attorney-General).

Speaker: CATHY HOPKINS.
Deputy Speaker: ERIC BENJAMIN.

Committee Chairmen

Access and Transport: JOHN CRANFIELD.
Civil Society, Tourism and Leisure: BERNICE OLSSON.
Economy and Finance: TARA THOMAS.
Education and Employment: ANTHONY GREEN.
Health and Social Welfare: CYRIL GUNNELL.
Home and International: DEREK THOMAS.
Infrastructure and Utilities: MERVYN YON.
Natural Resources, Development and Environment: RAYMOND WILLIAMS.

GOVERNMENT OFFICES

Office of the Governor: The Castle, Jamestown, STHL 1ZZ; tel. 2555; fax 2598; e-mail pagovernor@sainthelena.gov.sh; internet www.sainthelena.gov.sh.

Office of the Chief Secretary: The Castle, Jamestown, STHL 1ZZ; tel. 2470; fax 2598; e-mail ocs@cwimail.sh.

Office of the Financial Secretary: The Castle, Jamestown, STHL 1ZZ; tel. 2470; fax 2020; e-mail pafinancialsecretary@sainthelena.gov.sh.

Office of the Administrator of Ascension: The Residency, Georgetown, Ascension, ASCN 1ZZ; tel. 7000; fax 6152; e-mail aigenquiries@ascension.gov.ac; internet www.ascension-island.gov.ac.

Office of the Administrator of Tristan da Cunha: The Administrator's Office, Edinburgh of the Seven Seas, Tristan da Cunha, TDCU 1ZZ; tel. (satellite) 874-1445434; fax (satellite) 874-1445435; e-mail admin@tristandc.com; internet www.tristandc.com/administator.php.

Political Organizations

There are no political parties in Saint Helena. Elections to the Legislative Council, the latest of which took place in November 2009, are conducted on a non-partisan basis.

Judicial System

The legal system is derived from English common law and statutes. There is a Supreme Court and a Court of Appeal, and provision was made in the 2009 Constitution for the establishment of other subordinate courts. The Supreme Court is presided over by a Chief Justice. The Court of Appeal consists of a President and two or more Justices of Appeal. There is also a four-member Judicial Services Commission, presided over by the Chief Justice.

The Attorney-General of Saint Helena is the principal legal adviser to the Government of Saint Helena. The Attorney-General of Ascension and of Tristan da Cunha is the principal legal adviser to the Government of Ascension and to the Government of Tristan da Cunha and is the person for the time being holding or acting in the office of Attorney-General of St Helena. The courts of Ascension and of Tristan da Cunha are the Supreme Court of St Helena, the Court of Appeal of St Helena, and such courts subordinate to the Supreme Court as may be established by law.

Chief Justice: CHARLES W. EKINS.
Attorney-General: KENNETH BADDON.
Sheriff: GRETA PAT MUSK.

Religion

The majority of the population belongs to the Anglican Communion. Ascension forms part of the Anglican diocese of Saint Helena, which normally provides a resident chaplain who is also available to minister to members of other denominations. There is a Roman Catholic chapel served by visiting priests, as well as a small mosque. Adherents of the Anglican church predominate on Tristan da Cunha, which is within the Anglican Church of Southern Africa, and is under the jurisdiction of the Archbishop of Cape Town, South Africa.

CHRISTIANITY

The Anglican Communion

Anglicans are adherents of the Anglican Church of Southern Africa (formerly the Church of the Province of Southern Africa). The Metropolitan of the Province is the Archbishop of Cape Town, South Africa. St Helena forms a single diocese.

Bishop of Saint Helena: Rt Rev. JOHN SALT, Bishopsholme, POB 62, Saint Helena, STHL 1ZZ; tel. and fax 4471; e-mail bishop@helanta.sh; diocese f. 1859; has jurisdiction over the islands of Saint Helena and Ascension.

The Roman Catholic Church

The Church is represented in Saint Helena, Ascension and Tristan da Cunha by a Mission, established in August 1986. There were an estimated 100 adherents in the islands at 31 December 2007.

Superior: Rev. Fr MICHAEL MCPARTLAND (also Prefect Apostolic of the Falkland Islands); normally visits Tristan da Cunha once a year and Ascension Island two or three times a year; Rev. Fr MICHAEL DAVID GRIFFITHS, Sacred Heart Church, Jamestown, STHL 1ZZ; tel. and fax 2535.

Other Christian Churches

The Salvation Army, Seventh-day Adventists, Baptists, New Apostolics and Jehovah's Witnesses are active on the island.

BAHÁ'Í FAITH

There is a small Bahá'í community on the island.

The Bahá'í Community of St Helena: Moon Bldg, Napoleon St, Jamestown; tel. 3136; e-mail enquiries@sthelenabahai.org; internet www.sthelenabahai.org; f. 1954; Chair. BASIL GEORGE.

The Press

St Helena Herald: Saint Helena News Media Board, Broadway House, Jamestown, STHL 1ZZ; tel. 2612; fax 2802; e-mail sthelena.herald@cwimail.sh; internet www.news.co.sh; f. 1986; govt-sponsored, independent; weekly; Chief Exec. VERNON QUICKFALL; circ. 1,600.

The St Helena Independent: St Helena Media Productions Ltd, 2nd Floor, Association Hall, Main St, Jamestown, STHL 1ZZ; tel. 2660; e-mail independent@cwimail.sh; internet www.saint.fm; f. 2005; independent; weekly.

Broadcasting and Communications

TELECOMMUNICATIONS

Cable & Wireless (St Helena) PLC: POB 2, Bishops Rooms, Jamestown, STHL 1ZZ; tel. 2155; fax 2206; e-mail webmaster@helanta.sh; internet www.cw.com/sthelena; f. 1899; provides national and international telecommunications.

BROADCASTING

Cable & Wireless PLC: The Moon, Jamestown, STHL 1ZZ; tel. 2200; f. 1995; provides a 3-channel television service 24 hours daily from 5 satellite channels.

Saint FM: Association Hall, Main St, Jamestown, STHL 1ZZ; tel. 2660; e-mail fm@helanta.sh; internet www.saint.fm; f. 2004; independent FM radio station; also broadcasts on Ascension Island, Falkland Islands and Tristan da Cunha; Dir MIKE OLSSON.

Radio St Helena: Saint Helena Information Office, Broadway House, Jamestown, STHL 1ZZ; tel. 4669; fax 4542; e-mail radio.sthelena@cwimail.sh; internet www.sthelena.se/radioproject; independent service; providing broadcasts for 24 hours per day; local programming and relays of British Broadcasting Corporation World Service programmes; Station Man. GARY WALTERS.

Finance

BANK

Bank of Saint Helena: Post Office Bldg, Main St, Jamestown, STHL 1ZZ; tel. 2390; fax 2553; e-mail jamestown@sthelenabank.com; internet www.sainthelenabank.com; f. 2004; replaced the Government Savings Bank; total assets £42,369,292 (31 March 2010); 1 br. on Ascension; Chair. LYN THOMAS; Man. Dir ROSEMARY BARGO.

INSURANCE

Solomon & Co PLC: Jamestown, STHL 1ZZ; tel. 2380; fax 2423; e-mail generalenquiries@solomons.co.sh; internet www.solomons-sthelena.com; Solomon & Co operated an insurance agency on behalf of Royal SunAlliance Insurance Group during 1933–2002, until the latter co withdrew its interest from Saint Helena; negotiations for the foundation of a mutual insurance company on the island commenced in 2004; CEO MANDY PETERS.

Trade and Industry

GOVERNMENT AGENCY

St Helena Development Agency: 2 Main St, POB 117, Jamestown, STHL 1ZZ; tel. 2920; fax 2166; e-mail enquiries@shda.co.sh; internet www.shda.co.sh; f. 1995; Chair. GEORGE STEVENS; Man. Dir LINDA HOUSTON.

CHAMBER OF COMMERCE

St Helena Chamber of Commerce: POB 34, Jamestown, STHL 1ZZ; tel. 2258; fax 2598; e-mail secretary@chamberofcommerce.org.sh; internet www.chamberofcommerce.org.sh; 60 mems; Pres. STUART MOORS; Sec. BRENDA MOORS-CLINGHAM.

CO-OPERATIVE

St Helena Growers' Co-operative Society: Jamestown, STHL 1ZZ; tel. and fax 2511; vegetable marketing; also suppliers of agricultural tools, seeds and animal feeding products; 108 mems (1999); Chair. STEDSON FRANCIS; Sec. PETER W. THORPE.

Transport

There are no railways in Saint Helena.

AIR

The construction of an airport on Saint Helena was first proposed in 2002. Despite an initial commitment to bringing the airport into operation by 2012, in April 2009 the British Department for International Development announced a further consultation on future access to Saint Helena. In December 2009 Douglas Alexander, the British Secretary of State for International Development, announced that as a result of 'current economic conditions' the British Government had decided that it would not be appropriate to proceed with the airport project 'at this time'. However, a further analysis of potential cost savings to the airport contract which might be enabled by recent technological developments, and of options for funding the capital cost of the airport through a public-private partnership, was to be carried out during 2010. In July it was announced that construction of the airport would proceed, although no details of a timescale were immediately made available. A twice weekly Royal Air Force Tristar service between the United Kingdom and the Falkland Islands transits Ascension Island both southbound and northbound. There is a weekly US Air Force military service linking the Patrick Air Force Base in Florida with Ascension Island, via Antigua and Barbuda. There is no airfield on Tristan da Cunha.

ROADS

In 2002 there were 118 km of bitumen-sealed roads, and a further 20 km of earth roads, which can be used by motor vehicles only in dry weather. All roads have steep gradients and sharp bends.

SHIPPING

The St Helena Line Ltd serves Ascension Island with a two-monthly passenger/cargo service between Cardiff, in the United Kingdom, and Cape Town, in South Africa. A vessel under charter to the British Ministry of Defence visits the island monthly on its United Kingdom–Falkland Islands service. A US freighter from Cape Canaveral calls at three-month intervals. The St Helena Line Ltd, the MV *Hanseatic*, and MS *Explorer* and the SA *Agulhas* each visit Tristan da Cunha once each year, and two lobster concession vessels each make three visits annually, remaining for between two and three months. Occasional cruise ships also visit the island.

St Helena Line Ltd: Andrew Weir Shipping, Dexter House, 2 Royal Mint Court, London, EC3N 4XX, United Kingdom; tel. (20) 7265-0808; fax (20) 7481-4784; internet www.aws.co.uk; internet www.rms-st-helena.com; 5-year govt contract renewed in August 2006; service subsidized by the British Govt by £1.5m. annually; operates 2-monthly passenger/cargo services by the RMS *St Helena* to and from the United Kingdom and Cape Town, South Africa, calling at the Canary Islands, Ascension Island and Vigo, Spain, and once a year at Tristan da Cunha; also operates programme of shuttle services between Saint Helena and Ascension Island and the St Helena Liner Shipping Service; Chair. Garry Hopcroft.

Tourism

Although Saint Helena possesses flora and fauna of considerable interest to naturalists, as well as the house (now an important museum) in which the French Emperor Napoleon I spent his final years in exile, the remoteness of the island, which is a two-day sea voyage from Ascension Island, has inhibited the development of tourism. The potential construction of an airport on Saint Helena would greatly increase the island's accessibility to the limited number of visitors that can currently be accommodated. A total of 847 tourists visited Saint Helena in 2009. There are three hotels and a range of self-catering facilities. Small-scale eco-tourism is encouraged on Ascension Island, although accommodation is limited and all visits require written permission from the Administrator. Access is available by twice weekly flights operated from the United Kingdom by the Royal Air Force (see above), and by the RMS *St Helena*. Permission from the Administrator and the Island Council is required for visits to Tristan da Cunha. Facilities for tourism are limited, although some accommodation is available in island homes.

St Helena Tourism: Main St, Jamestown, STHL 1ZZ; tel. 2158; fax 2159; e-mail enquiries@tourism.gov.sh; internet www.sthelenatourism.com; f. 1998; provides general information about the island; Dir Pamela Young.

Education

Education is compulsory and free for all children between the ages of five and 15 years, although power to exempt after the age of 14 can be exercised by the Education Committee. The standard of work at the secondary comprehensive school is orientated towards the requirements of the General Certificate of Secondary Education and the General Certificate of Education Advanced Level of the United Kingdom. During the second half of the 1980s the educational structure was reorganized from a two-tier to a three-tier comprehensive system, for which a new upper-school building was constructed.

There is a free public library in Jamestown, financed by the Government and managed by a committee, and a mobile library service in the country districts.

SOUTH GEORGIA AND THE SOUTH SANDWICH ISLANDS

South Georgia, an island of 3,592 sq km (1,387 sq miles), lies in the South Atlantic Ocean, about 1,300 km (800 miles) east-south-east of the Falkland Islands. The South Sandwich Islands, which have an area of 311 sq km, lie about 750 km south-east of South Georgia.

The United Kingdom annexed South Georgia and the South Sandwich Islands in 1775. With a segment of the Antarctic mainland and other nearby islands (now the British Antarctic Territory), they were constituted as the Falkland Islands Dependencies in 1908. Argentina made formal claim to South Georgia in 1927, and to the South Sandwich Islands in 1948. In 1955 the United Kingdom unilaterally submitted the dispute over sovereignty to the International Court of Justice (based in the Netherlands), which decided not to hear the application in view of Argentina's refusal to submit to the Court's jurisdiction. South Georgia was the site of a British Antarctic Survey base (staffed by 22 scientists and support personnel) until it was invaded in April 1982 by Argentine forces, who occupied the island until its recapture by British forces three weeks later. The South Sandwich Islands were uninhabited until the occupation of Southern Thule in December 1976 by about 50 Argentines, reported to be scientists. Argentine personnel remained until removed by British forces in June 1982.

Under the provisions of the South Georgia and South Sandwich Islands Order of 1985, the islands ceased to be governed as dependencies of the Falkland Islands on 3 October 1985. The Governor of the Falkland Islands is, ex officio, Commissioner for the territory.

In May 1993, in response to the Argentine Government's decision to commence the sale of fishing licences for the region's waters, the British Government announced an extension, from 12 to 200 nautical miles, of its territorial jurisdiction in the waters surrounding the islands, in order to conserve crucial fishing stocks.

In September 1998 the British Government announced that it would withdraw its military detachment from South Georgia in 2000, while it would increase its scientific presence on the island with the installation of a permanent team from the British Antarctic Survey to investigate the fisheries around the island for possible exploitation. The small military detachment finally withdrew in March 2001. The British garrison stationed in the Falkland Islands would remain responsible for the security of South Georgia and the South Sandwich Islands.

Increased volcanic activity on Montagu Island, in the South Sandwich Islands, previously thought to be dormant, had been monitored closely by the British Antarctic Survey since 2001. In late 2005 Mount Belinda erupted, adding some 50 acres to the island's land area in just one month. The island is largely ice-covered and the eruption allowed scientists the rare opportunity to make direct observations of volcanic activity under ice sheets.

Budget revenue for 2009 amounted to £5.4m., while expenditure totalled £4.6m. The main sources of revenue are the sale of fishing licences (£4.1m.), incomes from visitor landing charges (£0.8m.), philatelic and commemorative coin sales, and customs and harbour duties.

At the close of the 2008/09 cruise ship season on 31 March 2009, South Georgia had recorded a total of 70 ship calls and some 7,700 passengers to the island. Greater numbers of visitors to this inhospitable territory—coupled with a growing recognition of the climate change phenomenon—prompted the Government to review its existing biosecurity policy in an effort to prevent the introduction, or translocation, of potentially destructive species of flora and fauna to the island. Furthermore, a major legislative review wasongoing in 2011, as a result of which the Government expected to implement changes to legislation governing tourism and visitor management.

The British Antarctic Survey maintains two research stations on South Georgia, at King Edward Point (eight winter personnel, 12 summer personnel in 2008/09) and Bird Island (four winter personnel, 10 summer personnel in 2008/09). In 2009/10 summer personnel at the two bases and the Signy research station in the South Orkney Islands amounted to 46.

Commissioner: Nigel Robert Haywood (took office on 16 October 2010).

Senior Executive Officer and Director of Fisheries: Dr Martin Collins (Stanley, Falkland Islands).

THE TURKS AND CAICOS ISLANDS

Introductory Survey

LOCATION, CLIMATE, LANGUAGE, RELIGION, FLAG, CAPITAL

The Turks and Caicos Islands consist of more than 30 low-lying islands forming the south-eastern end of the Bahamas chain of islands, and lying about 145 km (90 miles) north of Haiti. Eight islands are inhabited: Grand Turk and Salt Cay (both in the smaller Turks group to the east of the Caicos), South Caicos, Middle (Grand) Caicos, North Caicos, Providenciales (Provo), Pine Cay and Parrot Cay. The climate is warm throughout the year but tempered by constant trade winds. The average annual temperature is 27°C (82°F) and rainfall ranges from 530 mm (21 ins) in the eastern islands to 1,000 mm (40 ins) in the west. The official language is English, though some Creole is spoken by Haitian immigrants. Many Christian churches are represented, the largest denomination being the Baptist Union (36% of the population at the 2001 census). The flag is the British 'Blue Ensign', with the shield from the islands' coat of arms, bearing a shell, a lobster and a cactus, in the fly. The capital is Cockburn Town, on Grand Turk island.

CONTEMPORARY POLITICAL HISTORY

Historical Context

The Turks and Caicos Islands were first settled by Amerindian peoples. The islands were then inhabited by privateers, and were settled from Bermuda and by exiled 'Loyalists' from the former British colonies in North America. A Jamaican dependency from 1874 to 1959, the Turks and Caicos Islands became a separate colony in 1962, following Jamaican independence. After an administrative association with the Bahamas, the islands received their own Governor in 1972. The first elections under the present Constitution took place in 1976, and were won by the pro-independence People's Democratic Movement (PDM).

Domestic Political Affairs

In 1980 an agreement was made with the United Kingdom whereby, if the governing PDM won the 1980 elections, the islands would receive independence and a payment of £12m. However, lacking the leadership of J. A. G. S. McCartney, the Chief Minister (who had been killed in an aircraft accident in May), the PDM lost the election in November to the Progressive National Party (PNP), which is committed to continued dependent status. At a subsequent general election, in May 1984, the PNP, led by the Chief Minister, Norman Saunders, won a further term in office.

In March 1985 the Chief Minister, the Minister for Development and Commerce and a PNP member of the Legislative Council were arrested in Miami, Florida, USA, on charges involving illicit drugs and violations of the US Travel Act. All three men were subsequently convicted and imprisoned. Saunders was replaced as Chief Minister by Nathaniel Francis.

In July 1986 a commission of inquiry into allegations of arson and administrative malpractice concluded that Francis and two of his ministers were unfit for ministerial office; all three ministers resigned. In the same month the Governor dissolved the Government, and the Executive Council was replaced by an interim advisory council, comprising the Governor and four members of the former Executive Council. A constitutional commission was appointed in September to review the future administration of the islands.

A general election, preceding the return to ministerial rule, took place in March 1988, following the British Government's acceptance of the principal recommendations of the constitutional commission in the previous year. Under a new multi-member system of representation, the PDM won a majority of seats on the Legislative Council. Oswald O. Skippings, the leader of the PDM, was appointed Chief Minister. The new Constitution strengthened the reserve powers of the Governor, but otherwise the form of government was similar to the provisions of the 1976 Constitution.

In April 1991 a general election took place, at which the PNP defeated the PDM. Skippings was replaced as Chief Minister by C. Washington Misick, the leader of the PNP. However, the PDM was returned to office at a general election in January 1995. Derek Taylor, leader of the PDM, was appointed Chief Minister. The PDM increased its representation in the Legislative Council at a general election in March 1999.

A serious dispute arose between the Legislative Council and the Governor in August 1995, following the latter's decision to reappoint Kipling Douglas to the position of Chief Justice. Taylor, who claimed that Douglas did not enjoy the confidence of his Government, described the decision as provocative and disrespectful. Relations deteriorated in subsequent months, and in February 1996 a petition requesting the immediate removal of the Governor, signed by all members of the Government and opposition, was presented to the British Foreign and Commonwealth Office (FCO). The petition was rejected by the British Government, which deployed a frigate in the islands' waters and ordered 100 police officers to prepare for immediate transfer to the territory in the event of civil disturbance.

Constitutional reform

In April 2002 the Governor established a Constitutional Modernisation Review Body to discuss changes to the islands' Constitution. This all-party panel presented a report in September. Discussions on a new constitution took place in 2004 between representatives of the Turks and Caicos Islands and British Governments. Following further negotiations between government ministers in October 2005, it was agreed that a draft text of a modernized constitution would be drawn up by the FCO. This proposed document would be subject to approval by both the PDM and the PNP, after which a public consultation period would be held. Adoption of the amendments would be subject to approval by the Legislative Council.

In May 2002 the British Overseas Territories Act, having received royal assent in the United Kingdom in February, came into force and granted British citizenship rights to the people of its Overseas Territories, including the Turks and Caicos Islands. Under the new law, Turks and Caicos Islanders would be able to hold British passports and work in the United Kingdom and anywhere else in the European Union.

At a general election in April 2003 the PDM won seven of the 13 seats in the Legislative Council. The PNP took the remaining six seats, but challenged the results in two constituencies. By-elections were held in the two constituencies in August after evidence emerged of bribery and irregularities in voter registration lists; the PNP secured victory in both ballots and therefore wrested overall control of the Legislative Council from the PDM. Misick replaced Taylor as Chief Minister.

In spite of ongoing discussions regarding a new constitution, in April 2006 the Chief Minister met with members of the UN's Special Committee on Decolonization to discuss options for self-determination. The opposition questioned Misick's motives behind the talks. Misick subsequently issued a statement indicating that the PNP would not pursue independence during the constitutional discussions, nor would the matter feature as an objective of their electoral campaign ahead of the general election, scheduled for February 2007. A public consultation was conducted over a draft constitution, formulated pursuant to an agreement upon greater self-government for the territory, between United Kingdom and island representatives in October 2005, and approved by the Legislative Council on 28 June 2006. Following final submission to the FCO and endorsement by Queen Elizabeth II, the Council decreed the Turks and Caicos Constitutional Order 2006, adopting the new Constitution on 19 July. The Constitution was finally enacted on 9 August, when Chief Minister Misick and Deputy Chief Minister Floyd Hall were inaugurated as Premier and Deputy Premier, respectively. Former Chief Secretary Mahala Wynns was appointed to the new post of Deputy Governor; the assignment complied with a new constitutional requirement that the position be occupied by a 'belonger' of the Turks and Caicos Islands. Notable amendments under the new Constitution included the investiture of a unicameral parliament, which would replace and enlarge upon the former Legislative Council, and the inauguration of a Cabinet to replace the Executive Council. In accordance with a provision within the new Constitution, legislation affording the creation of two new constituencies on the island of Providenciales was ratified by the House of Assembly in January 2007.

A general election was held on 9 February 2007. The PNP was returned to office for a second term. Misick was reappointed Premier. The ballot followed a bitterly fought election campaign, in which the PDM made allegations of corruption against the ruling party.

In December 2008 Misick avoided a debate on a motion of no confidence submitted by the PDM as a result of a dispute over parliamentary procedure. Parliament was subsequently prorogued by the Governor, Gordon Wetherell, to be reconvened in April 2009. Later in December nine members of the ruling PNP, drafted a letter to Governor Wetherell requesting that Misick resign, citing a loss of confidence from legislators.

Deputy Premier Floyd Hall resigned on 13 February 2009, citing the legislative stalemate caused by the ongoing suspension of Parliament. Galmo Williams, the Minister for Home Affairs, had resigned the previous day. Misick announced that he would resign as Premier by the end of March, and that he would not be seeking re-election as leader of the PNP. Misick stood down on 23 March, at which point Williams was sworn in as Premier. Williams promptly announced the formation of a new Cabinet.

Recent developments: direct rule

The United Kingdom's House of Commons Foreign Affairs Committee (FAC) published a report in July 2008 regarding the adminis-

UNITED KINGDOM OVERSEAS TERRITORIES

tration of its Overseas Territories, in which it detailed claims of corruption and intimidation made by residents of the Turks and Caicos Islands. The Committee had received evidence from some 50 individuals, much of which had been submitted anonymously. The allegations of corruption referred to the sale of Crown land for unsustainable developments or for the personal gain of government members; nepotism in the distribution of development contracts and irregularities in the purchase of property for government use; the granting of 'belonger' status to individuals who were ineligible under the current law; and the misuse of public funds. The report criticized the Governor, who had failed to investigate the allegations of corrupt practice. Premier Misick denied the allegations and drew attention to anti-corruption legislation that had been introduced by his Government. However, a Commission of Inquiry into the allegations was established later that month. Applications made by some members of the legislature to limit the Commission's terms of reference were refused by the Supreme Court. In late February 2009 Sir Robin Auld issued the Commission of Inquiry's interim report, which referred to a 'high probability of systemic corruption and serious dishonesty', 'political amorality and general incompetence' and contained 24 recommendations, including the partial or full suspension of the Constitution and direct rule of the islands by the United Kingdom, acting through the Governor, with the advice of an Advisory Council. The report also recommended that criminal investigations should be instigated against Misick and four of his former cabinet ministers. Implementation of the report's recommendations were delayed owing to a legal challenge. By mid-August, however, this challenge had failed and on 14 August the British Government announced the imposition of direct rule from the United Kingdom, the partial suspension of the Constitution and the removal of the Premier and Cabinet. The House of Assembly was also suspended. The FCO announced its intention to hold elections in the territory no later than July 2011 and stated that its aim was to establish a lasting basis for good governance, sound financial management and sustainable development.

The Advisory Council immediately instituted a Stabilization Plan to reduce expenditure and increase revenue, as well as to lower the debt. At the end of August 2009 a Special Prosecutor was also appointed to look into possible criminal charges against the former PNP Government arising from the Commission of Inquiry's report. Former Premier Williams denounced the imposition of direct rule as a *coup d'état*. In early 2010 the FCO's Director of Overseas Territories indicated that following the elections in 2011, British government representatives would maintain an increased presence in the territory to ensure continuing good governance. The announcement called into question the plan to end direct rule following the ballot. A protest against British rule, held in March 2010 and supported by the PNP and the PDM, demonstrated the resentment harboured by some sections of the population.

The British Government announced in September 2010 that the 2011 elections would be postponed, citing a lack of progress on both the territory's reform programme and the investigation into alleged government corruption. Leaders of the PNP and the PDM, as well as the Caribbean Community and Common Market (CARICOM, see p. 219), expressed their opposition to the postponement of the ballot, and demonstrations were held during that month in protest against the delay. Further small-scale protest action, organized and funded by the PNP according to local media reports, was conducted in March 2011, and Providenciales airport was temporarily blockaded by demonstrators. It was expected that new elections would be held in 2012, although this was contingent upon eight 'milestones' being reached, including constitutional, governmental, electoral and financial reform, a return to fiscal stability, and progress in the investigation into alleged government corruption.

A process of constitutional reform was initiated by the British Government in early 2010. A contingent of constitutional experts was sent to the territory, and public consultations on the content of a revised constitution were held. Among the most important proposals for inclusion in the new charter were a reduction in the number of cabinet ministers, the withdrawal of trial by jury in certain circumstances, the abrogation of the Advisory National Security Council and a stipulation that a budget surplus must be maintained. It was also recommended that the four nominated seats in the House of Assembly be abolished. The final draft of the new constitution was expected to be released during 2011.

Further details regarding the alleged corruption perpetrated by the previous PNP administration emerged throughout 2010. Documents recovered from the Land Registry Department indicated that large plots of Crown land had been sold at vastly reduced rates to certain individuals, allegedly favoured PNP associates, who then rapidly divested them to foreign companies for an enormous profit. It was also revealed that Clayton Greene, the leader of the PNP, had provided legal services for one of the foreign firms involved in the scandal while serving as Speaker of the House of Assembly. Investigations were ongoing in early 2011, and reform of the land sale system (one of the eight 'milestones') was also under way.

The Turks and Caicos Islands

CONSTITUTION AND GOVERNMENT

The revised Constitution of 2006 (suspended since August 2009) provides for a Cabinet and a unicameral House of Assembly. Executive authority is vested in the British monarch and is exercised by the Governor (the monarch's appointed representative). The Governor is responsible for external affairs, internal security, defence, international financial services and the appointment of public officers; other matters are resolved by the Governor upon the advice of the Cabinet. The Governor is President of the Cabinet, which comprises nine members: one ex officio (the Attorney-General); the Premier; and six appointed by the Governor from among the elected members of the House of Assembly. The House of Assembly comprises 21 members: the Speaker; four nominated members; the ex officio member of the Cabinet and 15 members elected by universal adult suffrage.

REGIONAL AND INTERNATIONAL CO-OPERATION

The Turks and Caicos Islands are a member of the Caribbean Development Bank (see p. 224) and an associate member of the Caribbean Community and Common Market (CARICOM, see p. 219). The territory became an associate member of the Association of Caribbean States (see p. 445) in April 2006. The Turks and Caicos Islands are a member of the Commonwealth (see p. 230). As a dependency of the United Kingdom, the Turks and Caicos have the status of Overseas Territory in association with the European Union (EU, see p. 270).

ECONOMIC AFFAIRS

In 2009, according to UN estimates, the Turks and Caicos Islands' gross national income (GNI) was US $1,271m., equivalent to $35,422 per head. In 2007, according to official preliminary estimates, gross domestic product (GDP) was US $829m., equivalent to some $23,768 per head. During 2000–09, it was estimated, the population increased at an average annual rate of 8.5%. GDP increased, in real terms, by an annual average of 9.2% in 2000–07; growth was estimated at 11.3% in 2007.

Agriculture is not practised on any significant scale in the Turks Islands or on South Caicos (the most populous island of the territory). None the less, the sector (including fishing) contributed 1.0% to GDP in 2007, according to preliminary estimates, and engaged 1.2% of the employed labour force in that year. The other islands of the Caicos group grow some beans, maize and a few fruits and vegetables. There is some livestock-rearing, but the islands' principal natural resource is fisheries, which accounts for almost all commodity exports, the principal species caught being the spiny lobster (an estimated 380 metric tons in 2008) and the conch (an estimated 5,693 tons in that year). Conchs were being developed commercially (on the largest conch farm in the world), and there was potential for larger-scale fishing. Exports of lobster and conch earned US $4.2m. in 2008, accounting for 17.1% of total export earnings in that year. The sector's GDP increased, in real terms, by an annual average rate of 3.1% during 2000–07; the sector's GDP increased by 3.3% in 2007, according to preliminary estimates.

Industrial activity consists mainly of construction (especially for the tourism industry) and fish-processing. Industry contributed 22.9% to GDP in 2007, according to preliminary figures, and the sector engaged some 24.8% of the employed labour force in that year. The sector's GDP increased, in real terms, by an annual average rate of 13.1% during 2000–07; the sector's GDP increased by 14.8% in 2007, according to preliminary estimates.

Mining contributed some 1.3% of GDP in 2007, according to preliminary estimates, and the sector engaged 0.1% of the employed labour force in that year. The islands possess plentiful supplies of aragonite, but mineral fuels are imported (accounting for some 12.1% of the value of total imports in 2008) to satisfy energy requirements. The sector's GDP increased, in real terms, by an annual average rate of 17.6% during 2000–07; the sector's GDP increased by 19.9% in 2007, according to preliminary estimates.

Manufacturing contributed some 1.7% of GDP in 2007, according to preliminary estimates, and the sector engaged 1.3% of the employed labour force in that year. The sector's GDP decreased, in real terms, by an annual average rate of 0.8% during 2000–07; however, the sector's GDP increased by 5.8% in 2007, according to preliminary estimates.

Construction contributed some 16.4% of GDP in 2007, according to preliminary estimates, and the sector engaged 22.5% of the employed labour force in that year. The sector's GDP increased, in real terms, by an annual average rate of 17.6% during 2000–07; the sector's GDP increased by 19.9% in 2007, according to preliminary estimates.

The principal economic sector is the services industry, which in 2007 contributed an estimated 76.2% to GDP and engaged 73.9% of the employed labour force. The sector is dominated by tourism, which is concentrated on the island of Providenciales. The market is for wealthier visitors, mostly from the USA. Tourist arrivals increased from approximately 117,600 in 1999 to 264,887 in 2007, while tourism receipts were estimated at US $355.1m. in 2005. A new

UNITED KINGDOM OVERSEAS TERRITORIES

$40m. cruise ship terminal, capable of receiving large passenger liners, was inaugurated in February 2006. In 2007 nearly 380,000 cruise ship passengers visited the islands, compared with just 17,052 in 2004. The 'offshore' financial sector grew in the last two decades of the 20th century. In 2008 there were some 15,000 overseas companies registered in the islands. The sector's GDP increased, in real terms, by an annual average rate of 9.0% during 2000–07; the sector's GDP increased by 10.3% in 2007, according to preliminary estimates.

In 2008 the Turks and Caicos Islands recorded a trade deficit (including re-exports) of US $566.5m., and in 2007 the deficit was equivalent to 68.1% of GDP. This deficit is normally offset by receipts from tourism, aid from the United Kingdom and revenue from the 'offshore' financial sector. The USA is the principal trading partner (providing 99.3% of imports and receiving 99.9% of exports, in 2008), but some trade is conducted with the United Kingdom, Japan, and with neighbouring nations.

There was an overall budget deficit of US $33.4m. in 2007/08, and the deficit on the current account in 2006/07 was estimated to be equivalent to 3.5% of GDP in 2007. The total external public debt was $40.4m. in 2005. The rate of inflation, which stood at about 3.7% in 2007, is dependent upon the movement of prices in the USA, the islands' principal trading partner. The unemployment rate was recorded at some 5.4% in 2007. A large number of Turks and Caicos 'belongers' have emigrated, many to the Bahamas, especially in search of skilled labour. In July 2000 the Caribbean Development Bank (see p. 224) announced a loan to the Government of some $4m. to assist the Turks and Caicos Investment Agency.

The perceived stability of the Turks and Caicos Islands as an United Kingdom Overseas Territory was called into question following the suspension of the Constitution and imposition of direct rule from the United Kingdom in August 2009 following the discovery of systematic corruption in many levels of government. The Advisory Council that replaced the Cabinet set out debt reduction and revenue increase as its main economic priorities. The 'offshore' financial sector successfully rehabilitated its international reputation through the introduction, in 2002, of a supervisory body and the implementation of more stringent regulatory legislation. Although in 2009 the territory was included in the Organisation for Economic Co-operation and Development's (OECD, see p. 376) so-called 'grey list' of jurisdictions that had yet substantially to improve transparency in the financial sector, the islands secured their removal from the list 10 months later, after they concluded international tax information sharing agreements with 12 other nations. Despite a recovery in the tourism industry, the Ministry of Finance announced that real GDP (at market prices) had contracted by 11.1% in 2009, following several years of rapid expansion. The increase in visitor numbers continued during 2010, although the construction sector declined dramatically in that year and renewed growth in the economy was not expected in the short term. The large fiscal deficit and unsustainable debt burden were the main economic problems confronting the authorities in early 2011. However, a large proportion of the territory's debt was rescheduled in February, after the British Government agreed to act as guarantor on a low-interest US $260m. loan. Plans were also under way to lower the budget deficit—by rationalizing the civil service, reducing public sector salaries and reforming the tax system. Notably, the implementation of a value-added tax was expected by 2013/14. Economic growth in the islands—driven more by inward investment than by domestic production—remained highly dependent on external factors, and it remained to be seen if the imposition of direct rule from the United Kingdom, and the concomitant economic reform, would deter or encourage potential investors.

PUBLIC HOLIDAYS

2012: 1 January (New Year's Day), 12 March (for Commonwealth Day), 6 April (Good Friday), 9 April (Easter Monday), 28 May (National Heroes' Day), 9 June (Queen's Official Birthday), 1 August (Emancipation Day), 28 September (National Youth Day), 10 October (Columbus Day), 24 October (International Human Rights Day), 25–27 December (Christmas).

Statistical Survey

Source: Department of Economic Planning and Statistics, Ministry of Finance, South Base, Grand Turk; tel. 946-2801; fax 946-2557; e-mail info@depstc.org; internet www.depstc.org.

AREA AND POPULATION

Area: 948 sq km (366 sq miles). Note: Area includes low water level for all islands, but excludes area to high water mark.

Population: 7,413 at census of 12 May 1980; 11,465 at census of 31 May 1990; 19,886 (males 9,897, females 9,989) at census of 20 August 2001; *2011* (estimate): 42,375. *By Island* (2006, estimates): Grand Turk 5,718; South Caicos 1,118; Middle Caicos 307; North Caicos 1,537; Salt Cay 114; Parrot Cay 60; Providenciales 24,348.

Density (2011 estimate): 44.7 per sq km.

Population by Age and Sex (at 2001 census): *0–14:* 5,693 (males 2,736, females 2,957); *15–64:* 13,436 (males 6,826, females 6,610); *65 and over:* 758 (males 335, females 423); *Total* 19,886 (males 9,897, females 9,989) (Source: UN, *Demographic Yearbook*).

Principal Towns: Cockburn Town (capital, on Grand Turk), population 2,500 (1987 estimate); Cockburn Harbour (South Caicos), population 1,000. *Mid-2009* (UN estimate, incl. suburbs): Grand Turk 6,195 (Source: UN, *World Urbanization Prospects: The 2009 Revision*).

Births, Marriages and Deaths (2008): Live births 453 (birth rate 12.4 per 1,000); Marriages 486; Deaths 65 (death rate 1.8 per 1,000). *2010:* Crude birth rate 20.4; Crude death rate 4.2 (Source: Pan American Health Organization).

Life Expectancy (years at birth, 2010): 75.6 (males 73.3; females 78.1). Source: Pan American Health Organization.

Economically Active Population (2007, preliminary): Agriculture and fishing 237; Mining and quarrying 16; Manufacturing 246; Utilities 192; Construction 4,306; Wholesale and retail trade 1,729; Hotels and restaurants 4,065; Transport, storage and communications 846; Financial intermediation 515; Real estate, renting and business services 2,384; Public administration 2,298; Education, health and social work 771; Other community, social and personal services 1,190; Private household employment 376; *Sub-total* 19,171; Activities not adequately defined 416; *Total employed* 19,587; Unemployed 1,124; *Total labour force* 20,711.

HEALTH AND WELFARE

Total Fertility Rate (children per woman, 2010): 2.9.

Under-5 Mortality Rate (per 1,000 live births, 1997): 22.0.

Hospital Beds (per 1,000 head, 2008): 1.4.

Physicians (per 1,000 head, 2001): 7.3.

Health Expenditure (public, % of total, 2004): 12.6.

Health Expenditure (US $ per head, 2004): 741.2.

Access to Water (% of persons, 2008): 98.

Access to Sanitation (% of persons, 2004): 96.

Source: partly Pan American Health Organization.

For other sources and definitions see explanatory note on p. vi.

AGRICULTURE, ETC.

Fishing (metric tons, live weight, 2008): Capture 6,133 (Caribbean spiny lobster 380; Stromboid conchs 5,693); Aquaculture 0; *Total catch* 6,133.

Source: FAO.

INDUSTRY

Electric Energy (production, million kWh): 132 in 2005; 158 in 2006; 182 in 2007. Source: UN Industrial Commodity Statistics Database.

FINANCE

Currency and Exchange Rate: United States currency is used: 100 cents = 1 US dollar ($). *Sterling and Euro Equivalents* (31 December 2010): £1 sterling = US $1.565; €1 = US $1.336; $100 = £63.88 = €74.84.

Budget (US $ million, 2007/08): Total revenue and grants 280.31 (Current revenue 206.79, Capital revenue and grants 73.52); Total expenditure 313.73 (Current expenditure 235.85, Capital expenditure 77.89).

Gross Domestic Product (US $ million at constant 2000 prices): 481.9 in 2005; 568.1 in 2006; 632.0 in 2007 (preliminary).

Expenditure on the Gross Domestic Product (US $ million, 2007, preliminary): Government final consumption expenditure 143.0; Private final consumption expenditure 458.3; Gross capital formation 392.6; *Total domestic expenditure* 993.9; Exports of goods and services 522.6; *Less* Imports of goods and services 687.9; *GDP in market prices* 828.6.

Gross Domestic Product by Economic Activity (US $ million, 2007, preliminary): Agriculture and fishing 7.5; Mining and quarrying 10.0; Manufacturing 13.4; Utilities 26.4; Construction 125.5; Wholesale and retail trade 31.4; Hotels and restaurants 222.1;

UNITED KINGDOM OVERSEAS TERRITORIES

Transport, storage and communications 61.4; Financial intermediation 88.2; Real estate, renting and business activities 59.7; Public administration, defence and social security 61.8; Education 22.0; Health and social work 18.1; Other community, social and personal services 19.4; *Sub-total* 766.9; *Less* Financial intermediation services indirectly measured 59.3; *Gross value added in basic prices* 707.6; Taxes, *less* subsidies, on products 121.0; *GDP in market prices* 828.6.

Balance of Payments (US $ million, 2002): Exports of goods f.o.b. 8.7; Imports of goods f.o.b. −177.5; *Trade balance* −168.8; Exports of services 163.1; Imports of services −81.8; *Balance on goods and services* −87.5. Source: Caribbean Development Bank, *Social and Economic Indicators*.

EXTERNAL TRADE

Principal Commodities (US $ million, 2008, provisional): *Imports:* Food and live animals 63.3; Beverages and tobacco 17.7; Crude materials (inedible) except fuels 18.0; Mineral fuels, lubricants, etc. 71.6 (Petroleum and petroleum products 69.6); Chemicals and related products 37.5; Basic manufactures 126.1; Machinery and transport equipment 145.2 (Road vehicles 39.4); Miscellaneous manufactured articles 110.1; Total (incl. others) 591.3. *Exports:* Food and live animals 4.6 (Conchs 3.1; Lobsters 1.1); Machinery and transport equipment 16.8; Total exports 24.5. Note: Figures for exports exclude re-exports valued at 0.3.

Principal Trading Partners (US $ million, 2008, provisional): *Imports c.i.f.:* Bahamas 3.2; USA 587.3; Total (incl. others) 591.3. *Exports f.o.b.:* USA 24.5; Total (incl. others) 24.5. Note: Figures for exports exclude re-exports valued at 0.3.

TRANSPORT

Road Traffic (1984): 1,563 registered motor vehicles.

Shipping: *International Freight Traffic* (estimates in '000 metric tons, 1990): Goods loaded 135; Goods unloaded 149. *Merchant Fleet* (vessels registered at 31 December 2009): 7; Total displacement 1,386 grt. Sources: UN, *Monthly Bulletin of Statistics*; IHS Fairplay, *World Fleet Statistics*.

TOURISM

Tourist Arrivals ('000): 176.1 (of which USA 123.3) in 2005; 248.3 (of which USA 169.7) in 2006; 264.9 in 2007.

Tourism Receipts (US $ million, estimates): 275.6 in 2003; 317.9 in 2004; 355.1 in 2005.

Source: Caribbean Development Bank, *Social and Economic Indicators*.

COMMUNICATIONS MEDIA

Radio Receivers (1997): 8,000 in use.

Telephones (2009): 3,700 main lines in use.

Mobile Cellular Telephones (2008): 25,100 subscribers.

Non-daily Newspapers (1996): 1 (estimated circulation 5,000).

Internet Subscribers (2008): 3,000.

Sources: UNESCO, *Statistical Yearbook*; UN, *Statistical Yearbook*; International Telecommunication Union.

EDUCATION

Pre-primary (2005/06, unless otherwise indicated): 9 schools; 87 teachers (2004/05, estimate); 335 pupils.

Primary (2005/06): 14 schools; 126 teachers (state schools only); 2,353 pupils.

General Secondary (2005/06): 8 schools; 135 teachers (state schools only); 1,539 pupils. Note: In addition, 6 further private schools offered both primary and secondary education to 674 pupils in 2005/06.

Tertiary Education (2005/06): 2 schools; 257 pupils.

Special Education (2005/06): 2 schools; 99 pupils.

Pupil-teacher Ratio (primary education, UNESCO estimate): 15.0 in 2004/05. Source: UNESCO Institute for Statistics.

Adult Literacy Rate (UNESCO estimates): 99% (males 99%; females 98%) in 1998.

Sources: partly UNESCO Institute for Statistics; Caribbean Development Bank, *Social and Economic Indicators*.

The Turks and Caicos Islands

Directory

The Government

HEAD OF STATE

Queen: HM Queen ELIZABETH II.
Governor: GORDON WETHERELL (sworn in 5 August 2008).
Deputy Governor: (vacant).
Chief Executive: MARK CAPES.

ADVISORY COUNCIL

On 14 August 2009 the Government of the United Kingdom announced the imposition of direct rule on the Turks and Caicos Islands. This followed publication of the findings of a commission of inquiry charged with investigating allegations of widespread and systemic corruption and mismanagement in the governance of the territory. The islands were henceforth to be governed by the United Kingdom acting through the Governor and assisted by an Advisory Council.

Members: JOSEPH CONNOLLY, EDITH COX, THEOPHILUS DURHAM, EUGENE OTUONYE, DOREEN QUELCH-MISSICK, JOHN SMITH.

Ex officio Members: Gov. GORDON WETHERELL, MARK CAPES (Chief Executive), HUW SHEPHEARD (Attorney-General), DELTON JONES (Permanent Sec. of Finance), CAROLINE GARDNER (Chief Financial Officer).

GOVERNMENT OFFICES

Office of the Governor: Govt House, Waterloo, Grand Turk; tel. 946-2308; fax 946-2903; e-mail govhouse@tciway.tc.

Office of the Premier: Govt Sq., Grand Turk; tel. 946-2801; fax 946-2777.

Office of the Deputy Governor: South Base, Grand Turk; tel. 946-2702; fax 946-2886; e-mail cso@gov.tc.

Office of the Permanent Secretary: South Base, Grand Turk; tel. 946-2801; fax 946-2557; e-mail DJones@gov.tc.

Attorney-General's Chambers: South Base, Grand Turk; tel. 946-2096; fax 946-2588; e-mail attorneygeneral@tciway.tc; internet www.lawsconsolidated.tc.

HOUSE OF ASSEMBLY

Following the imposition of direct rule on the Turks and Caicos Islands in August 2009 (see above), the House of Assembly was suspended and plans were announced for the holding of fresh elections no later than July 2011, although this was later postponed.

Speaker: (vacant).
Clerk to the Councils: RUTH BLACKMAN.

Election, 9 February 2007

Party	Seats
Progressive National Party (PNP)	13
People's Democratic Movement (PDM)	2
Total	**15**

There is one ex officio member (the Attorney-General), four appointed members, and a Speaker (assisted by a Deputy Speaker).

Political Organizations

People's Democratic Movement (PDM): POB 309, Providenciales; tel. 231-6898; internet www.votepdm.com; f. 1975; favours internal self-govt and eventual independence; Chair. SHARLENE ROBINSON; Leader DOUGLAS PARNELL; Sec.-Gen. WILBUR CALEY.

Progressive National Party (PNP): Progress House, Airport Rd, Providenciales; tel. 941-8267; fax 946-8206; e-mail pnptci@gmail.com; internet www.mypnp.tc; supports full internal self-govt; Chair. DONHUE GARDINER; Leader CLAYTON GREENE.

United Democratic Party (UDP): Grand Turk; f. 1993; Leader WENDAL SWANN.

Judicial System

Justice is administered by the Supreme Court of the islands, presided over by the Chief Justice. There is a Chief Magistrate resident on Grand Turk, who also acts as Judge of the Supreme Court. There are also three Deputy Magistrates.

UNITED KINGDOM OVERSEAS TERRITORIES

The Turks and Caicos Islands

The Court of Appeal held its first sitting in February 1995. Previously the islands had shared a court of appeal in Nassau, Bahamas. In certain cases, appeals are made to the Judicial Committee of the Privy Council (based in the United Kingdom).

Judicial Department

Grand Turk; tel. 946-2114; fax 946-2720.
Chief Justice: GORDON WARD.
Supreme Court Judge: (Providenciales) RICHARD WILLIAMS.
Chief Magistrate: (Providenciales) JOAN JOYNER.

Religion

CHRISTIANITY

The Anglican Communion

Within the Church in the Province of the West Indies, the territory forms part of the diocese of Nassau and the Bahamas. The Bishop is resident in Nassau. According to the latest census (2001), around 10% of the population are Anglicans.

Anglican Church: St Mary's Church, Front St, Grand Turk; tel. 946-2289; internet bahamas.anglican.org; Archbishop Rev. LAISH Z. BOYD.

The Roman Catholic Church

The Bishop of Nassau, Bahamas (suffragan to the archdiocese of Kingston in Jamaica), has jurisdiction in the Turks and Caicos Islands as Superior of the Mission to the Territory (founded in June 1984). According to the 2001 census, around 11% of the population are Roman Catholics.

Roman Catholic Mission: Leeward Hwy, POB 340, Providenciales; tel. and fax 941-5136; e-mail info_rcm@catholic.tc; internet www.catholic.tc; churches on Grand Turk, South and North Caicos, and on Providenciales; 132 adherents in 1990 (according to census results); Chancellor Fr PETER BALDACCHINO.

Other Christian Churches

According to the 2001 census, some 36% of the population are Baptists, 12% belong to the Church of God, 9% are Methodists, 6% are Seventh-day Adventists and 2% are Jehovah's Witnesses.

Baptist Union of the Turks and Caicos Islands: South Caicos; tel. 946-3220; Gen. Sec. Rev. GOLDSTONE WILLIAMS.

Jehovah's Witnesses: Kingdom Hall, Intersection of Turtle Cove and Bridge Rd, POB 400, Providenciales; tel. 941-5583; e-mail englishprovo@yahoo.com.

Methodist Church: The Ridge, Grand Turk; tel. 946-2115.

New Testament Church of God: POB N-1708, Orea Alley, Grand Turk; tel. 324-2582; fax 324-7891; e-mail info@churchofgodbtci.org; internet www.churchofgodbtci.org.

Seventh-day Adventists: Grand Turk; tel. 946-2065; Pastor PETER KERR.

The Press

Times of the Islands Magazine: Lucille Lightbourne Bldg 7, POB 234, Providenciales; tel. and fax 946-4788; e-mail timespub@tciway.tc; internet www.timespub.tc; f. 1988; quarterly; circ. 10,000; Man. Editor KATHY BORSUK.

Turks and Caicos Free Press: Market Pl., POB 179, Providenciales; tel. 332-5615; fax 941-3402; e-mail freepress@tciway.tc; internet tcfreepress.com; f. 1991; publ. by Vox-Global Télématique; weekly; circ. 3,000; Editor Dr GILBERT MORRIS; Man. BARBARA SMITH.

Turks & Caicos Islands Real Estate Association Real Estate Magazine: Southwind Plaza, POB 234, Providenciales; tel. and fax 946-4788; e-mail timespub@tciway.tc; internet www.tcrea.com; publ. by Times Publ. Ltd; 3 a year; circ. 15,000; Man. Editor KATHY BORSUK.

Turks and Caicos Sun: Airport Plaza, Suite 5, POB 439, Providenciales; tel. 946-8542; fax 941-3281; e-mail turksandcaicossun@express.tc; internet www.suntci.com; f. 2005; publ. by Island Publishing Co Ltd; weekly; Publr and Editor-in-Chief HAYDEN BOYCE.

Turks and Caicos Weekly News: Leeward Hwy, Cheshire House, POB 52, Providenciales; tel. 946-4664; fax 946-4661; e-mail tcnews@tciway.tc; internet www.tcweeklynews.com; f. 1982; Editor W. BLYTHE DUNCANSON.

Where, When, How: Ad Vantage Ltd, J105 Regent Village, Grace Bay, Providenciales; tel. 946-4815; fax 941-3497; e-mail info@wwhtci.com; internet www.wherewhenhow.com; f. 1994; 5 a year; travel magazine; Co-Editor CHARLES ZDENEK; Co-Editor BRENDA ZDENEK; circ. 70,000 a year.

Broadcasting and Communications

TELECOMMUNICATIONS

Telecommunication Commission: Business Solutions Bldg, Leeward Hwy, Providenciales; tel. 946-1900; fax 946-1119; e-mail sales@tcitelecom.com; internet www.tcitelecom.com; f. 2004; regulates telecommunications; Telecommunications Officer JOHN WILLIAMS.

Digicel: Graceway House, Unit 207, Leeward Hwy, Providenciales; tel. 941-7600; fax 941-7601; e-mail tcicustomercare@digicelgroup.com; internet www.digiceltci.com; owned by an Irish consortium; granted licence in 2006 to provide mobile telecommunications services in Turks and Caicos; Chair. DENIS O'BRIEN; Country Man. KEVIN WHITE.

LIME: Cable & Wireless (TCI) Ltd, Leeward Hwy, POB 78, Providenciales; tel. 946-2200; fax 941-3051; e-mail cwtci@tciway.tc; internet www.time4lime.com; f. 1973; monopoly ended in Jan. 2006; fmrly Cable & Wireless; name changed as above 2008; CEO DAVID SHAW; Exec. Vice-Pres. (Turks and Caicos Islands) JOEL ABDINOOR.

Radio

Power 92.5 FM: Providenciales; tel. 628-9391; e-mail kenny@power925fm.com; internet www.power925fm.com.

Radio Providenciales: Leeward Hwy, POB 32, Providenciales; tel. 946-4496; fax 946-4108; commercial.

Radio Turks and Caicos (RTC): POB 69, Grand Turk; tel. 946-2010; fax 946-1600; e-mail rtcdirector@rtc107fm.com; internet www.rtc107fm.com; govt-owned; commercial; broadcasts 105 hrs weekly; Asst Dir LYNETTE THOMAS.

Radio Visión Cristiana Internacional: North End, South Caicos; tel. 946-6601; fax 946-6600; e-mail radiovision@tciway.tc; internet www.radiovision.net; commercial; Man. WENDELL SEYMOUR.

Television

Television programmes are available from a cable network, and broadcasts from the Bahamas can be received in the islands.

TCI New Media Network: Leeward Hwy, Providenciales; e-mail news@tcinewmedianetwork.tc; internet tcinewmedianetwork.tc; f. 2008; govt-owned; Gen. Man. AVA-DAYNE KERR.

Turks and Caicos Television: Pond St, POB 80, Grand Turk; tel. 946-1530; fax 946-2896.

WIV Cable TV: Tower Raza, Leeward Hwy, POB 679, Providenciales; tel. 946-4273; fax 946-4790; Chair. ROBERT BLANCHARD.

Finance

(cap. = capital; res = reserves; dep. = deposits; br(s). = branch(es); amounts in US $ unless otherwise indicated)

REGULATORY AUTHORITY

Financial Services Commission (FSC): Harry E. Francis Bldg, Pond St, POB 173, Grand Turk; tel. 946-2791; fax 946-2821; e-mail fsc@tciway.tc; f. 2002; regulates local and 'offshore' financial services sector; Man. Dir NEVILLE CADOGAN.

BANKING

Bordier International Bank and Trust Ltd: Caribbean Pl., Leeward Hwy, POB 5, Providenciales; tel. 946-4535; fax 946-4540; e-mail enquiries@bibt.com; internet www.bibt.com; Chair. FRANÇOIS BOHN; Man. ELISE HARTSHORN.

British Caribbean Bank: Governors Rd, POB 270, Providenciales; tel. 941-5028; fax 941-5029; e-mail info@bcbtci.com; internet www.bcbtci.com; fmrly Belize Bank, Turks & Caicos; Man. Dir ANDREW ASHCROFT.

FirstCaribbean International Bank (Bahamas) Ltd: Leeward Hwy, POB 698, Providenciales; tel. 946-2831; fax 946-2695; e-mail care@firstcaribbeanbank.com; internet www.firstcaribbeanbank.com; f. 2002 following merger of Caribbean operations of Barclays Bank PLC and CIBC; Barclays relinquished its stake to CIBC in June 2006; Exec. Chair. MICHAEL MANSOOR; CEO JOHN D. ORR.

Scotiabank (Canada): Cherokee Rd, POB 15, Providenciales; tel. 946-4750; fax 946-4755; e-mail bns.turkscaicos@scotiabank.com; Man. Dir DAVID TAIT; br. on Grand Turk.

Turks and Caicos Banking Co Ltd (TCBC): Duke St North, Cockburn Town, POB 123, Grand Turk; tel. 946-2368; fax 946-2365; e-mail services@tcbc.tc; internet www.turksandcaicos-banking.com; f. 1980; dep. 82.3m., total assets 92.7m. (Dec. 2009); Pres. ANTON J. B. FAESSLER; Gen. Man. DAVID J. BEE.

TRUST COMPANIES

Berkshire Trust Co Ltd: Caribbean Pl., POB 657, Providenciales; tel. 946-4324; fax 946-4354; e-mail berkshire.trust@tciway.tc; internet www.berkshire.tc; Pres. GORDON WILLIAMSON.

UNITED KINGDOM OVERSEAS TERRITORIES / The Turks and Caicos Islands

Chartered Trust Co: Town Centre Bldg, Mezzanine Floor, Butterfield Sq., POB 125, Providenciales; tel. 946-4881; fax 946-4041; e-mail reception@chartered-tci.com; internet www.chartered-tci.com; Man. Dir PETER A. SAVORY.

Meridian Trust Co Ltd: Caribbean Pl., Leeward Hwy, POB 599, Providenciales; tel. 941-3082; fax 941-3223; e-mail mtcl@tciway.tc; internet www.meridiantrust.tc; Man. Dir KEITH BURANT.

M & S Trust Co Ltd: Butterfield Sq., POB 260, Providenciales; tel. 946-4650; fax 946-4663; e-mail mslaw@tciway.tc; internet www.mslaw.tc/trusts.htm; Man. Dir TIMOTHY P. O'SULLIVAN; Man. STEVE ROSS.

Temple Trust Co Ltd: 228 Leeward Hwy, Providenciales; tel. 946-5740; fax 946-5739; e-mail info@templefinancialgroup.com; internet www.templefinancialgroup.com; f. 1985; CEO DAVID C. KNIPE.

INSURANCE

Turks and Caicos Islands National Insurance Board: Misick's Bldg, POB 250, Grand Turk; tel. 946-1048; fax 946-1362; internet www.tcinib.tc; f. 1992; 4 brs.

Turks and Caicos Association of Insurance Managers (TC-AIM): Southwinds Pl., Unit 6, Leeward Hwy, Providenciales; tel. 946-4987; fax 946-4621; internet turksandcaicos.tc/aim; f. 2000 as Asscn of Insurance Managers; name changed as above in 2003 when registered as a non-profit asscn; protects interests of domestic and 'offshore' insurance cos in the islands; Pres. GARY BROUGH; Treas. ROSS BLUMENTRITT.

Trade and Industry

GOVERNMENT AGENCIES

Financial Services Commission (FSC): see Finance.

General Trading Company (Turks and Caicos) Ltd: PMBI, Cockburn Town, Grand Turk; tel. 946-2464; fax 946-2799; shipping agents, importers, air freight handlers; wholesale distributor of petroleum products, wines and spirits.

Turks Islands Importers Ltd (TIMCO): Front St, POB 72, Grand Turk; tel. 946-2480; fax 946-2481; f. 1952; agents for Lloyds of London, importers and distributors of food, beer, liquor, building materials, hardware and appliances; Dir HUBERT MAGNUS.

DEVELOPMENT ORGANIZATION

Turks and Caicos Islands Investment Agency (TC Invest): Hon. Headley Durham Bldg, Church Folly, POB 105, Grand Turk; tel. 946-2058; fax 946-1464; e-mail tcinvest@tciway.tc; internet www.tcinvest.tc; f. 1974 as Devt Bd of the Turks and Caicos Islands; statutory body; devt finance for private sector; promotion and management of internal investment; Chair. LILLIAN MISICK; Pres. and CEO COLIN R. HEARTWELL.

CHAMBERS OF COMMERCE

Grand Turk Chamber of Commerce: POB 148, Grand Turk; tel. 946-2043; fax 946-2504; e-mail gtchamberofcomm@tciway.tc; f. 1974; 57 mem. cos; Pres. and Exec. Dir GLENNEVANS CLARKE; Hon. Sec. SHERLIN WILLIAMS.

North Caicos Chamber of Commerce: tel. 231-1232; Pres. FRANKLYN ROBINSON; Sec. LLEWYN HANDFIELD.

Providenciales Chamber of Commerce: POB 361, Providenciales; tel. 242-6418; fax 946-4582; e-mail provochamber@gmail.com; internet www.provochamber.com; f. 1991; 131 mems (2006); Pres. TINA FENIMORE; Vice-Pres. ALLAN HUTCHISON.

UTILITIES

Electricity and Gas

Atlantic (Fortis Turks and Caicos) Ltd: New Airport Rd, Airport Area, South Caicos; tel. and fax 946-3201; Fortis Inc (Bermuda) completed its acquisition of 100% shares in the co in Aug. 2006; sole provider of electricity in South Caicos; Pres. and CEO EDDINTON POWELL.

Provo Power Company (PPC) Ltd: Town Centre Mall, POB 132, Providenciales; tel. 946-4313; fax 946-4532; internet www.provopowercompany.com; Fortis Energy (Bermuda) completed its acquisition of 100% shares in the co, together with those of its sister co Atlantic Equipment and Power (Turks and Caicos) Ltd, in Aug. 2006; cos referred to collectively as Fortis Turks and Caicos; sole supplier of electricity to Providenciales, North Caicos and Middle Caicos; Pres. and CEO EDDINTON POWELL.

Turks and Caicos Utilities Ltd: Pond St, POB 80, Grand Turk; tel. 946-2402; fax 946-2896; e-mail ewiggins@wrbenterprises.com.

Water

Provo Water Co: Grace Bay Rd, POB 39, Providenciales; tel. and fax 946-5205; e-mail provowater@tciway.tc; owned by HAB Group.

Turks and Caicos Water Co: Provo Golf Clubhouse, Grace Bay Rd, POB 124, Providenciales; tel. 946-5126; fax 946-5127.

TRADE UNION

Turks and Caicos Service Workers Union: POB 369, Blue Mountain, Providenciales; tel. 3360; fax 8516; Pres. E. CONRAD HOWELL.

Transport

ROADS

There are 121 km (75 miles) of roads in the islands, of which 24 km, on Grand Turk, South Caicos and Providenciales, are surfaced with tarmac. A causeway linking the North and Middle Caicos islands was completed in 2007.

SHIPPING

There are regular freight services from Miami, FL, USA. The main sea ports are Grand Turk, Providenciales, Salt Cay and Cockburn Harbour on South Caicos. A new US $40m. cruise ship terminal in Grand Turk, with capacity for large passenger liners, opened in 2006.

Cargo Express Shipping Service Ltd: South Dock Rd, Providenciales; tel. 941-5006; fax 941-5062.

Seacair Ltd: Churchill Bldg, Front St, POB 170, Grand Turk; tel. 946-2591; fax 946-2226.

Tropical Shipping: c/o Cargo Express Services Ltd, South Dock Rd, Providenciales; tel. 941-5006; fax 941-5062; e-mail nbeen@tropical.com; internet www.tropical.com; Pres. RICK MURRELL.

CIVIL AVIATION

There are international airfields on Grand Turk, South Caicos, North Caicos and Providenciales, the last being the most important; there are also landing strips on Middle Caicos, Pine Cay, Parrot Cay and Salt Cay. An expansion project at Providenciales airport was under way and included a new terminal building and the lengthening of the runway in order to accommodate transatlantic flights. The project was scheduled for completion in 2013.

Civil Aviation Authority: Hibiscus Sq., POB 1120, Grand Turk; tel. 946-2137; fax 946-1659; e-mail cad@tciway.tc; Man. Dir THOMAS SWANN.

Air Turks and Caicos (2003) Ltd: 1 InterIsland Plaza, Old Airport Rd, POB 191, Providenciales; tel. 946-4181; fax 946-4040; e-mail info@flyairtc.com; internet www.airturksandcaicos.com; also operates *SkyKing Ltd*.

Caicos Caribbean Airlines: South Caicos; tel. 946-3283; fax 946-3377; freight to Miami (FL, USA).

Cairsea Services Ltd: Old Airport Rd, POB 138, Providenciales; tel. 946-4205; fax 946-4504; e-mail caisea@tciway.tc; internet www.cairsea.com; Man. Dir RODNEY THOMPSON.

Global Airways Ltd: POB 359, Providenciales; tel. 941-3222; fax 946-7290; e-mail global@tciway.tc; internet www.globalairways.tc; operates inter-island connections and Caribbean charter flights; Man. Dir LINDSEY GARDINER.

Turks Air Ltd: Providenciales; tel. and fax 946-4504; e-mail turksair@earthlink.net; twice weekly cargo service to and from Miami (USA); Grand Turk Local Agent CRIS NEWTON.

Turks and Caicos Airways Ltd: Providenciales International Airport, POB 114, Providenciales; tel. 946-4181; fax 946-4438; f. 1976 as Air Turks and Caicos; privatized 1983; scheduled daily inter-island service to each of the Caicos Islands, charter flights; Chair. ALBRAY BUTTERFIELD; Dir-Gen. C. MOSER.

Turks and Caicos Islands Airport Authority (TCIAA): Providenciales International Airport, Providenciales; tel. 946-4420; fax 941-5996; e-mail info@tciairports.com; internet www.tciairports.com/web; CEO JOHN T. SMITH.

Tourism

The islands' main tourist attractions are the numerous unspoilt beaches, and the opportunities for diving. Salt Cay has been designated a World Heritage site by UNESCO. Hotel accommodation is available on Grand Turk, Salt Cay, South Caicos, Parrot Cay, Pine Cay and Providenciales. In 2007 there were some 264,887 stop-over tourist arrivals and 379,936 cruise ship passengers visited the islands. In 2006 68.3% of stop-over tourists were from the USA. In 2007 there were 2,632 hotel rooms (some 87% of which were on Providenciales). Revenue from the sector in 2005 totalled an estimated US $355.1m.

Turks and Caicos Hotel and Tourism Association: POB 251, Ports of Call, Providenciales; tel. 941-5787; fax 946-4001; e-mail manager@turksandcaicoshta.com; internet www.turksandcaicoshta.com; fmrly Turks and Caicos Hotel Asscn; over 90 mem. orgs; Pres. KAREN WHITT; CEO CAESAR CAMPBELL.

Turks and Caicos Islands Tourist Board: Front St, POB 128, Grand Turk; tel. 946-2321; fax 946-2733; e-mail provo@turksandcaicostourism.com; internet www.turksandcaicostourism.com; f. 1970; br. in Providenciales; Dir RALPH HIGGS.

Defence

The United Kingdom is responsible for the defence of the Turks and Caicos Islands.

Education

Primary education, beginning at seven years of age and lasting seven years, is compulsory, and is provided free of charge in government schools. Secondary education, from the age of 14, lasts for five years, and is also free. In 2004/05, according to UNESCO estimates, 78% of children in the relevant age-group were enrolled in primary education, while the comparable ratio for secondary education was 70%. In 2005/06 there were 14 government primary schools and eight government secondary schools. In 2003 government budgetary recurrent expenditure on scholarships, education, grants and contributions was US $8.2m. (8.8% of total recurrent expenditure). According to the 2007/08 government budget communication, $19.3m. was to be allocated to tertiary education in the territory during that fiscal year.

THE UNITED STATES OF AMERICA

Introductory Survey

LOCATION, CLIMATE, LANGUAGE, RELIGION, FLAG, CAPITAL

The United States of America comprises mainly the North American continent between Canada and Mexico. Alaska, to the north-west of Canada, and Hawaii, in the central Pacific Ocean, are two of the 50 States of the USA. There is considerable climatic variation, with mean annual average temperatures ranging from 29°C (77°F) in Florida to −13.3°C (10°F) in Alaska. Average annual rainfall ranges from 1,831 mm (72.1 ins) in Arkansas to 191 mm (7.5 ins) in Nevada. Much of Texas, New Mexico, Arizona, Nevada and Utah is desert. The official language is English, although there are significant Spanish-speaking minorities. Christianity is the predominant religion. The national flag (proportions 10 by 19) has 13 alternating stripes (seven red and six white) with a dark blue rectangular canton, containing 50 white, five-pointed stars, in the upper hoist. The capital is Washington, DC.

CONTEMPORARY POLITICAL HISTORY

Historical Context

Concern at the spread of communist influence in Asia dominated US foreign policy during the 1960s and early 1970s. From 1961, until their termination in 1973 by President Richard Nixon, US military operations against communist forces in South Viet Nam led to considerable political division within the USA and were widely criticized internationally. Following a series of scandals involving Nixon and senior administration officials in allegations of corruption and obstruction of justice, known as the 'Watergate' affair, Nixon resigned in August 1974 and was replaced by the Vice-President, Gerald Ford. In November 1976 Jimmy Carter, a Democrat, was elected President. Domestically, economic recession and inflation preoccupied the Carter Administration, and the President's management of the economy was a decisive factor in his defeat by the Republican candidate, Ronald Reagan, in the 1980 presidential election.

Although economic recession and high unemployment persisted in the early period of the Reagan Administration, the Republicans retained their previous level of congressional representation in the November 1982 elections. With the resumption of economic growth in 1983, and its strong resurgence through 1984, unemployment and inflation fell, and in November Reagan was re-elected for a further four-year term, securing the largest majority of electoral votes in US history. However, the closing months of Reagan's presidency were clouded by political scandals involving senior presidential appointees.

Domestic Political Affairs

The Gulf War and the presidency of George Bush, 1989–93

At the November 1988 presidential election, Reagan was succeeded by his Vice-President, George Bush, although the Senate and House of Representatives both retained Democratic majorities. The initial months of the Bush Administration were dominated by concern over the formulation of effective measures to contain the federal budget deficit, and over the future course of arms reduction negotiations with the USSR (see Relations with the USSR and successor states).

Following the invasion of Kuwait by Iraqi forces on 2 August 1990, and the subsequent annexation of that country by Iraq, the US Government assumed a leading international role in the implementation of measures to bring about an Iraqi withdrawal. The imposition of mandatory economic sanctions against Iraq by the UN Security Council on 6 August was quickly followed by 'Operation Desert Shield', in which US combat troops and aircraft were dispatched to Saudi Arabia, at that country's request, to secure its borders against a possible attack by Iraq. An offer, subsequently repeated, by President Saddam Hussain of Iraq to link withdrawal from Kuwait with a resolution of other outstanding Middle East problems, was rejected, and in late August the UN Security Council endorsed the use of military action to enforce its economic sanctions. In early September President Bush and his USSR counterpart, Mikhail Gorbachev, jointly demanded an Iraqi withdrawal, although the USSR expressed reluctance to support military operations by the UN. In late September the UN Security Council intensified its economic measures against Iraq. However, the ineffectiveness both of economic sanctions and of diplomatic negotiation had become evident by late November, and the USSR gave its assent to the use of force against Iraq, although it did not participate in the multinational force that was now arrayed in the Persian (Arabian) Gulf region and included, under US command, air, sea and ground forces from the United Kingdom, France, Italy, Egypt, Morocco, Kuwait and the other Arab Gulf states. Jordan, which had sought to promote a negotiated settlement, was perceived by the US Government as sympathetic to Iraq, and US financial aid to that country was suspended.

On 29 November 1990 the UN Security Council authorized the use of 'all necessary means' to force Iraq to withdraw from Kuwait, unless it did so by 15 January 1991. By early January the USA had established a considerable military presence in the Gulf region, and on 17 January 'Operation Desert Storm' was launched, with massive air and missile attacks against Iraqi positions, both in Iraq and Kuwait. In the course of the conflict, more than 110,000 attacking air missions were flown over Kuwait and Iraq by multinational air forces, while naval support operations were conducted from the Gulf. In the following weeks severe damage was inflicted on Iraqi military and economic targets, while counter-attacks by its air force, and attempts to draw Israel into the conflict by launching missile attacks on population centres, proved ineffective. A ground offensive by the multinational force was launched on 23–24 February, and Iraqi positions were quickly overrun. Hostilities were suspended on 28 February. The Government of Iraq accepted cease-fire terms on 3 March, leaving the multinational forces in control of Kuwait, together with an area of southern Iraq, comprising about 15% of that country's total national territory. Troop withdrawals from the occupied area of Iraq commenced in March, with the remaining US troops evacuated in May, to be replaced by a UN peace-keeping force.

Following the termination of hostilities, in which 148 US troops died in combat, internal rebellions broke out within Iraq by groups opposed to President Saddam Hussain. The severity with which these were suppressed, particularly in the northern region among the Kurdish ethnic group, and the subsequent flight of refugees into neighbouring areas of Turkey and Iran, prompted large-scale international relief operations. The US Government was widely criticized for its refusal to support the anti-Government insurgents and to take action to depose Saddam Hussain. In May 1991 the USA began airlifting troops to northern Iraq to establish 'safe' enclaves, to which Kurdish refugees were encouraged to return. The US military continued to monitor events in these Kurdish areas from operational bases in Turkey and other strategic points in the region. Relations with Iraq remained tense following the discovery in November by UN representatives that President Saddam Hussain's regime was seeking to conceal its continuing development of nuclear weapons capability. In July 1992 contention arose between the Government of Iraq and the UN over the rights of UN observers to inspect Iraqi nuclear facilities, and in the following month the US Government sought to limit internal military operations by the Iraqi Government by imposing an air exclusion zone south of latitude 32°N. This was followed, in January 1993, by US participation in selective bombings of Iraqi missile sites.

Following the conclusion of the Gulf War in early 1991, Bush's political popularity fell sharply, amid growing public perception that the Government was assigning greater priority to foreign affairs than to addressing the problems of the US economy, which had been in recession since early 1989. In April 1992 serious rioting broke out in Los Angeles and spread briefly to several other cities. The underlying causes of the disorders were widely ascribed to the worsening economic and social plight of the impoverished urban black minority.

The 1992 presidential election campaign, in which Bush was opposed by Bill Clinton, a Democratic state governor, and Ross

Perot, a populist independent, was dominated by social and economic issues. Bush's record of economic management, particularly in relation to the persistence of federal budget deficits, provided the major line of attack by the opposing candidates. Voter turn-out, at 55%, was the highest at any presidential election since 1968, and gave a decisive majority, of 43% to 37%, to Clinton. Perot, whose campaign had concentrated on the question of federal deficit spending, obtained almost 19% of the popular vote.

The Clinton presidency, 1993–2001

The initial preoccupation of the Clinton Administration was the formulation of an economic recovery plan, to be phased over a five-year period, to reduce the federal budget deficit by means of increased taxation and economies in the cost of government, rather than by reduced levels of spending. Additional spending was planned for infrastructural projects and measures to stimulate economic activity. A major restructuring of the US health care system was also planned, and a commission to formulate proposals was placed under the chairmanship of President Clinton's wife, Hillary. Certain aspects of the economic recovery plan, particularly those relating to higher income tax and a new energy tax, encountered initial opposition in the Democrat-controlled Congress, but were eventually approved, in a modified form, by mid-1993. However, by this time the President's initial popularity had fallen sharply, owing in part to perceptions of indecisiveness by Clinton in formulating effective policies.

The collapse of Clinton's plans for health care reform following congressional opposition in 1994, together with increasing public concern about the domestic economy and the effectiveness of Clinton's policies on social issues (notably in the areas of welfare expenditure, law enforcement and the protection of traditional social values), led to a sharp rise in support for the conservative doctrines of politicians representing the right wing of the Republican Party. At congressional elections in November 1994, the Republicans gained control both of the Senate (for the first time since 1986) and the House of Representatives (which had been controlled by the Democrats since 1954). As a result, in 1995 serious divisions began to emerge between President Clinton and Congress. In June tensions arose over proposals to achieve a balanced federal budget. In November Clinton, in an effort to resolve the deadlock, refused to renew the temporary funding arrangements, causing an eight-day shutdown of all non-essential operations of the federal Government. Agreement on the 1995/96 budget was eventually reached in April 1996, although disagreements on the timetable for, and the method of achieving, a balanced budget remained unresolved.

Clinton decisively secured a second term in office in November 1996. The President declared the enhancement of educational standards to be a primary aim of his second term. Proposals were also announced to achieve further reductions in welfare dependency, by providing tax credits and other incentives to employers. Financial savings were to be achieved by reductions in defence expenditure, and by the implementation of additional cuts in spending on health care for the elderly. Clinton reiterated his intention, however, of seeking improved provisions for insured health care, and of achieving a balanced federal budget by 2002. Agreement between Clinton and the Republican congressional leadership on the general terms of these budgetary measures was reached in May 1997.

During his second term as President, Clinton was confronted by a number of allegations, which he consistently denied, of perjury and obstruction of justice arising from accusations of sexual harassment, dating from prior to 1992 and extending throughout his presidency. These matters were brought within the ambit of a congressionally mandated, independent counsel, Kenneth Starr, who began in 1994 to examine the legal ramifications of the 'Whitewater' affair (President Clinton and his wife were accused of financial irregularities in their alleged involvement in a company that collapsed in 1989, during Clinton's tenure as Governor of Arkansas). In January 1998 Starr was authorized by the Attorney-General to investigate whether a sexual relationship alleged by a former White House intern, Monica Lewinsky, had taken place with the President in 1995. Clinton vehemently denied any improper conduct with Lewinsky; however, in August 1998, following an offer of immunity from prosecution by Starr to Lewinsky, the President admitted that an inappropriate relationship had taken place, although he had at no time sought to obstruct legal processes. Starr's report to Congress alleged that Clinton had committed 11 offences of perjury and obstruction of justice, constituting grounds for his removal from office. No evidence, however, was offered of wrongdoing by Clinton in relation to the 'Whitewater' affair. In October the House of Representatives voted to commence an impeachment inquiry against the President, but in February 1999 the Senate acquitted Clinton on the first and second articles of impeachment. A subsequent attempt in the Senate to obtain a vote of censure on Clinton was unsuccessful.

In August 1998 bomb attacks on US embassy buildings in Nairobi, Kenya, and Dar es Salaam, Tanzania, claimed 258 lives, and were followed by US air missile attacks on a factory site in Khartoum, Sudan (which was alleged to be a manufactory of chemicals for use in toxic gases), and on targets in Afghanistan, which were stated by the US Government to be operational centres for Osama bin Laden, a fugitive Saudi Arabian-born Islamist activist whom the USA believed to be responsible for past assaults on US forces and facilities in Somalia, Yemen and Saudi Arabia. Bin Laden was also held responsible for terrorist operations within the USA, including the 1993 bombing of the World Trade Center in New York. In October 2001 four associates of bin Laden were sentenced to life imprisonment by a US court for their involvement in the bomb attacks in Nairobi and Dar es Salaam. Meanwhile, in September 1996 Clinton sanctioned missile strikes from US naval vessels in the Gulf at military targets in Iraq, in retaliation for attacks by Iraqi forces against Kurds in northern Iraq. In December 1998, following the termination by Iraq of international weapons inspections in its territory, the USA and the United Kingdom conducted further missile raids on Iraqi military sites.

Presidential vote of 2000: George W. Bush elected

A presidential election was held on 7 November 2000. Vice-President Al Gore was the Democratic Party candidate, while George W. Bush, the Governor of Texas and a son of former President Bush, was the Republican Party's nominee. Following voting, it emerged that the possession of an overall majority in the presidential Electoral College would depend on the 25 college mandates from the state of Florida, where the result of the ballot was in dispute. The state was initially declared in favour of Governor Bush, pending the result of a mandatory automated recount of the votes; however, the Democrats challenged the declaration (and the state government's refusal to permit the ballots to be recounted by electoral staff following the automated recount) in the Florida Supreme Court, claiming that a significant number of votes in certain counties had been incorrectly registered by the automated counting system. The Court ruled that the ballots in the counties concerned should be recounted by electoral staff and allowed an additional 12 days for this process to be completed. The US Supreme Court disallowed this ruling, however, and returned the matter to the Florida Supreme Court for further consideration. Only one county completed its 'manual' recount and the result remained in Governor Bush's favour (by 537 votes). The Democrats began further legal action, claiming that the importance of recounting all disputed ballots transcended time limits. The Florida Supreme Court upheld the appeal and ordered the recounting of some 45,000 disputed ballots. The Republicans challenged the verdict, claiming that no provision for such 'manual' recounts was made in the electoral legislation. The US Supreme Court narrowly upheld the Republican appeal. With all legal options exhausted, and with the Florida legislature having voted to endorse a list of Republican electors irrespective of the outcome of further legal action, Vice-President Gore conceded defeat in Florida (and thereby nationally) on 13 December. Final results subsequently indicated that Vice-President Gore obtained 48.4% of the valid votes cast, compared with 47.9% obtained by Governor Bush. Thus, the latter became the first contender since 1876 to win a majority in the Electoral College while losing the national popular ballot.

President Bush's first Cabinet contained several individuals who had served in his father's Administration, as well as one member of Clinton's Cabinet. His Government immediately suspended the implementation of a number of environmental regulations issued by Clinton shortly before his departure from office. The Administration's first budget, presented in February 2001, included provisions for reductions in levels of personal taxation.

Attacks of 11 September 2001

On 11 September 2001 four commercial passenger aircraft were hijacked shortly after take-off from Boston, New York and Washington, DC. The two aircraft originating in Boston, both bound for Los Angeles, were diverted to New York, and each was flown into one of the two towers of the World Trade Center, both of which subsequently collapsed. The third aircraft was flown into the Pentagon building (the headquarters of the Department of Defense) in Washington, DC, and the fourth aircraft, also apparently heading for Washington, DC, crashed in farmland near Pittsburgh, Pennsylvania. The death toll was eventually put at 2,752, including 266 passengers and crew (including the hijackers) on the four aircraft, 190 at the Pentagon, and the remainder in New York, principally those unable to escape from the towers before they collapsed, and members of the emergency services. On 13 September the Secretary of State, Gen. Colin Powell, identified Osama bin Laden and his al-Qa'ida organization, a network of fundamentalist Islamist militants, as responsible for the attacks. However, bin Laden, who was believed to be in Afghanistan, where he was harboured by the extremist Islamist Taliban regime, had already denied accusations that he had ordered the hijackings, although he expressed his approval of the attacks. In late 2002 an independent bipartisan inquiry, the National Commission on Terrorist Attacks Upon the United States, was established to investigate the circumstances surrounding the attacks. In March 2003 security forces in Rawalpindi, Pakistan, arrested the Kuwaiti-born Khalid Sheikh Mohammed, accused of being the operational planner behind the attacks, and released him into US custody for interrogation. In March 2006, in a court in Virginia, Moroccan-born Zacarias Moussaoui pleaded guilty to charges of conspiracy to commit acts of terrorism, in relation to the attacks. Moussaoui had pleaded guilty to conspiracy charges in July 2002, but subsequently retracted his plea. In May 2006 he was sentenced to life imprisonment without parole. In March 2007 Khalid Sheikh Mohammed, regarded as one of the principal agents of al-Qa'ida's operations, was tried by military commission, along with two other alleged key al-Qa'ida operatives. The US Department of Defense released a partial transcript of Sheikh Mohammed's trial at the detention centre in Guantánamo Bay, Cuba (see US-led military operations in Afghanistan), in which the suspect claimed involvement in 31 separate international terrorism plots and attacks, including orchestration of the 1993 and 2001 attacks on the World Trade Center, the beheading of US journalist Daniel Pearl in 2002 and numerous assassination attempts against international political leaders. However, speculation that such admissions had been obtained under duress, or torture, tarnished any belief in the international community that justice had been achieved and provoked further criticism of the interrogation methods employed at Guantánamo Bay. Charges brought by the US Government in February 2008 against five prisoners being held in Guantánamo Bay, including Khalid Sheikh Mohammed, elicited similar censure. The charges, for which military prosecutors were to seek the death penalty, related to the detainees' alleged involvement in the 2001 attacks and included conspiracy, murder, attacking civilians, destruction of property and terrorism. In November 2009 the Attorney-General, Eric Holder, announced that all five would be transferred to New York for a civilian trial (in which the death penalty would still be sought). The charges against the five within the military commissions were withdrawn in January 2010 in order to allow their future trial by a civilian court.

In the immediate wake of the attacks on New York and Washington, DC, President Bush declared that those responsible should be captured 'dead or alive'. Congress unanimously approved emergency anti-terrorism legislation, which made provision for increased military spending and US $20,000m. for reconstruction in New York, and adopted a resolution authorizing the President to use 'all necessary and appropriate force' against those who organized the attacks. Congress also approved the so-called 'Patriot Act' (Uniting and Strengthening America by Providing the Appropriate Tools Required to Intercept and Obstruct Terrorism—PATRIOT—Act of 2001), which was signed into law in October 2001, giving wide-ranging powers to the Government to investigate citizens and non-citizens alike. The Act was viewed by critics as a threat to civil liberties. (The Patriot Act was scheduled to expire at the end of 2005, but was temporarily extended by Congress until February 2006. A continuance of the measure, the USA Patriot Act Improvement and Reauthorization Act of 2005, was signed into law by the President in March 2006.) The Government began to form an international coalition against terrorism, for which most Western Governments pledged their support. The North Atlantic Treaty Organization (NATO) invoked Article Five of the NATO Charter (which states that an attack on a member state is an attack on all 19 members), which required members to assist the USA, according to judgement and resources; the Governments of the United Kingdom, France and Germany, among others, offered military and financial assistance. The Taliban regime in Afghanistan denied involvement in the terrorist attacks, and warned that it would retaliate if attacked. On 17 September 2001 the USA issued an ultimatum to the Taliban, via Pakistan (one of only three states with diplomatic links to the regime), to surrender bin Laden or face an imminent military assault. Several weeks of intense diplomatic activity ensued, during which time international support for the USA's so-called global 'war on terror' increased, and the US Government was apparently able to gather further evidence of the al-Qa'ida network's involvement in the attacks. The Taliban reportedly asked to see evidence of bin Laden's involvement in the attacks, a request rejected by the USA. Meanwhile, US military forces increased their presence in the region around Afghanistan. Pakistan and Uzbekistan agreed to grant the US-led forces use of their airbases for emergency operations, and Russia allowed access to its airspace for humanitarian missions. Saudi Arabia also granted access to its airspace.

US-led military operations in Afghanistan

On 2 October 2001 NATO declared that it had received evidence from the USA that confirmed bin Laden's responsibility for the terrorist attacks. On 7 October US and British armed forces commenced military operations ('Operation Enduring Freedom') against Taliban military targets and suspected al-Qa'ida training camps in Afghanistan. In addition to military strikes, aircraft released food and medicine parcels to Afghan civilians; leaflets were also dropped offering protection and a reward in return for information on the whereabouts of al-Qa'ida leaders. On 14 October a senior Taliban official offered to surrender bin Laden to a third country in return for a cessation of US bombing, if the USA provided evidence of his involvement in the terrorist attacks, an offer the USA rejected. The US-led forces co-ordinated operations with the military wing of the exiled Afghan Government, the United National Islamic Front for the Salvation of Afghanistan (UIFSA—also known as the Northern Alliance). During November the latter made substantial territorial gains in northern and western Afghanistan, including the Afghan capital, Kabul, and Mazar-i-Sharif, a strategically important town in the north. In late November US ground forces were deployed for the first time, near the southern city of Kandahar, in an attempt to locate bin Laden. Kandahar fell to the US-led forces in early December, leaving only localized areas of Taliban resistance; US forces subsequently intensified their search for bin Laden, who was believed to be in the Tora Bora caves near Jalalabad, in the east of the country. The USA refused, however, to deploy peacekeeping troops in Afghanistan to support the interim administration of Hamid Karzai, which replaced the Taliban regime in December, although it released previously withheld assets to his Government, and pledged financial aid to rebuild the country's infrastructure. In January 2002 the Bush Government pledged some US $296.8m. in funds for the reconstruction of Afghanistan.

In January 2002 the US military began transferring members of the Taliban and al-Qa'ida who had been captured in battle to the US naval base in Guantánamo Bay. Initially, the USA refused to grant the detainees (numbering almost 300) prisoner-of-war status under the Geneva Convention of 1949 (which guaranteed trial by court martial or a civilian court, as opposed to a military tribunal), prompting criticism from its coalition partners, which intensified following the publication of photographs showing prisoners shackled and blindfolded. In February, following pressure from the British and French Governments, President Bush accorded partial protection of the Convention to captured Taliban fighters (he denied full protection, claiming that the soldiers were members of an irregular militia); al-Qa'ida captives were offered no protection, as they were considered to be terrorists with no allegiance to any specific state or government. In June the Supreme Court ruled that, while the President as Commander-in-Chief had the power to detain enemy combatants, they were entitled to legal representation in a US federal court. The following day the first three prisoners from Guantánamo Bay appeared before a military tribunal.

In July 2004 the National Commission on Terrorist Attacks Upon the United States delivered its final report into intelligence failures in the months preceding the attacks of 11 September 2001. It asserted that both the Clinton and Bush Administrations had failed to realize the immediacy of the threat posed by the al-Qa'ida network. The report highlighted opportunities to uncover the plot that had been overlooked by both the Central Intelligence Agency (CIA) and the Federal Bureau of Investigation (FBI). However, it did not conclude that the attacks could have been prevented. It also found that, while Osama bin Laden had approved Khalid Sheikh Mohammed's plan in 1999, there was no evidence to link al-Qa'ida with Iraqi President Saddam Hussain. The report recommended, *inter alia*: the creation of a national director of intelligence with overall responsibility for all of the intelligence services; the formation of a national counter-terrorism centre to co-ordinate intelligence-gathering; a reduction in the number of congressional intelligence oversight committees; the establishment of an international network of intelligence-sharing; and the implementation of a national policy to address the threat of militant Islamism. On 17 December 2004, following its approval earlier in the month by both houses of Congress, President Bush enacted the Intelligence Reform and Terrorism Act, which drew on some of the recommendations of the Commission's report. The legislation was designed to restructure the security services and provided for a cabinet-level Director of National Intelligence, to be responsible for co-ordinating the activities of 15 different agencies, including the CIA and the FBI. In April 2005 Bush's nominee to the new post, the erstwhile US ambassador to Iraq, John D. Negroponte, was confirmed by the Senate. An internal investigation by the CIA into intelligence failings, concluded in January of that year, was particularly critical of its former director, George Tenet, who had resigned in June 2004.

Alleged torture of terrorist suspects

In November 2005 it was reported that US intelligence services maintained a network of secret prisons—referred to as 'black sites'—in locations that included eastern European Union (EU) countries. It was further alleged that terrorist suspects were taken from these prisons to countries where torture was tolerated, in a practice known as 'extraordinary rendition'. The following month Secretary of State Condoleezza Rice acknowledged the existence of rendition but denied any toleration of the torture of suspects. However, in January 2005 it had been revealed that, three years previously, the chief legal counsel to the President, Alberto Gonzales (who was appointed Attorney-General in January 2005), had issued a memorandum stating that the USA was not bound by the Geneva Conventions in its treatment of prisoners captured in Afghanistan. In another memorandum ordered by Gonzales in August 2002, it was proposed that CIA officers and other non-military personnel be exempted from a presidential directive for the humane treatment of prisoners. In February 2006 the UN Commission on Human Rights published a report that concluded that the methods used by the US military to interrogate prisoners at Guantánamo Bay amounted to torture, and appealed to the US Government to close the base and try the remaining detainees before courts on the US mainland. A military report to the Senate's armed forces committee in July found that treatment of the prisoners did not constitute torture, but that it was abusive and degrading. In December President Bush approved an amendment to ban the 'cruel, inhuman and degrading' treatment of prisoners, although he appended a presidential signing statement to the effect that the President's authority superseded the new legislation. Department of State officials were summoned to appear before the UN Committee Against Torture in Geneva, Switzerland, in May to answer enquiries relating to the alleged use of torture employed in extraordinary rendition. The Department of State delegation contended that it had sought assurances that detainees conveyed under this system would not be subjected to torture in their destination country and that US definitions of torture did not infringe those set out in the 1987 Convention. The UN concluded that interrogation methods involving 'waterboarding' (simulated drowning), sexual humiliation and the use of menacing dogs were unacceptable and should be eliminated. It also ruled that the detention of prisoners without charge for extended periods, the use of extraordinary rendition and reports of concealed prisons were issues of grave concern, and it urged the closure of the detention centre at Guantánamo Bay.

In June 2006 the US Supreme Court ruled that military tribunals established for the trial of prisoners at Guantánamo Bay contravened the US uniform code of military justice and Geneva Conventions, rejecting the Bush Administration's contention that the President's authority as Commander-in-Chief, and the resolution of Congress approved following the 11 September 2001 terrorist attacks, sanctioned the institution of such military tribunals. The Department of Defense issued a memorandum in July 2006 declaring that all prisoners at Guantánamo Bay and other US military detention centres world-wide would be protected under Article III of the Geneva Conventions, assuring humane treatment of and basic judicial defence for those facing trial. The announcement corrected previous assertions that the Military Commissions Act precluded invocation of Geneva Conventions articles. The Military Commissions Act of 2006, intended to 'bring to justice' terrorists and other unlawful enemy combatants by means of thorough, fair trials administered by military commissions, was approved by Congress in September and signed into law in the following month. In March 2007 an Australian, David Hicks (a convert to Islam) became the first detainee to be granted trial by such a commission at Guantánamo Bay and the first convicted of a terrorism offence since the camp's inauguration in 2002. An appeal by the legal representatives of approximately 60 Guantánamo detainees (facing similar military tribunals), contending that the prisoners had a constitutional right to contest their imprisonment in a US federal court, was rejected, by two votes to one, in the US Court of Appeal in February 2007. The Court's ruling stated that non-citizens without property or residency in the USA were not entitled to US constitutional rights. However, in June 2008 the Supreme Court issued a ruling that all detainees at Guantánamo Bay were entitled to challenge their detention through the US civilian courts. The decision did not bring to an end the military tribunals, which continued throughout 2008; however, in November a US court ruled that five Algerian detainees should be released from the prison camp after they successfully challenged their right to a civilian trial.

Alleged use of 'harsh interrogation' techniques, including waterboarding, caused controversy in October 2007, when a report by the *New York Times* claimed that the US Department of Justice had privately authorized their use by the CIA against terrorist suspects in 2005 while asserting that such methods did not contravene anti-torture legislation then before Congress. Later in the same month the Director of the CIA, Gen. Michael Hayden, defended the Agency's interrogation practices and use of extraordinary rendition as a lawful and indispensable means of obtaining information from suspects. However, on 6 December 2007—when an agreement was also reached by Congress negotiators on the terms of legislation to prohibit the use of 'harsh interrogation' techniques by the CIA—Hayden revealed that film tapes documenting the use of such procedures on two al-Qa'ida members in 2002 had been destroyed in November 2005, ostensibly to protect the identities of the CIA interrogators. Critics accused the Agency of destroying evidence that might provoke further allegations of torture in relation to their practices. A former CIA officer subsequently attested that waterboarding was used in the interrogation of Abu Zubaydah, the first high-ranking al-Qa'ida member to be captured after the terrorist attacks of 11 September 2001, and that he now considered the practice to constitute torture. In January 2008 a criminal investigation was launched by Attorney-General Michael B. Mukasey, and in February Hayden, for the first time, admitted the use of waterboarding on three al-Qa'ida detainees, including Khalid Sheikh Mohammed. He declared, however, that the method had not been used in the previous five years and that he had banned its use in 2006. Further, he did not rule out its future employment and admitted he was unsure of its legality under current laws. In March 2008 President Bush vetoed the legislation restricting 'harsh interrogation' techniques already approved by the House of Representatives in December 2007 and by the Senate in February 2008, claiming that such 'specialized interrogation procedures' were of proven effectiveness and, while not practised by the military, should remain available to the CIA. (For subsequent related developments, see the section on Legislative reform under the Obama Administration.)

Prelude to the 2003 invasion of Iraq

In September 2002 the Bush Administration outlined policies to address the new threats faced by the USA internationally in a National Security Strategy for the United States. In the same month the Republicans submitted a draft resolution to Congress, which would authorize President Bush to use 'any means necessary' to enforce existing UN resolutions against the regime of Saddam Hussain in Iraq and to defend US national interests by depriving Iraq of weapons of mass destruction. It was the first tangible evidence that the Administration was willing to deploy unilateral military action if the UN Security Council did not approve a new resolution authorizing military action against the Iraqi regime. The resolution was approved by Congress in October, with the provision that the Administration should first exhaust all available channels at the UN and other diplomatic

THE UNITED STATES OF AMERICA

means. As a result of US-led pressure, in November the UN Security Council passed unanimously Resolution 1441, which obliged Iraq, *inter alia*, to declare all weapons of mass destruction within 30 days, to comply with the UN Monitoring, Verification and Inspection Commission (UNMOVIC—the UN weapons inspectors, and successor to the UN Special Commission—UNSCOM), to allow UNMOVIC to resume its work within 45 days (UNSCOM had been expelled from Iraq in 1998), and to allow inspectors unrestricted access within Iraq. Later that month UNMOVIC resumed its operations and reported that the Iraqi Government was prepared to comply with Resolution 1441. In December Iraq presented its report on weapons of mass destruction to UNMOVIC; however, US officials declared Iraq to be in 'material breach' of Resolution 1441, for failing to comply with the demand for an accurate and complete account of its weapons programmes, and for resubmitting information that it had previously given to the UN. Following this development, the US and British Governments drew up a timetable to allow UNMOVIC to carry out intensified searches in early 2003, with the threat of military action against Saddam Hussain's regime for non-compliance.

In January 2003 some 70,000 US servicemen and -women joined the 60,000 troops already stationed in the Persian (Arabian) Gulf, and military exercises intensified. The French and German Governments expressed their opposition to any eventual conflict and called for a resolution to the problem by diplomatic means. However, the Administration took an increasingly uncompromising stance; President Bush stated that the USA would lead a 'coalition of the willing' if support was withheld by other UN Security Council members and its traditional allies. In February the USA, together with the United Kingdom, intensified its efforts to secure a second UN resolution that would authorize military intervention in Iraq; on 5 February Powell presented evidence of, *inter alia*, the alleged existence of weapons of mass destruction in Iraq, and possible links between Saddam Hussain's regime and al-Qa'ida. However, in mid-February UNMOVIC reported greater co-operation on the part of the Iraqi Government and that it had thus far failed to find any weapons of mass destruction. (On 13 February Saddam Hussain issued a presidential decree prohibiting weapons of mass destruction, although some al-Samoud missiles were found with a greater range than permitted under UN resolutions.) On 24 February the USA, with the United Kingdom and Spain, presented a draft resolution, reiterating that Iraq had been warned it would face serious consequences if it failed to disarm, and that it had failed to comply with Resolution 1441. In early March diplomatic efforts to resolve the crisis showed signs of breaking down when Russia and then France declared that they would employ their veto on any resolution leading to conflict, while the UN Secretary-General, Kofi Annan, questioned the legitimacy of a conflict in Iraq without UN approval. Nevertheless, Powell stated that the USA could go to war without a second UN resolution. UNMOVIC, meanwhile, reported that Iraq had destroyed part of its stock of al-Samoud missiles. An amended version of the draft for a second resolution was issued in mid-March and a deadline of 17 March given for Iraq to demonstrate full compliance with Resolution 1441. On 16 March President Bush, the British Prime Minister, Tony Blair, and the Spanish premier, José María Aznar, held an emergency summit in the Azores, Portugal, at the end of which the three leaders issued an ultimatum giving Saddam Hussain and his two sons 48 hours to leave Iraq or face invasion. The following day the USA, the United Kingdom and Spain decided not to seek a second UN resolution and condemned France for obstructing diplomatic efforts to reach a peaceful outcome. The President of France, Jacques Chirac, responded by criticizing the USA and the United Kingdom for making an 'unjustified' decision to resort to war, and for gravely undermining the UN. The USA announced that some 30 countries had expressed support for its 'coalition of the willing', although only the United Kingdom, Australia, the Czech Republic and Slovakia provided troops.

Iraqi regime of Saddam Hussain ousted

Shortly after the expiry of President Bush's 48-hour deadline, on 19 March 2003 US and British armed forces launched 'Operation Iraqi Freedom' to oust the regime of Saddam Hussain. A first wave of air-strikes against targets in the southern suburbs of the Iraqi capital, Baghdad, apparently aimed at leading members of the Iraqi regime (including the President himself), failed to achieve their target. Soon afterwards British and US forces crossed into Iraq from Kuwait and generally made a swift advance towards the capital. At the same time, a concerted campaign of massive air-strikes was launched by US-led forces against the key symbols of the Iraqi regime in and around Baghdad, including selected military bases, communications sites, government buildings and broadcasting headquarters. Government and military sites in other prominent Iraqi cities were targeted by the US-led coalition in subsequent days. The US and British forces adopted a simultaneous campaign of issuing leaflets and broadcasting radio messages, in an attempt to persuade Iraqi citizens to abandon their support for Saddam Hussain: their declared intention was that 'Operation Iraqi Freedom' would precipitate the disintegration of the regime 'from within'. By 9 April US forces reached the centre of Baghdad and on 1 May the conflict was officially declared over: Iraq did not formally offer its surrender. In mid-April US Gen. (retd) Jay Garner, Director of the USA's Office of Reconstruction and Humanitarian Assistance in Iraq (ORHA), was appointed Civil Administrator in Iraq, with the intention of overseeing the peaceful transition to civilian rule by Iraqi nationals. An Iraq Survey Group was established to investigate the presence of illegal weapons in the country. In early May a US diplomat, L. Paul Bremer, succeeded Garner as Civil Administrator. In July US special forces killed Saddam Hussain's sons, Uday and Qusay, in Mosul, and on 13 December US special forces captured Saddam Hussain himself, in the village of Ad-Dawr near his birthplace, Tikrit: he was accorded prisoner-of-war status and held in US custody, pending his trial by a court to be convened by the Iraqi Governing Council. Legal custody of Saddam Hussain was transferred to the new Iraqi Interim Government in June 2004, but he remained under US guard. The former Iraqi President's trial began in Baghdad in October 2005, and on 30 December 2006 Saddam Hussain was executed by hanging, following the rejection of his appeal against the death sentence imposed by the Supreme Iraqi Criminal Tribunal on 5 November.

In July 2003 the US Administration admitted that claims, made in January, that the regime of Saddam Hussain had attempted to procure uranium from several African countries as part of its nuclear programme were 'possibly inaccurate'. The claims had formed part of the argument for declaring war on Iraq. In October the Iraq Survey Group published its first report, which stated that although no weapons of mass destruction had been found thus far, there was evidence of weapons-related programmes. However, in January 2004 David Kay, the head of the Iraq Survey Group, resigned, stating that he did not believe that any stockpiles of weapons of mass destruction ever existed. Kay proposed the establishment of an independent inquiry into US intelligence on Iraqi weapons capability. The Survey Group left Iraq in January 2005. In an interim report to Congress in October 2004, Kay's successor, Charles Duelfer, concluded that Saddam Hussain had destroyed his stocks of weapons of mass destruction 10 years previously. In a report in March 2005, the Survey Group was critical of the restructuring proposed at the CIA and FBI and also criticized the agencies' failure to provide accurate information on the state of unconventional weapons in Iraq. In July 2004 a Senate intelligence committee concluded that the CIA had provided the Bush Administration with flawed intelligence before the invasion of Iraq. At that time the Secretary of Energy, Spencer Abraham, announced that US officials had removed 1.77 metric tons of enriched uranium from Iraq in the previous month.

In April 2004 photographs were published of US soldiers allegedly abusing prisoners at the Abu Ghraib prison near Baghdad. As further evidence of maltreatment continued to emerge, in May the Department of Defense revealed that in September 2003 investigations had begun into some 20 cases of the deaths or alleged torture of prisoners in US custody in Iraq; however, the military denied that there was any evidence of systematic maltreatment of detainees. President Bush publicly condemned the abuse of prisoners. The first prosecution of one of the soldiers involved began in the USA in June 2004. In August an internal military investigation directly implicated 27 soldiers in abuse at Abu Ghraib, while an independent civilian panel confirmed 66 out of some 300 reported cases of prisoner abuse in US-run prisons in Iraq, Afghanistan and at Guantánamo Bay. However, it did not find any systematic policy of abuse or instructions from senior military or government officials. In March 2005 it was announced that the USA was to hand over control of the prison to the Iraqi authorities. At that time in Iraq there were an estimated 10,000 prisoners at one British-run and three US-run prisons, including Abu Ghraib.

THE UNITED STATES OF AMERICA

Introductory Survey

Transfer of sovereignty in Iraq

In late June 2004 L. Paul Bremer officially handed over sovereignty to the Interim Government of Iraq. The event took place in secret two days ahead of schedule, amid fears of terrorist attacks. Full diplomatic relations were restored. The US Army announced plans to call up 5,600 retired and discharged soldiers to compensate for a lack of trained specialists. As part of the Disabled Soldier Support System, it also hoped to retain soldiers who had been wounded; in December it was estimated that 900 out of 9,300 soldiers injured in Iraq would be eligible for the programme. In January 2005 the Department of Defense revealed that it planned fundamentally to restructure the armed forces, diverting funds from costly weapons systems to manpower. At that time the cost of the military operation in Iraq had already exceeded US $200,000m. In July 2006 Muthanna became the first of Iraq's 18 provinces to be transferred from military control to the full responsibility of the Iraqi Government, signalling a measure of progress in the efforts to achieve stability. Despite fears of an escalation in sectarian violence, in September authority over the Iraqi armed forces was formally conferred upon the Government of Iraq by the US-led coalition.

The Administration resisted increasing pressure from 2005 to announce a timetable for the withdrawal of US troops from Iraq, and in June 2006 the Republican-controlled House of Representatives rejected a Democrat-sponsored resolution for such a schedule and upheld a non-binding covenant supporting the conflict as integral to the global 'war on terror'. The Senate echoed this sentiment, dismissing plans to withdraw most combat troops by the end of the year. Nevertheless, concerns about the misuse of reconstruction funding in Iraq, which precipitated the cancellation of contracts with US companies Parsons, Halliburton and Bechtel during 2006, provoked demands for an inquiry into the incidence of fraud and money-squandering during the execution of infrastructural projects. In June the Senate rejected such a resolution, although the Special Inspector General for Iraq Reconstruction (SIGIR) was, as of 30 April that year, pursuing 72 separate investigations into alleged fraudulence and profiteering by firms involved in the rebuilding efforts. In July the results of an audit into the practices of the United States Agency for International Development concluded that an accounting scheme had been employed to conceal overspending on reconstruction ventures in Iraq. The disclosure in November by *The New York Times* that President Bush had endorsed a military authorization bill in October, which included a provision for the disbanding of the Office of the SIGIR, precipitated outrage among Democrats who regarded the measure as an attempt to conceal the Administration's mismanagement of reconstruction funds.

The bipartisan Iraq Study Group (ISG) was established in March 2006 to conduct an assessment of the situation in Iraq and generate proposals for a revised US strategy towards resolution of the conflict. The ISG submitted its report to Congress in December, declaring the climate in Iraq to be 'grave and deteriorating', and cautioning that stability and democracy, as opposed to 'victory', should constitute the emphasis of future US military, diplomatic and political initiatives. The report delineated 79 recommendations for consideration by the President in formulating a new strategy for Iraq.

Despite the deployment of 15,600 US troops to Baghdad, the US military conceded in October 2006 that its efforts to secure the Iraqi capital had been unsuccessful, and the UN reported that the number of US and Iraqi fatalities was unremittingly high. In November the head of US Central Command and leader of US forces in the Middle East, Gen. John Abizaid, advised that additional US troops were required to train the Iraqi military forces. President Bush and his Iraqi counterpart, Nouri al-Maliki, pledged their intention for the expeditious transfer of responsibility from military to Iraqi government authority, with al-Maliki expressing his ambition for Iraqi forces to have secured full control of the country by June 2007, although no definite timetable was advanced.

Bush's new strategy for Iraq, 'A New Way Forward', was announced in January 2007. The new strategy was summarized as one that required greater commitment from the Iraqi Government to quell sectarian violence and establish democracy in the country through the attainment of a series of 'benchmarks', in return for US military reinforcements (numbering a further 21,500 troops) to assist in achieving the security and stability that would enable the Iraqi leaders to resume full responsibility for the territory. Bush cautioned that a withdrawal of US forces before this was accomplished would leave Iraq vulnerable to a 'contagion of violence' engulfing the whole region. Expansion of the USA's military capabilities was also requested, with the President asking Congress to authorize an increase of 92,000 personnel in the Army and Marine Corps over the next five years. The decision to expand US participation in what was increasingly regarded as a civil war met with strenuous opposition from Democrats and ignited intense debate in Congress in the succeeding weeks. None the less, dispatch of US reinforcements began in February 2007.

The US Administration indicated its willingness to participate in negotiations with neighbouring Iran and Syria towards resolving the crisis in Iraq, as had been recommended by the ISG report. Members of the UN Security Council, diplomats from all six of Iraq's neighbouring countries, representatives from three international organizations, and US delegates attended a conference convened by Iraqi leaders in March 2007 to discuss strategies for ending the violence in Iraq.

President Bush's proposed budget for 2008, presented in February 2007, incorporated a request for supplemental funding of US $93,400m. in 2008, and $141,000m. in 2009, to augment the Department of Defense's operations in the ongoing 'war on terror'. In March 2007 the House of Representatives voted in favour of emergency spending legislation that would provide $124,000m. for the funding of military operations in Iraq and Afghanistan over the next six months; however, attached to the provision was a timetable for the withdrawal, by 1 September 2008, of combat troops not devoted to security or training functions in Iraq. The Senate subsequently approved a similar bill allowing $122,000m. in emergency funding and stipulating withdrawal of US troops by an earlier deadline of 31 March 2008. Both versions of the legislation, in harmony with the President's stated new strategy, recommended that 'benchmarks' be reached by the Iraqi Government in order to guarantee continued US support. A final version received congressional approval in April 2007. However, in May the President vetoed the law, stating that setting a timetable for troop withdrawal would undermine military efforts and foster further insurgency in Iraq.

At a joint hearing of the House of Congress armed services and foreign affairs committees in September 2007, Gen. David Petraeus, the leader of US forces in Iraq, testified that the objectives of the 'surge' in troop numbers—30,000 extra US troops were dispatched to Iraq between February and June—were largely being met. He claimed that the tactic had reduced sectarian violence, and that in Anbar province in particular Sunni militias were now supporting US forces rather than presenting a hostile resistance. However, he acknowledged the ongoing difficulties of the situation and warned that a premature reduction in troop levels would have 'devastating consequences'. Petraeus advised that the US military presence could be scaled down in December 2007 and still further in July 2008, to the 2006 level of 130,000 troops. President Bush subsequently announced that 5,700 troops would be withdrawn from Iraq by the end of 2007 and a total of 21,500 by July 2008, in accordance with Petraeus's recommendations. Bush declined to give a timetable for a full withdrawal of troops, leading Democrats to criticize the scope of the plans. In February 2008 the President's 2009 federal budget presentation to Congress included a proposed 7.5% increase in spending on defence from 2008, to US $515,000m. An additional $70,000m. was allocated to fund the conflicts in Iraq and Afghanistan between the start of the fiscal year in October and January 2009. In a speech on 19 March 2008 in recognition of the fifth anniversary of the invasion of Iraq, Bush hailed the success of the 'surge' tactic amid criticism over the rising cost of the war. Estimates in this respect differed widely, with the non-partisan Congressional Budget Office placing the figure at $600,000m., while economist Joseph Stiglitz calculated that the total cost of the war for the USA alone would be $3,000,000m. Democrat consternation was further incited in April when Petraeus advocated a suspension in troop withdrawals after July in order to undertake a 45-day period of reassessment, as a result of which the President ordered an indefinite suspension to the exit, leaving a US force of around 140,000 combat personnel in the country from August. Petraeus was replaced as leader of US forces in Iraq by Gen. Raymond T. Odierno in September.

Bush's second presidential term, 2005–09

Presidential and legislative elections were held on 2 November 2004. The elections were notable for being the first in which unregulated, or so-called 'soft money', donations to the electoral campaigns of political parties from individuals, businesses and

THE UNITED STATES OF AMERICA

unions were banned. In the presidential ballot, President Bush was returned for a second term of office, taking some 51% of the popular vote. John Kerry, the Democratic challenger, conceded defeat before the final result was confirmed. In the concurrent legislative elections, the Republicans also increased their majority in both houses of Congress. The President was sworn in on 20 January 2005. His new Cabinet included Condoleezza Rice, hitherto Assistant to the President for National Security Affairs, as Secretary of State, and Alberto Gonzales, the President's former chief legal counsel, as Attorney-General. In February Bush presented a 2006 budget plan to Congress, which proposed reductions in funding to 12 out of 23 government agencies. Spending cuts targeted subsidies to farmers and health care payments to the poor and military veterans, as well as education and environment programmes. In May a presidential request for a further US $82,000m., principally towards continued military involvement in Afghanistan and Iraq, was approved by Congress.

In late August 2005 Hurricane Katrina caused extensive damage to the Gulf coast states of Louisiana, Mississippi and Alabama. Louisiana was the worst affected state: an estimated 80% of the city of New Orleans was flooded. On 2 September President Bush declared a state of emergency in 13 states to release some US $10,500m. in emergency funding; on the same day Congress approved legislation for emergency aid amounting to $51,800m. Damage to infrastructure was blamed for delays in delivering relief to those affected by the hurricane. The US Government appealed to the EU, NATO and the UN for crisis assistance. On 6 September the mayor of New Orleans ordered the evacuation of the entire city, some 480,000 people; however, an estimated 10,000 people, either unable or unwilling to move, remained in the city. More than 38,000 members of the National Guard were deployed in affected areas; 7,000 were deployed in New Orleans itself with orders to shoot to kill looters. They were joined by 8,500 soldiers on active duty. The impact of another hurricane, Hurricane Rita, along the Gulf coast at the end of September, further affected relief efforts. By August 2006 the official death toll as a result of Hurricane Katrina, the USA's deadliest natural disaster in almost 80 years, was 1,836; a further 135 people remained missing.

A report by the Government Accountability Office, published in February 2006, criticized government at all levels for its failure adequately to respond to the emergency. It found that relief efforts had been hampered by the absence of a clear chain of command, and compounded by insufficient planning and preparation; it also identified examples of waste and fraud in the appropriation of relief and reconstruction funds. Meanwhile, President Bush appealed to Congress for a further US $19,600m. towards reconstruction along the Gulf coast, particularly the strengthening of the protective levees around New Orleans. In August, however, it emerged that of the $110,000m. designated by Congress to the cause, only $44,000m. had been disseminated.

The Republican Party faced a series of corruption scandals in 2005–06. In September 2005 the Republican Majority Leader in the House of Representatives, Tom DeLay, was indicted on charges of having illegally financed Republican candidates in the 2002 election campaign. In October I. 'Scooter' Lewis Libby, chief of staff to Vice-President Dick Cheney, was indicted on charges that included obstruction of justice and perjury during an investigation into the leaking of the identity of CIA agent Valerie Plame in mid-2003. It was held that Plame's identity had deliberately been made public as a reprisal against her husband, Senator Joseph Wilson, a former US Ambassador to Iraq, who had publicly accused the Administration of making selective use of intelligence to justify the invasion of Iraq in 2003. The Libby trial commenced in January 2007, although neither Libby nor Vice-President Cheney, also implicated in the scandal, testified. In March Libby was convicted of four charges of perjury, and in June was sentenced to 30 months in prison. In the following month President Bush commuted Libby's sentence to a two-year probation period and a US $250,000 fine, after describing the original sentence as 'excessive'.

In March 2006 lobbyist Jack Abramoff was sentenced to 70 months' imprisonment, after pleading guilty to charges that included conspiracy to bribe public officials, fraud and tax evasion. The enactment of legislation banning members of Congress from accepting donations from lobbyists was approved by the Senate later that month, while a similar, although less far-reaching, law was narrowly approved by the House of Representatives in May.

At mid-term elections in November 2006, the Democrats secured control of both chambers of Congress. The Republican electoral defeat was regarded as indicative of citizens' loss of confidence in Bush's presidency, principally owing to the lack of progress in Iraq and escalating violence in Afghanistan, but also in regard to domestic policy, namely the perceived inadequacy of the federal Government's response to Hurricane Katrina, immigration policy, the erratic nature of economic recovery and the numerous cases of corruption within Republican ranks. Immediately following the elections, the Secretary of Defense, Donald Rumsfeld, ceded to demands for his resignation, citing the need for a 'fresh perspective' on the ongoing conflict in Iraq. Robert M. Gates, a former CIA Director, succeeded him. Rumsfeld had attracted international opprobrium for his apparent approval of 'harsh interrogation' techniques in the examination of terrorism suspects.

Further controversy involving the Republican Administration emerged in early 2007, after it was revealed that eight US state attorneys had been summarily dismissed under the direction of Attorney-General Alberto Gonzales. It was claimed that the dismissals were politically motivated, the majority having allegedly resulted from the attorneys' failure sufficiently to pursue accusations of voting irregularities against Democratic candidates in the November 2006 elections. Gonzales testified before the Senate Judiciary Committee in April 2007, when inconsistencies between his various statements regarding his knowledge of, and motivation for, the dismissals were found seriously to undermine his integrity as an impartial arbiter of justice. Several senior officials at the White House and the Department of Justice were implicated in the controversy and subsequently resigned. In September Gonzales finally stood down from office while maintaining that he had committed no wrongdoing. Michael B. Mukasey was confirmed by the Senate as the new Attorney-General in November.

There were a number of further resignations by key personnel in the Bush Administration in 2007–08. Al Hubbard announced his departure from the National Economic Council, of which he was the Director, in November 2007, at a time when the US economy was becoming increasingly unstable. In December Undersecretary of State for Public Diplomacy Karen Hughes became Bush's third adviser to vacate office in six months, following Counselor to the President Dan Bartlett in July and the President's Deputy Chief of Staff, Karl Rove, who relinquished his post in August, having been implicated in the controversy surrounding the dismissal of state attorneys earlier in the year. Housing and Urban Development Secretary Alphonso Jackson resigned in April 2008, amid an ongoing FBI investigation into allegations of favouritism in awarding housing contracts and as the US housing market continued to deteriorate. The crisis in the housing market moved Congress to approve legislation in mid-2008: the Housing and Economic Recovery Act provided for emergency funding for federal mortgage institutions and was intended to restore confidence in the sector.

Obama elected President

Presidential and congressional elections were held on 4 November 2008. Illinois senator Barack Obama had been selected as the Democratic Party's representative in June, thereby becoming its first African-American presidential candidate, after a long campaign in which he had defeated New York senator Hillary Clinton. Joseph Biden, the Delaware senator, was Obama's vice-presidential nominee. The Republican Party's presidential candidate, John McCain, selected the Governor of Alaska, Sarah Palin, as his running mate. In the event, Obama secured a clear victory, winning 52.9% of the valid votes cast and 365 electoral college votes, compared with McCain's 45.7% and 173 electoral college votes. The Democrats also performed well in the concurrently held congressional elections. The party increased its majority in the House of Representatives to 256 seats, and to at least 56 seats in the Senate (where elections to renew one-third of the seats were held), although it lacked the 60-member so-called 'super majority' required to overcome Republican delaying tactics in the latter. The result of the senate election in Minnesota was delayed owing to the closeness of the result. Following a lengthy legal process, the Democratic candidate, Al Franken, was declared the victor by a panel of state judges in March 2009, a ruling that was upheld by the Minnesota Supreme Court in June. Franken's victory, together with the defection, in April, of Arlen Specter of Pennsylvania from the Republican Party to the Democratic Party, increased the Democrats' representation in the Senate to 58. This, in effect, gave the Democrats the three-

THE UNITED STATES OF AMERICA

fifths' 'super majority', as the two independent senators routinely voted with the Democrats.

The search for a candidate to replace Obama in the Senate became the focus of increased media attention in late 2008, after it was alleged that the Governor of Illinois, Rod Blagojevich, had attempted to 'sell' the vacant seat to the highest bidder. Blagojevich was arrested on federal corruption charges in December. Blagojevich's nomination for the Senate, Roland Burris, was initially barred from taking his seat owing to his connections with the disgraced Governor, but was eventually sworn in on 15 January 2009; in the following month Burris admitted that he had been approached to fundraise for Blagojevich. Blagojevich was impeached on 27 January, and, following a unanimous vote in the Illinois state senate, was removed from office on 29 January; he was subsequently replaced by Lieutenant-Governor Patrick J. Quinn, III. In mid-August 2010 Blagojevich was convicted on just one of the 24 charges levelled against him, namely of lying to investigators; a mistrial was recorded in the remaining 23 charges, with the jury having been unable to reach consensus. A retrial on these 23 counts commenced in April 2011.

Obama was sworn in as President on 20 January 2009. Hillary Clinton was named Secretary of State in Obama's Cabinet, while Timothy F. Geithner was installed as Secretary of the Treasury, and Robert M. Gates, Secretary of Defense in the previous Bush Administration, was reappointed to that post. Obama's first choice for the commerce portfolio, Bill Richardson, was forced to withdraw in December 2008 owing to an ongoing investigation into financial irregularities, and a second nominee, Republican Judd Gregg, withdrew his candidacy in February 2009 after disagreements over economic policy; Gary F. Locke was subsequently confirmed as Secretary of Commerce in March. The President's candidate to take over the health and human services portfolio, former Senate majority leader Tom Daschle, had also retired from the nomination process at the end of January owing to tax discrepancies; Kathleen Sebelius was confirmed as Secretary of Health and Human Services at the end of April. Sonia Sotomayor became the first Hispanic American Associate Justice of the Supreme Court in August 2009, having been nominated to the post by Obama in May.

Legislative reform under the Obama Administration

One of the first priorities of the new Administration of Barack Obama was to gain congressional approval for a US $787,000m. economic stimulus programme aimed at alleviating the impact of the economic slowdown (see Economic Affairs). The series of measures, which included tax cuts, funding for infrastructural projects, the introduction of a cap on executive salaries, and several protectionist moves, was approved by Congress in February 2009. President Obama also announced a further $50,000m. in aid for homeowners struggling to meet mortgage payments. Obama's first State of the Union address to Congress, in January 2010, focused primarily on the economy, acknowledging the unpopularity of the rescue plan for financial institutions and identifying the creation of new jobs as his Administration's most important priority for 2010.

Shortly after taking office, President Obama had proposed a comprehensive reform of the health care system, with the aim of controlling rising costs, extending provision, improving the affordability of health insurance and increasing the accountability of health insurers. The House of Representatives and the Senate approved two separate, but broadly similar, health care reform bills in November and December 2009, respectively. However, the legislative process subsequently stalled, amid considerable opposition to the proposed changes from Republicans, who contended that the measures would, in fact, raise costs and entail excessive government intrusion. Moreover, the Democratic Party suffered a serious reverse on 19 January 2010, when it lost a special election for the senate seat in Massachusetts previously held by senior Democrat Edward Kennedy, himself a long-time proponent of universal health care coverage, who had died in August 2009 after almost 47 years in office: Republican Scott Brown, who opposed the health care bill, defeated the Democratic candidate, Martha Coakley. The victory of the Republican Party, which followed its defeat of the Democratic Party in gubernatorial elections in New Jersey and Virginia in November, reflected not only public uncertainty regarding Obama's health care proposals, but also discontent over the country's economic difficulties, and deprived the Democrats of their 'super majority' in the Senate.

Undeterred, Obama renewed his efforts to secure the congressional passage of health care reforms, and on 21 March 2010, by a margin of 219 votes to 212, the House of Representatives approved the bill adopted by the Senate in December 2009, despite unanimous Republican opposition. Under the legislation, which Obama signed into law two days later, health care provision was to be extended to an estimated 32m. currently uninsured US residents through the expansion of Medicaid, a federal programme for certain low-income categories, and the creation of state-based 'exchanges' offering subsidized insurance. In addition, health insurers would henceforth be prohibited from denying coverage to those with pre-existing medical conditions. Amendments to the legislation, submitted under the budget reconciliation process, which meant that they required the approval of only a simple majority of senators, had been adopted by both houses and signed by Obama by the end of the month. The Congressional Budget Office estimated that the implementation of the reforms would cost some US $938,000m. in 2010–19 and result in a net reduction in the federal budget deficit of $143,000m. over the same period.

Meanwhile, financial reforms continued in 2010. In March Obama enacted legislation providing tax incentives for businesses hiring unemployed workers and funding for infrastructure projects, following its approval by both chambers of Congress, and in July Obama pledged an end to taxpayer-funded bailouts as he signed into effect wide-ranging legislation that provided for a comprehensive overhaul of the financial regulatory system. *Inter alia*, the legislation afforded the Government new powers to shut down companies that were deemed to pose a threat to the national economy; granted enhanced powers to the Federal Reserve (the USA's central banking system), which was henceforth to be liable to greater congressional scrutiny; and offered greater protection to consumers from hidden borrowing fees and punitive rates of interest. The law was widely acclaimed as a second major legislative success for the Obama Administration, although Republicans contested that it would prove a burden on small banks and those companies and individuals reliant on them.

Upon taking office in January 2009, Obama had immediately instituted a 120-day hiatus on the military tribunals at Guantánamo Bay to allow for a thorough review of the situation. He also reiterated his pledge to close the prison camp within a year. The new President had already diverged significantly from the previous Administration by claiming that waterboarding constituted torture and by admitting the existence of secret CIA prisons. He also ordered that the CIA cease the torture of detainees. His decision was widely praised, although the presidential order stopped short of halting the CIA's right to use extraordinary rendition. However, in May Obama announced that military tribunals would be resumed for a number of detainees, following the implementation of measures to strengthen the legal rights of defendants, while others would be tried in US civilian courts. Later that month it emerged that Ahmed Ghailani, who was accused of involvement in the 1998 embassy bombings in Nairobi and Dar es Salaam, would be the first Guantánamo inmate to be tried by a US federal court. Ghailani's trial commenced in New York in June 2009, and in November 2010 he was convicted on one count of conspiracy to destroy US property with explosives but acquitted of 284 other counts of conspiracy and multiple murder charges, after the presiding judge ruled that the evidence of the main witness was not admissible because he had been held in a secret CIA prison 'under extreme duress'; nevertheless, Ghailani was sentenced to life imprisonment in January 2011.

Meanwhile, difficulties had arisen over the release of a number of Guantánamo detainees, some of whom were considered to be at risk of abuse if returned to their countries of origin. In addition, transfers of inmates to Yemen, where many of the prisoners originated, were suspended in January 2010, following a failed bombing attempt on a flight from the Netherlands' capital, Amsterdam, to Detroit, Michigan, on 25 December 2009 by a Nigerian who claimed to have been trained by al-Qa'ida in Yemen. (A review of the incident revealed a number of intelligence failures, concluding that the CIA and the National Counterterrorism Center had had access to sufficient information to have uncovered and potentially disrupted the plot; the Yemen-based al-Qa'ida in the Arabian Peninsula, which claimed responsibility for the failed attack, was subsequently designated a foreign terrorist organization by the US Administration.)

With Obama's self-imposed deadline for securing the closure of Guantánamo Bay long passed, hopes of securing its closure in the foreseeable future were dealt a severe blow in December 2010, when the House of Representatives voted to prohibit the Administration from transferring Guantánamo inmates to US soil for trial or detention. (Despite considerable opposition, Obama had ordered the preparation of a correction centre in Thomson, Illinois, for this purpose in December 2009.) A report partly declassified in December 2010, in which it was claimed that 81 of the 598 prisoners released thus far from Guantánamo Bay were known to have resumed involvement in terrorism-related activities, was cited by the Republicans as evidence of the need to provide for the continued detention of those prisoners whose release was deemed to be too dangerous but against whom there was insufficient presentable evidence for either a civilian or military trial. Some 174 detainees reportedly still remained at the camp at the end of 2010.

Continued engagement in Iraq and Afghanistan

In February 2009 President Obama reiterated his electoral pledge to withdraw all US combat troops from Iraq by the end of August 2010. US combat troops commenced their withdrawal from urban areas in Iraq on 30 June 2009, having formally transferred responsibility for security to Iraqi forces. Some US forces were to remain in the cities, in a non-combative capacity, to train, advise and support the Iraqi security forces, while others would participate in Iraqi-led operations outside urban areas. Total losses of US military personnel in Iraq had reached 4,321 by this time (increasing to 4,390 by the end of March 2010), while estimates of total Iraqi fatalities were a matter of dispute, ranging from 90,000 to as many as 600,000. By March, in which month Iraqi legislative elections were held, US troop numbers in Iraq had been reduced to about 96,000. In September 'Operation Iraqi Freedom' was renamed 'Operation New Dawn' to reflect the revised role of the US forces following the withdrawal from Iraq of all remaining US combat troops, two weeks ahead of schedule, in mid-August. All remaining US non-combat service personnel, who were estimated to number about 47,000 at early 2011, were scheduled to be withdrawn from the country by the end of that year.

Meanwhile, in February 2009 President Obama announced that a further 17,000 US troops would be deployed in Afghanistan. At the end of March Obama confirmed his Administration's shift in policy towards combating insurgency in Afghanistan and neighbouring Pakistan by announcing that an additional 4,000 troops were to be dispatched to the region to support the Afghan army and police force there. The shift towards counter-insurgency tactics—a break from the US Army's traditional doctrine—continued in the following month after Secretary of Defense Robert M. Gates announced that he had requested the resignation of Gen. David D. McKiernan as Commander of the International Security Assistance Force (ISAF), less than a year after his appointment; McKiernan was replaced in June by a veteran Special Operations commander, Lt-Gen. Stanley A. McChrystal, who was concomitantly promoted to the rank of general.

As the security situation in Afghanistan continued to deteriorate, a further 30,000 US troops were dispatched to that country in the first few months of 2010, in order to reinforce counter-insurgency operations and to allow an expansion in the training of the Afghan security forces, with the aim of being able to commence the phased withdrawal of US combat troops in July 2011. It was repeatedly emphasized, however, that the timetable for their departure would be flexible, depending on prevailing conditions. Meanwhile, Obama pledged continued assistance for Pakistan in its efforts to combat extremists. In February 2010 US-led coalition forces and Afghan troops initiated a major counter-insurgency operation in Afghanistan's Helmand province, 'Operation Moshtarak', which was described as the largest offensive since the Taliban regime was ousted in late 2001. In a notable change of approach, the offensive was widely publicized beforehand in order to warn the civilian population.

Obama made his first visit to Afghanistan as US President in late March 2010, addressing US troops and holding talks with his Afghan counterpart, Hamid Karzai. According to the Department of Defense, total losses of US military personnel in 'Operation Enduring Freedom' had reached 1,021 by this time, 943 deaths having occurred 'in or around' Afghanistan (which included deaths in Pakistan and Uzbekistan). In July Obama nominated Gen. David Petraeus as the new Commander of ISAF, in place of Gen. McChrystal, who had been recalled to Washington, DC, after negative comments pertaining to Vice-President Biden and other prominent figures within the Obama Administration were attributed to him in a prominent US publication.

As 2010 drew to a close, US officials noted positive developments arising from a long-anticipated surge on the Taliban stronghold of Qandahar, which had commenced in June, but cautioned that the true extent of any progress would remain unclear for some time. During a visit to Kabul in early January 2011, Vice-President Biden pledged a continuation of US assistance beyond 2014, exclusively in a training and supportive, rather than military, capacity; during his visit, Biden also claimed that Taliban momentum had been 'largely arrested' in key areas, including Helmand and Qandahar, but acknowledged that such gains were 'fragile and reversible'. (In July 2010 President Karzai announced details of ambitious plans for Afghan forces to have assumed control of all military and law enforcement operations throughout Afghanistan by 2014.) In March 2011 President Karzai named seven locations, including three provinces (Bamian, Kabul and Panjshir) and four cities (Herat, Kabul, Lashkar Gah and Mehter Lam), where the transfer of security responsibility to the Afghan authorities was scheduled to commence in July.

Recent developments: the 2010 mid-term elections

Despite the legislative achievements of the Obama Administration, the immense public goodwill that had greeted the President's election had all but dissipated by mid-2010. Obama's approval ratings languished at 41% in August, while the growing popularity of the 'Tea Party Movement'—a broad-based anti-Government movement on the right of the political spectrum that had emerged in 2009—was indicative of increasing dissatisfaction with continued economic hardship and the Administration's legislative agenda. The Tea Party Movement was credited by many observers with energizing the Republican Party, which was expected to make considerable gains at the 2010 mid-term elections.

The elections were held, as scheduled, on 2 November 2010, and, as expected the Democrats suffered heavy losses: the Republicans gained 63 seats in the House of Representatives (the largest change of seats in the House following a mid-term election since 1938), and won six seats in the Senate. With the Republicans reclaiming the House majority and the Senate remaining under Democrat control, it was widely anticipated that efforts by the Obama Administration to push through further legislative reform would require a much greater level of compromise in order to bridge the divide between the Democratic and Republican political agendas. An example of this was provided by a tax bill that was approved by both congressional chambers and signed into law in December 2010. The legislation, which provided for a two-year extension to tax reductions for the wealthiest Americans that had been introduced during the presidency of George W. Bush, was the result of a deal brokered between the Obama Administration and the Republicans, by which Obama rescinded his electoral pledge to eliminate the tax reductions in exchange for Republican support for an extension to benefits for 2m. unemployed and low-income earners.

In January 2011 Gabrielle Giffords, a Democratic member of the House of Representatives for Arizona, was critically injured in an apparent assassination attempt perpetrated by a lone gunman; six people, including a Chief Judge of the Arizona District Court, John M. Roll, were fatally shot and a further 13 others (including Giffords) were injured in the incident. The killing prompted enormous public debate on the increasing polarization and hostility present in US politics, with many commentators suggesting that the vitriolic nature of right-wing opposition to the Obama Administration, notably from supporters of the Tea Party Movement, helped to foster a culture of violent political enmity and may have contributed to Giffords' shooting. In a break from tradition designed to demonstrate congressional unity, rival Democrats and Republicans sat alongside one another during the President's State of the Union address later in that month. In his address Obama paid tribute to Giffords and appealed for a bipartisan effort to heal the divisions caused by 'sharply polarized' political debate.

Meanwhile, in December 2010 a federal judge in Virginia ruled that the health care reform legislation approved in March was unconstitutional since it overstepped the 'boundaries of congressional power'. In January 2011 the House of Representatives, with its new Republican majority, voted to repeal the legislation, although, as had been widely expected, the Democrat-controlled Senate voted to reject the repeal in early February. Meanwhile, in late January a second federal judge, in Florida, ruled that the health care reforms, specifically the requirement that all American citizens purchase health insurance, contravened the Constitution and should be rescinded. The Obama Administration dismissed the judgment as 'legal overreaching' and announced its intention to appeal against the ruling. Two other federal judges had rejected previous challenges to the legislation, the fate of which was expected ultimately to be decided by the Supreme Court in late 2011 or early 2012.

Differences in approach with regard to reducing the mounting federal budget deficit exacerbated divisions between the Democrats and the Republicans in early 2011. President Obama's draft budget for 2011/12, which was submitted to Congress in February 2011, proposed a range of deficit-reduction measures, including planned tax increases and a five-year freeze on non-military spending. However, the proposals were vehemently opposed by Republicans, who demanded a far more radical programme of spending cuts, including reductions in social spending, particularly on health care, as well as lower taxation to stimulate economic growth. An impasse over federal spending for the remainder of the 2011 fiscal year, which almost resulted in a 'shutdown' of government services, was finally resolved in April when the House approved a hard-fought compromise agreement. However, with Republicans, in particular those associated with the Tea Party Movement, continuing to demand ever-sharper reductions in public expenditure, lengthy negotiations were expected in mid-2011 before Obama's 2011/12 budget would be approved.

Controversy was generated in April 2011 by the announcement that Khalid Sheikh Mohammed (see Attacks of 11 September 2001, above) would be tried by a military commission at Guantánamo Bay, following congressional opposition to an earlier decision that he would stand trial in a civilian court in the USA. Obama had previously expressed doubts that a fair trial could be conducted under the military commission system. The Obama Administration suffered embarrassment later in the same month, when hundreds of classified US documents detailing conditions at Guantánamo Bay were released by the WikiLeaks organization (see Foreign Affairs—Other external relations). The documents contained evidence of the detention of suspects without charge and the imprisonment of innocent civilians.

At the beginning of May 2011 Osama bin Laden, the founder of al-Qa'ida and the FBI's 'most-wanted' terrorist target, was killed during a raid carried out by US special operations forces on a fortified compound in Abbottabad, Pakistan. Four other inhabitants of the compound, including one of bin Laden's sons, were reportedly killed during the operation. Following confirmation of his identity by DNA testing, bin Laden's body was buried at sea. The outcome of the operation resulted in a significant improvement in President Obama's domestic approval rating, according to several opinion polls. Furthermore, many observers suggested that the killing of bin Laden would provide the Administration with additional impetus in its efforts to extricate the USA from its military campaign in Afghanistan.

Immigration and Border Security

In January 2004 the US-Visit programme was implemented, requiring that all visa-holders entering the USA were electronically fingerprinted and photographed on arrival. By January 2005 the programme had been extended to 50 land border crossings and was scheduled to reach a further 115 by the end of that year. In April 2006 some 500,000 people in Los Angeles participated in a march in protest at restrictive new immigration legislation; other protest marches took place in Phoenix, Denver and Milwaukee. The legislation, approved by the House of Representatives in December 2005, made illegal immigration a criminal offence, and approved the Secure Border Initiative (SBI), which envisaged construction of 1,130 km (700 miles) of reinforced fencing along parts of the US–Mexican border, together with the implementation of surveillance cameras and motion sensors designed to act as a 'virtual fence' in those parts of the border without a physical barrier. The Senate ratified immigration legislation in May 2006 authorizing the establishment of a guest worker programme. Provisions were also made for immigrants to attain citizenship, subject to the satisfaction of certain criteria. In August the federal Government implemented 'Operation Jump Start', an immigration control initiative effected in the southern border regions, including Arizona, Texas, California and New Mexico. The initiative entailed the deployment of 6,000 National Guard personnel in support of the Border Patrol, and succeeded in curtailing the illegal border crossings by an estimated 30% by early 2007; 'Operation Jump Start' was formally concluded in July 2008. Meanwhile, during a visit by President George W. Bush to Mexico in March 2007, the Mexican President, Felipe Calderón Hinojosa, reiterated his opposition to the proposed security fence.

In his budget plan for 2010/11, which was submitted to Congress in February 2010, President Barack Obama proposed a reduction in expenditure on border security in order to increase spending on aviation security, in response to the failed aircraft bombing attempt of 25 December 2009 (see Domestic Political Affairs). In March 2010, after some 1,035 km (643 miles) of the border fence had been erected, the Secretary of Homeland Security, Janet Napolitano, announced a freeze on new SBI funding and diverted US $50m. of its approved funding to other uses, amid escalating public debate as to the potential effectiveness of the initiative: after more than $1,000m. spent on the project, just 53 miles of the border had been covered by the surveillance technology by the end of 2010. In August the House of Representatives approved the disbursement of some $600m. on an additional 1,500 Border Patrol agents, as well as two unmanned surveillance drones, in a development heralded by many observers as a return to more traditional border security measures. In January 2011 Napolitano announced the cancellation of the SBI project, pledging to formulate a new strategy that would be 'tailored to the unique needs of each border region', and which would offer 'a more effective balance between cost and capability'; details of the new region-specific proposals were expected to be announced later in the year. The number of illegal immigrants in the USA was reported to be relatively unchanged in 2010, at about 11.2m., compared with 11.1m. in 2009; a peak of about 12m. had been recorded in 2008.

Energy Security and Environmental Concerns

An energy policy report issued by the Administration of George W. Bush in May 2001, which included a proposal to introduce legislation authorizing exploratory drilling for oil in the Arctic National Wildlife Refuge in Alaska (ANWR), prompted criticism from the environmental lobby. In August the House of Representatives voted in favour of the proposal; however, the proposed legislation was rejected by the Senate in April 2002. The Administration subsequently introduced a provision to allow drilling to start in 2004, whereby federal revenue would be raised from the sale of leases to petroleum companies, but in March 2003 Congress removed the provision. In August the Government proposed further controversial amendments to regulations governing carbon emissions; under the new legislation, energy companies would no longer be required to install anti-pollution measures when upgrading equipment. The announcement prompted criticism from environmental groups. In March–April 2005 Congress narrowly approved a proposal to begin drilling in the ANWR. However, in its final version, the relevant legislation was part of a wider budget reconciliation bill that was only approved by both houses in December once the ANWR provision had been removed. In what appeared to be a repetition of the previous year's events, in March 2006 the Senate narrowly approved legislation that would permit the opening of parts of the ANWR to drilling; however, the outcome was again contingent on congressional approval of another budget reconciliation bill. Government proposals for the inclusion of the ANWR in the USA's Strategic Petroleum Reserve were presented in March 2007 as a means of expediting the long-debated exploitation of the Refuge for its oil wealth. Conversely, proposed legislation to designate the coastal region of the ANWR as a wilderness area to be permanently exempted from oil exploration was introduced to the Senate Natural Resources Committee for discussion in November, but was rejected before reaching the wider Senate. Despite ratification of minor amendments to existing ANWR legislation during that year, and the President's reiteration in April 2008 of the Refuge's potential as a resource for bolstering the Strategic Petroleum Reserve—with regard to the effects of escalating international oil prices upon the domestic economy—the existing restrictions were still in place when Barack Obama, who was strongly opposed to any future exploration of the ANWR, took office in January 2009. Although Obama announced proposals in March 2010 to expand offshore oil and gas exploration off the Atlantic coast, notably off Virginia, a reversal of his position on the ANWR seemed unlikely. According to the US Geological Survey, recoverable oil reserves in the ANWR were estimated at 10,400m. barrels of oil in 2005; at that time US oil consumption totalled about 20m. barrels per day.

An explosion in April 2010 on the *Deepwater Horizon* offshore drilling rig, which was operating for the United Kingdom-based company BP in an oilfield about 60 km south-east of the Louisiana coast, precipitated the largest ever accidental offshore oil spill globally. The equivalent of an estimated 4.9m. barrels of oil seeped into the Gulf of Mexico between the time of the explosion, on 20 April, and the eventual capping of the well, after a number of failed attempts, on 15 July; of this amount, only

THE UNITED STATES OF AMERICA

an estimated 800,000 barrels were captured during containment operations. The initial explosion claimed the lives of 11 oil workers and injured 17 others. In mid-May Obama established a bipartisan National Commission on the BP *Deepwater Horizon* Oil Spill and Offshore Drilling, which was charged with investigating the oil spill with a view to providing recommendations on how best to reduce the risk, and mitigate the impact, of any future spills as a result of offshore drilling. In a comprehensive report detailing the findings of its inquiry, which was published in early November, the Commission concluded that BP had not sacrificed safety in attempts to boost its profits but that some decisions had increased risks on the oil rig. Opinion polls conducted in June suggested that 59% of Americans disapproved of Obama's handling of the disaster, while 75% disapproved of how the federal Government in general had responded to the spill; complaints primarily centred on the belief that Obama had not taken a sufficiently firm line in dealing with BP, although the President did secure an agreement with the oil company committing to set up a US $20,000m. compensation fund from which to pay out damages to individuals and businesses affected by the oil spill; Obama also persuaded BP to create a separate $100m. fund from which to compensate oil rig employees who had been left unemployed as a result of the disaster.

Meanwhile, in March 2001 the withdrawal of support by the Bush Administration for the ratification process of the Kyoto Protocol on climate change (UN Environment Programme, see p. 65), claiming that it would be detrimental to US economic interests, had prompted stern condemnation from environmental campaigners and numerous foreign governments and international organizations. In February 2002 Bush proposed voluntary, less far-reaching, measures to reduce emissions of greenhouse gases. In response to the heightened international concern over global warming and the depletion of energy resources, President Bush signed the Energy Independence and Security Act in December 2007, increasing fuel-efficiency standards for passenger vehicles and stipulating that biofuels should account for 36,000m. gallons of motor fuel by 2022 in order to reduce the USA's dependence on imported petroleum. In his State of the Union address delivered in January 2008, Bush reaffirmed his commitment to combating climate change with initiatives including the establishment of a US $3,000m. international clean technology fund. He also urged Congress to approve a $150,000m. economic stimulus plan and to ensure that tax relief measures were made permanent.

Hopes of greater US co-operation in international efforts to counter the effects of man-made climate change were raised by Obama's election to the presidency, and in June 2009 the House of Representatives voted to commit the USA to reducing carbon emissions by 17% from 2005 levels by 2020 and by 83% by 2050; if approved by the Senate, the bill, which was hailed as the most important energy- and environment-related legislation in US history, would also provide for the establishment of a national 'cap and trade' system (an emissions trading programme with overall limits set by the federal Government). However, following the Democrats' loss of its 'super majority' in the Senate (see Domestic Political Affairs), the Obama Administration was forced to abandon the bill in June 2010, owing to continued opposition from Republican senators. In place of the abandoned bill, more limited legislation was proposed, the focus of which was on increasing firms' liability for oil spills, in response to public anger towards BP in the wake of the Gulf of Mexico spill. The new bill was approved by the House of Representatives in July. However, it remained stalled in the Senate at early 2011, with many Democrats blaming Republican senators for wilfully obstructing the passage of the bill in order to deny a major legislative success to the Obama Administration. Forced to adapt, Obama announced a moderated environmental strategy in his State of the Union address in January, which included a plan to double the percentage of US electricity derived from clean energy sources, from about 40% to 80% by 2035; investment in clean energy technology, the President argued, would 'strengthen our security, protect our planet, and create countless new jobs for our people'.

Foreign Affairs
Relations with Latin America

Ronald Reagan's Administration actively supported right-wing regimes in Latin America, where the US military occupation of Grenada in November 1983 attracted considerable international criticism. In December 1989, following the failure of an internal coup attempt that received non-military US support, the USA, under the presidency of Reagan's successor, George Bush, carried out an armed invasion of Panama and subsequently installed an elected government. US troops were withdrawn in February 1990. In Nicaragua the defeat of the Sandinista Government in a general election in February 1990 was followed by the resumption of cordial relations with the US Government.

The Administration of Bill Clinton made renewed efforts to restore to power Fr Jean-Bertrand Aristide, the first democratically elected President of Haiti, who had taken refuge in the USA following his overthrow by a military junta in 1991. An economic embargo imposed by the Organization of American States (OAS, see p. 391), together with implied threats of military intervention by the US Government, had failed to displace the military regime, and conditions within Haiti had led large numbers of refugees to seek asylum in the USA, many of whom were forcibly repatriated by the US authorities. In June 1994, following the imposition in the previous month of international sanctions against Haiti by the UN Security Council, Clinton announced the suspension of all commercial and financial transactions with Haiti. In September, following a diplomatic mission led by former President Carter, a UN-sponsored multinational force, composed almost entirely of US troops, arrived in Haiti with the agreement of the military junta, which relinquished power in October. US troops were withdrawn from the UN force in March 1995. In January 2004 the Administration of George W. Bush condemned attacks on thousands of demonstrators protesting against the Aristide Government. In March, in the face of growing violence and under international pressure, Aristide resigned and went into exile, although he claimed that he had been unconstitutionally removed from office by the USA. Several hundred US marines were deployed in Haiti in March–June 2004 as the vanguard of a multinational UN Stabilization Mission in Haiti to disarm rebel forces and stabilize the country. Following the earthquake that struck Haiti in January 2010, the USA dispatched some 12,000 military personnel to the country to assist in the distribution of relief supplies. In advance of the 2010–11 presidential and parliamentary elections, the first round of which was held in Haiti on 28 November 2010, the US Government donated US $14m. to support the staging of free and fair elections. Nevertheless, following the elections allegations of electoral malpractice and voting irregularities were raised both by opposition candidates and the international community. The decision of the US Administration to appeal for the modification of the first-round results—in line with recommendations made by an OAS 'Expert Verification Mission' that had been charged with investigating the polls—rather than calling for the holding of fresh elections, elicited severe criticism from some quarters, including a group of 19 Haitian and international policy and legal groups and human rights organizations, which issued a statement in February 2011 condemning the Administration's response to the apparently fraudulent elections.

Successive US Governments remained unwilling to restore relations with Cuba. Relations between the two countries deteriorated in March 1996, after two civilian aircraft carrying Cuban exiles protesting against the Government of Fidel Castro were shot down by the Cuban air force over international waters. In response, Clinton acceded to congressional demands to strengthen the US commercial and economic embargo that has been in force since 1962. Under the new measure, the Cuban Liberty and Solidarity (Helms-Burton) Act, the USA was to penalize foreign investors whose business in any way involved property in Cuba that was confiscated from US citizens following the 1959 revolution. In July 1996 a number of Canadian, Mexican and Italian companies were informed that sanctions were to be imposed on them under the Helms-Burton legislation, barring their senior executives and certain shareholders from visiting the USA. In response to intense international pressure, Clinton declared a temporary moratorium on certain provisions of the Helms-Burton Act, and in April 1997 the US Government and the EU, which had protested the measure, announced that a compromise had been agreed, subject to the abandonment by the US Government of certain sections of the Act. The moratorium on Title III of the Act was subsequently extended at six-monthly intervals and remained in operation in 2010. In late 2001 the USA lifted temporarily the trade embargo against Cuba to allow the purchase of food and medicines necessary for the reconstruction and aid effort following the devastation caused by Hurricane Michelle. In May 2002, however, the Bush Administration accused Cuba of maintaining a biological warfare programme and offering weapons technology to 'rogue states'. In April 2004 a

THE UNITED STATES OF AMERICA

Introductory Survey

motion, supported by the USA, condemning Cuba for human rights violations, was approved by the UN General Assembly; similar US-backed motions had been passed by the UN in 2002 and 2003. In April 2005 a milder, US-proposed motion requesting that the mandate of the UN's Special Rapporteur on Human Rights in Cuba be extended was approved by the General Assembly. In July Secretary of State Condoleezza Rice appointed Caleb McCarry Cuba Transition Co-ordinator, a position created at the behest of a special panel charged with directing the US Government's actions 'in support of a free Cuba' and hastening the end to Castro's presidency. Bilateral relations deteriorated further in 2007 following the release from a US prison of Luis Posada Carriles, who was wanted in Cuba on terrorism charges. The Cuban Government accused the Bush Administration of hypocrisy in its so-called 'war on terror'. In April 2009 the Administration of Barack Obama relaxed certain sanctions against Cuba, including travel restrictions on Cuban-American citizens and limits on remittances, and permitted US telecommunications companies to seek access to the Cuban market, prompting hopes of an amelioration in relations. However, the trade embargo remained in place and was renewed for a further year in September. Any improvement in relations was halted by the imprisonment in December of a US contractor on suspicion of espionage; Alan Gross had been arrested while working as a business and economic development consultant despite only possessing a tourist visa, but both he and the Obama Administration strenuously refuted the claims against him. In February 2011 the Cuban authorities announced that Gross was finally to be charged, with 'actions against the independence and territorial integrity of the state'. Meanwhile, the trade embargo was renewed for a further year in September 2010.

In December 1994 President Clinton proposed the formation, by 2006, of a Free Trade Area of the Americas (FTAA), comprising 34 countries of the Western hemisphere, although excluding Cuba. Negotiations were scheduled to conclude by January 2005, but stalled in November 2004; although it was agreed to resume talks in mid-2006, there had been no progress to this end by early 2011. Meanwhile, however, the Venezuelan President, Lt-Col (retd) Hugo Chávez Frías, had commenced implementation of an alternative free trade initiative for the Americas, the Bolivarian Alternative for the Americas (Alternativa Bolivariana para las Américas—ALBA), in direct challenge to the moribund FTAA. Relations between the Bush and Chávez Governments deteriorated markedly in the 2000s, and in September 2008 the Venezuelan President suspended diplomatic relations with the USA in solidarity with the Bolivian Government of Evo Morales. Morales had expelled the US ambassador, accusing him of fomenting opposition dissent in Bolivia. Secretary of State Hillary Clinton intimated in mid-2009 that the Obama Government wanted to improve relations with the left-wing administrations in Bolivia and Venezuela, and in June US-Venezuelan diplomatic relations were resumed.

In January 2000 the Clinton Administration announced an aid package for the Andean region worth US $1,300m., the largest ever aid programme for Latin America. The main portion of the programme, which became known as the 'Plan Colombia', was to provide some $860m. to Colombia, three-quarters of which was allocated to the security forces in that country, to aid with the ongoing war against drugs-trafficking. The size of the military component of the Plan caused controversy internationally, as did the proposed aerial destruction of crops in the region. The Bush Administration implemented an Andean Counterdrug Initiative in 2001 to complement Plan Colombia, the focus of which was on improving social and economic conditions in the region. Nevertheless, the objective remained the same: to reduce significantly the flow of drugs from the Andean region into the USA. An agreement signed by the USA and Colombia in October 2009, granting the US military access to seven Colombian bases, strengthened bilateral relations, but was criticized by other South American countries, most notably Venezuela. In February 2010 the Obama Administration proposed a reduction in funding for Plan Colombia in its budget plan for the 2011 fiscal year, partly on the grounds that the programme had progressed to less costly phases. Meanwhile, the USA signed bilateral free trade agreements with Colombia and Panama in 2006 and 2007, respectively, but both accords were still awaiting ratification by Congress in April 2011. In February the Secretary of the Treasury, Timothy Geithner, pledged the Obama Administration's commitment to ratifying the two agreements (together with a free trade pact with the Republic of Korea) before the end of 2011.

In response to the removal from power of the President of Honduras, José Manuel Zelaya Rosales, in June 2009 the Obama Administration withdrew some development aid and suspended military co-operation with the Central American state. Further aid to Honduras was cancelled in September, and the visas of the acting President, Roberto Micheletti Baín, and several other senior officials in his administration were revoked. However, the USA recognized the results of presidential and legislative elections held in Honduras in November, describing them as a 'necessary and important step forward', and the US Assistant Secretary of State for Western Hemisphere Affairs, Arturo Valenzuela, attended the inauguration of the new President, Porfirio Lobo Sosa, in January 2010. In March Secretary of State Hillary Clinton announced that US aid to Honduras would be restored and advocated the country's return to full participation in the OAS, its membership rights having been suspended since July 2009. Disbursement of US military and development aid to Honduras was restored from June 2010; however, at early 2011 Honduran membership to the OAS remained suspended.

President Obama embarked on a tour of Latin America in March 2011, visiting Brazil, Chile and El Salvador, with the aim of promoting economic co-operation and improved regional security. The tour commenced with a meeting between Obama and Brazilian President Dilma Vana Rousseff, emphasizing the growing economic and strategic importance of US relations with Brazil, Latin America's largest economic power. An agreement between the USA and Chile on nuclear energy was signed, while in El Salvador Obama pledged US $200m. to help to address the dramatic rise in violent crime in that country.

Relations with the USSR and successor states

A summit meeting in December 1989 between President George Bush and Soviet head of state Mikhail Gorbachev, in Valletta, Malta, marked the opening of a new era in US-Soviet relations. The withdrawal by the USSR in late 1989 and early 1990 from the exercise of direct political influence on the internal affairs of the countries of Eastern Europe was accompanied by a further improvement in US-Soviet relations, and by the implementation of programmes of US economic aid for several of the former Soviet 'client' states. In September 1990 the USA and USSR, with France and the United Kingdom (the other powers that occupied Germany at the end of the Second World War), formally agreed terms for the unification of the two post-war German states, which took effect in the following month. In July the USA, together with the world's six largest industrial democracies, agreed to provide the USSR with economic and technical assistance in undertaking a change-over to a market economy. This initiative was followed in November by the signing in Paris, France, by members of NATO and the Warsaw Pact, of a Treaty on Conventional Armed Forces in Europe (CFE), which provided for bilateral limits to be placed on the number of non-nuclear weapons sited between the Atlantic Ocean and the Ural Mountains. Immediately following the signing of the CFE Treaty, Presidents Bush and Gorbachev were present at a meeting of the Conference on Security and Co-operation in Europe (CSCE, now the Organization for Security and Co-operation in Europe—OSCE, see p. 385), at which the USA, the USSR and 32 other countries signed a charter declaring the end of the post-war era of confrontation and division in Europe. In July 1991 the USA and the USSR signed a Strategic Arms Reduction Treaty (START, renamed START I after negotiations commenced on START II—see below), providing for a 30% reduction in long-range nuclear weapons over a seven-year period.

In December 1991, following the replacement of the USSR by the Commonwealth of Independent States (CIS) comprising 11 of the former Soviet republics, the independence of each republic was recognized by the USA. In January 1992 a meeting was held between President Bush and President Boris Yeltsin of Russia, the dominant republic within the CIS. President Bush expressed concern that effective measures should be taken by the Russian Government to ensure that the nuclear weapons and related technical expertise of the former USSR did not become available to countries not in possession of nuclear weapons capability, or to nations in the Middle East or to the Democratic People's Republic of Korea (North Korea). At a subsequent meeting held in February, the Russian leader assured President Bush that immediate safeguards were in force, and that all short-range nuclear warheads would be moved into Russia from sites in other CIS republics by July. At a summit meeting held between Presidents Bush and Yeltsin in June in Washington, DC, agreement was reached on further substantial reductions in nuclear arms, under which, by 2003, total holdings of nuclear warheads would be reduced to less than one-half of the quotas contained in START.

Shortly before the transfer of the presidency to Bill Clinton in January 1993, Presidents Bush and Yeltsin met in Moscow to sign START II, which provided for the elimination by 2003 of almost 75% of all US and CIS-held nuclear warheads. Although ratified by the US Senate in 1993, START II remained unratified by the Russian legislature until April 2000. However, enactment of START II was contingent on the continuation of the Anti-Ballistic Missile (ABM) treaty (signed with the USSR in 1972). In December 2001 President George W. Bush announced the USA's intention to withdraw from the ABM Treaty after a six-month notice period, claiming that its adherence prevented the development of the US National Missile Defence (NMD) programme. (The NMD system, a network of ground- or sea-based interceptor rockets with the capability of destroying intercontinental ballistic missiles either accidentally launched or fired by a hostile power, was designed to replace the unrealized Strategic Defense Initiative, a space-based system of defences against nuclear attack, initiated by President Reagan in 1983.) Meanwhile, in November 2001, following a summit meeting in Washington, DC, President Bush and Russian President Vladimir Putin both pledged to reduce their nation's nuclear arsenals by approximately two-thirds over the following decade; a formal agreement, the Moscow Treaty, was signed in May 2002. In June the USA formally withdrew from the ABM. President Bush emphasized that the USA's withdrawal from the ABM would not undermine US-Russian relations. Russia immediately withdrew from START II, which had been effectively superseded by the treaty signed with the USA in the previous month.

The Administration of Barack Obama sought to improve US relations with Russia. In July 2009, during Obama's first official visit to Moscow since taking office, the President and his Russian counterpart, Dmitrii Medvedev, signed a joint understanding on the negotiation of a new nuclear arms control treaty to replace START I, which was due to expire at the end of 2009, and agreed to establish a bilateral presidential commission to enhance co-operation in areas including energy, counter-terrorism activities and drugs-trafficking. Furthermore, officials signed a new strategic framework for military co-operation, which had been suspended since August 2008 owing to the conflict between Russia and Georgia (q.v.), while the Russian Government also agreed to allow the USA to transport military personnel and equipment across its territory to Afghanistan. US-Russian relations were further improved in September 2009 when Obama announced the abandonment of plans initiated by his predecessor (and opposed by Russia) to construct missile defence facilities in the Czech Republic and Poland. However, the Administration intended to pursue other missile defence projects within Europe, using initially sea-based, but subsequently also land-based, interceptors, as was confirmed in a review of missile defence policy released by the Department of Defense in February 2010. None the less, in March Obama and Medvedev reached agreement on a replacement for START I and the Moscow Treaty of 2002, which would commit both Russia and the USA to reducing their deployed nuclear warheads from a maximum allowable number of 2,200 to 1,550 within seven years of the new treaty coming into force. In addition, the maximum numbers of launchers and missiles were to be limited to 800 and 700, respectively, and a new inspection and verification regime was to be established. The New START Treaty was signed by Obama and Medvedev in the Czech Republic in April 2010. Having been ratified by the US Senate in December and by the Russian legislature in January 2011, the treaty came into effect in February.

Relations with the People's Republic of China

In December 1992 relations with the People's Republic of China, which had been strained since 1989 by the Chinese Government's persistent suppression of political dissent, were revived by the removal of a US embargo on sales of military equipment. Hovever, relations with China pursued an uneven course under the Administration of Bill Clinton, owing to disagreements over trade matters and criticism by the USA of alleged abuses by the Chinese Government of human rights. Relations between the two countries declined sharply in February 1996, following US protests over Chinese military operations near Taiwan. Relations between the two countries were enhanced in October 1997 by a state visit to the USA by President Jiang Zemin, following which the US Government revoked a ban, in force since 1989, on the export of US nuclear technology to China. China, together with Russia and the USA, refused in December 1997 to sign an international treaty—the Ottawa Convention—banning the manufacture and use of anti-personnel land-mines; the US Government based its objection to the arrangements on its requirement for land-mines to protect its troops stationed in the Republic of Korea. (Following a review of land-mine policy, in February 2004 the Administration of George W. Bush announced that it would not sign the treaty and would continue to use, indefinitely, 'non-persistent' land-mines that would self-destruct or self-deactivate after a certain period of time.) Following the settlement in 1999 of a dispute over infringements of US copyright and other intellectual property rights, Chinese enhanced trading privileges were granted permanent status in 2000, opening the way for China to join the World Trade Organization (see p. 430). However, the accidental bombing by US aircraft of the Chinese diplomatic mission in the Yugoslav capital during NATO air attacks in May 1999 led to a period of strained relations, despite a subsequent apology and the payment of compensation by the US Government. In September 2001, in return for China's acceptance of its NMD programme (see Relations with the USSR and successor states), the USA pledged to keep China informed of its development and agreed to recognize that the Chinese might, in the future, want to resume nuclear weapons testing. The USA also urged China not to transfer ballistic missile technology to countries that the USA considered to be 'rogue states' (deemed by the Department of State to be those countries with the capabilities to use weapons of mass destruction without adherence to traditional international conventions).

President Barack Obama adopted a conciliatory approach during his first official visit to China, which took place in November 2009, emphasizing the need for joint action to confront global challenges. A joint statement, issued following Obama's talks with his Chinese counterpart, Hu Jintao, envisaged increased bilateral co-operation in areas such as climate change, security and trade. None the less, tensions arose in January 2010 when the Obama Administration confirmed plans to proceed with the sale of weapons to Taiwan under an agreement reached during George W. Bush's presidency. In retaliation, the Chinese Government announced its intention to suspend military exchanges with the USA, to review bilateral co-operation and to impose sanctions on US companies supplying the arms. US-Sino relations were further strained in February after Obama held a meeting with the Dalai Lama, the exiled spiritual leader of Tibet, in Washington, DC, despite Chinese objections. However, the USA and China agreed to restore full military ties in September. During an official visit to Washington, DC, by President Hu in January 2011, Obama urged the Chinese Government to take tougher action to improve China's human rights record, including in Tibet, and to open up substantive dialogue with the Dalai Lama; during his visit Hu made a rare acknowledgement that 'a lot still needs to be done in China in terms of human rights'. Following private talks between the two heads of state, the Obama Administration announced bilateral trade and investment deals worth an estimated US $45,000m. Meanwhile, Secretary of State Hillary Clinton urged the Chinese Government to support US efforts to counter the threat to world stability posed by alleged illicit nuclear programmes in North Korea and Iran.

Relations with North Korea

The prevention of nuclear proliferation, which remained a prime objective of US foreign policy, led in 1993 and early 1994 to a serious confrontation between the USA and the Democratic People's Republic of Korea (DPRK—North Korea). In March 1993 the DPRK, which is a signatory of the Nuclear Non-Proliferation Treaty (NPT) and is subject, by virtue of its membership of the International Atomic Energy Agency (IAEA, see p. 118), to the monitoring of its nuclear installations, refused to grant the IAEA inspectorate full access to its nuclear power facility. It cited as its reasons the existence of joint military exercises between the Republic of Korea (South Korea) and the USA and 'unjust acts' by the IAEA. The US Government stated that it had reason to suspect that the DPRK had been diverting nuclear plant material for the development of atomic weapons. In July President Bill Clinton visited South Korea, and warned the DPRK that any use of nuclear weapons by them would be met with military force. Despite increasing international pressure, and attempts at mediation by the UN, the DPRK repeatedly asserted its refusal to comply with the Treaty's inspection requirements. The crisis steadily worsened during early 1994, and in June the US Government, after seeking unsuccessfully to offer the DPRK economic aid, investment and diplomatic recog-

THE UNITED STATES OF AMERICA

nition, began to seek support for the imposition of UN economic sanctions. Later in the same month, following a visit to the DPRK by former President Carter (acting as an unofficial representative of the Government), the DPRK agreed to a temporary suspension of its nuclear programme, pending formal discussions with the US Government. These meetings were convened in July. Negotiations aimed at improving relations between the USA and the DPRK, and at fostering a political settlement between the DPRK and South Korea, were pursued throughout both Clinton Administrations. In March 1999 the US and DPRK Governments agreed on terms whereby US officials would receive unrestricted access to inspect DPRK nuclear facilities.

In January 2002 President George W. Bush described the DPRK, together with Iran and Iraq, as forming an 'axis of evil' that supported international terrorism and sought to develop weapons of mass destruction. Relations with the DPRK were severely strained in late 2002 when it emerged that the DPRK Government had resumed its nuclear energy programme, effectively breaking the accord signed with the USA in 1994. In October 2002 the DPRK demanded a treaty of non-aggression with the USA and asserted its right to possess nuclear weapons. In the following month the USA, South Korea, Japan and the EU suspended their supply of petroleum to the DPRK until its Government promised to terminate its nuclear weapons programme, although the DPRK denied it operated such a programme. However, in December it announced operations would resume at the Yongbyon nuclear plant, which was capable of producing weapons-grade plutonium. The USA considered that economic sanctions would be an effective means of containing North Korea, although this led to a more uncompromising stance from the DPRK, which said it would consider UN sanctions an 'act of war', and subsequently withdrew from the NPT in January 2003. In July the DPRK claimed that it had made enough plutonium to produce six nuclear bombs. In August six-party negotiations opened in the Chinese capital, Beijing, between the USA, the DPRK, the People's Republic of China, South Korea, Japan and Russia; however, little progress was achieved. In October President Bush announced that the USA would be prepared to offer security assurances to the DPRK in exchange for verifiable dismantling of any weapons programmes. In February 2004 a further round of six-party talks took place in Beijing. Talks in June ended unsuccessfully and in February 2005 the DPRK admitted for the first time that it possessed nuclear weapons. Talks eventually resumed in August, and the following month it appeared that a breakthrough had been made when the DPRK agreed in principle to end its weapons development programme in exchange for a civilian light-water reactor. However, the DPRK refused to begin dismantling its nuclear programme until it had received the reactor. Meanwhile, the US Administration alleged that the Banco Asia Delta in Macao, China, was laundering money on behalf of the DPRK Government and imposed a ban on transactions with the bank. The following month US authorities froze the assets of eight North Korean companies, which were accused of supporting the DPRK weapons programme. In October the US Department of Justice charged the DPRK with having forged millions of dollars worth of counterfeit US $100 bills—so-called 'Supernotes'—since 1989. The DPRK Government insisted that six-party negotiations would not resume until the economic sanctions against it were lifted.

In October 2006, after the DPRK conducted its first nuclear test, the USA entered into further talks, and in February 2007 significant progress appeared to have been made when the Government of the DPRK agreed to effect the disarmament programme agreed upon in 2005. The process was to begin with the closure of the nuclear reactor in Yongbyon within 60 days, but progress once again stalled when the DPRK missed a deadline at the end of 2007 by which it was due to give a full account of its nuclear activities. The DPRK eventually declared its nuclear activities in June 2008, and in October the country was removed from the US Department of State's list of state sponsors of terrorism. Nevertheless, six-party talks again broke down in December over verification of the disarmament programme, prompting the USA to suspend aid to the country. Tensions were heightened in April 2009, following the launch of a rocket by the DPRK. The condemnation of the UN Security Council prompted the North Korean Government (which claimed to have been placing a communications satellite into orbit) to annouce its permanent withdrawal from the six-party talks and the restoration of its nuclear facilities at Yongbyon. In June the Security Council adopted a resolution strengthening sanctions against the North Korean regime in response to the underground detonation of a nuclear device in May. Further nuclear tests conducted by the DPRK in July led to the imposition of sanctions against additional North Korean individuals and organizations. In August, following a meeting with North Korean leader Kim Jong Il in Pyongyang, the North Korean capital, former President Clinton secured the release of two US journalists who had been convicted in June of having illegally entered the DPRK from China and sentenced to 12 years' hard labour. In December Stephen Bosworth, the US Special Representative for North Korea Policy, visited the DPRK for the first time since his appointment in February, holding 'exploratory' discussions with the country's leaders (although not Kim Jong Il); Bosworth subsequently stated that a 'common understanding' on the importance of the disarmament process had been reached, although he had not secured a firm commitment on the DPRK's return to the six-party talks. Hopes of a resumption of the talks were raised by a statement broadcast on North Korean state television in January 2010, in which the DPRK appealed for an end to hostile relations with the USA and pledged its commitment to making the Korean peninsula a nuclear-free zone. However, hopes of a thawing in bilateral relations appeared to be quashed by the announcement in May that the US military was to participate in new naval exercises with South Korea, following the sinking, allegedly by a North Korean torpedo, of a South Korean military vessel in March, in which 46 South Korean sailors had been killed. The DPRK denied any involvement, and its state news agency counterclaimed that the USA had manipulated the incident to fabricate the appearance of North Korean involvement. The DPRK Government issued a bellicose warning to the Obama Administration in July, threatening to 'legitimately counter' the US-South Korean naval exercises with its 'powerful nuclear deterrence'.

Relations with the Middle East and North Africa

In the period following the Gulf War of 1990–91 (see Domestic Political Affairs) the US Government actively pursued initiatives to convene a regional conference to seek a permanent solution to the wider problems of the Middle East. In August 1991 Egypt, Israel, Jordan, Lebanon and Syria agreed to take part in such a conference, the opening session of which was convened in October. Successive negotiations failed to make any substantive progress, and traditionally close relations between Israel and the USA subsequently came under strain, following pressure by the US Government on Israel to suspend the construction of Jewish settlements in occupied territories, pending the eventual outcome of the peace negotiations.

During 1993 the Administration of Bill Clinton continued to foster efforts to promote a general resolution of tensions in the Middle East. With US assistance, but as a direct result of secret diplomatic mediation by Norway, the Palestine Liberation Organization (PLO) and the Government of Israel signed an agreement providing for Palestinian self-government in the Occupied Territories and for mutual recognition by Israel and the PLO. In January 1994, following a meeting held in Geneva, Switzerland, between Clinton and President Hafiz al-Assad of Syria, negotiations were initiated for a settlement between Israel and Syria. In December 1999, under Clinton's auspices, the first substantive negotiations since 1996 between the Governments of Israel and Syria took place in Washington, DC. In March 2000 the US Government sought to move towards a rapprochement with Iran with the announcement that it was to ease some of the trade sanctions against Iran that had been in force since 1979.

In his State of the Union address in January 2002, President George W. Bush described Iran and Iraq, together with the DPRK, as forming an 'axis of evil' that supported international terrorism and sought to develop weapons of mass destruction, and hinted that the USA was considering pre-emptive strikes against them. US allies warned against attacking states unless firm evidence of a link to terrorism could be found. In May the 'axis of evil' was extended to include Libya and Syria (as well as Cuba). The Bush Administration claimed that Libya and Syria had violated international weapons treaties. In December the Iranian Government denied US allegations of evidence of the secret manufacture of nuclear weapons. In September 2003 the USA supported an IAEA resolution establishing a deadline of the end of October for Iran to disclose full details of its nuclear programme and provide evidence that it was not developing nuclear weapons. In December Libya agreed to disclose and dismantle its programme to develop weapons of mass destruction and long-range ballistic missiles, following nine months of secret

THE UNITED STATES OF AMERICA

negotiations between the Libyan leader, Col Muammar al-Qaddafi, and US and British diplomats. In February 2004 the USA ended the restrictions on its citizens travelling to Libya, in place since 1981, and in June diplomatic relations were officially re-established between the two countries for the first time in 23 years; however, Libya was not removed from the US list of state sponsors of terrorism until May 2006. (In September 2008 Condoleezza Rice became the first US Secretary of State in 50 years to visit Libya.) In February 2005, in protest at what it believed to be Syria's role in the assassination of the Prime Minister of Lebanon, Rafiq Hariri, the USA removed its ambassador to Syria for consultations, and later demanded that all Syrian troops withdraw from Lebanon. The Administration of President Barack Obama sought to renew diplomatic relations with Syria, and in February 2010 Obama nominated a new US ambassador to Syria, Robert Ford, although his nomination was blocked by Republicans in the Senate throughout 2010. Obama forced through Ford's appointment during a congressional recess in January 2011. However, in March the US Administration condemned the excessive use of force by Syrian security forces against anti-Government and pro-democracy protesters. High-ranking members of the Syrian regime were subjected to a US assets freeze in April.

In April 2006 the Iranian President, Mahmoud Ahmadinejad, announced that Iran had successfully achieved the enrichment of uranium for civilian purposes. The Iranian Government claimed that the enriched uranium was not weapons-grade, but was, rather, to be used as nuclear fuel. In May a draft UN resolution was promulgated, under which France, Germany, the United Kingdom and the USA again urged Iran to arrest its nuclear enrichment programme and to abandon construction of a heavy-water reactor by the end of August, or face economic sanctions. In return for compliance, a portfolio of incentives was offered, including the provision of light-water nuclear reactors for electricity generation. However, in August Iran's Supreme Leader, Ayatollah Ali Khamenei, declared that the country's nuclear programme would continue, and at the end of that month the heavy-water plant became operational.

A resolution was approved by the UN Security Council in December 2006 imposing sanctions against Iran, which prevented the import or export of materials and technology associated with uranium enrichment enterprises and froze the financial assets of 12 Iranians and 10 institutions associated with the country's nuclear development programme. Nevertheless, in January 2007 Iran announced that production of nuclear fuel for industrial purposes was to commence imminently and declared its intention to enhance economic and military co-operation with Iraq. US suspicions that the Iranian Government was supplying Iraqi Shi'ite militants with ammunition and weapons appeared substantiated in February when US military officials in the Iraqi capital reported the seizure of explosives components manufactured in Iran; however, the Chairman of the Joint Chiefs of Staff, Gen. Peter Pace, later acknowledged that links between the bomb materials and the Iranian administration could not be unequivocally proven. Furthermore, the National Intelligence Estimate, published in December 2007 and compiled using information supplied by the USA's 16 intelligence agencies, reported with 'high confidence' that Iran had ceased its nuclear weapons programme in 2003 and had not recommenced such activities by mid-2007, although it continued to enrich uranium.

President Obama extended US trade and investment sanctions against Iran for a further year in March 2009, but later that month called for a 'new beginning' in relations between the two countries in a video message to the Iranian people and leadership. The President's policy of engagement was jeopardized in the following month, when a journalist with dual US-Iranian citizenship was convicted by an Iranian court of spying for the USA and sentenced to eight years' imprisonment. However, in what was regarded as a conciliatory gesture, the journalist was released in May and permitted to return to the USA, her sentence having been commuted to a two-year suspended term. Bilateral talks between the USA's Undersecretary of State for Political Affairs, William Burns, and Iran's chief nuclear negotiator, Saeed Jalili, in October represented the most senior-level direct engagement between the two countries since the Islamic Revolution of 1979. The talks took place on the sidelines of negotiations in Geneva on Iran's nuclear programme, involving representatives of the People's Republic of China, France, Germany, Russia and the United Kingdom, as well as the USA. However, the international negotiations reached an impasse in November, as Iran refused to accept a proposal that it transfer a large proportion of its enriched uranium to Russia and France for further processing to the level of enrichment required for medical research purposes and announced plans to expand its nuclear programme. Following protracted lobbying by the US Administration, in early June 2010 the UN Security Council adopted a resolution imposing further sanctions on Iran, owing to Iran's lack of compliance with previous resolutions related to its nuclear programme; the resolution expanded the scope of the existing arms embargo and tightened restrictions on certain financial and shipping enterprises. In the same month the US Congress approved the Comprehensive Iran Sanctions, Accountability, and Divestment Act of 2010, which Obama signed into law at the beginning of July; the law provided for, *inter alia*, the imposition against Iran of additional sanctions prohibiting specified foreign exchange, banking, and property transactions.

Meanwhile, following an escalation in the ongoing conflict in the Middle East, from early 2002 the USA intensified its efforts towards brokering a peace agreement between Israel and Palestine. In April Secretary of State Colin Powell visited Israel and held separate talks with the Israeli Prime Minister, Ariel Sharon, and with Palestinian President Yasser Arafat. However, the mission failed to bring about a cease-fire or the withdrawal of Israeli forces from Palestinian areas. In April 2003 President Bush presented both the Israeli and Palestinian Prime Ministers with an internationally sponsored 'roadmap' for peace, envisaging the phased creation of a sovereign Palestinian state. However, despite acceptance of the plan, Israel continued work on the construction of a 'security fence' in the disputed West Bank region, begun in mid-2002. In July 2003 the US Administration threatened to withhold almost US $10,000m. in essential loan guarantees unless construction of the fence ceased. Following approval by the Israeli Government of a further phase of construction, in November the US Congress cut $290m. from a total $1,400m. in loan guarantees to Israel as a penalty for the continuing expansion of Jewish settlements in the West Bank and Gaza. At a meeting between Bush and Sharon in Crawford, Texas, in April 2005, the President gave his support to Israel's planned withdrawal from the Gaza Strip, but criticized the continued expansion of Jewish settlements in the West Bank. In April 2006 the EU and USA suspended financial aid provisions to the Palestinian Authority (PA), under the leadership of the militant Hamas movement, in response to its continued refusal to recognize the state of Israel. The US Administration's failure to demand an immediate end to the Israeli military offensive against the radical Hezbollah movement in southern Lebanon that began in July also strained US-Lebanese relations. Instead, the Bush Administration appealed for joint Lebanese-Israeli negotiations to bring about a long-lasting cease-fire. The inauguration of a Fatah and Hamas coalition Government in Palestine in March 2007, while representing a significant advance towards reconciliation, did not herald any immediate improvement in US-Palestinian relations. At a Middle East peace conference held in Annapolis, Maryland, in November, Israeli Prime Minister Ehud Olmert and Palestinian President Mahmoud Abbas agreed mutually to a deadline of December 2008 for the formulation of a peace settlement. Bush demonstrated his continued commitment to the process in his final year in office by travelling to Israel and the West Bank in January 2008, his first visit to the area since becoming President.

However, the December 2008 deadline for a peace agreement was not met, and at the end of that month Israel initiated a major offensive against Hamas targets in the Gaza Strip that continued until mid-January 2009. The USA abstained from a vote at the UN Security Council earlier in January, at which a resolution calling for a cease-fire and a complete withdrawal of Israeli forces from the Strip was adopted. During separate meetings in Washington, DC, with the new Israeli Prime Minister, Binyamin Netanyahu, and Palestinian President Abbas in May President Obama sought to foster a revival of the stalled peace process and declared his commitment to a two-state solution. He also urged Israel to halt the expansion of settlements in the West Bank and East Jerusalem. In the following month, during his first official visit to the Middle East, Obama delivered a speech in Cairo, Egypt, in which he advocated a 'new beginning' in the relationship between the USA and Muslims world-wide, based on 'mutual interest and mutual respect'. While describing the USA's bond with Israel as 'unbreakable', the President also asserted that the situation for Palestinians was 'intolerable'. However, subsequent efforts by senior US diplomats, notably

THE UNITED STATES OF AMERICA

George Mitchell, the special envoy for the Middle East, to revive the peace process faltered over the settlements issue, and a tripartite meeting of Obama, Abbas and Netanyahu in New York in September also failed to result in a resumption of negotiations, as did talks between Obama and Netanyahu in Washington, DC, in November. Tensions in US-Israeli relations arose in March 2010, when the Israeli authorities' approval of plans to construct 1,600 new housing units in East Jerusalem overshadowed a visit to Israel by US Vice-President Joseph Biden and jeopardized a recent US-brokered agreement to hold indirect Israeli-Palestinian talks. In June Israel's ambassador to the USA spoke of a 'tectonic rift' developing between the two long-standing allies.

Direct negotiations between Netanyahu and Abbas, chaired by US Secretary of State Hillary Clinton, commenced in Washington, DC, in early September 2010—the first direct Israeli-Palestinian talks since December 2008—although Hamas refused to recognize their legitimacy. During September Obama urged the Israeli Government to extend the 10-month moratorium on settlement-building in the West Bank, which was due to expire later that month; however, Netanyahu was unwilling to implement a complete freeze on construction. A second round of direct negotiations took place in Sharm el-Sheikh, Egypt, and in Jerusalem, in mid-September. However, little progress was achieved with regard to substantive issues and, following the expiry of Israel's temporary settlement ban on 26 September, the PA suspended its involvement in the peace process.

Egypt has traditionally been one of the USA's firmest allies across the Middle East and North Africa region. The Obama Administration's response to protracted popular protests in Cairo and other major Egyptian cities from January 2011, the aim of which was to force the resignation of President Muhammad Hosni Mubarak, was at first markedly measured, with US officials compelled to balance expressions of support for the pro-democracy demonstrations with the offer of continued support for its long-standing ally Mubarak. However, Mubarak's eventual decision to tender his resignation in mid-February was hailed by Obama as a crucial moment in the 'wheel of history'. The US President congratulated the Egyptian people for taking the first step in determining their own future. He also urged the interim military Government to revoke Egypt's controversial state of emergency legislation, which had been in place almost continuously since 1967; amend the Constitution so that democratic principles were enshrined; and provide for the staging of free and fair elections.

Similar protests erupted in several other countries in the Middle East and North Africa during early 2011. In February Obama expressed concern at the violent response of the security forces to pro-democracy demonstrations in Bahrain, a key US ally due to its hosting of the US Navy's Fifth Fleet. Obama urged the Bahraini authorities to implement democratic reforms but did not condemn the deployment of Gulf Co-operation Council troops in the country to maintain order and security. The Obama Administration also denounced the use of violence against anti-Government demonstrators in Yemen; however, US criticism was tempered by the Yemeni Government's role as a strategic ally in the region, especially with regard to US-led anti-terrorism initiatives. The US response to the excessive use of state force to quell anti-Government protests and rebel attacks in Libya was more robust. In February Obama demanded that Libyan leader Col Muammar al-Qaddafi relinquish power, and sanctions against the Libyan regime, including an assets freeze, were imposed. On 17 March the USA gave its support to UN Security Council Resolution 1973, which endorsed the establishment of a 'no-fly zone' over Libya, and also played a leading role in the subsequent military intervention in that country.

Other external relations

By mid-1993 the crisis in the former Yugoslavia had assumed increased importance as a foreign policy issue, leading to disagreements between the USA and the Western European powers, which opposed US proposals to launch direct air strikes against military positions held by Bosnian Serbs. The US Administration, while avoiding any direct military commitment, gave its support, through NATO, to peace-keeping operations in Bosnia and Herzegovina. President Bill Clinton was unsuccessful, however, in efforts to secure the removal of the international embargo on arms sales to the Bosnian Muslims. In June 1994 the US Government endorsed proposals by EU countries for the tripartite partition of Bosnia and Herzegovina.

The reluctance of the Clinton Administration to participate directly in UN military operations in Bosnia and Herzegovina was modified in June 1995 with a statement by Clinton that US ground troops would be sent to Bosnia and Herzegovina in 'emergency' circumstances on a 'limited basis' if required to assist in the redeployment of existing UN forces, or to participate in monitoring an eventual peace settlement. In November, following US-sponsored negotiations held in Dayton, Ohio, a peace agreement was reached by the opposing sides. As part of its implementation, the US Government agreed to contribute 20,000 troops to a multinational supervisory force of 60,000 troops under the command of NATO. The USA committed about 8,500 troops in an extended NATO peace-keeping operation in Bosnia and Herzegovina until mid-1998, and about 1,000 soldiers served as part of NATO's Stabilization Force until December 2004.

In March 1999 the US Government initiated and led, under NATO auspices, a sustained campaign of missile raids on military and related installations in Serbia and Montenegro, in support of international demands that the President of the Federal Republic of Yugoslavia, Slobodan Milošević, desist from the mass expulsion of members of the ethnic Albanian population of the Serbian province of Kosovo. Following the military withdrawal of Serbian forces from Kosovo in June, US forces took a leading role in subsequent UN peace-keeping operations in the region.

Following a revival of contacts between the USA and Viet Nam, in May 1992 there was a partial relaxation of a trade embargo in force since 1975. In February 1994 the US Government lifted the remaining sanctions on trade with Viet Nam, and in the following July the USA established full diplomatic relations with that country.

In March 2006 an agreement was reached between President George W. Bush and India's premier, Manmohan Singh, during discussions in New Delhi, India, under the terms of which India would be permitted to purchase nuclear fuel and technology from the USA in return for the separation of its military and civilian nuclear programmes and consent for UN inspection of its civilian nuclear facilities. US assistance for the advancement of India's nuclear programme, together with those of Pakistan and Israel, had previously been denied under US law as the three were not signatories of the NPT. Amendments to the US Atomic Energy Act of 1954, permitting nuclear co-operation with India, were signed into law in December. The agreement was enacted by Bush in October 2008, following its approval by Congress and earlier endorsement by the IAEA.

Relations with Pakistan—regarded in the USA as vitally important due to that country's co-operation in combating Islamist militancy and its provision of logistical assistance to US-led coalition forces engaged in military operations in neighbouring Afghanistan—came under increasing strain during early 2011. Bilateral ties deteriorated in January due to the commencement in Pakistan of legal action against Raymond Davis, a CIA operative accused of shooting and killing two Pakistani men in Lahore. Davis claimed that he had been defending himself against an attempted robbery. US President Barack Obama asserted that Davis had diplomatic immunity and demanded his release. Following the payment of compensation to the victims' relatives, Davis was acquitted in March, prompting violent protests in Pakistan. Meanwhile, attacks by US 'drones' (unmanned aircraft) against militants within Pakistan also damaged relations between the two countries. The frequency of such operations, which frequently resulted in civilian casualties, had increased significantly since 2010. In April 2011 press reports claimed that the Pakistani Government had demanded a reduction in drone attacks and a curtailment of CIA operations in the country. In the same month the US Chairman of the Joint Chiefs of Staff, Adm. Michael Mullen, alleged that Pakistan's Directorate for Inter-Services Intelligence was colluding with militants in Afghanistan. The problematic nature of US-Pakistani relations was further illustrated by the covert operation carrried out by US special forces on Pakistani territory at the beginning of May in which al-Qa'ida founder Osama bin Laden was killed (see Domestic Political Affairs). While the Pakistani authorities welcomed bin Laden's demise, Prime Minister Yusuf Raza Gilani described the operation, which was carried out without consultation with the Pakistani authorities, as a violation of national sovereignty, and angrily rejected the widely held assumption that bin Laden's presence in the country must have been sanctioned by senior Pakistani officials.

An escalation in the conflict between Arab *Janjaweed* militia and ethnic groups in the Darfur region of Sudan, which had been ongoing since 2003, prompted protests in Washington, DC, and 18 other US cities in April 2006 to demand that the US Administration intervene to alleviate the humanitarian crisis there. In May the Darfur Peace Agreement—negotiated by the US Deputy Secretary of State, Robert B. Zoellick, African Union representatives and other foreign officials working in Nigeria—was signed between the Sudanese Government and a faction of the Sudan Liberation Army. In October President Bush signed the Darfur Peace and Accountability Act into law, imposing sanctions against those responsible for genocide, crimes against humanity and war crimes, supporting strategies to defend civilians and humanitarian exercises, and promoting peace initiatives in Darfur. The legislation was augmented by an executive order—forbidding transactions with, and receipt of property of, the Sudanese Government—which came into effect simultaneously. The order, while specifically prohibiting transactions relating to the oil and petrochemical industries of Sudan, made provision for limited trade to continue with non-governmental concerns in other regions of Sudan. Further sanctions were imposed against Sudan in 2007, excluding additional companies owned or operated by the Sudanese Government from the US financial system and blocking the assets of individuals accused of instigating violence in Darfur. In October 2010 President Obama renewed sanctions against Sudan for a further one-year period. The Obama Administration praised the successful and relatively peaceful execution of a referendum on the secession of Southern Sudan in mid-January 2011, during which an overwhelming majority approved the formation of a sovereign state in the south of the country; however, the US authorities continued to express concerns regarding the pace of progress on security and humanitarian issues in Darfur.

The USA attracted international criticism by its refusal to sign up to the terms of the International Criminal Court (ICC), established to try war criminals, which was inaugurated at The Hague, Netherlands, in March 2003. The USA defended its position by claiming that members of its military could be put on trial on political grounds, and, in response, in the same month, Congress approved the American Service Member and Citizen Protection Act, which would enable the USA to free, by force if necessary, any member of its military arrested by the ICC. In July the USA reduced military aid to some 35 countries that refused to sign agreements that would give US citizens immunity from prosecution. Following allegations of abuse and torture of Iraqi prisoners by US soldiers (see Domestic Political Affairs), in June 2004 the USA withdrew a proposed resolution at the UN Security Council to give US personnel immunity from prosecution at the ICC. By August 2006 some 101 Bilateral Immunity Agreements had been signed, exempting certain such US citizens from referral to the ICC. The deterioration of the situation in Darfur, Sudan, later that year prompted appeals that the US Administration endorse the jurisdiction of the ICC in prosecuting Sudanese leaders, indicating the USA's recognition of the Court's importance in administering international justice. In January 2008 legislation repealing the restrictions on military assistance to nations unwilling to enter into Bilateral Immunity Agreements was signed into law. Upon taking office, the Obama Administration initiated a full policy review of US-ICC relations. In November 2009 the USA attended an ICC assembly meeting in The Hague as an observer, the first time that it had participated in an ICC meeting since 2001. While the USA was not expected to accede to ICC membership in the short term, throughout 2010 and into early 2011 it repeatedly pledged its commitment to supporting the efforts of the Court to bring war criminals to justice.

In November 2010 WikiLeaks, an organization devoted to publishing leaked private and classified information, began to release a series of classified US diplomatic cables, allegedly secured through a source in the US Army. The documents contained candid assessments by US diplomats of foreign leaders and international affairs, as well as details of highly sensitive, private discussions with foreign officials. The cables emanated from more than 200 US overseas missions and caused significant embarrassment to the Government. US officials condemned the publication of the cables, claiming that this would damage relations with other countries, place US diplomats and soldiers in danger, and jeopardize future intelligence-gathering. Despite threats of legal action from US and other governments, WikiLeaks continued to release selected cables (of which it claimed to be in possession of over 250,000) in early 2011.

CONSTITUTION AND GOVERNMENT

The Constitution of the USA was adopted on 4 March 1789; 27 amendments have since been ratified, the most recent in 1992. The USA is a federal republic. Each of the 50 constituent states and the District of Columbia exercises a measure of internal self-government. Defence, foreign affairs, coinage, posts, the higher levels of justice, and internal security are the responsibility of the federal Government. The President is head of the executive and is elected for a four-year term by a college of representatives elected directly from each state. The President appoints the other members of the executive, subject to the consent of the Senate. Congress is the seat of legislative power and consists of the Senate (100 members) and the House of Representatives (435 members). Two senators are chosen by direct election in each state, to serve a six-year term, and one-third of the membership is renewable every two years. Representatives are elected by direct and universal suffrage for a two-year term. The number of representatives of each state in Congress is determined by the size of the state's population. Ultimate judicial power is vested in the Supreme Court, which has the power to disallow legislation and to overturn executive actions that it deems unconstitutional.

REGIONAL AND INTERNATIONAL CO-OPERATION

The USA is a member of the Organization of American States (see p. 391) and of the Inter-American Development Bank (see p. 333). Together with Mexico and Canada, the USA is a signatory to the North American Free Trade Agreement (see p. 367), which entered into force in 1994 and had been fully implemented by 2008. Agreement on a free trade accord, to be known as the Central American Free Trade Agreement (CAFTA), between the USA and Guatemala, Costa Rica, El Salvador, Honduras and Nicaragua was signed in May 2004 in Washington, DC. The Agreement, which was restyled DR-CAFTA following the inclusion of the Dominican Republic later that year, was ratified by Congress in July 2005 and signed by President George W. Bush in August. DR-CAFTA came into effect in El Salvador, Honduras, Nicaragua and Guatemala in 2006, in the Dominican Republic in 2007, and in Costa Rica in 2009. Discussions to establish a Free Trade Area of the Americas, first proposed in 1995, stalled in late 2004, and (although it was agreed in mid-2006 to resume talks) no progress had been made by April 2011.

The USA was a founder member of the UN in 1945 and is a permanent member of the UN Security Council; the headquarters of the organization are located in New York. As a contracting party to the General Agreement on Tariffs and Trade, the USA joined the World Trade Organization (see p. 430) on its establishment in 1995. The USA is also a member of the North Atlantic Treaty Organization (see p. 368) and of the Organisation for Economic Co-operation and Development (see p. 376), and participates in the Group of Eight (G8, see p. 460) leading industrialized nations and in the Group of Twenty (G20, see p. 451).

ECONOMIC AFFAIRS

In 2009, according to estimates by the World Bank, the USA's gross national income (GNI), measured at average 2007–09 prices, was US $14,502,626m., equivalent to $47,240 per head (or $46,730 on an international purchasing-power parity basis). During 2000–09, it was estimated, the population increased at an average annual rate of 0.9%, while gross domestic product (GDP) per head increased, in real terms, by an average of 0.6% per year. During the same period, according to UN estimates, overall GDP increased, in real terms, at an average annual rate of 1.6%; GDP grew by 0.4% in 2008, but declined by 2.6% in 2009.

Agriculture (including forestry, fishing and hunting) contributed 0.9% of GDP in 2009 and engaged 1.5% of the employed civilian population in 2008. The principal crops are hay, potatoes, sugar beet and citrus fruit, which, together with cereals, cotton and tobacco, are important export crops. In recent years the production and export of soybeans have also become significant. The principal livestock are cattle, pigs and poultry. Food and live animals provided an estimated 6.5% of total export revenue in 2010. The GDP of the sector increased, in real terms, by an average of 2.4% per year in 2000–09, according to UN estimates; sectoral GDP increased by 9.1% in 2008, but decreased by 9.2% in 2009.

Industry (including mining, manufacturing, construction and utilities) provided 18.6% of GDP in 2009 and engaged 19.9% of the employed civilian population in 2008. According to UN estimates, industrial GDP increased, in real terms, at an average annual rate of 0.1% in 2000–09; the sector's GDP decreased by 2.9% in 2008, but increased by 0.5% in 2009.

Mining and quarrying contributed 1.7% of GDP in 2009 and engaged 0.6% of the employed civilian population in 2008. The USA has significant mineral deposits, specifically of petroleum,

THE UNITED STATES OF AMERICA

Introductory Survey

natural gas, coal (with 238,308m. metric tons at the end of 2009, the USA had the largest proven recoverable reserves of coal in the world), copper, iron, silver and uranium. At the end of 2009 the USA's proven recoverable reserves of petroleum were 28,396m. barrels, equivalent to 2.1% of the world's proven oil reserves, and sufficient to sustain production at 2009 levels for about 11 years. Crude petroleum production averaged 7.2m. barrels per day (b/d) in 2009. The USA's proven recoverable reserves of natural gas were estimated at 6,927,887m. cu m at the end of 2009, and production in that year totalled 593,380m. cu m (second only to Russia). Crude materials (excluding fuels) accounted for an estimated 6.3% of total export revenue in 2010; mineral fuels accounted for a further 6.3% of the value of exports in that year. In real terms, the GDP of the sector (including utilities) decreased at an average annual rate of 0.3% during 2000–09, according to UN estimates; mining GDP declined by 0.8% in 2009.

Manufacturing contributed 11.2% of GDP in 2009 and engaged 10.9% of the employed civilian population in 2008. In 2009 the principal branches of manufacturing (measured by value of output) were chemical products (13.7%), computer and electronic equipment (13.0%), food, beverages and tobacco products (13.0%), motor vehicles and transport equipment (10.7%), fabricated metal products (7.7%), petroleum and coal products (7.6%), and machinery (7.1%). According to UN estimates, manufacturing GDP increased, in real terms, by an average of 1.1% per year in 2000–09; sectoral GDP for manufacturing decreased by 0.5% in 2009.

The construction sector contributed 3.8% of GDP in 2009 and engaged 7.5% of the employed labour force in 2008. During 2000–09, according to UN estimates, the GDP of the sector decreased at an average annual rate of 2.1%; construction GDP increased by 5.0% in 2009.

According to the US Energy Information Administration (EIA), the USA is the world's largest producer, consumer and net importer of energy. Energy is derived principally from domestic and imported hydrocarbons. The EIA estimated that in 2010 69.7% of total electricity production was provided by fossil fuels (coal 48.1%, natural gas 20.4% and petroleum 1.2%), 20.1% was provided by nuclear power, and some 9.8% was derived from renewable sources. In 2010 fuel imports amounted to an estimated 18.5% (petroleum and petroleum products 17.2%) of total merchandise import costs.

Services (including government services) provided 80.5% of GDP in 2009 and engaged 78.6% of the employed civilian population in 2008. The combined GDP of all service sectors rose, in real terms, at an average rate of 2.0% per year during 2000–09, according to UN estimates. Of non-government services subsectors, the contribution of professional and business services was most significant in 2008 (contributing 19.2% of the total GDP of non-government services). Services GDP decreased by 3.1% in 2009.

In 2009 the USA recorded a visible trade deficit of US $503,580m. (excluding military transactions), and there was a deficit of $378,430m. on the current account of the balance of payments. In 2010 the People's Republic of China was the principal provider of imports (supplying 19.1% of the total); other major suppliers were Canada, Mexico and Japan. Canada was the principal export market in that year, accounting for 19.4% of the total value of exports. Mexico was the USA's second largest export market in that year, followed by China and Japan. In 2010 machinery and transport equipment constituted the most significant category of both imports (accounting for 37.3% of the total value of imports) and exports (40.8% of the total).

A federal budget deficit of US $1,293,489m. was recorded for the financial year ending 30 September 2010, an amount equivalent to 8.8% of GDP in that year. The USA's general government gross debt was $11,896,590m. in 2009, equivalent to 84.3% of GDP. The annual rate of inflation averaged 2.4% in 2000–10.

Consumer prices increased by 1.7% in 2010. The rate of unemployment averaged 5.8% in 2008.

The US economy grew throughout the early 2000s, fuelled by robust consumer consumption. However, the country suffered an economic shock in late 2006 when the sub-prime mortgage crisis emerged: after house prices began to collapse in that year, many individuals were left unable to refinance mortgages as interest rates rose, leading to unprecedented levels of repossessions, and creating a nation-wide, and eventually global, 'credit crunch' as banks and mortgage lenders cut back on giving credit to customers and each other. The financial crisis intensified dramatically after the collapse of Lehman Brothers, an investment bank, and other financial ventures in September 2008, which led to fears of a complete breakdown of the financial sector. A government-backed rescue plan for the banks, valued at US $700,000m., was approved by Congress in October. Following the inauguration of President Barack Obama in January 2009, Congress approved a $787,000m. fiscal stimulus package in February, which included tax cuts for low- and middle-income households, as well as large-scale government spending. These measures contributed in large measure to a return to growth, of 1.6%, in the third quarter of 2009, following four successive quarters of negative growth; the rate of expansion accelerated to an impressive 5.0% in the following quarter, although GDP for the year as a whole contracted by 2.6%. In 2010 the economy expanded at a more subdued rate than had been anticipated; growth for the year as a whole was estimated at 2.9%. Meanwhile, in February 2010 Obama created a bipartisan National Commission on Fiscal Responsibility and Reform, which was charged with recommending measures to reduce the budgetary deficit to about 3% of GDP by 2015; partly as a result of the fiscal stimulus package, the deficit had expanded to the equivalent of 9.9% of GDP in 2009, from 3.2% in 2008. In November 2010 the National Commission on Fiscal Responsibility and Reform proposed a series of comprehensive spending cuts in order to tackle the deficit, which attracted much criticism across the political spectrum; included among the recommendations was an unexpected suggestion to reduce by one-third funding for the USA's overseas military bases and a proposed simplification of the tax code, which would involve the elimination of certain tax reduction provisions. Also in November a fresh round of quantitative easing was launched by the Federal Reserve; the central bank was to buy long-term Treasury security bonds worth some $600,000m. in an attempt to support the economic recovery. As part of the Administration's efforts to reduce the deficit, the President announced in his State of the Union address in January 2011 a five-year freeze on non-security domestic expenditure. However, new tax legislation adopted in December 2010 that extended for a further two years tax reductions for the wealthiest Americans (see Domestic Political Affairs) was expected to offset a significant proportion of gains from such deficit reduction measures. Meanwhile, unemployment rose from 4.8% in February 2008 to a peak of 10.1% in October 2009, before moderating gradually over the course of 2010 to 9.0% in January 2011.

PUBLIC HOLIDAYS*

2012: 1 January† (New Year's Day), 16 January (Martin Luther King Day), 20 February (Washington's Birthday/Presidents' Day), 28 May (Memorial Day), 4 July (Independence Day), 3 September (Labor Day), 8 October (Columbus Day), 12 November (for Veterans' Day), 22 November (Thanksgiving Day), 25 December (Christmas Day).

*Federal legal public holidays are designated by presidential proclamation or congressional enactment, but need not be observed in individual states, which have legal jurisdiction over their public holidays.

†As New Year's Day falls on a Sunday in 2012, the public holiday will be observed on 2 January 2012.

THE UNITED STATES OF AMERICA

Statistical Survey

Source (unless otherwise stated): Statistical Information Office, Population Division, Bureau of the Census, US Dept of Commerce, Washington, DC 20233-0001; internet www.census.gov.

Area and Population

AREA, POPULATION AND DENSITY

Area (sq km)	
Land	9,161,923
Water*	664,706
Total	9,826,630†
Population (census results)	
1 April 2000‡	
Males	138,053,563
Females	143,368,343
Total	281,421,906
1 April 2010	308,745,538
Density (per sq km) at census 2010§	33.7

* Comprises Great Lakes, and inland, territorial, and coastal waters.
† 3,794,083 sq miles.
‡ Excluding adjustment for underenumeration; the adjusted total was 281,424,602.
§ Land area only.

POPULATION BY AGE AND SEX
(population at census of 1 April 2000)

	Males	Females	Total
0–14	30,854,207	29,399,168	60,253,375
15–64	92,789,731	93,387,047	186,176,778
65 and over	14,409,625	20,582,128	34,991,753
Total	138,053,563	143,368,343	281,421,906

RACES
(2000 census)

	Number	%
White	211,460,626	75.14
Black	34,658,190	12.32
Asian	10,242,998	3.64
American Indian and Alaska Native	2,475,956	0.88
Native Hawaiian and Pacific Islander	398,835	0.14
Others*	22,185,301	7.88
Total	281,421,906	100.00

* Includes those of two or more races.

Hispanic or Latino population (all races): 35,305,818 (12.6%).

STATES
(population at census of 1 April 2010*)

State	Land area (sq km)	Residents	Density (per sq km)	Capital
Alabama	131,426	4,779,736	36.4	Montgomery
Alaska	1,481,347	710,231	0.5	Juneau
Arizona	294,312	6,392,017	21.7	Phoenix
Arkansas	134,856	2,915,918	21.6	Little Rock
California	403,933	37,253,956	92.2	Sacramento
Colorado	268,627	5,029,196	18.7	Denver
Connecticut	12,548	3,574,097	284.8	Hartford
Delaware	5,060	897,934	177.5	Dover
District of Columbia	159	601,723	3,784.4	Washington
Florida	139,670	18,801,310	134.6	Tallahassee
Georgia	149,976	9,687,653	64.6	Atlanta
Hawaii	16,635	1,360,301	81.8	Honolulu
Idaho	214,314	1,567,582	7.3	Boise
Illinois	143,961	12,830,632	89.1	Springfield
Indiana	92,895	6,483,802	69.8	Indianapolis
Iowa	144,701	3,046,355	21.1	Des Moines
Kansas	211,900	2,853,118	13.5	Topeka
Kentucky	102,896	4,339,367	42.2	Frankfort
Louisiana	112,825	4,533,372	40.2	Baton Rouge
Maine	79,931	1,328,361	16.6	Augusta
Maryland	25,314	5,773,552	228.1	Annapolis
Massachusetts	20,306	6,547,629	322.4	Boston
Michigan	147,121	9,883,640	67.2	Lansing
Minnesota	206,189	5,303,925	25.7	St Paul
Mississippi	121,488	2,967,297	24.4	Jackson
Missouri	178,414	5,988,927	33.6	Jefferson City
Montana	376,979	989,415	2.6	Helena
Nebraska	199,099	1,826,341	9.2	Lincoln
Nevada	284,448	2,700,551	9.5	Carson City
New Hampshire	23,227	1,316,470	56.7	Concord
New Jersey	19,211	8,791,894	457.6	Trenton
New Mexico	314,309	2,059,179	6.6	Santa Fe
New York	122,283	19,378,102	158.5	Albany
North Carolina	126,161	9,535,483	75.6	Raleigh
North Dakota	178,647	672,591	3.8	Bismarck
Ohio	106,056	11,536,504	108.8	Columbus
Oklahoma	177,847	3,751,351	21.1	Oklahoma City
Oregon	248,631	3,831,074	15.4	Salem
Pennsylvania	116,074	12,702,379	109.4	Harrisburg
Rhode Island	2,706	1,052,567	389.0	Providence
South Carolina	77,983	4,625,364	59.3	Columbia
South Dakota	196,540	814,180	4.1	Pierre
Tennessee	106,752	6,346,105	59.4	Nashville
Texas	678,051	25,145,561	37.1	Austin
Utah	212,751	2,763,885	13.0	Salt Lake City
Vermont	23,956	625,741	26.1	Montpelier
Virginia	102,548	8,001,024	78.0	Richmond
Washington	172,348	6,724,540	39.0	Olympia
West Virginia	62,361	1,852,994	29.7	Charleston
Wisconsin	140,663	5,686,986	40.4	Madison
Wyoming	251,489	563,626	2.2	Cheyenne
Total	9,161,923	308,745,538	33.7	

* Includes armed forces residing in each State.

PRINCIPAL TOWNS
(population at census of 1 April 2010)

New York	8,175,133	Las Vegas	583,756
Los Angeles	3,792,621	Oklahoma City	579,999
Chicago	2,695,598	Albuquerque	545,852
Houston	2,099,451	Tucson	520,116
Philadelphia	1,526,006	Fresno	494,665
Phoenix	1,445,632	Sacramento	466,488
San Antonio	1,327,407	Long Beach, CA	462,257
San Diego	1,307,402	Kansas City, MO	459,787
Dallas	1,197,816	Mesa City, AZ	439,041
San Jose	945,942	Virginia Beach, VA	437,994
Jacksonville	821,784	Atlanta	420,003
Indianapolis	820,445	Colorado Springs	416,427
San Francisco	805,235	Omaha	408,958
Austin	790,390	Cleveland	396,815
Columbus, OH	787,033	Tulsa	391,906
Fort Worth	741,206	Oakland	390,724
Charlotte	731,424	Minneapolis	382,578
Detroit	713,777	Wichita	382,368
El Paso	649,121	Arlington, TX	365,438
Memphis	646,889	New Orleans	343,829
Baltimore	620,961	Honolulu	337,256
Boston	617,594	Anaheim	336,265
Seattle	608,660	Tampa	335,709
Washington, DC (capital)	601,723	Santa Ana, CA	324,528
Nashville-Davidson	601,222	St Louis	319,294
Denver	600,158	Pittsburgh	305,704
Milwaukee	594,833	Cincinnati	296,943
Portland, OR	583,776	Toledo, OH	287,208

THE UNITED STATES OF AMERICA

BIRTHS, MARRIAGES, DEATHS

	Registered live births		Registered marriages		Registered deaths	
	Number ('000)	Rate (per 1,000)	Number ('000)	Rate (per 1,000)	Number ('000)	Rate (per 1,000)
2000	4,059	14.4	2,329	8.3	2,403	8.5
2001	4,026	14.1	2,345	8.2	2,416	8.5
2002	4,022	13.9	2,254	7.8	2,443	8.5
2003	4,090	14.1	2,245	7.7	2,448	8.4
2004	4,112	14.0	2,279	7.8	2,398	8.2
2005	4,143	14.0	2,249	7.6	2,448	8.3
2006	4,266	14.2	2,160*	7.4*	2,426	8.1
2007	4,316	14.3	2,205†	7.3†	2,424	8.0

* Data for Louisiana were not available.
† Provisional figures.

Source: National Center for Health Statistics, US Department of Health and Human Services.

Life expectancy (years at birth, WHO estimates): 78 (males 76; females 81) in 2008 (Source: WHO, *World Health Statistics*).

IMMIGRATION
(year ending 30 September)

Country of birth	2007/08	2008/09	2009/10
Europe	103,719	105,398	88,743
Bosnia-Herzegovina	1,491	1,501	946
Poland	8,354	8,754	7,643
Russia	11,695	8,238	6,718
Ukraine	10,813	11,223	8,477
United Kingdom	14,348	15,748	12,792
Asia	399,027	413,312	422,063
Bangladesh	11,753	16,651	14,819
China, People's Republic	80,271	64,238	70,863
India	63,352	57,304	69,162
Iran	13,852	18,553	14,182
Korea, Republic	26,666	25,859	22,227
Pakistan	19,719	21,555	18,258
Philippines	54,030	60,029	58,173
Taiwan	9,073	8,038	6,732
Thailand	6,637	10,444	9,384
Viet Nam	31,497	29,234	30,632
Africa	105,915	127,050	101,355
Egypt	8,712	8,844	8,978
Ethiopia	12,917	15,462	14,266
Nigeria	12,475	15,253	13,376
Somalia	10,745	13,390	4,558
North America, Central America and the Caribbean	393,253	375,236	336,602
Canada	15,109	16,140	13,328
Mexico	189,989	164,920	139,120
Caribbean			
Cuba	49,500	38,954	33,573
Dominican Republic	31,879	49,414	53,870
Haiti	26,007	24,280	22,582
Jamaica	18,477	21,783	19,825
Central America			
El Salvador	19,659	19,909	18,806
Guatemala	16,182	12,187	10,467
South America	98,555	102,878	87,187
Brazil	12,195	14,701	12,258
Colombia	30,213	27,849	22,406
Ecuador	11,663	12,128	11,492
Peru	15,184	16,957	14,247
Venezuela	10,514	11,154	9,409
Total (incl. others and unknown)	1,107,126	1,130,818	1,042,625

Source: US Department of Homeland Security, *Yearbook of Immigration Statistics*.

ECONOMICALLY ACTIVE POPULATION
(annual averages, civilian labour force, '000 persons aged 16 years and over)

	2006	2007	2008
Agriculture, hunting, forestry and fishing	2,206	2,095	2,168
Mining and quarrying	687	736	819
Manufacturing	16,377	16,302	15,904
Electricity, gas and water	1,186	1,193	1,225
Construction	11,749	11,856	10,974
Wholesale and retail trade; repair of motor vehicles, motorcycles and personal and household goods	21,328	20,937	20,585
Hotels and restaurants	9,474	9,582	9,795
Transport, storage and communications	6,269	6,457	6,501
Financial intermediation	7,254	7,306	7,279
Real estate, renting and business activities	18,105	18,802	18,489
Public administration and defence; compulsory social security	6,524	6,746	6,763
Education	12,522	12,828	13,169
Health and social work	17,416	17,834	18,233
Other services	13,332	13,371	13,458
Total employed	144,427	146,047	145,362
Unemployed	7,001	7,078	8,924
Total labour force	151,428	153,124	154,286
Males	81,255	82,136	82,519
Females	70,172	70,988	71,767

Source: ILO.

Health and Welfare

KEY INDICATORS

Total fertility rate (children per woman, 2008)	2.1
Under-5 mortality rate (per 1,000 live births, 2008)	8
HIV/AIDS (% of persons aged 15–49, 2007)	0.6
Physicians (per 1,000 head, 2000)	2.56
Hospital beds (per 1,000 head, 2005)	3.2
Health expenditure (2007): US $ per head (PPP)	7,285
Health expenditure (2007): % of GDP	15.7
Health expenditure (2007): public (% of total)	45.5
Total carbon dioxide emissions ('000 metric tons, 2007)	5,832,194.0
Carbon dioxide emissions per head (metric tons, 2007)	19.3
Human Development Index (2010): ranking	4
Human Development Index (2010): value	0.902

For sources and definitions, see explanatory note on p. vi.

Agriculture

PRINCIPAL CROPS
('000 metric tons)

	2007	2008	2009
Wheat	55,820	68,016	60,314
Rice, paddy	8,999	9,241	9,972
Barley	4,575	5,230	4,949
Maize	331,175	307,142	333,011
Oats	1,313	1,294	1,351
Sorghum	12,636	11,998	9,728
Potatoes	20,179	18,827	19,569
Sweet potatoes	820	837	883
Sugar cane	27,751	25,041	27,456
Sugar beet	31,912	24,386	26,779
Beans, dry	1,161	1,159	1,150
Soybeans (Soya beans)	72,858	80,749	91,417
Groundnuts, with shell	1,697	2,342	1,673
Sunflower seed	1,301	1,553	1,377
Rapeseed	650	656	669
Cabbages and other brassicas	911	942	909
Lettuce and chicory	4,360	4,015	4,104
Tomatoes	14,185	13,718	14,142
Cucumbers and gherkins	931	916	888

THE UNITED STATES OF AMERICA

—continued

	2007	2008	2009
Onions, dry	3,612	3,407	3,401
Peas, green	989	934	n.a.
String beans	979	997	958
Carrots and turnips	1,450	1,479	1,304
Maize, green	4,190	3,880	4,223
Watermelons	1,694	1,815	1,820
Cantaloupes and other melons	1,114	1,043	1,070
Oranges	6,917	9,141	8,281
Tangerines, mandarins, etc.	327	478	402
Lemons and limes	724	566	827
Grapefruit and pomelos	1,475	1,404	1,183
Apples	4,123	4,259	4,515
Pears	799	789	849
Peaches and nectarines	1,279	1,304	1,198
Plums and sloes	367	493	561
Strawberries	1,109	1,148	1,271
Grapes	6,403	6,640	6,412
Tobacco, unmanufactured	357	363	373

Aggregate production (may include official, semi-official or estimated data): Total cereals 415,125 in 2007, 403,541 in 2008, 419,810 in 2009; Total fruits (excl. melons) 25,088 in 2007, 27,762 in 2008, 27,116 in 2009; Total oilcrops 15,508 in 2007, 16,886 in 2008, 18,499 in 2009; Total roots and tubers 21,001 in 2007, 19,665 in 2008, 20,454 in 2009; Total vegetables (incl. melons) 38,506 in 2007, 37,252 in 2008, 37,813 in 2009.

Source: FAO.

LIVESTOCK
('000 head at 1 January)

	2007	2008	2009
Cattle	96,573	96,035	94,521
Pigs	62,516	65,909	67,148
Sheep	6,120	5,950	5,747
Horses*	9,500	9,500	n.a.
Chickens (million)*	2,050	2,059	n.a.
Turkeys (million)	267	273	250

* FAO estimates.

Source: FAO.

LIVESTOCK PRODUCTS
('000 metric tons)

	2007	2008	2009
Cattle meat	11,979	11,839	11,891
Sheep meat	83	82	80
Pig meat	9,951	10,599	10,442
Chicken meat	16,628	16,994	16,334
Cows' milk	84,189	86,159	85,859
Hen eggs	5,395	5,339	n.a.

Source: FAO.

Forestry

ROUNDWOOD REMOVALS
('000 cubic metres)

	2007	2008	2009
Sawlogs and veneer logs	223,000	189,199	159,620
Pulp wood	146,568	139,484	136,467
Other industrial wood	9,203	8,212	8,311
Fuel wood	46,358	43,614	40,437
Total	425,129	380,509	344,835

Source: FAO.

SAWNWOOD PRODUCTION
('000 cubic metres)

	2007	2008	2009
Coniferous	59,769	49,416	39,576
Broadleaved	25,608	23,454	22,423
Total	85,377	72,869	61,998

Source: FAO.

Fishing
('000 metric tons, live weight)

	2006	2007	2008
Capture	4,852.3	4,767.6	4,349.9
Humpback salmon	100.6	207.5	118.2
Pacific cod	235.3	221.5	224.1
Walleye pollock	1,542.6	1,390.8	1,032.5
North Pacific hake	258.8	206.5	241.1
Atlantic menhaden	183.9	215.5	187.7
Gulf menhaden	408.9	456.6	420.7
American sea scallop	222.9	220.8	202.3
Atlantic surf clam	145.0	151.5	138.6
Aquaculture	519.3*	525.3	500.1
Channel catfish	258.0	255.8	233.6
Total catch	**5,371.5***	**5,292.9**	**4,850.0**

* FAO estimate.

Note: Figures exclude aquatic plants (metric tons): 6,362 in 2006; 2,272 in 2007; 6,951 in 2008, and sponges (metric tons): 153.7 in 2006; 266.7 in 2007; 210.1 in 2008. Also excluded are aquatic mammals (recorded by number rather than weight); the number of whales and dolphins caught was: 324 in 2006; 626 in 2007; 260 in 2008. The number of seals and sea lions caught was: 1,830 in 2006; 1,645 in 2007; 1,608 in 2008. The number of American alligators caught was: 421,220 in 2006; 387,203 in 2007; 230,464 in 2008.

Source: FAO.

Mining
('000 metric tons, unless otherwise indicated)

	2006	2007	2008
Crude petroleum (million barrels)[1]	1,862	1,848	1,812
Natural gas (million cubic feet)[1,2]	19,410	20,196	21,112
Coal (million short tons)[1,3]	1,163	1,147	1,172
Iron ore[4]	52,700	50,900	53,500
Copper[5]	1,200	1,170	1,310
Lead[5]	419	434	399
Zinc[5]	699	769	748
Molybdenum (metric tons)[5]	59,800	57,000	55,900
Silver (metric tons)[5]	1,160	1,280	1,250
Uranium ('000 pounds)[1,6]	4,106	4,536	3,902
Gold (metric tons)[5]	252	238	233
Platinum group metals (kilograms):[5]			
Platinum	4,290	3,860	2,580
Palladium	14,000	12,800	11,600
Lime	21,000	20,200	19,800
Sand and gravel (million metric tons):			
Construction	1,330	1,240	1,040
Industrial	28,900	30,100	30,400
Stone, crushed (million metric tons)	1,780	1,650	1,440
Bentonite	4,940	4,820	5,030
Fuller's Earth	2,540	2,600	2,350
Kaolin	7,470	7,110	6,740
Phosphate rock[2]	30,100	29,700	30,200
Potash (a)[2,7]	2,400	2,600	2,400
Soda ash	11,000	11,100	11,300
Diatomite	799	687	764
Salt	40,600	45,500	47,600
Bromine (b)[7]	243	n.a.	n.a.

[1] Source: Energy Information Administration, US Department of Energy.
[2] Figures refer to marketable production.
[3] 1 short ton = 0.907185 metric tons.
[4] Figures refer to the gross weight of usable ore.
[5] Figures refer to metal content of ores and concentrates.
[6] Figures refer to gross weight of uranium oxide ore.
[7] Figures refer to the content of (a) K_2O or (b) bromine contained in minerals and compounds.

2009: Crude petroleum (million barrels) 1,957; Natural gas (million cubic feet) 21,604; Coal (million short tons) 1,075; Uranium ('000 pounds) 3,708.
2010: Crude petroleum (million barrels) 2,012; Natural gas (million cubic feet) 22,568; Uranium ('000 pounds, preliminary) 4,235.

Source (unless otherwise indicated): US Geological Survey.

THE UNITED STATES OF AMERICA

Industry

PRINCIPAL MANUFACTURES
(value of shipments in $ '000 million)

	2007	2008	2009
Food	589.9	650.0	628.6
Beverages and tobacco products	128.3	125.1	119.9
Wood products	102.0	87.8	65.4
Paper	176.1	179.2	161.8
Printing and related activities	103.4	98.6	83.9
Petroleum and coal products	615.5	769.7	497.9
Chemicals	724.1	738.7	628.9
Plastics and rubber products	210.4	200.7	171.2
Non-metallic mineral products	128.1	115.5	90.4
Primary metal industries	257.3	282.6	168.3
Fabricated metal products	345.3	358.3	281.3
Machinery	351.5	355.6	287.6
Computers and electronic products	403.0	383.9	328.0
Electrical equipment, appliances and components	129.7	130.3	106.7
Transportation equipment	744.9	672.8	545.0
Total (incl. others)	5,338.3	5,468.1	4,436.2

Source: Bureau of the Census, US Department of Commerce, *Annual Survey of Manufactures*.

Finance

CURRENCY AND EXCHANGE RATES

Monetary Units
100 cents = 1 United States dollar ($).

Sterling and Euro Equivalents (31 December 2010)
£1 sterling = US $1.565;
€1 = $1.336;
US $100 = £63.88 = €74.84.

FEDERAL BUDGET
('000 $ million, year ending 30 September)*

Revenue	2010	2011†	2012†
Individual income taxes	898.5	956.0	1,140.5
Corporation income taxes	191.4	198.4	329.3
Social insurance taxes and contributions	864.8	806.8	925.1
Excise taxes	66.9	74.1	103.1
Estate and gift taxes	18.9	12.2	13.6
Customs duties and fees	25.3	27.7	29.8
Miscellaneous receipts	96.8	98.4	86.1
Total	2,162.7	2,173.7	2,627.4

Expenditure	2010	2011†	2012†
National defence	693.6	768.2	737.5
International affairs	45.1	55.2	63.0
General science, space research and technology	31.0	33.4	32.3
Energy	11.6	27.9	23.4
Natural resources and environment	43.7	49.0	42.7
Agriculture	21.4	25.1	18.9
Commerce and housing credit	−82.3	17.4	23.6
Transportation	92.0	94.5	104.9
Community and regional development	23.8	25.7	25.7
Education, training, employment and social services	127.7	115.1	106.2
Health	369.1	387.6	373.8

Statistical Survey

Expenditure—*continued*	2010	2011†	2012†
Medicare	451.6	494.3	492.3
Income security	622.2	622.7	554.3
Social security	706.7	748.4	767.0
Veterans' benefits and services	108.4	141.4	124.7
Administration of justice	53.4	60.7	58.7
General government	23.0	32.1	31.1
Allowances	—	3.1	6.6
Net interest	196.2	206.7	241.6
Undistributed offsetting receipts	−82.1	−89.7	−99.6
Total	3,456.2	3,818.8	3,728.7

* Including social security and postal service receipts and expenditures, which are extrabudgetary.
† Estimates.

Sources: Office of Management and Budget, Executive Office of the President; and Financial Management Service, US Department of the Treasury.

STATE AND LOCAL GOVERNMENT FINANCES
($ million, fiscal years*)

Revenue	2005/06	2006/07	2007/08
From federal government	452,975	467,949	481,380
From state and local governments	2,289,176	2,604,695	2,179,095
General revenue from own sources	1,744,499	1,867,945	1,944,398
Taxes	1,205,667	1,283,283	1,330,412
Property	364,559	389,573	409,686
Sales and gross receipts	417,735	439,586	448,689
Individual income	268,667	289,827	304,627
Corporation income	53,081	60,592	57,810
Other	101,625	103,705	109,601
Charges and miscellaneous	538,833	584,662	613,987
Utility and liquor stores	131,636	141,234	146,385
Insurance trust revenue	413,040	595,516	88,312
Employee retirement	346,295	532,154	26,273
Unemployment compensation	36,989	34,186	34,489
Other	29,757	29,176	27,550
Total	2,742,151	3,072,645	2,660,475

Expenditure	2005/06	2006/07	2007/08
General expenditure	2,117,161	2,258,229	2,400,204
Education	728,917	774,373	826,063
Elementary and secondary	502,496	534,905	565,631
Institutions of higher education	191,589	204,706	223,294
Other	34,832	34,763	37,138
Libraries	10,462	10,789	11,611
Public welfare	367,397	384,769	404,624
Hospitals	109,001	118,876	128,853
Health	69,953	74,196	79,704
Social insurance administration	4,556	3,981	4,089
Veterans' services	992	1,031	1,083
Highways	136,502	144,713	153,515
Other transportations	23,965	26,263	27,807
Police	78,472	84,088	89,676
Fire protection	33,655	36,828	39,683
Correction	62,643	68,092	72,904
Protective inspection	13,312	14,250	14,937
Natural resources	25,283	28,717	29,917
Parks and recreation	34,667	37,526	40,646
Housing and community development	42,053	45,937	50,974
Sewerage	39,382	44,197	46,679
Solid waste management	22,701	22,819	23,757
Financial administration	37,675	39,631	40,995
Judicial and legal services	36,992	38,736	41,451
General public buildings	12,103	13,926	15,091

THE UNITED STATES OF AMERICA

Statistical Survey

Expenditure—continued	2005/06	2006/07	2007/08
Other government administration	23,649	27,103	29,460
Interest on general debt	86,162	93,586	100,055
Other and unallocable	116,668	123,802	126,630
Utility and liquor stores	174,520	189,330	199,287
Insurance trust expenditure	204,080	213,652	234,584
Unemployment compensation	28,097	28,934	35,568
Employee retirement	156,189	166,975	180,058
Other	19,794	17,744	18,958
Total†	**2,502,264**	**2,665,881**	**2,838,836**

* Figures refer to the fiscal year of individual state governments, normally ending 30 June, or, in the case of the following exceptions, ending on some date within the previous 12 months: the state government of Texas and Texas school districts (31 August); the state governments of Alabama and Michigan, all local governments in the District of Columbia, and Alabama school districts (30 September); and all state and local governments of New York (31 March).
† Including intergovernmental expenditure ($ million): 6,502 in 2005/06; 4,671 in 2006/07; 4,761 in 2007/08.

Source: Governments Division, Bureau of the Census, US Department of Commerce, *Survey of Government Finances*.

INTERNATIONAL RESERVES
($ '000 million at 31 December)

	2008	2009	2010
Gold (national valuation)	11.04	11.04	11.04
IMF special drawing rights	9.34	57.81	56.82
Reserve position in IMF	7.68	11.39	12.49
Foreign exchange	49.58	50.52	52.08
Total	**77.64**	**130.76**	**132.43**

Source: IMF, *International Financial Statistics*.

CURRENCY AND COIN IN CIRCULATION*
($ million at end of June)

	2008	2009	2010
Total	826,313.9	909,698.6	945,137.9

* Currency outside Treasury and Federal Reserve banks, including currency held by commercial banks.

Source: Financial Management Service, US Department of the Treasury.

COST OF LIVING
(Consumer Price Index for all urban consumers, average of monthly figures. Base: 1982–84 = 100, unless otherwise indicated)

	2008	2009	2010
Food and beverages	214.2	218.2	212.0
Housing	216.3	217.1	216.3
Clothing	118.9	120.1	119.5
Transport	195.5	179.3	193.4
Medical care	364.1	375.6	388.4
Recreation*	113.3	114.3	113.3
Education and communication*	123.6	127.4	129.9
Other goods and services	345.4	368.6	381.3
All items	**215.3**	**214.5**	**218.1**

* Base: December 1997 = 100.

Source: Bureau of Labor Statistics, US Department of Labor.

NATIONAL ACCOUNTS
($ '000 million at current prices)

National Income and Product

	2008	2009	2010
Compensation of employees	8,068.1	7,819.5	7,999.5
Operating surplus	3,322.8	3,294.9	3,641.0
Domestic factor incomes	**11,390.9**	**11,114.4**	**11,640.5**
Consumption of fixed capital	1,849.2	1,861.1	1,868.9
Statistical discrepancy	136.6	179.1	151.6
Gross domestic product (GDP) at factor cost	**13,376.7**	**13,154.6**	**13,661.0**
Taxes on production and imports	1,045.1	1,024.7	1,058.5
Less Subsidies on production and imports	52.8	60.3	59.0
GDP in purchasers' values	**14,369.1**	**14,119.0**	**14,660.4**
Factor income received from abroad	839.2	629.8	706.2
Less Factor income paid abroad	664.7	483.6	517.9
Gross national product (GNP)	**14,543.6**	**14,265.3**	**14,848.7**
Less Consumption of fixed capital	1,849.2	1,861.1	1,868.9
Net national product	**12,694.4**	**12,404.2**	**12,979.8**
Statistical discrepancy	−136.6	−179.1	−151.6
National income in market prices	**12,557.8**	**12,225.0**	**12,828.2**

Expenditure on Gross Domestic Product

	2008	2009	2010
Government final consumption expenditure	2,878.3	2,914.9	3,000.2
Private final consumption expenditure	10,104.5	10,001.3	10,349.1
Increase in stocks	−41.1	−127.2	71.7
Gross fixed investment	2,137.8	1,716.4	1,755.8
Total domestic expenditure	**15,079.5**	**14,505.4**	**15,176.8**
Exports of goods and services	1,843.4	1,578.4	1,837.5
Less Imports of goods and services	2,553.8	1,964.7	2,353.9
GDP in purchasers' values	**14,369.1**	**14,119.0**	**14,660.4**

Gross Domestic Product by Economic Activity*

	2007	2008	2009
Private industries	12,301.9	12,514.0	12,196.5
Agriculture, forestry, fishing and hunting	144.7	160.1	133.1
Agriculture	114.9	131.1	104.0
Forestry, fishing and related activities	29.8	29.0	29.2
Mining	254.2	317.1	240.8
Electricity, gas and water	248.8	262.6	268.1
Construction	657.2	623.4	537.5
Manufacturing	1,698.9	1,647.6	1,584.8
Wholesale trade	813.3	822.9	780.8
Retail trade	886.1	840.2	819.6
Transport and storage	405.4	418.7	389.5
Information	633.3	652.5	639.3
Finance and insurance	1,110.4	1,100.4	1,171.6
Real estate and rental and leasing	1,780.8	1,874.5	1,868.7
Professional and business services	1,700.5	1,768.8	1,701.3
Professional, scientific and technical services	1,028.7	1,093.6	1,068.5
Management of companies and enterprises	257.3	260.1	246.5
Administrative and waste management services	414.5	415.1	386.3
Education	137.3	147.0	154.9
Health care and social assistance	941.0	1,001.9	1,057.9
Arts, entertainment and recreation	134.4	135.2	127.3

THE UNITED STATES OF AMERICA

—continued	2007	2008	2009
Hotels and restaurants	410.8	400.2	385.8
Other private services	344.6	340.9	335.4
Government	1,759.9	1,855.1	1,922.5
Federal	552.3	580.2	611.5
General government	486.0	517.1	551.7
Government enterprises	66.2	63.1	59.9
State and local	1,207.6	1,274.9	1,311.0
General government	1,118.6	1,180.5	1,208.5
Government enterprises	89.1	94.4	102.5
GDP in purchasers' values	14,061.8	14,369.1	14,119.0

* Distribution is based on the 1997 North American Industry Classification System (NAICS), which differs from ISIC.

2007 ($ '000 million at current prices, revised figures): Business 10,771.4 (Farm 114.9); Households and institutions 1,685.8; General government 1,604.6 (State and local 1,118.6); Gross domestic product in purchasers' values 14,061.8.

2008 ($ '000 million at current prices, revised figures): Business 10,863.5 (Farm 131.1); Households and institutions 1,808.0; General government 1,697.6 (State and local 1,180.5); Gross domestic product in purchasers' values 14,369.1.

2009 ($ '000 million at current prices): Business 10,520.8 (Farm 104.0); Households and institutions 1,838.1; General government 1,760.2 (State and local 1,208.5); Gross domestic product in purchasers' values 14,119.0.

2010 ($ '000 million at current prices): Business 11,018.2 (Farm 124.5); Households and institutions 1,841.3; General government 1,801.0 (State and local 1,801.0); Gross domestic product in purchasers' values 14,660.4.

Source: Bureau of Economic Analysis, US Department of Commerce.

BALANCE OF PAYMENTS
($ '000 million)

	2007	2008	2009
Exports of goods f.o.b.	1,164.46	1,308.91	1,072.93
Imports of goods f.o.b.	1,984.60	−2,140.59	−1,576.51
Trade balance	−820.14	−831.68	−503.58
Exports of services	484.21	530.10	497.87
Imports of services	−366.16	−397.23	−369.20
Balance on goods and services	−702.10	−698.80	−374.91
Other income received	829.60	796.53	588.20
Other income paid	−730.05	−644.56	−466.78
Balance on goods, services and income	−602.55	−546.83	−253.49
Current transfers received	24.29	23.70	20.88
Current transfers paid	−139.84	−145.73	−145.82
Current balance	−718.10	−668.86	−378.43
Capital account (net)	0.38	6.01	−0.14
Direct investment abroad	−414.00	−351.14	−268.68
Direct investment from abroad	271.21	328.33	134.71
Portfolio investment assets	−390.75	285.88	−393.47
Portfolio investment liabilities	1,156.61	520.07	366.67
Financial derivatives (net)	6.22	−32.95	50.80
Other investment assets	−670.86	226.19	573.94
Other investment liabilities	679.83	−393.68	−195.74
Net errors and omissions	79.56	84.99	162.52
Overall balance	0.13	4.84	52.18

Source: IMF, *International Financial Statistics*.

FOREIGN AID
($ million, year ending 30 September)

	2003/04*	2004/05*	2005/06†
Multilateral assistance	1,464.7	1,702.8	1,797.2
Bilateral assistance	15,554.7	31,546.9	14,364.0
Military assistance	6,285.4	4,848.3	5,151.2

* Appropriated.
† Requested.

Source: US Agency for International Development.

External Trade

PRINCIPAL COMMODITIES
(distribution by SITC, $ million)

Imports	2008	2009	2010
Food and live animals	66,182.7	61,985.6	70,321.4
Mineral fuels, lubricants, etc.	491,884.7	271,739.2	353,540.0
Petroleum, petroleum products, etc.	443,830.5	249,024.3	329,635.3
Chemicals and related products	176,492.2	151,226.7	173,448.9
Basic manufactures	231,684.1	151,884.4	194,496.3
Machinery and transport equipment	721,174.9	569,950.2	714,084.3
General industrial machinery, equipment and parts	66,909.6	50,181.1	60,446.7
Office machines and automatic data-processing machines	96,526.4	91,097.8	113,471.8
Telecommunications and sound equipment	133,186.7	119,392.2	137,337.5
Other electrical machinery, apparatus, etc.	112,623.0	91,683.3	119,667.0
Motor vehicles	190,799.0	127,862.8	179,082.0
Miscellaneous manufactured articles	289,982.3	247,512.0	287,287.9
Clothing and accessories (excl. footwear)	78,893.3	69,326.4	78,523.0
Total (incl. others)	2,103,640.8	1,559,624.8	1,912,091.6

Exports	2008	2009	2010
Food and live animals	85,750.7	71,602.6	82,656.3
Crude materials (inedible) except fuels	76,462.0	61,695.7	81,045.4
Mineral fuels, lubricants, etc.	76,741.7	54,848.3	80,728.2
Chemicals and related products	179,736.6	159,892.0	189,089.4
Basic manufactures	124,764.4	94,720.1	119,486.9
Machinery and transport equipment	547,015.2	441,427.3	520,668.5
Power-generating machinery and equipment	36,007.2	30,438.4	35,971.9
Machinery specialized for particular industries	55,607.8	40,070.3	51,034.7
General industrial machinery, equipment and parts	59,013.8	48,764.5	56,502.3
Office machines and automatic data-processing machines	46,111.6	38,811.1	44,559.3
Telecommunication equipment, parts and accessories	40,604.7	36,114.6	42,458.4
Other electrical machinery, apparatus, etc.	105,917.0	85,566.2	104,991.5
Motor vehicles	106,535.4	69,806.5	95,026.9
Transport equipment	90,458.0	87,061.3	84,178.3
Miscellaneous manufactured articles	132,674.2	119,943.5	133,927.9
Professional, scientific and controlling instruments, etc.	49,119.0	44,806.0	51,778.2
Total (incl. others)	1,287,442.0	1,056,043.0	1,277,503.9

Source: Office of Trade and Industry Information (OTII), Manufacturing and Services, International Trade Administration, US Department of Commerce.

THE UNITED STATES OF AMERICA

PRINCIPAL TRADING PARTNERS
($ million)

Imports	2008	2009	2010
Brazil	30,452.9	20,069.6	23,918.1
Canada	339,491.4	226,248.4	276,477.8
China, People's Republic	337,772.6	296,373.9	364,943.8
France (incl. Monaco)	44,049.3	34,236.0	38,550.9
Germany	97,496.6	71,498.2	82,679.7
India	25,704.4	21,166.0	29,531.2
Ireland	31,346.5	28,100.6	33,897.8
Israel	22,335.8	18,744.4	20,974.9
Italy	36,135.0	26,429.8	28,463.2
Japan	139,262.2	95,803.7	120,347.8
Korea, Republic	48,069.1	39,215.6	48,859.6
Malaysia	30,736.1	23,282.6	25,904.7
Mexico	215,941.6	176,654.4	229,654.6
Nigeria	38,068.0	19,128.2	30,515.9
Russia	26,783.0	18,199.7	25,685.2
Saudi Arabia	54,747.4	22,053.1	31,420.1
Taiwan	36,326.1	28,362.1	35,906.8
Thailand	23,538.3	19,082.5	22,686.5
United Kingdom	58,587.4	47,479.9	49,755.5
Venezuela	51,423.6	28,059.0	32,774.7
Total (incl. others)	2,103,640.7	1,559,624.8	1,912,091.6

Exports	2008	2009	2010
Australia	22,218.6	19,599.3	21,803.3
Belgium	28,903.5	21,607.7	25,551.1
Brazil	32,298.7	26,095.5	35,357.4
Canada	261,149.8	204,658.0	248,194.1
China, People's Republic	69,732.8	69,496.7	91,878.3
France (incl. Monaco)	28,840.1	26,493.0	27,010.1
Germany	54,505.3	43,306.3	48,201.2
Hong Kong	21,498.6	21,050.5	26,569.3
India	17,682.1	16,441.4	19,222.7
Israel	14,486.9	9,559.4	11,271.5
Italy	15,460.8	12,268.0	14,191.4
Japan	65,141.8	51,134.2	60,545.5
Korea, Republic	34,668.7	28,611.9	38,843.8
Malaysia	12,949.5	10,403.3	13,981.9
Mexico	151,220.1	128,892.1	163,320.8
Netherlands	39,719.5	32,241.5	34,997.7
Saudi Arabia	12,484.2	10,792.2	11,591.0
Singapore	27,853.6	22,231.8	29,149.8
Switzerland	22,023.6	17,504.4	20,691.9
Taiwan	24,926.3	18,485.6	26,027.3
United Arab Emirates	14,417.4	12,210.9	11,638.3
United Kingdom	53,599.1	45,703.6	48,496.7
Total (incl. others)	1,287,442.0	1,056,043.0	1,277,503.9

Source: Office of Trade and Industry Information (OTII), Manufacturing and Services, International Trade Administration, US Department of Commerce.

Transport

RAILWAYS
(revenue traffic on class I railroads only)

	2002	2003	2004
Passengers carried ('000)*	23,269	24,595	25,215
Passenger-miles (million)*	5,314	5,680	5,511
Freight carried (million short tons)	2,207	2,240	2,398
Freight ton-miles ('000 million)	1,507	1,551	1,663

* AMTRAK passenger traffic only.

Source: Association of American Railroads, Washington, DC.

ROAD TRAFFIC
('000 motor vehicles registered at 31 December)

	2007	2008	2009
Passenger cars	135,933	137,079	134,880
Buses and coaches	834	843	842
Lorries (trucks) and vans	110,497	110,242	110,561
Motorcycles	7,138	7,753	7,930

Source: Federal Highway Administration.

INLAND WATERWAYS
(freight carried, million short tons)

	2007	2008	2009
Lake waterways	95.6	90.4	63.2
Coastal waterways	205.8	186.3	167.7
Internal waterways*	621.9	588.5	522.5
Total†	1,021.5	956.3	857.1

* Internal refers to freight moved solely within US boundaries, excluding traffic on the Great Lakes system. Figures also exclude waterway improvement materials and fish.
† Totals include intra-port and intra-territorial traffic.

Source: Waterborne Commerce Statistics Center, US Army Corps of Engineers.

OCEAN SHIPPING
Sea-going Merchant Vessels

	2001	2002	2003
Number:			
passenger	11	13	11
container	90	91	87
roll-on/roll-off	60	60	64
bulk	15	17	20
tanker	142	130	110
other*	136	132	124
Total	454	443	416
Capacity ('000 dwt):			
passenger	99	104	90
container	3,058	3,201	3,309
roll-on/roll-off	1,260	1,273	1,411
bulk	604	706	837
tanker	8,447	7,532	5,828
other*	2,362	2,162	1,818
Total	15,830	14,978	13,294

* Includes breakbulk, partial container, refrigerated cargo, barge carrier and specialized cargo vessels.

Source: Maritime Administration, US Department of Transportation.

Vessels Entered and Cleared in Foreign Trade in all Ports

	1998	1999	2000
Entered:			
number	61,417	58,374	60,064
displacement ('000 net tons)	619,071	621,204	672,834
Cleared:			
number	60,711	56,599	57,864
displacement ('000 net tons)	630,816	618,990	670,855

Source: Maritime Administration, US Department of Transportation.

THE UNITED STATES OF AMERICA

CIVIL AVIATION
(US airlines, revenue traffic on scheduled services)

	2003	2004	2005*
Number of departures ('000)	10,839	11,398	11,475
Domestic traffic:			
Passengers enplaned ('000)	592,412	640,683	670,152
Passenger-miles (million)	500,271	551,935	579,661
Freight ton-miles (million)†	12,342	12,756	12,634
Mail ton-miles (million)†	880	819	719
International traffic:			
Passengers enplaned ('000)	53,863	62,222	68,273
Passenger-miles (million)	156,638	181,743	199,326
Freight ton-miles (million)†	13,021	13,926	14,178
Mail ton-miles (million)†	492	477	476

* Provisional figures.
† Short tons (1 short ton = 0.907185 metric tons).

Source: Air Transport Association of America.

Tourism

FOREIGN VISITOR ARRIVALS
(by country of residence, '000)

	2008	2009	2010*
Australia	690	724	904
Canada	18,910	17,977	19,959
France	1,243	1,204	1,342
Germany	1,782	1,687	1,726
Italy	779	753	838
Japan	3,249	2,918	3,386
Korea, Republic	759	744	1,108
Mexico	13,686	13,229	13,423
United Kingdom	4,564	3,899	3,851
Total (incl. others)	57,937	54,962	59,745

* Preliminary.

Tourism receipts (incl. passenger transport, $ million): 141,713 in 2008; 121,071 in 2009; 134,400 in 2010.

Source: Office of Travel and Tourism Industries, International Trade Administration, US Department of Commerce.

Communications Media

	2007	2008	2009
Telephones ('000 main lines in use)	158,418.2	140,975.0	141,000.0
Mobile cellular telephones ('000 subscribers)	255,395.6	270,333.8	285,646.2
Internet users ('000)	231,505.5	230,632.8	245,433.8
Broadband subscribers ('000)	70,206.0	76,926.0	81,146.2

Personal computers: 240,500,000 (806.1 per 1,000) in 2006.

Television receivers ('000 in use): 267,000 in 2001.

Radio receivers ('000 in use): 570,000 in 1996 (estimate).

Books published (number of titles): 96,080 in 2000.

Daily newspapers (2001): 1,468 titles with average circulation of 55,600.

Sources: International Telecommunication Union; UN, *Statistical Yearbook*.

Education

ENROLMENT
('000 students at September of each year)

	2008	2009*	2010*
Public:			
elementary	34,286	34,505	34,730
secondary	14,980	14,807	14,657
higher	13,972	14,811	14,895
Private:			
elementary	4,574	4,580	4,582
secondary	1,395	1,389	1,382
higher*	5,131	5,617	5,655

* Projections.

Total elementary and secondary school teaching staff ('000): 3,674 (public 3,219, private 455) in 2008; 3,618 (public 3,161, private 457) in 2009 (projections); 3,634 (public 3,174, private 460) in 2009 (projections).

Total higher education teaching staff ('000, projections): 910 (public 603, private 306) in 2007; 927 (public 602, private 326) in 2008; 969 (public 633, private 336) in 2009.

Source: National Center for Education Statistics, US Department of Education.

Pupil-teacher ratio (primary education, UNESCO estimate): 13.7 in 2007/08 (Source: UNESCO Institute for Statistics).

Directory

The Executive

HEAD OF STATE

President: Barack Hussein Obama (took office 20 January 2009).
Vice-President: Joseph R. Biden, Jr.

THE CABINET
(May 2011)

The Government is formed by the Democratic Party.

Secretary of State: Hillary Rodham Clinton.
Secretary of the Treasury: Timothy F. Geithner.
Secretary of Defense: Robert M. Gates.
Attorney-General: Eric H. Holder, Jr.
Secretary of the Interior: Kenneth L. Salazar.
Secretary of Agriculture: Thomas J. Vilsack.
Secretary of Commerce: Gary Locke.
Secretary of Labor: Hilda L. Solis.
Secretary of Health and Human Services: Kathleen Sebelius.
Secretary of Housing and Urban Development: Shaun L. S. Donovan.
Secretary of Transportation: Raymond L. LaHood.
Secretary of Energy: Steven Chu.
Secretary of Education: Arne Duncan.
Secretary of Veterans Affairs: Gen. (retd) Eric K. Shinseki.
Secretary of Homeland Security: Janet Napolitano.

Officials with Cabinet Rank

Vice-President: Joseph R. Biden, Jr.
Chief of Staff to the President: William Daley.
Chair of the Council of Economic Advisers: Austan Goolsbee.
Director of the Office of Management and Budget: Jacob J. Lew.
US Trade Representative: Ronald Kirk.
Administrator of the Environmental Protection Agency: Lisa P. Jackson.
Director of National Intelligence: Lt-Gen. (retd) James R. Clapper, Jr.

THE UNITED STATES OF AMERICA

GOVERNMENT DEPARTMENTS

Department of Agriculture: 1400 Independence Ave, SW, Washington, DC 20250; tel. (202) 720-8732; fax (202) 720-9997; e-mail chris.mather@usda.gov; internet www.usda.gov; f. 1889.

Department of Commerce: 1401 Constitution Ave, NW, Washington, DC 20230; tel. (202) 482-2000; e-mail thesec@doc.gov; internet www.commerce.gov; f. 1913.

Department of Defense: 1400 Defense Pentagon, Washington, DC 20301-1400; tel. (703) 571-3343; fax (703) 428-1982; internet www.defense.gov; f. 1947.

Department of Education: 400 Maryland Ave, SW, 7E-247, Washington, DC 20202; tel. (202) 401-2000; fax (202) 401-0596; internet www.ed.gov; f. 1979.

Department of Energy: Forrestal Bldg, 1000 Independence Ave, SW, Washington, DC 20585; tel. (202) 586-5000; fax (202) 586-4403; e-mail the.secretary@hq.doe.gov; internet www.energy.gov; f. 1977.

Department of Health and Human Services: Hubert H. Humphrey Bldg, 200 Independence Ave, SW, Washington, DC 20201; tel. (202) 696-6162; fax (202) 690-8715; internet www.hhs.gov; f. 1980.

Department of Homeland Security: 1600 Pennsylvania Ave, NW, Washington, DC 20528; tel. (202) 282-8000; e-mail john.minnick@dhs.gov; internet www.dhs.gov; f. 2002.

Department of Housing and Urban Development: 451 Seventh St, SW, Washington, DC 20410; tel. (202) 708-1112; fax (202) 708-3106; internet www.hud.gov; f. 1965.

Department of the Interior: 1849 C St, NW, Washington, DC 20240; tel. (202) 208-3100; fax (202) 208-5048; e-mail feedback@ios.doi.gov; internet www.doi.gov; f. 1849.

Department of Justice: 950 Pennsylvania Ave, NW, Washington, DC 20530-0001; tel. (202) 514-2000; fax (202) 307-6777; e-mail askdoj@usdoj.gov; internet www.usdoj.gov; f. 1870; incl. the Office of the Attorney-Gen.

Department of Labor: Frances Perkins Bldg, 200 Constitution Ave, NW, Washington, DC 20210; tel. (202) 693-6000; fax (202) 693-6111; e-mail contact-ocio@dol.gov; internet www.dol.gov; f. 1913.

Department of State: 2201 C St, NW, Washington, DC 20520; tel. (202) 647-4000; fax (202) 647-6738; internet www.state.gov; f. 1789.

Department of Transportation: 1200 New Jersey Ave, SE, Washington, DC 20590; tel. (202) 366-4000; fax (202) 366-7202; e-mail dot.comments@dot.gov; internet www.dot.gov; f. 1967.

Department of the Treasury: 1500 Pennsylvania Ave, NW, Washington, DC 20220; tel. (202) 622-2000; fax (202) 622-6415; e-mail dcfo@do.treas.gov; internet www.ustreas.gov; f. 1789.

Department of Veterans Affairs: 810 Vermont Ave, NW, Washington, DC 20420; tel. (202) 273-6000; internet www.va.gov; f. 1989.

EXECUTIVE OFFICE OF THE PRESIDENT

The White House Office: 1600 Pennsylvania Ave, NW, Washington, DC 20500; tel. (202) 456-1414; fax (202) 456-2461; e-mail vice_president@whitehouse.gov; internet www.whitehouse.gov; coordinates activities relating to the President's immediate office; Chief of Staff to the Pres. WILLIAM DALEY.

Central Intelligence Agency: Office of Public Affairs, Washington, DC 20505; tel. (703) 482-0623; fax (703) 482-1739; internet www.cia.gov; f. 1947; Dir LEON E. PANETTA.

Council of Economic Advisers: Eisenhower Executive Office Bldg, 17th St and Pennsylvania Ave, NW, Washington, DC 20502; tel. (202) 395-5042; fax (202) 395-6958; internet www.whitehouse.gov/cea; f. 1946; Chair. AUSTAN GOOLSBEE.

Council on Environmental Quality: 722 Jackson Pl., Washington, DC 20503; tel. (202) 395-5750; fax (202) 456-0753; e-mail efoia@ceq.eop.gov; internet www.whitehouse.gov/ceq; f. 1969; Chair. NANCY SUTLEY.

Domestic Policy Council: Eisenhower Executive Office Bldg, Rm 469, 1600 Pennsylvania Ave, NW, Washington, DC 20500; tel. (202) 456-5594; fax (202) 456-2878; internet www.whitehouse.gov/dpc; f. 1993; fmrly a part of the Office of Policy Devt; includes the Office of Social Innovation and Civic Participation; Dir MELODY BARNES.

National Economic Council: Eisenhower Executive Office Bldg, Rm 235, 1600 Pennsylvania Ave, NW, Washington, DC 20502; tel. (202) 456-2800; fax (202) 456-2878; internet www.whitehouse.gov/nec; f. 1993; fmrly a part of the Office of Policy Devt; Dir GENE B. SPERLING.

National Security Council: Old Executive Office Bldg, 17th St and Pennsylvania Ave, NW, Washington, DC 20504; tel. (202) 456-1414; internet www.whitehouse.gov/nsc; f. 1947; Asst to the Pres. for Nat. Security Affairs TOM DONILON.

Office of Administration: Eisenhower Executive Office Bldg, 17th St, 1650 Pennsylvania Ave, NW, Washington, DC 20503; tel. (202) 456-2861; fax (202) 456-7921; internet www.whitehouse.gov/oa; f. 1977; Dir CAMERON MOODY.

Office of Faith-Based and Neighborhood Partnerships: The White House, 1600 Pennsylvania Ave, NW, Washington, DC 20502; tel. (202) 456-3394; e-mail whpartnerships@who.eop.gov; internet www.whitehouse.gov/ofbnp; f. 2001 as Office of Faith-Based and Community Initiatives; Dir JOSHUA DUBOIS.

Office of Management and Budget: 725 17th St, NW, Washington, DC 20503; tel. (202) 395-3080; fax (202) 395-3888; internet www.whitehouse.gov/omb; Dir JACOB J. LEW.

Office of National AIDS Policy: Eisenhower Executive Office Bldg, Rm 464, Washington, DC 20502; tel. (202) 456-4533; fax (202) 456-7315; e-mail aidspolicy@who.eop.gov; internet www.whitehouse.gov/onap/aids; Dir JEFFREY S. CROWLEY.

Office of National Drug Control Policy: POB 6000, Rockville, MD 20849-6000; tel. (202) 395-6700; fax (301) 519-5212; internet www.ondcp.gov; f. 1988; Dir R. GIL KERLIKOWSKE.

Office of Public Engagement and Intergovernmental Affairs: The White House, 1600 Pennsylvania Ave, NW, Washington, DC 20500; tel. (202) 456-1414; internet www.whitehouse.gov/ope; internet www.whitehouse.gov/eop/iga; includes the Council on Women and Girls and the Office of Urban Affairs; Dir, Public Engagement JON CARSON; Dir, Intergovernmental Affairs CECILIA MUÑOZ.

Office of Science and Technology Policy: 725 17th St, Rm 5228, NW, Washington, DC 20502; tel. (202) 456-7116; fax (202) 456-6021; e-mail info@ostp.gov; internet www.ostp.gov; f. 1993; Dir JOHN HOLDREN.

Office of the United States Trade Representative: Winder Bldg, 600 17th St, NW, Washington, DC 20508; tel. (202) 395-3230; fax (202) 395-6121; e-mail contactustr@ustr.eop.gov; internet www.ustr.gov; f. 1963; US Trade Rep. RONALD KIRK.

Office of the Vice-President: The White House, 1600 Pennsylvania Ave NW, Washington, DC 20501; tel. (202) 456-1414; fax (202) 456-2461; internet www.whitehouse.gov.

United States Mission to the United Nations: Press and Public Diplomacy Section, 140 East 45th St, New York, NY 10017; tel. (212) 415-4062; fax (212) 415-4053; e-mail usa@un.int; internet www.un.int/usa; US Ambassador to the United Nations Dr SUSAN RICE.

White House Military Office: Executive Office of the President, 1600 Pennsylvania Ave, NW, Washington, DC 20500; internet www.whitehouse.gov/whmo; areas of responsibility include Camp David (f. 1942) and Air Force One (f. 1962); Dir GEORGE D. MULLIGAN, Jr.

President and Legislature

PRESIDENT

Election, 4 November 2008

	Popular votes	% of popular votes	Electoral College votes
Barack Obama (Democrat)	69,456,897	52.92	365
John McCain (Republican)	59,934,814	45.66	173
Others*	1,865,617	1.42	—
Total	131,257,328	100.00	538

*Including write-in candidates, etc.

CONGRESS

Senate
(May 2011)

The Senate comprises 100 members. Senators' terms are for six years, one-third of the Senate being elected every two years.

President of the Senate: Vice-President JOSEPH R. BIDEN, Jr.

President Pro Tempore: DANIEL K. INOUYE.

Democrats: 51 seats.

Republicans: 47 seats.

Independents: 2 seats.

Majority Leader: HARRY M. REID.

Minority Leader: MITCH MCCONNELL.

THE UNITED STATES OF AMERICA

Members
(With political party and year in which term expires—on 3 January in all cases.)

Alabama
Jeff Sessions	Rep.	2015
Richard C. Shelby	Rep.	2017

Alaska
Mark Begich	Dem.	2015
Lisa Murkowski	Rep.	2017

Arizona
Jon Kyl	Rep.	2013
John McCain	Rep.	2017

Arkansas
Mark L. Pryor	Dem.	2015
John Boozman	Rep.	2017

California
Dianne Feinstein	Dem.	2013
Barbara Boxer	Dem.	2017

Colorado
Mark Udall	Dem.	2015
Michael F. Bennett	Dem.	2017

Connecticut
Joe I. Lieberman	Ind.-Dem.	2013
Richard Blumenthal	Dem.	2017

Delaware
Thomas Carper	Dem.	2013
Chris Coons	Dem.	2015

Florida
Bill Nelson	Dem.	2013
Marcio Rubio	Rep.	2017

Georgia
Saxby Chambliss	Rep.	2015
Johnny Isakson	Rep.	2017

Hawaii
Daniel K. Akaka	Dem.	2013
Daniel K. Inouye	Dem.	2017

Idaho
James Risch	Rep.	2015
Michael Crapo	Rep.	2017

Illinois
Richard J. Durbin	Dem.	2015
Mark Kirk	Rep.	2017

Indiana
Richard G. Lugar	Rep.	2013
Dan Coats	Rep.	2017

Iowa
Tom Harkin	Dem.	2015
Chuck Grassley	Rep.	2017

Kansas
Pat Roberts	Rep.	2015
Jerry Moran	Rep.	2017

Kentucky
Mitch McConnell	Rep.	2015
Rand Paul	Rep.	2017

Louisiana
Mary L. Landrieu	Dem.	2015
David Vitter	Rep.	2017

Maine
Olympia J. Snowe	Rep.	2013
Susan M. Collins	Rep.	2015

Maryland
Ben L. Cardin	Dem.	2013
Barbara A. Mikulski	Dem.	2017

Massachusetts
Scott P. Brown	Rep.	2013
John F. Kerry	Dem.	2015

Michigan
Debbie Stabenow	Dem.	2013
Carl Levin	Dem.	2015

Minnesota
Amy Klobuchar	Dem.	2013
Al Franken	Dem.	2015

Mississippi
Roger Wicker	Rep.	2013
Thad Cochran	Rep.	2015

Missouri
Claire McCaskill	Dem.	2013
Roy Blunt	Rep.	2017

Montana
Jon Tester	Rep.	2013
Max Baucus	Dem.	2015

Nebraska
E. Benjamin Nelson	Dem.	2013
Mike Johanns	Dem.	2015

Nevada
John E. Ensign	Rep.	2013
Harry M. Reid	Dem.	2017

New Hampshire
Jeanne Shaheen	Dem.	2015
Kelly Ayotte	Rep.	2017

New Jersey
Robert Menéndez	Dem.	2013
Frank R. Lautenberg	Dem.	2015

New Mexico
Jeff Bingaman	Dem.	2013
Robert Udall	Dem.	2015

New York
Kirsten E. Gillibrand	Dem.	2013
Charles E. Schumer	Dem.	2017

North Carolina
Kay Hagan	Dem.	2015
Richard Burr	Rep.	2017

North Dakota
Kent Conrad	Dem.	2013
John Hoeven	Rep.	2017

Ohio
Sherrod Brown	Dem.	2013
Rob Portman	Rep.	2017

Oklahoma
James M. Inhofe	Rep.	2015
Tom Coburn	Rep.	2017

Oregon
Jeff Merkley	Dem.	2015
Ronald L. Wyden	Dem.	2017

Pennsylvania
Robert P. Casey, Jr	Dem.	2013
Pat Toomey	Rep.	2017

Rhode Island
Sheldon Whitehouse, II	Dem.	2013
Jack Reed	Dem.	2015

South Carolina
Lindsey Graham	Rep.	2015
Jim DeMint	Rep.	2017

South Dakota
Tim Johnson	Dem.	2015
John Thune	Rep.	2017

Tennessee
Robert P. Corker	Rep.	2013
Lamar Alexander	Rep.	2015

Texas
Kay Bailey Hutchison	Rep.	2013
John Cornyn	Rep.	2015

Utah
Orrin G. Hatch	Rep.	2013
Mike Lee	Rep.	2017

Vermont
Bernard Sanders	Ind.	2013
Patrick J. Leahy	Dem.	2017

Virginia
James H. Webb, Jr	Dem.	2013
Mark R. Warner	Dem.	2015

Washington
Maria Cantwell	Dem.	2013
Patty Murray	Dem.	2017

THE UNITED STATES OF AMERICA

West Virginia
Joe Manchin	Dem.	2017
John D. (Jay) Rockefeller, IV	Dem.	2015

Wisconsin
Herb Kohl	Dem.	2013
Ron Johnson	Rep.	2017

Wyoming
John Barrasso	Rep.	2013
Mike B. Enzi	Rep.	2015

House of Representatives
(May 2011)

A new House of Representatives, comprising 435 members, is elected every two years.

Speaker: JOHN A. BOEHNER.

Republicans: 241 seats.

Democrats: 193 seats.

Vacant: 1 seat.

Majority Leader: ERIC CANTOR.

Minority Leader: NANCY PELOSI.

Election Commission

Federal Election Commission: 999 E St, NW, Washington, DC 20463; tel. (202) 694-1100; fax (202) 219-1043; e-mail director@fec.gov; internet www.fec.gov; f. 1975; independent; Chair. CYNTHIA L. BAUERLY.

Independent Agencies

Advisory Council on Historic Preservation: 1100 Pennsylvania Ave, NW, Suite 803, Old Post Office Bldg, Washington, DC 20004; tel. (202) 606-8503; fax (202) 606-8647; e-mail achp@achp.gov; internet www.achp.gov; f. 1966; Chair. MILFORD WAYNE DONALDSON; Exec. Dir JOHN M. FOWLER.

African Development Foundation: 1400 I St, NW, Suite 1000, Washington, DC 20005-2248; tel. (202) 673-3916; fax (202) 673-3810; e-mail info@adf.gov; internet www.adf.gov; Chair. JACK LESLIE; Pres. and CEO LLOYD O. PIERSON.

American Battle Monuments Commission: Courthouse Plaza II, Suite 500, 2300 Clarendon Blvd, Arlington, VA 22201-3367; tel. (703) 696-6900; fax (703) 696-6666; e-mail info@abmc.gov; internet www.abmc.gov; f. 1923; Sec. MAX CLELAND; Dir, Overseas Operations Brig.-Gen. (retd) STEVEN R. HAWKINS.

Appalachian Regional Commission: 1666 Connecticut Ave, NW, Washington, DC 20009-1068; tel. (202) 884-7700; fax (202) 884-7682; e-mail info@arc.gov; internet www.arc.gov; f. 1965; Fed. Co-Chair. EARL F. GOHL; Alt. Fed. Co-Chair. (vacant).

Commission on Civil Rights: 624 Ninth St, NW, Washington, DC 20425; tel. (202) 376-7700; fax (202) 376-7672; e-mail publications@usccr.gov; internet www.usccr.gov; f. 1957; Chair. MARTIN R. CASTRO; Staff Dir KIMBERLEY TOLHURST (acting).

Commission of Fine Arts: National Bldg Museum, Suite 312, 401 F St, NW, Washington, DC 20001-2728; tel. (202) 504-2200; fax (202) 504-2195; e-mail cfastaff@cfa.gov; internet www.cfa.gov; f. 1910; Chair. EARL A. POWELL, III; Sec. THOMAS LUEBKE.

Commodity Futures Trading Commission (CFTC): 3 Lafayette Centre, 1155 21st St, NW, Washington, DC 20581; tel. (202) 418-5000; fax (202) 418-5521; e-mail questions@cftc.gov; internet www.cftc.gov; f. 1974; Chair. GARY GENSLER.

Corporation for National and Community Service (CNS): 1201 New York Ave, NW, Washington, DC 20525; tel. (202) 606-5000; fax (202) 565-2799; e-mail info@cns.gov; internet www.nationalservice.gov; Chair. MARK GEARAN; CEO PATRICK ALFRED CORVINGTON.

Defense Nuclear Facilities Safety Board: 625 Indiana Ave, Suite 700, NW, Washington, DC 20004-2901; tel. (202) 694-7000; fax (202) 208-6518; e-mail mailbox@dnfsb.gov; internet www.dnfsb.gov; f. 1988; Chair. PETER S. WINOKUR; Gen. Man. BRIAN GROSNER.

Environmental Protection Agency: Ariel Rios Bldg, 1200 Pennsylvania Ave, NW, Washington, DC 20460; tel. (202) 272-0167; internet www.epa.gov; f. 1970; Admin. LISA P. JACKSON.

Equal Employment Opportunity Commission: 1801 L St, NW, POB 7033, Washington, DC 20507; tel. (202) 663-4900; fax (202) 663-4639; e-mail info@ask.eeoc.gov; internet www.eeoc.gov; f. 1965; Chair. JACQUELINE A. BERRIEN.

Directory

Export-Import Bank of the United States (Ex-Im Bank): see Finance—Banking.

Farm Credit Administration (FCA): 1501 Farm Credit Dr., McLean, VA 22102-5090; tel. (703) 883-4000; fax (703) 790-3260; e-mail info-line@fca.gov; internet www.fca.gov; f. 1933; Chair. and CEO LELAND A. STROM.

Federal Communications Commission (FCC): see Broadcasting and Communications.

Federal Deposit Insurance Corporation (FDIC): 550 17th St, NW, Washington, DC 20429; tel. (202) 736-0000; e-mail publicinfo@fdic.gov; internet www.fdic.gov; f. 1933; Chair. SHEILA C. BAIR; Dir THOMAS J. CURRY.

Federal Election Commission: see Election Commission.

Federal Emergency Management Agency: Federal Center Plaza, 500 C St, SW, Washington, DC 20472; tel. (202) 646-2500; fax (202) 646-2531; e-mail askfema@dhs.gov; internet www.fema.gov; f. 1979; part of the Dept of Homeland Security; Admin. WILLIAM CRAIG FUGATE.

Federal Home Loan Mortgage Corporation (Freddie Mac): 8200 Jones Branch Dr., MS 200, McLean, VA 22102-3110; tel. (703) 903-2000; internet www.freddiemac.com; f. 1970; CEO CHARLES E. HALDEMAN, Jr.

Federal Housing Finance Agency: 1700 G St, NW, 4th Floor, Washington, DC 20552; tel. (202) 796-5595; fax (202) 408-1435; e-mail fhfainfo@fhfa.gov; internet www.fhfa.gov; Dir EDWARD DEMARCO (acting).

Federal Labor Relations Authority (FLRA): 1400 K St, 4th Floor, NW, Washington, DC 20424; tel. (202) 218-7770; fax (202) 343-1007; e-mail solmail@flra.gov; internet www.flra.gov; f. 1978; Chair. CAROL WALLER POPE.

Federal Maritime Commission: see Transport—Ocean Shipping.

Federal Mediation and Conciliation Service: 2100 K St, NW, Washington, DC 20427; tel. (202) 606-8100; fax (202) 606-4251; e-mail foia@fmcs.gov; internet www.fmcs.gov; f. 1947; Dir GEORGE H. COHEN.

Federal National Mortgage Association (Fannie Mae): 3900 Wisconsin Ave, NW, Washington, DC 20016-2892; tel. (202) 752-7000; internet www.fanniemae.com; f. 1938; Pres. and CEO MICHAEL J. WILLIAMS.

Federal Reserve System: see Finance—Banking.

Federal Retirement Thrift Investment Board (FRTIB): 1250 H St, NW, Washington, DC 20005; tel. (202) 942-1600; fax (202) 942-1676; internet www.frtib.gov; f. 1986; Chair. ANDREW M. SAUL; Exec. Dir GREGORY T. LONG.

Federal Trade Commission: 600 Pennsylvania Ave, NW, Washington, DC 20580; tel. (202) 326-2222; fax (202) 326-2396; internet www.ftc.gov; f. 1914; Chair. JON LEIBOWITZ; Exec. Dir EILEEN HARRINGTON.

General Services Administration: 1800 F St, NW, Washington, DC 20405; tel. (202) 501-1231; fax (202) 501-1489; internet www.gsa.gov; f. 1949; Admin. MARTHA N. JOHNSON.

Inter-American Foundation: 901 North Stuart St, 10th Floor, Arlington, VA 22203; tel. (703) 306-4319; fax (703) 306-4365; e-mail info@iaf.gov; internet www.iaf.gov; f. 1969; provides grants to non-governmental and community-based orgs in Latin America and the Caribbean; Chair. JOHN P. SALAZAR; Pres. ROBERT N. KAPLAN.

Medicare Payment Advisory Commission (MedPAC): 601 New Jersey Ave, NW, Suite 9000, Washington, DC 20001; tel. (202) 220-3700; fax (202) 220-3759; e-mail webmaster@medpac.gov; internet www.medpac.gov; Chair. GLENN M. HACKBARTH; Exec. Dir MARK E. MILLER.

Merit Systems Protection Board: 1615 M St, NW, Washington, DC 20419; tel. (202) 653-7200; fax (202) 653-7130; e-mail mspb@mspb.gov; internet www.mspb.gov; f. 1979; Chair. SUSAN TSUI GRUNDMANN.

National Aeronautics and Space Administration (NASA): 300 E St, SW, Suite 5K39, Washington, DC 20546-0001; tel. (202) 358-0001; fax (202) 358-4338; e-mail info-center@hq.nasa.gov; internet www.nasa.gov; f. 1958; Admin. CHARLES F. BOLDEN, Jr.

National Archives and Records Administration: 8601 Adelphi Rd, College Park, MD 20740-6001; tel. (301) 837-1600; fax (301) 837-0483; internet www.archives.gov; f. 1934; Archivist of the United States DAVID FERRIERO.

National Capital Planning Commission: 401 Ninth St, NW, Suite 500, Washington, DC 20004; tel. (202) 482-7200; fax (202) 482-7272; e-mail info@ncpc.gov; internet www.ncpc.gov; f. 1924; Chair. L. PRESTON BRYANT, Jr; Exec. Dir MARCEL C. ACOSTA.

National Council on Disability: 1331 F St, NW, Suite 850, Washington, DC 20004-1107; tel. (202) 272-2004; fax (202) 272-2022; e-mail ncd@ncd.gov; internet www.ncd.gov; f. 1978; Chair. JONATHAN M. YOUNG; Exec. Dir AARON BISHOP.

THE UNITED STATES OF AMERICA

National Credit Union Administration: 1775 Duke St, Alexandria, VA 22314-3428; tel. (703) 518-6300; fax (703) 518-6660; e-mail boardmail@ncua.gov; internet www.ncua.gov; f. 1970; Chair. DEBBIE MATZ; Exec. Dir DAVID M. MARQUIS.

National Endowment for the Arts: 1100 Pennsylvania Ave, NW, Washington, DC 20506-0001; tel. (202) 682-5400; fax (202) 682-5639; e-mail webmgr@arts.endow.gov; internet www.arts.gov; f. 1965; Chair. ROCCO LANDESMAN.

National Endowment for the Humanities: 1100 Pennsylvania Ave, NW, Rm 503, Washington, DC 20506; tel. (202) 634-1121; e-mail info@neh.gov; internet www.neh.gov; f. 1965; Chair. JAMES A. LEACH.

National Labor Relations Board: 1099 14th St, NW, Washington, DC 20570-0001; tel. (202) 273-1000; fax (202) 273-4270; internet www.nlrb.gov; f. 1935; Chair. WILMA B. LIEBMAN.

National Mediation Board (NMB): 1301 K St, NW, Suite 250 East, Washington, DC 20005-7011; tel. (202) 692-5010; fax (202) 523-5080; internet www.nmb.gov; f. 1934; Chair. HARRY HOGLANDER.

National Science Foundation (NSF): 4201 Wilson Blvd, Arlington, VA 22230; tel. (703) 292-5111; e-mail info@nsf.gov; internet www.nsf.gov; f. 1950; supports basic scientific and engineering research and education; Chair. Dr RAY M. BOWEN; Dir Dr SUBRA SURESH.

National Transportation Safety Board: see Transport.

Nuclear Regulatory Commission (NRC): Office of Public Affairs, Washington, DC 20555; tel. (301) 415-8200; fax (301) 415-3716; e-mail opa@nrc.gov; internet www.nrc.gov; Chair. GREGORY B. JACZKO.

Occupational Safety and Health Review Commission (OSHRC): 1120 20th St, 9th Floor, NW, Washington, DC 20036-3457; tel. (202) 606-5398; fax (202) 606-5052; internet www.oshrc.gov; f. 1970; Chair. THOMASINA V. ROGERS.

Office of Government Ethics: 1201 New York Ave, NW, Suite 500, Washington, DC 20005-3917; tel. (202) 482-9300; fax (202) 482-9237; e-mail contactoge@oge.gov; internet www.usoge.gov; f. 1978; Dir ROBERT I. CUSICK.

Office of Personnel Management (OPM): Theodore Roosevelt Federal Bldg, 1900 E St, NW, Washington, DC 20415; tel. (202) 606-1800; fax (202) 606-2573; e-mail general@opm.gov; internet www.opm.gov; f. 1979; Dir JOHN BERRY.

Office of Special Counsel: 1730 M St, NW, Suite 300, Washington, DC 20036-4505; tel. (202) 254-3600; fax (202) 254-3711; e-mail adr@osc.gov; internet www.osc.gov; Special Counsel (vacant); Assoc. Special Counsel WILLIAM E. REUKAUF.

Peace Corps: Paul D. Coverdell Peace Corps HQ, 1111 20th St, NW, Washington, DC 20526; tel. (202) 692-2100; fax (202) 692-2101; e-mail webmaster@peacecorps.gov; internet www.peacecorps.gov; f. 1961; Dir AARON S. WILLIAMS.

Pension Benefit Guaranty Corporation: 1200 K St, NW, Suite 12201, Washington, DC 20005-4026; tel. (202) 326-4010; fax (202) 326-4016; e-mail participant.pro@pbgc.gov; internet www.pbgc.gov; f. 1974; Dir JOSHUA GOTBAUM.

Postal Rate Commission: 901 New York Ave, NW, Suite 200, Washington, DC 20268-0001; tel. (202) 789-6800; fax (202) 789-6891; e-mail prc-dockets@prc.gov; internet www.prc.gov; f. 1970; Chair. RUTH Y. GOLDWAY.

Railroad Retirement Board: 844 North Rush St, Chicago, IL 60611-2092; tel. (312) 751-4300; fax (312) 751-7154; e-mail opa@rrb.gov; internet www.rrb.gov; f. 1935; Chair. MICHAEL S. SCHWARTZ.

Securities and Exchange Commission: Station Pl., 100 F St, NE, Washington, DC 20549; tel. (202) 942-8088; e-mail publicinfo@sec.gov; internet www.sec.gov; f. 1935; Chair. MARY L. SCHAPIRO.

Selective Service System: 1515 Wilson Blvd, Arlington, VA 22209-2425; tel. (703) 605-4100; fax (703) 605-4106; e-mail information@sss.gov; internet www.sss.gov; f. 1940; Dir LAWRENCE G. ROMO.

Small Business Administration: 409 Third St, SW, Washington, DC 20416; tel. (202) 205-6650; fax (202) 205-6802; e-mail answerdesk@sba.gov; internet www.sba.gov; f. 1953; Admin. KAREN GORDON MILLS.

Smithsonian Institution: 1000 Jefferson Dr., SW, POB 37012, Washington, DC 20560-0001; tel. (202) 633-1000; e-mail info@si.edu; internet www.si.edu; f. 1846; Sec. G. WAYNE CLOUGH.

Social Security Administration: Office of Public Inquiries, Windsor Park Bldg, 6401 Security Blvd, Baltimore, MD 21235-0001; tel. (410) 965-3120; fax (410) 966-1463; internet www.ssa.gov; Commr MICHAEL J. ASTRUE.

Tennessee Valley Authority: 400 West Summit Hill Dr., Knoxville, TN 37902-1499; tel. (865) 632-2101; e-mail tvainfo@tva.gov; internet www.tva.gov; f. 1933; CEO and Pres. TOM KILGORE.

United States Agency for International Development (USAID): Ronald Reagan Bldg, 1300 Pennsylvania Ave, NW, Washington, DC 20523-0016; tel. (202) 712-4810; fax (202) 216-3524; e-mail pinquiries@usaid.gov; internet www.usaid.gov; f. 1961; Admin. Dr RAJIV SHAH.

United States Consumer Product Safety Commission: 4330 East-West Hwy, Bethesda, MD 20814-4408; tel. (301) 504-7923; fax (301) 504-0124; e-mail info@cpsc.gov; internet www.cpsc.gov; f. 1972; Chair. and Commr INEZ MOORE TENENBAUM; Exec. Dir KENNETH HINSON.

United States International Trade Commission: 500 E St, SW, Washington, DC 20436; tel. (202) 205-2000; fax (202) 205-2338; e-mail webmaster@usitc.gov; internet www.usitc.gov; f. 1916; Chair. DEANA TANNER OKUN.

United States Postal Service: 475 L'Enfant Plaza, SW, Washington, DC 20260-0010; tel. (202) 268-2000; fax (202) 268-4860; internet www.usps.com; f. 1970; Postmaster-Gen. and CEO JOHN (JACK) E. POTTER.

United States Trade and Development Agency (USTDA): 1000 Wilson Blvd, Suite 1600, Arlington, VA 22209-3901; tel. (703) 875-4357; fax (703) 875-4009; e-mail info@ustda.gov; internet www.ustda.gov; f. 1961; Dir LEOCADIA I. ZAK.

State Governments

(with expiration date of Governors' current term of office; legislatures at April 2011)

Alabama: Governor ROBERT J. BENTLEY (Rep.—Jan. 2015); Senate: Dem. 12, Rep. 22, Ind. 1; House: Dem. 39, Rep. 66.

Alaska: Governor SEAN R. PARNELL (Rep.—Jan. 2015); Senate: Dem. 10, Rep. 10; House: Dem. 16, Rep. 24.

Arizona: Governor JAN BREWER (Rep.—Jan. 2015); Senate: Dem. 9, Rep. 21; House: Dem. 20, Rep. 40.

Arkansas: Governor MIKE BEEBE (Dem.—Jan. 2015); Senate: Dem. 20, Rep. 15; House: Dem. 55, Rep. 44, Vacant 1.

California: Governor EDMUND G. (JERRY) BROWN (Dem.—Jan. 2015); Senate: Dem. 25, Rep. 15; Assembly: Dem. 52, Rep. 28.

Colorado: Governor JOHN HICKENLOOPER (Dem.—Jan. 2015); Senate: Dem. 20, Rep. 15; House: Dem. 32, Rep. 33.

Connecticut: Governor DANIEL P. (DAN) MALLOY (Dem.—Jan. 2015); Senate: Dem. 23, Rep. 13; House: Dem. 100, Rep. 51.

Delaware: Governor JACK MARKELL (Dem.—Jan. 2013); Senate: Dem. 14, Rep. 7; House: Dem. 26, Rep. 15.

Florida: Governor RICK SCOTT (Rep.—Jan. 2015); Senate: Dem. 12, Rep. 28; House: Dem. 39, Rep. 81.

Georgia: Governor NATHAN DEAL (Rep.—Jan. 2015); Senate: Dem. 20, Rep. 36; House: Dem. 66, Rep. 113, Ind. 1.

Hawaii: Governor NEIL ABERCROMBIE (Dem.—Jan. 2015); Senate: Dem. 24, Rep. 1; House: Dem. 43, Rep. 8.

Idaho: Governor C. L. (BUTCH) OTTER (Rep.—Jan. 2015); Senate: Dem. 7, Rep. 28; House: Dem. 13, Rep. 57.

Illinois: Governor PATRICK J. QUINN, III (Dem.—Jan. 2015); Senate: Dem. 35, Rep. 24; House: Dem. 64, Rep. 54.

Indiana: Governor MITCHELL (MITCH) E. DANIELS (Rep.—Jan. 2013); Senate: Dem. 13, Rep. 37; House: Dem. 40, Rep. 59, Undecided 1.

Iowa: Governor TERRY BRANSTAD (Rep.—Jan. 2015); Senate: Dem. 26, Rep. 24; House: Dem. 40, Rep. 60.

Kansas: Governor SAMUEL D. BROWNBACK (Rep.—Jan. 2015); Senate: Dem. 8, Rep. 32; House: Dem. 33, Rep. 92.

Kentucky: Governor STEVE BESHEAR (Dem.—Jan. 2012); Senate: Dem. 15, Rep. 22, Ind. 1; House: Dem. 58, Rep. 42.

Louisiana: Governor BOBBY JINDAL (Rep.—Jan. 2012); Senate: Dem. 19, Rep. 20; House: Dem. 49, Rep. 52, Ind. 4.

Maine: Governor PAUL LEPAGE (Rep.—Jan. 2015); Senate: Dem. 14, Rep. 20, Ind. 1; House: Dem. 72, Rep. 78, Ind. 1.

Maryland: Governor MARTIN O'MALLEY, Jr (Dem.—Jan. 2015); Senate: Dem. 35, Rep. 12; House: Dem. 98, Rep. 43.

Massachusetts: Governor DEVAL L. PATRICK (Dem.—Jan. 2015); Senate: Dem. 36, Rep. 4; House: Dem. 128, Rep. 31, Vacant 1.

Michigan: Governor RICK SNYDER (Rep.—Jan. 2015); Senate: Dem. 12, Rep. 26; House: Dem. 47, Rep. 63.

Minnesota: Governor MARK B. DAYTON (Democratic Farmer Labor Party—Jan. 2015); Senate: Dem. 30, Rep. 37; House: Dem. 62, Rep. 72.

Mississippi: Governor HALEY BARBOUR (Rep.—Jan. 2012); Senate: Dem. 25, Rep. 27; House: Dem. 72, Rep. 50.

Missouri: Governor JEREMIAH W. (JAY) NIXON (Dem.—Jan. 2013); Senate: Dem. 8, Rep. 26; House: Dem. 57, Rep. 106.

Montana: Governor BRIAN SCHWEITZER (Dem.—Jan. 2013); Senate: Dem. 22, Rep. 28; House: Dem. 32, Rep. 68.

THE UNITED STATES OF AMERICA

Nebraska: Governor Dave Heineman (Rep.—Jan. 2015); Legislature: unicameral body comprising 49 members elected on a non-partisan ballot and classed as senators.

Nevada: Governor Brian Sandoval (Rep.—Jan. 2015); Senate: Dem. 11, Rep. 10; Assembly: Dem. 26, Rep. 16.

New Hampshire: Governor John Lynch (Rep.—Jan. 2013); Senate: Dem. 5, Rep. 19; House: Dem. 102, Rep. 298.

New Jersey: Governor Chris Christie (Rep.—Jan. 2014); Senate: Dem. 24, Rep. 16; Assembly: Dem. 47, Rep. 33.

New Mexico: Governor Susana Martínez (Rep.—Jan. 2015); Senate: Dem. 27, Rep. 15; House: Dem. 37, Rep. 33.

New York: Governor Andrew M. Cuomo (Dem.—Jan. 2015); Senate: Dem. 30, Rep. 32; Assembly: Dem. 99, Rep. 51.

North Carolina: Governor Beverly (Bev) Perdue (Dem.—Jan. 2013); Senate: Dem. 19, Rep. 31; House: Dem. 52, Rep. 67, Ind. 1.

North Dakota: Governor John Hoeven (Rep.—Jan. 2013); Senate: Dem. 12, Rep. 35; House: Dem. 25, Rep. 69.

Ohio: Governor John Kasich (Rep.—Jan. 2015); Senate: Dem. 10, Rep. 23; House: Dem. 40, Rep. 59.

Oklahoma: Governor Mary Fallin (Rep.—Jan. 2015); Senate: Dem. 16, Rep. 32; House: Dem. 31, Rep. 70.

Oregon: Governor John Kitzhaber (Dem.—Jan. 2015); Senate: Dem. 16, Rep. 14; House: Dem. 30, Rep. 30.

Pennsylvania: Governor Tom Corbett (Rep.—Jan. 2015); Senate: Dem. 20, Rep. 30; House: Dem. 91, Rep. 112.

Rhode Island: Governor Lincoln D. Chafee (Ind.—Jan. 2015); Senate: Dem. 29, Rep. 8, Ind. 1; House: Dem. 65, Rep. 10.

South Carolina: Governor Nimrata (Nikki) Haley (Rep.—Jan. 2015); Senate: Dem. 19, Rep. 27; House: Dem. 48, Rep. 75, Vacant 1.

South Dakota: Governor Dennis Daugaard (Rep.—Jan. 2015); Senate: Dem. 5, Rep. 30; House: Dem. 19, Rep. 50, Ind. 1.

Tennessee: Governor Bill Haslam (Dem.—Jan. 2015); Senate: Dem. 13, Rep. 19, Vacant 1; House: Dem. 33, Rep. 64, Ind. 1, Vacant 1.

Texas: Governor Rick Perry (Rep.—Jan. 2015); Senate: Dem. 12, Rep. 19; House: Dem. 49, Rep. 101.

Utah: Governor Gary R. Herbert (Rep.—Jan. 2013); Senate: Dem. 7, Rep. 22; House: Dem. 17, Rep. 58.

Vermont: Governor Peter Shumlin (Dem.—Jan. 2013); Senate: Dem. 22, Rep. 8; House: Dem. 95, Rep. 48, Ind. and others 7.

Virginia: Governor Robert F. McDonnell (Rep.—Jan. 2014); Senate: Dem. 22, Rep. 18; House: Dem. 39, Rep. 59, Ind. 2.

Washington: Governor Christine O. Gregoire (Dem.—Jan. 2013); Senate: Dem. 27, Rep. 22; House: Dem. 56, Rep. 42.

West Virginia: Acting Governor Earl Ray Tomblin (Dem.—Jan. 2013); Senate: Dem. 28, Rep. 6; House: Dem. 65, Rep. 35.

Wisconsin: Governor Scott Walker (Rep.—Jan. 2015); Senate: Dem. 14, Rep. 19; Assembly: Dem. 38, Rep. 60, Ind. 1.

Wyoming: Governor Matt Mead (Rep.—Jan. 2015); Senate: Dem. 4, Rep. 26; House: Dem. 10, Rep. 50.

Political Organizations

Communist Party USA (CPUSA): 235 West 23rd St, 8th Floor, New York, NY 10011; tel. (212) 989-4994; fax (212) 229-1713; e-mail cpusa@cpusa.org; internet www.cpusa.org; f. 1919; mems in all 50 states, organized in over 40 states; Nat. Chair. Sam Webb; Exec. Vice-Chair. Jarvis Tyner.

Democratic National Committee: 430 South Capitol St, SE, Washington, DC 20003; tel. (202) 863-8000; fax (202) 863-8174; internet www.democrats.org; f. 1848; Nat. Chair. Donna Brazile (acting); Sec. Alice Travis Germond; Treas. Andrew Tobias.

The Green Party of the United States: 1623 Connecticut Ave, NW, POB 57065, Washington, DC 20037; tel. (202) 319-7191; fax (202) 289-5260; e-mail office@gp.org; internet www.gp.org; f. 2001; Sec. Holly Hart; Treas. Jeff Turner.

Libertarian Party: 2600 Virginia Ave, NW, Suite 200, Washington, DC 20037; tel. (202) 333-0008; fax (202) 333-0072; e-mail info@lp.org; internet www.lp.org; f. 1971; advocates individual freedom, smaller govt and fewer taxes; Nat. Chair. Mark Hinkle; Sec. Alicia Mattson; Treas. William Redpath.

Prohibition National Committee: Box 11, McConnellsburg, Pennsylvania, PA 17233; tel. (303) 237-4947; e-mail preachergene@comcast.net; internet www.prohibitionists.org; f. 1869; opposes the manufacture and sale of alcoholic drinks; opposes abortion, drug abuse and euthanasia; Nat. Chair. Toby Davis; Nat. Sec. Leroy Pletten; Treas. (vacant).

La Raza Unida Party (Partido Nacional La Raza Unida): POB 40376, Albuquerque, NM 87196; tel. (818) 365-6534; e-mail magonista66@yahoo.com; internet larazaunida.tripod.com; f. 1970; aims to achieve self-determination and greater govt representation for Latinos through electoral processes; four state groups, 100 local groups; Nat. Chair. Xenaro G. Ayala.

Republican National Committee: 310 First St, SE, Washington, DC 20003; tel. (202) 863-8500; fax (202) 863-8820; e-mail info@gop.com; internet www.gop.com; f. 1854; Chair., Nat. Cttee Reince Priebus; Co-Chair. Sharon Day; Sec. Demetra DeMonte; Treas. Tony Parker.

Social Democrats, USA: POB 5307, Johnston, PA 15904; tel. (814) 410-2542; e-mail info@socialdemocratsusa.org; internet www.socialdemocratsusa.org; f. 1972 following split from the Socialist Party USA (fmrly the Socialist Party of America, f. 1901); Pres. (vacant); Dir Gabriel McCloskey-Ross; Nat. Sec. Seamus Johnston.

Socialist Labor Party: POB 218, Mountain View, CA 94042-0218; e-mail socialists@slp.org; internet www.slp.org; f. 1876 as the Workingmen's Party; present name adopted in 1877; advocates collective ownership and democratic control of all industries and services through industrial unions; Nat. Sec. Robert Bills.

Socialist Party USA: A. J. Muste Bldg, 339 Lafayette St, Suite 303, New York, NY 10012; tel. and fax (212) 982-4586; e-mail natsec@sp-usa.org; internet socialistparty-usa.org; f. 1972 following split from the Socialist Party of America (f. 1901); Co-Chair. Andrea Pason, William Wharton; Nat. Sec. Greg Pason; 1,800 mems.

Socialist Workers Party: 306 West 37th St, 10th Floor, New York, NY 10018; tel. (212) 736-2540; fax (212) 244-4274; e-mail swpno@mac.com; f. 1938; communist; Nat. Sec. Jack Barnes.

Diplomatic Representation

EMBASSIES IN THE USA

Afghanistan: 2341 Wyoming Ave, NW, Washington, DC 20008; tel. 483-6410; fax 483-6488; e-mail press@embassyofafghanistan.org; internet www.embassyofafghanistan.org; Ambassador Eklil Hakimi.

Albania: 2100 S St, NW, Washington, DC 20008; tel. (202) 223-4942; fax (202) 628-7342; e-mail info@albanianembassy.org; internet www.albanianembassy.org; Ambassador Gilbert Galanxhi.

Algeria: 2118 Kalorama Rd, NW, Washington, DC 20008; tel. (202) 265-2800; fax (202) 667-2174; e-mail mail@algeria-us.org; internet www.algeria-us.org; Ambassador Abdallah Baali.

Andorra: 2 United Nations Plaza, 27th Floor, New York, NY 10017; tel. (212) 750-8064; fax (212) 750-6630; Ambassador Narcis Casal de Fonsdeviela.

Angola: 2100–2108 16th St, NW, Washington, DC 20009; tel. (202) 785-1156; fax (202) 822-9049; e-mail angola@angola.org; internet www.angola.org; Ambassador Josefina Perpétua Pitra Diakité.

Antigua and Barbuda: 3216 New Mexico Ave, NW, Washington, DC 20016; tel. (202) 362-5122; fax (202) 362-5225; e-mail embantbar@aol.com; Ambassador Deborah Mae Lovell.

Argentina: 1600 New Hampshire Ave, NW, Washington, DC 20009-2512; tel. (202) 238-6401; fax (202) 332-3171; internet www.embassyofargentina.us; Ambassador Alfredo Vicente Chiradía.

Armenia: 2225 R St, NW, Washington, DC 20008; tel. (202) 319-1976; fax (202) 319-2982; e-mail armpublic@speakeasy.net; internet www.armeniaemb.org; Ambassador Tatoul Markarian.

Australia: 1601 Massachusetts Ave, NW, Washington, DC 20036-2273; tel. (202) 797-3000; fax (202) 797-3168; internet www.usa.embassy.gov.au; Ambassador Kim Beazley.

Austria: 3524 International Court, NW, Washington, DC 20008-3035; tel. (202) 895-6700; fax (202) 895-6773; e-mail obwas@sysnet.net; internet www.austria.org; Ambassador Christian Prosl.

Azerbaijan: 2741 34th St, NW, Washington, DC 20008; tel. (202) 337-3500; fax (202) 337-5911; e-mail azerbaijan@azembassy.com; internet azembassy.com; Ambassador Yashar Aliyev.

Bahamas: 2220 Massachusetts Ave, NW, Washington, DC 20008; tel. (202) 319-2660; fax (202) 319-2668; e-mail bahemb@aol.com; Ambassador Cornelius A. Smith.

Bahrain: 3502 International Dr., NW, Washington, DC 20008; tel. (202) 342-1111; fax (202) 362-2192; e-mail ambsecretary@bahrainembassy.org; internet www.bahrainembassy.org; Ambassador Houda Erza Ebrahim Nonoo.

Bangladesh: 3510 International Dr., NW, Washington, DC 20008; tel. (202) 244-0183; fax (202) 244-2771; e-mail bdootwash@bdembassyusa.org; internet www.bdembassyusa.org; Ambassador Akramul Qader.

THE UNITED STATES OF AMERICA

Barbados: 2144 Wyoming Ave, NW, Washington, DC 20008; tel. (202) 939-9200; fax (202) 332-7467; e-mail washington@foreign.gov.bb; Ambassador JOHN BEALE.

Belarus: 1619 New Hampshire Ave, NW, Washington, DC 20009; tel. (202) 986-1604; fax (202) 986-1805; e-mail usa@belarusembassy.org; internet www.belarusembassy.org; Chargé d'affaires a.i. OLEG KRAVCHENKO.

Belgium: 3330 Garfield St, NW, Washington, DC 20008; tel. (202) 333-6900; fax (202) 333-3079; e-mail washington@diplobel.org; internet www.diplobel.us; Ambassador JAN MATTHYSEN.

Belize: 2535 Massachusetts Ave, NW, Washington, DC 20008; tel. (202) 332-9636; fax (202) 332-6888; e-mail ebwreception@aol.com; internet www.embassyofbelize.org; Ambassador NESTOR MENDEZ.

Benin: 2124 Kalorama Rd, NW, Washington, DC 20008; tel. (202) 232-6656; fax (202) 265-1996; e-mail info@beninembassyus.org; internet www.beninembassy.us; Ambassador SÈGBÉ CYRILLE OGUIN.

Bolivia: 3014 Massachusetts Ave, NW, Washington, DC 20008; tel. (202) 483-4410; fax (202) 328-3712; e-mail webmaster@bolivia-usa.org; internet www.bolivia-usa.org; Chargé d'affaires a.i. ERIKA DUEÑAS.

Bosnia and Herzegovina: 2109 E St, NW, Washington, DC 20037; tel. (202) 337-1500; fax (202) 337-1502; e-mail info@bhembassy.org; internet www.bhembassy.org; Ambassador MITAR KUDJUNDZIĆ.

Botswana: 1531-1533 New Hampshire Ave, NW, Washington, DC 20036; tel. (202) 244-4990; fax (202) 244-4164; e-mail sekgwa@botswanaembassy.org; internet www.botswanaembassy.org; Ambassador TEBELELO MAZILE SERETSE.

Brazil: 3006 Massachusetts Ave, NW, Washington, DC 20008-3634; tel. (202) 238-2805; fax (202) 238-2827; e-mail ambassador@brasilemb.org; internet www.brasilemb.org; Ambassador MAURO LUIZ IECKER VIEIRA.

Brunei: 3520 International Court, NW, Washington, DC 20008; tel. (202) 237-1838; fax (202) 885-0560; e-mail info@bruneiembassy.org; internet www.bruneiembassy.org; Ambassador Dato Paduka HAJI YUSOF HAJI ABDUL HAMID.

Bulgaria: 1621 22nd St, NW, Washington, DC 20008; tel. (202) 387-0174; fax (202) 234-7973; e-mail office@bulgaria-embassy.org; internet www.bulgaria-embassy.org; Ambassador ELENA POPTODOROVA.

Burkina Faso: 2340 Massachusetts Ave, NW, Washington, DC 20008; tel. (202) 332-5577; fax (202) 667-1882; e-mail ambawdc@verizon.net; internet www.burkina-usa.org; Ambassador PARMANGA ERNEST YONLI.

Burundi: 2233 Wisconsin Ave, NW, Suite 212, Washington, DC 20007; tel. (202) 342-2574; fax (202) 342-2575; e-mail burundiembassy@erols.com; internet www.burundiembassy-usa.org; Ambassador ANGELE NIYUHIRE.

Cambodia: 4530 16th St, NW, Washington, DC 20011; tel. (202) 726-7742; fax (202) 726-8381; e-mail cambodian_embassydc@hotmail.com; internet www.embassyofcambodia.org; Ambassador HEM HENG.

Cameroon: 2349 Massachusetts Ave, NW, Washington, DC 20008; tel. (202) 265-8790; fax (202) 387-3826; e-mail cdm@ambacam-usa.org; internet www.ambacam-usa.org; Ambassador JOSEPH FOE-ATANGANA.

Canada: 501 Pennsylvania Ave, NW, Washington, DC 20001; tel. (202) 682-1740; fax (202) 682-7726; e-mail washington-im-enquiry@international.gc.ca; internet www.canadainternational.gc.ca/washington; Ambassador GARY DOER.

Cape Verde: 3415 Massachusetts Ave, NW, Washington, DC 20007; tel. (202) 965-6820; fax (202) 965-1207; e-mail ambacvus@sysnet.net; internet www.virtualcapeverde.net; Ambassador MARIA DE FÁTIMA LIMA DA VEIGA.

Central African Republic: 1618 22nd St, NW, Washington, DC 20008; tel. (202) 483-7800; fax (202) 332-9893; e-mail centralafricwashington@yahoo.com; Ambassador STANISLAS MOUSSA-KEMBE.

Chad: 2401 Massachusetts Ave, NW, Washington, DC 20008; tel. (202) 462-4009; fax (202) 265-1937; e-mail info@chadembassy.us; internet chadembassy.us; Ambassador MAHAMOUD ADAM BÉCHIR.

Chile: 1732 Massachusetts Ave, NW, Washington, DC 20036; tel. (202) 785-1746; fax (202) 659-9624; e-mail embassy@embassyofchile.org; internet www.chile-usa.org; Ambassador ARTURO FERMANDOIS.

China, People's Republic: 3505 International Pl., NW, Washington, DC 20522; tel. (202) 495-2000; fax (202) 495-2138; e-mail chinaembassy_us@fmprc.gov.cn; internet www.china-embassy.org; Ambassador ZHANG YESUI.

Colombia: 2118 Leroy Pl., NW, Washington, DC 20008; tel. (202) 387-8338; fax (202) 232-8643; e-mail embassyofcolombia@colombiaemb,org; internet www.colombiaemb.org; Ambassador Dr GABRIEL SILVA LUJÁN.

Comoros: 866 United Nations Plaza, Suite 418, New York, NY 10017; tel. (212) 750-1637; fax (212) 750-1657; e-mail comun@undp.org; Ambassador MOHAMED TOIHIRI.

Congo, Democratic Republic: 1726 M St, NW, Suite 601, Washington, DC 20036; tel. (202) 234-7690; fax (202) 234-2609; e-mail ambassade@ambardcusa.org; internet www.ambardcusa.org; Ambassador FAIDA MITIFU.

Congo, Republic: 4891 Colorado Ave, NW, Washington, DC 20011; tel. (202) 726-5500; fax (202) 726-1860; e-mail info@embassyofcongo.org; Ambassador SERGE MOMBOULI.

Costa Rica: 2114 S St, NW, Washington, DC 20008; tel. (202) 234-2945; fax (202) 265-4795; e-mail embassy@costarica-embassy.org; internet www.costarica-embassy.org; Ambassador META SHANON FIGUERES BOGGS.

Côte d'Ivoire: 2424 Massachusetts Ave, NW, Washington, DC 20008; tel. (202) 797-0300; fax (202) 204-3967; e-mail info@ambacotedivoireusa.org; internet www.ambaci.us; Ambassador DAOUDA DIABATE.

Croatia: 2343 Massachusetts Ave, NW, Washington, DC 20008-2803; tel. (202) 588-5899; fax (202) 588-8936; e-mail public@croatiaemb.org; internet www.croatiaemb.org; Ambassador KOLINDA GRABAR-KITAROVIĆ.

Cuba: 'Interests section' in the Embassy of Switzerland, 2630 16th St, NW, Washington, DC 20009; tel. (202) 797-8518; fax (202) 797-0606; e-mail informacion1@sicuw.org; internet embacu.cubaminrex.cu/Default.aspx?tabid=8803; Counsellor JORGE ALBERTO BOLAÑOS SUÁREZ.

Cyprus: 2211 R St, NW, Washington, DC 20008; tel. (202) 462-5772; fax (202) 483-6710; e-mail info@cyprusembassy.net; internet www.cyprusembassy.net; Ambassador PAVLOS ANASTASIADES.

Czech Republic: 3900 Spring of Freedom St, NW, Washington, DC 20008; tel. (202) 274-9100; fax (202) 966-8540; e-mail washington@embassy.mzv.cz; internet www.mzv.cz/washington; Chargé d'affaires a.i. DANIEL KOŠTOVAL.

Denmark: 3200 Whitehaven St, NW, Washington, DC 20008-3616; tel. (202) 234-4300; fax (202) 328-1470; e-mail wasamb@um.dk; internet www.ambwashington.um.dk; Ambassador PETER TAKSOE-JENSEN.

Djibouti: 1156 15th St, NW, Suite 515, Washington, DC 20005; tel. (202) 331-0270; fax (202) 331-0302; Ambassador ROBLÉ OLHAYE.

Dominica: 3216 New Mexico Ave, NW, Washington, DC 20016; tel. (202) 364-6781; fax (202) 364-6791; e-mail embdomdc@aol.com; Ambassador HUBERT JOHN CHARLES.

Dominican Republic: 1715 22nd St, NW, Washington, DC 20008; tel. (202) 332-6280; fax (202) 265-8057; e-mail embassy@us.serex.gov.do; internet www.domrep.org; Ambassador ROBERT B. SALADIN SELIN.

Ecuador: 2535 15th St, NW, Washington, DC 20009; tel. (202) 234-7200; fax (202) 667-3482; e-mail embassy@ecuador.org; internet www.ecuador.org; Ambassador LUIS BENIGNO GALLEGOS CHIRIBOGA.

Egypt: 3521 International Court, NW, Washington, DC 20008; tel. (202) 895-5400; fax (202) 244-4319; e-mail Embassy@egyptembassy.net; internet www.egyptembassy.net; Ambassador SAMEH SHOUKRY.

El Salvador: 1400 16th St, NW, Suite 100, Washington, DC 20036; tel. (202) 265-9671; fax (202) 232-3763; e-mail correo@elsalvador.org; internet www.elsalvador.org; Ambassador FRANCISCO ALTSCHUL.

Equatorial Guinea: 2020 16th St, NW, Washington, DC 20009; tel. (202) 518-5700; fax (202) 518-5252; Ambassador PURIFICACIÓN ANGUE ONDO.

Eritrea: 1708 New Hampshire Ave, NW, Washington, DC 20009; tel. (202) 319-1991; fax (202) 319-1304; e-mail embassyeritrea@embassyeritrea.org; internet www.embassyeritrea.org; Chargé d'affaires a.i. BERHANE SOLOMON.

Estonia: 2131 Massachusetts Ave, NW, Washington, DC 20008; tel. (202) 588-0101; fax (202) 588-0108; e-mail info@estemb.org; internet www.estemb.org; Ambassador VÄINO REINART.

Ethiopia: 3506 International Dr., NW, Washington, DC 20008; tel. (202) 364-1200; fax (202) 587-0195; e-mail info@ethiopianembassy.org; internet www.ethiopianembassy.org; Chargé d'affaires a.i. GIRMA BIRRU.

Fiji: 2000 M St, NW, Suite 710, Washington, DC 20036; tel. (202) 466-8320; fax (202) 466-8325; e-mail info@fijiembassydc.com; internet www.fijiembassydc.com; Ambassador WINSTON THOMPSON.

Finland: 3301 Massachusetts Ave, NW, Washington, DC 20008; tel. (202) 298-5800; fax (202) 298-6030; e-mail sanomat.was@formin.fi; internet www.finland.org; Ambassador PEKKA LINTU.

France: 4101 Reservoir Rd, NW, Washington, DC 20007; tel. (202) 944-6000; fax (202) 944-6166; e-mail info@ambafrance-us.org; internet www.ambafrance-us.org; Ambassador FRANCOIS M. DELATTRE.

THE UNITED STATES OF AMERICA

Gabon: 2034 20th St, NW, Suite 200, Washington, DC 20009; tel. (202) 797-1000; fax (202) 983-1994; Ambassador CARLOS BOUNGOU.

The Gambia: Georgetown Plaza, 2233 Wisconsin Ave, NW, Suite 240, Washington, DC 20007; tel. (202) 785-1399; fax (202) 785-1430; e-mail info@gambiaembassy.us; internet www.gambiaembassy.us; Ambassador ALIEU MOMODOU NGUM.

Georgia: 2209 Massachusetts Ave, NW, Washington, DC 20008; tel. (202) 387-2390; fax (202) 387-0864; e-mail embgeo.usa@mfa.gov.ge; internet www.usa.mfa.gov.ge; Ambassador TEMUR YAKOBASHVILI.

Germany: 4645 Reservoir Rd, NW, Washington, DC 20007-1998; tel. (202) 298-4000; fax (202) 298-4249; internet www.germany.info; Ambassador KLAUS SCHARIOTH.

Ghana: 3512 International Dr., NW, Washington, DC 20008; tel. (202) 686-4520; fax (202) 686-4527; e-mail info@ghanaembassy.org; internet www.ghanaembassy.org; Ambassador DANIEL OHENE AGYEKUM.

Greece: 2217 Massachusetts Ave, NW, Washington, DC 20008; tel. (202) 939-1300; fax (202) 939-1324; e-mail greece@greekembassy.org; internet www.mfa.gr/washington; Ambassador VASSILIS KASKARELIS.

Grenada: 1701 New Hampshire Ave, NW, Washington, DC 20009; tel. (202) 265-2561; fax (202) 265-2468; internet www.grenadaembassyusa.org; Ambassador GILLIAN MARGARET SUSAN BRISTOL.

Guatemala: 2220 R St, NW, Washington, DC 20008; tel. (202) 745-4952; fax (202) 745-1908; e-mail embestadosunidos@minex.gob.gt; Ambassador FRANCISCO VILLAGRÁN DE LEÓN.

Guinea: 2112 Leroy Pl., NW, Washington, DC 20008; tel. (202) 986-4300; fax (202) 986-3800; Ambassador MORY KARAMOKO KABA.

Guinea-Bissau: POB 33813, Washington, DC 20033-3813; tel. and fax (301) 947-3958; embassy operations suspended since 2007; Ambassador (vacant).

Guyana: 2490 Tracy Pl., NW, Washington, DC 20008; tel. (202) 265-6900; fax (202) 232-1297; e-mail guyanaembassydc@verizon.net; Ambassador BAYNEY RAM KARRAN.

Haiti: 2311 Massachusetts Ave, Washington, DC 20008; tel. (202) 332-4090; fax (202) 745-7215; e-mail embassy@haiti.org; internet www.haiti.org; Ambassador LOUIS HAROLD JOSEPH.

Holy See: 3339 Massachusetts Ave, NW, Washington, DC 20008; tel. (202) 333-7121; fax (202) 337-4036; e-mail nuntiususa@nuntiususa.org; Apostolic Nuncio Most Rev. PIETRO SAMBI (Titular Archbishop of Bellicastrum).

Honduras: 3007 Tilden St, NW, Suite 4-M, Washington, DC 20008; tel. (202) 966-2604; fax (202) 966-9751; e-mail embassy@hondurasemb.org; internet www.hondurasemb.org; Ambassador JORGE RAMÓN HERNÁNDEZ ALCERRO.

Hungary: 3910 Shoemaker St, NW, Washington, DC 20008; tel. (202) 362-6730; fax (202) 966-8135; e-mail informacio.was@kum.hu; internet www.huembwas.org; Ambassador GYÖRGY SZAPÁRY.

Iceland: House of Sweden, Suite 509, 2900 K St, NW, Washington, DC 20007-1704; tel. (202) 265-6653; fax (202) 265-6656; e-mail icemb.wash@utn.stjr.is; internet www.iceland.org/us; Ambassador HJÁLMAR W. HANNESSON.

India: 2107 Massachusetts Ave, NW, Washington, DC 20008; tel. (202) 939-7000; fax (202) 265-4351; e-mail info2@indiagov.org; internet www.indianembassy.org; Ambassador MEERA SHANKAR.

Indonesia: 2020 Massachusetts Ave, NW, Washington, DC 20036-1084; tel. (202) 775-5200; fax (202) 775-5365; e-mail information@embassyofindonesia.org; internet www.embassyofindonesia.org; Ambassador DINO PATTI DJALAL.

Iran: 'Interests section' in the Embassy of Pakistan, 2209 Wisconsin Ave, NW, Washington, DC 20007; tel. (202) 965-4990; fax (202) 965-1073; e-mail requests@daftar.org; internet www.daftar.org; Dir ALI JAZINI.

Iraq: 3421 Massachusetts Ave, NW, Washington, DC 20007; tel. (202) 742-1600; fax (202) 462-5066; e-mail admin@iraqiembassy.us; internet www.iraqiembassy.us; Ambassador SAMIR SHAKIR MAHMOOD SUMAIDA'IE.

Ireland: 2234 Massachusetts Ave, NW, Washington, DC 20008; tel. (202) 462-3939; fax (202) 232-5993; e-mail embirlus@aol.com; internet www.embassyofireland.org; Ambassador MICHAEL COLLINS.

Israel: 3514 International Dr., NW, Washington, DC 20008; tel. (202) 364-5500; fax (202) 364-5566; e-mail info@washington.mfa.gov.il; internet www.israelemb.org; Ambassador MICHAEL OREN.

Italy: 3000 Whitehaven St, NW, Washington, DC 20008; tel. (202) 612-4400; fax (202) 518-2151; e-mail stampa.washington@esteri.it; internet www.ambwashingtondc.esteri.it; Ambassador GIULIO TERZI DI SANT'AGATA.

Jamaica: 1520 New Hampshire Ave, NW, Washington, DC 20006; tel. (202) 452-0660; fax (202) 452-0036; e-mail dcm@jamaicaembassy.org; internet www.jamaicaembassy.org; Ambassador AUDREY MARKS.

Japan: 2520 Massachusetts Ave, NW, Washington, DC 20008-2869; tel. (202) 238-6700; fax (202) 238-2184; e-mail jicc@embjapan.org; internet www.us.emb-japan.go.jp; Ambassador ICHIRO FUJISAKI.

Jordan: 3504 International Dr., NW, Washington, DC 20008; tel. (202) 966-2664; fax (202) 966-3110; e-mail hkjembassydc@jordanembassyus.org; internet www.jordanembassyus.org; Ambassador ALIA HATOUGH BOURAN.

Kazakhstan: 1401 16th St, NW, Washington, DC 20036; tel. (202) 232-5488; fax (202) 232-5845; e-mail zakh.embusa@verizon.net; internet www.kazakhembus.com; Ambassador ERLAN A. IDRISSOV.

Kenya: 2249 R St, NW, Washington, DC 20008; tel. (202) 387-6101; fax (202) 462-3829; e-mail information@kenyaembassy.com; internet www.kenyaembassy.com; Ambassador ELKANAH ODEMBO ABSALOM.

Korea, Republic: KORUS House, 2370 Massachusetts Ave, NW, Washington, DC 20008; tel. (202) 939-5600; fax (202) 797-0595; e-mail webmaster@dynamic-korea.com; internet www.dynamic-korea.com; Ambassador HAN DUK-SOO.

Kosovo: 1101 30th St, NW, Suite 330/340, Washington, DC 20007; tel. (202) 380-3581; fax (202) 380-3628; e-mail embassy.usa@ks-gov.net; Ambassador AVNI SPAHIU.

Kuwait: 2940 Tilden St, NW, Washington, DC 20008; tel. (202) 966-0702; fax (202) 966-0517; e-mail kio@kuwait-info.org; Ambassador Sheikh SALEM ABDULLAH JABER AS-SABAH.

Kyrgyzstan: 2360 Massachusetts Ave, NW, Washington, DC 20008; tel. (202) 449-9822; fax (202) 386 7550; e-mail consul@kgembassy.org; internet www.kgembassy.org; Ambassador MUKTAR DJUMALIEV.

Laos: 2222 S St, NW, Washington, DC 20008; tel. (202) 332-6416; fax (202) 332-4923; e-mail laoemb@verizon.net; internet www.laoembassy.com; Ambassador SENG SOUKHATHIVONG.

Latvia: 2306 Massachusetts Ave, NW, Washington, DC 20008; tel. (202) 328-2840; fax (202) 328-2860; e-mail embassy.usa@mfa.gov.lv; internet www.latvia-usa.org; Ambassador ANDREJS PILDEGOVICS.

Lebanon: 2560 28th St, NW, Washington, DC 20008; tel. (202) 939-6300; fax (202) 939-6324; e-mail info@lebanonembassyus.org; internet www.lebanonembassyus.org; Ambassador ANTOINE CHEDID.

Lesotho: 2511 Massachusetts Ave, NW, Washington, DC 20008; tel. (202) 797-5533; fax (202) 234-6815; e-mail lesothoembassy@verizon.net; internet www.lesothoemb-usa.gov.ls; Ambassador DAVID MOHLOMI RANTEKOA.

Liberia: 5201 16th St, Washington, DC 20011; tel. (202) 723-0437; fax (202) 723-0436; e-mail info@liberiaemb.org; internet www.embassyofliberia.org; Chargé d'affaires a.i. WILLIAM BULL.

Libya: Liaison Office, 2600 Virginia Ave, NW, Suite 705, Washington, DC 20037; tel. (202) 944-9601; fax (202) 944-9606; e-mail libya@libyanbureaudc.org; internet www.libyanbureaudc.org; Chief of Office (vacant).

Liechtenstein: 2900 K St, NW, Suite 602B, Washington, DC 20007; tel. (202) 331-0590; fax (202) 331-3221; e-mail tamara.brunhart@was.rep.llv.li; internet www.liechtenstein.li/fl-aussenstelle-washington; Ambassador CLAUDIA FRITSCHE.

Lithuania: 2622 16th St, NW, Washington, DC 20009; tel. (202) 234-5860; fax (202) 328-0466; e-mail info@ltembassyus.org; internet www.ltembassyus.org; Ambassador ŽYGIMANTAS PAVILIONIS.

Luxembourg: 2200 Massachusetts Ave, NW, Washington, DC 20008; tel. (202) 265-4171; fax (202) 328-8270; e-mail luxembassy.was@mae.etat.lu; internet washington.mae.lu; Ambassador JEAN-PAUL SENNINGER.

Macedonia: 2129 Wyoming Ave, NW, Washington, DC 20008; tel. (202) 667-0501; fax (202) 667-2131; e-mail usoffice@macedonianembassy.org; internet www.macedonianembassy.org; Ambassador Dr ZORAN JOLEVSKI.

Madagascar: 2374 Massachusetts Ave, NW, Washington, DC 20008; tel. (202) 265-5525; fax (202) 265-3034; e-mail malagasy.embassy@verizon.net; internet www.madagascar-embassy.org; Chargé d'affaires a.i. EULALIE NARISOLO RAVELOSOA.

Malawi: 1029 Vermont Ave, NW, Suite 1000, Washington, DC 20005; tel. (202) 721-0270; fax (202) 721-0288; e-mail info@malawiembassy-dc.org; internet www.malawiembassy-dc.org; Ambassador STEPHEN DICK TENNYSON MATENJE.

Malaysia: 3516 International Court, NW, Washington, DC 20008; tel. (202) 572-9700; fax (202) 572-9882; e-mail malwashdc@kln.gov.my; internet www.kln.gov.my/web/usa_washington; Ambassador Dr JAMALUDDIN JARJIS.

Maldives: 800 Second Ave, Suite 400E, New York, NY 10017; tel. (212) 599-6195; fax (212) 661-6405; e-mail info@maldivesembassy.us; internet www.maldivesembassy.us; Ambassador ABDUL GHAFOOR.

THE UNITED STATES OF AMERICA

Mali: 2130 R St, NW, Washington, DC 20008; tel. (202) 332-2249; fax (202) 332-6603; e-mail info@maliembassy.us; internet www.maliembassy.us; Ambassador MAMADOU TRAORE.

Malta: 2017 Connecticut Ave, NW, Washington, DC 20008; tel. (202) 462-3611; fax (202) 387-5470; e-mail maltaembassy.washington@gov.mt; internet www.mfa.gov.mt; Ambassador MARK MICELI-FARRUGIA.

Marshall Islands: 2433 Massachusetts Ave, NW, Washington, DC 20008; tel. (202) 234-5414; fax (202) 232-3236; e-mail info@rmiembassyus.org; internet www.rmiembassyus.org; Chargé d'affaires a.i. CHARLES R. PAUL.

Mauritania: 2129 Leroy Pl., NW, Washington, DC 20008; tel. (202) 232-5700; fax (202) 319-2623; e-mail info@mauritaniaembassy.us; internet mauritaniaembassy.us; Ambassador MOHAMED LEMINE EL HAYCEN.

Mauritius: 1709 N St, NW, Washington, DC 200036; tel. (202) 244-1491; fax (202) 966-0983; e-mail mauritius.embassy@verizon.net; Ambassador SOMDUTH SOBORUN.

Mexico: 1911 Pennsylvania Ave, NW, Washington, DC 20006; tel. (202) 728-1600; fax (202) 728-1698; e-mail mexembusa@sre.gob.mx; internet www.sre.gob.mx/eua; Ambassador ARTURO SARUKHAN CASA-MITJANA.

Micronesia: 1725 N St, NW, Washington, DC 20036; tel. (202) 223-4383; fax (202) 223-4391; e-mail firstsecretary@fsmembassydc.org; internet www.fsmembassydc.org; Ambassador YOSIWO P. GEORGE.

Moldova: 2101 S St, NW, Washington, DC 20008; tel. (202) 667-1130; fax (202) 667-1204; e-mail washington@mfa.md; internet www.embassyrm.org; Ambassador IGOR MUNTEANU.

Monaco: 3400 International Dr., NW, Suite 2K-100, Washington, DC 20008-3006; tel. (202) 234-1530; fax (202) 244-7656; e-mail embassy@monaco-usa.org; internet www.monaco-usa.org; Ambassador GILLES ALEXANDRE NOGHÈS.

Mongolia: 2833 M St, NW, Washington, DC 20007; tel. (202) 333-7117; fax (202) 298-9227; e-mail esyam@mongolianembassy.us; internet www.mongolianembassy.us; Ambassador KHASBAZARYN BEKHBAT.

Montenegro: 1610 New Hampshire Ave, NW, Washington, DC 20009; tel. (202) 234 6108; fax (202) 234 6109; e-mail usa@mfa.gov.me; Ambassador SRDAN DARMANOVIĆ.

Morocco: 1601 21st St, NW, Washington, DC 20009; tel. (202) 462-7979; fax (202) 265-0161; e-mail aafifi@moroccous.com; internet dcusa.themoroccanembassy.com; Ambassador AZIZ MEKOUAR.

Mozambique: 1525 New Hampshire Ave, NW, Washington, DC 20036; tel. (202) 293-7146; fax (202) 835-0245; e-mail embamoc@aol.com; internet www.embamoc-usa.org; Ambassador AMELIA MATOS SUMBANA.

Myanmar: 2300 S St, NW, Washington, DC 20008-4089; tel. (202) 332-3344; fax (202) 332-4351; e-mail pyi.thayar@verizon.net; internet www.mewashingtondc.com; Chargé d'affaires a.i. SOE PAING.

Namibia: 1605 New Hampshire Ave, NW, Washington, DC 20009; tel. (202) 986-0540; fax (202) 986-0443; e-mail info@namibiaembassyusa.org; internet www.namibianembassyusa.org; Ambassador MARTIN ANDJABA.

Nauru: 800 Second Ave, New York, NY 10017; tel. (212) 937-0074; fax (212) 937-0079; Ambassador MARLENE INEMWIN MOSES.

Nepal: 2131 Leroy Pl., NW, Washington, DC 20008; tel. (202) 667-4550; fax (202) 667-5534; e-mail info@nepalembassyusa.org; internet www.nepalembassyusa.org; Ambassador SHANKAR PRASAD SHARMA.

Netherlands: 4200 Linnean Ave, NW, Washington, DC 20008; tel. (202) 244-5300; fax (202) 362-3430; e-mail was@minbuza.nl; internet www.netherlands-embassy.org; Ambassador REGINA (RENÉE) JONES-BOS.

New Zealand: 37 Observatory Circle, NW, Washington, DC 20008; tel. (202) 328-4800; fax (202) 667-5227; e-mail info@nzemb.org; internet www.nzembassy.com/usa; Ambassador MICHAEL MOORE.

Nicaragua: 1627 New Hampshire Ave, NW, Washington, DC 20009; tel. (202) 939-6570; fax (202) 939-6545; e-mail nicaraguan.embassy@embanic.org; Ambassador FRANCISCO OBADIAH CAMPBELL HOOKER.

Niger: 2204 R St, NW, Washington, DC 20008; tel. (202) 483-4224; fax (202) 483-3169; e-mail infos@embassyofniger.org; internet www.embassyofniger.org; Ambassador AMINATA DJIBRILLA MAIGA TOURÉ.

Nigeria: 3519 International Court, NW, Washington, DC 20008; tel. (202) 986-8400; fax (202) 362-6541; e-mail babalola@nigeriaembassyusa.org; internet www.nigeriaembassyusa.org; Ambassador ADEBOWALE IBIBAPO ADEFUYE.

Norway: 2720 34th St, NW, Washington, DC 20008; tel. (202) 333-6000; fax (202) 337-0870; e-mail emb.washington@mfa.no; internet www.norway.org; Ambassador WEGGER CHRISTIAN STRØMMEN.

Oman: 2535 Belmont Rd, NW, Washington, DC 20008; tel. (202) 387-1980; fax (202) 745-4933; e-mail info@omaninfo.us; internet omanembassy.net; Ambassador HUNAINA SULTAN AHMED AL-MUGHAIRY.

Pakistan: 3517 International Court, NW, Washington, DC 20008; tel. (202) 243-6500; fax (202) 686-1534; e-mail info@embassyofpakistanusa.org; internet www.embassyofpakistanusa.org; Ambassador HUSAIN HAQQANI.

Palau: 1701 Pennsylvania Ave, NW, Suite 400, Washington, DC 20006; tel. (202) 452-6814; fax (202) 452-6281; e-mail info@palauembassy.com; internet www.palauembassy.com; Ambassador HERSEY KYOTA.

Panama: 2862 McGill Terrace, NW, Washington, DC 20008; tel. (202) 483-1407; fax (202) 483-8413; e-mail info@embassyofpanama.org; internet www.embassyofpanama.org; Ambassador MARIO ERNESTO JARAMILLO CASTILLO.

Papua New Guinea: 1779 Massachusetts Ave, NW, Suite 805, Washington, DC 20036; tel. (202) 745-3680; fax (202) 745-3679; e-mail info@pngembassy.org; internet www.pngembassy.org; Ambassador EVAN JEREMY PAKI.

Paraguay: 2400 Massachusetts Ave, NW, Washington, DC 20008; tel. (202) 483-6960; fax (202) 234-4508; e-mail secretaria@embaparusa.gov.py; internet www.embaparusa.gov.py; Ambassador RIGOBERTO GAUTO VIELMAN.

Peru: 1700 Massachusetts Ave, NW, Washington, DC 20036; tel. (202) 833-9860; fax (202) 659-8124; e-mail webadmin@embassyofperu.us; internet www.peruvianembassy.us; Ambassador LUIS MIGUEL VALDIVIESO MONTANO.

Philippines: 1600 Massachusetts Ave, NW, Washington, DC 20036-2274; tel. (202) 467-9300; fax (202) 467-9417; e-mail information@philippineembassy-usa.org; internet www.philippineembassy-usa.org; Ambassador JOSÉ CUISIA, Jr.

Poland: 2640 16th St, NW, Washington, DC 20009; tel. (202) 234-3800; fax (202) 328-6271; e-mail polemb.info@earthlink.net; internet www.polandembassy.org; Ambassador ROBERT KUPIECKI.

Portugal: 2012 Massachusetts Ave, NW, Washington, DC 20036; tel. (202) 350-5400; fax (202) 462-3726; e-mail info@embassyportugal-us.org; Ambassador NUNO FILIPE ALVES SALVADOR E BRITO.

Qatar: 2555 M St, NW, Washington, DC 20037-1305; tel. (202) 274-1600; fax (202) 237-0061; e-mail info@qatarembassy.net; internet www.qatarembassy.net; Ambassador ALI BIN FAHAD AL-HAJRI.

Romania: 1607 23rd St, NW, Washington, DC 20008; tel. (202) 232-4846; fax (202) 232-4748; e-mail office@roembus.org; internet washington.mae.ro; Ambassador ADRIAN COSMIN VIERITA.

Russia: 2650 Wisconsin Ave, NW, Washington, DC 20007; tel. (202) 298-5700; fax (202) 298-5735; e-mail russianembassy@mindspring.com; internet www.russianembassy.org; Ambassador SERGEI I. KISLYAK.

Rwanda: 1714 New Hampshire Ave, NW, Washington, DC 20009; tel. (202) 232-2882; fax (202) 232-4544; e-mail rwandaembassy@rwandaembassy.org; internet www.rwandaembassy.org; Ambassador JAMES KIMONYO.

Saint Christopher and Nevis: 3216 New Mexico Ave, NW, Washington, DC 20016; tel. (202) 686-2636; fax (202) 686-5740; e-mail info@embskn.com; internet www.embassy.gov.kn; Ambassador JACINTH LORNA HENRY-MARTIN.

Saint Lucia: OECS Bldg, 3216 New Mexico Ave, NW, Washington, DC 20016; tel. (202) 364-6792; fax (202) 364-6723; e-mail eofsaintlu@aol.com; Ambassador MICHAEL LOUIS.

Saint Vincent and the Grenadines: 3216 New Mexico Ave, NW, Washington, DC 20016; tel. (202) 364-6730; fax (202) 364-6736; e-mail mail@embvsg.com; internet www.embvsg.com; Ambassador LA CELIA PRINCE.

Samoa: 800 Second Ave, Suite 400J, New York, NY 10017; tel. (212) 599-6196; fax (212) 599-0797; e-mail samoa@un.int; Ambassador ALI'IOAIGA FETURI ELISAIA.

San Marino: 2650 Virginia Ave, NW, Washington, DC 20037; tel. (202) 250-1535; Ambassador PAOLO RONDELLI.

São Tomé and Príncipe: 1211 Connecticut Ave, NW, Suite 300, Washington, DC 20036; tel. (202) 775-2075; fax (202) 775-2077; e-mail stp@un.int; Ambassador OVIDIO MANUEL BARBOSA PEQUEÑO.

Saudi Arabia: 601 New Hampshire Ave, NW, Washington, DC 20037; tel. (202) 342-3800; fax (202) 944-5983; e-mail info@saudiembassy.net; internet www.saudiembassy.net; Ambassador ADEL BIN AHMED AL-JUBEIR.

Senegal: 2112 Wyoming Ave, NW, Washington, DC 20008; tel. (202) 234-0540; fax (202) 332-6315; Ambassador FATOU DANIELLE DIAGNE.

Serbia: 2134 Kalorama Rd, NW, Washington, DC 20008; tel. (202) 332-0333; fax (202) 332-3933; e-mail info@serbiaembusa.org; internet www.serbiaembusa.org; Ambassador VLADIMIR PETROVIĆ.

THE UNITED STATES OF AMERICA

Seychelles: 800 Second Ave, Suite 900c, New York, NY 10017; tel. (212) 972-1785; fax (212) 972-1786; Ambassador RONALD JEAN JUMEAU.

Sierra Leone: 1701 19th St, NW, Washington, DC 20009; tel. (202) 939-9261; fax (202) 483-1798; e-mail info@embassyofsierraleone.net; internet www.embassyofsierraleone.net; Ambassador BOCKARI KORTU STEVENS.

Singapore: 3501 International Pl., NW, Washington, DC 20008; tel. (202) 537-3100; fax (202) 537-0876; e-mail singemb_was@sgmfa.gov.sg; internet www.mfa.gov.sg/washington; Ambassador HENG CHEE CHAN.

Slovakia: 3523 International Court, NW, Suite 210, Washington, DC 20008; tel. (202) 237-1054; fax (202) 237-6438; e-mail emb.washington@mzv.sk; internet www.mzv.sk/washington; Ambassador PETER BURIAN.

Slovenia: 2410 California St, NW, Washington, DC 20008; tel. (202) 386-6610; fax (202) 386-6633; e-mail vwa@gov.si; internet www.washington.embassy.si; Ambassador ROMAN KIRN.

Solomon Islands: 800 Second Ave, Suite 400L, New York, NY 10017; tel. (212) 599-6192; fax (212) 661-8925; e-mail simny@solomons.com; Ambassador COLIN D. BECK.

South Africa: 3051 Massachusetts Ave, NW, Washington, DC 20008; tel. (202) 232-4400; fax (202) 265-1607; e-mail info@saembassy.org; internet www.saembassy.org; Ambassador EBRAHIM RASOOL.

Spain: 2375 Pennsylvania Ave, NW, Washington, DC 20037; tel. (202) 452-0100; fax (202) 833-5670; e-mail emb.washington@maec.es; internet www.maec.es/subwebs/embajadas/washington; Ambassador JORGE DEZCALLAR DE MAZARREDO.

Sri Lanka: 2148 Wyoming Ave, NW, Washington, DC 20008; tel. (202) 483-4025; fax (202) 232-7181; e-mail slembassy@slembassyusa.org; internet www.slembassyusa.org; Ambassador JALIYA WICKRAMASURIYA.

Sudan: 2210 Massachusetts Ave, NW, Washington, DC 20008; tel. (202) 338-8565; fax (202) 667-2406; e-mail info@sudanembassy.org; internet www.sudanembassy.org; Chargé d'affaires a.i. FATAH EL-RAHMAN ALI MOHAMED.

Suriname: 4301 Connecticut Ave, NW, Suite 460, Washington, DC 20008; tel. (202) 244-7488; fax (202) 244-5878; e-mail esuriname@covad.net; internet www.surinameembassy.org; Ambassador SUBHAS MUNGRA.

Swaziland: 1712 New Hampshire Ave, NW, Washington, DC 20009; tel. (202) 234-5002; fax (202) 234-8254; e-mail swaziland@compuserve.com; Ambassador ABEDNIGO MANDLA NTSHANGASE.

Sweden: 2900 K St, NW, Washington, DC 20007; tel. (202) 467-2600; fax (202) 467-2699; e-mail ambassaden.washington@foreign.ministry.se; internet www.swedenabroad.com/washington; Ambassador JONAS HAFSTRÖM.

Switzerland: 2900 Cathedral Ave, NW, Washington, DC 20008; tel. (202) 745-7900; fax (202) 387-2564; e-mail was.vertretung@eda.admin.ch; internet www.swissemb.org; Ambassador MANUEL SAGER.

Syria: 2215 Wyoming Ave, NW, Washington, DC 20008; tel. (202) 232-6316; fax (202) 265-4585; e-mail info@syrembassy.net; internet www.syrianembassy.us; Ambassador IMAD MOUSTAPHA.

Tajikistan: 1005 New Hampshire Ave, NW, Washington, DC 20037; tel. (202) 223-6090; fax (202) 223-6091; e-mail tajikistan@verizon.net; internet www.tjus.org; Ambassador ABDUJABBOR SHIRINOV.

Tanzania: 1232 22nd St, NW, Washington, DC 20037; tel. (202) 939-6125; fax (202) 797-7408; e-mail ubalozi@tanzaniaembassy-us.org; internet www.tanzaniaembassy-us.org; Ambassador MWANAIDI SINARE-MAAJAR.

Thailand: 1024 Wisconsin Ave, NW, Washington, DC 20007; tel. (202) 944-3600; fax (202) 944-3611; e-mail info@thaiembdc.org; internet www.thaiembdc.org; Ambassador KITTIPHONG NA RANONG.

Timor-Leste: 4201 Connecticut Ave, NW, Suite 504, Washington, DC 20008; tel. (202) 966-3202; fax (202) 966-3205; e-mail info@timorlesteembassy.org; internet www.timorlesteembassy.org; Ambassador CONSTÂNCIO DA CONCEIÇÃO PINTO.

Togo: 2208 Massachusetts Ave, NW, Washington, DC 20008; tel. (202) 234-4212; fax (202) 232-3190; e-mail info@togoembassy.us; internet www.togoembassy.us; Ambassador LIMBIYE EDAWE KADANGHA BARIKI.

Tonga: 250 East 51st St, New York, NY 10022; tel. (917) 369-1025; fax (917) 369-1024; Ambassador SONATANE TU'AKINAMOLAHI TAUMOEPEAU TUPOU.

Trinidad and Tobago: 1708 Massachusetts Ave, NW, Washington, DC 20036; tel. (202) 467-6490; fax (202) 785-3130; e-mail embttgo@erols.com; internet www.bordeglobal.com/ttembassy; Ambassador Dr NEIL PARSON.

Tunisia: 1515 Massachusetts Ave, NW, Washington, DC 20005; tel. (202) 862-1850; fax (202) 862-1858; Ambassador MUHAMMAD SALAH TKAYA.

Turkey: 2525 Massachusetts Ave, NW, Washington, DC 20008; tel. (202) 612-6700; fax (202) 612-6744; e-mail contact@turkishembassy.org; internet www.washington.emb.mfa.gov.tr; Ambassador NAMIK TAN.

Turkmenistan: 2207 Massachusetts Ave, NW, Washington, DC 20008; tel. (202) 588-1500; fax (202) 280-1003; e-mail turkmen@mindspring.com; internet www.turkmenistanembassy.org; Ambassador MERET B. ORAZOV.

Uganda: 5911 16th St, NW, Washington, DC 20011; tel. (202) 726-7100; fax (202) 726-1727; e-mail info@ugandaembassyus.org; internet www.ugandaembassy.com; Ambassador PEREZI KARUKUBIRO KAMUNANWIRE.

Ukraine: 3350 M St, NW, Washington, DC 20007; tel. (202) 333-0606; fax (202) 333-0817; e-mail mail@ukremb.com; internet www.mfa.gov.ua/usa; Ambassador OLEKSANDR MOTSYK.

United Arab Emirates: 3522 International Court, NW, Suite 400, Washington, DC 20008; tel. (202) 243-2400; fax (202) 243-2432; e-mail info@uaeembassy-usa.org; internet www.uae-embassy.org; Ambassador YOUSEF AL OTAIBA.

United Kingdom: 3100 Massachusetts Ave, NW, Washington, DC 20008; tel. (202) 588-6500; fax (202) 588-7850; e-mail britishembassyenquiries@gmail.com; internet ukinusa.fco.gov.uk; Ambassador Sir NIGEL SHEINWALD.

Uruguay: 1913 Eye St, NW, Washington, DC 20006; tel. (202) 331-1313; fax (202) 331-8142; e-mail uruwashi@uruwashi.org; internet www.uruwashi.org; Ambassador CARLOS A. GIANELLI DEROIS.

Uzbekistan: 1746 Massachusetts Ave, NW, Washington, DC 20036-1903; tel. (202) 887-5300; fax (202) 293-6804; e-mail info@uzbekistan.org; internet www.uzbekistan.org; Ambassador ILHOMJON T. NEMATOV.

Venezuela: 1099 30th St, NW, Washington, DC 20007; tel. (202) 342-2214; fax (202) 342-6820; e-mail despacho@venezuela-us.org; internet www.embavenez-us.org; Ambassador BERNARDO ALVAREZ HERRERA.

Viet Nam: 1233 20th St, NW, Suite 400, Washington, DC 20036; tel. (202) 861-0737; fax (202) 861-0917; e-mail info@vietnamembassy.us; internet www.vietnamembassy-usa.org; Ambassador LE CONG PHUNG.

Yemen: 2319 Wyoming Ave, NW, Washington, DC 20008; tel. (202) 965-4760; fax (202) 337-2017; e-mail information@yemenembassy.org; internet www.yemenembassy.org; Ambassador ABDULWAHAB ABDULLA AL-HAJJRI.

Zambia: 2419 Massachusetts Ave, NW, Washington, DC 20008; tel. (202) 265-9717; fax (202) 332-0826; e-mail embzambia@aol.com; internet www.zambiaembassy.org; Ambassador SHEILA SIWELA.

Zimbabwe: 1608 New Hampshire Ave, NW, Washington, DC 20009; tel. (202) 332-7100; fax (202) 483-9326; e-mail info33@zimbabwe-embassy.us; internet www.zimbabwe-embassy.us; Ambassador Dr MACHIVENYIKA TOBIAS MAPURANGA.

Judicial System

Each state has a judicial system structured similarly to the Federal system, with a Supreme Court and subsidiary courts, to deal with cases arising under State Law. These courts have jurisdiction in most criminal and civil actions. Each state has its own bar association of lawyers and its own legal code.

Supreme Court of the United States

Supreme Court Bldg, 1 First St, NE, Washington, DC 20543; tel. (202) 479-3211; fax (202) 479-2971; internet www.supremecourtus.gov.

The Supreme Court is the only Federal Court established by the Constitution. It is the highest court in the nation, comprising a Chief Justice and eight Associate Justices. Appointments, which are for life or until voluntary retirement, are made by the President, subject to confirmation by the US Senate.

Chief Justice: JOHN G. ROBERTS, Jr (appointed 2005).

Associate Justices: ANTONIN SCALIA (1986), ANTHONY M. KENNEDY (1988), CLARENCE THOMAS (1991), RUTH BADER GINSBURG (1993), STEPHEN G. BREYER (1994), SAMUEL A. ALITO, Jr (2006), SONIA SOTOMAYOR (2009), ELENA KAGAN (2010).

US Courts of Appeal

Administrative Office of the US Courts, Washington, DC 20544; tel. (202) 502-2600; internet www.uscourts.gov.

THE UNITED STATES OF AMERICA

The USA is divided into 12 judicial circuits, in each of which there is one Court of Appeals. The Court of Appeals for the Federal Circuit has nation-wide specialized jurisdiction.

Federal Courts hear cases involving federal law, cases involving participants from more than one state, cases involving crimes committed in more than one state, and civil or corporate cases that cross state lines. Federal District Courts, of which there are 94, are the courts of first instance for most federal suits.

Federal Circuit: RANDALL RAY RADER (Chief Judge), PAULINE NEWMAN, ALAN D. LOURIE, WILLIAM CURTIS BRYSON, ARTHUR J. GAJARSA, RICHARD LINN, TIMOTHY B. DYK, SHARON PROST, KIMBERLEY MOORE, KATHLEEN M. O'MALLEY, JIMMIE V. REYNA.

District of Columbia Circuit: DAVID B. SENTELLE (Chief Judge), DOUGLAS H. GINSBURG, KAREN LECRAFT HENDERSON, JUDITH W. ROGERS, DAVID S. TATEL, MERRICK B. GARLAND, JANICE ROGERS BROWN, THOMAS B. GRIFFITH, BRETT M. KAVANAUGH.

First Circuit (Maine, Massachusetts, New Hampshire, Rhode Island, Puerto Rico): SANDRA L. LYNCH (Chief Judge), JUAN R. TORRUELLA, MICHAEL BOUDIN, KERMIT V. LIPEZ, JEFFREY R. HOWARD, O. ROGERIEE THOMPSON.

Second Circuit (Connecticut, New York, Vermont): DENNIS JACOBS (Chief Judge), JOSÉ A. CABRANES, ROSEMARY S. POOLER, ROBERT A. KATZMANN, REENA RAGGI, RICHARD C. WESLEY, PETER W. HALL, DEBRA ANN LIVINGSTON, GERARD E. LYNCH, DENNY CHIN, RAYMOND J. LOHIER, Jr, SUSAN L. CARNEY.

Third Circuit (Delaware, New Jersey, Pennsylvania, Virgin Islands): THEODORE A. MCKEE (Chief Judge), DOLORES K. SLOVITER, ANTHONY J. SCIRICA, MARJORIE O. RENDELL, MARYANNE TRUMP BARRY, THOMAS L. AMBRO, JULIO M. FUENTES, D. BROOKS SMITH, D. MICHAEL FISHER, MICHAEL A. CHAGARES, KENT A. JORDAN, THOMAS M. HARDIMAN, JOSEPH A. GREENAWAY, Jr, THOMAS I. VANASKIE.

Fourth Circuit (Maryland, North Carolina, South Carolina, Virginia, West Virginia): WILLIAM B. TRAXLER, Jr (Chief Judge), J. HARVIE WILKINSON, III, PAUL V. NIEMEYER, DIANA GRIBBON MOTZ, ROBERT B. KING, ROGER L. GREGORY, DENNIS W. SHEDD, ALLYSON K. DUNCAN, G. STEVEN AGEE, ANDRE M. DAVIS, BARBARA M. KEENAN, JAMES A. WYNN, Jr, ALBERT DIAZ.

Fifth Circuit (Louisiana, Mississippi, Texas): EDITH H. JONES (Chief Judge), CAROLYN DINEEN KING, E. GRADY JOLLY, W. EUGENE DAVIS, JERRY E. SMITH, EMILIO M. GARZA, FORTUNATO P. BENAVIDES, CARL E. STEWART, JAMES L. DENNIS, EDITH BROWN CLEMENT, EDWARD C. PRADO, PRISCILLA R. OWEN, JENNIFER W. ELROD, LESLIE SOUTHWICK, CATHARINA HAYNES, JAMES E. GRAVES, Jr.

Sixth Circuit (Kentucky, Michigan, Ohio, Tennessee): ALICE M. BATCHELDER (Chief Judge), BOYCE F. MARTIN, Jr, DANNY J. BOGGS, KAREN NELSON MOORE, RANSEY GUY COLE, Jr, ERIC L. CLAY, JULIA SMITH GIBBONS, JOHN M. ROGERS, JEFFREY S. SUTTON, DEBORAH L. COOK, DAVID W. MCKEAGUE, RICHARD ALLEN GRIFFIN, RAYMOND M. KETHLEDGE, HELENE N. WHITE, JANE BRANSTETTER STRANCH.

Seventh Circuit (Illinois, Indiana, Wisconsin): FRANK H. EASTERBROOK (Chief Judge), RICHARD A. POSNER, JOEL M. FLAUM, MICHAEL S. KANNE, ILANA DIAMOND ROVNER, DIANE P. WOOD, ANN CLAIRE WILLIAMS, DIANE S. SYKES, JOHN DANIEL TINDER, DAVID F. HAMILTON.

Eighth Circuit (Arkansas, Iowa, Minnesota, Missouri, Nebraska, North Dakota, South Dakota): WILLIAM J. RILEY (Chief Judge), ROGER L. WOLLMAN, JAMES B. LOKEN, DIANA E. MURPHY, KERMIT E. BYE, MICHAEL J. MELLOY, LAVENSKI R. SMITH, STEVEN M. COLLOTON, RAYMOND W. GRUENDER, DUANE BENTON, BOBBY E. SHEPHERD.

Ninth Circuit (Alaska, Arizona, California, Guam, Hawaii, Idaho, Montana, Nevada, Northern Mariana Islands, Oregon, Washington): ALEX KOZINSKI (Chief Judge), MARY M. SCHROEDER, HARRY PREGERSON, STEPHEN REINHARDT, DIARMUID F. O'SCANNLAIN, PAMELA ANN RYMER, ANDREW J. KLEINFELD, SIDNEY R. THOMAS, BARRY G. SILVERMAN, SUSAN P. GRABER, M. MARGARET MCKEOWN, KIM MCLANE WARDLAW, WILLIAM A. FLETCHER, RAYMOND C. FISHER, RONALD M. GOULD, RICHARD A. PAEZ, MARSHA S. BERZON, RICHARD C. TALLMAN, JOHNNIE B. RAWLINSON, RICHARD R. CLIFTON, JAY S. BYBEE, CONSUELO M. CALLAHAN, CARLOS T. BEA, MILAN D. SMITH, Jr, SANDRA S. IKUTA, N. RANDY SMITH, MARY H. MURGUIA.

Tenth Circuit (Colorado, Kansas, New Mexico, Oklahoma, Utah, Wyoming): MARY BECK BRISCOE (Chief Judge), DEANELL REECE TACHA, PAUL J. KELLY, CARLOS F. LUCERO, MICHAEL R. MURPHY, HARRIS L. HARTZ, TERRENCE L. O'BRIEN, TIMOTHY M. TYMKOVICH, NEIL M. GORSUCH, JEROME A. HOLMES, SCOTT M. MATHESON, Jr.

Eleventh Circuit (Alabama, Florida, Georgia): JOEL F. DUBINA (Chief Judge), GERALD B. TJOFLAT, J. L. EDMONSON, SUSAN H. BLACK, EDWARD E. CARNES, ROSEMARY BARKETT, FRANK M. HULL, STANLEY MARCUS, CHARLES R. WILSON, WILLIAM H. PRYOR, Jr, BEVERLY BALDWIN MARTIN.

United States Court of Federal Claims
717 Madison Pl., NW, Washington, DC 20005; tel. (202) 357-6400; internet www.uscfc.uscourts.gov.

Judges: EMILY C. HEWITT (Chief Judge), FRANCIS M. ALLEGRA, LAWRENCE M. BASKIR, LAWRENCE J. BLOCK, SUSAN G. BRADEN, LYNN J. BUSH, EDWARD J. DAMICH, NANCY B. FIRESTONE, MARIAN BLANK HORN, CHARLES F. LETTOW, CHRISTINE ODELL COOK MILLER, GEORGE W. MILLER, MARGARET M. SWEENEY, THOMAS C. WHEELER, MARY ELLEN COSTER WILLIAMS, VICTOR J. WOLSKI.

US Court of International Trade
1 Federal Plaza, New York, NY 10278-0001; tel. (212) 264-2800; fax (212) 264-1085; internet www.cit.uscourts.gov.

Judges: DONALD C. POGUE (Chief Judge), GREGORY W. CARMAN, JANE A. RESTANI, EVAN J. WALLACH, JUDITH M. BARZILAY, DELISSA A. RIDGWAY, RICHARD K. EATON, TIMOTHY C. STANCEU, LEO M. GORDON.

United States Tax Court
400 Second St, NW, Washington, DC 20217; tel. (202) 521-0700; internet www.ustaxcourt.gov.

Judges: JOHN O. COLVIN (Chief Judge), MARY ANN COHEN, MAURICE B. FOLEY, JOSEPH H. GALE, JOSEPH R. GOEKE, DAVID GUSTAFSON, JAMES S. HALPERN, MARK V. HOLMES, DIANE L. KROUPA, L. PAIGE MARVEL, RICHARD T. MORRISON, ELIZABETH CREWSON PARIS, MICHAEL B. THORNTON, JUAN F. VASQUEZ, ROBERT A. WHERRY, Jr.

Religion

Christianity is the predominant religion. The largest single denomination is the Roman Catholic Church. Other major groups in terms of membership are the Baptist, Methodist, Lutheran and Orthodox churches. Numerous other beliefs are represented, the largest in terms of adherents being Judaism, Islam and Buddhism.

CHRISTIANITY

National Council of the Churches of Christ in the USA: 475 Riverside Dr., Suite 880, New York, NY 10115-0050; tel. (212) 870-2025; fax (212) 870-3112; e-mail webmaster@ncccusa.org; internet www.ncccusa.org; f. 1950; an ecumenical org. of 35 Protestant and Orthodox denominations, representing 100,000 congregations of c. 45m. mems; Pres. Rev. PEG CHEMBERLIN; Gen. Sec. Rev. Dr MICHAEL KINNAMON.

The Anglican Communion

The Episcopal Church in the USA: 815 Second Ave, New York, NY 10017-4564; tel. (212) 716-6000; fax (212) 697-5892; e-mail pboffice@episcopalchurch.org; internet www.iamepiscopalian.org; f. 1607; mem. of the Worldwide Anglican Communion and World Council of Churches; 7,200 parishes and missions; 2.4m. mems (2008); Presiding Bishop Most Rev. KATHARINE JEFFERTS SCHORI; Exec. Officer and Sec. Rev. Dr GREGORY S. STRAUB.

The Baptist Church

In 2008 there were an estimated 36.1m. Baptists in the USA.

American Baptist Association: 4605 North State Line Ave, Texarkana, TX 75503-2928; tel. (903) 792-2783; fax (903) 792-8128; e-mail bssc@abaptist.org; internet www.abaptist.org; f. 1905; 1,867 churches; 280,973 mems (2000); Pres. Dr NEAL CLARK.

American Baptist Churches in the USA (ABCUSA): POB 851, Valley Forge, PA 19482-0851; 588 North Gulph Rd, King of Prussia, PA 19406; tel. (610) 768-2000; fax (610) 768-2275; e-mail cathy.brubaker@abc-usa.org; internet www.abc-usa.org; f. 1907; mem. of the World Council of Churches; 5,538 churches (2010); 1.5m. mems (2010); Pres. FRANK CHRISTINE, Jr; Gen. Sec. Rev. Dr A. ROY MEDLEY.

Conservative Baptist Association of America: 3686 Stagecoach Rd, Unit F, Longmont, CO 80504-5660; tel. (720) 283-3030; fax (303) 772-5690; e-mail info@cbamerica.org; internet www.cbamerica.org; f. 1947; 1,200 churches; 200,000 mems; Nat. Exec. Dir Rev. STAN RIEB.

General Association of Regular Baptist Churches: 1300 North Meacham Rd, Schaumburg, IL 60173-4806; tel. (888) 588-1600; fax (847) 843-3757; internet www.garbc.org; 1,330 churches; 245,636 mems (2000); Nat. Rep. Rev. JOHN GREENING.

National Baptist Convention, USA: 1700 Baptist World Center Dr., Nashville, TN 37207; tel. (615) 228-6292; fax (615) 262-3917; e-mail president@nationalbaptist.com; internet www.nationalbaptist.com; f. 1880; mem. of the World Council of Churches; 9,000 churches; 5.0m. mems; Pres. Dr JULIUS R. SCRUGGS; Gen. Sec. CALVIN MCKINNEY.

Southern Baptist Convention: 901 Commerce St, Nashville, TN 37203-3629; tel. (615) 244-2355; fax (615) 742-8919; e-mail

THE UNITED STATES OF AMERICA

cpmissions@sbc.net; internet www.sbc.net; f. 1845; 42,972 churches; 16.4m. mems (2003); Pres. Dr BRYANT WRIGHT.

The Lutheran Church

In 2008 there were an estimated 8.7m. Lutherans in the USA.

Evangelical Lutheran Church in America: 8765 West Higgins Rd, Chicago, IL 60631; tel. (773) 380-2700; fax (773) 380-1465; e-mail info@elca.org; internet www.elca.org; f. 1988; mem. of the World Council of Churches; 10,448 churches; 4.7m. mems (2007); Presiding Bishop Rev. MARK STEPHEN HANSON; Sec. DAVID D. SWARTLING.

Lutheran Church—Missouri Synod: 1333 South Kirkwood Rd, St Louis, MO 63122-7295; tel. (314) 965-9000; fax (314) 996-1016; e-mail infocenter@lcms.org; internet www.lcms.org; f. 1847; 6,150 churches; 2.5m. mems (2007); Pres. Dr MATTHEW C. HARRISON; Sec. Dr RAYMOND HARTWIG.

The Methodist Church

In 2008 there were an estimated 11.4m. Methodists and Wesleyans in the USA.

African Methodist Episcopal Church: 500 Eighth Ave South, Nashville, TN 37203; tel. (615) 254-0911; fax (615) 254-0912; e-mail cio@ame-church.com; internet www.ame-church.com; f. 1816; mem. of the Churches Uniting in Christ and World Council of Churches; 4,174 churches; 2.5m. mems (1999); Sr Bishop JOHN R. BRYANT; Gen. Sec. Dr CLEMENT W. FUGH.

African Methodist Episcopal Zion Church: 3225 Sugar Creek Rd, POB 32843, Charlotte, NC 28269; tel. (704) 599-4630; e-mail admin@amez.org; internet www.amez.org; f. 1796; mem. of the Churches Uniting in Christ; 3,236 churches; 1.4m. mems (2003); Gen. Sec. Rev. Dr W. ROBERT JOHNSON, III.

United Methodist Church: POB 320, Nashville, TN 37202; e-mail umc@umcom.org; internet www.umc.org; f. 1968; mem. of the Churches Uniting in Christ and World Council of Churches; 34,892 churches; 8.2m. mems (2003); President of Council of Bishops Bishop GREGORY PALMER; Exec. Sec. ERNEST S. LYGHT.

The Orthodox Churches

Members of Eastern Orthodox churches numbered an estimated 824,000 in 2008.

Antiochian Orthodox Christian Archdiocese of North America (Greek Orthodox Patriarchate of Antioch and all the East): 358 Mountain Rd, POB 5238, Englewood, NJ 07631-3798; tel. (201) 871-1355; fax (201) 871-7954; e-mail archdiocese@antiochian.org; internet www.antiochian.org; f. 1895; mem. of the World Council of Churches; 210 churches; 82,374 mems (2000); Primate Metropolitan PHILIP (Saliba); Auxiliaries Bishop ANTOUN (Khouri), Bishop BASIL (Essey), Bishop JOSEPH (Zehlaoui), Bishop ALEXANDER (Mufarrij), Bishop MARK (Maymon), Bishop THOMAS (Joseph).

Armenian Apostolic Church of America: *Eastern Prelacy:* 138 East 39th St, New York, NY 10016; tel. (212) 689-7810; fax (212) 689-7168; e-mail email@armenianprelacy.org; internet www.armenianprelacy.org; *Western Prelacy:* 6252 Honolulu Ave, Suite 100, La Crescenta, CA 91214; tel. (818) 248-7737; fax (818) 248-7745; e-mail prelacy@aol.com; f. 1887; mem. of the World Council of Churches; 38 churches; 23,200 mems (2000); Prelate (Eastern Prelacy) Archbishop OSHAGAN CHOLOYAN; Prelate (Western Prelacy) Archbishop MOUSHEGH MARDIROSIAN.

Armenian Church of America: *Eastern Diocese:* 630 Second Ave, New York, NY 10016; tel. (212) 686-0710; fax (212) 779-3558; e-mail primate@armenianchurch.net; internet www.armenianchurch.net; *Western Diocese:* 3325 North Glenoaks Blvd, Burbank, CA 91504; tel. (818) 558-7474; fax (818) 558-6333; e-mail info@armenianchurchwd.com; internet www.armenianchurchwd.com; f. 1889; mem. of the World Council of Churches; 89 churches; 45,800 mems (2000); Primate (Eastern Diocese) Archbishop KHAJAG BARSAMIAN; Primate (Western Diocese) Archbishop HOVNAN DERDERIAN.

Greek Orthodox Archdiocese of America: 8–10 East 79th St, New York, NY 10075; tel. (212) 570-3500; fax (212) 774-0251; e-mail archdiocese@goarch.org; internet www.goarch.org; f. 1921 as Greek Orthodox Archdiocese of North and South America; mem. of the World Council of Churches; 540 churches; 1.5m. mems (2008); Primate Archbishop DIMITRIOS; Chancellor Bishop ANDONIOS (of Phasiane).

Orthodox Church in America: POB 675, Syosset, NY 11791-0675; tel. (516) 922-0550; fax (516) 922-0954; e-mail info@oca.org; internet www.oca.org; f. 1794; fmrly Russian Orthodox Greek Catholic Church of North America; mem. of the World Council of Churches; 567 churches; 103,000 mems (2009); Primate Metropolitan HERMAN; Chancellor Archpriest ALEXANDER GARKLAVS.

The Albanian, Bulgarian, Coptic, Romanian, Russian, Serbian, Syrian and Ukrainian Orthodox Churches are also represented.

The Presbyterian Church

In 2008 there were an estimated 4.7m. adherents of Presbyterian Churches.

Presbyterian Church in America: 1700 North Brown Rd, Lawrenceville, GA 30043-8143; tel. (678) 825-1000; fax (678) 825-1001; e-mail ac@pcanet.org; internet www.pcanet.org; f. 1973; 1,600 churches; 300,000 mems; Moderator HARRY L. REEDER, III; Stated Clerk Dr L. ROY TAYLOR.

Presbyterian Church (USA): 100 Witherspoon St, Louisville, KY 40202-1396; tel. (502) 569-5000; fax (502) 569-8080; e-mail presbytel@pcusa.org; internet www.pcusa.org; f. 1983; mem. of the Churches Uniting in Christ and World Council of Churches; 11,100 churches; 2.4m. mems (2007); Moderator CYNTHIA BOLBACH; Exec. Dir LINDA VALENTINE; Stated Clerk GRADYE PARSONS.

The Roman Catholic Church

In 2008 there were 194 dioceses, including 34 archdioceses, with some 57.2m. members.

United States Conference of Catholic Bishops: 3211 Fourth St, NE, Washington, DC 20017-1194; tel. (202) 541-3000; fax (202) 541-3322; internet www.usccb.org; f. 2001 by merger of the Nat. Conference of Catholic Bishops (f. 1966) and US Catholic Conference (f. 1966); Pres. Cardinal FRANCIS EUGENE GEORGE (Archbishop of Chicago); Gen. Sec. Mgr DAVID MALLOY.

Archbishops

Anchorage: ROGER L. SCHWIETZ.
Atlanta: WILTON D. GREGORY.
Baltimore: EDWIN F. O'BRIEN.
Boston: Cardinal SÉAN PATRICK O'MALLEY.
Chicago: Cardinal FRANCIS E. GEORGE.
Cincinnati: DENNIS M. SCHNURR.
Denver: CHARLES J. CHAPUT.
Detroit: ALLEN HENRY VIGNERON.
Dubuque: JEROME G. HANUS.
Galveston-Houston: Cardinal DANIEL N. DINARDO.
Hartford: HENRY J. MANSELL.
Indianapolis: DANIEL M. BUECHLEIN.
Kansas City in Kansas: JOSEPH F. NAUMAN.
Los Angeles: Cardinal JOSÉ HORACIO GÓMEZ.
Louisville: JOSEPH E. KURTZ.
Miami: THOMAS WENSKI.
Milwaukee: JEROME E. LISTECKI.
Mobile: THOMAS JOHN RODI.
Newark: JOHN JOSEPH MYERS.
New Orleans: GREGORY M. AYMOND.
New York: TIMOTHY M. DOLAN.
Oklahoma City: PAUL STAGG COAKLEY.
Omaha: GEORGE J. LUCAS.
Philadelphia: Cardinal JUSTIN F. RIGALI, STEFAN SOROKA (Ukrainian, Byzantine Rite).
Pittsburgh: (vacant).
Portland in Oregon: JOHN G. VLAZNY.
Saint Louis: ROBERT J. CARLSON.
Saint Paul and Minneapolis: JOHN CLAYTON NIENSTEDT.
San Antonio: GUSTAVO GARCÍA-SILLER.
San Francisco: GEORGE H. NIEDERAUER.
Santa Fe: MICHAEL J. SHEEHAN.
Seattle: JAMES PETER SARTAIN.
Washington: Cardinal DONALD W. WUERL.

Other Christian Churches

Assemblies of God: The General Council, 1445 North Boonville Ave, Springfield, MO 65802-1894; tel. (417) 862-2781; fax (417) 862-0133; e-mail generalsecretary@ag.org; internet www.ag.org; f. 1914; 810,000 mems in 2008; Gen. Supt GEORGE O. WOOD; Gen. Sec. JAMES T. BRADFORD.

Christian Church (Disciples of Christ) in the USA and Canada: 130 East Washington St, POB 1986, Indianapolis, IN 46206-1986; tel. (317) 635-3100; fax (317) 635-3700; e-mail news@cm.disciples.org; internet www.disciples.org; f. 1804; 3,754 congregations (2008); 691,160 mems (2008); mem. of the Churches Uniting in Christ and World Council of Churches; Gen. Minister and Pres. Rev. Dr SHARON E. WATKINS.

Christian Reformed Church in North America: 2850 Kalamazoo Ave, SE, Grand Rapids, MI 49560; tel. (616) 241-1691; fax (616)

THE UNITED STATES OF AMERICA

224-0803; e-mail crcna@crcna.org; internet www.crcna.org; f. 1857; Calvinist; 1,084 churches (2011); 255,700 mems (2011) (USA and Canada); Exec. Dir Rev. GERARD L. DYKSTRA.

Church of Christ: POB 472, Independence, MO 64051-0472; tel. (816) 833-3995; fax (816) 833-0210; e-mail cofctl@sbcglobal.net; internet www.churchofchrist-tl.org; f. 1830; Sec. Council of Apostles SMITH N. BRICKHOUSE; Gen. Church Sec. HARVEY E. SEIBEL.

Church of Christ, Scientist: 210 Massachusetts Ave, Boston, MA 02115; tel. (617) 450-2000; fax (617) 450-3554; e-mail info@churchofchristscientist.org; internet www.tfccs.com; f. 1879; 2,400 congregations world-wide; Pres. FUJIKO TAKAI.

Church of God in Christ: Mason Temple, 930 Mason St, Memphis, TN 38126; tel. (901) 947-9300; e-mail laity@cogic.org; internet www.cogic.org; f. 1907; 15,300 churches; 5.5m. mems (1991); Presiding Bishop CHARLES EDWARD BLAKE, Sr.

Church of Jesus Christ of Latter-day Saints (Mormon): 50 East North Temple, Salt Lake City, UT 84150; tel. (801) 240-1000; fax (801) 240-2033; internet www.lds.org; f. 1830; 12,112 wards and brs (congregations) in USA; c. 3.2m. mems in USA (2008); Pres THOMAS S. MONSON, HENRY B. EYRING, DIETER F. UCHTDORF.

Church of the Nazarene: 17001 Prairie Star Parkway, Lenexa, KS 66220; tel. (913) 577-0500; fax (913) 577-0848; e-mail gensec@nazarene.org; internet www.nazarene.org; f. 1908; 24,285 congregations; 1.9m. mems (2009); Gen. Sec. DAVID P. WILSON.

Friends United Meeting: 101 Quaker Hill Dr., Richmond, IN 47374-1980; tel. (765) 962-7573; fax (765) 966-1293; e-mail info@fum.org; internet www.fum.org; f. 1902; Quaker; mem. of the World Council of Churches; 44,000 mems (USA and Canada); Gen. Sec. SYLVIA GRAVES.

Jehovah's Witnesses: 25 Columbia Heights, Brooklyn, NY 11201-2483; tel. (718) 560-5000; internet www.watchtower.org; f. 1879; 12,494 congregations; c. 1.9m. mems (2008); Pres. DAN ADAMS.

Mariavite Old Catholic Church—Province of North America: 2803 10th St, Wyandotte, MI 48192-4994; tel. and fax (734) 281-3082; e-mail mariaviteocc@hotmail.com; f. 1930; 158 churches; 356,920 mems; Prime Bishop Most Rev. Archbishop Dr ROBERT R. J. M. ZABOROWSKI.

Reformed Church in America: 475 Riverside Dr., 18th Floor, New York, NY 10115-0001; tel. (212) 870-3071; fax (212) 870-2499; e-mail questions@rca.org; internet www.rca.org; f. 1628; Calvinist; mem. of the World Council of Churches; 1,000 churches (USA and Canada); 170,000 mems; Gen. Sec. Rev. WESLEY GRANBERG-MICHAELSON.

Seventh-day Adventists: 12501 Old Columbia Pike, Silver Spring, MD 20904-6600; tel. (301) 680-6400; fax (301) 680-6464; e-mail info@nad.adventist.org; internet www.nadadventist.org; f. 1863; 5,026 churches; 938,000 mems in 2008; Pres. DON SCHNEIDER; Sec. G. ALEXANDER BRYANT.

United Church of Christ: 700 Prospect Ave, Cleveland, OH 44115; tel. (216) 736-2100; fax (216) 736-2103; e-mail guessb@ucc.org; internet www.ucc.org; f. 1957; mem. of the Churches Uniting in Christ and World Council of Churches; 5,633 churches; 736,000 mems in 2007; Gen. Minister and Pres. Rev. GEOFFREY A. BLACK.

United Pentecostal Church International: 8855 Dunn Rd, Hazelwood, MO 63042-2211; tel. (314) 837-7300; fax (314) 837-7304; e-mail info@upci.org; internet www.upci.org; f. 1945 by merger of the Pentecostal Church, Inc, and Pentecostal Assemblies of Jesus Christ; 4,358 churches (USA and Canada); c. 600,000 mems; Gen. Supt Rev. Dr DAVID K. BERNARD; Gen. Sec. JERRY JONES.

BAHÁ'Í FAITH

At October 2010 there were an estimated 168,647 adherents of the Bahá'í faith in the mainland USA.

National Spiritual Assembly of Bahá'ís of the United States: External Affairs Office, 1320 19th St, NW, Suite 701, Washington, DC 20036-1610; tel. (202) 833-8990; fax (202) 833-8988; e-mail BahaisUS@usbnc.org; internet www.bahai.us; f. 1844 in Persia (Iran); Chair. JACQUELINE LEFT HAND BULL; Sec. KENNETH E. BOWERS.

BUDDHISM

In 2008 there were an estimated 1.2m. Buddhists in the USA.

Association of American Buddhists: 301 West 45th St, New York, NY 10036; tel. (212) 489-1075; e-mail iwanttoknow@buddhismonline.us; internet www.buddhismonline.us; f. 1980; 15 regional groups; Pres. Ven. Dr KEVIN R. O'NEIL.

Buddhist Association of the United States (BAUS): Chuang Yen Monastery, 2020 Route 301, Carmel, NY 10512; tel. (845) 225-1445; fax (845) 225-1485; internet www.baus.org; f. 1964; Pres. Ven. JI-XING.

Buddhist Churches of America: 1710 Octavia St, San Francisco, CA 94109-4341; tel. (415) 776-5600; fax (415) 771-6293; e-mail bcahq@pacbell.net; internet buddhistchurchesofamerica.org; f. 1899; Hongwanji-ha Jodo Shinshu denomination; c. 230,000 mems; Presiding Bishop SOCHO KOSHIN OGUI; Exec. Dir HENRY SHIBATA.

HINDUISM

In 2008 there were an estimated 582,000 Hindus in the USA.

Ramakrishna-Vivekananda Center: 17 East 94th St, New York, NY 10128; tel. (212) 534-9445; fax (212) 828-1618; e-mail rvcenternewyork@gmail.com; internet www.ramakrishna.org; f. 1933; teachings based on the system of Vedanta; Minister and Spiritual Leader SWAMI YUKTATMANANDA; Dir BARRY ZELIKOVSKY.

ISLAM

In 2008 there were an estimated 1.5m. Muslims in the USA.

Council of Masajid of United States (CMUS): 213 Patriots Path, Edison, NJ 08817; tel. (732) 985-3304; fax (732) 572-0486; e-mail dawud10@optonline.net; f. 1978; educational agency representing 650 local groups; Pres. DAWUD ASSAD.

Islamic Center of New York: 1711 Third Ave, New York, NY 10029-7303; tel. (212) 722-5234; fax (212) 722-5936; internet www.icnyu.org; f. 1966; Dir ZIYAD MONAYAIR.

Islamic Information Center: 529 14th St, Suite 1292, Washington, DC 20045; tel. (202) 347-6405; fax (202) 347-6406; internet www.islamicinformationcenter.org; f. 2002; provides accurate information on Islam to Muslims and non-Muslims; Chair. Imam SYED NAQVI.

Islamic Mission of America: 143 State St, Brooklyn, NY 11201; tel. (718) 875-6607; f. 1948; maintains an educational and training institute; 15,000 mems; Chair. MOHAMED KABBAJ; Dir Hajj D. A. HAROON.

JUDAISM

In 2008 there were an estimated 6.5m. Jews in North America.

American Jewish Congress: 115 East 57 St, Suite 11, New York, NY 10022; tel. (212) 879-4500; fax (212) 758-1633; e-mail contact@ajcongress.org; internet www.ajcongress.org; f. 1918; 50,000 mems; Chair. JACK ROSEN; Pres. RICHARD S. GORDON.

Central Conference of American Rabbis: 355 Lexington Ave, New York, NY 10017; tel. (212) 972-3636; fax (212) 692-0819; e-mail info@ccarnet.org; internet www.ccarnet.org; f. 1889; organized rabbinate of Reform Judaism; 1,840 mems; Pres. ELLEN WEINBERG DREYFUS.

The Rabbinical Assembly: 3080 Broadway, New York, NY 10027; tel. (212) 280-6000; fax (212) 749-9166; e-mail info@rabbinicalassembly.org; internet www.rabbinicalassembly.org; f. 1901; 1,550 mems; Pres. Rabbi GILAH DROR; Sec. Rabbi DEBRA NEWMAN KAMIN.

Union of Orthodox Jewish Congregations of America: 11 Broadway, New York, NY 10004; tel. (212) 563-4000; fax (212) 564-9058; e-mail info@ou.org; internet www.ou.org; f. 1898; 1,000 affiliated congregations representing c. 1.0m. mems; Chair. HARVEY BLITZ; Pres. STEVEN J. SAVITSKY.

Union for Reform Judaism: 633 Third Ave, New York, NY 10017-6778; tel. (212) 650-4000; fax (212) 650-4169; e-mail urj@urj.org; internet urj.org; f. 1873 as the Union of American Hebrew Congregations; present name adopted 2003; more than 900 affiliated congregations representing c. 1.5m. mems; Pres. Rabbi ERIC H. YOFFIE; Sr Vice-Pres. Rabbi DANIEL FREELANDER.

United Synagogue of Conservative Judaism: 820 Second Ave, New York, NY 10017-4504; tel. (212) 533-7800; fax (212) 353-9439; e-mail info@uscj.org; internet www.uscj.org; f. 1913; c. 700 affiliated congregations in North America representing c. 1.5m. mems; Pres. RICHARD SKOLNIK; Exec. Vice-Pres. Rabbi STEVEN WERNICK.

SIKHISM

In the mid-2000s there were an estimated 200,000 Sikhs in the USA.

Sikh Information Centre: POB 392, Lathrop, CA 95330; e-mail info@sikhinformationcentre.org; internet www.sikhinformationcentre.org.

The Press

The USA publishes more newspapers and periodicals than any other country. Most dailies give a greater emphasis to local news because of the strong interest in local and regional affairs and the decentralized structure of many government services. These factors, together with the distribution problem inherent in the size of the country, are responsible for the lack of national newspapers. In 2007 the Newspaper Association of America (NAA) estimated that some 48.4% of the adult population read a daily newspaper.

Most influential and highly respected among the few newspapers with a national readership are *USA Today*, the *New York Times*, the

THE UNITED STATES OF AMERICA

Washington Post, Los Angeles Times and *The Wall Street Journal* (the financial and news daily with editions in New York City, California, Illinois and Texas, and a European and an Asian edition).

In 2010, according to the Audit Bureau of Circulations, 22 daily newspapers had circulations (Mon.–Fri.) of over 250,000 copies. Among the largest of these, in order of daily circulation in 2008, were *The Wall Street Journal, USA Today, New York Times, Los Angeles Times, Washington Post, New York Daily News, New York Post, San Jose Mercury News, Chicago Tribune,* and *Houston Chronicle.*

In February 2010, according to the NAA, there were 1,408 daily newspapers, with a total circulation of 46.3m. copies per day at the end of September 2009. The Sunday edition is an important and distinctive feature of US newspaper publishing; many Sunday newspapers run to over 300 pages. In February 2010 there were 919 Sunday newspapers, with a total circulation of about 46.8m. at the end of September 2009. In 2005 there were 6,659 weekly newspapers.

The famous tradition of press freedom in the USA is grounded in the First Amendment to the Constitution, which declares that 'Congress shall make no law... abridging the freedom of speech or of the Press...', and confirmed in the legislations of many states, which prohibit any kind of legal restriction on the dissemination of news.

Legislation affecting the Press is both state and federal. A source of controversy between the Press and the courts has been the threat of the encroachment by judicial decrees on the area of courtroom and criminal trial coverage. In 1972 the Supreme Court ruled that journalists were not entitled to refuse to give evidence before grand juries on information they have received confidentially. Since then the frequent issuing of subpoenas to journalists and the gaoling of several reporters for refusing to disclose sources has led to many 'shield' bills being put before Congress and state legislatures demanding immunity for journalists from both federal and state jurisdiction.

In recent years, increased production costs have subjected the industry to considerable economic strain, resulting in mergers and take-overs, a great decline in competition between dailies in the same city, and the appearance of inter-city dailies catering for two or more adjoining centres. A consequence of these trends has been the steady growth of newspaper groups or chains.

The following are among the principal daily newspaper groups:

Advance Publications, Inc: 950 Fingerboard Rd, Staten Island, NY 10305-1453; tel. (212) 286-2860; fax (718) 981-1456; internet www.advance.net; Chair. and CEO SAMUEL I. (SI) NEWHOUSE, Jr; Pres. DONALD E. NEWHOUSE; interests in cable television and internet news websites; owns Condé Nast Publications, Parade Publications, Fairchild Publications and American City Business Journals, among others.

American Community Newspapers: 14875 Landmark Blvd, Suite 110, Dallas, TX 75254; tel. (972) 628-4080; fax (972) 801-3203; e-mail scarr@acnpapers.com; internet www.americancommunitynewspapers.com; CEO and Pres. RICHARD M. FRANKS; 100 publs (86 newspapers, incl. the Sun Newspapers group, and 14 speciality publs); combined circ. c. 1.4m.

Block Communications, Inc (BCI): 405 Madison Ave, Suite 2100, Toledo, OH 43604; tel. (419) 724-6212; fax (419) 724-6167; e-mail info@blockcommunications.com; internet www.blockcommunications.com; f. 1900; Chair. ALLAN J. BLOCK; Pres. GARY J. BLAIR; 2 daily newspapers, *The Pittsburgh Post-Gazette* and *The Toledo Blade*; also owns 2 cable cos, 5 television stations and a telephone co; interests in security, cable construction and advertising.

The Copley Press, Inc: 7776 Ivanhoe Ave, La Jolla, CA 92037; tel. (858) 454-0411; fax (858) 729-7629; internet www.copleynewspapers.com; f. 1928; Chair., Pres. and CEO DAVID C. COPLEY; 9 daily newspapers, incl. *The San Diego Union-Tribune*, 8 weekly newspapers and 1 bi-weekly newspaper; owns the Copley News Service syndicate (f. 1955).

Cox Media Group: 6205 Peachtree Dunwoody Rd, Atlanta, GA 30328; tel. (678) 645-0000; fax (678) 645-5002; e-mail brian.cooper@coxinc.com; internet www.coxmediagroup.com; f. 1898; Pres. SANDY SCHWARTZ; 8 daily newspapers, incl. *The Atlanta Journal-Constitution*, and 16 weekly newspapers; combined weekday circ. 1.2m., combined Sun. circ. 1.6m.

Dow Jones & Co Inc: 1 World Financial Center, 200 Liberty St, New York, NY 10281; tel. (212) 416-2000; fax (212) 416-3478; internet www.dowjones.com; f. 1882; acquired by News Corporation in December 2007; CEO LES HINTON; publs incl. *The Wall Street Journal*, the weekly financial magazine *Barron's* and the monthly *Far Eastern Economic Review*; also incl. the community newspaper subsidiary.

Dow Jones Local Media Group (ONI): POB 580, Middletown, NY 10940; tel. (845) 294-8181; e-mail dwaterman@ottaway.com; internet www.dowjoneslmg.com; f. 1936 as Ottaway Newspapers; merged with Dow Jones in 1970; present name adopted 2009; Exec. Chair. PATRICK J. PURCELL; 8 daily and 15 weekly newspapers; over 20 other publs; daily print circ. 282,000, Sun. circ. 316,000 (Oct. 2008).

Freedom Communications, Inc: 17666 Fitch, Irvine, CA 92614-6022; tel. (949) 253-2300; fax (949) 474-7675; e-mail info@link.freedom.com; internet www.freedom.com; Chair. JAMES D. DUNNING, Jr; CEO MITCHELL STERN; 33 daily newspapers, incl. *The Orange County Register*, and 77 weekly publs; combined weekday circ. c. 1m.; owns 8 television stations.

Gannett Co Inc: 7950 Jones Branch Dr., McLean, VA 22107; tel. (703) 854-6000; fax (703) 854-2046; e-mail gcishare@gannett.com; internet www.gannett.com; f. 1906; Chair., Pres. and CEO CRAIG A. DUBOW; 84 daily newspapers, incl. *USA Today, Detroit Free Press* and *The Arizona Republic*, c. 850 non-daily publs; combined weekday circ. 7.2m. (of which c. 2.1m. *USA Today*); owns 23 television stations broadcasting to 20m. households; owns and operates Newsquest Media Group (United Kingdom).

Hearst Corpn: Hearst Tower, 12th Floor, 300 West 57th St, New York, NY 10019; tel. (212) 649-4190; fax (212) 649-2108; e-mail lbagley@hearst.com; internet www.hearst.com; acquired Prime Time, Inc (publr, San Antonio region, Texas) in late 2006; acquired *Connecticut Post* and seven Connecticut weekly newspapers, and assumed control of three daily newspapers, in mid-2008; Chair. GEORGE R. HEARST, Jr; Vice-Chair. and CEO FRANK A. BENNACK, Jr; 15 daily newspapers, incl. the *Houston Chronicle* and *San Francisco Chronicle*, and 49 weekly newspapers; 14 monthly magazines incl. *Good Housekeeping, Cosmopolitan, O, The Oprah Magazine* and *Redbook*; owns or operates 29 television stations, broadcasting to 18% of the US market, and two radio stations; interests in cable networks, interactive media, business information publishing and real estate.

Lee Enterprises: 201 North Harrison St, Davenport, IA 52801-1939; tel. (563) 383-2100; e-mail information@lee.net; internet www.lee.net; f. 1890; Chair., Pres. and CEO MARY E. JUNCK; 49 daily newspapers (jt interest in further 4 dailies) and more than 300 weekly newspapers and speciality publs; combined weekday circ. 1.5m., combined Sunday circ. 1.8m.; interests in publishing and purchasing and distribution of raw materials.

The McClatchy Co: 2100 Q St, Sacramento, CA 95816-6899; tel. (916) 321-1855; fax (916) 321-1869; e-mail ptira@mcclatchy.com; internet www.mcclatchy.com; acquired Knight Ridder Inc in 2006; established 10 foreign news bureaux in that year; sold largest daily *Star Tribune* to Avista Capital Partners (New York) in early 2007; Chair., Pres. and CEO GARY B. PRUITT; 30 daily newspapers, incl. the *Miami Herald*, and community newspapers.

Media General, Inc: 333 East Franklin St, Richmond, VA 23219; tel. (804) 649-6000; e-mail etucker@mediageneral.com; internet www.mediageneral.com; Chair. J. STEWART BRYAN, III; Pres. and CEO MARSHALL N. MORTON; 21 daily newspapers, incl. *The Tampa Tribune, Richmond Times-Dispatch* and *Winston-Salem Journal*, as well as c. 200 weekly newspapers and other publs; owns 18 network-affiliated television stations.

MediaNews Group: 101 Colfax Ave, Suite 1100, Denver, CO 80202; tel. (303) 954-6360; fax (303) 954-6320; e-mail contact@medianewsgroup.com; internet www.medianewsgroup.com; Chair. and CEO WILLIAM DEAN SINGLETON; Pres. JOSEPH J. LODOVIC, IV; 54 daily newspapers, incl. *The Denver Post*; combined weekday circ. 2.4m., combined Sun. circ. 2.7m.; owns a television station in Anchorage, AK, and radio stations in Texas.

New York Times Co: 620 Eighth Ave, New York, NY 10018; tel. (212) 556-1234; internet www.nytco.com; Chair. ARTHUR O. SULZBERGER, Jr; Pres. and CEO JANET L. ROBINSON; 18 daily newspapers incl. *New York Times, The International Herald Tribune* and *The Boston Globe*; owns c. 50 internet websites; sold Broadcast Media Group to Oak Hill Capital Partners in May 2007.

E. W. Scripps Co: 312 Walnut St, 2800 Scripps Center, Cincinnati, OH 45202; POB 5380, Cincinnati, OH 45201; tel. (513) 977-3000; fax (513) 977-3024; e-mail corpcomm@scripps.com; internet www.scripps.com; Pres. and CEO RICHARD A. BOEHNE; 14 newspapers; owns the Scripps Howard News Service syndicate, 10 television stations, and 6 cable and satellite programming networks.

Tribune Publishing: 435 North Michigan Ave, Chicago, IL 60611; tel. (312) 222-9100; fax (312) 222-4760; e-mail gweitman@tribune.com; internet www.tribune.com; f. 1847; subsidiary of Tribune Co; merged with the Times Mirror Co in 2000; Tribune Co acquired by private investor in Dec. 2007; filed for Chapter 11 bankruptcy protection in Aug. 2010; Chair., Pres. and CEO (vacant); 8 daily newspapers incl. the *Chicago Tribune*, the *Los Angeles Times*, the *Baltimore Sun* and the Spanish-language newspaper *Hoy*; over 130 other publs; combined weekday circ. 2.3m., combined Sun. circ. 3.4m.; operates 23 television stations.

THE UNITED STATES OF AMERICA

PRINCIPAL DAILY AND SUNDAY NEWSPAPERS

Alabama

Birmingham News: 2201 Fourth Ave North, POB 2553, Birmingham, AL 35203; tel. (205) 325-4444; fax (205) 325-3278; e-mail tscarritt@bhamnews.com; internet www.bhamnews.com; f. 1888; Publr PAM SIDDALL; Editor THOMAS SCARRITT; circ. Mon. to Fri. 113,810, Sat. 113,702, Sun. 152,385.

Huntsville Times: 2317 South Memorial Parkway, Huntsville, AL 35801-5623; tel. (256) 532-4000; fax (256) 532-4213; e-mail kevin.wendt@htimes.com; internet www.htimes.com; f. 1910; Publr BOB LUDWIG; Editor KEVIN WENDT; circ. Mon. to Fri. 48,198, Sat. 48,220, Sun. 67,344.

Montgomery Advertiser: 425 Molton St, Montgomery, AL 36104; tel. (334) 262-1611; fax (334) 261-1521; e-mail editor@montgomeryadvertiser.com; internet www.montgomeryadvertiser.com; f. 1829 as *The Planter's Gazette*; subsidiary of Gannett Co, Inc, international news and information co (McLean, VA); Publr SAMUEL MARTIN; Exec. Editor WANDA S. LLOYD; circ. Mon. to Sat. 35,827, Sun. 44,120.

Press-Register: 304 Government St, POB 2488, Mobile, AL 36652-2488; tel. (251) 219-5614; fax (334) 219-5794; e-mail sjoynt@press-register.com; internet www.press-register.com; f. 1813; Pres. and Publr RICKY R. MATTHEWS; Editor and Vice-Pres. MIKE MARSHALL; circ. Mon. to Fri. 97,607, Sat. 91,811, Sun. 112,264.

Alaska

Anchorage Daily News: POB 149001, Anchorage, AK 99514-9001; tel. (907) 257-4305; fax (907) 257-4544; e-mail newsroom@adn.com; internet www.adn.com; f. 1946; Pres. and Publr PATRICK DOYLE; Senior Vice-Pres. and Editor PAT DOUGHERTY; circ. Mon. to Fri. 49,019, Sat. 46,709, Sun. 53,764.

Arizona

Arizona Daily Star: 4850 South Park Ave, POB 26807, Tucson, AZ 85726-6807; tel. (520) 573-4215; fax (520) 573-4200; e-mail jhumenik@azstarnet.com; internet www.azstarnet.com; f. 1877; Publr and Editor JOHN M. HUMENIK; Exec. Editor BOBBIE JO BUEL-CARTER; circ. Mon. to Fri. 108,612, Sat. 119,432, Sun. 150,256.

Arizona Republic: 200 East Van Buren St, POB 2244, Phoenix, AZ 85002; tel. (602) 444-8000; fax (800) 699-0732; e-mail comments@azcentral.com; internet www.azcentral.com/arizonarepublic; f. 1890; subsidiary of Gannett Co, Inc (McLean, VA) news group; Pres. and Publr JOHN ZIDICH; Vice-Pres. and Exec. Editor RANDY LOVELY; circ. Mon. to Fri. 351,207, Sat. 390,789, Sun. 510,500.

Arkansas

Democrat-Gazette: 121 East Capitol Ave, POB 2221, Little Rock, AR 72203; tel. (501) 378-3400; fax (501) 372-4765; e-mail ffellone@arkansasonline.com; internet www2.arkansasonline.com; f. 1819; morning; Publr WALTER E. HUSSMAN, Jr; Exec. Editor GRIFFIN SMITH; circ. Mon. to Fri. 185,222, Sat. 180,332, Sun. 267,849.

California

Bakersfield Californian: 1707 Eye St, Bakersfield, CA 93301; tel. (805) 395-7500; fax (805) 395-7519; internet www.bakersfield.com; f. 1866; Publr and Chair. VIRGINIA F. MOORHOUSE; Vice-Pres. and Exec. Editor JOHN ARTHUR; circ. Mon. to Fri. 47,191, Sat. 48,826, Sun. 55,840.

Daily Breeze: South Bay Tower, 21250 Hawthorne Blvd, Suite 170, Torrance, CA 90503; tel. (310) 540-5511; fax (310) 540-6272; e-mail newsroom@dailybreeze.com; internet www.dailybreeze.com; f. 1894; publ. by the Los Angeles Newspaper group (subsidiary of MediaNews Group); Mon. to Sat. evening, Sun. morning; Publr LINDA LINDUS; Man. Editor TONI SCIACQUA; circ. Mon. to Fri. 65,763, Sat. 67,709, Sun. 65,571.

Daily News: 21860 Burbank Blvd, Suite 200, Woodland Hills, POB 4200, CA 91367; tel. (818) 713-3000; fax (818) 713-0058; e-mail dnmetro@dailynews.com; internet www.dailynews.com; f. 1911; publ. by Los Angeles Newspaper Group; morning; Publr JACK KLUNDER; Editor CAROLINA GARCIA; circ. Mon. to Fri. 89,804, Sat. 90,800, Sun. 96,614.

Fresno Bee: 1626 E St, Fresno, CA 93786; tel. (559) 441-6233; fax (559) 441-6499; e-mail blumbye@fresnobee.com; internet www.fresnobee.com; f. 1922; Publr and Pres. WILLIAM H. FLEET; Senior Vice-Pres. and Exec. Editor BETSY LUMBYE; circ. Mon. to Fri. 118,978, Sat. 120,702, Sun. 140,392.

Investor's Business Daily: 12655 Beatrice St, Los Angeles, CA 90066; tel. (310) 448-6700; fax (310) 577-7301; e-mail ibdnews@investors.com; internet www.investors.com; f. 1984; morning; Publr WILLIAM J. O'NEILL; Editor-in-Chief WESLEY F. MANN; circ. Mon. to Fri. 131,959.

Los Angeles Times: 202 West First St, Los Angeles, CA 90012; tel. (213) 237-5000; fax (213) 237-7679; e-mail nancy.sullivan@latimes.com; internet www.latimes.com; f. 1881; Publr and CEO EDDY W. HARTENSTEIN; Editor RUSS STANTON; circ. Mon. to Fri. 616,606, Sat. 740,068, Sun. 941,914.

Modesto Bee: 1325 H St, POB 3928, Modesto, CA 95352; tel. (209) 578-2000; fax (209) 578-2207; e-mail ejohnston@modbee.com; internet www.modbee.com; f. 1884; Publr and Pres. ERIC JOHNSTON; Vice-Pres. and Editor MARK VASCHÉ; circ. Mon. to Fri. 64,772, Sat. 70,667, Sun. 73,650.

Oakland Tribune: 7677 Oakport St, Oakland, CA 94621; tel. (510) 208-6300; fax (510) 208-6477; e-mail mreynolds@bayareanewsgroup.com; internet www.oaklandtribune.com; f. 1874; publ. by Alameda Newspaper Group (subsidiary of MediaNews Group); Publr JOHN ARMSTRONG; Editor MARTIN REYNOLDS; circ. Mon. to Fri. 94,120, Sat. 85,170, Sun. 94,424.

Orange County Register: 625 North Grand Ave, POB 11626, Santa Ana, CA 92701-4347; tel. (877) 627-7009; fax (714) 796-3681; e-mail customerservice@ocregister.com; internet www.ocregister.com; Pres. and Publr TERRY HORNE; Editor KEN BRUSIC; circ. Mon. to Fri. 196,684, Sat. 229,069, Sun. 280,000.

Press Democrat: 427 Mendocino Ave, POB 569, Santa Rosa, CA 95402; tel. (707) 546-2020; fax (707) 521-5330; e-mail catherine.barratt@pressdemocrat.com; internet www.pressdemocrat.com; f. 1857; Publr BRUCE W. KYSE; Exec. Editor CATHERINE BARNETT; circ. Mon. to Fri. 62,093, Sat. 64,727, Sun. 66,392.

The Press-Enterprise: 3450 14th St, POB 792, Riverside, CA 92501; tel. (951) 684-1200; fax (951) 368-9022; e-mail feedback@pe.com; internet www.pe.com; f. 1878; publ. by A. H. Belo Corpn; morning; Publr and CEO RONALD R. REDFERN; Editor MARIA DE VARENNE; circ. Mon. to Fri. 114,556, Sat. 109,659, Sun. 119,209.

Press-Telegram: 300 Oceangate, Long Beach, CA 90844-0001; tel. (562) 435-1161; fax (562) 499-1277; e-mail rich.archbold@presstelegram.com; internet www.presstelegram.com; Publr LINDA LINDUS; Exec. Editor RICH ARCHBOLD; circ. Mon. to Fri. 69,761, Sat. 69,263, Sun. 68,477.

Sacramento Bee: 2100 Q St, POB 15779, Sacramento, CA 95852; tel. (916) 321-1000; fax (916) 321-1100; e-mail cdell@sacbee.com; internet www.sacbee.com; f. 1857; Pres. and Publr CHERYL DELL; Sr Vice-Pres. and Editor MELANIE SILL; circ. Mon. to Fri. 214,219, Sat. 231,150, Sun. 266,542.

San Bernardino Sun: 4030 North Georgia Blvd, San Bernardino, CA 92407; tel. (909) 889-9666; fax (909) 381-8741; e-mail nancy.kay@sbsun.com; internet www.sbsun.com; f. 1894; part of Los Angeles Media Group; Publr FRED HAMILTON; Exec. Editor FRANK PINE; circ. Mon. to Fri. 51,954, Sat. 54,892, Sun. 59,215.

San Diego Union-Tribune: 350 Camino de la Reina, San Diego, CA 92108; tel. (619) 299-3131; fax (619) 293-1896; e-mail letters@uniontrib.com; internet www.signonsandiego.com; f. 1868; acquired by private equity firm, Platinum Equity, in May 2009; Pres. and Publr EDWARD R. MOSS; Vice-Pres. and Editor JEFF LIGHT; circ. Mon. to Fri. 249,630, Sat. 287,637, Sun. 310,869.

San Francisco Chronicle: 901 Mission St, San Francisco, CA 94103; tel. (415) 777-1111; fax (415) 896-1107; e-mail letters@sfchronicle.com; internet www.sfgate.com; f. 1865; subsidiary of Hearst Communications; Publr and Pres. FRANK J. VEGA; Exec. Vice-Pres. and Editor WARD H. BUSHEE; circ. Mon. to Fri. 241,330, Sat. 224,100, Sun. 286,121.

San Francisco Examiner: 71 Stevenson, 2nd Floor, San Francisco, CA 94105; tel. (415) 359-2600; fax (415) 359-2766; e-mail dhussey@examiner.com; internet www.sfexaminer.com; f. 1887; publ. by Clarity Media Group; Publr JOHN WILCOX; Exec. Editor DEIRDRE HUSSEY; circ. Mon. to Fri. 70,000, Sat. 90,000 (2008).

San Jose Mercury News: 750 Ridder Park Dr., San Jose, CA 95190-0001; tel. (408) 920-5000; fax (408) 288-8060; e-mail dbutler@mercurynews.com; internet www.mercurynews.com; f. 1851; owned by MediaNews Group; Pres. and Publr MAC TULLY; Editor and Vice-Pres. DAVID J. BUTLER; circ. Mon. to Fri. 236,632, Sat. 202,125, Sun. 262,316.

Stockton Record: 530 East Market St, POB 900, Stockton, CA 95201; tel. (209) 943-6568; fax (209) 547-8186; e-mail newsroom@recordnet.com; internet www.recordnet.com; f. 1895; publ. by Dow Jones & Co; Publr ROGER COOVER; Editor MIKE KLOCKE; circ. Mon. to Fri. 42,821, Sat. 45,019, Sun. 48,935.

Colorado

Denver Post: 101 West Colfax Ave, Denver, CO 80202; tel. (303) 954-1010; fax (303) 820-1369; e-mail gmoore@denverpost.com; internet www.denverpost.com; f. 1892; Publr WILLIAM DEAN SINGLETON; Editor GREGORY MOORE; circ. Mon. to Fri. 333,675, Sat. 389,346, Sun. 486,976.

The Gazette: 30 South Prospect St, Colorado Springs, CO 80903; tel. (719) 632-5511; fax (719) 636-0202; e-mail liz.cobb@gazette.com;

THE UNITED STATES OF AMERICA

internet www.gazette.com; f. 1872; Pres. and Publr STEVE POPE; Editor and Vice-Pres. JEFF THOMAS; circ. Mon. to Fri. 85,305, Sat. 84,959, Sun. 94,801.

Connecticut

Connecticut Post: 410 State St, Bridgeport, CT 06604-4501; tel. (203) 333-0161; fax (203) 366-8158; e-mail edit@ctpost.com; internet www.connpost.com; f. 1883; Pres. and Publr JOHN J. DEAUGUSTINE; Editor TOM BADEN; circ. Mon. to Fri. 53,866, Sat. 41,768, Sun. 80,840.

Hartford Courant: 285 Broad St, Hartford, CT 06115; tel. (860) 241-6200; fax (860) 520-3176; e-mail nmeyer@courant.com; internet www.courant.com; f. 1764; Publr and CEO RICHARD GRAZIANO; Editor NAEDINE HAZELL (acting); circ. Mon. to Fri. 139,166, Sat. 132,222, Sun. 202,070.

New Haven Register: 40 Sargent Dr., New Haven, CT 06511; tel. (203) 789-5200; fax (203) 865-7894; e-mail mbrackenbury@nhregister.com; internet www.nhregister.com; f. 1812; Publr TOM WILEY; Editor JACK KRAMER; circ. Mon. to Fri. 75,547, Sat. 38,526, Sun. 100,486.

Waterbury Republican-American: American-Republican, Inc, 389 Meadow St, POB 2090, Waterbury, CT 06722-2090; tel. (203) 574-3636; fax (203) 596-9277; e-mail ghanisek@rep-am.com; internet www.rep-am.com; f. 1844; morning; Publr WILLIAM J. PAPE, II; Exec. Editor JONATHAN F. KELLOGG; circ. Mon. to Fri. 46,694, Sat. 44,418, Sun. 52,969.

Delaware

News Journal: POB 15505, Wilmington, DE 19850; tel. (302) 324-2500; fax (302) 856-3919; e-mail newsroom@newsjournal.com; internet www.delawareonline.com; f. 1871; publ. by Gannett Co Inc; Publr CURTIS W. RIDDLE; Exec. Editor DAVID LEDFORD; circ. Mon. to Fri. 92,538, Sat. 85,240, Sun. 113,467.

District of Columbia

Washington Post: 1150 15th St, NW, Washington, DC 20071; tel. (202) 334-6000; fax (202) 334-5693; internet www.washingtonpost.com; f. 1877; Chair. BOISFEUILLET JONES; Publr KATHARINE WEYMOUTH; Exec. Editor MARCUS BRAUCHLI, Jr; Man. Editors ELIZABETH SPAYD, RAJU NARISETTI; circ. Mon. to Fri. 578,482, Sat. 542,463, Sun. 797,679.

Washington Times: 3600 New York Ave, NE, Washington, DC 20002-1947; tel. (202) 636-3000; fax (202) 832-2982; e-mail yourletters@washingtontimes.com; internet www.washingtontimes.com; f. 1982; sold in 2010 to News World Media Devt group; Exec. Editor SAM DEALEY; circ. Mon. to Fri. 83,509, Sun. 43,889.

Florida

Daytona Beach News-Journal: 901 Sixth St, Daytona Beach, FL 32117; tel. (386) 252-1511; e-mail cory.lancaster@news-jrnl.com; internet www.news-journalonline.com; f. 1904; morning; CEO and Publr MICHAEL REDDING; Exec. Editor PAT RICE; circ. Mon. to Fri. 70,721, Sat. 77,391, Sun. 92,553.

Diario Las Américas: 2900 NW 39th St, Miami, FL 33142; tel. (305) 633-3341; fax (305) 635-7668; e-mail cartas@diariolasamericas.com; internet www.diariolasamericas.com; f. 1953; Spanish; Publr and Editor HORACIO AGUIRRE; circ. Mon. to Sat. 42,473, Sun. 44,951 (2009).

Florida Times-Union: 1 Riverside Ave, Jacksonville, FL 32202; POB 1949, Jacksonville, FL 32231; tel. (904) 359-4111; fax (904) 359-4478; e-mail rich.ray@jacksonville.com; internet jacksonville.com; f. 1864; Publr LUCY TALLEY; Editor FRANK DENTON; circ. Mon. to Fri. 117,416, Sat. 126,386, Sun. 166,843.

Florida Today: Cape Publs, Inc, POB 419000, Melbourne, FL 32941-9000; tel. (321) 242-3500; fax (321) 242-6601; internet www.floridatoday.com; f. 1966; morning; Publr and Pres. MARK MIKOLAJCZYK; Exec. Editor BOB STOVER; circ. Mon. to Fri. 72,838, Sat. 79,305, Sun. 100,176.

Ledger: 300 West Lime St, POB 408, Lakeland, FL 33802; tel. (863) 802-7000; fax (863) 802-7850; e-mail skip.perez@theledger.com; internet www.theledger.com; f. 1924; morning; Publr JEROME FERSON; Exec. Editor SKIP PEREZ; circ. Mon. to Fri. 54,991, Sat. 54,933, Sun. 70,617.

Miami Herald: 1 Herald Plaza, Miami, FL 33132-1693; tel. (305) 350-2111; fax (305) 376-5287; e-mail dwilson@miamiherald.com; internet www.miamiherald.com; f. 1910; Publr and Pres. DAVID LANDSBERG; Exec. Editor ANDERS GYLLENHAAL; circ. Mon. to Fri. 170,769, Sat. 137,854, Sun. 235,225.

News-Press: 2442 Dr Martin Luther King Jr Blvd, Fort Myers, FL 33901-3987; tel. (239) 335-0200; e-mail response@news-press.com; internet www.news-press.com; f. 1884; morning; Publr MEI-MEI CHAN; Exec. Editor TERRY EBERLE; circ. Mon. to Fri. 77,676, Sat. 83,136, Sun. 102,495.

Orlando Sentinel: 633 North Orange Ave, Orlando, FL 32801; tel. (407) 420-5000; fax (407) 420-5350; e-mail editor@orlandosentinel.com; internet www.orlandosentinel.com; f. 1876; morning; Publr HOWARD GREENBERG (acting); Editor CHARLOTTE HALL; circ. Mon. to Fri. 191,191, Sat. 198,304, Sun. 290,838.

Palm Beach Post: 2751 South Dixie Hwy, West Palm Beach, FL 33405; tel. (561) 820-4100; fax (561) 820-4407; internet www.palmbeachpost.com; f. 1916; Publr and Exec. Editor TIM BURKE; circ. Mon. to Fri. 122,611, Sat. 123,456, Sun. 154,046.

Pensacola News Journal: POB 12710, Pensacola, FL 32591; tel. (850) 435-8600; fax (850) 435-8633; e-mail news@pnj.com; internet www.pnj.com; f. 1889; Publr KEVIN DOYLE; Exec. Editor RICHARD A. SCHNEIDER; circ. Mon. to Fri. 44,776, Sat. 42,263, Sun. 60,312.

Sarasota Herald-Tribune: 1741 Main St, Sarasota, FL 34236; tel. (941) 953-7755; fax (941) 957-5276; internet www.heraldtribune.com; f. 1925; Publr DIANE MCFARLIN; Exec. Editor MIKE CONNELLY; circ. Mon. to Fri. 89,097, Sat. 89,031, Sun. 112,347.

St Petersburg Times: 490 First Ave South, POB 1121, St Petersburg, FL 33701; tel. (727) 893-8111; fax (727) 893-8675; e-mail custserv@sptimes.com; internet www.tampabay.com; f. 1884; division of Poynter Institute for Media Studies; Chair. and CEO PAUL TASH; Editor NEIL BROWN; circ. Mon. to Fri. 278,888, Sat. 270,071, Sun. 417,807.

Sun-Sentinel: 200 East Las Olas Blvd, Fort Lauderdale, FL 33301-2293; tel. (954) 356-4000; fax (954) 356-4559; e-mail emaucker@sun-sentinel.com; internet www.sun-sentinel.com; f. 1960; Publr HOWARD GREENBERG; Editor-in-Chief EARL MAUCKER; circ. Mon. to Fri. 180,273, Sat. 207,300, Sun. 263,409.

Tampa Tribune: 200 South Parker St, Tampa, FL 33606; POB 191, Tampa, FL 33601; tel. (813) 259-8225; fax (813) 254-4952; e-mail lomoto@tbo.com; internet www.tampatrib.com; f. 1893; morning; Publr and Pres. DENISE E. PALMER; Editor JANET COATS; circ. Mon. to Fri. 159,813, Sat. 170,261.

Georgia

Atlanta Journal-Constitution: 72 Marietta St, POB 4689, Atlanta, GA 30302-4689; tel. (404) 526-5151; fax (404) 526-5746; e-mail insideajc@ajc.com; internet www.ajc.com; f. 1950; morning; Publr MICHAEL JOSEPH; Editor JULIA WALLACE; circ. Mon. to Fri. 196,200, Sat. 210,214, Sun. 397,926.

Augusta Chronicle: 725 Broad St, POB 1928, Augusta, GA 30903-1928; tel. (706) 724-0851; fax (706) 823-3345; internet chronicle.augusta.com; f. 1785; Morris Communications Co, LLC; Publr WILLIAM S. MORRIS, III; Exec. Editor ALAN ENGLISH; circ. Mon. to Fri. 61,784, Sat. 66,571, Sun. 76,745.

Macon Telegraph: 120 Broadway, Macon, GA 31208; POB 4167, Macon, GA 31208; tel. (478) 744-4200; fax (478) 744-4663; e-mail smarshall@macon.com; internet www.macon.com; f. 1826; Publr GEORGE MCCANLESS; Exec. Editor SHERRIE MARSHALL; circ. Mon. to Fri. 49,845, Sat. 48,415, Sun. 65,086.

Savannah Morning News: 1375 Chatham Parkway, Savannah, GA 31401; POB 1088, Savannah, GA 31402-1088; tel. (912) 236-9511; fax (912) 234-6522; internet www.savannahnow.com; f. 1850; Publr MICHAEL C. TRAYNOR; Exec. Editor SUSAN CATRON, Jr; circ. Mon. to Fri. 51,456, Sat. 49,030, Sun. 64,308.

Hawaii

Honolulu Star-Advertiser: Restaurant Row, 7 Waterfront Plaza, Suite 210, 500 Ala Moana, Honolulu, HI 96813; tel. (808) 529-4747; fax (808) 529-4750; e-mail webmaster@staradvertiser.com; internet www.staradvertiser.com; f. 1882; known as Honolulu Star-Bulletin until 2010 when it bought Honolulu Advertiser (f. 1856) and present name adopted; owned by Black Press Ltd; Pres. and Publr DENNIS FRANCIS; Editor FRANK BRIDGEWATER; circ. Mon. to Fri. 109,479, Sat. 117,030, Sun. 123,411.

Idaho

Idaho Statesman: 1200 North Curtis Rd, POB 40, Boise, ID 83707; tel. (208) 377-6200; fax (208) 377-6449; e-mail vgowler@idahostatesman.com; internet www.idahostatesman.com; f. 1864; Publr MI-AI PARRISH; Editor and Vice-Pres. VICKI S. GOWLER; circ. Mon. to Fri. 52,444, Sat. 53,551, Sun. 73,247.

Illinois

Chicago Sun-Times: 350 North Orleans St, 10th Floor, Chicago, IL 60654; tel. (312) 321-3000; fax (312) 321-3084; e-mail aherrmann@suntimes.com; internet www.suntimes.com; f. 1948; Publr JOHN BARRON; Editor-in-Chief DONALD HAYNER; circ. Mon. to Fri. 268,803, Sat. 199,831, Sun. 247,416.

Chicago Tribune: 435 North Michigan Ave, Chicago, IL 60611-4041; tel. (312) 222-3232; fax (312) 222-4674; internet www.chicagotribune.com; f. 1847; publ. by Chicago Tribune Co; two sister

THE UNITED STATES OF AMERICA

newspapers: *RedEye* and *Hoy Chicago*; Publr TONY HUNTER; Editor GEROULD KERN; circ. Mon. to Fri. 452,145, Sat. 359,897, Sun. 794,350.

Daily Herald: 155 East Algonquin Rd, POB 280, Arlington Heights, IL 60006; tel. (847) 427-4300; fax (847) 427-4608; e-mail jbaumann@dailyherald.com; internet www.dailyherald.com; f. 1872; owned by Paddock Publications Inc; Publr and CEO DOUG RAY; Sr Vice-Pres. and Editor JOHN LAMPINEN; circ. Mon. to Fri. 106,287, Sat. 104,535, Sun. 115,504.

Journal Star: 1 News Plaza, Peoria, IL 61643; tel. (309) 686-3000; fax (309) 686-3296; e-mail kmauser@pjstar.com; internet www.pjstarpeoria.com; f. 1855; Publr KEN MAUSER; Man. Editor JOHN PLEVKA; circ. Mon. to Fri. 61,028, Sat. 65,506, Sun. 74,544.

Pantagraph: 301 West Washington St, POB 2907, Bloomington, IL 61702-2907; tel. (309) 829-9000; fax (309) 829-9104; e-mail jgerke@pantagraph.com; internet www.pantagraph.com; f. 1837; Publr RICHARD JOHNSTON; Editor MARK PICKERING; circ. Mon. to Fri. 40,759, Sat. 37,705, Sun. 43,954.

Rockford Register Star: 99 East State St, Rockford, IL 61104; tel. (815) 987-1200; fax (815) 987-1365; internet www.rrstar.com; f. 1888; acquired by GateHouse Media from Gannett Co in 2007; Publr PETER RICKER; Gen. Man. TOM LASLEY; circ. Mon. to Fri. 52,349, Sat. 41,343, Sun. 65,648.

State Journal-Register: 1 Copley Plaza, POB 219, Springfield, IL 62705-0219; tel. (217) 788-1300; fax (217) 788-1551; e-mail sjr@sj-r.com; internet www.sj-r.com; f. 1831; Publr WALT LAFFERTY; Exec. Editor JON BROADBOOKS; circ. Mon. to Fri. 50,071, Sat. 52,114, Sun. 60,277.

Indiana

Evansville Courier and Press: 300 East Walnut, POB 268, Evansville, IN 47713; tel. (812) 424-7711; fax (812) 422-8196; e-mail eccnewmedia@courierpress.com; internet www.courierpress.com; f. 1845; Publr and Pres. JACK PATE; Editor DAVID DIXON; circ. Mon. to Fri. 58,938, Sat. 57,111, Sun. 80,425.

Indianapolis Star: POB 145, Indianapolis, IN 46206-0145; tel. (317) 444-4000; fax (317) 633-1038; internet www.indystar.com; Publr and Pres. KAREN CROTCHFELT; Editor DENNIS R. RYERSON; circ. Mon. to Fri. 182,933, Sat. 167,151, Sun. 279,358.

Journal-Gazette: 600 West Main St, POB 88, Fort Wayne, IN 46801-0088; tel. (260) 461-8831; fax (219) 461-8648; e-mail jgnews@jg.net; internet www.journalgazette.net; f. 1863; publ. by Fort Wayne Newspapers; Publr JULIE INSKEEP; Editor CRAIG KLUGMAN; circ. Mon. to Fri. 63,046, Sat. 78,272, Sun. 105,462.

News-Sentinel: 600 West Main St, POB 100, Fort Wayne, IN 46802; tel. (260) 461-8324; fax (260) 461-8817; e-mail lmorris@news-sentinel.com; internet www.news-sentinel.com; f. 1833; publ. by Fort Wayne Newspapers; Publr MICHAEL J. CHRISTMAN; Editor KERRY HUBARTT; circ. Mon. to Fri. 20,635, Sat. 20,855.

Post-Tribune: 1433 East 83rd Ave, Merrillville, IN 46410; tel. (219) 648-3100; fax (219) 648-3249; internet www.post-trib.com; f. 1907; Publr LISA TATINA; Exec. Editor PAULETTE HADDIX; circ. Mon. to Fri. 46,140, Sat. 42,640, Sun. 45,230.

South Bend Tribune: 225 West Colfax Ave, South Bend, IN 46626; tel. (574) 235-6161; fax (574) 236-1765; e-mail sfunk@sbtinfo.com; internet www.southbendtribune.com; f. 1872; Publr and Editor DAVID C. RAY; circ. Mon. to Fri. 62,616, Sat. 69,842, Sun. 83,397.

The Times: 601 45th Ave, Munster, IN 46321; tel. (219) 933-3200; fax (219) 933-3249; e-mail dasher@nwitimes.com; internet www.thetimesonline.com; f. 1906; morning; Publr BILL MASTERSON, Jr; Exec. Editor WILLIAM NANGLE; circ. Mon. to Fri. 85,342, Sat. 82,593, Sun. 92,856.

Iowa

Cedar Rapids Gazette: 500 Third Ave, SE, Cedar Rapids, IA 52401; tel. (319) 398-8211; fax (319) 398-5846; e-mail steve.buttry@gazcomm.com; internet www.gazetteonline.com; f. 1883; Publr TIM McDOUGALL; Editor LYLE MULLER; circ. Mon. to Fri. 50,624, Sat. 58,794, Sun. 65,398.

Des Moines Register: 715 Locust St, POB 957, Des Moines, IA 50306-0957; tel. (515) 284-8000; fax (515) 268-2504; e-mail letters@dmreg.com; internet www.desmoinesregister.com; f. 1849; Pres. and Publr LAURA HOLLINGSWORTH; Editor CAROLYN WASHBURN; circ. Mon. to Fri. 113,597, Sat. 119,414, Sun. 206,138.

Quad-City Times: 500 East Third St, POB 3828, Davenport, IA 52801; tel. (563) 383-2200; fax (563) 383-2223; internet www.qctimes.com; f. 1855; division of Lee Enterprises, Inc; Publr JULIE BECHTEL; Exec. Editor JAN TOUNEY; circ. Mon. to Fri. 51,035, Sat. 52,567, Sun. 64,932.

Sioux City Journal: 515 Pavonia St, Sioux City, IA 51102; tel. (712) 293-4250; fax (712) 279-5059; internet www.siouxcityjournal.com; f. 1864; subsidiary of Lee Enterprises, Inc; Publr RON PETERSON; Editor MITCH PUGH; circ. Mon. to Sat. 36,927, Sun. 38,489.

Kansas

Topeka Capital-Journal: 616 SE Jefferson St, Topeka, KS 66607; tel. (785) 295-1111; fax (785) 295-1230; e-mail tomari.quinn@cjonline.com; internet www.cjonline.com; f. 1879; Publr MARK NUSBAUM; Man. Editor TOMARI QUINN; circ. Mon. to Fri. 39,013, Sat. 39,616, Sun. 47,889.

Wichita Eagle: 825 East Douglas Ave, POB 820, Wichita, KS 67201-0820; tel. (316) 268-6000; fax (316) 268-6438; e-mail wenews@wichitaeagle.com; internet www.kansas.com; f. 1872; Publr and Pres. WILLIAM SKIP HIDLAY; Editor SHERRY CHISENHALL; circ. Mon. to Fri. 73,716, Sat. 85,245, Sun. 113,579.

Kentucky

Courier-Journal: 525 West Broadway, Louisville, KY 40201-7431; POB 740031, Louisville, KY 40201; tel. (502) 582-4011; fax (502) 582-4200; e-mail publisher@courier-journal.com; internet www.courier-journal.com; f. 1868; Publr and Pres. ARNOLD GARSON; Exec. Editor BENNIE L. IVORY; circ. Mon. to Fri. 180,377, Sat. 165,320, Sun. 239,234.

Lexington Herald-Leader: 100 Midland Ave, Lexington, KY 40508-1999; tel. (859) 231-3475; e-mail tisaac@herald-leader.com; internet www.kentucky.com; f. 1860; Pres. and Publr TIM KELLY; Editor and Vice-Pres. PETER BANIAK; circ. Mon. to Fri. 102,324, Sat. 91,790, Sun. 115,816.

Louisiana

Advocate: POB 588, Baton Rouge, LA 70821-0588; tel. (225) 383-1111; fax (225) 388-0371; internet www.2theadvocate.com; f. 1904; morning; Publr DOUGLAS L. MANSHIP, Jr; Exec. Editor CARL REDMAN; circ. Mon. to Fri. 91,533, Sat. 89,869, Sun. 111,885.

The Times: 222 Lake St, POB 30222, Shreveport, LA 71101; tel. (318) 459-3200; e-mail pzanmill@gannett.com; internet www.shreveporttimes.com; f. 1872; subsidiary of Gannett Co, Inc; Publr PETE ZANMILLER; Exec. Editor AFRICA PRICE; circ. Mon. to Sat. 44,067, Sun. 55,844.

Times-Picayune: 3800 Howard Ave, New Orleans, LA 70125-1429; tel. (504) 826-3279; fax (504) 826-3700; e-mail pkovacs@timespicayune.com; internet www.nola.com/t-p; f. 1880; Publr ASHTON PHELPS, Jr; Editor JIM AMOSS; circ. Mon. to Fri. 157,068, Sat. 149,903, Sun. 170,502.

Maine

Bangor Daily News: 491 Main St, POB 1329, Bangor, ME 04401; tel. (207) 990-8000; fax (207) 941-9476; e-mail bdnnews@bangordailynews.net; internet www.bangordailynews.com; f. 1834; Publr RICHARD J. WARREN; Editor-in-Chief MICHAEL J. DOWD; circ. Mon. to Fri. 49,919, Sat. and Sun. 56,528.

Portland Press Herald: 1 City Center, 5th Floor, POB 1460, Portland, ME 04101-5009; tel. (207) 791-6650; fax (207) 791-6920; e-mail news@pressherald.com; internet pressherald.mainetoday.com; f. 1862; incorporates the *Maine Sunday Telegram* (circ. 82,979); Publr and Editor RICHARD L. CONNOR; Exec. Editor SCOTT WASSER; circ. Mon. to Fri. 55,813, Sat. 52,709.

Maryland

Baltimore Sun: 501 North Calvert St, POB 1377, Baltimore, MD 21278; tel. (410) 332-6000; fax (410) 752-6049; e-mail research@baltsun.com; internet www.baltimoresun.com; f. 1837; Publr, Pres. and CEO TIMOTHY E. RYAN; Editor and Sr Vice-Pres. MARY COREY; circ. Mon. to Fri. 210,098, Sat. 200,160, Sun. 351,243.

Massachusetts

Boston Globe: 135 Morrissey Blvd, POB 55819, Boston, MA 02205-5819; tel. (617) 929-2000; fax (617) 929-3192; e-mail comments@globe.com; internet bostonglobe.com; f. 1872; Publr CHRISTOPHER MAYER; Editor MARTIN D. BARON; circ. Mon. to Fri. 232,432, Sat. 229,321, Sun. 378,949.

Boston Herald: 1 Herald Sq., Boston, MA 02118; tel. (617) 426-3000; fax (617) 426-1896; e-mail letterstoeditor@bostonherald.com; internet www.bostonherald.com; f. 1825; Publr PATRICK PURCELL; Man. Editor JOE SCIACCA; circ. Mon. to Fri. 132,551, Sat. 108,019, Sun. 91,040.

Christian Science Monitor: 210 Massachusetts Ave, Boston, MA 02115; tel. (617) 450-2300; e-mail letters@csmonitor.com; internet www.csmonitor.com; f. 1908; publ. by The First Church of Christ, Scientist; Man. Publr JONATHAN WELLS; Editor-in-Chief MARY TRAMMELL; circ. Mon. to Fri. 47,951 (2009).

Lowell Sun: 491 Dutton St, Lowell, MA 01853; tel. (978) 458-7100; fax (978) 970-4600; e-mail moneil@lowellsun.com; internet www.lowellsun.com; f. 1878; Mon. to Fri. evening, Sat. and Sun. morning; Publr and Pres. MARK O'NEIL; Editor JAMES CAMPANINI; circ. Mon. to Fri. 44,218, Sat. 36,947, Sun. 49,539.

THE UNITED STATES OF AMERICA

Patriot Ledger: 400 Crown Colony Dr., POB 699159, Quincy, MA 02269-9159; tel. (617) 786-7200; fax (617) 786-7025; e-mail newsroom@ledger.com; internet www.patriotledger.com; f. 1837; mem. of the South of Boston Media Group; Mon. to Fri. evening, weekend; Publr RICK DANIELS; Editor CHAZY DOWALIBY; circ. Mon. to Fri. 43,136, Sat. and Sun. 50,256.

The Republican: 1860 Main St, Springfield, MA 01101; tel. (413) 788-1200; fax (413) 788-1301; e-mail garwady@repub.com; internet www.repub.com; f. 1824; fmrly Sunday Republican, merged with Union-News in 2003; Publr and CEO GEORGE ARWADY; Exec. Editor WAYNE E. PHANEUF; circ. Mon. to Fri. 67,181, Sat. 60,292, Sun. 102,015.

Worcester Telegram & Gazette: 20 Franklin St, POB 15012, Worcester, MA 01615-0012; tel. (508) 793-9100; fax (508) 767-9529; e-mail info@telegram.com; internet www.telegram.com; f. 1866; Publr BRUCE GAULTNEY; Editor LEAH LAMSON; circ. Mon. to Fri. 70,433, Sat. 74,024.

Michigan

Detroit Free Press: 615 West Lafayette Blvd, Detroit, MI 48226; tel. (313) 222-6400; fax (313) 222-5981; e-mail nlaughlin@freepress.com; internet www.freep.com; f. 1831; subsidiary of the Gannett Corpn, Inc; Mon. to Fri. morning, Sat. and Sun.; Publr and Vice-Pres. PAUL ANGER; Man. Editor JULIE TOPPING; circ. Mon. to Fri. 252,017, Sat. 224,429, Sun. 511,742.

The Detroit News: 615 West Lafayette Blvd, Detroit, MI 48226-3197; tel. (313) 222-2300; fax (313) 496-5400; e-mail jon.wolman@detnews.com; internet detnews.com; f. 1873; subsidiary co of MediaNews Group; Publr and Editor JONATHAN WOLMAN; Man. Editor DONALD W. NAUSS; circ. Mon. to Fri. 149,872, Sat. 134,983.

Flint Journal: 200 East First St, Flint, MI 48502-1925; tel. (810) 766-6100; fax (810) 767-7518; e-mail fj@flintjournal.com; internet www.flintjournal.com; f. 1876; Thur., Fri. and Sun. morning; Publr MATTHEW SHARP; Editor MARJORY RAYMER; circ. Thur. 60,075, Fri. 59,222, Sun. 74,375.

Grand Rapids Press: 155 Michigan St, NW, Grand Rapids, MI 49503-2302; tel. (616) 222-5818; e-mail dgaydou@grpress.com; internet www.mlive.com/grpress; f. 1890; Publr DAN GAYDOU; Editor PAUL M. KEEP; circ. Mon. to Fri. 99,642, Sat. 116,943, Sun. 158,355.

Kalamazoo Gazette: 401 South Burdick St, Kalamazoo, MI 49007; tel. (269) 345-3511; fax (269) 345-0583; e-mail jstephanak@kalamazoogazette.com; internet www.mlive.com/kgazette; f. 1883; Mon. to Fri. evening, Sat. and Sun. morning; Publr JAMES STEPHANAK; Editor REBECCA PIERCE; circ. Mon. to Fri. 45,940, Sat. 53,752, Sun. 62,044.

Lansing State Journal: 120 East Lenawee St, Lansing, MI 48919-0001; tel. (517) 377-1000; fax (517) 377-1298; e-mail publisher@lsj.com; internet www.lansingstatejournal.com; f. 1855; Pres. and Publr BRIAN PRIESTER; Exec. Editor MICHAEL HIRTEN; circ. Mon. to Fri. 44,888, Sat. 48,865, Sun. 68,344.

Oakland Press: 48 West Huron St, Pontiac, MI 48342; tel. (248) 332-8181; fax (248) 253-9986; e-mail glenn.gilbert@oakpress.com; internet www.theoaklandpress.com; f. 1843; Publr and Pres. KEVIN HAEZEBROECK; Exec. Editor GLENN GILBERT; circ. Mon. to Fri. 68,770, Sat. 67,786, Sun. 79,556.

Saginaw News: 100 South Michigan Ave, Saginaw, MI 48602; tel. (989) 776-9764; e-mail thenews@thesaginawnews.com; internet www.mlive.com/saginawnews; f. 1859; Thur., Fri. and Sun. morning; Publr MATTHEW SHARP; Exec. Editor JOHN P. HINER; circ. Thur. 27,581, Fri. 27,866, Sun. 39,156.

Minnesota

Duluth News Tribune: 424 West First St, Duluth, MN 55802; tel. (218) 723-5281; fax (218) 720-4120; e-mail news@duluthnews.com; internet www.duluthnewstribune.com; f. 1869; morning; Publr KEN BROWALL; Editor ROBIN WASHINGTON; circ. Mon. to Fri. 40,305, Sat. 40,082, Sun. 62,468 (2007).

Star Tribune: 425 Portland Ave South, Minneapolis, MN 55488; tel. (612) 673-4000; fax (612) 673-4359; internet www.startribune.com; f. 1920; filed for bankruptcy protection in 2009; Publr MIKE KLINGENSMITH; Editor and Sr Vice-Pres. NANCY BARNES; circ. Mon. to Fri. 295,438, Sat. 266,101, Sun. 493,027.

St Paul Pioneer Press: 345 Cedar St, St Paul, MN 55101; tel. (651) 222-1111; fax (651) 228-5500; e-mail bjohnson@pioneerpress.com; internet www.twincities.com; f. 1849; Publr GUY L. GILMORE; Vice-Pres. and Editor THOM FLADUNG; circ. Mon. to Fri. 193,054, Sat. 163,808, Sun. 254,010.

Mississippi

Clarion-Ledger: 201 South Congress St, Jackson, MS 39201; tel. (601) 961-7000; fax (601) 961-7211; e-mail publisher@clarionledger.com; internet www.clarionledger.com; f. 1954; Publr and Pres. LARRY WHITAKER; Exec. Editor RONNIE AGNEW; circ. Mon. to Fri. 65,300, Sat. 65,582, Sun. 78,192.

Missouri

Kansas City Star: 1729 Grand Blvd, Kansas City, MO 64108; tel. (816) 234-4741; fax (816) 234-4467; e-mail mfannin@kcstar.com; internet www.kansascity.com; f. 1880; Publr MARK ZIEMAN; Editor MIKE FANNIN; circ. Mon. to Fri. 216,446, Sat. 233,090, Sun. 314,449.

News-Leader: 651 Boonville Ave, Springfield, MO 65806; tel. (417) 836-1100; fax (417) 837-1381; e-mail rbates@news-leader.com; internet www.news-leader.com; f. 1933; morning; Publr LINDA RAMEY-GREIWE; Exec. Editor DAVID STOEFFLER; circ. Mon. to Sat. 43,277, Sun. 69,526.

St Louis Post-Dispatch: 900 North Tucker Blvd, St Louis, MO 63101; tel. (314) 657-3300; fax (314) 340-3050; e-mail generalmanager@stltoday.com; internet www.stltoday.com; f. 1878; Pres. and Publr KEVIN MOWBRAY; Editor ARNIE ROBBINS; circ. Mon. to Fri. 209,839, Sat. 215,718, Sun. 400,042.

Montana

Billings Gazette: POB 36300, Billings, MT 59107; tel. (406) 657-1200; fax (406) 657-1208; e-mail mgulledge@billingsgazette.com; internet billingsgazette.net; f. 1885; Publr MIKE GULLEDGE; Editor STEVE PROSINSKI; circ. Mon. to Sat. 40,518, Sun. 46,929.

Nebraska

Lincoln Journal Star: Journal Star Printing Co, 926 P St, POB 81609, Lincoln, NE 68508; tel. (402) 475-4200; fax (402) 473-7291; e-mail jmaher@journalstar.com; internet journalstar.com; f. 1867; morning; Publr JOHN F. MAHER; Editor MICHAEL NELSON; circ. Mon. to Fri. 74,208, Sat. 64,247, Sun. 76,646.

Omaha World-Herald: 1334 Douglas St, Omaha, NE 68102-1122; tel. (402) 444-1000; fax (402) 345-0183; e-mail mike.reilly@owh.com; internet www.omaha.com; f. 1885; CEO and Publr TERRY KROEGER; Exec. Editor MIKE REILLY; circ. Mon. to Fri. 152,522, Sat. 143,034, Sun. 184,923.

Nevada

Las Vegas Review-Journal: 1111 West Bonanza Rd, POB 70, Las Vegas, NV 89125; tel. (702) 383-0211; fax (702) 383-4676; e-mail afleming@reviewjournal.com; internet www.lvrj.com; f. 1908; Publr SHERMAN R. FREDERICK; Editor THOMAS MITCHELL; circ. Mon. to Fri. 174,876, Sat. 171,489, Sun. 197,312.

Reno Gazette-Journal: POB 22000, Reno, NV 89520-2000; tel. (775) 788-6200; fax (775) 788-6458; e-mail rgjfeedback@rgj.com; internet www.rgj.com; f. 1870; Publr TED POWER; Exec. Editor BERYL LOVE; circ. Mon. to Fri. 45,533, Sat. 43,422, Sun. 54,009.

New Hampshire

New Hampshire Union Leader, New Hampshire Sunday News: Union Leader Corpn, 100 William Loeb Dr., POB 9555, Manchester, NH 03108-9555; tel. (603) 668-4321; fax (603) 668-0382; e-mail publisher@unionleader.com; internet www.unionleader.com; f. 1863 (New Hampshire Union Leader); f. 1946 (New Hampshire Sunday News); Pres. and Publr JOSEPH W. MCQUAID; Editorial Vice-Pres. CHARLES PERKINS, III; circ. Mon. to Fri. 49,357, Sat. 29,482, Sun. 64,702.

New Jersey

Asbury Park Press: 3601 Hwy 66, POB 1550, Neptune, NJ 07754-1550; tel. (732) 922-6000; fax (732) 918-4818; e-mail lmarsh@app.com; internet www.app.com; f. 1879; Publr and Pres. THOMAS M. DONOVAN; Exec. Editor HOLLIS R. TOWNS; circ. Mon. to Fri. 114,655, Sat. 118,242, Sun. 161,079.

Courier-News: 92 East Main St, Suite 202, Somerville, NJ 08876-2319; internet www.mycentraljersey.com; f. 1884; Publr and Pres. WILLIAM C. HIDLAY; Man. Editor PAUL GRZELLA; circ. Mon. to Sat. 19,481, Sun. 23,103.

Courier-Post: 301 Cuthbert Blvd, POB 5300, Cherry Hill, NJ 08034; tel. (856) 663-6000; fax (856) 663-2831; e-mail thearon@courierpostonline.com; internet www.courierpostonline.com; f. 1875; Pres. and Publr TIM DOWD; Exec. Editor EUGENE E. WILLIAMS; circ. Mon. to Fri. 51,889, Sat. 59,311, Sun. 67,485.

Home News Tribune: 35 Kennedy Blvd, East Brunswick, NJ 08816; tel. (732) 246-5500; fax (732) 565-7208; e-mail hntmetro@thnt.com; internet www.mycentraljersey.com; f. 1879; Publr and Pres. WILLIAM C. HIDLAY; Exec. Editor PAUL GRZELLA; circ. Mon. to Sat. 36,480, Sun. 44,002.

Jersey Journal: 30 Journal Sq., Jersey City, NJ 07306; tel. (201) 653-1000; fax (201) 217-2455; e-mail jjletters@jjournal.com; internet www.jjournal.com; f. 1867; Publr KENDRICK ROSS; Editor JUDITH A. LOCORRIERE; circ. Mon. to Fri. 22,020, Sat. 23,312.

THE UNITED STATES OF AMERICA

The Record: 150 River St, Hackensack, NJ 07601-7172; tel. (201) 569-7100; fax (201) 457-2520; e-mail scandale@northjersey.com; internet www.northjersey.com; f. 1895; Publr STEPHEN A. BORG; Editor and Vice-Pres. FRANK SCANDALE; circ. Mon. to Fri. 158,105, Sat. 156,930, Sun. 178,584.

Star-Ledger: 1 Star-Ledger Plaza, Newark, NJ 07102-1200; tel. (973) 392-4040; e-mail jdennan@starledger.com; internet www.nj.com/starledger; f. 1917; Publr RICHARD VEZZA; Editor KEVIN WHITMER; circ. Mon. to Fri. 236,017, Sat. 194,552, Sun. 359,865.

The Times: 500 Perry St, POB 847, Trenton, NJ 08605; tel. (609) 989-5454; fax (609) 394-2819; e-mail bmalone@njtimes.com; internet www.nj.com/times; f. 1882; Publr BRIAN S. MALONE; Man. Editor KRISTIN J. BUCCI; circ. Mon. to Fri. 38,629, Sat. 38,119, Sun. 43,528.

Trentonian: 600 Perry St, Trenton, NJ 08618; tel. (609) 989-7800; fax (609) 393-6072; e-mail editor@trentonian.com; internet www.trentonian.com; f. 1946; Publr WILLIAM T. (BILL) MURRAY; Editor AARON NOBEL; circ. Mon. to Fri. 33,315, Sat. 28,232, Sun. 22,547.

New Mexico

Albuquerque Journal: Albuquerque Publishing Co, 7777 Jefferson St NE, Albuquerque, NM 87109; tel. (505) 823-3800; e-mail jangel@abqjournal.com; internet www.abqjournal.com; f. 1880; Publr T. H. LANG; Editor KENT WALZ; circ. Mon. to Fri. 95,469, Sat. 100,272, Sun. 123,387.

New York

Albany Times Union: Times Union, News Plaza, POB 15000, Albany, NY 12212; tel. (518) 454-5694; fax (518) 454-5628; e-mail jcrupi@timesunion.com; internet www.timesunion.com; f. 1856; Publr GEORGE HEARST, III; Exec. Editor REX SMITH; circ. Mon. to Fri. 74,895, Sat. 64,326, Sun. 141,210.

Buffalo News: 1 News Plaza, POB 100, Buffalo, NY 14240; tel. (716) 849-4444; fax (716) 856-5150; internet www.buffalonews.com; f. 1880; Publr STANFORD LIPSEY; Editor MARGARET M. SULLIVAN; circ. Mon. to Fri. 162,213, Sat. 163,179, Sun. 244,264.

Daily Gazette: 2345 Maxon Rd Ext., Schenectady, NY 12308; POB 1090, Schenectady, NY 12301-1090; tel. (518) 374-4141; fax (518) 395-3089; e-mail gazette@dailygazette.com; internet www.dailygazette.com; f. 1894; Publr and Editor JOHN E. N. HUME, III; Man. Editor JUDITH PATRICK; circ. Mon. to Fri. 55,318, Sat. 54,793, Sun. 54,793.

Democrat and Chronicle: 55 Exchange Blvd, Rochester, NY 14614-2001; tel. (585) 232-7100; fax (585) 258-3027; e-mail editor@democratandchronicle.com; internet www.democratandchronicle.com; f. 1833; Pres. and Publr ALI M. ZOIBI; Editor KAREN MAGNUSON; circ. Mon. to Fri. 122,588, Sat. 138,344, Sun. 179,992.

Newsday: 235 Pinelawn Rd, Melville, NY 11747; tel. (631) 843-2700; fax (516) 843-2953; e-mail editor@newsday.com; internet www.newsday.com; f. 1940; Publr FRED GROSER; Editor DEBBIE KRENEK; circ. Mon. to Fri. 334,809, Sat. 305,897, Sun. 394,909.

Post-Standard: Clinton Sq., POB 4915, Syracuse, NY 13221-4915; tel. (315) 470-0011; fax (315) 470-3081; e-mail mconnor@syracuse.com; internet post-standard.com; f. 1829; Editor and Publr STEPHEN A. ROGERS; Exec. Editor MICHAEL J. CONNOR; circ. Mon. to Fri. 89,819, Sat. 88,719, Sun. 142,627.

Press & Sun-Bulletin: 33 Lewis Rd, Binghamton, NY 13905-1044; tel. (607) 798-1234; fax (607) 798-1113; internet www.pressconnects.com; f. 1985; Publr SHERMAN M. BODNER; Exec. Editor CALVIN STOVALL; circ. Mon. to Fri. 38,682, Sat. 39,263, Sun. 54,914.

Times Herald-Record ('The Record'): 40 Mulberry St, POB 2046, Middletown, NY 10940; tel. (914) 341-1100; fax (914) 343-2170; e-mail dosenenko@th-record.com; internet www.recordonline.com; f. 1956; Publr JOE VANDERHOOF; Exec. Editor DEREK OSENENKO; circ. Mon. to Fri. 61,182, Sat. 60,904, Sun. 72,898.

New York City

New York Daily News: 450 West 33rd St, New York, NY 10001; tel. (212) 210-2100; fax (212) 682-4953; internet www.nydailynews.com; f. 1919; Publr MORTIMER B. ZUCKERMAN; Editor-in-Chief KEVIN CONVEY; circ. Mon. to Fri. 535,059, Sat. 416,007, Sun. 600,118.

New York Post: 1211 Ave of the Americas, New York, NY 10036-8790; tel. (212) 930-8000; fax (212) 930-8540; e-mail aaquilina@nypost.com; internet www.nypost.com; f. 1801; Publr PAUL V. CARLUCCI; Editor-in-Chief COL ALLAN; circ. Mon. to Fri. 525,004, Sat. 358,446, Sun. 333,958.

New York Times: 620 Eighth Ave, New York, NY 10018; tel. (212) 556-1234; e-mail public@nytimes.com; internet www.nytimes.com; f. 1851; Chair. and Publr ARTHUR OCHS SULZBERGER, Jr; Pres. and Gen. Man. SCOTT H. HEEKIN-CANEDY; Exec. Editor BILL KELLER; circ. Mon. to Fri. 951,063, Sat. 928,741, Sun. 1,376,230.

Staten Island Advance: 950 Fingerboard Rd, Staten Island, New York, NY 10305; tel. (718) 981-1234; fax (718) 981-5679; e-mail silverstein@siadvance.com; internet www.statenislandadvance.com; f. 1886; Mon. to Sat. evening, Sun. morning; Publr CAROLINE DIAMOND HARRISON; Editor BRIAN J. LALINE; circ. Mon. to Fri. 43,165, Sat. 42,022, Sun. 55,759.

The Wall Street Journal: 200 Liberty St, New York, NY 10281; tel. (212) 416-2000; e-mail wsj.ltrs@wsj.com; internet www.wsj.com; f. 1889; publ. by Dow Jones & Co Inc; morning; Chair. M. PETER MCPHERSON; CEO LES HINTON; Exec. Editor ALAN MURRAY; circ. Mon. to Fri. 2,092,523, Sat. and Sun. 1,913,284.

North Carolina

Charlotte Observer: 600 South Tryon St, POB 32188-28232, Charlotte, NC 28202-1842; tel. (704) 358-5000; fax (704) 358-5036; e-mail charlottefeedback@charlotteobserver.com; internet www.charlotteobserver.com; f. 1886; Publr and Pres. ANN CAULKINS; Editor RICK THAMES; circ. Mon. to Fri. 166,546, Sat. 193,258, Sun. 226,030.

Citizen-Times: 14 Ohenry Ave, POB 2090, Asheville, NC 28802; tel. (828) 252-5610; fax (828) 251-0585; e-mail pfernandez@citizen-times.com; internet www.citizen-times.com; f. 1870; morning; Publr and Pres. RANDY HAMMER; Exec. Editor PHIL FERNANDEZ; circ. Mon. to Fri. 35,823, Sat. 36,639, Sun. 51,425.

Fayetteville Observer: Fayetteville Publishing Co, 458 Whitfield St, POB 849, Fayetteville, NC 28302; tel. (910) 323-4848; fax (919) 486-3531; e-mail cbwell@fayobserver.com; internet www.fayobserver.com; f. 1816; morning; Publr CHARLES BROADWELL; Exec. Editor MIKE ARNHOLT; circ. Mon. to Fri. 55,412, Sat. 53,950, Sun. 58,080.

Greensboro News and Record: 200 East Market St, POB 20848, Greensboro, NC 27420-0848; tel. (336) 373-7000; fax (336) 373-7067; e-mail jrobinson@news-record.com; internet www.news-record.com; f. 1905; Publr and Pres. ROBIN SAUL; Exec. Editor JOHN ROBINSON; circ. Mon. to Fri. 67,625, Sat. 66,458, Sun. 89,275.

News and Observer: 215 South McDowell St, POB 191, Raleigh, NC 27602; tel. (919) 829-4500; fax (919) 829-4872; internet www.newsobserver.com; f. 1872; Publr ORAGE QUARLES, III; Exec. Editor JOHN DRESCHER; circ. Mon. to Fri. 137,804, Sat. 141,732, Sun. 188,030.

Winston-Salem Journal: 418 North Marshall St, POB 3159, Winston-Salem, NC 27102-3159; tel. (336) 727-7211; fax (336) 727-4071; e-mail mhall@journalnow.com; internet www.journalnow.com; Publr and Pres. JEFFREY GREEN; circ. Mon. to Fri. 64,750, Sat. 68,297, Sun. 80,892.

North Dakota

The Forum: 101 Fifth St North, Fargo, ND 58102; tel. (701) 235-7311; fax (701) 241-5406; e-mail support@inforum.com; internet www.inforum.com; f. 1878; Publr BILL M. MARCIL, Jr; Editor MATT VON PINNON; circ. Mon. to Fri. 49,897, Sat. 48,802, Sun. 53,052.

Ohio

Akron Beacon Journal: 44 East Exchange St, POB 640, Akron, OH 44308; tel. (330) 996-3000; fax (330) 996-3033; internet www.ohio.com; f. 1839; Publr ANDREA MATHEWSON; Editor BRUCE WINGES; circ. Mon. to Fri. 102,981, Sat. 119,224, Sun. 134,030.

Canton Repository: 500 Market Ave South, Canton, OH 44711-2112; tel. (330) 580-8300; fax (330) 454-5610; e-mail don.detore@cantonrep.com; internet www.cantonrep.com; f. 1815; Publr KEVIN M. KAMPMAN; Exec. Editor JEFF GAUGER; circ. Mon. to Fri. 61,036, Sat. 59,341, Sun. 71,935.

Cincinnati Enquirer: 312 Elm St, Cincinnati, OH 45202; tel. (513) 768-8000; fax (513) 768-8340; e-mail tcallinan@enquirer.com; internet news.cincinnati.com; f. 1841; Publr and Pres. MARGARET E. BUCHANAN; Editor TOM CALLINAN; circ. Mon. to Fri. 172,536, Sat. 165,873, Sun. 261,678.

Cleveland Plain Dealer: 1801 Superior Ave East, Cleveland, OH 44114-2198; tel. (216) 999-4800; fax (216) 999-6354; e-mail dasimmon@plaind.com; internet www.plaindealer.com; f. 1842; Pres. and Publr TERRANCE C. Z. EGGER; Editor SUSAN GOLDBERG; circ. Mon. to Fri. 267,888, Sat. 255,665, Sun. 362,394.

Columbus Dispatch: 34 South Third St, Columbus, OH 43215; tel. (614) 461-5000; fax (614) 461-7580; e-mail letters@dispatch.com; internet www.dispatch.com; f. 1871; Pres. MICHAEL FIORILE; Editor BEN MARRISON; circ. Mon. to Fri. 170,179, Sat. 218,026, Sun. 297,842.

Dayton Daily News: 1611 South Main St, Dayton, OH 45409; tel. (937) 222-5700; fax (937) 225-2489; e-mail kriley@coxohio.com; internet www.daytondailynews.com; Publr MICHAEL JOSEPH; Editor KEVIN RILEY; circ. Mon. to Fri. 102,357, Sat. 91,981, Sun. 141,808.

News-Herald: 7085 Mentor Ave, Willoughby, OH 44094; tel. (440) 951-0000; fax (440) 951-0917; e-mail lkessel@news-herald.com; internet www.news-herald.com; f. 1880; Mon. to Sat. evening,

THE UNITED STATES OF AMERICA

Sun. morning; Publr JEFF SUDBROOK; Exec. Editor TRICIA AMBROSE; circ. Mon. to Sat. 33,408, Sun. 39,912.

Toledo Blade: 541 North Superior St, Toledo, OH 43660; tel. (419) 724-6000; fax (419) 245-6191; e-mail luannsharp@theblade.com; internet www.toledoblade.com; f. 1835; Publr and Editor-in-Chief JOSEPH ZERBEY; Exec. Editor KURT FRANCK; circ. Mon. to Fri. 117,704, Sat. 117,837, Sun. 144,394.

The Vindicator: 107 Vindicator Sq., POB 780, Youngstown, OH 44501-0780; tel. (330) 747-1471; fax (330) 747-6712; e-mail bjagnow@vindy.com; internet www.vindy.com; Publr BETTY H. BROWN JAGNOW; Editor TODD FRANKO; circ. Mon. to Fri. 49,157, Sat. 55,288, Sun. 64,656.

Oklahoma

Daily Oklahoman: 9000 North Broadway, POB 25125, Oklahoma City, OK 73125; tel. (405) 475-3311; fax (405) 475-3183; internet www.newsok.com; f. 1894; Publr DAVID THOMPSON; Editor ED KELLEY; circ. Mon. to Fri. 151,264, Sat. 128,650, Sun. 207,081.

Tulsa World: 315 South Boulder Ave, POB 1770, Tulsa, OK 74103; tel. (918) 581-8300; fax (918) 581-8353; e-mail letters@tulsaworld.com; internet www.tulsaworld.com; f. 1906; Publr ROBERT E. LORTON, III; Exec. Editor JOE WORLEY; circ. Mon. to Fri. 101,508, Sat. 108,474, Sun. 140,971.

Oregon

The Oregonian: 1320 SW Broadway, Portland, OR 97201-3469; tel. (503) 221-8150; fax (503) 294-4193; e-mail s.rowe@news.oregonian.com; internet www.oregonian.com; f. 1850; Publr N. CHRISTIAN ANDERSON, III; Editor PETER BHATIA; circ. Mon. to Fri. 263,600, Sat. 265,330, Sun. 315,515.

The Register-Guard: 3500 Chad Dr., POB 10188, Eugene, OR 97440-2188; tel. (541) 485-1234; fax (541) 683-7631; e-mail tbaker@guardnet.com; internet www.registerguard.com; f. 1867; Publr and Editor TONY BAKER; circ. Mon. to Fri. 60,579, Sat. 63,851, Sun. 63,241.

Statesman Journal: 280 Church St, NE, POB 13009, Salem, OR 97309-3009; tel. (503) 399-6611; fax (503) 399-6706; e-mail bichurch@statesmanjournal.com; internet www.statesmanjournal.com; f. 1851; Publr and Pres. STEVE SILBERMAN; Exec. Editor BILL CHURCH; circ. Mon. to Fri. 39,075, Sat. 39,284, Sun. 46,776.

Pennsylvania

Bucks County Courier Times: 8400 Route 13, Levittown, PA 19057-5198; tel. (215) 949-4000; fax (215) 949-4177; e-mail pwalker@phillyburbs.com; internet www.phillyburbs.com; f. 1910; owned by Calkins Media Inc; Publr DALE LARSON; Exec. Editor PATRICIA S. WALKER; circ. Mon. to Fri. 48,958, Sun. 53,150.

Call Chronicle: POB 1260, Allentown, PA 18105; tel. (610) 820-6500; fax (610) 820-6693; f. 1921; Sun.; Publr GARY K. SHORTS; Exec. Editor LAWRENCE H. HYMANS; circ. 189,000.

The Morning Call: 101 North Sixth St, POB 1260, Allentown, PA 18105; tel. (610) 820-6553; fax (610) 820-6693; e-mail marie.herb@mcall.com; internet www.mcall.com; Publr and Pres. TIMOTHY E. RYAN; Editor and Vice-Pres. DAVID ERDMAN; circ. Mon. to Fri. 103,845, Sat. 88,169, Sun. 123,164.

Patriot-News: 812 Market St, Harrisburg, PA 17105; tel. (717) 255-8100; fax (717) 255-8456; internet www.patriot-news.com; f. 1854; Publr JOHN A. KIRKPATRICK; Exec. Editor DAVID NEWHOUSE; circ. Mon. to Fri.77,598, Sat. 72,768, Sun. 119,885.

Philadelphia Daily News: 400 North Broad St, POB 7788, Philadelphia, PA 19130; tel. (215) 854-5900; fax (215) 854-5910; e-mail dailynews.opinion@phillynews.com; internet www.philly.com; f. 1925; filed for Chapter 11 bankruptcy protection in Feb. 2009; bought by Philadelphia Media Networks in Sept. 2010; Publr GREGORY J. OSBERG; Man. Editor MICHAEL DAYS; circ. Mon. to Fri. 99,103, Sat. 63,092.

Philadelphia Inquirer: 400 North Broad St, POB 8263, Philadelphia, PA 19101; tel. (215) 854-2000; fax (215) 854-4974; e-mail mleary@phillynews.com; internet www.philly.com/inquirer; f. 1829; filed for Chapter 11 bankruptcy protection in Feb. 2009; bought by Philadelphia Media Networks in Sept. 2010; Publr GREGORY J. OSBERG; Acting Editor STAN WISCHNOWSKI; circ. Mon. to Fri. 356,189, Sat. 313,524, Sun. 517,807.

Pittsburgh Post-Gazette: 34 Blvd of the Allies, Pittsburgh, PA 15222; tel. (412) 263-1100; fax (412) 391-8452; e-mail ssmith@post-gazette.com; internet www.post-gazette.com; f. 1786; Chair., Publr and Editor-in-Chief JOHN ROBINSON BLOCK; Exec. Editor DAVID M. SHRIBMAN, Jr; circ. Mon. to Fri. 192,279, Sat. 173,947, Sun. 300,727.

Sunday News: Lancaster Newspapers, Inc, 8 West King St, POB 1328, Lancaster, PA 17608; tel. (717) 291-8811; fax (717) 399-6506; e-mail sunnews@lnpnews.com; internet www.lancasteronline.com/lol_pages/paper/sundaynews; f. 1923; Editor MARV ADAMS; circ. 97,538.

Tribune-Democrat: 425 Locust St, POB 340, Johnstown, PA 15907-0340; tel. (814) 532-5050; fax (814) 539-1409; e-mail cminemyer@tribdem.com; internet www.tribune-democrat.com; f. 1853; morning; Publr ROBIN QUILLON; Editor CHIP MINEMYER; circ. Mon. to Fri. 34,111, Sat. 33,800, Sun. 37,459.

Rhode Island

Providence Journal: 75 Fountain St, Providence, RI 02902-0050; tel. (401) 277-7000; fax (401) 277-7346; e-mail sareson@projo.com; internet www.projo.com; f. 1829; publ. by Belo Corpn; Publr HOWARD G. SUTTON; Exec. Editor THOMAS E. HESLIN; circ. Mon. to Fri. 99,573, Sat. 127,025, Sun. 141,688.

South Carolina

Greenville News: 305 South Main St, POB 1688, Greenville, SC 29602; tel. (864) 298-4100; fax (864) 298-4805; e-mail letters@greenvillenews.com; internet www.greenvilleonline.com; f. 1874; Publr STEVEN BRANDT; Pres. and Exec. Editor JOHN S. PITTMAN; circ. Mon. to Fri. 61,077, Sat. 63,324, Sun. 103,298.

The Post and Courier: 134 Columbus St, Charleston, SC 29403-4800; tel. (843) 577-7111; fax (843) 937-5579; e-mail mullins@postandcourier.com; internet www.charleston.net; f. 1803; Publr and Editor WILLAM E. HAWKINS; Man. Editor STEPHEN S. MULLINS; circ. Mon. to Fri. 88,939, Sat. 81,011, Sun. 95,289.

The State: 1401 Shop Rd, POB 1333, Columbia, SC 29202; tel. (803) 771-8380; fax (803) 771-8430; e-mail stateeditor@thestate.com; internet www.thestate.com; f. 1891; acquired by the McClatchy Co in 2006; Publr HENRY HAITZ, III; Exec. Editor MARK LETT; circ. Mon. to Fri. 83,392, Sat. 82,993, Sun. 105,872.

South Dakota

Argus Leader: 200 South Minnesota Ave, Sioux Falls, SD 57104; tel. (605) 331-2200; fax (605) 331-2294; e-mail jzimmerm@argusleader.com; internet www.argusleader.com; f. 1881; Publr RANDELL BECK; Exec. Editor MARICARROL KUETER; circ. Mon. to Sat. 35,970, Sun. 55,575.

Tennessee

Chattanooga Times-Free Press: 400 East 11th St, Chattanooga, TN 37403; tel. (423) 756-6900; fax (423) 757-6383; e-mail tgriscom@timesfreepress.com; internet www.timesfreepress.com; f. 1888; Pres. JASON TAYLOF; Exec. Editor J.TODD FOSTER; circ. Mon. to Fri. 76,526, Sat. 80,446, Sun. 97,729.

The Commercial Appeal: 495 Union Ave, Memphis, TN 38103; tel. (901) 529-2345; fax (901) 529-2522; internet www.commercialappeal.com; f. 1841; Pres. and Publr JOSEPH PEPE; Editor CHRIS PECK; circ. Mon. to Fri. 148,763, Sat. 102,560, Sun. 182,854.

Knoxville News-Sentinel: 2332 News Sentinel Dr., Knoxville, TN 37921-5731; tel. (865) 521-8181; fax (865) 342-8650; internet www.knoxnews.com; f. 1886; Publr PATRICK J. BIRMINGHAM; Editor JACK MCELROY; circ. Mon. to Fri. 100,441, Sat. 103,085, Sun. 126,527.

The Tennessean: 1100 Broadway St, Nashville, TN 37203; tel. (615) 259-8000; fax (615) 259-8093; e-mail eleifield@tennessean.com; internet www.tennessean.com; f. 1812; Publr CAROL HUDLER; Editor MARK SILVERMAN; circ. Mon. to Fri. 133,997, Sat. 140,763, Sun. 205,411.

Texas

Austin American-Statesman: 305 South Congress Ave, Austin, TX 78704; POB 670, Austin, TX 78767; tel. (512) 445-3500; fax (512) 445-3679; internet www.statesman.com; f. 1871; Publr MICHAEL VIVIO; Editor FRED ZIPP; circ. Mon. to Fri. 143,760, Sat. 138,450, Sun. 168,822.

Beaumont Enterprise: 380 Main St, POB 3071, Beaumont, TX 77701-2331; tel. (409) 833-3311; fax (409) 838-2857; e-mail tkelly@hearstnp.com; internet www.beaumontenterprise.com; f. 1880; Publr BILL OFFILL, II; Editor TIMOTHY M. KELLY; circ. Mon. to Sat. 28,939, Sun. 33,082.

Corpus Christi Caller-Times: 820 North Lower Broadway, POB 9136, Corpus Christi, TX 78469; tel. (361) 884-2011; fax (361) 886-3732; e-mail webmaster@caller.com; internet www.caller.com; f. 1883; Pres. and Publr DARRELL COLEMAN; Vice-Pres. and Editor SHANE FITZGERALD; circ. Mon. to Fri. 49,327, Sat. 47,618, Sun. 62,966.

Dallas Morning News: 508 Young St, Dallas, TX 75202; tel. (214) 977-8222; fax (214) 977-8319; e-mail bmong@dallasnews.com; internet www.dallasnews.com; f. 1885; publ. by Belo Corpn; Publr JAMES M. MORONEY, III; Editor ROBERT W. MONG, Jr; circ. Mon. to Fri. 260,659, Sat. 241,650, Sun. 373,031.

El Paso Times: Times Plaza, El Paso, TX 79901-1470; tel. (915) 546-6119; fax (915) 546-6415; e-mail cvlopez@elpasotimes.com; internet

THE UNITED STATES OF AMERICA

www.elpasotimes.com; f. 1881; Publr Sergio Salinas; Editor Chris V. Lopez; circ. Mon. to Fri. 72,251, Sat. 60,855, Sun. 84,001.

Fort Worth Star-Telegram: 400 West Seventh St, Fort Worth, TX 76102; tel. (817) 390-7761; fax (817) 390-7789; e-mail lnorder@star-telegram.com; internet www.star-telegram.com; f. 1909; Publr Gary Wortel; Exec. Editor Jim Witt; circ. Mon. to Fri. 165,252, Sat. 195,335, Sun. 249,676.

Houston Chronicle: 801 Texas Ave, Houston, TX 77002; POB 4260, Houston, TX 77210-4260; tel. (713) 362-7171; fax (713) 362-3575; e-mail online@chron.com; internet www.chron.com; f. 1901; Publr Jack Sweeney; Editor Jeff Cohen; circ. Mon. to Fri. 366,578, Sat. 344,216, Sun. 526,440.

Lubbock Avalanche-Journal: 710 Ave J, POB 491, Lubbock, TX 79401-1808; tel. (806) 762-8844; fax (806) 744-9603; e-mail terry.greenberg@lubbockonline.com; internet www.lubbockonline.com; f. 1900; Publr Stephen A. Beasley; Editor Terry Greenberg; circ. Mon. to Fri. 41,062, Sat. 41,974, Sun. 50,033.

San Antonio Express-News: 301 Ave E, San Antonio, TX 78205; tel. (210) 250-3000; fax (210) 250-3105; e-mail rrivard@express-news.net; internet www.mysanantonio.com; f. 1864; Publr Thomas A. Stephenson; Editor Robert Rivard; circ. Mon. to Fri. 146,230, Sat. 162,684, Sun. 258,309.

Utah

Deseret News: 30 East 100 South, POB 1257, Salt Lake City, UT 84110; tel. (801) 236-6000; fax (801) 237-2121; e-mail rhall@desnews.com; internet www.deseretnews.com; f. 1850; Pres. and CEO Clark Gilbert; Man. Editor Richard D Hall; circ. Mon. to Fri. 71,821, Sat. 70,173, Sun. 79,363.

Salt Lake Tribune: 90 South 400 West, Suite 700, Salt Lake City, UT 84101; tel. (801) 237-8742; fax (801) 257-8525; e-mail fitz@sltrib.com; internet www.sltrib.com; f. 1871; publ. by MediaNews Group; Publr Dean Singleton; Editor Nancy Conway; circ. Mon. to Fri. 113,474, Sat. 102,734, Sun. 129,898.

Standard-Examiner: 332 Standard Way, POB 12790, Ogden, UT 84412-2790; tel. (801) 625-4200; fax (801) 625-4508; e-mail ahowell@standard.net; internet www.standard.net; f. 1888; Publr Lee Carter; Exec. Editor Andy Howell; circ. Mon. to Fri. 60,164, Sat. 60,164, Sun. 66,006.

Vermont

Burlington Free Press: 191 College St, POB 10, Burlington, VT 05402-0010; tel. (802) 660-1897; fax (802) 660-1802; e-mail bhart@bfp.burlingtonfreepress.com; internet www.burlingtonfreepress.com; f. 1827; Publr James Fogler; Exec. Editor Michael Townsend; circ. Mon. to Sat. 32,993, Sun. 42,216.

Virginia

Daily Press: 7505 Warwick Blvd, Newport News, VA 23607; tel. (757) 247-4600; fax (757) 245-8618; e-mail egates@dailypress.com; internet www.dailypress.com; f. 1896; Publr Digby A. Solomon; Editor Ernest C. Gates; circ. Mon. to Fri. 64,479, Sat. 72,915, Sun. 90,914.

Richmond Times-Dispatch: 300 East Franklin St, POB 85333, Richmond, VA 23219; tel. (804) 649-6990; fax (804) 819-1216; e-mail letters@timesdispatch.com; internet www2.timesdispatch.com; f. 1850; Publr Thomas A. Silvestri; Exec. Editor Glenn Proctor; circ. Mon. to Fri. 125,011, Sat. 138,338, Sun. 171,510.

Roanoke Times: 201 West Campbell Ave, POB 2491, Roanoke, VA 24010-2491; tel. (540) 981-3211; fax (540) 981-3346; e-mail debbie.meade@roanoke.com; internet www.roanoke.com; Publr Debbie Meade; Editor Carole Tarrant; circ. Mon. to Fri. 78,622, Sat. 77,745, Sun. 91,186.

USA Today: 7950 Jones Branch Dr., McLean, VA 22108-0605; tel. (703) 276-3400; internet www.usatoday.com; f. 1982; Pres. and Publr David Hunke; Editor John Hillkirk; circ. Mon. to Fri. 2,113,725 (2009).

Virginian-Pilot: 150 West Brambleton Ave, POB 449, Norfolk, VA 23501-0449; tel. (757) 446-2000; fax (757) 446-2051; e-mail contactvp@pilotonline.com; internet thevirginianpilot.com; f. 1876; Publr and Pres. Maurice A. Jones; Man. Editor Maria Carillo; circ. Mon. to Fri. 160,609, Sat. 156,322, Sun. 179,986.

Washington

The Herald: 1213 California St, Everett, WA 98201; POB 930, Everett, WA 98206; tel. (425) 339-3435; fax (425) 339-3049; e-mail funk@herald.net; internet www.heraldnet.com; f. 1891; Publr Allen B. Funk; Exec. Editor Neal Pattison; circ. Mon. to Fri. 48,726, Sat. 43,635, Sun. 50,586.

News Tribune: 1950 South State St, POB 11000, Tacoma, WA 98411; tel. (253) 597-8742; fax (253) 597-8451; e-mail karen.peterson@thenewstribune.com; internet www.thenewstribune.com; f. 1883; Pres. and Publr David A. Zeeck; Exec. Editor Karen Peterson; circ. Mon. to Fri. 87,315, Sat. 84,158, Sun. 99,152.

Seattle Times: 1120 John St, POB 70, Seattle, WA 98111-0070; tel. (206) 464-2111; fax (206) 464-2261; e-mail pfoote@seattletimes.com; internet seattletimes.nwsource.com; f. 1896; Publr Frank A. Blethen; Exec. Editor David Boardman; circ. Mon. to Fri. 263,468, Sat. 237,681, Sun. 356,944.

Spokesman-Review: 999 West Riverside, POB 2160, Spokane, WA 99210-2160; tel. (509) 459-5000; fax (509) 459-3815; e-mail editor@spokesman.com; internet www.spokesman.com; f. 1883; Publr William Stacey Cowles; Editor Gary Graham; circ. Mon. to Fri. 76,291, Sat. 85,928, Sun. 95,939.

West Virginia

Charleston Daily Mail: 1001 Virginia St East, Charleston, WV 25301-2835; tel. (304) 348-5140; fax (304) 348-4847; e-mail dmnews@dailymail.com; internet www.dailymail.com; f. 1973; evening; Publr and Editor Nanya Friend; Man. Editor Brad McElhinny; circ. Mon. to Fri. 19,014.

Wisconsin

Green Bay Press-Gazette: 435 East Walnut St, POB 23430, Green Bay, WI 54305-3430; tel. (920) 435-4411; fax (920) 431-8499; e-mail jdye@greenbaypressgazette.com; internet www.greenbaypressgazette.com; f. 1915; bought by Gannett Co in 1980; Publr Kevin Corrado; Exec. Editor John Dye; circ. Mon. to Fri. 44,744, Sat. 55,382, Sun. 69,169.

Milwaukee Journal Sentinel: 333 West State St, POB 371, Milwaukee, WI 53201; tel. (414) 224-2000; fax (414) 224-2047; e-mail gstanley@journalsentinel.com; internet www.jsonline.com; f. 1837; Publr Elizabeth 'Betsy' Brenner; Editor Martin Kaiser; circ. Mon. to Fri. 186,433, Sat. 180,102, Sun. 328,247.

Post-Crescent: 306 West Washington St, POB 59, Appleton, WI 54911; tel. (920) 993-1000; fax (920) 733-1983; e-mail jmara@postcrescent.com; internet www.postcrescent.com; f. 1920; Mon. to Sat. evening, Sun. morning; Publr Genia Lovett; Exec. Editor Dan Flannery; circ. Mon. to Fri. 41,411, Sat. 47,416, Sun. 57,496.

Wisconsin State Journal: 1901 Fish Hatchery Rd, POB 8058, Madison, WI 53713; tel. (608) 252-6100; fax (608) 252-6119; e-mail wsjcity@madison.com; internet www.madison.com/wsj; f. 1839; Publr William K. Johnston; Sr Editor David Dombrowski; circ. Mon. to Fri. 91,575, Sat. 92,631, Sun. 125,039.

Wyoming

Star-Tribune: 170 Star Lane, POB 80, Casper, WY 82602; tel. (307) 266-0500; fax (307) 266-0568; e-mail nathan.bekke@trib.com; internet www.trib.com; f. 1891; Publr Nathan Bekke; Editor Chad Baldwin; circ. Mon. to Fri. 24,767, Sat. 24,270, Sun. 26,496.

SELECTED PERIODICALS

AARP The Magazine: 601 East St, NW, Washington, DC 20049; tel. (202) 434-3525; e-mail aarpmagazine@aarp.org; internet www.aarpmagazine.org; f. 1958 following merger of *My Generation* and *Modern Maturity*; publ. of the American Asscn of Retired Persons; 6 a year; general interest for the over-50s; Group Publr, Vice-Pres. and Publr Jim Fishman; Editor-in-Chief Hugh Delehanty; Editor Nancy Graham; circ. 23,721,626; AARP also publishes *AARP Bulletin* (11 a year, circ. 23,574,328) and *AARP Segunda Juventud* (quarterly, in Spanish and English).

Allure: 4 Times Sq., New York, NY 10036; tel. (212) 286-2860; fax (212) 286-4654; e-mail letters@allure.com; internet www.allure.com; f. 1991; publ. by Condé Nast Publs Inc; monthly; women's fashion and wellbeing; Vice-Pres. and Publr Agnes B. Chapski; Editor-in-Chief Linda Wells; circ. 1,082,873.

American Baby: 375 Lexington Ave, 9th Floor, New York, NY 10017-5514; tel. (212) 499-2000; fax (212) 499-2038; internet www.parents.com; f. 1986; 10 a year; Publr Richard Berenson; Editor Erin Crawford.

American Heritage: 416 Hungerford Dr., Suite 216, Rockville, MD 20850-4127; tel. (240) 453-0900; e-mail mail@americanheritage.com; internet www.americanheritage.com; f. 1949; 8 a year; US history; Pres. and Editor-in-Chief Edwin S. Grosvenor; Exec. Editor John F. Ross; circ. 318,571; American Heritage also publishes *American Heritage of Inventions and Technology* and quarterly African-American history and culture magazine *American Legacy*.

The American Legion Magazine: 700 North Pennsylvania St, POB 1055, Indianapolis, IN 46206-1055; tel. (317) 630-1298; fax (317) 630-1223; e-mail magazine@legion.org; internet www.legion.org; f. 1919; publ. of The American Legion; monthly; Editor Jeff Stoffer; circ. 2,346,264.

American Rifleman: NRA Publications, 11250 Waples Mill Rd, Fairfax, VA 22030; tel. (703) 267-1329; e-mail publications@nrahq

THE UNITED STATES OF AMERICA

.org; internet www.americanrifleman.org; f. 1885; official journal of the Nat. Rifle Asscn; monthly; Editor-in-Chief MARK A. KEEFE, IV; circ. 1,794,633.

American Teacher: 555 New Jersey Ave, NW, Washington, DC 20001-2079; tel. (202) 879-4430; fax (202) 783-2014; e-mail mailbox@aft.org; internet www.aft.org; f. 1916; publ. by American Federation of Teachers; 8 a year; Editor ROGER S. GLASS; circ. 919,000 (2009).

Architectural Digest: 4 Times Sq., New York, NY 10036; tel. (212) 286-2860; fax (212) 286-6905; e-mail jayson_goldberg@archdigest; internet www.architecturaldigest.com; f. 1920; monthly; Vice-Pres. and Publr GIULIO CAPUA; Editor-in-Chief MARGARET RUSSELL; circ. 840,995.

Arthritis Today: 1330 West Peachtree St, NW, Suite 100, Atlanta, GA 30309; tel. (404) 965-7635; e-mail atmail@arthritis.org; internet www.arthritistoday.org; f. 1987; publ. by the Arthritis Foundation; 6 a year; health and lifestyle magazine for sufferers of arthritis; Publr CINDY MCDANIEL; Editor-in-Chief MARCY O'KOON MOSS; circ. 681,911.

Barron's: 1211 Ave of the Americas, New York, NY 10036; tel. (212) 416-2000; e-mail editors@barrons.com; internet online.barrons.com; f. 1921; publ. by Dow Jones & Co, Inc, which was acquired by News Corpn in 2008; weekly; business and finance; Pres. and Editor EDWIN A. FINN, Jr; Man. Editor RICHARD RESCIGNO; circ. 310,180.

Better Homes and Gardens: 1716 Locust St, Des Moines, IA 50309-3023; tel. (515) 284-3000; fax (515) 284-3684; e-mail bhgeditor@meredith.com; internet www.bhg.com; f. 1922; publ. by Meredith Corpn; monthly; Vice-Pres. and Publr JAMES T. CARR; Editor-in-Chief GAYLE BUTLER; Exec. Editor KITTY MORGAN; circ. 7,644,011.

Bon Appétit: 6300 Wilshire Blvd, 10th Floor, Los Angeles, CA 90048; tel. (323) 965-3600; fax (323) 930-2369; internet www.bonappetit.com; f. 1955; monthly; Vice-Pres. and Publr PAUL JOWDY; Editor-in-Chief BARBARA FAIRCHILD; circ. 1,611,930.

Boys' Life: 1325 West Walnut Hill Lane, POB 152079, Irving, TX 75015-2079; tel. (972) 580-2263; fax (972) 580-2079; e-mail boyslifemagazine@netbsa.org; internet www.boyslife.org; f. 1911; publ. by Boy Scouts of America; monthly; Publr J. WARREN YOUNG; Editor-in-Chief J. D. OWEN; circ. 1,166,871.

Bloomberg BusinessWeek: 1221 Ave of the Americas, 43rd Floor, New York, NY 10120; tel. (212) 512-2511; e-mail lou_tosto@businessweek.com; internet www.businessweek.com; f. 1929; publ. by Bloomberg LP; weekly; business, finance and technology; Publr HUGH WILEY; Editor-in-Chief JOSH TYRANGIEL; circ. 921,340.

Car and Driver: 1585 Eisenhower Pl., Ann Arbor, MI 48108; tel. (734) 971-3600; fax (734) 971-9188; e-mail editors@caranddriver.com; internet www.caranddriver.com; f. 1956; publ. by Hachette Filipacchi Media US, Inc; Vice-Pres. and Publr JOHN C. DRISCOLL, Jr; Editor-in-Chief EDDIE ALTERMAN; circ. 1,326,350.

Catholic Digest: 1 Montauk Ave, Suite 200, POB 6015, New London, CT 06320-4967; tel. (800) 321-0411; fax (860) 572-0788; e-mail connors@catholicdigest.com; internet www.catholicdigest.com; f. 1936; monthly; Publr KATHLEEN STAUFFER; Editor DAN CONNORS; circ. 283,548 (2008).

Condé Nast Traveler: 4 Times Sq., 14th Floor, New York, NY 10036-6561; tel. (212) 286-2860; fax (212) 286-2094; e-mail beth_lusko@condenast.com; internet www.concierge.com/cntraveler; f. 1954; monthly; Publr CHRIS MITCHELL; Editor-in-Chief KLARA GLOWCZEWSKA; circ. 818,066.

Congressional Digest: Congressional Digest Corpn, POB 240, Boyds, MD 20841-0240; tel. (301) 916-1800; fax (240) 599-7679; e-mail info@congressionaldigest.com; internet www.congressionaldigest.com; f. 1921; monthly; Publr PAGE B. ROBINSON THOMAS; Editors SARAH ORRICK, ANTHONY ZURCHER.

Consumer Reports: 101 Truman Ave, Yonkers, NY 10703-1057; tel. (914) 378-2000; fax (914) 378-2900; e-mail pressroom@consumer.org; internet www.consumerreports.org; f. 1936; publ. by the Consumers Union; monthly; Editor-in-Chief KIM KLEMAN; Man. Editor ROBERT TIERNAN; circ. 4,000,000.

Consumers Digest: Consumers Digest Communications, 520 Lake Cook Rd, Suite 500, Deerfield, IL 60015; tel. (847) 607-3000; e-mail postmaster@consumersdigest.com; internet www.consumersdigest.com; f. 1959; 6 a year; Publr RANDY WEBER; circ. 1,200,000.

Cosmopolitan: 300 West 57th St, New York, NY 10019-3299; tel. (212) 649-3570; e-mail cosmo@hearst.com; internet www.cosmopolitan.com; f. 1886; monthly; women's interest; Publr DONNA KALAJIAN LAGANI; Editor-in-Chief KATE WHITE; circ. 3,046,229.

Country Home: 1716 Locust St, Des Moines, IA 50309; tel. (515) 284-2015; e-mail countryhome@meredith.com; internet www.countryhome.com; f. 1979; publ. by Meredith Corpn; 10 a year; lifestyle; Publr ANTHONY IMPERATO; Editor-in-Chief CAROL SHEEHAN; circ. 1,271,782.

Country Living: 300 West 57th St, New York, NY 10019-3788; tel. (212) 649-3500; e-mail countryliving@hearst.com; internet www.countryliving.com; f. 1978; monthly; Vice-Pres. and Publr CHRIS ALLEN; Editor-in-Chief SARAH GRAY MILLER; circ. 1,614,398.

Discover: 90 Fifth Ave, New York, NY 10011; tel. (212) 624-4800; fax (212) 624-4813; e-mail editorial@discovermagazine.com; internet www.discovermagazine.com; f. 1980; publ. by Kalmbach Publishing Co.; science and technology; Publr HENRY DONAHUE; Editor-in-Chief COREY S. POWELL; circ. 718,031.

Ebony: Johnson Publishing, 820 South Michigan Ave, Chicago, IL 60605-2191; tel. (312) 322-9200; fax (312) 322-0039; e-mail editors@ebony.com; internet www.ebonyjet.com/ebony; f. 1945; publ. by Johnson Publishing Co; monthly; African-American general interest; Editor-in-Chief AMY DUBOIS BARNETT; Man. Editor TERRY GLOVER; circ. 1,114,849.

Elks Magazine: 425 West Diversey Pkwy, Chicago, IL 60614-6196; tel. (773) 755-4740; fax (773) 755-4792; e-mail annai@elks.org; internet www.elks.org/elksmag; f. 1922; 10 a year; publ. by the Benevolent and Protective Order of Elks of the United States of America; Publr and Editor CHERYL T. STACHURA; Man. Editor ANNA L. IDOL; circ. 960,000 (2008).

Elle: 1633 Broadway, 44th Floor, New York, NY 10019; tel. (212) 767-5800; fax (212) 767-5980; internet www.elle.com; f. 1985; publ. by Hachette Filipacchi Media US, Inc; monthly; women's fashion; Sr Vice-Pres. and Group Publishing Dir ROBIN DOMENICONI; Editor-in-Chief ROBERTA MYERS; circ. 1,095,702.

Endless Vacation: 360 Lexington Ave, 19th Floor, New York, NY 10017; tel. (212) 481-3452; fax (212) 213-1287; e-mail barbara.peck@storyworldwide.com; internet www.endlessvacation.com; f. 1975; publ. by Resort Condominiums Int.; 5 a year; Publr BRIAN BRUNO; Editor BARBARA PECK; circ. 1,845,297 (2009).

Entertainment Weekly: 135 West 50th St, 3rd Floor, New York, NY 10020; tel. (212) 522-5600; fax (212) 522-4482; e-mail letters@ew.com; internet www.ew.com; f. 1990; Publr RAY CHELSTOWSKI; Editor-in-Chief JOHN HUEY; circ. 1,798,643.

ESPN RISE Magazine: SchoolSports, Inc, 971 Commonwealth Ave, Boston, MA 02215-1305; tel. (617) 779-9000; fax (617) 779-9100; e-mail feedback@risemag.com; internet www.risemag.com; f. 1997 as *SchoolSports Magazine*; acquired by ESPN in 2007; 9 a year; 25 regional edns distributed to c. 6,500 schools; sports and teenage active lifestyle; Editor-in-Chief JONATHAN SEGAL; circ. 1,012,586.

ESPN The Magazine: 19 East 34th St, New York, NY 10016; tel. (212) 515-1000; fax (212) 515-1275; e-mail ms_support@espn.go.com; internet insider.espn.go.com/insider/magazine; f. 1998; fortnightly; subsidiary of Walt Disney DIS; men's sports and lifestyle; Editor-in-Chief GARY BELSKY; circ. 2,073,813.

Esquire: 300 West 57th St, 21st Floor, New York, NY 10019-3797; tel. (212) 649-4020; fax (212) 649-4303; e-mail esquire@hearst.com; internet www.esquire.com; f. 1933; monthly; Vice-Pres. and Publr KEVIN O'MALLEY; Editor-in-Chief DAVID GRANGER; circ. 737,254.

Essence: 135 West 50th St, 4th Floor, New York, NY 10020; tel. (212) 642-0600; fax (212) 921-5173; e-mail info@essence.com; internet www.essence.com; f. 1970; monthly; African-American general interest; Editor-in-Chief ANGELA BURT-MURRAY; circ. 1,066,482.

Family Circle: 375 Lexington Ave, 9th Floor, New York, NY 10017-5514; tel. (212) 499-2000; fax (212) 499-6740; e-mail support@familycircle.com; internet www.familycircle.com; f. 1932; publ. by Meredith Corpn; every 3 weeks; Publr CAREY WITMER; Editor-in-Chief LINDA FEARS; circ. 3,849,673.

FamilyFun: Disney FamilyFun Group, 244 Main St, Northampton, MA 01060; tel. (413) 585-0444; fax (413) 587-9335; e-mail ellen.antoville@disney.com; internet familyfun.go.com; f. 1991; publ. by Disney Publishing Worldwide; monthly; general interest for families with young children; Editorial Dir ANN HALLOCK; Editor JON ADOLPH; circ. 2,117,159.

Family Handyman (Home Service Publications): 2915 Commers Dr., Suite 700, Eagan, MN 55121; tel. (651) 454-9200; fax (651) 994-2250; e-mail editors@thefamilyhandyman.com; internet www.rd.com/familyhandyman; f. 1951; publ. by Reader's Digest Asscn, Inc; 10 a year; Editor-in-Chief KEN COLLIER; circ. 1,142,799.

Fast Company: 7 World Trade Center, New York, NY 10007-2195; tel. (212) 389-5300; fax (212) 389-5496; e-mail loop@fastcompany.com; internet www.fastcompany.com; f. 1995; monthly; acquired by Mansueto Ventures LLC in 2005; global business practice; Publr HAROLD BOLLING; Editor-in-Chief ROBERT SAFIAN; circ. 737,982.

FHM: 110 Fifth Ave, New York, NY 10011; tel. (212) 201-6702; fax (212) 201-6965; e-mail andrew.ormson@emapmetrousa.com; internet www.fhmus.com; f. 2000; publ. by Emap Metro LLC; monthly; men's lifestyle, entertainment and fashion; Exec. Publr and Pres. DANA FIELDS; Editor-in-Chief SCOTT GRAMLING; circ. 1,250,275 (2006).

THE UNITED STATES OF AMERICA

Field & Stream: 2 Park Ave, New York, NY 10016-5601; tel. (212) 779-5000; fax (212) 779-5114; e-mail fsletters@time4.com; internet www.fieldandstream.com; f. 1895; publ. by Bonnier Corpn; 11 a year; Publr ERIC ZINCZENKO; Editor ANTHONY LICATA; circ. 1,260,769.

Fitness: 125 Park Ave, New York, NY 10017; tel. (212) 557-6600; e-mail eric.schwarzkopf@meredith.com; internet www.fitnessmagazine.com; f. 1992; acquired by Meredith Corpn in 2005; women's health and fitness; Publr LEE SLATTERY; Editor-in-Chief BETTY WONG; circ. 1,555,217.

Food & Wine: 1120 Ave of the Americas, New York, NY 10036; tel. (212) 382-5600; fax (212) 382-5879; e-mail christina.r.grdovic@aexp.com; internet www.foodandwine.com; f. 1978; publ. by American Express Publishing Corpn; monthly; Publr CHRISTINA R. GRDOVIC; Editor-in-Chief DANA COWIN; circ. 961,050.

Forbes: 60 Fifth Ave, New York, NY 10011-8802; tel. (212) 620-2200; fax (212) 620-1875; e-mail readers@forbes.com; internet www.forbes.com; f. 1917; fortnightly; Pres. and Editor-in-Chief STEVE FORBES; Publr RICHARD KARLGAARD; circ. 922,888.

Fortune: 1271 Ave of the Americas, New York, NY 10020; tel. (212) 522-1212; fax (212) 522-0810; e-mail letters@fortune.com; internet www.fortune.com; f. 1930; Man. Editor ANDREW SERWER; circ. 857,337.

Game Informer: 724 North First St, 3rd Floor, Minneapolis, MN 55401; tel. (612) 486-6100; fax (612) 486-6101; e-mail andy@gameinformer.com; internet www.gameinformer.com; f. 1991; owned by Sunrise Publs; monthly; computer gaming; Publr CATHY PRESTON; Editor-in-Chief ANDY MCNAMARA; circ. 4,364,170.

Glamour: 4 Times Sq., 16th Floor, New York, NY 10036; tel. (212) 286-2860; fax (212) 286-8336; e-mail letters@glamour.com; internet us.glamour.com; f. 1939; publ. by Condé Nast Publs Inc; monthly; Publr WILLIAM WACKERMANN; Editor-in-Chief CYNTHIA LEIVE; circ. 2,320,325.

Golf Digest: 20 Westport Rd, POB 850, Wilton, CT 06897; tel. (800) 438-0491; fax (203) 761-5135; e-mail editor@golfdigest.com; internet www.golfdigest.com; f. 1950; publ. by Condé Nast Publs Inc; monthly; Vice-Pres. and Publr THOMAS J. BAIR; Editor-in-Chief JERRY TARDE; circ. 1,676,792.

Golf Magazine: 2 Park Ave, New York, NY 10016-5601; tel. (212) 779-5000; fax (212) 779-5588; e-mail golfletters@golfonline.com; internet www.golf.com; f. 1959; publ. by Time Inc; monthly; Publr CHARLIE KAMMERER; Editor DAVID CLARKE; circ. 1,455,190.

Good Housekeeping: 300 West 57th St, New York, NY 10019-5288; tel. (212) 649-2000; fax (212) 265-3307; e-mail ghkletters@hearst.com; internet www.goodhousekeeping.com; f. 1885; monthly; Publr PATRICIA HAEGELE; Editor-in-Chief ROSEMARY ELLIS; circ. 4,427,964.

GQ: 4 Times Sq., New York, NY 10036; tel. (212) 286-6410; fax (212) 286-7969; internet us.gq.com; f. 1957; publ. by Condé Nast Publs Inc; monthly; men's lifestyle; Vice-Pres. and Publr PETER HUNSINGER; Editor-in-Chief JIM NELSON; circ. 947,519.

Guideposts: 39 Seminary Hill Rd, Carmel, NY 10512; tel. (212) 929-1300; fax (212) 929-9574; e-mail gpeditors@guideposts.org; internet www.guideposts.org; f. 1945; monthly; other publs incl. *Positive Thinking Magazine* (10 a year, circ. 335,000), *Angels on Earth* (6 a year, circ. 600,000) and *Guideposts Sweet 16* (6 a year); personal and spiritual development; Publr AMY MOLINERO; Editor-in-Chief EDWARD GRINNAN; circ. 2,026,433.

HANDY: 12301 Whitewater Dr., Minnetonka, MN 55343; tel. (952) 988-7294; fax (952) 988-7486; e-mail lokrend@namginc.com; internet www.handymanclub.com; f. 1993; publ. by North American Media Group Inc; official publ. of the Handyman Club of America; 6 a year; home improvement; Publr TOM SWEENEY; Editor LARRY OKREND; circ. 730,185.

Harper's Bazaar: 300 West 57th St, New York, NY 10019-3799; tel. (212) 903-5000; fax (212) 262-7101; e-mail bazaar@hearst.com; internet www.harpersbazaar.com; monthly; Publr VALERIE SALEMBIER; Editor-in-Chief GLENDA BAILEY; circ. 744,038.

Health: 2100 Lakeshore Dr., Birmingham, AL 35209; tel. (205) 445-6476; fax (205) 445-5123; e-mail health@timeinc.com; internet www.health.com; f. 1987; publ. by Southern Progress Corpn, a subsidiary of Time Inc; 10 a year; women's health and wellbeing; Publr and Vice-Pres. RENEE TULENKO; Editor-in-Chief ELLEN KUNES; circ. 1,391,627.

Highlights for Children: 803 Church St, Honesdale, PA 18431; tel. (570) 253-1080; fax (570) 251-7847; internet www.highlights.com; f. 1946; monthly; Editor-in-Chief CHRISTINE FRENCH CLARK; circ. 1,800,000 (2007).

Home: 1633 Broadway, 44th Floor, New York, NY 10019; tel. (212) 767-5518; e-mail homeeditor@hfnm.com; internet www.homemag.com; f. 1981; publ. by Hachette Filipacchi Media US Inc; 10 a year; home improvement and decoration; Vice-Pres. and Publr JOHN H. GRANT; Vice-Pres. and Editor-in-Chief DONNA SAPOLIN; circ. 828,630.

Hot Rod Magazine: 831 South Douglas St, El Segundo, CA 90245; e-mail hotrod@primedia.com; internet www.hotrod.com; f. 1948; monthly; Sr Vice-Pres. and Group Publr DOUG EVANS; Editor-in-Chief DAVID FREIBURGER; circ. 655,722.

House Beautiful: 300 West 57th St, 24th Floor, New York, NY 10019-5970; tel. (212) 903-5206; internet www.housebeautiful.com; f. 1896; monthly; Publr KATE KELLY SMITH; Editor-in-Chief NEWELL TURNER; circ. 906,349.

Inc.: 7 World Trade Center, New York, NY 10007-2195; tel. (212) 389-5300; fax (212) 389-5393; e-mail mail@inc.com; internet www.inc.com; f. 1987; acquired by Mansueto Ventures LLC in 2005; monthly; small business resources and advice; Publr JOHN TEBEAU; Editor-in-Chief JANE BERENTSON; circ. 712,647.

In Style: 1271 Ave of the Americas, New York, NY 10020; tel. (212) 522-1212; internet www.instyle.com; f. 1994; publ. by Time Inc; celebrity, women's lifestyle and fashion; Man. Editor CHARLA LAWHON; circ. 1,760,365.

In Touch Weekly: 270 Sylvan Ave, Englewood Cliffs, NJ 07632; tel. (201) 569-6699; fax (201) 569-3584; e-mail contactintouch@intouchweekly.com; internet www.intouchweekly.com; f. 2002; publ. by Bauer Publishing USA; weekly; celebrity and entertainment; Publr MARK OLTARSH; Editor-in-Chief MICHELLE LEE; circ. 810,189.

Jane: 750 Third Ave, New York, NY 10017; tel. (212) 630-4192; e-mail carlos_lamadrid@condenast.com; internet www.janemag.com; f. 1992; publ. by Condé Nast Publications; monthly; women's lifestyle; Vice-Pres. and Publr CARLOS LAMADRID; Editor-in-Chief BRANDON HOLLEY; circ. 706,561 (2005).

Jet: Johnson Publishing, 820 South Michigan Ave, Chicago, IL 60605-2191; tel. (312) 322-9200; fax (312) 322-0951; internet www.ebonyjet.com; f. 1951; weekly; African-American general interest; Editor-in-Chief MIRA LOWE; circ. 762,250.

Junior Scholastic: 557 Broadway, New York, NY 10012; tel. (212) 343-6100; fax (212) 343-6333; e-mail junior@scholastic.com; internet www2.scholastic.com; f. 1937; 18 a year; Editor LEE BAIER; circ. 615,000.

Kiplinger's Personal Finance: 1729 H St, NW, Washington, DC 20006-3904; tel. (202) 887-6400; fax (202) 331-8637; e-mail magazine@kiplinger.com; internet www.kiplinger.com; f. 1947; monthly; Editor JANET BODNAR; circ. 779,789.

Ladies' Home Journal: 125 Park Ave, New York, NY 10017-5599; tel. (212) 557-6600; fax (212) 455-1010; e-mail lhj@meredith.com; internet www.lhj.com; f. 1883; monthly; Publr JULIE PINKWATER; Editor-in-Chief SALLY LEE; circ. 3,831,072.

The Lion: 300 22nd St, Oak Brook, IL 60523-8842; tel. (630) 468-6729; fax (630) 571-1685; e-mail magazine@lionsclubs.org; f. 1918; 11 a year; business and professional; Editor JAY COPP; circ. 392,058.

Lucky: 4 Times Sq., 6th Floor, New York, NY 10036; tel. (212) 286-2860; fax (212) 286-4986; internet www.luckymag.com; f. 2000; publ. by Condé Nast Publs Inc; monthly; fashion and shopping; Vice-Pres. and Publr GINA SANDERS; Editor-in-Chief BRANDON HOLLEY; circ. 1,107,075.

Marie Claire: 300 West 57th St, 34th Floor, New York, NY 10019-1497; tel. (212) 649-5000; fax (212) 501-5050; e-mail marieclairepromo@hearst.com; internet www.marieclaire.com; f. 1994; monthly; Publr SUSAN D. PLAGEMANN; Editor-in-Chief JOANNA COLES; circ. 1,007,712.

Martha Stewart Living: 11 West 42nd St, 25th Floor, New York, NY 10036; tel. (212) 827-8000; fax (212) 827-8204; e-mail mstewart@marthastewart.com; internet www.marthastewart.com; f. 1991; publ. by Martha Stewart Living Omnimedia, Inc; monthly; lifestyle and general interest; Group Publr SALLY PRESTON; Editor-in-Chief VANESSA HOLDEN; circ. 2,057,960; other publs incl. *Everyday Food* (f. 2003, circ. 982,589).

Maxim: 1040 Ave of the Americas, New York, NY 10018; tel. (212) 302-2626; fax (212) 302-2631; e-mail editors@maximmag.com; internet www.maximonline.com; f. 1997; publ. by Alpha Media Group; monthly; men's lifestyle and general interest; Editorial Dir JAMES KAMINSKY; circ. 2,549,893.

MediZine Healthy Living: 500 Fifth Ave, Suite 1900, New York, NY 10110; tel. (212) 695-2223; fax (212) 695-2936; e-mail requestinfo@medizine.com; internet www.remedyhealthmedia.com; f. 1994; quarterly; health and wellbeing; other publs incl. *Remedy* (f. 1995, circ. 2,400,000) and *Diabetes Focus* (f. 2003, circ. 1,500,000); Editorial Dir DIANE UMANSKY; circ. 3,650,000 (2009).

Men's Fitness: 1 Park Ave, 10th Floor, New York, NY 10016; tel. (212) 545-4800; fax (212) 685-9644; e-mail jkimmel@amilink.com; internet www.mensfitness.com; f. 1985; publ. by AMI/Weider Publs; 10 a year; men's health, fitness and lifestyle; Publr MARC RICHARDS; Editor-in-Chief ROY S. JOHNSON; circ. 606,585.

Men's Health: 733 Third Ave, 15th Floor, New York, NY 10017; tel. (212) 573-0555; e-mail jon.hammond@rodale.com; internet www.menshealth.com; f. 1988; men's health and general interest; 10 a

THE UNITED STATES OF AMERICA

year; publ. by Rodale Inc; Vice-Pres. and Publr JACK ESSIG; Editor-in-Chief DAVID ZINCZENKO; circ. 1,917,411.

Men's Journal Magazine: 1290 Ave of the Americas, New York, NY 10104-0298; tel. and fax (212) 484-3429; e-mail vincent.krsulich@mensjournal.com; internet www.mensjournal.com; f. 1992; publ. by Wenner Media, Inc; monthly; men's general interest and active lifestyle; Publr FRANCIS X. FARRELL; Editor BRAD WIENERS; circ. 722,681.

Metropolitan Home: 1633 Broadway, 44th Floor, New York, NY 10019-6741; tel. (212) 767-5522; fax (212) 767-5636; e-mail metletters@hfnm.com; internet www.methome.com; f. 1981; publ. by Hachette Filipacchi Media US Inc; 10 a year; interior design and architecture; Publr DEBORAH BURNS; Editor-in-Chief DONNA WARNER; circ. 563,417.

Midwest Living: 1716 Locust St, Des Moines, IA 50309; tel. (515) 284-3000; fax (515) 284-2700; e-mail brian.kightlinger@meredith.com; internet www.midwestliving.com; f. 1987; publ. by Meredith Corpn; 6 a year; lifestyle with focus on US Midwest; Publr BRIAN KIGHTLINGER; Editor-in-Chief GREG PHILBY; circ. 966,784.

Money: Time & Life Bldg, Rockefeller Center, New York, NY 10020; tel. (212) 522-1210; fax (212) 522-0970; e-mail managing_editor@moneymail.com; internet money.cnn.com; f. 1972; monthly; Publr FRANK WALL; Man. Editor CRAIG MATTERS; circ. 1,928,179.

More: 125 Park Ave, New York, NY 10017-5529; tel. (212) 557-6600; fax (212) 455-1244; internet www.more.com; f. 1998; publ. by Meredith Corpn; 10 a year; women's lifestyle; Publr BRENDA SAGET DARLING; Editor-in-Chief LESLEY JANE SEYMOUR; circ. 1,307,215.

Motor Trend: 831 South Douglas St, El Segundo, CA 90245; tel. (323) 782-2220; internet www.motortrend.com; f. 1949; publ. by Primedia, Inc; monthly; Publr IRA GABRIEL; Editor-in-Chief ANGUS MACKENZIE; circ. 1,122,273.

National Enquirer: American Media, Inc, 4950 Communication Ave, Suite 100, Boca Raton, FL 3343; e-mail letters@nationalenquirer.com; internet www.nationalenquirer.com; f. 1926; publ. by American Media Inc; weekly; Publr DAVID J. PECKER; Exec. Editor BARRY LEVINE; circ. 956,095.

National Geographic Magazine: 1145 17th St, NW, Washington, DC 20036; tel. (212) 610-5500; fax (202) 775-6141; e-mail ngm@nationalgeographic.com; internet ngm.nationalgeographic.com; f. 1888; monthly; Pres. and CEO JOHN FAHEY; Editor-in-Chief CHRIS JOHNS; circ. 4,493,110.

National News: American Legion Auxiliary, 777 North Meridian St, 3rd Floor, Indianapolis, IN 46260; tel. (317) 569-4500; fax (317) 569-4502; e-mail nnpr@legion-aux.org; internet www.legion-aux.org; publ. of the American Legion Auxiliary (ALA); quarterly; Editor STEPHANIE L. HOLLOWAY; circ. 754,932 (June 2007).

The New Yorker: 4 Times Sq., New York, NY 10036-7448; tel. (212) 286-5400; fax (212) 286-4168; e-mail themail@newyorker.com; internet www.newyorker.com; f. 1925; publ. by Condé Nast Publs Inc; weekly; Publr LISA HUGHES; Editor DAVID REMNICK; circ. 1,034,602.

Newsweek: Newsweek Bldg, 251 West 57th St, New York, NY 10019-1894; tel. (212) 445-4000; fax (212) 445-5068; e-mail editors@newsweek.com; internet www.newsweek.com; f. 1933; weekly; Propr SIDNEY HARMAN; Editor (vacant); circ. 1,610,632.

Nick Jr. Family Magazine: 1515 Broadway, 32nd Floor, New York, NY 10036; tel. (212) 654-6198; fax (212) 846-1907; internet www.nickjr.com; f. 1999; subsidiary of Viacom Int. Inc; monthly; parenting; Editor-in-Chief FREDDI GREENBERG; circ. 431,136 (2009).

North American Hunter: 12301 Whitewater Dr., Minnetonka, MN 55343; tel. (320) 846-6090; fax (320) 846-6092; e-mail rsundberg@namginc.com; internet www.huntingclub.com; f. 1979; publ. by North American Media Group Inc; 8 a year; official publ. of the North American Hunting Club; hunting and conservation; Publr RICH SUNDBERG; Editor GORDY KRAHN; circ. 873,023.

O, The Oprah Magazine: 300 West 57th St, New York, NY 10019-5915; tel. (212) 903-5366; fax (212) 903-5388; e-mail omail@hearst.com; internet www.oprah.com/omagazine; f. 2001; monthly; Vice-Pres. and Publr JILL SEELIG; Editor-in-Chief SUSAN CASEY; circ. 2,394,303 (2009).

Organic Gardening: 400 South 10th St, Emmaus, PA 18098; tel. (610) 967-7711; fax (610) 967-8963; e-mail og@rodale.com; internet www.organicgardening.com; f. 1942; publ. by Rodale, Inc; 6 a year; Publr CHRIS LAMBIASE; Editor-in-Chief ETHNE CLARKE; circ. 351,713.

Outdoor Life: 2 Park Ave, 10th Floor, New York, NY 10016-5601; tel. (212) 779-5316; fax (212) 779-5118; e-mail amanda.mcnally@bonniercorp.com; internet www.outdoorlife.com; f. 1898; publ. by Bonnier Corpn; 10 a year; Editor-in-Chief TODD W. SMITH; Exec. Editor JOHN SNOW; circ. 774,444.

Outside: 400 Market St, Santa Fe, NM 87501; tel. (505) 989-7100; fax (505) 989-4700; e-mail letters@outsidemag.com; internet outside.away.com; f. 1976 as *Mariah*; publ. by Mariah Media Inc; monthly;

adventure travel and outdoor recreation; Chair. and Editor-in-Chief LAWRENCE J. BURKE; Vice-Pres. and Publr SCOTT PARMELEE; circ. 686,471.

Parenting: 2 Park Ave, New York, NY 10016; tel. (212) 779-5000; internet www.parenting.com; f. 1987; publ. by Bonnier Corpn; monthly; other publs incl. *Babytalk* (f. 1935, circ. 2,000,000); Editor-in-Chief SUSAN KANE; Publr GREG SCHUMANN; circ. 2,229,253.

Parents: 375 Lexington Ave, 10th Floor, New York, NY 10017-5514; tel. (212) 878-8700; fax (212) 986-2656; e-mail support@parents.com; internet www.parents.com; f. 1926; monthly; Publr DIANE NEWMAN; Editor-in-Chief DANA POINTS; circ. 2,202,324.

PC World: PC World Communications, 501 Second St, San Francisco, CA 94107; tel. (415) 243-0500; fax (415) 442-1891; e-mail pcwletters@pcworld.com; internet www.pcworld.com; f. 1982; publ. by PC World Communications, Inc, a subsidiary of International Data Group; monthly; computer technology; Sr Vice-Pres. and Publr MICHAEL CARROLL; Editor ED ALBRO; circ. 438,680.

People: Time & Life Bldg, 28th Floor, Rockefeller Center, 1271 Ave of the Americas, New York, NY 10020; tel. (212) 522-3347; fax (212) 522-0883; e-mail editor@people.com; internet www.people.com; f. 1974; publ. by Time Inc; weekly; celebrity and entertainment; Group Pres. PAUL CAINE; Man. Editor LARRY HACKETT; circ. 3,553,420.

Playboy: 680 North Lake Shore Dr., Chicago, IL 60611-4402; tel. (312) 751-8000; fax (312) 751-2818; e-mail edit@playboy.com; internet www.playboy.com/magazine-toc.html; f. 1953; monthly; men's interest; Publr LOUIS MOHN; Editor-in-Chief HUGH M. HEFNER; circ. 1,628,567.

Popular Mechanics: 300 West 57th St, New York, NY 10019-5899; tel. (212) 649-2000; e-mail popularmechanics@hearst.com; internet www.popularmechanics.com; f. 1902; monthly; Publr WILLIAM CONGDON; Editor-in-Chief JAMES B. MEIGS; circ. 1,219,094.

Popular Science: 2 Park Ave, 9th Floor, New York, NY 10016; tel. (212) 779-5000; fax (212) 779-5108; e-mail letters@popsci.com; internet www.popsci.com; f. 1872; publ. by Bonnier Corpn; monthly; Publr GREGG R. HANO; Editor MARK JANNOT; circ. 1,312,175.

Prevention: 400 South 10th St, Emmaus, PA 18098; tel. (610) 967-8045; fax (610) 967-9198; e-mail pvncustserv@rodale.com; internet www.prevention.com; f. 1950; publ. by Rodale Inc; monthly; Vice-Pres. and Editor-in-Chief DIANE SALVATORE; circ. 2,927,638.

Progressive Farmer: Lakeshore Park Plaza, 2204 Lakeshore Dr., Birmingham, AL 35209; tel. (205) 414-4700; fax (205) 414-4705; e-mail jodle@progressivefarmer.com; internet www.progressivefarmer.com; f. 1886; monthly; Publr ADRIAN BLAKE; Editor GREGG HILLYER; circ. 675,000 (2009).

Reader's Digest: Reader's Digest Rd, Pleasantville, NY 10570-7000; tel. (914) 238-1000; fax (914) 238-4559; internet www.rd.com; f. 1922; 10 a year; filed for Chapter 11 bankruptcy protection in Aug. 2009; Editor-in-Chief PEGGY NORTHROP; circ. 6,112,811.

Real Simple: Time and Life Bldg, 1271 Ave of the Americas, New York, NY 10020; tel. (212) 522-1212; fax (212) 467-1396; internet www.realsimple.com; f. 2000; publ. by Time Inc; monthly, plus two special issues; women's lifestyle and general interest; Exec. Producer HEIDI SCHOEMBS; Man. Editor KATHLEEN MURRAY HARRIS; circ. 2,014,781.

Redbook: 224 West 57th St, 6th Floor, New York, NY 10019-3796; tel. (212) 649-3450; fax (212) 581-8114; e-mail redbook@hearst.com; internet www.redbookmag.com; f. 1903; monthly; Vice-Pres. and Publr MARY E. MORGAN; Editor-in-Chief JILL HERZIG; circ. 2,226,356.

Road & Track: 1499 Monrovia Ave, Newport Beach, CA 92663-2752; tel. (949) 720-5300; fax (949) 631-2757; e-mail rtletters@hfmus.com; internet www.roadandtrack.com; f. 1947; monthly; Publr JOHN C. DRISCOLL, Jr; Editor-in-Chief MATT DELORENZO; circ. 709,087.

Rolling Stone: 1290 Ave of the Americas, 2nd Floor, New York, NY 10104-0298; tel. (212) 484-1616; fax (212) 484-3429; e-mail feedback@rollingstone.com; internet www.rollingstone.com; f. 1967; fortnightly; Publr JANN S. WENNER; Man. Editor WILL DANA; circ. 1,453,158.

Scholastic Parent & Child: 557 Broadway, New York, NY 10012; tel. (212) 343-6100; e-mail news@scholastic.com; internet teacher.scholastic.com/products/classmags/parent_child.htm; f. 1995; publ. by Scholastic Inc; 8 a year; Publr RISA CRANDALL; Editor-in-Chief NICK FRIEDMAN; circ. 1,313,701.

Scientific American: 415 Madison Ave, New York, NY 10017-1179; tel. (212) 451-8200; fax (212) 754-1138; e-mail editors@sciam.com; internet www.sciam.com; f. 1845; monthly; Vice-Pres. and Publr BRUCE BRANDFON; Exec. Editor MARIETTE DICHRISTINA; circ. 489,066.

Scouting Magazine: 1325 West Walnut Hill Lane, POB 152079, Irving, TX 75015-2079; tel. (972) 580-2000; fax (972) 580-2079; e-mail scole@netbsa.org; internet www.scoutingmagazine.org; f. 1913; publ. by Boy Scouts of America; 6 a year; Publr J. WARREN YOUNG;

THE UNITED STATES OF AMERICA

Editor-in-Chief J. D. Owen; Man. Editor Scott Daniels; circ. 1,011,593.

SELF Magazine: 4 Times Sq., 5th Floor, New York, NY 10036; tel. (212) 286-2860; fax (212) 286-6174; e-mail comments@self.com; internet www.self.com; f. 1979; publ. by Condé Nast Publs Inc; monthly; Vice-Pres. and Publr Laura McEwen; Editor-in-Chief Lucy Danziger; circ. 1,520,515.

Seventeen: 300 West 57th St, New York, NY 10019-1798; tel. (212) 649-2000; e-mail mail@seventeen.com; internet www.seventeen.com; f. 1944; publ. by Hearst Corpn; monthly; Publr Jayne Jamison; Editor-in-Chief Ann Shoket; circ. 2,048,781.

Shape: 1 Park Ave, 10th Floor, New York, NY 10016; tel. (212) 545-4800; fax (212) 252-1131; internet www.shape.com; f. 1981; publ. by American Media, Inc; women's health and fitness; Publr Sabine Feldmann; Editor-in-Chief Valerie Latona; circ. 1,650,752.

Sierra: 85 Second St, 2nd Floor, San Francisco, CA 94105; tel. (415) 977-5572; fax (415) 977-5794; e-mail sierra.mail@sierraclub.org; internet www.sierraclub.org/sierra; f. 1893; official publ. of the Sierra Club; 6 a year; nature and ecology; Editor-in-Chief Bob Sipchen; circ. 529,149.

SmartMoney: 1755 Broadway, 2nd Floor, New York, NY 10019; tel. (212) 765-7323; e-mail editors@smartmoney.com; internet www.smartmoney.com; f. 1992; jt venture of Dow Jones & Co, Inc and Hearst Corpn; Publr Bill Shaw; Editor-in-Chief Jonathan Dahl; circ. 815,934.

Smithsonian Magazine: 420 Lexington Ave, Suite 2335, New York, NY 10170; tel. (212) 916-1300; fax (212) 986-4259; e-mail bianchik@si.edu; internet www.smithsonianmag.com; f. 1970; monthly; Publr Kerry Bianchi; Editor Carey Winfrey; circ. 2,054,696.

Southern Living: 2100 Lakeshore Dr., Birmingham, AL 35209-6721; tel. (205) 877-6000; fax (205) 445-7523; internet www.southernliving.com; f. 1966; monthly; Vice-Pres. and Editor-in-Chief Eleanor Griffin; circ. 2,841,894.

Sporting News: POB 420235, Palm Coast, FL 32142-0235; tel. (646) 424-2227; fax (646) 424-2232; e-mail ebaker@sportingnews.com; internet www.sportingnews.com; f. 1886; acquired by American City Business Journals, Inc in 2006; 2 a month; Pres. and CEO Whitney Shaw; Editor John D. Rawlings; circ. 508,792.

Sports Illustrated: 1271 Ave of the Americas, 33rd Floor, New York, NY 10020-1339; tel. (212) 522-1212; fax (212) 522-0475; internet sportsillustrated.cnn.com; f. 1954; weekly; Editor Terry McDonnell; circ. 3,212,278.

Star: 1 Park Ave, 3rd Floor, New York, NY 10016; tel. (212) 743-6523; fax (212) 532-0940; e-mail djackson@starmagazine.com; internet www.starmagazine.com; f. 1974; weekly; Vice-Pres. and Publr David Jackson; Editor-in-Chief Candace Trunzo; circ. 946,480.

Sunset Magazine: 80 Willow Rd, Menlo Park, CA 94025-3691; tel. (650) 321-3600; fax (650) 327-5737; internet www.sunset.com; f. 1898; monthly; travel, home, garden, food and drink; Sr Vice-Pres. and Publr Kevin Lynch; Editor-in-Chief Katie Tamony; circ. 1,265,934.

TENNIS: 79 Madison Ave, 8th Floor, New York, NY 10016; tel. (212) 636-2700; fax (212) 636-2720; e-mail jwilliams@tennismagazine.com; internet www.tennis.com; f. 1965; acquired by Miller Publishing Group LLC in 1997; 8 a year; tennis, travel and lifestyle; Publr Jeff Williams; Editor Sarah Unke; circ. 605,428.

This Old House: 135 West 50th St, 10th Floor, New York, NY 10020; tel. (212) 522-9465; fax (212) 522-9435; e-mail toh_letters@thisoldhouse.com; internet www.thisoldhouse.com; f. 1995; publ. by Time Inc; 10 a year; home improvement; Editor J. Scott Omelianuk; circ. 992,621.

Time: Time & Life Bldg, Rockefeller Center, 1271 Ave of the Americas, New York, NY 10020-1393; tel. (212) 522-1212; fax (212) 522-0023; e-mail letters@time.com; internet www.time.com; f. 1923; weekly; Pres. and Publr Edward R. McCarrick; Man. Editor Richard Stengel; Deputy Man. Editor Michael Elliott; circ. 3,312,484.

Traditional Home: 125 Park Ave, New York, NY 10017; tel. (212) 557-6600; fax (212) 551-6914; e-mail traditionalhome@meredith.com; internet www.traditionalhome.com; f. 1978; publ. by Meredith Corpn; 8 a year; Publr Debra Brandt; Editor-in-Chief Ann Omvig Maine; circ. 972,928.

Travel & Leisure: 1120 Ave of the Americas, 10th Floor, New York, NY 10036-6770; tel. (212) 382-5600; fax (212) 768-1568; e-mail tlquery@amexpub.com; internet www.travelandleisure.com; f. 1971; monthly; Editor-in-Chief Nancy Novogrod; circ. 973,821.

TV Guide: 11 West 42nd St, New York, NY 10036; tel. (212) 852-7500; fax (212) 852-7323; internet www.tvguide.com; f. 1953; weekly; Sr Vice-Pres. and Publr Pete Haeffner; Editor-in-Chief Debra Birnbaum; circ. 2,093,124.

US News & World Report: 1050 Thomas Jefferson St, NW, Washington, DC 20007-3837; tel. (202) 955-2000; fax (202) 955-2685; e-mail letters@usnews.com; internet www.usnews.com; f. 1933; monthly; online only from Jan. 2011; Publr Kerry F. Dyer; Chair. and Editor-in-Chief Mortimer B. Zuckerman; Editor Brian Kelly; circ. 1,269,260.

US Weekly: 1290 Ave of the Americas, 2nd Floor, New York, NY 10104-0298; tel. (212) 484-1616; fax (212) 484-4242; e-mail letters@usmagazine.com; internet www.usmagazine.com; f. 1977; weekly; Publr Victoria Lasdon Rose; Editor-in-Chief Michael Steele; circ. 1,952,885.

Vanity Fair: 4 Times Sq., 7th Floor, New York, NY 10036; tel. (212) 286-2860; fax (212) 286-7036; e-mail vfmail@vf.com; internet www.vanityfair.com; f. 1983; publ. by Condé Nast Publs Inc; monthly; Publr Edward Menicheschi; Editor-in-Chief Graydon Carter; circ. 1,198,618.

VFW Magazine: 406 West 34th St, Kansas City, MO 64111-2736; tel. (816) 756-3390; fax (816) 968-1169; e-mail info@vfw.org; internet www.vfw.org; f. 1912; 11 a year; Editor Richard K. Kolb; circ. 1,362,177.

VIA: 3055 Oak Rd, Mail Stop W510, Walnut Creek, CA 94597; tel. (925) 279-2441; fax (925) 279-5654; e-mail viamail@viamagazine.com; internet www.viamagazine.com; f. 1917; publ. by the California State Automobile Asscn; 6 a year; travel, motoring, insurance; Editor Bruce Anderson; circ. 2,805,214.

VIBE: 215 Lexington Ave, New York, NY 10016; tel. (212) 231-7300; fax (212) 231-7400; internet www.vibe.com; f. 1993; acquired by Keith Glen Media from VIBE/Spin Ventures in 2006; monthly; urban music and culture; also publ. *VIBE Vixen* (quarterly, circ. 340,000); Publr Jeff Mazzacano; Editor-in-Chief Jermaine Hall; circ. 863,283.

Vogue: 4 Times Sq., 12th Floor, New York, NY 10036; tel. (212) 286-2810; fax (212) 286-8593; e-mail voguemail@aol.com; internet www.style.com/vogue; f. 1892; monthly; also publ. *Men's Vogue* (10 a year, circ. 368,898) and *Teen Vogue* (10 a year, circ. 1,017,125); Sr Vice-Pres. and Publishing Dir Thomas A. Florio; Editor Anna Wintour; circ. 1,215,027.

Weight Watchers Magazine: 11 Madison Ave, 17th Floor, New York, NY 10010; tel. (212) 589-2791; fax (212) 589-2600; internet www.weightwatchers.com; f. 1968; monthly; Publr Andrew Amill; Editor Kate Greer; circ. 1,313,239.

WHERE: c/o Morris Visitor Publications, 699 Broad St, Suite 500, Augusta, GA 30901; tel. (800) 680-4035; internet wheretraveler.com; f. 1936; monthly; int. visitor information; 23 regional edns; Group Publr Peter Blackwell; Editorial Dir Marq de Villiers; circ. 1,182,466.

Woman's Day: 1633 Broadway, 42nd Floor, New York, NY 10019; tel. (212) 767-6418; e-mail womansday@hfmus.com; internet www.womansday.com; f. 1931; owned by Hachette Filipacchi; 17 a year; women's general interest; Vice-Pres. and Publr Carlos Lamadrid; Editor-in-Chief Elizabeth Mayhew; circ. 3,919,488.

Woman's World: Bauer Publishing, 270 Sylvan Ave, Englewood Cliffs, NJ 07632; tel. (201) 569-6699; fax (201) 569-5303; e-mail gregslattery@baueradsales.com; f. 1981; publ. by Bauer Publishing USA; weekly; women's general interest; other publs include *First* (circ. 1,377,895), *J-14* (circ. 440,857) and *Life & Style Weekly* (circ. 528,294); Publr Greg Slattery; Editor-in-Chief Stephanie Saible; circ. 1,387,414.

Working Mother: Bonnier Corpn, 2 Park Ave, 10th Floor, New York, NY 10016; tel. (212) 219-7492; fax (212) 219-7448; internet www.workingmother.com; f. 1978; publ. by Working Mother Media, Inc; lifestyle magazine with focus on working mothers; Pres. Carol Evans; Editor-in-Chief Suzanne Riss; circ. 828,301.

NEWS AGENCIES

Associated Press (AP): 450 West 33rd St, New York, NY 10001; tel. (212) 621-1500; fax (212) 621-1679; e-mail info@ap.org; internet www.ap.org; f. 1846; Chair. William Dean Singleton; Pres. and CEO Tom Curley; c. 1,700 newspaper mems in the USA, 6,000 broadcast mems and over 8,500 subscribers abroad.

Bloomberg: 731 Lexington Ave, New York, NY 10022; tel. (212) 318-2000; fax (212) 893-5371; internet www.bloomberg.com; f. 1981; provides business data, news and analytics; Pres. and Dir Daniel L. Doctoroff; Editor-in-Chief Matthew Winkler.

Dow Jones News Service: 1155 Ave of the Americas, 7th Floor, New York, NY 10036; internet www.dowjones.com; parent co, Dow Jones & Co, acquired by News Corpn in 2008; CEO Les Hinton.

Jewish Telegraphic Agency, Inc (JTA): 330 Seventh Ave, 17th Floor, New York, NY 10001; tel. (212) 643-1890; fax (212) 643-8498; e-mail info@jta.org; internet www.jta.org; f. 1917; world-wide coverage of Jewish news; offices in Washington, DC, and Jerusalem, Israel; Pres. Elisa Spungen Bildner; Editor-in-Chief Ami Eden.

THE UNITED STATES OF AMERICA

Religion News Service: 1930 18th St, NW, Suite B2, Washington, DC 20009; tel. (202) 463-8777; fax (202) 463-0033; e-mail info@religionnews.com; internet www.religionnews.com; f. 1934; Editor KEVIN ECKSTROM.

United Media (UM): 200 Madison Ave, 4th Floor, New York, NY 10016; tel. (212) 293-8500; fax (212) 293-8505; e-mail cpuello@unitedmedia.com; internet unitedfeatures.com; f. 1978; licensing and syndication of news features; owned by The E. W. Scripps Co; Pres. and CEO DOUGLAS R. STERN; Sr Vice-Pres. and Gen. Man. LISA KLEM WILSON; Exec. Editor SUMA C. M. (Comics and Text).

> **Newspaper Enterprise Association, Inc:** tel. (212) 293-8500; fax (212) 293-8600; internet www.unitedfeatures.com; division of United Media.

> **Scripps-Howard News Service:** 1090 Vermont Ave, NW, Suite 1000, Washington, DC 20005; tel. (202) 408-1484; fax (202) 408-2062; e-mail copelandp@snhs.com; internet www.shns.com; division of United Media; Editor and Gen. Man. PETER COPELAND.

> **United Feature Syndicate, Inc:** tel. (212) 293-8500; fax (212) 293-8720; f. 1922; division of United Media.

United Press International (UPI): 1133 19th St, NW, Washington, DC 20036; tel. (202) 898-8000; fax (202) 898-8048; e-mail editorforms@upi.com; internet www.upi.com; f. 1907; Pres. NICHOLAS CHIAIA; Exec. Editor JOHN HENDEL; serves c. 1,000 newspaper clients world-wide.

NATIONAL ASSOCIATIONS

American Business Media: 675 Third Ave, Suite 415, 7th Floor, New York, NY 10017-5704; tel. (212) 661-6360; fax (212) 370-0736; e-mail info@abmmail.com; internet www.americanbusinessmedia.com; f. 1906; Chair. CHARLES MCCURDY; Pres. and CEO CLARK PETTIT, II; 350 mem. cos, 124 assoc. mems.

American Society of Magazine Editors (ASME): 810 Seventh Ave, 24th Floor, New York, NY 10019; tel. (212) 872-3700; fax (212) 906-0128; e-mail asme@magazine.org; internet magazine.org/asme; Pres. DAVID WILLEY; Chief Exec. SID HOLT; 850 mems.

Audit Bureau of Circulations (ABC): 48 West Seegers Rd, Arlington Heights, IL 60005-3913; tel. (224) 366-6939; fax (224) 366-6949; e-mail kammi.altig@accessabc.com; internet www.accessabc.com; f. 1914; Chair. MERLE K. DAVIDSON; Pres. and Man. Dir MICHAEL J. LAVERY; over 4,000 mems.

Council of Literary Magazines and Presses (CLMP): 154 Christopher St, Suite 3C, New York, NY 10014-9110; tel. (212) 741-9110; fax (212) 741-9112; e-mail info@clmp.org; internet www.clmp.org; f. 1967; provides services to non-commercial US literary magazines and presses; Exec. Dir JEFFREY LEPENDORF; 347 mems.

MPA—The Association of Magazine Media: 810 Seventh Ave, 24th Floor, New York, NY 10019; tel. (212) 872-3700; fax (212) 888-4217; e-mail mpa@magazine.org; internet www.magazine.org; f. 1919; fmrly Magazine Publishers of America; adopted present name in 2010; Chair. JACK H. GRIFFIN; Pres. and CEO NINA B. LINK; 200 mem. cos and 90 assoc. mems.

> **Publishers' Information Bureau:** 810 Seventh Ave, New York, NY 10019; tel. (212) 872-3722; fax (212) 753-2768; e-mail pib@magazine.org; internet www.magazine.org/pib; f. 1945; part of MPA; tracks advertising carried by consumer magazines; 250 mem. publs; Pres. WAYNE P. EADIE.

National Newspaper Association: 134 Neff Annex, POB 7540, Columbia, MO 65205-7540; tel. (573) 882-5800; fax (573) 884-5490; e-mail info@nna.org; internet www.nnaweb.org; f. 1885 as National Editorial Association; present name adopted 1964; Pres. ELIZABETH K. PARKER; over 2,700 mems.

Newspaper Association of America: 4401 Wilson Blvd, Suite 900, Arlington, VA 22203-1867; tel. (571) 366-1000; fax (571) 366-1195; internet www.naa.org; f. 1992; Chair. MARK G. CONTRERAS; Pres. and CEO JOHN F. STURM; more than 2,000 mems in USA and Canada accounting for over 87% of US daily newspaper circulation.

The Newspaper Guild: 501 Third St, NW, Washington, DC 20001-2797; tel. (202) 434-7177; fax (202) 434-1472; e-mail guild@cwa-union.org; internet www.newsguild.org; f. 1933; journalists' org., organ of the Communications Workers of America trade union; Pres. BERNARD J. LUNZER; Admin. Dir TIMOTHY SCHICK; over 34,000 mems in the USA, Puerto Rico and Canada.

Periodical & Book Association of America Inc: 481 Eighth Ave, Suite 826, New York, NY 10001; tel. (212) 563-6502; fax (212) 563-4098; e-mail lscott@pbaa.net; internet www.pbaa.net; Pres. JOSEPH GALLO; Exec. Dir LISA W. SCOTT; 110 mems.

Publishers

Abaris Books: 64 Wall St, Norwalk, CT 06850; tel. (203) 838-8625; fax (203) 857-0730; e-mail abaris@abarisbooks.com; internet www.abarisbooks.com; f. 1973; division of Opal Publishing Corpn; scholarly, fine art reference, philosophy; Publr ANTHONY S. KAUFMANN; Man. Editor J. C. WEST.

Abbeville Press, Inc: 137 Varick St, New York, NY 10013; tel. (212) 366-5585; fax (212) 366-6966; e-mail abbeville@abbeville.com; internet www.abbeville.com; f. 1977; fine arts and illustrated books; Pres. and Publr ROBERT E. ABRAMS.

Abingdon Press: 201 Eighth Ave South, POB 801, Nashville, TN 37202-0801; tel. (615) 749-6290; fax (615) 749-6512; e-mail orders@abingdonpress.com; internet www.abingdonpress.com; an imprint of The United Methodist Publishing House (f. 1789); religious; Vice-Pres. TAMMY GAINES.

Abrams: 115 West 18th St, New York, NY 10011; tel. (212) 206-7715; fax (212) 519-1210; e-mail abrams@abramsbooks.com; internet www.abramsbooks.com; f. 1949; acquired by Times Mirror Co in 1966; 7 imprints incl. Abrams Books (art, photography, design, architecture), Stewart, Tabori & Chang (f. 1981, cooking, design, gardening, crafts, pets, health, sports, and popular culture), Amulet Books (f. 2004, youth fiction and non-fiction) and Abrams Image (f. 2006, music, humour, reference, photography, design and popular culture); owned by Groupe de la Martinière, France; Pres. and CEO MICHAEL JACOBS.

AFB Press: 2 Penn Plaza, Suite 1102, New York, NY 10001; tel. (212) 502-7651; fax (917) 210-3979; e-mail press@afb.net; internet www.afb.org/store; publishing arm of the American Foundation for the Blind; books, journals, videos, and electronic materials on visual impairment for professionals, researchers and blind or visually impaired individuals and their families; Pres. and CEO CARL R. AUGUSTO; Dir and Editor-in-Chief NATALIE HILZEN.

Alfred Publishing Co, Inc: 16320 Roscoe Blvd, Suite 100, Van Nuys, CA 91410-0003; tel. (818) 892-2452; fax (818) 891-6252; e-mail info@alfred.com; internet www.alfred.com; f. 1922; educational music, methods and texts; Pres. MORTY MANUS; CEO STEVEN MANUS.

Andrews McMeel Publishing: c/o Simon & Schuster, Inc, 100 Front St, Riverside, NJ 08075; tel. (816) 932-6700; fax (816) 932-6706; e-mail licensing@amuniversal.com; internet www.andrewsmcmeel.com; f. 1970; humour, general trade; Pres. and CEO HUGH T. ANDREWS.

Augsburg Fortress, Publishers: 100 South Fifth St, POB 1209, Minneapolis, MN 55440; tel. (612) 330-3300; fax (612) 330-3455; e-mail info@augsburgfortress.org; internet www.augsburgfortress.org; f. 1890; publishing arm of the Evangelical Lutheran Church in America; religious (evangelical Lutheran) non-fiction; Pres. and CEO BETH LEWIS.

August House Inc, Publishers: 3500 Piedmont Rd, NE Suite 310, Atlanta, GA 30305; tel. (404) 442-4420; fax (404) 442-4435; e-mail ahinfo@augusthouse.com; internet www.augusthouse.com; f. 1979; Southern regional, history, humour and folklore; CEO STEVE FLOYD.

B&H Publishing Group: 127 Ninth Ave North, Nashville, TN 37234-0143; tel. (615) 251-5614; fax (615) 251-2701; e-mail miriam.evans@bhpublishinggroup.com; internet www.bhpublishinggroup.com; f. 1891; fmrly Broadman & Holman Publrs; present name adopted in 2006; religious (Protestant), fiction, non-fiction, reference and juvenile; Pres. SELMA WILSON; Publr DAVID SHEPHERD.

Baker Publishing Group: 6030 East Fulton Rd, Ada, MI 49301; tel. (616) 676-9185; fax (616) 676-9573; e-mail media@bakerbooks.com; internet www.bakerpublishinggroup.com; f. 1939; imprints incl. Brazos Press (Protestant and evangelical, Roman Catholic and Eastern Orthodox), Chosen Books (f. 1971, evangelical and charismatic Christian non-fiction), and Revell (Christian fiction and non-fiction); Pres. DWIGHT BAKER.

Ballantine Publishing Group: 1745 Broadway, New York, NY 10019; tel. (212) 572-2713; fax (212) 572-4912; e-mail bfi@randomhouse.com; internet www.randomhouse.com/rhpg; f. 1952; division of Random House Inc; fiction, non-fiction, reprints; Pres. GINA CENTRELLO.

Barnes and Noble Books: POB 111, Lyndhurst, NJ 07071; tel. (800) 962-6177; fax (212) 559-6910; e-mail customerservice@bn.com; internet www.barnesandnoble.com; f. 1873; division of Rowman & Littlefield Publrs, Inc; educational and general; Chair. LEONARD RIGGIO; CEO WILLIAM J. LYNCH.

Barron's Educational Series, Inc: 250 Wireless Blvd, Hauppauge, NY 11788; tel. (631) 434-3311; fax (631) 434-3723; e-mail barrons@barronseduc.com; internet www.barronseduc.com; f. 1945; general non-fiction, educational and juvenile; Chair. and CEO MANUEL H. BARRON; Pres. and Publr ELLEN SIBLEY.

Beacon Press: 25 Beacon St, Boston, MA 02108; tel. (617) 742-2110; fax (617) 723-3097; e-mail lriviere@beacon.org; internet www.beacon.org; f. 1854; dept of the Unitarian Universalist Asscn; world affairs, religion and general non-fiction; Dir HELENE ATWAN.

R. R. Bowker LLC: 630 Central Ave, New Providence, NJ 07974; tel. (888) 269-5372; fax (888) 286-1090; e-mail info@bowker.com;

THE UNITED STATES OF AMERICA

internet www.bowker.com; f. 1872; reference and bibliography; Pres. and CEO ANNIE CALLANAN.

Branden Books, Inc: POB 812094, Wellesley, MA 02482; tel. (781) 734-2046; fax (781) 790-1056; e-mail branden@brandenbooks.com; internet www.brandenbooks.com; f. 1909 as The Four Seasons Press; art, music, classics, fiction and non-fiction; Pres. MARGARET CASO; Editor and Treas. ADOLPH CASO.

George Braziller, Inc: 174 East, 74th St, New York, NY 10021; tel. (212) 737-9842; fax (212) 689-5405; e-mail georgebraziller@earthlink.net; internet www.georgebraziller.com; f. 1955; art, fiction and non-fiction; Publr GEORGE BRAZILLER.

Brookings Institution Press: 1775 Massachusetts Ave, NW, Washington, DC 20036-2103; tel. (202) 797-6000; fax (202) 536-3623; e-mail bibooks@brookings.edu; internet www.brookings.edu; f. 1927; economics, govt, foreign policy; Dir ROBERT L. FAHERTY.

Cambridge University Press: 32 Ave of the Americas, New York, NY 10013-2473; tel. (212) 924-3900; fax (212) 691-3239; e-mail information@cup.org; internet www.cambridge.org/us; scholarly; CEO STEPHEN BOURNE; Pres. RICHARD ZIEMACKI.

Catholic University of America Press: 620 Michigan Ave, NE, Washington, DC 20064; tel. (202) 319-5052; fax (202) 319-4985; e-mail cua-press@cua.edu; internet cuapress.cua.edu; f. 1939; scholarly; Dir and Editor-in-Chief DAVID J. MCGONAGLE.

Caxton Press: 312 Main St, Caldwell, ID 83605; tel. (208) 647-6465; fax (208) 459-7450; e-mail sgipson@caxtonpress.com; internet www.caxtonpress.com; f. 1903; Western Americana; Vice-Pres. and Publr SCOTT GIPSON.

Columbia University Press: 61 West 62nd St, New York, NY 10023; tel. (212) 459-0600; fax (212) 459-3678; e-mail cup_books@columbia.edu; internet www.columbia.edu/cu/cup; f. 1893; trade, educational, scientific and reference; Pres. and Dir JAMES D. JORDAN.

Concordia Publishing House (CPH): 3558 South Jefferson Ave, St Louis, MO 63118-3968; tel. (800) 325-3040; fax (800) 490-9889; e-mail order@cph.org; internet www.cph.org; f. 1869; publishing arm of the Lutheran Church—Missouri Synod; religious (Lutheran) children's books, devotionals and curriculum music; Pres. and CEO BRUCE G. KINTZ.

Cornell University Press: Sage House, 512 East State St, POB 250, Ithaca, NY 14850; tel. (607) 277-2338; fax (607) 277-2374; e-mail cupressinfo@cornell.edu; internet www.cornellpress.cornell.edu; f. 1869; scholarly, non-fiction; imprints incl. Comstock Publishing Associates, ILR Press and Fall Creek Books; Dir JOHN G. ACKERMAN.

CQ Press: 2300 N St, NW, Suite 800, Washington, DC 20037; tel. (202) 729-1900; fax (202) 729-1403; e-mail ahigginbotham@cqpress.com; internet www.cqpress.com; f. 1945; fmrly Congressional Quarterly Books; division of SAGE Publications; business, education and govt; directories; Pres. and Publr JOHN A. JENKINS.

The Creative Co: 123 South Broad St, POB 227, Mankato, MN 56001; tel. (507) 388-6273; fax (507) 388-2746; e-mail info@thecreativecompany.us; internet www.thecreativecompany.us; f. 1932; juvenile; Pres. TOM PETERSON.

F. A. Davis Co: 1915 Arch St, Philadelphia, PA 19103; tel. (215) 568-2270; fax (215) 568-5065; e-mail info@fadavis.com; internet www.fadavis.com; f. 1879; medical, nursing and allied health textbooks; Pres. ROBERT H. CRAVEN, Jr.

Dover Publications, Inc: 31 East Second St, Mineola, NY 11501; tel. (516) 294-7000; fax (516) 742-1401; internet www.doverpublications.com; f. 1941; trade, reprints, scientific, classics, language, arts and crafts; Pres. PAUL NEGRI.

Dufour Editions, Inc: POB 7, Chester Springs, PA 19425-0007; tel. (610) 458-5005; fax (610) 458-7103; e-mail info@dufoureditions.com; internet www.dufoureditions.com; f. 1949; literature, political science, humanities, music and history; Pres. CHRISTOPHER MAY.

Duke University Press: POB 90660, Duke University, Durham, NC 27708-0660; tel. (888) 651-0122; fax (888) 651-0124; e-mail bpublicity@dukeupress.edu; internet www.dukeupress.edu; f. 1921; scholarly; Editorial Dir KEN WISSOKER.

Duquesne University Press: 600 Forbes Ave, Pittsburgh, PA 15282; tel. (412) 396-6610; fax (412) 396-5984; e-mail wadsworth@duq.edu; internet www.dupress.duq.edu; f. 1927; scholarly; Dir SUSAN WADSWORTH-BOOTH; Production Editor KATHY MEYER.

Ediciones Universal: 3090 South West Eighth St, Miami, FL 33135; tel. (305) 642-3234; fax (305) 642-7978; e-mail ediciones@ediciones.com; internet www.ediciones.com; f. 1965; Spanish language fiction and non-fiction; Man. JUAN MANUEL SALVAT.

Elsevier: 11830 Westline Industrial Dr., St Louis, MO 63146; tel. (314) 453-6198; fax (314) 453-7095; e-mail usbkinfo@elsevier.com; internet www.elsevier.com; f. 1962; division of Reed Elsevier Group PLC; health sciences imprints incl. Butterworth-Heinemann (f. 1975, technology, medicine and management), Churchill Livingstone (f. 1972, medicine), Hanley & Belfus (f. 1984, medical textbooks and reference materials), Mosby (f. 1906, textbooks and reference materials on medicine, nursing, allied health and veterinary medicine), and W. B. Saunders Co (f. 1888, medicine); science and technology imprints incl. Academic Press (science, technology and business), Architectural Press (architecture), Focal Press (media technology), and Morgan Kaufmann (f. 1984, computing); CEO ERIK ENGSTROM.

Encyclopaedia Britannica, Inc: 331 North LaSalle St, Chicago, IL 60654; tel. (800) 621-3900; fax (800) 344-9624; e-mail international@eb.com; internet www.eb.com; f. 1768; encyclopaedias, atlases, dictionaries; Pres. JORGE CAUZ.

Facts On File Inc: 132 West 31st St, 17th Floor, New York, NY 10001; tel. (212) 896-4269; fax (917) 339-0323; e-mail custserv@factsonfile.com; internet www.infobasepublishing.com; f. 1941; acquired by Veronis Suhler Stevenson in 2005; imprints incl. Ferguson Publishing (f. 1907, children's reference), Chelsea House Publishers and World Almanac; non-fiction, reference and electronic databases; Publr MARK MCDONNELL.

Farrar, Straus and Giroux, Inc (FSG): 18 West 18th St, New York, NY 10011; tel. (212) 741-6900; fax (212) 633-9385; e-mail fsg.publicity@fsgbooks.com; internet us.macmillan.com/fsg.aspx; f. 1946; acquired by Holtzbrinck Publrs, LLC in 1994; imprints incl. Hill and Wang (f. 1956), Faber and Faber, Inc, and North Point Press; literature, international fiction, history, current affairs and science; Pres. JONATHAN GALASSI.

Fordham University Press: University Box L, Bronx, NY 10458-5172; tel. (718) 817-4795; fax (718) 817-4785; e-mail bkaobrien@fordham.edu; internet www.fordhampress.com; f. 1907; scholarly; Editorial Dir HELEN TARTAR.

W. H. Freeman & Co, Publishers: 41 Madison Ave, 37th Floor, New York, NY 10010; tel. (212) 576-9400; fax (212) 689-2383; e-mail international@whfreeman.com; internet www.whfreeman.com; f. 1946; part of Holtzbrinck Publrs, LLC; textbooks; Pres. ELIZABETH WIDDICOMBE.

Samuel French, Inc: 45 West 25th St, New York, NY 10010; tel. (212) 206-8990; fax (212) 206-1429; e-mail info@samuelfrench.com; internet www.samuelfrench.com; f. 1830; plays; Pres. and CEO LEON EMBRY.

Gale Cengage Learning: 27500 Drake Rd, Farmington Hills, MI 48331-3535; tel. (248) 669-4253; fax (248) 669-8064; e-mail lindsay.brown@cengage.com; internet gale.cengage.com; f. 1954; division of Cengage Learning; reference; Pres. GORDON T. MACOMBER.

Garland Science Publishing, Inc: 270 Madison Ave, New York, NY 10016; tel. (917) 351-7100; fax (212) 947-3027; e-mail info@garland.com; internet www.garlandscience.com; f. 1969; part of the Taylor & Francis Group; biology and chemistry textbooks; Vice-Pres. DENISE SCHANCK.

Genealogical Publishing Co: 3600 Clipper Mill Rd, Suite 260, Baltimore, MD 21211; tel. (410) 837-8271; fax (410) 752-8492; e-mail info@genealogical.com; internet www.genealogical.com; f. 1959; genealogy, immigration studies, heraldry and local history; Editor-in-Chief MICHAEL TEPPER.

The K. S. Giniger Co, Inc: 1045 Park Ave, New York, NY 10028; tel. and fax (212) 369-6692; f. 1965; general non-fiction; Pres. KENNETH S. GINIGER.

Greenwood Publishing Group, Inc: 88 Post Rd West, POB 5007, Westport, CT 06881; tel. (203) 226-3571; fax (203) 222-1502; e-mail webmaster@greenwood.com; internet www.greenwood.com; f. 1967; division of Reed Elsevier Group PLC; comprises Greenwood Press (reference), Heinemann (f. 1978, educational, teaching, professional development), Praeger Publrs (f. 1949, academic and general-interest non-fiction) and Libraries Unlimited (educational and reference); business reference and non-fiction; Pres. WAYNE SMITH.

Grove/Atlantic, Inc: 841 Broadway, New York, NY 10003-4793; tel. (212) 614-7850; fax (212) 614-7886; e-mail info@groveatlantic.com; internet www.groveatlantic.com; f. 1993 by merger of Grove Press and Atlantic Monthly Press (f. 1917); fiction, non-fiction, biography, history, social science, poetry; Pres. MORGAN ENTREKIN.

Hammond World Atlas Corpn: American Map-Langenscheidt Publishing Group, 15 Tyger River Dr., Duncan, SC 29334; tel. (864) 486-8289; fax (864) 486-0214; e-mail customerservice@americanmap.com; internet www.hammondmap.com; f. 1900; division of American Map-Langenscheidt Publishing Group; maps, atlases, cartography; Chair. and CEO STUART DOLGINS.

HarperCollins Publishers: 10 East 53rd St, New York, NY 10022; tel. (212) 207-7000; fax (212) 207-7759; e-mail orders@harpercollins.com; internet www.harpercollins.com; f. 1817; subsidiary of News Corpn; imprints incl. Amistad, Avon (f. 1941, romantic fiction), Avon A, Caedmon, Collins (general reference), Rayo (Latino culture) and William Morrow (f. 1926, fiction and non-fiction); fiction, non-fiction, religious, children's, medical, general; Pres. and CEO BRIAN MURRAY.

Harvard University Press: 79 Garden St, Cambridge, MA 02138; tel. (617) 495-2800; fax (401) 531-2801; e-mail contact_hup@harvard.edu; internet www.hup.harvard.edu; f. 1913; classics, fine arts,

THE UNITED STATES OF AMERICA

philosophy, science, medicine, law, literature, political science, religion, history and govt; Dir WILLIAM P. SISLER.

Hastings House/Daytrips Publishers: POB 908, Winter Park, FL 32790-0908; tel. (407) 339-3600; fax (407) 339-5900; e-mail hastings_daytrips@earthlink.net; internet www.hastingshousebooks.com; f. 1936; travel; Publr PETER LEERS.

Holiday House, Inc: 425 Madison Ave, New York, NY 10017; tel. (212) 688-0085; fax (212) 421-6134; e-mail info@holidayhouse.com; internet www.holidayhouse.com; f. 1935; juvenile; Pres. JOHN H. BRIGGS, Jr.

Holloway House Book Publishing Co: 8060 Melrose Ave, Los Angeles, CA 90046-7082; tel. (323) 653-8060; fax (323) 655-9452; e-mail info@psiemail.com; internet www.hollowayhousebooks.com; f. 1960; black experience and American Indian literature, gambling, fiction, non-fiction; CEO BENTLEY MORRISS.

Holmes & Meier Publishers, Inc: POB 943, Teaneck, NJ 07666; tel. (201) 833-2270; fax (201) 833-2272; e-mail info@holmesandmeier.com; internet www.holmesandmeier.com; f. 1969; imprints incl. Africana Publishing Co (f. 1969); history, political science, area studies, Africana, Judaica, foreign literature in translation, college texts and scholarly; Publr MIRIAM H. HOLMES.

Hoover Institution Press: 434 Galvez Mall, Stanford University, Stanford, CA 94305-6010; tel. (650) 723-3373; fax (650) 723-8626; internet www.hooverpress.org; f. 1962; scholarly; Assoc. Dir ERYN WITCHER.

Houghton Mifflin Harcourt: 222 Berkeley St, Boston, MA 02116; tel. (617) 351-5000; fax (617) 351-1125; e-mail corporate .communications@hmhpub.com; internet www.hmco.com; f. 1919 as Harcourt Inc; owned by Education Media and Publishing Group; fmrly Houghton Mifflin Riverdeep Group PLC; changed name in December 2007; general and educational; Interim CEO and CFO MICHAEL MULDOWNEY.

Indiana University Press: 601 North Morton St, Bloomington, IN 47404-3797; tel. (812) 855-8817; fax (812) 855-8507; e-mail iupress@indiana.edu; internet www.iupress.indiana.edu; f. 1950; trade and scholarly non-fiction; Dir JANET RABINOWITCH.

International Universities Press, Inc: 59 Boston Post Rd, Madison, CT 06443; tel. (203) 245-4000; fax (203) 245-0775; e-mail info@iup.com; internet www.iup.com; f. 1943; publrs of PsychoSocial Press; psychology, psychiatry, medicine, social sciences and journals; Exec. Vice-Pres. Dr MARGARET EMERY.

Islamic Books/Tahrike Tarsile Qur'ān, Inc: 80-08 51st Ave, Elmhurst, NY 11373-0115; tel. (718) 446-6472; fax (718) 446-4370; e-mail read@koranusa.org; internet www.koranusa.org; f. 1978; Koran and Islamic religious texts; Pres. AUN ALI KHALFAN.

Jewish Publication Society: 2100 Arch St, 2nd Floor, Philadelphia, PA 19103; tel. (215) 832-0600; fax (215) 568-2017; e-mail jewishbook@jewishpub.org; internet www.jewishpub.org; f. 1888; Judaica; CEO BARRY L. SCHWARTZ; Editor-in-Chief Dr ELLEN FRANKEL.

Johns Hopkins University Press: 2715 North Charles St, Baltimore, MD 21218-4363; tel. (410) 516-6900; fax (410) 516-6968; e-mail kk@press.jhu.edu; internet www.press.jhu.edu; f. 1878; social and physical sciences, humanities, health sciences, economics, literary criticism, history; Dir KATHLEEN KEANE.

Kendall/Hunt Publishing Co: 4050 Westmark Dr., POB 1840, Dubuque, IA 52004-1840; tel. (563) 589-1000; fax (563) 589-1046; e-mail orders@kendallhunt.com; internet www.kendallhunt.com; f. 1944; business and educational; CEO MARK FALB.

Krieger Publishing Co: 1725 Krieger Dr., Malabar, FL 32950; tel. (321) 724-9542; fax (321) 951-3671; e-mail info@krieger-pubishing.com; internet www.krieger-publishing.com; f. 1970; space technology, adult education, history and natural sciences; Pres. DONALD E. KRIEGER.

Loyola Press: 3441 North Ashland Ave, Chicago, IL 60657; tel. (773) 281-1818; fax (773) 281-0885; e-mail lane@loyolapress.com; internet www.loyolapress.com; f. 1912; owned by the Society of Jesus, Chicago Province; religious (Roman Catholic) education and language, religious trade and arts; Pres. GEORGE A. LANE.

McGraw-Hill Companies, Inc: 1221 Ave of the Americas, New York, NY 10020-1095; tel. (212) 904-2000; fax (614) 759-3749; e-mail customer.service@mcgraw-hill.com; internet www.mcgraw-hill.com; f. 1888; information texts and services for business, industry, govt and the general public; Chair., Pres. and CEO HAROLD MCGRAW, III.

Merriam-Webster Inc: 47 Federal St, POB 281, Springfield, MA 01102; tel. (413) 734-3134; fax (413) 731-5979; e-mail jwithgott@merriam-webster.com; internet www.merriam-webster.com; f. 1831; subsidiary of Encyclopaedia Britannica, Inc; dictionaries, reference; Pres. and Publr JOHN M. MORSE.

Michigan State University Press: Manly Miles Bldg, Suite 25, 1405 South Harrison Rd, East Lansing, MI 48823-5245; tel. (517) 355-9543; fax (517) 432-2611; e-mail msupress@msu.edu; internet msupress.msu.edu; f. 1947; scholarly; Dir GABRIEL DOTTO.

The MIT Press: 55 Hayward St, Cambridge, MA 02142-1493; tel. (617) 253-5646; fax (617) 258-6779; internet mitpress.mit.edu; f. 1932; computer sciences, architecture, design, linguistics, economics, philosophy, general science, neuroscience, cognitive science and engineering; Dir ELLEN W. FARAN.

Moody Publishers: 820 North LaSalle Blvd, Chicago, IL 60610; tel. (312) 329-2101; fax (312) 329-4157; e-mail pressinfo@moody.edu; internet www.moodypublishers.org; f. 1894; publishing division of Moody Bible Institute (f. 1886); religious; Vice-Pres., Publications GREG THORNTON.

National Academy Press (NAP): 500 Fifth St, NW, POB 285, Washington, DC 20055; tel. (202) 334-3180; fax (202) 334-2793; e-mail customer_service@nap.edu; internet www.nap.edu; f. 1863; division of Nat. Academy of Sciences; scientific and technical reports, abstracts, bibliographies, catalogues; Dir BARBARA KLINE POPE.

National Learning Corpn: 212 Michael Dr., Syosset, NY 11791; tel. (516) 921-8888; fax (516) 921-8743; e-mail info@passbooks.com; internet www.passbooks.com; f. 1967; professional and vocational study guides; Pres. MICHAEL P. RUDMAN.

New Directions Publishing Corpn: 80 Eighth Ave, New York, NY 10011; tel. (212) 255-0230; fax (212) 255-0231; e-mail editorial@ndbooks.com; internet www.ndpublishing.com; f. 1936; modern literature, poetry and criticism; Pres. PEGGY L. FOX; Publr BARBARA EPLER.

New York University Press: 838 Broadway, 3rd Floor, New York, NY 10003-4812; tel. (212) 998-2575; fax (212) 995-3833; e-mail information@nyupress.org; internet www.nyupress.org; f. 1916; scholarly and non-fiction; Dir STEVE MAIKOWSKI.

Northwestern University Press: 629 Noyes St, Evanston, IL 60208-4210; tel. (847) 491-2046; fax (847) 491-8150; e-mail nupress@northwestern.edu; internet www.nupress.northwestern.edu; f. 1958; scholarly and trade; Dir JANE BUNKER.

W. W. Norton & Co Inc: 500 Fifth Ave, New York, NY 10110; tel. (212) 354-5500; fax (212) 869-0856; e-mail srothbard@wwnorton.com; internet www.wwnorton.com; f. 1923; college textbooks, paperbacks, fiction and non-fiction; Pres. DRAKE MCFEELY.

NOVA Publications: 7342 Lee Hwy, No. 201, Falls Church, VA 22046; tel. and fax (703) 280-5383; e-mail novapublic@aol.com; internet www.members.aol.com/novapublic/index.htm; f. 1993; military history, political science, Russian and Middle Eastern studies; Publr ARNOLD C. DUPUY.

The Ohio State University Press: 180 Pressey Hall, 1070 Carmack Rd, Columbus, OH 43210-1002; tel. (614) 292-6930; fax (614) 292-2065; e-mail info@osupress.org; internet www.ohiostatepress.org; f. 1957; scholarly; Dir MALCOLM LITCHFIELD.

Ohio University Press: 19 Circle Dr., The Ridges, Athens, OH 45701-2979; tel. (740) 593-1154; fax (740) 593-4536; e-mail cunningh@ohio.edu; internet www.ohiou.edu/oupress; f. 1964; scholarly and regional studies; Editorial Dir GILLIAN BERCHOWITZ.

Open Court Publishing Co: 70 East Lake St, Suite 300, Chicago, IL 60601; tel. (312) 701-1720; fax (312) 701-1728; e-mail opencourt@caruspub.com; internet www.opencourtbooks.com; f. 1887; philosophy and general non-fiction; Pres. and Publr ANDRÉ CARUS.

Orbis Books: Price Bldg, POB 302, Maryknoll, NY 10545-0302; tel. (914) 941-7636; fax (914) 941-7005; e-mail orbisbooks@maryknoll.org; internet www.orbisbooks.com; f. 1970; owned by the Catholic Foreign Mission Society of America (Maryknoll); theology, religion and social concerns; Publr ROBERT ELLSBERG.

Oxford University Press, Inc: 198 Madison Ave, New York, NY 10016; tel. (212) 726-6000; fax (212) 677-1303; e-mail custserv.us@oup.com; internet www.oup.com/us; f. 1896; non-fiction, trade, religious, reference, college textbooks, medical and music; Pres. TIM BARTON.

Paladin Press: Gunbarrel Tech Center, 7077 Winchester Circle, Boulder, CO 80301-3505; tel. (303) 443-7250; fax (303) 442-8741; e-mail service@paladin-press.com; internet www.paladin-press.com; f. 1970; imprints incl. Sycamore Island Books and Flying Machines Press; military science and history; Chair. and Pres. PEDER C. LUND.

Paragon House: 1925 Oakcrest Ave, Suite 7, St Paul, MN 55113-2619; tel. (651) 644-3087; fax (651) 644-0997; e-mail paragon@paragonhouse.com; internet www.paragonhouse.com; f. 1982; academic non-fiction, university texts; Pres. GORDON L. ANDERSON.

Pearson Education: 1 Lake St, Upper Saddle River, NJ 07458; tel. (201) 236-7000; e-mail communications@pearsoned.com; internet www.pearsoned.com; imprints incl. Addison-Wesley, Allyn & Bacon, FT Prentice Hall, Scotts Foreman, Benjamin Cummings and Longman; educational; CEO JOHN FALLON.

Penguin Group (USA) Inc: 375 Hudson St, New York, NY 10014; tel. (212) 366-2000; fax (212) 366-2666; internet us.penguingroup

.com; f. 1996 by merger between Penguin Books USA and the Putnam Berkley Group; imprints incl. Ace Books (f. 1953, science fiction), Alpha (f. 1991, general reference), Avery (f. 1976, health, self-help, diet, and fitness), Berkley (f. 1955, mass-market and trade paperback), Dutton (f. 1852, fiction and non-fiction), Gotham (f. 2001, non-fiction), HP Books (automotive, photography, gardening, health and child care), Hudson Street Press (f. 2003, hardcover non-fiction), Jeremy P. Tarcher (f. 1976, non-fiction), NAL (f. 1948, paperback fiction), Penguin (f. 1936, paperback), Plume (f. 1970, paperback), Portfolio (f. 2001, business), Putnam (f. 1838, fiction and non-fiction), Riverhead (f. 1994, fiction), Sentinel (f. 2003, conservative), and Viking (f. 1925, fiction and non-fiction); CEO David Shanks; Pres. Susan Petersen Kennedy.

Pennsylvania State University Press: University Support Bldg I, Suite C, 820 North University Dr., University Park, PA 16802-1003; tel. (814) 865-1327; fax (814) 863-1408; e-mail info@psupress.org; internet www.psupress.org; f. 1956; scholarly non-fiction; Dir Patrick H. Alexander.

Presbyterian Publishing Corpn (PPC): 100 Witherspoon St, Louisville, KY 40202-1396; tel. (502) 569-5081; fax (502) 569-5113; e-mail customer_service@presbypub.com; internet www.ppcbooks.com; f. 1938; publishing arm of the Presbyterian Church (USA); imprints incl. Geneva Press (religious trade) and Westminster John Knox Press (f. 1938, non-denominational Christian, modern religious and scholarly); Pres. and Publr Marc Lewis.

Princeton University Press: 41 William St, Princeton, NJ 08540; tel. (609) 258-4900; fax (609) 258-6305; e-mail webmaster@press.princeton.edu; internet press.princeton.edu; f. 1905; scholarly; Dir Peter J. Dougherty; Editor-in-Chief Brigitta van Rheinberg.

Quite Specific Media Group Ltd: 7373 Pyramid Pl., Hollywood, CA 90046; tel. (323) 851-5797; fax (323) 851-5798; e-mail info@quitespecificmedia.com; internet www.quitespecificmedia.com; f. 1967; costume, design, fashion and performing arts; Publr Ralph Pine.

Rand McNally: 9855 Woods Dr., Skokie, IL 60076; tel. (847) 329-8100; fax (800) 934-3479; e-mail kconkey@reynoldsgroup.com; internet www.randmcnally.com; f. 1856; maps, atlases, travel guides and educational; Pres. and CEO Andrzej Wrobel.

Random House Publishing Group: 1745 Broadway, New York, NY 10019; tel. (212) 782-9000; fax (212) 572-8026; internet www.randomhouse.com; f. 2003 by merger of the Random House Trade Group and Ballantine Books Group; imprints incl. Random House Inc (f. 1925, originals, reprints, paperbacks, juvenile, series, textbooks), Ballantine Books (f. 1952, hardcover, trade and mass-market paperback), Del Rey (f. 1977, science fiction and fantasy), Modern Library (f. 1925, non-fiction and history), One World (f. 1991, multicultural), Presidio Press (military history), and Villard (f. 1983, general fiction and non-fiction); Chair. and CEO Markus Dohle; Pres. and Publr Gina Centrello.

Reader's Digest Association: Reader's Digest Rd, Pleasantville, NY 10570-7000; tel. (914) 238-1000; fax (914) 238-4559; internet www.rd.com; f. 1922; reference and non-fiction; Pres. and CEO Mary Berner.

Rizzoli International Publications: 300 Park Ave South, 3rd Floor, New York, NY 10010-5399; tel. (212) 387-3400; fax (212) 387-3535; e-mail comments@rizzoliusa.com; internet www.rizzoliusa.com; f. 1975; division of RCS Media Group (Italy); fine arts, performing arts, architecture; Pres. and CEO Marco Ausenda; Vice-Pres. and Publr Charles Miers.

Routledge: 270 Madison Ave, New York, NY 10016-0602; tel. (212) 216-7800; fax (212) 563-2269; e-mail info@taylorandfrancis.com; internet www.routledge.com; f. 1977; imprint of Taylor & Francis Group (q.v.); scholarly, professional, trade, humanities, social sciences; Pres. Emmett Dages.

Rutgers University Press: 100 Joyce Kilmer Ave, Piscataway, NJ 08854; tel. (732) 445-7762; fax (732) 445-7039; e-mail jwi@rutgers.edu; internet rutgerspress.rutgers.edu; f. 1936; trade, scholarly and regional; Dir Marlie Wasserman.

William H. Sadlier Inc: 9 Pine St, New York, NY 10005-1002; tel. (212) 227-2120; fax (212) 267-8696; e-mail BDingerJr@sadlier.com; internet www.sadlier.com; f. 1832; textbooks; Man. William Sadlier Dinger, Jr.

St Martin's Press Inc: 175 Fifth Ave, New York, NY 10010; tel. (212) 674-5151; fax (212) 420-9314; e-mail webmaster@stmartins.com; internet us.macmillan.com/smp.aspx; f. 1952; part of Holtzbrinck Publrs, LLC; general, scholarly, college textbooks, trade and mass-market; Pres. John Sargent.

Scarecrow Press, Inc: 4501 Forbes Blvd, Suite 200, Lanham, MD 20706; tel. (301) 459-3366; fax (301) 429-5748; e-mail customercare@rowman.com; internet www.scarecrowpress.com; f. 1950; subsidiary of Rowman & Littlefield, Inc; music, film, theatre, reference, textbooks, library and information science; Publr and Editorial Dir Edward Kurdyla.

Scholastic, Inc: 555 Broadway, New York, NY 10012; tel. (212) 343-6100; fax (212) 343-6930; e-mail customerservice@scholastic.com; internet www.scholastic.com; f. 1920; children's periodicals, textbooks, educational materials; Chair., Pres. and CEO M. Richard Robinson.

Simon & Schuster, Inc: 1230 Ave of the Americas, New York, NY 10020; tel. (212) 698-7000; fax (212) 698-7007; internet www.simonsays.com; f. 1924; part of the CBS Group; trade, juvenile, reference, educational, business and professional; imprints include Aladdin Paperbacks (juvenile fiction), Free Press (politics, history, religion, business, fiction), Howard Books (f. 1969, religion, gift books), Pocket Books (f. 1939, fiction), and Scribner (f. 1846, fiction); Pres. and CEO Carolyn Reidy.

Peter Smith Publisher, Inc: 5 Lexington Ave, Magnolia, MA 01930; tel. (978) 525-3562; fax (978) 525-3674; reprints; Pres. Mary Ann Lash.

Southern Illinois University Press: 1915 University Press Dr., Carbondale, IL 62901-4323; 1915 University Press Dr., SIUC Mail Code 6806, Carbondale, IL 62902-6806; tel. (618) 453-2281; fax (618) 453-1221; e-mail ladkins@siu.edu; internet www.siu.edu/~siupress; f. 1953; scholarly non-fiction; Dir Arthur M. (Lain) Adkins.

Springer: 233 Spring St, New York, NY 10013; tel. (212) 460-1500; fax (212) 460-1575; e-mail service-ny@springer.com; internet www.springer.com; f. 1964; part of Springer Science+Business Media; scientific, technical and medical; CEO Derk Haank.

Stanford University Press: 1450 Page Mill Rd, Palo Alto, CA 94304-1124; tel. (650) 723-9434; fax (650) 725-3457; e-mail info@www.sup.org; internet www.sup.org; f. 1925; Dir Geoffrey Burn.

State University of New York Press: 22 Corporate Woods Blvd, 3rd Floor Albany, NY 12211-2504; tel. (518) 472-5000; fax (518) 472-5038; e-mail info@sunypress.edu; internet www.sunypress.edu; f. 1966; scholarly and general interest; Exec. Dir Gary Dunham.

Sterling Publishing Co, Inc: 387 Park Ave South, New York, NY 10016; tel. (212) 532-7160; fax (212) 213-2495; e-mail publicity@sterlingpub.com; internet www.sterlingpub.com; f. 1949; subsidiary of Barnes and Noble, Inc; imprints incl. Lark Crafts and Hearst Books; non-fiction and illustrated; Chair. Burton H. Hobson.

Syracuse University Press: Suite 110, 621 Skytop Rd, Syracuse, NY 13244-5290; tel. (315) 443-5534; fax (315) 443-5545; e-mail supress@syr.edu; internet www.syracuseuniversitypress.syr.edu; f. 1943; scholarly; Dir Alice Randel Pfeiffer.

Taplinger Publishing Co Inc: POB 175, Marlboro, NJ 07746; tel. (305) 256-7880; fax (305) 256-7816; e-mail taplingerpub@yahoo.com; f. 1955; general fiction and non-fiction; Pres. Louis Strick.

Taylor & Francis Group: 270 Madison Ave, New York, NY 10016; tel. (212) 216-7800; fax (212) 564-7854; e-mail info@taylorandfrancis.com; internet www.taylorandfrancis.com; f. 1972; division of Informa PLC; imprints incl. CRC Press (f. 1913, reference, science, engineering and medicine), Garland Science Publishing (f. 1969, molecular biology, immunology and protein science textbooks), Routledge (q.v.), and Taylor & Francis Books (f. 1972, academic, science and reference); CEO Roger Horton.

Charles C. Thomas, Publisher: 2600 South First St, Springfield, IL 62794-9265; tel. (217) 789-8980; fax (217) 789-9130; e-mail books@ccthomas.com; internet www.ccthomas.com; f. 1927; textbooks and reference on education, medicine, psychology and criminology; Pres. Michael P. Thomas.

Tuttle Publishing: Airport Business Park, 364 Innovation Dr., North Clarendon, VT 05759-9436; tel. (802) 773-8930; fax (802) 773-6993; e-mail info@tuttlepublishing.com; internet tuttlepublishing.com; f. 1948; part of the Periplus Publishing Group; the Far East, particularly Japan, languages, art, crafts, martial arts, culture, juvenile, cookery; Publr Eric Oey.

United Nations Publications: United Nations Plaza, Room DC2-0853, New York, NY 10017; tel. (212) 963-8302; fax (212) 963-3489; e-mail publications@un.org; internet unp.un.org; f. 1946; world and national economies, international trade, social questions, human rights and international law; Chief of Section Christopher Woodthorpe.

University of Alabama Press: POB 870380, Tuscaloosa, AL 35487-0380; tel. (205) 348-5180; fax (205) 348-9201; e-mail sgriffit@uapress.ua.edu; internet www.uapress.ua.edu; f. 1945; scholarly; Dir Daniel J. J. Ross.

University of Alaska Press: 794 University Ave, Suite 220, POB 756240, Fairbanks, AK 99775; tel. (907) 474-5831; fax (907) 474-5502; e-mail fypress@uaf.edu; internet www.uaf.edu/uapress; f. 1967; scholarly regional non-fiction, history, anthropology of the circumpolar north; Chair. of Advisory Bd Patricia H. Partnow; Dir Joan Braddock.

University of Arizona Press: 355 South Euclid Ave, Suite 103, Tucson, AZ 85719; tel. (520) 621-1441; fax (520) 621-8899; e-mail uapress@uapress.arizona.edu; internet www.uapress.arizona.edu;

THE UNITED STATES OF AMERICA

f. 1959; scholarly, popular, regional and non-fiction; Dir KATHRYN CONRAD (acting).

University of Arkansas Press: McIlroy House, 105 N McIlroy Ave, Fayetteville, AR 72701; tel. (479) 575-3246; fax (479) 575-6044; e-mail cmoss@uark.edu; internet www.uapress.com; f. 1980; humanities, regional studies, natural history, African-American studies, Middle Eastern studies, poetry, civil rights studies and American history; Dir LARRY MALLEY.

University of California Press: 2120 Berkeley Way, Berkeley, CA 94704-1012; tel. (510) 642-4247; fax (510) 643-7127; e-mail askucp@ucpress.edu; internet www.ucpress.edu; f. 1893; academic and scholarly; Dir LYNNE WITHEY.

University of Chicago Press: 1427 East 60th St, Chicago, IL 60637; tel. (773) 702-7700; fax (773) 702-9756; e-mail publicity@press.uchicago.edu; internet www.press.uchicago.edu; f. 1891; scholarly and general; Dir GARRETT KIELY.

University of Georgia Press: 330 Research Dr., Athens, GA 30602-4901; tel. (706) 369-6130; fax (706) 369-6131; e-mail books@ugapress.uga.edu; internet www.ugapress.org; f. 1938; academic, scholarly, poetry, fiction, non-fiction and literary trade; Dir NICOLE MITCHELL.

University of Hawaii Press: 2840 Kolowalu St, Honolulu, HI 96822; tel. (808) 956-8255; fax (808) 988-6052; e-mail uhpbooks@hawaii.edu; internet www.uhpress.hawaii.edu; f. 1947; Asian, Pacific and Hawaiian studies; Dir WILLIAM H. HAMILTON.

University of Illinois Press: 1325 South Oak St, Champaign, IL 61820-6903; tel. (217) 333-0950; fax (217) 244-8082; e-mail uipress@uillinois.edu; internet www.press.uillinois.edu; f. 1918; scholarly and trade; Dir WILLIS G. REGIER.

University of Massachusetts Press: East Experiment Station, 671 North Pleasant St, POB 429, Amherst, MA 01004-0429; tel. (413) 545-2217; fax (413) 545-1226; e-mail info@umpress.umass.edu; internet www.umass.edu/umpress; f. 1963; scholarly; Dir BRUCE G. WILCOX.

University of Michigan Press: 839 Greene St, Ann Arbor, MI 48104-3209; tel. (734) 764-4388; fax (734) 615-1540; e-mail dshafer@umich.edu; internet www.press.umich.edu; f. 1930; academic, textbooks and paperbacks; Dir PHILIP POCHODA.

University of Minnesota Press: 111 Third Ave South, Suite 290, Minneapolis, MN 55401-5250; tel. (612) 627-1970; fax (612) 627-1980; e-mail ump@umn.edu; internet www.upress.umn.edu; f. 1925; scholarly and general; Dir DOUGLAS M. ARMATO.

University of Missouri Press: 2910 LeMone Blvd, Columbia, MO 65201; tel. (573) 882-7641; fax (573) 884-4498; e-mail upress@umsystem.edu; internet press.umsystem.edu; f. 1958; scholarly; Editor-in-Chief CLAIR WILLCOX.

University of Nebraska Press: 1111 Lincoln Mall, Lincoln, NE 68588-0630; tel. (402) 472-3581; fax (402) 472-6214; e-mail pressmail@unl.edu; internet www.nebraskapress.unl.edu; f. 1941; scholarly and general; Dir LADETTE RANDOLPH.

University of New Mexico Press: 1717 Roma NE, Albuquerque, NM 87106; tel. (505) 277-2346; fax (505) 277-3343; e-mail unmpress@unm.edu; internet www.unmpress.com; f. 1929; scholarly and regional studies; Dir LUTHER WILSON.

University of North Carolina Press: 116 South Boundary St, Chapel Hill, NC 27514-3808; tel. (919) 966-3561; fax (919) 966-3829; e-mail uncpress@unc.edu; internet www.uncpress.unc.edu; f. 1922; biography, regional and scholarly; Dir KATE D. TORREY.

University of Notre Dame Press: 310 Flanner Hall, Notre Dame, IN 46556; tel. (574) 631-6346; fax (574) 631-8148; e-mail undpress.1@nd.edu; internet www.undpress.nd.edu; f. 1949; humanities and social sciences; Man. Dir HARV HUMPHREY (acting).

University of Oklahoma Press: 2800 Venture Dr., Norman, OK 73069-8216; tel. (405) 325-2000; fax (405) 325-4000; e-mail presscs@ou.edu; internet www.oupress.com; f. 1928; scholarly; Editor-in-Chief CHARLES E. RANKIN; Dir B. BYRON PRICE.

University of Pennsylvania Press: 3905 Spruce St, Philadelphia, PA 19104-4112; tel. (215) 898-6261; fax (215) 898-0404; e-mail custserv@pobox.upenn.edu; internet www.pennpress.org; f. 1890; scholarly; Dir ERIC HALPERN.

University of Pittsburgh Press: Eureka Bldg, 3400 Forbes Ave, 5th Floor, Pittsburgh, PA 15260; tel. (412) 383-2456; fax (412) 383-2466; e-mail press@pitt.edu; internet www.upress.pitt.edu; f. 1936; scholarly; Dir CYNTHIA MILLER.

University of South Carolina Press: 718 Devine St, Columbia, SC 29208; tel. (803) 777-5245; fax (800) 868-0740; e-mail lmack@mailbox.sc.edu; internet www.sc.edu/uscpress; scholarly and regional studies; Dir CURTIS L. CLARK.

University of Tennessee Press: Conference Center Bldg, 600 Henley St, Suite 110, Knoxville, TN 37996-4108; tel. (865) 974-3321; fax (865) 974-3724; e-mail custserv@utk.edu; internet www.utpress.org; f. 1940; scholarly, regional, and literary fiction; Dir JENNIFER M. SILER.

University of Texas Press: POB 7819, Austin, TX 78713-7819; tel. (512) 471-7233; fax (512) 232-7178; e-mail utpress@uts.cc.utexas.edu; internet www.utexas.edu/utpress; f. 1950; general, scholarly non-fiction; Dir JOANNA HITCHCOCK.

University of Utah Press: J. Willard Marriott Library, Suite 5400, 295 South 1500 East, Salt Lake City, UT 84112-0860; tel. (801) 585-9786; fax (801) 581-3365; e-mail peter.delafosse@utah.edu; internet www.uofupress.com; f. 1949; scholarly, regional; Dir GLENDA COTTER.

University of Virginia Press: POB 400318, Charlottesville, VA 22904-4318; tel. (434) 924-3469; fax (434) 982-2655; internet www.upress.virginia.edu; f. 1963; scholarly non-fiction, literature, history, Victorian, African and Afro-American studies; Dir PENELOPE KAISERLIAN.

University of Washington Press: 4333 Brooklyn Ave, POB 50096, Seattle, WA 98145-5096; tel. (206) 543-4050; fax (206) 543-3932; e-mail uwpress@u.washington.edu; internet www.washington.edu/uwpress; f. 1920; general, scholarly, non-fiction and reprints; Dir PAT SODEN.

University of Wisconsin Press: 1930 Monroe St, 3rd Floor, Madison, WI 53711-2059; tel. (608) 263-1110; fax (608) 263-1132; e-mail uwiscpress@uwpress.wisc.edu; internet www.wisc.edu/wisconsinpress; f. 1936; scholarly and trade; Dir SHEILA LEARY.

University Press of America, Inc: 4501 Forbes Blvd, Suite 200, Lanham, MD 20706; tel. (301) 459-3366; fax (301) 429-5748; e-mail customercare@rowman.com; internet www.univpress.com; f. 1975; scholarly; Vice-Pres. STEPHEN DRIVER.

University Press of Florida: 15 North West 15th St, Gainesville, FL 32611-2079; tel. (352) 392-1351; fax (352) 392-0590; internet www.upf.com; f. 1945; general, scholarly, regional; Dir MEREDITH MORRIS-BABB.

University Press of Kansas: 2502 Westbrooke Circle, Lawrence, KS 66045-4444; tel. (785) 864-4154; fax (785) 864-4586; e-mail upress@ku.edu; internet www.kansaspress.ku.edu; f. 1946; scholarly; Dir FRED M. WOODWARD.

University Press of Kentucky: 663 South Limestone St, Lexington, KY 40508-4008; tel. (606) 257-8400; fax (606) 323-1873; e-mail smwrin2@email.uky.edu; internet www.kentuckypress.com; f. 1943; non-fiction, scholarly and regional; Dir STEPHEN M. WRINN.

University Press of Mississippi: 3825 Ridgewood Rd, Jackson, MS 39211-6492; tel. (601) 432-6205; fax (601) 432-6217; e-mail press@mississippi.edu; internet www.upress.state.ms.us; f. 1970; scholarly, non-fiction and regional; Dir LEILA W. SALISBURY.

University Press of New England: 1 Court St, Lebanon, NH 03766; tel. (603) 448-1533; fax (603) 448-7006; e-mail upneweb@dartmouth.edu; internet www.upne.com; f. 1970; scholarly; Dir MICHAEL P. BURTON.

Vanderbilt University Press: POB 1813, Nashville, TN 37235-1813; tel. (615) 322-3585; fax (615) 343-8823; e-mail vupress@vanderbilt.edu; internet www.vanderbiltuniversitypress.com; f. 1940; scholarly and trade; Dir MICHAEL AMES.

Wayne State University Press: 4809 Woodward Ave, Detroit, MI 48201-1309; tel. (313) 577-6120; fax (313) 577-6131; e-mail jane.hoehner@wayne.edu; internet wsupress.wayne.edu; f. 1941; scholarly; Dir JANE HOEHNER.

Westview Press: 2465 Central Ave, Boulder, CO 80301; tel. (303) 444-3541; e-mail westview.press@perseusbooks.com; internet www.perseusbooksgroup.com/westview; social sciences, humanities and science textbooks; f. 1975; part of the Perseus Books Group; Publr MARCUS BOGGS.

Wiley-Blackwell: 111 River St, Hoboken, NJ 07030-5774; tel. (201) 748-6000; fax (201) 748-6088; e-mail info@wiley.com; internet www.wiley.com; f. 1807; fmrly John Wiley and Sons, Inc; name changed as above in 2007; higher education, scientific, technical, medical, professional and trade; Chair. PETER B. WILEY; Pres. and CEO STEPHEN M. SMITH.

H. W. Wilson Co: 950 University Ave, Bronx, NY 10452; tel. (718) 588-8400; fax (718) 590-1617; e-mail custserv@hwwilson.com; internet www.hwwilson.com; f. 1898; reference and indices; Pres. and CEO HAROLD REGAN.

Wolters Kluwer Health: 530 Walnut St, 7th Floor, Philadelphia, PA 19106; tel. (215) 521-8300; internet www.wolterskluwerhealth.com; division of Wolters Kluwer; medical and scientific reference; imprints incl. Lippincott, Williams & Wilkins (f. 1792, dentistry, science, human and veterinary medicine); Pres. and CEO BOB BECKER.

Yale University Press: POB 209040, New Haven, CT 06520-9040; tel. (203) 432-0960; fax (203) 432-0948; e-mail language.yalepress@yale.edu; internet yalepress.yale.edu/yupbooks; f. 1908; scholarly; Dir JOHN DONATICH.

THE UNITED STATES OF AMERICA   *Directory*

GOVERNMENT PUBLISHING HOUSE

Government Printing Office: 732 North Capitol St, NW, Washington, DC 20401; tel. (202) 512-1800; fax (202) 512-2104; e-mail contactcenter@gpo.gov; internet www.gpo.gov; Public Printer WILLIAM J. BOARMAN.

ORGANIZATIONS AND ASSOCIATIONS

American Booksellers' Association (ABA): 200 White Plains Rd, Suite 600, Tarrytown, NY 10591; tel. (914) 591-2665; fax (914) 591-2720; e-mail info@bookweb.org; internet www.bookweb.org; f. 1900; 2,500 mems; Pres. MICHAEL TUCKER; CEO OREN TEICHER.

Association of American University Presses, Inc: 28 West 36th St, Suite 602, New York, NY 10018; tel. (212) 989-1010; fax (212) 989-0275; e-mail info@aaupnet.org; internet www.aaupnet.org; f. 1937; 125 mems; Exec. Dir PETER J. GIVLER.

The Children's Book Council, Inc: 54 West 39th St, 14th Floor, New York, NY 10018; tel. (212) 966-1990; fax (212) 966-2073; e-mail cbc.info@cbcbooks.org; internet www.cbcbooks.org; f. 1945; 75 mems; Chair. MEGAN TINGLEY.

Florida Publishers Association, Inc: POB 430, Highland City, FL 33846-0430; tel. and fax (836) 647-5951; e-mail fpabooks@aol.com; internet www.flbookpub.org; f. 1983; fmrly Nat. Asscn of Independent Publrs; 150 mems; Pres. CHRIS ANGERMANN.

Independent Book Publishers' Association (IBPA): 627 Aviation Way, Manhattan Beach, CA 90266; tel. (310) 372-2732; fax (310) 374-3342; e-mail info@ibpa-online.org; internet www.ibpa-online.org; f. 1983 as Publishers' Marketing Asscn; over 4,000 mem. publrs; Pres. FLORRIE BINFORD KICHLER; Exec. Dir TERRY NATHAN.

Independent Publishers Group: 814 North Franklin St, Chicago, IL 60610; tel. (312) 337-0747; fax (312) 337-5985; e-mail frontdesk@ipgbook.com; internet www.ipgbook.com; f. 1971; Pres. MARK SUCHOMEL; CEO CURT MATTHEWS.

Music Publishers Association of the US: 243 Fifth Ave, Suite 236, New York, NY 10016; tel. (212) 327-4044; e-mail admin@mpa.org; internet www.mpa.org; f. 1895; 80 mems; Pres. LAUREN KEISER.

Publishers Group West (PGW): 1700 Fourth St, Berkeley, CA 94710; tel. (510) 528-1444; fax (510) 528-3444; e-mail info@pgw.com; internet www.pgw.com; f. 1976; subsidiary of Publishers Group Worldwide; Vice-Pres. International Sales CHITRA BOPADIKAR.

Small Press Distribution: 1341 Seventh St, Berkeley, CA 94710-1409; tel. (510) 524-1668; fax (510) 524-0852; e-mail spd@spdbooks.org; internet www.spdbooks.org; f. 1969; distributes exclusively independently published literature; Exec. Dir JEFFREY LEPENDORF.

Small Publishers Association of North America (SPAN): 1618 West Colorado Ave, Colorado Springs, CO 80904; tel. (719) 475-1726; fax (719) 471-2182; e-mail span@spannet.org; internet www.spannet.org; f. 1996 to promote the profile and interests of independent publrs and authors; Exec. Dir SCOTT FLORA; over 1,000 mems.

Broadcasting and Communications

Federal Communications Commission (FCC): 445 12th St, SW, Washington, DC 20554; tel. (202) 418-0200; fax (202) 418-0232; e-mail fccinfo@fcc.gov; internet www.fcc.gov; f. 1934; regulates inter-state and foreign communications by radio, television, wire and cable; Chair. JULIUS GENACHOWSKI; Man. Dir STEVEN VANROEKEL.

TELECOMMUNICATIONS

Principal Telecommunications Networks

AT&T, Inc (American Telegraph and Telephone): 175 East Houston St, San Antonio, TX 78205; tel. (212) 387-5400; fax (212) 226-4935; internet www.att.com; f. 1885; bought by SBC Communications in Jan. 2005, merger completed and present name adopted in Nov. 2005; merged with the BellSouth Corpn in Dec. 2006, and acquired full ownership of Cingular Wireless; more than 150m. customers; Chair. and CEO RANDALL L. STEPHENSON.

Comcast Corpn: One Comcast Center, 1500 Market St, Philadelphia, PA 19103; tel. (215) 286-1700; e-mail corporate_communications@comcast.com; internet www.comcast.com; f. 1963 as American Cable Systems; renamed as above in 1969; acquired AT&T Broadband in 2002; acquired part of Adelphia Communications in 2006; acquired NBC Universal in 2011; largest cable operator and third largest telephone provider in USA; 23.2m. cable customers in 39 states and the District of Columbia, 16.4m. high-speed internet customers, 8.1m. voice customers; Chair. and CEO BRIAN L. ROBERTS; COO STEPHEN B. BURKE.

Frontier Communications: 3 High Ridge Park, Stamford, CT 06901-1390; tel. (203) 614-5600; fax (203) 614-4602; e-mail frontier@frontiercorp.com; internet www.czn.com; f. 1935; fmrly Citizens Communications Co; name changed as above in 2008; acquisition of Commonwealth Telephone Enterprises completed in March 2007; 3m. access lines in 24 states; Pres. and CEO MAGGIE WILDEROTTER; Exec. Vice-Pres. and COO DANIEL MCCARTHY.

Qwest Communications International, Inc: 1801 California St, Denver, CO 80202; tel. (303) 992-1400; fax (303) 896-8515; e-mail qnews@qwest.com; internet www.qwest.com; f. 1996; telephone and internet provider to 21.8m. customers in 14 states; acquired US West in 2000; Chair. and CEO EDWARD A. MUELLER; Exec. Vice-Pres. and COO TERESA A. TAYLOR.

SES AMERICOM: 4 Research Way, Princeton, NJ 08540-6684; tel. (609) 987-4000; fax (609) 987-4517; e-mail info.americom@ses-americom.com; f. 1975; fmrly GE American Communications, Inc; Pres. and CEO ROBERT BEDNAREK.

T-Mobile USA, Inc: 12920 South East 38th St, POB 53410, Bellevue, WA 98015-53410; internet www.t-mobile.com; f. 2002; US operating entity of T-Mobile International AG, owned by Deutsche Telekom AG (Germany); mobile cellular communications; 33.6m. customers; Pres. and CEO PHILIPP HUMM; 36,000 employees.

Verizon Communications: 140 West St, 29th Floor, New York, NY 10007; tel. (800) 621-9900; internet www.verizon.com; f. 2000 by merger of Bell Atlantic Corpn and GTE Corpn; divisions include Verizon Business, fmrly MCI, Inc; 140.3m. land lines in service; Chair. and CEO IVAN G. SEIDENBERG; Pres. and CEO (Verizon Wireless) LOWELL C. MCADAM.

Associations

United States Telecom Association (USTelecom): 607 14th St, NW, Suite 400, Washington, DC 20005; tel. (202) 326-7300; fax (202) 315-3603; e-mail membership@ustelecom.org; internet www.ustelecom.org; broadband association; Pres. and CEO WALTER B. MCCORMICK, Jr; Chair. STEVEN C. OLDHAM.

UTC—Utilities Telecom Council: 1901 Pennsylvania Ave, 5th Floor, NW, Washington, DC 20006; tel. (202) 872-0030; fax (202) 872-1331; e-mail utc@utc.org; internet www.utc.org; f. 1948; name changed from United Telecom Council in 2007; non-profit asscn representing telecommunications and information interests of public utilities, natural gas pipelines and other infrastructure cos and their strategic business partners; Pres. and CEO BILL MORONEY; Vice-Pres. (Operations) KATHLEEN FITZPATRICK.

BROADCASTING

The USA constitutes the world's biggest market for communications and broadcasting systems. The USA has the highest ratio of radio and television receivers per head of population of any country in the world. In 2004 radio sets were in use in 99% of homes and in 2008 there were an estimated 310m. television receivers in use. There were 7,853 cable systems in operation in 2008, serving an estimated 63.7m. basic cable subscribers. In 2009 72.1% of households with television receivers used video cassette recorders.

Radio

In 2004 there were 10,987 licensed commercial AM and FM radio stations operating in the USA. In 2004 the average US household had 8.0 radio sets in use.

Principal Domestic Networks

CBS RADIO: 40 West 57th St, New York, NY 10019; tel. (212) 846-3939; internet www.cbsradio.com; f. 1928; fmrly Infinity Broadcasting; division of CBS Corpn; owns CBS Radio Network serving more than 1,500 radio stations; operates 130 radio stations; Pres. and CEO DAN MASON.

Citadel Media Networks: 13725 Montfort Dr., Dallas, TX 75240; tel. (972) 991-9200; fax (214) 991-1071; e-mail omar.thompson@citcomm.com; internet www.citadelmedianetworks.com; f. 1944; fmrly ABC Radio Networks; name changed as above in 2009; fmrly wholly owned subsidiary of The Walt Disney Company; ABC Radio Business, as a spin-off concern of The Walt Disney Co, merged with a wholly owned subsidiary of Citadel Broadcasting Corpn in June 2007; 4,500 affiliated radio stations broadcasting five full service line networks; Pres. JOHN ROSSO; CEO FARID SULEMAN.

Clear Channel Radio: 200 East Basse Rd, San Antonio, TX 78209; tel. (210) 822-2828; e-mail lisacdollinger@clearchannel.com; internet www.clearchannel.com/radio; c. 800 radio stations; in July 2008 Clear Channel Communications (parent co) merged with a wholly owned subsidiary corpn of CC Media Holdings, Inc, the latter becoming overarching parent co; Pres. and CEO MARK MAYS.

National Public Radio (NPR): 635 Massachusetts Ave, NW, Washington, DC 20001; tel. (202) 513-2300; fax (202) 513-3329; e-mail achristopher@npr.org; internet www.npr.org; f. 1970; private, non-profit corpn providing programmes and support facilities to over 800 mem. stations nation-wide; also operates a global programme

THE UNITED STATES OF AMERICA

distribution service by radio, cable and satellite; Chair. DAVE EDWARDS; Pres. and CEO (vacant).

Westwood One, Inc: 1166 Ave of the Americas, 10th Floor, New York, NY 10036; tel. (212) 641-2000; e-mail david_hillman@westwoodone.com; internet www.westwoodone.com; f. 1934; managed by CBS Radio, Inc, fmrly Infinity Broadcasting; subsidiary of Viacom, Inc; largest domestic outsource provider of traffic-reporting services, broadcasting to 7,700 radio stations; produces and distributes national news, sports, talk, music and special event programmes, in addition to local news, sports, weather and other information programming; operates BLAISE, CBS, CNN Max, Navigator, NBC, NeXt, Source Max and WONE radio networks; Pres. and CFO ROD SHERWOOD.

Principal External Radio Services

American Forces Network Broadcast Center (AFN-BC): AFN Broadcast Center, 23755 Z St, Riverside, CA 92518; tel. (951) 413-2319; fax (951) 413-2227; e-mail larry.sichter@dma.mil; internet www.myafn.net; f. 1942; operated by Dept of Defense; provides encrypted US radio and TV programming in English exclusively to US military and Dept of Defense civilian personnel in 175 countries and aboard US Navy ships; Exec. Dir DAVID GEBHARDT (AFN Broadcast Center) (acting); Dir ANDREAS FRIEDRICH (AFRTS) (acting).

RFE/RL, Inc (Radio Free Europe/Radio Liberty): 1201 Connecticut Ave, NW, Suite 400, Washington, DC 20036; tel. (202) 457-6900; fax (202) 457-6992; e-mail zvanersm@rferl.org; internet www.rferl.org; f. 1950; private, non-profit corpn financed by Congress via the Broadcasting Board of Governors (BBG); broadcasts to 21 countries incl. Russia, Iran, Iraq, Afghanistan, Pakistan and the republics of Central Asia; c. 1,000 hours weekly in 28 languages; Chair. DENNIS MULHAUPT.

Voice of America: 330 Independence Ave, SW, Washington, DC 20237; tel. (202) 203-4959; fax (202) 203-4960; e-mail askvoa@voanews.com; internet www.voanews.com; f. 1942; govt-funded; broadcasts c. 1,500 hours weekly in 45 languages to all areas of the world via radio, television and the internet; serves more than 1,200 local affiliate stations and networks (radio, television and cable); Dir DANFORTH W. AUSTIN; Exec. Editor STEVE REDISCH.

Television

In 2008 commercial television stations numbered 1,353. The average US household had 2.8 television sets in use in January 2008.
All analogue broadcasting had ceased by 12 July 2009.

Principal Networks

ABC, Inc (American Broadcasting Co, Inc): 500 South Buena Vista St, Burbank, CA 91521-4551; tel. (818) 460-7477; e-mail netaudr@abc.com; internet abc.go.com; f. 1953; subsidiary of the Walt Disney Co since 1996; 10 owned and 226 affiliated stations; production through Touchstone Television, and Disney television content distribution through Buena Vista Television; Pres., ABC-owned Television Stations WALTER C. LISS; Pres., ABC Entertainment Group STEPHEN MCPHERSON.

C-SPAN (Cable-Satellite Public Affairs Network): 400 North Capitol St, Suite 650, Washington, DC 20001; tel. (202) 737-3220; fax (202) 737-3323; e-mail viewer@c-span.org; internet www.c-span.org; f. 1979; private, non-profit public service; earns its operating revenues through licence fees paid by cable and satellite systems offering the network to their customers; Chair. and CEO BRIAN LAMB; Co-Pres. and COO SUSAN SWAIN, ROBERT KENNEDY.

CBS Television Network (Columbia Broadcasting System Television Network): 51 West 52nd St, New York, NY 10019-6188; tel. (212) 975-4321; internet www.cbs.com; f. 1928; subsidiary of CBS Corpn; serves more than 200 affiliated stations; parent CBS Corpn subsidiary, CBS Television Stations Group, operates 39 stations, incl. 21 CBS, 11 The CW, 3 MyNetworkTV and 4 independents; CBS Corpn Pres. and CEO LESLIE MOONVES; Chair. SUMNER REDSTONE.

CNN (Cable News Network): 1 CNN Center, POB 105366, Atlanta, GA 30348; tel. (404) 827-1700; fax (404) 827-1099; e-mail public.information@turner.com; internet www.cnn.com; subsidiary of Time Warner; Pres. JONATHAN KLEIN; Pres., CNN News Group JIM WALTON.

FOX Broadcasting Co: 10201 West Pico Blvd, Los Angeles, CA 90035; tel. (310) 369-3716; fax (310) 969-3300; e-mail gaude.paez@fox.com; internet www.fox.com; f. 1986; subsidiary of News Corpn; more than 900 cable affiliations; Pres. KEVIN REILLY; Chair. PETER RICE.

NBC Universal Television Stations: 30 Rockefeller Plaza, New York, NY 10112; tel. (212) 664-4444; fax (212) 664-5830; e-mail feedback@nbcuni.com; internet www.nbcuni.com; f. 1926; subsidiary of NBC Universal; 51% stake in NBC Universal acquired by Comcast Corpn (q.v.) in 2011; 27 owned and over 200 affiliated stations; Pres. and CEO, NBC Universal JEFF ZUCKER; Chair., NBC Universal Television Entertainment JEFF GASPIN.

PBS (Public Broadcasting Service): 2100 Crystal Dr., Arlington, VA 22202; tel. (703) 739-5000; fax (703) 739-0775; e-mail cjohnson@pbs.org; internet www.pbs.org; f. 1969; non-profit-making; financed by private subscriptions and federal govt funds; owned and operated by the 356 public US television stations under 168 educational non-commercial licensees; Pres. and CEO PAULA KERGER; COO MICHAEL JONES.

Time Warner Cable, Inc (TWC): 290 Harbor Dr., Stamford, CT 06902-6732; tel. (203) 364-8203; fax (203) 328-0690; internet www.timewarnercable.com; cable television system serving c. 14.6m. subscribers in 28 states; acquired part of Adelphia Communications in 2005; 85.2% owned by Time Warner, Inc, following legal and structural separation of the two cos in March 2009; Chair., Pres. and CEO GLENN A. BRITT; COO LANDEL C. HOBBS.

Univision Network: 605 Third Ave, 12th Floor, New York, NY 10158-0180; tel. (212) 455-5200; fax (212) 867-6710; internet www.univision.com; f. 1961; subsidiary of Univision Communications, Inc; acquired by Broadcasting Media Partners, Inc, a group of private equity investors, in March 2007; Spanish-language television network; Pres., Univision Networks CESAR CONDE; Pres. and CEO, Univision Communications, Inc JOE UVA.

Associations

National Association of Broadcasters (NAB): 1771 N St, NW, Washington, DC 20036; tel. (202) 429-5300; fax (202) 429-4199; e-mail nab@nab.org; internet www.nab.org; f. 1922; trade asscn of radio and TV stations and networks; 8,300 mems; Chair. JOHN L. (JACK) SANDER; Pres. and CEO GORDON H. SMITH.

National Cable and Telecommunications Association (NCTA): 25 Massachusetts Ave, NW, Suite 100, Washington, DC 20001-1413; tel. (202) 222-2300; e-mail rstoddard@ncta.com; internet www.ncta.com; f. 1952 as Nat. Cable Television Asscn; represents cable operators for over 90% of customers and over 200 cable programme networks; internet and digital telephone service provider; c. 3,100 mems; Chair. PAT ESSER; Pres. and CEO KYLE MCSLARROW.

Finance

BANKING

Commercial Banking System

The US banking system is the largest and, in many respects, the most comprehensive and sophisticated in the world. Banking has, however, been largely subject to state rather than federal jurisdiction, and this has created a structure very different from that in other advanced industrial countries. In general, no bank may open branches or acquire subsidiaries in states other than that in which it is based, although in June 1985 the US Supreme Court ruled that federal legislation prohibiting interstate banks does not preclude state governments from permitting regional interstate banking. A number of such mergers have followed, although some states continue to restrict banks to a single branch, or to operating only in certain counties of the state. Federal anti-trust laws also limit mergers of banks within a state. The effect of these measures has been to preserve the independence of a relatively large number of banks. However, the influence of these banks has been increasingly challenged by the formation of several groupings of regional banks. Federal legislation permitting the operation of interstate branch banking networks and the provision of non-banking financial services was enacted in November 1999. In October 2003 the Bank of America announced the acquisition of FleetBoston Financial Corporation, in an agreement that was to create the second largest banking company in the world. Bank of America acquired Merrill Lynch and Co in January 2009. At the end of 2009 the restructured Bank of America operated more than 6,100 branch offices, and controlled total deposits of more than US $991,611m. The merger in 2004 of JP Morgan Chase & Co and Bank One Corporation established the second largest bank in the USA, with 2,798 branches and total assets in December 2009 of $2,031,989m.

Following the failure of a number of banks in the late 1980s, the Federal Deposit Insurance Corporation, a government-sponsored body that insures deposits in banks and acts as receiver for national and state banks that have been placed in receivership, was obliged to provide assistance for a large number of institutions. Many banks, meanwhile, have expanded their 'fee income' activities (such as sales of mutual fund investments) to offset declines in customer borrowing, particularly from the industrial and commercial sectors.

In 2008 the banking industry came under severe strain following the sharp contraction in world-wide credit markets and the declared bankruptcy, in September, of the financial services firm Lehman Brothers. The Emergency Economic Stabilization Act of 2008, ardb# THE UNITED STATES OF AMERICA

approved by Congress in October, provided some US $700,000m. of rescue aid to the US Treasury to redistribute in the markets. In the same month the Government subsequently announced that it would purchase equity stakes in nine of the largest financial institutions, at a cost of around $250,000m.

The possession of bank accounts and the use of banking facilities are perhaps more widespread among all regions and social groups in the USA than in any other country. This has influenced the formulation of monetary theory and policy, as bank credit has become a more important factor than currency supply in the regulation of the economy. The use of current accounts and credit cards is so common that many authorities claim that the USA can be regarded as, effectively, a cashless society.

Bank Holding Companies

Since 1956 bank holding companies, corporations that control one or more banks in the USA, have become significant elements in the banking system. The proportion of banks owned by holding companies increased from 62% in 1984 to 76% in 2000. In 2004 there were some 5,151 bank holding companies, of which 12% had financial holding company status.

Banking Activities Overseas

From the mid-1960s the leading banks rapidly expanded their overseas interests. At the end of 1960 there were only eight US banks operating foreign branches, mostly in Latin America and the Far East. The main factors behind this expansion were the geographical limitations imposed by law at home; the rapid expansion of US business interests abroad; the faster economic growth of certain foreign markets; and, finally, the profitability of the 'Eurodollar' capital markets. The expansion in the overseas activities of US banks reached a high point in 1984. Subsequently declining levels of profitability in this area have resulted in the closure of some overseas offices, although the aggregate total of assets held has continued to rise.

In 1981 the Federal Reserve Board sanctioned the establishment of domestic International Banking Facilities (IBF), permitting commercial banks within the US (including US branches and agencies of foreign banks) to transact certain types of foreign deposit and loan business free of reserve requirements and, in most cases, state income tax liability.

Federal Reserve System: 20th St and Constitution Ave, NW, Washington, DC 20551; tel. (202) 452-3000; fax (202) 452-3819; internet www.federalreserve.gov.

The Federal Reserve System, founded in 1913, comprises the Board of Governors, the Federal Open Market Committee, the Federal Advisory Council, the Consumer Advisory Council, the Thrift Institutions Advisory Council, the 25 branches of the 12 Federal Reserve Banks, together with all member banks.

The Board of Governors is composed of seven members appointed by the President of the United States with the advice and consent of the Senate.

The Reserve Banks are empowered to issue Federal Reserve notes fully secured by the following assets, alone or in any combination: (i) Gold certificates; (ii) US Government and agency securities; (iii) other eligible assets as described by statute; and (iv) Special Drawing Rights certificates. The Reserve Banks may discount paper for depository institutions and make properly secured advances to depository institutions. Federal Reserve Banks were established by Congress as the operating arms of the nation's central banking system. Many of the services performed by this network for depository institutions and for the Government are similar to services performed by banks and thrifts for business customers and individuals. Reserve Banks hold the cash reserves of depository institutions and make loans to them. They move currency and coin into and out of circulation, and collect and process millions of cheques each day. They provide banking services for the Treasury, issue and redeem government securities on behalf of the Treasury, and act in other ways as fiscal agent for the US Government. The Banks also take part in the primary responsibility of the Federal Reserve System, the setting of monetary policy, through participation on the Federal Open Market Committee.

The Comptroller of the Currency (see below) has primary supervisory authority over all federally chartered banks, and the banking supervisors of the States have similar jurisdiction over banks organized under State laws. State member banks are examined by the Federal Reserve.

In March 2004 some 2,900 commercial banks were members of the Federal Reserve System.

Board of Governors

Chairman: BEN S. BERNANKE.
Vice-Chairman: DONALD L. KOHN.
Governors: ELIZABETH A. DUKE, DANIEL K. TARULLO, KEVIN M. WARSH.
Secretary of the Board: JENNIFER J. JOHNSON.

Federal Reserve Banks

	Chairman	President
Boston	Henri A. Termeer	Eric S. Rosengren
New York	Lee C. Bollinger	William C. Dudley
Philadelphia	Charles P. Pizzi	Charles I. Plosser
Cleveland	Alfred M. Rankin, Jr	Sandra Pianalto
Richmond	Margaret E. McDermid	Jeffrey M. Lacker
Atlanta	Carol B. Tomé	Dennis P. Lockhart
Chicago	William C. Foote	Charles L. Evans
St Louis	Stephen H. Lipsten	James B. Bullard
Minneapolis	John W. Marvin	Narayana Kocherlakota
Kansas City	Paul DeBruce	Thomas M. Hoenig
Dallas	Herbert D. Kelleher	Richard W. Fisher
San Francisco	Douglas W. Shorenstein	John C. Williams

Comptroller of the Currency

1 Independence Sq., 250 E St, SW, Washington, DC 20219; tel. (202) 874-5000; e-mail publicaffairs3@occ.treas.gov; internet www.occ.treas.gov.

The Comptroller of the Currency has supervisory control over all federally chartered banks (see Federal Reserve System).

Comptroller: JOHN WALSH (acting).

Principal Commercial Banks

(cap. = total capital and reserves; dep. = deposits; m. = million; amounts in US dollars)

In general, only banks with a minimum of $2,000m. deposits are listed. In states where no such bank exists, that with the largest deposits is listed.

Alabama

Regions Bank: 1900 5th Ave North, Suite 300, POB 10247, Birmingham, AL 35203-2669; tel. (205) 326-5300; fax (205) 326-7779; internet www.regions.com; f. 1928; cap. 0.1m., dep. 108,492.0m. (Dec. 2010); Chair. ERNEST W. DEAVENPORT, Jr; Pres. and CEO O. B. GRAYSON HALL, Jr.

California

Bank of the West: 180 Montgomery St, San Francisco, CA 94104; tel. (415) 765-4800; fax (415) 434-3470; e-mail john.stafford@bankofthewest.com; internet www.bankofthewest.com; f. 1874; owned by BancWest Corpn; cap. 0.006m., dep. 46,328.9m. (Dec. 2010); Chair. and CEO J. MICHAEL SHEPHERD; Pres. and COO MAURA MARKUS; 663 brs.

California Bank and Trust: 11622 El Camino Real, Suite 200, San Diego, CA 92130; tel. (858) 793-7400; fax (858) 793-7438; e-mail info@calbanktrust.com; internet www.calbanktrust.com; f. 1998; cap. 265.2m., dep. 9,231.6m. (Dec. 2010); Pres. and CEO DAVID BLACKFORD.

City National Bank: 400 Roxbury Dr. North, Beverly Hills, CA 90210; tel. (310) 888-6000; fax (310) 888-6045; e-mail contact@cnb.com; internet www.cnb.com; f. 1954; cap. 90.0m., dep. 18,216.0m. (Dec. 2010); Chair. and CEO RUSSELL GOLDSMITH; Pres. CHRISTOPHER J. WARMUTH; 45 brs.

Union Bank NA: 400 California St, 1st Floor, San Francisco, CA 94104; tel. (415) 765-3434; fax (415) 765-3507; e-mail Investor.Relations@uboc.com; internet www.unionbank.com; f. 1996; fmrly Union Bank of California NA; name changed as above in 2008; cap. 604.6m., dep. 66,832.1m. (Dec. 2010); Pres. and CEO MASASHI OKA; 323 brs.

Connecticut

Citizens Bank, Connecticut: 237 Main St, Middletown, CT 06457; tel. (860) 638-4411; fax (860) 638-4444; e-mail intbank@citizensbank.com; internet www.citizensbank.com; f. 1996; a division of RBS Citizens NA since 2007; dep. 4,205.8m., total assets 4,617.0m. (Dec. 2006); Pres. RICHARD M. BARRY; 48 brs.

Florida

Northern Trust NA: 700 Brickell Ave, Miami, FL 33131; tel. (305) 372-1000; fax (305) 789-1106; internet www.northerntrust.com; f. 1982; cap. 34.1m., dep. 10,986.7m. (Dec. 2010); Chair., Pres. and CEO FREDERICK H. WADDELL.

Ocean Bank: 780 Northwest 42nd Ave, Miami, POB 441140, FL 33126; tel. (305) 442-2660; fax (305) 444-8153; e-mail obmail@oceanbank.com; internet www.oceanbank.com; f. 1982; cap. 8.5m., dep. 3,417.1m. (Dec. 2010); Pres. and CEO A. ALFONSO MACEDO; 21 brs.

THE UNITED STATES OF AMERICA

Georgia

SunTrust Bank: 303 Peachtree St, POB 4418, Atlanta, GA 30302; tel. (404) 588-7006; fax (404) 588-7094; internet www.suntrust.com; f. 1891; assumed all SunTrust Banks 2000; cap. 21.6m., dep. 137,167.5m. (Dec. 2010); Chair. and CEO James M. Wells, III; Pres. William H. Rogers, Jr; 1,694 brs in 12 states.

Hawaii

Bank of Hawaii: 111 South King St, Honolulu, HI 96813; tel. (888) 643-3888; fax (808) 537-8440; e-mail info@boh.com; internet www.boh.com; f. 1897; cap. 14.9m., dep. 11,966.2m. (Dec. 2010); Chair. and CEO Peter S. Ho.

First Hawaiian Bank: 999 Bishop St, Honolulu, HI 96813; tel. (808) 525-7000; fax (808) 525-8182; e-mail bfarias@fhb.com; internet www.fhb.com; f. 1858; cap. 16.2m., dep. 12,280.4m. (Dec. 2010); Chair. and CEO Donald G. Horner.

Illinois

First Midwest Bank: 1 Pierce Pl., Suite 1500, Itasca, IL 60143; tel. (630) 875-7450; fax (630) 875-7369; e-mail Investor.Relations@firstmidwest.com; internet www.firstmidwest.com; cap. 40.0m., dep. 6,888.6m. (Dec. 2010); Pres. and CEO Michael L. Scudder; 100 brs.

Harris National Association: 111 West Monroe St, 12th Floor, Chicago, IL 60603; tel. (312) 845-2028; fax (312) 845-2199; internet www.harrisbank.com; f. 1882 as N. W. Harris & Co; present name adopted 2005; owned by BMO Financial Group (Canada); cap. 199.9m., dep. 44,011.5m. (Dec. 2010); Pres. and CEO Ellen Costello; 280 brs in 3 states.

Northern Trust Co: 50 South LaSalle St, Chicago, IL 60603; tel. (312) 630-6000; fax (312) 444-5244; internet www.northerntrust.com; f. 1889; cap. 3.6m., dep. 62,082.5m. (Dec. 2010); Pres. and CEO Frederick H. Waddell.

Kentucky

First Capital Bank of Kentucky: 293 N. Hubbards Lane, Louisville, KY 40207; tel. (502) 895-5040; e-mail localroots@fcbok.com; internet www.fcbok.com; f. 1996; cap. 1.7m., dep. 392.4m. (Dec. 2010); Chair., Pres. and CEO H. David Hale.

Louisiana

Whitney National Bank: 228 St Charles Ave, New Orleans, LA 70130; tel. (504) 586-7562; fax (504) 586-7412; e-mail lgarza@whitneybank.com; internet www.whitneybank.com; f. 1883; cap. 3.4m., dep. 10,060.4m. (Dec. 2010); Chair. and CEO John C. Hope, III; 150 brs in 5 states.

Maryland

Provident Bank of Maryland: 114 East Lexington St, Baltimore, MD 21202-1725; tel. (410) 281-7000; fax (410) 277-2768; internet www.provbank.com; f. 1951; cap. 30.0m., dep. 5,675.6m. (Dec. 2007); Chair. and CEO Peter Martin.

Massachusetts

Citizens Bank, Massachusetts: 28 State St, Boston, MA 02109; tel. (617) 725-5500; fax (617) 725-5877; e-mail intbank@citizensbank.com; internet www.citizensbank.com; f. 1825; a division of RBS Citizens NA since 2007; dep. 30,403.2m., total assets 35,276.0m. (Dec. 2006); Chair., Pres. and CEO Robert E. Smyth.

Michigan

Citizens Bank: 328 South Saginaw St, Flint, MI 48502; tel. (313) 766-7500; fax (313) 768-6948; internet www.citizensonline.com; f. 1871; cap. 453.2m., dep. 8,789.9m. (Dec. 2010); Pres. and CEO Cathleen H. Nash.

Comerica Bank: Comerica Bank Tower, 1717 Main St, Dallas, TX 75201; tel. (800) 521-1190; fax (214) 462-6650; e-mail info@comerica.com; internet www.comerica.com; f. 1849; cap. 58.5m., dep. 45,241.7m. (Dec. 2010); Chair. and CEO Ralph W. Babb, Jr.

Minnesota

US Bank NA: 800 Nicollet Mall, Minneapolis, MN 55402; tel. (612) 303-0799; fax (612) 973-0838; e-mail international.banking@usbank.com; internet www.usbank.com; f. 1853; fmrly Firstar Bank NA, present name adopted in Aug. 2001; cap. 18.2m., dep. 255,832.6m. (Dec. 2010); Chair., Pres. and CEO Richard K. Davis; 2,851 brs.

Mississippi

Trustmark National Bank: 248 East Capitol St, POB 291, Jackson, MS 39201; tel. (601) 208-5111; fax (601) 949-2387; e-mail Trustmark@custhelp.com; internet www.trustmark.com; f. 1889; cap. 13.4m., dep. 8,087.1m. (Dec. 2010); Chair., Pres. and CEO Richard G. Hickson.

Missouri

Commerce Bank NA: 1000 Walnut St, POB 13686, Kansas City, MO 64106; tel. (816) 234-2000; fax (816) 234-2799; e-mail mymoney@commercebank.com; internet www.commercebank.com; f. 1865; cap. 10.2m., dep. 16,253.2m. (Dec. 2010); Chair., Pres. and CEO David W. Kemper.

Montana

First Interstate Bank of Montana NA: 401 North 31st St, Billings, MT 59101; tel. (406) 255-5000; e-mail investor.relations@fib.com; internet www.firstinterstatebank.com; f. 1891; dep. 4,008.0m., total assets 5,091.2m. (Dec. 2007); Chair. Thomas W. Scott; Pres. and CEO Lyle R. Knight.

Nebraska

First National Bank of Omaha: 1620 Dodge St, Omaha, NE 68197; tel. (402) 341-0500; fax (402) 633-3554; e-mail firstnational@fnni.com; internet www.firstnational.com; f. 1857; cap. 8.5m., dep. 11,322.2m. (Dec. 2010); Chair. Bruce R. Lauritzen; Pres. Daniel O'Neill; 37 brs.

New Hampshire

Citizens Bank, New Hampshire: 875 Elm St, Manchester, NH 03101; tel. (603) 634-7418; fax (603) 634-7481; e-mail intbank@citizensbank.com; internet www.citizensbank.com; f. 1853; a division of RBS Citizens NA since 2007; cap. 0.8m., dep. 9,250.3m. (Dec. 2006); Pres. Cathleen Schmidt; 76 brs.

New York

American Express Bank Ltd: American Express Tower, 23rd Floor, 200 Vesey St, New York, NY 10285-2300; tel. (212) 640-5000; fax (212) 693-1721; internet www.americanexpress.com; f. 1919; cap. 121.0m., dep. 12,992.0m. (Dec. 2006); Chair. and CEO Kenneth I. Chenault.

Bank of New York Mellon: 1 Wall St, New York, NY 10286; tel. (212) 495-1784; fax (212) 495-1398; e-mail comments@bankofny.com; internet www.bankofny.com; f. 1784; renamed as above after merger of Bank of New York Co and Mellon Financial Corpn in 2007; cap. 1,135.0m., dep. 153,923.0m. (Dec. 2010); Chair. and CEO Robert P. Kelly; Pres. Gerald L. Hassell.

Bank of Tokyo–Mitsubishi UFJ Trust Co: 1251 Ave of the Americas, New York, NY 10020-1104; tel. (212) 782-4000; fax (212) 782-6415; internet www.mufg.jp; f. 1955; cap. 132.9m., dep. 2,549.9m. (Dec. 2010); Chair. Takamune Okihara; Pres. and CEO Katsunori Nagayasu.

Citibank NA: 399 Park Ave, New York, NY 10043; tel. (212) 559-1000; fax (212) 223-2681; internet www.citibank.com; f. 1812; cap. 751.0m., dep. 972,076.0m. (Dec. 2010); CEO Eugene M. McQuade.

Deutsche Bank Trust Company Americas: 60 Wall St, New York, NY 10005; tel. (212) 250-2500; fax (212) 250-4429; internet www.db.com/usa; f. 1903; fmrly Bankers' Trust Co, present name adopted April 2002; cap. 3,627.0m., dep. 33,696.0m. (Dec. 2010); CEO, Americas Seth Waugh.

HSBC Bank USA, NA: 452 Fifth Ave, New York, NY 10018; tel. (212) 525-5000; fax (212) 525-6875; internet www.us.hsbc.com; f. 1999 following acquisition of Marine Midland Bank by Hongkong & Shanghai Banking Corpn; acquired Republic National Bank of New York in 2000; cap. 2.0m., dep. 153,750.5m. (Dec. 2010); Chair. Niall S. K. Booker; Pres. and CEO Irene Dorner.

JP Morgan Chase: 270 Park Ave, New York, NY 10017; tel. (212) 270-6000; internet www.jpmorganchase.com; f. 1982 as Chase Manhattan Bank USA; present name adopted 2005; cap. 1,785.0m., dep. 1,125,220.0m. (Dec. 2007); Chair. and CEO Jamed Dimon.

M&T Bank Corpn: 1 M & T Plaza, Buffalo, NY 14203-2399; tel. (716) 842-4200; fax (716) 842-5839; internet www.mtb.com; f. 1856; Mfrs' and Traders' Trust Co; cap. 120.6m., dep. 55,657.0m. (Dec. 2010); Chair. and CEO Robert G. Wilmers; 736 brs.

Trustco Bank: 1 Sarnowski Dr., Glenville, NY 12302; tel. (518) 377-3311; fax (518) 381-3668; internet www.trustcobank.com; cap. 29.4m., dep. 3,305.2m. (Dec. 2009); Chair., Pres. and CEO Robert J. McCormick.

United States Trust Co: 114 West 47th St, New York, NY 10036; tel. (212) 852-1000; fax (212) 995-5642; e-mail info@trust.com; internet www.ustrust.com; f. 1853; cap. 15.0m., dep. 9,585.5m. (Dec. 2006); Chair. and CEO Jeffrey S. Maurer.

THE UNITED STATES OF AMERICA

North Carolina

Bank of America NA: 100 South Tryon St, Charlotte, NC 28255; tel. (704) 386-5000; fax (704) 386-0981; internet www.bankamerica.com; f. 1904; cap. 3,020.0m., dep. 1,247,974.5m. (Dec. 2010); Chair. CHARLES HOLLIDAY, Jr; Pres. and CEO BRIAN T. MOYNIHAN.

Wachovia Bank NA: 301 South College St, Suite 4000, Charlotte, NC 28288-0013; tel. (704) 374-1246; internet www.wachovia.com; f. 1866; merged with Wells Fargo Bank in 2008; cap. 455.0m., dep. 549,062.0m. (Dec. 2008).

Ohio

Fifth Third Bank: 38 Fountain Square Plaza, Cincinnati, OH 45263; tel. (513) 579-5300; internet www.53.com; f. 1853; cap. 4.5m., dep. 90,391.0m. (Dec. 2010); Chair., Pres. and CEO KEVIN T. KABAT; 361 brs.

FirstMerit Bank NA: 3 Cascade Plaza, 7th Floor, Akron, OH 44308; tel. (330) 996-6300; fax (330) 384-7008; e-mail customerservice@firstmerit.com; internet www.firstmerit.com; cap. 57.6m., dep. 12,489.2m. (Dec. 2010); Chair. and CEO PAUL G. GREIG.

Huntington National Bank: 41 South High St, Columbus, OH 43287; tel. (614) 480-4685; fax (614) 480-5284; e-mail international@huntington.com; internet www.huntington.com; f. 1866; cap. 40.0m., dep. 47,158.0m. (Dec. 2010); Chair., Pres. and CEO STEVEN D. STEINOUR.

KeyBank NA: 127 Public Sq., Cleveland, OH 44114-1306; tel. (216) 689-3000; fax (216) 689-3683; e-mail KeyExpress@keybank.com; internet www.key.com; f. 1849; cap. 50.0m., dep. 73,417.4m. (Dec. 2010); Chair. and CEO HENRY L. MEYER, III.

National City Bank: 1900 East Ninth St, POB 94750, Cleveland, OH 44114-3484; tel. (216) 575-2000; fax (216) 575-9263; internet www.nationalcity.com; f. 1845; acquired by PNC in 2008; cap. 7.3m., dep. 121,790.3m. (Dec. 2008); Chair., Pres. and CEO PETER E. RASKIND; c. 1,300 brs.

Oklahoma

BancFirst: Suite 200, 101 North Broadway, POB 26788, Oklahoma City, OK 73102; tel. (405) 270-1000; fax (405) 270-1089; internet www.bancfirst.com; cap. 40.9m., dep. 4,339.3m. (Dec. 2010); Chair. and CEO H. E. RAINBOLT; Pres. DAVID RAINBOLT.

BOKF NA: Bank of Oklahoma Tower, POB 2300, Tulsa, OK 74192; tel. (918) 588-6000; fax (918) 588-6026; internet www.bok.com; f. 1933; wholly owned subsidiary of BOK Financial Corpn; fmrly Bank of Oklahoma NA; name changed as above in 2011; cap. 52.9m., dep. 15,488.2m. (Dec. 2010); Chair. GEORGE B. KAISER; Pres. and CEO STANLEY A. LYBARGER; 56 brs.

Pennsylvania

PNC Bank, NA: 1 PNC Plaza, 249 Fifth Ave, Pittsburgh, PA 15222-2707; tel. (412) 762-2000; fax (412) 762-5022; internet www.pnc.com; f. 1959; merged with National City Bank in Dec. 2008; cap. 740.1m., dep. 210,683.2m. (Dec. 2010); Chair. and CEO JAMES E. ROHR; Pres. JOSEPH C. GUYAUX; 854 brs.

Rhode Island

Citizens Bank, Rhode Island: 1 Citizens Plaza, Providence, RI 02903; tel. (401) 454-2441; fax (401) 455-5859; e-mail intbank@citizensbank.com; internet www.citizensbank.com; f. 1996; cap. 1.0m., dep. 12,272.2m. (Dec. 2006); Pres. EDWARD O. HANDY, III; 78 brs.

South Carolina

Carolina First Bank: 104 South Main St, Poinsett Plaza, 10th Floor, POB 1029, Greenville, SC 29602; tel. (864) 255-7900; fax (864) 241-1565; e-mail customerassistance@carolinafirst.com; internet www.carolinafirst.com; cap. 7.9m., dep. 10,558.8m. (Dec. 2009); part of The South Financial Group; Pres. and CEO H. LYNN HARTON; 110 brs.

South Dakota

Citibank (South Dakota) NA: 701 East 60th St, North, POB 6000, Sioux Falls, SD 57117; tel. (605) 331-2626; internet www.citibank.com; f. 1981; cap. 113.0m., dep. 114,614.2m. (Dec. 2010); Gen. Sec. DAVID L. ZIMBECK; Pres. KENDALL E. STORK.

Wells Fargo Bank NA: 101 North Phillips Ave, Sioux Falls, SD 57117; tel. (605) 575-7300; fax (605) 575-4815; e-mail ipb@wellsfargo.com; internet www.wellsfargo.com; f. 1960 as Wells Fargo Bank American Trust Co; fmrly Norwest Bank South Dakota NA, present name adopted in 2004; cap. 519.0m., dep.921,910.0m. (Dec. 2010); Pres. and CEO JOHN G. STUMPF; 3,000 brs.

Tennessee

First Tennessee Bank NA: 165 Madison Ave, 9th Floor, POB 84, Memphis, TN 38101-0084; tel. (901) 523-4420; fax (901) 523-4438; internet www.firsttennessee.com; f. 1864; subsidiary of First Horizon National Corpn; cap. 367.3m., dep. 19,649.7m. (Dec. 2010); Chair. MICHAEL D. ROSE; Pres. and CEO BRYAN JORDAN; 183 brs.

Texas

Frost National Bank: 100 West Houston St, POB 1600, San Antonio, TX 78296; tel. (210) 220-4011; e-mail frostbank@frostbank.com; internet www.frostbank.com; f. 1899; cap. 8.5m., dep. 15,223.3m. (Dec. 2010); Chair. and CEO RICHARD W. EVANS, Jr.

Virginia

Chevy Chase Bank, FSB: 7926 Jones Branch Dr., McLean, VA 22101; internet www.chevychasebank.com; f. 1955; merged with Capital One in July 2009; total assets 15,106.6m. (Sept. 2007); Pres. ROBERT D. BROEKSMIT, II.

Co-operative Bank

CoBank: 5500 South Quebec St, Greenwood Village, CO 80111; tel. (303) 740-4000; fax (303) 740-4366; e-mail webmaster@cobank.com; internet www.cobank.com; f. 1933; provides loan finance and domestic and international banking services for agricultural and farmer-owned co-operatives; cap. 2,220.1m., dep. 51,911.3m. (Dec. 2009); Chair. EVERETT DOBRINSKI; Pres. and CEO ROBERT B. ENGEL.

Trade Bank

Export-Import Bank of the United States (Ex-Im Bank): 811 Vermont Ave, NW, Washington, DC 20571; tel. (202) 565-3946; fax (202) 565-3380; e-mail info@exim.gov; internet www.exim.gov; f. 1934; independent agency since 1945; cap. subscribed by the US Treasury; finances and facilitates US external trade, guarantees payment to US foreign traders and banks, extends credit to foreign governmental and private concerns; cap. 1,000.0m. (Sept. 2009); Chair. and Pres. FRED P. HOCHBERG; Inspector-Gen. OSVALDO LUIS GRATACOS MUNET.

BANKING ASSOCIATIONS

There is a State Bankers Association in each state.

American Bankers Association: 1120 Connecticut Ave, NW, Washington, DC 20036; tel. (202) 663-5000; fax (202) 828-4547; e-mail custserv@aba.com; internet www.aba.com; f. 1875; Pres. and CEO EDWARD (ED) YINGLING; Chair. ARTHUR C. JOHNSON.

BAFT-IFSA: 1120 Connecticut Ave, NW, 5th Floor, Washington, DC 20036; tel. (202) 663-7575; fax (202) 663-5538; e-mail info@baft-ifsa.com; internet www.baft-ifsa.com; f. 1921; fmrly Bankers' Association for Finance and Trade (BAFT); merged with International Financial Services Asscn (IFSA) Jan. 2010 to form BAFT-IFSA; affiliated to the American Bankers Asscn; Chair. HOWARD F. BASCOM, Jr; CEO DONNA K. ALEXANDER.

Bank Administration Institute (BAI): 115 South LaSalle St, Suite 3300, Chicago, IL 60603-3801; tel. (312) 683-2464; fax (312) 683-2373; e-mail info@bai.org; internet www.bai.org; f. 1924; Chair. JOHN H. FREEMAN; Pres. and CEO DEBORAH L. BIANUCCI.

Independent Community Bankers of America: 1615 L St, NW, Suite 900, Washington, DC 20036; tel. (202) 659-8111; fax (202) 659-3604; e-mail info@icba.org; internet www.icba.org; f. 1930; Pres. and CEO CAMDEN R. FINE; c. 5,000 mems.

Mortgage Bankers Association of America: 1717 Rhode Island Ave, NW, Suite 400, Washington, DC 20036; tel. (202) 557-2700; e-mail info@mortgagebankers.org; internet www.mortgagebankers.org; f. 1914; Chair. ROBERT E. STORY, Jr; Pres. and CEO JOHN COURSON; 2,700 mems.

PRINCIPAL STOCK EXCHANGES

Boston Stock Exchange Inc: 100 Franklin St, Boston, MA 02110; tel. (617) 235-2000; internet www.bostonstock.com; f. 1834; Chair. and CEO MICHAEL J. CURRAN; 119 mems.

Chicago Stock Exchange: 1 Financial Pl., 440 South LaSalle St, Chicago, IL 60605; tel. (312) 663-2222; fax (312) 663-2721; e-mail info@chx.com; internet www.chx.com; f. 1882; Chair. MICHAEL H. KERR; CEO DAVID A. HERRON; 445 mems.

Nasdaq Stock Market Inc: 1 Liberty Plaza, 165 Broadway, New York, NY 10006; tel. (212) 401-8700; e-mail insidenasdaq@nasdaqomx.com; internet www.nasdaq.com; f. 1998 by the American Stock Exchange and the Nat. Asscn of Securities Dealers (NASD); incorporated the Boston Stock Exchange in 2008; world-wide electronic trading market; Chair. MERIT E. JANOW; CEO ERIC W. NOLL.

THE UNITED STATES OF AMERICA

National Stock Exchange SM (NSX): 440 South LaSalle St, Suite 2600, Chicago, IL 60605; tel. (312) 786-8803; fax (312) 939-7239; internet www.nsx.com; f. 1885; fmrly Cincinnati Stock Exchange, name changed as above in Nov. 2003; Chair. JAMES M. ANDERSON; CEO JOSEPH S. RIZZELLO.

NYSE Euronext (New York Stock Exchange Euronext): 11 Wall St, New York, NY 10005; tel. (212) 656-3000; fax (212) 656-5549; e-mail mmedina@nyx.com; internet www.nyse.com; f. 1792; incorporated the American Stock Exchange in 2009; Chair. JAN-MICHIEL HESSELS; CEO DUNCAN L. NIEDERAUER; 2,800 mems.

Philadelphia Stock Exchange (NASDAQ OMX PHLX): Stock Exchange Bldg, 1900 Market St, Philadelphia, PA 19103-3584; tel. (215) 496-5000; fax (215) 496-5460; e-mail info@phlx.com; internet www.nasdaqtrader.com; f. 1790; acquired by NASDAQ OMX Group, Inc in 2008; Pres. THOMAS A. WITTMAN; 505 mems.

INSURANCE
Principal Companies

Acacia Life Insurance Co: 7315 Wisconsin Ave, Bethesda, MD 20814-3202; tel. (301) 280-1000; fax (310) 280-1161; internet www.unificompanies.com; f. 1869; part of UNIFI Mutual Holding Co; life and health; Chair. and Dir BARBARA J. KRUMSIEK.

Allstate Corpn: 2775 Sanders Rd, Northbrook, IL 60062-6127; tel. (708) 402-5000; fax (708) 402-2351; e-mail directors@allstate.com; internet www.allstate.com; f. 1931; property and casualty, life, fire, indemnity; Chair., Pres. and CEO THOMAS J. WILSON.

American Family Insurance Group: 6000 American Pkwy, Madison, WI 53783-0001; tel. (608) 249-2111; internet www.amfam.com; f. 1927; life and annuities through subsidiary, American Family Life Insurance Co; property and casualty through eight other subsidiaries; Chair. and CEO DAVID R. ANDERSON; Pres. and COO JACK SALZWEDEL.

American Family Life Assurance Co of Columbus (AFLAC): 1932 Wynnton Rd, Columbus, GA 31999; tel. (706) 323-3431; e-mail news@aflac.com; internet www.aflac.com; f. 1955; life and health; Chair. and CEO DANIEL P. AMOS; Pres. KRISS CLONINGER, III.

American General Life and Accident Insurance Co: American General Center, MC 338N, Nashville, TN 37250; internet www.americangeneral.com; f. 1900; wholly owned subsidiary of American International Group, Inc (AIG); Pres. and CEO MATT WINTER.

American National Insurance Co: 1 Moody Plaza, Galveston, TX 77550-7999; tel. (409) 763-4661; fax (409) 763-4545; internet www.anico.com; f. 1905; operating in 50 states, the District of Columbia, Puerto Rico and American Samoa; life and health, annuities, property and casualty, credit insurance, and pension plan services; Chair. and CEO ROBERT L. MOODY, Sr; Pres. and COO G. RICHARD FERDINANDTSEN.

American United Life Insurance Co: 1 American Sq., POB 368, Indianapolis, IN 46206-0368; tel. (317) 285-2364; fax (317) 285-1931; internet www.aul.com; f. 1877; part of OneAmerica Financial Partners, Inc; owned by American United Mutual Insurance Holding Company (AUMIHC); life and health, annuities, Pres. and CEO DAYTON H. MOLENDORP.

Americo Life Insurance: POB 410288, Kansas City, MO 64141-0288; e-mail contactamerico@americo.com; internet www.americo.com; f. 1909; Pres. and CEO GARY L. MULLER.

Ameritas Life Insurance Corpn: 5900 O St, POB 81889, Lincoln, NE 68501-1889; fax (402) 467-7335; e-mail avlic@ameritas.com; internet www.ameritas.com; f. 1887 as Old Line Bankers Life Insurance Co of Nebraska (Bankers Life); adopted present name in 1988; part of UNIFI Mutual Holding Co; life and health; Chair., Pres. and CEO JOANN M. MARTIN.

Assurant: 1 Chase Manhattan Plaza, New York, NY 10005; tel. (212) 859-7000; fax (212) 859-5893; e-mail vera.carley@assurant.com; internet www.assurant.com; life and health; Chair. JOHN MICHAEL PALMS; Pres. and CEO ROBERT B. POLLOCK.

Auto-Owners Insurance Group: 6101 Anacapri Blvd, Lansing, MI 48917; tel. (517) 323-1200; fax (517) 323-8796; internet www.auto-owners.com; f. 1916; property and casualty through Auto-Owners Insurance Co and four other subsidiaries; life through Auto-Owners Life Insurance Co; Chair. and CEO R. H. SIMON.

Aviva USA Group: 7700 Mills Civic Parkway, West Des Moines, IA 50266; tel. (515) 362-3600; fax (515) 557-2625; e-mail steven.carison@avivausa.com; internet www.avivausa.com; f. 1896 as AmerUS group; life and health, annuities; subsidiaries: Aviva Life and Annuity Co (Des Moines, IA), Aviva Life and Annuity Co (Woodbury, NY); acquired by Aviva PLC in 2006; Pres. and CEO CHRISTOPHER LITTLEFIELD.

AXA-Equitable, Inc: 1290 Ave of the Americas, New York, NY; tel. (212) 554-1234; fax (212) 262-9019; internet www.axa-equitable.com; f. 1859; subsidiary of AXA Financial, Inc; life and health, annuities; Chair. and CEO CHRISTOPHER (KIP) CONDRON.

Baltimore Life Insurance Co: 10075 Red Run Blvd, Owings Mills, MD 21117-4871; tel. (410) 581-6600; fax (410) 581-6601; e-mail info@baltlife.com; internet www.baltlife.com; f. 1882; life and health; Chair. L. JOHN PEARSON; Pres. and CEO DAVID K. FICCA.

W. R. Berkley Corpn: 475 Steamboat Rd, Greenwich, CT 06830; tel. (203) 629-3000; fax (203) 629-3073; e-mail khorvath@wrberkley.com; internet www.wrberkley.com; f. 1967; property and casualty through subsidiaries, divided into five business sectors: regional, reinsurance, specialty, alternative markets and international; Chair. and CEO WILLIAM R. BERKLEY; Pres. and COO W. ROBERT BERKLEY, Jr.

Berkshire Hathaway, Inc: 3555 Farnam St, Omaha, NE 68131; tel. (402) 346-1400; e-mail berkshire@berkshirehathaway.com; internet www.berkshirehathaway.com; general insurance through Berkshire Hathaway Group; life insurance through subsidiary, Medical Protective, in Fort Wayne, IN; Chair. and CEO WARREN E. BUFFETT.

CIGNA Group Insurance: 2 Liberty Pl., 31st Floor, 1601 Chestnut St, Philadelphia, PA 19192; tel. (215) 761-1000; fax (215) 761-5588; internet www.cigna.com; f. 1982; part of CIGNA Corpn; life and health; Pres. and CEO DAVID M. CORDANI.

CNA Insurance: 333 South Wabash, Chicago, IL 60604; tel. (312) 822-5000; e-mail cna_help@cna.com; internet www.cna.com; part of Loews Corpn; property and casualty; Chair. and CEO THOMAS F. MOTAMED; Pres. and COO BOB LINDEMANN.

Combined Insurance Co of America (CICA): 1000 North Milwaukee Ave, Glenview, IL 60025; tel. (847) 953-2025; fax (847) 953-8070; e-mail Amy.Burrell-Tichy@combined.com; internet www.combinedinsurance.com; f. 1949; life and health; operates as Combined Life Insurance Co of New York in NY; Chair. and CEO DOUGLAS R. WENDT.

CNO Financial Group, Inc: 11825 North Pennsylvania St, Carmel, IN 46032; tel. (317) 817-6100; internet www.cnoinc.com; f. 1979; fmrly Conseco, Inc; present name adopted in 2010; life and health; subsidiaries: Conseco Life Insurance Co (IN), Conseco Insurance Co (IL), Conseco Variable Insurance Co (TX), Conseco Health Insurance Co (AZ), Conseco Senior Health Insurance Co (PA), Bankers Life & Casualty Co (Chicago, IL); Chair. R. GLENN HILLIARD; CEO C. JAMES PRIEUR.

Continental Casualty Co: CNA Plaza, 333 South Wabash Ave, Chicago, IL 60685-0001; tel. (312) 822-5000; fax (312) 822-6419; f. 1897; principal subsidiary of CNA; Chair. and CEO DENNIS H. CHOOKASZIAN.

The Continental Insurance Co: 180 Maiden Lane, New York, NY 10038-4925; tel. (212) 440-3000; fax (212) 440-3857; f. 1853; Chair. and CEO J. P. MASCOTTE.

Erie Insurance Group: 100 Erie Insurance Pl., Erie, PA 16530-0001; tel. (814) 451-5000; fax (814) 451-5060; internet www.erieinsurance.com; f. 1925; vehicle, home, commercial and life through network of independent agents; Chair. J. RALPH BORNEMAN, Jr; Pres. and CEO TERRENCE W. CAVANAUGH.

Farmers Insurance Group of Cos: 4680 Wilshire Blvd, Los Angeles, CA 90010-3807; tel. (213) 930-3200; fax (213) 932-3101; internet www.farmers.com; f. 1928; part of Farmers Group, Inc; owned by Zurich Financial Services; vehicle, home and life; operates in 41 states; subsidiaries: Farmers Insurance Exchange, Truck Insurance Exchange, Fire Insurance Exchange, Farmers New World Life Insurance Co (Mercer Island, WA); acquired Foremost Insurance Co (MI) in 2000; CEO ROBERT WOUDSTRA.

Federal Insurance Co: POB 1615, Warren, NJ 07061; tel. (908) 903-2000; internet www.chubb.com; CEO JOHN D. FINNEGAN.

Fidelity National Financial (FNF): 601 Riverside Ave, Jacksonville, FL 32204; tel. (888) 934-3354; internet www.fnf.com; principal subsidiaries: Fidelity National Title Group and Fidelity National Property and Casualty Insurance Group; Chair. WILLIAM P. FOLEY, II; CEO ALAN L. STINSON.

First American Corpn: 1 First American Way, Santa Ana, CA 92707; tel. (714) 250-3000; e-mail corporate.communications@firstam.com; internet www.firstam.com; f. 1889; Exec. Chair. PARKER S. KENNEDY; CEO DENNIS J. GILMORE.

General American Life Insurance Co: 1 Madison Ave, New York, NY 10010-3681; tel. (212) 578-2211; fax (212) 689-1980; internet www.metlife.com; f. 1933; wholly owned subsidiary of MetLife, Inc; Chair., Pres. and CEO KEVIN EICHNER.

Genworth Financial, Inc: 6620 West Broad St, Richmond, VA 23230; tel. (888) 436-9678; e-mail contactus@genworth.com; internet www.genworth.com; f. 1871 as The Life Insurance Co of Virginia; life, long-term care, annuities; Chair., Pres. and CEO MICHAEL D. FRAIZER.

Guarantee Life Co: 8801 Indian Hills Dr., Omaha, NE 68114-4066; tel. (402) 390-7300; fax (402) 390-7577; f. 1901; Sr Vice-Pres. RANDY BIGGERSTAFF.

THE UNITED STATES OF AMERICA

The Guardian Life Insurance Co of America: 7 Hannover Sq., New York, NY 10004; tel. (212) 598-8000; fax (212) 353-7034; e-mail marketcc@glic.com; internet www.guardianlife.com; f. 1860; life and health through 12 subsidiaries and affiliates; Pres. and CEO DENNIS J. MANNING.

Hanover Insurance Group, Inc: 440 Lincoln St, Worcester, MA 01653-0002; tel. (508) 855-1000; fax (508) 853-6332; e-mail abanek@hanover.com; internet www.hanover.com; f. 1852; fmrly operated as Allmerica Financial Life Insurance and Annuity Co, name changed as above in 2005; property and casualty; operates as The Hanover Insurance Co, and as Citizens Insurance Co of America in MI; Chair. MICHAEL P. ANGELINI; Pres. and CEO FREDERICK H. EPPINGER.

Hartford Financial Services Group, Inc: 1 Hartford Plaza, 690 Asylum Ave, Hartford, CT 06115; tel. (860) 547-5000; internet www.thehartford.com; f. 1810; vehicle, home, life, flood, property and casualty, group benefits, group reinsurance; Chair., Pres. and CEO LIAM E. MCGEE.

Integon General Insurance Corpn: 500 West Fifth St, Winston-Salem, NC 27102-3199; tel. (910) 770-2000; fax (910) 770-2122; f. 1920; part of GMAC Insurance Holdings, Inc since 1997.

John Hancock Life Insurance Co: 197 Clarendon St, POB 111, Boston, MA 02117; tel. (617) 572-6000; fax (617) 572-4539; e-mail investor_relations@manulife.com; internet www.johnhancock.com; f. 1862; owned by Manulife (Canada); Pres. and Gen. Man. STEVE FINCH, III.

Kansas City Life Insurance Co: 3520 Broadway, Kansas City, MO 64111; tel. (816) 753-7000; fax (816) 753-4902; internet www.kclife.com; f. 1895; life and health; operates in 48 states and the District of Columbia; subsidiaries: Old American Insurance Co, Sunset Life Insurance Co of America; Chair., Pres. and CEO R. PHILIP BIXBY.

Liberty Mutual Group, Inc: 175 Berkeley St, Boston, MA 02116; tel. (617) 357-9500; fax (617) 350-7648; internet www.libertymutual.com; f. 1912; subsidiaries: Liberty Life Assurance Co of Boston, Liberty Mutual Insurance Co, Liberty Mutual Fire Insurance Co and Employers Insurance Co of Wasusau; Chair., Pres. and CEO EDMUND F. KELLY.

Lincoln National Life Insurance Co: 350 Church St, Hartford, CT 06103; tel. (877) 275-5462; e-mail personalservicecenter@lfg.com; internet www.lfg.com; f. 1905; part of Lincoln National Corpn; life and health; Pres. and CEO DENNIS R. GLASS.

Manhattan Insurance Group: 10700 NW Freeway, Houston, TX 77092; tel. (860) 298-9343; fax (877) 626-4281; e-mail cs@manhattanlife.com; f. 1850; comprises Manhattan Life, Central United Life and Family Life Insurance; Chair. and CEO DAVID W. HARRIS.

Massachusetts Mutual Life Insurance Co (MassMutual): 1295 State St, Springfield, MA 01111-0001; tel. (413) 788-8411; fax (413) 744-6005; internet www.massmutual.com; f. 1851; part of Mass-Mutual Financial Group; mutual life and health; Chair. STUART H. REESE; Pres. and CEO ROGER W. CRANDALL.

Metropolitan Life Insurance Co (MetLife): 200 Park Ave, New York, NY 10166; tel. (212) 578-2211; fax (212) 689-1980; internet www.metlife.com; f. 1863; life and health; Chair., Pres. and CEO C. ROBERT HENRIKSON.

Minnesota Life Insurance Co: 400 Robert St North, St Paul, MN 55101; tel. (651) 665-3500; fax (651) 665-4488; internet www.minnesotamutual.com; f. 1880; affiliated to Securian Financial Group, Inc; life and health; Chair., Pres. and CEO ROBERT L. SENKLER.

Mutual of Omaha Insurance Co: Mutual of Omaha Plaza, Omaha, NE 68175; tel. (402) 342-7600; e-mail corporatesecretary@mutualofomaha.com; internet mutualofomaha.com; f. 1909; life and health; operating in 50 states, the District of Columbia, the US Virgin Is, Puerto Rico and Guam; Chair. and CEO DANIEL P. NEARY.

Nationwide Mutual Insurance Co: 1 Nationwide Plaza, Columbus, OH 43215-2220; tel. (614) 249-7111; e-mail casej6@nationwide.com; internet www.nationwide.com; f. 1925; property and casualty through 18 subsidiaries; life and retirement savings through 25 subsidiaries; also asset management and strategic investment; CEO STEVE RASMUSSEN; Exec. Vice-Pres. and COO MARK THRESHER.

New York Life Insurance Co: 51 Madison Ave, New York, NY 10010-1603; tel. (212) 576-7000; fax (212) 576-6794; e-mail infonyl@e-mail.com; internet www.newyorklife.com; f. 1845; life and health; Chair., Pres. and CEO THEODORE (TED) MATHAS.

The Northwestern Mutual Life Insurance Co: 720 East Wisconsin Ave, Milwaukee, WI 53202-4797; tel. (414) 271-1444; fax (414) 665-5739; internet www.nmfn.com; f. 1857; mutual life and health; Chair. and CEO JOHN E. SCHLIFSKE; Pres. GARY (SKIP) POLINER.

Old Line Life Insurance Co of America: POB 401, Milwaukee, WI 53201; tel. (414) 271-2820; fax (414) 283-5556; f. 1910; Pres. and CEO JAMES A. GRIFFIN.

Pacific Life Insurance Co: 700 Newport Center Dr., Newport Beach, CA 92660-6397; tel. (949) 219-3011; fax (949) 219-7614; e-mail info@pacificlife.com; internet www.pacificlife.com; f. 1868; life, annuities and mutual funds; Chair., Pres. and CEO JAMES T. MORRIS; Exec. Vice-Pres. and CFO KHANH T. TRAN.

Penn Mutual Life Insurance Co: 600 Dresher Rd, Horsham, PA 19044; tel. (215) 956-8000; fax (215) 956-7699; internet www.pennmutual.com; f. 1847; Chair. and CEO ROBERT E. CHAPPELL; Pres. EILEEN MCDONNELL.

Phoenix Life Insurance Co: 1 American Row, POB 5056, Hartford, CT 06102-5056; tel. (860) 403-5000; e-mail webmaster@phoenixwm.com; internet www.phoenixwm.com; f. 1851; life and health, annuities; operating in all states, the District of Columbia, Puerto Rico, the US Virgin Is and Canada; Chair. THOMAS J. JOHNSON; Pres. and CEO JAMES D. WEHR.

Pioneer Mutual Life Insurance Co: 101 North 10th St, Fargo, ND 58108; tel. (701) 297-5700; e-mail CorporateCommunications.CorpComm@oneamerica.com; internet www.oneamerica.com; f. 1868; part of OneAmerica Financial Partners, Inc, owned by American United Mutual Insurance Holding Co (AUMIHC); life and health, annuities; Pres. and CEO DAYTON H. MOLENDORP.

Principal Financial Group, Inc: 711 High St, Des Moines, IA 50392; tel. (515) 247-5111; fax (515) 235-5491; internet www.principal.com; f. 1879; life and health; Chair., Pres. and CEO LARRY D. ZIMPLEMAN.

The Progressive Group: 6300 Wilson Mills Rd, Mayfield Village, OH 44143; tel. (440) 461-5000; internet www.progressive.com; f. 1937; part of The Progressive Corpn; Chair. PETER B. LEWIS; Pres. and CEO GLENN M. RENWICK.

Protective Life Insurance Co: 2801 Hwy 280 South, Birmingham, AL 35223-2488; tel. (205) 268-1000; internet www.protective.com; f. 1907; part of Protective Life Insurance Corpn; life and health; Chair., Pres. and CEO JOHN D. JOHNS.

The Prudential Insurance Co of America: 751 Broad St, Newark, NJ 07102-3714; tel. (973) 802-6000; fax (973) 802-7277; e-mail investor.relations@prudential.com; internet www.prudential.com; f. 1875; life and health; Chair. and CEO JOHN R. STRANGFELD.

QBE Insurance Group: Wall Street Plaza, 88 Pine Street, New York, NY 10005; tel. (212) 422-1212; fax (212) 422-1313; internet www.qbeusa.com; CEO VINCE MCLENAGHAN.

SAFECO Corpn: Safeco Plaza, 4333 Brooklyn Ave, NE, Seattle, WA 98185-0001; tel. (206) 545-5000; fax (206) 548-7117; internet www.safeco.com; f. 1929; part of Liberty Mutual Group since 2008; subsidiaries: SAFECO Property and Casualty Insurance Cos, SAFECO Surety; Pres. MICHAEL HUGHES; Exec. Vice-Pres. and COO MATTHEW D. NICKERSON.

Security Mutual Life Insurance Co of New York: 100 Court St, POB 1625, Binghamton, New York, NY 13902-1625; tel. (607) 723-3551; e-mail hpalmer@smlny.com; internet www.smlny.com; f. 1886; life and health, annuities; operating in all states; Chair., Pres. and CEO BRUCE W. BOYEA.

Southwestern Life Insurance Co: 500 N Akard St, Dallas, TX 75201; tel. (214) 954-7111; fax (214) 954-7717; f. 1903; subsidiary of Southwestern Life Corpn.

StanCorp Financial Group: POB 711, Portland, OR 97207; tel. (503) 248-2700; fax (503) 321-7757; e-mail info@standard.com; internet www.standard.com; f. 1906; includes the Standard Insurance Company and Standard Life Insurance Company of New York; disability, group disability, group life, group dental, annuities; Chair. ERIC E. PARSONS; Pres. and CEO J. GREG NESS.

State Farm Insurance: 1 State Farm Plaza, Bloomington, IL 61710-0001; tel. (309) 766-2311; fax (309) 766-6169; internet www.statefarm.com; f. 1929; vehicle, fire, life and health insurance; Chair., Pres. and CEO EDWARD B. RUST, Jr.

State Life Insurance Co: 1 American Sq., POB 368, Indianapolis, IN 46206-0368; tel. (317) 681-5300; fax (317) 681-5492; internet www.oneamerica.com; f. 1894; part of OneAmerica Financial Partners, Inc, owned by American United Mutual Insurance Holding Company (AUMIHC); life and health, annuities; Chair., Pres. and CEO DAYTON H. MOLENDORP.

Teachers Insurance and Annuity Association-College Retirement Equities Fund (TIAA-CREF): 730 Third Ave, New York, NY 10017-3206; tel. (212) 916-6066; fax (212) 916-6088; e-mail trustees@tiaa-cref.org; internet www.tiaa-cref.org; f. 1918 (TIAA); f. 1952 (CREF); mutual life and health; Chair. RONALD L. THOMPSON; Pres. and CEO ROGER W. FERGUSON, Jr.

Thrivent Financial for Lutherans: 4321 North Ballard Rd, Appleton, WI 54919-0001; tel. (920) 734-5721; e-mail mail@thrivent.com; internet www.thrivent.com; life and health; Chair. KURT M. SENSKE; Pres. and CEO BRAD HEWITT.

Torchmark Corpn: 3700 South Stonebridge Dr., POB 8080, McKinney, TX 75070-8080; tel. (972) 569-4000; e-mail tmkir@

THE UNITED STATES OF AMERICA

torchmarkcorp.com; internet www.torchmarkcorp.com; life and health; principal subsidiaries: American Income Life Insurance Co (Waco, TX), First United American Life Insurance Co (Syracuse, NY), Globe Life And Accident Insurance Co (Oklahoma City, OK), Liberty National Life Insurance Co (Birmingham, AL), United American Insurance Co (McKinney, TX), United Investors Life Insurance Co (Birmingham, AL); Chair. and CEO Mark S. McAndrew; Exec. Vice-Pres. Gary L. Coleman.

Transamerica Corpn: 600 Montgomery St, Suite 2300, San Francisco, CA 94111-2725; tel. (415) 983-4000; fax (415) 983-4234; e-mail Nicole.Lorey@transamerica.com; internet www.transamerica.com; f. 1906; part of AEGON Insurance Group; life and health, annuities, reinsurance; subsidiaries: Transamerica Occidental Life Insurance Co, Transamerica Life Insurance Co, Transamerica Financial Life Insurance Co; Pres. Ron Wagley; Chair. Frank Herringer.

The Travelers Companies, Inc: 385 Washington St, Saint Paul, MN 55102; tel. (615) 310-7911; fax (651) 310-8204; internet www.travelers.com; f. 2004 as St Paul Travelers by merger of St Paul Coes and Travelers Property and Casualty Corpn; adopted current name in 2007; Chair., Pres. and CEO Jay S. Fishman.

Union Central Life Insurance Co: 1876 Waycross Rd, POB 40888, Cincinnati, OH 45240; tel. (513) 595-2200; fax (513) 595-2559; internet www.unioncentral.com; f. 1867; part of UNIFI Mutual Holding Co; life and health; Chair. John H. Jacobs; CEO Gary T. Huffman.

Unitrin, Inc: 1 East Wacker Dr., Chicago, IL 60601; tel. (312) 661-4600; e-mail mediarelations@unitrin.com; internet www.unitrin.com; life and health through Unitrin Life & Health Insurance Group (five subsidiaries); property and casualty through Unitrin Property & Casualty Insurance Group (19 subsidiaries); two further subsidiaries and five affiliated cos; Chair., Pres. and CEO Donald G. Southwell.

Unum Group: 1 Fountain Sq., Chattanooga, TN 37402; tel. (432) 294-1011; e-mail tawhite@unum.com; internet www.unumprovident.com; f. 1848; life and health; subsidiaries: Colonial Life Accident and Insurance Co, Paul Revere Life Insurance Co, Provident Life and Accident Insurance Co, Provident Life and Casualty Insurance Co, First Unum Insurance Co, and Unum Life Insurance Co of America; Chair. Jon S. Fossel; Pres. and CEO Thomas R. Watjen.

USAA: McDermott Bldg, 9800 Fredericksburg Rd, San Antonio, TX 78288; internet www.usaa.com; f. 1922; property and casualty through seven subsidiaries: United Service Automobile Asscn, USAA Casualty Insurance Co, USAA General Indemnity Co, Garrison Property and Casualty Insurance Co, USAA County Mutual Insurance Co, USAA Texas Lloyd's Co and USAA Ltd; life and annuities through two subsidiaries: USAA Life Insurance Co and USAA Life Insurance Company of New York (Highland Falls, NY); Chair. Lt-Gen. (retd) John H. Moellering; Pres. and CEO Josue (Joe) Robles, Jr.

Washington National Corporation: 300 Tower Pkwy, Lincolnshire, IL 60069; tel. (847) 793-3000; fax (847) 793-3737; f. 1911; Chair. and CEO Robert Patin.

Western & Southern Financial Group: 400 Broadway, Mail Station 90, Cincinnati, OH 45202; tel. (866) 832-7719; fax (513) 629-1220; internet www.westernsouthern.com; f. 1888; operating in 44 states; life and health; subsidiaries: Western and Southern Life Insurance Co, Western-Southern Life Assurance Co, Columbus Life Insurance Co, Integrity Life Insurance Co, Lafayette Life Insurance Co; Chair., Pres. and CEO John F. Barrett.

Zenith Insurance Co: 21255 Califa St, Woodland Hills, CA 91367; tel. (818) 713-1000; fax (818) 710-1860; e-mail corpcomm@thezenith.com; internet www.thezenith.com; holding co Zenith National Insurance Corpn, wholly owned subsidiary of Fairfax Financial Holdings Ltd; specializes in workers' compensation; subsidiary: ZNAT Insurance Co; Chair. and Pres. Stanley R. Zax.

INSURANCE ORGANIZATIONS

American Council of Life Insurance (ACLI): 101 Constitution Ave, NW, Washington, DC 20001-2133; tel. (202) 624-2000; fax (202) 624-2319; e-mail Media@acli.com; internet www.acli.com; f. 1976; 400 mem. cos; Chair. C. Robert Henrikson; Pres. and CEO Frank Keating, Jr.

American Institute of Marine Underwriters (AIMU): 14 Wall St, 21st Floor, New York, NY 10005-2145; tel. (212) 233-0550; fax (212) 227-5102; e-mail aimu@aimu.org; internet www.aimu.org; f. 1898; 105 mems; Chair. Dennis C. Marvin; Pres. James M. Craig.

American Insurance Association (AIA): 2101 L St, NW, Suite 400, Washington, DC 20037; tel. (202) 828-7100; fax (202) 293-1219; e-mail info@aiadc.org; internet www.aiadc.org; f. 1964; 300 mems; Pres. and CEO Leigh Ann Pusey.

Casualty Actuarial Society: 4350 North Fairfax Dr., Suite 250, Arlington, VA 22203; tel. (703) 276-3100; fax (703) 276-3108; e-mail office@casact.org; internet www.casact.org; f. 1914; 4,400 mems; Pres. Roger M. Hayne; Exec. Dir Cynthia R. Ziegler.

LIMRA International: 300 Day Hill Rd, Windsor, CT 06095; tel. (860) 688-3358; fax (860) 298-9555; e-mail customer.service@limra.com; internet www.limra.com; f. 1916; research and consultancy services for insurance cos; Chair. Dayton H. Molendorp; Pres. and CEO Robert A. Kerzner; 850 mems.

LOMA (Life Office Management Association): 2300 Windy Ridge Pkwy, Suite 600, Atlanta, GA 30339-8443; tel. (770) 951-1770; fax (770) 984-6417; e-mail askloma@loma.org; internet www.loma.org; f. 1924; 1,200 mem. cos; Pres. Robert A. Kerzner.

National Association of Health Underwriters (NAHU): 2000 North 14th St, Suite 450, Arlington, VA 22201; tel. (703) 276-0220; fax (703) 841-7797; e-mail info@nahu.org; internet www.nahu.org; Pres. Steven Selinsky; Exec. Vice-Pres. and CEO Janet Stokes Trautwein.

National Association of Life Underwriters: 2901 Telestar Court, Falls Church, VA 22042-1205; tel. (703) 770-8100; e-mail membersupport@naifa.org; internet www.naifa.org; 108,000 mems; CEO John J. Healy.

National Association of Mutual Insurance Cos (NAMIC): 3601 Vincennes Rd, POB 68700, Indianapolis, IN 46268-0700; tel. (317) 875-5250; fax (317) 879-8408; e-mail service@namic.org; internet www.namic.org; f. 1895; 1,400 mems; Chair. John T. Hill; Pres. and CEO Charles M. Chamness.

Reinsurance Association of America: 1445 New York Ave, NW, 7th Floor, Washington, DC 20005; tel. (202) 638-3690; fax (202) 638-0936; e-mail infobox@reinsurance.org; internet www.reinsurance.org; f. 1969; 35 mems; Pres. Franklin W. Nutter.

Trade and Industry

CHAMBER OF COMMERCE

US Chamber of Commerce: 1615 H St, NW, Washington, DC 20062-2000; tel. (202) 659-6000; fax (202) 463-5836; internet www.uschamber.com; f. 1912; mems: c. 3m. cos; over 100 US chambers of commerce in 91 countries; Pres. and CEO Thomas J. Donohue; Chair. Thomas D. Bell, Jr.

EMPLOYERS' ORGANIZATIONS

Chemicals

American Chemistry Council (ACC): 700 Second St, NE, Washington, DC 20002; tel. (202) 249-7000; fax (202) 249-6100; e-mail helpline@americanchemistry.com; internet www.americanchemistry.com; f. 1872; incl. the Plastics Division and Chlorine Chemistry Division; 136 mems; Pres. and CEO Calvin Dooley; Chief of Staff Dell Perelman.

American Pharmacists Association (APhA): 2215 Constitution Ave, NW, Washington, DC 20037; tel. (202) 628-4410; fax (202) 783-2351; e-mail scorbitt@aphanet.org; internet www.pharmacist.com; f. 1852; over 60,000 mems; Pres. Harold Godwin; Exec. Vice-Pres. and CEO Thomas E. Menighan.

American Plastics Council (APC): 1300 Wilson Blvd, Arlington, VA 22209; tel. (703) 741-5000; fax (703) 741-6093; internet www.americanplasticscouncil.org; affiliate of the American Chemistry Council; 13 mem. cos and 1 affiliated trade asscn; Pres. Rodney W. Lowman.

Consumer Specialty Products Association (CSPA): 900 17th St, NW, Suite 300, Washington, DC 20006; tel. (202) 872-8110; fax (202) 872-8114; e-mail info@cspa.org; internet www.cspa.org; f. 1914; fmrly Chemical Specialities Manufacturers Asscn; around 240 mems; Pres. Christopher Cathcart.

Drug, Chemical and Associated Technologies Association, Inc (DCAT): 1 Washington Blvd, Suite 7, Robbinsville, NJ 08691; tel. (609) 448-1000; fax (609) 448-1944; e-mail info@dcat.org; internet www.dcat.org; f. 1890; fmrly Drug, Chemical and Allied Trades Asscn; name changed as above in 2003; 350 mems; Pres. Joseph Principe; Exec. Dir Margaret M. Timony.

The Fertilizer Institute: Union Center Plaza, 820 First St, NE, Suite 430, Washington, DC 20002; tel. (202) 962-0490; fax (202) 962-0577; e-mail webmaster@tfi.org; internet www.tfi.org; f. 1883; 300 mem. orgs; Pres. Ford B. West.

National Community Pharmacists Association (NCPA): 100 Daingerfield Rd, Alexandria, VA 22314; tel. (703) 683-8200; fax (703) 683-3619; e-mail info@ncpanet.org; internet www.ncpanet.org; f. 1898; fmrly Nat. Asscn of Retail Druggists; more than 23,000 mems; Pres. Robert Greenwood; Exec. Vice-Pres. and CEO Douglas Hoey (acting).

Pharmaceutical Research & Manufacturers of America (PhRMA): 950 F St, NW, Suite 300, Washington, DC 20004; tel.

THE UNITED STATES OF AMERICA

(202) 835-3400; fax (202) 835-3414; internet www.phrma.org; f. 1958; 30 mems; Pres. and CEO JOHN CASTELLANI; Chair. of Bd JEFFREY B. KINDLER.

American Cleaning Institute (ACI): 1331 L St, NW, Suite 650, Washington, DC, 20005; tel. (202) 347-2900; fax (202) 347-4110; e-mail info@cleaninginstitute.org; internet www.cleaninginstitute.org; f. 1926; fmrly Soap and Detergent Asscn (SDA); c. 100 mems; Pres. and CEO ERNIE ROSENBERG.

Society of Chemical Manufacturers and Affiliates (SOCMA): 1850 M St, NW, Suite 700, Washington, DC 20036-5810; tel. (202) 721-4100; fax (202) 296-8120; e-mail info@socma.com; internet www.socma.com; f. 1921; fmrly Synthetic Organic Chemical Manufacturers' Asscn; renamed as above in 2009; 300 mem. cos; Chair. LARRY BROTHERTON; Pres. and CEO LAWRENCE SLOAN.

Construction
(see also Electricity, and Engineering and Machinery)

American Institute of Constructors (AIC): 700 North Fairfax St, Suite 510, POB 26334, Alexandria, VA 22314; tel. (703) 683-4999; fax (703) 527-3105; e-mail admin@aicnet.org; internet www.aicnet.org; f. 1971; 1,600 mems; Pres. MARK GIORGI; Sec. DAVID FLEMING.

Associated Builders and Contractors, Inc (ABC): 4250 North Fairfax Dr., 9th Floor, Arlington, VA 22203-1607; tel. (703) 812-2000; e-mail gotquestions@abc.org; internet www.abc.org; f. 1950; 24,000 mems; Chair. JAMES W. ELMER; Pres. and CEO M. KIRK PICKEREL.

Associated General Contractors of America (AGC) (AGC of America): 2300 Wilson Blvd, Suite 400, Arlington, VA 22201; tel. (703) 548-3118; fax (703) 548-3119; e-mail info@agc.org; internet www.agc.org; f. 1918; more than 32,000 mems; Pres. TED AADLAND; CEO CAROLYN COKER.

Associated Specialty Contractors, Inc (ASC): 3 Bethesda Metro Center, Suite 1100, Bethesda, MD 20814-5372; tel. (301) 657-3110; fax (301) 215-4500; e-mail dgw@necanet.org; internet www.assoc-spec-con.org; f. 1955 as the Council of Mechanical Specialty Contracting Industries, Inc; name changed in 1973; 9 mem. asscns; Pres. DANIEL G. WALTER; Chair. of Bd D. L. SMITH.

Building Stone Institute (BSI): POB 419, 5 Riverside Dr., Bldg 2, Chestertown, NY 12817; tel. (518) 803-4336; fax (518) 803-4338; e-mail barb@buildingstoneinstitute.org; internet www.buildingstoneinstitute.org; f. 1919; 400 mems; Pres. ROBERT HICKEN; Exec. Vice-Pres. JANE BENNETT.

Construction Specifications Institute (CSI): 110 South Union St, Suite 100, Alexandria, VA 22314; tel. (703) 684-0300; fax (703) 684-8436; e-mail csi@csinet.org; internet www.csinet.org; f. 1948; over 14,000 mems; Pres. DENNIS HALL; Exec. Dir and CEO WALTER T. MARLOWE.

Mechanical Contractors Association of America, Inc (MCAA): 1385 Piccard Dr., Rockville, MD 20850-4340; tel. (301) 869-5800; fax (301) 990-9690; e-mail mcaainfo@mcaa.org; internet www.mcaa.org; f. 1889; 2,500 mems; Pres. MARK A. ROGERS; CEO JOHN R. GENTILLE.

National Association of Home Builders of the US (NAHB): 1201 15th St, NW, Washington, DC 20005; tel. (202) 266-8200; fax (202) 266-8400; e-mail jhoward@nahb.org; internet www.nahb.org; f. 1942; 800 mem. asscns, 220,000 mems; Pres. and CEO GERALD M. HOWARD; Chair. of Bd ROBERT R. JONES.

National Association of Plumbing-Heating-Cooling Contractors (PHCC): 180 South Washington St, POB 6808, Falls Church, VA 22046; tel. (703) 237-8100; fax (703) 237-7442; e-mail naphcc@naphcc.org; internet www.phccweb.org; f. 1883; 4,000 mems; Pres. SKIP PFEFFER; Exec. Vice-Pres. GERARD J. KENNEDY, Jr.

National Ready Mixed Concrete Association (NRMCA): 900 Spring St, Silver Spring, MD 20910; tel. (301) 587-1400; fax (301) 585-4219; e-mail info@nrmca.org; internet www.nrmca.org; f. 1930; 1,000 mems; Chair. TIM BECKEN; Pres. ROBERT GARBINI.

National Tile Contractors Association (NTCA): 626 Lakeland East Dr., POB 13629, Jackson, MS 39236; tel. (601) 939-2071; fax (601) 932-6117; internet www.tile-assn.com; f. 1947; Exec. Dir BART BETTIGA; Chair. of Bd FRANK CANTO.

Tile Council of North America Inc (TCNA): 100 Clemson Research Blvd, Anderson, SC 29625; tel. (864) 646-8453; fax (864) 646-2821; e-mail info@tileusa.com; internet www.tileusa.com; f. 1945 as Tile Council of America; adopted current name in 2003; 130 mems; Exec. Dir ERIC ASTRACHAN.

US Green Building Council (USGBC): 2101 L St, NW, Suite 500, Washington, DC 20037; tel. (202) 828-7422; fax (202) 828-5110; e-mail info@usgbc.org; internet www.usgbc.org; over 6,400 mem. orgs; Pres. and CEO S. RICHARD FEDRIZZI; Chair. of Exec. Cttee TIM COLE.

Electricity
(see also Construction, Electronics and Technology, Engineering and Machinery Institute, and Trade and Industry—Utilities)

Edison Electric Institute (EEI): 701 Pennsylvania Ave, NW, Washington, DC 20004-2696; tel. (202) 508-5000; e-mail feedback@eei.org; internet www.eei.org; f. 1933; mems: nearly 200 investor-owned electric utility cos, more than 80 int. affiliates; mems generate about 70% of electricity produced by US utilities; Chair. RICHARD C. KELLY; Pres. THOMAS R. KUHN.

National Association of Electrical Distributors (NAED): 1181 Corporate Lake Dr., St Louis, MO 63132; tel. (314) 991-9000; fax (314) 991-3060; e-mail info@naed.org; internet www.naed.org; f. 1908; 2,900 mems; Pres. and CEO THOMAS NABER; Chair. JACK HENDERSON.

National Electrical Contractors Association (NECA): 3 Bethesda Metro Center, Suite 1100, Bethesda, MD 20814-5372; tel. (301) 657-3110; fax (301) 215-4500; internet www.necanet.org; f. 1901; 4,200 mems; Pres. REX FERRY; CEO JOHN M. GRAU.

National Electrical Manufacturers Association (NEMA) (Association of Electrical and Medical Imaging Equipment Manufacturers): 1300 North 17th St, Suite 1752, Rosslyn, VA 22209; tel. (703) 841-3200; fax (703) 841-5900; e-mail webmaster@nema.org; internet www.nema.org; f. 1926; c. 450 mem. cos; Chair. CHARLIE F. JERABEK; Pres. and CEO EVAN R. GADDIS.

Electronics and Technology

TechAmerica: North Bldg, Suite 600, 601 Pennsylvania Ave, NW, Washington, DC 20004; tel. (202) 682-9110; fax (202) 682-9111; e-mail anne.caliguiri@techamerica.org; internet www.techamerica.org; formed by the merger of AeA (fmrly American Electronics Asscn), Cyber Security Industry Alliance (CSIA), Information Technology Asscn of America (ITAA) and Government Electronics & Information Technology Asscn (GEIA); 1,200 mem. cos; Chair. HENRY STEININGER; CEO PHILIP J. BOND.

Electronic Industries Alliance: 2500 Wilson Blvd, Arlington, VA 22201-3834; tel. (703) 907-7500; fax (703) 907-7501; internet www.eia.org; f. 1924; 1,300 mem. cos; Chair. JOHN DENSLINGER; Pres. ROBERT WILLIS.

Institute of Electrical and Electronics Engineers, Inc (IEEE): 445 Hoes Lane, Piscataway, NJ 08854-4141; tel. (732) 981-0060; fax (732) 562-6380; e-mail contactcenter@ieee.org; internet www.ieee.org; f. 1963; more than 375,000 mems world-wide; Pres. and CEO PEDRO RAY; Exec. Dir JAMES PRENDERGAST.

IPC (Association Connecting Electronics Industries): 3000 Lakeside Dr., Suite 309, Bannockburn, IL 60015; tel. (847) 615-7100; fax (847) 615-7105; e-mail mcgude@ipc.org; internet www.ipc.org; f. 1957; 2,700 mem. cos; Chair. of Bd ROBERT J. FERGUSON; Pres. and CEO DENNIS P. MCGUIRK.

Telecommunications Industry Association (TIA): 2500 Wilson Blvd, Suite 300, Arlington, VA 22201; tel. (703) 907-7700; fax (703) 907-7727; e-mail tia@tiaonline.org; internet www.tiaonline.org; f. 1988; Chair. of Bd SHAWN OSBORNE; Pres. GRANT E. SEIFFERT.

Engineering and Machinery
(see also Electricity and Construction)

Air-Conditioning, Heating and Refrigeration Institute (AHRI): 2111 Wilson Blvd, Suite 500, Arlington, VA 22201; tel. (703) 524-8800; fax (703) 528-3816; e-mail ahri@ahrinet.org; internet www.ahrinet.org; f. 2007 by merger of the Air-Conditioning and Refrigeration Institute (ARI) and the Gas Appliance Mfrs Asscn (GAMA); more than 300 mems; Chair. RAY HOGLUND; Pres. STEPHEN R. YUREK.

American Council of Engineering Companies (ACEC): 1015 15th St, NW, 8th Floor, Washington, DC 20005-2605; tel. (202) 347-7474; fax (202) 898-0068; e-mail acec@acec.org; internet www.acec.org; f. 1909; more than 5,500 mem. cos; Chair. GERALD STUMP; Pres. and CEO DAVID A. RAYMOND.

American Institute of Chemical Engineers (AIChE): 3 Park Ave, New York, NY 10016-5991; tel. (203) 702-7660; fax (203) 775-5177; e-mail custserv@aiche.org; internet www.aiche.org; f. 1908; nearly 40,000 mems world-wide; Pres. HENRY T. (HANK) KOHLBRAND.

American Institute of Mining, Metallurgical and Petroleum Engineers, Inc: 8307 Shaffer Pkwy, Littleton, CO 80127-4012; tel. (303) 948-4255; fax (303) 948-4260; e-mail aime@aimehq.org; internet www.aimehq.org; f. 1871; five constituent socs representing more than 127,000 mems world-wide; Pres. IAN SADLER; Exec. Dir L. MICHELE LAWRIE-MUNRO (acting).

American Society of Civil Engineers (ASCE): 1801 Alexander Bell Dr., Reston, VA 20191-4400; tel. (703) 295-6300; fax (703) 295-6333; e-mail webmaster@asce.org; internet www.asce.org; f. 1852; more than 147,000 mems world-wide; Pres. BLAINE D. LEONARD; Exec. Dir PATRICK J. NATALE.

THE UNITED STATES OF AMERICA

American Society of Heating, Refrigerating and Air-Conditioning Engineers (ASHRAE): 1791 Tullie Circle, NE, Atlanta, GA 30329; tel. (404) 636-8400; fax (404) 321-5478; e-mail ashrae@ashrae.org; internet www.ashrae.org; f. 1894; 51,000 mems; Pres. LYNN G. BELLENGER; Exec. Vice-Pres. JEFF LITTLETON.

American Society of Naval Engineers, Inc: 1452 Duke St, Alexandria, VA 22314-3458; tel. (703) 836-6727; fax (703) 836-7491; e-mail asnehq@navalengineers.org; internet www.navalengineers.org; f. 1888; 5,000 mems; Pres. KATHLEEN E. HINTON; Exec. Dir Capt. (retd) DENNIS K. KRUSE.

Association of Coastal Engineers (ACE): c/o Angie Gross, Erickson Consulting Engineers, Inc, 7201 Delainey Ct, Sarasota, FL 34240; e-mail hugo@coastharborenq.com; internet www.coastalengineers.org; f. 1999; Pres. JOHN RAMSEY; Exec. Sec. ANGIE GROSS.

Association of Home Appliance Manufacturers (AHAM): 1111 19th St, NW, Suite 402, Washington, DC 20036; tel. (202) 872-5955; fax (202) 872-9354; e-mail info@aham.org; internet www.aham.org; f. 1915; Chair. MARK J. BISSELL; Pres. JOSEPH M. MCGUIRE.

AMT (The Association for Manufacturing Technology): 7901 Westpark Dr., McLean, VA 22102-4206; tel. (703) 893-2900; fax (703) 893-1151; e-mail amt@amtonline.org; internet www.amtonline.org; f. 1902; 370 mems; Pres. DOUGLAS K. WOODS.

Manufacturers Alliance/MAPI, Inc: 1600 Wilson Blvd, Suite 1100, 11th Floor, Arlington, VA 22209-2411; tel. (703) 841-9000; fax (703) 841-9514; e-mail info@mapi.net; internet www.mapi.net; f. 1933; more than 500 mems. cos; Pres. and CEO THOMAS J. DUESTERBERG; Chair. of Exec. Cttee TIMOTHY H. POWERS.

Petroleum Equipment Institute (PEI): POB 2380, Tulsa, OK 74101-2380; tel. (918) 494-9696; fax (918) 491-9895; e-mail info@pei.org; internet www.pei.org; f. 1951; over 1,600 mems world-wide; Pres. PETER WARD; Exec. Vice-Pres. ROBERT RENKES.

SAE International (Society of Automotive Engineers): 400 Commonwealth Dr., Warrendale, PA 15096-0001; tel. (724) 776-4841; fax (724) 776-0790; e-mail customerservice@sae.org; internet www.sae.org; f. 1905; over 121,000 mems world-wide; Pres. RICHARD KLEINE; CEO DAVID SCHUTT.

Society of Naval Architects and Marine Engineers (SNAME): 601 Pavonia Ave, Suite 400, Jersey City, NJ 07306-2907; tel. (201) 798-4800; fax (201) 798-4975; e-mail ccali-poutre@sname.org; internet www.sname.org; f. 1893; over 8,500 mems world-wide; Pres. R. KEITH MICHEL; Exec. Dir ERIK SEITHER.

United Engineering Foundation (UEF): POB 70, Mount Vernon, VA 22121-0070; tel. (973) 244-2328; fax (973) 882-5155; e-mail engfnd@aol.com; internet www.uefoundation.org; f. 1914; umbrella org. of engineering socs, incl. the American Institute of Chemical Engineers (AIChE), the American Institute of Mining Engineers (AIME), the American Society of Civil Engineers (ASCE), the American Society of Mechanical Engineers, and the Institute of Electrical and Electronics Engineers (IEEE); Pres. Dr ARTHUR W. WINSTON; Exec. Dir Dr DAVID L. BELDEN.

Food

American Bakers Association (ABA): 1350 I St, NW, Suite 700, Washington, DC 20005-3300; tel. (202) 789-0300; fax (202) 898-1164; e-mail info@americanbakers.org; internet www.americanbakers.org; f. 1897; Chair. ALLEN L. SHIVER; Pres. and CEO ROBB MACKIE.

American Beverage Association (ABA): 1101 16th St, NW, Washington, DC 20036-4803; tel. (202) 463-6732; fax (202) 659-5349; e-mail info@ameribev.org; internet www.ameribev.org; f. 1919; fmrly Nat. Soft Drink Asscn; 1,700 mems; Chair. LARRY D. YOUNG; Pres. and CEO SUSAN K. NEELY.

American Council for Food Safety and Quality: 710 Striker Ave, Sacramento, CA 95834; tel. (916) 561-5900; fax (916) 561-5910; e-mail samk@agfoodsafety.org; internet agfoodsafety.org; f. 1908; agricultural asscn (dried fruit and tree nuts); 51 mems; Pres. and CEO SAM KEIPER.

American Farm Bureau Federation (FB): 600 Maryland Ave, SW, Suite 1000W, Washington, DC 20024; tel. (202) 406-3600; fax (202) 406-3602; e-mail webmaster@fb.org; internet www.fb.org; f. 1919; 50 mem. states and Puerto Rico; Pres. BOB STALLMAN; Exec. Vice-Pres. RICHARD NEWPHER.

American Meat Institute: 1150 Connecticut Ave, NW, 12th Floor, Washington, DC 20036; tel. (202) 587-4200; fax (202) 587-4300; e-mail webmaster@meatami.com; internet www.meatami.com; f. 1906; 1,100 mems; Chair. JEFFREY ETTINGER; Pres. and CEO J. PATRICK BOYLE.

Commodity Markets Council (CMC): 1300 L St, NW, Suite 1020, Washington, DC 20005; tel. (202) 842-0400; fax (202) 789-7223; e-mail christine.cochran@commoditymkts.org; internet www.commoditymkts.org; f. 1930 as the National Grain Trade Council; reformed as two separate entities, CMC and the Transportation, Elevator and Grain Merchants Asscn, in 2006; 40 mems; Chair. CHARLES P. CAREY; Pres. CHRISTINE M. COCHRAN.

Distilled Spirits Council of the US, Inc (DISCUS): 1250 Eye St, NW, Suite 400, Washington, DC 20005; tel. (202) 628-3544; internet www.discus.org; f. 1973; 13 active mems and 23 affiliates; Pres. and CEO Dr PETER H. CRESSY.

Food Marketing Institute (FMI): 2345 Crystal Dr., Suite 800, Arlington, VA 22202; tel. (202) 452-8444; fax (202) 429-4519; e-mail fmi@fmi.org; internet www.fmi.org; f. 1977; 1,500 mem. cos; Chair. RICHARD N. JURGENS; Pres. and CEO LESLIE G. SARASIN.

Foodservice Sales and Marketing Association (FSMA): 9192 Red Branch Rd, Suite 200, Columbia, MD 21045; tel. (410) 715-4084; fax (410) 997-9387; e-mail info@fsmaonline.com; internet www.fsmaonline.com; f. 2003; Chair. of Bd BOB WATSON; Pres. and CEO RICK ABRAHAM.

Grocery Manufacturers of America, Inc (GMA): 1350 I St, NW, Suite 300, Washington, DC 20005; tel. (202) 639-5900; fax (202) 639-5932; e-mail info@gmaonline.org; internet www.gmaonline.org; f. 1908; over 200 mem. cos; Chair. RICHARD G. WOLFORD; Pres. and CEO PAMELA G. BAILEY (acting).

International Foodservice Distributors Association (IFDA): 1410 Spring Hill Rd, Suite 210, McLean, VA 22102; tel. (703) 532-9400; fax (703) 538-4673; internet www.ifdaonline.org; f. 1906; over 140 mems; Chair. MALCOLM R. SULLIVAN, Jr; Pres. and CEO MARK S. ALLEN.

National Association of Wheat Growers (NAWG): 412 Second St, NE, Suite 300, Washington, DC 20002-4993; tel. (202) 547-7800; fax (202) 546-2638; e-mail wheatworld@wheatworld.org; internet www.wheatworld.org; f. 1950; 20 affiliated mem. states; CEO DAREN COPPOCK.

National Beer Wholesalers Association (NBWA): 1101 King St, Suite 600, Alexandria, VA 22314-2944; tel. (703) 683-4300; fax (703) 683-8965; e-mail info@nbwa.org; internet www.nbwa.org; f. 1938; more than 2,850 mem. distributor cos; Chair. MITCH WATKINS; Pres. CRAIG A. PURSER.

National Cattlemen's Beef Association (NCBA): 9110 East Nichols Ave, Suite 300, Centennial, CO 80112; tel. (303) 694-0305; fax (303) 694-7372; e-mail membership@beef.org; internet www.beefusa.org; f. 1898; 33,000 mems, plus 44 cattle asscns and 50 breed and industry asscns; Pres. STEVE FOGLESONG; CEO FORREST ROBERTS.

National Confectioners Association of the US (NCA): 1101 30th St, Suite 200, Washington, DC 20007; tel. (202) 534-1440; fax (202) 337-0637; e-mail info@candyusa.com; internet www.candyusa.com; f. 1884; includes Chocolate Mfrs Asscn; 340 mems; Chair. MICHAEL F. GILMORE; Pres. LAWRENCE T. GRAHAM.

National Dairy Council (NDC): 10255 West Higgins Rd, Suite 900, Rosemount, IL 60018; tel. (847) 803-2000; fax (847) 803-2077; e-mail ndc@dairyinformation.com; internet www.nationaldairycouncil.org; f. 1915; 600 mems.

National Farmers (NFO): 528 Billy Sunday Rd, Suite 100, POB 2508, Ames, IA 50010; tel. (800) 247-2110; e-mail nfo@nfo.org; internet www.nfo.org; f. 1955; c. 35,000 mems; Chair. PAUL OLSON.

National Farmers Union (NFU): 20 F St NW, Suite 300, Washington, DC 20001; tel. (202) 554-1600; fax (202) 554-1654; e-mail lkendall@nfudc.org; internet www.nfu.org; f. 1902; 250,000 mems; Pres. ROGER JOHNSON.

National Frozen and Refrigerated Foods Association (NFRA): 4755 Linglestown Rd, Suite 300, POB 6069, Harrisburg, PA 17112; tel. (717) 657-8601; fax (717) 657-9862; e-mail info@nfraweb.org; internet www.nfraweb.org; f. 1945; over 400 mem. cos; Chair. GARY SPINAZZE; Pres. and CEO NEVIN B. MONTGOMERY.

National Grocers Association (NGA): 1005 North Glebe Rd, Suite 250, Arlington, VA 22201-5758; tel. (703) 516-0700; fax (703) 516-0115; e-mail info@nationalgrocers.org; internet www.nationalgrocers.org; f. 1982; 3,000 mems; Pres. and CEO PETER J. LARKIN.

National Meat Association (NMA): NMA East: 7757 Citation Dr., Marshall, VA 20115; NMA West: 1970 Broadway, Suite 825, Oakland, CA 94612; tel. (510) 763-1533; fax (510) 763-6186; e-mail staff@nmaonline.org; internet www.nmaonline.org; f. 1946; over 600 mems; Chair. BOB JENSEN; CEO BARRY CARPENTER.

North American Millers' Association (NAMA): 600 Maryland Ave, SW, Suite 825 West, Washington, DC 20024; tel. (202) 484-2200; fax (202) 488-7416; e-mail generalinfo@namamillers.org; internet www.namamillers.org; f. 1998; 48 mems and 28 assoc. mems; Chair. JOHN GILLCRIST; Pres. MARY WATERS.

United Fresh Fruit & Vegetable Association: 1901 Pennsylvania Ave, NW, Suite 1100, Washington, DC 20006; tel. (202) 303-3400; fax (202) 303-3433; e-mail united@unitedfresh.org; internet www.unitedfresh.org; f. 1904; 1,300 mems; Chair. STEFFANIE SMITH; Pres. and CEO THOMAS E. STENZEL.

THE UNITED STATES OF AMERICA

US Dairy Export Council (USDEC): 2101 Wilson Blvd, Suite 400, Arlington, VA 22201-3061; tel. (703) 528-3049; fax (703) 528-3705; e-mail info@usdec.org; internet www.usdec.org; f. 1995; 86 mems; Chair. LES HARDESTY; Pres. THOMAS M. SUBER.

Wine and Spirits Wholesalers of America, Inc (WSWA): 805 15th St, NW, Suite 430, Washington, DC 20005; tel. (202) 371-9792; fax (202) 789-2405; e-mail katrina@wswa.org; internet www.wswa.org; f. 1943; nearly 330 mem. cos; Chair. JOHN BAKER; Pres. and CEO CRAIG WOLF.

Iron and Steel

American Hardware Manufacturers Association (AHMA): 801 North Plaza Dr., Schaumburg, IL 60173-4977; tel. (847) 605-1025; fax (847) 605-1030; e-mail info@ahma.org; internet www.ahma.org; f. 1901; 500 mems; Pres. and CEO TIMOTHY S. FARRELL; Vice-Chair. WILLIAM P. FARRELL.

American Institute of Steel Construction (AISC): 1 East Wacker Dr., Suite 700, Chicago, IL 60601-1802; tel. (312) 670-2400; fax (312) 670-5403; e-mail ferch@aisc.org; internet www.aisc.org; f. 1921; Chair. DAVID HARWELL; Pres. ROGER E. FERCH.

American Iron and Steel Institute (AISI): 1140 Connecticut Ave, NW, Suite 705, Washington, DC 20036; tel. (202) 452-7100; e-mail webmaster@steel.org; internet www.steel.org; f. 1908; 24 mem. cos and 138 assoc. and affiliated mems; Chair. DANIEL DIMICCO; Pres. and CEO THOMAS J. GIBSON.

Steel Founders' Society of America (SFSA): 780 McArdle Dr., Unit G, Crystal Lake, IL 60014; tel. (815) 455-8240; fax (815) 455-8241; e-mail monroe@sfsa.org; internet www.sfsa.org; f. 1902; 80 mems; Exec. Vice-Pres. RAYMOND W. MONROE.

Steel Manufacturers Association (SMA): 1150 Connecticut Ave, NW, Suite 715, Washington, DC 20036; tel. (202) 296-1515; fax (202) 296-2506; e-mail cipicchio@steelnet.org; internet www.steelnet.org; 36 North American mem. cos and 129 assoc. mem. cos; Pres. THOMAS A. DANJCZEK.

Leather
(see also Textiles)

Leather Apparel Association (LAA): 4705 Center Blvd, Suite 806, Long Island City, NY 11109; tel. (718) 606-0767; fax (718) 606-6345; e-mail mbehar@leatherapparelassociation.com; internet www.leatherapparelassociation.com; f. 1990; over 100 mems; Pres. MORRIS GOLDFARB.

Leather Industries of America (LIA): 3050 K St, NW, Suite 400, Washington, DC 20007; tel. (202) 342-8497; fax (202) 342-8583; e-mail info@leatherusa.org; internet www.leatherusa.com; f. 1917; 55 mems; Pres. JOHN WITTENBORN.

Travel Goods Association (TGA): 301 North Harrison St, Suite 412, Princeton, NJ 08540-3512; tel. (609) 720-1200; fax (609) 720-0620; e-mail info@travel-goods.org; internet www.travel-goods.org; f. 1938; 300 mems; Chair. PETER COBB; Pres. MICHELE MARINI PITTENGER.

Lumber
(see also Paper)

American Forest and Paper Association (AF&PA): 1111 19th St, NW, Suite 800, Washington, DC 20036; tel. (202) 463-2700; fax (202) 463-2771; e-mail info@afandpa.org; internet www.afandpa.org; f. 1993; more than 157 mems; Pres. DONNA HARMAN.

APA–The Engineered Wood Association: 7011 South 19th St, Tacoma, WA 98466-5333; tel. (253) 565-6600; fax (253) 565-7265; e-mail help@apawood.org; internet www.apawood.org; f. 1933 as Douglas Fir Plywood Asscn; later became American Plywood Asscn; adopted current name 1994; 109 mems; Chair. JEFF WAGNER; Pres. DENNIS HARDMAN.

Forest Resources Association Inc: 600 Jefferson Plaza, Suite 350, Rockville, MD 20852-1150; tel. (301) 838-9385; fax (301) 838-9481; e-mail rlewis@forestresources.org; internet www.forestresources.org; f. 1934; 1,300 mems; Pres. R. LEWIS.

National Lumber and Building Material Dealers Association (NLBMDA): 2025 M St, NW, Suite 800, Washington, DC 20036-3309; tel. (202) 367-1169; fax (202) 367-2169; e-mail info@dealer.org; internet www.dealer.org; f. 1915; more than 6,000 mem. cos; Chair. DAN FESLER; Pres. and CEO MICHAEL O'BRIEN.

National Wooden Pallet and Container Association (NWPCA): 1421 Prince St, Suite 340, Alexandria, VA 22314-2805; tel. (703) 519-6104; fax (703) 519-4720; e-mail bscholnick@palletcentral.com; internet www.palletcentral.com; f. 1946; Chair. ROBERT WENNER; Pres. and CEO BRUCE N. SCHOLNICK.

North American Wholesale Lumber Association (NAWLA): 3601 Algonquin Rd, Suite 400, Rolling Meadows, IL 60008; tel. (847) 870-7470; fax (847) 870-0201; e-mail info@nawla.org; internet www.lumber.org; f. 1893; over 650 mems; Chair. GEORGE G. HUTCHISON; Pres. GARY F. VITALE.

Southern Forest Products Association: 2900 Indiana Ave, Kenner, LA 70065-4605; tel. (504) 443-4464; fax (504) 443-6612; e-mail mail@spfa.org; internet www.sfpa.org; f. 1915; c. 160 mem. orgs; Chair. ADRIAN BLOCKER; Pres. DIGGES MORGAN.

Western Wood Products Association (WWPA): Yeon Bldg, 522 South West Fifth Ave, Suite 500, Portland, OR 97204-2122; tel. (503) 224-3930; fax (503) 224-3934; e-mail info@wwpa.org; internet www.wwpa.org; f. 1964; c. 65 mem. orgs; Pres. and CEO MICHAEL R. O'HALLORAN.

Wood Products Manufacturers Association (WPMA): 175 State Rd East, POB 761, Westminster, MA 01473-0761; tel. (978) 874-5445; fax (978) 874-9946; e-mail woodprod@wpma.org; internet www.wpma.org; f. 1929; 664 mems; Pres. MAGGIE BRIGHAM; Exec. Dir PHILIP A. BIBEAU.

Metals and Mining
(see also Iron and Steel)

Aluminum Association, Inc: 1525 Wilson Blvd, Suite 600, Arlington, VA 22209; tel. (703) 358-2960; fax (703) 358-2961; e-mail lwilson@aluminum.org; internet www.aluminum.org; f. 1933; 82 mems; Pres. J. STEPHEN LARKIN.

American Zinc Association (AZA): 1750 K St, NW, Suite 700, Washington, DC 20006; tel. (202) 367-1151; fax (202) 367-2232; e-mail zincinfo@zinc.org; internet www.zinc.org; f. 1990; 10 regular mems, 14 affiliates; Exec. Dir GEORGE VARY.

ASM International: 9639 Kinsman Rd, Materials Park, OH 44073-0002; tel. (440) 338-5151; fax (440) 338-4634; e-mail customerservice@asminternational.org; internet asmcommunity.asminternational.org; f. 1913; fmrly the American Society for Materials; 40,000 mems world-wide; Pres. FREDERICK J. LISY; Man. Dir STANLEY C. THEOBALD.

Copper and Brass Fabricators Council, Inc: 3050 K St, NW, Suite 400, Washington, DC 20007; tel. (202) 833-8575; fax (202) 342-8451; e-mail copbrass@kelleydrye.com; f. 1964; 20 mem. cos; Pres. and Gen. Counsel DAVID A. HARTQUIST.

Copper Development Association, Inc (CDA): 260 Madison Ave, New York, NY 10016; tel. (212) 251-7200; fax (212) 251-7234; e-mail questions@cda.copper.org; internet www.copper.org; f. 1962; 65 mems; Pres. and CEO ANDREW G. KIRETA, Sr.

Fabricators and Manufacturers Association, International (FMA): 833 Featherstone Rd, Rockford, IL 61107; tel. (815) 399-8775; fax (815) 484-7701; e-mail info@fmanet.org; internet www.fmanet.org; f. 1970; more than 2,000 mems; Chair. JOHN KOSCHWANEZ; Pres. and CEO GERALD M. SHANKEL.

Manufacturing Jewelers and Suppliers of America, Inc (MJSA): 57 John L. Dietsch Sq., Attleboro Falls, MA 02763; tel. (401) 274-3840; fax (401) 274-0265; e-mail info@mjsa.org; internet www.mjsa.org; f. 1903; 1,800 mems; Chair. RICHARD POWERS; Pres. and CEO DAVID W. COCHRAN.

Metal Powder Industries Federation (MPIF): 105 College Rd East, 1st Floor, Princeton, NJ 08540-6692; tel. (609) 452-7700; fax (609) 987-8523; e-mail info@mpif.org; internet www.mpif.org; f. 1944; 6 feds of 300 corp. mems; Pres. MICHAEL C. LUTHERAN; Exec. Dir and CEO C. JAMES TROMBINO.

Mining and Metallurgical Society of America (MMSA): POB 810, Boulder, CO 80306-0810; tel. (303) 444-6032; e-mail contactmmsa@mmsa.net; internet www.mmsa.net; f. 1908; 340 mems; Exec. Dir BETTY L. GIBBS; Pres. MARK JORGENSEN.

National Mining Association (NMA): 101 Constitution Ave, NW, Suite 500 East, Washington, DC 20001-2133; tel. (202) 463-2600; fax (202) 463-2666; e-mail craulston@nma.org; internet www.nma.org; f. 1995; over 325 mem. cos; Pres. and CEO HAROLD P. QUINN, Jr.

Northwest Mining Association (NWMA): 10 North Post St, Suite 305, Spokane, WA 99201; tel. (509) 624-1158; fax (509) 623-1241; e-mail nwma_info@nwma.org; internet www.nwma.org; f. 1895; 1,800 mems; Pres. LUKE RUSSELL; Exec. Dir LAURA E. SKAER.

The Silver Institute: 888 16th St, NW, Suite 303, Washington, DC 20006; tel. (202) 835-0185; fax (202) 835-0155; e-mail info@silverinstitute.org; internet www.silverinstitute.org; f. 1971; 26 mems; Pres. ROQUE BENAVIDES; Exec. Dir MICHAEL DIRIENZO.

Paper
(see also Lumber)

Association of Independent Corrugated Converters (AICC): 113 South West St, POB 25708, Alexandria, VA 22313; tel. (703) 836-2422; fax (703) 836-2795; e-mail info@aiccbox.org; internet www.aiccbox.org; mems: 603 box-makers, 480 associates; Chair. KIM NELSON; Pres. A. STEVEN YOUNG.

NPTA Alliance: 401 North Michigan Ave, Suite 2200, Chicago, IL 60611-4267; tel. (312) 321-4092; fax (312) 673-6736; e-mail npta@

THE UNITED STATES OF AMERICA

gonpta.com; internet www.gonpta.com; f. 1903; fmrly Nat. Paper Trade Asscn, Inc; restructured Sept. 2007 to operate under management of SmithBucklin Corpn; 2,000 mems; Chair. FRED KFOURY, Jr; CEO NEWELL HOLT.

Paperboard Packaging Council (PPC): 1350 Main St, Suite 1508, Springfield, MA 01103-1628; tel. (413) 686-9191; fax (413) 747-7777; e-mail paperboardpackaging@ppcnet.org; internet www.ppcnet.org; f. 1929; unified with North American Packaging Association (NAPA) in 2010; Chair. STEVEN LEVKOFF; Pres. BEN MARKENS.

Petroleum and Fuel

American Association of Petroleum Geologists (AAPG): 125 West 15th St, POB 979, Tulsa, OK 74101-0979; tel. (918) 584-2555; fax (918) 560-2694; e-mail postmaster@aapg.org; internet www.aapg.org; f. 1917; 30,000 mems world-wide; Chair. DAVID G. RENSINK; Exec. Dir RICHARD D. FRITZ.

American Association of Petroleum Landmen (AAPL): 4100 Fossil Creek Blvd, Fort Worth, TX 76137-2791; tel. (817) 847-7700; fax (817) 847-7704; e-mail aapl@landman.org; internet www.landman.org; f. 1955; 7,000 mems and 43 affiliated asscns; Pres. STEVEN D. WENTWORTH; Exec. Vice-Pres. MARTIN SCHARDT.

American Petroleum Institute (API): 1220 L St, NW, Washington, DC 20005-4070; tel. (202) 682-8000; e-mail mediacenter@api.org; internet www.api.org; f. 1919; nearly 400 corporate mems; Pres. and CEO JACK GERARD; Vice-Pres. and Dir JIM CRAIG.

Association of Diesel Specialists (ADS): 400 Admiral Blvd, Kansas City, MO 64106; tel. (816) 285-0810; fax (847) 770-4952; e-mail info@diesel.org; internet www.diesel.org; more than 700 corp. and individual mems; Pres. CHUCK HESS; Exec. Dir DAVID FEHLING.

Coal Exporters' Association of the US, Inc: 101 Constitution Ave, NW, Suite 500, Washington, DC 20001-2133; tel. (202) 463-2654; fax (202) 833-9636; e-mail eschlecht@nma.org; f. 1945; 35 mems; Exec. Dir MOYA PHELLEPS.

Independent Petroleum Association of America (IPAA): 1201 15th St, NW, Suite 300, Washington, DC 20005; tel. (202) 857-4722; fax (202) 857-4799; e-mail webmaster@ipaa.org; internet www.ipaa.org; f. 1929; 6,000 mems; Chair. BRUCE VINCENT; Pres. and CEO BARRY RUSSELL.

National Ocean Industries Association (NOIA): 1120 G St, NW, Suite 900, Washington, DC 20005; tel. (202) 347-6900; fax (202) 347-8650; e-mail mkearns@noia.org; internet www.noia.org; f. 1972; over 300 mem. cos; Pres. RANDALL LUTHI.

National Petrochemical and Refiners' Association (NPRA): 1667 K St, NW, Suite 700, Washington, DC 20006; tel. (202) 457-0480; fax (202) 457-0486; e-mail info@npra.org; internet www.npradc.org; f. 1902; nearly 500 mems; Chair. WILLIAM KLESSE; Pres. CHARLES T. DREVNA.

Petroleum Marketers Association of America (PMAA): 1901 North Fort Myer Dr., Suite 500, Arlington, VA 22209-1604; tel. (703) 351-8000; fax (703) 351-9160; e-mail info@pmaa.org; internet www.pmaa.org; 47 mem. asscns; Chair. GERRY RAMM; Pres. DANIEL F. GILLIGAN.

Western States Petroleum Association (WSPA): 1415 L St, Suite 600, Sacramento, CA 95814; tel. (916) 498-7750; fax (916) 444-5745; internet www.wspa.org; f. 1907; 30 mem. cos; Pres. CATHERINE REHEIS-BOYD.

Printing and Publishing
(see also Publishers)

Association for the Suppliers of Printing, Publishing and Converting Technologies (NPES): 1899 Preston White Dr., Reston, VA 22091-4367; tel. (703) 264-7200; fax (703) 620-0994; e-mail npes@npes.org; internet www.npes.org; f. 1933; over 400 mem. cos; Chair. D. J. BURGESS; Pres. RALPH J. NAPPI.

Binding Industries Association International (BIA): 200 Deer Run Rd, Sewickley, PA 15143-2600; tel. (412) 259-1806; fax (412) 259-1800; e-mail jgoldstein@printing.org; internet www.printing.org/bia; f. 1955; 90 mems; Chair. RICHARD SENIOR; Man. JUSTIN GOLDSTEIN.

National Association for Printing Leadership (NAPL): 75 West Century Rd, Paramus, NJ 07652-1408; tel. (201) 634-9600; e-mail information@napl.org; internet www.napl.org; f. 1933; 150 assoc. mems; Chair. KEITH KEMP; Pres. and CEO JOSEPH P. TRUNCALE.

National Association of Printing Ink Manufacturers (NAPIM): 581 Main St, Suite 520, Woodbridge, NJ 07095; tel. (732) 855-1525; fax (732) 855-1838; e-mail napim@napim.org; internet www.napim.org; f. 1917; Exec. Dir JAMES E. COLEMAN.

Printing Industries of America, Inc/Graphic Arts Information Network (PIA/GATF): 200 Deer Run Rd, Sewickley, PA 15143; tel. (412) 741-6861; fax (412) 741-2311; e-mail printing@printing.org; internet www.printing.org; f. 1887 (PIA), 1924 (GATF); consolidated operations in 1999; more than 10,000 mem. cos; Chair. WILLIAM J. GIBSON; Pres. and CEO MICHAEL MAKIN.

Public Utilities
(see also Trade and Industry—Utilities)

American Public Power Association (APPA): 1875 Connecticut Ave, NW, Suite 1200, Washington, DC 20009-5715; tel. (202) 467-2900; fax (202) 467-2910; e-mail appanet@appanet.org; internet www.appanet.org; f. 1940; over 2,000 mem. utilities; Chair. LONNIE CARTER.

American Public Works Association (APWA): 2345 Grand Blvd, Suite 700, Kansas City, MO 64108-2625; tel. (816) 472-6100; fax (816) 472-1610; e-mail apwa@apwa.net; internet www.apwa.net; f. 1937; 29,000 mems; Pres. GEORGE CROMBIE; Exec. Dir PETER KING.

Rubber

Rubber Manufacturers Association (RMA): 1400 K St, NW, Suite 900, Washington, DC 20005-2043; tel. (202) 682-4800; e-mail info@rma.org; internet www.rma.org; f. 1915; over 100 mem. cos; Pres. and CEO Dr CHARLES A. CANNON.

Stone, Clay and Glass Products

Glass Association of North America (GANA): 2945 South West Jackson St, Suite 1500, Topeka, KS 66612-1200; tel. (785) 271-0208; fax (785) 271-0166; e-mail gana@glasswebsite.com; internet www.glasswebsite.com; f. 1994; 208 mems; Exec. Vice-Pres. WILLIAM M. YANEK.

National Glass Association (NGA): 8200 Greensboro Dr., Suite 302, McLean, VA 22102-3881; tel. (703) 342-5642; fax (703) 442-0630; e-mail administration@glass.org; internet www.glass.org; f. 1948; c. 3,000 mem. cos; Chair. STEVEN R. BURNETT; Pres. and CEO PHILIP J. JAMES.

National Stone, Sand and Gravel Association (NSSGA): 1605 King St, Alexandria, VA 22314; tel. (703) 525-8788; e-mail info@nssga.org; internet www.nssga.org; f. 2000 by merger of Nat. Aggregates Asscn and Nat. Stone Asscn; 950 mems; Pres. and CEO JENNIFER JOY WILSON.

Textiles

American Apparel and Footwear Association (AAFA): 1601 North Kent St, Suite 1200, Arlington, VA 22209; tel. (703) 524-1864; fax (703) 522-6741; e-mail mrust@apparelandfootwear.org; internet www.apparelandfootwear.org; f. 2000 following merger of American Apparel and Manufacturers Asscn and Footwear Industries of America; Chair. KILICK S. DATTA; Pres. and CEO KEVIN M. BURKE.

American Fiber Manufacturers Association, Inc (AFMA): 1530 Wilson Blvd, NW, Suite 690, Arlington, VA 22209; tel. (703) 875-0432; fax (703) 875-0907; e-mail afma@afma.org; internet www.fibersource.com; f. 1933; 34 mems; Pres. PAUL T. O'DAY.

Apparel Retailers of America: 325 Seventh St, Suite 1000, NW, Washington, DC 20004-2801; tel. (202) 347-1932; fax (202) 457-0386; f. 1916; 1,200 mems; Exec. Dir DOUGLAS W. WIEGAND.

National Council of Textile Organizations (NCTO): 910 17th St, NW, Suite 1020, Washington, DC 20006; tel. (202) 822-8028; fax (202) 822-8029; e-mail info@ncto.org; internet www.ncto.org; f. 2004; Chair. DAVID HASTINGS; Pres. CASS JOHNSON.

National Textile Association (NTA): 6 Beacon St, Suite 1125, Boston, MA 02108-3812; tel. (617) 542-8220; fax (617) 542-2199; e-mail info@nationaltextile.org; internet www.nationaltextile.org; f. 1854; fmrly Northern Textile Asscn and Knitted Textile Asscn; adopted current name in 2002; over 200 mems; Chair. ROGER BERKLEY; Pres. KARL SPILHAUS.

Tobacco

Tobacco Associates, Inc: 8452 Holly Leaf Dr., McLean, VA 22102-2225; tel. (703) 821-1255; fax (703) 821-1511; e-mail taw@tobaccoassociatesinc.org; internet www.tobaccoassociatesinc.org; f. 1947; Pres. KIRK WAYNE.

Tobacco Merchants Association of the United States (TMA): POB 8019, Princeton, NJ 08543-8019; tel. (609) 275-4900; fax (609) 275-8379; e-mail tma@tma.org; internet www.tma.org; f. 1915; 170 mems; Chair. JAMES H. STARKEY; Pres. FARRELL DELMAN.

Transport

Aerospace Industries Association of America, Inc (AIA): 1000 Wilson Blvd, Suite 1700, Arlington, VA 22209-3928; tel. (703) 358-1000; fax (703) 358-1012; e-mail alexis.allen@aia-aerospace.org; internet www.aia-aerospace.org; f. 1919; 107 mems and 183 assoc. mems; Chair. SCOTT C. DONNELLY; Pres. and CEO MARION C. BLAKEY.

Air Transport Association of America, Inc: see Civil Aviation—Associations.

THE UNITED STATES OF AMERICA   Directory

Alliance of Automobile Manufacturers (Auto Alliance): 1401 Eye St, NW, Suite 900, Washington, DC 20005; tel. (202) 326-5500; fax (202) 326-5598; internet www.autoalliance.org; f. 1999; asscn of 11 car and light truck mfrs; Pres. and CEO DAVE MCCURDY.

American Bureau of Shipping: see Ocean Shipping—Associations.

American Bus Association (ABA): 700 13th St, NW, Suite 575, Washington, DC 20005-5923; tel. (202) 842-1645; fax (202) 842-0850; e-mail abainfo@buses.org; internet www.buses.org; f. 1926; c. 3,250 mems; Pres. and CEO PETER J. PANTUSO.

American International Automobile Dealers' Association (AIADA): 211 North Union St, Suite 300, Alexandria, VA 22314; tel. (703) 519-7800; fax (703) 519-7810; e-mail goaiada@aiada.org; internet www.aiada.org; f. 1970; 11,000 mems; Pres. CODY LUSK.

American Public Transportation Association (APTA): 1666 K St, NW, Suite 1100, Washington, DC 20006; tel. (202) 496-4800; fax (202) 496-4324; e-mail info@apta.com; internet www.apta.com; f. 1882; 1,600 mems; Chair. MATTIE P. CARTER; Pres. WILLIAM W. MILLAR.

American Railway Engineering and Maintenance-of-Way Association (AREMA): 10003 Derekwood Lane, Suite 210, MD 20706; tel. (301) 459-3200; fax (301) 459-8077; e-mail amanstof@arema.org; internet www.arema.org; f. 1897; Exec. Dir and CEO Dr CHARLES H. EMELY.

American Short Line and Regional Railroad Association: see Railways—Associations.

American Trucking Associations (ATA): 2200 Mill Rd, Alexandria, VA 22314-4654; tel. (703) 838-1700; e-mail atamembership@trucking.org; internet www.truckline.com; f. 1933; 3,000 mems; Pres. and CEO WILLIAM GRAVES.

Association of American Railroads: see Railways—Associations.

Chamber of Shipping of America (CSA): see Ocean Shipping—Associations.

National Automobile Dealers Association (NADA): 8400 Westpark Dr., McLean, VA 22102-3522; tel. (703) 821-7000; e-mail nadainfo@nada.org; internet www.nada.org; f. 1917; over 19,700 mems; Pres. PHILLIP D. BRADY.

Owner/Operator Independent Drivers' Association (OOIDA): 1 North West OOIDA Dr., Grain Valley, MO 64029; tel. (816) 229-5791; e-mail webmaster@ooida.com; internet www.ooida.com; f. 1973; over 150,000 mems; Pres. JIM JOHNSTON.

Shipbuilders Council of America (SCA): 1455 F St, NW, Suite 225, Washington, DC 20005; tel. (202) 347-5462; fax (202) 347-5464; e-mail belliott@balljanik.com; internet www.shipbuilders.org; f. 1921; absorbed the American Waterways Shipyard Conference (f. 1976) in 1999; 41 mem. cos and 24 affiliate mems; Pres. MATTHEW PAXTON.

Miscellaneous

American Advertising Federation (AAF): 1101 Vermont Ave, NW, Suite 500, Washington, DC 20005-6306; tel. (202) 898-0089; fax (202) 898-0159; e-mail aaf@aaf.org; internet www.aaf.org; f. 1967; 40,000 mems, 200 corp. mems; Chair. FRANK COOPER; Pres. and CEO JAMES EDMUND DATRI.

American Association of Exporters and Importers (AAEI): 1050 17th St, NW, Suite 810, Washington, DC 20036; tel. (202) 857-8009; fax (202) 857-7843; e-mail hq@aaei.org; internet www.aaei.org; f. 1921; 1,200 mems; Chair. KARL RIEDI; Pres. and CEO MARIANNE ROWDEN.

American Marketing Association (AMA): 311 South Wacker Dr., Suite 5800, Chicago, IL 60606; tel. (312) 542-9000; fax (312) 542-9001; e-mail info@ama.org; internet www.marketingpower.com; f. 1937; nearly 40,000 mems; Chair. GEORGE DAY.

ASAE & the Center for Association Leadership (American Society of Association Executives): ASAE & The Center Bldg, 1575 I St, NW, Washington, DC 20005-1103; tel. (202) 371-0940; fax (202) 371-8315; e-mail pr@asaecenter.org; internet www.asaecenter.org; f. 1920; more than 22,000 mems in more than 11,000 orgs; provides resources, education and advocacy; Chair. KAREN L. HACKETT; Pres. and CEO JOHN H. GRAHAM.

Association of Equipment Manufacturers (AEM): 6737 West Washington St, Suite 2400, Milwaukee, WI 53214-5647; tel. (414) 272-0943; fax (414) 272-1170; internet www.aem.org; f. 2002; more than 800 mem. cos; Chair. CHUCK MARTZ; Pres. DENNIS SLATER.

Consumer Healthcare Products Association (CHPA): 900 19th St, NW, Suite 700, Washington, DC 20006; tel. (202) 429-9260; fax (202) 223-6835; e-mail efunderburk@chpa-info.org; internet www.chpa-info.org; f. 1881; more than 175 mem. and assoc. mem. cos; Chair. CHRISTOPHER D. DEWOLF; Pres. LYNDA A. SUYDAM.

Institute for Supply Management (ISM): 2055 East Centennial Circle, POB 22160, Tempe, AZ 85285-2160; tel. (408) 752-6276; fax (408) 752-7890; e-mail pnovak@ism.ws; internet www.ism.ws; f. 1915; more than 40,000 mems; Chair. SHELLEY STEWART, Jr; CEO PAUL NOVAK.

Motion Picture Association of America, Inc (MPAA): 1600 Eye St, NW, Washington, DC 20006; tel. (202) 293-1966; fax (202)296-7410; e-mail contactus@mpaa.org; internet www.mpaa.org; f. 1922; Chair. and CEO ROBERT PISANO (acting).

National Association of Manufacturers (NAM): 1331 Pennsylvania Ave, NW, Suite 600, Washington, DC 20004-1790; tel. (202) 637-3000; fax (202) 637-3182; e-mail manufacturing@nam.org; internet www.nam.org; f. 1895; 14,000 mems; Chair. MICHAEL E. CAMPBELL; Pres. and CEO JOHN ENGLER.

National Association of Realtors (NAR): 430 North Michigan Ave, Suite 500, Chicago, IL 60611-4087; fax (312) 329-8960; e-mail infocentral@realtors.org; internet www.realtor.org; f. 1908; 1.3m. mems; Pres. VICKI COX GOLDER; CEO DALE STINTON.

National Center for Manufacturing Sciences (NCMS): 3025 Boardwalk, Ann Arbor, MI 48108-3230; tel. (734) 995-0300; fax (734) 995-1150; e-mail bethb@ncms.org; internet www.ncms.org; f. 1986; Pres. and CEO RICHARD B. JARMAN; Chair. of Bd RALPH RESNICK.

National Cooperative Business Association (NCBA): 1401 New York Ave, NW, Suite 1100, Washington, DC 20005-2160; tel. (202) 638-6222; fax (202) 638-1374; e-mail info@ncba.coop; internet www.ncba.coop; f. 1916; 450 mems; Chair. MARTIN LOWERY; Pres. and CEO PAUL HAZEN.

National Retail Federation (NRF): 325 Seventh St, NW, Suite 1100, Washington, DC 20004-2802; tel. (202) 783-7941; fax (202) 737-2849; e-mail blackwellp@nrf.com; internet www.nrf.com; f. 1911; merged with American Retail Federation in 1990 and incorporated Apparel Retailers of America in 1995; mems: more than 100 state, nat. and trade orgs; Chair. TERRY J. LUNDGREN; Pres. and CEO MATT SHAY.

Personal Care Products Council: 1101 17th St, NW, Suite 300, Washington, DC 20036-4702; tel. (202) 331-1770; fax (202) 331-1969; e-mail publications@personalcarecouncil.org; internet www.personalcarecouncil.org; f. 1894; fmrly Cosmetic, Toiletry and Fragrance Asscn (CTFA); adopted current name 2007; more than 600 mem. cos; Chair. DAN BRESTLE; Pres. and CEO LEZLEE WESTINE.

Society of Manufacturing Engineers (SME): 1 SME Dr., Dearborn, MI 48121; tel. (313) 271-1500; fax (313) 425-3401; e-mail service@sme.org; internet www.sme.org; f. 1932; Exec. Dir MARK TOMLINSON.

UTILITIES
Regulatory Authority

Federal Energy Regulatory Commission (FERC): 888 First St, NE, Washington, DC 20426; tel. (202) 502-8004; e-mail customer@ferc.gov; internet www.ferc.gov; independent regulatory commission; Chair. JON WELLINHOFF.

Electricity

American Electric Power (AEP): 1 Riverside Plaza, Columbus, OH 43215-2372; tel. (614) 716-1000; e-mail jsloat@aep.com; internet www.aep.com; f. 1906 as the American Gas and Electricity Co; present name adopted 1958; electricity supplier to Arkansas, Indiana, Kentucky, Louisiana, Michigan, Ohio, Oklahoma, Tennessee, Texas, Virginia and West Virginia; Pres., Chair. and CEO MICHAEL G. MORRIS.

American Public Power Association: 1875 Connecticut Ave, NW, Suite 1200, Washington, DC 20009-5715; tel. (202) 467-2900; fax (202) 467-2910; e-mail mrufe@appanet.org; internet www.appanet.org; f. 1940; asscn of local publicly owned electric utilities; c. 2,000 mems; Chair. WILLIAM CARROLL; CEO MARK CRISSOM.

Association of Edison Illuminating Cos: 600 North 18th St, POB 2641, Birmingham, AL 35291-0992; tel. (205) 257-2530; fax (205) 257-2540; e-mail aeicdir@bellsouth.net; internet www.aeic.org; f. 1885; mems comprise 165 investor-owned public utilities, co-ops and municipal utility systems; Pres. DONALD J. SHIPPAR; Exec. Dir EARL B. PARSONS, Jr.

Edison Electric Institute: 701 Pennsylvania Ave, NW, Washington, DC 20004-2696; tel. (202) 508-5000; fax (202) 508-5759; e-mail news@eei.org; internet www.eei.org; f. 1933; mems comprise 184 investor-owned electric utility cos in the USA and 63 foreign mems; Chair. RICHARD C. KELLY; Pres. THOMAS R. KUHN.

Energy Telecommunications and Electrical Association (ENTELEC): 5005 West Royal Lane, Suite 116, Irving, TX 75063; tel. (888) 503-8700; fax (972) 915-6040; e-mail blaine@entelec.org; internet www.entelec.org; f. 1928 as the Petroleum Industry Electrical Asscn; changed name as above in 1978; 170 mems; Pres. JOEL PROCHASKA; Exec. Man. BLAINE SISKE.

National Rural Electric Co-operative Association: 4301 Wilson Blvd, Arlington, VA 22203; tel. (703) 907-5500; e-mail patrick.lavigne@nreca.coop; internet www.nreca.org; f. 1942; operates rural

THE UNITED STATES OF AMERICA

electric co-operative systems and public power distribution in 47 states; 900 mems; Pres. F. E. (WALLY) WOLSKI; CEO GLENN ENGLISH.

Gas

American Gas Association (AGA): 400 North Capitol St, NW, Suite 450, Washington, DC 20001; tel. (202) 824-7000; fax (202) 824-7115; e-mail ccussimanio@aga.org; internet www.aga.org; f. 1918; represents 195 local utility cos; Chair. ROBERT C. SKAGGS, Jr; Pres. and CEO DAVID N. PARKER.

American Public Gas Association (APGA): 201 Massachusetts Ave, NE, Suite C-4, Washington, DC 20002; tel. (202) 464-2742; fax (202) 464-0246; e-mail mhager@apga.org; internet www.apga.org; f. 1961; promotes efficiency among public gas systems; 700 mems; Chair. MARK BUSSMAN; Pres. and CEO BERT KALISCH.

Gas Technology Institute: 1700 South Mount Prospect Rd, Des Plaines, IL 60018; tel. (847) 768-0500; fax (847) 768-0501; e-mail businessdevelopmentinfo@gastechnology.org; internet www.gastechnology.org; f. 1976; fmrly Gas Research Institute; 175 mems; Chair. RANDALL BARNARD; Pres. and CEO DAVID CARROLL.

Natural Gas Supply Association: 1620 Eye St, NW, Suite 700, Washington, DC 20006; tel. (202) 326-9300; fax (202) 326-9330; internet www.ngsa.org; f. 1967; monitors legislation and economic issues affecting natural gas producers; Pres. R. SKIP HORVATH.

Water

American Water Works Association: 6666 West Quincy Ave, Denver, CO 80235-3098; tel. (303) 794-7711; fax (303) 347-0804; e-mail custsvc@awwa.org; internet www.awwa.org; f. 1881; 57,000 mems; Pres. JOSEPH MANTUA; Exec. Dir DAVID B. LAFRANCE.

The Water Research Foundation: 6666 West Quincy Ave, Denver, CO 80235-3098; tel. (303) 347-6100; fax (303) 730-0851; e-mail info@waterresearchfoundation.org; internet www.waterresearchfoundation.org; f. 1966; Chair. ROY WOLFE; Exec. Dir ROBERT RENNER.

Association of Metropolitan Water Agencies: 1620 I St, NW, Suite 500, Washington, DC 20006; tel. (202) 331-2820; fax (202) 785-1845; e-mail vandehei@amwa.net; internet www.amwa.net; f. 1981; 192 mems; Pres. JAMES MCDANIEL; Exec. Dir DIANE VANDE HEI.

National Association of Water Companies: 2001 L St, NW, Suite 850, Washington, DC 20036; tel. (202) 833-8383; fax (202) 331-7442; e-mail michael@nawc.com; internet www.nawc.org; f. 1895; privately owned and operated water cos; 161 mems; Pres. CHARLES V. FIRLOTTE; Exec. Dir MICHAEL DEANE.

National Rural Water Association: 2915 South 13th St, Duncan, OK 73533; tel. (580) 252-0629; fax (580) 255-4476; e-mail info@nrwa.org; internet www.nrwa.org; Pres. JOE LILES; Exec. Man. ROB JOHNSON.

TRADE UNIONS

In 2005 there were approximately 15.7m. union members in the USA, representing 12.5% of the civilian labour force.

Many trade unions based in the USA have members throughout North America. Approximately 30% of Canada's trade union members belong to unions having headquarters in the USA.

American Federation of Labor and Congress of Industrial Organizations (AFL-CIO): 815 16th St, NW, Washington, DC 20006; tel. (202) 637-5000; fax (202) 637-5058; internet www.aflcio.org; f. 1955; Pres. RICHARD L. TRUMKA; Sec.-Treas. LIZ SHULER; Exec. Vice-Pres. ARLENE HOLT BAKER; 56 affiliated unions with total membership of 11.5m. (2009).

AFL-CIO Affiliates
(with 50,000 members and over)

Amalgamated Transit Union: 5025 Wisconsin Ave, NW, Washington, DC 20016; tel. (202) 537-1645; fax (202) 244-7824; e-mail dispatch@atu.org; internet www.atu.org; f. 1892; Int. Pres. WARREN S. GEORGE; Int. Sec.-Treas. OSCAR OWENS; 160,000 mems (2007).

American Federation of Government Employees: 80 F St, NW, Washington, DC 20001; tel. (202) 737-8700; fax (202) 639-6490; e-mail comments@afge.org; internet www.afge.org; f. 1932; Nat. Pres. JOHN GAGE; Sec.-Treas. J. DAVID COX; 600,000 mems.

American Federation of Musicians of the United States and Canada: Paramount Bldg, Suite 600, 1501 Broadway, New York, NY 10036; tel. (212) 869-1330; fax (212) 764-6134; e-mail presoffice@afm.org; internet www.afm.org; f. 1896; Pres. RAY HAIR; Sec.-Treas. SAM FOLIO; 90,000 mems.

American Federation of State, County and Municipal Employees: 1625 L St, NW, Washington, DC 20036-5687; tel. (202) 429-1000; fax (202) 429-1293; internet www.afscme.org; f. 1936; Pres. GERALD W. MCENTEE; Sec.-Treas. LEE A. SAUNDERS; 1.6m. mems (2009).

American Federation of Teachers (AFT-AFL-CIO): 555 New Jersey Ave, NW, Washington, DC 20001; tel. (202) 879-4400; fax (202) 879-4556; internet www.aft.org; f. 1916; Pres. RANDI WEINGARTEN; Sec.-Treas. ANTONIA CORTESE; more than 1.4m. mems (2009).

American Federation of Television and Radio Artists: 260 Madison Ave, 7th Floor, New York, NY 10016-2401; tel. (212) 532-0800; fax (212) 545-1238; e-mail nyfilm@ios.com; internet www.aftra.com; f. 1937; Pres. BOB EDWARDS (acting); more than 70,000 mems (2007).

American Postal Workers Union: 1300 L St, NW, Washington, DC 20005; tel. (202) 842-4200; fax (202) 842-4297; internet www.apwu.org; f. 1971; Pres. WILLIAM BURRUS; Sec.-Treas. TERRY STAPLETON; more than 330,000 mems (2007).

Associated Actors and Artistes of America: 165 46th St West, New York, NY 10036; tel. (212) 869-0358; fax (212) 869-1746; f. 1919; Pres. THEODORE BIKEL; 6 nat. unions representing 125,000 mems.

Bakery, Confectionery, Tobacco Workers' and Grain Millers International Union: 10401 Connecticut Ave, Kensington, MD 20895; tel. (301) 933-8600; fax (301) 946-8452; e-mail bctgmwebmaster@bctgm.org; internet www.bctgm.org; f. 1999; Int. Pres. FRANK HURT; Sec.-Treas. DAVID B. DURKEE; 120,000 mems (2006).

Communications Workers of America: 501 Third St, NW, Washington, DC 20001; tel. (202) 434-1100; fax (202) 434-1279; internet www.cwa-union.org; f. 1939; Pres. LARRY COHEN; Sec.-Treas. JEFFREY A. RECHENBACH; over 700,000 mems (2010).

Glass Molders, Pottery, Plastics & Allied Workers International Union (AFL-CIO, CLC): 608 East Baltimore Pike, POB 607, Media, PA 19063-0607; tel. (610) 565-5051; fax (610) 565-0983; e-mail gmpiu@gmpiu.org; internet www.gmpiu.org; f. 1842; Pres. BRUCE SMITH; Sec.-Treas. WALTER THORN; 51,000 mems.

International Alliance of Theatrical Stage Employees, Moving Picture Technicians, Artists and Allied Crafts of the US, its Territories and Canada (IATSE): 1430 Broadway, 20th Floor, New York, NY 10018; tel. (212) 730-1770; fax (212) 730-7809; e-mail webmaster@iatse-intl.org; internet www.iatse-intl.org; f. 1893; Int. Pres. MATTHEW D. LOEB; Gen. Sec.-Treas. JAMES B. WOOD; 110,000 mems.

International Association of Bridge, Structural, Ornamental and Reinforcing Iron Workers: 1750 New York Ave, NW, Suite 400, Washington, DC 20006; tel. (202) 383-4800; fax (202) 638-4856; e-mail iwmagazine@iwintl.org; internet www.ironworkers.org; f. 1896; Gen. Pres. JOSEPH J. HUNT; Gen. Sec. WALTER W. WISE; 140,000 mems.

International Association of Fire Fighters: 1750 New York Ave, NW, Suite 300, Washington, DC 20006-5395; tel. (202) 737-8484; fax (202) 737-8418; e-mail tburn@iaff.org; internet www.iaff.org; f. 1918; Gen. Pres. HAROLD SCHAITBERGER; Sec.-Treas. THOMAS H. MILLER; 298,000 mems (2010).

International Association of Machinists and Aerospace Workers (IAM): 9000 Machinists Pl., Upper Marlboro, MD 20772-2687; tel. (301) 967-4500; fax (301) 967-4588; e-mail websteward@goiam.org; internet www.goiam.org; f. 1888; Int. Pres. R. THOMAS BUFFENBARGER; Gen. Sec.-Treas. WARREN L. MART; 720,000 mems (2010).

International Brotherhood of Boilermakers, Iron Ship Builders, Blacksmiths, Forgers and Helpers: 753 State Ave, Suite 570, Kansas City, KS 66101; tel. (913) 371-2640; fax (913) 281-8101; e-mail tracy.buck@boilermakers.org; internet www.boilermakers.org; f. 1880; Int. Pres. NEWTON B. JONES; Int. Sec.-Treas. WILLIAM T. CREEDEN; 100,000 mems.

International Brotherhood of Electrical Workers: 900 Seventh St, NW, Washington, DC 20001; tel. (202) 833-7000; fax (202) 728-7676; e-mail glenn_perusek@ibew.org; internet www.ibew.org; f. 1891; Int. Pres. EDWIN D. HILL; Int. Sec.-Treas. LINDELL K. LEE; c. 725,000 mems (2010).

International Longshoremen's Association: 17 Battery Pl., Suite 930, New York, NY 10004; tel. (212) 425-1200; fax (212) 425-2928; e-mail rhughes@ilaunion.org; internet www.ilaunion.org; f. 1892; Pres. RICHARD P. HUGHES, Jr; Sec.-Treas. ROBERT E. GLEASON; 65,000 mems.

International Union of Bricklayers and Allied Craftworkers: 620 F Street, NW, Washington, DC 20004; tel. (202) 783-3788; fax (202) 393-0219; e-mail askbac@bacweb.org; internet www.bacweb.org; f. 1865; Pres. JAMES BOLAND; Sec.-Treas. HENRY F. KRAMER.

International Union of Operating Engineers: 1125 17th St, NW, Washington, DC 20036; tel. (202) 429-9100; fax (202) 778-2616; internet www.iuoe.org; f. 1896; Gen. Pres. VINCENT J. GIBLIN; Gen. Sec.-Treas. CHRISTOPHER HANLEY; more than 400,000 mems in 138 local unions (2010).

International Union of Painters and Allied Trades: 1750 New York Ave, NW, Washington, DC 20006; tel. (202) 637-0700; f. 1887; Gen. Pres. MICHAEL E. MONROE; Sec.-Treas. JAMES A. WILLIAMS.

THE UNITED STATES OF AMERICA

International Union of Police Associations: 1549 Ringling Blvd, Suite 600, Sarasota, FL 34236; tel. (941) 487-2560; fax (941) 487-2570; e-mail iupa@iupa.org; internet www.iupa.org; f. 1954; Pres. SAMUEL A. CABRAL; Sec.-Treas. TIMOTHY A. SCOTT; 80,400 mems (2002).

Laborers' International Union of North America: 905 16th St, NW, Washington, DC 20006; tel. (202) 737-8320; fax (202) 737-2754; e-mail communications@liuna.org; internet www.liuna.org; f. 1903; Pres. TERENCE M. O'SULLIVAN; Gen. Sec.-Treas. ARMAND E. SABITONI; 500,000 mems (2010).

Marine Engineers' Beneficial Association (MEBA): 444 North Capitol St, NW, Suite 800, Washington, DC 20001; tel. (202) 638-5355; fax (202) 638-5369; e-mail mebahq@d1meba.org; internet www.d1meba.org; f. 1875; Pres. DON KEEFE; Sec.-Treas. BILL VAN LOO; 50,000 mems.

National Association of Letter Carriers (NALC): 100 Indiana Ave, NW, Washington, DC 20001-2144; tel. (202) 393-4695; fax (202) 737-1540; e-mail nalcinf@nalc.org; internet www.nalc.org; f. 1889; Pres. FREDRIC V. ROLANDO; Sec.-Treas. JANE E. BROENDEL; 300,058 mems (2006).

Office and Professional Employees International Union: 265 West 14th St, Suite 610, New York, NY 10011; tel. (212) 675-3210; fax (212) 727-3466; internet www.opeiu.org; f. 1945; Pres. MICHAEL GOODWIN; Sec.-Treas. NANCY WOHLFORTH; 125,000 mems.

Screen Actors Guild: 5757 Wilshire Blvd, Los Angeles, CA 90036-3600; tel. (323) 954-1600; fax (323) 549-6656; internet www.sag.org; f. 1933; Pres. KEN HOWARD; Sec.-Treas. AMY AQUINO; 20 brs and nearly 120,000 mems (2009).

Seafarers International Union of North America: 5201 Auth Way, Camp Springs, MD 20746; tel. (301) 899-0675; fax (301) 899-7355; e-mail webmaster@seafarers.org; internet www.seafarers.org; f. 1938; Pres. MICHAEL SACCO; Sec.-Treas. DAVID W. HEINDEL; 80,000 mems.

Sheet Metal Workers' International Association: 1750 New York Ave, NW, Washington, DC 20006; tel. (202) 783-5880; fax (202) 662-0894; e-mail info@smwia.org; internet www.smwia.org; f. 1888; Gen. Pres. MICHAEL J. SULLIVAN; Gen. Sec.-Treas. JOSEPH J. NIGRO; more than 150,000 mems (2009).

Transport Workers' Union of America (TWU): 1700 Broadway, 2nd Floor, New York, NY 10019; e-mail mailbox@twu.org; internet www.twu.org; f. 1934; Int. Pres. JAMES C. LITTLE; Sec.-Treas. JOSEPH C. GORDON; more than 200,000 mems (2009).

United Association of Journeymen and Apprentices of the Plumbing and Pipe Fitting Industry of the United States and Canada: 3 Park Pl., Annapolis, MD 21401; tel. (410) 269-2000; fax (410) 267-0262; internet www.ua.org; f. 1889; Gen. Pres. WILLIAM P. HITE; Gen. Sec.-Treas. PATRICK R. PERNO; more than 300,000 mems (2009).

United Automobile, Aerospace and Agricultural Implement Workers of America (UAW): Solidarity House, 8000 East Jefferson Ave, Detroit, MI 48214; tel. (313) 926-5000; fax (313) 823-6016; internet www.uaw.org; f. 1935; Pres. BOB KING; Sec.-Treas. DENNIS WILLIAMS; c. 386,677 active mems.

United Food and Commercial Workers International Union: 1775 K St, NW, Washington, DC 20006; tel. (202) 223-3111; internet www.ufcw.org; f. 1979; Int. Pres. JOSEPH T. HANSEN; Int. Sec.-Treas. ANTHONY M. PERRONE; 1.3m. mems.

United Mine Workers of America (UMWA): 18354 Quantico Gateway Dr., Suite 200, Triangle, VA 22172-1179; tel. (703) 291-2400; internet www.umwa.org; f. 1890; Int. Pres. CECIL E. ROBERTS; Int. Sec.-Treas. DANIEL J. KANE; 130,000 mems (1999).

United Steel, Paper and Forestry, Rubber, Manufacturing, Energy, Allied Industrial and Service Workers International Union (USW) (United Steelworkers): 5 Gateway Center, Pittsburgh, PA 15222; tel. (412) 562-2400; fax (412) 562-2445; e-mail webmaster@usw.org; internet www.usw.org; f. 1936; incorporated PACE International Union in 2005 and Independent Steelworkers Union in 2007; announced agreement in July 2008 to merge with Unite (United Kingdom) to create Workers Uniting; represents workers in the USA, Canada and the Caribbean; Int. Pres. LEO W. GERARD; Int. Sec.-Treas. STAN JOHNSON; 850,000 mems (2007).

United Transportation Union (UTU): 24950 Country Club Blvd, Suite. 340, North Olmsted, OH 44070-5333; tel. (216) 228-9400; fax (216) 228-5755; e-mail pr@utu.org; internet www.utu.org; f. 1969; formed strategic alliance with USW in July 2006; Int. Pres. MALCOLM B. FUTHEY, Jr; Gen. Sec. and Treas. KIM THOMPSON; 125,000 mems.

Utility Workers Union of America, AFL-CIO: 815 16th St, NW, Washington, DC 20006; tel. (202) 974-8200; fax (202) 974-8201; e-mail webmaster@uwua.net; internet www.uwua.net; f. 1945; Pres. D. MICHAEL LANGFORD; Sec.-Treas. GARY M. RUFFNER; over 50,000 mems (2010).

Independent Unions
(with 50,000 members and over)

American Nurses Association: 8515 Georgia Ave, Suite 400, Silver Spring, MD 20910; tel. (301) 628-5000; fax (301) 628-5001; e-mail ana@ana.org; internet www.nursingworld.org; f. 1896; publishes *The American Nurse* (6 a year) and *American Nurse Today* (6 a year); Pres. KAREN A. DALEY; 51 constituent mem. state asscns comprising 2.9m. mems.

Change to Win: 1900 L St, NW, Suite 900, Washington, DC 20036; tel. (202) 721-0660; fax (202) 721-0661; e-mail info@changetowin.org; internet www.changetowin.org; f. 2005 following split in the AFL-CIO; Int. Pres. JOSEPH HANSEN; Sec.-Treas. GERALYN LUTTY.

Affiliates with 5.5m mems and over include::

International Brotherhood of Teamsters: 25 Louisiana Ave, NW, Washington, DC 20001; tel. (202) 624-6800; fax (202) 624-6918; internet www.teamster.org; f. 1903; withdrew from AFL-CIO in 2005; Gen. Pres. JAMES P. HOFFA; Gen. Sec.-Treas. C. THOMAS KEEGEL; 1.4m. mems.

Service Employees' International Union (SEIU): 1800 Massachusetts Ave, NW, Washington, DC 20036; tel. (202) 730-7000; fax (202) 898-3304; e-mail media@seiu.org; internet www.seiu.org; f. 1921; withdrew from AFL-CIO in 2005; Pres. MARY KAY HENRY; Sec.-Treas. ELISIO MEDINA; 2.2m. mems (2010).

United Farm Workers: 29700 Woodford-Tehachapi Rd, POB 62, Keene, CA 93531; tel. (661) 823-6250; e-mail execoffice@ufw.org; internet www.ufw.org; f. 1962; Pres. ARTURO RODRIGUEZ; Sec.-Treas. SERGIO GUZMAN.

United Food and Commercial Workers International Union: 1775 K St, NW, Washington, DC 20006; tel. (202) 223-3111; internet www.ufcw.org; f. 1979; Int. Pres. JOSEPH T. HANSEN; Int. Sec.-Treas. ANTHONY M. PERRONE; 1.3m. mems.

Fraternal Order of Police: 701 Marriott Dr., Nashville, TN 37214; tel. (615) 399-0900; fax (615) 399-0400; e-mail pyoes@fop.net; internet www.fop.net; Nat. Pres. CHUCK CANTERBURY; Nat. Sec. PATRICK YOES; 325,000 mems.

International Longshore and Warehouse Union: 1188 Franklin St, 4th Floor, San Francisco, CA 94109-6800; tel. (415) 775-0533; fax (415) 775-1302; e-mail info@ilwu.org; internet www.ilwu.org; f. 1937; Pres. ROBERT MCELLRATH; Sec.-Treas. WILLIAM ADAMS; 59,500 mems (2006).

National Education Association of the United States: 1201 16th St, NW, Washington, DC 20036-3290; tel. (202) 833-4000; fax (202) 822-7974; internet www.nea.org; f. 1857; Pres. DENNIS VAN ROEKEL; Sec.-Treas. REBECCA PRINGLE; 3.2m. mems.

National Federation of Federal Employees: 805 15th St, NW, Suite 500, Washington, DC 20005; tel. (202) 216-4420; fax (202) 898-1861; e-mail guest@nffe.org; internet www.nffe.org; f. 1917; Pres. RICHARD N. BROWN; Sec.-Treas. JOHN M. PAOLINO; 120,000 mems (1999).

National Rural Letter Carriers' Association: 1630 Duke St, 4th Floor, Alexandria, VA 22314-3465; tel. (703) 684-5545; fax (703) 548-8735; internet www.nrlca.org; f. 1903; Pres. DON CANTRIEL; Sec.-Treas. CLIFFORD D. DAILING; 98,000 mems (1999).

National Treasury Employees Union: 1750 H St, NW, Washington, DC 20006; tel. (202) 572-5500; fax (202) 572-5644; e-mail nteu-pr@nteu.org; internet www.nteu.org; f. 1938; Nat. Pres. COLLEEN M. KELLEY; Exec. Vice-Pres. FRANK D. FERRIS; 150,000 mems.

Transport

Federal Transit Administration: East Bldg, 1200 New Jersey Ave, SE, Washington, DC 20590; tel. (202) 366-4043; e-mail fta.adaassistance@dot.gov; internet www.fta.dot.gov; Admin. PETER M. ROGOFF.

National Transportation Safety Board: 490 L'Enfant Plaza, SW, Washington, DC 20594; tel. (202) 314-6000; internet www.ntsb.gov; f. 1967; seeks to ensure that all types of transportation in the USA are conducted safely; carries out studies and accident investigations; Chair. DEBORAH A. P. HERSMAN.

Surface Transportation Board: 395 E St, SW, Washington, DC 20423-0001; tel. (202) 245-0245; fax (202) 565-9016; e-mail STBHelp@stb.dot.gov; internet www.stb.dot.gov; f. 1995 to succeed Interstate Commerce Commission; exercises regulatory authority over domestic surface common carriers; jurisdiction extends over rail, inland waterways and motorized traffic; Chair. DANIEL R. ELLIOTT, III.

Transportation Security Administration (TSA): 601 South 12th St, Arlington, VA 20598; tel. (866) 289-9673; e-mail tsa-contactcenter@dhs.gov; internet www.tsa.gov; f. 2001 to ensure

THE UNITED STATES OF AMERICA

the security of the country's transport system against possible terrorist attacks; 50,000 employees; Admin. JOHN S. PISTOLE.

RAILWAYS

In 2008 there were 151,410 km (94,082 miles) of Class I freight railroads, 26,860 km of regional freight railroads and 35,499 km of local freight railroads. In addition, there were 34,083 km of Amtrak passenger railroads.

Federal Railroad Administration: Dept of Transportation, 1200 New Jersey Ave, SE, Washington, DC 20590; tel. (202) 493-6024; fax (202) 493-6009; e-mail webmaster@fra.dot.gov; internet www.fra.dot.gov; f. 1966; part of the Dept of Transportation; formulates federal railway policies and administers and enforces safety regulations; Admin. JOSEPH C. SZABO.

Principal Companies

Alaska Railroad Corpn: 327 West Ship Creek Ave, Anchorage, AK 99510; tel. (907) 265-2300; fax (907) 265-2312; e-mail public_comment@akrr.com; internet www.akrr.com; f. 1912; independent corpn owned by the State of Alaska; year-round freight service and summer passenger service; operates 845 km of track; Pres. and CEO WILLIAM G. O'LEARY.

Amtrak (National Railroad Passenger Corpn): 60 Massachusetts Ave, NE, Washington, DC 20002; tel. (202) 906-3860; fax (202) 906-3306; internet www.amtrak.com; f. 1970; govt-funded private corpn operating inter-city passenger services over 33,796 track-km in 46 states; Chair. THOMAS C. CARPER; Pres. and CEO JOSEPH H. BOARDMAN.

BNSF Railway: 2650 Lou Menk Dr., Fort Worth, TX 76131-2830; tel. (913) 551-4479; fax (913) 551-4285; e-mail steven.forsberg@bnsf.com; internet www.bnsf.com; fmrly Burlington Northern Santa Fe Corpn; freight services; 51,498 track-km; Pres., Chair. and CEO MATTHEW K. ROSE.

Consolidated Rail Corpn (Conrail): 1717 Arch St, Philadelphia, PA 19103; tel. (215) 209-2000; e-mail info@conrail.com; internet www.conrail.com; f. 1976 by fed. govt merger of six bankrupt freight carriers; jtly owned by CSX (42%) and Norfolk Southern (58%); switching and terminal railroad operating in three locations: Northern New Jersey, Southern New Jersey/Philadelphia, and Detroit, MI; Pres. and COO RONALD L. BATORY.

CSX Transportation, Inc (Rail Transport): 500 Water St, Jacksonville, FL 32202; tel. (904) 359-3100; internet www.csx.com; f. 1980 by merger; operates 34,371 km of track (2005); Chair., Pres. and CEO MICHAEL J. WARD.

Kansas City Southern Railway Co: 427 West 12th St, Kansas City, MO 64105; tel. (816) 983-1303; internet www.kcsouthern.com; Chair. and CEO MICHAEL R. HAVERTY; Pres. and COO DAVID L. STARLING; operates 4,989 km of track.

Long Island Rail Road Co: Jamaica Station, Jamaica, NY 11435-4380; tel. (718) 558-7400; internet www.mta.info/lirr; f. 1834; operates 3,291 km of track (Dec. 2007); operated by the Metropolitan Transportation Authority—State of New York; Chair. H. DALE HEMMERDINGER; Exec. Dir and CEO ELLIOT G. SANDER.

Norfolk Southern Corpn: NS Tower, 3 Commercial Pl., Norfolk, VA 23510; tel. (757) 629-2600; fax (757) 664-5117; e-mail contactus@nscorp.com; internet www.nscorp.com; f. 1988; operates 37,600 miles of track (2008); Pres., Chair. and CEO C. WICK MOORMAN.

Pan Am Railways: 1700 Iron Horse Park, North Billerica, MA 01862; tel. (978) 663-1130; e-mail customerservice@panamrailways.com; internet www.panamrailways.com; frmly Guilford Rail System; name changed as above in 2006; Pres. DAVID FINK.

Union Pacific Railroad Co: 1400 Douglas St, Omaha, NE 68179; tel. (402) 544-5000; fax (402) 350-7362; internet www.uprr.com; f. 1897; division of Union Pacific Corpn; operates 52,143 km of track in 23 states; Pres. and CEO JAMES R. YOUNG.

Associations

American Short Line and Regional Railroad Association (ASLRRA): 50 F St, NW, Suite 7020, Washington, DC 20001; tel. (202) 628-4500; fax (202) 628-6430; e-mail aslrra@aslrra.org; internet www.aslrra.org; f. 1913; 875 mems; operates and maintains 29% of US rail mileage; Pres. and Treas. RICHARD F. TIMMONS.

Association of American Railroads: 425 Third St, SW, Suite 1000, Washington, DC 20024; tel. (202) 639-2100; fax (202) 639-2286; e-mail preilly@aar.org; internet www.aar.org; f. 1934; membership represents virtually all major railroads in the USA, Canada and Mexico, as well as rail industry products and services; oversees 173,000 miles of track; Pres. and CEO EDWARD R. HAMBERGER.

ROADS

In 2008 there were 75,238 km (46,751 miles) of interstate highway, 663,109 km of other national highway system roads and 5,767,873 km of other roads. Road network kilometres in that year totalled 6,506,220, of which some 67.4% was classified as paved.

Federal Highway Administration (FHWA): 1200 New Jersey Ave, SE, Washington, DC 20590; tel. (202) 366-4000; fax (202) 366-3244; internet www.fhwa.dot.gov; part of the Dept of Transportation; implements federal highway policy and promotes road safety; Admin. VICTOR M. MENDEZ.

National Highway Traffic Safety Administration (NHTSA): 1200 New Jersey Ave, SE, West Bldg, Washington, DC 20590; tel. (202) 366-9550; e-mail webmaster@nhtsa.dot.gov; internet www.nhtsa.dot.gov; f. 1970; part of the Dept of Transportation; Admin. DAVID L. STRICKLAND.

INLAND WATERWAYS

In 2009 there were some 40,749 km (25,320 miles) of navigable channels in the USA.

St Lawrence Seaway Development Corpn (SLSDC): US Dept of Transportation, 1200 New Jersey Ave, SE, W32-300, Washington, DC 20590; tel. (202) 366-0091; fax (202) 366-7147; e-mail tim.downey@sls.dot.gov; internet www.seaway.dot.gov; responsible for the operations and maintenance of sections of the St Lawrence Seaway within the territorial limits of the USA; Admin. COLLISTER JOHNSON, Jr.

Principal Companies

American Commercial Lines, Inc: 1701 East Market St, Jeffersonville, IN 47130; tel. (812) 288-0100; e-mail aclinfo@aclines.com; internet www.aclines.com; f. 1915; operates barge services on the Mississippi and Ohio rivers and tributaries to the Gulf Intracoastal Waterway; fleet of more than 2,700 barges and 125 towboats; Pres. and CEO MICHAEL P. RYAN.

Great Lakes Dredge & Dock Corpn: 2122 York Rd, Oak Brook, IL 60523; tel. (630) 574-3000; fax (630) 574-2909; internet www.gldd.com; f. 1890; dredging, marine construction and reclamation; operates tugboats, drillboats, carfloats, barges and dredges; 180 vessels; Pres. and CEO DOUGLAS B. MACKIE; CEO JONATHAN W. BERGER.

Great Lakes Fleet, Inc: 212 South 37th Ave, Suite 200, Duluth, MN 55807; tel. (218) 723-2420; fax (218) 723-2455; internet www.cn.ca/specialized/great_lakes/en_KFGreatLakes.shtml; Gen. Man. CHARLES PATTERSON, III; 8 vessels.

Associations

American Waterways Operators: 801 North Quincy St, Suite 200, Arlington, VA 22203; tel. (703) 841-9300; fax (703) 841-0389; internet www.americanwaterways.com; f. 1944; over 400 mems; Pres. and CEO THOMAS A. ALLEGRETTI.

Lake Carriers' Association: 20325 Center Ridge Rd, Suite 720, Rocky River, OH 44116; tel. (440) 333-4444; fax (440) 333-9993; e-mail info@lcaships.com; internet www.lcaships.com; f. 1892; 18 mem. cos; Pres. JAMES H. I. WEAKLEY.

National Waterways Conference, Inc: 4650 Washington Blvd, Suite 608, Arlington, VA 22201; tel. (703) 243-4090; fax (866) 371-1390; e-mail info@waterways.org; internet www.waterways.org; f. 1960; 200 mems; Chair. FRED CAVER; Pres. AMY W. LARSON.

OCEAN SHIPPING

At 31 December 2009 a merchant fleet of 6,546 vessels, with a total displacement of 12,017,750 grt, was registered in the USA.

Federal Maritime Commission: 800 North Capitol St, NW, Washington, DC 20573; tel. (202) 523-5725; fax (202) 523-0014; e-mail secretary@fmc.gov; internet www.fmc.gov; f. 1961 to regulate the water-borne foreign commerce of the USA; comprises 5 Commrs; Chair. RICHARD A. LIDINSKY, Jr; Man. Dir RONALD D. MURPHY.

Maritime Administration: 1200 New Jersey Ave, SE, Washington, DC 20590; tel. (202) 366-5807; e-mail pao.marad@dot.gov; internet www.marad.dot.gov; promotes the US Merchant Marine; administers subsidy programmes to ship operators; Maritime Administrator DAVID T. MATSUDA.

Principal Ports

The three largest ports in the USA, in terms of traffic handled, are the Port of South Louisiana, handling 224.0m. short tons in 2008, Houston (212.2m. tons in 2008) and New York/New Jersey (153.5m. tons in 2008). Many other large ports serve each coast, 10 of them handling more than 50m. tons of traffic in 2008. The deepening of channels and locks on the St Lawrence–Great Lakes Waterway, allowing the passage of large ocean-going vessels, has increased the importance of the Great Lakes ports, of which the largest, Duluth-Superior, handled some 45.3m. tons in 2008.

THE UNITED STATES OF AMERICA

Principal Companies

Alcoa Steamship Co, Inc: 201 Isabella St, Pittsburgh, PA 15212-5858; tel. (412) 553-4545; fax (412) 553-2624; bulk services worldwide; 5 vessels; Pres. R. S. HOSPODAR.

APL: 16220 North Scottsdale Rd, Suite 300, Scottsdale, AZ 85254; tel. (602) 586-4800; fax (602) 586-4861; e-mail global_marketing@apl.com; internet www.apl.com; f. 1848; serves east and west coasts of North America, Mexico, Caribbean Basin, Middle East and Far East; wholly owned subsidiary of Neptune Orient Lines (Singapore); 146 vessels; Pres. AIK MENG ENG.

Central Gulf Lines, Inc: 11 North Water St, Suite 18290, Mobile, AL 36602; tel. (251) 243-9228; e-mail wildkm@intship.com; Vice-Pres. KEVIN M. WILD.

Chevron Shipping Co: 6001 Bollinger Canyon Rd, San Ramon, CA 94583-5177; tel. (925) 842-1000; e-mail comment@chevron.com; internet www.chevron.com; f. 1895; subsidiary of Chevron Corpn; world-wide tanker services; regional offices in Houston, London, United Kingdom, and Singapore; 39 tankers; Chair. and CEO JOHN S. WATSON.

Colonial Marine Industries, Inc: Hamilton House, 26 East Bryan St, POB 9981, Savannah, GA 31412; tel. (912) 233-7000; fax (912) 232-8216; e-mail colonial@colonialmarine.com; internet www.colonialmarine.com; 5 vessels; Exec. Vice-Pres. RICHARD C. WIGGER.

Crowley Maritime Corpn: 555 12th St, Suite 2130, Oakland, CA 94607; tel. (510) 251-7500; fax (510) 251-7510; internet www.crowley.com; f. 1892; 280 vessels; Pres., Chair. and CEO THOMAS B. CROWLEY, Jr.

ETG Dorchester Ltd: 654 Madison Ave, New York, NY 10022; tel. (212) 813-9360; fax (212) 813-6390; e-mail info@etgglobal.com; internet www.etgglobal.com; 8 vessels; part of the Energy Transportation Group (ETG); provides LNG ship and shore management services; Chair. and CEO KIMBALL C. CHEN; Pres. and COO ALEX W. EVANS.

Horizon Lines: 4064 Colony Rd, Suite 200, Charlotte, NC; tel. (704) 973-7000; e-mail customercare@horizonlines.com; internet www.horizon-lines.com; f. 2001; Chair., Pres. and CEO CHARLES G. RAYMOND; 21 vessels.

Lykes Lines Ltd: 401 East Jackson St, Suite 3300, POB 31244, Tampa, FL 33631-3244; tel. (813) 276-4600; fax (813) 276-4873; f. 1997; routes from US Gulf and Atlantic ports to United Kingdom and northern Europe, Mediterranean and Africa.

Maritime Overseas Corpn: 511 Fifth Ave, New York, NY 10017; tel. (212) 953-4100; fax (212) 536-3735; manages c. 60 tankers and dry bulk carriers.

Matson Navigation Co: 555 12th St, Suite 700, Oakland, CA 94607; tel. (510) 628-4000; fax (510) 628-7380; e-mail general_info@matson.com; internet www.matson.com; f. 1901; container and other freight services between US west coast and Hawaii; container leasing worldwide; subsidiary of Alexander & Baldwin, Inc; 17 vessels; Pres. MATTHEW J. (MATT) COX.

OMI Corpn: 1 Station Pl., Stamford, CT 06902; tel. (203) 602-6700; fax (203) 602-6701; e-mail info@omicorp.com; internet www.omicorp.com; acquired by Teekay Corpn and A/S Dampskibsselskabet TORM in June 2007; 43 vessels; Chair. and CEO CRAIG H. STEVENSON, Jr; Pres. and COO ROBERT BUGBEE.

Stolt-Nielsen USA, Inc: 800 Connecticut Ave, 4th Floor, East Norwalk, CT 06854; tel. (203) 838-7100; fax (203) 299-0067; internet www.stolt-nielsen.com; over 130 tankers; Chair. CHRISTER OLSSON; CEO NIELS G. STOLT-NIELSEN.

Waterman Steamship Corpn: 1 Whitehall St, New York, NY 10004; tel. (212) 747-8550; fax (212) 747-8588; internet www.waterman-steamship.com; f. 1919; owned by International Shipholding Corpn.

Associations

American Bureau of Shipping: 16855 Northchase Dr., Houston, TX 77060; tel. (281) 877-5800; fax (281) 877-5803; e-mail abs-worldhq@eagle.org; internet www.eagle.org; f. 1862; 814 mems; Chair. and CEO ROBERT D. SOMMERVILLE; Pres. CHRISTOPHER WIERNICKI.

American Maritime Congress: Hall of the States, Suite G-50, 400 North Capitol St, NW, Washington, DC 20001; tel. (202) 347-8020; fax (202) 347-1550; e-mail diannelauer@americanmaritime.org; internet www.americanmaritime.org; f. 1977 as Joint Maritime Congress; adopted current name 1989; mems represent major US-flag ship operating cos; Chair. DON KEEFE; Pres. and CEO PHILLIP J. SHAPIRO.

Chamber of Shipping of America (CSA): 1730 M St, NW, Suite 407, Washington, DC 20036-4517; tel. (202) 775-4399; fax (202) 659-3795; e-mail omoore@knowships.org; internet www.knowships.org; fmrly American Institute of Merchant Shipping; 35 mem. cos; Pres. and CEO JOSEPH J. COX.

CIVIL AVIATION

Federal Aviation Administration: 800 Independence Ave, SW, Washington, DC 20591; tel. (202) 267-8738; fax (202) 267-5301; internet www.faa.gov; f. 1958; part of the Dept of Transportation; promotes safety in the air, regulates air commerce and assists in development of an effective national airport system; Administrator J. RANDOLPH BABBITT.

Principal Scheduled Companies

In 2009 there were 5,178 public-use airports in the USA. There were 95 registered air carriers operating in the USA in 2008; of these, 22 companies were classified as major carriers.

Alaska Airlines: 19300 International Blvd, POB 68900, Seattle, WA 98188; tel. (206) 433-3200; fax (206) 392-7750; internet www.alaskaair.com; f. 1932; scheduled passenger services to 59 cities in the USA, Canada and Mexico; Pres., Chair. and CEO WILLIAM S. AYER.

    Horizon Air: 19521 Pacific Hwy South, Seattle, WA 98188; tel. (206) 431-3647; e-mail support@horizonair.com; internet www.horizonair.com; f. 1981; serves 47 cities in the USA, Canada and Mexico; Pres. GLENN JOHNSON.

American Airlines, Inc: POB 619616, Dallas/Fort Worth Airport, TX 75261-9616; tel. (817) 967-1234; fax (817) 962-4162; internet www.aa.com; f. 1934; coast-to-coast domestic routes, and services to Canada, Hawaii, Mexico, the Caribbean, South America, Europe and the Far East; acquired Trans World Airlines in 2001; Chair. and CEO GERARD J. ARPEY; Pres. THOMAS W. HORTON.

Continental Airlines, Inc: 1600 Smith St, POB 4607, Houston, TX 77002; tel. (713) 324-5152; fax (713) 324-2637; e-mail geninfo@coair.com; internet www.continental.com; f. 1934; serves 133 US destinations and 132 int. destinations; Chair. GLENN F. TILTON; Pres. and CEO JEFFERY A. SMISEK.

Delta Air Lines, Inc: 1030 Delta Blvd, POB 20706, Atlanta, GA 30320-6001; tel. (404) 715-2600; internet www.delta.com; f. 1928; merged with Northwest Airlines in 2008; domestic and int. services to 351 destinations in 64 countries; CEO RICHARD H. ANDERSON; Pres. EDWARD BASTIAN.

Hawaiian Airlines, Inc: 3375 Koapaka St, G-350, Honolulu, HI 96819; tel. (808) 835-3700; fax (808) 835-3690; internet www.hawaiianair.com; f. 1929 as Inter-Island Airways Ltd; inter-island, US mainland and South Pacific services; Pres. and CEO MARK B. DUNKERLEY.

Southwest Airlines: POB 36647, Dallas, TX 75235-1647; tel. (214) 792-4223; internet www.southwest.com; f. 1971; scheduled services to 69 cities in 35 states; Pres., Chair. and CEO GARY KELLY.

United Airlines Corpn: POB 66100, Chicago, IL 60666; tel. (847) 700-9838; fax (847) 700-4081; internet www.united.com; f. 1931; domestic and int. services to over 200 destinations; Chair. GLENN F. TILTON; Pres. and CEO JEFFERY A. SMISEK.

US Airways, Inc: 4000 East Sky Harbor Blvd, Phoenix, AZ 85034; tel. (480) 693-0800; fax (480) 693-2300; internet www.usairways.com; f. 1939 as All-American Airways; merged with America West Airlines in 2005; scheduled passenger services to 208 destinations world-wide; Chair. and CEO DOUG PARKER; Pres. SCOTT KIRBY.

Associations

Air Transport Association of America, Inc (ATA): 1301 Pennsylvania Ave, NW, Suite 1100, Washington, DC 20004-1707; tel. (202) 626-4000; fax (202) 626-4181; e-mail ata@airlines.org; internet www.airlines.org; f. 1936; 17 US airlines mems, 3 non-US assoc. mems; Pres. and CEO JAMES C. MAY.

National Air Carrier Association: 1000 Wilson Blvd, Suite 1700, Arlington, VA 22209; tel. (703) 358-8060; fax (703) 358-8070; internet www.naca.cc; f. 1962; 15 mems; Pres. A. OAKLEY BROOKS.

National Air Transportation Association (NATA): 4226 King St, Alexandria, VA 22302; tel. (703) 845-9000; fax (703) 845-8176; internet www.nata.aero; f. 1940; approx. 2,000 mems; Chair. JAMES MILLER; Pres. JAMES. K. COYNE.

Regional Airline Association: 2025 M St, NW, Suite 800, Washington, DC 20036-3309; tel. (202) 367-1170; fax (202) 367-2170; e-mail raa@raa.org; internet www.raa.org; f. 1975; 34 mems; Chair. RUSSELL (CHIP) CHILDS; Pres. ROGER COHEN.

Tourism

In 2009 there were an estimated 54.9m. foreign visitors to the USA, a decrease of 5.3% compared with the previous year. Receipts from tourism in 2009 were estimated to total some US $120,300m.

American Society of Travel Agents: 1101 King St, Alexandria, VA 22314; tel. (703) 739-2782; fax (703) 684-8319; e-mail askasta@

THE UNITED STATES OF AMERICA

asta.com; internet www.asta.org; f. 1931; Pres. and Chair. CHRIS RUSSO; Vice-Pres. and Sec. K. HOPE WALLACE; over 20,000 mems.

Corporation for Travel Promotion: tel. (212) 332-3942; e-mail info@corporationfortravelpromotion.com; internet www.corporationfortravelpromotion.org; f. 2010; non-profit org. intended to promote the USA as a tourist destination; Chair. STEPHEN J. CLOOBECK.

Office of Travel and Tourism Industries: International Trade Administration, US Dept of Commerce, 14th and Constitution Ave, NW, Rm 1003, Washington, DC 20230; tel. (202) 482-0140; fax (202) 482-2887; e-mail tinet_info@ita.doc.gov; internet tinet.ita.doc.gov; f. 1996; fed. govt agency; analyses data and develops policy; Dir HELEN MARANO; Dep. Asst Sec. for Services JOEL SECONDY.

United States Travel Association: 1100 New York Ave, NW, Suite 450, Washington, DC 20005-3934; tel. (202) 408-8422; fax (202) 408-1225; internet www.ustravel.org; f. 2009 after merger between Travel Industry Association (f. 1941) and the Travel Business Roundtable; Pres. and CEO ROGER DOW; Chair. CAROLINE BETETA.

Defence

As assessed at November 2010, US armed forces totalled 1,563,996: army 639,063, air force 340,990, navy 336,289 and 204,056 marine corps; there was also a Coast Guard numbering 43,598 (not including civilians). At the same time active reservists totalled 871,240. Military conscription ended in 1973. The Strategic Air Command and Polaris nuclear submarines are equipped with nuclear weapons. The USA is a member of the North Atlantic Treaty Organization.

Defence expenditure: budgeted at US $768,200m. in 2010/11.
Chairman of the Joint Chiefs of Staff: Adm. MICHAEL MULLEN.
Chief of Staff of the Army: Gen. MARTIN E. DEMPSEY.
Chief of Staff of the Air Force: Gen. NORTON A. SCHWARTZ.
Chief of Naval Operations: Adm. GARY ROUGHHEAD.

Education

Education is primarily the responsibility of state and local governments, but some federal funds are available to help meet special needs at primary, secondary and higher education levels. Public education is free in every state from elementary school through high school. The period of compulsory education varies among states, but most states require attendance between the ages of seven and 16 years. In 2010 there were an estimated 34.7m. pupils enrolled in public primary schools and 14.7m. in public secondary schools. Private school enrolment was approximately 4.6m. at primary level and about 1.4m. at secondary level. In 2009 there were 4,409 degree-granting universities and colleges, with a total enrolment of an estimated 19.6m. students. Federal government expenditure on education (including training and employment programmes) was budgeted at an estimated US $115,100m. in 2010/11 (3.0% of total expenditure). Spending on education by state and local government in 2007/08 was $826,063m. (29.1% of total public expenditure).

UNITED STATES COMMONWEALTH TERRITORIES

There are two US Commonwealth Territories, the Northern Mariana Islands, in the Pacific Ocean, and Puerto Rico, in the Caribbean Sea. A Commonwealth is a self-governing incorporated territory that is an integral part of, and in full political union with, the USA.

THE NORTHERN MARIANA ISLANDS

Introductory Survey

LOCATION, CLIMATE, LANGUAGE, RELIGION, FLAG, CAPITAL

The Commonwealth of the Northern Mariana Islands comprises 14 islands (all the Marianas except Guam) in the western Pacific Ocean, about 5,300 km (3,300 miles) west of Honolulu (Hawaii). The temperature normally ranges between 24°C (75°F) and 30°C (86°F) in June–November, but is generally cooler and drier from December to May. The average annual rainfall is about 2,120 mm (84 ins). English, Chamorro and Carolinian are the official languages. The population is predominantly Christian, mainly Roman Catholic. The national flag of the United States of America (q.v.) is used by the Northern Mariana Islands. Six islands, including the three largest (Saipan, Tinian and Rota), are inhabited; the principal settlement and the administrative centre are on Saipan.

CONTEMPORARY POLITICAL HISTORY

Historical Context

The islands that comprise the Territory of the Northern Mariana Islands were first sighted by Europeans during the 1520s, and were claimed for Spain in 1565. They were sold to Germany in 1899, but control was transferred to Japan, which had taken the islands from Germany in 1914, by the League of Nations in 1921. During the Second World War the USA captured Saipan and Tinian from the Japanese, after fierce fighting in 1944, and the Northern Mariana Islands became a part of the Trust Territory of the Pacific Islands in 1947 (see the chapter on the Marshall Islands).

In June 1975 the Northern Mariana Islands voted for separate status as a US Commonwealth Territory, and in March 1976 President Gerald Ford of the USA signed the Northern Marianas Commonwealth Covenant. In October 1977 US President Jimmy Carter approved the Constitution of the Northern Mariana Islands, which provided for the former Marianas District to be internally self-governing from January 1978. In December 1977 elections took place for a bicameral legislature, a Governor and a Lieutenant-Governor. The gubernatorial election was won by Carlos Camacho of the Democratic Party, who took office in January 1978. The islanders also elected a Resident Representative (known as the 'Washington Representative') to promote their interests in the federal legislature in Washington, DC.

Domestic Political Affairs

In early 1982, following his defeat in the election held in late 1981, Camacho was replaced as Governor by Pedro (Pete) Tenorio of the Republican Party. The Northern Marianas were formally admitted to US Commonwealth status in November 1986, after the ending of the Trusteeship in the Territory. At the same time a proclamation issued by US President Ronald Reagan conferred US citizenship on the islands' residents.

At elections in late 1989 Republicans retained control of the governorship of the Northern Marianas and ousted a Democrat from the position of the islands' Resident Representative in Washington, DC. Lorenzo (Larry) De Leon Guerrero was elected Governor, following Pedro Tenorio's decision to resign. However, candidates of the Democratic Party won a majority of seats in the islands' House of Representatives.

Guerrero took office in January 1990. In December the UN Security Council voted to end the Trusteeship of the Northern Marianas, as well as that of two other Pacific Trust Territories. Although the decision to terminate the relationship had been taken in 1986, voting had been delayed. However, Governor Guerrero opposed the termination on the grounds that the new relationship would leave the islands subject to US law while remaining unrepresented in the US Congress.

At elections conducted in late 1991 Republicans regained a majority in the islands' House of Representatives (which had been enlarged by three seats), and in the Senate the Republican Party increased the number of its representatives to eight. Republicans retained their majority at elections to the House of Representatives in 1993. However, in the gubernatorial election a Democrat, Froilan Tenorio, was successful; Jesús Borja was elected as Lieutenant-Governor. Juan N. Babauta remained as the Northern Marianas' Resident Representative in Washington, DC.

The Territory's reputation was marred in April 1995 when the Government of the Philippines introduced a ban on its nationals accepting unskilled employment in the islands, owing to persistent reports of abuse and exploitation of immigrant workers. Meanwhile, the US Congress announced that it was to allocate US $7m. towards the enforcement of the islands' labour and immigration laws, following the publication of a report in late 1994 that alleged the repeated violations of these regulations, as well as widespread corruption among immigration officials and business leaders.

In May 1997 US President Bill Clinton informed Governor Tenorio of his intention to apply US immigration and minimum wage laws to the Territory, stating that labour practices in the islands were inconsistent with US values. In the previous month Democratic Congressman George Miller had proposed legislation (the Insular Fair Wage and Human Rights Act) in the US House of Representatives that would equalize the minimum wage level in the islands with that of the US mainland by 1999. The Territory's Government, which denied many of the claims of exploitation of immigrant workers, responded to the proposed legislation by successfully lobbying the Republican majority in the US House of Representatives to oppose the bill.

In January 1999 the Office of Insular Affairs (OIA) of the US Department of the Interior published a report in which it concluded that the Government's attempts to eradicate abuses of labour and immigration laws had been unsuccessful. In particular, the islands' administration was deemed to have failed to reduce the Territory's reliance on alien workers, to enforce US minimum wage laws and to curb evasions of trade legislation governing the export of garments to the USA. In the same month former employees of 18 US clothing retailers initiated legal action against the companies, which were accused of failing to comply with US labour laws in Saipan. In April 2000 a settlement was reached with the garment manufacturers, providing some US $8m. in compensation for the workers. The companies also agreed to conform to regulations established by an independent monitoring system in Saipan.

At the islands' legislative elections in November 1997 Republican candidates won 13 of the 18 seats in the House of Representatives and eight of the nine seats in the Senate. At the gubernatorial election, held concurrently, the incumbent Pedro Tenorio was successful, securing 46% of total votes. However, opponents of Tenorio subsequently initiated an unsuccessful legal challenge to his re-election on the grounds that his return to office constituted his third term as Governor, thereby violating the Constitution: this stated that a maximum of two gubernatorial terms could be served by any one individual, although the Constitution had been amended to include this provision only during the course of Tenorio's second term of office. Following legislative elections in November 1999, Democratic candidates held six of the 18 seats in the House of Representatives and two of the nine seats in the Senate.

In February 2000 the US Senate approved a bill granting permanent residency in the Northern Marianas to some 40,000 immigrant workers. However, the bill also included provisions for limiting the stay of all future guest workers. In December Governor Tenorio announced that he was to oppose the decision by the US Government to bring the Northern Marianas' labour and immigration laws under federal control; Tenorio argued that this would have a negative impact on the islands' economy. In May 2001, following intense lobbying by the Government of the Northern Marianas, the US Congress abandoned the bill. The issue of permanent residency for qualified immigrant workers re-emerged in 2007 with the introduction of minimum wage legislation (see below).

Legislative elections were held in November 2001, at which the Republican Party secured 12 seats in the House of Representatives, the Democratic Party won five and the newly formed Covenant Party

UNITED STATES COMMONWEALTH TERRITORIES

(founded by Benigno R. Fitial, hitherto a member of the Republican Party, to support his gubernatorial bid) took one. The Republican Party won six seats in the Senate, the Democratic Party two and the Covenant Party one. At the concurrent gubernatorial election Juan Babauta, the Republican Party candidate and former Washington Representative, won a convincing victory, securing 42.8% of the votes cast, defeating Fitial who received 24.4%. Babauta was inaugurated as Governor in January 2002, while Diego Benavente, the former Speaker of the House of Representatives, became Lieutenant-Governor.

In January 2002 the Supreme Court suspended deportation proceedings against an immigrant labourer working illegally in the Northern Marianas, after he appealed to the office of the UN High Commissioner for Refugees. The Court warned the Government that it might not be able to order the deportation of up to 10,000 of the Chinese, Sri Lankan and Bangladeshi workers in the Northern Marianas. In late 2002 the Government successfully resisted an attempt by the US Administration to place the Northern Mariana Islands' immigration and labour legislation under direct federal control. In September 2003 the Northern Mariana Islands announced the conclusion of a new immigration co-operation agreement with the US Department of the Interior, which removed the right of overseas political refugees in the Territory to seek asylum in the USA.

In May 2002 the issue of the Northern Marianas' working conditions was raised again by US Senator Edward Kennedy, who proposed a bill that would incrementally increase the minimum wage. In September seven further major US clothing retailers agreed to pay US $11.25m. in compensation to employees alleged to have suffered intolerable working conditions and poor rates of pay. The funds also included sponsorship of independent monitoring of labour conditions in the islands. The case was finally settled in April 2003, when a total of $20m. in compensation was ordered to be paid to the claimants. The Garment Oversight Board was constituted in June, with the authority to withdraw certification of working conditions in garment factories supplying major US clothing companies. In March 2004 the Board decertified one of the 26 participating garment manufacturers. In April more than 400 garment workers were referred to the Division of Immigration for probable deportation as a result of their non-compliance with a Fair Labor Standards Act civil action against garment manufacturers. Nevertheless, a delegate from the US Commission on Civil Rights concluded in May of that year that the situation of garment workers on Saipan appeared to be improving. However, owing to unfavourable external circumstances (see Economic Affairs), in 2005 about a dozen garment factories had ceased operations or reduced their work-force. In early April the repatriation of migrant workers no longer in employment began. In mid-2005 the minimum hourly wage in the Northern Marianas stood at $3.05, some 40% less than the rate prevailing on the US mainland. Legislation seeking to harmonize the minimum wage in the Northern Marianas with that of the USA was introduced in the US Senate in May. The legislation was criticized by the Speaker of the islands' House of Representatives, Benigno Fitial, who believed that the resultant rise in the minimum wage would place the Northern Marianas at a disadvantage with regional competitors. In July 2005, after further lobbying from the Government and the Saipan Chamber of Commerce, the Northern Marianas were excluded from minimum wage legislation that would have ensured equivalence with the US wage increase to $7.25 an hour. In January 2007 the Northern Marianas were finally included in the new legislation, while various tax concessions were provisionally approved to ease any losses incurred by small businesses as a result of the increase. The legislation also allowed qualified immigrant workers to apply for permanent residency. However, within the Northern Marianas, strong opposition to the federal legislation continued, as more garment factories closed down (see Economic Affairs).

In May 2002 the Government froze the assets of the Bank of Saipan, pending auditing of its accounts, after the institution's former Chairman was arrested for allegedly attempting to defraud the bank of more than US $6.6m. The bank, which was reported to hold substantial uninsured US government deposits, was placed in receivership and remained closed for 11 months. Following the bank's reopening in April 2003 with assets of some $12m., customers were permitted to retrieve a limited monthly quota of savings deposits. Four defendants were convicted in relation to the case in June.

In September 2002 Governor Babauta proposed reforms to reduce government expenditure. In November the Government announced plans for a US $40m. bond issue to cover the cost of compensating traditional landowners for the loss of property expropriated for government use, and in April 2003 draft legislation was proposed that would substantially reduce government personnel costs. However, in August credit ratings agencies expressed concerns that the Government's other outstanding debts, in particular those to the Northern Mariana Islands' Retirement Fund, would prevent full repayment of the bonds.

The Northern Mariana Islands

At the islands' legislative elections of 1 November 2003 the Covenant Party gained a majority in the House of Representatives, winning nine of the 18 seats. The Republican Party secured seven seats, the Democratic Party took one seat and an independent candidate won one seat. The Covenant Party won three seats in the Senate, the Republican Party took two and the Democratic Party won one; three independent candidates were also elected.

Several instances of corruption in public office were reported in 2003; in April Senator Ricardo S. Atalig was found guilty of illegally employing relatives of another Senator, José M. de la Cruz (who was suspended from office following his own conviction in July). In August 2004 the Superior Court convicted the chief financial officer of Tinian municipality, Romeo Atalig Diaz, in the first public corruption case lodged by the new anti-corruption unit of the Attorney-General's Office. However, the sentence imposed (fines totalling only US $2,800) was considered derisory by the local press.

At legislative elections held on 5 November 2005 the Covenant Party won eight seats in the House of Representatives, the Republican Party seven seats, the Democratic Party two seats and an independent candidate one seat. Following the election, the Covenant Party and the Republican Party each held three seats in the Senate, the Democratic Party had two seats and there was one independent senator. At the concurrent gubernatorial election Benigno Fitial of the Covenant Party and Timothy P. Villagomez, hitherto Vice-Speaker of the House, were elected Governor and Lieutenant-Governor, respectively, winning 3,809 votes (equivalent to 28.0% of valid votes cast). Independent Republican Heinz S. Hofschneider and his vice-gubernatorial candidate, David M. Apatang, received 3,710 votes (27.3%), while incumbent Governor Babauta and Lieutenant-Governor Diego Benavente garnered 3,610 votes (26.7%). The new Governor and Vice-Governor took office in January 2006.

In March 2006 Jack Abramoff, who was involved, along with other lobbyists and government officials, in transforming and impeding congressional action relating to the Northern Marianas (particularly with regard to the issue of the federal minimum wage—see above), was sentenced to five years and 10 months in prison on fraud and conspiracy charges, and ordered to pay restitution of more than US $21m. Abramoff and his law firm had reportedly received large sums of money from the Northern Marianas Government between 1995 and 2001.

Legislative elections were held on 3 November 2007, with the number of seats in the islands' House of Representatives having been increased to 20. The Republican Party regained a majority in the House of Representatives, securing 12 seats, while the Covenant Party won four seats, the Democratic Party one seat and independent candidates three seats. In the mid-term Senate elections, three incumbents (two independent candidates and one Covenant Party candidate) were re-elected to the three contested seats. The electorate also voted on several municipal and judicial posts, along with issues such as gaming.

In August 2008 Lieutenant-Governor Timothy Villagomez was indicted for conspiracy, wire fraud and theft, along with Tony Guerrero, former executive director of the Commonwealth Utilities Corporation (CUC). Also indicted were the Lieutenant-Governor's sister, Joaquina V. Santos, and James Santos, his brother-in-law and the islands' Secretary of Commerce. It was alleged in the indictment that Villagomez had presided over a scheme to misappropriate federal funds by exaggerating the cost of financial transactions with the CUC pertaining to the purchase of chemicals. James Santos resigned from office shortly after the indictment, and in April 2009 Villagomez resigned as Lieutenant-Governor after being convicted on corruption charges. Governor Fitial appointed Eloy Inos, hitherto the Secretary of the Department of Finance, as the new Lieutenant-Governor following consultations with the Senate in May.

Legislative elections were held on 7 November 2009. The Republican Party won only nine seats in the House of Representatives, compared with 12 at the 2007 poll; the Covenant Party secured seven seats and independent candidates won four seats, while the Democratic Party failed to secure representation. Four Republican Party candidates and two independent candidates were elected to the six Senate seats that were contested. At the concurrent gubernatorial election, Heinz Hofschneider of the Republican Party, along with his vice-gubernatorial candidate—Arnold Palacios, the Speaker of the House of Representatives—attracted the highest number of votes. However, owing to their failure to secure the stipulated 50% plus one of the votes, a second round of voting between Hofschneider and the second highest-polling candidate, the incumbent Governor Fitial, was contested on 23 November 2009. Following a short delay, it was announced in early December that Fitial, along with running mate Eloy Inos, had defeated Hofschneider and Palacios, by 6,610 votes to 6,240, to secure re-election to a second term as Governor and Lieutenant-Governor, respectively. (With effect from 2009, the Governor and Lieutenant-Governor's respective terms of office were extended, by an additional 12 months, to five years, so as to align future gubernatorial elections with federal elections in the USA.) Palacios was subsequently replaced as Speaker by former Governor Froilan Tenorio.

Economic concerns were prevalent during 2010. Poor performances by the tourism and garments industries resulted in a significant decline in government revenues. As a result of the widening fiscal deficit, the Government was forced to implement a range of austerity measures, including reductions in the working hours of public sector workers, and, with government coffers empty, employees were not paid on time on a number of occasions during mid-2010. A constitutional amendment adopted in 2009 required a balanced budget to be approved by the Legislature before the start of each fiscal year, with failure to do so resulting in the suspension of all but 'essential' government services. Following the Legislature's failure to approve the national budget for 2010/11 by the stipulated deadline of 30 September 2010, Governor Fitial declared a state of emergency on 1 October, and most public services and the employment of some 1,400 'non-essential' government workers (as determined by Fitial) were temporarily suspended pending approval of the budget. The two chambers were embroiled in a protracted dispute over a number of issues, including, most notably, the degree to which public employees' working hours should be reduced as part of measures to reduce the deficit, with the Senate arguing that a 12-hour reduction per payroll was sufficient and the House of Representatives insisting on a 16-hour reduction. On 8 October the Senate finally agreed to the House's demand, and, having been approved by both chambers, the budget was signed into effect by Fitial on the following day. Lieutenant-Governor Inos estimated that the 10-day impasse had saved the Government about US $750,000 in personnel costs.

Meanwhile, Froilan Tenorio introduced a bill to the House of Representatives seeking to legalize the operation of casinos on Saipan. Casinos had been legalized on Rota and Tinian, in 2007 and 1989, respectively. Tenorio argued that legalizing casinos on Saipan was the Northern Marianas' last remaining hope to improve the declining economy, and that without a casino government revenues would continue to decrease, necessitating further job losses and additional reductions in public sector working hours. Despite the public having rejected efforts to legalize casinos on Saipan twice previously, in 1979 and 2007, in August 2010 the House of Representatives approved Tenorio's bill. The bill was rejected by the Senate in September, with opponents of the draft legislation noting that the casinos on Rota and Tinian had not proven to be significant revenue-generating projects. However, a new version of the casino legalization bill was drafted by a House of Representatives committee in March 2011 and was expected to be formally introduced shortly thereafter. Meanwhile, the House approved another notable piece of legislation in November 2010 when it voted in support of a bill legalizing the use of cannabis for medicinal and recreational use among those aged 21 years and above. Proponents of the legislation, which also provided for the taxation of the commercial production and sale of cannabis, argued that it would boost tax revenue; however, critics noted that if the bill were to be enacted the Department of Public Health would forfeit federal grants amounting to about US $10m. annually. In the event, the Senate rejected the bill later in November.

Governor Fitial announced plans in December 2010 to merge the Covenant Party with the Republican Party; however, the proposal was rejected by the latter. Fitial subsequently declared that he would return to his former party; he duly rejoined the Republican Party in January 2011. In mid-January Eli Cabrera was elected Speaker of the House of Representatives, following Tenorio's resignation earlier in the month.

Relations with the Federal Government

In early 2004 the Northern Marianas requested provision for the appointment of a non-voting delegate to the US Congress from the islands. (Unlike other US territories such as American Samoa and Guam, the Northern Marianas had continued to be represented in the federal legislature by the islands' Resident Representative in Washington, DC.) In May 2008 US President George W. Bush approved the Consolidated Natural Resources Act of 2008 (introduced by the Senate in March of that year and approved by both chambers in April), which created a non-voting delegate seat for the Northern Marianas in the US House of Representatives, as well as providing for the Territory to be brought under federal immigration laws (subject to a transitional period scheduled to conclude on 31 December 2014). In November the congressional election was held to select the first delegate to represent the Northern Marianas in Washington. Gregorio Sablan, a former Democratic member of the islands' House of Representatives standing as an independent candidate, won the election with 2,474 votes, defeating his Republican rival, Pedro (Pete) Tenorio, who received 2,117 votes. The new delegate vowed to improve relations with the federal Government and was sworn into office in January 2009. Sablan was re-elected to a second two-year term in November 2010, defeating Joseph Camacho by 4,902 votes to 2,744. In January 2011 the US House of Representatives voted to rescind the 'symbolic' voting rights of territorial delegates in the 'Committee of the Whole House on the State of the Union', a means by which the House was able to expedite consideration of certain legislation, particularly amendments. Sablan, together with the Delegates from American Samoa, Guam, the District of Columbia, Puerto Rico and the Virgin Islands, expressed staunch opposition to the revocation of the privilege; the Northern Marianas' Delegate argued that it 'excludes us from even symbolic representation in our Government'. A few days later Democrats introduced a resolution to the House seeking to restore the territorial delegates' symbolic voting rights.

Meanwhile, in September 2008 Governor Benigno Fitial filed legal proceedings against the US Government intended to prevent the implementation, scheduled for June 2009, of the so-called 'federalization' process that would bring the Northern Marianas under federal immigration legislation. Fitial submitted a request to the US District Court for a permanent injunction against the US Administration on the basis that federalization would violate aspects of the islands' right to self-government. Although this request ultimately failed, a resolution adopted by the islands' House of Representatives in February 2009 urging the US Department of Homeland Security to delay the implementation of federalization for 180 days proved more successful: in April the USA announced the postponement, until November, of the implementation of federalization, a decision that was welcomed by Fitial. While still opposed to federalization, Fitial none the less acknowledged that the delay in its implementation would allow the Territory 'more time to meaningfully address the full implementation of this new federal law and minimize adverse economic impacts to our islands'. The transition to US immigration laws began as planned on 28 November. Partly in response to the ending of the islands' exemption from federal immigration and minimum wage laws, in a speech given during Commonwealth Covenant Day celebrations in March 2010, Fitial accused the federal Government of systematically suppressing the provisions originally enshrined in the Covenant that had been intended to protect the Northern Marianas' economy.

CONSTITUTION AND GOVERNMENT

Legislative authority is vested in the Northern Marianas Commonwealth Legislature, a bicameral body consisting of the Senate and the House of Representatives. There are nine senators, elected for four-year terms, and 20 members of the House of Representatives, elected for two-year terms. Executive authority is vested in the Governor, who is elected by popular vote for a five-year term. The Northern Marianas' first non-voting delegate to the US House of Representatives was elected in November 2008; previously, the Territory had been represented in the federal legislature by a Resident Representative ('Washington Representative').

REGIONAL AND INTERNATIONAL CO-OPERATION

The Commonwealth of the Northern Mariana Islands is a member of the Pacific Community (see p. 410) and an associate member of the UN's Economic and Social Commission for Asia and the Pacific (ESCAP, see p. 37).

ECONOMIC AFFAIRS

The Commonwealth of the Northern Mariana Islands' gross national income (GNI) was estimated by the Bank of Hawaii (BOH) to be US $696.3m. in 1999. GNI per head was estimated at $8,582. According to figures from the Secretariat of the Pacific Community, the population of the Northern Marianas decreased at an estimated average annual rate of 0.9% during 2005–10. The Territory's gross domestic product (GDP) was estimated to total $948.7m. in 2005, equivalent to $12,638 per head. Total reported business gross revenue (BGR—a measure of total revenues generated by business transactions that provides an indicator of economic performance in the absence of gross domestic product data, which the Government does not publish) was recorded at $1,552m. in 2009.

Agriculture is concentrated in small holdings, important crops being taro, sweet potatoes, coconuts, breadfruit, bananas and melons. Cattle-ranching is practised on Tinian. Vegetables, beef and pork are produced for export. There is little commercial fishing in the islands (the total catch was 231 metric tons in 2007), although there is a major transshipment facility at Tinian harbour. Agriculture (including forestry, fishing and mining) engaged 1.5% of the employed labour force, according to the census of 2000. Its commercial value as a sector is minimal, although FAO estimated that almost 23% of the total labour force were engaged in the sector in mid-2011, largely at subsistence level. In 2002 the sector accounted for only 0.1% of BGR.

Industry (including manufacturing and construction) engaged 47.2% of the employed labour force in 2000. Manufacturing alone engaged 31.4% of payroll workers, according to a US economic survey of island areas conducted in 2007. The principal manufacturing activity has been the garment industry, which grew rapidly after its establishment in the mid-1980s to become the islands' leading export sector. Manufacturers benefited from US regulations that permitted duty-free and quota-free imports from the

UNITED STATES COMMONWEALTH TERRITORIES

Commonwealth. Garment-manufacturing accounted for 23.6% of BGR in 2002, and overall exports of garments were worth US $1,017m. in 2000. However, following the liberalization of trade regulations in January 2005, which allowed developing countries to export garments to the USA, more than a dozen garment factories closed down. By 2008 the value of exports of garments had declined to $145.8m. In February 2009 Saipan's two remaining garment factories were closed down, bringing an end to production on the islands. Other small-scale manufacturing activities include handicrafts and the processing of fish and copra. Construction is very closely related to the tourist industry and demand for additional hotel capacity.

Service industries dominate the economy, particularly tourism. In 2000 services (including utilities) engaged 51.3% of the employed labour force, and accounted for 29.2% of BGR. According to the 2007 US economic census of island areas, some 21% of payroll workers were employed in hotels and restaurants. However, tourism receipts declined from US $430m. in 2001 to an estimated $225m. in 2002. Visitor numbers decreased from almost 600,000 in 2004 to 353,956 in 2009. In 2010, however, arrivals on Saipan, Tinian and Rota were reported to have risen to 370,091. Japan provided the majority (54%) of the islands' visitors in 2009. Other significant sources of tourists were the Republic of Korea (South Korea), Guam, the USA and the People's Republic of China. In 1995 a US company opened the Territory's first casino on Tinian (gambling being prohibited on other islands). The Northern Marianas were expected to receive some $12m. annually in revenue from this casino, and further large leisure industry developments were announced for Tinian in 2005. A second casino subsequently opened on Rota.

The Northern Marianas are dependent on imports, the value of which totalled US $267.2m. in 2000. The principal imports in that year were clothing (which accounted for 27.6% of the total), beverages, construction materials and automobiles and parts. In 1991 there was a trade deficit of $126.9m. In 2008 remittances from overseas workers and investments were valued at $76.8m.

The annual rate of inflation averaged 2.2% in 2000–09. Consumer prices increased by 3.6% in 2009. The rate of unemployment was estimated at 4.6% in 2003.

The Northern Mariana Islands have long benefited from their political association with the USA. However, the cessation of garment-manufacturing (see above) was estimated to have resulted in a 36% decline in employment during 2004–08. Tourism thus became the main source of income on the islands. The international financial crisis in the latter part of 2008 led to a decline in visitor arrivals. The situation was exacerbated by recessionary conditions in Japan, the Territory's principal source of tourists. In May 2011, furthermore, it was reported that 2,800 Japanese and 1,500 South Koreans had cancelled their holiday bookings, in response to the tsunami disaster in Japan two months previously, amid continuing fears of wider releases of radiation from a damaged nuclear power plant. The islands' hotels were obliged to curtail their operations in view of the decrease in visitor numbers. However, China (including Hong Kong) had meanwhile become the third largest source of visitors to the Northern Mariana Islands, after Japan and the Republic of Korea, and the inauguration of new flights from the Chinese cities of Shanghai and Guangzhou in May 2011 was expected significantly to boost tourist arrivals from mainland China. In April 2009 the islands received more than US $90m. in federal stimulus funding. In an attempt to reduce government expenditure, in March 2010 the House of Representatives approved a bill reducing by one hour the daily working hours of public sector employees; the austerity measure was expected to result in a 12.5% reduction in the Government's annual expenditure on personnel costs. Following the Legislature's failure to endorse the islands' 2010/11 budget, a state of emergency was declared in October 2010 and public services were suspended (see Domestic Political Affairs). In April 2011 it was reported that the Government planned a substantial reduction in budgetary spending for the next financial year. Expenditure of only $102m. was envisaged, in comparison with the outlay of $132m. originally proposed for 2011/12, representing less than 50% of the funding that had been available five years previously.

PUBLIC HOLIDAYS

2012 (provisional): 9 January (Commonwealth Day), 16 January (Martin Luther King Day), 20 February (Presidents' Day), 23 March (Covenant Day), 6 April (Good Friday), 28 May (Memorial Day), 4 July (Liberation Day), 3 September (Labor Day), 8 October (Commonwealth Cultural Day), 5 November (Citizenship Day), 12 November (for Veterans' Day), 22 November (Thanksgiving Day), 10 December (for Constitution Day), 25 December (Christmas Day).

Statistical Survey

Source: (unless otherwise stated): Department of Commerce, Central Statistics Division, POB 10007, Saipan, MP 96950; tel. 664-3000; fax 664-3001; internet www.commerce.gov.mp.

AREA AND POPULATION

Area: 457 sq km (176.5 sq miles). *By Island*: Saipan 120 sq km; Tinian 102 sq km; Rota 85 sq km; Pagan 48 sq km; Anatahan 32 sq km; Agrihan 30 sq km; Alamagan 11 sq km; Asuncion 7 sq km; Aguijan (Goat Is) 7 sq km; Sarigan 5 sq km; Guguan 4 sq km; Farallon de Pajaros 3 sq km; Maug 2 sq km; Farallon de Medinilla 1 sq km.

Population: 43,345 at census of 1 April 1990; 69,221 (males 31,984, females 37,237) at census of 1 April 2000. *By Island* (2000 census): Saipan 62,392; Rota 3,283; Tinian (with Aguijan) 3,540; Northern Islands 6. *Mid-2011* (Secretariat of the Pacific Community estimate): 63,517 (Source: Pacific Regional Information System).

Density (at mid-2011): 139.0 per sq km.

Population by Age and Sex (Secretariat of the Pacific Community estimates at mid-2011): *0–14:* 16,610 (males 8,785, females 7,825); *15–64:* 44,628 (males 22,259, females 22,369); *65 and over:* 2,279 (males 1,075, females 1,204); *Total* 63,517 (males 32,119, females 31,398) (Source: Pacific Regional Information System).

Ethnic Groups (2000 census): Filipino 18,141; Chinese 15,311; Chamorro 14,749; part-Chamorro 4,383; Total (incl. others) 69,221.

Principal Towns (population at 2000 census): San Antonio 4,741; Garapan (capital) 3,588; Koblerville 3,543; San Vincente 3,494; Tanapag 3,318; Chalan Kanoa 3,108; Kagman 3,026. Source: Thomas Brinkhoff, *City Population* (internet www.citypopulation.de).

Births and Deaths (2002): Registered live births 1,289 (birth rate 17.4 per 1,000); Registered deaths 164 (death rate 2.2 per 1,000). *2007* (estimates); Live Births 1,385; Deaths 140 (Source: UN, *Population and Vital Statistics Report*).

Employment (2000 census, persons aged 16 years and over): Agriculture, forestry, fisheries and mining 623; Manufacturing 17,398; Construction 2,785; Transport, communication and utilities 1,449; Trade, restaurants and hotels 9,570; Financing, insurance and real estate 1,013; Community, social and personal services 9,915; *Total employed* 42,753 (males 19,485, females 23,268); Unemployed 1,712 (males 888, females 824); *Total labour force* 44,465 (males 20,373, females 24,092). *2007* (US economic census, paid employment only, excl. public administration): Total employed 22,622 (Manufacturing 7,094; Wholesale and retail 3,642; Hotels and restaurants 4,772). *Mid-2011* (estimates): Agriculture, etc. 10,000; Total labour force 44,000 (Source: FAO).

HEALTH AND WELFARE

Key Indicators

Access to Water (% of persons, 2008): 98.

Access to Sanitation (% of persons, 2006): 94.

For sources and definitions, see explanatory note on p. vi.

AGRICULTURE, ETC.

Principal Crops (crops harvested for sale, '000 lb, 2007): Cassava 30.3; Taro 221.6; Yams 67.7; Sweet potatoes 352.3; Beans, yard long 40.2; Chinese cabbage 38.2; Cucumbers 93.8; Aubergines (Eggplant) 47.3; Pumpkins and squash 68.0; Watermelons 150.2; Bananas 146.9; Breadfruits 4.8; Papayas 50.7; Betel nuts 88.3; Coconuts 42.9; Ginger 1.5.

Livestock (2007): Cattle 1,395; Pigs 1,483; Goats 276; Poultry birds 12,390.

Livestock Products (sales of dozens, 2007): Hen eggs 195,510.

Fishing (metric tons, live weight, 2008): Total catch 292 (Parrotfishes 12; Skipjack tuna 195; Yellowfin tuna 15; Common dolphinfish 5; Scads 17; Other marine fishes 45). Source: FAO.

FINANCE

Currency and Exchange Rates: United States currency is used: 100 cents = 1 United States dollar (US $). *Sterling and Euro Equivalents* (31 December 2010): £1 sterling = US $1.565; €1 = US $1.336; US $100 = £63.88 = €74.84.

Federal Direct Expenditures (US $ million, year ending September 2009): Retirement and disability 34; Total (incl. others) 241 (Source: US Census Bureau, *Consolidated Federal Funds Report*).

Budget (US $ million, 2009): General fund revenue 154.7 (Taxes 112.6, Fees, charges and other revenues 30.0, Net transfers from other funds 12.1); Total expenditure 168.1.

UNITED STATES COMMONWEALTH TERRITORIES   The Northern Mariana Islands

Cost of Living (Consumer Price Index for Saipan; quarterly averages; base: 2000 = 100): All items 111.9 in 2007; 117.3 in 2008; 121.5 in 2009. Source: ILO.

Gross Domestic Product (US $ million in current prices): 1,073 in 2005; 1,007 in 2006; 962 in 2007 (Source: Bureau of Economic Analysis, US Department of Commerce).

Expenditure on the Gross Domestic Product (US $ million in current prices, 2007): Government consumption expenditure and gross investment 354; Personal consumption expenditure 566; Private fixed investment 22; *Total domestic expenditure* 942; Exports of goods and services 548; *Less* Imports of goods and services 529; *GDP in purchasers' values* 962 (Source: Bureau of Economic Analysis, US Department of Commerce).

EXTERNAL TRADE

Principal Commodities (US $ million): *Imports* (1997): Beverages 12.8; Tobacco 5.4; Automobiles (incl. parts) 42.1; Clothing 309.2; Total (incl. others) 836.2. *Exports* (2000): Total 1,000. *Value of Garment Exports* (US $ million): 486.5 in 2006; 307.6 in 2007; 145.8 in 2008.

Principal Trading Partners (US $ million, 1997): *Imports*: Guam 298.0; Hong Kong 200.5; Japan 118.3; Korea, Republic 80.6; USA 63.3; Total (incl. others) 836.2.

Sources: partly UN, *Statistical Yearbook for Asia and the Pacific* and *Statistical Yearbook*.

TRANSPORT

Road Traffic (registered motor vehicles, 2001): 17,900.

Shipping: *Registered Fleet* (2001): 1,029 vessels (791 fishing vessels); *Traffic* ('000 short tons, 1997): Goods loaded 184.1; Goods unloaded 425.9.

Civil Aviation (Saipan Int. Airport, year ending September 1999): 23,853 aircraft landings; 562,364 boarding passengers. *2007:* Passenger arrivals 470,013, Passenger departures 473,249. Source: Commonwealth Ports Authority.

TOURISM

Visitor Arrivals: 389,261 in 2007; 396,410 in 2008; 353,956 in 2009.

Visitor Arrivals by Country (2009): China, People's Republic (incl. Hong Kong) 29,814; Japan 191,111; Korea, Republic 89,132; USA (incl. Guam) 29,259; Total (incl. others) 353,956.

Tourism Receipts (US $ million): 407 in 1999; 430 in 2000; 225 in 2002 (approximate figure). Source: Bank of Hawaii, *Commonwealth of the Northern Mariana Islands Economic Report* (October 2003).

COMMUNICATIONS MEDIA

Radio Receivers (households with access, census of 2000): 10,684.

Television Receivers (estimate, 1995): 15,460 in use.

Telephones (main lines in use, 2009): 25,100.

Mobile Cellular Telephones (2004): 20,500 subscribers (Source: International Telecommunication Union).

EDUCATION

Pre-primary (2002/03, state schools, Headstart programme): 12 schools; 98 teachers; 606 pupils.

Primary (2002/03, state schools): 12 schools; 283 teachers; 5,849 students.

Secondary (2002/03, state schools): 9 schools; 248 teachers; 4,705 students.

Higher (2000/01): 1 college; 1,641 students (full- and part-time students).

Private Schools (2002/03): 18 schools; 186 teachers; 2,326 students.

Directory

The Government
(May 2011)

Governor: BENIGNO R. FITIAL (took office 9 January 2006; re-elected 23 November 2009).

Lieutenant-Governor: ELOY INOS.

DEPARTMENT SECRETARIES

Secretary of the Department of Finance: LARRISA LARSON.

Secretary of the Department of Community and Cultural Affairs: MELVIN FAISAO.

Secretary of the Department of Labor: GIL M. SAN NICOLAS.

Secretary of the Department of Lands and Natural Resources: IGNACIO DELA CRUZ.

Secretary of the Department of Public Lands: OSCAR M. BABAUTA.

Secretary of the Department of Public Works: MARTIN C. SABLAN.

Secretary of the Department of Commerce: SIXTO K. IGISOMAR (acting).

Commissioner of the Department of Public Safety: RAMON C. MAFNAS.

Secretary of the Department of Public Health: JOSEPH KEVIN P. VILLAGOMEZ.

GOVERNMENT OFFICES

Office of the Governor: Caller Box 10007, Capitol Hill, Saipan, MP 96950; tel. 664-2200; fax 664-2211; e-mail gov.frosario@saipan.com; internet cnmigov.net.

Department of the Interior, Office of Insular Affairs (OIA): Field Office of the OIA, Dept of the Interior, POB 502622, Saipan, MP 96950; tel. 234-8861; fax 234-8814; e-mail jeff.schorr@pticom.com; internet www.doi.gov/oia/Islandpages/cnmipage.htm; OIA representation in the Commonwealth; Field Representative JEFFREY SCHORR.

Department of Commerce: Caller Box 10007, Capitol Hill, Saipan, MP 96950; tel. 664-3000; fax 664-3067; e-mail deptcommerce@pticom.com; internet www.commerce.gov.mp.

Department of Community and Cultural Affairs: Capitol Hill, Saipan, MP 96950; tel. 664-2576; fax 664-2570; e-mail faisaom_dcca.deputysecretary@pticom.com.

Department of Finance: POB 5234, Capitol Hill, Saipan, MP 96950; tel. 664-1100; fax 664-1115; e-mail finance.edp@cnmiarra.net; internet www.cnmidof.net.

Department of Labor: POB 10007, Saipan, MP 96950; tel. 236-0900; fax 236-0991; e-mail webmaster@marianaslabor.net; internet www.marianaslabor.net.

Department of Lands and Natural Resources: Capitol Hill, Saipan, MP 96950; tel. 322-9830; fax 322-2633.

Department of Public Health: POB 500409 CK, 1 Hospital Way, Saipan, MP 96950; tel. 235-8950; fax 236-8756; e-mail joseph.kevin@dph.gov.mp; internet www.dph.gov.mp.

Department of Public Lands: POB 500380, Capitol Hill, Saipan, MP 96950; tel. 234-3751; fax 234-3755; e-mail dpl@dpl.gov.mp; internet www.dpl.gov.mp.

Department of Public Safety: Jose M. Sablan Bldg, POB 500791, Susupe, Saipan, MP 96950; tel. 664-9022; fax 664-9027; internet www.dps.gov.mp.

Department of Public Works: Caller Box 10007, Capitol Hill, Saipan, MP 96950; tel. 235-5827; fax 235-6346; e-mail dpwadmin@pticom.com; internet www.dpw.gov.mp.

Legislature

NORTHERN MARIANAS COMMONWEALTH LEGISLATURE

Legislative authority is vested in the Northern Marianas Commonwealth Legislature, a bicameral body consisting of the Senate and the House of Representatives. There are nine senators, elected for four-year terms, and 20 members of the House of Representatives, elected for two-year terms. The most recent legislative election was held on 7 November 2009. The Republican Party won nine seats in the House of Representatives, the Covenant Party seven seats and independent candidates four seats. Meanwhile, four Republican Party candidates and two independent candidates were elected to the six Senate seats that were contested.

Senate President: PAUL ATALIG MANGLONA.

Speaker of the House: ELI D. CABRERA.

Commonwealth Legislature: CNMI Legislative Bureau, POB 500586, Capitol Hill, Saipan, MP 96950; tel. 664-8954; fax 322-6840; e-mail semanp@cnmileg.gov.mp; internet www.cnmileg.gov.mp.

CONGRESS

Since 2008 the Northern Mariana Islands have been able to elect a non-voting Delegate to the US House of Representatives. The first

UNITED STATES COMMONWEALTH TERRITORIES — The Northern Mariana Islands

election for this position was held on 4 November 2008. At the election to the post in November 2010, incumbent Congressman Gregorio K. C. Sablan was re-elected for a two-year term.

Delegate of the Northern Mariana Islands: GREGORIO K. C. SABLAN, POB 504879 Saipan, MP 96950; tel. 323-2647; fax 323-2649; e-mail kilili@mail.house.gov; internet sablan.house.gov.

Election Commission

Commonwealth Election Commission: POB 500470, Saipan, MP 96950-0470; tel. 664-8683; fax 664-8689; e-mail info@votecnmi.gov.mp; internet www.votecnmi.gov.mp; Chair. FRANCES SABLAN; Exec. Dir ROBERT A. GUERRERO.

Political Organizations

Covenant Party: c/o Commonwealth Legislature, Capitol Hill, Saipan, MP 96950; Leader BENIGNO R. FITIAL; Chair. GREGORIO 'KACHUMA' CAMACHO.

Democratic Party of the Commonwealth of the Northern Mariana Islands, Inc: Saipan, MP 96950; tel. 234-7497; fax 233-0641; Pres. Dr CARLOS S. CAMACHO; Chair. LORENZO CABRERA.

Republican Party of the Northern Marianas: POB 500777, Saipan, MP 96950; tel. and fax 233-1288; e-mail dpwpio@vzpacifica.net; State Chair. DAVID ATTAO; Exec. Dir (vacant).

Judicial System

The judicial system in the Commonwealth of the Northern Mariana Islands (CNMI) consists of the Superior Court, the Commonwealth Supreme Court (which considers appeals from the Superior Court) and the Federal District Court. Under the Covenant, federal law applies in the Commonwealth, with some exceptions: for example, the CNMI is not part of the US Customs Territory, and it may enact its own taxation laws.

Chief Justice of the Commonwealth Supreme Court: MIGUEL S. DEMAPAN, POB 502165, Saipan, MP 96950.

Presiding Judge of the Superior Court: ROBERT C. NARAJA, POB 500307, Saipan, MP 96950.

Attorney-General: EDWARD T. BUCKINGHAM.

US Attorney: ALICIA GARRIDO LIMTIACO.

Public Defender: ADAM HARDWICKE.

Religion

The population is predominantly Christian, mainly Roman Catholic. There are small communities of Episcopalians (Anglicans—under the jurisdiction of the Bishop of Hawaii, in the USA) and Protestants.

CHRISTIANITY

The Roman Catholic Church

The Northern Mariana Islands comprise the single diocese of Chalan Kanoa, suffragan to the archdiocese of Agaña (Guam). The Bishop participates in the Catholic Bishops' Conference of the Pacific, based in Suva, Fiji. At 31 December 2007 there were 43,000 adherents, including temporary residents, in the Northern Mariana Islands.

Bishop of Chalan Kanoa: Most Rev. TOMAS AGUON CAMACHO, Bishop's House, Chalan Kanoa, POB 500745, Saipan, MP 96950; tel. 234-3000; fax 235-3002; e-mail diocese@pticom.com.

The Press

The weekly *Focus on the Commonwealth* is published in Guam, but distributed solely in the Northern Mariana Islands.

Marianas Observer: POB 502119, Saipan, MP 96950; tel. 233-3955; fax 233-7040; weekly; Publr JOHN VABLAN; Man. Editor ZALDY DANDAN; circ. 2,000.

Marianas Review: POB 501074, Saipan, MP 96950; tel. and fax 234-7160; f. 1979 as *The Commonwealth Examiner*; weekly; English and Chamorro; independent; Publr LUIS BENAVENTE; Editor RUTH L. TIGHE; circ. 1,700.

Marianas Variety: POB 6338, Tamuning 96931; tel. 234-9272; fax 234-9271; e-mail editor@mvariety.com; internet www.mvariety.com; Mon.–Fri.; English and Chamorro; independent; f. 1972; Publr ABED E. YOUNIS; Editor ZALDY DANDAN; circ. 8,000.

North Star: Chalan Kanoa, POB 500745, Saipan, MP 96950; tel. 234-3000; fax 235-3002; e-mail nstar@pticom.com; internet www.dioceseofchalankanoa.com; weekly; English and Chamorro; Roman Catholic; f. 1976; Publr Bishop TOMAS A. CAMACHO; Man. Editor Fr CELSO MAGBANUA, Jr; circ. 3,000.

Pacific Daily News (Saipan bureau): POB 500822, Saipan, MP 96950; tel. 234-6423; fax 234-5986; Publr LEE WEBBER; circ. 5,000.

Pacific Star: POB 505815 CHRB, Saipan, MP 96950; tel. 288-0746; fax 288-0747; weekly; Operational Man. NICK LEGASPI; circ. 3,000.

Pacifica: POB 502143, Saipan, MP 96950; monthly; Editor MIKE MALONE.

Saipan Tribune: CIC Centre, 2nd Floor, Beach Rd, Saipan; tel. 235-6397; fax 235-3740; e-mail editor.tribune@saipan.com; internet www.saipantribune.com; 2 a week; Publr LYNN KNIGHT; Editor JAYVEE L. VALLEJERA; circ. 3,500.

Broadcasting and Communications

TELECOMMUNICATIONS

Docomo Pacific Inc: Gualo Rai Commercial Center, Main Bldg, Gualo Rai, Middle Rd, Saipan; tel. 483-2273; fax 235-7640; e-mail service@guamcell.net; internet docomopacific.com/saipan; fmrly Saipan Cellular & Paging; name changed to SAIPANCELL Communications in 1992; present name adopted 2008; mobile cellular services; Pres. JAY SHEDD.

IT & E Overseas Inc: POB 500306 CK, Saipan, MP 96950; tel. 682-1060; fax 682-4555; internet www.pticom.com; fmrly Pacific Telecom Inc; name changed as above in 2009; mobile cellular and internet services; Pres. and CEO RICKY DELGADO.

BROADCASTING

Radio

Far East Broadcasting Co, Inc: POB 500209, Saipan, MP 96950; tel. 322-9088; fax 322-3060; e-mail saipan@febc.org; internet www.febc.org; f. 1946; non-commercial, religious broadcasts; Pres. GREGG HARRIS; Field Dir ROBERT L. SPRINGER.

KFBS-SW: POB 500209, Saipan, MP 96950; tel. 322-9088; fax 322-3060; e-mail saipan@febc.org; internet www.febc.org; f. 1946; international broadcasts in Chinese, Indonesian, Russian and Vietnamese; owned by Far East Broadcasting Co, Inc; Pres. GREGG HARRIS.

Inter-Island Communications, Inc: POB 500914, Saipan, MP 96950; tel. 234-7239; fax 234-0447; f. 1984; commercial; station KCNM-AM, or KZMI-FM in stereo; Gen. Man. HANS W. MICKELSON; Programme Dir KEN WARNICK; CEO ANGEL OCAMPO.

KRNM: POB 501250, Saipan, MP 96950; tel. 234-5498; fax 235-0915; internet www.krnm.org; f. 1994; public station based on Northern Marianas College campus; Gen. Man. CARL POGUE.

Magic 100.3: Magic Studio, 1st Floor, Naru Bldg, Susupe; tel. 234-5929; fax 286-5483; e-mail Kwaw100.3@Magic100Radio.com; internet www.magic100radio.com; contemporary music; Man. Dir LEO JUN GANACIAS.

Power 99: POB 10000, Saipan, MP 96950; tel. 235-7996; fax 235-7998; e-mail tpalacios@spbguam.com; Station Man. TINA PALACIOS; Gen. Man. CURTIS DANCOE.

The Rock 97.9: POB 10000, Saipan, MP 96950; tel. 235-7996; fax 235-7998; e-mail cdancoe@spbguam.com; Man. ALBERT JUAN.

Television

KMCV-TV: POB 501298, Saipan, MP 96950; tel. 235-6365; fax 235-0965; f. 1992; 52-channel commercial station, with 8 pay channels, broadcasting 24 hours a day; US programmes and local and international news; 5,650 subscribers; Gen. Man. WAYNE GAMBLIN.

Marianas CableVision: POB 501298, Saipan, MP 96950; tel. 235-4628; fax 235-0965; e-mail mcv.service@saipan.com; internet www.mcvcnmi.com; 55-channel cable service provider, broadcasting US and Pacific Rim programmes; Pres. JOHN CRUIKSHANK; Gen. Man. MARK BIRMINGHAM.

Finance

BANKING

Bank of Guam (USA): POB 500678, Saipan, MP 96950; tel. 233-5000; fax 233-5003; internet www.bankofguam.com; Gen. Man. MARCIE TOMOKANE; 5 brs.

Bank of Hawaii: Bank of Hawaii Bldg, El Monte Ave, Garapan, POB 500566, Saipan, MP 96950; tel. 237-2900; fax 322-4210; internet www.boh.com; Man. JOHN SHEATHER; 2 brs.

Bank of Saipan: POB 500690, Saipan, MP 96950; tel. 234-6260; fax 235-1802; e-mail bankofsaipan@gtepacifica.net; internet www.bankofsaipan.com; dep. US $23m. (Dec. 2004); Pres. JON BARGFREDE; 4 brs.

City Trust Bank: Gualo Rai, POB 501867, Saipan, MP 96950; tel. 235-7701; fax 234-8664; e-mail citytrustbank@ctbsaipan.com; Asst Vice-Pres. and Acting Man. MARIA LOURDES JOHNSON.

UNITED STATES COMMONWEALTH TERRITORIES

The Northern Mariana Islands

First Hawaiian Bank: Gualo Rai Commercial Center, Middle Rd, Gualo Rai, Saipan 96950; tel. 235-3090; fax 236-8936; internet www.fhb.com; Area Man. JUAN LIZAMA.

Guam Savings and Loan Bank: POB 503201, Saipan, MP 96950; tel. 233-2265; fax 233-2227; Gen. Man. GLEN PEREZ.

INSURANCE

Allied Insurance/Takagi and Associates, Inc: PPP 602, Box 10000, Saipan, MP 96950; tel. 233-2554; fax 670-2553; Gen. Man. PETER SIBLY.

Aon Insurance: Aon Insurance Micronesia (Saipan) Inc, POB 502177, Saipan, MP 96950; tel. 234-2811; fax 234-5462; e-mail rod.rankin@aon.com.au; internet www.aon.com/saipan; Communications Officer RODNEY RANKIN.

Associated Insurance Underwriters of the Pacific, Inc: POB 501369, Saipan, MP 96950; tel. 234-7222; fax 234-5367; e-mail aiup@pticom.com; Gen. Man. MAGGIE GEORGE.

Calvo's Insurance Underwriters, Inc: Oleai Centre Bldg, Saipan, MP 96950; tel. 234-5690; fax 234-5693; e-mail eli.buenaventura@calvosinsurance.com; internet www.calvosinsurance.com; affiliated to Tokio Marine & Nichido Fire Insurance Co, Japan; Man. ELI C. BUENAVENTURA.

Century Insurance (Tan Holdings Corpn): Century Insurance PMB 193, POB 10000, Saipan, MP 96950; tel. 234-0609; fax 234-1845; e-mail nel_matanguihan@cicspn.com; internet www.cicspn.com; Gen. Man. NEL MATANGUIHAN.

General Accident Insurance Asia Ltd (Microl Insurance): POB 502177, Saipan, MP 96950; tel. 234-2811; fax 234-5462; Man. Dir MICHAEL W. GOURLAY.

Marianas Insurance Co Ltd: POB 502505, Saipan, MP 96950-2505; tel. 234-5091; fax 234-5093; e-mail admin@marianasinsurance.com; internet www.marianasinsurance.com; f. 1989; Gen. Man. ROSALIA S. CABRERA.

Midland Insurance Underwriters, Inc: PMB 219, POB 10000, Capitol Hill, Saipan, MP 96950; tel. 235-3598.

Moylan's Insurance Underwriters (Int.), Inc: POB 500658, Saipan, MP 96950; tel. 234-6571; fax 234-8641; e-mail saipan@moylans.net; internet www.moylansinsurance.com; Branch Man. CATHY TENORIO.

Pacifica Insurance Underwriters Inc: POB 500168, Saipan, MP 96950; tel. 234-6267; fax 234-5880; e-mail piui@pacificains.com; internet www.pacificains.com; f. 1972; affiliated to Tokio Marine & Nichido Fire Insurance Co, Japan; Pres. NORMAN T. TENORIO.

Primerica Financial Services: POB 500964, Saipan, MP 96950; tel. 235-2912; fax 235-7910; Gen. Man. JOHN SABLAN.

Royal Crown Insurance: Royal Crown Bldg, Beach Road, Chalan LauLau, POB 10001, Saipan, MP 96950; tel. 234-2256; fax 234-2258.

StayWell Saipan, Inc: POB 502050, Saipan, MP 96950-2050; tel. 323-4260; fax 323-4263; e-mail saipan.office@staywellguam.com; internet www.staywellguam.com; Branch Man. ERIC PLINSKE.

Trade and Industry

GOVERNMENT AGENCIES

Commonwealth Development Authority: POB 502149, Wakins Bldg, Gualo Rai, Saipan, MP 96950; tel. 234-6245; fax 235-7147; e-mail administration@cda.gov.mp; internet www.cda.gov.mp; govt lending institution; funds capital improvement projects and private enterprises; offers tax incentives to qualified investors; Chair. PEDRO I. ITIBUS; Exec. Dir MANUEL A. SABLAN.

CHAMBER OF COMMERCE

Saipan Chamber of Commerce: Chalan Kanoa, POB 500806 CK, Saipan, MP 96950; tel. 233-7150; fax 233-7151; e-mail saipanchamber@saipan.com; internet www.saipanchamber.com; Pres. DOUGLAS BRENNAN; Exec. Dir KYLE CALABRESE.

EMPLOYERS' ASSOCIATIONS

Association of Commonwealth Teachers (ACT): POB 5071, Saipan, MP 96950; tel. and fax 256-7567; e-mail cnmiteachers@netscape.net; supports the teaching profession and aims to improve education in state schools.

Saipan Garment Manufacturers' Association (SGMA): POB 10001, Saipan, MP 96950; tel. 235-7699; fax 235-7899; e-mail sgmaemy@vzpacifica.net; Exec. Dir (vacant).

UTILITIES

Commonwealth Utilities Corporation (CUC): POB 501220, Saipan, MP 96950; tel. 235-7025; fax 235-6145; e-mail cucedp@gtepacifica.net; internet www.cucnmi.com; Exec. Dir ABE UTU MALAE.

TRADE UNION AND CO-OPERATIVES

International Brotherhood of Electrical Workers: c/o Micronesian Telecommunications Corpn, Saipan, MP 96950; local branch of US trade union based in Washington, DC.

The Mariana Islands Co-operative Association, and the Rota Producers and Tinian Producers Associations operate on the islands.

Transport

RAILWAYS

There have been no railways operating in the islands since the Japanese sugar industry railway, on Saipan, ceased operations in the Second World War.

ROADS

In 1991 there were 494 km (307 miles) of roads on the islands, 320 km (199 miles) of which are on Saipan. First grade roads constitute 135 km (84 miles) of the total, 99 km (62 miles) being on Saipan. There is no public transport, apart from a school bus system.

SHIPPING

The main harbour of the Northern Mariana Islands is the Port of Saipan, which underwent extensive renovation in the mid-1990s. There are also two major harbours on Rota and one on Tinian. Several shipping lines link Saipan, direct or via Guam, with ports in Japan, Asia, the Philippines, the USA and other territories in the Pacific.

Commonwealth Ports Authority (CPA): POB 501055, Saipan, MP 96950; tel. 237-6500; fax 234-5962; e-mail cpa.admin@pticom.com; internet www.cpa.gov.mp; Exec. Dir EDWARD DELEON GUERRERO.

Mariana Express Lines: POB 501937, CTS Bldg, Saipan, MP 96950; tel. 322-1690; fax 323-6355; e-mail desmond_aw@mariana-express.com; internet www.mariana-express.com; services between Saipan, Guam, Japan and Hong Kong; Man. DESMOND AW.

Saipan Shipping Co Inc (Saiship): Saiship Bldg, Charlie Dock, POB 500008, Saipan, MP 96950; tel. 322-9706; fax 322-3183; e-mail darlene_cabrera@saipanshipping.com; f. 1956; weekly barge service between Guam, Saipan and Tinian; monthly services to Japan and Micronesia; Gen. Man. DARLENE CABRERA.

Westpac Freight: POB 2048, Puerto Rico, Saipan, MP 96950; tel. 322-8798; fax 322-5536; e-mail westpac@gtepacifica.net; services between Saipan, Guam and the USA; Man. MICHIE CAMACHO.

CIVIL AVIATION

Air services are centred on the main international airport, Isley Field, on Saipan. There are also airports on Rota and Tinian.

Continental Micronesia: POB 508778, A.B. Won Pat International Airport, Tamuning, GU 96911, Guam; tel. 647-6595; fax 649-6588; internet www.continental.com; f. 1968, as Air Micronesia, by Continental Airlines (USA); name changed 1992; subsidiary of Continental Airlines; hub operations in Saipan and Guam; services throughout the region and to destinations in the Far East and mainland USA; Pres. CHARLES DUNCAN.

Freedom Air: POB 500239 CK, Saipan, MP 96950; tel. 234-8328; e-mail freedom@ite.net; internet www.freedomairguam.com; scheduled internal flights.

Tourism

Tourism is one of the most important industries in the Northern Mariana Islands, earning some US $225m. in 2002. In that year there were 4,313 hotel rooms. Most of the islands' hotels are Japanese-owned, and in 2009 more than 50% of tourists came from Japan. The Republic of Korea, the People's Republic of China and the USA are also important sources of tourists. The islands received a total of 396,410 visitors in 2008; tourist arrivals declined, to 353,956, in 2009. Arrivals on Saipan, Tinian and Rota were reported to have increased to 370,091 in 2010. The islands of Asuncion, Guguan, Maug, Managaha, Sarigan and Uracas (Farallon de Pajaros) are maintained as uninhabited reserves. Visitors are mainly attracted by the white, sandy beaches and the excellent diving conditions. There is also interest in the *Latte* or *Taga* stones (mainly on Tinian), pillars carved from the rock by the ancient Chamorros, and relics from the Second World War.

Hotel Association of the Northern Mariana Islands: POB 5075 CHRB, Saipan, MP 96950; tel. 233-6964; fax 233-1424; e-mail lynn_knight@tanholdings.com; internet www.saipanhotels.org; f. 1983; Chair. NICK NISHIKAWA.

UNITED STATES COMMONWEALTH TERRITORIES

Marianas Visitors Authority (MVA): POB 500861 CK, Saipan, MP 96950; tel. 664-3200; fax 664-3237; e-mail mva@mymarianas.com; internet www.mymarianas.com; f. 1976; responsible for the promotion and development of tourism in the Northern Mariana Islands; Chair. JERRY TAN; Man. Dir PERRY TENORIO.

Defence

The USA is responsible for the defence of the Northern Mariana Islands. The US Pacific Command is based in Hawaii (USA).

Education

School attendance is compulsory from six to 16 years of age. In 2002/03 there were 12 state primary schools, with a total of 5,849 pupils enrolled, and there were nine state secondary schools, with a total enrolment of 4,705 pupils. There was a total of 18 private schools, with a total enrolment of 2,326 pupils. There was one college of further education in 2000/01, with 1,641 students. Budgetary expenditure on education totalled US $49.6m. in 2000, equivalent to 22.0% of total government expenditure.

PUERTO RICO

Introductory Survey

LOCATION, CLIMATE, LANGUAGE, RELIGION, FLAG, CAPITAL

The Commonwealth of Puerto Rico comprises the main island of Puerto Rico, together with the small offshore islands of Vieques and Culebra and numerous smaller islets, lying about 80 km (50 miles) east of Hispaniola (Haiti and the Dominican Republic) in the Caribbean Sea. The climate is maritime-tropical, with an average annual temperature of 24°C (75°F) and a normal range between 17°C (63°F) and 36°C (97°F). The official languages are Spanish and English. Christianity is the dominant religion, and about 73% of the population are Roman Catholics. The flag (proportions 3 by 5) has five alternating red and white horizontal stripes of equal width, with a blue triangle, in the centre of which is a five-pointed white star, at the hoist. The capital is San Juan.

CONTEMPORARY POLITICAL HISTORY

Historical Context

Puerto Rico, also known as Borinquen (after the original Arawak Indian name Boriquen), was ruled by Spain from 1509 until 1898, when it was ceded to the USA at the conclusion of the Spanish–American War, and administered as an 'unincorporated territory' of the USA. In 1917 Puerto Ricans were granted US citizenship, and in 1947 Puerto Rico obtained the right to elect its own Governor. A Constitution, promulgated in 1952, assigned Puerto Rico the status of a self-governing 'Commonwealth', or 'estado libre asociado', in its relation to the USA.

The Partido Popular Democrático (PPD) held a majority in both chambers of the legislature from 1944 until 1968, when, following a split within the party, the Partido Nuevo Progresista (PNP), an advocate of statehood, won the governorship and legislative control. This followed a plebiscite in 1967, when 61% of voters had ratified a continuation of Commonwealth status in preference to independence (1%) or incorporation as a state of the USA (39%). In the general election of 1972 the PPD, under the leadership of Rafael Hernández Colón, regained the governorship and legislative control from the PNP, only to lose them again in 1976. The victorious PNP was led by Carlos Romero Barceló, who became Governor in January 1977.

Domestic Political Affairs

Romero Barceló, who had promised a referendum on statehood if re-elected for a further term in 1980, abandoned this plan following the election, in which he narrowly defeated former Governor Hernández Colón. The PPD, however, gained control of the legislature. The 1984 gubernatorial election, which was contested mainly on economic issues, was won by Hernández Colón by only 50,000 votes, with the PPD retaining substantial majorities in both legislative chambers. In September 1985 Romero Barceló was succeeded as leader of the PNP by Baltasar Corrada del Río.

A gubernatorial election, held in November 1988, resulted in the re-election of Hernández Colón. Electoral participation was unusually high, at almost 90%.

The question of eventual independence for Puerto Rico has been a politically sensitive issue for over 50 years. With the PPD supporting the continuation and enhancement of Commonwealth status and the PNP advocating Puerto Rico's inclusion as a state of the USA, mainstream party encouragement of independence aims has come mainly from the Partido Independentista Puertorriqueño (PIP) and other left-wing groups. There are two small, and occasionally violent, terrorist factions, the Ejército Popular Boricua (Los Macheteros), which operates in Puerto Rico, and the Fuerzas Armadas de Liberación Nacional (FALN), functioning principally on the US mainland.

In the 1988 election campaign, Corrada del Río, whose campaign was endorsed by the successful US presidential candidate, George Bush, advocated the admission of Puerto Rico as the 51st state of the USA, while Hernández Colón reiterated the traditional PPD policy of 'maximum autonomy' for Puerto Rico 'within a permanent union with the USA'. President Bush's open support of the statehood option was criticized by Hernández Colón and the PPD. In January 1989 Hernández Colón promised that a further plebiscite would be held. Although it was initially planned to hold this referendum in June 1991, in February the proposed legislation to make its result binding on the US Government failed to obtain sufficient support in the US Senate to allow it to proceed to full consideration by the US Congress.

In December 1991 the PPD Government organized a referendum on a proposal to adopt a charter of 'democratic rights', which included guarantees of US citizenship regardless of future change in Puerto Rico's constitutional status, and the maintenance of Spanish as the official language. The proposed charter was rejected by a margin of 53% to 45%. This result was widely interpreted as an indication that the majority of voters wished to retain Puerto Rico's Commonwealth status. Hernández Colón announced in January 1992 that he would not seek re-election in the gubernatorial election in November, and in the following month resigned as leader of the PPD. His successor as party leader, Victoria Muñoz Mendoza, was defeated in the election by the PNP candidate, Pedro Rosselló. The leadership of the PPD subsequently passed to Héctor Luis Acevedo.

Rosselló, who took office in January 1993, announced that a further referendum on Puerto Rico's future constitutional status would be held during the year. The Government proceeded with legislation rescinding the removal, in 1991, of English as an official language of the island. The referendum, which took place in November 1993, resulted in a 48% vote favouring the retention of Commonwealth status, with 46% of voters supporting accession to statehood and 4% advocating full independence.

Rosselló was re-elected as Governor at elections held in November 1996. The PNP retained control of both chambers of the legislature.

In March 1998 the US House of Representatives narrowly passed legislation providing for a referendum to determine the island's future status. Under the referendum plan, a vote in favour of statehood would oblige the US Congress to legislate for a 51st state during 1999, with Puerto Rico's admission to the union following within 10 years. In December 1998, however, the Puerto Rican electorate rejected the statehood proposal by a margin of 50% to 47%; 71% of eligible voters participated in the referendum. Rosselló described the result as a reflection of the PNP Government's decline in popularity over domestic issues, and indicated that he was to petition the US Congress to implement measures to facilitate the island's transition to statehood.

Sila María Calderón of the PPD was elected Governor in November 2000, narrowly defeating Carlos Pesquera of the PNP. The PPD also secured a majority in both the Senate and the House of Representatives in congressional elections. In July 2001 Calderón voiced support for a further referendum on the island's status during 2002. The Governor announced the creation of a 'Status Committee' to resolve the issue in July 2002; the Committee was to consist of representatives of the PPD, PNP and PIP, including Colón and Barceló.

Vieques

An extended period of public protest followed the accidental death, in April 1999, of a civilian security guard during routine US military exercises on the small offshore island of Vieques, the eastern section of which, covering a coastline of 32 km, was used by the US Navy as an ammunition testing range. With support from the PIP, groups of protesters promptly established camps on the firing range, compelling the US Navy temporarily to suspend these operations. Following extended negotiations between the Puerto Rican and US Governments, in January 2000 Rosselló and US President Bill Clinton announced that, in return for the resumption of naval exercises in which only dummy ammunition would be used, the US Administration would provide immediate development aid to Vieques of

US $40m. This figure would rise to $90m. if residents of the island would agree in a referendum to allow the US Navy to resume live ammunition testing, in which event the Navy would undertake to leave Vieques permanently by 2003. In May 2000, prior to a proposed unilateral resumption of naval exercises (using dummy ammunition), protests on Vieques intensified, and several hundred federal government agents were sent to remove the protesters forcibly. The US Navy subsequently declared a 5-km land and sea 'security area' around the island.

Upon taking office in 2001, Governor Calderón announced her administration's repudiation of the agreement on military activity on Vieques signed in January 2000 by Clinton and Rosselló. Military exercises on the island were resumed in April 2001, despite legal challenges and protests. In June the new US President, George W. Bush, announced that the US Navy would end military activity on the island by May 2003. Meanwhile, Calderón announced plans for a referendum on US military activity on Vieques to be held in July 2001; it was postponed until November, but was subsequently cancelled by the US Congress, which ordered the US military to remain on Vieques until an alternative location was found. The US Congress claimed that on-going tests were necessary as part of the US-led 'war on terror' following the terrorist attacks on Washington, DC, and New York in September. (A non-binding referendum had been held in July, in which 68% of voters were in favour of the immediate departure from the island of the US Navy.) Tests resumed in April 2002, amid protests from members of the PIP. In mid-2002 the PIP threatened to call a general strike and instigate a campaign of civil disobedience if the US Navy failed to leave the island by May 2003. The final scheduled bombing exercises took place in February 2003, and the US Navy withdrew from the island on 1 May. The firing range was to become a wildlife reserve. The last remaining base, at Ceiba, was closed on 31 March 2004. In 2006 environmental concerns were raised over underwater detonations carried out by the US Navy as part of its ongoing clean-up operations.

The Acevedo Vilá Government

Legislative and gubernatorial elections were held in November 2004. Aníbal Acevedo Vilá of the ruling PPD won the gubernatorial election with 48.4% of the ballot, while the PNP's candidate, former Governor Rosselló, attracted 48.2% of the votes cast. The third placed candidate, Rubén Berríos Martínez, representing the PIP, won 2.7%. Acevedo Vilá was duly sworn in as Governor on 2 January 2005. In the concurrently held legislative election, the PNP won a majority of seats in both the Senate and the House of Representatives.

In March 2005 both houses of the legislature unanimously approved legislation providing for a referendum in July on whether to petition the US Congress and President Bush to agree to honour the results of a further referendum on how the island's future status should be decided, to be held before the end of 2006. However, the following month, Governor Acevedo Vilá vetoed the legislation on the grounds that it did not make sufficient provision for the option of a constituent assembly, instead of a popular, binding referendum, to decide on the eventual status of the island.

Also in March 2005, there was widespread opposition to the decision by the US Territorial District Court of Puerto Rico to impose the death sentence on two convicted murderers. Capital punishment had been banned in the territory in 1930, a decision that had been upheld in 2000 by a ruling of the Supreme Court of Puerto Rico that it violated the island's Constitution. However, the ruling was subsequently overturned by the US Court of Appeals, which found that Puerto Rico was subject to US federal law and that the death penalty was applicable in certain cases; this decision was upheld by the US Supreme Court. In early April Acevedo Vilá wrote to the US Attorney-General requesting that the death penalty should not apply to residents of Puerto Rico. In May the jury serving on the trial moved to sentence the two men to life imprisonment.

In July 2005 Acevedo Vilá vetoed the proposed budget on the grounds that expenses were greater than income and that it was therefore unconstitutional. The Government continued to operate using the previous year's budget. However, in April 2006 Acevedo Vilá announced that the budget was insufficient to provide for the Government's operating expenses until the end of the financial year (30 June) and that non-essential public sector services would be suspended from 1 May unless the legislature approved an emergency loan, to fund the shortfall of US $740m., and the introduction of a 7% sales tax, to finance the loan repayments. The announcement prompted a protest march through San Juan in which more than 45,000 people participated. None the less, it was reported that 45 government agencies closed on 1 May, together with some 1,600 state schools, rendering some 95,760 workers temporarily unemployed. At a series of demonstrations in the capital, public sector employees demanded an early resolution to the impasse between the executive and the legislature. An emergency commission was established in May, composed of the Governor, members of the House of Representatives and banking agents, and mediated by the Archbishop of San Juan, Roberto Octavio González Nieves. The initiative resulted in an agreement to secure a loan and to replace excise tax with a general sales and use tax of 5.5%, with revenue to be divided between federal and local government. However, owing to inaccurate phrasing, the legislation that was enacted on 13 May authorized a combined sales tax of 7.0%. A petition filed by PNP deputies in early November requesting the Supreme Court to uphold the intended rate of tax was rejected and the law took effect later that month.

In December 2005 a US presidential task force on the status of Puerto Rico delivered its findings. It recommended that Congress approve legislation for a two-stage plebiscite to be held in Puerto Rico within a year. In the first stage, the people of Puerto Rico would be given the option to continue as part of the Commonwealth or to seek a change in status. In the event that they chose the latter, a second vote would be held on whether to be incorporated as a state within the USA or become an independent country. Irrespective of the outcome, any decision would have to be approved mutually by the US Congress and the Government of Puerto Rico. While the PNP and the PIP welcomed the report, it was criticized by Governor Acevedo Vilá and the PPD because it omitted autonomy as an option. In January 2006 both houses of the Puerto Rican legislature approved legislation calling on Congress to act on the recommendations of the task force. A series of proposed laws consistent with the findings of the task force was submitted to Congress throughout 2006, while a bill supported by Acevedo Vilá and the PPD was submitted in March 2007. The latter advocated that a constitutional convention choose one of three options: statehood, independence or a new or modified commonwealth status. The proposal provided for a referendum to be held on the recommended option, prior to its submission for debate in Congress.

Acevedo Vilá was the subject of corruption allegations in 2008 when an investigation by the Federal Bureau of Investigation (FBI) revealed details of improper campaign financing and tax fraud between 1999 and 2004. On 28 March 2008 the Governor was charged on 19 criminal counts relating to the use of illegally obtained donations to eliminate campaign debts and to pay for family holidays and other personal expenses. Among a further 12 associates also indicted were four businessmen from Philadelphia, Pennsylvania (USA), and a Puerto Rican business owner, who were accused of obtaining government contracts in return for making campaign donations. Acevedo Vilá pleaded not guilty to the charges and stated his intention to remain in office—and, indeed, stand for re-election in the November gubernatorial election—despite calls from opposition parties for his resignation. Following a federal court trial, Acevedo Vilá was cleared of all charges on 24 March 2009.

Gubernatorial and legislative elections were held on 4 November 2008. In the gubernatorial ballot, Luis Fortuño Burset of the PNP attracted 52.8% of the votes cast, defeating Acevedo Vilá, who won 41.3% of the ballot. The PNP also increased its representation in the Legislative Assembly at the expense of the PPD, securing a majority in both the Senate and the House of Representatives (22 of 27 senate seats and 37 of 51 lower-house seats). Voter turn-out was recorded at 78%. Fortuño was sworn in as Governor on 2 January 2009. His new cabinet included former Senate President Kenneth McClintock Hernández as Secretary of State. Fortuño's running mate, Pedro Pierluisi Urrutia, succeeded him as Resident Commissioner in Washington, DC.

Recent developments: Fortuño in office

Upon taking office, Fortuño announced a series of measures aimed at reducing the fiscal deficit. These included controversial plans to reduce the public sector work-force by some 30,000 employees, as well as to introduce widespread outsourcing of government functions and increase certain taxes. In June 2009 an estimated 100,000 people marched through San Juan to protest against the job losses. In a further attempt at reducing government expenditure, Fortuño announced plans in April 2010 to reduce the number of seats in the House of Representatives from 51 to 39 and in the Senate from 27 to 17. The proposals, which, if approved by the legislature would require a constitutional referendum, would save an estimated US $11m. The opposition PPD expressed concern at the plans, which it claimed would undermine democracy in Puerto Rico by removing representation from areas that traditionally have shown strong support for the PPD.

Puerto Rico's relations with the neighbouring US Virgin Islands deteriorated in late 2009 following the decision by international drinks producer Diageo to relocate its production facilities for the Captain Morgan's brand of rum to the territory. The decision by the company, which was a major employer in Puerto Rico, was expected to result in some 350 direct and 5,000 indirect job losses in the territory. The authorities in Puerto Rico had accused the US Virgin Islands Government of misusing their share of the federal rum tax revenue to persuade Diageo to relocate to the islands. The US Virgin Islands denied the claim and asserted that Puerto Rico was conducting a campaign of misinformation against the territory.

More than 890 people were murdered in Puerto Rico in 2009 and crime remained a concern for many Puerto Ricans. In early 2010 Fortuño announced that troops would accompany police in patrolling areas particularly affected by violent crime. In October 130 people,

UNITED STATES COMMONWEALTH TERRITORIES

Puerto Rico

including some 75 police officers, 12 prison officials and three members of the National Guard, were arrested in Puerto Rico by the FBI in connection with alleged drugs offences. The police corruption scandal was the largest such incident ever recorded in Puerto Rico, and the FBI operation involved the deployment of over 700 federal agents from the USA. Some commentators speculated that the low salaries paid to Puerto Rican police officers may have motivated some to turn to the illegal drugs industry to supplement their incomes.

In April 2010 the US House of Representatives voted in favour of a bill that would allow Puerto Ricans to determine their future relationship with the USA. It would provide for a referendum asking islanders if they wanted to change their political status. If the answer was no, eight years would elapse before the same question would be asked again. However, if the answer was yes, a second referendum would be held, offering a choice between statehood, independence or 'sovereignty in association with the United States'. Many observers, however, considered that it was unlikely that islanders, who were facing the imminent loss of important government subsidies and tens of thousands of jobs, would want to endanger their current relationship with the USA. The bill failed to receive approval by the US Senate during the 2009–11 congressional term and hence expired in January 2011. In March the US presidential task force on the status of Puerto Rico again recommended a two-stage referendum, to be conducted before the end of 2012.

CONSTITUTION AND GOVERNMENT

On 3 July 1950 the Congress of the United States of America adopted Public Law No. 600, which was to allow 'the people of Puerto Rico to organize a government pursuant to a constitution of their own adoption'. This Law was submitted to the voters of Puerto Rico in a referendum and was accepted in 1951. A new Constitution was drafted in which Puerto Rico was styled as a Commonwealth, or estado libre asociado, 'a state which is free of superior authority in the management of its own local affairs', though it remained in association with the USA. This Constitution, with its amendments and resolutions, was ratified by the people of Puerto Rico on 3 March 1952, and by the Congress of the USA on 3 July 1952. The Commonwealth of Puerto Rico was established on 25 July 1952.

The Constitution may be amended by a two-thirds' vote of the Puerto Rican Legislature and by the subsequent majority approval of the electorate.

Executive power is vested in the Governor, elected for a four-year term by universal adult suffrage. The Governor is assisted by an appointed cabinet. Legislative power is held by the bicameral Legislative Assembly, comprising the Senate (with 27 members) and the House of Representatives (51 members). Additional members may be assigned in each chamber to ensure adequate representation of minority parties. The members of both chambers are elected by direct vote for four-year terms. The Resident Commissioner, also elected for a four-year term, represents Puerto Rico in the US House of Representatives, but is permitted to vote only in committees of the House. Puerto Ricans are citizens of the USA, but those resident in Puerto Rico, while eligible to participate in national party primary elections, may not vote in presidential elections.

REGIONAL AND INTERNATIONAL CO-OPERATION

Puerto Rico holds associate status in the UN Economic Commission for Latin America and the Caribbean (ECLAC, see p. 41) and has observer status in the Caribbean Community and Common Market (CARICOM, see p. 219). Puerto Rico declined to accept associate status in the Association of Caribbean States (ACS), formed in 1994, on the grounds of opposition by the US Government to the inclusion of Cuba. In July 2001 Puerto Rico applied for associate membership of CARICOM; the USA criticized the move, emphasizing that it had authority over the island's foreign policy as long as Puerto Rico held Commonwealth status.

ECONOMIC AFFAIRS

In the fiscal year ending 30 June 2009, according to official estimates, Puerto Rico's gross national income (GNI) was US $62,759m., equivalent to approximately $15,800 per head. During 2000–09, it was estimated, the population increased at an average annual rate of 0.4%. According to UN figures, gross domestic product (GDP) per head increased, in real terms, by an average of 3.5% per year during 2000–09, while GDP decreased, in real terms, by an average of 0.3% per year over the same period. According to official figures, GDP decreased by an estimated 3.8% in 2009/10.

Agriculture, forestry and fishing contributed an estimated 0.7% of GDP in the fiscal year ending 30 June 2009, according to preliminary figures, and employed 1.5% of the working population in 2009/10. Dairy produce and other livestock products are the mainstays of the agricultural sector. The principal crops are fruits (principally plantains, bananas and oranges) and coffee. Cocoa cultivation has been successfully introduced, and measures to improve agricultural land use have included the replanting of some sugar-growing areas with rice and the cultivation of plantain trees over large areas of unproductive hill land. Commercial fishing is practised on a small scale. The GDP of the agricultural sector increased, in real terms, at an average rate of 3.1% per year between 2000 and 2009, according to UN estimates. Agricultural GDP fell by approximately 8.2% in 2009.

According to preliminary official figures, industry (including manufacturing, construction and mining) provided an estimated 49.3% of GDP in 2008/09 and employed 14.1% of the working population in 2009/10. Industrial GDP declined, in real terms, at an average annual rate of 0.2% between 2000 and 2009. It increased by 3.4% in 2009.

Puerto Rico has no commercially exploitable mineral resources, although deposits of copper and nickel have been identified. The sector provided less than 0.1% of GDP in 2008/09, according to official estimates.

Manufacturing is a significant source of income, accounting for an estimated 45.2% of GDP in 2008/09 and employing 9.2% of the working population in 2009/10. The principal branch of manufacturing in 2002/03, based on the value of output, was chemical products (accounting for 72.4% of the total sector), mainly drugs and medicines. Other important products were computers, electronic and electrical products (12.6%) and food products (6.0%). The GDP of the manufacturing sector decreased, in real terms, by a negligible amount per year between 2000 and 2009, according to UN estimates. The sector grew by 3.3% in 2009. In 2008/09 total electricity production was 23,579m. kWh.

The construction sector contributed as estimated 1.8% of GDP in 2008/09, and engaged 4.9% of the employed labour force in 2009/10. Between 2000 and 2009, according to UN estimates, the GDP of the sector declined at an average annual rate of 1.9%. Construction GDP decreased by 12.7% in 2008, but increased by 7.8% in 2009.

Services (including electricity, gas and water) provided an estimated 50.0% of GDP in 2008/09 and engaged 84.2% of the employed labour force in 2009/10 (including 23.7% employed by the Government). In real terms, the GDP of all service sectors increased at an average rate of 0.1% per year between 2000 and 2009. Services GDP declined by 0.5% in 2009. Tourism is of increasing importance; in 2008/09 tourist arrivals were estimated at 4.8m. visitors (including 1.2m. excursionists), generating revenue totalling US $3,472.8m. Visitors from the US mainland comprised almost 85% of the total number of visitors (excluding excursionists) in 2008/09.

In 2008/09 there was a visible trade surplus of US $18,032.0m. and a surplus of $67.4m. on the current account of the balance of payments. In 2008/09 the principal source of imports was the USA (responsible for 46.9% of the total value of imports), which was also the principal market for exports (71.6% of the total). Other important trading partners included Belgium, Germany, Ireland, Japan and the US Virgin Islands. The principal imports in that year were chemicals and related manufactures (particularly pharmaceuticals and medicines, which accounted for 33.4% of the total value of imports), petroleum and coal products and manufactured food products. The principal exports were manufactured chemical products (pharmaceuticals and medicines accounted for 69.0% of total value of exports), medical equipment and supplies and manufactured food products.

In 2008/09 there was a budget deficit of US $2,235.3m. (excluding other government fund financing), equivalent to 2.3% of GDP in that fiscal year. Puerto Rico's gross public debt at the end of the fiscal year to 30 June 2009 was an estimated $52,980.1m. The annual inflation rate averaged 2.8% in 2000–09. Consumer prices increased by an average of 0.3% in 2009. Puerto Rico is very densely populated, and unemployment has been a persistent problem, although, assisted by the growth in the tourism industry, the jobless rate declined during the 1990s. The average rate of unemployment was estimated at 16.0% in 2009/10.

Economic growth has been inhibited by the lack of an adequate infrastructure. Government programmes of industrial and taxation incentives, aimed at attracting US and foreign investors and encouraging domestic reinvestment of profits and long-term capital investment, have generated growth in the manufacturing and services sectors. The withdrawal by the USA of a number of important tax exemptions enjoyed by US and foreign investors from 1996 had a negative impact on the economy. In 2009 the incoming Governor, Luis Fortuño, inherited an economy in decline. The worsening global economic downturn, together with the already poor investment climate, exacerbated the economic situation. Fortuño declared a state of fiscal emergency, introducing measures to reduce the fiscal deficit. He announced drastic reductions in public sector employment, as well as freezes on salaries and social security benefits and tax increases. A fiscal stimulus programme was also introduced, in the hope of boosting investor confidence. However, higher unemployment and a concomitant decline in receipts from income tax placed considerable strain on the budget. According to official data, GDP declined by 3.8% in 2009/10, and the economy was expected to contract by a further 1.0% in 2010/11, the fifth consecutive year of recession in the territory. Economic activity was subdued throughout 2010, and the unemployment rate, at around 16%, remained high. A modest rate of growth, of 0.7%, was projected for 2011/12.

UNITED STATES COMMONWEALTH TERRITORIES

Puerto Rico

PUBLIC HOLIDAYS

2012: 1 January (New Year), 6 January (Epiphany), 9 January (Birthday of Eugenio María de Hostos), 16 January (Martin Luther King Day), 20 February (Presidents' Day), 22 March (Emancipation of the Slaves), 6 April (Good Friday), 16 April (Birthday of José de Diego), 28 May (Memorial Day), 4 July (US Independence Day), 16 July (Birthday of Luis Muñoz Rivera), 25 July (Constitution Day), 27 July (Birthday of José Celso Barbosa), 3 September (Labor Day), 8 October (Columbus Day), 11 November (Veterans' Day), 19 November (Discovery of Puerto Rico Day), 22 November (US Thanksgiving Day), 25 December (Christmas Day).

Statistical Survey

Source (unless otherwise stated): Puerto Rico Planning Board, POB 41119, San Juan, 00940-1119; tel. (787) 723-6200; internet www.jp.gobierno.pr.

Area and Population

AREA, POPULATION AND DENSITY

Area (sq km)	8,959*
Population (census results)	
1 April 2000	
Males	1,833,577
Females	1,975,033
Total	3,808,610
1 April 2010	3,725,789
Population (estimate at mid-year)†	
2011	3,989,133
Density (per sq km) at mid-2011	445.3

* 3,459 sq miles.
† Source: Population Division, US Census Bureau.

POPULATION BY AGE AND SEX
(population estimates at mid-2011)

	Males	Females	Total
0–14	383,748	367,484	751,232
15–64	1,270,557	1,366,417	2,636,974
65 and over	258,570	342,357	600,927
Total	1,912,875	2,076,258	3,989,133

Source: Population Division, US Census Bureau.

PRINCIPAL TOWNS
(population at 2010 census)

San Juan (capital)	395,326	Caguas	142,893
Bayamón	208,116	Guaynabo	97,924
Carolina	176,762	Arecibo	96,440
Ponce	166,327		

Source: Population Division, US Census Bureau.

BIRTHS, MARRIAGES AND DEATHS

	Registered live births		Registered marriages		Registered deaths	
	Number	Rate (per 1,000)	Number	Rate (per 1,000)*	Number	Rate (per 1,000)
2000	59,460	15.5	25,980	8.9	28,550	7.6
2001	55,983	14.6	28,598	7.4	28,794	7.5
2002	52,871	13.7	25,645	6.6	28,098	7.3

* Rates calculated using estimates of population aged 15 years and over.
Source: Department of Health, Commonwealth of Puerto Rico.

2003: Births 50,803 (birth rate 13.1 per 1,000); Deaths 28,356 (death rate 7.3 per 1,000).

2004: Births 51,239 (birth rate 13.2 per 1,000); Deaths 29,066 (death rate 7.5 per 1,000).

2005: Births 50,687 (birth rate 13.0 per 1,000); Deaths 29,702 (death rate 7.6 per 1,000).

2006: Births 48,744 (birth rate 12.4 per 1,000); Deaths 28,589 (death rate 7.2 per 1,000).

2007: Births 46,744 (birth rate 11.9 per 1,000); Deaths 29,292 (death rate 7.4 per 1,000).

2008 (preliminary): Births 45,687 (birth rate 12.1 per 1,000); Deaths 29,024 (death rate 7.3 per 1,000).

2009 (preliminary): Births 44,080 (birth rate 12.1 per 1,000); Deaths 28,173 (death rate 7.3 per 1,000).

Source: Department of Health, Commonwealth of Puerto Rico.

Life expectancy (years at birth): 79.1 (males 75.1; females 83.0) in 2010 (Source: Pan American Health Organization).

ECONOMICALLY ACTIVE POPULATION
('000 persons aged 16 years and over)

	2007/08	2008/09	2009/10
Agriculture, forestry and fishing	15	19	17
Mining	1	—	—
Manufacturing	129	112	102
Construction	82	68	54
Trade	257	244	240
Transportation, communication and other public utilities	54	58	57
Finance, insurance and real estate	43	43	41
Services	359	353	330
Government	279	271	261
Total employed	1,218	1,168	1,103
Unemployed	151	181	210
Total labour force	1,368	1,349	1,313

Health and Welfare

KEY INDICATORS

Total fertility rate (children per woman, 2010)	1.8
Under-5 mortality rate (per 1,000 live births, 2010)	8.3
Physicians (per 1,000 head, c. 2007)	2.2
Hospital beds (per 1,000 head, 2006)	3.1
Health expenditure (public, 2004): % of GDP	3.5

Source: mainly Pan American Health Organization.

For other sources and definitions see explanatory note on p. vi.

UNITED STATES COMMONWEALTH TERRITORIES   Puerto Rico

Agriculture

PRINCIPAL CROPS
('000 metric tons)

	2005	2006*	2007*
Tomatoes	18.7	18.7	18.8
Pumpkins, squash and gourds	14.3	14.3	14.3
Bananas	52.2	52.3	53.5
Plantains	76.4	77.0	80.0
Oranges	18.8	18.9	19.5
Guavas, mangoes and mangosteens	12.9	13.1	13.5
Pineapples	15.3	15.6	17.0
Coffee, green	7.9	8.0	8.1

* FAO estimates.

2008: Figures assumed to be unchanged from 2007 (FAO estimates). Note: No data were available for individual crops in 2009.

Aggregate production (may include official, semi-official or estimated data): Total fruits (excl. melons) 193.4 in 2005, 194.7 in 2006, 202.1 in 2007–09; Total roots and tubers 10.8 in 2005, 10.9 in 2006, 11.3 in 2007–09; Total vegetables (incl. melons) 45.5 in 2005, 45.5 in 2006, 45.8 in 2007–09.

Source: FAO.

LIVESTOCK
('000 head, year ending September, FAO estimates)

	2006	2007	2008
Asses	2	2	2
Cattle	378.0	380.0	380.0
Sheep	6.1	6.2	6.3
Goats	3.2	3.2	3.3
Pigs	48.7	50.0	50.0
Horses	6.5	6.5	6.6
Chickens	12,500	13,000	13,200

Note: No data were available for 2009.
Source: FAO.

LIVESTOCK PRODUCTS
('000 metric tons, FAO estimates)

	2006	2007	2008
Cattle meat	9.8	10.0	10.2
Pig meat	11.0	11.2	11.5
Chicken meat	50.0	50.0	50.0
Cows' milk	350.0	350.0	350.0
Hen eggs	11.2	11.5	11.5

Note: No data were available for 2009.
Source: FAO.

Fishing

(metric tons, live weight)

	2006	2007	2008
Capture	2,042	1,675	1,793
Groupers	24	20	19
Snappers and jobfishes	370	311	374
Seerfishes	53	35	32
Caribbean spiny lobster	148	123	142
Stromboid conchs	1,005	829	829
Aquaculture	266	44	44*
Tilapias	12	32	30*
Penaeus shrimps	237	0	0*
Total catch	2,308	1,719	1,837*

* FAO estimate.
Source: FAO.

Industry

SELECTED PRODUCTS
(year ending 30 June)

	1995/96	1996/97	1997/98*
Distilled spirits ('000 proof gallons)	25,343	36,292	33,471

* Preliminary.

Electric energy (million kWh): 23,935.2 in 2007/08; 22,610.9 in 2008/09; 23,578.7 in 2009/10.
Cement ('000 94-lb sacks): 37,173 in 2004; 36,847 in 2005; 36,910 in 2006 (Source: US Geological Survey).
Beer ('000 hectolitres): 317 in 1997; 263 in 1998; 259 in 1999 (Source: UN, *Industrial Commodity Statistics Yearbook*).

Finance

CURRENCY AND EXCHANGE RATES

Monetary Units
United States currency: 100 cents = 1 US dollar (US $).

Sterling and Euro Equivalents (31 December 2010)
£1 sterling = US $1.565;
€1 = US $1.336;
US $100 = £63.88 = €74.84.

BUDGET
(US $ '000, general government operations, year ending 30 June)

Revenue*	2006/07	2007/08	2008/09
Income tax	6,389,973	5,493,881	5,191,042
Excise tax	1,475,311	1,306,416	1,118,283
Sales and use tax	583,639	910,609	797,194
Other taxes	4,663	11,356	103,348
Charges for services	757,724	664,505	758,427
Intergovernmental transfers	5,029,854	4,419,109	5,580,153
Interest	148,638	66,894	25,928
Other revenue	334,501	258,275	540,854
Total	14,724,303	13,131,045	14,115,229

Expenditure	2006/07	2007/08	2008/09
General government services	2,313,735	1,568,296	1,363,118
Public safety	1,863,148	2,104,343	2,071,001
Health	1,940,520	2,345,115	2,761,868
Public housing and welfare	3,046,812	3,086,489	3,428,546
Education	4,356,304	4,419,176	5,048,612
Economic development	512,966	383,483	687,183
Intergovernmental transfers	426,352	368,837	425,418
Capital outlays	308,370	222,865	60,684
Principal on debt servicing	608,410	1,938,098	284,925
Interest	219,419	339,291	219,135
Total	15,596,036	16,775,993	16,350,490

* Excluding net financing (US $ '000): 1,865,572 in 2006/07; 3,704,835 in 2007/08; 3,019,238 in 2008/09.

Source: Department of the Treasury, Commonwealth of Puerto Rico.

COST OF LIVING
(Consumer Price Index; base: 2000 = 100)

	2007	2008	2009
Food (incl. beverages)	118.8	128.0	133.3
Fuel and light	138.9	159.7	149.0
Rent	112.9	117.3	117.3
Clothing (incl. footwear)	71.9	73.0	74.2
All items (incl. others)	121.3	127.6	128.0

Source: ILO.

UNITED STATES COMMONWEALTH TERRITORIES

Puerto Rico

NATIONAL ACCOUNTS
(US $ million at current prices, year ending 30 June)

Expenditure on the Gross Domestic Product

	2006/07	2007/08	2008/09*
Government final consumption expenditure	10,512.4	10,518.1	11,132.7
Private final consumption expenditure	51,949.3	54,561.0	55,564.6
Gross domestic investment	11,987.8	11,373.6	10,204.9
Net sales to the rest of the world	−14,929.0	−14,925.7	−14,143.3
Gross national product	59,520.5	61,527.0	62,758.9
Exports of goods and services } Less Imports of goods and services	28,884.0	31,398.9	32,949.3
GDP in purchasers' values	88,404.5	92,925.9	95,708.2

*Preliminary.

Gross Domestic Product by Economic Activity

	2006/07	2007/08	2008/09*
Agriculture	430.2	612.9	633.5
Mining†	61.4	62.0	54.6
Manufacturing	37,636.6	40,548.0	43,548.0
Utilities	2,214.4	2,114.6	2,123.1
Construction	1,965.4	1,928.7	1,727.1
Transportation	968.3	998.5	978.0
Trade	7,223.0	7,343.3	7,469.2
Finance, insurance and real estate	18,380.0	18,845.4	18,205.3
Other services	11,404.6	11,925.1	12,252.7
Government	8,584.9	8,762.2	9,254.2
Sub-total	88,868.4	93,140.7	96,245.7
Statistical discrepancy	−464.2	−214.9	−537.6
Total	88,404.5	92,925.9	95,708.2

*Preliminary.
† Mining includes only quarries.

BALANCE OF PAYMENTS
(US $ million, year ending 30 June)

	2006/07	2007/08	2008/09*
Merchandise exports	64,203.2	68,551.0	66,077.6
Merchandise imports	−51,040.5	−52,986.3	−48,045.6
Trade balance	13,162.7	15,564.7	18,032.0
Exports of services	6,696.4	6,941.4	6,569.1
Imports of services	−4,957.7	−5,033.4	−4,672.5
Balance on goods and services	14,901.4	17,472.7	19,928.6
Other income received	1,668.2	1,763.7	1,371.2
Other income paid	−31,498.6	−34,162.1	−35,443.1
Balance on goods, services and income	−14,929.0	−14,925.7	−14,143.3
Net transfers and interest	11,020.0	12,754.3	14,210.7
Current balance	−3,909.0	−2,171.4	67.4
Net capital movements	5,119.7	1,883.0	−32.5
Overall balance	1,210.7	−288.4	34.9

*Preliminary.

External Trade

PRINCIPAL COMMODITIES
(US $ million, year ending 30 June)

Imports	2006/07	2007/08	2008/09
Mining products	1,510.0	2,457.3	546.1
Manufacturing products	42,259.4	40,779.0	38,605.5
Food	2,440.6	2,627.7	2,955.6
Products of petroleum and coal	4,152.8	5,169.8	4,714.0
Chemical products	21,675.9	19,337.5	18,146.4
Basic chemicals	4,150.3	3,286.5	3,282.4
Pharmaceuticals and medicines	16,494.7	15,065.9	13,591.2
Machinery, except electrical	1,266.0	1,199.1	1,122.4
Computer and electronic products	2,932.8	2,986.2	2,829.2
Transport equipment	1,922.3	1,909.3	1,478.2
Motor vehicles	1,608.7	1,647.8	1,204.9
Miscellaneous manufacturing	1,617.9	1,605.6	1,512.0
Total (incl. others)	45,265.8	44,928.3	40,651.0

Exports	2006/07	2007/08	2008/09
Manufacturing products	59,378.1	63,229.9	60,098.4
Food	3,751.5	4,468.2	3,597.5
Chemicals	39,587.8	45,662.2	45,762.8
Pharmaceuticals and medicines	36,567.9	42,182.7	41,983.5
Computer and electronic products	6,885.0	4,083.5	3,197.2
Computers and peripheral equipment	4,023.0	2,274.0	1,596.6
Electrical equipment, appliances and components	1,281.4	1,558.3	1,241.7
Miscellaneous manufacturing	4,788.6	3,809.7	3,701.8
Medical equipment and supplies	4,675.2	3,732.6	3,649.6
Total (incl. others)	60,010.8	63,953.6	60,806.6

PRINCIPAL TRADING PARTNERS
(US $ million, year ending 30 June)

Imports	2004/05	2005/06	2006/07
Brazil	689.9	676.4	672.9
China, People's Republic	n.a.	566.7	644.9
Dominican Republic	643.9	596.4	485.7
Germany	828.0	903.0	871.9
Ireland	7,716.8	7,950.2	9,492.6
Japan	1,554.8	1,834.9	1,661.3
Nigeria	n.a.	n.a.	903.4
Singapore	956.7	592.7	612.2
United Kingdom	524.5	513.4	n.a.
USA	19,133.7	21,502.9	22,662.4
US Virgin Islands	1,264.7	1,486.1	1,377.5
Total (incl. others)	38,905.2	42,629.5	45,265.8

Exports	2004/05	2005/06	2006/07
Belgium	1,335.5	1,464.1	2,013.9
Dominican Republic	845.2	887.0	987.6
France	693.5	410.2	358.8
Germany	544.5	635.5	2,046.3
Italy	414.9	216.3	n.a.
Japan	n.a.	458.3	526.6
Netherlands	1,800.6	2,356.7	2,763.8
Singapore	608.0	849.7	1,119.2
Spain	n.a.	n.a.	353.6
United Kingdom	749.2	693.8	935.0
USA	46,703.0	49,651.8	46,324.0
Total (incl. others)	56,543.2	60,118.7	60,010.8

2007/08: *Imports:* USA 21,322.1; Total (incl. others) 44,928.3. *Exports:* USA 47,262.3; Total (incl. others) 63,953.6.

2008/09: *Imports:* USA 19,069.1; Total (incl. others) 40,651.0. *Exports:* USA 43,543.9; Total (incl. others) 60,806.6.

UNITED STATES COMMONWEALTH TERRITORIES   *Puerto Rico*

Transport

ROAD TRAFFIC
(motor vehicles registered at 31 December)

	2004	2006*	2007
Passenger cars	2,210,998	2,341,820	2,421,055
Buses and coaches	3,308	3,503	3,698
Lorries (trucks) and vans	36,063†	100,841	106,446
Motorcycles	31,770	91,082	115,865

* Data for 2005 were not available.
† Privately owned vehicles only.

Source: Federal Highway Administration, US Department of Transportation, *Highway Statistics*.

SHIPPING
(Port of San Juan, year ending 30 June)

	2007/08	2008/09	2009/10
Cruise passenger movements	1,496,853	1,236,121	1,185,780
Cruise ship calls	581	470	466
Cargo movements ('000 short tons)	9,395.9	8,272.9	7,949.0

Source: Puerto Rico Ports Authority.

CIVIL AVIATION
(year ending 30 June)

	2005/06	2006/07	2007/08
Luis Muñoz Marín International Airport			
Passenger movements ('000)	10,680.8	10,321.2	n.a.
Freight (million lbs)	541.0	521.4	n.a.
Regional airports			
Passenger movements ('000)	1,008.1	1,129.5	1,294.7
Freight (million lbs)	266.3	255.5	243.2

Source: Puerto Rico Ports Authority.

Tourism

(year ending 30 June)

	2006/07	2007/08	2008/09*
Total visitors ('000)	3,687.0	3,716.2	3,550.5
From USA	2,867.3	2,894.8	3,002.2
From US Virgin Islands	19.4	17.2	14.5
From elsewhere	800.3	804.3	533.8
Excursionists (incl. cruise passengers)	1,375.4	1,496.9	1,232.0
Expenditure (US $ million)	3,413.9	3,535.0	3,472.8

* Preliminary figures.

Communications Media

	2007	2008	2009
Telephones ('000 main lines in use)	1,012.9	949.4	905.7
Mobile cellular telephones ('000 subscribers)	2,431.5	2,543.6	2,712.2
Internet users ('000)	1,099.8	1,000.0	1,000.2
Broadband subscribers ('000)	182.2	426.3	426.3

Personal computers: 33,000 (8.4 per 1,000 persons) in 2005.
Television receivers ('000 in use): 1,270 in 1999.
Radio receivers ('000 in use): 2,840 in 1997.
Daily newspapers (1996): 3; average circulation ('000 copies) 475.
Non-daily newspapers (1988 estimates): 4; average circulation ('000 copies) 106.

Sources: UNESCO, *Statistical Yearbook*; UN, *Statistical Yearbook*; International Telecommunication Union.

Education

(public education at fall 2005, unless otherwise indicated)

	Institutes	Teachers	Enrolment
Elementary and secondary	1,523*	42,036	563,490
Post-secondary†	17‡	14,557§	67,990

* 2005/06.
† Excluding adult (enrolment 33,463 in 2005) and vocational education.
‡ 2006/07.
§ Four-year full-time equivalent teaching staff.

Adult and vocational education: 80 institutes (private only); 33,463 students enrolled (public only).

Source: National Center for Education Statistics, US Department of Education.

Private education (accredited private institutions, 2009/10 unless otherwise indicated): Institutes 145 (2003/04); Pre-primary enrolment 25,460; Elementary and secondary enrolment 99,817; Post-secondary enrolment 29,773 (Source: Consejo General de Educacíon, San Juan).

Adult literacy rate (UNESCO estimates): 90.1% (males 89.7%; females 90.4%) in 2008 (Source: UNESCO Institute for Statistics).

Pupil-teacher Ratio (primary education, UNESCO estimate): 11.7 in 2008/09.

Directory

The Government

HEAD OF STATE

President: BARACK HUSSEIN OBAMA (took office 20 January 2009).

EXECUTIVE
(May 2011)

The Government is formed by the Partido Nuevo Progresista (PNP).
Governor: LUIS G. FORTUÑO (took office 2 January 2009).
Secretary of State: KENNETH D. MCCLINTOCK HERNÁNDEZ.
Secretary of the Interior: MARCOS RODRÍGUEZ EMMA.
Secretary of Justice: GUILLERMO SOMOZA.
Secretary of the Treasury: JESÚS F. MÉNDEZ RODRÍGUEZ.
Secretary of Education: JESÚS RIVERA SÁNCHEZ.
Secretary of the Family: YANITSIA IRIZARRY MÉNDEZ.
Secretary of Labour and Human Resources: MIGUEL ROMERO LUGO.
Secretary of Transportation and Public Works: RUBÉN A. HERNÁNDEZ GREGORAT.
Secretary of Health: LORENZO GONZÁLEZ.
Secretary of Agriculture: JAVIER RIVERA AQUINO.
Secretary of Housing: MIGUEL HERNÁNDEZ-VIVONI.
Secretary of Natural and Environmental Resources: DANIEL JOSÉ GALÁN KERCADO.
Secretary of Consumer Affairs: LUIS GERALDO RIVERA MARÍN.
Secretary of Recreation and Sports: HENRY NEWMANN.
Secretary of Economic Development and Commerce: JOSÉ R. PÉREZ RIERA.
Secretary of Correction and Rehabilitation: CARLOS MOLINA RODRÍGUEZ.
Secretary of Organization and Public Policy: ALEJANDRO J. FIGUEROA.
Attorney-General: OBDULIO MELÉNDEZ.
Resident Commissioner in Washington: PEDRO PIERLUISI URRUTIA.

GOVERNMENT OFFICES

Office of the Governor: La Fortaleza, POB 9020082, PR 00902-0082; tel. (787) 721-7000; fax (787) 724-1472; e-mail secretariomail@fortaleza.gobierno.pr; internet www.fortaleza.gobierno.pr.

UNITED STATES COMMONWEALTH TERRITORIES   *Puerto Rico*

Department of Agriculture: Avda Fernández Juncos 1309, 2°, Parada 19 1/2, PR 00908-1163; POB 10163, Santurce, PR 00909; tel. (787) 721-2120; fax (787) 723-8512; e-mail enegron@da.gobierno.pr; internet www.agricultura.gobierno.pr.

Department of Consumer Affairs: Edif. Norte, 4°, Avda José de Diego, Parada 22, Centro Gubernamental Minillas, San Juan, PR 00940-1059; POB 41059, Minillas Station, Santurce, PR 00940; tel. (787) 722-7555; fax (787) 726-5707; e-mail confidencia@daco.gobierno.pr; internet www.daco.gobierno.pr.

Department of Correction and Rehabilitation: Avda Teniente Cesar Gonzalez, esq. Calle Juan Calaf 34, Urb. Industrial Tres Monjitas, San Juan, PR 00917; POB 71308, Río Piedras, PR 00936; tel. (787) 273-6464; fax (787) 792-7677; internet www.ac.gobierno.pr.

Department of Economic Development and Commerce: Avda Roosevelt 355, Suite 401, San Juan, PR 00936-2350; POB 362350, Hato Rey, PR 00918; tel. (787) 758-4747; fax (787) 753-6874; internet www.ddec.gobierno.pr.

Department of Education: Avda Teniente César González, esq. Calaf, Urb. Industrial Tres Monjitas, Hato Rey, PR 00919-0759; POB 190759, San Juan, PR 00917; tel. (787) 759-2000; fax (787) 250-0275; internet www.de.gobierno.pr.

Department of the Family: POB 11398, Santurce, San Juan, PR 00910-1398; tel. (787) 294-4900; fax (787) 294-0732; internet www.familia.gobierno.pr.

Department of Health: Edif. E altos, Área Centro Médico, Calle Maga, San Juan, PR 00936-8184; POB 70184, Rio Piedras, PR 00936; tel. (787) 765-2929; e-mail webmaster@salud.gov.pr; internet www.salud.gov.pr.

Department of Housing: Edif. Juan C. Cordero, Avda Barbosa 606, Rio Piedras, PR 00928-1365; Apdo 21365, San Juan, PR 00928-1365; tel. (787) 274-2527; fax (787) 758-9263; e-mail mcardona@vivienda.gobierno.pr; internet www.vivienda.gobierno.pr.

Department of Justice: Edif. Principal del Depto de Justicia, 11°, Calle Olimpo, esq. Axtmayer, Parada 11, No 601, Miramar, San Juan, PR 00902-0192; POB 9020192, San Juan, PR 00907; tel. (787) 721-2900; fax (787) 724-4770; e-mail aalamo@justicia.gobierno.pr; internet www.justicia.gobierno.pr; incl. the Office of the Attorney-General.

Department of Labour and Human Resources: Edif. Prudencio Rivera Martínez, Avda Muñoz Rivera 505, Hato Rey, PR 00918; POB 191020, San Juan, PR 00919-1020; tel. (787) 754-5353; fax (787) 756-1149; e-mail webmaster@dtrh.gobierno.pr; internet www.dtrh.gobierno.pr.

Department of Natural and Environmental Resources: Carretera 8838, Km 6.3, Sector El Cinco, Río Piedras, PR 00906-6600; POB 366147, San Juan, PR 00936; tel. (787) 999-2200; fax (787) 999-2303; e-mail webmaster@drna.gobierno.pr; internet www.drna.gobierno.pr.

Department of Recreation and Sports: Parque de Santurce, Calle Los Angeles, San Juan, PR 00902-3207; POB 9023207, Santurce, PR 00909; tel. (787) 721-2800; fax (787) 728-0313; e-mail mraffaele@drd.gobierno.pr; internet www.drd.gobierno.pr.

Department of State: Calle San José, esq. San Francisco, San Juan, PR 00902-3271; Apdo 9023271, San Juan, PR 00901; tel. (787) 722-2121; fax (787) 725-7303; e-mail estado@gobierno.pr; internet www.estado.gobierno.pr.

Department of Transportation and Public Works: Edif. Sur, 17°, Avda de Diego, Santurce, PR 00940-1269; POB 41269, Minillas Station, Santurce, PR 00940; tel. (787) 722-2929; fax (787) 725-1620; e-mail servciud@act.dtop.gov.pr; internet www.dtop.gov.pr.

Department of the Treasury: Edif. Intendente Ramírez, Parada 1, Paseo Covandonga 10, San Juan, PR 00902-4140; POB 9024140, San Juan, PR 00902; tel. (787) 722-0216; fax (787) 723-6213; e-mail infoserv@hacienda.gobierno.pr; internet www.hacienda.gobierno.pr.

Gubernatorial Election, 4 November 2008

Candidate	Votes	%
Luis G. Fortuño Burset (PNP)	1,025,945	52.84
Aníbal Acevedo Vilá (PPD)	801,053	41.26
Rogelio Figueroa García (PPR)	53,690	2.77
Edwin Irizarry Mora (PIP)	39,590	2.04
Total (incl. others)*	1,941,663	100.00

* Including 13,215 votes for write-in candidates, 3,282 blank votes and 4,888 invalid votes.

Legislature

LEGISLATIVE ASSEMBLY

Senate

President of the Senate: THOMAS RIVERA SCHATZ.

Election, 4 November 2008

Party	Seats
PNP	22
PPD	5
Total	27

House of Representatives

Speaker of the House: JENNIFFER GONZÁLEZ COLÓN.

Election, 4 November 2008

Party	Seats
PNP	37
PPD	14
Total	51

Election Commission

Comisión Estatal de Elecciones de Puerto Rico (CEE): Edif. Administrativo, Avda Arterial B 550, Hato Rey, San Juan, PR 00940-5552; POB 19555, San Juan, PR 00919; tel. (787) 777-8682; fax 296-0173; e-mail comentarios@cee.gobierno.pr; internet www.ceepur.org; f. 1977; independent; Pres. HÉCTOR CONTY; Dir YVONNE RIVERA PICORELLI.

Political Organizations

Frente Socialista: Buzón 69, POB 71325, San Juan, PR 00936; tel. (787) 617-7105; e-mail fs@frentesocialistapr.org; internet www.frentesocialistapr.org; f. 1990; mem. orgs incl. the Partido Revolucionario de los Trabajadores Puertorriqueños (PRTP—Los Macheteros) and Movimiento Socialista de Trabajadores; Spokesperson GUILLERMO DE LA PAZ VÉLEZ.

    Movimiento Socialista de Trabajadores (MST): POB 123, Río Piedras, PR 00123; e-mail info@bandera.org; internet www.bandera.org; f. 1982 by merger of the Movimiento Socialista Popular and Partido Socialista Revolucionario; pro-independence; mainly composed of workers and university students; Spokesperson SCOTT BARBÉS CAMINERO.

Movimiento Independentista Nacional Hostosiano (MINH): Of. Central, C25 NE339, San Juan, PR 00920; f. 2004 by merger of the Congreso Nacional Hostosiano and Nuevo Movimiento Independentista (fmr mems of the Partido Socialista Puertorriqueño); pro-independence; Co-Pres JOSÉ RIVERA SANTANA, HÉCTOR PESQUERA SEVILLANO.

Partido Independentista Puertorriqueño (PIP) (Puerto Rican Independence Party): Avda Roosevelt 963, San Juan, PR 00920-2901; tel. (787) 782-1430; fax (787) 782-2000; e-mail pipnacional@independencia.net; internet www.independencia.net; f. 1946; advocates full independence for Puerto Rico as a socialist-democratic republic; Leader RUBÉN BERRÍOS MARTÍNEZ; Exec. Pres. FERNANDO MARTÍN; Sec.-Gen. JUAN DALMAU RAMÍREZ; c. 6,000 mems.

Partido Nuevo Progresista (PNP) (New Progressive Party): POB 1992, Fernández Zuncos Station, San Juan 00910-1992; tel. (787) 289-2000; e-mail dannyls@caribe.net; internet www.pnp.org; f. 1967; advocates eventual admission of Puerto Rico as a federated state of the USA; Pres. LUIS G. FORTUÑO BURSET; c. 225,000 mems.

Partido Popular Democrático (PPD) (Popular Democratic Party): Avda Constitución 403, San Juan, PR 00906; POB 9065788, San Juan, PR 00906-5788; tel. (787) 725-7001; e-mail info@ppdpr.net; internet ppdpr.net; f. 1938; supports continuation and improvement of the present Commonwealth status of Puerto Rico; Pres. HÉCTOR J. FERRER RÍOS; Sec.-Gen. VÍCTOR SUÁREZ MELÉNDEZ; c. 950,000 mems.

Partido Puertorriqueños por Puerto Rico (Puerto Ricans for Puerto Rico—PPR): Calle Palma 1112, esq. con RH Tood, Santurce; POB 9858, San Juan, PR 00908; tel. (787) 340-4476; fax (787) 725-0001; e-mail contacto@popuertorico.com; internet www.porpuertorico.com; f. 2003 as an ecological ('green') party; formally registered as political party in 2007; promotes citizen participation, sustainable devt and quality of life; Pres. ROGELIO FIGUEROA.

UNITED STATES COMMONWEALTH TERRITORIES

Puerto Rican Republican Party: Suite 203, Avda Piñero 1629, San Juan, PR 00920; tel. (787) 462-7474; e-mail cchardon@goppr.org; internet www.goppr.org; Chair. CARLOS MÉNDEZ MARTÍNEZ; Exec. Dir RICARDO APONTE.

Puerto Rico Democratic Party: POB 19328, San Juan, PR 00910-3939; tel. (787) 274-2921; fax (787) 759-9075; Chair. ROBERTO PRATS.

Refundación Comunista Puerto Rico: Organización RC, POB 13362, San Juan, PR 00908-3362; e-mail refundacionpcp@yahoo.es; internet www.refundacioncomunistapr.com; f. 2001; Marxist-Leninist; pro-independence; maintains close relations with the Frente Socialista; Contact ABALLARDE ROJO.

Judicial System

The Judiciary is vested in the Supreme Court and other courts as may be established by law. The Supreme Court comprises a Chief Justice and, from 2011, up to nine Associate Justices, appointed by the Governor with the consent of the Senate. The lower Judiciary consists of Superior and District Courts and Municipal Justices equally appointed.

There is also a US Federal District Court, the judges of which are appointed by the President of the USA. Judges of the US Territorial District Court are appointed by the Governor.

Supreme Court of Puerto Rico

POB 2392, Puerta de Tierra, San Juan, PR 00902-2392; tel. (787) 724-3551; fax (787) 725-4910; e-mail buzon@tribunales.gobierno.pr; internet www.tribunalpr.org.

Chief Justice: FEDERICO HERNÁNDEZ DENTON.

Justices: FEDERICO HERNÁNDEZ DENTON, EDGARDO. RIVERA GARCÍA, LIANA FIOL MATTA, ANABELLE RODRÍGUEZ RODRÍGUEZ, ERICK V. KOLTHOFF CARABALLO, MILDRED G. PABÓN CHARNECO, RAFAEL L. MARTÍNEZ TORRES.

US District Court for the District of Puerto Rico

Clemente Ruiz-Nazario US Courthouse & Federico Degetau Federal Bldg, 150 Carlos Chardón St, Hato Rey, PR 00918; tel. (787) 772-3011; fax (787) 766-5693; internet www.prd.uscourts.gov.

Judges: AIDA M. DELGADO-COLÓN (Chief Judge), JOSÉ A. FUSTÉ, CARMEN C. CEREZO, DANIEL R. DOMÍNGUEZ, JAY A. GARCÍA-GREGORY, GUSTAVO A. GELPÍ, Jr, FRANCISCO A. BESOSA.

Religion

CHRISTIANITY

The Roman Catholic Church

Puerto Rico comprises one archdiocese and five dioceses. Some 73% of the population are Roman Catholics.

Bishops' Conference of Puerto Rico

POB 40682, San Juan, PR 00940-0682; tel. (787) 728-1650; fax (787) 728-1654; e-mail ceppr@coqui.net.

f. 1960; Pres. Mgr RUBÉN ANTONIO GONZÁLEZ MEDINA (Bishop of Caguas).

Archbishop of San Juan de Puerto Rico: Rt Rev. ROBERTO OCTAVIO GONZÁLEZ NIEVES, Arzobispado, Calle San Jorge 201, Santurce, POB 00902-1967; tel. (787) 725-4975; fax (787) 723-4040; e-mail cancilleria@arqsj.org.

Other Christian Churches

The Protestant churches active in Puerto Rico include the Episcopalian, Baptist, Presbyterian, Methodist, Seventh-day Adventist, Lutheran, Mennonite, Salvation Army and Christian Science.

Episcopal Church of Puerto Rico: POB 902, St Just, PR 00978; tel. (787) 761-9800; fax (787) 761-0320; e-mail iep@episcopalpr.org; internet www.episcopalpr.org; f. 1872; diocese of the Episcopal Church in the USA, part of the Anglican Communion; Leader Bishop Rt Rev. DAVID ANDRÉS ALVAREZ; 42,000 baptized mems.

Puerto Rico Council of Churches: Calle El Roble 54, Apdo 21343, Río Piedras, San Juan, PR 00928; tel. (787) 765-6030; fax (787) 765-5977; f. 1954 as the Evangelical Council of Puerto Rico; Pres. Rev. HÉCTOR SOTO; Exec. Sec. Rev. CRUZ A. NEGRÓN TORRES; 8 mem. churches.

BAHÁ'Í FAITH

National Spiritual Assembly: POB 11603, San Juan, PR 00910-2703; tel. (787) 763-0982; fax (787) 763-0982; e-mail bahaipr@prtc.net; internet www.bahaipr.org; f. 1972.

JUDAISM

There is a small Jewish community numbering around 2,500 adherents (less than 1% of the population).

Sha'are Zedek Synagogue-Community Center: Avda Ponce de León 903, Santurce, San Juan, PR 00907; tel. (809) 724-4157; fax (809) 722-4157; f. 1942; conservative congregation with 250 families; Rabbi GABRIEL FRYDMAN.

There is also a reform congregation with 60 families.

The Press

Puerto Rico has high readership figures for its few newspapers and magazines, as well as for mainland US periodicals. Several newspapers have a large additional readership among the immigrant communities in New York.

DAILIES
(m = morning; s = Sunday)

El Nuevo Día: Parque Industrial Amelia, Carretera 165, Guaynabo; POB 9067512, San Juan, PR 00906-7512; tel. (787) 641-8000; fax (787) 641-3924; e-mail laferre@elnuevodia.com; internet www.elnuevodia.com; f. 1970; Chair. and Editor MARÍA LUISA FERRÉ RANGEL; Pres. MARÍA EUGENIA FERRÉ RANGEL; Dir LUIS ALBERTO FERRÉ RANGEL; circ. 202,212 (m), 254,769 (s).

Primera Hora: Parque Industrial Amelia, Calle Diana Lote 18, Guaynabo, PR 00966; POB 2009, Cataño, PR 00963-2009; tel. (787) 641-5454; fax (787) 641-4472; e-mail servicios@primerahora.com; internet www.primerahora.com; Pres. and Editor ANTONIO LUIS FERRÉ; Dir JORGE CABEZAS; Gen. Man. JUAN MARIO ALVAREZ CARTAÑA; circ. 133,483 (m), 92,584 (Sat.).

The San Juan Star: POB 364187, San Juan, PR 00936-4187; tel. (787) 782-4200; fax (787) 783-5788; internet www.thesanjuanstar.com; f. 1959; English; Pres. and Publr GERRY ANGULO; Gen. Man. SALVADOR HASBÚN; circ. 50,000.

El Vocero de Puerto Rico: Apdo 7515, San Juan, PR 00906-7515; tel. (787) 721-2300; fax (787) 722-0131; e-mail opinion@vocero.com; internet www.vocero.com; f. 1974; Publr and Editor GASPAR ROCA; circ. 143,150 (m), 123,869 (Sat.).

PERIODICALS

BuenaVIDA: 1700 Fernández Juncos Ave, San Juan, PR 00909; tel. (787) 728-7325; f. 1990 as *Buena Salud*; monthly; health and fitness; Editor IVONNE LONGUEIRA; circ. 61,000.

Caribbean Business: 1700 Fernández Juncos Ave, San Juan, PR 00909-2938; POB 12130, San Juan, PR 00914-0130; tel. (787) 728-9300; fax (787) 726-1626; e-mail cbeditor@casiano.com; internet www.casiano.com/html/cb.html; f. 1973; weekly; business and finance; Man. Editor RAQUEL ROMÁN; circ. 45,000.

Educación: c/o Dept of Education, POB 190759, Hato Rey Station, San Juan, PR 00919; f. 1960; 2 a year; Spanish; Editor JOSÉ GALARZA RODRÍGUEZ; circ. 28,000.

La Estrella de Puerto Rico: 140 Roosevelt Bldg, Ave F. D. Roosevelt, Hato Rey, PR 00917; tel. (787) 754-4440; fax (787) 754-4457; e-mail myrna.lopez@periodicolaestrella.com; internet www.periodicolaestrella.com; f. 1983; weekly; Spanish and English; Editor-in-Chief FRANK GAUD; circ. 123,500.

Imagen: 1700 Fernández Juncos Ave, Stop 25, San Juan, PR 00909-2999; tel. (787) 728-4545; fax (787) 728-7325; e-mail imagen@casiano.com; internet www.casiano.com/html/imagen.html; f. 1986; monthly; women's interest; Editor ANNETTE OLIVERAS; circ. 80,000.

¡Qué Pasa!: Loiza St Station, POB 6338, San Juan, PR 00914; tel. (787) 728-3000; fax (787) 728-1075; e-mail manoly@casiano.com; internet www.casiano.com/html/quepasa.html; f. 1948; quarterly; English; publ. by Puerto Rico Tourism Co; official tourist guide; Editor RONALD FLORES; circ. 120,000.

Resonancias: Instituto de Cultura Puertorriqueña, Oficina de Publicaciones, Ventas y Mercadeo, POB 9024184, San Juan, PR 00902-4184; tel. (787) 724-4215; fax (787) 723-0168; e-mail revista@icp.gobierno.pr; internet www.icp.gobierno.pr; f. 2000; 2 a year; Spanish; Puerto Rican and general culture and music; Editor GLORIA TAPIA; circ. 3,000.

Revista Colegio de Abogados de Puerto Rico: POB 9021900, San Juan, PR 00902-1900; tel. (787) 721-3358; fax (787) 725-0330; e-mail carlosgil@prtc.net; f. 1914; quarterly; Spanish; law; Editor Lic. CARLOS GIL AYALA; circ. 10,000.

Revista del Instituto de Cultura Puertorriqueña: Oficina de Publicaciones, Ventas y Mercadeo, POB 9024184, San Juan, PR 00902-4184; tel. (787) 721-0901; e-mail revista@icp.gobierno.pr; internet www.icp.gobierno.pr; f. 1958; 2 a year; Spanish; arts, literature, history, theatre, Puerto Rican culture; Editor GLORIA TAPIA; circ. 3,000.

La Semana: Calle Cristóbal Colón, esq. Ponce de León, Casilla 6537, Caguas 00726-6537; tel. (787) 743-6537; e-mail gerentegeneral@lasemana.com; internet www.lasemana.com; weekly; f. 1963; Spanish; regional interest; Gen. Man. MARJORIE M. RIVERA RIVERA.

UNITED STATES COMMONWEALTH TERRITORIES

Puerto Rico

TeVe Guía: San Juan, PR; weekly; TV listings; circ. 470,000 (monthly).

La Torre: POB 23322, UPR Station, San Juan, PR 00931-3322; tel. (787) 758-0148; fax (787) 753-9116; e-mail ydef@hotmail.com; f. 1953; publ. by University of Puerto Rico; quarterly; literary criticism, linguistics, humanities; Editor YUDIT DE FERDINANDY; circ. 1,000.

Vea: POB 190240, San Juan, PR 00919-0240; tel. (787) 721-0095; fax (787) 725-1940; f. 1969; weekly; Spanish; TV, films and celebrities; Editor ENRIQUE PIZZI; circ. 92,000.

El Visitante: POB 41305, San Juan, PR 00940-1305; tel. (787) 728-3710; fax (787) 268-1748; e-mail director@elvisitante.biz; internet www.elvisitante.net; f. 1975; weekly; Roman Catholic; Dir JOSÉ R. ORTIZ VALLADARES; Editor Rev. EFRAÍN ZABALA; circ. 59,000.

Publishers

Ediciones Huracán Inc: 874 Baldorioty de Castro, San Juan, PR 00925; tel. (787) 763-7407; fax (787) 753-1486; e-mail edhucan@caribe.net; f. 1975; textbooks, literature, social studies, history; Pres. CARMEN RIVERA-IZCOA.

Editorial Académica, Inc: 67 Santa Anastacia St, El Vigía, Río Piedras, PR 00926; tel. (787) 760-3879; f. 1988; regional history, politics, government, educational materials, fiction; Dir FIDELIO CALDERÓN.

Editorial Cordillera, Inc: Of. 1A, Calle México 17, Hato Rey, PR 00917; tel. (787) 767-6188; fax (787) 767-8646; e-mail info@editorialcordillera.com; internet www.editorialcordillera.com; f. 1962; Puerto Rican history, culture and literature, educational, trade; Pres. PATRICIA GUTIÉRREZ; Sec. and Treas. ADOLFO R. LÓPEZ.

Editorial Cultural Inc: POB 21056, Río Piedras, San Juan, PR 00928; tel. (787) 765-9767; f. 1949; general literature and political science; Dir FRANCISCO M. VÁZQUEZ.

Instituto de Cultura Puertorriqueña: Oficina de Publicaciones, Ventas y Mercadeo, POB 9024184, San Juan, PR 00902-4184; tel. (787) 724-0700; fax (787) 723-0168; e-mail revista@icp.gobierno.pr; internet www.icp.gobierno.pr; f. 1955; literature, history, poetry, music, textbooks, arts and crafts; Dir GLORIA TAPIA.

University of Puerto Rico Press (EDUPR): POB 23322, UPR Station, Río Piedras, San Juan, PR 00931-3322; tel. (787) 250-0435; fax (787) 753-9116; e-mail info@laeditorialupr.com; internet www.laeditorialupr.com; f. 1947; general literature, children's literature, Caribbean studies, law, philosophy, science, educational; Exec. Dir MANUEL G. SANDOVAL BAÉZ.

Broadcasting and Communications

TELECOMMUNICATIONS

Junta Reglamentadora de Telecomunicaciones de Puerto Rico: Avda Roberto H. Todd 500, Parada 18, Santurce, San Juan, PR 00907-3981; tel. (787) 756-0804; fax (787) 756-0814; e-mail correspondencia@jrtpr.gobierno.pr; internet www.jrtpr.gobierno.pr; telecommunications regulator; Pres. SANDRA E. TORRES LÓPEZ.

Puerto Rico Telephone Co (PRTC): Avda Juan Ponce de León 562, Hato Rey; POB 360998, San Juan, PR 00936-0998; tel. (787) 782-8282; fax (787) 774-0037; internet www.telefonicapr.com; provides all telecommunications services in Puerto Rico; fmrly state-owned; acquired by America Móvil in 2007; Pres. and CEO ENRIQUE ORTIZ DE MONTELLANO RANGEL.

BROADCASTING

The only non-commercial stations are the radio station and the two television stations operated by the Puerto Rico Department of Education. The US Armed Forces also operate a radio station and three television channels.

Asociación de Radiodifusores de Puerto Rico (Puerto Rican Radio Broadcasters' Asscn): Caparra Terrace, Calle Delta 1305, San Juan, PR 00920; tel. (787) 783-8810; fax (787) 781-7647; e-mail prbroadcasters@centennialpr.net; f. 1947; Pres. MANUEL SANTIAGO SANTOS; Exec. Dir JOSÉ A. RIBAS DOMINICCI; 102 mems.

Finance

(cap. = capital; res = reserves; dep. = deposits; brs = branches; amounts in US dollars)

BANKING

Government Bank

Government Development Bank for Puerto Rico (Banco Gubernamental de Fomento para Puerto Rico—BGF): Roberto Sánchez Vilella Government Centre, Avda De Diego, Stop 22, Santurce, PR 00907; POB 42001, San Juan, PR 00940-2001; tel. (787) 722-2525; fax (787) 721-1443; e-mail gdbpr@bgf.gobierno.pr; internet www.gdb-pur.com; f. 1942; independent govt agency; acts as fiscal (borrowing) agent to the Commonwealth Govt and its public corpns and provides long- and medium-term loans to private businesses; equity 2,271.2m., dep. 9,447.9m. (June 2007); Pres. CARLOS M. GARCÍA; Chair. RAFAEL F. MARTÍNEZ MARGARIDA.

Autoridad para el Financiamiento de la Vivienda de Puerto Rico: Edif. Juan C. Cordero, Avda Barbosa 606, Río Piedras, PR 00919-0345; POB 71361, San Juan, PR 00936-8461; tel. (787) 765-7577; fax (787) 620-3521; f. 1961; fmrly Banco y Agencia de Financiamiento de la Vivienda de Puerto Rico; present name adopted in 2001; subsidiary of the Government Development Bank for Puerto Rico; finance agency; helps low-income families to purchase houses; Exec. Dir GEORGE R. JOYNER KELLY.

Commercial Banks

Banco Bilbao Vizcaya Argentaria Puerto Rico: 15th Floor, Torre BBVA, 258 Muñoz Rivera Ave, San Juan 00918; POB 364745, San Juan, PR 00936-4745; tel. (787) 777-2000; fax (787) 777-2999; internet www.bbvapr.com; f. 1967 as Banco de Mayagüez; taken over by Banco Occidental in 1979; merged with Banco Bilbao Vizcaya, S.A. in 1988; named changed from BBV Puerto Rico in 2000; cap. 138.7m., res, surplus and profits 387.5m., dep. 5,849.8m. (Dec. 2007); Pres. ANTONIO UGUINA; 65 brs.

Banco Popular de Puerto Rico: POB 362708, San Juan, PR 00936-2708; tel. (787) 724-3659; e-mail internet@bppr.com; internet www.bppr.com; f. 1893; cap. 7.0m., res, surplus and profits 1,811.0m., dep. 23,965.0m. (Dec. 2007); Chair. and CEO RICHARD L. CARRIÓN; Pres. DAVID H. CHAFEY, Jr; 195 brs.

Banco Santander Puerto Rico: Avda Ponce de León 207, Hato Rey, PR 00919; POB 362589, San Juan, PR 00936-0062; tel. (787) 759-7070; fax (787) 767-7913; e-mail jdiaz@bspr.com; internet www.santanderpr.com; f. 1976; cap. 106.2m., res, surplus and profits 504.6m., dep. 7,484.0m. (Dec. 2007); Pres. and CEO JUAN MORENO BLANCO; Chair. GONZALO DE LAS HERAS; 67 brs.

Citibank NA: Ochoa Bldg, 500 Tanca St, San Juan, PR 00901; tel. (787) 766-2323; internet www.latam.citibank.com/puertorico; 14 brs.

Doral Bank: Galería Paseos Mall, Grand Blvd Paseos, Suite 107, San Juan, PR 00926; tel. (787) 725-6060; fax (787) 725-6062; e-mail dbcw@doralbank.com; internet www.doralbank.com; cap. 400m., dep. 2,730m., assets 6,726m. (Dec. 2003); subsidiary of local bank-holding co, Doral Financial Corpn, which completed buyout negotiations with financial group, led by Bear Stearn Cos Inc (USA), in July 2007; 90% investor-owned, through Doral Holdings Delaware, LLC, since July 2007; CEO GLEN R. WAKEMAN; Chair. CALIXTO GARCÍA VELEZ; 37 brs.

FirstBank Puerto Rico: First Federal Bldg, Avda Ponce de León 1519, POB 9146, Santurce, PR 00908-0146; tel. (787) 729-8200; fax (787) 729-8139; internet www.firstbankpr.com; f. 1948, adopted current name in 1998; part of First BanCorp; cap. and res 368.3m., dep. 3,363.0m. (Dec. 2000); Chair. LUIS M. BEAUCHAMP; 45 brs.

Scotiabank de Puerto Rico: Plaza Scotiabank, Avda Ponce de León 273, esq. Calle Méjico, Hato Rey, PR 00918; POB 362230, San Juan, PR 00936-2230; tel. (787) 758-8989; fax (787) 766-7879; internet www.scotiabankpr.com; f. 1910; cap. 23.2m., res, surplus and profits 140.5m., dep. 1,354.1m. (Dec. 2007); Chair. PETER CARDINAL; Pres. and CEO TROY K. WRIGHT; 19 brs.

Savings Banks

Oriental Bank and Trust: Ave Fagot, esq. Obispado M-26, Ponce; tel. (787) 259-0000; fax (787) 259-0700; e-mail ofg@anreder.com; internet www.orientalonline.com; total assets 2,039m. (June 2001); Pres. and CEO JOSÉ ENRIQUE FERNÁNDEZ; Chair. JOSÉ J. GIL DE LAMADRID.

R & G Financial Corporation: POB 2510, Guaynabo, PR 00970; tel. (787) 766-6677; fax (787) 766-8175; internet www.rgonline.com; total assets 4,676m. (Dec. 2001); Pres. and CEO ROLANDO RODRÍGUEZ; Chair. JUAN AGOSTO-ALICEA.

Banking Organization

Puerto Rico Bankers' Association: Avda Ponce de León 208, Suite 1014, San Juan, PR 00918-1002; tel. (787) 753-8630; fax (787) 754-6022; e-mail info@abpr.com; internet www.abpr.com; Pres. RAFAEL BLANCO; Vice-Pres. JOSÉ DÍAZ.

INSURANCE

Atlantic Southern Insurance Co: POB 362889, San Juan, PR 00936-2889; tel. (787) 767-9750; fax (787) 764-4707; internet www.atlanticsouthern.com; f. 1945; Chair. DIANE BEAN SCHWARTZ; Pres. RAMÓN L. GALANES.

Caribbean American Life Assurance Co: Avda Ponce de Léon 273, Suite 1300, Scotiabank Plaza, San Juan, PR 00917; tel. (787)

250-1199; fax (787) 250-7680; internet www.calac.com; Pres. Iván C. López.

Cooperativa de Seguros Multiples de Puerto Rico: POB 363846, San Juan, PR 00936-3846; internet www.segurosmultiples.coop; general insurance; Pres. René A. Campos Carbonell.

La Cruz Azul de Puerto Rico: Carretera Estatal 1, Km 17.3, Río Piedras, San Juan, PR 00927; POB 366068, San Juan, PR 00936-6068; tel. (787) 272-9898; fax (787) 272-7867; e-mail scliente@cruzazul.com; internet www.cruzazul.com; Exec. Dir Marks Vidal.

FirstBank Insurance Agency, Inc: 1130 Muñoz Rivera Ave, POB 9146, San Juan, PR 00908-0146; tel. (787) 292-4380; fax (787) 292-4355; e-mail lymarie.torres@firstbankpr.com; internet www.firstbankpr.com; f. 2003; owned by First BanCorp; Pres. Víctor Santiago.

Great American Life Assurance Co of Puerto Rico: POB 363786, San Juan, PR 00936-3786; tel. (787) 758-4888; fax (787) 766-1985; e-mail galifepr@galifepr.com; known as General Accident Life Assurance Co until 1998; Pres. Artura Carión; Sr Vice-Pres. Edgardo Díaz.

National Insurance Co: POB 366107, San Juan, PR 00936-6107; tel. (787) 758-0909; fax (787) 756-7360; internet www.nicpr.com; f. 1961; subsidiary of National Financial Group; Chair., Pres. and CEO Carlos M. Benítez, Jr.

Pan American Life Insurance Co: POB 364865, San Juan, PR 00936-4865; tel. (787) 620-1414; fax (787) 999-1250; e-mail jortega@panamericanlife.com; internet www.panamericanlife.com; Regional Pres. Juan A. Ortega; Gen. Man. Maite Muñozguren.

Puerto Rican-American Insurance Co: POB 70333, San Juan, PR 00936-8333; tel. (787) 250-5214; fax (787) 250-5371; f. 1920; total assets 119.9m. (1993); Chair. and CEO Rafael A. Roca; Pres. Rodolfo E. Criscuolo.

Security National Life Insurance Co: POB 193309, Hato Rey, PR 00919; tel. (787) 753-6161; fax (787) 758-7409; Pres. Carlos Fernández.

Universal Insurance Group: Calle 1, Lote 10, 3°, Metro Office Park, Guaynabo; POB 2145, San Juan, PR 00922-2145; tel. (787) 793-7202; fax (787) 782-0692; internet www.universalpr.com; f. 1972; comprises Universal Insurance Co, Eastern America Insurance Agency and Caribbean Alliance Insurance Co; Chair. and CEO Luis Miranda Casañas.

There are numerous agents, representing Puerto Rican, US and foreign companies.

Trade and Industry

DEVELOPMENT ORGANIZATION

Puerto Rico Industrial Development Co (PRIDCO): POB 362350, San Juan, PR 00936-2350; Avda Roosevelt 355, Hato Rey, San Juan, PR 00918; tel. (787) 758-4747; fax (787) 764-1415; internet www.pridco.com; public agency responsible for the govt-sponsored industrial devt prog; Exec. Dir Javier Vásquez Morales.

CHAMBERS OF COMMERCE

Chamber of Commerce of Puerto Rico: 100 Calle Tetuán, Viejo San Juan, PR 00901; POB 9024033, San Juan, PR 00902-4033; tel. (787) 721-6060; fax (787) 723-1891; e-mail camarapr@camarapr.net; internet www.camarapr.org; f. 1913; Pres. Jorge Galliano; Exec. Vice-Pres. Edgardo Bigas Valladares; 1,800 mems.

Chamber of Commerce of the South of Puerto Rico: 65 Calle Isabel, POB 7455, Ponce, PR 00732-7455; tel. (787) 844-4400; fax (787) 844-4705; e-mail camarasur@prtc.net; internet www.camarasur.org; f. 1885; Pres. Mario R. Silvagnoli Guzmán; Exec. Dir Héctor E. López Palermo; 550 mems.

Chamber of Commerce of the West of Puerto Rico, Inc: Edif. Doral Bank, Of. 905, 101 Calle Méndez Vigo Oeste, POB 9, Mayagüez, PR 00680; tel. (787) 832-3749; fax (787) 832-4287; e-mail info@ccopr.com; internet www.ccopr.com; f. 1962; Pres. José A. Justiniano; 300 mems.

Puerto Rico/United Kingdom Chamber of Commerce: 1509 Lopez Landron, Suite 1100, San Juan, PR 00911; tel. (877) 721-0160; fax (787) 721-7333; e-mail iancourt1@cs.com; internet users.bivapr.net/iancourt; Chair. Dr Ian Court; 120 mems.

INDUSTRIAL AND TRADE ASSOCIATIONS

Home Builders' Association of Puerto Rico: Avda Ponce de León 1605, Condominium San Martín, Santurce, San Juan, PR 00909; tel. (787) 723-0279; Exec. Dir María Elena Cristy; 150 mems.

Pharmaceutical Industry Association of Puerto Rico (PIA-PR): City View Plaza, Suite 407, Guaynabo, PR 00968; tel. (787) 622-0500; fax (787) 622-0503; e-mail contact@piapr.com; internet www.piapr.com; Chair. Daneris Fernández; 19 mem. cos.

Puerto Rico Farm Bureau: Avda Ponce de León 1605, Suite 403, Condominium San Martín, Santurce, San Juan, PR 00909-1895; tel. (787) 721-5970; fax (787) 724-6932; f. 1925; Pres. Antonio Alvarez; over 1,500 mems.

Puerto Rico Manufacturers' Association (PRMA): Centro Internacional de Mercadeo, Torre II, Suite 702m, Carretera 165, Guaynabo, PR 00968; POB 195477, San Juan, PR 00919-5477; tel. (787) 759-9445; fax (787) 756-7670; e-mail prma_info@prma.com; internet www.prma.com; Pres. Josen Rossi; Exec. Vice-Pres. William Riefkohl.

Puerto Rico United Retailers Center: POB 190127, San Juan, PR 00919-0127; tel. (787) 641-8405; fax (787) 641-8406; e-mail cud@centrounido.com; internet www.centrounido.org; f. 1891; represents small and medium-sized businesses; Pres. Pedro L. Malave Aguiló; 20,000 mems.

UTILITIES

Electricity

Autoridad de Energía Eléctrica (AEE): POB 364267, San Juan, PR 00936-4267; tel. (787) 521-3434; fax (787) 521-4120; e-mail prensa@prepa.com; internet www.prepa.com; f. 1979; govt-owned electricity corpn; monopoly on power transmission and distribution ended in 2009; installed capacity of 4,404 MW; Exec. Dir Miguel Cordero López.

TRADE UNIONS

American Federation of Labor–Congress of Industrial Organizations (AFL–CIO): San Juan; internet www.afl-cio.org; Regional Dir Agustín Benítez; c. 60,000 mems.

Central Puertorriqueña de Trabajadores (CPT): POB 364084, San Juan, PR 00936-4084; tel. (787) 781-6649; fax (787) 277-9290; f. 1982; Pres. Federico Torres Montalvo.

Confederación General de Trabajadores de Puerto Rico: 620 San Antonio St, San Juan, PR 00907; f. 1939; Pres. Francisco Colón Gordiany; 35,000 mems.

Federación de Maestros de Puerto Rico (FMPR): Urb. El Caribe 1572, Avda Ponce de León, San Juan, PR 00926-2710; tel. (787) 766-1818; e-mail info@fmprlucha.org; internet www.fmprlucha.org; teachers' union; Pres. Rafael Feliciano.

Federación del Trabajo de Puerto Rico (AFL-CIO): POB S-1648, San Juan, PR 00903; tel. (787) 722-4012; f. 1952; Pres. Hipólito Marcano; Sec.-Treas. Clifford W. Depin; 200,000 mems.

Puerto Rico Industrial Workers' Union, Inc: POB 22014, UPR Station, San Juan, PR 00931; Pres. David Muñoz Hernández.

Sindicato Empleados de Equipo Pesado, Construcción y Ramas Anexas de Puerto Rico, Inc (Construction and Allied Trades Union): Calle Hicaco 95, Urb. Milaville, Río Piedras, San Juan, PR 00926; f. 1954; Pres. Jesús M. Agosto; 950 mems.

Sindicato de Obreros Unidos del Sur de Puerto Rico (United Workers' Union of South Puerto Rico): POB 106, Salinas, PR 00751; f. 1961; Pres. José Caraballo; 52,000 mems.

Unión General de Trabajadores de Puerto Rico: Apdo 29247, Estación de Infantería, Río Piedras, San Juan, PR 00929; tel. (787) 751-5350; fax (787) 751-7604; f. 1965; Pres. Juan G. Eliza-Colón; Sec.-Treas. Osvaldo Romero-Pizarro.

Unión de Trabajadores de la Industría Eléctrica y Riego de Puerto Rico (UTIER): POB 13068, Santurce, San Juan, PR 00908; tel. (787) 721-1700; e-mail utier@coqui.net; internet www.utier.org; Pres. Ricardo Santos Ramos; 6,000 mems.

Transport

RAILWAYS

In 2004 a 17-km urban railway (Tren Urbano), capable of carrying some 300,000 passengers per day, was inaugurated in greater San Juan. The railway took eight years to build and cost some US $2,150m. In 2007 plans were announced for a light-rail line to connect the urban area of Caguas with the Tren Urbano system, at a cost of US $450m. By mid-2011 construction on the project had still not commenced.

Alternativa de Transporte Integrado (ATI) (Integrated Transportation Alternative): San Juan; internet www.ati.gobierno.pr; govt agency; operates the Tren Urbano railway system.

Ponce and Guayama Railway: Aguirre, PR 00608; tel. (787) 853-3810; owned by the Corporación Azucarera de Puerto Rico; transports sugar cane over 96 km of track route; Exec. Dir A. Martínez; Gen. Supt J. Rodríguez.

ROADS

The road network totalled 26,186 km (16,271 miles) in 2009, of which some 94% was paved. A modern highway system links all cities and towns along the coast and cross-country. A highways authority oversees the design and construction of roads, highways and bridges.

Autoridad de Carreteras: Centro Gobierno Roberto Sánchez Vilella, Edif. Sur Avda de Diego 328, POB 42007, Santurce, San Juan, PR 00940-2007; tel. (787) 721-8787; fax (787) 727-5456; internet www.dtop.gov.pr/act; f. 1965; Exec. Dir LUIS TRINIDAD GARAY.

SHIPPING

There are 11 major ports on the island, the principal ones being San Juan, Ponce and Mayagüez. Other ports include Guayama, Guayanilla, Guánica, Yabucoa, Aguirre, Aguadilla, Fajardo, Arecibo, Humacao and Arroyo. San Juan, one of the finest and longest all-weather natural harbours in the Caribbean, is the main port of entry for foodstuffs and raw materials and for shipping finished industrial products. In 2009/10 it handled 7.9m. short tons of cargo. Under US cabotage laws all maritime freight traffic between the USA and Puerto Rico must be conducted using US-registered vessels. Passenger traffic is limited to tourist cruise vessels. Work on the US $84.4m. Port of the Americas 'megaport' was ongoing in 2011.

Autoridad de los Puertos (Puerto Rico Ports Authority): Calle Lindbergh, 64 Antigua Base Naval Miramar, San Juan, PR 00907; POB 362829, San Juan, PR 00936-2829; tel. (787) 723-2260; fax (787) 722-7867; e-mail webmaster@prpa.gobierno.pr; internet www.prpa.gobierno.pr; f. 1942 as the Autoridad de Transporte de Puerto Rico; present name adopted in 1955; manages and administers all ports and airports; Exec. Dir ALBERTO ESCUDERO MORALES.

CIVIL AVIATION

There are two international airports on the island (Luis Muñoz Marín at Carolina, San Juan, and Rafael Hernández at Aguadilla) and nine regional airports. There are also six heliports. In late 2010 the Government announced plans to transfer the management of Luis Muñoz Marín airport to the private sector in 2011.

Tourism

An estimated 3.6m. tourists visited Puerto Rico in 2008/09. In addition, there were an estimated 1.2m. excursionists. Almost 85% of all tourist visitors were from the US mainland. Tourism revenue was estimated at US $3,473m. in 2008/09. In 2010 there were approximately 12,000 guest rooms.

Compañía de Turismo (Puerto Rico Tourism Co): Edif. La Princesa, 2 Paseo La Princesa, POB 9023960, San Juan, PR 00902-3960; tel. (787) 721-2400; fax (787) 722-6238; e-mail drodriguez2@prtourism.com; internet www.gotopuertorico.com; f. 1970; Exec. Dir TERESTELLA GONZÁLEZ DENTON.

Puerto Rico Hotel & Tourism Association (PRHTA): Avda Ponce de León 165, Suite 301, San Juan, PR 00917-1233; tel. (787) 758-8001; fax (787) 758-8091; e-mail mtosses@prhta.org; internet www.prhta.org; more than 550 corporate mems; Pres. and CEO CLARISA JIMÉNEZ.

Defence

The USA is responsible for the defence of Puerto Rico. In 2003 the US Navy withdrew from Puerto Rico closing its bases at Roosevelt Roads and on the island of Vieques. Puerto Rico has a paramilitary National Guard of some 11,000 men, which is funded mainly by the US Department of Defense. The National Guard has served under US command in Iraq and has also been deployed to support domestic police operations.

Education

The public education system is centrally administered by the Department of Education. Education is compulsory for children between six and 16 years of age. In 2005/06 there were an estimated 563,490 pupils attending public day schools, and in 2009/10 there were an estimated 99,817 pupils attending private schools. The 12-year curriculum, beginning at five years of age, is subdivided into six grades of elementary school, three years at junior high school and three years at senior high school. Vocational schools at the high-school level and kindergartens also form part of the public education system. Instruction is conducted in Spanish, but English is a required subject at all levels. In 2004 there were five universities. The State University system consists of three principal campuses and six regional colleges. In 2005/06 there were some 67,990 students enrolled in higher education at public institutes (in addition, a further 33,463 were attending adult education courses), while 29,773 pupils were enrolled in private post-secondary institutions in 2009/10. In 2007/08 some US $4,432.9m. of general government expenditure was allocated to education (24.2% of total expenditure).

UNITED STATES EXTERNAL TERRITORIES

The External or Unincorporated Territories of the USA comprise the Pacific Territories of American Samoa and Guam, the Caribbean Territory of the US Virgin Islands, and a number of smaller islands.

AMERICAN SAMOA

Introductory Survey

LOCATION, CLIMATE, LANGUAGE, RELIGION, FLAG, CAPITAL

American Samoa comprises the seven islands of Tutuila, Ta'u, Olosega, Ofu, Aunu'u, Rose and Swains. They lie in the southern central Pacific Ocean, along latitude 14°S at about longitude 170°W, about 3,700 km (2,300 miles) south-west of Hawaii. The temperature normally ranges between 21°C (70°F) and 32°C (90°F), and the average annual rainfall is 5,000 mm (197 ins), the greatest precipitation occurring between December and March. English and Samoan, a Polynesian language, are spoken. The population is largely Christian, more than 50% being members of the Congregational Christian Church. The flag has a dark blue field, on which is superimposed a red-edged white triangle (with its apex at the hoist and its base at the outer edge of the flag), containing an eagle, representing the USA, grasping in its talons a yellow *fue* (staff) and *uatogi* (club), Samoan symbols of sovereignty. The capital is Pago Pago, on Tutuila (the officially designated seat of government is the village of Fagatogo).

CONTEMPORARY POLITICAL HISTORY

Historical Context

The Samoan islands were first visited by Europeans in the 1700s, but it was not until 1830 that missionaries from the London Missionary Society settled there. In 1878 the Kingdom of Samoa, then an independent state, gave the USA the right to establish a naval base at Pago Pago. The islands were also of interest to the United Kingdom and Germany, but the former withdrew in 1899, leaving the western islands for Germany to govern. The chiefs of the eastern islands ceded their lands to the USA in 1904, and the islands officially became an Unincorporated Territory of the USA in 1922.

Domestic Political Affairs

Until 1978 American Samoa was administered by a Governor, appointed by the US Government, with a legislature comprising the Senate and the House of Representatives. In November 1977 American Samoa's first gubernatorial election took place, and in January 1978 Peter Tali Coleman of the Republican Party, who had previously served in the position between 1956 and 1961, was inaugurated as the islands' first directly elected Governor. He was re-elected for a further term in November 1980, after three years in office instead of the prescribed four, in order to allow synchronization with mainland US elections in 1980. At the gubernatorial election of November 1984 A. P. Lutali of the Democratic Party was elected Governor and Eni Hunkin (who subsequently adopted the use of his chiefly name, Faleomavaega) became Lieutenant-Governor. The High Court of American Samoa had previously ruled that Coleman was ineligible to stand for election to a third successive term as Governor, as legislation restricted tenure by any individual to two successive terms. In October 1986 a constitutional convention completed a comprehensive redrafting of the American Samoan Constitution. However, the draft revision had yet to be submitted to the US Congress in the early 21st century. In April 2004 it was announced that the Political Status Study Commission was to examine the Territory's situation; the Commission concluded its investigations in 2006 and published a final report detailing its recommendations in January 2007. A series of constitutional conventions was subsequently held, most recently in mid-2010, at which proposed amendments to the Constitution were discussed—see below.

Meanwhile, American Samoa continued to be represented in the federal legislature by a non-voting delegate, the first election for this post having been held in 1981. The islands' Delegate was permitted to vote in committee but not on the floor of the US House of Representatives. In July 1988 the Territory's Delegate in Washington, DC, Fofo Sunia, announced that he would not seek re-election, as he was under official investigation for alleged financial mismanagement. In October he received a prison sentence for fraud. Eni Faleomavaega replaced Sunia as American Samoa's Delegate to the US House of Representatives in November. At the gubernatorial election held in November 1988 Republican Peter Coleman was returned to office for a third term as Governor, and Galea'i Poumele replaced Faleomavaega as Lieutenant-Governor. However, at the next gubernatorial election conducted in November 1992 Peter Coleman was defeated by A. P. Lutali. At elections to the House of Representatives in November 1994 about one-third of those members seeking re-election were defeated. Faleomavaega was re-elected as non-voting Delegate.

At gubernatorial and legislative elections in November 1996 only eight of the 18 members seeking re-election to the Fono (legislature) were successful. At a second round of voting the incumbent Lieutenant-Governor, the Democrat Tauese Sunia, was elected Governor with 51.3% of the votes cast, defeating Lealaifuaneva Peter Reid, Jr, who secured 48.7% of votes. Eni Faleomavaega was re-elected as Delegate to the US House of Representatives.

The decision in July 1997 by the Government of neighbouring Western Samoa to change the country's name to simply Samoa caused some controversy. Legislation approved in March 1998 by the Territory's House of Representatives stated that American Samoa should not recognize the new name, which was viewed by many islanders as serving to undermine their own Samoan identity. Also in response to the change of name, legislation prohibiting citizens of the former Western Samoa from owning land in American Samoa was approved. Nevertheless, some rapprochement followed. In August 2004 plans were announced for greater economic co-operation, and in November a twice-weekly air link commenced operations. However, concerns were expressed at the decision of the Samoan Government in March 2005 to require of American Samoan citizens travelling to Samoa a permit and a passport. In April a bilateral meeting was held in the Samoan capital, and leaders began negotiations on the issue of travel requirements. Meanwhile, in late March the Samoan Government announced plans to open a consulate in American Samoa; the consulate duly opened in mid-2006.

Meanwhile, in November 1998 Eni Faleomavaega was re-elected as the islands' Delegate to the US House of Representatives. At elections held on 7 November 2000 Democrat Tauese Sunia was narrowly re-elected as Governor, receiving 50.7% of the votes cast, compared with 47.9% for the independent candidate, Senator Lealaifuaneva. However, following the Chief Electoral Officer's refusal to allow a recount, as requested by Lealaifuaneva (who claimed that absentee ballots had not been properly handled), Lealaifuaneva filed a lawsuit against the Government; this was dismissed by the High Court in December. At the US congressional elections, held concurrently, no candidate received the necessary 50% majority, Eni Faleomavaega winning 45.7% of votes cast, compared with 30.3% for Gus Hannemann. A second round of polling took place on 21 November, when Faleomavaega was reported to have won 61.1% of the votes.

In September 2001 the islands' Senate approved a resolution urging discussion with the US Government with regard to the conferral of limited federal jurisdiction to the High Court of American Samoa, the only US territory without a sitting federal judge. A congressional public survey, conducted in the same month, registered wide popular support for a Federal Court and Public Prosecutor. At a meeting of the UN General Assembly in January 2002, the UN accepted American Samoa's request of May 2001 to be removed from the list of colonized territories. The Governor had sent a resolution to the UN Committee on Decolonization affirming American Samoa's wish to remain a US territory.

In September 2002 the Territory's immigration procedures were amended to give the Attorney-General, rather than the Immigration Board, the ultimate authority to grant permanent residency status to aliens. The House of Representatives of American Samoa also approved a resolution to repeal legislation automatically conferring US citizenship in the Territory to foreign parents. In the same month the Territory's intelligence agencies claimed that the Speaker of the House of Representatives, Tuanaitau Tuia, had used public funds to purchase a car and to finance private travel for his wife. Meanwhile, in June a former president of the Amerika Samoa Bank (now ANZ Amerika Samoa Bank) was convicted of fraud for his involvement in a scheme that had misappropriated US $75m. of investors' money. Further allegations of corruption in the banking sector followed in 2004.

In elections for American Samoa's Delegate to the US House of Representatives on 6 November 2002, Eni Faleomavaega won 41.3% of the votes cast, Fagafaga Daniel Langkilde secured 32.1% and Aumua Amata Coleman won 26.6%. Since none of the candidates received the requisite 50% of votes, Faleomavaega and Langkilde entered a second round of voting on 19 November, at which Faleomavaega secured an eighth term in office. In March 2003 Governor Tauese Sunia died while en route to Hawaii for medical treatment; Lieutenant-Governor Togiola Tulafono replaced him and appointed Ipulasi Aitofele Sunia, the late Governor's younger brother, as his deputy.

In December 2002 legislation was introduced that prohibited nationals of 23 countries deemed to present a terrorist threat from entering the Territory, unless they were granted special permission. Opposition groups in Fiji expressed their displeasure at the inclusion of their country on the list, owing to its large Muslim population.

In January 2003 the Senate approved a motion to begin expulsion hearings against Senator Faamausili Pola. Members of the chamber had already voted to remove him in September 2002, when it was alleged that he had not been elected according to Samoan tradition. In March 2003 it was reported that the South Korean owner of the Daewoosa Samoa clothing factory, Kil Soo Lee, had been convicted by a US court of trafficking in humans. (In July 2005 Lee was sentenced to 40 years' imprisonment; he subsequently appealed against his conviction, arguing that the USA did not have jurisdiction in American Samoa, but his appeal was dismissed in December 2006.) The mainly Vietnamese and Chinese factory employees had reportedly received very low wages, and their working conditions were described as appalling. The American Samoan High Court had previously ordered Daewoosa to pay workers US $3.5m. in compensation and fined the company an additional $290,000 in April 2002. In March 2004 Governor Tulafono announced plans for legislation that would allow prosecution of human-trafficking offences in the Territory, although little was immediately achieved to this end. In October 2009, however, a bill was introduced in the US Senate that, if approved, would finally render human-trafficking, as well as involuntary labour, a felony crime in American Samoa. At mid-2011 the bill remained pending, but it was hoped that it might be approved by the end of the year.

At the gubernatorial election held on 2 November 2004 incumbent Governor Togiola Tulafono of the Democratic Party received 48.4% of the votes cast in the first round of polling, while Afoa Moega Lutu obtained 39.4%. At the second round of voting, conducted on 16 November, Tulafono was re-elected, having secured 55.7% of the votes; Moega Lutu received 44.3%.

In October 2006 the minimum hourly wage for five industry categories was increased by between seven and nine cents. However, plans to raise the hourly rate for the cannery sector encountered strong opposition from the business community and from the Government itself, which argued that the decision would adversely affect companies' cost effectiveness. The tuna-canning industry, as the greatest source of revenue for the islands, was consequently able to exert significant pressure on wage levels. However, supporters of the decision pressed for a greater increase in order to attract and retain employees. Minimum wage legislation was brought under federal control in 2007, when it was envisaged that the minimum wage in the Territory would increase to US $7.25 per hour by 2014. This rise was to be implemented in phases, with variations among industries. A US delegation visited American Samoa in October 2010 on a fact-finding mission to investigate the effects of minimum wage increases on local residents and businesses.

Eni Faleomavaega, the incumbent Delegate to the US House of Representatives, was re-elected for an unprecedented 10th two-year term in office in November 2006, defeating his closest rival, Aumua Amata Coleman, by just 702 votes of the total of 11,033 cast. In February 2008 the Territory's House of Representatives endorsed an amendment to the Constitution that sought to confer ultimate legislative authority to the Fono in the event of the Governor's use of the veto.

The first stage of the gubernatorial election was held on 4 November 2008, when none of the four candidates obtained the requisite 50% of the votes cast to secure office. The second stage of the election therefore took place on 18 November and resulted in the re-election of incumbent Governor Togiola Tulafono, who received 6,590 votes, in comparison with the 5,084 votes received by rival candidate Utu Abe Malae. In the concurrent legislative election conducted on 4 November eight incumbents were re-elected to the Fono, including Speaker Savali Talavou, while the islands' only two female legislators lost their seats. Also held on 4 November was the election to determine American Samoa's Delegate to the US House of Representatives. Eni Faleomavaega was re-elected for an 11th consecutive term. American Samoan voters also participated in a referendum, coinciding with the elections of 4 November, on the issue of an amendment to the Constitution proposing to empower the Fono to overrule the Governor's power of veto; however, this was defeated by a narrow margin of only 22 votes.

A four-member delegation was dispatched to American Samoa by the US General Accountability Office in January 2010, with the explicit objective of identifying potential risks for American Samoa and the rest of the USA arising from existing customs and immigrations policies and practices. However, it was feared by some in the Territory that the visit was indicative of an intention on the part of the federal Government eventually to take control of American Samoa's customs and immigration systems.

During a forum on the subject of constitutional change in March 2010 Governor Tulafono expressed his personal belief that American Samoa would better benefit from the sort of relationship with the USA held by Palau under the latter's Compact of Free Association; the Governor noted that Palau's system of 'autonomous governance' allowed it to seek foreign aid, while American Samoa was able to seek only US funding, which, he argued, was an obstacle to the islands' development. A two-week constitutional convention was held in June–July, during which proposed amendments to the Constitution were discussed. The convention endorsed a series of proposals, including a new stipulation that members of the Fono should be US nationals of American Samoan ancestry, a proposal that provoked considerable censure owing to its perceived discriminatory and unconstitutional nature.

At a popular referendum held concurrently with legislative elections on 2 November 2010, the proposed amendments were rejected by a majority of voters: 7,410 voted against and 3,149 voted in favour of the changes. The handling of the referendum attracted considerable criticism; voters were given the option only to reject or to approve the entire list of proposed constitutional amendments, rather than being able to express an opinion on each individual proposal. In the legislative poll, six new representatives were elected to the Fono, while Speaker Savali Talavou was among those incumbents re-elected; Talavouwas re-elected as Speaker by the Fono in January 2011. Meanwhile, in an election for American Samoa's Delegate to the US House of Representatives, held concurrently with the legislative elections of November 2010, Eni Faleomavaega was re-elected, to a 12th consecutive term. In mid-November US Secretary of State Hillary Clinton made a brief official visit to Pago Pago at the end of a tour of the Asia-Pacific region; during her stay, Clinton acknowledged the 'close relationship' between the USA and American Samoa, and expressed appreciation for the 'long and noble history of sacrifice' by American Samoans serving within the US military. Clinton also expressed support for American Samoan hopes of securing membership of the Pacific Islands Forum (see p. 413).

In January 2011 the US House of Representatives voted to rescind the 'symbolic' voting rights of territorial delegates in the 'Committee of the Whole House on the State of the Union', a means whereby the House was able to expedite consideration of certain legislation, particularly amendments. Faleomavaega joined with the Delegates from Guam, the Northern Mariana Islands, the District of Columbia, Puerto Rico and the Virgin Islands to express opposition to the revocation of the privilege, arguing that American Samoans 'fight and die in disproportionate numbers in defence of our nation' and that the revocation of the territorial delegates' symbolic voting rights 'dishonours their service and demeans their sacrifice'. A few days later Democrats introduced a resolution to the House seeking to restore the territorial delegates' symbolic voting rights.

Corruption Issues

During 2003 several allegations of official corruption were made against government officials. In September an employee of the Territory's Office of Procurement was allowed to return to work despite a recent conviction in an insurance fraud case. In the same month the Senate ordered an official investigation into contracts awarded by Tafua Faau Seumanutafa, the Chief Procurement Officer, and senior officials from the Department of Health and Social Security and the Department of Education. In May 2004 Seumanutafa pleaded guilty in the Hawaii Federal District Court to one count of conspiracy to defraud the US Government, in a case that also implicated senior officials from the Department of Health and Social Security and the Department of Education. Also in May the Senate Select Investigative Committee issued subpoenas to several senators to testify in relation to alleged corruption in the allocation of government contracts. In September the Committee recommended that, while under investigation for alleged corruption, Lieutenant-Governor Ipulasi Aitofele Sunia be placed on leave and have his name removed from the list of candidates for the forthcoming gubernatorial election. Governor Tulafono claimed that the charges were politically motivated.

Meanwhile, in February 2004 the US Federal Bureau of Investigation (FBI) began an investigation into the alleged misuse of US government funds. In March 2005 the FBI effected an unannounced search of the government offices in Pago Pago, forbidding entry to the Governor, Lieutenant-Governor and Attorney-General for the duration of the operation. In mid-March the Government announced its intention to challenge the legality of the search warrants. In October

UNITED STATES EXTERNAL TERRITORIES

Dr Sili K. Sataua and Patolo Mageo, the former Directors of the Education and Human Resources Departments, respectively, were sentenced in a federal court in Honolulu, Hawaii, to custodial sentences following their conviction on corruption charges. In September 2007 Lieutenant-Governor Ipulasi Aitofele Sunia and Senator Tulifua Tini Lam Yuen were detained on federal charges of fraud, bribery and obstruction in relation to business transactions involving the Department of Education. Their trial commenced in January 2010 in the US federal court in Washington, DC. A mistrial was declared in February owing to the jury's inability to reach a unanimous verdict, and in April the federal court officially granted the US Department of Justice's motion to dismiss criminal charges against both men.

Natural Phenomena

The islands remained vulnerable to adverse weather phenomena. In May 2003 severe flooding and landslides led to the deaths of five people, and in the following month US President George W. Bush declared American Samoa a federal disaster area. In January 2004 a state of emergency was declared when a cyclone damaged the islands. The USA allocated US $12.5m. towards the relief effort. In February 2005 Cyclone Olaf caused extensive damage to the Territory's Manu'a islands, destroying numerous buildings and interrupting electricity supplies. An estimated 70 homes were destroyed in Manu'a, while some 200 houses suffered major damage. The islands' Governor subsequently declared a state of emergency. In early October 2009 US President Barack Obama declared both American Samoa and Samoa a federal disaster area, following a tsunami at the end of September, which had been caused by a massive submarine earthquake in the region of the Samoan islands; combined, the earthquake and tsunami resulted in 187 confirmed fatalities (34 in American Samoa, 149 in Samoa and four in Tonga) and caused extensive damage to properties and infrastructure.

CONSTITUTION AND GOVERNMENT

Executive power is vested in the Governor, who is elected by popular vote and has authority that extends to all operations within the Territory of American Samoa. The Governor has the power of veto with respect to legislation approved by the Fono (Legislature). The Fono comprises the Senate and the House of Representatives, with a President and a Speaker presiding over their respective divisions. The Senate is composed of 18 members, elected, according to Samoan custom, from local chiefs, or Matai, for a term of four years. The House of Representatives consists of 20 members, who are elected by popular vote for a term of two years, and a non-voting delegate from Swains Island. The Fono meets twice a year, in January and July, for not more than 45 days, and at such special sessions as the Governor may call. The Governor, who serves a four-year term, has the authority to appoint heads of government departments with the approval of the Fono. The islands' non-voting Delegate to the US House of Representatives is elected every two years.

REGIONAL AND INTERNATIONAL CO-OPERATION

American Samoa is a member of the Pacific Community (see p. 410), and is an associate member of the UN's Economic and Social Commission for Asia and the Pacific (ESCAP, see p. 37).

ECONOMIC AFFAIRS

In 2000, according to estimates by the American Samoa National Income and Product Accounts Task Force, American Samoa's gross national income (GNI), measured at constant 1999 prices, was about US $348.6m., equivalent to some $6,332 per head. Between 1973 and 1985, it was estimated, GNI increased, in real terms, at an average rate of 1.7% per year, with real GNI per head rising by only 0.1% per year. Gross domestic product (GDP) was estimated (at constant 1999 prices and allowing for statistical discrepancy) in 1999 at $444.2m. and in 2000 at $437.9m. In 2005, according to estimates by the Secretariat of the Pacific Community, American Samoa's GDP was $558.8m., equivalent to $9,041 per head. In 2000–09 the population increased by an average of 1.7% per year.

Agriculture, hunting, forestry and fishing engaged 28% of the total labour force in 2011, according to FAO estimates. According to estimates by the American Samoa National Income and Product Accounts Task Force, the sector (excluding fish-processing) accounted for 11.3% of GDP in 2002. Agricultural production provides little surplus for export. Major crops are coconuts, bananas, taro, pineapples, yams and breadfruit. Local fisheries are at subsistence level, but tuna-canning plants at Pago Pago process fish from US, Taiwanese and South Korean vessels. Canned tuna constituted some 98.4% of export revenue in 2005/06, when earnings reached US $431.5m.

Within the industrial sector, manufacturing activities engaged 35.3% of the employed labour force in 2000. Fish-canning is the dominant industry; in 2001 some 70% of those employed in these factories were guest workers from Samoa (formerly Western Samoa). According to official estimates, basic employment in fish-processing increased from 1,300 workers in 1975 to 4,546 in 2005. According to estimates by the American Samoa National Income and Product Accounts Task Force, fish-processing accounted for 22.3% of GDP in 2002. Other manufacturing activities include garment-manufacturing, meat-canning, handicrafts, dairy-farming, orchid-farming, and the production of soap, perfume, paper products and alcoholic beverages. The construction sector engaged 6.4% of the employed labour force in 2000.

Service industries engage a majority of the employed labour force in American Samoa (55.2% in 2000), and the sector contributed an estimated 51.5% of GDP in 2002, according to estimates by the American Samoa National Income and Product Accounts Task Force. The Government, supported by federal government grants, engaged almost 20% of all employed workers in 2005, according to official estimates. The tourist industry is developing slowly, and earned some US $10m. in 1998, although the number of tourist arrivals declined from 44,158 in 2000 to 25,347 in 2006. Of those, 44.6% were from Samoa, while 27.8% originated from the USA and 12.7% from New Zealand. The total number of tourist arrivals was reported to have decreased from 30,705 in 2009 to 29,060 in 2010.

In 2005/06 American Samoa recorded a visible trade deficit of US $140.7m. Most of American Samoa's trade is conducted with the USA (which supplied almost 40% of total imports). Other trading partners in 2005/06 included New Zealand (excluding items imported by the Government and goods by the fish-canning sector) and Singapore.

A fiscal deficit of US $10,484m. was recorded in the year to September 2006. The Government's proposed budget for 2008/09 budget represented an increase of 12% in comparison with the previous year's expenditure. The annual rate of inflation averaged 3.9% in 2000–06. Consumer prices increased by an average of 2.9% in 2006. An estimated 10.5% of the total labour force were unemployed in 2003.

Economic development has been hindered by the islands' remote location and the limited infrastructure. A controversial minimum wage structure, whereby American Samoa's minimum hourly rates of pay were considerably lower than the mainland USA, was largely attributed to the presence of the two tuna-canning plants, which together provided employment for almost one-half of the islands' labour force, thus exerting substantial influence over the setting of wage levels. However, the remit of US minimum wage legislation was extended to American Samoa from 2007. In December 2009 US President Barack Obama signed legislation postponing from May 2010 until September the implementation of the minimum wage increase. The closure of the COS Samoa Packing plant in September 2009, which resulted in the loss of about 2,000 jobs, together with retrenchment at the other tuna cannery, StarKist Samoa, had a major impact on the economy. In October 2010, however, agreement was reached on the sale of the COS plant to a US company, TriMarine, and in early 2011 fish-processing operations there were in the process of being resumed. Furthermore, by April 2011 the workforce of StarKist was reported to have been expanded to 2,000, supported by government tax concessions. In March 2009 it was announced that American Samoa was to receive US $19m. in federal economic stimulus funding, most of which was to be used to promote the conservation of energy in the islands. Economic assistance of $10.3m. was approved by the Federal Emergency Management Agency (FEMA) in February 2010, to facilitate the reconstruction of damaged public infrastructure following a devastating earthquake and tsunami in September 2009. In March 2011 it was reported that a newly endorsed 2% increase in personal income tax, being introduced in an attempt to reduce the government deficit, was to be backdated to 1 January. In addition to the regular flights from Hawaii, the launch by America West Jets of a new twice-weekly service between the US city of Los Angeles and Pago Pago, scheduled for late 2011, was expected to provide local employment opportunities, as well as attract more tourists to the islands.

PUBLIC HOLIDAYS

2012 (provisional): 2 January (for New Year's Day), 16 January (Martin Luther King Day), 20 February (Presidents' Day), 16 April (for Flag Day, commemorating the first raising of the US flag in American Samoa), 28 May (Memorial Day), 4 July (Independence Day), 3 September (Labor Day), 8 October (Columbus Day), 12 November (for Veterans' Day), 22 November (Thanksgiving Day), 25 December (Christmas Day).

Statistical Survey

Source (unless otherwise indicated): Statistics Division, Department of Commerce, Pago Pago, AS 96799; tel. 633-5155; fax 633-4195; internet www.spc.int/prism/Country/AS/ASindex.html.

AREA AND POPULATION

Area: 201 sq km (77.6 sq miles); *By Island* (sq km): Tutuila 137; Ta'u 46; Ofu 7; Olosega 5; Swains Island (Olohenga) 3; Aunu'u 2; Rose 1.

UNITED STATES EXTERNAL TERRITORIES

American Samoa

Population: 46,773 at census of 1 April 1990; 57,291 (males 29,264, females 28,027) at census of 1 April 2000. *By Island* (2000): Tutuila 55,400; Manu'a District (Ta'u, Olosega and Ofu islands) 1,378; Aunu'u 476; Swains Island (Olohenga) 37. *Mid-2011* (Secretariat of the Pacific Community estimate): 66,692 (Source: Pacific Regional Information System).

Density (mid-2011): 331.8 per sq km.

Population by Age and Sex (Secretariat of the Pacific Community estimates at mid-2011): *0–14:* 23,089 (males 11,947, females 11,142); *15–64:* 40,524 (males 20,643, females 19,881); *65 and over:* 3,080 (males 1,445, females 1,635); *Total* 66,692 (males 34,035, females 32,657) (Source: Pacific Regional Information System).

Ethnic Groups (2000 census): Samoan 50,545; part-Samoan 1,991; Asian 1,631; Tongan 1,598; Total (incl. others) 57,291.

Principal Towns (population at 2000 census): Tafuna 8,409; Nu'uuli 5,154; Pago Pago (capital) 4,278; Leone 3,568; Ili'ili 2,513.

Births, Marriages and Deaths (2006): Registered live births 1,442 (birth rate 21.6 per 1,000); Registered marriages 171; Registered deaths 267 (death rate 4.0 per 1,000). *2010:* Registered live births 1,542 (birth rate 23.5 per 1,000); Registered deaths 294 (death rate 4.5 per 1,000).

Life Expectancy (years at birth, 2007): 75.9 (Males 71.8; Females 80.3).

Economically Active Population (persons aged 16 years and over, 2000 census): Agriculture, hunting, forestry, fishing and mining 517; Manufacturing 5,900; Construction 1,066; Trade, restaurants and hotels 2,414; Transport, storage, communications and utilities 1,036; Financing, insurance, real estate and business services 311; Community, social and personal services 5,474; *Total employed* 16,718 (males 9,804, females 6,914); Unemployed 909 (males 494, females 415); *Total labour force* 17,627 (males 10,298, females 7,329) (Source: US Department of Commerce, *2000 Census of Population and Housing*). *2003* (estimates): Total employed 14,319; Unemployed 1,681; Total labour force 16,000 (Source: US Department of State). *2005* (official estimates): Basic employment 8,428 (Fish-processing 4,546, Government employment—supported by federal grants 3,282, Other 600); Non-basic employment 8,916; Total employment 17,344. *Mid-2011* (estimates): Agriculture, etc. 8,000; Total labour force 29,000 (Source: FAO).

AGRICULTURE, ETC.

Principal Crops ('000 metric tons, 2008, FAO estimates): Coconuts 4.7; Taro 9.0; Bananas 0.8. Note: No data were available for 2009.

Livestock (year ending September 2008, FAO estimates): Pigs 10,500; Cattle 110; Chickens 40,000. Note: No data were available for 2009.

Livestock Products (metric tons, 2009, unless otherwise indicated, FAO estimates): Pig meat 315; Chicken meat 24; Cows' milk 24; Hen eggs 30 (2008).

Fishing (metric tons, live weight, 2008): Total catch 4,451 (Albacore 3,589; Yellowfin tuna 336; Wahoo 135; Bigeye tuna 136).

Source: FAO.

INDUSTRY

Production (2007): Electric energy 196 million kWh. Source: UN Industrial Commodity Statistics Database.

FINANCE

Currency and Exchange Rates: United States currency is used: 100 cents = 1 United States dollar (US $). *Sterling and Euro Equivalents* (31 December 2010): £1 sterling = US $1.565; €1 = US $1.336; US $100 = £63.88 = €74.84.

Federal Direct Expenditures (US $ million, year ending September 2009): Retirement and disability payments 58; Grants 213; Total (incl. others) 368 (Source: US Census Bureau, *Consolidated Federal Funds Report*).

Budget (US $ '000, year ending September 2005): *Revenue:* Taxes 50,397; Licences and permits 1,160; Intergovernmental 111,783; Charges for services 8,438; Fines and fees 1,869; Total (incl. others) 182,015. *Expenditure:* General government 45,555; Public safety 11,827; Public works 5,801; Health and recreation 31,952; Education and culture 65,881; Economic development 20,083; Capital projects 7,411; Debt-servicing 3,989; Total 192,499.

Cost of Living (Consumer Price Index; base: 2000 = 100): All items (excl. rent) 116.1 in 2004; 122.1 in 2005; 125.7 in 2006. Source: ILO.

Gross Domestic Product (US $ million at current prices): 550 in 2005; 548 in 2006; 532 in 2007 (Source: Bureau of Economic Analysis, US Department of Commerce).

Expenditure on the Gross Domestic Product (US $ million at current prices, 2007): Government consumption expenditure and gross investment 229; Personal consumption expenditure 369; Private fixed investment 20; Change in private inventories –29; *Total domestic expenditure* 589; Exports of goods and services 511; *Less* Imports of goods and services 567; *GDP in purchasers' values* 532 (Source: Bureau of Economic Analysis, US Department of Commerce).

Gross Domestic Product by Economic Activity (US $ million at current prices, 2002): Agriculture and fishing (excl. fish-processing) 54.3; Fish-processing 107.3; Wholesale and retail trade 36.6; Government services 100.0; Other services 111.3; Other non-services 71.9; *Total* 481.4. Note: Recorded accounts are not available; figures represent the findings of the American Samoa National Income and Product Accounts Task Force, established to produce reliable economic statistics for the territory.

EXTERNAL TRADE

Principal Commodities (US $ million): *Imports* (excl. government purchases and cannery goods, year ending September 2006): Food 141.3 (Fish 74.4); Fuel and oil 35.8 (Diesel fuel 14.4); Textiles and clothing 6.6; Machinery and transport equipment 21.8 (Road motor vehicles and parts 13.7); Miscellaneous manufactured articles 113.7 (Tin plates 48.0); Construction materials 17.5; Total (incl. others) 341.5. *Exports:* Total exports 438.5 (Canned tuna 431.5; Pet food 7).

Principal Trading Partners (US $ million, year ending September 2006): *Imports* (excl. government purchases and cannery goods): Australia 8.4; Fiji 22.5; Japan 2.0; Korea, Republic 21.2; New Zealand 31.1; Samoa 17.0; Singapore 27.2; USA 133.4; Total (incl. others) 341.5. *Exports:* Total 438.5 (almost entirely to the USA).

TRANSPORT

Road Traffic ('000 registered motor vehicles, year ending September 2006): Passenger cars 7.8; Total 9.2.

International Sea-borne Shipping (freight traffic, '000 metric tons, year ending September 2006): Goods loaded 148; Goods unloaded 400.

Civil Aviation (Pago Pago Int. Airport, year ending September 2006): Flights 4,344; Passengers (excl. transit) 157,023 (Boarding 81,907, Disembarking 75,116); Transit 385; Freight and mail ('000 lb): Loaded 3,893, Unloaded 3,939.

TOURISM

Tourist Arrivals by Country (2006): Australia 950; China, People's Republic 439; Fiji 345; New Zealand 3,224; Philippines 230; Samoa 11,313; Tonga 450; United Kingdom 148; USA 7,037; Total (incl. others) 25,347. *2008:* Total arrivals 30,268.

Tourism Receipts (US $ million): 9 in 1996; 10 in 1997; 10 in 1998.

Source: World Tourism Organization.

COMMUNICATIONS MEDIA

Daily Newspapers (1996): 2; estimated circulation 5,000*.

Non-daily Newspapers (1996): 1; estimated circulation 3,000*.

Radio Receivers (1997): 57,000* in use.

Television Receivers (1999): 15,000* in use.

Telephones ('000 main lines in use, 2009): 10.4.

Mobile Cellular Telephones (2006): 8,525 subscribers.

*Sources: UNESCO, *Statistical Yearbook*; American Samoa Telecommunications Authority; International Telecommunication Union.

EDUCATION

Pre-primary (2006): 40 schools; 140 teachers; 2,038 pupils.

Primary (2006): 35 schools; 450 teachers; 11,100 pupils.

Secondary (2006): 12 high schools; 213 teachers; 5,074 pupils.

Higher (2006): American Samoa Community College 1,607 students.

Source: American Samoa Department of Education.

UNITED STATES EXTERNAL TERRITORIES

American Samoa

Directory

The Government
(May 2011)

Governor: TOGIOLA TALALELEI A. TULAFONO (took office March 2003, re-elected 16 November 2004 and 18 November 2008).
Lieutenant-Governor: FAOA IPULASI AITOFELE TOESE FITI SUNIA.

GOVERNMENT OFFICES

Governor's Office: Executive Office Bldg, 3rd Floor, Utulei, Pago Pago, AS 96799; tel. 633-4116; fax 633-2269; e-mail jacinta@americansamoa.gov; internet americansamoa.gov/governor.

Department of the Interior, Office of Insular Affairs (OIA): Field Office of the OIA, Dept of the Interior, POB 1725, Pago Pago, AS 96799; tel. 633-2800; fax 633-2415; internet www.doi.gov/oia/Islandpages/asgpage; Field Representative LYDIA FALEAFINE NOMURA.

Office of the Representative to the Government of American Samoa: Amerika Samoa Office, 1427 Dillingham Blvd, Suite 210, Honolulu, HI 96817, USA; tel. (808) 847-1998; fax (808) 847-3420; e-mail ahawaiioffice@aol.com; Representative SOLOALI'I FA'ALEPO, Jr.

Department of Administrative Services: American Samoa Government, Executive Office Bldg, Utulei, Pago Pago, AS 96799; tel. 633-4158; fax 633-1841; e-mail adminservices@americansamoa.gov; internet americansamoa.gov/departments/admin/department-administrative-services; Dir NU'UTAI SONNY THOMPSON.

Department of Agriculture: American Samoa Government, Executive Office Bldg, Utulei, Pago Pago, AS 96799; tel. 699-9272; fax 699-4031; e-mail agriculture@americansamoa.gov; internet americansamoa.gov/departments/agriculture/department-agriculture; Dir LEFITI AITULAGI PESE.

Department of Commerce: American Samoa Government, Executive Office Bldg, 2nd Floor, POB 1147, Utulei, Pago Pago, AS 96799; tel. 633-5155; fax 633-4195; e-mail doc@americansamoa.gov; internet americansamoa.gov/departments/doc/department-commerce; Dir FALESEU ELIU PAOPAO.

Department of Education: American Samoa Government, Executive Office Bldg, Utulei, Pago Pago, AS 96799; tel. 633-5237; fax 633-4240; e-mail webmaster@doe.as; internet www.doe.as; Dir Dr CLAIRE POUMELE.

Department of Health: American Samoa Government, Pago Pago, AS 96799; tel. 633-4606; fax 633-5379; e-mail publichealth@americansamoa.gov; internet americansamoa.gov/departments/doh/department-health; Dir ELISAPETA PONAUSUIA.

Department of Homeland Security: POB 4567, Pago Pago, AS 96799; tel. 633-2827; fax 633-2979; e-mail mrsala@americansamoa.gov; internet americansamoa.gov/asdhs/index.htm; Dir MICHAEL SALA.

Department of Human Resources: American Samoa Government, Executive Office Bldg, Utulei, Pago Pago, AS 96799; tel. 633-4485; fax 633-1139; e-mail hr@americansamoa.gov; internet americansamoa.gov/departments/hr/department-human-resources; Dir EVELYN VAITAUTOLU LANGFORD.

Department of Human and Social Services: American Samoa Government, Pago Pago, AS 96799; tel. 633-1187; fax 633-7449; e-mail hss@americansamoa.gov; internet americansamoa.gov/departments/dhss/department-human-social-services; Dir LEILUA STEVENSON.

Department of Legal Affairs: American Samoa Government, Executive Office Bldg, Utulei, Pago Pago, AS 96799; tel. 633-4163; fax 633-1838; e-mail legalaffairs@americansamoa.gov; internet americansamoa.gov/departments/legal-affairs/department-legal-affairs; Dir Attorney-General FEPULEA'I AFA RIPLEY, Jr.

Department of Local Government (Office of Samoan Affairs): American Samoa Government, Pago Pago, AS 96799; tel. 633-5201; fax 633-5590; e-mail localgov@americansamoa.gov; internet americansamoa.gov/departments/samoan-affairs/local-government; Dir TUFELE F. LI'AMATUA.

Department of Marine and Wildlife Resources: American Samoa Government, Executive Office Bldg, Utulei, Pago Pago, AS 96799; tel. 633-4456; fax 633-5944; e-mail marine@americansamoa.gov; internet americansamoa.gov/departments/mwr/department-marine-wildlife-resources; Dir UFAGAFA RAY TULAFONO.

Department of Parks and Recreation: American Samoa Government, Pago Pago, AS 96799; tel. 699-9614; fax 699-4427; e-mail parks@americansamoa.gov; internet americansamoa.gov/departments/parks/department-parks-recreation; Dir SAMANA SEMO VE'AVE'A.

Department of Planning and Budget: tel. 633-4201; fax 633-1148; e-mail budget@americansamoa.gov; internet americansamoa.gov/departments/budget/department-planning-budget; Dir MALEMO TAUSAGA.

Department of Port Administration: American Samoa Government, Pago Pago, AS 96799; tel. 633-4251; fax 633-5281; e-mail matagi.mcmoore@americansamoa.gov; internet americansamoa.gov/departments/port/department-port-administration; Dir MATAGI MAILO RAY MCMOORE.

Department of Procurement: American Samoa Government, Tafuna, AS 96799; tel. 699-1170; fax 699-2387; e-mail procurement@americansamoa.gov; internet americansamoa.gov/procurement/index.htm; Dir PAT TERVOLA.

Department of Public Information: American Samoa Government, Pago Pago, AS 96799; tel. 633-4191; fax 633-1044; e-mail kvzk@americansamoa.gov; internet americansamoa.gov/departments/kvzk/department-public-information; Dir PAOLO SIVIA SIVIA.

Department of Public Safety: American Samoa Government, Pago Pago, AS 96799; tel. 633-1111; fax 633-7296; e-mail publicsafety@americansamoa.gov; internet americansamoa.gov/departments/dps/department-public-safety; Dir TUAOLO M. E. FRUEAN.

Department of Public Works: American Samoa Government, Pago Pago, AS 96799; tel. 633-4141; fax 633-5958; e-mail publicworks@americansamoa.gov; internet americansamoa.gov/departments/dpw/department-public-works; Dir PUNAOFO TILEI.

Department of Treasury: American Samoa Government, Executive Office Bldg, Utulei, Pago Pago, AS 96799; tel. 633-4155; fax 633-4100; e-mail lmagalei@asg.as; internet americansamoa.gov/departments/treasury/department-treasury; Dir LOGOVI'I MAGALEI.

Department of Youth and Women's Affairs: American Samoa Government, Executive Office Bldg, Utulei, Pago Pago, AS 96799; tel. 633-2836; fax 633-2875; e-mail youthandwomen@americansamoa.gov; internet americansamoa.gov/departments/youth/youth-womens-affairs; Dir Leiataua Dr LEUGA TURNER.

Environmental Protection Agency: American Samoa Government, Executive Office Bldg, Utulei, Pago Pago, AS 96799; tel. 633-2304; fax 633-5801; e-mail toafa.vaiagae@asepa.gov; internet asepa.gov; Dir Fanuatele Dr TOA'FA VAIAGA'E.

Office of Protection and Advocacy for the Disabled: POB 3937, Pago Pago, AS 96799; tel. 633-2441; fax 633-7286; e-mail opad@americansamoa.gov; internet americansamoa.gov/departments/OPAD/office-protection-and-advocacy-disabled; Dir Dr LALOULU TAGOILELAGI.

Office of the Public Defender: American Samoa Government, Executive Office Bldg, 3rd Floor, Utulei, Pago Pago, AS 96799; tel. 633-1286; fax 633-4745; e-mail public_defender@americansamoa.gov; internet americansamoa.gov/departments/pd/public-defender; Dir RUTH RISCH.

Legislature

FONO

Senate

The Senate has 18 members, elected, according to Samoan custom, from local chiefs (*Matai*) for a term of four years.
President: GAOTEOTE PALAIE GAOTEOTE.

House of Representatives

The House has 20 members who are elected by popular vote for a term of two years, and a non-voting delegate from Swains Island.
Speaker: SAVALI TALAVOU ALE.

CONGRESS

Since 1980 American Samoa has been able to elect, for a two-year term, a Delegate to the Federal Congress, who may vote in committee but not on the floor of the House of Representatives. At the election to the post in November 2010, incumbent Congressman Eni F. Hunkin Faleomavaega was re-elected for a record 12th two-year term.

Delegate of American Samoa: ENI F. HUNKIN FALEOMAVAEGA, US House of Representatives, 2422 Rayburn House Office Bldg, Washington, DC 20515, USA; tel. (202) 225-8577; fax (202) 225-8757; e-mail faleomavaega@mail.house.gov; internet www.house.gov/faleomavaega.

Election Commission

Government Election Office: POB 3970, Pago Pago, AS 96799; tel. 699-3571; fax 699-3574; e-mail info@americansamoaelectionoffice

UNITED STATES EXTERNAL TERRITORIES

American Samoa

.org; internet www.americansamoaelectionoffice.org; Chief Election Officer SOLIAI T. FUIMAONO.

Political Organizations

While the USA's Democratic Party and the Republican Party have local chapters in American Samoa, most politicians in the Territory remain non-partisan.

Judicial System

The judicial system of American Samoa consists of the High Court, presided over by the Chief Justice and assisted by an Associate Justice (appointed by the Secretary of the Interior), and a local judiciary in the District and Village Courts. The judges for these local courts are appointed by the Governor, subject to confirmation by the Senate of the Fono. The High Court consists of three Divisions: Appellate, Trial, and Land and Titles. The Appellate Division has limited original jurisdiction and hears appeals from the Trial Division, the Land and Titles Division and from the District Court when it has operated as a court of record. The Trial Division has general jurisdiction over all cases. The Land and Titles Division hears cases involving land or *Matai* titles.

The District Court hears preliminary felony proceedings, misdemeanours, infractions (traffic and health), civil claims less than US $3,000, small claims, Uniform Reciprocal Enforcement of Support cases, and *de novo* trials from Village Courts. The Village Courts hear matters arising under village regulations and local customs.

Chief Justice of the High Court: MICHAEL KRUSE, Office of the Chief Justice, High Court, Pago Pago, AS 96799; tel. 633-1261; fax 633-1318; e-mail hcourt@samoatelco.com.

Associate Justice of the High Court: LYLE L. RICHMOND.

Attorney-General: FEPULEAI AFA RIPLEY, Jr.

Judges of the District Court: JOHN L. WARD II, ELVIS PATEA, POB 427, Pago Pago, AS 96799; tel. 633-1101; fax 633-5127.

Judge of the Village Court: FAISIOTA TAUANU'U, Pago Pago, AS 96799; tel. 633-1102.

Religion

The population is largely Christian, more than 50% being members of the Congregational Christian Church and about 20% being Roman Catholics.

CHRISTIANITY

American Samoa Council of Christian Churches: c/o CCCAS Offices, POB 1537, Pago Pago, AS 96799; f. 1985; six mem. churches; Pres. (vacant); Gen. Sec. Rev. ENOKA L. ALESANA (Congregational Christian Church in American Samoa).

The Roman Catholic Church

American Samoa comprises the single diocese of Samoa-Pago Pago, suffragan to the archdiocese of Samoa-Apia and Tokelau. At 31 December 2007 there were 15,000 adherents in the islands. The Bishop participates in the Catholic Bishops' Conference of the Pacific, based in Suva, Fiji.

Bishop of Samoa-Pago Pago: Rev. JOHN QUINN WEITZEL, Diocesan Pastoral Center, POB 596, Fatuoaiga, Pago Pago, AS 96799; tel. 699-1402; fax 699-1459; e-mail quinn@samoatelco.com.

The Anglican Communion

American Samoa is within the diocese of Polynesia, part of the Church of the Province of New Zealand. The Bishop of Polynesia is resident in Fiji.

Protestant Churches

Congregational Christian Church in American Samoa (CCCAS): POB 1537, Pago Pago, AS 96799; tel. 699-9810; fax 699-1898; e-mail cccasgs@samoatelco.com; internet www.efkas.org/; f. 1980; Gen. Sec. Rev. SAMUEL TIALAVEA; 40,000 mems (incl. congregations in New Zealand, Australia and USA) in 2004.

Other active Protestant groups include the Baptist Church, the Christian Church of Jesus Christ, the Methodist Church, Assemblies of God, Church of the Nazarene and Seventh-day Adventists. The Church of Jesus Christ of Latter-day Saints (Mormons) is also represented.

The Press

American Samoa Tribune: 5 a week; circ. 4,500 (2006).

News Bulletin: Department of Public Information, American Samoa Government, Pago Pago, AS 96799; tel. 633-5490; daily (Mon.–Fri.); English; non-commercial; Editor PHILIP SWETT; circ. 1,800.

Samoa Journal and Advertiser: POB 3986, Pago Pago, AS 96799; tel. 633-2399; weekly; English and Samoan; Editor MICHAEL STARK; circ. 3,000.

Samoa News: POB 909, Pago Pago, AS 96799; tel. 633-5599; fax 633-4864; e-mail webmaster@samoanews.com; internet www.samoanews.com; owned by Osini Faleatasi Inc dba Samoa News; 6 a week; English and Samoan; Publr VERA M. ANNESLEY; circ. 6,000.

Broadcasting and Communications

TELECOMMUNICATIONS

American Samoa Telecommunications Authority: Box M, Pago Pago, AS 96799; tel. 633-1126; internet www.samoatelco.com.

Blue Sky Communications: 478 Laufou Shopping Center, Pago Pago, AS 96799; tel. 699-2759; fax 699-6593; e-mail webmaster@bluesky.as; internet www.bluesky.as; mobile telecommunications provider; Pres. and CEO ADOLFO MONTENEGRO.

BROADCASTING

Radio

KSBS-FM (Island 92): POB 793, Pago Pago, AS 96799; tel. 633-7000; fax 622-5727; e-mail info@ksbsfm92.com; internet www.ksbsfm92.com; commercial; Gen. Man. ESTHER PRESCOTT.

V103: POB 6758, Pago Pago, AS 96799; tel. 633-7793; fax 633-4493; e-mail thepeople@wvuv.com; internet www.wvuv.com; fmr govt-administered station leased to Radio Samoa Ltd in 1975; commercial; English and Samoan; 24 hours a day; Gen. Man. JOEY CUMMINGS.

Television

KVZK-TV: POB 3511, Pago Pago, AS 96799; tel. 633-4191; fax 633-1044; e-mail kvzk@americansamoa.gov; f. 1964; govt-owned; non-commercial; English and Samoan; broadcasts 18 hours daily on two channels; Gen. Man. PAOLO SIVIA SIVIA; Technical Dir JEFFREY ALWIN.

Malama TV: Malama Communications, Inc, POB AB, Pago Pago 96799; tel. 699-5999; fax 699-6006; e-mail webmaster@malama.tv; internet malama.solupress.com.

Finance

(cap. = capital; dep. = deposits; m. = million; amounts in US dollars)

BANKING

Commercial Banks

ANZ Amerika Samoa Bank: POB 3790, Pago Pago, AS 96799; tel. 633-1151; fax 633-5057; internet www.anz.com.au/americansamoa; f. 1979; fmrly Amerika Samoa Bank; joined ANZ group in April 2001; Pres. and CEO DAVID WHITBY; 3 brs.

Bank of Hawaii (USA): POB 69, Pago Pago, AS 96799; tel. 633-4226; fax 633-2918; f. 1897; District Man. HOBBS LAWSON; 3 brs.

Development Bank

Development Bank of American Samoa: POB 9, Pago Pago, AS 96799; tel. 633-4031; fax 633-1163; e-mail dbasinfo@dbas.org; internet www.dbas.org; f. 1969; govt-owned and non-profit-making; Chair. (vacant); Pres. LOLO MOLIGA.

INSURANCE

American International Underwriters (South Pacific) Ltd: Pago Pago, AS 96799; tel. 633-4845.

Mark Solofa, Inc: POB 3149, Pago Pago, AS 96799; tel. 699-5902; fax 699-5904; e-mail marksalofainc@yahoo.com.

National Pacific Insurance Ltd: Centennial Bldg, POB 1386, Pago Pago, AS 96799; tel. 633-4266; fax 633-2964; e-mail contact@npipago.as; f. 1977; Country Man. JASON THOMAS.

Oxford Pacific Insurance Management: POB 1420, Pago Pago, AS 96799; tel. 633-4990; fax 633-2721; e-mail progressive_oxford@yahoo.com; f. 1977; represents major international property and life insurance cos; Pres. GREG F. DUFFY.

South Seas Financial Services Corporation: POB 1448, Pago Pago, AS 96799; tel. 633-7896; fax 633-7895; e-mail ssfs@samoatelco.com.

Trade and Industry

DEVELOPMENT ORGANIZATIONS

American Samoa Development Corporation: Pago Pago, AS 96799; tel. 633-4241; f. 1962; financed by private Samoan interests.

UNITED STATES EXTERNAL TERRITORIES

American Samoa Economic Advisory Commission: Pago Pago; Chair. JOHN WAIHEE.

Department of Commerce: see Government Offices; Dir FALESEU ELIU PAOPAO.

CHAMBER OF COMMERCE

Chamber of Commerce of American Samoa: POB 6758, Pago Pago, AS 96799; tel. 633-7793; fax 633-4493; e-mail info@amsamoachamber.com; internet www.amsamoachamber.com; 1979; Chair. JOEY CUMMINGS.

UTILITIES

American Samoa Power Authority: POB PPB, Pago Pago, AS 96799; tel. 699-1234; fax 699-4783; internet www.aspower.com; supplies water and electricity throughout the islands; also manages sewer and solid waste collection; Chair. ASAUA FUIMAONO; CEO ANDRA SAMOA.

Transport

ROADS

There are about 150 km (93 miles) of paved and 200 km (124 miles) of secondary roads. Non-scheduled commercial buses operate a service over 350 km (217 miles) of main and secondary roads. There were an estimated 8,100 registered motor vehicles in the islands in 2004.

SHIPPING

There are various passenger and cargo services from the US Pacific coast, Japan, Australia (mainly Sydney) and New Zealand that call at Pago Pago, which is one of the deepest and most sheltered harbours in the Pacific. Inter-island boats provide frequent services between Samoa and American Samoa.

PM&O Line: Suite 202, Fagatogo Sq., POB 5023, Pago Pago, AS 96799; tel. 633-4527; fax 633-4530; e-mail paige@blueskynet.as; f. 1978.

Polynesia Shipping: POB 1478, Pago Pago, AS 96799; tel. 633-1211; fax 633-1265.

Samoa Pacific Shipping: Samoan Sports Bldg, 1 Main St, Fagatogo, POB 1417, Pago Pago, AS 96799; tel. 633-4665; fax 699-4667; e-mail spsi@samoatelco.com; internet www.hamburgsud.com; f. 1988; Gen. Man. VA'A UITUALAGI.

CIVIL AVIATION

There is an international airport at Tafuna, 11 km (7 miles) from Pago Pago, and smaller airstrips on the islands of Ta'u and Ofu. International services are operated by Hawaiian Airlines and Polynesian Blue.

Samoa Aviation: POB 280, Pago Pago Int. Airport, Pago Pago, AS 96799; tel. 699-9106; fax 699-9751; f. 1986; operates service between Pago Pago and Samoa, Tonga and Niue; Pres. ANDRE LAVIGNE.

Tourism

The tourist industry is encouraged by the Government, but its development has been impeded by the cost and paucity of air services. A total of 29,060 tourists visited the islands in 2010, 1,645 fewer than in the previous year. The majority of tourists came from Samoa, the USA and New Zealand. The industry earned an estimated US $10m. in 1998.

American Samoa Visitors Bureau: POB 4240, Pago Pago, AS 96799; tel. 699-9805; fax 699-9806; e-mail info@americansamoa.travel; internet www.americansamoa.travel; Exec. Dir DAVID VAEAFE.

Office of Tourism: Convention Center, POB 1147, Tafuna, Pago Pago, AS 96799; tel. 699-9411; fax 699-9414; e-mail asgtourism@samoatelco.com; Deputy Dir VIRGINIA SAMUELU.

Pago Pago Visitors Association (PPVA): f. 2004; Pres. TOM DRABBLE.

Defence

The USA is responsible for the defence of American Samoa. The US Pacific Command is based in Hawaii, but the territory receives regular naval visits and assistance in surveillance of its waters.

Education

The Government's early childhood education division provides facilities for all children between three and five years of age. Education is compulsory for children between six and 18 years of age. The education system is based on the US pattern of eight years' attendance at an elementary school and four years' enrolment at a high school. In 2006 there were 11,100 pupils enrolled at the 35 primary schools and 5,074 at the 12 secondary schools. The American Samoa Community College had 1,607 students in 2006.

GUAM

Introductory Survey

LOCATION, CLIMATE, LANGUAGE, RELIGION, FLAG, CAPITAL

Guam is the southernmost and largest of the Mariana Islands, situated about 2,170 km (1,350 miles) south of Tokyo (Japan) and 5,300 km (3,300 miles) west of Honolulu (Hawaii, USA). The temperature normally ranges between 24°C (75°F) and 30°C (86°F) in June–November, but it is generally cooler and drier from December to May. The average annual rainfall is about 2,000 mm (79 ins). English is the official language, but Japanese and Chamorro, the local language, are also spoken. The principal religion is Christianity, the majority of the population being Roman Catholics. The national flag of the United States of America (q.v.) is used by Guam. The capital is Hagåtña (formerly Agaña).

CONTEMPORARY POLITICAL HISTORY

Historical Context

Members of a Spanish expedition, led by the Portuguese navigator Fernão Magalhães (Ferdinand Magellan), were the first Europeans to discover Guam, visiting the island in 1521. Guam was claimed by Spain in 1565, and the first Jesuit missionaries arrived three years later. The native Micronesian population is estimated to have declined from 100,000 in 1521 to fewer than 5,000 in 1741, owing largely to a combination of aggression by the Spaniards and exposure to imported diseases. The intermarrying of Micronesians, Spaniards and Filipinos resulted in the people now called Chamorros. Guam was ceded to the USA after the Spanish–American War of 1898. In 1941, during the Second World War, Guam was invaded by Japanese troops, but following fierce fighting the island was recaptured by US forces in 1944.

Guam became an Unincorporated Territory of the USA, under the jurisdiction of the US Department of the Interior, in 1950. The island continued to be administered by an appointed Governor. However, in 1970 the population of Guam chose its first directly elected Governor, Carlos Camacho of the Republican Party, and in 1972 a new law gave Guam the right to elect one Delegate to the US House of Representatives in Washington, DC. The Delegate was permitted to vote in committee but not on the floor of the House. In 1976, in a referendum held on the island, it was determined that Guam should maintain its close links with the USA, but that negotiations should be held to improve the island's status. In a further referendum, conducted in 1982, in which only 38% of eligible voters participated, the status of a Commonwealth, in association with the USA, was the most favoured of six options; this was supported by 48% of voters. In 1987, in a referendum on the provisions of a draft law aimed at conferring the status of Commonwealth on the Territory, voters approved the central proposal, while rejecting articles empowering the Guam Government to restrict immigration and granting the indigenous Chamorro people the right to determine the island's future political status. In a further referendum later in the year, both outstanding provisions were approved. Negotiations between the Guam Commission for Self Determination and the USA subsequently continued.

Domestic Political Affairs

Having won the gubernatorial election held in late 1974, Ricardo Bordallo of the Democratic Party took office as the island's Governor in January 1975. Bordallo was replaced in early 1979 by the Republican Paul McDonald Calvo, but he returned to the position in 1983, serving as Governor until January 1987. In February 1987 Bordallo was found guilty of charges of bribery, extortion and conspiracy to obstruct justice, and was sentenced to 30 years' imprisonment (later reduced to nine years) in April. In November Bordallo's wife, Madeleine, was elected to replace him as Senator (as the chamber's members were known) in the Guam Legislature. In October 1988

Ricardo Bordallo won an appeal and his sentence was cancelled. Bordallo was liable for imprisonment in the USA on charges of obstruction and attempting to influence witnesses, but in January 1990 he committed suicide. Madeleine Bordallo was the Democratic candidate at the gubernatorial election of November, when Republican Joseph Ada, who had replaced her husband as Governor in 1987, was re-elected. Concurrent elections to the Guam Legislature resulted in a Democratic majority of one seat.

At legislative elections in November 1992 the Democrats increased their representation to 14 of the 21 seats, while the Republicans secured only seven. Robert Underwood, the Democratic candidate, was elected as the island's Delegate to the US House of Representatives, replacing the Republican Ben Blaz.

In January 1994 the US Congress approved legislation providing for the transfer of 3,200 acres of land on Guam from federal to local control. This was a significant achievement for the Government of Guam, which had campaigned consistently for the return of 27,000 acres (20% of Guam's total area), appropriated by US military forces after the Second World War. However, Chamorro rights activists opposed the legislation, claiming that land should be transferred to the original landowners rather than to the Government of Guam.

At the gubernatorial election held in November 1994 the Democratic candidate, Carl Gutierrez, defeated his Republican opponent, Tommy Tanaka, winning 54.6% of total votes cast, while Madeleine Bordallo was elected to the post of Lieutenant-Governor. Legislative elections held concurrently also resulted in a Democratic majority, with candidates of the party securing 13 seats, while the Republicans won eight. Robert Underwood was re-elected unopposed as Delegate to the US House of Representatives.

Reports that Chamorro rights activists had initiated a campaign for independence from the USA were denied by the Governor in July 1995. However, in September Lieutenant-Governor Madeleine Bordallo expressed her support for the achievement of full autonomy for Guam and for the Chamorro people's desire for decolonization.

It was reported in 1995 that US President Bill Clinton had appointed a team of Commonwealth negotiators to review the draft Guam Commonwealth Act. Guam's self-styled Commission on Decolonization was established in 1997, headed by the Governor. A plebiscite on the political status of Guam was originally scheduled for November 2000 but was subsequently deferred, to coincide with the island's legislative and presidential elections scheduled for November 2004. However, in May 2004 legislation was drafted that would postpone the referendum until the number of Chamorro voters registered by the Guam Elections Committee had reached the requisite 50%.

At elections in November 1996 Republican members regained a majority in the Guam Legislature, winning 11 seats, while Democratic candidates secured 10 seats. In a concurrent referendum, voters approved a proposed reduction in the number of Senators from 21 to 15 (effective from November 1998), and plans to impose an upper limit (2.5% of total budgetary expenditure) on legislative expenses. However, a proposal to restrict the number of terms that Senators could seek to serve in the Legislature was rejected by voters. The island's Delegate to the US House of Representatives, Robert Underwood, was re-elected unopposed.

In June 1998 Underwood secured approval from the US authorities to change the spelling of Guam's capital from Agaña to Hagåtña. The change was effected in order to reflect more accurately the original Chamorro language name for the town.

Robert Underwood was re-elected, with 70.2% of the total votes cast, as Guam's Delegate to the US House of Representatives in November 1998. Concurrent gubernatorial and legislative elections resulted in the return to office of incumbent Governor Carl Gutierrez and of Lieutenant-Governor Madeleine Bordallo. (In December former Governor Joseph Ada alleged that Gutierrez's victory had been achieved by fraudulent means, and later in the month a Guam court invalidated the election result and ordered that a new poll be held. However, in February 1999 the Superior Court of Guam found that there had been no electoral malpractice, and confirmed the appointments of Gutierrez and Bordallo.) In elections to the Legislature, where the number of seats had been reduced from 21 to 15, a total of 12 candidates of the Republican Party and three candidates of the Democratic Party were elected as Senators.

At elections held in November 2000, Underwood was re-elected as Guam's Delegate to the US House of Representatives, winning 78.1% of votes cast. At the concurrent legislative election, eight candidates of the Republican Party and seven candidates of the Democratic Party were chosen.

Robert Underwood secured the Democratic nomination for the gubernatorial election scheduled for November 2002, but at the poll was defeated by the Republican candidate, Felix P. Camacho, who received 55.4% of the votes cast. Madeleine Bordallo was designated Guam's Delegate to the US House of Representatives. In the Legislature, nine Democratic candidates were elected as Senators, while the Republican party's representation decreased to six seats. Governor Camacho pledged to halt the widely perceived rise in corruption and misallocation of public funds on Guam.

Also in November 2002 the US Congress approved the Guam War Claims Review Commission Act, which provided for the creation of a body to investigate events that had followed the island's occupation by Japanese forces during the Second World War. Furthermore, the Commission was to determine whether the USA had offered the islanders sufficient compensation for their mistreatment prior to Guam's liberation in 1944. The War Claims Review Commission, appointed in September 2003, acknowledged the hardship and suffering of the people of Guam, their 'courageous loyalty to the USA' and the inequality in compensation payments with regard to similar claims. In March 2006 the Guam World War II Loyalty Recognition Act was reintroduced, thus apparently making significant progress in efforts to compel the federal Government to recompense Guam residents for their suffering during the 1940s. The legislation was approved by the US House of Representatives in May 2007; the Congressional Budget Office projected the cost of implementing the provisions of the bill during the period 2008–12 at almost US $130m. At mid-2011 the proposed legislation remained outstanding.

In July 2003, in response to the high costs incurred by a typhoon recovery programme, Delegate Madeleine Bordallo introduced a bill to amend the Organic Act of Guam (See Constitution and Government). The legislation attempted to empower the US Secretary of the Interior to waive Guam's outstanding federal debt, in order to offset social costs caused by migration to Guam from Compact of Free Association countries (see the chapter on the Marshall Islands). The measure was defeated, although the amended Compact of Free Association signed in December approved some US $14m. to offset Guam's migration costs and erased $157m. of debt owed to the US federal Government. New legislation seeking to amend the Organic Act of Guam, in order to grant the Territory greater autonomy from the US federal Government, was submitted to the Guam Legislature in February 2006. In the same month Governor Camacho announced his intention to restart negotiations on some $60.5m. of debt relief for Guam.

In May 2004, meanwhile, the US State Department's Radiation Exposure Compensation Program declared Guam eligible for compensation for the effects of nuclear tests carried out in the Pacific region during the 'Cold War' (the long period of mutual hostility between the USA and the Soviet Union). In April 2005 the US Congressional Committee to Assess the Scientific Information for the Radiation Exposure Screening and Education Program published a report recommending, in accordance with the wishes of the Guam delegation, that scientific criteria (including radiation measurements and analyses of public health data) be used for assessing eligibility for compensation, rather than geographical proximity to nuclear testing, which had determined eligibility hitherto. The report concluded that, although Guam had been exposed to radiation through wind-borne particles, this exposure had not significantly increased the incidence of cancers and other radiation-related illnesses. Future claims for compensation were therefore thought unlikely to succeed.

At the legislative election held on 2 November 2004 the Republican party secured a majority, winning nine of the 15 seats in the Guam Legislature; five Democrat incumbents were deposed. At a concurrently held plebiscite, a proposal to legalize casinos on the island was rejected. Later in the month a group of campaigners for the proposal filed an appeal in the Superior Court against the result of the election, alleging electoral malpractice.

Meanwhile, numerous investigations into allegations of official corruption were conducted. In April 2003 a former Republican Senator and gubernatorial candidate, Tommy Tanaka, pleaded guilty to charges of misprision of felony, which related to his alleged involvement in a fraudulent government contract. In the same month Joseph Mafnas, a former chief of the Guam police department, was indicted on forgery charges. However, the case against him foundered in September 2004 owing to the absence from the island of the key witness for the prosecution. In March 2004 former Governor Carl Gutierrez was tried for his involvement in a private property development scheme, which allegedly involved the misappropriation of public funds. All but two minor charges against him were dismissed by a Superior Court judge in April. Although in August charges ranging from theft by deception to official misconduct were filed against the former Governor, these were dismissed in early September. Gutierrez stood trial in June 2005 for alleged improper dealings relating to the island's retirement fund; he was acquitted of all charges in the following month, and in August announced his intention to contest the next gubernatorial election, scheduled for November 2006. However, in December 2005 new corruption charges connected to the retirement fund were filed against Gutierrez and others responsible for its operation. In January 2006 further charges were brought against the former Governor relating to his administration of the Guam Memorial Hospital. Meanwhile, in October 2005 Gutierrez's former Chief of Staff, Gil Shinohara, was convicted of conspiracy to commit fraud.

In an important decision in January 2006, the US House of Representatives approved an amendment to grant limited voting rights to the Delegate from Guam. Although the Delegate would be unable to vote on the final passage of legislation, the ruling would permit the island's envoy to cast a vote in the 'Committee of the Whole House on the State of the Union', a means by which the House expedites consideration of certain legislation, particularly amendments. The decision was expected to allow for more effective lobbying on the part of Guam's Delegate to Washington, DC, and the promotion of the islanders' views on a number of important issues within the federal system. However, in January 2011 the Republican-controlled House of Representatives voted to rescind the 'symbolic' voting rights of territorial delegates. Madeleine Bordallo joined with the Delegates from American Samoa, the Northern Mariana Islands, the District of Columbia, Puerto Rico and the Virgin Islands to express opposition to the revocation of the privilege, arguing that it rendered the House 'less transparent and less responsive to the American people'. A few days later Democrats introduced a resolution to the House seeking to restore the territorial delegates' voting rights in the Committee of the Whole House on the State of the Union.

Meanwhile, legislative and gubernatorial elections took place on 7 November 2006. Felix P. Camacho secured a second term as Governor, defeating Robert Underwood, who later filed an unsuccessful appeal at the US Supreme Court seeking clarification of the results, in a dispute over the exclusion of 'crossover' ballots from the valid votes. Michael W. Cruz was elected Lieutenant-Governor, replacing Kaleo Moylan. Madeleine Bordallo secured a third term as Delegate to the US House of Representatives. The Republicans retained control of the Guam Legislature, albeit with a decreased majority, winning eight seats, compared with the Democrats' seven; the incumbent Speaker, Republican Mark Forbes, was re-elected.

On 4 November 2008 legislative elections were held at which the Democrats won 10 of the 15 seats in the Guam Legislature. Three incumbent Republicans, including Speaker Mark Forbes, lost their seats. Judith Won Pat was subsequently appointed as the chamber's Speaker. The Democrats' increased majority was largely attributed to the party's opposition to the legalization of gambling in Tamuning, an initiative that appeared to be widely unpopular with the electorate. At a concurrent poll, Madeleine Bordallo won a fourth term as Delegate to the US House of Representatives.

US Secretary of State Hillary Clinton paid a brief visit to Guam in late October 2010 during a two-week official tour of the Asia-Pacific region. During her stay, Clinton met with Governor Camacho and other local officials and pledged her support for a proposal to waive visa requirements for Chinese and Russian nationals in a bid to boost Guam's tourism industry.

Meanwhile, in early September 2010 Edward (Eddie) Calvo, with Ray Tenorio as his running mate, was elected as the Republicans' candidate for the forthcoming gubernatorial election, defeating Lieutenant-Governor Cruz and running mate James Espaldon, in the party's primary poll. The incumbent Governor Camacho was constitutionally barred from seeking re-election to a third term in office. The Democrats' gubernatorial nomination was secured by the sole candidate, former Governor Carl Gutierrez—the first time that the Democrats' gubernatorial primary poll had been uncontested. The gubernatorial election was held on 2 November, concurrently with legislative and congressional delegate polls. After an initial vote count revealed a very closely contested poll, the election commission voted unanimously to recount all of the ballots, following which Eddie Calvo, the son of former Governor Paul McDonald Calvo, was proclaimed Governor, securing 20,066 votes (50.25% of the total) to Gutierrez's 19,579 (49.03%). Gutierrez's electoral team pledged to challenge the result, alleging that the ballots could have been tampered with. In the legislative poll, nine Democrats and six Republicans were elected. Madeleine Bordallo secured re-election to a fifth successive term as Delegate to the US House of Representatives.

Draft legislation was introduced by Senator Frank Blas, Jr in January 2011, which, if approved, would provide for the election of two Guam representatives to the US Senate. While critics noted that the legislation was unconstitutional, since only members of the federal union of the USA were entitled to send representatives to the Senate, Blas defended the bill, stating: 'Are we American citizens or not?... Is this an American possession or is this part of the United States...?'

Strategic Military Significance

Guam remains of vital strategic importance to the USA. In August 2001 the US Army announced plans to move some combat weaponry and equipment from Europe to storage bases in Guam, as well as in Taiwan and Hawaii, USA. During 2004–05 the US Air Force stationed several of its B-52 and B-2 bombers on Guam, following the construction of a new hangar on the island. In May 2005 the US Government announced plans substantially to increase military spending in 2005/06 in Guam, with some US $162m. allocated for new construction projects. Notwithstanding the concerns of some anti-war and Chamorro rights activists, the increased military presence on Guam was widely welcomed as a source of new investment and employment.

Rights activists continued to express their opposition after plans were revealed to relocate 8,000 US marines and their families from US bases in Japan, including the Futenma base in the Japanese city of Ginwan on the island of Okinawa, to Guam, as part of a broader agreement on the redeployment of US forces; the Futenma base itself was to be relocated within Okinawa, to the nearby, less populated city of Nago. While Japan was likely to bear much of the financial burden, US President George W. Bush submitted a proposed budget for 2008 that allocated US $345m. to military construction projects, including the relocation costs of the marines and their dependants. An agreement on the relocation of troops to Guam was concluded in May 2006, and legislation authorizing funding of some $6,000m. for the relocation had been approved by both chambers of the Japanese legislature by May 2007. The US Government had committed funding of $4,000m. for the realignment, which would also involve a reorganization of US troops within Japan. During a visit to the Territory in February 2007 US Vice-President Richard Cheney emphasized the strategic importance of Guam, while reports suggested that the inflow of funds related to the increased military presence might reach $15,000m. The relocation of troops, the implementation of which was expected to require as many as 15,000 skilled workers, was scheduled to begin in 2010, with a target completion date of 2014.

However, the assumption of the Japanese premiership by Yukio Hatoyama in September 2009 threatened to disrupt the process. Shortly after his inauguration, Hatoyama antagonized US officials by suggesting that the Japanese Government might conduct a review of the relocation pact agreed between the two countries in 2006. Such a review was confirmed following the election of Inamine Susumu as mayor of Nago, Okinawa, in January 2010; Hatoyama argued that Susumu's election reflected the local population's opposition to the plans to transfer the Futenma base to Nago since Susumu had campaigned on a platform of staunch opposition to the relocation. As a result, Hatoyama committed the Government to 'start from scratch' regarding the proposed relocation, both of the military base and of the troops, and to arrive at a final decision by the end of May. Some on Guam also remained sceptical about the benefits of the potential relocation, fearing that the influx might lead to an increase in violent crime and other social and environmental disturbances. However, despite the staging of a mass rally in Okinawa, in late April, at which some 100,000 demonstrators gathered to protest against the proposed relocation of the base within the prefecture, in early May Hatoyama conceded that resisting such a relocation was likely to prove impossible and urged the people of Okinawa to 'share the burden' of the base. Hatoyama attracted considerable criticism within Japan for his apparent vacillation over the Okinawa issue, which contributed to a decline in popularity that precipitated his resignation from the premiership in early June.

Hatoyama's replacement as Prime Minister, Naoto Kan, declared shortly after assuming office in June 2010 that he would maintain the controversial policy on Okinawa that his predecessor had been obliged to adhere to. However, a number of points of contention, including the extent of Japan's financial responsibility for the relocation of troops, the total cost of which was projected at US $10,270m., remained unresolved. (The Japanese Government had initially agreed to provide $2,800m., together with an additional $3,290m. in loans, with the US Government accounting for the remainder; however, in July it was reported that the USA had demanded that Japan assume responsibility for a greater share of the cost of the relocation, to the consternation of many Japanese.)

Meanwhile, in March 2009 the US Government announced that Guam was to receive US $45m. in funding for the modernization and maintenance of its military bases, as part of a federal plan of economic stimulus (see Economic Affairs). The US Government's proposed budget for 2010, submitted in May 2009, envisaged an allocation of $787m. towards military construction projects on Guam. A new naval hospital was to be built at a projected cost of $259m. In September Japan agreed to disburse $497.8m. for 2010/11 towards the transfer of troops to Guam, primarily to be allocated to the development of facilities and infrastructure on the island, including the construction of a fire station and a medical clinic. In the same month the US Department of Defense stated that the relocation of the troops would take until 2016 owing to a lack of facilities on Guam. As part of the ongoing effort to reduce the US military's presence in Okinawa, in January 2011 the USA and Japan agreed to relocate to Guam military drills involving 20 of the 50 F-15 fighter jets based in the Japanese prefecture. However, a final decision on the relocation of the Futenma military base was not expected until the second half of 2011.

The Environment and Natural Phenomena

In March 1998 delegates from several Pacific island nations and territories met in Hawaii to discuss methods of controlling the increasing population of brown tree snakes in Guam. The venomous reptile, which was accidentally introduced to the island (probably from the Solomon Islands) after the Second World War, had been responsible for frequent power cuts (as it was able to ascend electricity poles and short-circuit the lines), as well as for major environmental problems, notably the decimation of native bird, rodent and reptile populations. The US Geological Survey estimated the density of tree snakes on Guam to be roughly 13,000 per sq mile (nearly 5,020 per sq km) of forested land. By 2004 a team of 25 full-time snake-trappers and nine dog-handlers was capturing an estimated 6,000 tree snakes annually at Guam's five main ports (air and sea), but in September of that year plans were announced to reduce funding to this programme by nearly one-half. Also in September the US House of Representatives approved the Brown Tree Snake Control and Eradication Act, which allocated US $104m. of federal funds towards the elimination of Guam's snake population. In October, furthermore, the US Senate authorized expenditure of $77m., to be divided among Guam, Hawaii and other islands, for the purposes of snake eradication programmes. Subsequent allocations of additional federal funding for such programmes were approved; in June 2010 a further $2m. was made available. Madeleine Bordallo, Guam's Delegate to the US House of Representatives, noted that the funding would support efforts to focus on strategies to facilitate the reintroduction of threatened native species, including the ko'ko' (also known as the Guam Rail), a bird species extirpated from the island in the 1980s, its population having been destroyed by brown tree snakes. During the early 21st century the ko'ko was being bred in captivity and it was hoped that, once the local snake population was more effectively under control, the native bird might be successfully reintroduced to the island.

The island remained vulnerable to the impact of extreme weather formations. President George W. Bush declared the island a federal disaster area following Typhoon Chata'an in July 2002 and Super-typhoon Pongsona in December. Some 35,000 islanders were homeless in early 2003, and the US Government granted US $10m. towards the recovery effort.

CONSTITUTION AND GOVERNMENT

Guam is governed under the Organic Act of Guam of 1950, which gave the island statutory local power of self-government. Its inhabitants are citizens of the USA, although they are not permitted to vote in national elections. Guam's non-voting Delegate to the US House of Representatives is elected every two years. Executive power is vested in the Governor, who is elected by popular vote every four years. The heads of the executive departments are appointed by the Governor, with the consent of the Guam Legislature. The Legislature comprises 15 members, known as Senators, who are elected by popular vote every two years. It is empowered to enact legislation on local matters, including taxation and fiscal appropriations.

REGIONAL AND INTERNATIONAL CO-OPERATION

Guam is a member of the Pacific Community (see p. 410) and an associate member of the UN's Economic and Social Commission for Asia and the Pacific (ESCAP, see p. 37).

ECONOMIC AFFAIRS

In 2000, according to estimates by the Bank of Hawaii (BOH), Guam's gross national income (GNI), at current prices, was US $2,772.8m., equivalent to $16,575 per head. Between 1988 and 1993, it was estimated, GNI increased, in real terms, at an average rate of some 10% per year. GNI increased by 3.9% in 1994. Gross island product (GIP—the official measure of the Territory's economic performance) was officially estimated at some $3,700m. in 2005, equivalent to almost $22,700 per head. In 2000–09, according to World Bank figures, the population increased at an average annual rate of 1.5%.

Agriculture (including forestry, fishing and mining) engaged only an estimated 0.5% of the labour force in paid employment in December 2010, according to official payroll records. The principal crops cultivated on the island include watermelons, coconuts, cucumbers, gherkins, bananas, runner beans, aubergines (eggplants), squash, tomatoes and papaya. Livestock reared includes pigs, goats and poultry. The fishing catch totalled an estimated 302 metric tons in 2008, according to FAO.

The industrial sector accounted for some 15% of gross domestic product (GDP) in 1993. According to official figures, in 1995 construction contributed 12.6% of GIP. Manufacturing industries, including textile and garment production and boat-building, engaged an estimated 2.9% of the labour force in paid employment in December 2010, according to payroll records. Construction, which engaged 10.6% of the employed labour force in December 2010, is the dominant industrial activity, and this sector is closely related to the development of the tourist industry.

Service industries dominate the economy, engaging 86.0% of the labour force in paid employment in December 2010, according to payroll records. The federal and territorial Governments together employed 24.5% of workers at that time. According to official estimates, the services sector contributed 69.2% of GIP in 1995. Tourism is Guam's most important industry. Some 1,140,500 tourists visited the island in 2008, when 74.5% of visitors were from Japan. In comparison with the previous year, visitor arrivals were reported to have risen by 13.6% in 2010, to reach 1,196,295.

The Territory consistently records a visible trade deficit, and in 2008 this amounted to US $120m. Major imports in 2008 included motor cars (17.8% of the total value of imports), luggage items, clothing, perfumes and toilet water, beef, beer, sugared water, jewellery and watches. Exports in 2008 were dominated by motor cars (45.9% of the total value of exports) and fish. Singapore supplied 34.2% of total imports in 2002. Japan purchased 21.8% of the island's exports in 2008. Other important trading partners included the People's Republic of China, Germany, Hong Kong, the Republic of Korea, the Philippines, Singapore, the Federated States of Micronesia and Finland. Guam is a low-duty port, and is an important distribution point for goods destined for Micronesia. Re-exports constitute a high proportion of Guam's exports, major commodities being petroleum and petroleum products, iron and steel scrap, and eggs.

In the year ending September 2008 there was a surplus of US $59.0m. on the general fund budget. US federal Government expenditure in Guam totalled $1,396m. in 2008/09. The Government's total debt stood at $326.7m. at the end of the financial year 2003/04. The average annual rate of inflation was 4.6% in 2000–09. Consumer prices increased by 3.0% in 2010. Guam's unemployment rate stood at 8.3% in March 2007.

Guam continues to receive considerable financial support from the USA, particularly in the area of defence. The proposed relocation of US marines and their families from the Japanese island of Okinawa to Guam (see Contemporary Political History), and a further US military proposal to station a Global Strike Task Force at Andersen air force base on Guam, were crucial to the island's strategic planning. The forthcoming increase in Guam's population led to the drafting of plans for the establishment of a mass transit system, and in mid-2009 the USA pledged US $1,000m. to fund the construction of a new road between northern and southern Guam. In early 2009 the US Government allocated more than $140m. of its economic stimulus plan towards rebuilding military infrastructure and other projects in Guam. The modernization of the island's port was to be accorded priority. In addition to federal funding of $50.0m. from the US Department of Defense, in October 2010 the US Department of Agriculture announced that it had approved Guam's request for a loan of $54.5m. for the first phase of the upgrading of the port; of this sum, $29.5m. was to be provided by a private bank. US President Barack Obama allocated $566m. to military construction projects on Guam in his proposed budget for 2010/11. The island's economy was reported to have performed poorly in 2009, partly owing to deteriorating economic conditions in Japan, the Republic of Korea and the USA, important sources of visitors. Variations in exchange rates, notably the relative weakness of the South Korean currency, also affected the tourism industry in 2008–09. Following the tourism sector's recovery of 2010, the tsunami disaster in Japan in March 2011 was expected to lead to a considerable decline in tourist arrivals from that country in subsequent months. In April, with the aim of supporting the island's tourist industry, the Government of Guam issued a $90m. bond, which was to be repaid by means of receipts from a tax on hotel rooms. Of this total, $55m. was to be used for the financing of a new museum and cultural centre, along with other projects of benefit to the tourism sector.

PUBLIC HOLIDAYS

2012 (provisional): 2 January (for New Year's Day), 16 January (Martin Luther King Day), 20 February (Presidents' Day), 5 March (Guam Discovery Day), 6 April (Good Friday), 28 May (Memorial Day), 4 July (US Independence Day), 21 July (Liberation Day), 3 September (Labor Day), 8 October (Columbus Day), 2 November (All Souls' Day), 12 November (Veterans' Day), 22 November (Thanksgiving Day), 8 December (Immaculate Conception), 25 December (Christmas Day).

Statistical Survey

Sources (unless otherwise stated): Guam Bureau of Statistics and Plans, PO Box 2950, Hagåtña; tel. 472-4201; fax 477-1812; internet www.bsp.guam.gov.

AREA AND POPULATION

Area: 549 sq km (212 sq miles).

Population: 133,152 at census of 1 April 1990; 154,805 (males 79,181, females 75,624) at census of 1 April 2000. *Mid-2011* (Secretariat of the Pacific Community estimate): 192,090 (Source: Pacific Regional Information System).

Density (mid-2011): 349.9 per sq km.

UNITED STATES EXTERNAL TERRITORIES

Guam

Population by Age and Sex (Secretariat of the Pacific Community estimates at mid-2011): *0–14:* 50,967 (males 26,361, females 24,606); *15–64:* 127,892 (males 66,737, females 61,155); *65 and over:* 13,231 (males 6,335, females 6,896); *Total* 192,090 (males 99,433, females 92,657) (Source: Pacific Regional Information System).

Ethnic Groups (2000 census): Chamorro 57,297; Filipino 40,729; White 10,509; Other Asian 9,600; part-Chamorro 7,946; Chuukese 6,229; Total (incl. others) 154,805.

Regions (population at 2000 census): North 80,466; Central 45,382; South 28,957.

Principal Towns (population at 2000 census): Tamuning 10,833; Mangilao 7,794; Yigo 6,391; Astumbo 5,207; Barrigada 4,417; Hagåtña (capital) 1,122.

Births, Marriages and Deaths (2008 unless otherwise indicated, preliminary): Registered live births 3,466 (birth rate 19.7 per 1,000); Registered marriages (2005) 2,245 (marriage rate 13.3 per 1,000); Registered deaths 775 (death rate 4.4 per 1,000).

Life Expectancy (years at birth, estimates): 79.4 (males 77.0; females 82.1) in 2010.

Economically Active Population (persons aged 16 years and over, excl. armed forces, 2002 estimates): Agriculture, forestry, fishing and mining 290; Manufacturing 1,570; Construction 3,420; Transport, storage and utilities 4,590; Wholesale and retail trade 12,690; Finance, insurance and real estate 2,450; Public administration 16,500; Education, health and social services 14,510; *Total employed* 56,020; Unemployed 7,070; *Total labour force* 63,090. *2010* (payroll data at December, preliminary): Agriculture, forestry, fishing and mining 320; Manufacturing 1,790; Construction 6,660; Transport, storage and utilities 4,500; Wholesale and retail trade 13,710; Finance, insurance and real estate 2,650; Public administration 15,780; Other services 17,160; Total employed 62,570 (Source: Guam Department of Labor).

AGRICULTURE, ETC.

Principal Crops (metric tons, 2008 unless otherwise indicated, FAO estimates): Coconuts 53,200; Roots and tubers 2,630 (2009); Cucumbers and gherkins 400; Watermelons 2,500; Other melons 370; Bananas 350.

Livestock (head, year ending September 2008, FAO estimates): Chickens 210,000; Ducks 5,000; Pigs 5,200; Goats 700. Note: No data were available for 2009.

Livestock Products (metric tons, 2008, FAO estimates): Chicken meat 45; Hen eggs 750; Pig meat 150. Note: No data were available for 2009.

Fishing (metric tons, live weight, 2008): Common dolphinfish 16; Skipjack tuna 134; Other marine fishes 151; Total capture (incl. others) 302; Mozambique tilapia 100 (FAO estimate); Milkfish 40 (FAO estimate); Total aquaculture (incl. others) 162 (FAO estimate); *Total catch* 464 (FAO estimate).

Source: FAO.

INDUSTRY

Electric Energy (million kWh, estimates): 1,897 in 2005; 1,891 in 2006; 1,879 in 2007. Source: UN Industrial Commodity Statistics Database.

FINANCE

Currency and Exchange Rates: US currency is used. For details, see section on the Northern Mariana Islands.

Federal Direct Expenditures (US $ million, year ending September): 1,479 (Defence 507) in 2007; 1,533 (Defence 789) in 2008; 1,396 (Defence 567) in 2009. Source: US Census Bureau, *Consolidated Federal Funds Report.*

General Fund Budget (US $ million, year ending September 2008): *Revenue:* Taxes 443.0 (Income tax 254.1, Gross receipts 185.8, Other 3.1); Licences, fees and permits 5.6; Use of money and property 2.5; Federal contributions 45.3; Other 16.8; Total 513.2. *Expenditure:* General government 44.9; Public order 73.0; Public health 10.0; Community services 6.4; Recreation 3.3; Individual and collective rights 12.5; Public education 193.1; Economic development 3.6; Debt service 17.3; Total (incl. others) 454.2.

Cost of Living (Consumer Price Index; annual averages, base: October–December 2007 = 100): All items 104.3 in 2008; 106.1 in 2009; 109.3 in 2010.

Gross Domestic Product (US $ million at current prices): 4,100 in 2005; 4,176 in 2006; 4,280 in 2007 (Source: Bureau of Economic Analysis, US Department of Commerce).

Expenditure on the Gross Domestic Product (US $ million at current prices, 2007): Government consumption expenditure and gross investment 2,006; Personal consumption expenditure 2,783; Private fixed investment 180; *Total domestic expenditure* 4,969; Exports of goods and services 814; *Less* Imports of goods and services 1,504; *GDP in purchasers' values* 4,280 (Source: Bureau of Economic Analysis, US Department of Commerce).

Gross Island Product by Economic Activity (US $ million, 1995): Construction 379.02; Trade 622.86; Public administration 965.97; Other services 486.94; Other non-services 544.61; *Total* 2,999.40.

EXTERNAL TRADE

Principal Commodities (US $ million, 2008): *Imports f.o.b.:* Food and non-alcoholic beverages 66.5 (Meat and edible offal of beef 5.9; Meat and edible offal of poultry 4.7; Bread and bakery products 3.8; Water, containing sugar 8.2); Alcoholic beverages 8.5 (Malt beer 6.0); Home appliances, equipment, etc. 5.3; Transportation and parts 52.1 (Motor cars 40.0); Construction materials 14.4 (Structures of iron and steel 3.4); Men's and women's apparel 12.5; Plastics, leather and paper 28.9 (Travel goods, handbags, etc. 19.4); Miscellaneous manufactured imports 36.6 (Perfumes and toilet waters 8.0; Articles of jewellery 3.5; Watches 4.9); Total 224.9. *Exports (incl. re-exports) f.o.b.:* Food and non-alcoholic beverages 20.6 (Fish—fresh, chilled, frozen and preserved 19.2); Transportation and parts 49.8 (Motor cars 48.1); Construction materials 9.3 (Iron and steel 3.4; Aluminium waste, scraps, tubes and fittings 3.2); Plastics, leather and paper 5.0 (Travel goods, handbags, etc. 3.6); Miscellaneous manufactured imports 18.1 (Perfumes and toilet waters 3.8; Articles of jewellery 8.5; Watches 2.1); Total (incl. others) 104.9.

Principal Trading Partners: *Imports* (US $ '000, 2002): Australia 9,770; Hong Kong 36,240; Japan 96,450; Korea, Republic 9,688; New Zealand 5,520; Philippines 1,437; Singapore 180,076; Total (incl. others) 527,000 (Source: UN, *Statistical Yearbook for Asia and the Pacific*). *Exports* (US $ million, 2008): China, People's Republic 7.7; Finland 5.7; Germany 20.1; Hong Kong 15.1; Japan 22.9; Micronesia, Federated States 6.5; Philippines 6.0; Singapore 6.5; Total (incl. others) 104.9.

TRANSPORT

Road Traffic (registered motor vehicles, 2007): Private cars 65,062; Taxis 293; Buses 665; Goods vehicles 24,774; Motorcycles 1,545; Total (incl. others) 98,416. Source: Department of Revenue and Taxation, Government of Guam.

International Sea-borne Shipping (estimated freight traffic, '000 revenue tons, 2008): Goods loaded 213.7; Goods unloaded 1,269.6; Goods transshipped 576.5. *Merchant Fleet* (total displacement, '000 grt at 31 December 1992): 1 (Source: Lloyd's Register-Fairplay, *World Fleet Statistics*).

Civil Aviation (Guam International Airport): *Passengers* (year ending May 2008): Arrivals 933,364; Departures 934,263; Transit 285,762. *Cargo* (metric tons, 2008): Unloaded 17,528; Loaded 11,616. *Mail* (metric tons, 2008): Incoming 4,111; Outgoing 1,104. *Aircraft Movements* (year ending May 2008): 14,093. Source: Guam International Airport Authority.

TOURISM

Foreign Tourist Arrivals ('000): 1,211.7 in 2006; 1,225.0 in 2007; 1,140.5 in 2008.

Tourist Arrivals by Country of Residence ('000, 2008): Japan 849.8; Korea, Republic 110.5; Philippines 10.9; Taiwan 22.6; USA 52.8; Total (incl. others) 1,140.5. Source: World Tourism Organization.

Tourism Receipts (US $ million): 2,361 in 1998; 1,908 in 1999. Source: World Tourism Organization.

COMMUNICATIONS MEDIA

Radio Receivers (1997): 221,000 in use.

Television Receivers (1999): 110,000 in use.

Telephones (2009): 65,500 main lines in use.

Mobile Cellular Telephones (2008, estimate): 98,000 subscribers.

Internet Users (2009): 90,000.

Broadband Subscribers (2009): 3,000.

Daily Newspapers (1997): 1 (circulation 24,457).

Non-daily Newspapers (1988): 4 (estimated circulation 26,000).

Sources: International Telecommunication Union; UN, *Statistical Yearbook for Asia and the Pacific*.

UNITED STATES EXTERNAL TERRITORIES

EDUCATION

Institutions (2008/09): Primary (incl. kindergarten, grades 1–8) 44 (public 29, private 15); Secondary (grades 9–12) 11 (public 5, private 6).

Teachers (2005/06): Primary 1,917 (public 1,405, private 512); Secondary 1,108 (public 470, private 638).

Enrolment (2008/09 unless otherwise specified): Kindergarten (grades 1–5) 18,474 (public 13,851, private 4,623); Primary (grades 6–8) 9,241 (public 6,845, private 2,396); Secondary (grades 9–12) 12,160 (public 9,633, private 2,527); High school (graduates) 2,085 (public 1,492, private 593); Guam Community College (2005/06) 10,268; University of Guam 3,387.

Sources: Department of Education, Guam Community College, Office of Insular Affairs, *Guam Statistical Yearbook*; University of Guam.

Directory

The Government
(May 2011)

Governor: EDWARD B. CALVO (Republican—took office 3 January 2011).
Lieutenant-Governor: RAY TENORIO.

GOVERNMENT DEPARTMENTS

Government departments are located throughout the island.

Office of the Governor: POB 2950, Hagåtña, GU 96932; tel. 472-8931; fax 477-4826; e-mail governor@mail.gov.gu; internet governor.guam.gov.

Department of the Interior, Office of Insular Affairs (OIA): Hagåtña, GU 96910; tel. 472-7279; fax 472-7309; internet www.interior.gov/oia/Islandpages/gumpage.htm; Field Representative KEITH A. PARSKY.

Department of Administration: POB 884, Hagåtña, GU 96932; tel. 475-1101; fax 475-6788; e-mail doadir@mail.gov.gu; internet www.doa.guam.gov; Dir BENITA MANGLONA (acting).

Department of Agriculture: 163 Dairy Rd, Mangilao, GU 96913; tel. 734-3942; fax 734-6569; internet www.agriculture.guam.gov; Dir MARIQUITA TAITAGUE.

Department of Chamorro Affairs: POB 2950, Hagåtña, GU 96910; tel. 475-4278; fax 475-4227; internet www.dca.guam.gov; Pres. JOSEPH CAMERON.

Department of Corrections: POB 3236, Hagåtña, GU 96932; tel. 473-7021; fax 473-7009; internet www.doc.guam.gov; Dir JOSÉ A. SAN AGUSTIN.

Department of Education: POB DE, Hagåtña, GU 96932; tel. 475-0457; fax 472-5003; e-mail nbunderwood@gdoe.net; internet www.gdoe.net; Supt NERISSA BRETANIA UNDERWOOD.

Department of Integrated Services for Individuals with Disabilities: Suite 702, 238 Archbishop F. C. Flores St, Pacific News Bldg, Hagåtña, GU 96910; tel. 475-4646; fax 477-2892; internet www.disid.guam.gov; Dir BENITO S. SERVINO.

Department of Labor: 414 West Soledad Ave, GCIC Bldg, Hagåtña, GU 96910; tel. 475-7000; fax 475-7045; e-mail connent@ite.net; internet www.dol.guam.gov; Dir LEAH BETH NAHOLOWAA.

Department of Land Management: POB 2950, Hagåtña, GU 96932; tel. 649-5263; fax 649-5383; e-mail dlmdir@dlm.guam.gov; internet dlm.guam.gov; Dir ANISIA B. TERLAJE.

Department of Mental Health and Substance Abuse: tel. 647-5330; fax 649-6948; e-mail info@guamdmhsa.com; internet dmhsa.guam.gov; Dir WILFRED AFLAGUE (acting).

Department of Military Affairs: 430 Army Dr., Bldg 300, Barrigada; tel. 735-0406; fax 649-8775; internet dma.guam.gov; Dir Maj.-Gen. BENNY M. PAULINO.

Department of Parks and Recreation: 490 Chalan Palasyo, Agaña Heights, GU 96910; tel. 475-6296; fax 477-0997; e-mail parks@ns.gov.gu; internet www.dpr.guam.gov; Dir PETER CALVO (acting).

Department of Public Health and Social Services: 123 Chalan Kareta, Route 10, Mangilao, GU 96913-6304; tel. 735-7173; fax 734-5910; internet dphss.guam.gov; Dir JAMES GILLAN.

Department of Public Works: 542 North Marine Dr., Tamuning, GU 96913; tel. 646-3131; fax 649-6178; e-mail joanne.brown@dpw.guam.gov; internet www.dpw.guam.gov; Dir JOANNE M. BROWN.

Department of Revenue and Taxation: POB 23607, Guam Main Facility, GU 96921; tel. 635-1835; fax 633-2643; e-mail pinadm@revtax.gov.gu; internet www.guamtax.com; Dir JOHN P. CAMACHO.

Department of Youth Affairs: POB 23672, Guam Main Facility, GU 96921; tel. 735-5010; fax 734-7536; e-mail adonis.mendiola@dya.guam.gov; internet dya.guam.gov; Dir ADONIS MENDIOLA.

Legislature

GUAM LEGISLATURE

The Guam Legislature has 15 members, known as Senators, who are directly elected by popular vote for a two-year term. Elections took place on 2 November 2010, when the Democratic Party secured a majority of seats.

Speaker: JUDITH WON PAT.

CONGRESS

Guam elects a non-voting Delegate to the US House of Representatives. An election was held on 2 November 2010, when the Democratic candidate, Madeleine Z. Bordallo, was re-elected for a fifth term as Delegate.

Delegate of Guam: MADELEINE Z. BORDALLO, Cannon House Office Bldg, 427, Washington, DC 20515-5301, USA; tel. (202) 225-1188; fax (202) 226-0341; e-mail madeleine.bordallo@mail.house.gov; internet www.house.gov/bordallo.

Election Commission

Guam Election Commission: Guam Capital Investment Corpn Bldg, 414 West Soledad Ave, Suite 200, Hagåtña 96910; tel. 477-9791; fax 477-1895; e-mail director@gec.guam.gov; internet www.gec.guam.gov; Chair. FREDERICK J. HORECKY; Exec. Dir JOHN BLAS.

Political Organizations

The Territory has a two-party system, comprising local chapters of the US Democratic Party and Republican Party. However, at the local level, non-partisan candidates may seek election.

Judicial System

Attorney-General: LEONARDO M. RAPADAS.
US Attorney: ALICIA GARRIDO LIMTIACO.

Supreme Court of Guam: Suite 300, Guam Judicial Center, 120 West O'Brien Dr., Hagåtña, GU 96910; tel. 475-3162; fax 475-3140; e-mail justice@guamsupremecourt.com; internet www.justice.gov.gu/supreme.html; Chief Justice ROBERT J. TORRES, Jr.

District Court of Guam: 4th Floor, US Courthouse, 520 West Soledad Ave, Hagåtña, GU 96910; tel. 473-9180; fax 473-9118; e-mail judith_hattori@gud.uscourts.gov; internet www.gud.uscourts.gov; judge appointed by the President of the USA; the court has the jurisdiction of a federal district court and of a bankruptcy court of the USA in all cases arising under US law; appeals may be made to the Court of Appeals for the Ninth Circuit and to the US Supreme Court; Magistrate Judge JOAQUIN V. E. MANIBUSAN.

Superior Court of Guam: 120 West O'Brien Drive, Hagåtña, GU 96910; tel. 475-3250; internet www.justice.gov.gu/superior.html; judges are appointed by the Governor of Guam for an initial eight-year term and are thereafter retained by popular vote; the Superior Court has jurisdiction over cases arising in Guam other than those heard in the District Court; Presiding Judge ALBERTO C. LAMORENA, III.

There are also Probate, Traffic, Domestic, Juvenile and Small Claims Courts.

Religion

The majority of the population are Roman Catholic, but there are also members of the Episcopal (Anglican) Church, the Baptist churches and the Seventh-day Adventist Church. There are small communities of Muslims, Buddhists and Jews.

CHRISTIANITY

The Roman Catholic Church

Guam comprises the single archdiocese of Agaña. The Archbishop participates in the Catholic Bishops' Conference of the Pacific, based in Suva, Fiji, and the Federation of Catholic Bishops' Conferences of Oceania, based in Wellington, New Zealand. At 31 December 2007 there were 141,177 adherents in Guam.

Archbishop of Agaña: Most Rev. ANTHONY SABLAN APURON, Chancery Office, Cuesta San Ramón 96910B, Hagåtña, GU 96910; tel. 472-

UNITED STATES EXTERNAL TERRITORIES

6116; fax 477-3519; e-mail archbishop@mail.archdioceseofagana.com; internet www.archdioceseofagana.com.

BAHÁ'Í FAITH

National Spiritual Assembly: POB Box BA, Hagåtña, GU 96931; tel. 472-9100; fax 472-9101; e-mail nsamar@ite.net; mems resident in 19 localities in Guam and 10 localities in the Northern Mariana Islands.

The Press

NEWSPAPERS AND PERIODICALS

Bonita: POB 11468, Tumon, GU 96931; tel. 632-4543; fax 637-6720; f. 1998; monthly; Publr Imelda Santos; circ. 3,000.

Directions: POB 27290, Barrigada, GU 96921; tel. 635-7501; fax 635-7520; f. 1996; monthly; Publr Jerry Roberts; circ. 3,800.

Guam Business: POB 3191, Hagåtña, GU 96932; tel. 649-0883; fax 649-8883; e-mail glimpses@glimpsesofguam.com; internet www.guambusinessmagazine.com; f. 1983; quarterly; Publr Maureen N. Maratita; Man. Editor Frank Whitman; circ. 2,600.

Hospitality Guahan: POB 8565, Tamuning, GU 96931; tel. 649-1447; fax 649-8565; e-mail info@ghra.org; internet www.ghra.org; f. 1996; quarterly; circ. 3,000.

Marianas Business Journal: POB 3191, Hagåtña, GU 96932; tel. 649-0883; fax 649-8883; e-mail glimpses@glimpsesofguam.com; internet www.mbjguam.net; f. 2003; fortnightly; Publr Maureen N. Maratita; Editor Patricia Shook; circ. 3,000.

Pacific Daily News and Sunday News: POB DN, Hagåtña, GU 96932; tel. 472-1736; fax 472-1512; e-mail cblas@guampdn.com; internet www.guampdn.com; f. 1950; Publr Rindraty Limtiaco; Man. Editor David Crisostomo; circ. 28,520 (weekdays), 26,237 (Sunday).

The Pacific Voice: POB 2553, Hagåtña, GU 96932; tel. 472-6427; fax 477-5224; f. 1950; Sunday; Roman Catholic; Gen. Man. Terezo Mortera; Editor Rev. Fr Hermes Losbanes; circ. 6,500.

TV Guam Magazine: 237 Mamis St, Tamuning, GU 96911; tel. 646-4030; fax 646-7445; f. 1973; weekly; Publr Dina Grant; Man. Editor Emily Untalan; circ. 15,000.

NEWS AGENCY

United Press International (UPI) (USA): POB 1617, Hagåtña, GU 96910; tel. 632-1138; Correspondent Dick Williams.

Broadcasting and Communications

TELECOMMUNICATIONS

Guam Educational Telecommunication Corporation (KGTF): POB 21449, Guam Main Facility, Barrigada, GU 96921; tel. 734-2207; fax 734-3476; e-mail kgtfl2@ite.net; internet www.kgtf.org.

Guam Telephone Authority: 624 North Marines Corps Dr., POB 9008, Tamuning, GU 96913; tel. 644-4482; fax 649-4821; e-mail ask@gta.net; internet www.gta.net; acquired by TeleGuam Holdings LLC in Dec. 2004; CEO and Pres. Dan Moffat.

BROADCASTING

Radio

K-Stereo: 1868 Halsey Dr., Piti, GU 96915; tel. 477-9448; fax 477-6411; e-mail ksto@ite.net; operates on FM 24 hours a day; Pres. and Gen. Man. Edward H. Poppe.

KOKU-FM: 424 West O'Brien Drive, Julale Center, Hagåtña, GU 96910; tel. 477-5658; fax 472-7663; e-mail marketing@hitradio100.com; operates on FM 24 hours a day; Pres. Kurt S. Moylan; Marketing and Sales Man. Vince Limuaco.

KPRG FM: KPRG, UoG Station Mangilao, GU 96923; tel. 734-8930; fax 734-2958; e-mail kprg@kprg.org; internet www.kprg.org; operated by the University of Guam; news and music; Chair. Marie Mesa-Kerlin; Chairs Tod Thompson, Nick Captain; Gen. Man. Chris Hartig (acting).

Radio Guam (KUAM): 600 Harman Loop, Dededo, GU 96912; tel. 637-5826; fax 637-9865; e-mail generalmanager@kuam.com; internet www.kuam.com; f. 1954; operates on AM and FM 24 hours a day; Pres. Paul M. Calvo; Gen. Man. Joey Calvo.

Sorensen Media Group: Suite 800, 111 Chalan Santo Papa, Hagåtña, GU 96910; tel. 477-5700; fax 477-3982; e-mail rex@spbguam.com; internet www.pacificnewscenter.com; f. 1981; privately owned; Chair. and CEO Rex Sorensen.

Trans World Radio Pacific (TWR): POB CC, Hagåtña, GU 96932; tel. 477-9701; fax 477-2838; e-mail ktwr@twr.org; internet www.guam.net/home/twr; f. 1975; broadcasts Christian programmes on KTWR and one medium-wave station, KTWG, covering Guam and nearby islands, and operates five short-wave transmitters reaching most of Asia, Africa and the Pacific; Chair. Thomas J. Lowell; Pres. Dr David G. Tucker; Station Dir Michael Davis.

Television

KGTF—TV: POB 21449 Guam Main Facility, Barrigada, GU 96921; tel. 734-3476; fax 734-5483; e-mail kgtfl2@kgtf.org; internet www.kgtf.org; f. 1970; cultural, public service and educational programmes; Gen. Man. Shirley M. Suoza (acting); Operations Man. Benny T. Flores.

KTGM—TV: 692 Marine Dr., Tamuning 96911; tel. 649-8814; fax 649-0371.

KUAM—TV: 600 Harmon Loop, Dededo, Hagåtña, GU 96912; tel. 637-5826; fax 637-9865; e-mail generalmanager@kuam.com; internet www.kuam.com; f. 1956; operates channels 8 and 11; News Dir Sabrina Salas.

Finance

(cap. = capital; res = reserves; dep. = deposits; m. = million; brs = branches; amounts in US dollars)

BANKING

Commercial Banks

Allied Banking Corpn (Philippines): Suite 104, Bejess Commercial Bldg, 719 South Marine Drive, Tamuning, GU 96913; tel. 649-5001; fax 649-5002; e-mail abcguam@kuentos.guam.net; Asst Vice-Pres. Mario R. Palisoc; 1 br.

ANZ Guam Inc: 424 West O'Brien Dr., 112 Julale Shopping Center, Hagåtña, GU 96910; tel. 479-9000; fax 479-9092; internet www.anz.com/guam; mem. of ANZ Group; fmrly Citizens Security Bank (Guam) Inc, name changed as above in 2009; cap. US $8.5m., dep. US $148.7m. (Dec. 2010); CEO David McCall; 4 brs.

Bank of Guam: POB BW, 111 Chalan Santo Papa, Hagåtña, GU 96932; tel. 472-5300; fax 477-8687; e-mail customerservice@bankofguam.com; internet www.bankofguam.com; f. 1972; cap. 1.8m., dep. 904.3m. (Dec. 2010); Chair. Lourdes A. Leon Guerrero; Exec. Vice-Pres. William D. Leon Guerrero; 19 brs.

Bank of Hawaii (USA): 134 West Soledad Ave, Hagåtña, GU 96910; tel. 479-3500; fax 479-3893; Vice-Pres. Rodney Kimura; 3 brs.

BankPacific, Ltd: 151 Aspinall Ave, Hagåtña, GU 96910; tel. 472-6704; fax 477-1483; e-mail philipf@bankpacific.com; internet www.bankpacific.com; f. 1954; Pres. and CEO Philip J. Flores; Exec. Vice-Pres. Mark O. Fish; 4 brs in Guam; 1 br. in Palau; 1 br. in Northern Mariana Islands.

Citibank NA (USA): 402 East Marine Dr., Hagåtña, GU 96910; tel. 477-2484; fax 477-9441; internet www.citibank.com/guam; Country Man. Agustin Davalos; 2 brs.

First Commercial Bank (Taiwan): POB 2461, Hagåtña, GU 96932; tel. 472-6864; fax 477-8921; e-mail fcbgu@ite.net; Gen. Man. Jenn-Hwa Wang; 1 br.

First Hawaiian Bank (USA): Compadres Mall 562, Harmon Loop Rd, Dededo, GU 96912; tel. 632-9381; fax 637-9686; internet www.fhb.com; Regional Man. Laura-Lynn Dacanay; 3 brs.

HSBC Ltd: POB 27c, Hagåtña, GU 96932; tel. 647-8588; fax 646-3767; CEO Guy N. de B. Priestley; 2 brs.

Metropolitan Bank and Trust Co: 665 South Marine Drive, Tamuning, GU 96911; tel. 649-9555; fax 649-9558; e-mail mbguam@metrobank.com.ph; f. 1975; Sen. Man. Josephine M. Papelera.

Union Bank of California (USA): 194 Hernan Cortes Ave, POB 7809, Hagåtña, GU 96910; tel. 477-8811; fax 472-3284; Man. Kinji Suzuki; 2 brs.

INSURANCE

American National Insurance Co: POB 3340, Hagåtña, GU 96910; tel. 477-9600.

Chung Kuo Insurance Co: GCIC Bldg, Suite 707, 414 West Soledad Ave, Hagåtña, GU 96910; tel. 477-7696; fax 477-4788; e-mail chungkuo@ite.net; internet www.cki.com.tw.

Midland National Life Insurance Co: Winner Bldg, Suite 20n, Tamuning, GU 96911; tel. 649-0330; internet www.mnlife.com; f. 1906 as Dakota Mutual Life Insurance Company; name changed as above in 1925.

Moylan's Insurance Underwriters, Inc: Suite 102 Julale Shopping Center, 424 West O'Brien Dr., Hagåtña, GU 96910; tel. 477-8613; fax 477-1837; e-mail agana@moylans.net; internet www.moylansinsurance.com; Pres. Kurt S. Moylan; CEO Cesar Garcia.

Nanbo Insurance: 434 West O'Brien Dr., Hagåtña, GU 96910; tel. 477-9754; internet www.nanbo.com.

UNITED STATES EXTERNAL TERRITORIES

Guam

Pioneer Pacific Financial Services, Inc of Guam: POB EM, Hagåtña, GU 96910; tel. 477-6400.

Trade and Industry

DEVELOPMENT ORGANIZATION

Guam Economic Development Authority (GEDA): Guam International Trade Center Bldg, Suite 511, 590 South Marine Dr., Tamuning, GU 96913; tel. 647-4332; fax 649-4146; e-mail help@investguam.com; internet www.investguam.com; f. 1965; Admin. ANTHONY C. BLAZ.

CHAMBER OF COMMERCE

Guam Chamber of Commerce: Ada Plaza Center, Suite 101, 173 Aspinall Ave, POB 283, Hagåtña, GU 96932; tel. 472-6311; fax 472-6202; e-mail gchamber@guamchamber.com; internet www.guamchamber.com.gu; f. 1924; Chair. DAVID J. JOHN; Pres. DAVID P. LEDDY.

EMPLOYERS' ORGANIZATION

The Employers' Council: 718 North Marine Dr., Suite 201, East-West Business Center, Upper Tumon, GU 96913; tel. 649-6616; fax 649-3030; e-mail tecinc@teleguam.net; internet www.guamemployers.org; f. 1966; private, non-profit asscn providing management devt training and advice on personnel law and labour relations; Exec. Dir ANDY ANDRES.

UTILITIES

Electricity

Guam Energy Office: 548 North Marine Corps Dr., Tamuning, GU 96913; tel. 646-4361; fax 649-1215; e-mail lucybk@teleguam.net; internet www.guamenergy.com; Dir J. LAWRENCE M. CRUZ.

Guam Power Authority: POB 2977, Hagåtña, GU 96932; tel. 648-3225; fax 649-3290; e-mail webmaster@guampowerauthority.com; internet www.guampowerauthority.com; f. 1968; autonomous govt agency; supplies electricity throughout the island; Gen. Man. JOAQUIN FLORES.

Water

Guam Waterworks Authority: 578 North Marine Corps Dr., Tamuning, GU 96913-4111; tel. 647-2603; fax 646-2335; e-mail heidi@guamwaterworks.org; internet www.guamwaterworks.org; Gen. Man. Dr LEONARD J. OLIVE.

TRADE UNIONS

Many workers belong to trade unions based in the USA such as the American Federation of Government Employees and the American Postal Workers' Union.

Guam Federation of Teachers (GFT): Local 1581, POB 2301, Hagåtña, GU 96932; tel. 735-4390; fax 734-8085; e-mail mrector@gftunion.com; internet www.gftunion.com; f. 1965; affiliate of American Federation of Teachers; Pres. MATT RECTOR; 2,000 mems.

Guam Hotel and Restaurant Association: POB 8565, Tamuning, GU 96931; tel. 649-1447; fax 649-8565; e-mail president@ghra.org; internet www.ghra.org; 37 mem. restaurants and hotels; Pres. MARY P. TORRE.

Guam Landowners' Association: Hagåtña; Pres. ANTONY SABLAN; Sec. RONALD TEEHAN.

Transport

In September 2008 the Government announced that the sum of US $25m. was to be allocated to the creation of a mass transit network on the island, to accommodate the projected rise in the population that would result from the relocation of thousands of US marines to Guam.

ROADS

There are 885 km (550 miles) of public roads, of which some 675 km (420 miles) are paved. A further 685 km (425 miles) of roads are classified as non-public, and include roads located on federal government installations. In February 2009 a $140m. project to upgrade the island's road network was announced. In the same month the US Government announced that it was committing $1,000m. to fund a new road to link US military facilities in northern and southern Guam. The works were expected to be completed by 2014.

SHIPPING

Apra, on the central western side of the island, is one of the largest protected deep-water harbours in the Pacific. Plans for the modernization of the port were under way in 2009.

Port Authority of Guam: 1026 Cabras Highway, Suite 201, Piti, GU 96925; tel. 477-5931; fax 477-4445; e-mail webmaster@portguam.com; internet www.portguam.com; f. 1975; government-operated port facilities; Gen. Man. PEDRO A. LEON GUERRERO, Jr.

Ambyth, Shipping and Trading, Inc: 1026 Cabras Highway, Piti, GU 96915; tel. 477-7250; fax 472-1264; e-mail ops@ambyth.guam.net; internet www.ambyth.com; agents for all types of vessels and charter brokers; Pres. ALFRED LAM; Gen. Man. ANDREW MILLER.

Atkins, Kroll, Inc: 443 South Marine Dr., Tamuning, GU 96913; tel. 649-6410; fax 646-9592; e-mail atkins_kroll@akguam.com; internet www.akguam.com; f. 1914; vehicle distribution; Pres. DAN CAMACHO.

COAM Trading Co Ltd: PAG Bldg, Suite 110, 1026 Cabas Highway, Piti, GU 96925; tel. 477-1737; fax 472-3386.

Dewitt Moving and Storage: Suite 100, 165-1, Guerrero St, Tamuning, GU 96913; tel. 648-1800; fax 648-0034; e-mail ezdewitt@dewittguam.com; internet www.dewittguam.com; Pres. JOHN BURROWS.

Guam Shipping Agency: POB GD, Hagåtña, GU 96932; tel. 477-7381; fax 477-7553; Gen. Man. H. KO.

Interbulk Shipping (Guam) Inc: Bank of Guam Bldg, Suite 502, 111 Chalan Santo Papa, Hagåtña, GU 96910; Man. S. GYSTAD.

Maritime Agencies of the Pacific Ltd: Piti, GU 96925; tel. 477-8500; fax 477-5726; e-mail rehmapship@kuentos.guam.net; f. 1976; agents for fishing vessels, cargo, dry products and construction materials; Pres. ROBERT E. HAHN.

Pacific Navigation System: POB 7, Hagåtña, GU 96910; f. 1946; Pres. KENNETH T. JONES, Jr.

Seabridge Micronesian, Inc: 1026 Cabras Highway, Suite 114, Piti, GU 96925; tel. 477-7345; fax 477-6206; Gen. Man. PAUL L. BLAS.

Sea-Land Service, Inc: POB 8897, Tamuning, GU 96931; tel. 475-8100; internet www.horizon-lines.com; CEO CHARLES RAYMOND.

Tucor Services: 180 Guerrero St, Harmon Industrial Park, POB 6128, Tamuning, GU 96911; tel. 646-6947; fax 646-6945; e-mail boll@tucor.com; general agents for numerous dry cargo, passenger and steamship cos; Pres. MICHELLE BOLL.

CIVIL AVIATION

Guam is served by A. B. Won Pat International Airport.

Guam International Airport Authority: POB 8770, Tamuning, GU 96931; tel. 646-0300; fax 646-8823; e-mail lizb@guamairport.net; internet www.guamairport.com; Chair. MARTIN GERBER; Exec. Man. MARY C. TORRES (acting).

Asia Pacific Airlines (APA): POB 24858, Guam Main Facility, Barrigada, Guam 96921; fax 647-8440; e-mail info@flyapa.com; internet www.flyapa.com; f. 1999; affiliate of Tan Holdings Corpn (Commonwealth of the Northern Mariana Islands); cargo; serving Guam, Hawaii (USA), Hong Kong, Marshall Islands, Federated States of Micronesia, Palau and the Philippines.

Continental Micronesia Airlines: POB 8778, Tamuning, GU 96931; tel. 645-8182; internet www.continental.com; f. 1968, as Air Micronesia, by Continental Airlines (USA); hub operations in Guam and Saipan (Northern Mariana Islands); services throughout the region and to destinations in the Far East and the mainland USA; Pres. CHARLES DUNCAN.

Freedom Air: POB 1578, Hagåtña, GU 96932; tel. 647-8359; fax 646-7488; e-mail freedom@ite.net; internet www.freedomairguam.com; f. 1974; Man. Dir JOAQUIN L. FLORES, Jr.

Tourism

Tourism is the most important industry on Guam. Visitor arrivals were reported to have increased by 13.6% in 2010, to total 1,196,295. Most visitors are from Japan, the Republic of Korea, the USA and Taiwan. The majority of Guam's hotels are situated in, or near to, Tumon, where amenities for entertainment are well-developed. Numerous sunken wrecks of aircraft and ships from Second World War battles provide interesting sites for divers. There were 7,561 hotel rooms on Guam in 2004.

Guam Visitors Bureau: 401 Pale San Vitores Rd, Tumon, GU 96913; tel. 646-5278; fax 646-8861; e-mail guaminfo@visitguam.org; internet www.visitguam.org; Chair. DAVID B. TYDINGCO; Gen. Man. ERNIE A. GALITO (acting).

Defence

Guam is an important strategic military base for the USA. In 2004 a new hangar for B-52 and B-2 bombers was completed. In May 2005 the US Government announced plans substantially to increase military spending in 2005/06 in Guam, with some US $162m. allocated for new construction projects. As assessed at November 2010, 2,982 members of the US Air Force were stationed on Guam, in addition to a US naval base. As part of a wider programme of

Education

School attendance is compulsory from six to 16 years of age. There were 44 kindergarten and primary schools (29 public, 15 private) and 11 secondary schools (five public, six private) operating on the island in 2008/09. In that year total enrolment at kindergarten schools amounted to 18,474 students; the comparable figures for primary and secondary schools were 9,241 and 12,160 students, respectively. Enrolment in tertiary education has expanded in recent years, with 10,268 students enrolled at the Guam Community College for 2005/06 and 3,387 students enrolled at the University of Guam for 2008/09. In 2000 the rate of adult illiteracy was estimated at 1.0%. Government expenditure on public education was US $193.1m. in 2007/08 (equivalent to 42.5% of total expenditure).

THE UNITED STATES VIRGIN ISLANDS

Introductory Survey

LOCATION, CLIMATE, LANGUAGE, RELIGION, FLAG, CAPITAL

The United States Virgin Islands consists of three main inhabited islands (St Croix, St Thomas and St John) and about 50 smaller islands, mostly uninhabited. They are situated at the eastern end of the Greater Antilles, about 64 km (40 miles) east of Puerto Rico in the Caribbean Sea. The climate is tropical, although tempered by the prevailing easterly trade winds. The temperature averages 26°C (79°F), with little variation between winter and summer. The humidity is low for the tropics. English is the official language, but Spanish and Creole are also widely used. The people of the US Virgin Islands are predominantly of African descent. There is a strong religious tradition, and most of the inhabitants are Christians, mainly Protestants. The flag (proportions 2 by 3) is white, with a modified version of the US coat of arms (an eagle holding an olive branch in one foot and a sheaf of arrows in the other, with a shield, comprising a small horizontal blue panel above vertical red and white stripes, superimposed), between the letters V and I, in the centre. The capital is Charlotte Amalie, on the island of St Thomas.

CONTEMPORARY POLITICAL HISTORY

Historical Context

The Virgin Islands, originally inhabited by Carib and Arawak Indians, were discovered by Europeans in 1493. The group subsequently passed through English, French, and Dutch control, before the western islands of St Thomas and St John, colonized by Denmark after 1670, and St Croix, purchased from France in 1733, became the Danish West Indies. In 1917 these islands, which are strategically placed in relation to the Panama Canal, were sold for US $25m. by Denmark to the USA. They now form an unincorporated territory of the USA. Residents of the US Virgin Islands are US citizens, but cannot vote in presidential elections, if resident in the islands. The US Virgin Islands is represented in the US House of Representatives by one popularly elected Delegate, who is permitted to vote only in committees of the House.

Domestic Political Affairs

The inhabitants of the islands were granted a measure of self-government by the Organic Act, as revised in 1954, which created the elected 15-member Senate. Since 1970 executive authority has been vested in the elected Governor and Lieutenant-Governor. In the first gubernatorial election, in 1970, the Republican incumbent, Melvin Evans, retained office. In 1974 Cyril E. King, leader of the Independent Citizens' Movement (a breakaway faction of the Democratic Party), was elected Governor. On King's death in 1978, the former Lieutenant-Governor, Juan Luis, was elected Governor. He was returned to power in the 1982 election. The governorship passed to the Democratic Party with the election of Alexander Farrelly in 1986. Farrelly was re-elected Governor in 1990, and in the 1994 elections was succeeded by an Independent, Dr Roy Schneider. The governorship was regained by a Democrat, Charles Turnbull, in the 1998 elections. Turnbull was re-elected to the post in 2000 and 2002. The Democrats retained the governorship in 2006, with the election of John deJongh, Jr (Turnbull was constitutionally precluded from standing for a third consecutive term of office).

In February 2005 a 7,000-signature petition was submitted to the US Congress by residents of St Croix, in support of making the island a separate US External Territory from St Thomas and St John. Organizers of the petition claimed that such a move would generate more federal funding for the island, which was affected by a higher unemployment rate than the other two islands, despite being the location for one of the world's largest petroleum refineries. In May the Territorial Government brought a court case against the owners of the Hovensa LLC oil refinery (see Economic Affairs) and the defunct St Croix Alumina plant for contaminating the sole groundwater supply on St Croix. Both companies had reached an agreement with the US Environmental Protection Agency (EPA) in 2001 to clean up petroleum spillages; according to the EPA, some 2m. gallons of petroleum leaked into the local aquifer between 1978 and 1991.

In March 2002 the islands were removed from the Organisation for Economic Co-operation and Development's list of 'unco-operative' tax havens, after pledging to improve the transparency of its financial services sector by the end of 2005. In May 2007 the territory's Delegate to Congress, Donna M. Christensen, presented legislation for the institution of a Chief Financial Officer in the territory to function as an independent arbiter upon government fiscal policy. Although a similar law had been approved earlier, Christensen proposed a number of amendments to it. It was hoped that the new legislation would encourage greater co-operation between the Governor and Legislative Assembly towards reducing the fiscal deficit, and would facilitate and enhance the transparency of financial policy. A number of financial scandals earlier in the year had foregrounded the necessity of financial services regulatory reform: in May former director of the Department of Planning and Natural Resources Division of Environmental Protection Hollis L. Griffin was given a custodial sentence at the federal court in Atlanta, Georgia, after being convicted of conspiring to defraud the islands' Government of US $1.4m. Furthermore, an economic development programme, implemented by the Territorial Government, that permitted firms operating in the islands to reduce their tax payments by up to 90%, was discovered to have been exploited in March, when four individuals, including one islander, were charged with tax evasions amounting to US $74m. Following initial reports in 2003 that the programme was being used as a means of tax evasion, the US Federal Government had imposed restrictions on the tax incentive scheme in 2004. In February 2007 the US Inland Revenue Service announced that the financial affairs of 8,500 high-salaried residents of the US Virgin Islands would be subjected to increased scrutiny. In April Alric Simmonds, Deputy Chief of Staff to erstwhile Governor Turnbull, was indicted on charges of embezzlement, conversion of government property and grand larceny. He was sentenced to eight years' imprisonment in June 2008.

Combating crime and terrorism was a stated objective of Governor deJongh's administration. An anti-crime initiative was announced in February 2007; measures included an increase in the size of the police force and establishment of a forensic facility. Specialized police professionals from external US police jurisdictions were also to be drafted in to support and instruct existing personnel. A previous scheme, the Blue Lightning Marine unit (based on St Thomas), was to be reinstated to address the problems of guns- and drugs-trafficking and illegal immigrant incursions through coastal patrols. In March 2008 deJongh submitted legislation to abolish the Drug Enforcement Bureau and to redirect funding to the police department, which had proved to be more successful in targeting drugs-trafficking. Despite the enhanced crime prevention measures, the murder rate continued to rise, reaching a record 56 in 2009, before increasing further to 66 in 2010.

Constitutional review

Since 1954 there have been five attempts to redraft the Constitution to give the US Virgin Islands greater autonomy. Each draft has, however, been rejected by a referendum. The US Government has expressed the view that it would welcome reform, if approved by the residents, as long as it was economically feasible and did not affect US national security. A non-binding referendum on the islands' future status in 1993 produced support of 80% for retaining the islands' existing status, with 14% favouring full integration with the USA and 5% advocating the termination of US sovereignty. The result of the referendum was, however, invalidated by the low turn-out: only 27% of registered voters took part, falling short of the 50% participation required for the referendum to be valid. Subsequent legislation to create a constitutional convention was presented to the US Virgin Islands Senate, and in 2000 a committee of the US House of Representatives began consideration of a range of measures to enlarge the scope of local self-government in the territory. In November 2004 Governor Turnbull approved legislation allowing the creation of a further constituent assembly to redraft the Constitution.

Progress towards formulating a new constitution for the territory was furthered in July 2007, when a Fifth Constitutional Convention was assembled to commence work upon the drafting of a new document. A final draft would require the approval of two-thirds of all convention delegates before being put before the Governor for approval. The Governor was then legally obliged to present the document to the US Congress for scrutiny and, ultimately, presidential approval, after which the amended draft would put to a referendum. The Convention presented a proposed constitution for consideration by the Governor in June 2009. Governor deJongh objected to several clauses in the document, claiming that it did not recognize the supremacy of the US Constitution, and was therefore invalid. In particular, he opposed proposals that the Governor and Lieutenant-Governor be native or ancestral Virgin Islanders and that native or ancestral citizens be granted property tax exemptions, as well as a provision allowing only native or ancestral Virgin Islanders the right to vote on constitutional amendments. In spite of his objections, the constitution was forwarded to the US Congress, which began discussion of the document in March 2010. However, the charter was rejected by Congress in June on the grounds that certain provisions within the document were in contravention of the US Constitution and federal law. Concerns were specifically raised over the benefits that would be bestowed upon native or ancestral citizens and the failure of the draft constitution to acknowledge US sovereignty over the islands. Congress requested that the Fifth Constitutional Convention review and modify the clauses in question.

Rum dispute

In November 2010 a rum distillery that would supply the international drinks producer Diageo with rum for its Captain Morgan brand was inaugurated in St Croix. Production at the distillery, which began in November 2010, was expected to reach 20m. proof gallons per year. The project was part of an agreement reached between the Government and Diageo in 2009: the US Virgin Islands authorities agreed to finance construction of the plant in return for receiving an estimated $3,000m. in additional excise revenue over the 30-year duration of the contract. A similar accord with drink producer Fortune Brands was reached in October: the Government would meet the necessary costs in expanding and improving the company's Cruzan Rum distillery on the islands, including construction of a waste water treatment facility, in exchange for a guarantee that the rum producer would maintain a presence in the territory for 30 years. The Puerto Rican Government protested at Diageo's decision to relocate to the US Virgin Islands, claiming that the Virgin Islands had misappropriated federal excise taxes collected on rum revenues to persuade the company to move to the territory, a claim the Government vehemently denied.

A memorandum of understanding was signed in September 2010 by the US Virgin Islands and the Organisation of Eastern Caribbean States. The agreement envisaged greater co-operation in the areas of security, economic development, disaster management and environmental protection.

Recent developments: 2010 gubernatorial election

John deJongh was re-elected as Governor in an election held on 2 November 2010, attracting 56.3% of the votes cast. Kenneth Mapp, an independent and the only other candidate, received 43.6% of the ballot. Donna Christensen was re-elected as the territory's Delegate to the US Congress. Governor deJongh was inaugurated on 6 January 2011; he reiterated his commitment to addressing crime and boosting economic activity on the islands.

CONSTITUTION AND GOVERNMENT

The Government of the US Virgin Islands is organized under the provisions of the Organic Act of the Virgin Islands, passed by the US Congress in 1936 and revised in 1954 and 1984. Executive power is vested in the Governor, elected for four years by universal suffrage. Legislative power is vested in a unicameral, 15-member body.

ECONOMIC AFFAIRS

According to estimates by the US Bureau of Economic Analysis, the islands' gross domestic product (GDP) in 2007 was US $4,580m., equivalent to about $39,915 per head. GDP increased, in real terms, at an average rate of 2.9% per year during 2002–07. In 2000–09 the population increased at an average annual rate of 0.1%. Growth in 2008 was estimated at 2.8%.

Most of the land is unsuitable for large-scale cultivation, but tax incentives have encouraged the growing of vegetables, fruit and cereals, which are produced for local consumption. The islands are heavily dependent on links with the US mainland. There are no known natural resources, and, because of limited land space and other factors, the islands are unable to produce sufficient food to satisfy local consumption. Most goods are imported, mainly from the mainland USA. According to the 2000 census figures, 0.7% of the economically active population were engaged in agriculture, forestry, fishing and mining. According to FAO estimates, however, the sector engaged around 18.0% of the labour force in mid-2011.

Industry (including construction and mining) engaged some 13.3% of the non-agricultural labour force in 2009, according to official figures. The manufacturing sector employed 4.9% of the employed labour force in 2009. The main branch of manufacturing is petroleum-refining.

Services (including public administration) employed some 86.6% of the non-agricultural labour force in 2009, according to official figures, of which about 30% were employed in public administration. Tourism, which is estimated to account for more than 30% of GDP, is the mainstay of the islands' income and employment, and provides the major source of direct and indirect revenue for other service sectors (including trade and transport). The emphasis is on the visiting cruise ship business and the advantages of duty-free products for tourist visitors. In 2010 visitor arrivals (including excursionists and cruise passengers) totalled 2.5m.; in 2009 visitor expenditures amounted to US $1,467.5m. In 2011 work was ongoing on a number of construction projects related to the tourism industry, including a $63m. recreation centre on St Thomas and the addition of a cruise ship dock at St Croix harbour. Planned construction of a $500m. casino and resort on St Croix, approved in 2005, was yet to begin in 2011.

St Croix has one of the world's largest petroleum refineries, Hovensa LLC (a joint venture between the US oil company Amerada Hess and Petróleos de Venezuela, SA), which had a production capacity of almost 500,000 barrels per day (b/d) in 2009. In response to stricter environmental controls, in 2005 the company began work on a US $400m. desulphurization unit. In January 2007 four solar power sites on St Thomas, constructed by residents with government funding, were certified by the Energy Office as suitable power generation units from which the Water and Power Authority might purchase energy that was surplus to the residents' requirements. Efforts have been made to introduce labour-intensive and non-polluting manufacturing industries. Rum is an important product; in late 2010 Diageo inaugurated a distillery that was expected to produce 20m. proof gallons annually. In 2009 the Government also agreed to fund expansion of the existing Cruzan Rum distillery. Federal excise taxes collected on rum exports to the USA (the so-called 'cover over' programme) returned $106.8m. of revenue in 2009.

In 1999 the Territorial Government introduced a Five-Year Strategic and Financial Operating Plan to reduce government expenditure and enhance the effectiveness of procedures for revenue collection. In 2009 there was a budget deficit of $27.4m. In 2005/06 the islands' debt amounted to some $1,150m., equivalent to $10,272 per head. The average rate of unemployment stood at 8.1% in 2010.

In 2009 the islands recorded a trade deficit of US $561.6m. In that year the USA provided 11.1% of imports and took 87.3% of exports. Venezuela was also a major source of imports. Of total exports to the USA in 2009, some 85.6% were refined petroleum products. Crude petroleum accounted for 68.9% of the islands' total imports in that year.

Owing to the islands' heavy reliance on imported goods, local prices and inflation are higher than on the mainland, and the islands' economy was dependent on that of the USA. From 2009 the economy, particularly the tourism and construction sectors, was adversely affected by the global economic downturn, while lower tax receipts put government finances under strain. In June 2009 the legislature approved borrowing of US $250m. to meet budget shortfalls, and in early 2010 the Governor submitted a further borrowing request to the Legislative Assembly, to cover the projected shortfall of $170m. Economic activity remained subdued in 2010 owing to weak domestic demand and a slow recovery in the USA, the territory's main trading partner. The unemployment rate rose in 2010 to 8.1% (from 6.9% in 2009) and was expected to remain at that level during 2011. Nevertheless, an increase in tourist numbers in 2010 was welcomed, and a gradual economic recovery was forecast for 2011–12. Further budget shortfalls of $75m. and $132m. were projected by Governor deJongh in 2011 and 2012, respectively, and in February 2011 he submitted a series of austerity measures to the Senate. The proposals included tax increases and a freeze in public sector salaries.

PUBLIC HOLIDAYS

2012: 1 January (New Year's Day), 6 January (Three Kings' Day), 16 January (Martin Luther King Day), 20 February (Presidents' Day), 31 March (Transfer Day), 6–9 April (Easter), 28 May (Memorial Day), 18 June (Organic Act Day), 3 July (Danish West Indies Emancipation Day), 4 July (US Independence Day), 26 July (Hurricane Supplication Day), 3 September (Labor Day), 8 October (Columbus Day/Puerto Rico Friendship Day), 15 October (Virgin Islands Thanksgiving Day), 1 November (Liberty Day), 11 November (Veterans' Day), 22 November (US Thanksgiving Day), 25 December (Christmas).

UNITED STATES EXTERNAL TERRITORIES

The United States Virgin Islands

Statistical Survey

Sources (unless otherwise stated): Office of Public Relations, Office of the Governor, Charlotte Amalie, VI 00802; tel. (340) 774-0294; fax (340) 774-4988; Bureau of Economic Research, Dept of Economic Development and Agriculture, 1050 Norre Gade No. 5, Suite 301, Charlotte Amalie, VI 00802; POB 6400, Charlotte Amalie, VI 00804; tel. (340) 774-8784; e-mail dhazell@usviber.org; internet www.usviber.org.

AREA AND POPULATION

Area: 347.1 sq km (134 sq miles): St Croix 215 sq km (83 sq miles); St Thomas 80.3 sq km (31 sq miles); St John 51.8 sq km (20 sq miles).

Population: 101,809 at census of 1 April 1990; 108,612 (males 51,684, females 56,748) at census of 1 April 2000. *By Island* (2000 census): St Croix 53,234, St Thomas 51,181, St John 4,197 (Source: US Census Bureau). *2008* (resident population): St Croix 57,351; St Thomas 55,138; St John 4,522; Total 117,011. *Mid-2011* (UN estimate): 109,114 (Source: UN, *World Population Prospects: The 2008 Revision*).

Density (at mid-2011): 314.4 per sq km.

Population by Age and Sex ('000, UN estimates at mid-2011): *0–14:* 22,367 (males 11,484, females 10,883); *15–64:* 70,478 (males 32,981, females 37,497); *65 and over:* 16,269 (males 7,173, females 9,096); *Total* 109,114 (males 51,638, females 57,476) (Source: UN, *World Population Prospects: The 2008 Revision*).

Principal Towns (population at census of 1 April 2000): Charlotte Amalie (capital) 11,004; Christiansted 2,637; Frederiksted 732. Source: Thomas Brinkhoff, *City Population* (internet www.citypopulation.de).

Births and Deaths (2006, preliminary): Registered live births 1,431 (birth rate 13.2 per 1,000); Registered deaths 629 (death rate 5.8 per 1,000) (Source: US National Center for Health Statistics). *2010:* Birth rate 11.5 per 1,000; Death rate 7.0 per 1,000 (Source: Pan American Health Organization).

Life Expectancy (years at birth, estimates): 79.2 (males 76.1; females 82.4) in 2010. Source: Pan American Health Organization.

Economically Active Population (persons aged 16 years and over, 2000 census): Agriculture, forestry, fishing, hunting and mining 324; Manufacturing 2,754; Construction 4,900; Wholesale trade 912; Retail trade 6,476; Transportation, warehousing and utilities 3,321; Information 931; Finance, insurance, real estate, rental and leasing 2,330; Professional, scientific, management, administrative and waste management services 3,058; Educational, health, and social services 6,742; Arts, entertainment, recreation, accommodation and food services 7,351; Public administration 4,931; Other services 2,535; *Total employed* 46,565 (Source: US Bureau of the Census). *2009* (number of waged and salaried jobs, official figures): Construction and mining 2,179; Manufacturing 2,220; Transportation, warehouses and utilities 1,613; Wholesale and retail trade 6,807; Financial activities 2,458; Leisure and hospitality 6,875; Information 777; Other services 9,117; Federal government 991; Territorial government 12,009; Total 45,046. *2010* (civilians only, annual averages): Total employed 47,268, Unemployed 4,145; Total labour force 51,413.

HEALTH AND WELFARE

Total Fertility Rate (children per woman, 2010): 1.8.
Under-5 Mortality Rate (per 1,000 live births, 2010): 9.8.
Physicians (per 1,000 head, 2003): 1.47.
Hospital Beds (per 1,000 head, 1996): 18.7.
Source: Pan American Health Organization.
For definitions, see explanatory note on p. vi.

AGRICULTURE, ETC.

Livestock (2008, FAO estimates): Cattle 8,100; Sheep 3,250; Pigs 2,650; Goats 4,100; Chickens 40,000. Note: No data were available for 2009.

Fishing (metric tons, live weight, 2008): Total catch (all capture) 1,075 (Groupers 36; Snappers, jobfishes, etc. 127; Grunts, sweetlips, etc. 38; Parrotfishes 170; Surgeonfishes 36; Triggerfishes, durgons, etc. 49; Caribbean spiny lobster 121; Stromboid conchs 327).

Source: FAO.

INDUSTRY

Production ('000 metric tons unless otherwise indicated, 2002, estimates): Jet fuels 1,745; Motor spirit (petrol) 2,654; Kerosene 91; Gasdiesel (distillate fuel) oil 5,725; Residual fuel oils 3,550; Liquefied petroleum gas 164; Electric energy (2007) 1,070 million kWh. Source: UN, *Industrial Commodity Statistics Yearbook* and Database.

FINANCE

Currency and Exchange Rates: 100 cents = 1 United States dollar (US $). *Sterling and Euro Equivalents* (31 December 2010): £1 sterling = US $1.5655; €1 = US $1.3362; US $100 = £63.88 = €74.84.

Budget (US $ million, 2009): Operating budget 848.6 (Net revenues from taxes, duties and other sources 468.2); Rum excise taxes (Federal remittance) 106.8; Direct Federal expenditures 876.

Cost of Living (Consumer Price Index; base: 2001 = 100): All items 117.6 in 2006; 123.3 in 2007; 132.1 in 2008.

Gross Domestic Product (US $ million at current prices): 4,240 in 2005; 4,298 in 2006; 4,580 in 2007 (Source: Bureau of Economic Analysis, US Department of Commerce).

EXTERNAL TRADE

Total Trade (US $ million): *Imports:* 12,251.0 in 2007; 17,861.3 in 2008; 10,289.9 in 2009. *Exports:* 12,961.8 in 2007; 17,249.4 in 2008; 9,728.3 in 2009. Note: The main import is crude petroleum (7,085.9m. in 2009), while the principal exports are refined petroleum products (8,327.3m. in 2009).

Trade with the USA (US $ million): *Imports:* 1,261.0 in 2007; 1,214.6 in 2008; 1,139.3 in 2009. *Exports:* 12,182.1 in 2007; 14,496.3 in 2008; 8,495.3 in 2009.

TRANSPORT

Road Traffic (registered motor vehicles, 2008): 64,469.

Shipping: Freight Imports ('000 metric tons) 1,056 in 2002; 879 in 2003; 979 in 2004. *Cruise Ship Arrivals:* 687 in 2008; 621 in 2009; 680 in 2010. *Passenger Arrivals:* 1,757,067 in 2008; 1,582,264 in 2009; 1,858,946 in 2010.

Civil Aviation (visitor arrivals): 678,140 in 2008; 664,249 in 2009; 691,558 in 2010.

TOURISM

Visitor Arrivals ('000): 2,435.2 in 2008 (arrivals by air 678.1, cruise ship passengers 1,757.1); 2,219.2 in 2009 (arrivals by air 646.3, cruise ship passengers 1,572.9); 2,480.2 in 2010 (arrivals by air 699.7, cruise ship passengers 1,780.4).

Visitor Receipts (US $ million, 2009): Total receipts 1,467.5 (tourists 961.2, excursionists 506.2).

COMMUNICATIONS MEDIA

Radio Receivers (1997): 107,100 in use.
Television Receivers (1999): 71,000 in use.
Telephones (2009): 75,000 main lines in use.
Personal Computers: 3,000 (27.4 per 1,000 persons) in 2005.
Mobile Cellular Telephones (2009): 80,300 subscribers.
Internet Users (2009): 30,000.
Broadband Subscribers (2009, estimate): 9,000.
Daily Newspapers (1996): 3 titles; average circulation 42,000 copies.
Non-daily Newspapers (1988, estimates): 2; average circulation 4,000 copies.

Sources: UNESCO, *Statistical Yearbook*; International Telecommunication Union.

EDUCATION

Pre-primary (1992/93, unless otherwise indicated): 62 schools; 121 teachers; 4,714 students (2000).

Elementary (1992/93, unless otherwise indicated): 62 schools; 790 teachers (public schools only); 11,728 students (2005).

Secondary: 541 teachers (public schools only, 1990); 5,022 students (2005).

Higher Education: 266 teachers (2003/04); 2,610 students (2004).

Sources: UNESCO, *Statistical Yearbook*; US Bureau of the Census.

UNITED STATES EXTERNAL TERRITORIES

Directory

The Government

HEAD OF STATE

President: BARACK HUSSEIN OBAMA (took office 20 January 2009).

EXECUTIVE
(May 2011)

The Government is formed by the Democratic Party of the Virgin Islands.

Governor: JOHN DE JONGH, Jr (took office 1 January 2007; re-elected 2 November 2010).
Lieutenant-Governor: GREGORY R. FRANCIS.
Commissioner of Agriculture: LOUIS E. PETERSON, Jr.
Commissioner of Education: Dr LAVERNE TERRY.
Commissioner of Finance: ANGEL DAWSON, Jr.
Commissioner of Health: JULIA SHEEN-AARON.
Commissioner of Human Services: CHRISTOPHER FINCH.
Commissioner of Labor: ALBERT BRYAN, Jr.
Commissioner of Licensing and Consumer Affairs: WAYNE L. BIGGS, Jr.
Commissioner of Planning and Natural Resources: ALICIA BARNES.
Commissioner of Police: NOVELLE E. FRANCIS, Jr.
Commissioner of Property and Procurement: LYNN A. MILLIN MADURO.
Commissioner of Public Works: DARRYL SMALLS.
Commissioner of Sports, Parks and Recreation: ST CLAIRE N. WILLIAMS.
Commissioner of Tourism: BEVERLY NICHOLSON-DOTY.
Attorney-General: VINCENT FRAZER.
US Virgin Islands Delegate to the US Congress: DONNA M. CHRISTENSEN.

GOVERNMENT OFFICES

Office of the Governor: Government House, 21–22 Kongens Gade, Charlotte Amalie, VI 00802; tel. (340) 774-0001; fax (340) 774-1361; e-mail contact@governordejongh.com; internet www.governordejongh.com.

Office of the Lieutenant-Governor: Government Hill, 18 Kongens Gade, Charlotte Amalie, VI 00802; tel. (340) 774-2991; fax (340) 774-6953; internet www.ltg.gov.vi.

Department of Agriculture: Estate Lower Love, Kingshill, St Croix, VI 00850; tel. (340) 774-5182; fax (340) 774-1823; e-mail lpeters@uvi.edu.

Department of Education: 1834 Kongens Gade, Charlotte Amalie, VI 00802-6746; tel. (340) 774-0100; fax (340) 779-7153; e-mail lterry@doe.vi; internet www.doe.vi.

Department of Finance: GERS Bldg, 2nd Floor, 76 Kronprindsens Gade, Charlotte Amalie, VI 00802; tel. (340) 774-4750; fax (340) 776-4028; e-mail aedawson@dof.gov.vi.

Department of Health: 1303 Hospital Ground Suite 10, Charlotte Amalie, St Thomas, VI 00802; tel. (340) 774-0117; fax (340) 777-4001; e-mail julia.sheen@usvi-doh.org; internet www.healthvi.org.

Department of Human Services: Knud Hansen Complex, Bldg A, 1303 Hospital Ground, Charlotte Amalie, VI 00802; tel. (340) 774-0930; fax (340) 774-3466; internet www.dhs.gov.vi.

Department of Justice: GERS Bldg, 2nd Floor, 34–38 Kronprindsens Gade, Charlotte Amalie, VI 00802; tel. (340) 774-5666; fax (340) 774-9710; e-mail vfrazer@doj.vi.gov; internet doj.vi.gov.

Department of Labor: 53A–54AB Kronprindsens Gade, St Thomas, VI 00803-2608; tel. (340) 776-3700; fax (340) 774-5908; e-mail customersupport@vidol.gov; internet www.vidol.gov.

Department of Licensing and Consumer Affairs: Property & Procurement Bldg, 1 Sub Base, Rm 205, Charlotte Amalie, St Thomas, VI 00802; tel. (340) 774-3130; fax (340) 776-0675; e-mail dlcacommissioner@dlca.gov.vi; internet www.dlca.gov.vi.

Department of Planning and Natural Resources: Cyril E. King Airport, Terminal Bldg, 2nd Floor, Suite 6, 8100 Lindberg Bay, St Thomas, VI 00802; tel. (340) 774-3320; fax (340) 775-5706; e-mail robertmathes@dpnr.gov.vi; internet www.dpnr.gov.vi.

Department of Police: Alexander Farrelly Criminal Justice Center, Charlotte Amalie, St Thomas, VI 00802; tel. (340) 774-2211; fax (340) 715-5517; e-mail police.commissioner@vipd.gov.vi; internet www.vipd.gov.vi.

Department of Property and Procurement: Property & Procurement Bldg No. 1, 3rd Floor, Sub Base, Charlotte Amalie, VI 00802; tel. (340) 774-0828; fax (340) 777-9587; e-mail lmillin@pnpvi.org; internet www.pnpvi.org.

Department of Public Works: Bldg No. 8, Sub Base, Charlotte Amalie, VI 00802; tel. (340) 776-4844; fax (340) 774-5869; e-mail darryl.smalls@dpw.vi.gov.

Department of Sports, Parks and Recreation: Property & Procurement Bldg No. 1, Sub Base, 2nd Floor, Rm 206, Charlotte Amalie, VI 00802; tel. (340) 774-0255; fax (340) 774-4600; e-mail info@dspr.vi; internet www.dspr.vi.

Department of Tourism: POB 6400, St Thomas, VI 00804; tel. (340) 774-8784; fax (340) 774-4390; e-mail info@usvitourism.vi; internet www.visitusvi.com.

Legislature

LEGISLATIVE ASSEMBLY
Senate

President of the Senate: LOUIS PATRICK HILL.

Election, 4 November 2008

Party	Seats
Democrats	10
Independent Citizens' Movement	2
Independent	3
Total	15

Election Commission

Election Board: Election Systems of the Virgin Islands, POB 1499, Kingshill, St Croix, VI 00851-1499; tel. (340) 773-1021; fax (340) 773-4523; e-mail electionsys@unitedstates.vi; internet www.vivote.gov; Supervisor of Elections JOHN ABRAMSON, Jr; brs on St Thomas and St John.

Political Organizations

Democratic Party of the Virgin Islands: POB 502578, St Thomas Democratic District, VI 00805-2578; tel. (340) 643-4600; affiliated to the Democratic Party of the USA; Chair. CECIL R. BENJAMIN, Jr.

Independent Citizens' Movement (The ICM Party, VI): POB 305188, St Thomas, VI 00803-5188; tel. (340) 772-9524; f. 1968; Chair. Sen. TERRENCE NELSON.

Republican Party of the Virgin Islands: 6067 Questa Verde, Christiansted, St Croix, VI 00820-4485; tel. (340) 332-2579; e-mail info@virepublicanwomen.com; internet www.vigop.com; f. 1948; affiliated to the Republican Party of the USA since 1952; Chair. HERBERT SCHOENBOHM; Exec. Dir WARREN COLE.

Judicial System

Supreme Court of the Virgin Islands: No. 161B, Crown Bay, St Thomas, VI 00802; tel. (340) 774-2237; fax (340) 774-2258; e-mail administrative.services@visupremecourt.org; internet www.visupremecourt.org; f. 2007; assumed jurisdiction for all appeals formerly administered by the Superior Court; highest local appellate body, established to administer justice independently of the US federal justice system; judges are appointed by the Governor.

Judges: RHYS S. HODGE (Chief Judge), IVE ARLINGTON SWAN, MARIA M. CABRET.

Superior Court of the Virgin Islands: Alexander A. Farrelly Justice Center, 5400 Veteran's Dr., St Thomas, VI 00802; tel. (340) 774-6680; fax (340) 776-9889; e-mail court.administrator@visuperiorcourt.org; internet www.visuperiorcourt.org; f. 1976 as the Territorial Court of the Virgin Islands; name officially changed in 2004; jurisdiction over all local civil actions and criminal matters; court in St Croix also; judges are appointed by the Governor.

Judges: DARRYL DEAN DONOHUE (Presiding), ISHMAEL A. MEYERS, BRENDA J. HOLLAR, AUDREY L. THOMAS, PATRICIA D. STEELE, JULIO A. BRADY, JAMES S. CARROLL, MICHAEL C. DUNSTON, HAROLD W. L. WILLCOCKS, ADAM G. CHRISTIAN.

US Federal District Court of the Virgin Islands: Division of St Thomas/St John: 5500 Veteran's Dr., Charlotte Amalie, St Thomas, VI 00802-6424; Division of St Croix: 3013 Estate Golden Rock, Christiansted, St Croix, VI 00820-4355; tel. (340) 774-0640; fax (340) 774-1293; internet www.vid.uscourts.gov; jurisdiction in civil, criminal and federal actions; judges are appointed by the President of the USA with the advice and consent of the Senate.

Judges: CURTIS V. GOMEZ (Chief Judge), RAYMOND L. FINCH.

Religion

The population is mainly Christian. The main churches with followings in the islands are Baptist, Roman Catholic, Episcopalian, Lutheran, Methodist, Moravian and Seventh-day Adventist. There is also a small Jewish community, numbering around 900 adherents.

CHRISTIANITY

The Roman Catholic Church

The US Virgin Islands comprises a single diocese, suffragan to the archdiocese of Washington, DC, USA. Some 28% of the population are Roman Catholics.

Bishop of St Thomas: Most Rev. HERBERT A. BEVARD, Bishop's Residence, 29A Princesse Gade, POB 301825, Charlotte Amalie, VI 00803-1825; tel. (340) 774-3166; fax (340) 774-5816; e-mail chancery@islands.vi; internet www.catholicvi.com.

The Anglican Communion

Episcopal Diocese of the Virgin Islands: Bishop: Rt Rev. AMBROSE GUMBS, POB 7488, St Thomas, VI 00801; tel. (340) 776-1797; fax (340) 777-8485; internet www.episcopalvi.org.

The Press

Pride Magazine: 22A Norre Gade, POB 7908, Charlotte Amalie, VI 00801; tel. (340) 776-4106; f. 1983; monthly; Editor JUDITH WILLIAMS; circ. 4,000.

St Croix Avis: La Grande Princesse, Christiansted, St Croix, VI 00820; tel. (340) 773-2300; f. 1944; morning; Editor RENA BROADHURST-KNIGHT; circ. 10,000.

St John Tradewinds: The Marketplace, Office Suites II, Office 104, POB 1500, Cruz Bay, St John, VI 00831; tel. (340) 776-6496; fax (340) 693-8885; e-mail editor@tradewinds.vi; internet www.stjohnnews.com; f. 1972; weekly; Publr MALINDA NELSON; circ. 2,500.

Virgin Islands Daily News: 9155 Estate Thomas, VI 00802; tel. (340) 774-8772; fax (340) 776-0740; e-mail dailynews@vipowernet.net; internet www.virginislandsdailynews.com; f. 1930; acquired from Innovative Communication Corpn by Times-Shamrock Communications, USA in 2008; morning; CEO and Exec. Editor JASON ROBBINS; circ. 15,000.

Virgin Islands Source: St Thomas; tel. (340) 777-8144; fax (340) 777-8136; e-mail source@viaccess.net; internet www.visource.com; f. 1998; comprises the *St Thomas Source*, *St Croix Source* and *St John Source*; daily; digital; Publr SHAUN A. PENNINGTON.

Broadcasting and Communications

TELECOMMUNICATIONS

Innovative Telephone: Bjerget House, POB 1730, St Croix, VI 00821; tel. (340) 777-7700; fax (340) 777-7701; e-mail webmaster@iccvi.com; internet www.innovativetelephone.com; f. 1959 as Virgin Islands Telephone Corpn (Vitelco); acquired by Innovative Communication Corpn in 1987; present name adopted in 2001; provides telephone services throughout the islands; launched internet service, Innovative PowerNet, in 1999; Pres. and CEO CLARKE GARNETT (acting).

Innovative Wireless: 4006 Estate Diamond, Christiansted, St Croix, VI 00820; fax (340) 778-6011; internet www.vitelcellular.com; f. 1989 as VitelCellular; subsidiary of Innovative Communication Corpn; mobile cellular telecommunications; Man. Dir BEULAH JONIS (acting).

RADIO

WDHP 1620 AM, WRRA 1290 AM, WAXJ 103.5 FM: 79A Castle Coakley, Christiansted, St Croix, VI 00820; tel. (340) 719-1620; fax (340) 778-1686; e-mail wrra@islands.vi; internet www.reefbroadcasting.com; operated by Reef Broadcasting, Inc; commercial; English; broadcasts to the US and British Virgin Islands, Puerto Rico and the Eastern Caribbean; Owner and Gen. Man. HUGH PEMBERTON.

WEVI (Power 101.7 WeVi-FM): 2C Hogensborg, Frederiksted, St Croix, VI 00840; POB 892, Christiansted, VI 00821; tel. (340) 719-9384; e-mail aw@frontlinemissions.org; internet www.wevifm.net; operated by FrontLine Missions International, Inc; non-commercial; Christian programming; English, Spanish and Creole/Patois.

WGOD: 22A, Estate Dorothea, POB 305012, Charlotte Amalie, St Thomas, VI 00803; tel. (340) 774-4498; fax (340) 777-9978; internet wgodradio.org; operated by Moody Broadcasting Network, USA; commercial; Christian religious programming; Pres. Rev. REYNALD CHARLES; Gen. Man. MARIE RHYMER-MARTIN.

WIUJ: POB 2477, St Thomas, VI 00803; e-mail information@wiuj.com; internet www.wiuj.com; operated by V. I. Youth Development Radio, Inc; non-commercial; educational and public service programmes; Gen. Man. LEO MORONE.

WJKC (Isle 95-FM), WMNG (Mongoose), WVIQ (Sunny): 5020 Anchor Way, POB 25680, Christiansted, St Croix, VI 00824; tel. (340) 773-0995; fax (340) 770-9093; e-mail jkc@viradio.com; internet www.isle95.com; f. 1982; commercial; Gen. Man. JONATHAN K. COHEN.

WSTA (Lucky 13): 121 Sub Base, POB 1340, St Thomas, VI 00804; tel. (340) 774-1340; fax (340) 776-1316; e-mail addie@wsta.com; internet www.wsta.com; f. 1950; acquired by Ottley Communications Corpn in 1984; commercial; Owner and Gen. Man. ATHNIEL C. OTTLEY.

WVGN: 8000 Nisky Centre, Suite 714, St Thomas, VI 00802; tel. (800) 275-6437; e-mail info@wvgn.org; internet www.wvgn.org; f. 2002; operated by Caribbean Community Broadcasting Co; non-commercial; news and public affairs programming; affiliated to NBC, USA; CEO KEITH BASS; Gen. Man. LORRAINE BAA-ELISHA.

WVWI (Radio One), WVJZ (Jamz), WWKS (Kiss), WIVI (Hitz) (Ackley Media Group Stations): POB 302179, St Thomas, VI 00803-2179; tel. (340) 776-1000; fax (340) 776-5357; e-mail info@amg.vi; internet www.amg.vi; f. 1962; acquired from Knight Quality Stations by Ackley Media Group in 2006; commercial; Pres. and CEO GORDON P. ACKLEY.

WZIN (Buzzrocks): Nisky Mall Center, PMB 357, St Thomas, VI 00802; tel. (340) 776-1043; fax (340) 775-446; e-mail cristy@buzzrocks.com; internet www.buzzrocks.com; operated by Pan Caribbean Broadcasting, Inc; commercial; Gen. Man. ALAN FRIEDMAN.

Other radio stations include: WIVH, WMYP (Latino 98.3 FM), WSTX (Magic 97X), and WYAC (Voice of the Virgin Islands).

TELEVISION

Innovative Cable Television (St Croix, St Thomas, St John): 4006 Estate Diamond, Christiansted, St Croix, VI 00820; POB 6100, St Thomas, VI 00804; fax (340) 778-6011; e-mail info@iccvi.com; internet www.innovativecable.com; f. 1997 following acquisition of St Croix Cable TV (f. 1981); subsidiary of Innovative Communication Corpn; acquired Caribbean Communication Corpn in 1998; comprises TV2 (f. 2000); broadcasts to seven Caribbean islands and France; Pres. and Gen. Man. JENNIFER MATARANGAS-KING.

WSVI-TV8 (Channel 8): Sunny Isle Shopping Center, POB 6000, Christiansted, St Croix, VI 00823; tel. (340) 778-5008; fax (340) 778-5011; e-mail channel8@wsvitv.com; internet www.wsvi.tv; f. 1965; operated by Alpha Broadcasting Corpn; affiliated to ABC, USA; one satellite channel and one analogue translator.

WTJX-TV (Public Television Service): POB 808, St Croix, VI 00820; tel. (340) 773-3337; fax (340) 773-4555; e-mail pphipps@wtjxtv.org; internet www.wtjxtv.org; f. 1968; educational and public service programmes; affiliated to PBS, USA; broadcasts on one terrestrial and four digital (cable) channels; broadcasts to the US and British Virgin Islands and Puerto Rico; Chair. RAÚL CARRILLO; Exec. Dir OSBERT POTTER.

Finance

BANKING

Banco Popular of the Virgin Islands: 193 Altona and Welgunst, Charlotte Amalie, VI 00802; tel. (340) 693-2702; fax (340) 693-2782; e-mail internet@bppr.com; internet www.bancopopular.com; Chair. RICHARD L. CARRIÓN; 8 brs.

Bank of Nova Scotia (Scotiabank): 214C Altona and Welgunst, POB 420, Charlotte Amalie, VI 00804; tel. (340) 774-0037; fax (340) 693-5994; e-mail lawrence.aqui@scotiabank.com; internet www.usvi.scotiabank.com; Vice-Pres. LAWRENCE AQUI; Man. ALLAN TOBIN; 10 brs.

Bank of St Croix: POB 24240, Gallows Bay, St Croix 00824; tel. (340) 773-8500; fax (340) 773-8508; e-mail info@bankofstcroix.com; internet www.bankofstcroix.com; f. 1994; CEO JAMES BRISBOIS; 1 br.

FirstBank of Puerto Rico: POB 3126, St Thomas, VI 00803; tel. (340) 774-2022; fax (340) 776-1313; acquired First Virgin Islands Federal Savings Bank in 2000 and Virgin Islands Community Bank in Jan. 2008; Pres. and CEO JAMES E. CRITES; 2 brs.

Virgin Islands Community Bank: 12–13 King St, Christiansted, St Croix, VI 00820; tel. (340) 773-0440; fax (340) 773-4028; internet www.vibank.org/vicbank.html; acquired by FirstBank of Puerto Rico in Jan. 2008; Pres. and CEO MICHAEL J. DOW; 3 brs.

INSURANCE

A number of mainland US companies have agencies in the Virgin Islands.

Trade and Industry

GOVERNMENT AGENCY

US Virgin Islands Economic Development Authority: Government Development Bank Bldg, 1050 Norre Gade No. 5, POB 305038, St Thomas, VI 00803; tel. (340) 774-8104; e-mail edc@usvieda.org; internet www.usvieda.org; semi-autonomous body comprising Government Devt Bank, Economic Devt Commission, Industrial Park Devt Corpn, Small Business Devt Agency and the Enterprise Zone programme; offices in St Thomas and St Croix; Chair. ALBERT BRYAN, Jr; CEO PERCIVAL CLOUDEN.

CHAMBERS OF COMMERCE

St Croix Chamber of Commerce: 3009 Orange Grove, Suite 12, Christiansted, St Croix, VI 00820; tel. (340) 718-1435; fax (340) 773-8172; e-mail info@stxchamber.org; internet www.stxchamber.org; f. 1924; Pres. SCOT F. McCHAIN; Exec. Dir MICHAEL DEMBECK; 300 mems.

St Thomas-St John Chamber of Commerce: 6–7 Dronningens Gade, POB 324, Charlotte Amalie, VI 00804; tel. (340) 776-0100; fax (340) 776-0588; e-mail chamber@islands.vi; Pres. THADDEUS BAST; Exec. Dir JOSEPH S. AUBAIN; c. 700 mems.

UTILITIES

Regulatory Authority

Virgin Islands Energy Office: 4101 Estate Mars Hill, Frederiksted, St Croix, VI 00840; tel. (340) 713-8436; fax (340) 772-0063; e-mail dbuchanan@vienergy.org; internet www.vienergy.org; Dir BEVAN R. SMITH, Jr.

Electricity and Water

Virgin Islands Water and Power Authority (WAPA): POB 1450, Charlotte Amalie, VI 00804-1450; tel. (340) 774-3552; fax (340) 774-3422; internet www.viwapa.vi; f. 1964; public corpn; manufactures and distributes electric power and desalinated sea water; Chair. CHERYL BOYNES-JACKSON; CEO HUGO HODGE, Jr; c. 50,000 customers.

Transport

ROADS

The islands' road network totals approximately 855.5 km (531.6 miles).

SHIPPING

The US Virgin Islands are a popular port of call for cruise ships. The bulk of cargo traffic is handled at a container port on St Croix. A passenger and freight ferry service provides frequent daily connections between St Thomas and St John and between St Thomas and Tortola (British Virgin Islands). In 2004 the Port Authority approved a US $9.3m. project to expand freight, vehicle and passenger facilities at Red Hook. A $150m. marina restoration project on St Thomas, completed in 2006, included provision for 'mega-yacht' docking facilities in addition to conventional moorings, which, it was hoped, would invigorate the cruise ship industry.

Virgin Islands Port Authority: POB 301707, Charlotte Amalie, VI 00803-1707; tel. (340) 774-1629; fax (340) 774-0025; e-mail info@viport.com; internet www.viport.com; f. 1968; semi-autonomous govt agency; maintains, operates and develops marine and airport facilities; Exec. Dir KENN HOBSON (acting).

CIVIL AVIATION

There are airports on St Thomas and St Croix, and an airfield on St John. Seaplane services link the three islands. The runways at Cyril E. King Airport, St Thomas, and Alexander Hamilton Airport, St Croix, can accommodate intercontinental flights.

Tourism

The islands have a well-developed tourism infrastructure, offering excellent facilities for fishing, yachting and other aquatic sports. A National Park covers about two-thirds of St John. There were 4,948 guest rooms in 2009, 3,809 of which were in hotels. Visitors from the US mainland comprised 83.7% of hotel guests in that year. In 2010 there were some 2.5m. visitors to the islands, of whom 699,700 were stop-over tourists and 1.8m. were cruise ship passengers. Visitor expenditure amounted to US $1,467.5m. in 2009.

St Croix Hotel Association: POB 24238, St Croix, VI 00824; tel. (340) 773-7117; fax (340) 773-5883.

US Virgin Islands Hotel and Tourism Association: POB 2300, Charlotte Amalie, St Thomas, VI 00803; tel. (340) 774-6835; fax (340) 774-4993; e-mail stsjhta@vipowernet.net; internet www.virgin-islands-hotels.com; Chair. MARC LANGEVIN.

Defence

The USA is responsible for the defence of the United States Virgin Islands.

Education

The public education system in the US Virgin Islands comprises a State Education Agency and two Local Education Agencies, serving the St Thomas/St John District and the St Croix District. Education is compulsory up to the age of 16 years. It generally comprises eight years at primary school and four years at secondary school. There are two high schools, three middle schools and 13 elementary schools in St Thomas/St John District, while the district of St Croix has two high schools, three middle schools, 10 elementary schools and an alternative and a vocational school. In 2009 there were 15,493 students enrolled at public elementary and secondary schools, while in 2008 a total of 6,907 students were enrolled at private schools. The University of the Virgin Islands, with campuses on St Thomas and St Croix, had 2,602 full- and part-time students in 2009. The proposed budget for 2010/11 allocated US $40.9m. in federal funds to the Department of Education.

OTHER UNITED STATES TERRITORIES

Baker and Howland Islands

The Baker and Howland Islands lie in the Central Pacific Ocean, about 2,575 km (1,600 miles) south-west of Honolulu, Hawaii; they comprise two low-lying coral atolls without lagoons, and are uninhabited. Both islands were mined for guano in the late 19th century. Settlements, known as Meyerton (on Baker) and Itascatown (on Howland), were established by the USA in 1935, but were evacuated during the Second World War, owing to Japanese air attacks. The islands are National Wildlife Refuges, and since 1974 have been administered by the US Fish and Wildlife Service. In 1990 legislation before Congress proposed that the islands be included within the boundaries of the State of Hawaii. In January 2009 President George W. Bush established by proclamation the Pacific Remote Islands Marine National Monument, which included Baker and Howland Islands. The islands are administered by the US Department of the Interior, US Fish and Wildlife Service, Refuge Complex Office, POB 50167, Honolulu, Hawaii 96850; internet www.fws.gov.

Jarvis Island

Jarvis Island lies in the Central Pacific Ocean, about 2,090 km (1,300 miles) south of Hawaii. It is a low-lying coral island and is uninhabited. The island was mined for guano in the late 19th century. A settlement, known as Millersville, including a weather station for the benefit of trans-Pacific aviation, was established by the USA in 1935, but was evacuated during the Second World War. Legislation before Congress in 1990 proposed that the island be included within the State of Hawaii. In January 2009 Jarvis Island became part of the Pacific Remote Islands Marine National Monument (see above). The island is a National Wildlife Refuge and is administered by the US Department of the Interior, US Fish and Wildlife Service (details as above, under Baker and Howland Islands).

Johnston Atoll

Johnston Atoll lies in the Pacific Ocean, about 1,319 km (820 miles) west-south-west of Honolulu, Hawaii. It comprises Johnston Island, Sand Island (uninhabited) and two man-made islands, North (Akua) and East (Hikina), with a total area of 2.6 sq km (1 sq mile). Johnston Atoll was designated a Naval Defense Sea Area and Airspace Reservation in 1941, and is closed to public access. In 1985 construction of a chemical weapons disposal facility began on the atoll, and by 1990 it was fully operational. In 1989 the US Government agreed to remove artillery shells containing more than 400 metric tons of nerve gas from the Federal Republic of Germany, and destroy them on Johnston Island. In late 1991, following expressions of protest to the US Government by the nations of the South Pacific Forum (now Pacific Islands Forum, see p. 413), together with many environmental groups, a team of scientists visited the chemical disposal facility to monitor the safety and environmental impact of its activities. In May 1996 it was reported that all nerve gases stored on the atoll had been destroyed. However, 1,000 tons of chemical agents remained contained in land-mines, bombs and missiles at the site. In December 2000 it was announced that the destruction of the remaining stock of chemical weapons had been completed (the original deadline for the destruction of 40,000 weapons stored on the island had been August 1995). The closure and decontamination of the facility was completed in 2004; in June of that year all military personnel left and control of the Atoll was transferred to the US Fish and Wildlife Service, which has reported its intention eventually to create a nature reserve on the atoll. In March 2005 the Department of Defense announced the termination of the Air Force mission in Johnston Atoll. A facility capable of performing atmospheric tests of nuclear weapons remains operational on the atoll. The atoll had an estimated population of 173 in 1990, although this increased to approximately 1,000, mainly military, personnel during weapons disposal operations in previous years. In January 2009 Johnston Atoll became part of the Pacific Remote Islands Marine National Monument (see above, under Baker and Howland Islands). Johnston Atoll falls under the jurisdiction of the Department of the Interior, US Fish and Wildlife Service (details as above, under Baker and Howland Islands). Operational control is the responsibility of the US Air Force. Permission to land on Johnston Island must be obtained from the US Air Force. The residing military commander of Johnston Island acts as the agent for the Defense Threat Reduction Agency (DTRA).

Kingman Reef

Kingman Reef lies in the Pacific Ocean, about 1,500 km (925 miles) south-west of Hawaii, and comprises a reef and shoal measuring about 8 km (5 miles) by 15 km (9.5 miles). In 2000 administrative control was transferred from the US Navy to the Department of the Interior. In 2001 the waters around the reef were designated a National Wildlife Refuge, under the jurisdiction of the US Fish and Wildlife Service (details as above, under Baker and Howland Islands). In January 2009 Kingman Reef became part of the Pacific Remote Islands Marine National Monument (see above, under Baker and Howland Islands).

Midway Atoll

Midway Atoll lies in the northern Pacific Ocean, about 1,850 km (1,150 miles) north-west of Hawaii. A coral atoll, it comprises Sand Island, Eastern Island and several small islets within the reef, and has a total area of about 5 sq km (2 sq miles). The islands had a population of 2,200 in 1983, but by 1990 this had declined to 13. Since the transfer of the islands' administration from the US Department of Defense to the Department of the Interior in October 1996, limited tourism is permitted. There is a National Wildlife Refuge on the Territory, which is home to many species of birds. In March 2011 it was reported that thousands of seabirds, including albatrosses and other endangered species, had been killed by the tsunami that followed the powerful earthquake of the east coast of Japan. Legislation before Congress in 1990 proposed the inclusion of the Territory within the State of Hawaii. The islands are administered by the US Department of the Interior, US Fish and Wildlife Service (details as above, under Baker and Howland Islands).

Navassa Island

Navassa Island lies in the Caribbean Sea, about 160 km (100 miles) south of Guantánamo Bay, Cuba, and 65 km (40 miles) west of Haiti. It is a raised coral island with a limestone plateau and has an area of 5.2 sq km (2 sq miles). The island is uninhabited. Navassa became a US Insular Area in 1857, and was mined throughout the late 19th century, under the Navassa Phosphate Co. All mining activities were terminated in 1898. In 1996 the US Coast Guard ceased operations of the island's lighthouse, and in January 1997 the Office of Insular Affairs (under the control of the US Department of the Interior) assumed control of the island. A research expedition undertaken in mid-1998 revealed the presence of numerous undiscovered plant and animal species, many of which were thought to be unique to the island. Visits to the island and its surrounding waters were subsequently prohibited, pending further assessment of the island's environment. In December 1999 administrative responsibility for Navassa passed wholly to the US Department of the Interior, US Fish and Wildlife Service (details as above, under Baker and Howland Islands); however, control over political matters was retained by the Office of Insular Affairs.

Palmyra

Palmyra lies in the Pacific Ocean, about 1,600 km (1,000 miles) south of Honolulu, Hawaii. It comprises some 50 low-lying islets, has a total area of 100 ha, is uninhabited and is privately owned. Since 1961 the Territory has been administered by the US Department of the Interior. In 1990 legislation before Congress proposed the inclusion of Palmyra within the boundaries of the State of Hawaii. In mid-1996 it was announced that the owners (the Fullard-Leo family in Hawaii) were to sell the atoll to a US company, which, it was believed, planned to establish a nuclear waste storage facility in the Territory. The Government of neighbouring Kiribati expressed alarm at the proposal, and reiterated its intention to seek the reinclusion of the atoll within its own national boundaries. However, in June one of the Hawaiian Representatives to the US Congress proposed legislation in the US House of Representatives to prevent the establishment of such a facility, and a US government official subsequently announced that the atoll would almost certainly not be used for that purpose. Palmyra was purchased by The Nature Conservancy (internet www.tnc.org) in December 2000. Designated a National Wildlife Refuge, the lagoons and surrounding waters within the 12 nautical mile zone of US territorial seas were transferred to the US Fish and Wildlife Service (details as above, under Baker and Howland Islands) in January 2001; the US Fish and Wildlife Service subsequently undertook negotiations to purchase part of the 680 acres of emergent lands owned by The Nature Conservancy. In November 2005 an international team of scientists joined with The Nature Conservancy to establish a new station on the Palmyra Atoll in order to undertake environmental research. In January 2009 Palmyra became part of the Pacific Remote Islands Marine National Monument (see above, under Baker and Howland Islands).

Wake Island

Wake Island lies in the Pacific Ocean, about 2,060 km (1,280 miles) east of Guam. It is a coral atoll comprising the three islets of Wake, Wilkes and Peale, with an area less than 8 sq km (3 sq miles) and a population estimated to be almost 2,000 in 1988. Legislation before Congress in 1990 proposed the inclusion of the islands within the Territory of Guam. However, the Republic of the Marshall Islands, some 500 km (310 miles) south of Wake, exerted its own claim to the atoll (called Enenkio by the Micronesians), which is a site of great importance for the islands' traditional chiefly rituals. Plans by a US company, announced in 1998, to establish a large-scale nuclear waste storage facility on the atoll were condemned by environmentalists and politicians in the region. In August 2006 Hurricane Ioke severely damaged much of the island's infrastructure. The US Air Force had previously evacuated all 188 residents. In January 2009 Wake Island became part of the Pacific Remote Islands Marine National Monument (see above, under Baker and Howland Islands). Since 1972 the group has been administered by the US Department of Defense, Department of the Air Force (Pacific/East Asia Division), The Pentagon, Washington, DC 20330; tel. (202) 694-6061; fax (703) 696-7273; internet www.af.mil.

URUGUAY

Introductory Survey

LOCATION, CLIMATE, LANGUAGE, RELIGION, FLAG, CAPITAL

The Eastern Republic of Uruguay lies on the south-east coast of South America, with Brazil to the north and Argentina to the west. The climate is temperate, with an average temperature of 14°C–16°C (57°F–61°F) in winter and 21°C–28°C (70°F–82°F) in summer. The language is Spanish. There is no state religion but Roman Catholicism is predominant. The national flag (proportions 2 by 3) has nine horizontal stripes (five white and four blue, alternating), with a square white canton, containing a yellow sun with 16 alternating straight and wavy rays, in the upper hoist. The capital is Montevideo.

CONTEMPORARY POLITICAL HISTORY

Historical Context

After independence, gained in 1825, domestic politics in Uruguay became dominated by two parties: the Colorados ('reds' or Liberals) and the Blancos ('whites' or Conservatives, subsequently also known as the Partido Nacional). Their rivalry resulted in frequent outbreaks of civil war in the 19th century: the names derive from the flags of the 1836 civil war. From 1880 to 1958 the governing Partido Colorado was led by the Batlle family. Owing to the progressive policies of José Batlle y Ordóñez, Colorado President in 1903–07 and in 1911–15, Uruguay became the first welfare state in Latin America. During 1951–66 the presidency was in abeyance, being replaced by a collective leadership.

Domestic Political Affairs

In December 1967 Jorge Pacheco Areco assumed the presidency. His period in office was notable for massive increases in the cost of living, labour unrest and the spectacular exploits of the Tupamaro urban guerrilla movement. In March 1972 Pacheco was succeeded by Juan María Bordaberry Arocena, a Colorado, who won the presidential election in November 1971. The army took complete control of the campaign against the Tupamaros, and by late 1973 had suppressed the movement. Military intervention in civilian affairs led, in 1973, to the closure of the Congreso (Congress) and its replacement by an appointed 25-member Council of State (subsequently increased to 35 members). The Partido Comunista and other left-wing groups were banned; repressive measures, including strict press censorship, continued. In September 1974 army officers were placed in control of the major state-owned enterprises.

President Bordaberry was deposed by the army in June 1976 because of his refusal to countenance any return to constitutional rule. In July the recently formed Council of the Nation elected Aparicio Méndez Manfredini to the presidency for five years. Despite the Government's announcement that there would be a return to democracy, persecution of opponents continued; some 6,000 political prisoners were thought to be in detention in 1976.

President Méndez introduced constitutional amendments, known as Institutional Acts, to consolidate the internal situation and to create a 'new order'. By 1980 severe economic problems made the army anxious to return executive responsibility to civilian politicians. However, a new proposed constitution, under which the armed forces would continue to be involved in all matters of national security, was rejected by voters in a plebiscite in November. The military leadership was therefore forced to amend the draft document in consultation with leaders of the recognized political parties, and in September 1981 a retired army general, Gregorio Alvarez Armellino, was appointed by the Joint Council of the Armed Forces to serve as President during the transition period to full civilian government.

The Government's reluctance to permit greater public freedom and to improve observance of human rights caused serious unrest throughout 1983. Popular discontent was further aroused by the rapid deterioration of the economy and by the effect of the end of military rule in Argentina. In August the authorities suspended all public political activity and reserved the right to impose a new constitution without consultation, insisting, however, that the original electoral timetable would be maintained. The political opposition responded by threatening to boycott the elections and by uniting with proscribed groups to hold a national day of protest. In September the first organized labour protest for 10 years was supported by 500,000 workers.

Political agitation increased during 1984, and the Government threatened to postpone the elections, planned for 25 November, unless the political parties agreed to its proposals for constitutional reform. Tensions increased in June, following the return from exile and subsequent arrest of Ferreira Aldunate, the proposed presidential candidate of the Partido Nacional. Following talks between the Government, the Partido Colorado and the Unión Cívica (a Christian democratic party), in which the parties obtained several important concessions, including the right to engage in political activity, in August the parties (with the exception of the Partido Nacional) agreed to the Government's proposals. The Government confirmed that elections would take place, and all restrictions on political activity were withdrawn.

At elections in November 1984 the Partido Colorado, led by Dr Julio María Sanguinetti Cairolo, secured a narrow victory over the opposition. Sanguinetti was inaugurated on 1 March 1985, as was a Government of national unity, incorporating representatives of the other parties. Concurrently, various outlawed organizations, including the Partido Comunista, were legalized. All political prisoners were released under an amnesty law later in the month. The new Government announced its commitment to reversing the economic recession; however, its efforts to address the crisis were hampered by frequent industrial stoppages.

A major political issue in 1986 was the investigation into alleged violations of human rights by the armed forces during the military dictatorship. In August the Government proposed legislation that would offer an amnesty for all military and police personnel accused of this type of crime, in accordance with a pact made with the armed forces that human rights trials would not take place. In October the draft legislation was rejected by opposition parties, but in December a revised law (the Ley de Caducidad, or Statute of Limitations Law) was approved, which brought an end to current military trials and made the President responsible for any further investigations. The law was widely opposed and in February 1987 a campaign was initiated to organize a petition containing the signatures of at least 25% of the registered electorate, as required by the Constitution, in order to force a referendum on the issue. The campaign was supported principally by human rights groups, trade unions and the centre-left coalition, the Frente Amplio (FA). A referendum duly took place in April 1989, at which a total of 53% of the votes were cast in favour of maintaining the amnesty law.

The presidential and legislative elections in November 1989 resulted in victory (for the first time since 1962) for the Partido Nacional. In the presidential election, Luis Alberto Lacalle, the party's main candidate (the electoral code permitted each party to present more than one candidate), received 37% of the votes, while his closest rival, Jorge Batlle Ibáñez of the Partido Colorado, won 30%. However, the Partido Nacional failed to obtain an overall majority in the Congreso, thus compelling the President-elect to seek support from a wider political base. Immediately before taking office, in March 1990, he announced the conclusion of an agreement, the 'coincidencia nacional', between the two principal parties, whereby the Partido Colorado undertook to support proposed legislation on economic reform, in return for the appointment of four of its members to the Council of Ministers.

Labour unrest intensified during the early 1990s. The trade union confederation, the Plenario Intersindical de Trabajadores—Convención Nacional de Trabajadores (PIT—CNT), organized a series of general strikes in support of demands for wage increases and in opposition to government austerity measures and privatization plans. Opposition from within the ruling coalition to the planned sale of state enterprises became apparent in May 1991, when former President Sanguinetti, the leader of the Partido Colorado's Foro Batllista faction, withdrew his support from the Government, thus forcing the resignation of the faction's sole representative in the Council of Ministers. Reservations were also expressed by elements of the Partido Nacional. In September, none the less, the privatization legislation was narrowly approved by the Congreso. In response, the opposition FA, with the support of another political organization, Nuevo Espacio, and the trade unions, began a campaign to overrule the legislature by way of a referendum. In October 1992, in a special poll, some 30% of the electorate voted for a full referendum to be held on the partial amendment of the Government's privatization legislation. At the referendum, held in December, 72% of voters supported the proposal for a partial repeal of the legislation. The vote was also widely recognized as a vote of censure against the President's economic policy, and in particular his determination to keep public sector wage increases to a minimum.

Emergence of a third political force

The presidential and legislative elections in November 1994 were notable for the emergence of a third political force to rival the traditional powers of the Partido Nacional and the Partido Colorado. The Encuentro Progresista (EP)—a predominantly left-wing alliance principally comprising the parties of the FA, as well as dissidents of the Partido Nacional and other minor parties—secured 31% of the votes in the presidential poll, as did the Partido Nacional, while the Partido Colorado won a narrow victory, with 33% of the vote. Sanguinetti, the leading presidential candidate of the Partido Colorado, was pronounced President-elect; he indicated his intention to appoint a broadly based Council of Ministers in order to ensure legislative support for his administration.

In early 1995, following talks with opposition parties, the Partido Colorado established a 'governability pact' with the Partido Nacional, providing for a coalition Government. The Council of Ministers contained six members of the Partido Colorado, four from the Partido Nacional, one Unión Cívica member, and one representative from the Partido por el Gobierno del Pueblo (Lista 99), which had contested the elections in alliance with Sanguinetti's Foro Batllista faction of the Partido Colorado, and whose leader, Hugo Batalla, had been elected as Sanguinetti's Vice-President.

In July 1995 the Government and the opposition reached an agreement on the reform of the electoral system. Under the existing system, known as the Ley de Lemas, parties were permitted to present more than one presidential candidate, with the leading candidate in each party assuming the total number of votes for candidates in that party. According to the proposed reform, each party would present one candidate, selected by means of an internal election, and, in the event of no candidate securing an absolute majority, a second round of voting would be conducted. Notwithstanding a degree of opposition from elements of the FA, in October 1996 President Sanguinetti finally secured the necessary two-thirds' support in the legislature for the reform, which also accorded greater autonomy to municipal administrations and established a framework for environmental protection. The amendments were approved by 51% of voters in a plebiscite held in December, and came into effect in January 1997.

In May 1997 some 20,000 civilians staged a rally in the capital to demand that the Government and the armed forces provide information on the whereabouts of as many as 140 people who had 'disappeared' during the military dictatorship. In December President Sanguinetti issued a decree that granted an amnesty to 41 former army officers who had been dismissed from service during the dictatorship, owing to their political beliefs. In May 1999 some 15,000 people participated in a further march in support of demands that the authorities account for the disappearance of friends and relatives during the military dictatorship.

The presidential and legislative elections of October 1999 confirmed the end of the traditional dominance of the Partido Colorado and the Partido Nacional. The Encuentro Progresista—Frente Amplio (EP—FA) became the largest single party in both the Cámara de Representantes (Chamber of Representatives) and the Cámara de Senadores (Senate). The Partido Colorado largely maintained its representation, while support for the Partido Nacional declined considerably. Tabaré Ramón Vázquez Rosas, a former Mayor of Montevideo and the candidate of the EP—FA, won 39% of the vote, compared with 31% for Batlle, representing the Colorados and 21% for Lacalle of the Partido Nacional. However, Batlle defeated Vázquez in a second round of voting on 28 November, aided by the support of the Partido Nacional. Following his inauguration on 1 March 2000, President Batlle appointed a new Council of Ministers, allocating eight portfolios to the Partido Colorado and five to the Partido Nacional.

In early 2000 Batlle held several meetings with Vázquez, in an apparent attempt to achieve a degree of rapprochement with the left, and also committed himself to resolving the issue of the 'disappeared', in marked contrast to his predecessor, Sanguinetti, who had consistently resisted pressure to investigate their fate. In April 2000 Batlle dismissed Gen. Manuel Fernández, one of the country's most senior army officials, after he sought to justify the military repression of the 1970s. In August Batlle announced the formation of a commission, composed of representatives from the Government, the opposition, the Church and the victims' families, to investigate the fate of 164 people who 'disappeared' during the military dictatorship. The unexpected dismissal in January 2001 of Gen. Juan Geymonat, Commander-in-Chief of the Armed Forces, was interpreted as a first step in a military reform programme advocated by Batlle. In October 2002 the Commission reported its preliminary findings that 26 of the 33 'disappeared' Uruguayan citizens under its investigation had been murdered by Argentine and Uruguayan military officers.

Against a background of ongoing economic recession, the Batlle administration encountered opposition to its policies from organized labour groups from 1999. In June 2000 a general strike was organized by the PIT—CNT to demand increased action on unemployment and more finance for education and health care, as well as to protest against emergency legislation, approved that month, which would allow the partial privatization of some public services, including the railways and the ports. A more widespread strike was held in December to protest at the same issues. However, an attempt by the EP—FA to force a referendum on the controversial law in February 2001 failed, owing to a lack of public support.

Financial crisis and 2004 elections

The financial crisis in neighbouring Argentina of December 2001–January 2002 caused additional economic hardship in Uruguay, with continued rural unrest and political and trade union opposition to the austerity measures introduced by the Government. In May the Argentine Government's imposition of severe restrictions on bank withdrawals prompted many Argentine citizens holding assets in Uruguay to access their funds, precipitating a crisis in Uruguay's financial system. In late June the Government was forced to abandon exchange rate controls in order to maintain the peso uruguayo's competitiveness against the devalued Argentine and Brazilian currencies. However, by late July, following a 30% decline in the peso's value in relation to the US dollar, and amid rising concerns over the viability and transparency of the banking sector, substantial numbers of Uruguayans also began to withdraw their deposits. In an attempt to avert a financial collapse, the Government instructed all banking institutions in Uruguay to close for a period of four days and introduced emergency economic measures, which included an increase in taxation on salaries and pensions. Three state-owned banks were placed under direct government administration, and restrictions were imposed on their customers' access to long-term foreign exchange deposits. The Government successfully sought an immediate loan of US $1,500m. from the USA to prevent a severe deterioration in international reserves and in November agreement was reached with the IMF on stand-by loans totalling some $2,800m., to be disbursed in 2002 and 2003. Nevertheless, as a result of the financial crisis, in late July Alberto Bensión, the Minister of Economy and Finance, was forced to resign, having lost the support of the Partido Nacional. He was succeeded by Alejandro Atchugarry, a prominent member of the Partido Colorado.

The financial crisis led to a greater willingness within the Partido Nacional to reconsider its association with the Partido Colorado. In November 2002 the Partido Nacional terminated discussions on a new 'governability pact' between the two parties, removed its five ministers from the Government and withdrew from the ruling coalition, leaving the FA as the largest political bloc in the Congreso. President Batlle subsequently appointed non-partisan ministers to the vacant posts and a limited rationalization of ministries was effected.

In November 2002 it was announced that the three suspended state-run banks were to be merged into one: in March 2003 the Nuevo Banco Comercial began operations. The incorporation of the new bank coincided with the resumption of IMF disbursements, suspended in November owing to the Government's perceived lack of progress on the restructuring of the banking sector. (In January 2005 the International Court of Arbitration of the International Chamber of Commerce, see p. 339 ruled that Uruguay must pay US $100m., in addition to legal expenses and accrued interest, to foreign investors in the liquidated Banco Comercial.)

In August 2003 a series of strikes was held by public sector workers to protest at the Government's reform programme, in particular at plans to increase private sector participation in the economy. In June the EP—FA succeeded in gaining parliamentary approval for a referendum to be held on the proposed partial privatization of the state-run fuel, cement and alcohol monopoly, the Administración Nacional de Combustible, Alcohol y Portland. In the referendum, held in December, some 62% voted to repeal the controversial legislation; the high level of opposition was widely interpreted as a further expression of public dissatisfaction with the Batlle administration.

At the presidential election in October 2004 Tabaré Vázquez, the candidate of the EP—FA—Nueva Mayoría (as the grouping became known until late 2005), won the presidency in the first round of voting, with 50.7% of the ballot. His nearest rival, Jorge Larrañaga, the Partido Nacional candidate, obtained some 34.1% of the votes. The EP—FA—Nueva Mayoría coalition also made gains in the concurrent legislative elections, winning a majority in both chambers. The Partido Colorado's representation fell sharply, while the Partido Nacional became the second largest party in both chambers. The EP—FA—Nueva Mayoría's electoral campaign had centred on pledges to increase social spending dramatically, to effect a radical reform of the tax and pension systems, and to retain state control over utilities and services.

Concurrently with the presidential election, a referendum was held on a proposal that the water industry remain under state control. The proposal was supported by the EP—FA—Nueva Mayoría, but opposed by the incumbent Colorado administration. In the poll, 64.5% of those voting were in favour of the water sector remaining under state control.

The Vázquez presidency, 2005–10

President Vázquez took office on 1 March 2005. He notably appointed Danilo Astori of the Asamblea Uruguay as Minister of Economy and Finance. The appointment of Astori, an orthodox economist on the right wing of the EP—FA—Nueva Mayoría (renamed the FA in late 2005), was widely interpreted as an attempt to strengthen investor confidence in a broadly left-wing administration. It had been announced in February that the new administration would receive cross-party support for its economic policies (in addition to the support already pledged for its policies on education and foreign affairs), but both opposition parties withdrew their support for the Government's economic policies in mid-March in protest at their allocation of positions on the governing bodies of state banks, companies and quasi-autonomous agencies, which, they considered, fell short of the number traditionally allocated to members of the opposition.

An immediate priority of the new Government was to eradicate poverty; to this end, in March 2005 President Vázquez announced the Plan de Atención Nacional de Emergencia Social, a programme of social spending, expected to total some US $200m. over two years. The following day the new Minister of National Defence, Azucena Berruti, announced that the Government had begun investigations into the 'disappearances' that occurred during the years of military rule. In August the heads of Uruguay's armed forces submitted to the President a report admitting the kidnap, torture and murder of political dissidents, and purportedly detailing the whereabouts of their remains. Information in the report led to the exhumation in November of the bodies of two dissidents murdered by members of the air force. Earlier that month Vázquez had proposed legislation seeking to amend the Ley de Caducidad of 1986 in order to facilitate prosecution of members of the military for human rights abuses committed during military rule. In December 35 unidentified corpses were exhumed from a cemetery in a town near the Brazilian border.

The investigation of human rights abuses allegedly committed during the military dictatorship continued during 2006–07. In May 2006 six former Uruguayan military officers were arrested in connection with the 'disappearance' and presumed murder in 1976 of María Claudia García, the daughter of the Argentine poet Juan Gelman, following an extradition request from Argentina. The arrests represented the first occasion on which any individuals had faced legal action for their alleged role in the torture and murder of dissidents during the period of military repression in the 1970s. In November 2006 former President Bordaberry and his then foreign minister, Juan Carlos Blanco, were charged with the abduction and murder of four opponents of the authorities in 1976. Furthermore, in February 2007 a former officer of senior rank in the Uruguayan military was arrested in Brazil, and his extradition to Uruguay sought, on charges relating to the murders of three dissidents in 1976, as well as the 'disappearance' of García. In December former President Alvarez was arrested and charged, along with two army captains, with the forced disappearance of up to 40 dissidents in 1978, during which time he was Commander-in-Chief of the Army. Alvarez's arrest was facilitated by legislation, adopted in September 2006, which established that acts of forced disappearance were considered to be ongoing, and were therefore not excluded from prosecution by the Ley de Caducidad. In October 2009 Alvarez was found guilty of the murder of 37 people and sentenced to 25 years' imprisonment. Former President Bordaberry received a 30-year prison sentence in February 2010, having been convicted of the murder of two opposition supporters and of the disappearance of nine others. The Inter-American Court of Human Rights ruled in February 2011 that the Uruguayan state was responsible for the 'disappearance' of García and urged the Government to prosecute those involved.

In November 2008 a law to allow abortion without restriction in the first 12 weeks of pregnancy was approved by the Cámara de Senadores, despite vociferous opposition from the Roman Catholic Church. However, Vázquez promptly vetoed the legislation (to which he was ethically opposed), leading the Partido Socialista del Uruguay (PS) to criticize the President for placing his personal beliefs before the will of the party. Vázquez subsequently resigned from the PS. Vázquez also suffered a reverse in November when the FA party delegation nominated the outspoken and flamboyant José (Pepe) Mujica (a senator and erstwhile Tupamaro guerrilla), of the Movimiento de Participación Popular (MPP), as the coalition's official candidate for the presidential election due in October 2009. Vázquez openly favoured Danilo Astori as his successor.

Meanwhile, in April 2009 the legislature approved plans to hold a referendum (in October, concurrently with the presidential and legislative elections) to reform the Constitution in order to allow Uruguayan emigrants to vote in elections from 2014. It was estimated that as many as 600,000 Uruguayans lived abroad; critics of the proposed reform noted that of these, the majority were believed to be supporters of the FA. A referendum to consider whether to repeal the Ley de Caducidad was also to be held concurrently, following the presentation of some 325,000 signatures (far exceeding the requisite 250,000) to the Congreso in April. In March the FA had won a non-binding vote in the Congreso declaring the Ley de Caducidad unconstitutional, and in October, considering the case of the alleged murder in 1974 of an opponent of the military Government, the Supreme Court also ruled that the law was unconstitutional.

Recent developments: Mujica in office

The FA narrowly retained its majority in both chambers of the Congreso in the legislative elections, which were held on 25 October 2009, securing 50 of the 99 seats in the Cámara de Representantes and 16 in the 30-seat Cámara de Senadores. The Partido Nacional won 30 seats in the lower chamber and nine in the upper, while the Partido Colorado increased its representation to 17 and five seats, respectively. The Partido Independiente obtained the remaining two seats in the Cámara de Representantes. In the concurrent presidential election, Mujica secured 48.0% of the votes cast, followed by Lacalle, again the Partido Nacional's candidate, with 29.1%, and Pedro Bordaberry of the Partido Colorado, with 17.0%. Two other candidates contested the election, in which 89.9% of the electorate participated. Mujica defeated Lacalle in a second round of voting on 29 November, winning 52.4% of the ballot. A turn-out of 89.2% was recorded. Mujica's victory was partly attributed to the popularity of outgoing President Vázquez and to the strong performance of the economy under the latter's FA administration. During the electoral campaign Mujica had pledged to continue Vázquez's moderate left-wing policies.

In the two referendums conducted on 25 October 2009, both initiatives were rejected by the electorate: 63.1% voted against permitting emigrants to vote in elections from 2014 and 52.6% opposed a repeal of the Ley de Caducidad. None the less, the Supreme Court's ruling earlier that month (see above), that the amnesty law was unconstitutional, set a significant precedent for future cases concerning human rights abuses allegedly committed during the military dictatorship.

Mujica was inaugurated as President on 1 March 2010. He declared that his priorities would be to improve education, to eradicate extreme poverty, to guarantee energy supplies, to maintain security and to reduce bureaucracy in public administration. Ministerial positions in the new Government were divided among the various constituent parties of the FA, with the majority of the more strategic portfolios, including the interior, foreign affairs and national defence, allocated to the MPP.

The FA suffered a defeat in the regional elections conducted in May 2010. The ruling coalition only managed to gain control of five of the 19 contested departments (including the key administration of Montevideo), while the Partido Nacional won 12 and the Partido Colorado two.

A corruption scandal within the navy was exposed in August 2010, involving the disappearance of around US $7m. Most of the funds had ostensibly been used to purchase naval vessels, but these ships were subsequently found to be non-existent. The Government acted promptly to address the structural inadequacies within the navy that had facilitated these so-called 'phantom purchases', and legal action commenced against some 25 senior naval officers, including a former naval commander. In late 2010 Minister of National Defence Luis Rosadilla stated that details of an extensive military reform programme would be revealed during 2011.

Despite the results of the October 2009 referendum and fervent opposition from the Partido Nacional and the Partido Colorado, in September 2010 the FA proposed a reinterpretation of several key clauses within the Ley de Caducidad, which would effectively invalidate the law and facilitate the resumption of legal action against those accused of committing human rights abuses during the military dictatorship. This proposal was adopted by the Cámara de Representantes in October, although approval by the Cámara de Senadores was pending in early 2011. In November 2010 the Supreme Court again declared the Ley de Caducidad unconstitutional, while later that month, in an unprecedented move against a serving officer in the military, Gen. Miguel Dalmao was charged in connection with the alleged murder of left-wing activist Nibia Sabalsagaray in 1974.

Throughout the second half of 2010 the country was disrupted by widespread industrial action, primarily led by public sector workers appealing for improved salaries and conditions. The labour unrest culminated in November, when 12 different trade unions declared strikes. However, public opinion surveys showed that the majority of the population opposed the strike action, and Mujica's high approval ratings allowed him to resist the unions' demands.

Foreign Affairs

In 1991 the Governments of Argentina, Brazil, Paraguay and Uruguay agreed to create a common market of the 'Southern Cone' countries, the Mercado Común del Sur (Mercosur, see p. 425). The Treaty of Asunción allowed for the dismantling of trade barriers between the four countries, and entered full operation in 1995. However, in February 2002, following the drastic reduction in exports to other Mercosur member states as a result of the devaluation of the Argentine peso at the beginning of that year, President Batlle declared that Uruguay would begin bilateral free trade negotiations with the USA. In January 2007 the two countries signed a trade and investment framework, which was regarded as a step towards eventual free trade agreement negotiations.

In April 2002 Uruguay severed diplomatic relations with Cuba, citing insults by the Cuban Government after Uruguay sponsored a motion, which was adopted by the UN Human Rights Commission, calling on Cuba to improve its civil and political rights record. Diplomatic relations were restored, however, following the inauguration of the Vázquez administration in March 2005.

Relations with Argentina were strained from 2005, when a Finnish company began construction of a cellulose plant in the Uruguayan city of Fray Bentos near the River Uruguay, which separates the two countries. The Argentine Government expressed concerns over the environmental impact of this plant and of a further mill scheduled to be built nearby. The two plants were expected to generate some US $1,800m. of investment in Uruguay. (Construction of the second plant was cancelled in 2006 as a result of the dispute, although the company responsible later announced that it would build the mill at a different location.) In January 2006 Argentine demonstrators blocked the three bridges spanning the river in protests that were tolerated by the Argentine authorities, drawing condemnation from the Uruguayan Government. Demonstrations, attended by some 10,000 people claiming that the project would cause serious environmental damage, continued in the Argentine city of Gualeguaychú. The dispute escalated in May when the Argentine Government initiated proceedings at the International Court of Justice (ICJ) on the grounds that the project would contravene the Statute of the River Uruguay treaty, signed by the two countries in 1975. The ICJ declined to order the suspension of construction of the mills in July, but in January 2007 also rejected a request by the Government of Uruguay to order Argentina to end the ongoing blockade of major roads and bridges between the two countries. Uruguay had claimed that Argentina's protests were resulting in economic hardship for Uruguay and had caused a loss of revenue of some $800m., much of this in the form of lost earnings from tourism. Bilateral relations improved slightly in April following mediation by Spain, as a result of which both countries declared their willingness to reach a resolution to the impasse. None the less, in November President Vázquez authorized the recently inaugurated mill to begin production, provoking condemnation from Argentina, and temporarily closed the border between the countries in anticipation of violent protests. Argentine demonstrations continued to impede cross-border traffic in 2008, prompting an official complaint from Uruguay regarding the damage caused to its economy. The ICJ issued its ruling on the dispute in April 2010, concluding that Uruguay had breached its procedural obligations under the Statute of the River Uruguay treaty to inform Argentina of its plans for the construction of the mills, but had not violated its environmental obligations. The Court rejected Argentina's request for the dismantling of the plant in operation and for compensation for alleged damage to its economy. After losing the support of the Argentine Government, the demonstrators finally ended their blockade in June. The signing by both nations in November of a technical agreement on monitoring pollution levels in the River Uruguay signified a mutually satisfactory conclusion to the long-running dispute.

CONSTITUTION AND GOVERNMENT

Uruguay is a republic comprising 19 departments. Under the 1966 Constitution, executive power is held by the President, who is directly elected by universal adult suffrage for a five-year term. The President is assisted by the Vice-President and the appointed Council of Ministers. Legislative power is vested in the bicameral Congreso, comprising the Cámara de Senadores (Senate) and the Cámara de Representantes (Chamber of Representatives), also directly elected for five years. The President, the Vice-President, the Senators (who number 31, including the Vice-President, who is automatically allocated a seat as President of the Cámara de Senadores) and the 99 Deputies are elected nationally. Judicial power is exercised by the five-member Supreme Court of Justice and by tribunals and local courts.

REGIONAL AND INTERNATIONAL CO-OPERATION

Uruguay is a member of the Inter-American Development Bank (see p. 333), of the Asociación Latinoamericana de Integración (see p. 359), of the Sistema Económico Latinoamericano (see p. 448), of the Mercado Común del Sur (Mercosur, see p. 425) and of the Organization of American States (see p. 391). In December 2004 Uruguay was one of 12 countries that were signatories to the agreement creating the South American Community of Nations (Comunidad Sudamericana de Naciones), intended to promote greater regional economic integration. A treaty for the community—referred to as the Union of South American Nations (Unión de Naciones Suramericanas) since its reinvention in April 2007—was initialled in May 2008, with full functionality of economic union tentatively scheduled for 2019.

Uruguay was a founder member of the UN in 1945. As a contracting party to the General Agreement on Tariffs and Trade, Uruguay joined the World Trade Organization (see p. 430) on its establishment in 1995.

ECONOMIC AFFAIRS

In 2009, according to estimates by the World Bank, Uruguay's gross national income (GNI), measured at average 2007–09 prices, was US $31,312m., equivalent to $9,360 per head (or $12,910 per head on an international purchasing-power parity basis). During 2000–09, it was estimated, the population increased at an average annual rate of 0.1%, while gross domestic product (GDP) per head increased, in real terms, by an average 2.9% per year. According to official figures, overall GDP increased, in real terms, at an average annual rate of 6.2% in 2005–10; GDP increased by 8.5% in 2010.

Agriculture (including forestry and hunting) contributed 9.4% of GDP in 2010, according to preliminary official figures. Some 11.1% of the active labour force was employed in the sector in mid-2011, according to FAO estimates. The principal crops are rice, sugar cane, wheat, barley, potatoes, sorghum and maize. Livestock-rearing, particularly sheep and cattle, is traditionally Uruguay's major economic activity. Food and live animals provided 33.1% of export revenues in 2009, while exports of crops and vegetable products provided a further 27.1% in the same year. According to World Bank figures, agricultural GDP increased at an average annual rate of 2.9% per year in 2000–09; sectoral GDP increased by 0.1% in 2009.

Industry (including mining, manufacturing, construction and power) contributed 27.3% of GDP in 2010, according to preliminary official figures, and employed 21.5% of the working population in 2003. Industrial GDP increased at an average annual rate of 5.7% in 2005–10; industrial GDP increased by 9.4% in 2010.

Uruguay has few mineral resources and no proven hydrocarbon reserves. Accordingly, mining and quarrying (including fishing) only contributed 0.5% of GDP in 2010, and employed 0.1% of the working population in 2003. Apart from the small-scale extraction of building materials, industrial minerals and semi-precious stones, there has been little mining activity, although gold deposits are currently being developed. The GDP of the mining sector declined at an average annual rate of 9.1% in 2005–10; mining GDP rose by 4.6% in 2010.

Manufacturing contributed 15.0% of GDP in 2010, according to preliminary official figures, and employed 14.6% of the working population in 2003. The principal branches of manufacturing were food products, beverages and tobacco, chemicals, metal products, machinery and equipment, and textiles, clothing and leather products. Manufacturing GDP increased at an average annual rate of 6.3% in 2005–10. Manufacturing GDP increased by 3.7% in 2010.

Construction contributed 8.2% of GDP in 2010, according to preliminary official figures, and employed 6.7% of the working population in 2003. Construction GDP increased at an average annual rate of 5.9% in 2005–10; the sector expanded by 4.3% in 2010.

Energy is derived principally from hydroelectric power (85.6% of total electricity production in 2007). The first natural gas pipeline between Uruguay and Argentina, with an operating capacity of 4.9m. cu ft per day, began operating in 1998. A second natural gas pipeline between Uruguay and Argentina, the Gasoducto Cruz del Sur (GCDS—Southern Cross pipeline), with a transportation capacity of 180m. cu ft per day, was completed in 2002. Imports of mineral fuels and lubricants comprised 24.4% of the value of total imports in 2009. In August 2005 the Venezuelan President, Hugo Chávez, agreed to supply Uruguay with petroleum on preferential terms for the next 25 years.

The services sector contributed 63.3% of GDP in 2010, according to preliminary official figures, and engaged 73.9% of the working population in 2003. Tourism is a significant source of foreign exchange, earning a provisional US $1,180m. in 2008. The GDP of the services sector increased at an average annual rate of 6.9% in 2005–10, according to preliminary figures. The GDP of the services sector increased by 8.1% in 2010.

In 2009 Uruguay recorded an estimated visible trade deficit of US $271.1m., and there was a surplus of $214.5m. on the current account of the balance of payments. In 2009 the principal source of imports was Argentina (23.6%); other major suppliers were Brazil, the People's Republic of China, the USA and Russia. Brazil was the principal market for exports (20.4%) in that year; other major recipients were Argentina, the People's Republic of China and Russia. The main exports in 2009 were live animals and animal products and crops and vegetable products. The principal imports in that year were mineral products and machinery, appliances and related products.

In 2009 there was a budgetary deficit of 45,564m. pesos uruguayos, equivalent to some 6.4% of GDP. Uruguay's general government gross debt was 431,319m. pesos uruguayos in 2009, equivalent to 60.7% of GDP. At the end of 2008 Uruguay's total external debt was US $11,049m., of which $10,044m. was public and publicly guaranteed debt. In 2007 the cost of debt-servicing was equivalent to 14.6% of the value of exports of goods, services and income. The average annual rate of inflation was 8.7% in 2000–10. Consumer prices increased by 6.7% in 2010. Some 9.1% of the labour force was unemployed in 2007.

Social welfare expenditure increased dramatically under the Government of Tabaré Vázquez (2005–10), partly funded by sustained economic growth and increased foreign investment, as well as by radical tax reforms. Between 2004 and 2008 the level of poverty fell from 31.9% to 21.7%. Foreign investment in the country grew significantly in 2008, as did exports, partly as a result of operations commencing at the Botnia paper mill. Uruguay fared relatively well in the wake of the international financial crisis. GDP growth slowed in 2009, but, at 2.6%, according to preliminary figures, was higher than anticipated. Foreign direct investment declined by an estimated 38% in 2009, and the fiscal deficit widened owing to increased expenditure and lower revenues. The Government of José Mujica, which took office in March 2010, pledged to continue the economic policies pursued by Vázquez. Real GDP expanded by an estimated 8.5% in 2010. This impressive performance was driven by increased domestic economic activity, a recovery in demand and prices for Uruguayan exports, and an upsurge in tourist numbers. Unemployment reached its lowest recorded level, at 5.4%, in December 2010, with full employment reported in some sectors, although rising inflation was a concern. Additional employment opportunities were expected to be generated by the construction of a new $1,900m. pulp mill, plans for which were announced by the Government in January 2011. The mill represented the largest foreign investment project in Uruguay's history and was forecast to transform the country into a cellulose exporter of international significance. The IMF projected further GDP growth of 5.0% in 2011.

PUBLIC HOLIDAYS

2012: 1 January (New Year's Day), 6 January (Epiphany), 20–21 February (Carnival), 2–6 April (Holy Week), 22 April (for Landing of the 33 Patriots), 1 May (Labour Day), 21 May (for Battle of Las Piedras), 19 June (Birth of José Artigas), 18 July (Constitution Day), 25 August (National Independence Day), 15 October (for Discovery of America and Battle of Sarandí), 2 November (All Souls' Day), 25 December (Christmas Day).

Many businesses close for the entirety of Carnival week (20–24 February 2012).

URUGUAY

Statistical Survey

Sources (unless otherwise stated): Instituto Nacional de Estadística, Río Negro 1520, 11100 Montevideo; tel. (2) 9027303; internet www.ine.gub.uy; Banco Central del Uruguay, Avda Juan P. Fabini, esq. Florida 777, Casilla 1467, 11100 Montevideo; tel. (2) 9085629; fax (2) 9021634; e-mail info@bcu.gub.uy; internet www.bcu.gub.uy; Cámara Nacional de Comercio y Servicios del Uruguay, Edif. Bolsa de Comercio, Rincón 454, 2°, Casilla 1000, 11000 Montevideo; tel. (2) 9161277; fax (2) 9161243; e-mail info@cncs.com.uy; internet www.cncs.com.uy.

Area and Population

AREA, POPULATION AND DENSITY

Area (sq km)	
Land area	175,016
Inland water	1,199
Total	176,215*
Population (census results)†	
22 May 1996	3,163,763
May–July 2004	
Males	1,565,533
Females	1,675,470
Total	3,241,003
Population (official estimates at mid-year)	
2009	3,344,938
2010	3,356,584
2011	3,368,595
Density (per sq km) at mid-2011	19.2

* 68,037 sq miles.
† Excluding adjustment for underenumeration.

POPULATION BY AGE AND SEX
(official estimates at mid-2011)

	Males	Females	Total
0–14	382,929	366,171	749,100
15–64	1,063,791	1,096,541	2,160,332
65 and over	180,891	278,272	459,163
Total	1,627,611	1,740,984	3,368,595

DEPARTMENTS
(population estimates at mid-2011)

	Area (sq km)	Population	Density (per sq km)	Capital
Artigas	11,928	79,265	6.6	Artigas
Canelones	4,536	531,770	117.2	Canelones
Cerro Largo	13,648	91,403	6.7	Melo
Colonia	6,106	120,945	19.8	Colonia del Sacramento
Durazno	11,643	62,589	5.4	Durazno
Flores	5,144	25,765	5.0	Trinidad
Florida	10,417	71,117	6.8	Florida
Lavalleja	10,016	62,047	6.2	Minas
Maldonado	4,793	154,287	32.2	Maldonado
Montevideo	530	1,335,484	2,519.8	Montevideo
Paysandú	13,922	116,678	8.4	Paysandú
Río Negro	9,282	56,813	6.1	Fray Bentos
Rivera	9,370	113,064	12.1	Rivera
Rocha	10,551	70,316	6.7	Rocha
Salto	14,163	129,381	9.1	Salto
San José	4,992	111,761	22.4	San José de Mayo
Soriano	9,008	88,944	9.9	Mercedes
Tacuarembó	15,438	97,547	6.3	Tacuarembó
Treinta y Tres	9,529	49,419	5.2	Treinta y Tres
Total	175,016*	3,368,595	19.2	

* Land area only.

PRINCIPAL TOWNS
(population at 22 May 1996 census)

Montevideo (capital)	1,378,707	Mercedes		50,800
Salto	93,420	Maldonado		50,420
Paysandú	84,160	Melo		47,160
Las Piedras	66,100	Tacuarembó		42,580
Rivera	63,370			

Mid-2010 ('000, incl. suburbs, UN estimate): Montevideo 1,635 (Source: UN, *World Urbanization Prospects: The 2009 Revision*).

BIRTHS, MARRIAGES AND DEATHS*

	Registered live births		Registered marriages		Registered deaths	
	Number	Rate (per 1,000)	Number	Rate (per 1,000)	Number	Rate (per 1,000)
2002	51,953	15.7	14,073	4.3	31,628	9.6
2003	50,631	15.3	14,147	4.3	32,587	9.9
2004	50,052	15.2	13,123	4.0	32,222	9.8
2005	46,944†	14.2†	13,075	4.0	32,319†	9.8†
2006	47,410†	14.2†	12,415	3.7	31,056†	9.4†
2007	47,373	14.3	12,771	3.8	33,706†	10.3†
2008	53,199	16.0	12,180	3.7	31,363	9.4
2009	47,152	14.1	11,080	3.3	32,179	9.6

* Data are tabulated by year of registration rather than by year of occurrence and have not been adjusted to take account of the most recent census.
† Preliminary.

Life expectancy (years at birth, WHO estimates): 75 (males 72; females 79) in 2008 (Source: WHO, *World Health Statistics*).

ECONOMICALLY ACTIVE POPULATION
(ISIC major divisions, '000 persons aged 14 years and over, urban areas)

	2001	2002	2003
Agriculture, hunting, forestry and fishing	45.4	43.7	46.9
Mining and quarrying	1.3	1.2	1.2
Manufacturing (incl. electricity, gas and water)	167.1	154.2	151.1
Construction	87.9	77.4	69.6
Trade, restaurants, hotels and repair of vehicles and household goods	240.8	228.9	225.4
Transport, storage and communications	66.8	62.4	61.1
Financing, insurance, real estate and business services	97.4	96.5	91.0
Public administration and defence, compulsory social security	85.1	86.9	91.2
Education	57.2	62.2	61.6
Health and social work	72.5	76.7	76.7
Community, social and personal services	56.2	52.2	54.8
Private households with employed persons	98.5	96.0	100.9
Sub-total	—	—	1,031.7
Activities not adequately defined	—	—	0.3
Total employed	1,076.2	1,038.3	1,032.0
Males	617.7	597.9	589.7
Females	458.5	440.4	442.3
Unemployed	193.2	211.3	208.5
Total labour force	1,269.4	1,250.1	1,240.5

Source: ILO.

2007 ('000 persons aged 14 years and over, estimates): Total employed 1,482; Unemployed 149; Total labour force 1,631 (males 913, females 718).

Mid-2011 ('000, estimates): Agriculture, etc. 185; Total labour force 1,665 (Source: FAO).

URUGUAY

Health and Welfare

KEY INDICATORS

Total fertility rate (children per woman, 2008)	2.1
Under-5 mortality rate (per 1,000 live births, 2008)	16
HIV/AIDS (% of persons aged 15–49, 2007)	0.6
Physicians (per 1,000 head, 2002)	3.7
Hospital beds (per 1,000 head, 2006)	2.9
Health expenditure (2007): US $ per head (PPP)	916
Health expenditure (2007): % of GDP	8.0
Health expenditure (2007): public (% of total)	74.0
Total carbon dioxide emissions ('000 metric tons, 2007)	6,214.1
Carbon dioxide emissions per head (metric tons, 2007)	1.9
Human Development Index (2010): ranking	52
Human Development Index (2010): value	0.765

For sources and definitions, see explanatory note on p. vi.

Agriculture

PRINCIPAL CROPS
('000 metric tons)

	2007	2008	2009
Wheat	697.1	1,288.0	1,844.4
Rice, paddy	1,145.7	1,330.0	1,287.2
Barley	310.2	405.5	464.1
Maize	337.8	334.7	269.8
Oats	21.1	19.0	54.4
Sorghum	162.8	151.2	324.2
Potatoes	118.4	106.6	102.3
Sweet potatoes	70.0	22.0	18.6
Sugar cane	293.2	334.1	359.0*
Sunflower seed	43.1	54.2	50.6
Tomatoes	41.5	28.5	37.0
Onions, dry	40.0	19.6	25.6
Carrots and turnips	23.9	24.9	22.5
Oranges	186.3	128.9	n.a.
Tangerines, mandarins, clementines and satsumas	117.7	88.5	n.a.
Lemons and limes	37.7	40.0	n.a.
Apples	66.9	51.3	n.a.
Pears	18.7	15.8	n.a.
Peaches and nectarines	17.6	18.6	n.a.
Grapes	133.0	112.9	87.5

* FAO estimate.

Aggregate production ('000 metric tons, may include official, semi-official or estimated data): Total cereals 2,677.5 in 2007, 3,531.4 in 2008, 4,247.2 in 2009; Total fruits (excl. melons) 595.3 in 2007, 467.9 in 2008, 442.5 in 2009; Total vegetables (incl. melons) 179.7 in 2007, 150.9 in 2008, 163.4 in 2009.

Source: FAO.

LIVESTOCK
('000 head, year ending September)

	2006	2007	2008
Cattle	12,437	12,368	12,657
Sheep	11,087	10,323	9,559
Pigs	240	245	235
Horses	525	427	427*
Chickens*	14,000	14,000	16,000

* FAO estimate(s).
Source: FAO.

LIVESTOCK PRODUCTS
('000 metric tons)

	2006	2007	2008
Cattle meat*	600.0	560.0	588.0
Sheep meat†	31.0	27.0	27.0
Pig meat	18.5	21.1	20.9
Chicken meat†	60.4	50.1	75.3
Cows' milk	1,620.0	1,576.0	1,422.0
Hen eggs	42.3*	47.6	58.3
Wool, greasy	46.7	45.6	45.0†

* Unofficial figure(s).
† FAO estimate(s).

2009 (FAO estimates): Chicken meat 75.3; Cows' milk 1,425.0.

Source: FAO.

Forestry

ROUNDWOOD REMOVALS
('000 cubic metres, excl. bark)

	2007	2008	2009
Sawlogs and veneer logs	1,168	1,150	1,030
Pulpwood	3,929	6,080	5,146
Other industrial wood	14	14	14
Fuel wood	2,062	2,210	2,210
Total	7,173	9,454	8,400

Source: FAO.

SAWNWOOD PRODUCTION
('000 cubic metres, incl. railway sleepers)

	2007	2008	2009
Coniferous (softwood)	109	105	102
Broadleaved (hardwood)	199	179	162
Total	308	284	264

Source: FAO.

Fishing

('000 metric tons, live weight)

	2006	2007	2008
Capture	134.0	108.7	110.7
Argentine hake	31.2	30.6	34.1
Striped weakfish	10.0	8.9	11.2
Whitemouth croaker	28.9	27.7	28.1
Argentine anchovy	12.9	n.a.	n.a.
Castaneta	3.9	1.0	4.4
Rays, stingrays and mantas	2.8	3.6	1.9
Argentine shortfin squid	16.3	15.9	10.9
Aquaculture	0.0	0.0	0.0
Total catch	134.0	108.8	110.7

Note: Figures exclude aquatic mammals, recorded by number rather than by weight. The number of South American fur seals and sea lions caught was: 35 in 2006; 88 in 2007; 63 in 2008.

Source: FAO.

URUGUAY

Mining

('000 metric tons, unless otherwise indicated)

	2007	2008	2009*
Gold (kg)	2,820	2,182	1,690
Gypsum	1,150*	1,150*	1,150
Feldspar (metric tons)	2,500	2,500	2,500

* Estimate(s).

Source: US Geological Survey.

Industry

SELECTED PRODUCTS
('000 metric tons, unless otherwise indicated)

	2005	2006	2007
Raw sugar*	6	6	6
Wine	89.2	95.9	94.0
Motor spirit (petrol, '000 barrels)†	1,830	1,850	1,850
Kerosene ('000 barrels)†	67	100	100
Distillate fuel oils ('000 barrels)†	8,476	8,500	8,500
Residual fuel oils ('000 barrels)†	3,650	3,650	3,650
Cement (hydraulic)†	620	620	620
Electric energy (million kWh)	7,683	5,618	9,424

* Unofficial figures.
† US Geological Survey estimates.

Sources: FAO; US Geological Survey; UN Industrial Commodity Statistics Database.

2008 ('000 barrels, unless otherwise indicated): Motor spirit (petrol) 1,850; Kerosene 100; Distillate fuel oil 8,500; Residual fuel oils 3,650; Cement (hydraulic) 620,000 metric tons (Source: US Geological Survey).

2009 ('000 barrels, unless otherwise indicated, estimates): Motor spirit (petrol) 1,850; Kerosene 100; Distillate fuel oil 8,500; Residual fuel oils 3,650; Cement (hydraulic) 620,000 metric tons (Source: US Geological Survey).

Finance

CURRENCY AND EXCHANGE RATES

Monetary Units
100 centésimos = 1 peso uruguayo.

Sterling, Dollar and Euro Equivalents (31 December 2010)
£1 sterling = 31.457 pesos;
US $1 = 20.094 pesos;
€1 = 26.850 pesos;
1,000 pesos uruguayos = £31.79 = $49.77 = €37.24.

Average Exchange Rate (pesos per US $)
2008   20.949
2009   22.568
2010   20.059

Note: On 1 March 1993 a new currency, the peso uruguayo (equivalent to 1,000 former new pesos), was introduced.

Statistical Survey

CENTRAL GOVERNMENT BUDGET*
(million pesos uruguayos)

Revenue	2007	2008	2009
Tax revenue	113,947	132,986	144,880
Taxes on income, profits, etc.	22,724	33,499	36,049
Individual taxes	9,638	15,780	16,613
Corporate taxes	11,952	5,867	2,847
Taxes on property	8,276	8,941	10,552
Domestic taxes on goods and services	75,868	82,010	88,160
General sales, take-over or value-added tax	61,119	69,578	73,977
Taxes on international trade and transactions	3,275	4,182	4,330
Taxes on leisure activities	52	59	65
Other taxes and rates	3,752	4,295	5,724
Non-tax revenue	8,347	7,240	9,559
Transfers	3,700	4,368	6,066
Other income	938	1,891	2,284
Total	**126,932**	**146,485**	**162,789**

Expenditure	2004	2005	2006
General public services	23,204	25,519	28,230
Government administration	13,444	15,058	16,290
Defence	4,376	4,660	5,187
Public order and safety	5,385	5,801	6,753
Special and community services	37,148	38,747	58,271
Education	11,873	12,573	14,392
Health	6,521	7,135	8,654
Social security and welfare	16,817	17,109	32,375
Housing and community amenities	1,259	1,371	2,029
Recreational, cultural and religious affairs	679	559	821
Economic affairs and services	3,353	5,931	6,435
Fuel and energy	186	179	194
Agriculture, fishing, forestry and hunting	1,421	2,033	1,584
Mining and mineral resources	253	273	275
Transport and communications	2,530	2,728	3,725
Other economic services	964	718	657
Debt-servicing and governmental transfers	22,805	20,322	24,289
Total	**88,510**	**90,519**	**117,225**

* Figures represent the consolidated accounts of the central Government, which include social security revenue and expenditure.

2007: Total expenditure 133,728.
2008: Total expenditure 155,686.
2009: Total expenditure 178,543.

General government finances (consolidated accounts of general government, million pesos uruguayos, preliminary figures): *Revenue:* Total 173,315 (taxes 157,913) in 2006; Total 201,035 (taxes 184,322) in 2007; Total 225,173 in 2008. *Expenditure:* Total 180,122 (social security 54,720) in 2006; Total 206,193 (social security 59,897) in 2007; Total 231,646 in 2008.

INTERNATIONAL RESERVES
(US $ million at 31 December)

	2008	2009	2010
Gold	7	9	12
IMF special drawing rights	4	385	378
Reserve position in the IMF	—	—	97
Foreign exchange	6,349	7,644	7,257
Total	**6,360**	**8,038**	**7,744**

Source: IMF, *International Financial Statistics*.

URUGUAY

MONEY SUPPLY
(million pesos uruguayos at 31 December)

	2007	2008	2009
Currency outside depository corporations	18,892.5	21,406.7	24,306.0
Transferable deposits	71,624.0	98,811.7	97,072.6
Other deposits	125,875.9	163,607.5	155,599.1
Securities other than shares	6,661.0	2,943.3	2,193.1
Broad money	223,053.4	286,769.3	279,170.8

Source: IMF, *International Financial Statistics*.

COST OF LIVING
(Consumer Price Index for Montevideo; base: March 1997 = 100)

	2008	2009	2010
Food and beverages	292.0	310.0	331.3
Housing	279.2	309.0	336.3
Clothing and footwear	166.3	174.2	177.4
Transport and communications	255.6	260.7	266.2
All items (incl. others)	257.3	275.4	293.9

NATIONAL ACCOUNTS
(million pesos uruguayos at current prices, preliminary figures)

Expenditure on the Gross Domestic Product

	2008	2009	2010
Government final consumption expenditure	77,449.2	92,209.6	102,649.8
Private final consumption expenditure	459,827.5	486,698.9	554,188.4
Increase in stocks	11,978.5	−11,578.8	−7,380.7
Gross fixed capital formation	133,506.3	133,198.3	151,629.0
Total domestic expenditure	682,761.5	700,528.1	801,086.5
Exports of goods and services	190,270.7	188,757.6	208,879.5
Less Imports of goods and services	−219,896.6	−182,401.7	−202,281.0
GDP in market prices	653,135.6	706,883.3	807,685.1
GDP at constant 2005 prices	516,834.4	530,175.9	575,069.4

Gross Domestic Product by Economic Activity

	2008	2009	2010
Agriculture, hunting and forestry	60,142.4	58,003.9	66,102.9
Fishing and mining	3,275.7	3,162.4	3,287.1
Manufacturing	104,118.0	102,313.4	105,798.1
Electricity, gas and water	3,954.7	10,427.9	25,557.6
Construction	42,248.8	49,601.3	58,170.2
Trade, restaurants and hotels	98,107.1	101,799.2	116,215.1
Transport, storage and communications	47,574.5	49,063.3	54,271.7
Finance and insurance	27,129.1	29,552.7	34,007.6
Real estate and business services	88,581.0	101,712.4	117,338.5
Public administration and defence; compulsory social security	31,893.5	38,120.2	41,560.3
Other community, social and personal services	78,523.1	92,220.6	102,603.4
Sub-total	585,547.8	635,977.3	724,912.5
Less Financial intermediation services indirectly measured	15,577.6	17,233.0	19,725.8
Gross value added in basic prices	570,070.2	618,744.3	705,186.7
Taxes, less subsidies, on products	83,165.4	88,139.0	102,498.4
GDP in market prices	653,135.6	706,883.3	807,685.1

BALANCE OF PAYMENTS
(US $ million)

	2007	2008	2009
Exports of goods f.o.b.	5,099.9	7,095.5	6,388.9
Imports of goods f.o.b.	−5,645.4	−8,806.7	−6,660.0
Trade balance	−545.5	−1,711.3	−271.1
Exports of services	1,833.5	2,276.4	2,168.3
Imports of services	−1,130.0	−1,462.8	−1,133.7
Balance on goods and services	158.0	−897.6	763.5
Other income received	885.0	757.5	519.8
Other income paid	−1,400.9	−1,493.8	−1,208.5
Balance on goods, services and income	−357.9	−1,633.9	74.8
Current transfers received	164.6	187.7	177.5
Current transfers paid	−27.1	−39.3	−37.8
Current balance	−220.5	−1,485.5	214.5
Capital account (net)	3.7	0.2	—
Direct investment abroad	−89.4	10.9	−1.5
Direct investment from abroad	1,329.5	1,809.4	1,261.7
Portfolio investment assets	195.2	−54.8	−707.3
Portfolio investment liabilities	955.3	−502.9	−2.7
Other investment assets	−2,027.5	44.1	−2,096.2
Other investment liabilities	1,143.1	1,495.4	1,979.5
Net errors and omissions	−284.1	915.6	938.9
Overall balance	1,005.4	2,232.3	1,586.9

Source: IMF, *International Financial Statistics*.

External Trade

PRINCIPAL COMMODITIES
(US $ million, preliminary)

Imports c.i.f.	2007	2008	2009
Food industry products; beverages, tobacco, alcohol and vinegars	257.0	373.2	388.5
Mineral products	1,303.5	2,820.2	1,708.7
Mineral fuels, petroleum and petroleum products	1,274.5	2,769.0	1,684.3
Chemicals and related products	841.0	1,171.7	850.2
Fertilizers	215.9	304.8	156.4
Plastics and plastic products; rubber and manufactures thereof	458.6	575.7	441.7
Plastics and plastic products	349.2	424.3	340.4
Textiles and textile manufactures	235.9	312.5	286.2
Base metals and metal manufactures	281.4	409.5	312.8
Machinery and appliances, electrical materials, audio-visual recording and reproducing apparatus	967.2	1,457.6	1,331.5
Nuclear reactors, boilers, etc. machinery and apparatus	535.7	867.3	803.6
Transport equipment	457.9	882.9	603.8
Automobiles, tractors, cycles, parts and accessories	453.4	711.0	591.6
Total (incl. others)	5,627.7	9,069.4	6,906.7

URUGUAY

Exports f.o.b.	2007	2008	2009
Live animals and animal products	1,492.2	2,110.6	1,780.8
Chilled beef products	229.1	319.0	213.1
Frozen beef products	566.8	877.4	739.3
Fish, crustaceans, molluscs and preparations thereof	171.2	192.2	164.9
Dairy products and birds' eggs	353.1	455.4	384.0
Crops and vegetable products	747.0	1,229.5	1,460.0
Rice	280.0	444.3	461.2
Food industry products; beverages, tobacco, alcohol and vinegars	154.6	143.7	152.9
Mineral products	211.1	210.1	84.5
Chemicals and related products	236.5	320.3	293.0
Plastics and plastic products; rubber and manufactures thereof	246.7	301.7	255.2
Pelts, skins, hides and products thereof	339.9	289.1	189.3
Hides and leathers	305.0	258.4	170.1
Wood, charcoal, cork, etc. and products thereof	247.4	421.6	333.7
Textiles and textile manufactures	306.8	289.6	244.0
Total (incl. others)	4,517.5	5,948.9	5,385.5

PRINCIPAL TRADING PARTNERS
(US $ million)

Imports c.i.f.	2007	2008	2009
Argentina	1,254.8	2,250.0	1,628.3
Brazil	1,314.3	1,618.0	1,459.8
Canada	19.3	192.7	27.0
Chile	77.3	101.9	99.6
China, People's Republic	540.2	908.3	819.1
France (incl. Monaco)	83.7	102.4	82.7
Germany	112.0	141.6	167.6
India	49.4	74.5	47.5
Iran	1.1	1.3	0.8
Italy	94.0	117.3	119.2
Japan	60.9	88.7	73.2
Korea, Republic	59.8	94.9	52.5
Mexico	83.8	119.5	97.5
Russia	195.6	955.2	255.8
Spain	71.5	94.0	83.4
United Kingdom	42.9	56.0	52.4
USA	413.2	530.1	563.7
Venezuela	637.6	647.1	523.6
Total (incl. others)	5,627.7	9,069.4	6,906.7

Exports f.o.b.	2007	2008	2009
Argentina	445.7	506.5	345.6
Brazil	731.6	988.0	1,099.1
Canada	72.0	32.6	37.2
Chile	107.9	134.0	81.2
China, People's Republic	163.4	171.5	234.0
France (incl. Monaco)	35.4	34.0	28.5
Germany	205.5	212.2	158.9
Iran	29.6	101.6	25.4
Israel	45.5	83.1	60.7
Italy	100.1	143.4	115.1
Japan	32.3	43.9	5.1
Mexico	207.2	176.8	134.7
Netherlands	94.1	162.4	119.3
Paraguay	77.3	106.7	84.5
Russia	112.9	332.3	217.6
Spain	147.5	240.2	151.3
United Kingdom	120.5	172.3	142.6
USA	493.1	214.4	177.3
Venezuela	97.1	235.4	187.5
Total (incl. others)	4,517.5	5,941.9	5,385.5

Transport

RAILWAYS
(traffic)

	2002	2003	2004
Passenger-km (million)	8	11	11
Net ton-km (million)	178	188	297

Source: UN, *Statistical Yearbook*.

ROAD TRAFFIC
(motor vehicles in use at 31 December)

	1995	1996	1997
Passenger cars	464,547	485,109	516,889
Buses and coaches	4,409	4,752	4,984
Lorries and vans	41,417	43,656	45,280
Road tractors	12,511	14,628	15,514
Motorcycles and mopeds	300,850	328,406	359,824

Source: International Road Federation, *World Road Statistics*.

2005: Passenger cars and vans 523,866; Coaches and minibuses 6,990; Lorries and road tractors 77,364; Motorcycles and mopeds 473,967.

2006: Passenger cars and vans 553,204; Coaches and minibuses 7,049; Lorries and road tractors 83,958; Motorcycles and mopeds 536,220.

SHIPPING

Merchant Fleet
(registered at 31 December)

	2007	2008	2009
Number of vessels	127	130	129
Total displacement ('000 grt)	111.5	108.8	109.3

Source: IHS Fairplay, *World Fleet Statistics*.

CIVIL AVIATION
(traffic on scheduled services)

	2004	2005	2006
Kilometres flown (million)	9.3	7.7	7.6
Passenger-km (million)	1,075.9	979.6	940.4
Total ton-km (million)	4.5	4.3	4.2

Source: UN Economic Commission for Latin America and the Caribbean, *Statistical Yearbook*.

URUGUAY

Tourism

ARRIVALS BY NATIONALITY*

	2006	2007	2008
Argentina	975,027	908,116	1,025,574
Brazil	228,353	286,319	300,791
Chile	43,800	43,219	39,236
Germany	14,421	14,923	16,499
Italy	15,334	16,642	17,267
Mexico	16,261	16,747	14,778
Paraguay	21,670	23,888	27,708
Peru	10,975	13,637	12,396
Spain	31,332	33,075	32,332
United Kingdom	15,684	13,310	14,397
USA	62,834	64,933	68,369
Total (incl. others)	1,824,340	1,815,281	1,997,884

* Figures refer to arrivals at frontiers of visitors from abroad, including Uruguayan nationals permanently resident elsewhere.

Tourism receipts (US $ million, incl. passenger transport): 711 in 2006; 931 in 2007; 1,180 in 2008.

Source: World Tourism Organization.

Communications Media

	2007	2008	2009
Telephones ('000 main lines in use)	965.2	959.3	953.4
Mobile cellular telephones ('000 subscribers)	3,004.3	3,507.8	3,802.0
Internet users ('000)	968	1,340	1,855
Broadband subscribers ('000)	243.5	244.5	n.a.

Personal computers: 450,000 (136.1 per 1,000 persons) in 2005.

Television receivers (2000): 1,770,000 in use.

Radio receivers (1997): 1,970,000 in use.

Book production (1996): 934 titles.

Daily newspapers (1996): 36 (estimated average circulation 950,000).

Sources: UNESCO, *Statistical Yearbook*; UN, *Statistical Yearbook*; International Telecommunication Union.

Education

(2007, unless otherwise indicated)

	Institutions	Teachers	Students
Pre-primary	1,405	3,984	106,878
Primary	2,395	18,884	348,579
Secondary: general	436	25,168*†	213,550
Secondary: vocational	131	n.a.	70,184
University and equivalent institutions*‡	6	7,723	72,100

* Public education only.
† 2003.
‡ 2005.

Students (2008): Pre-primary 109,654; primary 342,498; secondary: vocational 70,110.

Pupil-teacher ratio (primary education, UNESCO estimate): 15.5 in 2006/07 (Source: UNESCO Institute for Statistics).

Adult literacy rate (UNESCO estimates): 98.2% (males 97.8%; females 98.5%) in 2008 (Source: UNESCO Institute for Statistics).

Directory

The Government

HEAD OF STATE

President: José Alberto Mujica Cordano (took office on 1 March 2010).

Vice-President: Danilo Astori (AU).

COUNCIL OF MINISTERS
(May 2011)

A coalition of the Movimiento de Participación Popular (MPP), the Asamblea Uruguay (AU), the Partido Comunista de Uruguay (PCU), the Partido Socialista del Uruguay (PS), the Vertiente Artiguista (VA) and one Independent.

Minister of the Interior: Eduardo Bonomi Varela (MPP).
Minister of Foreign Affairs: Luis Leonardo Almagro Lemes (MPP).
Minister of National Defence: Luis Rosadilla (MPP).
Minister of Social Development: Ana María Vignoli (PCU).
Minister of Economy and Finance: Fernando Lorenzo (AU).
Minister of Industry, Energy and Mining: Roberto Kreimerman (PS).
Minister of Livestock, Agriculture and Fishing: Tabaré Aguerre (Ind.).
Minister of Tourism and Sport: Dr Héctor Lescano (AP).
Minister of Transport and Public Works: Enrique Pintado (AU).
Minister of Labour and Social Security: Eduardo Brenta (VA).
Minister of Education and Culture: Ricardo Ehrlich (MPP).
Minister of Public Health: Daniel Olesker (PS).
Minister of Housing, Territorial Regulation and the Environment: Graciela Muslera (MPP).
Director of the Planning and Budget Office: Gabriel Frugoni (MPP).
Secretary to the Presidency: Alberto Raúl Breccia Guzzo.
Pro-Secretary to the Presidency: Daniel Cánepa.

MINISTRIES

Office of the President: Casa de Gobierno, Plaza Independencia 710, Torre Ejecutiva, 1° y 2°, 11000 Montevideo; tel. (2) 1502647; fax (2) 9171121; e-mail sci@presidencia.gub.uy; internet www.presidencia.gub.uy.

Ministry of Economy and Finance: Colonia 1089, 3°, 11100 Montevideo; tel. (2) 7122910; fax (2) 7122919; e-mail seprimef@mef.gub.uy; internet www.mef.gub.uy.

Ministry of Education and Culture: Reconquista 535, 9°, 11000 Montevideo; tel. (2) 9161174; fax (2) 9161048; e-mail centrodeinformacion@mec.gub.uy; internet www.mec.gub.uy.

URUGUAY

Ministry of Foreign Affairs: Palacio Santos, Avda 18 de Julio 1205, 11100 Montevideo; tel. (2) 9021010; fax (2) 9021349; e-mail webmaster@mrree.gub.uy; internet www.mrree.gub.uy.

Ministry of Housing, Territorial Regulation and the Environment: Zabala 1432, esq. 25 de Mayo, 11000 Montevideo; tel. (2) 9170710; fax (2) 9163914; e-mail ministro@mvotma.gub.uy; internet www.mvotma.gub.uy.

Ministry of Industry, Energy and Mining: Paysandú s/n, esq. Avda Libertador Brig. Gral Lavalleja, 4°, Montevideo; tel. (2) 9002600; fax (2) 9021245; e-mail ministro@miem.gub.uy; internet www.miem.gub.uy.

Ministry of the Interior: Mercedes 993, 11100 Montevideo; tel. (2) 9089024; fax (2) 9023142; e-mail secmin@minterior.gub.uy; internet www.minterior.gub.uy.

Ministry of Labour and Social Security: Juncal 1511, 4°, Planta Baja, 11000 Montevideo; tel. (2) 9162681; fax (2) 9162708; e-mail consultas@mtss.gub.uy; internet www.mtss.gub.uy.

Ministry of Livestock, Agriculture and Fishing: Avda Constituyente 1476, 1°, 11200 Montevideo; tel. (2) 4126326; fax (2) 4184051; e-mail ministro@mgap.gub.uy; internet www.mgap.gub.uy.

Ministry of National Defence: Edif. General Artigas, Avda 8 de Octubre 2628, Montevideo; tel. (2) 4872828; fax (2) 4814833; e-mail rrpp.secretaria@mdn.gub.uy; internet www.mdn.gub.uy.

Ministry of Public Health: Avda 18 de Julio 1892, 11100 Montevideo; tel. (2) 4000101; fax (2) 4085360; e-mail comunicaciones@msp.gub.uy; internet www.msp.gub.uy.

Ministry of Social Development: Avda 18 de Julio 1453, esq. Dr Javier Barrios Amorín, 2°, 11200 Montevideo; tel. and fax (2) 4000302; e-mail ministra@mides.gub.uy; internet www.mides.gub.uy.

Ministry of Tourism and Sport: Rambla 25 de Agosto 1825, esq. Yacaré s/n, Montevideo; tel. (2) 1885100; fax (2) 9162487; e-mail webmaster@mintur.gub.uy; internet www.mintur.gub.uy.

Ministry of Transport and Public Works: Rincón 561, 11000 Montevideo; tel. (2) 9160509; fax (2) 9162883; e-mail difusion@mtop.gub.uy; internet www.mtop.gub.uy.

Planning and Budget Office: Plaza Independencia 710, Torre Ejecutivo, 11000 Montevideo; tel. (2) 1503581; fax (2) 2099730; e-mail direccion@opp.gub.uy; internet www.opp.gub.uy.

President and Legislature

PRESIDENT

Election, 25 October and 29 November 2009

Candidate	First round % of vote	Second round % of vote
José Alberto Mujica Cordano (Frente Amplio)	47.96	52.39
Luis Alberto Lacalle de Herrera (Partido Nacional)	29.07	43.51
Pedro Bordaberry Herrán (Partido Colorado)	17.02	—
Pablo Mieres Gómez (Partido Independiente)	2.49	—
Raúl Rodríguez da Silva (Asamblea Popular)	0.67	—
Invalid votes	2.79	4.10
Total	100.00	100.00

CONGRESO

Cámara de Senadores
(Senate)

President: Vice-Pres. DANILO ASTORI.

Election, 25 October 2009

Party	Seats
Frente Amplio	16
Partido Nacional	9
Partido Colorado	5
Total*	30

*An additional seat is reserved for the Vice-President, who sits as President of the Senate.

Cámara de Representantes
(Chamber of Representatives)

President: IVONNE PASSADA.

Election, 25 October 2009

Party	Seats
Frente Amplio	50
Partido Nacional	30
Partido Colorado	17
Partido Independiente	2
Total	99

Election Commission

Corte Electoral: Ituzaingó 1467, Montevideo; tel. (2) 9158950; fax (2) 9165088; e-mail corelect@adinet.com.uy; internet www.corteelectoral.gub.uy; f. 1967; Pres. Dr RONALD HERBERT.

Political Organizations

Alianza Libertadora Nacionalista: Montevideo; extreme right-wing; Leader OSVALDO MARTÍNEZ JAUME.

Asamblea Popular Izquierda Unida: Avda Daniel Fernández Crespo 1910 bis, esq. La Paz, Montevideo; tel. (2) 9290861; internet www.asambleapopular.webcindario.com; f. 2008; extreme left-wing; mems include:

  Movimiento de Defensa de los Jubilados: Leader HÉCTOR MORALES.

  Movimiento 26 de Marzo: Durazno 1118, 11200 Montevideo; tel. (2) 9023903; e-mail paginaweb@26demarzo.org.uy; internet www.26demarzo.org.uy; f. 1971; socialist; Pres. EDUARDO RUBIO; Sec.-Gen. FERNANDO VÁZQUEZ.

  Partido Comunista Revolucionario: e-mail pcruruguay@yahoo.com; internet www.pcr.org.uy; Sec.-Gen. RICARDO COHEN.

  Partido Humanista: Avda 18 de Julio 907, local 3 de Galería Caubarrere, Montevideo; tel. 098001969 (mobile); e-mail partidohumanistauy@gmail.com; internet partidohumanistauy.jimdo.com; Leader DANIEL ROCCA.

Frente Amplio (FA): Colonia 1367, 2°, 11100 Montevideo; tel. (2) 9026666; e-mail comunicacion@frenteamplio.org.uy; internet www.frenteamplio.org.uy; f. 1971; left-wing grouping; Pres. JORGE BROVETTO; mems include:

  Alianza Progresista 738 (AP): Colonia 1831, Montevideo; tel. and fax (2) 4016365; e-mail a738@adinet.com.uy; internet alianza738.com.uy; f. 1998; left-wing; Leader RODOLFO NIN NOVOA.

  Asamblea Uruguay (AU): Carlos Quijano 1273, Montevideo; tel. (2) 9032121; fax (2) 9241147; e-mail info@2121.org.uy; internet www.2121.org.uy; f. 1994; centre-left; Leader DANILO ASTORI.

  Frente Izquierda de Liberación (FIDEL): Mercedes 1244, Montevideo; tel. (2) 9087530; e-mail contacto@fidel.com.uy; internet www.fidel.com.uy; f. 1962; socialist; Sec.-Gen. DOREEN IBARRA.

  Movimiento de Participación Popular (MPP): Mercedes 1368, 11200 Montevideo; tel. (2) 9088900; fax (2) 9032248; e-mail info@mppuruguay.org.uy; internet www.mpp.org.uy; f. 1989; grouping of left-wing parties incl. MLN—Tupamaros (see below); Leader LUCÍA TOPOLANSKY.

  Movimiento de Liberación Nacional (MLN)—Tupamaros: Tristán Narvaja 1578, 11200 Montevideo; tel. (2) 4092298; fax (2) 4099957; e-mail mln@chasque.apc.org; internet www.chasque.net/mlnweb; f. 1962; radical socialist; during 1962–73 the MLN, operating under its popular name of the Tupamaros, conducted a campaign of urban guerrilla warfare until it was defeated by the Armed Forces in late 1973; following the return to civilian rule, in 1985, the MLN announced its decision to abandon its armed struggle; legally recognized in May 1989; Sec.-Gen. JOSÉ ALBERTO MUJICA CORDANO.

  Nuevo Espacio: Eduardo Acevedo 1615, 11200 Montevideo; tel. (2) 4026990; fax (2) 4026989; e-mail internacionales@nuevoespacio.org.uy; internet www.nuevoespacio.org.uy; f. 1994; social-democratic; allied to the FA since Dec. 2002; moderate left-wing; Leader RAFAEL MICHELINI; Sec. EDGARDO CARVALHO.

  Partido Comunista de Uruguay (PCU): Río Negro 1525, 11100 Montevideo; tel. (2) 9017171; fax (2) 9011050; e-mail comitecentral@webpcu.org; f. 1920; Sec.-Gen. EDUARDO LORIER; c. 42,000 mems.

URUGUAY

Partido Socialista del Uruguay (PS): Casa del Pueblo, Soriano 1218, 11100 Montevideo; tel. (2) 9013344; fax (2) 9082548; e-mail info@ps.org.uy; internet www.ps.org.uy; f. 1910; Pres. REINALDO GARGANO; Sec.-Gen. EDUARDO (LALO) FERNÁNDEZ.

Partido por la Victoria del Pueblo (PVP): Mercedes 1469, esq. Tacuarembó, Montevideo; tel. (2) 4020370; e-mail info@pvp.org.uy; internet www.pvp.org.uy; f. 1975 in Buenos Aires, Argentina; left-wing; Sec.-Gen. (vacant); Spokesman ANGEL VERA.

Vertiente Artiguista (VA): San José 1191, 11200 Montevideo; tel. (2) 9000177; e-mail vertient@vertiente.org.uy; internet portal.vertiente.org.uy; f. 1989; left-wing; Leader ENRIQUE RUBIO.

Partido Azul Demócrata (PA): Paul Harris 1722, Montevideo; tel. and fax (2) 6016327; e-mail hablacon@partidoazul.s5.com; internet www.partidoazul.s5.com; liberal; f. 1993; Leader Dr ROBERTO CANESSA; Gen. Sec. Ing. ARMANDO VAL.

Partido Colorado: Andrés Martínez Trueba 1271, 11100 Montevideo; tel. (2) 4090180; e-mail info@partidocolorado.com.uy; internet www.partidocolorado.com.uy; f. 1836; Sec.-Gen. PEDRO BORDABERRY HERRÁN; factions include:

  Foro Batllista: Col. 1243, 11100 Montevideo; tel. (2) 9030154; e-mail info@forobatllista.com; internet www.forobatllista.com; Leader Dr JULIO MARÍA SANGUINETTI CAIROLO.

  Lista 15: Leader JORGE LUIS BATLLE IBÁÑEZ.

  Vanguardia Batllista: Casa de Vanguardia, Paysandú 1333, entre Ejido y Curiales, Montevideo; tel. (2) 9027779; e-mail albertoscavarelli@yahoo.com; internet www.scavarelli.com; f. 1999; Sec.-Gen. Dr ALBERTO SCAVARELLI.

Partido Demócrata Cristiano (PDC): Aquiles Lanza 1318 bis, 11100 Montevideo; tel. and fax (2) 9030704; e-mail pdc@chasque.apc.org; internet www.chasque.apc.org/pdc; f. 1962; fmrly Unión Cívica del Uruguay; allied to the Alianza Progresista since 1999; Pres. Dr HÉCTOR LESCANO; Sec.-Gen. JUAN A. ROBALLO.

Partido Independiente: Avda 18 de Julio 2015, Montevideo; tel. (2) 4020120; e-mail info@partidoindependiente.org; internet www.partidoindependiente.org.uy; Leader PABLO MIERES GÓMEZ.

Partido Nacional (Blanco): Juan Carlos Gómez 1384, Montevideo; tel. (2) 9163831; fax (2) 9163758; e-mail partidonacional@partidonacional.com.uy; internet www.partidonacional.com.uy; f. 1836; Exec. Pres. LUIS ALBERTO LACALLE DE HERRERA; Sec.-Gen. ALBERTO ZUMARÁN; tendencies within the party include:

  Alianza Nacional: Avda 18 de Julio 2060, Montevideo; tel. (2) 4022020; e-mail info@alianzanacional.com.uy; internet alianzanacional.com.uy; Leader JORGE LARRAÑAGA.

  Concordia Nacional 747: Avda 18 de Julio 2139, esq. Juan Paullier, Montevideo; tel. (2) 4014320; internet www.concordianacional.com.uy.

  Consejo Nacional Herrerista: Leader LUIS ALBERTO LACALLE DE HERRERA.

  Desafío Nacional: Leader JUAN ANDRÉS RAMÍREZ.

  Línea Nacional de Florida: Leader ARTURO HEBER.

Partido del Sol: Peatonal Yi 1385, 11000 Montevideo; tel. (2) 9001616; fax (2) 9006739; e-mail partidodelsol@adinet.com.uy; internet www.partidodeluruguay.org; ecologist, federal, pacifist; Leader HOMERO MIERES.

Unión Cívica: Montevideo; tel. (2) 9005535; e-mail info@unioncivica.org; internet www.dreamsmaker.com.uy/trabajos/union-civica; f. 1912; recognized Christian Democrat faction, split from the Partido Demócrata Cristiano in 1980; Leader W. GERARDO AZAMBUYA.

Diplomatic Representation

EMBASSIES IN URUGUAY

Argentina: Cuareim 1470, 11800 Montevideo; tel. (2) 9028166; fax (2) 9028172; e-mail emargrou@adinet.com.uy; internet emb-uruguay.mrecic.gov.ar; Ambassador MIGUEL DANTE DOVENA.

Bolivia: Dr Prudencio de Peña 2469, entre Campbell y Ponce, Casilla 11600, 11300 Montevideo; tel. (2) 7083573; fax (2) 7080066; e-mail embouy@adinet.com; Ambassador SALVADOR RIC RIERA.

Brazil: Blvd Artigas 1328, 11300 Montevideo; tel. (2) 7072119; fax (2) 7072086; e-mail montevideu@brasemb.org.uy; internet www.brasil.org.uy; Ambassador JOÃO CARLOS DE SOUZA-GOMES.

Canada: Plaza Independencia 749, Of. 102, 11100 Montevideo; tel. (2) 9022030; fax (2) 9022029; e-mail mvdeo@international.gc.ca; internet www.canadainternational.gc.ca/uruguay; Ambassador FRANCIS TRUDEL.

Chile: 25 de Mayo 575, Montevideo; tel. (2) 9164090; fax (2) 9164083; e-mail echileuy@netgate.com.uy; Ambassador JUAN EDUARDO BURGOS SANTANDER.

China, People's Republic: Miraflores 1508, esq. Pedro Blanes Viale, Carrasco, Casilla 18966, Montevideo; tel. (2) 6016126; fax (2) 6018508; e-mail embchina@adinet.com.uy; internet uy.china-embassy.org; Ambassador QU SHENGWU.

Colombia: Edif. Tupí, Juncal 1305, 18°, esq Buenos Aires, 11000 Montevideo; tel. (2) 9161592; fax (2) 9161594; e-mail embajada@colombia.com.uy; internet www.colombia.com.uy; Ambassador MARÍA CLARA ISAZA MERCHÁN.

Costa Rica: Roque Graseras 740, entre Solano Antuña y Juan María Pérez, Casilla 12242, Montevideo; tel. (2) 7116408; fax (2) 7120872; e-mail embarica@adinet.com.uy; Ambassador MARCO VINICIO VARGAS PEREIRA.

Cuba: Cristóbal Echevarriarza 3471, Montevideo; tel. (2) 6232803; fax (2) 6232805; e-mail emcuburu@adinet.com.uy; internet embacu.cubaminrex.cu/uruguay; Ambassador CARMEN ZILIA PÉREZ MAZÓN.

Dominican Republic: Tomás de Tezanos 1186, entre Arturo Prat y Miguel Grau, 11300 Montevideo; tel. (2) 6287766; fax (2) 6289655; e-mail embajadomuruguay@adinet.com.uy; Ambassador DANIEL GUERRERO TAVERAS.

Ecuador: Juan María Pérez 2810, Montevideo; tel. (2) 7110448; fax (2) 7102492; e-mail embajadaecuador@netgate.com.uy; Ambassador EMILIO IZQUIERDO MIÑO.

Egypt: Avda Brasil 2663, 11300 Montevideo; tel. (2) 7096412; fax (2) 7080977; e-mail embassy.montevideo@mfa.gov.eg; Ambassador MOHAMED ABOU ELDAHAB.

El Salvador: Arq. Raúl Lerena Acevedo 1453, Punta Gorda, 11300 Montevideo; tel. (2) 6134143; fax (2) 6199473; e-mail embasuy@dedicado.net.uy; Ambassador VLADIMIRO P. VILLALTA.

France: Avda Uruguay 853, Casilla 290, 11100 Montevideo; tel. (2) 7050000; fax (2) 7050110; e-mail ambafranceuruguay@gmail.com; internet www.ambafranceuruguay.org; Ambassador JEAN-CHRISTOPHE POTTON.

Germany: La Cumparsita 1435, Plaza Alemania, Casilla 20014, 11200 Montevideo; tel. (2) 9025222; fax (2) 9023422; e-mail info@montevideo.diplo.de; internet www.montevideo.diplo.de; Ambassador KARL-OTTO KÖNIG.

Greece: Blvr José G. Artigas 1231, 11600 Montevideo; tel. (2) 4089224; fax (2) 4020360; e-mail gremb.mvd@mfa.gr; internet www.mfa.gr/montevideo; Ambassador LOUIS-ALKIVIADIS ABATÍS.

Guatemala: Costa Rica 1538, Carrasco, Montevideo; tel. and fax (2) 6012225; fax (2) 6014057; e-mail embaguate-uruguay@minex.gob.gt; Ambassador JUAN JOSÉ BARRIOS TARACENA.

Holy See: Blvd Artigas 1270, Casilla 1503, 11300 Montevideo (Apostolic Nunciature); tel. (2) 7072016; fax (2) 7072209; e-mail nuntius@adinet.com.uy; Apostolic Nuncio Most Rev. ANSELMO GUIDO PECORARI (Titular Archbishop of Populonia).

Iran: Blvr Artigas 531, Montevideo; tel. (2) 7116657; fax (2) 7116659; e-mail embajada.iran@adinet.com.uy; Ambassador HOJJATOLLAH SOLTANI.

Israel: Blvr Artigas 1585, 11200 Montevideo; tel. (2) 4004164; fax (2) 4095821; e-mail info@montevideo.mfa.gov.il; internet montevideo.mfa.gov.il; Ambassador DORI GOREN.

Italy: José Benito Lamas 2857, Casilla 268, 11300 Montevideo; tel. (2) 7084916; fax (2) 7084148; e-mail ambasciata.montevideo@esteri.it; internet www.ambmontevideo.esteri.it; Ambassador MASSIMO ANDREA LEGGERI.

Japan: Blvr Artigas 953, 11300 Montevideo; tel. (2) 4187645; fax (2) 4187980; e-mail embjapon@adinet.com.uy; internet www.uy.emb-japan.go.jp; Ambassador KENICHI SAKUMA.

Korea, Republic: Edif. World Trade Center, Avda Luis Alberto de Herrera 1248, Torre 2, 10°, Montevideo; tel. (2) 6289374; fax (2) 6289376; e-mail koemur@gmail.com; internet ury.mofat.go.kr; Ambassador CHOI YEON-CHOONG.

Lebanon: Avda General Rivera 2278, Montevideo; tel. (2) 4086640; fax (2) 4086365; e-mail embliban@adinet.com.uy; Chargé d'affaires a.i. NMEIR NOUREDDINE.

Mexico: 25 de Mayo 512/514 esq. Treinta y Tres, 11100 Montevideo; tel. (2) 9166034; fax (2) 9166098; e-mail embajada-mexico@embamex.com.uy; internet www.sre.gob.mx/uruguay; Ambassador CASSIO LUISELLI FERNÁNDEZ.

Netherlands: Leyenda Patria 2880, Of. 202, 2°, Casilla 1519, 11000 Montevideo; tel. (2) 7112956; fax (2) 7113301; e-mail mtv@minbuza.nl; internet www.holanda.org.uy; Ambassador H. E. C. M. (RASHA) TER BRAACK.

Panama: Juan Benito Blanco 3388, Montevideo; tel. (2) 6230301; fax (2) 6230300; e-mail empanuru@netgate.com.uy; Ambassador DIGNA M. DONADO F.

Paraguay: Blvr Artigas 1256, Montevideo; tel. (2) 7072138; fax (2) 7083682; e-mail embapur@netgate.com.uy; Chargé d'affaires a.i. CARLOS SCAVONE GODOY.

URUGUAY

Peru: Obligado 1384, 11300 Montevideo; tel. (2) 7076862; fax (2) 7077793; e-mail emba8@embaperu.org.uy; internet www.angelfire.com/country/embaperu; Ambassador José Emilio Romero Cevallos.

Portugal: Avda Dr Francisco Soca 1128, Apto 701, 11300 Montevideo; tel. (2) 7084061; fax (2) 7096456; e-mail embport@montevideu.dgaccp.pt; internet www.embajadadeportugal.com.uy; Ambassador Luís João de Sousa Lorvão.

Romania: Echevarriarza 3452, Casilla 12040, 11000 Montevideo; tel. (2) 6220135; fax (2) 6220685; e-mail ambromvd@adinet.com.uy; Ambassador Gheorghe Petre.

Russia: Blvr España 2741, 11300 Montevideo; tel. (2) 7081884; fax (2) 7086597; e-mail embaru@montevideo.com.uy; internet www.uruguay.mid.ru; Ambassador Serguey N. Koshkin.

South Africa: Dr Gabriel Otero 6337, Carrasco, 11300 Montevideo; tel. (2) 6017591; fax (2) 6003165; e-mail montevideo.general@foreign.gov.za; Ambassador Anthony Leon (resident in Argentina).

Spain: Avda Libertad 2738, 11300 Montevideo; tel. (2) 7086010; fax (2) 7083291; e-mail emb.montevideo@mae.es; internet www.maec.es/embajadas/montevideo; Ambassador Aurora Díaz-Rato Revuelta.

Switzerland: Ing. Federico Abadie 2936/40, 11°, Casilla 12261, 11300 Montevideo; tel. (2) 7115545; fax (2) 7115031; e-mail vertretung@mtv.rep.admin.ch; internet www.eda.admin.ch/montevideo; Ambassador Hans-Ruedi Bortis.

United Kingdom: Marco Bruto 1073, Casilla 16024, 11300 Montevideo; tel. (2) 6223630; fax (2) 6223650; e-mail ukinuruguay@gmail.com; internet ukinuruguay.fco.gov.uk; Ambassador Patrick Mullee.

USA: Lauro Muller 1776, 11200 Montevideo; tel. (2) 4187777; fax (2) 4188611; e-mail webmastermvd@state.gov; internet uruguay.usembassy.gov; Chargé d'affaires a.i. Thomas Lloyd.

Venezuela: Iturriaga 3589, esq. Tomás de Tezanos, Puerto Buceo, Montevideo; tel. (2) 6221262; fax (2) 6282530; e-mail despacho@embvenezuelauy.org; internet www.embvenezuelauy.org; Ambassador Julio Ramón Chirino Rodríguez.

Judicial System

The Supreme Court of Justice comprises five members appointed at the suggestion of the executive, for a period of five years. It has original jurisdiction in constitutional, international and admiralty cases, and hears appeals from the appellate courts, of which there are seven, each with three judges.

Cases involving the functioning of the state administration are heard in the ordinary Administrative Courts and in the Supreme Administrative Court, which consists of five members appointed in the same way as members of the Supreme Court of Justice.

In Montevideo there are 19 civil courts, 10 criminal and correctional courts, 19 courts presided over by justices of the peace, three juvenile courts, three labour courts and courts for government and other cases. Each departmental capital, and some other cities, have a departmental court; each of the 224 judicial divisions has a justice of the peace.

The administration of justice became free of charge in 1980, with the placing of attorneys-at-law in all courts to assist those unable to pay for the services of a lawyer.

Supreme Court of Justice

H. Gutiérrez Ruiz 1310, Montevideo; tel. (2) 9001041; fax (2) 902350; e-mail secparga@poderjudicial.gub.uy; internet www.poderjudicial.gub.uy.

President of the Supreme Court of Justice: Leslie Van Rompaey.

Supreme Administrative Court: Mercedes 961, 11100 Montevideo; tel. (2) 9013090; fax (2) 9080539; e-mail sgianarelli@tca.gub.uy; internet www.tca.gub.uy.

Religion

Under the Constitution, the Church and the State are declared separate and toleration for all forms of worship was proclaimed. Roman Catholicism predominates.

CHRISTIANITY

Federación de Iglesias Evangélicas del Uruguay: Avda 8 de Octubre 3324, 11600 Montevideo; tel. and fax (2) 4875907; e-mail fieu@dcd.com.uy; internet www.chasque.net/obra/skontakt.htm; f. 1956; eight mem. churches; Pres. Oscar Bolioli; Sec. Obed Bodyajian.

The Roman Catholic Church

Uruguay comprises one archdiocese and nine dioceses. Some 71% of the population are Roman Catholics.

Bishops' Conference

Conferencia Episcopal Uruguaya, Avda Uruguay 1319, 11100 Montevideo; tel. (2) 9002642; fax (2) 9011802; e-mail ceusecre@adinet.com.uy; internet www.iglesiauruguaya.com.

f. 1972; Pres. Rt Rev Carlos María Collazzi Irazábal (Bishop of Mercedes).

Archbishop of Montevideo: Most Rev. Nicolás Cotugno Fanizzi, Arzobispado, Treinta y Tres 1368, Casilla 356, 11000 Montevideo; tel. (2) 9158127; fax (2) 9158926; e-mail info@arquidiocesis.net; internet www.arquidiocesis.net.

The Anglican Communion

Uruguay constitutes a diocese in the Province of the Southern Cone of America. The presiding Bishop of the Iglesia Anglicana del Cono Sur de América is the Bishop of Northern Argentina.

Bishop of Uruguay: Rt Rev. Miguel Tamayo Zaldívar, Centro Diocesano, Reconquista 522, Casilla 6108, 11000 Montevideo; tel. (2) 9159627; fax (2) 9162519; e-mail mtamayo@netgate.com.uy; internet www.uruguay.anglican.org.

Other Churches

Baptist Evangelical Convention of Uruguay: Mercedes 1487, 11100 Montevideo; tel. and fax (2) 2167012; e-mail suspasos@adinet.com.uy; f. 1948; 4,500 mems; Pres. Dr Juan Carlos Otormín.

Iglesia Adventista (Adventist Church): Castro 167, Montevideo; f. 1901; 4,000 mems; Principal Officers Dr Guillermo Durán, Dr Alexis Piro.

Iglesia Evangélica Metodista en el Uruguay (Evangelical Methodist Church in Uruguay): San José 1457, 11200 Montevideo; tel. (2) 4136552; fax (2) 4136554; e-mail iemu@adinet.com.uy; internet www.gbgm-umc.org/iemu; f. 1878; 1,193 mems (1997); Pres. Rev. Oscar Bolioli.

Iglesia Evangélica Valdense (Waldensian Evangelical Church): Avda 8 de Octubre 3039, 11600 Montevideo; tel. and fax (2) 4879406; e-mail ievm@internet.com.uy; f. 1952; 15,000 mems; Pastor Alvaro Michelin Salomón.

Iglesia Pentecostal Unida Internacional en Uruguay (United Pentecostal Church International in Uruguay): Helvecia 4032, Piedras Blancas, 12200 Montevideo; tel. (2) 5133618; e-mail lrodrigu@montevideo.com.uy; internet members.tripod.com/~lrodrigu; Pastor Luis Rodríguez.

Primera Iglesia Bautista (First Baptist Church): Avda Daniel Fernández Crespo 1741, Casilla 5051, 11200 Montevideo; tel. (2) 4098744; fax (2) 4094356; e-mail piebu@adinet.com.uy; f. 1911; 314 mems; Pastor Lemuel J. Larrosa.

Other denominations active in Uruguay include the Iglesia Evangélica del Río de la Plata and the Iglesia Evangélica Menonita (Evangelical Mennonite Church).

BAHÁ'Í FAITH

National Spiritual Assembly of the Bahá'ís: Blvr Artigas 2440, 11600 Montevideo; tel. (2) 4875890; fax (2) 4802165; e-mail bahai@multi.com.uy; f. 1938; mems resident in 140 localities.

The Press

DAILIES

Montevideo

El Diario Español: Cerrito 551–555, Casilla 899, 11000 Montevideo; tel. (2) 9159481; fax (2) 9157389; e-mail marcelo.reinante@eldiarioespanol.com.uy; f. 1905; morning (except Monday); newspaper of the Spanish community; Editor Marcelo Reinante; circ. 20,000.

Diario Oficial: Avda 18 de Julio 1373, Montevideo; tel. (2) 9085042; fax (2) 9023098; e-mail impo@impo.com.uy; internet www.impo.com.uy; f. 1905; biweekly; publishes laws, official decrees, parliamentary debates, judicial decisions and legal transactions; Dir-Gen. Gonzalo Reboledo.

El Observador: Cuareim 2052, 11800 Montevideo; tel. (2) 9247000; fax (2) 9248698; e-mail elobservador@observador.com.uy; internet www.observa.com.uy; f. 1991; morning; Chief Editor Gabriel Preyra; circ. 26,000.

El País: Zelmar Michelini 1287, 4°, 11100 Montevideo; tel. (2) 9020115; fax (2) 9020464; e-mail cartas@elpais.com.uy; internet www.elpais.com.uy; f. 1918; morning; supports the Partido Nacional; Editor Martín Aguirre Regules; circ. 106,000.

URUGUAY

La República: Avda Gral Garibaldi 2579, 11600 Montevideo; tel. (2) 4873565; fax (2) 4873824; e-mail ffasano@chasque.net; internet www.larepublica.com.uy; f. 1988; morning; Editor FEDERICO FASANO MERTENS; Gen. Man. PABLO FASANO MÁRQUEZ; circ. 25,000.

Ultimas Noticias: Paysandú 1179, 11100 Montevideo; tel. (2) 9020452; fax (2) 9024669; e-mail contacto@ultimasnoticias.com.uy; internet www.ultimasnoticias.com.uy; f. 1981; evening (except Saturday); owned by Impresora Polo; Publr Dr ALPHONSE EMANUILOFF-MAX; circ. 25,000.

Florida

El Heraldo: Independencia 824, 94000 Florida; tel. (35) 22229; fax (35) 24546; e-mail elheraldo@elheraldo.com.uy; internet www.diarioelheraldo.com.uy; f. 1919; morning; independent; Dir ALVARO RIVA REY; circ. 20,000.

Maldonado

Correo de Punta del Este: Calle 33 y Sarandi 800 bis, 20000 Maldonado; tel. and fax (42) 235633; e-mail gallardo@adinet.com.uy; internet www.diariocorreo.com; f. 1993; morning; Editor MARCELO GALLARDO; circ. 2,500.

Paysandú

El Telégrafo: Avda 18 de Julio 1027, 60000 Paysandú; tel. (722) 3141; fax (722) 7999; e-mail correo@eltelegrafo.com; internet www.eltelegrafo.com; f. 1910; morning; independent; Dir FERNANDO A. BACCARO; circ. 8,500.

Salto

El Pueblo: Avda 18 de Julio 151, entre Artigas y Rivera, Salto; tel. (733) 4133; e-mail dipueblo@adinet.com.uy; internet www.diarioelpueblo.com.uy; f. 1959; morning; Dir ADRIANA MARTÍNEZ.

PERIODICALS

Montevideo

Brecha: Avda Uruguay 844, 11100 Montevideo; tel. (2) 9025042; fax (2) 9020388; e-mail brecha@brecha.com.uy; internet www.brecha.com.uy; f. 1985; weekly; politics, current affairs; Dir GABRIEL PAPA; Editor-in-Chief ROBERTO LÓPEZ BELLOSO; circ. 8,500.

Búsqueda: Avda Uruguay 1146, 11100 Montevideo; tel. (2) 9021300; fax (2) 9022036; e-mail info@busqueda.com.uy; internet www.busqueda.com.uy; f. 1972; weekly (Thurs.); independent; politics and economics; Dir CLAUDIO PAOLILLO; circ. 25,000.

Charoná: Gutiérrez Ruiz 1276, Of. 201, Montevideo; tel. (2) 9086665; e-mail administracion@charona.com; internet www.charona.com; f. 1968; fortnightly; children's; Dir SERGIO BOFFANO; circ. 25,000.

Crónicas Económicas: Avda Libertador Brig.-Gen. Lavalleja 1532, Montevideo; tel. (2) 9004790; fax (2) 9020759; e-mail cronicas@netgate.com.uy; internet www.cronicas.com.uy; f. 1981; weekly; independent; business and economics; Dirs JULIO ARIEL FRANCO, WALTER HUGO PAGÉS, JORGE ESTELLANO.

El Derecho Digital: Montevideo; tel. (2) 4099643; e-mail ddu@elderechodigital.com.uy; internet www.elderechodigital.com.uy; legal; Dir LUIS FERNANDO IGLESIAS; Editor FERNANDO VARGAS.

El Diario Medico: Avda 18 de Julio 1485, 2°, Montevideo; tel. and fax (2) 4083797; e-mail eldiariomedico@eldiariomedico.com.uy; internet www.eldiariomedico.com.uy; f. 1997; health; Dir ELBIO D. ALVAREZ.

Guambia: Rimac 1576, 11400 Montevideo; tel. and fax (2) 6132703; e-mail info@guambia.com.uy; internet www.guambia.com.uy; f. 1983; monthly; satirical; Dir and Editor ANTONIO DABEZIES.

La Justicia Uruguaya: Avda 25 de Mayo 555, Apto 404, 11000 Montevideo; tel. (2) 9157587; fax (2) 9159721; e-mail lajusticiauruguaya@lju.com.uy; internet www.lajusticiauruguaya.com.uy; f. 1940; bimonthly; jurisprudence; Dirs EDUARDO ALBANELL MARTINO, ADOLFO ALBANELL MARTINO (Editor); circ. 3,000.

Marketing Directo: Guaná 2237 bis, 11200 Montevideo; tel. (2) 650602; fax (2) 4087221; e-mail consumo@adinet.com.uy; internet www.ciecc.org; f. 1988; monthly; Dir EDGARDO MARTÍNEZ ZIMARIOFF; circ. 9,500.

Opinar: Río Negro 1192/60, Montevideo; tel. 099686125 (mobile); e-mail cgarcia@opinar.com; internet www.opinar.com.uy; communist; Dir TABARÉ VIERA DUARTE; Editor CÉSAR GARCÍA ACOSTA.

Patria: Montevideo; e-mail semanariopatria@gmail.com; internet www.patria.com.uy; weekly; organ of the Partido Nacional; right-wing; Dir LUIS A. HEBER; Editor Dr JOSÉ LUIS BELLANI.

Propiedades: Bvar. España 2586, Montevideo; tel. (2) 7118384; fax (2) 7121674; e-mail redaccion@revistapropiedades.com.uy; internet www.revistapropiedades.com.uy; f. 1987; construction and real estate; Dir JULIO C. VILLAMIDE.

Uruguay Natural: Ibiray 2293, 11300 Montevideo; tel. (2) 7114900; fax (2) 7123421; e-mail info@uruguaynatural.com.uy; internet www.uruguaynatural.com.uy; tourism; Pres. JAVIER SANTOMÉ SOSA DIAS; Dir FERNANDO ROJO SANTANA.

Voces: Chaná 2389, Montevideo; tel. (2) 4018298; e-mail vocesfa@montevideo.com.uy; internet www.vocesfa.com.uy; political; Editor ALFREDO GARCÍA.

PRESS ASSOCIATIONS

Asociación de Diarios del Uruguay: Río Negro 1308, 6°, 11100 Montevideo; f. 1922; Pres. GUILLERMO SCHECK.

Asociación de la Prensa Uruguaya: San José 1330, Montevideo; tel. and fax (2) 9013695; e-mail apu@adinet.com.uy; internet www.apu.org.uy; f. 1944; Pres. DANIEL LEMA; Sec.-Gen. RÚBEN HERNÁNDEZ.

Publishers

Autores Uruguayos: Paysandú 1561, 11200 Montevideo; e-mail mensajes@autoresuruguayos.com.uy; internet www.autoresuruguayos.com; publishes works by Uruguayan authors; Man. ADRIANA DOS SANTOS.

Editorial Arca: Ana Monterroso de Lavalleja 2231, Montevideo; tel. (2) 24097514; fax (2) 24099788; e-mail arcaeditorial@adinet.com.uy; internet www.arcaeditorial.com; f. 1963; general literature, social science and history; Man. Dir GABRIELA MÁRQUEZ.

Ediciones de la Banda Oriental: Gaboto 1582, 11200 Montevideo; tel. (2) 4083206; fax (2) 4098138; e-mail info@bandaoriental.com.uy; internet www.bandaoriental.com.uy; f. 1961; general literature; Man. Dir HEBER RAVIOLO.

CENCI—Uruguay (Centro de Estadísticas Nacionales y Comercio Internacional): Juncal 1327D, Of. 1603, Casilla 1510, 11000 Montevideo; tel. (2) 9152930; fax (2) 9154578; e-mail cenci@cenci.com.uy; internet www.cenci.com.uy; f. 1956; economics, statistics; Dir KENNETH BRUNNER.

Editorial y Librería Jurídica Amalio M. Fernández SRL: 25 de Mayo 589, 11000 Montevideo; tel. and fax (2) 9151782; e-mail amflibrosjurid@movinet.com.uy; f. 1951; law and sociology; Man. Dir CARLOS W. DEAMESTOY.

Editorial La Flor del Itapebí: 26 de Marzo 1185/201, Montevideo; fax (2) 7091620; e-mail itapebi@chasque.apc.org; internet www.itapebi.com.uy; f. 1991; cultural, technical, educational.

Fundación de Cultura Universitaria: 25 de Mayo 568, Casilla 1155, 11000 Montevideo; tel. (2) 9161152; fax (2) 9152549; e-mail ventas@fcu.com.uy; internet www.fcu.com.uy; f. 1968; law and social sciences; Pres. Dr MARCELO VIGO.

Hemisferio Sur: Buenos Aires 335, Casilla 1755, 11000 Montevideo; tel. (2) 9164515; fax (2) 9164520; e-mail editorial@hemisferiosur.com; internet www.hemisferiosur.com; f. 1951; agronomy and veterinary science.

Editorial Idea: Misiones 1424, 5°, 11000 Montevideo; tel. (2) 9165456; fax (2) 9150868; e-mail vescovi@fastlink.com.uy; law; Dir Dr GUILLERMO VESCOVI.

Librería Linardi y Risso: Juan C. Gómez 1435, 11000 Montevideo; tel. (2) 9157129; fax (2) 9157431; e-mail lyrbooks@linardiyrisso.com.uy; internet www.linardiyrisso.com.uy; f. 1944; general; Man. Dirs ALVARO RISSO, ANDRÉS LINARDI.

Editorial Medina SRL: Gaboto 1521, Montevideo; tel. (2) 4085800; f. 1933; general; Pres. MARCOS MEDINA VIDAL.

A. Monteverde & Cía, SA: Treinta y Tres 1475, Casilla 371, 11000 Montevideo; tel. (2) 9152939; fax (2) 9152012; f. 1879; educational; Man. Dir LILIANA MUSSINI.

Mosca Hermanos SA: Avda 18 de Julio 1578, 11300 Montevideo; tel. (2) 4093141; fax (2) 4088059; e-mail info@mosca.com.uy; internet www.mosca.com.uy; f. 1888; general; Pres. Lic. ZSOLT AGARDY.

Librería Selecta Editorial: Guayabo 1865, 11200 Montevideo; tel. (2) 4086989; fax (2) 4086831; f. 1950; academic books; Dir FERNANDO MASA.

Ediciones Trilce: Durazno 1888, 11200 Montevideo; tel. (2) 4127662; fax (2) 4127722; e-mail trilce@trilce.com.uy; internet www.trilce.com.uy; f. 1985; science, politics, history.

Vintén Editor: Hocquart 1771, 11804 Montevideo; tel. (2) 2090223; internet vinten-uy.com; poetry, theatre, history, art, literature.

PUBLISHERS' ASSOCIATION

Cámara Uruguaya del Libro: Juan D. Jackson 1118, 11200 Montevideo; tel. (2) 4015732; fax (2) 4011860; e-mail camurlib@adinet.com.uy; f. 1944; Pres. ERNESTO SANJINÉS; Man. ANA CRISTINA RODRÍGUEZ.

URUGUAY

Broadcasting and Communications

TELECOMMUNICATIONS

Regulatory Authority

Unidad Reguladora de Servicios de Comunicaciones (URSEC): Uruguay 988, Casilla 11100, Montevideo; tel. (2) 9028082; fax (2) 9005708; e-mail webmaster@ursec.gub.uy; internet www.ursec.gub.uy; regulates telecommunications and postal sectors; Pres. JAIME IGORRA.

Service Providers

Administración Nacional de Telecomunicaciones (ANTEL): Complejo Torre de las Telecomunicaciones, Guatemala 1075, Montevideo; e-mail antel@antel.com.uy; internet www.antel.com.uy; f. 1974; state-owned; Pres. EDGARDO CARVALHO; Gen. Man. JOSÉ LUIS SALDÍAS.

ANCEL: Pablo Galarza 3537, Montevideo; internet www.ancel.com.uy; f. 1974; state-owned mobile telephone co.

CTI Móvil: Montevideo; internet www.cti.com.uy; owned by América Móvil, SA de CV (Mexico); mobile cellular telephone services; launched wireless services in Dec. 2004.

Movistar Uruguay: Avda Constituyente, Edif. Torre el Gaucho, 1467 Montevideo; tel. (2) 4087502; internet www.movistar.com.uy; owned by Telefónica Móviles, SA (Spain); mobile telephone services.

BROADCASTING

Regulatory Authority

Asociación Nacional de Broadcasters Uruguayos (ANDEBU): Carlos Quijano 1264, 11100 Montevideo; tel. (2) 9021525; fax (2) 9021540; e-mail andebu@internet.com.uy; internet www.andebu.com.uy; f. 1933; 101 mems; Pres. CARLOS FALCO; Vice-Pres. Dr WALTER C. ROMAY.

Radio

El Espectador: Río Branco 1481, 11100 Montevideo; tel. (2) 9023531; fax (2) 9083192; e-mail ventas@espectador.com.uy; internet www.espectador.com; f. 1923; commercial; Gen. Man. ESTELA BARTOLIC.

FM del Sol: Plaza Independencia 753, Of. 201, 2°, Montevideo; tel. (2) 9032225; e-mail marketing@fmdelsol.com; internet www.fmdelsol.com.

Radio Carve: Mercedes 973, 11100 Montevideo; tel. (2) 9026162; fax (2) 9020126; e-mail carve@sadrep.com.uy; internet www.carve850.com.uy; f. 1928; commercial; Dir HÉCTOR CARLOS VERA.

Radio Montecarlo: Avda 18 de Julio 1224, 1°, 11100 Montevideo; tel. (2)9014433; fax (2) 9017762; e-mail cx20@radiomontecarlo.com.uy; internet www.radiomontecarlo.com.uy; f. 1924; commercial; Dir DANIEL ROMAY.

Radio Sarandí: Enriqueta Compte y Riqué 1250, 11800 Montevideo; tel. (2) 2082612; fax (2) 2036906; e-mail direccion@sarandi690.com.uy; internet www.radiosarandi.com.uy; f. 1931; commercial; Pres. RAMIRO RODRÍGUEZ VALLAMIL RIVIERE.

Radio Universal: Avda 18 de Julio 1220, 3°, 11100 Montevideo; tel. (2) 9032222; fax (2) 9026050; e-mail info@22universal.com; internet www.22universal.com; f. 1929; commercial; Pres. OSCAR IMPERIO.

Radiodifusión Nacional SODRE: Sarandí 430, 11000 Montevideo; tel. (2) 957865; fax (2) 9161933; e-mail direccionradios@sodre.gub.uy; internet www.sodre.gub.uy; f. 1929; state-owned; operates radio stations: Radio Clásica 650 AM, Radio Uruguay 1050 AM, Emisora del Sur 94.7 FM and Babel 97.1 FM; Dir SERGIO SACOMANI.

In 2002 there were some 16 AM and six FM radio stations in the Montevideo area. In addition, there were approximately 41 AM and 56 FM radio stations outside the capital.

Television

The Uruguayan Government holds a 10% stake in the regional television channel Telesur (q.v.), which began operations in 2005 and is based in Caracas, Venezuela.

Canal 4 Monte Carlo: Paraguay 2253, 11800 Montevideo; tel. (2) 9244444; fax (2) 9247929; e-mail webmontecarlotv@montecarlotv.com.uy; internet www.canal4.com.uy; f. 1961; Dir HUGO ROMAY SALVO.

SAETA TV—Canal 10: Dr Lorenzo Carnelli 1234, 11200 Montevideo; tel. (2) 4102120; fax (2) 4009771; internet www.canal10.com.uy; f. 1956; Pres. JORGE DE FEO.

SODRE (Servicio Oficial de Difusión Radiotelevisión y Espectáculos): Blvr Artigas 2552, 11600 Montevideo; tel. (2) 4806448; fax (2) 4808515; e-mail direccion@tveo.com.uy; internet www.sodre.gub.uy; f. 1963; Pres. NELLY GOITIÑO.

Teledoce Televisora Color—Canal 12: Enriqueta Compte y Riqué 1276, 11800 Montevideo; tel. (2) 2083555; fax (2) 2037623; e-mail latele@teledoce.com; internet www.teledoce.com; f. 1962; Gen. Man. (vacant).

Tevé Ciudad: Javier Barrios Amorín 1460, Montevideo; tel. (2) 4001908; fax (2) 4029369; e-mail griselda.diaz@imm.gub.uy; internet www.teveciudad.com; f. 1996; state-owned; Gen. Dir GRISELDA DÍAZ LARREA.

Finance

BANKING

(cap. = capital; res = reserves; dep. = deposits; m. = million; brs = branches; amounts in pesos uruguayos unless otherwise indicated)

State Banks

Banco Central del Uruguay: Avda Juan P. Fabini 777, Casilla 1467, 11100 Montevideo; tel. (2) 9085629; fax (2) 9021634; e-mail info@bcu.gub.uy; internet www.bcu.gub.uy; f. 1967; note-issuing bank, also controls private banking; cap. 1,547.7m., res −13,844.4m., dep. 103,138.6m. (Dec. 2005); Pres. MARIO BERGARA DUQUE; Dir JORGE LUIS GAMARRA SEBASTIÁN.

Banco Hipotecario del Uruguay (BHU): Avda Daniel Fernández Crespo 1508, Montevideo; tel. (2) 4090000; fax (2) 4090782; e-mail info@bhu.net; internet www.bhu.net; f. 1892; state mortgage bank; in 1977 assumed responsibility for housing projects in Uruguay; Pres. JORGE POLGAR.

Banco de la República Oriental del Uruguay (BROU): Cerrito y Zabala 351, 11000 Montevideo; tel. (2) 9150157; fax (2) 9162064; e-mail broupte@adinet.com.uy; internet www.brounet.com.uy; f. 1896; cap. 12,517.6m., res 2,825.1m., dep. 124,856.8m. (Dec. 2006); Pres. FERNANDO CALLOIA RAFFO; Gen. Man. FERNANDO JORAJURÍA; 117 brs.

Principal Commercial Banks

ABN AMRO Bank Uruguay NV: Julio Herrera y Obes 1365, Casilla 888, 11100 Montevideo; tel. (2) 9031073; fax (2) 9025011; internet www.abnamro.com.uy; f. 1952; owned by ABN AMRO Bank NV (Netherlands); Country Rep. FRANCISCO DI ROBERTO, Jr; 24 brs.

Banco Bilbao Vizcaya Argentaria Uruguay SA (BBVA): 25 de Mayo 401, esq. Zabala, 11000 Montevideo; tel. (2) 9161444; fax (2) 9162821; internet www.bbvabanco.com.uy; f. 1968; fmrly Unión de Bancos del Uruguay, and later Banesto Banco Uruguay, SA and Banco Francés Uruguay, SA; adopted current name in 2000 following merger with Banco Exterior de América, SA; cap. 883.0m., res 674.1m., dep. 10,336.3m. (Dec. 2005); Pres. TOMÁS DEANE; Vice-Pres. and Gen. Man. ANGEL SORIA; 14 brs.

Banco Galicia Uruguay, SA: Edif. World Trade Center, Luis A. Herrera 1248, 22°, Montevideo; tel. (2) 6281230; e-mail contactenos@bancogalicia.com.uy; internet www.bancogalicia.com.uy; f. 1999.

Banco Surinvest SA: Rincón 530, 11000 Montevideo; tel. (2) 9160177; fax (2) 9160241; e-mail bancosurinvest@surinvest.com.uy; internet www.surinvest.com.uy; f. 1981 as Surinvest Casa Bancaria; name changed as above 1991; cap. 249.3m., res 71.4m., dep. 2,351.2m. (Dec. 2004); Gen. Man. ALBERTO A. MELLO.

Crédit Uruguay Banco SA: Rincón 500, 11000 Montevideo; tel. (2) 9150095; fax (2) 9164282; internet www.credituruguay.com.uy; f. 1998 as Banco Acac SA; adopted current name 2004; bought by BBVA (q.v.) in April 2011; cap. 413.4m., res 18.4m., dep. 11,616.1m. (Dec. 2005); Pres. GERMÁN VILLAR; Gen. Man. MARCELO OTEN.

Discount Bank (Latin America), SA: Rincón 390, 11000 Montevideo; tel. (2) 9164848; fax (2) 9160890; e-mail mensajes@discbank.com.uy; internet www.discbank.com.uy; f. 1978; owned by Israel Discount Bank of New York (USA); cap. US $12.8m., res $0.62m., dep. $179.3m. (Dec. 2002); Pres. and Chair. REUVEN SPIEGEL; Dir and Gen. Man. VALENTIN D. MALACHOWSKI; 4 brs.

HSBC Bank (Uruguay), SA: Ituzaingó 1389, 11000 Montevideo; tel. (2) 9153395; fax (2) 9160125; f. 1995; owned by HSBC Bank PLC (United Kingdom); CEO ALAN WILKINSON.

Nuevo Banco Comercial, SA (NBC): Misiones 1399, CP 11000 Montevideo; tel. (2) 1401300; fax (2) 1401185; e-mail servicioalcliente@nbc.com.uy; internet www.nbc.com.uy; f. 2003 by merger of Banco Comercial, Banco La Caja Obrera and Banco de Montevideo; fmrly state-owned, privatized in June 2006; dep. US $923m., total assets $1,153m. (July 2006); Pres. ERNEST BACHRACH; Gen. Man. JOSÉ FUENTES; 46 brs.

Credit Co-operative

There are several credit co-operatives, which permit members to secure small business loans at preferential rates.

URUGUAY

Federación Uruguaya de Cooperativas de Ahorro y Crédito (FUCAC): Blvr Artigas 1472, Montevideo; tel. and fax (2) 7088888; e-mail info@fucac.com.uy; internet www.fucac.com.uy; f. 1972; Pres. CARLOS ALBERTO ICASURIAGA SAMANO; Gen. Man. JAVIER HUMBERTO PI LEÓN.

Development Bank

Banco Bandes Uruguay: Sarandí 402, CP 111000, Montevideo; tel. (2) 9160100; fax (2) 9153904; internet www.bandes.com.uy; owned by the Banco de Desarrollo Económico y Social (BANDES) of Venezuela.

Bankers' Association

Asociación de Bancarios del Uruguay (Bankers' Association of Uruguay—AEBU): Camacuá 575, Montevideo; tel. (2) 9161060; e-mail secprensa@aebu.org.uy; internet www.aebu.org.uy; f. 1945; 7 mem. banks; Dir OSCAR JORGE VISSANI.

STOCK EXCHANGE

Bolsa de Valores de Montevideo: Edif. Bolsa de Comercio, Misiones 1400, 11000 Montevideo; tel. (2) 9165051; fax (2) 9161900; e-mail info@bolsademontevideo.com.uy; internet www.bolsademontevideo.com.uy; f. 1867; 75 mems; Pres. IGNACIO ROSPIDE.

INSURANCE

From mid-1994, following the introduction of legislation ending the state monopoly of most types of insurance, the Banco de Seguros del Estado lost its monopoly on all insurance except life, sea transport and fire risks, which have been traditionally open to private underwriters.

AIG Uruguay Compañía de Seguros, SA (USA): Colonia 993, 1°, Montevideo; tel. (2) 9000330; fax (2) 9084552; e-mail aig.uruguay@aig.com; internet www.aig.com; f. 1996; all classes; Gen. Man. JORGE FERRANTE.

Alico Compañía de Seguros de Vida, SA (USA): 18 de Julio 1738, Montevideo; tel. (2) 4033939; fax (2) 4033938; e-mail alico@alico.com.uy; internet www.alico.com; f. 1996; life; Gen. Man. JUAN ETCHEVERRY.

Banco de Seguros del Estado: Avda Libertador 1465, Montevideo; tel. (2) 9089303; fax (2) 9017030; e-mail directorio@bse.com.uy; internet www.bse.com.uy; f. 1912; state insurance org.; all risks; Pres. ENRIQUE ROIG CURBELO; Gen. Man. CARLOS VALDÉS.

Compañía de Seguros Aliança da Bahia Uruguay, SA (Brazil): Río Negro 1394, 7°, Montevideo; tel. (2) 9021086; fax (2) 9021087; e-mail avivo@netgate.com.uy; f. 1995; transport; Gen. Man. BERNARDO VIVO.

Mapfre Compañía de Seguros, SA (Spain): Blvr Artigas 459, Montevideo; tel. and fax (2) 7116595; e-mail info@mapfre.com.uy; internet www.mapfre.com.uy; f. 1994; general; Gen. Man. DIEGO SOBRINI.

Porto Seguro, Seguros del Uruguay SA (Brazil): Blvr Artigas 2025, Montevideo; tel. (2) 4028000; fax (2) 4030097; e-mail admin@portoseguro.com.uy; internet www.portoseguro.com.uy; f. 1995; property; Pres. LEANDRO SUÁREZ.

Real Uruguaya de Seguros SA (Netherlands): Avda 18 de Julio 988, Montevideo; tel. (2) 9025858; fax (2) 9024515; e-mail realseguros@abnamro.com; internet www.realseguros.com.uy; f. 1900; life and property; part of the ABN AMRO Group; Gen. Man. JOSÉ LUIZ TOMAZINI.

Royal & SunAlliance Seguros, SA (United Kingdom): Peatonal Sarandí 620, Montevideo; tel. (2) 9170505; fax (2) 9170490; internet www.royalsunalliance.com.uy; f. 1997; life and property; Dir Dr JUAN QUARTINO.

Surco, Compañía Cooperativa de Seguros: Blvr Artigas 1320, Montevideo; tel. (2) 7090089; fax (2) 7077313; e-mail surco@surco.com.uy; internet www.surco.com.uy; f. 1995; insurance co-operative; all classes; Gen. Man. ANDRÉS ELOLA.

L'UNION de Paris Compañía Uruguaya de Seguros, SA (France): Misiones 1549, Montevideo; tel. (2) 9160850; fax (2) 9160847; e-mail gabriel.penna@lunion.com.com.uy; internet www.lunion.com.uy; f. 1897 as L'Union IARD; present name adopted 2004; general; Gen. Man. GABRIEL PENNA.

INSURANCE ASSOCIATION

Asociación Uruguaya de Empresas Aseguradoras (AUDEA): Juncal 1305, Of. 1901, 11000 Montevideo; tel. (2) 9161465; fax (2) 9165991; e-mail audea@adinet.com.uy; Pres. MANUEL RODRÍGUEZ; Gen. Man. MAURICIO CASTELLANOS.

Trade and Industry

GOVERNMENT AGENCIES

Administración Nacional de Combustibles, Alcohol y Portland (ANCAP): Payasandú y Avda del Libertador Brig.-Gen. Lavalleja, 11100 Montevideo; tel. (2) 9020608; fax (2) 9021136; e-mail webmaster@ancap.com.uy; internet www.ancap.com.uy; f. 1931; deals with transport, refining and sale of petroleum products, and the manufacture of alcohol, spirits and cement; tanker services, also river transport; Pres. RAÚL SENDIC; Sec.-Gen. MIGUEL A. TATO.

Oficina de Planeamiento y Presupuesto de la Presidencia de la República: Plaza Independencia 710, 11000 Montevideo; tel. (2) 4872110; fax (2) 2099730; e-mail direccion@opp.gub.uy; internet www.opp.gub.uy; f. 1967; responsible for the implementation of devt plans; co-ordinates the policies of the various ministries; advises on the preparation of the budget of public enterprises; Dir GABRIEL FRUGONI; Sub-Dir JERÓNIMO ROCA.

Uruguay XXI (Instituto de Promoción de Inversiones y Exportaciones de Bienes y Servicios): Rincón 518/528, 11100 Montevideo; tel. (2) 9153838; fax (2) 9163059; e-mail info@uruguayxxi.gub.uy; internet www.uruguayxxi.gub.uy; f. 1996; govt agency to promote economic investment and export; Exec. Dir ROBERTO VILLAMIL; Gen. Man. ROBERTO BENNETT.

DEVELOPMENT ORGANIZATIONS

Corporación Nacional para el Desarrollo (CND): Rincón 528, 7°, Casilla 977, 11000 Montevideo; tel. (2) 9162800; fax (2) 9159662; e-mail cnd@cnd.org.uy; internet www.cnd.org.uy; f. 1985; national devt corpn; mixed-capital org.; obtains 60% of funding from state; Pres. LUIS PORTO; Gen. Man. PABLO GUTIÉRREZ.

Asociación Nacional de Micro y Pequeños Empresarios (ANMYPE): Miguelete 1584, Montevideo; tel. (2) 9241010; e-mail info@anmype.org.uy; internet www.anmype.org.uy; promotes small businesses; f. 1988; Pres. ALEXIS VERA; Sec. SUSANA CRESPO.

Asociación Nacional de Organizaciones No Gubernamentales Orientadas al Desarrollo: Avda del Libertador 1985 esq. 202, Montevideo; tel. and fax (2) 9240812; e-mail anong@anong.com.uy; internet www.anong.org.uy; f. 1992; umbrella grouping of devt NGOs; Pres. ANA LAURA SCARENZIO; Sec. MARCELO VENTOS.

Centro Interdisciplinario de Estudios sobre el Desarrollo, Uruguay (CIEDUR): 18 de Julio 1645-7, 11200 Montevideo; tel. and fax (2) 4084520; e-mail ciedur@ciedur.org.uy; internet www.ciedur.org.uy; f. 1977; devt studies and training; Pres. ALMA ESPINO; Exec. Sec. ALFREDO BLUM.

Fundación Uruguaya de Cooperación y Desarrollo Solidario (FUNDASOL) (Uruguayan Foundation for Supportive Co-operation and Development): Blvr Artigas 1165, esq. Maldonado, 11200 Montevideo; tel. (2) 4002020; fax (2) 4081485; e-mail consultas@fundasol.org.uy; internet www.fundasol.org.uy; f. 1979; Pres. EDUARDO PIETRA; Gen. Man. JORGE NAYA.

CHAMBERS OF COMMERCE

Cámara de Industrias del Uruguay (Chamber of Industries): Avda Italia 6101, 11500 Montevideo; tel. (2) 6040464; fax (2) 6040501; e-mail ciu@ciu.com.uy; internet www.ciu.com.uy; f. 1898; Pres. DIEGO BALESTRA; Gen. Man. MIGUEL VILARIÑO.

Cámara Nacional de Comercio y Servicios del Uruguay (National Chamber of Commerce): Edif. Bolsa de Comercio, Rincón 454, 2°, Casilla 1000, 11000 Montevideo; tel. (2) 9161277; fax (2) 9161243; e-mail info@cncs.com.uy; internet www.cncs.com.uy; f. 1867; 1,500 mems; Pres. ALFONSO VARELA; Man. Dr CLAUDIO PIACENZA.

Cámara Mercantil de Productos del País (Chamber of Commerce for Local Products): Avda General Rondeau 1908, 1°, 11800 Montevideo; tel. (2) 9240644; fax (2) 9244701; e-mail info@camaramercantil.com.uy; internet www.camaramercantil.com.uy; f. 1891; 180 mems; Pres. CHRISTIAN BOLZ; Gen. Man. GONZALO GONZÁLEZ PIEDRAS.

EMPLOYERS' ORGANIZATIONS

Asociación de Importadores y Mayoristas de Almacén (Importers' and Wholesalers' Asscn): Edif. Bolsa de Comercio, Of. 317/319, Rincón 454, 11000 Montevideo; tel. (2) 9156103; fax (2) 9160796; e-mail fmelissari@nidera.com.uy; f. 1926; 52 mems; Pres. FERNANDO MELISSARI.

Asociación Rural del Uruguay (ARU): Avda Uruguay 864, 11100 Montevideo; tel. (2) 9020484; fax (2) 9020489; e-mail aru@netgate.com.uy; internet www.aru.com.uy; f. 1871; 1,800 mems; Pres. MANUEL LUSSICH TORRENDEL; Gen. Man. Dr GONZALO ARROYO FACELLO.

Federación Rural: Avda 18 de Julio 965, 1°, 11100 Montevideo; tel. (2) 9005583; fax (2) 9004791; e-mail fedrural@gmail.com; internet

URUGUAY

Directory

www.federacionrural.org; f. 1915; 2,000 mems; Pres. Miguel Bidegain.

Unión de Exportadores del Uruguay (Uruguayan Exporters' Asscn): Avda Uruguay 917, 1°, esq. Convención, 11100 Montevideo; tel. (2) 9170105; fax (2) 9165967; e-mail info@uruguayexporta.com; internet www.uruguayexporta.com; Pres. Alejandro Bzurovski; Exec. Sec. Teresa Aishemberg.

UTILITIES

Electricity

Administración Nacional de Usinas y Transmisiones Eléctricas (UTE): Palacio de la Luz, Paraguay 2431, 10°, 11100 Montevideo; tel. (2) 2003424; fax (2) 2037082; e-mail ute@ute.com.uy; internet www.ute.com.uy; f. 1912; autonomous state body; sole purveyor of electricity until 1997; Pres. Gonzalo Casaravilla; Gen. Man. Alejandro Perroni.

Gas

Conecta: Avda Giannattasio, Km 20, 800 Ciudad de la Costa, Canelones, Montevideo; tel. (2) 6826817; fax (2) 6006732; internet www.conecta.com.uy; gas distribution; Dir Francisco Llano.

MontevideoGas: Plaza Independencia 831, 10°, 11000 Montevideo; tel. (2) 9017454; e-mail mlcoitino@montevideogas.com.uy; internet www.montevideogas.com.uy; gas producers and service providers; Pres. Clovis Correa; Gen. Man. Pedro Borges.

Water

Aguas de la Costa: Calle 1 y 20, La Barra, Maldonado; tel. (42) 771930; fax (42) 771932; e-mail adlcosta@adinet.com.uy; internet www.aguasdelacosta.com.uy; subsidiary of Aguas de Barcelona (Spain); operating in Uruguay since 1994; contract due to expire in 2019; management of water supply in Maldonado Dept.

Obras Sanitarias del Estado (OSE): Carlos Roxlo 1275, 11200 Montevideo; tel. (2) 4001151; fax (2) 4088069; e-mail info@ose.com.uy; internet www.ose.com.uy; f. 1962; processing and distribution of drinking water, sinking wells, supplying industrial zones of the country; Pres. Jorge Carlos Colacce Molinari.

TRADE UNION

Plenario Intersindical de Trabajadores—Convención Nacional de Trabajadores (PIT—CNT): Jackson 1283, 11200 Montevideo; tel. (2) 4096680; fax (2) 4004160; e-mail pitcnt@adinet.com.uy; internet www.pitcnt.org.uy; f. 1966; org. comprising 83 trade unions, 17 labour federations; 320,000 mems; Pres. Jorge Castro; Exec. Sec. Juan Castillo.

Transport

Dirección Nacional de Transporte: Rincón 575, 5°, 11000 Montevideo; tel. and fax (2) 9163122; e-mail infodnt@dnt.gub.uy; internet www.dnt.gub.uy; co-ordinates national and inter-national transport services; Gen. Man. Felipe Martín.

RAILWAYS

Administración de los Ferrocarriles del Estado (AFE): Avda Rondeau 1921, esq. Lima, Montevideo; tel. (2) 9243924; e-mail secretariogeneral@afe.com.uy; internet www.afe.com.uy; f. 1952; state org.; 3,002 km of track connecting all parts of the country; there are connections with the Argentine and Brazilian networks; passenger services ceased in 1988; passenger services linking Montevideo with Florida and Canelones were resumed in mid-1993; Pres. Alejandro Orellano; Gen. Man. José Nunes.

ROADS

In 2008 Uruguay had an estimated 8,696 km of motorways (forming the densest motorway network in South America), connecting Montevideo with the main towns of the interior and the Argentine and Brazilian frontiers. There was also a network of approximately 40,000 km of paved roads under departmental control.

Corporación Vial del Uruguay, SA: Rincón 528, 5°, 11000 Montevideo; tel. (2) 9162680; fax (2) 9170114; e-mail cvu@cnd.org.uy; internet www.cvu.com.uy; road construction agency; 100% owned by the Corporación Nacional para el Desarrollo; Pres. Luis Porto; Gen. Man. Patricia de Santis.

INLAND WATERWAYS

There are about 1,250 km of navigable waterways, which provide an important means of transport.

Nobleza Naviera, SA: Avda General Rondeau 2257, Montevideo; tel. (2) 9243222; fax (2) 9243218; e-mail nobleza@netgate.com.uy; operates cargo services on the River Plate, and the Uruguay and Paraná rivers; Chair. Américo Deambrosi; Man. Dir Doris Ferrari.

SHIPPING

Administración Nacional de Puertos (ANP): Rambla 25 de Agosto de 1825 160, Montevideo; tel. (2) 9151441; fax (2) 9161704; e-mail presidencia@anp.com.uy; internet www.anp.com.uy; f. 1916; national ports admin; Pres. Alberto Díaz; Gen. Mans Osvaldo Tabacchi, Schubert Méndez.

Prefectura Nacional Naval: Edif. Comando General de la Armada, 4°, Rambla 25 de Agosto de 1825 s/n, esq. Maciel, Montevideo; tel. (2) 29152210; fax (2) 29160022; e-mail premo_imdg@armada.mil.uy; internet mercanciaspeligrosas.com.uy; f. 1829; maritime supervisory body, responsible for rescue services, protection of sea against pollution, etc.; Sec.-Gen. Rear-Adm. Oscar Debali de Palleja.

Navegación Atlántida, SA: Río Branco 1373, 11100 Montevideo; tel. (2) 9084449; f. 1967; ferry services for passengers and vehicles between Argentina and Uruguay; Pres. H. C. Pietranera.

Transportadora Marítima de Combustibles, SA (TRAMACO, SA): Rincón 540, Puerta Baja, Montevideo; tel. (2) 9165754; fax (2) 9165755; e-mail tramaco@tramaco.com.uy; owned by the Christopherson Group; Pres. Jorge Fernández Baubeta.

CIVIL AVIATION

Civil aviation is controlled by the Dirección General de Aviación Civil and the Dirección General de Infraestructura Aeronáutica. The main airport is at Carrasco, 21 km from Montevideo, and there are also airports at Paysandú, Rivera, Salto, Melo, Artigas, Punta del Este and Durazno.

Aeromás, SA: Avda de las Américas 5120, Montevideo; tel. (2) 6046359; e-mail aeromas@aeromas.com; internet www.aeromas.com; private hire, cargo, and air ambulance flights; internal mass transit services to Salto, Paysandú, Rivera, Tacuarembó and Artigas; f. 1983; Dir Daniel Dalmás.

Primeras Líneas Uruguayas de Navegación Aérea (PLUNA): Colonia 1013, 9°, 11000 Montevideo; tel. (2) 9013559; fax (2) 9020231; e-mail presidenciapluna@adinet.com.uy; internet www.flypluna.com; f. 1936; nationalized 1951; partially privatized in 1994; 75% stake acquired by Leadgate Investment Corpn in 2007; operates international services to Argentina, Brazil, Chile, El Salvador, Paraguay, Spain and the USA; Pres. Carlos Bouzas.

Tourism

The sandy beaches and woodlands on the coast and the grasslands of the interior, with their variety of fauna and flora, provide the main tourist attractions. About 51% of tourists came from Argentina and 15% from Brazil in 2008. Uruguay received an estimated 2.0m. visitors in that year, while tourism revenues totalled a provisional US $1,180m.

Asociación Uruguaya de Agencias de Viajes (AUDAVI): Río Branco 1407, Of. 205, 11100 Montevideo; tel. (2) 9012326; fax (2) 9021972; e-mail audavi@netgate.com.uy; internet www.audavi.com.uy; f. 1951; 100 mems; Pres. Giorgio Valenti; Man. Ledo Silva.

Cámara Uruguaya de Turismo: San José 942, 2°, Of. 4, 11200 Montevideo; tel. and fax (2) 9000453; internet camtur.com.uy; Pres. Luis Borsari.

Uruguay Natural: Rambla 25 de Agosto de 1825, esq. Yacaré, Montevideo; tel. (2) 1885100; e-mail webmaster@mintur.gub.uy; internet www.uruguaynatural.com; f. 2003; state-run tourism promotion agency; Dir-Gen. Dr Antonio Carámbula.

Defence

As assessed at November 2010, Uruguay's Armed Forces consisted of 24,621 volunteers between the ages of 18 and 45 who contract for one or two years of service. There was an army of 16,234, a navy of 5,403 and an air force of 2,984. There were also paramilitary forces numbering 818.

Defence Budget: an estimated 9,340m. pesos uruguayos in 2011.

Commander-in-Chief of the Army: Lt-Gen. Jorge Washington Rosales Sosa.

URUGUAY

Commander-in-Chief of the Navy: Adm. ALBERTO LAUREANO CARAMÉS SILVEIRA.

Commander-in-Chief of the Air Force: Brig.-Gen. WASHINGTON R. MARTÍNEZ.

Education

All education, including university tuition, is provided free of charge. Education is officially compulsory for six years between six and 14 years of age. Primary education begins at the age of six and lasts for six years. Secondary education, beginning at 12 years of age, lasts for a further six years, comprising two cycles of three years each. In 2007 primary enrolment included 98% of children in the relevant age-group (males 97%; females 98%), while the equivalent ratio for secondary enrolment was 68% (males 64%; females 71%). The programmes of instruction are the same in both public and private schools and private schools are subject to certain state controls. There are six universities in Uruguay, including the state Universidad de la República. Central government expenditure on education in 2006 was 14,392m. pesos uruguayos (12.3% of central government spending).

UZBEKISTAN

Introductory Survey

LOCATION, CLIMATE, LANGUAGE, RELIGION, FLAG, CAPITAL

The Republic of Uzbekistan is located in Central Asia. It is bordered by Kazakhstan to the north, Turkmenistan to the south-west, Kyrgyzstan to the east, Tajikistan to the south-east and Afghanistan to the south. The climate is marked by extreme temperatures and low levels of precipitation. Summers are long and hot with average temperatures in July of 32°C (90°F); daytime temperatures often exceed 40°C (104°F). During the short winter there are frequent severe frosts, and temperatures can fall as low as −38°C (−36°F). The official language is Uzbek. Islam is the predominant religion. Most Uzbeks are Sunni Muslims, principally of the Hanafi school, although there are small communities of Salafis; Sufism is relatively well established in southern Uzbekistan. There are also Orthodox Christians among the Slavic communities. The national flag (proportions 1 by 2) consists of five unequal horizontal stripes of (from top to bottom) light blue, red, white, red and light green, with a white crescent and 12 white stars near the hoist on the top stripe. The capital is Tashkent (Toshkent).

CONTEMPORARY POLITICAL HISTORY

Historical Context

Soviet power was first established in parts of Uzbekistan in November 1917. In April 1918 the Turkestan Autonomous Soviet Socialist Republic (ASSR), covering a vast region in Central Asia, was proclaimed, but Soviet forces withdrew against opposition from the local *basmachi* movement, the White Army and a British expeditionary force. Soviet power was re-established in September 1919, although armed opposition continued until the early 1920s. The khanates of Buxoro (Bukhara) and Xiva (Khiva) became nominally independent Soviet republics in 1920, but by 1924 they had been incorporated into the Turkestan ASSR. On 27 October 1924 the Uzbek Soviet Socialist Republic (SSR) was established (until 1929 it included the Tajik ASSR—now Tajikistan). In May 1925 the Uzbek SSR became a constituent republic of the Union of Soviet Socialist Republics (USSR). In 1936 Qoraqalpog'iston (Karakalpakstan) was transferred from the Russian Federation to the Uzbek SSR, retaining its status as a nominally autonomous viloyat (oblast or region).

The National Delimitation of the Central Asian republics of 1924–25 established an Uzbek nation state for the first time. Literacy rose from 3.8% in 1926 to 52.5% in 1932. Muslim establishments were closed, and clergy were persecuted.

Under the first two Five-Year Plans (1928–38), however, there was considerable economic growth, aided by the immigration of skilled workers from within the USSR. Although economic expansion continued after the Second World War (during which Uzbekistan's industrial base had been enlarged by the transfer of industries from the war zone), most Uzbeks continued to lead a traditional rural lifestyle, affected only by the huge increase in the amount of cotton grown in the republic.

Greater freedom of the press was permitted in the late 1980s, facilitated by the policies of the Soviet leader, Mikhail Gorbachev, which allowed discussion of previously unexamined aspects of Uzbek history and contemporary ecological and economic concerns. The over-irrigation of land to feed the vast cotton-fields had caused both salination of the soil and, most importantly, the desiccation of the Aral Sea.

Environmental problems and the status of the Uzbek language were among the concerns on which Uzbekistan's first independent political movement, Unity (Birlik), campaigned. However, the movement remained unregistered and was unsuccessful in the 1989 elections to the USSR's Congress of People's Deputies; nevertheless, its campaign led to the adoption of legislation declaring Uzbek to be the official language of the republic in October of that year.

On 18 February 1990 elections were held to the 500-seat Uzbekistani Supreme Soviet (Supreme Council—legislature), which came to be dominated by the Communist Party of the Uzbek SSR (CPU), not least as members of Unity were not permitted to stand. The new Supreme Soviet convened in March and elected Islam Karimov, the First Secretary (leader) of the CPU, to the newly created post of executive President.

Domestic Political Affairs

In April 1991 Uzbekistan agreed, with eight other Soviet republics, to sign a new Union Treaty to reconstitute the USSR. However, on 19 August, the day before the signing was to take place, there was an attempt to stage a coup by conservative communists in Moscow, the Russian and Soviet capital. President Karimov only expressed his opposition to the coup once it became clear that it had failed. On 31 August an extraordinary session of the Supreme Soviet voted to declare an independent Republic of Uzbekistan. The CPU voted to dissociate itself from the Communist Party of the Soviet Union, and in November restructured itself as the People's Democratic Party of Uzbekistan (PDPU), still under Karimov's leadership.

On 21 December 1991 Karimov and 10 other republican leaders agreed to dissolve the USSR and establish the Commonwealth of Independent States (CIS, see p. 238). On 29 December a direct presidential election was held in Uzbekistan, at which Karimov won a reported 86% of the total votes cast. His sole rival (winning 12% of the votes) was Muhammad Salih, the leader of the Freedom (Erk) party, which had been established as an offshoot of Unity in 1990. At a concurrent referendum, 98.2% of participants voted to endorse Uzbekistan's independence.

Under Karimov's leadership, there was widespread repression of opposition groups. A new Constitution, adopted on 8 December 1992, enshrined the concept of state secularism, but formal provisions for a democratic multi-party system, freedom of expression and the observance of human rights were largely ignored, in practice. It also provided for a new, smaller legislature, the 250-member Oliy Majlis (Supreme Assembly), to take effect from elections due to be held in late 1994. On the day of the adoption of the new Constitution three leading opposition members were seized by Uzbekistani security police in the Kyrgyzstani capital, Bishkek, and charged with sedition. One day later Unity was banned. Media regulation was intensified: in mid-1993 the Government ordered all newspapers and periodicals to re-register with the State Committee for the Press, and permitting registration only to organs of the state and government.

Similarly, only the PDPU and its ally, Progress of the Fatherland (PF), were permitted to register for the elections to the Oliy Majlis. At the elections, held on 25 December 1994 (with further rounds of voting, where required, on 8 and 22 January 1995), the PDPU won 69 of the 250 seats, and the PF secured 14. The remaining 167 deputies elected had been nominated by local councils rather than by political parties; the majority of these deputies (some 120) were members of the PDPU, and thus the party's domination of the Majlis was retained. Some 94% of eligible voters were reported to have participated in the elections.

In January 1995 Karimov announced that the formation of blocs in the Oliy Majlis was to be permitted. In February a new political party, the Justice Social Democratic Party of Uzbekistan (Adolat), was registered; it immediately declared its intention to establish such a parliamentary faction. A referendum held in March produced a 99.6% vote in favour of extending Karimov's presidential term, originally scheduled to end in 1997, until 2000, when parliamentary elections were due to be held. In May two new political formations, both of which were reported to be pro-Government, emerged: the National Revival Democratic Party (Milliy Tiklanish) and the People's Unity Movement (Xalq Birligi). Both were officially registered in June. In December 1995 O'tkir Sultonov, hitherto the Minister of Foreign Economic Relations, replaced Abdulkhashim Mutalov as Prime Minister. In June 1996 Karimov resigned from his position as Chairman of the PDPU.

During 1996 Karimov began to advocate the creation of a political opposition to the PDPU, and in December the Oliy Majlis approved a new law on political parties, which prohibited the organization of parties on a religious or ethnic basis and compelled prospective parties to provide evidence that they had

5,000 members drawn from a majority of Uzbekistan's administrative regions.

In late 1997 there was an upsurge of violence, attributed to groups of Islamist activists, in the densely populated Farg'ona (Fergana) valley in eastern Uzbekistan. In November the deputy head of the administration of Namangan Viloyat (region) was assassinated, and in December four police officers were killed; government troops arrested hundreds of suspects. The Government's campaign against Islamist militancy intensified in early 1998. In February the Ministry of Foreign Affairs appealed to the Pakistani Government to extirpate military training camps in that country, where Uzbeks were allegedly being trained in dissident activities. (Pakistan denied the existence of any such camps.) In May the Oliy Majlis adopted legislation that severely limited the activities of religious organizations and Karimov declared to the Majlis that he would be prepared personally to execute members of Islamist groups found guilty of terrorism. In May–July several suspected militant Islamists were sentenced to terms of imprisonment, and a member of an Islamist organization was sentenced to death following his conviction for the murder of five people and for his role in the training of militants in Afghanistan. In January 1999 five men allegedly linked with a former *imam* of a mosque in Tashkent, who had been in hiding since early 1998, were found guilty of attempting to overthrow the Government and establish an Islamist state. Meanwhile, in June 1998 new legislation was adopted banning the purchase, sale or exchange of land.

In February 1999 a series of bombs exploded in the centre of Tashkent, killing an estimated 15 people. Following the trial, in June, of 22 people suspected of involvement in the bomb attacks (which officials claimed were intended to bring about the assassination of the President), six of the accused were sentenced to death, and the other defendants received lengthy prison sentences. In August six members of the banned Freedom party were given prison sentences of between eight and 15 years for their involvement in the bombings. In November the Tashkent region was infiltrated by a group of about 15 armed militants, who shot three police officers and three civilians. (It was alleged that the group, who were subsequently killed by security forces, had been trained in the separatist Chechen Republic, Russia, and had entered Uzbekistan from Kyrgyzstan.) Following the violence, Karimov appealed to the Organization for Security and Co-operation in Europe (OSCE, see p. 385) to assist Uzbekistan in combating international terrorism.

At elections to the Oliy Majlis, held on 5 and 19 December 1999, the PDPU obtained 48 seats, more than any other party, while non-partisan local council nominees obtained a total of 110 seats. The rate of voter participation at the first round was reported to be some 93.5%. The OSCE had sent only a limited number of observers to the elections, since all of the parties participating were pro-Government, two opposition parties having been prevented from contesting.

President Karimov secured 91.9% of the votes cast at the presidential election held on 9 January 2000, according to official figures, compared with the 4.2% attributed to his sole opponent, the leader of the PDPU, Abdulkhafiz Jalolov. Karimov was duly inaugurated for another five-year term on 22 January. Both the OSCE and the US Government criticized the election (in which 95% of the registered electorate were reported to have participated) as undemocratic, as opposition parties had been barred from nominating candidates.

The trial of 12 people accused of involvement in the bomb attacks of February 1999 opened in October 2000. In November the spiritual leader of the proscribed Islamic Movement of Uzbekistan (IMU), Tohir Yuldosh, and his field commander, Jumaboy Hojiyev (known as Juma Namangoniy), were sentenced to death *in absentia*. The remaining 10 defendants (including, *in absentia*, Salih) were sentenced to between 12 and 20 years' imprisonment. In June 2001 10 further Islamist militants were reported to have received prison sentences for attempting to overthrow the Government.

The perceived threat of militant Islamist movements intensified in the latter half of 2001, following the suicide attacks in the USA on 11 September (see below), and Uzbekistan's decision to co-operate with the USA in its attempts to form an international coalition to combat the al-Qa'ida organization of Osama bin Laden (elements of which were harboured by the de facto ruling Taliban militia in Afghanistan). It was widely believed that Karimov expected to secure strategic benefits from such co-operation, notably the suppression of the IMU and the moderation of international criticism of his Government's position on economic reforms and human rights. There were frequent allegations of the torture and arrest of suspected members of the IMU and Hizb-ut-Tahrir al-Islami (Hizb-ut-Tahrir—the Party of Islamic Liberation), a clandestine, transnational organization, which sought to re-establish a caliphate, apparently solely through peaceful means, and which was alleged to enjoy significant support in Uzbekistan and neighbouring countries, particularly in the Farg'ona valley region. In October an estimated 5,000–7,000 members of the IMU (which both the UN and the USA identified as a terrorist organization) were reported to be fighting alongside Taliban forces in Afghanistan.

Constitutional amendments introduced in 2002

On 27 January 2002 a referendum took place to seek approval for proposed constitutional amendments. Some 91.6% of the electorate participated, of whom 93.7% approved the reorganization of the legislature on a bicameral basis, while 91.8% endorsed the extension of the presidential term from five to seven years. The amendments also prescribed that elections to all offices of state were henceforth to be held in the third week of December in the year in which the term of office expired, thereby extending Karimov's existing presidential mandate by a further 11 months, until December 2007.

In April 2003 the Oliy Majlis approved constitutional amendments permitting the redistribution of authority within the Government, with effect from the next legislative elections, including the prohibition of the same person from serving simultaneously as President and Prime Minister, with the latter leading the Cabinet of Ministers. In addition, a law granting former presidents both lifelong immunity from prosecution and permanent membership of the Senat (Senate), the new upper legislative chamber, was endorsed.

On 11 December 2003 the Oliy Majlis confirmed the appointment of Shavkat Mirziyoyev, who had substantial experience in the agricultural sector, as Prime Minister. His predecessor, Sultonov became a Deputy Prime Minister, with responsibility for the energy, petroleum and chemicals sectors.

On 28–29 March 2004 three police officers were killed in two separate shooting incidents in Tashkent; on 29 March two bombings, seemingly by suicide bombers, in the city's Chorsu market resulted in further casualties. It was also reported that 10 people had been killed and 26 injured after bombs exploded in an apartment block, which police alleged was being used as a base for the manufacture of explosives, in Buxoro. On 30 March security forces carried out a raid in Tashkent, during which at least 16 suspected militant Islamists and three police officers were killed. A further bomb attack on 1 April killed one person and prompted the Government temporarily to close the country's land borders. By July some 85 people suspected of involvement in the attacks had been arrested. In August 15 of the accused were sentenced to between six and 18 years' imprisonment; in October a further 23 militants were sentenced to between three and 18 years' imprisonment. In July 2005 another 20 men were given gaol sentences for their involvement in the attacks.

Meanwhile, in July 2004 seven people were killed as a result of suicide bomb attacks in Tashkent outside the Israeli and US embassies and outside the Office of the Prosecutor-General. President Karimov accused Hizb-ut-Tahrir of bearing primary responsibility. In December the Office of the Prosecutor-General declared that all three of the suicide bombers had been Kazakhstani citizens.

In November 2004 riots erupted in Qoqand in the Farg'ona valley, where some 5,000–10,000 people were protesting against the introduction of new laws affecting market traders; the protests spread to markets in other towns in Uzbekistan, including Buxoro. In December human rights groups and opposition parties gathered outside the US embassy, urging the USA to encourage the Uzbekistani Government to promote democracy and respect for human rights in Uzbekistan, after three opposition parties (Unity, Freedom and the Free Peasants' Party) were denied permission to put forward candidates for the legislative elections scheduled for the end of the month.

Elections to the Qonunchilik palatasi (Legislative Chamber), the 120-seat lower chamber of the new bicameral legislature, were held on 26 December 2004, with a second round of voting on 9 January 2005 in the 58 constituencies in which no candidate had obtained an absolute majority of votes cast. All five parties permitted to participate in the elections supported Karimov. The Movement of Entrepreneurs and Businessmen—Liberal Democratic Party of Uzbekistan, established in late 1993 and led by Muhammadjon Ahmadjonov, obtained 41 seats. The PDPU obtained 28 seats, the Self-Sacrificers' National Democratic

UZBEKISTAN

Party 18, the National Revival Democratic Party 11 and the Justice Social Democratic Party 10. The rate of voter participation at the first round was an estimated 85.1%. Several ministerial changes were effected in late 2004 and early 2005. On 14 January 2005 President Karimov announced the appointment of 16 members of the Senat, and regional council members elected a further 84 senators on 17–20 January. The inaugural session of the chamber took place on 27 January.

Violence in Andijon

Political tensions intensified in early 2005, particularly in the Farg'ona valley, as a result of dissatisfaction at widespread poverty, the influence of the political upheaval in neighbouring Kyrgyzstan in March (see the chapter on Kyrgyzstan), and discontent at restrictions on trade and on the freedom of association. From February daily peaceful protests, sometimes attended by up to 1,000 people, took place outside a court in Andijon, where 23 local business executives had been brought to trial on charges of belonging to a prohibited Islamist organization, Akramiya, which was alleged to have broken away from Hizb-ut-Tahrir. All 23 denied the charges brought against them. In the early hours of 13 May, several days before the trial was due to conclude, a group of armed men stormed the gaol in Andijon, and released as many as 2,000 prisoners, including the 23 alleged members of Akramiya. Armed rebels took control of the regional administration building in the city later that day, and several thousand people gathered in the main square, protesting against both the trial of the alleged militants and economic difficulties. Heavily armed state security forces, including troops in tanks, entered Andijon and opened fire on the demonstrators. The exact number of people killed was disputed, because of the strict restrictions placed on both media coverage and access to the region by foreign diplomatic representatives or members of non-governmental organizations (NGOs). Protests continued in Andijon later in the month, and unrest was reported in Qorasuv, on the border with Kyrgyzstan south-east of Andijon, where local Islamist rebels seized control of the local administration and reopened a border crossing that had been closed since 2000. State forces subsequently recaptured the town. Meanwhile, Kyrgyzstan reported that it had registered more than 500 Uzbekistani refugees in the immediate aftermath of the violence in Andijon.

President Karimov rejected requests by the international community for an independent investigation into the events in Andijon. In July 2005 the Prosecutor of Andijon Viloyat announced that 187 people had been killed as a result of the violence, including 94 terrorists, 57 civilians, 20 law-enforcement officials and 11 soldiers; in contrast, independent reports claimed that as many as 1,000 people had been killed. In September the Office of the Prosecutor-General issued a report stating that foreign-based Islamists had staged the violence, and claiming that earlier in the year Kyrgyzstan-based instructors had trained some 70 militant Islamists in terrorist techniques. In August Karimov approved a decree abolishing capital punishment, which was to take effect from 1 January 2008.

In September 2005 the First Deputy Prosecutor-General suggested that 'external forces' had instructed Western journalists to publish false information about the events in Andijon in the foreign media. Individuals and organizations that provided accounts undermining the credibility of the Government's version of events were subject to official harassment, including, in some cases, expulsion from the country or imprisonment. In October the European Union (EU, see p. 270) imposed sanctions on Uzbekistan (including a ban on travel to EU states by officials suspected of involvement in the shooting of civilians in Andijon, and an embargo on the export of weaponry), owing to the Government's refusal either to permit an international investigation into events at Andijon or to bring those who had perpetrated the killings to trial. (These sanctions were extended in November 2006 and again in May 2007.) By December 2005 more than 150 people had been imprisoned for their involvement in the Andijon protests; in November the USA and the Office of the UN High Commissioner for Human Rights expressed concern that some of the convicted defendants had not been permitted a fair trial, and about the alleged use of torture to extract confessions. In February 2006 the Government approved a resolution that made journalists deemed to be interfering in internal affairs or insulting Uzbekistani citizens liable to prosecution. In March the authorities requested that the UN High Commission for Refugees vacate its offices in Uzbekistan.

Meanwhile, frequent government and security personnel changes continued to be effected. In June 2005 the First Deputy Head of the Military Intelligence Directorate, Lt-Col Sanjar Ismoilov, was arrested on suspicion of spying for Russia; he was sentenced to 20 years' imprisonment in January 2006. In November 2005 Karimov dismissed the Minister of Defence, Qodir G'ulomov, who was subsequently succeeded by Ruslan Mirzayev. (G'ulomov was given a five-year suspended prison sentence in July 2006 for offences committed during his term of office.) Later in November 2005 Rustam Azimov was appointed as Minister of Finance. In December the Minister of Internal Affairs, Zokirjon Almatov—whom the EU held responsible for overseeing the violent repression of the protests in Andijon—resigned, citing ill health. He was succeeded in January 2006 by Bahodir Matlyubov. In late 2006 several hokims (regional governors) were replaced.

The arrest of human rights activists and political dissidents continued unabated in 2006–07. The operations in Uzbekistan of several NGOs were terminated at the behest of a Tashkent court, ostensibly owing to alleged financial offences and engagement in improper activities. In August 2006 the trial commenced in Tashkent of a popular musician and songwriter, Dodokhon Hasan, who was accused of defaming the President. In mid-September the apparent disappearance of Jamshid Karimov, formerly a reporter for the United Kingdom-based Institute for War and Peace Reporting (IWPR) and a nephew of President Karimov, was reported; it was subsequently announced that he had been detained at a psychiatric hospital in Samarqand. Another former IWPR reporter, Ulughbek Haydarov, was convicted of extortion in October and sentenced to six years' imprisonment. A human rights activist, Umida Niyazova, was convicted on charges of illegal cross-border smuggling and sentenced to seven years' imprisonment in May 2007, although this was subsequently commuted to a three-year suspended sentence. In June the six-year prison sentence of another human rights activist, Gulbahor Turayeva, convicted in April by an Andijon court for distributing press material that threatened public order, was also reduced on appeal to a three-year suspended sentence.

Meanwhile, in March 2007 the Qonunchilik palatasi approved legislation (initially proposed by President Karimov in November 2006) recognizing the existence of parliamentary factions, each of which was hitherto to be consulted by the President before the appointment of a Prime Minister or a regional hokim. Provision was made for parliamentary factions to designate themselves as officially forming the role of opposition (although by 2011 no faction had done so, and those parties which represented substantive opposition to Karimov's administration remained proscribed), while the responsibilities of President and Prime Minister were more strictly defined than hitherto. The new provisions, which some observers suggested might be intended to bring about the eventual introduction of a parliamentary system of government, were to enter into effect from January 2008. In September 2007 the Central Election Commission announced that a presidential election was to take place on 23 December. Karimov subsequently confirmed that he would contest the election, despite a constitutional provision restricting the President to two consecutive terms in office; the authorities maintained that the extension of the presidential term to seven years from 2002 effectively meant that Karimov's previous terms in office would not be taken into account for the purposes of this restriction. In October EU foreign ministers, while extending the embargo on the export of armaments to Uzbekistan for a further year, adopted a decision to suspend for a period of six months the travel restrictions on senior Uzbekistani officials, including the Minister of Defence, with the stated aim of encouraging the authorities to improve the human rights situation in the country. Prior to the poll, a number of human rights activists were arrested.

On 23 December 2007 Karimov was re-elected President, receiving some 88.1% of votes cast (the other three candidates permitted to contest the election were all considered to be loyal to Karimov); the rate of voter participation was officially recorded as 90.6%. An observer mission from the Office for Democratic Institutions and Human Rights of the OSCE stated that the poll had failed to meet democratic standards. At the end of December Karimov appointed Azimov (who retained the finance portfolio) as First Deputy Prime Minister, responsible for the Economic Sector and Foreign Economic Relations. In January 2008, following the removal of the Speaker of the lower legislative chamber, Erkin Halilov, for abuse of office, Dilorom Tashmuhamedova (who had contested the presidential election as a candidate of Adolat) was elected to the post. In April the EU extended for a further six months the suspension of the travel

UZBEKISTAN

sanctions on Uzbekistani officials. In the same month a prominent poet and human rights activist, Yusuf Juma, was sentenced to five years' imprisonment for resisting arrest (after staging a protest at the detention of one of his sons). In June Ahmadjon Odilov, a former opposition figure who had been imprisoned in 1984 and was believed to be the longest-serving political prisoner in the country, was released. Also in June 2008 a prominent human rights activist was granted early release. In September Karimov dismissed Ruslan Mirzayev as Minister of Defence; he was succeeded by Qobul Berdiyev. In October a summit meeting of EU ministers of foreign affairs issued a declaration stating that the travel ban on Uzbekistani officials would officially end in the following month (although the embargo on the export of armaments was to remain in place), as a result in the improved observance of human rights in Uzbekistan. In the same month an independent journalist was imprisoned for 10 years.

Recent developments: the 2009/10 legislative elections

In July 2009 a government reorganization was implemented. The hitherto Minister of the Economy, Botir Xo'jayev, became a Deputy Prime Minister, being succeeded in his former position by Sunatilla Bekenov. Several other new appointments were made. In late August at least three people were killed in a series of shootings involving the security forces and unidentified gunmen in Tashkent.

Legislative elections were held on 27 December 2009, with a second round of voting on 10 January 2010 in 39 constituencies in which no candidate had secured more than 50% of the votes cast. In accordance with a revised version of the electoral law, approved in 2008, the Ecological Movement of Uzbekistan automatically received 15 reserved seats; the four remaining parties participating in the elections were supporters of the Karimov regime. The rate of participation by the electorate at the first round was 87.8%. The Movement of Entrepreneurs and Businessmen—Liberal Democratic Party of Uzbekistan obtained 53 seats, the PDPU 32, the National Revival Democratic Party 31 and the Justice Social Democratic Party 19.

In mid-July 2010 G'ulomjon Ibragimov was appointed Deputy Prime Minister, responsible for Geology, Fuel and Energy and the Chemical, Petrochemical and Metallurgical Industries, in place of Ergash Shaismatov. In late October Bekenov was succeeded as Minister of the Economy by Ravshan G'ulomov. Concerns about freedom of expression in Uzbekistan were heightened in October, when an Uzbekistani freelance journalist, Abdumalik Boboev, who worked as a correspondent for the US state-funded Voice of America radio service, was tried on various charges including slander and the dissemination of materials harmful to social stability. The USA placed diplomatic pressure upon Uzbekistan to release Boboev without charge, and, although the criminal code provided for imprisonment for the charges upon which Boboev was found guilty later in the month, he was instead fined 18.1m. sum.

In mid-November President Karimov presented two items of draft legislation concerning the constitutional balance of powers for parliamentary discussion; the proposals provided, first, for presidential powers to be transferred to the Chairman of the Senate in the event of the incapacity of the Head of State, and, second, for prime ministerial candidates to be nominated by the leader of the party with most legislative deputies. The legislature, moreover, was to be granted the right to undertake votes of no confidence in the Government. Some observers described these measures, along with the appointment of a new hokim in Samarqand in December (replacing a close ally of Mirziyoyev), as representing an assertion of Karimov's authority, in particular over that of the incumbent Prime Minister. In late December Vladimir Norov was dismissed as Minister of Foreign Affairs; he was succeeded by Elyor G'aniyev, who retained his existing duties as Deputy Prime Minister, responsible for Foreign Economic Activities, the Attraction of Foreign Investment and the Localization of Production, while Galina Saidova was appointed to G'aniyev's former position as Minister of Foreign Economic Relations, Investment and Trade. In March 2011 new appointments were made to the positions of Minister of National Education and Minister of Higher and Secondary Specialized Education.

Foreign Affairs

Regional relations

Uzbekistan's closest relations are with the neighbouring Central Asian republics—Kazakhstan, Kyrgyzstan, Tajikistan and Turkmenistan. In September 1997 a Central Asian peacekeeping battalion participated, with troops from the USA and other countries, in military manoeuvres, which were held in Uzbekistan and elsewhere in the region under the auspices of NATO's 'Partnership for Peace' (see p. 371) programme of military co-operation. (Uzbekistan had joined the programme in 1994.) In November 2008, however, the Eurasian Economic Community (EURASEC, see p. 447) officially confirmed that it had been informed of Uzbekistan's decision to suspend its membership of the organization.

Uzbekistan was a member, alongside the People's Republic of China, Kazakhstan, Kyrgyzstan, Russia and Tajikistan, of the Shanghai Five, founded in 1996 to address border disputes, and acceded to that organization's successor, the Shanghai Co-operation Organization (SCO, see p. 462), signing the Shanghai Convention on Combating Terrorism, Separatism and Extremism. The organization subsequently established a regional anti-terrorism centre, located in Tashkent.

In June 2006 it was announced that Uzbekistan had commenced participation in the Collective Security Treaty Organization (CSTO, see p. 459), the successor organization to the CIS Collective Security Treaty (from which Uzbekistan had withdrawn in March 1999). In March 2008 the Oliy Majlis officially approved Uzbekistan's full membership of the CSTO (which also comprised Armenia, Belarus, Kazakhstan, Kyrgyzstan, Russia and Tajikistan).

In October 1998 Uzbekistan and Kazakhstan signed a Treaty of Eternal Friendship and agreed on a seven-year programme of bilateral economic co-operation. In November 2001 the two countries signed a treaty demarcating most of their common border. However, the demarcation of certain areas, including the villages of Bagys and Turkestanets, remained unresolved. The majority of citizens in Bagys were ethnic Kazakhs, and it had been hoped that the land, hitherto leased to Uzbekistan, would be returned to Kazakhstan following independence. In December residents declared an 'Independent Kazakh Republic of Bagys', and elected a president and legislature. The Uzbekistani security forces subsequently arrested a number of activists, and in April 2002 it was reported that troops had barricaded the villages. In September a new agreement delimiting the Kazakhstani–Uzbekistani border was signed by the countries' Presidents. However, at the end of 2002 Uzbekistan closed its border with Kazakhstan. The creation of a working group to finalize the demarcation of the border was announced in August 2003. However, following the arrests of Kazakhstani citizens in connection with a series of bombings in Uzbekistan in mid-2004, in January 2005 representatives from the Uzbekistani Ministry of Defence reportedly announced that they considered Kazakhstan to be a potential military adversary and a base for armed groups opposed to the Uzbekistani regime. In the same month the Uzbekistani authorities announced proposals for the demolition of settlements along the border, apparently in response to cross-border smuggling. Demonstrations in February by residents demanding compensation for the destruction of their homes were met with a promise from the hokim (governor) of Tashkent Viloyat that an assessment of property values in the village would be conducted with the view of providing the residents with compensation. In March President Karimov and the President of Kazakhstan, Nursultan Nazarbayev, agreed to establish a working group to create a future free trade zone.

Relations with Kyrgyzstan worsened in September 2000, when Uzbekistani government forces planted land-mines along the Kyrgyzstani–Uzbekistani border, apparently without having informed Kyrgyzstani border guards, in order to prevent insurgents from entering Uzbekistan. Although it was announced in June 2001 that the mines were to be removed, there were claims in September that the laying of mines was continuing. As a result, the Kyrgyzstani legislature refused to ratify an agreement with Uzbekistan on arms supplies. Relations were again strained in mid-2005, when the Kyrgyzstani Government refused to return a large number of refugees who had fled there from Uzbekistan following the violence in Andijon in May (see above). In July more than 400 refugees were deported from Kyrgyzstan to Romania, which Uzbekistan condemned as a violation of international law, while there were subsequent reports that refugees repatriated to Uzbekistan had been tortured. In August Uzbekistan annulled a bilateral agreement to supply natural gas to Kyrgyzstan. In the following month Uzbekistan issued a report accusing Kyrgyzstan of having permitted extremist Islamists to use bases in that country to foment unrest in Andijon. In August 2006 Kyrgyzstan deported some of the Andijon refugees to Uzbekistan. In early 2007 a bilateral agreement providing for visa-free travel between the two countries took effect. In late May 2009 a police officer was reportedly killed in a suicide bombing in Andijon, and a police post in the town of Khanabad was attacked by a group of armed men. Kyrgyzstani officials denied Uzbekistani claims that the assailants had entered Uzbekistan from Kyrgyzstan. Bilateral relations were further strained in June, when Uzbekistan began digging trenches in disputed areas along the joint border, ostensibly to prevent incursions by militants. The outbreak of inter-ethnic violence in southern regions of Kyrgyzstan, following the uprising there in April 2010 (see the chapter on Kyrgyzstan), in which ethnic Uzbeks were targeted, and several hundred were killed, caused further tensions in relations. By June Uzbekistan had permitted some 100,000 ethnic Uzbek refugees from Kyrgyzstan, particularly from the Osh region, enter Kyrgyzstan, and was also supplying humanitarian assistance to its neighbour.

In September 2000 Turkmenistan and Uzbekistan signed a treaty demarcating their 1,867-km border. In December 2002 Turkmenistani special forces entered the Uzbekistani embassy in the Turkmenistani capital, Aşgabat, purportedly in order to investigate reports that it was harbouring Boris Shikhmuradov, whom the Turkmenistani authorities blamed for an assassination attempt against that country's President, Saparmyrat Niyazov. Uzbekistan's ambassador to Turkmenistan was subsequently declared *persona non grata*, on the grounds that he had offered support to Shikhmuradov. The Uzbekistani authorities denied the allegations and reacted with hostility; open confrontation rapidly led to the deployment of troops from both countries along their mutual border, and an associated increase in border security. In November 2004 Presidents Karimov and Niyazov met for their first presidential summit in more than four years, in Buxoro, where they signed three bilateral agreements, pertaining to friendship, mutual trust and co-operation; they included simplifying regulations concerning cross-border travel for residents of border zones (where cross-border smuggling and related shooting incidents had become problematic in recent years), and a framework for sharing regional water resources. The Presidents declared that all bilateral issues had been resolved, and in January 2005 Uzbekistan appointed a new ambassador to Turkmenistan. President Karimov made an official visit to Turkmenistan in October 2007, meeting the President installed earlier in that year, Gurbanguly Berdymuhamedov.

Uzbekistan dispatched troops to Tajikistan in 1992, as part of a CIS peace-keeping contingent, and tightened border controls with Tajikistan in an attempt to prevent the civil conflict in that country from extending into Uzbekistan (see the chapter on Tajikistan). In August 1997 Uzbekistan agreed to act as one of the guarantors of a peace accord reached between the Tajikistani Government and opposition forces two months earlier. During a visit to Uzbekistan in January 1998 President Imamali Rakhmonov (later Rakhmon) of Tajikistan met Karimov, and the two leaders expressed their opposition to religious extremism. In February agreement on restructuring Tajikistan's debt to Uzbekistan was reached. In August 1999 the Uzbekistani Government accused Tajikistan of allowing militant groups to operate from its territory. From August 2000 armed Islamist militants made a series of incursions into the section of the Farg'ona valley in Uzbekistan from Tajikistan, and entered into conflict with government forces. By September, however, the remaining militants were reported to have been killed by government troops. In the mean time, Uzbekistan, which had begun laying land-mines along its border with Tajikistan from mid-2000, in an effort to prevent cross-border incursions by Islamist insurgents, officially informed Tajikistan of its actions only in May 2001, although relations subsequently improved. President Rakhmonov met President Karimov in Uzbekistan in December; while no border agreement was reached, it was announced that the crossing between the Penjakent district in Tajikistan and Samarqand Viloyat, in Uzbekistan, was to reopen. At a meeting of the Tajikistani and Uzbekistani Prime Ministers in February 2002, an agreement on border-crossing procedures was reached. The continued influx of illegal drugs from Tajikistan also threatened relations. Later in the year the Presidents of the two countries agreed on the demarcation of more than 85% of the two countries' shared borders.

Tajikistani-Uzbekistani relations deteriorated sharply following the suspension at the beginning of 2009 of Turkmenistan's electricity exports to Tajikistan, in response to the failure of Tajikistan and Uzbekistan to agree a transit rate. Tajikistan accused Uzbekistani state utility Uzbekenergo of interrupting deliveries of Turkmenistani electricity, and threatened to limit the amount of water flowing downstream to Uzbekistan, in order to maintain levels in its reservoirs (Tajikistan is a principal supplier of water to Uzbekistan). An additional matter of contention between the two countries was the planned construction of a hydroelectric plant at Roghun, in central Tajikistan, which was strongly opposed by Uzbekistan, owing to concerns regarding the potential impact of the project on its own water supplies. Later in January Karimov and Russian President Dmitrii Medvedev issued a joint declaration, stating that any hydro-engineering projects with transboundary implications were required to meet international laws and standards. However, in February Karimov unexpectedly announced that Uzbekistan was prepared to reconsider its opposition to the project, provided that international auditors verified its viability. On 19 February First Deputy Prime Minister Azimov visited Tajikistan to attend the first bilateral high-level commission meeting in seven years; it was reported that negotiations resulted in agreement on a debt repayment schedule, and on a protocol regarding a reservoir in northern Tajikistan, although a number of the fundamental issues remained unresolved. In March an agreement was reached between the national airlines of Uzbekistan and Tajikistan on the resumption of direct flights (suspended since 1992) between Tashkent and the Tajikistani capital, Dushanbe. However, relations with Tajikistan again deteriorated from late 2009, as rail traffic from Uzbekistan into Tajikistan (including non-military supplies being sent to the US-led troops in Afghanistan) was repeatedly disrupted. The Tajikistani Prime Minister Oqil Oqilov accused Uzbekistan of deliberately causing delays in transit, so as to disrupt Tajikistani agriculture, and as an expression of continued discontent concerning the construction of the Roghun hydroelectric plant (which had the potential substantially to alter the energy market of Central Asia), but Uzbekistan maintained that the cause of the delays was purely technical. However, in April 2010 it was reported that a spokesman for the Uzbekistani state railways company had announced that the Government had issued a secret decree ordering the prevention of the passage of Tajikistani transit cargo through Uzbekistan. Moreover, in early 2010 a series of protests was organized in various cities in Uzbekistan, seemingly with official endorsement, ostensibly to protest against pollution allegedly being produced at the Tajikistani state-owned Talco aluminium plant in Tursunzade, western Tajikistan, and in late July some 1,400 people participated in a demonstration in Surxondaryo Viloyat organized by the Ecological Movement of Uzbekistan (a quasi-state organization with reserved parliamentary representation since the previous year) against the pollution from the plant.

Relations with Russia have been intermittently strained by concerns regarding Uzbekistan's ethnic Russian population (an estimated 5.5% of the population in 1996). Uzbekistan has repeatedly refused to grant dual citizenship to its Russian minority, and since independence many thousands of these Russians have emigrated. In October 1998 Russia, Uzbekistan and Tajikistan signed a pact offering mutual military assistance, especially against 'the threat of religious extremism'; at the same time Russia and Uzbekistan signed a number of inter-governmental agreements. Russia supported the Uzbekistani Government's official report on the events in Andijon in May 2005. Uzbekistan forged closer relations with Russia in 2005, as relations of both Uzbekistan and Russia with Western countries notably worsened, and in November Karimov and the Russian President, Vladimir Putin, signed a bilateral agreement providing for co-operation in trade and security, the use of military facilities and efforts to combat drugs-trafficking and terrorism. The two countries also agreed to provide support to the other in the event that one of them came under attack. In January 2009 Russian President Dmitrii Medvedev (who had succeeded Putin in May 2008) undertook a state visit to Uzbekistan to discuss issues of bilateral co-operation. Uzbekistan provided assurances that it would only export gas by way of Russia, and offered to increase the volume of gas to be allocated for purchase by Russia to an annual quota of 31,000m. cu m, after Russia agreed that the purchases would be made at market rates; additionally, the Russian energy company LUKoil was to invest some US $5,000m. in Uzbekistan's gas sector over the following seven years. In April 2010 President Karimov visited Moscow, Russia, where he again met Medvedev.

Relations with the People's Republic of China improved in the 1990s, and in July 1996 Jiang Zemin became the first Chinese President to visit Uzbekistan; a joint declaration on bilateral relations and co-operation was signed. China and Uzbekistan signed further co-operation agreements in November 1999, including a joint communiqué on the development of bilateral relations. In October 2000 the two countries signed an agreement on combating terrorism.

Uzbekistan's concerns for the security of the Central Asian region were augmented by the long-standing civil war and the growth of radical forms of Islamism in Afghanistan. In the early 1990s President Burhanuddin Rabbani of Afghanistan claimed that Uzbekistan was providing military and financial assistance to the Afghan (and ethnic Uzbek) militia leader Gen. Abdul Rashid Dostam, whose forces controlled parts of northern Afghanistan. In 1994 Uzbekistan denied any military involvement in Afghanistan. At a summit meeting attended by representatives of Russia and the Central Asian republics in October 1996, Karimov confirmed that no military assistance would be accorded to Gen. Dostam, but declared that Dostam's forces provided the only defence for the Central Asian republics against the Taliban militant Islamist grouping. Following the defeat of Dostam's forces in May 1997, increased numbers of troops were deployed along the border with Afghanistan. In late 1997 the Uzbekistani Government denied having facilitated the return of Gen. Dostam to Afghanistan from exile in Turkey. In October 2000 Gen. Dostam rejected allegations that his troops fought alongside Uzbekistani government forces in August–September to repel incursions by Islamist militants. Relations with the de facto ruling Taliban regime in Afghanistan deteriorated after it granted political asylum to Jumaboy Hojiyev, the field commander of the IMU.

Following the suicide attacks in the USA in September 2001, and the commencement of US-led military action in Afghanistan, in October Uzbekistan began to deploy troops on the Uzbekistani–Afghan border. The Uzbekistani Government was reluctant to accept refugees from Afghanistan, even though 1.5m. of them were ethnic Uzbeks, citing security concerns. Initially, the Government also refused to open the border to allow humanitarian aid to reach Afghanistan. However, following the military successes of the anti-Taliban forces in November, the Government opened the 'Friendship Bridge', the only transit point into Afghanistan, in the following month. At an official summit of the heads of the Central Asian states in Tashkent in December 2001 (at which Turkmenistan was not represented), the leaders declared their support for the new Afghan Interim Administration, which was established following the defeat of the Taliban regime. In March 2002 the leaders of Uzbekistan and Afghanistan pledged jointly to combat terrorism and the drugs trade; the IMU, for example, remained a threat to both countries.

Other external relations

Relations with the USA improved noticeably in the late 1990s, and during a visit to Tashkent in April 2000 the US Secretary of State had affirmed the USA's willingness to assist Uzbekistan in combating the spread of Islamist extremism. Following the suicide attacks on the USA of 11 September 2001 (see the chapter on the USA), relations improved further. Uzbekistan's decision to support the US-led 'coalition against global terrorism' was of great strategic importance to the USA, which hoped to benefit from access to the country's transportation facilities. In late September the Uzbekistani Government confirmed that US military aircraft had landed at an airfield near Tashkent. In early October Uzbekistan and the USA signed a co-operation agreement, whereby Uzbekistan agreed to make its airbases available for use in humanitarian and 'search-and-rescue' operations during the US-led aerial bombardment of targets in Afghanistan. The USA also agreed that it would enter into urgent negotiations should Uzbekistan's security be threatened.

In November 2001 Uzbekistan and the USA signed a number of agreements pledging to improve bilateral relations and to increase economic co-operation. Further bilateral agreements on political, economic and military co-operation were signed in January and March 2002, and Karimov visited the USA in March. Disagreements over Uzbekistan's lack of progress in democratic reform and human rights practices led the USA to reduce its aid programme by US $18m. in July 2004. In October the US Drug Enforcement Agency and Uzbekistan's Ministry of Internal Affairs, together with Azerbaijan, Georgia, Kazakhstan, Kyrgyzstan, Moldova, Russia, Tajikistan and Ukraine, initiated an operation to control the flow of illegal drugs.

Following the violence in Andijon in May 2005, the USA urged Uzbekistan to allow an international inquiry to be undertaken. In June a spokesman from the US Department of State stated that witnesses had reported the killing of hundreds of civilians by Uzbekistani government forces. Uzbekistan subsequently imposed restrictions on the USA's use of the Qarshi-Khanabad ('K-2') military base, which had been used by the USA since October 2001 to support military and other operations in Afghanistan (see above); Uzbekistan also proposed that the USA withdraw from the airbase. In July 2005 the SCO issued a statement demanding that deadlines be imposed on the use of military bases in Central Asia by Western countries for operations in Afghanistan. Later in the month, following discussions with the USA, Uzbekistan renounced the agreement under which the USA was permitted to use the Qarshi-Khanabad airbase, and the last US military aircraft left the base in November. After Kyrgyzstan announced the closure of the US airbase on its territory that had been used by forces operating in Afghanistan in February 2009, it was reported that US and Uzbekistani officials were engaged in negotiations on an arrangement to allow US forces to return to the Qarshi-Khanabad base. In early April Uzbekistan signed an agreement with the USA allowing the use of Uzbekistani territory for the transit of non-military supplies to Afghanistan. In mid-August the Uzbekistani Minister of Defence and the head of US Central Command signed a bilateral agreement on military educational exchanges and training. In December 2010 the US Secretary of State, Hillary Clinton, visited Tashkent, where she signed an agreement on scientific and technical co-operation between the USA and Uzbekistan.

CONSTITUTION AND GOVERNMENT

Under the terms of the Constitution of 8 December 1992, Uzbekistan is a secular, democratic presidential republic. The directly elected President is Head of State and also holds supreme executive power. In April 2002 the Oliy Majlis (Supreme Assembly) adopted a resolution extending the presidential term from five to seven years, with immediate effect. The Government (Cabinet of Ministers) is subordinate to the President, who appoints the Prime Minister, Deputy Prime Ministers and Ministers (subject to the approval of the legislature). The highest legislative body is the bicameral Oliy Majlis. The Majlis may be dissolved by the President (with the approval of the Constitutional Court). The Oliy Majlis comprises the 150-member lower chamber, the Qonunchilik palatasi Kengashi (Legislative Chamber), whose members are directly elected for a five-year term, except for 15 seats that are reserved for members of the Ecological Movement of Uzbekistan. The upper chamber, the Senat (Senate), is composed of 84 members indirectly elected by regional Council members and 16 citizens appointed by the President. Judicial power is independent of government. Judges of higher courts (the Constitutional Court, the Supreme Court and the High Economic Court) are nominated by the President and confirmed by the Oliy Majlis. Uzbekistan is divided into 12 Viloyats (regions), the city of Toshkent (Tashkent), and one sovereign republic (Qoraqalpog'iston).

REGIONAL AND INTERNATIONAL CO-OPERATION

Uzbekistan is a member of the Commonwealth of Independent States (CIS, see p. 238), the Shanghai Co-operation Organization (SCO, see p. 462), the Economic Co-operation Organization (ECO, see p. 264) and the Organization for Security and Co-operation in Europe (OSCE, see p. 385).

Uzbekistan joined the UN in 1992. The country has observer status at the World Trade Organization (WTO, see p. 430).

ECONOMIC AFFAIRS

In 2009, according to the World Bank, Uzbekistan's gross national income (GNI), measured at average 2007–09 prices, was US $30,535m., equivalent to $1,100 per head (or $2,890 per head on an international purchasing-power parity basis). During 2000–09, it was estimated, the population increased by an annual average of 1.3%, while gross domestic product (GDP) per head increased, in real terms, at an average annual rate of 5.4%. Overall GDP increased, in real terms, by an average of 6.8% per year in 2000–09. According to the Asian Development Bank (ADB, see p. 202), growth was 7.0% in 2009.

In 2009, according to the World Bank, agriculture (including forestry) contributed 20.9% of GDP; the agricultural sector employed 29.1% of the working population in 2005. Some 60% of the country's land is covered by desert and steppe, while the remainder comprises fertile valleys watered by two major river systems. The massive irrigation of arid areas has greatly increased production of the major crop, cotton, but has caused devastating environmental problems (most urgently the desiccation of the Aral Sea). Uzbekistan is among the five largest producers of cotton in the world, and the crop accounted for 27.5% of the value of total exports in 2000. Other major crops include grain, rice, vegetables and fruit. Since independence the Government has striven to reduce the area under cultivation for cotton in order to produce more grain. Private farming was legalized in 1992, and by 1996 more than 98% of agricultural production originated in the non-state sector. According to World Bank figures, during 2000–09 agricultural GDP increased, in real terms, by an annual average of 6.2%. Agricultural GDP increased by 6.8% in 2010, according to the ADB.

According to the World Bank, industry (including mining, manufacturing, utilities and construction) contributed 32.0% of GDP in 2009. It provided 13.2% of total employment in 2005. According to World Bank figures, during 2000–09 industrial GDP increased by an average of 5.1% annually, in real terms. Sectoral GDP increased by 8.3% in 2010, according to the ADB.

Uzbekistan is well endowed with mineral deposits, in particular gold, natural gas, petroleum and coal. At the end of 2009 Uzbekistan had sufficient proven recoverable reserves of natural gas to maintain output at 2009 levels for a little over 26 years, and enough petroleum for over 15 years. There are large reserves of silver, copper, lead, zinc and tungsten, and Uzbekistan is one of the world's largest producers of uranium and gold. In 2008 some 2,757 metric tons of uranium ore was produced; all uranium mined is exported. The Murantau mine, in the Kyzyl-kum desert, was reportedly the world's largest single open-cast gold mine, and produced a reported 74% of Uzbekistan's estimated output in 2003. In 2004 Oxus Gold and the Uzbekistani Government officially opened a further gold-mining complex in Amantaytau, 30 km from the Murantau mine. Each party had a 50% share in the mine, which had estimated reserves of some 1,400 tons.

The manufacturing sector contributed 11.8% of GDP in 2009, according to the World Bank. Significant investment has been directed to the expansion of the raw-materials processing industry. According to the World Bank, manufacturing GDP grew at an average of 2.8% per year in 2000–09. Sectoral GDP increased by 6.0% in 2009.

The construction sector contributed 5.7% of GDP in 2008, according to the ADB. The sector employed some 7.5% of the working population in 2000, according to official figures.

Uzbekistan is self-sufficient in natural gas, crude petroleum and coal, and became a net exporter of crude petroleum in 1995. Energy products accounted for 4.2% of the value of imports in 2000. The opening of two petroleum refineries, which had a total refining capacity of 173,000 barrels per day (b/d), significantly increased Uzbekistan's hydrocarbons capacity. In 2007 70.6% of electricity was generated by natural gas, 11.3% by petroleum and 13.1% by hydroelectric power.

According to the World Bank, the services sector contributed 47.1% of GDP in 2009. It employed 57.7% of the working population in 2005. According to World Bank figures, during 2000–09 the GDP of the services sector increased, in real terms, by an average of 8.5% annually. Services GDP increased by 11.6% in 2010, according to the ADB.

In 2007, according to preliminary IMF figures, Uzbekistan recorded a visible trade surplus of US $2,296m., and there was a surplus of $4,267m. on the current account of the balance of payments. In 2009 the principal source of imports was Russia (accounting for 23.6% of the total value of imports). Other major suppliers were the People's Republic of China, the Republic of Korea, Germany and Ukraine. Ukraine was the main market for exports in that year (accounting for 29.9% of the total value of exports); other important purchasers were Russia, Turkey, Kazakhstan, Bangladesh and China. The principal exports in 2000 were cotton fibre, energy products, metals and food products. The main imports in that year were machinery and equipment, chemicals and plastics, food products and metals. By 2000 trade with republics of the former USSR represented only about 35% of Uzbekistan's total trade, compared with some 83% in 1990.

In 2007, according to preliminary figures, Uzbekistan's overall budget surplus (including extrabudgetary operations) was 419,000m. sum (equivalent to 1.5% of GDP). Uzbekistan's general government gross debt was 5,385,550m. sum in 2009, equivalent to 11.2% of GDP. At the end of 2008 Uzbekistan's total external debt was US $3,995.0m., of which $3,156.0m. was public and publicly guaranteed debt. Inflation declined at an annual average rate of 1.6% in 2000–09, according to ADB figures. The rate of inflation was 0.6% in 2009. According to the ADB, in 2008 some 17,000 people (0.2% of the economically active population) were registered as unemployed, although the actual level was believed to be considerably higher.

Uzbekistan's economy, in which the extraction of mineral resources and the production of cotton both play an important role, experienced a downturn in the aftermath of the dissolution of the USSR, but recovered markedly during the 2000s. In the mid-2000s numerous initiatives to increase the output of natural gas were announced; in 2004 the Russian state-controlled natural gas company Gazprom and the Uzbekistani company Uzbekneftgazkurilish agreed a 15-year production-sharing agreement at the Shakhpakhty gas and condensate field. In January 2006 Uzbekistan signed a production-sharing agreement with Gazprom for three further natural gas fields. Meanwhile, the Government announced initiatives that were intended to help diversify the economy. In early 2008 the unified tax rate for micro- and small businesses and the corporate income tax rate for banks were both reduced. In 2010 President Karimov announced that the following year was to be designated a 'year of small businesses and entrepreneurship', and also announced numerous projects for the modernization of the industrial sector during 2011–15. Remittances from nationals living in Russia provided an estimated 13% of GDP in 2008. However, owing to the global economic downturn, many Uzbekistani migrant workers were compelled to return to Uzbekistan because of unemployment. In response to the downturn, in late 2008 a crisis-prevention programme for 2009–12 was adopted. In December 2008 the Government created a free industrial-economic zone in Navoiy Viloyat, offering tax and customs preferences to foreign investors. By late 2010 among those companies that had declared an intention to invest in the zone were the automobile manufacturers General Motors (of the USA) and the airline Korean Air (of the Republic of Korea). In 2010 a joint venture company, Mercedes-Benz Buses Central Asia, was established by Daimler (of Germany) and the Uzbekistani state-controlled O'zavtosanoat, to construct buses for the domestic market and for export. In 2009 overall GDP growth remained high, at 7.0%, according to the ADB, and government figures indicated that foreign direct investment increased by 80%, compared with the previous year. In 2010 GDP growth of 8.5% was recorded, according to government figures, and a similar level of growth was forecast for 2011.

PUBLIC HOLIDAYS

2012: 1 January (New Year's Day), 14 January (Defenders of the Native Land Day), 8 March (International Women's Day), 21 March (Navruz Bairam, Spring Holiday), 9 May (Memorial and Respect Day), 1 September (Independence Day), 18 August* (Ruza Hayit, Id al-Fitr or end of Ramadan), 1 October (Teachers' and Instructors' Day), 25 October* (Kurban Hayit, Id al-Adha or Feast of the Sacrifice), 8 December (Constitution Day).

* These holidays are dependent on the Islamic lunar calendar and may vary by one or two days from the dates given.

UZBEKISTAN

Statistical Survey

Principal source (unless otherwise indicated): The State Committee of the Republic of Uzbekistan on Statistics, 100077 Tashkent, Mustaqillik maydoni 63; tel. (71) 150-50-01; fax (71) 150-50-88; e-mail Gks@stat.uz; internet www.stat.uz

Area and Population

AREA, POPULATION AND DENSITY

Area (sq km)	447,400*
Population (census results)†	
17 January 1979	15,389,307
12 January 1989	
Males	9,784,156
Females	10,025,921
Total	19,810,077
Population (official estimates at 1 January)	
2008	27,100,000
2009	27,555,300
2010	28,000,800
Density (per sq km) at 1 January 2010	62.6

* 172,740 sq miles.
† Figures refer to *de jure* population. The *de facto* total at the 1989 census was 19,905,158.

POPULATION BY AGE AND SEX
(UN estimates at mid-2011)

	Males	Females	Total
0–14	4,014,648	3,871,443	7,886,091
15–64	9,436,371	9,555,798	18,992,169
65 and over	520,394	712,101	1,232,495
Total	13,971,413	14,139,342	28,110,755

Source: UN, *World Population Prospects: The 2008 Revision*.

POPULATION BY ETHNIC GROUP
(1996, rounded estimates)

	%
Uzbek	80.0
Russian	5.5
Tajik	5.0
Kazakh	3.0
Kara-Kalpak	2.5
Tatar	1.5
Others	2.5
Total	100.0

Source: Ministry of Health, Tashkent.

ADMINISTRATIVE DIVISIONS
(1996, rounded figures, official estimates)

	Area (sq km)	Population	Density (per sq km)	Capital city (with population)
Sovereign Republic:				
Qoraqalpog'iston	165,600	1,400,000	8.5	Nukus (236,700)
Viloyats				
Andijon	4,200	1,899,000	452.1	Andijon (303,000)
Buxoro	39,400	1,384,700	35.2	Buxoro (263,400)
Farg'ona	6,800	2,597,000	381.9	Farg'ona (214,000)
Jizzax	20,500	910,500	44.4	Jizzax (127,200)
Namangan	7,900	1,862,000	235.7	Namangan (341,000)
Navoiy	110,800	767,500	6.9	Navoiy (128,000)
Qashqadaryo	28,400	2,029,000	71.4	Qarshi (177,000)
Samarqand	16,400	2,322,000	141.6	Samarqand (366,000)
Sirdaryo	5,100	648,100	127.1	Guliston (54,000)
Surxondaryo	20,800	1,676,000	80.6	Termiz (95,000)
Tashkent*	15,300	4,450,000	290.9	Tashkent (2,100,000)
Xorazm	6,300	1,200,000	190.5	Urgench (135,000)
Total	447,400	23,145,800	51.7	

* Including Tashkent City, which subsequently assumed a separate administrative status.

Source: Government of Uzbekistan.

PRINCIPAL TOWNS
(estimated population at 1 January 2001)

Tashkent (the capital)	2,137,218	Farg'ona	183,037
Namangan	391,297	Margilan	149,646
Samarqand	361,339	Chirchik	141,742
Andijon	338,366	Urgench	138,609
Buxoro	237,361	Navoiy	138,082
Nukus	212,012	Jizzax	131,512
Qarshi	204,690	Termiz	116,467
Qoqand	197,450	Olmaliq	113,114

Source: UN, *Demographic Yearbook*.

Mid-2010 ('000, incl. suburbs, UN estimate): Toshkent (Tashkent) 2,210 (Source: UN, *World Urbanization Prospects: The 2009 Revision*).

BIRTHS, MARRIAGES AND DEATHS

	Registered live births		Registered marriages		Registered deaths	
	Number	Rate (per 1,000)	Number	Rate (per 1,000)	Number	Rate (per 1,000)
2005	533,500	20.3	184,000	7.0	140,600	5.4
2006	555,900	20.9	208,500	7.8	139,600	5.3
2007	608,900	22.6	254,200	9.4	137,400	5.1
2008	646,400	23.6	249,000	9.1	137,500	5.0
2009	649,700	23.3	277,600	10.0	130,700	4.7

Note: Numbers are rounded to the nearest 100.

Life expectancy (years at birth, WHO estimates): 68 (males 66; females 71) in 2008 (Source: WHO, *World Health Statistics*).

UZBEKISTAN

EMPLOYMENT
(annual averages, '000 persons)

	1998	1999	2000
Agriculture*	3,467	3,213	3,083
Industry†	1,114	1,124	1,145
Construction	573	640	676
Transport and communications	362	370	382
Trade and catering‡	717	735	754
Other services	1,976	2,042	2,042
Housing, public utilities and personal services	235	240	246
Health care, social security, physical culture and sports	502	538	567
Education, culture and art	1,073	1,094	1,120
Banking and insurance	50	48	51
General administration	111	122	126
Information and computer services	5	—	—
Total (incl. others)	8,800	8,885	8,983

* Including forestry.
† Comprising manufacturing (except printing and publishing), mining and quarrying, electricity, gas, water, logging and fishing.
‡ Including material and technical supply.

Source: Centre for Economic Research, Tashkent, *Uzbek Economic Trends*.

2005 ('000 persons): Total employed 10,196 (Agriculture 2,970, Industry 1,348, Other 5,879) (Source: Asian Development Bank).

Total employed ('000 persons): 10,467 in 2006; 10,735 in 2007; 11,035 in 2008 (Source: Asian Development Bank).

Unemployed ('000 persons registered): 28 in 2005; 26 in 2006; 23 in 2007; 17 in 2008 (Source: Asian Development Bank).

Mid-2011 ('000, estimates): Agriculture, etc. 2,729; Total labour force 13,079 (Source: FAO).

Health and Welfare

KEY INDICATORS

Total fertility rate (children per woman, 2008)	2.3
Under-5 mortality rate (per 1,000 live births, 2008)	38
HIV/AIDS (% of persons aged 15–49, 2007)	0.1
Physicians (per 1,000 head, 2005)	2.7
Hospital beds (per 1,000 head, 2005)	5.2
Health expenditure (2007): US $ per head (PPP)	121
Health expenditure (2007): % of GDP	5.0
Health expenditure (2007): public (% of total)	46.1
Access to water (% of persons, 2008)	87
Total carbon dioxide emissions ('000 metric tons, 2007)	115,994.9
Carbon dioxide emissions per head (metric tons, 2007)	4.3
Human Development Index (2010): ranking	102
Human Development Index (2010): value	0.617

For sources and definitions, see explanatory note on p. vi.

Agriculture

PRINCIPAL CROPS
('000 metric tons)

	2007	2008	2009
Wheat	6,197.4	6,146.5	6,637.7
Rice, paddy	198	110	194
Barley*	90	157	210
Maize	206	228	231
Sorghum*	14	15	20
Potatoes	1,188	1,399	1,525
Broad beans, horse beans, dry*	8	8	11
Sunflower seed*	7	12	13
Safflower seed	4†	4†	n.a.
Sesame seed	18†	18†	n.a.
Seed cotton	3,716	3,716	2,940†
Cabbages and other brassicas*	400	447	486
Tomatoes*	1,680	1,930	2,110
Cucumbers and gherkins*	285	318	350
Onions, dry*	602	728	795
Garlic*	40	45	49
Carrots and turnips*	815	910	995

Statistical Survey

—continued	2007	2008	2009
Watermelons	840	981	1,071
Apples*	503	585	635
Pears*	55	61	65
Apricots*	230	265	290
Sweet cherries*	55	61	67
Peaches and nectarines*	68	75	82
Plums and sloes*	59	65	70
Grapes	880	791	900
Tobacco, unmanufactured	19†	19†	n.a.
Jute	20†	20†	n.a.

* Unofficial figures.
† FAO estimate.

Aggregate production ('000 metric tons, may include official, semi-official or estimated data): Total cereals 6,749 in 2007, 6,706 in 2008, 7,358 in 2009; Total roots and tubers 1,188 in 2007, 1,399 in 2008, 1,525 in 2009; Total vegetables (incl. melons) 5,510 in 2007, 6,199 in 2008, 6,776 in 2009; Total fruits (excl. melons) 2,149 in 2007, 2,194 in 2008, 2,426 in 2009.

Source: FAO.

LIVESTOCK
('000 head at 1 January)

	2007	2008	2009
Horses	162*	168	175
Cattle	7,043	7,458	8,025
Camels*	17	17	17
Pigs	92	92*	92*
Sheep†	10,383	10,625	11,405
Goats†	2,040	2,000	2,154
Chickens	24,220	25,100†	29,100†
Turkeys†	360	400	400

* FAO estimate(s).
† Unofficial figure(s).
Source: FAO.

LIVESTOCK PRODUCTS
('000 metric tons)

	2007	2008	2009
Cattle meat*	551.0	586.0	623.0
Sheep meat*	83.0	88.0	93.0
Pig meat*	18.0	19.0	20.0
Chicken meat*	22.4	24.0	25.0
Cows' milk*	5,061.0	5,387.0	5,732.4
Goats' milk*	36.4	39.0	46.2
Hen eggs*	121.2	132.9	148.7
Other poultry eggs*	3.2	3.5	3.9
Honey	2.2†	2.2†	n.a.
Wool, greasy	22.4	23.8	25.0

* Unofficial figures.
† FAO estimate.
Source: FAO.

Fishing

(metric tons, live weight)

	2006	2007*	2008*
Capture	3,400	2,802	2,800
Common carp	1,140	950	950
Crucian carp	188	155	155
Roach	223	180	180
Silver carp	180	145	143
Aquaculture	3,800	3,424	3,418
Common carp	266	210	200
Crucian carp	19	16	20
Grass carp (White amur)	190	170	170
Silver carp	3,268	2,980	2,980
Bighead carp	57	48	48
Total catch	7,200	6,226	6,218

* FAO estimates.
Source: FAO.

UZBEKISTAN

Mining

(metric tons unless otherwise indicated)

	2006	2007	2008
Coal ('000 metric tons)*	3,126	3,282	2,400
Crude petroleum ('000 metric tons)†	3,007	3,017	2,533
Natural gas ('000 million cu m)	63	65	68
Copper ore‡§	95,000	92,000	92,000
Molybdenum ore‡§	600	600	500
Silver ore (kilograms)‡§	83,000	83,000	83,000
Gold (kilograms)‡§	84,000	85,000	85,000
Kaolin ('000 metric tons)	251	250§	250§
Fluorspar	88	90§	90§
Uranium ore (metric tons)‡	2,677	2,736	2,757

* Including lignite and brown coal.
† Including gas condensate.
‡ Figures refer to the metal content of ores.
§ Estimated production.

Source: US Geological Survey.

Crude petroleum ('000 metric tons): 4,781 in 2008; 4,455 in 2009 (Source: BP, *Statistical Review of World Energy*).

Natural gas (excl. flared or recycled, million cu m): 62,172 in 2008; 64,434 in 2009 (Source: BP, *Statistical Review of World Energy*).

Industry

SELECTED PRODUCTS

('000 metric tons unless otherwise indicated)

	2006	2007	2008
Flour	1,348.7	1,440.7	1,425.6
Sugar (granulated)	170.6	170.9	254.3
Flour	1,348.7	1,440.7	1,425.6
Sugar (granulated)	170.6	170.9	254.3
Beer ('000 hectolitres)	n.a.	1,041.3	1,194.7
Vodka and other spirits ('000 hectolitres)	651.4	766.7	856.6
Cigarettes, etc. (million)	7,903	8,729	10,461
Cotton yarn	143.7	150.3	136.1
Knitwear articles ('000 pieces)	28,889	30,883	29,163
Sulphuric acid	833.1	976.9	924.4
Chemical fertilizers	940.9	1,022.1	1,064.9
Motor spirit (petrol)	1,368.6	1,405.9	1,464.1
Gas-diesel (distillate fuel) oils	1,436.8	1,393.8	1,287.2
Residual fuel oils	895.6	688.5	539.5
Lubricating oils	255.9	302.3	261.2
Kerosene	358.9	300.0	361.7
Cement	5,582.9	6,042.5	6,647.0
Window glass ('000 sq m)	10,546.3	11,952.0	12,412.0
Finished steel	585.7	619.6	685.7
Refrigerators and freezers (units)	5,044	10,774	6,218
Television receivers ('000)	90.6	93.5	n.a.
Motor cars	140,080	171,809	195,038
Buses	n.a.	1,116	1,556
Tractors	2,872	2,411	2,437
Tractor cultivators	1,572	1,562	1,773
Electric energy (million kWh)	49,300	48,950	50,100

Finance

CURRENCY AND EXCHANGE RATES

Monetary Units
100 teen = 1 sum.

Sterling, Dollar and Euro Equivalents (31 December 2010)
£1 sterling = 2,567.4 sum;
US $1 = 1,640.0 sum;
€1 = 2,191.4 sum;
10,000 sum = £3.89 = $6.10 = €4.56.

Average Exchange Rate (sum per US $)
2000   236.61
2001   423.31
2002   769.50

Note: Prior to the introduction of the sum (see below), Uzbekistan used a transitional currency, the sum-coupon. This had been introduced in November 1993 to circulate alongside (and initially at par with) the Russian (formerly Soviet) rouble. Following the dissolution of the USSR in December 1991, Russia and several other former Soviet republics retained the rouble as their monetary unit. The Russian rouble ceased to be legal tender in Uzbekistan from 15 April 1994.

On 1 July 1994 a permanent currency, the sum, was introduced to replace the sum-coupon at 1 sum per 1,000 coupons. The initial exchange rate was set at US $1 = 7.00 sum. Sum-coupons continued to circulate, but from 15 October 1994 the sum became the sole legal tender. On 15 October 2003 the sum became fully convertible.

CONSOLIDATED BUDGET

('000 million sum)

Revenue	2006	2007*	2008†
Tax revenue	4,365	5,870	6,791
Taxes on incomes and profits	1,293	1,758	2,002
Taxes on property	276	349	438
Taxes on goods and services	2,623	3,470	4,104
VAT	1,142	1,682	2,001
Excises	881	1,017	1,170
Customs duties	173	293	248
Other budget revenue	333	522	317
Social security contributions	1,253	1,761	2,650
Road fund and other extra-budgetary revenue	273	355	412
Education development tax	233	365	431
Grants	62	50	30
Total	6,519	8,922	10,632

Expenditure‡	2006	2007*	2008†
Socio-cultural expenditure	2,169	2,906	3,910
Social safety net	1,735	2,283	3,400
Low income support	366	397	620
Pension and employment fund	1,369	1,886	2,780
Pension fund	1,335	1,841	2,726
Employment fund	35	45	54
Economy	594	678	915
Public authorities and administration	124	176	243
Public investment	532	627	847
Interest expenditure	74	172	103
Other expenditure in the budget	879	1,138	1,078
Road fund	204	270	349
Extra-budgetary expenditure financed by grants	62	50	30
Statistical discrepancy	—	155	—
Total	6,374	8,455	10,875

* Preliminary.
† Projected.
‡ Excluding net lending ('000 million): 40 in 2006; 48 in 2007 (preliminary); −90 in 2008 (projected).

Source: IMF, *Republic of Uzbekistan: 2008 Article IV Consultation-Staff Report; Public Information Notice on the Executive Board Discussion; and Statement by the Executive Director for the Republic of Uzbekistan* (July 2008).

UZBEKISTAN

Statistical Survey

INTERNATIONAL RESERVES
(US $ million at 31 December)

	2002	2003	2004
Gold (national valuation)	505.8	558.0	418.5
IMF special drawing rights	1.1	0.1	0.0
Foreign exchange	709.8	1,101.2	1,728.0
Total	1,215.0	1,659.3	2,146.5

Total reserves (US $ million at 31 December): 2,895.0 in 2005; 4,459.0 in 2006; 7,413.0 in 2007 (preliminary); 10,145.0 in 2008 (preliminary).

Source: Asian Development Bank.

MONEY SUPPLY
('000 million sum at 31 December)

	2006	2007*	2008*
Currency outside banks	1,495	2,048	2,528
Demand deposits at deposit money banks	491	1,061	1,415
Total money	1,986	3,109	3,943

* Preliminary.

Source: Asian Development Bank.

COST OF LIVING
(Consumer Price Index; base: previous year = 100)

	2007	2008	2009
Food	103.3	102.7	103.2
Other goods	108.4	107.7	108.0
All items	106.8	107.8	108.4

Source: Asian Development Bank.

NATIONAL ACCOUNTS
('000 million sum at current prices, preliminary)

Expenditure on the Gross Domestic Product

	2006	2006	2008
Final consumption expenditure	15,231.7	19,678.5	23,704.2
Households	11,521.6	14,853.7	17,915.4
Non-profit institutions serving households			
General government	3,710.1	4,824.9	5,788.8
Gross capital formation	3,838.3	6,144.1	7,129.0
Gross fixed capital formation	3,838.3	5,987.3	7,080.4
Acquisitions, less disposals, of valuables			
Changes in inventories	—	156.8	48.6
Total domestic expenditure	19,070.0	25,822.6	30,833.2
Exports of goods and services	8,541.7	11,406.8	13,661.6
Less Imports of goods and services	6,852.4	9,043.2	10,705.2
GDP in market prices	20,759.3	28,186.2	33,789.6

Gross Domestic Product by Economic Activity

	2006	2007	2008
Agriculture and forestry	5,003.0	6,116.4	7,974.3
Mining and quarrying			
Manufacturing	4,587.8	6,764.7	7,523.8
Electricity, gas and water			
Construction	1,058.7	1,550.2	1,745.8
Trade	1,972.1	2,649.5	3,165.0
Transport and communications	2,366.6	3,128.7	3,807.0
Finance			
Public administration	3,861.2	5,299.0	6,228.6
Other services			
GDP at factor cost	18,849.4	25,508.5	30,444.4
Indirect taxes	1,909.9	2,677.7	3,345.2
Less Subsidies			
GDP in purchasers' values	20,759.3	28,186.2	33,789.6

Source: Asian Development Bank.

BALANCE OF PAYMENTS
(US $ million)

	2005	2006	2007*
Exports of goods f.o.b.	4,757	5,615	8,026
Imports of goods f.o.b.	−3,310	−3,841	−5,730
Trade balance	1,446	1,774	2,296
Export of services	659	775	965
Import of services	−790	−828	−1,007
Balance on goods and services	1,315	1,721	2,254
Income (net)	−24	41	62
Current transfers (net)	658	1,171	1,951
Current balance	1,949	2,933	4,267
Capital account (net)	31	−116	−104
Foreign direct and portfolio investment (net)	88	195	739
Existing public and publicly-guaranteed debt (net)	−241	−347	−213
Commercial non-guaranteed debt (net)	34	43	273
Foreign assets of commercial banks (net)	—	−290	−433
Other capital and statistical discrepancy	−1,093	−854	−2,430
Adjustment	—	—	56
Overall balance	768	1,564	2,155

* Preliminary.

Source: IMF, *Republic of Uzbekistan: 2008 Article IV Consultation-Staff Report; Public Information Notice on the Executive Board Discussion; and Statement by the Executive Director for the Republic of Uzbekistan* (July 2008).

External Trade

PRINCIPAL COMMODITIES
(US $ million)

Imports f.o.b.	1998	1999	2000
Chemicals and plastics	407.2	363.0	399.5
Metals	303.6	245.4	253.5
Machinery and equipment	1,553.7	1,393.5	1,044.1
Food products	512.2	408.1	361.1
Energy products	16.3	66.6	112.7
Total (incl. others)	3,288.7	3,110.7	2,696.4

Exports f.o.b.	1998	1999	2000
Cotton fibre	1,361.0	883.7	897.1
Chemicals and plastics	51.7	101.8	93.4
Metals	180.7	138.9	216.7
Machinery and equipment	146.6	103.2	111.8
Food products	111.9	206.7	176.4
Energy products	277.8	371.5	335.2
Total (incl. others)	3,528.2	3,235.8	3,264.7

Source: Center for Economic Research, Tashkent, *Uzbek Economic Trends*.

2006 (US $ million, official estimates): Total imports 4,395.9; total exports 6,389.8.

2007 (US $ million, official estimates): Total imports 5,235.6; total exports 8,991.5.

2008 (US $ million, official estimates): Total imports 7,504.1; total exports 11,572.9.

UZBEKISTAN

PRINCIPAL TRADING PARTNERS
(US $ million)

Imports	2007	2008	2009
Belarus	102.4	151.9	115.2
China, People's Republic	842.6	1,405.1	1,687.7
Germany	395.9	498.3	504.7
Kazakhstan	388.8	443.9	388.3
Korea, Republic	823.1	1,234.9	1,080.3
Kyrgyzstan	83.1	255.3	223.4
Russia	1,901.9	2,298.3	1,966.0
Tajikistan	95.7	109.3	n.a.
Turkey	247.6	370.8	307.0
Ukraine	381.5	654.8	446.8
USA	97.6	330.6	107.1
Total (incl. others)	6,452.3	9,153.0	8,314.7

Exports	2007	2008	2009
Bangladesh	257.9	353.0	340.5
China, People's Republic	330.3	300.4	283.5
Iran	134.2	169.5	158.9
Japan	147.6	287.9	94.0
Kazakhstan	362.6	414.0	362.2
Poland	619.0	46.9	25.5
Russia	1,330.8	1,189.6	695.1
Tajikistan	194.5	137.7	120.4
Turkey	558.0	528.0	375.5
Ukraine	496.4	1,925.7	1,491.6
Total (incl. others)	6,124.0	7,007.5	4,986.8

Note: Data reflect the IMF's direction of trade methodology and, as a result, the totals may not be equal to those presented for trade in commodities.

Source: Asian Development Bank.

Transport

RAILWAYS
(traffic)

	2002	2003	2004
Passenger-km (million)	2	2	2
Freight ton-km (million)	18	19	18

Source: UN, *Statistical Yearbook*.

2008: Passengers carried (intercity) 13.0m.; passengers carried (urban electrical) 123.1m.; freight carried 62,900,000 metric tons.

CIVIL AVIATION
(estimated traffic on scheduled services)

	2004	2005	2006
Kilometres flown (million)	44	42	42
Passengers carried ('000)	1,588	1,639	1,665
Passenger-km (million)	4,454	4,409	4,599
Total ton-km (million)	486	479	483

Source: UN, *Statistical Yearbook*.

2007: Passengers carried ('000) 1,940.4 (Source: World Bank, World Development Indicators database).

2008: Passengers carried ('000) 2,033.9 (Source: World Bank, World Development Indicators database).

Tourism

FOREIGN VISITOR ARRIVALS
('000, incl. excursionists)

Region of origin	2006	2007	2008
Africa	2.0	2.0	2.5
Americas	6.0	8.0	8.0
East Asia and the Pacific	295.9	442.7	578.6
Europe	215.6	370.4	385.2
Middle East	30.0	50.0	55.0
South Asia	10.0	30.0	40.0
Total	559.5	903.1	1,069.3

Tourism receipts (US $ million, excl. passenger transport): 43 in 2006; 51 in 2007; 64 in 2008.

Source: World Tourism Organization.

Communications Media

	2007	2008	2009
Telephones ('000 main lines in use)	1,822.1	1,849.6	1,856.6
Mobile cellular telephones ('000 subscribers)	5,691.5	12,375.3	16,417.9
Internet users ('000)	2,015.0	2,469.0	4,689.0
Broadband subscribers ('000)	19.2	66.0	88.7

Source: International Telecommunication Union.

Book production: 1,003 titles and 30,914,000 copies in 1996 (Source: UNESCO, *Statistical Yearbook*).

Daily newspapers: 3 titles and 75,000 copies (average circulation) in 1996; 5 titles in 2004 (Sources: UNESCO, *Statistical Yearbook*; UNESCO Institute for Statistics).

Non-daily newspapers: 350 titles and 1,404,000 copies (average circulation) in 1996 (Source: UNESCO, *Statistical Yearbook*).

Other periodicals: 81 titles and 684,000 copies (average circulation) in 1996 (Source: UNESCO, *Statistical Yearbook*).

Radio receivers ('000 in use): 10,800 in 1997 (Source: UNESCO, *Statistical Yearbook*).

Television receivers ('000 in use): 7,000 in 2001 (Source: International Telecommunication Union).

Personal computers: 830,000 (31.3 per 1,000 persons) in 2006 (Source: International Telecommunication Union).

Education

(2007 unless otherwise indicated)

	Schools	Teachers	Students
Pre-primary	6,423	96,100*	571,200
Primary	} 9,816†	} 463,100‡	1,905,693*
Secondary: general			5,715,100‡
teacher training	n.a.	2,464§	35,411§
vocational	1,052‡	7,900*	214,500*
Higher	63‖	18,400*	263,600‖
Universities	20*	n.a.	131,100*

* 1994/95.
† Including 20 evening schools.
‡ 2006.
§ 1993.
‖ 2004.

Sources: UNESCO, *Statistical Yearbook* and Center for Economic Research, Tashkent.

Pupil-teacher ratio (primary education, UNESCO estimate): 17.1 in 2008/09 (Source: UNESCO Institute for Statistics).

Adult literacy rate (UNESCO estimates): 99.2% (males 99.5%; females 98.9%) in 2008 (Source: UNESCO Institute for Statistics).

Directory

The Government

HEAD OF STATE

President of the Republic: ISLAM A. KARIMOV (elected by Supreme Soviet 24 March 1990; term of office extended by popular referendum 26 March 1995; re-elected 9 January 2000 and 23 December 2007; inaugurated 16 January 2008).

CABINET OF MINISTERS
(May 2011)

Prime Minister: SHAVKAT M. MIRZIYOYEV.

First Deputy Prime Minister, Minister of Finance, responsible for Macroeconomic Development, Structural Economic Transformation and Integrated Regional Development: RUSTAM S. AZIMOV.

Deputy Prime Minister, responsible for Municipal Services, Transport, Capital Works and the Construction Industry: BOTIR A. XO'JAYEV.

Deputy Prime Minister, responsible for Geology, Fuel and Energy and the Chemical, Petrochemical and Metallurgical Industries: G'ULOMJON I. IBRAGIMOV.

Deputy Prime Minister, Chairman of O'zavtosanoat Joint-Stock Co, responsible for the Development of Machine Construction, the Electro-technical and Aviation Industries and the Standardization of Production: ULUG'BEK U. ROZUKULOV.

Deputy Prime Minister, responsible for Education, Health, Social Welfare, Information Systems and Telecommunications: ABDULLA N. ARIPOV.

Deputy Prime Minister, Minister of Foreign Affairs, responsible for Foreign Economic Activities, the Attraction of Foreign Investment and the Localization of Production: ELYOR M. G'ANIYEV.

Deputy Prime Minister, Chairman of the Committee of Women of Uzbekistan: FARIDA SH. AKBAROVA.

Minister of the Economy: RAVSHAN A. G'ULOMOV.

Minister of Labour and Social Protection: AKTAM A. XAITOV.

Minister of Culture and Sports: (vacant).

Minister of Internal Affairs: BAHODIR A. MATLYUBOV.

Minister of Foreign Economic Relations, Investment and Trade: GALINA K. SAIDOVA.

Minister of Defence: QOBUL R. BERDIYEV.

Minister of Higher and Specialized Secondary Education: BAXODIR YU. XODIYEV.

Minister of National Education: AVAZJON R. MARAHIMOV.

Minister of Agriculture and Water Resources: ZAFAR SH. RUZIEV.

Minister of Justice: RAVSHAN A. MUXITDINOV.

Minister of Health: ADXAM I. IKRAMOV.

Minister of Emergency Situations: TURSINXON A. XUDAYBERGANOV.

Note: The Constitution provides for the Chairman of the Council of Ministers of the Republic of Qoraqalpog'iston to serve as an ex officio member of the Council of Ministers of the Republic of Uzbekistan. Since March 2006 this position has been held by BAXODIR YANGIBOYEV. The following are also members of the Council of Ministers: the Chairman of the State Tax Committee, the Chairman of the State Customs Committee and the Chairmen of the State Committees on: the Management of State Property; Geology and Mineral Resources; Statistics; Demonopolization and the Development of Competition; Architecture and Construction; Land Resources, Geodesy, Cartography and the State Cadastre; and the Protection of the Environment.

MINISTRIES

Office of the President: 100163 Tashkent, O'zbekiston shoh ko'ch. 43; tel. (71) 239-54-04; fax (71) 239-53-25; e-mail presidents_office@press-service.uz; internet www.press-service.uz.

Office of the Cabinet of Ministers: 100078 Tashkent, Mustaqillik maydoni 5; tel. (71) 239-82-95; fax (71) 239-84-63; internet www.gov.uz.

Ministry of Agriculture and Water Resources: 100004 Tashkent, A. Navoiy ko'ch. 4; tel. (712) 241-00-42; fax (712) 244-23-97; e-mail info@agro.uz; internet www.agro.uz.

Ministry of Culture and Sport: 100159 Tashkent, Mustaqillik maydoni 5; tel. (71) 139-83-31; fax (71) 139-46-11; e-mail madaniyat@sport.uz; internet www.madaniyat.sport.uz.

Ministry of Defence: 100000 Tashkent, Ak. Abdullaev ko'ch. 100; tel. (71) 133-03-30; fax (71) 268-48-67.

Ministry of the Economy: 100003 Tashkent, O'zbekiston shoh ko'ch. 45A; tel. (71) 232-63-20; fax (71) 232-63-72; e-mail info@mineconomy.uz; internet www.mineconomy.uz.

Ministry for Emergency Situations: 100084 Tashkent, Yunusobod tumani, Kichik xalka yo'li 4; tel. (71) 239-16-85; fax (71) 239-44-14; e-mail it@mchs.uz; internet www.mchs.uz.

Ministry of Finance: 100008 Tashkent, Mustaqillik maydoni 5; tel. (71) 233-70-73; fax (71) 244-56-43; e-mail info@mf.uz; internet www.mf.uz.

Ministry of Foreign Affairs: 100029 Tashkent, O'zbekiston shoh ko'ch. 9; tel. (71) 233-64-75; fax (71) 239-15-17; e-mail letter@mfa.uz; internet www.mfa.uz.

Ministry of Foreign Economic Relations, Investment and Trade: 100029 Tashkent, Shevchenko ko'ch. 1; tel. and fax (71) 238-51-00; e-mail secretary@mfer.uz; internet www.mfer.uz.

Ministry of Health: 100011 Tashkent, A. Navoiy ko'ch. 12; tel. (71) 242-16-91; fax (71) 244-10-33; e-mail minzdrav@med.uz; internet www.minzdr.uz.

Ministry of Higher and Specialized Secondary Education: 100095 Tashkent, 2-Chimboy ko'ch. 96; tel. and fax (71) 246-01-95; e-mail mhsse@edu.uz; internet www.edu.uz.

Ministry of Internal Affairs: 100029 Tashkent, Yu. Rajaby ko'ch. 1; tel. (71) 233-66-46; fax (71) 233-38-82; e-mail info@mvd.uz; internet www.mvd.uz.

Ministry of Justice: 100047 Tashkent, Sayilgoh ko'ch. 5; tel. (71) 233-13-05; fax (71) 233-48-44; e-mail info@minjust.gov.uz; internet www.minjust.uz.

Ministry of Labour and Social Security: 100100 Tashkent, A. Avloniy ko'ch. 20A; tel. and fax (71) 239-41-12; e-mail axborot@mintrud.uz; internet www.mintrud.uz.

Ministry of National Education: 100078 Tashkent, Mustaqillik maydoni 5; tel. (71) 239-17-35; fax (71) 239-42-14; e-mail press@mno.uz; internet www.uzedu.uz.

President

Presidential Election, 23 December 2007

Candidate	Votes	%
Islam Karimov (Movement of Entrepreneurs and Businessmen—Liberal Democratic Party of Uzbekistan)	13,008,357	88.10
Asliddin Rustamov (People's Democratic Party of Uzbekistan)	468,064	3.17
Dilorom Tashmuhamedova (Justice Social Democratic Party of Uzbekistan)	434,111	2.94
Akmal Saidov (Independent)	420,815	2.85
Total*	14,765,444	100.00

*Including 434,097 invalid votes (2.94% of the total).

Legislature

The Oliy Majlis (Supreme Assembly) is a bicameral legislative body, comprising the 100-member upper chamber, the Senat (Senate), and the 150-member lower chamber, the Qonunchilik palatasi (Legislative Chamber).

Qonunchilik palatasi
(Legislative Chamber)

100008 Tashkent, Xalqlar Do'stligi shoh ko'ch. 1; tel. (71) 239-87-07; fax (71) 239-41-51; internet www.parliament.gov.uz.

Speaker: DILOROM H. TASHMUHAMEDOVA.

UZBEKISTAN

General Election, 27 December 2009 and 10 January 2010

Parties and groups	Seats
Movement of Entrepreneurs and Businessmen—Liberal Democratic Party of Uzbekistan	53
People's Democratic Party of Uzbekistan	32
National Revival Democratic Party of Uzbekistan (Milliy Tiklanish)	31
Justice Social Democratic Party of Uzbekistan (Adolat)	19
Total*	**150**

*Including 15 seats reserved for members of the Ecological Movement of Uzbekistan.

Senat
(Senate)

100029 Tashkent, Mustaqillik maydoni 6; tel. (71) 238-26-66; fax (71) 238-29-01; e-mail info@senat.uz; internet www.senat.uz.

Of the 100 members of the chamber, 84 members are indirectly elected by regional Council members and 16 are appointed by the President of the Republic. Following the indirect elections of senators, conducted on 20–22 January 2010, the presidential appointees to the Senat were announced on 22 January.

Speaker: ILGIZAR M. SOBIROV.

Election Commission

Central Election Commission (O'zbekiston Respublikasi Markaziy Saylov Kommissiyasi): 100000 Tashkent; tel. (71) 239-15-72; fax (71) 239-43-91; internet www.elections.uz; mems approved by the Oliy Majlis; Chair. MIRZO-ULUG'BEK E. ABDUSALOMOV.

Political Organizations

Following Uzbekistan's independence (achieved in August 1991), the ruling People's Democratic Party of Uzbekistan (PDPU—the successor to the Communist Party of the Uzbek SSR) took increasingly repressive measures against opposition and Islamist parties. A new law on political parties was approved in 1996; among other provisions, the law prohibited the establishment of parties on a religious or ethnic basis and stipulated a minimum membership, per party, of 5,000 people (with stipulation that membership be distributed across the country's regions). The Movement of Entrepreneurs and Businessmen—Liberal Democratic Party of Uzbekistan, which effectively succeeded the PDPU as the 'party of power' in the 2000s (although the PDPU continued to play a substantial role in national life), continued to implement similarly restrictive policies. From February 2004 the minimum membership requirement was increased to 20,000 people. The Ecological Movement of Uzbekistan, founded in 2008, has a reserved allocation of 15 seats in the Oliy Majlis, with effect from the legislative elections of December 2009–January 2010. Since independence a number of opposition elements have been based abroad, particularly in Russia.

Ecological Movement of Uzbekistan (O'zbekiston Ekologik Harakati): 100000 Tashkent, Bunyodkor ko'ch. 1A; tel. (71) 227-44-95; fax (71) 245-96-32; e-mail info@eco.uz; internet www.eco.uz; f. 2008; holds legal entitlement to 15 reserved seats in the Oliy Majlis; Chair. BORIY B. ALIXONOV.

Free Peasants' Party (Ozod Dehqonlar partiyasi—Ozod Dehqonlar): 100000 Tashkent; f. 2003; denied registration; Exec. Sec. of Political Council NIGORA HIDOYATOVA; Ideological Leader BABUR MALIKOV (in USA).

Freedom Democratic Party of Uzbekistan (O'zbekiston Erk Demokratik Partiyasi—Erk): 100055 Tashkent, Ipakchi ko'ch. 38; tel. (71) 220-65-30; e-mail admin@uzbekistanerk.org; internet www.uzbekistanerk.com; f. 1990; banned in 1993; Chair. MUHAMMAD SALIH (based in Norway).

Justice Social Democratic Party of Uzbekistan ('Adolat' Sotsial Demokratik Partiyasi—Adolat): 100043 Tashkent, Novza ko'ch. 14; tel. and fax (71) 245-50-67; internet www.adolat.uz; f. 1995; advocates respect of human rights, improvement of social justice and consolidation of democratic reform; supports President Karimov; Pres. ISMOIL SAIFNAZAROV; 77,210 mems (2009).

Movement of Entrepreneurs and Businessmen—Liberal Democratic Party of Uzbekistan (Tadbirkorlar va Ishbilarmonlar Harakati—O'zbekiston Liberal Demokratik Partiyasi—O'zlidep): 100015 Tashkent, Mirobod tumani, Nukus ko'ch. 73A; tel. (71) 255-27-99; fax (71) 255-62-11; e-mail uzlidep@intal.uz; internet www.uzlidep.uz; f. 2003; supports President Karimov; Chair. MUXAMMADYUSUF M. TESHABAEV; 161,758 members (Aug. 2009).

National Revival Democratic Party of Uzbekistan (O'zbekiston Milliy Tiklanish Demokratik Partiyasi—Milliy Tiklanish): 100000 Tashkent, A. Navoiy ko'ch. 30; tel. (71) 239-45-77; fax (71) 239-45-53; internet www.new.uzmtdp.uz; f. 1995; supports President Karimov; merged with Self-Sacrificers' National Democratic Party 2008; Leader AXTAM S. TURSUNOV; 108,390 mems (Aug. 2009).

People's Democratic Party of Uzbekistan (O'zbekiston Xalq demokratik partiyasi): 100029 Tashkent, Mustaqillik maydoni 5/1; tel. (71) 239-83-11; fax (71) 233-59-34; internet www.xdp.uz; f. 1991; successor to Communist Party of the Uzbek SSR; Chair. of Bd LATIF GULYAMOV; 346,800 mems (Jul. 2009).

Unity People's Movement Party ('Birlik' Xalq Harakati Partiyasi—Birlik): c/o Union of Writers of Uzbekistan, 100000 Tashkent, Neru ko'ch. 1; tel. (71) 233-63-74; e-mail postmaster@harakat.net; internet www.birlik.net; f. 1988; leading opposition group, banned in 1992; registered as a social movement; refused registration as a political party 2004; Chair. Prof. ABDURAKHIM PULAT; Sec.-Gen. VASILA INOYATOVA.

The militant Islamist group **Islamic Movement of Uzbekistan (IMU)** was founded in 1999. It was banned by the Uzbek Government in 1999 and its leaders sentenced to death *in absentia* in 2000. The IMU's activities were believed to have been seriously curtailed after the death of one its leaders during the US-led military campaign in Afghanistan that commenced in late 2001. The transnational militant Islamist **Hizb-ut-Tahrir al-Islami (Party of Islamic Liberation)** was believed to operate in Uzbekistan. As in neighbouring states, the organization was proscribed in Uzbekistan. Another Islamist organization, **Akromiya**, also banned, was founded in 1996 by AKROM YO'LDOSHEV, who received a 17-year sentence of imprisonment in 1999 for involvement in terrorist activity.

Diplomatic Representation

EMBASSIES IN UZBEKISTAN

Afghanistan: 100000 Tashkent, Kichik Beshyog ko'ch. 79; tel. (71) 134-84-32; fax (71) 234-84-65; e-mail afgemuz@mail.tps.uz; Ambassador BARYALAI SABIR BARYA.

Algeria: 100000 Tashkent, Beshog'aynilar ko'ch. 46; tel. (71) 235-52-99; fax (71) 235-21-99; Ambassador RAMDANE MEKDOUD.

Azerbaijan: 100000 Tashkent, Sharq Tongi ko'ch. 25; tel. (71) 273-61-67; fax (71) 273-26-58; e-mail sefiruz@gmail.com; internet www.azembassy.uz; Ambassador NAMIQ ABBASOV.

Bangladesh: 100015 Tashkent, Vasit Vaxidov ko'ch. 33; tel. (71) 150-21-18; fax (71) 120-67-11; e-mail bdoottas@yahoo.com; internet www.bangladeshembtashkent.uz; Ambassador MOHAMMED IMRAN.

Belarus: 100047 Tashkent, Ya. G'ulomov ko'ch. 75; tel. (71) 120-75-11; fax (71) 120-72-53; e-mail uzbekistan@belembassy.org; internet www.uzbekistan.belembassy.org; Ambassador IGOR S. SOKOL.

Bulgaria: 100031 Tashkent, Rakatboshi ko'ch. 52; tel. (71) 258-48-88; fax (71) 120-33-73; e-mail misiyabg@bcc.com.uz; internet www.mfa.bg/bg/68/; Ambassador ILKO D. SLAVCHEV.

China, People's Republic: 100047 Tashkent, Ya. G'ulomov ko'ch. 79; tel. (71) 233-80-88; fax (71) 233-47-35; e-mail chinaemb@bcc.com.uz; internet uz.china-embassy.org; Ambassador YU HONGJUN.

Czech Republic: 100041 Tashkent, Navnixol ko'ch. 6; tel. (71) 120-60-71; fax (71) 120-60-75; e-mail tashkent@embassy.mzv.cz; internet www.mzv.cz/tashkent; Ambassador ROBERT KOPECKÝ.

Egypt: 100115 Tashkent, Chilonzor ko'ch. 53A; tel. (71) 120-50-08; fax (71) 120-64-52; e-mail egyptianembassytashkant@yahoo.com; Ambassador ABDULKADIR AL-HASHSHAB MOHAMAD.

France: 100041 Tashkent, Oxunboboev ko'ch. 25; tel. (71) 233-53-82; fax (71) 233-62-10; e-mail presse@ambafrance-uz.org; internet www.ambafrance-uz.org; Ambassador FRANÇOIS GAUTHIER.

Georgia: 100170 Tashkent, Polkovnik A. Muxitdinov ko'ch. 6; tel. (71) 262-62-43; fax (71) 262-91-39; e-mail tashkent.emb@mfa.gov.ge; internet www.uzbekistan.mfa.gov.ge; Ambassador GIORGI KUBLASHVILI.

Germany: 100017 Tashkent, Sh. Rashidov ko'ch. 15, POB 4337; tel. (71) 120-84-40; fax (71) 120-66-93; e-mail info@taschkent.diplo.de; internet www.taschkent.diplo.de; Ambassador WOLFGANG NEUN.

Holy See: 100000 Tashkent, Musakhanov ko'ch. 80/1; tel. and fax (71) 233-70-25; Apostolic Nuncio (vacant).

India: 100000 Tashkent, Qarabuloq ko'ch. 15–16; tel. (71) 140-09-83; fax (71) 140-09-99; e-mail indhoc@buzton.com; internet www.indembassy.uz; Ambassador (vacant).

Indonesia: 100000 Tashkent, Ya. G'ulomov ko'ch. 73; tel. (71) 232-02-36; fax (71) 220-65-40; e-mail tashkent@indonesia.embassy.uz;

UZBEKISTAN

internet www.kbri-tashkent.go.id; Ambassador Asruchin Mohamad.

Iran: 100007 Tashkent, Parkent ko'ch. 20; tel. (71) 268-69-68; fax (71) 220-67-61; e-mail iriemuz@hotmail.com; Ambassador Mohammad Gholamali Keshavarzzadeh.

Israel: 100000 Tashkent, A. Qaxxor ko'ch. 3; tel. (71) 120-58-09; fax (71) 120-58-12; e-mail ambassador-sec@tashkent.mfa.gov.il; internet tashkent.mfa.gov.il; Ambassador Hillel Neuman.

Italy: 100031 Tashkent, Yusuf Xos Xojib ko'ch. 40; tel. (71) 252-11-19; fax (71) 220-66-06; e-mail segreteria.tashkent@esteri.it; internet www.ambtashkent.esteri.it; Ambassador Giovanni Ricciulli.

Japan: 100047 Tashkent, S. Azimov ko'ch., 1-tor 28; tel. (71) 120-80-60; fax (71) 120-80-77; internet www.uz.emb-japan.go.jp; Ambassador Yoshihisa Kuroda.

Jordan: 100000 Tashkent, Dipvilla, Farxod ko'ch. 9; tel. (71) 274-24-79; fax (71) 140-11-44; e-mail jordanembuzb@mail.ru; Chargé d'affaires a.i. Muwaffaq Mohammad Ahmed Ajlouni.

Kazakhstan: 100015 Tashkent, Chexov ko'ch. 23; tel. (71) 252-16-54; fax (71) 252-16-50; e-mail info@kazembassy.uz; internet www.kazembassy.uz; Ambassador Boribai Jeksembin.

Korea, Democratic People's Republic: 100000 Tashkent, Usmon Nosir ko'ch. 95A; tel. (71) 250-59-44; fax (71) 250-27-99; Ambassador Lee Don Pal.

Korea, Republic: 100000 Tashkent, Afrosiyob ko'ch. 7; tel. (71) 252-31-51; fax (71) 140-02-48; e-mail uzkoremb@mofat.go.kr; internet uzb.mofat.go.kr; Ambassador Chon De-Wan.

Kuwait: 100000 Tashkent, Batumskaya ko'ch. 2; tel. (71) 120-58-88; fax (71) 120-84-96; Ambassador Khalaf Budhair.

Kyrgyzstan: 100000 Tashkent, X. Samatova ko'ch. 30; tel. (71) 237-47-94; fax (71) 220-72-94; e-mail erkindik@sarkor.uz; Ambassador Anvarbek M Mokeyev.

Latvia: 100000 Tashkent, A. Lashkarbegi ko'ch. 16A; tel. (71) 237-22-15; fax (71) 120-70-36; e-mail embassy.uzbekistan@mfa.gov.lv; Ambassador Igors Apokins.

Malaysia: 100031 Tashkent, M. Yaqubova ko'ch. 30; tel. (71) 256-30-27; fax (71) 252-30-71; e-mail maltskent@kln.gov.my; internet www.kln.gov.my/web/uzb_tashkent; Ambassador Abdul Aziz Bin Harun.

Pakistan: 100115 Tashkent, Kichik Xalqa Yo'li ko'ch. 15; tel. (71) 248-86-49; fax (71) 120-49-21; e-mail parepuzb2006@yahoo.co; internet www.mofa.gov.pk/uzbekistan; Ambassador Mohammad Waheed-ul-Hasan.

Poland: 100084 Tashkent, Firdavsiy ko'ch. 66; tel. (71) 120-86-50; fax (71) 120-86-51; e-mail ambasada@bcc.com.uz; internet www.taszkent.polemb.net; Ambassador (vacant).

Romania: 100000 Tashkent, Rejametov ko'ch. 44A; tel. (71) 252-63-55; fax (71) 120-75-67; e-mail romanian_embassy@sarkor.uz; internet www.romania.uz; Chargé d'affaires a.i. Florin Alin Barbu.

Russia: 100015 Tashkent, Nukus ko'ch. 83; tel. (71) 120-35-02; fax (71) 120-35-09; e-mail embassy@russia.uz; internet www.russia.uz; Ambassador Vladimir L. Tyurdenev.

Saudi Arabia: 100000 Tashkent, Bobur ko'ch. 3 A; tel. (71) 281-51-01; fax (71) 281-51-06; e-mail uzemb@mofa.gov.sa; Ambassador Ibrahim Mansour al-Mansour.

Slovakia: 100070 Tashkent, Kichik Beshyog ko'ch. 38; tel. (71) 159-01-02; fax (71) 140-03-39; e-mail emb.tashkent@mzv.sk; internet www.tashkent.mfa.sk; Ambassador Jozef Mačisák.

Switzerland: 100070 Tashkent, Sh. Rustaveli ko'ch., tupik 1/4; tel. (71) 120-67-38; fax (71) 120-62-59; e-mail tas.vertretung@eda.admin.ch; internet www.eda.admin.ch/tashkent; Ambassador Anne Bauty.

Tajikistan: 100000 Tashkent, A. Kaxxor ko'ch., 6-chi tor, 61; tel. (71) 254-99-66; fax (71) 254-89-69; e-mail tajembasy_uz@mail.ru; Ambassador Muzaffar Huseinov.

Turkey: 100000 Tashkent, Ya. G'ulomov ko'ch. 87; tel. (71) 113-03-00; fax (71) 113-03-33; e-mail turemb@bcc.com.uz; internet tashkent.emb.mfa.gov.tr; Ambassador Mehmet Sertac Sunmezai.

Turkmenistan: 100000 Tashkent, Afrosiab ko'ch. 19; tel. (71) 256-94-02; fax (71) 256-94-03; Ambassador Soltan Pirmuhamedov.

Ukraine: 100000 Tashkent, Ya. G'ulomov ko'ch. 68; tel. (71) 236-08-12; fax (71) 233-10-89; e-mail ukremb@albatros.uz; internet www.mfa.gov.ua/uzbekistan; Ambassador Yurii V. Savchenko.

United Kingdom: 100000 Tashkent, ul. Ya. G'ulomov ko'ch. 67; tel. (71) 120-15-00; fax (71) 120-15-20; e-mail brit@emb.uz; internet ukinuzbekistan.fco.gov.uk; Ambassador Rupert Joy.

USA: 100093 Tashkent, Moyqurg'on ko'ch. 3, Yunusobod District; tel. (71) 120-54-50; fax (71) 120-63-35; e-mail tashkentinfo@state.gov; internet uzbekistan.usembassy.gov; Chargé d'affaires Duane C. Butcher.

Viet Nam: 100000 Tashkent, Sh. Rashidov ko'ch. 100; tel. (71) 234-03-93; fax (71) 120-62-65; e-mail dsqvntas@online.ru; Ambassador Le Van Toan.

Judicial System

Supreme Court (O'zbekiston Respublikasi Oliy sud): 100000 Tashkent, A. Qodiriy ko'ch. 1; tel. and fax (71) 244-62-93; internet www.supcourt.uz; Chair. Buritosh M. Mustafaev.

Office of the Prosecutor-General: 100000 Tashkent, Ya. G'ulomov ko'ch. 66; tel. (71) 233-20-66; Prosecutor-Gen. Rashidjon H. Qodirov.

Constitutional Court (Konstitutsiyaviy sud): 100087 Tashkent, Mustaqillik maydoni 6; tel. (71) 239-80-20; fax (71) 239-86-36; e-mail interconcourt@sarkor.uz; Chair. (vacant); Dep. Chair. Bakhtiyar Mirbabaev.

Supreme Economic Court (Oliy Xo'jalik Sudi): 100097 Tashkent, Cho'ponota ko'ch. 6; tel. (71) 267-36-18; fax (71) 273-84-78; e-mail economical-court@sarkor.uz; internet www.economical-court.uz; Chair. Dilmurad A. Mirzakarimov.

Religion

The Constitution of 8 December 1992 stipulates that, while there is freedom of worship and expression, there may be no state religion or ideology. A new law on religion was adopted in May 1998, which severely restricted the activities of religious organizations.

The most widespread religion in Uzbekistan is Islam; the majority of ethnic Uzbeks are Sunni Muslims (Hanafi school), but the number of Salafi communities is increasing. At 1 October 2002 there were 1,965 Islamic organizations registered in Uzbekistan, including 11 educational institutions. Most ethnic Slavs in Uzbekistan are adherents of Orthodox Christianity; there were 36 Russian Orthodox organizations registered in Uzbekistan at October 2002. At the end of 1993 there were some 32,000 Jews in Uzbekistan; many Jews have since emigrated to Israel.

State Committee for Religious Affairs: 100159 Tashkent, Mustaqillik 5; tel. and fax (71) 239-17-63; e-mail info@religions.uz; internet www.religions.uz; f. 1992; Chair. Artikbek Yusupov (acting).

ISLAM

Muslim Board of Uzbekistan (O'zbekiston Musulmonlari Idorasi): 100002 Tashkent, Zarkainar ko'ch. 103, Madrese 'Barakhan'; tel. (71) 240-39-33; fax (71) 240-08-31; internet www.muslim.uz; f. 1943 (as Muslim Board of Central Asia and Kazakhstan, covering the Kazakh, Kyrgyz, Tajik, Turkmen and Uzbek SSRs); Chair. Chief Mufti Usmonxon Olimov.

CHRISTIANITY

Roman Catholic Church

The Church is represented in Uzbekistan by an Apostolic Administration, established in April 2005. There were an estimated 4,000 adherents at 31 December 2008.

Apostolic Administrator: Most Rev. Jerzy Maculewicz (Titular Bishop of Nara), 100047 Tashkent, Musahanov ko'ch. 80/1; tel. (71) 233-70-25; fax (71) 233-70-35; e-mail adm.ap@mail.ru; internet catholic.uz.

Russian Orthodox Church (Moscow Patriarchate)

Eparchy of Tashkent and Central Asia (Moscow Patriarchate)—Orthodox Church of Central Asia: 100047 Tashkent, S. Azimov ko'ch. 22/3D; tel. (71) 233-33-21; fax (71) 236-79-39; e-mail church@albatros.uz; internet www.pravoslavie.uz; Metropolitan of Tashkent and Central Asia Vladimir (Ikim); has jurisdiction over Kyrgyzstan, Tajikistan and Uzbekistan.

JUDAISM

Chief Rabbi: Rabbi David Gurevich, 100100 Tashkent, Shohzhahon ko'ch. 30; tel. (71) 252-59-78; fax (71) 220-64-31; e-mail jewish@jewish.uz; internet www.jewish.uz.

The Press

The publications listed below are in Uzbek, unless otherwise stated.

UZBEKISTAN

REGULATORY AUTHORITY

Uzbek Agency for Press and Information (O'zAAA) (O'zbekiston Aloqa Va Axborotlashtirash Agentligi): 100011 Tashkent, Navoiy ko'ch. 28A; tel. (71) 238-41-07; fax (71) 239-87-82; e-mail info@aci.uz; internet aci.uz; f. 2002; Gen. Dir Hakim A. Mukhitdinov.

PRINCIPAL NEWSPAPERS

XXI ASR (21st Century): 100000 Tashkent, Nukus ko'ch. 73A; tel. and fax (371) 281-40-17; fax (371) 215-63-80; e-mail axborotXXIasr@yahoo.com; internet www.21asr.uz; f. 2003; in Uzbek; weekly; Chief Editor Mirodil Abdurahmonov.

Adolat (Justice): 100043 Tashkent, Novza ko'ch. 14; tel. and fax (71) 245-50-67; f. 1995; organ of the Justice Social Democratic Party of Uzbekistan (Adolat) (q.v.); weekly; Editor Tohtamurod Toshev; circ. 5,900.

Biznes-vestnik Vostoka (Business Herald of the East): 100029 Tashkent, Buxoro ko'ch. 26; tel. (71) 232-27-30; fax (71) 236-00-55; e-mail bvv-info@mail.ru; f. 1991; 2 a week; in Russian; economic and financial news; also weekly English edition, *BVV Business Report*; circ. 8,000.

Ekonomicheskoye Obozreniye (Economic Survey): 100070 Tashkent, Usman Nosir ko'ch., 1 tupik, 5; tel. (71) 150-02-02; fax (71) 361-45-48; e-mail review@cer.uz; internet www.review.uz; f. 1998; weekly; economics, politics, civil society, finance.

Inson va Qonun (Person and Law): 100047 Tashkent, Sayilgoh ko'ch. 5; tel. (71) 233-95-31; e-mail info@press-iq.uz; internet www.minjust.uz/uz/group.scm?groupId=4146; weekly; organ of the Ministry of Justice (q.v.); Editor-in-Chief Ko'chqor Norqobil.

Ma'rifat (Enlightenment): 100000 Tashkent, Matbuotchilar ko'ch. 32; tel. (71) 233-50-55; e-mail mariat@ars-inform.uz; internet www.marifat.uz; f. 1931; 2 a week; in Uzbek and Russian; Editor Khalim Saidov; circ. 33,000 (2006).

Mulkdor (The Proprietor): 100083 Tashkent, Buyuk Turon ko'ch. 41; tel. (71) 239-21-96; f. 1994; weekly; Editor-in-Chief Mirodil Abdurakhmanov; circ. 10,000.

Novyi Vek (New Age): 100060 Tashkent, Movarounnaxr ko'ch. 19; tel. (71) 233-48-55; fax (71) 233-76-84; f. 1992; fmrly *Kommercheskii Vestnik* (Commerical Herald); in Russian; weekly; Editor Valerii Niyazmatov; circ. 22,000.

O'zbekiston Adabiyoti va San'ati (Literature and Art of Uzbekistan): 100000 Tashkent, Matbuotchilar ko'ch. 32; tel. (71) 233-52-91; f. 1956; weekly; organ of the Union of Writers of Uzbekistan; Editor Akhmajon Meliboyev; circ. 10,300.

O'zbekiston ovozi/ Golos Uzbekistana (Voice of Uzbekistan): 100000 Tashkent, Matbuotchilar ko'ch. 32; tel. 236-55-17; fax 233-72-83; e-mail info@uzbekistonovozi.uz; internet www.uzbekistonovozi.uz; f. 1918; Uzbek and Russian edns; organ of the People's Democratic Party of Uzbekistan; Editor-in-Chief Safar Ostonov.

Postda/ Na postu: 100029 Tashkent, Yu. Rajaby ko'ch. 1; tel. (71) 254-37-91; fax (71) 232-05-51; e-mail postda08@mail.ru; f. 1930; in Uzbek and Russian; military; weekly; Editor Z. Nematov.

Pravda Vostoka (Truth of the East): 100000 Tashkent, Matbuotchilar ko'ch. 32; tel. (71) 236-57-12; fax (71) 233-70-98; e-mail pvbox@mail.ru; internet www.pv.uz; f. 1917; 5 a week; in Russian; organ of the Cabinet of Ministers; Editor Abbaskhan Usmanov; circ. 16,000.

Savdogar (The Trader): 100000 Tashkent, Buyuk Turon ko'ch. 41; tel. (71) 233-34-55; f. 1992; economy and commerce; Editor Muhammad Orazmetov; circ. 17,000.

Sport: 100167 Tashkent, E. Bobohon ko'ch. 67A; tel. (71) 244-17-37; fax (71) 244-06-69; f. 1932; Editor Haydar Akbarov; circ. 8,490.

Toshkent Haqiqati/ Tashkentskaya Pravda (Tashkent Truth): 100000 Tashkent, Matbuotchilar ko'ch. 32; tel. (71) 233-64-95; fax (71) 233-58-85; internet www.th.uz; f. 1954; 2 a week; Uzbek and Russian edns; Editor Fatkhiddin Mukhitdinov; circ. 19,000 (Uzbek edn), 6,400 (Russian edn).

Turkiston (Turkestan): 100083 Tashkent, Matbuotchilar ko'ch. 32; tel. (71) 233-95-97; f. 1925 as *Yash Leninchy* (Young Leninist), renamed as above 1992; 2 a week; organ of the Kamolot Asscn of Youth of Uzbekistan; Editor Gafar Khatomov; circ. 8,000 (2010).

UzReport: 100000 Tashkent, Buxoro ko'ch. 26; tel. (71) 232-27-29; fax (71) 236-00-55; e-mail info@corp.uzreport.com; internet www.uzreport.com; online only; in Uzbek, Russian and English; business, economics; f. 1999.

Vatanparvar (The Patriot): 100000 Tashkent, Ak. Abdullaev ko'ch. 100; tel. (71) 269-82-43; fax (71) 269-82-28; f. 1992; fmrly *Frunzevets* (Supporter of Frunze); publ. by Ministry of Defence (q.v.); weekly.

Xalk So'zi/ Narodnoye Slovo (People's Word): 100000 Tashkent, Matbuotchilar ko'ch. 32; tel. (71) 233-15-22; e-mail info@narodnoeslovo.uz; internet www.narodnoeslovo.uz; f. 1991; Uzbek and Russian edns; 5 a week (Uzbek), weekly (Russian); organ of the Oliy Majlis and the Cabinet of Ministers; Editor Abbaskhon Usmanov; circ. 41,580 (Uzbek edn), 12,750 (Russian edn).

Xamkor/ Delovoi Partner/ Business Partner: 100084 Tashkent, Amir Temir ko'ch. 107A; tel. (71) 138-59-77; fax (71) 138-58-23; f. 1990; weekly; Uzbek, Russian and English edns; circ. 4,735.

Xurriiat (Freedom): 100000 Tashkent; tel. (71) 244-25-06; fax (71) 244-36-16; e-mail amir@uzpac.uz; f. 1996; weekly; independent; circ. 5,000.

PRINCIPAL PERIODICALS

Monthly, unless otherwise indicated.

Erk (Freedom): 100055 Tashkent, Ipakchi ko'ch. 38; tel. (71) 220-65-30; e-mail erkgazetasi@yahoo.com; organ of Freedom Democratic Party of Uzbekistan (Erk) (q.v.); f. 1991; 4 a month; Uzbek and Russian edns; circ. 5,300 (2007).

Fan va turmush/ Nauka i Zhizn Uzbekistana (Science and Life): 100052 Tashkent, Ya. G'ulomov ko'ch. 70; tel. (71) 233-50-33; fax (71) 236-00-37; e-mail shuhrat@astrin.uzsci.net; f. 1933 as *Sosialistik ilm va Texnika* (Socialist Science and Technology); every 2 months; Uzbek and Russian edns; publ. by the Fan (Science) Publishing House; popular scientific; Editor Prof. Shuxrat A. Egamberdiev; circ. 28,000.

Guliston: 100000 Tashkent, Buyuk Turon ko'ch. 41; tel. (71) 236-78-90; f. 1925; present name adopted 1967; every 2 months; sociopolitical, literary; Editor-in-Chief Azim Suyun; circ. 4,000.

Gulxan (Bonfire): 100129 Tashkent, Navoiy ko'ch. 30; tel. (71) 236-78-85; f. 1929; monthly; illustrated juvenile fiction; Editor Ashurali Dzhuraev; circ. 26,000.

Guncha (Small Bud): 700129 Tashkent, Navoiy ko'ch. 30; tel. (71) 236-78-80; e-mail guncha_2010@bk.ru; internet www.guncha.uz; f. 1958; monthly; illustrated; for pre-school-age children; Editor Dilfuza Shomalikova; circ. 35,000.

Ijtimoij fikr/ Obshchestvennoe mneniye. Prava Cheloveka (Public Opinion. Human Rights): 100029 Tashkent, Mustaqilliq maidoni 5/3; tel. (71) 239-84-29; fax (71) 239-85-48; e-mail info@ijtimoiy-fikr.uz; internet www.ijtimoiy-fikr.uz; f. 1998; 4 a year; in Uzbek, Russian and English; publ. by the Republican Centre for the Study of Public Opinion and National Human Rights Centre; Editor Amal H. Saidov.

Jahon Adabiyoti (World Literature): 100129 Tashkent, Navoiy ko'ch. 30; tel. (71) 244-41-60; fax (71) 244-41-61; f. 1997; Editor Mupriyrat Mupzaeb; circ. 2,000.

Oila va zhamiiat (Family and Society): 100129 Tashkent, Navoiy ko'ch. 30; tel. and fax (71) 139-40-12; e-mail womancomitet@mail.ru; internet www.womancomitet.narod.ru; f. 1991; weekly; publ. by Women's Committee of Uzbekistan; in Uzbek.

San'at (Art): 100029 Tashkent, Mustaqilliq maidoni 2; tel. (71) 239-44-51; fax (71) 239-46-86; e-mail bientash@globalnet.uz; internet sanat.orexca.com; f. 1997; 4 a year; publ. by Academy of the Arts of Uzbekistan; Uzbek, Russian and English edns; illustrated journal about the arts and crafts; Editor-in-Chief Juliya Syrtsova.

Saodat (Happiness): 100083 Tashkent, Buyuk Turon ko'ch. 41; tel. (71) 233-68-10; f. 1925; 8 a year; women's popular; Editor Oidin Khajiyeva; circ. 70,000.

Sikhat-salomatlik (Health): 100000 Tashkent, Parkent ko'ch. 51; tel. (71) 268-17-54; f. 1990; every 2 months; Editor Damin A. Asadov; circ. 36,000.

Tafakkur (Contemplation): 100000 Tashkent, Movaraunnakhr ko'ch.; f. 1994; 4 a year; literary; organ of the (state-controlled) Republican Committee for Spirituality and Enlightenment; Editor-in-Chief Erkin A'zam.

NEWS AGENCIES

Jahon (World) Information Agency: 100029 Tashkent, O'zbekiston shoh ko'ch. 9; tel. (71) 233-65-91; fax (71) 220-64-43; e-mail aajahon@mfa.uz; internet jahon.mfa.uz; information agency of Ministry of Foreign Affairs; Dir Abror Gulyamov.

Press-UZ.info: Tashkent; e-mail admin@press-uz.info; internet www.press-uz.info; f. 2005; independent; news from Uzbekistan, Central Asia and Russia, in Uzbek, Russian and English.

Uzbekistan National News Agency (UzA): 100000 Tashkent, Buyuk Nuron ko'ch. 41; tel. (71) 233-16-22; fax (71) 233-24-45; internet www.uza.uz; Dir Mamatskul Khazratskulov.

Publishers

Uzbek Agency for Press and Information: 100129 Tashkent, A. Navoiy ko'ch. 30; tel. (71) 244-32-87; fax (71) 244-14-84; e-mail ozmaa@uzpak.uz; internet www.uzapi.gov.uz; f. 2002; mass media,

UZBEKISTAN

press and information exchange; printing, publishing and distribution of periodicals; Gen. Dir BABUR ALIMOV.

Chulpon (Morning Star) Publishers: 100129 Tashkent, A. Navoiy ko'ch. 30; tel. (71) 239-13-75; fax (71) 244-20-52; e-mail chulpan@sarkor.uz; internet www.chulpon.uz; Dir R. ZAPAROV.

Fan (Science) Publishers: 100047 Tashkent, Ya. G'ulomov ko'ch. 70/102; tel. (71) 233-69-61; scientific books and journals; Dir N. T. KHATAMOV.

Gafur Gulom Publishing House: 100129 Tashkent, A. Navoiy ko'ch. 30; tel. (71) 244-22-53; fax (71) 241-35-47; f. 1957; fiction, the arts; books in Uzbek, Russian and English; Dir MIZROB M. BURONOV; Editor-in-Chief NAZIRA J. JURAYEVNA.

Mekhnat (Labour) Publishers: 100129 Tashkent, A. Navoiy ko'ch. 30; tel. (71) 244-22-27; f. 1985; Dir RUSTAM A. MIRZAYEV.

O'qituvchi (Teacher) Publishing-Printing and Creative House: 100129 Tashkent, A. Navoiy ko'ch. 30; tel. and fax (71) 244-26-89; f. 1936; literary textbooks, education manuals, popular science, juvenile; Dir R. O. MIRZAYEV.

O'zbekiston Milliy Entsiklopediyasi (Uzbekistan National Encyclopedias): 100129 Tashkent, A. Navoiy ko'ch. 30; tel. (71) 244-34-38; fax (71) 244-24-91; e-mail ume2@yandex.ru; internet www.ensiklopediya.uz; f. 1997; encyclopedias, dictionaries and reference books; Dir N. TUKHLIYEV.

O'zbekiston (Uzbekistan) Publishing and Printing Creative House: 100129 Tashkent, A. Navoiy ko'ch. 30; tel. (71) 244-34-01; fax (71) 244-38-10; e-mail aptpk@ars-inform.uz; f. 2004; politics, economics, law, history, art, illustrated, manuals and textbooks for schools and higher educational institutes; Dir ZAIR T. ISADJANOV; Editor-in-Chief SHOMUXITDIN SH. MANSUROV.

Yozuvchi (Writer) Publishers: 100129 Tashkent, A. Navoiy ko'ch. 30; tel. (71) 244-29-97; f. 1990; Dir M. U. TOICHIYEV.

Broadcasting and Communications

TELECOMMUNICATIONS

Communications and Information Agency of Uzbekistan (O'zbekiston Aloqa va Axborotlashtirish Agentligi): 100011 Tashkent, A. Navoiy ko'ch. 28A; tel. (71) 233-65-03; fax (71) 239-87-82; e-mail info@aci.uz; internet www.aci.uz; Dir-Gen. ABDULLA N. ARIPOV.

Service Providers

Coscom: 100031 Tashkent, V. Vaxidov ko'ch. 118; tel. (71) 252-15-51; fax (71) 220-72-65; e-mail inform@coscom.uz; internet www.coscom.uz; f. 1996; Uzbekistani-US jt venture; mobile cellular telecommunications.

Unitel (Beeline): 100000 Tashkent, Buxoro ko'ch. 1; tel. (71) 233-33-30; fax (71) 232-12-22; internet www.beeline.uz; f. 1996; fmrly Daewoo Unitel; subsidiary of VympelKom-Bilain (Russia); mobile cellular telecommunications; more than 1m. subscribers (2007).

Uzbektelecom: 100000 Tashkent, Amir Temur ko'ch. 24; tel. (71) 233-42-59; fax (71) 236-01-88; e-mail uztelecom@intal.uz; internet www.uztelecom.uz; f. 2000; provides local, regional and international telecommunications services; partial privatization pending; Gen. Dir KH. A. MUKHITDINOV.

Uzdunrobita: 100000 Tashkent, Amir Temur ko'ch. 24; tel. (97) 130-01-01; fax (97) 130-01-05; e-mail office@uzdunrobita.com.uz; internet www.uzdunrobita.uz; f. 1991; mobile cellular telecommunications; 74% owned by Mobile Telesystems (Russia); Gen. Dir BEKHZOD AKHMEDOV.

BROADCASTING

State Television and Radio Broadcasting Company of Uzbekistan (UZTELERADIO): 100011 Tashkent, A. Navoiy ko'ch. 69; tel. (71) 233-81-06; fax (71) 244-16-60; e-mail uztele@tkt.uz; local broadcasts, as well as relays from Egypt, France, India, Japan, Russia and Turkey; Chair. ALISHER KHUJAYEV.

Television

Kamalak Television: 100084 Tashkent, Amir Temur ko'ch. 109; tel. (71) 237-51-77; fax (71) 220-62-28; e-mail kam.tv@kamalak.co.uz; f. 1992; jt venture between State Television and Radio Broadcasting Company and a US company; satellite broadcasts; relays from France, Germany, India, Russia, the United Kingdom and the USA; Gen. Dir PULAT UMAROV.

Uzbekistan Television and Radio Company (Uzteleradio): 100011 Tashkent, A. Navoiy ko'ch. 69; tel. (71) 233-81-06; fax (71) 244-16-60; e-mail uztcint@hotmail.com; four local programmes as well as relays from Russia, Kazakhstan, Egypt, India and Turkey; Chair. ALISHER KHADJAYEV.

Finance

(cap. = capital; res = reserves; dep. = deposits; m. = million; amounts in Uzbek sum, unless otherwise stated; brs = branches)

BANKING

A reform of the banking sector was begun in 1994. A two-tier system was introduced, consisting of the Central Bank and about 30 commercial banks. An association of commercial banks was established in 1995 to co-ordinate the role of commercial banks in the national economy. At the end of 2002 there were reported to be 35 banks in Uzbekistan, of which 13 were under private ownership.

Central Bank

Central Bank of the Republic of Uzbekistan: 100001 Tashkent, O'zbekiston shoh ko'ch. 6; tel. and fax (71) 252-57-39; e-mail webmaster@cbu.st.uz; internet www.cbu.uz; f. 1991; Chair. of Bd FAIZULLA M. MULLAJONOV.

State Commercial Bank

National Bank for Foreign Economic Activity of the Republic of Uzbekistan (NBU) (O'zbekiston Respublikasi Tashqi Iqtisodiy Faoliyat Milliy Banki): 100047 Tashkent, Oxunbabaev ko'ch. 23; tel. (71) 137-59-70; fax (71) 133-32-00; e-mail webmaster@central.nbu.com; internet eng.nbu.com; f. 1991; cap. 22,386m., res 500,230m., dep. 2,046,165m. (Dec. 2008); Chair. SAIDAKHMAT B. RAKHIMOV; 95 brs.

State Joint-Stock Commercial Banks

Asaka—Specialized State Joint-Stock Commercial Bank: 100015 Tashkent, Nukus ko'ch. 67; tel. (71) 120-81-11; fax (71) 120-86-91; e-mail contact@asakabank.com; internet www.asakabank.com; f. 1995; cap. 40,701.9m., res 18,284.5m., dep. 1,255,219.9m. (Dec. 2008); 66.7% owned by Ministry of Finance; Chair. KAHRAMON T. ARIPOV; 27 brs.

Ipoteka Commercial Mortgage Bank: 100000 Tashkent, Pushkin ko'ch. 17; tel. (71) 233-11-22; fax (71) 150-89-35; e-mail info@ipotekabank.uz; internet www.ipotekabank.uz; f. 2005 by merger of UzJilSberBank and Zaminbank; cap. 30,417.7m., res 22,571.0m., dep. 402,897.4m. (Dec. 2007); Chair. of Bd ABDURASUL ABDULLAYEV; 38 brs.

Other Banks

Agrobank: 100096 Tashkent, Mukimi ko'ch. 43; tel. (71) 120-88-33; fax (71) 150-53-95; e-mail headoffice@agrobank.uz; internet www.agrobank.uz; f. 1995; cap. 75,751.7m., res 4,801.0m., dep. 818,804.3m. (Dec. 2008); fmrly Paxta Bank; present name adopted 2009; Chair. ABDURAXMAT BOYMURATOV; 187 brs.

Aloqabank: 100015 Tashkent, Tolstoy ko'ch. 1A; tel. (71) 252-78-74; fax (71) 252-75-11; e-mail alokauz@uzpak.uz; internet www.alokabank.uz; f. 1995; cap. 12,574.8m., dep. 21,190.2m., total assets 102,090.7m. (Dec. 2007); Chair. ABDULLA N. ARIPOV; 12 brs, 28 sub-brs (2007).

HamkorBank: 170111 Andijon, Babura ko'ch. 85; tel. (74) 224-76-88; fax (74) 224-73-83; e-mail info@hamkorbank.uz; internet www.hamkorbank.uz; f. 1991; Chair. SHAHRUH HAKIMOV; 25 brs.

Ipak Yuli Bank (Silk Road Bank): 100017 Tashkent, Kodiriy ko'ch. 2; tel. (71) 120-00-09; fax (71) 120-34-43; e-mail info@ipakyulibank.com; internet www.ipakyulibank.com; f. 2000; cap. 16,873.4m., dep 270,681.6m., total assets 302,328.3m. (Dec. 2008); Chair. of Bd RUSTAMBEK R. RAHIMBEKOV.

Microkreditbank: 100096 Tashkent, Lutfiy ko'ch. 14; tel. (71) 273-28-11; fax (71) 273-05-89; e-mail office@mikrokreditbank.uz; internet www.mikrokreditbank.uz; f. 2006; micro-credit bank; Chair. JAMSHED SAYFIDDINOV.

O'zsanoatkurilishbank (Uzpromstroibank) (Uzbek Industrial and Construction Bank): 100000 Tashkent, Shaxrisab ko'ch. 3; tel. (71) 120-45-01; fax (71) 233-34-26; e-mail info@uzpsb.uz; internet www.uzpsb.uz; f. 1922; cap. 47,822.6m., res 438.4m., dep. 674,482.2m. (Dec. 2007); Chair. of Managing Bd ABDURASUL N. ABDULLAEV; 49 brs, 100 sub-brs.

Qishloq Qurilish Bank (Rural Construction Bank): 100060 Tashkent, Lahuti ko'ch. 38; tel. and fax (71) 133-42-25; f. 2009 on basis of Galla Bank.

Savdogarbank: 100060 Tashkent, S. Barak ko'ch. 78; tel. (71) 281-30-29; fax (71) 256-56-71; internet www.savdogarbank.uz; Chair. MURSURMON N. NURMAMATOV.

Trustbank: 100038 Tashkent, A. Navoiy ko'ch. 7; tel. (71) 244-76-22; fax (71) 244-76-61; e-mail info@trustbank.uz; internet www.trustbank.uz; f. 1994; cap. 6,946.3m., dep. 198,503.9m., total assets 215,059.6m. (Dec. 2008); Chair. ILHOM F. SOLIYEV; 2 brs.

Turonbank: 100011 Tashkent, Abay 4A; tel. (71) 700-55-55; fax (71) 244-25-81; e-mail info@turonbank.uz; internet www.turonbank.uz;

UZBEKISTAN

f. 1990; cap. US $8m., res $1.7m., dep. $10.7m. (Jan. 2008); Chair. of Bd DANIYOR B. ARIFJANOV; 18 brs.

Uzbekistan-Turkish UT Bank: 100043 Tashkent, Xalqlar Do'stligi ko'ch. 15B; tel. (71) 273-83-25; fax (71) 220-63-62; e-mail utbank@utbk.com; internet www.utbk.com; f. 1993; 50% owned by Paxta Bank, 50% owned by Türkiye Cumhuriyeti Ziraat Bankası (Agricultural Bank of the Turkish Republic); cap. 2,608.8m., res 5,629.3m., dep. 45,408.0. (Dec. 2007); Chair. AZIM TANGIRBERDIEV.

INSURANCE

Ark Sug'urta: 100000 Tashkent, Pushkin ko'ch. 88; tel. (71) 267-73-19; fax (71) 267-70-28; e-mail info@arksugurta.uz; internet www.arksugurta.uz; f. 1991; life and non-life; Dir-Gen. ZAFAR O. TURSUNOV.

Ishonch: 100027 Tashkent, Xojaev ko'ch. 1 A; tel. and fax (71) 238-69-65; e-mail info@ishonch-iic.uz; internet www.ishonch-iic.uz; f. 1996; life and non-life; Dir-Gen. MIRSHAMSIDDIN M. XIKMATILLAEV.

Kalofat: 100000 Tashkent, Mustaqillik maydoni 5, 9th Floor; tel. (71) 233-26-98; fax (71) 233-38-49; internet www.kalofatdask.uz; f. 1997; life and non-life; Dir-Gen. SHERALI B. IMAMOV.

O'zbekinvest (Uzbekinvest) National Export–Import Insurance Co: 100017 Tashkent, Istiqlol ko'ch. 49; tel. (71) 235-78-01; fax (71) 235-94-09; e-mail office@uzbekinvest.uz; internet www.insurance.uz; f. 1994, restructured 1997; jt venture with American International Group (AIG—USA); cap. US $60m.; Dir-Gen. FAKHRITDIN SAIDAKHMEDOV.

Standard Insurance Group: 100015 Tashkent, Kunaev ko'ch. 25; tel. (71) 250-99-99; fax (71) 150-01-01; e-mail info@ingo.uz; internet www.sig-insurance.uz; f. 2005; non-life; Dir-Gen. UMUD U. KAMILOV.

Temir Yo'llari Sug'urta: 100060 Tashkent, Amir Temur ko'ch. 19; tel. (71) 236-01-68; fax (71) 233-05-31; e-mail mail@tys.uz; internet www.tys.uz; f. 2002; owned by O'zbekiston Temir Yo'llari (Uzbekistan State Railway Co); non-life; Dir-Gen. SUNNAT UMAROV.

COMMODITY EXCHANGE

Tashkent Republican Commodity and Raw Materials Exchange: 100003 Tashkent, O'zbekiston shoh ko'ch. 53; tel. (71) 239-83-77; fax (71) 239-83-92; Chair. of Bd NABIHON S. SAMATOV.

STOCK EXCHANGE

Tashkent Republican Stock Exchange (UZSE) (Respublika Fond Birjasi 'Toshkent'): 100047 Tashkent, Buxoro ko'ch. 10; tel. (71) 236-07-40; fax (71) 233-32-31; e-mail info@uzse.uz; internet www.uzse.uz; f. 1994; Chair. BAKHTIYOR I. KHUDOYAROV.

Trade and Industry

GOVERNMENT AGENCIES

Foreign Investment Agency: 100077 Tashkent, Buyuk Ipak Yuli ko'ch. 75; tel. (71) 268-77-05; fax (71) 267-07-52; e-mail afi@mail.uznet.net; Gen. Dir SHAZIYATOV S. SHOAZIZ.

State Committee for De-monopolization and the Development of Competition (O'zbekiston Respublikasi Monopoliadan Chiqarish va Raqobatni Rivojlantirish Davlat Qo'mitasi): 100011 Tashkent, A. Navoiy ko'ch. 18A; tel. (71) 239-15-42; e-mail devonhona@antimon.uz; internet www.antimon.uz; Chair. BAIMUROD S. ULASHOV (acting).

State Committee for the Management of State Property (State Property Committee): 100003 Tashkent, O'zbekiston shoh ko'ch. 55; tel. (71) 239-44-46; fax (71) 259-20-37; e-mail ves@gki.uz; internet www.gki.uz; f. 1994; Chair. DILSHOD O. MUSAEV.

CHAMBER OF COMMERCE

Chamber of Commerce and Industry of Uzbekistan (O'zbekiston Respublikasi Savdo-Sanoat Palatasi): 100047 Tashkent, Buxoro ko'ch. 6; tel. (71) 150-60-00; fax (71) 150-60-09; e-mail info@chamber.uz; internet www.chamber.uz; f. 1996; present name adopted 2004; Chair. ALISHER SHAIHOV.

STATE HYDROCARBONS COMPANY

Uzbekneftegaz (Uzbekistani Petroleum and Natural Gas Co): 100047 Tashkent, Akhunbabayev ko'ch. 21; tel. (71) 233-57-57; fax (71) 236-77-71; e-mail nhk@uzneftegaz.uz; internet www.uzneftegaz.uz; f. 1999; national petroleum and gas corpn; Dir SHOKIR N. FAYZULLAEV.

TRADE UNIONS

Federation of Trade Unions of Uzbekistan: 100000 Tashkent; Chair. of Council KHULKAR JAMALOV.

Transport

RAILWAYS

There were 3,645 km of track in 2007.

O'zbekiston Temir Yo'llari (Uzbekistan State Railway Co): 100060 Tashkent, T. Shevchenko ko'ch. 7; tel. (71) 238-80-00; fax (71) 233-45-49; e-mail gajk@uzrailway.uz; internet www.uzrailway.uz; f. 1994; state-owned joint-stock co; Chair. of Bd ACHILBAY ZH. RAMATOV.

Toshkent metropoliteni (Tashkent Metro): 100027 Tashkent, O'zbekiston shoh ko'ch. 93A; tel. (71) 232-38-52; fax (71) 233-66-81; e-mail metro@sarkor.uz; f. 1977; three lines with total length of 36 km, and fourth line under construction; Chair. M. A. ODILOV.

ROADS

In 1999 the total length of the road network was estimated at 81,600 km, of which 87.3% was paved.

CIVIL AVIATION

There is an international airport at Tashkent.

Uzbekistan Airways (Uzbekiston Havo Yollari): 100061 Tashkent, A. Timur ko'ch. 41; tel. and fax (71) 140-46-23; e-mail info@uzairways.com; internet www.uzairways.com; f. 1992; Dir-Gen. VALERIY TYAN.

Tourism

The country has more than 4,000 historical monuments, many of which are associated with the ancient 'Silk Road'. Uzbekistan received an estimated 1,069,300 foreign visitors (including excursionists) in 2008, when tourism receipts (excluding passenger transport) totalled US $64m.

Uzbektourism: 100047 Tashkent, Xorazm ko'ch. 47; tel. (71) 233-54-14; fax (71) 233-80-68; e-mail info@uzbektourism.uz; internet www.uzbektourism.uz; f. 1992; Chair. ZAHID L. XAKIMOV.

Defence

The establishment of Uzbekistani national armed forces was initiated in 1992. As assessed at November 2010, active armed forces numbered some 67,000, comprising an army of 50,000 and an air force of some 17,000. There were also paramilitary forces numbering up to 20,000 (comprising a 1,000-strong National Guard attached to the Ministry of Defence and up to 19,000 troops attached to the Ministry of Internal Affairs). Compulsory military service lasts for 12 months. In July 1994 Uzbekistan joined the North Atlantic Treaty Organization (NATO) 'Partnership for Peace' programme.

Defence Expenditure: Budgeted at 1,420,000m. sum in 2010.

Joint Chief of Staff of the Armed Forces: Maj.-Gen. V. MAHMUDOV.

Education

In the 1990s a greater emphasis on Uzbek history and literature was introduced in the education system. In 2006 some 89.2% of pupils were educated in Uzbek. Primary education, beginning at seven years of age, lasts for four years. Secondary education, beginning at 11 years of age, lasts for seven years, comprising a first cycle of five years and a second cycle of two years. In 2006/07 enrolment at primary schools was equivalent to 95% of children in the relevant age-group. In the same year secondary enrolment included 92% of children in the relevant age-group. In 2007 some 5.7m. pupils were enrolled in general secondary schools. A total of 263,600 students were enrolled at 63 institutions of higher education in 2004. The 2006 budget allocated 1,285,078.5m. sum (29.8% of total budgetary expenditure) to education.

VANUATU

Introductory Survey

LOCATION, CLIMATE, LANGUAGE, RELIGION, FLAG, CAPITAL

The Republic of Vanuatu comprises an irregular archipelago of 83 islands in the south-west Pacific Ocean, lying about 1,000 km (600 miles) west of Fiji and 400 km (250 miles) north-east of New Caledonia. The group extends over a distance of about 1,300 km (808 miles) from north to south. The islands have an oceanic tropical climate, with a season of south-east trade winds between May and October. Winds are variable, with occasional cyclones for the rest of the year, and annual rainfall varies between 2,300 mm (90 ins) in the south and 3,900 mm (154 ins) in the north. In Port Vila, in the centre of the group, mean temperatures vary between 22°C (72°F) and 27°C (81°F). The national language is Bislama, ni-Vanuatu pidgin. There are many Melanesian languages and dialects. English, French and Bislama are the official languages. Most of the inhabitants (about 80%) profess Christianity, of which a number of denominations are represented. The national flag (proportions 3 by 5) consists of two equal horizontal stripes, red above green, on which are superimposed a black-edged yellow horizontal 'Y' (with its base in the fly) and, at the hoist, a black triangle containing two crossed yellow mele leaves encircled by a curled yellow boar's tusk. The capital is Port Vila, on the island of Efate.

CONTEMPORARY POLITICAL HISTORY

Historical Context

During the 19th century the New Hebrides (now Vanuatu) were settled by British and French missionaries, planters and traders. The United Kingdom and France established a Joint Naval Commission for the islands in 1887. The two countries later agreed on a joint civil administration, and in 1906 the territory became the Anglo-French Condominium of the New Hebrides (Nouvelles-Hébrides). Under this arrangement, there were three elements in the structure of administration: the British National Service, the French National Service and the Condominium (Joint) Departments. Each power was responsible for its own citizens and other non-New Hebrideans who chose to be 'ressortissants' of either power. Indigenous New Hebrideans were not permitted to claim either British or French citizenship. This resulted in two official languages, two police forces, three public services, three courts of law, three currencies, three national budgets, two resident commissioners in Port Vila (the capital) and two district commissioners in each of the four Districts.

Domestic Political Affairs

Local political initiatives began after the Second World War, originating in New Hebridean concern over the alienation of native land. More than 36% of the New Hebrides was owned by foreigners. Na-Griamel, one of the first political groups to emerge, had its source in cult-like activities. In 1971 the leaders of Na-Griamel petitioned the UN to prevent further sales of land at a time when areas were being sold to US interests for development as tropical tourist resorts. In 1972 the New Hebrides National Party was formed, with support from Protestant missions and covert support from British interests. In response, French interests formed the Union des Communautés Néo-Hébridaises in 1974. In that year discussions in the United Kingdom resulted in the replacement of the Advisory Council, established in 1957, by a Representative Assembly of 42 members, of whom 29 were directly elected in November 1975. The Assembly did not hold its first full working session until November 1976, and it was dissolved in early 1977, following a boycott by the National Party, which had changed its name to the Vanuaaku Pati (VP) in 1976. However, the VP reached an agreement with the Condominium powers on new elections for the Representative Assembly, based on universal suffrage for all seats.

In 1977, at a conference in France involving British, French and New Hebridean representatives, it was announced that the islands would become independent in 1980, following a referendum and elections. The VP boycotted this conference, as it demanded immediate independence. The VP also boycotted the elections in November 1977, and declared a 'People's Provisional Government'. Nevertheless, a reduced Assembly of 39 members was elected, and a measure of self-government was introduced in early 1978. A Council of Ministers and the office of Chief Minister (occupied by Georges Kalsakau) were created, and the French, British and Condominium Services began to be replaced by a single New Hebrides Public Service. In December a Government of National Unity was formed, with Father Gérard Leymang as Chief Minister and Father Walter Lini (the VP President) as Deputy Chief Minister.

At elections in November 1979 the VP won 26 of the 39 seats in the Assembly. The outcome of the election led to rioting by supporters of Na-Griamel on the island of Espiritu Santo, who threatened non-Santo 'foreigners'. However, the new Assembly elected Lini as Chief Minister. In June 1980 Jimmy Stevens, the leader of Na-Griamel, declared Espiritu Santo independent of the rest of the New Hebrides, styling it the 'Independent State of Vemarana'. Members of his movement, allegedly assisted by French *colons* (immigrants) and supported by private US business interests, moved to the coast and imprisoned government officers and police, who were later released together with other European and indigenous public servants. British Royal Marines were deployed as a peace-keeping force, prompting strong criticism by the French authorities, which would not permit the United Kingdom's unilateral use of force on Espiritu Santo.

However, in mid-July 1980 agreement was reached between the two Condominium powers and Lini, and the New Hebrides became independent within the Commonwealth, under the name of Vanuatu, as planned, on 30 July. The first President was the former Deputy Chief Minister, George Kalkoa, who adopted the surname Sokomanu ('leader of thousands'), although the post was largely ceremonial. Lini became Prime Minister. The Republic of Vanuatu signed a defence pact with Papua New Guinea, and in August units of the Papua New Guinea Defence Force replaced the British and French troops on Espiritu Santo and arrested the Na-Griamel rebels.

At a general election in November 1983 the VP retained a majority in Parliament, taking 24 of the 39 seats. Sokomanu remained as President and Lini as Prime Minister. In February 1984 Sokomanu resigned as President, after pleading guilty in court to the late payment of road taxes, but he was re-elected in the following month. In October 1987 the Government expelled the French ambassador (see Foreign Affairs). The envoy was alleged to have provided 'substantial financial assistance' to the opposition Union of Moderate Parties (UMP). Parliament was expanded to 46 seats for the general election held in December. Of these, the VP won 26 seats, the UMP 19 and the Fren Melanesia Pati one. Lini retained the premiership. Following the election, the Secretary-General of the VP, Barak Sope, unsuccessfully challenged Lini for the party presidency, but later accepted a portfolio in the Council of Ministers.

In May 1988 a government decision to abolish a local land corporation, which had been a principal source of patronage for Sope, prompted a demonstration in Port Vila by Sope's supporters. Serious rioting ensued, in which one person was killed and several others injured. Lini accused Sope of being instrumental in provoking the riots, and subsequently dismissed him from the Council of Ministers. In July Sope and four colleagues resigned from the VP, and were subsequently dismissed from Parliament at Lini's behest. In addition, 18 members of the UMP were dismissed after they had boycotted successive parliamentary sittings in protest against the expulsions. In September Sope and his colleagues announced the formation of a new political party, the Melanesian Progressive Pati (MPP), and in October the VP expelled 128 of its own members for allegedly supporting the new party. In October the Court of Appeal ruled as unconstitutional the dismissal from Parliament of Sope and his colleagues, and reinstated them, but upheld the expulsion of the 18 members of the UMP. In November Sope resigned from Parliament, citing loss of confidence in its Speaker. In December President Sokomanu dissolved Parliament and announced that Sope would act as interim Prime Minister, pending a general election scheduled for February 1989. Lini immediately denounced Sokomanu's actions, and the Governments of Australia, New Zealand and Papua New Guinea refused to recognize the interim Government. The islands' police force remained loyal to Lini, and later in December 1988 Sokomanu, Sope and other members of the interim Government were arrested and charged with treason. In 1989 Sokomanu was sentenced to six years' imprisonment, and Sope and the then leader of the parliamentary opposition, Maxime Carlot Korman, received five-year terms, for seditious conspiracy and incitement to mutiny. However, representatives of the International Commission of Jurists, who had been present at the trials, criticized the rulings, and in April the Court of Appeal overruled the original judgment, citing insufficient evidence for the convictions. Fred Timakata, the former Minister of Health, replaced Sokomanu as President in January 1989.

The removal of Walter Lini and subsequent events

Diminishing support for Lini's leadership led to the approval in August 1991 of a motion of no confidence in Lini as party leader at the VP's congress. Donald Kalpokas, the Secretary-General of the VP, was unanimously elected to replace Lini as President of the party. In September a motion of no confidence in the premiership of Lini was narrowly approved in Parliament, and Kalpokas was elected Prime Minister. Subsequently, Lini, with the support of a substantial number of defectors from the VP, formed the National United Party (NUP). At a general election in December the UMP secured 19 seats, while the VP and NUP each won 10 seats, the MPP four, and Tan Union, Fren Melanesia and Na-Griamel one each. The leader of the UMP, Maxime Carlot Korman, was appointed Prime Minister, and a coalition Government was formed by the UMP and the NUP.

At a presidential election in February 1994 neither the UMP's candidate, Father Luc Dini, nor Father John Bani, who was supported by the opposition, attained the requisite two-thirds of total votes cast. The election was rescheduled for March. The VP subsequently agreed to vote with the ruling UMP, in return for a guaranteed role in a future coalition government. As a result of this agreement, the UMP's candidate, Jean-Marie Leye, was elected to the presidency with 41 votes. The VP subsequently withdrew its support for the UMP when Carlot refused to offer the party more than one ministerial post.

In May 1994 the 'breakaway' members of the NUP who had remained in their ministerial posts, Sethy Regenvanu, Edward Tabisari and Cecil Sinker, were expelled from the party. They subsequently formed a new grouping, the People's Democratic Party (PDP), and later in that month signed an agreement with the UMP to form a new coalition Government, the third since the election of December 1991. The UMP-PDP coalition held a total of 26 legislative seats.

In October 1994 the Supreme Court granted the Government a restraining order against further actions by the President, pending the hearing of an application to the Supreme Court to overrule several of the President's recent decisions. Members of the Government and judiciary had become increasingly alarmed by Leye's exercise of his presidential powers, which had included orders to free 26 criminals and to appoint a convicted criminal as police commissioner.

In April 1995 Carlot attracted strong criticism from the Vanuatu-based regional news agency, Pacnews, when he dismissed two senior government officials for making comments critical of the Government; moreover, the journalists who reported the comments were threatened with dismissal. The Prime Minister's increasing reputation for intolerance of criticism was compounded by allegations that, as part of his Government's policy of reducing the number of employees in the public service, civil servants believed to be opposition sympathizers were among the first to lose their jobs.

At a general election held in November 1995, 20 of the 50 seats in the newly enlarged Parliament were won by the Unity Front coalition, the anglophone grouping led by Donald Kalpokas, which incorporated the VP, the MPP, the Tan Union and the NUP. The UMP secured 17 seats. A period of intense political manoeuvring followed the election, as the two main parties sought to form coalitions with other members in an attempt to secure a parliamentary majority. The situation was compounded by the emergence of two factions within the UMP, one comprising the supporters of Carlot and another led by Serge Vohor (the party's President). The Carlot faction of the UMP and the Unity Front both sought the political allegiance of the NUP. The latter's decision to accept the offer of a coalition with the UMP effectively excluded the Unity Front (the grouping with the largest number of seats) from the Government, and, in protest, its members boycotted the opening of Parliament in December, thus preventing a vote on the formation of a new government taking place. At a subsequent parliamentary session, Vohor was elected as Prime Minister, despite continuing allegations of irregularities in the election of senior members of the Government.

In early February 1996 seven dissident UMP members of Parliament proposed a motion of no confidence in Vohor, supported by 22 other opposition members. However, Vohor announced his resignation as Prime Minister, thus preventing the vote from taking place. A parliamentary session to elect a new premier was abandoned as a result of a boycott by supporters of Vohor, who was reported to have retracted his resignation. However, at a further sitting, Carlot was elected Prime Minister.

In July 1996 a report published by the national ombudsman revealed a serious financial scandal, involving the issuing of 10 bank guarantees with a total value of US $100m. The Minister of Finance, Barak Sope, who had issued the guarantees in April, had been persuaded by an Australian financial adviser, Peter Swanson, that the scheme could earn the country significant revenue. Swanson, who left Vanuatu after securing the guarantees, was subsequently traced and charged with criminal offences relating to his dealings with Sope. (In February 1998 the Supreme Court found Swanson guilty on seven charges arising from the scandal, sentencing him to 18 months' imprisonment.) Carlot, meanwhile, rejected demands for his resignation for his compliance with the scheme and resisted considerable pressure to dismiss Sope and the Governor of the Reserve Bank of Vanuatu. In the following month, however, Sope was dismissed following his defection to the opposition.

In an attempt to restore a measure of political stability, Carlot appealed for reconciliation among the various political groups in the country in August 1996 and invited members of the opposition to join the Government. The opposition responded by reiterating its demand for Carlot's resignation, and in September a motion of no confidence in the Government was approved and Vohor was elected Prime Minister. Vohor's coalition Government comprised the pro-Vohor faction of the UMP, the NUP, the MPP, Tan Union and Fren Melanesia. A new Council of Ministers, in which Sope was appointed Deputy Prime Minister, was announced in mid-October.

Also in October 1996 a dispute over unpaid allowances, dating from 1993, led members of the 300-strong Vanuatu Mobile Force (VMF—the country's paramilitary force) briefly to abduct the President and Deputy Prime Minister to demand a settlement. Both Leye and Sope expressed sympathy for the VMF members. Sope was replaced as Deputy Prime Minister by Donald Kalpokas, and Father Walter Lini was appointed Minister of Justice. Following a further incident in November 1996 in connection with the pay dispute, in which an official from the Department of Finance was abducted and allegedly assaulted, Lini ordered the arrest of more than one-half of the members of the VMF. About 30 members were detained and charged with criminal offences. In June 1999 18 VMF members were charged with the kidnapping of a number of government officers in 1996; one was convicted.

In March 1997 a memorandum of agreement was signed between the VP, the NUP and the UMP, the three parties of the newly formed governing coalition. However, the defection in May of five NUP members of Parliament, including two cabinet ministers, to the VP led to the party's expulsion from the Government. As a result, a new coalition, comprising the UMP, the MPP, Tan Union and Fren Melanesia, was formed. The nomination of the new Council of Ministers was controversial, owing to the appointment of Sope to the position of Deputy Prime Minister and Minister of Commerce, Trade and Industry. Sope had been described in January by the national ombudsman, Marie-Noëlle Ferrieux-Patterson (in a further report on the financial scandal of the previous year), as unfit for public office. Ferrieux-Patterson also criticized the recent appointment of Willie Jimmy as Minister of Finance. In July legal action was initiated to recover the estimated US $300,000 of public funds paid in 1993 by Jimmy, together with Carlot, as compensation to the 23 members dismissed from Parliament following their boycott of the legislature in 1988.

In September 1997 Vohor dismissed Jimmy from his position as Minister of Finance, apparently owing to a dispute between Jimmy and the Prime Minister over the latter's decision to remove several areas of responsibility from the finance portfolio. The dispute intensified the disunity within the UMP, which had now come to comprise three factions, led respectively by Vohor, Carlot and Jimmy. In November Parliament approved legislation to repeal the Ombudsman Act and the Government announced that it was to establish a commission of inquiry to determine if the ombudsman had exceeded her constitutional powers. However, President Leye refused to promulgate the new law on the grounds that it was unconstitutional, and he referred it to the Supreme Court. Later in the month Carlot filed a motion of no confidence in Vohor's Government. When Vohor attempted to withdraw all proposed legislation in order to prevent debate on the motion, Leye announced the dissolution of Parliament. However, the Supreme Court revived the parliamentary session in December. The matter was referred to the Court of Appeal, which in January 1998 ordered the immediate dissolution of Parliament. Following Leye's announcement of a forthcoming general election, Carlot announced the formation of the Vanuatu Republikan Pati (VRP).

The Governments of Donald Kalpokas and Barak Sope

At a general election held on 6 March 1998, the VP won 18 of the 52 seats in the newly enlarged Parliament, the UMP secured 12, the NUP won 11, the MPP obtained six, the John Frum Movement secured two, the VRP obtained one, and independent candidates won two seats. In mid-March the VP and the NUP agreed to form a coalition Government, with the support of Carlot (the VRP's sole representative) and one independent member. At the end of the month Donald Kalpokas was elected Prime Minister with 35 parliamentary votes, defeating Vohor (who secured 17). Kalpokas also assumed three ministerial portfolios, including that for Foreign Affairs, while Lini, who was appointed to the revived post of Deputy Prime Minister, also became Minister of Justice and Internal Affairs.

In June 1998, despite strong opposition, notably from the UMP, Parliament approved a new 'leadership code'. Regarded as a crucial element in ensuring greater accountability and transparency in public life, the code defined clear guide-lines for the conduct of state officials (including a requirement that all public figures submit an annual declaration of assets to Parliament), and laid down strict penalties for those convicted of corruption. Shortly before, the Supreme Court upheld the repeal of the Ombudsman Act, as approved by Parliament in November 1997. The Kalpokas Government emphasized its commitment to strengthening the role of the ombudsman, stating that new legislation governing the office would be prepared. Although the ombudsman was to continue to function in the mean time, in early August 1998 Ferrieux-Patterson issued a statement in which she expressed concern that her powers of jurisdiction had been diminished.

In October 1998 Kalpokas expelled the NUP from the governing coalition, following reports that the party's leader, Lini (who died in February 1999), had organized a series of meetings with prominent members of the opposition, with the aim of forming a new coalition government that would exclude the VP. NUP ministers were largely replaced by members of the UMP faction led by Jimmy, which included the Deputy President of the party, Vincent Boulekone, and its Secretary-General, Henri Taga; one ministerial post was allocated to the John Frum Movement. In March 1999 Father John Bani was chosen by the electoral college to succeed Jean-Marie Leye as President of Vanuatu.

The governing coalition was threatened in August 1999 by a decision by the National Council of the UMP to oppose participation in the Government. The Council issued a directive to the 17 members of Jimmy's faction to resign from the Kalpokas administration. Following their refusal to comply with the directive, the National Council acted to suspend the members in October. However, later in that month the suspensions were overruled by the Supreme Court. The two factions of the UMP had previously attempted reunification, but negotiations had stalled over the demands of Vohor's faction for two of the four ministerial positions held by Jimmy's faction. (The UMP achieved reunification in November 2000.)

At the end of August 1999 four by-elections took place, three of which were won by opposition parties, thus eliminating the Government's majority in Parliament. In November the Government staged a boycott of Parliament to avoid a proposed vote of no confidence by opposition parties against the Kalpokas administration. However, the subsequent defection to the opposition of an independent representative, followed by that of the Minister of Health, forced the resignation of Kalpokas prior to a no confidence motion on 25 November. The Speaker, Edward Natapei, announced his resignation shortly afterwards, and Paul Ren Tari of the NUP was elected as his replacement. The leader of the MPP, Barak Sope, was elected to lead a new Government the same day; he secured 28 votes compared with the 24 votes gained by Natapei as the newly appointed President of the VP. Sope formed a coalition Government, comprising the MPP, the NUP, the Vohor faction of the UMP, the VRP and the John Frum Movement. The new Council of Ministers included Vohor as Minister of Foreign Affairs and Carlot as Minister of Lands and Mineral Resources, both of whom, with Sope, had been the subject of critical reports by the ombudsman.

In May 2000 Parliament approved controversial legislation (the Public Services Amendment Bill and the Government Amendment Bill) giving the Government direct power to appoint and dismiss public servants. The opposition criticized the changes, claiming that they contravened the principles of the Comprehensive Reform Programme (a range of economic measures supported by the Asian Development Bank—ADB, see p. 202). President John Bani subsequently referred both pieces of legislation to the Supreme Court, which, in August, ordered that he approve them. The ADB reacted strongly to the development, arguing that it allowed for political bias in the public sector, and threatened to withhold further funds from Vanuatu. The bank's stance served to perpetuate an ongoing dispute between the organization and the Vanuatu Government, which had often expressed the view that the bank imposed harsh conditions in return for its finance. Also in August Deputy Prime Minister Reginald Stanley resigned, following his alleged involvement in a serious assault on two people and in causing criminal damage to property while under the influence of alcohol. He was replaced by the Minister of Trade Development, James Bule.

In September 2000 the opposition leader, Edward Natapei, invited the Vohor faction of the UMP to join the opposition and form a new government. Vohor declined, saying that his priority was the stability of the current Government. The resignation of a VP member in October prevented the success of a motion of no confidence in the Prime Minister. In January 2001 the Government deported Mark Neil-Jones, the publisher of an independent newspaper, *Trading Post*, on the grounds of instigating instability in the country. (The *Trading Post* had recently published several critical articles about the Government.) However, the Supreme Court reversed the decision, declaring that the deportation order was illegal, and Neil-Jones was allowed to return to the country.

The Government of Edward Natapei

In late January 2001 three members of the UMP resigned from the party, further reducing the Government's majority. The Government's problems intensified in March after the withdrawal of the UMP from the ruling coalition. Opposition attempts to vote on a motion of no confidence were delayed as Sope initiated legal action against the motion, and the Speaker, Paul Ren Tari, refused to allow the vote while legal action was pending. The Chief Justice, however, ordered the vote to proceed, and, after further postponements by the Speaker, the Sope Government was voted out of office in April. A new Government, led by Edward Natapei of the VP, was elected. The incoming administration, a coalition of the VP and UMP, was duly sworn in; Vohor was appointed Deputy Prime Minister. In May Parliament held an extraordinary session to debate a motion to remove Ren Tari as Speaker because of his conduct during the political crisis. Ren Tari responded by suspending Natapei, along with five other cabinet ministers, for breaching parliamentary procedure. Despite an order by the Chief Justice that they be allowed to return to Parliament to continue the extraordinary session, Ren Tari refused to open the legislature while he appealed to the Supreme Court against the order. In response, Ren Tari and his two deputies were arrested and charged with sedition. A new Speaker, Donald Kalpokas, President of the UMP, was elected, thus reducing Natapei's majority in Parliament to one. In September Sope tabled a motion of no confidence against the ruling coalition, but the opposition was defeated.

In November 2001 Sope was ordered to appear in court to answer charges that he had forged two government-supported Letters of Guarantee, worth US $23m., while he was Prime Minister. Sope was convicted of fraud in July 2002 and sentenced to three years' imprisonment. It was alleged soon afterwards that New Zealand had interfered in Vanuatu's internal affairs by funding the investigation that had led to Sope's conviction.

In March 2002 Parliament was dissolved after the Supreme Court ruled that its four-year term had expired. Natapei remained in charge of an interim Government until the general election, scheduled for early May. Also in March it was announced that the newly established People's Progressive Party (PPP) and Fren Melanesia were to form a coalition with the ruling NUP to contest the forthcoming election. It was reported that the general election was to be monitored by an independent group of observers. The future of the Comprehensive Reform Programme was widely perceived to be the main issue in the electoral campaign.

The general election was held on 2 May 2002. A total of 327 candidates contested the 52 seats available in Parliament. A record 138 candidates stood as independents, prompting Natapei to comment prior to the election that for Vanuatu to attain political stability the electoral constituency should vote only for party candidates. After some uncertainty, it was announced that the UMP had won 15 seats in the new Parliament and that the VP had secured 14. However, in accordance with the terms of the coalition agreement, the VP was permitted to nominate the next Prime Minister. The new Government was formed in early June, with Natapei as Prime Minister.

In August 2002, following the controversial appointment of Mael Apisai as Vanuatu's new police commissioner, disaffected police officers staged a raid during which they arrested Apisai, Attorney-General Hamilton Bulu and 14 other senior civil servants on charges of seditious conspiracy. Following an investigation, the charges were abandoned owing to a lack of evidence. Prime Minister Natapei subsequently assumed the police and VMF portfolios from the Minister of Internal Affairs, Joe Natuman, in what was thought to be an attempt to distance Natuman from some members of the police force, with whom he had reportedly become too closely involved. Later in the month members of the paramilitary VMF surrounded the police headquarters in Port Vila to serve arrest warrants on 27 of those who had been involved in the raid, including the acting police commissioner, Holis Simon, and the commander of the VMF, Api Jack Marikembo. Shortly afterwards, in an attempt to bring an end to hostilities, the Government signed an agreement with representatives from the police department and the VMF during a traditional Melanesian reconciliation ceremony. The police officers involved, who had been suspended from their posts, were reinstated, the police and the VMF undertook to make no further arrests, and it was agreed that Apisai's appointment would be reviewed by a newly appointed police services commission. At the same time it was decided that the allegations of conspiracy that had been brought against the 15 officials initially arrested would be considered by the judicial authorities. A new acting police commissioner, Lt-Gen. Arthur Coulton, was then appointed.

In October 2002 it was announced that the charges against 18 of those arrested in connection with the August raid would be abandoned, leaving eight senior officers to face trial on charges of mutiny and incitement to mutiny. In December four of these police officers were found guilty by the Supreme Court on charges of mutiny, incitement to mutiny, kidnapping and false imprisonment and were given suspended two-year prison sentences. In the same month police intervened to prevent former Prime Minister Sope from reclaiming his seat in Parliament, claiming that this was nullified by his conviction for fraud in July, despite receiving a pardon in November from President Bani. The pardon, which Bani stated he had made on the grounds of Sope's poor health, provoked widespread public opposition and led the Government to announce the appointment of a commission of inquiry to investigate the President's decision. However, in November 2003, at a by-election to the seat vacated by his conviction for fraud, Sope was re-elected.

In April 2003 the election of Ham Lini (brother of Walter Lini, the late founder of the NUP) as President of the NUP led to the signing of a memorandum of understanding inviting that party to join the coalition Government. The NUP was expected to assume three ministerial portfolios (including finance) in a development that observers believed might lead to the reunification of the NUP with the VP (the two were a single political organization until the split of 1991). However, in late April the NUP rejected the VP's offer and announced its intention to remove the Government in a motion of no confidence. A further attempt to propose a motion of no confidence in the Government led Natapei to remove the UMP from the ruling coalition in a reorganization of cabinet portfolios in November. The party was replaced in the coalition by members of the NUP, the PPP, the Green Confederation Party and independents. Continued instability within the coalition prompted three further cabinet reorganizations during the first three months of 2004.

In April 2004 former Speaker Alfred Maseng Nalo was sworn in as Vanuatu's new President, having defeated 31 other candidates during four rounds of voting. However, it was subsequently revealed that Maseng was serving a suspended prison sentence, having been convicted of misappropriation and receiving property dishonestly, and in May the Supreme Court ruled that Maseng should be removed from office. Kalkot Mataskelekele was elected in his stead in August. Meanwhile, pre-empting a vote of no confidence against the Government, which held a minority of seats in Parliament, the Council of Ministers dissolved Parliament in June.

The Governments of Serge Vohor and Ham Lini

A general election was held on 6 July 2004, at which no single party won an overall majority and 25 new members were elected, including many independent candidates. However, the validity of the election was jeopardized by an incident on Tanna in which ballot boxes *en route* to Port Vila for processing were ambushed and burnt. More than 40 people were arrested in connection with the incident, including the acting Minister of Finance, Jimmy Nickelim of the VP. In late July Serge Vohor was elected Prime Minister, defeating Ham Lini by 28 votes to 24. A Council of Ministers composed of five political groups and several independents was appointed shortly afterwards. However, the stability of the new administration was threatened by rumours of shifting allegiances and reports that several members were being persuaded to cross the floor of Parliament. Despite these suggestions, an opposition motion of no confidence in the new Government, proposed in September, was defeated, with Vohor's administration securing the support of 31 of the 52 members. Further doubts over Vohor's ability to continue as Prime Minister were raised when the country's police commissioner attempted to arrest him on charges of contempt, following comments made in Parliament accusing the Chief Justice, Vincent Lunabeck, of being unduly influenced by a desire to please foreign interests. However, the Supreme Court dismissed the charges against Vohor in an appeal.

The Prime Minister became the focus of further serious controversy in November 2004 when he announced the establishment of diplomatic relations with Taiwan. The announcement, which Vohor defended by claiming that Taiwan's assistance was necessary to cover the budgetary deficit, was made only weeks after the Prime Minister had made an official visit to the People's Republic of China during which he had reiterated Vanuatu's allegiance to that country. The Council of Ministers, which had not given the necessary approval of the agreement with Taiwan, responded by demanding that Vohor renounce recognition of Taiwan or dismiss the entire cabinet. Controversy increased following reports that Vohor had assaulted the Chinese ambassador when questioned over the legitimacy of the Taiwanese flag flying in Port Vila. A parliamentary vote of no confidence in Vohor in December was approved by 35 votes to 14. Ham Lini was elected Prime Minister and subsequently appointed a cabinet that included five former ministers who had withdrawn their support for and voted against Vohor.

Lini's Government reversed the policy of the previous administration regarding Taiwan, and in July 2005 the Minister for Home Affairs made an official visit to China to sign a co-operation agreement providing for technical, logistical and financial support for the Vanuatu Police Force. Lini effected a cabinet reorganization in the same month. Further changes to the Council of Ministers reflected the decision of five opposition members to join the Green Confederation Party, led by the Minister of 'Finance, Moana Carcasses Kalosil. Their defection resulted in the Green Confederation Party becoming Lini's most significant partner in the governing coalition. In a further cabinet reorganization in November, Moana Carcasses was replaced as Minister of Finance by Willie Jimmy, hitherto Minister of Lands, Geology and Mines. In a further reallocation of portfolios announced in March 2006, Dunstan Hilton replaced Barak Sope as Minister of Agriculture, following reports that the former Prime Minister had been conducting negotiations aimed at attempting to oust the incumbent, Ham Lini, from office. In the same month the Prime Minister defeated by 30 parliamentary votes to 20 a motion of no confidence, which had been presented by the opposition partly as a result of criticism of the Government's handling of a trade dispute with Fiji.

In late 2006 activists of the Vete association, which comprised inhabitants of Tongoa, vandalized unoccupied government buildings in Port Vila to publicize their campaign for land ownership rights. Vete claimed that prior to the declaration of areas of the capital as public land, no customary owner had been named. In December it was reported that members of Vete were occupying several empty government buildings. In March 2007 allegations of witchcraft, following the death of a woman, led to civil unrest in outlying areas of Port Vila, with migrants from two islands engaging in violence that resulted in three fatalities and some 150 arrests. A two-week state of emergency was declared.

The conflict provoked renewed public debate about internal migration in Vanuatu.

In May 2007 the Minister of Agriculture, Forestry and Fisheries, Marcellino Pipite, was dismissed, having been accused of disloyalty to the Government; he was replaced by Donna Brounie. Following further cabinet changes in June, the VP was removed from the governing coalition and replaced by the UMP, the President of which, former premier Vohor, was appointed Minister of Infrastructure and Public Utilities. The VP had reportedly allied itself with the UMP in the latter's attempt to oust the Government in a motion of no confidence, but the UMP subsequently retracted the motion. Vohor himself was dismissed in July, allegedly having been involved in an altercation with a government official. At the same time, the Deputy Prime Minister and Minister for Foreign Affairs and External Trade, Sato Kilman, and the Minister of Sports and Youth Development, Dunstan Hilton, both of the PPP, were removed from office owing to allegations of fraud (in August Hilton was reported to have been charged in a fraud case involving funds misappropriated from the National Bank of Vanuatu). The VP rejoined the Government, and its members were allocated major portfolios including that of home affairs. The former Prime Minister and VP President, Edward Natapei, assumed the role of Deputy Prime Minister and resumed the infrastructure and public utilities portfolios. In August 2008 Maxime Carlot Korman, the Minister of Lands, was obliged to answer a bribery charge relating to a land lease in Lelepa, but he was subsequently cleared of the charge owing to lack of evidence.

Natapei's return to office

Parliamentary elections took place on 2 September 2008, when more than 300 candidates contested the 52 seats. About one-third of the incumbent members of Parliament lost their seats at the poll, including Barak Sope, the former Prime Minister, and Willie Jimmy, hitherto the Minister of Finance. The VP won 11 seats, thus obtaining the largest representation in Parliament, followed by the NUP with eight seats, the UMP with seven and the VRP, also with seven. A brief period of uncertainty ensued, with both Edward Natapei, leader of the VP, and Maxime Carlot Korman, leader of the VRP, claiming to have enough support to form a government. On 22 September Natapei was elected Prime Minister after obtaining 27 parliamentary votes, while Carlot received 25. The former Minister of Foreign Affairs and External Trade, George Wells, was elected Speaker of Parliament. Natapei appointed outgoing Prime Minister Ham Lini as his Deputy Prime Minister. Within days of its formation Carlot led a motion of no confidence against the Natapei administration. However, before the motion could be presented to Parliament, in early October the Prime Minister effected a cabinet reorganization, in order to accommodate three members of the UMP, including party President Serge Vohor, who returned to his former position as Minister of Infrastructure and Public Utilities. The Natapei Government was thus able to defeat the subsequent motion of no confidence by 31 votes to 20. In March 2009 former Deputy Prime Minister Sato Kilman replaced Carlot as Leader of the Opposition. In April a by-election was held in the constituency of Tanna, following the conviction on bribery charges of an independent member of Parliament, Judah Issac, and his campaign team.

In June 2009 the Speaker, George Wells, was expelled from the NUP after accusing James Bule, the Minister of Trade and Commerce and a fellow member of the NUP, of misappropriating funds intended for copra farmers. Wells then joined the opposition, along with three other members of the legislature. In the same month the opposition parties brought a motion of no confidence against the Government, citing the allegedly missing copra subsidies. Before the motion was debated Harry Iauko (a VP member who had reportedly been voting with the opposition) was appointed Minister of Lands, Geology and Mines, and the Supreme Court declared invalid the election (in the previous September) of four members of Parliament (including the Minister of Foreign Affairs and External Trade, Bakoa Kaltonga), in response to a petition by Barak Sope alleging that the four had bribed and threatened voters. The Government defeated the motion of no confidence (by 28 votes to 18). Parliament then voted to remove Wells from the office of Speaker, and he was replaced by Carlot.

President Mataskelekele's term of office expired in August 2009. In September, in the third round of the ensuing presidential election, Iolu Abbil Johnson (who had held office as the minister responsible for internal affairs shortly after independence) was successful, defeating 14 other candidates. In November, anticipating another motion of no confidence, Natapei reorganized the Council of Ministers, bringing opposition members, from the Green Confederation Party and from the PPP, into the Government to replace members of the NUP and VRP. Ham Lini was replaced as Deputy Prime Minister by Sato Kilman, who was also appointed Minister of External Trade, while Moana Carcasses Kalosil became the new Minister of Internal Affairs. The Minister of Lands, Geology and Mines, Harry Iauko, was removed from office following allegations of malpractice concerning sales of land. Later in November the Speaker, Carlot, declared that Natapei had forfeited his parliamentary seat, because he had been absent from three consecutive sittings without giving written notice (while attending the Commonwealth Heads of Government Meeting). In early December, however, the Chief Justice ruled that Carlot's decision had been unconstitutional and had no legal effect. Later in December a vote of no confidence in the Government (the fifth since Natapei took office in September 2008) was defeated. After rejecting on technical grounds several attempts by the Government to remove him from the office of Speaker, in January 2010 Carlot resigned, and his predecessor, George Wells, was re-elected to the office. Meanwhile, in December 2009 the Secretary-General of the National Council of Chiefs, Selwyn Garu, deplored the cost of the recent political rivalries in terms of finance and the waste of parliamentary time.

In April 2010, at the VP Congress, Natapei's leadership was challenged by Iauko, and the party was reported to have split into two rival factions. The formation of a new political party, the Land and Justice Party, was announced in November. Led by Ralph Regenvanu, the new party aimed primarily to protect customary land ownership and to address the issue of foreign ownership of local businesses

On 2 December 2010 Natapei was ousted from the premiership in a parliamentary vote of no confidence; 31 of the 52 parliamentary members voted in support of the motion, which was reported to have been filed in response to Natapei's attempted suspension from Parliament of five opposition legislators, as well as his failure to agree to Fiji's assumption of the rotating chairmanship of the Melanesian Spearhead Group (MSG—see Foreign Affairs). Natapei was replaced by Deputy Prime Minister Kilman, who pledged to ensure that the abrupt change of leadership would not lead to any political instability. Considerable concern was prompted by the exclusion of the media and general public, upon the instruction of the Speaker, from the parliamentary session during which the motion of no confidence was debated.

Recent developments: the Kilman Government, its removal and reinstatement

The composition of a new coalition Government was announced on 7 December 2010; Ham Lini was appointed Deputy Prime Minister and Minister of Trade; George Wells assumed responsibility for foreign affairs, relinquishing the position of Speaker, and Moana Carcasses Kalosil was allocated the finance portfolio. In mid-December the opposition filed a motion of no confidence in Kilman's Government. During Prime Minister Kilman's absence from the country, Deputy Prime Minister Lini dismissed Willie Lop, the newly appointed Minister of Internal Affairs, and replaced him with Dunstan Hilton, hitherto the Minister of Justice and Social Affairs; the justice portfolio was reallocated to Alfred Carlot. Before the opposition's motion of no confidence could be debated, Kilman effected a further cabinet reorganization on 21 December, this time incorporating members of the UMP within the coalition Government; new appointments included that of UMP President Serge Vohor, who became Minister of Infrastructure and Public Utilities, while Minister of Justice and Social Affairs Alfred Carlot was among the recent appointees removed from office.

A report accusing Harry Iauko of involvement in corruption during his tenure as Minister of Lands, Geology and Mines was submitted to Prime Minister Kilman by the former Director-General of the Ministry in January 2011; a number of other senior officials of the ministry were also incriminated. Kilman was reported to have offered assurances that the allegations would be fully investigated and appropriate action taken if the accused were found to have committed any wrongdoing. Transparency International urged the Vanuatu Government to appoint a Commission of Inquiry to examine comprehensively the claims made in the report.

In mid-February 2011 Vohor and two other cabinet ministers, namely Minister of Education Charlot Salwai, the Vice-

President of the UMP, and VRP Secretary-General Marcellino Pipite, who had been returned to the agriculture portfolio in mid-December 2010, resigned in protest against the failure of Kilman to allocate additional cabinet posts to the UMP and the VRP. Pre-empting a parliamentary vote of no confidence in his administration, Kilman effected a further cabinet reorganization later in February. While the UMP declared its intention to rejoin the opposition, Pipite returned to the Government as Minister of Education; Harry Iauko was transferred to the public utilities portfolio. A few days later the opposition, no longer commanding sufficient support to oust Kilman, withdrew its motion of no confidence against the premier. Some members of the opposition claimed that the Government had bribed some parliamentary members into withdrawing support for the motion.

The issue of press freedom came to the fore in early March 2011 when Marc Neil-Jones, now publisher of the *Daily Post* newspaper, was physically assaulted in his workplace by several men who he claimed were led by Harry Iauko; Iauko later admitted to having stormed into Neil-Jones's office, stating that he had been angry about articles printed in the *Daily Post* alleging his involvement in fraudulent land deals. Iauko was charged with assault in early April. Meanwhile, in mid-March Ralph Regenvanu, who had been appointed Minister of Lands and Natural Resources in February, was transferred to the justice portfolio, while Alfred Carlot was appointed as the new Minister of Lands and Natural Resources in his place.

On 24 April 2011 the Government of Kilman was removed from office following a parliamentary motion of no confidence, which was narrowly approved by 26 votes to 25. Serge Vohor was thus returned to the premiership, six years after his removal from office. On the following day the incoming Prime Minister announced the composition of the new Council of Ministers; Joshua Kalsakau of the VLP was appointed Deputy Prime Minister, while assuming concurrent responsibility for the portfolios of infrastructure and public utilities, and Joe Natuman, who had been responsible for the foreign affairs portfolio during the premiership of Natapei, was returned to that post.

However, Vanuatu's political upheavals continued. On 13 May 2011 the Court of Appeal overruled Vohor's election as Prime Minister and reinstated Kilman in the post, upholding the latter's appeal against the legitimacy of his removal from office. Kilman had contended that his removal by a simple majority was unconstitutional, arguing that an absolute majority (a minimum of 27 of the 52 parliamentary members' votes, i.e. one more than Vohor had received) was required. Having secured the support of 27 members, Kilman was able to defeat a subsequent parliamentary motion of no confidence. The reinstated Prime Minister appointed Alfred Carlot as his Minister of Foreign Affairs, and Steven Kalsakau of the UMP replaced Carlot as his Minister of Lands and Natural Resources. The internal affairs portfolio was allocated to George Wells of the National Community Association Party (NCAP), in place of the PPP's Dunstan Hilton.

Foreign Affairs

Regional relations

In March 1988 Vanuatu signed an agreement with Papua New Guinea and Solomon Islands to form the Melanesian Spearhead Group (MSG), which aimed to preserve Melanesian cultural traditions and to lobby for independence from French rule for New Caledonia. In 1994 the MSG concluded an agreement providing for the gradual establishment of a free trade area encompassing the three countries. Fiji joined the group in 1996. In March 2006 the MSG met in Port Vila to discuss several issues concerning regional trade and security. Vanuatu had been accused of breaching the group's agreement by restricting its markets through the imposition of export licences for the sale of kava and other commodities. Negotiations were also taking place regarding the construction in Vanuatu of a permanent headquarters for the MSG Secretariat. In March 2007 the members of the MSG adopted a formal constitution at a meeting in Vanuatu. A diplomatic dispute arose in July 2010 when ni-Vanuatu Prime Minister Edward Natapei, the outgoing chairman of the MSG, refused to agree to Fiji's scheduled assumption of the rotating chairmanship and cancelled a planned meeting of the Group at which the transfer of leadership was due to have taken place; Natapei argued that the MSG was founded on democratic ideals and that allowing Fiji's unelected Prime Minister, Frank Bainimarama (see the chapter on Fiji), to chair the Group would thus be an affront to its core principles. In the following months the Vanuatu Government denied speculation that its stance on the issue had been formulated in response to pressure from Australia and New Zealand to oppose Fijian leadership of the MSG, with the Vanuatu Minister of Foreign Affairs stressing that its position was based exclusively on the 'unconstitutionality' of an unelected leader chairing the Group. Nevertheless, Fiji was permitted to assume the chairmanship following the ousting from office of Natapei in December (see Domestic Political Affairs). Incoming premier Sato Kilman expressed his determination to improve relations between Vanuatu and Fiji.

In August 2005 it was announced that discussions had taken place between the Prime Ministers of Vanuatu and Solomon Islands on the possibility of establishing an agreement governing border control and a patrol system. The issues were discussed amid concerns regarding drugs- and people-trafficking, money-laundering, and other border-related crime. It was hoped that a system of mutual co-operation similar to that operating between Solomon Islands and Papua New Guinea might be established. In December 2006 approximately 10 ni-Vanuatu police officers joined international peace-keeping forces in Timor-Leste. A memorandum of understanding signed between the two countries in March 2011 would allow the Vanuatu Government to recruit nursing staff from Solomon Islands in a bid to combat a persistent shortage of nursing staff within Vanuatu. Both countries pledged their commitment further to enhance co-operation in health and other services.

In April 2009 the Minister of Foreign Affairs and External Trade, Bakoa Kaltonga, announced that High Commissions were to be established in Malaysia, New Zealand and Fiji, as part of the Government's plans to strengthen relations with the countries of the Asia-Pacific region. Vanuatu was expected to open a High Commission in Australia in the second half of 2011.

Like other small Pacific island nations, Vanuatu has a close relationship with Australia and New Zealand, which are important trading partners and sources of financial and technical assistance. In April 2009 the Australian Minister for Trade, Simon Crean, visited Vanuatu for discussions with the Government regarding the negotiation of a free trade agreement, known as PACER Plus, by Australia, New Zealand and the Pacific islands. The Vanuatu Government was reported to be supportive of the proposed agreement, although in December the Governor of the Reserve Bank of Vanuatu, Odo Tevi, suggested that such an agreement would be disadvantageous to Vanuatu's producers. In May of the same year Vanuatu and Australia concluded a development partnership agreement. During 2009 Australia and New Zealand both committed funds for road construction and maintenance in Vanuatu, and for the provision of free primary education for all children by 2012. A tax information exchange agreement was signed by Vanuatu and Australia in April 2010. In July of that year Australia's Governor-General, Quentin Bryce, visited Vanuatu to attend celebrations intended to commemorate the 30th anniversary of Vanuatu's accession to independence. The Australian Government granted $A66m. in official development assistance to Vanuatu for 2010/11.

The People's Republic of China is an important provider of development assistance (despite a temporary rift over Vanuatu's recognition of Taiwan in 2004—see Domestic Political Affairs). In September 2009 China provided a new jointly owned fish-processing plant near Port Vila, and this was expected to allow Vanuatu's economy to benefit from fish caught within its territorial waters but hitherto processed elsewhere. Two Chinese naval vessels docked at Port Vila in August 2010, the first time that Chinese ships had visited Vanuatu; the four-day 'goodwill visit' was intended to enhance bilateral military relations. In October Vanuatu halted the issuing of visas in China after claims that ni-Vanuatu passports were being sold on the 'black market' in that country, for around US $5,000 each. Henceforth, Chinese nationals seeking a visa for travel to Vanuatu would have to apply directly to the ni-Vanuatu authorities.

Vanuatu has repeatedly reaffirmed its support for dialogue on the issue of the desire for independence of the Indonesian province of Papua (see the chapter on Indonesia). In June 2010 the Vanuatu legislature adopted a motion appealing for the International Court of Justice (ICJ) to investigate the legality of the region's incorporation within Indonesia in the 1960s.

Other external relations

Vanuatu has had an uneasy relationship with France, the former joint colonial power. In 1981 the French ambassador to Vanuatu was expelled following the deportation from the neighbouring French territory of New Caledonia of the VP Secretary-General, who had been due to attend an assembly of the New Caledonian Independence Front. France immediately withdrew aid to Vanuatu, but this was subsequently restored and a new ambas-

VANUATU

Introductory Survey

sador was appointed. However, the French ambassador was expelled again in 1987, for allegedly providing 'substantial financial assistance' to Vanuatu's opposition parties. In response to the expulsion, the French Government again announced that it would withdraw aid to Vanuatu. Maxime Carlot Korman, Vanuatu's first francophone Prime Minister, made an official visit to France in May 1992, and the two countries fully restored diplomatic relations in October. In July, however, the Carlot Government reaffirmed its support for the Kanak independence movement in New Caledonia, following threats by Walter Lini to withdraw from the Government unless Carlot's pro-French policies were modified. Improved relations with France were confirmed in 1993 with the signing of a bilateral co-operation agreement. In mid-1995 the Carlot Government was virtually alone in the region in failing to condemn France's resumption of nuclear tests in French Polynesia. The opposition criticized the Government's stance as not reflecting the views of the vast majority of ni-Vanuatu. In 2006, during a 'France-Oceania' meeting of regional leaders, the Governments of France and Vanuatu and the administration of New Caledonia concluded a tripartite agreement on co-operation. Under this agreement, assistance to Vanuatu during 2009 included the provision of improved television transmitters and a new sound system for the Parliament building. A long-standing disagreement over the sovereignty of the small, uninhabited Matthew and Hunter islands, situated between Vanuatu and New Caledonia, caused renewed controversy in January 2010, when the Minister of Internal Affairs, Moana Carcasses Kalosil, was criticized by opposition politicians for suggesting that France and Vanuatu should establish a condominium over the islands. The Maritime Zone Amendment Act, approved by the Vanuatu legislature in June, referred to Matthew and Hunter islands as 'within and part of the sovereign state of the Republic of Vanuatu'. In December Prime Minister Edward Natapei warned that if France were not prepared to open a dialogue over ownership of the disputed islands Vanuatu would be forced to refer the matter to the ICJ.

In February 2009 a government delegation travelled to the US city of New York for a meeting of the UN Economic and Social Council (ECOSOC, see p. 21) to present a case against recommendations that Vanuatu's status be raised from that of Least Developed Country (LDC) to Developing Country. The change in status would lead to the loss of a number of economic privileges, including special treatment in areas such as trade and foreign aid. In mid-2011 Vanuatu still retained LDC status. In March 2009 the Government re-entered negotiations on its accession to the World Trade Organization (WTO, see p. 430), initiated in 1995 but subsequently suspended. In early May 2011 the WTO Working Party on Vanuatu's accession approved the country's accession arrangements, which were expected formally to be adopted later in that month; Vanuatu would then have six months in which to ratify the agreement before acceding to the Organization 30 days later. However, the benefits of membership were questioned by some local non-governmental organizations. Meanwhile, in December 2009 the European Union released US $1.06m. in budgetary support for Vanuatu as part of a recently agreed economic reform programme to encourage good governance and improved services.

CONSTITUTION AND GOVERNMENT

Vanuatu is a republic. Under the 1980 Constitution, legislative power is vested in the unicameral Parliament, with 52 members who are elected by universal adult suffrage for four years. The President is the head of state, elected for a five-year term by an electoral college consisting of Parliament and the Presidents of the Regional Councils. Executive power is vested in the Council of Ministers, appointed by the Prime Minister and responsible to Parliament. The Prime Minister is elected by and from members of Parliament. Judicial power is exercised by Magistrates' and Island Courts and the Supreme Court. The Court of Appeal is constituted by two or more judges of the Supreme Court sitting together. The six provincial authorities are Malampa, Penama, Sanma, Shefa, Tafea and Torba.

REGIONAL AND INTERNATIONAL CO-OPERATION

Vanuatu is a member of the Pacific Community (see p. 410), the Pacific Islands Forum (see p. 413), the Asian Development Bank (ADB, see p. 202) and the UN's Economic and Social Commission for Asia and the Pacific (ESCAP, see p. 37). The country is a signatory of the South Pacific Regional Trade and Economic Agreement (SPARTECA, see p. 414) and of the Lomé Conventions and the successor Cotonou Agreement (see p. 327) with the European Union. Vanuatu is also a member of the Melanesian Spearhead Group, along with Fiji, Papua New Guinea and Solomon Islands; a free trade agreement concluded by members grants most-favoured nation status for all trading transactions.

Vanuatu joined the UN in 1981 and is a member of the Commonwealth and the Organisation Internationale de la Francophonie (La Francophonie). The country was expected to join the World Trade Organization (WTO, see p. 430) in mid-2011.

ECONOMIC AFFAIRS

In 2009, according to estimates by the World Bank, Vanuatu's gross national income (GNI), measured at average 2007–09 prices, was US $628m., equivalent to $2,620 per head (or $4,290 per head on an international purchasing-power parity basis). During 2000–09, it was estimated, the population increased at an average annual rate of 2.6%, while gross domestic product (GDP) per head decreased, in real terms, by an average of 0.6% per year. Overall GDP increased, in real terms, at an average annual rate of 3.2% in 2000–09. According to the Asian Development Bank (ADB), GDP increased by 4.0% in 2009 and by 3.0% in 2010.

The agricultural sector (including forestry and fishing) contributed 20.7% of GDP in 2008, according to the ADB, compared with some 40% in the early 1980s. According to UN figures, the GDP of the agricultural sector was estimated to have increased at an average annual rate of 2.8% in 2000–09. The sector's GDP increased by 1.7% in 2009 and by 2.2% in 2010, according to the ADB. About 29.9% of the employed labour force was estimated to be engaged in agricultural activities in mid-2011, according to FAO estimates. Coconuts, cocoa and coffee are grown largely for export. In 2008 copra provided 30.3% of total export earnings and coconut oil 20.4%. Yams, taro, cassava, breadfruit and vegetables are cultivated for subsistence purposes. Cattle, pigs, goats and poultry are the country's principal livestock, and beef is a significant export commodity. The forestry industry is also important, with timber having become a major export item. The Government derives substantial revenue from the sale of fishing rights to foreign fleets. In October 2005 the Government and the People's Republic of China signed an agreement that provided for the financing of the establishment of a new fish-processing plant near Port Vila. The facility would also be available for processing other products for export, such as beef.

The industrial sector (including manufacturing, utilities and construction) contributed about 9.7% of GDP in 2008, according to the ADB, although only 3.5% of the employed labour force were engaged in the sector in 1989. In 2000–09, according to UN figures, the GDP of the industrial sector was estimated to have decreased at an average annual rate of 0.2%. Compared with the previous year, industrial GDP increased by 6.9% in 2009 and by 9.2% in 2010, according to the ADB.

According to the ADB, manufacturing, which contributed about 4.2% of GDP in 2008, is mainly concerned with the processing of agricultural products. In 2000–09, according to the UN figures, the GDP of the manufacturing sector increased at an average annual rate of 1.3%. The country's first kava extraction plant (for the manufacture of alcoholic beverages) was opened in 1998. However, in 2001 a ban was imposed on kava imports by several countries in Europe, owing to health concerns.

Various mineral deposits have been identified. These include manganese on the island of Efate, and there are reserves of gold, copper and petroleum around the islands of Malekula and Espiritu Santo. In March 2006 an agreement was signed by the Vanuatu Government to allow a Swiss-US company to extract manganese and to export the commodity.

According to the ADB, construction activity alone contributed 3.2% of GDP in 2008. According to UN figures, during 2000–09 construction GDP decreased at an average annual rate of 3.7%; the sector grew by 27.5% in 2008, but declined by 7.3% in 2009.

Electricity generation is largely thermal. Long-term plans focus on the potential of renewable resources. Imports of mineral fuels comprised 16.7% of the value of total imports in 2008.

The economy depends heavily on the services sector, which accounted for 69.5% of GDP in 2008, according to the ADB. According to UN figures, in 2000–09 the GDP of the services sector was estimated to have increased at an average annual rate of 4.4%. According to the ADB, the GDP of the services sector increased by 3.8% in 2009 and by 4.4% in 2010. Tourism, 'offshore' banking facilities and a shipping registry, providing

VANUATU

a 'flag of convenience' to foreign-owned vessels, make a significant contribution to the country's income. In 2009 a total of 225,493 foreign tourists visited Vanuatu, including 124,818 cruise-ship arrivals (in comparison with 106,138 arrivals by sea in the previous year). A further increase in total visitor arrivals was reported in 2010, when numbers were estimated to have risen to 237,648. Revenue from tourism was estimated at US $142m. in 2007.

In 2009 Vanuatu recorded a visible trade deficit of US $177.0m., and there was a deficit of $14.7m. on the current account of the balance of payments. In 2008 the principal sources of imports were Australia (28.1%); other major suppliers were New Zealand, Fiji and Singapore. In that year principal source for exports was New Caledonia was (accounting for 9.8% of the total); other major purchasers were Japan and New Zealand. The principal imports in 2008 were machinery and transport equipment, mineral fuels and lubricants, and food and live animals. Copra (which provided 30.3% of total export earnings), coconut oil (20.3%) and kava (13.7%) were the main export commodities in 2008.

Budget estimates for 2009 projected a deficit of 3,910m. vatu, excluding grants from abroad in that year totalling 4,529m. vatu. The Government envisaged a near-balanced budget in 2010. Australia, New Zealand, France, the United Kingdom and Japan are significant sources of development assistance. In 2010/11 Australia budgeted for aid of $A66.4m. In the same year development assistance from New Zealand was projected at $NZ19.0m. Vanuatu's total external debt reached US $138.1m. at the end of 2008, of which US $102.0m. was long-term public and publicly guaranteed debt. In that year the cost of debt-servicing was estimated to be equivalent to 1.4% of the value of exports of goods, services and income. The annual rate of inflation averaged 2.9% in 2000–09. Consumer prices increased by 3.4% in 2010, according to the ADB.

Vanuatu's economic development has been curtailed by the slow pace of reform, weak infrastructure and dependence on the agricultural sector, which is vulnerable to adverse weather conditions. Another important factor is the relatively high rate of population growth: in the early 21st century the country's GDP per head was estimated to be below the level of the mid-1980s. Opportunities for overseas employment have traditionally been limited. Since 2007, however, the establishment of schemes permitting Pacific islanders to work in the New Zealand and Australian horticultural industries have provided wider opportunities for ni-Vanuatu. In March 2006 Vanuatu and the US Millennium Challenge Corporation signed an agreement providing the country with a grant of US $65.9m., to be disbursed between 2007 and 2011, for the purpose of financing various infrastructural projects. A major challenge for successive governments has been the need to address the problem of hardship in rural areas, where access to basic services has remained very limited. The relative strength of the economy of Australia (the leading source of visitors), combined with the political instability in neighbouring Fiji, led to an increase in tourist arrivals in 2009. However, although arrivals by cruise-ship of short-stay visitors continued to rise, the number of tourists arriving by air was reported to have decreased in 2010. It was hoped that the availability of additional flights from Australia, together with the strength of that country's currency, would reverse the decline in the latter category of visitors. Inflationary pressures moderated somewhat in 2010, but by early 2011 upward pressure on consumer prices was reported to be increasing, as a result of the higher costs of fuel and other essential commodities. Despite the deterioration in global economic conditions, GDP growth was maintained in 2008–10, largely owing to the steady performance of the tourism sector. GDP was forecast by the ADB to expand for the ninth consecutive year in 2011, to reach 4.2%. Vanuatu's accession to the World Trade Organization (WTO, see p. 430), scheduled for 2011 following the successful completion of negotiations in May, was expected to lead to the country's closer integration into the global economy and to yield major benefits in the longer term.

PUBLIC HOLIDAYS

2012 (provisional): 2 January (for New Year's Day), 21 February (Father Walter Lini Day), 5 March (Custom Chief's Day), 6–9 April (Easter), 1 May (Labour Day), 17 May (Ascension Day), 24 July (Children's Day), 30 July (Independence Day), 15 August (Assumption), 5 October (Constitution Day), 29 November (Unity Day), 25 December (for Christmas Day), 26 December (Family Day).

Statistical Survey

Source (unless otherwise indicated): National Statistics Office, Ministry of Finance and Economic Management, PMB 9019, Port Vila; tel. (678) 22110; fax (678) 24583; e-mail stats@vanuatu.com.vu; internet www.spc.int/prism/country/vu/stats.

AREA AND POPULATION

Area: 12,190 sq km (4,707 sq miles); *By Island* (sq km): Espiritu Santo 4,010; Malekula 2,024; Efate 887; Erromango 887; Ambrym 666; Tanna 561; Pentecost 499; Epi 444; Ambae 399; Vanua Lava 343; Gaua 315; Maewo 300.

Population: 186,678 at census of 16 November 1999; 234,023 (males 119,090, females 114,933) at census of 16 November 2009. *Mid-2011* (Secretariat of the Pacific Community estimate): 251,304 (Source: Pacific Regional Information System). *By Island* (mid-1999, official estimates): Espiritu Santo 31,811; Malekula 19,766; Efate 43,295; Erromango 1,554; Ambrym 7,613; Tanna 26,306; Pentecost 14,837; Epi 4,706; Ambae 10,692; Vanua Lava 2,074; Gaua 1,924; Maewo 3,385. Source: partly Pacific Regional Information System.

Density (mid-2011): 20.6 per sq km.

Population by Age and Sex (Secretariat of the Pacific Community estimates at mid-2011): *0–14:* 93,731 (males 48,274, females 45,457); *15–64:* 148,559 (males 75,162, females 73,397); *65 and over:* 9,014 (males 4,623, females 4,391); *Total* 251,304 (males 128,059, females 123,245) (Source: Pacific Regional Information System).

Principal Towns (population at 2009 census): Port Vila (capital) 44,039; Luganville (Santo) 13,156.

Births and Deaths (annual averages, 2005–10, UN estimates): Birth rate 30.4 per 1,000; Death rate 5.0 per 1,000. Source: UN, *World Population Prospects: The 2008 Revision.*

Life Expectancy (years at birth, WHO estimates): 69 (males 68; females 70) in 2008. Source: WHO, *World Health Statistics.*

Economically Active Population (census of May 1989): Agriculture, forestry, hunting and fishing 40,889; Mining and quarrying 1; Manufacturing 891; Electricity, gas and water 109; Construction 1,302; Trade, restaurants and hotels 2,712; Transport, storage and communications 1,030; Financing, insurance, real estate and business services 646; Community, social and personal services 7,891; *Sub-total* 55,471; Activities not adequately defined 11,126; *Total labour force* 66,597 (males 35,692, females 30,905). *1999 Census* (persons aged 15 to 64 years): Subsistence farmers 51,309; Total employed (incl. others) 75,110; Unemployed (seeking work) 1,260; Total labour force 76,370 (males 42,072, females 34,298). *Mid-2011* (estimates): Agriculture, etc. 40,000; Total labour force 134,000 (Source: FAO).

HEALTH AND WELFARE

Key Indicators

Total Fertility Rate (children per woman, 2008): 4.0.

Under-5 Mortality Rate (per 1,000 live births, 2008): 33.

Physicians (per 1,000 head, 2004): 0.1.

Hospital Beds (per 1,000 head, 2005): 4.1.

Health Expenditure (2007): US $ per head (PPP): 145.

Health Expenditure (2007): % of GDP: 3.6.

Health Expenditure (2007): public (% of total): 76.3.

Access to Water (% of persons, 2008): 83.

Access to Sanitation (% of persons, 2008): 53.

Total Carbon Dioxide Emissions ('000 metric tons, 2007): 102.6.

Carbon Dioxide Emissions Per Head (metric tons, 2007): 0.4.

Human Development Index (2007): ranking: 126.

Human Development Index (2007): value: 0.693.

For sources and definitions, see explanatory note on p. vi.

VANUATU

Statistical Survey

AGRICULTURE, ETC.

Principal Crops ('000 metric tons, 2008 unless otherwise indicated, FAO estimates): Coconuts 308; Roots and tubers 45.0 (2009); Vegetables and melons 11.5 (2009); Bananas 14.5; Groundnuts, with shell 2.6; Maize 0.8.

Livestock ('000 head, year ending September 2008, FAO estimates): Cattle 175; Pigs 89; Goats 19; Horses 3; Chickens 804. Note: No data were available for 2009.

Livestock Products (metric tons, 2009 unless otherwise indicated, FAO estimates): Cattle meat 2,560; Pig meat 3,366 (2008); Chicken meat 460; Cows' milk 2,900 (2008); Hen eggs 340.

Forestry ('000 cu m, 2009): *Roundwood Removals* (excl. bark): Sawlogs and veneer logs 28; Fuel wood 91; Total 119. *Sawnwood Production* (all broadleaved, incl. railway sleepers): Total 28.

Fishing ('000 metric tons, live weight, 2008): Marine fishes 60.6 (Skipjack tuna 38.9; Yellowfin tuna 10.6; Bigeye tuna 2.9; Albacore 5.8); Marine crustaceans 250.0 (FAO estimate); Total catch (incl. others) 60.9.

Source: FAO.

FINANCE

Currency and Exchange Rates: Currency is the vatu. *Sterling, Dollar and Euro Equivalents* (30 November 2010): £1 sterling = 148.712 vatu; US $1 = 95.770 vatu; €1 = 124.482 vatu; 1,000 vatu = £6.72 = $10.44 = €8.03. *Average Exchange Rate* (vatu per US $): 102.44 in 2007; 101.33 in 2008; 106.74 in 2009.

Budget (million vatu, 2009): *Revenue:* Tax revenue 10,855; Other current revenue 1,445; Capital assets 6; Total 12,306, excluding grants from abroad (4,529). *Expenditure:* Current expenditure 13,245; Capital expenditure 2,971; Total (incl. others) 16,215. Source: Asian Development Bank.

International Reserves (US $ million at 31 December 2010): IMF special drawing rights 2.39; Reserve position in IMF 3.84; Foreign exchange 155.15; *Total* 161.38. Source: IMF, *International Financial Statistics*.

Money Supply (million vatu at 31 December 2010): Currency outside depository corporations 4,542; Transferable deposits 17,591; Other deposits 34,407; *Broad money* 56,539. Source: IMF, *International Financial Statistics*.

Cost of Living (Consumer Price Index; base: 2005 = 100): All items 118.5 in 2007; 124.2 in 2008; 129.8 in 2009. Source: ILO.

Gross Domestic Product (million vatu at constant 1983 prices): 17,906 in 2005; 19,236 in 2006; 20,550 in 2007.

Expenditure on the Gross Domestic Product (million vatu at current prices, 2008): Government final consumption expenditure 9,360; Private final consumption expenditure 36,671; Gross fixed capital formation 19,779; Increase in stocks 690; Statistical discrepancy 1,441; *Total domestic expenditure* 67,941; Exports of goods and services 30,016; *Less* Imports of goods and services 35,204; *GDP in purchasers' values* 62,753. Source: Asian Development Bank.

Gross Domestic Product by Economic Activity (million vatu at current prices, 2008): Agriculture, forestry and fishing 11,722; Mining 24; Manufacturing 2,380; Electricity, gas and water 1,300; Construction 1,797; Wholesale and retail trade 9,563; Transport, storage and communications 5,979; Finance and insurance 4,795; Public administration 7,964; Others 11,032; *Sub-total* 56,556; Taxes, less subsidies, on products 8,394; *Less* Imputed bank service charge 2,198; *GDP in purchasers' values* 62,753. Source: Asian Development Bank.

Balance of Payments (US $ million, 2009): Exports of goods 53.6; Imports of goods –230.5; *Trade balance* –177.0; Exports of services and income 261.5; Imports of services and income –141.4; *Balance on goods, services and income* –56.9; Current transfers received 44.4; Current transfers paid –2.2; *Current balance* –14.7 (incl. adjustments); Capital account (net) 32.2; Direct investment (net) 28.9; Portfolio investment (net) –0.9; Other investments (net) –16.8; Net errors and omissions –7.6; *Overall balance* 21.1. Source: Asian Development Bank.

EXTERNAL TRADE

Principal Commodities (million vatu, 2008): *Imports c.i.f.* (excl. imports for re-export): Food and live animals 4,452; Beverages and tobacco 806; Mineral fuels, lubricants, etc. 4,818; Chemicals 2,033; Basic manufactures 4,162; Machinery and transport equipment 8,924; Miscellaneous manufactured articles 2,484; Total (incl. others) 28,850. *Exports f.o.b.* (excl. re-exports): Cocoa 241; Copra 1,079; Beef 385; Timber 80; Coconut oil 727; Shells 43; Kava 487; Total (incl. others) 3,566.

Principal Trading Partners (million vatu, 2008): *Imports c.i.f.* (excl. imports for re-export): Australia 8,099; Fiji 3,005; France 1,320; Japan 1,348; New Zealand 3,830; Singapore 1,492; Total (incl. others) 28,850. *Exports f.o.b.* (excl. re-exports): Australia 126; European Union countries 783; Japan 241; New Caledonia 350; New Zealand 194; Total (incl. others) 3,566.

TRANSPORT

Road Traffic ('000 motor vehicles in use, 2001, estimates): Passenger cars 2.6; Commercial vehicles 4.4. Source: UN, *Statistical Yearbook*.

Shipping: *Merchant Fleet* (registered at 31 December 2009): Vessels 445; Total displacement ('000 grt) 2,144.6 (Source: IHS Fairplay, *World Fleet Statistics*). *International Sea-borne Freight Traffic* ('000 metric tons, 1990, estimates): Goods loaded 80; Goods unloaded 55 (Source: UN, *Monthly Bulletin of Statistics*).

Civil Aviation (traffic on scheduled services, 2006): Kilometres flown (million) 3; Passengers carried ('000) 117; Passenger-km (million) 241; Total ton-km (million) 23. Source: UN, *Statistical Yearbook*.

TOURISM

Foreign Tourist Arrivals: 81,345 in 2007; 90,657 in 2008; 100,675 in 2009. Note: Figures refer to arrivals by air only; arrivals from cruise-ships were: 85,737 in 2007; 106,138 in 2008; 124,818 in 2009.

Tourist Arrivals by Country of Residence (2009): Australia 64,909; New Caledonia 9,155; New Zealand 12,606; Other Pacific 3,707; Europe 4,891; North America 2,549; Total (incl. others) 100,675.

Tourism Receipts (US $ million, incl. passenger transport): 104 in 2005; 109 in 2006; 142 in 2007 (Source: World Tourism Organization).

COMMUNICATIONS MEDIA

Radio Receivers (1997): 62,000 in use*.

Television Receivers (1999): 2,000 in use†.

Telephones (2009): 7,200 main lines in use‡.

Mobile Cellular Telephones (2009): 126,500 subscribers‡.

Internet Users (2009): 17,000‡.

Broadband Subscribers (2009): 500‡.

Personal Computers: 3,000 (13.9 per 1,000 persons) in 2005‡.

Non-daily Newspapers (2004): 1 (estimated circulation 3,000)*.

* Source: UNESCO, *Statistical Yearbook*.
† Source: UN, *Statistical Yearbook*.
‡ Source: International Telecommunication Union.

EDUCATION

Pre-primary (1992, unless otherwise indicated): 252 schools; 49 teachers (1980); 5,178 pupils.

Primary (2007, unless otherwise indicated): 374 schools (1995); 1,614 teachers (2002); 38,026 pupils.

Secondary (2007, unless otherwise indicated): 27 schools (1995); 591 teachers (2002); 15,132 students.

Tertiary (2002): 2,124 students.

Secondary (Teacher Training): 1 college (1989); 13 teachers (1983); 124 students (1991).

Pupil-teacher Ratio (primary education, UNESCO estimate): 23.8 in 2006/07 (Source: UNESCO Institute for Statistics).

Adult Literacy Rate (UNESCO estimates): 81.3% (males 83.0%; females 79.5%) in 2008 (Source: UNESCO Institute for Statistics).

VANUATU

Directory

The Government

HEAD OF STATE

President: Iolu Abbil Johnson (appointed 2 September 2009).

COUNCIL OF MINISTERS
(May 2011)

The Government includes members of the Green Confederation Party, the Land and Justice Party (LJP), the National Community Association Party (NCAP), the People's Progressive Party (PPP), the Union of Moderate Parties (UMP), the Vanuaaku Party (VP), the Vanuatu Republikan Pati (VRP) and the National United Party (NUP).

Prime Minister and Minister for Public Service: Sato Kilman (PPP).
Deputy Prime Minister and Minister of Trade, Industry and Tourism: Ham Lini (NUP).
Minister of Foreign Affairs: Alfred Carlot (VRP).
Minister of Infrastructure and Public Utilities: Harry Lauko (VP).
Minister of Internal Affairs: George Wells (NCAP).
Minister of Justice and Social Affairs: Ralph Regenvanu (LJP).
Minister of Agriculture, Quarantine, Forestry and Fisheries: James Ngwango (PPP).
Minister of Health: Don Ken (Ind.).
Minister of Education: Marcellino Pipite (VRP).
Minister of Finance and Economic Management: Moana Carcasses Kalosil (Green Confederation Party).
Minister of Lands and Natural Resources: Steven Kalsakau (UMP).
Minister of Ni-Vanuatu Business Development and Co-operatives: Esmon Sae (NUP).
Minister of Youth Sports and Training: Morkin Stevens (NUP).

MINISTRIES AND DEPARTMENTS

Prime Minister's Office: PMB 9053, Port Vila; tel. 22413; fax 26301; internet www.governmentofvanuatu.gov.vu.
Deputy Prime Minister's Office: PMB 9056, Port Vila; tel. 27045; fax 27832.
Ministry of Agriculture, Quarantine, Forestry and Fisheries: PMB 9039, Port Vila; tel. 23406; fax 26498.
Ministry of the Comprehensive Reform Programme: POB 9088, Port Vila; tel. 25816; fax 25815.
Ministry of Co-operative and Ni-Vanuatu Business Development: PMB 9056, Port Vila; tel. 26220; fax 25677.
Ministry of Education: PMB 9028, Port Vila; tel. 22309; fax 24569.
Ministry of Finance and Economic Management: PMB 9058, Port Vila; tel. 23032; fax 27937.
Ministry of Foreign Affairs and External Trade: PMB 9051, Port Vila; tel. 27045; fax 27832.
Ministry of Health: PMB 9042, Port Vila; tel. 22545; fax 26113.
Ministry of Infrastructure and Public Utilities: PMB 9057, Port Vila; tel. 22790; fax 27714.
Ministry of Internal Affairs: PMB 9036, Port Vila; tel. 22252; fax 27064.
Ministry of Justice and Social Welfare: PMB 9036, Port Vila; tel. 22252; fax 27064.
Ministry of Lands and Natural Resources: PMB 9090, Port Vila; tel. 22892; fax 27708; e-mail molvanuatu@gmail.com; internet www.mol.gov.vu.
Ministry of Sports and Youth Development: POB 9006, Port Vila; tel. 25298; fax 26879.
Ministry of Trade, Industry, Commerce and Tourism: PMB 9056, Port Vila; tel. 25674; fax 25677.

Legislature

PARLIAMENT

Speaker: Maxime Carlot Korman.

General Election, 2 September 2008

	Seats
Vanuaaku Pati	11
National United Party	8
Union of Moderate Parties	7
Vanuatu Republikan Pati	7
People's Progressive Party	4
Green Confederation Party	2
Others	9
Independents	4
Total	**52**

Election Commission

Vanuatu Electoral Commission: PMB 033, Port Vila; tel. 23914; fax 26681; Principal Electoral Officer Martin Tete.

Political Organizations

Efate Laketu Party: Port Vila; f. 1982; regional party, based on the island of Efate.
Green Confederation Party: POB 538, Port Vila; tel. 7778069; e-mail moanakalosil6@gmail.com; f. 2001; est. by breakaway group of the UMP; Leader Moana Carcasses Kalosil.
Land and Justice Party: Port Vila; f. 2010; aims to protect customary land ownership and to address issue of foreign ownership of local businesses; Leader Ralph Regenvanu.
Melanesian Progressive Pati (MPP): POB 39, Port Vila; tel. 23485; fax 23315; f. 1988; est. by breakaway group of the VP; Chair. Barak Sope; Sec.-Gen. Georges Calo.
National Community Association Party (NCAP): Port Vila; f. 1996; advocates land reform.
National Democratic Party (NDP): Port Vila; f. 1986; advocates strengthening of links with France and the United Kingdom; Leader John Naupa.
National United Party (NUP): Port Vila; f. 1991; est. by supporters of Walter Lini, following his removal as leader of the VP; Pres. Ham Lini; Sec.-Gen. Willie Titongoa.
People's Democratic Party (PDP): Port Vila; f. 1994; est. by breakaway faction of the NUP.
People's Progressive Party (PPP): Port Vila; f. 2001; formed coalition with the NUP and Fren Melanesia to contest 2002 elections; Pres. Sato Kilman; Sec.-Gen. Willie Lop.
Tu Vanuatu Kominiti: Port Vila; f. 1996; espouses traditional Melanesian and Christian values; Leader Hilda Lini.
Union of Moderate Parties (UMP): POB 698, Port Vila; f. 1980; Pres. Serge Vohor; Vice-Pres. Charlot Salwai.
Vanuaaku Pati (VP) (Our Land Party): POB 472, Port Vila; tel. 22584; f. 1971; est. as the New Hebrides National Party; advocates 'Melanesian socialism'; Pres. Edward Natapei; First Vice-Pres. Iolu Abbil Johnson; Sec.-Gen. Sela Molisa.
Vanuatu Independent Alliance Party (VIAP): Port Vila; f. 1982; supports free enterprise; Leaders Thomas Seru, George Worek, Kalmer Vocor.
Vanuatu Independent Movement: Port Vila; f. 2002; Pres. Willie Tasso.
Vanuatu Labour Party (VLP): Port Vila; f. 1986; trade-union based; Leader Joshua Kalsakau.
Vanuatu Progressive Development Party: Epi; f. 2011; promotes devt in rural sector; Pres. Robert Bohn; Sec.-Gen. Peter Mawa.
Vanuatu Republikan Pati (VRP): Port Vila; f. 1998; est. by breakaway faction of the UMP; Leader Maxime Carlot Korman; Sec.-Gen. Marcellino Pepite.

The Na-Griamel (Leader Frankley Stevens), Namangie Aute Tan Union (Leader Vincent Bulekone) and Fren Melanesia (Leader Albert Ravutia) represent rural interests on the islands of Espiritu Santo and Malekula. The John Frum Movement represents interests on the island of Tanna.

VANUATU

Directory

Diplomatic Representation

EMBASSIES AND HIGH COMMISSIONS IN VANUATU

Australia: Winston Churchill Ave, POB 111, Port Vila; tel. 22777; fax 23948; e-mail australia_vanuatu@dfat.gov.au; internet www.vanuatu.highcommission.gov.au; High Commissioner JEFF ROACH.

China, People's Republic: PMB 9071, Rue d'Auvergne, Nambatu, Port Vila; tel. 23598; fax 24877; e-mail publicinfo@chinese-embassy.com.vu; internet vu.china-embassy.org; Ambassador CHENG SHUPING.

France: Kumul Highway, POB 60, Port Vila; tel. 28700; fax 28701; e-mail ambafra@vanuatu.com.vu; internet www.ambafrance-vu.org; Ambassador FRANÇOISE MAYLIÉ.

New Zealand: La Casa d'Andrea e Luciano, Rue Pierre Lamy St, POB 161, Port Vila; tel. 22933; fax 22518; e-mail kiwi@vanuatu.com.vu; internet www.nzembassy.com/vanuatu; High Commissioner BILL DOBBIE.

Judicial System

The Supreme Court has unlimited jurisdiction to hear and determine any civil or criminal proceedings, and is the court of first instance in constitutional matters. It consists of the Chief Justice, appointed by the President of the Republic after consultation with the Prime Minister and the leader of the opposition, and three other judges, who are appointed by the President of the Republic on the advice of the Judicial Service Commission. The Court of Appeal is constituted by two or more judges of the Supreme Court sitting together.

Magistrates' Courts have limited jurisdiction to hear and determine any civil or criminal proceedings. Island Courts have been established in several local government regions, and are constituted when three justices are sitting together to exercise civil or criminal jurisdiction, as defined in the warrant establishing the court. A magistrate nominated by the Chief Justice acts as Chairman. The Island Courts are competent to rule on land disputes.

In 2001 legislation was introduced to establish a new Land Tribunal, in order to expedite the hearing of land disputes. The tribunal was to have three levels, and no cases were to go beyond the tribunal and enter either the Supreme Court or the Island Courts.

Chief Justice of the Supreme Court: VINCENT LUNABEK, PMB 041, rue de Querios, Port Vila; tel. 22420; fax 22692.

Public Prosecutor: KAYLEEN TAVOA.

Attorney-General: ISHMAEL KALSAKAU.

Religion

Most of Vanuatu's inhabitants profess Christianity. Presbyterians form the largest Christian group (with about one-half of the population being adherents), followed by Anglicans and Roman Catholics.

CHRISTIANITY

Vanuatu Christian Council: POB 13, Luganville, Santo; tel. 03232; f. 1967; est. as New Hebrides Christian Council; five mem. churches, two observers; Chair. (vacant); Sec. Rev. JOHN LIU.

The Roman Catholic Church

Vanuatu forms the single diocese of Port Vila, suffragan to the archdiocese of Nouméa (New Caledonia). At 31 December 2007 there were an estimated 32,500 adherents in the country. The Bishop participates in the Catholic Bishops' Conference of the Pacific, based in Fiji.

Bishop of Port Vila: JOHN BOSCO BAREMES, Evêché, POB 59, Port Vila; tel. 22640; fax 25342; e-mail catholik@vanuatu.com.vu.

The Anglican Communion

Anglicans in Vanuatu are adherents of the Church of the Province of Melanesia, comprising eight dioceses: Vanuatu (which also includes New Caledonia), Banks and Torres and six dioceses in Solomon Islands. The Archbishop of the Province is the Bishop of Central Melanesia, resident in Honiara, Solomon Islands. In 1985 the Church had an estimated 16,000 adherents in Vanuatu.

Bishop of Vanuatu: Fr JAMES LIGO, Bishop's House, POB 238, Luganville, Santo; tel. 37065; fax 36026.

Bishop of Banks and Torres: Rt Rev. NATHAN TOME, Bishop's House, POB 19, Toutamwat, Torba Province.

Protestant Churches

Presbyterian Church of Vanuatu (Presbitirin Jyos long Vanuatu): POB 150, Port Vila; tel. 27184; fax 23650; f. 1948; 56,000 mems (1995); Moderator Pastor BANI KALSINGER; Assembly Clerk Pastor FAMA RAKAU.

Other denominations active in the country include the Apostolic Church, the Assemblies of God, the Churches of Christ in Vanuatu and the Seventh-day Adventist Church.

BAHÁ'Í FAITH

National Spiritual Assembly of the Bahá'ís of Vanuatu: POB 1017, Port Vila; tel. 22419; e-mail nsavanuatu@vanuatu.com.vu; f. 1953; Sec. CHARLES PIERCE; mems resident in 233 localities.

The Press

Hapi Tumas Long Vanuatu: POB 1292, Port Vila; tel. 23642; fax 23343; quarterly tourist information; English; Publr MARC NEIL-JONES; circ. 12,000.

Pacific Island Profile: Port Vila; f. 1990; monthly; general interest; English and French; Editor HILDA LINI.

Port Vila Presse: 1st Floor, Raffea House, POB 637, Port Vila; tel. 22200; fax 27999; e-mail marke@presse.com.vu; internet www.presse.com.vu; f. 2000; daily; English and French; Publr MARKE LOWEN; Editor RICKY BINIHI.

Vanuatu Daily Post: POB 1292, Port Vila; tel. 23111; fax 24111; e-mail tpost@vanuatu.com.vu; internet www.dailypost.vu; daily; English; Publr MARC NEIL-JONES; Editor ROYSON WILLIE; circ. 2,000.

Vanuatu Weekly: PMB 049, Port Vila; tel. 22999; fax 22026; f. 1980; weekly; govt-owned; Bislama, English and French; circ. 1,700.

Vanuatu Wikli Post: f. 2008; weekly; Bislama; Editor RICKY BINIHI.

Viewpoints: Port Vila; weekly; newsletter of Vanuaaku Pati; Editor PETER TAURAKOTO.

Wantok Niuspepa: POB 1292, Port Vila; tel. 23642; fax 23343.

Broadcasting and Communications

TELECOMMUNICATIONS

Digicel Vanuatu: PMB 9103, Ellouk Plateau, Port Vila; tel. 27692; fax 27865; e-mail customercarevanuatu@digicelgroup.com; internet www.digicelvanuatu.com; Gen. Man. TANYA MENZIES.

Telecom Vanuatu Ltd (TVL): POB 146, Port Vila; tel. 22185; fax 22628; e-mail sales@tvl.net.vu; internet www.tvl.vu; f. 1989; national and international telecommunications services; Man. Dir MICHEL DUPUIS.

BROADCASTING

Radio

Vanuatu Broadcasting and Television Corpn (VBTC): PMB 049, Port Vila; tel. 22999; fax 22026; internet www.vbtc.com.vu; fmrly Government Media Services, name changed in 1992; Gen. Man. FRED VUROBARAVU; Chair. GODWIN LIGO.

Radio Vanuatu: PMB 049, Port Vila; tel. 22999; fax 22026; f. 1966; govt-owned; broadcasts in English, French and Bislama; Dir JOE BOMAL CARLO.

Television

Vanuatu Broadcasting and Television Corpn (VBTC): see Radio.

Television Blong Vanuatu: PMB 049, Port Vila; f. 1993; govt-owned; French-funded; broadcasts for four hours daily in French and English; Gen. Man. CLAUDE CASTELLY; Programme Man. GAEL LE DANTEC.

Finance

(cap. = capital; res = reserves; dep. = deposits; brs = branches; amounts in vatu unless otherwise indicated)

BANKING

Central Bank

Reserve Bank of Vanuatu: PMB 9062, Port Vila; tel. 23333; fax 24231; e-mail enquiries@rbv.gov.vu; internet www.rbv.gov.vu; f. 1981; est. as Central Bank of Vanuatu; name changed as above in 1989; govt-owned; cap. 100.0m., res 613.6m., dep. 7,722.1m. (Dec. 2006); Gov. ODO TEVI.

VANUATU

Development Bank

Development Bank of Vanuatu: Rue de Paris, POB 241, Port Vila; tel. 22181; fax 24591; f. 1979; govt-owned; Man. Dir AUGUSTINE GARAE.

National Bank

National Bank of Vanuatu: POB 249, Rue de Paris, Port Vila; tel. 22201; fax 27227; e-mail nationalbank@vanuatu.com.vu; internet www.nbv.vu; f. 1991; est. upon assumption of control of Vanuatu Co-operative Savings Bank; govt-owned; cap. 600m., dep. 7,793.5m. (Dec. 2008); Chair. DUDLEY ARU; Man. Dir BOB HUGHES; 21 brs.

Foreign Banks

ANZ Bank (Vanuatu) Ltd: PMB 9003, Port Vila; tel. 26355; fax 22230; e-mail vanuatu@anz.com; internet www.anz.com/vanuatu; f. 1971; cap. 3.7m., res 317.7m., dep. 24,734.2m. (Sept. 2003); Man. Dir GAYLE STAPLETON; brs in Port Vila and Luganville.

European Bank Ltd (USA): International Bldg, Fr Walter Lini Highway, POB 65, Port Vila; tel. 27700; fax 22884; e-mail info@europeanbank.net; 'offshore' and private banking; cap. US $0.75m., res US $1.25m., dep. US $44.76m. (Dec. 2008); Chair. THOMAS MONTGOMERY BAYER; Pres. ROBERT MURRAY BOHN.

Westpac Banking Corporation (Australia): Lini Highway, Port Vila; tel. 22084; fax 24773; e-mail westpacvanuatu@westpac.com.au; internet www.westpac.vu; Man. R. B. WRIGHT; 2 brs.

Financial Institutions

The Vanuatu Financial Centre Association: POB 1128, Port Vila; tel. 23410; fax 23405; e-mail VFCA@vanuatu.com.vu; internet www.fca.vu; f. 1980; group of banking, legal, accounting and trust cos administering 'offshore' banking and investment; Chair. MARK STAFFORD; Sec. THOMAS BAYER.

Vanuatu Financial Services Commission (VFSC): Bougainville St, PMB 9023, Port Vila; tel. 22247; fax 22242; e-mail info@vfsc.vu; internet www.vfsc.vu; f. 1993; regulation and supervision of non-banking financial services; Commr GEORGE ANDREWS.

INSURANCE

Pacific Insurance Brokers: POB 229, Port Vila; tel. 23863; fax 23089.

QBE Insurance (Vanuatu) Ltd: La Casa D'Andrea Bldg, POB 186, Port Vila; tel. 22299; fax 23298; e-mail info.van@qbe.com; Gen. Man. GEOFFREY R. CUTTING.

Trade and Industry

GOVERNMENT AGENCY

Vanuatu Investment Promotion Authority: PMB 9011, Port Vila; tel. 24096; fax 25216; e-mail ataritambe@vanuatu.gov.vu; internet www.investinvanuatu.com; fmrly the Vanuatu Investment Board, name changed as above in 2000; CEO SMITH TEBU.

CHAMBER OF COMMERCE

Chamber of Commerce and Industry of Vanuatu: POB 189, Port Vila; tel. 27543; fax 27542; e-mail vancci@vanuatu.com.vu; internet www.vanuatuchamber.org; Pres. JACQUES NIOTEAU.

MARKETING BOARD

Vanuatu Commodities Marketing Board: POB 268, Luganville, Santo; f. 1982; sole exporter of major commodities, including copra, kava and cocoa; plans to cease operations were mooted in mid-2010; Chair. JACK LOWANI.

UTILITIES

Utilities Regulatory Authority: Port Vila, Efate; internet www.ura.gov.vu; f. 2008; regulates electricity and water supply; Pres. JOHNSON NAVITI MARAKIPULE.

Union Electrique du Vanuatu (Unelco Vanuatu Ltd): POB 26, rue Winston Churchill, Port Vila; tel. 22211; fax 25011; e-mail unelco@unelco.com.vu; f. 1939; private org. contracted for the generation and supply of electricity in Port Vila, Luganville, Tanna and Malekula, and for the supply of water in Port Vila; fully owned subsidiary of GDF Suez, France; Dir-Gen. JEAN FRANÇOIS BARBEAU.

TRADE UNIONS

Vanuatu Council of Trade Unions (VCTU): POB 287, Port Vila; tel. 26903; fax 23679; e-mail carlo@vanuatu.com.vu; Pres. OBED MASINGIOW; Sec.-Gen. EPHRAIM KALSAKAU.

National Union of Labour: Port Vila.

The principal trade unions, of which the majority were reported to be inactive at mid-2010, include:

Oil and Gas Workers' Union: Port Vila; f. 1984.

Vanuatu Airline Workers' Union: Port Vila; f. 1984.

Vanuatu National Workers Union: PMB 9089, Port Vila; tel. 23679; fax 26903; Nat. Sec. EPHRAIM KALSAKAU.

Vanuatu Public Service Association: Port Vila.

Vanuatu Teachers' Union: Port Vila; Gen. Sec. CHARLES KALO; Pres. WILFRED LEO.

Vanuatu Waterside, Maritime and Allied Workers' Union: Port Vila.

Transport

ROADS

There are about 1,070 km of roads, of which 54 km, mostly on Efate Island, are sealed.

SHIPPING

The principal ports are Port Vila and Luganville. Various shipping lines operate services to Vanuatu. At the end of 2009 the merchant fleet comprised 445 vessels, with a total displacement of 2,144,600 grt. A shipping registry, based in Singapore, provides a 'flag of convenience' to foreign-owned vessels.

Vanuatu Maritime Authority: POB 320, Marine Quay, Port Vila; tel. 23128; fax 22949; e-mail iantchichine@vma.com.vu; domestic and international ship registry, maritime safety regulator; Commissioner of Maritime Affairs JOHN T. ROOSEN; Chair. LENNOX VUTI.

Ports and Harbour Department: PMB 9046, Port Vila; tel. 22339; fax 22475; e-mail nhamish@vanet.com; Harbour Master Capt. LUKE BEANDI; Dir NORRIS HAMISH.

Burns Philp (Vanuatu) Ltd: POB 27, Port Vila.

Ifira Shipping Agencies Ltd: POB 68, Port Vila; tel. 22929; fax 22052; f. 1986; Man. Dir CLAUDE BOUDIER.

Sami Ltd: Kumul Highway, POB 301, Port Vila; tel. 24106; fax 23405.

South Sea Shipping: POB 84, Port Vila; tel. 22205; fax 23304.

Vanua Navigation Ltd: POB 44, Port Vila; tel. 22027; f. 1977; est. by the Co-operative Federation and Sofrana Unilines; Chief Exec. GEOFFREY J. CLARKE.

CIVIL AVIATION

The principal airports are Bauerfield (Efate, for Port Vila) and Pekoa (Espiritu Santo, for Luganville). There are airstrips on all Vanuatu's principal islands, and also an international airport at White Grass on Tanna. In 2000 it was announced that a further three airports were to be built on the islands of Pentecost, Malekula and Tanna. Major improvements providing for the accommodation of larger aircraft at both Bauerfield and Pekoa airports began in 2000. Moreover, in September 2000 plans for a new international airport at Teouma (Efate) were announced, with finance from a private Thai investor. In late 2003 plans for the construction of an international air terminal at Pekoa (Espiritu Santo) costing US $1.6m. were announced.

Civil Aviation Authority: POB 131, Port Vila; tel. 25111; fax 25532.

Air Vanuatu: 3rd Floor, Air Vanuatu House, Rue de Paris, Port Vila; tel. 23838; fax 23250; e-mail sales@airvanuatu.com.vu; internet www.airvanuatu.com; f. 1981; govt-owned national carrier since 1987; regular services between Port Vila and Sydney, Brisbane and Melbourne (Australia), Nadi (Fiji), Nouméa (New Caledonia), Auckland (New Zealand) and Honiara (Solomon Islands); CEO JOSEPH LALOYER.

Dovair: Port Vila; privately owned; operates domestic services.

Tourism

Tourism is an important source of revenue. Visitors are attracted by the islands' scenery and rich local customs. There were some 120 hotels and guest houses in 2003, providing more than 1,300 rooms. In 2010 foreign visitor arrivals (including cruise-ship passengers) were estimated to have increased by more than 5% to reach 237,648. The majority of visitors are from Australia and New Zealand. Receipts from tourism totalled some US $142m. in 2007. The development of the tourist industry has hitherto been concentrated on the islands of Efate, Espiritu Santo and Tanna, but other islands are also being promoted.

Vanuatu Hotels and Resorts Association: POB 5151, Port Vila; tel. 22040; fax 27579; internet www.vanuatuhotelsandresortsassociation.com; Chair. FAHAD HAYAT.

Vanuatu Tourism Office: Lini Highway, POB 209, Port Vila; tel. 22685; fax 23889; e-mail tourism@vanuatu.com.vu; internet www.vanuatutourism.com; Gen. Man. ANNIE NIATU; Chair. BEN TARI.

Defence

Upon Vanuatu's achievement of independence in 1980, a defence pact with Papua New Guinea was signed. A 300-strong paramilitary force, the Vanuatu Mobile Force, exists. In 2003 Vanuatu sent 50 defence personnel to join the Australian-led regional intervention force in Solomon Islands. In 2007 the Government allocated 1,380m. vatu for defence, equivalent to 11.7% of total recurrent budgetary expenditure.

Education

In 2009 the central Government launched a policy to provide free primary education from the beginning of the 2010 school year. The policy, which was made possible with financial assistance from Australia and New Zealand, was in response to evidence that many children were denied access to education because their parents could not afford school fees. At 2007 it was estimated that 87% of children between the ages of six and 11 were enrolled at primary institutions. Secondary education begins at 12 years of age, and comprises a preliminary cycle of four years and a second cycle of three years. In 2007 there were 38,026 pupils enrolled in primary schools (which numbered 374 in 1995) and 15,132 pupils attended the country's secondary schools (which numbered 27 in 1995). Vocational education and teacher-training are also available.

An extension centre of the University of the South Pacific was opened in Port Vila in 1989. Students from Vanuatu can also receive higher education at the principal faculties of that university (in Suva, Fiji), in Papua New Guinea or in France.

In 2004 the country's first pre-school (the Vila North Model Pre-School) was opened. The pre-school, which had been built with funding of 5.6m. vatu from the European Union, was to have a staff of four teachers and was expected to serve as a centre for training other pre-school teachers.

The 2007 budget allocated an estimated 3,156m. vatu to education (26.7% of total recurrent expenditure by the central Government).

THE VATICAN CITY
(THE HOLY SEE)

Introductory Survey

LOCATION, CLIMATE, LANGUAGE, RELIGION, FLAG

The State of the Vatican City is situated entirely within the Italian capital, Rome, on the right bank of the Tiber river. It covers an area of 0.44 sq km (0.17 sq miles). The climate is Mediterranean, with warm summers and mild winters (see Italy). Italian and Latin are the official languages. Roman Catholicism is the official religion. The state flag, which is square, consists of two vertical stripes of yellow and white, with the papal coat of arms superimposed on the white stripe.

HISTORY

For a period of nearly 1,000 years, dating roughly from the time of Charlemagne to the year 1870, the Popes ruled much of the central Italian peninsula, including the city of Rome. During the process of unification, the Kingdom of Italy gradually absorbed these States of the Church, the process being completed by the entry into Rome of King Victor Emmanuel's troops in September 1870. From 1860 to 1870 many attempts had been made to induce the Pope, Pius IX, to surrender his temporal possessions. Since, however, he regarded them as a sacred trust from a higher power, to be guarded on behalf of the Church, he refused to do so. After the entry of the Royal Army into Rome, he retired to the Vatican from where no Pope emerged again until the ratification of the Lateran Treaty of 11 February 1929. By the Law of Guarantees of May 1871, Italy attempted to stabilize the position of the Papacy by recognizing the Pope's claim to use of the Palaces of the Lateran and the Vatican, the Papal villa of Castelgandolfo, and their gardens and annexes, and to certain privileges customary to sovereignty. This unilateral arrangement was not accepted by Pius IX, and his protest against it was repeated constantly by his successors.

In 1929 two agreements were made with the Italian Government—the Lateran Treaty and the Concordat. By the terms of the Lateran Treaty, the Holy See was given exclusive power and sovereign jurisdiction over the State of the Vatican City, which was declared neutral and inviolable territory. Financial compensation was also given for the earlier losses. Under the Concordat, Roman Catholicism became the state religion of Italy, with special privileges defined by law. The new Italian Constitution of 1947 reaffirmed adherence to the Lateran Treaty. In December 1978 the two sides agreed on a draft plan for a new Concordat, under which Catholicism would cease to be the official Italian state religion and most of the Catholic Church's special privileges in Italy would be removed. The revised version was signed in February 1984.

In 1917 the first legal code, the Code of Canon Law (Codex Iuris Canonici), was devised for the Catholic Church. In 1963 a pontifical commission was inaugurated to investigate possible reforms to the law, and in 1981 the Pope received more than 70 cardinals and bishops who had prepared the new code's 1,752 rules. Revisions included a reduction in the number of cases meriting excommunication and a general relaxing of penalties, with increased emphasis on the importance of the laity within the Church. The code was ratified in January 1983, and came into force in November.

In October 1978 Cardinal Karol Wojtyła (then Archbishop of Kraków, Poland) became the first non-Italian Pope since the 16th century, taking the name John Paul II. Security surrounding the Pontiff was tightened considerably after an attempt on his life in May 1981 and another in May 1982. An Italian parliamentary inquiry, which published its findings in March 2006, concluded that the 1981 attempt was orchestrated by the former USSR.

In April 1984 Pope John Paul II announced a major reshuffle of offices in the Roman Curia, which included the delegation of most of his responsibility for the routine administration of the Vatican City to the Secretariat of State. In July 1988 a number of reforms to the Curia were introduced. These consolidated the power of the Secretariat of State, as well as reorganizing some of the Congregations and Pontifical Commissions.

In February 1987 Italian judges issued a warrant for the arrest of Archbishop Paul Marcinkus, the Chairman of the Istituto per le Opere di Religione ('Vatican Bank'), and two other bank officials for alleged involvement in the fraudulent bankruptcy of the Banco Ambrosiano in Milan, which collapsed in 1982. In July 1987, however, the Italian Supreme Court cancelled the warrants for the arrest of the three bank officials, stating that the Vatican stood outside Italian jurisdiction and that, according to the Lateran Treaty, Italy did not have the right to interfere in the affairs of the central organs of the Roman Catholic Church. In May 1988, following an appeal, the Archbishop's immunity was endorsed by the Constitutional Court. In March 1989 the Vatican announced a wide-ranging reorganization of the Istituto per le Opere di Religione, by abolishing the post of Chairman, held by Marcinkus, and appointing a commission of five cardinals, nominated by the Pope, to preside over the bank, assisted by a committee of financial experts. Archbishop Marcinkus retired from papal service in October 1990 and died in February 2006.

In March 1998 the Vatican released its long-awaited 'definitive statement' condemning anti-Semitism and anti-Judaism, and repenting for Roman Catholic passivity during the Nazi Holocaust. However, a number of high-ranking Jewish officials expressed disappointment in the document and demanded an explicit apology for the attitude of Pope Pius XII and the Roman Catholic Church's failure to speak out, at the time, against Nazi atrocities. In March 2000, during a service in St Peter's Basilica in Rome, despite misgivings expressed by some theologians that such a statement would undermine the Church's authority, the Pope made a comprehensive and unprecedented plea for forgiveness for the 'past sins of the Church', including racial and ethnic discrimination and Christian mistreatment of minorities, women and native peoples. However, in July 2001 a panel of Catholic and Jewish historians was forced to halt its study of the Church's role in the Holocaust when the Vatican refused it access to files on Pope Pius XII, prompting allegations that the Vatican was seeking to conceal potentially damaging evidence. Following further pressure, however, archives covering the years 1922–39 were released in February 2003.

In February 2001 the Constitution, dating back to the Lateran Treaty of 1929, was replaced by a new Basic Law incorporating a number of constitutional amendments made over the years. The Basic Law clarified the distinction between the legislative, executive and judicial branches.

In November 2001 Pope John Paul II issued an apology to victims of sexual abuse perpetrated by members of the Catholic clergy. Furthermore, in January 2002 new regulations were published by the Vatican, outlining the appropriate method of dealing with cases of alleged sexual abuse, notably against children, by members of the clergy. However, in mid-2002, in the most significant scandal to affect the Roman Catholic Church in many years, it was revealed that Cardinal Bernard Law, the Archbishop of Boston, Massachusetts, USA, had protected a number of priests who faced accusations of sexual misconduct against children. Hundreds of priests in the USA resigned or were subsequently suspended or sued in the wake of more than 200 allegations of sexual abuse involving members of the clergy in the Boston area. In April the Pope summoned 13 US cardinals to the Vatican to discuss the crisis. A 'zero tolerance' policy adopted by the US Conference of Catholic Bishops in June was subsequently rejected by the Vatican; a somewhat altered charter, which provided for the eventual dismissal of any priests found guilty of sexual abuse in a church tribunal, was accepted by the Vatican in December. Victims' groups were disappointed with the revisions, however, which reintroduced a 10-year statute of limitation on accusations. Following the filing of 450 lawsuits against Cardinal Law's archdiocese and the petition of 58 Boston priests, Law resigned in December 2002.

THE VATICAN CITY

Following a long period of ill health, Pope John Paul II died on 2 April 2005 at the age of 84. Only St Peter and Pius IX, in the mid-19th century, had enjoyed longer papacies. More than 3m. people visited the Vatican City in the period between the death of John Paul II and his funeral, which took place on 8 April and was attended by around 200 world leaders. By the time of his death, John Paul II had canonized 482 saints (more than all his predecessors combined since the 16th century), performed 1,338 beatifications and created 232 cardinals.

The conclave to elect a new Pope began on 18 April 2005 and was attended by 115 of the 117 cardinals of voting age (under 80 years old). On 19 April Cardinal Joseph Ratzinger of Germany was elected as the Supreme Pontiff, and took the name Benedict XVI. Ratzinger, who was aged 78 years, was hitherto the Dean of the College of Cardinals, the Prefect of the Congregation for the Doctrine of the Faith and President of the International Theological Commission and of the Pontifical Biblical Commission. The new Pope's inauguration as the 265th Roman pontiff took place on 24 April. Benedict XVI subsequently reappointed the officials of the Roman Curia, who had, according to custom, ceased to hold their offices on the death of John Paul II. In May Benedict announced the commencement of the process of beatification of John Paul II, waiving the five-year delay normally required after a person's death. In his first addresses as Pope, Benedict pledged to continue his predecessor's attempts to improve ties with other Christian denominations and with other religions. In October the first synod of Benedict XVI's papacy took place, at which the celibacy of the priesthood was reaffirmed.

In early 2006 it was reported that the Pope had decided to stop using one of his nine official titles, that of Patriarch of the West; this was regarded as a gesture of reconciliation towards the Orthodox churches. On 24 March Benedict appointed 15 new cardinals. Notable among the appointees was Joseph Zen Zekiun, Bishop of Hong Kong and an outspoken critic of the Chinese Government.

In September 2006 Cardinal Angelo Sodano retired as Secretary of State and was replaced by Cardinal Tarcisio Bertone, hitherto Archbishop of Genoa, Italy, while Cardinal Edmund Szoka was replaced as President of the Pontifical Commission for the Vatican City State and of the Governorate of the Vatican City State by Most Rev. Giovanni Lajolo, who had been Secretary of State for Relations with States—in effect the minister responsible for foreign affairs. Most Rev. Dominique Mamberti was appointed Secretary of State for Relations with States. In November 2007 Pope Benedict appointed 23 new cardinals (including Lajolo), of whom 18 were of voting age, thus bringing the number of cardinals eligible to vote in the conclave to elect a new pontiff to 121.

In January 2009 it was announced that legislation enacted in Italy would henceforth not automatically be incorporated into Vatican law, as had hitherto been the case; instead, each law would be considered on an individual basis prior to adoption. The Vatican stated that the decision had been motivated by the number and instability of Italian laws, as well as their increasing 'contrast with the inviolable principles of the Church'.

In 2010 the Vatican was subject to renewed pressure following a series of allegations of sexual abuse of children perpetrated by clergy in several countries, notably Belgium, Ireland, Germany and the USA. In March, in a pastoral letter to Roman Catholics in Ireland, Benedict XVI issued an unprecedented apology to victims of abuse; the issue had caused outrage in Ireland following the publication in November 2009 of the findings of an official inquiry into abuse in the Archdiocese of Dublin in 1975–2004, which had led to the resignation of four bishops. Later in March 2010 the Pope was personally implicated in a number of abuse scandals for the first time, following various allegations that, as Archbishop of Munich and subsequently as Prefect of the Congregation for the Doctrine of the Faith, he had failed to take disciplinary action against priests in Germany and the USA accused of abusing children. In June the creation was announced of an Apostolic Visitation (an investigation at the most senior level) concerning abuse in Ireland: the investigation was to be led by the former Archbishop of Westminster, Cardinal Cormac Murphy-O'Connor.

In June 2010 it was reported that Cardinal Crescenzio Sepe, the Archbishop of Naples, was under investigation for an allegedly corrupt property transaction, made in 2004, while he was Prefect of the Congregation for the Evangelization of Peoples (commonly known as Propaganda Fide, the shorter version of its former title); Sepe had been removed from his post as Prefect in 2006, and a new Prefect, Cardinal Ivan Dias, had been appointed by Pope Benedict with a mandate to introduce more transparent management of the large property assets used to finance the work of Propaganda Fide. In September 2010 the President of the Istituto per le Opere di Religione, Ettore Gotti Tedeschi, and the bank's Director-General, Paolo Cipriani, were placed under investigation, following the seizure by the Italian financial authorities of €23m. that had been deposited in an Italian bank for onward transfer: the transaction allegedly failed to comply with Italian regulations intended to prevent money-laundering. The Vatican Secretariat of State issued a statement expressing complete confidence in the two officials, and declaring that the problem was due to a misunderstanding. It pointed out that the Vatican had been making efforts to achieve greater financial transparency, and to comply with international standards, as stipulated by the Organisation for Economic Co-operation and Development (OECD, see p. 376), in order to combat money-laundering and the financing of terrorism. In late December Pope Benedict announced the creation of a new Financial Information Authority (FIA) to supervise the Vatican's financial operations and to ensure compliance with international regulations on financial transparency and the prevention of illegal transactions. New Vatican legislation on the prevention of money-laundering, the financing of terrorism, fraud and counterfeiting, which had been agreed in a Monetary Convention concluded with the European Union (EU, see p. 270) in December 2009, came into effect at the beginning of April 2011. Meanwhile, in October 2010 the European Commission recommenced investigations (originally begun in 2005) into the exemption from taxation of church-owned property in Italy, following an official complaint by an Italian political party, Radicali Italiani, that the exemption contravened the regulations of the EU on unfair competition.

In June 2010 Pope Benedict announced the creation of the Pontifical Council for Promoting the New Evangelization, to be presided over by Archbishop Salvatore (Rino) Fisichella, with the aim of countering what was perceived to be the increasingly secular nature of society in Western developed countries. In July a Swiss bishop, Kurt Koch, was nominated as the President of the Pontifical Council for Promoting Christian Unity. In November 24 new cardinals were created (including Bishop Koch). The late Pope John Paul II was beatified in a ceremony on 1 May 2011.

Foreign Affairs

The Vatican's prominence in international affairs increased from the late 1980s. In July 1989 diplomatic relations with Poland, severed in 1945, were restored. The Vatican had hitherto maintained no diplomatic relations with Eastern European governments under communist rule, except for Yugoslavia. During the early 1990s diplomatic relations were restored or established with many former communist states, including with the USSR in 1990. In 1992 full diplomatic relations were restored, after more than 120 years of discord, between the Vatican and Mexico. In December 1993 the Vatican and Israel signed a mutual-recognition agreement, which led to the establishment of full diplomatic ties and the exchange of ambassadors in September 1994. Meanwhile, in February 1994 the Vatican established diplomatic relations with Jordan, in an apparent move to strengthen links with the Arab world to counterbalance its recent recognition of Israel. Similarly, in October of that year the Vatican instituted 'official relations' with the Palestine Liberation Organization.

Diplomatic relations between the Vatican and the People's Republic of China had been severed in 1951 following the communists' accession to power in Beijing. In August 1999 China vetoed plans for Pope John Paul II to visit Hong Kong later that year, owing to the Vatican's diplomatic ties with Taiwan. In January 2000 the state-controlled Patriotic Church in Beijing ordained five bishops in a ceremony timed to upstage official papal ordinations in the Vatican City. Relations further deteriorated following the Pope's announcement in September 2000 that he was to canonize 120 western and Chinese Catholics killed in China between 1648 and 1930. However, in October 2001 Pope John Paul II issued an apology to China for the sins committed by Christians against the country; an appeal was also made for diplomatic relations between the two states to be restored. Informal talks recommenced in early 2003, but were adversely affected by the outspoken anti-Government stance of Hong Kong's Bishop (later Cardinal), Joseph Zen Ze-kiun. Following the accession of Benedict XVI, there appeared to be a growing emphasis on the need to improve Sino-Vatican relations, although the ordination of a series of bishops by the Patriotic Church in April and May 2006 provoked criticism from the Pope. In July 2007 an open letter addressed to Chinese Catholics on behalf of the Pope called for 'respectful and constructive' relations. In September the Vatican approved the ordination of a bishop by the Patriotic Church, allaying fears that efforts toward reconciliation would be undermined by the death earlier that month of a Vatican-appointed bishop, John Han Dingxiang, while in detention by the Chinese authorities.

In February 2000 the Vatican and the Palestinian (National) Authority signed an historic agreement on joint interests, which appealed for a peaceful solution, through dialogue, to the Israeli-Palestinian conflict, and called for an internationally guaranteed special statute for the city of Jerusalem that safeguarded freedom of religion and conscience. The Israeli Government criticized the accord as representing unwelcome 'interference' by the Vatican in the ongoing Middle East peace talks. In early 2000 the Pope undertook a millennial pilgrimage to some of the principal biblical sites of the Middle East, visiting Egypt in February (the first visit by a pontiff to that country) and Israel, Jordan and the West Bank in March. Pope John Paul II's six-day visit to the politically volatile Holy Land constituted the first papal visit to that region for 36 years. In 2002 an agreement was signed by the Vatican and the Turkish Government, promoting religious dialogue between Muslims and Christians.

In mid-2001 Pope John Paul II undertook visits to Greece and Syria, the first by a Roman pontiff since the division of Christianity into eastern and western churches. During his visit to Greece, the Pope attempted to heal the historic rift between the Roman Catholic and Orthodox churches by presenting an apology to the Orthodox community for wrongs committed over the centuries by the Roman Catholic Church. The Pope, despite not being granted the consent of the Russian Orthodox Patriarch, also visited Ukraine, where he called for an end to the 1,000-year schism between Roman Catholicism and the Orthodox Church in Ukraine and, by extension, the Russian Orthodox Church. The leaders of the Orthodox Church in Ukraine refused to meet the Pope, although his visit attracted much popular support.

Tensions between the Roman Catholic Church and the Russian Orthodox Church increased in February 2002 when the Vatican announced that the four apostolic administrations in Russia (officially considered to be temporary) had become dioceses. This move was interpreted by representatives of the Russian Orthodox Church as the establishment of an alternative church within the country, and a few days later a visit to Russia by the Head of the Pontifical Council for the Promotion of Christian Unity, Cardinal Walter Kasper, was cancelled by the Russian Orthodox Church.

In November 2002 John Paul II became the first pontiff to address the Italian Parliament, symbolically closing the Vatican's territorial dispute with Italy. His speech advocated institutional recognition by the European Union (EU, see p. 270) of Europe's Christian heritage. This followed an ultimately unsuccessful call in October for Christianity to be enshrined in the proposed EU constitution. In June 2004 John Paul II publicly criticized the lack of reference to Christianity in the approved text of the EU constitutional treaty, and in early 2005 the Vatican again criticized the increasing secularization of the EU. In 2007 Pope Benedict XVI also criticized the Italian Government for its plans to give homosexual and unmarried couples equal legal status with married couples.

During late 2002 and early 2003 Pope John Paul II was prominent in opposing the prospect of US-led military intervention to remove the regime of Saddam Hussain in Iraq, urging a diplomatic resolution to the crisis. Papal envoys were sent to Baghdad, Iraq, and Washington, DC. This was followed in March 2003 by an historic five-day meeting with a delegation from Israel's Chief Rabbinate.

Pope John Paul II visited Switzerland in June 2004, where it was announced that diplomatic relations, which had been severed in 1873, were to be restored. In mid-2004 the Pope continued his policy of engagement with the Orthodox churches, which included the return of a copy of the icon 'Our Lady of Kazan' to Moscow. On 1 July the Pope issued a joint statement with Patriarch Bartholomew I of Constantinople, the Orthodox Patriarch in Istanbul, Turkey, confirming their commitment to dialogue between the Roman Catholic and Orthodox churches.

Tensions between the Vatican and the Muslim world increased in September 2006 after Benedict XVI delivered a lecture at the University of Regensburg, Germany, in the course of which he quoted a medieval Byzantine emperor as saying that the Prophet Muhammad had contributed only 'evil and inhuman' things to the world. The Pope's remarks provoked widespread protest in Muslim countries. Benedict later apologized for causing offence, stating that the quotation did not reflect his personal belief. In November Benedict visited Turkey, where he was praised by Muslims for facing Mecca while praying in the Blue Mosque in Istanbul. He also held a joint service with Patriarch Bartholomew I, a gesture that was regarded as an attempt to heal the divisions between the Roman Catholic and Greek Orthodox churches. In May 2007 it was announced that the Pontifical Council for Inter-Religious Dialogue was to be restored, thereby reversing a decision in March 2006 to place it under the direction of the Pontifical Council for Culture. (The decision to downgrade the Council, which had previously been led by an expert on Islamic affairs, had been criticized by Muslim leaders.) King Abdullah of Saudi Arabia visited the Vatican in November 2007 for talks with the Pope, representing the first meeting between a Saudi monarch and a pontiff. It was subsequently revealed that the discussions had focused on inter-faith relations and the 'necessity of finding a just solution' to the Israeli–Palestinian conflict. In March 2008 Benedict XVI received a delegation of Muslim religious leaders at the Vatican. The talks were organized after the publication in October 2007 of an open letter to the Pope, in which 138 Muslim leaders had urged increased co-operation between Roman Catholic and Muslim religious leaders. In an attempt to further inter-faith relations, in November 2008 the Vatican hosted a three-day conference of Roman Catholic and Muslim scholars, at which the Pope urged political and religious leaders to co-operate in efforts to protect the freedom of conscience and of worship. In January 2011 Egypt recalled its ambassador to the Vatican, after Pope Benedict had condemned recent violent attacks on Christians in Egypt and Iraq and urged the respective Governments to adopt measures to protect religious minorities. In the same month Al-Azhar, a prominent Egyptian scholarly institution, announced the suspension of its dialogues with the Vatican, hitherto held twice a year, claiming that the Pope had made negative comments concerning Islam in his response to attacks on Christians.

Relations between the Holy See and Israel have frequently been strained, despite continued efforts to resolve disputes (most notably concerning Pius XII's attitude to the Holocaust) since the establishment of diplomatic relations in 1993. In January 2009 the decision of Benedict XVI to rehabilitate four bishops who had been excommunicated in 1988 provoked severe criticism from world leaders and jeopardized efforts to improve relations with Israel, owing to the fact that one of the bishops, Richard Williamson, had denied the existence of gas chambers at the Nazi concentration camps. The Vatican subsequently claimed that Benedict XVI had not been aware of Williamson's views, and demanded that he recant them before taking up his appointment as a bishop in the Roman Catholic Church. In early May Pope Benedict XVI spent five days in Israel and the West Bank. In a speech in Tel-Aviv, the Pope condemned anti-Semitism as 'totally unacceptable' and, during a visit to the Yad Vashem Holocaust museum in Jerusalem, he repudiated denial of the Holocaust. However, he was criticized by a number of Israeli political leaders for failing to express sufficient remorse for the Nazi persecution of the Jews.

CONSTITUTION AND GOVERNMENT

The State of the Vatican City came into existence with the Lateran Treaty of 1929. The Holy See (a term designating the papacy, i.e. the office of the Pope, and thus the central governing body of the Roman Catholic Church) is a distinct, pre-existing entity. Both entities are subjects of international law. On 22 February 2001 a new Basic Law replaced the former Constitution dating back to the 1929 Lateran Treaty.

The Vatican City State is under the temporal jurisdiction of the Pope, the Supreme Pontiff elected for life by a conclave comprising members of the Sacred College of Cardinals. The Pope holds all legislative, executive and judicial power. Legislative power is vested in the Pontifical Commission for the Vatican State, which comprises a Cardinal President and six other cardinals, nominated by the Pope for a five-year period. Executive power is vested in the President of the Pontifical Commission (who is also the President of the Governorate of the Vatican City State), who is assisted by a Secretary-General. The State Councillors, including one General Councillor and eight other Councillors, are nominated by the Pope for a five-year period, and assist in the drawing-up of laws and report to the Pontifical Commission. Judiciary power is vested in a number of Tribunals and the Apostolic Penitentiary, who exercise their judicial authority in the name of the Pope. The Pontiff exclusively retains the right to grant pardons and amnesties.

THE VATICAN CITY

REGIONAL AND INTERNATIONAL CO-OPERATION

The Holy See has permanent observer status at a number of international organizations, including the UN, the World Trade Organization (WTO, see p. 430) and the Council of Europe (see p. 250).

ECONOMIC AFFAIRS

The official population of the Vatican City was 793 at March 2011, comprising 572 citizens of the Vatican City (including non-residents) and 221 resident non-citizens; the total resident population was 444. Its inhabitants are of many nationalities, representing the presence of the Roman Catholic Church throughout the world. The papal guards, who numbered 86 in 2011, are of Swiss nationality.

The Vatican City has no agricultural land and no industry. For its income, the Holy See is chiefly reliant on four sources: the Istituto per le Opere di Religione (the 'Vatican Bank'); interest on its financial investments; receipts from tourism, including profits from the Vatican museums and from the sale of postage stamps, publications and souvenirs; and voluntary contributions, known as 'Peter's Pence' (Obolo di San Pietro). The euro is used as currency, and the Vatican City issues its own euro coins.

No official annual accounts for the Holy See were published until 1979, when an annual budgetary deficit of US $20.1m. was revealed. The deficit continued to increase in subsequent years until 1991, when a peak of $87.5m. was reached. In April of that year a meeting was held in the Vatican, attended by representatives of bishops' conferences throughout the world, which discussed ways of reducing the deficit through systematic contributions from local dioceses. The deficit declined in 1992, and small surpluses were returned for the remainder of the 1990s. The budget for 2001, in contrast, showed the first deficit since 1993, of $3.1m., as a result of a general slowdown in the global economy following the suicide attacks in the USA on 11 September 2001; by 2003 the deficit had increased to $22.5m., although surpluses were again recorded in the following three years. In 2007 the Holy See recorded a budget deficit of some $13.5m., owing largely to the significant decline of the US dollar against the euro; 'Peter's Pence' contributions in that year (not included in the consolidated budget) totalled $79.8m. Contributions fell to $75.8m. in 2008, largely as a result of the global economic crisis; however, the Holy See's budget deficit in that year was reduced to €0.9m. Meanwhile, the Governorate of the Vatican City State, the accounts of which were also excluded from the consolidated budget of the Holy See, recorded a deficit of €15.3m. In 2009 the Holy See recorded expenditure of €254.2m. and income of €250.1m., resulting in a budget deficit of €4.1m. In that year 'Peter's Pence' contributions amounted to US $82.5m.

In 2008 a total of 1,894 people were employed in the Vatican City. In addition to staffing costs, principal destinations for expenditure are the Vatican Radio and *L'Osservatore Romano*, the Vatican newspaper, which regularly incur losses, which reached a combined figure of US $22.9m. in 2007. The establishment of new diplomatic missions from the late 1980s onwards (see History) entailed considerable capital expenditure for the papacy, and incurred $37m. in expenses in 2001.

The Istituto per le Opere di Religione is reported to have consistently returned an operating profit, although much of the revenue generated by it in the 1980s was used to repay the creditors remaining from the collapse of Banco Ambrosiano in 1982. New legislation concerning greater transparency in financial transactions, in compliance with international standards, came into effect in April 2011 (see History).

Directory

Government

THE GOVERNMENT OF THE VATICAN CITY STATE

Head of State

His Holiness Pope BENEDICT XVI (elected 19 April 2005).

Pontifical Commission for the Vatican City State

Cardinal GIOVANNI LAJOLO (President).
Cardinal GIOVANNI BATTISTA RE.
Cardinal JOSÉ SARAIVA MARTINS.
Cardinal JEAN-LOUIS TAURAN.
Cardinal RENATO RAFFAELE MARTINO.
Cardinal ATTILIO NICORA.
Cardinal LEONARDO SANDRI.

State Councillors

Prof. CESARE MIRABELLI (General Councillor).
There are 10 additional councillors.

Governorate of the Vatican City State

President: Cardinal GIOVANNI LAJOLO.
Secretary-General: Most Rev. CARLO MARIA VIGANÒ (Titular Archbishop of Ulpiana).
Vice-Secretary-General: Rt Rev. GIORGIO CORBELLINI (Titular Bishop of Abula).

THE SUPREME PONTIFF

His Holiness Pope Benedict XVI (Joseph Ratzinger), Bishop of Rome, Vicar of Christ, Successor of the Prince of the Apostles, Supreme Pontiff of the Universal Church, Primate of Italy, Archbishop and Metropolitan of the Province of Rome, Sovereign of the Vatican City State, Servant of the Servants of God, acceded on 19 April 2005 as the 265th Roman pontiff.

THE SACRED COLLEGE OF CARDINALS AND THE ROMAN CURIA

Members of the Sacred College of Cardinals are created by the Pope. The cardinals are divided into three orders: Bishops, Priests and Deacons. Under the decree of November 1970, *Ingravescentem Aetatem*, only cardinals under 80 years of age have the right to enter the conclave for the election of the Pope. Cardinals who reside in Rome, Italy, as the Pope's immediate advisers are styled Cardinals 'in Curia'. The Roman Curia acts as the Papal court and the principal administrative body of the Church. The College of Cardinals derives from the Church's earliest days. In March 1973 Pope Paul VI announced that the number of cardinals permitted to participate in the conclave would be limited to 120. This was increased to 135 by Pope John Paul II in February 2001. At 18 April 2005, as the conclave to elect John Paul II's successor began, there were 183 cardinals, of whom 117 were under the age of 80; 115 cardinals participated in the conclave. Following Benedict XVI's third consistory on 20–21 November 2010, in February 2011 there were 201 cardinals, of whom 117 were of voting age. There are six Cardinal Bishops, who are in titular charge of suburban sees of Rome. The order of Cardinal Bishops also includes the additional four Cardinals of Patriarchal Sees of Oriental Rites. Cardinal Priests occupy titular churches in Rome founded soon after Christianity originated. The administration of the Church's affairs is undertaken through the Secretariat of State and the Council for the Public Affairs of the Church, under the Cardinal Secretary of State, and through a number of Congregations, each under the direction of a cardinal or senior member of the Church, as well as through Tribunals, Offices, Commissions and Secretariats for special purposes.

The 'Apostolic Constitution' (*Regimini Ecclesiae Universae*), published in August 1967 and effective from 1 March 1968, reformed the Roman Curia. Among the changes were the creation of new organs and the restructuring of the Secretariat of State. In 1969 the Congregation of Rites was divided into two Congregations—one for Divine Worship and the other for the Causes of Saints. The Congregation for the Discipline of the Sacraments and the Congregation for Divine Worship were amalgamated in 1975, but separated again in 1984.

In July 1988 further reforms of the Curia were introduced. The Secretariat of State was divided into two sections: the first section dealing with 'General Affairs' and the second 'Relations with States'. The Congregation for Divine Worship was again amalgamated with the Congregation for the Discipline of the Sacraments.

Members in order of precedence:

Cardinal Bishops

ANGELO SODANO (Italy—Titular Bishop of Albano and of Ostia and Dean of the College of Cardinals).

THE VATICAN CITY

Roger Etchegaray (France—Titular Bishop of Porto-Santa Rufina and Vice-Dean of the College of Cardinals).
Giovanni Battista Re (Italy—Titular Bishop of Sabina-Poggio Mirteto).
Francis A. Arinze (Nigeria—Titular Bishop of Velletri-Segni).
Tarcisio Bertone (Italy—Titular Bishop of Frascati, Secretary of the Secretariat of State and Chamberlain of the Apostolic Chamber).
José Saraiva Martins (Portugal—Titular Bishop of Palestrina).

Cardinal Bishops of Patriarchal Sees of Oriental Rites

Nasrallah Pierre (Boutros) Sfeir (Lebanon—Maronite Patriarch of Antioch).
Ignace Moussa I Daoud (Syria).
Emmanuel III Delly (Iraq—Chaldean Patriarch of Babylon).
Antonios Naguib (Egypt—Coptic Patriarch of Alexandria).

Cardinal Priests

Eugênio de Araújo Sales (Brazil).
Luis Aponte Martínez (Puerto Rico).
Paulo Evaristo Arns (Brazil).
William Wakefield Baum (USA).
Marco Cé (Italy).
Franciszek Macharski (Poland).
Michael Michai Kitbunchu (Thailand).
Alexandre do Nascimento (Angola).
Godfried Danneels (Belgium).
Thomas Stafford Williams (New Zealand).
Carlo Maria Martini (Italy).
Józef Glemp (Poland).
Joachim Meisner (Germany—Archbishop of Cologne).
Duraisamy Simon Lourdusamy (India).
Miguel Obando Bravo (Nicaragua).
Ricardo Jamin Vidal (Philippines).
Henryk Roman Gulbinowicz (Poland).
Jozef Tomko (Slovakia).
Andrzej Maria Deskur (Poland).
Paul Joseph Jean Poupard (France).
Friedrich Wetter (Germany).
Silvano Piovanelli (Italy).
Adrianus Johannes Simonis (Netherlands).
Bernard Francis Law (USA—Archpriest of the Patriarchal Liberian Basilica of Santa Maria Maggiore).
Giacomo Biffi (Italy).
Eduardo Martínez Somalo (Spain).
Achille Silvestrini (Italy).
José Freire Falcão (Brazil).
Alexandre José Maria dos Santos (Mozambique).
Giovanni Canestri (Italy).
Simon Ignatius Pimenta (India).
Edward Bede Clancy (Australia).
Edmund Casimir Szoka (USA).
László Paskai (Hungary).
Christian Wiyghan Tumi (Cameroon—Archbishop of Douala).
Edward Idris Cassidy (Australia).
Nicolás de Jesús López Rodríguez (Dominican Republic—Archbishop of Santo Domingo).
José Tomás Sánchez (Philippines).
Virgilio Noè (Italy).
Fiorenzo Angelini (Italy).
Roger Michael Mahony (USA—Archbishop of Los Angeles).
Anthony Joseph Bevilacqua (USA).
Camillo Ruini (Italy).
Ján Chryzostom Korec (Slovakia).
Henri Schwéry (Switzerland).
Georg Maximilian Sterzinsky (Germany).
Miloslav Vlk (Czech Republic).
Carlo Furno (Italy).
Julius Riyadi Darmaatmadja (Indonesia).
Jaime Lucas Ortega y Alamino (Cuba—Archbishop of San Cristóbal de la Habana).
Gilberto Agustoni (Italy).
Emmanuel Wamala (Uganda).
William Henry Keeler (USA).
Jean-Claude Turcotte (Canada—Archbishop of Montréal).
Ricardo María Carles Gordó (Spain).
Adam Joseph Maida (USA—Superior of the Cayman Islands).
Vinko Puljić (Bosnia and Herzegovina—Archbishop of Vrhbosna, Sarajevo).
Juan Sandoval Iñiguez (Mexico—Archbishop of Guadalajara).
Kazimierz Świątek (Belarus).
Ersilio Tonini (Italy).
Jorge Arturo Augustin Medina Estévez (Chile).
Darío Castrillón Hoyos (Colombia).
Lorenzo Antonetti (Italy).
James Francis Stafford (USA).
Salvatore De Giorgi (Italy).
Serafim Fernandes de Araújo (Brazil).
Antonio María Rouco Varela (Spain—Archbishop of Madrid).
Aloysius Matthew Ambrozic (Canada).
Dionigi Tettamanzi (Italy—Archbishop of Milan).
Polycarp Pengo (Tanzania—Archbishop of Dar-es-Salaam).
Christoph Schönborn (Austria—Archbishop of Vienna).
Norberto Rivera Carrera (Mexico—Archbishop of Mexico City).
Francis Eugene George (USA—Archbishop of Chicago).
Paul Shan Kuo-hsi (Taiwan).
Giovanni Cheli (Italy).
Marian Jaworski (Ukraine).
Jānis Pujats (Latvia—Archbishop of Rīga).
Agostino Cacciavillan (Italy).
Sergio Sebastiani (Italy).
Zenon Grocholewski (Poland—Prefect of the Congregation for Catholic Education and Grand Chancellor of the Pontifical Gregorian University).
Jorge María Mejía (Argentina).
Walter Kasper (Germany).
Ivan Dias (India).
Geraldo Majella Agnelo (Brazil—Archbishop of São Salvador de Bahia).
Pedro Rubiano Sáenz (Colombia).
Theodore Edgar McCarrick (USA).
Desmond Connell (Ireland).
Audrys Juozas Bačkis (Lithuania—Archbishop of Vilnius).
Francisco Javier Errázuriz Ossa (Chile—Archbishop of Santiago de Chile).
Julio Terrazas Sandoval (Bolivia—Archbishop of Santa Cruz de la Sierra).
Wilfrid Fox Napier (South Africa—Archbishop of Durban).
Óscar Andrés Rodríguez Maradiaga (Honduras—Archbishop of Tegucigalpa).
Bernard Agré (Côte d'Ivoire).
Juan Luis Cipriani Thorne (Peru—Archbishop of Lima).
Francisco Alvarez Martínez (Spain).
Cláudio Hummes (Brazil).
Jorge Mario Bergoglio (Argentina—Archbishop of Buenos Aires).
José da Cruz Policarpo (Portugal—Patriarch of Lisbon).
Severino Poletto (Italy).
Cormac Murphy-O'Connor (United Kingdom).
Edward Michael Egan (USA).
Lubomyr Husar (Ukraine—Archbishop-Major of Kyiv-Halyč, Byzantine Ukrainian Rite).
Karl Lehmann (Germany—Bishop of Mainz).
Jean Marcel Honoré (France).
Roberto Tucci (Italy).
Crescenzio Sepe (Italy—Archbishop of Naples).
Angelo Scola (Italy—Patriarch of Venice).
Anthony Olubunmi Okogie (Nigeria—Archbishop of Lagos).
Bernard Louis Auguste Panafieu (France).
Gabriel Zubeir Wako (Sudan—Archbishop of Khartoum).
Carlos Amigo Vallejo (Spain).
Justin Francis Rigali (USA—Archbishop of Philadelphia).
Keith Michael Patrick O'Brien (United Kingdom—Archbishop of St Andrews and Edinburgh).
Eusébio Oscar Scheid (Brazil).

THE VATICAN CITY

ENNIO ANTONELLI (Italy—President of the Pontifical Council for the Family).
PETER KODWO APPIAH TURKSON (Ghana—President of the Pontifical Council for Justice and Peace).
TELESPHORE PLACIDUS TOPPO (India—Archbishop of Ranchi).
GEORGE PELL (Australia—Archbishop of Sydney).
JOSIP BOZANIĆ (Croatia—Archbishop of Zagreb).
JEAN-BAPTISTE PHAM MINH MÂN (Viet Nam—Archbishop of Ho Chi Minh City).
RODOLFO QUEZADA TORUÑO (Guatemala—Archbishop of Guatemala City).
PHILIPPE XAVIER IGNACE BARBARIN (France—Archbishop of Lyon).
PÉTER ERDŐ (Hungary—Archbishop of Esztergom-Budapest).
MARC OUELLET (Canada—Prefect of the Congregation for Bishops and President of the Pontifical Commission for Latin America).
AGOSTINO VALLINI (Italy—Vicar-General of His Holiness for the Diocese of Rome and Archpriest of the Lateran Patriarchal Archbasilica).
JORGE LIBERATO UROSA SAVINO (Venezuela—Archbishop of Caracas—Santiago de Venezuela).
GAUDENCIO BORBON ROSALES (Philippines—Archbishop of Manila).
JEAN-PIERRE BERNARD RICARD (France—Archbishop of Bordeaux).
ANTONIO CAÑIZARES LLOVERA (Spain—Prefect of the Congregation for Divine Worship and the Discipline of the Sacraments).
NICHOLAS CHEONG JIN-SUK (Republic of Korea—Archbishop of Seoul).
SEAN PATRICK O'MALLEY (USA—Archbishop of Boston).
STANISŁAW DZIWISZ (Poland—Archbishop of Kraków).
CARLO CAFFARRA (Italy—Archbishop of Bologna).
JOSEPH ZEN ZE-KIUN (Hong Kong).
SEÁN BAPTIST BRADY (Ireland—Archbishop of Armagh).
LLUÍS MARTÍNEZ SISTACH (Spain—Archbishop of Barcelona).
ANDRÉ ARMAND VINGT-TROIS (France—Archbishop of Paris).
ANGELO BAGNASCO (Italy—Archbishop of Genoa).
THÉODORE-ADRIEN SARR (Senegal—Archbishop of Dakar).
OSWALD GRACIAS (India—Archbishop of Mumbai).
FRANCISCO ROBLES ORTEGA (Mexico—Archbishop of Monterrey).
DANIEL NICHOLAS DINARDO (USA—Archbishop of Galveston-Houston).
ODILO PEDRO SCHERER (Brazil—Archbishop of São Paulo).
JOHN NJUE (Kenya—Archbishop of Nairobi).
ESTANISLAO ESTEBAN KARLIC (Argentina).
MEDARDO JOSEPH MAZOMBWE (Zambia).
RAÚL EDUARDO VELA CHIRIBOGA (Ecuador).
LAURENT MONSENGWO PASINYA (Democratic Republic of the Congo—Archbishop of Kinshasa).
PAOLO ROMEO (Italy—Archbishop of Palermo).
DONALD WILLIAM WUERL (USA—Archbishop of Washington, DC).
RAYMUNDO DAMASCENO ASSIS (Brazil—Archbishop of Aparecida).
KAZIMIERZ NYCZ (Poland—Archbishop of Warsaw).
ALBERT MALCOLM RANJITH PATABENDIGE DON (Sri Lanka—Archbishop of Colombo).
REINHARD MARX (Germany—Archbishop of Munich and Freising).
JOSÉ MANUEL ESTEPA LLAURENS (Spain).

Cardinal Deacons

JEAN-LOUIS TAURAN (France—President of the Pontifical Council for Inter-Religious Dialogue).
RENATO RAFFAELE MARTINO (Italy).
FRANCESCO MARCHISANO (Italy).
JULIÁN HERRANZ CASADO (Spain—President of the Disciplinary Commission of the Roman Curia).
JAVIER LOZANO BARRAGÁN (Mexico).
ATTILIO NICORA (Italy—President of the Administration of the Patrimony of the Apostolic See).
GEORGES MARIE MARTIN COTTIER (Switzerland).
STANISŁAW KAZIMIERZ NAGY (Poland).
WILLIAM JOSEPH LEVADA (USA—Prefect of the Congregation for the Doctrine of the Faith, President of the Pontifical Biblical Commission, President of the International Theological Commission, President of the Pontifical Commission 'Ecclesia Dei').
BRÁZ DE AVIZ (Brazil—Prefect of the Congregation for Institutes of Consecrated Life and for Societies of Apostolic Life).
ANDREA CORDERO LANZA DI MONTEZEMOLO (Italy).
ALBERT VANHOYE (France).

LEONARDO SANDRI (Argentina—Prefect of the Congregation for the Oriental Churches).
JOHN PATRICK FOLEY (USA—Pro Grand Master of the Equestrian Order of the Holy Sepulchure of Jerusalem).
GIOVANNI LAJOLO (Italy—President of the Governorate of the Vatican City State, President of the Pontifical Commission for Vatican City State).
PAUL JOSEF CORDES (Germany).
ANGELO COMASTRI (Italy—President of the Fabric of St Peter).
STANISŁAW RYŁKO (Poland—President of the Pontifical Council for the Laity).
RAFFAELE FARINA (Italy—Archivist of the Vatican Secret Archives).
GIOVANNI COPPA (Italy).
ANGELO AMATO (Italy—Prefect of the Congregation for the Causes of Saints).
ROBERT SARAH (Guinea—President of the Pontifical Council 'Cor Unum').
FRANCESCO MONTERISI (Italy—Archpriest of the Patriarchal Basilica of San Paolo Fuori-le-Mura).
FORTUNATO BALDELLI (Italy—Major Penitentiary of the Apostolic Penitentiary).
RAYMOND LEO BURKE (USA—Prefect of the Apostolic Signatura).
KURT KOCH (Switzerland—President of the Pontifical Council for Promoting Christian Unity).
PAOLO SARDI (Italy—Vice-Chamberlain Emeritus of the Apostolic Chamber).
MAURO PIACENZA (Italy—Prefect of the Congregation for the Clergy).
VELASIO DE PAOLIS (Italy—President of the Prefecture for the Economic Affairs of the Holy See).
GIANFRANCO RAVASI (Italy—President of the Pontifical Council for Culture).
ELIO SGRECCIA (Italy).
WALTER BRANDMÜLLER (Germany).
DOMENICO BARTOLUCCI (Italy).

THE ROMAN CURIA

Secretariat of State: Palazzo Apostolico Vaticano, 00120 Città del Vaticano; tel. (06) 69883913; fax (06) 69885255; e-mail vati026@relstat-segstat.va; Sec. of State Cardinal TARCISIO BERTONE.

First Section—General Affairs: Segreteria di Stato, 00120 Città del Vaticano; tel. (06) 69883438; fax (06) 69885088; e-mail vati023@genaff-segstat.va; Asst Sec. of State Most Rev. GIOVANNI ANGELO BECCIU (Titular Archbishop of Roselle).

Second Section—Relations with States: Segreteria di Stato, 00120 Città del Vaticano; tel. (06) 69883014; fax (06) 69885364; e-mail vati032@relstat-segstat.va; Sec. Most Rev. DOMINIQUE MAMBERTI (Titular Archbishop of Sagona).

Congregations

Congregation for the Doctrine of the Faith: Piazza del S. Uffizio 11, 00120 Città del Vaticano; tel. (06) 69895911; fax (06) 69883409; e-mail cdf@cfaith.va; concerned with questions of doctrine and morals; examines doctrines and gives a judgement on them; Prefect Cardinal WILLIAM JOSEPH LEVADA; Sec. Most Rev. LUIS FRANCISCO LADARIA FERRER (Titular Archbishop of Thibica).

Congregation for the Oriental Churches: Palazzo del Bramante, Via della Conciliazione 34, 00193 Rome, Italy; tel. (06) 69884281; fax (06) 69884300; e-mail cco@orientchurch.va; f. 1862; exercises jurisdiction over all persons and things pertaining to the Oriental Rites; Prefect Cardinal LEONARDO SANDRI; Sec. Most Rev. ANTONIO CYRIL VASIL (Titular Archbishop of Ptolemais in Libya).

Congregation for Divine Worship and the Discipline of the Sacraments: Palazzo delle Congregazioni, Piazza Pio XII 10, 00120 Città del Vaticano; tel. (06) 69884316; fax (06) 69883499; considers all questions relating to divine worship, liturgy and the sacraments; Prefect Cardinal ANTONIO CAÑIZARES LLOVERA; Sec. Most Rev. JOSEPH AUGUSTINE DI NOIA (Titular Archbishop of Oregon City).

Congregation for the Causes of Saints: Palazzo delle Congregazioni, Piazza Pio XII 10, 00193 Rome, Italy; tel. (06) 69884247; fax (06) 69881935; e-mail vati335@csaints.va; concerned with proceedings relating to beatification and canonization; Prefect Cardinal ANGELO AMATO (Titular Archbishop of Sila); Sec. Most Rev. MARCELLO BARTOLUCCI (Titular Archbishop of Mevania).

Congregation for the Bishops: Palazzo delle Congregazioni, Piazza Pio XII 10, 00193 Rome, Italy; tel. (06) 69884217; fax (06) 69885303; e-mail vati076@cbishops.va; designed for the preparation of matters for the erection and division of dioceses and the election of Bishops and for dealing with Apostolic Visitations; Prefect Cardinal

THE VATICAN CITY

Marc Ouellet; Sec. Most Rev. Manuel Monteiro de Castro (Titular Archbishop of Beneventum).

Congregation for the Evangelization of Peoples: Palazzo di Propaganda Fide, Piazza di Spagna 48, 00187 Rome, Italy; tel. (06) 69879299; fax (06) 69880118; e-mail cepsegreteria@evangel.va; exercises ecclesiastical jurisdiction over missionary countries; Prefect Cardinal Fernando Filoni (Titular Archbishop of Volturnum).

Congregation for the Clergy: Palazzo delle Congregazioni, Piazza Pio XII 3, 00193 Rome, Italy; tel. (06) 69884151; fax (06) 69884845; e-mail clero@cclergy.va; internet www.clerus.org; has jurisdiction over the life and discipline of the clergy and its permanent formation; parishes, chapters, pastoral and presbyteral councils; promotes catechesis and the preaching of the Word of God; deals with economic questions related to the compensation of the clergy and the patrimony of the Church; Prefect Cardinal Mauro Piacenza (Titular Archbishop of Victoriana).

Congregation for Institutes of Consecrated Life and for Societies of Apostolic Life: Palazzo delle Congregazioni, Piazza Pio XII 3, 00193 Rome, Italy; tel. (06) 69884128; fax (06) 69884526; e-mail civcsva@religiosi.va; promotes and supervises practice of evangelical counsels, according to approved forms of consecrated life, and activities of societies of apostolic life; Prefect Cardinal Franc Rodé; Sec. Most Rev. Joseph William Tobin (Titular Archbishop of Obba).

Congregation for Catholic Education: Palazzo delle Congregazioni, Piazza Pio XII 3, 00193 Rome, Italy; tel. (06) 69884167; fax (06) 69884172; e-mail cec@cec.va; f. 1588; concerned with the direction, temporal administration and studies of Catholic universities, seminaries, schools and colleges; Prefect Cardinal Zenon Grocholewski; Sec. Most Rev. Jean-Louis Bruguès.

Tribunals

Apostolic Penitentiary: Palazzo della Cancelleria, Piazza della Cancelleria 1, 00186 Rome, Italy; tel. (06) 69887526; fax (06) 69887557; e-mail regente@apostpnt.va; internet www.penitenzieria.va; Major Penitentiary Cardinal Fortunato Baldelli; Regent Rt Rev. Giovanni Francesco Girotti (Titular Bishop of Meta).

Supreme Tribunal of the Apostolic Signatura: Palazzo della Cancelleria, Piazza della Cancelleria 1, 00120 Città del Vaticano; tel. (06) 69887520; fax (06) 69887553; e-mail apost.segnatura@tribsgna.va; Prefect Cardinal Raymond Leo Burke; Sec. Rt Rev. Frans Daneels.

Tribunal of the Roman Rota: Palazzo della Cancelleria, Piazza della Cancelleria 1, 00186 Rome, Italy; tel. (06) 69887502; fax (06) 69887554; Dean Rt Rev. Antoni Stankiewicz (Titular Bishop of Nova Petra).

Pontifical Councils

Pontifical Council for the Laity: Piazza S. Calisto 16, 00153 Rome, Italy; tel. (06) 69887322; fax (06) 69887214; e-mail pcpl@laity.va; advises and conducts research on lay apostolic initiatives; Pres. Cardinal Stanisław Ryłko (Titular Archbishop of Novica); Sec. Rt Rev. Josef Clemens (Titular Bishop of Segerme).

Pontifical Council for Promoting Christian Unity: Via della Conciliazione 5, 00193 Rome, Italy; tel. (06) 69884083; fax (06) 69885365; e-mail office1@chrstuni.va; f. 1964; Pres. Cardinal Kurt Koch; Sec. Rt Rev. Brian Farrell (Titular Bishop of Abitinae).

Pontifical Council for the Family: Piazza S. Calisto 16, 00153 Rome, Italy; tel. (06) 69887243; fax (06) 69887272; e-mail pcf@family.va; Pres. Cardinal Ennio Antonelli; Sec. Rt Rev. Jean Laffitte (Titular Bishop of Entrevaux).

Pontifical Council for Justice and Peace: Piazza S. Calisto 16, 00153 Rome, Italy; tel. (06) 69879911; fax (06) 69887205; e-mail pcjustpax@justpeace.va; promotes social justice, human rights, peace and development in needy areas; Pres. Cardinal Peter Kodwo Appiah Turkson; Sec. Rt Rev. Mario Toso (Titular Bishop of Bisarcio).

Pontifical Council 'Cor Unum': Cor Unum, Via della Conciliazione 5, 00193 Rome, Italy; tel. (06) 69889411; fax (06) 69887301; e-mail corunum@corunum.va; f. 1971; cares for the needy, promotes human fellowship; Pres. Cardinal Robert Sarah.

Pontifical Council for the Pastoral Care of Migrants and Itinerant People: Piazza S. Calisto, 00120 Città del Vaticano; tel. (06) 69887131; fax (06) 69887111; e-mail office@migrants.va; f. 1970; Pres. Most Rev. Antonio Maria Vegliò (Titular Archbishop of Eclano); Sec. Most Rev. Joseph Kalathiparambil (Titular Bishop of Calicut).

Pontifical Council for Health Pastoral Care: Via della Conciliazione 3, 00193 Rome, Italy; tel. (06) 69883138; fax (06) 69883139; e-mail opersanit@hlthwork.va; Pres. Most Rev. Zigmunt Zimowski; Sec. Rt Rev. José Luis Redrado Marchite (Titular Bishop of Ofena).

Pontifical Council for Legislative Texts: Palazzo delle Congregazioni, Piazza Pio XII 10, 00193 Rome, Italy; tel. (06) 69884008; fax (06) 69884710; e-mail vati100@legtxt.va; f. 1984; publishes *Communicationes* journal twice yearly; Pres. Most Rev. Francesco Coccopalmerio (Titular Archbishop of Celiana); Vice-Pres. Most Rev. Bruno Bertagna (Titular Archbishop of Drivasto); Sec. Rt Rev. Juan Ignacio Arrieta Ochoa de Chinchetru (Titular Bishop of Civitate).

Pontifical Council for Inter-Religious Dialogue: Via della Conciliazione 5, 00193 Rome, Italy; tel. (06) 69884321; fax (06) 69884494; e-mail dialogo@interrel.va; f. 1964; Pres. Cardinal Jean-Louis Tauran; Sec. Most Rev. Pier Luigi Celata (Titular Archbishop of Doclea).

Pontifical Council for Culture: Via della Conciliazione 5, 00193 Rome, Italy; tel. (06) 69893811; fax (06) 69887368; e-mail cultura@cultura.va; merged with Pontifical Council for Dialogue with Non-Believers in 1993; promotes understanding and dialogue between the Church, people from the field of learning, artists and non-believers; Pres. Cardinal Gianfranco Ravasi.

Pontifical Council for Social Communications: Via della Conciliazione 5, 00120 Città del Vaticano; tel. (06) 69891800; fax (06) 69891840; e-mail pccs@pccs.va; internet www.pccs.va; f. 1948; examines the relationship between the media and religious affairs; manages radio, TV, film and photographic work in the Vatican; Pres. Most Rev. Claudio Maria Celli (Titular Archbishop of Cluentum).

Pontifical Council for Promoting the New Evangelization: f. 2010; Pres. Most Rev. Salvatore (Rino) Fisichella (Titular Archbishop of Vicohabentia); Sec. Most Rev. José Octavio Ruiz Arenas.

Pontifical Commissions and Committees

Pontifical Commission for the Cultural Heritage of the Church: Via della Conciliazione 5, 00193 Rome, Italy; tel. (06) 69885640; fax (06) 69884621; e-mail beniculturali@beniculturali.va; f. 1988; Pres. Cardinal Gianfranco Ravasi (Titular Archbishop of Villamagna in Proconsulari).

Pontifical Biblical Commission: Palazzo del Sant'Uffizio, 00120 Città del Vaticano; tel. (06) 69884682; e-mail vati419@cfaith.va; Prefect Cardinal William Joseph Levada.

Pontifical Commission of Sacred Archaeology: Palazzo del Pontificio Istituto di Archeologia Cristiana, Via Napoleone III 1, 00185 Rome, Italy; tel. (06) 4465610; fax (06) 4467625; e-mail pcas@arcsacra.va; Pres. Cardinal Gianfranco Ravasi.

Pontifical Commission 'Ecclesia Dei': Palazzo della Congregazione per la Dottrina della Fede, Piazza del S. Uffizio 11, 00120 Città del Vaticano; tel. (06) 69885213; fax (06) 69883412; e-mail eccdei@ecclsdei.va; internet www.ecclesiadei-commissio.org; Pres. Cardinal William Joseph Levada.

Pontifical Commission for Latin America: Palazzo di San Paolo, Via della Conciliazione 1, 00193 Rome, Italy; tel. (06) 69883131; fax (06) 69884260; e-mail pcal@latinamer.va; Pres. Cardinal Marc Ouellet; Vice-Pres. (vacant).

International Theological Commission: Palazzo della Congregazione per la Dottrina della Fede, Piazza del S. Uffizio 11, 00193 Rome, Italy; tel. (06) 69895965; Pres. Cardinal William Joseph Levada; Sec.-Gen. Fr Charles Morerod.

Pontifical Committee for International Eucharistic Congresses: Palazzo S. Calisto 16, 00120 Città del Vaticano; tel. (06) 69887366; fax (06) 6987154; e-mail eucharistcongress@org.va; Pres. Most Rev. Piero Marini (Titular Archbishop of Martirano).

Pontifical Committee of Historical Sciences: Palazzo delle Congregazioni, Piazza Pio XII 3, 00193 Rome, Italy; tel. (06) 69884618; fax (06) 69873014; e-mail pcss@scienstor.va; Pres. Mgr Bernard Ardura; Sec. Rev. Prof. Cosimo Semeraro.

Archives of the Second Vatican Council: c/o Archivio Segreto Vaticano, 00120 Città del Vaticano; tel. (06) 69883314; fax (06) 69885574; e-mail asv@asv.va; Dir Rt Rev. Sergio Pagano (Titular Bishop of Celene).

Commission for Lawyers: Palazzo della Cancelleria, Piazza della Cancelleria 1, 00186 Rome, Italy; tel. (06) 69887523; fax (06) 698887557; f. 1988; Pres. Cardinal Raymond Leo Burke.

Disciplinary Commission of the Roman Curia: Palazzo delle Congregazioni, Piazza Pio XII 10, 00120 Città del Vaticano; tel. (06) 69884008; fax (06) 69884710; e-mail herranz@org.va; Pres. Rt Rev. Giorgio Corbellini.

Offices

Apostolic Chamber: Palazzo Apostolico, 00120 Città del Vaticano; tel. (06) 69883554; Chamberlain of the Holy Roman Church Cardinal Tarcisio Bertone; Vice-Chamberlain Most Rev. Santos Abril y Castelló (Titular Archbishop of Tamada).

Administration of the Patrimony of the Apostolic See: Palazzo Apostolico, 00120 Città del Vaticano; tel. (06) 69893403; fax (06)

THE VATICAN CITY

69883141; e-mail apsa-ss@apsa.va; f. 1967; Pres. Cardinal ATTILIO NICORA; Sec. Most Rev. DOMENICO CALCAGNO.

Labour Office of the Apostolic See: Via della Conciliazione 1, 00193 Rome, Italy; tel. (06) 69884449; fax (06) 69883800; e-mail ulsa1@ulsa.va; Pres. Rt Rev. GIORGIO CORBELLINI (Titular Bishop of Abula).

Prefecture for the Economic Affairs of the Holy See: Palazzo delle Congregazioni, Largo del Colonnato 3, 00193 Rome, Italy; tel. (06) 69884263; fax (06) 69885011; e-mail rmpaess@econaffr.va; f. 1967; Pres. Cardinal VELASIO DE PAOLIS; Sec. (vacant).

Prefecture of the Papal Household: 00120 Città del Vaticano; tel. (06) 69883114; fax (06) 69885863; f. 1967; responsible for domestic administration and organization; Prefect Most Rev. JAMES MICHAEL HARVEY (Titular Archbishop of Memphis); Regent PAOLO DE NICOLÒ (Titular Bishop of Mariana in Corsica).

Office of the Liturgical Celebrations of the Supreme Pontiff: Palazzo Apostolico, 00120 Città del Vaticano; tel. (06) 69883253; fax (06) 69885412; Master Mgr GUIDO MARINI.

Central Statistical Office of the Church: Palazzo Apostolico, 00120 Città del Vaticano; tel. (06) 69883493; fax (06) 69883816; e-mail vformenti@statistica.va; Dir Mgr VITTORIO FORMENTI.

Holy See Press Office: Via della Conciliazione 54, 00120 Città del Vaticano; tel. (06) 698921; fax (06) 69885178; internet www.vatican.va; Dir Fr FEDERICO LOMBARDI; Vice-Dir Fr CIRO BENEDETTINI.

Pontifical Administration of the Patriarchal Basilica of San Paolo Fuori-le-Mura: 00120 Città del Vaticano; tel. (06) 5409374; fax (06) 54074049; e-mail spbasilica@org.va; Archpriest Cardinal FRANCESCO MONTERISI (Titular Archbishop of Alba Maritima).

Diplomatic Representation

DIPLOMATIC MISSIONS IN ROME ACCREDITED TO THE HOLY SEE

Albania: Via Silla 7/1, 00192 Rome, Italy; tel. (06) 39754085; fax (06) 39733150; e-mail embassy.vatican@mfa.gov.al; Ambassador RROK LOGU.

Angola: Palazzo Odeschalchi, Piazza SS. Apostoli 81, 00166 Rome, Italy; tel. (06) 69190650; fax (06) 69788483; Ambassador ARMINDO FERNANDES DO ESPÍRITO SANTO VIEIRA.

Argentina: Via del Banco di Santo Spirito 42, 00186 Rome, Italy; tel. (06) 68801701; fax (06) 6879021; e-mail essed@mrecic.gov.ar; Ambassador JUAN PABLO CAFIERO.

Australia: Via Paola 24/10, 00186 Rome, Italy; tel. (06) 6877688; fax (06) 6896255; e-mail holysee.embassy@dfat.gov.au; internet www.holysee.embassy.gov.au; Ambassador TIM FISCHER.

Austria: Via Reno 9, 00198 Rome, Italy; tel. (06) 853725; fax (06) 8543058; e-mail vatikan-ob@bmeia.gv.at; Ambassador ALFONS KLOSS.

Belgium: Via Giuseppe de Notaris 6A, 00197 Rome, Italy; tel. (06) 3224740; fax (06) 3226042; e-mail romeholysee@diplobel.fed.be; internet www.diplomatie.be/vaticanfr; Ambassador CHARLES GHISLAIN.

Benin: Rome, Italy; Ambassador COMLANVI THÉODORE LOKO.

Bolivia: Via di Porta Angelica 15/2, 00193 Rome, Italy; tel. (06) 6874191; fax (06) 6874193; e-mail embolivat@rdn.it; Ambassador CARLOS FEDERICO DE LA RIVA GUERRA.

Bosnia and Herzegovina: Piazzale Clodio 12, 00195 Rome, Italy; tel. (06) 39742411; fax (06) 39742484; e-mail embvavat@tin.it; Ambassador JASNA KRIVOŠIĆ PRPIĆ.

Brazil: Via della Conciliazione 22, 00193 Rome, Italy; tel. (06) 6875252; fax (06) 6872540; e-mail embaixada@vatemb.it; internet www.vatemb.it; Ambassador LUIZ FELIPE DE SEIXAS CORRÊA.

Bulgaria: Via di Porta Angelica 63, 00193 Rome, Italy; tel. (06) 6875717; fax (06) 6865233; e-mail ambulvat@yahoo.it; internet www.mfa.bg/bg/117; Ambassador NIKOLA IVANOV KADULOV.

Cameroon: Via Gregorio VII 58, 00165 Rome, Italy; tel. (06) 39918492; fax (06) 68806283; e-mail ambacamsaintsiege@yahoo.fr; Ambassador ANTOINE ZANGA.

Canada: Palazzo Pio, Via della Conciliazione 4D, 00193 Rome, Italy; tel. (06) 68307316; fax (06) 68806283; e-mail vatcn@international.gc.ca; internet www.canadainternational.gc.ca/holy_see-saint_siege; Ambassador ANNE LEAHY.

Chile: Piazza Risorgimento 55, 00192 Rome, Italy; tel. (06) 6861232; fax (06) 6874992; e-mail echileva@uni.net; Ambassador FERNANDO ZEGERS SANTA CRUZ.

Colombia: Via Cola di Rienzo 285/4B, 00192 Rome, Italy; tel. (06) 3211681; fax (06) 3211703; e-mail estasede@minrelext.gov.co; Ambassador CÉSAR MAURICIO VELÁSQUEZ OSSA.

Congo, Democratic Republic: Via del Castro Pretorio 28/2, 00185 Rome, Italy; tel. (06) 45447860; Ambassador JEAN-PIERRE HAMULI MUPENDA.

Costa Rica: Via G.B. Benedetti 3, 00197 Rome, Italy; tel. and fax (06) 80660390; e-mail embcr.vaticano@iol.it; Ambassador FERNANDO FELIPE SANCHEZ CAMPOS.

Côte d'Ivoire: Via Sforza Pallavicini 11, 00193 Rome, Italy; tel. (06) 6877503; fax (06) 6867925; e-mail ambaco.va@hotmail.it; Ambassador KOUAMÉ BENJAMIN KONAN.

Croatia: Via della Conciliazione 44, 00193 Rome, Italy; tel. (06) 6877000; fax (06) 6877003; e-mail velrhvat@tin.it; internet va.mfa.hr; Ambassador FILIP VUČAK.

Cuba: Via Aurelia 137/12B, 00165 Rome, Italy; tel. (06) 39366680; fax (06) 636685; e-mail embajada@cubassede.com; Ambassador EDUARDO DELGADO BERMÚDEZ.

Cyprus: Piazza Farnese 44, Scala A, Int. 1, 00186 Roma, Italy; tel. (06) 6865758; fax (06) 68803756; e-mail embcyprusholysee@tin.it; Ambassador GEORGIOS F. POULIDES.

Czech Republic: Via Crescenzio 91/1B, 00193 Rome, Italy; tel. (06) 6874694; fax (06) 6879731; e-mail vatican@embassy.mzv.cz; internet www.mzv.cz/vatican; Ambassador PAVEL VOŠALÍK.

Dominican Republic: Lungotevere Marzio 3, 00186 Rome, Italy; tel. and fax (06) 6864084; e-mail embajadardss@tiscali.it; Ambassador VICTOR GRIMALDI CÉSPEDES.

Ecuador: Via di Porta Angelica 64, 00193 Rome, Italy; tel. (06) 6897179; fax (06) 68892786; e-mail mecuadorsantasede@ecuaemss.it; Ambassador LUIS DOSITEO LATORRE TAPIA.

Egypt: Piazza della Città Leonina 9, 00193 Rome, Italy; tel. (06) 6865878; fax (06) 6832335; e-mail ambegyptvatican@tiscali.it; Ambassador LAMIA ALI HAMADA MEKHEMAR.

El Salvador: Via Panama 22/2, 00198 Rome, Italy; tel. (06) 8540538; fax (06) 85301131; e-mail embasalssede@iol.it; Ambassador MANUEL BARRERA ROBERTO LÓPEZ.

France: Villa Bonaparte, Via Piave 23, 00186 Rome, Italy; tel. (06) 42030900; fax (06) 42030968; e-mail ambfrssg@tin.it; internet www.france-vatican.org; Ambassador STANISLAS LEFEBVRE DE LABOULAYE.

Gabon: Piazzale Clodio 12, 00195 Rome, Italy; tel. (06) 39721584; fax (06) 39724847; Ambassador FIRMIN MBOUTSOU.

Georgia: Via Emilia 25, 00187 Rome, Italy; tel. and fax (06) 42010664; e-mail vatican.emb@mfa.gov.ge; internet vatican.mfa.gov.ge; Ambassador KETEVAN BAGRATION-MUKHRANBATONI.

Germany: Via di Villa Sacchetti 4–6, 00197 Rome, Italy; tel. (06) 809511; fax (06) 80951227; internet www.vatikan.diplo.de; Ambassador WALTER JÜRGEN SCHMID.

Greece: Via Giuseppe Mercalli 6, 00197 Rome, Italy; tel. (06) 8070786; fax (06) 8079862; e-mail grembassyvat@grembassyvat.191.it; Ambassador MILTIADIS HISKAKIS.

Guatemala: Piazzale Gregorio VII 65A, 00165 Rome, Italy; tel. (06) 6381632; fax (06) 39376981; e-mail embsantasede@minex.gob.gt; Ambassador ALFONSO ROBERTO MATTA FAHSEN.

Haiti: Via de Villa Patrizi 5B, 00161 Rome, Italy; tel. (06) 44242749; fax (06) 44236637; Ambassador CARL-HENRI GUITEAU.

Honduras: Via Boezio 45, 00193 Rome, Italy; tel. and fax (06) 6876051; e-mail honvati@fastwebnet.it; Ambassador ALEJANDRO EMILIO VALLADARES LANZA.

Hungary: Piazza Girolamo Fabrizio 2, 00161 Rome, Italy; tel. (06) 4402167; fax (06) 4402312; e-mail mission.vat@kum.hu; Ambassador GÁBOR GYŐRIVÁNYI.

Indonesia: Via Marocco 10, 00144 Rome, Italy; tel. (06) 59290049; fax (06) 54221292; e-mail info@indonesiavatican.it; internet www.vatican.deplu.go.id; Chargé d'affaires a.i. LUSY SURJANDARI.

Iran: Via Bruxelles 57, 00198 Rome, Italy; tel. (06) 8552494; fax (06) 8547910; e-mail chalac@libero.it; Ambassador ALI AKBAR NASERI.

Iraq: Via della Camilluccia 355, 00135 Rome, Italy; tel. (06) 30111140; fax (06) 35506416; e-mail ftkemb@iraqmofamail.net; Ambassador HABEEB HADI AL-SADR.

Ireland: Villa Spada, Via Giacomo Medici 1, 00153 Rome, Italy; tel. (06) 5810777; fax (06) 5895709; internet www.embassyofirelandholysee.it; Ambassador NOEL FAHEY.

Israel: Via Michele Mercati 12, 00197 Rome, Italy; tel. (06) 36198690; fax (06) 36198626; e-mail info-vat@holysee.mfa.gov.il; internet vatican.mfa.gov.il; Ambassador MORDECHAY LEWY.

Italy: Palazzo Borromeo, Viale delle Belle Arti 2, 00196 Rome, Italy; tel. (06) 3264881; fax (06) 3201801; e-mail amb.scv@esteri.it; Ambassador FRANCESCO MARIA GRECO.

Japan: Via Virgilio 30, 00193 Rome, Italy; tel. (06) 6875828; fax (06) 68807543; Ambassador HIDEKAZU YAMAGUCHI.

Korea, Republic: Via della Mendola 109, 00135 Rome, Italy; tel. (06) 3314505; fax (06) 3314522; Ambassador THOMAS HAN HONG-SOON.

THE VATICAN CITY

Lebanon: Via di Porta Angelica 15, 00193 Rome, Italy; tel. (06) 6833512; fax (06) 6833507; e-mail amb.libano@tin.it; Ambassador GEORGES CHAKIB AL-KHOURI.

Libya: Via Orazio 31B, 00193 Rome, Italy; tel. (06) 97605051; fax (06) 45433476; Sec. of the People's Bureau ABD AL-HAFID GADDUR.

Lithuania: Corso Vittorio Emanuele II 308, 00186 Rome, Italy; tel. (06) 68192858; fax (06) 68809596; e-mail amb.va@urm.lt; internet va.mfa.lt; Ambassador VYTAUTAS ALIŠAUSKAS.

Luxembourg: Via Casale di S. Pio V 20, 00165 Rome, Italy; tel. (06) 660560; fax (06) 66056309; e-mail siebenaler@dehon.it; Ambassador PAUL DÜHR.

Macedonia, former Yugoslav Republic: Via di Porta Cavalleggeri 143, 00165 Rome, Italy; tel. (06) 635878; fax (06) 634826; e-mail vatican@mfa.gov.mk; Ambassador GJOKO GJORGJEVSKI.

Mexico: Via Ezio 49/3, 00192 Rome, Italy; tel. (06) 3230360; fax (06) 3230361; e-mail embamex-s.sede@mclink.it; internet portal.sre.gob.mx/vaticano; Ambassador HÉCTOR FEDERICO LING ALTAMIRANO.

Monaco: Largo Nicola Spinelli 5, 00198 Rome, Italy; tel. (06) 8414357; fax (06) 8414507; e-mail ambmonacovat@alice.it; Ambassador JEAN-CLAUDE MICHEL.

Montenegro: Via Crescenzio 97/II, 00193 Rome, Italy; tel. (06) 68134897; fax (06) 68130569; e-mail ambmont.vat@hotmail.it; Ambassador ANTUN SBUTEGA.

Morocco: Via delle Fornaci 203, 00165 Rome, Italy; tel. (06) 39388398; fax (06) 6374459; e-mail sifamavat@marocco.191.it; Ambassador ALI ACHOUR.

Netherlands: Piazza della Città Leonina 9, 00193 Rome, Italy; tel. (06) 6868044; fax (06) 6879593; e-mail vat@minbuza.nl; Chargé d'affaires a.i. JOS DOUMA.

Nicaragua: Via Luigi Luciani 42/1A, 00197 Rome, Italy; tel. (06) 32600265; fax (06) 3207249; e-mail embanicsantasede@tin.it; Ambassador JOSÉ CUADRA CHAMORRO.

Panama: Largo di Torre Argentina 11/28, 00186 Rome, Italy; tel. (06) 68809764; fax (06) 68809812; e-mail embapass@tiscalinet.it; Ambassador DELIA CÁRDENAS CHRISTIE.

Paraguay: Via Ugo Bartolomei 23B, int. 1, 00136 Rome, Italy; tel. (06) 39751368; fax (06) 39745063; e-mail embapar.vaticano@mre.gov.py; Chargé d'affaires a.i. CARLOS VERA AGUILERA.

Peru: Via di Porta Angelica 63, 00193 Rome, Italy; tel. (06) 68308535; fax (06) 6896059; e-mail embaperuva@tin.it; Ambassador ALFONSO DÁMASO ANTONIO RIVERO MONSALVE.

Philippines: Via Paolo VI 29, 00193 Rome, Italy; tel. (06) 68308020; fax (06) 6834076; e-mail embholysee@philvatican.it; Ambassador MERCEDES TUASON.

Poland: Via dei Delfini 16/3, 00186 Rome, Italy; tel. (06) 6990958; fax (06) 6990978; e-mail polamb.wat@agora.it; Ambassador HANNA SUCHOCKA.

Portugal: Villa Lusa, Via S. Valentino 9, 00197 Rome, Italy; tel. (06) 8091581; fax (06) 8077585; e-mail embportugalvatican@tiscalinet.it; Ambassador MANUEL TOMÁS FERNANDES PEREIRA.

Romania: Via Panama 92, 00198 Rome, Italy; tel. (06) 8541802; fax (06) 8554067; e-mail ambasciata@vatican.mae.ro; internet vatican.mae.ro; Ambassador BOGDAN TĂTARU-CAZABAN.

Russia: Via della Conciliazione 10, 00193 Rome, Italy; tel. (06) 6877078; fax (06) 6877168; e-mail russsede@libero.it; Ambassador NIKOLAY SADCHIKOV.

San Marino: Piazza G. Winckelmann 12, 00162 Rome, Italy; tel. (06) 86321798; fax (06) 8610814; e-mail amb-sanmarino@libero.it; Ambassador SANTE CANDUCCI.

Senegal: Via dei Monti Parioli 51, 00197 Rome, Italy; tel. (06) 3218892; fax (06) 3203624; e-mail senvat@iol.it; Ambassador FÉLIX OUDIANE.

Serbia: Via dei Monti Parioli 20, 00197 Rome, Italy; tel. (06) 3200099; fax (06) 3204530; e-mail amb.serbia.vatican@ambroma.com; Ambassador VLADETA JANKOVIĆ.

Slovakia: Via dei Colli della Farnesina 144, 00135 Rome, Italy; tel. (06) 36715234; fax (06) 36715237; e-mail emb.vatican@mzv.sk; internet www.mzv.sk/vatikan; Ambassador JOZEF DRAVECKÝ.

Slovenia: Via della Conciliazione 10, 00193 Rome, Italy; tel. (06) 6833009; fax (06) 68307942; e-mail vva@gov.si; Ambassador MAJA MARIJA LOVRENČIČ SVETEK.

Spain: Palazzo di Spagna, Piazza di Spagna 57, 00187 Rome, Italy; tel. (06) 6784351; fax (06) 6784355; e-mail emb.santasede@mae.es; internet www.maec.es/embajadas/santasede; Ambassador MARÍA JESÚS FIGA LÓPEZ-PALOP.

Taiwan (Republic of China): Via della Conciliazione 4D, 00193 Rome, Italy; tel. (06) 68136206; fax (06) 68136199; e-mail taiwan@embroc.it; internet www.taiwanembassy.org/va; Ambassador LARRY YU-YUAN WANG.

Timor Leste: Via Cavour 285, 5° Int. 10, 00184 Rome, Italy; tel. (06) 47824537; fax (06) 47883366; e-mail servicio.administracao@embtimorvaticano.it; Ambassador JUSTINO MARIA APARÍCIO GUTERRES.

Turkey: Via Lovanio 24/1, 00198 Rome, Italy; tel. (06) 85508601; fax (06) 85508660; e-mail vatibe@libero.it; Ambassador KENAN GÜRSOY.

Ukraine: Via G. Bessarione 8, Int. 3, 00165 Rome, Italy; tel. (06) 39378800; fax (06) 39375884; e-mail emb_va@mfa.gov.ua; internet www.mfa.gov.ua/vatican; Ambassador TETIANA IZHEVSKA.

United Kingdom: Via XX Settembre 80A, 00187 Rome, Italy; tel. (06) 42204000; fax (06) 42204205; e-mail holysee@fco.gov.uk; internet www.ukinholysee.fco.gov.uk; Chargé d'affaires a.i. GEORGE EDGAR.

USA: Villa Domiziana, Via delle Terme Deciane 26, 00153 Rome, Italy; tel. (06) 46743428; fax (06) 5758346; e-mail vaticaninfo@mail.usembassy.it; internet vatican.usembassy.gov; Ambassador Dr MIGUEL HUMBERTO DÍAZ.

Uruguay: Via Antonio Gramsci 9/14, 00197 Rome, Italy; tel. (06) 3218904; fax (06) 3613249; e-mail uruvati@tin.it; Ambassador MARIO JUAN BOSCO CAYOTA ZAPPETTINI.

Venezuela: Via Antonio Gramsci 14, 00197 Rome, Italy; tel. (06) 3225868; fax (06) 36001505; e-mail evidano@iol.it; Ambassador IVÁN GUILLERMO RINCÓN URDANETA.

Ecclesiastical Organization

The organization of the Church consists of:

(1) Patriarchs, Archbishops and Bishops in countries under the common law of the Church.

(2) Abbots and Prelates 'nullius dioceseos'.

(3) Vicars Apostolic and Prefects Apostolic in countries classified as Missionary and under Propaganda, the former having Episcopal dignity.

The population of the world adhering to the Roman Catholic faith, according to official estimates, was 1,166m. at 31 December 2008.

Among the Pope's official titles until early 2006, when Pope Benedict XVI decided no longer to use it, was that of Patriarch of the West. There are five other Patriarchates of the Latin Rite—Jerusalem, the West Indies, the East Indies, Lisbon and Venice. The Eastern Catholic Churches each have Patriarchs: Alexandria for the Coptic Rite; Babylon for the Chaldean Rite; Cilicia for the Armenian Rite; and Antioch for the Syrian, Maronite and Melkite Rites.

At 31 December 2009 there were 2,812 residential sees—13 patriarchates, four senior archbishoprics, 539 metropolitan archbishoprics, 77 archbishoprics and 2,179 bishoprics. Of the 2,086 titular sees (92 metropolitan archbishoprics, 91 archbishoprics and 1,903 bishoprics), 1,086 are filled by bishops who have been given these titles, but exercise no territorial jurisdiction. Other territorial divisions of the Church include 48 prelacies, 11 territorial abbacies, 24 exarchates of the Eastern Church, 35 military ordinariates, 83 apostolic vicariates, 41 apostolic prefectures, nine apostolic administrations and nine missions 'sui iuris'. In January 2011 the Personal Ordinariate of Our Lady of Walsingham was established to accommodate former Anglican clergy and adherents in England and Wales.

The Press

Acta Apostolicae Sedis: Periodical Dept, Libreria Editrice Vaticana, 00120 Città del Vaticano; tel. (06) 69883529; fax (06) 69884716; e-mail mariasic2@publish.va; internet www.libreriaeditricevaticana.com; f. 1909; official bulletin issued by the Holy See; monthly, with special editions on special occasions; the record of Encyclicals and other Papal pronouncements, Acts of the Congregations and Offices, nominations, etc.; circ. 6,000.

Annuario Pontificio: Libreria Editrice Vaticana, Via del Tipografia, 00120 Città del Vaticano; tel. (06) 69883493; fax (06) 69885088; e-mail segreteria.lev@lev.va; official year book edited by Central Statistical Office; Dir Mgr VITTORIO FORMENTI.

L'Osservatore Romano: Tipografica Vaticana, Via del Pellegrino, 00120 Città del Vaticano; tel. (06) 69883461; fax (06) 69883675; e-mail ornet@ossrom.va; internet www.vatican.va/news_services/or/home_ita.html; f. 1861; an authoritative daily newspaper in Italian; its special columns devoted to the affairs of the Holy See may be described as semi-official; the news service covers religious matters and, in a limited measure, general affairs; weekly editions in English, French, German, Italian, Portuguese and Spanish; monthly editions in Polish; Editor-in-Chief GIOVANNI MARIA VIAN; Man. Editor CARLO DE LUCIA; circ. (Italian daily) 20,000.

Pro Dialogo: Via della Conciliazione 5, 00193 Rome, Italy; tel. (06) 69884321; fax (06) 69884494; e-mail dialogo@interrel.va; 3 a year; publ. by the Pontifical Council for Inter-Religious Dialogue.

THE VATICAN CITY

Statistical Yearbook of the Church: Central Statistical Office of the Church, Palazzo Apostolico, 00120 Città del Vaticano; tel. (06) 69883493; fax (06) 69883816; e-mail vformenti@statistica.va; Dir Mgr VITTORIO FORMENTI.

NEWS AGENCY

Agenzia Internazionale FIDES: Palazzo 'de Propaganda Fide', Via di Propaganda 1C, 00187 Rome, Italy; tel. (06) 69880115; fax (06) 69880107; e-mail fides@fides.va; internet www.fides.org; f. 1927; handles news of missions throughout the world and publishes a weekly bulletin in 6 languages (circ. 3,000), provides a daily news service by e-mail; Dir LUCA DE MATA.

Publishers

Biblioteca Apostolica Vaticana: Cortile del Belvedere, 00120 Città del Vaticano; tel. (06) 69879411; fax (06) 69884795; e-mail bav@vatlib.it; internet www.vaticanlibrary.va; f. 1451; philology, classics, history, catalogues; Librarian of the Holy Roman Church Cardinal RAFFAELE FARINA.

Libreria Editrice Vaticana: Via della Posta, 00120 Città del Vaticano; tel. (06) 69884834; fax (06) 69884716; e-mail lev@publish.va; internet www.libreriaeditricevaticana.com; f. 1926; religion, philosophy, literature, art, Latin philology, history; Pres. Mgr GUISEPPE SCOTTI; Dir Rev. GIUSEPPE COSTA.

Tipografia Vaticana (Vatican Press): Via della Tipografia, 00120 Città del Vaticano; tel. (06) 69883506; fax (06) 69884570; e-mail tipvat@tipografia.va; f. 1587; religion, theology, education, juveniles, natural and social sciences; prints *Acta Apostolicae Sedis* and *L'Osservatore Romano*; Dir-Gen. Rev. ELIO TORRIGIANI.

Broadcasting and Communications

RADIO

Radio Vaticana was founded in 1931 and is situated within the Vatican City. A transmitting centre, inaugurated by Pius XII in 1957, is located at Santa Maria di Galeria, about 20 km north-west of the Vatican. Under a special treaty between the Holy See and Italy, the site of this centre, which covers 420 ha, enjoys the same extra-territorial privileges as are recognized by international law for the diplomatic headquarters of foreign states.

The station operates an all-day service, normally in 40 languages, but with facilities for broadcasting liturgical and other religious services in additional languages, including Latin.

The purpose of Radio Vaticana is to broadcast papal teaching, to provide information on important events in the Roman Catholic Church, to express the Catholic point of view on problems affecting religion and morality, and, above all, to form a continuous link between the Holy See and Roman Catholics throughout the world.

Radio Vaticana: Palazzo Pio, Piazza Pia 3, 00120 Città del Vaticano; tel. (06) 69883551; fax (06) 69883237; e-mail sedoc@vatiradio.va; internet www.vaticanradio.org; f. 1931; Dir-Gen. Rev. Fr FEDERICO LOMBARDI; Tech. Dir SANDRO PIERVENAZI; Administrative Dir ALBERTO GASBARRI; Dir of Programmes Rev. Fr ANDREJ KOPROWSKI.

TELEVISION

Centro Televisivo Vaticano (CTV) (Vatican Television Centre): Via del Pellegrino, 00120 Città del Vaticano; tel. (06) 69885467; fax (06) 69885192; e-mail ctv@ctv.va; f. 1983; produces and distributes programmes about the Pope and the Vatican City; Pres. Archbishop CLAUDIO MARIA CELLI; Dir-Gen. Rev. Fr FEDERICO LOMBARDI.

Finance

Financial Information Authority (FIA): 00120 Città del Vaticano; f. 2010; est. by Pope Benedict XVI as an autonomous and independent body; supervises adherence to international regulations to prevent money-laundering and the financing of terrorism; responsible for co-operation with foreign authorities; Chair. Cardinal ATTILIO NICORA; Dir FRANCESCO DE PASQUALE.

Istituto per le Opere di Religione (IOR): 00120 Città del Vaticano; tel. (06) 69883354; fax (06) 69883809; e-mail dige@sistonet.org; f. 1887; renamed in 1942; oversees the distribution of capital designated for religious works; it takes deposits from religious bodies and Vatican residents; governed by a Board of Superintendence comprising 5 financial experts, overseen by a commission of 5 cardinals; Pres. Prof. ETTORE GOTTI TEDESCHI; Dir-Gen. PAOLO CIPRIANI; Commission mems Cardinals TARCISIO BERTONE, ATTILIO NICORA, JEAN-LOUIS TAURAN, TELESPHORE PLACIDUS TOPPO, ODILO PEDRO SCHERER.

Lay Employees' Association

In 1989 Pope John Paul II agreed to establish a Labour Council to settle any disputes between the Holy See and its lay employees.

Associazione Dipendenti Laici Vaticani (Association of Vatican Lay Workers): Via della Posta, 00120 Città del Vaticano; tel. (06) 69885343; fax (06) 69884400; f. 1979; aims to safeguard the professional, legal, economic and moral interests of its members; Sec.-Gen. ALESSANDRO CANDI; 320 mems.

Transport

There is a small railway (863 m) which runs from the Vatican into Italy. It began operating in 1934 and now carries supplies and goods. There is also a heliport used by visiting heads of state and Vatican officials.

VENEZUELA

Introductory Survey

LOCATION, CLIMATE, LANGUAGE, RELIGION, FLAG, CAPITAL

The Bolivarian Republic of Venezuela lies on the north coast of South America, bordered by Colombia to the west, Guyana to the east and Brazil to the south. The climate varies with altitude from tropical to temperate; the average temperature in Caracas is 21°C (69°F). The language is Spanish. There is no state religion, but some 85% of the population is Roman Catholic. The national flag (proportions 2 by 3) has three horizontal stripes of yellow, blue and red, with eight five-pointed white stars, arranged in an arc, in the centre of the blue stripe. The state flag has, in addition, the national coat of arms (a shield bearing a gold wheat sheaf in the first division, a panoply of swords, an indigenous bow and arrow quiver, a machete, flags and a lance in the second, and a white running horse in the base, flanked by branches of laurel and palm and with two cornucopias at the crest) in the top left-hand corner. The capital is Caracas.

CONTEMPORARY POLITICAL HISTORY

Historical Context

Venezuela was a Spanish colony from 1499 until 1821 and, under the leadership of Simón Bolívar, achieved independence in 1830. The country was governed principally by dictators until 1945, when a military-civilian coup replaced Isaías Medina Angarita with Rómulo Betancourt as head of a revolutionary junta. Col (later Gen.) Marcos Pérez Jiménez seized power in December 1952 and took office as President in 1953. He remained in office until 1958, when he was overthrown by a military junta under Adm. Wolfgang Larrazábal. Betancourt was elected President in the same year.

Domestic Political Affairs

A new Constitution was promulgated in 1961. Three years later President Betancourt became the first Venezuelan President to complete his term of office. Dr Raúl Leoni was elected President in December 1963. Supporters of former President Pérez staged an abortive military uprising in 1966. Dr Rafael Caldera Rodríguez became Venezuela's first Christian Democratic President in March 1969. He achieved some success in stabilizing the country politically and economically, although political assassinations and abductions committed by underground organizations continued into 1974. At elections in December 1973 Carlos Andrés Pérez Rodríguez, candidate of Acción Democrática (AD), the main opposition party, was chosen to succeed President Caldera. The new Government invested heavily in agriculture and industrial development, creating a more balanced economy, and also undertook to nationalize important sectors. The presidential election of December 1978 was won by the leader of the Partido Social-Cristiano (Comité de Organización Política Electoral Independiente—COPEI), Dr Luis Herrera Campíns. In 1981 a deteriorating economic situation provoked social unrest and a succession of guerrilla attacks. At a presidential election in December 1983, the AD candidate, Dr Jaime Lusinchi, was elected. The AD also won the majority of seats in the Congreso Nacional.

At elections conducted in December 1988, AD candidate Carlos Andrés Pérez Rodríguez became the first former President to be re-elected. However, the AD lost its overall majority in the Congreso Nacional. President Pérez implemented a series of adjustments designed to halt Venezuela's economic decline. These measures provoked rioting throughout the country in late February. The Government introduced a curfew and suspended various constitutional rights in order to quell the disturbances, but it was estimated that some 246 people had died during the protests. In early March the curfew was revoked, and all constitutional rights were restored, after wages had been increased and the prices of some basic goods were frozen.

In May 1989 popular opposition to the Government's austerity programme became co-ordinated by the country's largest trade union, the Confederación de Trabajadores de Venezuela (CTV), which organized a 24-hour general strike (the first for 31 years) in favour of the introduction of pro-labour reforms. In May 1991 a controversial new labour law came into effect, providing for a severance benefit scheme and a social security system. In the second half of that year a series of widespread and often violent demonstrations and strikes were staged to protest against monthly increases in the price of petrol, or to demand, *inter alia*, wage increases, the reintroduction of price controls on basic goods, and the suspension of planned public sector redundancies.

On 4 February 1992 an attempt to overthrow the President by rebel army units was defeated by armed forces loyal to the Government. The rebels, identified as members of the 'Movimiento Bolivariano Revolucionario 200' (MBR-200), attempted to occupy the President's office, the Miraflores palace, and his official residence, but were forced to capitulate. Simultaneous rebel action in the cities of Maracay, Valencia and Maracaibo ended when one of the leaders of the coup, Lt-Col Hugo Rafael Chávez Frías, broadcast an appeal for their surrender. More than 1,000 soldiers were arrested, and 33 officers were subsequently charged. A number of constitutional guarantees were immediately suspended, and press and television censorship was imposed to exclude coverage of Chávez, who had received considerable passive popular support. The rebels' stated primary reasons for staging the insurrection were the increasing social divisions and uneven distribution of wealth resulting from government economic policy, and widespread corruption in public life. Immediately following the attempted coup Pérez authorized a 50% increase in the minimum wage and a 30% increase in the pay of middle-ranking officers of the armed forces. He also announced plans to bring forward a US $4,000m. social project, aimed at improving health care, social welfare and education.

In March 1992 Pérez announced a series of proposed political and economic reforms, including the introduction of legislation for immediate reform of the Constitution. In addition, the President announced the suspension of increases in the price of petrol and electricity, and the reintroduction of price controls on a number of basic foodstuffs and on medicine. In that month, in an effort to broaden the base of support for his Government, Pérez appointed two members of COPEI to the Council of Ministers. Full constitutional rights were finally restored in April. Nevertheless, widespread protests against government austerity measures and alleged official corruption continued in September and October.

On 27 November 1992 a further coup attempt, reported to have been instigated by members of MBR-200, was suppressed by forces loyal to the Government. A videotaped statement by the imprisoned Lt-Col Chávez, transmitted from a captured government-owned television station, urged Venezuelans to stage public demonstrations in support of the rebels. Principal air force bases were seized, and rebel aircraft attacked the presidential palace and other strategically important installations. The Government introduced a state of emergency and suspended the Constitution. Sporadic fighting continued into the following day, but by 29 November order had been restored and some 1,300 rebel members of the armed forces had been arrested. The curfew imposed during the coup was ended at the beginning of December, and further constitutional rights were restored later in the month. Popular discontent with the Government was reflected further in regional and municipal elections held in December, which resulted in significant gains for COPEI. In March 1993 the Supreme Court annulled the rulings of an extraordinary summary court martial, which had been established by presidential decree to try those implicated in the attempted coup of November 1992, on the grounds that the court was unconstitutional. Those sentenced by the court were to be retried by an ordinary court martial.

In May 1993 an extraordinary joint session of the Congreso Nacional voted to endorse a Supreme Court ruling that sufficient evidence existed for Pérez to be prosecuted on corruption charges. The charges concerned allegations that Pérez, and two former government ministers, had, in 1989, embezzled US $17m. from a secret government fund. Pérez was subsequently suspended from office and, in accordance with the terms of the Constitution, replaced by the President of the Senado, pending the election by the Congreso Nacional of an interim

VENEZUELA

President. On 5 June the Congreso Nacional elected Ramón José Velásquez, an independent senator, as interim President. In August the Congreso Nacional approved legislation enabling Velásquez to introduce urgent economic and financial measures by decree in order to address the growing economic crisis. In late August a special session of the Congreso Nacional voted in favour of the permanent suspension from office of Pérez, regardless of the outcome of the legal proceedings being conducted against him.

1993 elections

The presidential and legislative elections of December 1993 proceeded peacefully. Dr Rafael Caldera Rodríguez, the candidate of the newly formed Convergencia Nacional (CN), was elected President (having previously held office in 1969–74). However, the CN secured only minority representation in the Congreso Nacional. Caldera took office in February 1994. In that month the AD and COPEI established a pact using their combined majority representation in the Congreso Nacional in order to gain control of the major legislative committees. In response, Caldera warned that he would dissolve the legislature and organize elections to a Constituent Assembly should the government programme encounter obstructions in the Congreso Nacional. Also in February, in an attempt to consolidate relations with the armed forces, Caldera initiated proceedings providing for the release and pardon of all those charged with involvement in the coup attempts of February and November 1992.

In June 1994 the Government announced that it was to assume extraordinary powers, in view of the deepening economic crisis and the virtual collapse of the banking sector. Six articles of the Constitution were suspended; these concerned guarantees including freedom of movement, freedom from arbitrary arrest, and the right to own property and to engage in legal economic activity. The Government also announced the introduction of price controls and a single fixed exchange rate. Later that month Caldera issued a decree placing the financial system under government control. Of those banks affected by the crisis, 10 were closed permanently; the majority of those still operational were to be returned to private control. In July the Congreso Nacional voted to restore five of the six suspended constitutional guarantees. Despite protest, the Government promptly reintroduced the suspensions. Later that month, however, the legislature endorsed emergency financial measures, including an extension of price controls and the strengthening of finance sector regulation, as a precursor to the restoration of full constitutional guarantees, which were finally restored in July. In September 1997 the Congreso Nacional approved an 'enabling law' ('ley habilitante') that conferred extraordinary powers on President Caldera to enact legislation by decree, in order to facilitate the implementation of emergency economic measures designed to reduce the huge fiscal deficit and to accelerate social security reforms.

The legislative elections of November 1998 were won by the Polo Patriótico, an alliance of small, mainly left-wing parties led by the Movimiento V República (MVR). The MVR had been founded in the previous year by the leader of the attempted coup of February 1992, Lt-Col (retd) Chávez; its electoral success was widely considered to reflect the popular rejection of apparent corruption in the country's major political parties.

Hugo Chávez elected President, 1998

In the light of the MVR's success in the legislative poll, prior to the presidential election the AD and COPEI withdrew their support for their respective candidates and united in support of independent candidate Henrique Salas Römer, hoping to forestall the loss of their long-standing political predominance. However, Chávez, who styled himself as a radical left-wing populist, promising social revolution and constitutional reform, was elected President on 6 December 1998, ahead of Salas Römer.

Chávez immediately announced plans for elections to a Constituent Assembly to draft a new constitution, and asked the Congreso to pass a new enabling law to allow him to implement an extensive restructuring of public administration and a comprehensive economic recovery programme. Chávez was inaugurated as President on 2 February 1999. At the end of February he announced details of an ambitious emergency social improvement plan (the Plan Bolívar 2000) to rehabilitate public property and land through voluntary civil and military action. Such pledges (together with a promise that the armed forces would not be used against the civilian population) prompted a series of rural and urban public land occupations, none of which was forcibly ended.

In April 1999 the Congreso approved the enabling law. On 25 April a national referendum, organized to ascertain levels of popular support for the convening of a Constituent Assembly and the regulations governing the election of such a body, demonstrated 82% support for the Assembly and 80% support for Chávez's proposals for electoral procedures. (The successful endorsement of the proposals was, however, qualified by the 60% rate of voter abstention.) Elections to the National Constituent Assembly (ANC) in July resulted in an outright victory for the Polo Patriótico. The leadership of COPEI and of the AD subsequently resigned. The ANC was formally inaugurated and by late August had assumed most functions of the opposition-controlled Congreso Nacional; the Congreso itself was put into recess indefinitely. In response, the opposition accused the Government of establishing a de facto dictatorship. Chávez justified the control of the legislature, executive and judiciary as necessary in order to eradicate corruption and implement social reforms. A Judicial Emergency Commission was also appointed in August with the task of investigating the notoriously corrupt judicial system. (By November 200 judges had been dismissed or suspended.) In response, the Supreme Court President resigned. In September the ANC and the Congreso Nacional signed an agreement of political co-existence that guaranteed the full functioning of the legislative branch from 2 October until a new constitution entered into force.

The draft of the new Constitution was signed by the ANC on 19 November 1999 and was approved by 71% of the popular vote in a referendum held on 15 December. The 350-article Constitution, which renamed the country the Bolivarian Republic of Venezuela, was promulgated on 30 December. It extended the President's term from five to six years, eliminated the Senado, permitted more state intervention in the economy, reduced civilian supervisory powers over the military, guaranteed the Government's oil monopoly and strengthened minority rights. The Constitution also promoted public participation by giving the electorate the right to remove elected officials from office by referendum and to annul all but a handful of key laws with an absolute majority. The monitoring of such election processes was to be carried out by an independent National Electoral Council (Consejo Nacional Electoral—CNE). The Congreso Nacional was officially dissolved on 4 January 2000.

New elections for the President, governors, legislators and mayors, as stipulated under the new Constitution, were scheduled for May 2000. The ANC was dissolved in January after it formally delegated its powers to a newly created 21-member Legislative Commission, which was designated as an interim body until the formation of a new Asamblea Nacional. On 25 May, three days before voting was scheduled to take place, the Tribunal Supremo de Justicia suspended the elections, citing technical faults with the electronic voting system. Elections for the President, national legislators and governors were eventually held on 30 July, separate from the local elections, which were postponed until December. Despite the weak economic situation, popular support for the President, especially from the poorest sections of society, remained strong: Chávez won 60% of the valid votes cast in the presidential poll, compared with the 38% of the ballot polled by Francisco Arias Cárdenas. At the concurrent election to the new, 165-seat Asamblea Nacional, the ruling MVR secured a majority, although short of the three-fifths' majority required to appoint members of the judiciary and the Attorney-General and Comptroller-General.

In November 2000 Chávez's powers were further enhanced when the Asamblea Nacional approved a new enabling law, allowing the President to decree, without legislative debate, a wide range of laws (in areas including public finance and land reform) for one year. In the same month the legislature approved controversial legislation that assigned the power to appoint important government posts, such as Attorney-General, Ombudsman (Defensor del Pueblo) and senior judges, to a 15-member congressional committee that was dominated by members of the ruling party.

In May 2001 thousands of petroleum and steel workers went on strike to demand recognition of trade union rights. In late November the opposition-controlled CTV allied itself with the country's largest business association, Fedecámaras (Federación Venezolana de Cámaras y Asociaciones de Comercio y Producción), to demand a nation-wide general strike. Fedecámaras was protesting against a recently decreed series of 49 laws (adopted using the enabling law, thereby bypassing legislative scrutiny); these measures included land reform legislation allowing the Government to expropriate land it deemed unproductive, and a hydrocarbons law, which increased royalties on the petroleum industry. The CTV objected to the hydrocarbons law, claiming that it threatened foreign investment and jobs.

In early 2002 Chávez appointed to his Council of Ministers several co-conspirators in the 1992 military coup attempt. The cabinet reorganization was interpreted by many as a move to the left that would increase political instability. In February four military officials, in separate statements, publicly demanded that Chávez resign, leading to further anti-Government protests and counter-demonstrations in support of the Government. In the same month, in the face of increasing economic uncertainty, the Government abandoned the fixed currency exchange regime and allowed the bolívar to float freely, in an attempt to halt mass capital flight.

In March 2002 business leaders, trade union leaders and representatives of the Catholic Church signed a pact calling for, inter alia, the installation of a government of national unity. At the same time, industrial unrest continued to escalate. Following the appointment of a new management board of the state petroleum company Petróleos de Venezuela, SA (PDVSA), several thousand PDVSA managers marched through Caracas in protest, claiming that the appointments were politically motivated. On 9 April a 48-hour general strike was organized by the CTV and Fedecámaras. It was subsequently announced that the strike would continue indefinitely, and on 11 April more than 150,000 people marched on the presidential palace to demand Chávez's resignation. In the subsequent clashes outside the Miraflores palace between protesters, government supporters and the security forces, 20 people were killed and more than 100 injured.

Failed coup of April 2002

On 12 April 2002 a group of senior military officers announced that President Chávez had resigned amid allegations that pro-Government loyalists had fired on opposition protesters. It later emerged that Chávez had, in fact, refused to resign and that, in effect, a military coup had taken place. The military conspirators appointed Pedro Carmona, the President of Fedecámaras, interim President, while Chávez was held incommunicado. On assuming power, Carmona dissolved the Asamblea Nacional and the Tribunal Supremo de Justicia and pronounced Chávez's Bolivarian Constitution to be null and void. The removal from office by the military of an elected head of state was immediately condemned by many Governments in the region; however, in contrast, the US Administration of George W. Bush blamed the crisis on Chávez and refused to call his ousting from power a coup. Thousands of pro-Chávez and pro-democracy supporters took to the streets to demand Chávez's reinstatement, while many senior military officers also expressed their continued loyalty to the deposed President. In the face of threats by officers loyal to Chávez to attack the presidential palace, Carmona resigned; Vice-President Cabello was sworn in as interim President on 13 April. Chávez returned to the Miraflores palace within hours and, in a televised ceremony, resumed his presidential powers, less than two days after he was ousted.

On reassuming the presidency, as a gesture of reconciliation, Chávez announced the resignation of the disputed PDVSA board of directors. He also declared that there would be no persecution of those who had supported his removal from office. Nevertheless, Carmona and 100 military personnel were arrested. (Carmona escaped from house arrest and was subsequently granted asylum in Colombia.) In late April 2002 the Asamblea Nacional approved the establishment of a Truth Commission to investigate the events surrounding the coup attempt. (In October 2004 eight people were convicted and sentenced to prison terms of between three and six years for their roles in the uprising.)

The country's political and economic situation continued to deteriorate in mid-2002. In August the Supreme Court ruled that there was insufficient evidence to prosecute four senior members of the military who had participated in the failed coup attempt in April. (However, this ruling was overturned in March 2005.) In October the opposition and its allies in the CTV and Fedecámaras called a one-day strike, which brought much of Venezuela to a halt. On 23 October a group of 14 senior military officers, many of whom had been involved in April's failed coup, declared themselves in rebellion against the Chávez Government, occupying a square in eastern Caracas, where they were joined by hundreds of opposition activists. More than 100 junior officers later also expressed their rejection of Chávez's policies and joined the protest. All of the officers involved were subsequently dismissed from the armed forces. In an attempt to find a constitutional solution to the ongoing political crisis, 12 representatives of the opposition and the Government began round-table discussions, sponsored by the Organization of American States (OAS, see p. 391), in early November. The talks failed to make any immediate progress, however, and in late November the opposition, the CTV and Fedecámaras announced that a general strike would be held from 2 December to force President Chávez to call fresh elections or submit to a referendum. The general strike lasted a further nine weeks. The majority of large businesses and international companies observed the stoppage, although small shopkeepers and public transport continued to operate throughout. The strike had a particularly severe impact on the oil industry. The majority of managers and administrative staff at PDVSA observed the strike, and the company was obliged to declare force majeure on its exports of crude petroleum and petroleum products. The President of PDVSA, Alí Rodríguez Araque, sought to restart the industry by replacing the strikers with new staff, contract workers and retired employees. He eventually dismissed 18,000 of PDVSA's previous 33,000 full-time work-force for observing the strike, and production reportedly recovered to pre-strike levels by late March 2003.

In January 2003 President Chávez suspended trading in the national currency, the bolívar, in response to the economic crisis. Early the following month it was announced that the bolívar was to be pegged to the US dollar, and that price controls were to be introduced on basic food items. Although the Government refused to negotiate on the issue of early elections, discussions between the two sides, suspended at the start of the strike, resumed in late January. The opposition, which had combined under the Coordinadora Democrática (CD) grouping, presented an estimated 4m. signatures in support of early elections. In mid-February the Government and opposition representatives signed an agreement to seek to reduce political tension in Venezuela. This was immediately thrown into question, however, when the following day police arrested the President of Fedecámaras, Carlos Fernández Pérez, on charges including treason, relating to his role in organizing the strike. A warrant was also issued for his fellow strike leader, the President of the CTV, Carlos Ortega, who went into hiding and later obtained political asylum in Costa Rica. The opposition immediately accused President Chávez of authoritarianism. In March an appeals court ordered the release without charge of Fernández Pérez, ruling that there was no evidence against him.

Presidential recall referendum

In April 2003, following further OAS-sponsored negotiations, the Government and opposition agreed in principle that a referendum on the Chávez Government could be held if the opposition succeeded in collecting 2.4m. signatures in support of a vote. The agreement was finalized in May. The signatures collected by the opposition were to be verified by the CNE. However, since the Asamblea Nacional was unable to agree on appointments to the electoral body, responsibility passed, as stipulated by the Constitution, to the Tribunal Supremo de Justicia, which appointed, in August, a new head of the electoral authority, as well as four other board members. One week earlier opposition parties had submitted a 2.4m.-signature petition to the CNE demanding a recall referendum. However, in early September the new board of the electoral authority ruled that the petition was not valid, as some of the signatures had been collected more than six months before the date on which a referendum could be held. Furthermore, in late September the CNE issued a new and more stringent set of referendum guidelines, which stipulated that, in the case of a binding presidential recall referendum, a President would then only be removed from office if a greater proportion of the electorate voted against him than had supported him in the most recent election (in the case of Chávez in the 2000 ballot, this would be greater than 59.7% of the votes). Also, if there were insufficient valid signatures collected (20% of the electorate, equivalent to some 2.4m. voters), no further recall petitions would be permitted during that President's term of office.

In October 2003 the CD presented a new recall referendum request to the CNE. In response, the MVR announced that it intended to compile more than 40 recall petitions on opposition deputies and state governors. The CNE ruled that any recall referendums would be restricted to members of the Asamblea Nacional and federal Government. The CNE was scheduled to announce the validity of both sets of petitions by the end of December. However, a series of technical problems and doubts over the validity of some petitions led to delays, provoking civil unrest in which eight protesters were killed in February 2004.

Finally, following further delays, in June the CNE ruled that the number of valid signatures collected was sufficient to force a presidential recall referendum. The Government accepted this ruling, and the poll was duly held on 15 August. The motion to recall the President was defeated, with 59% of valid votes cast against Chávez's removal from office. The rate of participation was 70% of the electorate. Despite assertions by international observers that the ballot had been conducted fairly, the CD disputed the result. In September the CNE rejected the CD's appeal against the referendum result, citing a lack of evidence.

In January 2005 President Chávez signed a decree initiating a 90-day review process into both the level of productivity on privately owned land and into the validity of its ownership. Local authorities were granted powers to expropriate estates deemed unproductive by the review for redistribution to landless farmers. The number of 'unproductive' estates was estimated at over 500, according to a preliminary government survey. In January 2006 the Government took control of 32 oilfields under private operation, in accordance with its policy of revising all private sector contracts for hydrocarbon exploitation in order to give the government-owned PDVSA a majority stake.

At elections to the Asamblea Nacional on 4 December 2005 the ruling MVR secured an overwhelming number of seats. The government victory was primarily owing to the boycott of the ballot by the main opposition parties, which claimed that the electronic voting system could not guarantee voters' anonymity. As a result, voter participation was estimated at just 25%. However, observers from the European Union (EU, see p. 270) and the OAS declared the elections to be free and transparent.

The Government announced further measures under its so-called Bolivarian social reform programme in early 2006. In March it was stated that 150,000 new homes were to be built during the year to begin to address the housing crisis among impoverished sectors of society. In April a programme costing US $24m. to extend basic services to some 77,000 people living in rural areas was announced. Moreover, in November new measures aimed at extending access to higher education and at providing dental care for the poor were introduced. The Government's ongoing revision of its hydrocarbons operations also continued. In April the state assumed control of seven oilfields operated by foreign petroleum companies, five of which were relinquished under legislation introduced in 2001 and two of which were retaken without the agreement of the companies currently operating the sites. Further amendments to the hydrocarbon laws, approved in May 2006, provided for an increase in royalties required from foreign companies operating Venezuelan oilfields from one-sixth to one-third.

Re-election of Chávez, 2006

At the presidential election held on 3 December 2006 Chávez was decisively re-elected with 62.9% of the vote. The opposition's unity candidate, Manuel Rosales Guerrero, the Governor of Zulia, secured 36.9% of votes cast. Observers from the EU declared themselves to be generally satisfied with the conduct of the election and praised the high rate of participation (some 75% of registered voters took part). The victory was seen as a strong endorsement of the Government's Bolivarian programme of social reform, and of Chávez himself, as a charismatic and popular national leader. Shortly after the election it was announced that the MVR was to be dissolved and replaced by a new political organization, the Partido Socialista Unido de Venezuela (PSUV), which was intended to unite the various left-wing parties allied to the Government. In January 2007 the Asamblea Nacional approved a wide-ranging enabling law granting the President powers to legislate by decree for a period of 18 months in 11 areas, including the reform of state institutions and public services. The law was intended, in particular, to facilitate one of the stated priorities of the new administration, the return to state ownership of privatized industries (particularly in the telecommunications, electricity and hydrocarbons sectors). To this end, in February the Government agreed the terms of the purchase of shares in Electricidad de Caracas, and in May it bought a majority share in the telecommunications concern Compañía Anónima Nacional Teléfonos de Venezuela. In June PDVSA gained control of petroleum operations in the Orinoco Belt, a large reserve of heavy crude petroleum, by acquiring majority stakes in four joint ventures with foreign companies. Two further companies refused to renegotiate their contracts with PDVSA, and the projects in which they were involved came under full state ownership.

The Government's announcement in December 2006 that it would not renew the broadcasting licence of Radio Caracas Televisión (RCTV), Venezuela's oldest television station, upon its expiry in May 2007 was condemned by numerous international media organizations. Chávez cited the station's support for the brief coup of 2002 and the anti-Government bias of its news reporting as reasons for the decision. The station duly ceased broadcasting in May and was replaced by a state-owned channel, Televisora Venezolana Social; however, RCTV recommenced broadcasting via cable in July by means of its US-based subsidiary, RCTV International.

In August 2007 Chávez presented the Asamblea Nacional with a proposal to amend 33 articles of the 1999 Constitution. The most significant of the amendments would have removed the restriction limiting the President to two consecutive terms in office—allowing him to be re-elected indefinitely—and increased the presidential term from six to seven years. The revised Constitution would, *inter alia*, have abolished the autonomy of the central bank and placed the country's international reserves under government control, defined a political role for the armed forces, and reduced the maximum working day from eight to six hours. In November the Asamblea Nacional approved Chávez's proposed amendments, along with a further 36 proposed by the legislature. A referendum was held on 2 December on the two sets of amendments, both of which were rejected. Gen. Raúl Isaías Baduel, a former close ally of Chávez who had retired as Minister of National Defence in July, had been prominent in his opposition to the reforms, claiming that it would have amounted to a coup. (Baduel was arrested in April 2009 on corruption charges; he claimed that his detention was politically motivated. Nevertheless, Baduel was convicted of corruption in May 2010 and received an eight-year gaol term.)

The appointment by Chávez of more moderate figures to the Council of Ministers in January 2008 was seen as a response to the Government's referendum defeat. Meanwhile, in April Chávez announced that the Government would take control of the cement industry in Venezuela, in order to guarantee supplies for state housing construction programmes. Majority stakes in two of the three main cement companies were purchased in August; however, in the same month, following its failure to negotiate a take-over of the Venezuelan operations of the Mexican firm Cemex, the Government seized and expropriated the firm's plants and offices by force.

In May 2008 Chávez used his powers under the enabling law of January 2007 to enact a law on intelligence and counter-intelligence by decree. The new legislation was criticized by the opposition and human rights organizations, in particular for an article that established prison terms of up to four years for any person who refused to co-operate with the intelligence services. In response, the President conceded that mistakes had been made, and announced that the law had been repealed. On 31 July Chávez made further use of the enabling law—just before it was scheduled to expire—to promulgate 26 decrees, many of which introduced measures that had been included in the proposed constitutional reforms rejected in 2007. Several of the new laws increased state control over the economy, notably in the area of food security.

More than 65% of the registered electorate voted in municipal and gubernatorial elections in November 2008, representing the highest turn-out ever recorded in local elections. Although PSUV candidates were elected to governorships in 17 of the 22 contested states, the opposition's gain of three of the most populous states, in addition to the two it already held, was seen as a significant challenge to the pro-Chávez hegemony across the country.

In December 2008 Chávez initiated another attempt to remove the restriction on presidential re-election, asking PSUV members to gather signatures in support of the necessary constitutional amendment. In an effort to widen support for the initiative, in early January 2009 the President proposed that term limits should be abolished for all popularly elected offices, including governors, mayors and deputies. Later in that month the Asamblea Nacional approved, subject to referendum, Chávez's proposed amendments to five articles of the Constitution that would enable re-election to all posts. A referendum was duly held on 15 February, at which the amendments were approved by 55% of valid votes cast. Some 70% of the electorate participated in the poll. Immediately after the result was announced, Chávez confirmed his intention to stand in the presidential election due in 2012.

In March 2009, following an investigation begun at Chávez's request, the Attorney-General issued an arrest order against Manuel Rosales, who was accused of having embezzled public funds while he was Governor of Zulia. The opposition leader denied the charges, which he denounced as politically motivated, and fled to Peru, claiming that the Venezuelan judicial system would not afford him a fair trial; the Peruvian Government swiftly granted him political asylum, prompting Venezuela to recall its ambassador to that country in protest.

Further nationalization moves

The Government made further moves to increase its control over the economy and public administration in the months following the referendum. In late February 2009 Chávez ordered the National Guard to take control of all rice-processing plants, in order to ensure that they complied with government regulations requiring 60% of their output to be basic rice sold at fixed prices. Shortly afterwards, in early March, the Government established more stringent regulations on food production, increasing to 80% the proportion of rice that producers were to sell at regulated prices and setting similar quotas on other basic foodstuffs; on the following day Chávez announced the expropriation of a rice mill belonging to the US multinational corporation Cargill, accusing it of failing to meet production quotas, and threatened other food producers with nationalization if they similarly contravened the regulations. In mid-March the Asamblea Nacional approved legislation allowing the President to reassume the administration of strategic infrastructure, including ports, airports and roads, from state governments (to which control had been devolved in 1999). Chávez subsequently ordered the armed forces to take control of three major ports—Puerto Cabello, Guamache and Maracaibo—and an airport, all in states governed by the opposition. Furthermore, in April the Asamblea Nacional approved a law allowing the President to appoint a Head of Government of the Capital District (comprising the largest of Caracas's five municipalities), to whom most of the budget hitherto assigned to the metropolitan authority would be transferred; Jaqueline Faría, the President of state-owned mobile telephone operator Movilnet, was subsequently appointed to the post. The new arrangements were widely regarded as being intended to diminish the authority of the recently elected opposition Mayor of the metropolitan district, Antonio Ledezma. In May the Government began the nationalization of all companies providing services to the petroleum and gas industry, taking control of terminals and boats on Lake Maracaibo; several steel and iron companies were also brought under state control that month. The Government nationalized the Banco de Venezuela, the country's third largest bank, in July.

In June 2009 a total of 14 opposition parties, including the AD, COPEI, the pro-Chávez Por la Democracia Social (PODEMOS) and Primero Justicia, announced the formation of an alliance, the Mesa de la Unidad Democrática (MUD). The group presented a letter to the OAS, protesting against electoral legislation under consideration in the Asamblea Nacional, which it claimed was intended to favour the ruling PSUV. In early July Ledezma and 12 supporters commenced a hunger strike in the OAS office in Caracas with the stated aim of attracting attention to 'democratic instability' in Venezuela. The strike was ended after some five days, when the OAS Secretary-General, José Miguel Insulza, agreed to meet Ledezma. However, Insulza insisted that he could not intervene in internal Venezuelan affairs

The announcement in July 2009 that 34 radio stations were to be closed and more than 130 investigated for their alleged failure to comply with regulations was condemned by opposition politicians and others, who accused the Government of infringing the right to freedom of speech. The closure of a further 29 stations on similar grounds was announced in September. The Government rejected accusations that media organizations deemed to be critical of Chávez's administration were being specifically targeted. Meanwhile, various official investigations were initiated into the private cable television channel Globovisión, which frequently criticized the Government.

At the beginning of August 2009 the Asamblea Nacional approved the electoral reforms opposed by the MUD. Changes included a reduction in the number of deputies to be elected by proportional representation (from 40% of the total to 30%), a provision permitting two different political parties to nominate the same candidate (once as an individual and once through a party list), and the revision of electoral districts. Later that month controversial legislation on education was also adopted, as thousands of demonstrators, including academics, students, teachers, trade unionists and members of the clergy, protested outside the legislative building. Opponents of the new law, which excluded religious teaching from the curriculum and centralized state control over education, claimed that it promoted the 'indoctrination' of pupils with socialist ideology, although the Minister of Education, Héctor Navarro, insisted that it would provide equal access to education for all citizens. A few days later legislation allowing the seizure of unused or underused land or buildings for 'social purposes' was approved. An anti-Government demonstration took place in Caracas in early September in protest against the education reforms and the closure of radio stations, while government supporters also held a rally on the same day.

Legislation was approved in October 2009 according legal status to the Bolivarian National Militia, formed by the President in 2008, thus allowing it to be allocated budget funds. The Militia, in which foreigners were permitted to serve, was expected to provide logistical support for the next legislative elections, which were subsequently scheduled for 26 September 2010. Opinion polls in late 2009 indicated that the popularity of Chávez and the PSUV had declined in recent months, amid economic difficulties, rationing of electricity and water supplies (imposed in response to shortages caused by a severe drought) and concerns regarding levels of violent crime, although it was not apparent that this had resulted in increased support for the opposition. In December a new national police force, the Bolivarian National Police, was launched and the salaries of police officers increased substantially as part of an effort to reduce crime levels. Meanwhile, the Government assumed control of a total of eight private banks in November and December, citing liquidity deficiencies and administrative irregularities. Ricardo Fernández Barrueco, the owner of four of the banks, was charged with violating various banking regulations, and further arrests within the financial sector followed. The detention of Arné Chacón, the President of Banco Real, prompted the resignation of his brother, Jesse Chacón, as Minister of Science, Technology and Intermediate Industries. The authorities subsequently introduced measures to strengthen the regulation of the banks. In January 2010 Chávez unexpectedly announced a devaluation of the bolívar, with the introduction of a secondary rate of exchange for non-essential goods, in an attempt to increase revenues from oil exports and stimulate domestic production. He also ordered the expropriation of a French-Colombian supermarket chain, which he accused of raising prices unlawfully.

Several government changes were effected in January 2010, following the dismissal of the Minister of Electric Energy, Angel Rodríguez, in response to complaints regarding the implementation of the electricity rationing plan, and the resignations, for personal reasons, of Vice-President Carrizalez and Yuvirí Ortega, the Minister of the Environment (and Carrizalez's wife). The Minister of the Economy and Finance, Alí Rodríguez Araque, was appointed Minister of Electric Energy, while Jorge Giordani, Minister of Planning, was additionally assigned the finance portfolio. There was speculation that the resignation of Carrizalez had been prompted by his disagreement with a decision temporarily to suspend the broadcasting licences of six cable television channels, including RCTV International, after they refused to transmit state announcements and presidential speeches, as required under media regulations. The suspension prompted protests in several cities, including Mérida, where two students were killed and more than 20 police officers injured in violent clashes. Elías José Jaua Milano assumed Carrizales's vice-presidential post in addition to his existing position as Minister of Agriculture and Lands, while Carlos Mata Figueroa was allocated the defence portfolio. Alejandro Hitcher Marvaldi was appointed to replace Ortega. In February, in a futher sign of dissent within the ruling party, the Governor of the state of Lara, Henri Falcón, defected from the PSUV to join a minor allied organization, Patria Para Todos (PPT), publishing an open letter to Chávez in which he expressed concern regarding a lack of communication between the President and regional leaders. Meanwhile, Chávez announced the creation of a peasant militia force, within the Bolivarian National Militia, which was to operate within rural areas. Chávez also promulgated legislation aimed at decentralizing powers from state and municipal administrations to local 'communal councils'. In accordance with this, the Consejo Federal de Gobierno (Federal Council of Government—comprising ministers, local governors and mayors, and communal council members) was established in May. The opposition criticized these measures, claiming that they would instead reinforce central authority and undermine the power and resources of elected local officials.

Chávez effected a cabinet reorganization in June 2010 following the resignations of several ministers who were planning to participate in the upcoming legislative elections. Jennifer Josefina Gil became Minister of Education, while responsibility for agriculture and lands was transferred from Vice-President Jaua to Juan Carlos Loyo Hernández; the main portfolios remained unaltered.

Guillermo Zuloaga, President of the private television station Globovisión, was charged with illegal business practices in June 2010, in relation to his operation of two motor vehicle companies. Zuloaga, who was believed to have fled the country, claimed that this accusation was motivated by the authorities' disapproval of Globovisión's anti-Government programming. Later that month the Government seized the Banco Federal, presided over by Nelson Mezerhane, another Globovisión senior executive, owing to alleged violations of banking regulations, and in the process the state procured the bank's minority shareholding in Globovisión. Legislation was adopted in August that prohibited banks from investing in media companies.

Recent developments: the 2010 legislative elections

Elections to the Asamblea Nacional were held on 26 September 2010. The PSUV maintained its legislative dominance, with 98 seats (one seat short of the 60% majority needed to grant Chávez decree powers), but the opposition MUD registered a strong performance, securing 65 seats; the remaining two seats were won by PPT. The rate of participation by the electorate was recorded at 66.5%. Although the PSUV and the MUD attracted virtually the same number of votes, modifications to constituency boundaries and the voting system (implemented earlier in the year) ensured that the ruling party obtained a disproportionate number of seats. Nevertheless, the PSUV still lost ground to the opposition, principally because of public concern over the ailing economy, electricity rationing (which had ended in June, although power outages continued) and crime. The death in August of Franklin Brito, a farmer who had conducted a lengthy hunger strike to protest against the seizure of his land in 2003 as part of the Government's land reform programme, also undermined the PSUV.

A state of emergency was declared in several regions in late 2010 due to widespread flooding that caused at least 36 deaths and extensive damage to housing, infrastructure and farmland. In December a new enabling law, conferring decree powers upon the President for one-and-a-half years, was adopted. Chávez claimed that this was necessary to allow him to respond effectively to the crisis, but these new powers also gave him the ability to advance his legislative agenda without the approval of the new Asamblea Nacional, which was inaugurated in January 2011, prompting opposition condemnation. The Asamblea's position was further weakened by the introduction of new rules limiting the number of times that the legislature would be convened and restricting the length of speeches, allegedly to increase efficiency. Meanwhile, a flurry of legislation was approved by the outgoing Asamblea, including controversial laws to regulate radio, television and internet output, which critics claimed would be used to suppress anti-Government media outlets. By early 2011 Chávez had only promulgated three decrees, all of which were related to the flooding.

Foreign Affairs
Regional relations

In 1982 Venezuela refused to renew the 1970 Port of Spain Protocol, which declared a 12-year moratorium on the issue of Venezuela's claim to a large area of Guyana to the west of the Essequibo river. In 1985 Venezuela and Guyana requested UN mediation in an attempt to resolve their dispute over the Essequibo region. A UN mediator was appointed in 1989; however, negotiations remained deadlocked. The dispute resurfaced in 1999 when Guyana granted offshore oil concessions in the disputed waters to foreign oil firms, and in October of that year President Hugo Chávez renewed Venezuela's claim to the Essequibo region. The tension escalated in 2000 when Guyana gave preliminary approval to the installation of a US satellite-launching facility in the disputed area. In 2004 Chávez met his Guyanese counterpart, Bharrat Jagdeo; although no progress was made on resolving the dispute, the Venezuelan Government indicated its willingness to 'authorize' Guyanese mineral exploration in the Essequibo region. In 2005 Guyana signed the PetroCaribe energy accord with Venezuela, granting Guyana preferential terms for purchasing Venezuelan petroleum. In July 2010 Chávez and Jagdeo concluded a number of trade agreements and agreed to restart UN-mediated negotiations on their territorial dispute, which had been in abeyance since 2007.

Venezuela also has a claim to some islands in the Netherlands Antilles, and a territorial dispute with Colombia concerning maritime boundaries in the Gulf of Venezuela. In 1989 an agreement was reached with Colombia on the establishment of a border commission to negotiate a settlement for the territorial dispute. In 1990 both countries signed the 'San Pedro Alejandrino' document, pledging to implement the commission's proposals.

Periodic incursions into Venezuelan territory by Colombian combatants and criminal elements continually strained relations with Colombia. Despite agreements signed by both countries in 1997 and 2000 to increase co-operation in policing the border area, clashes between the Venezuelan military and Colombian guerrillas were frequent. Tensions were exacerbated in 2000, owing to Chávez's public opposition to the military component of 'Plan Colombia' (Colombia's US-supported anti-drugs strategy) and accusations by Colombia that Venezuela was covertly aiding the guerrilla forces. In November 2000 Colombia briefly recalled its ambassador to Venezuela after a representative of the Fuerzas Armadas Revolucionarias de Colombia—Ejército del Pueblo (FARC) was allowed to speak in the Venezuelan Asamblea Nacional. In March 2001 Venezuela refused to extradite to Colombia a member of a guerrilla group accused of hijacking an aircraft in 1999. The Venezuelan Government continued to demand improvements to border security arrangements, following confrontations with armed Colombian groups in December 2003 and September 2004 that resulted in the deaths of several Venezuelan soldiers. In a public demonstration of amity, Chávez met his Colombian counterpart Alvaro Uribe in Cartagena, Colombia, in November 2004 to discuss border security and economic co-operation. However, relations were severely strained in December following the arrest by the Colombian authorities of Rodrigo Granda Escobar, the supposed international spokesperson of the FARC. It was subsequently alleged by the Venezuelan Government that Granda, although ultimately arrested in Cúcuta, Colombia, was first kidnapped in Caracas by Venezuelan and Colombian agents in the pay of the Colombian Government and with the collusion of US intelligence services; the Uribe and US Governments denied any involvement. In consequence, the Venezuelan ambassador to Colombia was recalled in January 2005 and restrictions on trade and passage between the two countries were imposed by the Chávez Government. Following an expression of regret by the Colombian Government in January and a visit to Caracas by President Uribe in February, relations between the two countries were normalized. Relations were strengthened in September following the Colombian authorities' refusal of political asylum to seven Venezuelan military officials and one diplomat accused of participating in the failed coup attempt of April 2002. However, in 2005 and early 2006 the Colombian and US Governments repeatedly expressed concern over Venezuela's rapid military expansion, which, it was argued, would upset the military balance of the region.

In August 2007 Uribe engaged Chávez in negotiating with FARC leaders in respect of the release of hostages held by the guerrilla group. However, Uribe abruptly cancelled Chávez's mediation attempt in November, accusing him of making contact with senior Colombian military officers against his orders; nevertheless, the Venezuelan President's subsequent role in securing the release of two of the hostages in January 2008 led to a slight improvement in relations. Chávez strongly condemned Uribe following Colombia's incursion into Ecuadorean territory in March, during which time a senior FARC commander was killed; in response to the incident Chávez ordered the closure of the Venezuelan embassy in the Colombian capital, Bogotá, and sent troops to the Colombian border. Uribe subsequently alleged that evidence gathered during the raid indicated that Chávez had aided the FARC, and threatened to prosecute him in the International Criminal Court. However, formal diplomatic relations were swiftly restored a few days later after Chávez mediated a rapprochement between Uribe and the Ecuadorean President, Rafael Correa Delgado, at a Rio Group summit in the Dominican Republic. In June, in a reversal of his previous declarations in support of the rebels, Chávez publicly urged the FARC to end its armed struggle and release all its remaining hostages. The personal animosity between Chávez and Uribe was put aside in the following month when the two Presidents held a cordial meeting in Venezuela. However, relations between Venezuela and Colombia deteriorated in July 2009, after it emerged that Colombia was negotiating an agreement with the USA (signed in October) to allow US troops access to its military bases. Tensions increased later that month, when the Colombian Vice-President accused Venezuela of supplying weapons to the FARC, prompting Chávez to sever diplomatic relations with Colombia and threaten to halt imports of Colombian goods. In November, following the signature of the agreement between Colombia and the USA, which the Venezuelan Government claimed represented a threat to Venezuela's security, Chávez ordered the deployment of 15,000 troops at the border with Colombia, citing increased violence by Colombian paramilitary groups. Increasingly aggressive rhetoric from Chávez subsequently prompted Colombia to lodge an official complaint with the UN Security Council. Critics of Chávez accused him of orchestrating the diplomatic row in order to deflect attention from domestic difficulties. During the first half of 2010 fresh allegations of Venezuelan-FARC links emerged from various sources, including senior US officials. On 22 July, at an OAS summit meeting, Colombian officials publicly accused the Venezuelan Government of providing shelter to large numbers of FARC guerrillas. Chávez immediately dismissed these claims and severed diplomatic relations with Colombia. However, tensions eased in August following the inauguration of new Colombian President Juan Manuel Santos Calderón, who, in contrast to Uribe, intended to take a more conciliatory stance towards Venezuela. During their first meeting on 10 August Chávez and Santos agreed to restore diplomatic relations and establish a number of joint committees to discuss economic and security concerns. A second round of constructive talks in November resulted in the signing of several economic accords, and an agreement on combating cross-border drugs-trafficking was concluded in January 2011.

Following his election in December 1998, President Chávez announced that his administration would seek greater integration in large regional organizations such as the Caribbean Community and Common Market (CARICOM, see p. 219) and the Southern Common Market (Mercado Común del Sur—Mercosur, see p. 425). In September 2005 Chávez launched PetroCaribe, an initiative to promote energy integration and offer preferential prices for petroleum in the Caribbean region. Venezuela was admitted to Mercosur in July 2006, but its entry was subject to ratification by the group's existing members; by early 2011 Venezuela's accession had yet to be ratified by the legislature of Paraguay.

President Chávez made closer relations with Cuba a priority, and in October 2000 Chávez and the Cuban Head of State, Fidel Castro Ruz, signed a co-operation agreement allowing the export of oil to Cuba on preferential terms. From 2003 improved relations between the two countries led to increased Cuban assistance for the Government's social welfare programmes, and Venezuela continued to support Cuba's integration into regional trade associations. In December 2009 Venezuela and Cuba signed a series of accords on economic co-operation, reportedly worth some US $3,200m., which notably granted Venezuela increased involvement in petroleum exploration off the Cuban coast. The preferential oil export deal, signed in 2000, was extended in November 2010 for a further 10 years.

Venezuela's relations with Mexico deteriorated in November 2005 at the Summit of the Americas in Mar del Plata, Argentina, owing to President Chávez's strident denunciation of an initiative promoted by Mexican President Vicente Fox Quesada for a free trade area of the Americas. The Venezuelan ambassador to Mexico was recalled later that month, as was the Mexican ambassador to Venezuela. Relations with Mexico improved after Felipe Calderón Hinojosa took office as President of that country in late 2006, and in August 2007 an exchange of ambassadors marked the restoration of full diplomatic relations.

Other external relations

Relations between Venezuela and the USA (the main purchaser of Venezuelan crude petroleum) deteriorated markedly following the election of Chávez. In 2000 Chávez refused to authorize US drugs-surveillance flights over Venezuela. Furthermore, the President's close relationship with Fidel Castro led to further estrangement from the USA. Bilateral relations further deteriorated after the US Administration of George W. Bush refused to condemn the short-lived military ousting of Chávez in April 2002. Relations with the USA remained hostile during the 2000s, owing in large part to Chávez's sustained personal criticism of President Bush and his outspoken rhetoric against US 'imperialism'. In April 2005 Venezuela suspended its military exchange programmes with the USA. In August of that year Chávez suspended co-operation with the US Drug Enforcement Agency (DEA), following its repeated criticism of Venezuela's counter-narcotics policies. Chávez accused DEA agents of spying on Venezuela and the US Government responded by 'decertifying' Venezuela for non-compliance in fulfilling its obligations to combat the trade in illegal drugs. None the less, in January 2006 Venezuela agreed to renew some co-operation with the DEA, although US agents from the organization were not to be allowed on Venezuelan territory. In the following month Venezuela expelled a US naval attaché in Venezuela, accusing him of espionage. The following day the USA expelled a Venezuelan diplomat in response. Meanwhile, from 2005 members of the Government, including President Chávez, repeatedly alleged that the USA was planning to invade Venezuela in order to secure its supply of petroleum; the USA dismissed the allegation as unsubstantiated and accused Chávez of seeking to destabilize the region by expanding its military capability so significantly. During 2006 the Venezuelan Government continued to strengthen its armed forces, purchasing military aircraft from Russia as well as 100,000 assault rifles. In March the US authorities announced an embargo on all commercial arms sales to Venezuela. The US Government continued to express concern regarding Venezuela's close relations with countries including Cuba, Libya and Iran, with whose Government Chávez publicly stated his commitment to co-operate in the field of nuclear energy. In September 2008 Venezuela expelled the US ambassador, Patrick Duddy, and recalled its own ambassador from the USA, in solidarity with Bolivia, which had just carried out a similar action as part of an ongoing dispute. The US Administration of Barack Obama, which took office in January 2009, sought to improve bilateral relations, and in June US-Venezuelan diplomatic relations were formally resumed. However, the agreement signed by the USA and Colombia in October, granting the US military access to seven Colombian bases (see above), strained relations between the USA and Venezuela. In the previous month US Secretary of State Hillary Clinton had expressed concern about Venezuelan weapons purchases, following the conclusion of a new arms agreement between Venezuela and Russia (see below) during a tour by Chávez of several countries, including Libya and Iran. Venezuela demonstrated increased co-operation with the USA during mid-2010 by extraditing a number of alleged drugs-traffickers. However, relations were strained by a dispute over the USA's designated ambassador to Venezuela, Larry Palmer. Chávez expressed dissatisfaction in August at Palmer's recent criticism of the Venezuelan armed forces and the policies of the Venezuelan Government, and in the following month Chávez officially protested against Palmer's nomination as ambassador. This position was reiterated in December, when Chávez stated that Palmer would be ejected if he attempted to enter Venezuela. Later that month, in retaliation, the US authorities rescinded the visa of the Venezuelan ambassador to the USA.

President Chávez has sought to strengthen Venezuela's alliance with Russia. Chávez visited Russia in July 2008 to sign co-operation agreements in the fields of energy and defence. Russian President Dmitrii Medvedev paid a return visit to Venezuela in November (the first by a Russian leader) as part of a wider tour of Latin America, and promised Russian assistance to enable Venezuela to build its first nuclear power plant. Coinciding with Medvedev's visit, a Russian naval squadron visited Venezuelan waters and participated in joint exercises with the Venezuelan navy. During a visit to Russia in September 2009, Chávez announced that Venezuela would recognize the separatist Georgian territories of Abkhazia and South Ossetia as independent sovereign states (becoming only the third country to do so after Russia and Nicaragua), while the Russian Government agreed to loan Venezuela some US $2,200m. over a period of seven years for the purchase of tanks and missiles. An accord on joint petroleum exploration in Venezuelan territory was also signed. Further bilateral agreements, mainly again in the areas of energy and defence, were signed during a visit to Venezuela by Russian Prime Minister Vladimir Putin in April 2010. Chávez travelled to Russia in October, during another controversial foreign tour that included visits to Iran, Libya, Syria and Belarus. A preliminary agreement on the construction of a nuclear power plant in Venezuela was signed, generating unease in the USA. However, the Venezuelan Government cancelled this project in March 2011, following the serious damage caused to two nuclear plants in Fukushima, Japan, by a devastating tsunami earlier that month.

Chávez was notable as one of the few world leaders in early 2011 to support publicly Libyan leader Col Muammar al-Qaddafi during his regime's violent attempts to suppress anti-Govern-

VENEZUELA

Introductory Survey

ment protests. Chávez was critical of the subsequent UN-supported military intervention in Libya, in which the USA played a prominent role.

CONSTITUTION AND GOVERNMENT

Venezuela is a federal republic comprising 23 states, a Capital District and 72 Federal Dependencies. Under the Constitution, which was promulgated on 30 December 1999, legislative power is held by the unicameral Asamblea Nacional (National Assembly). Executive authority rests with the President. The President is elected for six years by universal adult suffrage. The President has extensive powers, and is assisted by a Council of Ministers. Each state has a directly elected executive governor and an elected legislature. Judicial power is exercised by the Supreme Tribunal of Justice (Tribunal Supremo de Justicia) and by the other tribunals.

REGIONAL AND INTERNATIONAL CO-OPERATION

Venezuela is a member of the Inter-American Development Bank (see p. 333), of the Latin American Integration Association (Asociación Latinoamericana de Integración, see p. 359), of the Latin American Economic System (Sistema Económico Latinoamericano, see p. 448) and of the Organization of American States (see p. 391). Venezuela is an associate member of the Southern Common Market (Mercado Común del Sur—Mercosur, see p. 425); its admittance to full membership in July 2006 remained subject to ratification by Paraguay in early 2011. In December 2004 Venezuela was one of 12 countries that were signatories to the agreement creating the South American Community of Nations (Comunidad Sudamericana de Naciones), intended to promote greater regional economic integration. A treaty for the community—renamed the Union of South American Nations (Unión de Naciones Suramericanas) in April 2007—was initialled in May 2008, with full functionality of economic union tentatively scheduled for 2019. In April 2006 the Venezuelan, Cuban and Bolivian heads of state signed a trade agreement, the Bolivarian Alternative for the Americas (Alternativa Bolivariana para las Américas—ALBA), intended to be an alternative to the stalled Free Trade Area of the Americas, advanced by the USA. ALBA was renamed the Bolivarian Alliance for the Peoples of our America (Alianza Bolivariana para los Pueblos de Nuestra América) in June 2009. A new monetary unit, the Sistema Unico de Compensación Regional (Sucre), intended to be used for electronic payments between ALBA member states, was introduced from 2010, initially just between Venezuela and Cuba.

Venezuela was a founder member of the UN in 1945. As a contracting party to the General Agreement on Tariffs and Trade, Venezuela joined the World Trade Organization (see p. 430) on its establishment in 1995. Venezuela is also a member of the Organization of the Petroleum Exporting Countries (see p. 405).

ECONOMIC AFFAIRS

In 2009, according to estimates by the World Bank, Venezuela's gross national income (GNI), measured at average 2007–09 prices, was US $288,111m., equivalent to $10,150 per head (or $12,370 per head on an international purchasing-power parity basis). During 2000–09, it was estimated, the population increased by an annual average of 1.7%, while gross domestic product (GDP) per head decreased, in real terms, at an average of 1.8% per year. Overall GDP increased, in real terms, by an average annual rate of 3.5% in 2000–09; according to preliminary government figures, GDP fell by 3.3% in 2009 and by a further 1.4% in 2010.

According to the World Bank, agriculture (including hunting, forestry and fishing) contributed an estimated 4.0% of GDP in 2005 and engaged 8.5% of the employed labour force in 2008. The principal crops are sugar cane, bananas, maize, rice, plantains, oranges, sorghum and cassava. Cattle are the principal livestock. According to the World Bank, agricultural GDP increased by an estimated annual average of 3.4% during 2000–08. The sector's GDP decreased, in real terms, by 3.9% in 2007, but increased by 1.1% in 2008.

Industry (including mining, manufacturing, petroleum-related activities, construction and power) contributed a preliminary 40.4% of GDP in 2010 and engaged 23.1% of the employed labour force in 2008. According to official estimates, industrial GDP rose by an annual average of 0.8% during 2000–10. However, sectoral GDP decreased, in real terms, by a preliminary 3.3% in 2010.

Mining and quarrying (including petroleum and petroleum-related activities) contributed a preliminary 13.7% of GDP in 2010, but mining and quarrying engaged only 0.9% of the employed labour force in 2008. Petroleum and petroleum-related products provided 95.8% of export revenues in 2009. At the end of 2008 proven reserves totalled 99,400m. barrels, although if heavy and extra-heavy crude petroleum reserves were included, Venezuela's total reserves were estimated to be considerably higher. Production averaged 2.4m. barrels per day in 2009. As well as large reserves of petroleum, Venezuela has substantial deposits of natural gas, coal, diamonds, gold, zinc, copper, lead, silver, phosphates, manganese and titanium. The GDP of the mining sector declined by an estimated average of 1.7% per year in 2000–10; the sector declined, in real terms, by a preliminary 0.4% in 2010.

Manufacturing contributed a preliminary 16.9% of GDP in 2010 and engaged approximately 12.0% of the employed labour force in 2008. The most important sectors were food products, transport equipment, industrial chemicals and iron and steel. According to official estimates, manufacturing GDP increased by an annual average of 1.9% during 2000–10. The sector's GDP decreased, in real terms, by a preliminary 3.4% in 2010.

Construction contributed a preliminary 7.3% of GDP in 2010 and engaged approximately 9.7% of the employed labour force in 2008. The sectoral GDP increased by an annual average of 3.2% during 2000–10; it decreased, in real terms, by a preliminary 7.1% in 2010.

Energy is derived principally from domestic supplies of petroleum and coal, and from hydroelectric power. Hydroelectric power provided 73.4% of electricity production in 2008, according to the US Energy Information Administration, with thermal generation supplying the remainder. Imports of mineral fuels comprised 1.3% of the total value of merchandise imports in 2009.

The services sector (excluding hotels and restaurants) contributed a preliminary 59.6% of GDP in 2010 and engaged some 68.4% of the employed labour force in 2008. The sector increased by an annual average of 3.3% in 2000–10. Sectoral GDP decreased, in real terms, by a preliminary 11.8% in 2010.

In 2009 Venezuela recorded a visible trade surplus of US $19,153m., and there was a surplus of $8,561m. on the current account of the balance of payments. In 2009 the principal source of imports (27.3%) was the USA; other major suppliers were Colombia, the People's Republic of China and Brazil. The USA was also the principal market for exports (32.0% in 2008); other major purchasers were the Netherlands Antilles and Brazil. The principal exports in 2009 were mineral fuels, lubricants and related materials (95.8%). The principal imports in 2009 were machinery and transport equipment (34.4%), chemicals, basic manufactures, food and live animals and miscellaneous manufactured articles.

There was a budgetary deficit of 12,967,600m. bolívares in 2007. Venezuela's general government gross debt was 254,739m. bolívares in 2009, equivalent to 36.4% of GDP. Venezuela's total external debt was US $50,229.0m. at the end of 2008, of which $29,925.0m. was public and publicly guaranteed debt. In that year the cost of servicing the debt was equivalent to 5.6% of the value of exports of goods, services and income. The average annual rate of inflation was 21.6% in 2000–09. Consumer prices increased by an annual average of 28.1% in 2010. An estimated 6.9% of the labour force were unemployed in March 2009.

Venezuela's economy is largely dependent on the petroleum sector and is therefore particularly vulnerable to fluctuations in global oil prices. The administration of Hugo Chávez has done little to diversify the economy away from oil, exports of which account for some 95% of export revenues. From 2004 the Government consolidated its policy of increased state intervention; it also increased petroleum taxes and royalties and in January 2006 appropriated 32 privately operated oilfields. The nationalization of parts of the telecommunications and electricity sectors, of the cement industry, of companies providing services to the petroleum and gas sector, and of transport infrastructure notably followed in 2007–08, and in 2009 the Government assumed control of eight banks. From mid-2008 international oil prices suffered serious decreases. As a result, the economy contracted by 3.3% in 2009, with a sharp decline in oil-related GDP, of 7.2%. Furthermore, the Government's policy of heightened state intervention continued to deter investment. In January 2010, in an effort to increase oil revenues and stimulate domestic production, the bolívar was devalued and a dual exchange rate system introduced; oil-related GDP expanding

VENEZUELA

marginally, by 0.2%, in 2010. The Government continued its nationalization programme throughout that year, notably purchasing numerous companies in the agricultural and construction sectors, in accordance with Chávez's goals of boosting food production and addressing a chronic shortage of housing. Following the end of the drought, in June 2010 Chávez removed the restrictions on electricity usage (which had seriously undermined industrial activity) and pledged funding for thermoelectric schemes to prevent an over-reliance on hydroelectric plants. In spite of the economy benefiting from rising oil prices during 2010, real annual GDP contracted by an estimated 1.4%. Inflation, recorded at 27.2% in 2010, remained a problem, and another currency devaluation in January 2011 was expected to generate additional inflationary pressure. Oil prices were projected to increase further during 2011, and the IMF forecast a resumption of GDP growth in that year, albeit of just 0.5%.

PUBLIC HOLIDAYS

2012: 1 January (New Year's Day), 20–21 February (Carnival), 5 April (Maundy Thursday), 6 April (Good Friday), 19 April (Declaration of Independence), 1 May (Labour Day), 24 June (Battle of Carabobo), 5 July (Independence Day), 24 July (Birth of Simón Bolívar and Battle of Lago de Maracaibo), 12 October (Day of Indigenous Resistance), 25 December (Christmas).

Banks and insurance companies also close on: 6 January (Epiphany), 19 March (St Joseph), Ascension Day (17 May 2012), 29 June (SS Peter and Paul) and 8 December (Immaculate Conception).

Statistical Survey

Sources (unless otherwise stated): Instituto Nacional de Estadística (formerly Oficina Central de Estadística e Informática), Edif. Fundación La Salle, Avda Boyacá, Caracas 1050; tel. (212) 782-1133; fax (212) 782-2243; e-mail ocei@platino.gov.ve; internet www.ine.gov.ve; Banco Central de Venezuela, Avda Urdaneta, esq. de las Carmelitas, Caracas 1010; tel. (212) 801-5111; fax (212) 861-0048; e-mail mbatista@bcv.org.ve; internet www.bcv.org.ve.

Area and Population

AREA, POPULATION AND DENSITY

Area (sq km)	916,445*
Population (census results)	
20 October 1990†	18,105,265
30 October 2001‡	
Males	11,402,869
Females	11,651,341
Total	23,054,210
Population (official postcensal estimates at mid-year)§	
2009	28,384,132
2010	28,833,845
2011	29,277,736
Density (per sq km) at mid-2011	31.9

* 353,841 sq miles.
† Excluding Indian jungle population and adjustment for underenumeration, estimated at 6.7%.
‡ Excluding Indian jungle population, enumerated at 183,143 in a separate census of indigenous communities in 2001. Also excluding adjustment for underenumeration, estimated at 6.7%.
§ Based on results of 2001 census, including Indian jungle population and adjustment for underenumeration.

POPULATION BY AGE AND SEX
(postcensal estimates at mid-2011)

	Males	Females	Total
0–14	4,346,471	4,159,325	8,505,796
15–64	9,528,349	9,518,606	19,046,955
65 and over	798,582	926,403	1,724,985
Total	14,673,402	14,604,334	29,277,736

ADMINISTRATIVE DIVISIONS
(official postcensal estimates at mid-2011)

	Area (sq km)	Population	Density (per sq km)	Capital
Capital District	433	2,109,166	4,871.1	Caracas
Amazonas	177,617	157,293	0.9	Puerto Ayacucho
Anzoátegui	43,300	1,574,505	36.4	Barcelona
Apure	76,500	520,508	6.8	San Fernando
Aragua	7,014	1,758,873	250.8	Maracay
Barinas	35,200	821,635	23.3	Barinas
Bolívar	240,528	1,648,110	6.9	Ciudad Bolívar
Carabobo	4,650	2,365,665	508.7	Valencia
Cojedes	14,800	324,260	21.9	San Carlos
Delta Amacuro	40,200	166,907	4.2	Tucupita
Falcón	24,800	966,127	39.0	Coro
Guárico	64,986	802,540	12.3	San Juan de los Morros
Lara	19,800	1,909,846	96.5	Barquisimeto
Mérida	11,300	907,938	80.3	Mérida
Miranda	7,950	3,028,965	381.0	Los Teques
Monagas	28,900	926,478	32.1	Maturín
Nueva Esparta	1,150	462,480	402.2	La Asunción
Portuguesa	15,200	942,555	62.0	Guanare
Sucre	11,800	975,814	82.7	Cumaná
Táchira	11,100	1,263,628	113.8	San Cristóbal
Trujillo	7,400	765,964	103.5	Trujillo
Vargas	1,497	342,845	229.0	La Guaira
Yaracuy	7,100	646,598	91.1	San Felipe
Zulia	63,100	3,887,171	61.6	Maracaibo
Federal Dependencies	120	1,865	15.5	—
Total	916,445	29,277,736	31.9	—

PRINCIPAL TOWNS
(city proper, estimated population at 1 July 2000)

Caracas (capital)	1,975,787	Mérida	230,101
Maracaibo	1,764,038	Barinas	228,598
Valencia	1,338,833	Turmero	226,084
Barquisimeto	875,790	Cabimas	214,000
Ciudad Guayana	704,168	Baruta	213,373
Petare	520,982	Puerto la Cruz	205,635
Maracay	459,007	Los Teques	183,142
Ciudad Bolívar	312,691	Guarenas	170,204
Barcelona	311,475	Puerto Cabello	169,959
San Cristóbal	307,184	Acarigua	166,720
Maturín	283,318	Coro	158,763
Cumaná	269,428		

Mid-2010 ('000, incl. suburbs, UN estimates): Caracas 3,090; Maracaibo 2,192; Valencia 1,770; Barquisimeto 1,180; Maracay 1,057 (Source: UN, *World Urbanization Prospects: The 2009 Revision*).

VENEZUELA

BIRTHS, MARRIAGES AND DEATHS*

	Registered live births Number	Rate (per 1,000)	Registered marriages Number	Rate (per 1,000)	Registered deaths Number	Rate (per 1,000)
2001	529,552	23.2	81,516	3.3	107,867	5.0
2002	492,678	22.9	73,163	2.9	105,388	5.0
2003	555,614	22.6	74,562	2.9	118,562	5.0
2004	637,799	22.3	74,103	2.8	110,946	5.0
2005	665,997	22.0	86,093	3.2	110,301	5.0
2006	646,225	21.8	89,772	3.2	115,348	5.1
2007	615,371	21.5	93,003	3.4	118,594	5.1
2008	581,480	21.3	93,741	3.4	124,062	4.4

* Figures for numbers of births and deaths exclude adjustment for under-enumeration. Rates are calculated using adjusted data.

Life expectancy (years at birth, WHO estimates): 75 (males 71; females 78) in 2008 (Source: WHO, *World Health Statistics*).

ECONOMICALLY ACTIVE POPULATION
(labour force survey, '000 persons aged 15 years and over, 2008)*

	Males	Females	Total
Agriculture, hunting, forestry and fishing	920.1	85.8	1,005.9
Mining and quarrying	91.2	15.6	106.8
Manufacturing	985.4	431.0	1,416.4
Electricity, gas and water	42.8	11.9	54.7
Construction	1,099.9	53.9	1,153.7
Wholesale and retail trade, restaurants and hotels	1,340.2	1,468.8	2,808.9
Transport, storage and communications	943.1	99.4	1,042.5
Financing, insurance, real estate business services	386.2	227.8	614.0
Community, social and personal services	1,440.1	2,193.7	3,633.8
Sub-total	7,248.9	4,587.9	11,836.8
Activities not adequately defined	15.5	10.7	26.3
Total employed	7,264.4	4,598.6	11,863.1
Unemployed	506.3	366.6	872.9
Total labour force	7,770.7	4,965.2	12,736.0

* Figures exclude members of the armed forces.

Source: ILO.

Health and Welfare

KEY INDICATORS

Total fertility rate (children per woman, 2008)	2.5
Under-5 mortality rate (per 1,000 live births, 2008)	18
HIV/AIDS (% of persons aged 15–49, 2005)	0.7
Physicians (per 1,000 head, 2001)	1.94
Hospital beds (per 1,000 head, 2003)	0.9
Health expenditure (2007): US $ per head (PPP)	697
Health expenditure (2007): % of GDP	5.8
Health expenditure (2007): public (% of total)	46.5
Access to water (% of persons, 2004)	83
Access to sanitation (% of persons, 2004)	68
Total carbon dioxide emissions ('000 metric tons, 2007)	165,414.9
Carbon dioxide emissions per head (metric tons, 2007)	6.0
Human Development Index (2010): ranking	75
Human Development Index (2010): value	0.696

For sources and definitions, see explanatory note on p. vi.

Agriculture

PRINCIPAL CROPS
('000 metric tons)

	2006	2007	2008
Rice, paddy	1,122.9	1,054.9	1,360.6
Maize	2,336.8	2,570.9	2,995.7
Sorghum	584.4	382.1	377.0
Potatoes	454.1	456.7	421.0
Cassava (Manioc)	489.0	416.9	430.2
Yautia (Cocoyam)	86.0	79.7	84.0
Yams	87.2	88.6	84.8
Sugar cane	9,322.9	9,690.8	9,448.2
Coconuts	173.4	190.7	154.1
Oil palm fruit	307.4	327.8	327.8*
Cabbages and other brassicas	101.4	100.3	100.2
Tomatoes	195.9	209.4	199.3
Chillies and peppers, green	101.1	124.1	152.2
Onions, dry	255.0	256.2	272.9
Carrots and turnips	211.6	221.0	211.0
Watermelons	150.7	206.0	171.6
Cantaloupes and other melons	131.6	207.5	188.1
Bananas	509.0	512.2	383.8
Plantains	335.3	390.3	496.5
Oranges	377.9	389.8	382.6
Tangerines, mandarins, etc.	93.0	67.2	70.1
Lemons and limes	49.6	57.8	54.7
Guavas, mangoes and mangosteens	74.4	67.8	57.2
Avocados	58.7	83.3	71.8
Pineapples	356.9	363.1	358.8
Papayas	151.4	132.0	128.0
Coffee, green	74.3	70.3	72.0

* FAO estimate.

Aggregate production ('000 metric tons, may include official, semi-official or estimated data): Total cereals 4,044 in 2006, 4,008 in 2007, 4,734 in 2008–09; Total roots and tubers 1,175 in 2006, 1,097 in 2007, 1,064 in 2008–09; Total vegetables (incl. melons) 1,391 in 2006, 1,578 in 2007, 1,540 in 2008–09; Total fruits (excl. melons) 2,217 in 2006, 2,289 in 2007, 2,231 in 2008–09.

Source: FAO.

LIVESTOCK
('000 head, year ending September)

	2006	2007	2008
Horses*	500	510	510
Asses*	440	440	440
Mules*	72	72	72
Cattle	16,629	16,854	16,988
Pigs	3,196	3,216	3,312
Sheep	544	555	566
Goats	1,362	1,386	1,415
Chickens*	117,242	103,577	115,551

* FAO estimates.

Note: No data were available for 2009.

Source: FAO.

LIVESTOCK PRODUCTS
('000 metric tons)

	2006	2007	2008
Cattle meat	515.9	480.9	483.0
Pig meat	137.1	154.4	163.7
Chicken meat	734.9	780.1	802.3
Cows' milk	1,590.6	1,727.5	2,220.2
Hen eggs	169.5	153.7	157.5

2009 (FAO estimate): Pig meat 167.0.

Source: FAO.

VENEZUELA

Forestry

ROUNDWOOD REMOVALS
('000 cubic metres, excl. bark)

	2007	2008*	2009*
Sawlogs, veneer logs and logs for sleepers	1,289	1,428	1,428
Pulpwood	847	920	920
Fuel wood*	3,925	3,968	4,011
Total	6,061	6,316	6,359

* FAO estimates.
Source: FAO.

SAWNWOOD PRODUCTION
('000 cubic metres, incl. railway sleepers)

	2006	2007	2008*
Coniferous (softwood)	538	598	670
Broadleaved (hardwood)	300	250	280
Total	838	848	950

* Unofficial figures.
2009: Production assumed to be unchanged from the year 2008 (FAO estimates).
Source: FAO.

Fishing

('000 metric tons, live weight)

	2006	2007	2008
Capture*	315.3	256.4	295.4
Freshwater fishes*	41.8	33.3	24.8
Sea catfishes*	7.8	5.6	10.8
Round sardinella	80.0	60.0	36.2*
Skipjack tuna	26.6	20.4	28.4
Yellowfin tuna	24.9	29.2	25.6
Marine crabs*	8.3	5.9	11.5
Ark clams*	52.0	49.0	64.5
Aquaculture*	23.4	20.0	18.6
Whiteleg shrimp	21.2	17.7	16.0
Total catch*	338.7	276.3	314.0

* FAO estimate(s).
Note: Figures exclude crocodiles, recorded by number rather than by weight. The number of spectacled caimans caught was: 60,864 in 2006; 23,201 in 2007; 15,489 in 2008.
Source: FAO.

Mining

('000 metric tons unless otherwise indicated)

	2007	2008	2009*
Hard coal	7,457	7,457	7,500
Crude petroleum ('000 barrels)	953,745	936,590	936,600
Natural gas (million cu metres)†	32,100	31,500	32,000
Iron ore: gross weight	20,700	20,650	14,900
Iron ore: metal content	15,200	15,200	15,200
Nickel ore (metric tons)‡	20,000	20,000	20,000
Bauxite	5,500	5,500	5,500
Gold (kilograms)‡	10,092	10,100	10,100
Phosphate rock	400	400	400
Salt (evaporated)	350	350	350
Diamonds (carats): Gem	45,000	45,000	45,000
Diamonds (carats): Industrial	70,000	70,000	70,000

* Estimated production.
† Figures refer to the gross volume of output: estimated marketed production (in million cu metres) was: 28,500 in 2007; 24,000 in 2008–09.
‡ Figures refer to the metal content of ores and concentrates.
Source: US Geological Survey.

Industry

PETROLEUM PRODUCTS
('000 barrels)

	2004	2005*	2006*
Motor spirit (petrol)	131,929	75,000	85,000
Kerosene	179	120	120
Jet fuel	29,412	32,000	32,000
Distillate fuel oils	109,555	109,000	109,000
Residual fuel oils	101,481	90,000	90,000

* Estimated production.
2007–09: Figures assumed to be unchanged from 2006 (estimates).
Source: US Geological Survey.

SELECTED OTHER PRODUCTS
('000 metric tons, unless otherwise indicated)

	2005	2006	2007
Raw sugar*	690	700	700
Cement††	10,000	11,000	11,000
Crude steel†	4,907	4,900‡	5,000‡
Aluminium†	615	610‡	610‡
Electric energy (million kWh)*	105,990	112,266	114,852

* UN Industrial Commodity Statistics Database.
† Data from US Geological Survey.
‡ Estimate(s).
2008–09 (estimates): Cement 11,000; Crude steel 5,000; Aluminium 610.
Source: US Geological Survey.

VENEZUELA

Statistical Survey

Finance

CURRENCY AND EXCHANGE RATES

Monetary Units
100 céntimos = 1 bolívar fuerte.

Sterling, Dollar and Euro Equivalents (31 December 2010)
£1 sterling = 4.060 bolívares fuertes;
US $1 = 2.594 bolívares fuertes;
€1 = 3.465 bolívares fuertes;
10 bolívares fuertes = £2.46 = $3.86 = €2.89.

Average Exchange Rate: From 1 March 2005 to 8 January 2010 the national currency was pegged to the US dollar at a fixed rate of US $1 = 2.147 bolívares fuertes. From 8 January 2010, when the currency was devalued, a dual fixed rate of US $1 = 2.6 bolívares fuertes for some essential goods (including foods and medicines), and US $1 = 4.3 bolívares fuertes for others, was established

Note: Venezuela adopted a new currency, the bolívar fuerte, equivalent to 1,000 of the former currency, on 1 January 2008; this became the sole legal tender from the end of June of the same year. Most of the relevant historical data in this survey continue to be presented in terms of Venezuelan bolívares.

BUDGET
('000 million bolívares, preliminary figures)

Revenue	2005	2006	2007
Current revenue	114,385.3	147,865.9	161,881.8
Tax revenue	36,756.2	49,056.5	62,670.2
Taxes on income	7,086.1	12,155.5	17,208.8
Social security contributions	1,889.9	2,743.4	4,217.6
Other	27,780.2	34,157.5	41,243.8
Non-tax revenue	77,599.7	98,801.6	99,211.6
State petroleum company surplus	53,181.0	64,725.6	74,902.5
Transfers	29.3	7.8	—
Capital revenue	27.5	0.5	—
Total revenue	114,412.8	147,866.5	161,881.8

Expenditure*	2005	2006	2007
Current expenditure	64,842.6	94,617.7	109,721.8
Operating expenditure	16,779.6	27,759.0	31,000.2
Wages and salaries	11,594.3	16,270.5	20,852.9
Interest and commission on public debt	9,046.1	8,223.0	8,036.7
Transfers	38,463.3	57,420.5	69,852.0
Other current expenditure	553.7	1,215.2	832.9
Capital expenditure	34,867.9	55,935.9	63,153.9
Acquisition of fixed capital	11,967.9	17,666.9	24,550.9
Capital transfers	22,900.0	38,269.0	38,603.0
Extrabudgetary expenditure	1,415.7	1,894.4	518.6
Total expenditure	101,126.1	152,448.0	173,394.4

* Excluding net lending (preliminary figures): 835.0 in 2005; 1,275.6 in 2006; 1,455.0 in 2007.

CENTRAL BANK RESERVES
(US $ million at 31 December)

	2008	2009	2010
Gold (national valuation)	9,201	13,297	16,363
IMF special drawing rights	21	3,511	3,449
Reserve position in IMF	496	505	496
Foreign exchange	32,581	17,687	9,192
Total	42,299	35,000	29,500

Source: IMF, *International Financial Statistics*.

MONEY SUPPLY
(million bolívares fuertes at 31 December)

	2006	2007	2008
Currency outside banks	13	17	22
Demand deposits at commercial banks	93,437	115,961	147,572
Total (incl. others)	107,746	135,827	171,799

Demand deposits at commercial banks: 188,939 in 2009; 263,050 in 2010.

Source: IMF, *International Financial Statistics*.

COST OF LIVING
(Consumer Price Index for Caracas; base: 2000 = 100)

	2006	2007	2008
Food	399.3	506.3	738.0
Clothing and footwear	203.3	232.5	283.1
Rent	192.5	205.1	214.0
All items (incl. others)	289.8	343.9	452.1

2009: Food 958.3; All items (incl. others) 581.4.

All items (Consumer Price Index for whole country; base: 2008 = 100): 121.9 in 2009; 156.2 in 2010.

Source: ILO.

NATIONAL ACCOUNTS
('000 million bolívares at constant 1997 prices, preliminary)

Expenditure on the Gross Domestic Product

	2008	2009	2010
Final consumption expenditure	51,028.1	49,895.8	49,214.0
Households			
Non-profit institutions serving households	41,862.8	40,521.6	39,595.3
General government	9,165.3	9,374.2	9,618.7
Gross capital formation	23,950.2	19,157.1	19,190.1
Gross fixed capital formation. Acquisitions, *less* disposals, of valuables	18,568.3	17,054.9	16,305.5
Changes in inventories*	5,381.9	2,102.2	2,884.6
Total domestic expenditure	74,978.3	69,052.9	68,404.1
Exports of goods and services	10,280.7	8,956.4	7,845.8
Less Imports of goods and services	27,332.0	21,986.6	20,985.9
GDP in market prices	57,927.0	56,022.7	55,264.0

* Including statistical discrepancy.

Gross Domestic Product by Economic Activity

	2008	2009	2010
Petroleum-related activities	6,974.8	6,471.4	6,483.2
Non-petroleum activities	47,046.9	46,123.8	45,277.6
Mining and quarrying	346.1	307.4	266.2
Manufacturing	9,221.1	8,633.9	8,343.1
Electricity and water	1,240.2	1,292.9	1,214.4
Construction	3,884.3	3,890.8	3,613.1
Wholesale and retail trade; repair of motor vehicles, motorcycles and personal and household goods	6,204.3	5,687.7	5,339.6
Transport and storage	2,196.4	2,009.3	1,957.8
Communications	2,807.6	3,083.2	3,369.5
Financial intermediation and insurance	2,561.4	2,500.8	2,377.4

VENEZUELA

Statistical Survey

—continued	2008	2009	2010
Real estate, renting and business activities	5,488.2	5,376.5	5,313.0
Community, social and personal services	3,193.9	3,292.8	3,313.2
Government services	6,455.1	6,610.7	6,781.7
Others*	3,448.3	3,437.8	3,388.6
Sub-total	54,021.7	52,595.2	51,760.8
Less Financial intermediation services indirectly measured	2,705.1	2,688.6	2,487.4
Gross value added in basic prices	51,316.6	49,906.6	49,273.4
Taxes on products *Less* Subsidies on products	6,610.3	6,116.0	5,990.6
GDP in market prices	57,927.0	56,022.7	55,264.0

*Including agriculture and hotels and restaurants.

BALANCE OF PAYMENTS
(US $ million)

	2007	2008	2009
Exports of goods f.o.b.	69,010	95,138	57,595
Imports of goods f.o.b.	−46,031	−49,482	−38,442
Trade balance	22,979	45,656	19,153
Exports of services	1,767	2,162	2,005
Imports of services	−8,719	−10,516	−9,622
Balance on goods and services	16,027	37,302	11,536
Other income received	10,194	8,063	2,313
Other income paid	−7,727	−7,365	−4,965
Balance on goods, services and income	18,494	38,000	8,884
Current transfers received	346	345	357
Current transfers paid	−777	−953	−680
Current balance	18,063	37,392	8,561
Direct investment abroad	−30	−1,273	−1,834
Direct investment from abroad	1,008	350	−3,105
Portfolio investment assets	−1,559	2,747	3,928
Portfolio investment liabilities	4,127	299	5,003
Financial derivatives (net)	−5	—	—
Other investment assets	−29,440	−29,363	−24,484
Other investment liabilities	4,225	2,602	5,909
Net errors and omissions	−1,746	−3,302	−4,785
Overall balance	−5,357	9,452	−10,807

Source: IMF, *International Financial Statistics*.

External Trade

PRINCIPAL COMMODITIES
(US $ million)

Imports f.o.b.	2007	2008	2009
Food and live animals	2,441.8	6,764.3	5,493.1
Cereals and cereal preparations	590.5	1,489.6	1,041.2
Chemicals and related products	3,572.6	6,496.0	6,629.2
Medicinal and pharmaceutical products	1,184.2	1,813.5	2,361.9
Medicaments (incl. veterinary)	890.0	1,408.5	1,841.5
Basic manufactures	3,972.8	7,212.8	5,749.0
Textile yarn, fabrics, etc.	744.5	1,470.4	1,266.0
Machinery and transport equipment	16,206.8	18,487.1	13,296.1
Machinery specialized for particular industries	1,437.0	2,617.4	2,079.8
General industrial machinery equipment and parts	2,108.2	3,593.3	2,975.8
Office machines and automatic data processing machines	1,228.6	1,414.5	1,023.2

Imports f.o.b.—continued	2007	2008	2009
Telecommunications and sound recording and reproducing equipment	2,999.6	3,159.1	2,019.9
Telecommunications equipment parts and accessories	1,850.1	2,550.1	1,626.0
Transmission apparatus for radio-telephony, radio-telegraphy, etc.	1,273.0	1,898.1	1,161.3
Transmission apparatus incorporating reception apparatus	1,267.1	1,884.7	1,158.2
Other electrical machinery, apparatus, etc.	1,608.4	2,769.5	2,217.5
Road vehicles	5,258.6	3,101.1	1,056.9
Passenger motor vehicles (except buses)	2,874.7	1,138.6	65.1
Miscellaneous manufactured articles	3,542.8	5,895.3	4,295.4
Articles of apparel and clothing accessories	797.4	1,641.4	851.4
Total (incl. others)	41,911.0	47,450.1	38,676.6

Exports f.o.b.	2006	2008*	2009
Mineral fuels, lubricants and related materials	56,818.4	78,199.5	54,232.2
Petroleum, petroleum products and related materials	56,617.7	77,882.2	54,201.8
Crude petroleum	56,228.5	61,005.6	35,844.0
Basic manufactures	2,983.6	2,874.6	1,445.9
Iron and steel	1,691.7	1,703.6	904.8
Total (incl. others)	61,385.2	83,477.8	56,583.1

*Data for 2007 exports were not available.

Source: UN, *International Trade Statistics Yearbook*.

PRINCIPAL TRADING PARTNERS
(US $ million)

Imports f.o.b.	2007	2008	2009
Argentina	966.7	1,152.2	873.9
Brazil	3,003.4	4,275.5	3,396.4
Canada	373.2	807.2	539.4
Chile	619.8	1,213.3	877.8
China, People's Republic	2,076.3	4,527.5	4,034.5
Colombia	3,729.5	6,903.4	4,417.6
France (incl. Monaco)	376.3	486.4	423.2
Germany	701.2	1,420.1	1,258.5
Italy	707.5	1,172.0	1,018.9
Japan	874.6	764.5	624.5
Korea, Republic	608.5	557.0	320.2
Mexico	1,569.7	2,202.9	1,461.1
Panama	1,617.9	1,018.4	930.7
Spain	686.1	953.2	794.8
USA	8,462.2	12,651.3	10,545.4
Total (incl. others)	41,911.0	47,450.1	38,676.6

Exports f.o.b.	2006	2008*
Brazil	1,410.5	1,808.3
Canada	631.9	141.6
Chile	887.3	1,167.4
Colombia	585.6	929.6
Netherlands	1,211.9	1,193.1
Netherlands Antilles	3,516.8	13,198.1
Spain	1,914.2	1,603.4
United Kingdom	776.7	1,190.4
USA	31,268.7	26,750.5
Total (incl. others)	61,385.2	83,477.8

*Data for 2007 exports were not available.

2009: Total exports 56,583.1.

Source: UN, *International Trade Statistics Yearbook*.

VENEZUELA

Statistical Survey

Transport

RAILWAYS
(traffic)

	1994	1995	1996
Passenger-kilometres (million)	31.4	12.5	0.1
Net ton-kilometres (million)	46.8	53.3	45.5

Net ton-kilometres (million): 54 in 1997; 79 in 1998; 54 in 1999; 59 in 2000; 81 in 2001; 32 in 2002; 12 in 2003; 22 in 2004.

Source: UN, *Statistical Yearbook*.

ROAD TRAFFIC
('000 motor vehicles in use)

	2002	2003	2004
Passenger cars	2,092	2,173	2,466
Commercial vehicles	615	630	677

Source: UN, *Statistical Yearbook*.

2007 ('000 motor vehicles in use): Passenger cars 2,952,129; Buses and coaches 40,440; Lorries and vans 1,051,443 (Source: IRF, *World Road Statistics*).

SHIPPING
Merchant Fleet
(registered at 31 December)

	2007	2008	2009
Number of vessels	327	333	338
Total displacement ('000 grt)	1,068.8	1,016.4	1,021.0

Source: IHS Fairplay, *World Fleet Statistics*.

CIVIL AVIATION
(traffic on scheduled services)

	2004	2005	2006
Kilometres flown (million)	57.4	59.4	61.2
Passenger-km (million)	2,468.9	2,578.7	2,635.0
Freight ton-km (million)	0.6	2.1	2.1

Source: UN Economic Commission for Latin America and the Caribbean.

Tourism

ARRIVALS BY NATIONALITY

	2006	2007	2008
Argentina	26,287	26,863	26,055
Belgium	3,594	3,443	3,708
Brazil	45,438	55,133	58,539
Canada	28,014	26,670	25,870
Chile	15,020	15,359	15,424
Colombia	84,293	79,735	77,417
France	23,487	25,036	23,026
Germany	37,089	37,686	37,719
Italy	53,177	56,005	52,131
Mexico	18,011	19,146	17,405
Netherlands	18,129	19,985	17,651
Peru	27,671	28,259	26,720
Portugal	19,561	20,160	19,466
Spain	65,894	75,301	66,649
Trinidad and Tobago	18,682	18,468	14,870
United Kingdom	24,057	25,446	27,180
USA	88,825	90,074	86,982
Total (incl. others)	747,930	770,567	744,709

Tourism receipts (US $ million, incl. passenger transport): 843 in 2006; 894 in 2007; 984 in 2008.

Source: World Tourism Organization.

Communications Media

	2007	2008	2009
Telephones ('000 main lines in use)	5,195.1	6,417.8	6,866.6*
Mobile cellular telephones ('000 subscribers)	23,820.1	27,414.4	28,123.6*
Internet users ('000)	5,760.8	7,277.6	8,918.0
Broadband subscribers ('000)	857.8	1,092.3	1,343.3*

*Preliminary.

Personal computers ('000 in use, 2005): 2,475,000 (93.1 per 1,000 persons) in 2005.

Radio receivers ('000 in use, 1997, estimate): 10,750.

Television receivers ('000 in use, 2001): 10,750.

Book production (titles, 1997): 3,851*.

Daily newspapers (2004): 92 (estimated average circulation 2,450,000).

*First editions only.

Sources: UNESCO Institute for Statistics; UN, *Statistical Yearbook*; International Telecommunication Union.

Education

(2003/04)

	Institutions	Teachers	Students*
Pre-school	14,857†	59,178	984,224
Basic education:			
grades 1–6	17,521†	172,322	3,449,579
grades 7–9	4,667†	109,437	1,383,891
Further education:			
general	3,362†	56,458	501,243
professional		8,844	68,372
Adult education	2,402	43,660	506,301
Special needs	1,999	8,723	317,687
Universities	48	51,459	626,837
Other higher	120‡	30,664	447,513‡

* Excluding students in out-of-school education: 720,726 in 2003/04.

† Data may be duplicated for institutions where education is offered at more than one level. The total number of pre-school, basic and further educational establishments in 2003/04 was 24,634.

‡ Estimate.

Sources: Ministry of Education, Caracas; National Council of Universities, Caracas.

2007/08 (UNESCO estimates): *Teachers:* Pre-primary 79,019; Primary 212,425; Secondary 217,516; Tertiary 122,525. *Pupils:* Pre-primary 1,183,816; Primary 3,439,199; Secondary 2,224,214; Tertiary 2,109,331 (Source: UNESCO Institute for Statistics).

Pupil-teacher ratio (primary education, UNESCO estimate): 16.2 in 2007/08 (Source: UNESCO Institute for Statistics).

Adult literacy rate (UNESCO estimates): 95.2% (males 95.4%; females 94.9%) in 2007 (Source: UNESCO Institute for Statistics).

VENEZUELA

Directory

The Government

HEAD OF STATE

President of the Republic: Lt-Col (retd) HUGO RAFAEL CHÁVEZ FRÍAS (took office 2 February 1999; re-elected 30 July 2000 and 3 December 2006).

COUNCIL OF MINISTERS
(May 2011)

The Government is formed by the Partido Socialista Unido de Venezuela.

Executive Vice-President: ELÍAS JOSÉ JAUA MILANO.
Minister of the Interior and Justice: TAREK EL AISSAMI.
Minister of Agriculture and Lands: JUAN CARLOS LOYO HERNÁNDEZ.
Minister of Health: EUGENIA SADER CASTELLANOS.
Minister of Planning and Finance: JORGE A. GIORDANI.
Minister of Science, Technology and Intermediate Industries: RICARDO MENÉNDEZ PRIETO.
Minister of Energy and Petroleum: RAFAEL DARÍO RAMÍREZ CARREÑO.
Minister of Foreign Affairs: NICOLÁS MADURO MOROS.
Minister of Electric Energy: ALÍ RODRÍGUEZ ARAQUE.
Minister of Basic Industry and Mining: JOSÉ SALAMAT KHAN FERNÁNDEZ.
Minister of Defence: Gen. CARLOS MATA FIGUERO.
Minister of Trade: RICHARD SAMUEL CANÁN.
Minister of Labour and Social Security: MARÍA CRISTINA IGLESIAS.
Minister of Food: CARLOS OSORIO ZAMBRANO.
Minister of Education: MARYANN HANSON FLORES.
Minister of Tourism: ALEJANDRO FLEMING CABRERA.
Minister of University Education: YADIRA CÓRDOVA.
Minister of Housing and Habitat: RICARDO MOLINA PEÑALOZA.
Minister of the Environment: ALEJANDRO HITCHER MARVALDI.
Minister of Communes and Social Protection: ISIS OCHOA CAÑIZALES.
Minister of Communication and Information: ANDRÉS IZARRA.
Minister of Sport: HÉCTOR RODRÍGUEZ CASTRO.
Minister of Culture: FRANCISCO (FARRUCO) SESTO NOVAS.
Minister of Indigenous Peoples: NICIA MARINA MALDONADO.
Minister of Women's Affairs and Gender Equality: NANCY PÉREZ SIERRA.
Minister of Transport and Communications: FRANCISCO JOSÉ GARCÉS DA SILVA.
Minister of State for Public Banking: HUMBERTO RAFAEL ORTEGA DÍAZ.
Minister of the Office of the Presidency: FRANCISCO JOSÉ AMELIACH ORTA.
Permanent Secretary: CARLOS GRANADILLO.

MINISTRIES

Ministry of Agriculture and Lands: Avda Urdaneta, entre esq. Platanal a Candilito, a media cuadra de la Plaza la Candelaria, Parroquia la Candelaria, Caracas; tel. (212) 509-0347; e-mail pda2007@mat.gob.ve; internet www.mat.gob.ve.

Ministry of Basic Industry and Mining: Torre Las Mercedes, 9°, Avda La Estancia, Urb. Chuao, Caracas; tel. (212) 950-0311; fax (212) 950-0286; e-mail webmaster@mibam.gob.ve; internet www.mibam.gob.ve.

Ministry of Communes and Social Protection: Edif. INCE, Avda Nueva Granada, Apdo 10340, Caracas 1040; tel. (212) 603-2396; internet www.mpcomunas.gob.ve.

Ministry of Communication and Information: Torre Ministerial, 9° y 10°, Avda Universidad, esq. el Chorro, Caracas 1010; tel. (212) 505-3322; e-mail contactenos@mci.gob.ve; internet www.mci.gob.ve.

Ministry of Culture: Edif. Archivo General de la Nación, Avda Panteón, Foro Libertador, Caracas; tel. (212) 509-5600; e-mail mppc@ministeriodelacultura.gob.ve; internet www.ministeriodelacultura.gob.ve.

Ministry of Defence: Edif. 17 de Diciembre, planta baja, Base Aérea Francisco de Miranda, La Carlota, Caracas; tel. (212) 908-1264; fax (212) 237-4974; e-mail prensamd@mindefensa.gov.ve; internet www.mindefensa.gob.ve.

Ministry of Education: Edif. Sede del MPPE, Mezzanina, esq. de Salas a Caja de Agua, Parroquia Altagracia, Caracas 1010; tel. (212) 569-4111; e-mail atencionsocial@me.gob.ve; internet www.me.gob.ve.

Ministry of Electric Energy: Caracas.

Ministry of Energy and Petroleum: Edif. Petróleos de Venezuela, Torre Oeste, Avda Libertador con Avda Empalme, La Campiña, Porroquia El Recreo, Caracas; tel. (212) 708-7581; fax (212) 708-7598; e-mail atencionalpublico@menpet.gob.ve; internet www.menpet.gob.ve.

Ministry of the Environment: Torre Sur Plaza, 25°, Centro Simón Bolívar, Caracas 1010; tel. (212) 408-1111; internet www.minamb.gob.ve.

Ministry of Food: Edif. Las Fundaciones, Avda Andrés Bello, Caracas; tel. (212) 395-7474; e-mail oirp@minal.gob.ve; internet www.minal.gob.ve.

Ministry of Foreign Affairs: Torre MRE, al lado del Correo de Carmelitas, Avda Urdaneta, Caracas 1010; tel. (212) 806-4400; fax (212) 861-2505; e-mail web.master@mre.gov.ve; internet www.mre.gov.ve.

Ministry of Health: Edif. Sur, 8°, Avda Baralt, Centro Simón Bolívar, El Silencio, Caracas 1010; tel. (212) 408-0033; fax 483-2560; e-mail mpps@mpps.gob.ve; internet www.msds.gov.ve.

Ministry of Housing and Habitat: Torre Este, 50°, Parque Central, Caracas 1010; tel. (212) 201-5551; internet www.mvh.gob.ve.

Ministry of Indigenous Peoples: Antiguo Edif. Sudeban, Avda Universidad, esq. Traposos, 8°, Caracas 1010; tel. (212) 543-1599; fax (212) 543-3100; e-mail atencionlindigena@minpi.gob.ve; internet www.minpi.gob.ve.

Ministry of the Interior and Justice: Edif. Ministerio del Interior y Justicia, esq. de Platanal, Avda Urdaneta, Caracas 1010; tel. (212) 506-1101; fax (212) 506-1559; e-mail webmaster@mij.gov.ve; internet www.mij.gov.ve.

Ministry of Labour and Social Security: Torre Sur, 5°, Centro Simón Bolívar, Caracas 1010; tel. (212) 481-1368; fax (212) 483-8914; internet www.mintra.gov.ve.

Ministry of Planning and Finance: Edif. Ministerio de Finanzas, esq. Carmelitas, Avda Urdaneta, Caracas 1010; tel. (212) 802-1000; e-mail webmaster@mpd.gob.ve; internet www.mpd.gob.ve.

Ministry of the Presidency: Palacio de Miraflores, final Avda Urdaneta, esq. de Bolero, Caracas; tel. (212) 806-3111; fax (212) 806-3229; e-mail dggcomunicacional@presidencia.gob.ve; internet www.presidencia.gob.ve.

Ministry of Science, Technology and Intermediate Industries: Torre MCT, Avda Universidad, esq. El Chorro, Caracas; tel. (212) 555-7410; fax (212) 555-7504; e-mail mcti@mcti.gob.ve; internet www.mct.gob.ve.

Ministry of Sport: Sede Principal, Avda Intercomunal Montalban, Urb. Montalbán, La Vega, Caracas 1020; tel. (212) 443-2682; fax (212) 443-3224; internet www.mindeporte.gob.ve.

Ministry of Tourism: Edif. Mintur, Avda Francisco de Miranda con Avda Principal de la Floresta, Municipio Chacao, Caracas; tel. (212) 208-4651; e-mail auditoria@mintur.gob.ve; internet www.mintur.gob.ve.

Ministry of Trade: Torre Oeste de Parque Central, entrada por el Nivel Lecuna, Avda Lecuna, Caracas 1010; tel. (212) 509-6861; fax (212) 574-2432; e-mail ministro@milco.gob.ve; internet www.milco.gob.ve.

Ministry of Transport and Communications: Caracas; internet www.mtc.gob.ve.

Ministry of University Education: Torre Ministerial, 1°–7°, Avda Universidad, esq. el Chorro, Caracas 1010; tel. (212) 596-5270; fax (212) 569-5261; e-mail webmaster@mppeu.gob.ve; internet www.mppeu.gob.ve.

Ministry of Women's Affairs and Gender Equality: Caracas.

State Agencies

Consejo de Defensa de la Nación (Codena): Edif. 2, 2°, Fuerte Tiuna, Caracas; tel. (212) 690-3222; e-mail secodena@codena.gob.ve; internet www.codena.gob.ve; national defence council; Sec.-Gen. Gen. VIVIAM ANTONIO DURÁN GARCÍA.

Contraloría General de la República (CGR): Edif. Contraloría, Avda Andrés Bello, Guaicaipuro, Caracas 1050; tel. (212) 508-3111;

VENEZUELA
Directory

e-mail atencionciudadano@cgr.gov.ve; internet www.cgr.gob.ve; national audit office for Treasury income and expenditure, and for the finances of the autonomous institutes; Comptroller-Gen. CLODOSBALDO RUSSIÁN UZCÁTEGUI.

Defensoría del Pueblo: Edif. Defensoría del Pueblo, 8°, Avda México, Plaza Morelos, Los Caobos, Caracas; tel. (212) 575-4703; fax (212) 575-4467; e-mail prensadefensoria@hotmail.com; internet www.defensoria.gob.ve; acts as an ombudsman and investigates complaints between citizens and the authorities; Ombudsman GABRIELA DEL MAR RAMÍREZ.

Procuraduría General de la República: Paseo Los Ilustres con Avda Lazo Martí, Santa Mónica, Caracas; tel. (212) 597-3300; e-mail webmaster@pgr.gov.ve; internet www.pgr.gob.ve; Procurator-Gen. GLADYS MARÍA GUTIÉRREZ ALVARADO.

President

Election, 3 December 2006

Candidates	Votes	% of total
Lt-Col (retd) Hugo Rafael Chávez Frías (Movimiento V República*)	7,309,080	62.84
Manuel Antonio Rosales Guerrero (Un Nuevo Tiempo)	4,292,466	36.91
Others	28,606	0.25
Total†	11,630,152	100.00

* Dissolved in December 2006 and replaced by the Partido Socialista Unido de Venezuela (PSUV).
† In addition, there were 160,245 blank or spoiled ballots.

Legislature

ASAMBLEA NACIONAL
(National Assembly)

President: LUIS FERNANDO SOTO ROJAS.
First Vice-President: ARISTÓBULO ISTÚRIZ ALMEIDA.
Second Vice-President: BLANCA ROSA EEKHOUT GÓMEZ.
General Election, 26 September 2010

Party	Seats
Partido Socialista Unido de Venezuela (PSUV)	98
Mesa de Unidad Democrática (MUD)*	65
Patria para Todos (PPT)	2
Total	165

*A coalition grouping of opposition parties formed to contest the election.

Election Commission

Consejo Nacional Electoral (CNE): Edif. Poder Electoral, antigua torre Teleport, 3°, Plaza Venezuela, Paseo Colón, Caracas; tel. (212) 576-2399; fax (212) 576-5603; internet www.cne.gov.ve; f. 2002; Pres. TIBISAY LUCENA RAMÍREZ.

Political Organizations

Acción Democrática (AD): Casa Nacional Acción Democrática, Calle Los Cedros, La Florida, Caracas 1050; internet www.acciondemocratica.org.ve; f. 1936 as Partido Democrático Nacional; adopted present name and obtained legal recognition in 1941; social democratic; member of opposition coalition Mesa de Unidad Democrática (MUD) formed to contest the Sept. 2010 election; Pres. ISABEL CARMONA DE SERRA; Sec.-Gen. HENRY RAMOS ALLUP.

Alianza Bravo Pueblo: Caracas; e-mail alianzabravopueblo@gmail.com; oppositionist; merged with Visión Emergente in 2010; Pres. JOSÉ ZABALA; Nat. Sec. ALCIDES PADILLA.

La Causa Radical (La Causa R): Santa Teresa a Cipreses, Residencias Santa Teresa, 2°, Ofs 21 y 22, Caracas; tel. (212) 545-7002; f. 1971; radical democratic; member of opposition coalition Mesa de Unidad Democrática (MUD) formed to contest the Sept. 2010 election; Leader ANDRÉS VELÁSQUEZ; Sec.-Gen. DANIEL SANTOLO.

Convergencia Nacional (CN): Edif. Tajamar, 2°, Of. 215, Parque Central, Avda Lecuna, El Conde, Caracas 1010; tel. (212) 578-1177; fax (212) 578-0363; e-mail jjcaldera@convergencia.org.ve; internet www.convergencia.org.ve; f. 1993; Leader Dr RAFAEL CALDERA RODRÍGUEZ; Gen. Co-ordinator JUAN JOSÉ CALDERA.

Movimiento Demócrata Liberal: Quinta El Encuentro, 1°, Avda de Santa Eduvigis, entre 5a y 6a transversal, Caracas; tel. (212) 442-3956; fax (212) 471-3856; e-mail info@democrataliberales.org; internet www.democrataliberales.org; liberal opposition party; Political Dir MARCO POLESEL.

Movimiento Republicano (MR): Reynaldo Hahn 1606, Urb. Santa Mónica, Caracas; tel. (212) 693-2937; e-mail elrepublicano.ve@gmail.com; internet movimientorepublicano.blogspot.com; f. 1997; Pres. CARLOS PADILLA; Sec.-Gen. MANUAL RIVAS.

Movimiento al Socialismo (MAS): Quinta Alemar, Avda Valencia, Las Palmas, Caracas 1050; tel. (212) 793-7800; fax (212) 761-9297; e-mail asamblea07@cantv.net; f. 1971 by PCV dissidents; opposition democratic-socialist party; split in 1997 over issue of support for presidential campaign of Hugo Chávez; member of opposition coalition Mesa de Unidad Democrática (MUD) formed to contest the Sept. 2010 election; Pres. NICOLÁS SOSA; Sec.-Gen. JOSÉ ANTONIO ESPAÑA.

Partido Comunista de Venezuela (PCV): Edif. Cantaclaro, Calle Jesús Faría, esq. de San Pedro a San Francisquito, Parroquia San Juan, Caracas; tel. (212) 484-0061; fax (212) 481-9737; internet www.pcv-venezuela.org; f. 1931; Pres. JERÓNIMO CARRERA; Sec. OSCAR FIGUERA.

Partido Social-Cristiano (Comité de Organización Política Electoral Independiente) (COPEI): El Bosque, Avda Principal El Bosque, cruce con Avda Gloria Quinta Cujicito, Chacao, Caracas; tel. (212) 731-4746; fax (212) 731-4953; e-mail info@copeivenezuela.com; internet www.copeivenezuela.com; f. 1946; Christian democratic; member of opposition coalition Mesa de Unidad Democrática (MUD) formed to contest the Sept. 2010 election; Pres. ROBERTO ENRÍQUEZ; Sec.-Gen. JESÚS ALBERTO BARRIOS.

Partido Socialista Unido de Venezuela (PSUV): Calle Lima, cruce con Avda Libertador, Los Caobos, Caracas; tel. (212) 782-3808; fax (212) 782-9720; e-mail contacto@psuv.org.ve; internet www.psuv.org.ve; f. 2007; successor party to the Movimiento V República (dissolved Dec. 2006); promotes Bolivarian revolution; Pres. Lt-Col (retd) HUGO RAFAEL CHÁVEZ FRÍAS.

Patria Para Todos (PPT): Calle Montevideo, Quinta Plaza, Calle Maripérez, Plaza Venezuela, Caracas; tel. (212) 578-3098; fax (212) 577-4545; e-mail partidoppt@gmail.com; internet www.ppt.org.ve; f. 1997; breakaway faction of La Causa Radical; revolutionary humanist party; Nat. Sec.-Gen. JOSÉ ALBORNOZ.

Por la Democracia Social (PODEMOS): Caracas; f. 2001 by dissident mems of MAS (q.v.); abandoned support for the Govt in 2007; member of opposition coalition Mesa de Unidad Democrática (MUD) formed to contest the Sept. 2010 election; Leader ISMAEL GARCÍA.

Primero Justicia: Centro Comercial Chacaíto, Of. 26A, Urb. San Soucy, Caracas; tel. (212) 952-9733; e-mail pjelhaltillo@cantv.net; internet www.primerojusticia.org.ve; f. 2000; member of opposition coalition Mesa de Unidad Democrática (MUD) formed to contest the Sept. 2010 election; Nat. Co-ordinator JULIO ANDRÉS BORGES; Nat. Sec. CARLOS GUILLERMO AROCHA.

Proyecto Venezuela (PRVZL): e-mail administrador@vpvonline.com; f. 1998; humanist party; Leader HENRIQUE SALAS RÖMER; Sec.-Gen. CARLOS BERRIZBEITIA.

Un Nuevo Tiempo (UNT): Edif. Montral, Avda Principal de Las Palmas, Municipio Libertador, Caracas; tel. (212) 425-1239; e-mail prensa@partidounnuevotiempo.org; internet www.partidounnuevotiempo.org; f. 2005; opposes Pres. Chávez; member of opposition coalition Mesa de Unidad Democrática (MUD) formed to contest the Sept. 2010 election; Exec. Pres. OMAR BARBOZA; Exec. Sec. ENRIQUE OCHOA ANTICH.

OTHER ORGANIZATIONS

Asociación Civil Queremos Elegir: Edif. Industrial, 4°, Avda Sucre, Los Dos Caminos, Municipio Sucre, Caracas; tel. (212) 286-9785; e-mail info@queremoselegir.org; internet www.queremoselegir.org; f. 1991; opposition grouping promoting citizens' rights; mem. of Alianza Cívica de la Sociedad Venezolana; Principal Co-ordinator ELÍAS SANTANA.

Comité de Familiares Víctimas de los Sucesos de Febrero y Marzo de 1989 (COFAVIC): Edif. El Candil, 1°, Of. 1-A, Avda Urdaneta, esq. El Candilito, Apdo 16150, La Candelaria, Caracas 1011-A; tel. (212) 572-9631; fax (212) 572-9908; e-mail cofavic@cofavic.org.ve; internet www.cofavic.org.ve; f. 1989 as an asscn of relatives of those who had died in demonstrations of Feb.–March; promotes human rights; Exec. Dir LILIANA ORTEGA.

Súmate: Torre A, 5°, Avda Francisco de Miranda, Centro Plaza, Caracas; tel. (212) 285-4562; e-mail info@sumate.org; internet www

VENEZUELA

.sumate.org; f. 2002; opposition grouping promoting citizens' rights; Dir María Corina Machado.

Diplomatic Representation

EMBASSIES IN VENEZUELA

Algeria: 8a Transversal con 3a Avda, Quinta Azahar, Urb. Altamira, Caracas 1062; tel. (212) 263-2092; fax (212) 261-4254; e-mail ambalgcar@cantv.net; Ambassador Rachid Bladehane.

Argentina: Edif. Fedecámaras, 3°, Avda El Empalme, El Bosque, Apdo 569, Caracas; tel. (212) 731-3311; fax (212) 731-2659; e-mail evene@cancilleria.gov.ar; internet www.venezuela.embajada-argentina.gov.ar; Ambassador Alicia Amalia Castro.

Austria: Edif. Torre D&D, Piso PT, Of. PTN, Avda Orinoco, entre Mucuchíes y Perijá, Urb. Las Mercedes, Apdo 61381, Caracas 1060-A; tel. (212) 999-1211; fax (212) 993-2753; e-mail caracas-ob@bmeia.gv.at; internet www.aussenministerium.at/caracas; Ambassador Thomas Schuller-Götzburg.

Barbados: Edif. Los Frailes, 5°, Of. 501, Avda Principal de Chuao, Chuao, Apdo 68829, Caracas 1060; tel. (212) 992-0545; fax (212) 991-0333; e-mail caracas@foreign.gov.bb; Ambassador Sandra Phillips.

Belarus: Quinta Campanera, 3a Transversal (Calle Aveledo) con Avda 7, Urb. Los Chorros, Municipio Sucre, Caracas 1071; tel. (212) 239-2760; fax (212) 239-0419; e-mail venezuela@belembassy.org; internet www.venezuela.belembassy.org; Ambassador Gurinovich Valentin Arkadjevich.

Belgium: 10a Transversal con 9a Transversal, Apdo del Este 61550, Altamira, Caracas 1060; tel. (212) 263-3334; fax (212) 261-1333; e-mail caracas@diplobel.fed.be; internet www.diplomatie.be/caracas; Ambassador Jean-Paul Warnimont.

Bolivia: Edif. Los Llanos, 1°, Avda Francisco Zolano, esq. San Gerónimo, Zabana Grande, Caracas; tel. (212) 263-3015; fax (212) 261-3386; e-mail embaboliviaven@hotmail.com; internet www.embajada-boliviana-venezuela.com; Chargé d'affaires a.i. Jorge Alvarado Rivas.

Brazil: Avda Mohedano con Calle Los Chaguaramos, Centro Gerencial Mohedano, 6°, La Castellana, Caracas 1060; tel. (212) 918-6000; fax (212) 261-9601; e-mail brasembcaracas@embajadabrasil.org.ve; internet www.brasil.org.ve; Ambassador José Antonio Marcondes de Carvalho.

Bulgaria: Quinta Sofía, Calle Las Lomas, Urb. Las Mercedes, Apdo 68389, Caracas; tel. (212) 993-2714; fax (212) 993-4839; e-mail embulven@gmail.com; internet www.mfa.bg/en/21; Ambassador Ventzislav Anguelov Ivanov.

Canada: Edif. Embajada de Canadá, Avda Francisco de Miranda con Avda Sur, Altamira, Apdo 62302, Caracas 1060-A; tel. (212) 600-3101; fax (212) 261-8741; e-mail crcas@international.gc.ca; internet www.canadainternational.gc.ca/venezuela; Ambassador Paul Gibbard.

Chile: Edif. Torre La Noria, 10°, Of. 10A, Paseo Enrique Eraso, Urb. Las Mercedes, Caracas; tel. (212) 992-3378; fax (212) 992-0614; e-mail echileve@cantv.net; internet www.embachileve.org; Chargé d'affaires a.i. Axel Cabrera Martínez.

China, People's Republic: Avda El Paseo, Quinta El Oriente, Prados del Este, Caracas; tel. (212) 977-4949; fax (212) 978-0876; e-mail embcnven@cantv.net; internet ve.chineseembassy.org; Ambassador Zhao Rongxian.

Colombia: Torre Credival, 11°, 2A Calle de Campo Alegre con Avda Francisco de Miranda, Apdo 60887, Caracas; tel. (212) 216-9596; fax (212) 261-1358; e-mail ecaracas@minrelext.gov.co; Ambassador (vacant).

Costa Rica: Edif. For You, 11°, Avda San Juan Bosco, entre 1a y 2a Transversal, Urb. Altamira, Chacao, Apdo 62239, Caracas; tel. (212) 267-1104; fax (212) 265-4660; e-mail embaricavene@yahoo.com.mx; Ambassador Manuel Vladimir de la Cruz de Lemos.

Cuba: Calle Roraima, entre Río de Janeiro y Choroní, Chuao, Caracas 1060; tel. (212) 991-6661; fax (212) 993-5695; e-mail embajadorcubavzl@cantv.net; internet embacu.cubaminrex.cu/venezuela; Ambassador Rogelio Polanco Fuentes.

Czech Republic: Calle Los Cedros, Quinta Isabel, Urb. Country Club, Altamira, Caracas 1060; tel. (212) 261-8528; fax (212) 266-3987; e-mail caracas@embassy.mzv.cz; internet www.mfa.cz/caracas; Ambassador Stanislav Slavický.

Dominica: Caracas; Ambassador Dr Philbert Aaron.

Dominican Republic: Edif. Argentum, Ofs 1 y 2, 2a Transversal, entre 1a Avda y Avda Andrés Bello, Los Palos Grandes, Caracas 1060; tel. (212) 283-3709; fax (212) 283-3965; e-mail embajadominicana@cantv.net; Ambassador Jaime Durán Hernández.

Ecuador: Centro Andrés Bello, Torre Oeste, 13°, Avda Andrés Bello, Maripérez, Apdo 62124, Caracas 1060; tel. (212) 265-0801; fax (212) 264-6917; e-mail embajadaecuador@cantv.net; Ambassador Gen. (retd) Ramón Torres.

Egypt: Calle Caucagua con Calle Guaicaipuro, Quinta Maribel, Urb. San Román, Municipio Baruta, Apdo 49007, Caracas 1042-A; tel. (212) 992-6259; fax (212) 993-1555; e-mail embassy.caracas@mfa.gov.eg; internet www.mfa.gov.eg/Caracas_Emb; Ambassador Ali Saleh Mourad.

El Salvador: Avda Nicolás Copérnico, Quinta Cuscatlán, Urb. Valle Arriba, Sector Los Naranjos, Municipio Baruta, Miranda, Caracas; tel. (212) 991-4472; fax (212) 959-3920; e-mail embasalve@cantv.net; Ambassador Romnán Antonio Moyorga Quiroz.

Finland: Edif. Atrium, 1°, Calle Sorocaima, El Rosal, Caracas; tel. (212) 952-4111; fax (212) 952-7536; e-mail sanomat.car@formin.fi; internet www.finland.org.ve; Ambassador Mikko Pyhälä.

France: Calle Madrid con Avda Trinidad, Las Mercedes, Apdo 60385, Caracas 1060; tel. (212) 909-6500; fax (212) 909-6630; e-mail infos@francia.org.ve; Ambassador Jean-Marc Laforet.

The Gambia: 4a Avda con 8a Transversal, Quinta La Paz, Urb. Los Palos Grandes, Chacao, Caracas; tel. (212) 285-2554; fax (212) 285-6250; Ambassador Bala Garba Jahumpa.

Germany: Torre La Castellana, 10°, Avda Eugenio Mendoza, cruce con Avda José Angel Lamas, La Castellana, Apdo 2078, Caracas 1010-A; tel. (212) 219-2500; fax (212) 261-0641; e-mail info@caracas.diplo.de; internet www.caracas.diplo.de; Ambassador Georg-Clemens Dick.

Greece: Quinta Maryland, Avda Principal del Avila, Alta Florida, Caracas 1050; tel. (212) 730-3833; fax (212) 731-0429; e-mail gremb.car@mfa.gr; Ambassador Anastassios Petrovas.

Grenada: Avda Norte 2, Quinta 330, Los Navajos del Cafetal, Caracas; tel. (212) 985-5461; fax (212) 985-6391; e-mail egrenada@cantv.net; internet www.grenadaembassycaracas.org; Ambassador George MacLeish.

Guatemala: Avda de Francisco de Miranda, Torre Dozsa, 1°, Urb. El Rosal, Caracas; tel. (212) 952-5247; fax (212) 954-0051; e-mail embaguat@cantv.net; Ambassador Erick Molina.

Guyana: Quinta 'Roraima', Avda El Paseo, Prados del Este, Apdo 51054, Caracas 1050; tel. (212) 977-1158; fax (212) 976-3765; e-mail embaguy@cantv.net; Ambassador Geoffrey da Silva.

Haiti: Quinta Flor 59, Avda Las Rosas, La Florida, Caracas; tel. (212) 730-7220; fax (212) 730-4605; Chargé d'affaires a.i. Christian Toussaint.

Holy See: Avda La Salle, Los Caobos, Apdo 29, Caracas 1010-A (Apostolic Nunciature); tel. (212) 781-8939; fax (212) 793-2403; e-mail nunapos@cantv.net; Apostolic Nuncio Most Rev. Pietro Parolin (Titular Archbishop of Acquapendente).

Honduras: Edif. Banco de Lara, 8°, Of. B2, Avda Principal de la Castellana con 1a Transversal de Altamira, La Castellana, Apdo 68259, Caracas; tel. (212) 264-0606; fax (212) 263-4379; e-mail honduven@cantv.net; Chargé d'affaires a.i. Fernando Suárez Lovo.

India: Quinta Tagore, No. 12, Avda San Carlos, La Floresta, Apdo 61585, Caracas; tel. (212) 285-7887; fax (212) 286-5131; e-mail info@embindia.org; internet www.embindia.org; Ambassador Lal Dingliana.

Indonesia: Quinta 'Indonesia', Avda El Paseo, con Calle Maracaibo, Prados del Este, Apdo 80807, Caracas 1080; tel. (212) 976-2725; fax (212) 976-0550; e-mail kbricaracas1@yahoo1.com; internet www.caracas.deplu.go.id; Ambassador Alfred T. Palembangan.

Iran: Quinta Ommat, Calle Kemal Atatürk, Urb. Valle Arriba, Apdo 68460, Caracas; tel. (212) 992-3575; fax (212) 992-9989; e-mail embairanve@cantv.net; Ambassador Shahin Rosta Mkthani.

Iraq: Quinta Babilonia, Avda Nicolás Copérnico con Calle Los Malabares, Urb. Valle Arriba, Caracas; tel. (212) 993-3446; fax (212) 993-0819; e-mail crcemb@iraqmfamail.com; Chargé d'affaires a.i. Fakhri Al Essa.

Italy: Edif. Atrium PH, Calle Sorocaima, entre Avdas Tamanaco y Venezuela, El Rosal, Apdo 3995, Caracas 1060; tel. (212) 952-7311; fax (212) 952-4960; e-mail ambcaracas@esteri.it; internet www.ambcaracas.esteri.it; Ambassador Paolo Serpi.

Jamaica: Edif. Los Frailes, 5°, Calle La Guairita, Urb. Chuao, Caracas 1062; tel. (212) 916-9055; fax (212) 991-5708; e-mail embjaven@cantv.net; Ambassador Clinton Stone.

Japan: Edif. Bancaracas, 10°, Avda San Felipe con 2a Transversal, La Castellana, Caracas; tel. (212) 261-8333; fax (212) 261-6780; e-mail ajapon@genesisbci.net; internet www.ve.emb-japan.go.jp; Ambassador Shuji Shimokoji.

Korea, Republic: Avda Francisco de Miranda, Centro Lido, Torre B, 9°, Ofs 91-B y 92-B, El Rosal, Caracas; tel. (212) 954-1270; fax (212) 954-0619; e-mail venezuela@mofat.go.kr; internet ven.mofat.go.kr; Ambassador Kim Joo-Teck.

VENEZUELA

Kuwait: Quinta El-Kuwait, Avda Las Magnolias con Calle Los Olivos, Los Chorros, Caracas; tel. (212) 235-3864; fax (212) 238-1752; e-mail caracas@mofa.gov.kw; Ambassador Yousef Hussain Al-Gabandi.

Lebanon: Edif. Embajada del Líbano, Prolongación Avda Parima, Colinas de Bello Monte, Calle Motatán, Caracas 1041; tel. (212) 751-5943; fax (212) 753-0726; e-mail emblibano@cantv.net; Ambassador Charbel Wehbe.

Malaysia: Centro Profesional Eurobuilding, 6°, Ofs 6D-G, Calle La Guairita, Apdo 65107, Chuao, Caracas 1060; tel. (212) 992-1011; fax (212) 992-1277; e-mail malcaracas@kln.gov.my; internet www.embajadamalasia.com; Ambassador Ramlan Kimin.

Mexico: Edif. Forum, Calle Guaicaipuro con Principal de las Mercedes, 5°, El Rosal, Chacao, Apdo 61371, Caracas; tel. (212) 952-5777; fax (212) 952-3003; e-mail mexico@embamex.com.ve; internet www.embamex.com.ve; Ambassador Jesús Mario Chacón Carrillo.

Netherlands: Edif. San Juan, 9°, Avda San Juan Bosco con 2a Transversal de Altamira, Caracas; tel. (212) 276-9300; fax (212) 276-9311; e-mail car@minbuza.nl; internet www.mfa.nl/car; Ambassador Johannes Gerardus Van Vloten Dissevetl.

Nicaragua: Avda El Paseo, Quinta Doña Dilia, Prados del Este, Caracas; tel. (212) 977-3289; fax (212) 977-3973; e-mail spoveda@cancilleria.gob.ni; Ambassador Ramón Enrique Leets Castillo.

Nigeria: Calle Chivacoa cruce con Calle Taría, Quinta Leticia, Urb. San Román, Apdo 62062, Chacao, Caracas 1060-A; tel. (212) 993-1520; fax (212) 993-7648; e-mail embnig@cantv.net; Ambassador Charles Nduka Onianwa.

Norway: Centro Lido, Torre A-92A, Avda Francisco de Miranda, El Rosal, Apdo 60532, Chacao, Caracas 1060-A; tel. (212) 953-0269; fax (212) 953-6877; e-mail emb.caracas@mfa.no; internet www.noruega.org.ve; Ambassador Ingunn Klepsvik.

Panama: Edif. Los Frailes, 6°, Calle La Guairita, Chuao, Apdo 1989, Caracas; tel. (212) 992-9093; fax (212) 992-8107; e-mail empanve@cantv.net; Ambassador Pedro Pereira.

Paraguay: Quinta Helechales, 4a Avda, entre 7a y 8a Transversal, Urb. Altamira, Municipio Chacao, Caracas; tel. and fax (212) 267-5543; e-mail embaparven@cantv.net; Ambassador Augusto Ocampos Caballero.

Peru: Edif. San Juan, 5°, Avda San Juan Bosco con 2a Transversal, Altamira, Caracas; tel. (212) 264-1483; fax (212) 265-7592; e-mail leprucaracas@cantv.net; Ambassador José Romero Cevallos.

Philippines: 5a Transversal de Altamira, Quinta Filipinas, Altamira, Municipio Chacao, Caracas 1060; tel. (212) 266-4725; fax (212) 266-6443; e-mail caracas@embassyph.com; Ambassador Jocelyn Batoon-García.

Poland: Quinta Ambar, Calle Nicolás Copérnico, Sector Los Naranjos, Valle Arriba, Apdo 62293, Chacao, Caracas; tel. (212) 991-1461; fax (212) 992-2164; e-mail ambcarac@cantv.net; internet www.caracas.polemb.net; Ambassador Krzysztof Jacek Hinz (also serves Guyana).

Portugal: Torre La Castellana, 3°, Avda Eugénio Mendoza, cruce con Calle José Angel Lamas, Urb. La Castellana, Caracas 1062; tel. (212) 263-2529; fax (212) 267-9766; e-mail embajadaportugal@cantv.net; Ambassador Mário Alberto Lino da Silva.

Qatar: Avda Principal Lomas El Mirador, Quinta Alto Claro, Municipio Baruta, Caracas; tel. (212) 993-7925; fax (212) 993-2917; e-mail qatarven@cantv.net; Ambassador Rashid Mubarak Al-Kuwari.

Romania: 4a Avda de Altamira, entre 8a y 9a Transversales, Quinta Guardatinajas 49-19, Chacao, Caracas; tel. (212) 261-9480; fax (212) 263-5697; e-mail secretariat.amb@gmail.com; Chargé d'affaires a.i. Elena Lincan.

Russia: Quinta Soyuz, Calle Las Lomas, Las Mercedes, Apdo 60313, Caracas; tel. (212) 993-4395; fax (212) 993-6526; e-mail rusemb@cantv.net; internet www.venezuela.mid.ru; Ambassador Vladimir F. Zaemsky.

Saudi Arabia: Calle Andrés Pietri, Quinta Makkah, Los Chorros, Caracas 1071; tel. (212) 239-0290; fax (212) 239-6494; e-mail veemb@mofa.gov.sa; Ambassador Abdelrahman bin Abdulaziz bin Sulaiman Abanamy.

South Africa: Edif. Atrium PH-1A, Sorocaima con Avda Venezuela, Urb. El Rosal, Chacao, Apdo 2613, Caracas 1064; tel. (212) 952-0026; fax (212) 952-0277; e-mail embajador.caracas@foreign.gov.za; Ambassador Bheki Wisdom Gila.

Spain: Avda Mohedano entre 1a y 2a Transversal, La Castellana, Apdo 62297, Caracas; tel. (212) 263-2855; fax (212) 261-0892; e-mail emb.caracas@maec.es; internet www.maec.es/embajadas/caracas; Ambassador Juan Ramón Serrat Cuenca-Romero.

Sudan: Caracas; Ambassador Abdurrahman Ahmed Klalid Sharfi.

Suriname: 4a Avda entre 7a y 8a Transversal, Quinta 41, Altamira, Caracas; Apdo 61140, Chacao, Caracas; tel. (212) 261-2724; fax (212) 263-9006; e-mail emsurl@cantv.net; Ambassador Samuel Pawironadi.

Switzerland: Centro Letonia, Torre Ing-Bank, 15°, Avda Eugenio Mendoza y San Felipe, La Castellana, Apdo 62555, Chacao, Caracas 1060-A; tel. (212) 267-9585; fax (212) 267-7745; e-mail car.vertretung@eda.admin.ch; internet www.eda.admin.ch/caracas; Ambassador Markus-Alexander Antonietti.

Syria: Avda Casiquiare, Quinta Damasco, Colinas de Bello Monte, Caracas; tel. (212) 753-5375; fax (212) 751-6146; Ambassador Ghassan Suleiman Abbas.

Trinidad and Tobago: Quinta Poshika, 3a Avda entre 7 y 8 Transversales, Altamira, Municipio Chacao, Caracas; tel. (212) 261-5796; fax (212) 261-9801; e-mail embassytt@cantv.net; Ambassador Razia Ali.

Turkey: Calle Kemal Atatürk, Quinta Turquesa 6, Valle Arriba, Apdo 62078, Caracas 1060-A; tel. (212) 991-0075; fax (212) 992-0442; e-mail turkishemb@cantv.net; internet karakas.be.mfa.gov.tr; Ambassador Nihat Akyol.

United Kingdom: Torre La Castellana, 11°, Avda Principal La Castellana, Caracas 1061; tel. (212) 263-8411; fax (212) 267-1275; e-mail britishembassy@internet.ve; internet ukinvenezuela.fco.gov.uk; Ambassador Catherine Elizabeth Nettleton.

USA: Calle Suapure con Calle F, Urb. Colinas de Valle Arriba, Caracas 1080; tel. (212) 975-6411; fax (212) 975-6710; e-mail embajada@state.gov; internet caracas.usembassy.gov; Chargé d'affaires a.i. John Caulfield.

Uruguay: Torre Seguros Altamira, 4°, Of. D y E, 4a Avda de los Palos Grandes, Apdo 60366, Caracas 1060-A; tel. (212) 285-3549; fax (212) 286-6777; e-mail uruvene@cantv.net; Ambassador Jorge Ernesto Mazzarovich Severi.

Viet Nam: 9a Transversal, entre 6a y 7a Avdas, Quinta Las Mercedes, Urb. Altamira, Chacao 1060-025, Caracas; tel. (212) 635-7402; fax (212) 264-7324; e-mail embavive@yahoo.com.vn; internet www.vietnamembassy-venezuela.org; Ambassador Tran Thanh Huan.

Judicial System

The judicature is headed by the Supreme Tribunal of Justice, which replaced the Supreme Court of Justice after the promulgation of the December 1999 Constitution. The judges are divided into penal and civil and mercantile judges; there are military, juvenile, labour, administrative litigation, finance and agrarian tribunals. In each state there is a superior court and several secondary courts which act on civil and criminal cases. A number of reforms to the judicial system were introduced under the Organic Criminal Trial Code of March 1998. The Code replaced the inquisitorial system, based on the Napoleonic code, with an adversarial system in July 1999. In addition, citizen participation as lay judges and trial by jury was introduced, with training financed by the World Bank.

SUPREME TRIBUNAL OF JUSTICE

The Supreme Tribunal comprises 32 judges appointed by the Asamblea Nacional for 12 years. It is divided into six courts, each with three judges: political-administrative, civil, constitutional, electoral, social and criminal. When these act together the court is in full session. It has the power to abrogate any laws, regulations or other acts of the executive or legislative branches conflicting with the Constitution. It hears accusations against members of the Government and high public officials, cases involving diplomatic representatives and certain civil actions arising between the State and individuals.

Tribunal Supremo de Justicia

Final Avda Baralt, esq. Dos Pilitas, Foro Libertador, Caracas 1010; tel. (212) 801-9178; fax (212) 564-8596; e-mail cperez@tsj.gov.ve; internet www.tsj.gov.ve.

President: Luisa Estella Morales Lamuño.

President of the Constitutional Court: Luisa Estella Morales Lamuño.

President of the Political-Administrative Court: Evelyn Margarita Marrero Ortíz.

President of the Court of Civil Cassation: Yris Armenia Peña de Andueza.

President of the Court of Penal Cassation: Ninoska Queipo Briceño.

President of the Court of Social Cassation: Omar Alfredo Mora Díaz.

President of the Electoral Court: Jhannett María Madríz Sotillo.

Attorney-General: Luisa Ortega Díaz.

VENEZUELA

Religion

Roman Catholicism is the religion of the majority of the population, but there is complete freedom of worship.

CHRISTIANITY

The Roman Catholic Church

For ecclesiastical purposes, Venezuela comprises nine archdioceses, 24 dioceses and three Apostolic Vicariates. There are also apostolic exarchates for the Melkite and Syrian Rites. Some 88% of the population are Roman Catholics.

Latin Rite

Bishops' Conference

Conferencia Episcopal de Venezuela, Prolongación Avda Páez, Montalbán, Apdo 4897, Caracas 1010; tel. (212) 471-6284; fax (212) 472-7029; e-mail prensa@cev.org.ve; internet www.cev.org.ve.
f. 1985; statutes approved in 2000; Pres. Most Rev. UBALDO RAMÓN SANTANA SEQUERA (Archbishop of Maracaibo).

Archbishop of Barquisimeto: Most Rev. ANTONIO JOSÉ LÓPEZ CASTILLO, Arzobispado, Venezuela con Calle 29 y 30 Santa Iglesia Catedral, Nivel Sótano, Barquisimeto 3001; tel. (251) 231-3446; fax (251) 231-3724; e-mail arquidiocesisdebarquisimeto@hotmail.com.

Archbishop of Calabozo: MANUEL FELIPE DÍAZ SÁNCHEZ, Arzobispado, Calle 4, No 11–82, Apdo 954, Calabozo 2312; tel. (246) 871-0483; fax (246) 871-2097; e-mail el.real@telcel.net.ve.

Archbishop of Caracas (Santiago de Venezuela): Cardinal JORGE LIBERATO UROSA SAVINO, Arzobispado, Plaza Bolívar, Apdo 954, Caracas 1010-A; tel. (212) 542-1611; fax (212) 542-0297; e-mail arzobispado@cantv.net.

Archbishop of Ciudad Bolívar: Most Rev. MEDARDO LUIS LUZARDO ROMERO, Arzobispado, Avda Andrés Eloy Blanco con Calle Naiguatá, Apdo 43, Ciudad Bolívar 8001; tel. (285) 654-4960; fax (285) 654-0821; e-mail arzcb@cantv.net.ve.

Archbishop of Coro: Most Rev. ROBERTO LÜCKERT LEÓN, Arzobispado, Calle Federación esq. Palmasola, Apdo 7342, Coro; tel. (268) 251-7024; fax (268) 251-1636; e-mail dioceco@reaccium.ve.

Archbishop of Cumaná: Most Rev. DIEGO RAFAEL PADRÓN SÁNCHEZ, Arzobispado, Calle Bolívar 34 con Catedral, Apdo 134, Cumaná 6101-A; tel. (293) 431-4131; fax (293) 433-3413; e-mail dipa@cantv.net.

Archbishop of Maracaibo: Most Rev. UBALDO RAMÓN SANTANA SEQUERA, Arzobispado, Calle 95, entre Avdas 2 y 3, Apdo 439, Maracaibo; tel. (261) 722-5351; fax (261) 721-0805; e-mail ubrasan@hotmail.com.

Archbishop of Mérida: Most Rev. BALTAZAR ENRIQUE PORRAS CARDOZO, Arzobispado, Avda 4, Plaza Bolívar, Apdo 26, Mérida 5101-A; tel. (274) 252-5786; fax (274) 252-1238; e-mail arquimer@latinmail.com.

Archbishop of Valencia: Most Rev. REINALDO DEL PRETTE LISSOT, Arzobispado, Avda Urdaneta 100-54, Apdo 32, Valencia 2001-A; tel. (241) 858-5865; fax (241) 857-8061; e-mail arqui_valencia@cantv.net.

Melkite Rite

Apostolic Exarch: Rt Rev. GEORGES KAHHALÉ ZOUHAÏRATY, Iglesia San Jorge, Final 3a Urb. Montalbán II, Apdo 20120, Caracas; tel. (212) 472-5367; fax (212) 443-0131; e-mail georgeskhhale@cantv.net.

Syrian Rite

Apostolic Exarch: HIKMAT BEYLOUNI, Parroquia Nuestra Señora de la Asunción, 1A Calle San Jacinto, Apdo 11, Maracay; tel. (243) 235-0821; fax (243) 235-7213.

The Anglican Communion

Anglicans in Venezuela are adherents of the Episcopal Church in the USA, in which the country forms a single, extra-provincial diocese attached to Province IX.

Bishop of Venezuela: Rt Rev. ORLANDO DE JESÚS GUERRERO, Avda Caroní 100, Apdo 49-143, Colinas de Bello Monte, Caracas 1042-A; tel. (212) 753-0723; fax (212) 751-3180; e-mail iglanglicanavzla@cantv.net.

Protestant Churches

Convención Nacional Bautista de Venezuela: Avda Santiago de Chile 12–14, Urb. Los Caobos, Caracas 1050; Apdo 61152, Chacao, Caracas 1060-A; tel. (212) 782-2308; fax (212) 781-9043; e-mail cnbv@telcel.net.ve; internet www.cnbv.org.ve; f. 1951; Pres. Rev. IVÁN MARTÍNEZ; Dir-Gen. Rev. ALEXANDER MONTERO.

Iglesia Evangélica Luterana en Venezuela: Apdo 68738, Caracas 1062-A; tel. and fax (212) 264-1868; e-mail iglesia_ielv@cantv.net; internet ielv.tripod.com; Pres. AKOS V. PUKY; 4,000 mems.

JUDAISM

Confederación de Asociaciones Israelitas de Venezuela: Avda Washington, al lado del Hotel Avila, San Bernardino, Caracas; tel. (212) 551-0368; fax (212) 551-0377; internet www.caiv.org; f. 1966; federation of five Jewish orgs; Pres. ABRAHAM LEVY BENSHIMOL.

ISLAM

Mezquita Sheikh Ibrahim bin-Abdulaziz bin-Ibrahim: Calle Real de Quebrada Honda, Los Caobos, Caracas; tel. (212) 577-7382; f. 1994; Leader OMAR KADWA.

BAHÁ'Í FAITH

National Spiritual Assembly of the Bahá'ís: Colinas de Bello Monte, Apdo 49133, Caracas; tel. and fax (212) 751-7669; e-mail aenbaven@telcel.net.ve; internet www.bci.org/venezuela; f. 1961; mems resident in 954 localities.

The Press

PRINCIPAL DAILIES

Caracas

The Daily Journal: Avda Principal de Boleíta Norte, Apdo 76478, Caracas 1070-A; tel. (212) 237-9644; fax (212) 232-6831; e-mail redaccion@dj.com.ve; internet www.dj.com.ve; f. 1945; morning; English; Chief Editor RUSSELL M. DALLEN, Jr.

Diario 2001: Edif. Bloque DeArmas, 2°, final Avda San Martín cruce con Avda La Paz, Caracas; tel. (212) 406-4111; fax (212) 443-4961; e-mail contacto@dearmas.com; internet www.2001.com.ve; f. 1973; Pres. MARTÍN DE ARMAS S.; Dir ISRAEL MÁRQUEZ.

El Diario de Caracas: Calle Los Laboratorios, Torre B, 1°, Of. 101, Los Ruices, Caracas 1070; tel. (212) 238-0386; e-mail editor@eldiariodecaracas.net; internet www.eldiariodecaracas.net; f. 2003; distributed free of charge; Editor JULIO AUGUSTO LÓPEZ.

Meridiano: Edif. Bloque DeArmas, final Avda San Martín cruce con Avda La Paz, Caracas 1010; tel. (212) 406-4040; fax (212) 442-5836; e-mail meridian@dearmas.com; internet www.meridiano.com.ve; f. 1969; morning; sport; Pres. MARTÍN DE ARMAS S.; Dir VÍCTOR JOSÉ LÓPEZ.

El Mundo: Torre de la Prensa, 4°, Plaza del Panteón, Apdo 1192, Caracas; tel. (212) 596-1911; fax (212) 596-1478; e-mail olugo@cadena-capriles.com; internet www.elmundo.com.ve; f. 1958; morning; independent; economics and business; Pres. MIGUEL ANGEL CAPRILES LÓPEZ; Dir OMAR LUGO.

El Nacional: Avda Principal de Los Cortijos de Lourdes con 3a Transversal, Caracas 1071-A; tel. (212) 203-3243; fax (212) 203-3158; e-mail contactenos@el-nacional.com; internet www.el-nacional.com; f. 1943; morning; right-wing; independent; Pres. and Editor MIGUEL HENRIQUE OTERO.

El Nuevo País: Pinto a Santa Rosalía 44, Caracas; tel. (212) 541-5211; fax (212) 545-9675; e-mail enpais1@telcel.net.ve; f. 1988; Dir and Editor RAFAEL POLEA.

Reporte (Diario de la Economía): Edif. Jimmy, 1°, Of. 6, California con Mucuchíes, Urb. Las Mercedes, Caracas 1060; tel. (212) 993-3505; e-mail diarioreporte@yahoo.com; internet www.diarioreportedelaeconomia.com; f. 1988; Pres. TANNOUS GERGES.

TalCual: Edif. Menegrande, 5°, Of. 51, Avda Francisco de Miranda, Caracas; tel. (212) 286-7446; fax (212) 232-7446; e-mail tpetkoff@talcualdigital.com; internet www.talcualdigital.com; f. 2000; evening; right-wing; Pres. TEODORO PETKOFF; Editor-in-Chief MAYE PRIMERA.

Ultimas Noticias: Torre de la Prensa, 3°, Plaza del Panteón, Apdo 1192, Caracas; tel. (212) 596-1911; fax (212) 596-1433; e-mail edrangel@cadena-capriles.com; internet www.ultimasnoticias.com.ve; f. 1941; morning; independent; Pres. MIGUEL ANGEL CAPRILES LÓPEZ; Dir ELEAZAR DÍAZ RANGEL.

El Universal: Edif. El Universal, Avda Urdaneta, esq. de Animas, Apdo 1909, Caracas; tel. (212) 505-2314; fax (212) 505-3710; e-mail consejoeditorial@eluniversal.com; internet www.eluniversal.com; f. 1909; morning; Dir ANDRÉS MATA OSORIO; Chief Editor ELIDES ROJAS.

Vea: Edif. San Martín, Sótano Uno, Parque Central, Caracas 1010; tel. (212) 516-1004; fax (212) 578-3031; e-mail webmaster@diariovea.com.ve; internet www.diariovea.com.ve; f. 2003; morning; left-wing; Dir GUILLERMO GARCÍA PONCE; Editor-in-Chief MERCEDES ORDUÑO.

VENEZUELA

Barcelona

El Norte: Avda Intercomunal Jorge Rodríguez, Sector Las Garzas, Grupo UP, Entre el Banco Exterior y el BOD, Barcelona; tel. (281) 286-2484; e-mail fmartinez@elnorte.com.ve; internet www.elnorte.com.ve; f. 1989; morning; Dir ALBERTINA PETRICCA; Exec. Dir FERNANDO MARTÍNEZ.

Barquisimeto

El Impulso: Avda Los Comuneros, entre Avda República y Calle 1a, Urb. El Parque, Apdo 602, Barquisimeto; tel. (251) 250-2222; fax (251) 250-2129; e-mail reaccion@elimpulso.com; internet www.elimpulso.com; f. 1904; morning; independent; Dir and Editor CARLOS CARMONA.

El Informador: Edif. El Informador, Carrera 21, esq. Calle 23, Barquisimeto; tel. (251) 231-1811; fax (251) 231-0624; e-mail mauriciogomez@elinformador.com.ve; internet www.elinformador.com.ve; f. 1968; morning; Dir-Gen. MAURICIO GÓMEZ SIGALA.

Ciudad Bolívar

El Bolivarense: Calle Igualdad 26, Apdo 91, Ciudad Bolívar; tel. (414) 893-4443; fax (285) 632-5667; e-mail publicidad@elbolivarense.com; f. 1957; morning; independent; Dir ÁLVARO NATERA.

El Expreso: Paseo Gáspari con Calle Democracia, Ciudad Bolívar; tel. and fax (285) 632-0334; e-mail webmaster@diarioelexpreso.com.ve; internet www.diarioelexpreso.com.ve; f. 1969; morning; independent; Dir LUIS ALBERTO GUZMÁN.

Maracaibo

Panorama: Avda 15, No 95–60, Apdo 425, Maracaibo; tel. (261) 725-6888; fax (261) 725-6911; e-mail editor@panodi.com; internet www.panodi.com; f. 1914; morning; independent; Pres. ESTEBAN PINEDA BELLOSO; Editorial Dir MARÍA INÉS DELGADO; circ. 16,000.

Maracay

El Aragüeño: Calle 3a Oeste con Avda 1 Oeste, Urb. Ind. San Jacinto, Maracay; tel. (243) 235-9018; fax (243) 235-7866; e-mail el-aragueno@cantv.net; internet www.el-aragueno.com; f. 1972; morning; Editors ROSELYS PEÑA, PEDRO ELÍAS HERNÁNDEZ.

El Periodiquito: Calle Páez Este 178, Maracay; tel. (243) 322-1422; fax (243) 233-6987; e-mail redaccion@elperiodiquito.com; internet www.elperiodiquito.com; f. 1986; Pres. RAFAEL RODRÍGUEZ R.; Editor-in-Chief YHOSSELINE LUNA GALLARDO.

El Siglo: Edif. 'El Siglo', Avda Bolívar Oeste 244, La Romana, Maracay; tel. (243) 554-9521; fax (243) 554-5154; e-mail direccion@elsiglo.com.ve; internet www.elsiglo.com.ve; f. 1973; morning; independent; Editor TULIO CAPRILES.

Puerto la Cruz

El Tiempo: Edif. Diario El Tiempo, Avda Municipal 153, Puerto La Cruz; tel. (281) 260-0600; fax (281) 260-0660; e-mail buzon@eltiempo.com.ve; internet www.eltiempo.com.ve; f. 1958; independent; Dir and Editor GIOCONDA DE MÁRQUEZ.

San Cristóbal

Diario Católico: Carrera 4a, No 3–41, San Cristóbal; tel. (276) 343-2819; fax (276) 343-4683; e-mail catolico@truevision.net; internet www.diariocatolico.com.ve; f. 1924; morning; Catholic; Man. Dir Mgr JOSÉ LAUREANO BALLESTEROS BLANCO.

Diario La Nación: Edif. La Nación, Calle 4 con Carrera 6 bis, La Concordia, Apdo 651, San Cristóbal; tel. (276) 346-4263; fax (276) 346-5051; e-mail lanacion@lanacion.com.ve; internet www.lanacion.com.ve; f. 1968; morning; independent; Editor JOSÉ RAFAEL CORTEZ.

El Tigre

Antorcha: Edif. Antorcha, Avda Francisco de Miranda, El Tigre; tel. (283) 235-2383; fax (283) 235-3923; e-mail yurbina@diarioantorcha.com; internet www.diarioantorcha.com; f. 1954; morning; independent; Pres. and Editor ANTONIO BRICEÑO AMPARÁN.

Valencia

El Carabobeño: Edif. El Carabobeño, Avda Universidad, Urb. La Granja, Naguanagua, Valencia; tel. (241) 867-2918; fax (241) 867-3450; e-mail website@el-carabobeno.com; internet www.el-carabobeno.com; f. 1933; morning; Dir EDUARDO ALEMÁN PÉREZ.

Notitarde: Edif. Carabobo, Avda Boyacá, entre Navas Spínola y Flores, Valencia; tel. (241) 850-1666; fax (241) 850-1534; e-mail lauodr@notitarde.com; internet www.notitarde.com; evening; Dir LAURENTZI ODRIOZOLA ECHEGARAY.

SELECTED PERIODICALS

Artesanía y Folklore de Venezuela: C. C. Vista Mar, Local 20, Urbaneja, Lecherías, Estado Anzoátegui; tel. and fax (212) 286-2857; e-mail ismandacorrea@cantv.net; handicrafts and folklore; Dir ISMANDA CORREA.

Automóvil de Venezuela: Avda Caurimare, Quinta Expo, Colinas de Bello Monte, Caracas 1050; tel. (212) 751-1355; fax (212) 751-1122; e-mail ortizauto@gmail.com; internet www.automovildevenezuela.com; f. 1961; monthly; automotive trade; circ. 6,000; Editor MARÍA A. ORTIZ.

Barriles: Centro Parque Carabobo, Torre B, 20°, Of. 2003, Avda Universidad, La Candelaria, Caracas; e-mail informaciones@camarapetrolera.org; publ. of the Cámara Petrolera de Venezuela; Editor HAYDÉE REYES.

Business Venezuela: Torre Credival, Avda de Campo Alegre, Apdo 5181, Caracas 1010-A; tel. (212) 263-0833; fax (212) 263-2060; e-mail yrojas@venamcham.org; internet www.bvonline.com.ve; every two months; business and economics journal in English; published by the Venezuelan-American Chamber of Commerce and Industry; Editor-in-Chief CARLOS TEJERA.

ComputerWorld Venezuela: Edif. Marystella, Avda Carabobo, El Rosal, Caracas; tel. (212) 952-7427; fax (212) 953-3950; e-mail cernic@cwv.com.ve; internet www.cwv.com.ve; Editor CLELIA SANTAMBROGIO.

Dinero: Torre Sur, 1°, Centro Comercial El Recreo, Avda Venezuela, Caracas 1050; tel. (212) 750-5011; fax (212) 750-5005; e-mail mcastillo@gep.com.ve; internet www.dinero.com.ve; monthly; business and finance; Dir SALVATORE LOMONACO.

Exceso: Edif. Karam, Avda Urdaneta, 5°, Caracas; tel. (212) 564-1702; fax (212) 564-6760; e-mail baf-exceso@cantv.net; lifestyle; Dir BEN AMÍ FIHMAN; Editor ARMANDO COLL.

Gerente Venezuela: Avda Orinoco 3819, entre Muchuchies y Monterrey, Las Mercedes, Caracas 1060; tel. (212) 267-3733; fax (212) 267-6583; business and management; Editor LUIS RODÁN; circ. 15,000.

Nueva Sociedad: Edif. IASA, 6°, Of. 606, Plaza La Castellana, Apdo 61712, Caracas; tel. (212) 265-9975; fax (212) 267-3397; e-mail nuso@nuso.org; internet www.nuso.org; f. 1972; Latin American affairs; Dir JOACHIM KNOOP.

Producto: Torre Sur, 1°, Centro Comercial El Recreo, Avda Venezuela, Caracas 1050; tel. (212) 750-5011; fax (212) 750-5005; e-mail mcastillo@producto.com.ve; internet www.producto.com.ve; f. 1983; monthly; business; Editor ERNESTO LOTITTO.

Quinto Día: Avda Principal de Los Ruices con Avda Rómulo Gallegos, Residencia Los Almendros, nivel mezzanina, Of. 5, Los Ruices, Caracas; tel. (212) 237-9809; fax (212) 239-2955; e-mail acarrera@quintodia.com; internet www.quintodia.com; weekly; current affairs; Dir CARLOS CROES.

La Razón: Edif. Valores, Sótano 'A', Avda Urdaneta, esq. de Urapal, Apdo 16362, La Candelaria, Caracas; tel. (212) 578-3143; fax (212) 578-2397; e-mail larazon@internet.ve; internet www.larazon.net; weekly, on Sun.; independent; Dir PABLO LÓPEZ ULACIO.

La Red: Urb. Vista Alegre, Calle 7, Quinta Luisa Amelia, Caracas; tel. (212) 472-0703; fax (212) 471-7749; e-mail vdiaz@lared.com.ve; internet www.lared.com.ve; f. 1996; information technology; Editor LUIS MANUEL DÁVILA.

Ronda: Edif. Bloque DeArmas, final Avda San Martín cruce con Avda La Paz, Caracas 1020; tel. (212) 406-4018; fax (212) 406-4018; e-mail martinjr@dearmas.com; fortnightly; celebrities and entertainment; Dir JENNIFER MIRANDA.

Sic: Edif. Centro de Valores, esq. de Luneta, Centro Gumilla, Caracas; tel. (212) 564-9803; fax (212) 564-7557; e-mail sic@gumilla.org; internet www.gumilla.org; f. 1938; Compañía de Jesús; monthly; liberal Jesuit publ; Dir ARTURO PERAZA.

Tendencia: Torre Tendencia, 5°, Avda El Milagro, Sector Gonzaga, Maracaibo; tel. (261) 743-7674; fax (261) 742-0960; e-mail kmanrique@tendencia.com; internet www.tendencia.com; every two months; lifestyle; Dir E. PATRICIO PARDO.

Variedades: Edif. Bloque DeArmas, 6°, final Avda San Martín cruce con Avda La Paz, Caracas 1020; tel. (212) 406-4390; fax (212) 451-0762; e-mail jfeijoo@dearmas.com; f. 1963; monthly; women's interest; Dir MARÍA JESÚS RODRÍGUEZ.

VenEconomía: Edif. Gran Sabana, 1°, Avda Abraham Lincoln 174, Blvr de Sabana Grande, Caracas 1050; tel. (212) 761-8121; fax (212) 762-8160; e-mail editor@veneconomia.com; internet www.veneconomia.com; f. 1982; weekly and monthly edns; Spanish and English; business, economic and political issues; Editor ROBERT BOTTOME.

Zeta: Pinto a Santa Rosalía 44, Apdo 14067, Santa Rosalía, Caracas; tel. (212) 541-5211; fax (212) 545-9675; e-mail enpaiscolumna@hotmail.com; f. 1974; weekly; politics and current affairs; Dir JURATE ROSALES; Editor RAFAEL POLEO.

VENEZUELA

PRESS ASSOCIATIONS

Asociación de Prensa Extranjera en Venezuela (APEX): Hotel Caracas Hilton, Torre Sur, 3°, Of. 301, Avda México, Caracas; tel. (212) 503-5301; fax (212) 576-9284; e-mail caracashilton@hotmail.com; Pres. PHILIP GUNSON.

Bloque de Prensa Venezolano (BEV): Edif. El Universal, 5°, Of. C, Avda Urdaneta, Caracas; tel. (212) 561-7704; fax (212) 561-9409; e-mail contacto@bloquedeprensavenezolano.com; internet www.bloquedeprensavenezolano.com; asscn of newspaper owners; Pres. Dr DAVID NATERA FEBRES.

Colegio Nacional de Periodistas (CNP): Casa Nacional del Periodista, 2°, Avda Andrés Bello, Caracas; tel. and fax (212) 781-7601; e-mail colegiodeperiodistasjdn@yahoo.com; internet www.cnp.org.ve; journalists' asscn; Pres. WILLIAM ECHEVERRÍA; Sec.-Gen. SILVIA ALEGRETT.

STATE PRESS AGENCY

Agencia Bolivariana de Noticias: Avda Bolívar, Torre Oeste, 16°, Parque Central, Caracas; tel. (212) 572-6543; fax (212) 571-0563; internet www.abn.info.ve; fmrly Venpress; Pres. FREDDY FERNÁNDEZ TORRES.

Publishers

Armitano Editores, CA: Centro Industrial Boleita Sur, 4a Transversal de Boleita, Apdo 50853, Caracas 1070; tel. (212) 234-2565; fax (212) 234-1647; e-mail armiedit@telcel.net.ve; internet www.armitano.com; art, architecture, ecology, botany, anthropology, history, geography; Pres. ERNESTO ARMITANO.

Colegial Bolivariana, CA: Edif. COBO, 1°, Avda Diego Cisneros (Principal), Los Ruices, Apdo 70324, Caracas 1071-A; tel. (212) 239-1433; fax (212) 239-6502; internet www.co-bo.com; f. 1961; general, educational; Dir ANTONIO JUZGADO ARIAS.

Ediciones Ekaré: Edif. Banco del Libro, Avda Luis Roche, Altamira Sur, Caracas 1062; tel. (212) 264-7615; fax (212) 263-3291; e-mail editorial@ekare.com.ve; internet www.ekare.com; f. 1978; children's literature; Pres. CARMEN DIANA DEARDEN; Exec. Dir MARÍA FRANCISCA MAYOBRE.

Editora Ferga, CA: Torre Bazar Bolívar, 5°, Of. 501, Avda Francisco de Miranda, El Marqués, Apdo 16044, Caracas 1011-A; tel. (212) 239-1564; fax (212) 234-1008; e-mail ddex1@ibm.net; internet www.ddex.com; f. 1971; Venezuelan Exporters' Directory; Dir NELSON SÁNCHEZ MARTÍNEZ.

Fundación Biblioteca Ayacucho: Centro Financiero Latino, 12°, Ofs 1, 2 y 3, Avda Urdaneta, Animas a Plaza España, Apdo 14413, Caracas 1010; tel. (212) 561-6691; fax (212) 564-5643; e-mail biblioayacucho@cantv.net; internet www.bibliotecayacucho.gob.ve/fba; f. 1974; literature; Pres. HUMBERTO MATA.

Fundación Bigott: Casa 10-11, Calle El Vigia, Plaza Sucre, Centro Histórico de Petare, Caracas 1010-A; tel. (212) 272-2020; fax (212) 272-5942; e-mail contacto@fundacionbigott.com; internet www.fundacionbigott.com; f. 1936; Venezuelan traditions, environment, agriculture; Admin. Co-ordinator NELSON REYES.

Fundación Editorial Salesiana: Avda Andrés Bello, Paradero a Salesianos 6, Apdo 369, Caracas; tel. (212) 571-6109; fax (212) 574-9451; e-mail gerenciales@cantv.net; internet www.salesiana.com.ve; f. 1960; education; Pres. LUCIANO STÉFANI.

Fundarte: Edif. Tajamar P. H., Avda Lecuna, Parque Central, Apdo 17559, Caracas 1015-A; tel. (212) 573-1719; fax (212) 574-2794; internet www.fundarte.gob.ve; f. 1975; literature, history; Pres. ALFREDO GOSEN; Dir ROBERTO LOVERA DE SOLA.

Editorial González Porto: Sociedad a Traposos 8, Avda Universidad, Caracas; Pres. Dr PABLO PERALES.

Ediciones IESA: Edif. IESA, 3°, Final Avda IESA, San Bernardino, Apdo 1640, Caracas 1010-A; tel. (212) 555-4504; e-mail ediesa@iesa.edu.ve; internet www.iesa.edu.ve/publicaciones/ediciones; f. 1984; economics, business; Assoc. Dir JOSÉ MALAVÉ.

Ediciones María Di Mase: Caracas; f. 1979; children's books; Pres. MARÍA DI MASE; Gen. Man. ANA RODRÍGUEZ.

Monte Avila Editores Latinoamericana, CA: Centro Simón Bolívar, La Torre Norte, 22°, El Silencio, Caracas; tel. (212) 265-6020; fax (212) 263-8783; e-mail editorial@monteavila.gob.ve; internet www.monteavila.gob.ve; f. 1968; general; Pres. CARLOS NOGUERA.

Nueva Sociedad: Edif. IASA, 6°, Of. 606, Plaza La Castellana, Apdo 61712, Chacao, Caracas 1060-A; tel. (212) 265-0593; fax (212) 267-3397; e-mail nuso@nuevasoc.org.ve; internet www.nuevasoc.org.ve; f. 1972; social sciences; Dir DIETMAR DIRMOSER.

Directory

Ediciones Panamericanas EP, SRL: Edif. Freites, 2°, Avda Libertador cruce con Santiago de Chile, Apdo 14054, Caracas; tel. (212) 782-9891; Man. JAIME SALGADO PALACIO.

Oscar Todtmann Editores: Avda Libertador, Centro Comercial El Bosque, Local 4, Caracas 1050; tel. (212) 763-0881; fax (212) 762-5244; science, literature, photography; Dir CARSTEN TODTMANN.

Vadell Hermanos Editores, CA: Edif. Golden, Avda Sur 15, esq. Peligro a Pele el Ojo, Caracas; tel. (212) 572-3108; fax (212) 572-5243; e-mail edvadell1@cantv.net.ve; internet www.vadellhermanos.com; f. 1973; science, social science; Gen. Man. MANUEL VADELL GRATEROL.

Ediciones Vega, SRL: Edif. Odeon, Plaza Las Tres Gracias, Los Chaguaramos, Caracas 1050-A; tel. (212) 662-2092; fax (212) 662-1397; f. 1965; educational; Man. Dir FERNANDO VEGA ALONSO.

PUBLISHERS' ASSOCIATION

Cámara Venezolana del Libro: Centro Andrés Bello, Torre Oeste, 11°, Of. 112-0, Avda Andrés Bello, Caracas 1050-A; tel. (212) 793-1347; fax (212) 793-1368; f. 1969; Pres. HANS SCHNELL; Sec. ISIDORO DUARTE.

Broadcasting and Communications

TELECOMMUNICATIONS

Regulatory Authority

Comisión Nacional de Telecomunicaciones (CONATEL): Avda Veracruz con Cali, Edif. Conatel, 6°, Las Mercedes, Municipio Baruta, Caracas; tel. (212) 909-0510; fax (212) 993-6122; e-mail conatel@conatel.gov.ve; internet www.conatel.gov.ve; regulatory body for telecommunications; Dir-Gen. PEDRO ROLANDO MALDONADO MARÍN.

Major Service Providers

AT&T Venezuela: Edif. Centro Banaven, Avda La Estancia A, Chuao, Caracas 1060; internet www.att.com.

Compañía Anónima Nacional Teléfonos de Venezuela (CANTV): Edif. NEA, 20, Avda Libertador, Caracas 1010-A; tel. (212) 500-3016; fax (212) 500-3512; e-mail amora@cantv.com.ve; internet www.cantv.net; privatized in 1991; renationalized in 2007; Pres. SOCORRO HERNÁNDEZ.

 Movilnet: Edif. NEA, 20, Avda Libertador, Caracas 1010-A; tel. (202) 705-7901; e-mail info@movilnet.com.ve; internet www.movilnet.com.ve; f. 1992; mobile cellular telephone operator; owned by CANTV; 6.3m. subscribers (June 2006); Pres. MANUEL FERNÁNDEZ.

Digicel, CA: Caracas; internet www.digicel.com.ve; owned by Banco Santander Central Hispano of Spain; fixed-line telecommunications; 110,200 subscribers (June 2006).

Digitel TIM: Caracas; tel. (212) 280-5902; fax (212) 280-5943; e-mail 0412empres@digitel.com.ve; internet www.digitel.com.ve; f. 2000; mobile cellular telephone operator; owned by Telecom Italia, Italy; 2.4m. subscribers (June 2006); Pres. OSWALDO CISNEROS.

Intercable: Avda La Pedregosa Sur, cruce con Avda Los Próceres, Tapias; e-mail jguerrero@multimedios.net; internet www.intercable.net/default.asp; cable, internet and telecommunications services; Dir JUAN GERARDO GUERRERO.

Movistar: Edif. Parque Cristal, Torre Oeste, Avda Francisco Miranda, 14°, Los Palos Grandes, Caracas 1062; tel. (582) 201-8200; internet www.movistar.com.ve; f. 2005; subsidiary of Telefónica Móviles (Spain); 6.5m. subscribers (June 2006); Pres. LUIS MALVIDO.

NetUno: Edif. Insenica II, planta baja, Calle 7, La Urbina, Caracas; tel. (212) 710-0404; e-mail atccaracas@netuno.net; internet www.netuno.net; f. 1995; voice, data and video transmission services; Pres. GILBERT MINIONIS.

Telecom Venezuela: Torre Fondo Común, 5°, Avda Andrés Bello, Caracas; tel. (212) 393-2931; e-mail eauverana@cvgtelecom.com.ve; internet www.telecom.gob.ve; f. 2004 as CVG Telecomunicaciones, CA; present name adopted Aug. 2007; state-owned telecommunications co; Pres. CARMEN LEONOR MÁRQUEZ; Man. EVELYN AUVERANA.

Telecomunicaciones Gran Caribe: Caracas; f. 2007; owned by Telecom Venezuela (60%) and Transbit of Cuba (40%); construction and operation of 1,550 km fibre-optic cable connecting La Guaira (Venezuela) and Siboney (Cuba); Pres. WILFREDO MORALES.

BROADCASTING

Regulatory Authorities

Cámara Venezolana de la Industria de Radiodifusión: Avda Antonio José Istúriz entre Mohedano y Country Club, La Castellana, Caracas; tel. (212) 261-1651; fax (212) 261-4783; e-mail camradio@

VENEZUELA

camradio.org.ve; internet www.camradio.org; Pres. NELSON BELFORT.

Cámara Venezolana de Televisión por Suscripción: Edif. Banco Venezolano de Crédito, Avda Londres con Avda Principal de Las Mercedes, Caracas; tel. and fax (212) 993-7553; e-mail cavetesu@cavetesu.org.ve; internet www.cavetesu.org.ve; regulatory body for private stations; Pres. MARIO SEIJAS.

Radio

Radio Nacional de Venezuela (RNV): Final Calle Las Marías, entre Chapellín y Country Club, La Florida, Caracas 1050; tel. (212) 730-6022; fax (212) 731-1457; e-mail infornv@rnv.gob.ve; internet www.rnv.gov.ve; f. 1936; state broadcasting org.; 15 stations; Dir HELENA SALCEDO.

There are also 20 cultural and some 500 commercial stations.

Television

Government Stations

Telesur (Televisora del Sur): Edif. Telesur, Calle Vargas con Calle Santa Clara, Urb. Boleíta Norte, Caracas; tel. (212) 600-0202; e-mail contactenos@telesurtv.net; internet www.telesurtv.net; f. 2005; jtly owned by Govts of Venezuela (51%), Argentina (20%), Cuba (19%) and Uruguay (10%); regional current affairs and general interest; Pres. Lt (retd) ANDRÉS IZARRA; Vice-Pres. ARAM AHARONIAN.

Televisora Venezolana Social—Canal 2 (TVes): Quinta Thaizza, Avda Principal Augusto César Sandino con 10a Transversal, Maripérez, Municipio Libertador, Caracas; tel. (212) 781-8069; e-mail info@tves.com.ve; internet tvestv.blogspot.com; f. May 2007 to replace private channel RCTV (q.v.); govt-owned; Pres. LIL RODRÍGUEZ.

Venezolana de Televisión (VTV)—Canal 8: Edif. VTV, Avda Principal Los Ruices, Caracas; tel. (212) 207-1220; fax (212) 239-8102; e-mail web@vtv.gob.ve; internet www.vtv.gob.ve; f. 1964; 26 relay stations; Vice-Pres. VANESSA DAVIES.

ViVe TV (Visión Venezuela): Edif. Biblioteca Nacional, AP-4, Final Avda Panteón, Foro Libertador, Altagracia, Caracas; tel. (212) 505-1611; e-mail webmaster@vive.gob.ve; internet www.vive.gob.ve; f. 2003; govt-run cultural channel; Pres. RICARDO MÁRQUEZ.

Private Stations

Corporación Venezolana de Televisión (Venevisión)—Canal 4: Edif. Venevisión, final Avda La Salle, Colinas de los Caobos, Apdo 6674, Caracas; tel. (212) 708-9224; fax (212) 708-9535; e-mail mponce@venevision.com.ve; internet www.venevision.net; f. 1961; privately owned; Pres. GUSTAVO CISNEROS.

Globovisión—Canal 33: Quinta Globovisión, Avda Los Pinos, Urb. Alta Florida, Caracas; tel. (212) 730-2290; fax (212) 731-4380; e-mail info@globovision.com; internet www.globovision.com; f. 1994; 24-hour news and current affairs channel; Pres. GUILLERMO ZULOAGA; Dir-Gen. (vacant).

Meridiano Televisión: Caracas; e-mail opina@dearmas.com; internet www.meridiano.com.ve; f. 1997; sports programming; Pres. MARTÍN DE ARMAS; Dir-Gen. JUAN ANDRÉS DAZA.

Radio Caracas Televisión (RCTV): Edif. RCTV, Dolores a Puente Soublette, Quinta Crespo, Caracas; tel. (212) 401-2222; fax (212) 401-2647; e-mail marriaga@rctv.net; internet www.rctv.net; f. 1953; fmrly broadcast on terrestrial channel as Radio Caracas Televisión—Canal 2; ceased broadcasting in May 2007; subsidiary RCTV International (based in Miami, FL, USA) recommenced broadcasting in Venezuela via cable in July 2007; broadcasting licence of RCTV Internacional temporarily suspended in Jan. 2010; Pres. MARCEL GRANIER.

Televén—Canal 10 (Televisión de Venezuela): Edif. Televén, 4a Transversal con Avda Rómulo Gallegos, Urb. Horizonte, Apdo 1070, Caracas; tel. (212) 280-0011; fax (212) 280-0204; e-mail aferro@televen.com; internet www.televen.com; f. 1988; privately owned; Pres. OMAR CAMERO ZAMORA.

Televisora Andina de Mérida (TAM)—Canal 6: Edif. Imperador, Entrada Independiente, Avda 6 y 7, Calle 23, Mérida 5101; tel. and fax (274) 251-0660; f. 1982; regional channel; Pres. Most Rev. BALTAZAR ENRIQUE PORRAS CARDOZO.

VALE TV (Valores Educativos Televisión)—Canal 5: Quinta VALE TV, final Avda La Salle, Colinas de los Caobos, Caracas 1050; tel. (212) 793-9215; fax (212) 708-9743; e-mail info@valetv.com; internet www.valetv.com; f. 1998; Pres. JORGE CARDENAL L. UROSA SAVINO.

Zuliana de Televisión—Canal 30: Edif. 95.5 América, Avda 11 (Veritas), Maracaibo; tel. (265) 641-0355; fax (265) 641-0565; e-mail elregionalredac@iamnet.com; Pres. GILBERTO URDANETA FIDOL.

Zuvisión: Maracaibo; f. 2007; regional channel for the state of Zulia; Pres. RAFAEL URDANETA.

Finance

(cap. = capital; res = reserves; dep. = deposits; m. = million; brs = branches; amounts in bolívares unless otherwise indicated)

BANKING

Regulatory Authorities

Corporación de la Banca Pública (CBP): Caracas; f. 2009 to oversee all state-owned financial institutions; Supt EDGAR HERNÁNDEZ BEHRENS.

Superintendencia de Bancos (SUDEBAN): Edif. Centro Empresarial Parque del Este, Avda Francisco de Miranda, Urb. La Carlota, Municipio Sucre del Estado Miranda, Apdo 6761, Caracas; tel. (212) 280-6933; fax (212) 238-2516; e-mail sudeban@sudeban.gob.ve; internet www.sudeban.gob.ve; regulates banking sector; Supt EDGAR HERNÁNDEZ BEHRENS.

Central Bank

Banco Central de Venezuela: Avda Urdaneta, esq. de Carmelitas, Caracas 1010; tel. (212) 801-5111; fax (212) 861-0048; e-mail info@bcv.org.ve; internet www.bcv.org.ve; f. 1940; bank of issue and clearing house for commercial banks; granted autonomy 1992; controls international reserves, interest rates and exchange rates; cap. 10m., res 131,188,625m., dep. 73,298,601m. (Dec. 2007); Pres. and Chair. NELSON JOSÉ MERENTES DÍAZ; 2 brs.

Commercial Banks

Banco del Caribe, CA: Edif. Banco del Caribe, 1°, Dr Paúl a esq. Salvador de León, Apdo 6704, Carmelitas, Caracas 1010; tel. (212) 505-5103; fax (212) 562-0460; e-mail producto@bancaribe.com.ve; internet www.bancaribe.com.ve; f. 1954; cap. 201,000m., res 469,639m., dep. 6,701,991m. (Dec. 2008); Founding Pres. JUAN CARLOS DAO; Pres. MIGUEL IGNACIO PURROY; 70 brs and agencies.

Banco Caroní: Edif. Multicentro Banco Caroní, Vía Venezuela, Puerto Ordaz, Estado Bolívar; tel. (286) 950-5200; fax (286) 920-0995; e-mail contactenos.caroni@bancocaroni.com.ve; internet www.bancocaroni.com.ve; Pres. ARÍSTIDES MAZA TIRADO.

Banco de Comercio Exterior (Bancoex): Central Gerencial Mohedano, 1°, Calle Los Chaguaramos, La Castellana, Caracas 1060; tel. (212) 265-1433; fax (212) 265-6722; e-mail exports@bancoex.com; internet www.bancoex.com; f. 1997 principally to promote non-traditional exports; state-owned; cap. US $200m.; Pres. VÍCTOR ALVAREZ.

Banco Exterior, CA—Banco Universal: Edif. Banco Exterior, 1°, Avda Urdaneta, esq. Urapal a Río, Candelaria, Apdo 14278, Caracas 1011-A; tel. (212) 501-0211; fax (212) 501-0745; e-mail lperez@bancoexterior.com; internet www.bancoexterior.com; f. 1958; cap. 85,050m., res 84,518m., dep. 7,550670m. (Dec. 2008); Chair. JOSÉ LORETO ARISMENDI; Pres. RAÚL BALTAR ESTÉVEZ; 70 brs.

Banco Federal, CA: Torre Federal, Avda Venezuela, Urb. El Rosal, Caracas; tel. (268) 51-4011; e-mail masterbf@bancofederal.com; internet www.bancofederal.com; f. 1982; operations suspended June 2010; Pres. NELSON MEZERHANE; Exec. Pres. ROGELIO TRUJILLO.

Banco de Fomento Regional Coro, CA: Avda Manaure, entre Calles Falcón y Zamora, Coro, Falcón; tel. (268) 51-4421; f. 1950; transferred to private ownership in 1994; Pres. ABRAHAM NAÍN SENIOR URBINA.

Banco Guayana, CA: Edif. Los Bancos, Avda Guayana con Calle Caura, Puerto Ordaz, Bolívar; e-mail atencion.cliente@bancoguayana.net; internet www.bancoguayana.net; f. 1955; state-owned; Pres. OSCAR EUSEBIO JIMÉNEZ AYESA; Exec. Pres. BERNARDO KABCHE.

Banco Industrial de Venezuela, CA: Torre Financiera BIV, Avda Las Delicias de Sabana Grande, cruce con Avda Francisco Solano López, Caracas 1010; tel. (212) 952-4051; fax (212) 952-6282; e-mail webmaster@biv.com.ve; internet www.biv.com.ve; f. 1937; 98% state-owned; cap. 9,840m., res 278,645m., dep. 8,600,674m. (Dec. 2006); Pres. LUIS QUIARO; 60 brs.

Banco Occidental de Descuento Banco Universal, CA: Calle 77, esq. Avda 17, Maracaibo 4001, Apdo 695, Zulia; tel. (261) 759-3011; fax (261) 594-9811; e-mail atclient@bodinternet.com; internet www.bodinternet.com; f. 1957; transferred to private ownership in 1991; cap. 169,674m., res 970,738m., dep. 13,824,285m. (Dec. 2008); Pres. VÍCTOR J. VARGAS IRAUSQUIN; Exec. Pres. TOMÁS NIEMBRO CONCHA; 17 brs.

Banco Standard Chartered: Edif. Banaven, Torre D, 5°, Of. D52, Avda la Estancia, Chuao, Caracas 1060A; tel. (212) 993-0522; fax (212) 993-3130; internet www.standardchartered.com/ve; f. 1980 as Banco Exterior de los Andes y de España; current name adopted in 1998 following acquisition by Standard Chartered Bank (United Kingdom); representative office only; CEO JOHN LETO; 3 brs.

Banco de Venezuela, SA: Torre Banco de Venezuela, 16°, Avda Universidad, esq. Sociedad a Traposos, Apdo 6268, Caracas 1010-A;

VENEXUELA

tel. (212) 501-3333; fax (212) 501-2570; e-mail bancodevenezuela@banvenez.com; internet www.bancodevenezuela.com; f. 1890; nationalized in July 2009; cap. 40,524m., res 496,464m., dep. 16,837,805m. (Dec. 2006); Pres. HUMBERTO RAFAEL ORTEGA DÍAZ; 242 brs.

Banesco Banco Universal, CA: Edif. Banesco, 12°, Avda Guaicaipura con Avda Principal de Las Mercedes, Caracas; tel. (212) 952-4972; fax (212) 952-7124; e-mail atclient@banesco.com; internet www.banesco.com; cap. 1,050,000.0m., res 465,000.0m., dep. 32,749,000.0m. (Dec. 2008); Chair. JUAN CARLOS ESCOTET RODRÍGUEZ; Exec. Pres. LUIS XAVIER LUJÁN PUIGBÓ.

BBVA Banco Provincial, SA: Centro Financiero Provincial, 27°, Avda Vollmer con Avda Este O, San Bernadino, Apdo 1269, Caracas 1011; tel. (212) 504-5098; fax (212) 574-9408; e-mail calidad@provincial.com; internet www.provincial.com; f. 1952; 55.14% owned by Banco Bilbao Vizcaya Argentaria, 26.27% owned by Grupo Polar; cap. 1,078,274.7m., res 1,091,213.4m., dep. 17,131,652.6m. (Dec. 2007); Pres. LEÓN HENRIQUE COTTIN; Exec. Pres. PEDRO RODRÍGUEZ SERRANO.

Bicentenario Banco Universal: Caracas; internet www.banfoandes.com.ve; f. 2009 by merger of Banco Bolívar, Banco Confederado, Banfoandes and Banco Central; BaNorte incorporated in Jan. 2010; state-owned; Pres. KIMLEN CHANG DE NEGRÓN.

Corp Banca, CA Banco Universal: Torre Corp Banca, Plaza la Castellana, Chacao, Caracas 1060; tel. (212) 206-3333; fax (212) 206-4950; e-mail calidad@corpbanca.com.ve; internet www.corpbanca.com.ve; f. 1969; fmrly Banco Consolidado, current name adopted in 1997; cap. 40,000m., res 47,740m., dep. 2,754,500m. (Dec. 2006); Chair. JORGE SELUME ZAROR; CEO MARIO CHAMORRO; 116 brs.

Mercantil CA Banco Universal: Edif. Mercantil, 35°, Avda Andrés Bello 1, San Bernardino, Apdo 789, Caracas 1010-A; tel. (212) 503-1111; fax (212) 503-1075; e-mail mercan24@bancomercantil.com; internet www.bancomercantil.com; f. 1925; cap. 268,060m., res 208,730m., dep. 28,807,177m. (Dec. 2008); Chair. and CEO Dr GUSTAVO A. MARTURET; 309 brs.

Unibanca Banco Universal, CA: Torre Grupo Unión, Avda Universidad, esq. El Chorro, Apdo 2044, Caracas; tel. (212) 501-7031; fax (212) 563-0986; internet www.unibanca.com.ve; f. 2001 by merger of Banco Unión (f. 1943) and Caja Familia; Pres. Dr IGNACIO SALVATIERRA; Vice-Pres. JOSÉ Q. SALVATIERRA; 174 brs.

Venezolano de Crédito, SA—Banco Universal: Edif. Banco Venezolano de Crédito, Avda Alameda, San Bernadino, Caracas 1011; tel. (212) 806-6111; fax (212) 541-2757; e-mail info@venezolano.com; internet www.venezolano.com; f. 1925 as Banco Venezolano de Crédito, SACA; name changed as above in 2001; cap. 69,888m., res 118,846m., dep. 3,811,053m. (Dec. 2008); Pres. Dr OSCAR GARCÍA MENDOZA; 95 brs in Venezuela and abroad.

Development Banks

Banco de Desarrollo Económico y Social de Venezuela (BANDES): Torre Bandes, Avda Universidad, Traposos a Colón, Caracas 1010; tel. (212) 505-8010; fax (212) 505-8030; e-mail apublicos@bandes.gov.ve; internet www.bandes.gov.ve; state-owned; Pres. EDMÉE BETANCOURT DE GARCÍA.

Banco de Desarrollo de la Mujer (BANMUJER): Edif. Sudameris, planta baja, Avda Urdaneta, entre Plaza España y esq. de Animas, Caracas 1010; tel. (212) 564-3015; fax (212) 564-4087; e-mail banmujer@cantv.net; internet www.banmujer.gob.ve; f. 2001; state-owned bank offering loans to women; Pres. NORA CASTAÑEDA.

Banco del Pueblo Soberano, CA: Edif. El Gallo de Oro, Gradillas a San Jacinto Parroquia Catedral, Caracas; tel. (212) 505-2800; fax (212) 505-2995; e-mail abarrera@bancodelpueblo.gob.ve; internet www.bancodelpueblo.gob.ve; f. 1999; microfinance; Pres. DARÍO ENRIQUE BAUTE DELGADO.

Banco del Sur: Caracas; e-mail atencionalcliente@delsur.com.ve; internet www.delsur.com.ve; f. 2007 by Govts of Argentina, Bolivia, Brazil, Ecuador, Paraguay, Uruguay and Venezuela; regional devt bank; brs in Buenos Aires (Argentina) and La Paz (Bolivia); Pres. CÉSAR NAVARRETE.

Fondo de Desarrollo Microfinanciero (FONDEMI): Edif. Sudameris, 2°, Avda Urdaneta con Fuerzas Armadas, esq. Plaza España, Caracas 1030; tel. (212) 287-7611; fax (212) 287-7658; e-mail fondemi@fondemi.gob.ve; internet www.fondemi.gob.ve; f. 2001; microfinancing devt fund; Pres. ISA MERCEDES SIERRA FLORES.

Banking Association

Asociación Bancaria de Venezuela: Torre Asociación Bancaria de Venezuela, 1°, Avda Venezuela, El Rosal, Caracas; tel. (212) 951-4711; fax (212) 951-3696; e-mail abvinfo@asobanca.com.ve; internet www.asobanca.com.ve; f. 1959; 49 mems; Pres. JUAN CARLOS ESCOTET; Exec. Dir LARRY M. DE CRACCO.

STOCK EXCHANGE

Bolsa de Valores de Caracas, CA: Edif. Atrium, Nivel C-1, Calle Sorocaima entre Avdas Tamanaco y Venezuela, Urb. El Rosal, Apdo 62724-A, Caracas 1060-A; tel. (212) 905-5511; fax (212) 952-2640; e-mail bvc@bolsadecaracas.com; internet www.bolsadecaracas.com; f. 1947; 65 mems; Pres. NELSON ORTIZ CUSNIER.

INSURANCE

Supervisory Board

Superintendencia de Seguros: Edif. Torre del Desarollo, PH, Avda Venezuela, El Rosal, Chacao, Caracas 1060; tel. (212) 905-1611; fax (212) 953-8615; e-mail sudeseg@sudeseg.gob.ve; internet www.sudeseg.gob.ve; Supt JOSÉ LUÍS PÉREZ.

Principal Insurance Companies

Adriática, CA de Seguros: Edif. Adriática de Seguros, Avda Andrés Bello, esq. de Salesianos, Caracas; tel. (212) 571-5702; fax (212) 571-0812; e-mail adriatica@adriatica.com.ve; internet www.adriatica.com.ve; f. 1952; Pres. FRANÇOIS THOMAZEAU; Exec. Vice-Pres. GHISLAIN FABRE.

Avila, CA de Seguros: Edif. Torre Británica de Seguros, PH, Avda José Felix Sosa, Urb. El Dorado, Altamira, Chacao, Caracas; tel. (212) 238-2470; fax (212) 239-9743; f. 1936; Pres. RAMÓN RODRÍGUEZ; Vice-Pres. JUAN LUIS CASAÑAS.

Bolivariana de Seguros: Caracas; f. 2010; state-owned; Pres. JESÚS TOVAR JIMÉNEZ.

Carabobo, CA de Seguros: Edif. Mene Grande, 7°, Avda Francisco de Miranda, Urb. Los Palos Grandes, Caracas; tel. (212) 620-7193; fax (212) 620-7320; e-mail aehernandez@seguroscarabobo.com; internet www.seguroscarabobo.com; f. 1955; Pres. PAUL FRAYND; Gen. Man. ANDRÉS HERNÁNDEZ.

Mapfre La Seguridad, CA de Seguros: Calle 3A, Frente a La Torre Express, La Urbina Sur, Apdo 473, Caracas 1010; tel. (212) 213-8000; fax (212) 204-8751; e-mail endirecto@mapfre.com.ve; internet www.mapfre.com.ve; f. 1943; owned by Seguros Mapfre (Spain); Pres. ARISTÓBULO BAUSELA.

La Occidental, CA de Seguros: Edif. Seguros Occidental, Avda 4 (Bella Vista) esq. con Calle 71, No 10126, Maracaibo, Zulia; tel. (261) 796-2226; fax (261) 796-2293; e-mail clientes@laoccidental.com; internet www.laoccidental.com; f. 1956; Pres. TOBÍAS CARRERO NÁCAR; Dir CARLOS MONÍZ ROCHA.

La Oriental, CA de Seguros: Torre Oriental de Seguros, Avda Venezuela, entre Calle Sojo y Avda Sorocaima, Urb. El Rosal, Chacao, Caracas 1060; tel. (212) 905-9999; fax (212) 905-9652; internet www.laoriental.com; f. 1975; Pres. GONZALO LAURÍA ALCALÁ.

Seguros Los Andes, CA: Edif. Central, 5°, Avda San Felipe, entre 1a y 2a Transversal, La Castellana, Caracas; tel. (276) 266-5020; fax (276) 340-2596; internet www.seguroslosandes.com; Pres. RAMÓN RODRÍGUEZ.

Seguros Caracas de Liberty Mutual, CAV: Torre Seguros Caracas C-4, Centro Comercial El Parque, Avda Francisco de Miranda, Los Palos Grandes, Caracas; tel. (212) 209-9111; fax (212) 209-9556; e-mail informatica@seguroscaracas.com; internet www.seguroscaracas.com; f. 1943; Pres. ROBERTO SALAS; Regional Man. ANDRÉS VERROCCHI.

Seguros Catatumbo, CA: Edif. Seguros Catatumbo, Avda 4 (Bella Vista), No 77–55, Apdo 1083, Maracaibo; tel. (261) 700-5555; fax (261) 216-0037; e-mail mercado@seguroscatatumbo.com; internet www.seguroscatatumbo.com; f. 1957; cap. 9,300m. (2003); Pres. ERNESTO PINEDA HERNÁNDEZ; Dir-Gen. RAFAEL ARRAGA HUERTA.

Seguros Mercantil, CA: Edif. Seguros Mercantil, Avda Libertador con calle Andrés Galarraga, Chacao, Caracas; tel. (212) 276-2000; fax (212) 276-2596; e-mail cat@segurosmercantil.com; internet www.segurosmercantil.com; f. 1988; acquired Seguros Orinoco in 2002; Pres. ALBERTO BENSHIMOL; Gen. Man. MARÍA SILVIA RODRÍGUEZ FEO.

Seguros Nuevo Mundo, SA: Torre Nuevo Mundo, Avda Luis Roche con 3a Transversal, Urb. Altamira, Apdo 2062, Caracas; tel. (212) 201-1111; fax (212) 201-1428; e-mail luis.sanelli@nuevomundo.com.ve; internet www.nuevomundo.com.ve; f. 1856; cap. 100m. (2003); Pres. RAFAEL PEÑA ALVAREZ; Sec. JUAN CARLOS TRIVELLA.

Seguros La Previsora, CNA: Torre La Previsora, Avda Abraham Lincoln, Sábana Grande, Caracas; tel. (212) 709-1555; fax (212) 709-1976; internet www.previsora.com; f. 1914; nationalized in Dec. 2009; Pres. ALBERTO QUINTANA; Exec. Vice-Pres. JUAN CARLOS MALDONADO.

Seguros Venezuela, CA: Edif. Seguros Venezuela, 8° y 9°, Avda Francisco de Miranda, Urb. Campo Alegre, Caracas; tel. (212) 901-7111; fax (212) 901-7218; e-mail carmen.guillen@segurosvenezuela.com; internet www.segurosvenezuela.com; f. 1948; part of American International group; Exec. Pres. ENRIQUE BANCHIERI ORTIZ.

VENEZUELA

Universitas de Seguros, CA: Edif. Impres Médico, 2°, Avda Tamanaco, El Rosal, Caracas; tel. (212) 951-6711; fax (212) 901-7506; e-mail tbarrera@universitasdeseguros.com; internet www.universitasdeseguros.com; cap. 6,500m; Pres. ANA TERESA FERRINI.

Insurance Association

Cámara de Aseguradores de Venezuela: Torre Taeca, 2°, Avda Guaicaipuro, Urb. El Rosal, Apdo 3460, Caracas 1010-A; tel. (212) 952-4411; fax (212) 951-3268; e-mail rrpp@camaraseg.org; internet www.camaraseg.org; f. 1951; 42 mems; Pres. GONZALO LAURIA ALCALA; Exec. Pres. ALESIA RODRIGUÉZ PARDO.

Trade and Industry

GOVERNMENT AGENCIES

Comisión de Administración de Divisas (CADIVI): Antiguo Edif. PDVSA Servicios, 6°, Avda Leonardo Da Vinci, Los Chaguaramos, Caracas; tel. (212) 606-3904; fax (212) 606-3026; e-mail info@cadivi.gov.ve; internet www.cadivi.gob.ve; f. 2003; regulates access to foreign currency; Pres. WILLIAM CONTRERAS.

Corporación Venezolana de Guayana (CVG): Edif. General, 2°, Avda La Estancia, Apdo 7000, Chuao, Caracas; tel. (212) 992-1813; fax (212) 993-4306; e-mail presidenciaccs@cvg.com; internet www.cvg.com; f. 1960 to organize devt of Guayana area, particularly its metal ore and hydroelectric resources; Pres. JOSÉ SALAMAT KHAN FERNÁNDEZ (Minister of Basic Industry and Mining); 15 subsidiaries; 18,000 employees.

Instituto Nacional de Tierras (INTI): Quinta La Barranca, Calle San Carlos, Urb. Vista Alegre, Caracas; tel. (212) 574-8554; fax (212) 576-2201; internet www.inti.gob.ve; f. 1945 as Instituto Agrario Nacional (IAN); present name adopted in 2001; established under Agrarian Law to assure ownership of the land to those who worked on it; now authorized to expropriate and redistribute idle or unproductive lands; Pres. JUAN CARLOS LOYO.

Instituto Nacional de la Vivienda: Torre Inavi, Avda Francisco de Miranda, Chacao, Caracas; tel. (212) 206-9279; e-mail comunica@inavi.gov.ve; internet www.inavi.gob.ve; f. 1975; administers govt housing projects; Pres. PABLO JOSÉ PEÑA CHAPARRO; Gen. Man. ALDO REYES CHACÓN.

Mercal, CA: Edif. Torres Seguros Orinoco, Avda Fuerzas Armadas, esq. Socarras, Caracas; tel. (212) 564-3856; e-mail fosorio@correo.mercal.gob.ve; internet www.mercal.gob.ve; responsible for marketing agricultural products; fmrly Corporación de Mercadeo Agrícola; Pres. Lt-Col FÉLIX OSORIO GUZMÁN.

Ministry of Energy and Petroleum: see The Government—Ministries.

Superintendencia de Inversiones Extranjeras (SIEX): Edif. La Perla, esq. La Bolsa a Mercaderes, 3° y 5°, Capitolio, Caracas 1010; tel. (212) 483-6666; fax (212) 484-4368; e-mail siexdespacho@cantv.net; internet www.siex.gob.ve; f. 1974; supervises foreign investment in Venezuela; Supt MANUEL FIGUEROA.

DEVELOPMENT ORGANIZATIONS

Fondo para el Desarrollo Agrario Socialista (FONDAS): Edif. FONDAFA, esq. Salvador de León a Socarras, La Hoyada, Caracas; tel. (212) 542-3570; fax (212) 542-5887; internet www.fondas.gob.ve; f. 1974; devt of agriculture, fishing and forestry; Pres. RICARDO JAVIER SÁNCHEZ.

Fondo de Desarrollo Microfinanciero (FONDEMI): see Finance—Development Banks.

Instituto de Desarrollo de la Pequeña y Mediana Industria (INAPYMI): Torre Británica, 14°, 15°, 16° y planta baja, Avda José Felix Sosa, Altamira Sur, Caracas; tel. (212) 276-9511; e-mail zcarrillo@inapymi.gob.ve; internet www.inapymi.gob.ve; f. 2001; govt agency; promotes the devt of small and medium-sized industries; Pres. PATRICIA FEBLES MONTES; Exec. Dir ZAIDA MARÍA CARRILLO.

CHAMBERS OF COMMERCE AND INDUSTRY

Federación Venezolana de Cámaras y Asociaciones de Comercio y Producción (Fedecámaras): Edif. Fedecámaras, Avda El Empalme, Urb. El Bosque, Apdo 2568, Caracas; tel. (212) 731-1711; fax (212) 730-2097; e-mail presidencia@fedecamaras.org.ve; internet www.fedecamaras.org.ve; f. 1944; 307 mems; Pres. NOEL ALVAREZ C.; Gen. Man. GILBERTO DELGADO G.

Cámara de Comercio, Industria y Servicios de Caracas: Edif. Cámara de Comercio de Caracas, 8°, Avda Andrés Eloy Blanco 215, Los Caobos, Caracas; tel. (212) 571-3222; fax (212) 571-0050; e-mail comunicaciones@lacamaradecaracas.org.ve; internet www.lacamaradecaracas.org.ve; f. 1893; 650 mems; Pres. Dr DIANA MAYORAL; Exec. Dir VÍCTOR MALDONADO.

Cámara Venezolano-Americana de Industria y Comercio (Venamcham): Torre Credival, 10°, Of. A, 2a Avda Campo Alegre, Apdo 5181, Caracas 1010-A; tel. (212) 263-0833; fax (212) 263-2060; e-mail venam@venamcham.org; internet www.venamcham.org; f. 1950; Pres. CARLOS HENRIQUE BLOHM; Gen. Man. CARLOS TEJERA.

There are chambers of commerce and industry in all major provincial centres.

EMPLOYERS' ORGANIZATIONS

Caracas

Asociación Nacional de Industriales Metalúrgicos y de Minería de Venezuela (AIMM): Centro Empresarial Senderos, 3°, Ofs 302 y 303A, Avda Principal Los Cortijos de Lourdes, 2a Transversal, Sucre, Caracas 1071; tel. and fax (212) 237-5169; e-mail aimmv@cantv.net; internet www.aimm-ven.org; metallurgy and mining; Pres. EDUARDO GARMENDIA; Exec. Dir MARÍA GRACIELA FERREIRA.

Asociación Textil Venezolana: Edif. Textilera Gran Colombia, Calle el Club 8, Los Cortijos de Lourdes, Caracas; tel. (212) 238-1744; fax (212) 239-4089; f. 1957; textiles; Pres. DAVID FIHMAN; 68 mems.

Asociación Venezolana de Exportadores (AVEX): Centro Comercial Concresa, Of. 435, 2°, Prados del Este, Avda Río Caura, Baruta, Caracas; tel. (212) 979-5042; fax (212) 979-4542; e-mail asistentedepresidencia@avex.com.ve; internet www.avex.com.ve; Pres. ALBA GUEVARA; Gen. Man. MARÍA ISABEL SÁEZ.

Cámara Petrolera: Torre Domus, 3°, Of. 3-A, Avda Abraham Lincoln con Calle Olimpo, Sábana Grande, Caracas; tel. (212) 794-1222; fax (212) 793-8529; e-mail informacion@camarapetrolera.org; internet www.camarapetrolera.org; f. 1978; asscn of petroleum-sector cos; Pres. MAURICIO CANARD MENDOZA; Exec. Dir RONALD RIVAS.

Confederación Nacional de Asociaciones de Productores Agropecuarios (FEDEAGRO): Edif. Casa de Italia, planta baja, Avda La Industria, San Bernardino, Caracas 1010; tel. (212) 571-4035; fax (212) 573-4423; e-mail fedeagro@fedeagro.org; internet www.fedeagro.org; f. 1960; agricultural producers; 133 affiliated asscns; Pres. PEDRO RIVAS ISMAYEL.

Confederación Venezolana de Industriales (CONINDUSTRIA): Edif. CIEMI, Avda Principal de Chuao, Caracas 1061; tel. (212) 991-2116; fax (212) 991-7737; e-mail conindustria@conindustria.org; internet www.conindustria.org; asscn of industrialists; Pres. CARLOS LARRAZABAL; Exec. Pres. ISMAEL PÉREZ VIGIL.

Federación Nacional de Ganaderos de Venezuela (FEDENAGA): Avda Urdaneta, Centro Financiero Latino, 18°, Ofs 18-2 y 18-4, La Candelaria, Caracas; tel. (212) 563-2153; fax (212) 564-7273; e-mail fedenagat@cantv.net; internet www.fedenaga.org; f. 1962; cattle owners; Pres. MANUEL CIPRIANO HEREDIA C.

Unión Patronal Venezolana del Comercio: Edif. General Urdaneta, 2°, Marrón a Pelota, Apdo 6578, Caracas; tel. (582) 561-7025; fax (582) 561-4321; trade; Sec. H. ESPINOZA BANDERS.

Other Towns

Asociación de Comerciantes e Industriales del Zulia (ACIZ): Edif. Los Cerros, 9°, Calle 77 con Avda 3c, Apdo 91, Maracaibo, Zulia; tel. (261) 91-7064; fax (261) 92-0907; e-mail info@aciz.org; f. 1941; traders and industrialists; Pres. DANIEL HÓMEZ.

Asociación Nacional de Cultivadores de Algodón (ANCA) (National Cotton Growers' Association): Edif. Portuguesa, Avda Los Pioneros, Sector Aspiga-Acarigua; tel. (255) 621-5111; fax (255) 621-4368; e-mail anca@asoanca.com; Pres. CONCEPCIÓN QUIJADA G.

Asociación Nacional de Empresarios y Trabajadores de la Pesca: Cumaná; fishermen's org.

Unión Nacional de Cultivadores de Tabaco: Urb. Industrial La Hamaca, Avda Hustaf Dalen, Maracay; tobacco growers.

STATE HYDROCARBONS COMPANIES

PDVSA Petróleo SA: Edif. Petróleos de Venezuela, Torre Este, Avda Libertador, La Campiña, Apdo 169, Caracas 1010-A; tel. (212) 708-4743; fax (212) 708-4661; e-mail saladeprensa@pdvsa.com; internet www.pdvsa.com; f. 1975; responsible for petrochemical sector since 1978 and for devt of coal resources in western Venezuela since 1985; in 1997 the three operating branches (Lagoven SA, Maraven SA and Corpoven SA) were reintegrated to form PDVSA Petróleo y Gas; in 2001 gas related activity passed to PDVSA Gas; state-owned, under control of the Ministry of Energy and Petroleum; Pres. RAFAEL DARÍO RAMÍREZ CARREÑO (Minister of Energy and Petroleum); Vice-Pres. of Exploration and Production EULOGIO DEL PINO; Vice-Pres. of Refining ASDRÚBAL CHÁVEZ; the following are subsidiaries of PDVSA:

Bariven, SA: Edif. PDVSA Los Chaguaramos, 6°, Avda Leonardo Da Vinci, Urb. Los Chaguaramos, Apdo 1889, Caracas 1010-A; tel.

VENEZUELA

(212) 606-4060; fax (212) 606-2741; handles the petroleum, petrochemical and hydrocarbons industries' overseas purchases of equipment and materials.

Corporación Venezolana del Petróleo (CVP): Edif. Pawa, Calle Cali con Avda Veracruz, Las Mercedes, Caracas; f. 1960, reformed 2003; responsible for PDVSA's negotiations with other petroleum cos.

Deltaven, SA: Edif. PDVSA Deltaven, Avda Principal de La Floresta, La Floresta, Caracas 1060; tel. (212) 208-1111; f. 1997; markets PDVSA products and services within Venezuela.

Intevep, SA: Centro de Investigación y Apoyo Tecnológico, Edif. Sede Central, Urb. Santa Rosa, Sector El Tambor, Los Teques, Apdo 76343, Caracas 1070-A; tel. (212) 330-6011; fax (212) 330-6448; f. 1973 as Fundación para la Investigación de Hidrocarburos y Petroquímica; present name adopted in 1979; research and devt br. of PDVSA.

Palmaven: Avda Principal de la Urbina, Torre Olimpia, 7°, Caracas; tel. (212) 204-4511; sustainable devt agency of PDVSA; Man. Dir EDDIE RAMÍREZ.

PDV Marina: Edif. Petróleos de Venezuela Refinación, Suministro y Comercio, Torre Oeste, 9°, Avda Libertador, La Campiña, Apdo 2103, Caracas 1010-A; tel. (212) 708-1111; fax (212) 708-2200; f. 1990; responsible for the distribution, by ship, of PDVSA products.

PDVSA Gas: Edif. Sucre, Avda Francisco de Miranda, La Floresta, Caracas; tel. (212) 208-6212; fax (212) 208-6288; e-mail messina@pdvsa.com; f. 1998; gas exploration and extraction; Pres. WUILMAN PAREIRA.

Pequiven (Petroquímica de Venezuela, SA): Zona Industrial Municipal Sur, Avda 73, con Calle 79B, Valencia, Carabobo; tel. (241) 839-4665; e-mail deinterespequiven@pequiven.com; internet www.pequiven.com; f. 1956 as Instituto Venezolano de Petroquímica; became Pequiven in 1977; involved in many joint ventures with foreign and private Venezuelan interests for expanding petrochemical industry; active in regional economic integration; an affiliate of PDVSA from 1978 until 2005; thereafter state-owned, under Ministry of Energy and Petroleum; Pres. CLARK INCIARTE.

UTILITIES

Electricity

Corporación Eléctrica Nacional (Corpoelec): Edif. Centro Eléctrico Nacional, Avda Sanz, Urb. El Marqués, Sucre, Caracas; tel. (212) 280-8111; internet www.corpoelec.gob.ve; f. 2007; generation, transmission, distribution and marketing of electric power and energy; incorporated Edelca, La Nueva Electricidad de Caracas, ENELVEN, ENELCO, ENELBAR, CADAFE, GENEVAPCA, ELEBOL, ELEVAL, Seneca, ENAGAS, TURBOVEN into one corpn in 2010; state-owned; Chair. HIPÓLITO IZQUIERDO GARCÍA; Dir (Generation) JESÚS RANGEL; Dir (Distribution) KHALED ORTÍZ VILLEGAS; Dir (Commercial) JAVIER ALVARADO OCHOA.

CADAFE (Compañía de Administración y Fomento Eléctrico): Edif. Centro Eléctrico Nacional, 14°, Avda Sanz, Urb. El Marqués, Sucre, Caracas; tel. (212) 280-8583; fax (212) 280-8667; e-mail dirgestion@cadafe.com.ve; internet www.cadafe.com.ve; f. 1958; electricity transmission.

La Electricidad de Caracas (EDC): Edif. La Electricidad de Caracas, Avda Vollmer, Urb. San Bernadino, Apdo 2299, Caracas 1010-A; tel. (212) 502-2111; e-mail info@edc-ven.com; internet www.laedc.com.ve; supplies electricity to Caracas.

Electrificación del Caroní, CA (Edelca): Edif. General, planta baja, Avda La Estancia, Chuao, Caracas; tel. (212) 950-2111; fax (212) 950-2808; e-mail asuntos-publicos@edelca.com.ve; internet www.edelca.com.ve; supplies some 70% of the country's electricity.

Enelbar (Energía Eléctrica de Barquisimeto): Edif. Sede, Avda Francisco de Miranda, Carora, Barquisimeto; tel. (251) 239-4050; internet www.enelbar.com.ve.

Enelco (Energía Eléctrica de la Costa Oriental): Edif. Sumnistro, Calle Rosario 32, Urb. La Rosa, Cabimas, Miranda; tel. (264) 370-5555; e-mail atencionalcliente@enelco.com.ve; internet www.enelco.com.ve; electricity services to the eastern coast of the Lago de Maracaibo region.

Enelven (Energía Eléctrica de Venezuela): Calle 77, entre Avda 10 y 11, Maracaibo; tel. (261) 790-3800; e-mail asuntospublicos@enelven.com.ve; internet www.enelven.gob.ve.

Gas

ENAGAS (Ente Nacional del Gas): Calle Panamá con Avda Libertador, 8°, Urb. Los Caobos, Caracas; tel. (212) 706-6654; fax (212) 706-6471; e-mail presidencia@enagas.gov.ve; internet www.enagas.gob.ve; f. 1999; subsidiary of Corpoelec; Pres. JORGE LUIS SÁNCHEZ.

Water

Hidroven: Edif. Hidroven, Avda Augusto César Sandino con 9a Transversal, Maripérez, Caracas; tel. (212) 781-4778; fax (212) 781-6424; e-mail ngamboa@cantv.net; internet www.hidroven.gov.ve; national water co; owns Hidroandes, Hidrocapital, Hidrocaribe, Hidrofalcon, Hidrolago, Hidrollanos, Hidropaez, Hidrosuroeste, Aguas de Monagas, Aguas de Ejido, Hidrolara, Aguas de Anaco, Aguas de Cojedes, Aguas de Mérida, Aguas de Apure, Aguas de Yaracuy, Aguas de Portuguesa; Pres. CRISTÓBAL FRANCISCO ORTIZ; Vice-Pres. FRANCISCO DURÁN.

Compañía Anónima Hidrológica de la Región Capital (Hidrocapital): Edif. Hidrocapital, Avda Augusto César Sandino con 9a Transversal, Maripérez, Caracas; tel. (212) 793-1638; fax (212) 793-6794; internet www.hidrocapital.com.ve; f. 1992; operates water supply in Federal District and states of Miranda and Vargas; Pres. ALEJANDRO HITCHER.

TRADE UNIONS

About one-quarter of the labour force in Venezuela belongs to a trade union. Most unions in Venezuela are legally recognized. The country's union movement is strongest in the public sector.

Confederación de Trabajadores de Venezuela (CTV) (Confederation of Venezuelan Workers): Edif. José Vargas, 17°, Avda Este 2, Los Caobos, Caracas; tel. (212) 574-1049; e-mail ctv@ctv.org.ve; internet www.ctv.org.ve; f. 1936; largest trade union confederation; principally active in public sector; Chávez Govt disputes legitimacy of election of CTV leadership; Pres. CARLOS ALFONSO ORTEGA CARVAJAL; Sec.-Gen. MANUEL JOSÉ COVA FERMÍN; 26 regional and 57 industrial feds.

Fedepetrol: union of petroleum workers; Pres. RAFAEL ROSALES.

Federación Campesina (FC): peasant union; CTV affiliate; Leader RUBÉN LANZ.

Fetrametal: union of metal workers; Leader JOSÉ MOLLEGAS.

Fuerza Bolivariana de Trabajadores (FBT): f. 2000; pro-Govt union.

Unión Nacional de Trabajadores (UNT): f. 2003; pro-Govt federation; Nat. Co-ordinators STALIN PÉREZ BORGES, ORLANDO CHIRINO.

Other trade union federations include the Alianza Sindical Independiente (ASI), the Central Unitaria de Trabajadores de Venezuela (CUTV), the Confederación de Sindicatos Autónomos de Venezuela (CODESA) and the Confederación General de Trabajadores de Venezuela (CGT).

Transport

RAILWAYS

The 1999 Constitution included provision for renovation of the national rail network. In 2006 a 41.4-km railway line from Caracas to Cúa was opened. A 173.7-km railway line linking Puerto Cabello to Acarigua was also in operation. In 2011 a line linking Puerto Cabello and La Encrucijada in the centre of the country was completed and was expected to commence operations in 2012, as was a 468-km line connecting Anaco and Tinaco. Other lines under construction included: a 252.5-km line connecting San Juan de los Moros and San Fernando de Apure; a 44.3-km line linking Acarigua and Turén; and a 201-km line between Chaguaramas and Cabruta.

CVG Ferrominera Orinoco, CA: Edif. Administrativo, Vía Caracas, Puerto Ordaz, Apdo 399, Bolívar; tel. (286) 930-3775; fax (286) 930-3783; e-mail contacto@ferrominera.com; internet www.ferrominera.com; f. 1976; part of state-owned Corporación Venezolana de Guayana (see Trade and Industry—Government Agencies); operates two lines, San Isidro mine–Puerto Ordaz (316 km) and El Pao–Palua (55 km), for transporting iron ore; Pres. RADWAN SABBAGH.

Ferrocarril de CVG Bauxilum—Operadora de Bauxita: Edif. Administrativo, Avda Fuerzas Armadas, Zona Industrial Matanzas, Ciudad Guayana, Bolívar; tel. (286) 950-6271; fax (286) 950-6270; e-mail asuntos.publicos@bauxilum.com.ve; internet www.bauxilum.com; f. 1989; state-owned; operates line linking Los Pijiguaos with river Orinoco port of Gumilla (52 km) for transporting bauxite; Pres. JOSÉ CHINA.

Instituto de Ferrocarriles del Estado (IFE): Edif. Torre Británica de Seguros, 7° y 8°, Avda José Félix Sosa, Urb. Altamira, Chacao, Caracas 1062-A; tel. (212) 201-8736; fax (212) 201-8902; e-mail tlopez@ife.gob.ve; internet www.ife.gob.ve; state co; Pres. FRANKLIN PÉREZ COLINA.

CA Metro de Caracas: Multicentro Empresarial del Este, Edif. Miranda, Torre B, 7°, Avda Francisco de Miranda, Calle Los Maristas, Apdo 61036, Caracas; tel. (212) 206-7111; fax (212) 266-3346; e-mail sugerencias@metrodecaracas.com.ve; internet www.metrodecaracas.com.ve; f. 1976 to supervise the construction and use of the underground railway system; services began in 1983; state-owned; Pres. HAIMAN EL TROUDI.

ROADS

In 2004 there were an estimated 96,200 km of roads, of which 32,300 km were paved. Responsibility for road maintenance generally lies with state governments; however, legislation adopted in 2009 allowed the central Government to take control of motorways and major roads, as well as ports and airports.

INLAND WATERWAYS

Instituto Nacional de Canalizaciones: Edif. INC, Calle Caracas, al lado de la Torre Diamen, Chuao, Caracas; tel. (212) 908-5106; fax (212) 959-6906; e-mail atencionalciudadano@incanal.gov.ve; internet www.incanal.gov.ve; f. 1952; semi-autonomous institution; Pres. JUAN CARLOS FERRER SÁNCHEZ; Vice-Pres. SEGUNDO RAMÓN JUSTO PINTO.

SHIPPING

There are 13 major ports, 34 petroleum and mineral ports and five fishing ports. The main ports for imports are La Guaira, the port for Caracas, and Puerto Cabello, which handles raw materials for the industrial region around Valencia. Maracaibo is the chief port for the petroleum industry. Puerto Ordaz, on the Orinoco River, was also developed to deal with the shipments of iron from Cerro Bolívar.

Consolidada de Ferrys, CA (CONFERRY): Edif. Conferry, Planta Baja, Of. Comercial, Avda Terranova con Llano Adentro, Porlamar, Isla de Margarita; tel. (295) 263-9878; fax (295) 263-8372; internet www.conferry.com; f. 1970; ferry services to Margarita island; Pres. RODOLFO JOSÉ TOVAR MATA.

Corpoven, SA: Edif. Petróleos de Venezuela, Avda Libertador, La Campiña, Apdo 61373, Caracas 1060-A; tel. (212) 708-1111; fax (212) 708-1833; Pres. Dr ROBERTO MANDINI; Vice-Pres. JUAN CARLOS GÓMEZ; 2 oil tankers.

Lagoven, SA: Edif. Lagovén, Avda Leonardo da Vinci, Los Chaguaramos, Apdo 889, Caracas; tel. (212) 606-3311; fax (212) 606-3637; f. 1978 as a result of the nationalization of the petroleum industry; fmrly Creole Petroleum Group; transports crude petroleum and by-products between Maracaibo, Aniba and other ports in the area; Pres. B. R. NATERA; Marine Man. P. D. CAREZIS; 10 tankers.

Transpapel, CA: Edif. Centro, 11°, Of. 111, Centro Parque Boyaca, Avda Sucre, Los Dos Caminos, Apdo 61316, Caracas 1071; tel. (212) 283-8366; fax (212) 285-7749; e-mail nmaldonado@cantv.net; f. 1985; Chair. GUILLERMO ESPINOSA F.; Man. Dir Capt. NELSON MALDONADO.

CIVIL AVIATION

There are two adjacent airports 13 km from Caracas: Maiquetía for domestic and Simón Bolívar for international services. There are 11 international airports.

Regulatory Authority

Instituto Nacional de Aeronáutica Civil: Torre Británica, Urb. Altamira Sur, Avda José Félix Sosa, Chacao, Caracas 1060; tel. (212) 277-4411; e-mail contacto@inac.gov.ve; internet www.inac.gov.ve; f. 2005; Pres. JOSÉ LUIS MARTÍNEZ BRAVO.

National Airlines

Aeropostal (Alas de Venezuela): Torre Polar Oeste, 22°, Avda Paseo Colón, Plaza Venezuela, Los Caobos, Caracas 1051; tel. (212) 708-6211; fax (212) 782-6323; e-mail corporativa@aeropostal.com; internet www.aeropostal.com; f. 1933; transferred to private ownership in Sept. 1996, acquired by Venezuelan/US consortium Corporación Alas de Venezuela; domestic services and flights to destinations in the Caribbean, South America and the USA; Pres. and CEO DOUGLAS VÁSQUEZ ORELLANA.

Aserca Airlines: Edif. Aserca Airlines, Avda Andrés Eloy Blanco, Calle 137-C, Urb. Prebo I, Valencia; tel. (241) 237-111; fax (241) 220-210; e-mail rsv@ascercaairlines.com; internet www.asercaairlines.com; f. 1968; domestic services and flights to Caribbean destinations; Pres. SIMEÓN GARCÍA; Dir-Gen. ORLAN VILORIA.

Consorcio Venezolano de Industrias Aeronáutica y Servicios Aéreos, SA (CONVIASA): Aeropuerto Internacional de Maiquetía, Edif. Sector 6.3, Avda Intercomunal, Adyacente a Tránsito Terrestre, Maiquetía; tel. (212) 303-7332; e-mail mercadeo@conviasa.aero; internet www.conviasa.aero; f. 2004; state-owned; Pres. JESÚS RAFAEL VIÑAS GARCÍA.

LASER (Línea Aérea de Servicio Ejecutivo Regional): Torre Bazar Bolívar, 8°, Avda Francisco de Miranda, El Marqués, Caracas; tel. (212) 202-0100; fax (212) 235-8359; internet www.laser.com.ve; f. 1994; scheduled and charter passenger and cargo services to domestic and international destinations; Pres. INOCENCIO ALVAREZ; Gen. Man. JORGE ANDRADE HIDALGO.

Línea Turística Aereotuy, CA: Edif. Gran Sábana, 5°, Blvd de Sábana Grande, Apdo 2923, Carmelitas, Caracas 1050; tel. (212) 761-6231; fax (212) 762-5254; e-mail tuysales@etheron.net; internet www.tuy.com; f. 1982; operates on domestic and international routes; Pres. PETER BOTTOME; Gen. Man. JUAN C. MÁRQUEZ.

Santa Barbara Airlines: Edif. Tokay, 3°, Calle 3- B, La Urbina, Caracas; tel. (212) 204-4400; fax (212) 242-3260; e-mail atc@sbairlines.com; internet www.sbairlines.com; f. 1995; domestic and international services; Pres. JORGE ALVAREZ MÉNDEZ.

Tourism

In 2008 Venezuela received an estimated 744,709 tourists. Receipts from tourism in that year amounted to US $984m. An estimated 90% of tourists visit the island of Margarita, while only 20% of tourists visit the mainland.

Asociación Venezolana de Agencias de Viajes y Turismo (AVAVIT): Caracas; e-mail turvspecialtours@cantv.net; internet www.avavit.com; Pres. ELIAS M. RAJBE S.

Instituto Nacional de Turismo (INATUR): Hotel Caracas Hilton, Torre Sur, 4°, Of. 424, Caracas; tel. (212) 576-4193; fax (212) 576-5138; e-mail inatur@inatur.gob.ve; internet www.inatur.gob.ve; f. 2001; govt tourism devt agency; Pres. YEAN LUIS DURÁN; Exec. Dir ANTONIO SALVUCHI.

Venezolana de Turismo, SA (VENETUR): Edif. Mintur, Avda Francisco de Miranda con Avda Principal de La Floresta, Torre Norte, 3°, Municipio Chacao, Caracas; tel. (212) 208-4812; fax (212) 208-8160; e-mail informacion@venetur.gob.ve; internet www.venetur.gob.ve; govt tourism promotion agency; Dir JORGE GONZÁLEZ VÁSQUEZ.

Defence

As assessed at November 2010, the armed forces numbered 115,000 men: an army of 63,000, a navy of 17,500 (including an estimated 7,000 marines), an air force of 11,500 and a National Guard of 23,000. In October 2009 legal status was accorded to a fifth unit of the armed forces, the Bolivarian National Militia, and in February 2010 the creation was announced within the National Militia of a peasant force. There was also an army reserve numbering 8,000. Military service is selective and the length of service varies by region for all services. The President is Commander-in-Chief of the Armed Forces.

Defence Budget: 8,600m. bolívares in 2010.

Commander-General of the National Gaurd: Maj. Gen. LUÍS MOTTA DOMÍNGUEZ.

Commander-General of the Navy: Adm. CARLOS MÁXIMO ANIASI TURCHIO.

Commander of the Army: Maj.-Gen. EUCLIDES AMADOR CAMPOS APONTE.

Commander-General of the Air Force: Maj.-Gen. JORGE AREVALO OROPEZA PERNALETE.

Education

Primary education in Venezuela is free and compulsory between the ages of six and 15 years. Secondary education begins at the age of 15 years and lasts for a further two years. In 2008 enrolment at primary schools included 90% of children in the relevant age-group, while the equivalent ratio for secondary enrolment was 69% (males 66%; females 74%). In 2003/04 there were 48 universities. In 2003 the Government, with assistance from Cuba, initiated Misión Robinson, a project intended to eradicate illiteracy and innumeracy in Venezuela. Expenditure by the central Government on education and sport was an estimated 29,601.6m. bolívares in 2004.

VIET NAM

Introductory Survey

LOCATION, CLIMATE, LANGUAGE, RELIGION, FLAG, CAPITAL

The Socialist Republic of Viet Nam is situated in South-East Asia, bordered to the north by the People's Republic of China, to the west by Laos and Cambodia, and to the east by the South China Sea. The climate is humid during both the hot summer and the relatively cold winter, and there are monsoon rains in both seasons. Temperatures in Hanoi are generally between 13°C (55°F) and 33°C (91°F). The language is Vietnamese. The principal religion is Buddhism. There are also Daoist, Confucian, Hoa Hao, Caodaist and Christian (mainly Roman Catholic) minorities. The national flag (proportions 2 by 3) is red, with a large five-pointed yellow star in the centre. The capital is Hanoi.

CONTEMPORARY POLITICAL HISTORY

Historical Context

Cochin-China (the southernmost part of Viet Nam) became a French colony in 1867. Annam and Tonkin (central and northern Viet Nam) were proclaimed French protectorates in 1883. Later all three were merged with Cambodia and Laos to form French Indo-China. Throughout the French colonial period, but especially after 1920, nationalist and revolutionary groups operated in Viet Nam, the best organized of which was the Vietnamese Revolutionary Youth League, founded by Ho Chi Minh. The League was succeeded in 1930 by the Communist Party of Indo-China, also led by Ho Chi Minh.

In September 1940 Japanese forces began to occupy Viet Nam, although (Vichy) France retained administrative authority, and in June 1941 the nationalists formed the Viet Nam Doc Lap Dong Minh Hoi (Revolutionary League for the Independence of Viet Nam), or Viet Minh. In March 1945 French control was ended by a Japanese coup. Following Japan's surrender in August, Viet Minh forces entered Hanoi, and on 2 September the new regime proclaimed independence as the Democratic Republic of Viet Nam (DRV), with Ho Chi Minh as President. The Communist Party, formally dissolved in 1945, continued to be the dominant group within the Viet Minh Government. In March 1946, after French forces re-entered Viet Nam, an agreement between France and the DRV recognized Viet Nam as a 'free' state within the French Union. However, the DRV Government continued to seek complete independence. Negotiations with France broke down, and full-scale hostilities began in December 1946.

In March 1949 the French established the State of Viet Nam in the South. Meanwhile, in the North the Viet Minh was dissolved in 1951, and the Communists formed the Dang Lao Dong Viet Nam (Viet Nam Workers' Party), with Ho Chi Minh as Chairman of the Central Committee. After the defeat of French forces at Dien Bien Phu in May 1954, terms for a cease-fire were settled in Geneva, Switzerland. Agreements signed in July provided for the provisional partition of Viet Nam into two military zones, with French forces south of latitude 17°N and DRV forces in the north. Later in 1954 the French withdrew from South Viet Nam. Ngo Dinh Diem became Prime Minister of the State of Viet Nam, and in 1955, following a referendum, proclaimed himself President of the Republic of Viet Nam. He thereby deposed Bao Dai, Emperor of Viet Nam from 1932 until his forced abdication in 1945, who had become Head of the State of Viet Nam in 1949. (The former Emperor died in exile in France in 1997.) Ngo Dinh Diem refused to participate in elections envisaged by the Geneva agreement. In the DRV Ho Chi Minh was succeeded as Prime Minister by Pham Van Dong in 1955, but remained head of state and party Chairman.

Domestic Political Affairs

The anti-communist regime in the South was opposed by former members of the Viet Minh, who became known as the Viet Cong. Ngo Dinh Diem was overthrown by a coup in November 1963, and a series of short-lived military regimes held power until June 1965, when some stability was restored by the National Leadership Committee, with Lt-Gen. Nguyen Van Thieu as Chairman and Air Vice-Marshal Nguyen Cao Ky as Prime Minister. In 1967 Gen. Nguyen Van Thieu was elected President, with Marshal Nguyen Cao Ky as Vice-President; in 1971, after a division with the latter, the President was re-elected unopposed.

From 1959 the DRV actively assisted the insurgent movement in South Viet Nam, supporting the establishment there of the communist-dominated National Liberation Front (NLF) in December 1960. In 1961 the USA joined the war on the side of the anti-communist regime in the South, later bombing the North extensively from 1965 to 1968. In November 1968 peace talks between the four participants in the Viet Nam War began in Paris, France, but remained deadlocked as the fighting continued. In June 1969 the NLF formed the Provisional Revolutionary Government (PRG) in the South. Ho Chi Minh died in September 1969: he was succeeded as head of state by Ton Duc Thang, while political leadership passed to Le Duan, First Secretary of the Viet Nam Workers' Party since 1960.

In 1972 PRG and North Vietnamese forces launched a major offensive in South Viet Nam, and US bombing of the North was renewed with greater intensity. In January 1973 a peace agreement was finally signed in Paris, providing for a cease-fire in the South, the withdrawal of US forces, the eventual peaceful reunification of the whole country, and US aid to the Government in the North to assist in reconstruction. US troops withdrew, and in December 1974 combined PRG and North Vietnamese forces began a final offensive, taking the southern capital, Saigon, in April 1975. By May the new regime was in complete control of the South.

While South Viet Nam, under the PRG, remained technically separate from the DRV, effective control of the whole country passed to Hanoi. In July 1976 the country's reunification was proclaimed under the name of the Socialist Republic of Viet Nam, and Saigon was renamed Ho Chi Minh City. A new Government was appointed, dominated by members of the former Government of the DRV but including some members of the PRG. In December Le Duan was appointed General Secretary of the Communist Party of Viet Nam (formerly the Viet Nam Workers' Party). President Ton Duc Thang died in March 1980. A new Constitution was adopted in December of that year. Truong Chinh was appointed President of the Council of State (head of state) in July 1981, but real power remained with Le Duan.

Le Duan died in July 1986, and was succeeded as General Secretary of the Communist Party by Truong Chinh. At the Sixth Party Congress, held in December, the country's three most senior leaders, Truong Chinh, Pham Van Dong and Le Duc Tho, announced their retirement from the party Political Bureau (Politburo). However, they continued to attend politburo meetings in an advisory capacity. Truong Chinh and Pham Van Dong retained their respective posts as President of the Council of State and Chairman of the Council of Ministers (Prime Minister) until 1987, and Le Duc Tho continued to wield considerable political influence until his death in October 1990. The Congress appointed Nguyen Van Linh, a long-standing party official, as General Secretary of the Party.

In February 1987 an extensive government reorganization involved the dismissal of 12 ministers, as well as the merger or restructuring of several ministries, apparently with a view to the implementation of economic reforms. An election to the National Assembly took place in April. There were 829 candidates for the 496 seats (compared with 613 candidates at the previous election). In June the new Assembly elected Vo Chi Cong and Pham Hung, both former Vice-Chairmen of the Council of Ministers, to the posts of President of the Council of State and Chairman of the Council of Ministers respectively. Although a veteran of the struggle with the South, and reputedly a strict conservative, Pham Hung gave his support to the programme of economic reform, referred to as doi moi (renovation), initiated by Nguyen Van Linh. The new liberalism of the regime was demonstrated by the release in September of 480 political prisoners from 're-education' camps, as part of an amnesty for more than 6,600 prisoners on the anniversary of independence from France in 1945. In February 1988 more than 1,000 political prisoners were released. In March Pham Hung died. The Council of State appointed Vo Van Kiet, a Vice-Chairman of the Council of

VIET NAM

Introductory Survey

Ministers and the Chairman of the State Commission for Planning, as acting Chairman of the Council of Ministers.

At the meeting of the National Assembly in June 1988, members from the South took the unprecedented step of nominating the reformist Vo Van Kiet to oppose the Central Committee's more conservative candidate, Do Muoi (ranked third in the Politburo), in the election for the chairmanship of the Council of Ministers. Do Muoi was elected to the position, but Vo Van Kiet received unexpectedly strong support. Despite his reputation, Do Muoi declared his commitment to the advancement of reform. Widespread dissatisfaction with the condition of the economy led to the removal of hundreds of cadres from government posts in a 'purification' of the party. In an attempt to improve international relations, and thus secure much-needed Western aid, Viet Nam amended its Constitution in December, removing derogatory references to the USA, the People's Republic of China, France and Japan. In March 1989 a reorganization of senior economic ministers adjusted the balance further towards reform and strengthened the position of Nguyen Van Linh.

In August 1989 68 members of a US-based exiles' movement, the National Front for the Liberation of Viet Nam, were arrested while crossing from Thailand into Laos. Viet Nam formally protested to Thailand for supporting the group, which had allegedly attempted to incite a rebellion in southern Viet Nam, although the Thai Government denied involvement. In January 1990 38 suspected rebels were extradited to Viet Nam; in October they were sentenced to long terms of imprisonment.

Municipal elections to provincial and district councils took place in November 1989. Under new legislation, candidates who were not members of the Communist Party were allowed to participate for the first time. In December the National Assembly approved legislation imposing new restrictions on the press: the appointment of editors became subject to government approval, and journalists were required to reveal sources of information on request. Open dissension towards Communist Party policy also became a criminal offence. In late 1989 progress towards political reform under *doi moi* was adversely affected by government concern regarding the demise of socialism in Eastern Europe. At a meeting of the Central Committee in March 1990, disagreement on the issue of political pluralism resulted in the dismissal of a member of the Politburo, Tran Xuan Bach, who had openly advocated reform.

In the second half of 1990 the Government dismissed or brought charges against more than 18,000 officials, in an attempt to eradicate corruption. In December the Central Committee produced draft political and economic reports, reaffirming the party's commitment to socialism and to the process of economic liberalization, which were to be submitted to the next Party Congress. In the same month Bui Tin, the deputy editor of the official organ of the Communist Party, *Nhan Dan*, criticized government policy. He was subsequently expelled from the Politburo and dismissed as deputy editor. Following a request by the Central Committee for public comment on the reports, in early 1991 the party journal, *Tap Chi Cong San* (Communist Review), published articles by prominent intellectuals that severely criticized the reports and questioned the effectiveness of the socialist system. The Communist Party subsequently increased surveillance of dissidents and instructed the press to publish retaliatory articles condemning party critics. In June the Communist Party Congress approved the reports. It elected Do Muoi to replace Nguyen Van Linh as General Secretary of the Party; seven members of the Politburo were removed from their posts, including Nguyen Van Linh, although he, together with Pham Van Dong and the President of the Council of State, Vo Chi Cong, remained in the Central Committee in an advisory capacity. At a session of the National Assembly held in late July and early August, the reformist Vo Van Kiet was elected to replace Do Muoi as Chairman of the Council of Ministers. In addition, the National Assembly studied proposals, made by a constitutional commission, for amendments to the Constitution.

A new draft Constitution was published in December 1991 and, after being reviewed in public discussions, was adopted by the National Assembly in April 1992. Like the previous (1980) Constitution, it emphasized the central role of the Communist Party; however, the new document stipulated that the party must be subject to the law. While affirming adherence to a state-regulated socialist economy, the new Constitution guaranteed protection for foreign investment in Viet Nam, and permitted foreign travel and overseas investment for Vietnamese. Land was to remain the property of the State, although the right was granted to procure long-term leases, which could be inherited or sold. The National Assembly was to be reduced in number, but was to have greater power. The Council of State was to be replaced by a single President as head of state, to be responsible for appointing (subject to the approval of the National Assembly) a Prime Minister and senior members of the judiciary. The new Constitution was to enter into effect after the July 1992 general election.

The ninth National Assembly, 1992–97

In July 1992 a total of 601 candidates contested 395 seats in the National Assembly. Almost 90% were members of the Communist Party: although independent candidates (i.e. not endorsed by the Viet Nam Fatherland Front—the grouping of mass organizations, such as trade unions, affiliated to the Communist Party) were for the first time permitted to seek election, in the event only two were deemed to qualify, and neither was elected.

At the first session of the ninth National Assembly, in September 1992, the conservative Gen. Le Duc Anh (a member of the Politburo and a former Minister of Defence) was elected to the new post of executive President. Vo Van Kiet was appointed Prime Minister (the equivalent of his former post) by the Assembly in October. Only four ministers, all of whom had been implicated in corruption scandals, were not reappointed. During 1993 the Government emphasized its determination to continue progress towards a market-led economy and to encourage foreign investment. However, there was no tolerance of political dissent. In August 14 people were sentenced to terms of imprisonment, after having been convicted of conspiring to overthrow the Government, and in November several Buddhist monks were imprisoned for allegedly inciting anti-Government demonstrations. In January 1994 four new members were appointed to the Politburo, including the Minister of Foreign Affairs, Nguyen Manh Cam, and 20 new members (all under the age of 55) were elected to the Communist Party's Central Committee. In June the National Assembly approved a labour law that guaranteed the right to strike (providing that the 'social life of the community' was not adversely affected). Strikes followed in some southern provinces, and in August the first incident of industrial action in Hanoi was reported. At the fourth Congress of the Fatherland Front, in August, a new, 200-member Central Committee was elected. Elections to provincial and district councils took place during December 1994.

In February 1995 a prominent human rights organization, Amnesty International, protested to the Vietnamese Government about the recent detention of members of the anti-Government Unified Buddhist Church of Viet Nam. In August the People's Court of Ho Chi Minh City sentenced nine political activists, who had attempted to organize pro-democracy conferences, to terms of imprisonment. (Two of those sentenced, who held joint US-Vietnamese nationality, were released in November following a request from the US Government.) In October the National Assembly adopted an extensive civil code (drafted over a period of 10 years), guaranteeing the rights of the individual and enshrining existing rights concerning land usage and inheritance of property. In November two former prominent members of the Communist Party, Do Trung Hieu and Hoang Minh Chinh, were sentenced to custodial terms on charges of damaging national security: The former had been involved with an organization demanding political pluralism, while the latter had published articles urging the restoration of senior party officials removed in the 1960s.

In April 1996 the Central Committee of the Communist Party released draft reports on political and economic policy, which were to be submitted to the Eighth Communist Party Congress at the end of June, indicating that the party intended to maintain state control of the economy (while remaining committed to economic growth) and to continue to reject political pluralism. Also in April the Vice-Chairman of the National Assembly was dismissed from the Politburo and from the Communist Party; it was reported that he had been accused of treason in connection with the Viet Nam War. In June the Congress elected a new, 170-member Central Committee and an expanded (19-member) Politburo. A five-member Standing Board, which included Do Muoi, Le Duc Anh and Vo Van Kiet, was created. In November 12 ministers were dismissed in an extensive cabinet reorganization. Later in the month Le Duc Anh withdrew temporarily from politics, owing to ill health: this prompted considerable speculation regarding the eventual leadership succession. In subsequent months Lt-Gen. Le Kha Phieu, a member of the new Standing Board, came to the fore as a likely successor to Do Muoi as General Secretary of the Communist Party. Widely seen as a conservative, Le Kha Phieu was expected to seek an increased

VIET NAM

political role for the military. Le Duc Anh returned to active politics in April 1997.

In December 1996 the Politburo issued a directive requiring the establishment of Communist Party cells in all foreign-invested enterprises. In January 1997 an unprecedentedly high-profile corruption case was brought to trial: the case involved former senior officials of Tamexco (an import-export company owned by the Communist Party), along with officials from Vietcombank (the state foreign trade bank) and the financial sector. The 20 defendants were accused of a range of financial crimes, principally embezzlement of socialist property. In late January four death sentences were pronounced, together with one sentence of life imprisonment, two suspended sentences and a combined total of 103 years' imprisonment for the remaining defendants. In February a judge of the Supreme People's Court was sentenced to two years' imprisonment, having been found to have abused a position of influence for personal gain, and was thus the first member of Viet Nam's judiciary to be convicted of corruption.

In May 1997 substantial amendments to the criminal code were approved by the National Assembly in respect of corruption, bribery, child abuse and drugs-trafficking. The acceptance of bribes in excess of 50m. dông, and possession of 5 kg of opium or 100 grams of heroin, became crimes punishable by death or life imprisonment; increased penalties were introduced for first-time offenders in cases of corruption. In the same month a group of 22 people, including police, customs and border officials, stood trial for drugs-trafficking: all were convicted, with eight sentenced to death and eight to life imprisonment. In July, following what was reported as Viet Nam's first terrorism trial, two people were sentenced to death, and three others to life imprisonment, having been convicted of involvement in a bomb attack in Ho Chi Minh City in October 1994. Official reports stated that the defendants were members of the National Resistance Front for the Restoration of Viet Nam, which was alleged to have issued death threats to foreign nationals who had established businesses in Viet Nam.

The 10th National Assembly, 1997–2002

Elections to the 10th National Assembly took place on 20 July 1997. A record 663 candidates contested 450 seats (expanded from 395 seats). Under a modified selection process, 112 non-Communist Party members registered as potential candidates. However, following rigorous screening procedures, only 11 independent ('self-nominated') candidates qualified to contest the elections, of whom three secured seats in the Assembly. Do Muoi was among senior figures who did not seek re-election, and, in total, fewer than one-third of the members of the outgoing Assembly returned to office. At the first session of the new National Assembly in late September, Tran Duc Luong, hitherto a Deputy Prime Minister, was elected as President in succession to Le Duc Anh, who, owing to continued ill health, did not seek re-election. The Assembly subsequently endorsed the appointment of Nguyen Thi Binh as Vice-President, Nong Duc Manh as Chairman of the National Assembly Standing Committee, and Phan Van Khai as Prime Minister. (Vo Van Kiet had also stepped down.) A reorganization of the Cabinet was approved at the end of September: the new Cabinet included an increased number of Deputy Prime Ministers, each of whom held a wide portfolio of responsibilities. In October Do Que Luong was appointed acting Governor of the State Bank of Viet Nam (a cabinet post), following the refusal of the National Assembly to re-elect the incumbent Cao Si Kiem, deemed responsible for recent corruption scandals in the banking sector.

Reports emerged during September 1997 of violent unrest in the northern province of Thai Binh. The unrest, which had begun in May and intensified in June as hundreds of farmers protested against taxes and local corruption, had remained largely unreported earlier in the year as the province had been closed to foreign journalists. There was violence in November in the predominantly Roman Catholic province of Dong Nai, in southern Viet Nam, as thousands of protesters demonstrated against corruption in local government and attempts to confiscate church land. At the end of November the Government pledged to provide financial aid to Thai Binh province, and in February 1998 President Luong made an official tour of the province. In July more than 30 people were sentenced to terms of imprisonment for their involvement in the previous year's violent unrest in Thai Binh.

In December 1997 Le Kha Phieu was elected to succeed Do Muoi as General Secretary of the Central Committee of the Communist Party. At the same time Do Muoi, Le Duch Anh and Vo Van Kiet resigned from the Politburo; all three were subsequently appointed as advisers to the Central Committee. Four new members were elected to the Politburo, and in January 1998 the election by the Politburo of a new Standing Board, comprising Le Kha Phieu, Tran Duc Luong, Phan Van Khai, Nong Duc Manh and Pham The Duyet, was announced. The new appointments were widely perceived to reflect the consolidation of the conservative tendency within the leadership, to the detriment of reformists, among them the Prime Minister. In March, in an illustration of the Government's commitment to countering corruption, the Communist Party announced that in 1997 it had disciplined and expelled some 18,000 members, and sentenced 469 to terms of imprisonment. Further members of the party were reported to have been disciplined over corruption-related offences in July.

In a general amnesty announced by the Government to mark Viet Nam's National Day on 2 September 1998, more than 5,000 prisoners, including four of the country's most prominent dissidents—Doan Viet Hoat, Nguyen Dan Que, Thich Quang Do and Thich Tue Sy—were released from detention; however, the release of at least two of the dissidents was reported to be dependent upon their immediate exile from Viet Nam. In October amnesty was granted to a further 2,630 prisoners. In the same month the former editor-in-chief of *Doanh Nghiep*, Nguyen Hoang Linh, was convicted of 'abusing freedom and democratic rights to violate the interests of the State', following the publication in his newspaper of articles detailing alleged government corruption; Nguyen Hoang Linh was sentenced to more than 12 months' imprisonment, but, having already been detained for that length of time while awaiting trial, was released almost immediately. Also in October the Special Rapporteur on religious intolerance of the UN Commission on Human Rights, Abdelfattah Amor, visited Viet Nam to investigate assertions made by the Vietnamese authorities that greater freedom of religious expression was being afforded in the country. However, at the end of his visit, Amor stated that his investigation had been obstructed by government officials and that he had been prevented from meeting key religious dissidents.

In January 1999 the leadership of the Communist Party announced that it had expelled Gen. (retd) Tran Do from the party in response to his explicit criticism of the establishment. His expulsion caused renewed speculation about party divisions, and also set the precedent for the continued suppression of political dissent. In March the prominent writer and geophysicist, Nguyen Thanh Giang, whose critiques of the Communist Party were reported to have been widely disseminated both within Viet Nam and abroad, was arrested on the grounds of 'propagandizing against the socialist regime'; he was released in May, but reportedly remained under house arrest. In September the trial opened of 24 members of the dissident People's Action Party, charged with 'exiting the country illegally for the purpose of undermining the people's administration'; all 24 defendants were subsequently convicted and sentenced to terms of imprisonment ranging from two to 20 years. Prior to the trial Le Kha Phieu, speaking at the Seventh Plenum of the Eighth Party Central Committee in August, had emphasized the Communist Party's opposition to political pluralism.

In 1999 the issue of corruption remained a major source of concern for the Communist Party. The trial of 74 people accused of smuggling (more than one-half of whom were reported to be former government officials) opened in March, with two of the defendants later being sentenced to death, and the remainder to terms of imprisonment. In May 77 businessmen, bankers and government officials appeared in court charged with the fraudulent procurement of state loans; in August six of the defendants were sentenced to death (although two of these subsequently had their sentences commuted to life imprisonment), and the remainder to various terms of imprisonment. In December, in a further demonstration of the efforts of the Communist Party to address corruption, Deputy Prime Minister Ngo Xuan Loc was dismissed from the Cabinet following his implication in a corrupt land deal related to a private-sector project. However, in April 2000 he was reinstated to a government post and resumed responsibility for the sectors connected to the initial accusations against him, thus attracting speculation as to the extent of the Government's attempts to eliminate corruption. In September 2001 eight officials were tried on charges of fraud in Hanoi in connection with the land deal. One businessman received a 20-year prison sentence; the remaining defendants were either released or sentenced to prison terms of nine months or less.

In November 2000 Communist Party documents divulged to the US-based human rights group Freedom House emphasized the leadership's level of concern regarding the increasing number of ethnic minorities converting to Christianity, and the fear that religion would be used by the USA and other countries to undermine communism in Viet Nam. In December the Minister of National Defence, Lt-Gen. Pham Van Tra, instructed the army not to become depoliticized, and to remain vigilant and safeguard the Communist Party and the socialist system.

The Ninth Party Congress was held in April 2001, and resulted in the election of a new 150-member Central Committee, 15-member Politburo and nine-member Secretariat. Nong Duc Manh was appointed General Secretary, replacing Le Kha Phieu, who was accused of using military intelligence against party members and of slowing the pace of reforms. Phieu had agreed to step down under pressure from the Central Committee. Nong Duc Manh, who was rumoured to be the illegitimate son of Ho Chi Minh, was the first ethnic Tay to attain such a senior position. Some 84 members of the previous Central Committee were re-elected. President Tran Duc Luong and Prime Minister Phan Van Khai retained their party posts, but former President Le Duc Anh, former Prime Minister Vo Van Kiet and former General Secretary Do Muoi lost their positions as senior advisers to the Central Committee upon the abolition of the posts. Manh was believed to favour economic reforms and greater democracy, the latter a major theme at the Congress. However, the Congress reiterated its commitment to socialism as a means to national industrialization and modernization. In June 2001 Nguyen Van An, a member of the Politburo, was elected to the chairmanship of the National Assembly, succeeding Nong Duc Manh.

Meanwhile, ethnic violence broke out in the Central Highland provinces of Gia Lai and Dak Lak in February 2001, as local hill minorities (known as Montagnards) protested against perceived injustices caused by the migration of ethnic Vietnamese from the densely populated coastal regions and by the deforestation resulting from the establishment of coffee plantations. Some 5,000 protesters in the provincial capitals of Pleiku and Buon Ma Thuot, respectively, attacked state offices and blocked roads. The Vietnamese authorities deployed troops, riot police, water cannon and helicopters to quell the unrest, and injuries were reported on both sides. Some 20 people were arrested in connection with instigating the violence, which was attributed to 'extremists' seeking to use religion to foment unrest. The protesters had demanded autonomy, freedom to practise their Protestant religion, the return of ancestral lands confiscated for use as coffee plantations and the right to preserve their traditional way of life. The Ministry of Public Security accused the US-based Montagnard Foundation of organizing the violence, stating that several of those arrested were former members of the United Front for the Liberation of Oppressed Races (FULRO), a guerrilla unit that had close links to the US military and Central Intelligence Agency (CIA) during the Viet Nam War. The Vietnamese authorities also stated that during 2000 there had been several incursions into the country by agents of Free Viet Nam, a movement based in Thailand.

In March 2001 the authorities denounced a Catholic priest, Nguyen Van Ly, for writing to the US Congress and urging it not to ratify a bilateral trade agreement, owing to human rights abuses in Viet Nam. In October Nguyen Van Ly was sentenced to 15 years in prison after a court convicted him of undermining national unity and contravening a detention order. (His sentence was reduced by five years in July 2003 and by a further five years in June 2004, and in February 2005 he was released from prison, having been granted amnesty. However, he was imprisoned again in March 2007—see The 11th National Assembly, 2002–07.) Exiled Vietnamese Buddhist leaders also claimed that their followers in Viet Nam were routinely harassed. In September 2001 Ho Tan Anh, leader of the Buddhist Youth Movement, burnt himself to death in protest at the restrictions that had been imposed upon his organization. In the same month 14 Montagnards received sentences of between six and 12 years' imprisonment for participating in the protests of February. In October a further six men were convicted of distributing propaganda and inciting ethnic unrest in the city of Buon Ma Thuot during the disturbances.

A critical report issued by the international organization Human Rights Watch in April 2002 warned of further violence in the Central Highlands if the Government continued to implement its repressive policies towards ethnic minorities. In November 2002 it was alleged that the Government had executed three Montagnards in the previous month, reportedly owing to their involvement in the violence of February 2001. In December 2002 a further eight people were convicted of charges of undermining national unity, having allegedly aided people attempting to leave the region following the violence. In January 2003, according to Human Rights Watch, 70 Montagnards were known to be imprisoned in Viet Nam owing to their political or religious beliefs. In April a report issued by Human Rights Watch claimed that government persecution of the Montagnards had escalated since January. In May 15 Montagnards were convicted of causing social disorder during the protests of February 2001 and sentenced to lengthy prison terms. In April 2004 Human Rights Watch again accused the Vietnamese Government of repression, following reports that a rally held by Montagnards in that month in Dak Lak province, in protest against land confiscation and religious persecution, had been violently suppressed by government officials. Human Rights Watch claimed that at least 10 Montagnards had been killed, although the Vietnamese Government insisted that only two people had died. In May Human Rights Watch reported that the Vietnamese authorities had arrested a number of Montagnard church leaders, as well as Montagnards with relatives in the USA. In August nine Montagnards, who were alleged to be former members of the FULRO, were convicted of fomenting disorder and undermining national unity during the demonstrations of February 2001 and thereafter. They were sentenced to prison terms of between five and 12 years.

In December 2001 the National Assembly gave its approval to several constitutional amendments, including one allowing politicians to instigate mid-term votes of no confidence if they considered any minister to be performing unsatisfactorily. The amendments were intended to encourage the development of Viet Nam's market economy and improve democracy, thus facilitating the country's further integration into the international community.

It was reported in January 2002 that the Communist Party had approved a decree authorizing the police to engage in the destruction of publications that had not been approved by the party. Books written by several leading dissidents, including Gen. Tran Do, had subsequently been destroyed. In March the Politburo was reported to have established a special investigation into allegations that more than 50 government officials had colluded in organized crime. Several of those accused were reported to have accepted bribes to protect a gang whose alleged leader, Truong Van Cam, also known as Nam Cam, was undergoing investigation on murder charges. As the investigation continued, more than 100 government officials and an estimated 50 police officers were implicated; two members of the Central Committee (the Director-General of the state radio station Voice of Viet Nam, Tran Mai Hanh, and Pham Sy Chien) were expelled from the Communist Party in July owing to their involvement. In November the Deputy Minister of Public Security, Maj.-Gen. Haong Ngoc Nhat, was dismissed from his position and demoted in rank, owing to his alleged complicity. In January 2003 the director of the Economic Commission of the Politburo, Truong Tan San, became the most senior member of the Communist Party to be punished in relation to the investigation; he was formally reprimanded for 'dereliction of duty' during his tenure as secretary of the party in Ho Chi Minh City in 1996–2000.

Meanwhile, in March 2002 the Communist Party decided that it would formally permit its members to engage in private business, indicating the Government's desire to encourage the expansion of the role of the private sector within the economy. In April 59 people went on trial in Ho Chi Minh City charged with embezzling state assets and violating commercial law in connection with the Chinese-owned Viet Hoa bank. In the following month all those tried were found guilty of the charges against them; 43 were sentenced to prison terms of varying lengths, while the remainder were given suspended sentences. The trial was widely perceived to constitute a further attempt on the part of the Government to take firm action against corruption.

The 11th National Assembly, 2002–07

Elections to the 11th National Assembly took place on 19 May 2002. The 498 seats available were contested by 759 candidates, only 13 of whom were independent. Non-Communist Party candidates won 51 seats and independents two, the remainder being secured by party members. In July and August the newly elected National Assembly held its first session, during which significant reorganizations of both the Standing Committee and the Cabinet were approved. Three new ministries were created as part of the extensive reorganization, in which Vu Khoan, the former Minister of Trade, was promoted to the position of Deputy

Prime Minister. President Tran Duc Luong, Prime Minister Phan Van Khai and the Chairman of the National Assembly, Nguyen Van An, were all formally re-elected to their posts, while Truong My Hoa succeeded Nguyen Thi Binh as Vice-President.

In November 2002 Le Chi Quang, a lawyer, was convicted of committing 'acts of propaganda' against the State, after allegedly publishing material critical of the Government on the internet. He was sentenced to a four-year prison term (but was released early, in June 2004, to serve a three-year term of house arrest). In December 2002 another dissident, Nguyen Khac Toan, was sentenced to 12 years in prison, having been convicted of using the internet for espionage purposes; he was subsequently granted amnesty and released in January 2006. In March 2003 the dissident Nguyen Dan Que, who had spent over 18 years in prison for campaigning for improved democracy and human rights in Viet Nam and had been freed five years previously, was arrested again after publishing an essay on the internet concerning Viet Nam's control of the media. In July 2004 he was sentenced to a 30-month prison term, but was granted amnesty and released in February 2005, one of an estimated 12 political or religious prisoners to be granted early release during the course of that year. Meanwhile, at the Seventh Plenum of the Central Committee of the Communist Party held in January 2003, a resolution intended to increase the Party's control over religious affairs was approved. At the Plenum Nguyen Van Chi was appointed to the Party Secretariat.

In February 2003 the trial of Nam Cam and 154 other defendants on a number of charges, including murder, organized gambling, bribery, drugs-trafficking and extortion, began in Ho Chi Minh City. Among the defendants were 21 former state and government officials. The hearings constituted Viet Nam's largest corruption trial to date. In June Nam Cam was convicted of all the charges against him and sentenced to death. In the same month many more defendants in the trial were convicted of the charges against them, including Tran Mai Hanh, who received a 10-year prison term, and Pham Sy Chien, who was to serve a six-year sentence. Five other defendants were given death sentences. In June 2004 Nam Cam and four of his co-defendants were executed by firing squad, the death sentence of the fifth having been commuted to life imprisonment.

In April 2003 Prime Minister Phan Van Khai held talks with Thich Huyen Quang, leader of the anti-Government Unified Buddhist Church of Viet Nam, who had been held under house arrest since the group was proscribed almost 20 years previously. While the meeting was welcomed by international diplomats, there was speculation that the Communist Party might use it to respond to continued criticism of its human rights record, while avoiding making any more substantial reforms. In May Thich Huyen Quang was permitted to meet with his deputy, Thich Quang Do, for only the third time in 21 years. In June Thich Quang Do was released from house arrest, two months before the end of his two-year sentence. In the same month, however, Pham Hong Son, a doctor, was sentenced to a 13-year prison term, to be followed by three years of house arrest, having been found guilty of charges of espionage and disseminating false information about the State on the internet. The Government later reduced the length of his prison sentence to five years. In October a one-day 'stand-off' was reported to have taken place in Binh Dinh province between government security forces and supporters of the Unified Buddhist Church of Viet Nam, following an attempt by Thich Huyen Quang and Thich Quang Do to depart for Ho Chi Minh City. In November both the US House of Representatives and the European Parliament approved resolutions condemning the continuing official repression of non-recognized religious organizations in Viet Nam and calling for the release of Thich Huyen Quang.

In November 2003 the trial opened in Hanoi of two former junior agriculture ministers, Nguyen Thien Luan and Nguyen Quang Ha, together with La Thi Kim Oanh, the former director of a company controlled by the Ministry of Agriculture and Rural Development, and five other officials, on embezzlement charges. The opening of the trial was televised as part of the Government's ongoing campaign to combat corruption. In December all those tried were found guilty of the charges against them. La Thi Kim Oanh was sentenced to death, while the remaining defendants received prison sentences of various lengths. Meanwhile, in the same month former journalist Nguyen Vu Binh was sentenced to a seven-year prison term, having been convicted of espionage charges. (Nguyen Vu Binh was granted a presidential amnesty in June 2007, shortly before a visit by the Vietnamese President to the USA, which had pressed for the dissident's release.) In June 2004 the National Assembly approved the dismissal of the Minister of Agriculture and Development, Le Huy Ngo, on the grounds that he had failed adequately to monitor his subordinates and organizations under his administration in connection with the embezzlement case; he was replaced by Cao Duc Phat.

In March 2004 police arrested four members of the Mennonite Church, which was not officially recognized by the Government, after scuffles broke out when a number of Mennonites attempted to photograph police officers who were posted outside the headquarters of the Church. In June Nguyen Hong Quang, the Secretary-General of the Mennonite Church in Viet Nam, was also arrested for his involvement in the incident, and a sixth church member was detained the following month. In November Quang was sentenced to three years' imprisonment for preventing officials from carrying out their duties, while the five other defendants received custodial sentences of between nine months and two years.

Two veteran dissidents, Tran Van Khue, a retired academic, and Pham Que Duong, a military historian, were sentenced to 19 months' imprisonment in July 2004, having been convicted of abusing democratic freedoms to undermine the interests of the State. Both men had posted articles critical of the Government on the internet. However, they were released at the end of the month, as they had been in detention since December 2002. In late July 2004 the Minister of Posts and Telecommunications, Do Trung Ta, issued new regulations aimed at controlling access to the internet by allowing internet service providers to suspend contracts with cafés that allowed customers to view pornographic websites or those deemed to threaten national security. In August a special police unit was established to combat internet crime and prevent the spread of banned materials.

Also in July 2004 the President promulgated an Ordinance on Beliefs and Religions, which came into effect in November. A coalition of non-recognized Protestant churches condemned the new law, which, while upholding the right of citizens to freedom of religious belief, decreed that only state-authorized clergy be entitled to preach and only within defined territorial jurisdictions. The ordinance also provided for the suspension of religious activities that were deemed to jeopardize national security, public order or national unity. In February 2005 it was reported that the Government had issued a decree allowing outlawed Protestant churches to operate if they renounced connections to the FULRO.

Details emerged in September 2004 of a major corruption scandal in which local textile companies had been allegedly obliged to pay large bribes to trade officials in order to secure export quotas to the USA. Some 19 people were subsequently arrested in connection with the case; the most prominent of these was Deputy Minister of Trade Mai Van Dau, who was charged with abuse of power and dismissed from the Government in November. Mai Van Dau's trial was conducted in March 2007: the former Deputy Minister of Trade was convicted of receiving bribes and sentenced to 14 years' imprisonment, while 12 other defendants received sentences ranging from one year to 17 years; Mai Van Dau's sentence was reduced to 12 years in June. Meanwhile, in November 2004 the National Assembly approved new legislation on national security, which stipulated the principles of security policy and the powers and responsibilities of the agencies in charge of national security.

In December 2004 two retired state physicists, Tran Van Luong and Nguyen Thi Minh Hoan, were sentenced, respectively, to 21 months' and eight months' imprisonment for sending to state agencies documents and petitions that were critical of the Government and the Communist Party. In January 2005 the Government announced that 8,323 prisoners, including six political dissidents and 33 foreigners, were to be released in an amnesty to mark Tet (the lunar New Year). In March the Government issued a decree aimed at tightening control over demonstrations and banning unauthorized gatherings. It was reported that the decree required the approval in advance of all gatherings not organized by the Communist Party or state organs.

It was reported in June 2005 that, according to the Ministry of Public Security, 176,534 economic crimes had been exposed in the 12 previous years; 9,960 of those were said to be related to corruption. In November the National Assembly ratified a long-awaited Anti-Corruption Law, the terms of which required all officials, and their close relatives, to disclose fully their assets. There was considerable scepticism as to how effectively this would be enforced, especially in view of the protection given to the authorities by state control of the media. In the previous month the deputy head of the State Inspectorate's department of economic inspection, Luong Cao Khai, was arrested amid claims that he had accepted bribes and had abused his position to provide relatives with employment; in November 2007 he was convicted of the charges against him and sentenced to 21 years' imprisonment, while two other former senior officials from the State Inspectorate received shorter custodial terms for accepting bribes.

In April 2006 the Minister of Transport and Communications, Dao Dinh Binh, tendered his resignation from the Cabinet, following allegations concerning an apparent misappropriation of state funds by staff members within his ministry. It was claimed that officials had stolen money allocated to construction projects and had accepted numerous bribes. Binh announced that he would accept full responsibility for the actions of those employed in his ministry. The Deputy Minister of Transport and Communications, Nguyen Viet Tien, was arrested in connection with the embezzlement of state funds. In August 2007 eight people were sentenced to between seven and 13 years' imprisonment for their involvement in the scandal, while a ninth defendant received a suspended two-year term. Criminal charges against Nguyen Viet Tien were withdrawn in March 2008.

The 10th Communist Party Congress was held in late April 2006, during which elections were held for a new 160-member Central Committee, 14-member Politburo and eight-member Secretariat. Nong Duc Manh was retained as General Secretary of the Party; five other members of the previous Politburo also secured re-election. President Tran Duc Luong, Prime Minister Phan Van Khai and Chairman of the National Assembly Standing Committee, Nguyen Van An, all announced that they were to resign, thus preparing the way for a younger generation of officials to assume prominent positions within the party leadership. The Congress reaffirmed its commitment to socialism, announced its aim of Viet Nam achieving the status of a developed country by 2020 and adopted the Report and Five-Year Plan of Action on Socio-economic Development Goals for 2006–10; the issue of corruption within the party was also given considerable focus, with General Secretary Manh vowing in his opening speech to 'intensify' the fight against it. In June 2006, at its annual session, the National Assembly formally approved the resignations of Tran Duc Luong, Phan Van Khai and Nguyen Van An. Phan Van Kai's nominee, Nguyen Tan Dung, was confirmed as Prime Minister, while Nguyen Minh Triet succeeded Tran Duc Luong as President. Nguyen Phu Trong was elected Chairman of the National Assembly Standing Committee. Soon after, a cabinet reorganization was approved: Minister of Finance Nguyen Sinh Hung, who had been promoted to the position of Deputy Prime Minister, was replaced by Vu Van Ninh, while another Deputy Prime Minister, Pham Gia Khiem, took additional charge of the foreign affairs portfolio. Among the new appointees were Truong Vinh Trong as Deputy Prime Minister and Lt-Gen. Phung Quang Thanh as Minister of National Defence (to replace Lt-Gen. Pham Van Tra following his retirement); however, several other ministers retained their portfolios. Vu Khoan, who had retired from the post of Deputy Prime Minister, was later appointed as the Prime Minister's special envoy for foreign affairs.

At the end of June 2006 the new Prime Minister's decision to waive possible disciplinary action against the retiring former Minister of Transport and Communications, Dao Dinh Binh, encountered significant, although unsuccessful, opposition within the National Assembly. In October it appeared that the campaign against corruption was progressing, with the establishment of the Central Steering Committee for Corruption Prevention and Control, chaired by Nguyen Tan Dung. The committee, which was created to oversee and co-ordinate national anti-corruption operations, would have the power to suspend government officials for unlawful practices. In the following month the Government was reported to have established a department to address the issue of corruption, as part of the General Directorate of Police, with links to the Ministry of Public Security.

Meanwhile, in August 2006 Pham Hong Son (see above) was one of thousands of prisoners freed under an amnesty to commemorate National Day in the following month. In November seven people, three of them US nationals, were convicted on terrorism charges and sentenced to 15 months' imprisonment. In the same month the USA's decision to remove Viet Nam from its list of 'countries of particular concern' in relation to religious freedom provoked criticism from Thich Quang Do. Although the decision recognized the country's progress towards greater religious freedom, reports of cases against dissidents continued: in March 2007 the Catholic priest Father Nguyen Van Ly (see Political Refugees and Economic Migrants) was convicted of disseminating information against the State and sentenced to eight years' imprisonment. None the less, relations between the Vietnamese Government and the Roman Catholic Church were improving. In January 2007 Nguyen Tan Dung became the first Vietnamese Prime Minister to visit the Vatican, where he held talks with Pope Benedict XVI, and in March a delegation from the Vatican visited Viet Nam to discuss the possibility of establishing full diplomatic relations. Moreover, during 2007 the Government's Committee for Religious Affairs granted operating licences to several additional religions, including the Mennonite Church, the Baptist Church and the Bahá'í faith.

Recent developments: the 12th National Assembly, 2007–11

Elections to the 12th National Assembly held on 20 May 2007 were contested by 875 candidates, including 30 independents. Of the 493 deputies elected, only one was an independent, while a further 42 were non-Communist Party members. A high turnout, of 99.6%, was recorded. Earlier that month several pro-democracy activists were convicted of spreading propaganda intended to undermine the State, including two human rights lawyers, Nguyen Van Dai and Le Thi Cong Nhan, who were sentenced to terms of five years and four years, respectively; both were also to serve four years and three years under house arrest subsequent to their release from prison. The sentence of both lawyers was reduced by one year on appeal in November. (Although rights organizations welcomed the release, as scheduled, of Le Thi Cong Nhan, in March 2010, and of Nguyen Van Dai, in March 2011, such groups appealed to the Vietnamese Government for their immediate and unconditional release from house arrest.)

The first session of the newly elected National Assembly commenced in July 2007. Nguyen Minh Triet, Nguyen Tan Dung and Nguyen Phu Trong were all re-elected to their respective positions as President, Prime Minister and Chairman of the National Assembly Standing Committee, while Nguyen Thi Doan succeeded Truong My Hoa as Vice-President. In early August the National Assembly endorsed a cabinet reorganization, which included a reduction in the number of ministries from 26 to 22 and the appointment of Hoang Trung Hai and Nguyen Thien Nhan, both relatively young and with economic backgrounds, as additional Deputy Prime Ministers (joining Nguyen Sinh Hung, Pham Gia Khiem and Truong Vinh Trong), with Nguyen Thien Nhan also remaining Minister of Education and Training. The incumbent Ministers of National Defence, Public Security, Finance and Foreign Affairs all remained in the Cabinet, while new appointees were allocated responsibility for some of the less strategic portfolios. A reduction in the term of the 12th National Assembly from five years to four years was also approved. Meanwhile, hundreds of peasant farmers from the Mekong River Delta protested in Ho Chi Minh City in July against the seizure of their land and alleged abuse of legislation on land usage by local government officials; a smaller demonstration also took place in Hanoi. Deputy Prime Minister Truong Vinh Trong urged local leaders to conduct a swift investigation into the farmers' complaints.

Six political activists, including one French, one Thai and two US nationals, were arrested in Ho Chi Minh City in November 2007, reportedly after participating in pro-democracy discussions. The US and French citizens were members of the US-based Viet Tan (Vietnam Reform Party), which stated that its aim was to promote democratic reform in Viet Nam through peaceful means, although it was described as a terrorist organization by the Vietnamese state media. Six days later two other US nationals were detained for allegedly attempting to enter Viet Nam with a firearm; Viet Tan denied any link to them. They were freed in mid-December, as were the French citizen and one of the two US members of Viet Tan, following international demands for their release, although the others remained in detention. Meanwhile, rising inflation provoked labour unrest in late 2007 and early 2008, with large increases in food prices being of particular concern.

In July 2008 thousands of people attended the funeral of Thich Huyen Quang, the leader of the outlawed Unified Buddhist Church of Viet Nam. The authorities, under international pressure, had permitted the ceremony to proceed despite having earlier condemned the dissident's supporters as 'extremist elements disguised as Buddhist monks'. In September it was reported that the Government had threatened to take legal action against the Archbishop of Hanoi, Joseph Ngo Quang Kiet, and four other senior Roman Catholic priests in a dispute over two pieces of land in the capital that the Church claimed to own. Church officials asserted that the State had illegally confiscated the land in 1954 after independence from France and that they had documentation proving continuing church ownership of the land; for its part, the Government stated that the land had been officially signed over to the city authorities in 1962 and that the disputed areas were now public parks. In March 2009 seven Roman Catholics, who had taken part in demonstrations in Hanoi in August and September in the previous year to protest against the Government's alleged confiscation of the land, received suspended prison sentences of between 12 and 15 months on charges of public order offences and damage to public property.

In October 2008 a respected investigative journalist, Nguyen Viet Chien, who worked for the daily newspaper *Thanh Nien*, was sentenced to two years' imprisonment after being found guilty of 'abusing freedom and democratic rights' during his investigation into the 2006 government corruption case involving the Ministry of Transport and Communications. Another journalist, Nguyen Van Hai of the daily *Tuoi Tre*, having pleaded guilty, was sentenced to two years' re-education without detention on the same charges. Although the Vietnamese press remained generally deferential to the authorities, the Government's treatment of the two journalists prompted unprecedented criticism from the Vietnamese media on the grounds that it would discourage further action against corruption. The issue of government corruption came to the fore again in January 2009 when the former Deputy Chief of the Government Office, Vu Dinh Thuan, was charged with embezzlement and abuse of power. Thuan had been in charge of the so-called Project 112, a flawed plan to computerize Viet Nam's administrative system that had been abandoned in April 2007, and, together with the project secretary, Luong Cao Son, was alleged to have misappropriated some 1,000m. dông of allocated funds. Both men were convicted in January 2010; Thuan was sentenced to five years' imprisonment on charges of 'abuse of power', while Son, who was deemed to have been the main instigator of the crime, was sentenced to a six-year prison term, as was Nguyen Thuy Ha, the director of an information and technology company. A further 20 defendants were also convicted of involvement in the scandal, and received sentences of between 18 months' probation and 30 months' imprisonment.

Further human rights concerns were prompted by an apparent intensification of government efforts to suppress dissident activity. In June 2009 prominent human rights lawyer Le Cong Dinh was arrested and charged with propaganda against the State; in December this was amended to the more serious charge of subversion. (It was widely postulated that Dinh's arrest was due to an article that he had written, questioning government plans for a bauxite-mining operation by a Chinese company in the Central Highlands region.) In January 2010 Dinh and three other pro-democracy activists were convicted of subversion, having been found to have colluded with 'Vietnamese reactionary groups and hostile forces in exile'; Dinh was sentenced to five years' imprisonment, while his three co-defendants received prison terms ranging from five to 16 years. The rights organization Amnesty International urged the release of the men, whom it described as 'prisoners of conscience'. (Appeals subsequently lodged by the four were rejected in May; the sentences of all but one of the defendants were upheld, with that of the fourth reduced by 18 months.) Later in January dissident writer Pham Thanh Nghien was convicted of disseminating anti-state propaganda and sentenced to four years' imprisonment, to be followed by a three-year period of house arrest. Nghien had been arrested in September 2008 for attempting to stage a peaceful protest in response to having been assaulted following a visit to a human rights activist. In October 2009 three dissidents were sentenced by a Hanoi court to prison terms of between three and four years after being convicted of writing defamatory material against the State; in the same month a further six people were imprisoned for between two and six years, having been convicted by a Haiphong court on similar charges of producing anti-state propaganda. In December Tran Anh Kim, a former army officer who had confessed to joining the outlawed Democratic Party of Viet Nam, was convicted of 'working to overthrow the people's administration' and sentenced to five-and-a-half years' imprisonment; as in the case of Le Cong Dinh, the subversion charge against Tran was raised from the lesser charge of anti-state propaganda shortly before the commencement of his trial. Following repeated pleas by Western governments and international human rights organizations, Father Nguyen Van Ly was released from prison in March 2010, having been granted a one-year suspension of his sentence owing to the deteriorating state of his health; the priest had suffered two strokes during 2009. A number of rights groups, including Amnesty International, launched campaigns to prevent the scheduled return to prison, in March 2011, of Father Nguyen. At the beginning of May Father Nguyen was reported to remain under house arrest pending a final decision as to whether he would be returned to prison to serve the remainder of his sentence.

Four land rights petitioners, all members of the outlawed Viet Tan, were arrested at various locations around Viet Nam in July–August 2010 and were subsequently charged with subversion. Viet Tan alleged that the four, who remained in detention at mid-2011, had been denied legal representation and visits from relatives. Vi Duc Hoi, formerly a member of the Communist Party, was arrested in October 2010 and imprisoned for eight years (to be followed by five years under house arrest) in January 2011, following his conviction on the charge of disseminating anti-state propaganda; the activist, who had been expelled from the Communist Party in 2007 after urging democratic reforms from 2006, had appealed for an end to one-party rule and the introduction of a democratic, multi-party political system. Cu Huy Ha Vu, a prominent dissident whose father had been a cabinet minister during the presidency of Ho Chi Minh, was arrested in November 2010; he was convicted in April 2011 of disseminating anti-state propaganda, having similarly advocated an end to communist rule and the establishment of a multi-party system, and was sentenced to seven years' imprisonment, to be followed by a three-year period of house arrest. Cu Huy Ha Vu's conviction, which followed two thwarted attempts to sue Prime Minister Nguyen Tan Dung over a mining project that the former alleged would be harmful to the environment, led to concern within the US Administration of President Barack Obama, which expressed reservations regarding the 'apparent lack of due process' during the one-day trial.

In December 2010 the US House of Representatives adopted a resolution appealing for the redesignation of Viet Nam as a 'country of particular concern' with regard to violations of religious freedoms. The Vietnamese Ministry of Foreign Affairs vehemently dismissed the contents of the resolution as being inaccurate and lacking in objectivity. In its annual global report published in January 2011, Human Rights Watch also urged the US Government to return Viet Nam to its list of 'countries of particular concern' with regard to religious freedoms, alleging that the Vietnamese Government continued to harass peaceful worshippers of religions other than those officially recognized by the state. The report also claimed that the Vietnamese Government had further intensified its suppression of dissent during 2010 in advance of the 11th Communist Party Congress (held earlier in January 2011—see below), and that incidents of police brutality were widespread and well documented.

At the end of February 2011 prominent human rights activist Nguyen Dan Que was again arrested, on charges of 'directly violating the stability and strength of the people's government', after posting a message on an internet forum in which he urged opponents of the Government to stage a popular revolution akin to those that had successfully overthrown the respective Governments of Tunisia and Egypt earlier in the year. Following widespread criticism from local and international rights organizations, including Amnesty International, the pro-democracy dissident, who had appealed for 'a new, free, democratic, humane and progressive Viet Nam', was released on bail a few days later. Three US citizens of Vietnamese origin, all members of Viet Tan, were arrested in Ho Chi Minh City in March after attending a peaceful protest against state corruption and land rights; although all three had been released without charge by the end of the month, rights groups pointed to their arrest as a further indication of the Government's refusal to tolerate expressions of dissent.

Meanwhile, the 11th Communist Party Congress was held in January 2011, during which a new 175-member Central Committee (with an additional 25 alternate members), 14-member Politburo and 10-member Secretariat were elected. The inclusion within the new Central Committee of a higher proportion of representatives from provincial areas engendered some hope that the issue of growing income disparity between urban and rural areas across Viet Nam might be afforded greater prominence during the coming five-year period. The reappointment to the Politburo of Nguyen Tan Dung, who was reported to have defeated a leadership challenge from Truong Tan Sang (a member of the Politburo since 1996, who also secured re-election to the Bureau), prepared the way for his likely reconfirmation as Prime Minister by the National Assembly later in the year, despite concerns about his management of the economy; Truong Tan Sang was expected to be confirmed as State President. Seven other members of the previous Politburo were also re-elected. Nguyen Phu Trong was elected General Secretary of the Party, in place of Nong Duc Manh who had previously announced his resignation from the position; Nguyen Phu Trong relinquished his previous position as Chairman of the National Assembly Standing Committee. Four new members were elected to the Secretariat. A number of short- and long-term plans were adopted during the Congress, including national strategies on socio-economic development for 2011–20 and on political policies and tasks for 2011–15. During the Congress, party leaders acknowledged that the issue of public corruption and abuse of power had significantly constrained the pace of national development and needed effectively to be addressed to ensure strong economic performance. In somewhat critical assessments of the country's current progress to this end, Truong Tan Sang noted that some senior party leaders continued to 'lack example in morality and lifestyle', while Nguyen Phu Trong declared in his opening statement: 'Quality, efficiency and competitiveness remain low. Bureaucracy, corruption, wastefulness, social vices, moral and lifestyle degradation have not been prevented.'

The final session of the 12th National Assembly was convened in late March 2011. Elections for the 500 seats of the 13th National Assembly (for the period 2011–16) were held on 22 May. Of the 827 candidates, 14.3% were reported to be non-members of the Communist Party. The inaugural session of the new National Assembly was due to convene in mid-July.

Political Refugees and Economic Migrants

By the end of 1976 Viet Nam had established diplomatic relations with many countries, including all of its South-East Asian neighbours. However, tension arose over the growing number of Vietnamese refugees (particularly ethnic Chinese) arriving in Thailand and other nearby countries. In 1979 more than 200,000 fled Viet Nam, and in July an international conference was convened in Geneva to discuss the situation. The Orderly Departure Programme, sponsored by the Office of the UN High Commissioner for Refugees (UNHCR, see p. 71), whereby Viet Nam agreed to legal departures, was negotiated, and by the end of 1988 about 140,000 people had left the country in this way. However, illegal departures continued, and the increasing reluctance of Western countries to provide resettlement opportunities led to a meeting in Malaysia in March 1989, at which representatives of 30 nations were present and a comprehensive programme of action was drafted. Members of the Association of Southeast Asian Nations (ASEAN, see p. 206) subsequently ceased to accept refugees for automatic resettlement and planned to institute a screening procedure to distinguish genuine refugees from economic migrants. A similar procedure had been in effect since June 1988 in Hong Kong, and an agreement had been signed in November, whereby Viet Nam agreed to accept voluntary repatriation of refugees from Hong Kong, funded by UNHCR and the United Kingdom, with UN supervision to protect the returning refugees from punitive measures by the Vietnamese Government.

In June 1989 a UN-sponsored conference adopted the so-called Comprehensive Action Plan that had been drafted in March, introducing the desired screening procedures to distinguish political refugees from economic migrants (who might be forcibly repatriated if efforts to secure their voluntary return proved unsuccessful). In December the United Kingdom forcibly repatriated a group of 51 Vietnamese from Hong Kong, provoking international criticism; this policy was abandoned as a result both of opposition by the USA and of Viet Nam's refusal to accept further deportations. However, in July 1990 the USA accepted in principle the 'involuntary' repatriation of refugees classed as economic migrants who did not actively oppose deportation. In September the United Kingdom, Viet Nam and UNHCR reached an agreement whereby the Vietnamese Government would no longer refuse refugees who had been repatriated 'involuntarily'. In May 1992 the United Kingdom and Viet Nam signed an agreement providing for the compulsory repatriation of all economic migrants from Hong Kong. In 1991–95 some 66,132 Vietnamese were voluntarily repatriated, while an additional 1,562 were forcibly returned. In January 1996 ASEAN member states, including Viet Nam, agreed that all Vietnamese residing in South-East Asian refugee camps (apart from those in Hong Kong) would be repatriated by the end of June of that year. (China had already indicated that all Vietnamese refugees in Hong Kong should be returned prior to the transfer of the territory to Chinese sovereignty in June 1997.) In March 1996 UNHCR announced that it would suspend funding of Vietnamese refugee camps from the end of June. In April a new initiative, proposed by the US Government in an effort to accelerate the repatriation programme, whereby refugees who returned to Viet Nam would be eligible to apply for settlement in the USA under a new screening process, was received with caution by the Vietnamese authorities. By February 1997 Malaysia, Singapore, Indonesia and Thailand had closed their camps, following the repatriation of all Vietnamese refugees from those countries, leaving Hong Kong as the only South-East Asian country with a significant number (12,000 in November 1996). In December 1996 repatriates were prohibited from engaging in any type of political activity, and from January 1997 anti-communist activists and critics of the Government were banned from returning to Viet Nam. In mid-June the main Vietnamese detention centre in Hong Kong was closed. However, the scheduled repatriation of all remaining Vietnamese (estimated at some 1,600 people qualifying as refugees and 700 non-refugees) before the end of the month was not achieved. In July 1999 Hong Kong announced that the Vietnamese who remained in the territory—estimated to number around 1,400, some classed as refugees, others as 'stateless' persons—would be given permanent residency in Hong Kong; the last remaining camp for Vietnamese refugees in Hong Kong was closed in May 2000.

Following the unrest in the Central Highlands in February 2001 (see Domestic Political Affairs), many Montagnards fled over the border into Cambodia, where they were accommodated in two camps situated in the provinces of Mondol Kiri and Rotanak Kiri. By December the camps housed 805 refugees, who sought a supervised return to the Highlands, accompanied by a guarantee that they would be given permission to reoccupy their ancestral lands. In January 2002 Viet Nam and Cambodia signed a joint repatriation agreement with UNHCR, and in February 15 refugees left the camps to return to their home in Kon Tum province. Later in the same month the Vietnamese Government criticized UNHCR for the delay in the repatriation of the refugees (of whom there were now more than 1,000). A deadline of 30 April 2002 for the completion of the repatriation process had been imposed. The programme was later suspended, as UNHCR claimed that by imposing the deadline the Government was undermining the voluntary nature of returns. In March UNHCR announced its withdrawal from the agreement, owing to the frequent intimidation of both refugees and UN staff at the camps. Its decision was precipitated by an incident in which more than 400 Vietnamese had crossed the border into Cambodia and threatened inmates and staff at the Mondol Kiri camp. Following the termination of the agreement, the US Government stated that it was prepared to offer asylum to the refugees who remained in Cambodia. The Cambodian Government announced in April that, while it would authorize the resettlement of the Montagnard refugees in the USA, it planned to close down the camps housing the refugees and cease its provision of asylum within one month.

Following the repression of a protest rally in the Central Highland province of Dak Lak in April 2004 (see Domestic Political Affairs), there was a further influx of Montagnards into Cambodia. In January 2005 UNHCR and the Governments of Cambodia and Viet Nam signed an agreement on the resettlement to third countries or the repatriation to Viet Nam of some 750 Montagnards in Cambodia. The Vietnamese Government guaranteed that returnees would not be punished, discriminated against or prosecuted for their departure. In March the first group of 43 Montagnards who had opted for repatriation returned to Viet Nam; by that time a further 297 had decided to accept resettlement in third countries, including the USA, Finland and Canada. In December 2010 the Cambodian Government ordered UNHCR to close its centre for Montagnard refugees in Phnom-Penh, the Cambodian capital, by 1 January 2011, insisting that there was no reason for the refugees' continued stay in Cambodia, citing Viet Nam's economic progress and absence of armed conflict in Montagnard areas. The Cambodian Government subsequently agreed to an extension to the deadline, until 15 February, in order to allow more time to resettle or repatriate the 62 Montagnards remaining at the centre. Human Rights Watch urged the Cambodian Government to remain mindful of the fact that, regardless of the centre's closure, as a party to the 1951 UN Convention Relating to the Status of Refugees, Cambodia had 'a clear obligation to ensure that future Montagnard asylum-seekers are permitted to enter a refugee screening process that is fair and based on international standards'. A spokesperson for the Vietnamese Ministry of Foreign Affairs stated in late February 2011 that the Vietnamese Government 'highly valued' the Cambodian Government's decision to close the camp.

Foreign Affairs
Regional relations

Relations with Kampuchea (known as Cambodia until 1976 and again from 1989) deteriorated during 1977, and in December Viet Nam launched a major offensive into eastern Kampuchea. Sporadic fighting continued, and in December 1978 Viet Nam invaded Kampuchea in support of elements opposed to the regime of the Khmers Rouges (see the chapter on Cambodia). By January 1979 the Government of Pol Pot had been overthrown and a pro-Vietnamese regime was installed. The invasion prompted much international criticism, and in February Chinese forces launched a punitive attack across the border into Viet Nam. Peace talks began in April but made little progress, and in March 1980 they were suspended by China. In March 1983 Viet Nam rejected a five-point peace plan, proposed by China, aimed at resolving the dispute over Kampuchea. In 1984 Chinese and Vietnamese troops engaged in heavy fighting, accusing each other of persistent border violations. China refused to normalize relations with Viet Nam until the withdrawal of Vietnamese troops from Kampuchea. Throughout 1986 and 1987 further armed clashes between Vietnamese and Chinese soldiers occurred on the Sino-Vietnamese border. Both sides denied responsibility for initiating the attacks. In early 1988 the tension between the two countries was exacerbated by the re-emergence of conflict over the Spratly Islands in the South China Sea, when the Vietnamese Government alleged that China had dispatched warships to the islands. (For many years the sovereignty of the islands had been contested, not only by Viet Nam and China, which engaged in military conflict over the issue in 1974, but also by the neighbouring states of Brunei, Malaysia, the Philippines and Taiwan.)

In March 1984 Viet Nam agreed in principle that it would eventually withdraw its troops from Kampuchea, and in August 1985 it was announced that all Vietnamese troops would be withdrawn by 1990. An eight-point peace plan, proposed by Kampuchean resistance leaders in March 1986 (involving the installation of a quadripartite government in Kampuchea, to be followed by UN-supervised elections), was rejected by Viet Nam. Viet Nam's urgent need of Western aid, together with increasing pressure from the USSR, prompted an announcement in May 1988 that Viet Nam would withdraw 50,000 (of an estimated total of 100,000) troops from Kampuchea by the end of the year. The Vietnamese military high command left Kampuchea in June, placing the remainder of the Vietnamese forces under Kampuchean control.

In April 1989 the Vietnamese Government and the Heng Samrin regime in Kampuchea declared that Vietnamese troops would withdraw by September even if a political settlement had not been reached, on condition that military assistance to the three other Kampuchean factions also ceased by that date. China responded that it would halt military aid to the Khmers Rouges only after a complete withdrawal of Vietnamese troops had been verified. The Vietnamese Government claimed that the withdrawal of troops had been completed by the end of September. However, the absence of a UN commission to verify the troops' departure led to claims by the Government-in-exile of Democratic Kampuchea that a number of troops remained in the country, while ASEAN, China and the USA initially refused to recognize the alleged withdrawal. In July 1990 the USA finally acknowledged that all troops had been withdrawn.

In September 1990 secret negotiations took place between Viet Nam and China, during which the Vietnamese endorsed a new UN Security Council agreement to resolve the conflict in Cambodia (q.v.). It was widely believed that the Chinese had promised an improvement in Sino-Vietnamese relations in exchange for Vietnamese support for the UN plan. In October 1991 Viet Nam was a signatory to a peace agreement whereby an interim Supreme National Council was established in Cambodia, representing all four factions there, as a prelude to the holding of UN-supervised elections. The agreement allowed immediate progress towards ending Viet Nam's diplomatic and economic isolation (see below). During 1992–93 there were several massacres of civilians of Vietnamese origin living in Cambodia. In January 1995 the First Prime Minister of Cambodia, Prince Norodom Ranariddh, visited Viet Nam for discussions. In November of that year Viet Nam accused the Cambodian Government of supporting a dissident Vietnamese movement, based in Phnom-Penh. In January 1996 it was reported that Cambodian troops had opened fire in a southern border area; Cambodia subsequently claimed that Vietnamese forces had made incursions into Cambodian territory. Discussions between Vietnamese and Cambodian government officials on the border issue took place in April and May, and in March 1997 Viet Nam and Cambodia signed an agreement on bilateral co-operation in combating crime.

In 2000 security officials from Viet Nam and Cambodia signed a number of agreements aimed at combating drugs-trafficking and strengthening border controls. In November 2005 Viet Nam and Cambodia signed a supplementary border treaty to an existing one concluded in 1985; under the new agreement, the demarcation of the border between the two countries was to be finalized by the end of 2008. However, owing to technical problems, such as unclear maps drawn up during colonial times, and to flooding, work on demarcation progressed slowly and the projected date for its completion was postponed until 2012. In May 2008 a new body, the Vietnam-Laos-Cambodia Economic Co-operation and Development Association, was established in Hanoi; its initial membership of 500 organizations, individuals and enterprises was expected to double by 2012. Relations were further strengthened in December 2009 by the signing of bilateral co-operation agreements on power generation, industry, mining and maritime transport, and by the signing, at a conference co-hosted by the Vietnamese Ministry of Planning and Investment and the Cambodian Development Council later in December, of more than 60 further agreements and contracts, intended to promote Vietnamese investment in Cambodia and estimated to be worth some US $6,000m. Bilateral trade was expected to reach $2,300m. in 2010. At a joint investment promotion conference co-chaired by the Vietnamese and Cambodian respective premiers in Phnom-Penh in April 2011, it was announced that the two countries were targeting an increase in bilateral trade to $6,500m. by 2015. Meanwhile, in March 2010 a new 70-km road extending from the Vietnamese province of Gia Lai, in the Central Highlands region, to the Cambodian province of Ratanak Kiri was opened to traffic. The Vietnamese Deputy Prime Minister, Truong Vinh Trong, and Cambodian Prime Minister Hun Sen presided over the inauguration of the project, which they hailed as a symbol of burgeoning bilateral relations.

Meanwhile, following the conclusion of the Cambodian peace agreement in October 1991, Vo Van Kiet and Do Muoi paid an official visit to China in November, during which normal diplomatic relations were restored and agreements were concluded on trade and on border affairs. Further agreements were signed in March 1992 on the resumption of transport and communications links (severed in 1979), and on the reopening of border posts. In May 1992 Viet Nam protested to China when the latter unilaterally granted exploration rights to a US petroleum company in an area of the South China Sea regarded by Viet Nam as part of its continental shelf; several more protests were lodged later in the year over the presence of Chinese vessels in disputed areas. In November the Chinese Premier, Li Peng, made an official visit to Viet Nam (the first visit by a Chinese head of government since 1971): new agreements on economic, scientific and cultural co-operation were signed, and the two Governments agreed to accelerate negotiations on disputed territory that had begun in the previous month. In October 1993 Viet Nam and China concluded an agreement to avoid the use of force when resolving territorial disputes. In November 1994 the two countries agreed to co-operate in seeking an early resolution to all border disputes. During an official visit by Do Muoi to China in November 1995, it was agreed that rail links between the two countries would be restored (they were subsequently reopened in February 1996). In April 1996 the state-owned petroleum company, Petrovietnam, signed a joint exploration contract with a US enterprise that covered part of the South China Sea where the Chinese Government had granted exploration rights in May 1992. In May 1996 China agreed to abide by the UN Convention on the Law of the Sea, which provided for international arbitration, but at the same time announced a new delineation of its sea border, attracting criticism from Viet Nam and other nations in the region.

In March 1997 Chinese vessels entered Vietnamese waters around the disputed Spratly Islands and were believed to be carrying out exploratory activities. China defended its actions, declaring a legitimate claim to the territory. In April China agreed to hold talks with Viet Nam over the issue; however, China withdrew the vessels before the discussions took place, stating that its operation in the area had been completed. In May China ratified the opening to traffic of a sea route between north-eastern Viet Nam and China. In October 1998 Phan Van Khai made an official visit to China, during which it was agreed that Viet Nam and China would increase efforts to reach a settlement on their various border disputes; in November, however, Viet Nam reiterated its territorial claim to the disputed Spratly Islands. In December 1999 a formal border treaty was signed by Viet Nam and China. Vietnamese leaders travelled to China in June 2000 to attend an ideological symposium on methods of introducing market reforms without incurring any loss of political control. The visit was regarded as a major improvement in bilateral relations, and was followed by a second symposium in Hanoi in November. The two countries also made further progress in delineating their mutual land border, which took effect from July 2000, and finalized their border in the Gulf of Tonkin in late December, the latter agreement demarcating their economic and fishing zones. Chinese military delegations visited Viet Nam in July 2000 and February 2001 to enhance military co-operation, and President Tran Duc Luong visited China in December 2000 and 2001. In February 2002 Chinese President Jiang Zemin paid an official visit to Viet Nam, his second since the restoration of normal bilateral relations in 1991. His visit coincided with campaigns mounted by several dissidents expressing concern over the agreements that had been signed to demarcate the Sino-Vietnamese border. An ongoing dispute over fishing rights in the Gulf of Tonkin prevented the ratification of any agreement to delineate the shared maritime boundary. During Jiang Zemin's visit modest agreements on technical and economic co-operation were signed, and the framework was agreed for a Chinese loan of US $12m. to Viet Nam. In April 2002 it was reported that the two countries had begun demarcating their land border. In November of that year, following an ASEAN summit meeting attended by China, a declaration was issued outlining a code of conduct to be observed by those countries contesting the Spratly Islands. It was hoped that the agreement would end Viet Nam's dispute with China over the issue. However, China strongly opposed Viet Nam's decision, in March 2004, to allow tourists to visit the Spratly Islands, claiming that the tours infringed its territorial sovereignty.

Viet Nam and China accelerated efforts to delineate their border in early 2005, and an 11th round of talks was held on the issue in Hanoi in February and March. In October Viet Nam and China agreed to conduct joint military patrols of the Gulf of Tonkin. Later that month Chinese President Hu Jintao made a three-day state visit to Viet Nam, during which he met with President Tran Duc Luong and General Secretary of the Central Committee of the Communist Party Nong Duc Manh. Bilateral relations were discussed, as were issues of regional and international concern, and both countries pledged to work together to promote mutual trust and encourage further bilateral co-operation. President Nguyen Minh Triet visited China in May 2007, holding talks with Hu Jintao and Premier Wen Jiabao. Several agreements on co-operation were signed during the visit, including nine economic accords. Notably, a joint working group was established to formulate a five-year plan for the further development of bilateral economic and trade co-operation. Border issues were also addressed, with Presidents Nguyen and Hu pledging to complete the demarcation of the 1,350-km land border in 2008 and to accelerate negotiations on the delineation of boundaries in the Gulf of Tonkin. However, the territorial dispute in the South China Sea continued to provoke tensions, and in July 2007 a Chinese naval vessel fired on Vietnamese fishing boats near the Spratly Islands, sinking one boat; one fisherman died in the incident and several others were injured. In November, moreover, Viet Nam protested after China conducted naval exercises near the Paracel Islands, and in the following month Vietnamese students demonstrated outside China's embassy in Hanoi and its consulate in Ho Chi Minh City, following reports that China was to create a new municipality incorporating the Spratly and Paracel Islands. In July 2008 Viet Nam announced that it intended to continue with a joint petroleum exploration project with ExxonMobil in disputed waters in the South China Sea, despite a warning from China to the US energy company to cancel the agreement. In December the Chinese and Vietnamese Governments announced that, following four days of negotiations in Hanoi, the demarcation of the land border had been completed as scheduled. Three formal border agreements were signed by the two countries in November 2009 and took effect in July 2010: a protocol on border demarcation and landmark-planting; an agreement on border management regulations; and an agreement on border-gates and their management Both countries hailed the implementation of the agreements as the formal conclusion to the 36-year land border dispute and an important 'milestone' in bilateral relations; an agreement to form a joint land border committee was also announced. Meanwhile, in 2009 China was Viet Nam's largest trade partner, with two-way trade valued at US $17,238.4m.

In commemoration of the 60th anniversary of the establishment of diplomatic relations, the year 2010 was designated as the 'China-Viet Nam Friendship Year'. However, relations continued to be impeded by ongoing tensions over the disputed Spratly and Paracel Islands. In June a Chinese tourism development plan incorporating the disputed Spratly and Paracel Islands was denounced by the Vietnamese Government, which restated its belief that Viet Nam held 'indisputable sovereignty' over both archipelagos. In July the two countries agreed to address 'properly' their maritime territory issues, as well as to expand political, economic, trade and cultural ties, and to enhance co-operation on regional and international issues. However, in August the Vietnamese Government issued a demand that China 'immediately cease violating Viet Nam's sovereignty. . . in the East Sea' in response to reports that Chinese vessels had, since May, been conducting oil and gas exploration activities off the coast of Tri Ton Island, part of the Paracel Islands. Tensions were significantly exacerbated by the arrest in mid-September of nine Vietnamese fishermen in the South China Sea by the Chinese authorities; following forthright demands from the Vietnamese Government that China grant their 'immediate and unconditional' release; the fishermen were released in mid-October. The first direct flights between Ho Chi Minh City and Beijing were inaugurated in December; it was hoped that the new route would facilitate an expansion in bilateral trade and tourism.

The Cambodian peace agreement of 1991 allowed Viet Nam to initiate closer relations with ASEAN member states: Vo Van Kiet visited Indonesia, Thailand and Singapore in late 1991 and Malaysia, Brunei and the Philippines in early 1992; agreements on economic co-operation were concluded with these countries, including guarantees of protection for future investment by them in Viet Nam. In July 1992 Viet Nam signed the ASEAN agreement (of 1976) on regional amity and co-operation, and in July 1995 became a full member of the organization. In September 1992 an agreement was signed with Singapore on the mutual provision of 'most-favoured nation' trading status. In April 1995 Viet Nam, Thailand, Laos and Cambodia signed an agreement providing for the establishment of the Mekong River Commission (see p. 448), which was to co-ordinate the sustainable development of the resources of the Lower Mekong River basin. In October 1997 Viet Nam and Thailand reached an agreement to demarcate their maritime boundary, following a series of incidents between Vietnamese and Thai fishing vessels. In December 1998 Viet Nam hosted the sixth summit meeting of the heads of state and government of the ASEAN grouping of countries. During 2000 Viet Nam reaffirmed sovereignty over the Spratly and Paracel Islands, but reassured ASEAN that it was committed to a peaceful solution to the territorial dispute through multilateral negotiations. It was hoped that the declaration of November 2002, which established a code of conduct to be adhered to by the claimants of the islands, would provide such a solution. Vietnamese and Laotian officials held several meetings during the course of 2000, and Viet Nam provided assistance to Laos in its fight against ethnic Hmong rebels. In November 2001 President Tran Duc Long held talks with President Gloria Macapagal Arroyo while on an official visit to the Philippines. The two countries agreed to the enhancement of economic relations and to co-operation in trade, investment and tourism. In February 2002 the Prime Minister met with the Prime Ministers of Cambodia and of Laos in Ho Chi Minh City. The three countries agreed to promote co-operation in the development of tourism and infrastructure within the 'development triangle'. In February 2004 the first joint meeting of the Cabinets of Viet Nam and Thailand took place. During the meeting, several co-operation agreements were signed concerning various social and economic issues. Prime Minister Phan Van Khai paid a four-day visit to Singapore (the largest foreign investor in Viet Nam) in March, during which a comprehensive co-operation framework document was signed. Following the announcement also in March that Viet Nam intended to allow tourists to begin visiting the Spratly Islands, the first tour took place in April, despite opposition from other claimants to the disputed islands. In May Viet Nam announced that it was renovating a disused runway on one of the islands to further its tourism plans. As part of efforts to strengthen relations with other ASEAN member states, particularly in the area of economic co-operation, Vietnamese Prime Minister Nguyen Tan Dung visited Brunei, Indonesia, Myanmar, the Philippines and Singapore in August 2007. In February 2008 Viet Nam, Cambodia and Laos concluded a draft agreement on defining the intersection point of their borders. In the following month Viet Nam ratified the new ASEAN Charter, which codified the principles and purposes of the Association and had been signed in November 2007 at the 13th summit meeting in Singapore. Viet Nam initially opposed the inclusion of a human rights mechanism in the Charter, but later agreed to the provision. Viet Nam assumed the annually rotating chair of ASEAN in January 2010. An agreement committing the respective legislative bodies of Viet Nam and Indonesia to increased collaboration and visit exchanges was signed in the Indonesian capital, Jakarta, in March. During a visit to Hanoi by Philippine President Benigno Aquino in October, Aquino and Vietnamese President Nguyen Minh Triet concluded a number of agreements, including separate memoranda of understanding (MOUs) on defence and education.

In January 1992 a Japanese government mission visited Viet Nam to negotiate the repayment of Vietnamese debts, and in November Japan (which—although a principal trading partner—had hitherto imposed a ban on official economic co-operation) began to provide financial assistance to Viet Nam. By the end of the 2000s Japan was the largest source of Official Development Assistance (ODA) to Viet Nam; Japanese ODA to Viet Nam reached 155,000m. yen in the 2009 fiscal year. In March 1999 Prime Minister Phan Van Khai made an official visit to Japan. During 2000 Viet Nam and Japan also strengthened their defence links, with the aim of promoting regional security. In June 2001 Phan Van Khai paid a further visit to Japan. In May 2008 Viet Nam and Japan signed a co-operation agreement on the use of nuclear energy, under the terms of which Japan pledged to help Viet Nam to prepare and plan for the introduction of nuclear energy. During a visit to Hanoi by Japanese Prime Minister Naoto Kan in October 2010, Vietnamese premier Nguyen Tan Dung thanked Kan for Japan's continued financial contribution to Viet Nam's economic and social development. In a joint statement the two leaders underscored the importance of ongoing bilateral co-operation in the fields of, *inter alia*, energy and climate change, and noted that the Vietnamese Government had decided to choose Japan as its 'cooperation partner' in the proposed construction of two reactors at a second planned nuclear plant in Viet Nam's Ninh Thuan province; however, no formal agreement to this end was reported to have been signed. The statement also revealed that the two countries had agreed to co-operate in the exploration for, and the mining, development and production of, rare earth minerals within Viet Nam that were vital to the manufacture of high-tech merchandise.

Relations with the USA

From 1984 Viet Nam indicated that it would welcome a return to normal diplomatic relations with the USA, but the latter rejected any re-establishment of relations until agreements were made concerning the return to the USA of the remains of US soldiers 'missing in action' (MIA) from Viet Nam, and the proposed resettlement in the USA of some 10,000 Vietnamese 'political prisoners'. A number of senior US officials visited Hanoi during 1985 and 1986 for discussions about missing soldiers (estimated to total 1,797), and Viet Nam arranged for the return of some of the remains. In September 1987 the Vietnamese Government agreed to investigate the fate of some 70 soldiers who were believed to have been captured alive, while the US Government, in turn, agreed to facilitate humanitarian aid for Viet Nam from US charities and private groups, which had hitherto been illegal. In July 1988 Viet Nam agreed in principle to the resettlement of former political detainees in the USA or elsewhere. In early 1991 a US representative was stationed in Hanoi to supervise inquiries into MIA, the first official US presence in Viet Nam since 1975. In April 1991 the USA proposed a four-stage programme for the resumption of normal diplomatic relations with Viet Nam, conditional on Vietnamese co-operation in reaching a diplomatic settlement in Cambodia and in accounting for the remaining MIA. Following the conclusion of the peace agreement on Cambodia in October, Viet Nam made a plea for the removal of the US economic embargo, and in November discussions on the establishment of normal trade relations began. In early 1992 the US Government agreed to provide humanitarian aid for Viet Nam, but refused to end the economic embargo, reiterating that relations would not fully return to normal until after the UN-supervised elections in Cambodia, due to take place in early 1993. The embargo was renewed for another year in September 1992, although in December the US Government announced that US companies would now be allowed to open offices and sign contracts in Viet Nam, in anticipation of a future removal of the embargo. In July 1993 the new administration of President Bill Clinton revoked the US veto on assistance from the IMF and the World Bank for Viet Nam. In September the USA permitted US companies to take part in projects in Viet Nam that were financed by international aid agencies. The trade embargo was finally removed in February 1994.

In January 1995 Viet Nam and the USA signed an agreement permitting the two countries to establish liaison offices in each other's capitals (these were opened immediately) and which resolved a long-standing dispute concerning former US diplomatic properties seized by the Vietnamese authorities in 1975. The establishment of full diplomatic relations was announced in July 1995. In May 1996 Clinton formally ended Viet Nam's official classification as a combat zone. In March 1997 military relations were established between the two countries. In April Douglas Peterson was appointed as the first US ambassador to Viet Nam, and in May Le Van Bang was formally appointed the first Vietnamese ambassador to the USA. In June Madeleine Albright became the first US Secretary of State to visit the country since the end of the Viet Nam War. During a visit to Washington, DC, in November by the Vietnamese Minister of Planning and Investment, an agreement was signed to promote greater economic co-operation. This was facilitated in March 1998, when Clinton signed a waiver to the 'Jackson-Vanik amendment' to 1974 US trade legislation, which restricted trade with communist countries. (In August 1999 the US House of Representatives voted in favour of an extension of the waiver of the amendment for Viet Nam.) In September 1998 the Vietnamese Deputy Prime Minister and Minister of Foreign Affairs, Nguyen Manh Cam, made an official visit to the USA. In July 1999 Viet Nam and the USA reached agreement in principle on the establishment of normal trade relations. Madeleine Albright made another official visit to Viet Nam in September. In March 2000 the US Secretary of Defense, William Cohen, made the first visit to Viet Nam by a US Secretary of Defense since the end of the Viet Nam War.

Although in early 2000 the US Government continued to refuse to acknowledge the responsibility of the chemical defoliant Agent Orange, sprayed in large quantities over areas of Viet Nam by the USA during the Viet Nam War, for widespread health problems (including birth defects) among the Vietnamese, Cohen, during his visit in March, reportedly indicated that the US Government would be willing to conduct joint research with the Vietnamese Government into the effects of the chemical. In May the US House of Representatives approved a resolution calling for the release of all political and religious prisoners in Viet Nam, a motion that was criticized as 'impudent interference' by Viet Nam. A landmark bilateral trade agreement between the USA and Viet Nam was signed in Washington, DC, in 2000, preparing the way for an increase in exports to, and investment from, the USA. The agreement was subject to an annual review by the US Congress. US President Bill Clinton made a highly significant visit to Viet Nam in November, the first since a brief stop-over by Richard Nixon in 1969. Although warmly received by the Vietnamese people, Clinton's calls for greater freedoms were rebuffed by General Secretary Le Kha Phieu, who defended the socialist system. In March 2001 Viet Nam accused US-based groups of fomenting the recent unrest in the Central Highlands (see above). In April a helicopter carrying nine Vietnamese and seven US citizens, searching for the remains of MIA, crashed in the highlands, killing all on board. Some 1,498 US servicemen and 300,000 Vietnamese remained unaccounted for in Viet Nam.

Following the September 2001 attacks on the USA (see the chapter on the USA) the Vietnamese Government expressed its support for the US-led 'war on terror'. In October the severe penalty imposed on the dissident Roman Catholic priest Father Nguyen Van Ly (see above) accelerated the passage of the Viet Nam Human Rights Act through the US House of Representatives. The act was intended to make US non-humanitarian aid to

Viet Nam conditional upon the improvement of its human rights record, thus antagonizing the Vietnamese Government; however the act was subsequently blocked and never voted on in the Senate. (The act was reintroduced and approved again by the US House of Representatives in July 2004, but subsequently stalled in the Senate. The House of Representatives adopted another version of the act in September 2007.) In November 2001 the National Assembly finally ratified the bilateral trade agreement, marking the complete restoration of normal relations between the two countries. In March 2002 Vietnamese and US scientists attended an unprecedented joint conference in Hanoi, at which the effects of Agent Orange were discussed. As a result, the two countries formally agreed to conduct joint research into the effects of the defoliant. However, relations with the USA threatened to deteriorate once more when the US Government expressed its concern for the safety of refugees returning to the Central Highlands from Cambodia. In March 2002, following the collapse of Viet Nam's agreement with UNHCR, the USA offered asylum to those refugees who remained in Cambodia. In the same month relations were further strained when the US Government issued a critical report on Viet Nam's human rights record.

In early 2003 the Vietnamese Government condemned the US-led campaign to oust the regime of Saddam Hussain in Iraq. However, in November relations improved when Minister of National Defence Lt-Gen. Pham Can Tra visited Washington, DC, and held talks with US Secretary of Defense Donald Rumsfeld. In the same month a US frigate spent four days in the port of Ho Chi Minh City, the first visit to Viet Nam by a US warship since the end of the Viet Nam War in 1975. In December 2003 an aviation agreement was signed with the USA, enabling direct flights between the two countries for the first time; the first US flight arrived in Ho Chi Minh City in December 2004. During a visit to Viet Nam in February 2004 Adm. Thomas Fargo, head of the US Pacific Command, reportedly became the first foreign official to visit the naval base at Da Nang. In January, meanwhile, an independent organization, the Vietnam Association for Victims of Agent Orange, submitted a lawsuit to the US Federal Court, on behalf of three Vietnamese people who had been affected by the defoliant, against the US companies that were responsible for its manufacture. The lawsuit was the first of its kind to have been filed. In March 2005, however, the US Federal Court dismissed the lawsuit, ruling that there was no legal basis for the claims of the plaintiffs. In February 2008 an appeal against the judgment was rejected. The Vietnam Association for Victims of Agent Orange condemned the decision and announced its intention to file an appeal with the US Supreme Court.

In September 2004 the US Secretary of State designated Viet Nam as a 'country of particular concern' under the International Religious Freedom Act for particularly severe violations of religious freedom. (Viet Nam was removed from the list in November 2006.) The Department of State again urged the Vietnamese Government to release prisoners detained for their religious beliefs and to reopen churches closed in the Central Highlands. The designation was denounced by the Vietnamese Government, which lodged an official protest with the US Government. In June 2005 Prime Minister Phan Van Khai, accompanied by a delegation of government officials, made an official state visit to the USA. He thus became the most senior Vietnamese official to visit the USA since the end of the Viet Nam War three decades previously. During his visit, he met with US President George W. Bush. Among the issues discussed were Viet Nam's application to join the World Trade Organization (WTO, see p. 430), human rights, religious freedom and corporate development. In May 2006 the two countries signed a bilateral trade agreement, marking the final stage of Viet Nam's accession to the WTO. US Secretary of Defense Rumsfeld's visit to Viet Nam in June was followed by a visit from President Bush in November. In December the US Congress approved legislation permitting 'permanent normal trade relations' with Viet Nam. It appeared that progress was being made with regard to the ongoing Agent Orange issue when the Bush Administration approved funding of US $400,000 towards a $1m. study into the decontamination of its former base in Da Nang in February 2007. In June Nguyen Minh Triet became the first Vietnamese head of state to visit the USA since the end of the Viet Nam War. Nguyen held talks with President Bush during the visit, and several bilateral economic agreements were signed, including a Trade and Investment Framework Agreement (TIFA). However, while the two Presidents were meeting, hundreds of protesters, including many Vietnamese exiles, demanded the release of Vietnamese political prisoners. The first ministerial-level meeting on the TIFA took place in Washington, DC, in December, focusing on Viet Nam's implementation of its WTO commitments, following its accession to that organization in January, as well as measures to expand bilateral trade and investment relations. In June 2008 Prime Minister Nguyen Tan Dung visited the USA, where he had discussions with President Bush in the fourth bilateral meeting between Vietnamese and US leaders in as many years. During Nguyen's visit, he and Bush agreed to launch negotiations on a potential bilateral investment agreement; the first round of negotiations was held in Washington, DC, in December 2008, followed by a second round in Hanoi in July 2009. In the latter year the USA was the largest foreign investor in Viet Nam, and bilateral trade stood at $15,271.4m. Despite the global economic deceleration in 2008/09, US merchandise exports to Viet Nam increased by about 11% in 2009. In early August 2010 the 15th anniversary of the restoration of normal diplomatic relations was commemorated by a port visit to Viet Nam by a US war vessel, a visit that reflected burgeoning military links between the two countries, which held their first senior-level defence dialogue in mid-August. However, rumours that the Vietnamese Government was considering entering into a military alliance with the USA were categorically denied in late August by the Vietnamese Vice-Minister of Defence. Meanwhile, during a visit to Hanoi in the previous month, US Secretary of State Hillary Clinton stated that resolution of the dispute over ownership of the Spratly Islands was 'pivotal' to regional stability as well as to US and Vietnamese national interests and offered US mediation in efforts to resolve the issue; the offer provoked an irate response from the Chinese Government, which accused the US Administration of interference in regional affairs.

Relations with Russia

Following the dissolution of the USSR at the end of 1991, the Vietnamese Government pursued close relations with its successor states, particularly Russia. In June 1994 Vo Van Kiet visited Russia, Ukraine and Kazakhstan to discuss economic and defence co-operation issues. In February 1997 Russia announced plans further to develop its defence links with Viet Nam, and in November of that year the Russian Prime Minister, Viktor Chernomyrdin, paid an official visit to Viet Nam; Tran Duc Luong made a reciprocal visit to Russia in August 1998. The Russian Deputy Prime Minister, Viktor Khristenko, visited Viet Nam in July 2000 to discuss Russian involvement in oil and gas development, and Viet Nam's outstanding 11,000m. rouble Soviet-era debt. Agreement on the latter was reached in September, when it was arranged that Viet Nam would repay Russia US $1,700m. over 23 years, mostly in the form of business concessions. In February–March 2001 the Russian President, Vladimir Putin, became the first Russian (or Soviet) head of state to visit Viet Nam. The two countries agreed to strengthen co-operation in economic, energy, and military and defence matters, and proclaimed a new 'strategic partnership'. In May 2002 control of the former Soviet naval base at Cam Ranh Bay, in central Viet Nam, was formally transferred to the Vietnamese Government, two years ahead of the agreed date.

In May 2004 President Tran Duc Luong visited Russia and held talks with President Putin on bilateral relations, focusing particularly on expanding economic co-operation. Both leaders confirmed their commitment to the 'strategic partnership'. In April 2007 Russia and Viet Nam reached agreement in principle on reducing barriers to bilateral trade, and in June the two countries initialled an MOU on Russia's bid for accession to the WTO, which Viet Nam had joined in January 2007. Trade and investment were also the main areas of discussion during visits by Prime Minister Nguyen Tan Dung to Russia, the Czech Republic and Poland in September. During a state visit to Russia in October 2008, President Nguyen Minh Triet stressed that Viet Nam wished to increase co-operation with Russia in all areas, including the media, education, and the oil and gas sectors; Nguyen's proposal to establish a joint Vietnamese-Russian university was welcomed by his Russian counterpart. During a visit to Moscow in December 2009, Prime Minister Nguyen Tan Dung announced that Viet Nam had concluded a US $2,000m. deal agreeing to purchase submarines from Russia. A further agreement, concluded in February 2010, provided for the supply to Viet Nam of 12 Russian fighter aircraft in 2011–12 at an estimated cost of $1,000m. During a visit to Hanoi by Russian President Dmitrii Medvedev in October 2010, an agreement was signed on the construction, by state firm Russian Atomic Energy Corp, of Viet Nam's first nuclear power plant, to be located in Ninh Thuan province, in a deal reported to be worth around $5,000m. Construction of the plant was due to commence in 2014, with completion scheduled by 2020. Meanwhile, the delivery of eight Russian fighter jets purchased by Viet Nam under an earlier arrangement was anticipated in 2011.

Other external relations

In the late 1990s Viet Nam developed closer links with India, ostensibly because of mutual concerns about China. The Indian Minister of Defence visited Viet Nam in March 2000 and signed a wide-ranging defence agreement that would allow Viet Nam to train the Indian army in jungle warfare and counter-insurgency methods, and India to assist in the modernization of the Vietnamese military. The two countries also agreed to take action to combat piracy in the South China Sea. The Indian Minister of External Affairs, Jaswant Singh, and Prime Minister Atal Bihari Vajpayee made separate visits to Viet Nam in November 2000 and January 2001, respectively, and agreed to co-ordinate their positions in the Non-aligned Movement (see p. 461), South-South Co-operation and regional forums. India's Oil and Natural Gas Company became an investor in Viet Nam's Nam Con Son gas field in 2000, and India pledged some US $238m. of investment in the Vietnamese petroleum and gas industries. In September 2001 the Minister of Foreign Affairs, Nguyen Dy Nien, visited India, and in March 2002 Vice-President Nguyen Thi Binh also visited the country to discuss the possibility of closer bilateral co-operation. Relations were further strengthened in July 2007 by a state visit to India by Prime Minister Nguyen Tan Dung, during which a joint declaration was signed on the establishment of a 'strategic partnership' between India and Viet Nam, covering bilateral co-operation in the areas of politics, the economy, security, defence, culture, science and technology. In March 2008 the Vietnamese Minister of Public Security, Le Hong Anh, and the Indian Minister of Home Affairs, Shivraj Patil, signed an MOU on bilateral co-operation in combating international terrorism and drugs-trafficking. The Indian President, Pratibha Devisingh Patil, held talks with President Nguyen Minh Triet regarding the expansion of economic relations between the two countries in November 2008 during her first official visit to Viet Nam. Defence links were bolstered by the visit to India of the Vietnamese Minister of National Defence, Gen. Phung Quang Thanh, in November 2009. Prime Minister Nguyen Tan Dung was reported in April 2010 to have instructed the Vietnam Airlines Corporation to open direct air routes between Viet Nam and India; he also envisaged the establishment of a bilateral business association. In the following month the two countries announced an agreement to create a joint committee to promote co-operation in, inter alia, trade, investment and technology. Preparations for the launch of the Viet Nam-India Business Forum were well advanced at mid-2011.

In October 1990 the European Community (EC, now the European Union—EU, see p. 270) announced the restoration of diplomatic relations with Viet Nam. The EC-Vietnam Joint Commission, a forum for senior-level discussions on political and economic developments in the EU and Viet Nam, was established in 1996; continuing to meet once every two years, the Commission was convened in Hanoi in November 2009. Meanwhile, in June 2008 the first session of negotiations on a Partnership and Co-operation Agreement (PCA) between Viet Nam and the EU took place in Brussels, Belgium. The PCA was to be a comprehensive agreement covering a broad range of areas for dialogue and co-operation in the political, economic, development, social and cultural fields. A further eight rounds of negotiations had been held by September 2010, following which a draft agreement was initialled by both sides in October. A final agreement was expected to be signed in 2011. Meanwhile, relations with the EU were further enhanced in March 2010 by the visit to Hanoi of the EU Commissioner for Trade, Karel De Gucht, during which De Gucht and Prime Minister Nguyen Tan Dung formally agreed to initiate negotiations on a bilateral free trade agreement. Preliminary technical preparations were under way at mid-2011, with talks expected officially to commence in the second half of the year.

Meanwhile, in October 1991 a group of industrialized countries, led by France, agreed to assist Viet Nam in paying its arrears to the IMF, thereby enabling it to qualify for future IMF loans (which nevertheless remained dependent on the approval of the USA, as the IMF's principal vote-holder). In February 1993 the French President, François Mitterrand, made an official visit to Viet Nam (the first Western head of state to do so since the country's reunification). France's Geopetrol oil company formed part of a consortium to develop Vietnamese offshore oil and gas deposits. In October 2002 President Tran Duc Luong paid the first visit to France by a Vietnamese leader since the establishment of diplomatic relations with that country in 1973. French President Jacques Chirac made an official visit to Viet Nam in October 2004, attending the fifth biennial Asia-Europe Meeting, which took place in Hanoi. Several agreements on bilateral co-operation were signed during the visit, and Chirac pledged his country's support for Viet Nam's (ultimately successful) bid to join the WTO.

Prime Minister Nguyen Tan Dung visited Germany, Ireland and the United Kingdom in March 2008, agreeing with his counterparts in the three countries to strengthen bilateral co-operation in a range of areas. In June 2009 National Assembly Chairman Nguyen Phu Trong made an official visit to Budapest, Hungary, during which he and his Hungarian counterpart, Szili Katalin, signed a co-operation agreement pledging to increase co-operation between their respective national assemblies. During a visit to the United Kingdom in September 2010, the Vietnamese Deputy Prime Minister and Minister of Foreign Affairs, Pham Gia Khiem, and the British Secretary of State for Foreign and Commonwealth Affairs, William Hague, signed a Strategic Partnership Agreement; this upgrading of relations was expected greatly to benefit British businesses looking to invest in Viet Nam, and to facilitate closer co-operation on countering organized crime, as well as allowing a continuation of the two states' 'frank dialogue' on human rights.

CONSTITUTION AND GOVERNMENT

The 1992 Constitution declares the supremacy of the Communist Party. Legislative power is vested in the National Assembly, which has 500 members and is elected for a five-year term by universal adult suffrage. The President, elected by the National Assembly from among its members, is the head of state and Commander-in-Chief of the armed forces. The President appoints a Prime Minister (from among the members of the National Assembly, and subject to their approval), who forms a government (again, subject to ratification by the National Assembly). The country is divided into provinces and municipalities, which are subordinate to the central government. Local government is entrusted to locally elected People's Councils.

REGIONAL AND INTERNATIONAL CO-OPERATION

Viet Nam is a member of the Association of Southeast Asian Nations (ASEAN, see p. 206), the Asia-Pacific Economic Co-operation (APEC, see p. 197), the Asian Development Bank (ADB, see p. 202), the UN's Economic and Social Commission for Asia and the Pacific (ESCAP, see p. 37) and the Mekong River Commission (see p. 448).

Viet Nam became a member of the UN in 1977, and was admitted to the World Trade Organization (WTO, see p. 430) in 2007. Viet Nam participates in the Group of 77 (G77, see p. 447) developing nations, and is also a member of the International Labour Organization (ILO, see p. 138) and the Non-aligned Movement (see p. 461).

ECONOMIC AFFAIRS

In 2009, according to estimates by the World Bank, Viet Nam's gross national income (GNI), measured at average 2007–09 prices, was US $87,979m., equivalent to $1,010 per head (or $2,850 per head on an international purchasing-power parity basis). During 2000–09, it was estimated, the population increased at an average annual rate of 1.3%, while gross domestic product (GDP) per head increased, in real terms, by an average of 5.9% per year. Overall GDP increased, in real terms, at an average annual rate of 7.3% in 2000–09. According to the Asian Development Bank (ADB), GDP grew by 5.3% in 2009 and by 6.8% in 2010.

In 2009 agriculture (including forestry and fishing) contributed an estimated 20.9% of GDP in 2009 and engaged 48.2% of the employed labour force. The staple crop is rice. Viet Nam is also a major producer of coffee; this commodity accounted for 4.2% of export revenue in 2007. Other important cash crops include sugar cane, groundnuts, cashew nuts, rubber, tea and cotton. According to the ADB, exports of wood and wood products increased from US $1,943m. in 2006 to $2,404m. in 2007, when they accounted for 5.3% of total export earnings. Livestock-rearing and fishing are also important. In 2007 marine products accounted for some 8.3% of export revenues. According to figures from the ADB, agricultural GDP increased at an average annual rate of 3.7% in 2000–09; the sector's GDP expanded by 1.8% in 2009 and by 2.8% in 2010.

In 2009 industry (comprising manufacturing, mining and quarrying, construction and utilities) contributed an estimated 40.2% of GDP. In 2009 the industrial sector engaged an estimated 19.6% of the labour force. According to figures from the ADB, industrial GDP increased at an average annual rate of 9.2% in 2000–09. The industrial sector's GDP expanded by 5.5% in 2009 and by 7.7% in 2010.

In 2009 mining and quarrying contributed an estimated 10.0% of GDP. The mining sector engaged only 1.0% of the labour force in 2009. Viet Nam's principal mineral exports are petroleum and coal. Tin, zinc, iron, antimony, chromium, natural phosphates, bauxite and gold are also mined. Significant reserves of offshore natural gas were discovered in 1993. In 2008 exports of mineral fuels accounted for 20.3% of total merchandise exports. According to figures from the ADB, mining GDP increased at an average annual rate of 2.3% in 2000–09. Mining GDP decreased by 3.8% in 2008, but increased by 7.6% in 2009.

Manufacturing contributed an estimated 20.1% of GDP in 2009, and in that year the sector accounted for 14.3% of employment. Manufacturing activities include food-processing, textiles, footwear, chemicals and electrical goods. Manufacturing GDP increased at an average annual rate of 10.7% in 2000–09. The sector's GDP expanded by 9.8% in 2008 and by 2.8% in 2009.

Construction contributed an estimated 6.6% of GDP in 2009, in which year the sector engaged 5.6% of the labour force. According to figures from the ADB, construction GDP increased at an average annual rate of 9.7% in 2000–09. The sector's GDP contracted by 0.4% in 2008, but expanded by 11.4% in 2009.

Energy is derived principally from hydroelectric power, which in 2007 accounted for 43.0% of the total electricity produced. Other sources are natural gas (32.1%), coal (21.4%) and petroleum (3.5%). In 2008 fuel imports accounted for 15.8% of the value of total merchandise imports. In February 2009 Viet Nam's first petroleum refinery, at Dung Quat, became operational. In 2006 the Government announced its intention to construct a 2,000-MW nuclear power plant by 2020.

The services sector contributed an estimated 38.8% of GDP in 2009, in which year it employed 32.2% of the labour force. Tourism is an important source of foreign exchange; receipts from tourism totalled US $3,926m. in 2008. The number of tourist arrivals rose from 3.8m. in 2009 to 5.0m. in 2010. According to figures from the ADB, the GDP of the services sector increased by an average of 7.3% per year in 2000–09. The sector's GDP rose by 6.6% in 2009 and by 7.5% in 2010.

In 2009 Viet Nam recorded a visible trade deficit of US $8,306m. The deficit on the current account of the balance of payments in that year was $6,116m. In 2009 the People's Republic of China was Viet Nam's principal source of imports, supplying 16.5% of total imports; other major sources were Singapore, Japan, the Republic of Korea and Thailand. The principal market for exports in that year was the USA (which accounted for 21.4%); other important purchasers were Japan and China. The principal exports in 2008 were mineral fuels (20.3%), food and live animals, machinery and transport equipment, and basic manufactures. In 2008 the principal imports were machinery and transport equipment (27.8%), basic manufactures, mineral fuels, chemicals and related products, food and live animals, and crude materials (inedible) except fuels.

In 2011 budgetary expenditure was forecast at 519,279,000m. dông, with revenue projected at 398,679,000m. dông. The fiscal deficit was initially projected at the equivalent of 5.3% of GDP for that year, but this projection was subsequently revised downwards to less than 5.0%. Viet Nam's total external debt was estimated by the ADB at US $27,929m. in 2009. In that year the cost of servicing the debt was equivalent to 7.5% of the value of exports of goods and services, rising to 8.5% in 2010. The annual rate of inflation averaged 7.4% in 2000–08. According to the ADB, the rate of inflation reached 6.9% in 2009 and 9.2% in 2010. In 2010 an estimated 4.4% of the labour force were unemployed.

The process of *doi moi* (renovation) was initiated in 1990 with the objective of transforming Viet Nam's centralized economy into a market-orientated system. Viet Nam's accession to the World Trade Organization (WTO, see p. 430) in January 2007 greatly improved the country's investment potential. However, owing to the deterioration in global economic conditions, foreign direct investment declined from US $9,279m. in 2008 to $6,900m. in 2009, rising only slightly in 2010. Having eased somewhat in 2009, inflationary pressures had increased again by the latter months of 2010 (in part owing to a depreciation of the Vietnamese currency) and were expected to accelerate in 2011. It was feared that the pressure on prices for essential commodities would jeopardize the substantial progress achieved in recent years with regard to the reduction of poverty among the population (the incidence of poverty reportedly having decreased from 12.3% in 2009 to 10.6% in 2010). The Government therefore hoped to raise its provision for social security programmes in 2011. The acceleration of economic growth in 2010 was attributed largely to the recovery in external demand; the value of exports rose by more than 26%. The ADB predicted that economic growth would be sustained in 2011, albeit at a more moderate pace, forecasting that GDP would expand by 6.1%. The Vietnamese Government remained committed to its programme of privatization ('equitization'), although in 2010 the relative weakness of the stock market continued to impede plans to transfer state assets to the private sector. Meanwhile, Viet Nam's international credit ratings were downgraded by some agencies, owing to uncertainty with regard to the Government's potential liabilities, as demonstrated in late 2010 when a state-owned shipping group defaulted on the repayment of a loan. Nevertheless, long-term prospects remained favourable. The Socio-Economic Development Strategy for 2011–20 projected annual GDP growth of 7%–8%. In February 2011 the Government announced a range of policy measures, with the objective of curtailing inflation, improving economic stability and restoring investor confidence,. These included the implementation of a more stringent monetary policy and the reduction of the fiscal deficit (see above) through the imposition of restrictions on public expenditure.

PUBLIC HOLIDAYS

2012: 2 January (for New Year's Day), 23–26 January (Tet, lunar new year)*, 3 February (Founding of the Communist Party), 2 April (Hung Kings Day)*, 30 April (Liberation of Saigon), 1 May (Labour Day), 3 September (for National Day).

* Varies according to the lunar calendar.

VIET NAM

Statistical Survey

Statistical Survey

Sources (unless otherwise stated): General Statistics Office of Viet Nam, 2 Hoang Van Thu, Ba Dinh District, Hanoi; tel. (4) 7332997; e-mail banbientap@gso.gov.vn; internet www.gso.gov.vn; Communist Party of Viet Nam, 1 Hoang Van Thu, Hanoi; e-mail cpv@hn.vnn.vn; internet www.cpv.org.vn.

Area and Population

AREA, POPULATION AND DENSITY

Area (sq km)	331,051.4*
Population (census results)	
1 April 1999	76,323,173
1 April 2009	
Males	42,413,143
Females	43,433,854
Total	85,846,997
Density (per sq km) at 2009 census	259.3

* 127,819.7 sq miles.

POPULATION BY AGE AND SEX
(UN estimates at mid-2011)

	Males	Females	Total
0–14	11,377,633	10,692,168	22,069,801
15–64	30,782,321	31,396,173	62,178,494
65 and over	2,350,291	3,377,186	5,727,477
Total	44,510,245	45,465,527	89,975,772

Source: UN, *World Population Prospects: The 2008 Revision*.

ADMINISTRATIVE DIVISIONS
(2009 census)

	Area (sq km)	Population ('000)	Density (per sq km)
Red River Delta	21,063.1	19,584.3	930
Hanoi	3,344.6	6,451.9	1,929
Vinh Phuc	1,231.8	999.8	812
Bac Ninh	822.7	1,024.5	1,245
Quang Ninh	6,099.0	1,145.0	188
Hai Duong	1,650.2	1,705.1	1,033
Haiphong	1,522.1	1,837.2	1,207
Hung Yen	923.5	1,127.9	1,221
Thai Binh	1,567.4	1,781.8	1,137
Ha Nam	860.2	784.1	912
Nam Dinh	1,652.5	1,828.1	1,106
Ninh Binh	1,389.1	899.0	647
North East	57,893.9	8,331.4	144
Ha Giang	7,945.8	724.5	91
Cao Bang	6,724.6	507.2	75
Bac Kan	4,859.4	293.8	60
Tuyen Quang	5,870.4	724.8	123
Lao Cai	6,383.9	614.6	96
Yen Bai	6,899.5	740.4	107
Thai Nguyen	3,526.2	1,123.1	319
Lang Son	8,323.8	732.5	88
Bac Giang	3,827.8	1,554.1	406
Phu Tho	3,532.5	1,316.4	373
North West	37,444.8	2,722.1	73
Dien Bien	9,562.9	490.3	51
Lai Chau	9,112.3	370.5	41
Son La	14,174.4	1,076.1	76
Hoa Binh	4,595.2	785.2	171
North Central Coast	51,524.6	10,070.2	195
Thanh Hoa	11,133.4	3,400.6	305
Nghe An	16,490.7	2,912.0	177
Ha Tinh	6,025.6	1,227.0	204
Quand Binh	8,065.3	844.9	105
Quang Tri	4,747.0	598.3	126
Thua Thien-Hué	5,062.6	1,087.4	215
South Central Coast	33,192.3	7,032.8	212
Da Nang	1,283.4	887.4	691
Quang Nam	10,438.4	1,422.3	136
Quang Ngai	5,152.7	1,216.8	236
Binh Dinh	6,039.6	1,486.5	246
Phu Yen	5,060.6	862.2	170
Khanh Hoa	5,217.6	1,157.6	222
Central Highlands	54,640.6	5,115.1	94
Kon Tum	9,690.5	430.1	44
Gia Lai	15,536.9	1,274.4	82
Dak Lak	13,125.4	1,733.6	132
Dak Nong	6,515.6	489.4	75
Lam Dong	9,772.2	1,187.6	122
South East	34,773.5	15,799.5	454
Ninh Thuan	3,358.0	565.0	168
Binh Thuan	7,810.4	1,167.0	149
Binh Phuoc	6,874.4	873.6	127
Tay Ninh	4,049.2	1,066.5	263
Binh Duong	2,695.2	1,481.6	550
Dong Nai	5,903.4	2,486.2	421
Ba Ria-Vung Tau	1,987.4	996.7	502
Ho Chi Minh City	2,095.5	7,162.9	3,418
Mekong River Delta	40,518.5	17,191.4	424
Long An	4,493.8	1,436.1	320
Tien Giang	2,484.2	1,672.3	673
Ben Tre	2,360.2	1,255.9	532
Tra Vinh	2,295.1	1,003.0	437
Vinh Long	1,479.1	1,024.7	693
Dong Thap	3,375.4	1,666.5	494
An Giang	3,536.8	2,142.7	606
Kien Giang	6,346.3	1,688.2	266
Can Tho	1,401.6	1,188.4	848
Hau Giang	1,601.1	757.3	473
Soc Trang	3,311.8	1,292.9	390
Bac Lieu	2,501.5	856.5	342
Ca Mau	5,331.6	1,206.9	226
Total	331,051.4	85,847.0	259

PRINCIPAL TOWNS
(excl. suburbs, estimated population at mid-1992)

Ho Chi Minh City (formerly Saigon)	3,015,743*	Nam Dinh	171,699
Hanoi (capital)	1,073,760	Qui Nhon	163,385
Haiphong	783,133	Vung Tau	145,145
Da Nang	382,674	Rach Gia	141,132
Buon Ma Thuot	282,095	Long Xuyen	132,681
Nha Trang	221,331	Thai Nguyen	127,643
Hué	219,149	Hong Gai	127,484
Can Tho	215,587	Vinh	112,455
Cam Pha	209,086		

* Including Cholon.

Source: UN, *Demographic Yearbook*.

Mid-2010 (incl. suburbs, '000 persons, UN estimates): Ho Chi Minh City 6,167; Hanoi 2,814 (refers to urban population in city districts); Haiphong 1,970 (Source: UN, *World Urbanization Prospects: The 2009 Revision*).

BIRTHS AND DEATHS
(annual averages, UN estimates)

	1995–2000	2000–05	2005–10
Birth rate (per 1,000)	21.3	19.1	17.3
Death rate (per 1,000)	5.7	5.3	5.4

Source: UN, *World Population Prospects: The 2008 Revision*.

Life expectancy (years at birth, WHO estimates): 73 (males 70; females 75) in 2008 (Source: WHO, *World Health Statistics*).

VIET NAM

EMPLOYMENT
('000 persons aged 15 years and over, averages at mid-year)

	2007	2008	2009*
Agriculture, hunting and forestry	22,696.6	22,705.5	23,022.0
Fishing	1,672.8	1,742.2	1,766.5
Mining and quarrying	406.8	446.0	477.4
Manufacturing	6,103.0	6,523.1	6,851.2
Power and utilities	201.6	232.3	262.6
Construction	2,320.9	2,476.4	2,692.8
Wholesale and retail trade; repair of motor vehicles, motor cycles and personal and household goods	4,984.1	5,131.5	5,285.2
Hotels and restaurants	766.6	793.7	811.6
Transport, storage and communications	1,146.6	1,167.0	1,207.9
Financial intermediation	197.7	210.3	219.6
Scientific activities and technology	25.3	25.7	26.7
Real estate, renting and business activities	203.4	240.2	267.4
Public administration and defence; compulsory social security	1,688.2	1,771.9	1,819.0
Education and training	1,277.8	1,338.7	1,370.2
Health and social work	361.9	381.9	391.5
Recreational, cultural and sporting activities	128.5	128.7	128.9
Activities of the Communist Party and of membership organizations	181.7	210.3	205.3
Community, social and personal service activities and private households with employed persons	844.5	935.4	937.6
Total employed	**45,208.0**	**46,460.8**	**47,743.6**

* Preliminary figures.

Unemployed (million persons): 2.3 in 2006; 2.0 in 2007; 2.4 in 2008 (Source: Asian Development Bank).

Health and Welfare

KEY INDICATORS

Total fertility rate (children per woman, 2008)	2.1
Under-5 mortality rate (per 1,000 live births, 2008)	14
HIV/AIDS (% of persons aged 15–49, 2007)	0.5
Physicians (per 1,000 head, 2002)	0.6
Hospital beds (per 1,000 head, 2005)	2.6
Health expenditure (2007): US $ per head (PPP)	183
Health expenditure (2007): % of GDP	7.1
Health expenditure (2007): public (% of total)	39.3
Access to water (% of persons, 2008)	94
Access to sanitation (% of persons, 2008)	75
Total carbon dioxide emissions ('000 metric tons, 2007)	111,286.7
Carbon dioxide emissions per head (metric tons, 2007)	1.3
Human Development Index (2007): ranking	116
Human Development Index (2007): value	0.725

For sources and definitions, see explanatory note on p. vi.

Agriculture

PRINCIPAL CROPS
('000 metric tons)

	2006	2007	2008
Rice, paddy	35,850	35,943	38,725
Maize	3,855	4,303	4,531
Potatoes*	370	370	370
Sweet potatoes	1,461	1,438	1,324
Cassava (Manioc)	7,783	8,193	9,396
Sugar cane	16,720	17,397	16,128
Beans, dry*	158	158	158
Cashew nuts, with shell	1,092	1,208	1,191
Soybeans (Soya beans)	258	276	269
Groundnuts, with shell	462	510	534
Coconuts	1,001	1,035	1,086

—continued	2006	2007	2008
Cabbages and other brassicas*	700	700	700
Onions, dry*	225	225	225
Watermelons*	420	420	420
Bananas*	1,350	1,355	1,355
Oranges*	601	601	601
Guavas, mangoes and mangosteens*	370	370	370
Pineapples*	470	470	470
Coffee, green	985	1,251†	1,067†
Tea	151	164	175
Tobacco, unmanufactured	42	32	32*
Natural rubber	555	606	660

* FAO estimate(s).
† Unofficial figure.

2009: Rice, paddy 38,896; Maize 4,382; Cassava (Manioc) 8,557; Sugar cane 15,246; Soybeans 214; Coffee, green 1,176 (unofficial figure).

Aggregate production ('000 metric tons, may include official, semi-official or estimated data): Total cereals 39,706 in 2006, 40,248 in 2007, 43,258 in 2008, 43,279 in 2009; Total roots and tubers 9,613 in 2006, 10,000 in 2007, 11,090 in 2008, 10,251 in 2009; Total vegetables (incl. melons) 7,991 in 2006–09; Total fruits (excl. melons) 5,716 in 2006, 5,721 in 2007–09.

Source: FAO.

LIVESTOCK
('000 head, year ending September)

	2007	2008	2009
Horses	103.5	121.0	n.a.
Cattle	6,724.7	6,337.7	6,103.3
Buffaloes	2,996.4	2,897.7	2,886.6
Pigs	26,560.7	26,701.6	27,627.7
Goats	1,777.6	1,483.5	n.a.
Chickens	158,200	173,110	196,140
Ducks	67,800	75,190	84,060

Source: FAO.

LIVESTOCK PRODUCTS
('000 metric tons)

	2007	2008	2009
Cattle meat	206.1	194.0*	189.0*
Buffalo meat*	109.7	106.0	105.6
Pig meat	2,553.0	2,470.0*	2,553.0*
Chicken meat	358.8	448.2	518.3
Duck meat*	81.6	82.0	80.6
Cows' milk	234.4	262.2	278.2
Buffaloes' milk*	32.0	32.0	32.0
Hen eggs*	223	247	309
Silk-worm cocoons*	3.0	3.0	n.a.

* FAO estimate(s).
Source: FAO.

Forestry

ROUNDWOOD REMOVALS
('000 cubic metres, excl. bark)

	2006	2007	2008
Sawlogs, veneer logs and logs for sleepers*	2,200	2,150	2,450
Pulpwood	1,291	1,920	2,500
Other industrial wood	1,380	1,380	900
Fuel wood*	26,151	22,000	22,000
Total*	**31,022**	**27,450**	**27,850**

* FAO estimates.

2009: Production assumed to be unchanged from 2008 (FAO estimates).

Source: FAO.

VIET NAM

SAWNWOOD PRODUCTION
('000 cubic metres, incl. railway sleepers)

	2007	2008	2009
Total (all broadleaved)	4,500	5,000	5,000

Source: FAO.

Fishing

('000 metric tons, live weight)

	2006	2007	2008
Capture*	1,970.6	2,020.4	2,087.5
Freshwater fishes	136.2	133.6	129.9
Marine fishes	1,377.5	1,413.0	1,454.8
Prawns and shrimps	108.6	111.4	113.3
Cephalopods	200.0*	211.6	227.7
Aquaculture*	1,657.7	2,085.4	2,461.7
Freshwater fishes*	1,157.0	1,530.3	1,467.3
Giant tiger prawns	150.0*	170.0*	324.6
Marine molluscs*	146.2	170.5	170.0
Total catch*	3,628.3	4,105.8	4,549.2

* FAO estimate(s).

Note: Figures exclude aquatic plants ('000 metric tons, all aquaculture): 36 in 2006; 38 in 2007; 36 in 2008.

Source: FAO.

Mining

('000 metric tons unless otherwise indicated)

	2006	2007	2008
Crude petroleum ('000 barrels)	123,194	116,741	109,291
Natural gas (million cubic metres)*	7,000	7,080	7,944
Coal (anthracite)	38,778	42,483	39,777
Chromium ore—gross weight	73.0	103.8	55.9
Ilmenite—gross weight†	605	550	550
Gold (kilograms)†	2,500	3,000	3,000
Kaolin†	650	650	650
Barite (metric tons)	90,000	90,000	80,000†
Phosphate rock:			
gross weight	1,232	1,523	2,099
P_2O_5 content†	365	390	400
Salt (unrefined)	842	857	847

* Gross production.
† Estimate(s).

Source: US Geological Survey.

Industry

SELECTED PRODUCTS
('000 metric tons unless otherwise indicated)

	2007	2008	2009*
Raw sugar	1,558.2	1,611.0	1,772.1
Beer (million litres)	1,655.3	1,847.2	2,013.0
Cigarettes ('000 million packets)	4.5	4.4	4.9
Fabrics (million metres)	700.4	1,076.4	1,087.2
Chemical fertilizers	2,499.4	2,459.4	2,396.0
Insecticides	58.3	59.4	60.0
Soap	408.6	452.4	524.1
Cement	37,102	40,009	47,900
Crude steel	4,612	5,001	5,252
Paint	204.4	200.5	203.2
Footwear (million pairs)	213.2	169.2	192.9
Ready-made clothes (million pieces)	1,936.1	2,045.0	2,290.0

* Preliminary figures.

Electric energy (million kWh): 64,147 in 2007; 72,100 in 2008; 80,700 in 2009 (Source: Asian Development Bank).

Finance

CURRENCY AND EXCHANGE RATES

Monetary Units
100 xu = 1 new dông.

Sterling, Dollar and Euro Equivalents (29 October 2010)
£1 sterling = 30,143.5 dông;
US $1 = 18,932.0 dông;
€1 = 26,234.1 dông;
100,000 new dông = £3.32 = $5.28 = €3.81.

Average Exchange Rate (new dông per US $)
2007   16,105.1
2008   16,302.3
2009   17,065.1

Note: The new dông, equivalent to 10 former dông, was introduced in September 1985.

BUDGET
('000,000 million dông)

Revenue (incl. grants)	2005	2006	2007*
Tax revenue	166.2	210.3	231.4
Corporate income tax	71.7	100.8	99.0
Individual income tax	4.2	5.2	6.1
Tax on the transfer of properties	2.8	3.4	3.8
Value-added tax (VAT)	45.7	54.8	78.9
Excises	15.7	17.1	17.1
Taxes on international trade	23.6	26.3	23.8
Other taxes	2.3	2.8	2.7
Non-tax and capital revenue	48.5	50.3	47.5
Fees and charges	21.0	23.1	23.1
Income from natural resources	21.9	20.2	19.9
Capital revenues	0.9	1.5	0.8
Grants	2.3	3.6	3.0
Total	217.1	264.2	281.9

VIET NAM

Statistical Survey

Expenditure (cash basis)†	2005	2006	2007*
Current expenditure	155.0	181.5	221.3
General administrative services	16.8	19.0	24.8
Economic services	12.8	15.0	16.3
Social services	77.3	91.4	97.3
Education	29.1	33.8	38.1
Health	10.7	12.7	14.7
Social subsidies	23.6	28.7	26.8
Other services (incl. defence)	13.8	16.3	17.8
Interest on public debt	7.0	8.9	11.7
Capital expenditure	72.0	86.1	99.5
Total	226.9	267.6	320.7

* Forecasts.

† Excluding off-budget investment expenditure ('000,000 million dông): 39.4 in 2005; 33.7 in 2006; 39.4 in 2007 (forecast).

Source: IMF, *Vietnam: Statistical Appendix* (December 2007).

2007 ('000 billion dông, revised): *Revenue:* Tax revenue 269 (Oil revenues 79, Non-oil tax revenues 190); Non-tax and capital revenues 53; Total 322 (excl. grants 6). *Expenditure:* Government expenditure 336; Other expenditure 14; Total 350 (Source: IMF, *Vietnam: 2010 Article IV Consultation—Staff Report and Public Information Notice*—September 2010).

2008 ('000 billion dông, estimates): *Revenue:* Tax revenue 368 (Oil revenues 90, Non-oil tax revenues 278); Non-tax and capital revenues 53; Total 421 (excl. grants 9). *Expenditure:* Government expenditure 410; Other expenditure 33; Total 443 (Source: IMF, *Vietnam: 2010 Article IV Consultation—Staff Report and Public Information Notice*—September 2010).

2009 ('000 billion dông, budgeted figures): *Revenue:* Tax revenue 345 (Oil revenues 64, Non-oil tax revenues 282); Non-tax and capital revenues 40; Total 385 (excl. grants 5). *Expenditure:* Government expenditure 456; Other expenditure 74; Total 529 (Source: IMF, *Vietnam: 2010 Article IV Consultation—Staff Report and Public Information Notice*—September 2010).

INTERNATIONAL RESERVES
(US $ million at 31 December)

	2007	2008	2009
Gold (market valuation)	268.3	285.7	356.1
IMF special drawing rights	7.6	8.2	419.7
Foreign exchange	23,471.8	23,882.0	16,027.4
Total	23,747.7	24,175.9	16,803.2

2010: IMF special drawing rights 412.5.

Source: IMF, *International Financial Statistics*.

MONEY SUPPLY
('000 million dông at 31 December)

	2007	2008	2009
Currency outside banks	220,514	236,848	293,225
Demand deposits at banks	214,653	196,470	271,988
Total money	435,168	433,318	565,213

Source: IMF, *International Financial Statistics*.

COST OF LIVING
(Consumer Price Index; base: previous year = 100)

	2008	2009	2010
Food	136.6	108.7	110.7
Beverages and tobacco	110.8	109.6	108.2
Clothing (incl. footwear)	110.3	108.9	106.9
Household goods	109.1	108.5	105.4
Housing and construction	120.5	103.5	114.7
Transport and communications	116.0	n.a.	n.a.
Education	104.2	105.7	110.4
All items (incl. others)	123.0	106.9	109.2

NATIONAL ACCOUNTS
('000 million dông at current prices)

Expenditure on the Gross Domestic Product

	2007	2008	2009
Government final consumption expenditure	69,247	90,904	104,540
Private final consumption expenditure	740,615	1,000,972	1,102,279
Increase in stocks	55,598	75,759	59,800
Gross fixed capital formation	437,702	513,987	572,526
Total domestic expenditure	1,303,162	1,681,622	1,839,144
Exports of goods and services	879,461	1,157,178	1,132,688
Less Imports of goods and services	1,060,763	1,383,006	1,304,350
Sub-total	1,121,860	1,455,794	1,667,481
Statistical discrepancy	21,855	29,243	-9,092
GDP in purchasers' values	1,143,715	1,485,038	1,658,389
GDP at constant 1994 prices	461,344	490,459	516,568

Gross Domestic Product by Economic Activity

	2007	2008	2009
Agriculture, forestry and fishing	232,586	329,886	346,786
Mining and quarrying	111,700	146,607	165,310
Manufacturing	243,142	302,136	333,166
Electricity, gas and water	39,869	47,169	58,592
Construction	79,712	95,696	110,255
Trade	156,442	212,139	244,933
Transport, storage and communications	51,118	66,359	72,412
Finance	20,756	27,215	31,617
Public administration	94,578	113,856	128,904
Other community, social and personal services	113,812	143,975	166,414
Total	1,143,715	1,485,038	1,658,389

Source: Asian Development Bank.

BALANCE OF PAYMENTS
(US $ million)

	2007	2008	2009
Exports of goods f.o.b.	48,561	62,685	57,096
Imports of goods f.o.b.	-58,999	-75,467	-65,402
Trade balance	-10,438	-12,782	-8,306
Exports of services	6,030	7,041	5,656
Imports of services	-6,785	-7,956	-6,886
Balance on goods and services	-11,193	-13,697	-9,536
Other income received	1,166	1,357	753
Other income paid	-3,356	-5,758	-3,781
Balance on goods, services and income	-13,383	-18,098	-12,564
Current transfers (net)	6,430	7,311	6,448
Current balance	-6,953	-10,787	-6,116
Direct investment abroad	-184	-300	-700
Direct investment from abroad	6,700	9,579	7,600
Portfolio investment (net)	6,243	-578	128
Other investment assets	2,623	677	-305
Other investment liabilities	2,348	2,963	5,146
Net errors and omissions	-565	-1,080	-13,509
Overall balance	10,212	474	-7,756

Source: IMF, *International Financial Statistics*.

VIET NAM

External Trade

SELECTED COMMODITIES
(distribution by SITC, US $ million)

Imports c.i.f.	2006	2007	2008
Food and live animals	2,299	3,280	4,525
Beverages and tobacco	145	183	269
Crude materials (inedible) except fuels	2,084	2,741	4,006
Mineral fuels, etc.	6,699	8,744	12,330
Animal and vegetable fats, and oils	254	473	636
Chemicals and related products	6,317	8,369	10,298
Basic manufactures	12,164	17,062	20,113
Machinery and transport equipment	10,806	17,860	22,425
Miscellaneous manufactured goods	2,244	2,737	3,384
Total (incl. others)	44,891	62,765	80,714

Exports f.o.b.	2006	2007	2008
Food and live animals	7,509	9,192	12,164
Crude materials (inedible) except fuels	1,845	2,200	2,492
Mineral fuels, etc.	9,709	10,061	12,751
Basic manufactures	2,926	3,976	6,398
Machinery and transport equipment	4,195	5,601	7,368
Total (incl. others)	39,826	48,561	62,685

PRINCIPAL TRADING PARTNERS
(US $ million)

Imports c.i.f.	2007	2008	2009
China, People's Republic	12,710.0	15,652.1	13,198.5
Hong Kong	1,950.7	2,633.3	3,564.7
Japan	6,188.9	n.a.	7,170.2
Korea, Republic	5,340.4	7,066.3	6,241.4
Malaysia	2,289.9	2,596.1	2,161.3
Singapore	7,613.7	9,392.5	7,689.0
Thailand	3,744.2	4,905.6	5,132.7
USA	1,700.5	2,635.3	3,418.4
Total (incl. others)	62,764.7	80,713.8	79,896.9

Exports f.o.b.	2007	2008	2009
Australia	3,802.2	4,225.2	2,447.6
China, People's Republic	3,646.1	4,535.7	4,039.9
Germany	1,854.9	2,073.4	2,359.6
Japan	6,090.0	8,537.9	6,326.5
Korea, Republic	1,243.4	1,784.4	1,576.1
Malaysia	1,555.0	1,955.3	1,706.8
Philippines	965.1	1,824.7	1,739.9
Singapore	2,234.4	2,659.7	2,062.3
USA	10,104.5	11,868.5	11,853.0
Total (incl. others)	48,561.4	62,685.1	55,400.5

Note: Data reflect the IMF's direction of trade methodology and, as a result, the totals may not be equal to those presented for trade in commodities.

Source: Asian Development Bank.

Transport

RAILWAYS
(traffic)

	2007	2008	2009*
Passengers carried (million)	11.6	11.3	11.0
Passenger-km ('000 million)	4.7	4.6	4.1
Freight carried (million metric tons)	9.1	8.5	8.1
Freight ton-km ('000 million)	3.9	4.2	3.8

* Preliminary figures.

ROAD TRAFFIC

	2007	2008	2009*
Passengers carried (million)	1,473.0	1,629.0	1,818.7
Passenger-km ('000 million)	49.4	54.2	59.7
Freight carried (million metric tons)	403.4	455.9	494.6
Freight ton-km ('000 million)	24.6	28.0	30.3

* Preliminary figures.

Commercial vehicles ('000 in use): 49.4 in 1998; 57.8 in 1999; 69.9 in 2000 (Source: UN, *Statistical Yearbook*).

INLAND WATERWAYS

	2007	2008	2009*
Passengers carried (million)	144.5	143.0	148.2
Passenger-km ('000 million)	3.2	3.2	3.4
Freight carried (million metric tons)	135.3	133.0	135.7
Freight ton-km ('000 million)	22.2	24.9	25.4

* Preliminary figures.

SHIPPING

Merchant Fleet
(registered at 31 December)

	2007	2008	2009
Number of vessels	1,235	1,312	1,415
Total displacement ('000 grt)	2,529.6	2,993.1	3,451.1

Source: IHS Fairplay, *World Fleet Statistics*.

International Sea-Borne Shipping
(freight traffic)

	2006	2007	2008*
Freight carried (million metric tons)	42.7	49.0	59.7
Freight ton-km ('000 million)	70.5	83.8	125.7

* Preliminary figures.

VIET NAM

CIVIL AVIATION
(traffic on scheduled services)

	2006	2007	2008
Domestic:			
Passengers carried ('000)	4,313.5	5,478.4	6,820.9
Passenger-km (million)	3,551.9	4,685.6	5,541.0
Freight carried ('000 metric tons)	73.2	86.5	83.7
Freight ton-km (million)	81.2	94.7	88.3
International:			
Passengers carried ('000)	3,132.0	3,419.2	3,379.1
Passenger-km (million)	9,264.7	9,996.0	10,611.3
Freight carried ('000 metric tons)	47.6	43.1	47.7
Freight ton-km (million)	188.2	185.2	207.3

Tourism

TOURIST ARRIVALS BY COUNTRY OF RESIDENCE

Country	2006	2007	2008
Australia	172,519	227,300	234,760
Cambodia	154,956	150,655	n.a.
China, People's Republic	516,286	558,719	650,055
France	132,304	182,501	182,048
Japan	383,896	411,557	392,999
Korea, Republic	421,741	475,535	449,237
Laos	33,980	31,374	n.a.
Malaysia	105,558	145,535	174,008
Singapore	104,947	127,040	158,405
Taiwan	274,663	314,026	303,527
Thailand	123,804	160,747	183,142
United Kingdom	84,264	105,918	n.a.
USA	385,654	412,301	417,198
Total (incl. others)	3,583,486	4,171,564	4,253,740

2009: Australia 218,461; China, People's Republic 527,610; France 174,525; Japan 359,231; Korea, Republic 362,115; Malaysia 166,284; Taiwan 271,643; Thailand 152,633; USA 403,930; Total (incl. others) 3,772,359.

2010: Australia 278,155; China, People's Republic 905,360; France 199,351; Japan 442,089; Korea, Republic 495,902; Malaysia 211,337; Taiwan 334,007; Thailand 222,839; USA 430,993; Total (incl. others) 5,049,855.

Source: Viet Nam National Administration of Tourism.

Tourism receipts (US $ million, excl. passenger transport): 3,200 in 2006; 3,477 in 2007; 3,926 in 2008 (Source: World Tourism Organization).

Communications Media

	2007	2008	2009
Telephones ('000 main lines in use)	11,165.6	14,767.6	17,427.4
Mobile cellular telephones ('000 subscribers)	45,024.0	74,872.3	98,224.0
Internet users ('000)	17,872.0	7,277.6	23,382.3
Broadband subscribers ('000)	1,294.1	1,092.3	3,214.2

Personal computers: 8,118,000 (96.5 per 1,000 persons) in 2006.
Radio receivers ('000 in use): 8,200 in 1997.
Television receivers ('000 in use): 14,750 in 2000.
Book production: 11,455 titles (166,500,000 copies) in 2001.
Daily newspapers: 5 (with estimated circulation of 450,000 copies) in 1999.
Non-daily newspapers: 80 in 2004.

Sources: partly International Telecommunication Union; UN, *Statistical Yearbook*; UNESCO, *Statistical Yearbook*.

Education

(2008/09 unless otherwise indicated)

	Institutions	Teachers ('000)	Students (million)
Pre-primary	12,265	144.5	2.9
Primary†	15,172	355.2	6.9
Lower secondary†	10,064	317.2	5.2
Upper secondary†	2,267	146.3	2.8
Universities and colleges†*	403	65.1	1.8

* 2009/10.
† Preliminary figures.

Pupil-teacher ratio (primary education, UNESCO estimate): 19.5 in 2008/09 (Source: UNESCO Institute for Statistics).

Adult literacy rate (UNESCO estimates): 92.5% (males 95.1%; females 90.2%) in 2008 (Source: UNESCO Institute for Statistics).

Directory

In October 2008 telephone numbers in many regions were expanded by one digit; however, full details of the changes were not immediately available.

The Government

HEAD OF STATE

President: NGUYEN MINH TRIET (appointment approved by the 11th National Assembly on 27 June 2006; re-elected 25 July 2007).
Vice-President: NGUYEN THI DOAN.

CABINET
(May 2011)

The Cabinet is formed by Dang Cong San Viet Nam (the Communist Party of Viet Nam).
Prime Minister: NGUYEN TAN DUNG.
Standing Deputy Prime Minister: NGUYEN SINH HUNG.
Deputy Prime Minister and Minister of Foreign Affairs: PHAM GIA KHIEM.
Deputy Prime Ministers: NGUYEN THIEN NHAN, TRUONG VINH TRONG, HOANG TRUNG HAI.
Minister of National Defence: Gen. PHUNG QUANG THANH.
Minister of Public Security: LE HONG ANH.
Minister of Justice: HA HUNG CUONG.
Minister of Finance: VU VAN NINH.
Minister of Labour, War Invalids and Social Affairs: NGUYEN THI KIM NGAN.
Minister of Health: NGUYEN QUOC TRIEU.
Minister of Education and Training: PHAM VU LUAN.
Minister of Culture, Sports and Tourism: HOANG TUAN ANH.
Minister of Construction: NGUYEN HONG QUAN.
Minister of Transport: HO NGHIA DUNG.
Minister of Home Affairs: TRAN VAN TUAN.
Minister of Agriculture and Rural Development: CAO DUC PHAT.
Minister of Industry and Trade: VU HUY HOANG.
Minister of Planning and Investment: VO HONG PHUC.
Minister of Science and Technology: HOANG VAN PHONG.
Minister of Natural Resources and the Environment: PHAM KHOI NGUYEN.
Minister of Information and Communication: LE DOAN HOP.
Chief Government Inspector: TRAN VAN TRUYEN.
Minister, Chairman of the Committee for Ethnic Minority Affairs: GIANG SEO PHU.
Minister, Chairman of the Government Office: NGUYEN XUAN PHUC.

VIET NAM

MINISTRIES AND COMMITTEES

Ministry of Agriculture and Rural Development: 2 Ngoc Ha, Ba Dinh District, Hanoi; tel. (4) 38468161; fax (4) 38454319; e-mail webmaster@agroviet.gov.vn; internet www.agroviet.gov.vn.

Ministry of Construction: 37 Le Dai Hanh, Hai Ba Trung District, Hanoi; tel. (4) 39760271; fax (4) 39762153; e-mail vanphong@moc.gov.vn; internet www.moc.gov.vn.

Ministry of Culture, Sports and Tourism: 51–53 Ngo Quyen, Hoan Kiem District, Hanoi; tel. (4) 39439915; fax (4) 39439009; e-mail phongthongtin@cinet.gov.vn; internet www.cinet.gov.vn.

Ministry of Education and Training: 49 Dai Co Viet, Hai Ba Trung District, Hanoi; tel. (4) 38692397; fax (4) 38694085; e-mail bogddt@moet.edu.vn; internet www.moet.gov.vn.

Ministry of Finance: 28 Tran Hung Dao, Hoan Kiem District, Hanoi; tel. (4) 22202828; fax (4) 22208091; e-mail support@mof.gov.vn; internet www.mof.gov.vn.

Ministry of Foreign Affairs: 1 Ton That Dam, Ba Dinh District, Hanoi; tel. (4) 37992000; fax (4) 38231872; e-mail banbientap@mofa.gov.vn; internet www.mofa.gov.vn.

Ministry of Health: 138A Giang Vo, Ba Dinh District, Hanoi; tel. (4) 62732273; fax (4) 38464051; e-mail byt@moh.gov.vn; internet www.moh.gov.vn.

Ministry of Home Affairs: 37A Nguyen Binh Khiem, Hai Ba Trung District, Hanoi; tel. (4) 39764116; fax (4) 39781005; e-mail websitemaster@moha.gov.vn; internet www.moha.gov.vn.

Ministry of Industry and Trade: 54 Hai Ba Trung, Hoan Kiem District, Hanoi; tel. (4) 22202222; fax (4) 22202525; e-mail bbt@moit.gov.vn; internet www.moit.gov.vn.

Ministry of Information and Communication: 18 Nguyen Du, Hanoi; tel. (4) 39435602; fax (4) 38263477; e-mail otonghop@mic.gov.vn; internet mic.gov.vn.

Ministry of Justice: 60 Tran Phu, Ba Dinh District, Hanoi; tel. (4) 37332802; fax (4) 38431431; e-mail banbientap@moj.gov.vn; internet www.moj.gov.vn.

Ministry of Labour, War Invalids and Social Affairs: 12 Ngo Quyen, Hoan Kiem District, Hanoi; tel. (4) 38248913; fax (4) 38248036; e-mail lasic@molisa.gov.vn; internet www.molisa.gov.vn.

Ministry of National Defence: 7 Nguyen Tri Phuong, Ba Dinh District, Hanoi; tel. (69) 534223; fax (69) 532090.

Ministry of Natural Resources and the Environment: 83 Nguyen Chi Thanh, Dong Da District, Hanoi; tel. (4) 38343911; fax (4) 37736892; e-mail baotainguyenmoitruong@gmail.com; internet www.monre.gov.vn.

Ministry of Planning and Investment: 6B Hoang Dieu, Ba Dinh District, Hanoi; tel. (4) 38433360; fax (80) 48473; e-mail banbientap@mpi.gov.vn; internet www.mpi.gov.vn.

Ministry of Public Security: 44 Yet Kieu, Hoan Kiem District, Hanoi; tel. (4) 38226602; fax (4) 39420223.

Ministry of Science and Technology: 39 Tran Hung Dao, Hoan Kiem District, Hanoi; tel. (4) 39437056; fax (4) 39439733; e-mail bbt@most.gov.vn; internet www.most.gov.vn.

Ministry of Transport: 80 Tran Hung Dao, Hoan Kiem District, Hanoi; tel. (4) 39424015; fax (4) 39423291; e-mail vpmot@mt.gov.vn; internet www.mt.gov.vn.

Committee for Ethnic Minority Affairs: 80 Phan Dinh Phung, Ba Dinh District, Hanoi; tel. (4) 38431876; fax (4) 38230235; e-mail banbientap@cema.gov.vn; internet www.cema.gov.vn.

Government Inspection Committee: 220 Doi Can, Ba Dinh District, Hanoi; tel. (80) 43490; fax (80) 48493; e-mail ttcp@thanhtra.gov.vn; internet www.thanhtra.gov.vn.

NATIONAL DEFENCE AND SECURITY COUNCIL

President: Nguyen Minh Triet.

Vice-President: Nguyen Tan Dung.

Members: Nguyen Phu Trong, Pham Gia Khiem, Phung Quang Thanh, Le Hong Anh.

Legislature

QUOC HOI
(National Assembly)

Elections for the 13th National Assembly were held on 22 May 2011. The new Assembly was to comprise 500 members.

Standing Committee

Chairman: Nguyen Phu Trong.

Vice-Chairmen: Nguyen Duc Khien, Uong Chu Luu, Tong Thi Phong, Huynh Ngoc Son.

Political Organizations

COMMUNIST PARTY

Dang Cong San Viet Nam (Communist Party of Viet Nam): 1A Hung Vuong, Hanoi; e-mail dangcongsan@cpv.org.vn; internet www.cpv.org.vn; f. 1976; ruling party; fmrly the Viet Nam Workers' Party (f. 1951 as the successor to the Communist Party of Indo-China, f. 1930); Cen. Cttee of 175 full mems and 25 alternate mems elected at 11th National Congress held in Jan. 2011; 14-mem. Politburo and four-mem. Secretariat elected (see below); 3.6m. mems; Gen. Sec. of Cen. Cttee Nguyen Phu Trong.

Political Bureau (Politburo)

Members: Le Hong Anh, Ngo Van Du, Nguyen Tan Dung, Le Thanh Hai, Nguyen Sinh Hung, Dinh The Huynh, Pham Quang Nghi, Tong Thi Phong, Nguyen Xuan Phuc, Tran Dai Quang, To Huy Rua, Truong Tan Sang, Gen. Phung Quang Thanh, Nguyen Phu Trong.

Secretariat

Members: Truong Hoa Binh, Ha Thi Khiet, Ngo Xuan Lich, Nguyen Thi Kim Ngan.

OTHER POLITICAL ORGANIZATIONS

Ho Chi Minh Communist Youth Union: 62 Ba Trieu, Hanoi; tel. (4) 62631874; fax (4) 62631875; e-mail vanphongtwd@doantn.vn; internet doanthanhnien.vn; f. 1931; 4m. mems; First Sec. Vo Van Thuong.

People's Action Party (PAP): POB 4752, San Jose, CA 95150-4752, USA; e-mail dang@ndhd.net; internet www.dndhd.org; Chair. Nguyen Si Binh.

Viet Nam Fatherland Front: 46 Trang Thi, Hanoi; tel. (4) 9287401; e-mail ubmttqvn@mattran.org.vn; internet www.mattran.org.vn; f. 1930; replaced the Lien Viet (Viet Nam National League), the successor to Viet Nam Doc Lap Dong Minh Hoi (Revolutionary League for the Independence of Viet Nam) or Viet Minh; in 1977 the original org. merged with the National Front for the Liberation of South Viet Nam and the Alliance of National, Democratic and Peace Forces in South Viet Nam to form a single front; 200-mem. Cen. Cttee; Pres. Presidium of Cen. Cttee Huynh Dam; Gen. Sec. Nong Duc Manh.

Vietnam Women's Union (VWU): 39 Hang Chuoi, Hanoi; tel. (4) 9713436; fax (4) 9713143; internet hoilhpn.org.vn; f. 1930; 13m. mems; Pres. Nguyen Thi Thanh Hoa.

Diplomatic Representation

EMBASSIES IN VIET NAM

Algeria: 13 Phan Chu Trinh, Hanoi; tel. (4) 38253865; fax (4) 38260830; e-mail ambalghanoi@ambalgvn.org.vn; internet www.ambalgvn.org.vn; Ambassador Chérif Chikhi.

Argentina: Office Tower, 8th Floor, Daeha Business Centre, 360 Kim Ma, Ba Dinh District, Hanoi; tel. (4) 38315262; fax (4) 38315577; e-mail embarg@hn.vnn.vn; internet www.embargentina.org.vn; Ambassador Alberto J. Kaminker.

Australia: 8 Dao Tan, Ba Dinh District, Hanoi; tel. (4) 37740100; fax (4) 37740111; e-mail austemb@fpt.vn; internet www.vietnam.embassy.gov.au; Ambassador Allaster Cox.

Austria: Prime Centre, 8th Floor, 53 Quang Trung, Hai Ba Trung District, Hanoi; tel. (4) 39433050; fax (4) 39433055; e-mail hanoi-ob@bmeia.gv.at; internet www.bmeia.gv.at/botschaft/hanoi; Ambassador Dr Georg Heindl.

Bangladesh: Vuon Dao Compound, Villa D6B-05, 675 Lac Long Quan, Tay Ho District, Hanoi; tel. (4) 37716625; fax (4) 37716628; e-mail bdoothn@netnam.org.vn; internet www.bangladeshembassy.vn; Ambassador Supradip Chakma.

Belarus: 52 Tay Ho, Tay Ho District, Hanoi; tel. (4) 38290494; fax (4) 37197125; e-mail vietnam@belembassy.org; internet www.vietnam.belembassy.org; Ambassador Valeriy E. Sadoho.

Belgium: Hanoi Towers, 9th Floor, 49 Hai Ba Trung, Hanoi; tel. (4) 39346179; fax (4) 39346183; e-mail Pub.Hanoi@diplobel.fed.be; internet www.diplomatie.be/hanoi; Ambassador Hubert Cooreman.

Brazil: Villa D6-07, 14 Thuy Khue, Tay Ho District, Hanoi; tel. (4) 38430817; fax (4) 38432542; e-mail vetbrem@vnn.vn; Ambassador João de Mendonça Lima Neto.

Brunei: Villa 8 & 9, 44/8 Van Bao, Van Phuc Diplomatic Quarter, Ba Dinh District, Hanoi; tel. (4) 7262001; fax (4) 7262010; e-mail bruemviet@hn.vnn.vn; Ambassador Dato Paduka Haji Mahadi bin Wasli.

VIET NAM

Bulgaria: Van Phuc Quarter, 5 Nui Truc, Hanoi; tel. (4) 38452908; fax (4) 38460856; e-mail bgremb@fpt.vn; internet www.mfa.bg/bg/22; Ambassador GEORGI KONSTANTINOV VASSILIEV.

Cambodia: 71A Tran Hung Dao, Hanoi; tel. (4) 8253788; fax (4) 9423225; e-mail arch@fpt.vn; Ambassador HUL PHANY.

Canada: 31 Hung Vuong, Hanoi; tel. (4) 37345000; fax (4) 37345049; e-mail hanoi@international.gc.ca; internet www.canada international.gc.ca/vietnam; Ambassador DEBORAH CHATSIS.

Chile: Villa C8–D8, 14 Thuy Khue, Tay Ho District, Hanoi; tel. (4) 39351147; fax (4) 38430762; e-mail embajada1@chile.org.vn; internet chileabroad.gov.cl/vietnam; Ambassador FERNANDO URRUTIA.

China, People's Republic: 46 Hoang Dieu, Hanoi; tel. (4) 38453736; fax (4) 38232826; e-mail eossc@hn.vnn.vn; internet vn.chineseembassy.org; Ambassador SUN GUOXIANG.

Cuba: 65A Ly Thuong Kiet, Hanoi; tel. (4) 9424775; fax (4) 9422426; e-mail embacuba@fpt.vn; internet embacuba.cubaminrex.cu/vietnam; Ambassador FREDESMÁN TURRÓ GONZÁLEZ.

Czech Republic: 13 Chu Van An, Hanoi; tel. (4) 38454131; fax (4) 38233996; e-mail hanoi@embassy.mzv.cz; internet www.mfa.cz/hanoi; Ambassador MICHAL KRÁL.

Denmark: 19 Dien Bien Phu, Hanoi; tel. (4) 38231888; fax (4) 38231999; e-mail hanamb@um.dk; internet www.ambhanoi.um.dk; Ambassador JOHN NIELSEN.

Egypt: 63 To Ngoc Van, Quang An, Tay Ho District, Hanoi; tel. (4) 8294999; fax (4) 8294997; e-mail arabegypt@ftp.vn; Ambassador MUHAMMAD R. K. EL-TAIFY.

Finland: Central Bldg, 6th Floor, Suite 63, 31 Hai Ba Trung, Hanoi; tel. (4) 38266788; fax (4) 38266766; e-mail sanomat.han@formin.fi; internet www.finland.org.vn; Ambassador PEKKA HYVÖNEN.

France: 57 Tran Hung Dao, Hanoi; tel. (4) 39445700; fax (4) 39445717; e-mail ambafrance.hanoi@diplomatie.gouv.fr; internet www.ambafrance-vn.org; Ambassador JEAN-FRANÇOIS GIRAULT.

Germany: 29 Tran Phu, Hanoi; tel. (4) 38453836; fax (4) 38453838; e-mail info@hanoi.diplo.de; internet www.hanoi.diplo.de; Ambassador ROLF SCHULZE.

Hungary: Daeha Business Centre, 12th Floor, 360 Kim Ma, Ba Dinh District, Hanoi; tel. (4) 37715714; fax (4) 37715716; e-mail mission.hoi@kum.hu; internet www.mfa.gov.hu/kulkepviselet/vn; Ambassador LÁSZLÓ VIZI.

India: 58–60 Tran Hung Dao, Hanoi; tel. (4) 38244990; fax (4) 38244998; e-mail embassyindia@fpt.vn; internet www.indembassy.com.vn; Ambassador RANJIT RAE.

Indonesia: 50 Ngo Quyen, Hanoi; tel. (4) 38253353; fax (4) 38259274; e-mail komhan@hn.vnn.vn; internet www.deplu.go.id/hanoi; Ambassador PITONO PURNOMO.

Iran: 54 Tran Phu, Ba Dinh District, Hanoi; tel. (4) 8232068; fax (4) 8232120; e-mail embiri@fpt.vn; internet www.iranembassy.org.vn; Ambassador JAVAD GHAVAM SHAHIDI.

Iraq: 66 Tran Hung Dao, Hanoi; tel. (4) 39424141; fax (4) 39424055; e-mail hanemb@iraqmfamail.com; Ambassador FARIS ABD AL-KARIM ZAARAWI.

Ireland: Vincom City Towers, 8th Floor, 191 Ba Trieu, Hai Ba Trung District, Hanoi; tel. (4) 39743291; fax (4) 39743295; e-mail irishembassyhanoi@dfanet.ie; internet www.embassyofireland.vn; Ambassador MAEVE COLLINS.

Israel: 68 Nguyen Thai Hoc, Dong Da, Hanoi; tel. (4) 38433140; fax (4) 38435760; e-mail info@hanoi.mfa.gov.il; internet hanoi.mfa.gov.il; Ambassador AMNON EFRAT.

Italy: 9 Le Phung Hieu, Hoan Kiem District, Hanoi; tel. (4) 38256256; fax (4) 38267602; e-mail ambasciata.hanoi@esteri.it; internet www.ambhanoi.esteri.it; Ambassador ANDREA PERUGINI.

Japan: 27 Lieu Giai, Ba Dinh District, Hanoi; tel. (4) 38463000; fax (4) 38463043; e-mail soumuhan@vnn.vn; internet www.vn.emb-japan.go.jp; Ambassador YASUAKI TANIZAKI.

Korea, Democratic People's Republic: 25 Cao Ba Quat, Hanoi; tel. (4) 8453008; fax (4) 8231221; e-mail emb.dprk@hn.vnn.vn; Ambassador KIM CHANG IL.

Korea, Republic: Daeha Business Centre, 4th Floor, 360 Kim Ma, Ba Dinh District, Hanoi; tel. (4) 38315111; fax (4) 38315117; e-mail koreambviet@mofat.go.kr; internet hanquocngaynay.com; Ambassador HA CHAN-HO.

Kuwait: Hanoi; tel. (4) 9330609; fax (4) 9330611; e-mail hanoi@mofa.gov.kw; Ambassador HAMAD SALEH AL-JUTAILI.

Laos: 22 Tran Binh Trong, Hai Ba Trung, Hanoi; tel. (4) 9424576; fax (4) 8228414; internet www.embalaohanoi.gov.la; Ambassador SOUNTHONE SAYACHAK.

Libya: A3 Van Phuc Residential Quarter, Kim Ma, Hanoi; tel. (4) 8453379; fax (4) 8454977; e-mail libpbha@yahoo.com; Secretary SALEM ALI SALEM DANNAH.

Malaysia: 43–45 Dien Bien Phu, Ba Dinh District, Hanoi; tel. (4) 37343836; fax (4) 37343832; e-mail malhanoi@kln.gov.my; internet www.kln.gov.my/web/vnm_hanoi; Ambassador LIM KIM ENG.

Mexico: 14 Thuy Khue, T-11, Hanoi; tel. (4) 38470948; fax (4) 38470949; e-mail embvietnam@sre.gob.mx; internet www.sre.gob.mx/vietnam; Ambassador (vacant).

Mongolia: Villa 6, Van Phuc Diplomatic Quarter, Hanoi; tel. (4) 38453009; fax (4) 38454954; e-mail mongembhanoi@vnn.vn; Ambassador PALAMYN SÜNDEV.

Morocco: 9 Chu Van, Ba Dinh District, Hanoi; tel. (4) 37345586; fax (4) 37345589; e-mail embassymorocco.hanoi@fpt.vn; Ambassador EL HOUCINE FARDANI.

Myanmar: 298A Kim Ma, Hanoi; tel. (4) 38453369; fax (4) 38452404; e-mail mevhan@fpt.vn; Ambassador KHIN MAUNG SOE.

Netherlands: Daeha Office Tower, 6th Floor, 360 Kim Ma, Ba Dinh District, Hanoi; tel. (4) 38315650; fax (4) 38315655; e-mail han@minbuza.nl; internet www.netherlands-embassy.org.vn; Ambassador JOZEF WILLEM SCHEFFERS.

New Zealand: Level 5, 63 Ly Thai To, Hanoi; tel. (4) 38241481; fax (4) 38241480; e-mail nzembhan@fpt.vn; internet www.nzembassy.com/viet-nam; Ambassador HEATHER RIDDELL.

Norway: Vincom City Towers, Blk B, 10th Floor, 191 Ba Trieu, Hanoi; tel. (4) 39742930; fax (4) 39743301; e-mail emb.hanoi@mfa.no; internet www.norway.org.vn; Ambassador STÅLE TORSTEIN RISA.

Pakistan: 44/2 Van Bao, Van Phuc Diplomatic Quarter, Hanoi; tel. (4) 37262251; fax (4) 37262253; e-mail parepvietnam@yahoo.com; internet www.mofa.gov.pk/vietnam; Ambassador SHAHID M. G. KIANI.

Panama: 17F, 191 Ba Trieu, Hai Ba Trung, Hanoi; tel. (4) 9365213; Ambassador EDUARDO ANTONIO YOUNG VIRZI.

Philippines: 27B Tran Hung Dao, Hanoi; tel. (4) 39437873; fax (4) 39435760; e-mail hnpe2000@gmail.com; internet www.hanoipe.org; Ambassador JERRIL G. SANTOS.

Poland: 3 Chua Mot Cot, Hanoi; tel. (4) 38452027; fax (4) 38236914; e-mail hanoi.amb.sekretariat@msz.gov.pl; internet www.hanoi.polemb.net; Ambassador ROMAN IWASZKIEWICZ.

Romania: 5 Le Hong Phong, Hanoi; tel. (4) 38452014; fax (4) 38430922; e-mail romambhan@fpt.vn; Ambassador DUMITRU OLARU.

Russia: 191 La Thanh, Hanoi; tel. (4) 38336991; fax (4) 38336995; e-mail moscow.vietnam@hn.vnn.vn; internet www.vietnam.mid.ru; Ambassador ANDREI GRIGORIEVICH KOVTUN.

Saudi Arabia: Regus Hanoi Opera House, 2nd Floor, 63 Ly Thai To, Hoan Kiem District, Hanoi; tel. (4) 39366722; fax (4) 39367401; Ambassador SALAH AHMAD SARHAN.

Singapore: 41–43 Tran Phu, Hanoi; tel. (4) 38489168; fax (4) 38489178; e-mail singemb_han@sgmfa.gov.sg; internet www.mfa.gov.sg/hanoi; Ambassador SIMON WONG WIE KUEN.

South Africa: Central Bldg, 3rd Floor, 31 Hai Ba Trung, Hanoi; tel. (4) 9362000; fax (4) 9361991; e-mail admin.hanoi@foreign.gov.za; Ambassador RATUBATSI SUPER MOLOI.

Spain: Daeha Business Centre, 15th Floor, 360 Kim Ma, Ba Dinh District, Hanoi; tel. (4) 37715207; fax (4) 37715206; e-mail embajadaesp@vnn.vn; internet www.maec.es/subwebs/embajadas/hanoi; Ambassador FERNANDO CURCIO RUIGÓMEZ.

Sri Lanka: 55B Tran Phu, Ba Dinh District, Hanoi; tel. (4) 37341894; fax (4) 37341897; e-mail slembvn@fpt.vn; internet www.slembvn.org; Ambassador KALAHE GAMAGE IVAN AMARASINGHE.

Switzerland: 44B Ly Thuong Kiet, Central Office Bldg, 15th Floor, Hanoi; tel. (4) 39346589; fax (4) 39346591; e-mail han.vertretung@eda.admin.ch; internet www.eda.admin.ch/hanoi; Ambassador JEAN-HUBERT LEBET.

Thailand: 63–65 Hoang Dieu, Hanoi; tel. (4) 38235092; fax (4) 38235088; e-mail thaiemhn@netnam.org.vn; Ambassador ANUSON CHIVANNO.

Turkey: 4 Da Tuong, Hoan Kiem District, Hanoi; tel. (4) 38222460; fax (4) 38222458; e-mail turkeyhn@fpt.vn; internet hanoi.emb.mfa.gov.tr; Ambassador ATES OKTEM.

Ukraine: 6B Le Hong Phong, Ba Dinh District, Hanoi; tel. (4) 37344484; fax (4) 37344497; e-mail emb_vn@mfa.gov.ua; internet www.mfa.gov.ua/vietnam; Ambassador IVAN DOVGANYCH.

United Arab Emirates: 44/3 Van Bao, Van Phuc Diplomatic Quarter, Ba Dinh District, Hanoi; tel. (4) 37264545; fax (4) 37262020; e-mail feedback@uaeembassy.vn; internet uaeembassy.vn; Ambassador Sheikh AHMED ALI AL-MUALLA.

United Kingdom: Central Bldg, 4th Floor, 31 Hai Ba Trung, Hanoi; tel. (4) 39360500; fax (4) 39360561; e-mail behanoi02@vnn.vn; internet ukinvietnam.fco.gov.uk; Ambassador Dr ANTHONY STOKES.

USA: Rose Garden Tower, 3rd Floor, 170 Ngoc Khanh, Hanoi; tel. (4) 38505000; fax (4) 38505120; e-mail hanoiac@state.gov; internet vietnam.usembassy.gov; Ambassador MICHAEL W. MICHALAK.

VIET NAM

Venezuela: 368 Lac Long Quan, Tay Ho District, Hanoi; tel. (4) 7588891; fax (4) 7588893; e-mail embavenezhanoi@yahoo.com; Ambassador JORGE JOSÉ RONDÓN UZCÁTEGUI.

Judicial System

The Supreme People's Court in Hanoi is the highest court and exercises civil and criminal jurisdiction over all lower courts. The Supreme Court may also conduct trials of the first instance in certain cases. There are People's Courts in each province and city which exercise jurisdiction in the first and second instance. Military courts hear cases involving members of the People's Army and cases involving national security. In 1993 legislation was adopted on the establishment of economic courts to consider business disputes. The observance of the law by ministries, government offices and all citizens is the concern of the People's Organs of Control, under a Supreme People's Organ of Control. The Chief Justice of the Supreme People's Court and the Chief Procurator of the Supreme People's Organ of Control are elected by the National Assembly, on the recommendation of the President.

Chief Justice of the Supreme People's Court: TRUONG HOA BINH, 48 Ly Thuong Kiet, Hanoi.

Chief Procurator of the Supreme People's Organ of Control: TRAN QUOC VUONG.

Religion

Traditional Vietnamese religion included elements of Indian and all three Chinese religions: Mahayana Buddhism, Daoism and Confucianism. Its most widespread feature was the cult of ancestors, practised in individual households and clan temples. Various Buddhist sects belong to the 'new' religions of Caodaism and Hoa Hao. The Protestant and Roman Catholic Churches are also represented. In 2007 operating licences were granted to several additional religious groups, including the Mennonite Church, the Baptist Church and the Bahá'í faith.

BUDDHISM

In the North a Buddhist organization, grouping Buddhists loyal to the Democratic Republic of Viet Nam, was established in 1954. In the South the United Buddhist Church was formed in 1964, incorporating several disparate groups, including the 'militant' An-Quang group (mainly natives of central Viet Nam), the group of Thich Tam Chau (mainly northern emigrés in Saigon) and the southern Buddhists of the Xa Loi temple. In 1982 most of the Buddhist sects were amalgamated into the state-approved Viet Nam Buddhist Church (which comes under the authority of the Viet Nam Fatherland Front). The number of adherents was estimated at 10m. in 2005, approximately 12% of the total population. The Unified Buddhist Church of Viet Nam is an anti-Government organization.

Viet Nam Buddhist Church: Pres. Exec. Council Most Ven. THICH TRI TINH; Gen. Sec. THICH MING CHAU.

Unified Buddhist Church of Viet Nam: Leader Patriarch THICH QUANG DO.

CAODAISM

Formally inaugurated in 1926, this is a syncretic religion based on spiritualist seances with a predominantly ethical content, but sometimes with political overtones. There are 13 different sects, of which the most politically involved (1940–75) was that of Tay Ninh. Another sect, the Tien Thien, was represented in the National Liberation Front from its inception. There were an estimated 2.4m. adherents in 2005, resident mainly in the South.

Leader: Cardinal THAI HUU THANH.

CHRISTIANITY

In 2005 the number of Christian adherents represented an estimated 7.2% of the total population.

The Roman Catholic Church

The Roman Catholic Church has been active in Viet Nam since the 17th century, and since 1933 has been led mainly by Vietnamese priests. Many Roman Catholics moved from North to South Viet Nam in 1954–55, but some remained in the North. The total number of adherents was estimated at 6,089,223 in December 2007, representing 6.9% of the population. For ecclesiastical purposes, Viet Nam comprises three archdioceses and 23 dioceses.

Bishops' Conference

Conférence Episcopale du Viet Nam, 22 Tran Phu, Khank Hoa, Nha Trang; tel. (58) 822842; fax (58) 815494; e-mail vangia@dng.vnn.vn. f. 1980; Pres. Most Rev. PIERRE NGUYEN VAN NHON (Bishop of Da Lat).

Archbishop of Hanoi: Most Rev. JOSEPH NGO QUANG KIET, Archevêché, 40 Pho Nha Chung, Hanoi; tel. (4) 8254424; fax (4) 9285073; e-mail ttgmhn@hn.vnn.vn.

Archbishop of Ho Chi Minh City: Cardinal JEAN-BAPTISTE PHAM MINH MÂN, Archevêché, 180 Nguyen Dinh Chieu, Ho Chi Minh City 3; tel. (8) 9303828; fax (8) 9300598.

Archbishop of Hué: Most Rev. ETIENNE NGUYEN NHU THE, Archevêché, 6 Nguyen Truong To, Hué; tel. (54) 824937; fax (54) 833656; e-mail tgmhue@dng.vnn.vn.

Committee for Solidarity of Patriotic Vietnamese Catholics: 59 Trang Thi, Hanoi; Pres. Rev. VUONG DINH AI.

The Protestant Church

Introduced in 1920 with 500 adherents; the total number was estimated at 500,000 in 2005.

HOA HAO

A new manifestation of an older religion called Buu Son Ky Huong, the Hoa Hao sect was founded by Nguyen Phu So in 1939. There were an estimated 1.6m. adherents in 2005.

ISLAM

The number of Muslims was estimated at 65,000 in 2005.

The Press

The Ministry of Information and Communication supervises the activities of newspapers, news agencies and periodicals.

DAILIES

Hanoi

Le Courrier du Viet Nam: 33 Le Thanh Tong, Hanoi; tel. (4) 38252096; fax (4) 38258368; e-mail courrier@vnagency.com.vn; internet lecourrier.vnagency.com.vn; French; publ. by the Viet Nam News Agency; Editor-in-Chief HOANG LAN HUONG.

Dan Tri (Intellectual People's Standard): 2/48 Giang Vo, Dong Da District, Hanoi; tel. (4) 37366491; fax (4) 37366490; e-mail dantri@dantri.com.vn; internet www.dantri.com.vn; f. 1982, fmrly known as *Tin Tuc* (News); publ. by the Viet Nam News Agency; afternoon; Vietnamese; Editor-in-Chief HUY HOAN PHAM.

Hanoi Moi (New Hanoi): 44 Le Thai To, Hoan Kiem District, Hanoi; tel. (4) 38253067; fax (4) 39287445; e-mail webmaster@hanoimoi.com.vn; internet www.hanoimoi.com.vn; f. 1976; organ of Hanoi Cttee of the Communist Party of Viet Nam; Editor HO QUANG LOI; circ. 35,000.

Lao Dong (Labour): 52B Nguyen Thi Dinh, Trung Hoa, Cau Giay, Hanoi; tel. (4) 35562295; fax (4) 35562275; e-mail webmaster@laodong.com.vn; internet www.laodong.com.vn; f. 1929; organ of the Viet Nam General Confederation of Labour; Editor-in-Chief VUONG VAN VIET; circ. 80,000.

Nhan Dan (The People): 71 Hang Trong, Hoan Kiem District, Hanoi; tel. (4) 38254231; fax (4) 38255593; e-mail toasoan@nhandan.org.vn; internet www.nhandan.org.vn; f. 1946; official organ of the Communist Party of Viet Nam; Editor-in-Chief THUAN HUU; circ. 220,000.

Nong Nghiep Viet Nam (Viet Nam Agriculture): 1059 Hongha, Hoan Kiem, Hanoi; tel. (4) 38256492; fax (4) 38252923; e-mail baonnvn@hn.vnn.vn; internet www.nongnghiep.vn; f. 1987; fmrly a weekly publ; Editor-in-Chief LE NAM SON.

Quan Doi Nhan Dan (People's Army): 7 Phan Dinh Phung, Hanoi; tel. (4) 37471748; fax (4) 37474913; e-mail dientubqd@gmail.com; internet www.qdnd.vn; f. 1950; organ of the armed forces; Editor NGUYEN LE PHUC; circ. 80,000.

Thanh Nien: 248 Cong Quynh, District 1, Ho Chi Minh City; tel. (8) 39255738; fax (8) 39255901; e-mail admin@thanhniennews.com; internet www.thanhniennews.com; f. 1986; flagship publication of the Viet Nam National Youth Federation; Chief Editor NGUYEN QUANG THONG.

Viet Nam Economic Times: 96 Hoang Quoc Viet, Cau Giay District, Hanoi; tel. (4) 37552060; fax (4) 37552046; e-mail editor@vneconomy.vn; internet vneconomy.vn; f. 1994; in Vietnamese (with monthly edn in English); Editor-in-Chief Prof. DAO NGUYEN CAT; Dep. Editor-in-Chief NGUYEN THI VAN ANH; circ 38,900.

Viet Nam News: 11 Tran Hung Dao, Hanoi; tel. (4) 39332316; fax (4) 39332311; e-mail vnnews@vnagency.com.vn; internet vietnamnews.vnanet.vn; f. 1991; English; publ. by the Viet Nam News Agency; Editor-in-Chief TRAN MAI HUONG; circ. 60,000.

VIET NAM

Ho Chi Minh City

Sai Gon Giai Phong (Liberated Saigon): 399 Hong Bang, Ward 14, District 5, Ho Chi Minh City; tel. (8) 39294092; fax (8) 39294083; e-mail sggponline@sggp.org.vn; internet www.sggp.org.vn; f. 1975; organ of Ho Chi Minh City Cttee of the Communist Party of Viet Nam; Editor-in-Chief Tran The Tuyen; circ. 100,000.

Saigon Times: 35 Nam Ky Khoi Nghia, District 1, Ho Chi Minh City; tel. (8) 38295936; fax (8) 38294294; e-mail sgt@thesaigontimes.vn; internet www.thesaigontimes.vn; f. 1991; Vietnamese and English; business issues; Editor-in-Chief Tran Thi Ngoc Hue.

PERIODICALS

Dai Doan Ket (Great Unity): 66 Ba Trieu, Hanoi; tel. (4) 38228303; fax 38228547; e-mail toasoan@baodaidoanket.com.vn; internet www.daidoanket.vn; f. 1977; weekly; organ of the Viet Nam Fatherland Front; Editor Dinh Duc Lap.

Dau Tu: 47 Quan Thanh, Ba Dinh, Hanoi; tel. (4) 38450537; fax (4) 38235281; e-mail baodautu.vn@gmail.com; internet baodautu.vn/portal/public/vir/trangchu; 3 a week; business newspaper publ. in Vietnamese; Editor-in-Chief Dr Nguyen Anh Tuan; circ. 40,000.

Dau Tu Chung Khoan: 47 Quan Thanh, Ba Dinh, Hanoi; tel. (4) 98450537; fax (4) 38430969; e-mail tinnhanhchungkhoan@vir.com.vn; internet www.tinnhanhchungkhoan.vn; weekly; stock market news publ. in Vietnamese; Editor-in-Chief Dr Nguyen Anh Tuan; circ. 50,000.

Giao Duc Thoi Dai (People's Teacher): 29B Ngo Quyen, Hoan Kiem District, Hanoi; tel. (4) 39369800; fax (4) 39345611; e-mail gdtddientu@gmail.com; internet www.gdtd.vn; f. 1959; weekly; organ of the Ministry of Education and Training; Chief Editor Dr Nguyen Danh Binh.

Giao Thong-Van Tai (Communications and Transport): 1 Nha Tho, Hoan Kiem, Hanoi; tel. (4) 9286763; fax (4) 8255387; e-mail toasoan@giaothongvantai.com.vn; internet giaothongvantai.com.vn; f. 1962; weekly; Thur.; organ of Ministry of Transport; Editor Nguyen Van Luu; circ. 30,000.

Hoa Hoc Tro (Pupils' Flowers): 5 Hoa Ma, Hanoi; tel. (4) 8211065; internet www.hoahoctro.vn; weekly; Chief Editor Nguyen Huy Loc; circ. 150,000.

Khoa Hoc Ky Thuat Kinh Te The Gioi (World Science, Technology and Economy): 5 Ly Thuong Kiet, Hanoi; tel. (4) 8252931; f. 1982; weekly.

Khoa Hoc va Doi Song (Science and Life): 70 Tran Hung Dao, Hanoi; tel. (4) 8253427; f. 1959; weekly; Editor-in-Chief Tran Cu; circ. 30,000.

Nghe Thuat Dien Anh (Cinematography): 65 Tran Hung Dao, Hanoi; tel. (4) 8262473; f. 1984; fortnightly; Editor Dang Nhat Minh.

Nguoi Cong Giao Viet Nam (Vietnamese Catholic): 59 Trang Thi, Hanoi; tel. (4) 8256242; f. 1984; weekly; organ of the Cttee for Solidarity of Patriotic Vietnamese Catholics; Editor-in-Chief So Chi.

Nguoi Dai Bieu Nhan Dan (People's Deputy): 35 Ngo Quyen, Hanoi; tel. (4) 08046231; fax (4) 08046659; e-mail ndbnd@hn.vnn.vn; f. 1988; bi-weekly; disseminates resolutions of the National Assembly and People's Council; Editor-in-Chief Ho Anh Tai (acting); circ. 2m.

Nguoi Hanoi (The Hanoian): 19 Hang Buom, Hanoi; tel. (4) 8255662; f. 1984; Editor Vu Quan Phuong.

Nha Bao Va Cong Luan (The Journalist and Public Opinion): 59 Ly Thai To, Hanoi; tel. (4) 8253609; fax (4) 8250797; f. 1985; monthly review; organ of the Viet Nam Journalists' Asscn; Editor-in-Chief Phan Duoc Toan; circ. 40,000.

Outlook: 11 Tran Hung Dao, Hanoi; tel. (4) 8222884; fax (4) 9424908; e-mail vnnews@vnagency.com.vn; internet vietnamnews.vnanet.com.vn; f. 2002; monthly news magazine; Editor-in-Chief Tran Mai Huong; circ. 6,000.

Phu Nu (Woman): Vietnam Women's Union, International Relations Dept, 39 Hang Chuoi, Hanoi; e-mail VWUnion@netnam.org.vn; f. 1997; fortnightly; women's magazine; circ. 100,000.

Phu Nu Thu Do (Capital Women): 72 Quan Su, Hanoi; tel. (4) 8247228; fax (4) 8223989; f. 1987; weekly; magazine of the Hanoi Women's Union; Editor-in-Chief Mai Thuc.

Phu Nu Viet Nam (Vietnamese Women): 39 Hang Chuoi, Hanoi; tel. (4) 8253500; weekly; magazine of the Vietnam Women's Union; Editor-in-Chief Phuong Minh.

Suc Khoe Va Doi Song (Health and Life): 138A Giang Vo, Ba Dinh District, Hanoi; tel. (4) 38461684; fax (4) 38443144; e-mail tranyenchau@gmail.com; internet http://suckhoedoisong.vn; f. 1961; weekly; published by the Ministry of Health; Editor-in-Chief Tran Si Tuan; circ. 45,000.

Tap Chi Cong San (Communist Review): 28 Tran Binh Trong Thanh, Hanoi; tel. (4) 9429753; fax (4) 9429754; e-mail baodientu@tccs.org.vn; internet www.tapchicongsan.org.vn; f. 1955 as *Hoc Tap*; fortnightly; political and theoretical organ of the Communist Party of Viet Nam; Editor-in-Chief Dr Vu Van Phuc; circ. 50,000.

Tap Chi Nghien Cuu Van Hoc (Literature Research Magazine): 20 Ly Thai To, Hanoi; tel. (4) 8252895; e-mail tcvapmail@vnn.vn; monthly; published by the Institute of Literature; Editor-in-Chief Phan Trong Thuong.

Tap Chi San Khau (Theatre Magazine): 51 Tran Hung Dao, Hanoi; tel. (4) 9434423; fax (4) 9434293; e-mail trongkhoi@hn.vnn.vn; f. 1973; monthly; Editor Ngo Thao.

Tap Chi Tac Pham Van Hoc: 65 Nguyen Du, Hanoi; tel. (4) 8252442; f. 1987; monthly; organ of the Viet Nam Writers' Asscn; Editor-in-Chief Nguyen Dinh Thi; circ. 15,000.

Tap Chi Tu Tuong Van Hoa (Ideology and Culture Review): Hanoi; f. 1990; organ of the Central Committee Department of Ideology and Culture; Editor Pham Huy Van.

The Thao Van Hoa (Sports and Culture): 5 Ly Thuong Kiet, Hanoi; tel. (4) 8267043; fax (4) 8264901; f. 1982; weekly; Editor-in-Chief Nguyen Huu Vinh; circ. 100,000.

The Thao Viet Nam (Viet Nam Sports): 5 Trinh Hoai Duc, Hanoi; tel. (4) 35625457; fax (4) 35625455; e-mail baottvn@yahoo.com; internet www.thethaovietnam.com.vn; f. 1968; weekly; Editor Hoang Dur.

Thieu Nhi Dan Toc (The Ethnic Young): 5 Hoa Ma, Hanoi; tel. (4) 9317133; bi-monthly; Editor Pham Thanh Long; circ. 60,000.

Thieu Nien Tien Phong (Young Pioneers): 5 Hoa Ma, Hanoi; tel. (4) 39713133; fax (4) 38215710; e-mail toasoan@thieunien.vn; internet www.thieunien.vn; 3 a week; Editor Vu Quang Vinh; circ. 210,000.

Thoi Bao Kinh Te Viet Nam: 175 Nguyen Thai Hoc, Hanoi; tel. (4) 8452411; fax (4) 8432755; f. 1993; 2 a week; Editor-in-Chief Pavef Daonguyencat; circ. 37,000.

Thoi Trang Tre (New Fashion): 12 Ho Xuan Huong, Hanoi; tel. (4) 8254032; fax (4) 8226002; f. 1993; monthly; Editor Vu Quang Vinh; circ. 80,000.

Thuong Mai (Commerce): 100 Lo Duc, Hanoi; tel. (4) 8263150; f. 1990; weekly; organ of the Ministry of Industry and Trade; Editor Tran Nam Vinh.

Tien Phong (Vanguard): 15 Ho Xuan Huong, Hanoi; tel. (4) 8264031; fax (4) 8225032; f. 1953; four a week; organ of the Ho Chi Minh Communist Youth Union and of the Forum of Vietnamese Youth; Editor Duong Xuan Nam; circ. 165,000.

Van Hoa (Culture and Arts): 26 Dien Bien Phu, Hanoi; tel. (4) 8257781; f. 1957; fortnightly; Editor Phi Van Tuong.

Van Nghe (Arts and Letters): 17 Tran Quoc Toan, Hanoi; tel. (4) 8264430; f. 1949; weekly; organ of the Vietnamese Writers' Union; Editor Huu Thinh; circ. 40,000.

Van Nghe Quan Doi (Army Literature and Arts): 4 Ly Nam De, Hanoi; tel. (4) 8254370; f. 1957; monthly; Editor Nguyen Tri Huan; circ. 50,000.

Viet Nam Business Forum: 9 Dao Duy Anh, 4th Floor, Dong Da District, Hanoi; tel. (4) 35743985; fax (4) 35743063; e-mail vbfhn@hn.vnn.vn; internet vibforum.vcci.com.vn; f. 1995; weekly magazine in English; publ. by the Viet Nam Chamber of Commerce and Industry; Editor-in-Chief Doan Duy Khuong.

Viet Nam Courier: 5 Ly Thuong Kiet, Hanoi; tel. (4) 8261847; fax (4) 8242317; weekly; English; publ. by the Viet Nam News Agency; Editor-in-Chief Nguyen Duc Giap.

Viet Nam Cultural Window: 46 Tran Hung Dao, Hanoi; tel. (4) 38253841; fax (4) 38269578; e-mail vncw@hn.vnn.vn; f. 1998; every 2 months; English; Dir Tran Doan Lam.

Viet Nam Investment Review (VIR): 47 Quan Thanh, Ba Dinh, Hanoi; tel. (4) 38450537; fax (4) 38457937; e-mail vir.hn@vir.com.vn; internet www.vir.com.vn; f. 1990; weekly; business newspaper publ. in English; Editor-in-Chief Dr Nguyen Anh Tuan; circ 40,000.

Vietnam Pictorial: 11 Tran Hung Dao, Hanoi; tel. (4) 39332303; fax (4) 39332291; e-mail vietnamvnp@gmail.com; f. 1954; monthly online, in Vietnamese, English, French, Chinese, Japanese, Spanish and Russian; fmrly Viet Nam Review; Editor-in-Chief Nguyen Thang; circ. 138,000.

Viet Nam Renovation: Hanoi; f. 1994; quarterly magazine on reform of the agricultural sector; in Vietnamese, Chinese and English.

Viet Nam Social Sciences: 27 Tran Xuan Soan, Hanoi; tel. (4) 9784578; fax (4) 9783869; e-mail 21.6.tapchikhxh@fpt.vn; f. 1984; every 2 months; publ. in English and Vietnamese; organ of Viet Nam Social Academy; Editor-in-Chief Dr Le Dinh Cuc.

Vietnamese Studies: 46 Tran Hung Dao, Hanoi; tel. (4) 38253841; fax (4) 38269578; e-mail thegioi@hn.vnn.vn; internet www.thegioipublishers.com.vn; f. 1964; quarterly; English and French edns; Dir and Chief Editor Dr Tran Doan Lam.

VIET NAM

NEWS AGENCY

Viet Nam News Agency (VNA): 79 Ly Thuong Kiet, Hoan Kiem District, Hanoi; tel. (4) 38255443; fax (4) 38252984; e-mail btk@vnanet.vn; internet www.vnanet.vn; f. 1945; mem. of Organization of Asian and Pacific News Agencies; Gen. Dir TRAN MAI HUONG.

PRESS ASSOCIATION

Viet Nam Journalists' Association (VJA): 59 Ly Thai To, Hanoi; tel. (4) 39386270; fax (4) 38250797; e-mail hnbvietnam@gmail.com; internet www.vja.org.vn; f. 1950; asscn of editors, reporters and photographers working in the press, radio, television and news agencies; 17,000 mems (2008); Pres. NGUYEN CHU NHAC; Vice-Pres. HA MINH HUE.

Publishers

Am Nhac Dia Hat (Music) Publishing House: 61 Ly Thai To, Hoan Kiem District, Hanoi; tel. (4) 8256208; f. 1986; produces cassettes, videocassettes, books and printed music; Dir PHAM DUC LOC.

Cong An Nhan Dan (People's Public Security) Publishing House: 167 Mai Hac De, Hai Ba Trung District, Hanoi; tel. (4) 8260910; f. 1981; cultural and artistic information, public order and security; Dir PHAM VAN THAM.

Giao Thong Van Tai (Communications and Transport) Publishing House: 80B Tran Hung Dao, Hanoi; tel. (4) 39423346; fax (4) 38224784; e-mail nxbgtvt@fpt.vn; f. 1983; managed by the Ministry of Transport; 350 titles annually; Dir LE TU GIANG.

Khoa Hoc Va Ky Thuat (Science and Technology) Publishing House: 70 Tran Hung Dao, Hanoi; tel. (4) 9424786; fax (4) 8220658; e-mail nxbkhkt@hn.vnn.vn; internet www.nxbkhkt.com.vn; f. 1960; scientific and technical works, guide books, dictionaries, popular and management books; Dir Prof. Dr TO DANG HAI.

Khoa Hoc Xa Hoi (Social Sciences) Publishing House: 61 Phan Chu Trinh, Hanoi; tel. (4) 8255428; f. 1967; managed by the Institute of Social Science; Dir Dr NGUYEN DUC ZIEU.

Kim Dong Publishing House: 55 Quang Trung, Hanoi; tel. (4) 9434730; fax (4) 8229085; e-mail kimdong@hn.vnn.vn; internet www.nxbkimdong.com.vn; f. 1957; children's; managed by the Ho Chi Minh Communist Youth Union; Dir PHAM QUANG VINH; Editor-in-Chief LE THI DAT.

Lao Dong (Labour) Publishing House: 54 Giang Vo, Hanoi; tel. (4) 8515380; f. 1945; translations and political works; managed by the Viet Nam Gen. Confed. of Labour; Dir LE THANH TONG.

My Thuat (Fine Arts) Publishing House: 44B Hamlong, Hanoi; tel. (4) 39449076; fax (4) 39436133; e-mail ngandangminh@yahoo.com.vn; f. 1987; managed by the Plastic Arts Workers' Asscn; Dir NGAN DANG THI BICH.

Nha Xuat Ban Giao Duc (Education) Publishing House: 81 Tran Hung Dao, Hanoi; tel. (4) 8220801; fax (4) 9422010; e-mail vanphong@nxbgd.vn; internet www.nxbgd.com.vn; f. 1957; managed by the Ministry of Education and Training; Dir NGO TRAN AI; Editor-in-Chief NGUYEN QUY THAO.

Nha Xuat Ban Hoi Nha Van (Writers' Association) Publishing House: 65 Nguyen Du, Hoan Kiem District, Hanoi; tel. and fax (4) 8222135; f. 1957; managed by the Vietnamese Writers' Asscn; Editor-in-Chief and Dir (acting) NGO VAN PHU.

Nong Nghiep (Agriculture) Publishing House: DH 14, Phuong Mai Ward, Dong Da District, Hanoi; tel. (4) 8523887; f. 1976; managed by the Ministry of Agriculture and Rural Devt; Dir DUONG QUANG DIEU.

Phu Nu (Women) Publishing House: 16 Alexandre De Rhodes, Hanoi; tel. (4) 8294459; f. 1957; managed by the Vietnamese Women's Union; Dir TRAN THU HUONG.

Quan Doi Nhan Dan (People's Army) Publishing House: 25 Ly Nam De, Hanoi; tel. (4) 8255766; managed by the Ministry of National Defence; Dir DOAN CHUONG.

San Khau (Theatre) Publishing House: 51 Tran Hung Dao, Hanoi; tel. (4) 8264423; f. 1986; managed by the Stage Artists' Asscn.

Su That (Truth) Publishing House: 24 Quang Trung, Hanoi; tel. (4) 8252008; fax (4) 8251881; f. 1945; Marxist-Leninist classics, politics and philosophy; managed by the Communist Party of Viet Nam; Dir TRAN NHAM.

Thanh Nien (Youth) Publishing House: 270 Nguyen Dinh Chieu, District 3, Hanoi; tel. and fax (4) 8222612; f. 1954; managed by the Ho Chi Minh Communist Youth Union; Dir BUI VAN NGOI.

The Duc The Thao (Physical Education and Sports) Publishing House: 7 Trinh Hoai Duc, Hanoi; tel. (4) 8256155; f. 1974; managed by the Ministry of Culture, Sports and Tourism; Dir NGUYEN HIEU.

The Gioi Publishers: 46 Tran Hung Dao, Hanoi; tel. (4) 8253841; fax (4) 8269578; e-mail thegioi@hn.vnn.vn; internet www.thegioipublishers.com.vn; f. 1957; foreign language publs; managed by the Ministry of Culture, Sports and Tourism; Dir and Chief Editor Dr TRAN DOAN LAM.

Thong Ke (Statistics) Publishing House: 96 Thuy Khe, Hanoi; tel. (4) 8257814; f. 1980; managed by the Gen. Statistics Office; Dir NGUYEN DAO.

Van Hoa (Culture) Publishing House: 43 Lo Duc, Hanoi; tel. (4) 8253517; f. 1971; managed by the Ministry of Culture, Sports and Tourism; Dir QUANG HUY.

Van Hoc (Literature) Publishing House: 19 Nguyen Truong To, Ba Dinh, Hanoi; tel. (4) 8294783; fax (4) 8294781; f. 1948; managed by the Ministry of Culture, Sports and Tourism; Dir NGUYEN VAN CU.

Xay Dung (Building) Publishing House: 37 Le Dai Hanh, Hanoi; tel. (4) 8268271; fax (4) 8215369; f. 1976; managed by the Ministry of Construction; Dir NGUYEN LUONG BICH.

Y Hoc (Medicine) Publishing House: 4 Le Thanh Ton, Phan Chu Trinh, Hoan Kiem District, Hanoi; tel. (4) 8255281; e-mail xuatbanyhoc@netnam.vn; managed by the Ministry of Health; Dir HOANG TRONG QUANG.

PUBLISHERS' ASSOCIATION

Viet Nam Publishers' Association (Hoi Xuat Ban Viet Nam): Lo 2, B15, My Dinh 1, Tu Liem District, Hanoi; tel. and fax (4) 62872645; e-mail thuytp1803@gmail.com; Dir LE VAN TINH.

Broadcasting and Communications

TELECOMMUNICATIONS

Directorate General for Posts and Telecommunications (DGPT): Department of Science-Technology and International Cooperation, 18 Nguyen Du, Hanoi; tel. (4) 8226580; fax (4) 8226590; industry regulator; Sec.-Gen. Dr MAI LIEM TRUC.

Board of the Technical and Economic Programme on Information Technology: 39 Tran Hung Dao, Hanoi; e-mail nyenet@itnet.gov.vn; Gen. Dir Dr DO VAN LOC.

Electricity of Viet Nam Telecommunications Co (EVN Telecom): 30A, Pham Hong Thai, Ba Dinh District, Hanoi; tel. (4) 22232323; fax (4) 22286868; internet www.evntelecom.com; provides fixed and cellular telephone services, as well as broadband internet services.

Hanoi Telecommunications Co (Hanoi Telecom): 2 Chua Boc, Dong Da District, Hanoi; tel. (3) 35729833; fax (4) 35729834; e-mail info@hanoitelecom.com; internet www.hanoitelecom.com; f. 2005; cellular telephone service provider; Chair. PHAM NGOC LANG.

Saigon Post and Telecommunications Service Corpn: 199 Dien Bien Phu, Binh Thanh District, Ho Chi Minh City; tel. (8) 54040608; fax (8) 54040609; e-mail info@spt.vn; internet www.spt.vn; f. 1995; partially state-owned; nation-wide post and telecommunications services; Chair. TRAN THI NGOC BINH; Pres. PHAM NGOC TUAN.

Viet Nam Military Electronics and Telecommunications Corpn (Viettel): 1 Giang Van Minh, Ba Dinh District, Hanoi; tel. (4) 62556789; fax (4) 62996789; e-mail gopy@viettel.com.vn; internet www.viettel.com.vn; f. 1998; offers range of post and telecommunication services, including cellular, 3G, telephone and broadband internet services; CEO TONG VIET TRUNG.

Viet Nam Posts and Telecommunications Corpn (VNPT): VNPT Bldg, 57 Huynh Thuc Khang, Dong Da District, Hanoi; tel. (3) 35775104; fax (3) 37741093; e-mail vnpt_website@vnpt.com.vn; internet www.vnpt.com.vn; f. 1995; state-owned communications co; Chair. PHAM LONG TRAN; Pres. and CEO VU TUAN HUNG.

Viet Nam Mobile Telecommunication Services Co (MobiFone): Lot VP1, Yen Hoa Ward, Cau Giay District, Hanoi; tel. (4) 37831733; e-mail webmaster@mobifone.com.vn; internet www.mobifone.com.vn; f. 1993; mobile cellular telephone service provider; Dir PHAM NGOC MINH.

Viet Nam Telecommunication Services Co (VinaPhone): 1 Nam Thanh Cong, Lot A, Dong Da District, Hanoi; tel. (4) 8358816; fax (4) 7731745; internet www.vinaphone.com.vn; f. 1996; provides mobile cellular telephone services; Man. Dir LAM HOANG VINH.

Vietnam Power Telecommunications Co (VP Telecom): Hanoi; f. 2004; cellular telephone service provider.

RADIO

Voice of Viet Nam (VOV): 58 Quan Su, Hanoi; tel. (4) 39344231; fax (4) 39344230; e-mail toasoan@vovnews.vn; internet www.vov.org.vn; f. 1945; four domestic channels in Vietnamese; two foreign service channels in English, Japanese, French, Khmer, Laotian,

VIET NAM   *Directory*

Spanish, Thai, Cantonese, Mandarin, Indonesian, Vietnamese and Russian; Dir-Gen. Dr VU VAN HIEN.

TELEVISION

Viet Nam Television (VTV): 43 Nguyen Chi Thanh, Hanoi; tel. (4) 8354992; fax (4) 8350882; e-mail webmaster@vtv.org.vn; internet www.vtv.org.vn; television was introduced in South Viet Nam in 1966 and in North Viet Nam in 1970; broadcasts from Hanoi (via satellite) to the whole country, the Asia region, Western Europe and North America; Vietnamese, French, English; Dir-Gen. Dr VU VAN HIEN.

Vietnam Multimedia Corpn (Vietnam Television Corpn—VTC): 8 Duong Tam Trinh, Hanoi; e-mail vtcvod@vtc.vn; internet www.vtc.com.vn; controlled by the Ministry of Information and Communication; Dir TAN THAI MINH.

Finance

(cap. = capital; res = reserves; dep. = deposits; m. = million; brs = branches; amounts in new đồng unless otherwise indicated)

BANKING

In 2010 the Vietnamese banking system comprised five state-owned commercial banks, one policy bank, five joint-venture banks, 48 foreign bank branches, 37 joint-stock commercial banks and 1,016 local credit funds, supervised by the Central People's Credit Fund. From March 2006 foreign banks were for the first time allowed to offer a full range of banking services.

Central Bank

State Bank of Viet Nam: 49 Ly Thai To, Hanoi; tel. (4) 39343327; fax (4) 39349569; e-mail webmaster@sbv.gov.vn; internet www.sbv.gov.vn; f. 1951; central bank of issue; provides a national network of banking services and supervises the operation of the state banking system; Gov. NGUYEN VAN GIAU; 61 brs and sub-brs.

State Banks

Bank for Investment and Development of Vietnam (BIDV): BIDV Tower, 35 Hang Voi, Hoan Kiem District, Hanoi; tel. (4) 22205544; fax (4) 22200399; e-mail bidv@hn.vnn.vn; internet www.bidv.com.vn; cap. 10,498,568m., res 5,651,721m., dep. 220,150,826m. (Dec. 2009); Chair. TRAN BAC HA; Gen. Dir TRAN ANH TUAN.

Housing Bank of Mekong Delta (MHB): 9 Vo Van Tan, District 3, Ho Chi Minh City; tel. (8) 39302501; fax (8) 39302506; e-mail webmaster@mhb.com.vn; internet www.mhb.com.vn; f. 1997; cap. 823,394m., res 337,948m., dep. 30,000,745m. (Dec. 2009); Chair. HUYNH NAM DUNG.

Joint Stock Commercial Bank for Foreign Trade of Viet Nam (Vietcombank): 198 Tran Quang Khai, Hanoi; tel. (4) 9343137; fax (4) 8269067; e-mail webmaster@vietcombank.com.vn; internet www.vietcombank.com.vn; f. 1963; authorized to deal in foreign currencies and all other international banking business; undergoing equitization in mid-2005; cap. 12,146,020m., res 1,460,250m., dep. 230,485,478m. (Dec. 2009); Chair. NGUYEN HOA BINH; Dir-Gen. NGUYEN PHUOC THANH; 23 brs.

Vietnam Bank for Agriculture and Rural Development (VBARD): 2 Lang Ha, Ba Dinh District, Hanoi; tel. (4) 8313717; fax (4) 8313719; e-mail webmaster@agribank.com.vn; internet www.agribank.com.vn; f. 1988; cap. 11,283,171m., res 7,418,666m., dep. 376,625,401m. (Dec. 2009); Chair. NGUYEN THE BINH; Gen. Dir PHAM THANH TAN; 2,200 brs.

Vietnam Joint Stock Commercial Bank for Industry and Trade (VietinBank): 108 Tran Hung Dao, Hanoi; tel. (4) 39421030; fax (4) 39421032; internet www.vietinbank.vn; f. 1987; fmrly Industrial and Commercial Bank of Viet Nam (Incombank); authorized to receive personal savings, extend loans, issue stocks and invest in export-orientated cos and jt ventures with foreign interests; cap. 11,252,973m., res 482,829m., dep. 172,347,747m. (Dec. 2009); Chair. PHAM HUY HUNG; Gen. Dir PHAM XUAN LAP; 150 brs.

Joint-Stock and Other Banks

Asia Commercial Bank: 442 Nguyen Thi Minh Khai, District 3, Ho Chi Minh City; tel. (8) 39290999; fax (8) 38343269; e-mail acb@acb.com.vn; internet www.acb.com.vn; f. 1993; Chair. TRAN XUAN GIA; Pres. LY XUAN HAI.

CBD (Codo Rural Share Commercial Bank): Co Do, Thoi Dong, O Mon, Can Tho Province; tel. (71) 61642; Dir TRAN NGOC HA.

DS Bank (Dongthap Commercial Joint-Stock Bank): 48 Rad 30/4, Cao Lanh Town, Dong Thap Province; tel. (67) 51441; fax (67) 51878; Dir HOANG VAN TU.

Ficombank (Denhat Joint-Stock Commercial Bank): 715 Tran Hung Dao, Ward 1, District 5, Ho Chi Minh City; tel. (8) 39237128; fax (8) 39234314; internet www.ficombank.com.vn; CEO NGUYEN NGOC THINH.

Indovina Bank Ltd: 46–50 Pham Hong Thai, District 1, Ho Chi Minh City; tel. (8) 38224995; fax (8) 38230131; e-mail support@indovinabank.com.vn; internet www.indovinabank.com.vn; f. 1990; jt venture of Cathay United Bank (Taiwan) and VietinBank; also has brs in Hanoi, Haiphong, Binh Duong, Can Tho and Dong Nai; cap. US $25m., res $3.4m., dep. $151m. (Dec. 2004); Chair. ROGER MING HSIEN LEE; Gen. Dir JAN YEI-FONG; 9 brs.

Maritime Commercial Joint Stock Bank: 88 Lang Ha, Dong Da District, Hanoi; tel. (4) 37718989; fax (4) 37718899; e-mail msb@msb.com.vn; internet www.msb.com.vn; f. 1991; cap. 3,000,000m., res 370,752m., dep. 54,314,306m. (Dec. 2009); Chair. LE THI LIEN; Gen. Dir TRAN ANH TUAN; 9 brs.

Phuong Nam Commercial Joint-Stock Bank (Southern Bank): 279 Ly Thuong Kiet, District 11, Ho Chi Minh City; tel. (8) 38663890; fax (8) 38663891; e-mail icsc@southernbank.com.vn; internet www.southernbank.com.vn; f. 1993; cap. 2,949,318m., dep. 31,758,689m. (Dec. 2009); Chair. MACH THIEU DUC.

Sacombank (Saigon Thuong Tin Commercial Joint-Stock Bank): 266–268 Nam Ky Khoi Nghia, Ward 8, District 3, Ho Chi Minh City; tel. (8) 39320420; fax (8) 39320424; e-mail info@sacombank.com.vn; internet www.sacombank.com.vn; f. 1991; became the first bank to list on the Securities Trading Centre in July 2006; cap. 8,078,178m., res 2,210,823m., dep. 83,943,435m. (Dec. 2009); Chair. DANG VAN THANH; CEO TRAN XUAN HUY.

Saigon Bank for Industry and Trade: 2C Pho Duc Chinh, District 1, Ho Chi Minh City; tel. (8) 39143183; fax (8) 39143193; e-mail webadmin@saigonbank.com.vn; internet www.saigonbank.com.vn; cap. 1,500,715m., res 223,928.1m., dep. 9,096,920.7m. (Dec. 2009); specializes in trade and industry activities; Chair. NGUYEN PHUC MINH; Dir-Gen. TRAN THI VIET ANH; 32 brs.

Shinhanvina Bank: 100 Nguyen Thi Minh Khai, Ward 6, District 3, Ho Chi Minh City; tel. (8) 38291581; fax (8) 38211648; internet www.shinhanvina.com.vn; f. 1993; jt venture between Vietcombank and Korea First Bank; fmrly known as Chohung Vina Bank; cap. US $30.0m., res $3.3m., dep. $181.5m. (Dec. 2007); Chair. PHU THAI VU; CEO CHOI HEUNG YEON.

Southeast Asia Commercial Joint Stock Bank (SeABank): 25 Tran Hung Dao, Hoan Kiem, Hanoi; tel. (4) 39448688; fax (4) 39448689; e-mail seabank@seabank.com.vn; internet www.seabank.com.vn; f. 1994; cap. 5,068,600m., res 141,552m., dep. 24,646,214m. (Dec. 2009); Chair. NGUYEN THI NGA.

VID Public Bank: Prime Bldg Centre, 7th Floor, 53 Quang Trung, Hanoi; tel. (4) 9438999; fax (4) 9439005; e-mail vidservice@vnn.vn; internet www.vidpublicbank.com.vn; f. 1992; jt venture between Bank for Investment and Devt of Viet Nam and Public Bank Bhd (Malaysia); commercial bank; cap. US $20m. (2001); Chair. TRAN ANH TUAN (acting); Gen. Dir KONG CHEE FIRE; 7 brs.

Vietnam Export-Import Commercial Joint-Stock Bank (Vietnam Eximbank): 7 Le Thi Hong Gam, District 1, Ho Chi Minh City; tel. (8) 38210055; fax (8) 38296063; e-mail website@eximbank.com.vn; internet www.eximbank.com.vn; f. 1989; est. as Vietnam Export Import Bank; present name adopted 1992; authorized to undertake banking transactions for the production and processing of export products and export-import operations; cap. 12,526,947m., res 377,856m., dep. 49,517,147m. (Dec. 2009); Chair. LE HUNG DUNG; Dir-Gen. TRUONG VAN PHUOC; 124 brs and offices.

Viet Nam Technological and Commercial Joint-Stock Bank (Techcombank): 70–72 Ba Trieu, Hoan Kiem District, Hanoi; tel. (4) 39446368; fax (4) 39446362; internet www.techcombank.com.vn; cap. 5,400,417m., res 525,719m., dep. 84,104,081m. (Dec. 2009); Chair. HO HUNG ANH; Gen. Dir NGUYEN DUC VINH.

VinaSiam Bank: 2 Pho Duc Chinh, District 1, Ho Chi Minh City; tel. (8) 38210630; fax (8) 38210585; e-mail vsb@vsb.com.vn; internet www.vinasiambank.com; f. 1995; jt venture between Bank for Agriculture and Rural Devt, Siam Commercial Bank (Thailand) and Charoen Pokphand Group (Thailand); cap. US $20.0m., res. $1.1m., dep. $37.2m. (Dec. 2005); Chair. LE VAN SO; Gen. Man. VIROJ THANAPITAK.

VP Bank (Viet Nam Commercial Joint-Stock Bank for Private Enterprises): 8 Le Thai To, Hoan Kiem District, Hanoi; tel. (4) 39288869; fax (4) 39288867; internet www.vpb.com.vn; cap. 2,117,474m., res 301,046m., dep. 23,974,394m. (Dec. 2009); Chair. NGO CHI DUNG; Gen. Dir NGUYEN HUNG.

STOCK EXCHANGES

Hanoi Stock Exchange (HNX): 81 Tran Hung Dao, Hoan Kiem, Hanoi; tel. (4) 39360750; fax (4) 39347818; e-mail marketinfo@hnx.vn; internet www.hnx.vn; f. 2005; est. as Hanoi Securities Trading

Centre; renamed as above 2009; 382 listed stocks (May 2011); CEO Tran Van Dzung.

Ho Chi Minh Stock Exchange: 45–47 Ben Chuong Duong, District 1, Ho Chi Minh City; tel. (8) 38217713; fax (8) 38217452; internet www.hsx.vn; f. 2000; fmrly Securities Trading Centre; name changed as above in 2007; Chair. Nguyen Doan Hung.

Supervisory Body

State Securities Commission: 164 Tran Quang Khai, Hanoi; tel. (4) 39340750; fax (4) 39340739; e-mail banbientap@ssc.gov.vn; internet www.ssc.gov.vn; f. 1997; responsible for developing the capital markets, incl. the establishment of a stock exchange; 13 mems; Chair. Bang Vu.

INSURANCE

In September 2006 there were 22 insurance companies operating in the country.

Aon Vietnam Ltd: Suites 1403–07, 14th Floor, Vietcombank Tower, 198 Tran Quang Khai, Hoan Kiem District, Hanoi; tel. (4) 38260832; fax (4) 38243983; e-mail vu_my_lan@aon-asia.com; internet www.aon.com/vietnam; f. 1993; fmrly Inchibrok Insurance; Man. Dir Vu My Lan.

Bao Long (Nha Rong Joint-Stock Insurance Co): 185 Dien Bien Phu, Dakao Ward, District 1, Ho Chi Minh City; tel. (8) 8239219; fax (8) 8239223; internet www.nharonginsurance.com; Dir Tran Van Binh.

Bao Minh Insurance Co (Ho Chi Minh City Insurance Co): 26 Ton That Dam, District 1, Ho Chi Minh; tel. (8) 38294180; fax (8) 38294185; e-mail baominh@baominh.com.vn; internet www.baominh.com.vn; f. 1994; non-life; Chair. and CEO Vinh Duc Tran; Gen. Dir Le Van Thanh.

Baoviet (Viet Nam Insurance Co): 35 Hai Ba Trung, Hoan Kiem District, Hanoi; tel. (4) 38262774; fax (4) 38257188; e-mail bvvn@baoviet.com.vn; internet www.baoviet.com.vn/bvvn.asp; f. 1965; property and casualty, personal accident, liability and life insurance; total assets 8,817,000m. đông (2004); Chair. Le Quang Binh; CEO Tran Trong Phuc.

Dai-ichi Life Insurance Co of Vietnam Ltd: 3rd Floor, Saigon Riverside Office Center, 2a–4a, Ton Duc Thang, District 1, Ho Chi Minh City; tel. (8) 38291919; fax (8) 38293131; e-mail info@dai-ichi-life.com.vn; internet www.dai-ichi-life.com.vn; f. 2007; Chair. and CEO Takashi Fujii.

Manulife (Vietnam) Ltd: Manulife Plaza, 75 Hoang Van Thai, Tan Phu Ward, District 7, Ho Chi Minh City; tel. (8) 54166888; fax (8) 54161818; e-mail manulifevn_info@manulife.com; internet www.manulife.com.vn; f. 1999; fmrly Chinfon-Manulife Life Insurance Co Ltd; first wholly foreign-owned life insurance co to operate in Viet Nam; Gen. Dir Carl Gustini.

Petrolimex Joint-Stock Insurance Co (PJICO Insurance): 532 Lang Ha, Dong Da District, Hanoi; tel. (4) 37760867; fax (4) 37760868; e-mail pjico@petrolimex.com.vn; internet www.pjico.com.vn; f. 1995; non-life insurance; Chair. Nguyen Van Tien; Gen. Dir Nguyen Anh Dung.

PetroVietnam Insurance Joint Stock Corpn (PVI): 154 Nguyen Thai Hoc, Ba Dinh District, Hanoi; tel. (4) 37335588; fax (4) 37336284; e-mail contact@pvi.com.vn; internet www.pvi.com.vn; f. 1996; non-life insurance; Chair. Nguyen Anh Tuan; Gen. Dir Bui Van Thuan.

Viet Nam International Assurance Co (VIA): Sun Red River Bldg, 6th Floor, 23 Phan Chu Trinh, Hoan Kiem District, Hanoi; tel. (4) 39330704; fax (4) 39330706; e-mail hn@via.com.vn; internet www.via.com.vn; f. 1996; jt-venture co, 51% owned by Baoviet, 49% owned by Tokio Marine and Nichido Fire Insurance Co (Japan); non-life insurance and reinsurance for foreign cos; Marketing Man. Vu Thi Kim Chi.

INSURANCE ASSOCIATION

Association of Vietnamese Insurers: 8th Floor, 141 Le Duan, Hanoi; tel. (4) 39412063; fax (4) 39422601; internet www.avi.org.vn; Chair. Trinh Quang Tuyen.

Trade and Industry

GOVERNMENT AGENCIES

State Financial and Monetary Council (SFMC): f. 1998; established to supervise, review and resolve matters relating to national financial and monetary policy.

Vietrade (Viet Nam Trade Promotion Agency): 20 Ly Thuong Kiet, Ba Dinh District, Hanoi; tel. (4) 39347628; fax (4) 39344260; e-mail vietrade@vietrade.gov.vn; internet www.vietrade.gov.vn; part of the Ministry of Industry and Trade; responsible for state management, co-ordination and implementation of trade and trade-related investment promotion and development activities; Dir-Gen. Do Thang Hai.

Vinacontrol (The Viet Nam Superintendence and Inspection Joint Stock Co): 54 Tran Nhan Tong, Hanoi; tel. (4) 39433840; fax (4) 39433844; e-mail vinacontrolvn@hn.vnn.vn; internet www.vinacontrol.com.vn; f. 1957; brs in all main Vietnamese ports and trade centres; controls quality and volume of exports and imports and transit of goods, and conducts inspections, sampling and testing of deliveries and production processes; price, assets and enterprise valuation, marine survey, damage survey, claim settling and adjustment; Chair. Bui Duy Chinh; Gen. Dir Mai Tien Dung; 600 employees.

CHAMBER OF COMMERCE

VCCI (Viet Nam Chamber of Commerce and Industry): 9 Dao Duy Anh, 4th Floor, Hanoi; tel. (4) 35742022; fax (4) 35742020; e-mail webmaster@vcci.com.vn; internet www.vcci.com.vn; f. 1963; offices throughout Viet Nam; promotes business and investment between foreign and Vietnamese cos; organizes exhibitions, provides information etc.; represents foreign applicants for patents and trade mark registration; helps domestic and foreign businesses to settle disputes by negotiation or arbitration; Pres. and Chair. Dr Vu Tien Loc; Sec.-Gen. Pham Gia Tuc; assoc. orgs: Viet Nam Int. Arbitration Centre, Viet Nam General Average Adjustment Cttee, Advisory Bd.

Viet Nam International Arbitration Centre (VIAC): 9 Dao Duy Anh, 6th Floor, Dong Da District, Hanoi; tel. (4) 35744001; fax (4) 35743001; e-mail viac-vcci@hn.vnn.vn; internet www.viac.org.vn; f. 1993; adjudicates in disputes concerning both domestic and international economic relations.

INDUSTRIAL AND TRADE ORGANIZATIONS

Agrex Saigon (Agricultural Products and Foodstuffs Export Co): 58 Vo Van Tan, District 3, Ho Chi Minh City; tel. (8) 39303186; fax (8) 38725194; e-mail tt-agr@hcm.fpt.vn; internet www.agrexsaigon.com.vn; f. 1976; exports agricultural produce, coffee, frozen foods and aquatic products; imports agricultural and industrial materials, machinery and equipment, and consumer goods; Gen. Dir Le Thi My Linh; 1,200 employees.

Agrimex (Viet Nam National Agricultural Products Corpn): 173 Hai Ba Trung, District 3, Ho Chi Minh City; tel. (8) 8241049; fax (8) 8291349; e-mail agrimex@hcm.fpt.vn; f. 1956; imports and exports agricultural products; Gen. Dir Nguyen Bach Tuyet.

Airimex (General Civil Aviation Import-Export and Forwarding Co): 414 Nguyen Van Cu, Gia Lam, Long Bien District, Hanoi; tel. (4) 38271939; fax (4) 38271925; e-mail contact@airimex.vn; internet www.airimex.vn; f. 1989; imports and exports aircraft, spare parts and accessories for aircraft and air communications; Gen. Dir Pham Doa Hong.

An Giang Afiex Co (An Giang Agriculture and Foods Import and Export Co): 25/40 Tran Hung Dao, Long Xuyen Town, An Giang Province; tel. (76) 932985; fax (76) 932981; e-mail xnknstpagg@hcm.vnn.vn; internet www.afiex-seafood.com.vn; f. 1992; mfr and sale of agricultural products, also beverages; Dir Pham Van Bay.

Artexport–Vietnam (Viet Nam Handicrafts and Art Articles Export-Import Joint Stock Co): 2a Pham Su Manh, Hanoi; tel. (4) 38266576; fax (4) 38259275; e-mail ducquantri@artexport.com.vn; internet www.artexport.com.vn; f. 1964; deals in craft products and art articles; Gen. Dir Do Van Khoi.

B12 Petroleum Co: Cai Lan, Bay Chay Sub-District, Ha Long City, Quang Ninh Province; tel. (33) 846360; fax (33) 846349; internet www.b12petroleum.com.vn; distribution of petroleum products; Dir Vu Ngoc Hai.

Barotex (Viet Nam Investment and Trading Joint Stock Co): 100 Thai Thinh, Dong Da District, Hanoi; tel. (4) 38573428; fax (4) 38573036; e-mail info@barotex.com.vn; internet www.barotex.com.vn; f. 1971; specializes in art and handicrafts made from natural materials, sports shoes, ceramic and lacquer wares, gifts and other housewares, fibres, agricultural and forest products; Gen. Dir Ta Quoc Toan.

Bim Son Cement Co: Badinh, Bimson Town, Thanh Hoa Province; tel. (37) 3824242; fax (37) 3824046; e-mail ktkh_bs@yahoo.com; internet www.ximangbimson.com.vn; mfr of cement; Dir Nguyen Nhu Khue.

Binh Tay Import-Export Joint Stock Co (BITEX): 110–112 Hau Giang, District 6, Ho Chi Minh City; tel. (8) 9604325; fax (8) 9602478; e-mail bitexvn@bitexvn.com; trade in miscellaneous goods; Dir Nguyen Van Thien.

Centrimex (Viet Nam National General Import-Export Corpn): 247 Giang Vo, Dong Da District, Hanoi; tel. (58) 8512986; fax (58) 8512974; e-mail centrimexhn@fpt.vn; internet www.centrimexhn.com.vn; f. 1986; exports and imports goods for five provinces in the south-central region of Viet Nam; Gen. Dir Hoang Dinh Dung.

VIET NAM — Directory

Coalimex (Vinacomin Coal Import-Export Joint Stock Co): 47 Quang Trung, Hanoi; tel. (4) 9423166; fax (4) 9422350; e-mail coalimex@fpt.vn; internet www.coalimex.com.vn; f. 1982; exports coal, imports mining machinery and equipment; Gen. Dir PHAM HONG KHANH.

Cocenex (Central Production Import-Export Corpn): 80 Hang Gai, Hanoi; tel. (4) 8254535; fax (4) 8294306; f. 1988; Gen. Dir BUI THI THU HUONG.

Coffee Supply, Processing and Materials Co: 38B Nguyen Bieu, Nha Trang City, Khanh Hoa Province; tel. (58) 21176; coffee mfr.

Cokyvina (Post and Telecommunication Equipment Import-Export Service Corpn): 178 Trieu Viet Vuong, Hai Ba Trung, Hanoi; tel. (4) 39781323; fax (4) 39782368; e-mail info@cokyvina.com.vn; internet www.cokyvina.com.vn; f. 1987; imports and exports telecom equipment, provides technical advice on related subjects, undertakes authorized imports, jt ventures, jt co-ordination and co-operation on investment with foreign and domestic economic orgs; Dir NGUYEN KIM KY.

Constrexim (Viet Nam Construction Investment and Export-Import Holdings Corpn): 39 Nguyen Dinh Chieu, Hai Ba Trung, Hanoi; tel. (4) 2812000; fax (4) 7820176; e-mail constrexim@fpt.vn; internet www.constrexim.com.vn; f. 1982; exports and imports building materials, equipment and machinery; undertakes construction projects in Viet Nam and abroad, and production of building materials with foreign partners; also involved in investment promotion and project management, real estate development, and human resources development and training; Gen. Dir DO MANH VU.

Culturimex (State Enterprise for the Export and Import of Works of Art and other Cultural Commodities): 22B Hai Ba Trung, Hanoi; tel. (4) 8252226; fax (4) 8259224; e-mail namson@fpt.vn; f. 1988; exports cultural items and imports materials for the cultural industry; Gen. Dir NGUYEN LAI.

Dau Tieng Rubber Corpn: Dau Tieng Townlet, Dau Tieng District, Binh Duong Province; tel. (650) 561847; fax (650) 561488; e-mail vanphong@caosudautieng.com.vn; internet www.caosudautieng.com.vn; f. 1981; planting, processing and export of natural rubber; Man. Dir LE VAN KHOA.

Epco Ltd (Export Import and Tourism Co Ltd): 1 Nyuyen Thuong Hien, District 3, Ho Chi Minh City; tel. (8) 8324392; fax (8) 8324744; f. 1986; processes seafood; tourism and hotel business; Gen. Dir NGUYEN LOC RI.

Foodcosa (Food Co Ho Chi Min City): 57 Nguyen Thi Minh Khai, District 1, Ho Chi Minh City; tel. (8) 39309184; fax (8) 39304552; e-mail info@foodcosa.vn; internet www.foodcosa.vn; mfr and distributor of food products (rice, instant noodles, porridge, sauces, biscuits); Dir NGO VAN TAN; 3,500 employees.

Forexco Quang Nam (Quang Nam Forest Products Export Joint Stock Co): Xa Dien Ngoc, Dien Ban District, Quangnam Province; tel. (510) 3944073; fax (510) 3843619; e-mail forexcoqnam@dng.vnn.vn; internet forexco.com.vn; f. 1986; mfr and exporter of furniture and other wood products; Gen. Dir PHAM PHU THONG.

Garmex Saigon (Saigon Garment Manufacturing Import-Export Co): 236/7 Nguyen Van Luong, Ward 17, Go Vap District, Ho Chi Minh City; tel. (8) 39844822; fax (8) 39844746; e-mail gmsg@hcm.fpt.vn; internet www.garmexsaigon-gmc.com; f. 1993; garment production and export; Pres. LE QUANG HUNG; Man. Dir NGUYEN AN.

Genecofov (General Co of Foods and Services): 64 Ba Huyen Thanh Quan, District 3, Ho Chi Minh City; tel. (8) 9325366; fax (8) 9325428; e-mail gecofov@hcm.fpt.vn; f. 1956; import and export of food products, handicrafts and ceramics, garage services, vehicle trading; under the Ministry of Trade; Dir TO VAN PHAT.

Generalexim (Viet Nam National General Export-Import Corpn): 46 Ngo Quyen, Hoan Kiem, Hanoi; tel. (4) 38264009; fax (4) 38259894; e-mail gexim@generalexim.com.vn; internet www.generalexim.com.vn; f. 1981; export and import on behalf of production and trading organizations, also garment processing for export and manufacture of toys; Gen. Dir HOANG TUAN KHAI.

Generalimex (General II Import-Export Joint Stock Co): 212/1 Nguyen Trai, District 1, Ho Chi Minh City; tel. (8) 62907517; fax (8) 62907518; e-mail generalimex@generalimex.com.vn; internet www.generalimex.com.vn; exports of agricultural products and spices, imports of machinery, vehicles, chemicals and fertilizers; Gen. Dir NGUYEN VAN HOANG.

Haprosimex (Hanoi General Production and Import-Export Company): Km 11, National Highway 1A, Van Dien, Hanoi; tel. (4) 8618341; fax (4) 8615390; e-mail business@hapro.com.vn; internet www.hapro.com.vn; specializes in handicrafts, textiles, clothing and agricultural and forestry products; Gen. Dir NGUYEN MINH TUAN.

Hatien 1 Cement Joint Stock Co: 360 Ben Chuong Dong, P. Cau Kho, District 1, Ho Chi Minh City; tel. (8) 38368363; fax (8) 38361278; e-mail hatien1@hatien1.com.vn; internet www.hatien1.com.vn; mfr of cement; Dir NGUYEN NGOC ANH.

Hatien Cement Co No 2: Kien Luong Town, Ha Tien, Kien Giang Province; tel. (77) 53004; fax (77) 53005; e-mail xmht2@vnn.vn; internet www.xmht2.com; mfr of cement; Dir NGUYEN MANH.

Haugiang Petrolimex (Haugiang Petrol and Oil Co): 21 Cach Mang Thang 8, Can Tho City, Can Tho Province; tel. (71) 21657; fax (71) 12746; distributor of fuel; Dir TRINH MANG THANG.

Hoang Thach Cement Co: Minh Tan Hamlet, Kinh Mon, Hai Durong; tel. (32) 3821092; fax (32) 3821098; e-mail contact@ximanghoangthach.com; internet www.ximanghoangthach.com.vn; sale of construction materials; Dir NGOC BINH DAO.

Intimex Import-Export Corpn: 96 Tran Hung Dao, Hanoi; tel. (4) 39423529; fax (4) 39424250; e-mail intimex@hn.vnn.vn; internet www.intimexco.com; f. 1979; exports mainly agricultural products and processed items; imports mainly consumer goods, motorcycles and raw materials, machinery and equipment for the construction industry; Chair. NGUYEN THI NGA; Gen. Dir HOANG HOANG HANH.

Lefaso (Viet Nam Leather and Footwear Asscn): 160 Hoang Hoa Tham, Tay Ho, Hanoi; tel. (4) 37281560; fax (4) 37281561; e-mail hhdg@hn.vnn.vn; internet www.lefaso.org.vn; f. 1990 to promote external trade relations, to provide technical support and technological training and to disseminate market information; Chair. NGUYEN DUC THUAN; Gen. Sec. NGUYEN THI TONG.

Machinoimport (Viet Nam Machinery and Spare Parts Co): 8 Trang Thi, Hoan Kiem, Hanoi; tel. (4) 8253703; fax (4) 8254050; e-mail machinokhdt@hn.vnn.vn; internet www.machinoimport.com.vn; f. 1956 as Vietnam National Machinery Export-Import Corpn; reorganized in 2003; controlled by Ministry of Industry and Trade; imports and exports machinery, spare parts and tools; consultancy, investment, jt-venture, and manufacturing services; comprises 12 cos; Chair. NGUYEN TRAN DAT; Gen. Dir TRAN DUC TRUONG.

Marine Supply (Marine Technical Materials Import-Export and Supplies): 276A Da Nang, Ngo Quyen, Haiphong; tel. (31) 847308; fax (31) 845159; f. 1985; imports and exports technical materials for marine transportation industry; Dir PHAN TRANG CHAN.

Mecanimex (Viet Nam National Mechanical Products Export-Import Co): 37 Trang Thi, Hoan Kiem District, Hanoi; tel. (4) 8257459; fax (4) 9349904; e-mail mecahn@fpt.vn; internet mecanimex.com.vn; exports and imports mechanical products and hand tools; Gen. Dir TRAN BAO GIOC.

Nafobird (Viet Nam Forest and Native Birds, Animals and Ornamental Plants Export-Import Enterprises): 64 Truong Dinh, District 3, Ho Chi Minh City; tel. (8) 8290211; fax (8) 8293765; f. 1987; exports native birds, animals and plants, and imports materials for forestry; Dir VO HA AN.

Naforimex (Hanoi Forest Products Export-Import and Production Corpn): 19 Ba Trieu, Hoan Kiem District, Hanoi; tel. (4) 8261255; fax (4) 8259264; e-mail naforimexhanoi@fpt.vn; f. 1960; imports chemicals, machinery and spare parts for the forestry industry and water supply network; exports oils, forest products, gum benzoin and resin; CEO NGUYEN BA HUNG.

Nitagrex (Ninh Thuan Agricultural Products Import-Export Co): 158 Bac Ai, Do Vinh Ward, Phan Rang Thap Cham, Ninh Thuan Province; tel. (68) 888779; fax (68) 888842; e-mail nitagrex@hcm.vnn.vn; internet www.nitagrex.com.vn; f. 1999; production and export of agricultural products; import of consumer goods, transport vehicles and agricultural materials and equipment; Gen. Dir DAO VAN CHAN.

Packexport (Viet Nam National Packaging Technology and Import-Export Co): 31 Hang Thung, Hanoi; tel. (4) 8262792; fax (4) 8269227; e-mail packexport-vn@vnn.vn; f. 1976; manufactures packaging for domestic and export demand, and imports materials for the packaging industry; Gen. Dir TRINH LE KIEU.

Petec Trading and Investment Corpn: 194 Nam Ky Khoi Nghia, District 3, Ho Chi Minh City; tel. (8) 39303633; fax (8) 39305686; e-mail petectonghop@hcm.vnn.vn; internet www.petec.com.vn; f. 1981; imports equipment and technology for oil drilling, exploration and oil production; exports crude petroleum, rice, coffee and agricultural products; invests in silk, coffee, financial and transport sectors; Chair. and CEO NGUYEN MINH TRUC.

Petrol and Oil Co (Zone 1): Duc Gliang Town, Gia Lam, Hanoi; tel. (4) 8271400; fax (4) 8272432; sales of oil and gas; Dir PHAN VAN DU.

Petrolimex (Viet Nam National Petroleum Corpn): 1 Kham Thien, Dong Da District, Hanoi; tel. (4) 38512603; fax (4) 38519203; e-mail xttm@petrolimex.com.vn; internet www.petrolimex.com.vn; f. 1956; import, export and distribution of petroleum products and liquefied petroleum gas; Chair. NGUYEN THANH SON; Dir-Gen. BUI NGOC BAO.

Petrolimex Saigon Petroleum Co (Zone 2): 15 Le Duan, District 1, Ho Chi Minh City; tel. (8) 8292081; fax (8) 8222082; sales of petroleum products; Dir TRAN VAN THANG.

Petrovietnam (The Viet Nam Oil and Gas Corpn): 18 Lang Ha, Ba Dinh, Hanoi; tel. (4) 38252526; fax (4) 38265942; e-mail info@pvn.vn; internet www.petrovietnam.com.vn; f. 1975; exploration and production of petroleum and gas; Chair. DINH LA THANG; Pres. and CEO PHUNG DINH THUC.

VIET NAM
Directory

Saigon Beer Alcohol Beverage Corpn (Sabeco): 6 Hai Ba Trung, Ben Nghe District, Ho Chi Minh City; tel. (8) 38294083; fax (8) 38296856; e-mail biasaigon@sabeco.com.vn; internet www.sabeco.com.vn; producer of beer; Pres. NGUYEN ANH DZUNG.

Seaco (Sundries Electric Appliances Co): 64 Pho Duc Chinh, District 1, Ho Chi Minh City; tel. (8) 8210961; fax (8) 8210974; deals in miscellaneous electrical goods; Dir MAI MINH CUONG.

Seaprodex Hanoi (Hanoi Sea Products Export-Import Co): 20 Lang Ha, Dong Da, Hanoi; tel. (4) 38345678; fax (4) 38354125; e-mail seahn@seaprodexhanoi.com.vn; internet www.seaprodexhanoi.com.vn; Dir LE CONG DUC.

Seaprodex Saigon (Ho Chi Minh City Sea Products Import-Export Corpn): 87 Ham Nghi, District 1, Ho Chi Minh City; tel. (8) 38214186; fax (8) 39142236; e-mail seaprodexsg@seaprodexsg.com; internet www.seaprodexsg.com; f. 1978; exports frozen and processed sea products; imports machinery and materials for fishing and processing; Gen. Dir NGUYEN DUY DUNG.

SJC (Saigon Jewellery Co): 115 Nguyen Cong Tru, District 1, Ho Chi Minh City; tel. (8) 39144056; fax (8) 39144057; e-mail info@sjc.com.vn; internet www.sjc.com.vn; f. 1998; manufacturing, processing and trading of gold, gemstones, silver and jewellery; Man. Dir NGUYEN THANH LONG.

Technimex JSC (Technology Import-Export Joint Stock Company): 70 Tran Hung Dao, Hoan Kiem District, Hanoi; tel. (4) 7519423; fax (4) 3778220; e-mail technimex@hn.vnn.vn; internet www.technimexvn.com; f. 1982 under the name Viet Nam Technology Import-Export Corpn; name changed as above in 2001; exports and imports machines, equipment, instruments, etc.; Dir NGUYEN HUY BINH.

Technoimport (Viet Nam National Complete Equipment and Technics Import-Export Corpn): 16–18 Trang Thi, Hanoi; tel. (4) 38254974; fax (4) 38254059; e-mail technohn@netnam.vn; internet technoimport.vn; f. 1959; imports and exports equipment, machinery, transport equipment, spare parts, materials and various consumer commodities; exports products by co-investment and jt-venture enterprises; provides consulting services for trade and investment, transport and forwarding services; acts as import-export brokering and trading agents; Gen. Dir VU CHU HIEN.

Terraprodex (Corpn for Processing and Export-Import of Rare Earth and Other Specialities): 35 Dien Bien Phu, Hanoi; tel. (4) 8232010; fax (4) 8256446; f. 1989; processing and export of rare earth products and other minerals; Dir TRAN DUC HIEP.

Thanglong Minerals and Metals Co Ltd: 127 Khuat Duy Tien, Hanoi; tel. (4) 35535218; fax (4) 35532669; e-mail thanglong@thanglongcastiron.com; internet www.thanglongcastiron.com; fmrly Viet Nam National Minerals Export Import Corpn; exports cast iron products; imports pig iron and crude steel; Gen. Dir LE THI MINH.

Tocontap Saigon (Saigon Sundries Export-Import Joint Stock Co): 35 Le Quy Don, District 3, Ho Chi Minh City; tel. (8) 39325687; fax (8) 39325963; e-mail info@tocontapsaigon.com; internet www.tocontapsaigon.com; f. 1956; imports and exports apparel, agricultural products, art and handicrafts and sundries; Gen. Dir LE THI THANH HUONG.

Tracimexco (Transport Investment Co-operation and Import-Export Corpn): 22 Phan Dinh Giot, Ward 2, Tan Binh District, Ho Chi Minh City; tel. (8) 8442247; fax (8) 8445240; e-mail tralico@hn.vnn.vn; internet www.tracimexco.com.vn; fmrly Vietranscimex; exports and imports specialized equipment and materials for transportation and communication; Gen. Dir PHAM QUANG VINH.

Vama (Viet Nam Automobile Manufacturers' Association): Viglacera Bldg, 8th Floor, Me Tri Ward, Tu Liem District, Hanoi; tel. (4) 35536893; fax (4) 35536841; e-mail vama.office@gmail.com; internet www.vama.org.vn; f. 2000; 18 mems; Chair. AKITO TACHIBANA.

Vasep (Viet Nam Asscn of Seafood Exporters and Producers): Lot 218A, 6 An Kanh, An Phu Ward, District 2, Ho Chi Minh City; tel. (8) 62810432; fax (8) 62810450; e-mail vasep@fpt.vn; internet www.vasep.com.vn; f. 1998; exports seafood products; provides essential market information to Viet Nam's seafood industry; organizes and implements activities designed to develop and promote the industry; Chair. TRAN THIEN HAI.

Vegetexco (Viet Nam National Vegetables and Fruit Export-Import Corpn): 2 Pham Ngoc Thach, Dong Da District, Hanoi; tel. (4) 5744592; fax (4) 8523926; e-mail vegetexcovn@fpt.vn; internet www.vegetexcovn.com.vn; f. 1971; exports fresh and processed vegetables and fruit, spices and flowers, and other agricultural products; imports vegetable seeds and processing materials; Gen. Dir LE VAN ANH.

Vicem (Viet Nam Cement Industry Corpn—Vinacement): 228 Le Duan, Dong Da District, Hanoi; tel. (4) 8512425; fax (4) 8512778; e-mail banbt@vinacement.com.vn; internet www.vicem.vn; f. 1980; manufactures and exports cement and clinker; Chair. LE VAN CHUNG; Gen. Dir NGUYEN NGOC ANH.

Viet Nam Dairy Products JS Company (VINAMILK): 10 Tan Trao, Ward Tan Phu, District 7, Ho Chi Minh City; tel. (8) 54155555; fax (8) 54161226; e-mail vinamilk@vinamilk.com.vn; internet www.vinamilk.com.vn; f. 1976; producer of dairy products; Dir MAI KIEU LIEN.

Vietnam Rubber Group: 236 Nam Ky Khoi Nghia, District 3, Ho Chi Minh City; tel. (8) 9327857; fax (8) 9327341; merged with Rubexim (rubber export-import corpn) in 1991; fmrly known as GERUCO; manages and controls the Vietnamese rubber industry, including the planting, processing and trading of natural rubber and rubber wood products; also imports chemicals, machinery and spare parts for the industry; Chair. TRAN NGOC THANH; Dir-Gen. LE QUANG THUNG.

Vietrans (Viet Nam National Foreign Trade Forwarding and Warehousing Corpn): 13 Ly Nam De, Hoan Kiem District, Hanoi; tel. (4) 38457417; fax (4) 38455829; e-mail info@vietrans.com.vn; internet vietrans.com.vn; f. 1970; agent for forwarding and transport of exports and imports, diplomatic cargoes and other goods, warehousing, shipping and insurance; Gen. Dir THAI DUY LONG.

Viettronimex (Viet Nam Electronics Import-Export Corpn): 74–76 Nguyen Hue, District 1, Ho Chi Minh City; tel. (8) 8298201; fax (8) 8294873; e-mail vtr@hcm.vnn.vn; internet viettronimex.com.vn; f. 1981; imports and exports electronic goods; Dir NGUYEN HUU THINH.

Vigecam (Viet Nam General Corpn of Agricultural Materials): 16 Ngo Tat To, Dong Da District, Hanoi; tel. and fax (4) 37478890; e-mail info@vigecam.vn; internet www.vigecam.vn; exports and imports agricultural products; Gen. Dir TRAN VAN KANH.

Viglacera (Viet Nam Glass and Ceramics Corpn): 16–17 Viglacera Bldg, 1 Thang Long, Ward Me Tri, Tu Liem, Hanoi; tel. (4) 5536660; fax (4) 5536671; e-mail vgc@hn.vnn.vn; internet www.viglacera.com.vn; f. 1974; mfr of building materials; Gen. Dir NGUYEN ANH TUAN.

Vimedimex II (Vimedimex Medi-Pharma Joint Stock Co): 602/45D Dien Bien Phu, Ward 22, Binh Thanh District, Ho Chi Minh City; tel. (8) 38990164; fax (8) 38990165; e-mail info@vietpharm.com.vn; internet www.vietpharm.com.vn; f. 1984; exports and imports medicinal and pharmaceutical materials and products, medical instruments; Gen. Dir NGUYEN TIEN HUNG.

Vimico (Viet Nam National Minerals Corpn): 562 Nguyen Van Cu, Gia Lam District, Hanoi; tel. (8) 8770010; fax (8) 8770006; e-mail vimico@hn.vnn.vn; internet www.vimicovn.com; Chair. VU XUAN KHOAT; Gen. Dir NGO VAN TROI.

Vinacafe (Viet Nam National Coffee Import-Export Corpn): 211–213 Tran Huy Lieu, Ward 8, Phu Nuan District, Ho Chi Minh City; tel. (8) 54495514; fax (8) 54495513; e-mail vinacafe@hn.vnn.vn; internet www.vinacafe.com.vn; f. 1995; state-owned; exports coffee, and imports equipment and chemicals for coffee production; Chair. Dr DOAN DINH THIEM.

Vinachem (Viet Nam National Chemical Corpn): 1A Trang Tien, Hoan Kiem District, Hanoi; tel. (4) 38240551; fax (4) 38252995; e-mail info@vinachem.com.vn; internet www.vinachem.com.vn; f. 1969; production, import and export of chemicals and fertilizers; Chair. NGUYEN QUOC TUAN; Pres. and CEO NGUYEN DINH KHANG.

Vinachimex (Viet Nam National Chemicals Import-Export Corpn): 4 Pham Ngu Lao, Hanoi; tel. (4) 8256377; fax (4) 8257727; f. 1969; exports and imports chemical products, minerals, rubber, fertilizers, machinery and spare parts; Dir NGUYEN VAN SON.

Vinacomin (Viet Nam National Coal-Mineral Industries Group): 226 Le Duan, Dong Da District, Hanoi; tel. (4) 5180141; fax (4) 8510724; e-mail info@vinacomin.vn; internet www.vinacomin.vn; f. 2005; est. following merger of Vietnam Coal Corpn and Vietnam Minerals Corpn; subsidiaries include Vinacomin Port Co; coal and bauxite mining, shipbuilding, automobile manufacturing, tourism, financing, and power generation in thermal power plants; Gen. Dir TRAN XUAN HOA.

Vinafilm (Viet Nam Film Import, Export and Film Service Corpn): 73 Nguyen Trai, Dong Da District, Hanoi; tel. (4) 8244566; f. 1987; export and import of films and videotapes; film distribution; organization of film shows and participation of Vietnamese films in international film festivals; Gen. Man. NGO MANH LAN.

Vinafimex (Viet Nam National Agricultural Produce and Foodstuffs Import and Export Corpn): 58 Ly Thai To, Hanoi; tel. (4) 8255768; fax (4) 8255476; e-mail fime@hn.vnn.vn; internet www.vinafimex.com.vn; f. 1984; exports cashews, peanuts, coffee, rubber and other agricultural products, and garments; imports malt, fertilizer, insecticide, seeds, machinery and equipment, etc.; Pres. NGUYEN TOAN THANG; Gen. Dir NGUYEN VAN THANG.

Vinafood Hanoi (Hanoi Food Import-Export Co): 6 Ngo Quyen, Hoan Kiem District, Hanoi; tel. (4) 8256771; fax (4) 8258528; f. 1988; exports rice, maize, tapioca; imports fertilizers, insecticides, wheat and wheat flour; Dir NGUYEN DUC HY.

Vinalivesco (Vietnam National Livestock Corpn): 519 Minh Khai, Hai Ba Trung District, Hanoi; tel. (4) 38621814; fax (4) 38623645;

VIET NAM

e-mail vilico@vilico.vn; internet vilico.vn; f. 1996; imports and exports animal and poultry products, animal feeds and other agro-products, and foodstuffs; Gen. Dir NGUYEN VAN KHAC.

Vinapimex (Viet Nam Paper Corpn): 25A Ly Thuong Kiet, Hanoi; tel. (4) 8260143; fax (4) 8260381; f. 1995; production and marketing of paper; Pres. and CEO VO SY DONG.

Vinaplast (Viet Nam Plastics Corpn): 92–94 Ly Tu Trong, District 1, Ho Chi Minh City; tel. (8) 39453301; fax (8) 39453298; e-mail vinaplast@vinaplast.com.vn; internet www.vinaplast.com.vn; f. 1976; import and export of products for plastic processing industry; production and trade of plastic products; Gen. Dir NGUYEN KHAC LONG.

Vinasteel (Viet Nam National Steel Corpn): D2 Ton That Tung, Dong Da District, Hanoi; tel. (4) 8525537; fax (4) 8262657; distributor of metal products; Dir NGO HUY PHAN.

Vinataba (Viet Nam National Tobacco Corpn): 25A Ly Thuong Kiet, Hoan Kiem District, Hanoi; tel. (4) 8265778; fax (4) 8265777; internet www.vinataba.com.vn; mfr of tobacco products; Chair. NGUYEN THAI SINH; Gen. Dir NGUYEN NAM HAI.

Vinatea (Viet Nam National Tea Development Investment and Export-Import Co): 92 Vo Thi Sau, Hanoi; tel. (4) 6226990; fax (4) 6226991; e-mail info@vinatea.com.vn; internet www.vinatea.com.vn; exports tea, imports tea-processing materials; Gen. Dir NGUYEN THIEN TOAN.

Vinatex (Viet Nam National Textile and Garment Corpn): 25 Ba Trieu, Hoan Kiem District, Hanoi; tel. (4) 38257700; fax (4) 38262269; e-mail vinatexhn@vinatex.com.vn; internet www.vinatex.com; f. 1995; imports raw material, textile and sewing machinery, spare parts, accessories, dyestuffs; exports textiles, ready-made garments, carpets, jute, silk; Gen. Dir VU DUC GIANG.

Vitas (Viet Nam Tea Association): 92 Vo Thu Sau, Hai Ba Trung District, Hanoi; tel. (4) 36250908; fax (4) 36251801; e-mail vitas@fpt.vn; internet www.vitas.org.vn; f. 1988; promotes the trading and marketing of tea products; offers advice and information, both to the Govt and to farmers, regarding development schemes and policies; Chair. and Pres. NGUYEN VAN THU.

Vocarimex (National Co for Vegetable Oils, Aromas, and Cosmetics of Viet Nam): 58 Nguyen Binh Khiem, District 1, Ho Chi Minh City; tel. (8) 8294513; fax (8) 8290586; e-mail vocar@hcm.vnn.vn; internet www.vocarimex.com; f. 1976; producing and trading vegetable oils, oil-based products and special industry machinery; packaging; operating port facilities; Gen. Dir DO NGOC KAI.

Xunhasaba (Viet Nam State Corpn for Export and Import of Books, Periodicals and other Cultural Commodities): 32 Hai Ba Trung, Hanoi; tel. (4) 38262989; fax (4) 38252860; e-mail xunhasaba@hn.vnn.vn; internet www.xunhasaba.com.vn; f. 1957; exports and imports books, periodicals, postage stamps, greetings cards, calendars and paintings; Dir HA TRIEU KIEN.

UTILITIES

Electricity

Electricity of Viet Nam (EVN): 18 Tran Nguyen Han, Hanoi; tel. (4) 8249508; fax (4) 8249461; e-mail vp@evn.com.vn; internet www.evn.com.vn; produces, transmits and distributes electrical power; Chair. DAO VAN HUNG; Pres. and CEO PHAM LE TANH.

Power Co No 1 (PC1): 20 Tran Nguyen Han, Hoan Kiem, Hanoi; tel. (4) 8255074; fax (4) 8244033; e-mail anhdn@pc1.com.vn; manages the generation, transmission and distribution of electrical power in northern Viet Nam; Dir DO VAN LOC.

Power Co No 3 (PC3): 315 Trung Nu Vuong, Hai Chau District, Da Nang; tel. (511) 621028; fax (511) 625071; f. 1975; manages the generation, transmission and distribution of electrical power in central Viet Nam; Gen. Dir TA CANH.

Southern Power Corpn (EVN SPC): 72 Hai Ba Trung, District 1, Ho Chi Minh City; tel. (8) 22200350; fax (8) 22200352; fmrly Power Co No 2; reorg. and renamed as above in early 2010; manages the distribution of electrical power in southern Viet Nam; Gen. Dir NGUYEN THANH DUY.

Water

Hanoi Water Business Co: 44 Yen Phu, Hanoi; tel. (4) 8293179; fax (4) 8294069; f. 1954; responsible for the supply of water to Hanoi and its five urban and two suburban districts; Dir-Gen. NHU HAI NGUYEN.

Saigon Water Corpn (SAWACO): 1 Cong Truong Quoc Te, District 3, Ho Chi Minh City; tel. (8) 38291974; fax (8) 38241644; e-mail hcmcwater@hcm.vnn.vn; f. 1966; manages the water services and water construction works of Ho Chi Minh City; Gen. Dir DINH PHU TRAN.

CO-OPERATIVES

Viet Nam Co-operative Alliance (VCA): 77 Nguyen Thai Hoc, Ba Dinh District, Hanoi; tel. (4) 8431689; fax (4) 8431883; e-mail admin@vca.org.vn; internet www.vca.org.vn; f. 1993; fmrly Viet Nam Co-operatives Council; Pres. DAO XUAN CAN.

TRADE UNIONS

Tong Lien doan Lao dong Viet Nam (Vietnam General Confederation of Labour): 82 Tran Hung Dao, POB 627, Hanoi; tel. (4) 9421794; fax (4) 9423781; e-mail doingoaitld@hn.vnn.vn; internet www.congdoanvn.org.vn; f. 1929; merged in 1976 with the South Viet Nam Trade Union Fed. for Liberation; 6m. mems; 20 affiliated unions; Pres. DANG NGOC TUNG; Vice-Pres. NGUYEN HOA BINH.

Cong Doan Nong Nghiep Cong Nghiep Thu Pham Viet Nam (Viet Nam Agriculture and Food Industry Trade Union): Hanoi; f. 1987; 550,000 mems.

National Union of Building Workers: 12 Cua Dong, Hoan Kiem, Hanoi; tel. (4) 38253781; fax (4) 38281407; e-mail cdxdvn12@gmail.com; f. 1957; Pres. NGUYEN VAN BINH.

Vietnam National Union of Industrial Workers: 54 Hai Ba Trung, Hanoi; tel. (4) 9344426; fax (4) 8245306; f. 1997; Pres. VU TIEN SAU.

Vietnam National Union of Post and Telecoms Workers: 30 Hang Chuoi, Hai Ba Trung, Hanoi; tel. (4) 9713514; fax (4) 9720236; f. 1947; Chair. HOANG HUY LOAT.

Transport

RAILWAYS

In 2007 the Government approved plans to construct a new rail link between Hanoi and Ho Chi Minh City, which would reduce the journey time from 29 hours to less than 10 hours. However, in June 2010, owing to concerns over the cost, the National Assembly voted to postpone the project. In 2008 construction commenced of a metro system in Ho Chi Minh City. The 19.7-km route was due for completion in 2014.

Duong Sat Viet Nam (DSVN) (Viet Nam Railways): 118 Le Duan, Hanoi; tel. (4) 8220537; fax (4) 9422866; e-mail dsvn@vr.com.vn; internet www.vr.com.vn; 2,600 km of main lines (1996); lines in operation are: Hanoi–Ho Chi Minh City (1,726 km), Hanoi–Haiphong (102 km), Hanoi–Dong Dang (167 km), Hanoi–Lao Cai (296 km), Hanoi–Thai Nguyen (75 km), Thai Nguyen–Kep–Bai Chay (106 km); Chair. and Gen. Dir Dr NGUYEN HUU BANG.

ROADS

In 2007 there were an estimated 160,089 km of roads, of which 13,554 km were highways and 31,575 km were secondary roads. In 2006 an upgrade of National Highway No. 2, linking An Giang province in Viet Nam to Takeo province in Cambodia, was completed. In the following year the Government announced plans to upgrade the section of National Highway No. 1 in the central province of Thua Thien-Hué; construction was scheduled for completion in 2010.

SHIPPING

The principal port facilities are at Haiphong, Da Nang and Ho Chi Minh City. At the end of 2008 the Vietnamese merchant fleet (1,415 vessels) had a combined displacement totalling 3,451,100 grt.

Transport and Chartering Corpn (Vietfracht): 74 Nguyen Du, Hai Ba Trung, Hanoi; tel. (4) 38228915; fax (4) 39423679; e-mail vfhan@vietfracht.com.vn; internet www.vietfracht.com.vn; f. 1963; ship broking, chartering, ship management, shipping agency, international freight forwarding; logistic and consultancy services, import-export services; Pres. TRAN VAN QUY; Gen. Dir NGO XUAN HONG.

Viet Nam National Shipping Lines (Vinalines): Ocean Park Bldg, 1 Dao Duy Anh, Phuong Mai Quarter, Dang Da District, Hanoi; tel. (4) 35770825; fax (4) 35770850; e-mail vnl@vinalines.com.vn; internet www.vinalines.com.vn; f. 1996; 27 subsidiaries and 36 associated companies; import and export of maritime materials and equipment, shipping agency and repair, construction, hotels, tourism, warehousing and logistics services; Chair. DUONG CHI DUNG.

Viet Nam Ocean Shipping Agency Corporation (VOSA Corpn): Unit 801, Harbour View Tower, 35 Nguyen Hue, District 1, Ho Chi Minh City; tel. (8) 39141490; fax (8) 39140423; e-mail vosagroup@hcm.vnn.vn; internet www.vosagroup.com; f. 1957; fmrly the Viet Nam Ocean Shipping Agency; controlled by Vinalines; in charge of merchant shipping; arranges ship repairs, salvage, passenger services, air and sea freight forwarding services; offices throughout Viet Nam; Dir-Gen. TRAN DUNG KHANG.

Viet Nam Ocean Shipping Joint Stock Co (VOSCO) (Cong Ty Van Tai Duong Bien Viet Nam): 215 Tran Quoc Toan, Ngo Quyen

VIET NAM

District, Haiphong; tel. (31) 3731090; fax (31) 3731007; e-mail pid@vosco.vn; drycargo@vosco.vn; internet www.vosco.com.vn; controlled by the Viet Nam General Dept of Marine Transport; Gen. Dir BUI VIET HOAI.

Viet Nam Sea Transport and Chartering Co (Vitranschart): 428 Nguyen Tat Thanh, Ward 18, District 4, Ho Chi Minh City; tel. (8) 39404271; fax (8) 39404711; e-mail vtc-hcm@vitranschart.com.vn; internet www.vitranschart.com.vn; Dir VO PHUNG LONG.

Viet Nam Shipbuilding Industry Group (Vinashin): 172 Ngo Quyen, Hanoi; tel. (4) 37711212; fax (4) 37711535; e-mail contact@vinashin.com.vn; internet www.vinashin.com.vn; f. 1972; shipbuilding and ship repair, marine transport and trade services; Chair. NGUYEN HONG TRUONG; Gen. Dir TRUONG VAN TUYEN.

CIVIL AVIATION

Viet Nam's principal airports are Tan Son Nhat International Airport (located 6 km north of Ho Chi Minh City) and Noi Bai International Airport (Hanoi), which handle both overseas and domestic traffic. By 2010 the Government aimed to expand the annual capacity of Tan Son Nhat to 30m. passengers and 1m. metric tons of freight. A third international airport is located at Da Nang, and an international terminal was inaugurated at Can Tho in January 2011, following the upgrading of that airport's facilities. In 2004 plans were announced for the construction of a new international airport at Long Thang, in Dong Nai province; work on the project was expected to commence in 2011. The airport, with a projected passenger capacity of 20m. a year, was to have four runways and four terminals, the first of which were scheduled to become operational in 2015. As of late 2006 there were 20 domestic airports in Viet Nam, including Ca Mau, Con Son, Chu Lai and Nha Trang.

Jetstar Pacific Airlines: 112 Hong Ha, Tan Binh District, Ho Chi Minh City; tel. (8) 38450092; fax (8) 38450085; internet www.jetstar.com/vn/vi/index.aspx; f. 1991; fmrly Pacific Airlines; present name adopted 2008; 70% owned by Viet Nam's State Capital Investment Corpn and 27% owned by Qantas (Australia); operates low-cost domestic flights; Chair. LE SONG LAI.

Viet Nam Airlines: 200 Nguyen Son, Long Bien District, Hanoi; tel. (4) 38320320; fax (4) 38722375; internet www.vietnamairlines.com; fmrly the Gen. Civil Aviation Admin. of Viet Nam, then Hang Khong Viet Nam; privatization plans mooted; operates domestic passenger services from Hanoi and from Ho Chi Minh City to the principal Vietnamese cities, and international services to 18 countries; Pres. and CEO PHAM NGOC MINH; Chair. NGUYEN SY HUNG.

Tourism

Tourist arrivals increased from 3.8m. in 2009 to 5.0m. in 2010. Of these, the largest proportion in 2010 was from the People's Republic of China (18%); other important sources of visitors include the Republic of Korea, Japan and the USA. Revenue from tourism totalled US $3,926m. in 2008.

Viet Nam National Administration of Tourism (VNAT): 80 Quan Su, Hanoi; tel. (4) 39423998; fax (4) 39424115; e-mail titc@vietnamtourism.gov.vn; internet www.vietnamtourism.com; f. 1960; Chair. NGUYEN VAN TUAN.

Hanoi Tourism Service Co (HANOI TOSERCO): 273 Kim Ma, Hanoi; tel. (4) 7262626; fax (4) 7262571; e-mail hanoitoserco@hn.vnn.vn; internet www.tosercohanoi.com; f. 1988; manages the devt of tourism, hotels and restaurants in the capital, and other services incl. staff training; Dir TRAN TIEN HUNG.

Tong Cong ty Du lich Sai Gon (Saigon Tourist Holding Co): 23 Le Loi, District 1, Ho Chi Minh City; tel. (8) 8225887; fax (8) 8291026; e-mail saigontourist@sgtourist.com.vn; internet www.saigon-tourist.com; f. 1975; holding co controlling 11 tour operators, 56 hotels, 10 resorts and 24 restaurants; Gen. Dir NGUYEN HUU THO.

Defence

As assessed at November 2010, the total strength of the armed forces was an estimated 482,000: army 412,000; navy 40,000; air force 30,000. Men are subject to a two-year minimum term of compulsory military service between 18 and 35 years of age. Paramilitary forces number in excess of 5m. and include the urban People's Self Defence Force and the rural People's Militia. Border defence troops number an estimated 40,000.

Defence Expenditure: Budgeted at US $2,410m. for 2010.

Commander-in-Chief of the Armed Forces: NGUYEN MINH TRIET.

Chief of General Staff (Army): DO BA TY.

Commander of the Navy: Vice-Adm. NGUYEN VAN HIEN.

Education

Primary education, which is compulsory, begins at six years of age and lasts for five years. Secondary education, beginning at the age of 11, lasts for up to seven years, comprising a first cycle of four years and a second cycle of three years. In 2004/05 enrolment in primary schools included 87.7% of children in the relevant age-group, while enrolment in secondary schools included 69.3% of children in the relevant age-group. In 2008/09 a total of 2.9m. pupils attended pre-primary institutions, at which 144,500 teachers were employed. In 2009/10 a total of 6.9m. pupils attended primary schools, at which 355,200 teachers were employed; and 8m. students were enrolled in secondary level institutions, at which 463,500 teachers were employed. In 1989 Viet Nam's first private college since 1954, Thang Long College, was opened in Hanoi to cater for university students. In 1999/2000 total enrolment at tertiary level was equivalent to 9.7% of students in the relevant age-group (males 11.2%; females 8.1%). In 2009/10, according to preliminary official figures, 1.8m. students were enrolled within a total of some 403 universities and colleges, at which 65,100 teachers were employed. Of total planned budgetary expenditure by the central Government in 2007, 38,100,000m. dông (11.9% of total expenditure) was allocated to education.

YEMEN
Introductory Survey

LOCATION, CLIMATE, LANGUAGE, RELIGION, FLAG, CAPITAL

The Republic of Yemen is situated in the south of the Arabian peninsula, bounded to the north by Saudi Arabia, to the east by Oman, to the south by the Gulf of Aden, and to the west by the Red Sea. The islands of Perim and Kamaran at the southern end of the Red Sea, the island of Socotra, at the entrance to the Gulf of Aden, and the Kuria Muria islands, near the coast of Oman, are also part of the Republic. The climate in the semi-desert coastal strip is hot, with high humidity and temperatures rising to more than 38°C (100°F); inland, the climate is somewhat milder, with cool winters and relatively heavy rainfall in the highlands. The eastern plateau slopes into desert. The language is Arabic. The population is almost entirely Muslim, and mainly of the Sunni Shafi'a sect. The national flag (proportions 2 by 3) has three equal horizontal stripes, of red, white and black. The capital is San'a.

CONTEMPORARY POLITICAL HISTORY

Historical Context

The Republic of Yemen was formed in May 1990 by the amalgamation of the Yemen Arab Republic (YAR) and the People's Democratic Republic of Yemen (PDRY). The YAR (from 1967 also known as North Yemen) had formerly been a kingdom. When Turkey's Ottoman Empire was dissolved in 1918, the Imam Yahya, leader of the Zaidi community, was left in control. In 1948 Yahya was assassinated in a palace coup, when power was seized by forces opposed to his feudal rule. However, Yahya's son, Ahmad, defeated the rebel forces to become Imam. In 1958 Yemen and the United Arab Republic (Egypt and Syria) formed a federation called the United Arab States, though this was dissolved in 1961. The Imam Ahmad died in September 1962 and was succeeded by his son, Muhammad. Less than a week later army officers, led by Col (later Marshal) Abdullah al-Sallal, removed the Imam and proclaimed the YAR. Civil war ensued between royalist forces, supported by Saudi Arabia, and republicans, aided by Egyptian troops. The republicans prevailed and Egyptian forces withdrew in 1967. In November President Sallal was deposed by a Republican Council.

The People's Republic of Southern Yemen, comprising Aden and the former Protectorate of South Arabia, was formed on 30 November 1967. Aden had been under British rule since 1839, and the Protectorate was developed by a series of treaties between the United Kingdom and local leaders. Prior to the British withdrawal, two rival factions, the National Liberation Front (NLF) and the Front for the Liberation of Occupied South Yemen, fought for control. The Marxist NLF eventually prevailed and assumed power as the National Front (NF). The country's first President, Qahtan al-Sha'abi, was forced out of office in June 1969, when a Presidential Council, led by Salem Rubayi Ali, took power. Muhammad Ali Haitham became Prime Minister. In November 1970, on the third anniversary of independence, the country was renamed the PDRY. In May 1971 a provisional Supreme People's Council (SPC) was established as the national legislature. In August Haitham was replaced as Prime Minister by Ali Nasser Muhammad. Following the introduction of repressive measures against dissidents by the Government after independence, more than 300,000 Southern Yemenis fled to the YAR. Backed by Saudi Arabia and Libya, many of the refugees joined mercenary organizations, aimed at the overthrow of the Marxist regime in Southern Yemen, and conducted cross-border raids.

Intermittent fighting, beginning in early 1971, flared into open warfare between the two Yemens in October 1972, with the YAR receiving aid from Saudi Arabia and the PDRY being supplied with Soviet arms. A cease-fire was arranged in the same month, under the auspices of the League of Arab States (Arab League, see p. 361), and soon afterwards both sides agreed to the union of the two Yemens within 18 months. The union was not, however, implemented.

Domestic Political Affairs

On 13 June 1974 a 10-member Military Command Council (MCC) seized power in the YAR, under the leadership of the pro-Saudi Lt-Col Ibrahim al-Hamadi. Mohsin al-Aini was appointed Prime Minister, but was replaced by Abd al-Aziz Abd al-Ghani in January 1975. An unsuccessful pro-royalist coup was reported in August. Al-Hamadi subsequently attempted to reduce the influence of the USSR, and endeavoured to re-equip the army with US weapons, making use of financial assistance from Saudi Arabia. In October 1977, however, al-Hamadi was killed by unknown assassins in San'a. Another member of the MCC, Lt-Col Ahmad bin Hussain al-Ghashmi, took over as Chairman, and martial law was imposed. In February 1978 the MCC appointed a Constituent People's Assembly, and in April the Assembly elected al-Ghashmi President of the Republic. The MCC was then dissolved.

In June 1978 the proposed union of the two Yemens was seriously hampered when President al-Ghashmi of the YAR was assassinated by a bomb carried in the suitcase of a PDRY envoy. In the following month the Constituent People's Assembly elected a senior military officer, Lt-Col (later Gen., and subsequently Field Marshal) Ali Abdullah Saleh, as President of the YAR. During recriminations that followed the assassination, President Rubayi Ali of the PDRY was deposed and executed by opponents within the ruling party, which had been known as the United Political Organization—National Front (UPO—NF) since its merger with two smaller parties in October 1975. The Prime Minister, Ali Nasser Muhammad, became interim Head of State. Two days after the overthrow of Rubayi Ali, it was announced that the UPO—NF had agreed to form a Marxist-Leninist 'vanguard' party. At the constituent congress of this Yemen Socialist Party (YSP), held in October 1978, Abd al-Fattah Ismail, who favoured uncompromising Marxist policies, became Secretary-General. A new SPC was elected in December and appointed Ismail to be Head of State. In April 1980 Ali Nasser Muhammad replaced Ismail as Head of State, Chairman of the Presidium of the SPC and Secretary-General of the YSP, while retaining the post of Prime Minister; his posts were confirmed at an extraordinary congress of the YSP in October.

Renewed fighting broke out between the YAR and the PDRY in February and March 1979, when the National Democratic Front (NDF), an alliance of disaffected YAR politicians, won the support of the PDRY and began a revolt. Later in the same month, however, at a meeting between the North and South Yemeni Heads of State in Kuwait, arranged by the Arab League, an agreement was signed pledging unification of the two states. Following a series of meetings, in December 1981 the two sides signed a draft Constitution for a unified state and established a joint YAR/PDRY Yemen Council to monitor progress towards unification. NDF forces rebelled again in 1982, but they were defeated and forced over the border into the PDRY.

In May 1983 President Saleh submitted his resignation at an extraordinary meeting of the Constituent People's Assembly, declaring his intention to nominate himself for a presidential election. His five-year term of office was due to end in July. However, he was nominated and unanimously re-elected by the Assembly for a further five-year term. Elections to the Assembly itself, scheduled for early 1983, were postponed.

In the PDRY, President Muhammad relinquished the post of Prime Minister in February 1985, nominating the Minister of Construction, Haidar Abu Bakr al-Attas, as his successor (while retaining his other senior posts). The former President, Abd al-Fattah Ismail, returned from exile in the USSR in the same month, and was reappointed to the Secretariat of the YSP's Central Committee. At the party's third General Congress, in October, President Muhammad was re-elected to the posts of Secretary-General of the YSP and of its Political Bureau for a further five years. However, his control over the party was weakened by the enlargement of the Political Bureau from 13 members to 16 (including his rival, Ismail), and by an increase in membership of the Central Committee from 47 to 77, to incorporate a number of his critics.

On 13 January 1986 President Muhammad attempted to eliminate his opponents in the Political Bureau: his personal guard opened fire on six members who had assembled for a meeting with the President. Three were killed, and three escaped, including Ismail (who was, however, officially declared to have been killed in subsequent fighting). Muhammad was reported to have left Aden for his tribal stronghold in Abyan province, to the east of the city. In Aden itself, rival elements of the armed forces fought for control, causing widespread destruction, and the conflict quickly spread to the rest of the country, despite diplomatic efforts by the USSR. Apparently prompted by reports of massacres by President Muhammad's supporters, the army intervened decisively, turning back pro-Muhammad tribesmen from Abyan who were advancing on Aden. On 24 January al-Attas, the Prime Minister, who had been abroad when the troubles began, was named by the YSP Central Committee as head of an interim administration in Aden, and Muhammad was stripped of all his party and state posts; he reportedly fled to Ethiopia. An estimated 5,000 people died in the conflict. A new Government of the PDRY was formed in February. Al-Attas was confirmed as President, Chairman of the Presidium of the SPC and Secretary-General of the YSP Political Bureau. The former Deputy Prime Minister and Minister of Fisheries, Dr Yasin Said Numan, was named as Prime Minister. The new Council of Ministers contained only three members of the previous Government. In March a general amnesty was proclaimed, inviting supporters of Muhammad to return from the YAR, where some 10,000 of them had sought refuge. In October a general election took place for a 111-member SPC. Al-Attas was unanimously elected Chairman of the YSP. In December the Supreme Court sentenced Muhammad to death, *in absentia*, for treason; 34 other men received the same sentence, although it was only carried out in five cases.

In July 1988 the first general election took place in the YAR for 128 seats in the new 159-member Consultative Council, which replaced the non-elected Constituent People's Assembly. The remaining 31 seats were filled by presidential decree. More than 1m. people registered to vote and more than 1,200 candidates contested the poll. Approximately 25% of the elective seats were won by candidates sympathetic to the Muslim Brotherhood, a militant Islamist organization. Later in the month President Saleh was re-elected by the Consultative Council for a third five-year term, winning 96% of the votes. Al-Ghani was reappointed Prime Minister.

The first session of the joint YAR/PDRY Yemen Council (which had been established in 1981) was held in San'a in August 1983 and discussed the state of progress towards unification. These sessions were scheduled to take place every six months and to alternate between San'a and Aden. A joint committee on foreign policy met for the first time in March 1984 in Aden. In July 1986 Presidents Saleh of the YAR and al-Attas of the PDRY met for the first time in Libya to discuss unification.

In May 1988 the Governments of the YAR and the PDRY agreed to withdraw troops from their mutual border and to create a demilitarized zone, covering an area of 2,200 sq km, between Marib and Shabwah, where they intended to carry out joint projects involving exploration for petroleum. The movement of citizens between the two states was also to be facilitated. In July a programme of wide-ranging political and economic reforms was introduced in the PDRY, indicating the country's intention to create a free-market economy. In November President Saleh and the Secretary-General of the Central Committee of the YSP, Ali Salim al-Baid, signed an agreement to unify the two states. On 1 December 1989 a draft Constitution for the unified state was published: it was to be ratified by both countries within six months, and was subsequently to be approved by a referendum.

Yemeni unification

The first joint meeting of the two Councils of Ministers was held in San'a in January 1990 and resulted in restrictions on travel between the two countries being rescinded. In February President Saleh held talks with King Fahd of Saudi Arabia, who pledged his official support for the unification of the YAR and the PDRY. However, opposition to unification developed in the YAR in early 1990. The Muslim Brotherhood, which believed that *Shari'a* (Islamic) law should be enshrined in the Constitution of the unified state (as in the YAR Constitution), condemned the draft Constitution, which was based principally, but not solely, on *Shari'a* law, and advocated a boycott of the referendum on the Constitution. In the PDRY, meanwhile, there were demonstrations by women, who feared that the increasing influence of Islamist militancy might jeopardize their freedom, and demanded that their existing rights in the secular Republic be guaranteed in the new Constitution.

In May 1990 the armed forces of the YAR and the PDRY were declared to be technically dissolved, prior to their unification, and it was announced that they were to be withdrawn from their respective capitals to designated military zones. In the same month a draft law embodying the freedom of the press was signed. The unification of the YAR and the PDRY was proclaimed on 22 May, six months ahead of the agreed deadline, apparently in order to counter the threat to the unification process posed by disruption in the north of the YAR. The unification agreement had been ratified on the previous day by both countries' legislatures. The new country was to be known as the Republic of Yemen, with San'a as its political capital and Aden its economic and commercial centre. President Saleh of the YAR became President of the new state, while al-Baid was elected Vice-President. The President of the PDRY, al-Attas, became Prime Minister, leading a transitional coalition Council of Ministers with 39 members, of whom 20 were from the YAR (members of the General People's Congress—GPC—a broad grouping of supporters of President Saleh) and 19 from the PDRY (all members of the YSP, under the continued leadership of al-Baid). A five-member Presidential Council (chaired by Saleh) was formed, together with a 45-member advisory council. The two legislatures were amalgamated to form the House of Representatives, pending elections to be held after a 30-month transitional period; an additional 31 members, including opponents of the YAR and PDRY governments, were nominated by President Saleh. In September it was reported that more than 30 new political parties had been formed since unification. The Yemeni Congregation for Reform (al-Islah), an Islamic grouping with considerable support in the House of Representatives, was regarded as the most influential of the new parties.

In May 1991 the people of Yemen voted in a referendum on the Constitution for the unified state. Religious fundamentalists and sympathizers, including al-Islah members, had urged a boycott of the referendum, owing to the proposed role of Islam. Those who participated in the referendum approved the new Constitution by a large majority, although less than 50% of the electorate registered to vote. Members of al-Islah and other opposition groups claimed that irregularities in the voting procedure had invalidated the result.

During late 1991 and early 1992 the deteriorating economic situation prompted domestic unrest. A shooting incident in San'a in October 1991 led to two days of rioting, in which nine people were believed to have died. In March 1992 workers in some parts of the country held a one-day strike, in support of demands for salary increases and the establishment of a job creation programme for the estimated 850,000 returnees from Saudi Arabia (see below). In December at least 15 people were killed in riots in several towns, apparently caused by a sharp rise in consumer prices.

At legislative elections held on 27 April 1993, an estimated 4,730 candidates contested the 301 elective seats in the House of Representatives, of whom approximately 30% were affiliated to political parties. International observers were largely satisfied with the conduct of the elections. The GPC secured 123 of the 300 seats for which results were announced. Al-Islah won 62 seats, and the YSP 56, with independents securing 47 of the remaining seats. In May the two former ruling parties, the GPC and YSP, agreed to merge, thereby creating a single political group with an overall majority in the new House of Representatives. The subsequent election of al-Islah's leader, Sheikh Abdullah bin Hussain al-Ahmar, as Speaker of the House was regarded as a concession to his party, the influence of which had been weakened by the merger. At the end of the month, however, a 31-member coalition Government was announced, including representatives of all three leading parties. Al-Attas was reappointed Prime Minister.

In August 1993 the YSP leader, al-Baid, ceased to participate in the political process and withdrew from San'a to Aden. This followed a visit to the USA, apparently without the approval of President Saleh, for talks with the US Vice-President, Al Gore. Al-Baid claimed that Saleh had made no attempt to halt the numerous armed attacks by northern officials on southerners, and claimed that as many as 150 YSP members had been assassinated since unification. He also protested at what he perceived to be the increasing marginalization of the south, particularly with regard to the distribution of petroleum revenues. In October the House of Representatives elected a new five-member Presidential Council, and later in the month the Council, in the absence of al-Baid, re-elected Saleh as its Chairman, and, accordingly, as President of the Republic of Yemen, for a further four-year term. Al-Baid was unanimously re-elected as Vice-President, but was not sworn in.

The political deadlock persisted into November 1993. Reports emerged that the armed forces of the former YAR and the PDRY (which had failed to integrate since unification) were being deployed along the former frontier. In September al-Baid, who remained in Aden, had submitted an 18-point programme of conditions for his return to San'a. Although President Saleh accepted the programme in December, there was no indication of any improvement in the political situation. In January 1994, following Jordanian mediation, representatives of the main political parties signed a 'Document of Pledge and Agreement' designed to resolve the crisis. In February Saleh and al-Baid signed the document, which contained certain security guarantees, as well as providing for a degree of decentralization, and for a review of the Constitution and of the country's economic policies. Nevertheless, both leaders remained active in mustering support for their positions throughout the region. At the same time there were reports of clashes between rival army units.

Civil war and the declaration of the Democratic Republic of Yemen

In March 1994 Saleh and al-Baid held talks in Oman, but at the end of the month al-Baid refused to attend a meeting of the Presidential Council, which he had boycotted since August 1993. At the end of April 1994 the First Deputy Prime Minister, Hassan Muhammad Makki, was wounded during an assassination attempt in San'a. A series of pitched battles followed between battalions stationed in the territory of their former neighbour. On 5 May President Saleh declared a 30-day state of emergency, and dismissed al-Baid from his position as Vice-President, together with four other southern members of the Government, including Salim Muhammad. On the same day missile attacks were launched against economic and military targets, including San'a, Aden and other main airports. On 9 May Saleh announced that al-Attas had been replaced as Prime Minister by the Minister of Industry, Muhammad Said al-Attar, and that the Minister of Petroleum and Minerals had also been replaced. By this time fighting had become concentrated around Aden, and along the former north–south frontier. Several thousand southern reservists were mobilized, as the forces of the former YAR attempted to isolate and capture Aden. Meanwhile, President Saleh rejected appeals for a negotiated settlement to the civil war, and demanded that al-Baid surrender.

On 22 May 1994, the fourth anniversary of the unification of Yemen, al-Baid, in a televised address, declared the independence of a new Democratic Republic of Yemen (DRY), with Aden as its capital. He also announced the formation of a Presidential Council, with himself as President and Abd al-Rahman al-Jifri, the leader of the League of the Sons of Yemen (LSY), as Vice-President. The composition of the Council reflected al-Baid's need to achieve a consensus of the different political and tribal groups of the former PDRY. Saleh denounced the secession as illegitimate, and offered an amnesty to all in the PDRY who rejected it, with the exception of 16 YSP leaders (including al-Baid).

At the beginning of June 1994, with the northern army attacking Aden on three fronts to the north and east of the city, the UN Security Council adopted Resolution 924, demanding a cease-fire and the resumption of dialogue in Yemen, and ordering the dispatch of a UN commission of inquiry to the region. Although welcomed by the authorities in Aden, the resolution was initially rejected by the Government in San'a, which urged the Arab League to support the unity of Yemen. Subsequently, however, the San'a Government declared itself positively disposed towards the resolution.

On 1 June 1994 the House of Representatives voted to extend the state of emergency for a further 30 days. On the following day al-Baid announced the composition of a DRY Government, in which al-Attas was to be Prime Minister and Minister of Finance. Although most of the ministers were from the YSP, the Government contained a range of religious, political and tribal representatives. As northern forces made further territorial gains around Aden, it was reported that al-Baid had transferred his centre of operations to Mukalla, east of Aden. On 7 July Aden came under the control of Saleh's troops. Many of the southern secessionist leaders fled to neighbouring Arab states, and it was officially announced that the civil war had ended. Al-Baid was believed to have requested political asylum in Oman. In March 1998 al-Baid, al-Attas and three other rebel leaders were sentenced to death *in absentia*.

According to official sources, 931 civilians and soldiers were killed, and 5,000 wounded, in the civil war, although this was generally regarded as a conservative estimate. President Saleh immediately undertook measures to consolidate his position and bring stability to the country, ending the state of emergency and reiterating the general amnesty; by August 1994, when the amnesty expired, more than 5,000 Yemenis had returned to the country. In the same month, in an attempt to undermine the strength of southern military units loyal to the YSP, President Saleh announced that party membership would no longer be permitted within the armed forces. In September, moreover, Saleh introduced amendments to the Constitution intended to strengthen his position further: the Presidential Council was abolished, and in future the President would be elected by universal suffrage. *Shari'a* would also serve as the basis of all legislation. On 1 October Saleh was re-elected President; he appointed Abd al-Rabbur Mansur Hadi as his deputy, and Abd al-Aziz Abd al-Ghani (hitherto a member of the Presidential Council) as Prime Minister. In the new Council of Ministers, members of the GPC retained the key portfolios, the YSP was denied representation and al-Islah was rewarded for its allegiance during the civil war by the allocation of nine ministerial posts. In a reorganization of the Council of Ministers in June 1995, the GPC increased its share of portfolios at the expense of independents, leading to a Government composed entirely of GPC and al-Islah members. Also in June President Saleh was re-elected Chairman of the GPC at the party's first general assembly since 1988.

In July 1994 UN-sponsored negotiations between the Yemeni leadership and the secessionists proved inconclusive. President Saleh announced that any further discussions would have to be conducted in Yemen, effectively terminating dialogue, as the YSP leaders remained in exile. In August a faction of the YSP in Yemen declared itself the new party leadership. In October, nevertheless, exiled leaders of the YSP announced the formation of a coalition, the National Opposition Front, which included former Prime Minister al-Attas and Abd al-Rahman al-Jifri, leader of the LSY. The role of the YSP in Yemeni politics subsequently diminished considerably. In February 1995 another opposition grouping, the Democratic Coalition of Opposition, was formed, embracing 13 political parties and organizations, including a faction of the YSP and the LSY.

Developments following the civil war

The economic repercussions of the civil war on the population were significant, particularly in the south. During March and April 1994, following the devaluation of the riyal (YR) and the doubling of the price of fuel, demonstrators clashed with police in Aden, San'a and Dhamar, resulting in three deaths and more than 50 arrests. The activities of militant Islamists, meanwhile, posed an additional threat to internal stability. In September some 20 people were reportedly killed in clashes with the security forces in Abyan province, following the destruction of three Muslim saints' shrines by Islamists who deemed them idolatrous.

The results of elections, conducted on 27 April 1997, demonstrated a decisive victory for the GPC, which increased its parliamentary representation from 123 to 187 seats. Al-Islah secured 53 seats (compared with 62 in 1993), and independent candidates won 54 seats. The remaining seats were shared between Nasserite and Baathist parties. The GPC's position was further consolidated by the stated intention of 39 newly elected independent deputies to demonstrate parliamentary allegiance to the GPC.

Al-Ghani presented his Government's resignation in May 1997. Two days later Faraj Said bin Ghanim, a political independent, was appointed Prime Minister. All but four of the new ministers were GPC members. In April 1998 bin Ghanim resigned; the Deputy Prime Minister and Minister of Foreign Affairs, Abd al-Karim al-Iryani, was appointed Prime Minister, announcing his new Government in May. A substantial increase in the price of petrol and basic foodstuffs in June led to public demonstrations in which more than 50 people died. In September a series of explosions in Yemen was attributed by the Government to 'foreign elements'.

The suppression of lawlessness, which had been exacerbated by the widespread ownership of weapons dating from the period of internal unrest, was a persistent domestic problem in the late

1990s. A number of armed kidnappings, frequently of tourists, attracted international attention during 1997–98, and in December 1998 16 foreign tourists were taken hostage; four were later killed during an attempt to release them. Yemen was criticized for failing to warn foreign embassies of an increased terrorist threat to tourists and for its precipitate use of force to free the hostages. In May 1999 three of the kidnappers, who belonged to the Islamic Aden-Abyan Army, a small extremist Islamist movement, were sentenced to death. Two of the death sentences were later commuted to life imprisonment, and in October the leader of the Islamic Aden-Abyan Army, Zein al-Abidine al-Mihdar, was executed. His was the first execution under legislation, enacted in August 1998, providing for the use of capital punishment in kidnapping cases. In August 1999 eight British citizens and two Algerians, who were reported to have links to the Islamic Aden-Abyan Army, were found guilty of plotting terrorist attacks on British targets in Aden, receiving sentences of up to seven years' imprisonment. (In October 2002 the Islamic Aden-Abyan Army attacked a French supertanker, the *Limburg*, off the coast of Yemen. A spokesman for the group declared the attack, which killed a crew member, to be revenge for the execution of al-Mihdar.)

On 23 September 1999 the first direct presidential election was held in Yemen. Saleh was re-elected, winning 96.3% of the votes; his only opponent was Najib Qahtan al-Sha'bi, a member of the GPC who stood as an independent. The election, which was boycotted by the YSP, was criticized for its lack of a credible candidate to oppose President Saleh.

Some internal instability was reported in 1999, with a number of bomb explosions in San'a. In April 2000 15 YSP officials were arrested in Abyan governorate and the Secretary-General was arrested at San'a airport on his return to the country. Kidnappings continued throughout 1999 and early 2000, involving hostages from a number of Western nations; all were released unharmed. However, in June 2000 a Norwegian diplomat was killed during a police operation to release him and his son from kidnappers in San'a. In October Hatim Muhsin bin Farid, the alleged new leader of the Islamic Aden-Abyan Army, was sentenced to a seven-year term of imprisonment, having been convicted of kidnapping charges. Owing to a lack of evidence, he was cleared of charges relating to his leadership of the movement and to the possession of heavy weapons.

In mid-October 2000 a suicide bomb attack on a US destroyer, the USS *Cole*, in Aden harbour, as a result of which 17 US naval personnel were killed, was linked by many commentators to the escalating crisis in the Middle East. The Yemeni authorities responded by arresting several Islamist militants, including leading members of Islamic Jihad from Yemen, Egypt, Algeria and other Arab states. The USA blamed agents of Osama bin Laden, the Saudi-born fundamentalist Islamist believed at that time to be based in Afghanistan, for the attack, and claimed to have evidence that the two suicide bombers were Saudi nationals. Only days after the USS *Cole* bombing, the British embassy in San'a was the target of an attack, although it was unclear as to whether the two incidents were linked. (In July 2001 four Yemenis were found guilty of plotting and orchestrating the embassy bombing, and sentenced to between four and 15 years' imprisonment.)

In November 2000 Yemen and the USA signed an anti-terrorism agreement whereby the Yemeni authorities agreed to allow the US Federal Bureau of Investigation to assist in investigations into the USS *Cole* explosion, and to extradite any persons accused of involvement in terrorism against foreign targets. It was announced in the following month that investigations into the bombing had been completed and that six Yemeni nationals would stand trial in early 2001. In January, however, the Yemeni Government agreed to a postponement of the trial, following a request by US officials for more time to gather additional evidence. A further two Yemenis entering the country from Afghanistan were detained in February; another three suspects were reportedly arrested in April. In November a Yemeni newspaper published claims that the individual suspected of planning the attack had subsequently sought refuge in Afghanistan. The man was named as Muhammad Omar al-Harazi, and was also believed to have been one of the principal organizers of the 1998 attacks on the US embassies in Kenya and Tanzania. In February 2002 it was reported that the trial of eight of the suspects in the bombing of the USS *Cole* had been postponed at the request of the US authorities because of the possibility that new information about the case would be obtained during interrogation of al-Qa'ida (see below) and Taliban prisoners captured by US military forces in Afghanistan in late 2001. Two senior al-Qa'ida operatives believed to have been responsible for planning the attack on the USS *Cole* were arrested by US forces and Pakistani police in November 2002 and April 2003, respectively. In April 2003 10 of the Yemenis accused of involvement in the USS *Cole* attack escaped from a high-security prison; two of the fugitives were captured in May, and charged with the murder of US military personnel. The remaining eight, in addition to one further suspect, were reportedly captured in March 2004. In September two men (a Yemeni and a Saudi) were sentenced to death for their role in the attack. Four other Yemeni nationals received prison sentences of between five and 10 years. In February 2005 an appeal court ruling upheld one of the death sentences, but commuted the other to 15 years in prison and reduced the sentence of one of the other men from eight to five years.

In January 2001 the formation of a new opposition grouping, the Opposition Co-ordination Council, was announced in Yemen. The bloc, which included the YSP, was created in anticipation of the forthcoming municipal elections, Yemen's first since unification, which were held on 20 February. A national referendum was held concurrently on proposed amendments to the Constitution that would extend the President's term of office from five to seven years and the mandate of the House of Representatives from four to six years, abolish the right of the President to issue decree laws when parliament is not in session, and provide for the creation of a 111-member Consultative Council. According to official sources, 77.5% of voters endorsed the constitutional changes. There were claims of electoral irregularities and harassment of opposition candidates, and violent clashes were reported (principally between supporters of the GPC and those of al-Islah) in which, according to certain sources, up to 45 people were killed. The elections were boycotted by some opposition parties and were criticized by human rights groups, which claimed that the President and the GPC were seeking to consolidate their dominant position at the expense of further democratization.

In March 2001 President Saleh dismissed Prime Minister Abd al-Karim al-Iryani and declared the formation of a new Government, to be led by the former Deputy Prime Minister and Minister of Foreign Affairs, Abd al-Qadir Bajammal. The new Council of Ministers was composed exclusively of GPC members and included Yemen's first female minister. In April the President elected a new Consultative Council, which for the first time included three female politicians.

The 2003 parliamentary elections

In early 2003 22 political parties were registered for a parliamentary election, which was held on 27 April. The GPC recorded another decisive victory, winning 228 of the 301 seats, while al-Islah secured 47 seats, independents 14 and the YSP seven. (Final results were published following three by-elections held in July.) Voter turn-out was a reported 76% of the electorate. The European Union (EU, see p. 270) expressed its satisfaction with the elections, but the US-based National Democratic Institute for International Affairs claimed that the electoral process was flawed, citing instances of under-age voting, ballot-buying and inappropriate behaviour by security forces. Opposition parties threatened to boycott the new parliament after widespread claims of ballot-rigging, fraud and intimidation. None the less, on 10 May the President re-appointed Bajammal as Prime Minister. Bajammal's new Council of Ministers included 17 new appointees, among them a Minister of Human Rights, Amat al-Alim al-Susua, although the key portfolios of defence, the interior, petroleum and mineral resources, and foreign affairs remained unchanged.

Meanwhile, also in May 2003 President Saleh declared an amnesty for five exiled southern secessionist leaders who had been sentenced to death *in absentia* in 1998. In June 2003 the House of Representatives endorsed a government proposal that Yemen's counter-terrorism organization should become a separate department overseen by the Ministry of the Interior; the resources allocated to the unit were also increased. In July security forces killed six suspected Islamist militants during an operation in Abyan province, where alleged members of the Islamic Aden-Abyan Army had taken refuge after attacking a military detachment. The Government had previously maintained that the Islamic Aden-Abyan Army had ceased to exist following the execution of its leader in 1999.

In June 2004 the Director of the Ministry of Religious Endowments and Guidance stated that the authorities would not allow Islamist parties to share control over state-controlled mosques

YEMEN

and use them as platforms to preach extremism. Firm measures would be taken against imams who preached opposition to the Government and incited worshippers to violence. Later that month the Council of Ministers ordered the closure of all unlicensed religious schools in an effort to combat extremism, and stated that an extensive review of religious education in public schools was urgently needed to ensure that teaching about Islam advocated moderation.

As part of efforts to combat violence and extremism, the Government stated in 2003 that it had spent over US $32m. since 2002 purchasing weapons on sale on the open market and seeking to persuade ordinary citizens to sell their weapons to the authorities. (According to the Government, 60m.–80m. guns were owned by the country's population, which numbered some 19m.) An initiative endorsed by President Saleh to prevent the public from carrying firearms resulted in riots in February 2005, in which five people died in northern Yemen. Saudi Arabia had recently complained to Yemen over reports of the smuggling of arms into the kingdom, and in 2004 began the construction of a 'separation wall' along the Saudi–Yemeni border (see below).

In late 2005 and 2006 a series of kidnappings further undermined Yemen's image abroad. Meanwhile, in July 2005 at least 39 people were killed in severe riots in San'a, Aden and several other towns in protest against the Government's decision to remove subsidies on fuel and the consequent doubling in the price of petroleum products. The GPC accused opposition parties of instigating the riots after they publicly criticized the price increases. The opposition denied the allegations and condemned the killing of civilians by security forces. At the end of July the Government announced a partial reduction in fuel prices.

Despite having announced in July 2005 that he would not seek re-election to the presidency in September 2006, President Saleh was re-elected as Chairman of the GPC in December 2005, prompting speculation that he would in fact continue in office. Saleh effected a comprehensive reorganization of the Council of Ministers, which was increased in size, to 34 members (including two new female ministers), in February 2006. The ministers in charge of the key portfolios of defence, oil, finance and planning were all removed from their posts; however, the Minister of the Interior, Maj.-Gen. Dr Rashad Muhammad al-Alimi, who had been under pressure following the escape of 23 suspected al-Qa'ida sympathizers (including Jamal al-Badawi, who had been convicted for the bombing of the USS *Cole* in 2000) from a San'a prison earlier in the month, was promoted to Deputy Prime Minister. The President claimed that the changes would add new impetus to the process of economic and political reform, although the opposition suggested that the reorganization was targeted at strengthening the regime before the forthcoming presidential and municipal elections.

The 2006 presidential election

The presidential election was held on 20 September 2006, with turn-out estimated at approximately 65% of the 9.2m. registered voters. As widely predicted, Saleh, who had rescinded his statement that he would not seek re-election, was chosen to serve another seven-year term, attracting 77.2% of the total ballot, according to official results published by the Supreme Commission for Elections and Referendums (SCER). Saleh's primary opponent, Faisal bin Shamlan of the Joint Meeting Parties (JMP—a recently formed opposition bloc comprising five Islamist and leftist parties, including the YSP, al-Islah and the al-Haq party), garnered 21.8% of the ballot, although Shamlan's supporters rejected the results, claiming that he had received at least 40% of all votes; three other candidates each won less than 0.5% of the total number of votes cast. The SCER acknowledged that tens of thousands of votes had been discounted due to 'voter error'; however, the Minister of Foreign Affairs, Abu Bakr al-Kurbi, denied claims of electoral fraud. (One week prior to the polls at least 51 people died, and more than 230 were injured, during a stampede at an election campaign rally for the incumbent Saleh.) EU election observers reported that the presidential and municipal elections had been conducted in a reasonably free and fair manner, but identified a number of problems, particularly with regard to voter registration and the use of state resources to promote the ruling party. The JMP agreed to accept the election results on the condition that the Government enter into negotiations on electoral reform.

In September 2006 the Ministry of the Interior announced that security forces had foiled two co-ordinated suicide attacks intended to destroy oil facilities in Marib and Hadramout. Security guards identified vehicles laden with explosives at both locations, and destroyed the vehicles before they reached their intended targets, killing all four assailants and one security guard. In October it was reported that security forces had killed two of the 23 suspected al-Qa'ida sympathizers who had escaped from prison in February during a gun battle on the outskirts of San'a. In November a militant Islamist group calling itself 'al-Qa'ida in Yemen' issued a statement via the internet in which it claimed responsibility for the attempted bombing of oil facilities.

A presidential decree was issued at the end of March 2007 appointing Ali Muhammad Mujawar, hitherto Minister of Electricity, as Prime Minister, to replace Bajammal, whose dismissal was reported to be the result of weak anti-corruption policies. A new Council of Ministers was formed in early April. Key portfolios remained unchanged, with the Ministers of Foreign Affairs, Defence, the Interior, Information, and Oil and Minerals all being retained. The Ministry of Expatriate Affairs was reintroduced, to be headed by Saleh Hassan Sumi'e, and there were 11 other new appointments, including those of Noman Taher al-Souhaibi as Minister of Finance and Abd al-Qader Ali Hilal as Minister of Local Administration. Addressing the new cabinet for the first time, President Saleh urged ministers to: adopt a tougher stance against corruption; abandon nepotism; tackle rising inflation; and improve living standards.

The threat to national security posed by purported Islamist militants also increased in 2007. A suicide bomber drove an explosives-laden car into a convoy of tourist vehicles in Marib in early July, killing eight Spanish tourists and two local drivers. Several arrests were made in connection with the attack, for which the Government held al-Qa'ida responsible. By this time a total of nine of the 23 suspected al-Qa'ida sympathizers who had escaped from prison in February 2006 had apparently surrendered to the authorities; five had been killed in various clashes with the Yemeni security forces; one had been killed by US forces in Somalia; one was under arrest in Kenya; and seven—including Nasir al-Wuhayshi (reported to be the new leader of al-Qa'ida in Yemen), Kassem al-Raimi (who, together with al-Wuhayshi, was believed to have been involved in the July 2007 attack) and Jamal al-Badawi—remained at large. In August three al-Qa'ida militants were killed by Yemeni security forces. Al-Badawi surrendered to the Yemeni authorities in October; initial reports that he had been placed under house arrest, after declaring his allegiance to President Saleh, and was effectively at liberty prompted criticism from the USA, although in December a statement from the Ministry of the Interior insisted that he remained in custody. In November 32 people were found guilty of planning the attacks on oil facilities in Marib and Hadramout in September 2006 and sentenced to prison terms of between two and 15 years; six of those convicted, including al-Raimi and al-Wuhayshi, had been tried *in absentia*, while four other defendants were acquitted owing to a lack of evidence.

Thousands of military and security officers who had been forced to retire after the civil war in 1994 demonstrated in Aden in July 2007, demanding to be allowed to return to work and to be paid wages for the intervening years. A few days earlier President Saleh had ordered the return to service of more than 600 officers, but this was regarded as inadequate by the protesters, some of whom advocated the redivision of Yemen. Unrest persisted in the south of the country in the following months, provoked not only by the issue of the military retirees, but also by economic concerns. In mid-August sit-ins were staged outside local government buildings in several towns in protest against water shortages, increases in consumer prices, unemployment, poverty and corruption; it was reported that more than 10,000 people participated in Taiz. Further demonstrations took place in Aden and Mukalla, the capital of Hadramout, in early September, during which 40 protesters were reportedly arrested on suspicion of treason for chanting secessionist slogans. Six people were believed to have been killed in clashes between the security forces and protesters in Aden and Lahij in October. Meanwhile, in a renewed effort to improve security and reassure foreign investors and tourists, in late August the Ministry of the Interior decided to enforce a ban on carrying firearms in San'a and provincial capitals, noting that some 5,000 people had been killed and 18,500 others injured in gun-related incidents during the previous three years. (By late April 2008 more than 100,000 weapons had been confiscated under the initiative.)

Sheikh Abdullah bin Hussain al-Ahmar, Speaker of the House of Representatives since 1993 and Chairman of al-Islah, died in December 2007. Yahya Ali al-Ra'ei, of the GPC, was elected to succeed al-Ahmar as Speaker in February 2008, while Sheikh Muhammad Ali al-Yadoumi became Chairman of al-Islah.

Clashes between government forces and al-Houthi rebels continued in Saada in early 2008 (see The Al-Houthi Rebellion), resulting in deaths on both sides, while further demonstrations against the perceived marginalization of the south took place in Aden and other southern towns. At the same time a series of attacks and bomb explosions, mainly targeting Western interests, exacerbated tensions. In mid-January 2008 two Belgian tourists and their Yemeni driver were killed in Hadramout by gunmen who ambushed their convoy. Another al-Qa'ida-affiliated group, calling itself Jund al-Yaman (Soldiers of Yemen), later claimed responsibility for the attack, as well as that perpetrated against Spanish tourists in July 2007. A grenade attack believed to have been aimed at the US embassy in San'a wounded 13 pupils at a neighbouring school, as well as several soldiers, in March 2008. In early April three explosions took place at a residential compound housing Western workers in the capital, but no injuries were reported. Two days later the US embassy announced that it was evacuating non-essential personnel from Yemen. In mid-April three police officers were killed in a bomb attack in Marib, and later that month there were two explosions in San'a near the Italian embassy.

Public unrest in the south of the country intensified in late March 2008, as large demonstrations degenerated into rioting in the provinces of Aden, Lahij and al-Dali. The protesters had various demands, ranging from an improvement in living standards to the secession of south Yemen, while youths claimed that the authorities had reneged on promises to offer them employment in the army. In response, the Government heightened security in the region and arrested those believed to be organizing the rallies. The Prime Minister stated that 283 people had been detained in connection with the disturbances between 30 March and 9 April, but that 161 had been released. Several members of the YSP were reported to be among those arrested.

Gubernatorial elections were held for the first time on 17 May 2008, governors having hitherto been appointed by the President. The electorate consisted of almost 7,500 elected members of local councils in the 20 governorates and the capital, with the Ministry of Local Administration reporting a turn-out of 87%. With the JMP opting to boycott the elections, the GPC secured the mayoralty of San'a and all governorships except three that were won by independent candidates, in al-Baida, Marib and al-Jawf. However, the election result in al-Jawf was subsequently overturned by the Government, amid allegations that the successful candidate had links to al-Houthi militants; an alternative Governor, selected by the Government, was appointed in June.

Immediately following the gubernatorial elections, President Saleh effected a reorganization of the Council of Ministers, in which Rashad al-Alimi, hitherto Deputy Prime Minister and Minister of the Interior, was allocated the newly expanded post of Deputy Prime Minister for Defence and Security Affairs. Mutahar al-Masri, Governor of Saada, was appointed Minister of the Interior, and there were changes to a further seven cabinet posts. The local administration portfolio was added to al-Alimi's responsibilities in November 2008, following the resignation of Abd al-Qader Ali Hilal. Hilal, who had been responsible for the post-conflict reconstruction programme in Saada, was under investigation for alleged close links with both al-Houthi followers and al-Islah.

Postponement of the 2009 legislative elections

The failure of the Government and the opposition to reach agreement on electoral reform led to an escalating political crisis in 2008. The opposition, dissatisfied with the Government's apparent reluctance to introduce promised revisions, refused to participate in the appointment of new commissioners to the SCER, which was due to review voter registration lists, prompting fears that the legislative elections scheduled for April 2009 might be delayed. Despite lengthy negotiations throughout 2007–08, in August 2008 an electoral reform bill was rejected by the GPC-dominated House of Representatives; the Government blamed the JMP's refusal to participate in the SCER for the rejection. A new SCER, formed without opposition involvement, appointed 35,000 teachers to sub-committees tasked with undertaking a comprehensive revision of the voter registry, beginning in November. However, as opposition parties appealed for a boycott of the registration process, which they claimed was illegitimate, sub-committees were hindered in their activities by protests in most governorates, and there were reports of attacks on committee members. Violent clashes between police and protesters intensified throughout November, and numerous opposition activists were reportedly arrested. In late November the House of Representatives voted to delay the forthcoming municipal elections, which had been due to be held in April 2009. Meanwhile, the Government continued to insist that the legislative polls would proceed as scheduled, urging the opposition parties to participate. However, in late February 2009, after negotiations between the Government and the JMP, the House of Representatives voted overwhelmingly to postpone the elections until 27 April 2011, before which time, it was hoped, agreement could be reached on the reform of the electoral system.

In November 2008 a new secessionist movement, the Southern Liberation Council, was formed in southern Yemen, and appealed for a boycott of the (subsequently postponed) legislative elections due to take place in April 2009. There were further disturbances in Aden, Lahij and al-Dali in January 2009, as demonstrations organized by supporters of the so-called Southern Movement (an increasingly separatist group led by former military officers) once again escalated into violent clashes with security forces. Rioting followed a demonstration in Mukalla, in Hadramout, in late April, leading to the arrests of at least 50 protesters. After the provincial authorities established additional military checkpoints in Lahij, apparently in violation of a prior agreement, armed confrontation between separatist militants and security forces erupted in early May. After five days of fighting in the Radfan region, in which up to eight people, including several soldiers, were killed, a truce was arranged and a mediation committee was charged with resolving the crisis. Meanwhile, in April the Ministry of the Interior initiated proceedings to remove the immunity from prosecution of two parliamentary deputies, most notably Nasser al-Khabji, a YSP deputy and alleged leader of the Southern Movement in Lahij, whom it accused of violating the Constitution. In an effort to suppress media coverage of the conflict in the south, the Ministry of Information issued a directive in early May banning the publication of any material deemed harmful to national unity. Seven newspapers were ordered to suspend operations, and existing copies of their publications were seized by the authorities. The offices of the independent daily *Al-Ayyam* were reportedly surrounded by security forces, preventing distribution of the newspaper.

There was growing domestic and international concern about the rise in militant Islamist activity in Yemen from 2008. Observers speculated that successful counter-terrorism operations in neighbouring Saudi Arabia were resulting in the migration of al-Qa'ida-affiliated groups into Yemen. A security officer was killed in Sayoun, in Hadramout, in a suicide bombing in July 2008, for which al-Qa'ida claimed responsibility. In August, also in Hadramout, two government troops and five suspected al-Qa'ida militants were killed in a confrontation in Tarim. Later in August security officials arrested 30 alleged al-Qa'ida members in the same governorate, and at the end of the month the arrest was announced of Khalid Abd al-Nabi, reported to be the leader of the Islamic Aden-Abyan Army. On 17 September a car bomb was detonated outside the US embassy in San'a and armed militants attacked the heavily fortified building from a second car. Responsibility for the attack, in which at least 16 people were killed, including all six militants as well as security guards and civilian bystanders, was initially claimed by an organization calling itself Islamic Jihad in Yemen. Six men were arrested in October on suspicion of membership of the terrorist cell responsible for the US embassy bombing and the subsequent issuing of threats to attack other embassies in San'a. The Yemeni authorities also accused the suspects of collaborating with the Israeli intelligence service; the Israeli Government strongly denied any involvement. Of the six suspects detained, three were released, while the remaining three were found guilty of offences including espionage and fraud in March 2009; two of those convicted were sentenced to three and five years' imprisonment, respectively, the third receiving the death penalty.

The first detainee at the US military detention camp at Guantánamo Bay, Cuba, to be convicted by a US military court was a Yemeni citizen. Salim Hamdan, who had worked as a driver for Osama bin Laden, was found guilty in August 2008 of providing material support for terrorism and sentenced to five-and-a-half years' imprisonment. Having been in US custody since 2001, Hamdan was transferred to a prison in Yemen in November 2008 and released in January 2009. Another Yemeni detainee at the camp, Ali Hamza Ahmad al-Bahlul, was sentenced to life imprisonment on terrorism charges in November 2008. The strategic importance of Yemen as a base for jihadist activity in the region was underlined in late January 2009, when, in video footage posted on the internet, al-Qa'ida announced the merger of its Saudi Arabian and Yemeni operations, forming an entity known as al-Qa'ida in the Arabian Peninsula (AQAP). The authorities in Yemen responded by strengthening their counter-terrorism operations and increasing security co-operation with Saudi Arabia. In March a list of 154 wanted militants, including many who were also sought by Saudi Arabia, was issued by the Yemeni Ministry of the Interior. In the same month the trial began of 16 suspected members of Jund al-Yaman who were accused of perpetrating the attacks against Spanish and Belgian tourists in July 2007 and January 2008, as well as several other attacks on foreign interests in San'a. Four South Korean tourists and a Yemeni guide were killed in a suicide bombing at a popular tourist site at Shibam, in Hadramout, in mid-March 2009. A second attack, a few days later, targeted a delegation of South Korean government officials and bereaved relatives of the tourists killed at Shibam; none of the group, which reportedly included the South Korean ambassador, was injured.

On 12 June 2009 nine foreign nationals connected to a Dutch aid agency, including seven Germans, were kidnapped in Saada province. Three female hostages were found dead a few days after their abduction. The Government initially blamed the al-Houthi movement. However, this was strongly denied by the rebels, and German investigators working on the case subsequently stated their conviction that the newly formed AQAP was more likely the responsible party. In January 2010, in advance of a visit to Yemen by the German Minister of Foreign Affairs, Guido Westerwelle, the authorities announced that they had evidence that the remaining hostages were still alive. In mid-May the Saudi authorities announced that two of the remaining German hostages had been found alive near the border between Saudi Arabia and Yemen.

Meanwhile, in mid-June 2009 security officials announced the arrest of a Saudi national, Hassan Hussain bin Alwan, purported to be the chief financier to AQAP. In mid-July six suspected AQAP militants were sentenced to death in a Yemeni court. Another 10 suspects, including four Syrians and a Saudi national, were sentenced to terms of imprisonment of up to 15 years. The militants were convicted of perpetrating 13 attacks in Yemen over two years, including the murder of two Belgian tourists in January 2008 and the attack on the US embassy in March of that year.

Growing civil unrest in the southern provinces

Fuelled by the Government's rejection of its demands, and harsh repression of its activities, the Southern Movement gained considerable momentum in 2009, as the formerly disparate grouping began to coalesce into a unified political movement with significant popular support and an overtly separatist agenda. From April there was growing tension in the region as several demonstrations, attended by thousands of protesters, escalated into violent clashes with the security forces. In May Ali Salim al-Baid, the exiled former leader of the 1994 southern secession, announced his intention to play a leading role in the movement. Up to 16 people were killed, including 10 security officers, and more than 30 injured in violent clashes involving armed separatists and security forces following an unauthorized political rally in Zinjibar, Abyan province, in July 2009. The rally had been organized by Tareq al-Fadhli, an influential tribal leader, previously loyal to President Saleh, who had announced his support for the Southern Movement in April. The offices of the GPC in Zinjibar were damaged in a bomb attack in late July; on the same day four soldiers were killed in an ambush in Abyan province. By now, more than 40 people had reportedly been killed in civil unrest since late April.

Large anti-Government demonstrations, at which the flag of the former PDRY was increasingly visible, continued during the latter part of 2009. Meanwhile, the separatist leadership continued to reject allegations of associations with AQAP, which had been growing since Nasir al-Wuhayshi, the leader of the militant Islamist group, had declared his support for the Southern Movement in May. Five people were killed in clashes between demonstrators and security forces at a rally in Ataq, in Shabwa province, on 25 November. Following reports of the murder of two civilians of northern Yemeni origin, the Government initiated a major clampdown on separatist activity, arresting around 200 separatist supporters in Aden and banning public demonstrations to mark the anniversary of the British withdrawal from Aden and southern Yemeni independence scheduled for 30 November.

On 17 December 2009 security forces, supported by air-strikes, launched a raid on an alleged AQAP training camp in the southern Abyan province. According to official sources, more than 30 militants were killed and 17 captured in the operation. However, human rights groups alleged that numerous civilians had been killed in the attack. (In early March 2010 a parliamentary committee reported that 42 civilians, predominantly women and children, had been killed in the raid. The Government issued an apology and resolved to pay compensation to the families of those killed.) In the following week two AQAP commanders reportedly addressed an anti-Government rally, attended by supporters of the Southern Movement, close to the site of the raid. While there was no consensus on the extent of any co-operation between AQAP and militant groups active in Yemen's northern and southern regional conflicts, most observers concluded that AQAP was likely to be exploiting the widespread political instability in order to expand its influence in the country. In mid-December the US authorities repatriated six Yemeni detainees from Guantánamo Bay; however, more than 90 Yemeni nationals remained in detention in the US facility.

Renewed civil unrest erupted in the south in late February 2010 following the proclamation by al-Fadhli of a new campaign of demonstrations and civil disobedience to achieve independence. Large protests were held in Abyan, al-Dali, Lahij and Hadramout provinces in late February to coincide with a regional donors' conference on Yemen, taking place under the auspices of the Co-operation Council for the Arab States of the Gulf (the Gulf Co-operation Council—GCC, see p. 243) in Riyadh, Saudi Arabia, at the end of that month. Security forces used tear gas and live ammunition in an effort to curtail the demonstrations. The unrest grew more violent in the following months, with increasing reports of armed attacks by separatist militants, bomb explosions in public buildings, kidnappings, and mass arrests of demonstrators. Much of the unrest centred on al-Dali, where 30 separatist prisoners escaped from prison following a bomb attack in early April, and where a general strike shut down all business activity in the city in mid-April. According to the Ministry of the Interior, by mid-April 18 people had been killed and 120 injured in civil unrest in the southern provinces since the beginning of the year.

International concern regarding security in Yemen

A failed attempt by a Nigerian jihadist to detonate explosives aboard a passenger aircraft in Detroit, Michigan, USA, on 25 December 2009 provoked renewed international concern about Yemen's reputation as a safe haven for Islamist militant groups. Omar Farouk Abdulmutallab had studied Arabic in San'a during 2004–05, and had reportedly been trained and equipped by AQAP during a second visit to Yemen in 2009. It was widely claimed that he had been 'radicalized' through his contact with Anwar al-Awlaki, a US-born Islamic scholar believed to be living in Yemen, who was wanted by the US authorities for his role as a proselytizer for al-Qa'ida. On 28 December AQAP claimed responsibility for the attempted bombing, stating that the mission had been instigated to avenge US support for recent security operations against jihadists in Yemen. In early January 2010 the authorities in the USA and the United Kingdom announced plans to fund a special counter-terrorism unit within Yemen's police force. Shortly after the announcement, the embassies of the USA, the United Kingdom and France in San'a were temporarily closed, following reports of direct threats from AQAP. Reports that the US Administration was preparing for direct military intervention in Yemen were refuted by the Government in San'a. Yemeni security forces launched a series of operations against suspected AQAP militants during January. Following two raids in mid-January, the security authorities claimed to have killed several senior AQAP commanders and to have captured the group's deputy leader, Said Ali al-Shihri, a Saudi national; however, the subsequent release of an audio recording in which a voice purporting to be that of al-Shihri claimed to have orchestrated the attempted aircraft bombing of Abdulmutallab, appeared to confirm that the former remained at large. In late January the British Secretary of State for Foreign and Commonwealth Affairs, David Miliband, chaired an international conference in London, United Kingdom, on the political and economic crises in Yemen, attended by the ministers responsible for foreign affairs of key regional and international partners, as well as representatives of international organizations. An intergovernmental grouping, the Friends of Yemen, was established to support political reform and economic development in the country. The inaugural meeting of the international grouping was held in Abu Dhabi, United Arab Emirates, in March.

In April 2010 the British ambassador to Yemen narrowly avoided injury when a suicide bomber targeted his convoy in San'a. The attacker himself was killed and three other people were injured in the incident, which prompted the temporary closure of the British embassy. The Yemeni Ministry of the Interior attributed the attack to AQAP. Following the provision of US intelligence, 30 foreign nationals domiciled in Yemen, some of whom had links to the San'a Institute for the Arabic Language, where Omar Farouk Abdulmutallab had studied, were arrested in June. In the same month Hamza Saleh al-Dayan, one of 23 prisoners who had escaped from a San'a gaol in February 2006 (see The 2003 parliamentary elections), surrendered to the authorities; al-Dayan was thought to have been responsible for a number of violent attacks, including that perpetuated against Spanish tourists in July 2007 (see The 2006 presidential election). A number of attacks suspected to have been carried out by AQAP were reported in mid-2010, including an ambush at a high-security prison in Aden, in which 14 people were killed and a small number of inmates released, in June, and an attack on a government building in Zinjibar, in Abyan governorate, in which a further 11 people were killed and three others injured, in July.

Concerns about the threat posed to international security by elements within Yemen were exacerbated at the end of August 2010 when two Yemeni nationals were arrested on board a flight from Chicago, Illinois, USA, to Amsterdam, Netherlands; the two men were alleged to have been conducting a trial run of a planned terrorist attack, after a number of suspicious items were discovered in their hand luggage. In October a grenade attack on a British embassy vehicle in the capital, and a separate incident in which a French national was fatally shot and a British national was seriously injured when a gunman opened fire at the compound of Austrian oil company OMV, further fuelled concerns about the targeting of Westerners and Western interests in Yemen.

The interception at airports in the United Kingdom and Dubai, United Arab Emirates, of two Chicago-bound air freight packages containing bombs, which had originated in Yemen, prompted renewed anxiety about Yemeni involvement in international terrorist activity in late October 2010. The foiled attack, which was discovered with the assistance of Saudi intelligence, was attributed to AQAP, with Ibrahim Asiri, a Saudi citizen who was reported to have entered Yemen in mid-2006 and subsequently to have become a member of AQAP, named by the US authorities as the suspected bomb maker. President Saleh declared that Yemen was 'determined to continue fighting terrorism and al-Qa'ida in co-operation with its partners' but warned the Administration of US President Barack Obama against interference in Yemen's internal affairs by targeting al-Qa'ida operatives within Yemen in drone attacks. The US Government continued to deny any involvement in such attacks.

The arrest on unknown charges of Hassan Bamoum, a prominent leader of the Southern Movement, sparked angry protests in al-Dali and several other southern towns in November 2010. Protesters tried to break into a prison in al-Dali, while four soldiers were injured when a military checkpoint in the town was attacked. In January 2011 AQAP senior leader Nasir al-Wuhayshi was reported to have been killed in an air-strike in December 2010; however, considerable doubt surrounded the reports, and rumours of his death remained unconfirmed at mid-2011. In January of that year it was reported that 1,030 members of the Yemeni security forces had been killed or injured by AQAP militants or the Southern Movement during 2010; of these, 178 had been killed.

Recent developments: increasing opposition disaffection, and popular protests

An amendment to the electoral law, which stipulated that the SCER be composed of judges, rather than parliamentary delegates as had hitherto been the case, was approved by the GPC-dominated legislature in December 2010, prompting members of the opposition to stage a sit-in protest in parliament amid claims that the Government and its allies had 'put an end to the national dialogue' and were engaged in a 'conspiracy' against efforts towards meaningful political reform. Some members of the opposition threatened to boycott the postponed legislative elections, due to be held on 27 April 2011. In mid-December 2010 the Government underscored its commitment to the staging of elections as scheduled, with or without opposition participation. However, in March 2011 the SCER announced that the elections were again to be postponed, until later in the year, to allow additional time for electoral rolls to be revised. Meanwhile, in January 2011 Saleh, to the consternation of the opposition, proposed a constitutional amendment that would allow him to stand for re-election in the presidential election in 2013.

In January 2011 the Minister of Oil and Minerals, Amir Salim al-Aidarous, was suspended, together with the Executive Director of the Yemen Petroleum Company, Omar Muhammad Ismail al-Arhabi, following fuel shortages that had led to large queues at petrol stations and considerable public anger. Later that month the Minister of Industry and Trade, Yahya al-Mutawakil, was dismissed and replaced by Hisham Sharaf; no reason was offered for al-Mutawakil's dismissal.

In mid-January 2011 protests erupted in Yemen, seemingly inspired by recent popular demonstrations in Tunisia that had precipitated the ouster of President Zine al-Abidine Ben Ali (see the chapter on Tunisia). Several thousand people participated in a demonstration within the grounds of San'a University to demand the removal from power of President Saleh. A female Islamic activist, Tawakel Karman, who was reported to have organized the protest, was arrested. Two days later Saleh pledged to step down as President upon the expiry of his second term in 2013, and dismissed widespread speculation that he planned to effect a dynastic succession by handing over power to his son. Saleh announced a series of measures intended to pacify critics of the Government, including the reduction by one-half of the rate of income tax, an increase in public sector wages and controls on price inflation. However, further protests were staged in various locations around the capital and elsewhere in the country in late January, at which tens of thousands of demonstrators chanted anti-Government slogans, and appealed for an end to corruption and ineffective economic policies.

Addressing an emergency session of the legislature shortly before a planned 'day of rage', organized by the political opposition and civil society groups, in early February 2011, President Saleh reiterated his pledge to seek neither to extend his term of office beyond 2013 nor to pass power to his son and urged the opposition to halt all planned protests, rallies and sit-ins, since 'the interests of the country come before our personal interests'. Saleh also announced a series of welfare reforms and tax relief measures. While the opposition welcomed the President's pledges, the 'day of rage' proceeded as planned on the following day, with an estimated 20,000 protesters amassing in the streets of the capital to reject publicly Saleh's offer to stand down upon the expiry of his term in 2013 and to demand his immediate resignation. Thousands of pro-Government demonstrators also gathered in the capital, to pledge their support to Saleh; clashes were reported between the two camps of supporters and at least 20 people were arrested. There were widespread reports of the use of force by the authorities in their efforts to disperse crowds of anti-Government protesters in the capital and elsewhere, and in mid-February 2011 the first fatalities since the start of the protests were reported, including that of a 16-year-old girl who was alleged to have been shot by security forces in the al-Shikh district of Aden. On the following day two students were reported to have been killed and two others injured when security forces opened fire on protesters near their encampment outside the grounds of San'a University. In early March at least 80 people were injured when the authorities opened fire on protesters outside San'a University; one person subsequently died of his injuries.

Meanwhile, in mid-February 2011 an offer by President Saleh to hold talks at which 'legitimate' demands would be heard was rejected by the opposition, which stated its refusal to enter into negotiations until the Government desisted from using excessive force against protesters. In early March Saleh announced plans to change to a parliamentary system of government, pledging to hold a popular referendum on the issue later in the year; however, the overture was rapidly dismissed by the opposition and protesters continued to demand the President's immediate resignation. Meanwhile, the Government appeared to have initiated a crackdown on Western journalists, and in mid-March four journalists working for US media were arrested and deported; no official reason was given for their removal from the country, but, with only a few foreign journalists remaining in Yemen at that time, it was feared that the authorities were preparing for a violent escalation of efforts to suppress the anti-Government protests. Also in mid-March the Governor of Marib was seriously injured when he was stabbed in the neck while trying to disperse a crowd of demonstrators outside the local government headquarters. By that time some 30 protesters were reported to have been killed in clashes with the authorities. On 14 March the Minister of Endowments and Religious Guidance, Hamoud al-Hitar, was removed from office; Hamoud Muhammad Abad, hitherto Minister of Youth and Sports, was appointed to replace him, and was in turn succeeded by Arif Awad al-Zoka.

On 18 March 2011 52 protesters were killed and hundreds of others were wounded when unidentified gunmen in civilian clothes opened fire from rooftops on a large group of protesters as they observed morning prayers at their encampment outside San'a University; the security forces denied any involvement in the incident, with the Government blaming local citizens, who also denied any culpability. Later that day President Saleh declared a state of emergency, for a period of 30 days, and also announced the creation of a committee of inquiry to investigate the massacre, as well as other incidents that had led to fatalities during the protests. In the days that followed an increasing number of defections from the GPC, including that of senior army commanders, was reported, prompting speculation that a military coup might be imminent and precipitating violent clashes between defecting military personnel and forces remaining loyal to Saleh. Other prominent defectors included the Minister of Human Rights, Huda Abd al-Latif al-Ban, who cited the 'unnatural situation that human rights face in Yemen' as a result of 'a system that doesn't respect people's rights and freedoms', as well as the Minister of Tourism, and a number of prominent diplomats, including the Yemeni ambassador to the UN. Saleh's declaration of emergency rule was approved by parliament, by 160 votes to four, on 23 March. However, opponents of the Government claimed that the GPC had overstated the number of members present during the parliamentary session at which the vote was conducted, alleging that, with the opposition, independents and defectors from the GPC all boycotting the session, just 133 legislators had been present—a quorum of more than 50% of the 301-seat parliament was required for a vote to be valid. The GPC denied the accusation. Meanwhile, on 20 March Saleh dismissed the Council of Ministers, although Prime Minister Mujawar and his administration were requested to remain in office on an interim basis pending the formation of a new government.

On 24 March 2011 Saleh was reported to have accepted a five-point plan for the transition of power proposed by the opposition that envisaged the formation of a government of national unity and a committee to draft a new constitution, the holding of a constitutional referendum, the implementation of new electoral legislation, and the staging of parliamentary and presidential elections, all by the end of the year. However, in advance of mass rival rallies organized by anti-Government protesters and Saleh's supporters on the following day, President Saleh stated that, while he was prepared to hand over power, he would do so only to 'safe hands' and urged his supporters to 'stand firm', suggesting that he did not in fact intend to observe the opposition-proposed transition plan, concerns that were heightened in early April when Saleh declared: 'I pledge to sacrifice my blood and everything I hold valuable for the sake of my great people'. Meanwhile, on 29 March 150 people were killed and around 80 others injured following explosions at a munitions factory in the southern town of Jaar; the authorities attributed responsibility for the incident to AQAP.

From early April 2011 the GCC member states initiated diplomatic efforts to bring an end to the ongoing impasse between President Saleh and the opposition. In a statement released on 7 April, Qatari Prime Minister Sheikh Hamad bin Jasim bin Jaber Al Thani announced that the GCC hoped to finalize a deal that would provide for the transfer of power to Vice-President Maj.-Gen. Abd al-Rabbuh Mansur al-Hadi at the head of an interim government, while offering guarantees of safe protection for Saleh and his family. However, Saleh rejected the proposal, dismissing it as 'blatant interference in Yemeni affairs'. In mid-April a number of those who had defected from the ruling party, reportedly including al-Ban and former Minister of Tourism Nabil Hassan al-Faqih, formed a new political group, the Justice and Development Bloc, to oppose violence against the protesters. On 21 April the GCC proposed a new mediation plan, under the terms of which both sides would agree to the immediate cessation of protests and Saleh, who would be offered immunity from prosecution, would step down within one month of signing the accord, having appointed an opposition leader to head a national unity government that would prepare for a presidential election within two months of Saleh's resignation; members of the GPC would account for one-half of the new government, members of the opposition coalition would comprise 40%, while the remaining 10% would comprise members of non-affiliated political groupings. Following a meeting with a GCC delegation, Saleh formally accepted the proposal on 23 April. Members of the opposition also accepted the plan, but nevertheless voiced doubts that Saleh would honour the terms of the accord. Indeed, the month passed without an announcement that Saleh had signed the agreement. On 28 April at least eight people were reported to have been killed after security forces opened fire on a demonstration near the San'a Trade Centre; sources reported by the UN suggested in early May that at least 135 people had been killed since the outbreak of unrest in January. Later that month the Qatari Government withdrew from the GCC delegation, citing its frustration with Saleh's refusal to co-operate. However, talks continued, and on 18 May it was announced that a similar agreement had been reached. Representatives of the opposition parties duly signed the agreement, as did some members of the GPC, but it subsequently emerged that Saleh had demanded that the opposition representatives attend the presidential residence before giving his formal assent. On 22 May the GCC suspended its mediation efforts.

The Al-Houthi Rebellion

In June 2004 violent clashes took place in the mountainous north-western province of Saada between the security forces and supporters of a militant Zaidi cleric, Hussain al-Houthi, leader of Al-Shabab al-Mo'men (Believing Youth). The authorities alleged that al-Houthi's movement had formed its own militia near the border with Saudi Arabia and had launched attacks against government buildings and mosques in Saada. Although the group appeared to be motivated by opposition to the USA and Israel and to have a militant Islamist agenda, it was not thought to have links to al-Qa'ida. Reports estimated that al-Houthi had some 3,000 armed supporters, of whom some 200–300 had been killed since the conflict began, with hundreds of rebels wounded or arrested. In September al-Houthi himself was killed by members of the security forces; the Government declared this development to have effectively ended the uprising. However, renewed fighting broke out with followers of the cleric in April 2005; five Yemeni soldiers and eight members of Al-Shabab al-Mo'men were understood to have been killed. On 12 April it was reported that the conflict had decreased in intensity and that government forces were seeking al-Houthi's relatives, in particular his brother, Abd al-Malik al-Houthi, and his father, Badr al-Din al-Houthi, who were believed to have acceded to the leadership of the movement. After several months of relative peace, fighting broke out again in November when two days of conflict reportedly left 16 rebels and eight government soldiers dead.

Renewed violence broke out in the province of Saada in early 2007, with a series of clashes between insurgents led by Abd al-Malik al-Houthi and government forces. President Saleh issued an ultimatum warning of a full military campaign against the rebels if they did not surrender their weapons, and thousands of additional troops were subsequently deployed to the region. Following an escalation of the violence in late February, in early March it was reported that more than 500 people, including more than 400 troops, had died in the fighting since the beginning of the year.

Following mediation by Qatar, in mid-June 2007 the Government and the leaders of the al-Houthi rebellion reached a cease-fire agreement, which required the rebels to relinquish their weapons and the Government to release imprisoned rebels, fund reconstruction efforts in areas affected by the fighting and facilitate the return to their homes of displaced people (estimated at more than 50,000 by the International Committee of the Red Cross—ICRC); in addition, Abd al-Malik al-Houthi, two of his brothers and another rebel leader were to move to the Qatari capital, Doha, for an unspecified period of exile. However, later that month it was reported that the rebel leaders remained in Saada and that insurgents were continuing to attack government troops in the province, amid some dissent within the al-Houthi movement regarding the accord with the Government. The rebels had apparently issued a new set of demands, most notably the return of the body of Hussain al-Houthi (who had been killed by the security forces in 2004).

The cease-fire between government forces and al-Houthi insurgents in Saada was breached in October 2007, when at least three armed rebels and one soldier were killed in clashes resulting from the rebels' refusal to surrender their weapons. Four soldiers died in further fighting later that month after al-Houthi supporters reportedly attacked a police station.

With the security situation in Saada deteriorating further, the Qatari Government renewed its efforts to mediate between the Yemeni Government and the al-Houthi insurgents, and at the beginning of February 2008 a document was signed outlining measures for the implementation of the initial agreement reached in June 2007; the full details of the new accord were not disclosed. Some progress in restoring stability in Saada was achieved in the following weeks. In mid-February 2008 it was reported that hostilities had ceased and that the rebels had freed two military commanders who had been captured in January. Furthermore, by early March the Government had released 376 detainees arrested in connection with the rebellion. However, the Government subsequently accused the rebels of violating the cease-fire agreement and of killing a detainee whom they had recently abducted, and sporadic violence resumed. Fighting broke out between al-Houthi followers and al-Bakhtan tribesmen in Saada in early April, after the pro-Government tribe accused the rebels of killing one of its members two months previously; more than 20 people died in the confrontations. In mid-April a GPC member of the House of Representatives, Saleh al-Hindi Daghsan, was killed, together with his son and a bodyguard, in an ambush carried out by unknown gunmen in Saada. Later that month Abd al-Malik al-Houthi asserted that efforts to implement the peace agreement had failed, owing to the Government's refusal to withdraw its forces from the areas in which they were deployed during the conflict with the rebels. A few days later further clashes resulted in the deaths of eight al-Houthi insurgents and three soldiers. In early May at least 15 people were killed and up to 60 injured in a bombing at a mosque frequented by military personnel in Saada. Abd al-Malik al-Houthi denied claims of his followers' involvement in the incident.

In July 2008 President Saleh announced that the conflict with the al-Houthi militants had ended, adding that the combatants were engaged in constructive dialogue. Despite this pronouncement, there were continued reports of sporadic violence in the region. In August Abd al-Malik al-Houthi was reported to have accepted the President's 10-point proposal for a final settlement of the conflict, which was believed to encompass most of the terms of the Qatari-mediated agreement of 2007. In September 2008 the Government established a Saada Reconstruction Fund and announced a four-year strategy to rehabilitate the war-ravaged province. The cost of the reconstruction plan was estimated at US $500m., and the authorities appealed for international donors to contribute a significant proportion. According to the Ministry of Local Administration, more than 6,000 houses, 900 farms, 80 schools and 90 mosques had been destroyed or damaged during the four-year conflict. In addition to the hundreds of fatalities caused by the fighting, thousands of people had been displaced, many of whom were living in poor conditions in makeshift refugee camps. Several international non-governmental organizations, including the ICRC and Médecins sans frontières, endeavoured to bring medical and other humanitarian aid into affected areas, although all reported severe difficulties in delivering aid, mainly owing to ongoing instability.

During the first half of 2009 the truce in Saada province appeared increasingly fragile, as both government and rebel sources released reports of clashes between the two sides. Furthermore, al-Houthi representatives alleged that the Government was sending substantial military reinforcements into the area in preparation for a new offensive. Renewed fighting erupted in late July; at least seven Yemeni soldiers were killed during rebel attacks on army bases in Saada province. In early August al-Houthi militants ousted government troops from several towns and seized control of a strategic military post on the highway linking Saada with San'a. On 11 August the Government launched 'Operation Scorched Earth', a campaign of intensive aerial, missile and artillery strikes against insurgent positions in the region. Dozens of militants and civilians were reportedly killed during the opening days of the campaign, as rebel strongholds came under heavy bombardment from jet fighters and tanks. According to the office of the UN High Commissioner for Refugees (UNHCR), an estimated 35,000 people were displaced during the first two weeks of the operation. On 21 August President Saleh issued a cease-fire proposal that required the rebels to accept six conditions for peace: the release of all civilian and military prisoners; withdrawal from occupied areas and reinstatement of local government control; the reopening of roads and clearing of checkpoints and land-mines; the surrender of weapons and equipment seized during the conflict; the cessation of incursions into Saudi territory; and a commitment to abide by the Constitution. The al-Houthi leadership rejected the proposed terms.

Official sources reported on 23 August 2009 that at least 100 rebels, including two senior commanders, had been killed during an anti-insurgent operation in the Harf Sufyan district of Amram province, to the south of Saada. At the beginning of September a cease-fire initiative proposed by the rebels was flatly rejected by the Government, and intensive ground operations and air-strikes continued. President Saleh subsequently alleged that the rebels were receiving financial support from groups within Iran and from supporters of Iraqi Shi'a cleric Moqtada al-Sadr. Conversely, al-Houthi representatives increasingly complained of Saudi Arabian collaboration in the Government's campaign, claiming that Yemeni troops had been granted access to Saudi territory in order to outflank rebel positions. It was reported in mid-September that more than 85 civilians had been killed when Yemeni forces launched air-strikes against a refugee camp in Harf Sufyan. The incident provoked widespread condemnation from international human rights groups; however, details of the attack were not confirmed in official government sources. (The Government subsequently launched an investigation into the incident; however, by mid-2011 no findings had been made public.) On 20 September 2009 government forces repelled a rebel assault on their headquarters in Saada; more than 140 al-Houthi militants were reportedly killed in the battle. Nevertheless, despite vast advantages in troop numbers and equipment, the Government's goal of securing a swift and decisive victory looked increasingly uncertain. (During 'Operation Scorched Earth' the Government reportedly deployed up to 40,000 troops to the region, as well as mobilizing numerous irregular tribal militias.)

In October 2009 Yahya Badr al-Din al-Houthi, an exiled parliamentary deputy and a brother of the rebellion's leader, having been stripped of his parliamentary immunity, was placed on trial, *in absentia*, on charges of fomenting rebellion. Yahya was convicted of involvement in the rebellion in April 2010 and sentenced to 15 years' imprisonment; however, he remained in exile in Germany. Meanwhile, at the end of October 2009 the authorities apprehended an Iranian-crewed vessel reportedly transporting a shipment of weapons to the al-Houthi rebels.

In early November 2009, following an exchange of gunfire between al-Houthi militants and Saudi border guards, in which at least one guard was killed, Saudi Arabia launched a campaign of air-strikes and ground offensives against rebel targets in the Saudi–Yemeni border region. In mid-November Saudi Arabia enforced a naval blockade along Yemen's northern coast to prevent the supply of weapons and fighters to the rebel movement. The Saudi intervention exacerbated the already serious humanitarian crisis in north-western Yemen: in mid-November there were reported to be in excess of 170,000 internally displaced people in the region, with aid agencies reporting difficulties in delivering humanitarian supplies, while thousands of people were also evacuated from villages on the Saudi Arabian side of the border; furthermore, reports indicated that the air-strikes had claimed a high number of civilian fatalities.

Despite incurring heavy casualties while under sustained attack from government forces to the south and Saudi forces in the border areas, the militants continued a campaign of guerrilla warfare. On 22 December 2009 Saudi Arabia announced the end of major combat operations, stating that full control of the border region had been regained. At that time, 73 Saudi troops had been killed and 26 were missing since the commencement of the operation in early November. A truce offered to the Saudi authorities by the rebels, who stated that all fighters had been withdrawn from the kingdom's territory, was rejected in mid-January 2010. Although heavy fighting between government forces and the militants persisted in early February, a truce based on recognition of the six-point agenda proposed by the Government in August 2009 was initiated on 11 February 2010, after Abd al-Malik al-Houthi had announced his readiness to negotiate a cease-fire with the Government in late January; four regional joint committees, comprising Government and al-Houthi representatives, were established to oversee the implementation of the truce. Although the truce remained intact at mid-2011, sporadic violent incidents had continued to be reported throughout 2010 and into 2011, and analysts expressed concern regarding the Government's failure to address the underlying causes of the conflict. The Al-Houthi leadership expressed its support for the ongoing anti-Government protest movement (see Domestic Political Affairs). In late March 2011 al-Houthi rebels were reported to have seized control of the majority of Saada, causing the local Governor to flee; Faris Man'a declared himself to be in charge of the town and that control over the northern area had been 'achieved for the sake of toppling this regime'. Clashes between al-Houthi rebels and tribespeople loyal to President Saleh were reported throughout March and April, prompting fears of full-scale civil war.

Foreign Affairs

Relations with Saudi Arabia

Relations with Saudi Arabia deteriorated as a result of Yemen's initially strong opposition to the presence of foreign armed forces in the Gulf and to the ambiguous stance it had subsequently adopted in this respect. Apparently in retaliation, Saudi Arabia announced in September 1990 that it had withdrawn the privileges that Yemeni workers had previously enjoyed. This resulted in an exodus from Saudi Arabia of some 850,000 Yemeni workers during October and November, which caused widespread economic and social disruption. The expulsion and consequent return to Yemen of the workers not only caused a reduction in the country's income from remittances, but also led to a serious increase in unemployment. During 1995, at negotiations proceeding from the February 1995 memorandum of understanding (MOU—see below) it was reported that the Saudi authorities had agreed to allow Yemenis sponsored by Saudi nationals to seek employment in the kingdom. In 1998 Saudi Arabia began issuing visas to Yemeni workers.

The Governments of Yemen and Saudi Arabia held negotiations concerning the demarcation of their common border during 1992–94; however, in December 1994 Yemen accused Saudi Arabia of trespassing on Yemeni territory and alleged that three of its soldiers had been killed during clashes earlier in that month. Further clashes were reported in January 1995 following the failure of the two countries to renew the 1934 Ta'if agreement (renewable every 20 years), which delineated their existing frontier. Intense mediation by Syria culminated in a joint statement in mid-January 1995, in which Yemen and Saudi Arabia pledged to cease all military activity in the border area. It was subsequently announced that the demarcation of the disputed border would be undertaken by a joint committee. In February the Yemeni and Saudi Governments signed an MOU that reaffirmed their commitment to the Ta'if agreement and provided for the establishment of six joint committees to delineate the land and sea borders and develop economic and commercial ties. In June President Saleh led a high-ranking delegation to Saudi Arabia, constituting the first official visit to that country since February 1990. The two Governments expressed their satisfaction with the MOU and pledged their commitment to strengthening economic, commercial and cultural co-operation.

Friction between Yemen and Saudi Arabia over border claims was revived in 1997, and in May 1998 it was reported that Saudi Arabia had occupied an uninhabited island in the Red Sea regarded by Yemen as within its national boundaries. In the same month Saudi Arabia sent a memorandum to the UN stating that it did not recognize the 1992 border agreement between Yemen and Oman and claiming that parts of the area involved were Saudi Arabian territory. The Saudi objection to the accord was widely believed to be related to its attempts to gain land access to the Arabian Sea, via a corridor between Yemen and Oman, which it had thus far been denied in its negotiations with Yemen. In July 1998 Yemen submitted a memorandum to the Arab League refuting the Saudi claim to the land, and stating that the Saudi protests contravened the Ta'if agreement signed by that country. In the same month three Yemeni troops were killed during fighting with a Saudi border patrol on the disputed island of Duwaima in the Red Sea; Saudi Arabia claimed its actions on the island were in self-defence and that, under the Ta'if agreement, three-quarters of the island belonged to Saudi Arabia. Meanwhile, bilateral discussions continued and the Saudi Minister of Foreign Affairs visited Yemen at the end of July. The Yemeni Prime Minister cancelled a planned visit to Saudi Arabia in October 1999, reportedly owing to the failure of the two Governments to agree on the issues to be discussed.

Despite reported clashes in the border area during 1999, however, relations continued to improve. In June 2000, at a ceremony in Riyadh, Saudi Arabia, the Saudi Arabian and Yemeni ministers responsible for foreign affairs signed a final border treaty demarcating their joint land and sea border. The treaty incorporated both the 1934 Ta'if agreement and the 1995 MOU, although it failed to define the eastern section of the Saudi–Yemeni land frontier. The two countries also agreed to further economic, commercial and cultural ties, and each pledged not to permit its territory to be used as a base for political or military aggression against the other. Renewed tensions surfaced in early 2004 after the Saudi Government began construction of a 'separation wall' along the border that some considered to be in violation of the treaty of June 2000 on border demarcation. The construction of the wall reflected unease on the part of the Saudis regarding the capacity of the Yemeni authorities to maintain their own border security. In June 2006 the Saudi and Yemeni ministers responsible for internal affairs signed an agreement on the final demarcation of their shared border.

Following the formation of AQAP in early 2009 (see Domestic Political Affairs), the Saudi Arabian authorities became increasingly concerned about the concentration of militant Islamist activity in ungoverned areas of Yemen. President Saleh held talks on regional security issues and bilateral relations with King Abdullah ibn Abd al-Aziz Al Sa'ud in Riyadh in June 2009. Saudi anxiety concerning jihadist activity in Yemen appeared to be confirmed in August, when a failed attempt to assassinate the kingdom's security chief, Prince Muhammad ibn Nayef, in Jeddah, Saudi Arabia, was attributed to AQAP. The growing lawlessness in Yemen's northern border region during 2009, exacerbated by the al-Houthi conflict, led to a significant expansion of Saudi military capacity in the region, which culminated in a military campaign against northern Yemeni rebels from November (see The Al-Houthi Rebellion). A meeting of the Saudi-Yemeni Co-operation Council in Riyadh in March 2010 led to the signing of a number of agreements concerning Saudi-funded energy, health, education and humanitarian projects in Yemen. Following several weeks of anti-Government protests from January 2011 (see Domestic Political Affairs), President Saleh dispatched the Minister of Foreign Affairs, Abu Bakr al-Kurbi, to Riyadh in mid-March, reportedly to seek Saudi military assistance to tackle the escalating civil unrest. It was not immediately clear whether the Saudi Government acceded to the request.

Other external relations

An agreement on the long-disputed former PDRY–Omani border was signed in San'a in October 1992 and ratified in December. Demarcation was completed in June 1995. Oman withdrew an estimated 15,000 troops from the last of the disputed territories on the Yemeni border in July 1996, in accordance with the 1992 agreement. In May 1997 officials from both countries signed the demarcation maps at a ceremony in Muscat, Oman. In January 2004 the two countries signed an agreement on their sea border during wider discussions over the establishment of a joint free trade zone.

The Iraqi invasion of Kuwait in August 1990 proved problematic for the Yemeni Government, as the economy was heavily dependent on trade with, and aid from, Iraq, and also on aid from Saudi Arabia, which was host to a considerable number of Yemeni expatriate workers. In December Yemen assumed the chair of the UN Security Council (which rotates on a monthly basis), and the Government increased its efforts to mediate in the Gulf crisis. It was, however, unable to prevent the outbreak of war, despite a peace plan, presented in January 1991, and further diplomatic initiatives. Yemen condemned the US-led military offensive against Iraq, and large demonstrations were held in support of Iraq. Later in January it was confirmed that US aid to Yemen was to be suspended indefinitely, apparently as a result of Yemen's policy towards Iraq, although reduced US economic aid was resumed in August. Yemen continued to support Iraq, and in December 1998 it requested an Arab League summit on Iraq and appealed for an end to the sanctions. The Yemeni Government expressed its concerns regarding the US-led military operations against Iraqi air defence targets in 1999–2002.

Following the suicide attacks apparently perpetrated by Osama bin Laden's al-Qa'ida network against New York and Washington, DC, USA, on 11 September 2001, the Yemeni Government arrested a number of suspected Islamist militants and froze the assets of individuals and organizations deemed to have links with al-Qa'ida. In December up to 30 people (including about 19 soldiers) were reportedly killed during clashes in the central Marib governorate, when local residents apparently fought to prevent the Yemeni security forces from arresting a group of alleged militants. (President Saleh had, during a visit to Washington, DC, in November, been presented with a list of suspected al-Qa'ida members residing in Yemen.) Meanwhile, at least 100 foreign students enrolled at the country's Islamic institutes were said to have been arrested on charges of violating residency requirements. In January 2002 the US embassy in San'a was closed amid fears of an imminent terrorist attack; two grenades were thrown at the building in March, although no injuries were reported. There were reports in March that the US Administration was considering the deployment of several hundred US troops to Yemen to assist the authorities in their struggle against militant Islamist organizations. In April an explosion was reported close to the home of a leading security official involved in the search for al-Qa'ida militants; a previously unknown group styled the al-Qa'ida Sympathizers was suspected of having carried out the bombing. Despite increasing popular resentment towards US activities in the Middle East among Yemenis, President Saleh continued to co-operate with the USA over anti-terrorism initiatives, and in November an unmanned US aircraft killed six men in northern Yemen believed to have links with al-Qa'ida. In December three US missionaries were murdered by a Yemeni who confessed to having links with bin Laden's network.

In February 2002 President Saleh was reported to have warned the US Government that a US-led attack on the regime of Saddam Hussain in Iraq, as part of its 'war on terror', would jeopardize the continued support of its traditional allies in the Arab region. However, Saleh was careful to emphasize his own ongoing efforts to persuade the Iraqi authorities to accept the return of UN weapons inspectors. When the US-led military campaign commenced in Iraq in March 2003, some 30,000 protesters, some of them armed, marched on the US embassy in San'a. Public resentment also continued to increase towards President Saleh's regime, as a result of its perceived co-operation with the USA. In June, however, the Director of the US Federal Bureau of Investigation, Robert Mueller, met Saleh in Aden to discuss further co-operation on security and intelligence. In September the human rights organization Amnesty International released a report claiming that the authorities were holding some 200 people without trial in an effort to assuage US concerns that Yemen was not co-operating fully with the 'war on terror'. In November Muhammad Hamdi al-Ahdal, who, according to the USA, had been among the 20 most significant al-Qa'ida members still at large, was captured by security forces; al-Ahdal was suspected of having organized the bombings of the USS *Cole* in 2000 and the French petroleum tanker the *Limburg* in 2002 (see above). Another reported senior al-Qa'ida operative, who had apparently survived a US attempt to assassinate him in 2002, was arrested by security forces in March 2004.

In March 2004 Yemen welcomed the signing of an interim constitution in Iraq, describing it as a step towards Iraq recovering its sovereignty, but continued to press for the USA and its allies to withdraw their forces from the country. In August the Minister of Foreign Affairs confirmed that Yemen was preparing a peace-keeping force for Iraq under mandates from the Arab League and the UN, but would only send the troops should the US-led coalition forces withdraw from Iraq. Discussions held between Saleh and US President George W. Bush in May 2007, during a visit by the Yemeni President to Washington, DC, focused on efforts to combat terrorism and developments in the Middle East, as well as bilateral relations. In September 2008 the US embassy in San'a was the target of another violent attack (see above), in which at least 16 people were killed, although no embassy staff were reported to have been injured in the incident.

Media reports in December 2010 claimed that the USA had launched four clandestine cruise missile strikes in the previous 12 months, which had killed 40 suspected terrorists but had also claimed the lives of more than 200 civilians. The online release by the WikiLeaks organization of a series of leaked classified US diplomatic cables from late 2010 appeared to indicate the existence of an agreement whereby the Administration of US President Barack Obama offered covert military support to target suspected terrorists in Yemen in exchange for the Yemeni Government claiming responsibility for the air-strikes in order to shield the US Administration from external criticism; in one such communiqué, President Saleh was quoted as having said 'we'll continue saying the bombs are ours, not yours', while another cable suggested that the USA had provided emergency supplies of weapons as well as intelligence to support Saudi military action against al-Houthi rebels (see The Al-Houthi Rebellion) in late 2009, despite a denial of any military involvement at the time by US Department of State spokespersons.

During a visit to San'a in January 2011, the first visit to the Yemeni capital by a US Secretary of State in two decades, Hillary Clinton stressed that the issue of AQAP militants operating in Yemen was an 'urgent concern' for the Obama Administration and declared that the Administration sought to 'broaden dialogue' and enhance bilateral ties beyond those of a military nature.

In March US Secretary of Defence Robert Gates noted his 'concern' about the authorities' handling of the anti-Government protest movement (see Domestic Political Affairs) but stressed that it was not his place to discuss Yemeni internal affairs. However, US rhetoric in response to widespread reports of the excessive use of force to quell the protesters became increasingly firm and outspoken, and US media reported in early April that the Obama Administration had told Yemeni officials that Saleh's position had become 'untenable'.

In November 1995 there were reports that Eritrean troops had attempted to land on the Red Sea island of Greater Hanish, one of three islands (the others being Lesser Hanish and Zuqar) claimed by both Yemen and Eritrea. The attempted invasion had apparently been prompted by Yemen's announced intention to develop Greater Hanish as a tourist resort, and its subsequent refusal to comply with an Eritrean demand that the island be evacuated. Negotiations in Yemen and Eritrea failed to defuse the crisis, and on 15 December fighting broke out between the two sides, resulting in the deaths of six Eritrean and three Yemeni soldiers. On 17 December Yemen and Eritrea agreed to a cease-fire. None the less, fighting was renewed the following day and Eritrean forces succeeded in occupying Greater Hanish. The cease-fire was adhered to thenceforth, and some 180 Yemeni soldiers (captured during the fighting) were released at the end of the month.

In May 1996, following French mediation, it was announced that Yemen and Eritrea would sign an arbitration agreement, whereby both countries would renounce the use of force and submit their dispute to an international tribunal. France subsequently undertook to observe and supervise military movements in the area around the disputed islands. Eritrean troops occupied Lesser Hanish in mid-August, but were withdrawn later in the month after representations by France and a UN Security Council edict to evacuate the island forthwith. At a meeting held in Paris, France, in October, representatives of Eritrea and Yemen confirmed that they would submit the dispute to an international tribunal. In October 1998 the tribunal ruled that Yemen had sovereignty over Greater and Lesser Hanish, and all islands to their north-west, while Eritrea had sovereignty over the Mohabaka islands. The court recommended that the fishing traditions around the islands be maintained, thereby granting access to the Hanish islands to Eritrean and Yemeni fishermen. Both countries accepted the ruling, and shortly afterwards they agreed to establish a joint committee to strengthen bilateral co-operation. A final ruling on the Hanish islands, issued by the tribunal in December, delineated the joint maritime border as the median line between their mainland coastlines. In June 2003 a number of Yemeni fishing boats and 133 crew members were arrested by Eritrean naval patrols in the area around the Hanish islands. Although the men were released in July, the development was an indication of increased tension between the countries since the decision of the tribunal.

In December 2003 Yemen consolidated its improved relations with two of its neighbours to the west, Sudan and Ethiopia, with the establishment of the Tripartite San'a Co-operation Forum. Eritrea, however, accused the group of collaborating against it.

In May 2007 the staging of a demonstration intended to protest against perceived Iranian and Libyan interference in Yemeni domestic affairs was prevented by the Ministry of the Interior, provoking outrage among, in particular, many in Saada, who were angered by alleged Iranian and Libyan support for those rebels loyal to al-Houthi who were thought to be responsible for much of the violence in that region. A few days previously Yemen had recalled its ambassadors from both countries. The Iranian and Libyan Governments both denied any involvement in the rebellion in Saada and sought to ease tensions with Yemen. Later in May the Libyan leader dispatched an envoy to San'a to deliver a letter to President Saleh expressing support for the Yemeni Government's efforts to quash the insurgency, and in July Muhammad Reza Baqeri, the Iranian Deputy Foreign Minister for Arab and African Affairs, visited Yemen in an effort to improve bilateral relations. However, in November 2008 Rashad al-Alimi, Yemen's Deputy Prime Minister for Defence and Security Affairs, alleged that al-Houthi militants were receiving training and support from Iran. Two Yemeni citizens were convicted in April 2009 of spying for Iran and sentenced to death. The intensification of the Government's conflict with the al-Houthi militants from August led to increased tensions with Iran. Reports that the security authorities had apprehended an Iranian shipment of arms destined for the rebels, in October, were vehemently denied by the Iranian authorities. Trial proceedings against a further four Yemenis, accused of spying for Iran on behalf of the al-Houthi movement, commenced in April 2010; the defendants denied the charges against them and alleged that they had been tortured while in police custody. The trial of three further Yemenis on charges of spying for Iran commenced in February 2011.

President Saleh sought to mediate in the dispute that arose between rival Palestinian political factions the Islamic Resistance Movement (Hamas) and Fatah after Hamas had seized control of the Gaza Strip in June 2007. In March 2008 the Yemeni President brokered a reconciliation agreement, the San'a Declaration, which was signed by the two organizations (see the chapter on the Palestinian Autonomous Areas). The launch of Israel's military offensive against Hamas targets in the Gaza Strip in late December 2008 led to angry demonstrations throughout Yemen. Protesters angered by Egypt's perceived support for Israel stormed the Egyptian consulate in Aden, causing serious damage. President Saleh attended the Arab Economic, Social and Development Summit in Kuwait in January 2009, at which he presented proposals for the formation of a union of Arab states.

Since the mid-1990s President Saleh has increasingly sought to widen the range of Yemen's international contacts, particularly in relation to aid and co-operation agreements. In November 1997, on an official visit to the United Kingdom (during which a co-operation agreement was signed with the EU), President Saleh made a formal application for Yemen to join the Commonwealth (see p. 230). Saleh made a state visit to the People's Republic of China in February 1998, during which extensive agreements were negotiated for Yemen to receive technical and economic assistance. In early 2000 Saleh made official visits to Canada, the USA, Italy and Iran; at the same time Yemen repeatedly denied reports that it had had secret contacts with Israel and that it was seeking to normalize relations with that country. At a meeting held in London, United Kingdom, in November 2006, international donors pledged some US $5,000m. in development assistance for Yemen; however, the IMF noted in August 2010 that only a small portion of this pledged amount had been disbursed hitherto. Meanwhile, in August 2007 Yemen signed a 10-year development partnership agreement with the United Kingdom. In late February 2011 the British Government announced that it was almost to double its aid to Yemen from £46.7m. in 2011 to £90m. by 2015, on the condition that Yemen meet a series of targets, including the holding of free and fair elections and the promotion of economic reforms; a British government spokesperson identified Yemen as 'a major priority for British aid' and expressed the hope that the planned increase would facilitate a move towards 'a more stable and prosperous future' for the Middle Eastern country, while also suggesting that the Saleh administration needed to do more to counter the threat posed to domestic and international security by AQAP and other terrorist elements within Yemen.

CONSTITUTION AND GOVERNMENT

A draft Constitution for the united Republic of Yemen, based on that endorsed by the Yemen Arab Republic (YAR) and the People's Democratic Republic of Yemen (PDRY) in December 1981, was published in December 1989; it was approved by a popular referendum held on 15–16 May 1991. Legislative power is vested in the House of Representatives, with 301 members directly elected by universal adult suffrage. Under the revised Constitution, the President of the Republic (head of state) is to be elected directly by voters for a period of seven years, renewable once. The President appoints a Council of Ministers, headed by a Prime Minister.

REGIONAL AND INTERNATIONAL CO-OPERATION

Yemen is a member of the League of Arab States (Arab League, see p. 361) and is currently pursuing membership of the Co-operation Council for the Arab States of the Gulf (the Gulf Co-operation Council—GCC, see p. 243). Since unification in 1990, Yemen has been represented at the UN as a single member. (The Yemen Arab Republic joined the organization in September 1947, and the People's Democratic Republic of Yemen in December 1967.) The country has observer status at the World Trade Organization (WTO, see p. 430), membership of which organization was applied for in 2000. It also participates in the Organization of the Islamic Conference (OIC, see p. 400).

ECONOMIC AFFAIRS

In 2009, according to estimates by the World Bank, Yemen's gross national income (GNI), measured at average 2007–09 prices, was US $25,026m., equivalent to $1,060 per head (or $2,340 per head on an international purchasing-power parity basis). During 2000–09, it was estimated, the population increased at an average annual rate of 2.9%, while gross domestic product (GDP) per head increased, in real terms, by an average of 0.9% per year. According to the World Bank, overall GDP increased, in real terms, at an average annual rate of 3.9% in 2000–09. GDP grew by 4.7% in 2009, according to provisional official estimates.

Agriculture (including forestry and fishing) contributed an estimated 12.2% of GDP in 2009, and the sector engaged 35.1% of the working population in 2005/06. According to FAO estimates, however, the sector engaged some 37.8% of the total labour force in mid-2011. The principal cash crops are coffee, cotton and fruits. Subsistence crops include sorghum, wheat, barley and potatoes. However, cultivation of the amphetamine-like narcotic qat has displaced other crops in many areas. Livestock-rearing (particularly in the east and north) and fishing are also important activities. Official estimates indicated an average annual growth rate of 5.8% in 2000–09. Real agricultural GDP increased by 5.6% in 2009, according to provisional estimates.

Industry (including mining, manufacturing, construction and power) contributed an estimated 32.3% of GDP in 2009, and 18.5% of the working population were employed in the sector in 2005/06. According to estimates, industrial GDP decreased at an average annual rate of 1.0% in 2000–09. Real industrial GDP was provisionally estimated to have declined by 1.4% in 2009.

Mining and quarrying contributed an estimated 18.8% of GDP in 2009, and employed only 0.4% of the working population in 2005/06. Yemen's proven petroleum reserves totalled 2,670m. barrels at the end of 2009, sufficient to maintain production at that year's levels for more than 24 years. Petroleum production averaged 298,000 barrels per day (b/d) during 2009. The value of exports of petroleum and petroleum products accounted for 88.4% of the value of total exports in 2009. There are also significant reserves of natural gas: proven reserves at the end of 2009 were 490,000m. cu m. Salt and gypsum are also exploited on a large scale. It was announced in late 2008 that the country's first gold mine was to be established at Haddah, on the border with Saudi Arabia. In addition, there are deposits of copper, lead, zinc, sulphur and molybdenum. The GDP of the mining sector decreased at an estimated average annual rate of 5.1% in 2000–09; real mining GDP contracted by 6.6% in 2009, according to provisional estimates.

The manufacturing sector contributed an estimated 8.2% of GDP in 2009; in 2005/06 some 5.5% of the working population were employed in the sector. The most important branches of manufacturing are food-processing, petroleum refining, construction materials (particularly cement and iron and steel), paper and paper products, and traditional light industries (including textiles, leather goods and jewellery). Production of liquefied natural gas (LNG) commenced in October 2009. Real growth in manufacturing GDP was estimated at an average of 4.1% annually in 2000–09; according to provisional estimates, the sector's real GDP increased by 4.5% in 2009.

Construction contributed an estimated 4.5% of GDP in 2009, and employed 12.1% of the working population in 2005/06. The real GDP of the sector increased at an estimated average annual rate of 9.6% in 2000–09; construction GDP grew by some 5.8% in 2009, according to provisional estimates.

Some domestic energy requirements are served by locally produced petroleum, but the country is somewhat reliant on fuel imports (particularly petroleum from other producers in the region). Imports of fuel and energy comprised 20.9% of the value of total imports in 2009. The northern and southern electricity grids were linked in 1997.

The services sector contributed an estimated 55.5% of GDP in 2009, and employed 46.4% of the working population in 2005/06. A free trade zone at Aden was inaugurated in May 1991. Security concerns have undermined Yemen's attractiveness as a destination for tourists and investment. The real GDP of the services sector increased at an estimated average annual rate of 8.9% in 2000–09; real services GDP expanded by 7.3% in 2009, according to provisional estimates.

In 2009 Yemen recorded a visible trade deficit of US $2,012.8m., and there was a deficit of $2,564.9m. on the current account of the balance of payments. In 2009 the principal source of imports (9.9%) was the United Arab Emirates (UAE);

other major suppliers were the People's Republic of China, the USA, Japan and Saudi Arabia. In that year China was the main export destination (25.2%). Other important export markets were Thailand, India, Singapore, South Africa, the UAE and Japan. The principal exports in 2009 were mineral fuels and lubricants (89.5%). The main imports in that year were food and live animals (especially cereals and cereal preparations), machinery and transport equipment, and mineral fuels and lubricants.

A preliminary budget deficit of YR 567,300m. was recorded in 2009. Yemen's general government gross debt was YR 2,601,820m. in 2009, equivalent to 51.0% of GDP. Total external debt at the end of 2008 was estimated to be US $6,257.9m., of which $5,679.1m. was public and publicly guaranteed debt. In that year the cost of debt-servicing was equivalent to 2.4% of the value of exports of goods, services and income. The annual rate of inflation averaged 12.1% in 2000–08, according to ILO figures; consumer prices increased by 7.0% in 2008. The rate of unemployment was estimated at 14.6% of the labour force in 2009.

In view of the near-exhaustion of Yemen's petroleum reserves, diversification of the economy remained a priority if Yemen's high level of poverty and the needs of a rapidly expanding population were to be addressed. The commencement of output by a new LNG plant in late 2009 was expected to prove a significant new source of revenue, but this would be insufficient to offset an eventual loss of oil income. Beyond the hydrocarbons sector, substantial investment in infrastructure, as well as effective efforts to alleviate security concerns, were required to facilitate development of the tourism industry. Security concerns also remain to be resolved in the maritime sector, and have notably been a disincentive to offshore exploration for hydrocarbons, while severe shortages of water have impeded diversification in the agriculture sector. Although the global financial crisis from late 2008 had a limited impact on economic growth, Yemen's fiscal deficit widened to US $2,300m. in 2009, considerably in excess of the $1,960m. originally forecast; the larger-than-anticipated deficit was attributed to declining foreign investment, as well as decreased oil and gas revenues owing to reduced output and lower oil prices. In August 2010 the IMF approved a three-year Extended Credit Facility (ECF) for Yemen, which was intended to support the Yemeni Government's efforts to diversify the economy, restructure government finances, alleviate poverty, and bolster foreign investment inflows. The ECF arrangement, which provided for the disbursement of $368m. over a three-year period, of which $52.8m. was made available immediately, targeted a reduction in the fiscal deficit from about 10% of GDP in 2009 to approximately 3.5% by 2013, which was to be achieved by, *inter alia*, reducing fuel subsidies, containing non-essential current expenditure, and implementing a series of tax policy and administration reforms, including the elimination of the majority of existing income tax and customs duty exemptions, which, it was hoped, would reduce the country's reliance on the hydrocarbons sector. The IMF stressed that support from the international donor community would be 'vital' if Yemen's development programme were to achieve tangible success. Data released in April 2011 indicated that most major economic sectors, including oil, tourism, and national and foreign investments, as well as the foreign exchange rate, had been significantly disrupted by the ongoing anti-Government protests (see Contemporary Political History). The IMF forecast a slowing in GDP growth to 3.4% in 2011, from an estimated 8.0% in 2010. Meanwhile, inflation eased significantly in 2009, decreasing from an annual average of 19.0% in 2008 to just 5.4% in 2009, as the global economic slowdown precipitated a reduction in food and other commodity prices. However, according to Central Bank data, the rate of inflation accelerated to an annual average of 9.8% in 2010, and stood at 12.5% at year-end, increasing further to 12.9% in January 2011, as food prices rose.

PUBLIC HOLIDAYS

2012: 1 January (New Year's Day), 4 February* (Mouloud, Birth of the Prophet), 1 May (Labour Day), 22 May (National Day of the Republic—Unification Day), 19 July* (Ramadan begins), 18 August* (Id al-Fitr, end of Ramadan), 26 September (National Day—Establishment of the Yemen Arab Republic), 14 October (Revolution Day), 25 October* (Id al-Adha, Feast of the Sacrifice), 14 November* (Muharram, Islamic New Year), 30 November (Independence Day—Establishment of the People's Republic of Southern Yemen).

* These holidays are dependent on the Islamic lunar calendar and may vary by one or two days from the dates given.

Statistical Survey

Sources (unless otherwise indicated): Republic of Yemen Central Statistical Organization, POB 13434, San'a; tel. (1) 250619; fax (1) 250664; e-mail csoi@y.net.ye; internet www.cso-yemen.org; Central Bank of Yemen, POB 59, Ali Abd al-Mughni St, San'a; tel. (1) 274314; fax (1) 274360; e-mail cbyh@y.net.ye; internet www.centralbank.gov.ye.

Area and Population

AREA, POPULATION AND DENSITY

Area (sq km)	536,869*
Population (census results)	
16 December 1994†	14,587,807
16 December 2004‡	
Males	10,036,953
Females	9,648,208
Total	19,685,161
Population (UN estimates at mid-year)§	
2009	23,580,220
2010	24,255,928
2011	24,943,950
Density (per sq km) at mid-2011	46.5

* 207,286 sq miles.
† Excluding adjustment for underenumeration.
‡ Population is *de jure*.
§ Source: UN, *World Population Prospects: The 2008 Revision*.

POPULATION BY AGE AND SEX
(UN estimates at mid-2011)

	Males	Females	Total
0–14	5,450,548	5,251,964	10,702,512
15–64	6,880,368	6,758,307	13,638,675
65 and over	276,064	326,699	602,763
Total	12,606,980	12,336,970	24,943,950

Source: UN, *World Population Prospects: The 2008 Revision*.

PRINCIPAL TOWNS
(population at 1994 census)

San'a (capital)	954,448	Hodeida	298,452
Aden	398,294	Mukalla	122,359
Taiz	317,571	Ibb	103,312

Source: UN, *Demographic Yearbook*.

Mid-2010 ('000, incl. suburbs, UN estimate): San'a 2,342 (Source: UN, *World Urbanization Prospects: The 2009 Revision*).

YEMEN

BIRTHS, MARRIAGES AND DEATHS
(annual averages, UN estimates)

	1995–2000	2000–05	2005–10
Birth rate (per 1,000)	42.9	38.6	37.1
Death rate (per 1,000)	10.1	8.6	7.4

Source: UN, *World Population Prospects: The 2008 Revision.*

Registered births: 256,288 in 2007; 309,373 in 2008; 271,269 in 2009.

Registered deaths: 24,449 in 2007; 30,463 in 2008; 31,914 in 2009.

Marriages (2002, estimate): 10,934 (Source: UN, *Demographic Yearbook*).

Life expectancy (years at birth, WHO estimates): 64 (males 63; females 66) in 2008 (Source: WHO, *World Health Statistics*).

EMPLOYMENT
(persons aged 15 years and over, 2005/06)

	Males	Females	Total
Agriculture, hunting and forestry	1,260,796	113,797	1,374,593
Fishing	31,506	—	31,506
Mining and quarrying	14,225	735	14,959
Manufacturing	200,339	21,799	222,138
Electricity, gas and water	18,466	308	18,773
Construction	485,048	816	485,864
Trade, restaurants and hotels	641,117	9,697	650,814
Transport, storage and communications	235,681	3,796	239,477
Hotels and Restaurants	72,992	1,063	74,054
Finance, insurance and real estate	37,368	2,539	39,907
Education	196,594	49,535	246,129
Health and social welfare	38,146	16,763	54,909
Personal and social services	72,163	5,282	77,445
Public administration and defence	436,802	16,730	453,532
Private households with employed persons	15,196	8,106	23,302
Sub-total	3,756,438	250,967	4,007,404
Unspecified	73,363	68,679	142,043
Total	3,829,801	319,646	4,149,447

Mid-2011 (estimates in '000): Agriculture, etc. 2,358; Total labour force 6,243 (Source: FAO).

Health and Welfare

KEY INDICATORS

Total fertility rate (children per woman, 2008)	5.2
Under-5 mortality rate (per 1,000 live births, 2008)	69
HIV/AIDS (% of persons aged 15–49, 2003)	0.1
Physicians (per 1,000 head, 2004)	0.3
Hospital beds (per 1,000 head, 2006)	0.7
Health expenditure (2007): US $ per head (PPP)	104
Health expenditure (2007): % of GDP	3.9
Health expenditure (2007): public (% of total)	39.6
Access to water (% of persons, 2008)	62
Access to sanitation (% of persons, 2008)	52
Total carbon dioxide emissions ('000 metric tons, 2007)	21,958.4
Carbon dioxide emissions per head (metric tons, 2007)	1.0
Human Development Index (2010): ranking	133
Human Development Index (2010): value	0.439

For sources and definitions, see explanatory note on p. vi.

Agriculture

PRINCIPAL CROPS
('000 metric tons)

	2007	2008	2009
Wheat	219	170	222
Barley	35	27	23
Maize	87	66	56
Millet	88	74	62
Sorghum	601	377	312
Potatoes	249	264	278
Chick-peas	63	58	51
Sesame seed	23	24	24
Seed cotton	23	24	25
Tomatoes	233	240	251
Cucumbers and gherkins	14	15	n.a.
Chillies and peppers, green*	17	17	n.a.
Onions, dry	191	203	216
Garlic*	8	8	n.a.
Beans, green*	3	3	n.a.
Carrots and turnips	14	15	n.a.
Okra	21	22	n.a.
Watermelons	162	166	n.a.
Cantaloupes and other melons	27	30	n.a.
Bananas	120	129	132
Oranges	129	131	113
Tangerines, mandarins, etc.	21	22	22
Grapes	126	127	129
Mangoes, mangosteens and guavas	369	388	405
Dates	54	55	57
Papayas	23	24	25
Coffee, green	18	19	19
Tobacco, unmanufactured	21	22	n.a.

* FAO estimates.

Aggregate production ('000 metric tons, may include official, semi-official or estimated data): Total cereals 1,029 in 2007, 714 in 2008, 674 in 2009; Total roots and tubers 249 in 2007, 264 in 2008, 278 in 2009; Total vegetables (incl. melons) 744 in 2007, 772 in 2008, 797 in 2009; Total fruits (excl. melons) 937 in 2007, 974 in 2008, 981 in 2009.

Source: FAO.

LIVESTOCK
('000 head, year ending September)

	2007	2008	2009
Horses*	3	3	n.a.
Asses*	500	500	n.a.
Cattle	1,495	1,531	1,567
Camels	365	373	384
Sheep	8,589	8,889	9,087
Goats	8,414	8,708	8,883
Chickens (million)*	51,000	51,000	58,000

* FAO estimates.

Source: FAO.

LIVESTOCK PRODUCTS
('000 metric tons)

	2007	2008	2009
Cattle meat	81.9	90.2	99.4
Sheep meat	26.8	28.9	30.7
Goat meat	26.1	29.6	31.6
Chicken meat	129.5	135.6	139.7
Camels' milk*	18.1	18.0	18.0
Cows' milk	248.3	272.2	n.a.
Sheep's milk	35.0	39.0	42.1
Goats' milk	45.4	49.3	52.3
Hen eggs	53.6†	56.4†	n.a.
Wool, greasy*	7.0	7.0	7.0

* FAO estimates.
† Unofficial figure.

Source: FAO.

YEMEN

Forestry

ROUNDWOOD REMOVALS
('000 cubic metres, excl. bark, estimates)

	2007	2008	2009
Total (all fuel wood)	395	410	425

Source: FAO.

Fishing

('000 metric tons, live weight of capture)

	2006	2007	2008
Demersal percomorphs*	13.2	14.2	8.1
Indian oil sardine*	19.3	18.0	17.7
Yellowfin tuna	19.2	15.8	13.7
Pelagic percomorphs*	101.5	63.0	34.0
Sharks, rays and skates, etc.*	12.6	12.4	5.5
Cuttlefish and bobtail squids	16.8	9.5	6.0
Total catch (incl. others)*	229.7	179.9	127.1

* FAO estimates.
Source: FAO.

Mining

('000 metric tons, unless otherwise indicated)

	2007	2008	2009
Crude petroleum	16,262	14,368	14,046
Natural gas (million cu m)*	29,200	30,000	30,000
Salt	61	65	65
Gypsum (crude)	92	100	100

* Gross production.

Sources: BP, *Statistical Review of World Energy*; US Geological Survey.

Industry

SELECTED PRODUCTS
('000 barrels unless otherwise indicated)

	2007	2008	2009
Mineral water (million litres)	340*	401*	n.a.
Soft drinks (million litres)	229*	270*	n.a.
Cigarettes (million packets)	177*	215*	n.a.
Liquefied petroleum gas ('000 metric tons)	817	758	n.a.
Motor spirit*	5,110	5,110	5,110
Kerosene*	4,052	4,052	4,052
Distillate fuel oils*	7,775	7,775	7,775
Residual fuel oils*	3,723	3,723	14,750
Cement ('000 metric tons)	1,728	2,111	2,118
Paints ('000 litres)	38,347*	47,551*	n.a.
Plastic bags (metric tons)	31,562*	39,768*	n.a.
Electric energy (million kWh)	6,027	6,546	6,749

* Estimated figure(s).

Source: partly US Geological Survey.

Finance

CURRENCY AND EXCHANGE RATES

Monetary Units
100 fils = 1 Yemeni riyal (YR).

Sterling, Dollar and Euro Equivalents (29 October 2010)
£1 sterling = YR 340.89;
US $1 = YR 214.10;
€1 = YR 296.68;
YR 1,000 = £2.93 = $4.67 = €3.37.

Average Exchange Rate (YR per US $)
2007   198.953
2008   199.764
2009   202.847

Note: The exchange rate of US $1 = YR 9.76, established in the YAR in 1988, remained in force until February 1990, when a new rate of $1 = YR 12.01 was introduced. Following the merger of the two Yemens in May 1990, the YAR's currency was adopted as the currency of the unified country. In March 1995 the official exchange rate was amended from YR 12.01 to YR 50.04 per US dollar. The rate has since been adjusted. From mid-1996 data refer to a market-determined exchange rate, applicable to most private transactions.

CENTRAL GOVERNMENT BUDGET
(YR '000 million)

Revenue*	2007	2008	2009†
Oil and gas	947.9	1,456.3	744.5
Exports	486.4	837.3	377.7
Domestic revenues	461.5	619.0	366.8
Non-oil revenues	466.5	522.3	511.4
Tax revenues	315.4	371.4	406.0
Non-tax revenues	151.1	150.9	105.4
Total	1,414.4	1,978.6	1,255.9

Expenditure	2007	2008	2009†
Current expenditure	1,352.5	1,866.5	1,476.3
Civil wages and salaries	494.5	578.0	559.3
Materials and services	202.2	192.4	192.1
Interest	97.4	125.9	127.1
Domestic	87.3	115.0	113.8
Foreign	10.1	10.9	13.3
Transfers and subsidies	533.5	940.4	568.6
Current transfers	125.8	175.1	171.6
Subsidies	407.7	765.3	397.0
Other current expenditure	24.9	29.8	29.2
Capital development expenditure	310.0	300.4	297.8
Net lending	71.0	54.7	69.8
Total	1,733.5	2,221.6	1,843.9

* Excluding grants received (YR '000 million): 14.7 in 2007; 14.2 in 2008; 20.7 in 2009 (preliminary).
† Preliminary figures.

INTERNATIONAL RESERVES
(US $ million at 31 December)

	2008	2009	2010
Gold (national valuation)	46.1	57.4	74.4
IMF special drawing rights	0.4	313.6	280.5
Foreign exchange	8,110.9	6,622.0	5,587.8
Total	8,157.4	6,993.0	5,942.7

Source: IMF, *International Financial Statistics*.

MONEY SUPPLY
(YR million at 31 December)

	2008	2009	2010
Currency outside banks	472,225	532,372	547,284
Demand deposits at commercial banks	151,636	165,915	175,592
Total money (incl. others)	680,159	758,561	786,560

Source: IMF, *International Financial Statistics*.

YEMEN

Statistical Survey

COST OF LIVING
(Consumer Price Index; base: 2000 = 100)

	2006	2007	2008
Food	269.5	317.9	323.2
Rent	146.8	152.0	189.5
Clothing	120.0	126.2	141.6
All items (incl. others)	211.6	232.8	249.1

Source: ILO.

NATIONAL ACCOUNTS
(YR million at current prices)

National Income and Product

	2006	2007*	2008†
Domestic factor incomes	4,395,830	5,087,984	6,399,920
Consumption of fixed capital	272,055	322,058	401,871
Gross domestic product (GDP) at factor cost	4,667,885	5,410,042	6,801,791
Indirect taxes, *less* subsidies	−172,706	−265,478	−598,745
GDP in purchasers' values	4,495,179	5,144,564	6,203,046
Factor income from abroad (net)	−229,593	−254,068	−360,983
Gross national product (GNP)	4,265,586	4,890,497	5,842,063
Less Consumption of fixed capital	272,055	322,058	401,871
National income in purchasers' values	3,993,531	4,568,439	5,440,192
Other transfers from abroad (net)	258,691	269,180	410,540
National disposable income	4,252,222	4,837,619	5,850,732

Expenditure on the Gross Domestic Product

	2006	2007*	2008†
Government final consumption expenditure	585,071	757,593	821,810
Private final consumption expenditure	2,773,653	3,278,958	3,972,443
Changes in stocks	369,821	432,692	485,191
Gross fixed capital formation	751,524	990,122	1,223,406
Total domestic expenditure	4,480,069	5,459,366	6,502,850
Exports of goods and services	1,549,130	1,544,316	2,033,922
Less Imports of goods and services	1,534,019	1,859,117	2,333,726
GDP in purchasers' values	4,495,179	5,144,564	6,203,046
GDP at constant 2000 prices	2,380,299	2,491,775	2,604,037

2009 (preliminary estimates): Government final consumption expenditure 852,570; Private final consumption expenditure 4,769,554; Changes in stocks −251,261; Gross fixed capital formation 1,280,926; *Total domestic expenditure* 6,651,789; Exports of goods and services 1,419,177; *Less* Imports of goods and services 2,001,369; *GDP in purchasers' values* 6,069,598; *GDP at constant 2000 prices* 2,726,529.

Gross Domestic Product by Economic Activity

	2006	2007*	2008†
Agriculture, hunting, forestry and fishing‡	415,600	503,487	605,928
Mining and quarrying	1,410,545	1,499,488	1,939,485
Manufacturing	249,349	309,842	374,517
Electricity, gas and water	30,228	36,403	41,283
Construction	195,228	214,187	240,590
Trade, restaurants and hotels	763,311	941,524	1,120,372
Transport, storage and communications	563,957	591,237	689,192
Finance, insurance, real estate and business services	368,498	415,397	472,655
Government services	408,850	530,102	604,434
Other community, social and personal services	49,690	54,382	60,958
Private non-profit services and services to households	3,788	4,113	4,700
Sub-total	4,549,044	5,100,162	6,154,115
Import duties (net)	36,135	44,402	48,931
GDP in purchasers' values	4,495,179	5,144,564	6,203,046

* Provisional.
† Preliminary estimates.
‡ Including production of qat.

2009 (preliminary estimates): Agriculture, hunting, forestry and fishing (incl. production of qat) 732,577; Mining and quarrying 1,132,921; Manufacturing 493,974; Electricity, gas and water 44,247; Construction 271,808; Trade, restaurants and hotels 1,355,995; Transport, storage and communications 744,679; Finance, insurance, real estate and business services 568,666; Government services 597,681; Other community, social and personal services 65,035; Private non-profit services and services to households 5,380; *Sub-total* 6,012,964; Import duties (net) 56,634; *GDP in purchasers' values* 6,069,598.

BALANCE OF PAYMENTS
(US $ million)

	2007	2008	2009
Exports of goods f.o.b.	7,049.5	8,976.9	5,855.0
Imports of goods f.o.b.	−7,490.3	−9,333.8	−7,867.8
Trade balance	−440.8	−356.9	−2,012.8
Exports of services	723.8	1,205.4	1,237.2
Imports of services	−1,867.1	−2,347.6	−2,132.8
Balance on goods and services	−1,584.1	−1,499.1	−2,908.5
Other income received	384.9	321.3	115.0
Other income paid	−1,735.1	−2,236.6	−1,286.3
Balance on goods, services and income	−2,934.2	−3,414.4	−4,079.8
Current transfers received	1,474.5	2,223.0	1,628.3
Current transfers paid	−48.6	−59.8	−113.4
Current balance	−1,508.3	−1,251.2	−2,564.9
Capital account (net)	94.2	19.3	—
Direct investment from abroad	917.3	1,554.6	129.2
Portfolio investment assets	−8.5	−44.0	−13.5
Other investment assets	−87.8	157.1	−574.9
Other investment liabilities	−73.7	−137.7	142.1
Net errors and omissions	465.4	55.8	1,589.6
Overall balance	−201.3	353.9	−1,292.4

Source: IMF, *International Financial Statistics*.

YEMEN

External Trade

PRINCIPAL COMMODITIES
(distribution by SITC, US $ million)

Imports c.i.f.	2007	2008	2009
Food and live animals	1,894.3	2,334.8	2,295.4
Meat and meat preparations	137.5	132.2	182.1
Dairy products and bird eggs	211.1	225.3	191.8
Cereal and cereal preparations	953.9	1,369.8	1,219.2
Sugars, sugar preparations and honey	224.8	226.7	274.8
Beverages and tobacco	87.5	108.6	138.5
Mineral fuels and lubricants	1,824.3	3,036.7	1,922.3
Petroleum and petroleum products	1,824.2	3,027.0	1,914.0
Animal and vegetable oils and fats	132.6	148.4	108.6
Chemicals and related products	610.8	669.2	634.4
Medicinal and pharmaceutical products	228.1	246.1	243.5
Basic manufactures	1,319.7	1,288.1	1,234.6
Non-metallic mineral manufactures	172.8	163.3	162.2
Iron and steel	573.2	476.8	545.8
Machinery and transport equipment	2,044.1	2,445.9	2,147.8
Power-generating machinery and equipment	253.7	379.7	171.1
Machinery specialized for particular industries	383.5	262.4	270.3
General industrial machinery, equipment and parts	256.0	534.1	272.0
Telecommunications, sound recording and reproducing equipment	197.9	79.4	133.9
Electrical machinery, apparatus and appliances	221.5	286.5	200.8
Road vehicles	647.8	803.6	924.4
Passenger motor vehicles (excl. buses)	370.6	524.0	593.2
Miscellaneous manufactured articles	507.3	376.9	587.1
Total (incl. others)	8,510.7	10,546.2	9,184.8

Exports f.o.b.	2007	2008	2009
Food and live animals	295.9	360.7	337.5
Mineral fuels and lubricants	5,698.1	6,728.9	5,599.7
Petroleum and petroleum products	5,698.0	6,728.9	5,533.4
Petroleum oils and oils obtained from bituminous minerals, crude	4,972.8	5,879.9	5,034.5
Basic manufactures	34.9	34.1	53.5
Machinery and transport equipment	131.0	344.6	145.0
Road vehicles	52.5	147.7	64.7
Total (incl. others)	6,298.9	7,583.8	6,259.0

Source: UN, *International Trade Statistics Yearbook*.

PRINCIPAL TRADING PARTNERS
(distribution by SITC, US $ million)

Imports c.i.f.	2007	2008	2009
Armenia	195.5	60.1	n.a.
Australia	77.9	304.0	329.0
Brazil	194.5	197.3	341.6
China, People's Republic	773.8	790.7	855.1
Egypt	134.7	138.8	147.7
France (incl. Monaco)	234.4	209.2	263.5
Germany	263.6	252.5	276.2
India	385.7	461.8	340.3
Indonesia	153.2	107.9	80.9
Italy	127.1	202.8	111.7
Japan	464.4	507.0	518.7
Korea, Republic	152.6	202.4	192.6
Kuwait	424.6	660.8	398.1
Malaysia	156.7	259.5	208.0
Netherlands	67.3	397.8	299.8
Pakistan	81.1	92.4	89.2

Imports c.i.f.—continued	2007	2008	2009
Russia	197.1	127.3	117.6
Saudi Arabia	428.1	448.5	461.6
Somalia	74.2	48.0	n.a.
Switzerland-Liechtenstein	597.7	295.3	430.2
Thailand	149.3	226.6	265.1
Turkey	191.3	236.1	364.3
United Arab Emirates	966.1	1,881.8	912.2
United Kingdom	118.3	101.3	98.2
USA	649.9	769.1	588.2
Total (incl. others)	8,510.7	10,546.2	9,184.8

Exports f.o.b.	2007	2008	2009
Australia	0.1	0.2	0.1
China, People's Republic	1,317.1	2,369.8	1,577.8
Djibouti	22.8	16.4	n.a.
Egypt	48.7	24.5	23.1
France (incl. Monaco)	57.7	29.8	23.1
Germany	13.5	33.7	17.6
India	1,015.5	608.7	1,259.8
Iraq	24.1	18.2	13.2
Italy	30.8	13.0	n.a.
Japan	406.7	113.4	341.9
Korea, Democratic People's Rep.	0.1	1.3	0.0
Korea, Republic	224.3	478.2	36.3
Kuwait	127.5	188.4	96.7
Malaysia	39.1	108.6	5.2
Netherlands	1.4	1.4	31.2
Saudi Arabia	105.2	139.0	162.6
Singapore	75.9	151.9	432.4
Somalia	36.4	42.6	41.8
South Africa	260.4	208.0	393.7
Switzerland-Liechtenstein	433.9	185.2	17.9
Thailand	1,235.1	1,819.9	1,148.9
United Arab Emirates	399.3	574.1	361.8
United Kingdom	11.2	20.6	27.2
USA	217.7	70.3	26.5
Total (incl. others)	6,298.9	7,583.8	6,259.0

Source: UN, *International Trade Statistics Yearbook*.

Transport

ROAD TRAFFIC
(vehicles in use at 31 December)

	1994	1995	1996
Passenger cars	227,854	229,084	240,567
Buses and coaches	2,712	2,835	3,437
Goods vehicles	279,154	279,780	291,149

2004: Private cars 285,335; Taxi cars 36,371; Buses 22,214; Lorries 127,213; Motorcycles 64,845.

Source: IRF, *World Road Statistics*.

2007 (registered vehicles): Private cars 273,867; Taxi cars 97,766.

SHIPPING

Merchant Fleet
(registered at 31 December)

	2007	2008	2009
Number of vessels	47	48	50
Total displacement ('000 grt)	29.2	30.0	32.8

Source: IHS Fairplay, *World Fleet Statistics*.

YEMEN

International Sea-borne Freight Traffic
('000 metric tons unless otherwise indicated, excluding dhows)

	2007	2008	2009
Vessels called (number)	3,328	3,119	2,831
Dry cargo:*			
goods loaded	388	423	400
goods unloaded	7,105	6,446	7,006
Oil products:			
goods loaded	5,045	5,612	5,146
goods unloaded	10,135	11,364	11,541

* Excluding livestock and vehicles.

CIVIL AVIATION
(traffic on scheduled services)

	2004	2005	2006
Kilometres flown (million)	22	24	22
Passengers carried ('000)	1,022	1,083	978
Passenger-km (million)	2,473	2,812	2,815
Total ton-km (million)	282	320	291

Source: UN, *Statistical Yearbook*.

Passenger carried ('000): 2,023 in 2007; 2,240 in 2008; 2,272 in 2009.

Freight carried (metric tons): 19,220 in 2007; 25,166 in 2008; 22,054 in 2009.

Tourism

TOURISM ARRIVALS

	2007	2008	2009
Africa	10,485	10,836	16,418
Sudan	2,451	2,275	3,190
Americas	17,613	18,118	25,493
Europe	33,079	35,489	43,493
France	5,388	5,123	6,141
Germany	2,551	5,477	4,257
Italy	3,418	2,937	2,749
United Kingdom	8,892	9,128	13,844
Middle East	278,238	300,750	296,906
Egypt	11,921	10,263	14,293
Iraq	2,997	2,283	3,447
Jordan	6,159	6,604	7,880
Saudi Arabia	162,537	176,305	163,000
Syria	9,896	8,436	10,792
Total (incl. others)	379,390	404,497	433,921

Tourism receipts (US $ million): 425 in 2007; 886 in 2008; 903 in 2009.

Communications Media

	2007	2008	2009
Telephones ('000 main lines in use)	1,022	961	997
Mobile cellular telephones ('000 subscribers)	4,349	6,445	8,313
Internet users ('000)	1,116	1,579	2,349
Broadband subscribers ('000)	11	26	54

Personal computers: 600,000 (27.7 per 1,000 persons) in 2006.

Source: International Telecommunication Union.

Radio receivers ('000 in use): 1,050 in 1997.

Television receivers ('000 in use): 5,200 in 2000.

Daily newspapers: 6 titles (total circulation 83,300 copies) in 2004.

Sources: UN, *Statistical Yearbook*; UNESCO, *Statistical Yearbook*; UNESCO Institute for Statistics.

Education

(2008/09 unless otherwise indicated)

	Schools	Teachers	Males	Females	Total
Pre-primary*	63	615	4,911	4,272	9,183
Primary	11,816	111,621	2,498,675	1,828,775	4,327,450
Secondary	321	6,766	374,317	206,512	580,829
Higher	16*	7,052	178,390	77,735	256,125

* 2004/05 figure(s).

Adult literacy rate (UNESCO estimates): 60.9% (males 78.9%; females 42.8%) in 2008 (Source: UNESCO Institute for Statistics).

Directory

The Government

HEAD OF STATE

President: Field Marshal ALI ABDULLAH SALEH (took office 24 May 1990; re-elected 1 October 1994, 23 September 1999 and 20 September 2006).

Vice-President: Maj.-Gen. ABD AL-RABBUH MANSUR AL-HADI.

COUNCIL OF MINISTERS
(May 2011)

On 20 March 2011 President Ali Abdullah Saleh dismissed the Council of Ministers, amid ongoing protests against his governing regime in towns across Yemen, including the capital, San'a. (However, the administration of Prime Minister Ali Muhammad Mujawar was to remain in office on an interim basis pending the formation of a new government.) A number of senior government representatives, including Minister of Human Rights Huda Abd al-Latif al-Ban, Minister of Tourism Nabil Hassan al-Faqih and the country's ambassador to the UN, had resigned the previous week in protest against measures implemented by the security forces to quell the unrest. On 18 March President Saleh had imposed a 30-day state of emergency after 52 people were reported to have been shot dead by unidentified forces at a protest gathering in San'a; Saleh denied that forces loyal to the Government had been responsible. Mediation efforts led by the Co-operation Council for the Arab States of the Gulf (Gulf Co-operation Council) from late April resulted in an agreement over a transition to political reform, under the terms of which Saleh would step down within one month, having appointed an opposition leader to head a national unity government; members of the Saleh's General People's Congress (GPC) would account for one-half of the new administration and members of the opposition coalition 40%, while the remaining 10% would comprise members of non-affiliated political groups. Despite securing the approval of opposition representatives and of some GPC members, by late May Saleh had yet to sign the agreement.

Prime Minister: ALI MUHAMMAD MUJAWAR.

Deputy Prime Minister for Defence and Security Affairs and Minister of Local Administration: Maj.-Gen. Dr RASHAD MUHAMMAD AL-ALIMI.

Deputy Prime Minister for Economic Affairs and Minister of Planning and International Co-operation: ABD AL-KARIM ISMAIL AL-ARHABI.

Deputy Prime Minister for Local Authority Affairs: Sadiq Ahmin Abu Ras.
Minister of the Interior: Maj.-Gen. Mutahar Rashad al-Masri.
Minister of Finance: Noman Taher al-Souhaibi.
Minister of Oil and Minerals: Amir Salim al-Aidarous.
Minister of Social Affairs and Labour: Amat al-Razzak Ali Hamad.
Minister of Human Rights: (vacant).
Minister of Transport: Khalid Ibrahim al-Wazir.
Minister of Information: Hassan Ahmad al-Lawzi.
Minister of Foreign Affairs: Abu Bakr al-Kurbi.
Minister of Expatriate Affairs: Ahmad Musaead Hussein.
Minister of Electricity and Energy: Awadh Sa'ad al-Suqatri.
Minister of Legal Affairs: Rashad Ahmad al-Rassas.
Minister of Religious Endowments and Guidance: Hamoud Muhammad Abad.
Minister of Culture: Muhammad Abu Bakr al-Maflahi.
Minister of Agriculture and Irrigation: Mansour Ahmad al-Houshabi.
Minister of Industry and Trade: Hisham Sharaf.
Minister of Public Health and Population: Abd al-Karim Ras'e.
Minister of Education: Abd al-Salam al-Jawfi.
Minister of Fisheries: Muhammad Saleh Shamlan.
Minister of Justice: Ghazi Shayef al-Aghbari.
Minister of Higher Education and Scientific Research: Saleh Ali Basorra.
Minister of Technical Education and Vocational Training: Ibrahim Omar Hajri.
Minister of Tourism: (vacant).
Minister of the Civil Service and Social Security: Dr Yahya al-Shuaibi.
Minister of Communications and Information Technology: Kamal Hussein al-Jabri.
Minister of Defence: Brig.-Gen. Muhammad Nasser Ahmad Ali.
Minister of Public Works and Highways: Omar Abdullah al-Kurshumi.
Minister of Water and the Environment: Abd al-Rahman al-Iryani.
Minister of Youth and Sports: Arif Awad al-Zoka.
Minister of State for Parliament and Shoura Council Affairs: Ahmad Muhammad al-Kuhlani.
Minister of State and Mayor of San'a: Abd al-Rahman al-Aqwa.
Minister of State: Abd al-Qader Ali Hilal.
Minister of State: Abd al-Rahman Tarmoum.

MINISTRIES

Ministry of Agriculture and Irrigation: POB 2805, San'a; tel. (1) 282962; fax (1) 289509; internet www.agricultureyemen.com.
Ministry of Communications and Information Technology: POB 17045, San'a; tel. (1) 331469; fax (1) 333420; e-mail mtit@mtit.gov.ye; internet www.mtit.gov.ye.
Ministry of Culture: San'a; tel. (1) 235461; fax (1) 251557; e-mail moc@y.net.ye; internet www.mocyemen.com.
Ministry of Defence: POB 1399, San'a; tel. (1) 252374; fax (1) 252378.
Ministry of Education: San'a; tel. (1) 274548; fax (1) 274555; e-mail moetele@yemen.net.ye; internet www.moe.gov.ye.
Ministry of Electricity and Energy: POB 11422, San'a; tel. (1) 326191; fax (1) 326214; e-mail yempec@y.net.ye.
Ministry of Expatriate Affairs: San'a; tel. (1) 402643; fax (1) 400710; e-mail info@iayemen.org; internet www.iayemen.org.
Ministry of Finance: POB 190, San'a; tel. (1) 260365; fax (1) 263040; e-mail support@mofyemen.net; internet www.mof.gov.ye.
Ministry of Fisheries: San'a; tel. (1) 268583; fax (1) 263182.
Ministry of Foreign Affairs: POB 1994, San'a; tel. (1) 276612; fax (1) 286618; e-mail mofa1@mofa.gov.ye; internet www.mofa.gov.ye.
Ministry of Industry and Trade: POB 22210, San'a; tel. (1) 252345; fax (1) 252337; e-mail info@moitye.net; internet www.moit.gov.ye.
Ministry of Information: POB 3040, San'a; tel. (1) 274011; fax (1) 282004; e-mail yemen-info@y.net.ye.
Ministry of the Interior: POB 4991, San'a; tel. (1) 274147; fax (1) 332511; e-mail moi@yemen.net.ye; internet www.moi.gov.ye.
Ministry of Legal Affairs: POB 1192, San'a; tel. (1) 402213; fax (1) 402695; e-mail legal@y.net.ye; internet www.legalaffairs.gov.ye.
Ministry of Local Administration: POB 2198, San'a; tel. (1) 252532; fax (1) 251513; internet www.molayemen.com.
Ministry of Oil and Minerals: POB 81, San'a; tel. (1) 202306; fax (1) 202314; e-mail mom@y.net.ye; internet www.mom.gov.ye.
Ministry of Planning and International Co-operation: POB 175, San'a; tel. (1) 250713; fax (1) 250662; e-mail kamalmasoud@hotmail.com; internet www.mpic-yemen.org.
Ministry of Public Health and Population: POB 274160, San'a; tel. (1) 252193; fax (1) 252247; e-mail his@moh.gov.ye; internet www.mophp-ye.org.
Ministry of Public Works and Highways: San'a; tel. (1) 262602; fax (1) 262609; e-mail info@mpwh-ye.net; internet www.mpwh-ye.net.
Ministry of Social Affairs and Labour: San'a; tel. (1) 274921; fax (1) 262806.
Ministry of Technical Education and Vocational Training: POB 25235, San'a; tel. (1) 406287; fax (1) 469043; e-mail mtevt@yemen.net.ye; internet www.mtevt.info.
Ministry of Tourism: POB 5607, San'a; tel. (1) 251033; fax (1) 251034; e-mail tourism@yementourism.com; internet www.yementourism.com/gov.
Ministry of Transport: POB 2781, San'a; tel. (1) 260903; fax (1) 260901; e-mail mot@yemen.net.ye; internet www.mot.gov.ye.
Ministry of Water and the Environment: San'a; tel. (1) 418290; fax (1) 418282; internet www.mweye.org.
Ministry of Youth and Sports: POB 2414, San'a; tel. (1) 472901; fax (1) 472900; e-mail hamod.obad@yahoo.com.

President and Legislature

PRESIDENT

Presidential Election, 20 September 2006

Candidates	Valid votes cast	% of valid votes
Field Marshal Ali Abdullah Saleh	4,149,673	77.17
Faisal bin Shamlan	1,173,025	21.81
Fathi al-Azab	24,524	0.46
Yassin Abdo Saeed Nu'man	21,642	0.40
Ahmad al-Majidi	8,324	0.15
Total	**5,377,188***	**100.00**

* Excluding 648,580 invalid votes.

House of Representatives

POB 623, San'a; tel. (1) 272761; fax (1) 276099; e-mail parliament.SG@y.net.ye.
Speaker: Yahya Ali al-Ra'ei.

General Election, 27 April 2003

Party	Seats*
General People's Congress (GPC)	228
Yemeni Congregation for Reform (al-Islah)	47
Independents	14
Yemen Socialist Party (YSP)	7
Nasserite Unionist Popular Organization	3
Arab Socialist Baath Party	2
Total	**301**

* Includes the results of three by-elections held in July 2003.

Election Commission

Supreme Commission for Elections and Referendums (SCER): San'a; tel. (1) 202325; e-mail scer@y.net.ye; internet www.scer.org.ye; f. 2001; Chair. Khaled A. al-Sharif.

Political Organizations

In the former PDRY the Yemen Socialist Party (YSP) was the only legal political party until December 1989, when the formation of opposition parties was legalized. There were no political parties in the former YAR. The two leading parties that emerged in the unified Yemen were the General People's Congress and the YSP. During 1990 an estimated 30–40 further political parties were reported to have been formed, and in 1991 a law regulating the formation of political parties was approved. Following the civil war from May to

July 1994, President Saleh excluded the YSP from the new Government formed in October. There were 22 registered political parties in April 2003.

General People's Congress (GPC): San'a; e-mail gpc@y.net.ye; internet www.almotamar.net; f. 1982; a broad grouping of supporters of President Saleh; Chair. Field Marshal ALI ABDULLAH SALEH; Vice-Chair. Maj.-Gen. ABD AL-RABBUH MANSUR HADI; Sec.-Gen. ABD AL-LATIF AL-ZAYANI.

Al-Haq: San'a; f. 1995; conservative Islamic party; operates within the JMP opposition coalition; Sec.-Gen. HASSAN MUHAMMAD ZAID.

Joint Meeting Parties (JMP): San'a; f. 2006 as a coalition of five parties incl. al-Haq, al-Islah and the YSP; a sixth party, the Arab Socialist Baath Party, joined in 2008; Chair. YASIN SAID NO'MAN.

League of the Sons of Yemen (Rabitat Abna' al-Yemen—RAY): Aden; e-mail services@ray-party.org; internet www.ray-party.org; f. 1951; represents interests of southern tribes; Chair. OMAR ABDULLAH AL-JIFRI; Sec.-Gen. MOHSEN BIN FARID MUHAMMAD ABU BAKR.

Nasserite Unionist Popular Organization: Aden; tel. (1) 536497; e-mail alwahdawinet@hotmail.com; internet www.alwahdawi.net; f. 1989 as a legal party; operates within the JMP opposition coalition; Sec.-Gen. SULTAN AL-ATWANI.

National Opposition Council: San'a; a coalition of eight small opposition parties.

Yemen Socialist Party (YSP): San'a; f. 1978 to succeed the United Political Organization—National Front (UPO—NF); fmrly Marxist-Leninist 'vanguard' party based on 'scientific socialism'; has Political Bureau and Cen. Cttee; mem. of the JMP opposition coalition; Chair. YASIN SAID NO'MAN.

Yemeni Congregation for Reform (al-Islah): POB 23090, San'a; tel. (1) 213281; fax (1) 213311; e-mail an84a@hotmail.com; internet www.al-islah.net; f. 1990 by mems of the legislature, other political figures and tribal leaders; seeks constitutional reform based on Islamic law; a leading mem. of the JMP opposition coalition; Chair. Sheikh MUHAMMAD ALI AL-YADOUMI; Sec.-Gen. ABD AL-WAHAB AL-ANISI.

Other parties in Yemen include the **Arab Socialist Baath Party**; the **Federation of Popular Forces**; the **Liberation Front Party**; the **Nasserite Democratic Party**; the **National Democratic Front**; the **National Social Party**; the **Popular Nasserite Reformation Party**; the **Social Green Party**; the **Yemen League**; the **Yemeni Unionist Congregation Party**; and the **Yemeni Unionist Rally Party**.

Diplomatic Representation

EMBASSIES IN YEMEN

Algeria: POB 509, 67 Amman St, San'a; tel. (1) 206350; fax (1) 209688; Ambassador ABDELWAHAB ABU ZAHER.

Bulgaria: POB 1518, Asr, St 4, Residence 5, San'a; tel. (1) 208469; fax (1) 207924; e-mail bgemb_yem@y.net.ye; internet www.mfa.bg/en/37/; Chargé d'affaires BORIS BORISOV.

China, People's Republic: POB 482, az-Zubairy St, San'a; tel. (1) 275337; fax (1) 275341; e-mail chinaem@y.net.ye; internet ye.china-embassy.org; Ambassador LIU DENGLIN.

Cuba: POB 15256, St 6B, Blk 9, House 3, Safia Zone, nr Amman St, San'a; tel. (1) 442321; fax (1) 442322; e-mail embacubayemen@y.net.ye; Ambassador BUENAVENTURA REYES ACOSTA.

Czech Republic: POB 2501, Safiya Janoobia, St 16, House 6, San'a; tel. (1) 440946; fax (1) 440762; e-mail sanaa@embassy.mzv.cz; Ambassador JOZEF VRABEC.

Djibouti: POB 3322, 6 Amman St, San'a; tel. (1) 445236; fax (1) 445237; e-mail youssouf@y.net.ye; Ambassador SAHAL ISMAIL NAUR.

Egypt: POB 1134, Gamal Abd al-Nasser St, San'a; tel. (1) 275948; fax (1) 274196; Ambassador MUHAMMAD MORSY MUHAMMAD AWAD.

Eritrea: POB 11040, Western Safia Bldg, San'a; tel. (1) 209422; fax (1) 214088; Ambassador MOUSA YASSIN SHEIKH ALDDIN.

Ethiopia: POB 234, Al-Hamadani St, San'a; tel. (1) 208833; fax (1) 213780; e-mail ethoembs@y.net.ye; Ambassador HASAN ABDULLAH ALI.

France: POB 1286, cnr Sts 2 and 21, San'a; tel. (1) 268888; fax (1) 269160; e-mail sanaa@ambafrance-ye.org; internet www.ambafrance-ye.org; Ambassador JOSEPH SILVA.

Germany: POB 2562, Hadda, San'a; tel. (1) 413174; fax (1) 413179; e-mail info@sanaa.diplo.de; internet www.sanaa.diplo.de; Ambassador MICHAEL KLOR-BERCHTOLD.

India: POB 1154, Bldg 12, Djibouti St, San'a; tel. (1) 441251; fax (1) 441257; e-mail indiaemb@y.net.ye; internet www.eoisanaa.com.ye; Ambassador AUSAF SAYEED.

Indonesia: POB 19873, Bldg 16, Beirut St, Haddah, San'a; tel. (1) 427210; fax (1) 427212; e-mail indosan@y.net.ye; Ambassador NOUR AL-AULIA'A.

Iran: POB 1437, Haddah St, San'a; tel. (1) 413552; fax (1) 414139; e-mail iriranemb@y.net.ye; Ambassador MAHMOUD ALI ZADA.

Iraq: POB 498, South Airport Rd, San'a; tel. (1) 440184; fax (1) 440187; e-mail snaemb@iraqmofamail.net; Ambassador ASAAD ALI YASEEN.

Italy: POB 1152, Haddah St No. 131, San'a; tel. (1) 432587; fax (1) 432590; e-mail ambasciata.sanaa@esteri.it; internet www.ambsanaa.esteri.it; Ambassador ALESSANDRO FALLAVOLLITA.

Japan: POB 817, Haddah Area, San'a; tel. (1) 423700; fax (1) 417850; internet www.ye.emb-japan.go.jp; Ambassador MITSUNORI NAMBA.

Jordan: POB 2152, Hadat Damascus St, San'a; tel. (1) 413276; fax (1) 414516; e-mail sanaa@fm.gov.jo; Ambassador AHMAD ALI JARADAT.

Korea, Democratic People's Republic: POB 1209, al-Hasaba, Mazda Rd, San'a; tel. (1) 232340; Ambassador CHANG MYONG SON.

Korea, Republic: POB 5005, San'a; tel. (1) 431801; fax (1) 431806; e-mail yemen@mofat.go.kr; internet yem.mofat.go.kr/eng/af/yem/main; Ambassador PARK KYU-OCK.

Kuwait: POB 3746, South Ring Rd, San'a; tel. (1) 268876; fax (1) 268875; Ambassador FAHD SAAD SAEED AL-MAI'A.

Lebanon: POB 38, St 12, San'a; tel. (1) 203959; fax (1) 201120; e-mail lebem@y.net.ye; Ambassador HASSAN FOUAD ABI ASKAR.

Libya: POB 1506, Ring Rd, St 8, House 145, San'a; Secretary of Libyan Brotherhood Office MUSTAFA HWAIDI.

Malaysia: POB 16157, San'a; tel. (1) 429781; fax (1) 429783; e-mail malsanaa@kln.gov.my; internet www.kln.gov.my/perwakilan/yemen; Ambassador Dato' ABDUL SAMAD OTHMAN.

Mauritania: POB 19383, No. 6, Algeria St, San'a; tel. (1) 264188; fax (1) 215926; Ambassador MOHAMED AL-AMEEN AL-SALIM OULD AL-DAH.

Morocco: Faj Attan, Hay Assormi, ave Beyrouth, San'a; tel. (1) 426628; fax (1) 426627; e-mail sifama_sanaa@hotmail.com; Ambassador MUHAMMAD HAMMA.

Netherlands: POB 463, off 14th October St, San'a; tel. (1) 421800; fax 421035; e-mail saa@minbuza.nl; internet www.holland.com.ye; Ambassador R. H. BUIKEMA.

Oman: POB 6163, 14th October St, al-Gala Quarter, Bldg 2, Khormaskar, San'a; tel. (1) 208874; fax (1) 204586; e-mail sanaa@mofa.gov.om; Ambassador ABDULLAH BIN HAMAD AL-BADI.

Pakistan: POB 2848, Ring Rd, off Haddah St, San'a; tel. (1) 248814; fax (1) 248866; e-mail pakembassy@yemen.net.ye; internet www.pakistanembassyyemen.com; Ambassador Dr SYED KHAWAJA ALQAMA.

Qatar: POB 19717, San'a; tel. (1) 304640; fax (1) 304645; e-mail sanaa@mofa.gov.qa; Ambassador JASIM BIN ABD AL-AZIZ AL-BUAINAIN.

Russia: POB 1087, 26 September St, San'a; tel. (1) 278719; fax (1) 283142; e-mail remb@y.net.ye; internet www.rusemb-ye.org; Ambassador SERGEI KOZLOV.

Saudi Arabia: POB 1184, Zuhara House, Hadda Rd, San'a; tel. (1) 240429; Ambassador ALI BIN MUHAMMAD AL-HAMDAN.

Somalia: San'a; tel. (1) 208864; Ambassador MUHAMMAD DAWARE.

Spain: POB 7108, San'a; tel. (1) 429899; fax (1) 429893; e-mail emb.sanaa@maec.es; Ambassador FRANCISCO JAVIER HERGUETA GARNICA.

Sudan: POB 2561, 82 Abou al-Hassan al-Hamadani St, San'a; tel. (1) 265231; fax (1) 265234; Ambassador AWAD HUSSEIN AHMED ZARROUG.

Syria: POB 494, Hadda Rd, Damascus St 1, San'a; tel. (1) 414891; Ambassador ABD AL-GHAFOUR SABOUNI.

Tunisia: POB 2561, Diplomatic Area, St 22, San'a; tel. (1) 471845; fax (1) 471840; Ambassador TAWFIQ JABER.

Turkey: POB 18371, al-Safiya, San'a; tel. (1) 430480; fax (1) 430484; e-mail turkbe@yemen.net.ye; internet sanaa.emb.mfa.gov.tr; Ambassador MEHMET DÖNMEZ.

United Arab Emirates: POB 2250, Ring Rd, San'a; tel. (1) 248778; fax (1) 248779; Ambassador ABDULLAH MATAR AL-MAZROUEI.

United Kingdom: POB 1287, 938 Thaher Himiyar St, East Ring Rd, San'a; tel. (1) 308100; fax (1) 302454; e-mail BritishEmbassySanaa@fco.gov.uk; internet ukinyemen.fco.gov.uk; Ambassador JONATHAN WILKS.

USA: POB 22347, Sa'awan St, Sheraton Hotel District, San'a; tel. (1) 7552000; fax (1) 303182; e-mail passanaa@state.gov; internet yemen.usembassy.gov; Ambassador GERALD M. FEIERSTEIN.

Judicial System

Yemen's Constitution guarantees the independence of the judiciary and identifies Islamic law (*Shari'a*) as the basis of all laws.

Yemen is divided into 20 governorates in addition to the Capital Secretariat of San'a (a municipality), each of which is further divided into districts. Each district has a Court of First Instance in which all cases are heard by a single magistrate. Appeals against decisions of the Courts of First Instance are referred to a Court of Appeal. Each governorate has a Court of Appeal with four divisions: Civil, Criminal, Matrimonial and Commercial, each of which consists of three judges.

The Supreme Court of the Republic, which sits in San'a, rules on matters concerning the Constitution, appeals against decisions of the Courts of Appeal and cases brought against members of the legislature. The Supreme Court has eight divisions, each of which consists of five judges.

The Supreme Judicial Council supervises the proper function of the courts, and its Chairman is the President of the Republic.

Religion

ISLAM

The majority of the population are Muslims. Most are Sunni Muslims of the Shafi'a sect, except in the north-west of the country, where Zaidism (a moderate sect of the Shi'a order) is the dominant persuasion.

CHRISTIANITY

The Roman Catholic Church

Apostolic Vicariate of Southern Arabia: POB 54, Abu Dhabi, United Arab Emirates; tel. (2) 4461895; fax (2) 4465177; e-mail vicapar@eim.ae; f. 1889; fmrly Apostolic Vicariate of Arabia; renamed as above, following reorganization in 2011; responsible for a territory comprising the UAE, Oman and Yemen, with an estimated 650,000 Roman Catholics (31 December 2010); Vicar Apostolic PAUL HINDER (Titular Bishop of Macon, Georgia, resident in the UAE); Vicar Delegate for Yemen Rev. GEORGE PUDUSSERY.

The Anglican Communion

Within the Episcopal Church in Jerusalem and the Middle East, Yemen forms part of the diocese of Cyprus and the Gulf. The Anglican congregations in San'a and Aden are entirely expatriate; the Bishop in Cyprus and the Gulf is resident in Cyprus, while the Archdeacon in the Gulf is resident in Bahrain.

HINDUISM

There is a small Hindu community.

The Press

Legislation embodying the freedom of the press in the unified Republic of Yemen was enacted in May 1990. The lists below include publications that appeared in the YAR and the PDRY prior to their unification in May 1990.

DAILIES

Al-Ayyam: POB 648, al-Khalij al-Imami, Crater, Aden; tel. (2) 255170; fax (2) 255692; e-mail editor@al-ayyam-yemen.com; internet www.al-ayyam.info; f. 1958; Editor HISHAM BASHRAHEEL.

Al-Jumhuriya: Taiz Information Office, Taiz; tel. (4) 216748; Arabic; Deputy Editor ZAID MUHAMMAD AL-GHABIRI; circ. 100,000.

Al-Rabi' 'Ashar Min Uktubar (14 October): POB 4227, Crater, Aden; f. 1968; not publ. on Sat; Arabic; Editorial Dir FAROUQ MUSTAFA RIFAT; Chief Editor MUHAMMAD HUSSAIN MUHAMMAD; circ. 20,000.

Al-Sharara (The Spark): POB 4227, Crater, Aden; Arabic; circ. 6,000.

Al-Thawra (The Revolution): POB 2195, San'a; tel. (1) 262626; fax (1) 274139; e-mail contact@althawranews.net; internet www.althawranews.net; Arabic; govt-owned; Editor MUHAMMAD AL-ZORKAH; circ. 110,000.

PERIODICALS

Almotamar Net: San'a; tel. (1) 208934; fax (1) 402983; e-mail editing@almotamar.net; internet www.almotamar.net; online news organ of the General People's Congress; Editor-in-Chief ABD AL-MALIK AL-FUAIDI.

Attijarah (Trade): POB 3370, Hodeida; tel. (3) 213784; fax (3) 211528; e-mail hodcci@y.net.ye; monthly; Arabic; publ. by Hodeida Chamber of Commerce.

Al-Balagh: San'a; tel. (1) 280581; fax (1) 280584; internet www.al-balagh.net; Arabic; weekly; Editor ABDULLAH IBRAHIM.

Al-Bilad (The Country): POB 1438, San'a; weekly; Arabic; centre-right; Editor-in-Chief ABD AL-MALIK AL-FAISHANI.

Dar al-Salam (Peace): POB 1790, San'a; tel. (1) 272946; f. 1948; weekly; Arabic; political, economic and general essays; Editor ABDULLAH MUKBOOL AL-SICGUL.

Al-Hares: Aden; fortnightly; Arabic; publ. by Ministry of the Interior; circ. 8,000.

Al-Hikma (Wisdom): POB 4227, Crater, Aden; monthly; Arabic; publ. by the Writers' Union; circ. 5,000.

Al-Mithaq (The Charter): San'a; weekly; organ of the Gen. People's Congress.

Al-Ra'i al-'Am (Public Opinion): POB 293, San'a; tel. (1) 253785; fax (1) 223378; e-mail alraialaam2002@yahoo.com; internet www.alraialaam.com.ye; weekly; independent; Editor KAMAL ALUFI.

Ray: Aden; tel. (1) 400532; internet www.ray-yem.com; Arabic; organ of League of the Sons of Yemen.

Al-Risalah: POB 55777, 26 September St, Taiz; tel. (4) 214215; fax (4) 221164; e-mail alaws@y.net.ye; f. 1968; weekly; Arabic; publ. by Assalam Trading Houses.

Al-Sahwa (Awakening): POB 11126, Hadda Rd, San'a; tel. (1) 247892; fax (1) 269218; e-mail aa230317@yahoo.com; internet www.alsahwa-yemen.net; weekly; publ. by Yemeni Congregation for Reform (al-Islah); Editor-in-Chief MUHAMMAD YOUSUFI.

Sawt al-Yemen (Voice of Yemen): POB 302, San'a; weekly; Arabic.

Al-Shoura: POB 15114, San'a; tel. (1) 251106; fax (1) 251104; e-mail shoura@y.net.ye; internet www.y.net.ye/shoura; circ. 15,000.

Al-Thawry (The Revolutionary): POB 4227, Crater, Aden; internet www.althawry.org; weekly, on Sat.; Arabic; organ of Cen. Cttee of Yemen Socialist Party.

26 September: POB 17, San'a; tel. (1) 262626; fax (1) 274139; e-mail 26sept@yemen.net.ye; internet www.26september.info; armed forces weekly; Editor-in-Chief ALI AL-SHATIR; circ. 25,000.

Al-Wahda al-Watani (National Unity): Al-Baath Printing House, POB 193, San'a; tel. (1) 77511; f. 1982; fmrly Al-Omal; monthly; Editor MUHAMMAD SALEM ALI; circ. 40,000.

Al-Wahdawi: POB 13010, San'a; tel. (1) 536497; e-mail alwahdawinet@hotmail.com; internet www.alwahdawi.net; weekly; organ of Nasserite Unionist Popular Org.

Yemen Observer: POB 19183, San'a; tel. (1) 505466; fax (1) 260504; e-mail contact@yobserver.com; internet www.yobserver.com; f. 1996; twice-weekly; English; publ. by Yemen Observer Publishing House; Editor-in-Chief ZAID AL-ALAYA'A.

Yemen Post: POB 15531, San'a; tel. (1) 450262; fax (1) 450262; e-mail editor@yemenpost.net; internet www.yemenpost.net; f. 2007; English; weekly; Editor-in-Chief HAKIM AL-MASMARI.

The Yemen Times: POB 2579, Hadda St, San'a; tel. (1) 268661; fax (1) 268276; e-mail yementimes@yementimes.com; internet www.yementimes.com; f. 1990; Mon. and Thur.; English; privately owned; Editor-in-Chief NADIA AL-SAQQAF; circ. 30,000.

Yemen Today: POB 19183, San'a; tel. (1) 248444; fax (1) 260504; e-mail info@yemen-today.com; internet www.yemen-today.com; f. 2007; monthly; English; politics and current affairs; publ. by Yemen Observer Publishing House; Man. Editor DAVID MACDONALD.

Yemeni Women: POB 4227, Crater, Aden; monthly; circ. 5,000.

PRESS ASSOCIATION

Yemeni Journalists Syndicate: San'a; internet yemenjournalist.org; Chair. YASSIN AL-MASOUDI; Sec.-Gen. MARWAN AL-DAMMAJ.

NEWS AGENCY

Yemen News Agency (SABA): Five Story Office Bldg and Printing Plant, al-Jama'ah al-Arabia St, al-Hasaba, San'a; tel. (1) 252944; fax (1) 251586; e-mail info@sabanews.net; internet www.sabanews.net; f. 1990 by merger of Saba News Agency and Aden News Agency following reunification of Yemen; mem. of the Fed. of Arab News Agencies and of the Non-Aligned News Agencies; Editor-in-Chief NASR TAHA MUSTAFA.

Publishers

Armed Forces Printing Press: POB 17, San'a; tel. (1) 274240; publishes *26 September*.

14 October Corpn for Printing, Publishing, Distribution and Advertising: POB 4227, Crater, Aden; under control of the Ministry of Information; publs include *Al-Rabi' 'Ashar Min Uktubar*; Chair. AHMAD AL-HUBAISHI.

Al-Thawrah Corpn: POB 2195, San'a; fax (1) 251505; Chair. M. R. AL-ZURKAH.

YEMEN   *Directory*

Yemen Observer Publishing House: POB 19183, San'a; tel. (1) 248444; fax (1) 260504; e-mail contact@yobserver.com; internet www.yobserver.com; f. 1996; publs include *Yemen Observer* and *Yemen Today*; Publr FARIS ABDULLAH SANABANI.

PUBLISHERS' ASSOCIATION

Yemeni Publishers' Association: f. 2008; Man. Dr NABIL ABADI.

Broadcasting and Communications

TELECOMMUNICATIONS

HiTs-Unitel (Y): San'a; tel. (700) 700111; internet www.y-gsm.com; f. 2007; provides mobile telephone services; Chair. NADER KALAI; CEO IMAD HAMAD.

MTN Yemen: POB 4562, San'a; e-mail ashahidi@mtn.com.ye; internet www.mtn.com.ye; f. 2000 as Spacetel Yemen; renamed as above in 2006, following merger of MTN Group Ltd with Investcom LLC; provides mobile services; CEO RAED AHMAD.

Public Telecommunications Corpn: POB 17045, Airport Rd, al-Jiraf, San'a; tel. and fax (1) 331109; e-mail ptc@yemen.net.ye; internet www.ptc.gov.ye; state-owned; Dir-Gen. MUHAMMAD AL-KASSOUS.

Yemen International Telecommunications Co (TeleYemen): POB 168, al-Tahreer Area, San'a; tel. (1) 7522000; fax (1) 270848; e-mail teleyemen@y.net.ye; internet www.teleyemen.com.ye; f. 1990 as a jt venture with Cable and Wireless PLC (United Kingdom); wholly owned by Public Telecommunications Corpn since 2003; provides fixed-line, mobile and internet services; CEO HESHAM AL-ALAILI.

Yemen Mobile Co: San'a; internet www.yemenmobile.com.ye; f. 2004 as a subsidiary of Yemen Int. Telecommunications Co (TeleYemen); initial public offering of 45% of shares in 2006; provides mobile services; Chair. ALI NAJI NASRI; CEO SADEK MUHAMMAD MOUSLEH; 1.9m. subscribers (2009).

Yemen Co for Mobile Telephony (SabaFon): POB 18550, San'a; e-mail website@sabafon.com; internet www.sabafon.com; f. 2001; shareholders include Al-Ahmar Group For Trade, the Iran Foreign Investment Co and Batelco (Bahrain); provides mobile services; Chair. Sheikh HAMID AL-AHMAR; CEO TARIK AL-HAIDARY.

BROADCASTING

Yemen Radio and Television Corpn: POB 2182, San'a; tel. (1) 230654; fax (1) 230761; e-mail info@yemenradio.net; internet www.yemenradio.net; state-controlled; operates two television channels and eight regional radio stations for San'a, Taiz, Mukalla, Aden, Lahij, Sayoun, Hodeida and Abyan; Chair. ABDULLAH AL-ZALAB; Gen. Man. AHMAD T. SHAYANY.

Finance

(cap. = capital; res = reserves; dep. = deposits; m. = million; brs = branches; amounts in Yemeni riyals unless otherwise indicated)

BANKING

Central Bank

Central Bank of Yemen: POB 59, Ali Abd al-Mughni St, San'a; tel. (1) 274314; fax (1) 274360; e-mail cbyh@y.net.ye; internet www.centralbank.gov.ye; f. 1971; merged with Bank of Yemen in 1990; cap. 6,000m., res 275,871m., dep. 773,681m. (Dec. 2009); Gov. MUHAMMAD AWAD BIN HUMAM; Dep. Gov. MUHAMMAD AL-RUBIDI; 20 brs.

Principal Banks

Co-operative and Agricultural Credit Bank (CACBANK): POB 2015, Banks Complex, al-Zubairy St, San'a; tel. and fax (1) 250009; e-mail info@cacbank.com.ye; internet www.cacbank.com.ye; f. 1976; cap. 9,000m., res 1,155m., dep. 210,921m. (Dec. 2009); Chair. MEHDAR ABDULLAH AL-SAGGAF; 54 brs.

International Bank of Yemen YSC: POB 4444, 106 al-Zubairy St, San'a; tel. (1) 407000; fax (1) 407020; e-mail info@ibyemen.com; internet www.ibyemen.com; f. 1980; commercial bank; 75% private Yemeni interests; 25% foreign shareholders; cap. 7,000m., res 1,099m., dep. 132,753m. (Dec. 2009); Chair. HAYEL A. HAQ BESHER (acting); Gen. Man. AHMAD T. N. AL-ABSI; 19 brs.

Islamic Bank of Yemen for Finance and Investment: POB 18452, Mareb Yemen Insurance Co Bldg, al-Zubairy St, San'a; tel. (1) 206117; fax (1) 206116; internet www.islbank.com; f. 1996; savings, commercial, investment and retail banking; cap. 3,568m., res 1,449m., dep. 12,616m. (Dec. 2009); Chair. ABD AL-KAREM AL-ASWADI; Man. Dir KHALED AL-DUSARI; 5 brs.

National Bank of Yemen: POB 5, Arwa Rd, Crater, Aden; tel. (2) 253753; fax (2) 252325; e-mail nby.ho@y.net.ye; internet www.nbyemen.com; f. 1970 as Nat. Bank of South Yemen; reorg. 1971; 100% state-owned; cap. 9,000m., res 3,074m., dep. 90,387m. (Dec. 2009); Chair. and Gen. Man. ABD AL-RAHMAN MUHAMMAD AL-KUHALI; 28 brs.

Shamil Bank of Yemen and Bahrain: POB 19382, Haddah St, San'a; tel. (1) 411847; fax (1) 411848; e-mail shamilbank@y.net.ye; internet www.sbyb.net; f. 2002; cap. 6,000m., res 112m., dep. 24,541m. (Dec. 2009); Chair. AHMAD ABUBAKER OMER BAZARA.

Tadhamon International Islamic Bank: POB 2411, al-Saeed Commercial Bldg, al-Zubairy St, San'a; e-mail tib@y.net.ye; internet www.tiib.com; f. 1995 as Yemen Bank for Investment and Devt; became Tadhamon Islamic Bank in 1996; name changed as above in 2002; cap. 20,000m., res 30,399m., dep. 68,999m. (Dec. 2009); Chair. ABD AL-GABBAR HAYEL SAID; CEO RAFIQ N. SCHWARZ; 21 brs.

Yemen Bank for Reconstruction and Development (YBRD): POB 541, 26 September St, San'a; tel. (1) 270483; fax (1) 271684; e-mail ybrdho@y.net.ye; internet www.ybrd.com.ye; f. 1962; 51% state-owned; 49% owned by public shareholders; cap. 9,500m., res 2,653m., dep. 103,323m. (Dec. 2009); Chair. HUSSAIN FADHL MUHAMMAD; Gen. Man. ABD AL-NASER NOMAN AL-HAG; 43 brs.

Yemen Commercial Bank (YCB): POB 19845, al-Rowaishan Bldg, al-Zubairy St, San'a; tel. (1) 277224; fax (1) 277291; e-mail info@ycb.com.ye; internet www.ycb.com.ye; f. 1993; cap. 6,653m., res 523m., dep. 70,769m. (Dec. 2009); Chair. Sheikh MUHAMMAD BIN YAHYA AL-ROWAISHAN; Chief Exec. and Gen. Man. AYED AL-MASHNI; 13 brs.

INSURANCE

Aman Insurance Co (YSC): POB 1133, al-Zubairy St, San'a; tel. (1) 202106; fax (1) 209452; e-mail akil@amaninsurance-ye.com; internet www.y.net.ye/amaninsurance; all classes of insurance; Chair. MUHAMMAD ABDULLAH AL-SUNIDAR; Man. Dir AKIL AL-SAKKAF.

Mareb Yemen Insurance Co: POB 2284, al-Zubairy St, San'a; tel. (1) 206111; fax (1) 206118; e-mail maryinsco74@y.net.ye; internet www.marebinsurance.com.ye; f. 1974; all classes of insurance; cap. 150m.; Chair. and CEO ALI MUHAMMAD HASHIM; Gen. Man. ALI ABD AL-RASHID.

Saba Yemen Insurance Co: POB 19214, Ishaq Bldg, al-Zubairy St, San'a; tel. (1) 240908; fax (1) 240943; e-mail saba-ins@y.net.ye; internet www.saba-insurance.com; f. 1990; all classes of insurance; cap. 400m. (Jan. 2006); Chair. Sheikh MUHAMMAD BIN YAHIAH AL-ROWAISHAN; Man. Dir MUHAMMAD HUSSEIN ZAWIYAH.

Trust Yemen Insurance and Reinsurance Co: POB 18392, San'a; tel. (1) 425007; fax (1) 412570; e-mail trust-yemen@y.net.ye; internet www.trustgroup.net/Main; f. 1995; all classes of insurance; Chair. ALI DHIB; Gen. Man. HUSSAIN AYYOUB.

United Insurance Co: POB 1883, al-Saeed Commercial Bldg, 2nd Floor, al-Zubairy St, San'a; tel. (1) 555555; fax (1) 214012; e-mail uuicyemen@uicyemen.com; internet www.uicyemen.com; f. 1981; general and life insurance; cap. 400m. (2005); Chair. AHMAD SAID; Gen. Man. TAREK A. HAYEL SAID.

Al-Watania Insurance Co (YSC): POB 15497, al-Kasr St, San'a; tel. (1) 272874; fax (1) 272924; e-mail alwatania-ins@y.net.ye; internet www.alwataniains.com; f. 1993; all classes of insurance; cap. 100m. (2005); Exec. Chair. YOUSUF ABD AL-WADUD SAID.

Yemen General Insurance Co (SYC): POB 2709, YGI Bldg, 25 Algiers St, San'a; tel. (1) 442489; fax (1) 442492; e-mail ygi-san@y.net.ye; internet www.yginsurance.com; f. 1977; all classes of insurance; cap. 500m. (2005); Chair. ABD AL-GABBAR THABET; Gen. Man. BAKIR AL-MUNSHI.

Yemen Insurance Co: POB 8437, San'a; tel. (1) 272806; fax (1) 274177; e-mail sanaa@yemenins.com; internet yemenins.com; f. 1990; all classes of insurance; cap. 100m.; Chair. MUHAMMAD MUBARAK ADHBAN; Gen. Man. KHALID BASHIR TAHIR.

Yemen Insurance and Reinsurance Co: POB 456, Aden; tel. (2) 54286; fax (2) 57336; e-mail yireico@y.net.ye; f. 1969; Lloyd's Agents; cap. 5m.; Gen. Man. HUSSAIN AL-HADDAD.

Trade and Industry

GOVERNMENT AGENCIES

General Investment Authority (GIAY): POB 19022, al-Quds St, San'a; tel. (1) 262962; fax (1) 262964; e-mail info@giay.org; internet www.investinyemen.gov.ye; f. 1992; promotes and facilitates strategic investment in Yemen; Chair. SALEH MUHAMMAD SAID AL-ATTAR.

YEMEN

Yemen Economic Corpn: POB 1207, San'a; tel. (1) 262501; fax (1) 262508; e-mail yeco@yeco.biz; internet www.yeco.biz; f. 1973; promotes and facilitates investment and development across various sectors of the economy; Gen. Man. ALI MUHAMMAD AL-KUHLANI.

DEVELOPMENT ORGANIZATIONS

Agricultural Research and Extension Authority: POB 87148, Dhamar; tel. (6) 423913; fax (6) 423914; e-mail area@yemen.net.ye; internet www.area.gov.ye; Chair. Dr ISMAIL A. MUHARRAM.

Social Fund for Development (SFD): POB 15485, Fij Attan, San'a; tel. (1) 449669; fax (1) 449670; e-mail sfd@sfd-yemen.org; internet www.sfd-yemen.org; f. 1997; autonomous devt agency, governed by a bd of dirs representing the Govt, NGOs and the private sector, chaired by the Prime Minister.

Tihama Development Authority: POB 3792, Doreihemy Rd, Hodeida; e-mail arcechodeida@y.net.ye; agricultural devt agency under the supervision of the Ministry of Agriculture and Irrigation; Chair. MUHAMMAD YAHIA AL-GASHAM.

Yemen Free Zone Public Authority: POB 5842, Aden; tel. (2) 241210; fax (2) 221237; e-mail yfzpa@y.net.ye; internet www.yemenfreezone.com; f. 1991; supervises creation of a free zone for industrial investment; Vice-Chair. ABD AL-GALIL SHAIF AL-SHAIBI.

CHAMBERS OF COMMERCE

Chamber of Commerce and Industry—Aden: POB 473, Crater 101, Aden; tel. (2) 251104; fax (2) 255446; e-mail info@adenchamber.org; internet www.adenchamber.org; f. 1886; 7,708 mems (July 2006); Chair. MUHAMMAD OMER BAMASHMUS; Dir-Gen. G. AHMAD HADI SALEM.

Federation of Chambers of Commerce: POB 16992, San'a; tel. (1) 232445; fax (1) 221765; e-mail moh-saeed@fycci.org; internet www.fycci.org; Chair. MUHAMMAD ABDO SAID AN'AM; Dir-Gen. MUHAMMAD AL-MAITAMI.

Hadramout Chamber of Commerce and Industry: POB 8302, Main St, Mukalla City, Hadramout; tel. (5) 353258; fax (5) 303437; e-mail hdramoutchamber@y.net.ye; Chair. OMER A. R. BAJARASH.

Hodeida Chamber of Commerce: POB 3370, 20 al-Zubairy St, Hodeida; tel. (3) 217401; fax (3) 211528; e-mail hodcci@y.net.ye; f. 1960; 6,500 mems; cap. YR 10m.; Dir NABIL AL-WAGEEH.

Ibb Chamber of Commerce and Industry: POB 70004, Ibb; tel. (4) 404868; fax (4) 403893.

Saadah Chamber of Commerce and Industry: POB 3754-2566, Saadah; tel. (7) 521524; fax (7) 513671; Chair. MUHAMMAD R. JARMAN.

San'a Chamber of Commerce and Industry: Airport Rd, al-Hasabah St, POB 195, San'a; tel. (1) 232361; fax (1) 232412; e-mail sanaacomyemen@y.net.ye; f. 1963; over 15,000 mems; Pres. Al-Haj HUSSAIN AL-WATARI; Gen. Man. ABDULLAH H. AL-RUBAIDI.

Taiz Chamber of Commerce and Industry: POB 5029, Chamber St, Taiz; tel. (4) 210580; fax (4) 212335; e-mail taizchamber@y.net.ye; internet www.taizchamber.com; f. 1962; 5,600 mems; Chair. AHMED HAYEL SAID; Dir MOFID A. SAIF.

Thamar Chamber of Commerce and Industry: POB 87010, Thamar; tel. (5) 502200; fax (6) 501191.

STATE ENTERPRISES

While the Government is committed to privatization in all areas of trade and industry, there are still numerous state-owned enterprises:

General Corpn for Foreign Trade and Grains: POB 710, San'a; tel. (1) 202361; fax (1) 209511; f. 1976; Dir-Gen. ABD AL-RAHMAN AL-MADWAHI.

General Corpn for Manufacturing and Marketing of Cement: POB 1920, San'a; tel. (1) 215691; fax (1) 263168; Chair. AMIN ABD AL-WAHID AHMAD.

National Co for Foreign Trade: POB 90, Crater, Aden; tel. (2) 42793; fax (2) 42631; f. 1969; incorporates main foreign trading businesses (nationalized in 1970) and arranges their supply to the National Co for Home Trade; Gen. Man. AHMAD MUHAMMAD SALEH (acting).

National Co for Home Trade: POB 90, Crater, Aden; tel. (2) 41483; fax (2) 41226; f. 1969; marketing of general consumer goods, building materials, electrical goods, motor cars and spare parts, agricultural machinery, etc.; Man. Dir ABD AL-RAHMAN AL-SAILANI.

National Dockyards Co: POB 1244, Hedjuff, Aden; tel. (2) 244503; fax (2) 241681; f. 1969; maintenance and repair of ships and vessels; marine engineering; Man. Dir ABDULLAH ALI MUHAMMAD.

Yemen Drug Co for Industry and Commerce (YEDCO): POB 40, San'a; tel. (1) 370210; fax (1) 370209; e-mail yedco@y.net.ye; import, maufucture and distribution of pharmaceutical products, chemicals, medical supplies, baby foods and scientific instruments; Chair. MUHAMMAD AL-KOHLANI; Gen. Man. MUHAMMAD ALI AL-KADIR.

Yemen Trading and Construction Co: POB 1092, San'a; tel. (1) 264005; fax (1) 240624; e-mail ytcc@y.net.ye; f. 1979; initial cap. YR 100m.; Gen. Man. GHASSAN AMIN KASSIM.

STATE HYDROCARBONS COMPANIES

General Corpn for Oil and Mineral Resources: San'a; f. 1990; state petroleum co; Pres. AHMAD BARAKAT.

Ministry of Oil and Minerals: POB 81, San'a; tel. (1) 202306; fax (1) 202314; e-mail mom@y.net.ye; internet www.mom.gov.ye; responsible for the refining and marketing of petroleum products, and for prospecting and exploitation of indigenous hydrocarbons and other minerals; subsidiaries include:

Aden Refinery Co: POB 3003, Aden 110; tel. (2) 376214; fax (2) 376600; e-mail info@arc-ye.com; internet www.arc-ye.com; f. 1952; operates petroleum refinery; capacity 8.6m. metric tons per year; operates two general tankers and one chemical tanker; Exec. Dir FATHI SALEM ALI; Refinery Man. MUHAMMAD YESLAM.

Petroleum Exploration and Production Authority (PEPA): POB 7196, Haddah St, San'a; tel. (1) 442630; fax (1) 442632; e-mail pepa-expo.com@y.net.ye; internet www.pepa.com.ye; f. 1990; manages petroleum concessions; Chair. NASSER ALI AL-HOMADY.

Safer Exploration and Production Operations Co: POB 481, San'a; tel. (1) 416080; e-mail webmaster@sepocom.com; internet www.sepocye.com; f. 1997; operation of Marib/Al-Jawf Blk 18 since 2005; Exec. Man. MUHAMMAD HUSSAIN AL-HAJ.

Yemen Co for Investment in Oil and Minerals: POB 11993, San'a; tel. (1) 203925; fax (1) 203923; e-mail yicom@y.net.ye; internet www.yicom.net; promotes investment in new exploration areas; supervises operators in several exploration blocks; Exec. Gen. Man. Eng. ALI AL-KADI.

Yemen Gas Co: al-Raqas St, San'a; internet www.yemengasco.com; f. 1993 as Gen. Gas Corpn; renamed as above 1996; 100% govt-owned; production and distribution of LPG; Deputy Dir NAJEEB AL-OUD.

Yemen General Oil and Gas Corporation: POB 19137, San'a; tel. (1) 446857; fax (1) 446417; e-mail info@yogc.com.ye; internet www.yogc.com.ye; f. 1996; Exec. Dir ABD AL-KADER SHAEA.

Yemen National Oil Co: POB 5050, Ma'alla, Aden; importer and distributor of petroleum products; Gen. Man. MUHAMMAD ABD HUSSEIN.

Yemen Oil Refinery Co: POB 15203, San'a; tel. and fax (1) 218962; e-mail info@yorco.net; internet www.yorco.net; f. 1996; operates petroleum refinery at Marib; Gen. Man. Eng. MUSAD AHMAD AL-SUBARI.

Yemen Petroleum Co: tel. (1) 444046; fax (1) 447691; internet www.ypcye.com; f. 1961; responsible for marketing of oil in domestic market; Exec. Dir OMAR MUHAMMAD ISMAIL AL-ARHABI.

Yemen LNG Co Ltd: POB 15347, San'a; tel. (1) 438000; fax (1) 428042; e-mail pr@yemenlng.com; internet www.yemenlng.com; f. 2005; shareholders include Total SA (France—39.62%), Hunt Oil (USA—17.22%), Yemen Gas Co (16.73%), SK Corpn (Repub. of Korea—9.55%); operates a two-train LNG plant in Marib region; Chair. AMIR SALIM AL-AIDAROUS (Minister of Oil and Minerals); Gen. Man. JOEL FORT.

UTILITIES

Electricity

Public Electricity Corpn: POB 178, Airport Rd, San'a; tel. (1) 328141; fax (1) 328150; e-mail ypecnt@y.net.ye; Man. Dir ABD AL-MONIM MUTAHAR.

Water

General Authority for Rural Water Supply Projects (GARWSP): San'a; govt agency responsible for water supply in rural areas.

National Water Resources Authority (NWRA): POB 8944, Amran St, al-Hassaba, San'a; tel. (1) 231733; e-mail info@nwra-yemen.org; internet www.nwra-yemen.org; govt agency responsible for management of water resources; Chair. SALEM HASSAN BASHUEB.

National Water and Sewerage Authority (NWSA): POB 104, San'a; tel. (1) 250158; fax (1) 251536; e-mail NWSA@y.net.ye; govt agency responsible for water supply in urban areas.

TRADE UNIONS

Agricultural Co-operatives Union: POB 649, San'a; tel. (1) 270685; fax (1) 274125.

General Confederation of Workers: POB 1162, Ma'alla, Aden; f. 1956; affiliated to WFTU; 35,000 mems; Pres. RAJEH SALEH NAJI; Gen. Sec. ABD AL-RAZAK SHAIF.

Trade Union Federation: San'a; Pres. ALI SAIF MUQBIL.

Transport

RAILWAYS
There are no railways in Yemen.

ROADS
In 1996 Yemen had a total road network of 64,725 km, including 5,234 km of main roads and 2,474 km of secondary roads. In 2006 there were an estimated 73,200 km of roads; some 13.7% of the road network was paved.

General Corpn for Roads and Bridges: POB 1185, al-Zubairy St, Asir Rd, San'a; tel. (1) 202278; fax (1) 209571; e-mail gcrb@y.net.ye; responsible for maintenance and construction.

Yemen Land Transport Co: POB 279, Taiz St, San'a; tel. (1) 262108; fax (1) 263117; f. 1961; incorporates fmr Yemen Bus Co and all other public transport of the fmr PDRY; oversees provision of public transport; scheduled for privatization; Chair. YAHYA AHMED AL-KOHLANI; Gen. Man. SALEH ABDULLAH ABD AL-WALI.

SHIPPING
Aden is the main port. Aden Main Harbour has 28 first-class berths. In addition, there is ample room to accommodate vessels of light draught at anchor in the 18-ft dredged area. There is also 800 ft of cargo wharf accommodating vessels of 300 ft length and 18 ft draught. Aden Oil Harbour accommodates four tankers of 57,000 metric tons and up to 40 ft draught. A long-term concession to operate Aden Container Terminal and nearby Ma'alla Container Terminal, in partnership with the Gulf of Aden Port Corporation, was signed by Dubai Ports World, of the United Arab Emirates, in late 2005 and came into effect in November 2008, incorporating an estimated US $220m. upgrade programme; this was expected to increase the annual capacity from 700,000 containers in 2007 to 1.5m. containers by 2012. Total container throughput at Aden was 265,459 20-ft equivalent units in 2009. Hodeida port, on the Red Sea, also handles a considerable amount of traffic. The port of Bal Haf has been developed to accommodate natural gas liquefaction and export facilities; shipments commenced in late 2009. Al-Mukalla port, in Hadramout province, is an important regional centre for trade, fishing and shipbuilding. Plans to develop a new industrial port at Dhabah, also in Hadramout, were announced in 2009.

At 31 December 2009 Yemen's merchant fleet comprised 50 vessels, with a combined displacement of some 32,800 grt.

Regulatory and Port Authorities

Maritime Affairs Authority: POB 19395, San'a; tel. (1) 414412; fax (1) 414645; e-mail MAA-HeadOffice@y.net.ye; internet www.maa.gov.ye; f. 1990 as Public Corpn for Maritime Affairs; renamed as above 2001; protection of the marine environment; registration of ships; implementation of international maritime conventions; Capt. ABDULLAH IBRAHIM ABKAR AL-NEGRI.

Yemen Arabian Sea Ports Corpn: POB 50793, al-Mukalla, Hadramout; tel. (5) 305560; fax (5) 303508; e-mail info@portofmukalla.com; internet www.portofmukalla.com; management and supervision of ports at al-Mukalla and Socotra; Chair. ABD AL-HAFEDH AL-QUAITI.

Yemen Gulf of Aden Ports Corpn: POB 1316, Tawahi, Aden; tel. (2) 202666; fax (2) 203521; e-mail info@portofaden.net; internet www.portofaden.net; f. 1888; management and supervision of Port of Aden and other ports in the western Gulf of Aden; Chair. Capt. MUHAMMAD ISHAQ; Port Officer Capt. SHAKEEB M. ABD AL-WAHED.

Yemen Red Sea Ports Corpn: Hodeidah; tel. (3) 211603; fax (3) 211561; e-mail chirman@hodport.com; internet www.portofhodeidah.com; management and supervision of the Port of Hodeidah as the main port and ports of Mokha and Saleef as secondary ports.

Principal Shipping Companies

Atlas Shipping and Transport Co Ltd: POB 3182, Hodeida; tel. (3) 202053; fax (3) 202057; e-mail atlas@atlasye.com; internet www.atlasye.com; f. 1998; subsidiary of Al-Hadha Group; shipping agents, cargo, bunkering.

Al-Bukari Shipping Co Ltd: POB 3358, Hodeida; tel. (3) 222888; fax (3) 211741; e-mail bukari@y.net.ye; internet www.bukarishipping.com; f. 1978; shipping agents, stevedoring, cargo, bunkering; Man. Dir SULEIMAN H. AL-BUKARI.

Elkirshi Shipping and Stevedoring Co: POB 3813, al-Hamdi St, Hodeida; tel. (3) 204448; fax (3) 241199; operates at ports of Hodeida, Mocha and Salif; Contact FATHI ALI MUHAMMAD.

Gulf of Aden Shipping Co: POB 1439, Tawahi, Aden; tel. (2) 202175; fax (2) 202559; e-mail almansoob@y.net.ye; internet www.almansoob.com.ye; cargo operations, arranges crew changes, bunkers and repairs.

Hodeida Shipping and Transport Co Ltd: POB 3337, Hodeida; tel. (3) 228543; fax (3) 228533; e-mail hodship_1969@y.net.ye; internet www.hodship.aden.com.ye; f. 1969; shipping agents, stevedoring, Lloyd's agents; clearance, haulage, land transportation, cargo and vessel surveys; Chair. MUHAMMAD ABDO THABET.

Middle East Shipping Co Ltd (Mideast): POB 3700, Hayel Saeed Bldg, al-Tahreer St, Hodeida; tel. (3) 203977; fax (3) 203910; e-mail mideast@mideastshipping.com; internet www.mideastshipping.com; f. 1962; Chair. ABD AL-WASA HAYEL SAID; Gen. Man. AHMAD GAZEM SAID; brs in Mocha, Aden, Taiz, Mukalla, San'a, Salif, Ras Isa, al-Shihr.

National Shipping Co: POB 1228, Steamer Point, Aden; tel. 733553888 (mobile); fax (2) 202644; e-mail natship@y.net.ye; shipping, bunkering, clearing and forwarding, and travel agents; Dir-Gen. MOHSEN SALEM BIN BREIK.

Saba Shipping and Stevedoring Co Ltd: POB 3378/3173, Meena St, Hodeida; tel. (3) 226628; fax (3) 211588; e-mail sabaship@y.net.ye; internet www.sabashipping.com; f. 1983; shipping agents, stevedoring, cargo, bunkering.

CIVIL AVIATION
There are six international airports—San'a International (13 km from the city), Aden Civil Airport (at Khormaksar, 11 km from the port of Aden), al-Ganad (at Taiz), Mukalla (Riyan), Seyoun and Hodeida. Work on the third and final phase of a US $500m. expansion of San'a international airport was expected to be completed in 2011.

Civil Aviation and Meteorology Authority: POB 1042, San'a; tel. (1) 274717; fax (1) 274718; e-mail hasconst@cama.gov.ye; internet www.cama.gov.ye; supervisory body for civil aviation and meteorology affairs; Chair. HAMED AHMAD FARAG.

Felix Airways: Al-Hasaba St, Airport Rd, San'a; tel. (1) 252992; fax (1) 252989; e-mail hassan.thabet@felixairways.com; internet www.felixairways.com; f. 2008; 75% owned by Islamic Corpn for the Devt of the Private Sector, 25% by Yemen Airways; low-cost carrier providing domestic services from San'a and Aden and regional services to the United Arab Emirates, Oman, Saudi Arabia and Djibouti; CEO Eng. MUHAMMAD ABDULLAH AL-ARASHA; Chair. Sheikh SALEH AL-AWAJI.

Yemen Airways (Yemenia): POB 1183, Airport Rd, San'a; tel. (1) 232400; fax (1) 252991; e-mail info@yemenia.com; internet www.yemenia.com; f. 1961 as Yemen Airlines; nationalized as Yemen Airways Corpn 1972; present name adopted 1978; merged with airlines of fmr PDRY in 1996; owned 51% by Yemeni Govt and 49% by Govt of Saudi Arabia; scheduled for privatization; supervised by a ministerial cttee under the Ministry of Transport; internal services and external services to more than 30 destinations in the Middle East, Asia, Africa, Europe and the USA; Chair. and CEO ABD AL-KALEK S. AL-KADI.

Tourism

Yemen boasts areas of beautiful scenery, a favourable climate, and towns of historic and architectural importance. UNESCO has named San'a, Shibam and Zabid as World Heritage sites because of their cultural significance; in 2008 the Socotra Archipelago was added to the list of World Heritage sites as a natural landmark. However, the growth of tourism has, in recent years, been hampered by political instability, with a number of foreign tourists being victims of fatal attacks and kidnappings. In 2009 some 433,921 tourists visited Yemen; tourism receipts totalled US $903m. in that year.

Association of Yemen Tourism and Travel Agencies: San'a; e-mail ysaleh@y.net.ye; internet www.aytta.org.ye; f. 1996; Chair. YAHYA M. A. SALEH.

General Authority of Tourism: POB 129, San'a; tel. (1) 252319; fax (1) 252317; e-mail gtda@gtda.gov.ye; internet www.gtda.gov.ye; Chair. MUTAHAR TAQI.

Yemen Tourism Promotion Board: POB 5607, 48 Amman St, San'a; tel. (1) 251033; fax (1) 251034; e-mail ytpb@yementourism.com; internet www.yementourism.com; f. 1999; Exec. Dir AHMAD AL-BIEL.

Defence

The armed forces of the former YAR and the PDRY were officially merged in May 1990, but by early 1994 the process had not been completed and in May civil war broke out between the forces of the two former states, culminating in victory for the North. In October President Saleh announced plans for the modernization of the armed forces, which would include the banning of party affiliation in the security services and armed forces, and in March 1995 the full merger of the armed forces was announced.

Supreme Commander of the Armed Forces: Field Marshal ALI ABDULLAH SALEH.

Chief of the General Staff: Brig.-Gen. AHMAD ALI AL-ASHWAL.

YEMEN

Defence Budget (2010): YR 448,000m.
Military Service: conscription (formerly three years) ended in May 2001, although two-year conscription to paramilitary service still exists.
Total Armed Forces (as assessed at November 2010): 66,700: army 60,000; navy 1,700; air force 3,000; air defence 2,000.
Paramilitary Forces: an estimated 50,000-strong Ministry of the Interior Force, at least 20,000 tribal levies, and a coast guard of about 1,200.

Education

Primary education in Yemen is compulsory between the ages of six and 15. Secondary education, beginning at 15, lasts for a further three years. In the 2007/08 academic year enrolment at primary schools included 73% of children in the relevant age-group (boys 79%; girls 66%). Enrolment at secondary schools in 2004/05 was equivalent to just 37% of students in the appropriate age-group (males 49%; females 26%). In 2004/05 9,183 pupils were in pre-primary education. In 2008/09 some 4,327,450 pupils attended primary institutions. There were some 580,829 pupils in secondary education in that year. In 2008/09 some 256,125 students were enrolled at public and private universities. In 2007 public expenditure on education amounted to an estimated YR 229,861m., equivalent to 14.4% of total government spending (excluding loan repayments). A Basic Education Development project, for which the World Bank provided a loan of US $65m., aims to increase enrolment in primary schools to 85% over 40 years.

ZAMBIA

Introductory Survey

LOCATION, CLIMATE, LANGUAGE, RELIGION, FLAG, CAPITAL

The Republic of Zambia is a land-locked state in southern central Africa, bordered to the north by Tanzania and the Democratic Republic of the Congo, to the east by Malawi and Mozambique, to the south by Zimbabwe, Botswana and Namibia, and to the west by Angola. The climate is tropical, modified by altitude, with average temperatures from 18°C to 24°C (65°F–75°F). The official language is English. The principal African languages are Nyanja, Bemba, Tonga, Lozi, Lunda and Luvale. Christians comprise an estimated 50% of the population and are roughly divided between Protestants and Roman Catholics. A sizeable proportion of the population follow traditional animist beliefs. Most Asians are Muslims, although some are Hindus. The national flag (proportions 2 by 3) is green, with equal red, black and orange vertical stripes in the lower fly corner, and an orange eagle in flight in the upper fly corner. The capital is Lusaka.

CONTEMPORARY POLITICAL HISTORY

Historical Context

In 1924 control of Northern Rhodesia was transferred from the British South Africa Company to the Government of the United Kingdom. In 1953 the protectorate united with Southern Rhodesia (now Zimbabwe) and Nyasaland (now Malawi) to form the Federation of Rhodesia and Nyasaland. In 1962, following a campaign of civil disobedience organized by the United National Independence Party (UNIP), in support of demands that Northern Rhodesia be granted independence, the British Government introduced a new Constitution, which provided for a limited African franchise. In December 1963 the Federation was formally dissolved. Northern Rhodesia, which was henceforth known as Zambia, became an independent republic within the Commonwealth on 24 October 1964, with the leader of UNIP, Dr Kenneth Kaunda, as the country's first President.

Following its accession to power, the Kaunda administration supported African liberation groups operating in Southern Rhodesia (then known as Rhodesia) and Mozambique; repeated clashes along the border with both countries were reported, while incidents of internal political violence, particularly in the Copperbelt region, also occurred. In December 1972 Zambia was declared a one-party state. Kaunda, the sole candidate, was re-elected to the presidency in 1978, 1983 and 1988.

Domestic Political Affairs

In May 1990 Kaunda announced that a popular referendum on the subject of multi-party politics would take place in October of that year, and that supporters of such a system (which Kaunda and UNIP opposed) would be permitted to campaign and hold public meetings. Accordingly, in July the Movement for Multi-party Democracy (MMD), an unofficial alliance of political opponents of the Government, was formed. The MMD, which was led by a former government minister, Arthur Wina, and the Chairman of the Zambian Congress of Trade Unions (ZCTU), Frederick Chiluba, swiftly gained widespread public support. Later in July Kaunda announced that the referendum was to be postponed until August 1991, to facilitate the registration of a large section of the electorate. In September 1990, however, following the proposals by Kaunda that a multi-party political system be reintroduced, that multi-party elections be organized by October 1991, that the national referendum be abandoned, and that a commission be appointed to revise the Constitution, the National Council of UNIP endorsed plans for multi-party legislative and presidential elections, and accepted the recommendations of a parliamentary committee regarding the restructuring of the party.

In December 1990 constitutional amendments were adopted that permitted the formation of other political associations to contest the forthcoming elections. The MMD was subsequently granted official recognition. In early 1991 several prominent members of UNIP resigned from the party and declared their support for the MMD, while the ZCTU officially transferred allegiance to the MMD. Several other opposition movements were also established.

In June 1991 the constitutional commission presented a series of recommendations, including the creation of the post of Vice-President, the expansion of the National Assembly to 150 members and the establishment of a constitutional court. Kaunda accepted the majority of the proposed constitutional amendments, which were subsequently submitted for approval by the National Assembly. The MMD, however, rejected the draft, and announced that it would boycott the forthcoming elections if the National Assembly accepted the proposals. In July, following discussions between Kaunda, Chiluba and delegates from seven other political associations, Kaunda agreed to suspend the review of the draft Constitution in the National Assembly pending further negotiations. Subsequent discussions between the MMD and UNIP resulted in the establishment of a joint commission to revise the draft Constitution. In late July Kaunda conceded to opposition demands that ministers be appointed only from the National Assembly and that proposals for a constitutional court be abandoned. A provision granting the President the power to impose martial law was also rescinded.

On 2 August 1991 the National Assembly formally adopted the new Constitution. At the UNIP congress in the same month Kaunda was unanimously re-elected as President of the party. Kaunda also announced the dissociation of the armed forces from UNIP; senior officers in the armed forces were subsequently obliged to retire from the party's Central Committee. In September Kaunda officially dissociated UNIP from the State; workers in the public sector were henceforth prohibited from engaging in political activity.

On 31 October 1991 Chiluba, with 75.8% of votes cast, defeated Kaunda in the presidential election. In the concurrent legislative elections, contested by 330 candidates representing six political parties, the MMD secured 125 seats in the National Assembly, while UNIP won the remaining 25 seats; only four members of the previous Government were returned to the National Assembly. Kaunda's failure to secure re-election was attributed to widespread perceptions of economic mismanagement by his administration. On 2 November Chiluba was inaugurated as President. He appointed Levy Mwanawasa, a constitutional lawyer, as Vice-President and Leader of the National Assembly, and formed a new Cabinet. Chiluba subsequently initiated a major restructuring of the civil service and of parastatal organizations, as part of efforts to reverse the country's significant economic decline and eradicate widespread corruption among officials.

Divisions within the MMD became apparent in August 1993, when 15 prominent members (11 of whom held seats in the National Assembly) resigned from the party: they accused the Government of protecting corrupt cabinet ministers and of failing to respond to numerous reports linking senior party officials with the illegal drugs trade. Their opposition to the Government was consolidated later in the month by the formation of a new political group, the National Party (NP). In November Chiluba appointed a 22-member commission to revise the Constitution; it was announced that the draft document was to be submitted for approval by a Constituent Assembly, and subsequently by a national referendum. At partial elections for 10 of the 11 vacated seats in the National Assembly, which took place in November 1993 and April 1994, the MMD regained five seats, while the NP secured four and UNIP took one. The remaining seat was secured by UNIP at a by-election in December. Meanwhile, in July 1994 Mwanawasa resigned as Vice-President, citing long-standing differences with Chiluba, and was subsequently replaced by Brig.-Gen. Godfrey Miyanda.

In June 1995 some members of the Constitutional Review Commission rejected a final draft of the Constitution, objecting, in particular, to restrictions on the independent press, and on public gatherings and demonstrations; they claimed that the four members of the Commission who had prepared the draft had taken payments from the Government, and accused the Chairman of complicity with the authorities. Later that month, however, the draft Constitution was submitted for approval. At the end of June Kaunda was elected President of UNIP and announced his intention of seeking re-election to the state presidency, despite provisions in the draft Constitution that effectively debarred his candidature. At by-elections in 13 constituencies in September–October 1995, the MMD secured seven seats, and UNIP six. In October the Minister for Legal Affairs announced that Kaunda had not officially relinquished Malawian citizenship until 1970 (and had therefore governed illegally for six years), and that he had not obtained Zambian citizenship through the correct procedures. However, following widespread reports that the authorities intended to deport Kaunda, the Government ordered security forces to suspend investigations into the former President's citizenship (apparently owing to fears of civil unrest).

In January 1996 seven opposition parties, including UNIP and the NP, established an informal alliance to campaign in favour of democratic elections and the establishment of a Constituent Assembly to approve the draft Constitution by a process of national consensus. Opposition parties subsequently demanded that the Government abandon the draft Constitution and negotiate with them regarding electoral reform. Later that month UNIP deputies withdrew from a parliamentary debate on the draft, which was subsequently approved by a large majority in the National Assembly. On 28 May the Constitution was officially adopted by Chiluba. In early June Western donor governments suspended aid to Zambia, in protest at the constitutional provisions that effectively precluded Kaunda from contesting the presidency, while Kaunda announced that he intended to defy the ban.

Chiluba's second term

In August 1996 Chiluba and Kaunda met for discussions, as part of a programme of dialogue between the Government and opposition parties. Following Kaunda's decision to boycott a scheduled second round of discussions in September, the Government made minor concessions regarding the conduct of forthcoming elections, including assurances that votes would be counted at polling stations and that the Electoral Commission (appointed by Chiluba) would be independent; UNIP's request that the elections be conducted according to the 1991 Constitution was rejected. In mid-October 1996 Chiluba dissolved the National Assembly and announced that presidential and legislative elections would take place on 18 November. UNIP, still dissatisfied with the electoral system, announced its intention to boycott the elections and organize a campaign of civil disobedience; by early November a further six political parties had also decided to boycott the elections. There was widespread criticism of the voter registration process, in which fewer than one-half of the estimated 4.6m. eligible voters had been listed.

Despite appeals for a postponement, the elections were held as planned, and Chiluba and the MMD were returned to power by a large majority. In the presidential election Chiluba defeated the four other candidates with 72.5% of the valid votes cast. His nearest rival (with only 12.5%) was Dean Mung'omba of the Zambia Democratic Congress (ZADECO), an erstwhile opponent of Chiluba within the MMD. The MMD secured 131 of the 150 seats in the National Assembly. Of the eight other parties that contested the elections, only the NP (five seats), ZADECO (two seats) and Agenda for Zambia (AZ—two seats) won parliamentary representation, with independent candidates taking the remaining 10 seats.

Chiluba was inaugurated for a second presidential term on 21 November 1996. Amid demands for his resignation and for fresh elections to be held, Chiluba dissolved the Cabinet and placed the military on alert at the end of the month. In early December a new Government was appointed, although the main portfolios remained largely unchanged.

Political tension increased in the second half of 1997 and in August Kaunda and Roger Chongwe, the leader of the Liberal Progressive Front, were shot and wounded (Chongwe seriously) when the security forces opened fire on an opposition gathering in Kabwe, north of Lusaka. Kaunda's subsequent allegation that the shooting was an assassination attempt organized by the Government was strongly denied by Chiluba. On 28 October 1997 rebel army officers briefly captured the national television and radio station from where they proclaimed the formation of a military regime. The attempted coup was swiftly suppressed by regular military units; 15 people were arrested during the operation. Allegations by Kaunda that the Government had orchestrated the coup in order to be in a position to detain prominent members of the opposition were repeated by other opposition figures after Chiluba declared a state of emergency on 29 October, providing for the detention for 28 days without trial of people suspected of involvement in the attempted coup.

Chiluba carried out an extensive cabinet reshuffle in early December 1997. Observers interpreted the transfer to lesser cabinet posts of Miyanda and of Benjamin Mwila, hitherto the Minister of Defence, as an attempt to forestall the emergence of potential rivals to Chiluba within the MMD. Lt-Gen. Christon Tembo, hitherto the Minister of Mines and Mineral Development, replaced Miyanda as Vice-President.

On 25 December 1997 Kaunda was arrested under emergency powers and imprisoned, shortly after his return to Zambia from more than two months abroad. Numerous regional and international Governments expressed serious concern at the detention of Kaunda. On the following day Kaunda was placed under house arrest at his home in Lusaka. He was arraigned in court in January 1998, and in mid-February he was formally notified that he was to stand trial for 'misprision of treason', on the grounds that he had failed to report in advance to the authorities details allegedly known to him of the attempted coup of October 1997. Meanwhile, in late January 1998 the National Assembly voted to extend the state of emergency for a further three months; Chiluba eventually revoked the state of emergency on 17 March, following pressure from external donors. Also in March, Chiluba effected a minor cabinet reshuffle, most notably dismissing the Minister of Finance and Economic Development, Ronald Penza. In April 80 people who were being detained in connection with the attempted coup, including Kaunda and Mung'omba, were committed to summary trial in the High Court. Kaunda was released from detention in June, after charges against him were withdrawn, apparently owing to lack of evidence.

In November 1998 Penza was murdered at his home by a gang of masked men. Shortly afterwards five of the six suspects were shot dead by police officers, who claimed the motive for Penza's murder was robbery, although it was reported that nothing had been stolen. The police action, and Chiluba's subsequent approval of legislation providing for Zambia's intelligence service to be armed, were of considerable concern to human rights organizations. In December Mung'omba was granted bail, as no witnesses had provided evidence against him since his detention on charges of treason following the failed coup attempt of October 1997.

At the end of March 1999 the High Court delivered its judgment in a case concerning Kaunda's citizenship, declaring him to be a stateless person. The following day Kaunda appealed to the Supreme Court against the ruling, and later that day he escaped a reported assassination attempt, when a group of armed men opened fire on his car. In April five opposition parties, including the AZ and ZADECO, formed a new alliance, the Zambia Alliance for Progress (ZAP). However, the authorities refused to register the ZAP on the grounds that its constituent parties had not been dissolved. The ZAP initially disputed the ruling and announced its intention to appeal to the High Court, but in August ZADECO formally announced its dissolution, thus effectively losing its parliamentary seat.

In September 1999 59 soldiers were sentenced to death for their part in the failed coup against the Chiluba administration in October 1997. A further soldier was sentenced to 21 years' imprisonment for concealing information regarding the coup attempt from the authorities, while another eight soldiers were acquitted of charges of treason, owing to lack of evidence. In October 1999 55 of the soldiers sentenced to death launched an appeal against the convictions.

In March 2000 Kaunda announced his resignation as President of UNIP and his retirement from active politics. At an extraordinary congress, which was convened in Ndola in May, Francis Nkhoma, a former governor of the Bank of Zambia, was elected to replace Kaunda as President of UNIP, while Kaunda's son, Tilyenji, became the party's new Secretary-General.

In May 2000 the Minister of the Environment and Natural Resources and MMD National Treasurer, Benjamin Mwila, announced that he intended to stand in the presidential election scheduled for 2001; Chiluba had previously prohibited members of his Cabinet from publicly discussing their potential candidacy for the presidency upon the expiry of the two terms permitted to him by the Constitution. Mwila was subsequently dismissed from the Government and expelled from the MMD. In July Mwila and a number of other MMD members formed a new political movement, the Republican Party (RP); Mwila reiterated his intention to seek election to the presidency. The RP merged with the ZAP in February 2001, Mwila becoming leader of the new movement, known as the Zambia Republican Party (ZRP).

In early 2001 a number of prominent figures in the MMD publicly advocated Chiluba's election to a third presidential term, despite such an event being prohibited by the Constitution. Chiluba, while declining to reveal his intentions, was reported to have expressed a willingness to listen to the outcome of any public debate on the issue. Opposition parties and some leading MMD members (including Tembo) demanded that Chiluba announce that he would not seek re-election. In April, amid increasing controversy, a convention of the MMD approved a motion removing the stipulation that the party's President should serve a maximum of two five-year terms. Tembo, Miyanda and seven other ministers expressed their opposition to the convention's decision and were expelled from the party; their supporters subsequently alleged that intimidation by supporters of Chiluba had caused some who opposed the motion not to attend the conference. Several Western donor governments also expressed their opposition to Chiluba's re-election. In April Tilyenji Kaunda was elected as the President of UNIP.

In May 2001 a motion to impeach Chiluba for misconduct, proposed by two MMD deputies, was signed by more than one-third of the members of the National Assembly. The following day Chiluba announced that he would not seek re-election and dissolved the Cabinet. A new Cabinet was appointed some days later, with the ministers who had opposed Chiluba all being replaced—Tembo was succeeded as Vice-President by Enoch Kavindele, the Vice-President of the MMD and hitherto Minister of Health. In July the recently established Forum for Democracy and Development (FDD) won a by-election in Lusaka, occasioned by the resignation of Tembo after his expulsion from the MMD; violent confrontations between rival supporters from the MMD and FDD were reported. Meanwhile, Miyanda had established a further opposition party, the Heritage Party (HP).

The MMD adopted former Vice-President Mwanawasa as its presidential candidate in August 2001. Later that month seven opposition parties, including UNIP and the FDD, agreed to form a government of national unity following the forthcoming legislative elections, in order to provide effective opposition in the event of the MMD securing the presidency. In September Michael Chilufya Sata resigned as Minister without Portfolio and as National Secretary of the MMD, in protest at the nomination of Mwanawasa as presidential candidate. He subsequently formed a new political party, the Patriotic Front (PF). In October Tembo was elected as President of the FDD and as that party's candidate in the forthcoming presidential election.

The 2001 elections

The presidential and legislative elections took place on 27 December 2001. On 1 January 2002 (the scheduled date for the announcement of the election results) violent confrontations took place between anti-Government demonstrators and the security forces in Lusaka and Kitwe, amid allegations that the MMD had engaged in electoral fraud and voter intimidation. Mwanawasa was officially declared President the following day, with 29.2% of the valid votes cast, narrowly defeating Anderson Mazoka, the leader of the United Party for National Development (UPND, established in 1998), who secured 27.2%, while Tembo won 13.2% and Tilyenji Kaunda 10.1%. The High Court had rejected a petition for the further postponement of the declaration of the results by opposition parties, which were demanding an investigation into their allegations. The MMD secured 69 of the 150 elective seats in the National Assembly (and subsequently all eight of the seats nominated by the President); the UPND became the second largest party in the National Assembly, with 49 seats. Other parties to gain legislative representation were UNIP (with 13 seats), the FDD (12 seats), the HP (four seats), and the PF and the ZRP (one seat each); one independent candidate was also elected.

Although the MMD held only 77 of the 158 seats in the National Assembly, Mwanawasa refused to form a coalition with any of the opposition parties to ensure a working majority, and appointed a new Cabinet in early January, retaining many ministers from the previous administration. Kavindele remained Vice-President; Katele Kalumba was appointed as Minister of Foreign Affairs, while Mwanawasa assumed the defence portfolio himself.

In July 2002 the Minister of Foreign Affairs and the Chief Justice resigned, apparently in response to pressure from Mwanawasa, exerted in what was regarded as an attempt to rid the administration of corrupt officials. Later that month the National Assembly voted to remove Chiluba's immunity from prosecution, pending a review by the High Court, in order to allow his trial on charges of corruption to proceed. Mwanawasa offered Chiluba a full pardon, on condition that he return the assets he was alleged to have embezzled. The decision to remove his immunity was upheld by the High Court in August. In February 2003 the Supreme Court ruled that Chiluba's immunity could not be restored, and a few days later he was arrested and charged with stealing more than US $2m. of public funds while President.

In August 2003 Chiluba, who had been released on bail following his arrest in February, was rearrested and charged with the theft of US $29.7m. while in office. In October, amid an intensification of demands for political reform, President Mwanawasa convened a four-day national conference. The principal opposition parties and reformist civil organizations refused to participate in the conference, however. In December two concurrent trials of Chiluba commenced. The former President was reportedly arraigned on 264 charges of stealing a total of some $40m., in collaboration, in some instances, with other former government officials. In March 2004 Nevers Mumba, Vice-President since May 2003, announced that about 150 former government officials and businessmen linked to Chiluba's administration were under investigation in connection with the theft of public funds. By January 2005 the charges against Chiluba had been reduced to six counts of theft of some $488,000. In November 2006 a magistrates' court ruled that Chiluba was not fit to stand trial because of a chronic heart condition. The court ordered the release of his passport so that he could undergo medical treatment in South Africa. In August 2009 Chiluba was formally cleared of all charges, with a judge ruling that the funds he was accused of embezzling could not be traced to government sources. Meanwhile, a civil case against Chiluba (which had been initiated in the United Kingdom by Minister for Legal Affairs George Kunda) concluded in May 2007; Chiluba was found guilty of embezzling $46m. of public funds and was ordered to return the stolen money. However, in August 2010 the Zambian High Court dismissed the British judgment as legally unenforceable within Zambia, prompting criticism from the PF and US officials. The Government's subsequent failure to appeal against the High Court ruling raised doubts about the authorities' willingness to address high-level corruption. In December the High Court acquitted Regina Chiluba, the wife of the former President, of corruption, overruling a 2009 judgment that declared her guilty of embezzling state funds.

Mwanawasa re-elected

Mwanawasa, who had focused during the election campaign upon his Government's economic reforms and anti-corruption drive, secured a second presidential term on 28 September 2006, with 43.0% of the votes cast. Sata, the populist candidate of the PF, took 29.4%, while Hakainde Hichilema of the opposition United Democratic Alliance (UDA) coalition, won 25.3%. Voter turn-out was estimated at 70.8%. Sata alleged electoral fraud, claiming that as many as 400,000 votes appeared not to have been counted in areas where he had expected to win support. Clashes between PF supporters and the security forces broke out in Lusaka when the Electoral Commission of Zambia (ECZ) announced that Sata had fallen from first place to third in interim vote counts. Protesters threw stones at police who responded with tear gas and by firing live ammunition into the air. The subsequent violence, which lasted two days, and allegations of irregularities contrasted with the voting on election day, which international observers proclaimed took place in a generally efficient and transparent manner. In concurrently held parliamentary elections, the MMD took 72 seats, the PF won 43 and the UDA secured 26. Voting in two constituencies was postponed until 26 October, owing to the deaths of candidates.

Mwanawasa was in sworn in as President on 3 October 2006 and a new Cabinet was announced a few days later: Rupiah Banda was named as Vice-President, while Mundia Sikatana and George Mpombo were appointed to the foreign affairs and defence portfolios, respectively. In December Sata was arrested for allegedly making a false declaration of his assets before the presidential election; however, the charges were dropped later that month.

In February 2007 a High Court judge ruled that Zambia must pay a substantial sum to a so-called 'vulture fund' (companies that buy up the debt of poor nations cheaply when it is about to be written off, then sue for the full value of the debt plus interest). British Virgin Islands-based Donegal International paid less than US $4m. for a debt Zambia owed, but sued Zambia for a $42m. repayment. There were concerns that such funds were eradicating the benefits that international debt relief was envisaged to bring to poor countries.

In March 2007 police demolished some 250 houses in Lusaka that the authorities maintained were built without official approval. The Government announced that it was the beginning of a campaign to eradicate corruption in the way land plots were distributed. Earlier that month the Minister of Lands, Gladys Nyirongo, was dismissed for allocating plots of land to family members; in April Minister of Information and Broadcasting Services Vernon Mwaanga was removed from office. In May a further governmental reorganization was effected in which Minister of Health Angela Chifire was replaced by Brig.-Gen. Brian Chituwo, hitherto Minister of Science, Technology and Vocational Training. In August Minister of Foreign Affairs Mundia Sikatana was replaced by Kabinga Pande in another cabinet reshuffle. Pande was succeeded at the Ministry of Tourism, the Environment and Natural Resources by Michael Kaingu.

Recent developments: Banda replaces Mwanawasa

In late June 2008 President Mwanawasa suffered a stroke prior to the African Union (AU, see p. 183) summit in Egypt and was transferred to a hospital in Paris, France, for treatment. However, in mid-August his condition deteriorated suddenly and on 19 August 2008 his death was announced. Vice-President Banda replaced him as acting head of state, as stipulated in the Constitution, and was subsequently selected by the MMD to contest the presidential election, which was to be held on 30 October. (The successful candidate would serve the remainder of Mwanawasa's presidential term, which was to expire in October 2011.) At the election, which took place as scheduled, Banda narrowly defeated Sata, again representing the PF, winning 40.6% of the votes to Sata's 38.6%; Hichilema took third place in the ballot with 20.0% of the votes cast. AU monitors declared the election to be free and fair, but Sata refused to accept the result, alleging vote-rigging, and petitioned the Supreme Court for a recount; he withdrew this request in March 2009. On 1 November 2008 police used tear gas to suppress a demonstration in Lusaka, where Sata's supporters marched through deprived areas of the capital and set fire to market stalls. In mid-November 38 people were arrested when violent protests broke out in the city of Kitwe; demonstrators attacked a police station and set cars alight, apparently in response to the arrest of Frank Bwalya, a priest and manager of a Catholic radio station that had been critical of Banda's Government.

Meanwhile, Banda was sworn in as President on 2 November 2008 and later that month he appointed a new Cabinet in which George Kunda, Minister of Justice since 2001, was appointed to the vice-presidency while retaining responsibility for the justice portfolio. There were several new additions to the Government; most notably Dr Situmbeko Musokotwane, a former senior central bank official, was appointed as Minister of Finance and National Planning, and Kapemmbwa Simbao was named as Minister of Health, replacing Chituwo, who became Minister of Agriculture and Co-operatives. Banda pledged that his administration would prioritize the elimination of poverty and would take steps to improve performance in the agricultural, mining, energy and tourism sectors. In a minor government reshuffle in March 2009 Banda appointed Peter Daka as Minister of Lands, replacing Ronald Muykuma, who was named as Minister of Presidential Affairs. Gabriel Namulambe succeeded Daka as Minister of Science, Technology and Vocational Training. In July Minister of Defence George Mpombo resigned from office, and was succeeded by Kalombo Mwansa, formerly Minister of Home Affairs; Lameck Mangani was appointed to replace Mwansa. In September the death was announced of Bennie Tetamashimba, the Minister of Local Government and Housing, following a short illness. He was replaced by Eustarkio Kazonga, hitherto Deputy Minister of Defence, in November. Further minor changes to the composition of the Government were effected in January 2010 with the appointment of Brig.-Gen. Brian Chituwo as Minister of Minister of Science, Technology and Vocational Training; Daka assumed Chituwo's agriculture and co-operatives portfolio, while Gladys Lundwe became Minister of Lands.

Meanwhile, as preparations for the 2011 presidential and legislative elections began, in June 2009 the PF and the UPND announced the formation of an electoral alliance. Despite occupying opposite ends of the political spectrum, the two parties agreed to co-operate at all policy levels, and in March 2010 they confirmed their intention to field a joint presidential candidate in the forthcoming election. However, by early 2010 it had become apparent that the two parties had little policy direction in common, and that their sole shared goal was the removal of the MMD from power. The fragile coalition finally collapsed in March 2011 after the UPND announced its withdrawal from the pact. Deep divisions over the selection of a single presidential candidate had proven to be insurmountable. Meanwhile, in late 2009 disaffected members of the UPND formed the Alliance for Democracy and Development, under the interim presidency of Douglas Shing'andu, while in March 2010 the formation of a further opposition movement, the National Restoration Party, was announced.

In May 2010 Banda replaced Minister of Home Affairs Lameck Mangani with Mukondo Lungu. During the same month Katele Kalumba was found guilty of corruption while serving as Minister of Finance and National Planning (1999–2002) and received a five-year gaol term. Former Minister of Defence George Mpombo was imprisoned for two months in August after being convicted of failing to honour a cheque that he had written in December 2009; the PF accused Banda of exerting pressure on the judiciary to ensure the conviction of Mpombo, a prominent critic of the President. Meanwhile, Banda implemented a minor cabinet reshuffle in September.

In January 2011 violent clashes erupted in Western Province between the police and demonstrators demanding greater autonomy and even the complete secession of the region from Zambia. (The lands comprising Western Province, formerly known as Barotseland, had been autonomous before being incorporated into the Zambian state at independence.) Three deaths were reported, and the authorities detained nearly 125 protesters, some of whom were charged with treason. Banda accused the demonstrators of fomenting disunity within the state, but commentators noted that a lack of government investment in the poverty-ridden Western Province had acted as a catalyst for the unrest.

Foreign Affairs

In 1986 South African troops launched attacks on alleged bases of the African National Congress of South Africa (ANC) in Zambia; a number of foreigners and Zambian citizens were subsequently arrested in Zambia on suspicion of spying for South Africa. In August of that year Zambia undertook to impose economic sanctions against South Africa, and the South African Government retaliated by temporarily enforcing trade restrictions on Zambia. Further attacks on ANC targets took place during 1987–89. During the 1980s President Kaunda's support for the Governments of Angola and Mozambique resulted in attacks on Zambian civilians by Angolan rebels (with assistance from the Governments of South Africa and the USA) and by Mozambican rebels (also allegedly supported by South Africa). In September 1992 the Governments of Zambia and Angola signed a security agreement providing for common border controls. In early 1996 Zambia contributed some 1,000 troops to the UN Angola Verification Mission. Zambia consistently denied allegations, made by the Angolan Government in 1997–98, that it was providing military and logistical support to the Angolan rebel movement, União Nacional para a Independência Total de Angola (UNITA).

In early 1999, however, tension between the two countries intensified as the accusations resurfaced and a bomb severely damaged the Angolan embassy in Lusaka. In March the Angolan Government delivered a letter to the UN explaining its accusations against Zambia. The Zambian Government again refuted all allegations against it. In April, however, relations appeared to have improved, when both countries were reported to have signed an agreement aimed at resolving their differences, under the mediation of Swaziland's King Mswati III. In June the Zambian and Angolan Governments signed a further agreement, which provided for the reactivation of the joint permanent commission on defence and security and the organization of a summit between Chiluba and the Angolan President, José Eduardo dos Santos. In December it was reported that Angolan jets had bombed Zambian territory in pursuit of UNITA rebels, and in January 2000 it was announced that some 21,000 Angolan refugees had entered Zambia since October 1999. During January–February 2000 UNITA rebels carried out a series of raids on Zambian villages, which prompted Chiluba to announce that he would not permit UNITA troops to operate from Zambia. In February, following the convention of the joint permanent commission on defence and security to discuss the security situation along the common border, both sides resolved to strengthen measures against UNITA forces operating in the common border area.

In February 2001 the Governments of Zambia, Angola and Namibia agreed to establish a tripartite mechanism for political and security co-operation in an attempt to improve security on their joint borders. However, armed Angolans raided three Zambian villages close to the border in November, reportedly abducting some 100 Zambians and subsequently killing seven of them; Zambian forces claimed to have killed 10 Angolans in retaliation. Reports in the Zambian press attributed the attacks on the villages to the Angolan armed forces, which admitted occupying UNITA bases in the area, but claimed to have observed UNITA rebels crossing the border shortly before the attacks. At the end of 2002 there were 188,436 Angolan refugees in Zambia, compared with 218,154 at the beginning of the year; by the end of 2008, according to the office of the UN High Commissioner for Refugees (UNHCR), that figure had been reduced to 27,131. In July 2007 some 100 Angolan refugees refused to be repatriated until the Zambian Government paid wages due for construction work carried out in 2003. The refugees had been employed on a casual basis by a government agency that had since been dissolved. Other refugees had returned to Angola in late 2006 without receiving their wages, despite being assured that they would receive payment.

In early March 1997 the Zambian Government appealed for international assistance in coping with the influx of refugees fleeing the civil conflict in Zaire (now the Democratic Republic of the Congo—DRC); by March some 6,000 Zairean refugees had arrived in Zambia. In January 1998 Zambia and the DRC agreed to establish a joint permanent commission on defence and security. During late 1998 and early 1999 the Zambian Government was involved in regional efforts to find a political solution to the conflict in the DRC, after a rebellion was mounted against the Government in August 1998; President Chiluba was appointed to co-ordinate peace initiatives on the crisis by the Southern African Development Community (SADC, see p. 420) and the Organization of African Unity (OAU, now the AU, see p. 183). Meanwhile, thousands of Congolese entered Zambia, fleeing the renewed fighting, prompting the Government to appeal to the international community for immediate assistance to cope with the refugees, who, by then, reportedly numbered more than 30,000. In addition, several hundred DRC soldiers crossed into Zambia seeking refuge, but were subsequently repatriated. At a summit held in Lusaka during June–July 1999 a cease-fire document was formulated, providing for the withdrawal of foreign forces from the DRC and for political reform in the country. The accord was signed by the President of the DRC and the leaders of the five other countries involved in the conflict in July, and by rebel leaders in August. In March 2004 it was reported that more than 1,000 DRC nationals had entered Zambia, fleeing renewed fighting between government and rebel forces in south-eastern DRC. At the end of 2006 there were more than 64,000 refugees living in UNHCR refugee camps in Zambia, of whom 43,788 were from the DRC. In addition, UNHCR estimated that a further 75,000 refugees (including 49,000 Angolans) had settled among the Zambian population. According to UNHCR over 7,000 refugees from the DRC were repatriated between May and December 2007, and almost 10,000 were returned home in 2008. In October 2008 Zambia closed its border to refugees arriving from the DRC, owing to heavy fighting in the east of the country.

Relations with Zimbabwe deteriorated following the disputed presidential election in that country in March 2008. Mwanawasa, in his capacity as Chairman of SADC, had been highly critical of the conduct of Mugabe's ZANU—PF and had proposed the postponement of the second round of polling in view of the worsening situation in Zimbabwe. Mwanawasa also denounced the outcome of the run-off as undemocratic and unacceptable; however, his forthright stance was not endorsed by most other SADC leaders. The installation of a power-sharing government in Zimbabwe in February 2009 resulted in an improvement in relations and in May Banda pledged his support for Zimbabwe's economic recovery plan during a four-day visit to that country.

In February 2007 Chinese President Hu Jintao announced new investment worth US $800m. in Zambia after talks in Lusaka with President Mwanawasa. The two leaders stated that a special economic zone would be created in Zambia's copper-mining area in Chambishi, north of Lusaka, where Chinese firms could operate without paying import or value-added taxes. Part of Zambia's bilateral debt to the People's Republic of China was also written off. Further economic accords were concluded in early 2010, and China also agreed to assist in the construction of a new sports stadium in the Zambian capital. Additional funding was pledged by China in August in support of a large-scale power project. Chinese investment in Zambia during 2010 totalled over $1,000m. and was forecast to exceed $2,000m. in 2011. However, China's increasing economic presence within Zambia also led to accusations that Chinese business owners were exploiting the local labour force. Miners protesting against low salaries and dangerous working conditions at a coal mine in the south of the country were allegedly fired upon by the mine's Chinese managers in October 2010, resulting in injuries being sustained by 11 workers. Two Chinese men were subsequently arrested and accused of attempted murder. The shooting caused widespread public outrage, and President Banda was forced to appeal for calm amid rising anti-Chinese sentiments.

CONSTITUTION AND GOVERNMENT

Under the provisions of the Constitution, which was formally adopted in May 1996, Zambia is a multi-party state. Executive power is vested in the President, who is the constitutional Head of State. Legislative power is vested in a National Assembly, which comprises 158 members, of whom 150 are elected by universal adult suffrage, and eight nominated by the President. The President and the National Assembly are elected simultaneously by universal adult suffrage for a five-year term. The maximum duration of the President's tenure of office is limited to two five-year terms. The President governs with the assistance of a Vice-President and a Cabinet, whom he appoints from members of the National Assembly. The Constitution also provides for a 27-member House of Chiefs, which represents traditional tribal authorities. Each of Zambia's nine provinces has a minister, who is appointed by the President. In September 2009 the National Constitutional Conference approved an increase in the number of members of the National Assembly from 158 to 280. Also approved was a proposal to have 240 of those members elected by simple majority, 30 members elected by proportional representation and a maximum of 10 nominated by the President.

REGIONAL AND INTERNATIONAL CO-OPERATION

Zambia is a member of the African Union (see p. 183), of the Southern African Development Community (see p. 420) and of the Common Market for Eastern and Southern Africa (see p. 228).

Zambia became a member of the UN in 1964. As a contracting party to the General Agreement on Tariffs and Trade, Zambia joined the World Trade Organization (WTO, see p. 430) on its establishment in 1995. Zambia participates in the Group of 77 (G77, see p. 447) developing countries.

ECONOMIC AFFAIRS

In 2009, according to estimates by the World Bank, Zambia's gross national income (GNI), measured at average 2007–09 prices, was US $12,560m., equivalent to $970 per head (or $1,280 per head on an international purchasing-power parity basis). During 2000–09, it was estimated, the population increased at an average annual rate of 2.4%, while gross domestic product (GDP) per head increased, in real terms, by an average of 2.9% per year. Overall GDP increased, in real terms, at an average annual rate of 5.4% in 2000–09; growth in 2009 was 6.3%.

Agriculture (including forestry and fishing) contributed 20.9% of GDP in 2009, according to the African Development Bank (AfDB). According to the 2000 census, 71.6% of those employed were engaged in the sector. However, in 2006 only 11.7% of those in paid employment were engaged in agriculture. The principal crops are sugar cane, maize, cassava, cotton, wheat, sweet potatoes and groundnuts. Millet, rice, sorghum, tobacco, sunflower seeds and horticultural produce are also cultivated. Cattle-rearing remains important. During 2000–09, according to the World Bank, agricultural GDP increased by an average of 0.7% per year. Agricultural GDP decreased by 0.1% in 2009.

Industry (including mining, manufacturing, construction and power) contributed 32.8% of GDP in 2009, according to the AfDB, and engaged 22.7% of all those in paid employment in 2006. According to the World Bank, industrial GDP grew at an average annual rate of 9.6% in 2000–09. Industrial GDP increased by 17.6% in 2009.

In 2009 mining and quarrying contributed 1.3% of GDP, according to the AfDB, and engaged 5.5% of those in paid employment in 2006. According to the UN, exports of copper contributed 67.0% of the value of total exports in 2009. Output of copper ore increased from 514,000 metric tons in 2006 to 697,000 tons in 2009. Cobalt is also an important export, while coal, gold, emeralds, amethyst, limestone and selenium are also mined. In addition, Zambia has reserves of phosphates, fluorspar and iron ore. During 2002–06, according to the IMF, mining GDP increased by an estimated average of 8.1% per year. Mining GDP increased by 15.7% in 2009, according to the AfDB.

According to the AfDB, manufacturing contributed 9.3% of GDP in 2009. The sector engaged 11.6% of those in paid employment in 2006. The principal manufacturing activities are food-processing, the smelting and refining of copper and other metals, vehicle assembly, petroleum-refining, and the production of fertilizers, explosives, textiles, bottles, batteries, bricks and copper wire. During 2000–09, according to the World Bank, manufacturing GDP increased at an average annual rate of 5.2%. Manufacturing GDP increased by 5.1% in 2009.

Construction contributed 19.4% of GDP in 2009, according to the AfDB. The sector engaged only 3.0% of those in paid employment in 2006. During 2002–06, according to the IMF, construction GDP increased at an average annual rate of 19.4%. Sectoral GDP grew by 15.6% in 2009, according to the AfDB.

Energy is derived principally from hydroelectric power (99.4% in 2007), in which Zambia is self-sufficient. Imports of mineral fuels accounted for 13.9% of the value of merchandise imports in 2009. In an effort to address the problem of power shortages and expand availability of electricity, the construction was planned of three new hydroelectric plants during 2009–15, for which a financing requirement of some US $1,200m. was anticipated.

In 2009, according to the AfDB, the services sector contributed 46.3% of GDP. The sector engaged 65.6% of those in paid employment in 2006. According to the World Bank, the GDP of the services sector increased by an average of 6.2% per year in 2000–09. Services GDP increased by 10.9% in 2008, but decreased by 2.9% in 2009.

In 2009 Zambia recorded a trade surplus of US $905.7m., but there was a deficit of $703.1m. on the current account of the balance of payments. In 2009 the principal source of imports (40.0%) was South Africa; other major suppliers were the Democratic Republic of the Congo (DRC) and Kuwait. The principal market for exports in that year was Switzerland-Liechtenstein (accounting for 47.0% of the total); other significant purchasers were the People's Republic of China, South Africa, and the DRC. The principal export in 2009 was copper, which accounted for 67.0% of the total; metalliferous ore and metal scrap, and food and live animals were also important exports. The principal imports in that year were machinery and transport equipment, petroleum and chemicals and related products.

In 2009 there was an overall budgetary deficit of K2,395,000m., equivalent to 3.7% of GDP. A budgetary deficit of K1,941,000m. was projected by the IMF in 2010. Zambia's general government gross debt was K17,881,550m. in 2009, equivalent to 27.2% of GDP. Zambia's total external debt was US $2,986.4m. at the end of 2008, of which $1,166.7m. was public and publicly guaranteed debt. In that year the cost of servicing the debt was equivalent to 3.2% of the value of exports of goods, services and income. In 2000–10 the average annual rate of inflation was 15.4%. Consumer prices increased by 8.5% in 2010.

In the mid-2000s Zambia experienced a period of robust economic growth, attributable principally to the impact of high international prices for its major export, copper, in conjunction with extensive debt relief and the consolidation of economic restructuring under the supervision of the IMF and the World Bank. Zambia's economy successfully withstood the negative impact of the global economic slowdown, which resulted in lower copper prices from late 2008 and job losses in the industry. Increased production in the mining and agricultural sectors during late 2009, combined with the recovery of copper prices, led to GDP expansion of 6.3% in that year, according to the IMF. Rising demand for copper prompted a significant increase in output during 2010, while the agricultural sector enjoyed another year of robust production, and buoyant activity in the construction and tourism sectors was also reported. Furthermore, there was a strong resurgence in levels of foreign direct investment throughout 2010, with the manufacturing and mining industries attracting most of this capital, and the IMF estimated that GDP grew by 7.6% during the year. Under the Sixth National Development Plan (2011–15), the Government aimed to increase expenditure on poverty-reduction programmes and infrastructural investment, while promoting economic growth and diversification. With copper prices expected to remain high, the IMF forecast further GDP growth of 6.8% in 2011. Zambia's medium-term prospects were also encouraging, due to continued large-scale investment in the copper industry and the scheduled commencement of a comprehensive exploration of petroleum and gas reserves in 2011.

PUBLIC HOLIDAYS

2012: 1 January (New Year's Day), 8 March (International Women's Day), 11 March (Youth Day), 6–9 April (Easter), 1 May (Labour Day), 25 May (African Freedom Day, anniversary of OAU's foundation), 2 July (Heroes' Day), 3 July (Unity Day), 6 August (Farmers' Day), 24 October (Independence Day), 25 December (Christmas Day).

Statistical Survey

Source (unless otherwise indicated): Central Statistical Office, POB 31908, Lusaka; tel. (21) 1211231; internet www.zamstats.gov.zm.

Area and Population

AREA, POPULATION AND DENSITY

Area (sq km)	752,612*
Population (census results)	
25 October 2000	9,885,591
15 October 2010 (preliminary)	
Males	6,394,455
Females	6,652,053
Total	13,046,508
Density (per sq km) at 2010 census	17.3

* 290,585 sq miles.

POPULATION BY AGE AND SEX
(UN estimates at mid-2011)

	Males	Females	Total
0–14	3,146,680	3,113,494	6,260,174
15–64	3,446,579	3,461,242	6,907,821
65 and over	188,891	228,475	417,366
Total	6,782,150	6,803,211	13,585,361

Note: Estimates not adjusted to take account of results of 2010 census.
Source: UN, *World Population Prospects: The 2008 Revision.*

ZAMBIA

PROVINCES
(2010 census, preliminary)

	Area	Population	Density
Central	94,394	1,267,803	13.4
Copperbelt	31,328	1,958,623	62.5
Eastern	69,106	1,707,731	24.7
Luapula	50,567	958,976	19.0
Lusaka	21,896	2,198,996	100.4
Northern	147,826	1,759,600	11.9
North-Western	125,826	706,462	5.6
Southern	85,283	1,606,793	18.8
Western	126,386	881,524	7.0
Total	752,612	13,046,508	17.3

PRINCIPAL TOWNS
(population at 2000 census)

Lusaka (capital)	1,084,703	Lundazi		236,833
Kitwe	376,124	Petauke		235,879
Ndola	374,757	Choma		204,898
Chipata	367,539	Solwezi		203,797
Chibombo	241,612	Mazabuka		203,219

Mid-2010 (incl. suburbs, UN estimate): Lusaka 1,450,759 (Source: UN, *World Urbanization Prospects: The 2009 Revision*).

BIRTHS AND DEATHS
(annual averages, UN estimates)

	1995–2000	2000–05	2005–10
Birth rate (per 1,000)	45.1	44.6	43.2
Death rate (per 1,000)	19.0	20.2	17.5

Source: UN, *World Population Prospects: The 2008 Revision*.

Life expectancy (years at birth, WHO estimates): 48 (males 47; females 49) in 2008 (Source: WHO, *World Health Statistics*).

EMPLOYMENT
(Usually active population aged 12 years and over at 2000 census)

Agriculture, hunting, forestry and fishing	2,014,028
Mining and quarrying	36,463
Manufacturing	77,515
Electricity, gas and water	11,016
Construction	36,790
Wholesale and retail trade; restaurants and hotels	190,354
Transport, storage and communicationws	53,736
Financial, insurance, real estate and business services	29,151
Community, social and personal services	363,375
Total	2,812,428

Source: ILO.

2006 (persons in paid employment, labour force survey, January): Agriculture, forestry and fishing 56,139; Mining and quarrying 26,253; Manufacturing 55,709; Electricity and water 12,399; Construction 14,343; Wholesale and retail trade 65,012; Transport and communications 19,378; Finance and insurance 54,032; Public administration 176,062; *Total* 479,327 (Source: IMF, *Zambia: Statistical Appendix*, January 2008).

Mid-2011 ('000, estimates): Agriculture, etc. 3,325; Total labour force 5,308 (Source: FAO).

Health and Welfare

KEY INDICATORS

Total fertility rate (children per woman, 2008)	5.8
Under-5 mortality rate (per 1,000 live births, 2008)	148
HIV/AIDS (% of persons aged 15–49, 2007)	15.2
Physicians (per 1,000 head, 2004)	0.1
Hospital beds (per 1,000 head, 2004)	2.2
Health expenditure (2007): US $ per head (PPP)	79
Health expenditure (2007): % of GDP	6.2
Health expenditure (2007): public (% of total)	57.7
Access to water (% of persons, 2008)	60
Access to sanitation (% of persons, 2008)	49
Total carbon dioxide emissions ('000 metric tons, 2007)	2,689.4
Carbon dioxide emissions per head (metric tons, 2007)	0.2
Human Development Index (2010): ranking	150
Human Development Index (2010): value	0.395

For sources and definitions, see explanatory note on p. vi.

Agriculture

PRINCIPAL CROPS
('000 metric tons)

	2007	2008	2009
Wheat	115.8	113.2	195.5
Rice, paddy	18.3	24.0*	41.9*
Maize	1,366.2	1,445.7	1,887.0*
Millet	21.7	39.2	49.0*
Sorghum	12.8	11.4	21.8*
Potatoes	14.5†	10.5	n.a.
Sweet potatoes	67.5†	67.5*	100.0†
Cassava (Manioc)	1,100†	1,100*	900†
Sugar cane	2,500†	2,500†	n.a.
Soybeans (Soya beans)	12*	12†	12†
Groundnuts, with shell*	60	71	121
Sunflower seed*	8	8	8
Seed cotton†	140	140	140
Onions, dry	27†	27†	n.a.
Tomatoes	25†	25†	n.a.
Tobacco, unmanufactured	48†	48†	n.a.

* Unofficial figure(s).
† FAO estimate(s).

Aggregate production ('000 metric tons, may include official, semi-official or estimated data): Total cereals 1,537 in 2007, 1,636 in 2008, 2,198 in 2009; Total pulses 24 in 2007–09; Total roots and tubers 1,015 in 2007, 890 in 2008, 1,011 in 2009; Total vegetables (incl. melons) 292 in 2007–09; Total fruits (excl. melons) 105 in 2007–09.

Source: FAO.

LIVESTOCK
('000 head, year ending September, FAO estimates)

	2005	2006	2007
Cattle	2,900	2,800	2,850
Sheep	190	195	200
Goats	1,950	1,950	2,000
Pigs	345	340	340
Chickens	32,000	30,000	30,000

2008: Figures assumed to be unchanged from 2007 (FAO estimates). Note: No data were available for 2009.

Source: FAO.

LIVESTOCK PRODUCTS
('000 metric tons, FAO estimates)

	2005	2006	2007
Cattle meat	59.2	57.6	58.4
Pig meat	11.2	11.0	11.0
Chicken meat	39.0	36.5	36.5
Cows' milk	84.0	81.0	84.0
Hen eggs	46.8	46.4	46.9
Cattle hides	7.8	7.6	7.7

2008–09: Production assumed to be unchanged from 2007 (FAO estimates).

Source: FAO.

ZAMBIA

Forestry

ROUNDWOOD REMOVALS
('000 cubic metres, FAO estimates)

	2007	2008	2009
Sawlogs, veneer logs and logs for sleepers	245	245	245
Other industrial wood	1,080	1,080	1,080
Fuel wood	8,705	8,840	8,978
Total	10,030	10,165	10,303

Source: FAO.

SAWNWOOD PRODUCTION
('000 cubic metres, incl. railway sleepers, FAO estimates)

	1995	1996	1997
Coniferous (softwood)	300	230	145
Broadleaved (hardwood)	20	15	12
Total	320	245	157

1998–2009: Figures assumed to be unchanged from 1997 (FAO estimates).
Source: FAO.

Fishing

('000 metric tons, live weight)

	2006	2007	2008
Capture	60.2	73.5	79.4
Dagaas	7.7	9.5	7.9
Other freshwater fishes	52.6	64.1	71.5
Aquaculture	5.2	5.9	5.6
Three-spotted tilapia	1.9	2.1	2.0
Total catch	65.4	79.4	85.0

Note: Figures exclude crocodiles, recorded by number rather than weight. The number of Nile crocodiles caught was: 39,804 in 2006; 37,305 in 2007; 21,897 in 2008.
Source: FAO.

Mining

(estimates)

	2007	2008	2009
Coal ('000 metric tons)	220	220	220
Copper ore ('000 metric tons)*	508	546	697
Cobalt ore (metric tons)*	7,500	6,900	2,300
Amethysts ('000 kilograms)	1,300	900	1,400

* Figures refer to the metal content of ore.
Source: US Geological Survey.

Industry

SELECTED PRODUCTS
('000 metric tons unless otherwise indicated)

	2007	2008	2009
Cement	650	700	880
Copper (unwrought): smelter	224	232	330
Copper (unwrought): refined	430	415	405
Cobalt (refined, metric tons)	4,335	3,991	1,500
Raw sugar	237	n.a.	n.a.
Electric energy (million kWh)	9,853	n.a.	n.a.

Sources: US Geological Survey; UN Industrial Commodity Statistics Database.

Finance

CURRENCY AND EXCHANGE RATES

Monetary Units
100 ngwee = 1 Zambian kwacha (K).

Sterling, Dollar and Euro Equivalents (31 December 2010)
£1 sterling = 7,508.30 kwacha;
US $1 = 4,796.11 kwacha;
€1 = 6,408.56 kwacha;
10,000 Zambian kwacha = £1.33 = $2.09 = €1.56.

Average Exchange Rate (Zambian kwacha per US $)
2008   3,745.66
2009   5,046.11
2010   4,797.14

CENTRAL GOVERNMENT BUDGET
(K '000 million)*

Revenue	2009	2010†	2011‡
Tax revenue	9,661	11,764	14,562
Income tax	5,073	6,109	7,414
Excise taxes	1,024	1,397	1,711
Value-added tax (VAT)	2,475	2,940	3,796
Customs duty	1,089	1,318	1,641
Non-tax revenue	654	722	447
Total§	10,315	12,486	15,009

Expenditure	2009	2010†	2011‡
Current expenditure	11,924	13,229	14,564
Wages and salaries	5,274	6,281	6,735
Goods and services	3,188	3,581	3,957
Interest payments	1,033	1,151	1,270
Other current expenditure	2,429	2,215	2,602
Capital expenditure	2,808	3,507	4,128
Domestic arrears payments	278	269	67
Total	15,010	17,005	18,759

* The budgetary out-turn includes a statistical discrepancy of K311,000m. in 2009.
† Programmed figures.
‡ Projections.
§ Excluding grants received (K '000 million): 2,611 in 2009; 2,579 in 2010 (programmed); 2,258 in 2011 (projection).

Source: IMF, *Zambia: Fifth Review Under the Three-Year Arrangement Under the Extended Credit Facility, Requests for Waiver of Nonobservance of Performance Criterion and Modification of Performance Criteria, and Financing Assurances Review* (December 2010).

INTERNATIONAL RESERVES
(excl. gold, US $ million at 31 December)

	2008	2009	2010
IMF special drawing rights	10.6	637.6	625.2
Foreign exchange	1,085.0	1,254.4	1,468.5
Total	1,095.6	1,892.1	2,093.7

Source: IMF, *International Financial Statistics*.

MONEY SUPPLY
(K '000 million at 31 December)

	2007	2008	2009
Currency outside depository corporations	1,299.8	1,609.3	1,579.6
Transferable deposits	5,818.3	6,881.2	7,517.1
Other deposits	3,281.3	4,324.6	4,700.2
Broad money	10,399.5	12,815.1	13,796.9

Source: IMF, *International Financial Statistics*.

ZAMBIA

COST OF LIVING
(Consumer Price Index; low-income group; base: 2000 = 100)

	2001	2002	2003
Food (incl. alcohol and tobacco)	118.9	151.1	184.5
Clothing and footwear	120.5	139.4	168.8
Fuel and rent	121.4	145.1	176.5
All items (incl. others)	121.4	148.4	180.1

Food (incl. alcohol and tobacco): 214.7 in 2004; 254.5 in 2005; 267.1 in 2006; 281.1 in 2007; 319.9 in 2008; 365.5 in 2009.

All items: 212.5 in 2004; 251.4 in 2005; 274.1 in 2006; 303.3 in 2007; 341.1 in 2008; 386.8 in 2009; 419.6 in 2010.

Source: ILO.

NATIONAL ACCOUNTS
(K '000 million at current prices)

Expenditure on the Gross Domestic Product

	2006	2007	2008
Government final consumption expenditure	7,941.5	8,794.0	11,093.0
Private final consumption expenditure	17,238.2	24,600.8	26,356.6
Changes in inventories	505.3	510.0	550.0
Gross fixed capital formation	9,447.0	9,852.0	17,004.0
Total domestic expenditure	35,132.0	43,756.8	55,003.6
Exports of goods and services	14,842.8	18,450.0	18,041.0
Less Imports of goods and services	11,414.0	16,012.0	17,966.0
GDP in purchasers' values	38,560.8	46,194.8	55,078.8

Gross Domestic Product by Economic Activity

	2007	2008	2009
Agriculture, hunting, forestry and fishing	9,139.5	10,863.8	13,469.9
Mining and quarrying	2,037.2	2,227.6	805.4
Manufacturing	4,487.4	5,125.0	6,011.3
Electricity, gas and water	1,345.0	1,512.4	1,804.9
Construction	6,692.7	8,811.4	12,468.2
Wholesale and retail trade, restaurants and hotels	8,749.7	10,128.2	11,553.7
Transport and communications	1,984.4	2,248.9	2,312.9
Finance and insurance, real estate and business services	6,325.4	7,648.0	9,263.9
Public administration and defence	1,258.3	1,446.1	1,482.8
Other services	3,065.8	4,019.0	5,158.9
Sub-total	45,085.4	54,030.4	64,331.9
Less Imputed bank service charge	2,096.0	2,592.0	3,205.4
Indirect taxes, less subsidies	3,205.4	3,640.4	3,199.5
GDP in purchasers' values	46,194.8	55,078.8	64,326.0

Source: African Development Bank.

BALANCE OF PAYMENTS
(US $ million)

	2007	2008	2009
Exports of goods f.o.b.	4,509.8	4,961.7	4,319.1
Imports of goods f.o.b.	−3,610.6	−4,554.3	−3,413.4
Trade balance	899.2	407.4	905.7
Export of services	273.4	299.6	240.9
Import of services	−914.8	−906.5	−705.4
Balance on goods and services	257.8	−199.5	441.2
Other income received	35.2	29.5	5.5
Other income paid	−1,512.4	−1,428.9	−1,368.2
Balance on goods, services and income	−1,228.3	−1,598.8	−921.6
Current transfers received	356.8	349.4	255.5
Current transfers paid	−95.9	−110.3	−37.0
Current account	−967.4	−1,359.7	−703.1

—*continued*	2007	2008	2009
Capital account (net)	222.8	230.0	237.3
Direct investment from abroad	1,323.9	938.6	699.2
Portfolio investment liabilities	41.8	−6.1	−79.2
Other investment assets	−1,130.3	−509.9	−3.2
Other investment liabilities	607.9	393.4	149.8
Net errors and omissions	−61.9	11.0	565.4
Overall balance	36.8	−302.7	866.1

Source: IMF, *International Financial Statistics*.

External Trade

PRINCIPAL COMMODITIES
(US $ million)

Imports c.i.f.	2007	2008	2009
Food and live animals	127.0	150.2	145.7
Crude materials except fuels	189.9	592.2	398.5
Mineral fuels and lubricants	488.7	810.7	528.6
Petroleum and petroleum products	468.5	788.4	514.9
Petroleum oils and oils obtained from bituminous minerals, crude	226.5	481.9	430.8
Chemicals and related products	543.3	757.5	709.0
Medicinal and pharmaceutical products	97.9	162.5	157.4
Basic manufactures	645.7	742.2	617.2
Iron and steel	202.4	196.0	148.2
Machinery and transport equipment	1,706.8	1,644.5	1,085.8
Machinery specialized for particular industries	557.9	485.0	318.2
General industrial machinery, equipment and machine parts	313.0	244.5	170.6
Electrical machinery, apparatus, appliances and electrical parts	200.5	196.2	128.8
Road vehicles	371.7	476.4	272.7
Miscellaneous manufactured articles	178.8	214.8	195.9
Total (incl. others)	4,007.0	5,060.5	3,792.6

Exports f.o.b.	2007	2008	2009
Food and live animals	254.0	201.2	220.8
Beverages and tobacco	65.1	79.8	94.1
Crude materials except fuels	377.2	839.7	584.3
Metalliferous ore and metal scrap	294.3	779.2	511.6
Chemicals and related products	81.3	72.3	87.3
Basic manufactures	3,640.2	3,678.6	3,071.9
Non-ferrous metals	3,283.6	3,275.8	2,890.7
Copper	3,280.1	3,270.9	2,889.0
Machinery and transport equipment	107.4	142.6	138.8
Total (incl. others)	4,617.5	5,098.7	4,312.1

Source: UN, *International Trade Statistics Yearbook*.

ZAMBIA

PRINCIPAL TRADING PARTNERS
(US $ million)

Imports c.i.f.	2007	2008	2009
China, People's Repub.	239.7	227.2	178.0
Congo, Democratic Repub.	127.9	534.7	486.7
Finland	55.2	50.6	14.8
France (incl. Monaco)	117.5	40.8	15.5
Germany	81.4	66.7	59.1
India	164.9	191.6	130.9
Japan	51.9	86.7	66.4
Kenya	78.4	80.4	78.0
Kuwait	0.1	513.7	401.0
Mozambique	59.9	53.0	33.9
Netherlands	77.1	34.8	31.0
South Africa	1,898.5	2,154.0	1,516.0
Sweden	89.4	61.6	34.2
Tanzania	23.6	47.6	33.7
United Arab Emirates	254.5	123.5	109.7
United Kingdom	160.8	157.2	136.0
USA	65.2	72.2	50.7
Zimbabwe	111.7	107.1	56.9
Total (incl. others)	4,007.0	5,060.5	3,792.6

Exports f.o.b.	2007	2008	2009
Belgium	46.5	54.8	55.9
China, People's Repub.	189.0	286.9	482.6
Congo, Democratic Repub.	245.9	287.1	300.9
Egypt	232.0	384.8	106.5
France-Monaco	53.3	1.8	2.0
India	52.1	32.6	49.4
Japan	37.3	41.6	2.2
Korea, Repub.	94.2	68.9	77.0
Malawi	31.2	63.0	73.2
Malaysia	54.2	10.8	0.0
Netherlands	50.1	126.6	42.4
Pakistan	48.4	28.9	30.9
Saudi Arabia	216.4	90.5	118.1
South Africa	555.3	528.4	394.7
Switzerland-Liechtenstein	1,951.7	2,537.3	2,027.2
Tanzania	73.0	31.9	34.5
Thailand	273.8	99.8	23.7
United Arab Emirates	49.3	23.7	141.0
United Kingdom	55.5	115.1	87.2
Zimbabwe	81.6	64.1	84.3
Total (incl. others)	4,617.5	5,098.7	4,312.1

Source: UN, *International Trade Statistics Yearbook*.

Transport

ROAD TRAFFIC
(estimates, '000 motor vehicles in use at 31 December)

	1994	1995	1996
Passenger cars	123	142	157
Lorries and vans	68	74	81

2007: Passenger cars 131; Buses 4; Lorries and vans 76; Motorcycles 7.

Source: IRF, *World Road Statistics*.

CIVIL AVIATION
(traffic on scheduled services)

	2004	2005	2006
Kilometres flown (million)	2	2	2
Passengers carried ('000)	50	54	59
Passenger-km (million)	16	17	19
Total ton-km (million)	1	2	2

Source: UN, *Statistical Yearbook*.

2007: Passengers carried ('000) 61.1 (Source: World Bank, World Development Indicators database).

2008: Passengers carried ('000) 62.5 (Source: World Bank, World Development Indicators database).

Tourism

TOURIST ARRIVALS BY NATIONALITY

	2006	2007	2008
Australia	14,617	9,389	14,517
South Africa	100,286	125,231	95,415
Tanzania	74,039	92,732	106,284
United Kingdom	57,119	66,858	46,516
USA	38,800	39,127	33,870
Zimbabwe	194,639	278,010	226,428
Total (incl. others)	756,860	897,413	811,775

Tourism receipts (US $ million, excl. passenger transport): 110 in 2006; 138 in 2007; 146 in 2008.

Source: World Tourism Organization.

Communications Media

	2007	2008	2009
Telephones ('000 main lines in use)	91.8	90.6	90.3
Mobile cellular telephones ('000 subscribers)	2,639.0	3,539.0	4,406.7
Internet users ('000)	599.7	700.4	816.2
Broadband subscribers ('000)	4.0	5.7	8.0

Personal computers: 131,000 (11.2 per 1,000 persons) in 2005.
Radio receivers ('000 in use): 1,436 in 1999.
Television receivers ('000 in use): 540 in 2001.
Daily newspapers: 4 (average circulation 55,000 copies) in 2004.

Sources: UNESCO, *Statistical Yearbook*; UNESCO Institute for Statistics; UN, *Statistical Yearbook*; International Telecommunication Union.

Education

(2008/09 unless otherwise indicated)

	Institutions	Teachers	Students
Primary	4,221*	48,075†	2,840,540
Secondary	n.a.	29,148†	707,744
Tertiary	n.a.	n.a.	24,553‡

* 1998 figure.
† 2007/08 figure.
‡ 1999/2000 estimate.

Source: UNESCO Institute for Statistics.

Pupil-teacher ratio (primary education, UNESCO estimate): 60.5 in 2007/08 (Source: UNESCO Institute for Statistics).

Adult literacy rate (UNESCO estimates): 70.7% (males 80.6%; females 61.0%) in 2008 (Source: UNESCO Institute for Statistics).

Directory

The Government

HEAD OF STATE

President: RUPIAH BANDA (took office 2 November 2008).

THE CABINET
(May 2011)

President: RUPIAH BANDA.
Vice-President and Minister of Justice: GEORGE KUNDA.
Minister of Home Affairs: MUKONDO LUNGU.
Minister of Foreign Affairs: KABINGA PANDE.
Minister of Defence: KALOMBO MWANSA.
Minister of Finance and National Planning: Dr SITUMBEKO MUSOKOTWANE.
Minister of Commerce, Trade and Industry: FELIX MUTATI.
Minister of Agriculture and Co-operatives: EUSTARKIO KAZONGA.
Minister of Communications and Transport: GEOFFREY LUNGWANGWA.
Minister of Energy and Water Development: KENNETH KONGA.
Minister of Tourism, the Environment and Natural Resources: CATHERINE NAMUGALA.
Minister of Education: DORA SILIYA.
Minister of Science, Technology and Vocational Training: PETER DAKA.
Minister of Health: KAPEMMBWA SIMBAO.
Minister of Local Government and Housing: Dr BRIAN CHITUWO.
Minister of Works and Supply: GABRIEL NAMULAMBE.
Minister of Community Development and Social Services: MICHAEL KAINGU.
Minister of Sport, Youth and Child Development: KENNETH CHIPUNGU.
Minister of Lands: GLADYS LUNDWE.
Minister of Labour and Social Security: AUSTIN LIATO.
Minister of Mines and Mineral Development: MAWELL MWALE.
Minister of Information and Broadcasting Services: RONNIE SHIKAPWASHA.
Minister of Gender and Development: SARAH SAYIFWANDA.
Minister of Presidential Affairs: RONALD MUYKUMA.
There were, in addition, 26 Deputy Ministers.

MINISTRIES

Office of the President: POB 30135, Lusaka 10101; tel. (21) 1260317; fax (21) 1254545; internet www.statehouse.gov.zm.

Ministry of Agriculture and Co-operatives: Mulungushi House, Independence Ave, Nationalist Rd, POB RW50291, Lusaka; tel. (21) 1213551.

Ministry of Commerce, Trade and Industry: 9th and 10th Floor, Nasser Rd, POB 31968, Lusaka 10101; tel. (21) 1228301; fax (21) 1226984; internet www.mcti.gov.zm.

Ministry of Communications and Transport: Fairley Rd, POB 50065, Lusaka; tel. (21) 151444; fax (21) 151795; internet www.mct .gov.zm.

Ministry of Community Development and Social Services: Fidelity House, POB 31958, Lusaka; tel. (21) 1228321; fax (21) 1225327.

Ministry of Defence: POB 31931, Lusaka; tel. (21) 1252366.

Ministry of Education: Civic Center Area, Plot 89, cnr Mogadishu and Chimanga Rds, POB 50093, Lusaka 10101; tel. (21) 1250855; fax (21) 1250760; internet www.moe.gov.zm.

Ministry of Energy and Water Development: Mulungushi House, Independence Ave, Nationalist Rd, POB 36079, Lusaka; tel. and fax (21) 1252589; internet www.mewd.gov.zm.

Ministry of Finance and National Planning: Finance Bldg, POB 50062, Lusaka; tel. (21) 1252121; fax (21) 1251078; e-mail info@ mofnp.gov.zm; internet www.mofnp.gov.zm.

Ministry of Foreign Affairs: POB RW50069, Lusaka; tel. (21) 1252718; fax (21) 1222440.

Ministry of Gender and Development: Lusaka.

Ministry of Health: Ndeke House, POB 30205, Lusaka; tel. (21) 1253040; fax (21) 1253344; internet www.moh.gov.zm.

Ministry of Home Affairs: POB 32862, Lusaka; tel. (21) 1213505.

Ministry of Information and Broadcasting Services: Independence Ave, POB 51025, Lusaka; tel. and fax (21) 1235410; internet www.mibs.gov.zm.

Ministry of Justice: Fairley Rd, POB 50106, 15101, Ridgeway, Lusaka; tel. (21) 1228522.

Ministry of Labour and Social Security: Lechwe House, Freedom Way, POB 32186, Lusaka; tel. (21) 1212020; internet www.mlss .gov.zm.

Ministry of Lands: POB 50694, Lusaka; tel. (21) 1252288; fax (21) 1250120; internet www.ministryoflands.gov.zm.

Ministry of Local Government and Housing: Church Rd, POB 50027, Lusaka; tel. (21) 1250528; fax (21) 1252680; e-mail ps@mlgh .gov.zm; internet www.mlgh.gov.zm.

Ministry of Mines and Mineral Development: Chilufya Mulenga Rd, POB 31969, 10101 Lusaka; tel. (21) 1235323; fax (21) 1235346.

Ministry of Science, Technology and Vocational Training: Maxwell House, Los Angeles Blvd, POB 50464, Lusaka; tel. (21) 1252911; fax (21) 1252951; e-mail psmstvt@mstvt.gov.zm; internet www.mstvt.gov.zm.

Ministry of Sport, Youth and Child Development: Memaco House, POB 50195, Lusaka; tel. (21) 1227158; fax (21) 1223996.

Ministry of Tourism, the Environment and Natural Resources: 3rd Floor, Kwacha House, POB 34011, Cairo Rd, Lusaka 10101; tel. (21) 1223931; fax (21) 1223930; e-mail info@mtenr.gov .zm; internet www.mtenr.gov.zm.

Ministry of Works and Supply: POB 50003, Lusaka; tel. (21) 1253088; fax (21) 1253404.

President and Legislature

PRESIDENT

Presidential Election, 30 October 2008

Candidate	Votes	% of votes
Rupiah Banda (MMD)	718,359	40.63
Michael Sata (PF)	683,150	38.64
Hakainde Hichilema (UDA)	353,018	19.96
Brig.-Gen. Godfrey Miyanda (HP)	13,683	0.77
Total	1,768,210	100.00

NATIONAL ASSEMBLY

Speaker: AMUSAA KATUNDA MWANAMWAMBWA.

General Election, 28 September 2006*

Party	Seats
Movement for Multi-party Democracy (MMD)	75
Patriotic Front (PF)	43
United Democratic Alliance (UDA)†	26
Independents	3
United Liberal Party (ULP)	2
National Democratic Focus (NDF)	1
Total	150

* Includes the results of voting in two constituencies where the elections were postponed until 26 October 2006, owing to the deaths of candidates.

† Coalition of the Forum for Democracy and Development (FDD), the United National Independence Party (UNIP) and the United Party for National Development (UPND).

House of Chiefs

The House of Chiefs is an advisory body which may submit resolutions for debate by the National Assembly. There are 27 Chiefs, four each from the Northern, Western, Southern and Eastern Provinces, three each from the North-Western, Luapula and Central Provinces, and two from the Copperbelt Province.

ZAMBIA

Election Commission

Electoral Commission of Zambia (ECZ): Elections House, Haile Selassie Ave, POB 50274, Longacres, Lusaka; tel. (21) 1253155; fax (21) 1253884; e-mail elections@electcom.org.zm; internet www.elections.org.zm; f. 1996; independent; Chair. FLORENCE MUMBA; Dir DAN KALALE.

Political Organizations

Agenda for Change (AfC): POB 37119, Lusaka; e-mail agenda@zambia.co.zm; internet www.agenda123.com; f. 1995; Pres. Prof. HENRY KYAMBALESA; Nat. Chair. DARROH P. CHOONGA.

Alliance for Democracy and Development (ADD): f. 2009; Interim Pres. DOUGLAS SHING'ANDU.

Citizens Democratic Party (CDP): POB 37277, Lusaka; tel. 975642011; fax 967052011; e-mail citizens@thecitizensdemocraticparty.com; internet www.thecitizensdemocraticparty.com.

Democratic Party (DP): Plot C4, President Ave (North), POB 71628, Ndola; f. 1991; Pres. EMMANUEL MWAMBA.

Heritage Party (HP): POB 51055, Lusaka; f. 2001 by expelled mems of the MMD; Pres. Brig.-Gen. GODFREY MIYANDA.

Movement for Multi-party Democracy (MMD): POB 30708, Lusaka; tel. (21) 1250177; fax (21) 1252329; e-mail mmd@zamtel.zm; internet www.mmdzam.org; f. 1990; governing party since Nov. 1991; Pres. RUPIAH BANDA; Nat. Sec. KATELE KALUMBA.

National Democratic Focus: Lusaka; f. 2006 to contest the presidential election; Acting Chair. NEVERS MUMBA (RP).

All Peoples' Congress Party (APC): Lusaka; f. 2005 by fmr mems of the FDD; Pres. WINRIGHT K. NGONDO.

Party for Unity, Democracy and Development (PUDD): Lusaka; f. 2004 by fmr mems of the MMD; Pres. (vacant).

Reform Party (RP): Lusaka; f. 2005 by fmr mems of the MMD; Pres. NEVERS MUMBA; Nat. Chair. EVA SANDERSON; Sec.-Gen. CLEMENT MICHELO.

Zambia Democratic Conference (ZADECO): Lusaka; f. 1998 as the Zambia Democratic Congress Popular Front by fmr mems of the Zambia Democratic Congress; disbanded in 1999; reformed after 2001 election by fmr mems of the ZAP; Pres. Rev. Dr DAN PULE.

Zambia Republican Party (ZRP): Lusaka; f. 2001 by merger of the Republican Party (f. 2000) and the Zambia Alliance for Progress (f. 1999); Gen. Sec. SILVIA MASEBO; Nat. Chair. BEN KAPITA.

National Leadership for Development (NLD): POB 34161, Lusaka; f. 2000; Pres. Dr YOBERT K. SHAMAPANDE.

National Party (NP): POB 37840, Lusaka 10101; tel. (21) 18491431; e-mail nationalparty1993@yahoo.com; f. 1993; by fmr mems of the MMD; promotes human rights; Pres. Rev. RICHARD KAMBULU; Sec.-Gen. NDANISO BANDA.

National Restoration Party (NAREP): 43 Nalikwanda Rd, Woodlands, Lusaka; tel. (21) 1260336; e-mail info@newzambia.org; internet www.newzambia.org; f. 2010; Pres. ELIAS CHIPIMO; Sec.-Gen. JONATHAN ZULU.

Patriotic Front (PF): Farmers House, POB 320015, Lusaka; tel. 96768080 (mobile); fax (21) 1228661; internet www.pf.com.zm; f. 2001 by expelled mems of the MMD; Pres. MICHAEL CHILUFYA SATA; Sec.-Gen. GUY SCOTT.

United Democratic Alliance (UDA): Kenneth Kaunda House, Cairo Rd, Lusaka; f. 2006 to contest that year's elections; Nat. Chair. TILYENJI KAUNDA (FDD).

Forum for Democracy and Development (FDD): POB 35868, Lusaka; f. 2001 by expelled mems of the MMD; Pres. EDITH NAWAKWI; Chair. SIMON ZUKAS.

United National Independence Party (UNIP): POB 30302, Lusaka; tel. (21) 1221197; fax (21) 1221327; f. 1959; sole legal party 1972–90; Pres. TILYENJI KAUNDA; Nat. Chair. KEN KAIRA.

United Party for National Development (UPND): POB 33199, Lusaka; internet www.upnd.org; f. 1998; incl. fmr mems of the Progressive People's Party and Zambia Dem. Party; Pres. HAKAINDE HICHILEMA.

Unity Party for Democrats (UPD): POB RW28, Ridgeway, Lusaka; f. 1997; Pres. MATHEW PIKITI.

Zambia Alliance for Progress (ZAP): Lusaka; f. 1999; re-registered as ZAP in 2001 after splitting from Zambia Republican Party; Pres. (vacant).

Diplomatic Representation

EMBASSIES AND HIGH COMMISSIONS IN ZAMBIA

Angola: Plot 108, Great East Rd, Northmead, POB 31595, 10101 Lusaka; tel. (21) 1134764; fax (21) 1221210; Ambassador PEDRO DE MORAIS NETO.

Botswana: 5201 Pandit Nehru Rd, Diplomatic Triangle, POB 31910, 10101 Lusaka; tel. (21) 1250555; fax (21) 1250804; High Commissioner T. DITLHABI-OLIPHANT.

Brazil: 4 Manenekela Road, Woodlands, Lusaka; tel. (21) 1252171; fax (21) 1253203; e-mail brasemblusaca@iconnect.zm; Ambassador JOSAL LUIZ PELLEGRINO.

Canada: Plot 5199, United Nations Ave, POB 31313, 10101 Lusaka; tel. (21) 1250833; fax (21) 1254176; e-mail lsaka@international.gc.ca; internet www.canadainternational.gc.ca/zambia-zambie; High Commissioner PIERRE-PAUL PERRON.

China, People's Republic: Plot 7430, United Nations Ave, Longacres, POB 31975, 10101 Lusaka; tel. (21) 1251169; fax (21) 1251157; e-mail chinaemb_zm@mfa.gov.cn; Ambassador LI QIANGMIN.

Congo, Democratic Republic: Plot 1124, Parirenyatwa Rd, POB 31287, 10101 Lusaka; tel. and fax (21) 1235679; Ambassador JOHNSON WA BINANA.

Cuba: 5574 Mogoye Rd, Kalundu, POB 33132, 10101 Lusaka; tel. (21) 1291308; fax (21) 1291586; e-mail ambassador@iconnect.zm; internet emba.cubaminrex.cu/zambiaing; Ambassador FRANCISCO JAVIER VIAMONTES CORREA.

Denmark: 5219 Haile Selassie Ave, POB 50299, Lusaka; tel. (21) 1254277; fax (21) 1254618; e-mail lunamb@um.dk; internet www.amblusaka.um.dk/en; Ambassador THOMAS NEWHOUSE TRIGG SCHJERBECK.

Egypt: Plot 5206, United Nations Ave, Longacres, POB 32428, Lusaka 10101; tel. (21) 1250229; fax (21) 1252213; Ambassador SALAH ED-DIN ABDEL SADEK.

Finland: Haile Selassie Ave, opp. Ndeke House, Longacres, POB 50819, 15101 Lusaka; tel. (21) 1251988; fax (21) 1253783; e-mail sanomat.lus@formin.fi; internet www.finland.org.zm; Ambassador SINIKKA ANTILA.

France: Mpile Bldg, 74 Independence Ave, POB 30062, 10101 Lusaka; tel. (21) 1251322; fax (21) 1254475; e-mail france@ambafrance-zm.org; internet www.ambafrance-zm.org; Ambassador OLIVIER RICHARD.

Germany: Plot 5209, United Nations Ave, POB 50120, 15101 Ridgeway, Lusaka; tel. (21) 1250644; fax (21) 1254014; e-mail info@lusaka.diplo.de; internet www.lusaka.diplo.de; Ambassador FRANK MEYKE.

Holy See: 283 Los Angeles Blvd, POB 31445, 10101 Lusaka; tel. (21) 1251033; fax (21) 1250601; e-mail nuntius@coppernet.zm; Apostolic Nuncio Most Rev. NICOLA GIRASOLI (Titular Archbishop of Egnazia Appula).

India: 1 Pandit Nehru Rd, POB 32111, 10101 Lusaka; tel. (21) 1253159; fax (21) 1254118; e-mail hoc.lusaka@mea.gov.in; internet www.hcizambia.com; High Commissioner ASHOK KUMAR.

Ireland: 6663 Katima Mulilo Rd, Olympia Park, POB 34923, 10101 Lusaka; tel. (21) 1290650; fax (21) 1290482; e-mail iremb@zamnet.zm; internet www.embassyofireland.co.zm; Ambassador TONY COTTER.

Italy: Plot 5211, Embassy Park, Diplomatic Triangle, POB 50497, Lusaka; tel. (21) 1250781; fax (21) 1254929; e-mail ambasciata.lusaka@esteri.it; internet www.amblusaka.esteri.it; Chargé d'affaires a.i. Dr GUIDO BILANCINI.

Japan: Plot 5218, Haile Selassie Ave, POB 34190, 10101 Lusaka; tel. (21) 1251555; fax (21) 1254425; e-mail jez@zamtel.zm; internet www.zm.emb-japan.go.jp; Ambassador (vacant).

Kenya: 5207 United Nations Ave, POB 50298, 10101 Lusaka; tel. (21) 1250722; fax (21) 1253829; e-mail kenhigh@zamnet.zm; High Commissioner LAZARUS O. AMAYO.

Libya: 251 Ngwee Rd, off United Nations Ave, Longacres, POB 35319, 10101 Lusaka; tel. (21) 1253055; fax (21) 1251239; Ambassador KHALIFA OMER SWIEXI.

Malawi: 31 Bishops Rd, Kabulonga, POB 50425, Lusaka; tel. (21) 1265768; fax (21) 1265765; e-mail mhcomm@iwayafrica.com; High Commissioner Dr CHRISSIE MUGHOGHO.

Mozambique: Kacha Rd, Plot 9592, POB 34877, 10101 Lusaka; tel. (21) 1220333; fax (21) 1220345; e-mail embamoc.zambia@minec.gov.mz; High Commissioner MARIA LEOCÁDIA TIVANE MATE.

Namibia: 30B Mutende Rd, Woodlands, POB 30577, 10101 Lusaka; tel. (21) 1260407; fax (21) 1263858; e-mail namibia@coppernet.zm; High Commissioner MARTIN SHALLI.

ZAMBIA

Netherlands: 5208 United Nations Ave, POB 31905, 10101 Lusaka; tel. (21) 1253819; fax (21) 1253733; e-mail lus@minbuza.nl; internet www.netherlandsembassy.org.zm; Ambassador HARRY MOLENAAR.

Nigeria: 5203 Haile Selassie Ave, Diplomatic Triangle, Longacres, POB 32598, Lusaka; tel. (21) 1229860; fax (21) 1223791; High Commissioner FOLAKE BELLO.

Norway: cnr Birdcage Walk and Haile Selassie Ave, Longacres, POB 34570, 10101 Lusaka; tel. (21) 1252188; fax (21) 1253915; e-mail emb.lusaka@mfa.no; internet www.norway.org.zm; Chargé d'affaires a.i. TORE HOVEN.

Russia: Plot 6407, Diplomatic Triangle, POB 32355, 10101 Lusaka; tel. (21) 1252120; fax (21) 1253582; Ambassador BORIS MALAKHOV.

Saudi Arabia: 27BC Leopards Hill Rd, Kabulonga, POB 34411, 10101 Lusaka; tel. (21) 1266861; fax (21) 1266863; e-mail saudiemb@uudial.zm; Ambassador HASSAN ATTAR.

Serbia: Independence Ave 5216, POB 33379, 10101 Lusaka; tel. (21) 1250235; fax (21) 1253889; e-mail serbianemba@zamnet.zm; Chargé d'affaires a.i. MIRKO MANOJLOVIĆ.

Somalia: G3/377A Kabulonga Rd, POB 34051, Lusaka; tel. (21) 1262119; Ambassador (vacant).

South Africa: D26, Cheetah Rd, Kabulonga, Private Bag W369, Lusaka; tel. (21) 1260999; fax (21) 1263001; e-mail sahcadmin@samnet.zm; High Commissioner MOSES MABOKELA CHIKANE.

Sudan: 31 Ng'umbo Rd, Longacres, POB RW179X, 15200 Lusaka; tel. (21) 1252116; fax (21) 1252448; e-mail sudemblsk@hotmail.com; Ambassador SABIT ABBEY ALLEY.

Sweden: Haile Selassie Ave, POB 50264, 10101 Lusaka; tel. (21) 1251711; fax (21) 1254049; e-mail ambassaden.lusaka@foreign.ministry.se; internet www.swedenabroad.com/lusaka; Ambassador MARIE ANDERSSON DE FRUTOS.

Tanzania: Ujamaa House, Plot 5200, United Nations Ave, POB 31219, 10101 Lusaka; tel. (21) 1253222; fax (21) 1254861; e-mail tzreplsk@zamnet.zm; High Commissioner GEORGE MWANJABALA.

United Kingdom: Plot 5210, Independence Ave, POB 50050, 15101 Ridgeway, Lusaka; tel. (21) 1423200; fax (21) 1423291; internet ukinzambia.fco.gov.uk; Jt High Commissioner CAROLYN DAVIDSON, THOMAS CARTER.

USA: cnr Independence and United Nations Aves, POB 31617, Lusaka; tel. (21) 1250955; fax (21) 1252225; internet zambia.usembassy.gov; Ambassador MARK CHARLES STORELLA.

Zimbabwe: 11058 Haile Selassie Ave, Longacres, POB 33491, 10101 Lusaka; tel. (21) 1254012; fax (21) 1227474; e-mail zimzam@coppernet.zm; Ambassador LOVEMORE MAZEMO.

Judicial System

The judicial system of Zambia comprises a Supreme Court, composed of a Chief Justice, a Deputy Chief Justice and five Justices; a High Court comprising the Chief Justice and 30 Judges; Senior Resident and Resident Magistrates' Courts, which sit at various centres; and Local Courts, which deal principally with customary law, but which also have limited criminal jurisdiction.

Supreme Court of Zambia

Independence Ave, POB 50067, Ridgeway, Lusaka; tel. (21) 1251330; fax (21) 1251743.

Chief Justice: ERNEST SAKALA.

Deputy Chief Justice: IREEN MAMBILIMA.

Supreme Court Judges: LOMBE CHIBESAKUNDA, DENNIS CHIRWA, PETER CHITENGI, FLORENCE MUMBA, SANDSON SILOMBA.

Religion

CHRISTIANITY

Council of Churches in Zambia: Church House, Cairo Rd, POB 30315, Lusaka; tel. (21) 1229551; fax (21) 1224308; e-mail info@ccz.org.zm; f. 1945; Chair. Rt Rev. THUMA HAMUKANG'ANDU (Brethren in Christ Church); Gen. Sec. JAPHET NDHLOVU; 22 mem. churches and 18 affiliate mem. orgs.

The Anglican Communion

Anglicans are adherents of the Church of the Province of Central Africa, covering Botswana, Malawi, Zambia and Zimbabwe. The Church comprises 15 dioceses, including five in Zambia. The Archbishop of the Province is the Bishop of Upper Shire in Malawi. There are an estimated 80,000 adherents in Zambia.

Bishop of Central Zambia: Rt Rev. DEREK G. KAMUKWAMBA, POB 70172, Ndola; tel. (21) 2612431; fax (21) 2615954; e-mail adcznla@zamnet.zm.

Bishop of Eastern Zambia: Rt Rev. WILLIAM MUCHOMBO, POB 510154, Chipata; tel. and fax (21) 6221294; e-mail dioeastzm@zamnet.zm.

Bishop of Luapula: Rt Rev. ROBERT MUMBI, POB 710210, Mansa, Luapula.

Bishop of Lusaka: Rt Rev. DAVID NJOVU, Bishop's Lodge, POB 30183, Lusaka; tel. (21) 1264515; fax (21) 1262379; e-mail angdiolu@zamnet.zm.

Bishop of Northern Zambia: Rt Rev. ALBERT CHAMA, POB 20798, Kitwe; tel. (21) 2223264; fax (21) 2224778; e-mail dionorth@zamnet.zm.

Protestant Churches

At mid-2000 there were an estimated 2.7m. Protestants.

African Methodist Episcopal Church: Carousel Bldg, Lumumba Rd, POB 36628, Lusaka; tel. 955708031; fax (21) 1225067; Presiding Elder Rev. PAUL KAWIMBE; 440 congregations, 880,000 mems.

Baptist Church: Lubu Rd, POB 30636, Lusaka; tel. (21) 1253620.

Baptist Mission of Zambia: Baptist Bldg, 3062 Great East Rd, POB 50599, 15101 Ridgeway, Lusaka; tel. (21) 1222492; fax (21) 1227520; internet bmoz.org.

Brethren in Christ Church: POB 630115, Choma; tel. (21) 3320228; fax (21) 3320127; e-mail biccz@zamtel.zm; internet www.bic.org; f. 1906; Bishop Rev. T. HAMUKANG'ANDU; 180 congregations, 19,526 mems.

Evangelical Lutheran Church in Zambia: Plot No. 145-4893, Mpezeni Rd, POB 37701, 10101 Lusaka; tel. 97787584; fax (21) 1224023; e-mail elcza_head@yahoo.com; Senior Pastor Rev. ALFRED CHANA; 2,210 mems (2010).

Reformed Church in Zambia: POB 38255, Lusaka; tel. (21) 1295369; e-mail info@rczsynod.co.zm; internet www.rczsynod.co.zm; f. 1899; African successor to the Dutch Reformed Church mission; Gen. Sec. Rev. WILLIAM ZULU (acting); 147 congregations, 400,000 mems.

Seventh-day Adventist Church: Plot 9221, cnr Burma Rd and Independence Ave, POB 36010, Lusaka; tel. and fax (21) 1254036; e-mail lcsdac@zamnet.zm; internet www.lcsdac.net.zm; f. 1905; Pres. Dr CORNELIUS MULENGA MATANDIKO; Sec. HARRINGTON SIMUI AKOMBWA; 534,126 mems.

United Church of Zambia: Synod Headquarters, Nationalist Rd at Burma Rd, POB 50122, Lusaka; tel. (21) 1250641; fax (21) 1252198; e-mail uczsynod@zamnet.zm; f. 1965; Synod Bishop Rev. MUTALE MULUMBWA (Interim Synod Bishop); Gen. Sec. Rev. Prof. TEDDY KALONGO; c. 3m. mems.

Other denominations active in Zambia include the Assemblies of God, the Church of Christ, the Church of the Nazarene, the Evangelical Fellowship of Zambia, the Kimbanguist Church, the Presbyterian Church of Southern Africa, the Religious Society of Friends (Quakers) and the United Pentecostal Church. At mid-2000 there were an estimated 2m. adherents professing other forms of Christianity.

The Roman Catholic Church

Zambia comprises two archdioceses and eight dioceses. The number of adherents in the country was equivalent to 30% of the total population.

Bishops' Conference

Catholic Secretariat, Unity House, cnr Freedom Way and Katunjila Rd, POB 31965, 10201 Lusaka; tel. (21) 1262613; fax (21) 1262658; e-mail zec@zamnet.zm.

f. 1984; Pres. Rt Rev. LUNGU GEORGE COSMOS ZUMAIRE (Bishop of Chipata).

Archbishop of Kasama: Most Rev. JAMES SPAITA, Archbishop's House, POB 410143, Kasama; tel. (21) 4221248; fax (21) 4222202; e-mail archkasa@zamtel.zm.

Archbishop of Lusaka: Most Rev. TELESPHORE GEORGE MPUNDU, 41 Wamulwa Rd, POB 32754, 10101 Lusaka; tel. (21) 1255973; fax (21) 1255975; e-mail adlarch@zamnet.zm.

ISLAM

There are about 10,000 members of the Muslim Association in Zambia.

BAHÁ'Í FAITH

National Spiritual Assembly: Sekou Touré Rd, Plot 4371, Private Bag RW227X, Ridgeway 15102, Lusaka; tel. and fax (21) 1254505; f. 1952; Sec.-Gen. MARGARET K. LENGWE; mems resident in 1,456 localities.

ZAMBIA

The Press

DAILIES

The Post: 36 Bwinjimfumu Rd, Rhodespark, Private Bag E352, Lusaka; tel. (21) 1231092; fax (21) 1229271; e-mail post@post.co.zm; internet www.postzambia.com; f. 1991; privately owned; Editor FRED M'MEMBE; circ. 29,000.

The Times of Zambia: Kabelenga Ave, POB 70069, Ndola; tel. and fax (21) 2614469; e-mail times@zamtel.zm; internet www.times.co.zm; f. 1943; govt-owned; English; Deputy Editor-in-Chief DAVEY SAKALA; circ. 25,000.

Zambia Daily Mail: Zambia Publishing Company, POB 31421, Lusaka; tel. (21) 1225131; fax (21) 1225881; internet www.daily-mail.co.zm; f. 1968; govt-owned; English; Man. Editor EMMANUEL NYIRENDA; circ. 40,000.

PERIODICALS

The Challenge: Mission Press, Chifubu Rd, POB 71581, Ndola; tel. (21) 2680456; fax (21) 2680484; e-mail info@missionpress.org; internet www.missionpress.org; f. 1999; quarterly; English; social, educational and religious; Roman Catholic; edited by Franciscan friars; Dir Fr MIHA DREVENSEK; circ. 5,000.

Chipembele Magazine: POB 30255, Lusaka; tel. (21) 1254226; six a year; publ. by Wildlife Conservation Soc. of Zambia; circ. 20,000.

Farming in Zambia: POB 50197, Lusaka; tel. (21) 1213551; f. 1965; quarterly; publ. by Ministry of Agriculture and Co-operatives; Editor L. P. CHIRWA; circ. 3,000.

Imbila: POB RW20, Lusaka; tel. (21) 1217254; e-mail mambue2002@zanis.org.zm; f. 1953; monthly; publ. by Zambia Information Services; Bemba; Editor ALFRED M ZULU; circ. 20,000.

Intanda: POB RW20, Lusaka; tel. (21) 1219675; f. 1958; monthly; publ. by Zambia Information Services; Tonga; Editor J. SIKAULU; circ. 6,000.

Konkola: Zambia Consolidated Copper Mines Ltd, PR Dept, POB 71505, Ndola; tel. (21) 2640142; f. 1973 as *Mining Mirror*; monthly; English; Editor G. MUKUWA; circ. 30,000.

The Lowdown: Lusaka; internet www.lowdown.co.zm; f. 1995; monthly; English; Editor HEATHER CHALCRAFT.

Lukanga News: POB 919, Kabwe; tel. (21) 5217254; publ. by Zambia Information Services; Lenje; Editor J. H. N. NKOMANGA; circ. 5,500.

National Mirror: Multimedia Zambia, 15701 Woodlands, POB 320199, Lusaka; tel. (21) 1263864; fax (21) 1263050; f. 1972; fortnightly; news, current affairs and foreign affairs; publ. by Multimedia Zambia; Editor SIMON MWANZA; circ. 40,000.

Ngoma: POB RW20, Lusaka; tel. (21) 1219675; monthly; Lunda, Kaonde and Luvale; publ. by Zambia Information Services; Editor B. A. LUHILA; circ. 3,000.

Speak Out!: POB 70244, Ndola; tel. (21) 2612241; fax (21) 2620630; e-mail speakout@zamnet.zm; f. 1984; six a year; Christian; aimed at youth readership up to 35 years; Man. Editor CONSTANTIA TREPPE; circ. 25,000.

The Sportsman: POB 31762, Lusaka; tel. (21) 1214250; f. 1980; monthly; Man. Editor SAM SIKAZWE; circ. 18,000.

Sunday Express: Lusaka; f. 1991; weekly; Man. Editor JOHN MUKELA.

Sunday Times of Zambia: Kabelenga Ave, POB 70069, Ndola; tel. (21) 1614469; fax (21) 2617096; e-mail times@zamtel.zm; internet www.times.co.zm/sunday; f. 1965; owned by UNIP; English; Man. Editor ARTHUR SIMUCHOBA; circ. 78,000.

Tsopano: POB RW20, Lusaka; tel. (21) 1217254; f. 1958; monthly; publ. by Zambia Information Services; Nyanja; Editor S. S. BANDA; circ. 9,000.

Workers' Voice: POB 20652, Kitwe; tel. (21) 2211999; f. 1972; fortnightly; publ. by Zambia Congress of Trade Unions.

Youth: POB 30302, Lusaka; tel. (21) 1211411; f. 1974; quarterly; publ. by UNIP Youth League; Editor-in-Chief N. ANAMELA; circ. 20,000.

Zambia Government Gazette: POB 30136, Lusaka; tel. (21) 1228724; fax (21) 1224486; f. 1911; weekly; English; official notices.

NEWS AGENCY

Zambia News Agency (ZANA): Mass Media Complex, 2nd Floor, Alick Nkhata Rd, POB 30007, Lusaka; tel. (21) 1219673; fax (21) 1251631; e-mail zana@zamnet.zm; internet www.zana.gov.zm; f. 1969; Dir LEWIS MWANANGOMBE; Editor-in-Chief VILLIE LOMBANYA; headquarters in Lusaka and nine regional offices.

PRESS ASSOCIATION

Press Association of Zambia (PAZA): Bishops Rd, Multi-Media Centre, POB 37065, Lusaka; tel. (21) 1263595; fax (21) 1263110; f. 1983; Pres. ANDREW SAKALA; Vice-Pres. AMOS CHANDA.

Zambia Union of Journalists: Lusaka; Pres. ANTHONY MULOWA; Sec.-Gen. BOB SIANJALIKA.

Publishers

Africa: Literature Centre, POB 21319, Kitwe; tel. (21) 2210765; fax (21) 2210716; general, educational, religious; Dir JACKSON MBEWE.

African Social Research: Institute of Economic and Social Research, University of Zambia, POB 32379, Lusaka; tel. (21) 1294131; fax (21) 1253952; social research in Africa; Editor MUBANGA E. KASHOKI.

Bookworld Ltd: Plot 10442, off Lumumba Rd, POB 31838, Lusaka; tel. (21) 1230606; fax (21) 1230614; e-mail bookworld@realtime.zm.

Daystar Publications Ltd: POB 32211, Lusaka; f. 1966; religious; Man. Dir S. E. M. PHEKO.

Directory Publishers of Zambia Ltd: Mabalenga Rd, POB 30963, Lusaka; tel. (21) 1257133; fax (21) 1257137; e-mail dpz@coppernet.zm; f. 1958; trade directories; Gen. Man. W. D. WRATTEN.

Multimedia Zambia: Woodlands, POB 320199, Lusaka; tel. and fax (21) 1261193; f. 1971; religious and educational books, audio-visual materials; Exec. Dir EDDY MUPESO.

University of Zambia Press (UNZA Press): POB 32379, 10101 Lusaka; tel. (21) 1292269; fax (21) 1253952; f. 1938; academic books, papers and journals.

Zambia Educational Publishing House: Chishango Rd, POB 32708, 10101 Lusaka; tel. (21) 1222324; fax (21) 1225073; f. 1967; educational and general; Man. Dir BENIKO E. MULOTA.

GOVERNMENT PUBLISHING HOUSES

Government Printer: POB 30136, Lusaka; tel. (21) 1228724; fax (21) 1224486; official documents and statistical bulletins.

Zambia Information Services: POB 50020, Lusaka; tel. (21) 1219673; state-controlled; Dir BENSON SIANGA.

PUBLISHERS' ASSOCIATION

Booksellers' and Publishers' Association of Zambia: POB 31838, Lusaka; tel. (21) 1222647; fax (21) 1225195; Chair. RAY MUNAMWIMBU; Sec. BASIL MBEWE.

Broadcasting and Communications

REGULATORY AUTHORITY

Zambian Communications Authority: Plot 3141, cnr Lumumba and Buyantanshi Rds, POB 36871, Lusaka; tel. (21) 1241236; fax (21) 1246701; e-mail info@caz.zm; internet www.caz.zm; f. 1994; Acting CEO RICHARD MWANZA.

TELECOMMUNICATIONS

Airtel Zambia Ltd: POB 320001, Nyerere Rd, Woodlands, Lusaka; tel. (21) 1250707; e-mail customerservice.zm@zain.com; internet africa.airtel.com/zambia; f. 1997 as ZamCell Ltd; fmrly Celtel Zambia, subsequently Zain Zambia, present name adopted 2010; mobile cellular telephone operator; Man. Dir FAYAZ KING; c. 500,000 subscribers.

MTN (Zambia) Ltd: Plot 1278, Lubuto Rd, Rhodespark, POB 35464, Lusaka; tel. 966750750 (mobile); fax 966257732 (mobile); e-mail mtn@mtnzambia.co.zm; internet www.mtnzambia.co.zm; f. 1997 as Telecel (Zambia) Ltd; acquired by MTN Group, South Africa, in 2005; mobile cellular telecommunications provider; CEO PER ERIKSSON; 152,000 subscribers (2006).

Zambia Telecommunications Co Ltd (ZAMTEL): Provident House, Buteko Ave, POB 71660, Ndola; tel. (21) 2611111; fax (21) 2615855; e-mail zamtel@zamtel.zm; internet www.zamtel.zm; 75% owned by Lap Green Networks, Libya; operates Cell-Z cellular network (f. 1995); Chair. BASIL SICHALI; Man. Dir MUKELA MUYUNDA.

BROADCASTING

Zambia National Broadcasting Corpn: Mass Media Complex, Alick Nkhata Rd, POB 50015, Lusaka; tel. (21) 1252005; fax (21) 1254013; e-mail lukundosa@yahoo.com; internet www.znbc.co.zm; f. 1961; state-owned; two national radio stations (Radio 1 and Radio 2) and one line-of-rail station (Radio 4); television broadcasts along the line of rail, from Livingstone to Chililabombwe; services in

ZAMBIA

English and seven Zambian languages; Dir-Gen. JULIANA MWILA (acting).

Radio

Breeze FM: POB 511178, Chipata; tel. (21) 6221175; fax (21) 6221823; e-mail breezefm@zamtel.zm; internet www.breezefm.com; f. 2003; Nyanja and English; community-based commercial radio; broadcasts to the Eastern Province; signal is also received in parts of north-west Malawi and border areas of Tete Province in Mozambique; Man. Dir MIKE DAKA.

Educational Broadcasting Services: Headquarters: POB 50231, Lusaka; tel. (21) 1251724; radio broadcasts from Lusaka; audio-visual aids service from POB 50295, Lusaka; Controller MICHAEL MULOMBE.

Radio Chikaya: POB 530290, Lundazi; tel. (6) 480080; e-mail rchikaya@zamtel.zm.

Radio Chikuni: Private Bag E702, POB 660239, Monze; tel. and fax (32) 50708; e-mail chikuni@sat.signis.net; internet www.chikuniradio.org.

Radio Icengelo: Plot 5282, Mwandi Cres., Riverside, POB 20694, Kitwe; tel. (2) 220478; fax (2) 229305; e-mail radioice@zamtel.zm; Man. WILBROAD MWAPE.

Radio Maria Zambia: POB 510307, Chipata; tel. and fax (21) 6221154; e-mail info.zam@radiomaria.org; internet www.radiomaria.org; f. 1999; Dir MWANZA GABRIEL KWAKU.

Radio Phoenix: Private Bag E702, Lusaka; tel. (21) 1223581; fax (21) 1226839; e-mail rphoenix@zamnet.zm; internet www.radiophoenixzambia.com; commercial radio station; Chair. ERROL T. HICKEY.

Yatsani Radio: Leopards Hill Rd, Bauleni Catholic Church, POB 320147, Lusaka; tel. (21) 1261082; fax (21) 1265842; internet yatsani.com; f. 1999; owned by the Archdiocese of Lusaka; Roman Catholic religious community; broadcasts to Lusaka; Dir Most Rev. MEDARDO JOSEPH MAZOMBWE (Archbishop of Lusaka).

Television

Educational Broadcasting Services: (see Radio).

Muvi Television: Plot No. 17734, Nangwenya Rd, POB 33932, Lusaka; tel. (21) 1253171; fax (21) 1257351; e-mail frontoffice@muvitv.com; internet www.muvitv.com.

Finance

(cap. = capital; auth. = authorized; res = reserves; dep. = deposits; m. = million; br(s). = branch(es); amounts in kwacha)

BANKING

In 2010 there were 18 commercial banks, 24 microfinance institutions and one development bank in Zambia. From 2 January 2007 all banks operating in Zambia were required to have capital of not less than K12,000m. in order to receive a banking licence or to continue to function.

Central Bank

Bank of Zambia: Bank Sq., Cairo Rd, POB 30080, 10101 Lusaka; tel. (21) 1228888; fax (21) 1225652; internet www.boz.zm; f. 1964; bank of issue; cap. 10,020m., res 317,538m., dep. 5,460,206m. (Dec. 2009); Gov. and Chair. Dr CALEB M. FUNDANGA; br. in Ndola.

Commercial Banks

Finance Bank Zambia Ltd: 2101 Chanik House, Cairo Rd, POB 37102, 10101 Lusaka; tel. (21) 1229733; fax (21) 1227290; e-mail fbz@financebank.co.zm; internet www.financebank.co.zm; f. 1986 as Leasing Finance Bank Ltd; name changed as above 1988; the Bank of Zambia took possession of the Finance Bank Zambia Ltd in 2010 and initiated its sell-off process in 2011; cap. 3,630m., res 9,320m., dep. 823,894m. (Dec. 2006); Interim CEO LEONARD HAYNES; 33 brs and 10 agencies.

National Savings and Credit Bank: Plot 248B, Cairo Rd, POB 30067, Lusaka; tel. (21) 1227534; fax (21) 1223296; e-mail natsave@zamnet.zm; internet www.natsave.co.zm; f. 1972; state-owned; total assets 6,598m. (Dec. 1998); Chair. FRANK NGAMBI; Man. Dir CEPHAS CHABU (acting).

Zambia National Commercial Bank PLC (ZANACO): POB 33611, Plot 33454 Cairo Rd, Lusaka; tel. (21) 1228979; fax (21) 1223106; e-mail support@zanaco.co.zm; internet www.zanaco.co.zm; f. 1969; 50.8% govt-owned; cap. 11,550m., res 189,142m., dep.. 2,296,000m. (Dec. 2009); Chair. Dr MUTUMBA BULL LAWANIKA; Man. Dir MARTYN H. SCHOUTEN; 41 brs.

Foreign Banks

Bank of China (Zambia) Ltd (China): Amandra House, Ben Bella Rd, POB 34550, Lusaka; tel. (21) 1235349; fax (21) 1235350; e-mail service_zm@bank-of-china.com; f. 1997; cap. and res 5,731m., total assets 73,237m. (Dec. 2001); Chair. PING YUE; Gen. Man. HONG XINSHENG.

Barclays Bank Zambia PLC (United Kingdom): Kafue House, Cairo Rd, POB 31936, Lusaka; tel. (21) 1228858; fax (21) 1226185; e-mail barclays.zambia@barclays.com; internet www.africa.barclays.com; f. 1971; cap. 91,109m., res 247,794m., dep. 2,857,304m. (Dec. 2009); Chair. JACOB SIKAZWE; Man. Dir SAVIOUR CHIBIYA; 5 brs.

Citibank Zambia Ltd (USA): Citibank House, Cha Cha Cha Rd, POB 30037, Southend, Lusaka; tel. (21) 1229025; fax (21) 1226264; internet www.citibank.co.zm; f. 1979; cap. 1,000.0m., res 23,655.7m., dep. 1,100,772.6m. (Dec. 2009); Man. Dir SAVIOR CHIBIYA; 1 br.

Ecobank Zambia: 22768 Thabo Mbeki Rd, POB 30705, Lusaka; tel. (21) 1250056; fax (21) 1250171; e-mail ecobankzm@ecobank.com; internet www.ecobank.com; Chair. PETRONELLA N. MWANGALA; Man. Dir CHARITY LUMPA.

Indo-Zambia Bank (IZB): Plot 6907, Cairo Rd, POB 35411, Lusaka; tel. (21) 1224653; fax (21) 1225090; e-mail izb@zamnet.zm; internet www.izb.co.zm; f. 1984; cap. 15,000.0m., res 38,591.9m., dep. 767,161.3m. (March 2010); Chair. ORLENE Y. MOYO; Man. Dir CYRIL PATRO; 9 brs.

Stanbic Bank Zambia Ltd: Woodgate House, 6th Floor, Cairo Rd, POB 32111, Lusaka; tel. (21) 1229285; fax (21) 1225380; e-mail stanbic@zamnet.zm; internet www.stanbicbank.co.zm; f. 1971; wholly owned by Standard Bank Investment Corpn; cap. 7,700m., res 172,526m., dep. 2,160,400m. (Dec. 2009); Chair. V. CHITALU; Man. Dir L. F. KALALA; 7 brs.

Standard Chartered Bank Zambia PLC: Standard House, Cairo Rd, POB 32238, Lusaka; tel. (21) 1229242; fax (21) 1225337; internet www.standardchartered.com/zm; f. 1971; 90% owned by Standard Chartered Holdings (Africa) BV, the Netherlands; 10% state-owned; cap. 2,048m., res 23,657m., dep. 2,589,288m. (Dec. 2009); Chair. GEORGE SOKOTA; Man. Dir MIZINGA MELU; 16 brs.

Development Banks

Development Bank of Zambia: Development House, Katondo Rd, POB 33955, Lusaka; tel. (21) 1228576; fax (21) 1222821; e-mail projects@dbz.co.zm; internet www.dbz.co.zm; f. 1973; 99% state-owned; cap. and res 7,580.0m., total assets 145,976.6m. (March 1998); Chair. NAMUKULO MUKUTU; Man. Dir ABRAHAM MWENDA; 2 brs.

Banking Association

Bankers' Association of Zambia: POB 34810, Lusaka; tel. (21) 1234255; fax (21) 1233046; e-mail bazsecretariat@coppernet.zm; Chair. MIZINGA MELU.

STOCK EXCHANGE

Lusaka Stock Exchange (LuSE): Exchange Bldg, 3rd Floor, Central Park, Cairo Rd, POB 34523, Lusaka; tel. (21) 1228391; fax (21) 1225969; e-mail info@luse.co.zm; internet www.luse.co.zm; f. 1994; Chair. FRIDAY NDHLOVU; Gen. Man. BEATRICE NKANZA.

INSURANCE

In 2010 there were 15 licensed insurance companies in Zambia: two reinsurance companies, eight general insurance companies and five long-term insurance companies.

African Life Assurance Zambia: Mukuba Pension House, 4th Floor, Dedan Kimathi Rd, POB 31991; tel. (21) 1225452; fax (21) 1225435; e-mail customercare@african-life.com.zm; f. 2002; life insurance; CEO STEVE WILLIAMS.

Goldman Insurance Ltd: Zambia National Savings and Credit Bank Bldg, 2nd Floor, Cairo Rd, Private Bag W395, Lusaka; tel. (21) 1235234; fax (21) 1227262; e-mail goldman@zamnet.zm; internet www.goldman.co.zm; f. 1992; CEO M. N. RAJU.

Madison Insurance Co Ltd: Plot 255, Kaleya Rd, Roma, POB 37013, Lusaka; tel. (21) 1295311; fax (21) 1295320; internet www.madisonzambia.com; f. 1992; general and micro-insurance; Chair. DAVID A. R. PHIRI; Man. Dir LAWRENCE S. SIKUTWA.

NICO Insurance Zambia Ltd (NIZA): 1131 Parirenyatwa Rd, Fairview, POB 32825, Lusaka; tel. (21) 1222862; fax (21) 1222863; e-mail nicozam@zamnet.zm; internet www.nicomw.com/zambia; f. 1997; subsidiary of NICO Group, Malawi; general insurance; Chair. JOHN MWANAKATWE; Gen. Man. TITUS KALENGA.

Professional Insurance Corpn Zambia Ltd (PICZ): Finsbury Park, Kabwe Roundabout, POB 34264, Lusaka; tel. (21) 1227509; fax (21) 1222151; e-mail customerservice@picz.co.zm; internet www.picz.co.zm; f. 1992; Chair. R. L. MATHANI; Man. Dir ASHOK CHAWLA.

ZAMBIA

Zambia State Insurance Corpn Ltd: Premium House, Independence Ave, POB 30894, Lusaka; tel. (21) 1229343; fax (21) 1222263; e-mail zsic@zsic.co.zm; internet www.zsic.co.zm; f. 1968; transfer to private sector pending; Chair. ALBERT WOOD; Man. Dir IRENE MUYENGA.

ZIGI Insurance Co Ltd: Mukuba Pension House, 5th Floor, POB 37782, Lusaka; tel. (21) 1226835; fax (21) 1231564; e-mail zigi@zamnet.zm; f. 1998; Chair. and CEO SAVIOUR H. KONIE.

Regulatory Authority

Pensions and Insurance Authority: Private Bag 30X, Ridgeway, Lusaka; tel. (21) 1293533; fax (21) 1293530; e-mail pia@pia.org.zm; internet www.pia.org.zm; f. 2005; Chair. CHABUKA JEROME KAWESHA.

Trade and Industry

GOVERNMENT AGENCY

Zambia Development Agency: Privatisation House, Nasser Rd, POB 30819, Lusaka; tel. (21) 1220177; fax (21) 1225270; e-mail zda@zda.org.zm; internet www.zda.org.zm; f. 2006 by merger of the Zambia Privatisation Agency, the Zambia Investment Centre, the Export Board of Zambia, the Zambia Export Processing Zones Authority and the Small Enterprises Development Board; operational in July 2007; 262 cos privatized by mid-2006, 22 privatizations pending; Dir-Gen. and CEO ANDREW CHIPWENDE.

Zambia Revenue Authority: Lusaka; internet www.zra.org.zm; f. 1994; Dir-Gen. WISDOM NEKAIRO.

DEVELOPMENT ORGANIZATION

Industrial Development Corpn of Zambia Ltd (INDECO): Indeco House, Buteko Place, POB 31935, Lusaka; tel. (21) 1228026; fax (21) 1228868; f. 1960; auth. cap. K300m.; taken over by the Nat. Housing Authority in May 2005; Chair. R. L. BWALYA; Man. Dir S. K. TAMELÉ.

CHAMBERS OF COMMERCE

Zambia Association of Chambers of Commerce and Industry: Great East Rd, Showgrounds, POB 30844, Lusaka; tel. (21) 1252483; fax (21) 1253020; e-mail secretariat@zacci.co.zm; internet www.zacci.org.zm; f. 1938; Chair. HANSON SINDOWE; CEO JUSTIN M. CHISULO; 10 district chambers, 8 trade assocs, 35 corporate mems.

Member chambers and associations include:

Chamber of Mines of Zambia: POB 22100, Kitwe; tel. (21) 2214122; f. 1941 as Northern Rhodesia Chamber of Mines; replaced by the Copper Industry Service Bureau 1965–2000; represents mining employers; 19 mems; Pres. NATHAN CHISHIMBA; Gen. Man. FREDERICK BANTUBONSE.

Zambia Association of Manufacturers: POB 30036, Lusaka; tel. (21) 1242780; fax (21) 1222912; e-mail babbar@zamnet.zm; f. 1985; Chair. D. BABBAR; 180 mems.

Chamber of Small and Medium Business Associations.

INDUSTRIAL AND TRADE ASSOCIATIONS

Tobacco Board of Zambia (TBZ): POB 31963, Lusaka; tel. (21) 1288995; fax (21) 1287118; e-mail tbz@zamnet.zm; promotes, monitors and controls tobacco production; CEO AVEN MUVWENDE.

Zambia Farm Employers' Association (ZFEA): Farmers' Village, Lusaka Agricultural and Commercial Showgrounds, POB 30395, Lusaka; tel. (21) 1252649; fax (21) 1252648; e-mail znfu@zamnet.zm; Chair. R. DENLY; 350 mems.

Other associations include: the Bankers Asscn of Zambia; the Cotton Asscn of Zambia; the Environmental Conservation Asscn of Zambia; the Insurance Brokers Asscn of Zambia; the Kapenta Fishermen Asscn; the National Aquaculture Asscn of Zambia; the National Council for Construction; the Poultry Asscn of Zambia; the Tobacco Asscn of Zambia; the Wildlife Producers Asscn of Zambia; the Young Farmers Clubs of Zambia; the Zambia Asscn of Clearing and Forwarding; the Zambia Asscn of Manufacturers; the Zambia Coffee Growers Asscn; the Zambia Export Growers Asscn; and Zambian Women in Agriculture.

EMPLOYERS' ORGANIZATION

Zambia Federation of Employers (ZFE): Electra House, 1st Floor, Cairo Rd, POB 31941, Lusaka; e-mail zfe@zamnet.zm; internet www.zfe.co.zm; f. 1966; Pres. ALFRED MASUPHA.

UTILITIES

Electricity

Copperbelt Energy Corpn PLC (CEC): Private Bag E835, Postnet No. 145, Chindo Rd, Kabulonga, Lusaka; tel. (21) 1261647; fax (21) 1261640; e-mail info@cec.com.zm; internet www.cecinvestor.com; f. 1997 upon privatization of the power div. of Zambia Consolidated Copper Mines; privately owned co supplying power generated by ZESCO to mining cos in the Copperbelt; Exec. Chair. HANSON SINDOWE.

ZESCO (Zambia Electricity Supply Corpn) Ltd: Stand 6949, Great East Rd, POB 33304, Lusaka; tel. (21) 1226084; fax (21) 1222753; e-mail mchisela@zesco.co.zm; internet www.zesco.co.zm; f. 1970; state-owned; Chair. KWALELA LAMASWALA; Man. Dir RHODNIE P. SISALA.

CO-OPERATIVE

Zambia Co-operative Federation Ltd: Co-operative House, Cha Cha Cha Rd, POB 33579, Lusaka; tel. 2220157; fax 2222516; f. 1973; agricultural marketing; supply of agricultural chemicals and implements; cargo haulage; insurance; agricultural credit; auditing and accounting; property and co-operative devt; Chair. B. TETAMASHIMBA; Man. Dir G. Z. SIBALE.

TRADE UNIONS

Zambia Congress of Trade Unions (ZCTU): Solidarity House, Oxford Rd, POB 20652, Kitwe; tel. (21) 2211999; fax (21) 2228284; e-mail zctu@microlink.zm; f. 1965; Pres. LEONARD HIKAUMBA; Sec.-Gen. ROY MWABA; c. 350,000 mems (2007).

Affiliated Unions

Airways and Allied Workers' Union of Zambia: Lusaka International Airport, 2nd Floor, Terminal Bldg, POB 30175, 10101 Lusaka; Pres. F. MULENGA; Gen. Sec. B. CHINYANTA.

Civil Servants' & Allied Workers' Union of Zambia (CSAWUZ): Plot 5045A, Mumbwa Rd, POB 50160, Lusaka; tel. and fax (21) 1287106; e-mail csuz@zamnet.zm; f. 1975; Chair. L. C. HIKAUMBA; Gen. Sec. DARISON CHAALA; 35,000 mems.

Guards Union of Zambia (GUZ): POB 21882, Kitwe; tel. (21) 2216189; e-mail uni-africa@union-network.org; f. 1972; Chair. D. N. S. SILUNGWE; Gen. Sec. MICHAEL S. SIMFUKWE; 13,500 mems.

Hotel Catering Workers' Union of Zambia: POB 35693, Lusaka; Chair. IAN MKANDAWIRE; Gen. Sec. STOIC KAPUTU; 9,000 mems.

Mineworkers' Union of Zambia (MUZ): POB 20448, Kitwe; tel. (21) 2214022; Pres. CHARLES MUKUKA; Sec.-Gen. OSWELL MUNYENYEMBE; 50,000 mems.

National Union of Building, Engineering and General Workers (NUBEGW): City Sq., Millers Bldg, Plot No. 1094, POB 21515, Kitwe; tel. (21) 2224468; fax (21) 2661119; e-mail nubegw@zamtel.zm; Chair. LUCIANO MUTALE (acting); Gen. Sec. P. N. NZIMA; 18,000 mems.

National Union of Commercial and Industrial Workers (NUCIW): 17 Obote Ave, POB 21735, Kitwe; tel. (21) 2228607; fax (21) 2225211; e-mail nuciw@zamtel.zm; f. 1982; Chair. I. M. KASUMBU; Gen. Sec. JOHN M. BWALYA; 16,000 mems.

National Union of Communication Workers: POB 70751, 92 Broadway, Ndola; tel. (21) 2611345; fax (21) 2614679; e-mail nucw@zamtel.zm; Pres. PATRICK KAONGA; Gen. Sec. CLEMENT KASONDE; 4,700 mems.

National Union of Plantation and Agricultural Workers: POB 80529, Kabwe; tel. (21) 5224548; e-mail nupawhq@yahoo.com; Pres. MUDENDA RISHER; Gen. Sec. MULENGA MUKUKA; 15,155 mems.

National Union of Public Services' Workers (NUPSW): POB 32523, Lusaka; tel. (21) 1227451; fax (21) 1287105; e-mail znslib@zamtel.zm; Gen. Sec. DAVIS J. CHINGONI.

National Union of Transport and Allied Workers (NUTAW): Cha Cha Cha House, Rm 4, 1st Floor, POB 30068, Cario Rd, Lusaka; tel. (21) 1214756; e-mail sapphiri2005@yahoo.com; Pres. PATRICK C. CHANDA; Gen. Sec. SAM A. P. PHIRI.

Railway Workers' Union of Zambia: POB 80302, Kabwe; tel. (21) 5224006; Chair. H. K. NDAMANA; Gen. Sec. BENSON L. NGULA; 10,228 mems.

University of Zambia and Allied Workers' Union: POB 32379, Lusaka; tel. (21) 1213221; f. 1968; Chair. BERIATE SUNKUTU; Gen. Sec. SAINI PHIRI.

Zambia Electricity Workers' Union: POB 70859, Ndola; f. 1972; Chair. COSMAS MPAMPI; Gen. Sec. ADAM KALUBA; 3,000 mems.

Zambia Graphical and Allied Workers' Union (ZAGRAWU): POB 290346, Ndola; tel. and fax (21) 2614457; e-mail zatawu@yahoo.com; Gen. Sec. DAVID S. MWABA.

ZAMBIA

Zambia National Farmers' Union: ZNFU Head Office, Tiyende Pamodzi Rd, opp. Polo Grounds, Farmers' Village, Zambia Agricultural and Commercial Showgrounds, POB 30395, Lusaka; tel. (21) 1252649; fax (21) 1252648; e-mail znfu@zamnet.zm; internet www.znfu.org.zm; Exec. Dir SONGOWAYO ZYAMBO.

Zambia National Union of Teachers: POB 31914, Lusaka; tel. (21) 1214623; fax (21) 1214624; e-mail znut@microlink.zm; Chair. RICHARD M. LIYWALII; Gen. Sec. ROY MWABA; 2,120 mems.

Zambia Union of Journalists: POB 30394, Lusaka; tel. (21) 1227348; fax (21) 1221695; e-mail zuj.zambia@yahoo.com; Vice-Pres. MORGAN CHONYA; Gen. Sec. NIGEL MULENGA.

Zambia Union of Local Government Officers: f. 1997; Pres. ISAAC MWANZA.

Zambia United Local Authorities Workers' Union (ZULAWU): Mugala House, POB 70575, Ndola; tel. (21) 2615022; Chair. ABRAHAM M. MUTAKILA; Gen. Sec. AMON DAKA (acting).

Principal Non-Affiliated Union

Zambian African Mining Union: Kitwe; f. 1967; 40,000 mems.

Transport

RAILWAYS

The total length of railways in Zambia was 2,162 km (including 891 km of the Tanzania–Zambia railway) in 2000. There are two major railway networks: the Zambia Railways network, which traverses the country from the Copperbelt in northern Zambia and links with the National Railways of Zimbabwe to provide access to South African ports, and the Tanzania–Zambia Railway (Tazara) network, linking New Kapiri-Mposhi in Zambia with Dar es Salaam in Tanzania. In June 2002 plans were announced to rebuild the Benguela railway, linking Zambian copper mines with the Angolan port of Lobito. It was announced in 2003 that a line would be built linking the Zambian port of Mpulungu to the Tazara network. In April 2005 Northwest Railways undertook to develop a new line between Chingola, in the Copperbelt Province, and Lumwana, in the North-Western Province. It was anticipated that the line could eventually be linked to the Benguela railway. In August 2010 a 27-km railway line linking Chipata with Mchinji, Malawi was inaugurated. There were plans to link Mulobezi with the Namibian railway system.

Tanzania–Zambia Railway Authority (Tazara): POB T01, Mpika; Head Office: POB 2834, Dar es Salaam, Tanzania; tel. (21) 4370684; fax (21) 4370228; f. 1975; operates passenger and freight services linking New Kapiri-Mposhi, north of Lusaka, with Dar es Salaam in Tanzania, a distance of 1,860 km, of which 891 km is in Zambia; jtly owned and administered by the Govts of Tanzania and Zambia; Chair. SALIM H. MSOMA; Man. Dir AKASHAMBATWA MBIKUSITA-LEWANIKA.

Zambia Railways Ltd: cnr Buntungwa St and Ghana Ave, POB 80935, Kabwe; tel. (21) 5222201; fax (21) 5224411; f. 1967; Chair. B. NONDE; Man. Dir GÖRAN MALMBERG.

ROADS

In 2001 there was a total road network of 91,440 km, including 4,222 km of main roads and 8,948 km of secondary roads. The main arterial roads run from Beitbridge (Zimbabwe) to Tunduma (the Great North Road), through the copper-mining area to Chingola and Chililabombwe (hitherto the Zaire Border Road), from Livingstone to the junction of the Kafue river and the Great North Road, and from Lusaka to the Malawi border (the Great East Road). In 1984 the 300-km BotZam highway linking Kazungula with Nata, in Botswana, was formally opened. A 1,930-km main road (the TanZam highway) links Zambia and Tanzania.

Road Development Agency: POB 50003, Lusaka; tel. (21) 1253801; fax (21) 1253404; e-mail rda_hq@roads.gov.zm; internet www.rda.org.zm; f. 2002; fmrly Dept of Roads; CEO ERASMUS CHILUNDIKA.

CIVIL AVIATION

In 1984 there were 127 airports, aerodromes and airstrips. An international airport, 22.5 km from Lusaka, was opened in 1967.

National Airports Corpn Ltd (NACL): Airport Rd, 10101 Lusaka; tel. (21) 1271313; fax (21) 1271048; e-mail nacl@zamnet.zm; internet www.lun.aero; f. 1973; air cargo services; Man. Dir ROBINSON MISITALA (acting).

Proflight Zambia: Site 15B, Private Hangars, Lusaka International Airport, POB 30536, Lusaka; tel. (21) 1271032; fax (21) 1271139; e-mail reservations@proflight-zambia.com; internet www.proflight-zambia.com; f. 2004; Chair. TONY IRWIN.

Zambezi Airlines: Petroda House, 2nd Floor, Great East Rd, Rhodes Park, POB 35470, Lusaka; tel. (21) 1257606; fax (21) 1257631; e-mail info@flyzambezi.com; internet www.flyzambezi.com; f. 2008; Chair. Dr MAURICE JANGULO; CEO DON MACDONALD.

Tourism

Zambia's main tourist attractions, in addition to the Victoria Falls, are its wildlife, unspoilt scenery and diverse cultural heritage; there are 19 national parks and 36 game management areas. In 2008 811,775 tourists visited Zambia; tourism receipts totalled US $146m. in that year.

Tourism Council of Zambia: 55–56 Mulungushi International Conference Centre, POB 36561, Lusaka; tel. (21) 1291788; fax (21) 1290436; e-mail secretariat.tcz@iconnect.zm; internet www.tcz.org.zm; f. 1997; Exec. Dir VICTOR INAMBWAE.

Zambia National Tourist Board: Century House, Lusaka Sq., POB 30017, Lusaka; tel. (21) 1229087; fax (21) 1225174; e-mail zntb@zambiatourism.org.zm; internet www.zambiatourism.com; Chair. ERROL HICKEY; Man. Dir CHANDA CHARITY LUMPA.

Defence

As assessed at November 2010, Zambia's armed forces officially numbered about 15,100 (army 13,500 and air force 1,600). Paramilitary forces numbered 1,400. Military service is voluntary. There is also a National Defence Force, responsible to the Government. In 2009 some 600 Zambian troops were stationed abroad, attached to UN missions in Africa and Asia; of these, 49 were serving as observers.

Defence Expenditure: Estimated at K1,330,000m. for 2009.

Commander of the Army: Lt-Gen. WISDOM LOPA.

Commander of the Air Force: Lt-Gen. ANDREW SAKALA.

Education

Between 1964 and 1979 enrolment in schools increased by more than 260%. Primary education, which is compulsory, begins at seven years of age and lasts for seven years. Secondary education, beginning at the age of 14, lasts for a further five years, comprising a first cycle of two years and a second of three years. According to UNESCO estimates, in 2008/09 91% of children (90% of boys; 92% of girls) in the relevant age group attended primary schools, while enrolment at secondary schools included 46% of children (51% of boys; 42% of girls) in the relevant age group. There are two universities: the University of Zambia at Lusaka, and the Copperbelt University at Kitwe (which is to be transferred to Ndola). There are 14 teacher training colleges. In 2005 expenditure on education was K1,062.0m. The 2006 budgetary allocation was K1,647.0m., some 26.9% of the overall budget. The Government recruited an additional 8,000 teachers in 2005 and had recruited a further 5,000 by mid-2010.

ZIMBABWE

Introductory Survey

LOCATION, CLIMATE, LANGUAGE, RELIGION, FLAG, CAPITAL

The Republic of Zimbabwe is a land-locked state in southern Africa, with Mozambique to the east, Zambia to the north-west, Botswana to the south-west and South Africa to the south. The climate is tropical, modified considerably by altitude. Average monthly temperatures range from 13°C (55°F) to 22°C (72°F) on the Highveld, and from 20°C (68°F) to 30°C (86°F) in the low-lying valley of the Zambezi river. The rainy season is from November to March. The official languages are English, ChiShona and SiNdebele. About 55% of the population are Christians. A large number of the African population follow traditional beliefs, while the Asian minority comprises both Muslims and Hindus. The national flag (proportions 1 by 2) has seven equal horizontal stripes, of green, gold, red, black, red, gold and green, with a white triangle, bearing a red five-pointed star on which a gold 'Great Zimbabwe bird' is superimposed, at the hoist. The capital is Harare.

CONTEMPORARY POLITICAL HISTORY

Historical Context

In 1923 responsibility for Southern Rhodesia (now Zimbabwe) was transferred from the British South Africa Company to the Government of the United Kingdom, and the territory became a British colony. It had full self-government (except for African interests and some other matters) under an administration controlled by European settlers. African voting rights were restricted.

In 1953 the colony united with two British protectorates, Northern Rhodesia (now Zambia) and Nyasaland (now Malawi), to form the Federation of Rhodesia and Nyasaland. A new Constitution, which ended most of the United Kingdom's legal controls and provided for a limited African franchise, came into effect in November 1962. At elections in December the Prime Minister, Sir Edgar Whitehead, lost power to the Rhodesian Front (RF), a coalition of white opposition groups committed to maintaining racial segregation. The leader of the RF, Winston Field, became Prime Minister.

As a result of pressure from African nationalist movements in Northern Rhodesia and Nyasaland, the Federation was dissolved in December 1963. African nationalists were also active in Southern Rhodesia: Joshua Nkomo formed the Zimbabwe African People's Union (ZAPU), which was declared an unlawful organization in September 1962. ZAPU split in July 1963, and a breakaway group, led by the Rev. Ndabaningi Sithole, formed the Zimbabwe African National Union (ZANU) in August. Robert Mugabe became Secretary-General of ZANU.

In April 1964 Field was succeeded as Prime Minister of Southern Rhodesia by his deputy, Ian Smith. The new regime rejected British conditions for independence, including acceptance by the whole Rhodesian population and unimpeded progress to majority rule. In August ZANU was banned. After Northern Rhodesia became independent as Zambia in October, Southern Rhodesia became generally (although not officially) known as Rhodesia. On 5 November 1965 a state of emergency (to be renewed annually) was declared, and on 11 November Smith made a unilateral declaration of independence (UDI) and proclaimed a new Constitution, naming the country Rhodesia. The British Government regarded Rhodesia's independence as unconstitutional and illegal, and no other country formally recognized it. The United Kingdom terminated all relations with Rhodesia, while the UN applied economic sanctions. Both ZAPU and ZANU took up arms against the RF regime.

Following a referendum in June 1969, Rhodesia was declared a republic in March 1970. The 1969 Constitution provided for a bicameral Legislative Assembly, comprising a 23-member Senate and a 66-member House of Assembly (50 Europeans and 16 Africans). The President had only formal powers, and Smith remained Prime Minister. The RF won all 50 European seats in the House of Assembly in 1970, 1974 and 1977.

In November 1971 the British and Rhodesian Governments agreed on draft proposals for a constitutional settlement, subject to their acceptability to the Rhodesian people 'as a whole'. In December the African National Council (ANC), led by Bishop Abel Muzorewa, was formed to co-ordinate opposition to the plan. In December 1974, however, the Rhodesian Government and leaders of four nationalist organizations (including ZAPU, ZANU and the ANC) agreed the terms of a cease-fire, conditional on the release of African political detainees and on the convening of a constitutional conference in 1975. The African organizations agreed to unite within the ANC, with Muzorewa as President. Mugabe opposed the incorporation of ZANU into the ANC, and in mid-1975 left Rhodesia for neighbouring Mozambique, where he took control of ZANU's external wing, and challenged Sithole's leadership of the party. In September the ANC split into rival factions, led by Muzorewa and Nkomo. Constitutional talks between the Government and the Nkomo faction began in December 1975, but were abandoned in March 1976. In September, under pressure from South Africa, Smith announced his Government's acceptance of proposals leading to majority rule within two years. In late 1976 representatives of the RF, the African nationalists and the British Government met to discuss the transition to majority rule. The nationalists were led by Muzorewa, Sithole, Nkomo and Mugabe (by then the recognized leader of ZANU). Nkomo and Mugabe adopted a joint position as the Patriotic Front (PF).

In January 1977 Angola, Botswana, Mozambique, Tanzania and Zambia (the 'front-line' states) declared their support for the PF. Smith rejected British proposals for an interim administration, and received a mandate from the RF to repeal racially discriminatory laws and to seek agreement with such African factions as he chose. In November Smith accepted the principle of universal adult suffrage, and talks on an internal settlement were initiated with Muzorewa's United African National Council (UANC), Sithole's faction of the ANC and the Zimbabwe United People's Organization, led by Chief Jeremiah Chirau. These talks led to the signing of an internal settlement on 3 March 1978, providing for an interim power-sharing administration to prepare for independence on 31 December. The proposals were rejected by the PF and by the UN Security Council. In May 1978 the newly created Executive Council, consisting of Smith, Sithole, Muzorewa and Chirau, ordered the release of all political detainees in an attempt to bring about a cease-fire.

In January 1979 a 'majority rule' Constitution, with entrenched safeguards for the white minority, was approved by the House of Assembly and endorsed by a referendum of European voters. In April elections to the new House of Assembly (the first by universal adult suffrage) were held in two stages: for 20 directly elected European members (chosen by non-African voters only) and then for 72 African members (chosen by the whole electorate). The elections were boycotted by the PF. The UANC emerged as the majority party, with 51 seats, while the RF won all 20 seats for whites. In May the new Parliament elected Josiah Gumede as President. Muzorewa became Prime Minister of the country (renamed Zimbabwe Rhodesia) in June. In accordance with the Constitution, Muzorewa formed a government of national unity, including European members (Smith became Minister without Portfolio). However, international recognition was not forthcoming, and UN sanctions remained in force.

New impetus for a lasting and internationally recognized settlement followed the Commonwealth Conference in Zambia in August 1979. In September a Rhodesian Constitutional Conference in London, United Kingdom, was attended by delegations under Muzorewa and the joint leaders of the PF. The PF reluctantly agreed to special representation for the whites under the proposed new Constitution, which was eventually accepted by both parties; complete agreement was reached on transitional arrangements in November, and a cease-fire between the guerrillas of the PF and the Rhodesian security forces was finalized the following month. On 11 December the Zimbabwe Rhodesia Parliament voted to renounce independence and to revert to the status of a British colony, as Southern Rhodesia. Illegal rule ended on the following day, when Parliament was dissolved, the President, Prime Minister and Cabinet resigned, and the British-appointed Governor, Lord Soames, was vested with full executive and legislative authority for the duration of the transition to legal independence. The United Kingdom immediately revoked economic sanctions.

Lord Soames ended the ban on the two wings of the PF (ZAPU and ZANU) and ordered the release of most of the detainees who were held under the 'emergency powers' laws. Elections to a new House of Assembly proceeded in February 1980 (again in two stages) under the supervision of a British Electoral Commissioner. Mugabe's ZANU—PF emerged as the largest single party, winning 57 of the 80 African seats; Nkomo's PF—ZAPU took 20 seats and the UANC only three. In a separate poll of white voters, the RF secured all 20 reserved seats. The new state of Zimbabwe became legally independent, within the Commonwealth, on 18 April, with Rev. Canaan Banana as President (with largely ceremonial duties) and Mugabe as Prime Minister, at the head of a coalition Government.

Domestic Political Affairs

Relations within the new Government were strained, particularly between Mugabe and Nkomo. The latter was removed from the Cabinet, with two PF colleagues, in February 1982, under suspicion of plotting against Mugabe. By May 1984 the RF, now restyled the Republican Front, retained only seven of the 20 seats reserved for whites, the remaining 13 being held by independents. In July the RF was renamed the Conservative Alliance of Zimbabwe (CAZ), and opened its membership to all races.

There were several outbreaks of violence prior to a general election in June–July 1985. ZANU—PF was returned to power with an increased majority, winning 63 of the 79 'common roll' seats in the House of Assembly (and an additional seat at a by-election in August). ZAPU won 15 seats, retaining its traditional hold over Matabeleland, and ZANU—Sithole took a single seat. The UANC failed to gain representation. Of the 20 seats reserved for whites, 15 were secured by the CAZ. However, the CAZ was not represented in the new Cabinet.

During mid-1985 a large number of ZAPU officials were detained for questioning about dissident activity in Matabeleland. The failure, in August 1987, of talks aimed at uniting ZANU and ZAPU led to renewed rebel activity, whereupon the Government took steps to prevent ZAPU from functioning effectively. Furthermore, ZANU declined to endorse seven ZAPU-nominated candidates for the parliamentary seats made vacant in September by the abolition of seats reserved for whites (see below). In December Mugabe and Nkomo finally signed an agreement of unity, which was ratified by both parties in April 1988. In January 1988 Nkomo was appointed as one of the Senior Ministers in the President's Office, and two other ZAPU officials were given government posts. Following the unity agreement, there was a significant improvement in the security situation in Matabeleland. However, the state of emergency remained in force, owing to incursions into eastern Zimbabwe by the Mozambican rebel movement, the Resistência Nacional Moçambicana (Renamo, see Foreign Affairs, below).

Two major constitutional reforms were enacted during 1987. In September the reservation for whites of 20 seats in the House of Assembly and 10 seats in the Senate was abolished, as permitted by the Constitution, subject to a majority vote in the House. In October the 80 remaining members of the House of Assembly elected 20 candidates, who were nominated by ZANU, including 11 whites, to fill the vacant seats in the House of Assembly until the next general election. In the same month Parliament approved the replacement of the ceremonial presidency by an executive presidency. The post of Prime Minister was to be incorporated into the presidency. President Banana (who, as the only candidate, had been sworn in for a second term of office as President in April 1986) retired in December 1987, and at the end of that month Mugabe (the sole candidate) was inaugurated as Zimbabwe's first executive President.

In December 1989 ZANU and ZAPU merged to form a single party, named the Zimbabwe African National Union—Patriotic Front (ZANU—PF). The united party aimed to establish a one-party state with a Marxist-Leninist doctrine. Mugabe was appointed President of ZANU—PF, while Nkomo became one of its two Vice-Presidents.

Presidential and parliamentary elections were held concurrently in March 1990; at these elections legislation approved in late 1989 came into effect, abolishing the Senate and increasing the number of seats in the House of Assembly from 100 to 150 (of which 120 were to be directly elected; 12 were to be allocated to presidential nominees, 10 to traditional Chiefs and eight to provincial governors). Mugabe won nearly 80% of all votes cast at the presidential election and at the parliamentary elections ZANU—PF secured 117 of the 120 elective seats in the House of Assembly. Although ZANU—PF won an outright victory, only 54% of the electorate voted, and representatives of the ruling party were accused of intimidating voters. Following the elections Nkomo was appointed as one of two Vice-Presidents (the other being Simon Muzenda, also a Vice-President of ZANU—PF), and remained one of the Senior Ministers in the President's Office. In August 1990 the state of emergency was finally revoked.

In March 1992 the House of Assembly approved legislation (the Land Acquisition Act) that permitted the compulsory acquisition of land by the Government; this was intended to facilitate the redistribution of land ownership from Europeans (who owned about one-third of farming land in early 1992) to Africans. In May 1993 the Government published a list of properties allotted for transfer to the State under the Act, provoking a strong protest from the white-dominated Commercial Farmers' Union (CFU). The High Court subsequently ruled against three white farmers who had attempted to prove that the confiscation of their land was unconstitutional. A lack of available funds impeded the progress of the Government's land resettlement programme.

ZANU—PF won an overwhelming victory at legislative elections in April 1995, receiving more than 82% of the votes cast and securing 118 of the 120 elective seats in the House of Assembly (55 of which were uncontested). The remaining two elective seats were taken by ZANU—Ndonga (formerly ZANU—Sithole). Following the allocation of nominated and reserved seats, ZANU—PF controlled 148 of the total 150 seats. However, only 54% of the electorate voted, and the elections were boycotted by eight opposition groups, including the Zimbabwe Unity Movement. In mid-April Mugabe appointed a reorganized and enlarged Cabinet; Nkomo and Muzenda remained as Vice-Presidents.

Mugabe retained the presidency at an election in March 1996, winning 92.7% of the votes cast. Turn-out was, however, low. In late March Mugabe was sworn in for a third term as President. In October it was announced that ZANU—PF was abandoning Marxism-Leninism as its guiding principle and in August the Government had announced that the independence war veterans (an increasingly powerful lobby) would be awarded a number of substantial, unbudgeted benefits.

Land resettlement

In October 1997 Mugabe announced that the pace of the land resettlement programme would be accelerated, declaring that the constitutional right of white commercial farmers to receive full and fair compensation for confiscated land would not be honoured and (unsuccessfully) challenging the United Kingdom, in its role as former colonial power, to take responsibility for assisting them. A list of 1,503 properties to be reallocated forthwith was published in November. In January 1998, however, the IMF stipulated on an assurance from the Mugabe administration that it would respect the Constitution during the land resettlement procedure as a condition for the release of financial assistance; such an assurance was eventually given in March, when it was announced that 120 farms would be acquired in the near future in exchange for full and fair compensation. In August Mugabe introduced the second phase of the programme, to resettle 150,000 families on 1m. ha of land each year for the next seven years. Under pressure from Western donors, the Government agreed to reduce its plans, and was restricted to using 118 farms that it had already been offered. In November, however, 841 white-owned farms were ordered to be confiscated by the state: compensation was to be deferred. Pressure exerted by the IMF in light of a forthcoming release of aid brought an assurance from Mugabe that his administration would not break agreements for a gradual land reform programme; however, at the end of March 1999 the President contravened the agreement when he announced a new plan to acquire a further 529 white-owned farms. Mugabe accused the USA and the United Kingdom of 'destabilizing' Zimbabwe through their alleged control over the IMF, which was delaying financial assistance to the country. In May the Government agreed a plan that aimed to resettle 77,700 black families on 1m. ha by 2001. Some of this land was to come from the 118 farms that had already been offered. The remainder would be the result of uncontested acquisitions under the Government's reduced list of 800 farms for compulsory purchase. The plan was to be partially funded by the World Bank, and was broadly accepted by the white landowners' association.

Meanwhile, labour unrest escalated in December 1997, when a general strike was organized by the Zimbabwe Congress of Trade

Unions (ZCTU), in protest at the imposition by the Government of three unpopular new taxes in order to finance the provision of benefits to war veterans (see above); the authorities capitulated, withdrawing two of the taxes immediately. Shortly after the demonstrations had subsided, Morgan Tsvangirai, the Secretary-General of ZCTU, was attacked in his office by unknown assailants. The weak Zimbabwe currency and soaring food prices aggravated the nation-wide mood of discontent. In January 1998 riots erupted in most of the country's urban areas in protest at rises in the price of maize meal, the staple food. In response Mugabe agreed to withdraw the most recent price increase. However, the army was deployed to suppress the disturbances and was authorized to open fire on protesters; nine people were reportedly killed and some 800 rioters were arrested. The ZCTU organized a further two-day strike in March, to protest against the continuing rise in living costs.

In October 1998 the Government discussed potential amendments to Zimbabwe's Constitution with an opposition grouping, the National Constitutional Assembly (NCA). In March 1999 Mugabe appointed a commission of inquiry to make recommendations for a new constitution. The NCA refused to participate, owing to the alleged high risk of presidential manipulation.

An international constitutional conference was held in November 1999, but several experts suspected that the draft constitution had already been written, and that they had been invited primarily to give the process global credibility. In late November a document bearing no relation to that prepared by the 400-member constitutional commission, a drafting committee overseen by ZANU—PF having deleted crucial clauses (particularly relating to the reduction of the President's powers and the introduction of a parliamentary system), was declared to have been 'adopted by acclamation', despite vigorous protests. In January 2000 Mugabe announced that a referendum on the new constitution would take place on 12–13 February. Confusion before the polls over such issues as eligibility to vote and the location of polling stations was believed by the opposition to have been orchestrated by ZANU—PF to maximize Mugabe's chances of victory. Despite fears that a lack of supervision of the ballot had led to widespread irregularities on ZANU—PF's part, 54.6% of the 26% of the electorate who participated in the polls voted to reject the draft constitution. The level of participation was highest in urban areas where support for the recently formed opposition party, the Movement for Democratic Change (MDC), led by Tsvangirai, was strong.

The Government embarked on a campaign to restore its popularity prior to the June 2000 legislative elections. Illegal occupations of white-owned farms by black 'war veterans' (many of whom, too young to have taken part in the war of independence, were suspected of having been paid to participate), which began in late February, were rumoured to have been organized by the Government in an attempt to regain support through the land issue. Occupations increased, and the police also failed to take steps to evict the protesters; Mugabe repeatedly denied that his administration was behind the occupations, but made no secret of his support for them. The international community condemned the Government's increasingly militant stance, which also extended to the treatment of the opposition, in particular the MDC, which was subjected to a campaign of intimidation and aggression. In May Mugabe signed a law allowing the seizure of 841 white-owned farms without compensation and the following month a list was published of 804 farms that were to be confiscated. Farmers were to be granted approximately one month to contest the list.

Prior to legislative elections, which took place on 24–25 June 2000, there were reports of violence towards observers, and a UN team, sent to co-ordinate the polls, was recalled following obstruction by the Government. The authorities also refused to permit the accreditation of some 200 foreign monitors. ZANU—PF secured 48.6% of the votes cast and 62 of the 120 elective seats in the House of Assembly, the MDC won 47.0% of the ballot and 57 seats, while ZANU—Ndonga received one seat. Morgan Tsvangirai failed to win his constituency, as did the Ministers of Justice and Home Affairs. There were reports of widespread irregularities in the polls, which international observers declared not to have been free and fair. The MDC announced that it was to submit 10 dossiers listing alleged incidents of electoral fraud to the High Court. In total, the MDC challenged the results in 37 constituencies. In April 2001 the Court announced that results in two constituencies, including that contested by Tsvangirai, were to be nullified and new elections held; the MDC had previously abandoned proceedings relating to two other constituencies, and had been defeated in its challenge to the result in another. In June one further result was nullified, and one upheld.

Shortly after the legislative elections, Mugabe announced that some 500 additional white-owned farms would be appropriated for resettlement. In December 2000 a court ruling upheld previous opinions that declared the appropriation of white-owned farms without compensation payments to be unlawful, and urged the Government to produce a feasible land-reform programme by June 2001; Mugabe announced that sufficient white-owned land had been appropriated for resettlement, but repeated his assertion that he would not accept court-imposed impediments to any further land-reform measures. Negotiations between the Government and farmers' representatives resumed in January 2001.

International isolation

In March 2001 the Commonwealth announced that it would send a delegation comprising the foreign ministers of Australia, Barbados and Nigeria to Zimbabwe for discussions with the Government. Mugabe refused to meet the delegation, however, claiming that the decision had been inspired by the United Kingdom. Similar criticisms were made of an attempt by the European Union (EU, see p. 270) to establish a dialogue with Zimbabwe regarding its record on human rights. In early June Mugabe urged war veterans to intensify the occupation of white-owned farms, and in the following days attacks against such farms throughout the country were reported to have increased, causing the death of at least one farm worker. The Zimbabwean Government criticized US and British media coverage of the events, and in mid-June it imposed severe restrictions on journalists visiting the country. Later that month the Government listed a further 2,030 farms for compulsory acquisition, and in August the Minister of Lands, Agriculture and Rural Development announced the Government's intention to appropriate 8.3m. ha of commercial farmland. Further unrest occurred later that month in the north of the country, where approximately 100 white-owned farms were reported to have been evacuated following attacks by war veterans.

In early September 2001 a meeting of Commonwealth ministers was convened in Abuja, Nigeria, to discuss Mugabe's land resettlement programme; it was agreed that illegal farm seizures would cease and that international donors would compensate white farmers for the distribution of their land to landless black families. The agreement was broadly supported by both ZANU—PF and the MDC. By the end of September, however, more than 20 new farm invasions were reported to have taken place, resulting in several deaths, and talks between the Government and the CFU collapsed. Mugabe's intention to disregard the terms of the Abuja agreement became apparent in early October, when he ordered the Supreme Court to recognize the land reform programme as legal, reversing the ruling of December 2000; widespread criticism was directed at the Government for its manipulation of the judiciary. Commonwealth ministers and officials visited Zimbabwe later in October 2001 to monitor the Government's adherence to the Abuja agreement, but failed to persuade the Government to comply with its terms. Government repression intensified in November, when it amended the Land Act by decree. According to the revised legislation, any farm issued with a 'notice of acquisition' would become the property of the state with immediate effect; previously, a farm owner had been served 90 days' notice.

In November 2001 the Government ordered *The Daily News* to close its offices, alleging financial irregularities; it was widely believed, however, that the measure was taken to suppress criticism of the Government. The editor of that newspaper was charged with false reporting and undermining the Government in October 2002, under the Public Order and Security Act (see below), and resigned in December.

International concern regarding the situation in Zimbabwe intensified at the end of 2001. South African President Thabo Mbeki expressed doubts about whether conditions were suitable for a free and fair presidential election (scheduled to be held in March 2002), and the Commonwealth Ministerial Action Group on the Harare Declaration, meeting in London, United Kingdom, in late December 2001, warned the Zimbabwean Government that it risked suspension from the organization unless it ended violent land seizures and political intimidation of the media and opposition groups. Despite Zimbabwe's growing isolation in the international community, in January 2002 further controversial legislation, aimed at suppressing opposition to Mugabe, was introduced: the Public Order and Security Bill prohibited the publication of documents that incited public disorder or undermined the security services, and banned public gatherings that incited rioting; the General Laws Amendment Bill prohibited foreign and independent missions from monitoring the elections, and forbade voter education (the Bill was repealed by the Supreme Court in February, following a challenge from the MDC); and the Access to Information Bill made it an offence for foreign news services to report from Zimbabwe unless authorized by the Zimbabwean Government. The EU finally imposed so-called 'smart' sanctions on Zimbabwe in mid-February, after the leader of its electoral observer mission was expelled from the country. The sanctions included an embargo on the sale of arms to Zimbabwe, the suspension of €128m. of aid scheduled to be disbursed during 2002–07, and the freezing of the assets of 19 Zimbabwean officials, including Mugabe, who were also prohibited from visiting any EU state; the USA imposed similar measures several days later. In July the EU applied the sanctions to a further 53 people, including all cabinet members. The EU extended sanctions for a further 12 months in February 2003, although Mugabe attended the Franco-African summit in Paris, France, later that month. The USA also extended its sanctions to more than 70 senior officials in March 2003.

The presidential election took place on 9–10 March 2002, but voting was extended to 11 March by the High Court, in response to a request from the MDC, which had claimed that the number of polling stations in areas with strong MDC support was inadequate, and that certain stations had closed on 10 March before many people had been able to vote. Mugabe was declared the winner on 13 March, with 56.2% of the valid votes cast; Tsvangirai secured 42.0%. Independent observers were divided in their judgement of whether the election was free and fair; most observers from African countries declared the election result legitimate, while the Norwegian delegation (the only European representatives) and independent Zimbabwean observers condemned the result and reported widespread electoral fraud and intimidation of the electorate and of observers by members of ZANU—PF. The MDC claimed that a number of its agents had been abducted from certain polling stations and detained by the police. Tsvangirai mounted a legal challenge to have the results declared null and void; however, after a protracted case, the High Court eventually ruled against him in 2005 and the Supreme Court dismissed his application in February 2006.

Prior to the presidential election the Commonwealth had nominated the Nigerian President, Olusegun Obasanjo, Mbeki and the Australian Prime Minister, John Howard, to consider the conduct of the election and to formulate the organization's response. Mbeki and Obasanjo visited Zimbabwe following the election and urged Mugabe and the MDC to form a government of national unity; however, the MDC refused to co-operate unless the election was reheld. The Commonwealth suspended Zimbabwe from meetings of the organization for one year in mid-March 2002, stating that the election result had been undermined by politically motivated violence and that conditions did not permit the free will of the electorate to be expressed. (The suspension was extended for a further nine months in March 2003.) Immediately after the election the Government enacted the Access to Information and Protection of Privacy Act, which required all journalists reporting in Zimbabwe to be approved by the state; seven journalists had been detained under the Act by early May 2002. In April the NCA organized demonstrations in support of demands for a new constitution and a re-run of the presidential election, at which more than 80 demonstrators were arrested. Violence directed at supporters of the MDC intensified following the election, allegedly committed by ZANU—PF supporters, and more than 50 people were reported to have been killed between the election and the end of April.

Land seizures also escalated, and in late March 2002 the Government listed almost 400 white-owned farms for compulsory acquisition, bringing the area scheduled for redistribution to the black population to around 85% of total commercial farmland. In June Mugabe issued an order listing some 2,900 white-owned farms for seizure; farmers were obliged to cease working their land in June, or face up to two years' imprisonment, and to leave their properties by August. Some 860 farmers had vacated their properties by the deadline, while 1,700 refused to leave. (Some 300 had left their farms temporarily to avoid confrontation.) In a speech in August Mugabe stated that white farmers who were 'loyal' to the Government had the option of staying, although later that month it was reported that almost 200 farmers had been arrested for refusing to leave their properties, while others had gone into hiding. In September the Land Acquisition Act was amended to allow the eviction of white farmers within seven days, as opposed to the 90 days previously required.

Opposition to Mugabe

In April 2002 ZANU—PF and the MDC engaged in talks in an effort to end the political crisis, but negotiations collapsed in the following month when ZANU—PF withdrew, citing the MDC's petition to the High Court seeking to overturn the election results, which ZANU—PF regarded as unlawful. In August Mugabe dissolved his Cabinet and appointed a new Government a few days later, retaining several ministers from the previous administration. In February 2003, following their arrest the previous year, the trial of Tsvangirai and two other senior MDC officials for allegedly plotting to assassinate Mugabe began in Harare, but was adjourned until May. In March the MDC led a 'mass action' against the Government, aimed at forcing it to repeal what the party called repressive legislation and to release political prisoners; the Government claimed that the MDC had detonated bombs in Kadoma, south-west of Harare, and it was reported that up to 500 members of the opposition had been arrested and many more driven from their homes and beaten. In early June Tsvangirai was arrested at the conclusion of further demonstrations against the Government organized by the MDC, reportedly in connection with statements he had made in May; he was released on bail in late June.

In September 2003 the closure of *The Daily News*, owing to the failure of its publisher to register with the Government's Media and Information Commission (MIC), provoked international condemnation. A court ruling that the newspaper should be allowed to resume publication, pending the result of an application that it had made to register with the MIC, was initially disregarded by the police. Publication of *The Daily News* did subsequently resume, despite the refusal of the MIC to grant it a licence, but was suspended again in February 2004 when the Supreme Court confirmed that its unlicensed appearance was illegal. (By early 2005 four newspapers had been closed under the Access to Information and Protection of Privacy Act: *The Daily News*, the *Daily News on Sunday*, *The Tribune* and *The Weekly Times*. However, *The Daily News*, along with four other newspapers, was awarded a new operating licence in May 2010 and began publishing again in early 2011.)

From October 2003 increased concern was expressed at divisions within the Commonwealth over the political crisis in Zimbabwe. The decision, taken at a meeting of Commonwealth Heads of Government held in Abuja, Nigeria, in December, to extend Zimbabwe's suspension from the organization indefinitely, until the country had restored democracy and the rule of law, confirmed the existence of a rift between African Commonwealth members and their Western counterparts. The 12 members from southern Africa criticized the decision, and Mbeki claimed that other Commonwealth members had failed to understand the question of land ownership in Zimbabwe and that they were mistaken in their belief that the presidential election held in Zimbabwe in 2002 had been unfair. Zimbabwe, for its part, announced its decision to withdraw from the Commonwealth shortly before the conclusion of the Heads of Government meeting.

In January 2004, giving evidence for the first time in his trial for treason, Tsvangirai denied that he had ever plotted to assassinate President Mugabe or to overthrow the Government. Tsvangirai was acquitted of the assassination charges in mid-October 2004; the outstanding treason charge was finally dropped in August 2005. Meanwhile, in February 2004 the EU renewed sanctions imposed upon the Mugabe regime, extending the travel ban and assets freeze to cover a total of 95 Zimbabwean officials, and in March the USA imposed a further series of sanctions on Zimbabwe, notably targeting government-owned enterprises.

In late 2004 a power struggle developed within ZANU—PF. There was speculation that Mugabe was actively assigning key posts in the administration to members of his own Zezuru clan, replacing members of the majority Karanga clan. In December the country's voting constituencies were redrawn, reportedly increasing the number of seats available in traditional ZANU—PF strongholds, while reducing those available in areas where the MDC commanded popular support.

According to provisional results of the legislative elections held on 31 March 2005, Mugabe's ruling ZANU—PF party won 78 of the 120 seats available, taking 56.4% of the vote. The opposition MDC took 41 seats, with 42.1% of the votes cast. Under the Constitution, the President could allocate 12 seats in the House of Assembly to candidates of his choosing and appoint the eight provincial governors; a further 10 seats were reserved for tribal chiefs, also loyal to Mugabe. The overall results therefore gave ZANU—PF a two-thirds' majority in the Assembly which would allow Mugabe to amend the Constitution. International observers from the African Union (AU, see p. 183) and the Southern African Development Community (SADC, see p. 420) endorsed the results; observers from the Commonwealth, the EU and the USA were not invited, owing to their perceived hostility towards the Mugabe Government. The Governments of Malawi, Mozambique, South Africa and Zambia were among those who accepted the elections as free and fair; however, the results were dismissed by Australia, the EU and the USA. (The observers from the AU later reversed their opinion and called for investigations into allegations of electoral fraud.) The MDC contested the results, citing electoral irregularities in 76 out of the 120 constituencies, and claimed that it should, in fact, have won 94 seats. In mid-April the MDC released a report alleging that some 134,000 people had been turned away from polling stations and that ballot boxes had been filled with votes for ZANU—PF after the polls had closed. The MDC filed petitions at the Electoral Court challenging the results in 13 constituencies. Meanwhile, the outgoing Minister responsible for Land Reform and Resettlement, John Nkomo, announced that white farmers who had lost their farms during the resettlement programme would be compensated for the value of assets and improvements but not for the land itself, which the Government maintained was the responsibility of the United Kingdom. It was estimated that the white population in Zimbabwe had fallen from 200,000 in 2000 to around 25,000 at March 2005; of these some 500 were farmers.

The EU renewed its sanctions against Zimbabwe in February 2005, but in early April Italy was obliged to allow Mugabe to travel through the country to the Vatican City in order to attend the funeral of the Supreme Pontiff of the Roman Catholic Church, Pope John Paul II. The Zimbabwe Government exploited international treaties which obliged countries to allow foreign government officials to travel to international organizations hosted within those countries. In July the Governor of the Reserve Bank of Zimbabwe, Gideon Gono, and acting Minister of Finance Herbert Murerwa both attended a meeting of the IMF in New York, USA, despite sanctions which otherwise would have prevented them travelling to that country, while in October Mugabe attended a conference of the Food and Agriculture Organization in Rome, Italy.

In April 2005 Mugabe announced his new Government. The former Zimbabwean ambassador to the United Kingdom, Simbarashe Mumbengegwi, was appointed Minister of Foreign Affairs, while Murerwa was confirmed as Minister of Finance. Sixteen ministers retained their portfolios, including Patrick Chinamasa as Minister of Justice, Legal and Parliamentary Affairs. Didymus Mutasa was appointed Minister of State for National Security and head of the Central Intelligence Organization, and in mid-May also assumed overall responsibility for the land redistribution programme.

In late May 2005 the Government launched Operation Murambatsvina ('Sweep Away the Rubbish'), which targeted black market trading—principally in foreign currency and fuel—and 'general lawlessness'. The MDC claimed that it was a punitive action against the urban poor who had voted against ZANU—PF in the elections in March. Shanty towns were razed to the ground in Harare and other major cities, including Bulawayo and Gweru. The operation attracted widespread international condemnation and, according to a report by UN-Habitat published in late July, some 700,000 people were made homeless; however, the Government refused offers of humanitarian aid. In late June President Mugabe announced that some Z.$3,000,000m. was to be spent on new housing and commercial premises under a three-year redevelopment programme entitled Operation Garikai/Hlalani Kuhle. (In September 2006 the human rights organization Amnesty International reported that the Government had not met its housing obligations as just 3,325 new homes had been built, while 92,460 had been demolished.) In late 2005 Vice-President Mujuru announced the official end of Operation Murambatsvina and appealed for humanitarian aid.

In late August 2005 the House of Assembly approved legislation which provided for a number of changes to the Constitution and which was also to conclude the land redistribution programme: courts would no longer be able to hear appeals on land acquisition and once listed for appropriation land would immediately become state property. (However, in early 2006 banks were still refusing to extend loans to resettled farmers because they were not in possession of the title deeds to the land.) Under the bill it became a criminal offence for Zimbabweans to endorse sanctions or military action against their country, and the Zimbabwe Electoral Commission (ZEC) was established in place of the Electoral Supervisory Commission. In addition, the legislation provided for the reintroduction of a 66-member Senate (abolished in 1990) as the second chamber of the legislature; senatorial elections were held in late November 2005. The MDC was deeply divided over the issue of participating in the elections. Tsvangirai opposed electoral participation, advocating mass protests and 'democratic resistance'; however, a faction led by the party's Secretary-General, Welshman Ncube, fielded 26 candidates. ZANU—PF won 43 of the 50 elected seats, receiving 73.7% of the vote; MDC candidates took the remaining seven seats, with 20.3% of the vote. The MDC effectively split in two, with a 'pro-Senate' faction electing Arthur Mutumbara as its leader in February 2006. The rump of the party re-elected Tsvangirai as its President in late March.

In July 2006 five senior members of the MDC were injured in an attack as they left the Harare suburb of Mabvuku. A statement from the pro-Senate faction blamed the attack on Tsvangirai. However, Tsvangirai's spokesman suggested that the attack was the work of government agents attempting to sow division within the party. In late December Lovemore Madhuku, the Chairman of the NCA, was the victim of an arson attack on his home; the NCA alleged that it was the third attempt on Madhuku's life in four years and the attack occurred as the organization was mobilizing supporters to resist a proposed extension of Mugabe's term in office until 2010. An alliance of 23 opposition parties, church and civic groups had agreed to unite under the 'Save Zimbabwe' banner to campaign against any such extension.

Financial decline

Meanwhile, in March 2006 the IMF postponed a decision to expel Zimbabwe after it repaid US $120m. of its debt to the fund and pledged to clear its remaining obligations by November. In December the IMF recommended sharp reductions in public spending to lower inflation (the annual rate was recorded as 1,594% in January 2007) as well as the reform of exchange rates, the liberalization of price controls, the removal of restrictions on current account payments and the strengthening of private property rights. In August 2006 the Reserve Bank of Zimbabwe unexpectedly devalued the Zimbabwe dollar by 59.3%, and removed three zeros from the currency in an attempt to stem both corruption and hyperinflation. New banknotes were introduced later that month, which led to the seizure of more than $50m. worth of old banknotes at roadblocks and border posts in a crackdown on money launderers. In June the People's Republic of China had signed an agreement worth $1,300m. with Zimbabwe to help relieve an acute shortage of energy. In exchange for chrome from Zimbabwe, Chinese companies agreed to build new coal mines and three thermal power stations in the Zambezi valley on the Zambian border. In December Zimbabwe opened talks with China regarding a US $2,000m. loan in an attempt to secure much needed funding to boost its rapidly deteriorating economy.

In February 2007 President Mugabe dismissed Murerwa, and made a number of other changes to the Cabinet. Murerwa had been involved in a prolonged public disagreement with Gono over economic policies, and had also been subjected to sustained criticism with regard to the subsidizing of the prices of grain, fuel and electricity; Mugabe had also denounced a number of Murerwa's decisions as 'disastrous'.

Between November 2006 and February 2007 more than 31,000 people were arrested in a major police crackdown, known as Operation Chikorokoza Chapera ('The End of Illegal Gold Dealings'). With the rate of unemployment reportedly standing at more than 80%, many Zimbabweans had turned to gold- or diamond-prospecting following the collapse of commercial agriculture. In February the Government had announced that the last white farmers, numbering some 400, could remain on their land long enough to harvest their crops, even though the deadline to leave had passed. In the previous month the US-based Famine Early Warning System had predicted that Zimbabwe was likely to record a shortfall in maize of some 850,000 metric tons in 2007.

In mid-February 2007 police used tear gas and water cannons to prevent an MDC rally from proceeding in Harare, despite the organization obtaining a High Court order allowing the rally to take place. In late February anti-Government protesters took control of Budiriro township in Harare for several hours, setting up roadblocks of boulders and burning tyres. Political tensions intensified further when Tsvangirai was arrested in mid-March, along with five other members of the MDC, after riot police violently dispersed a 'Save Zimbabwe' prayer meeting in Harare's Highfield township. One activist was killed by the police and Tsvangirai suffered severe injuries while in police custody. The Government stated that the rally breached a recently introduced three-month ban on political gatherings. The incident provoked widespread international condemnation and demands for the release of those detained. Following an SADC summit in Dar es Salaam, Tanzania, in late March, it was announced that Mbeki had agreed to mediate between the MDC and the Zimbabwean Government; however, there were further reports of the mistreatment of MDC activists in police custody, provoking renewed opposition protests and repeated calls for Mugabe to relinquish the presidency. Nevertheless, in early April ZANU—PF declared that Mugabe would stand as the party's candidate in the 2008 presidential election. In mid-May 2007 Zimbabwe was elected to lead the UN Commission on Sustainable Development, prompting widespread objections from EU and US officials, who had opposed Zimbabwe's candidacy and questioned the nation's ability to assume such a role.

In early June 2007 constitutional amendments were proposed that would allow the legislative elections to be brought forward to coincide with the presidential election in 2008, harmonizing the presidential and parliamentary terms of office. The proposals also contained provisions for amendments to the structure of the House of Assembly and the Senate. The MDC opposed the proposals, which would, *inter alia*, allow the House of Assembly to nominate a new President should the incumbent stand down; under the existing structure, new elections would be required if the presidency were vacated. The MDC continued to be weakened by divisions between party members and in July 2007 it was announced that the two factions planned to field separate candidates in the presidential and legislative elections. Meanwhile, South African-led mediation between the MDC and ZANU—PF faltered amid worsening political and economic conditions; however, Mbeki denied that negotiations would collapse.

The 2008 elections

On 30 October 2007 a number of changes to the Constitution were officially adopted. With effect from the 2008 elections, the House of Assembly was to be enlarged to comprise 210 directly elected members, while the total number of members of the Senate was to be increased to 93. Of these, 60 were to be directly elected, five were to be nominated by the President and 10 seats were reserved for provincial governors; the remaining 18 were to include the President and the Deputy President of the Council of Chiefs and 16 traditional Chiefs. The presidential term was reduced to five years. However, talks between ZANU—PF and the opposition failed to produce any agreement on electoral procedures and negotiations continued.

In January 2008 Mugabe confirmed that presidential and legislative elections would be held concurrently on 29 March, resulting in complaints from the opposition which continued to demand further electoral and constitutional reforms. The MDC announced that it was to organize a mass protest against the Government's decision not to delay elections, claiming that Mugabe had reneged on agreements reached during the earlier talks mediated by Mbeki. In February Simba Makoni, a senior member of ZANU—PF who had served as Minister of Finance and Economic Development in 2000–02, announced his intention to challenge Mugabe for the presidency; Makoni was later expelled from the ruling party.

Presidential and legislative elections took place as scheduled on 29 March 2008. According to results released by the ZEC, the faction of the MDC led by Tsvangirai (MDC—T) secured 99 of the 210 seats in the House of Assembly, while ZANU—PF took 97 seats; the MDC faction led by Mutambara (MDC—M) secured 10 seats. However, no immediate announcement was made regarding the outcome of the presidential poll. Widespread irregularities were reported and observers expressed concern that the delay in releasing official results was allowing the ruling party to manipulate ballot papers. A recount of the legislative votes in 23 constituencies—the majority of which had been awarded to the MDC after the first count—commenced in mid-April. Following completion of the recount, the ZEC confirmed that the original results remained unchanged. In mid-May it was reported that ZANU—PF had filed legal petitions challenging the results in 53 constituencies, while the MDC had challenged the election of 52 deputies. Provisional results of the senatorial elections indicated that ZANU—PF had secured 30 of the 60 directly elected seats in the upper chamber; the MDC—T took 24 seats, while the MDC—M won six.

On 2 May 2008 the ZEC released results of the disputed presidential election, according to which Tsvangirai secured 47.9% of the votes cast, while Mugabe took 43.2%. Makoni was placed third with 8.3%. As no candidate secured the requisite 50% of the votes, a second round of voting was to be conducted. Following an alleged campaign of violent intimidation of MDC supporters by ZANU—PF loyalists, Tsvangirai refused to confirm his participation in the run-off. On 10 May, however, Tsvangirai, who had temporarily relocated to South Africa, announced that he would take part in the second round. Nevertheless, the Chairman of the ZEC expressed doubt that the run-off would take place within three weeks of the declaration of the election results, as stipulated by the Electoral Law, and in mid-May it was announced that the second round would take place on 27 June. Tsvangirai withdrew his candidacy shortly before the election, claiming he was unwilling to ask his supporters to vote amid the increasing violence in which some 80 MDC members were reported to have been killed. On 23 June the UN Security Council issued a statement condemning the actions of ZANU—PF and ruled that a free and fair ballot would be 'impossible'. The UN Secretary-General, Ban Ki-Moon, expressed his support for the postponement of the second round; however, the run-off proceeded as scheduled with Mugabe as the sole candidate. On 29 June the ZEC announced that Mugabe had secured 85.5% of votes cast in the second round of voting and he was sworn in for a sixth term as President. However, turn-out was low and the MDC claimed that ZANU—PF had been coercing people to vote; Tsvangirai appealed to the international community to denounce the results.

Recent developments: the Interparty Political Agreement

Following an AU summit held in Sharm el-Sheikh, Egypt, on 29 June–1 July 2008, African leaders failed to condemn the result of the presidential election, instead appealing to Mugabe and Tsvangirai to enter into negotiations to establish a government of national unity; by contrast, Western observers insisted that Mugabe should be removed from power and that financial assistance to Zimbabwe would be dependent on the formation of a government led by Tsvangirai. The AU's stance also appeared divided as it later emerged that several members, including Nigeria and Senegal, wished to see a government formed on the basis of the results of the first round of the election, won by Tsvangirai. In August Lovemore Moyo of the MDC was elected Speaker of the House of Assembly, strengthening that party's position. However, following protracted negotiations involving SADC mediation, a power-sharing agreement was concluded in September. Under the terms of the so-called Interparty Political Agreement (IPA), Mugabe was to remain as President with executive authority and would chair the 31-member Cabinet (which would evaluate and adopt all government policies and approve all international agreements) and the National Security Council, while Tsvangirai would be appointed Prime Minister, also with executive authority, and would chair the Council of Ministers, which was to consist of all cabinet ministers and would 'ensure that the Prime Minister properly discharges his responsibility to oversee the implementation of the work of government and assesses the implementation of Cabinet decisions'. The IPA also stipulated that there would be no reversal of the land redistribution policy. Meanwhile, in mid-March 2008 Mugabe had signed a controversial indigenization law requiring 51% of all companies operating in Zimbabwe to be owned by black Zimbabweans. The legislation also banned mergers and restructuring of businesses unless the majority share was owned by black interests.

Further lengthy negotiations regarding the composition of the Cabinet followed, again mediated by Mbeki and SADC, and in early February 2009 the House of Assembly and the Senate approved a number of transitional amendments to the Constitution. These confirmed the arrangements agreed under the IPA and also stipulated the division of senior roles among the three signature parties. Mugabe and/or ZANU—PF was to nominate two Vice-Presidents, while provision was made for the appointment of two Deputy Prime Ministers, one from the MDC—T and one from the MDC—M. On 11 February Tsvangirai was inaugurated as Prime Minister and Thokozani Khupe and Arthur Mutambara were sworn in as First and Second Deputy Prime Ministers, respectively. The installation of the Cabinet was delayed slightly, owing to late changes to the list of appointments and the MDC—T questioning a number of nominations by ZANU—PF. The original agreement, providing for a 31-member cabinet, was amended to allow ZANU—PF and the MDC—T to share responsibility for the Ministry of Home Affairs. Kembo Mohadi was nominated for ZANU—PF, while Giles Mutsekwa represented the MDC—T in that ministry. Eventually 35 ministers were sworn in on 13 February 2009 with ZANU—PF allocated a total of 17 ministers in the new Cabinet, including Mumbengegwi, who retained the foreign affairs portfolio, and Chinamasa who remained Minister of Justice and Legal Affairs. Emmerson Mnangwagwa was named Minister of Defence. The MDC—T had 15 representatives in the Government, most notably Tendai Biti as Minister of Finance and Elton Mangoma as Minister of Economic Planning and Development. The MDC—M held three portfolios. Shortly before the inauguration ceremony, the designated Deputy Minister of Agriculture, Roy Bennett, of the MDC—T, was arrested and charged with treason. His detention delayed proceedings and threatened to undermine the projected image of unity within the Government, which was already viewed by many analysts with extreme suspicion. In early March the Supreme Court ordered his release on bail.

In early March 2009 Tsvangirai was involved in a car accident in which his wife died. Despite rumours of ZANU—PF involvement in the incident, Tsvangirai insisted later that he suspected no foul play and Mugabe attended the funeral, offering his condolences and declaring his intention to co-operate in the power-sharing Government. However, in April Mugabe's commitment was called into question when he unilaterally announced that the ZANU—PF-controlled Ministry of Transport would absorb the functions hitherto carried out by the Minister of Information and Communications Technology, Nelson Chamisa of the MDC—T. Earlier that month the Government adopted a 100-day renewal plan aimed at improving ties with Western nations, in particular the USA and the United Kingdom. The Government also pledged to restore human rights, address security concerns, stabilize the economy, adopt a new constitution and review media legislation that prevented independent local and international media from operating freely within Zimbabwe. In early April it was announced that the Government had appointed a 25-member parliamentary committee to supervise the process of drafting a new constitution, which would include nation-wide consultation; it was envisaged that the new document would then be submitted for approval at a national referendum.

In May 2009 a court in Harare revoked the bail of 18 prominent human rights activists, including Jestina Mukoko, the director of the Zimbabwe Peace Project, who had been charged in December 2008 with conspiring to overthrow Mugabe's Government. Following protests by Tsvangirai, who declared that the case threatened the stability of the power-sharing agreement, they were again granted bail, pending the beginning of their trial. During June 2009 Tsvangirai visited the USA and several European states, in an effort to secure financial support for economic reconstruction. It was reported that US President Barack Obama had pledged only US $73m. in conditional aid to Zimbabwe and expressed continued concerns over democracy and human rights in the country. In total, only about $150m. in humanitarian and transitional assistance had been pledged to Zimbabwe, reflecting the international community's lack of confidence in the reconciliation process, in view of the delays in the implementation of the IPA. In July a constitutional convention in Harare degenerated into clashes between ZANU—PF and MDC delegates, which were suppressed by special police; the convention was resumed on the following day, under police supervision. In August Joseph Msika, a Vice-President in the Government and ZANU—PF, died, after becoming ill in June. (In December he was succeeded in both posts by John Nkomo, hitherto Minister of State in the President's Office.) In September the Supreme Court ruled that the case against Mukoko and nine other defendants was inadmissible, owing to their abduction by state agents and alleged torture while in custody.

In September 2009 a high-level EU delegation visited Zimbabwe for the first time since the imposition of sanctions; senior EU officials indicated that further progress was required in ending human rights violations in the country before the removal of sanctions. In October a court in Mutare ruled that Roy Bennett be returned to prison; Tsvangirai subsequently announced that the MDC would suspend participation in government meetings until the resolution of Bennett's detention and a number of other outstanding issues within the power-sharing arrangements. Although Bennett was again released on bail two days later, his trial, on charges of funding the purchase of armaments, began in early November. Tsvangirai agreed to end the MDC boycott of government meetings, following the intervention of SADC (with new South African President Jacob Zuma succeeding Mbeki as the principal mediator); however, the MDC issued an ultimatum that Mugabe implement the power-sharing agreement fully within 30 days to avert the collapse of the Government. Meanwhile, in late October Manfred Nowak, the UN Special Rapporteur on Torture, announced that he would recommend action against Zimbabwe, after he was detained on arrival at Harare airport and deported. At the end of 2009 a Zimbabwean Farmers' rights group, Justice for Agriculture, stated that the seizure of farms, which often involved attacks on white farmers, had increased dramatically since the establishment of the coalition Government in February, and were frequently perpetrated by senior members of ZANU—PF, and political and military officials. In January 2010 a Supreme Court in Pretoria, South Africa, granted permission to three white Zimbabwean farmers to take legal action against the Zimbabwe Government over loss of farmlands, in accordance with a SADC ruling in November 2008. Reports of further illegal occupations of white-owned farms continued throughout 2010.

In early 2010 ongoing negotiations between ZANU—PF, the MDC—T and the MDC—M on power-sharing issues were reported to be at an impasse, while the programme to draft a new constitution had been suspended owing to lack of funding. In February the EU issued a statement extending the sanctions in force against Zimbabwe for a further year, citing lack of progress in implementing the IPA (although the Union had ended restrictive measures against some officials and corporations previously associated with Mugabe's administration). In early March President Obama also announced the extension of travel and financial restrictions against Mugabe and other officials for a further year. In the same month the High Court upheld the election of Lovemore Moyo as parliamentary Speaker in August 2008, rejecting a challenge on grounds of procedural violations by former Minister of Information Jonathan Moyo. Later in March 2010 Zuma continued mediation efforts in Harare to resolve the impasse between the government parties; however, Mugabe demanded the removal of all sanctions prior to any concessions and rejected the MDC's demands, which were, principally, for Bennett's inauguration as Deputy Minister of Agriculture, the allocation of five provincial governorships to the MDC, and the replacement of Gono (who had been reappointed as Governor of the Reserve Bank for a further five-year term in November 2008) and the Attorney-General. At the end of March 2010 Mugabe inaugurated the country's first Human Rights Commission, chaired by a former senior Commonwealth official, and a new Electoral Commission; under the terms of the IPA, elections had been scheduled to take place within two years of its signature.

In March 2010 Mugabe's controversial indigenization law, which required companies operating in Zimbabwe to transfer 51% of their shareholdings to black Zimbabweans within five years, entered into force. The MDC—T's opposition to the legislation exacerbated the existing tensions within the Government. Critics argued that the indigenization programme acted as a huge deterrent to investors, a claim supported during 2010 by the low levels of investment recorded and the withdrawal of several foreign-owned firms from the country. By early 2011, with the details still not finalized, much uncertainty remained regarding the implementation of the indigenization legislation.

Meanwhile, Bennett was acquitted of all charges by the High Court in May 2010, and the Supreme Court upheld this judgment in March 2011 following the initiation of an appeal by the state. Tsvangirai effected a reorganization of MDC—T cabinet ministers in June 2010; most notably, Theresa Makone became the MDC—T's representative in the shared Ministry of Home Affairs. Supported by EU funding, a nation-wide public consultation scheme regarding the drafting of the new constitution began in the same month. However, the outreach campaign was disrupted by escalating political violence (predominantly directed against MDC—T followers), which Tsvangirai accused ZANU—PF of orchestrating. Further divisions between the two parties were created by Mugabe's unilateral moves throughout the year to appoint high-ranking public officials. Mugabe rejected Tsvangirai's demands to be consulted on the appointments and claimed that his actions had been lawful. In late 2010 Mugabe began publicly to advocate the holding of new elections in 2011, and he was announced as ZANU—PF's presidential candidate in December. However, with the constitutional drafting process running behind schedule, and limited progress reported on other vital political reforms, it appeared unlikely that the legal framework necessary to guarantee free and fair elections would be in place by 2011. Tsvangirai vehemently opposed a fresh ballot governed by existing legislation since it was weighted unfairly in ZANU—PF's favour and pledged to boycott a poll conducted under these circumstances.

Welshman Ncube, the Minister of Industry and Commerce, replaced Arthur Mutambara as leader of the smaller MDC faction in January 2011. The EU and the USA renewed their existing sanctions against Zimbabwe for one year in February and March, respectively. The EU criticized the slow pace of reform and continuing politically motivated violence. Zimbabwe attracted further international censure in February, when 46 people were arrested and accused of treason for holding a meeting to discuss the popular uprisings in Tunisia and Egypt that had resulted in the overthrow of the long-standing Presidents of those nations earlier in the year. The police claimed that those arrested were planning a similar revolt to unseat Mugabe, an allegation rejected by the detainees. In the following month 40 of those charged were released on the grounds of insufficient evidence. Meanwhile, Elton Mangoma, the MDC—T Minister of Energy and Power Development and a close associate of Tsvangirai, was detained by the police in March and charged with corruption. The MDC—T criticized the arrest, while Mangoma's lawyer claimed that his client was an innocent victim of a 'harassment campaign' organized by ZANU—PF.

Foreign Affairs
Regional relations
Zimbabwe severed diplomatic relations with South Africa in September 1980 and subsequently played an important role in international attempts to stabilize southern Africa and to end apartheid in South Africa. In July 1987 the Cabinet rejected a proposal by Mugabe to impose sanctions against South Africa, and the Government opted instead for less stringent economic measures. South Africa is believed to have been responsible for intermittent attacks during the 1980s against the then banned African National Congress of South Africa (ANC) in Zimbabwe. A meeting between President Mugabe and a South African government official in April 1991 (following the implementation of a programme of political reforms by President F. W. de Klerk of South Africa in February 1990) constituted the first direct contact between the Zimbabwean and South African Governments since 1980. The two countries re-established diplomatic relations following the holding of the first democratic elections in South Africa in April 1994, and in March 1997 a mutual defence co-operation agreement was concluded. Relations deteriorated in 1998, owing to South Africa's opposition to Zimbabwe's military intervention in the civil war in the Democratic Republic of the Congo (DRC—see below). Relations were also strained from 1999, owing to Zimbabwe's increasingly negative economic and political circumstances (see above). By May 2000 the increasingly turbulent land reform situation in Zimbabwe had adversely affected South Africa's economy, prompting Mbeki to appeal to foreign donors to fund the transfer of white-owned land to black farmers. Following his election in May 2009, South African President Jacob Zuma succeeded Mbeki as the Chairman of SADC and principal mediator in negotiations between the government parties in Zimbabwe (see above).

During the 1980s and early 1990s Zimbabwe provided support to the Mozambican Government against Renamo rebels; in late 1992–early 1993, under the terms of the peace agreement in Mozambique (q.v.), Zimbabwean troops, who had been stationed in Mozambique since 1982, were withdrawn. During the mid-1990s a group of armed Zimbabwean dissidents, known as the Chimwenjes, were reportedly active in western Mozambique. In January 1996 the Mozambican Government announced its intention to expel the rebels, and in January 1997 an accord was signed by representatives of Mozambique and Zimbabwe on the co-ordination of activities against the rebels. Plans for the repatriation of some 145,000 Mozambican refugees were announced in March 1993; this scheme, co-ordinated by the Office of the UN High Commissioner for Refugees, was completed by May 1995.

Following an SADC summit in Harare in August 1998, the Zimbabwean Government dispatched troops and arms to the DRC to support the regime of President Laurent-Désiré Kabila against advancing rebel forces. The Zimbabwe and DRC Governments announced a plan in September 1999 to establish a joint diamond and gold marketing venture to finance the war. Nevertheless, in early 2000 the Zimbabwean Government was reportedly unable to pay allowances to its troops fighting in the region, owing to the critical shortage of foreign currency (see above). Public opinion was further turned against the continuation of the conflict in February when heavy rains and a cyclone struck Mozambique and neighbouring provinces of eastern Zimbabwe. There was a desperate shortage of helicopters, which were needed to bring aid to those affected, owing to their deployment in the DRC. The war also caused tensions between Zimbabwe and the IMF, the latter suspending assistance partly because of Zimbabwe's false accounting of expenses relating to the conflict. Following a number of positive developments in the lengthy peace process between the DRC Government and the rebels, the last Zimbabwean troops, from an initial deployment of around 11,000, withdrew from the DRC in October 2002.

In March 2004, at the international airport in Harare, the Zimbabwean authorities detained 70 men alleged to be involved in a plot to overthrow the Government of Equatorial Guinea, after impounding the aircraft in which 67 of them had travelled from South Africa. South African government officials suggested that the suspected mercenaries had landed in Harare en route to Equatorial Guinea in order to collect weapons, although the company that had chartered the aircraft insisted that the men had stopped to obtain mining-related supplies before flying to Burundi and the DRC to work as security guards. Later that month the 70 defendants appeared in a prison court near Harare, charged with a number of offences, including conspiring against the Government of Equatorial Guinea and violating immigration laws. In June Zimbabwe and Equatorial Guinea agreed to open embassies in their respective capitals and it was reported that President Mugabe had agreed to extradite the 70 men accused of involvement in the coup plot in exchange for petroleum to the value of US $1,200m. Simon Mann, a South African-based British security consultant and the alleged leader of the coup plot, was convicted in September of attempting illegally to procure weapons and was sentenced to seven years' imprisonment (subsequently reduced to four) in Zimbabwe. At the completion of that sentence in 2007, the Equato-Guinean authorities sought to extradite Mann in order to undergo further legal proceedings. That request was granted by a Zimbabwean judge in May and in early February 2008 Mann was transported to custody in Equatorial Guinea.

Other external relations
Relations between the United Kingdom and Zimbabwe remained strained throughout 2000 and 2001. In September 2002, at the UN World Summit on Sustainable Development in South Africa, tensions increased when Mugabe criticized the British Prime Minister, Tony Blair, for his part in imposing EU sanctions on Zimbabwe and for interfering in the country's domestic politics; later that month the Government informed British diplomats that they could not leave Harare without permission from the Ministry of Foreign Affairs. In November Mugabe imposed a ban on senior British officials, including Blair, from travelling to Zimbabwe; the measure was taken in response to the United Kingdom's introduction of a requirement for Zimbabwean nationals to apply for a visa in order to visit that country. The British Prime Minister, Gordon Brown, boycotted a summit of EU and African states held in Lisbon, Portugal, in December 2007, in opposition to Mugabe's attendance. Relations between the United Kingdom and Zimbabwe deteriorated further following the disputed presidential election of 2008 (see above); however an improvement was expected as a result of the installation of a power-sharing administration in February 2009. In June Prime Minister Tsvangirai visited the United Kingdom, in an effort to secure financial assistance, meeting Prime Minister Brown, who (in common with other European government leaders) was reluctant to extend large-scale funds in view of lack of progress in the power-sharing agreement. In March 2010 Brown rejected demands by South African President Jacob Zuma, issued during an official visit to the United Kingdom, for the removal of the EU sanctions in force against Zimbabwe.

Iranian President Mahmoud Ahmadinejad made a controversial visit to Zimbabwe in April 2010. During his trip a series of bilateral co-operation accords were signed and Mugabe pledged his support for Iran's contentious nuclear power plans. However, the MDC—T labelled Ahmadinejad's presence in Zimbabwe a 'scandal' and boycotted the discussions amid fears that closer ties with Iran would damage relations with Western nations. Iran approved a €40m. loan for Zimbabwe in July to support a variety of economic development schemes in the country.

ZIMBABWE

CONSTITUTION AND GOVERNMENT

Under the terms of the 1980 Constitution (as subsequently amended), legislative power is vested in the President and a bicameral Parliament, consisting of a House of Assembly and a Senate. The House of Assembly comprises 210 members, who are directly elected by universal adult suffrage. Members of the House of Assembly serve for five years. The Senate comprises 93 members, 60 of whom are directly elected by universal adult suffrage (six in each of the 10 Provinces), five are appointed by the President, 10 are provincial governors, two are the President and the Deputy President of the Council of Chiefs and 16 are traditional Chiefs. Members of the Senate serve for five years.

Following the unanimous approval of the Zimbabwe Amendment (No. 19) Bill by the House of Assembly and the Senate on 5 February 2009, certain transitional amendments were made to the 1980 Constitution, pertaining to the Interparty Political Agreement signed on 15 September 2008. These stated that the President, the Prime Minister and the Cabinet shall all exercise executive authority. The Office of the President shall continue to be occupied by Robert Gabriel Mugabe, who chairs the Cabinet and the National Security Council and formally appoints the Vice-Presidents, the Prime Minister, the Deputy Prime Ministers, ministers and deputy ministers. Following consultation with the Vice-Presidents, the Prime Minister and the Deputy Prime Ministers, he also allocates ministerial portfolios. The Office of the Prime Minister shall be occupied by Morgan Tsvangirai, who chairs the Council of Ministers and is Deputy Chairperson of the Cabinet. There shall be two Vice-Presidents nominated by the President and/or the Zimbabwe African National Union—Patriotic Front (ZANU—PF). There shall be two Deputy Prime Ministers, one from the Movement for Democratic Change—Tsvangirai (MDC—T) and one from the Movement for Democratic Change—Mutambara (MDC—M). Provision is made for the nomination of ministers and deputy ministers by ZANU—PF, the MDC—T and the MDC—M. The President shall, at his discretion, appoint five persons to the existing positions of presidential senatorial appointments. An additional six appointed senatorial posts shall be created and filled by persons appointed by the President, four of whom shall be nominated by MDC—T and two by the MDC—M. The Cabinet, *inter alia*, evaluates and adopts all government policies and the consequential programmes and approves all international agreements. The Council of Ministers, which consists of all Cabinet ministers, ensures that the Prime Minister properly discharges his responsibility to oversee the implementation of the work of government and assesses the implementation of Cabinet decisions.

REGIONAL AND INTERNATIONAL CO-OPERATION

Zimbabwe is a member of the Southern African Development Community (see p. 420), which aims to promote closer economic integration among its members, and also belongs to the Common Market for Eastern and Southern Africa (see p. 228).

Zimbabwe became a member of the UN in 1980 and was admitted to the World Trade Organization (WTO, see p. 430) in 1995. Zimbabwe participates in the Group of 15 (G15, see p. 447) and the Group of 77 (G77, see p. 447) developing countries. Zimbabwe joined the Commonwealth (see p. 230) in 1980, but was suspended from the organization in 2002 and announced its withdrawal from the Commonwealth in 2003.

ECONOMIC AFFAIRS

In 2005, according to the World Bank, Zimbabwe's gross national income (GNI), measured at average 2003–05 prices, was US $4,467m., equivalent to $360 per head. During 2000–09, it was estimated, the population increased at an average annual rate of 0.1%, while gross domestic product (GDP) per head decreased, in real terms, by an average of 5.4% per year during 2000–05. Overall GDP decreased, in real terms, at an average annual rate of 5.8% in 2000–07, according to the African Development Bank (AfDB); GDP declined by 3.3% in 2007, and by 9.9% in 2008.

Agriculture (including forestry and fishing) contributed 17.5% of GDP in 2009, according to UN figures, and engaged 15.5% of the employed labour force in 2004. According to FAO estimates, however, the sector was estimated to employ 55.8% of the total labour force in mid-2011. The principal cash crops are tobacco (which accounted for an estimated 13.5% of export earnings in 2004), maize, cotton, coffee and sugar. In addition, wheat, soybeans and groundnuts are cultivated. Beef production was traditionally an important activity; however, at December 2004 the Cattle Producers' Association reported that the commercial beef herd numbered fewer than 125,000 head of cattle, down from 1.4m. in 2000. Agricultural output has declined significantly since the farm invasions that took place from the late 1990s (see Contemporary Political History). Zimbabwe's cereals deficit in 2007 was estimated at some 1m. metric tons. Of a maize requirement of 1.8m. tons, the country's own harvest was in the region of 300,000 tons, and the Government undertook to distribute a further 400,000 tons. The UN World Food Programme estimated that some 5.1m. Zimbabweans would require emergency food assistance in the first quarter of 2009. According to UN figures, in 2000–09 agricultural GDP declined by an average of 6.3% per year. Agricultural GDP decreased by 15.3% in 2008, but increased by 4.8% in 2009.

Industry (including mining, manufacturing, construction and power) contributed 20.8% of GDP in 2009, according to UN estimates, and engaged 22.2% of the employed labour force in 2004. During 2000–09, according to the UN, industrial GDP decreased at an average annual rate of .5%. Industrial GDP declined by 15.1% in 2008, but increased by 5.1% in 2009.

Mining contributed 1.8% of GDP and engaged 5.0% of the employed labour force in 2004. Nickel, gold (much of which is illegally smuggled out of the country), and asbestos are the major mineral exports. Chromium ore, copper, silver, emeralds, lithium, tin, iron ore, cobalt, magnesite, niobium, tantalum, limestone, phosphate rock, coal and diamonds are also mined. In October 1999 the discovery of significant diamond deposits in Zimbabwe was announced; in 2003 Rio Tinto opened Zimbabwe's second diamond mine, at Murowa, near Zvishavane. In 2003 Anglo Platinum announced its intention to mine reserves of platinum ore located at Unki, on the Great Dyke. Zimbabwe also has large reserves of kyanite and smaller reserves of zinc and lead. In 2004 the export of minerals comprised an estimated 36.0% of the value of total exports. Mining GDP declined by 29.7% in 2008, according to the AfDB.

Manufacturing contributed 15.9% of GDP in 2009, according to UN estimates, and engaged 13.6% of the employed labour force in 2004. The most important sectors, measured by gross value of output, are food-processing, metals (mainly ferrochrome and steel), chemicals and textiles. According to the Confederation of Zimbabwe Industries, 840 manufacturing companies closed between 2000 and 2003. During 2000–09, according to UN figures, manufacturing GDP decreased by an average of 7.6% per year. Manufacturing GDP declined by 14.3% in 2008, but increased by 4.8% in 2009.

Construction contributed 1.3% of GDP in 2009, according to UN estimates, and engaged 2.5% of the employed labour force in 2004. According to the UN, construction GDP decreased by an average of 14.6% per year during 2000–09. It declined by 15.9% in 2008, but increased by 5.3% in 2009.

In 2007 56.8% of Zimbabwe's electricity production was derived from hydroelectric power, and 43.0% from coal. Imports of mineral fuels comprised an estimated 12.9% of the value of total imports in 2009. In 2002 Zimbabwe purchased 24.2% of its electrical energy from neighbouring countries. In 2007 the supply of electricity to households was rationed to four hours per day, and frequent power cuts were reported in subsequent years.

The services sector contributed 61.8% of GDP in 2009, according to UN estimates, and engaged 62.4% of the employed labour force in 2004. During 2000–09 the GDP of the services sector decreased at an average annual rate of 5.6%. Services GDP declined by 18.7% in 2008, but increased by 9.4% in 2009.

In 2009, according to IMF estimates, Zimbabwe had a visible trade deficit of US $1,607m., while there was a deficit of $1,323m. on the current account of the balance of payments. In 2009 South Africa was the principal source of imports (60.5%); other major source of imports were the USA, and Botswana. South Africa was also the principal market for exports (52.5%) in that year; other major purchasers were the Netherlands and Switzerland. The principal exports in 2009 were printed books, newspapers and pictures, plants and cut flowers, tobacco and tobacco refuse, and nickel and nickel articles. The main imports in that year were road vehicles, fuel and petroleum and related products, and cereals.

In 2009 there was an estimated budgetary deficit of US $123m. Zimbabwe's general government gross debt was Z.$4,142m. in 2009, equivalent to 89.7% of GDP. At the end of 2007 Zimbabwe's external debt totalled US $5,293m., of which US $3,735m. was long-term public debt. In 2008 external debt was estimated to be equivalent to 189% of GDP. The annual rate of inflation averaged 478.2% in 2000–07, according to ILO. Consumer prices increased by an annual average of 6,723.1% in 2007. By October 2008 the year-on-year rate of inflation had reached 231m.%; however, following the declaration in January 2009 of a number of foreign currencies (including the US dollar, the euro, the British pound sterling, the South African rand and the Botswana pula) as legal tender in Zimbabwe, consumer prices were reported to have declined by 3.1%. According to official figures, 6.0% of the total labour force were unemployed in 1999, although the actual rate was believed to be significantly greater: according to the Zimbabwe Congress of Trade Unions, some 80% of the labour force were unemployed in early 2007.

From 1999 the Zimbabwean economy entered a period of significant decline, and by the late 2000s the country was suffering hyperinflation, extremely high levels of unemployment, and a chronic shortage of foreign exchange to finance essential imports. This was attributed by international humanitarian groups to the Government's land redistribution and urban clearance programmes (see Contemporary Political History), which had contributed to a widening of disparities in incomes and impeded the access of vulnerable groups to adequate food supplies, education, water, sanitation and health care. Despite the discharge of arrears to the IMF's General Resources Account (GRA) in February 2006, and the consequent annulment of proceedings for the compulsory withdrawal of Zimbabwe from the Fund, Zimbabwe remained in substantial arrears to the IMF. In 2008 hyperinflation increased to an extent that the Zimbabwe dollar became virtually worthless (despite a redenomination in August), contributing to widespread food shortages that prompted the UN World Food Programme to launch an appeal for humanitarian assistance in October. Real GDP contracted by 18.9% in that year, according to the IMF. In January 2009 the authorities legalized the use of selected foreign currencies in the country in order to combat the spiralling inflation. Consumer prices subsequently fell steadily and financial conditions improved, resulting in increased short-term capital inflows and investment. (The multi-currency system was to be maintained until 2012.) A new power-sharing Government, which was installed in February under a political agreement reached in September 2008, began to implement economic reforms. Efforts by new Prime Minister Morgan Tsvangirai in June 2009 to secure international aid for economic reconstruction met with only limited success, owing to continuing doubts of the US and European Governments concerning the implementation of the power-sharing agreement. In September the IMF provided funds of US $400m. to Zimbabwe, as part of a Group of 20 leading industrialized and developing nations (G20) agreement to assist member states. A reported increase in attacks against white farmers and landowners during 2009 presented a continued deterrent to foreign investment. In early 2010 it was reported that ZANU—PF opposed recommendations by the African Development Bank that the country apply for Highly Indebted Poor Country status, in order to obtain relief on debt of some $5,700m. owed to international lending institutions, which hampered any government reconstruction efforts. In February the IMF restored Zimbabwe's voting rights (which had been suspended in 2003); the Fund stated that, although Zimbabwe was henceforth eligible to use resources from its GRA, it would not be able to access support under the facility until it settled arrears of $140m. to its Poverty Reduction and Growth Trust. Legislation to reform the Reserve Bank of Zimbabwe, the policies of which had been widely held responsible for contributing to the hyperinflation, was approved in April 2010. Real GDP grew by 5.9% in that year according to IMF estimates. The economy was buoyed by the recovery of international commodity markets, which had driven up the prices of key Zimbabwean exports such as gold and platinum, while clement weather conditions had led to a resurgence in agricultural production (particularly in the tobacco sector). However, the country's enormous debt burden was restricting development and the slow pace of political reform meant that donors were still unwilling to commit significant funding to the Government. There were also indications that the entry into force in March of contentious indigenization legislation, which involved the phased transfer of 51% of all company shareholdings to black Zimbabweans, had dampened inflows of foreign direct investment. The unemployment rate was estimated at around 95% in mid-2010. Meanwhile, the Government was hindered in its attempts to commence potentially lucrative exports of diamonds from the country's Marange fields due to its failure to secure full accreditation through the Kimberley Process Certification Scheme (KPCS) because of allegations that the military forces controlling the fields had committed extensive human rights abuses. Limited trading was allowed to proceed from July, but by early 2011 KPCS endorsement had still not been received. It was expected that the mining and agricultural sectors would continue to drive growth in 2011, and the IMF projected further GDP expansion of 4.5% in that year.

PUBLIC HOLIDAYS

2012: 1 January (New Year's Day), 18 April (Independence Day), 6–9 April (Easter), 1 May (Workers' Day), 25 May (Africa Day, anniversary of OAU's foundation), 11 August (Heroes' Day), 12 August (Defence Forces National Day), 22 December (National Unity Day), 25–26 December (Christmas).

Statistical Survey

Source (unless otherwise stated): Central Statistical Office, Ministry of Finance, Blocks B, E and G, Composite Bldg, cnr Samora Machel Ave and Fourth St, Private Bag 7705, Causeway, Harare; tel. (4) 706681; fax (4) 728529; internet www.mofed.gov.zw.

Area and Population

AREA, POPULATION AND DENSITY

Area (sq km)	390,757*
Population (census results)	
18 August 1997	11,789,274
17 August 2002†	
Males	5,634,180
Females	5,997,477
Total	11,631,657
Population (UN estimates at mid-year)‡	
2009	12,522,784
2010	12,644,041
2011	12,834,257
Density (per sq km) at mid-2011	32.8

* 150,872 sq miles.
† Source: UN, *Population and Vital Statistics Report*.
‡ Source: UN, *World Population Prospects: The 2008 Revision*.

POPULATION BY AGE AND SEX
(UN estimates at mid-2011)

	Males	Females	Total
0–14	2,507,997	2,491,885	4,999,882
15–64	3,483,730	3,820,259	7,303,989
65 and over	227,095	303,291	530,386
Total	6,218,822	6,615,435	12,834,257

Source: UN, *World Population Prospects: The 2008 Revision*.

ZIMBABWE

PRINCIPAL TOWNS
(population at census of August 1992)

Harare (capital)	1,189,103	Masvingo	51,743
Bulawayo	621,742	Chinhoyi (Sinoia)	43,054
Chitungwiza	274,912	Hwange (Wankie)	42,581
Mutare (Umtali)	131,367	Marondera (Marandellas)	39,384
Kwekwe (Que Que)	75,425	Zvishavane (Shabani)	32,984
Gweru (Gwelo)	128,037	Redcliff	29,959
Kadoma (Gatooma)	67,750		

Mid-2010 ('000, incl. suburbs, UN estimate): Harare 1,631,594 (Source: UN, *World Urbanization Prospects: The 2009 Revision*).

BIRTHS AND DEATHS
(annual averages, UN estimates)

	1995–2000	2000–05	2005–10
Birth rate (per 1,000)	32.0	30.3	30.0
Death rate (per 1,000)	14.8	18.7	16.2

Source: UN, *World Population Prospects: The 2008 Revision*.

2006: Birth rate 30.0 per 1,000; Death rate 17.4 per 1,000 (Source: African Development Bank).

2007: Birth rate 30.0 per 1,000; Death rate 16.7 per 1,000 (Source: African Development Bank).

2008: Birth rate 29.9 per 1,000; Death rate 16.0 per 1,000 (Source: African Development Bank).

2009: Birth rate 29.8 per 1,000; Death rate 15.3 per 1,000 (Source: African Development Bank).

Life expectancy (years at birth, WHO estimates): 42 (males 42; females 42) in 2008 (Source: WHO, *World Health Statistics*).

ECONOMICALLY ACTIVE POPULATION
(sample survey, persons aged 15 years and over, 1999)

	Males	Females	Total
Agriculture, hunting, forestry and fishing	1,215,661	1,584,839	2,800,500
Mining and quarrying	46,946	3,367	50,313
Manufacturing	283,090	94,667	377,757
Electricity, gas and water	10,158	n.a.	10,158
Construction	98,908	6,659	105,567
Trade, restaurants and hotels	154,198	178,341	332,539
Transport, storage and communications	93,289	8,288	101,577
Financing, insurance, real estate and business services	100,425	20,749	121,174
Community, social and personal services	320,020	258,505	578,525
Sub-total	2,322,695	2,155,415	4,478,110
Activities not adequately defined	63,052	124,286	187,338
Total employed	2,385,747	2,279,701	4,665,448
Unemployed	187,142	110,669	297,811
Total labour force	2,572,889	2,390,370	4,963,259

2004 ('000 employees, annual average): Agriculture, hunting, forestry and fishing 154; Mining and quarrying 50; Manufacturing 136; Electricity, gas and water 11; Construction 25; Trade, restaurants and hotels 114; Transport, storage and communications 38; Financing, insurance, real estate and business services 38; Public administration 68; Education 151; Health 26; Domestic 102; Other services 88; *Total employed* 999 (Source: IMF, *Zimbabwe: Selected Issues and Statistical Appendix*—October 2005).

Mid-2011 (estimates in '000): Agriculture, etc. 3,177; Total labour force 5,690 (Source: FAO).

Health and Welfare

KEY INDICATORS

Total fertility rate (children per woman, 2008)	3.4
Under-5 mortality rate (per 1,000 live births, 2008)	96
HIV/AIDS (% of persons aged 15–49, 2007)	15.3
Physicians (per 1,000 head, 2004)	0.2
Hospital beds (per 1,000 head, 2006)	3.0
Health expenditure (2007): US $ per head (PPP)	20
Health expenditure (2007): % of GDP	8.9
Health expenditure (2007): public (% of total)	46.3
Access to water (% of persons, 2008)	82
Access to sanitation (% of persons, 2008)	44
Total carbon dioxide emissions ('000 metric tons, 2007)	9,629.0
Carbon dioxide emissions per head (metric tons, 2007)	0.8
Human Development Index (2010): ranking	169
Human Development Index (2010): value	0.140

For sources and definitions, see explanatory note on p. vi.

Agriculture

PRINCIPAL CROPS
('000 metric tons)

	2006	2007	2008
Wheat	242	149	31
Barley	54	48	48*
Maize	1,485	953	496
Millet	63	44	37
Sorghum	101	76	75
Potatoes*	40	40	40
Cassava (Manioc)*	190	192	192
Beans, dry	30	30	30*
Sugar cane*	3,100	3,000	3,100
Soybeans (Soya beans)	71	112	105†
Groundnuts, with shell	83	125	79†
Sunflower seed	17	26	23†
Oranges*	93	93	93
Bananas*	85	85	85
Coffee, green	5†	5*	5*
Tea*	22	22	22
Tobacco, unmanufactured	44.5	79.0	79.0*
Cotton lint	72†	80*	80*

* FAO estimate(s).
† Unofficial figure.

2009: Wheat 40 (FAO estimate); Soybeans 110 (unofficial figure); Sunflower seed 10 (unofficial figure).

Aggregate production ('000 metric tons, may include official, semi-official or estimated data): Total cereals 1,948 in 2006, 1,273 in 2007, 691 in 2008, 699 in 2009; Total roots and tubers 233 in 2006, 235 in 2007–09; Total vegetables (incl. melons) 181 in 2006, 191 in 2007–09; Total fruits (excl. melons) 244 in 2006, 245 in 2007–09.

Source: FAO.

LIVESTOCK
('000 head, year ending September, FAO estimates)

	2006	2007	2008
Horses	28.0	28.0	28.0
Asses	112	112	112
Cattle	5,050	5,010	5,020
Sheep	410	390	610
Pigs	615	620	625
Goats	3,120	3,320	3,100
Chickens	28,000	30,000	32,000

Note: No data were available for 2009.

Source: FAO.

ZIMBABWE

LIVESTOCK PRODUCTS
('000 metric tons, FAO estimates)

	2007	2008	2009
Cattle meat	103.5	104.0	n.a.
Goat meat	14.8	13.8	13.8
Pig meat	30.0	30.3	30.3
Chicken meat	56.9	61.0	61.0
Cows' milk	388	389	n.a.
Hen eggs	28	28	28

Source: FAO.

Forestry

ROUNDWOOD REMOVALS
('000 cubic metres, excl. bark, FAO estimates)

	2007	2008	2009
Sawlogs, veneer logs and logs for sleepers	578	578	578
Pulpwood	81	81	81
Other industrial wood	112	112	112
Fuel wood	8,461	8,543	8,626
Total	9,232	9,314	9,397

Source: FAO.

SAWNWOOD PRODUCTION
('000 cubic metres, incl. railway sleepers)

	2004*	2005	2006
Coniferous (softwood)	354	594	533
Broadleaved (hardwood)	43	22	32
Total	397	617	565

* FAO estimates.

2007–09: Production assumed to be unchanged from 2006 (FAO estimates).

Source: FAO.

Fishing

('000 metric tons, live weight)

	2004	2005	2006*
Capture	10.5*	10.4*	10.5
Tilapias	1.0*	1.0*	1.0
Other freshwater fishes	1.6*	1.6*	1.6
Dagaas	7.9*	7.8	7.9
Aquaculture	3.0	2.5	2.5
Tilapias	3.0	2.5	2.5
Total catch	13.5*	12.9*	13.0

* FAO estimate(s).

2007–08: Catch assumed to be unchanged from 2006 (FAO estimates).

Note: Figures exclude aquatic animals, recorded by number rather than weight. The number of Nile crocodiles caught was: 60,185 in 2004; 69,374 in 2005; 80,873 in 2006; 64,490 in 2007; 81,554 in 2008.

Source: FAO.

Mining

('000 metric tons, unless otherwise indicated)

	2007	2008	2009
Asbestos	85	11	5
Chromium ore	614.5	442.6	193.7*
Coal	2,080	1,947	1,750*
Cobalt ore (metric tons)†	100*	85	74
Copper ore‡	2.7	2.8	3.6*
Gold (kilograms)	6,750	3,579	4,965
Iron ore	79	2	n.a.
Limestone*	50	50	40
Magnesite (metric tons)	1,814	2,549	449
Nickel ore (metric tons)	8,582	6,354	4,858*
Phosphate rock	46.1	21.1	20.0*
Silver (kilograms)*	250	150	200

* Estimated figure(s).
† Figures include metal content of compounds and salts and may include cobalt recovered from nickel-copper matte.
‡ Figures refer to the metal content of ores and concentrates.

Source: US Geological Survey.

Industry

SELECTED PRODUCTS
('000 metric tons unless, otherwise indicated)

	2007	2008	2009*
Coke (metallurgical)	400*	112	43
Cement*	400	400	700
Ferro-chromium	187.3	145.4	72.2
Crude steel	23	10	20
Refined copper—unwrought (metric tons)	6,798	3,072	3,000
Refined nickel—unwrought (metric tons)*	14,000	13,700	6,000

* Estimated figure(s).

Source: US Geological Survey.

Raw sugar ('000 metric tons): 430 in 2005; 446 in 2006; 349 in 2007 (Source: UN Industrial Commodity Statistics Database).

Electric energy (net production, million kWh): 10,269 in 2005; 9,776 in 2006; 9,180 in 2007 (Source: UN Industrial Commodity Statistics Database).

Finance

CURRENCY AND EXCHANGE RATES

Monetary Units
100 cents = 1 Zimbabwe dollar (Z.$).

Sterling, US Dollar and Euro Equivalents (31 December 2008)
£1 sterling = Z.$7,143,221.60;
US $1 = Z.$4,900,000.00;
€1 = Z.$6,819,326.81;
Z.$10,000 = £0.0014 = US $0.0020 = €0.0015.

Average Exchange Rate (Z.$ per US dollar)
2008   6,715,420.00

Note: On 1 August 2008 a redenomination of the Zimbabwe dollar was introduced whereby 10,000m. of the former currency was revalued at 1 dollar. In January 2009, in order to address the diminishing value of the national currency, a number of foreign currencies (including the US dollar, the euro, the British pound sterling, the South African rand and the Botswana pula), were also declared legal tender in Zimbabwe. A further massive redenomination of the Zimbabwe dollar was announced in February (whereby 1,000,000m. of the former currency was to be revalued at 1 dollar), but in April of the same year it was announced that legal use of the national currency was to be suspended for at least one year.

ZIMBABWE

BUDGET
(US $ million)

Revenue	2007	2008*	2009†
Tax revenue	193	128	765
Personal income tax	56	22	111
Corporate income tax	33	18	81
Other direct taxes	17	3	28
Customs	12	45	220
Excise	8	6	65
Value-added tax	62	32	251
Other taxes	5	2	10
Non-tax revenue	9	5	115
Total	202	133	880

Expenditure‡	2007	2008*	2009†
Current expenditure	305	241	1,005
Salaries and wages	89	52	278
Interest payments	125	139	163
Foreign	122	138	162
Domestic	3	1	1
Grants and transfers	49	18	178
Other current expenditure	29	32	385
Capital expenditure	70	14	182
Total	375	255	1,187

* Estimates.
† Projections.
‡ Excluding net lending (US $ million): 9 in 2007; 3 in 2008 (estimate); 62 in 2009 (projected).

Source: IMF, *Zimbabwe: 2009 Article IV Consultation-Staff Report; Public Information Notice on the Executive Board Discussion; and Statement by the Executive Director for Zimbabwe* (May 2009).

2008 (US $ million, revised estimates): *Revenue:* Tax revenue 128; Non-tax revenue 5; Total revenue 133. *Expenditure:* Current expenditure 240; Capital expenditure 14; Net lending 3; Total expenditure (incl. net lending) 257 (Source: IMF, *Zimbabwe: 2010 Article IV Consultation—Staff Report; Staff Supplement; Public Information Notice on the Executive Board Discussion; and Statement by the Executive Director for Zimbabwe* (July 2010)).

2009 (US $ million, revised estimates): *Revenue:* Tax revenue 883; Non-tax revenue 51; Budget grants 41; Total revenue (incl. grants) 975. *Expenditure:* Current expenditure 1,052; Capital expenditure 45; Net lending 1; Total expenditure (incl. net lending) 1,098 (Source: IMF, *Zimbabwe: 2010 Article IV Consultation—Staff Report; Staff Supplement; Public Information Notice on the Executive Board Discussion; and Statement by the Executive Director for Zimbabwe* (July 2010)).

INTERNATIONAL RESERVES
(US $ million at 31 December)

	2000	2001	2002
Gold*	45.4	27.5	22.7
IMF special drawing rights	0.2	—	—
Reserve position in IMF	0.4	0.4	0.4
Foreign exchange	192.5	64.3	82.9
Total	238.5	92.2	106.0

*Valued at a market-related price which is determined each month.

2003–10: Reserve position in IMF 0.5.
2009: IMF special drawing rights 361.3.
2010: IMF special drawing rights 254.0.

Source: IMF, *International Financial Statistics*.

MONEY SUPPLY
(Z.$ '000 million at 31 December)

	2005	2006	2007
Currency outside banks	9,876	228,064	73,074,687
Demand deposits at deposit money banks	34,048	404,965	350,998,729
Total money (incl. others)	44,746	636,799	425,445,154

Note: The value of the Zimbabwe dollar has not been adjusted retrospectively to reflect subsequent redenominations.

Source: IMF, *International Financial Statistics*.

COST OF LIVING
(Consumer Price Index; base: 2000 = 100)

	2005	2006	2007
Food	27,900	316,000	23,620,200
All items (incl. others)	28,300	316,600	21,602,000

Source: ILO.

NATIONAL ACCOUNTS

Expenditure on the Gross National Product
(US $ million at current prices, estimates)

	2005	2006	2007
Government final consumption expenditure	142.52	215.94	204.67
Private final consumption expenditure	3,503.53	4,173.46	3,746.44
Gross capital formation	150.47	683.86	826.06
Total domestic expenditure	3,796.52	5,073.26	4,777.17
Exports of goods and services	1,458.18	1,715.97	1,370.60
Less Imports of goods and services	1,836.60	1,845.95	1,416.00
GDP in purchasers' values	3,418.09	4,943.28	4,731.77

Gross Domestic Product by Economic Activity
(Z.$ million, at factor cost)

	2004	2005	2006
Agriculture, hunting, forestry and fishing	3,543	23,494	155,807
Mining and quarrying	5,038	34,722	239,307
Manufacturing	7,774	46,901	282,960
Electricity and water	1,661	6,739	27,343
Construction	666	1,138	15,262
Trade, restaurants and hotels	13,187	47,204	168,978
Transport, storage and communications	6,070	8,244	20,744
Finance, insurance and real estate	3,819	13,095	42,428
Government services	744	2,263	6,885
Other services	4,194	12,324	37,265
Sub-total	46,969	196,124	996,979
Less Imputed bank service charges	330	663	1,331
GDP at factor cost	46,365	195,463	995,648
Indirect taxes, less subsidies	2,688	9,615	34,413
Total	49,053	205,078	1,030,061

Source: African Development Bank.

2007 (US $ million): Agriculture, hunting, forestry and fishing 613; Mining, manufacturing and utilities 701 (Manufacturing 569); Construction 49; Wholesale, retail trade, restaurants and hotels 280; Transport, storage and communications 282; Other services 1,571; *Total, all industries* 3,497 (Source: UN, National Accounts Main Aggregates Database).

2008 (US $ million): Agriculture, hunting, forestry and fishing 532; Mining, manufacturing and utilities 600 (Manufacturing 489); Construction 41; Wholesale, retail trade, restaurants and hotels 235; Transport, storage and communications 236; Other services 1,340; *Total, all industries* 2,985 (Source: UN, National Accounts Main Aggregates Database).

2009 (US $ million): Agriculture, hunting, forestry and fishing 564; Mining, manufacturing and utilities 628 (Manufacturing 512); Construction 43; Wholesale, retail trade, restaurants and hotels 260; Transport, storage and communications 259; Other services 1,475; *Total, all industries* 3,229 (Source: UN, National Accounts Main Aggregates Database).

ZIMBABWE

BALANCE OF PAYMENTS
(US $ million, estimates)

	2008	2009
Exports of goods f.o.b.	1,633	1,625
Imports of goods f.o.b.	−2,630	−3,232
Trade balance	−997	−1,607
Non-factor services (net)	−206	−32
Balance on goods and services	−1,203	−1,639
Investment income (net)	−368	−387
Balance on goods, services and income	−1,571	−2,026
Private transfers (net)	625	703
Current balance	−945	−1,323
Official transfers (net)	73	156
Direct investment (net)	44	105
Portfolio investment (net)	—	250
Long-term capital (net)	−174	−179
Short-term capital (net)	192	295
IMF special drawing rights liabilities	—	519
Net errors and omissions	187	206
Overall balance	−624	29

Source: IMF, *Zimbabwe: 2010 Article IV Consultation—Staff Report; Staff Supplement; Public Information Notice on the Executive Board Discussion; and Statement by the Executive Director for Zimbabwe* (July 2010).

External Trade

PRINCIPAL COMMODITIES
(US $ million)

Imports f.o.b.	2007	2008	2009
Cereals	187.6	215.7	220.7
Maize	150.3	169.9	104.9
Animal, vegetable fats and oils, cleavage products, etc.	22.6	47.1	118.5
Safflower, sunflower/cottonseed oil and fractions	12.6	33.3	96.0
Mineral fuels, oils, distillation products, etc.	588.0	320.2	454.2
Petroleum and related products	559.2	266.1	334.8
Fertilizers	106.2	184.5	86.9
Mixtures of nitrogen, phosphorous and potassium fertilizers	65.6	164.6	50.8
Articles of iron and steel	61.1	91.6	110.0
Structures (rods, angle, plates) of iron and steel	8.2	39.3	51.5
Copper and copper articles	270.6	3.2	6.1
Nickel and nickel articles	43.0	108.0	138.7
Nuclear reactors, boilers, machinery, etc.	466.3	299.9	300.8
Vehicles other than railway, tramway	440.1	445.3	533.7
Tractors	139.1	74.2	51.8
Trucks, motor vehicles used for the transport of goods	151.8	200.4	269.5
Total (incl. others)	3,441.7	2,831.8	3,526.8

Exports	2007	2008	2009
Live trees, plants, bulbs, roots, cut flowers etc.	201.1	185.8	334.2
Edible vegetables, roots and tubers	143.9	37.3	2.9
Frozen vegetables	106.6	12.3	2.0
Sugars and sugar confectionery	45.7	42.6	78.5
Cane or beet sugar and chemically pure sucrose, in solid form	35.2	39.3	73.5
Tobacco and manufactured tobacco substitutes	278.3	127.4	276.2
Tobacco and tobacco refuse	210.6	99.9	241.8
Ores, slag and ash	215.6	137.3	181.2
Nickel ores and concentrates	209.3	132.7	170.5
Printed books, newspapers, pictures etc.	369.0	64.6	435.5
Cotton	107.8	146.4	114.4
Raw cotton	88.7	88.0	102.4
Pearls, precious stones, metals, coins, etc.	143.3	23.5	129.6
Gold unwrought or in semi-manufactured forms	120.3	8.1	102.1
Iron and steel	417.7	61.4	43.7
Ferro-alloys	401.3	47.5	30.9
Nickel and nickel articles	396.0	166.3	266.3
Nickel matte and nickel oxide sinters	199.8	149.1	251.8
Unwrought nickel	194.5	16.7	14.6
Electrical, electronic equipment	25.8	65.0	26.4
Vehicles other than railway, tramway	205.9	87.4	10.8
Cars (incl. station wagons)	144.1	9.7	1.4
Optical, photo, technical, medical, etc. apparatus	1.0	79.5	0.3
Furniture, lighting, signs, prefabricated buildings	125.9	17.6	15.7
Total (incl. others)	3,308.4	1,693.9	2,269.0

Source: Trade Map-Trade Competitiveness Map, International Trade Centre, www.intracen.org/marketanalysis.

PRINCIPAL TRADING PARTNERS
(US $ million)

Imports f.o.b.	2007	2008	2009
Botswana	409.0	214.8	198.6
China, People's Repub.	215.9	138.1	128.8
Germany	48.9	52.2	38.7
India	40.8	33.4	27.0
Kuwait	167.9	11.1	80.5
Malawi	171.6	24.3	6.7
Mauritius	9.6	5.7	43.5
Mozambique	125.0	81.7	145.1
Netherlands	35.8	15.0	8.3
South Africa	1,534.2	1,758.9	2,132.2
United Kingdom	106.6	67.4	70.7
USA	123.3	113.6	275.1
Zambia	109.8	61.9	91.3
Total (incl. others)	3,441.7	2,831.8	3,526.8

ZIMBABWE

Exports f.o.b.	2007	2008	2009
Belgium	28.4	37.1	61.0
Botswana	201.0	157.0	36.9
China, People's Repub.	63.8	37.5	54.2
Congo, Democratic Repub.	84.1	14.8	14.7
France (incl. Monaco)	9.3	33.2	6.4
Germany	39.0	6.4	8.6
Italy	26.6	48.3	46.5
Lesotho	4.6	1.2	25.6
Malawi	57.7	72.7	29.9
Mozambique	431.4	41.1	98.2
Netherlands	153.1	169.3	187.8
Russia	48.6	4.8	7.7
Singapore	25.7	32.3	22.6
South Africa	1,239.1	711.3	1,192.2
Switzerland (incl. Liechtenstein)	133.5	33.2	169.6
United Kingdom	245.4	57.8	56.7
USA	78.0	20.8	10.0
Zambia	124.4	70.1	82.7
Total (incl. others)	3,308.4	1,693.9	2,269.0

Source: Trade Map-Trade Competitiveness Map, International Trade Centre, www.intracen.org/marketanalysis.

Transport

RAIL TRAFFIC
(National Railways of Zimbabwe, including operations in Botswana)

	1998	1999	2000
Total number of passengers ('000)	1,787	1,896	1,614
Revenue-earning metric tons hauled ('000)	12,421	12,028	9,422
Gross metric ton-km (million)	9,248	8,962	6,953
Net metric ton-km (million)	4,549	4,375	3,326

ROAD TRAFFIC
('000 motor vehicles in use, estimates)

	1998	1999	2000
Passenger cars	540	555	573
Commercial vehicles	37	38	39

2002: Passenger cars 570,866; Lorries and vans 84,456; Motorcycles 45.

CIVIL AVIATION
(traffic on scheduled services)

	2004	2005	2006
Kilometres flown (million)	6	7	10
Passengers carried ('000)	225	243	239
Passenger-km (million)	500	553	671
Total ton-km (million)	67	74	76

Source: UN, *Statistical Yearbook*.

2007: Passengers carried ('000) 254.7 (Source: World Bank, World Development Indicators database).

2008: Passengers carried ('000) 264.4 (Source: World Bank, World Development Indicators database).

Tourism

VISITOR ARRIVALS BY NATIONALITY

	2006	2007	2008
Australia and New Zealand	20,023	18,947	20,201
Botswana	86,117	227,777	147,780
Canada and USA	36,855	31,412	37,754
Malawi	78,039	111,177	63,597
Mozambique	114,988	94,290	118,117
South Africa	1,516,135	1,362,982	936,727
United Kingdom	22,045	22,295	22,778
Zambia	146,143	301,265	346,344
Total (incl. others)	2,286,572	2,508,255	1,955,596

Tourism receipts (US $ million, incl. passenger transport): 338 in 2006; 365 in 2007; 294 in 2008.

Source: World Tourism Organization.

Communications Media

	2007	2008	2009
Telephones ('000 main lines in use)	345.0	348.0	385.1
Mobile cellular telephones ('000 subscribers)	1,225.7	1,654.7	2,991.0
Internet users ('000)	1,351.0	1,421.0	1,422.0
Broadband subscribers ('000)	15.2	17.0	18.0

Personal computers: 865,000 (69.4 per 1,000 persons) in 2006.

Radio receivers ('000 in use): 4,488 in 1999.

Television receivers ('000 in use): 410 in 2000.

Daily newspapers: 2 (average circulation 209,000 copies) in 1996; 3 in 2004.

Sources: UNESCO, *Statistical Yearbook*; UNESCO Institute for Statistics; UN, *Statistical Yearbook*; International Telecommunication Union.

Education

(2002/03, unless otherwise indicated)

	Institutions*	Teachers	Students
Pre-primary	n.a.	19,588	448,124
Primary	4,699	64,001†	2,445,520†
Secondary	1,539	33,964	831,488†
Tertiary	n.a.	2,072‡	49,645‡

* 1998 figures.
† 2005/06.
‡ 2008/09.

Source: mainly UNESCO Institute for Statistics.

Pupil-teacher ratio (primary education, UNESCO estimate): 38.2 in 2005/06 (Source: UNESCO Institute for Statistics).

Adult literacy rate (UNESCO estimates): 91.4% (males 94.4%; females 88.8%) in 2008 (Source: UNESCO Institute for Statistics).

Directory

The Government

HEAD OF STATE

President: ROBERT GABRIEL MUGABE (took office 31 December 1987; re-elected March 1990, 16–17 March 1996, 9–11 March 2002 and 27 June 2008).

THE CABINET
(May 2011)

The Cabinet comprises representatives of the Zimbabwe African National Union—Patriotic Front (ZANU—PF), the Movement for Democratic Change—Tsvangirai (MDC—T) and the Movement for Democratic Change—Mutambara (MDC—M).

Vice-President (ZANU—PF): JOHN NKOMO.
Vice-President (ZANU—PF): JOYCE MUJURU.
Prime Minister (MDC—T): MORGAN TSVANGIRAI.
First Deputy Prime Minister (MDC—T): THOKOZANI KHUPE.
Second Deputy Prime Minister (MDC—M): ARTHUR MUTAMBARA.
Minister of Agriculture, Mechanisation and Irrigation Development (ZANU—PF): JOSEPH MADE.
Minister of Constitutional and Parliamentary Affairs (MDC—T): ERIC MATINENGA.
Minister of Defence (ZANU—PF): EMMERSON MNANGWAGWA.
Minister of Economic Planning and Development (MDC—T): TAPIWA MASHAKADA.
Minister of Education, Sports and Culture (MDC—M): DAVID COLTART.
Minister of Energy and Power Development (MDC—T): ELTON MANGOMA.
Minister of the Environment and Natural Resources (ZANU—PF): FRANCIS NHEMA.
Minister of Finance (MDC—T): TENDAI BITI.
Minister of Foreign Affairs (ZANU—PF): SIMBARASHE MUMBENGEGWI.
Minister of Health and Child Welfare (MDC—T): HENRY MADZORERA.
Minister of Higher and Tertiary Education (ZANU—PF): I. STANISLAUS GORERAZVO MUDENGE.
Minister of Home Affairs (ZANU—PF): KEMBO MOHADI.
Minister of Home Affairs (MDC—T): THERESA MAKONE.
Minister of Industry and Commerce (MDC—M): WELSHMAN NCUBE.
Minister of Information and Communications Technology (MDC—T): NELSON CHAMISA.
Minister of Justice and Legal Affairs (ZANU—PF): PATRICK ANTHONY CHINAMASA.
Minister of Labour (MDC—T): PAULINE MPARIWA.
Minister of Lands and Rural Resettlement (ZANU—PF): HERBERT MURERWA.
Minister of Local Government (ZANU—PF): Dr IGNATIUS MORGAN CHIMINYA CHOMBO.
Minister of Media, Information and Publicity (ZANU—PF): WEBSTER SHAMU.
Minister of Mines (ZANU—PF): OBERT MPOFU.
Minister of National Housing and Social Amenities (MDC—T): GILES MUTSEKWA.
Minister of Public Service (MDC—T): ELPHAS MUKONOWESHURO.
Minister of Public Works (MDC—T): JOEL GABUZA.
Minister of Regional Integration and International Trade (MDC—M): PRISCILLA MISIHAIRABWI.
Minister of Science and Technology (MDC—T): HENERI DZINOTYIWEI.
Minister of Small and Medium Enterprises and Co-operative Development (ZANU—PF): SITHEMBISO NYONI.
Minister of State Enterprises and Parastatals (MDC—T): GORDON MOYO.
Minister of State for National Security in the President's Office (ZANU—PF): SYDNEY SEKERAMAYI.
Minister of State for Presidential Affairs (ZANU—PF): DIDYMUS MUTASA.
Minister of State in the Prime Minister's Office (MDC—T): JAMESON TIMBA.
Minister of State in the Prime Minister's Office (MDC—T): SEKAI MASIKANA HOLLAND.
Minister of Tourism and the Hospitality Industry (ZANU—PF): WALTER MZEMBI.
Minister of Transport and Infrastructural Development (ZANU—PF): NICHOLAS GOCHE.
Minister of Water Resources (MDC—T): SAMUEL SIPEPA NKOMO.
Minister of Women's Affairs, Gender and Community Development (ZANU—PF): OLIVIA MUCHENA.
Minister of Youth Development, Indigenization and Empowerment (ZANU—PF): SAVIOR KASUKUWERE.

In addition, there are 15 deputy ministers, eight from ZANU—PF, six from the MDC—T and one from the MDC—M.

The Constitution provides for the Attorney-General to serve as an ex officio member of the Cabinet.

MINISTRIES

Office of the President: Munhumutapa Bldg, Samora Machel Ave, Private Bag 7700, Causeway, Harare; tel. (4) 707091.
Office of the Vice-Presidents: Munhumutapa Bldg, Samora Machel Ave, Private Bag 7700, Causeway, Harare; tel. (4) 707091.
Ministry of Agriculture, Mechanisation and Irrigation Development: Ngungunyana Bldg, Private Bag 7701, Causeway, Harare; tel. (4) 700596; fax (4) 734646; internet www.moa.gov.zw.
Ministry of Defence: Defence House, cnr Kwame Nkuruma and 3rd Sts, Harare; tel. (4) 700155; fax (4) 727501; internet www.mod.gov.zw.
Ministry of Economic Planning and Development: New Complex Bldg, Government Composite Offices, cnr 3rd St and Samora Machel Ave, Harare; e-mail moed@gta.gov.zw; internet www.mofed.gov.zw.
Ministry of Education, Sports and Culture: Ambassador House, Union Ave, POB CY121, Causeway, Harare; tel. (4) 734051; fax (4) 707599; internet www.moesc.gov.zw.
Ministry of Energy and Power Development: Chaminuka Bldg, Private Bag 7758, Causeway, Harare; tel. (4) 733095; fax (4) 797956; e-mail energy@gta.gov.zw; internet www.energy.gov.zw.
Ministry of the Environment and Natural Resources: Kaguvi Bldg, 12th Floor, cnr 4th St and Central Ave, Private Bag 7753, Causeway, Harare; tel. (4) 701681; fax (4) 252673; e-mail metlib@zarnet.ac.zw; internet www.met.gov.zw.
Ministry of Finance: Blocks B, E and G, Composite Bldg, cnr Samora Machel Ave and Fourth St, Private Bag 7705, Causeway, Harare; tel. (4) 738603; fax (4) 792750; internet www.mofed.gov.zw.
Ministry of Foreign Affairs: Munhumutapa Bldg, Samora Machel Ave, POB 4240, Causeway, Harare; tel. (4) 727005; fax (4) 705161; internet www.zimfa.gov.zw.
Ministry of Health and Child Welfare: Kaguvi Bldg, Fourth St, POB CY198, Causeway, Harare; tel. (4) 730011; fax (4) 729154; internet www.mohcw.gov.zw.
Ministry of Higher and Tertiary Education: Government Composite Bldg, cnr Fourth St and Samora Machel Ave, Union Ave, POB UA275, Harare; tel. (4) 796440; fax (4) 790923; e-mail thesecretary@mhet.ac.zw; internet www.mhet.ac.zw.
Ministry of Home Affairs: Mukwati Bldg, 11th Floor, cnr Fourth St and Livingstone Ave, Private Bag 7703, Causeway, Harare; tel. (4) 703641; fax (4) 707231; e-mail moha@gvt.co.zw; internet www.moha.gov.zw.
Ministry of Industry and Commerce: Mukwati Bldg, Fourth St, Private Bag 7708, Causeway, Harare; tel. (4) 702731; fax (4) 729311; internet www.miit.gov.zw.
Ministry of Information and Communications Technology: Linquenda House, Baker Ave, POB CY825, Causeway, Harare; tel. (4) 703894; fax (4) 707213.
Ministry of Justice and Legal Affairs: New Government Complex, cnr Samora Machel Ave and 4th St, Private Bag 7751, Causeway, Harare; tel. (4) 774620; fax (4) 772999; internet www.justice.gov.zw.
Ministry of Local Government: Mukwati Bldg, Fourth St, Private Bag 7755, Causeway, Harare; tel. (4) 7282019; fax (4) 708493; internet www.mlgpwud.gov.zw.
Ministry of Mines: ZIMRE Centre, 6th Floor, cnr Leopold Takawira St and Kwame Nkrumah Ave, Private Bag 7709, Causeway, Harare; tel. (4) 777022; fax (4) 777044; e-mail minsec@technopark.co.zw; internet www.mines.gov.zw.

ZIMBABWE

Ministry of Public Service: Compensation House, cnr Central Ave and Fourth St, Private Bag 7707, Causeway, Harare; tel. (4) 790871; fax (4) 794568; e-mail mpslsw@gta.gov.zw; internet www.pslsw.gov.zw.

Ministry of Transport and Infrastructural Development: Kaguvi Bldg, 4th Central Ave, POB 595, Causeway, Harare; tel. (4) 252396; fax (4) 726661; e-mail angiekaronga@yahoo.co.uk; internet www.transcom.gov.zw.

Ministry of Water Resources: Kurima House, cnr Nelson Madela Ave and Fourth St, Private Bag CY 7767, Harare; tel. (4) 700596; fax (4) 738165; internet www.water.gov.zw.

Ministry of Youth Development, Indigenization and Empowerment: ZANU—PF Bldg, Private Bag 7762, Causeway, Harare; tel. (4) 734691; fax (4) 732709; e-mail mydgec@zarnet.ac.zw; internet www.mydgec.gov.zw.

PROVINCIAL GOVERNORS
(May 2011)

Bulawayo: CAIN MATHEMA.
Harare: DAVID KARIMANZIRA.
Manicaland: CHRISTOPHER MUSHOHWE.
Mashonaland Central: MARTIN DINHA.
Mashonaland East: AENEAS CHIGWEDERE.
Mashonaland West: FABER CHIDARIKIRE.
Masvingo: TITUS MALULEKE.
Matabeleland North: THOKOZILE MATHUTHU.
Matabeleland South: ANGELINE MASUKU.
Midlands: JAISON MACHAYA.

President and Legislature

PRESIDENT

Presidential Election, First Round, 29 March 2008

Candidate	Votes	% of valid votes
Morgan Tsvangirai	1,195,562	47.87
Robert Gabriel Mugabe	1,079,730	43.24
Simba Herbert Makoni	207,470	8.31
Langton Towungana	14,503	0.58
Total	**2,497,265**	**100.00**

Presidential Election, Second Round, 27 June 2008, provisional results

Candidate	Votes	% of valid votes
Robert Gabriel Mugabe	2,150,269	90.21
Morgan Tsvangirai*	233,000	9.78
Total†	**2,383,629**	**100.00**

* Tsvangirai announced his withdrawal from the second round of voting on 22 June; however, the Zimbabwe Election Commission stated that the Constitution necessitated that the run-off take place and Tsvangirai's name remained on the ballot papers.
† Excludes 131,481 spoiled ballots.

HOUSE OF ASSEMBLY

Speaker: LOVEMORE MOYO.
General Election, 29 March 2008, provisional results

Party	Votes	% of votes	Seats
MDC—Tsvangirai	1,041,176	42.99	99
ZANU—PF	1,110,649	45.86	97
MDC—Mutambara	202,259	8.35	10
Independents	54,254	2.24	1
Others	13,635	0.56	—
Total	**2,421,973**	**100.00**	**207***

* Voting was postponed in three constituencies, owing to the deaths of candidates.

SENATE

Speaker: EDNA MADZONGWE.
General Election, 29 March 2008, provisional results

Party	Seats
ZANU—PF	30
MDC—Tsvangirai	24
MDC—Mutambara	6
Total	**60***

* In addition to the 60 directly elective seats, five are held by nominees of the President, 10 by provincial governors, two by the President and the Deputy President of the Council of Chiefs and 16 by traditional Chiefs.

Election Commission

Zimbabwe Electoral Commission (ZEC): Century House East, PMB 7782, Causeway, Harare; tel. (4) 759130; fax (4) 781903; e-mail zecpr@gta.gov.zw; internet www.zimbabweelectoralcommission.org; f. 2005; the President appoints eight members, four of whom must be women, and also the Chair. in consultation with the Judicial Service Commission and the Committee on Standing Rules and Orders for a six-year term; superseded and replaced the Electoral Supervisory Commission (abolished Aug. 2005); responsible for establishing constituency boundaries, voter registration and conducting elections; Chair. SIMPSON MTAMBANENGWE.

Political Organizations

Christian Democratic Party: Leader WILLIAM GWATA.

Committee for a Democratic Society (CODESO): f. 1993; Karanga-supported grouping, based in Matabeleland; Leader SOUL NDLOVU.

Federal Democratic Union: f. 2008; Leader PAUL SIWELA.

Forum Party of Zimbabwe (FPZ): POB 74, Bulawayo; f. 1993; conservative; Pres. (vacant).

General Conference of Patriots: Harare; f. 1998; opposes the Govt; aims to organize and direct dissent; Leader OBEY MUDZINGWA.

Movement for Democratic Change—Mutambara (MDC—M): Harare; e-mail a.mutambara@mdczim.com; internet www.mdczim.com; f. 2005; Pres. Prof. ARTHUR MUTAMBARA; Sec.-Gen. Prof. WELSHMAN NCUBE.

Movement for Democratic Change—Tsvangirai (MDC—T): Harvest House, 6th Floor, cnr Angwa St and Nelson Mandela Ave, Harare; tel. (4) 770708; fax (4) 780302; e-mail mdcnewsbrief@gmail.com; internet www.mdc.co.zw; f. 1999; split into two factions in 2005; allied to Zimbabwe Congress of Trade Unions; Pres. MORGAN TSVANGIRAI; Sec.-Gen. TENDAI BITI.

National Progressive Alliance: f. 1991; Chair. CANCIWELL NZIRAMASANGA.

United National Federal Party (UNFP): Harare; f. 1978; conservative; seeks a federation of Mashonaland and Matabeleland; Leader Chief KAYISA NDIWENI.

United People's Party (UPP): f. 2006; Leader DANIEL SHUMBA.

Zimbabwe Active People's Unity Party: Bulawayo; f. 1989; Leader NEWMAN MATUTU NDELA.

Zimbabwe African National Union—Ndonga (ZANU—Ndonga): POB UA525, Union Ave, Harare; tel. and fax (4) 481180; f. 1977; breakaway faction from ZANU, also includes fmr mems of United African Nat. Council; supports free market economy; Nat. Chair. REKETAI MUSHIWEKUFA SEMWAYO; Sec.-Gen. EDWIN C. NGUWA.

Zimbabwe African National Union—Patriotic Front (ZANU—PF): cnr Rotten Row and Samora Machel Ave, POB 4530, Harare; tel. (4) 753329; fax (4) 774146; f. 1989 by merger of PF—ZAPU and ZANU—PF; Pres. ROBERT GABRIEL MUGABE; Vice-Pres SIMON VENGAYI MUZENDA, JOHN NKOMO; Nat. Chair. SIMON KHAYA MOYO.

Zimbabwe Congress Party: Harare; f. 1994; Pres. KENNETH MANO.

Zimbabwe Development Party: Harare; Leader KISINOTI MUKWAZHE.

Zimbabwe Federal Party (ZFPO): Stand 214, Nketa 6, P.O. Nkulumane, Bulawayo; f. 1994; aims to create national federation of five provinces; Leader RICHARD NCUBE.

Zimbabwe Integrated Programme: f. 1999; seeks economic reforms; Pres. Prof. HENEDI DZINOCHIKIWEYI.

ZIMBABWE

Zimbabwe People's Democratic Party: POB 4001, Harare; e-mail mail@zpdp.org; internet www.zpdp.org; f. 1991; Chair. ISABEL SHANANGURAI MADANGURE; Sec.-Gen. DUDLEY GURA.

Zimbabwe Progressive People's Democratic Party: Harare; Leader TAFIRENYIKA MUDAVANHU.

Zimbabwe Unity Movement (ZUM): f. 1989 by a breakaway faction from ZANU—PF; merged with United African National Council in 1994; Leader EDGAR TEKERE.

Zimbabwe Youth in Alliance: Leader MOSES MUTYASIRA.

Diplomatic Representation

EMBASSIES IN ZIMBABWE

Algeria: 8 Pascoe Ave, Belgravia, Harare; tel. (4) 791773; fax (4) 701125; e-mail offambalch@utande.co.zw; internet www.algerianembassy-harare.org; Ambassador LAZHAR SOUALEM.

Angola: 26 Speke Ave, POB 3590, Harare; tel. (4) 770075; fax (4) 770077; Ambassador FILIPE FELISBERTO MONIMAMBU.

Australia: 1 Green Close, Borrowdale, Harare; POB 4541, Harare; tel. (4) 852471; fax (4) 870566; e-mail zimbabwe.embassy@dfat.gov.au; internet www.zimbabwe.embassy.gov.au; Ambassador MATTHEW NEUHAUS.

Austria: 13 Duthie Rd, Alexandra Park, POB 4120, Harare; tel. (4) 702921; fax (4) 705877; e-mail harare-ob@bmeia.gv.at; Ambassador Dr MARIA MOYA-GÖTSCH.

Bangladesh: 9 Birchenough Rd, POB 3040, Harare; tel. (4) 727004; Ambassador NASIMA HAIDER.

Botswana: 22 Phillips Ave, Belgravia, POB 563, Harare; tel. (4) 729551; fax (4) 721360; Ambassador GLADYS KOKORWE.

Brazil: Old Mutual Centre, 9th Floor, Jason Moyo Ave, POB 2530, Harare; tel. (4) 790740; fax (4) 790754; e-mail brasemb@ecoweb.co.zw; internet www.brazil.org.zw; Ambassador RAUL DE TAUNAY.

Bulgaria: 15 Maasdorp Ave, Alexandra Park, POB 1809, Harare; tel. (4) 730509; fax (4) 732504; e-mail bgembhre@ecoweb.co.zw; Ambassador CHRISTO TEPAVITCHAROV.

Canada: 45 Baines Ave, POB 1430, Harare; tel. (4) 252181; fax (4) 252186; e-mail hrare@international.gc.ca; internet www.canadainternational.gc.ca/zimbabwe; Ambassador BARBARA RICHARDSON.

China, People's Republic: 30 Baines Ave, POB 4749, Harare; tel. and fax (4) 794155; e-mail chinaemb_zw@mfa.gov.cn; internet www.chinaembassy.org.zw; Ambassador XIN SHUNKANG.

Congo, Democratic Republic: 5 Pevensey Rd, Highlands, POB 2446, Harare; tel. (4) 481172; fax (4) 796421; e-mail harare@embadrcongo.co.zw; internet www.embadrcongo.co.zw; Ambassador MAWAMPANGA MWANA NANGA.

Cuba: 5 Phillips Ave, Belgravia, POB A1196, Harare; tel. (4) 790126; fax (4) 707998; e-mail cuba.embassy@cubanembassy.co.zw; internet emba.cubaminrex.cu/zimbabweing; Ambassador COSME TORRES ESPINOSA.

Czech Republic: 4 Sandringham Dr., Alexandra Park, GPO 4474, Harare; tel. (4) 700636; fax (4) 720930; e-mail harare@embassy.mzv.cz; internet www.mzv.cz/harare; Chargé d'affaires LUDĚK ZAHRADNÍČEK.

Egypt: 7 Aberdeen Rd, Avondale, POB A433, Harare; tel. (4) 303445; fax (4) 303115; Ambassador GAMEEL SAEED FAYED.

Ethiopia: 14 Lanark Rd, Belgravia, POB 2745, Harare; tel. (4) 701514; fax (4) 701516; e-mail emb@ecoweb.co.zw; Ambassador ADBI DALAL MOHAMMED.

France: Bank Chambers, 11th Floor, 74–76 Samora Machel Ave, POB 1378, Harare; tel. (4) 703216; fax (4) 730078; e-mail web.harare@diplomatie.gouv.fr; internet www.ambafrance-zw.org; Ambassador FRANÇOIS PONGE.

Germany: 30 Ceres Rd, Avondale, POB A1475, Harare; tel. (4) 308655; fax (4) 303455; e-mail botschaft_harare@gmx.de; internet www.harare.diplo.de; Ambassador Dr ALBRECHT CONZE.

Ghana: 11 Downie Ave, Belgravia, POB 4445, Harare; tel. (4) 700982; fax (4) 707076; e-mail ghanaembassy@zol.co.zw; Ambassador JAMES OKOE NAADJIE.

Greece: 8 Deary Ave, Belgravia, POB 4809, Harare; tel. (4) 793208; fax (4) 703662; e-mail grembha@ecoweb.co.zw; Ambassador MICHAEL KOUKAKIS.

Holy See: 5 St Kilda Rd, Mount Pleasant, POB MP191, Harare (Apostolic Nunciature); tel. (4) 744547; fax (4) 744412; e-mail nunzim@zol.co.zw; Apostolic Nuncio Most Rev. GEORGE KOCHERRY (Titular Archbishop of Othona).

India: 12 Natal Rd, Belgravia, POB A620, Harare; tel. (4) 795955; fax (4) 722324; e-mail ambassador@embindia.org.zw; Ambassador V. ASHOK.

Indonesia: 3 Duthie Ave, Belgravia, POB CY 69, Causeway, Harare; tel. (4) 251799; fax (4) 796587; e-mail indohar@ecoweb.co.zw; internet www.indonesia-harare.org; Ambassador EDDY POERWANA.

Iran: 8 Allan Wilson Ave, Avondale, POB A293, Harare; tel. (4) 726942; Ambassador MOHAMMAD POUR-NAJAF.

Italy: 7 Bartholomew Close, Greendale North, POB 1062, Harare; tel. (4) 498190; fax (4) 498199; e-mail ambasciata.zimbabwe@esteri.it; internet www.ambharare.esteri.it; Ambassador STEFANO MOSCATELLI.

Japan: Social Security Centre, 4th Floor, cnr Julius Nyerere Way and Sam Nujoma St, POB 2710, Harare; tel. (4) 250025; fax (4) 250111; internet www.zw.emb-japan.go.jp; Ambassador MORITA KOICHI.

Kenya: 95 Park Lane, POB 4069, Harare; tel. (4) 704820; fax (4) 723042; Ambassador Prof. JOHN ABDUBA.

Korea, Democratic People's Republic: 102 Josiah Chinamano Ave, Greenwood, POB 4754, Harare; tel. (4) 724052; Ambassador AN HUI JONG (resident in South Africa).

Kuwait: 1 Bath Rd, Avondale, POB A485, Harare; Ambassador ABDALLAH JUMA ABDALLAH AS-SHARHAN.

Libya: 124 Harare St, POB 4310, Harare; tel. (4) 728381; Ambassador TAHER AL-MAQRAHI.

Malawi: 9–11 Duthie Rd, Alexandra Park, POB 321, Harare; tel. (4) 798584; fax (4) 799006; e-mail malahigh@africaonline.co.zw; Ambassador Prof. RICHARD PHOYA.

Malaysia: 40 Downie Ave, Avondale, POB 5570, Harare; tel. (4) 334413; fax (4) 334415; e-mail malharare@kln.gov.my; Ambassador CHEAH CHOONG KIT.

Mozambique: 152 cnr Herbert Chitepo Ave and Leopold Takawira St, POB 4608, Harare; tel. (4) 253871; fax (4) 253875; e-mail emba@embamoc.org.zw; Ambassador VICENTE MEBUNIA VELOSO.

Netherlands: 2 Arden Rd, Highlands, POB HG601, Harare; tel. (4) 776701; fax (4) 776700; e-mail har@minbuza.nl; Ambassador JOSEPH WETERINGS.

Nigeria: 36 Samora Machel Ave, POB 4742, Harare; tel. (4) 253900; fax (4) 253877; e-mail ngrharamb@yahoo.com; internet www.nigeriaharare.co.zw; Ambassador ADEKUNLE OLADOKUN ADEYANJU.

Norway: 5 Lanark Rd, Belgravia, POB A510, Avondale, Harare; tel. (4) 252426; fax (4) 252430; e-mail emb.harare@mfa.no; internet www.norway.org.zw; Ambassador GUNNAR FØRELAND.

Pakistan: 314 Pipendale Rd, Barrowadalf, Harare; tel. (4) 762018; fax (4) 794264; e-mail pahichar@yahoo.com; Ambassador RIFFAT IQBAL.

Poland: 16 Cork Rd, Belgravia, POB 3932, Harare; tel. (4) 253442; fax (4) 253710; Ambassador MARCIN KUBIAK.

Portugal: 12 Harvey Brown Ave, Milton Park, Harare; tel. (4) 253023; fax (4) 253637; e-mail embport@harare.dgaccp.pt; Ambassador JOÃO DA CÂMARA.

Romania: 105 Fourth St, POB 4797, Harare; tel. (4) 700853; fax (4) 725493; e-mail romemb@cybersatafrica.com; Chargé d'affaires a.i. FLORICĂ BARBU.

Russia: 70 Fife Ave, POB 4250, Harare; tel. (4) 701957; fax (4) 795932; e-mail russianembassy@zol.co.zw; internet www.zimbabwe.mid.ru; Ambassador SERGEI KRYUKOV.

South Africa: 7 Elcombe Rd, Belgravia, POB A1654, Harare; tel. (4) 753147; fax (4) 749657; e-mail admin@saembassy.co.zw; Ambassador VUSI MAVIMBELA.

Spain: 16 Phillips Ave, Belgravia, POB 3300, Harare; tel. (4) 250740; fax (4) 795261; e-mail emb.harare@mae.es; Ambassador PILAR FUERTES FERRAGUT.

Sudan: 4 Pascoe Ave, Harare; tel. (4) 700111; fax (4) 703450; e-mail sudan@africaonline.co.zw; internet www.sudaniharare.org.zw; Ambassador HASSAN AHMED FAGEERI.

Sweden: 32 Aberdeen Rd, Avondale, POB 4110, Harare; tel. (4) 302636; fax (4) 302236; e-mail ambassaden.harare@foreign.ministry.se; internet www.swedenabroad.com/harare; Ambassador ANDERS LIDÉN.

Switzerland: 15 Fleetwood Rd, Alexandra Park, POB 3440, Harare; tel. (4) 745682; fax (4) 745465; e-mail har.vertretung@eda.admin.ch; internet www.eda.admin.ch/harare; Ambassador ALEXANDER WITTWER.

Tanzania: Ujamaa House, 23 Baines Ave, POB 4841, Harare; tel. (4) 792714; fax (4) 792747; e-mail tanrep@icon.co.zw; Ambassador ADADI RAJABU.

United Kingdom: 3 Norfolk Rd, Mount Pleasant, POB 4490, Harare; tel. (4) 338800; fax (4) 338829; e-mail consular.harare@fco.gov.uk; internet ukinzimbabwe.fco.gov.uk/en; Ambassador MARK CANNING.

ZIMBABWE

USA: 172 Herbert Chitepo Ave, POB 3340, Harare; tel. (4) 250593; fax (4) 796488; e-mail hararepas@state.gov; internet harare.usembassy.gov; Ambassador CHARLES AARON RAY.

Zambia: Zambia House, cnr Union and Julius Nyerere Aves, POB 4698, Harare; tel. (4) 773777; Ambassador SIPULA KABANJE.

Judicial System

The legal system is Roman-Dutch, based on the system which was in force in the Cape of Good Hope on 10 June 1891, as modified by subsequent legislation.

The Supreme Court

Harare.

Has original jurisdiction in matters in which an infringement of Chapter III of the Constitution defining fundamental rights is alleged. In all other matters it has appellate jurisdiction only. It consists of the Chief Justice, a Deputy Chief Justice and such other judges of the Supreme Court, being not less than two, as the President may deem necessary.

Chief Justice: GODFREY CHIDYAUSIKU.
Deputy Chief Justice: LUKE MALABA.
Other Judges: W. SANDURA, RITA MAKARAU.

The High Court

Harare.

Consists of the Chief Justice, the Judge President, and such other judges of the High Court as may from time to time be appointed.

Judge President: GEORGE CHIWESHE.

Other Judges: SUSAN MAVANGIRA, LAVENDER MAKONI, BEN HLATSHWAYO, NICHOLAS MATHONSI, ANDREW MUTEMA, GARAINESU MAWADZE.

Below the High Court are Regional Courts and Magistrates' Courts with both civil and criminal jurisdiction presided over by full-time professional magistrates. The Customary Law and Local Courts Act, adopted in 1990, abolished the village and community courts and replaced them with customary law and local courts, presided over by chiefs and headmen; in the case of chiefs, jurisdiction to try customary law cases is limited to those where the monetary values concerned do not exceed Z.$1,000 and in the case of a headman's court Z.$500. Appeals from the Chiefs' Courts are heard in Magistrates' Courts and, ultimately, the Supreme Court. All magistrates now have jurisdiction to try cases determinable by customary law.

Attorney-General: JOHANNES TOMANA.

Religion

AFRICAN RELIGIONS

Many Zimbabweans follow traditional beliefs.

CHRISTIANITY

About 55% of the population are Christians.

Zimbabwe Council of Churches: 128 Mbuya Nehanda St, POB 3566, Harare; tel. (4) 772043; fax (4) 773650; e-mail zcc@africaonline.co.zw; f. 1964; Pres. Rt Rev. Dr WILSON SITSHEBO; Gen. Sec. DENSEN MAFIYANI; 24 mem. churches, nine assoc. mems.

The Anglican Communion

Anglicans are adherents of the Church of the Province of Central Africa, covering Botswana, Malawi, Zambia and Zimbabwe. The Church comprises 15 dioceses, including five in Zimbabwe. The current Archbishop of the Province is the Bishop of Northern Zambia. The Church had an estimated 320,000 members at mid-2000.

Bishop of Central Zimbabwe: Rt Rev. ISHMAEL MUKUWANDA, POB 25, Gweru; tel. (54) 21030; fax (54) 21097; e-mail diocent@telconet.co.zw.

Bishop of Harare: Rt Rev. CHAD NICHOLAS GANDIYA, 9 Monmouth Rd, Avondale, Harare; tel. (4) 308042; e-mail diohrecpca@ecoweb.co.zw.

Bishop of Manicaland: PETER HATENDI (acting), 113 Herbert Chitepo St, Mutare; tel. (20) 64194; fax (20) 63076; e-mail diomani@syscom.co.zw; internet www.anglicandioceseofmanicaland.co.zw.

Bishop of Masvingo: Rt Rev. GODFREY TOANEZVI, POB 1421, Masvingo; tel. (39) 362536; e-mail anglicandiomsv@comone.co.zw.

Bishop of Matabeleland: Rt Rev. CLEOPHAS LUNGA, POB 2422, Bulawayo; tel. (9) 61370; fax (9) 68353; e-mail clunga@aol.com.

The Roman Catholic Church

For ecclesiastical purposes, Zimbabwe comprises two archdioceses and six dioceses. The number of adherents was equivalent to an estimated 10% of the total population.

Zimbabwe Catholic Bishops' Conference (ZCBC)
Catholic Secretariat, Causeway, 29 Selous Ave, POB 8135, Harare; tel. (4) 705368; fax (4) 705369; internet www.zcbc.co.zw. f. 1969; Pres. Most Rev. ROBERT C. NDLOVU (Archbishop of Harare).

Archbishop of Bulawayo: Most Rev. ALEX THOMAS KALIYANIL, cnr Lobengula St and 9th Ave, POB 837, Bulawayo; tel. (9) 63590; fax (9) 60359; e-mail archdbyo@mweb.co.zw.

Archbishop of Harare: Most Rev. ROBERT C. NDLOVU, Archbishop's House, 66 Fifth St, POB CY330, Causeway, Harare; tel. (4) 727386; fax (4) 721598; e-mail hrearch@zol.co.zw.

Other Christian Churches

At mid-2000 there were an estimated 4.8m. adherents professing other forms of Christianity.

Dutch Reformed Church in Zimbabwe (Nederduitse Gereformeerde Kerk): 35 Samora Machel Ave, POB 503, Harare; tel. (4) 774738; fax (4) 774739; e-mail pvanvuuren@mango.zw; f. 1895; 11 congregations in Zimbabwe and two in Zambia; Chair. Rev. PIETER F. J. VAN VUUREN; Sec. Rev. J. HAASBROEK; 1,245 mems.

Evangelical Lutheran Church: 7 Lawley Rd, POB 2175, Bulawayo; tel. (9) 254991; fax (9) 254993; e-mail elczhead@mweb.co.zw; f. 1903; Sec. Rt Rev. L. M. DUBE; 150,000 mems (2009).

Greek Orthodox Church: POB 2832, Harare; tel. (4) 744991; fax (4) 744928; e-mail zimbabwe@greekorthodox-zimbabwe.org; internet www.greekorthodox-zimbabwe.org; Archbishop GEORGE.

Methodist Church in Zimbabwe: POB CY71, Causeway, Harare; tel. (4) 250523; fax (4) 723709; e-mail methodistconn@zol.co.zw; f. 1891; Presiding Bishop Rev. SIMBARASHE SITHOLE; Sec. of Conference Rev. AMOS NDHLUMBI.

United Congregational Church of Southern Africa: 40 Jason Moyo St, POB 2451, Bulawayo; tel. (9) 63686; internet www.uccsa.org.za/zimbabwe-synod; Chair. Rev. B. MATHEMA (acting); Sec. Rev. MAJAHA NTHLIZIYO.

United Methodist Church: POB 3408, Harare; tel. (4) 704127; f. 1890; Bishop of Zimbabwe ABEL TENDEKAYI MUZOREWA; 45,000 mems.

Among other denominations active in Zimbabwe are the African Methodist Church, the African Methodist Episcopal Church, the African Reformed Church, the Christian Marching Church, the Church of Christ in Zimbabwe, the Independent African Church, the Presbyterian Church (and the City Presbyterian Church), the United Church of Christ, the Zimbabwe Assemblies of God and the Ziwezano Church.

JUDAISM

The Jewish community numbered 897 members at 31 December 1997; by 2006 that number had fallen to around 300.

Zimbabwe Jewish Board of Deputies: POB 1954, Harare; tel. (4) 702507; fax (4) 702506; Pres. P. STERNBERG; Sec. E. ALHADEFF.

BAHÁ'Í FAITH

National Spiritual Assembly: POB GD380, Greendale, Harare; tel. (4) 495945; fax (4) 744611; internet www.bahai.co.zw; Nat. Sec. DEREK SITHOLE; f. 1970; mems resident in 57 clusters.

The Press

DAILIES

In early 2011 there were five daily newspapers in Zimbabwe.

The Chronicle: 9th Ave and George Silundika St, POB 585, Bulawayo; tel. (9) 888871; fax (9) 888884; e-mail editor@chronicle.co.zw; internet www.chronicle.co.zw; f. 1894; publ. by govt-controlled co Zimpapers; circulates throughout south-west Zimbabwe; English; Editor INNOCENT GORE; circ. 25,000 (2004).

The Daily News: 18 Sam Nujoma St and cnr Speke Ave, Harare; tel. (4) 753027; fax (4) 753024; internet www.dailynews.co.zw; publ. by Associated Newspapers of Zimbabwe; English; publ. suspended Sept. 2003; Editor NQOBILE NYATHI; CEO SAM SIPEPA NKOMO; Chair. STRIVE MASIYIWA; circ. c. 80,000 (2003).

The Herald: POB 396, Harare; tel. (4) 795771; fax (4) 700305; internet www.herald.co.zw; f. 1891; publ. by govt-controlled co Zimpapers; English; Editor PIKIRAYI DEKETEKE; circ. c. 60,000 (2006).

NewsDay: Harare; tel. (4) 773839; e-mail newsday@zimind.co.zw; internet www.newsday.co.zw; f. 2009; owned by ZimInd Publrs (Pvt) Ltd; Editor-in-Chief VINCENT KAHIYA.

ZIMBABWE

Directory

The Zimbabwe Mail: e-mail editor@thezimbabwemail.com; internet www.thezimbabwemail.com; f. 2011; Exec. Chair. LEIGHTON MUSHANINGA; Man. Editor NKULULEKO NDLOVU.

WEEKLIES

Financial Gazette: Coal House, 5th Floor, cnr Nelson Mandela Ave and Leopold Takawira St, Harare; tel. (4) 781571; fax (4) 781578; e-mail schamunorwa@fingaz.co.zw; internet www.fingaz.co.zw; f. 1969; publ. by ZimInd Publrs (Pvt) Ltd; affiliated to the ZANU—PF party; Editor-in-Chief SUNSLEEY CHAMUNORWA; Gen. Man. JACOB CHISESE; circ. c. 40,000 (2004).

Indonsakusa/Ilanga: c/o CNG, POB 6520, Harare; tel. (4) 796855; fax (4) 703873; publ. by Community Newspaper Group (Mass Media Trust); distributed in north and south Matabeleland; circ. c. 10,000.

Kwayedza: POB 396, Harare; tel. (4) 795771; fax (4) 791311; internet www.kwayedza.co.zw; publ. by govt-controlled co Zimpapers; f. 1985; ChiShona; Editor GERVASE M. CHITEWE; circ. c. 15,000 (2003).

Manica Post: POB 960, Mutare; tel. (20) 61212; fax (20) 61149; internet www.manicapost.com; f. 1893; publ. by govt-controlled co Zimpapers; English; Editor PAUL MAMBO; circ. 15,000 (2004).

Mashonaland Guardian/Telegraph: c/o CNG, POB 6520, Harare; tel. (4) 796855; fax (4) 703873; publ. by Community Newspaper Group (Mass Media Trust); distributed in Mashonaland; circ. c. 10,000.

Masvingo Mirror: POB 1214, Masvingo; tel. (39) 64372; fax (39) 64484; independent; Editor NORNA EDWARDS.

Masvingo Star: 2–3 New Market Centre, R. Tangwena Ave, POB 138, Masvingo; tel. and fax (39) 63978; publ. by Community Newspaper Group (Mass Media Trust); English; distributed in Masvingo province; Editor (vacant); circ. c. 10,000.

Midlands Observer: POB 533, Kwekwe; tel. (55) 22248; fax (55) 23985; e-mail nelson_mashiri@yahoo.com; f. 1953; weekly; English; Editor R. JARIJARI; circ. 20,000.

North Midlands Gazette: POB 222, Kadoma; tel. and fax (68) 3731; f. 1912; Editor C. B. KIDIA.

The Standard: 1st Block, 3rd Floor, Ernst and Young Bldg, 1 Kwame Nkrumah Ave, POB 661730, Kopje, Harare; tel. (4) 773930; fax (4) 798897; internet www.thestandard.co.zw; f. 1997; publ. by ZimInd Publrs (Pvt) Ltd; Sun.; Exec. Chair. and CEO TREVOR NCUBE; Editor NEVANJI MADANHIRE; circ. 42,000 (2004).

Sunday Mail: POB 396, Harare; tel. (4) 795771; fax (4) 700305; internet www.sundaymail.co.zw; f. 1935; publ. by govt-controlled co Zimpapers; English; Chair. THOMAS SITHOLE; Editor WILLIAM CHIKOTO; circ. 110,000 (2004).

Sunday News: POB 585, Bulawayo; tel. (9) 540071; fax (9) 540084; f. 1930; publ. by govt-controlled co Zimpapers; English; Editor BREZHNEV MALABA; circ. 30,000 (2004).

The Times: c/o CNG, POB 6520, Harare; tel. (4) 796855; fax (4) 703873; f. 1897; fmrly *The Gweru Times*; publ. by Community Newspaper Group (Mass Media Trust); distributed in Mashonaland; English; circ. c. 5,000.

uMthunywa (The Messenger): 9th Ave and George Silundika St, POB 585 Bulawayo; tel. (9) 880888; fax (9) 888884; e-mail advertising@chronicle.co.zw; internet www.umthunywa.co.zw; f. 2004; SiNdebele; publ. by govt-controlled co Zimpapers; Editor BHEKITHEMBA J. NCUBE.

The Vanguard: Zimbabwe National Students' Union, 21 Wembley Cres., Eastlea, Harare; tel. (4) 788135; e-mail zinasu@gmail.com; internet www.zinasu.org/vanguards/latest.html; publ. by the Zimbabwe Nat. Students' Union.

Zimbabwe Independent: Zimind Publishers (Pvt) Ltd, Suites 23/24, 1 Union Ave, POB BE1165, Belvedere, Harare; e-mail trevorn@mg.co.za; internet www.theindependent.co.zw; f. 1996; publ. by ZimInd Publrs (Pvt) Ltd; English; Publr TREVOR NCUBE; Editor VINCENT KAHIYA; circ. 30,500 (2005).

The Zimbabwean: POB 248, Hythe, SO45 4WX, United Kingdom; tel. (23) 8084-8694; e-mail feedback@thezimbabwean.co.uk; internet www.thezimbabwean.co.uk; f. 2005; independent; publ. in the United Kingdom and South Africa; focus on news in Zimbabwe and life in exile; Publr and Editor WILF MBANGA.

Zimbabwean Government Gazette: POB 8062, Causeway, Harare; official notices; Editor L. TAKAWIRA.

PERIODICALS

The Agenda: Information Department, 348 Herbert Chitepo Ave, Harare; tel. (4) 736338; fax (4) 721146; e-mail info@nca.org.zw; internet www.nca.org.zw; f. 1997; publ. by the Nat. Constitutional Assembly; quarterly; civil rights issues.

Chamber of Mines Journal: Stewart House, North Wing, 4 Central Ave, POB 712, Harare; tel. (4) 702841; fax (4) 707983; publ. by Thomson Publs; monthly.

Chaminuka News: POB 650, Marondera; f. 1988; publ. by Community Newspaper Group (Mass Media Trust); fortnightly; English and ChiShona; distributed in Manicaland and Mashonaland North provinces; Editor M. MUGABE; circ. c. 10,000.

Indonsakusa: Hwange; f. 1988; monthly; English and SiNdebele; Editor D. NTABENI; circ. 10,000.

The Insider: Insider Publications, POB FM 415, Famona, Bulawayo; tel. (11) 789-739; e-mail charlesrukuni@insiderzim.com; internet www.insiderzim.com; f. 1990; monthly; digital newsletter; news and current affairs; Editor and Publr CHARLES RUKUNI.

Mahogany: POB UA589, Harare; tel. (4) 752063; fax (4) 752062; f. 1980; 6 a year; English; women's interest; Editor TENDAI DONDO; circ. 240,000.

Masiye Pambili (Let Us Go Forward): POB 591, Bulawayo; tel. (9) 75011; fax (9) 69701; e-mail tcdept@citybyo.co.zw; f. 1964; 2 a year; English; Editor M. NYONI; circ. 25,000.

Moto (Fire): POB 890, Gweru; tel. (54) 24886; fax (54) 28194; e-mail mot@hnetzim.wn.apc.org; f. 1959; monthly; publ. by govt-controlled co Zimpapers; banned in 1974; relaunched in 1980 as a weekly newspaper, then in magazine format in 1982; Roman Catholic; Editor SYDNEY SHOKO; circ. 22,000.

Mukai-Vukani Jesuit Journal for Zimbabwe: Jesuit Communications, 1 Churchill Ave, Alexandra Park, POB 949, Southerton, Harare; tel. (4) 744571; fax (4) 744284; e-mail owermter@zol.co.zw; internet www.jescom.co.zw; 4–6 a year; Catholic; Editor Fr OSKAR WERMTER; circ. 2,500.

New Farmer: Herald House, cnr George Sikundika and Sam Nujoma Sts, POB 55, Harare; tel. (4) 708296; fax (4) 702400; e-mail advertising@chronicle.co.zw; internet www.newfarmer.co.zw; f. 2002; publ. by govt-controlled co Zimpapers; weekly; English; Editor GEORGE CHISOKO.

The Outpost: POB HG106, Highlands; tel. (4) 724571; fax (4) 703631; e-mail theoutpostmag@yahoo.com; f. 1911; publ. of the Zimbabwe Republic Police; monthly; English; Editor MOSES MOYO; circ. c. 27,000 (2005).

Railroader: National Railways of Zimbabwe, cnr Fife St and 10th Ave, POB 596, Bulawayo; tel. (9) 363716; fax (9) 363502; f. 1952; publ. by Nat. Railways of Zimbabwe; monthly; Editor M. GUMEDE; circ. 10,000.

Southern African Political and Economic Monthly (SAPEM): Southern Africa Political Economy Series Trust, 2–6 Deary Ave, Belgravia, POB MP111, Mt Pleasant, Harare; tel. (4) 252962; fax (4) 252964; f. 1987; monthly; publ. by the SAPES Trust; incorporating *Southern African Economist*; Editor-in-Chief KHABELE MATLOSA; circ. 16,000.

Trends: 9th Ave and George Silundika St, POB 585 Bulawayo; tel. (09) 880888; fax (09) 888884; e-mail advertising@chronicle.co.zw; internet www.zimtrends.co.zw; f. 2003; publ. by govt-controlled co Zimpapers; monthly; English; leisure and entertainment; Editor EDWIN DUBE.

The Worker: ZCTU, Chester House, 9th Floor, Speke Ave and Third St, POB 3549, Harare; tel. (4) 794742; fax (4) 728484; e-mail info@zctu.co.zw; publ. by the Zimbabwe Congress of Trade Unions; News Editor BRIGHT CHIBVURI.

Zambezia: University of Zimbabwe Publications, POB MP203, Mount Pleasant, Harare; tel. (4) 303211; fax (4) 333407; e-mail uzpub@admin.uz.ac.zw; internet www.uz.ac.zw/publications; publ. by the Univ. of Zimbabwe; 2 a year; humanities and general interest; Editor Dr ZIFIKILE MGUNI-GAMBAHAYA.

Zimbabwe Agricultural Journal: Dept of Research and Specialist Services, 5th St, Extension, POB CY594, Causeway, Harare; tel. (4) 704531; fax (4) 728317; f. 1903; 6 a year; Editor R. J. FENNER; circ. 2,000.

The Zimbabwe Farmer: POB 1683, Harare; tel. (4) 736836; fax (4) 749803; monthly; fmrly *Tobacco News*; present name adopted in 2003; publ. by Thomson Publs; Editor D. MILLER; circ. 2,000.

Zimbabwe National Army Magazine: Ministry of Defence, Defence House, cnr Kwame Nkuruma Ave and 3rd St, Harare; tel. (4) 700316; f. 1982; 4 a year; Dir of Communications Col LIVINGSTONE CHINEKA; circ. 5,000.

Zimbabwean Travel: Herald House, cnr George Sikundika and Sam Nujoma Sts, POB 55, Harare; tel. (4) 708296; fax (4) 702400; e-mail advertising@chronicle.co.zw; internet www.zimtravel.com; f. 2003; publ. by govt-controlled co Zimpapers; monthly; English; Editor NOMSA NKALA.

NEWS AGENCY

NewZiana (Pvt) Ltd: Mass Media House, 19 Selous Ave, POB CY511, Causeway, Harare; tel. (4) 251754; fax (4) 794336; internet

ZIMBABWE

www.newziana.co.zw; f. 1981 as Zimbabwe Inter-Africa News Agency; present name adopted in 2003; owned by govt-controlled co Multimedia Investment Trust (fmrly Zimbabwe Mass Media Trust); operates 10 community newspapers; CEO MUNYARADZI MATANYAIRE.

Publishers

Academic Books (Pvt) Ltd: POB 567, Harare; tel. (4) 755408; fax (4) 781913; educational; Editorial Dir IRENE STAUNTON.

Amalgamated Publications (Pvt) Ltd: POB 1683, Harare; tel. (4) 736835; fax (4) 749803; f. 1949; trade journals.

Anvil Press: POB 4209, Harare; tel. (4) 751202; fax (4) 739681; f. 1988; general; Man. Dir PAUL BRICKHILL.

The Argosy Press: POB 2677, Harare; tel. (4) 755084; magazine publrs; Gen. Man. A. W. HARVEY.

Baobab Books (Pvt) Ltd: POB 567, Harare; tel. (4) 665187; fax (4) 665155; general, literature, children's.

The Bulletin: POB 1595, Bulawayo; tel. (9) 78831; fax (9) 78835; fmrly Directory Publrs Ltd; educational; CEO BRUCE BEALE.

College Press Publishers (Pvt) Ltd: 15 Douglas Rd, POB 3041, Workington, Harare; tel. (4) 754145; fax (4) 754256; f. 1968; educational and general; Man. Dir B. B. MUGABE.

Harare Publishing House: Chiremba Rd, Hatfield, Harare; tel. (4) 570342; f. 1982; Dir Dr T. M. SAMKANGE.

HarperCollins Publishers Zimbabwe (Pvt) Ltd: Union Ave, POB UA201, Harare; tel. (4) 721413; fax (4) 732436; Man. S. D. MCMILLAN.

Longman Zimbabwe (Pvt) Ltd: POB ST125, Southerton, Harare; tel. (4) 62711; fax (4) 62716; f. 1964; general and educational; Man. Dir N. L. DLODLO.

Mambo Press: Senga Rd, POB 779, Gweru; tel. (54) 24017; fax (54) 21991; f. 1958; religious, educational and fiction in English and African languages.

Modus Publications (Pvt) Ltd: Modus House, 27–29 Charter Rd, POB 66070, Kopje, Harare; tel. (4) 738722; Man. Dir ELIAS RUSIKE.

Munn Publishing (Pvt) Ltd: POB UA460, Union Ave, Harare; tel. (4) 481048; fax (4) 7481081; Man. Dir I. D. MUNN.

Standard Publications (Pvt) Ltd: POB 3745, Harare; Dir G. F. BOOT.

Southern African Printing and Publishing House (SAPPHO): 109 Coventry Rd, Workington, POB MP1005, Mount Pleasant, Harare; tel. (4) 621681; fax (4) 666061; internet www.zimmirror.co.zw; Editor-in-Chief Dr IBBO MANDAZA.

University of Zimbabwe Publications: University of Zimbabwe, POB MP203, Mount Pleasant, Harare; tel. (4) 303211; fax (4) 333407; e-mail uzpub@admin.uz.ac.zw; internet www.uz.ac.zw/publications; f. 1969; Dir MUNANI SAM MTETWA.

Zimbabwe Newspapers (1980) Ltd (Zimpapers): POB 55, Harare; tel. (4) 704088; fax (4) 702400; e-mail theherald@zimpapers.co.zw; internet www.herald.co.zw; f. 1981; 51% state-owned; publ. the newspapers *The Herald*, *The Sunday Mail*, *The Manica Post*, *The Chronicle*, *The Sunday News*, *Kwayedza*, *Umthunywa* and *The Southern Times* (based in Namibia); and magazines incl. *Zimbabwean Travel*, *Trends Magazine* and *New Farmer Magazine*; Chair. HERBERT NKALA; Group CEO JUSTIN MUTASA.

ZPH Publishers (Pvt) Ltd: 183 Arcturus Rd, Kamfinsa, GD510, Greendale, Harare; tel. (4) 497548; fax (4) 497554; e-mail tafi@zph.co.zw; f. 1982 as Zimbabwe Publishing House Ltd; Chair. BLAZIO G. TAFIREYI.

Broadcasting and Communications

TELECOMMUNICATIONS

Econet Wireless Zimbabwe: Econet Park, No. 2 Old Mutare Rd, Msasa, POB BE1298, Belvedere, Harare; tel. (4) 486121; fax (4) 486120; e-mail enquiry@econet.co.zw; internet www.econet.co.zw; f. 1998; mobile cellular telecommunications operator; Chair. TAWANDA NYAMBIRAI; CEO DOUGLAS MBOWENI.

Net.One Ltd: POB CY579, Causeway, Harare; tel. (4) 707138; e-mail marketing@netone.co.zw; internet www.netone.co.zw; f. 1998; state-owned; mobile cellular telecommunications operator; Chair. CALLISTUS NDLOVU; CEO REWARD KANGAI.

Posts and Telecommunication Regulatory Authority (POTRAZ): Block A, Emerald Park, 30 The Chase, Mt Pleasant, POB MP 843, Harare; tel. (4) 333032; fax (4) 333041; e-mail the.regulator@potraz.gov.zw; internet www.potraz.gov.zw; fmrly Post

Directory

and Telecommunications Corpn; Chair. DAVIDSON CHIROMBO (acting); Dir-Gen. CHARLES SIBANDA.

Telecel Zimbabwe: 148 Seke Rd, Graniteside, POB CY232, Causeway, Harare; tel. (4) 748321; fax (4) 748328; e-mail info@telecelzim.co.zw; internet www.telecel.co.zw; f. 1998; 60% owned by Telecel Int. and 40% owned by Empowerment Corpn; mobile cellular telecommunications operator; Chair. JAMES MAKAMBA; Man. Dir AIMABLE MPORE.

TelOne: Runhare House, 107 K. Nkrumah Ave, POB CY331, Causeway, Harare; tel. (4) 798111; fax (4) 700474; e-mail webmaster@telone.co.zw; internet www.telone.co.zw; state-owned; sole fixed-line telecommunications operator; Man. Dir HAMPTON MHLANGA (acting).

BROADCASTING

There are four govt-controlled radio stations (National FM, Power FM, Radio Zimbabwe and Spot FM) and one television station. Radio Voice of the People was established as an alternative to state broadcasting. An independent radio station, SW Radio Africa, broadcasts to Zimbabwe from London, United Kingdom. Since 2003 Voice of America has broadcast a weekday news and entertainment programme (Studio 7) from the USA in ChiShona, English and SiNdebele.

Regulatory Authority

Zimbabwe Media Commission: Harare; f. 2009 to introduce media reforms; Chair. GODFREY MAJONGA.

Radio

Feba Radio: 69 Central Ave, POB A300, Avondale, Harare; tel. (4) 708207; e-mail info@feba.co.zw; internet www.feba.co.zw; Nat. Dir KURAI MADZONGA.

Voice of the People (VOP): POB 5750, Harare; tel. (4) 707123; e-mail voxpop@ecoweb.co.zw; internet www.vopradio.co.zw; f. 2000 by fmr ZBC staff; broadcasts one hour per day; relayed by Radio Netherlands transmitters in Madagascar; news and information in ChiShona, SiNdebele and English; Chair. DAVID MASUNDA; Exec. Dir JOHN MASUKU.

Zimbabwe Broadcasting Corpn: Broadcasting Center, Pocket Hill, POB HG444, Highlands, Harare; tel. and fax (4) 498940; e-mail zbc@zbc.co.zw; internet www.zbc.co.zw; f. 1957; programmes in English, ChiShona, SiNdebele and 14 minority languages, incl. Chichewa, Venda and Xhosa; broadcasts a general service (mainly in English), vernacular languages service, light entertainment, and educational programmes; Editor-in-Chief CHRISTINA TARUVINGA.

Television

Zimbabwe Broadcasting Corpn: (see Radio).

The main broadcasting centre is in Harare, with a second studio in Bulawayo. ZBC-TV is broadcast 24 hours per day, while a second channel (ZBC Channel 2) was launched in May 2010.

Finance

(cap. = capital; res = reserves; dep. = deposits; m. = million; br(s). = branch(es); amounts in Zimbabwe dollars unless otherwise indicated)

BANKING

In 2010 there were 15 commercial banks, six merchant banks, three discount houses and four building societies in Zimbabwe. From 11 December 2008 commercial banks, merchant banks and discount houses operating in Zimbabwe were required to have a minimum capital of US $12.5m., US $10m. and US $5m., respectively.

Central Bank

Reserve Bank of Zimbabwe: 80 Samora Machel Ave, POB 1283, Harare; tel. (4) 703000; fax (4) 707800; e-mail rbzmail@rbz.co.zw; internet www.rbz.co.zw; f. 1964 as Reserve Bank of Rhodesia; bank of issue; cap. 2m., res 89,161,333m., dep. 471,625,968m. (Dec. 2007); Gov. Dr GIDEON GONO.

Commercial Banks

Barclays Bank of Zimbabwe Ltd: Barclays House, cnr First St and Jason Moyo Ave, POB 1279, Harare; tel. (4) 758281; fax (4) 752913; e-mail barmkt@africaonline.co.zw; internet www.barclays.com/africa/zimbabwe; f. 1912; commercial and merchant banking; cap. 1,000m., res 18,123m., dep. 125,836m. (Dec. 2004); Chair. Dr ROBBIE MATONGO MUPAWOSE; 44 brs.

CBZ Bank Ltd (CBZ): Union House, 60 Kwame Nkrumah Ave, POB 3313, Harare; tel. (4) 748050; e-mail info@cbz.co.zw; internet www.cbz.co.zw; state-owned; f. 1980 as Bank of Credit and Com-

ZIMBABWE

Directory

merce Zimbabwe Ltd; renamed Commercial Bank of Zimbabwe Ltd in 1991; present name adopted 2005; cap. and res 2,551m., total assets 36,057m. (Dec. 2001); Chair. L. ZEMBE; CEO Dr J. P. MANGUDYA; 27 brs.

FBC Bank Ltd: FBC Centre, Marketing and Public Relations Division, 45 Nelson Mandela Ave, POB 1227, Harare; tel. (4) 783204; fax (4) 783440; e-mail info@fbc.co.zw; internet www.fbc.co.zw/bank; f. 1997; cap. 1,000m., res 11,035,000m., dep. 39,946,000m. (Dec. 2007); Chair. DAVID W. BIRCH; Man. Dir JOHN MUSHAYAVANHU.

Kingdom Bank Ltd: 3rd Floor, Karigamombe Centre, 53 Samora Machel Ave, POB CY 3205, Harare; tel. (4) 749400; fax (4) 755201; e-mail kmb@kingdom.co.zw; internet www.kingdom.co.zw; f. 1997; res US $20.4m., dep. US $46.7m. (Dec. 2009); CEO LYNN MUKONOWESHURO.

Stanbic Bank Zimbabwe Ltd: Stanbic Centre, 1st Floor, 59 Samora Machel Ave, POB 300, Harare; tel. (4) 759471; fax (4) 751324; e-mail zimbabweinfo@stanbic.com; internet www.stanbicbank.co.zw; f. 1990 as ANZ Grindlays Bank; acquired by Standard Bank Investment Corpn in 1992; total assets US $201,387 (Dec. 2009); Chair. S. MOYO; Man. Dir JOSHUA TAPAMBGWA; 16 brs.

Standard Chartered Bank Zimbabwe Ltd: Mutual Centre, 2nd Floor, POB 373, Harare; tel. (4) 52852; fax (4) 752609; internet www.standardchartered.com/zw/; f. 1983; cap. US $0.8m., res US $26.5m., dep. US $26.5m. (Dec. 2009); Chair. H. P. MKUSHI; CEO WASHINGTON MATSAIRA; 28 brs.

Zimbabwe Banking Corpn Ltd (Zimbank): Zimbank House, Speke Ave and First St, POB 3198, Harare; tel. (4) 757471; fax (4) 757497; e-mail finhold@finhold.co.zw; internet www.finhold.co.zw; f. 1951; state-owned; cap. 102m., res 178,293m., dep. 821,214m. (Sept. 2004); Chair. RICHARD CHEMIST HOVE; Group CEO ELISHA N. MUSHAYAKARARA; 35 brs.

Development Banks

African Export-Import Bank (Afreximbank): Eastgate Bldg, 3rd Floor, Gold Bridge (North Wing), Second St, POB 1600, Causeway, Harare; tel. (4) 729751; fax (4) 729756; e-mail info@afreximbank.com; internet www.afreximbank.com; Pres. and Chair. J. L. EKRA.

Infrastructure Development Bank of Zimbabwe (IDBZ): 99 Rotten Row, Harare; tel. (4) 750171; fax (4) 774225; e-mail enquiries@zdb.co.zw; internet www.idbz.co.zw; f. 2005, to replace Zimbabwe Development Bank (ZDB); CEO CHARLES CHIKAURA.

Merchant Banks

African Banking Corpn of Zimbabwe Ltd (ABC): ABC House, 1 Endeavour Cres., Mount Pleasant Business Park, Mount Pleasant, POB 2786, Harare; tel. (4) 369260; fax (4) 369939; e-mail abczw@africanbankingcorp.com; internet www.africanbankingcorp.com; f. 1956 as Rhodesian Acceptances Ltd; name changed to First Merchant Bank of Zimbabwe Ltd in 1990; merged with Heritage Investment Bank in 1997; present name adopted in 2002; subsidiary of ABC Holdings Ltd, Botswana; cap. and res 36.8m., total assets 475.6m. (Dec. 2001); Chair. O. M. CHIDAWU; Man. Dir F. M. DZANYA; 1 br.

Genesis Investment Bank Ltd: Corner Hse, 2nd Floor, 29 Samora Machel Ave, Harare; tel. (4) 703551; fax (4) 705491; e-mail gib@genesis-zim.com; f. 1995; fmrly Trade and Investment Bank Ltd, present name adopted 2002; cap. and res 32m., total assets 421m. (Dec. 1997); Chair. M. F. DANDATO; Acting CEO BRIGHT MAYERE.

MBCA Bank Ltd: Old Mutual Centre, 14th Floor, cnr Third St and Jason Moyo Ave, POB 3200, Harare; tel. (4) 701636; fax (4) 708005; e-mail mbcabank@mbca.co.zw; internet www.mbca.co.zw; f. 1956; res US $11.2m., US $72.8m., total assets US $91m. (Dec. 2009); Chair. V. W. ZIREVA; Man. Dir MBERIKWAZVO C. CHITAMBO.

NMB Bank Ltd: Unity Court, 4th Floor, cnr Union Ave and First St, POB 2564, Harare; tel. (4) 759651; fax (4) 759648; e-mail enquiries@nmbz.co.zw; internet www.nmbz.co.zw; f. 1993; fmrly Nat. Merchant Bank of Zimbabwe; cap. 0.3m., res 8,017m., dep. 51,128m. (Dec. 2006); Chair. Dr GIBSON MANYOWA MANDISHONA; CEO Dr DAVID T. HATENDI; 10 brs.

Standard Chartered Merchant Bank Zimbabwe Ltd: Standard Chartered Bank Bldg, cnr Second St and Nelson Mandela Ave, POB 60, Harare; tel. (4) 708585; fax (4) 725667; f. 1971; cap. and res 78m., dep. 83m. (Dec. 1998); Chair. BARRY HAMILTON; Man. Dir EBBY ESSOKA.

Tetrad Investment Bank: Block 5, 1st Floor, Arundel Office Park, Norfolk Rd, Mt Pleasant, Harare; tel. (4) 704271; fax (4) 338400; internet www.tetrad.co.zw; f. 1995; res US $11.3m., dep. US $9.6m., total assets US $22.0m.; Chair. A. S. CHATIKOBO; Man. Dir E. E. CHIKAKA.

Discount Houses

African Banking Corpn Securities Ltd: 69 Samora Machel Ave, POB 3321, Harare; tel. (4) 752756; fax (4) 790641; cap. and res 68m. (Dec. 1999); fmrly Bard Discount House Ltd; Chair. N. KUDENGA; Man. Dir D. DUBE.

The Discount Co of Zimbabwe (DCZ): 70 Park Lane, POB 3424, Harare; tel. (4) 705414; fax (4) 731670; cap. and res 8.9m., total assets 377.4m. (Feb. 1995); Man. Dir PETER MUKUNGA.

Intermarket Discount House: Unity Court, 5th Floor, Union Ave, POB 3290, Harare.

National Discount House Ltd: MIPF House, 5th Floor, Central Ave, Harare; tel. (4) 700771; fax (4) 792927; internet www.ndh.co.zw; cap. and res 168.4m., total assets 2,365.2m. (Dec. 2000); Chair. EDWIN MANIKAI; Man. Dir LAWRENCE TAMAYI.

Banking Organizations

Bankers' Association of Zimbabwe (BAZ): Kuwana House, 4th Floor, Union Ave and First St, POB UA550, Harare; tel. (4) 728646; f. 1992; Pres. JOHN MUSHAYAVANHU; Dir SIJABULISO T. BIYAM.

Institute of Bankers of Zimbabwe: Centre Block, Second Floor, Suite 13, 1 Union Ave, POB UA521, Harare; tel. (4) 752474; fax (4) 750281; e-mail info@iobz.co.zw; internet www.iobz.co.zw; f. 1973; Chair. S. MALABA; Pres. STEVE GWASIRA; Dir T. BIYAM; 7,000 mems.

STOCK EXCHANGE

Zimbabwe Stock Exchange: Chiyedza House, 5th Floor, cnr First St and Kwame Nkrumah Ave, POB UA234, Harare; tel. (4) 736861; fax (4) 791045; f. 1946; Chair. G. MHLANGA; CEO EMMANUEL MUNYUKWI.

INSURANCE

Export Credit Guarantee Corpn of Zimbabwe (Pvt): 6 Earles Rd, Alexandra Park, POB CY2995, Causeway, Harare; tel. and fax (4) 744644; e-mail ecgc@telco.co.zw; internet www.ecgc.co.zw; f. 1999 as national export credit insurance agency; also provides export finance guarantee facilities; 100% owned by Reserve Bank of Zimbabwe; Chair. J. A. L. CARTER; Man. Dir RAPHAEL G. NYADZAYO.

Credit Insurance Zimbabwe (Credsure): Credsure House, 69 Sam Nujoma St, POB CY1584, Causeway, Harare; tel. (4) 706101; fax (4) 706105; e-mail headoffice@credsure.co.zw; export credit insurance; Man. Dir BRIAN HILLEN-MOORE.

Fidelity Life Assurance of Zimbabwe (Pvt) Ltd: 66 Julius Nyerere Way, POB 435, Harare; tel. (4) 750927; fax (4) 751723; f. 1977; 52% owned by Zimre Holdings Ltd; pensions and life assurance; Chair. J. P. MKUSHI; Man. Dir SIMON B. CHAPAREKA.

NICOZ Diamond: Insurance Centre, 30 Samora Machel and Leopold Takawira Ave, POB 1256, Harare; tel. (4) 704911; fax (4) 704134; e-mail enquiries@nicozdiamond.co.zw; internet www.nicozdiamond.co.zw; f. 2003 by merger of National Insurance Co of Zimbabwe and Diamond Insurance of Zimbabwe; Chair. PHINEAS S. CHINGONO; Man. Dir GRACE MURADZIKWA.

Old Mutual PLC: POB 70, Highlands, Harare; tel. (4) 308400; fax (4) 308467; e-mail info@oldmutual.co.zw; internet www.oldmutual.co.zw; f. 1845; life and general insurance, asset management and banking services; Chair. M. J. LEVETT; CEO J. H. SUTCLIFFE.

ZB Life Assurance Ltd: ZB House, 10th Floor, 46 Speke Ave, POB 3198, Harare; tel. (4) 751168; fax (4) 757141; e-mail info@zb.co.zw; internet www.zb.co.zw; f. 1964 as Intermarket Life Assurance; subsidiary of ZB Financial Holdings Ltd; Man. Dir AMBROSE G. CHINEMBIRI.

Zimnat Lion Insurance Co Ltd: Zimnat House, cnr Nelson Mandela Ave and Third St, POB CY1155, Causeway, Harare; tel. (4) 707581; fax (4) 793441; e-mail enquiries@zimnatlion.co.zw; internet www.zimnatlion.co.zw; f. 1998 by merger of Zimnat Insurance Co Ltd and Lion of Zimbabwe Insurance; merged with AIG Zimbabwe in 2005; short-term insurance; Chair. NYAJEKA BOTHWELL; Man. Dir ELISHA K. MOYO.

Trade and Industry

GOVERNMENT AGENCIES

Industrial Development Corpn of Zimbabwe (IDC): 93 Park Lane, POB CY1431, Causeway, Harare; tel. (4) 706971; fax (4) 250385; e-mail pr@idc.co.zw; internet www.idc.co.zw; f. 1963; state investment agency; Gen. Man. MIKE NDUDZO.

State Enterprises Restructuring Agency (SERA): Cecil House, 1st Floor, cnr Jason Moyo Ave and Third St, Private Bag 7728, Causeway, Harare; tel. (4) 729164; fax (4) 726317; e-mail communications@sera.co.zw; internet www.sera.co.zw; f. 1999 as

ZIMBABWE

Privatisation Agency of Zimbabwe; named changed as above in 2005; CEO ANDREW N. BVUMBE.

Zimbabwe Investment Authority (ZIA): Investment House, 109 Rotten Row, POB 5950, Harare; tel. (4) 757931; fax (4) 773843; e-mail info@zia.co.zw; internet www.zia.co.zw; f. 2007 by merger of Zimbabwe Investment Centre and the Export Processing Zones Authority; promotes domestic and foreign investment; CEO RICHARD MBAIWA.

ZimTrade: 904 Premium Close, Mt Pleasant Business Park, POB 2738, Harare; tel. (4) 369330; fax (4) 369244; e-mail info@zimtrade.co.zw; internet www.zimtrade.co.zw; f. 1991; national export promotion org.; Chair. J. D. CHIGARU; CEO HERBERT CHAKANYUKA.

DEVELOPMENT ORGANIZATIONS

Alternative Business Association (ABA): Stand No. 15295, cnr First St and Eighth Cres., Sunningdale, Harare; tel. (4) 589625; fax (4) 799600; f. 1999 to address urban and rural poverty; programme areas include: agriculture, micro-mining, cross-border trade, micro-enterprise devt and micro-finance; Dir ISRAEL MABHOU.

Indigenous Business Development Centre (IBDC): Pocket Bldg, 1st Floor, Jason Moyo Ave, POB 3331, Causeway, Harare; tel. (4) 748345; f. 1990; Pres. BEN MUCHECHE; Sec.-Gen. ENOCH KAMUSHINDA.

Indigenous Business Women's Organisation (IBWO): 73B Central Ave, POB 3710, Harare; tel. (4) 702076; fax (4) 614012; Pres. JANE MUTASA.

Zimbabwe Human Rights NGO Forum: Blue Bridge, 8th Floor, Eastgate, POB 9077, Harare; tel. (4) 250511; fax (4) 250494; e-mail admin@hrforum.co.zw; internet www.hrforumzim.com; f. 1998; provides legal and 'psycho-social' assistance to the victims of organized violence; comprises 16 mem. orgs.

Zimbabwe Women's Bureau: 43 Hillside Rd, POB CR 120, Cranborne, Harare; tel. (4) 747809; fax (4) 707905; e-mail zwbtc@africaonline.co.zw; f. 1978; promotes entrepreneurial and rural community devt; Dir BERTHA MSORA.

CHAMBERS OF COMMERCE

Manicaland Chamber of Industries: 91 Third St, POB 92, Mutare; tel. (20) 61718; f. 1945; Pres. KUMBIRAI KATSANDE; 60 mems.

Mashonaland Chamber of Industries: POB 3794, Harare; tel. (4) 772763; fax (4) 750953; f. 1922; Pres. CHESTER MHENDE; 729 mems.

Matabeleland Chamber of Industries: 104 Parirenyatwa St, POB 2317, Bulawayo; tel. (9) 60642; fax (9) 60814; f. 1931; Pres. FELIX TSHUMA; 75 mems (2003).

Midlands Chamber of Industries: POB 213, Gweru; tel. (54) 2812; Pres. Dr BILL MOORE; 50 mems.

Zimbabwe National Chamber of Commerce (ZNCC): ZNCC Business House, 42 Harare St, POB 1934, Harare; tel. (4) 749335; fax (4) 750375; e-mail info@zncchq.co.zw; internet www.zncc.co.zw; f. 1983; represents small and medium businesses; Pres. TRUST CHIKOHORA; Acting CEO KIPSON GUNDANI; 2,500 mems; 8 brs.

INDUSTRIAL AND TRADE ASSOCIATIONS

Chamber of Mines of Zimbabwe: Stewart House, North Wing, 4 Central Ave, POB 712, Harare; tel. (4) 702841; fax (4) 707983; f. 1939 by merger of the Rhodesian Chamber of Mines (Bulawayo) and Salisbury Chamber of Mines; Pres. VICTOR GAPARE.

Confederation of Zimbabwe Industries (CZI): 31 Josiah Chinamano Ave, POB 3794, Harare; tel. (4) 251490; fax (4) 252424; e-mail cmsileya@czi.co.zw; internet www.czi.org.zw; f. 1957; Pres. KUMBIRAI KATSANDE; CEO CLIFFORD M. SILEYA.

Specialized affiliate trade associations include:

CropLife Zimbabwe: POB MP712, Mount Pleasant, Harare; tel. (4) 487211; fax (4) 487242; e-mail graeme.reid@bayer.co.zw; internet www.croplifeafrica.org; fmrly Agricultural Chemical Industry Asscn; Chair. MAX MAKUVISE.

Furniture Manufacturers' Association: c/o CZI, 31 Josiah Chinamano Ave, POB 3794, Harare; Pres. MATT SNYMAN.

Zimbabwe Association of Packaging: 17 Coventry Rd, Workington, Harare; tel. (4) 753800; fax (4) 882020.

Construction Industry Federation of Zimbabwe: Conquenar House, 256 Samora Machel Ave East, POB 1502, Harare; tel. (4) 746661; fax (4) 746937; e-mail cifoz@comone.co.zw; Pres. GILBERT MATIKA; CEO MARTIN CHINGAIRA; c. 460 mems.

Grain Marketing Board (GMB): Dura Bldg, 179–187 Samora Machel Ave, POB CY77, Harare; tel. (4) 701870; fax (4) 251294; e-mail marketing@gmbdura.co.zw; internet www.gmbdura.co.zw; f. 1931; responsible for maintaining national grain reserves and ensuring food security; CEO SAMUEL MUVUTI (acting).

Indigenous Petroleum Group of Zimbabwe (IPGZ): Harare; f. 2004 following split from Petroleum Marketers' Asscn of Zimbabwe; Chair. HUBERT NYAMBUYA; represents 68 importers.

Minerals Marketing Corpn of Zimbabwe (MMCZ): 90 Mutare Rd, Msasa, POB 2628, Harare; tel. (4) 487200; fax (4) 487161; e-mail administrator@mmcz.co.zw; internet www.mmcz.co.zw; f. 1982; sole authority for marketing of mineral production (except gold); Chair. MERCY MKUSHI (acting); Gen. Man. and CEO ONESIMO MAZAI MOYO.

Petroleum Marketers' Association of Zimbabwe (PMAZ): 142 Samora Machel Ave, Harare; tel. (4) 797556; represents private importers of petroleum-based products; Chair. GORDON MUSARIRA.

Timber Council of Zimbabwe: Conquenar House, 256 Samora Machel Ave, POB 3645, Harare; tel. (4) 746645; fax (4) 746013; Exec. Dir MARTIN DAVIDSON.

Tobacco Growers' Trust (TGT): POB AY331, Harare; tel. (4) 781167; fax (4) 781722; f. 2001; manages 20% of tobacco industry foreign exchange earnings on behalf of Reserve Bank of Zimbabwe; affiliated orgs include Zimbabwe Tobacco Asscn and Zimbabwe Farmers' Union; Chair. WILFANOS MASHINGAIDZE; Gen. Man. ALBERT JAURE.

Tobacco Industry and Marketing Board: POB 10214, Harare; tel. (4) 613310; fax (4) 613264; internet www.timb.co.zw; f. 1936; Chair. NJODZI MACHIRORI; CEO STANLEY MUTEPFA.

Tobacco Trade Association: c/o 4–12 Paisley Rd, POB ST180, Southerton, Harare; tel. (4) 773858; fax (4) 773859; e-mail tta@zol.co.zw; f. 1948; represents manufacturers and merchants.

Zimbabwe National Traditional Healers' Association (ZINATHA): Red Cross House, 2nd Floor, Rm 202, 98 Cameron St, POB 1116, Harare; tel. and fax (11) 606771; f. 1980; certifies and oversees traditional healers and practitioners of herbal medicine through the Traditional Medical Practitioners Council; promotes indigenous methods of prevention and treatment of HIV/AIDS; Pres. Prof. GORDON CHAVUNDUKA; 55,000 mems (2004).

Zimbabwe Tobacco Association (ZTA): 108 Prince Edward St, POB 1781, Harare; tel. (4) 796931; fax (4) 791855; e-mail fctobacco@zta.co.zw; internet www.zta.co.zw; f. 1928; represents growers; Pres. ANDREW FERREIRA; CEO RODNEY AMBROSE; c. 5,500 mems.

EMPLOYERS' ASSOCIATIONS

Commercial Farmers' Union (CFU): Agriculture House, cnr Adylinn Rd and Marlborough Dr., Marlborough; POB WGT390, Westgate, Harare; tel. (4) 309800; fax (4) 309849; e-mail aisd3@cfu.co.zw; internet www.cfu.co.zw; f. 1942; Pres. DOUGLAS TAYLOR-FREEME; Dir HENDRIK W. OLIVIER; 1,200 mems.

Cattle Producers' Association (CPA): Agriculture House, cnr Adylinn Rd and Marlborough Dr., Marlborough; POB WGT390, Westgate, Harare; tel. and fax (4) 309837; e-mail livestock@cfuzim.org; Chair. MARYNA ERASMUS.

Coffee Growers' Association: Agriculture House, cnr Adylinn Rd and Marlborough Dr., Marlborough; POB WGT390, Westgate, Harare; tel. and fax (4) 750238; e-mail pres@cfu.co.zw; f. 1961; Chair. T. GIFFORD; Dir H. OLIVIER.

Commercial Cotton Growers' Association: Agriculture House, cnr Adylinn Rd and Marlborough Dr., Marlborough; POB WGT390, Westgate, Harare; tel. (4) 309800; fax (4) 309849; f. 1951; Chair. NEVILLE BROWN.

Crops Association: Agriculture House, cnr Adylinn Rd and Marlborough Dr., Marlborough; POB WGT390, Westgate, Harare; tel. (4) 309843; fax (4) 309850; e-mail copa@cfu.co.zw; comprises the Commercial Oilseeds Producers' Asscn (COPA), the Zimbabwe Cereal Producers' Asscn (ZCPA) and the Zimbabwe Grain Producers' Asscn (ZGPA); Chair. DENNIS LAPHAM; Man. (Crops) GEORGE HUTCHISON; represents c. 800 producers.

National Association of Dairy Farmers: Agriculture House, cnr Adylinn Rd and Marlborough Dr., Marlborough; POB WGT390, Westgate, Harare; tel. (4) 309800; fax (4) 309837; e-mail livestock@cfuzim.org; f. 1953; CEO ROB J. VAN VUUREN; 174 mems.

Ostrich Producers' Association of Zimbabwe (TOPAZ): Agriculture House, cnr Adylinn Rd and Marlborough Dr., Marlborough; POB WGT390, Westgate, Harare; tel. (4) 309800; fax (4) 309862; Chair. CEDRIC WILDE; Exec. Dir CLARE DAVIES.

Zimbabwe Association of Tobacco Growers (ZATG): Agriculture House, cnr Adylinn Rd and Marlborough Dr., Marlborough; POB WGT390, Westgate, Harare; f. 2001; Pres. JULIUS NGORIMA; CEO CANAAN RUSHIZHA; 1,500 mems.

Zimbabwe Poultry Association (Commercial Poultry Producers' Association): Agriculture House, cnr Adylinn Rd and Marlborough Dr., Marlborough; POB WGT390, Westgate, Harare; tel. (4) 309800; fax (4) 309849; Chair. PETER DRUMMOND; represents c. 200 producers.

Employers' Confederation of Zimbabwe (EMCOZ): Stewart House, 4 Central Ave, 2nd Floor, POB 158, Harare; tel. (4) 739647; fax (4) 739630; e-mail emcoz@emcoz.co.zw; Pres. DAVID GOVERE; Exec. Dir JOHN W. MUFUKARE.

Horticultural Promotion Council (HPC): 12 Maasdorp Ave, Alexandra Park; POB WGT290, Westgate, Harare; tel. (4) 745492; fax (4) 745480; Chief Exec. BASILIO SANDAMU; represents c. 1,000 producers.

> **Export Flower Growers' Association of Zimbabwe (EFGAZ):** 12 Maasdorp Ave, Alexandra Park; POB WGT290, Westgate, Harare; tel. (4) 725130; fax (4) 795303; e-mail exflower@icon.co.zw; Dir MARY DUNPHY; c. 300 mems.

National Employment Council for the Construction Industry of Zimbabwe: St Barbara House, Nelson Mandela Ave and Leopold Takawira St, POB 2995, Harare; tel. (4) 773966; fax (4) 773967; CEO STANLEY R. MAKONI; represents over 19,000 mem. cos (2002).

National Employment Council for the Engineering and Iron and Steel Industry: Adven House, 5th Floor, cnr Inez Terrace and Speke Ave, POB 1922, Harare; tel. (4) 775144; fax (4) 775918; f. 1943; Gen. Sec. E. E. SHARPE.

Timber Producers' Federation (TPF): Fidelity Life Centre, 4th Floor, H. Chitepo St, POB 1736, Mutare; tel. and fax (20) 60959; e-mail lmubaiwa@mweb.co.zw; CEO LOYD MUBAIWA.

Zimbabwe Association of Consulting Engineers (ZACE): 16 Murandy Sq. East, POB HG836, Highlands, Harare; tel. and fax (4) 746010; e-mail zace@mango.zw.

Zimbabwe Building Contractors' Association: Caspi House, Block C, 4 Harare St, Harare; tel. (4) 780411; represents small-scale building contractors; CEO CONCORDIA MUKODZI.

Zimbabwe Commercial Farmers' Union (ZCFU): 53 Third St, Mutare; tel. (20) 67163; fmrly Indigenous Commercial Farmers' Union; Pres. TREVOR GIFFORD; Dir JOHN MAUTSA; represents c. 11,000 black farmers (2003).

Zimbabwe Farmers' Union (ZFU): POB 3755, Harare; tel. (4) 704763; fax (4) 700829; Pres. SILAS HUNGWE; Exec. Dir KWENDA DZAVIRA; represents c. 200,000 small-scale black farmers (2002).

UTILITIES

Electricity

Rural Electrification Agency (REA): Office 720, 7th Floor, Megawatt House, 44 Samora Machel Ave, Private Bag 250A, Harare; tel. (4) 700666; fax (4) 707667; e-mail emidzi@zesa.co.zw; internet www.rea.co.zw; f. 2002; manages the Rural Electrification Fund to expand and accelerate the electrification of rural areas; Chair. Dr SYDNEY ZIKUZO GATA; CEO EMMANUEL MIDZI.

ZESA Holdings (Pvt) Ltd: 25 Samora Machel Ave, POB 377TA, Harare; tel. (4) 774508; fax (4) 774542; e-mail pr@zesa.net; internet www.zesa.co.zw; f. 2002 following restructure of Zimbabwe Electricity Supply Authority; operates one hydroelectric and four thermal power stations; CEO BEN RAFEMOYO; dependable generation capacity of 1,700 MW.

> **Zimbabwe Electricity Transmission Co (ZETCO):** Electricity Centre, 8th Floor, 25 Samora Machel Ave, POB 1760, Harare; tel. (4) 774508; fax (4) 756179; e-mail zetconews@zetco.co.zw; internet www.zetco.org; f. 2002; develops, operates and maintains transmission infrastructure; Man. Dir (vacant).

Zimbabwe Electricity Regulatory Commission (ZERC): Century Towers, 14th Floor, 45 Samora Machel Ave, POB CY2585, Causeway, Harare; tel. (4) 780010; fax (4) 250696; e-mail admin@zerc.co.zw; internet www.zerc.co.zw; f. 2004 to oversee the unbundling from ZESA of the Zimbabwe Power Co, the Zimbabwe Electricity Transmission Co and the Zimbabwe Electricity Distribution Co; Dir-Gen. MAVIS CHIDZONGA.

Oil

National Oil Company of Zimbabwe (Pvt) Ltd (NOCZIM): NOCZIM House, 100 Leopold Takawira St, POB CY223, Causeway, Harare; tel. (4) 748543; fax (4) 748525; responsible for importing liquid fuels; Chair. CHARLES CHIPATO; Man. Dir ZVINECHIMWE CHURA.

Water

Zimbabwe National Water Authority (ZINWA): POB CY1215, Causeway, Harare; tel. and fax (4) 793139; e-mail mtetwa@utande.co.zw; f. 2001; fmrly Dept of Water, privatized in 2001; construction of dams, water supply, resources planning and protection; Chief Exec. ALBERT MUYAMBO.

TRADE UNIONS

Zimbabwe Congress of Trade Unions (ZCTU): Chester House, 9th Floor, Speke Ave and Third St, POB 3549, Harare; tel. (4) 794742; fax (4) 728484; internet www.zctu.co.zw; f. 1981 by merger of the African Trade Union Congress, the Nat. African Trade Union Congress, the Trade Union Congress of Zimbabwe, the United Trade Unions of Zimbabwe, the Zimbabwe Fed. of Labour and the Zimbabwe Trade Union Congress; co-ordinating org. for trade unions; Pres. LOVEMORE MATOMBO; Sec.-Gen. WELLINGTON CHIBEBE; c. 70,000 mems (2007).

In 2005 there were 35 affiliated unions. Affiliates with over 3,000 mems include:

Associated Mineworkers of Zimbabwe (AMWZ): St. Andrew's House, 4th Floor, Leopold Takawira St and Samora Machel Ave, POB 384, Harare; tel. (4) 700287; fax (4) 706543; e-mail amwz@mweb.co.zw; Nat. Pres. TINAGO EDMUND RUZIVE; 10,000 mems (2002).

Commercial Workers' Union of Zimbabwe (CWUZ): CWUZ House, 15 Sixth Ave, Parktown; POB 3922 Harare; tel. (4) 664701; Pres. TAITUS MAGAYA; Gen. Sec. LOVEMORE MUSHONGA (acting); 22,000 mems (2003).

Communication and Allied Services Workers' Union of Zimbabwe (CASWUZ): Morgan House, 4th Floor, G. Silundika Ave, POB 739, Harare; tel. (4) 794763; e-mail caswuz@africaonline.co.zw; fmrly the Zimbabwe Post and Telecommunication Workers' Union; present name adopted 2002; Gen. Sec. REWARD S. MUSIWOKUWAYA; 5,700 mems (2002).

Federation of Food and Allied Workers' Union of Zimbabwe (FFAWUZ): Gorlon House, 3rd Floor, 7 Jason Moyo Ave, cnr Harare St, POB 4211, Harare; tel. (4) 757600; fax (4) 748482; e-mail ffawuzdick@mweb.co.zw; f. 1962; Gen. Sec. UNGANAI DICKSON TARUSENGA; 7,300 mems (2010).

General Agricultural and Plantation Workers' Union (GAPWUZ): POB 1952, Harare; tel. (4) 734141; fax (4) 797918; e-mail alb@cfu.co.zw; Gen. Sec. GERTRUDE HAMBIRA; 5,000 mems (2002).

National Engineering Workers' Union (NEWU): St Barbara House, cnr Nelson Mandela Ave and Leopold Takawira St, Harare; tel. (4) 759597; fax (4) 759598; e-mail information@newu.org.zw; Pres. ISAAC MATONGO; Gen. Sec. JAPHET MOYO; 9,000 mems (2002).

National Union of Clothing Industry Workers (NUCI): Union House, 139A Lobengula St with 13th Ave, POB RY28, Raylton, Bulawayo; tel. (9) 64432; fax (9) 71089; Gen. Sec. FRED MPOFU; 4,500 mems (2002).

Progressive Teachers' Union of Zimbabwe (PTUZ): 14 McLaren Rd, Milton Park, Harare; POB CR620, Cranborne, Harare; tel. (4) 757746; fax (4) 741937; e-mail ptuz@mweb.co.zw; f. 1997; Pres. TAKAVAFIREI ZHOU; Sec.-Gen. RAYMOND MAJONGWE; 12,000 mems (2002).

Public Service Association: PSA House, 9 Livingstone Ave, POB 179, Harare; tel. (4) 792542; fax (4) 704971; e-mail psahq@mweb.co.zw; f. 1919; Pres. CECILIA ALEXANDER-KHOWA; Exec. Sec. EMMANUEL MUTAKURA TICHAREVA; 12,500 mems (2011).

Civil Service Employees' Association (CSEA): PSA House, 3rd floor, 9 Livingstone Ave, POB CY202, Causeway, Harare; tel. (4) 701123; fax (4) 707208; e-mail civilsea@africaonline.co.zw; f. 1966; represents public sector employees; Pres. MASIMBA KADZIMU; Gen. Sec. GEORGE NASHO WILSON; 5,000 mems (2006).

Zimbabwe Amalgamated Railway Workers' Union (ZARU): Unity House, 13th Ave, Herbert Chitepo St, POB 556, Bulawayo 10; tel. (9) 60948; Gen. Sec. GIDEON P. SHOKO; 7,000 mems (2002).

Zimbabwe Banks and Allied Workers' Union (ZIBAWU): 1 Meredith Dr., Eastlea, POB 966, Harare; tel. (4) 703744; e-mail bankunion@zol.co.zw; Pres. GEORGE KAWENDA; Gen. Sec. COLLEN GWIYO; 4,560 mems (2002).

Zimbabwe Catering and Hotel Workers' Union (ZCHWU): Nialis Bldg, 1st Floor, Manyika, POB 3913, Harare; tel. (4) 753338; 8,500 mems (2002).

Zimbabwe Chemical, Plastics and Allied Workers' Union (ZCPAWU): St Andrew's House, 2nd Floor, Leopold Takawira St and Samora Machel Ave, POB 4810, Harare; tel. (4) 796533; Gen. Sec. F. P. GOMBEDZA; 3,723 mems (2002).

Zimbabwe Construction and Allied Trades Workers' Union (ZCAWU): St Barbara House, Office 306, cnr Nelson Mandela Ave and Leopold Takawira St, POB 1291, Harare; tel. (4) 750159; fax (4) 773967; Gen. Sec. CHARLES GUMBO; 3,000 mems (2002).

Zimbabwe Electricity and Energy Workers' Union (ZEEWU): Crossroads House, 43 Julius Nyere Way, POB 5537, Harare; tel. and fax (4) 724430; e-mail zeewu@comone.co.zw; Pres. ANGELINE CHITAMBO; 3,075 mems (2002).

Zimbabwe Furniture, Timber and Allied Trades Union (ZFTATU): St Andrew's House, 4th Floor, Samora Machel Ave, POB 4793, Harare; tel. (4) 728056; fax (4) 737686; e-mail invioftbb@yahoo.com; Gen. Sec. L. CHISHAKWE; 3,500 mems (2002).

Zimbabwe Graphical Workers' Union (ZGWU): 6 Harare St, POB 494, Harare; tel. (4) 775627; fax (4) 775727; represents employees in the printing and packaging industries; Gen. Sec. MADZIVO CHIMHUKA; 5,000 mems (2005).

Zimbabwe Leather Shoe and Allied Workers' Union (ZLSAWU): POB 4450, Harare; tel. (4) 727925; fax (4) 727926; Gen. Sec. ISIDORE MANHANDO ZINDOGA; 6,745 mems (2002).

Zimbabwe Textile Workers' Union (ZTWU): 50 Jason Moyo Ave, Pockets Bldg, 2nd Floor, South Wing, Hillside, POB 10245, Harare; tel. (4) 770226; fax (4) 758233; e-mail ztwu@mweb.co.zw; Gen. Sec. SILAS KUVEYA; 11,636 mems (2004).

Zimbabwe Tobacco Industry Workers' Union (ZTIWU): St Andrew's House, 2nd Floor, Samora Machel Ave, POB 2757, Harare; tel. (4) 702339; Gen. Sec. ESTEVAO CUMBULANE; 3,000 mems (2002).

Zimbabwe Urban Councils Workers' Union (ZUCWU): POB CY 1859, Causeway, Harare; tel. (4) 729412; f. 1990; represents workers in engineering, housing and community services, health and emergency services, and clerical and treasury services; Pres. SIMON TAYALI; Gen. Sec. MOSES TSHIMKENI-MAHLANGU; 10,200 mems (2003).

Zimbabwe Federation of Trade Unions (ZFTU): Makombe Complex, Causeway, Harare; f. 1996 as alternative to ZCTU; 23 affiliated unions (2006); Gen. Sec. ADAMS VERENGA.

Affiliated unions include:

Zimbabwe Teachers' Union (ZITU): POB GV1, Glen View, Harare; tel. (4) 692454; fax (4) 708929; f. 2002; Gen. Sec. SIMPLISIO K. MATUMBA.

Non-affiliated Unions

Zimbabwe National Students' Union (ZINASU): 53 Hebert Chitepo Ave, Harare; tel. (4) 788135; fax (4) 793246; e-mail zinasu@gmail.com; internet www.zinasu.org; represents students in more than 43 tertiary institutions; Pres. CLEVER BERE; Nat. Co-ordinator BENJAMIN NYANDORO; c. 260,000 mems (2006).

Zimbabwe Nurses' Association (ZINA): 47 Livingstone Ave, POB 2610, Harare; tel. and fax (4) 700479; e-mail zimnurse@mweb.co.zw; f. 1980; Pres. DOREEN CHORUMA; 4,500 mems (2003).

Zimbabwe Teachers' Association (ZIMTA): POB 1440, Harare; tel. (4) 728438; fax (4) 791042; e-mail zimta@telco.co.zw; Pres. TENDAI CHIKOWORE; Sec.-Gen. RICHARD GUNDANI (acting); 55,000 mems (2004).

Transport

RAILWAYS

In 2008 the rail network totalled 2,583 km, of which 313 km was electrified. Trunk lines run from Bulawayo south to the border with Botswana, connecting with the Botswana railways system, which, in turn, connects with the South African railways system; north-west to the Victoria Falls, where there is a connection with Zambia Railways; and north-east to Harare and Mutare connecting with the Mozambique Railways' line from Beira. From a point near Gweru, a line runs to the south-east, making a connection with the Mozambique Railways' Limpopo line and with the Mozambican port of Maputo. A connection runs from Rutenga to the South African Railways system at Beitbridge. A 320-km line from Beitbridge to Bulawayo was opened in 1999. In 2010 plans were announced for the construction of a railway line in northern Zimbabwe running to the border with Zambia, which would eventually be linked with the southern Zambian town of Kafue.

National Railways of Zimbabwe (NRZ): cnr Fife St and 10th Ave, POB 596, Bulawayo; tel. (9) 363716; fax (9) 363502; internet www.nrz .co.zw; f. 1899; reorg. 1967; privatization under way; Chair. Brig. DOUGLAS NYIKAYARAMBA; Gen. Man. Air Commodore MIKE TICHAFA KARAKADZAI.

ROADS

In 2002 the road system in Zimbabwe totalled an estimated 97,267 km; some 18,481 km of the total network was paved. In December 2005 tollgates were introduced at the borders to raise funds to maintain the road network.

CIVIL AVIATION

AirZim operates an effective monopoly over air travel and transport within Zimbabwe. International and domestic air services connect most of the larger towns.

Civil Aviation Authority of Zimbabwe (CAAZ): Harare Int. Airport Terminal, Level 3, Private Bag CY7716, Causeway, Harare; tel. (4) 585073; fax (4) 585112; e-mail ais@caaz.co.zw; internet www .caaz.co.zw; f. 1999; operates eight airports incl. Harare Int. Airport and Joshua Mqabuko Nkomo Int. Airport (fmrly Bulawayo Airport); CEO DAVID CHAWOTA.

Air Zimbabwe (Pvt) Ltd (AirZim): POB AP1, Harare Airport, Harare; tel. (4) 575111; fax (4) 575068; internet www.airzimbabwe .com; f. 1967; scheduled domestic and international passenger and cargo services to Africa, Australia and Europe; plans were announced in April 2006 to separate operations, creating the new cos Air Zimbabwe Technical, Air Zimbabwe Cargo, Nat. Handling Services and Galileo Zimbabwe, in addition to Air Zimbabwe; Chair. JONATHAN KADZURA; CEO Dr PETER CHIKUMBA.

Tourism

The principal tourist attractions are the Victoria Falls, the Kariba Dam, and the Hwange Game Reserve and National Park. Zimbabwe Ruins, near Fort Victoria, and World's View, in the Matapos Hills, are also of interest. There is climbing and trout-fishing in the Eastern Districts, around Umtali. In 2008 some 2.0m. tourists visited Zimbabwe; revenue from tourism in that year totalled US $294m.

Zimbabwe Tourism Authority (ZTA): Samora Machel Ave, POB CY286, Causeway, Harare; tel. (4) 752570; fax (4) 758826; e-mail info@ztazim.co.zw; internet www.zimbabwetourism.co.zw; f. 1984; promotes tourism domestically and from abroad; Chair. EMMANUEL FUNDIRA; CEO KARIKOGA KASEKE.

Associations licensed by the ZTA include:

Safari Operators Association of Zimbabwe (SOAZ): 18 Walter Hill Ave, Eastlea, Harare; tel. (4) 702402; fax (4) 707306; e-mail soaz@mweb.co.zw; internet www.soaz.net; f. 2006; Chair. EMMANUEL FUNDIRA.

Defence

As assessed at November 2010, total armed forces numbered about 29,000: 25,000 in the army and 4,000 in the air force. Paramilitary forces comprise a police force of 19,500 and a police support unit of 2,300.

Defence Expenditure: Budgeted at US $98.3m. in 2010.

Commander-in-Chief of the Armed Forces: Pres. ROBERT GABRIEL MUGABE.

Head of the Armed Forces: Lt-Gen. CONSTANTINE CHIWENGA.

Commander of the Zimbabwe National Army: Lt-Gen. PHILLIP V. SIBANDA.

Education

Primary education, which begins at six years of age and lasts for seven years, is free and has been compulsory since 1987. Secondary education begins at the age of 13 and lasts for six years. According to UNESCO estimates, in 2005/06 enrolment at primary schools included 90% of children in the relevant age-group (males 89%; females 91%), while the comparable ratio for secondary enrolment was just 38% of children (males 39%; females 37%) in the same school year. In 2008/09 some 49,645 students were enrolled in tertiary institutions. There are two state-run universities, the University of Zimbabwe, which is located in Harare, and the University of Science and Technology, at Bulawayo. There are also two private universities, Africa University in Mutare and Solusi University in Figtree. Education was allocated Z.$6,800,000m. by the central Government in the budget for 2005, equivalent to 24.7% of total expenditure for that year.

INDEX OF TERRITORIES IN VOLUMES I AND II

	Page
Abu Dhabi	4670
Afghanistan	513
Ajman	4670
Åland Islands	1775
Albania	540
Alderney	4755
Algeria	560
American Samoa	4920
Andorra	587
Angola	594
Anguilla	4764
Antarctic Territory, Australian	715
Antarctic Territory, British	4778
Antarctica	612
Antigua and Barbuda	614
Argentina	624
Armenia	653
Aruba	3336
Ascension	4815
Ashmore Islands	715
Australia	671
Australian Antarctic Territory	715
Austria	717
Azad Kashmir	3553
Azerbaijan	746
Bahamas	765
Bahrain	776
Baker Island	4940
Bangladesh	797
Barbados	824
Barbuda	614
Belarus	834
Belau (see Palau)	
Belgium	854
Belize	883
Bermuda	4770
Bhutan	910
Bolivia	927
Bonaire	3332
Bosnia and Herzegovina	948
Botswana	974
Bouvetøya	3489
Brazil	989
Brecqhou	4755
British Antarctic Territory	4778
British Indian Ocean Territory	4778
British Virgin Islands	4779
Brunei	1024
Bulgaria	1036
Burkina Faso	1056
Burma (see Myanmar)	
Burundi	1073
Caicos Islands	4821
Cambodia	1091
Cameroon	1114
Canada	1133
Cape Verde	1175
Cartier Island	715
Cayman Islands	4786
Central African Republic	1184
Ceuta	4195
Chad	1200
Channel Islands	4752
Chile	1219
China, People's Republic	1244

	Page
China, Republic (see Taiwan)	
Christmas Island	706
Cocos Islands	709
Colombia	1326
Comoros	1351
Congo, Democratic Republic	1363
Congo, Republic	1383
Cook Islands	3385
Coral Sea Islands Territory	715
Costa Rica	1399
Côte d'Ivoire	1416
Croatia	1439
Cuba	1460
Curaçao	3343
Cyprus	1483
Czech Republic	1507
Democratic People's Republic of Korea	2625
Democratic Republic of the Congo	1363
Denmark	1528
Diego Garcia (see British Indian Ocean Territory)	
Djibouti	1566
Dominica	1576
Dominican Republic	1585
Dronning Maud Land	3490
Dubai	4670
East Timor (see Timor-Leste)	
Ecuador	1602
Egypt	1625
El Salvador	1657
Equatorial Guinea	1673
Eritrea	1684
Estonia	1697
Ethiopia	1716
Falkland Islands	4793
Faroe Islands	1553
Federated States of Micronesia	3110
Fiji	1736
Finland	1752
Former Yugoslav republic of Macedonia	2904
France	1780
French Guiana	1825
French Polynesia	1860
French Southern and Antarctic Territories	1885
Fujairah	4670
Futuna Islands	1878
Gabon	1899
Gambia	1915
Georgia	1929
Germany	1954
Ghana	2000
Gibraltar	4799
Gilgit-Baltistan	3553
Great Britain	4690
Greece	2020
Greenland	1559
Grenada	2042
Grenadines	3891
Guadeloupe	1832
Guam	4926
Guatemala	2051
Guernsey	4752
Guinea	2070
Guinea-Bissau	2087
Guyana	2102

www.europaworld.com

5127

INDEX OF TERRITORIES IN VOLUMES I AND II

Territory	Page
Haiti	2114
Heard Island	716
Herm	4755
Herzegovina	948
Holy See	4992
Honduras	2134
Hong Kong	1291
Howland Island	4940
Hungary	2151
Iceland	2170
India	2184
Indian Ocean Territory, British	4778
Indonesia	2245
Iran	2286
Iraq	2322
Ireland	2358
Islands of the Bailiwick of Guernsey	4756
Isle of Man	4759
Israel	2383
Italy	2427
Ivory Coast (see Côte d'Ivoire)	
Jamaica	2463
Jan Mayen	3489
Japan	2479
Jarvis Island	4940
Jersey	4756
Jethou	4755
Johnston Atoll	4940
Jordan	2528
Kazakhstan	2571
Keeling Islands	709
Kenya	2591
Kingman Reef	4940
Kiribati	2616
Korea, Democratic People's Republic	2625
Korea, Republic	2654
Kosovo	2689
Kuwait	2702
Kyrgyzstan	2723
Laos	2743
Latvia	2759
Lebanon	2777
Lesotho	2808
Liberia	2822
Libya	2840
Liechtenstein	2864
Lihou	4755
Lithuania	2872
Luxembourg	2892
Macao	1313
Macedonia, former Yugoslav republic	2904
Madagascar	2923
Malawi	2942
Malaysia	2959
Maldives	2998
Mali	3010
Malta	3028
Man, Isle of	4759
Marshall Islands	3039
Martinique	1840
Mauritania	3048
Mauritius	3064
Mayotte	1847
McDonald Islands	716
Melilla	4200
Mexico	3080
Micronesia, Federated States	3110
Midway Atoll	4940

Territory	Page
Miquelon	1874
Moldova	3118
Monaco	3139
Mongolia	3146
Montenegro	3171
Montserrat	4806
Morocco	3180
Mozambique	3205
Myanmar	3223
Namibia	3253
Nauru	3271
Navassa Island	4940
Nepal	3280
Netherlands	3306
Nevis	3871
New Caledonia	1886
New Zealand	3354
Nicaragua	3400
Niger	3418
Nigeria	3436
Niue	3393
Norfolk Island	711
North Korea	2625
Northern Ireland	4690
Northern Mariana Islands	4901
Norway	3463
Oman	3491
Pakistan	3507
Palau	3554
Palestinian Autonomous Areas	3562
Palmyra	4940
Panama	3592
Papua New Guinea	3611
Paraguay	3634
People's Republic of China	1244
Peru	3652
Peter I Øy	3490
Philippines	3676
Pitcairn Islands	4812
Poland	3718
Portugal	3742
Príncipe	3917
Puerto Rico	4908
Qatar	3768
Ras al-Khaimah	4670
Republic of China (see Taiwan)	
Republic of the Congo	1383
Republic of Korea	2654
Réunion	1852
Romania	3786
Ross Dependency	3380
Russian Federation	3811
Rwanda	3853
Saba	3334
Saint-Barthélemy	1873
Saint Christopher and Nevis	3871
Saint Helena, Ascension and Tristan da Cunha	4815
Saint Lucia	3880
Saint-Martin	1873
Saint Pierre and Miquelon	1874
Saint Vincent and the Grenadines	3891
Samoa	3900
San Marino	3910
São Tomé and Príncipe	3917
Sark	4755
Saudi Arabia	3927
Senegal	3952

INDEX OF TERRITORIES IN VOLUMES I AND II

Territory	Page
Serbia	3976
Seychelles	4001
Sharjah	4670
Sierra Leone	4009
Singapore	4026
Sint Eustatius	3334
Sint Maarten	3350
Slovakia	4053
Slovenia	4072
Solomon Islands	4088
Somalia	4103
South Africa	4122
South Georgia	4820
South Korea	2654
South Sandwich Islands	4820
South Sudan (see Sudan)	
Spain	4156
Spanish North Africa	4195
Sri Lanka	4206
St Kitts (Saint Christopher)	3871
Sudan	4235
Suriname	4260
Svalbard	3487
Swaziland	4272
Sweden	4287
Switzerland	4313
Syria	4339
Taiwan	4367
Tajikistan	4399
Tanzania	4418
Thailand	4438
Timor-Leste	4473
Tobago	4521
Togo	4492
Tokelau	3380
Tonga	4510

Territory	Page
Trinidad and Tobago	4521
Tristan da Cunha	4815
Tunisia	4539
Turkey	4559
'Turkish Republic of Northern Cyprus'	1483
Turkmenistan	4596
Turks and Caicos Islands	4821
Tuvalu	4613
Uganda	4620
Ukraine	4640
Umm al-Qaiwain	4670
United Arab Emirates	4670
United Kingdom	4690
United States of America	4828
United States Virgin Islands	4934
Uruguay	4942
Uzbekistan	4961
Vanuatu	4979
Vatican City	4992
Venezuela	5002
Viet Nam	5028
Virgin Islands, British	4779
Virgin Islands, US	4934
Wake Island	4941
Wallis and Futuna Islands	1878
Western Samoa (see Samoa)	
Yemen	5059
Zambia	5085
Zimbabwe	5102